TITAN BOOK

in association w

PRICE GUIDE PROD

presents

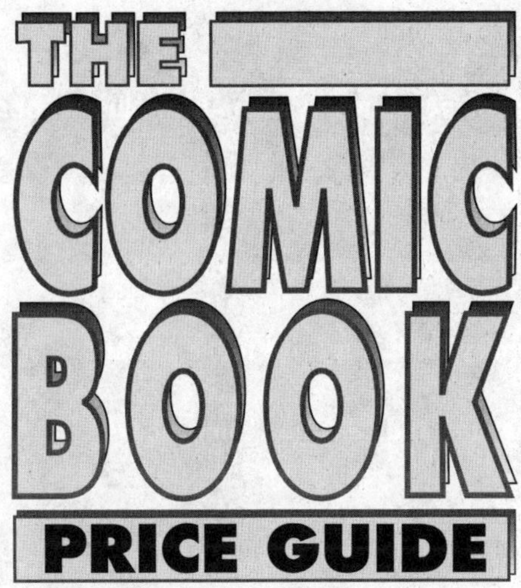

1997/98 EDITION

by DUNCAN McALPINE
(COMPILER AND EDITOR)

with John Skoulides

Editor (British Section)
STEVE HOLLAND

Honorary Editor
ALAN AUSTIN

Editor (Titan Books)
SIMON FURMAN

The Comic Book Price Guide Hall of Fame
BOB OVERSTREET

The indispensable reference companion for British fans, collectors and dealers

- Based on the original 1983 guide by Alan Austin, Justin Ebbs and Gary Fox
- Completely updated, revised and expanded from the UK Price Guide #7
- Fully illustrated throughout with classic comic covers
- DC and Marvel comics listed from 1938 to the present
- Independent, American and Canadian comic books
- Graphic novels and trade paperbacks
- British comics and annuals
- Features on the grading, preservation, storage and handling of comics
- Collectors' information for Marvel, DC and Independents
- Prices for each comic in three grades in both $US and £UK, plus the differing formats, page-counts, rarity and distribution
- Major artists' and writers' work, back-ups, reprints, secondary features
- First appearances index plus cross-overs and tie-ins
- Eight page colour section featuring selected classic first appearances
- Top 50 rarest comics in the world
- Top 100 comics and titles for DC, Marvel and Independents
- New revised Trading and Bubble Gum Card guide

EDITOR'S FOREWORD

It has been an incredibly busy year for me, with the Comicana shop in Barnet, directing an opera, and still trying to renovate the family house in Muswell Hill. The time will come when I don't have to rush upstairs to the attic with my wife's Le Creuset set of saucepans every time it rains. Quite how much longer I can wear so many hats remains to be seen, particularly with some film and television projects in the pipeline. Writing this book is getting easier in some ways (the help and effort I have got from Simon Furman at Titan Books has been tremendous) but it still remains a very complex reference work and sometimes there are just not enough hours in the day to do what I want with it. I hope you enjoy the book and appreciate the work that has gone into it.

The most exciting event for me has been the launch of "Comicana" on the Sci-Fi Channel. For years, ever since I first touted a treatment called "Comix Scene" around the corridors of power at the BBC in 1988, I have wanted to see a regular platform for comics to reach a wider audience outside comic shops, marts and conventions. I am absolutely indebted to Terry Marsh at the Sci-Fi Channel Europe. She took a chance and commissioned the series when money was tight and when a first regular programme ever devoted entirely to comic books was very much an unknown quantity. It is a small beginning, but as I write this, we have just filmed Show Three at UKCAC and we were delighted at the comments and feedback we were getting about the show. Money is so tight in television generally, let alone in cable and satellite, that we have to think twice about getting a cab if it's possible to walk to an interview with the camera. But we do the best we can because we and the Sci-Fi Channel believe in the potential of "Comicana".

A mention here then for the production personnel: Abigail Harvey who cares about the success of "Comicana" as Executive Producer as passionately as I do, for which I thank her very much; Peter Brown who calls the shots, calms the nerves and entertains us all with stories of errant animals up the Zambezi; Andrew Herring who points the camera, clears the pix and is the world expert on acid funk jazz and Jamiroquai; Karen Pritchard as researcher and ace news-hound who keeps all the boys in order; Caroline Tudor who fronts it all with her own zappy style and groovy hair, and can memorise any amount of last minute script changes that I thrust upon her with astonishing ease; there's the lovely Clive and Toby on studio days who light and film us and, apart from cunningly disguising my grey bits, they contribute massively to the slick and gloss of the programme. And, of course, there's Emma and Sue, legal eagles George and Michaela, my main man in New York David Armstrong and the very nice girl on the front desk.

But, most of all there is you, the audience. If want more of "Comicana", if you want to see features that interest you, if you want to hear what your favourite creator has to say, if there are issues and items of news that you feel are important, don't just sit there but write to: 77 Charlotte Street, London W1P 2DD. Easy. Give "Comicana" the voice that you want to hear.

My thanks list is important, as ever. Louise, my better half, for all her help and encouragement. My children Benjamin and Ella for scribbling all over my computer-printouts. And John Skoulides, without whom this book would not have been possible (he in turn would like to say thank you to Rick Appleby for constant research help).

A very special mention must be reserved for David Dupont and Helen Sawyer for their typesetting and design and a thousand other little jobs that you don't see and they receive no recognition for.

Major thanks also to Steve Holland, compiler of the new-look British section which is now more streamlined, comics and television orientated and has a specially designed Classics Illustrated listing that is all the more informative.

The roll call of thanks goes on to all the main and other contributors and market reporters who are credited elsewhere in this book. I look forward to the day when the contributors' listing runs into many pages.

The people at Titan Books cannot go without recognition. My thanks to Nick Landau, Katy Wild and Simon Furman in particular in his role as editor and scribe, Ruth Cole and Siobhan Flynn and anybody else who has been involved in the production of this book including Bob Kelly in the Studio. Howard Hughes, Colin Clarke, Kelvin, Brian and all at Commercial Colour Press know they have my thanks and it has been a pleasure doing a seventh book with them.

While Alan Austin never seeks the limelight, I once again acknowledge him as the founding father of price guides in this country and his rightful place as "The Guv'nor".

I seem to spend so much of my time mentioning Bob Overstreet as the author of the very first price guide for comic books. And rightly so, for all he has done for this industry.

Penultimate thanks to Tony Petrou for all his work on the computing side. I acknowledge the amount of work he has done to make this book the best it can possibly be. And thanks also to his better half Demi for her hospitality when we're working late into the night . And "hi" to their new son Christopher.

My final thanks are reserved for the cover artists Paul Neary and Bryan Hitch and especially to DC Comics for allowing the use of Batman on the cover which is a particular thrill for me.
Read and enjoy.

Duncan McAlpine

This book is dedicated to my father-in-law Dr. Stanley Craven who died in the early hours of January 7th. A quite brilliant mind and affable nature that has been so tragically taken away from us. We're thinking of you Stan.

CONTRIBUTORS TO THE 1997/98 EDITION

MAIN CONTRIBUTORS TO THE 1997/98 EDITION

RICK APPLEBY • JULES BURT • DAVE FINN • RON HALL • DARRYL JONES • GEORGE LESSITER • MALCOLM PHILLIPS • JOHN PIRES • GRANT RYMER

MARKET REPORTERS TO THE 1997/98 EDITION

MANNY AMARIO • RICK APPLEBY • MARTIN BEESON • KENNETH BURNS • DAVE & SUSAN FINN • TOMMY HOODLESS • DAVE HOPKINS • DARRYL JONES • MARK LAST • CHRIS RICE • ALAN SCOTT • STEVE WREN

OTHER CONTRIBUTORS/SPECIAL THANK YOUs TO THE 1997/98 EDITION

ROB BARROW (Fantasy Trading Card Company) • COLIN CAMPBELL (Comics Warehouse) • SHAUN FINNIE • MIKE GOULD • IAN HOLMES • TIM O'DONNELL • S. KUMAR • DAVID ROACH • BARRY RONESS (Fantasy Trading Card Company) • MARCUS SIEMASKO • DEZ SKINN (Comics International) • MICHAEL STANWYCK • SURESH TOLAT (Casson & Beckman) • GEOFF WEST (Conquistador)

ABOUT THE COVER

Most people know that I am a great Batman fan and indeed many of my friends would say that it's to the point of obsession. There is no doubt that for me Batman is the most powerful and resonant comic book character and judging by the number of times he has been re-invented by some of the best writers and artists in the business, I'm not alone in that thinking. Having done much to promote Batman in one form or another over the years, I am thrilled that DC Comics has granted us the use of Batman for the cover of this book, in what promises to be a spectacular year for the Caped Crusader with the release of the new Batman film, surely the biggest movie of the four. And I am thrilled that two top British professionals in the guise of Bryan Hitch and Paul Neary, ably assisted by colourist Robin Riggs, have put together a fittingly stunning cover, proving once again the calibre of British talent.

Cover illustration by Bryan Hitch, Paul Neary and Robin Riggs.

DISCLAIMER

The views expressed by the contributors are not necessarily those of the Editor and Publishers. Every care is taken to ensure that the contents of this book are accurate but the Editor and Publishers assume no responsibility for errors whatsoever. Whilst extreme care and prior conditions acceptance are used when accepting and publishing advertisements, the Editor and Publishers cannot accept any responsibilty whatsoever for copyright infringement and plagiarism. All illustrations reproduced within the pages of The Comic Book Price Guide for Great Britain remain the property of their respective copyright holders and are used in an information, news and comparative capacity. No infringement of copyright is intended.

THE COMIC BOOK PRICE GUIDE 1997/98
ISBN 1 85286 794 9

Published by Titan Books, 42–44 Dolben Street, London SE1 0UP

First Edition April 1997

10 9 8 7 6 5 4 3 2 1

WARNING

IN ORDER TO HELP PREVENT THE UNLAWFUL COPYING AND REPRODUCTION OF ANY SECTION OF THE PRICE GUIDE LISTINGS, INFORMATIONAL DEVICES HAVE BEEN PLACED THROUGHOUT THE TEXT KNOWN ONLY TO THE EDITOR. THESE DEVICES ARE NOT INTENTIONALLY MISLEADING AND NOR DO THEY AFFECT THE VALUE OF ANY GIVEN COMIC. THEY ARE HOWEVER INSTANTLY RECOGNISABLE SHOULD THE NEED AND OCCASION ARISE.

CORRESPONDENCE, CORRECTIONS AND ADDITIONAL INFORMATION

PLEASE ADDRESS ALL COMMUNICATIONS TO THE EDITORIAL ADDRESS: PRICE GUIDE PRODUCTIONS, PO BOX 10793 LONDON N10 3NF

DESIGN AND TYPESETTING XENDO, 167 FERNHEAD ROAD, LONDON W9 3ED

PRINTING COMMERCIAL COLOUR PRESS, 116-118 WOODGRANGE ROAD, FOREST GATE, LONDON E7 OEW. TEL: (0181) 519 1919

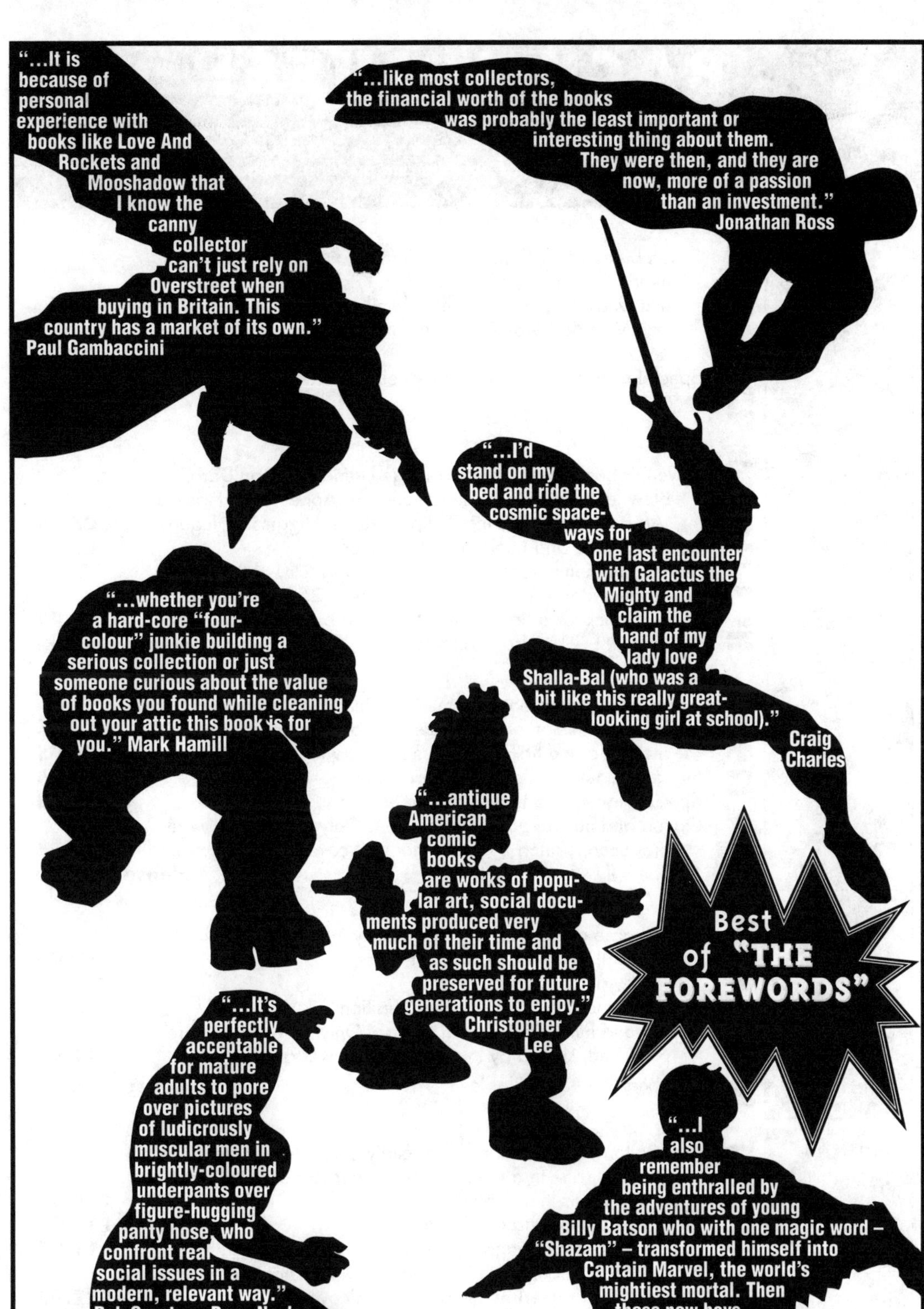
"...It is because of personal experience with books like Love And Rockets and Mooshadow that I know the canny collector can't just rely on Overstreet when buying in Britain. This country has a market of its own."
Paul Gambaccini
"...like most collectors, the financial worth of the books was probably the least important or interesting thing about them. They were then, and they are now, more of a passion than an investment."
Jonathan Ross
"...I'd stand on my bed and ride the cosmic space-ways for one last encounter with Galactus the Mighty and claim the hand of my lady love Shalla-Bal (who was a bit like this really great-looking girl at school)."
Craig Charles
"...whether you're a hard-core "four-colour" junkie building a serious collection or just someone curious about the value of books you found while cleaning out your attic this book is for you." Mark Hamill
"...antique American comic books are works of popular art, social documents produced very much of their time and as such should be preserved for future generations to enjoy."
Christopher Lee
Best of "THE FOREWORDS"
"...It's perfectly acceptable for mature adults to pore over pictures of ludicrously muscular men in brightly-coloured underpants over figure-hugging panty hose, who confront real social issues in a modern, relevant way."
Rob Grant Doug Naylor
"...I also remember being enthralled by the adventures of young Billy Batson who with one magic word – "Shazam" – transformed himself into Captain Marvel, the world's mightiest mortal. Then these new boys, Superman and Batman came along..."
Colin Baker

BACK ISSUES!

To celebrate our team-up with Titan Books, Price Guide Productions is pleased to present back copies of all the Price Guides produced from #2 to date (#1 sold out), in mint, unsigned, signed and special editions. Who knows? These variations may themselves become collector's items! They make fascinating reading and comparing and stocks are limited. ***Please enclose a flat fee of £2.50 per order for postage and packing. Cheques/PO's payable to Price Guide Productions.***

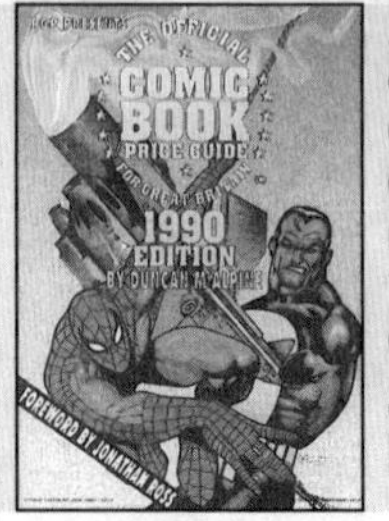

Nº 2 (1990)

Simon Bisley cover featuring Spiderman and the Punisher! Interior pin-ups by Ewins & Lloyd, Kitson and Ridgeway; first typeset Guide in the new familiar format. The days when Iron Man #55 was £4.00 and New Mutants #87 wasn't even out yet! **£6.95**
Special signed and hand-stamped edition **£7.95**

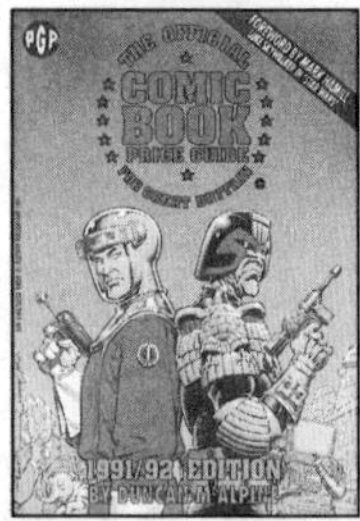

Nº 3 (1991)

Dave Gibbons cover featuring Judge Dredd and Dan Dare. New features include the famous First Appearance Index and Artist Gallery featuring Philips & Kane, Higgins & Hughes **£7.95**
Special signed and hand-stamped edition **£8.95**
Signed and numbered Limited Edition. Only 250 of these were produced and some very low numbers (25-100) have been kept back for a first come, first served basis **£9.95**
Numbers #1–#10 also available **please enquire**

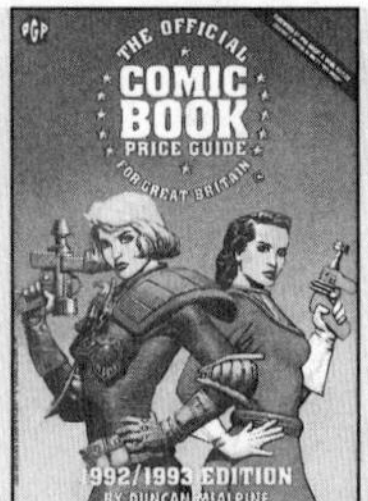

Nº 4 (1992)

Sean Philips cover featuring the "girlfriends" of Dredd and Dare—Judge Anderson and Dr. Jocelyn Peabody! Special colour section for the first time and many new features **£8.95**
Signed by author and cover artist **£9.95**
Special signed and hand-stamped edition **£9.95**
Signed and numbered Limited Edition. Only 50 of these were produced, signed by the author and cover artist **£10.95**
Numbers #1–#5 available **please enquire**

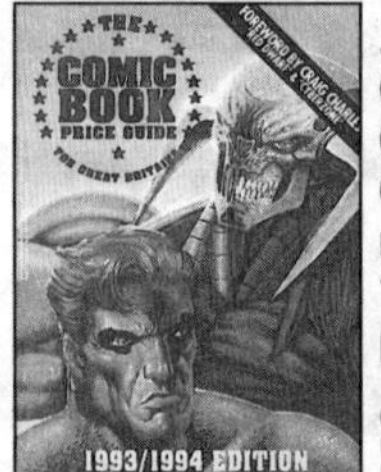

Nº 5 (1993)

Liam Sharpe cover featuring the unlikely team-up of Death's Head (a robot) and Magnus Robot Fighter **£9.95**
Signed by author and cover artist **£10.95**
Special signed and hand-stamped edition **£10.95**
Signed and numbered Limited Edition. Only 50 of these were produced, signed by the author and cover artist **£11.95**
Numbers #1–#5 available **please enquire**

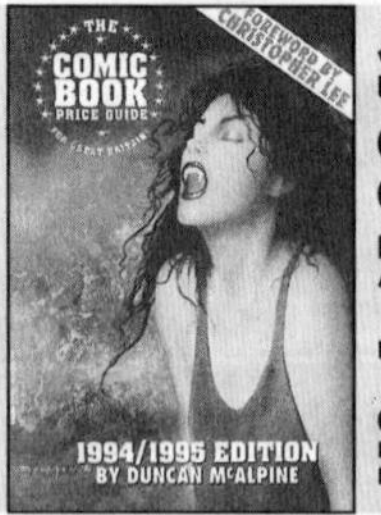

Nº 6 (1994)

John Bolton cover featuring a specially created character called "Liliana", one in a long line of vampiresses from the depths of the artist's imagination **£10.95**
Signed by author and cover artist **£11.95**
Special signed and hand-stamped edition **£11.95**
Signed and numbered Limited Edition. Only 50 of these were produced, signed by the author and cover artist **£12.95**
Numbers #1–#5 available **please enquire**

Guide #7 (1996) with a stunning Sabretooth cover by Gary Frank. First dual priced edition with prices in pounds and dollars **£12.95**
Special signed (by author) edition with dedication of your choice **£13.95**

Price Guide Productions • P.O. Box 10793 • London N10 3NF

CONTENTS

Editor's Foreword 3
Best of The Forewords 5
Contents 7
Abbreviations 9

GENERAL INTRODUCTION **11**
Multiples of Guide 14
The Repair & Restoration of Comic Books 15
Storage of Comic Books 16
Pricing Structures 16
An Introduction to Grading 18
Percentage Chart 19
Defects Chart 19
Collecting Batman by Duncan McAlpine 23
First Appearance Index 30
Top Ten Hot Babes of 1996 50
Origins Index 53
Star Wars Action Figure Price Guide 57
Death Index 63
Comic Book Price Guide Dealers' Market Reports 67
Succeeding In Business/Self Assessment by Suresh Tolat 75
Reprint Index 77
Signed and Numbered Limited Editions by Grant Rymer 81
The Top Fifty Rarest Comics 86
Top 20 Most Valuable Comics 91
Under-valued Comics by Dave Finn 92
Early Works of Artists 94
Top 100 Best Selling Comics for 1996 99
Top 100 UK DC Comics 100
Top 100 US DC Comics 101
Top 100 UK Marvel Comics 102
Top 100 US Marvel Comics 103
Top 100 UK Independent Comics 104
Top 100 US Independent Comics 105
Top 100 UK DC Titles 106
Top 100 US DC Titles 109
Top 100 UK Marvel Titles 110
Top 100 US Marvel Titles 111
Top 100 UK Independent Titles 112
Top 100 US Independent Titles 113
Top 100 UK Titles 114
Top 100 US Titles 115
Top 100 UK Comics 116
Top 100 US Comics 117
Top 50 Comics Differential DC Comics and ranges £UK to $US 119
Top 50 Comics Differential DC Comics and ranges $US to £UK 120
Top 50 Comics Differential Marvel Comics and ranges £UK to $US 121
Top 50 Comics Differential Marvel Comics and ranges $US to £UK 122

Top 50 Comics Differential Independent Comics and ranges £UK to $US 123
Top 50 Comics Differential Independent Comics and ranges $US to £UK 124
Top 50 Comics Differential Comics and ranges £UK to $US 125
Top 50 Comics Differential Comics and ranges $US to £UK 126
Selected Further Reading 127

COLOUR SECTION **129**
The Trading Card Guide (with assistance from Barrie Roness, Rob Barrow & Ron Hall) 137
Bubble Gum Card Section by Duncan McAlpine (with assistance from Peter Rice & Ron Hall) 156

AMERICAN COMICS GUIDE **163**
The Historical Ages of Comic Books 164
An Introduction to DC Comics 168
DC Market Report 169
An Introduction to Marvel Comics 175
Marvel Market Report 176
An Introduction to Independent Comics 181
DC, Marvel & Independent Comics – Points to Remember 182
AMERICAN COMICS LISTING 183
The British & American Market – a Comparison 715

BRITISH COMICS GUIDE **720**
An Introduction to British Comics by Steve Holland 722
Points to Remember 726
BRITISH COMICS LISTING 727

ADVERTISEMENTS **793**

ABBREVIATIONS AND TERMINOLOGY USED IN THIS GUIDE

Arrival Date	pencil markings on the cover of a comic that indicate when that comic was received by the distributor or news-stand dealer to be sold on the news-stand. The date is usually two months prior to the cover date. Much more of a U.S. market phenomenon and concern
Ashcan	a prototype comic put together by a publisher to secure title and format copyright. Usually new black and white covers stapled around an existing comic
Baxter	a type of high quality heavier stock white paper
B&W	Black and White artwork
Bi-Monthly	published every two months
Bi-Weekly	published every two weeks
Bondage cover	usually shows a glamorous female bound and/or gagged
Bookshelf Format	Marvel's equivalent of DC's Prestige Format: a special edition of a comic that approaches a graphic novel
Bronze Age	generally accepted to be the period of comics from 1970-1980. More widely used in America than the U.K.
Cameo	a brief appearance by a character (comic book or real) in a comic story. Usually defined as being 2 or 3 panels only.
(c)or(cy)	the copyright date or copyright year on an otherwise undated publication
CCA	The Comics Code Authority that issued a Seal of Approval on most mainstream comics from April 1955
Digest	a paperback collected edition, smaller than regular comic size, most usually reprints. 4" x 6"
DS	double size: an issue with twice the number of pages than a normal size comic ie. 64 pages
Dust Shadow	when an edge of a comic, front or back cover, is exposed to a layer of dust over the years, leaving a dark shadow
Embossed	when a pattern is pressed into a cover to form a raised surface
Film	a film adaptation or a comic based on concepts from a film.
1st	first appearance, of a character or of a character in that title. Can also be used for objects, places etc.
flashback	a sequence injected into a story either by the narrators or a character remembering or re-telling the story in some part
Foil cover	a special coloured cover on card-stock paper with a "metallic" sheen
Foxing	tiny red-brown or red-orange spores in paper caused by damp. This is most prevalent on Golden Age and some Silver Age material
GA	Golden Age, commonly accepted to be 1938–1945.
Graphic Novel	paperback or hardback special edition of a comic, high production value text, art and reproduction. Term first coined by Will Eisner in the late 1970s. Usually 8" x 11" in size.
holo-grafix cover	a silver-shard printed effect on a cover that produces different colours radiating outward as the cover is rolled around in a light source
intro	introducing (usually a character)
JLA	Justice League of America
JLI	Justice League International
JSA	Justice Society of America
Late Golden Age	the period of comics from 1945-1949
Late Silver Age	the period of comics from 1966-1969
LD	Limited Distribution in the UK. Applies mainly to post 1970 comics. More recently denotes the fact that a high demand item has sold quickly and is scarce in its availability
less common	a term that is still being tested referring to a noticeable scarcity of a comic that was previously thought not to be scarce
LSH	Legion of Super-Heroes
Mag	Magazine format or size
Mando	a type of high-quality paper
Marvel Chipping	a defect peculiar to Marvel comics of the 1950s and 1960s in the trimming process that resulted in chips out of the right edge of the cover
Mature Readers	a comic labelled for Mature Readers; not intended for children
Modern Age	generally accepted to be from 1980 to the present day
MS	Mini or Maxi-series: an intentionally finite series
Mylar	inert plastic protective sleeve, stiffer and safer for storage purposes than an ordinary plastic bag
ND	Not Distributed in the UK
nn	No number: an unnumbered issue
OS	one-shot: a single issue, not part of a series
Pre Golden Age	the period of comics from 1933-1938

Pre Silver Age	the period of comics from 1950 -1955
Prestige Format	DC's equivalent of Marvel's Bookshelf Format: a special edition of a comic approaching a graphic novel
Printing defect	faults with a comic as a result of the production process. These include spine and cover wrinkles, extra paper "tags" on pages folded back in, pages still joined at top/bottom edges etc. While these still affect the grade of the comic, they are different from Grading Defects which occur as a result of wear and tear
Quarterly	published every three months
Rare	comics that are seldom seen in collections that come to light or are offered for sale in shops or on lists. Rarity may be due to original distribution or production circumstances. Applies readily to both new and old comics
re-done	a story re-told with new artwork
SA	Silver Age, 1956-1965
Scarce	a comic that is generally harder to obtain than most owing to original distribution circumstances. Applies mostly to pre 1970s comics
Scarcer	a comic that is noticeably not around for no apparent reason. Usually applied to newer comics and is a term that is still being tested like "less common"
Splash page	usually the first story art page, one single panel
Squarebound	a comic glue-bound with a square spined cover
sub crease	a vertical crease caused when a comic was folded in half for subscription mailing
3-D comic	comic produced in two colour tinted layers which produces a three-dimensional effect when viewed through special glasses
Toy	a comic title based on a toy product
Trade paperback	a 7"x10" paperback collection of a series of chosen stories, usually reprints
TV	a comic based on a Television show
Very Scarce	a comic that is harder to obtain than a Scarce issue, usually as a result of a production fault like a lost shipment or distribution inequality between US and UK. Also factors of high collector interest. Applies more readily to pre 1970 comics but can occasionally be used for newer comics
Very Rare	a comic that almost never turns up owing to original distribution or production reasons coupled with original and subsequent high collector interest resulting in many copies staying in collections for years away from the general circulation
X-over	Cross-over, when a character appears in another character's title so that the narrative directly continues. These occasions are usually multi-part stories and all parts are necessary to enjoy the full narrative

EXAMPLES OF USAGE

Neal Adams, Wrightson art	contains artwork by Adams and Wrightson, but not on the same strip
Neal Adams/Wrightson art	Neal Adams pencils, inked by Wrightson
Superman,Batman in 24	both appear in issue 24 in different stories
Superman/Batman in 24	both co-star in a story in issue 24
FEATURES	new stories, previously unpublished
REPRINT FEATURES	stories, often back-ups, which have been previously published elsewhere

ERRORS AND FURTHER INFORMATION

Although assembled directly from personal observations wherever possible, a project of this complexity will inevitably contain errors. If you find any inaccuracies or omissions in the body of the text or in any of the featured articles, please write and tell us, so that corrections can be made; any contributions will be credited in the next edition.

FOR THOSE SENDING A SUBSTANTIAL BODY OF INFORMATION, THE BEST 5 WILL RECEIVE A SPECIAL SIGNED AND NUMBERED COPY OF THE GUIDE. THESE 5 COPIES WILL BE UNIQUE.

Have we omitted an artist whose work you feel should be noted, or ignored a title of collector interest? With your suggestions and help, the 1998/9 edition can be more complete and comprehensive. We would also like to hear from you if you have a particular field of knowledge; Canadian comics or British reprints of American material, for instance.

PLEASE WRITE WITH ANY COMMENTS OR SUGGESTIONS TO:

PRICE GUIDE PRODUCTIONS,PO BOX 10793,LONDON N10 3NF.

Always check the editorial address before sending any form of correspondence.

GENERAL INTRODUCTION

WELCOME to the 8th edition of the Comic Book Price Guide. This is in more ways than one a completely new book, having a re-designed front section, over 75,000 records updated and over 1,000 titles added since the last Guide. Once again we are delighted to bring you what we believe is The Guide's most important feature: that of dual-pricing for both the British and American markets. The dollar prices in this book are not simply a conversion of the British value. Wherever possible each individual record has been considered and a current market value that is generally relevant for the United States has been entered. It will be noticed therefore that many US prices far exceed UK prices – in some exceptional circumstances by as much as 500%! In the Top 100s section, you will find a list of some notable comparative prices. We are also delighted that a Star Wars figures Guide has been compiled by Jules Burt of Purple Haze Comics in Plymouth which we hope will be the basis of a future stand-alone publication.

For those not familiar with the history of the British Guide, particularly American dealers and collectors who may be seeing this book for the first time, this is how it went. The British Price Guide assumes its pedigree from the very fine pioneering work done by British dealer and fanzine editor Alan Austin (still in my opinion "The Guv'nor"), Justin Ebbs and Gary Fox, the 4th edition of which was released in 1982. In 1989, the 5th edition was released when myself and Lance Rickman assumed the agony and the ecstasy of production. We achieved what they said could not be done and moved the Guide into a new stage of professional packaging and widespread exposure.

Much experience was gained and after having taken over the sole responsibility of producing the Guide, the 6th Edition came out in April 1990 with a new look, a new format (professionally typeset) and a more comprehensive listing. Just to confuse matters I decided to establish a numbering sequence for this and future Guides, settling on a Number 2 as it was the second one that I had done. Number 3 came out in April 1991 with 30% more back-issue information and listings extended even further back into the early Silver Age. Numbers 4, 5 and 6 followed with number 7 being the first published by Titan Books. This book is number 8.

This Guide, as with every other Guide that we have done, must be seen very much as a work-in-progress, a basis upon which to build for the future.

Where The Guide used to be divided into 4 sections of D.C., MARVEL, INDEPENDENTS and BRITISH with a general introduction to each, it was decided that all the American comics would be listed alphanumerically with the section on British comics remaining separate at the end.

The British section is compiled by Mr. Steve Holland with help from a number of his associates and overseen by me. It has been reduced somewhat this year as many early 20th Century items remain static in price year after year and many of these have a very limited collectability. The new section concentrates on that particular area of science fiction and TV related material starting more or less with The Eagle in 1950. A more definitive British stand-alone volume is in the works. Watch this space!

The pricing rationale for so vast and complex a subject is continually evolving, as is more fully explained under the section PRICING STRUCTURE. Where the mechanics of the mathematics might necessarily break down, particularly with reference to more recent comics, a certain amount of judgement and common sense must be used. The more recent

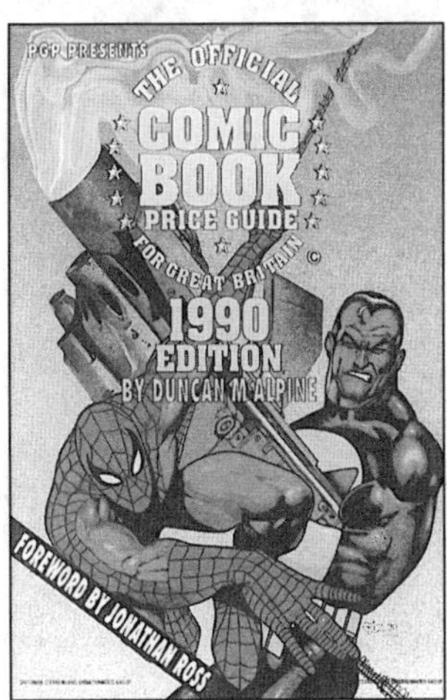

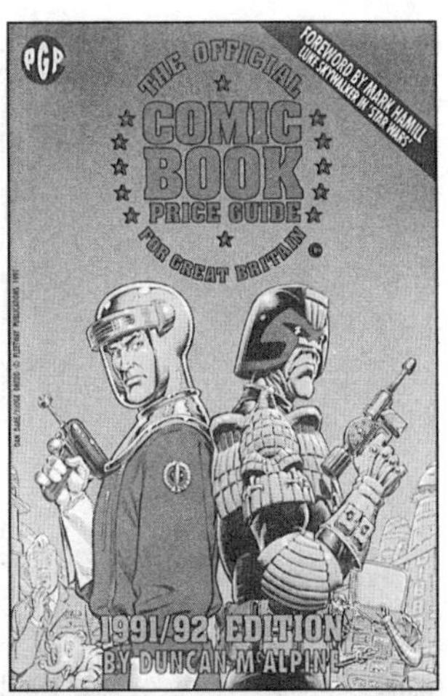

the comic, the less the margin between the near-mint and mint, to the point where they become more or less the same. And where the mathematics used to produce unsightly values like £13.20 or £3.60, we have devised a rounding up and rounding down formula to make for whole numbers in the Good and Fine columns.

As shall no doubt be repeated elsewhere, **IF A COMIC IS GRADED ACCURATELY AND FAIRLY, THE INFORMATION IN THIS BOOK WILL PROVIDE EXACTLY WHAT IT INTENDS – A GUIDE.**

COLLECTING COMIC BOOKS

The collecting of comic books (or PANELOLOGY, to use the more scientific term) is at once fascinating and frustrating, exhaustive and rewarding, both creatively and often financially. Many people rediscover their interest in comics in later years (wishing Mother hadn't "thrown that pile of comics out, dear...") while others start collecting young and carry on building up their collections. This General Introduction highlights certain points worth remembering when buying new or old comics either on a regular basis or for the first time. This introduction is also written with the British market very much in mind though most of its points are universally applicable.

COMIC SHOPS AND SHOP ETIQUETTE

Brand new comics at the newsagent or in specialist shops are not necessarily in MINT condition. They are more likely to be so at the comic shops rather than news-stands or newsagents as most comic shops individually bag their new comics but they should still be checked for proper cut and trim, no creases or corners folded over, no ink stains inside or any other defects that may arise from packaging and delivery. When handling a shop's back-issue stock, a certain amount of care should be exercised. Individual comics are usually in alphabetical and numerical order in back-issue boxes and should not be shuffled around. Don't bend comics backwards to see the covers or thrust them carelessly back into place as you could be causing damage far in excess of the amount you will eventually spend. Comics should not be removed from bags without first checking with a member of staff as some dealers prefer to open and re-seal the bags themselves. Thoughtless customers soon become unpopular in any shop while careful browsers are universally welcomed.

BUYING NEW COMICS AND BACK ISSUES

When buying back issues it is worth making a detailed "wants list" of a defined area of collecting, be it titles or characters, themes or artists. **ABOVE ALL ELSE, IT PAYS TO SHOP AROUND** as prices can vary tremendously and with patience a good deal can be obtained. Having said that, it is also worthwhile concentrating on one shop or one dealer to build up a rapport and relationship that may lead to more personal service and better deals. It is also a good idea to budget strictly and collect within one's means, though this often proves to be the greatest point of frustration and even more so if one chooses to collect higher condition (and therefore higher priced) comics. Collectors are becoming more and more aware of grading and condition and many set a minimum acceptable grade or improve the general condition of a collection by gradual replacement (upgrading). As ever, it is all a matter of personal choice as some prefer to collect entire runs of high-grade comics and others just want to read the comics and stories whatever their condition.

PROFIT OR FUN?

As in any other dealing there is a certain element of financial speculation in the market where current fashions, hyped-up demand and limited supplies can realise quick profits for the well-informed investor. Recent market reports in American publications indicate that more and more businessmen are treating Golden Age comics especially as an easily-negotiable and high-return investment.

A personal collection, however, that is seen only in terms of capital investment is all too easy to mismanage. Potential profit can become actual loss and the pleasure of collecting and dealing can often turn to disappointment. **ABOVE ALL ELSE, I BELIEVE THAT COMICS ARE MEANT PRIMARILY FOR FUN AND ENJOYMENT,** to be read and appreciated for what they are and to be collected and dealt in on that basis. Any financial gain is purely a bonus and a reassurance that money can be well invested if so desired.

SELLING YOUR COLLECTION

When it comes to selling, a vendor has two courses of action – sell to a dealer or sell the comics yourself. Selling to a shop or dealer cuts out a lot of time and hassle but with their overheads and profit margins to consider, only a certain percentage – sometimes around half and often a lot less – of a comics' market value will be given. Some may take comics in trade against purchase of other items but again percentages will be lower as any comics they take still have to be processed and sold. Selling comics yourself can be time consuming and involve certain costs but may realise higher gains.

Advertisements in fan publications and stalls at comic marts and conventions are the usual way of reaching potential customers. The disadvantage is that the rarer or the most popular comics will sell quite quickly, leaving you with a less saleable collection of low-interest titles.

STARTING A BUSINESS

(see also the article written by Suresh Tolat further on in this book)

With the continued growth of comics in this country as an industry it is tempting for a novice collector to start up in business, assuming that all dealers make huge profits and keep the best items for themselves. All too often a prized collection is used to start up a fledgling business with the best of intentions only to see it frittered away and wasted.

If there is an intention to turn collecting into a business or just start one having observed from the outside, it is essential to seek professional advice. Banks should provide all the information you need on finances and distribution companies will help you (or should do!) with stock control. Either way, a few points to bear in mind may help. These points are fairly obvious to most people but worth re-iterating nonetheless.

1) Have a very clear idea of your intended target-market and the size of your operation.
2) Have a very clear and professional business plan set out for at least 18 months ahead.
3) Have a very clear idea of your intended image or logo design and how you are going to advertise yourself. There is an awful lot of competition out there! You need to get your name known.
4) Be sure that you are well versed in the current state of the market. There are a number of magazines and books that are essential reading such as Comics International, Previews, Overstreet's Fan and Krause Publications' Comic Buyers Guide.
5) Be sure that you can afford the proper amount of time to your business, no matter how small or side-line. All dealers will tell you that everything takes longer than one might think. Be prepared for some long hours!
6) Seek advice from dealers, particularly those who have been established for some time but realise that they are not going to give away their trade secrets that they may have learned after years of hard work.
7) Try to find a new way of doing things, offering a level of service that makes you stand out from the rest.
8) Be approachable from other dealers in terms of doing business as things often come about after a chance meeting or conversation.
9) If employing others, make sure you are definite and clear in your relationship with them. Too often friends can fall out, particularly over money!
10) Above all else, approach your business with common sense and if in doubt, talk to someone.

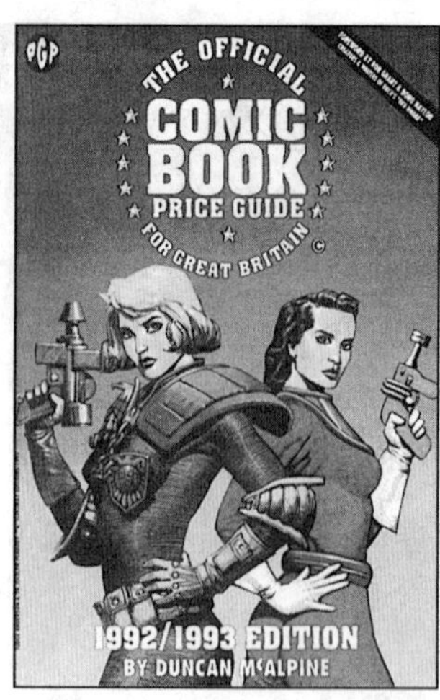

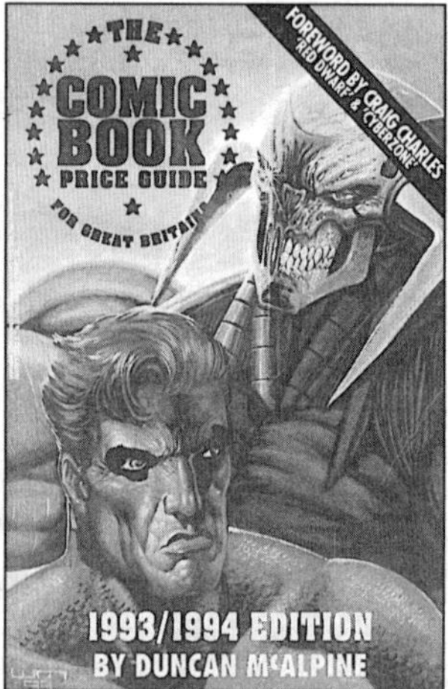

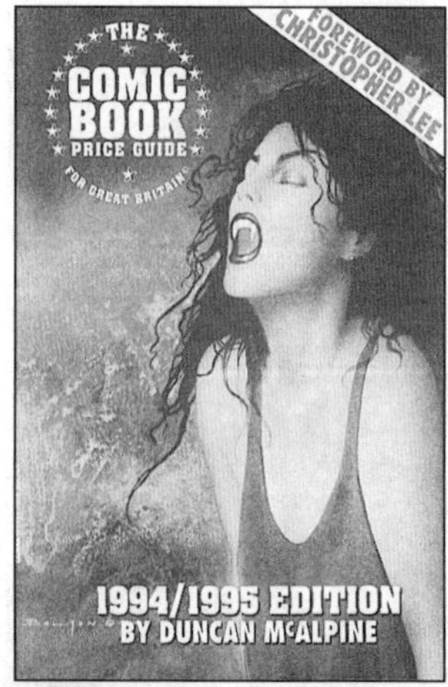

These are by no means hard and fast rules to easy success but they are obvious considerations worth stating here. As such, there is no formal training to be a comics dealer, though a knowledge of financial matters coupled with expertise in a particular field is obviously advantageous.

THE DISTRIBUTION AND SCARCITY OF COMICS

The relative scarcity of certain comics owing to original production factors or distribution patterns are denoted throughout the Guide very carefully. While it is impossible to ascribe actual numbers to the various terms that are used, every effort—through consultation and comparison—has been made to be accurate, though the scarcity and distribution of some issues remains contentious. Below is a list of generally accepted terms in the U.K. market in order of degree of scarcity.

L.D.

LIMITED OR LOW DISTRIBUTION IN THE U.K.

This is a term for the purposes of this book that applies to the U.K. market and should be noted by American dealers and collectors. A good example of **L.D.** would be D.C.'s Crisis on Infinite Earths #1 which had a generally lower than usual distribution around the U.K. and as it didn't turn up in all the newsagents it was a little harder to get in some areas. **L.D.** is a term that generally applies to comics after 1970 or thereabouts.

Please note however that owing to the number of specialist shops throughout the UK and more U.K. dealers bringing back quantities of material from U.S. conventions, the concept of Low Distribution of a comic through all the normal outlets has lost much of its meaning in the last few years. The term **L.D.** is now more often applied to a high-demand item that sells out very quickly, is therefore immediately sought after by fans and collectors and does not often turn up in collections bought by dealers a few months later.

N.D.

NON OR NOT DISTRIBUTED IN THE U.K.

to the usual network of newsagents. These comics are thus harder to obtain than Low Distributed comics. This term is most traditionally applicable to certain 1970s comics. American dealers and collectors will note throughout this book that there are quite a few comics with this **N.D.** accreditation. There have, however, always been **N.D.** comics as far as the U.K. market is concerned, in fluctuating degrees, as prior to the mid 1970s there were no large-scale distributors of comics so an **N.D.** comic then was considerably harder to obtain. More recently, with an increase in the distribution of the **N.D.** issues to the specialist shops, they have become a little easier to obtain so the concept of **NON DISTRIBUTED** has increasingly less meaning but because they are still imported on a comparatively limited basis, generally by air freight or mail order by dealers and collectors, they still remain scarce in the general circulation. An example in the U.K. market would be the run of Amazing Spiderman #121-214 which were not distributed in the U.K at the time of publication in order not to clash with the Marvel U.K reprints of the original U.S. Spiderman stories that began in 1972 (see Mighty World of Marvel and Spiderman Comics Weekly in the British section).

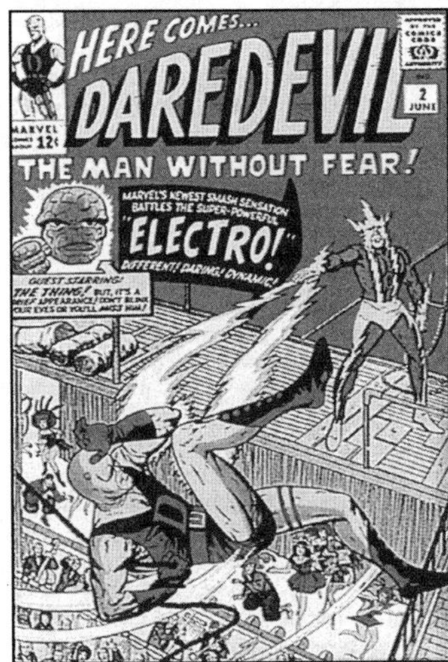

Daredevil #2 – Scare in the U.K.

Strange Tales #130 – Very Scarce in the U.K.

Amazing Spiderman #19 – Rare in the U.K.

SCARCE IN THE U.K.

A TERM GENERALLY APPLIED TO PRE 1970s COMICS

as those being harder to come by than most. Actual numbers of a particular issue are difficult to determine. The problem with applying the term is deciding whether a comic is scarce owing to original circumstances (like missing shipments to the U.K. of American Flagg #19) or to popularity and demand and therefore collectors sitting on copies leaving fewer in circulation. I believe that both reasons make the use of the term valid. It may be noted that the terms **L.D.** and **SCARCE** are virtually inter-changeable as they both mean more or less the same thing. I prefer to use **SCARCE** for older items such as Fantastic Four #51 (i.e. pre 1970) and L.D. for more recent ones such as Fantastic Four #286 (i.e. post 1970) as concerns and awareness of limited distribution and indeed the coining of the term are more recent phenomena. In some instances a comic can, however, be **SCARCE** as well as **N.D.** in the U.K. market and as such may also be called **VERY SCARCE.**

VERY SCARCE IN THE U.K.

HARDER TO OBTAIN THAN SCARCE AND MAY BE VIRTUALLY INTER-CHANGEABLE WITH THE LATER TERM N.D. SCARCE.

Once again the use of the term **VERY SCARCE** would be for older items, that is, pre 1970s comics. An indication of this particular degree comes when back issue collections are bought by shops or dealers and the same recurring numbers of certain titles are missing for one reason or another. Silver Surfer (1st Series) #4 is a good example. Being a thicker issue at 68 pages than a regular comic with a cross-over appearance of Thor and considered a collectible even cult title, Silver Surfer #4 is a comic that is generally deemed VERY SCARCE in the U.K. market. A newer comic that I would rather call N.D. **SCARCE** in the U.K. market would be Captain America King Size Annual #4, not distributed to UK news-agents and scarce even over in America owing perhaps to a production problem or high demand/lower print run at the time.

RARE IN THE U.K.

HARDER STILL TO OBTAIN THAN ANY OF THE ABOVE.

These comics do not often turn up in bought collections in the U.K. and are rarely seen for sale in comics shops or on Mailing lists. Classic examples in the U.K. market would be Avengers #9, Fantastic Four #7, Spiderman #18 and Uncanny X-Men #8. It is a term that, owing to its minimal use, may be applied to older as well as newer comics.

VERY RARE IN THE U.K.

ALMOST IMPOSSIBLE TO OBTAIN AND NOT EVEN SEEN BY THE MAJORITY OF PEOPLE IN ANY CONDITION.

Once again it is a term that may be applied to any comic regardless of its age, so a newer example may be the G.I. Joe Treasury Edition and older examples would be issues of certain esoteric romance or humour titles. In particular it would refer to Golden Age comics, some examples can be counted in tens and twenties on both sides of the Atlantic (see The Top 50 Rarest Section). Certainly as far as very old or very expensive Golden Age material goes, most of it would be classed as rare or very rare in the U.K. Whatever contentions and arguments remain, all the terms from **SCARCE to VERY RARE** must be used with extreme caution in order to preserve their meaning. **THE INDISCRIMINATE AND UNINFORMED USE OF THE TERMS RENDERS THEM WORTHLESS** as it must be remembered that any degrees of scarcity of any comic must take into consideration the picture of the market as a whole and not the local absence of something in any one area.

Journey Into Mystery #109 – Very Rare in the U.K.

Iron Man #67 – ND in the U.K.

Amazing Spiderman #251 – LD in the U.K.

CENTS OR PENCE?

The majority of comics in circulation in the U.K. have cover prices in old (that is pre-1971 decimalization examples like 9d or 10d) or new pence (that is post 1971 decimalization examples like 6p or 15p) either imprinted in the top left or right-hand corners or ink-stamped somewhere on the cover. Comics distributed in America always have their prices in cents. Over the last few years comics set for distribution in the U.K. have both sets of prices. Some collectors prefer to have cents copies of comics as a mark of a kind of purism. Other collectors prefer to have pence copies because that is what they may remember reading as children. Comic dealers in this country generally do not distinguish between the two although in the case of earlier or more sought-after issues cents copies are sought after/valued more. It is in the case of RARE or KEY books that this difference becomes more marked. A genuinely near-mint copy of Amazing Spiderman #1 for example is listed in this guide at £12,000. A near-mint cents copy of the same comic would be valued much more highly. One reason for this is that the American market does not very highly regard pence copies of comics, though this varies tremendously from dealer to dealer. Indeed it has been noticed particularly in the last year that more and more British priced copies of Silver Age material are appearing on American dealers' lists with anything from about a 25% less price tag to actual parity with a presumably cents copy of the same comic.

It would be a fallacy to say that the one comic is inferior to the other. **BOTH ARE ESSENTIALLY EXACTLY THE SAME,** appearing on the same paper printed at the same time on the same machine on the same day. A pence-priced (or black) plate would have been substituted towards the end of the print run of each comic to print up the overseas-market issues for distribution. One cannot be said to be an inferior reprint of the other (for more expansion on this matter, see the article dealing with the differences between the U.K. and U.S. markets to be found further on in this book)

Broadly speaking the question of cents or pence does not matter for the vast majority of comics. It is only really of importance on rare or key issues and even then only on older items and there seems to be a traditional 20–25% difference in price although this is very approximate: as has been already indicated American dealers generally regard pence copies as inferior and will not trade in them or if they do they will offer very low percentages. Whether this situation will change depends on the usual factors of supply and demand. If unrestored, high grade copies of key issues are demanded, where else can American dealers go apart from pence copies if the supply of unrestored cents copies is drying up? Time will tell.

KEY ISSUES

The term **KEY ISSUE** means a comic that features an important event like the first appearance of a character, the origin story of a character or an issue that is historically important as the first of its type. Very often it is the first issue of a character's title. The term originated in America and as such American dealers and collectors have found an almost innumerable number of Keys, particularly in recent years. At times it seems that any excuse is found to make an individual comic that much more valuable, particularly one that was not selling in any great number before! An example would be issues of DC's Omega Men featuring the first appearances of a character called Lobo which for years were consigned to the depths of bargain boxes. The situation is such that the terms "Major Keys" and "Minor Keys" has become prevalent. This Guide's position is that where possible it draws attention to these issues but takes this opportunity to urge caution with any comics that appear to be artificially inflated for no apparent reason. It is difficult to know where to draw the line at calling a comic a "key issue" and how far one should go in paying for a desired item. Once again it is a matter of personal choice. If new to collecting comics it would be wise to seek expert advice.

Those Key issues that have been established as such for some time however may be prized as items of great interest. Showcase #4 as the comic that re-introduced the Golden Age hero The Flash in a new, or Silver Age, incarnation and the first appearances of The Fantastic Four, Spiderman, The Hulk and Thor or even a more modern instance of the first appearance of the new X-Men in Giant Size X-Men #1 for example are all well established Key issues and in top condition are able to command multiples of Guide.

MULTIPLES OF GUIDE

The concept of "multiples of Guide" again originated in America when a particular collection called the Mile High Collection (later renamed, and rightly so, The Edgar Church Collection) came to light in 1977. A collection of 22,000 comics from the late 1930s to the early 1950s was discovered in Denver, Colorado. The overall condition of these comics was of an unprecedented high grade owing to the very favourable storage conditions and the fact that they were all part of the same collection, bought as new and ageing together, gave these comics a unique feel rather than a collection assimilated over the years of varying grades and degrees of deterioration (for more information on this and other pedigree collections, see The Photo-Journal Guide to Comic Books Volume 1 by Ernie Gerber, am excellent and breath-taking set of books). The comics were immediately sold at twice the listed price in the then edition of the American Overstreet Guide. They changed hands over the years at ever spiralling multiples. One American dealer/ collector sold a large number to another at four times Guide across the board, no matter what the comic or condition. In this way the Mile High Collection assumed a certain pedigree. Other notable high grade collections have since been discovered – The San Francisco, The Larsen, The Denver and The Allentown are considered to be the next best in roughly that order and in most cases (but not all) the Key issues such as Detective Comics #27 (featuring the first appearance of Batman) or Batman #1 and Superman #1 etc. have been of the highest order in terms of condition. These collections often come with a certificate of authentication or are easily identifiable by certain characteristics or markings and as such represent some of the best copies available of a particular issue on the world market and as such have excellent investment potential. They are all for the most part Golden Age collections, that is, featuring comics from the Golden Age of comic book heroes from the late 1930s to the late 1940s.

The most significant collection of recent years has been the White Mountain Collection of high

More Fun Comics #59 from the Edgar Church Collection.
Note the detail of "D-7-28" marked in distributor's crayon pencil top left of the cover. Most comics from this collection have variations on this coding and as such this is the identifying mark.

grade Silver Age comics, much of which was sold at a San Diego Comicon. Key issues from this such as Spiderman #1 and Showcase #22 (1st Silver Age Green Lantern) have commanded multiples of Guide prices. A copy of Fantastic Four #1 was recently listed at a staggering $60,000!

What this has meant for the discerning collector has been an increased awareness and valuation of comics that are in unusually nice condition, genuinely Very Fine or Near Mint. While Key issues in pedigree collections may command prices at three and four times the listed Guide price, comics that turn up individually in very high grade may vary as widely in price and as such more and more research is being done for this Guide to draw attention to particular issues. Key issues that are offered in unusually high grade but may not be from a pedigree collection may command prices over and above the listed Guide price (say Guide and a quarter or Guide and a half) though not in the accepted levels of 2 to 5 times Guide that the top pedigree collections can command. Outstanding examples of "multiple if Guide" are seven times Guide for a More Fun #52 (1st appearance of The Spectre) one particular year and more recently eight times Guide for an All Star Comics #8 (1st Wonder Woman).

A very noticeable distinction between the U.K. and U.S. markets is that in the former there is a marked resistance to the concept of multiples of Guide. This has been particularly true in the last couple of years. This point is discussed further in the article on the U.K. and U.S. markets and also under PRICING STRUCTURES.

Having taken all the above into consideration above all else this Guide advises those who are new to the field of collecting comics that it is essential to seek out professional advice before parting with large sums of money.

FAKES AND FORGERIES

Inevitably where vast amounts of money are concerned, the problem of fakes and forgeries come into their own, particularly as the technology for the repair and restoration of comics gains in expertise and capability every year. It is unlikely that Silver and Golden Age forgeries can be created from scratch though there have been instances over the years of File Copies of key issues being created with elaborate stamps and approval ticks and signatures. Much of this is the subject of debate and speculation. Where possible and where known, details are given of forged comics that have appeared such as the counterfeit Cerebus the Aardvark #1 or Teenage Mutant Ninja Turtles #1. No value is given to these comics, as is the case quite rightly so with American guides.

THE REPAIR AND RESTORATION OF COMIC BOOKS

The repair and upgrading of comic books is still in its infancy in the U.K. That is to say that while it is a multi-million dollar industry in America, the full-time professional repair of comic books in the U.K. is unheard of. The healthy market in America for Golden Age comics particularly from 1938-1948 means that there is a demand for repairing and effectively upgrading poorer condition copies of comics, very much more so for origin, first appearance or key issues. Comics purchased for hundreds of dollars and repaired for hundreds could be sold for thousands. This has led to a marked back-lash against restoration from time to time in the U.S. and a definite air of suspicion in the U.K. and certainly on both sides of the Atlantic against unskilled hack-jobs that even detract from the value of the comic in its original if poor condition. There is now a very definite distinction between comics that have been repaired by an amateur (often abbreviated in American catalogues by **rep.**) and those that have been professionally restored (often abbreviated as **rest.**). It is worthwhile for U.K. collectors and dealers for that matter getting hold of American catalogues and listings for examples of grading terminology and indications of restoration.

It is the intention of this Guide to produce in the near future a Restoration Guide for key issues in Heavy, Moderate and Light Restoration. Watch this space!

The more skilled and recognised work of the person who pioneered the restoration of comics Bill Sarrill, and today people like Susan Ciccione, Mark Wilson, Matt Wilson and Jef Hinds are generally held in esteem (as far as this author is concerned anyway). An argument for controlled restoration is that it may enhance and preserve an otherwise deteriorating comic for future appreciation and historical value. For example, if a comic has severe staple rust, should those staples be removed and the paper around that general area be restored to order to prevent further deterioration? An excellent publication that goes into greater depth on the subject is The Grading Guide by Bob Overstreet and is fully recommended by this publication.

All of this is not to say that restored comic books are in any way fakes or counterfeits. It merely depends on the amount of restoration and more importantly that both buyer and seller are fully aware and honest about the extent. It would be fair to say that American collectors are more experienced in recognising and understanding restoration than British collectors are. But British collectors are becoming more aware of the situation as there is more documentation available and there are increasing numbers of British attendees at American conventions. Either way it is important when buying or selling special Gold and Silver Age comics, particularly for those people located in the U.K. market, to be aware of the restoration industry in general and to recognise what to look for.

SOME RESTORATION TERMS

For those unsure what to look for in a repaired or restored comic, these are some of the more common areas:

STAPLE REINFORCEMENT – White Typex-like or transparent glue around the staples, usually on the inside front cover. The cover itself may have a certain stiff feeling when being opened and closed.

COLOUR TOUCHING – Difficult to detect if done by a professional. Look at colour differences in the darker areas of the cover and particularly the spine. If any touch-ups have been done with a felt tip pen, these will show through on the inside of the cover. This Guide very much takes the attitude that if you have a comic with a worn spine or cover creases, **DO NOT USE FELT-TIP PENS!** Leave well alone. You will only make the comic less attractive.

TEAR REPAIR – The closing of tears in covers and pages using paper fibres or glue. Professional tear repair can be almost undetectable to the naked eye. Amateur attempts using glue or tiny pieces of magic tape can usually be easily spotted.

TRIMMING – Where edges have been trimmed to even them up and lessen or hide original Marvel Chipping. This is considered to be a very serious defect and once again this Guide urges that if you have a comic that has even a tiny amount of Marvel chipping, even removing one or two millimetres from any edge of the covers will ultimately detract from that comic. Leave well alone.

DEACIDIFYING – Where browning pages have been lightened or even whitened with chemicals. A slight chemical smell usually gives the game away though techniques have become very sophisticated and some would argue that controlled deacidification can benefit the long term life of a comic. Either way, such restoration should be thoroughly researched by a prospective client and only carried out by a professional. U.K. collectors should talk to people like Bill Cole of Bill Cole Enterprises in America for more information.

BLEACHING – Where covers are lightened to give an almost unnatural white appearance. General

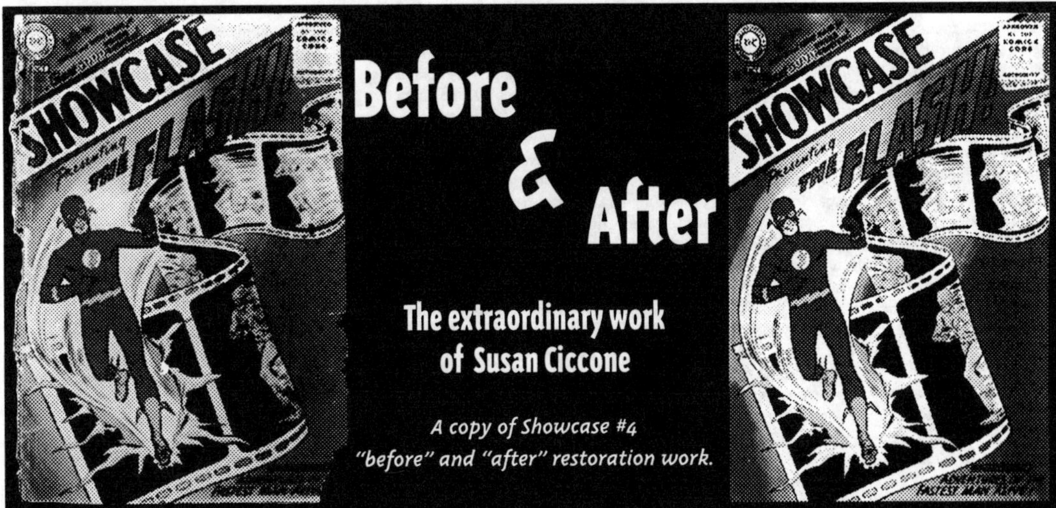

Before & After

The extraordinary work of Susan Ciccone

A copy of Showcase #4 "before" and "after" restoration work.

considered to be more risky and less desirable than deacidifying as bleach physically weakens paper fibres. Again thorough information should be sought before embarking on this course of action.

SPINE REINFORCEMENT – Where there was once a spine- roll and it has been pressed out and weaker paper has had to be reinforced with acrylic and/ or paper often giving a much stiffer feel to the covers. There are arguments for and against such a course of action if a comic is falling apart and deemed worth preserving. Once again, professional advice should be sought.

The number of restored comic books in circulation in the U.K. market is very low so this information is not meant to be alarmist. It simply means that one should exercise caution if buying a key issue for a lot of money. Again one should seek professional advice if one is unsure or unused to spotting restoration. This question of restoration only really applies to Golden and Silver Age comics. There would be little point in spending a fortune on restoring a £10 or $15 copy of X-Men. Thus an informed buyer can buy with confidence and the informed collector or dealer always has the choice of preserving certain comic books if so desired.

This Guide does not encourage amateur restoration using such things as felt tips and glue, magic tape and paper whatsoever. It also fully condemns the practice of restoration carried out for purely financial purposes, a "get rich quick" mentality, and the practice of deliberately ignoring or understating degrees of restoration by both dealers and collectors.

STORAGE OF COMIC BOOKS

Storing and preserving a collection becomes more difficult the larger it becomes but a small amount of care is worthwhile in the long run. Many shops and dealers at marts and conventions sell their new comics and back issues in plastic bags and this is the most simple method of preservation. Plastic bags for all sizes of comics can now be bought, quite cheaply, for all comics from Digest to Treasury. The best type to use is 250 gauge with a one inch flap at the top which provides an almost air-tight seal. THE SEAL SHOULD NOT BE COMPLETELY AIR-TIGHT as this has been known to cause chemical reactions among the inks and acids in comic book pages. A plastic bag will afford good protection from the usual effects of dust, dirt, wear and tear but they should be changed every two or three years as certain polymers can react with the acids, inks and paper. One should avoid the use of freezer bags bought from supermarkets and food stores.

A more ideal solution, and particularly for more valuable comics, is the use of Mylar bags which are chemically inert, stiff, clear plastic sleeves, some with flaps at the top. They are available from certain comic shops and mail order companies and come in three basic sizes for Marvel, DC and Golden Age comic books but they can be prohibitively expensive for collections running into thousands. A lighter and cheaper version called Mylites is available for bulk storage. There are a number of U.K. and U.S. suppliers, some of which can be found advertising in this book. Backing boards can also be used to help store comics but these should be of the acid-free variety and ordinary cardboard should be avoided at all costs. Please note that there are many different types of bags and backing boards available today so it is important to check that they are acid-free if claimed to be so. In the case of backing boards, the board ideally should be double-sided white or of food-board quality that companies like Birds Eye might use to package their food products. Avoid any boards with obvious wood-chips in them as this is commonly called box-board and is not acid-free. Beware putting a comic in a plastic bag and then into a Mylar with a backing board. There are some types of bag which will "crinkle" and give a wavy effect to the cover of the comic when viewed – very annoying when you've bagged hundreds of comics in this way! As ever, professional advice should be sought. Several comic shops sell custom-made comic boxes which are easily transportable, store around 150 bagged comics and can be stacked easily. There are also longer "coffin boxes" which can store up to 300 bagged comics. For the most part both types of boxes are not completely acid-free.

Other alternatives are ring binders with clear plastic sleeves may be used to store more valuable items (which themselves should be in Mylar bags) and bulk collections can be stored in wooden boxes or on wooden shelving units, again avoiding cardboard boxes at all times as the acids in these will react with the paper over a period of time. Ideally comics should be stored vertically in Mylars with acid-free backing boards in wooden or acid-free boxes. They may be stacked individually in horizontal piles but without the stiffness of Mylars or backing boards the top ones will tend to curl over and spine rolls may develop. Comics should also be kept in a dark, cool atmosphere with a reasonable amount of humidity. A dry atmosphere or too much sunlight can turn comics brown and then brittle in a comparatively short space of time. With careful storage comics will keep their freshness and colour for years to come. Careful storage is the key but remember that Mylars and acid-free backing boards are an aid to collecting, not an absolute necessity. Common sense can be just as valuable in the long term (and much cheaper in the short!)

As mentioned above in SOME RESTORATION TERMS, comics can be de-acidified but it is a complex and often expensive business (though Bill Cole Enterprises in America is constantly researching much cheaper and effective methods of de-acidification) that involves soaking the individual pages or hanging each page for spraying with specially prepared solutions. Covers of comics pose a special problem owing to the varied composition of the papers used. SUCH PROCEDURES SHOULD BE LEFT TO EXPERTS.

PRICING STRUCTURES

The question I most often get asked (not unreasonably) if how do you work out the prices? Most of those who ask realise that it is not just a matter of making them up out of the blue or taking last year's book and adding 10 percent (wish it was sometimes!)

As a GUIDE only, all the prices contained herein are necessarily approximations based on observations in comic shops and marts all over the U.K., mail order lists and catalogues from both U.K. and U.S. dealers (many thanks to those who send theirs such as Justin Ebbs of Just Comics and Mike Goldman of Motor City Comics for example), the collective knowledge of a great number of authoritative people who advise me every year and my own experience of well over twenty-five years as a collector.

The process of deciding prices has very much developed into an on-going situation all year round with detailed scrutiny before any publication.

The actual process of pricing is an enormous task, sometimes simple but more often than not complicated with revisions and revisions of revisions. My main man and Assistant Editor John Skoulides and I go through the entire Guide from A to Z and discuss each and every price where possible. Obviously there are some one-shots and titles that just do not change in value year after year. But they still get a glance – it's amazing how a typo can creep in one year or an issue be lost another when it's been quite alright before. The 35 megabytes of data get manipulated around and transferred from machine to machine so many times and moved back and forth in the typesetting so often that it's inevitable one record or segment of a record is altered or lost. Necessarily there are other titles that need hours of discussion and it has not been unknown to spend a ludicrous amount of time discussing one issue! (Incredible Hulk #1 or Giant Size X-Men #1 are good examples of heated debate). After an eight hour session with both our machines side by side, many packets of biscuits consumed and far too many cups of tea, we both feel like never doing another Price Guide ever again. But then we arrange to meet again on Tuesday and do it all over again on another small section...

Our ambition is to have a regular Board of Advisors both from the U.K and U.S. and regular questionnaires to have maximum dealer and collector involvement in putting together an annual U.K. Price Guide. All this takes time and money and probably a larger set up than just we two. It is hoped with Titan Books taking over the packaging and administration of this book, more time can be spent on research and true national input.

The rationale behind pricing is a little more complex than the process itself. We are helped enormously by the decision to print prices in both pounds and dollars. We can see immediately the context of every issue which is exactly what a Guide is all about – context and thereby a rough guide to values.

There is no doubt in our minds that prices for Golden Age material in the U.K. are dictated by the American market. The Overstreet Price Guide has been long established and the market for Golden Age comics in the U.S. seems to be as healthy as it's always been. The market in the U.K. is quite small (and is possibly growing smaller?) as every year more and more Golden Age comics go up in value and thus in the higher grades out of most people's price ranges. If a British collector wants to purchase a Golden Age comic and more precisely a high grade key or pedigree issue, then they will probably have to pay American market rates plus a bit more. For the purposes of this book, we have used our judgement to estimate current American market values based on as many written, verbal and professional sources at our disposal and arrived by conversion at a British value. Whether comics would actually sell at these values and indeed sell on a regular basis is another matter, another book. But it is a starting point. A Guide price.

Some would argue that it should be more difficult to buy Golden Age comic in the U.K. than in the U.S and by and large that is probably true. Does it therefore follow that the British value of most Golden Age comics should be that much more than the American market value owing to factors of rarity, popularity and availability? The answer again is probably yes but one must also take into account the size of the market for Golden Age comics in the U.K., of a size that may negate the rarity/ popularity/ availability factor. The old adage of a comic's value being that which someone is prepared to pay for it comes very much into play. Thus this book's very general rationale for Golden Age material is a reasonable parity of prices with some of the more straightforward titles and issues, a lesser U.K. value after dollar/pound conversion on some of the more lesser titles and issues and a greater U.K. value on some of the most popular titles and issues after conversion (all the above assumes exact parity in grading which is another question entirely and yet another book!). Within these very general parameters there are going to be exceptions owing to character and creator considerations.

The same sort of rationale is used for Silver Age comics up to official distribution in the U.K. from the November 1959 cover date. Thereafter the question of cents priced U.S. copies and pence priced U.K.

copies of the same comic come into play. For many collectors in the U.K. the cents/pence distinction as we have already stated does not matter. But for some it does. And particularly for American dealers and collectors considering British pence priced copies. And particularly on key issues.

Our rationale changes with comics in the 70s where so many Marvels were officially Not Distributed in the U.K. at the time. Or with how War and Romance comics are generally valued in the U.K. as opposed to the U.S. Or how "hot book" trends may happen in the U.S. first, peak higher and faster there than in the U.K. or how the trend may last longer in the U.K. than in the U.S.

Our rationale therefore has to be flexible from decade to decade, trend to trend, title to title, comic to comic. It may be noticed throughout this book that in our judgement, some British pound values are over a converted American dollar prices when there are factors of popularity and/or rarity. On the other hand there are many instances of the British pound price being half the converted American dollar price and sometimes even less than that! These cases have been judged individually and can be found by studying the prices carefully. The overall conclusion that this book has come to is that at present American market values are generally higher across the board than British market values and that in the last year a great number of Silver Age values have fallen in the U.K., particularly in the Good and Fine grades.

It may be noticed that many of the ratios between Good, Fine and Near Mint have changed (anything from a 1:3:5 right up to a 1:3:17). Each one has been judged individually and they will keep altering and evolving as we observe the general prices between lower and higher grades. The overall effect of our ratio changes is that prices on Good and Fine material in the U.K. market have remained largely static since the last U.K. price guide whilst the values on Near Mint material have risen. We will have to monitor the situation to see if this trend continues.

The most complex part of pricing rationale but often the most enjoyable is discussing and establishing relationships between characters, issues and titles. For example, there is a year on year relationship between Flash, Green Lantern and Justice League of America from DC Comics where generally speaking, one title traditionally sells better in back-issue terms than another in the U.K. A character like the Hobgoblin may be more highly valued for a time and for whatever reason in the U.S. than in the U.K. or issues like the Silver Surfer Moebius series may be valued more highly in the U.K. than in the U.S. as it seems to be much harder to find in shops and collections in the U.K.

It is for these reasons, and many more besides, that we feel our Price Guide for American Comic Books should have prices in both pounds and dollars. We welcome any correspondence on the subject at the editorial address.

There are obviously design considerations when dealing with so many more figures and we have tried to make the book as clear and user-friendly as possible. Again we welcome any comments on the subject.

THE BRITISH SECTION

The British section is compiled by Mr. Steve Holland, as has already been noted. The production process requires many telephone calls as he sends me a disk/printout which then passes back and forth as I amend from my own collection and collecting experiences. Steve himself calls upon a large number of people at his end. It is hoped to restrict the British section in future Guides to TV, film and sci-fi/comics related material and to list everything in a more comprehensive stand alone British Comics Guide. This process has already started and will continue.

It must be noted that collectors of British comics do not use precisely the same system of grading as used for American material and few British comics of any significant age survive in exceptionally high grade. In view of this, British comics' collectors tend to use a hybrid of terms that are used for books and paperbacks as well as American comics. For further information, see the introduction to the British section. For the purposes

Showcase # 94 – price ratio 1:3:6

Showcase # 50 – price ratio 1:3:7

Showcase # 3 – price ratio 1:3:8

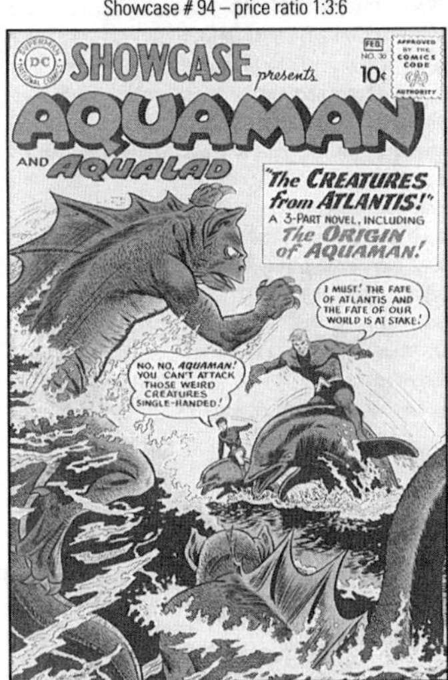

Showcase # 30 – price ratio 1:3:9

Showcase # 1 – price ratio 1:3:10

Showcase # 8 – price ratio 1:3:16

of this book, a single Near Mint price in pounds sterling is listed and a percentage chart can be used to work out prices on lower grades. On some of the more well known titles like Dandy and Beano, an attempt has been made to show a Good and Fine price as copies that come onto the U.K. market are in these low or mid grades. We hope in future Guides to show many more titles with values in three grades and, where applicable, values in dollars as well.

AN INTRODUCTION TO GRADING

The most difficult, contentious and eternally frustrating aspect of comic-book collecting is grading. For collector and dealer alike it is essential to grade the condition of a comic book fairly and accurately in order to determine its true value and worth. As the collecting trend in today's market seems to be more and more discerning as fandom becomes more and more knowledgeable, accuracy on the higher grades becomes even more essential.

As grading is very much a subjective exercise it is all too easy for the novice (and indeed the experienced collector) to allow wishful thinking and optimism to influence the appearance of a comic book and make it better than it really is. One man's idea of Mint may be very different from another's! The stricter and harder one becomes, even to the point of under-grading, the more secure one can feel in selling comics and the happier one can be in collecting. It is worth re-evaluating one's grading criteria from time to time in order to become the more expert. Accurate and consistent grading only comes with experience. One exercise the novice may undertake could be to take a comic from each of the recognised grades and lay them side by side in order to appreciate more fully and put into perspective the varying degrees of wear and tear.

THE PROCESS OF GRADING

1) Open the comic and grade from the inside out. Lie it on a flat surface or hold it in the cup of the hand. Do not bend back or flatten out. Check the centrefold is there and attached by both staples. Check for missing pages, panels or coupons cut, tears in pages, writing or stains. Check outer edges of pages for browning/brittleness. One may check the comic smell for signs of dampness or acidity.
2) Check inside front and back covers, particularly turning the cover to see how it strains against the staples and may have torn. Older comics in particular often have staples slightly out of line. They also tended not to use stainless steel staples so rust is more prevalent. Check for unusual whiteness as against the page colour which may indicate cover-bleaching and stain removal. Check for any staple reinforcement.
3) Check back cover for tears and/or pieces out. Check wear or any soiling along the spine.
4) Check front cover. This is the most important part of the comic as it is most seen when displayed and liable to the most wear. The areas of most common wear are around the staples and at the corners. Check for any cracks of chipping along the right hand edge. Hold it up to the light and check for cover gloss and any indentations. Check dark blue/black areas for any signs of colour touch-up.
5) Finally assess the overall appearance of the comic, checking for tightness and squareness of trim. Many comics were off-cut or had off-centre staples where the cover art wraps a little round to the back cover. Eye appeal is what can often influence initial grading but is also vitally important as a final assessment.

These steps should be adhered to generally to treat all comics with respect but need only be exhaustively followed on more important items.

If one feels that grading is important or not, above all read and enjoy.

GRADING FOR BEGINNERS

Having been through the process of examining your comic book, the hard part comes with arriving at an accurate grade. Every comic has an accurate grade which can be arrived at by asking the right questions. As a beginner you might find yourself being a little vague and saying "It's about VG or a Fine/NM copy". Spot-on grading only comes with practice. If you are just starting out it is worth getting these approximations in your head to give an overall picture:

MINT	Perfect
NEAR MINT	Nearly perfect
VERY FINE	Very nice condition
FINE	Above average
VERY GOOD	Average
GOOD	Below average
FAIR	Well worn
POOR.	Very tatty

Practising with a stack of comics and sorting them out into these eight different piles is a very useful exercise and one that experts should do from time to time.

THE GRADING DEFINITIONS

Having got used to rough approximations, the next step is exact definition. The accepted grades of condition for comic books and their fuller definitions are as follows:

MINT (M)

Perfect and as new, REGARDLESS OF AGE, with full cover gloss and lustre and white, crisp pages. No printing or cutting defects, off-centre covers or staples. No marks on the cover whatsoever, not even an official distributors stamp, even if it is neatly done (note: American Guides seem to allow this - why?)

As with coins or stamps, MINT really means uncirculated or untouched and as such the only MINT comics would be those kept on file at the various comic companies (and not all of these are untouched - quite the reverse!) or those comics issued in plastic bags and unopened. Either way a comic would have to be in quite spectacular condition to qualify for this grade. Even new comics on the rack at news-stands or comic shops are not necessarily Mint. They have been handled, transported, stacked and handled again even before they reach the shelves. Please note that there is no such grade as NEAR MINT/MINT or MINT MINUS. A comic is either mint or it isn't. The true rarity of this grade cannot be emphasised enough.

PERMISSIBLE FAULTS: *None*

NEAR MINT (NM)

Almost perfect and as new. White pages. Tight, flat and clean with only extremely light stress marks at a staple or staples or the smallest of creases at a corner or on the spine. No marks on cover except perhaps an official distributors stamp or mark in pencil and even then very neatly done. Please note that this is still an extremely high and very scarce grade.

PERMISSIBLE FAULTS: *You have to look very carefully and even then there should be no more than one, perhaps two very minor defects. Among the most common are:*

Extremely light stress around the staples.
The smallest corner crease.

NOT PERMISSIBLE FAULTS:

Any page discolouration
Anything missing
Anything added
Any degree of spine roll
Any writing anywhere apart from very neat arrival date (preferably in pencil)

Even within these strict confines, a spectacular copy may be referred to as a NM+ (a NM++ is taking things a bit far) and a comic that is very nice but just not quite up to being a Near Mint may be referred to as a Near Mint- (similarly NM-- stretches the point beyond being a useful grading term).

VERY FINE (VF OR VFN)

Very slight wear beginning to show owing to an accumulation of very minor defects. This is a comic that has been read carefully a few times and stored away with due care and attention. Most of the cover lustre remaining and still clean, flat and tight with only the tiniest spine wear or perhaps nick at top and bottom. No major cover marks or creases. A light crease up to about half an inch. Pages may be off-white but in no way yellowing or beginning to brown. Very Fine means a copy with excellent eye appeal.

PERMISSIBLE FAULTS: *Minimal wear is apparent at first sight. One or two very minor faults are allowed. Some of the most common permissible defects are:*

A light cover crease up to about half an inch
Off white pages
Slight staple discolouration (but no rust)
One or two corners with slight rounding
Some minimal cover surface wear

NOT PERMISSIBLE FAULTS:

Yellowing pages or any worse than that
Staple rust
Any writing apart from neat arrival date or some other such small neat initial/figure
Anything missing apart from a slight nick in the spine top or bottom
Spine roll although "white spine" where the comic is still absolutely flat but the printing process has wrapped the cover around so that a slight edge of the cover illustration shows on the right edge of the back cover or a white edge has wrapped around from the back cover to show on the left edge of the front cover

Within these quite strict confines, a nice looking comic may be referred to as a VFN+ and one that is quite sharp but may have a noticeable defect that starts to offend the eye may be referred to as a VFN-.

FINE (FN)

The basic minimum for most collectors, a comic with wear showing on edges, slight spine creases or stress around the staples. Still clean and flat with no major marks major or writing on cover or inside. Some cover gloss or lustre remaining. Pages may be yellowing slightly but not browning or brown edges. Above-average, read quite a few times and stored away with some concern though not necessarily in ideal conditions. This is the most widely used (and abused) grade.

PERMISSIBLE FAULTS: *No major defects but an accumulation of a few minor defects instantly apparent. Some of the permissible faults are:*

A couple of cover creases or one or up to an inch or so
Some small spine creases
Pages may have a yellow tinge to them but in no way tanning
Small neat writing or name
Staple discolouration but not rusty
Tiniest piece or chip may be out of a page or the cover
Slightest spine roll
Slight corner knock or impact

NOT PERMISSIBLE FAULTS:

Heavy creases
Any tanning of pages or worse
Very noticeable writing
Coupon or puzzle completing
Staple rust
Piece out of page or cover bigger than a chip
Anything other than the slightest spine roll
Any water mark/ripple/damage
Anything other than a slight stain either to the cover or inside
Big corner crunch or book crease
No tape of any description or size

There is obviously a lot more room for manoeuvre in this grade than with any of the above as far as combinations of minor defects goes, but the overall eye appeal of the comic must be above average with a good amount of gloss or lustre left on the cover

VERY GOOD (VG)

An average, second-hand, obviously read copy with marks and minor defects. Printing lustre almost gone but not soiled or stained. Worn along spine with possible spine-roll or slightly loose staples. Pages may be yellowing with signs of browning around the edges. The cover could have minor tear or crease or there could be a loose centre-fold. NO PAGES OR PARTS MISSING. No coupons or panels cut

PERMISSIBLE FAULTS: *An average used comic which many collectors regard as the bare minimum as nothing major is actually missing. An accumulation of defects, one or two moderate. Some accepted defects in this grade are:*

Moderate cover creasing
Tanning or slightly browning pages
Some cover writing but not scribble
Rust spots on staple
Cover detached from one staple
Small piece out of page or cover, fingernail sized
Moderate spine roll
Water stain but not rippling
Corner crunch or small book crease
Small tape repair evident
Some tape removal evident
Coupon or small puzzle completed
Centrefold loose

NOT PERMISSIBLE FAULTS:

Heavy cover creasing
Brown pages
Cover or interior scribble, especially with a felt tip
Rusty staples
Cover detached
Any piece out bigger than a fingernail size
Heavy spine roll
Water rippling or water damage
Heavy book crease
Moderate tape evident
Major tape removal
Major amateur colouring in
Centrefold missing, panels or coupons cut

GOOD (G)

A well read copy with minor tears or splits, soiled and marked, rolled spine and creases. Tape repairs to the staples or spine but STILL COMPLETE and acceptable. Collectible mostly as a reading copy only. Please note that this grade is very misleading – "good" is basically a very low grade. Please also note that it is the condition in which the large majority of 50s and 60s collections that come out of attic rooms and old boxes. They would not have been consciously stored away in plastic bags and the damper climate of some areas in the U.K. and indeed the U.S. generally often results in rusty staples and a damp, musty smell to the comic and very often browning pages.

PERMISSIBLE FAULTS: *An accumulation of defects, one or two quite major ones. Some of the accepted defects in this grade are*

Generally heavy creasing
Browning (but not brittle) pages
General writing (but not heavy scribble or graffiti)
Rusty staples (but not staining the immediate paper area)
Piece out of cover or page about thumb-nail size
Heavy spine roll
Light water rippling (but not damage)
Subscription crease
Moderate tape evident
Major tape removal (but only leaving stain, no tears or print removed)

NOT PERMISSIBLE FAULTS: *Panels or coupons cut*
Anything worse than the above lists of faults

It must be stressed again that while a Good comic may have lots of faults and one or two quite major, there is NOTHING SUBSTANTIAL MISSING. The pages may even be quite discoloured and may have lost their suppleness but in no way are they brittle.

FAIR (F) OR FAIRLY GOOD (FG)

Very worn and soiled with possible small chunks out of spine or cover. Some tears and heavy creases and marks or writing on cover/inside. A couple of extra staples as cover was detached at some time. No pages out but a panel and/or a coupon may be out or clipped. The pages are brown and bordering on the brittle.

NOT PERMISSIBLE FAULTS:

Brittleness
Page(s) out
Coverless
Lots of extra staples
Heavy brown tape

This grade of comic is basically a mess and is only really collectible as a rare item because no better one exists or as a filler to complete a run until something better comes along which shouldn't be too hard.

POOR (P)

Well damaged and heavily soiled. Not collectible unless it is something very rare or very special. Very worn, torn, brittle, water-damaged, heavily brown-taped spine, absolute mess and may be incomplete – watch out for coupons cut out or pin-up pages missing, no centrefold or no back cover.

Please note that A MISSING PAGE IS A VERY SERIOUS DEFECT, PARTICULARLY A STORY PAGE AND EVEN IF THE REST OF THE COMIC APPEARS TO BE ANYTHING FROM NEAR MINT DOWNWARDS, THIS DEFECT DEVALUES IT DRASTICALLY.

COVERLESS(C)

These turn up regularly, particularly as older comics but they have little value beyond reading copies, even if the interior is white and clean which it usually isn't. Only collectible as extremely rare or old curiosity items or research material. Having said that some people love them. Having a coverless Batman #1 in your collection may be the only way you'll ever afford one. It's great for pure reading value. While it is difficult to ascribe a universally held valuation formula, they may be offered at about one quarter to one sixth of the good price.

With the advances in restoration, coverless copies do have an added attraction in that it is sometimes possible to match up covers and coverless copies. I remember an advert where the covers of Batman #1 were advertised for $500 and that was some time ago.

PERCENTAGE CHART

For quick calculation of values other than the GOOD:FINE: NEAR MINT columns in this book, a percentage chart is offered for use. Percentage charts have been used by dealers for years and recently made more public by the work people like Gary Ochiltree (Board Member) of Krypton Komics in the U.K. in particular.

This is only a rough guide to the percentage breakdowns between the main grades so that Poors, Fairs and in-between plus and minus grades may be calculated.

PLEASE NOTE THAT PARTICULARLY IN GRADING RARE OR KEY ISSUES, PLUS AND MINUS SIGNS ALONG WITH THE GRADES IS ACCEPTABLE as it may more closely define that grade as being a Very Fine- copy or a Fine+ and these have been built into this chart. Obviously the difference is minimal but enough to make a difference to the experienced eye and more particularly when there are large sums of money involved. There is no such thing (in my opinion) as Very Fine++ or any other such excesses. POOR and FAIR are not usually given the distinction of being either plus or minus. It would be absurd to distinguish between a Poor+ and a Fair-, even on the most expensive and sought after comics.

The established top grade for the purpose of Guide values is Near Mint or a figure of 100% from which the other grades can be calculated.

GRADE	Percentage of Near Mint Guide Price
MINT	120-200%+
NEAR MINT+	110%
NEAR MINT	100%
NEAR MINT-	90%
VERY FINE+	80%
VERY FINE	75%
VERY FINE-	70%
FINE+	65%
FINE	60%
FINE-	50%
VERY GOOD+	40%
VERY GOOD	35%
VERY GOOD-	30%
GOOD+	25%
GOOD	20%
GOOD-	15%
FAIR	10%
POOR	5%
COVERLESS	3.75%

FOR CENTS COPIES OF LONG-ESTABLISHED KEY ISSUES ADD 20-25% ONLY IF IN VERY HIGH GRADE (VF+ or better) (and see Multiples of Guide section).

This is a ROUGH GUIDE only and allows only for working with newer comics (in a ratio of 1:3:5) published for the most part from 1980 or so onwards. As many collectors and most new collectors nowadays concentrate on these comics, particularly at the beginning of their collecting, it is a useful chart with which to practice.

Other percentages charts for other ratios would need to be calculated if exact figures are needed. For example, comics in a 1:3:9 ratio would have Poor as 2.5% of Near Mint, not 5%.

Rather than write out all percentage charts for all ratios used in this book and beyond (a 1:3:20 ratio can't be far way), one may use The Hundred Scale which is favoured by many collectors and dealers, particularly in America. The very rough percentages can be used as follows for all comic books generally:

MINT =	100%
NEAR MINT (inc. +/-) =	90–99%
VERY FINE (inc. +/-) =	75–89%
FINE (inc. +/-) =	55–74%
VERY GOOD (inc. +/-) =	35–54%
GOOD (inc. +/-) =	15–34%
FAIR =	5–14%
POOR =	1–4%

While these percentages are useful for rough calculations, on major issues where considerable sums are involved, differences of hundreds and even thousands of pounds or dollars could result from approximation. This Guide would advise accuracy and that means working out the ratio and calculating the exact percentage for the exact grade accordingly.

DEFECTS CHART

This is more difficult to quantify as the whole area of grading is at best subjective and can vary tremendously with the type, number and cumulative effect of the various defects common to most comics.

As a ROUGH GUIDE (with thanks to David Hern of Wonderworld for pioneering work) the following twelve tables demonstrate the most common areas of defect that a comic is likely to have and the varying degrees of that defect and how those degrees account for a final grade.

A drop of a FULL GRADE would be from say VERY FINE to FINE+.

A drop of a half a grade would be from say VERY FINE- to FINE+.

1 PAGE COLOUR	PENALTY	GRADE
White	–	NM
Off White	6	NM-
Cream	16	VF+
Slight Yellowing	28	VF-
Yellowing and/or Shaded Edges	33	FN+
Light Tan and /or Darker Edges	38	FN
Light Brown and/or Brown Edges	56	VG+
Generally Brown	63	VG
Very Brown	78	G
Brittle	88	FR
Very Brittle	93	PR

e.g A brittle comic should not be graded more than FAIR even if it appears NM at first glance.

2 SPINE WEAR	PENALTY	GRADE
None	–	NM
1/2 Tiny Creases	16	VF+
Very Light Wear/Creases	28	VF-
Medium Wear/Creases	38	FN
Heavy Wear/Creases	63	VG
Very Slight Spine Roll	28	VF-
Spine Roll	38	FN
Heavy Spine Roll	63	VG
Tiny Spine Tear Top and/or Bottom	23	VF
Spine Split Top and/or Bottom	38	FN
Half Spine Split	63	VG
Major Spine Split	78	G

e.g. A comic with a heavy spine roll should not be graded more than a VG even if otherwise perfect.

NM (100)
NM- (90-99)
VF+ (80-89)
VF (75-79)
VF- (70-74)
FN+ (65-69)
FN (60-64)
FN- (50-59)
VG+ (40-49)
VG (35-39)
VG- (30-34)
G+ (25-29)
G (20-24)
G- (15-19)
FR (10-14)
PR (5-9)
PR and/or COVERLESS (1-4) (and any minus values)

3 TEAR(S) COVER(S)/INTERIOR	PENALTY	GRADE
No tears	–	NM
Tiny Tear – no more than 2mm	6	NM-
Small Tear(s) – totalling 3-10mm	28	VF-
Tear(s) – totalling 11-20mm	33	FN+
Larger Tear(s) – totalling 21-30mm	46	FN-
Major Tear(s) – totalling 31-50mm	63	VG
Torn generally – Covers	78	G
Torn generally – Covers and Interior	88	FR
Ripped through Comic	93	PR

e.g. A comic even with two small tears anywhere and no more than 10mm each should not grade above VF-

4 PIECES MISSING COVER/INTERIOR	PENALTY	GRADE
Nothing Missing	–	NM
Tiny Chip – but less than 2mm square	23	VF
Small Chip – 3-5 mm square	23	VF
Chip – 6-9 mm square	28	VF-
Half Thumbnail Size – 10x10 mm	33	FN+
Thumbnail Size – 20x20 mm	38	FN
Chunk from Cover/Coupon Clipped	63	VG
Ad Page/Pin Up Page Missing	88	FR
Story Page/Back Cover Missing	93	PR
Covers Missing	98	Coverless!
Marvel Chipping – 1 edge	38	FN
Heavy Marvel Chipping – 2/3 Edges	63	VG

e.g. A comic with a coupon or panel cut out should grade no more than a VG even if otherwise perfect.

5 COVER(S) DEFECTS – GENERAL	PENALTY	GRADE
Unmarked	–	NM
Small Writing – Neat up to 5x20 mm - Cover/Interior	28	VF-
Larger Writing – Neat up to 5x50 mm - Cover Interior	46	FN-
Some Scrawl: Felt Tip/Marker Pen	63	VG
Major Scrawl: Felt Tip/Marker Pen	78	G
Stain - less than 10 mm diameter	28	VF-
Stain – 11-50 mm diameter	38	FN
Stain – more than 50mm diameter	63+	VG or less
Non-Removable Sticky Label	23	VF
Label Stain/Discolouration	28	VF-
Foxing – Light	28	VF-
Foxing – Heavy	46	FN-

6 STAPLE DEFECTS	PENALTY	GRADE
Perfectly Centred/New Staples	–	NM
One Staple Missing	16	VF+
One Staple Detached	28	VF-
Both Staples Detached/Loose Cover	63	VG
Light Rust on Staple(s)	38	FN
Rust/Rust Stain Spine/Interior	63	VG
Heavy Rust/Staining	78	G
Staples Off-centre from Spine – 2 mm into Back or Front Cover	23	VF
Re-stapled correctly	28	VF-
Re-stapled incorrectly	38	FN
Extra Staples in Spine	46	FN-
Extra Staples through Spine	68	VG-

7 COVER CREASE(S)

	PENALTY	GRADE
No Crease(s)	–	NM
Tiny Crease(s) – totalling 10 mm or less	6	NM-
Light Crease(s) – totalling 11-20 mm	23	VF
Crease(s) – totalling 21-50 mm	33	FN+
Heavier Crease(s) – totalling 51-100mm	38	FN
General Crease(s) – 101-249 mm	46	FN-
Subscription Crease (250 mm) – unflattened	56	VG+
Heavy Subscription Crease – flattened	68	VG-
Subscription Crease – unflattened	78	G
Heavy Subscription Crease – unflattened	93	PR

e.g. A comic with a subscription crease, even if flattened out affects the whole comic no more than VG+

8 COVER COLOURS/GLOSS

	PENALTY	GRADE
Full Colour/Full Gloss	–	NM
Most Gloss Remaining (75%)	6	NM-
Half Gloss Remaining (50%)	28	VF-
Some Gloss Remaining (25%)	33	FN+
Gloss Obviously Gone (particularly early 1960s)	46	FN-
Slightly Fading Colours (sun damage)	28	VF-
Fading Colours (sun damage)	38	FN
Extreme Fading Colours	63	VG
Colour Flakes Off at Staple	23	VF
Colour Flakes Off along Spine	28	VF-
Cover Re-glossed – Professionally	38	FN
Cover Bleached – Professionally	38	FN

e.g. If a comic has a very faded cover, it should not grade above a VG. Sun damage causes brittleness.

NM	NM-	VF+	VF	VF-	FN+	FN	FN-	VG+	VG	VG-	G+	G	G-	FR	PR	PRand/or COVERLESS
(100)	(90-99)	(80-89)	(75-79)	(70-74)	(65-69)	(60-64)	(50-59)	(40-49)	(35-39)	(30-34)	(25-29)	(20-24)	(15-19)	(10-14)	(5-9)	(1-4) (and any minus values)

9 TAPE DEFECTS

	PENALTY	GRADE
No Tape	–	NM
Tiny Piece – 10 mm or less	28	VF-
Small Piece – 11 to 50 mm	38	FN
Larger Piece – 51 to 100 mm	56	VG+
Taped Spine – Scotch or Magic Tape	73	G+
Taped Spine – Sellotape	83	G-
Taped Spine + Edges Cover	88	FR
Taped Spine + Edges Yellowed/Brown	93	PR
Tiny Patch Torn Off by Tape	46	FN-
Patch Torn Off by Tape	63	VG
Large Patch Torn Off by Tape	88	FR
Glue Patch After Tape Removal	38	FN

e.g. A comic with a part taped spine (say 100 mm) should not grade more than a VG+ at best

10 MISCELLANEOUS DEFECTS

	PENALTY	GRADE
Edge with Ink Spots (Usually red or blue)	28	VF-
Ink Staining along one edge	33	FN+
Heavy Ink Staining/Onto Cover	46	FN-
Slightly Trimmed Edge – usually top	63	VG
Heavily Trimmed Edges	88	FR
Slight Water Mark	33	FN+
Water Stain (Brown-edged)	46	FN-
Water Soak (slightly crinkled)	68	VG-
Water Soaked (rippled)	88	FR
Sun/Dust Shadow Cover(s) – slight	28	VF-
Sun/Dust Shadow Cover(s) – medium	38	FN
Sun/Dust Shadow Cover(s) – heavy	68	VG-

e.g. A comic with its edges trimmed, usually to hide severe chipping, affects the whole comic no better than FAIR. Some Golden Age are trimmed by 5 mm.

11 MISCELLANEOUS DEFECTS (2)

	PENALTY	GRADE
Rubber Stamp – ink smudged	23	VF
Popular Book Centre Stamp	28	VF-
Popular Book Centre Stamps	46	FN-
Cover Off Centre ("white spine")	23	VF
Centre Fold Missing	93	PR
Slight Drawing/Colouring In	46	FN-
Drawing/Colouring In on figures etc	68	VG-
Much Drawing and Graffiti	83	G-
Spine Glue Stain – tape removed	56	VG+
General Indentations – held up to the light	46	FN-
General Soiling/Dirt – usually worst on back cover	46	FN-

12 RESTORATION (see Section)

	PENALTY	GRADE
Restored to appear NM (Professional)	Assume 1/2 grade less	NM-
Restored to appear VF (Professional)	"	VF-
Restored to appear FN (Professional)	Assume 1 grade less	VG+
Restored to appear VG (Professional)	"	G+
Amateur Repair – felt tip colour touch	46 or +	FN- or less
Amateur Repair – tear mending	46 or +	FN- or less
Amateur Repair – trimming	63 or +	VG or less
Amateur Repair – re-stapling	28 or +	VF- or less
Amateur Repair – tape removal	46 or +	FN-orless
Amateur Repair - different back cover	78 or +	G- or less
Amateur Repair - pages from different comics	78 or +	G or less

The problem with any grading assessment whether using charts or not is the cumulative effects of the problem areas on a comic. It is easier to grade a comic with minimal damage (say a tiny crease at one corner making a Near Mint comic a Near Mint Minus) than a comic with multiple wounds (is a spine rolled comic with white pages and a tiny piece of tape inside, better or worse than a comic with a light subscription crease, very white pages and a small piece out of the back cover?)

It is suggested that the tables may be reasonably used thus:

IF A COMIC HAS ONLY ONE NOTICEABLE DEFECT:
Find the degree of that defect and read across the page to find the grade.(e.g. if there is only a tiny chip = deduct 6 points = NM-)

IF THE COMIC HAS TWO OR THREE MINOR DEFECTS:
Add up the penalties and refer to the middle column and read off the grade there.(e.g. the comic has off white pages and a slight spine roll which means 6 + 28 = 34 deducted from 100 = 66 = FN+)

IF THE COMIC HAS MULTIPLE DEFECTS:
Take the one most serious penalty and read across the page to find the grade.(e.g. the comic is brittle with light rust on the staples and small tears and large writing. Penalties are 88 + 38 + 28 + 46 = 200. A brittle penalty makes it no better than a FAIR to start with and the other defects would probably push it into the POOR category therefore.)

THESE TABLES MAY BE USED PURELY FOR PRACTISING AND RECOGNISING THE NUMBER OF FAULTS A COMIC MAY HAVE, THEIR RELATIVE SEVERITY AND HOW THAT AFFECTS THE OVERALL FINAL GRADE. DON'T WORRY TOO MUCH IF YOU END UP WITH HUGE MINUS NUMBERS AND THEREFORE NO GRADE TO READ OFF. AT LEAST PRACTICE IN GRADING IS BEING ACQUIRED.

Once an assessment of the defect (if any) and thus grade has been made, then by using this book sensibly, a true Price Guide price or Price Guide value may be arrived at.

These are by no means hard and fast rules but do give some idea of the relative degrees of seriousness of damage that a comic may suffer over the years and the complexity that grading has reached now that there are comics in the hundreds of thousands of pounds and dollars. These charts are meant not just for the benefit of dealers new and old but also for fans and collectors.

Remember that it is the whole book that needs to be graded and not just the front cover. More and more attention is being paid to the interior whiteness and freshness of comic books. It also it cannot be stressed enough that MINT MEANS MINT, REGARDLESS OF AGE. New comics bought at shops or the newsagents are not necessarily mint. Older comics should not be more lightly graded because of the fact that they are simply older no matter how tempting it may be. Thus an Action Comics #1 **should** be graded as one would an Action Comics #701. The scarcity of an old or rare comic is reflected in its value or price. At the end of the day a comic is only really worth what someone is prepared to pay for it and as such any formal prices are merely arbitrary. Guide prices serve to be just that: a guide to pricing and valuing a comic once the conditions of the certain recognised grades have been examined.

Some last grading points to remember as stressed in the above tables:

1) The term Pristine Mint occasionally arises and seems more popular in America than in the U.K. This would mean something that is unusually mint and could only really apply to a file copy that has hardly if ever been opened. As such comics of this sort hardly ever appear on the market and I would tend to disregard this grade.
2) Comics that appear to be of a high grade but have very brown or brittle pages should not be graded above fair. A comic is brittle if flakes of paper fall easily from it or if a corner can be folded over and it comes away with little or no effort. See the section on the storage of comic books.
3) A comic that has at one time been water-soaked (usually owing to being brought across on a ship as ballast) cannot be graded above fair condition, possibly very good minus if the damage is very slight.
4) Subscription copies (where a comic has been folded lengthways for mailing) should be noted even though after a period of time they may have been flattened out.
5) Finally, a comic should only be graded after careful consideration of the whole book, not just at first glance. Ideally, a second opinion should be sought on rare or important issues.

Superboy # 49 –
an example of FAIR condition

Superboy# 47 –
an example of POOR condition

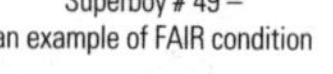

SPECIFICATIONS

FOR THE SERIOUS STATISTICS & TRIVIA FREAKS ONLY

Total number of DC comics	21,540
Total number of Marvel comics	20,246
Total number of Independent comics	35,359
Total number of DC/Marvel comics	41,786
Total number of DC/Marvel/Independent comics	77,145

Total number of DC titles	1,235
Total number of Marvel titles	1,518
Total number of Independent titles	4,426
Total number of DC/Marvel titles	2,753
Total number of DC/Marvel/Independent titles	7,179

Total value of DC comics	£2,760,321.95	$4,197,556.25
Total value of Marvel comics	£691,419.65	$1,092,135.10
Total value of Independent comics	£728,971.05	$1,115,508.90
Total value of DC/Marvel comics	£3,451,741.60	$5,289,691.35
TOTAL VALUE OF DC/MARVEL/ INDEPENDENT COMICS	**£4,180,712.65**	**$6,405,200.25**

COLLECTING BATMAN

or How Long Does It Take To Put Together A Set Of Batman?

Duncan McAlpine

At the beginning of 1974 I bought a copy of Batman #254 from my local newsagents, and though I didn't realise it at the time, it was a purchase that would have a profound and enduring effect on my comics collecting career. It was the first of those 100-page Super Spectaculars of the time, and had a selection of stories going back to the Golden Age. I was inspired, and from then on started collecting Golden Age comics (mostly Batman) seriously. In those days, when decent-shaped copies of the early numbers could still be bought for between £5 and £50, it was not too difficult to put together a set of Batman from issue #30 on and end up with only a few missing. For this reason, the cover of issue **#254** will forever be engraved on my memory.

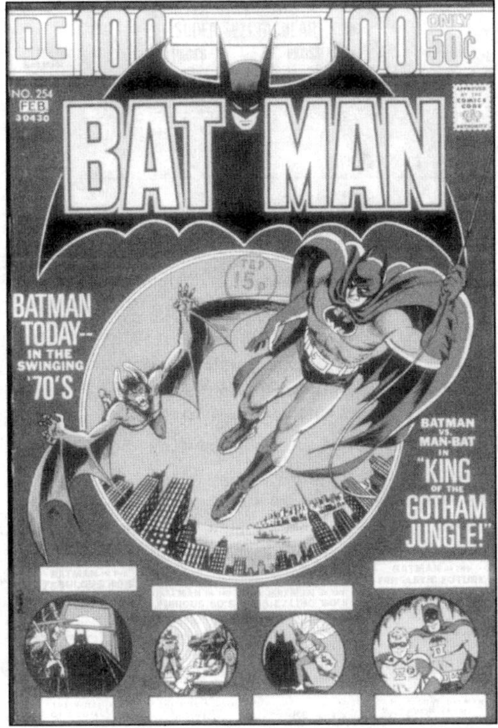

BATMAN #254

For anyone collecting Batman comics specifically, the most daunting aspect is the amount of material available. Complete sets of Batman and Detective Comics have long been out of the question (I was within about 30 issues of Detective Comics until houses and families took over). If I was to offer any advice to people who have been collecting Batman comics for a while, or have even just started, it would be the same — collect what you most like and can afford. I'd like to list some collecting highlights from the last fifty or so years, some obvious and some not so obvious. Incidentally, each decade of Batman used to have its own unofficial title: The Fabulous Forties, The Furious Fifties, The Sizzling Sixties and The Swinging Seventies. I wonder what epithets they would choose for the last two decades?

The Golden Age of Batman is beyond the pockets of most collectors, which though understandable, is a crying shame. Fortunately DC Comics have gradually got it into their heads to reprint much of this material. The hardcover Batman Archives feature Detective Comics #27-86 and show the development of Bob Kane's at times rather simplistic, cartoon-style, artwork in contrast to the detail and perspectives of Jerry Robinson and the first signs of Dick Sprang's rounded, accentuated, style that gave The Joker an impossible grin and Batman the physique of Charles Atlas. Golden Age reprints can also be found in 80-page giants, Limited Collector's Edition tabloids and reprint titles like Wanted and Secret Origins. Another source of Golden Age stargazing can be had from *The Photo-Journal Guide to Comic Books*. The first two-volume set has something like 22,000 covers to slobber over. Volume One has all the Batman covers from #1 to #140 and Detective Comics from #1 to #254 unbroken. Many copies of this book have been remaindered and it may still be possible to pick up a Volume One for £20 or £25. A bargain.

Personal favourites on the Batman title before #100 include the fantastic cover on issue #11 by Kane and Robinson, where Batman slugs The Joker against a background of playing cards. #17 is one of those highly patriotic war issues with Batman and Robin astride an American Eagle urging the public to buy US War Bonds. Interestingly, when they did it again on issue #30, the cover image was not quite so glorious. The reality of war had set in, and this was reflected in the tone of that particular cover. No more glorious eagles swooping to victory but rather the handing of a new gun to a beleaguered G.I. under fire.

Covers and stories of the late 1940s are very similar in tone to the corresponding years of Superman, and in my opinion form the nadir of Batman's adventures. Mind you, even covers where Batman is ice-skating and falls through a bat-shaped hole in the frozen pond (#39) or an issue later where The Joker walks under a ladder and a bucket of goo falls on his head compare quite favourably with the silliness of Superman juggling and a falling club breaking on his head (#47) or the most powerful super-hero of them all yelping in pain as one of Lois Lane's rock-hard cookies falls on his toe (#51). Early purchases in my Batman collection include issue #41, which had the first science fiction cover and featured pointy-eared aliens capturing a rocket-packed Dynamic Duo, and #59, a very striking cover featuring the Bat-Plane in outer space and the Bat-Signal cast from Earth onto the moon. We are talking one powerful beam of light that can shine a quarter of a million miles and cast a bat-signal hundreds of miles across! The science content of these science-fiction stories was minimal to say the least, but they have their own charm. However, a story like The Robot Cop of Gotham City in #70 was much more deliberately predictive and pre-dated RoboCop by some 40 years!

BATMAN: THE DARK KNIGHT RETURNS

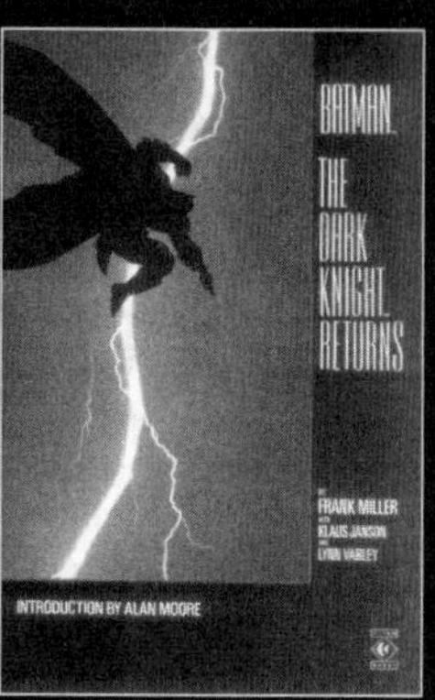

Few Batman stories have the sheer impact of Frank Miller's revisionary treatment of the character, a dark and sombre look at the twilight of a tortured hero that single-handedly redefined an American myth and in the process reshaped the face of modern comics. Miller's mix of cinematic storytelling and adult themes struck a chord that resonated far beyond the comics' world and introduced the concept of comics-as-literary-form to a hitherto dismissive general public.

The Dark Knight Returns set a standard to which many have since aspired but few have equalled (certainly, none bettered). Ignoring the conventions and structure of standard Batman fare, and in a pre-Elseworlds era with none of the latitude now extended to DC's creators, Miller presented readers with darker, more ambivalent anti-hero, and a warrior's semi-mythic rite of passage in a world sliding towards chaos and self-destruction.

Batman is forced to emerge from a self-imposed retirement to re-establish some sort of order, not simply in a city ruled by street gangs and terrorised by madmen, but in his own, directionless, life. Bereft of The Batman, his avenging angel of the night, Bruce Wayne is a shell of a man, self-destructively feeding on his own impotent anger. So the Dark Knight is born again, risen from the ashes for a last reckoning. Final, fateful, encounters with Superman, Two-Face and The Joker are woven together seamlessly to mark the twilight of the DC age of heroes.

It's worth noting that, while ten years have passed since The Dark Knight Returns was first published, its impact is as strong as ever. The recent 10th Anniversary edition looks as fresh and vital as ever, making it the one real 'must-read' for neophyte and fan alike.

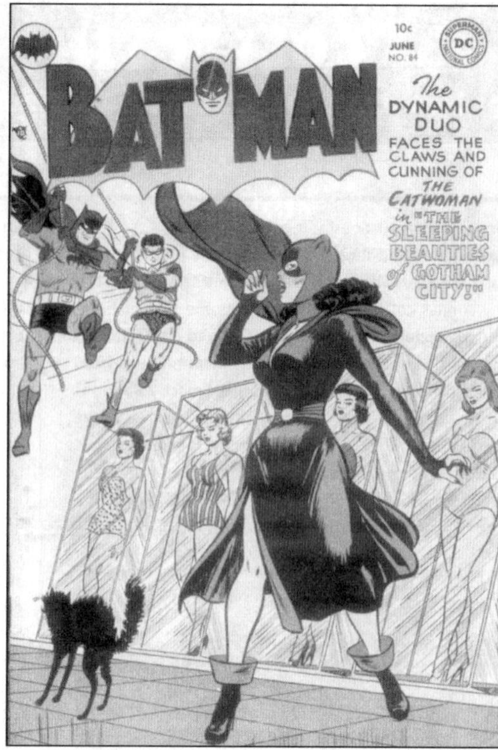

BATMAN #84

My favourite cover from this early to mid Fifties period is **#84**, showing Catwoman in her classic Golden Age costume with split skirt, cape and cowl against a white background, with her cat arching its back as Batman and Robin swoop in on bat-ropes attached who knows where. I've only ever seen one true Near Mint copy of this. I paid three times Guide for it and spent the next three years trying to justify such an outrageous expense to myself! One of the quirkiest issues from the late Fifties period is #92 with the introduction of Bat-Hound. There is something absurd and wonderful in the thought of a dog thinking to itself that in order to fight crime effectively a disguise is needed. Thus a custom-built (by whom? The dog?) mask is suspended in such a way that Ace the Bat-Hound can slip into it at the first sign of trouble. They don't write comics like that anymore.

Comics from the mid to late Fifties can be bought for £30 to £50 in around Good condition and for my money represent excellent reading and collecting value. The same cannot be said of issue #100, surely one of the most over-priced comics of them all. True enough, there is a very striking cover showing a selection of past issues but at over £300 for a Fine copy, this is a prime example of a comic that has suffered from American hype and market forces. The stories are nothing special, hardly an appropriate way to celebrate 100 issues. But back then anniversary issues were treated very much like just another number. The same is true of Superman #100, though the latter is harder to find.

Late Fifties' and early Sixties' issues are as much in demand in the States as they are in the UK, but it is a matter of finding them. Most dealers' catalogues or boxes at marts will have very few issues before #200 and certainly even fewer in top condition. Issues between #120 and #150 were not really old enough to reprint in the 80-page Giants and Batman Annuals so it is just a matter of picking these issues up where you can. There are some intriguing covers and stories. Batman #113 has the first science-fiction story for a long while and presaged a theme running through Batman comics that lasted up to the 'new look' in 1964. For some collectors this era of Batman typifies the character at his worst, fighting pink fluffy aliens on planets with two suns. For others this range of comics represents a fascinating refection of the times, when America and Russia were reaching out into space and when cult status B-movies were all the rage at the drive-ins.

Batman #121 may be one to watch as it features Mr Zero who was the basis for the Batman TV show's Mr Freeze (and who will be played by Arnold Schwarzenegger in the new Batman movie, Batman & Robin, this year). The last two issues that I found between #100 and #200 were numbers #135 and #163, which I believe are significantly scarce in the UK, certainly in high grade.

The first 'new look' Batman issue was **#164** cover-dated June 1964, though Detective Comics #327 a month earlier coined the 'new look' phrase on the cover. This presumably meant getting away from the overtly cartoony style of the artwork and ditching scenarios in outer space. Though successful in the latter, the artwork varied tremendously in quality. In the letters page for issue #164, the editors draw attention to the new look "...Batcave, Batmobile and Hot-Line, the more realistic illustrative appearance of Batman and Robin...". A yellow background was also added to the Bat-Symbol on Batman's chest. The official line from DC Comics at the present time is that the 'new look' marked the moment between the Golden Age and Silver Age versions of Batman, although the Silver Age had started eight years previously in 1956 with Showcase #4. It is worth putting issues #163 and #164 together to note the differences in style.

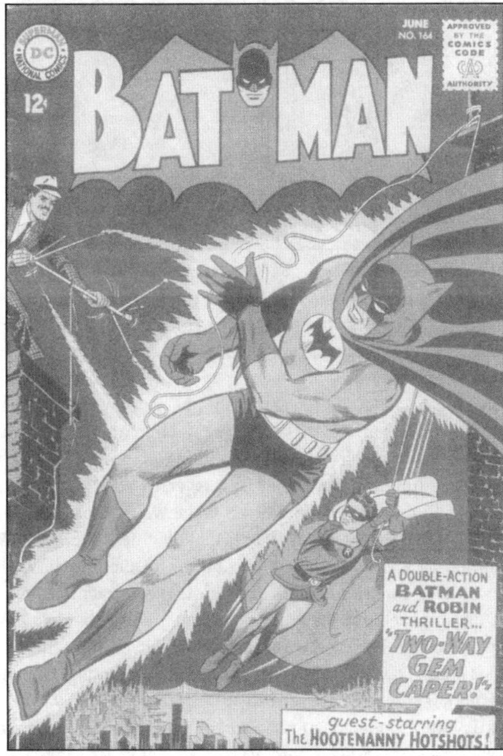

BATMAN #164

I think that the first Batman comic I ever bought (or rather was bought for me at the tender age of 5) was #169. The second half of the Sixties was a very exciting time for Batman, with the TV show all the rage. The best bit was the cliff-hanger at the end of most episodes. Would Batman escape that dastardly trap? Would he be forced to marry Catwoman? Along with all the merchandise (if only I'd kept the box for my Batmobile on Christmas Day 1967, but then what children did?), Batman was everywhere. A commonplace marketing strategy now but unheard of thirty years ago. Prompted by the TV show, The Riddler was back (#171), an issue which is gaining in collectibility once more after something of a slump. A high grade copy with that pink cover is one of the most eye-catching of comic covers and perfectly in tune with the garish pop-art style of the times. Speaking of pop-art styles, can there be a more fabulous and ridiculous villain than The Eraser in issue #188? He's a very snappy dresser and his main weapon seems to be pencil-sharp winkle-picker shoes. A villain that should have been in the TV show.

BATMAN: YEAR ONE

Miller again, this time punching big holes in the mythos of Batman's origin and early years, aided and abetted by artist David Mazzuchelli's starkly dynamic storytelling. This is Batman from the ground up, remade and remodelled for a more demanding, post-Dark Knight, audience.

What's most notable about this hugely enjoyable re-telling (re-invention) of the Batman legend, is how much of the new groundwork laid here became accepted as the definitive article by Batman readers and creators alike. From Catwoman's decidedly different back story through the fleshing out of Harvey Dent (later Two-Face) as Gotham's Assistant DA to the introduction of resident crimelord 'The Roman' (the focus of the current Batman: The Long Halloween), Miller managed to lay on just enough to tease the imagination and demand further exploration.

For those just embarking on a crash course in Batman appreciation, this provides the perfect introduction to the character and supporting cast, and yet is also never less than a well fleshed-out, well rounded story. Years Two and Three (and quite possibly Four and Five) followed, but the freshness of the original could simply not be touched. A fine example this of remaining reverential and indeed respectful to the source material but knowing where work is needed; where to prune and where to embellish.

BATMAN: A DEATH IN THE FAMILY

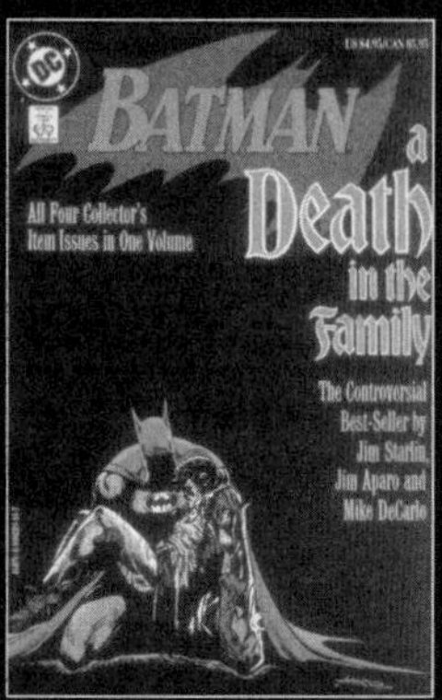

This really has all the elements for a really cracking Batman story. The death of a major character (Jason Todd's Robin), the return of The Joker (always something special), tragedy, triumph and all that jazz. So why, you have to wonder, does it all fall so flat?

Is it simply because no-one, not even the talented Batman writers of the time, could really generate much in the way of empathy for the Jason Todd character? He was, after all, the immediate successor to what many readers considered to be the one true Robin (namely Dick Grayson, who had grown up by this point and become Nightwing), and suffered their resentment accordingly. Or is it perhaps that Batman's reaction is pretty much as blasé as the reader's? Even after Robin's death, we never really get a sense that Bruce Wayne is either grief-stricken, vengeful or even driven (in fact, if anything, he seems less so than usual). In the final analysis, however, you have to lay the blame squarely at the door of whoever decided to turn this 'event' into a readers' poll, the comics equivalent of one of those TV talent shows where the audience sit with key pads ready to punch A, B or C. It reduces any sort of pathos to Monty Pythonesque farce, and in so doing breaks the cardinal rule of reminding the reader of a comic's two-dimensional status.

Ultimately, this is one of those stories that is worth reading for all the wrong reasons, and so a final word of warning. If you're going to start a Batman collection somewhere, don't make it here!

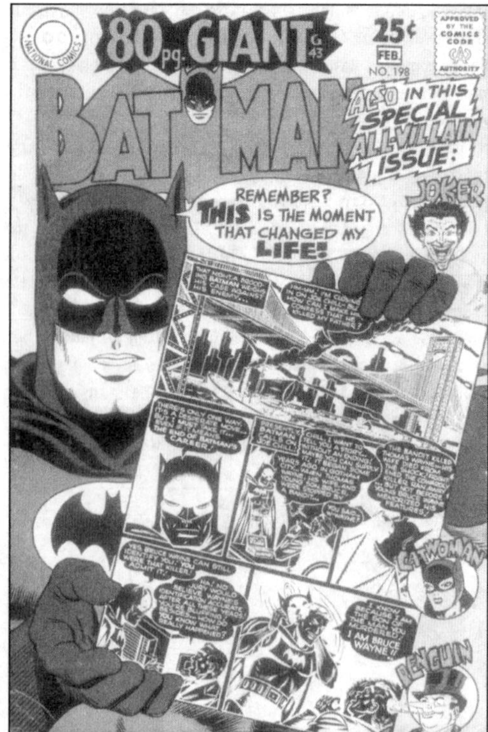

BATMAN #198

The 80-page Giants came out thick and fast with issues #176, #182, #185, #187, #193, #198, #203 and #208. It seems that DC had realised they had a substantial back catalogue and that it was a cheap way of charging 25 cents for a comic with far less proportional cost than their regular 32-page issues. Of these 80-pagers, **#198** is notoriously hard to find and I remember that being the case even when it first came out. The main reason was that the comic was an all-villain issue and also reprinted Batman's origin from #47. The eye-catching cover shows Batman holding up a page from the story itself (but reversed out) where he reveals his identity to Joe Chill, the man who murdered Bruce Wayne's parents. Great issue! Equally difficult to find in high grade is #176, though it does show up in low grade quite a lot in the UK and is well worth picking up for the last story, The Joker's Utility Belt, with Dick Sprang's artwork at its best. This is a reprint from issue #73 and has the usual scenario of the time with Batman and Robin in some fiendish trap (a conveyor belt – The Joker was big on thematic entrapments). Of course, The Joker finds himself hoisted on his own petard – or should that be belt?

Issue #200 has always been a disappointment for me. A terrific cover featuring Neal Adams-rendered Batman and Robin figures overlaying a collage of past covers. But the story inside is nothing special. It features The Scarecrow, who is not exactly a top Batman villain, though there are cameo appearances from The Joker and The Penguin. The only anniversary feature is a reprint of the first page from Detective Comics #27. Issues #213, #218 and #223 were the last of the square-bound Giant issues and it was around this time that Batman started changing again. After thirty years of Batman and Robin, suddenly the Caped Crusader was going solo. Robin was off to college and the Batcave was closed down.

But there was excitement in all the confusion. An appearance by The Beatles in issue #222. Some terrific covers by Neal Adams, like on issue #219 (which also featured a Neal Adams back-up Christmas story), and particularly issue **#227**, which paid homage to the ultimate Batman cover from Detective Comics #31.The introduction of a fascinating arch-nemesis for Batman in the shape of Ra's Al Ghul in Batman #232, a difficult issue to find in high grade. Neal Adams re-introducing Two-Face after twenty years in #234. The classic Ra's Al Ghul two-parter from issues #243 and #244, with covers and art by Neal Adams, and one of my favourite comics of all time, Batman #251, with Neal Adams' rendition of The Joker. A great cover with Batman pinned to a giant Ace of Spades card, held by an emblematic giant Joker bestriding Gotham City. The interior sequence where Batman is trapped in a tank with a shark is straight out of those fiendish traps of the Forties, but it is almost perfectly story-boarded for a modern day big budget film.

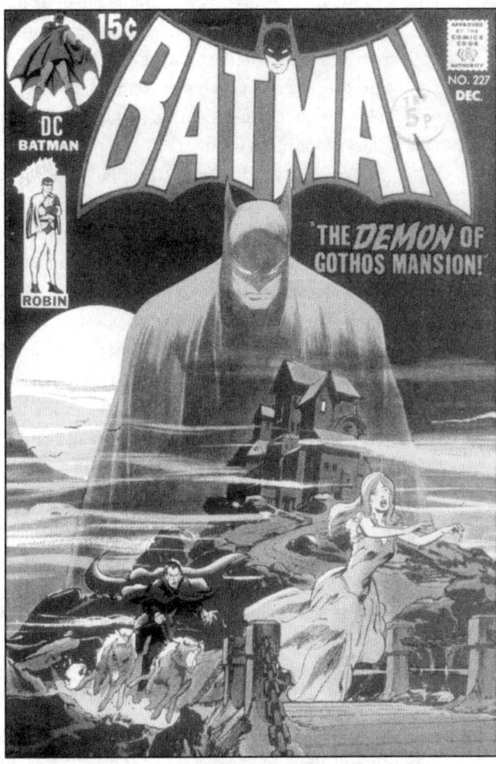

BATMAN #227

Batman meets The Shadow in #253 and then the run of 100-page Super Spectaculars starts. A Neal Adams story in #255. The Catwoman in her awful Seventies costume in #256. The Joker in #260 (a very highly priced comic in the US, in common with all Joker appearances) and the difficult to find #262, which was 68 pages before reverting back to the regular size with #263. For those just starting to get into collecting Batman, this is the period that I would recommend. There are some great characters and covers and most of all a transition from Sixties pop-art (Zap! Kapow!) to something a little harder edged. Issues in good condition should only cost between one and two pounds, and as such represent excellent reading value. Those interested in investment and that dread word 'speculation' can have fun trying to find these issues in top shape. The 52-page issues from #234 to #242 are becoming increasingly hard to find and the awkward #238, which is a 100-pager, is rarely seen on dealers' lists. Of course these Giant issues were not very well distributed at the time, as Thorp and Porter had regulation size shipping packets and half or less of the usual number of issues would fit in. All the newsagents that I could reasonably get to had only one copy each of the 100-page Super Spectaculars, sometimes none at all. I remember it being particularly difficult to find issue #238.

The latter half of the Seventies are traditionally difficult for the Batman run, and most dealers' lists have conspicuous gaps in the numbers from #265 to #295. I would recommend this period for the beginnings of multi-part stories (The Underworld Olympics in issues #272–275 and The High Tribunal of Crime in #291–294 for example) and, if you can find them of course, issues in good condition should be a pound or less. Issue #266 sees the return of Catwoman after a long absence and she returns to wearing her old 1940s costume (just love that split skirt!). Issue #274 is an interesting one, at least in America anyway. Cover-dated April 1976, in common with most Marvel and DC comics that month it carried a card centrespread advertising Mark Jewelers (the same sort of centrespread had appeared two years earlier in many titles), and was only

BATMAN: KNIGHTFALL

In the wake of the very popular (and media soaked) Death of Superman storyline, DC decided to do the same for their other flagship hero (with almost as much success). The unthinkable happens, Bruce Wayne is crippled by the supervillain known as Bane and a successor is found to carry the mantle of The Batman.

It's done very credibly, beginning with a mass breakout from Arkham Asylum and subsequent round up that leaves The Batman on the verge of total exhaustion. Enter Bane, a pumped-up WWF reject (or something like that) and the mastermind behind all the chaos, exit Bruce Wayne, his back broken in a move that looks suspiciously (reinforcing the previous suspicion re Bane) like a body slam. With Wayne (all but) out of the picture, the Azrael character (introduced in the Sword of Azrael storyline) is promoted to the big league, and proceeds to... well, read it and find out. This, and the subsequent KnightQuest and KnightsEnd stories, pretty much set the tone for the sort of multi-part, cross-title (within the Batman 'family' of comics) that have characterised Batman in the nineties (Contagion, Legacy, Prodigal et al), and this, it has to be said, is the best example. The only minor niggle is that it's a relatively minor player like Bane who bests Batman. Somehow it should have been The Joker, just as it should have been Lex Luthor who 'killed' Superman.

It's curious to note that the role of Bane in the upcoming Batman & Robin movie will be played by Jeep Swenson, a professional wrestler. I mention this only in passing.

distributed via the direct sales market to specialist shops. These titles, including Batman #274, are coming to be treated as variant issues, and yet the insert is merely an advertisement! Surely an example of variant-mania gone mad! The only positive benefit that this card insert had for these comics (though it should not affect the value!) is that it tended to keep the comic flatter for longer and thereby help keep its high grade. Issue #300 is not the easiest comic to find and is often missing when back issue collections are brought in. It's a 48-page issue with a full-length story set in the near future and art by Walt Simonson. Though distributed in the UK at the time it was quite hard to find – again, the strict sizes of the importer's packages were to blame.

Issues #301 to #400 correspond to the months from late 1978 to early 1987, and represent a fairly static period in the development of Batman's character and supporting cast. Exceptions to this rule are a very strong story arc from #330–335 featuring the return of Talia and Ra's Al Ghul, and the memorable Catwoman issues of #323–324 and #332–335, where Batman and Catwoman became romantically linked (until Catwoman's 'disappearance' in #382). These issues were all the rage during the second Batman movie thanks to Michelle Pfeiffer strutting her stuff, and as a result, many of these are still locked away in collections and are noticeably scarce in the marketplace. Jason Todd was introduced as the new Robin, an event which caused less of a stir than perhaps one might have expected. Maybe fans couldn't quite accept this brash new kid on the block and certainly his demise was ignominious to say the least. Batman **#400** was an excellent issue and was much sought after at the time of its release in October 1986. Batman was suddenly a hot property again, thanks mostly to the release of Batman: The Dark Knight Returns (see feature). This mini-series by Frank Miller became the hottest book of the year and perhaps one of the very first to offer the chance of speculation. I remember (somewhat shamefacedly now) clearing out the West End shops of 102 copies and selling them on at up to £15.

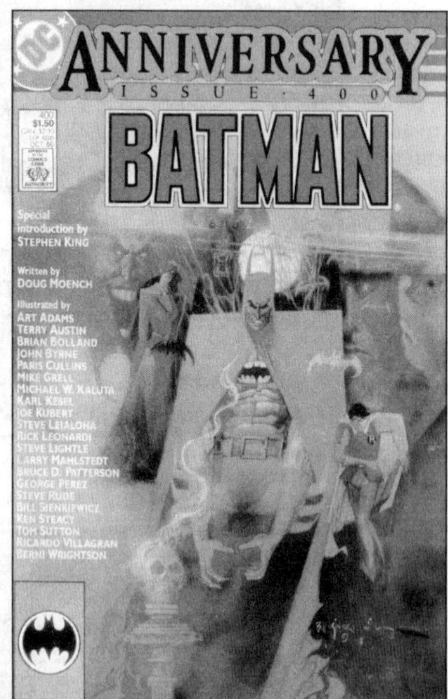

BATMAN #400

After the generally dull Batman-in-the-300s, and hot on the heels of Batman #400, came Frank Miller's and David Mazzuchelli's Batman: Year One storyline (see feature) in issues #404 to #407. While this type of storyline is done to death now, this was the first time a first year in the life of a superhero had been explored in this way. It was a fresh and exciting re-telling of the origin of Batman and a particularly interesting new angle on the origin of Catwoman, with Selina Kyle as a leather-clad sado-masochistic prostitute. A far cry from the society jewel thief of the 1940s incarnation.

The Ten Nights of the Beast story-line from #417 to 420 was also very hot and in-demand when it first came out. Batman was pitted against a new and more vicious foe in the shape of the KGB Beast. As drawn by Mike Zeck, the material may look pretty pale in comparison to some of today's stories, but at the time it was thought to be cutting edge, and The Beast a rising star in the Batman rogue's gallery. Prices are now well down on these issues and the story has been reprinted in trade paperback form by Titan Books, so you can judge for yourself.

The biggest storyline towards the end of the 1980s was the death of the Jason Todd/Robin character in issue #428. At the time, the death of a relatively major character was quite an event and DC Comics had the idea of using a telephone-voting system to decide Jason Todd's fate. The story goes that a group of University students called The Twerpies rigged their computers to dial in at regular intervals with the tag line 'Kill The Twerp!', and thus the death of Jason Todd was assured. Though the issues are readily available these days, there was a time when the first part of the storyline (#426) hit the £15 mark. Hard to believe now. Again, Batman: A Death in the Family (see feature) has been reprinted in trade paperback form by Titan, so readers new to Batman can read at leisure without paying a fortune.

The Eighties had not expired before a new Robin was found, as part of a Year Three storyline beginning with issue #436. As you might have guessed, there was something of a sense of overkill by now, and while DC may have expected these comics to be hot and generate the back issue demand that Year One and Ten Nights of The Beast had, it was not to be. The only saving grace of this very early 1990s period was a nice little run of Brian Bolland covers from #445-447.

Nothing special to report in the issues forming the latter half of the 400s until we come to the KnightFall storyline (see feature). Beginning in issue #492, it was an attempt at following up on the success of the Death of Superman storyline – an unexpectedly huge hit for DC Comics and a national news story both sides of the Atlantic. At the time there was brisk back-issue trade and genuine interest, but there was also a certain inevitability about it all. There was no way Bruce Wayne would remain in a wheelchair forever and the impact of Azrael (in the four issue mini-series Batman: Sword of Azrael) was more down to the artwork by Joe Quesada than the character himself. With the whole storyline reprinted in trade paperback form, it is very accessible and the back issues from #492 to #500 are in plentiful supply. Even the platinum edition of #492 is around. At its height it cost a minimum of $30 to buy in the States and £50 was not unheard of in the UK. Now you can pick it up for a fiver. Just goes to show how volatile the premium market can be and how easy it is to overpay.

BATMAN #520

The KnightQuest and KnightsEnd storylines immediately following #500 very much smacked of overkill and there was no discernible excitement at the time. Bruce Wayne found a cure for spine damage and returned as Batman in #515 which also came in a nice all-black cover Collector's Edition. Mr Freeze made a return appearance in #525, neatly coinciding with the announcement that he was to be one of the major villains in the new Batman movie.

The last year or so of the Batman title has been of a consistent quality. Kelley Jones as the main artist has defined Batman as a more terrifying creature of the night and the costume has become almost entirely black (from #515) with barbed spikes on boots and gauntlets. The ears are impossibly long. The cover of **#520** probably sums up the look of Batman better than any other illustration. It is difficult to tell the gargoyle from the bat as the costume appears to be a shapeless shroud and Batman squats atop a Gotham City building like some hunchback. It will be interesting to see how long this look will last with the film drawing ever nearer and merchandising and product recognition being brought to bear.

There has also been a resurgence in popular villains. Killer Croc in #521–522, The Scarecrow in #524, Two-Face in #527–528. The Joker has been promised. There was an interesting editorial announcement in issue #535 by Denny O'Neill. After the successful Contagion and Legacy storylines that ran through all the Batman comics and related titles like Azrael, Catwoman and Robin, O'Neill announced that for at least the next year there would be more concentration on single issue stories and that multi-part stories would only run a maximum of three issues. There was a nicely ironic '1 of 1' emblem on the cover of #535. In part this was a practical move by DC, as crossovers and multi-part stories involve considerable consultation time with other editors and creative staff, but it also gives the title a chance to find itself, to breathe and develop. It will be an interesting time for the Batman title as it heads towards its 550th issue, especially now, with strength of storyline and character development the prime considerations rather than gimmick covers and marketing strategies. A refreshing time indeed.

When the credits come up on the fourth Batman film and you decide to embark on your Batman comic collection, try not to be daunted by the 550 issues, all the related titles, specials, annuals and one-shots. The joy is that there is so much material to choose from that collections are much more thematic than complete-run oriented. It is possible to collect with regard to certain artists or characters and a run of Batman may be seen as #400 up or even #500 up. For the novice collector there is a wealth of information about comics in price guides and updates so informed judgements can be made about which issues to purchase and whether or not it is worth spending five pounds on a particular issue because it is 'hot'. While speculation has its many evils the one benefit is that so much recent material is available and in good condition thanks to advances in archive and storage accessories. It's always cheaper somewhere and while putting together a complete run of Batman may be out of the question, a run of the last hundred issues is very easy.

The very last Batman comic (or at least a much better copy than the one I had from when I was five) that I had to buy to complete my run was issue **#169**. And that was this year.

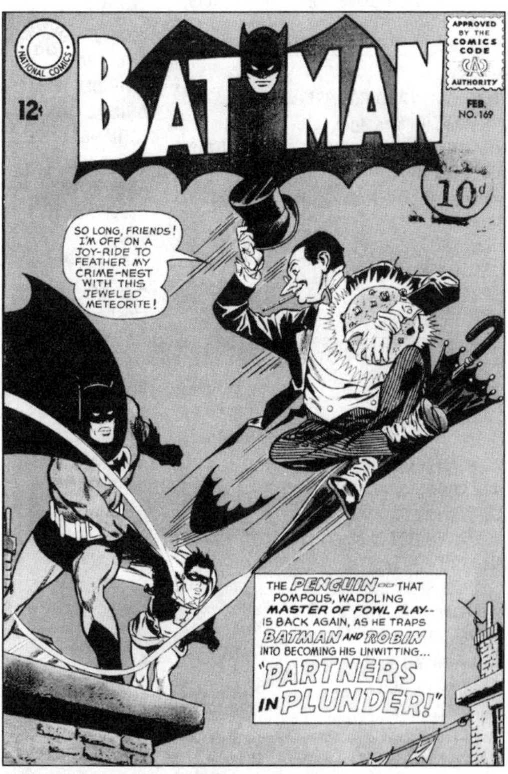

BATMAN #169

FIRST APPEARANCE INDEX

Below is the latest version of our First Appearance Index, a feature first brought to you by this publication. If there are any corrections or omissions please feel free to contact the Editorial address.

A.I.M.
STRANGE TALES #146....JULY 1966
ABEL
HOUSE OF SECRETS #61....JULY/AUGUST 1963
ABIGAIL ARCANE
SWAMP THING #2....FEBRUARY 1973
ABOMINATION
TALES TO ASTONISH #90....APRIL 1967
ABRA KADABRA
FLASH (1st Series) #128....MAY 1962
ABSORBING MAN
JOURNEY INTO MYSTERY #114....MARCH 1965
ADAM STRANGE
SHOWCASE #17....DECEMBER 1958
ADAMANTIUM
AVENGERS #66....JULY 1969
ADRIAN CHASE (Vigilante)
NEW TEEN TITANS, THE (1st Series) #23....SEPTEMBER 1982
ADULT LEGION
SUPERMAN #147....AUGUST 1961
AGATHA HARKNESS
FANTASTIC FOUR #94....JANUARY 1970
AGENT 13
TALES OF SUSPENSE #75....MARCH 1966
AGENT LIBERTY
SUPERMAN (2nd Series) #60....OCTOBER 1991
AGON
THOR #148....JANUARY 1968
AGUILA
POWER MAN AND IRON FIST #58....AUGUST 1979
AIR WAVE (Golden Age)
DETECTIVE COMICS #60....FEBRUARY 1942
AIR WAVE (Modern)
GREEN LANTERN #100....JANUARY 1978
AIREO
FANTASTIC FOUR #47....FEBRUARY 1966
AIRWALKER
FANTASTIC FOUR #120....MARCH 1972
ALCHEMIST
LEGION OF SUPER-HEROES #24....DECEMBER 1991
ALFRED
BATMAN #16....APRIL/MAY 1942
ALICIA MASTERS
FANTASTIC FOUR #8....NOVEMBER 1962
ALL STAR SQUADRON
ALL STAR SQUADRON #1....SEPTEMBER 1981
ALL WINNERS SQUAD
ALL WINNERS COMICS #19....AUTUMN 1946
ALLATOU
MARVEL SPOTLIGHT #18....APRIL 1974
ALPHA FLIGHT
X-MEN, THE UNCANNY #120....APRIL 1979
ALPHA PRIMITIVES
FANTASTIC FOUR #47....FEBRUARY 1966
AMAZING MAN
ALL STAR SQUADRON #23....JULY 1983
AMAZO
BRAVE AND THE BOLD, THE #30....JULY 1960
AMBUSH BUG
DC COMICS PRESENTS #52....DECEMBER 1992
AMERICAN EAGLE
MARVEL TWO IN ONE ANNUAL #6....1981
AMERICAN SCREAM
SHADE, THE CHANGING MAN (2nd Series) #1....JUNE 1990
AMETHYST
LEGION OF SUPER-HEROES (1st Series) #298....APRIL 1983
AMPHIBIAN
AVENGERS #145....MARCH 1976
ANACONDA
MARVEL TWO IN ONE #64....JUNE 1980
ANCIENT ONE
STRANGE TALES #111....AUGUST 1963
ANDROMEDA (DC)
LEGION OF SUPER-HEROES....DECEMBER 1991
ANDROMEDA (Marvel)
DEFENDERS #146....AUGUST 1985
ANGAR THE SCREAMER
DAREDEVIL #100....JUNE 1973
ANGEL (Archangel)
X-MEN, THE UNCANNY #1....SEPTEMBER 1963
ANGEL (Golden Age)
MARVEL COMICS #1....OCT/NOV 1939
ANGEL AND THE APE
SHOWCASE #77....AUGUST 1968
ANGLE MAN
WONDER WOMAN #70....NOVEMBER 1954
ANIMAL MAN
STRANGE ADVENTURES #180....SEPTEMBER 1965
ANNIHILUS
FANTASTIC FOUR ANNUAL #6....NOVEMBER 1968
ANT BOY
ANT BOY #1....1984
ANT MAN
TALES TO ASTONISH #27....JANUARY 1962
ANT MAN II
MARVEL PREMIERE #47....APRIL 1981
ANTHRO
SHOWCASE #74....MAY 1968
ANTON ARCANE
SWAMP THING #2....FEBRUARY 1973
APARITION
LEGION OF SUPER-HEROES #25....DECEMBER 1991
APOCALYPSE
X-FACTOR #5....JUNE 1986
APOKOLIPS
NEW GODS, THE #1....FEB/MAR 1971
APOLLO
THOR #301....NOVEMBER 1980
AQUABOY
SUPERBOY #171....JANUARY 1971
AQUAGIRL
AQUAMAN #33....JUNE 1967
AQUALAD
ADVENTURE COMICS #269....FEBRUARY 1960
AQUAMAN (Golden Age)
MORE FUN COMICS #73....NOVEMBER 1941
AQUAMAN (Silver Age)
ADVENTURE COMICS #260....MAY 1959
AQUARIAN
ADVENTURE INTO FEAR #17....OCTOBER 1973
ARABIAN KNIGHT
INCREDIBLE HULK #257....MARCH 1981
ARAK
WARLORD #48....AUGUST 1981
ARCADE
MARVEL TEAM UP #65....JANUARY 1978
ARCHANGEL
X-FACTOR #24....JANUARY 1988
ARCHER & ARMSTRONG
ARCHER & ARMSTRONG #0....JUNE 1992
ARCHIE
PEP COMICS #22....DECEMBER 1941
ARES
THOR #129....JUNE 1966
ARION
WARLORD #55....MARCH 1982
ARKON
AVENGERS #75....APRIL 1970
ARMADILLO
CAPTAIN AMERICA #308....AUGUST 1985
ARMORINES
X-O MANOWAR #25....NOVEMBER 1993
ARON THE ROGUE WATCHER
CAPTAIN MARVEL #39....FEBRUARY 1975
ARTEMIS
THOR #129....JUNE 1966
ASGARD
JOURNEY INTO MYSTERY #85....OCTOBER 1962
ASMODEUS
FANTASTIC FOUR #117....DECEMBER 1971
ASP
CAPTAIN AMERICA #309....SEPTEMBER 1985
ASTRA
X-MEN, THE UNCANNY #107....NOVEMBER 1977
ASTROBOY
SHONEN MAGAZINE (Japan) #1....1951
ASTRONOMER
SILVER SURFER (3rd Series) #4....OCTOBER 1987
ATARI FORCE
NEW TEEN TITANS, THE (1st Series) #27....JANUARY 1983
ATHENA
THOR #164....MAY 1969
ATOM (Golden Age)
ALL AMERICAN COMICS #19....OCTOBER 1940
ATOM (Silver Age)
SHOWCASE #34....OCTOBER 1961
ATOMIC KNIGHTS
STRANGE ADVENTURES #117....JUNE 1960

ATOMIC SKULL
SUPERMAN #323 .... MAY 1978
ATTILAN
FANTASTIC FOUR #47 .... FEBRUARY 1966
ATTUMA
FANTASTIC FOUR #33 .... DECEMBER 1964
AUNT AGATHA
BATMAN #89 .... FEBRUARY 1955
AURON
GREEN LANTERN #141 .... JUNE 1981
AURORA
X-MEN, THE UNCANNY #120 .... APRIL 1979
AVALANCHE
X-MEN, THE UNCANNY #141 .... JANUARY 1981
AVENGERS
AVENGERS #1 .... SEPTEMBER 1963
AVENGERS MANSION
AVENGERS #2 .... NOVEMBER 1963
AVIUS
FANTASTIC FOUR #129 .... DECEMBER 1972
AWESOME ANDROID
FANTASTIC FOUR #15 .... JUNE 1963
AZRAEL (Jean Paul Valley)
BATMAN: SWORD OF AZRAEL #1 .... OCTOBER 1992
AZREAL
NEW TEEN TITANS, THE (1st Series) #52 .... MAY 1985
BABE
ATARI FORCE #1 .... JANUARY 1984
BABY HUEY
CASPER #1 .... SEPTEMBER 1949
BADGER
BADGER #1 .... OCTOBER 1983
BALDER
JOURNEY INTO MYSTERY #85 .... OCTOBER 1962
BANE
VENGEANCE OF BANE SPECIAL .... JANUARY 1993
BANSHEE
X-MEN, THE UNCANNY #28 .... JANUARY 1967
BAPHOMET
MARVEL SPOTLIGHT #15 .... JANUARY 1974
BARBARUS
X-MEN, THE UNCANNY #62 .... NOVEMBER 1969
BARON BEDLAM
BATMAN AND THE OUTSIDERS #1 .... AUGUST 1983
BARON BLITZKRIEG
WORLD'S FINEST #246 .... AUGUST 1977
BARON BLOOD
INVADERS #7 .... JULY 1976
BARON EARTH
WARLORD #55 .... MARCH 1982
BARON MORDO
STRANGE TALES #111 .... AUGUST 1963
BARON STRUCKER
SGT. FURY AND HIS HOWLING COMMANDOS #5 .... JANUARY 1964
BARON ZEMO I
AVENGERS #4 .... MARCH 1964
BARON ZEMO II
CAPTAIN AMERICA #168 .... DECEMBER 1973
BAT LASH
SHOWCASE #76 .... JULY 1968
BATGIRL (New)
DETECTIVE COMICS #359 .... JANUARY 1967
BATGIRL (Old)
BATMAN #139 .... APRIL 1961
BAT-GYRO
DETECTIVE COMICS #31 .... SEPTEMBER 1939
BAT-HOUND
BATMAN #92 .... JUNE 1955
BATMAN (Golden Age)
DETECTIVE COMICS #27 .... MAY 1939
BATMAN (Silver Age)
DETECTIVE COMICS #327 .... MAY 1964
(**Note:** DC's official line debateable however)
BATMAN AND THE OUTSIDERS
BRAVE AND THE BOLD, THE #200 .... JULY 1983
BAT-MITE
DETECTIVE COMICS #267 .... MAY 1959
BATMOBILE
BATMAN #5 .... SPRING 1941
BATROC THE LEAPER
TALES OF SUSPENSE #76 .... APRIL 1966
BAT-SUBMARINE
BATMAN #86 .... SEPTEMBER 1954
BATTALION
TEAM TITANS #2 .... OCTOBER 1992
BATTLESTAR
CAPTAIN AMERICA #341 .... MAY 1988
BATWOMAN
DETECTIVE COMICS #233 .... JULY 1956
BEAST
X-MEN, THE UNCANNY #1 .... SEPTEMBER 1963
BEAST BOY
DOOM PATROL #99 .... NOVEMBER 1965
BEETLE
STRANGE TALES #123 .... AUGUST 1964
BELASCO
KA-ZAR THE SAVAGE #11 .... FEBRUARY 1982
BELATHAUZER
DEFENDERS #59 .... MAY 1978
BEL-DANN
X-MEN, THE UNCANNY #137 .... SEPTEMBER 1980
BELIT
GIANT SIZE CONAN #1 .... SEPTEMBER 1974
BETA RAY BILL
THOR #337 .... NOVEMBER 1983
BEYONDER
SECRET WARS II #1 .... JULY 1985
BIG BARDA
MISTER MIRACLE #4 .... SEPT/OCT 1971
BIG BERTHA
WEST COAST AVENGERS #46 .... JULY 1988
BIG MAN AND THE ENFORCERS
AMAZING SPIDERMAN #10 .... MARCH 1964
BIG SIR
FLASH (1st Series) #338 .... OCTOBER 1984
BINARY
X-MEN, THE UNCANNY #164 .... DECEMBER 1982
BISHOP
X-MEN, THE UNCANNY #282 .... NOVEMBER 1992
BIZARRO (Modern)
MAN OF STEEL #5 .... AUGUST 1986
BIZARRO (Silver Age)
SUPERBOY #68 .... OCTOBER 1956
BIZARRO BATMAN
WORLD'S FINEST #156 .... MARCH 1966
BIZARRO FLASH
LOIS LANE, SUPERMAN'S GIRLFRIEND #74 .... MAY 1967
BIZARRO KRYPTO
SUPERBOY #82 .... JULY 1960

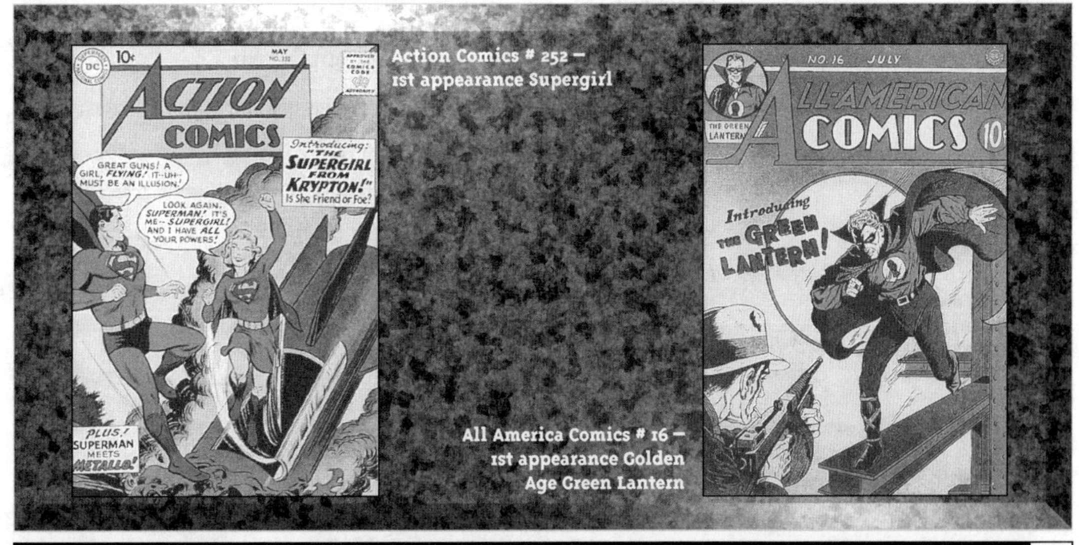

Action Comics # 252 – 1st appearance Supergirl

All America Comics # 16 – 1st appearance Golden Age Green Lantern

BIZARRO LANA LANG
ADVENTURE COMICS #292 ....JANUARY 1962
BIZARRO LEGION
ADVENTURE COMICS #329.........FEBRUARY 1965
BIZARRO LOIS LANE
ACTION COMICS #255 ....AUGUST 1959
BIZARRO LUCY LANE
ADVENTURE COMICS #292 ....JANUARY 1962
BIZARRO MXYZPTLK
ADVENTURE COMICS #286 ....JULY 1961
BIZARRO SUPERGIRL
SUPERMAN #140 ....OCTOBER 1960
BIZARRO TITANO
ADVENTURE COMICS #295 ....APRIL 1962
BLACK ARCHER
SQUADRON SUPREME #10..................JUNE 1986
BLACK BOLT
FANTASTIC FOUR #45.................DECEMBER 1965
BLACK CANARY (Golden Age)
FLASH COMICS #86..........................AUGUST 1941
BLACK CANARY (Silver Age)
JUSTICE LEAGUE OF
AMERICA #75...................................OCTOBER 1969
BLACK CANARY (Modern)
DETECTIVE COMICS #554 ....SEPTEMBER 1985
BLACK CAT
AMAZING SPIDERMAN #194................JULY 1979
BLACK CAT (Golden Age)
POCKET COMICS #1 ....AUGUST 1941
BLACK CONDOR
CRACK COMICS #1 ....MAY 1940
BLACK CONDOR (Modern)
BLACK CONDOR #1 ....JUNE 1992
BLACK CROW
CAPTAIN AMERICA #292 ....APRIL 1984
BLACK GOLIATH
BLACK GOLIATH #1 ....FEBRUARY 1976
BLACK HOOD
PEP COMICS #48.......................................MAY 1944
BLACK HOOD (Golden Age)
TOP NOTCH COMICS #9 ....OCTOBER 1940
BLACK KNIGHT I
MARVEL SUPER-HEROES #17..NOVEMBER 1968
BLACK KNIGHT II
TALES TO ASTONISH #52 ....FEBRUARY 1964
BLACK KNIGHT III
AVENGERS #48...............................JANUARY 1968
BLACK LIGHTNING
BLACK LIGHTNING #1..........................APRIL 1977
BLACK MANTA
AQUAMAN #35 ....SEPT/OCT 1967
BLACK MASK
BATMAN #368 ....JANUARY 1984
BLACK ORCHID
ADVENTURE COMICS #428 ..JULY/AUGUST 1973
BLACK ORCHID (New)
BLACK ORCHID #1.......................DECEMBER 1988
BLACK PANTHER (Golden Age)
STARS AND STRIPES COMICS #3.......JUNE 1941
BLACK PANTHER
FANTASTIC FOUR #52..............................JULY 1966
BLACK PIRATE
SENSATION COMICS #1...............JANUARY 1942
BLACK QUEEN
NEW MUTANTS #9 ....NOVEMBER 1983
BLACK RACER
NEW GODS, THE #3 ....JUNE/JULY 1971

BLACK SPIDER
DETECTIVE COMICS #463 ....SEPTEMBER 1976
BLACK TERROR
TOTAL ECLIPSE #3.......................DECEMBER 1988
BLACK TOM CASSIDY
X-MEN, THE UNCANNY #101 ....OCTOBER 1976
BLACK WIDOW
TALES OF SUSPENSE #52 ....APRIL 1964
BLACK WIDOW (Golden Age)
MYSTIC COMICS #4 ....AUGUST 1940
BLACKFIRE
NEW TEEN TITANS, THE
(1st Series) #23 ....SEPTEMBER 1982
BLACKHAWK
MILITARY COMICS #1 ....AUGUST 1941
BLACKLASH
IRON MAN #146 ....MAY 1981
BLACKOUT I
NOVA, THE MAN CALLED #19 ....JUNE 1978
BLACKOUT II
GHOST RIDER (2nd Series) #2..............JUNE 1990
BLADE
TOMB OF DRACULA #10..........................JULY 1973
BLASTAAR
FANTASTIC FOUR #62..............................MAY 1967
BLAZE
MARVEL SPOTLIGHT #5 ....MARCH 1972
BLIMP
SHOWCASE #62............................MAY/JUNE 1966
BLIZZARD
IRON MAN #86 ....MAY 1976
BLOB
X-MEN, THE UNCANNY #3 ....JANUARY 1964
BLOCKBUSTER (Silver Age)
DETECTIVE COMICS #345..........NOVEMBER 1965
BLOCKBUSTER (Modern)
STARMAN #9..APRIL 1989
BLOK
SUPERBOY #253...JULY 1979
BLOOD BROTHERS
IRON MAN #55 ....FEBRUARY 1972
BLOOD STONE
MARVEL PRESENTS #1 ....OCTOBER 1975
BLOODSHOT
ETERNAL WARRIOR #4...............DECEMBER 1992
BLOODSPORT
SUPERMAN (2nd Series) #4 ....APRIL 1987
BLUE BEETLE (Charlton)
BLUE BEETLE (Charlton) #18.......FEBRUARY 1955
BLUE BEETLE (Golden Age)
MYSTERY MEN #1 ....AUGUST 1939
BLUE BEETLE (Modern)
CAPTAIN ATOM (Charlton) #83
....NOVEMBER 1966
BLUE BOLT
BLUE BOLT #1...JUNE 1940
BLUE DEVIL
FIRESTORM THE NUCLEAR MAN,
THE FURY OF #24....................................JUNE 1984
BLUE EAGLE
SQUADRON SUPREME #2............OCTOBER 1985
BLUE KRYPTONITE
SUPERMAN #140 ....OCTOBER 1960
BLUE SHIELD
DAZZLER #5..JULY 1981
BOLT
BLUE DEVIL #6............................NOVEMBER 1984

BOMBA
BOMBA, THE JUNGLE BOY #1.....SEPT/OCT 1967
BOOMER
SECRET WARS II #5 ....NOVEMBER 1985
BOOMERANG
TALES TO ASTONISH #81 ....JULY 1966
BOOSTER GOLD
BOOSTER GOLD #1 ....FEBRUARY 1986
BOUNCING BOY
ACTION COMICS #276.............................MAY 1961
BOY COMMANDOS
DETECTIVE COMICS #64 ....JUNE 1942
BRAIN DRAIN
ALPHA FLIGHT #109 ....JUNE 1992
BRAINIAC (Silver Age)
ACTION COMICS #242 ....JULY 1958
BRAINIAC (Modern)
SUPERMAN, THE ADVENTURES OF #438
....JULY 1988
BRAINIAC 5 (Silver Age)
ACTION COMICS #276.............................MAY 1961
BRAINIAC 5 (Modern)
LEGION OF SUPER-HEROES #24
....DECEMBER 1991
BRAINSTORM
JUSTICE LEAGUE OF
AMERICA #32 ....DECEMBER 1964
BRONZE TIGER
RICHARD DRAGON, KUNG FU
FIGHTER #1 ....APRIL/MAY 1975
BROOD
X-MEN, THE UNCANNY #155 ....MARCH 1982
BROTHER BLOOD
NEW TEEN TITANS, THE
(1st Series) #21 ....JULY 1982
BROTHER POWER
BROTHER POWER THE GEEK #1....SEP/OCT 1968
BROTHER VOODOO
STRANGE TALES #173...........................APRIL 1974
BROTHERS GRIMM
IRON MAN #188 ....NOVEMBER 1984
BUCKY
CAPTAIN AMERICA COMICS #1......MARCH 1941
BUCKY II
MARVEL PREMIERE #30.........................JUNE 1976
BUDAN
MARVEL TWO-IN-ONE #71..........JANUARY 1981
BULLDOZER
DEFENDERS #17...........................NOVEMBER 1974
BULLET
DAREDEVIL #250..............................JANUARY 1988
BULLSEYE
NICK FURY, AGENT OF
SHIELD #15 ....NOVEMBER 1969
BUMBLEBEE
TEEN TITANS #48 ....JUNE 1977
BUN-DALL
CAPTAIN MARVEL #45.............................JULY 1976
BUSHMASTER
CAPTAIN AMERICA #310 ....OCTOBER 1985
BUSHWACKER
DAREDEVIL #249..........................DECEMBER 1987
BUTCHER
BUTCHER #1 ....MAY 1990
B'WANA BEAST
SHOWCASE #66 ....JAN/FEB 1967
CABLE
NEW MUTANTS #87 ....MARCH 1990

CAIN
HOUSE OF MYSTERY #175 ......JULY/AUGUST 196
CALIBAN
X-MEN, THE UNCANNY #148..........AUGUST 1981
CALLISTO
X-MEN, THE UNCANNY #169 ....MAY 1983
CALYPSO
AMAZING SPIDERMAN #209.......OCTOBER 1980
CANNONBALL
MARVEL GRAPHIC NOVEL #4..........................1982
CAPTAIN AMERICA (Golden Age)
CAPTAIN AMERICA COMICS #1......MARCH 1941
CAPTAIN AMERICA (Silver Age)
AVENGERS #4.......................................MARCH 1964
CAPTAIN ATLAS
QUASAR #10...MAY 1990
CAPTAIN ATOM (Charlton)
SPACE ADVENTURES #33 ....MARCH 1960
CAPTAIN ATOM (DC)
CAPTAIN ATOM #1.............................MARCH 1987
CAPTAIN BOOMERANG
FLASH (1st Series) #117 ....DECEMBER 1960
CAPTAIN BRITAIN
CAPTAIN BRITAIN #1 ....OCTOBER 13TH 1976
(American Guides note!)
CAPTAIN BRITAIN (1st US appearance)
MARVEL TEAM UP #66................FEBRUARY 1978
CAPTAIN CARROT
NEW TEEN TITANS, THE
(1st Series) #16...............................FEBRUARY 1982
CAPTAIN COLD
SHOWCASE #8 ....JUNE 1957
CAPTAIN COMET
STRANGE ADVENTURES #9 ....JUNE 1951
CAPTAIN COMMANDO
PEP COMICS #30...............................AUGUST 1942
CAPTAIN FREEDOM (Golden Age)
SPEED COMICS #13 ....MAY 1941
CAPTAIN FREEDOM (Modern)
AMERICOMICS #1..........................JANUARY 1983
CAPTAIN GEORGE STACY
AMAZING SPIDERMAN #56.........JANUARY 1968
CAPTAIN MARVEL (Female)
AMAZING SPIDERMAN ANNUAL #16...........1982
CAPTAIN MARVEL (Kree)
MARVEL SUPER-HEROES #12...DECEMBER 1967
CAPTAIN MARVEL (M.F. Enterprises)
CAPTAIN MARVEL #1.............................APRIL 1966
CAPTAIN MARVEL (Modern)
SHAZAM, A NEW BEGINNING #1......APRIL 1987
CAPTAIN MARVEL (Shazam)
WHIZ COMICS #2..........................FEBRUARY 1940
CAPTAIN MARVEL Jnr
WHIZ COMICS #25 ....DECEMBER 1941
CAPTAIN PARAGON
BILL BLACK'S FUN COMICS #1
....DECEMBER 1982
CAPTAIN SAVAGE
SGT. FURY AND HIS HOWLING
COMMANDOS #10....................NOVEMBER 1964
CAPTAIN STORM
CAPTAIN STORM #1 ....MAY/JUN 1964
CAPTAIN STRONG
ACTION COMICS #421.....................MARCH 1973
CAPTAIN THUNDER
FLASH COMICS (Fawcett) #1 ....JANUARY 1940
CAPTAIN UNIVERSE
MICRONAUTS #8 ....AUGUST 1979
CARDIAC
AMAZING SPIDERMAN #344.....FEBRUARY 1991
CARNAGE
AMAZING SPIDERMAN #361 ....APRIL 1992
CARRION
SPECTACULAR SPIDERMAN #25
....DECEMBER 1978
CAT
THE CAT #1 ....NOVEMBER 1972
CATHERINE COBERT
JUSTICE LEAGUE EUROPE #1.............APRIL 1989
CAT-MAN
DAREDEVIL #10................................OCTOBER 1965
CATMAN
DETECTIVE COMICS #311 ....JANUARY 1963
CAT-MAN II
DAREDEVIL #157 ....MARCH 1979
CATSEYE
NEW MUTANTS #16...............................JUNE 1984
CATSPAW
LEGION OF SUPER-HEROES #33
....SEPTEMBER 1992
CATWOMAN (Golden Age) called The Cat
BATMAN #1 ....SPRING 1940
CATWOMAN (Silver Age)
LOIS LANE, SUPERMAN'S
GIRLFRIEND #70..........................NOVEMBER 1966
CATWOMAN (Modern)
BATMAN #406...APRIL 1987
CAVALIER
DETECTIVE COMICS #81...........NOVEMBER 1943
CAVE CARSON
BRAVE AND THE BOLD, THE #31
....SEPTEMBER 1960
CELESTIAL – ARISHEM THE JUDGE
ETERNALS, THE #2............................AUGUST 1976
CELESTIAL – ESON THE SEARCHER
ETERNALS, THE #9..............................MARCH 1977
CELESTIAL – GAMMENON THE GATHERER
ETERNALS, THE #4 ....OCTOBER 1976
CELESTIAL – HARGEN THE MEASURER
ETERNALS, THE #9..............................MARCH 1977
CELESTIAL – JEMIAH THE ANALYZER
ETERNALS, THE #7..........................JANUARY 1977
CELESTIAL – NEZARR THE CALCULATOR
ETERNALS, THE #9..............................MARCH 1977
CELESTIAL – ONE ABOVE ALL
ETERNALS, THE #7..........................JANUARY 1977
CELESTIAL – ONEG THE PROBER
ETERNALS, THE #9..............................MARCH 1977
CELESTIAL – TEFRAL THE SURVEYOR
ETERNALS, THE #7..........................JANUARY 1977
CELESTIAL – ZIRAN THE TESTER
ETERNALS, THE #18.....................DECEMBER 1977
CERBERUS
SUPERMAN: THE MAN OF STEEL #1...JULY 1991
CEREBRO
X-MEN, THE UNCANNY #7 ......SEPTEMBER 1964
CEREBUS THE AARDVARK
CEREBUS #1...................................DECEMBER 1977
CERISE
EXCALIBUR #47 ....FEBRUARY 1992
CHALLENGERS OF THE UNKNOWN
SHOWCASE #6 ....FEBRUARY 1957
CHAMELEON
AMAZING SPIDERMAN #1 ....MARCH 1963
CHAMELEON BOY
ACTION COMICS #267 ....AUGUST 1960
CHAMPION
MARVEL TWO IN ONE ANNUAL #7...............1982

Amazing Spiderman # 2
1st appearance The Vulture

Avengers # 57
1st appearance The Vision

CHAMPIONS
CHAMPIONS #1....OCTOBER 1975
CHANGELING
X-MEN, THE UNCANNY #36....SEPTEMBER 1967
CHANGELING (formerly Beast Boy)
NEW TEEN TITANS #1....NOVEMBER 1980
CHARLIE 27
MARVEL SUPER-HEROES #18....JANUARY 1969
CHECKMATE
ACTION COMICS #598....MARCH 1988
CHEETAH (Marvel)
CAPTAIN MARVEL #48....JANUARY 1977
CHEETAH I
WONDER WOMAN #6....AUTUMN 1943
CHEETAH II
WONDER WOMAN #274....JANUARY 1981
CHEETAH III
WONDER WOMAN #9....OCTOBER 1987
CHEMICAL KING
ADVENTURE COMICS #354....MARCH 1967
CHEMO
SHOWCASE #39....JULY/AUG 1962
CHIRON
FANTASTIC FOUR #129....DECEMBER 1972
CHLOROPHYLL KID
ADVENTURE COMICS #306....MARCH 1963
CHOD
X-MEN, THE UNCANNY #107....NOVEMBER 1977
CHOP-CHOP
MILITARY COMICS #3....OCTOBER 1941
CHRONOS
ATOM, THE #3....OCT/NOV 1962
CHTHON
AVENGERS #187....SEPTEMBER 1979
CIRCUS OF CRIME
DAREDEVIL #118....FEBRUARY 1975
CITADEL
GREEN LANTERN #136....JANUARY 1981
CLAW
CLAW THE UNCONQUERED #1....MAY/JUN 1975
CLAYFACE I
DETECTIVE COMICS #40....JUNE 1940
CLAYFACE II
DETECTIVE COMICS #298....DECEMBER 1961
CLAYFACE III
DETECTIVE COMICS #478....JULY/AUGUST 1978
CLAYFACE IV
OUTSIDERS #21....JULY 1987
CLEA
STRANGE TALES #126....NOVEMBER 1964
CLETUS KASADY
AMAZING SPIDERMAN #345....MARCH 1991
CLIFF STEELE (Robotman)
MY GREATEST ADVENTURE #80
....OCTOBER 1963
CLOAK AND DAGGER
PETER PARKER, THE SPECTACULAR
SPIDERMAN #64....MARCH 1982
CLOCK KING
WORLD'S FINEST COMICS #111....AUGUST 1960
COBRA
JOURNEY INTO MYSTERY #98
....NOVEMBER 1963
COLLECTOR
AVENGERS #28....MAY 1966
COLLEEN WING
MARVEL PREMIERE #14....MARCH 1974

COLOSSAL BOY
ACTION COMICS #267....AUGUST 1960
COLOSSUS
X-MEN GIANT-SIZE #1....SUMMER 1975
COLOUR KID
ADVENTURE COMICS #342....MARCH 1966
COMBAT KELLY
COMBAT KELLY #1....JUNE 1967
COMET
ACTION COMICS #347....MARCH 1967
COMMANDER KRAKEN
SUB-MARINER #27....JULY 1970
COMMISSIONER GORDON
DETECTIVE COMICS #27....MAY 1939
COMPOSITE SUPERMAN
WORLD'S FINEST #142....JUNE 1964
COMPUTO (Silver Age)
ADVENTURE COMICS #340....JANUARY 1966
COMPUTO (Modern)
LEGION OF SUPER-HEROES ANNUAL #1....1982
CONAN THE BARBARIAN
CONAN THE BARBARIAN #1....OCTOBER 1970
CONCRETE
DARK HORSE PRESENTS #1....JULY 1986
CONGO BILL
ACTION COMICS #37....JUNE 1941
CONGORILLA
ACTION COMICS #248....JANUARY 1959
CONSTRICTOR
INCREDIBLE HULK #212....JUNE 1977
CONTEMPLATOR
MARVEL TREASURY SPECIAL #1....1974
CONTROLLER
IRON MAN #12....APRIL 1969
COPPERHEAD (DC)
BRAVE AND THE BOLD, THE #78
....JUNE/JULY 1968
COPPERHEAD (Marvel)
CAPTAIN AMERICA #337....JANUARY 1988
CORONA
SPECTACULAR SPIDERMAN #176....MAY 1991
CORRUPTOR
NOVA, THE MAN CALLED #4....DECEMBER 1976
CORSAIR
X-MEN, THE UNCANNY #107....NOVEMBER 1977
COSMIC BOY
ADVENTURE COMICS #247....APRIL 1958
COSMIC CUBE
TALES OF SUSPENSE #79....JULY 1966
COTTONMOUTH
CAPTAIN AMERICA #310....OCTOBER 1985
COUGAR
COUGAR, THE #1....APRIL 1975
COUNT NEFARIA
AVENGERS #13....FEBRUARY 1965
COUNT VIRTIGO
WORLD'S FINEST #251....JUNE/JULY 1978
CRAZY NATE
GUARDIANS OF THE GALAXY #17
....OCTOBER 1991
CREATURE COMMANDOES
WEIRD WAR TALES #93....NOVEMBER 1980
CREEPER
SHOWCASE #73....MAR/APRIL 1968
CRIME-BUSTER
NOVA, THE MAN CALLED #13....DECEMBER 1977
CRIMEMASTER
AMAZING SPIDERMAN #26....JULY 1965

CRIMSON
X-FACTOR #54....MAY 1990
CRIMSON AVENGER
DETECTIVE COMICS #20....OCTOBER 1938
CRIMSON COMMANDO
X-MEN, THE UNCANNY #215....MARCH 1987
CRIMSON DYNAMO
TALES OF SUSPENSE #46....OCTOBER 1963
CRIMSON DYNAMO II
TALES OF SUSPENSE #52....APRIL 1964
CRIMSON DYNAMO III
IRON MAN #21....JANUARY 1970
CRIMSON DYNAMO IV
CHAMPIONS, THE #8....OCTOBER 1976
CRIMSON DYNAMO V
IRON MAN #109....APRIL 1978
CRIMSON FOX
JUSTICE LEAGUE EUROPE #6
....SEPTEMBER 1989
CROSSBONES
CAPTAIN AMERICA #360....OCTOBER 1989
CROSSFIRE
DNAGENTS #10....MARCH 1984
CROSSFIRE (Marvel)
MARVEL TWO IN ONE #52....JUNE 1979
CRUSADER
THOR #330....MARCH 1983
CRUSADER (Formerly old Marvel Boy)
FANTASTIC FOUR #164....NOVEMBER 1975
CRUSADERS
INVADERS #14....MARCH 1977
CRYSTAL
FANTASTIC FOUR #45....DECEMBER 1965
CRYSTAR
CRYSTAR, SAGA OF #1....MAY 1983
CUTTHROAT
MARVEL TEAM UP #89....JANUARY 1980
CYBELE
ETERNALS, THE (Limited Series) #1
....OCTOBER 1985
CYBER
MARVEL COMICS PRESENTS #85....1991
CYBORG
DC COMICS PRESENTS #26....OCTOBER 1980
CYBORG SUPERMAN (Hank Henshaw)
ADVENTURES OF SUPERMAN #465....MAY 1990
CYCLONE
AMAZING SPIDERMAN #143....APRIL 1975
CYCLOPS
X-MEN, THE UNCANNY #1....SEPTEMBER 1963
CYPHER
NEW MUTANTS #13....MARCH 1984
DAGOTH
MARVEL PREMIERE #7....MARCH 1973
DAILY BUGLE
AMAZING SPIDERMAN #1....MARCH 1963
DAILY PLANET
ACTION COMICS #23....APRIL 1940
DAIMON HELLSTROM (see Son of Satan)
DAREDEVIL
DAREDEVIL #1....APRIL 1964
DARKHAWK
DARKHAWK #1....MARCH 1991
DARKOTH
FANTASTIC FOUR #142....JANUARY 1974
DARKSEID
JIMMY OLSEN, SUPERMAN'S PAL #134
....DECEMBER 1970

DARKSTAR
CHAMPIONS, THE #7 .... AUGUST 1976
DARKSTARS
DARKSTARS #1 .... OCTOBER 1992
DAWNSTAR
SUPERBOY #226 .... APRIL 1977
DAZZLER
X-MEN, THE UNCANNY #130 ..... FEBRUARY 1980
DEADLINE
STARMAN #15 .... OCTOBER 1989
DEADLY EARNEST
ALPHA FLIGHT #7 .... FEBRUARY 1984
DEADMAN
STRANGE ADVENTURES #205
.... SEPTEMBER 1967
DEADPOOL
NEW MUTANTS #98 .... FEBRUARY 1991
DEADSHOT
BATMAN #59 .... JUN/JULY 1950
DEADSHOT (Modern)
DETECTIVE COMICS #474
.... NOVEMBER/DECEMBER 1977
DEATH
CAPTAIN MARVEL #27 .... FEBRUARY 1974
DEATH
SANDMAN (2nd Series) #8 .... AUGUST 1989
DEATH ADDER
MARVEL TWO IN ONE #64 .... JUNE 1980
DEATH THROWS
CAPTAIN AMERICA #317 .... MAY 1986
DEATHBIRD
MS. MARVEL #9 .... SEPTEMBER 1977
DEATHLOK
ASTONISHING TALES #25 .... AUGUST 1974
DEATH'S HEAD
DRAGON'S CLAWS
(Back cover story) #3 .... SEPTEMBER 1988
DEATHSTALKER
DAREDEVIL #114 .... OCTOBER 1974
DEATHSTROKE THE TERMINATOR
NEW TEEN TITANS, THE
(1st Series) #2 .... DECEMBER 1980
DEATHURGE
MARVEL TWO IN ONE #71 .... JANUARY 1981
DEATHWATCH
GHOST RIDER (2nd Series) #1 .... MAY 1990
DEFENDERS
MARVEL FEATURE #1 .... DECEMBER 1971
DEMOGOBLIN
WEB OF SPIDERMAN #86 .... MARCH 1992
DEMOLITION MAN
CAPTAIN AMERICA #328 .... APRIL 1987
DEMON
DEMON, THE #1 .... AUG/SEPT 1978
DESAAD
FOREVER PEOPLE #2 .... APRIL/MAY 1971
DESPERO
JUSTICE LEAGUE OF AMERICA #1
.... OCT/NOV 1960
DESTINY
X-MEN, THE UNCANNY #141 .... JANUARY 1981
DESTINY FOX
GHOSTLY HAUNTS #39 .... JULY 1974
DESTROYER
JOURNEY INTO MYSTERY #118 .... JULY 1965
DESTROYER DUCK
DESTROYER DUCK #1 .... FEBRUARY 1982

DESTRUCTOR
DESTRUCTOR #1 .... FEBRUARY 1975
DETECTIVE CHIMP
REX THE WONDER DOG #4 .... JUL/AUG 1952
DEVIL DINOSAUR
DEVIL DINOSAUR #1 .... APRIL 1978
DEVOS
FANTASTIC FOUR #359 .... DECEMBER 1991
DIABLO
FANTASTIC FOUR #30 .... SEPTEMBER 1964
DIAL H FOR HERO
HOUSE OF MYSTERY #156 .... JANUARY 1966
DIAMOND LIL
ALPHA FLIGHT #11 .... JUNE 1984
DIAMONDBACK
CAPTAIN AMERICA #310 .... OCTOBER 1985
DICK TRACY (1st in comics)
POPULAR COMICS #1 .... FEBRUARY 1936
DIONYSUS
THOR #129 .... JUNE 1966
DOC SAMSON
INCREDIBLE HULK #141 .... JULY 1971
DOC SAVAGE
DOC SAVAGE MAGAZINE #1 1933
DOCTOR ALCHEMY
SHOWCASE #14 .... JUNE 1958
DOCTOR ECLIPSE (Fred Bender)
SOLAR, MAN OF THE ATOM #15
.... NOVEMBER 1992
DOCTOR SPECTRO
CAPTAIN ATOM (Charlton) #79 .... MARCH 1966
DOLL MAN
FEATURE COMICS #27 .... DECEMBER 1939
DOLPHIN
SHOWCASE #79 .... JANUARY 1969
DOMINATORS
ADVENTURE COMICS #361 .... OCTOBER 1967
DOMINIC FORTUNE
MARVEL PREVIEW #2 1975
DOMINO
NEW MUTANTS #98 .... FEBRUARY 1991
DOMINO II
X-FORCE #8 .... MARCH 1992
DOMINUS
FANTASTIC FOUR #131 .... FEBRUARY 1973
DONALD PEARCE
X-MEN, THE UNCANNY #132 .... APRIL 1980
DOOM PATROL
MY GREATEST ADVENTURE #80
.... OCTOBER 1963
DOOMSDAY
SUPERMAN: THE MAN OF STEEL #18
.... DECEMBER 1983
DORMAMMU
STRANGE TALES #126 .... NOVEMBER 1964
DOROTHY SPINNER
DOOM PATROL (2nd Series) #14
.... NOVEMBER 1988
DOVE
HAWK AND THE DOVE #1 .... AUG/SEPT 1968
DOVE II
HAWK AND DOVE MINI SERIES #1
.... OCTOBER 1988
DR. DEMONICUS
GODZILLA #4 .... NOVEMBER 1972
DR. DOOM
FANTASTIC FOUR #5 .... JULY 1962

DR. FATE (Golden Age)
MORE FUN COMICS #55 .... MAY 1940
DR. FATE (Silver Age)
JUSTICE LEAGUE OF AMERICA #21
.... AUGUST 1963
DR. FATE (Female)
DOCTOR FATE #25 .... FEBRUARY 1991
DR. FAUSTUS
CAPTAIN AMERICA #107 .... NOVEMBER 1968
DR. LIGHT
CRISIS ON INFINITE EARTHS #4 .... JULY 1985
DR. MALUS
SPIDERWOMAN #30 .... SEPTEMBER 1980
DR. MIDNIGHT (new)
INFINITY INC. #21 .... DECEMBER 1985
DR. MID-NITE
ALL AMERICAN COMICS #25 .... APRIL 1941
DR. MIRAGE
SHADOWMAN #16 .... AUGUST 1992
DR. OCCULT
NEW FUN COMICS #6 .... OCTOBER 1935
DR. OCTOPUS
AMAZING SPIDERMAN #3 .... MAY 1963
DR. PHOSPHOROUS
DETECTIVE COMICS #469 1976
DR. POLARIS
GREEN LANTERN #21 .... JUNE 1962
DR. SOLAR
DR SOLAR, MAN OF THE ATOM #1
.... OCTOBER 1962
DR. SPECTRUM
AVENGERS #85 .... FEBRUARY 1971
DR. STRANGE
STRANGE TALES #110 .... JULY 1963
DR. WHO
MARVEL PREMIERE #57 .... DECEMBER 1980
DRAAGA
SUPERMAN, THE ADVENTURES OF #454
.... MAY 1989
DRACULA
TOMB OF DRACULA #1 .... APRIL 1972
DRAGON MAN
FANTASTIC FOUR #35 .... FEBRUARY 1965
DRAGONMAGE
LEGION OF SUPER-HEROES #33
.... SEPTEMBER 1992
DREADKNIGHT
IRON MAN #101 .... AUGUST 1977
DREAM GIRL
ADVENTURE COMICS #317 .... FEBRUARY 1964
DREAM QUEEN
ALPHA FLIGHT #56 .... MARCH 88
D'SPAYRE
MARVEL TEAM UP #68 .... APRIL 1978
DUO DAMSEL
ADVENTURE COMICS #340 .... JANUARY 1966
DUPLICATE BOY
ADVENTURE COMICS #324 .... AUGUST 1964
DWELLER IN DARKNESS
THOR #229 .... NOVEMBER 1974
DYNAMO BOY
ADVENTURE COMICS #330 .... MARCH 1965
EASY COMPANY
OUR ARMY AT WAR #81 .... APRIL 1959
ECLIPSO
HOUSE OF SECRETS #61 .... JULY/AUGUST 1963
EEL
STRANGE TALES #112 .... SEPTEMBER 1963

EGG HEAD
TALES TO ASTONISH #38...........DECEMBER 1962
EGO
THOR #132....................................SEPTEMBER 1966
EL DIABLO (DC)
ALL-STAR WESTERN #2.................OCT/NOV 1970
EL JAGUAR
DAREDEVIL #120.......................................APRIL 1975
ELASTIC LAD
JIMMY OLSEN, SUPERMAN'S PAL #31
....SEPTEMBER 1958
ELASTI-GIRL
MY GREATEST ADVENTURE #80
....OCTOBER 1963
ELECTRO
AMAZING SPIDERMAN #9.......NOVEMBER 1963
ELECTRON
X-MEN, THE UNCANNY #107...NOVEMBER 1977
ELEKTRA
DAREDEVIL #168.............................JANUARY 1981
ELEMENT GIRL
METAMORPHO #10..........................JAN/FEB 1967
ELEMENT LAD
ADVENTURE COMICS #307.................APRIL 1963
ELFQUEST
FANTASY QUARTERLY #1.................SPRING 1978
ELONGATED MAN
FLASH (1st Series) #112...............APRIL/MAY 1960
ELRIC OF MELVINBONE
CEREBUS #4...JUNE 1978
E-MAN
E-MAN #1..OCTOBER 1973
EMERALD PRINCESS
ADVENTURE COMICS #352..........JANUARY 1967
EMMA FROST
X-MEN, THE UNCANNY #129.......JANUARY 1980
EMPATH
NEW MUTANTS #16..................................JUNE 1984
ENCHANTRESS
JOURNEY INTO MYSTERY #103.........APRIL 1964
ENEMY ACE
OUR ARMY AT WAR #151...........FEBRUARY 1965
ERADICATOR
ADVENTURES OF SUPERMAN #455...JUNE 1989
ETERNAL WARRIOR
SOLAR, MAN OF THE ATOM #10..........JUNE 1992
ETERNITY
STRANGE TALES #138...............NOVEMBER 1965
EVIL STAR
GREEN LANTERN #37............................JUNE 1965
EXCALIBUR
EXCALIBUR SPECIAL EDITION........................1987
EXECUTIONER
JOURNEY INTO MYSTERY #103.........APRIL 1964
EXTERMINATOR (becomes Deathstalker)
DAREDEVIL #39.......................................APRIL 1968
EYSIUS
CAPTAIN MARVEL #59..............NOVEMBER 1978
FACELESS CREATURE
STRANGE ADVENTURES #124.....JANUARY 1961
FALCON (Golden Age)
PEP COMICS #1..............................JANUARY 1940
FALCON
CAPTAIN AMERICA #117.........SEPTEMBER 1969
FALCONA
INCREDIBLE HULK ANNUAL #1...OCTOBER 1968
FALZON
INHUMANS #3..............................FEBRUARY 1976

FANDRAL
JOURNEY INTO MYSTERY #119.....AUGUST 1965
FANG
X-MEN, THE UNCANNY #107...NOVEMBER 1977
FANTASTIC FOUR
FANTASTIC FOUR #1...................NOVEMBER 1961
FASTBAK
NEW GODS, THE #5.........................OCT/NOV 1971
FATAL FIVE
ADVENTURE COMICS #352..........JANUARY 1967
FELIX FAUST
JUSTICE LEAGUE OF AMERICA #10
....MARCH 1962
FENRIS
X-MEN, THE UNCANNY #200....DECEMBER 1985
FENRIS WOLF
JOURNEY INTO MYSTERY #114.......MARCH 1965
FERAL
NEW MUTANTS #99...........................MARCH 1991
FER-PORR
CAPTAIN MARVEL #37...............DECEMBER 1974
FERRO
LEGION OF SUPER-HEROES #24
....DECEMBER 1991
FERRO LAD
ADVENTURE COMICS #346....................JULY 1966
FIDDLER
ALL-FLASH #32.................................DEC/JAN 1947
FIGHTING AMERICAN
FIGHTING AMERICAN #1...........APRIL/MAY 1954
FIN
DARING MYSTERY #7..........................APRIL 1941
FIN FANG FOOM
STRANGE TALES #89.......................OCTOBER 1961
FIRE
SUPER FRIENDS #25.......................OCTOBER 1979
FIRE LAD
ADVENTURE COMICS #306..............MARCH 1963
FIREARM
FIREARM #1...............................SEPTEMBER 1993
FIREBIRD
INCREDIBLE HULK #265............NOVEMBER 1981
FIREBUG
BATMAN #318...............................DECEMBER 1979
FIREHAWK
FIRESTORM THE NUCLEAR MAN,
THE FURY OF #17.............................OCTOBER 1973
FIRELORD
THOR #225...JULY 1974
FIRESTAR
X-MEN, THE UNCANNY #193.................MAY 1985
FIRESTORM
FIRESTORM #1....................................MARCH 1978
FIXER
STRANGE TALES #141.................FEBRUARY 1966
FLAG SMASHER
CAPTAIN AMERICA #312...........DECEMBER 1985
FLAIDERMAUS
FANTASTIC FOUR #129..............DECEMBER 1972
FLAMEBIRD (Jimmy Olsen)
SUPERMAN #158.........................DECEMBER 1962
FLAMING CARROT
VISIONS #1...1977
FLASH (Golden Age)
FLASH COMICS #1..........................JANUARY 1940
FLASH (Silver Age)
SHOWCASE #4..................................SEP/OCT 1956

FLASH (Modern)
CRISIS ON INFINITE EARTHS #12...MARCH 1986
FLY
FLY, ADVENTURES OF THE #1.........AUGUST 1959
FLY-GIRL
FLY, ADVENTURES OF THE #14
....SEPTEMBER 1961
FOES FROM KRYPTON
SUPERMAN #65......................JULY/AUGUST 1950
FOOLKILLER I
MAN-THING #3...................................MARCH 1974
FOOLKILLER II
OMEGA THE UNKNOWN #8..................MAY 1977
FOREIGNER
WEB OF SPIDERMAN #15.....................JUNE 1986
FOREVER PEOPLE
FOREVER PEOPLE #1.......................FEB/MAR 1971
FORGE
X-MEN, THE UNCANNY #184..........AUGUST 1984
FORGOTTEN ONE
ETERNALS, THE #13.................................JULY 1977
FOX
BLUE RIBBON COMICS #4...................JUNE 1940
FRANKENSTEIN'S MONSTER
FRANKENSTEIN,
THE MONSTER OF #1............................APRIL 1973
FRANKIE RAYE
FANTASTIC FOUR #164..............NOVEMBER 1975
FRANKLIN STORM
FANTASTIC FOUR #31.....................OCTOBER 1964
FRED BENDER (Dr. Eclipse)
SOLAR #14...OCTOBER 1992
FREEDOM FIGHTERS
JUSTICE LEAGUE OF
AMERICA #107................................JANUARY 1977
FREEDOM FORCE
X-MEN, THE UNCANNY #199...NOVEMBER 1985
FRENZY
X-FACTOR #4..MAY 1986
FRIGHTFUL FOUR
FANTASTIC FOUR #36........................MARCH 1965
FROG MAN
MARVEL TEAM UP #121...........SEPTEMBER 1982
GABRIEL
FANTASTIC FOUR #120.......................MARCH 1972
GAEA
DOCTOR STRANGE (2nd Series) #6
....FEBRUARY 1975
GALACTUS
FANTASTIC FOUR #48.........................MARCH 1966
GAMBIT
X-MEN, THE UNCANNY #266..........AUGUST 1990
GAMORA
STRANGE TALES #180.............................MAY 1975
GANGBUSTER
SUPERMAN, THE ADVENTURES OF #434
....SEPTEMBER 1987
GARDENER
MARVEL TEAM UP #55......................MARCH 1977
GARGOYLE
DEFENDERS #94.......................................APRIL 1981
GARRYN BEK
INVASION #1...1988
GARV
L.E.G.I.O.N. #15..MAY 1990
GATECRASHER
EXCALIBUR SPECIAL EDITION #1..................1987

GEB
THOR #241 ....NOVEMBER 1975
GEE
POWER PACK #1 ....AUGUST 1984
GEIRRODUR
JOURNEY INTO MYSTERY #101
....................FEBRUARY 1964
GENERAL GLORY
JUSTICE LEAGUE AMERICA #46
....................JANUARY 1991
GENTLEMEN GHOST
ATOM, THE #43 ....JUNE/JULY 1969
GEO-FORCE
BRAVE AND THE BOLD, THE #200 ....JULY 1983
GEOMANCER (Geoff)
SOLAR, MAN OF THE ATOM #10..........JUNE 1992
GHAUR
ETERNALS, THE (Limited Series) #2
....................NOVEMBER 1985
GHOST
IRON MAN #219 ....JUNE 1987
GHOST PATROL
FLASH COMICS #29....................MAY 1942
GHOST RIDER (Western)
GHOST RIDER #1 ....FEBRUARY 1967
GHOST RIDER I (Johnny Blaze)
MARVEL SPOTLIGHT #5 ....MARCH 1972
GHOST RIDER II (Daniel Ketch)
GHOST RIDER (2nd Series) #1 ....MAY 1990
GHOST RIDER OF 31ST CENTURY
GUARDIANS OF THE GALAXY #13 ......JUNE 1991
GIANT MAN
TALES TO ASTONISH #49..........NOVEMBER 1963
GIANT MAN II
MARVEL TWO IN ONE #54 ....AUGUST 1979
GIBBON
AMAZING SPIDERMAN #110
....................SEPTEMBER 1971
GIDEON
NEW MUTANTS #98....................FEBRUARY 1991
GILGAMESH
ETERNALS, THE #13....................JULY 1977
GIZMO
DOMINO CHANCE #7 ....DECEMBER 1984
GLADIATOR
DAREDEVIL #18....................JULY 1966
GLADIATOR II
X-MEN, THE UNCANNY #107 ...NOVEMBER 1977
GLAMOR
VISION AND SCARLET WITCH
(2nd Series) #4....................JANUARY 1986
GLORIAN
INCREDIBLE HULK #191...........SEPTEMBER 1975
GLYTRA
FANTASTIC FOUR #240....................MARCH 1982
G'NORT
JUSTICE LEAGUE INTERNATIONAL #10
....................FEBRUARY 1988
GODIVA
NEW TEEN TITANS ANNUAL
(2nd Series) #3 1987
GOLD BUG
LUKE CAGE, HERO FOR HIRE #41 ....MARCH 1977
GOLD KRYPTONITE
ADVENTURE COMICS #299 ....AUGUST 1962
GOLDEN GLIDER
FLASH #250....................JUNE 1977
GOLDEN GORILLA (Becomes Congorilla)
ACTION COMICS #224 ....JANUARY 1957
GOLDFACE
GREEN LANTERN #28....................APRIL 1964
GOLEM
STRANGE TALES #174 ....JUNE 1974
GOLIATH
AVENGERS #28 ....MAY 1966
GOLIATH II
AVENGERS #63 ....APRIL 1969
GOLIATH III
IRON MAN ANNUAL #7 1985
GORGON
FANTASTIC FOUR #44................NOVEMBER 1965
GORILLA GRODD
FLASH (1st Series) #106..............APRIL/MAY 1959
GOSSAMER
LEGION OF SUPER-HEROES #24
....................DECEMBER 1991
GRANDMASTER
AVENGERS #69 ....OCTOBER 1969
GRAPPLERS
MARVEL TWO IN ONE #54 ....AUGUST 1979
GRAVITON
AVENGERS #158 ....APRIL 1977
GREEN ARROW
MORE FUN COMICS #73............NOVEMBER 1941
GREEN FLAME
SUPER FRIENDS #42....................MARCH 1981
GREEN GOBLIN I
AMAZING SPIDERMAN #14 ....APRIL 1964
GREEN GOBLIN II
AMAZING SPIDERMAN #136
....................SEPTEMBER 1975
GREEN GOBLIN III
AMAZING SPIDERMAN #176.......JANUARY 1978
GREEN HORNET (Golden Age)
GREEN HORNET COMICS #1 .....DECEMBER 1940
GREEN KRYPTONITE
SUPERMAN #61 ....NOV/DEC 1949
GREEN LANTERN (Golden Age)
ALL AMERICAN COMICS #16................JULY 1940
GREEN LANTERN (Silver Age)
SHOWCASE #22 ....SEP/OCT 1959
GREEN LANTERN CORPS
GREEN LANTERN #9 ....NOV/DEC 1961
GREENBERG THE VAMPIRE
BIZARRE ADVENTURES #29.....NOVEMBER 1981
GREGORY GIDEON
FANTASTIC FOUR #34....................JANUARY 1965
GREMLIN
INCREDIBLE HULK #163 ....MAY 1973
GRENDEL
COMICO PRIMER #2....................1982
GREY GARGOYLE
JOURNEY INTO MYSTERY #107 .....AUGUST 1964
GRIM GHOST
SENSATION COMICS #1...............JANUARY 1942
GRIM REAPER
AVENGERS #52....................MAY 1968
GRIMJACK
STARSLAYER #10 ....NOVEMBER 1983
GRIZZLY
AMAZING SPIDERMAN #139....DECEMBER 1974
GRONK
MARVEL TWO IN ONE #71...........JANUARY 1981
GROO THE WANDERER
DESTROYER DUCK #1 ....FEBRUARY 1982
GUARDIAN (Golden Age)
STAR SPANGLED COMICS #7 ....APRIL 1942

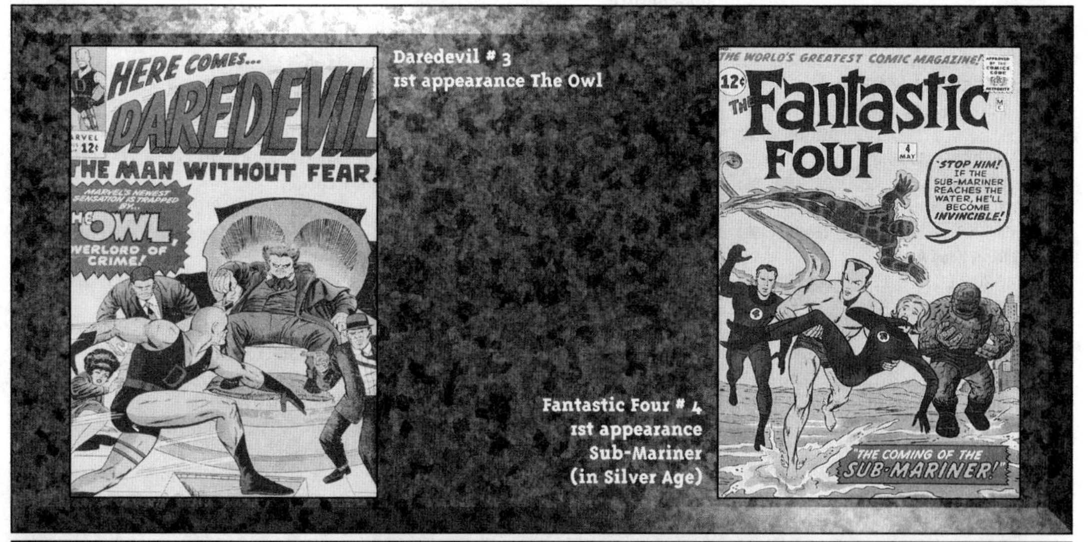

Daredevil # 3
1st appearance The Owl

Fantastic Four # 4
1st appearance
Sub-Mariner
(in Silver Age)

GUARDIAN (DC)
TEEN TITANS #44 ....JANUARY 1973
GUARDIAN (Marvel)
ALPHA FLIGHT #2....................SEPTEMBER 1983
GUARDIAN II
ALPHA FLIGHT #32 ....MARCH 1986
GUARDIANS OF THE GALAXY
MARVEL SUPER-HEROES #18......JANUARY 1969
GUARDIANS OF THE UNIVERSE
GREEN LANTERN #1..............JULY/AUGUST 1960
GUARDSMAN
IRON MAN #43....................DECEMBER 1971
GUARDSMAN II
IRON MAN #97....................APRIL 1977
GULLIVAR JONES
CREATURES ON THE LOOSE #16.....MARCH 1972
GUNNER & SARGE
ALL AMERICAN MEN OF WAR #67................1958
GUY GARDNER
GREEN LANTERN #59....................MARCH 1968
GWEN STACY
AMAZING SPIDERMAN #31......DECEMBER 1965
GYPSY MOTH
SPIDERWOMAN #10....................JANUARY 1979
H.A.R.D. CORPS
HARBINGER #10....................OCTOBER 1992
HACKER
HACKER FILES #1....................AUGUST 1992
HALO
BATMAN & THE OUTSIDER #1.......AUGUST 1983
HAMMER & ANVIL
INCREDIBLE HULK #182.............DECEMBER 1974
HAMMERHEAD
AMAZING SPIDERMAN #113.......OCTOBER 1972
HANGMAN
WEREWOLF BY NIGHT #11.......NOVEMBER 1973
HANNIBAL KING
TOMB OF DRACULA #25...............OCTOBER 1974
HARBINGER
HARBINGER #1....................JANUARY 1992
HARLEQUIN (Golden Age)
ALL AMERICAN COMICS #89
....................SEPTEMBER 1947
HARLEQUIN
TEEN TITANS #48....................JUNE 1977
HATEMONGER I
FANTASTIC FOUR #21................DECEMBER 1963
HAVOK
X-MEN, THE UNCANNY #56 ....MAY 1969
HAWK AND DOVE (Silver Age)
HAWK AND DOVE MINI SERIES #1
....................OCTOBER 1988
HAWK AND DOVE (Modern)
SHOWCASE #75....................JUNE 1968
HAWKEYE
TALES OF SUSPENSE #57 ....SEPTEMBER 1964
HAWKGIRL (Golden Age)
ALL STAR COMICS #5....................JUN/JUL 1941
HAWKGIRL (Silver Age)
BRAVE AND THE BOLD, THE #34.....MARCH 1961
HAWKMAN (Golden Age)
FLASH COMICS #1 ....JANUARY 1940
HAWKWOMAN (Modern)
HAWKWORLD (Limited Series) #1...................1989
HEATWAVE
FLASH (1st Series) #140 ....NOVEMBER 1963
HECKLER
HECKLER #1....................SEPTEMBER 1992

HECTOR HAMMOND
GREEN LANTERN #5....................APRIL 1961
HEIMDALL
JOURNEY INTO MYSTERY #85.....OCTOBER 1962
HELA
JOURNEY INTO MYSTERY #102.......MARCH 1964
HELIO
MARVEL TWO IN ONE #71............JANUARY 1981
HELLBLAZER (John Constantine)
SWAMP THING #37....................JUNE 1985
HELLCAT (Formerly The Cat)
AVENGERS #144....................FEBRUARY 1976
HELLFIRE CLUB
X-MEN, THE UNCANNY #129.......JANUARY 1980
HELLGRAMITE
ACTION COMICS #673 ....JANUARY 1992
HELLSTORM
AVENGERS WEST COAST #14
....................NOVEMBER 1986
HENRY PETER GYRICH
AVENGERS #168....................FEBRUARY 1978
HENRY PYM
TALES TO ASTONISH #27.............JANUARY 1962
HEPHAESTUS
THOR ANNUAL #5....................1976
HER
MARVEL TWO IN ONE #61................MARCH 1980
HERA
THOR #129....................JUNE 1966
HERBIE
FORBIDDEN WORLDS #73 ....JAN/FEB 1957
HERBIE THE ROBOT
FANTASTIC FOUR #209....................AUGUST 1979
HERCULES
JOURNEY INTO MYSTERY ANNUAL #1.........1965
HERMES
THOR #129....................JUNE 1966
HIGH EVOLUTIONARY
THOR #134 ....NOVEMBER 1966
HIM
FANTASTIC FOUR #67 ....OCTOBER 1967
HIPPOLYTE
ALL STAR COMICS #8 ....DEC/JAN 1941
HOBGOBLIN
AMAZING SPIDERMAN #238...........MARCH 1983
HOBGOBLIN II
AMAZING SPIDERMAN #289..............JUNE 1987
HOCUS & POCUS
ACTION COMICS #83 ....APRIL 1945
HOGUN THE GRIM
JOURNEY INTO MYSTERY #119.....AUGUST 1965
HOP HARRIGAN
ALL AMERICAN COMICS #1................APRIL 1939
HORUS
THOR #240....................OCTOBER 1975
HOUNGAN
NEW TEEN TITANS, THE
(1st Series) #14....................DECEMBER 1981
HOURMAN (Golden Age)
ADVENTURE COMICS #48................MARCH 1940
HOURMAN (Silver Age)
JUSTICE SOCIETY OF AMERICA #21
....................AUGUST 1963
HOURMAN (Modern)
INFINITY INC. #20....................NOVEMBER 1985
HOWARD THE DUCK
FEAR #19....................DECEMBER 1973

HULK (Green)
INCREDIBLE HULK #2....................JULY 1962
HULK (Grey)
INCREDIBLE HULK #1 ....MAY 1962
HULK (Modern Green Skin)
INCREDIBLE HULK #377................JANUARY 1991
HULK (Modern Grey Skin)
INCREDIBLE HULK #324................OCTOBER 1986
HULK 2099
2099 UNLIMITED #1 ....SEPTEMBER 1993
HULKBUSTERS
INCREDIBLE HULK #317....................MARCH 1985
HUMAN TARGET
ACTION COMICS #419 ....DECEMBER 1972
HUMAN TOP
TALES TO ASTONISH #50...........DECEMBER 1963
HUMAN TORCH (Golden Age)
MARVEL COMICS #1....................OCT/NOV 1939
HUMAN TORCH (Silver Age)
FANTASTIC FOUR #1..................NOVEMBER 1961
HUNTRESS (Marvel)
MARVEL SUPER ACTION #1 ....MAY 1977
HUNTRESS (Golden Age)
SENSATION COMICS #68 ....AUGUST 1947
HUNTRESS (Modern)
ALL STAR COMICS #69...................NOV/DEC 1978
HUSSAR
X-MEN, THE UNCANNY #137
....................SEPTEMBER 1980
HYDRA
STRANGE TALES #135 ....AUGUST 1965
HYDROMAN
AMAZING SPIDERMAN #212.......JANUARY 1981
HYENA
FIRESTORM #4....................AUG/SEPT 1978
HYPERION
AVENGERS #85....................FEBRUARY 1971
IBIS THE INVINCIBLE
WHIZ COMICS #1....................FEBRUARY 1940
ICE
SUPER FRIENDS #9....................JANUARY 1977
ICE CREAM SOLDIER
OUR ARMY AT WAR #85..................AUGUST 1959
ICE MAN
LEGION #32....................OCTOBER 1991
ICEMAN
X-MEN, THE UNCANNY #1 ......SEPTEMBER 1963
IG'NEA
LEGION #30....................AUGUST 1991
IKARIS
ETERNALS, THE #1 ....JULY 1976
IKTHALON
MARVEL SPOTLIGHT #14 ....DECEMBER 1973
ILLUSION
VISION AND SCARLET WITCH
(2nd Series) #4....................JANUARY 1986
IMMORTUS
AVENGERS #10....................NOVEMBER 1964
IMPERIAL GUARD
X-MEN, THE UNCANNY #107 ...NOVEMBER 1977
IMPOSSIBLE MAN
FANTASTIC FOUR #11 ....FEBRAURY 1963
IMPOSSIBLE WOMAN
MARVEL TWO IN ONE #60 ....FEBRUARY 1980
IMPULSE
X-MEN, THE UNCANNY #107 ...NOVEMBER 1977
IN-BETWEENER
WARLOCK #10....................DECEMBER 1975

INFERIOR FIVE
SHOWCASE #62....MAY/JUNE 1966
INFERNO
LEGION OF SUPER-HEROES #24
....DECEMBER 1991
INFINITY GAUNTLET
THANOS QUEST #2....OCTOBER 1990
INFINITY INC.
ALL STAR SQUADRON #25....SEPTEMBER 1983
INHERITOR
INCREDIBLE HULK #149....MARCH 1972
INHUMANS
FANTASTIC FOUR #45....DECEMBER 1965
INJUSTICE LEAGUE
JUSTICE LEAGUE INTERNATIONAL #23
....JANUARY 1989
INJUSTICE SOCIETY
ALL STAR COMICS #37
....OCTOBER/NOVEMBER 1947
INSECT QUEEN (Lana Lang)
SUPERBOY #124....OCTOBER 1965
INTERGALACTIC VIGILANTE SQUADRON
ADVENTURE COMICS #237....JUNE 1957
INTERLOPER
DEFENDERS #147....SEPTEMBER 1985
INVADERS
AVENGERS #71....DECEMBER 1969
INVISIBLE KID
ACTION COMICS #267....AUGUST 1960
INVISIBLE KID (new)
LEGION OF SUPER-HEROES ANNUAL #1....1982
INVISIBLE WOMAN
FANTASTIC FOUR #1....NOVEMBER 1961
IRON FIST
MARVEL PREMIERE #15....JUNE 1974
IRON MAJOR
OUR ARMY AT WAR #158....SEPTEMBER 1965
IRON MAN
TALES OF SUSPENSE #39....MARCH 1963
IRON MAN II (Jim Rhodes)
IRON MAN #170....MAY 1983
IRON MAN 2020
AMAZING SPIDERMAN ANNUAL #20
....NOVEMBER 1986
IRON MONGER
IRON MAN #166....JANUARY 1983
IRON WOLF
WEIRD WORLDS #8....OCT/NOV 1973
IRONCLAD
INCREDIBLE HULK #254....DECEMBER 1980
ISAAC
CAPTAIN MARVEL #32....JULY 1974
ISIS (Marvel)
THOR #280....FEBRUARY 1979
ISIS (DC)
SHAZAM #25....OCTOBER 1976
IVAR, TIMEWALKER
ARCHER & ARMSTRONG/
ETERNAL WARRIOR #8....MARCH 1993
J. JONAH JAMESON
AMAZING SPIDERMAN #1....MARCH 1963
JACK FROST
MARVEL PREMIERE #29....APRIL 1976
JACK OF HEARTS
DEADLY HANDS OF KUNG FU #23....APRIL 1976
JACK O'LANTERN
MACHINE MAN #19....FEBRUARY 1991
JACK O'LANTERN II
CAPTAIN AMERICA #396....JANUARY 1992
JACKAL
AMAZING SPIDERMAN #129....FEBRUARY 1974
JADE
ALL STAR SQUADRON #25....SEPTEMBER 1983
JAGUAR
ADVENTURES OF THE
JAGUAR #1....SEPTEMBER 1961
JAMES RHODES
IRON MAN #120....MARCH 1979
JARELLA
INCREDIBLE HULK #140....JUNE 1971
JASON TODD
DETECTIVE COMICS #524....MARCH 1983
JEAN DeWOLFF
MARVEL TEAM UP #48....AUGUST 1976
JERICHO
NEW TEEN TITANS, THE
(1st Series) #42....MAY 1984
JESTER
DAREDEVIL #42....JULY 1968
JETSTREAM
NEW MUTANTS #16....JUNE 1984
JEWEL KRYPTONITE
ACTION COMICS #310....MARCH 1964
JIGSAW
AMAZING SPIDERMAN #161....OCTOBER 1976
JIMMY OLSEN
ACTION COMICS #6....NOVEMBER 1938
JINX
NEW TEEN TITANS, THE
(1st Series) #56....JULY 1985
JOCASTA
AVENGERS #162....AUGUST 1977
JOE POTATO
DETECTIVE COMICS #594....NOVEMBER 1988
JOHN CONSTANTINE
SWAMP THING, SAGA OF THE #37....JUNE 1985
JOHN JAMESON
AMAZING SPIDERMAN #1....MARCH 1963
JOHN STEWART
GREEN LANTERN #87....DEC/JAN 1972
JOHNNY QUICK
MORE FUN COMICS #71....SEPTEMBER 1941
JOHNNY THUNDER
FLASH COMICS #1....JANUARY 1940
JOKER
BATMAN #1....SPRING 1940
JONAH HEX
ALL STAR WESTERN #10....FEB/MAR 1972
J'ONN J'ONZZ (see Martian Manhunter)
JUBILEE
X-MEN, THE UNCANNY #244....MAY 1989
JUDOMASTER (Charlton)
SPECIAL WAR SERIES #4....NOVEMBER 1965
JUDOMASTER (DC)
CRISIS ON INFINITE EARTHS #6
....SEPTEMBER 1985
JUGGERNAUT
X-MEN, THE UNCANNY #12....JULY 1965
JUGHEAD
PEP COMICS #22....DECEMBER 1941
JUSTICE LEAGUE AMERICA
LEGENDS #6....APRIL 1987
JUSTICE LEAGUE EUROPE
JUSTICE LEAGUE AMERICA #24....MARCH 1989
JUSTICE LEAGUE INTERNATIONAL
JUSTICE LEAGUE INTERNATIONAL #24....????
JUSTICE LEAGUE OF AMERICA
BRAVE AND THE BOLD, THE #28....MARCH 1960
JUSTICE SOCIETY OF AMERICA
ALL STAR COMICS #3....WINTER 1940
JUSTICE SOCIETY OF AMERICA (Silver Age)
JUSTICE LEAGUE OF AMERICA #21
....AUGUST 1963
JUSTIN HAMMER
IRON MAN #120....MARCH 1979
KALIBAN
FANTASTIC FOUR #117....DECEMBER 1971
KAMANDI
KAMANDI THE LAST BOY ON EARTH #1
....OCT/NOV 1972
KANG
AVENGERS #8....SEPTEMBER 1964
KANGAROO
AMAZING SPIDERMAN #81....FEBRUARY 1970
KANJAR RO
JUSTICE LEAGUE OF AMERICA #3
....FEBRUARY/MARCH 1961
KARATE KID
ADVENTURE COMICS #346....JULY 1966
KARKAS
ETERNALS, THE #8....FEBRUARY 1977
KARMA
MARVEL TEAM UP #100....DECEMBER 1980
KARNAK
FANTASTIC FOUR #45....DECEMBER 1965
KARNILLA
JOURNEY INTO MYSTERY #107....AUGUST 1964
KATANA
BRAVE AND THE BOLD, THE #200....JULY 1983
KA-ZAR (Golden Age)
MARVEL COMICS #1....OCT/NOV 1939
KA-ZAR (Silver Age)
X-MEN, THE UNCANNY #10....MARCH 1965
KESTREL
HAWK AND DOVE MINI
Series #1....OCTOBER 1988
KEY, THE
JUSTICE LEAGUE OF
AMERICA #41....DECEMBER 1965
KHORYPHOS
ETERNALS, THE (Limited Series) #1
....OCTOBER 1985
KID ETERNITY
HIT COMICS #25....DECEMBER 1942
KID FLASH
FLASH (1st Series) #110....DEC/JAN 1960
KID QUANTAM
LEGION OF SUPER-HEROES #33
....SEPTEMBER 1992
KIERROK
X-MEN, THE UNCANNY #96....DECEMBER 1975
KILG%RE
FLASH (2nd Series) #3....AUGUST 1987
KILLER CROC
BATMAN #357....JANUARY 1984
KILLER SHRIKE
RAMPAGING HULK #1....JANUARY 1977
KILLOWAT
NEW TEEN TITANS ANNUAL #7....1991
KILLRAVEN
AMAZING ADVENTURES VOL 2 #18....MAY 1973

KILOWOG
GREEN LANTERN CORPS #201............JUNE 1986
KING COBRA (see Cobra)
KING KULL
CREATURES ON THE LOOSE #10.....MARCH 1971
KINGPIN
AMAZING SPIDERMAN #50..................JULY 1967
KITTY PRYDE
X-MEN, THE UNCANNY #129.......JANUARY 1980
KLAW
FANTASTIC FOUR #53......................AUGUST 1966
KNICK KNACK
CAPTAIN AMERICA #317........................MAY 1986
KOBRA
KOBRA #1 ....FEB/MAR 1976
KOFI
POWER PACK #16.......................NOVEMBER 1985
KOLE
NEW TEEN TITANS, THE
(2nd Series) #8 ....MAY 1985
KONG
KONG THE UNTAMED #1................JUN/JUL 1975
KORATH THE PURSUER
QUASAR #32 ....MARCH 1992
KORVAC
DEFENDERS GIANT SIZE #3.....NOVEMBER 1974
KRANG
FANTASTIC FOUR ANNUAL #1.........................1963
KRAVEN THE HUNTER
AMAZING SPIDERMAN #15..................MAY 1964
KREE
FANTASTIC FOUR #65 ....AUGUST 1967
KRO
ETERNALS, THE #1..................................JULY 1976
KRONUS
IRON MAN #55 ....FEBRUARY 1972
KRYPTO THE SUPER DOG
ADVENTURE COMICS #210..............MARCH 1955
KRYPTONITE KID
SUPERBOY #83..........................SEPTEMBER 1960
KURGO
FANTASTIC FOUR #7 ....OCTOBER 1962
KURSE
SECRET WARS II #4........................OCTOBER 1985
KYLUN
EXCALIBUR #2............................NOVEMBER 1988
L.E.G.I.O.N.
INVASION #2..MARCH 1989
LADY BLACKHAWK
BLACKHAWK #133.........................FEBRUARY 1958
LADY DEATHSTRIKE
ALPHA FLIGHT #33..................................APRIL 1986
LADY JANE
SWAMP THING, SAGA OF THE #119....MAY 1992
LADY QUARK
CRISIS ON INFINITE EARTHS #4..........JULY 1985
LADY SHIVA
RICHARD DRAGON,
KUNG FU FIGHTER #5.................DECEMBER 1975
LANA LANG
SUPERBOY #10...............................SEPT/OCT 1949
LAVA MEN
JOURNEY INTO MYSTERY #97.....OCTOBER 1963
LEADER
TALES TO ASTONISH #62..........DECEMBER 1964
LEGION
NEW MUTANTS #25..........................MARCH 1985

LEGION OF MONSTERS
MARVEL PREMIERE #28.............FEBRUARY 1976
LEGION OF SUBSTITUTE HEROES
ADVENTURE COMICS #306..............MARCH 1963
LEGION OF SUPER HEROES
ADVENTURE COMICS #247.................APRIL 1958
LEGION OF SUPER VILLAINS
SUPERMAN #147 ....OCTOBER 1961
LEGIONNAIRES
LEGION OF SUPER-HEROES
(3rd Series) #34............................DECEMBER 1991
LEMURIA
SUB-MARINER #9.........................JANUARY 1969
LEONUS
INCREDIBLE HULK ANNUAL #1...OCTOBER 1968
LEVIATHAN
LEGION OF SUPER-HEROES #24
....DECEMBER 1992
LEX LUTHOR (Golden Age)
ACTION COMICS #23 ....APRIL 1940
LEX LUTHOR (Silver Age)
ADVENTURE COMICS #271 ....APRIL 1960
LEX LUTHOR (Modern)
MAN OF STEEL #2..................................JUNE 1986
LEX LUTHOR II
ACTION COMICS #670.....................AUGUST 1992
LIBERTY LEGION
MARVEL PREMIERE #29...................MARCH 1976
LIGHTMASTER
SPECTACULAR SPIDERMAN #3
....FEBRUARY 1977
LIGHTNING LAD
ADVENTURE COMICS #247 ....APRIL 1958
LIGHTNING LASS
ADVENTURE COMICS #308....................MAY 1963
LIGHTRAY
NEW GODS, THE #1 ....FEB/MAR 1971
LIGHTSPEED
POWER PACK #1 ....AUGUST 1984
LILANDRA
X-MEN, THE UNCANNY #105
....SEPTEMBER 1977
LILITH (Dracula's Daughter)
CHILLERS GIANT SIZE #1......................JUNE 1974
LITTLE AUDREY
LITTLE AUDREY #1 ....APRIL 1948
LITTLE DOT
SAD SACK COMICS #1.............SEPTEMBER 1949
LITTLE LULU
FOUR COLOUR #74..................................JUNE 1945
LIVING LASER
AVENGERS #34...........................NOVEMBER 1966
LIVING LIGHTNING
AVENGERS WEST COAST #63......OCTOBER 1990
LIVING MONOLITH
MARVEL TEAM UP #69 ....MAY 1978
LIVING MUMMY
SUPERNATURL THRILLERS #5........AUGUST 1973
LIVING PHAROAH
X-MEN, THE UNCANNY #54................APRIL 1969
LIVING TRIBUNAL
STRANGE TALES #157 ....JUNE 1967
LIZ TWOYOUNGMAN
ALPHA FLIGHT #5........................DECEMBER 1983
LIZARD
AMAZING SPIDERMAN #6 ....AUGUST 1963
LLYRA
SUB-MARINER #32....................DECEMBER 1970

LOBO
OMEGA MEN #3..JUNE 1983
LOCKHEED
X-MEN, THE UNCANNY #166 .....FEBRUARY 1983
LOCKJAW
FANTASTIC FOUR #45.................DECEMBER 1965
LOIS LANE
ACTION COMICS #1 ....JUNE 1938
LOKI
JOURNEY INTO MYSTERY #85.....OCTOBER 1962
LONGSHOT
LONGSHOT #1 ....SEPTEMBER 1985
LOOTER
AMAZING SPIDERMAN #36 ....MAY 1966
LORD CHAOS (Marvel)
MARVEL TWO IN ONE ANNUAL #2
....FEBRUARY 1977
LORD CHAOS (DC)
NEW TEEN TITANS ANNUAL (2nd Series) #7
....1991
LORD SATANIS
ACTION COMICS #527 ....JANUARY 1982
LORD SATANUS
ADVENTURES OF
SUPERMAN #493 ....AUGUST 1992
LORELEI
THOR #339 ....JANUARY 1984
LORI LEMARIS
SUPERMAN #127 ....FEBRUARY 1959
LOSERS
G.I. COMBAT #138..............................OCT/NOV 1969
LUCIFER
X-MEN, THE UNCANNY #9..........JANUARY 1965
LUDI
DOCTOR STRANGE (2nd Series) #35 ..JUNE 1979
LUKE CAGE
LUKE CAGE, HERO FOR HIRE #1...........JUNE 1972
LUNA
FANTASTIC FOUR #240......................MARCH 1982
LUNATIK
DEFENDERS #56............................FEBRUARY 1978
LUPO
X-MEN, THE UNCANNY #62.....NOVEMBER 1969
MARVEL FAMILY
CAPTAIN MARVEL ADVENTURES #18
....DECEMBER 1942
MACE
LUKE CAGE, HERO FOR HIRE #3...OCTOBER 1972
MACHETE
CAPTAIN AMERICA #302............FEBRUARY 1985
MACHINE MAN
2001: A SPACE ODYSSEY #8 ....JULY 1977
MACHINESMITH
MARVEL TWO IN ONE #47...........JANUARY 1979
MAC-RONN
CAPTAIN MARVEL #49......................MARCH 1977
MAD DOG
DEFENDERS #125........................NOVEMBER 1983
MAD HATTER (Golden Age)
BATMAN #49.......................................OCT/NOV 1948
MAD HATTER (Silver Age)
DETECTIVE COMICS #230 ....APRIL 1956
MAD THINKER
FANTASTIC FOUR #15 ....JUNE 1963
MADAME MASQUE
IRON MAN #17 ....SEPTEMBER 1969
MADAME WEB
AMAZING SPIDERMAN #210...NOVEMBER 1980

MADCAP
CAPTAIN AMERICA #307 .... JULY 1985

MAD-DOG
DEFENDERS #125 .... NOVEMBER 1983

MADISON JEFFRIES
ALPHA FLIGHT #16 .... NOVEMBER 1984

MADMAN
BLUE BEETLE #3 .... AUGUST 1986

MAELSTROM
MARVEL TWO IN ONE #71 .... JANUARY 1981

MAELSTROM'S MINIONS
MARVEL TWO IN ONE #71 .... JANUARY 1981

MAGE
GRENDEL #16 .... JANUARY 1988

MAGIC
X-MEN, THE UNCANNY #107 ... NOVEMBER 1977

MAGMA
NEW MUTANTS #8 .... OCTOBER 1983

MAGNETO
X-MEN, THE UNCANNY #1 ...... SEPTEMBER 1963

MAGNUS ROBOT FIGHTER
MAGNUS, ROBOT FIGHTER #1 .. FEBRUARY 1963

MAGPIE
MAN OF STEEL #3 .... JULY 1986

MAGUS
NEW MUTANTS #18 .... AUGUST 1984

MAHA YOGI
X-MEN, THE UNCANNY #47 .... AUGUST 1968

MAJOR MAPLE LEAF
ALPHA FLIGHT #106 .... MARCH 1992

MAJOR MYNAH
ATOM #37 .... JUN/JUL 1968

MAJOR VICTORY
GUARDIANS OF THE GALAXY #20
.... JANUARY 1992

MAKKARI
ETERNALS, THE #5 .... NOVEMBER 1976

MAKOTH
THOR #148 .... JANUARY 1968

MALEVOLENCE (Mephisto's Daughter)
GUARDIANS OF THE GALAXY #7
.... DECEMBER 1990

MAN APE
AVENGERS #62 .... MARCH 1969

MAN BAT
DETECTIVE COMICS #400 .... JUNE 1970

MAN WOLF
AMAZING SPIDERMAN #124
.... SEPTEMBER 1973

MAN-BEAST
THOR #134 .... NOVEMBER 1966

MANDARIN
TALES OF SUSPENSE #50 .... FEBRUARY 1964

MANDRAKE THE MAGICIAN
KING COMICS #1 .... APRIL 1936

MANDRILL
SHANNA THE SHE-DEVIL #4 .... JUNE 1973

MANDROID
AVENGERS #94 .... NOVEMBR 1971

MANGA KHAN
JUSTICE LEAGUE INTERNATIONAL #14
.... JUNE 1988

MANHUNTER (Golden Age)
ADVENTURE COMICS #73 .... APRIL 1942

MANHUNTER (Modern)
DETECTIVE COMICS #437 .... OCT/NOV 1973

MANHUNTER II (Golden Age)
POLICE COMICS #8 .... MARCH 1942

MANHUNTER II (Modern)
MANHUNTER #1 .... JULY 1988

MANHUNTERS
FIRST ISSUE SPECIAL #5 .... AUGUST 1975

MANO
ADVENTURE COMICS #352 .... JANUARY 1967

MANSLAUGHTER
DEFENDERS #134 .... AUGUST 1984

MANTA
X-MEN, THE UNCANNY #137 .. SEPTEMBER 1980

MAN-THING
SAVAGE TALES #1 .... MAY 1971

MANTIS
AVENGERS #112 .... JUNE 1973

MANTRA
MANTRA #1 .... JULY 1993

MARAK
FANTASTIC FOUR #240 .... MARCH 1982

MARINNA
ALPHA FLIGHT #1 .... AUGUST 1983

MARK MERLIN
HOUSE OF SECRETS #23 .... AUGUST 1958

MARSHAL LAW
MARSHAL LAW #1 .... OCTOBER 1987

MARTIAN MANHUNTER
DETECTIVE COMICS #225 .... NOVEMBER 1955

MARTINEX
MARVEL SUPER-HEROES #18 ...... JANUARY 1969

MARVEL GIRL
X-MEN, THE UNCANNY #1 ...... SEPTEMBER 1963

MARVEL MAN (later Quasar)
CAPTAIN AMERICA #217 .... JANUARY 1978

MARY JANE WATSON
AMAZING SPIDERMAN #42 ..... NOVEMBER 1966

MARY MARVEL
CAPTAIN MARVEL ADVENTURES #18
.... DECEMBER 1942

MASS MASTER
POWER PACK #1 .... AUGUST 1984

MASTER
ALPHA FLIGHT #2 .... SEPTEMBER 1983

MASTER D'ARQUE
SHADOWMAN #8 .... DECEMBER 1992

MASTER OF KUNG FU
MARVEL SPECIAL EDITION #15 .. JANUARY 1974

MASTER ORDER
MARVEL TWO IN ONE ANNUAL #2
.... FEBRUARY 1977

MASTER PANDEMONIUM
AVENGERS WEST COAST #4 .... JANUARY 1986

MASTERMIND
X-MEN, THE UNCANNY #4 .... MARCH 1964

MASTERS OF EVIL
AVENGERS #272 .... NOVEMBER 1986

MATTER EATER LAD
ADVENTURE COMICS #303 .... DECEMBER 1962

MAVERICK
X-MEN (2nd Series) #5 .... FEBRUARY 1992

MAXIE ZEUS
DETECTIVE COMICS #483 .... APRIL 1979

MAXIMA
ACTION COMICS #645 .... SEPTEMBER 1989

MAXIMUS
FANTASTIC FOUR #47 .... FEBRUARY 1966

MAYHEM
CLOAK AND DAGGER, THE MUTANT
MISADVENTURES OF #5 .... JULY 1989

MEDUSA
FANTASTIC FOUR #36 .... MARCH 1965

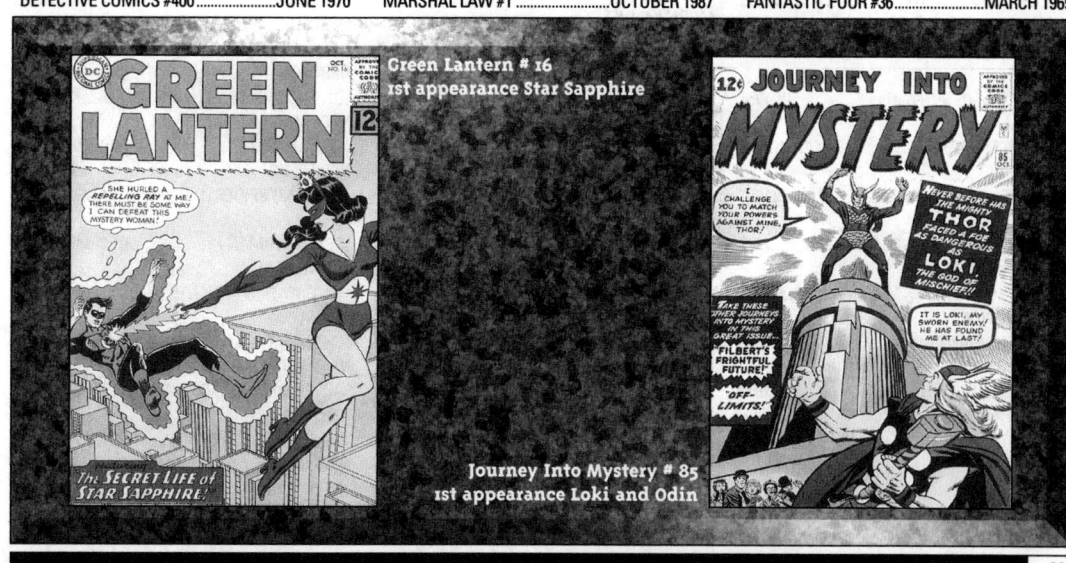

Green Lantern # 16
1st appearance Star Sapphire

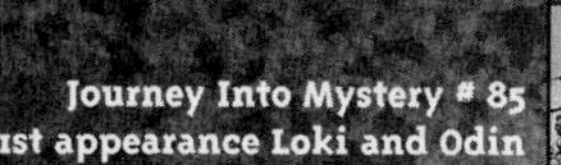
Journey Into Mystery # 85
1st appearance Loki and Odin

MEGGAN
NEW MUTANTS ANNUAL #2 ....OCTOBER 1986
MELTER
TALES OF SUSPENSE #47..........NOVEMBER 1963
MENTALLO
STRANGE TALES #141 ....FEBRUARY 1966
MENTO
DOOM PATROL #91 ....DECEMBER 1964
MENTOR
IRON MAN #5.............................SEPTEMBER 1968
MEPHISTO
SILVER SURFER (1st Series) #3.....OCTOBER 1968
MERA
AQUAMAN #11 ....SEPT/OCT 1963
MERBOY
WONDER WOMAN #107......................APRIL 1959
MERCENARIES
G.I. COMBAT #244...1981
MESMERO
X-MEN, THE UNCANNY #49..........OCTOBER 1968
METAL MEN
SHOWCASE #37.......................................APRIL 1962
METALLO (Silver Age)
ACTION COMICS #252.............................MAY 1959
METALLO (1970s)
SUPERMAN #310 ....APRIL 1977
METAMORPHO
BRAVE AND THE BOLD, THE #57
....DECEMBER 1964
METRON
NEW GODS, THE #1 ....FEB/MAR 1971
MEVERICK
X-MEN (2nd Series) #6 ....MARCH 1992
MIDAS
IRON MAN #17...........................SEPTEMBER 1969
MIDGARD SERPENT
THOR #127 ....APRIL 1966
MIDGET
X-MEN, THE UNCANNY #107 ...NOVEMBER 1977
MIDNIGHT SUN
SILVER SURFER (3rd Series) #29
....NOVEMBER 1989
MIGHTY CRUSADERS
MIGHTY CRUSADERS #1 ....NOVEMBER 1965
MILLIE THE MODEL
MILLIE THE MODEL #1? ....WINTER 1945
MIME
BATMAN #412..................................OCTOBER 1987
MIMIC
X-MEN, THE UNCANNY #19.................APRIL 1986
MINERVA
CAPTAIN MARVEL #49.......................MARCH 1977
MIRAGE (DC)
NEW TEEN TITANS ANNUAL #7.......................1991
MIRAGE (Marvel)
MARVEL GRAPHIC NOVEL #4...........................1982
MIRROR MASTER
FLASH (1st Series) #105............FEB/MARCH 1955
MISS AMERICA
AVENGERS GIANT-SIZE #1.............AUGUST 1974
MISSING LINK
INCREDIBLE HULK #105..........................JULY 1968
MISTER FANTASTIC
FANTASTIC FOUR #1 ....NOVEMBER 1961
MISTER FEAR I
DAREDEVIL #6................................FEBRUARY 1965
MISTER FEAR II
DAREDEVIL #54 ....JULY 1969

MISTER FEAR III
DAREDEVIL #91 ....SEPTEMBER 1972
MISTER FEAR IV
MARVEL TEAM UP #92..........................APRIL 1980
MISTER HYDE
JOURNEY INTO MYSTERY #99..DECEMBER 1963
MISTER MIRACLE
MISTER MIRACLE #1 ....MAR/APRIL 1971
MISTER MIRACLE II
MISTER MIRACLE (2nd Series) #15.......MAY 1990
MISTER SINISTER
X-MEN, THE UNCANNY #221..SEPTEMBER 1987
MISTY KNIGHT
MARVEL PREMIERE #20 ....FEBRUARY 1975
MOCKINGBIRD
MARVEL TEAM UP #95............................JULY 1980
MODAM
QUASAR #9 ....APRIL 1990
MODOK
TALES OF SUSPENSE #94 ....OCTOBER 1967
MODRED THE MYSTIC
MARVEL CHILLERS #1 ....OCTOBER 1975
MODRED THE MYSTIC (re-introduced)
DARKOLD #3 ....DECEMBER 1992
MOJO
LONGSHOT #3 ....NOVEMBER 1985
MOJO II
X-MEN ANNUAL (2nd Series) #1 1992
MOLE MAN
FANTASTIC FOUR #1..................NOVEMBER 1961
MOLECULE MAN
FANTASTIC FOUR #20................NOVEMBER 1963
MOLTEN MAN
AMAZING SPIDERMAN #28....SEPTEMBER 1965
MONARCH
ARMAGEDDON 2001 #1 ....MAY 1991
MON-EL (VALOR)
SUPERBOY #89 ....JUNE 1961
MONGOOSE
THOR #391 ....MAY 1988
MONGUL (Modern)
ADVENTURES OF SUPERMAN #454.....MAY 1989
MONITOR
NEW TEEN TITANS, THE (1st Series) #21
....JULY 1982
MOON KNIGHT
WEREWOLF BY NIGHT #32 ....MAY 1976
MOONBOY
DEVIL DINOSAUR #1 ....APRIL 1978
MOONDRAGON
IRON MAN #54.................................JANUARY 1973
MOONSTONE
INCREDIBLE HULK #228 ....OCTOBER 1978
MORAG
AVENGERS #133.................................MARCH 1975
MORBIUS
AMAZING SPIDERMAN #101....DECEMBER 1970
MORDRU
ADVENTURE COMICS #369....................JUNE 1968
MORGAN EDGE
JIMMY OLSEN #133 ....OCTOBER 1970
MORGAN LE FAY
SPIDERWOMAN #2...MAY 1978
MOTHER NIGHT
CAPTAIN AMERICA #123....................MARCH 1970
MR. AMERICA
ACTION COMICS #33....................FEBRUARY 1941

MR. BONES
INFINITY INC. #16..JULY 1985
MR. ELEMENT
SHOWCASE #13...APRIL 1958
MR. HYDE
JOURNEY INTO MYSTERY #99..DECEMBER 1963
MR. MIND
CAPTAIN MARVEL ADVENTURES #22
....MARCH 1943
MR. MIND (Modern)
SHAZAM #2 ....APRIL 1973
MR. MONSTER
VANGUARD ILLUSTRATED #7 1984
MR. MXYZPTLK (Golden Age)
SUPERMAN #30 ....SEP/OCT 1944
MR. MXYZPTLK (Silver Age)
SUPERMAN #131 ....AUGUST 1959
MR. MXYZPTLK (Modern)
SUPERMAN (2nd Series) #11 ...NOVEMBER 1987
MR. TERRIFIC
SENSATION COMICS #1 ....JANUARY 1942
MR. X
VORTEX #2 1983
MR. Z
SUPERMAN #51...............................JANUARY 1991
MS. MARVEL
MS. MARVEL #1 ....JANUARY 1977
MS. MARVEL II
THING, THE #35 ....MAY 1986
MULTIPLE MAN
FANTASTIC FOUR GIANT SIZE #4
....FEBRUARY 1975
MYSTERIO
AMAZING SPIDERMAN #13............MARCH 1964
MYSTIQUE
MS. MARVEL #18..JULY 1978
NADAR
MARVEL TWO IN ONE #71...........JANUARY 1981
NAMORA
MARVEL MYSTERY COMICS #82...........MAY 1947
NAMORITA
SUB-MARINER #50.....................................JUNE 1972
N'ASTIRH
X-FACTOR #32 ....SEPTEMBER 1988
NEBULA
AVENGERS #257 ....AUGUST 1985
NEBULO
INCREDIBLE HULK ANNUAL #1 ...OCTOBER 1968
NEBULON
DEFENDERS #13 ....MAY 1974
NECROM
EXCALIBUR #45.............................DECEMBER 1991
NED LEEDS
AMAZING SPIDERMAN #18 ....AUGUST 1964
NEEDLE
SPIDERWOMAN #9 ....DECEMBER 1978
NEGATIVE MAN
MY GREATEST ADVENTURE #80 ....JUNE 1963
NEKRA
SHANNA THE SHE-DEVIL #4 ....JUNE 1973
NEMESIS KID
ADVENTURE COMICS #346 ....JULY 1966
NEPTUNE
TALES TO ASTONISH #70 ....AUGUST 1965
NEW GODS
NEW GODS, THE #1 ....FEB/MAR 1971
NEW MUTANTS
MARVEL GRAPHIC NOVEL #4...........................1982

NEW TEEN TITANS
DC COMICS PRESENTS #26..........OCTOBER 1981
NEW WARRIORS
THOR #411 ....NOVEMBER 1989
NEWSBOY LEGION (Golden Age)
STAR SPANGLED COMICS #7...............APRIL 1942
NEWSBOY LEGION (Silver Age)
JIMMY OLSEN, SUPERMAN'S PAL #133
....OCTOBER 1969
NEXT MEN
DARK HORSE PRESENTS #54
....SEPTEMBER 1991
NICK FURY
SGT. FURY AND HIS HOWLING
COMMANDOS #1 ....MAY 1963
NICK FURY (As Agent of SHIELD)
STRANGE TALES #135 ....AUGUST 1965
NIGHT THRASHER
THOR #411 ....NOVEMBER 1989
NIGHTCRAWLER
X-MEN GIANT-SIZE #1....................SUMMER 1975
NIGHTGIRL
ADVENTURE COMICS #306..............MARCH 1963
NIGHTHAWK
AVENGERS #69 ....OCTOBER 1969
NIGHTHAWK II
AVENGERS #85...............................FEBRUARY 1971
NIGHTMAN
THE STRANGERS #1...............................JUNE 1993
NIGHTMARE
STRANGE TALES #110..............................JULY 1963
NIGHTMASTER
SHOWCASE #82 ....MAY 1969
NIGHTRIDER
NEW TEEN TITANS ANNUAL #7.......................1991
NIGHTSHADE (Marvel)
CAPTAIN AMERICA #164 ....AUGUST 1973
NIGHTSHADE
CAPTAIN ATOM (Charlton) #82SEPTEMBER 1966
NIGHTWING (Dick Grayson)
NEW TEEN TITANS, THE
(1st Series) #43..JUNE 1984
NIGHTWING (Superman)
SUPERMAN #158.........................DECEMBER 1962
NIKKI
MARVEL PRESENTS #4 ....APRIL 1976
NIMBUS
ADVENTURE COMICS #67............OCTOBER 1941
NIMROD
X-MEN, THE UNCANNY #191 ....MARCH 1985
NINGAL
CHAMBER OF CHILLS #4...........DECEMBER 1951
NINJAK (as Colin King)
BLOODSHOT #6..JULY 1993
NITRO
CAPTAIN MARVEL #34.............SEPTEMBER 1974
NOMAD I
CAPTAIN AMERICA #180...........DECEMBER 1974
NOMAD II
CAPTAIN AMERICA #261 ....SEPTEMBER 1981
NOMAN
THUNDER AGENTS #1................NOVEMBER 1965
NORMAN OSBORN
AMAZING SPIDERMAN #37 ....JUNE 1966
NORTHSTAR
X-MEN, THE UNCANNY #120..............APRIL 1979
NORTHWIND
ALL STAR SQUADRON #25 ......SEPTEMBER 1983

NOVA
THE MAN CALLED NOVA #1....SEPTEMBER 1976
NOVA II
FANTASTIC FOUR #244 ....JULY 1982
NTH MAN
MARVEL COMICS PRESENTS #25
....AUGUST 1989
NUKE
DEFENDERS #112............................OCTOBER 1982
NUKLO
AVENGERS GIANT SIZE #1.............AUGUST 1974
NUKLON
ALL STAR SQUADRON #25 ......SEPTEMBER 1983
NULL THE LIVING DARKNESS
DEFENDERS #103 ....JANUARY 1982
NUT
THOR #241 ....NOVEMBER 1975
OBSIDIAN
ALL STAR SQUADRON #25 ......SEPTEMBER 1983
OCEAN MASTER
AQUAMAN #29..................................SEP/OCT 1966
ODDBALL
HAWKEYE #3...............................NOVEMBER 1983
ODIN
JOURNEY INTO MYSTERY #85.....OCTOBER 1962
OLYMPIA
ETERNALS, THE #5 ....NOVEMBER 1976
OLYMPUS
THOR ANNUAL #1 1965
OMAC
OMAC #1 ....SEP/OCT 1974
OMEGA
OMEGA THE UNKNOWN #1 ....MARCH 1976
OMEGA FLIGHT
ALPHA FLIGHT #11 ....JUNE 1984
OMEGA MEN
GREEN LANTERN #141 ....JUNE 1981
OMEGA RED
X-MEN (2nd Series) #4..................JANUARY 1992
ORACLE
X-MEN, THE UNCANNY #107 ...NOVEMBER 1977
ORION
NEW GODS, THE #1 ....FEB/MAR 1971
ORKA
SUB-MARINER #23 ....MARCH 1970
OSIRIS
THOR #240.......................................OCTOBER 1975
OSWALD THE RABBIT
NEW FUN COMICS #1 ....FEBRUARY 1935
OUTLAW KID
OUTLAW KID #1 ....SEPTEMBER 1954
OUTSIDER
DETECTIVE COMICS #334 ....DECEMBER 1964
OVERMIND
FANTASTIC FOUR #111 ....JUNE 1971
OWL
DAREDEVIL #3......................................AUGUST 1964
PALADIN
DAREDEVIL #150............................JANUARY 1978
PANTHA
NEW TITANS #73 ....FEBRUARY 1991
PARASITE I
ACTION COMICS #340 ....AUGUST 1966
PARASITE II
FIRESTORM THE NUCLEAR MAN,
THE FURY OF #58 ....APRIL 1987
PATCHWORK MAN
SWAMP THING #2.........................FEBRUARY 1973

PEACEMAKER
FIGHTIN' 5 #40..............................DECEMBER 1966
PENGUIN (Golden Age)
DETECTIVE COMICS #58.............DECEMBER 1941
PENGUIN (Silver Age)
BATMAN #155 ....MAY 1963
PEREGRINE
CONTEST OF CHAMPIONS #1 ....JUNE 1982
PERRY WHITE
SUPERMAN #7 ....NOV/DEC 1940
PERSUADER
ADVENTURE COMICS #352 ....JANUARY 1967
PESTILENCE
ALPHA FLIGHT #36 ....JULY 1986
PETE ROSS
SUPERBOY #86...............................JANUARY 1961
PHAEDER
MARVEL TWO IN ONE #71............JANUARY 1981
PHANTOM
KING COMICS #61 ....MAY 1941
PHANTOM EAGLE
MARVEL SUPER-HEROES #16
....SEPTEMBER 1968
PHANTOM GIRL
ACTION COMICS #276.............................MAY 1961
PHANTOM LADY
POLICE COMICS #1 ....AUGUST 1941
PHANTOM STRANGER (Golden Age)
PHANTOM STRANGER #1...........AUG/SEPT 1952
PHANTOM ZONE
ADVENTURE COMICS #283 ....APRIL 1961
PHASTOS
ETERNALS, THE (Limited Series) #1
....OCTOBER 1985
PHOBIA
NEW TEEN TITANS, THE (1st Series) #14
....DECEMBER 1981
PHOBIUS
MARVEL TWO IN ONE #71............JANUARY 1981
PHOENIX (Jean Grey)
X-MEN, THE UNCANNY #101 ....OCTOBER 1976
PHOENIX (Rachel Summers)
X-MEN, THE UNCANNY #141 ....JANUARY 1981
PIED PIPER
FLASH (1st Series) #106............................MAY 1959
PIEFACE
GREEN LANTERN #2 ....OCTOBER 1960
PILEDRIVER
DEFENDERS #17..........................NOVEMBER 1974
PINYON
FANTASTIC FOUR #129 ....DECEMBER 1972
PIP THE TROLL
STRANGE TALES #179............................APRIL 1975
PIPER
X-MEN, THE UNCANNY #62 .....NOVEMBER 1969
PISKAS
FANTASTIC FOUR #131 ....FEBRUARY 1973
PLANTMAN
STRANGE TALES #113 ....OCTOBER 1963
PLANTMASTER
ATOM #1 ....JUNE/JULY 1962
PLASMUS
NEW TEEN TITANS, THE
(1st Series) #14 ....DECEMBER 1981
PLASTIC MAN (Golden Age)
POLICE COMICS #1...........................AUGUST 1941
PLASTIC MAN (Silver Age)
PLASTIC MAN #1 ....NOV/DEC 1966

PLASTIC MAN (Modern)
PLASTIC MAN (2nd Series) #1 ....NOVEMBER 1988
PLUNDERER
DAREDEVIL #12....JANUARY 1966
PLUTO
THOR #127 ....APRIL 1966
POISON IVY
BATMAN #181....JUNE 1966
POLAR BOY
ADVENTURE COMICS #306....MARCH 1963
POLARIS
X-MEN, THE UNCANNY #49....OCTOBER 1968
PORCUPINE
TALES TO ASTONISH #48 ....OCTOBER 1963
POSSESSOR
THOR #235....MAY 1975
POW WOW SMITH
DETECTIVE COMICS #151 ....SEPTEMBER 1949
POWER GIRL
ALL STAR COMICS #58....JAN/FEB 1976
POWER MAN
LUKE CAGE, HERO FOR HIRE #1 ....JUNE 1972
POWER MAN (Erik Josten)
AVENGERS #21 ....OCTOBER 1965
POWER PACK
POWER PACK #1 ....AUGUST 1984
POWER PRINCESS
DEFENDERS #112....OCTOBER 1982
PRANKSTER
ACTION COMICS #51 ....AUGUST 1942
PREDATOR
PREDATOR #1....JUNE 1989
PRIME
PRIME #1....JUNE 1993
PRINCE EVILLO
ADVENTURE COMICS #350....NOVEMBER 1966
PRINCE RA-MAN (formerly Mark Merlin)
HOUSE OF SECRETS #73 ....JULY/AUGUST 1965
PRINCESS PROJECTRA
ADVENTURE COMICS #346 ....JULY 1966
PRINCESS PYTHON
AMAZING SPIDERMAN #22....DECEMBER 1964
PROFESSOR AMOS FORTUNE
JUSTICE LEAGUE OF AMERICA #6 ....AUGUST/SEPTEMBER 1961
PROFESSOR POWER
MARVEL TEAM UP #117 ....MAY 1982
PROFESSOR WARREN
AMAZING SPIDERMAN #31....DECEMBER 1965
PROFESSOR X
X-MEN, THE UNCANNY #1 ....SEPTEMBER 1963
PROFESSOR ZOOM
FLASH #139....1963
PROJECTA
ADVENTURE COMICS #346 ....JULY 1966
PROPHET
YOUNGBLOOD #2....AUGUST 1992
PROTEUS
X-MEN, THE UNCANNY #126 ....OCTOBER 1979
PROTOTYPE
PRIME #3....AUGUST 1993
PROWLER
AMAZING SPIDERMAN #78....NOVEMBER 1969
PSYCHO MAN
FANTASTIC FOUR ANNUAL #5....1967
PSYCHO PIRATE (Golden Age)
ALL STAR COMICS #23....WINTER 1944
PSYCHO PIRATE (Silver Age)
SHOWCASE #56....MAY/JUNE 1965
PSYLOCKE
NEW MUTANTS ANNUAL #2 ....OCTOBER 1986
PUCK
ALPHA FLIGHT #1....AUGUST 1983
PUFF ADDER
CAPTAIN AMERICA #337 ....JANUARY 1988
PUMA
AMAZING SPIDERMAN #256 ....SEPTEMBER 1984
PUNISHER
AMAZING SPIDERMAN #129....FEBRUARY 1974
PUPPET MASTER
FANTASTIC FOUR #8....NOVEMBER 1962
PURPLE GIRL
ALPHA FLIGHT #41 ....OCTOBER 1986
PURPLE MAN
DAREDEVIL #4....DECEMBER 1964
PYRA
KAMANDI THE LAST BOY ON EARTH #31 ....JULY 1975
PYRO
X-MEN, THE UNCANNY #141 ....JANUARY 1981
QUAGMIRE
SQUADRON SUPREME #5 ....JANUARY 1986
QUANTUM
WEST COAST AVENGERS #12 ....SEPTEMBER 1986
QUANTUM QUEEN
ADVENTURE COMICS #375 ....DECEMBER 1968
QUASAR
INCREDIBLE HULK #234 ....APRIL 1979
QUASIMODO
FANTASTIC FOUR ANNUAL #4....1966
QUESTION
BLUE BEETLE (Charlton) #1 ....JUNE 1967
QUICKSAND
THOR #392....JUNE 1988
QUICKSILVER
X-MEN, THE UNCANNY #4 ....MARCH 1964
QUISLET
LEGION OF SUPER-HEROES (2nd Series) #14....SEPTEMBER 1985
QUISP
AQUAMAN #1....FEBRUARY 1962
R J BRANDE
ADVENTURE COMICS #350....NOVEMBER 1966
RACHEL SUMMERS (becomes Phoenix)
X-MEN, THE UNCANNY #141 ....JANUARY 1981
RADIOACTIVE MAN
JOURNEY INTO MYSTERY #93 ....JUNE 1963
RAGE
AVENGERS #326....NOVEMBER 1990
RAGMAN
RAGMAN #1 ....AUG/SEP 1976
RAI
MAGNUS, ROBOT FIGHTER (2nd Series) #5 ....OCTOBER 1991
RAINBOW RAIDER
FLASH (1st Series) #286....JUNE 1980
RAMA-TUT
FANTASTIC FOUR #19....OCTOBER 1963
RAMPAGE
SUPERMAN [2nd Series] #7 ....JULY 1987
RAMROD
DAREDEVIL #103....SEPTEMBER 1973
RANCOR
GUARDIANS OF THE GALAXY #8 ....JANUARY 1991
RANDAC
THOR #147 ....DECEMBER 1967
RA'S AL G'HUL
BATMAN #232....APRIL 1971
RATTLER
CAPTAIN AMERICA #310....OCTOBER 1985
RAVEN
DC COMICS PRESENTS #26....OCTOBER 1980
RAWHIDE KID
RAWHIDE KID #1 ....MARCH 1955
RAY, THE
THE RAY #1 ....FEBRUARY 1992
RAZORBACK
SPECTACULAR SPIDERMAN #13 ....DECEMBER 1977
RAZOR-FIST
MASTER OF KUNG FU #29....JUNE 1975
REAPER
BATMAN #237 ....DECEMBER 1971
RED BEE
HIT COMICS #1 ....JULY 1940
RED GHOST
FANTASTIC FOUR #13 ....APRIL 1963
RED GUARDIAN
AVENGERS #43....AUGUST 1968
RED RAVEN (Golden Age)
RED RAVEN COMICS #1 ....AUGUST 1940
RED RAVEN (Modern)
X-MEN, THE UNCANNY #44 ....MAY 1968
RED RONIN
GODZILLA #7 ....FEBRUARY 1973
RED SKULL (Golden Age)
CAPTAIN AMERICA COMICS #1....MARCH 1941
RED SKULL (Silver Age)
TALES OF SUSPENSE #65....MAY 1965
RED SONJA
CONAN THE BARBARIAN #23 ....MARCH 1973
RED SOPHIA
CEREBUS #3....APRIL 1978
RED STAR
TEEN TITANS #18 ....DECEMBER 1968
RED TORNADO (Golden Age)
ALL AMERICAN COMICS #20...NOVEMBER 1940
RED TORNADO (Silver Age)
JUSTICE LEAGUE OF AMERICA #64 ....AUGUST 1968
RED TORNADO (Modern)
JUSTICE LEAGUE OF AMERICA #3 1985
RED WOLF I
MARVEL SPOTLIGHT #1 ....NOVEMBER 1971
RED WOLF II
AVENGERS #80....SEPTEMBER 1970
REDSTONE
SQUADRON SUPREME #9....MAY 1986
REDWING
NEW TEEN TITANS ANNUAL #7....1991
REJECT
ETERNALS, THE #8 ....FEBRUARY 1977
REX THE WONDER DOG
REX THE WONDER DOG #1 ....JAN/FEB 1952
RHINO
AMAZING SPIDERMAN #41 ....OCTOBER 1966
RICHIE RICH
LITTLE DOT #1 ....SEPTEMBER 1953

RICK JONES
INCREDIBLE HULK #1 ....MAY 1962
RIDDLER (Golden Age)
DETECTIVE COMICS #140 ....OCTOBER 1948
RIDDLER (Silver Age)
BATMAN #171 ....MAY 1965
RINGER
DEFENDERS #51 ....SEPTEMBER 1977
RINGMASTER
CAPTAIN AMERICA COMICS #5 ....AUGUST 1941
RINTRAH
DOCTOR STRANGE (2nd Series) #81 ....FEBRUARY 1987
RIP HUNTER
SHOWCASE #20 ....JUNE 1959
ROBIN (Carrie Kelly)
BATMAN THE DARK KNIGHT RETURNS #2 ....APRIL 1986
ROBIN (Dick Grayson)
DETECTIVE COMICS #38 ....APRIL 1940
ROBIN (Jason Todd)
BATMAN #369 ....FEBRUARY 1984
ROBIN (Timothy Drake)
BATMAN #442 ....DECEMBER 1989
ROBOCOP
ROBOCOP #1 ....OCTOBER 1987
ROBOTMAN (Golden Age)
STAR SPANGLED COMICS #7 ....APRIL 1942
ROBOTMAN (Silver Age)
MY GREATEST ADVENTURE #80 ....JUNE 1963
ROBOTMAN (Modern)
SHOWCASE #94 ....AUGUST/SEPTEMBER 1977
ROCK PYTHON
CAPTAIN AMERICA #342 ....JUNE 1988
ROCKET RACCOON
MARVEL PREVIEW #7 1975
ROCKET RACER
AMAZING SPIDERMAN #172 ....SEPTEMBER 1977
ROCKET RED
GREEN LANTERN CORPS #209 ....FEBRUARY 1987
ROCKETEER
STARSLAYER #1 ....FEBRUARY 1982
ROGUE
AVENGERS ANNUAL #10 1981
ROGUE'S GALLERY
FLASH (1st Series) #155 ....FEBRUARY 1965
ROH KAR
BATMAN #78 ....AUGUST/SEPTEMBER 1953
ROM
ROM #1 ....DECEMBER 1979
ROMA
X-MEN, THE UNCANNY #225 ....JANUARY 1988
ROMNAR
INCREDIBLE HULK ANNUAL #1 ....OCTOBER 1968
RONAN THE ACCUSER
FANTASTIC FOUR #65 ....AUGUST 1967
ROND VIDAR
ADVENTURE COMICS #349 ....OCTOBER 1966
ROSE
AMAZING SPIDERMAN #253 ....JUNE 1984
ROSE AND THORN
LOIS LANE, SUPERMAN'S GIRLFRIEND #105 ....OCTOBER 1970
ROULETTE
NEW MUTANTS #16 ....JUNE 1984
ROY RAYMOND
DETECTIVE COMICS #153 ....NOVEMBER 1949
ROYAL FLUSH GANG
JUSTICE LEAGUE OF AMERICA #43 1966
RUNNER
DEFENDERS #143 ....MAY 1985
RYNDA
THOR #148 ....JANUARY 1968
SABRA
INCREDIBLE HULK #256 ....FEBRUARY 1981
SABRETOOTH
IRON FIST #14 ....APRIL 1977
SANDMAN (1970s)
SANDMAN #1 ....WINTER 1974
SANDMAN DC (Golden Age)
ADVENTURE COMICS #40 ....JULY 1939
SANDMAN DC (Golden Age in Silver Age)
JUSTICE LEAGUE OF AMERICA #46 ....AUGUST 1966
SANDMAN (DC Modern)
SANDMAN (2nd Series) #1 ....JANUARY 1989
SANDMAN (former Marvel villain)
AMAZING SPIDERMAN #4 ....JUNE 1963
SANDY
ADVENTURE COMICS #69 ....DECEMBER 1941
SARACEN
PUNISHER WAR JOURNAL #25 ....DECEMBER 1990
SARGON THE SORCERER
ALL AMERICAN COMICS #26 ....MAY 1941
SASQUATCH
X-MEN, THE UNCANNY #120 ....APRIL 1979
SATANNA
VAMPIRE TALES #2 ....DECEMBER 1973
SATANNISH
DOCTOR STRANGE (1st Series) #174 ....NOVEMBER 1968
SATURN GIRL
ADVENTURE COMICS #247 ....APRIL 1958
SATURNINE
GHOST RIDER #76 ....JANUARY 1983
SAURON
X-MEN, THE UNCANNY #60 ....AUGUST 1969
SAVAGE DRAGON
MEGATON #3 1983
SCALPHUNTER
WEIRD WESTERN TALES #39 ....MARCH/APRIL 1977
SCARECROW (DC)
WORLD'S FINEST #3 ....AUTUMN 1941
SCARECROW (Marvel)
TALES OF SUSPENSE #51 ....MARCH 1964
SCARLET WITCH
X-MEN, THE UNCANNY #4 ....MARCH 1964
SCHEMER
AMAZING SPIDERMAN #83 ....APRIL 1970
SCORPION
AMAZING SPIDERMAN #20 ....OCTOBER 1964
SCOURGE
IRON MAN #194 ....MAY 1985
SEA DEVILS
SHOWCASE #27 ....AUGUST 1960
SEBASTIAN SHAW
X-MEN, THE UNCANNY #129 ....JANUARY 1980
SECRET SIX
SECRET SIX #1 ....APRIL/MAY 1968
SECRET SOCIETY OF SUPER-VILLAINS
SECRET SOCIETY OF SUPER-VILLAINS #1 ....MAY/JUNE 1976
SEEKER
FANTASTIC FOUR #46 ....JANUARY 1966

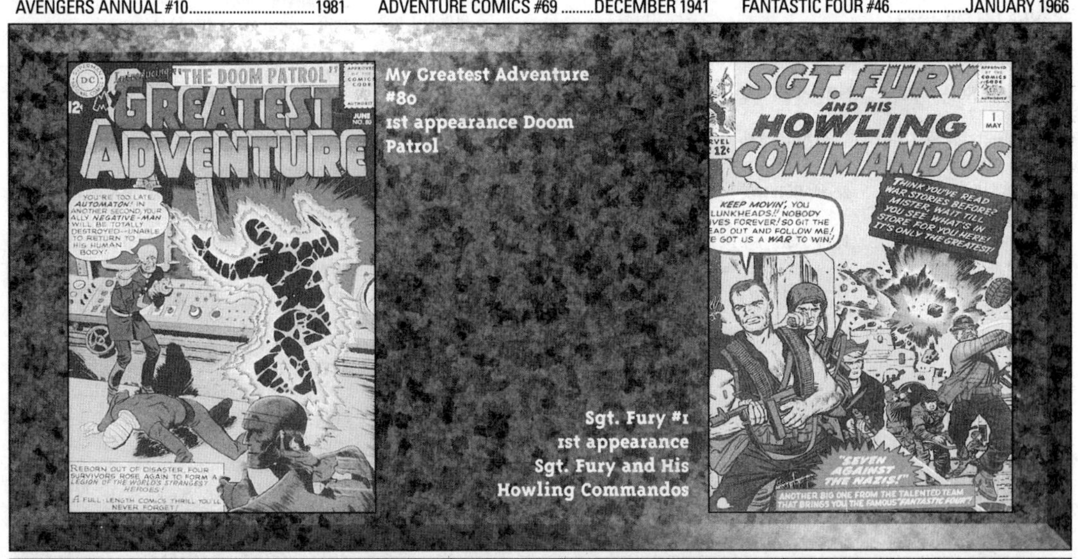

My Greatest Adventure #80 1st appearance Doom Patrol

Sgt. Fury #1 1st appearance Sgt. Fury and His Howling Commandos

SELENE
NEW MUTANTS #9 ....NOVEMBER 1983
SENSOR GIRL
LEGION OF SUPER-HEROES
(2nd Series) #14 ....SEPTEMBER 1985
SENTINELS
X-MEN, THE UNCANNY #14 .....NOVEMBER 1965
SENTRY
FANTASTIC FOUR #64 ....JULY 1967
SERPENT SOCIETY
CAPTAIN AMERICA #310 ....OCTOBER 1985
SERSI
STRANGE TALES #109 ....JUNE 1963
SET
CONAN THE BARBARIAN #7 ....JULY 1971
SETH
THOR #240 ....OCTOBER 1975
SEVEN SOLDIERS OF VICTORY
LEADING COMICS #1 ....WINTER 1941
SGT. BILKO
SGT. BILKO #1 ....MAY/JUNE 1957
SGT. BULLET & THE BRAVOS
G.I. COMBAT #264 ....APRIL 1984
SGT. FURY
SGT. FURY AND HIS HOWLING
COMMANDOS #1 ....MAY 1963
SGT. ROCK
OUR ARMY AT WAR #81 ....APRIL 1959
SHADE, THE CHANGING MAN
SHADE, THE CHANGING MAN #1
....JUN/JULY 1977
SHADOW (DC)
SHADOW, THE #1 ....OCT/NOV 1973
SHADOW KING
X-MEN, THE UNCANNY #117 ....JANUARY 1979
SHADOW LASS
ADVENTURE COMICS #366 ....MARCH 1968
SHADOW THIEF
HAWKWORLD #5 ....OCTOBER 1990
SHADOWCAT
X-MEN, THE UNCANNY #129 ....JANUARY 1980
SHADOWHAWK
YOUNGBLOOD #2 ....AUGUST 1992
SHADOWMAN
X-O MANOWAR #4 ....APRIL 1992
SHANNA THE SHE-DEVIL
SHANNA THE SHE-DEVIL #1 .....DECEMBER 1972
SHAPER OF WORLDS
INCREDIBLE HULK #155 ....SEPTEMBER 1972
SHARK
GREEN LANTERN #24 ....OCTOBER 1963
SHARON CARTER
TALES OF SUSPENSE #75 ....MARCH 1966
SHATTERSTAR
INHUMANS #3 ....FEBRUARY 1976
SHAZAM
SHAZAM #1 ....FEBRUARY 1973
SHE HULK
SHE HULK, THE SAVAGE #1 ....FEBRUARY 1980
SHI'AR
X-MEN, THE UNCANNY #97 ....JANUARY 1976
SHIELD (organization)
STRANGE TALES #135 ....AUGUST 1965
SHIELD (Silver Age)
ADVENTURES OF THE FLY #8..SEPTEMBER 1960
SHINING KNIGHT
ADVENTURE COMICS #66 ....SEPTEMBER 1941

SHIVA
WOLVERINE #50 ....JANUARY 1992
SHOCK
DAREDEVIL #315 ....APRIL 1993
SHOCKER
AMAZING SPIDERMAN #46 ....MARCH 1967
SHOOTING STAR
INCREDIBLE HULK #265 ....NOVEMBER 1981
SHRINKING VIOLET
ACTION COMICS #276 ....MAY 1961
SHROUD
SUPER-VILLAIN TEAM-UP #5 ....APRIL 1976
SIDEWINDER
MARVEL TWO IN ONE #64 ....JUNE 1980
SIF
JOURNEY INTO MYSTERY #102 ....MARCH 1964
SIGNALMAN
BATMAN #112 ....DECEMBER 1957
SILENT KNIGHT
BRAVE AND THE BOLD, THE #1
....AUG/SEPT 1955
SILVER BANSHEE
ACTION COMICS #595 ....DECEMBER 1987
SILVER SABLE
AMAZING SPIDERMAN #265 ....JUNE 1985
SILVER SAMURAI
DAREDEVIL #111 ....JULY 1974
SILVER SHADE
FIRESTORM THE NUCLEAR MAN,
THE FURY OF #53 ....NOVEMBER 1986
SILVER SURFER
FANTASTIC FOUR #48 ....MARCH 1966
SILVER SWAN
WONDER WOMAN (2nd Series) #15..APRIL 1988
SILVERMANE
AMAZING SPIDERMAN #73 ....JUNE 1969
SINESTRO
GREEN LANTERN #7 ....JUL/AUG 1961
SINISTER SIX
AMAZING SPIDERMAN ANNUAL #1 1963
SIRYN
SPIDERWOMAN #37 ....APRIL 1981
SIVANA
WHIZ COMICS #1 ....FEBRUARY 1940
SKIDS
X-FACTOR #7 ....AUGUST 1986
SKRULLS
FANTASTIC FOUR #2 ....JANUARY 1962
SKULL THE SALAYER
SKULL THE SLAYER #1 ....AUGUST 1975
SKY PIRATE
GREEN LANTERN #27
.....................................AUGUST/SEPTEMBER 1947
SLEEPWALKER
SLEEPWALKER #1 ....JUNE 1991
SLIGGUTH
MARVEL PREMIERE #5 ....NOVEMBER 1972
SLUDGE
SLUDGE #1 ....OCTOBER 1993
SLUG
CAPTAIN AMERICA #325 ....JANUARY 1987
SLYDE
AMAZING SPIDERMAN #272 ....JANUARY 1986
SMART ALEC
ALPHA FLIGHT #7 ....FEBRUARY 1984
SMASHER
X-MEN, THE UNCANNY #107 ...NOVEMBER 1977

SMUGGLER
SPECTACULAR SPIDERMAN #49
....DECEMBER 1980
SNAPPER CARR
BRAVE AND THE BOLD #28
....FEBRUARY/MARCH 1960
SOLOMUN GRUNDY
ALL AMERICAN COMICS #59 ....JULY 1944
SON OF SATAN
MARVEL SPOTLIGHT #12 ....OCTOBER 1973
SONAR
GREEN LANTERN #14 ....JULY 1962
SONS OF THE TIGER
DEADLY HANDS OF KUNG-FU #1 ....APRIL 1974
SOVIET SUPER-SOLDIERS
INCREDIBLE HULK #258 ....APRIL 1981
SPACE CABBIE
MYSTERY IN SPACE #26 ....JUNE/JULY 1955
SPACE PHANTOM
AVENGERS #2 ....NOVEMBER 1963
SPACE RANGER
SHOWCASE #15 ....AUGUST 1958
SPACENIGHTS
ROM #1 ....DECEMBER 1979
SPAWN
SPAWN #1 ....MAY 1992
SPECTRE (Golden Age)
MORE FUN COMICS #52 ....FEBRUARY 1940
SPECTRE (Silver Age)
SHOWCASE #60 ....JAN/FEB 1966
SPEED DEMON
AMAZING SPIDERMAN #222...NOVEMBER 1981
SPEED RACER
DAI KAMIKAZE #1 ....JUNE 1987
SPEEDBALL
AMAZING SPIDERMAN ANNUAL #22
....1988
SPEEDY
MORE FUN COMICS #73 ....NOVEMBER 1941
SPHINX
NOVA, THE MAN CALLED #6 ......FEBRUARY 1977
SPIDERMAN
AMAZING FANTASY #15 ....AUGUST 1962
SPIDERMAN (Black Costumed)
AMAZING SPIDERMAN #252 ....MAY 1984
SPIDERMAN (Cosmic Powered)
SPECTACULAR SPIDERMAN #158
....DECEMBER 1989
SPIDERMAN 2099
AMAZING SPIDERMAN #365 ....AUGUST 1992
SPIDERWOMAN
MARVEL SPOTLIGHT #32 ....FEBRUARY 1977
SPIDERWOMAN II
SECRET WARS #7 ....NOVEMBER 1984
SPIRAL
LONGSHOT #1 ....SEPTEMBER 1985
SPIRIT OF '76
INVADERS #14 ....MARCH 1977
SPITFIRE
INVADERS #12 ....JANUARY 1977
SPYMASTER
IRON MAN #33 ....JANUARY 1971
SQUADRON SUPREME
AVENGERS #85 ....FEBRUARY 1971
STARJAMMERS
UNCANNY X-MEN #104 ....APRIL 1977
SRO-HIMM
CAPTAIN MARVEL #37 ....DECEMBER 1974

STALKER
STALKER #1....................JUNE/JULY 1975
STALLIOR
INCREDIBLE HULK ANNUAL #1...OCTOBER 1968
STAR SAPPHIRE
GREEN LANTERN #16....................OCTOBER 1962
STAR SPANGLED KID
ACTION COMICS #40....................SEPTEMBER 1941
STAR THIEF
WARLOCK #14....................OCTOBER 1976
STARBOLT
X-MEN, THE UNCANNY #107...NOVEMBER 1977
STARBOY
ADVENTURE COMICS #282....................MARCH 1961
STARFIRE
DC COMICS PRESENTS #26....................OCTOBER 1980
STARFOX
IRON MAN #55....................FEBRUARY 1972
STARHAWK
DEFENDERS #27....................SEPTEMBER 1975
STARLIGHT
QUASAR #19....................FEBRUARY 1991
STARLORD
MARVEL PREVIEW #4....................1975
STARMAN (Golden Age)
ADVENTURE COMICS #61....................APRIL 1941
STARMAN (Silver Age)
JUSTICE LEAGUE OF AMERICA #29
....................AUGUST 1964
STARMAN (1970s)
FIRST ISSUE SPECIAL #12....................MARCH 1976
STARMAN (Modern)
STARMAN #1....................OCTOBER 1988
STARRO
BRAVE AND THE BOLD, THE #28.....MARCH 1960
STARSLAYER
STARSLAYER #1....................FEBRUARY 1982
STEALTH
L.E.G.I.O.N. #1....................FEBRUARY 1989
STEEL (John Henry Irons)
ADVENTURES OF SUPERMAN #500..APRIL 1993
STILT MAN
DAREDEVIL #8....................JUNE 1965
STINGRAY
SUB-MARINER #19....................NOVEMBER 1969
STONE BOY
ADVENTURE COMICS #306....................MARCH 1963
STORM
X-MEN GIANT-SIZE #1....................SUMMER 1975
STRANGER
X-MEN, THE UNCANNY #11....................MAY 1965
STRATA
INVASION #2....................MARCH 1989
STRIPSEY
ACTION COMICS #40....................SEPTEMBER 1941
STRONG GUY
NEW MUTANTS #29....................JULY 1985
STRYFE
NEW MUTANTS #87....................MARCH 1990
STUART'S RAIDERS
G.I. COMBAT #257....................SEPTEMBER 1983
SUB MARINER (Golden Age)
MOTION PICTURE FUNNIES
WEEKLY #1....................OCTOBER 1939
SUB MARINER (Silver Age)
FANTASTIC FOUR #4....................MAY 1962
SUDDEN DEATH
HAWK AND DOVE, THE #5....................OCTOBER 1989

SUICIDE SQUAD (New)
LEGENDS #2....................DECEMBER 1986
SUN EATER
ADVENTURE COMICS #352....................JANUARY 1967
SUNBOY
ADVENTURE COMICS #290.......NOVEMBER 1961
SUNDER
X-MEN, THE UNCANNY #169....................MAY 1983
SUNFIRE
X-MEN, THE UNCANNY #64....................JANUARY 1970
SUNSPOT
MARVEL GRAPHIC NOVEL #4....................1982
SUPER BABY
SUPERBOY #8....................MAY/JUNE 1950
SUPER PATRIOT
CAPTAIN AMERICA #323....................NOVEMBER 1986
SUPER SKRULL
FANTASTIC FOUR #18....................SEPTEMBER 1963
SUPER-ADAPTOID
TALES OF SUSPENSE #82....................OCTOBER 1966
SUPERBOY
MORE FUN COMICS #101....................JAN/FEB 1945
SUPERBOY II (Kid Clone)
ADVENTURES OF SUPERMAN #500..APRIL 1993
SUPERBOY ROBOT
ADVENTURE COMICS #251....................AUGUST 1958
SUPERFRIENDS
SUPERFRIENDS #1....................NOVEMBER 1976
SUPERGIRL
ACTION COMICS #252....................MAY 1959
SUPERGIRL (Matrix)
SUPERMAN #16....................APRIL 1988
SUPERMAN (Golden Age)
ACTION COMICS #1....................JUNE 1938
SUPERMAN (Modern)
MAN OF STEEL #1....................JUNE 1986
SUPERMAN EMERGENCY SQUAD
JIMMY OLSEN, SUPERMAN'S PAL #48
....................OCTOBER 1960
SUPERMAN ROBOT
ADVENTURE COMICS #265....................OCTOBER 1959
SUPERMONKEY
SUPERBOY #76....................NOVEMBER 1959
SUPER-SABRE
X-MEN, THE UNCANNY #215....................MARCH 1987
SUPERWOMAN
DC COMICS PRESENTS ANNUAL #2....................1983
SUPREME INTELLIGENCE
FANTASTIC FOUR #64....................JULY 1967
SURTUR
JOURNEY INTO MYSTERY #97.....OCTOBER 1963
SWAMP THING
HOUSE OF SECRETS #92....................JUNE/JULY 1971
SWARM
SPECTACULAR SPIDERMAN #36
....................OCTOBER 1979
SWORDSMAN
AVENGERS #19....................AUGUST 1965
TALISMAN I
ALPHA FLIGHT #19....................FEBRUARY 1985
TALISMAN II
ALPHA FLIGHT #38....................SEPTEMBER 1986
TARANTULA
AMAZING SPIDERMAN #134....................JULY 1974
TAROT
NEW MUTANTS #16....................JUNE 1984
TASKMASTER
AVENGERS #196....................JUNE 1980

TATTERDEMALION
WEREWOLF BY NIGHT #9........SEPTEMBER 1973
TEAM AMERICA
CAPTAIN AMERICA #269....................MAY 1982
TEAM TITANS
NEW TEEN TITANS ANNUAL #7....................1991
TEEN TITANS
BRAVE AND BOLD #54....................JUNE/JULY 1964
TEENAGE MUTANT NINJA TURTLES
GOBBLEDYGOOK #1....................1984
TELEPATH
L.E.G.I.O.N. #15....................MAY 1990
TELLUS
LEGION OF SUPER-HEROES
(2nd Series) #14....................SEPTEMBER 1985
TEMPEST
X-MEN, THE UNCANNY #107...NOVEMBER 1977
TEMPTRESS
MISTER E #1....................JUNE 1991
TERMINUS
FANTASTIC FOUR #269....................AUGUST 1984
TERRA I
NEW TEEN TITANS, THE
(1st Series) #28....................FEBRUARY 1983
TERRA II
NEW TITANS ANNUAL #7....................1991
TERRA MAN
SUPERMAN #249....................MARCH 1972
TERRAX
FANTASTIC FOUR #211....................OCTOBER 1979
TEXAS TWISTER
FANTASTIC FOUR #177....................DECEMBER 1976
THANOS
IRON MAN #55....................FEBRUARY 1972
THAROC
ADVENTURE COMICS #352....................JANUARY 1967
THENA
ETERNALS, THE #5....................NOVEMBER 1976
THING
FANTASTIC FOUR #1....................NOVEMBER 1961
THONGOR
CREATURES ON THE LOOSE #22.....MARCH 1973
THOR (Don Blake)
JOURNEY INTO MYSTERY #83.......AUGUST 1962
THOR (Beta Ray Bill)
THOR #337....................NOVEMBER 1983
THOR OF THE FUTURE (Dargo)
THOR #384....................OCTOBER 1987
THORN
LOIS LANE, SUPERMAN'S
GIRLFRIEND #105....................OCTOBER 1970
THRAXTON
FANTASTIC FOUR ANNUAL #12....................1977
3-D MAN,
MARVEL PREMIERE #35....................APRIL 1977
THUNDER AGENTS
THUNDER AGENTS #1....................NOVEMBER 1965
THUNDERBALL
DEFENDERS #17....................NOVEMBER 1974
THUNDERBIRD
X-MEN GIANT-SIZE #1....................SUMMER 1975
THUNDERBIRD II
NEW MUTANTS #16....................JUNE 1984
THUNDERBOLT (Peter Cannon)
THUNDERBOLT #1....................JANUARY 1966
THUNDRA
FANTASTIC FOUR #129....................DECEMBER 1972

TICK, THE
TICK #1 .... JUNE 1988
TIGER SHARK
SUB-MARINER #5 .... SEPTEMBER 1968
TIGRA (formerly The Cat)
CREATURES GIANT SIZE #1 .... JULY 1974
TIM DRAKE
BATMAN #440 .... OCTOBER 1989
TIM HUNTER
THE BOOKS OF MAGIC #1 1990
TIMBER WOLF
ADVENTURE COMICS #327 .... DECEMBER 1964
TIMBERIUS
INCREDIBLE HULK ANNUAL #1 ... OCTOBER 1968
TIME TRAPPER
ADVENTURE COMICS #321 .... JUNE 1964
TINKERER
AMAZING SPIDERMAN #2 .... APRIL 1963
TITANIA
SECRET WARS #3 .... JULY 1984
TITANIUM MAN
TALES OF SUSPENSE #69 .... SEPTEMBER 1965
TITANO THE SUPER APE
SUPERMAN #127 .... APRIL 1959
TOAD
X-MEN, THE UNCANNY #4 .... MARCH 1964
TOM THUMB
SQUADRON SUPREME #9 .... MAY 1986
TOMAHAWK
STAR SPANGLED COMICS #69 .... JUNE 1947
TOMAR-RE
GREEN LANTERN #6 .... JUNE 1961
TOMBSTONE
WEB OF SPIDERMAN #35 .... FEBRUARY 1988
TOMMY TOMORROW
REAL FACTS COMICS #6 .... JAN/FEB 1947
TOP
FLASH (1st Series) #122 .... AUGUST 1961
TORO (Golden Age)
HUMAN TORCH #2 .... AUTUMN 1940
TORO (Modern)
SUB-MARINER #14 .... JUNE 1969
TORPEDO
DAREDEVIL #126 .... AUGUST 1975
TOYMAN (Golden Age)
ACTION COMICS #64 .... SEPTEMBER 1943
TOYMAN (Modern)
SUPERMAN (2nd Series) #13 .... JANUARY 1988
TRAPSTER
FANTASTIC FOUR #38 .... MAY 1965
TRAUMA
INCREDIBLE HULK #394 .... JANUARY 1992
TRIAD
LEGION OF SUPER-HEROES #24
.... DECEMBER 1991
TRICKSTER
FLASH (1st Series) #113 .... JULY 1960
TRINITY
NEW TITANS ANNUAL #6 1990
TRIPLICATE GIRL
ACTION COMICS #276 .... MAY 1961
TRITON
FANTASTIC FOUR #45 .... DECEMBER 1965
TROIA
NEW TITANS #55 .... JUNE 1989
TUROK
FOUR COLOR #596 .... DECEMBER 1954
TUROK (Modern)
MAGNUS, ROBOT FIGHTER
(2nd Series) #12 .... MAY 1992
TWEEDLEDEE AND TWEEDLEDUM
DETECTIVE COMICS #74 .... APRIL 1943
TWO FACE (Golden Age)
DETECTIVE COMICS #66 .... AUGUST 1942
TWO FACE (Modern)
BATMAN #234 .... JUNE 1971
TWO GUN KID
TWO GUN KID #1 .... MARCH 1948
TYPHOID MARY
DAREDEVIL #254 .... MAY 1988
TYRANNUS
INCREDIBLE HULK #5 .... JANUARY 1963
ULIK
THOR #137 .... FEBRUARY 1967
ULTIMUS
THOR #209 .... MARCH 1973
ULTRA BOY
SUPERBOY #98 .... JULY 1962
ULTRON
AVENGERS #55 .... AUGUST 1968
ULTRON AS CRIMSON COWL
AVENGERS #54 .... JULY 1968
UMAR
STRANGE TALES #150 .... NOVEMBER 1966
UNA
MARVEL SUPER-HEROES #12 ... DECEMBER 1967
UNICORN
TALES OF SUSPENSE #56 .... AUGUST 1964
UNION JACK I (Lord Falsworth)
INVADERS #7 .... JULY 1976
UNION JACK II (Brian Falsworth)
INVADERS #8 .... SEPTEMBER 1976
UNION JACK III (Joey Chapman)
CAPTAIN AMERICA #254 .... FEBRUARY 1981
UNIVERSO
ADVENTURE COMICS #349 .... OCTOBER 1966
UNKNOWN SOLDIER
STAR SPANGLED WAR STORIES #151
.... JUNE/JULY 1970
UNUS
X-MEN, THE UNCANNY #8 .... NOVEMBER 1964
URSA MAJOR
INCREDIBLE HULK #258 .... APRIL 1981
USAGENT
CAPTAIN AMERICA #323 .... NOVEMBER 1986
USAGI YOJIMBO
ALBEDO #1 .... JUNE 1985
VALDA
ARAK #3 .... NOVEMBER 1981
VALKYRIE
AVENGERS #87 .... APRIL 1971
VAMP
CAPTAIN AMERICA #217 .... JANUARY 1978
VAMPIRELLA
VAMPIRELLA #1 .... SEPTEMBER 1969
VANDAL SAVAGE (Golden Age)
GREEN LANTERN #10 .... WINTER 1943
VANDAL SAVAGE (Silver Age)
FLASH (1st Series) #137 .... JUNE 1963
VANGUARD
IRON MAN #109 .... APRIL 1978
VANISHER
X-MEN, THE UNCANNY #2 .... NOVEMBER 1963
VELVET TIGER
DETECTIVE COMICS #518 .... SEPTEMBER 1982
VENOM
AMAZING SPIDERMAN #300 .... MAY 1987
VENUS
SUB-MARINER #57 .... JANUARY 1973
VERMIN
CAPTAIN AMERICA #272 .... AUGUST 1982
VESTA
THOR #301 .... NOVEMBER 1980
VICKI VALE
BATMAN #45 .... FEBRUARY/MARCH 1948
VIGILANTE (Golden Age)
ACTION COMICS #42 .... NOVEMBER 1941
VIGILANTE II (Modern)
NEW TEEN TITANS ANNUAL
(1st Series) #2 1982
VIGILANTE III (female)
DEATHSTROKE THE TERMINATOR #10
.... MAY 1992
VIKING PRINCE
BRAVE AND THE BOLD, THE #1 .. AUG/SEPT 1955
VINDICATOR
UNCANNY X-MEN #120 .... APRIL 1979
VINDICATOR II
ALPHA FLIGHT #32 .... MARCH 1986
VIPER
CAPTAIN AMERICA #110 .... FEBRUARY 1969
VISHANTI
MARVEL PREMIERE #5 .... NOVEMBER 1972
VISION
AVENGERS #57 .... OCTOBER 1968
VIXEN
ACTION COMICS #521 .... JULY 1981
VOLCANA
SECRET WARS #3 .... JULY 1984
VRIL DOX
INVASION! #1 .... FEBRUARY 1989
VULTURE I
AMAZING SPIDERMAN #2 .... APRIL 1963
WANDERERS
ADVENTURE COMICS #375 .... DECEMBER 1968
WARLOCK (Cocoon)
FANTASTIC FOUR #66 .... SEPTEMBER 1967
WARLOCK (Him)
FANTASTIC FOUR #67 .... OCTOBER 1967
WARLOCK (New Mutants)
NEW MUTANTS #18 .... AUGUST 1984
WARLORD
FIRST ISSUE SPECIAL #8 .... NOVEMBER 1975
WARP
NEW TEEN TITANS, THE
(1st Series) #14 .... DECEMBER 1981
WARPATH
NEW MUTANTS #16 .... JUNE 1984
WARSTAR
X-MEN, THE UNCANNY #137 .. SEPTEMBER 1980
WARSTRIKE
MANTRA #1 .... JULY 1993
WARWOLVES
EXCALIBUR SPECIAL EDITION #1 1987
WASP
TALES TO ASTONISH #44 .... JUNE 1963
WATCHER
FANTASTIC FOUR #13 .... APRIL 1963
WAVERIDER
ARMAGEDDON 2001 #1 .... MAY 1991
WEAPON ALPHA (becomes Vindicator)
UNCANNY X-MEN #109 .... FEBRUARY 1978

WEAPON OMEGA
ALPHA FLIGHT #102....................NOVEMBER 1991
WEATHER WIZARD
FLASH (1st Series) #110.................JANUARY 1960
WEB, THE
FLYMAN #36..MARCH 1966
WENDIGO
INCREDIBLE HULK #162 ....APRIL 1973
WEREWOLF
MARVEL SPOTLIGHT #2............DECEMBER 1971
WHIPLASH
TALES OF SUSPENSE #97 ....JANUARY 1968
WHIPLASH II
MARVEL COMICS PRESENTS #49..................1990
WHIRLWIND
AVENGERS #46..............................NOVEMBER 1968
WHIRLYBATS
DETECTIVE COMICS #257 ....JULY 1958
WHITE BISHOP
X-MEN, THE UNCANNY #129.......JANUARY 1980
WHITE KRYPTONITE
ADVENTURE COMICS #279 ....DECEMBER 1960
WHITE QUEEN
X-MEN, THE UNCANNY #129.......JANUARY 1980
WHITE WITCH
ADVENTURE COMICS #351 ....DECEMBER 1966
WHIZZER (Golden Age)
USA COMICS #1 ....AUGUST 1941
WHIZZER (Modern)
AVENGERS GIANT-SIZE #1.............AUGUST 1974
WIDGET
EXCALIBUR #1 ....OCTOBER 1988
WILDCAT
SENSATION COMICS #1...............JANUARY 1941
WILDCAT II (female)
CRISIS ON INFINITE EARTHS #6
....SEPTEMBER 1985
WILDCHILD
ALPHA FLIGHT #11 ....JUNE 1984
WILD DOG
WILD DOG #1...............................SEPTEMBER 1987
WIZARD
STRANGE TALES #102...............NOVEMBER 1962
WIZARD WORLD
WARLORD #28..............................DECEMBER 1979

WOLFSBANE
MARVEL GRAPHIC NOVEL #4...........................1982
WOLVERINE
INCREDIBLE HULK #180.................OCTOBER 1974
WONDER GIRL
WONDER WOMAN #107 ....JULY 1961
WONDER GIRL (as Teen Titan)
BRAVE AND THE BOLD, THE #60
....JUNE/JULY 1965
WONDER MAN
AVENGERS #9 ....OCTOBER 1964
WONDER TOT
WONDER WOMAN #122..........................MAY 1961
WONDER WOMAN (Golden Age)
ALL STAR COMICS #8 ....DEC/JAN 1941
WONDER WOMAN (Silver Age)
WONDER WOMAN #105.......................APRIL 1959
WONDER WOMAN (Modern)
WONDER WOMAN (2nd Series) #1
....FEBRUARY 1987
WONG
STRANGE TALES #110...............................JULY 1963
WOODGOD
MARVEL PREMIERE #31..................AUGUST 1976
WRECKER
THOR #148 ....JANUARY 1968
WYATT WINGFOOT
FANTASTIC FOUR #50.................................MAY 1966
X
DARK HORSE COMICS #8 ....MARCH 1993
XEMNU
JOURNEY INTO MYSTERY #62
....NOVEMBER 1959
X-FACTOR
AVENGERS #263 ....JANUARY 1986
X-FORCE
NEW MUTANTS #100............................APRIL 1991
X-KRYPTONITE
ACTION COMICS #261 ....FEBRUARY 1960
X-MEN
UNCANNY X-MEN #1...............SEPTEMBER 1963
X-O MANOWAR
X-O MANOWAR #1........................FEBRUARY 1992
X-RAY VISION
ACTION COMICS #18.................NOVEMBER 1939

X-TERMINATORS
X-TERMINATORS #1 ....OCTOBER 1988
YELLOW CLAW
CAPTAIN AMERICA #165 ....SEPTEMBER 1973
YELLOWJACKET
AVENGERS #59...............................DECEMBER 1968
YELLOWJACKET II
AVENGERS #264....................................MARCH 1986
Y'GARON
DRACULA GIANT SIZE #2.........SEPTEMBER 1974
YON-ROGG
MARVEL SUPER-HEROES #12...DECEMBER 1967
YOUNG ALLIES
YOUNG ALLIES #1 ....SUMMER 1941
YOUNGBLOOD
MEGATON EXPLOSION..........................JUNE 1987
ZARAN
MASTER OF KUNG FU #77.....................JUNE 1979
ZARATHOS
MARVEL SPOTLIGHT #5 ....MARCH 1972
ZAREK
MARVEL SUPER-HEROES #12...DECEMBER 1967
ZATANNA
HAWKMAN #4.....................................OCT/NOV 1964
ZATARA
ACTION COMICS #1 ....JUNE 1938
ZODIAC
AVENGERS #72.................................JANUARY 1970
ZOM
STRANGE TALES #156 ....MAY 1967
ZURAS
ETERNALS, THE #5......................NOVEMBER 1976
ZZAXX
INCREDIBLE HULK #166 ....AUGUST 1973

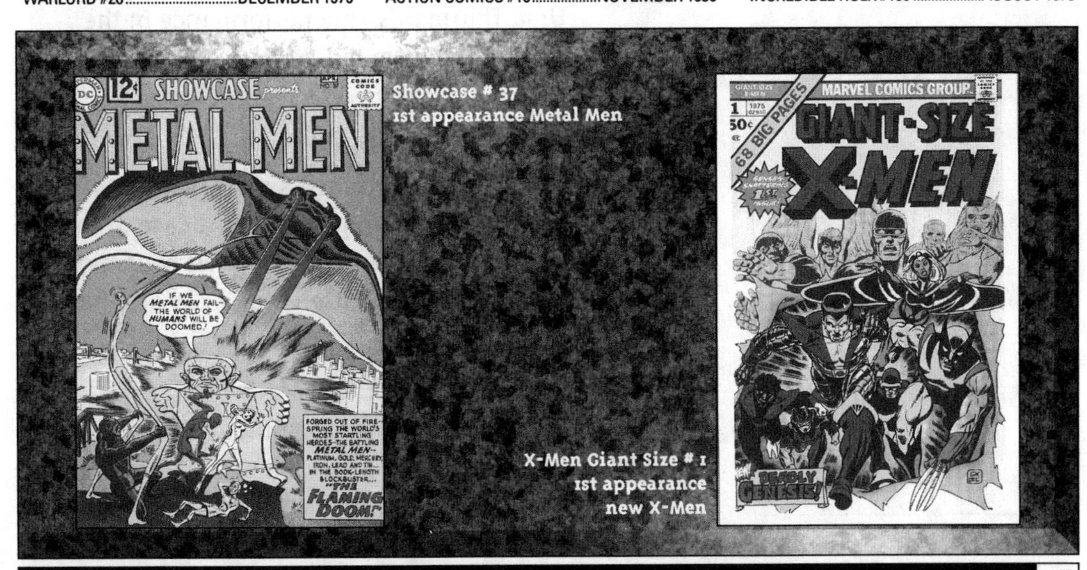

Showcase # 37
1st appearance Metal Men

X-Men Giant Size # 1
1st appearance
new X-Men

TOP TEN

In past editions, we've tended to take a leisurely (and by no means unpleasant) saunter through the past thirty-five years or so of 'Hot Babes', bringing you an all-time top fifty of the most curvaceous and pheromone-inducing creations ever to grace the comic page. We felt, though, that it was time for a change, that a more hands-on approach to the subject was needed to reflect the change in the industry's growing relationship with the 'Hot Babe'.

From the deeply dishy to the downright deadly, the role of the female comics character has seen something of a renaissance in the last few years. The libidinous fervour of creator and

10 ELEKTRA

Miller's lithe and lethal femme fatale is reborn (again) in a new, ongoing series, proving beyond a doubt that her attraction is not all Greek to a large slice of the comics buying public. A bullseye, and no mistake!

9 SAVANT

If any confirmation were needed that looks and intelligence are what every man craves, then look no further. She's got IQ and SA in abundance, and though outwardly reserved we hear she can be a bit of a wildC.A.T.

8 POISON IVY

Taking a leaf out of Batman's book, we're fairly crawling up the walls in anticipation of Uma Thurman's vine performance in the upcoming *Batman and Robin* film. She's sure to grow on you.

7 WONDER WOMAN

The Amazonian princess really set the world aflame in 1996. In fact, it was a case of first degree Byrne for many an unwary comic buyer who'd forgotten their special asbestos-coated mylar.

THE INVISIBLE WOMAN

Not seen for some time on the chart, Susan Richards makes a sudden reappearance at number six, the winds of change having left her in a more Lee-ward situation. Fantastic!

HOTTEST BABES

fan alike seems to have driven this particular sub-genre into a sales force all of its own. So, all in the cause of furthering frontiers, stretching the material, and proving that we have the legs to outlast any other related publications, we are proud to present the Top Ten Hottest Babes of 1996 (personal opinions only!).

Using very few criteria, beyond the appreciative passing of eye over printed page, we've compiled a top ten that (maybe) reflects each character's overall exposure during the past twelve months. In the best tradition of such endeavours, we will announce the results in the reverse order...

5 **SUPERGIRL**

Let's be Frank here, it's two for the price of one. Supergirl and Linda Danvers, all in one super-charged package. For double the thrills, there's no beating this dynamic duo.

4 **SCULLY**

Well, how could we not include 'the world's seXiest woman'... even if we are only dealing in two-dimensions here? The FBI's no-non-sense investigator is Topps. Trust us.

3 **NANCY CALLAHAN**

Though the Guide is hardly pulp fiction, it'd be a sin to exclude one of the real movers and shakers of 1996, and this exotic dancer is in at number three with a bullet.

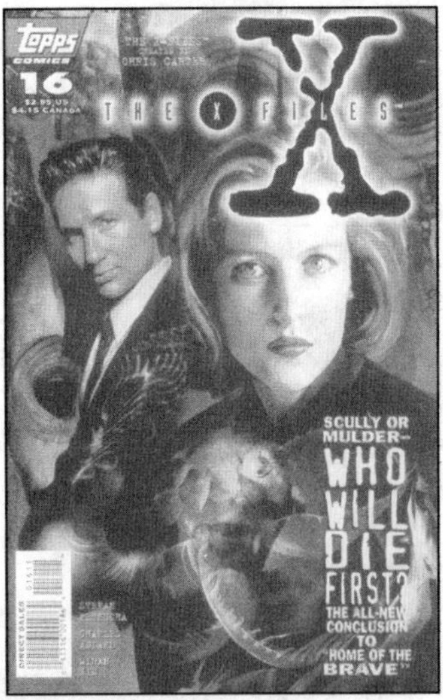

2 **BARB WIRE**

Thanks to Pammy, Barb got all the exposure she could have wished for... and more. It went right to the wire this year, but she'll have to settle for the big two. And yes, we are going to call her babe!

1 **WITCHBLADE**

After a spell in the wilderness, the lady with the arcane armour shows she's still got a real cutting edge, and what's more she knows how to use it. The top babe from Top Cow... magic!

BACK ISSUES!

To celebrate our team-up with Titan Books, Price Guide Productions is pleased to present back copies of all the Price Guides produced from #2 to date (#1 sold out), in mint, unsigned, signed and special editions. Who knows? These variations may themselves become collector's items! They make fascinating reading and comparing and stocks are limited. ***Please enclose a flat fee of £2.50 per order for postage and packing. Cheques/PO's payable to Price Guide Productions.***

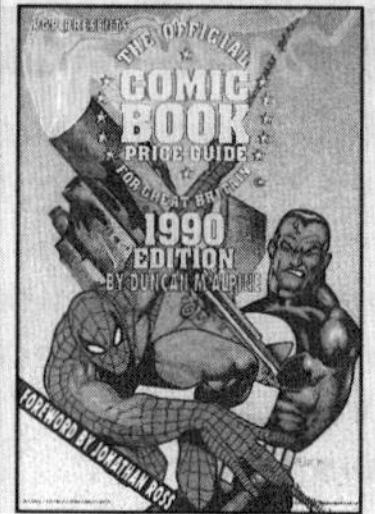

Nº 2 (1990)

Simon Bisley cover featuring Spiderman and the Punisher! Interior pin-ups by Ewins & Lloyd, Kitson and Ridgeway; first typeset Guide in the new familiar format. The days when Iron Man #55 was £4.00 and New Mutants #87 wasn't even out yet! **£6.95**

Special signed and hand-stamped edition **£7.95**

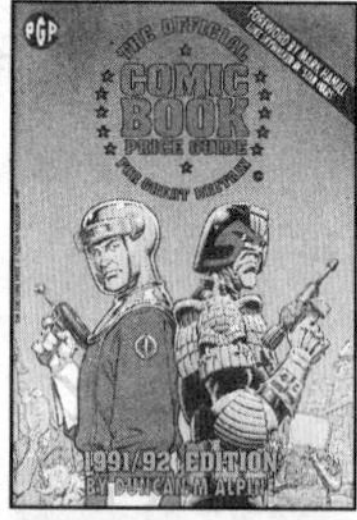

Nº 3 (1991)

Dave Gibbons cover featuring Judge Dredd and Dan Dare. New features include the famous First Appearance Index and Artist Gallery featuring Philips & Kane, Higgins & Hughes **£7.95**

Special signed and hand-stamped edition **£8.95**

Signed and numbered Limited Edition. Only 250 of these were produced and some very low numbers (25-100) have been kept back for a first come, first served basis **£9.95**

Numbers #1–#10 also available **please enquire**

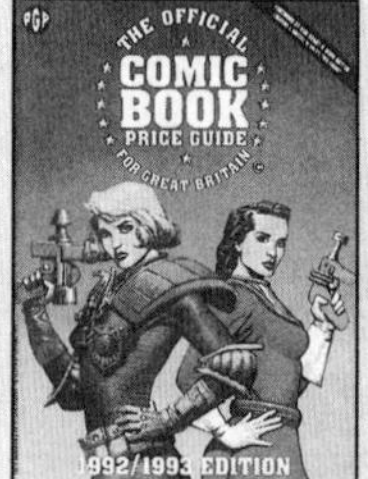

Nº 4 (1992)

Sean Philips cover featuring the "girlfriends" of Dredd and Dare—Judge Anderson and Dr. Jocelyn Peabody! Special colour section for the first time and many new features **£8.95**

Signed by author and cover artist **£9.95**

Special signed and hand-stamped edition **£9.95**

Signed and numbered Limited Edition. Only 50 of these were produced, signed by the author and cover artist **£10.95**

Numbers #1–#5 available **please enquire**

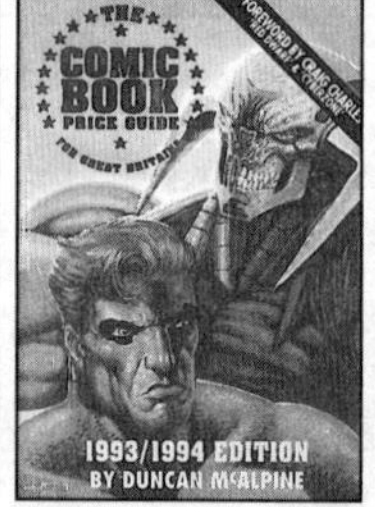

Nº 5 (1993)

Liam Sharpe cover featuring the unlikely team-up of Death's Head (a robot) and Magnus Robot Fighter **£9.95**

Signed by author and cover artist **£10.95**

Special signed and hand-stamped edition **£10.95**

Signed and numbered Limited Edition. Only 50 of these were produced, signed by the author and cover artist **£11.95**

Numbers #1–#5 available **please enquire**

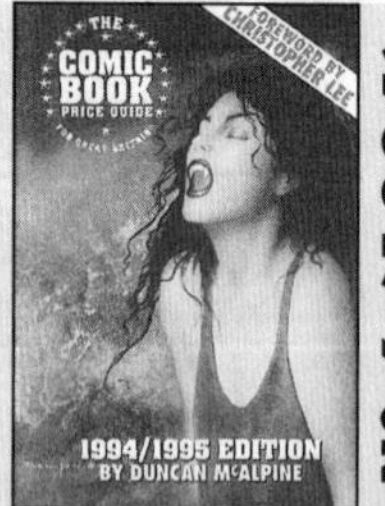

Nº 6 (1994)

John Bolton cover featuring a specially created character called "Liliana", one in a long line of vampiresses from the depths of the artist's imagination **£10.95**

Signed by author and cover artist **£11.95**

Special signed and hand-stamped edition **£11.95**

Signed and numbered Limited Edition. Only 50 of these were produced, signed by the author and cover artist **£12.95**

Numbers #1–#5 available **please enquire**

Guide #7 (1996) with a stunning Sabretooth cover by Gary Frank. First dual priced edition with prices in pounds and dollars **£12.95**

Special signed (by author) edition with dedication of your choice **£13.95**

Price Guide Productions • P.O. Box 10793 • London N10 3NF

ORIGINS INDEX

(Foundation work by ANDY KYTHREOTIS)

Below is a work-in-progress listing of the first and/or most detailed origins of selected characters. Very often the origin of a character comes along with his or her first appearance but that is not always the case. Indeed comic publishers often delight in producing a more detailed "secret origin" story years later. While there are many characters missing from our list, at least it gives some idea and where to look to read up about your favourites.

We hope to expand this feature in a number of ways. Our first objective is to give first origin story and most detailed origin story to every character that appears in the First Appearance Index. Our second objective is to list all subsequent origin retellings for major characters like Batman, Superman and Spiderman for example. *Any volunteers?* Any further information may be sent to the editorial address.

ABOMINATION
- TALES TO ASTONISH #90 .... APRIL 1967

ABSORBING MAN
- JOURNEY INTO MYSTERY #114 ..... MARCH 1965

ADAM WARLOCK
- MARVEL PREMIERE #1 .... APRIL 1972
- STRANGE TALES #178 .... FEBRUARY 1975

ADAM STRANGE
- SHOWCASE #17 .... DECEMBER 1958
- ADAM STRANGE MINI-SERIES #1-3 .... MAR/MAY 1990

AIRWALKER
- THOR #306 .... APRIL 1981

ALFRED
- BATMAN #16 .... APR/MAY 1943

ALPHA FLIGHT
- ALPHA FLIGHT #2 .... SEPTEMBER 1983

ANCIENT ONE
- STRANGE TALES #148 .... SEPTEMBER 1966

ANGAR THE SCREAMER
- DAREDEVIL #101 .... JULY 1973

ANGEL (Archangel)
- X-MEN, THE UNCANNY #54 .... APRIL 1969

ANIMAL MAN
- STRANGE ADVENTURES #180 .... SEPTEMBER 1965

ANNIHILUS
- FANTASTIC FOUR #140 .... NOVEMBER 1973

ANT-MAN
- TALES TO ASTONISH #27 .... JANUARY 1962

ANT MAN II
- MARVEL PREMIERE #47-48 .... APRIL 1981

APOCALYPSE
- X-FACTOR #24 .... JANUARY 1988

AQUAMAN (Golden Age)
- MORE FUN COMICS #73 .... NOVEMBER 1941

AQUAMAN (Silver Age)
- ADVENTURE COMICS #260 .... MAY 1959

ARABIAN KNIGHT
- INCREDIBLE HULK (2nd) #257 .... MARCH 1981

ARCADE
- UNCANNY X-MEN #124 .... AUGUST 1979

ATOM (Golden Age)
- ALL STAR SQUADRON ANNUAL #1 1982

ATOM (Silver Age)
- SHOWCASE #34 .... OCTOBER 1961

AVENGERS
- AVENGERS #1 .... SEPTEMBER 1963

BALDER THE BRAVE
- JOURNEY INTO MYSTERY #106 .... JULY 1964

BARON BLOOD
- INVADERS #9 .... OCTOBER 1976

BARON MORDO
- STRANGE TALES #115 .... DECEMBER 1963

BARON STRUCKER
- SGT. FURY AND HIS HOWLING COMMANDOS #5 ..... JANUARY 1964

BARON ZEMO I
- CAPTAIN AMERICA #168 .... DECEMBER 1973

BATGIRL
- DETECTIVE COMICS #359 .... JANUARY 1967
- SECRET ORIGINS (2nd Series) #20 .... NOVEMBER 1987

BAT-MITE
- DETECTIVE COMICS #267 .... MAY 1959

BATMAN
- DETECTIVE COMICS #33 .... NOVEMBER 1939
- BATMAN #47 .... JUN/JUL 1947
- BATMAN #200 .... MARCH 1968
- BATMAN #404 .... FEBRUARY 1987
- SECRET ORIGINS (2nd Series) #6 .... SEPTEMBER 1986

BATWOMAN
- DETECTIVE COMICS #233 .... JULY 1956

BATTLESTAR
- CAPTAIN AMERICA #334 .... OCTOBER 1988

BATWOMAN
- DETECTIVE COMICS #233 .... JULY 1956

BEAST
- X-MEN, THE UNCANNY #15 .... DECEMBER 1965

BEAST BOY
- DOOM PATROL #100 .... JANUARY 1966

BEETLE
- STRANGE TALES #123 .... AUGUST 1964

BELASCO
- KA-ZAR THE SAVAGE #11 .... FEBRUARY 1982

BETA RAY BILL
- THOR #337 .... NOVEMBER 1983

BINARY
- X-MEN, THE UNCANNY #164 .... DECEMBER 1982

BIZARRO
- SUPERBOY #68 .... OCTOBER 1956

BLACK BOLT
- THOR #148 .... JANUARY 1968

BLACK CAT
- AMAZING SPIDERMAN #195 .... AUGUST 1979

BLACK CONDOR
- BLACK CONDOR, THE #11 .... APRIL 1993

BLACKHAWK
- BLACKHAWK #164 .... SEPTEMBER 1961

BLACK PANTHER
- FANTASTIC FOUR #53 .... AUGUST 1966
- AVENGERS #87 .... APRIL 1971

BLACK WIDOW
- AVENGERS #44 .... SEPTEMBER 1968

BLADE
- TOMB OF DRACULA #13 .... OCTOBER 1973

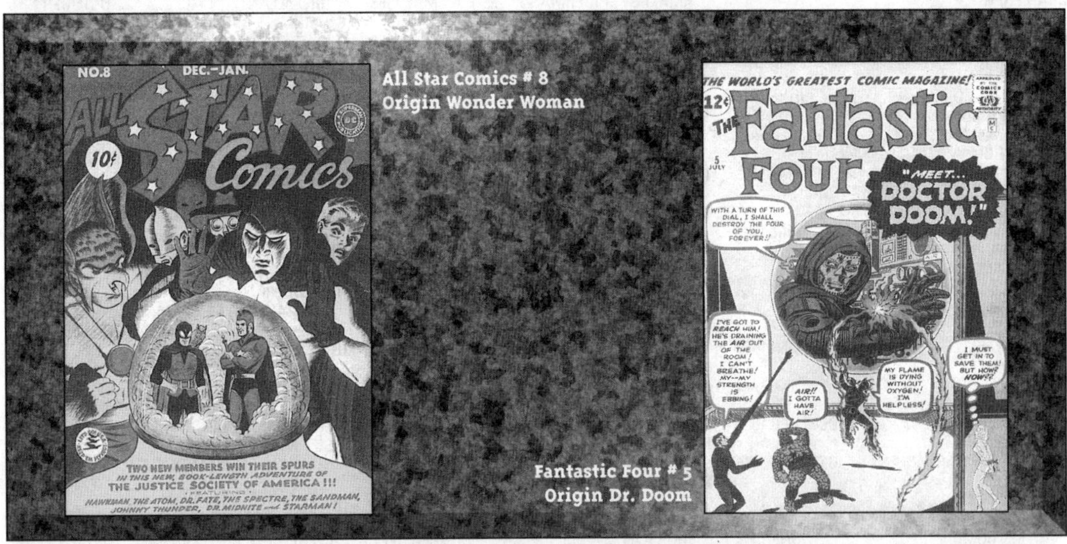

All Star Comics # 8
Origin Wonder Woman

Fantastic Four # 5
Origin Dr. Doom

BLASTAAR
MARVEL TWO IN ONE #75 .... MAY 1981
BLOOD STONE
MARVEL PRESENTS #2 .... DECEMBER 1975
BOOMER
SECRET WARS II #5 .... NOVEMBER 1985
BOOMERANG
TALES TO ASTONISH #81 .... JULY 1966
BOOSTER GOLD
BOOSTER GOLD #6 .... JULY 1986
BOUNCING BOY
ADVENTURE COMICS #301 .... OCTOBER 1962
BOY COMMANDOES
DETECTIVE COMICS #64 .... JUNE 1942
BRAINIAC (Silver Age)
ACTION COMICS #242 .... JULY 1958
SUPERMAN #167 .... FEBRUARY 1964
BROTHER VOODOO
STRANGE TALES #169 .... SEPTEMBER 1973
BROTHERS GRIMM
IRON MAN #187 .... OCTOBER 1984
BULLSEYE
DAREDEVIL #131 .... JUNE 1976
BUSHMASTER
CAPTAIN AMERICA ANNUAL #10 1991
CANNONBALL
MARVEL GRAPHIC NOVEL #4 1982
CAPTAIN AMERICA (Golden Age)
CAPTAIN AMERICA COMICS #1 .... MARCH 1941
CAPTAIN AMERICA (Silver Age)
TALES OF SUSPENSE #63 .... MARCH 1965
CAPTAIN AMERICA #109 .... JANUARY 1969
CAPTAIN ATOM
CAPTAIN ATOM #1 .... MARCH 1987
CAPTAIN BOOMERANG
FLASH (1st Series) #117 .... DECEMBER 1960
CAPTAIN BRITAIN (US)
MARVEL TEAM UP #65 .... JANUARY 1978
CAPTAIN COLD
SHOWCASE #8 .... JUNE 1957
CAPTAIN COMET
STRANGE ADVENTURES #9 .... JUNE 1951
CAPTAIN MARVEL (Kree)
MARVEL SUPER-HEROES #18 .... JANUARY 1969
CAPTAIN STORM
CAPTAIN STORM #1 .... MAY/JUN 1964
CARRION
SPECTACULAR SPIDERMAN #31 .... MAY 1979
CATWOMAN (Golden Age)
BATMAN #62 .... DEC/JAN 1951
CATWOMAN (Modern)
BATMAN #404-406 .... FEB/APR 1987
CHALLENGERS OF THE UNKNOWN
SHOWCASE #6 .... FEBRUARY 1957
CHAMELEON
AMAZING SPIDERMAN #307
.... DECEMBER 1987
CHAMPIONS
CHAMPIONS, THE #1 .... OCTOBER 1975
CHIEF
DOOM PATROL #88 .... JUNE 1964
CLAYFACE I
DETECTIVE COMICS #40 .... JUNE 1940
SECRET ORIGINS
(2nd Series) #44 .... SEPTEMBER 1989
CLAYFACE II
DETECTIVE COMICS #298 .... DECEMBER 1961
CLEA
DOCTOR STRANGE (2nd Series) #8-9
.... APRIL 1975
CLOAK AND DAGGER
CLOAK AND DAGGER (Limited series) #4
.... JANUARY 1984
COBRA
JOURNEY INTO MYSTERY #98
.... NOVEMBER 1963
COLOSSUS
X-MEN, THE UNCANNY #122 .... JUNE 1979
COMET THE SUPER-HORSE
ACTION COMICS #293 .... OCTOBER 1962
CONAN
CONAN THE BARBARIAN #1 .... OCTOBER 1970
CONCRETE
CONCRETE #3 .... JULY 1987
CONGO BILL
ACTION COMICS #37 .... JUNE 1941

CORSAIR
X-MEN, THE UNCANNY #156 .... APRIL 1982
CREEPER
SHOWCASE #73 .... APRIL 1968
CRUSADER
THOR #330 .... MARCH 1983
CYBORG
NEW TEEN TITANS, THE (1st Series) #7
.... MAY 1981
CYCLOPS
X-MEN, THE UNCANNY #38 .... NOVEMBER 1967
DAREDEVIL
DAREDEVIL #1 .... APRIL 1964
DAREDEVIL #53 .... JUNE 1969
DARKHAWK
DARKHAWK #1 .... MARCH 1991
DARKSTAR
INCREDIBLE HULK (2nd) #259 .... MAY 1981
DAZZLER
DAZZLER #1 .... JULY 1981
DEADMAN
STRANGE ADVENTURES #205
.... SEPTEMBER 1967
DEATHLOK
ASTONISHING TALES #25 .... AUGUST 1974
DEATHSTROKE THE TERMINATOR
NEW TEEN TITANS, THE (1st Series) #44
.... JULY 1984
DEFENDERS
MARVEL FEATURE #1 .... DECEMBER 1971
DEMON
DEMON #1 .... AUG/SEPT 1978
DESPERO
JUSTICE LEAGUE OF AMERICA (1st)#1
.... OCT/NOV 1960
DON BLAKE
THOR #158 .... NOVEMBER 1968
DOOM PATROL
DOOM PATROL #86 .... MARCH 1964
DOOM PATROL
MY GREATEST ADVENTURE #80
.... OCTOBER 1963
DORMAMMU
DOCTOR STRANGE (2nd Series) #71
.... APRIL 1986
DR. DOOM
FANTASTIC FOUR #5 .... JULY 1962
FANTASTIC FOUR ANNUAL #2 1964
DR DROOM
AMAZING ADVENTURES #1 .... JUNE 1961
DR. DESTINY
JUSTICE LEAGUE OF AMERICA #5 .... JULY 1961
DR. DOOM
FANTASTIC FOUR ANNUAL #2 1964
DR. FATE (Golden Age)
MORE FUN COMICS #67 .... MAY 1941
DR. OCTOPUS
AMAZING SPIDERMAN #3 .... MAY 1963
DR. POLARIS
GREEN LANTERN #21 .... JUNE 1963
DR. SOLAR
DR. SOLAR, MAN OF THE ATOM #1
.... OCTOBER 1962
DR. STRANGE
STRANGE TALES #115 .... DECEMBER 1963
DOCTOR STRANGE #169 .... JUNE 1968
DRAX THE DESTROYER
IRON MAN #55 .... FEBRUARY 1972
DREAM QUEEN
ALPHA FLIGHT #67 .... FEBRUARY 1989
ELECTRO
AMAZING SPIDERMAN #9 .... NOVEMBER 1963
ELEKTRA
DAREDEVIL #168 .... JANUARY 1981
ELONGATED MAN
FLASH ANNUAL (1st Series) #1 1963
EXCALIBUR
EXCALIBUR SPECIAL EDITION #1 1987
FALCON
CAPTAIN AMERICA #117 .... SEPTEMBER 1969
FANTASTIC FOUR
FANTASTIC FOUR #1 .... NOVEMBER 1961
FIN FANG FOOM
STRANGE TALES #89 .... OCTOBER 1961
FIRELORD
THOR #306 .... APRIL 1981

FIRESTAR
FIRESTAR #1-4 .... MARCH 1986
FIRESTORM
FIRESTORM #1 .... MARCH 1978
FLASH (Golden Age)
FLASH COMICS #1 .... JANUARY 1940
FLASH (Silver Age)
SHOWCASE #4 .... SEPT/OCT 1956
FLASH (Modern Age)
FLASH #110 .... DEC/JAN 1960
FOOLKILLER I
MAN THING (1st Series) #3 .... MARCH 1974
FOOLKILLER II
OMEGA THE UNKOWN #8 .... MAY 1977
GAEA
THOR ANNUAL #10 1982
GALACTUS
THOR #162 .... MARCH 1969
THOR #168/169 .... SEPT/OCT 1969
GARGOYLE
DEFENDERS #95 .... MAY 1981
GEE
POWER PACK #1 .... AUGUST 1984
GHOST RIDER I
MARVEL SPOTLIGHT (1st Series) #5
.... MARCH 1972
GIANT MAN II
LUKE CAGE, POWER MAN #24 .... APRIL 1975
GLORIAN
INCREDIBLE HULK #267 .... JANUARY 1982
GREEN ARROW (Silver Age)
ADVENTURE COMICS #256 .... JANUARY 1959
SECRET ORIGINS (2nd Series) #38
.... MARCH 1989
GREEN GOBLIN I
AMAZING SPIDERMAN #40 .... SEPTEMBER 1966
GREEN GOBLIN II
AMAZING SPIDERMAN #126
.... NOVEMBER 1974
GREEN GOBLIN III
AMAZING SPIDERMAN #176 .... JANUARY 1978
GREEN LANTERN (Golden Age)
ALL-AMERICAN COMICS #16 .... JULY 1940
GREEN LANTERN (Silver Age)
SHOWCASE #22 .... SEPT/OCT 1959
GREEN LANTERN (John Stewart)
GREEN LANTERN #185 .... FEBRUARY 1985
GREEN LANTERN (Kyle Rayner)
GREEN LANTERN (2nd Series) #50
.... MARCH 1994
GREMLIN
ROM #44 .... JULY 1983
GRENDEL
COMICO PRIMER #2 1982
GUARDIAN
ALPHA FLIGHT #2 .... SEPTEMBER 1983
GUARDIAND OF OA
GREEN LANTERN #40 .... OCTOBER 1965
GUARDIANS OF THE GALAXY
MARVEL SUPER-HEROES #18 .... JANUARY 1969
GYPSY MOTH
SPIDERWOMAN #48 .... JUNE 1982
HANNIBAL KING
TOMB OF DRACULA #25 .... OCTOBER 1974
HAVOK
X-MEN #54 .... MARCH 1969
HAWKEYE
AVENGERS #19 .... AUGUST 1965
HAWKMAN (Golden Age)
FLASH COMICS #1 .... JANUARY 1940
HAWKMAN (Silver Age)
BRAVE AND THE BOLD #34 .... MARCH 1961
HOBGOBLIN
SPECTACULAR SPIDERMAN #85
.... DECEMBER 1983
HOBGOBLIN II
WEB OF SPIDERMAN #48 .... MARCH 1989
HOURMAN (Golden Age)
ADVENTURE COMICS #48 .... MARCH 1940
HOWLING COMMANDOS
SGT. FURY AND HIS
HOWLING COMMANDOS #34
.... SEPTEMBER 1966
HULK
INCREDIBLE HULK (1st) #1 .... MAY 1962
INCREDIBLE HULK #102 .... APRIL 1968

ICEMAN
X-MEN, THE UNCANNY #44-46 ... MAY 1968
IMPOSSIBLE MAN
FANTASTIC FOUR #11 ... FEBRUARY 1963
INFINITY INC.
ALL-STAR SQUADRON #26 ... OCTOBER 1983
INHUMANS
THOR #146 ... NOVEMBER 1967
INTERLOPER
DEFENDERS #152 ... FEBRUARY 1986
INVISIBLE WOMAN
FANTASTIC FOUR #1 ... NOVEMBER 1961
IRON FIST
MARVEL PREMIERE #15 ... JUNE 1974
POWERMAN & IRON FIST #54 ... DECEMBER 1978
IRON MAN
TALES OF SUSPENSE #39 ... MARCH 1963
IRON MAN #47 ... JUNE 1972
JACK OF HEARTS
DEADLY HANDS OF KUNG-FU #29 ... OCTOBER 1976
JOHNNY QUICK
ADVENTURE COMICS #142 ... JULY 1949
JOKER
DETECTIVE COMICS #168 ... FEBRUARY 1951
BATMAN: THE KILLING JOKE ... 1988
JUGGERNAUT
X-MEN, THE UNCANNY #12 ... JULY 1965
JUSTICE LEAGUE OF AMERICA
JUSTICE LEAGUE OF AMERICA #9 ... JANUARY 1962
JUSTICE SOCIETY OF AMERICA
ALL STAR COMICS #3 ... WINTER 1940
KA-ZAR (Silver Age)
DAREDEVIL #13 ... APRIL 1966
KAMANDI
KAMANDI THE LAST BOY ON EARTH #1 ... OCT/NOV 1972
KARATE KID
SUPERBOY #210 ... SEPTEMBER 1975
KID ETERNITY
HIT COMICS #25 ... DECEMBER 1942
KID FLASH
FLASH (1st Series) #110 ... DEC/JAN 1960
KID PSYCHO
SUPERBOY #125 ... DECEMBER 1965
KILLER MOTH)
BATMAN #63 ... DEC/JAN 1952
KRAVEN THE HUNTER
AMAZING SPIDERMAN #15 ... MAY 1964
KULL
KULL THE CONQUEROR #1 ... JUNE 1971
LEADER
TALES TO ASTONISH #63 ... JANUARY 1965
LEGION
NEW MUTANTS #28 ... JUNE 1985
LEGION OF SUPER-HEROES
ADVENTURE COMICS #247 ... APRIL 1958
LEX LUTHER (Silver Age)
ADVENTURE COMICS #271 ... APRIL 1960
SUPERMAN #292 ... OCTOBER 1976
LIZARD
AMAZING SPIDERMAN #6 ... AUGUST 1963
LOKI
JOURNEY INTO MYSTERY #112 ... JANUARY 1965
JOURNEY INTO MYSTERY #115 ... APRIL 1965
LORI LEMARIS
SUPERMAN (2nd Series) #12 .. DECEMBER 1987
LONGSHOT
LONGSHOT #1-6 ... SEPTEMBER 1965
LUKE CAGE
LUKE CAGE, HERO FOR HIRE #1 ... JUNE 192
MACHETE
CAPTAIN AMERICA #302 ... FEBRUARY 1985
MACHINESMITH
CAPTAIN AMERICA #249 ... SEPTEMBER 1980
MADAME WEB
AMAZING SPIDERMAN #210 ... NOVEMBER 1980
MADCAP
CAPTAIN AMERICA #309 ... SEPTEMBER 1985
MADROX
GIANT SIZE FANTASTIC FOUR #4 ... DECEMBER 1974
MAELSTROM
QUASAR #21 ... APRIL 1991
MAGMA
NEW MUTANTS #8-11 ... OCTOBER 1983
MAGNETO
X-MEN, THE UNCANNY #161 ... SEPTEMBER 1982
MAN APE
AVENGERS #62 ... MARCH 1969
MAN BAT
DETECTIVE COMICS #400 ... JUNE 1970
SECRET ORIGINS #39 ... APRIL 1989
MAN-THING
SAVAGE TALES #1 ... MAY 1971
MANDARIN
TALES OF SUSPENSE #62 ... FEBRUARY 1965
MANSLAUGHTER
DEFENDERS #152 ... FEBRUARY 1986
MANTIS
AVENGERS #123 ... MAY 1974
MARRINA
ALPHA FLIGHT #2-4 ... SEPTEMBER 1983
MARTIAN MANHUNTER
DETECTIVE COMICS #225 ... NOVEMBER 1955
DETECTIVE COMICS #231 ... MAY 1956
MARVEL BOY
FANTASTIC FOUR #165 ... DECEMBER 1975
MARVEL GIRL
BIZARRE ADVENTURES #27 ... JULY 1981
MASTER
ALPHA FLIGHT #3 ... OCTOBER 1983
MASTER PANDEMONIUM
WEST COAST AVENGERS #9 ... JUNE 1986
MENTOR
CAPTAIN MARVEL #29 ... APRIL 1974
METAL MEN
METAL MEN #27 ... AUGUST 1967
METAMORPHO
BRAVE AND THE BOLD, THE #57 ... DECEMBER 1964
MIRAGE
AMAZING SPIDERMAN #156 ... MAY 1976
MISS AMERICA
MARVEL PREMIERE #29 ... APRIL 1976
MISTER FANTASTIC
FANTASTIC FOUR #1 ... NOVEMBER 1961
MISTER HYDE
JOURNEY INTO MYSTERY #99 ... DECEMBER 1963
MODOK
CAPTAIN AMERICA #133 ... JANUARY 1971
MODRED THE MYSTIC
MARVEL CHILLERS #1 ... OCTOBER 1975
MOLE MAN
FANTASTIC FOUR #1 ... NOVEMBER 1961
MOLECULE MAN
FANTASTIC FOUR #20 ... NOVEMBER 1963
MOLTEN MAN
AMAZING SPIDERMAN #28 ... SEPTEMBER 1965
MOON KNIGHT
MOON KNIGHT #1 ... NOVEMBER 1980
MOONBOY
DEVIL DINOSAUR #1 ... APRIL 1978
MOONDRAGON
DAREDEVIL #105 ... NOVEMBER 1973
MOONSTONE
INCREDIBLE HULK (2nd) #228 ... OCTOBER 1978
MORBIUS
AMAZING SPIDERMAN #102 ... JANUARY 1971
MR. AMERICA
ACTION COMICS #33 ... FEBRUARY 1941
MR. MIRACLE
MISTER MIRACLE #9 ... JULY 1972
MR. MXYZTPLK (Golden Age)
SUPERMAN #30 ... SEPT/OCT 1944
MR. MXYZPTLK (Modern)
SUPERMAN (2nd Series) #11 ... NOVEMBER 1987
MS. MARVEL
MS. MARVEL #2 ... FEBRUARY 1977
MS. AMERICA
MARVEL COMICS #49 ... NOVEMBER 1943
MYSTERIO
SPECTACULAR SPIDERMAN #51 ... FEBRUARY 1981

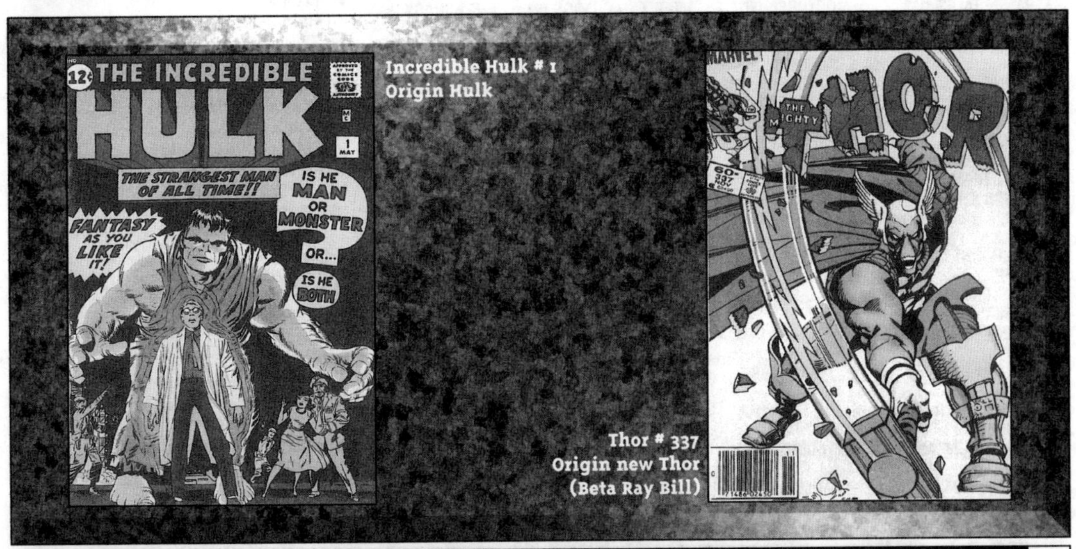

Incredible Hulk # 1
Origin Hulk

Thor # 337
Origin new Thor
(Beta Ray Bill)

N'ASTIRH
NEW MUTANTS #71....................JANUARY 1989
NAMORA
MARVEL COMICS #82....................AUGUST 1947
NAMORITA
SUB-MARINER #51..............................JULY 1972
NEBULON
DEFENDERS #14..................................JUNE 1974
NICK FURY AGENT OF SHIELD
STRANGE TALES #135....................AUGUST 1965
STRANGE TALES #159....................AUGUST 1967
NIGHT THRASHER
NEW WARRIORS #2......................AUGUST 1990
NIGHTCRAWLER
GIANT SIZE X-MEN #1.................SUMMER 1975
NIGHTHAWK
SQUADRON SUPREME #7.............MARCH 1986
NIGHTHAWK II
DAREDEVIL #62..............................MARCH 1970
NIKKI
MARVEL PRESENTS #4......................APRIL 1976
NITRO
CAPTAIN MARVEL #34..........SEPTEMBER 1974
NORTHSTAR
ALPHA FLIGHT #10...............................MAY 1984
NOVA
NOVA, THE MAN CALLED #1
....SEPTEMBER 1976
NOVA II
FANTASTIC FOUR #238...............JANUARY 1982
OCEAN MASTER
BRAVE AND THE BOLD #82...........MARCH 1969
ODIN
JOURNEY INTO MYSTERY #97........OCTOBER 1963
THOR #294 ....APRIL 1980
OMAC
OMAC #1.......................................SEPT/OCT 1974
OMEGA
DEFENDERS #77.......................NOVEMBER 1979
ORKA
SUB-MARINER #23.........................MARCH 1970
OVERMIND
FANTASTIC FOUR #115...............OCTOBER 1971
OWL
DAREDEVIL #3................................AUGUST 1964
PARASITE I
ACTION COMICS #340....................AUGUST 1966
PHANTOM ZONE
SUPERBOY #104 ....APRIL 1963
PHOENIX (Jean Grey)
CLASSIC X-MEN #8..............................APRIL 1987
PIED PIPER
FLASH #106..MAY 1959
PILEDRIVER
DEFENDERS #18.......................DECEMBER 1974
PIP THE TROLL
WARLOCK #12.......................................APRIL 1976
PLANTMAN
STRANGE TALES #113.................OCTOBER 1963
POLARIS
X-MEN, THE UNCANNY #49-52
....OCTOBER 1968
PORCUPINE
TALES TO ASTONISH #48...........OCTOBER 1963
POWER GIRL
SHOWCASE #97.........................FEBRUARY 1970
PROFESSOR POWER
MARVEL TEAM UP #118......................JUNE 1982
PROFESSOR X
X-MEN, THE UNCANNY #12...............JULY 1965
PUCK
ALPHA FLIGHT #32..........................MARCH 1986
PUNISHER
MARVEL PREVIEW #2....................................1975
PUPPET MASTER
MARVEL TEAM UP #6....................JANURY 1973
QUASAR
QUASAR #1-2...................................AUGUST 1989
QUASIMODO
FANTASTIC FOUR ANNUAL #4......................1966
QUICKSILVER
X-MEN, THE UNCANNY #4............MARCH 1964
RAGE
AVENGERS #328...........................JANUARY 1991
RAMA-TUT
FANTASTIC FOUR #19..................OCTOBER 1963

RED RAVEN
MARVEL PREMIERE #29.....................APRIL 1976
RED SKULL (Silver Age)
TALES OF SUSPENSE #66..................JUNE 1965
RED TORNADO
SECRET ORIGINS (2nd Series) #29
....AUGUST 1988
REVERSE FLASH
FLASH (1st Series) #139................AUGUST 1963
RHINO
AMAZING SPIDERMAN #41.......OCTOBER 1966
ROBIN
(Dick Grayson)
DETECTIVE COMICS #38....................APRIL 1940
SECRET ORIGINS #50 (2nd Series)
....AUGUST 1990
ROBIN (Jason Todd)
BATMAN #408..JUNE 1987
ROCKETEER
STARSLAYER #2...................................APRIL 1982
ROM
ROM #1......................................DECEMBER 1979
SANDMAN (Golden Age)
ADVENTURE COMICS #40...................JULY 1939
SANDMAN (Marvel)
AMAZING SPIDERMAN #84................MAY 1970
SASQUATCH
ALPHA FLIGHT #9................................APRIL 1984
SCORPION
AMAZING SPIDERMAN #20.......OCTOBER 1964
SGT. FURY)
SGT. FURY #89.......................................JULY 1971
SHADOWCAT
X-MEN, THE UNCANNY #129.....JANUARY 1980
SHANG-CHI
DEADLY HANDS OF KUNG-FU #1 .....APRIL 1974
SHE-HULK
SHE HULK, THE SAVAGE #1......FEBRUARY 1980
SHINING KNIGHT
ADVENTURE COMICS #66.....SEPTEMBER 1941
ADVENTURE COMICS #127...............APRIL 1948
SHROUD
SUPER-VILLAIN TEAM-UP #7......AUGUST 1976
SILVER SABLE
WEB OF SPIDERMAN ANNUAL #5..............1989
SILVER SURFER
MARVEL SAGA..........................DECEMBER 1987
SINESTRO
GREEN LANTERN #7.....................JUL/AUG 1961
SNAKE EYES
G.I. JOE #26.......................................AUGUST 1984
SNAPPER CARR
BRAVE AND THE BOLD #28...........MARCH 1960
SOLOMON GRUNDY
ALL AMERICAN COMICS #61.....OCTOBER 1944
SON OF SATAN
MARVEL SPOTLIGHT #12...........OCTOBER 1973
SPECTRE
MORE FUN COMICS #52...........FEBRUARY 1940
SPIDERMAN
AMAZING FANTASY #15...............AUGUST 1962
SPIDERMAN 2099
SPIDERMAN 2099 #1-3...........NOVEMBER 1992
STARBOY
ADVENTURE COMICS #282...........MARCH 1961
STARMAN (Golden Age)
ADVENTURE COMICS #61 ....APRIL 1941
STARMAN (Modern)
STARMAN #42.............................JANUARY 1992
STAR SAPPHIRE
GREEN LANTERN #16..................OCTOBER 1962
STREAKY THE SUPER-CAT
ACTION COMICS #261..............FEBRUARY 1960
STORM
X-MEN, THE UNCANNY #102.......DECEMBER 1976
STRANGER
FANTASTIC FOUR #116...........NOVEMBER 1971
STRYFE
X-FORCE #17.............................DECEMBER 1992
SUB MARINER (Silver Age)
FANTASTIC FOUR #4.............................MAY 1962
SUB-MARINER #1.................................MAY 1968
SUB-MARINER (Golden Age)
MARVEL COMICS #1....................OCT/NOV 1939
SUNBOY
ADVENTURE COMICS #290.....NOVEMBER 1961

SUPER SKRULL
FANTASTIC FOUR #18............SEPTEMBER 1963
SUPERBOY
MORE FUN COMICS #101............JAN/FEB 1945
SUPERGIRL
ACTION COMICS #252..........................MAY 1959
SUPERMAN (Golden Age)
ACTION COMICS #1..............................JUNE 1938
SECRET ORIGINS #1 (2nd Series).....APRIL 1986
SWAMP THING
SWAMP THING #1...................NOVEMBER 1972
TEEN TITANS
BRAVE AND THE BOLD, THE #54
....SEPTEMBER 1964
TERRAX
FANTASTIC FOUR #211..............OCTOBER 1979
THANOS
CAPTAIN MARVEL #33..................AUGUST 1974
THING
FANTASTIC FOUR #1................NOVEMBER 1961
THOR
JOURNEY INTO MYSTERY #83.....AUGUST 1962
TITANO THE SUPER-APE
SUPERMAN ANNUAL (2nd Series) #1
....AUGUST 1987
TOMBSTONE
SPECTACULAR SPIDERMAN #139....JUNE 1988
TRICKSTER
FLASH (1st Series) #113.......................JULY 1960
TWO-GUN KID
TWO-GUN KID #60...................NOVEMBER 1962
TWO FACE
DETECTIVE COMICS #66...............AUGUST 1942
TYPHOID MARY
DAREDEVIL #254....................................MAY 1988
ULTRA BOY
SUPERBOY #98..JULY 1962
ULTRON
AVENGERS #58..........................NOVEMBER 1968
UNKNOWN SOLDIER
UNKNOWN SOLDIER #1..........DECEMBER 1988
VANDAL SAVAGE
GREEN LANTERN (Golden Age) #10
....WINTER 1943
VENOM
AMAZING SPIDERMAN #300..............MAY 1987
VIGILANTE (Golden Age)
ACTION COMICS #42..............NOVEMBER 1941
VIKING PRINCE
BRAVE AND THE BOLD #23..................MAY 1959
VISION
AVENGERS #58..........................NOVEMBER 1968
WARLORD
FIRST ISSUE SPECIAL #8.........NOVEMBER 1975
WASP
TALES TO ASTONISH #44....................JUNE 1963
WATCHER
TALES OF SUSPENSE #53.....................MAY 1964
WAVERIDER
ARMAGEDDON 2001 #1..........................MAY 1991
WEREWOLF BY NIGHT
MARVEL SPOTLIGHT #2...........DECEMBER 1971
WHITE TIGER
DEADLY HANDS OF
KUNG-FU #20...............................JANUARY 1976
WOLVERINE
MARVEL COMICS PRESENTS #72................1991
WOLVERINE
WOLVERINE #50............................JANUARY 1992
WONDER GIRL
WONDER WOMAM #105...................APRIL 1959
WONDER WOMAN (Golden Age)
ALL STAR COMICS #8...................DEC/JAN 1941
WONDER WOMAN (Modern)
WONDER WOMAN (2nd Series) #1
....FEBRUARY 1987
X-MEN
X-MEN, THE UNCANNY #1....SEPTEMBER 1963

STAR WARS ACTION FIGURE Price Guide

JULES BURT & GEORGE LESSITER
Purple Haze Comics

Hello and welcome to the 'Star Wars Universe'.

Well what can we say? The prices are going up and up due to more and more people wanting Star Wars items. This might have something to do with the fact that more people are remembering the great toys that were brought out for the Star Wars Trilogy and wanting to get them again. Also, with the confirmation that George Lucas will be releasing another trilogy in 2001, the anticipation for new figures and toys is tremendous!

For anyone who's new to collecting Star Wars toys a brief history lesson in the figures and accessories is in order, as it can get very complicated.

The figures and accessories were manufactured from 1977 to 1985. In America all the toys were manufactured by Kenner Inc. and in the U.K they were manufactured by Palitoy. For our European friends Meccano, Harbert and Top Toys had the rights for the Star Wars line until 'The Empire Strikes Back' was released and then Europe had the Palitoy range the same as Britain. For 'Return Of The Jedi' the whole of Europe got standard Tri-Logo cards.

Not all the figures and accessories were officially released in Britain, however they were all imported to meet the demand in the toy shops.

In this guide we will list the figures and accessories in production order.

The first twenty one figures were released on a 'Star Wars' card. They were also available later on 'Empire' cards and lastly on 'Return' cards. The reason for this is that each time a new film came out the toys were repackaged to make them current and to tie-in with the latest film - hence better sales.

Also of interest to collectors is the American only 'Power Of The Force' cards, which were released in 1985 to try to help sell the line. Old figures were re-released and new ones issued. All came with a special collector's coin.

This affected the collectors' market, with carded figures on an original 'Star Wars' card usually commanding the highest prices.The exception are those figures which were only released on 'Power Of The Force' cards. These are among the rarest Star Wars figures of all. It is also the same for the accessories.

To accurately put a price on a figure or toy you have to be able to grade it properly. In this guide we have used the following grades: MINT ON MINT CARD **(MOMC)**, MINT IN MINT BOX **(MIMB)** and LOOSE-COMPLETE **(LOOSE)**.

MOMC: The figure should still be on its original cardboard backing card and sealed in the plastic bubble. The card should have NO creases in it and still be shiny and fresh regardless of its age. The bubble should not have any cracks or stress lines and should be dust-free and not be yellowed or sun-bleached. MINT ON MINT CARD means the same condition as when the toy left the factory, with no signs of wear and tear evident. Any slight defect, such as a corner crease or a slight tear would affect the overall appearance of the toy and hence downgrade the price.

MIMB: The toy is still in its original box and has never been played with. All instructions and stickers are intact and unspoiled. The box must be fresh and glossy without any dents or tears. MINT IN MINT BOX means a perfect toy that looks as if you bought it brand new yesterday from your local toyshop. Any marks or imperfections will affect the value of the MIMB price

LOOSE: The figure or toy is not in it's original card or box but still in perfect condition. All of the accessories (i.e.; clothes, weapons and staffs) are intact and are also in perfect condition. All the working parts on the figure or toy should be stiff and show no signs of stress. Any markings or stickers should be as new and not worn. LOOSE means a perfect figure or toy that could just have been opened but never played with.

STORAGE: The ideal way to store carded figures is by bagging them in protective comic bags. Then store the figures vertically in a comic box. For boxed accessories the same applies but beware when stacking toys on top of each other – an AT-AT is a lot heavier than the Land Of The Jawas playset. Many a crushed box could have been saved if stored properly.

The main things to avoid are heat, light, damp or humidity as these will very quickly turn your precious collectibles into something no one's going to want in twenty year's time. You have been warned!

All prices are in UK pounds.

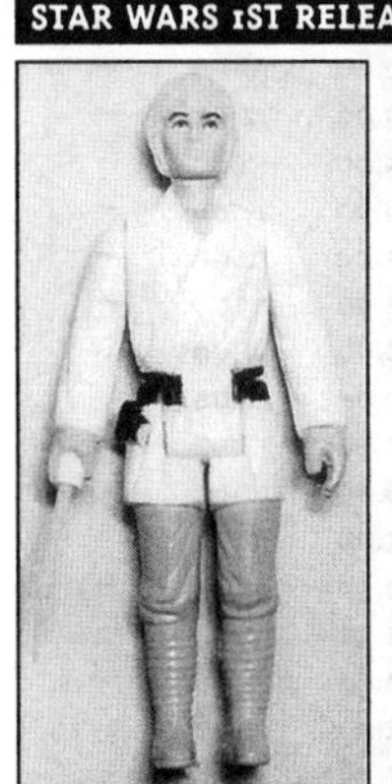

STAR WARS 1ST RELEASE 1978 3¾" FIGURES	LOOSE	SW 12	20/21	EMP	JEDI	TRI	POTF
Luke-Blonde Hair	10.00	200.00	160.00	125.00	90.00	70.00	–
Luke-Brown Hair	14.00	225.00	140.00	125.00	55.00	70.00	–
Princess Leia	17.50	190.00	170.00	180.00	225.00	100.00	–
Han Solo-Small Head	25.00	325.00	–	–	–	100.00	–
Han Solo-Large Head	8.00	375.00	265.00	150.00	85.00	75.00	–
C-3PO	10.00	90.00	65.00	35.00	25.00	30.00	–
R2-D2	15.00	90.00	65.00	30.00	55.00	35.00	–
Stormtrooper	4.50	140.00	95.00	50.00	30.00	25.00	100.00
Ben Kenobi-White Hair	8.00	140.00	80.00	50.00	30.00	30.00	70.00
Ben Kenobi-Grey Hair	8.00	140.00	80.00	50.00	30.00	30.00	–
Darth Vader	6.00	125.00	65.00	40.00	30.00	25.00	60.00
Chewbacca	4.00	125.00	60.00	40.00	30.00	20.00	50.00
Jawa-Plastic Cape (Beware of bootlegs!!!)	175.00	1100.00	–	–	–	–	–
Jawa	8.00	125.00	60.00	45.00	35.00	30.00	50.00
Sand People	5.00	150.00	90.00	65.00	40.00	35.00	–
Death Squad Comm	7.00	135.00	70.00	65.00	45.00	50.00	–

STAR WARS 2ND RELEASE 1979 3¾" FIGURES	LOOSE	20/21	EMP	JEDI	TRI	POTF
Death Star Droid	10.00	95.00	90.00	50.00	35.00	—
Greedo	6.00	95.00	80.00	40.00	35.00	
Hammerhead	6.00	90.00	75.00	50.00	35.00	—
Luke X-Wing	5.00	100.00	80.00	50.00	45.00	65.00
Power Droid	10.00	90.00	85.00	35.00	35.00	—
R5-D4	10.00	85.00	75.00	40.00	30.00	—
Snaggletooth	8.00	85.00	65.00	35.00	30.00	—
Snaggletooth-Blue	120.00					
(Only released with Sears Creature Cantina, approx 20,000 made)						
Walrusman	5.00	90.00	80.00	45.00	35.00	—
Boba Fett	6.00	400.00	170.00	95.00	90.00	—

THE EMPIRE STRIKES BACK 1ST RELEASE 1980 3¾" FIGURES	LOOSE	EMP	JEDI	TRI	POTF
Lando Calrissian-No Teeth	4.00	35.00	30.00	30.00	
Lando Calrissian-With Teeth	4.00	35.00	30.00	30.00	
Leia Bespin-Turtle Neck	5.00	85.00	45.00	35.00	
Leia Bespin-Crew Neck	5.00	65.00	45.00	35.00	
Imperial Snowtrooper.	4.50	35.00	30.00	30.00	
Han Solo Hoth	2.50	35.00	35.00	30.000	
Luke Bespin-Blonde Hair	12.00	95.00	55.00	45.00	
Luke Bespin-Brown Hair	12.00	95.00	55.00	45.00	
Rebel Soldier	2.00	20.00	20.00	15.00	
Bespin Guard-White	2.00	35.00	20.00	15.00	
Bespin Guard-Black	2.00	25.00	35.00	15.00	
Bossk	3.50	50.00	30.00	25.00	
FX-7	4.00	30.00	30.00	25.00	
IG-88	4.50	50.00	40.00	35.00	

THE EMPIRE STRIKES BACK 2ND RELEASE 1981 3¾" FIGURES	LOOSE	EMP	JEDI	TRI	POTF
2-1B	4.50	30.00	25.00	20.00	—
Yoda-Orange Snake	12.00	40.00	—	—	—
Yoda-Brown Snake	12.00		35.00	25.00	160.00
Ugnaught	5.00	25.00	25.00	18.00	—
Dengar	3.50	25.00	25.00	18.00	—
Lobot	2.50	15.00	15.00	12.50	—
Han Solo Bespin	4.50	45.00	35.00	25.00	—
Leia Hoth	4.50	30.00	25.00	25.00	—
Imperial Commander	3.00	17.50	15.00	18.00	—
AT-AT Driver	2.50	17.50	15.00	18.00	150.00
Rebel Commander	2.50	17.50	15.00	18.00	—
4-LOM	3.50	90.00	20.00	18.00	—

THE EMPIRE STRIKES BACK 3RD RELEASE 1982 3¾" FIGURES	LOOSE	EMP	JEDI	TRI	POTF
C3-PO Removable Arms and Legs	5.00	25.00	20.00	17.50	55.00
Luke Hoth	4.00	25.00	25.00	18.00	—
AT-AT Commander	2.00	17.50	17.50	15.00	—
Cloud Car Pilot	17.50	45.00	35.00	55.00	—
TIE Fighter Pilot	3.50	45.00	35.00	25.00	—
Zuckuss	3.50	27.50	20.00	18.00	—
R2-D2 Sensorscope	8.00	20.00	20.00	18.00	—

THE RETURN OF THE JEDI 1ST RELEASE 1983 3¾" FIGURES	LOOSE	JEDI	TRI	POTF
Luke Jedi-Blue Saber	40.00	95.00	60.00	125.00
Luke Jedi-Green Saber	20.00	50.00	45.00	—
Leia in Boushh Disguise	5.00	30.00	18.00	—
Nein Numb	3.00	15.00	12.00	—
Emp.Royal Guard	3.50	15.00	10.00	—
Ree-Yees	1.75	10.00	12.00	—
Lando Skiff Guard	4.00	15.00	10.00	—
Chief Chirpa	2.50	12.50	10.00	—
Klaatu	2.00	10.00	10.00	—
Rebel Commando	2.00	15.00	10.00	—
Biker Scout	3.50	15.00	12.50	35.00
Gamorrean Guard	2.00	10.00	15.00	95.00
Logray	1.50	15.00	10.00	—
Squid Head	1.50	12.50	10.00	—
Admiral Ackbar	2.50	12.50	10.00	—
General Madine	1.50	10.00	8.00	—
Bib Fortuna	1.50	12.50	10.00	—
Weequay	1.50	10.00	8.50	—

THE RETURN OF THE JEDI 2ND RELEASE 1984 3¾" FIGURES	LOOSE	JEDI	TRI	POTF
Klaatu Skiff Guard	2.00	12.50	10.00	–
Nikto	2.00	2.00	10.00	185.00
Prune Face	2.00	12.00	10.00	–
AT-ST Driver	3.00	12.00	10.00	35.00
B-Wing Pilot	4.00	12.00	10.00	10.00
8D8	2.50	15.00	10.00	–
Teebo	3.00	15.00	10.00	85.00
Wicket W. Warrick	3.50	15.00	10.00	55.00
Rancor Keeper	5.00	10.00	8.00	–
Emperor	2.50	15.00	10.00	30.00
Han In Trench Coat	5.00	30.00	17.50	170.00
Leia Combat Poncho	5.00	25.00	17.50	55.00
Paploo	12.00	25.00	25.00	25.00
Lumat	12.00	25.00	25.00	25.00
Rebo Band	25.00	75.00	50.007	–

POWER OF THE FORCE 1985 RELEASE 3¾" FIGURES	LOOSE	TRI	POTF
Yak Face	75.00	195.00	500.00
EV-9D9	45.00	65.00	85.00
R2-D2 Pop-Up Saber	55.00	65.00	100.00
Han In Carbonite	70.00	125.00	150.00
Warok	12.00	15.00	20.00
Imperial Dignitary	17.50	45.00	75.00
Romba	12.00	25.00	30.00
Barada	40.00	50.00	60.00
Lando General Pilot	25.00	40.00	55.00
Anakin Skywalker	12.00	35.00	425.00
Luke Stormtrooper	65.00	90.00	125.00
Imperial Gunner	55.00	85.00	100.00
Luke Battle Poncho	25.00	45.00	55.00
A-Wing Pilot	17.50	45.00	55.00
Amanaman	45.00	75.00	135.00

12" FIGURES 1979–1980	LOOSE	SW	EMP	JEDI	TRI	POTF
Chewbacca	50.00	100.00	–			
C-3Po	35.00	85.00	–			
Ben Kenobi	85.00	190.00	–			
Jawa	30.00	100.00	–			
R2-D2	30.00	85.00	–			
Stormtrooper	55.00	190.00	–			
Han Solo	160.00	325.00	–			
Boba Fett	60.00	225.00	195.00			
IG-88	170.00		425.00L			

DROIDS AND EWOKS

Another spin-off of the Star Wars trilogy was the animated series of Droids and Ewoks. 3¾" figures from both these series were released in 1985 along with the 'Power Of The Force' line. Like their movie counterparts they all came with a special collector's coin. These figures were not officially sold in the U.K and are quite scarce, especially loose.

DROIDS ANIMATED SERIES 1985 3¾" FIGURES	LOOSE	DROIDS
R2-D2	10.00	25.00
C-3PO	10.00	25.00
A-Wing Pilot	17.50	90.00
Boba Fett	6.00	125.00
Jann Tosh	6.00	15.00
Jord Duscat	6.00	15.00
Kea Moll	6.00	15.00
Kez-Iban	6.00	15.00
Sise Fromm	8.00	20.00
Thall Joben	6.00	15.00
Tir Fromm	15.00	40.00
Uncle Gundy	6.00	10.50

EWOKS ANIMATED SERIES 1985 3¾" FIGURES	LOOSE	EWOKS
Dulok Shaman	6.00	11.00
Dulok Scout	6.00	11.00
King Gorneesh	6.00	11.00
Logray	6.00	11.00
Ugrah	6.00	11.00
Wicket W.Warrick	6.00	11.00

ACCESSORIES 1977	LOOSE	SW
Early Bird Envelope	–	150.00
Set of four Early Bird figures in plastic box	150.00	200.00

ACCESSORIES 1978	LOOSE	SW	EMP
Mail-In Action Stand	40.00	135.00	135.00
X-Wing	20.00	55.00	–
TIE Fighter	25.00	60.00	–
Land Speeder	17.50	45.00	–

ACCESSORIES 1979	LOOSE	SW	EMP	JEDI
Death Star (U.S.)	45.00	110.00	–	–
Death Star (U.K.)	100.00	350.00	–	–
Droid Factory	30.00	60.00	120.00	–
Cantina Cafe	25.00	60.00	–	–
As above with Blue Snaggletooth figure	125.00	235.00	–	–
Land Of The Jawas	30.00	55.00	150.00	–
Patrol Dewback	25.00	60.00	80.00	–
Millinium Falcon	30.00	160.00	75.00	50.00
Imperial Transport (Talking)	30.00	65.00	65.00	–
Darth Vader's TIE Fighter	35.00	55.00	–	–
Death Star Escape Set	45.00	85.00	–	–
Sonic Controlled Land Speeder	85.00	300.00	–	–

ACCESSORIES 1980	LOOSE	EMP	JEDI
Imperial Attack Base	35.00	55.00	–
Vader's Star Destroyer	25.00	85.00	–
Hoth Ice Planet Set	25.00	55.00	–
Tauntaun	15.00	30.00	–
Twin Pod Cloud Car	30.00	55.00	–
Imperial Troop Transport (Non-Talking)	25.00	65.00	–
Snow Speeder	25.00	55.00	40.00

ACCESSORIES 1981	LOOSE	EMP	JEDI
Turret And Probot Set	40.00	65.00	–
AT-AT	45.00	85.00	60.00
Slave 1	25.00	60.00	45.00
Dagobah Playset	35.00	60.00	–
Cloud City Playset	95.00	250.00	–
MTV-7	5.00	15.00	12.50
PDT-8	5.00	12.50	8.00
MCL-3	5.00	15.00	12.50

ACCESSORIES 1982	LOOSE	EMP	JEDI
INT-4	5.00	12.00	8.00
CAP-2	5.00	12.00	8.00
Radar Laser Cannon	3.50	8.00	5.00
Tri-Pod Laser Cannon	3.50	8.00	5.00
Vehicle Maintenance Energiser	3.50	8.00	5.00
Hoth Wampa	8.00	20.00	–
Tauntaun-Open Belly	12.50	25.00	–
X-Wing With Battle Damage	15.00	50.00	37.50
Scout Walker	15.00	45.00	30.00
Rebel Transport	15.00	45.00	30.00

ACCESSORIES 1983	LOOSE	JEDI
AST-5	3.50	10.00
ISP-6	5.00	15.00
Speeder Bike	6.50	15.00
Jabba's Palace Playset	25.00	45.00
Jabba's Dungeon With 3 Figures	35.00	65.00
Y-Wing	35.00	75.00
TIE Fighter-Battle Damaged	35.00	50.00
Ewok Village	20.00	50.00

ACCESSORIES 1984	LOOSE	JEDI
Desert Sail Skiff	6.00	10.00
Endor Forest Ranger	5.00	10.00
Ewok Assualt Catapult	6.00	12.00
Ewok Glider	6.00	12.00
Rancor Monster	15.00	25.00
B-Wing Fighter	35.00	65.00
TIE Interceptor	35.00	65.00

Imperial Shuttle	125.00	300.00
Jabba's Dungeon With 3 POTF Figures	125.00	200.00

POWER OF THE FORCE ACCESSORIES 1985	LOOSE	POTF
Tatooine Skiff	165.00	400.00
Ewok Battle Wagon	30.00	55.00
One-Man Sand Skimmer	25.00	50.00
Imperial Sniper	27.50	55.00
Security Scout	25.00	50.00

DROIDS ACCESSORIES 1985	LOOSE	DROIDS
A-Wing Fighter	125.00	350.00
Imperial Side Gunner	17.50	40.00
ATL Interceptor	17.50	40.00

CARRYING CASES FOR 3¾" FIGURES	MIMB
Mini Action Figure Case With Star Wars Scenes	25.00
Mini Action Figure Case With Empire Scenes	25.00
Mini Action Figure Case With Jedi Scenes	100.00
Darth Vader Case	35.00
C-3PO Case	45.00
Chewbacca Bandolier Strap	12.50
Laser Rifle Case	40.00

1995

1995 marked the return of the Star Wars figure in a big way. Once again, toy shops around the world are filled with all the favourite characters from the trilogy. Collectors and kids alike have come to accept these new versions as a continuation of the originals and if anything, are collecting them even more passionately.

POWER OF THE FORCE 1995 RELEASE 4" FIGURES	LOOSE	US CARD	TRI	TRI with thx flyer
Ben Kenobi.-Long saber,Head shot	5.00	30.00	20.00	–
Ben Kenobi-Long saber,Full figure shot	5.00	30.00	15.00	20.00
Ben Kenobi-Short saber,Full figure shot	5.00	7.50	5.00	–
Chewbacca	2.50	7.50	5.00	10.00
C-3PO	2.50	7.50	5.00	10.00
Darth Vader-Long saber	2.50	10.00	15.00	–
Darth Vader-Short saber in long tray	2.50	10.00	12.50	15.000
Darth Vader-Short saber	2.50	7.50	5.00	–
Han Solo	2.50	7.50	–	10.00
Luke Skywalker-Long saber	2.50	15.00	10.00	15.00
Luke Skywalker-Short saber	2.50	7.50	5.00	–
Princess Leia	10.00	40.00	25.00	95.00
R2-D2	2.50	7.50	5.00	10.00
Stormtrooper	2.50	12.50	7.50	12.50
Han Solo in Stormtrooper Disguise- GU.S. Mail Order preminum only (Comes in plain white box).	25.00	30.00	–	
Toys 'R' Us Classic Edition 4 Pack	16.00	65.00	–	–

POWER OF THE FORCE 1996 RELEASE 4" FIGURES	LOOSE	US CARD	TRI
Boba Fett-Half Circle on hand	7.50	25.00	17.500
Boba Fett-Full Circle on hand	2.50	10.00	7.50
Han Solo Hoth Outfit-Open hand	2.50	10.00	7.50
Han Solo Hoth Outfit-Closed hand	2.50	7.50	5.00
Lando Calrissian	2.50	7.50	5.00
Luke in X-Wing Outfit-Long saber	3.50	15.00	10.00
Luke in X-Wing Outfit-Short saber,Long tray	2.50	12.50	7.50
Luke in X-Wing Outfit-Short saber	2.50	7.50	5.00
Luke in Dagobah Outfit-Long saber	3.50	15.00	10.00
Luke in Dagobah Outfit-Short saber,Long tray	2.50	12.50	7.50
Luke in Dagobah Outfit-Short saber	2.50	7.50	5.00
TIE Fighter Pilot-With 'Warning' sticker	2.50	20.00	–
TIE Fighter Pilot-With 'Warning' printed	2.50	7.50	5.00
Yoda the Jedi Master	2.50	7.50	5.00

POWER OF THE FORCE-SHADOWS OF THE EMPIRE 1996 RELEASE 4" FIGURES	LOOSE	US CARD	TRI
Chewbacca in Bounty Hunter Disguise	2.50	7.50	5.00
Dash Rendar	2.50	7.50	5.00
Han Solo in Carbonite-'With freezing chamber'	2.50	12.50	–
Han Solo in Carbonite-'With carbonite block'	2.50	10.00	5.00
Leia in Boush Disguise	2.50	7.50	5.00
Luke Skywalker Jedi Knight-Brown Tunic	5.00	17.50	–
Luke Skywalker Jedi Knight-Black Tunic	2.50	7.50	5.00

Prince Xizor	2.50	7.50	5.000
IG-88 Vs. Boba Fett 2 Pack	5.00	20.00	10.00
Prince Xizor Vs. Darth Vader 2 Pack	5.00	20.00	10.00

POWER OF THE FORCE 1996 RELEASE 4" FIGURES	LOOSE	US CARD	TRI
Death Star Gunner	2.50	7.50	5.00
Greedo	2.50	7.50	5.00
Hammerhead	2.50	7.50	5.00
Jawas 2 Pack	2.50	7.50	5.00
Luke Skywalker in Stormtrooper Disguise	2.50	7.50	5.00
Stormtrooper in Tantooine Outfit	2.50	7.50	5.00
Tusken Raider	2.50	7.50	5.00

POWER OF THE FORCE-DELUXE 1996 RELEASE 4" FIGURES WITH ACCESSORIES	LOOSE	US CARD	TRI
Crowd Control Stormtrooper	5.00	20.00	10.00
Han Solo With Smugglers Flight Gear	5.00	20.00	10.00
Luke Skywalker With Desert Sports Skiff	5.00	20.00	10.00

POWER OF THE FORCE 1996 RELEASE 12" FIGURES	LOOSE	US BOX WITH DARK BLUE INSERT
Ben Kenobi-Black Boots	10.00	40.00
Darth Vader	10.00	20.00
Han Solo	10.00	20.00
Luke Skywalker	10.00	20.00

POWER OF THE FORCE 1996 RELEASE 12" FIGURES	LOOSE	US BOX WITH LIGHT BLUE INSERT
Ben Kenobi-Brown Boots	10.00	50.00
Ben Kenobi-Black Boots	10.00	40.00
Darth Vader	10.00	20.00
Han Solo	10.00	20.00
Luke Skywalker	10.00	20.00

POWER OF THE FORCE 1997 RELEASE 12" FIGURES	LOOSE	US BOX
Boba Fett	10.00	20.00
Chewbacca	10.00	20.00
Lando Calrissian	10.00	20.00
Luke Skywalker in Bespin Outfit	10.00	20.00
Luke Skywalker in X-Wing Outfit	10.00	20.00
Princess Leia	10.00	20.00
Stormtrooper	10.00	20.00
Tusken Raider	10.00	20.00

VECHICLES AND ACCESSORIES 1995 RELEASE	LOOSE	US BOX	TRI BOX
Landspeeder	5.00	20.00	10.00
Imperial AT-ST	7.50	25.00	15.00
Millenium Falcon	25.00	60.00	50.00
TIE Fighter	7.50	25.00	15.00
X-Wing Fighter	7.50	25.00	15.00

VECHICLES AND ACCESSORIES 1996 RELEASE	LOOSE	US BOX	TRI BOX
Imperial Speeder Bike with Biker Scout Figure	5.00	15.00	10.00
Rebel Snowspeeder	7.50	20.00	12.50
Dash Rendar's Outrider	5.00	15.00	–
Slave One	15.00	30.00	–

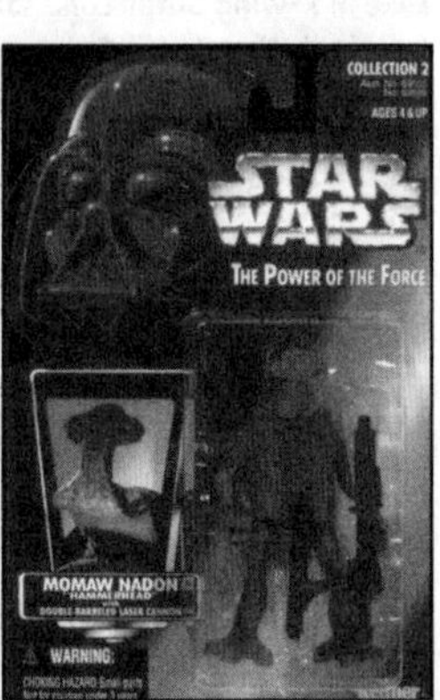

DEATH INDEX

Foundation work by Andy Kythreotis

Below is a work-in-progress listing of the first deaths of selected characters (Note: Some of these characters have since been resurrected). We hope to expand this feature to include subsequent rebirths/new incarnations in future editions. Any further information may be sent to the editorial address.

ADAM CRAY
SUICIDE SQUAD #62 .... FEBRUARY 1992

AGATHA HARKNESS
VISION & SCARLET WITCH (2nd Series) #3 .... DECEMBER 1985

AIRWALKER
THOR #306 .... APRIL 1981

AMAHL FAROUK
X-MEN, THE UNCANNY #117 .... JANUARY 1979

ANCIENT ONE
MARVEL PREMIERE #10 .... SEPTEMBER 1973

ANGLE-MAN
CRISIS ON INFINITE EARTHS #11 .... FEBRUARY 1986

AQUABABY
AQUAMAN 57 .... AUGUST/SEPT 1977

AQUAGIRL
CRISIS ON INFINTE EARTHS #10 .... JANUARY 1986

ARTEMIS
WONDER WOMAN [2nd Series] #100 .... JULY 1995

AUNT MAY
AMAZING SPIDERMAN #400 .... APRIL 1995

AURON
SUPERMAN #509 .... FEBRUARY 1994

BALDER
THOR #274 .... AUGUST 1978

BANDIT
CRISIS ON INFINITE EARTHS #12 .... MARCH 1986

BARON BLOOD
CAPTAIN AMERICA #254 .... FEBRUARY 1981

BARON STRUCKER
STRANGE TALES #158 .... JULY 1967

BARON ZEMO I
AVENGERS #15 .... APRIL 1965

BASILISK
FANTASTIC FOUR #289 .... APRIL 1986

BATMAN (Earth 2)
ADVENTURE COMICS #462 .... OCTOBER 1979

BATWOMAN
DETECTIVE COMICS #485 .... JUNE 1979

BELIT
CONAN THE BARBARIAN #100 .... JULY 1979

BEN PARKER
AMAZING FANTASY #15 .... AUGUST 1962

BEYONDER
SECRET WARS II #9 .... MARCH 1986

BIG MAN
AMAZING SPIDERMAN #52 .... SEPTEMBER 1967

BLACK KNIGHT I
MARVEL SUPER HEROES #17 .... NOVEMBER 1968

BLACK KNIGHT II
AVENGERS #47 .... DECEMBER 1968

BLACK OUT
AVENGERS #277 .... APRIL 1987

BLIZZARD
AMAZING SPIDERMAN ANNUAL #20 .... NOVEMBER 1986

BLOOD STONE
RAMPAGING HULK #8 .... AUGUST 1977

BLUE STREAK
CAPTAIN AMERICA #318 .... JUNE 1986

BUCKY
AVENGERS #4 .... MARCH 1964

CAPTAIN GEORGE STACY
AMAZING SPIDERMAN #90 .... NOVEMBER 1970

CAPTAIN MARVEL (Kree)
MARVEL GRAPHIC NOVEL #1 1982

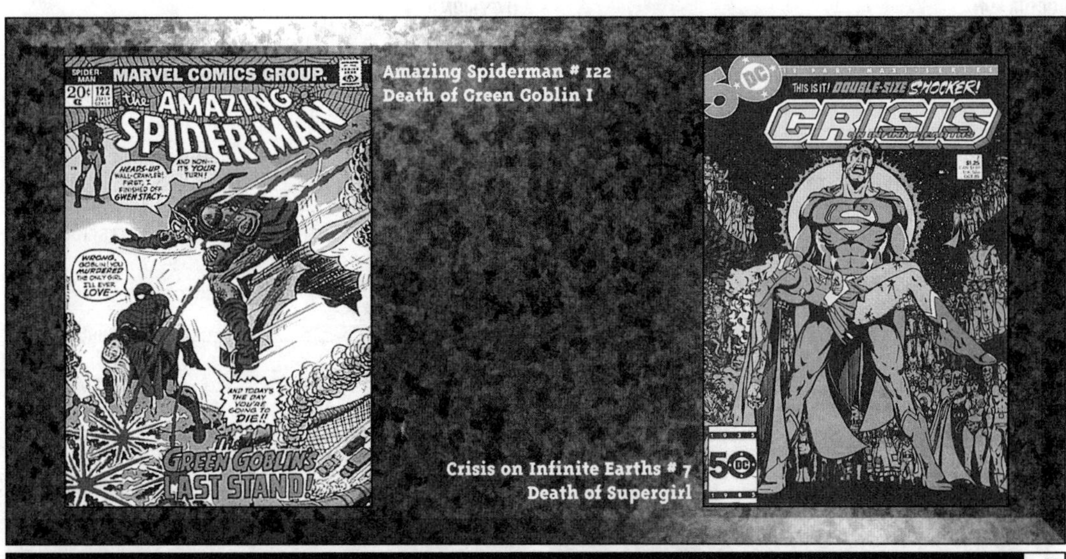

Amazing Spiderman # 122
Death of Green Goblin I

Crisis on Infinite Earths # 7
Death of Supergirl

CAPTAIN STACY
AMAZING SPIDERMAN #90 .... NOVEMBER 1970
CAPTAIN STORM
LOSERS SPECIAL #1 1985
CARRION
SPECTACULAR SPIDERMAN #31 .... MAY 1979
CASCADE
SOVEREIGN SEVEN #2 .... AUGUST 1995
CHANGELING
X-MEN, THE UNCANNY #42 .... MARCH 1968
CHEETAH (Marvel)
CAPTAIN AMERICA #319 .... JULY 1986
CHEMO
CRISIS ON INFINITE EARTHS #10 .... JANUARY 1986
CHUCK
BLACKHAWK #250 .... JAN/FEB 1977
CLAYFACE II
CRISIS ON INFINITE EARTHS #12 .... MARCH 1986
COMMANDER KRAKEN
CAPTAIN AMERICA #319 .... JULY 1986
COMMANDER STEEL
ECLIPSO #13 .... NOVEMBER 1993
COUNT NEFARIA
IRON MAN #116 .... NOVEMBER 1978
CREEPER
ECLIPSO #13 .... NOVEMBER 1993
CRUSHER
IRON MAN #6 .... OCTOBER 1968
CYCLONE
CAPTAIN AMERICA #319 .... JULY 1986
DARKOTH
FANTASTIC FOUR #194 .... MAY 1978
DEATH ADDER
CAPTAIN AMERICA #318 .... JUNE 1986
DEATHLOK
MARVEL TWO-IN-ONE #54 .... AUGUST 1979
DEATHSTALKER
DAREDEVIL #158 .... APRIL 1979
DESTINY
SUB-MARINER #7 .... NOVEMBER 1968
DOCTOR MIDNIGHT
ECLIPSO #13 .... NOVEMBER 1993
DOCTOR OCTOPUS
SPECTACULAR SPIDERMAN #221 .... FEBRUARY 1995
DOCTOR SUN
FANTASTIC FOUR #327 .... JUNE 1989
DOOM PATROL
DOOM PATROL #121 .... SEPT/ OCT 1968
DOVE
CRISIS ON INFINITE EARTHS #12 .... MARCH 1986
DRACULA (Marvel)
DOCTOR STRANGE (2nd series) #62 .... JANUARY 1985
DRAX THE DESTROYER
AVENGERS #220 .... JUNE 1982
EEL
GHOST RIDER (1st Series) #21 .... JANUARY 1977
EGGHEAD
AVENGERS #230 .... APRIL 1983
ELEKTRA
DAREDEVIL #181 .... APRIL 1982
ELEMENT GIRL
METAMORPHO #10 .... FEBRUARY 1967
ENFORCER
IRON MAN #194 .... MAY 1985
EXECUTIONER
THOR #362 .... DECEMBER 1985

FAORA
SUPERMAN (2nd Series) #22 .... OCTOBER 1988
FAFNIR
THOR #343 .... MAY 1984
FERRO LAD
ADVENTURE COMICS #353 .... FEBRUARY 1967
FIREBRAND
CAPTAIN AMERICA #319 .... JULY 1986
FLASH (Silver Age)
CRISIS ON INFINITE EARTHS #8 .... NOVEMBER 1985
FOOLKILLER I
MAN-THING #4 .... APRIL 1974
GAMORA
AVENGERS ANNUAL #7 1977
GARGOYLE I
INCREDIBLE HULK (1st) #1 .... MAY 1962
GENERAL ZOD
SUPERMAN (2nd Series) #22 .... OCTOBER 1988
GOLDEN EAGLE
NEW TITANS ##72 .... JANUARY 1991
GRAND DIRECTOR
CAPTAIN AMERICA #236 .... AUGUST 1979
GREEN ARROW (Earth-2)
CRISIS ON INFINITE EARTHS #12 .... MARCH 1986
GREEN GOBLIN I
AMAZING SPIDERMAN #122 .... JULY 1973
GRIM REAPER
VISION & SCARLET WITCH (2nd Series) #2 .... NOVEMBER 1985
GUARDIAN
ALPHA FLIGHT #12 .... JULY 1984
GUNNER & SARGE
LOSERS SPECIAL #1 1985
GWEN STACY
AMAZING SPIDERMAN #121 .... JUNE 1973
HAMMER & ANVIL
MARVEL FANFARE #29 .... NOVEMBER 1986
HANGMAN
BIZARRE ADVENTURES #31 .... MARCH 1982
HATEMONGER I
SUPER VILLAIN TEAM UP #17 .... JUNE 1976
HOBGOBLIN (Ned Leeds)
AMAZING SPIDERMAN #289 .... MAY 1987
HUNTRESS (Golden Age)
CRISIS ON INFINITE EARTHS #12 .... MARCH 1986
HYPERION II
SQUADRON SUPREME #8 .... APRIL 1986
IMPERIAL HYDRA
STRANGE TALES #141 .... FEBRUARY 1966
INVISIBLE KID
SUPERBOY #203 .... AUGUST 1974
IRIS ALLEN (West)
FLASH #275 .... JULY 1979
IT, THE LIVING COLOSSUS
INCREDIBLE HULK (2nd) #244 .... FEBRUARY 1980
JACKAL
AMAZING SPIDERMAN #149 .... OCTOBER 1976
JANICE CORD
IRON MAN #22 .... FEBRUARY 1970
JARELLA
INCREDIBLE HULK (2nd) #205 .... NOVEMBER 1976
JEAN DeWOLFF
SPECTACULAR SPIDERMAN #107 .... OCTOBER 1985
JERICHO
NEW TITANS #83 .... FEBRUARY 1992
JOCASTA
MARVEL TWO IN ONE #93 .... NOVEMBER 1982

JONAH HEX
JONAH HEX SPECTACULAR ... AUTUMN 1978
JOHNNY CLOUD
CRISIS ON INFINITE EARTHS #3 ... JUNE 1985
KANGAROO
AMAZING SPIDERMAN #126 ... NOVEMBER 1974
KARATE KID
LEGION OF SUPER-HEROES (3rd Series) #4 ... FEBRUARY 1990
KIBER THE CRUEL
BLACK PANTHER #13 ... JANUARY 1979
KID CASSIDY
GUNHAWKS #6 ... AUGUST 1973
KID PSYCHO
CRISIS ON INFINITE EARTHS #3 ... JUNE 1985
KILLOWOG
GREEN LANTERN [2nd Series] #50 ... MARCH 1994
KOLE
CRISIS ON INFINITE EARTHS #12 ... MARCH 1986
KORVAC
AVENGERS #178 ... DECEMBER 1978
LADY DORMA
SUB-MARINER #37 ... MAY 1971
LETHA
CAPTAIN AMERICA #319 ... JULY 1986
LIGHTNING LAD
ADVENTURE COMICS #304 ... JANUARY 1963
LILITH
DOCTOR STRANGE (2nd Series) #62 ... JANUARY 1985
LORI LEMARIS
CRISIS ON INFINITE EARTHS #12 ... MARCH 1986
MA & PA KENT
SUPERMAN #161 ... MAY 1963
MAJOR VICTORY
ECLIPSO #13 ... NOVEMBER 1993
MALEKITH THE ACCURSED
THOR #367 ... MAY 1986
MANHUNTER (Paul Kirk)
DETECTIVE COMICS #443 ... NOVEMBER 1974
MARIKO
WOLVERINE #57 ... AUGUST 1992
MARK HAZZARD
MARK HAZZARD: MERC ANNUAL #1 ... NOVEMBER 1987
MARK SHAW: MANHUNTER
ECLIPSO #13 ... NOVEMBER 1993
MARVEL BOY
FANTASTIC FOUR #165 ... DECEMBER 1975
MAULER I
DAREDEVIL #167 ... DECEMBER 1980
MEGATAK
THOR #359 ... SEPTEMBER 1985
MELTER
AVENGERS #263 ... FEBRUARY 1986
MIDGARD SERPENT
THOR #380 ... JUNE 1987
MIKE MURDOCK
DAREDEVIL #41 ... JUNE 1968
MIMIC
INCREDIBLE HULK (2nd) #161 ... MARCH 1973
MIRAGE I
CAPTAIN AMERICA #319 ... JULY 1986
MISS AMERICA
GIANT SIZE AVENGERS #1 ... AUGUST 1974
MOCKINGBIRD
WEST COAST AVENGERS 100 ... NOVEMBER 1993
MODOK
CAPTAIN AMERICA #313 ... JANUARY 1986
MONITOR
CRISIS ON INFINITE EARTHS #4 ... JULY 1985
MR. TERRIFIC
JUSTICE LEAGUE OF AMERICA #172 ... NOVEMBER 1979
NEBULON
AVENGERS ANNUAL #11 ... 1982
NEMESIS KID
LEGION OF SUPER-HEROES (2nd Series) #5 ... DECEMBER 1984
NICK FURY
DOUBLE EDGE OMEGA ... 1995
NIGHTHAWK (Marvel)
DEFENDERS #106 ... APRIL 1982
NIGHTHAWK (DC Western)
CRISIS ON INFINITE EARTHS #3 ... JUNE 1985
NIGHTHAWK II
DEFENDERS #106 ... APRIL 1982
NUKE
SQUADRON SUPREME #3 ... NOVEMBER 1985
OBADIAH STANE
IRON MAN #200 ... NOVEMBER 1985
OMEGA
OMEGA THE UNKNOWN #10 ... JULY 1977

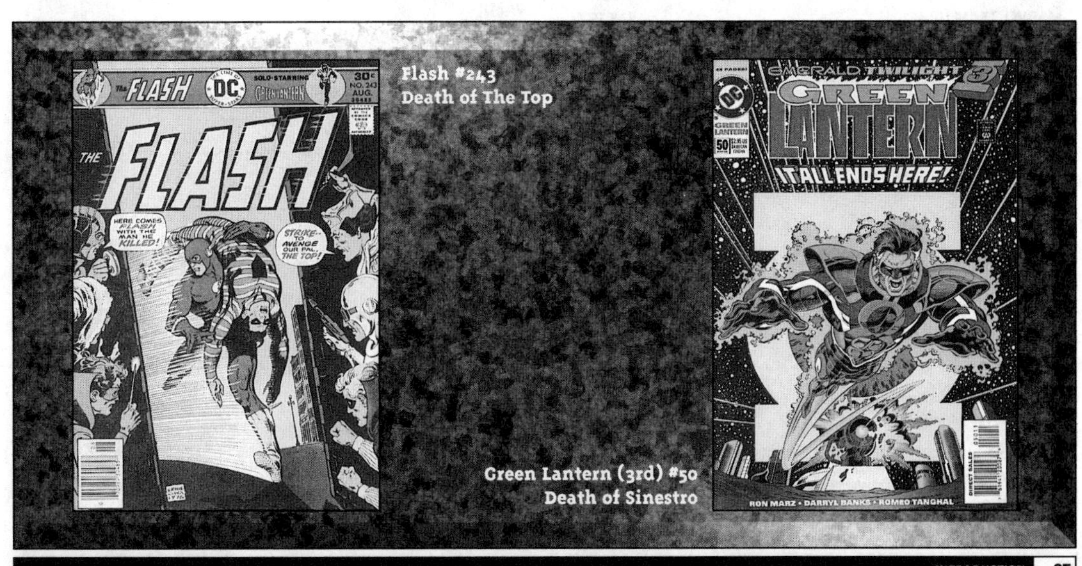

Flash #243
Death of The Top

Green Lantern (3rd) #50
Death of Sinestro

PATRIOT
CAPTAIN AMERICA #285 ... SEPTEMBER 1983
PEACEMAKER
ECLIPSO #13 ... NOVEMBER 1993
PHOENIX (Jean Grey)
X-MEN, THE UNCANNY #137 ... SEPTEMBER 1980
PIP THE TROLL
MARVEL TWO IN ONE ANNUAL #2 ... FEBRUARY 1977
PORCUPINE
CAPTAIN AMERICA #315 ... MARCH 1986
PROFESSOR POWER
CAPTAIN AMERICA #338 ... FEBRUARY 1988
PSIMON
CRISIS ON INFINITE EARTHS #10 ... JANUARY 1986
QUEX-UL
SUPERMAN (2nd Series) #22 ... OCTOBER 1988
QUINCY HARKER
TOMB OF DRACULA #70 ... AUGUST 1979
RAVEN
NEW TITANS #84 ... MARCH 1992
RED BEE
ALL-STAR SQUADRON #35 ... JULY 1984
RED GUARDIAN I
AVENGERS #44 ... SEPTEMBER 1968
RED RAVEN
SUB-MARINER #26 ... JUNE 1970
RED RYAN
CHALLENGERS OF THE UNKNOWN #55 ... MAY 1967
RED SKULL (Silver Age)
CAPTAIN AMERICA #300 ... DECEMBER 1984
REVERSE FLASH (Professor Zoom)
FLASH #324 ... AUGUST 1983
RINGER
CAPTAIN AMERICA #319 ... JULY 1986
ROBIN (Golden Age)
CRISIS ON INFINITE EARTHS #12 ... MARCH 1986
ROBIN II (Jason Todd)
BATMAN #428 ... SEPTEMBER 1988
SATANA
MARVEL TEAM UP #81 ... MAY 1979
SHARON CARTER
CAPTAIN AMERICA #237 ... SEPTEMBER 1979
SINESTRO
GREEN LANTERN [2nd Series] #50 ... MARCH 1994
SLIM STRYKER
G.I. COMBAT #244 ... AUGUST 1982
SNOWBIRD
ALPHA FLIGHT #44 ... JANUARY 1987
SOLARR
POWERMAN AND IRON FIST #113 ... JANUARY 1985
SPHINX
THING, THE #34 ... APRIL 1986
SPIRIT OF '76
WHAT IF (1st Series) #4 ... AUGUST 1977
SPYMASTER
IRON MAN #220 ... JULY 1987
STEVE TREVOR
WONDER WOMAN #180 ... JAN/FEB 1969
STICK
DAREDEVIL #190 ... JANUARY 1983
SUNBURST
CRISIS ON INFINITE EARTHS #12 ... MARCH 1986
SUPERBOY (original)
LEGION OF SUPER-HEROES (2nd Series) #38 ... SEPTEMBER 1987
SUPERGIRL (original)
CRISIS ON INFINITE EARTHS #7 ... OCTOBER 1985
SUPERMAN (Modern) (Since revived)
SUPERMAN (2nd Series) #75 ... JANUARY 1993
SWORDSMAN
GIANT SIZE AVENGERS #2 ... OCTOBER 1974
TARANTULA
AMAZING SPIDERMAN #236 ... JANUARY 1983
TERRA
NEW TEEN TITANS ANNUAL (1st Series) #3 ... 1983
TERRAX
FANTASTIC FOUR #260 ... DECEMBER 1983
THANOS (Since revived)
MARVEL TWO IN ONE ANNUAL #2 ... FEBRUARY 1977
THUNDERBIRD
X-MEN, THE UNCANNY #95 ... OCTOBER 1975
THUNDERBOLT
POWERMAN AND IRON FIST #62 ... APRIL 1980
TITANIA
MARVEL TWO IN ONE #54 ... AUGUST 1979
TOM THUMB
SQUADRON SUPREME #9 ... MAY 1986
TOMAR-RE
GREEN LANTERN #198 ... MARCH 1986
TOP
FLASH #243 ... AUGUST 1976
TORO
SUB-MARINER #14 ... JUNE 1969
TORPEDO
ROM #50 ... JANUARY 1984
TORQUE
HARBINGER #6 ... JUNE 1992
UNION JACK I (Lord Falsworth)
CAPTAIN AMERICA #254 ... FEBRUARY 1981
VAMP
CAPTAIN AMERICA #319 ... JULY 1986
VIBE
JUSTICE LEAGUE OF AMERICA #258 ... JANUARY 1987
VIGILANTE (Modern)
VIGILANTE #50 ... FEBRUARY 1988
WARLOCK
AVENGERS ANNUAL #7 ... NOVEMBER 1977
WARLOCK (New Mutants)
NEW MUTANTS #95 ... NOVEMBER 1990
WASP
MARVEL SUPER-HERO SECRET WARS #6 ... OCTOBER 1984
WHIZZER
VISION & SCARLET WITCH (1st series) #2 ... NOVEMBER 1985
WILDCAT II
ECLIPSO #13 ... NOVEMBER 1993
WRAITH
AMAZING SPIDERMAN #277 ... JUNE 1986
ZURAS
THOR #300 ... OCTOBER 1980

MARKET REPORTS

A new look to market reports for this edition (though we'd welcome old vs new style feedback from readers), with a topic by topic breakdown (as opposed to a store-by-store overview), done Q&A style. Otherwise, the feature remains essentially the same, with reports (as up-to-date as possible) on the current state of the market, what's hot and what's not, and predictions for the year to come. Comic shop owners and Forbidden Planet buyers around the country kindly donated their time and efforts to let us know just what's happening out there on the front line. This is what they had to say...

YOUR VIEW OF 1996 IN GENERAL

(Dave Hopkins at Nostalgia & Comics, Birmingham) *"Not too bad. There doesn't seem to be such a glut of material on the shelves, and I definitely think Marvel did the right thing by thinning out their line."*

(Darryl Jones at Silver Acre Comics, Chester) *"A strong year for the back-issue market, and while demand has been good across the whole range of the comics spectrum, the big surprise for me was the high demand for lesser priced items, with the collectors veering towards quantity rather than quality."*

(Alan Scott at Adventure Into Comics, London) *"Steady, but sales figures showed little real improvement on last year. Back issue sales suffered, as opposed to new titles, re-vamps, one-shots, mini-series, and crossovers, all of which performed well."*

(Tommy Hoodless at Imagination Station, Carlisle) *"Marvel seem to have got their title count about right, while DC seem to be adding new titles every month. Kingdom Come was my best seller, closely followed by DC Versus Marvel (not as good, but a whole lot of fun). Dark Horse comics were strong sellers, Image less so. For sheer consistency of sales, small Independents are my year's winners."*

(Martin Beeson at Ace Comics, Colchester) *"Sales of Independents have increased as a result of Marvel's fall in status and quality. DC comics sold well, but over the year – as they pumped out too many titles – the overall turnover faltered. A lesson to be learned, perhaps. Strangehaven, Stray Bullets, Strangers In Paradise and Kurt Busiek's Astro City all proved that quality sells."*

(Manny Amario at Whatever Comics, Maidstone) *"Retail-wise, both our stores had a good year, figures showing a marked increase in sales. However, the previously flourishing attendance at Comic Marts seems to be down. Which is a shame."*

(Steve Wren at Forbidden Planet, Newcastle) *"A complex year, with falling comic sales being offset by increases in turnover in other stock areas. Diamond's increasing influence on the market has led to concerns about a monopoly of supply. Comics-wise, it's a time to retrench, consolidate and hope for consistently high standards of new product."*

(Kenneth Burns at A-1 books & comics, Glasgow) *"Gone are the days of just putting out comics on the shelves and watching them disappear, you really have to know your market and work hard to keep your customers happy. Crossovers and specials did help sales figures, but how long this will wash with people is not clear. On the whole, though, not as stressed as the last few years."*

(Mark Last at Forbidden Planet, Coventry) *"A good year in all with a steady swing back to quality rather than quantity."*

(Rick Appleby at Dream Comics, New Barnet) *"In three words –*

Strangehaven #3 — Stray Bullets #11 — Kingdom Come #3

a real challenge! Distribution changes and subsequent mistakes have made collecting comics a real nightmare. We, like many other retailers, have had to consider very carefully what titles to stock and in what numbers. 'Sell-through' has become the buzz word, ie: order enough for you regular customers and that's it. Gone are the days when a retailer could afford the luxury of carrying extra stock."

(Chris Rice at Forbidden Planet, Head Office) *"This has been a very odd year in comics, following the implosion started by Marvel last year and the absorption of Capital by Diamond. Editorially, there have never been so many quality comics available, and – most importantly – we've finally discarded the collector mentality that almost destroyed the market. The only way to go from here is up."*

DO YOU SENSE AN UPSWING IN THE MARKET, OR ARE REPORTS OF A RECOVERY EXAGGERATED?

(Martin Beeson) *"Greatly exaggerated. Sales are fairly constant but people still only have a fixed amount they're willing to spend on comics each month. To really expand, I'm having to move into other areas like tele-fantasy and Gaming cards."*

(Steve Wren) *"At best some titles are holding their own, but I see no upswing in the near future. In general terms, recovery has not yet reached the North-East, a view shared by other retailers in the 'entertainment' industry."*

(Rick Appleby) *"No upswing at present. Sales are steady if anything, with the odd success story here and there. Whether the industry grows from here depends on many factors and remains to be seen."*

(Kenneth Burns) *"There's not much of an upswing in the UK, it just looks that way because there are less comic shops now and the same number of people buying comics. Owners are certainly having to work harder: doing marts, mail-order and travelling more."*

(Chris Rice) *"The amount of comics retailers in the States is dwindling at an alarming rate, a trend that is thankfully not reflected to such an extent here. Whether this is down to a widening of stock (with many stores deciding they cannot live on comics alone) or the loyalty of UK readers isn't clear, although I'd plump for the latter."*

(Mark Last) *"Comics buying does seem to be on the up, thanks mainly to lines like Vertigo and Helix that have drawn in readers from other markets. TV and film adaptations have also helped in this respect."*

(Manny Amario) *"I sense a slight upswing in the market, but I wouldn't go as far as to call it a recovery. Not yet anyway."*

(Dave Hopkins) *"I don't sense an upswing in the market as a whole, but Marvel's Heroes Reborn push did create a new surge of interest. Will it last? Probably not."*

(Darryl Jones) *"My personal view is that the back issue market is very strong and getting stronger, but for those dealing in advance orders alone – wear a crash helmet!"*

(Tommy Hoodless) *"Not an upswing, no. But I would describe the current climate as stable."*

(Alan Scott) *"I can't see a change at all, and all the new titles, crossovers, etc., have had a detrimental effect on back-issue sales (where a retailer can actually turn a reasonable profit)."*

WHICH ESTABLISHED/NEW TITLES HAVE BEEN YOUR BIGGEST SELLERS?

(Rick Appleby) *"Established – Spawn, Gen 13, X-Men (family), Batman and Superman (family). New – Preacher, Witchblade, Weapon Zero and Darkchylde."*

(Steve Wren) *"Established – X-Men, Uncanny X-Men, Sandman, Wolverine, and Preacher . New – Marvel Versus DC, Onslaught, Kingdom Come, Fantastic Four and The Dreaming ."*

(Kenneth Burns) *"Established – X-Men titles (buoyed up considerably by the Onslaught storyline), Preacher (one of the hottest comics on our shelves), Batman, Spawn and Gen 13 . Not much, though, in the way of new titles apart from Saint of Killers, Aztek (surprisingly) and (best of all) Hitman."*

(Alan Scott) *"Established – Wolverine, X-Men, Batman and Spawn . New – all the Heroes Reborn titles and The Curse of Spawn ."*

(Manny Amario) *"Established – X-Men (and all sister titles), Preacher and Spawn . New – Dawn, DV8, Kingdom Come and The Fantastic Four ."*

(Tommy Hoodless) *"Established – Superman titles, Batman, Star Wars, X-Men, Uncanny X-Men and Sin City . New – Kingdom Come, Preacher, Supergirl, X-Files, Gen 13."*

(Mark Last) *"Established – almost all X-Men titles, Vertigo sales are rising, Preacher especially. Spawn is a consistent good seller, as are Dark Horse's Star Wars titles. New – Top Cow are going from strength to strength with the likes of The Darkness and Witchblade. Vertigo's The Dreaming did surprisingly well, and almost anything new by Garth Ennis sells."*

(Martin Beeson) *"Established – X-Men, Batman, Star Wars, Sin City, Starman. New – Hitman, Kingdom Come, Supergirl, JLA, Sin City That Yellow Bastard. The Heroes Reborn titles all sold well."*

(Darryl Jones) *"Established – Marvel's mainline titles seem to remain strong year in, year out, while The X-Files also provided a high return. New – the new issue market is very volatile at present, and where a new book used to be in demand for the best part of a year, now you're lucky if the interest lasts the month."*

(Dave Hopkins) *"Established – any X-Men or related titles, Batman, The X-Files, Spawn and Spider-Man. New – Kingdom Come, Sin City That Yellow Bastard, Gen 13. "*

HOW HAS THE YEAR BEEN FOR DC COMICS?

(Darryl Jones) *"DC seem to care more about the comics they publish, and it's been a good year for Vertigo, with demand for Preacher still rising."*

(Mark Last) *"Very good. New titles have generated a lot of interest (Supergirl, Nightwing, JLA) and standard of art and story has been high. Helix started off quietly, but is now gaining a solid readership."*

(Chris Rice) *"DC have had a generally good year, and for us at least it's been the year of Ennis. However, they're still putting out too many titles (Takion, Mr. Miracle, Eradicator... the list goes on) and could do with a Marvel-style strip down. They can't hope to successfully introduce new characters out of the blue without a talented writer to back them up."*

(Alan Scott) *"Quality stories (Elseworlds in particular) have made for a good year, with Vertigo showing particularly strongly. Overall, a slight improvement on last year, saleswise."*

(Dave Hopkins) *"Fairly average, with Batman titles staying fairly consistent and Kingdom Come selling well. But the Superman titles have tailed off, with nothing very new or exciting to stimulate interest."*

(Martin Beeson) *"Very good up until August, but it now seems they are churning out too many titles again. If this continues, I see sales dropping off. Haven't they learned?"*

(Steve Wren) *"Kingdom Come has shown there is a real appetite among buyers for excellence. Where DC have expanded upon their core characters and mythos, interest remains strong. Other lines are solid rather than spectacular."*

(Rick Appleby) *"Steady. Getting the product out on time with a high quality of content (eg; Impulse, Flash, Aquaman, Preacher, Kingdom Come) and not resorting to variant covers has helped. High quality = word of mouth = high sales. Final Night is also worthy of a mention."*

(Manny Amario) *"Very good. Kingdom Come, Supergirl and Preacher have shown DC's commitment to excellence."*

(Tommy Hoodless) *"This year's Annuals were very poor saleswise, with readers unimpressed by the story content. Whereas Kingdom Come and Preacher, they couldn't get enough of."*

(Kenneth Burns) *"From my side of the counter, things look very good. They're one step away from being the biggest force in comics, and are always looking to help the retailer."*

HOW HAS THE YEAR BEEN FOR MARVEL COMICS?

(Manny Amario) *"Also very good. The Onslaught storyline boosted sales considerably. Still, it has to be said, some of Marvel's output, like The World of 2099, seems almost purposefully bad."*

(Tommy Hoodless) *"Reasonably good. Steady sales. The Onslaught storyline had potential but faded towards the end. A shame really, because it started out so well."*

(Steve Wren) *"Concentrating on producing good, solid, if not spectacular, core titles, particularly The X-Men, has proved a sensible response to market realities. Distribution-wise, it's been a nightmare."*

(Kenneth Burns) *"The exchange rate makes Marvel comics the dearest on the shelves, and their re-ordering system is terrible. That said, however, the company is doing much better than it was at the start of the year."*

(Rick Appleby) *"Aside from the Onslaught storyline everything else is old hat! Only the really die-hard Marvel fans are buying their product. Anyone want a Spider-clone?"*

(Martin Beeson) *"The higher sales that Onslaught brought with it are now starting to fade. In general, it seems their customer base has become younger, more fickle, and less interested in the history of the titles."*

(Alan Scott) *"A case of swings and roundabouts, with the increase in sales for Heroes Reborn, one-shots and mini-series offset by a fall in the regular titles."*

(Chris Rice) *"Editorially, Marvel are the strongest they've been in years. The stripped down line has been well received, and improved sales have reflected this. The main event of the year was obviously Onslaught, with X-titles selling well above average. Standout of the year was Mark Waid and Ron Garney on Captain America, the best run this title has ever had."*

(Dave Hopkins) *"For all the bad press they get, Marvel still sell really well, so they must be doing something right. The Onslaught storyline and Heroes Reborn have both done very well for them."*

(Mark Last) *"I feel Marvel are putting all their eggs in one basket when it comes to the X-Men. A lot of smaller titles such as Ghost Rider are suffering through inferior writers and artists, and this could be their undoing."*

(Darryl Jones) *"Marvel the company just don't seem to care anymore, about their product or their readers, and it shows."*

[It's worth noting that many of these replies were received before the announcement that Marvel had filed for Chapter 11 bankruptcy. Their decision to go down this route through the courts is, by their own admission, a way of buying themselves some time for financial reorganisation, but how successful this tactic will be, only time will tell.]

HOW HAS THE YEAR BEEN FOR IMAGE COMICS?

(Chris Rice) *"As well as their internal problems, sales have dropped on all their titles, with the exception of the mighty Spawn. Todd McFarlane can seem to do no wrong, with Curse of Spawn almost selling as well as Spawn. At Wildstorm things are not quite so rosy, with only DV8 proving a solid hit. Most improved was Top Cow, The Darkness a grade A Spawn-sized hit."*

(Steve Wren) *"The 'bad girl' bandwagon has now derailed, taking a lot of Image with it. Generally, an Image title will sell well for its first five or six issues and then, when the drop in quality becomes apparent, sink without trace. Hazard wins my award for worst new comic this year!"*

(Mark Last) *"A mixed year, with studios coming and going, but somehow the company still manages to draw in a regular following of fans. It's nice to see they're starting to expand beyond just superhero titles."*

(Rick Appleby) *"Good. The popularity of Spawn and Gen 13 continues, while Kurt Busiek's Astro City has received deserved success. The exception is the Liefeld-produced stuff – is anyone buying this? Then again, given his recent 'divorce' from Image, the point seems academic."*

(Darryl Jones) *"They've maintained a generally high standard, with Spawn and Witchblade their bestsellers. Gen 13 seems to be cooling down while DV8 hots up."*

(Kenneth Burns) *"In January, Image were fast catching up with the big boys, but as the year has gone on they've slipped away, stagnated. But who knows? Perhaps by the end of next year they'll be doing all of Marvel's comics!"*

(Martin Beeson) *"More and more low quality pap being pumped out has translated into lower and lower sales. Extreme titles are almost unsellable. Apart from Spawn and Gen 13, it's the 'imports' like Bone and Kurt Busiek's Astro City that have been the best performers for them."*

(Alan Scott) *"In Image's case, more titles only mean that customers tend to discard one in favour of the other."*

(Dave Hopkins) *"Do they really have to fire out so much product? The list of duds is becoming almost embarrassingly long. That said, Spawn, Gen 13, Witchblade and, to a lesser extent, The Maxx and Savage Dragon, all sell well."*

(Manny Amario) *"Key titles like Spawn and Witchblade show no sign of flagging, but the likes of Hazard and Backlash are really slowing down now. DV8 was the best new title from Image for quite a while, nail on the head job."*

(Tommy Hoodless) *"Pretty sad. Outside of Spawn, Gen 13 and Kurt Busiek's Astro City, nothing really moves. Even Alan Moore's name generates only slight interest."*

HOW HAS THE YEAR BEEN FOR THE OTHER INDEPENDENTS?

(Martin Beeson) *"On the whole, sales have improved, but Capital's demise has caused problems for many of them in terms of cashflow (thereby causing delays in publication). Caliber titles have shown the biggest improvement."*

(Rick Appleby) *"There's been much interest in the likes of Stray Bullets and Strangers in Paradise, as well as the Sirius range of titles. Poison Elves is also popular. Recent enquiries for the Broadway titles is encouraging."*

(Tommy Hoodless) *"Sin City, The X-Files and Dawn always do well, Tarzan Versus Predator was a good mover. It's a shame, though, more interest isn't shown in the smaller press. With the glut of product from the bigger companies, these tend to get overlooked."*

(Steve Wren) *"Dark Horse's licensed titles continue to perform well, with Fantagraphics (Hate, Eightball) and Kitchen Sink (Crow titles, From Hell) clocking up good sales as well. Some titles (Hepcats, Strangers in Paradise) failed to live up to their hype."*

(Darryl Jones) *"Topps always impress me and this year has been no exception. Zorro sold well and Mars Attacks! looks set to do the same."*

(Kenneth Burns) *"Not too shabby by any means. Topps have had a good year with The X-Files and Tekno's Phage was a good seller for me."*

(Mark Last) *"Steady, with Caliber and Maximum Press showing a great increase in their sales."*

(Dave Hopkins) *"Dark Horse have really found their niche, and they fill it well. The so-called 'alternatives': Strangers in Paradise, Hate and Stray Bullets (among others) don't seem to be able to steadily build sales and interest."*

(Manny Amario) *"Ash, The Crow, Lady Death, Dawn, Strangers in Paradise... the list goes on. Plenty of output and some strong sellers among them. Dark Horse, with Sin City and the amazing Storyteller, continue to lead the field."*

(Chris Rice) *"While Caliber have quietly been producing a large amount of high quality material, including War of the Worlds and Jinx, things seem to have just gone quiet at Dark Horse (their only substantial hits being Sin City and Star Wars comics). Sirius are actually the most major minor company for me, with the year's real gem coming in the shape of Poison Elves."*

HOW IS THE BACK ISSUES MARKET HOLDING UP, AND WHICH TITLES, IF ANY, ARE MOST IN DEMAND?

(Kenneth Burns) *"We don't do much by way of Golden Age material, and of the Silver Age only Spider-Man titles remain a good bet. The late 80s and early 90s titles are the best sellers, with Gen 13 and Preacher the two hottest. It's really been the year of dealers throwing everything under £3 into a box marked 50p, working on the 'better than nothing' principle."*

(Mark Last) *"X-Men titles from the last few years still seem to sell well, but anything earlier than that just doesn't seem as sought after. Affordable seems to be the key word in the back issue market these days."*

(Dave Hopkins) *"The back issue market seems to be tailing off, certainly as far as we're concerned. Recent 'hot' issues tend to do well, but the trouble is they don't tend to stay 'hot' for very long."*

(Manny Amario) *"Back issue demand in general is not bad, but you just can't predict what the next customer will ask for. I've been asked for some very odd things of late, so it's as well I stock odd things. Silver Age Amazing Spider-Mans, Sergeant Fury issues (including #1), Uncanny X-Men #94 and Kirby stuff from the 70s, stuff from across the spectrum really. We sold two high grade copies of Giant Size X-Men #1 in as many weeks."*

(Martin Beeson) *"We seldom sell Golden/Silver Age titles these days, with most of our back issue business coming from the last three years. Back issue sales accounted for only about 2–3% of our business this year, as opposed to 20–25% just two years ago."*

(Alan Scott) *"We do move some Silver Age titles – Spider-Man, Uncanny X-Men, Daredevil, Showcase, Batman – but only at reduced prices. Over the year, back issue sales have inevitably suffered due to the flood of new titles."*

(Rick Appleby) *"Our most popular back issue era is the 90s!! But seriously, the (aforementioned) stock problems for retailers have had an adverse effect on back issue prices. Low orders plus high demand mean that prices jump sharply on recent 'hot' titles. Readers think dealers are profiteering from this situtaion, but that is not the case. Silver Age titles are still in demand, but customers expect high grades at mid or low grade prices. I'd be happy to oblige if I could buy the books accordingly!"*

(Tommy Hoodless) *"Interest in Silver Age back issues is slight, usually just Amazing Spider-Man, Fantastic Four, and Uncanny X-Men. Here in the North-West, there's very little demand for any title more than about five years old."*

(Steve Wren) *"Apart from some very high quality and very rare Silver and Golden Age titles, the back issue market is, quite frankly, dead. What interest there is, is restricted to recent (last two years) issues."*

(Darryl Jones) *"Trying to graph sales and trends in the back issue market is hard, but collectors do seem to be trying to buy up 70s titles before they get too expensive. Golden Age and Silver Age titles are always fairly strong, but in the last few months of 1996 things really went ballistic. We sold a vf restored copy of Detective Comics #1 and sales on big titles were generally excellent."*

WE'VE SEEN THE END OF SWAMP THING AND SANDMAN, HOW DO YOU SEE THE FUTURE FOR VERTIGO?

(Mark Last) *"Pretty much guaranteed, I'd say. With quality comics like Preacher and The Invisibles, and mini-series such as Terminal City, they have a huge following and seem to be reaching new audiences all the time."*

(Kenneth Burns) *"More titles, more adult-orientation, more blood, more Preacher equals a whole lot more sales."*

(Manny Amario) *"Even with the loss of Swampy and Sandman, Vertigo still have some of the best mature reader titles on the shelves. With the likes of Hellblazer, Books of Magic, The Dreaming and Preacher still going strong, I see the imprint being around for some time yet."*

(Martin Beeson) *"I don't think Vertigo depends on Sandman and Swamp Thing. Preacher has stepped in to fill any gap they left. This is far and away the strongest of DC's imprints."*

(Tommy Hoodless) *"With Preacher and The Dreaming filling the void left by those two titles the future looks set to remain strong."*

(Chris Rice) *"The obvious star, and worthy successor to Sandman and Swamp Thing, is, of course, Preacher. Nothing I can say that hasn't been said before. The Dreaming, after a strong start, seems to be declining a little, while House of Secrets is their best new book for a long time. Of the mini-series, Flex Mentallo was superb and Girl was good, silly, gory fun."*

(Steve Wren) *"I doubt they'll ever have a hit like Sandman again, but if the quality of titles like Preacher and The Dreaming continues we'll continue to sell a proportionately higher quantity of Vertigo titles than other FP shops. The only real danger is a 'fossilising' of creativity into a clichéd 'Vertigo style'."*

(Dave Hopkins) *"All depends how long they hang on to Garth Ennis. But seriously, the Vertigo line is now strong enough to keep going on the name alone. They do need good regular books to replace the outgoing titles, although Swamp Thing was fading anyway."*

(Rick Appleby) *"Uncertain. How much can Garth Ennis get away with?"*

(Darryl Jones) *"I think the mature reader titles will continue to do well in the near future, but interest in Preacher may reduce due to the high price of back issues."*

"SAME AS IT NEVER WAS" OR SAME AS IT EVER WAS? HOW MUCH INTEREST HAS THE RE-LAUNCH OF THE ACCLAIM SUPERHEROES GENERATED WITH YOUR CUSTOMERS?

[In this case, the question proved to be a lot longer than most of the answers we received. Here are a selection of these, which do actually speak volumes...]

(Darryl Jones) *"Acclaim, who are they?"* (Alan Scott) *"No interest – no surprise."* (Tommy Hoodless) *"Absolute Zero."* (Dave Hopkins) *"Not a lot."* (Steve Wren) *"Who, in all honesty, cares?"*

OF THE MULTI-TITLE COMPANY STORY ARCS, WHICH HAS BEEN THE BEST RECEIVED?

(Alan Scott) *"Legacy for best story, but Onslaught for sales (Marvel customers are still wary of trying DC books)."*

(Darryl Jones) *"Both the Onslaught and Legion Quest storylines were good sellers, but Contagion outsold them."*

(Steve Wren) *"Contagion boosted Bat-sales like nothing else this year, while Onslaught also did very well for the titles involved."*

(Tommy Hoodless) *"Contagion, basically because it was a great ride. Fast and furious, you couldn't wait for the next instalment. That's what comics should be all about."*

(Mark Last) *"Onslaught went beyond all expectations, especially for the non-'X' titles involved (which are otherwise severely under-ordered), whereas Contagion and Legacy seemed to annoy a lot of people with their 'too many titles' syndrome."*

(Kenneth Burns) *"All the crossovers sold well, and helped sell copies of normally hard-to-shift titles, but I didn't notice anyone exactly running into the shop to sing their praises either."*

[And votes for Onslaught from Martin Beeson, Chris Rice, Manny Amario, Rick Appleby *and* Dave Hopkins.*]*

THE GLUT OF INTER-COMPANY CROSSOVERS CONTINUES. OVERKILL, OR IS THERE A LEGITIMATE AND ENDURING DEMAND HERE?

(Tommy Hoodless) *"Overkill. The rate at which the companies are turning these out now, there's nothing to look forward to. What used to be an event, once every few years, is now a cynical marketing ploy, every few weeks."*

(Mark Last) *"There is a limit to the amount of inter-company crossovers the market will tolerate, but judging by continuing customer demand, that has not yet been reached."*

(Manny Amario) *"Too many too soon will inevitably kill the excitement. I mean, do we really need a Ghost Rider/Green Arrow X-over? Now, Wolverine/Lobo, that would be cool."*

(Martin Beeson) *"Whereas there's still a legitimate demand for DC/Marvel crossovers, sales on the Image/Marvel crossovers are stone cold. Unless there's a significant reduction in the number of crossovers, the sales value of these titles will die a death."*

(Dave Hopkins) *"You can definitely have too much of a good thing, and like most things in comics these days, there's too much of this about. The DC/Marvel crossover was nice, but the All Access series just pushed it too far."*

(Alan Scott) *"Overkill. The current glut of these titles is killing back issue sales across the board, and this is where retailers really need sales to make a living."*

(Steve Wren) *"People can spot second division bandwagon-jumping a mile off, and that's exactly what the Image/Marvel crossovers are. This sort of ploy fools no-one, as the poor sales on these titles bear out."*

(Kenneth Burns) *"As long as they sell, then they're worth doing. Personally, I think one day there will be no DC, no Marvel, and no Image, just one big company run by Warner Bros."*

Darkness #1 | DC Access #1 | Avengers (2nd) #1

(Rick Appleby) *"Definitely overkill! Crossovers used to 'longed for', nowadays nobody much cares, especially for the more absurd team-ups. Tomoe vs Witchblade? Help!"*

HAS THE MUCH LAUDED RETURN OF THE IMAGE FOUNDERS TO MARVEL HAD A POSITIVE OR NEGATIVE EFFECT ON SALES?

(Alan Scott) *"The early, all-hype, sales on Heroes Reborn titles are losing steam rapidly. A lot of customers who regularly followed the original (pre-Heroes Reborn) titles simply didn't bother with the re-vamped books."*

(Steve Wren) *"While not exactly spectacular, early sales on the Heroes Reborn titles were at least good. However, interest – especially in the Rob Liefeld books – is dropping sooner rather later."*

(Tommy Hoodless) *"On Fantastic Four and Iron Man, very positive, and I expect the interest to be maintained. However, after good initial sales on Captain America and Avengers, these are now firmly in the toilet. I suspect most copies were bought out of curiosity, and then dropped like hot bricks."*

(Rick Appleby) *"No difference to sales, an initial 'curiosity' surge but that's about it. Another case of a short term fix to a long term problem."*

(Darryl Jones) *"My initial reaction, on hearing that Marvel were handing four key titles over to Image, was utter disbelief. But having now seen Fantastic Four and Iron Man, I believe I may have been hasty in predicting their immediate demise. In fact, they're probably doing a better job than Marvel were."*

(Kenneth Burns) *"Whatever else Marvel are, they're not stupid. This whole relaunch was designed to get X-Men fans to buy the titles, and in the short term this has worked. In the case of Avengers and Captain America, however, unless the comics get better fast, it won't last."*

(Chris Rice) *"They've sold incredibly well, on a par with the X-books, and even better than expected (at least initially). Liefeld's Captain America is, well, pretty bad, and the signs are that sales are dropping off. On the flipside, Jim Lee's Fantastic Four is actually growing in sales."*

(Manny Amario) *"Sales have been strong, and I expect them to continue... up to the point the Image creators leave the titles. Still, they can always cross them over with the 'X' titles to boost sales."*

(Martin Beeson) *"Very much a short term affair, I'm afraid. But then interest in the whole Marvel line is declining, so why should these titles be any exception?"*

(Dave Hopkins) *"I don't expect the current 'highs', in sales terms, to be long lasting. Let's face it, Rob Liefeld has a knack for starting out well and fading fast, so the smart money would be on either Iron Man or Fantastic Four to have any staying power."*

(Mark Last) *"Though the 'event' produced a huge amount of interest and exceptionally high sales on early issues, the general view is that it's a novelty, and I'm highly sceptical about the long term."*

ARE TRADING CARDS STILL A FORCE TO BE RECKONED WITH, OR IS INTEREST WANING?

(Steve Wren) *"It depends on the type of card. Sales on cards based on media licences are still huge, but other cards (fantasy art, sports, etc) are dead. Sales on comic-based cards vary in relation to the performance of the source titles."*

(Manny Amario) *"Trading Cards still have a place in the market, though some, like The X-Files cards, are stronger sellers than others. Collectable Gaming cards, like the Magic series, also still do very well."*

(Darryl Jones) *"We only started dealing extensively in Trading Cards this year, but the response from our customers has been good. That said, the sales were mainly confined to Star Trek, Babylon 5, Star Wars and The X-Files."*

(Tommy Hoodless) *"As far as this region goes, Trading Cards have never really been a force to be reckoned with. If only more companies would take a leaf out of Comic Images' book and keep the price down. Topps' recent ID4 cards were priced competitively, and – surprise, surprise – they sold very well."*

[Opinion among the other Market Reporters was pretty much divided down the middle, with Mark Last and Alan Scott leaning towards the 'interest waning' side of things, and Dave Hopkins and Kenneth Burns still dealing with 'a force to be reckoned with'. Martin Beeson reported good sales of Gaming cards, but little else.]

WHAT'S HOT AND WHAT'S NOT IN RELATED MERCHANDISE?

(Martin Beeson) *"Horrible word, 'hot'. I've always felt it's been used to exploit people's greed and need to keep up with current trends. However, The X-Files, Star Trek and Star Wars merchandise does sell well. Friends is top of our list, though."*

(Kenneth Burns) *"More cheap or mid-priced superhero action figures are needed, as these always sell well. I'd like to see a Captain America figure and a set of Gen 13 team-members."*

(Mark Last) *"Action figures are the hottest comics-related, merchandise at the moment, due to the generally very high standard of detail and quality."*

(Darryl Jones) *"Again, this is a market I've tended not to have much to do with the past, but this year I was pleasantly surprised with the response to a new stock of Batman and Star Wars figures."*

(Steve Wren) *"I could sell a cheese sandwich if it had an 'X' on it. Licensed material is still a big seller, though comic-related T-shirts, posters and the like are just not moving. Strangely, while it's no longer considered 'cool' to be seen wearing a Sandman T-shirt, cheesy 70s Marvel T-shirts are in. Kids today, eh?"*

(Tommy Hoodless) *"Though T-shirts, mugs and calendars (on subjects like Babylon 5, The X-Files, and Star Trek) are hot, audio tapes, caps and CDs (on similar subjects) are not."*

WHAT TRENDS FROM THE PAST YEAR DO YOU SEE DEVELOPING OR FADING, AND WHAT ARE YOUR TIPS AND FORECASTS FOR 1997?

(Dave Hopkins at Nostalgia & Comics, Birmingham) *"The X-Files is tailing off, as is the whole 'women with big breasts carrying big guns' thing (thankfully). As for '97, I'd like to see (though whether we will or not is uncertain) a wider variety of comics and more emphasis on the writing. Also, Trading Cards that look good, and are worth buying on that strength alone (rather than being another set of The X-Files or X-Men)."*

(Rick Appleby at Dream Comics, New Barnet) *"Publishers need to be more open about the use of variant covers to boost sales, so fans and dealers can order accordingly. My advice for readers – take out a standing order for your books, make certain you get them. Hunt out the bargain boxes, there's plenty of good stuff around (why pay £10 for a 'limited, exclusive, variant, foil edition cover' when you can have ten other comics?). Let's get back to collecting for reading's sake rather than perceived 'worth'. Finally, a big thank you to all our customers for their continued support."*

(Chris Rice at Forbidden Planet, Head Office) *"The real downside of the year has been that, for perhaps the first time, the business and politics sides of the comics industry have been obvious even to the casual reader. With things such as Rob Liefeld's heavily publicised split from Image and Marvel's current money troubles, the actual comics and stories are becoming just another business asset, even to a hardened fanboy like myself. Either it's getting harder to appreciate a comic on its own merits or I am taking things waaay too seriously."*

(Darryl Jones at Silver Acre Comics, Chester) *"On the way out, I'd have to say The X-Files, while up and coming are definitely Mars Attacks!, Babylon 5 and 1960s and 1970s Trading Cards. I expect the back-issue market to grow steadily in 1997, and (boring-but-true) the hottest comic of the year will be the one you enjoyed reading most. Have a great year!"*

(Alan Scott at Adventure Into Comics, London) *"Judging from the way this year's gone, and the number of retail outlets that have closed their doors, the outlook for 1997 looks decidedly shaky. I just hope things improve. My hot tips for 1997 are The Darkness, Witchblade, and JLA."*

(Tommy Hoodless at Imagination Station, Carlisle) *"The X-Files bubble has got to burst soon, mainly due to the level of market saturation at present. It's a sad fact, but that's the way many of my customers feel. The titles I've a good feeling for in '97 are The Darkness, Kurt Busiek's Astro City, Batman: The Long Halloween, Supergirl, Elektra, Storyteller and Leave It To Chance. The cynical part of me sees a whole lot more inter-company crossovers. I hope to be proved wrong."*

(Martin Beeson at Ace Comics, Colchester) *"Gathering pace is the growth of the 'short term interest' reader, more prone to impulse buying than following any one comic for any length of time. For 1997, I see a need for shops to diversify their range of comics, which in turn means a growth in sales of Independents. If all else fails, there will always be TV spin-offs to bolster sales, if you look for them."*

(Manny Amario at Whatever Comics, Maidstone) *"Customers are simply not prepared to pay the very high cover prices any more. Thankfully, many publishers seem to be aware of this trend and have lowered prices on some titles. A return to comics being fun, without costing you an arm and a leg, would be good. The Darkness, The X-Files and possibly Shadowman are ones to watch in 1997."*

(Steve Wren at Forbidden Planet, Newcastle) *"While I see the comics themselves static in terms of sales, toys, models and merchandise will continue to become a larger part of the product mix for those who can afford them. 1997 is the 20th Anniversary of Star Wars, and we should be riding that renewed wave of interest all year. Marvel will continue their modest expansion, DC will expand too quickly, and, if there's any justice, Jim Shooter will be elected US President!"*

(Kenneth Burns at A-1 books & comics, Glasgow) *"A good year ahead for DC, Topps and Homage, I think, both in comic and profit terms. Likewise for Marvel and Chaos. As far as the market goes, I think this year is a pretty good indicator of the year to come, with a lot of people just carefully treading water."*

(Mark Last at Forbidden Planet, Coventry) *"Nostalgia for '70s comics is on the up, and I see a lot of characters being reintroduced by both DC and Marvel. Mini-series, as opposed to ongoing series, seem to be the way forward. Increasingly, I think, Marvel will go to outside studios (such as Top Cow) for their artwork needs and Rob Liefeld will disappear from the industry altogether as a major player."*

The following market report which was too late to be included in the Q&A format is from Dave and Sue Finn of Incognito Comics, Kent

Is it really time for another market report for the UK Guide? I suppose it is. As usual my thanks go to Duncan for allowing us to give one and all a little insight into how this wonderful industry of ours affects us down in Kent in Incognito. Once more, it's been a very volatile year, and as we write this, we've just been advised that Marvel has filed for bankruptcy in the US. Food for thought eh? They'll survive, but will the industry? Here's what we know.

THE PLATINUM OR PRE-GOLDEN AGE [1933-1938]

Never really had to mention this time period before, but in the last year we've finally been able to obtain and sell a quantity of these pre-hero comics.. Before Superman arrived in 1938, most comic books in America consisted largely of crime and mystery stories, mixed in with a selection of funny strips. Many of the super-hero creators cut their artistic teeth in these comics. For instance, before Superman, Siegel and Shuster created the strip Federal Men, which ran in various comic books. The prices of most Platinum Age books is remarkably cheap, compared to the later super-hero comics.

Sales from this period include: Detective Comics #1, Fine, Restored, £15000.00; Detective Comics #2, Fine, Restored, £4500.00; Detective Comics #6, Good, £500.00 (a steal!); Detective Comics #19 and #26, both in Fine/Fine+, Restored, at £1800.00 the pair; And New Adventure Comics #19. VG-, £400.00. New Adventure Comics is one of those confusing titles that was called New Comics from issues #1 to #11, then New Adventure Comics from #12 to #31 and then Adventure Comics from issue #32 onwards. Phew! Purchases in this period also included early More Fun issues including #8, #13, #29 and #30, and New Comics #3.

THE GOLDEN AGE [1938-1945]

As each year passes more and more collectors seem to buy Golden Age books from us. Most books from this early age are very nostalgic, especially as World War II was raging across the world. Comic books were extensively used to boost morale, encourage the purchase of War Bonds to buy weapons. Paper drives to recycle for victory led to a great many comics from this period being destroyed, increasing scarcity. Some comics even carried adverts encouraging children to destroy their comics for the war effort. Some of the best covers ever seen were war covers. Check out Batman #17 and Superman#14 as two classic examples. 1996 was definitely our best year yet for Golden Age sales. Some of note were: Captain America Comic #8, VF- restored, £800.00; Marvel Mystery Comics #11, Good, £275.00; All Star Comics #15, VG+, £400.00; Batman #40, Fine, £300.00; Batman #73, VF-, £300.00.

THE SILVER AGE [1956-1969]

Once again, the Silver Age market is a strong, steady one with only a gradual market increase and certainly none of the hysterics of a few years ago. This market has settles. Sales are steady except for those elusive VF+ or better cents copies. When these surface, there's always a bit of feeding frenzy. There are still a great may collectors of these comics. As always, Amazing Spider-Man, Avengers and X-Men lead the way for Marvel, while at DC its Batman, Detective and The Brave and The Bold. Some of our best sellers were still very low grade key issues, especially with the Marvels. In the last year we have sold copies of Daredevil #1, Avengers #1, Fantastic Four #1, Justice league of America #1, Atom #1, X-Men #1 and many other keys, in Fair to Good condition, or at below Guide prices. Notable Silver Age sales include: Fantastic Four #1, VG, £1495.00; Avengers #1, VG-, £250.00; Silver Surfer #1, NM, £300.00; Fantastic Four #48, VF+, £350.00; Amazing Spider-man 1, VG-, £995.00; Amazing Fantasy #15, VG-, £1100.00.

THE BRONZE AGE [1970-1975]

1996 was quite a strong year for Bronze Age books. Most main run titles Marvels sell consistently, especially the ND issues. Marvel and Dc horror titles from this period have also seen an increase in popularity, along with the Marvel anthology titles, such as Marvel Premiere and Marvel Spotlight. Incredible Hulk #181, X-Men #94 and Giant Size X-Men #1 can be contained no more. For so long the prices of these three books have been dropping behind the American Guide prices. No more. In the last year we have been asking, and receiving, prices for these books that are finally on par with the American market. Copies of these three books in NM have fetched £325.00, £325.00 and £350.00 respectively. American prices for these three are now touching $500.00. One peculiar glitch. Late last year we sold three copies of Amazing Spider-man #129 in grades from VF to NM in two weeks to three different customers. Sales of Punisher appearances had all but stopped up to that time. Is he going to be hot again?... Nah! The Defenders are still gradually improving in popularity, with #1 and #10 the most sought after. Neal Adams, Barry Smith, Jim Steranko and Jack Kirby books from this period are still high in demand.

INDEPENDENTS

Every issue of Spawn continues to sell well. Image back-issues in general are steady sellers. Older Indies still have their fans though. Cerebus just keeps on selling. We probably obtain about 2 copies of Cerebus #1 per year (which isn't bad considering the print run was only 2000). The first UK Guide listed this book at £250.00. With the exception of the second Guide, where there was a slight increase in value to £275.00, the price of Cerebus #1 has halved over the seven guides published before this one. Guide Seven lists it at £120.00. Does this mean that Cerebus #1 is half as desirable as it was? Or is it twice as easy to obtain? No. Cerebus #1 is one of the most requested Indie comics we have ever known, and certainly one of the hardest to find. We have sold two Cerebus Number Ones at £395.00 in the last year. That's over tripe Guide! The last book was in stock about a fortnight, and now has a happy home in Norway, of all places, with a delighted new owner. I wonder what it's Guide price is this year

Even in an uncertain world, there still seems to be just as many new publishers trying to push their titles. 1996 has seen a few good Indie titles emerge from the pack, such as Witchblade, especially the Medieval Spawn/Witchblade mini-series. Darkness, the Witchblade spin-off also shows promise. Marvel's Heroes Reborn quartet are selling merrily, though whoever thought that taking Mark Waid off Captain America was a good idea, really needs his bumps felt. Have you noticed that the variant cover has become the gimmick of the year, reaching as far afield as the Uncanny X-Men. Whatever next; foil, holographic, wrap-around, die-cut card stock covers? Again?... All our customers want to pay for what is a good read, not a cover that you can see your face in for double the usual price of the regular comic! When will publishers ever learn. People have a finite amount to spend on comics, and generally they prefer as much story for their cash as they can get. Preacher continues to push itself to extremes. The Invisible have made a return. DC still rules the roost with Vertigo titles. DC's Helix on the other hand is dead in the water. The core DC hero titles are still on an upswing, especially The Flash and Supergirl. Supergirl #1 still sells strongly at about £5.00. The new Grant Morrison JLA is also proving a hit, even among the die-hard JLA fans. If the writers make a comic work and sell on the "adult" Vertigo titles, stick them on the super-hero comics. Makes sense... I think.

The Bad Girls are beginning to wane, except for the previously mentioned Witchblade and Joe Linsner's Dawn. A number of fake Cry For Dawn Number Ones are know to be circulating in the States and some will no doubt end up over here. Beware!

Well that's it for now. It's still an uncertain world out there. To make this industry work, customers, retailers, distributors and publishers need to pull together. As Bill and Ted once said... Be excellent to each other... and party on!

[FINALLY, A BIG THANK YOU TO ALL OUR MARKET REPORTERS. IT'S NICE TO SEE THAT WHILE 1996 WAS EVIDENTLY A TOUGH YEAR, THERE'S STILL ENOUGH OPTIMISM OUT THERE TO INSPIRE CONFIDENCE IN THE FUTURE.]

Spawn #1 | Witchblade #11 | JLA #1

"SUCCEEDING IN BUSINESS"

SURESH TOLAH

Casson Beckman (Chartered Accountants & Business Advisers)

One of the successes of recent years has been the comic industry which has continued to grow with many new businesses starting up. However, in many cases, it is the enthusiastic collector who has started up by using his own collection as his initial stock without proper planning. Not surprisingly these businesses fail so I set out below the main points that should be considered before taking the step of setting up your own business:—

1. Consider whether to start in business full time or initially trade on a part time basis with a view to eventually trading full time. It is essential to ensure that you have sufficient time to devote to your business.
2. Prepare a business plan which should cover the following:-
   - a Target market
   - b Site of business/Mail Order
   - c Cash flow forecasts
   - d Sources of capital
   - e Division of profits (if applicable)
   - f Promotion methods/advertising.
3. Consider whether to be self-employed (or in a partnership) or whether to set up a Limited Company. Self employment has its advantages with regard to expenses but a Limited Company gives more protection. If a partnership is set up, there should be a formal partnership agreement which sets out the specific duties of each partner and their profit shares.
4. Ensure that you have a good knowledge of the current state of the market and that you read all the relevant trade magazines. In addition, establish good contacts amongst other dealers who have been trading for some time as they can often give practical advice.
5. Ensure that proper bookkeeping records are kept so that accounts can easily be prepared. With the advent of Self Assessment, it is essential that all documentation to back up income and expenses are kept. Sight of these can be requested by the Inland Revenue.
6. Ensure that you have proper professional advice at the outset from your bank manager/ accountant/ solicitor rather than when problems are encountered.

Once you have decided to commence in business, the following should be informed as soon as possible:—

1 THE INLAND REVENUE

They must be advised of your change of status and you should write to your own tax district advising them of this. If you have no tax district at present, then you should write to your local tax district who will then send you the appropriate forms for completion to enable them to set up the appropriate records. The time limit for notification is six months from the end of the tax year e.g. for the year 1996/97 notification must take place by 5 October 1997. The penalty for non-notification is a tax geared one but this can be eliminated if all the tax for the year 1996/97 is paid by 31 January 1998.

In addition, if you have not done so before, you will have to submit a tax return detailing your income and claim for allowances to your Inspector of Taxes on an annual basis. The appropriate tax return form, together with the relevant supporting schedules that may be required, will be forwarded to you once you have notified the Revenue of your change in status.

2 THE DEPARTMENT OF SOCIAL SECURITY

This Government Office is responsible for dealing with National Insurance Contributions. You are required to notify them when you start a business to enable them to calculate the contributions that should be paid. If you are self employed, you will normally have to pay the flat rate Class 2 National Insurance Contributions. In addition, Class 4 National Insurance Contributions have to be paid on your profits between certain pre-defined limits.

3 THE CUSTOMS AND EXCISE

Normally you only have to register for VAT once your turnover reaches a certain level (at present £48,000). However, as comics are zero rated for Value Added Tax purposes, it is advantageous to register voluntarily as this means that VAT on most expenses incurred can be reclaimed from the Customs and Excise. This then assists with cashflow as, once satisfied, the Customs and Excise will make repayments on a monthly basis.

SELF ASSESSMENT

Self Assessment is the new way of working out and paying tax. It applies to people who receive tax returns and also to those who are liable to pay tax but have not been issued with a tax return. The Revenue have carried out a massive advertising campaign to ensure that the public are aware of this new regime. However, this new regime is much more stringent than before and I would draw your attention to the following:—

a The new tax return in itself is much larger than before. Whilst the basic return comprises of eight foolscap pages, it may be necessary for a number of additional schedules to be completed.

b Action will be required promptly as, if you require the Revenue to calculate your tax liability, your tax return must be submitted by 30 September 1997. However, if you wish to do the calculation yourself (using the Revenue's own form) the deadline is 31 January 1998.

c If a Tax Return is not submitted by 31 January 1998, there is now an automatic penalty of £100. If the Return is still outstanding six months later, there is a further penalty of £100 and, in addition, the Inspector may seek a penalty of up to £60 per day.

d At present, if tax is paid late, interest will be charged. However, in future, the Collector of Taxes will be entitled to make surcharges on the following basis:—

- **i** 5% on any tax for the previous tax year which is unpaid by 28 February.
- **ii** A further 5% surcharge on any amounts still unpaid by 31 July.
- **iii** If the Tax Return is not submitted and the tax is not paid by 31 January, the Inspector will merely estimate the amount of tax and surcharge which he believes to be due and collect this along with the fixed penalty.

e Under Self Assessment, it is now absolutely essential for taxpayers to retain records to back up their tax return for at least five years after it has been filed. There is a penalty for failing to keep proper records of up to £3,000 (which would be charged if there was a history of serious failure or deliberate destruction of records).

f The Inland Revenue have now indicated that they are allocating more resources to tax investigations and, without doubt, cash businesses will become targets. Under Self Assessment, the Inspector of Taxes no longer has to have reasonable grounds for opening an investigation into an individual's affairs and may now challenge tax returns entirely at random. This is why it is so essential for proper business records to be kept.

g Employers now face an extra burden as there are specific dates by which they must provide their employees with certain information about their pay, benefits and tax liability.

Obviously, the above is by no means an exhaustive list of points as each individual's circumstances should be considered on its own merits. Should you have any further queries relating to Self Assessment, please do not hesitate to write to me or alternatively send me a fax (details below). Whilst you will appreciate that it is impossible for me to give responses to queries on an individual basis, I propose to deal with any queries that may be of general interest in the Comic Book Price Guide magazine.

CASSON BECKMAN is a medium sized firm of Chartered Accountants and Business Advisers who have a specialist department dealing with the entertainment industry.

SURESH TOLAT qualified as a Chartered Accountant in 1982. He is an Assistant Manager in our Tax Division and, being a keen comic collector, has a specialist knowledge of this industry.

Casson Beckman, Hobson House, 155 Gower Street, London WC1E 6BJ Tel. 0171 387 2888 Fax. 0171 388 0600

REPRINT INDEX

compiled by the author while sifting through his collection one day

Below is a list-in-progress of key issues that can be found reprinted elsewhere and usually at much less cost to the collector. This index is designed with budgeting in mind, as very often collectors may wish to own an original first issue or appearance but it proves financially impossible. Many of the classic stories have been reprinted at some time or another and for the novice it is a valuable way of learning about the great heroes and villains and their backgrounds. Happy reading!

ACTION #1
(origin Superman only) .... Secret Origins (1st) 1

ACTION #242
(Brainiac origin) .... Superman Annual 2

ACTION #252
(Supergirl origin) .... Superman Annual 1
.... Action Comics 334
.... Secret Origins (1st) 2
(Metallo origin) .... Superman Annual 2

ACTION #267
(3rd Legion) .... Action Comics 334

ADVENTURE #40
(1st GA Sandman) .... Justice League of America 94

ADVENTURE #48
(1st Hourman) .... Justice League of America 96

ADVENTURE #61
(1st GA Starman) .... Justice League of America 94

ADVENTURE #210
(1st Krypto) .... Superboy 165

ADVENTURE #247
(1st Legion) .... Superman Annual 6
.... Secret Origins (1st) 6
.... Adventure 491

ADVENTURE #260
(Aquaman origin) .... Eighty Page Giant 8

ADVENTURE #267
(2nd Legion) .... Adventure 491

ADVENTURE #271
(Luthor origin) .... Eighty Page Giant 10

ADVENTURE #290
.... Superboy 147

ALL STAR COMICS #8
(GA Wonder Woman origin) .... Wonder Woman 196

AMAZING FANTASY #15
(origin/1st Spiderman) .... Marvel Tales Annual 1
.... Marvel Tales 137
.... Amazing Fantasy 15 Reprint

AMAZING SPIDERMAN #1
(cover story) .... Spiderman Annual 1
.... Spiderman Annual 6
(lead story) .... Spiderman Annual 2
.... Marvel Tales 138

AMAZING SPIDERMAN #2
.... Marvel Tales 139

AMAZING SPIDERMAN #3
.... Marvel Collectors Item Classics 1
.... Marvel Tales 140

AMAZING SPIDERMAN #4
.... Marvel Collectors Item Classics 2
.... Marvel Tales 141

AMAZING SPIDERMAN #5
.... Marvel Tales 142

AMAZING SPIDERMAN #6
.... Marvel Tales 3
.... Marvel Tales 143

AMAZING SPIDERMAN #14
.... Marvel Tales 9
.... Marvel Tales 151

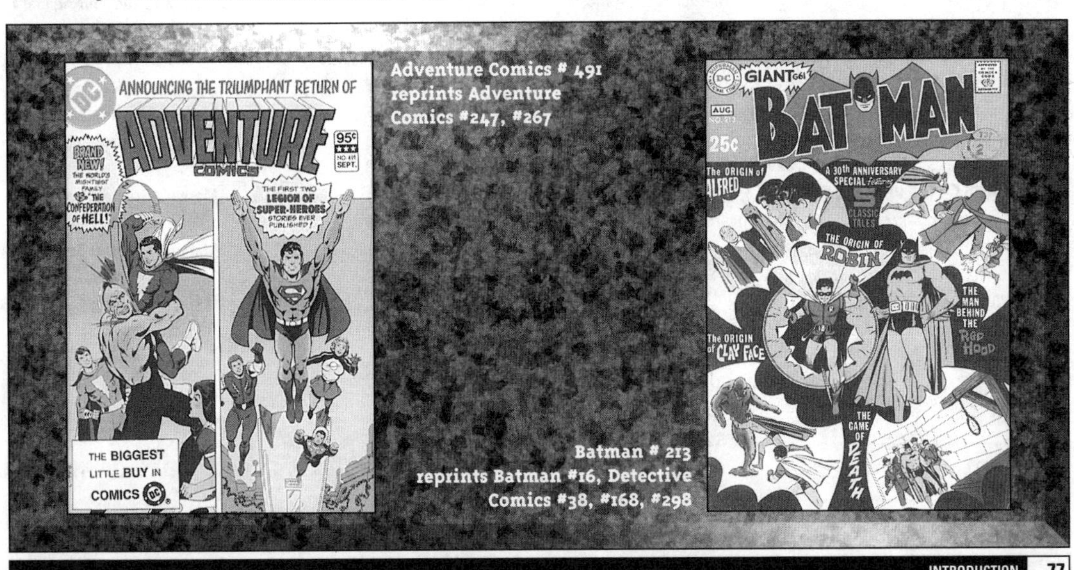

Adventure Comics # 491 reprints Adventure Comics #247, #267

Batman # 213 reprints Batman #16, Detective Comics #38, #168, #298

AMAZING SPIDERMAN #50
..........Marvel Tales 36
AMAZING SPIDERMAN #100
..........Marvel Tales 251
AMAZING SPIDERMAN #129
(1st Punisher)..........Marvel Tales 106
..........Marvel Tales 209
AMAZING SPIDERMAN ANNUAL #1
..........Spiderman Annual 6
AVENGERS #1
..........Marvel Tales Annual 2
AVENGERS #2
..........Marvel Super-Heroes (1st) 1
AVENGERS #3
..........Marvel Super-Heroes (1st) 21
AVENGERS #4
..........Avengers Annual 3
..........Captain America 400
AVENGERS #57
..........Marvel Super-Action 18
AVENGERS #58
..........Marvel Super-Action 19
BATMAN #16
(1st Alfred)..........Batman 213
BATMAN #47
(origin)..........Batman 198
..........Batman and Other DC Classics 1
BRAVE AND THE BOLD #28
..........Justice League of America 39
BRAVE AND THE BOLD #29
..........Justice League of America 48
BRAVE AND THE BOLD #30
..........Justice League of America 39
BRAVE AND THE BOLD #34
(1st SA Hawkman)..........Brave and the Bold 113
BRAVE AND THE BOLD #54
..........DC 100 Page Super Spectacular 21
BRAVE AND THE BOLD #60
..........Superboy 185
CAPTAIN AMERICA #100
..........Marvel Super Action 1
CAPTAIN AMERICA #110
..........Marvel Super Action (2nd) 12
CAPTAIN AMERICA #111
..........Marvel Super Action (2nd) 13
CHALLENGERS OF THE UNKNOWN #1
..........Challengers of the Unknown 64,65
CHALLENGERS OF THE UNKNOWN #2
..........Challengers of the Unknown 76
DAREDEVIL #1
..........Marvel Super-Heroes (1st) 1
DAREDEVIL #2
..........Marvel Super-Heroes (1st) 22
DAREDEVIL #3
..........Marvel Super-Heroes (1st) 23
DAREDEVIL #4
..........Marvel Super-Heroes (1st) 24
DETECTIVE #27
(1st Batman)..........Detective 387
..........Detective 627
DETECTIVE #31
(1st Batarang)..........DC 100 Page Spectacular 14
DETECTIVE #32
..........DC 100 page Spectacular 14
DETECTIVE #33
(origin Batman)..........Secret Origins (1st) 1
DETECTIVE #37
..........Batman 237
DETECTIVE #38
(origin Robin)..........Secret Origins (1st) 7
..........Batman 213
DETECTIVE #66
(1st Two Face)..........DC 100 Page Spectacular 20
DETECTIVE #68
(2nd part Two Face)..........DC 100 Page Spectacular 20
DETECTIVE #168
(1st Joker origin)..........Batman 213
DETECTIVE #225
..........Secret Origins Annual 1
..........World's Finest 175
DETECTIVE #233
..........Batman Annual 4
DETECTIVE #298
(Clayface II)..........Batman 213
DOCTOR STRANGE #169
(origin retold)..........Doctor Strange (2nd Series) 21
FANTASTIC FOUR #1
..........Fantastic Four Annual 1
..........Fantastic Four 1 Reprint
FANTASTIC FOUR #2
..........Marvel Collectors Item Classics 1
FANTASTIC FOUR #3
..........Marvel Collectors Item Classics 2
FANTASTIC FOUR #4
..........Marvel Collectors Item Classics 3
FANTASTIC FOUR #5
..........Fantastic Four Annual 2
FANTASTIC FOUR #6
..........Fantastic Four Annual 3
FANTASTIC FOUR #25
..........Fantastic Four Annual 4
FANTASTIC FOUR #26
..........Fantastic Four Annual 4
FANTASTIC FOUR #48
..........Marvel's Greatest Comics 35
..........Marvel Treasury Edition 2
FANTASTIC FOUR #49
..........Marvel's Greatest Comics 36
FANTASTIC FOUR #50
..........Marvel's Greatest Comics 37
FANTASTIC FOUR #66
..........Marvel's Greatest Comics 49
FANTASTIC FOUR #67
..........Marvel's Greatest Comics 50
FLASH #105
..........Eighty Page Giant 4
FLASH #106
..........Flash Annual 1
FLASH #107
..........Flash 160

FLASH #108

....Flash 196

FLASH #110

(cover story)..Eighty Page Giant 4

(Kid Flash)..Flash Annual 1

FLASH #112

....Flash Annual 1

FLASH #123

....Eighty Page Giant 9

FLASH #129

....Flash 169

FLASH #137

....Flash 213

GHOST RIDER #1

....Original Ghost Rider (2nd Series) 8

GREEN LANTERN #1

....Wanted 1

....Secret Origins Annual 1

HOUSE OF SECRETS #61

....Action Comics #411

HOUSE OF SECRETS #92

....Swamp Thing 33

HULK #1

....Marvel Tales Annual 1

HULK #102

....Marvel Super-Heroes (1st) 56

HULK #180

....Incredible Hulk and Wolverine 1

HULK #181

....Incredible Hulk and Wolverine 1

IRON MAN AND SUB-MARINER #1

....Marvel Double Feature 17

JOURNEY INTO MYSTERY #83

....Marvel Tales Annual 1

....Thor 432

JOURNEY INTO MYSTERY #84

....Marvel Tales 3

JOURNEY INTO MYSTERY #85

....Journey into Mystery Annual 1

JUSTICE LEAGUE OF AMERICA #1

....Justice League of America 58

JUSTICE LEAGUE OF AMERICA #2

....Justice League of America 48

JUSTICE LEAGUE OF AMERICA #3

....Justice League of America 48

JUSTICE LEAGUE OF AMERICA #4

....Justice League of America 67

JUSTICE LEAGUE OF AMERICA #9

....Eighty Page Giant 8

....Justice League of America 97

JUSTICE LEAGUE OF AMERICA #21

....DC 100 Page Spectacular 6

LOIS LANE #1

....Superman Annual 1

....Lois Lane 77

MARVEL COMICS #1

....Fantasy Masterpieces 9

MARVEL SPOTLIGHT #5

....Original Ghost Rider (2nd Series) 1

MARVEL SPOTLIGHT #12

....Original Ghost Rider (2nd Series) 10

MILITARY COMICS #1

(1st Blackhawk)..Secret Origins (1st) 6

MORE FUN #52

(origin Spectre)..Secret Origins (1st) 5

MORE FUN #53

(origin Spectre)..Secret Origins (1st) 5

MORE FUN #73

(origin Aquaman)..Secret Origins (1st) 7

MY GREATEST ADVENTURE #80

(1st Doom Patrol)..Batman 238

MYSTERY IN SPACE #75

(Early JLA X-over)..Strange Adventures 235

OUR ARMY AT WAR #81

(1st Sgt. Rock)..Our Army At War 280

POLICE COMICS #1

....DC Special #15

SENSATION COMICS #1

(Wildcat story)..Secret Origins (1st) #3

SGT. FURY #1

....Marvel Tales Annual 1

....Sgt. Fury 167

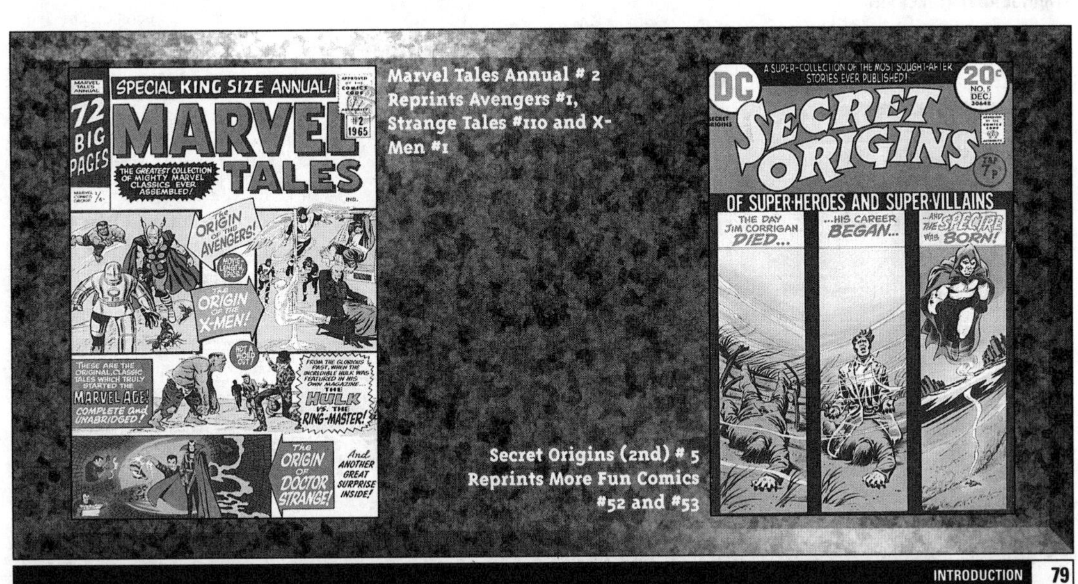

Marvel Tales Annual # 2 Reprints Avengers #1, Strange Tales #110 and X-Men #1

Secret Origins (2nd) # 5 Reprints More Fun Comics #52 and #53

SGT FURY #13
............Special Marvel Edition 11
SHOWCASE #4
............Secret Origins Annual 1
............Secret Origins (1st) 1
............Flash 215
SHOWCASE #6
(part only)............Secret Origins Annual 1
SHOWCASE #7
............Challengers of the Unknown 75
SHOWCASE #11
............Challengers of the Unknown 80
SHOWCASE #12
............Challengers of the Unknown 77
SHOWCASE #13
(cover story)............Eighty Page Giant 4
SHOWCASE #13
(Mr. Element)............Flash Annual 1
SHOWCASE #14
(cover story)............Eighty Page Giant 4
SHOWCASE #15
(1st Space Ranger)............DC Superstars 8
SHOWCASE #17
............Secret Origins Annual 1
SHOWCASE #22
............Secret Origins (1st) 2
SHOWCASE #23
............Green Lantern 88
SHOWCASE #34
(1st Atom)............Eighty Page Giant 8
............Secret Origins (1st) 2
SHOWCASE #37
............Flash 214
SILVER SURFER #1
............Fantasy Masterpieces (2nd) 1
SILVER SURFER #4
............Fantasy Masterpieces (2nd) 4
STRANGE ADVENTURES #180
............Adventure Comics 412
STRANGE ADVENTURES #184
............Adventure Comics 414
STRANGE ADVENTURES #190
............Adventure Comics 415
STRANGE ADVENTURES #195
............Adventure Comics 420
STRANGE ADVENTURES #201
............Adventure Comics 421
STRANGE TALES #89
............Fantasy Masterpieces 2
STRANGE TALES #101
............Marvel Tales 3
............Human Torch 1
STRANGE TALES #110
............Marvel Tales 2
............Marvel Collector's Item Classics 3
............Marvel Tales 137
STRANGE TALES #115
(origin Dr. Strange)............Marvel Tales Annual 2
SUB-MARINER #1
............Tales to Astonish (2nd) 1
SUPERBOY #68
(Bizarro origin)............Superman Annual 2
SUPERBOY #86
............Eighty Page Giant 11
SUPERBOY #89
............Superboy 129
SUPERMAN #30
(1st GA Mr. Mxyztplk)............Superman 183
............Lois Lane 123
SUPERMAN #76
............World's Finest 179
SUPERMAN #123
............Superman Annual 6
............Superman 217
SUPERMAN #127
(Titano)............Superman Annual 2
(Titano)............Superman 239
(Lori Lemaris)............Eighty Page Giant 14
(Lori Lemaris)............Superman 217
SUPERMAN #141
............Superman 232
SUPERMAN #146
(life story)............Eighty Page Giant 8
SUPERMAN #147
............Superboy 147
SUPERMAN #149
............Superman 193
TALES OF SUSPENSE #39
............Marvel Tales Annual 1
TALES OF SUSPENSE #49
............Giant Size Iron Man 1
TALES TO ASTONISH #35
............Marvel Tales Annual 1
TALES TO ASTONISH #44
(origin/1st Wasp)............Marvel Feature 8
TALES TO ASTONISH #93
............Marvel Super-Heroes (1st) 48
THOR #126
............Marvel Spectacular 1
WONDER WOMAN #1
............Secret Origins (1st) 3
WONDER WOMAN #105
............Secret Origins Annual 1
WORLD'S FINEST #94
............Secret Origins Annual 1
............World's Finest 179
X-MEN #1
............Marvel Tales Annual 2
............X-Men 1 Reprint
............Amazing Adventures (3rd Series) 1,2
X-MEN #2
............Marvel Super-Heroes (1st) 21
............Amazing Adventures (3rd Series) 3,4
X-MEN #3
............Marvel Super-Heroes (1st) 22
............Amazing Adventures (3rd Series) 5,6
X-MEN #4
............Marvel Super-Heroes (1st) 23
............Amazing Adventures (3rd Series) 7,8

Signed & Numbered Limited Editions

GRANT RYMER

and again with a grateful assist from GEOFF WEST of Conquistador.

Welcome again to the most unique section of the U.K. Price Guide and especially to all the new American readers.

The editions listed here are not of the kind currently being produced by certain American companies which are ordinary copies of the comics except for the signature and a Certificate of Authenticity. Rather, the editions listed here are those which have been specifically printed in order to be signed. There is a strictly limited print run, most commonly between one and two thousand copies. Many have new covers, a new art plate for the signature and new editorials.

The books in the Signed and Numbered Limited Edition Hardbacks section are also different from their respective trade paperback or previous hardback editions. Almost all have a new plate set in the frontispiece and in some cases a slipcase, expanded stories, sketch pages and text pages by the artist and author respectively. The plate is usually a unique piece of art with spaces specifically for signatures, the number of the copy and the total number of copies printed.

Currently, the two main publishers of Signed and Limited Editions are Graphitti Designs and Dark Horse Publishing. Dark Horse only publish editions from work already previously published by themselves, either in comic or trade paperback format. Graphitti on the other hand publish a wide variety of material from companies ranging from DC to Epic, Pacific Comics to First Publishing. Graphitti publish no comics in their own right.

In the past a significant number of editions were also published by Eclipse and Kitchen Sink.

The Signed and Numbered Limited Edition Hardback represents the very pinnacle of production in the comics industry. They are produced very much for the connoisseur and in general feature the finest material the comics medium has to offer.

As investments they are not for the recent breed of "comics speculator". They tend to hold their value well but owing to the high initial cost and with few exceptions they tend to appreciate slowly. That said, once sold out from the publisher, prices can vary greatly owing to what some fans will pay for an edition they particularly want.

Also included in this section are Signed and Numbered Limited Edition trading cards, portfolios, trade paperbacks and prints. Both the prints and portfolios sections should be regarded as only a small sample of what is a vast body of work.

MARKET OVERVIEW

Well it's been another big year for the comics' industry. Marvel filing for Chapter 11 bankruptcy, Rob Liefeld being kicked out of Image and a general downward spiral in the circulation of many titles. There have been some high points. The excellent **Kingdom Come** which is sure to end up as a Signed and Numbered Limited Edition before long and continued great runs on **Starman, Preacher** and **Hitman** which probably won't.

However, with the market being as it is at the moment, there have been very few high priced editions this year. In fact there were only 6 new signed and numbered limited editions produced. Two of them were by Frank Miller and three were Star Wars related.

Best of the bunch was **Batman: The Dark Knight Returns** 10th Anniversary Edition. Produced by DC Comics, their first without Graphitti, this superb volume is slip-cased and not only contains the four part story but also a sketch book, the original script and a book of press cuttings so you can read about what was the Dark Knight phenomenon at the time. Although limited to 10,000 copies (!) it quickly sold out and is proving hard to re-order. It just goes to show the influence that this ground-breaking series has even now.

Also released was the third Sin City volume **Sin City: The Big Fat Kill**. Again a slipcase edition, this volume, although perhaps artistically inferior to the first two books, boasts another fine story about "the town without pity".

With Star Wars on everybody's lips, Dark Horse Comics released **Star Wars: Dark Empire II** by the same creative team as the first volume and also **Star Wars: Droids** featuring C-3PO and R2-D2. **Star Wars: The Art of Dave Dorman** is a book of his paintings and painted comics' covers and was released by Friedlander.

Lastly, there is **Queen of Hearts** by Jim Silke featuring paintings of 50s pin-up model Betty Page in an A4 sized volume.

That's it for now. Till next time.

GRAPHITTI EDITIONS

Number/Title		Print Run	Value
1.	THE ROCKETEER	1,000	£175.00
2.	NEXUS	1,000	£90.00
3.	ELRIC OF MELNIBONE	2,000	£35.00
4.	GRENDEL: DEVIL BY THE DEED	2,000	£170.00
5.	THE RETURN OF MR. X	1,500	£35.00
6.	ELRIC: SAILOR ON THE SEAS OF FATE	1,800	£35.00
7.	AMERICAN FLAGG! SOUTHERN COMFORT	2,000	£35.00
8.	RIO	1,500	£25.00
9.	NIGHT AND THE ENEMY	1,500	£25.00
10.	AMERICAN FLAGG! HARD TIMES	1,800	£30.00
11.	GRENDEL: DEVIL'S LEGACY	2,000	£65.00
12.	MOEBIUS 1	1,500	£35.00
13.	MOEBIUS 2	1,500	£35.00
14.	MOEBIUS 3	1,500	£45.00
15.	SOMEPLACE STRANGE	1,200	£30.00
16.	ELEKTRA ASSASSIN	2,000	£80.00
17.	AMERICAN FLAGG! STATE OF THE UNION	1,800	£35.00
18.	MOONSHADOW	1,200	£75.00
19.	GRENDEL: THE DEVIL INSIDE	1,200	£75.00
20.	THE GROO CHRONICLES	1,500	£35.00
21.	HELLRAISER 1	1,500	£30.00
	HELLRAISER 1	500	£55.00
22.	MOEBIUS 4: BLUEBERRY	1,500	£35.00
23.	MOEBIUS 5: BLUEBERRY	1,500	£35.00
24.	MOEBIUS 6: YOUNG BLUEBERRY	1,500	£35.00
25.	MARSHALL LAW	1,500	£35.00
26.	PLASTIC FORKS	1,200	£35.00
27.	STRANGE ADVENTURES (not yet released)		
28.	MELTDOWN: HAVOC AND WOLVERINE	2,000	£40.00
29.	ELEKTRA LIVES AGAIN	2,500	£40.00
30.	STRAY TOASTERS (not yet released)		
31.	ELRIC: THE WEIRD OF THE WHITE WOLF	1,200	£35.00
32.	HELLRAISER II	1,500	£30.00
	HELLRAISER II	500	£55.00
33.	AKIRA BOOK 1 (not signed)	1,500	£35.00
34.	THE CROW	1,000?	£80.00

35.	MOEBIUS 7	1,500	£30.00
36.	MOEBIUS 8	1,500	£35.00
37.	MOEBIUS 9	1,500	£35.00
38.	HELLRAISER III	1,000	£30.00
	HELLRAISER III	500	£55.00
39.	AKIRA BOOK 2 (not signed)	1,500	£35.00
40.	CHAOS & METALLIC DREAMS (working title) (not yet released)		
41.	HELLRAISER IV (may be cancelled)		
42.	MYTHOLOGY OF AN ABANDONED CITY	500	£40.00
43.	MADMAN (not yet released)		
44.	AKIRA BOOK 4 (not signed)	1,500	£35.00
45.	AKIRA BOOK 5 (not signed)	1.500	£35.00
46.	AKIRA BOOK 6 (not signed) (was due for release Summer 1994)		
47.	MARVELS	8,500	£40.00
48.	MADMAN (Two Volumes, slipcased)	1,500	£60.00
49.	MOEBIUS 10 (no release date as yet)		

NOTES ON THE GRAPHITTI SECTION

1) All of the Hellraiser volumes have two versions. Version 1 is signed by various creators who worked on the series and is limited to 1,500 copies (except Volume III which is 1,000 copies). Version 2 is signed by various creators plus Clive Barker. It is leather-bound and is limited to 500 copies.

2) Although all volumes of Akira are officially listed as unsigned, there are very limited quantities (between 12 and 15 copies) of Books 1-3 which are signed. Apparently Otomo did not want to get involved in the "commercialism" of signing all the copies.

3) Strange Adventures was delayed owing to the death of Harvey Kurtzman and although he has not signed all the copies, Graphitti say that he has signed "enough" and while it should have been released in late 1994, there is no sign of it yet.

4) Stray Toasters has been indefinitely delayed and, as yet, no release date has been announced.

5) Graphitti's first ever edition of The Rocketeer had a "sub-set"; as well as the books numbered 1–1,000 there were 26 additional copies numbered A–Z. These were created as artists' proofs and gifts for people involved in the production of the book.

DC COMICS

(NN)	BATMAN: THE DARK KNIGHT RETURNS 10th ANNIVERSARY EDITION (in slipcase)	10,000	£70.00

GRAPHITTI/DC CO-PRODUCTIONS

Number/Title		Print Run	Value
(NN)	BATMAN: THE DARK KNIGHT RETURNS	4,000	£225.00
(NN)	HISTORY OF THE DC UNIVERSE	2,000	£25.00
(NN)	ENEMY ACE: WAR IDYLL	1,000	£50.00

NOTES ON THE GRAPHITTI/DC SECTION

1) Although the plates in Enemy Ace: War Idyll are numbered to 2,000 a last minute decision was taken to produce only 1,000 copies. It is also of note that the volume itself is designed to be a replica of the diary kept by the main character of the story.

2) Batman: The Dark Knight Returns also has a "sub-set" which again is numbered A - Z. These copies are additionally signed by Lynn Varley and Klaus Janson.

GRAPHITTI/IMAGE CO-PRODUCTIONS

Number/Title		Print Run	Value
1.	SHADOWHAWK	5,000	£45.00
2.	SAVAGE DRAGON	5,000	£45.00

NOTES ON THE GRAPHITTI/IMAGE SECTION

1) Owing to the splintered nature of the various studios publishing under the Image Comics banner, there is no "official" agreement between the two companies. It does however seem likely that there will be more editions following the two already released.

DARK HORSE EDITIONS

Title	Print Run	Value
ALIENS: VOLUME 1 (Slipcase)	1,500	£100.00
ALIENS: VOLUME 2	2,500	£45.00
ALIENS: EARTH WAR	2,000	£30.00
ALIENS: TRIBES	1,200	£50.00
ALIENS Vs. PREDATOR (Slipcase)	1,000	£55.00
BOOK OF THE NIGHT (Slipcase)	500	£40.00
CONCRETE: SHORT STORIES	2,000	£30.00
DON MARTIN'S DROLL BOOK	500	£40.00
GIVE ME LIBERTY	2,000	£80.00
HARD BOILED	2,000	£80.00
HELLBOY	2,000	£75.00
PREDATOR: VOLUME 1	2,500	£40.00
QUEEN OF HEARTS	1,200	£70.00
SIN CITY (Slipcase)	1,000	£60.00
SIN CITY: BIG FAT KILL (Slipcase)	1,000	£75.00
STAR WARS: DARK EMPIRE (Slipcase)	1,000	£105.00
STAR WARS: DARK EMPIRE II	1,000	£75.00
STAR WARS: DROIDS	1,000	£70.00
TERMINATOR: TEMPEST (Slipcase)	1,500	£50.00
THE COMPLETE ALIENS	500	£200.00

ECLIPSE EDITIONS

Title	Print Run	Value
ALEX TOTH'S ZORRO	350	£50.00
APPLESEED BOOK 1: THE PROMETHEAN CHALLENGE	230	£50.00
APPLESEED BOOK 2: PROMETHEUS UNBOUND	300	£40.00
APPLESEED BOOK 3: THE SCALES OF PROMETHEUS	300	£40.00
ARIANE AND BLUEBEARD	300	£25.00
BOB KANE'S BATMAN	2,500	£80.00
CLIVE BARKER, ILLUSTRATOR	1,000	£40.00
DIRTY PAIR: BIOHAZARDS	850	£35.00
DIRTY PAIR: DANGEROUS ACQUAINTANCES	850	£35.00
DR. WATCHSTOP: ADVENTURES IN TIME & SPACE	350	£25.00
FUN WITH REID FLEMING	300	£55.00
THE HOBBIT	600	£100.00
JACK KIRBY TREASURY VOLUME 2	500	£60.00
LARRY MARDER'S BEANWORLD	300	£25.00
OPERA	300	£25.00
PANDEMONIUM	350	£20.00
PIGEONS FROM HELL	1,000	£25.00
SABRE (10TH ANNIVERSARY EDITION)	500	£30.00
THE SACRED AND THE PROFANE	500	£30.00
SCOUT: THE FOUR MONSTERS	1,750	£30.00
SCOUT: MOUNT FIRE	750	£30.00
SILVERHEELS	750	£25.00
THE SISTERHOOD OF STEEL	300	£20.00
SOMERSET HOLMES	750	£25.00
SWORDSMEN AND SAURIANS	175	£200.00
TECUMSEH!	250	£40.00
TOADSWART D'AMPLESTONE	250	£20.00
VALKYRIE: PRISONER OF THE PAST	250	£20.00
VALKYRIE: THE RETURN OF THE VALKYRIE	250	£20.00
ZOT!	450	£30.00

NOTES ON THE ECLIPSE SECTION

1) Some of the above limitations have yet to be verified so the above list should not be taken as 100% accurate. The majority of Eclipse's signed editions are clothbound.

2) Alex Toth's Zorro is a two volume set in one slipcase.

3) The Hobbit volume comes boxed.

KITCHEN SINK EDITIONS

Title	Print Run	Value
A CONTRACT WITH GOD (Eisner. 1st print)	600	£50.00
A CONTRACT WITH GOD (2nd Print)	600	£25.00
A LIFE FORCE (Eisner)	1,250	£20.00
BILL SIENKIEWICZ SKETCHBOOK	2,000	£25.00
CADILLACS AND DINOSAURS	1,500	£30.00
CITY PEOPLE (Eisner)	1,500	£20.00
CURSE OF THE MOLEMEN	1,000	£20.00
DINOSAUR SHAMEN	1,500	£20.00
DREAMER (Eisner)	750	£20.00
FLASH GORDON	750	£35.00
FROM AARGH TO ZAP	1,250	£40.00
HYPNOTIC TALES	250	£30.00
SPIRIT CASEBOOK (Eisner)	1,750	£25.00
STEVE RUDE SKETCHBOOK	1,200	£30.00
THE ART OF WILL EISNER	1,000	£40.00
THE BUILDING (Eisner)	750	£25.00
THE CITY (Eisner)	600	£30.00
THE HEART OF THE STORM (Eisner)	900	£25.00
WILL EISNER READER	600	£25.00
WILL EISNER SKETCHBOOK	1,000	£30.00

NOTES ON KITCHEN SINK SECTION

1) As can be seen from the above Kitchen Sink's limited editions have concentrated on the talents of Will Eisner. Of the 19 books listed above, 11 of them are Eisner editions.

EDITIONS BY OTHER COMPANIES

Title	Print Run	Publisher	Value
ART OF JACK DAVIS	750	Starburst	£26.00
ART OF JACK KIRBY	1,000	Blue Rose Press	£75.00
ART OF MOEBIUS	100	Byron Press	£85.00
BERNIE WRIGHTSON: A LOOK BACK			
(Original)	250	Land of Enchantment	£350.00
(Reprint)	250	Land of Enchantment	£195.00
[both the above with slipcase]			
BRAT PACK	1,000	King Hell/Tundra	£35.00
COMICS AND STORIES (Slipcase)	750	?	£65.00
COMPLETE ELFQUEST (Pini)	1,000	Warp Graphics	£150.00
COMPLETE ROBERT CRUMB #1-9	400	Fantagraphics	£55.00
COMPLETE STAR WARS			
(Williamson/Goodwin)	2,500	Russ Cochran	£140.00
CYCLE OF THE WEREWOLF	150	?	£300.00
DANCING NEKKID WITH ANGELS			
(Cruse)	1,250	?	£25.00
DONALD DUCK: 50 YEARS OF			
HAPPY FRUSTRATION	700	3 Ducks	£80.00
DRACULA (J.J. Muth)	1,000	NBM	£40.00
DRAWINGS & MONOTYPES			
(Kent Williams)	1,000	Tundra	£35.00
E. R. BURROUGHS LIBRARY OF			
ILLUSTRATION (this edition comes with slipcase)	2,000	Russ Cochran	£250.00
ELFQUEST			
#1 (Pini)	1,500	Warp Graphics	£80.00
#2-4 (Pini)	1,500	Warp Graphics	£45.00
THE FINE ART OF WALT DISNEY'S			
DONALD DUCK (Barks) (half the print run were burgundy bound, half were blue bound) (This edition comes with slipcase)	1,850	Another Rainbow	£1,000.00
FOEMINA (Manara)	1,200	Glittering Images	£95.00
FOREVER WAR #1,2,3 (Slipcase)			
(Marvano)	300	NBM	£100.00
FRANKENSTEIN (Wrightson/King)	250	?	£300.00
FUTURE DAY (Gene Day)	530	?	£25.00
GINGER FOX (O'Connell)	1,200	Comico	£25.00
GOLDEN AGE OF TARZAN (Hogarth)	2,000	Chelsea House	£180.00
HERNANDEZ BROTHERS			
SKETCHBOOK #1	750	Fantagraphics	£35.00
HERNANDEZ BROTHERS			
SKETCHBOOK #2	1,000	Fantagraphics	£25.00
HYPNOTIC TALES	250	?	£30.00
ILLUSTRATED HARLAN ELLISON	3,000	?	£35.00
INDIAN SUMMER (Manara)	500	Catalan	£50.00
JUST TEASING (Dave Stevens)	1,500	?	£50.00
LAW & CHAOS (Pini)	1,000	Warp Graphics	£30.00
LIGHTSHIP (Jim Burns)	250	?	£25.00
LORD OF THE RINGS (1 volume)	250	Unwin/Allen	£195.00
LORD OF THE RINGS (3 volume set)	250	Unwin/Allen	£250.00
LOVE & ROCKETS Volumes 1-3			
(1st print) each	400	Fantagraphics	£50.00
(2nd print) each	600	Fantagraphics	£30.00
Volumes 4-8 each	600	Fantagraphics	£40.00
MAGE VOLUME #1	1,500	Donning	£100.00
MAGE VOLUME #2	1,500	Donning	£60.00
MAGE VOLUME #3 (these three volumes come with slipcase)	1,500	Donning	£60.00
MAUS 1,2 (Slipcase)			
(Spiegleman)	300	Pantheon	£150.00
MELTING POT	500	?	£35.00
METROPOLIS (Kaluta)	1,000	Donning	£40.00
MICKEY MOUSE IN COLOUR			
(Barks and Gottfredson)	2,500	Another Rainbow	£175.00
MOCKBA (Moebius)	1,500	Stardom	£60.00
NO MAN'S LAND	500	Tundra	£40.00
PHOTO JOURNAL GUIDE TO COMICS			
Vol 1,2 each	900	Gerber	£145.00
Vol 3,4 each	2,500	Gerber	£75.00
PRIME	5,000	Malibu	£30.00
QUADRANT	1,000	Malibu Graphics	£40.00
RAY BRADBURY CHRONICLES			
Vol 1-5 each	1,200	NBM	£35.00
REAPER OF LOVE (Wrightson)	1,200	Fantagraphics	£30.00
ROBERT CRUMB SKETCHBOOK			
#1	400	Fantagraphics	£55.00
#2	400	Fantagraphics	£55.00
#3	400	Fantagraphics	£55.00
SATAN'S TEARS	1,000	?	£30.00
SPACEHAWK	250	Archival	£40.00
STAR WARS: THE ART OF DAVE DORMAN			
	2,500	F.P.G.	£55.00
THIEF OF BAGDAD (Russell)	1,000	Donning	£35.00
UNCLE SCROOGE			
McDUCK (Barks)	5,000	Celestial Arts	£250.00
VAMPIRE LESTAT	2,000	Innovation	£40.00
VIAMOUR (Moebius)	200	L'Atelier	£200.00

NOTES ON OTHER COMPANIES SECTION

1) The Complete Robert Crumb is an ongoing series and the ten volumes published so far cover his work up to the mid 1970s.

2) The remarkable thing about the Ray Bradbury Chronicles is that as well as being signed by Mr. Bradbury himself, barring death, the five volumes are each signed by every creator who ever worked on them.

3) No Man's Land is a companion volume to Graphitti's Enemy Ace book, containing the research, background material and sketches produced by writer/artist George Pratt in the making of Enemy Ace: War Idyll.

4) There are two different signed and numbered editions of Quadrant.

5) Geoff Darrow's Comics & Stories is a French edition and there is very little text. It also contains a magazine.

SIGNED AND NUMBERED LIMITED EDITION TRADE PAPERBACKS

Title	Print run	Publisher	Value
CEREBUS: FLIGHT	?	Aardvark	£20.00

CEREBUS: JAKA'S STORY	435	Aardvark	£20.00
CEREBUS: MOTHERS AND DAUGHTERS I	?	Aardvark	£17.00
CEREBUS: MOTHERS AND DAUGHTERS II	?	Aardvark	£17.00
FROM THE DARKNESS	300	Malibu Graphics	£20.00
SABRE	?	Eclipse	£15.00

SIGNED AND NUMBERED LIMITED EDITION TRADING CARDS

Title	Print run	Publisher	Value
FAUST (Vigil & Quinn)			
Gold Hologram	1,000	Rebel Studios	£20.00

SIGNED AND NUMBERED LIMITED EDITION PRINTS

Title	Print run	Value
A BAD NIGHT FOR NINJAS (2 prints - Jim Lee)	2,500	£75.00
ALIEN (John Bolton)	1,500	£75.00
ALIEN VS. PREDATOR (Dave Dorman)	1,500	£75.00
ANGEL (Bill Sienkiewicz)	201	£135.00
AVIATOR (Moebius)	150	£125.00
BETTY BATH (Dave Stevens)	395	£170.00
BLIND NARCISSUS (Jones)	1,000	£200.00
DARK MISTS (Richard Corben)	200	£20.00
DEVIL'S FOOD (Olivia)	250	£595.00
DINOSAUR (Mark Schultz)	250	£125.00
DOC SAVAGE: SQUEAKING GOBLIN (Bama)	150	£60.00
WORLD'S FAIR GOBLIN (Bama)	150	£60.00
PIRATE OF THE PACIFIC (Bama)	150	£60.00
SEA ANGEL (Bama)	150	£60.00
MYSTIC MULLAH (Bama)	150	£60.00
RED SNOW (Bama)	150	£60.00
DRACULA (Jon J. Muth)	200	£75.00
DRAGON SLAYER (Jones)	275	£45.00
DREAMS OF AN ANCIENT WORLD (Corben)	500	£30.00
FRANKENSTEIN 1. THE MONSTER (Wrightson)	300	£20.00
2. THE BED (Wrightson)	300	£20.00
3. THE BOAT (Wrightson)	300	£20.00
4. THE WINDOW (Wrightson)	300	£20.00
5. THE RAIN (Wrightson)	300	£20.00
6. THE CLIFF (Wrightson)	300	£20.00
FRANKENSTEIN Embossed 1 (Wrightson)	275	£45.00
Embossed 2 (Wrightson)	275	£45.00
FREDER'S DREAMS (Mike Kaluta)	450	£40.00
GREEN HORNET (Jim Steranko)	1,500	£55.00
GRENDEL: WAR CHILD (Matt Wagner)	1,000	£30.00
HARD BOILED 1 (Darrow, Miller, Legris)	100	£55.00
HARD BOILED 2 (Darrow, Miller)	400	£95.00
KING KONG (Dave Stevens)	1,000	£85.00
LABYRINTH (Richard Corben)	250	£30.00
LADIES AND GENTLEMEN...MIMI RODAN (Dave Stevens)	850	£75.00
LA FEMME ET FELINE (Olivia)	40	£150.00
MAD (Harvey Kurtzman)	750	£195.00
MITRAS (B. Windsor Smith)	350	£130.00
MIDNIGHT GROVE (Charles Vess)	75	£75.00
MIDNIGHT READER (Howard Chaykin)	325	£45.00
MEMENTOS (Bernie Wrightson)	600	£40.00
MISTER X (Dean Motter)	295	£55.00
NIMUE THE ENCHANTRESS (B. Windsor Smith)	100	£300.00
ODE TO A SCOTTISH PRAYER (Wrightson)	450	£50.00
PHARAGONESIA (Moebius)	50	£75.00
PYSCHE (B. Windsor Smith)	1,000	£75.00
PURRFECT MEMORIES (Spiderman, 2 prints.Charles Vess)	2,500	£55.00
RETURN OF VALKYRIE (Jim Steranko)	1,500	£45.00
RUINS (George Pratt)	300	£20.00
SCORCHER (Dave Stevens)	750	£95.00
SIBYL (B. Windsor Smith)	850	£95.00
SMOOTHIES (Olivia)	255	£350.00
SONNET (Jon J. Muth)	200	£50.00
STEALER OF SOULS (Mike Kaluta)	300	£40.00
STREET CASINO (Will Eisner)	800	£35.00
THE ACTRESS AND THE BISHOP (B. Bolland)	500	£65.00
THE BOOK OF SAMOTHRACE (B.W. Smith)	1,000	£65.00
THE CRYSTAL GATE (Moebius)	300	£125.00
THE DESIRE (Moebius)	150	£75.00
THE EMISSARY (Mike Kaluta)	100	£80.00
THE GHOUL (Edwards)	990	£20.00
THE GUN (Moebius)	200	£60.00
THE LAST ATLANTEAN (B. Windsor Smith)	960	£40.00
THE LATE TRAIN (Will Eisner)	800	£35.00
THE MAMMOTH (Arthur Suydam)	450	£50.00
THE SHADOW ABLAZE (Mike Kaluta)	2,500	£35.00
THE STREET (Moebius, Darrow)	100	£100.00
THE UNDYING WIZARD (Jones)	275	£45.00
THE VOLCANO (Moebius)	200	£85.00
THREE WOMEN (Dave Stevens)	850	£80.00
TURF WAR (Will Eisner)	800	£35.00
VAMPIRELLA (Dave Stevens)	850	£85.00
VIRTUE TRIUMPHANT (John Bolton)	500	£20.00
WEREWOLF (John Bolton)	1,000	£20.00
WHISPER (Dave McKean)	201	£135.00
WIZARD'S DREAMS (Richard Corben)	500	£25.00
YAQUI (Moebius)	175	£90.00

NOTES ON THE PRINTS SECTION

1) Purrfect Memories are two complimentary prints featuring Spiderman and Black Cat. There are 2,500 copies of each print but the value as listed is for the set of two.

2) A Bad Night for Ninjas is also a two print set, this time featuring Punisher and Wolverine. There are 2,500 copies of each print but the value as listed is for the set of two.

SIGNED AND NUMBERED LIMITED PORTFOLIOS

Title	Plates	Print Run	Value
BLUEBERRY PORTFOLIO (Moebius)	15 (c)	800	£75.00
BRIAN BOLLAND PORTFOLIO	6 (b&w)	666	£35.00
CITY OF FIRE (Moebius/Darrow)	11 (c)	950	£300.00
CRY FOR DAWN 1 (Linsner)	8 (b&w)	1,500	£40.00
EDGAR ALLEN POE (Wrightson)	8 (c)	2,000	£50.00
FANTASTIC ISLANDS (B.W. Smith)	4 (b&w)	1,000	£85.00
FRANKENSTEIN (Wrightson)	6 (b&w)	1,000	£100.00
FRANKENSTEIN II (Wrightson)	6 (b&w)	2,000	£60.00
FRANKENSTEIN III	6 (b&w)	1,000	£50.00
INDIAN SUMMER (Milo Manara)	2 (c)	999	£165.00
JEFF JONES FANTASY COLLECTION	8 (c)	275	£55.00
JOHN BOLTON PORTFOLIO	6 (b&w)	888	£20.00
KUBLA KHAN (Frank Frazetta)	5 (b&w)	1,500	£95.00
PUNISHER PORTFOLIO 1 (Zeck)	6 (b&w)	600	£85.00
PUNISHER PORTFOLIO 2 (Zeck)	6 (b&w)	600	£25.00
ROBERT E. HOWARD (B.W.S)	5 (c)	920	£125.00
SANDRA PORTFOLIO (Milo Manara)	8 (c)	600	£95.00
SIBYLA (B. Windsor Smith)	5 (c)	1,000	£75.00
STARSTRUCK PORTFOLIO (Kaluta)	6 (b&w)	1,000	£20.00
THE CITY PORTFOLIO (Eisner)	6 (t/t)	1,200	£55.00
DRAWINGS OF BARRY WINDSOR SMITH	8 (b&w)	750	£95.00
THE FOUR AGES (B. Windsor Smith)	4 (b/i)	1,000	£85.00
THE PIN-UP COLLECTION (Olivia)	12 (c)	4,000	£200.00
THE SPIRIT PORTFOLIO (Eisner)	11 (c)	1,500	£95.00
THE STAND PORTFOLIO (Wrightson)	12 (b&w)	1,200	£50.00
TOUR DU MONDE (Moebius)	48 (c)	300	£235.00
TUPENNT CONAN (B.Windsor Smith)	6 (b&w)	1,000	£175.00
WATCHMEN (Gibbons, Moore)	12 (c)	2,000	£75.00
WOMEN OF THE AGES (Frazetta)	6 (b&w)	1,500	£95.00
7 WONDERS OF THE ANCIENT WORLD (Krenkel)	7 (c)	1,000	£60.00

NOTES ON THE PORTFOLIO SECTION

KEY: (c) colour (b&w) black and white (b/i) black on ivory (t/t) two tone

1) Of the 4,000 copies of Olivia's The Pin Up Collection, half were sold to Japan leaving only 2,000 copies for Europe and the U.S.A.

2) Tour Du Monde comes in a deluxe rubber-covered folder.

3) The five plates in the Robert E. Howard Portfolio feature: Conan, Toth Amon, Red Sonja, Bran Mak Morn and Soloman Kane.

4) The Stand Portfolio comes in a black and gold embossed folder and the Drawings of Barry Windsor Smith comes in a deluxe box folder.

5) Both of the Punisher Portfolios are French editions, one of which was later reprinted by Marvel in an unsigned, colour format.

6) Many of the above portfolios come in either an illustrated folder or an illustrated envelope. As previously stated, the above list covers only a fraction of the signed and numbered portfolios produced.

7) The City of Fire Portfolio is one of the most important portfolios of the 1980s. It comes in a hardcover, deluxe box folder which is embossed in yellow and red.

SIGNED AND NUMBERED LIMITED EDITION COMICS

Title/Number	Print Run	Publisher	Value
ACHILLES STORM #4	999	Aja Blue	£4.95
CRY FOR DAWN #3	1,500	C.F.D.	£40.00
CRY FOR DAWN #4	1,500	C.F.D.	£40.00
CRY FOR DAWN #5	1,500	C.F.D	£40.00
CRY FOR DAWN #6	1,500	C.F.D	£35.00
CRY FOR DAWN #7	2,000	C.F.D	£30.00
CRY FOR DAWN #8	2,000	C.F.D.	£60.00
CRY FOR DAWN #9	2,000	C.F.D.	£35.00
DAWN #1 (Look Sharp)	1,000	Sirius	£25.00
DAWN #1 (White Trash)	1,000	Sirius	£25.00
DAWN #2	5,000	Sirius	£25.00
DAWN #3	1,500	Sirius	£25.00
DRAMA #1	2,000	Sirius	£25.00
EO #1	2,000	Rebel Studios	£40.00
FAUST #1	1,900	Northstar	£60.00
FAUST #6	1,900	Northstar	£50.00
THE MAXX ASHCAN #1	?	Image	£10.00
NIGHT VISIONS #1	3,000	Rebel Studios	£3.95
NORTHSTAR #1	1,000	Northstar	£70.00
OMEGA #1	1,900	Northstar	£50.00
PITT ASHCAN #1	5,500	Image	£10.00
PITT ASHCAN OLIVE #2	1,800	Image	£12.95
PITT ASHCAN BLACK #2	1,800	Image	£10.00
PITT ASHCAN PLATINUM #2	1,800	Image	£10.00
VAMPIRE LESTAT #1-12	1,000	Innovation	£45.00

NOTES ON THE COMICS SECTION

1) Cry for Dawn #8 is the "fan club" edition, available only through the fan club and almost impossible to find in this country. Cry for Dawn #6 is the only issue of the title, in both the regular and signed & numbered editions not to feature Dawn on the cover.

2) Copies of Omega #1 were recalled and destroyed by Northstar following threatened legal action by Marvel Comics over copyright infringement. The initial print run was 1,900 but it is unknown how many of these survived. The comic eventually reappeared as The Omen.

3) All of the Image ashcans are "mini" comics with coloured card covers and black and white interiors.

4) The twelve issues of Vampire Lestat come in a slipcase which also contains The Vampire Companion #1 and 2.

5) Dawn is in a signed envelope with a sketch on it. Both editions of Dawn #1 are signed on certificates but have totally new covers.

Dawn #1 Limited Edition (White Trash Edition)

Dawn #3 Limited Edition

THE TOP 50 RAREST COMICS

Below is an excercise that I carried out to determine the Top 50 rarest comic books. It is based on personal observation with some advice from a few friends and collectors. The numbers are "best guesses" at the time of going to press. I recently noticed another Action Comics ashcan advertised by Pacific Comics Exchange, citing only three copies in existence.Therefore more information, particularly from American dealers, would be most welcome.

POS./TITLE/NUMBER	DATE	COPIES KNOWN

1) AMAZING MYSTERY FUNNIES 1940? 1

Discovered by Mark Wilson in America, it has the same cover as Amazing Man #23 from Centaur Comics but it has no number. The reason is unclear.

1) ALL STAR COMICS (ASH CAN) 1940 1

This comic was discovered by Jon Warren in America. It is an "ash can" copy or a publisher's in-house facsimile of a proposed new title and used to secure the name and design of the title. Most ash can comics have black and white covers stapled to an already existing coverless comic. Some ash cans are completely black and white throughout. This particular ash can shows what was to be the cover for DC's Flash Comics #1 (January 1940).

1) BLOOD IS THE HARVEST 1950 1

This was issued by the Cathetical Guild as less than a comic and more of an illustrated pamphlet against Communism. It is known in three forms and this is the black and white un-trimmed version.

4) IS THIS TOMORROW? 1947 2

Issued by the Cathetical Guild, a forerunner to Blood is the Harvest and the theme of Communists taking over America. This is the black and white advance copy. It is more of an educational pamphlet than a recognized comic book.

5) ACTION COMICS ASHCAN 1938 3

This is the black and white ash can comic that was used to secure the title and design of Action Comics that was to feature the first appearance of Superman. The cover shows a pirate type figure in head and shoulders close up brandishing a cutlass. This cover was eventually used in full colour for Action Comics #3, August 1938. A copy was on view for sale at the 1991 San Diego Comicon.

5) SYNDICATE COMICS FEATURES 1937 3

Discovered by Mark Wilson in 1990, this comic was designed to promote the character Dan Hastings to all the newspaper comic sections. Dated November 1937, this 4 page comic has artwork by Fred Guardineer who did much work for other major companies. Look for his cover art on early issues of Action Comics. The front is done in green and red ink, the interior is black and white. The size is much larger than normal comic size at 17" by 11". All three known copies are in VG condition.

5) THRILL COMICS 1939 3

Fawcett Publications came up with an idea for a comic called Flash Comics starring Captain Thunder in 1939. The race was on to secure copyright. DC Comics (or National Periodical Publications as they were then known) beat Fawcett to it by publishing their own Flash Comics #1 cover dated January 1940. This Thrill Comics is an in-house ash can comic, re-titled from a second ash can Fawcett Flash Comics (same cover illustration of Captain Thunder snapping free from chains – see 19) to try and salvage the character of Captain Thunder. Unfortunately in December 1939 Better/Nedor Publications filed for a title which was to appear cover dated February 1940 called Thrilling Comics so Fawcett had to change to Whiz Comics which eventually came out in February 1940 as well.

5) FEATURE BOOK (POPEYE) 1937 3

Issued by David McKay Publications, this hundred page comic had no number on the cover but was later issued as number 3, same interior but a different cover. It featured black and white newspaper reprints but unlike the ash cans, it is more of a recognized, proper comic. of the three known copies in existence, one is high grade and the other two are much lower grade.

9) SLAM BANG COMICS 1940 3 to 4

An ash can black and white produced by Fawcett to secure the title which appeared in 1940 (cover dated March). There is no cover illustration but the announcement "Featuring the episode adventures of Ibis the Invincible...". Estimated number of copies is difficult to confirm. The 1st Sotheby's catalogue for the sale dated Wednesday December 18th 1991 had an example on offer and claimed it was the only copy in existence which seems unlikely. Further research is obviously needed though it does seem to be the rarest of this type of ash-can.

10) IF THE DEVIL WOULD TALK 1958 4

Issued by the Cathetical Guild, it treats of the threat of worldly temptations. This is a black and white, small size version of the original colour version. More of a pamphlet than a comic.

11) FLASH COMICS VOL 1 #1 1939 4 to 5

This was the black and white ash can copy produced by DC to secure the title in the race with Fawcett (see 5). It is cover dated December 1939 and reprints the cover from DC's Adventure Comics #41 with an underwater scene of a shark attacking a drowning man.

11) FLASH COMICS 1939 4 to 5

This was the first (of three) black and white ash can copy produced by Fawcett in the race to secure the title (see 5 and 8). The cover has no illustration but rather the announcement "..featuring the episode adventures of Golden Arrow..". A copy was offered for sale at the 1st Sotheby's auction in December 1991. Other characters included Captain Thunder, Ibis and Dan Dare (not the British one!).

11) FIVE CENT COMICS 1940 4 to 5

An ash can black and white produced by Fawcett cover dated February to secure a title which appeared in May 1940 as Nickel Comics featuring Bulletman. This copy has no cover illustration, only the announcement "Featuring the episode adventures of Dan Dare, brilliant young free-lance detective..". A copy was offered for sale in the 1st Sotheby's auction in December 1991.

11) NICKEL COMICS 1940 4 to 5

An ash can black and white copy produced by Fawcett to secure the idea of comics sold at 5 cents and indeed that title (see 10). There is no cover illustration but an announcement of "Featuring the episode adventures of Scoop Smith, daring young newspaper reporter..". A copy was offered for sale in the 1st Sotheby's auction in December 1991.

11) WORLD'S BEST 1939 4 to 5

This is another ash can comic cover dated February 1941 in order to secure copyright for the title of World's Best Comics which appeared in Spring 1941 and became World's Finest Comics with issue 2. The cover is a black and white reprint of Action Comics #29 showing Superman rescuing a bound and gagged Lois Lane from the back of a gangster's car. The interior is also made up from stock reprints from DC's inventory at the time.

16) WOW (1ST SERIES) #2 1936 4 to 7

Sub-titled What a Magazine, this 52 page comic is magazine size and features characters like Fu Manchu and Popeye and artwork elsewhere featured is by Will Eisner. All copies of this four issue series are very rare but this is the rarest.

17) BLOOD IS THE HARVEST 1950 5

Issued by the Cathetical Guild announcing the impending threat of Communism, this is the black and white version of the original colour issue. More of a pamphlet than a comic. One of these has surfaced in un-trimmed condition (see entry #2).

18) DOUBLE ACTION COMICS 1940 5 to 7

Dated January 1940 with a black and white interior, the colour cover is a reprint of Adventure Comics #37. It is not an ash can comic ie. it was distributed on the news-stands though issue 1 is thought to exist as an ash can as an experiment for Action Comics #1 that appeared in June 1938 (see Action Funnies - entry No. 5 above). The style of the words "Action" and "Comics" is very similar to what actually appeared on the comic that launched Superman.

19) FLASH COMICS 1939 8

This was the second (of three) black and white ash can copy produced by Fawcett in the race for the title (see entries 5,11,11). Thinking that they had secured the title, a cover illustration of Captain Thunder was drawn, snapping free from chains whilst being attacked by two thugs. When the existence of DC's own ash can Flash became known (see entry 11), Fawcett hastily re-drew the title to Thrill Comics (see entry 5). A copy was offered for sale at the 1st Sotheby's auction in December 1991. A copy was also sold in the U.K. in early 1994 for £18,000 in a cash and trade deal. It was apparently the best surviving copy.

20) MARVEL MYSTERY COMICS 1943/44 9

This 128 page comic was published during the classic Marvel Mystery Comics run which ended at issue 92 in June 1949. The interior is black and white, reprinting two Captain America stories and two other Marvel Mystery stock stories. It has the colour cover of Marvel Mystery Comics #33. It was possibly an experiment to produce some kind of annual to accompany the series cover priced at 25 cents. One estimate of known copies puts it as low as three.

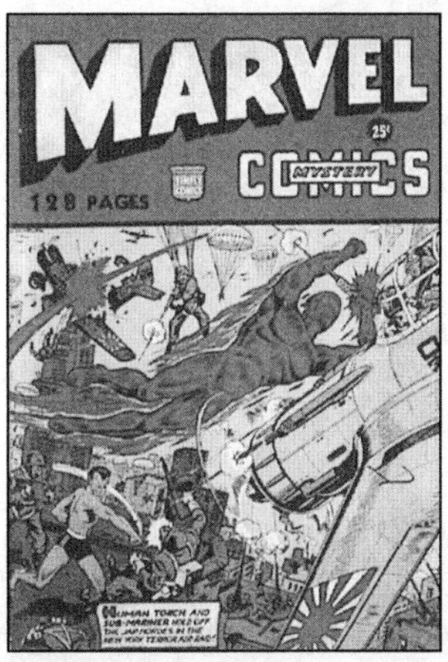

20) FEATURE BOOK (DICK TRACY) 1937 9

Like the other no number Feature Book with Popeye (see no. 5), this was later reprinted as Feature Book #4 with a new cover dated August 1937. It is 100 pages long.

22) ALL NEW #15 1947 9 to 10

Smaller than standard comic size, it was distributed through the mail only (see Stuntman #3). Joe Palooka and Black Cat appear. Black and white cover and interior. Estimates vary between 4 and 15 copies in existence.

23) FAMOUS FUNNIES (SERIES 1)#1 1933 10

This was the first recognisable comic book sold. Funnies On Parade and Famous Funnies A Carnival of Comics were given away. It was reprinted from a combination of these latter two comics and historians estimate about 35,000-40,000 were printed to be sold in chain stores throughout the U.S. Estimates vary between 8 and 12 copies in existence with 1 in strict NM condition which would bring at least 50% more than Guide values.

23) COMICS MAGAZINE #1 1936 10

Cover dated May 1936 this much under-rated comic contains Dr. Mystic, The Occult Detective by Siegel and Shuster as the inventory for this comic was sold by DC Comics from the pages of their magazine More Fun Comics. This first ever origin of a super-hero continues in the pages of DC's More Fun Comics #14. Dr. Mystic is a Superman prototype as his costume resembles Superman's and he can fly. Even though Superman appeared in 1938, the idea had been evolving as early as 1934.

23) NEW COMICS #2 1936 10

Cover dated January this comic is thought to be one of the rarest DC comics though others would disagree citing anything from 21 to 50 copies. Federal Men by Siegel and Shuster begins, a strip that went on to feature in Comics Magazine.

23) NEW FUN #2 1935 10

Cover dated March this is the second DC comic published and it is thought to be the rarest; certainly it has the tradition of being the hardest to find.

23) STUNTMAN #3 1946 10

This comic is smaller than standard comic size at 5" by 8". It was distributed through the mail only rather than sold on news-stands. It was only discovered to exist a few years ago.

23) DANGER TRAIL #3 1950 10

Cover dated November/December this comic is only very recently thought to be the rarest pre-Silver Age comic. The whole short-lived title (5 issues) is hard to come by in any condition. It is unusual for being the most recent comic book in this listing.

23) FAMOUS FUNNIES #2 1934 10

Published by Eastern Colour Printing Company, these comics contain all reprints from the Sunday funny pages like Mutt and Jeff and Joe Palooka.

23) FAMOUS FUNNIES #9 1935 10

Same as above. All these early Famous Funnies are very difficult to come by in any grade, let alone anything approaching high grade.

31) COMICS MAGAZINE #2 1936 10 to 12

Cover dated June 1936 this comic features Federal Men by Siegel and Shuster. It is thought to be as rare as issue #1 but unlikely. These are only educated guesses by those that know.

32) MORE FUN #9 1936 12

This is the first comic sized issue of the title as the previous issues 7 and 8 were a slightly larger 8" by 10". Issues 1-6 were New Fun Comics before title changed with issue 7. Cover dated March.

33) BLOOD IS THE HARVEST 1950 13

This is the original educational pamphlet as published by the Cathetical Guild. A black and white version became available (see entry No. 17) and un untrimmed version as well (see entry No. 1).

33) DETECTIVE COMICS #3 1937 13

Considered the rarest of the pre-Batman Detective Comics (#1-26), this is cover-dated May, exactly two years before the first appearance of Batman. Lovely cover by Creig Flessel of an escaped convict caught in a yellow search-light. Estimated copies vary from a lower value of 6 to an upper value of 20.

35) BIG BOOK OF FUN COMICS 1936 14

The 1st ever DC annual dated Spring 1936. Estimates very from as little as 5 copies to 23 copies which goes to show how difficult it is to calculate exactly the number of extant copies of any of these books. 1 is known in strict NM condition which would bring at least 50% in addition to the estimated value given here.

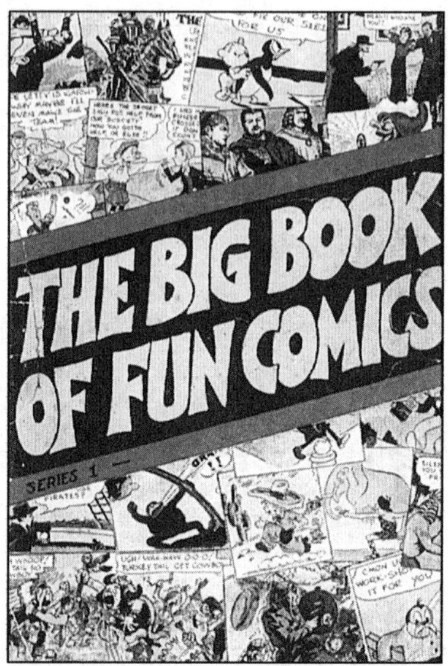

36) NEW FUN #6 1935 15

Cover-dated October, this is the first appearance of the Superman prototype Dr. Occult by Siegel and Shuster.

37) GREEN GIANT #1 1940 16

An experimental comic published by Moreau Publications to utilize a printing press of theirs. With no price on the cover it probably never got as far as the distribution stage. Estimates vary from 12 to 20 copies in existence. 3 are known in strict NM condition which would bring at least 50% more than any Guide values.

37) NEW FUN #1 1935 17

Cover-dated February, this is the first DC comic ever published. The title became More Fun with issue 7. Estimates of copies in existence run between 10 and 24 hence the average value of 17. There is one (1) known copy in Very Fine to Near Mint condition and it could bring double the current Guide value.

37) WOW COMICS #1 1936 17

Dated July, this is the magazine format from Henle Publishing sub-titled What a Magazine! (see No. 16). Estimated extant copies vary but only slightly from a lower limit of 15 to an upper limit of 20. The tightness of the range suggests that this comic is fairly well documented in its rarity value.

40) MORE FUN #8 1936 18

A slightly larger than standard comic (as was More Fun 7) at 10" by 12". Estimates of rarity vary from 15 to 20 copies but with another report citing parameters 21 to 50 though this is thought to be questionable. More information is obviously needed.

41) WOW COMICS #3 1936 20

Another in the short-lived magazine format series sub-titled What a Magazine!. The only reliable estimate at the moment suggests 20 copies though further research is needed.

42) DETECTIVE PICTURE STORIES #1 1936 22

One of the experts asked cites this as an extremely important comic as The Comics Magazine Co. and DC Comics raced to publish a comic devoted to a single theme. An ad appeared in New Comics #11 (December 1936) that Detective Comics #1 was appearing but it actually appeared three months after Detective Picture Stories #1, dated December 1936. Estimates vary from 15 to 30 copies in existence from three sources while another source seems way off the mark citing anywhere between 50 and 200 copies.

43) DETECTIVE COMICS #2 1937 23

Dated April 1937, another very rare pre-Batman Detective comic. Very distinctive cover illustration of a ugly thug's face in close up. Estimates of rarity vary tremendously from as few as 6 up to 35 copies though both of these seem extreme. A middle ground figure has been chosen.

44) NEW ADVENTURE COMICS #13 1937 25

One reliable source puts this at about 25 copies and this is the figure chosen for now. Another source claims it to be much rarer at under 5 copies but this seems a little extreme.

44) IF THE DEVIL WOULD TALK 1950 25

Educational pamphlet rather than really a comic book from the Cathetical Guild. Estimates run from between 20 to 30 copies so 25 has been chosen. The 1958 version is much rarer at 6 known copies and the black and white at 4 known copies.

46) MORE FUN #7 1936 26

Slightly over-sized comic at 10" by 12" as was More Fun #8. Estimated copies from as low as 7 to as high as 45. One estimate went as high as 50 but in view of one estimate of 7 and one of 10, the figure of 50 is discounted for now. 2 copies are known to exist in strict Near Mint and would bring at least 50% more above the suggested value here. Title was previously New Fun Comics #1-6.

47) BOY EXPLORERS #2 1946 27

Like Stuntman #3 and All New #15, this was a small size black and white comic distributed through the mail only and not on sale at news-stands. The only estimates available ranged between 20 and 35 copies so a middle figure has been chosen.

48) DETECTIVE COMICS #1 1937 30

The comic that gave DC its initials and in the race for the first comic with one theme (see entry No. 42). Estimates from sources said 20,25,30 and 35 copies respectively with one not so committal at 21-50 copies. A mid range value of 30 has been chosen for now. Sporting a beautiful Fu Manchu chinaman cover, probably by Creig Flessel, only one (1) known copy exists in Near Mint condition and could bring double the current Guide value. One more copy in this country came to the author's attention at the end of 1993, though the total estimated number has been left alone.

48) FAMOUS FUNNIES #1 1934 30

Not to be confused with Famous Funnies (Series 1) #1. This comic was the first regular monthly news-stand comic as number 2 came out one month later and so on. Two sources independently agreed on 30 extant copies while another went as low and as vague as 6 to 10 copies. For the moment the figure of 30 has been chosen. Two (2) copies are known to exist in Near Mint condition and would bring at least 50% above the current Guide value.

48) FUNNY PICTURE STORIES #1 1936 30

From The Comics Magazine Company a funnies anthology that was taken over by Centaur Publications with issue 6. Two estimates put extant copies from 25 to 35 copies so 30 was chosen. A third unconfirmed estimate suggests 21 to 50 copies.

OTHER RAREST COMIC BOOKS JUST OUTSIDE THE TOP 50 ARE:

DETECTIVE COMICS #4
has been suggested from 11-20 copies

FLASH GORDON #5
at about 30-40 copies as it was distributed through the mail like Stuntman #3, Boy Explorers #2 and All New #15

NEW FUN #3
which could be anywhere between 11 and 45 copies

NEW FUN #4
could be anywhere between 21 and 50 copies

MORE FUN #11, #15, #22 and #23
may have anywhere between 11 and 50 copies

NEW COMICS #3, #6, #11

and
NEW ADVENTURE COMICS #12, #14, #16, #18, #19, #22 AND #23
have been suggested by one source at 11–20 copies

CAPTAIN MARVEL THRILL BOOK
has been cited at 25 copies but as yet unconfirmed

NEW BOOK OF COMICS #2
at a possible 35 copies

NEW BOOK OF COMICS #1
at about 42 copies

JUMBO COMICS #1, CENTURY OF COMICS AND WOW COMICS #4
at a possible 40 copies each

FAMOUS FUNNIES (CARNIVAL OF COMICS), JUMBO COMICS #7 AND NEW COMICS #1
at a possible 50 copies each

ALL AMERICAN COMICS #16
at about 50–60 copies.

All the above information is at best mostly speculation based on observation by myself, what I have in my own collection, what I know for a fact are in other people's collections both here and in the America and informed guesses by a number of top American dealers, all of whom I credit and thank for their participation. No doubt when more information becomes available, positions in the Top 50 will alter.

THOSE AMERICAN DEALERS WHO ASSISTED IN THIS SURVEY WERE:

GARY CARTER, STEPHEN FISHLER, ERNST GERBER (and his invaluable Photo-Journals), **SEAN LINKENBACK, JAMES PAYETTE, JON WARREN** and **MARK WILSON** and a special mention for **BOB OVERSTREET** and his excellent Price Guide which pioneered the work of cataloguing the rarest comics in the world.

Even though many of the comics are very rare items indeed it does not necessarily make them the most valuable comics. Indeed only two (Detective Comics #1 and New Fun #1) feature in the Top 50 Rarest and Top 20 Most Valuable. The Top 20 most valuable comics in the U.K. market are valued according to those known to have been sold or offered for sale. A Near Mint price has been calculated on extant copies, known popularity of the characters and comics and educated guesses. Please note that the order may differ from that generally accepted in America as certain characters are less popular here than there. The values may be subject to variations of up to 20% either way.

Very high grade copies (Very Fine or better) of this Top Ten from "named" collections (**Note**: these are the only fully recognised and well documented "named" or "pedigree" collections: Mile High, San Francisco, Larsen, Allentown, Denver, Kansas City) may bring up to 50% more. Unrestored Near Mint copies from named collections may bring 100% more. Thus if ever the Mile High Action #1 or the Larsen Detective #27 ever came on the market, a genuine six figure sum in cash could easily be achieved. The continued success of the most recent Sotheby's and Christie's auctions in New York reinforce this belief.

The Top 20 Most Valuable Comics

Estimated values are guide prices only.
Please note that copies from named collections and copies sold at auction MAY command multiples of Guide.

RANK	COMIC/NUMBER	ESTIMATED TOTAL COPIES KNOWN	COPIES KNOWN IN U.K.	ESTIMATED U.K. VALUE IN UNRESTORED NEAR MINT
1	ACTION COMICS #1	100–125 with 4 NM	6 (in varying grades)	£100,000–£115,000
2	DETECTIVE COMICS #27	75–125 with 3 NM	7 (in varying grades, 2 heavily restored)	£90,000–£106,000
3	SUPERMAN #1	175–225 with 3 NM	12 (in varying grades, 3 heavily restored)	£65,000–£80,000
4	MARVEL COMICS #1	75–125 with 4 NM	3 (in varying grades)	£50,000–£65,000
5	DETECTIVE COMICS #1	25–35 with 1 NM	5 (in varying grades)	£40,000–£53,500
6	BATMAN #1	275–350 with 15 NM	10 (in varying grades)	£35,000–£45,000
7	WHIZ COMICS #1	125–175 with 3 NM	2 (in lower grades)	£32,750–£42,750
8	ALL AMERICAN #16	50–60 with 3 NM	2 (in lower grades)	£32,500–£42,500
9	CAPTAIN AMERICA #1	150–200 with 8 NM	5 (in varying grades)	£31,675–£41,675
10	NEW FUN #1	10–25 with 1 VF/NM	None known in U.K.	£30,000–£40,000
11	MORE FUN COMICS #52	60–70 with 3 NM	2 (1 grade not known, the other VG range)	£27,350–£37,350
12	FLASH COMICS #1	125–150 with 7 NM	4 (2 in higher grades, 1 very low grade, 1 heavily restored)	£25,000–£35,000
13	MORE FUN COMICS #53	60–70 with 3 NM	2 (1 in high grade,1 in low grade)	£21,700–£26,700
14	DETECTIVE COMICS #33	75–100 with 7 NM	3 (all high grade)	£19,000–£24,000
15	ADVENTURE COMICS #40	50–60 with 1 NM	2 (in varying grades)	£18,350–£23,350
15	ALL STAR COMICS #3	150–175 with 6 NM	5 (2 in high grade, 2 restored and 1 in low grade)	£18,350–£23,350
17	DETECTIVE COMICS #38	80–100 with 9 NM	4 (in varying grades)	£16,675–£21,675
18	CAPTAIN MARVEL ADVENTURES #1	130–150 with 3 NM	1 (grade not known)	£15,000–£20,000
19	DETECTIVE COMICS #29	75–100 with 6 NM	2 (both grades not known)	£12,350–£17,350
19	DETECTIVE COMICS #31	75–100 with 6 NM	5 (2 in high grade, 3 not known)	£12,350–£17,350

From last year's chart, there have been rises in position for Action Comics #1 over Detective Comics #27 for the coveted position of Most Valuable Comic and that trend may well continue for the next few years. Batman #1 and Whiz #1 overtake All American #16. More Fun #53 and Detective #33 overtake Adventure Comics #40. Detective Comics #29 and #31 assume the same pricing and position.

It will be noticed that the value range is very generous with an upper limit of the Guide price in this book. While it is very likely that an individual may reasonably expect to pay more than the Guide price stated, one must take into consideration the size of the market in the U.K. for this sort of material and that deals and discounts would be expected by a purchaser with serious money. The market in the U.K.for these books is almost exclusively driven by the U.S market and as such the popularity of books may differ. For example, Adventure Comics #40 is not such a popular Wants List item in the U.K. as it may be in the U.S. so it's actual market value in the U.K. may be less than the figure stated. Please note that the numbers of copies known in the U.K. are known to myself personally. There may be others around yet to be documented. The high grade copies known to me are a mixture of unrestored and restored copies. THE VALUES GIVEN ARE FOR UNRESTORED COPIES ONLY. RESTORED COPIES WOULD BE LESS VALUABLE, DEPENDING ON THE AMOUNT OF RESTORATION AND (INCREASINGLY NOW) THE PERSON RESPONSIBLE FOR THAT RESTORATION AND THE DOCUMENTATION THAT GOES WITH THE COMIC. A RESTORED COMIC WITHOUT DOCUMENTATION WOULD OBVIOUSLY BE LESS VALUABLE. We are in the process of putting together a Restoration Guide for key books which will feature in the next U.K. Price Guide.

It is important to remember that values are calculated on the basis of known availability should anyone suddenly decide to invest that sort of money and the very rare actual sale. Necessarily there are very few known collectors aspiring to such heights at this present time so such prices may be treated with due consideration.

With the number of these key Golden Age comics being professionally (and unprofessionally!) restored, the unrestored comic will advance into a super-league of its own.

THIS GOES TO SHOW THAT WHAT MAKES A COMIC VALUABLE APART FROM CONDITION IS THE FACTOR OF THE FAME OF THE CHARACTER COUPLED WITH RARITY AS SECONDARY. DETECTIVE #27 SHOWS THAT COMICS DO NOT NECESSARILY NEED TO BE FIRST ISSUES THOUGH THIS IS A CONTRIBUTORY FACTOR. IN ANY EVENT SUCH COMICS ARE HIGHLY PRIZED AS REMARKABLE PIECES OF POPULAR ART AND CULTURAL CONSCIOUSNESS AND ONE HOPES THAT THEY WILL BE DULY LOOKED AFTER FOR FUTURE GENERATIONS TO ENJOY.

UNDER-VALUED COMICS

Dave Finn of Incognito Comics

Listed here are a few personal thoughts on the current and anticipated value of selected comics that have come to mind in the last year. They are in no particular order of preference or value.

GOLDEN AGE AND POST GOLDEN AGE COMICS

MASK COMICS 2 (Rural Home Publications)

Much scarcer than issue 1, sporting possibly on of the best L. B. Cole covers ever. A steal at current Guide prices, and up til now only increasing modestly in price each year.

SPECIAL EDITION COMICS (Fawcett)

This is a pre-issue 1 Captain Marvel Adventures by any other name, but due to editorial shenanigans, it was published with no number, and was consequently followed by a regular issue 1. Special Edition Comics currently guides almost a quarter of Captain Marvel Adventures 1. Surely it should be on a more level price pegging?

ALL-WINNERS COMICS 19 (Timely)

The scarce first appearance of the All-Winners Squad. Very scarce, very sought after and very under-valued. Interest is increasing, as will the price on this key issue.

FLASH COMICS 104 (DC)

The last in the original Flash series, and probably the rarest. Prices are high on this one, but demand continues to outstrip availability. Issues 100 to 103 are cheaper, but are just as rare.

DETECTIVE COMICS 8 (DC)

All of the pre-Batman Detective Comics are undervalued, except perhaps Detective Comics 1. I've highlighted issue 8, as its Mr Chang cover is copied almost exactly on the cover of Atomic Comics 1 (Green Publishing), eight years later in 1945.

MARVEL MYSTERY COMICS (ANNUAL?) (Timely)

Presumed as an Annual, but not numbered. Only three copies of this comic are known to exist. The contents are three previously released comics in a 132 page squarebound comic. Most Timely collectors will never even see, let alone own, one of these! A super Schomberg cover from Marvel Mystery Comics 33 adds to the desirability.

SILVER AGE COMICS

BATMAN 181

First appearance of Poison Ivy. Currently eight times cheaper than Batman 171 (the first Silver Age appearance of The Riddler). With Poison Ivy scheduled for the new Batman and Robin movie, watch for demand, and price to rice. Copies should contain a bound-in poster.

BATMAN 121

First appearance of Mr Zero (Mr Freeze). A scarce comic at the best of times. Once more, demand will certainly increase when Arnie plays this character in the new Bat-film.

SHOWCASE 17

First appearance of Adam Strange. There has definitely been an increase in interest in science-fiction comics in the last year or so. This comic in high-grade, without colour touch to its black cover is a very scarce item.

HOUSE OF SECRETS 1 (NPP/DC)

Just inside the Silver Age, this comic is rarely seen in the UK. Mystery and suspense comics, like the sci-fi books are increasingly in demand.

AMAZING SPIDERMAN 18 (Marvel)

Scarcer than you think in the UK. Most copies seen in the UK have come from the States in the last few years. Cameo appearances galore and the first appearance of Ned Leeds (who becomes the Hobgoblin) increase the interest. Most copies found will be cents copies.

Special Edition Comics #1 | All-Winners Comics #19 | Flash Comics # 104

BRONZE AGE COMICS

SUPERMAN'S PAL JIMMY OLSEN 134 (DC)

First appearance of Darkseid, one of Kirby's and DC's greatest villains.

GIANT SIZE X-MEN 1 (Marvel)

First appearance of the new X-Men team. We are asked for more copies of this comic in NM than any other. Demand is very, very high, and this has been reflected in rising prices. Copies with a truly "square" squarebound spine and a bright white cover are extremely rare. This has been reflected in a large price increase recently.

FANTASTIC FOUR 112 (Marvel)

One of the finest Marvel covers of the time, and they had to make the background black! This comic is incredibly rare in VF+ or better, without a single spine stress mark. We managed to obtain a pence copy in NM, which sold very quickly to a collector who normally would only buy cents copies!

MODERN COMICS

CEREBUS 1

Grossly undervalued. Only 2000 of these were ever printed. One of the scarcest and most popular Indies.

STAR WARS DROIDS AND EWOKS COMICS

From the Marvel Star Comics kiddies imprint. A completist's nightmare. Guiding last year at 60p and 50p respectively, these elusive items sold well at four times last year's Guide price – a whopping £2 each!

MARS ATTACKS (Topps)

All series. It's another film tie-in causing an increase in demand. Tim Burton's new movie is creating great interest in these issues.

GRENDEL

Devil's Vagary (from the Comico Collection slipcase). Another very tricky book to obtain.

Detective Comics # 8

Marvel Mystery Comics Annual

Showcase # 17

Amazing Spiderman # 18

Fantastic Four# 112

Cerebus The Aardvark # 1

EARLY WORKS OF ARTISTS

Below is a Work-in-progress list of the early works of 16 of the hottest artists currently working in the comics industry. The first five entries for all the artists have been placed in chronological order with the remaining entries in ALPHABETICAL ORDER ONLY. When time permits all will be put into order to illustrate their developing technique.

1 JOHN BYRNE

1 **FLINTSTONES (2nd Series) ....37 (1st Professional Work)**
2 **E-MAN (1st Series) 6,7**
3 **DRACULA GIANT SIZE.....5 (1st Work for Marvel)**
4 **E-MAN (1st Series).......................................9**
5 **DOOMSDAY PLUS ONE....................................1**
6 ACTION COMICS 584-600
7 ALPHA FLIGHT 1-28
8 ART OF JOHN BYRNE ....nn
9 ATOM, POWER OF THE 6
10 AVENGERS, THE 164-166,181-191,233
11 AVENGERS ANNUAL, THE ....13 (inks)
12 BATMAN...400 (1 page only)
13 BATMAN 3-D GRAPHIC ALBUM ....nn
14 BATMAN: UNTOLD LEGEND OF THE 1
15 BIG BYRNE BOOK..nn
16 BIZZARE ADVENTURES 31
17 CAPTAIN AMERICA 247-255,350
18 CHRISTMAS WITH THE SUPER-HEROES 2
19 CHAMPIONS, THE...11-15, 17 (inks)
20 CHARLTON BULLSEYE...1,2,4,5
21 CLASSIC X-MEN 15-47
22 CRAZY (2nd Series)...88
23 CRITICAL ERROR 1
24 DAREDEVIL...138
25 DARK HORSE PRESENTS.......................................54-57
26 DANGER UNLIMITED..1-4
27 DOOMSDAY PLUS ONE 2-12
28 DOOMSDAY SQUAD 1-7
29 E-MAN (1st Series) 10
30 E-MAN 2nd Series...................................1 (1 page Byrne)
31 EMERGENCY (2nd Series)..1
32 FANTASTIC FOUR........209-218,220,221,232-293,358 (Pin-up)
33 FANTASTIC FOUR ANNUAL..17-19
34 FANTASTIC FOUR ROAST 1
35 FANTASTIC FOUR SPECIAL EDITION 1
36 FLINTSTONES (2nd Series) 42
37 GHOST RIDER (1st Series) 20
38 GREEN LANTERN CORPS ANNUAL 3
39 GREEN LANTERN: GANTHET'S TALE 1
40 HERBIE (2nd Series)..2-5
41 HEROES FOR HOPE STARRING THE X-MEN ....nn
42 HOT AND COLD HEROES 1
43 HOWARD THE DUCK (2nd Series)..................7 (1 page Byrne)
44 HULK (2nd Series) ....314-319,393 (contains Byrne Hulk in flashback)
45 HULK ANNUAL (2nd Series) 7
46 INDIANA JONES, FURTHER ADVENTURES OF 1,2
47 IRON FIST..1-15
48 IRON MAN 118
49 IRON MAN ANNUAL ....10 (Pin-up)
50 JOHN BYRNE'S 2112 GRAPHIC NOVEL................................nn
51 JUDGE DREDD'S CRIME FILES 1
52 LEGENDS (Limited Series) 1-6
53 MAN OF STEEL 1-6
54 MARVEL CHILLERS 6
55 MARVEL COMICS PRESENTS 18,79
56 MARVEL FANFARE.......................................29,45 (Pin up),48
57 MARVEL PREMIERE 25,47,48
58 MARVEL PREVIEW 11
59 MARVEL SAGA, THE 3
60 MARVEL TALES 193-198,201-208
61 MARVEL TEAM UP 53-55,59-70,75,79,100
62 MARVEL TWO-IN-ONE 43,50,53-55
63 MARVEL YEAR IN REVIEW 2
64 NAMOR, THE SUB-MARINER..1-25
65 NEW MUTANTS...75
66 NEW TEEN TITANS ANNUAL (2nd Series).................................2
67 NEXT MEN..0 -present
68 OMAC (2nd Series) 1-4
69 OUTSIDERS, THE...11
70 PHOENIX - THE UNTOLD STORY 1
71 POWERMAN 48-50
72 PREVIEWS 3rd Series ....1 -present
73 ROG 2000, THE COMPLETE...nn
74 ROM...74 (inks)
75 SAN DIEGO CONVENTION COMIC ART ....1992 nn
76 SECRET ORIGINS ANNUAL..1
77 SHE HULK, THE SENSATION..........................1-8,31-46,48-50
78 SHE HULK TRADE PAPERBACK...nn

79 SILVER SURFER (2nd Series)..........1
80 SPACE 1999..........3-7
81 SPECTACULAR SPIDERMAN..........58
82 SPIDERMAN, THE AMAZING..........189,190,206
83 SPIDERMAN, THE AMAZING ANNUAL..........13
84 SPIRIT MAGAZINE, THE..........30
85 STAR BRAND, THE..........10-19
86 STARLORD, THE SPECIAL EDITION..........1
87 SUPERMAN (1st Series)..........400 (1 page only)
88 SUPERMAN (2nd Series)..........1-17,19-22,50 (Co-artist)
89 SUPERMAN ANNUAL (2nd Series)..........2
90 SUPERMAN ANNUAL, THE ADVENTURES OF..........2
91 SUPER VILLAIN CLASSICS..........1
92 THING, THE..........2 (inks),7
93 WEST COAST AVENGERS..........42-57
94 WEST COAST AVENGERS ANNUAL..........4
95 WHAT IF...? (1st Series)..........36
96 WHAT THE -?!..........2,6
97 WHEELIE AND THE CHOPPER BUNCH..........1-7
98 WOLVERINE..........17-23 (Co-artist)
99 X-FACTOR ANNUAL..........4
100 X-MEN, THE UNCANNY..........108,109,111-143,273 (Co-artist)
101 X-MEN, THE UNCANNY ANNUAL..........3 (1 page only)

2 GREG CAPULLO

1 **GORE SHRIEK ....4 (1st published work ?)**
2 **AVENGERS SPOTLIGHT 39**
3 **DAREDEVIL 286**
4 **WHAT IF (2nd Series) 2**
5 **WHAT IF (2nd Series) 8**
6 Angela..........1-3
7 Beck & Caul..........4 (cover art only)
8 Cyberforce Universe..........1 (Pin-up only)
9 Deathmate..........Black
10 Endless Gallery, The..........1 (Pin-up only)
11 Evil Ernie..........0 (cover art only)
12 Fantastic Four Annual..........23
13 Impossible Man Summer Fun Special..........1
14 Lynch Mob..........1-4 (cover art only)
15 Magneto..........0 (Pin-up only)
16 Quasar..........18-25
17 Quasar..........27-29, 31-32, 35-38
18 Quasar..........30, 33-34 (cover art only)
19 Rack & Pain..........1-4 (cover art only)
20 Spawn..........16-20
21 Spawn..........23-24, 26-37, 39, 41, 43
22 Stryfe's Strike File..........1
23 Taboo..........8
24 Violator..........2 (Pin-up only)
25 Violator..........3
26 What If (2nd Series)..........15 cover art only
27 X-Force..........14 cover art only
28 X-Force..........15-25
29 X-Force..........26-27 cover art only
30 X-Men Unlimited..........1 Pin-up only

3 GARY FRANK

1 **TOXIC! ....19 (cover art only/1st published work ?)**
2 **TOXIC! ....22 (cover art only)**
3 **TOXIC! 25**
4 **OVERKILL 1**
5 **HULK, THE INCREDIBLE ....400 (Pin-up only)**
6 Batman: Dark Knight Gallery..........1 (Pin-up only)
7 Black Canary..........1
8 Bullets and Bracelets..........1
9 Codename Genetix..........4 (cover art only)
10 Dark Angel..........6
11 Deaths Head, the Incomplete..........2 (cover art only)
12 Deaths Head, the Incomplete..........11 (cover art only)
13 Doctor Strange..........82
14 Godwheel..........1
15 Hulk, The Incredible..........401-402 (cover art only)
16 Hulk, The Incredible..........403-411
17 Hulk, The Incredible..........413-414
18 Hulk, The Incredible..........416-418
19 Hulk, The Incredible..........420-423
20 Hulk, The Incredible..........425
21 Marvel Swimsuit Special..........1995 (Pin-up only)
22 Motormouth..........1-4
23 Motormouth..........6
24 Sabretooth Special..........1
25 Stormwatch..........15-16 (Pin-up only)
26 Ultraverse: Year Two..........(cover art only)
27 What If (2nd Series)..........80 (cover art only)
28 WildC.A.T.S. Sorcebook..........1-2 (Pin-up only)
29 X-Men: Prime..........1

4 TRENT KANIUGA

1 **HALL OF HEROES ....1 (1st published work ?)**
2 **CREED ....1 (1st Series)**
3 **BLOODFIRE/HELLINA 1**
..........(Variant Cover/cover art only
4 **DEADBOLT 1**
5 **HELLINA: WICKED WAYS 1**
6 Creed..........1-present

7 Catfight: Dream Warrior ....1 (cover art only)
8 Minotaur ....1 (cover art only)
9 Snowman ....1 (Pin-up only)

5 SAM KIETH

1 **COMICO PRIMER ....4 (1st Professional Work)**
2 **MAGE ....6-15 (inks)**
3 **ADOLESCENT RADIOACTIVE BLACKBELT HAMSTERS 6-9**
4 **TARGET AIRBOY 1**
5 **MANHUNTER (DC) ....1-3 (inks)**
6 ALIENS: EARTH WAR 1-4
7 CRITTERS 8
8 DARKER IMAGE 1
9 EPICURUS THE SAGE 1,2
10 G.I. JOE ....120 (Art on G.I.Joe Dossier)
11 HULK (2nd Series) 368
12 I BEFORE E 1
13 MARVEL COMICS PRESENTS 85-92,100,117-122
14 MARVEL SUPERHEROES 1992 HOLIDAY SPECIAL 1
15 MAXX 1-present
16 MR. MONSTER ATTACKS 1,2
17 RAW MEDIA MAGS 1
18 ROBOTECH: THE NEW GENERATION ....5 (inks)
19 SANDMAN (2nd Series) 1-5
20 SECRET ORIGINS SPECIAL 1
21 WOLVERINE: MARVEL COLLECTOR'S EDITION 1

6 DALE KEOWN

1 **SAMURAI (1st Series) ....13-16 ....(1st Professional work)**
2 **DRAGONRING (2nd Series) 9,13,15**
3 **DRAGONFORCE 1-13**
4 **WARLOCK ....5 (1st Series)16,17**
5 **NTH MAN ....8 (1st Work for Marvel)**
6 DRAGONFORCE CHRONICLES 1-5
7 HULK (2nd Series) ....367 (1st work on Hulk)
8 HULK (2nd Series) 369-377,379,381-388,390-393,395-398,400
9 PITT 1-present
10 YOUNGBLOOD 4

7 ERIK LARSEN

1 **MEGATON ....1-4 ....(1st Professional Work /black and white)**
2 **FEM FORCE 6**
3 **DNAGENTS, THE NEW 13-16**
4 **SPIDERMAN, THE AMAZING ....287 ....(1st work on Spiderman, 1st Marvel art)**
5 **SECRET ORIGINS (2nd Series) 13**
6 CHAMPIONS (2nd Series) 1
7 DOOM PATROL (2nd Series) 6-15
8 DOOM PATROL/SUICIDE SQUAD SPECIAL 1
9 EXCALIBUR: AIR APPARENT 1
10 MARVEL COMICS PRESENTS 1-38,48-50
11 OUTSIDERS 27-28
12 PUNISHER 21-25
13 SAVAGE DRAGON 1-4
14 SAVAGE DRAGON (ongoing) 1-4
15 SAVAGE DRAGON VS SAVAGE MEGATON MAN 1
16 SPIDERMAN (2nd Series) 15,18-23
17 SPIDERMAN, THE AMAZING 324,327,329-344,346-350
18 TEEN TITANS SPOTLIGHT 10,15
19 THOR 385
20 WHAT THE -?! 5

8 JIM LEE

1 **SAMURAI SANTA ....1 (1st Professional Work?)**
2 **ALPHA FLIGHT ....51 1st Professional Work for Marvel**
3 **SOLO AVENGERS ....1 (2nd Work for Marvel)**
4 **ALPHA FLIGHT 53,55-62,64**
5 **PUNISHER WAR JOURNAL 1-12**
6 CLASSIC X-MEN ....39 (2nd work on X-Men)
7 DAREDEVIL ANNUAL ....4 (2nd 4 produced)
8 DARKER IMAGE 1
9 DEATHBLOW 1-3
10 DEATHMATE PROLOGUE
11 DEATHMATE BLACK
12 MARVEL COMICS PRESENTS 33
13 MARVEL ILLUSTRATED SWIMSUIT SPECIAL ....nn (Pin-up only)
14 MARVEL UNIVERSE (2nd Series) ....17 (Illustration only)
15 PUNISHER ANNUAL 2
16 PUNISHER WAR JOURNAL 17-19
17 ST. GEORGE 8
18 WHAT THE -?! 5
19 WILDCATS ....0 (Sold Together with the WildC.A.T.S TPB)
20 WILDC.A.T.S 1-4

21 WILDC.A.T.S 1-present
22 X-MEN, THE UNCANNY 248,256-258,267-278,286
23 X-MEN (2nd Series) 1-11
24 X-MAN ANNUAL (2nd Series) 1

9 ROB LIEFELD

1 MEGATON EXPLOSION 1
1st Work (college magazine)
2 MEGATON 5,8
3 EX-MUTANTS SHATTERED EARTH 4,5
4 WARLORD....................131 (1st Work for DC)
5 HAWK AND DOVE MINI 1-5
6 BRIGADE ....1 (inks)
7 DARKER IMAGE 1-present
8 MARVEL COMICS PRESENTS 51-53
9 MARVEL COMICS PRESENTS 85,86
10 MARVEL UNIVERSE (2nd Series) ....20 (Illustration only)
11 NEW MUTANTS 87-91,93-96,98-100
12 NEW MUTANTS ANNUAL ....5, 7 (pin-up)
13 SECRET ORIGINS (2nd Series) 28
14 SPIDERMAN, THE AMAZING ANNUAL 23
15 SUPREME ....1,2 (inks)
16 WHAT IF...? (2nd Series) 7
17 X-FORCE 1-9
18 X-FACTOR ....40 (1st work for Marvel)
19 X-MEN, THE UNCANNY ....245 (1st work on X-Men)
20 YOUNGBLOOD 0-4

10 JOSEPH MICHAEL LINSNER

1 CONTINUM ....1 (1st published work ?)
2 CRY FOR DAWN 1
3 CRY FOR DAWN 2
4 CRY FOR DAWN 3
5 CRY FOR DAWN ....4 (cover art only)
6 Amazing Heroes Swimsuit ....5 (cover art only)
7 Angry Christ Comics ....1 (trade paperback)
8 Coven of Angels ....1 (cover art only)
9 Cadillacs and Dinosaurs: The Wild Ones ..1-3 (cover art only)
10 Coven of Angels ....1 (cover art only)
11 Cry for Dawn 5-9
12 Crypt of Dawn 1
13 Dark Fantasies ....1 (cover art only)
14 Dracula Chronicles ....1-3 (cover art only)
15 Dawn ....½
16 Dawn 1-5
17 Drama 1
18 Deadworld: Necropolis ....1 (cover art only)
19 Eleven or One 1
20 Fang ....1 (cover inks only)
21 Girlie Show ....1 (Pin-ups only)
22 Justice League Quarterly ....13 (cover art only)
23 Lady Death & the Women of Chaos Galary 1.......(Pin-up only)
24 Lady Death in Lingerie ....(1 Pin-up only)
25 Paradox ....1 (cover art only)
26 Poison Elves ....1 (cover art only)
27 Razor ....½ (cover art only)
28 Razor ....5 (cover art only)
29 Razor & Shi Special ....1 (cover art only)
30 Razor Swimsuit Special ....(Pin-up only)
31 Razor; the Suffering ....1-2 (cover art only)
32 Safety Belt Man ....4 (backup)
33 Subtle Violents 1
34 Tears of Dawn ....1 (Signed & Numbered Ltd. Edition)
35 Utterly Strange Stories 1
36 Villain & Hero 1
37 Zorro (Topps) ....11 (cover art only)

11 TODD MCFARLANE

1 COYOTE ....11-13 (1st Professional work)
2 INFINITY INC. ....14-16 (1st Work for DC)
3 ALL STAR SQUADRON 47
4 INFINTY INC. 17-21
5 INFINITY INC. ANNUAL....................1
6 BATMAN/SPAWN ....nn
7 BORN TO BE WILD 1
8 DAREDEVIL 241
9 DETECTIVE COMICS 576-578
10 G.I. JOE 60
11 HULK (2nd Series) 330-334,336-345
12 INDIANA JONES AND THE LAST CRUSADE 2
13 INFINITY INC. 22-37
14 INVASION 1-2
15 'MAZING MAN SPECIAL 3
16 SPAWN 1-15, 21-present
17 SPECTACULAR SPIDERMAN ANNUAL 9,10
18 SPIDERMAN (2nd Series) 1-16
19 SPIDERMAN, THE AMAZING 298-323,325,328
20 SPITFIRE AND THE TROUBLESHOOTERS 4
21 WHAT THE -?! 3

12 GEORGE PEREZ

1 **ASTONISHING TALES..25 (1st Professional work)**
2 **CREATURES ON THE LOOSE .....33 (1st Full work)**
3 **CREATURES ON THE LOOSE34,35,36-37 (Co-artist)**
4 **AVENGERS..141-144**
5 **AVENGERS 147-151**
6 ACTION COMICS 600,643-645,647-652
7 ACTION COMICS ANNUAL..2
8 ADVENTURES OF SUPERMAN 462
9 ALIEN WORLDS (1st Series)..7
10 ALIEN WORLDS (2nd Series) 1
11 ALL STAR SQUADRON ANNUAL ....3 (Co-artist)
12 AVENGERS, THE
...............154,155,160-162,167,168,171,172,194-196,198-202
13 AVENGERS ANNUAL, THE..6,8
14 BATMAN AND OTHER DC CLASSICS....................................1
15 BEST OF DC, THE 24
16 CRISIS ON INFINITE EARTHS 1-12
17 DC COMICS PRESENTS 26,61
18 DEADLY HANDS OF KUNG-FU 6-8,12,19-21,30
19 FANTASTIC FOUR.........164-167,170-172,176-178,184-188,191,192
20 FANTASTIC FOUR ANNUAL..14
21 FLASH (1st Series)................................289 (1st work for DC)
22 FLASH (1st Series)............................290-293 (Back-ups only)
23 HEROES AGAINST HUNGER ....1 (2pgs only)
24 HISTORY OF THE DC UNIVERSE 1,2
25 HULK: FUTURE IMPERFECT..1,2
26 INFINTY GAUNTLET.......................................1-3,4 (Co-artist)
27 INHUMANS 1-4,8
28 JUSTICE LEAGUE OF AMERICA.............184,185,192-197,200
29 LOGANS RUN (Marvel)..1-5
30 MARVEL COMICS SUPER SPECIAL..4
31 MARVEL FANFARE..10-13
32 MARVEL ILLUSTRATED SWIMSUIT SPECIAL..nn (Pin-up only)
33 MARVEL PREMIERE 45,46
34 MARVEL PREVIEW ....12 (2 pages)
35 MARVEL TWO-IN-ONE...................................56-58,60,63-65
36 NEW TEEN TITANS................................1-4,6-34,37-47,49-50
37 NEW TEEN TITANS (2nd Series) 1-5,50-61
38 NEW TEEN TITANS ANNUAL 1,2
39 NEW TEEN TITANS DRUG AWARENESS CAMPAIGN ....nn (1)
40 POWERMAN 27
41 SECRET ORIGINS (2nd Series) 50
42 SECRET ORIGINS ANNUAL (2nd Series) 3
43 TALES OF THE TEEN TITANS 1-4
44 WALLY WOOD'S THUNDER AGENTS.............................1,2,4
45 WONDER WOMAN (2nd Series) 1-24
46 WONDER WOMAN ANNUAL (2nd Series)............................1
47 WORLD'S FINEST COMICS ....300 (Co-artist)
48 X-MEN, THE UNCANNY ANNUAL..3

13 STEVEN PLATT

1 **AGENT THREE ZERO 1.....(1st Professional Work)**
2 **MOON KNIGHT..55**
3 **MOON KNIGHT..56**
4 **MOON KNIGHT..57**
5 **MOON KNIGHT.......................58 (cover only)**
6 MOON KNIGHT...59 (cover only)
7 MOON KNIGHT 60
8 PROPHET ....4A (cover only)
9 PROPHET 5
10 SUPREME ....25 (cover only)

14 WHILCE PORTACIO

1 **ALIEN LEGION...6-8 (inks/1st Professional Work)**
2 **LONGSHOT....................................1-6 (inks)**
3 **STAR WARS ....107 (Co-artist)**
4 **STRIKEFORCE MORITURI 10**
5 **STRIKEFORCE MORITURI 16**
6 ALPHA FLIGHT ....39-46 (inks), 47 (Co-inks), 49 (inks),
....50 (Co-artist), 51-54 (inks)
7 DAREDEVIL ANNUAL.................................4 (2nd 4 produced)
8 LEGION OF THE NIGHT 1,2
9 PUNISHER..8-18
10 POWER PACK 46
11 WETWORKS 1-present
12 WHAT THE -?! 5
13 X-FACTOR..63-69
14 X-MEN, THE UNCANNY ....201 (1st work on X-Men)
15 X-MEN, THE UNCANNY 281-286,289,290

15 JOE QUESADA

1 **SPELLJAMER COMICS 8-13**
2 **RAY...............................1-6 (6 layouts only)**
3 **BATMAN: SWORD OF AZRAEL......................1-3**
4 **SLEEPWALKER 12**
5 **SAN DIEGO CONVENTION COMIC ART 1992 .....nn**
6 CRUCIBLE 1,2
7 DEATHMATE EPILOGUE 6
8 NINJAK..1-3
9 X-FACTOR 87-present
10 X-FACTOR ANNUAL..7

Top 100 Best Selling Comics 1996

1 DC VS MARVEL #1
2 X-MEN OMEGA
3 SPAWN #37
4 MUTANTS: THE AMAZING X-MEN #4
5 SPAWN #32
6 MUTANTS: THE ASTONISHING X-MEN #4
7 MUTANTS: THE AMAZING X-MEN #3
8 SPAWN #38
9 WEAPON X #4
10 MUTANTS: THE ASTONISHING X-MEN #3
11 MUTANTS: THE AMAZING X-MEN #2
12 MUTANTS: GENERATION NEXT #4
13 GEN 13 #6
14 MUTANTS: THE ASTONISHING X-MEN #2
15 SPAWN #36
16 MUTANTS: THE AMAZING X-MEN #1
17 WEAPON X #3
18 SPAWN #34
19 GAMBIT & THE X-TERNALS #4
20 WEAPON X #2
21 GEN 13 #1
22 SPAWN #35
23 MUTANTS: NEXT GENERATION #3
24 MUTANTS: THE ASTONISHING X-MEN #1
25 SPAWN: BLOOD FEUD #1
26 GAMBIT & THE X-TERNALS #3
27 X-MEN #42
28 FACTOR X #4
29 X-MAN #4
30 SPAWN #27
31 X-MEN #43
32 WEAPON X #1
33 GEN 13 #5
34 BATMAN: MAN-BAT #1
35 SPAWN #33
36 UNCANNY X-MEN #322
37 GEN 13 #4
38 GAMBIT & THE X-TERNALS #2
39 FACTOR X #3
40 MUTANTS: GENERATION NEXT #2
41 SUPERMAN #100 COLLECTORS' EDITION
42 X-MEN CHRONICLES #2
43 X-MEN PRIME #1
44 LADY DEATH: IN LINGERIE #1
45 SPAWN #31
46 X-MAN #3
47 SPAWN #28
48 GEN 13 #3
49 SPAWN: BLOOD FEUD #2
50 X-CALIBRE #4
51 X-CALIBRE #3
52 CYBLADE/SHI SPECIAL: BATTLE FOR INDEPENDENTS
53 SPAWN #30
54 MUTANTS: GENERATION NEXT #1
55 UNCANNY X-MEN #323
56 SPAWN #29
57 WOLVERINE #91
58 GEN 13 #2 - DIRECT MARKET
59 SPAWN: BLOOD FEUD #3
60 SPAWN: BLOOD FEUD #4
61 FACTOR X #2
62 X-MAN #2
63 X-CALIBRE #2
64 VIOLATOR/BADROCK #2
65 X-UNIVERSE #1
66 GAMBIT & THE X-TERNALS #1
67 SHI/CYBLADE SPECIAL #1
68 X-UNIVERSE #2
69 FACTOR X #1
70 GENERATION X #6
71 SUPERMAN: THE MAN OF STEEL #50
72 GENERATION X #5
73 SOVEREIGN SEVEN #1
74 X-MAN #5
75 X-MAN #1
76 X-MAN #6
77 AMAZING SPIDERMAN #400 ENHANCED
78 X-MEN CHRONICLES #1
79 WITCHBLADE #1
80 SUPERMAN #106
81 ADVENTURES OF SUPERMAN #529
82 X-CALIBRE #1
83 BATMAN #525
84 ANGELA #2
85 BATMAN #524
86 SUPERMAN #107
87 SOVEREIGN SEVEN #3
88 ACTION COMICS #715
89 LADY DEATH II #1
90 ADVENTURES OF SUPERMAN #530
91 ACTION COMICS #716
92 GREEN LANTERN/SILVER SURFER
93 X-FORCE #44
94 SUPERMAN: THE MAN OF STEEL #51
95 SPIDERMAN #61
96 GLORY/AVENGELYNE #1
97 BATMAN #526
98 DAWN #1
99 X-FACTOR #112
100 DETECTIVE COMICS #691

Top 100 U.K. DC Comics

Rank	Title	Price
1	ACTION COMICS #1	£113500.00
2	DETECTIVE COMICS #27	£106675.00
3	SUPERMAN (1st Series) (ADVENTURES OF SUPERMAN) #1	£80000.00
4	DETECTIVE COMICS #1	£53500.00
5	BATMAN #1	£45000.00
6	ALL-AMERICAN COMICS #16	£42500.00
7	MORE FUN COMICS #1	£40000.00
8	MORE FUN COMICS #52	£37350.00
9	FLASH COMICS #1	£35000.00
10	MORE FUN COMICS #53	£26700.00
11	DETECTIVE COMICS #33	£24000.00
12	ADVENTURE COMICS #40	£23350.00
	ALL-STAR COMICS #3	£23350.00
14	DETECTIVE COMICS #38	£21675.00
15	ALL-STAR COMICS #8	£20000.00
	MORE FUN COMICS #6	£20000.00
17	GREEN LANTERN (1st Series) #1	£19350.00
18	NEW YORK WORLD'S FAIR #1	£18750.00
19	SHOWCASE #4	£18700.00
20	MORE FUN COMICS #2	£18675.00
21	SENSATION COMICS #1	£18350.00
22	DETECTIVE COMICS #29	£17350.00
	DETECTIVE COMICS #31	£17350.00
24	ACTION COMICS #2	£16750.00
25	ADVENTURE COMICS #48	£15000.00
26	ADVENTURE COMICS #1	£13350.00
	WONDER WOMAN #1	£13350.00
28	DETECTIVE COMICS #2	£11700.00
29	DETECTIVE COMICS #28	£11675.00
30	ADVENTURE COMICS #73	£10500.00
31	NEW YORK WORLD'S FAIR #2	£10250.00
32	NEW BOOK OF COMICS #1	£10000.00
	SHOWCASE #8	£10000.00
34	WORLD'S FINEST COMICS (1st Series) #1	£9700.00
35	MORE FUN COMICS #3	£9350.00
	MORE FUN COMICS #4	£9350.00
	MORE FUN COMICS #5	£9350.00
	MORE FUN COMICS #73	£9350.00
39	ALL-AMERICAN COMICS #17	£9250.00
40	ALL-AMERICAN COMICS #19	£9250.00
41	MORE FUN COMICS #55	£9100.00
42	ACTION COMICS #3	£9000.00
43	ADVENTURE COMICS #61	£8350.00
	ALL-STAR COMICS #1	£8350.00
	DETECTIVE COMICS #3	£8350.00
46	ADVENTURE COMICS #72	£8250.00
	ALL-FLASH #1	£8250.00
49	BATMAN #2	£8000.00
	MORE FUN COMICS #14	£8000.00
50	SUPERMAN (1st Series) (ADVENTURES OF SUPERMAN) #2	£7350.00
51	ACTION COMICS #7	£7000.00
52	NEW BOOK OF COMICS #2	£6675.00
53	MORE FUN COMICS #54	£6500.00
54	ALL-AMERICAN COMICS #25	£6250.00
55	ACTION COMICS #10	£6000.00
	ADVENTURE COMICS #2	£6000.00
	ALL-AMERICAN COMICS #18	£6000.00
	COMIC CAVALCADE #1	£6000.00
	DETECTIVE COMICS #8	£6000.00
60	BATMAN #3	£5500.00
61	ACTION COMICS #4	£5350.00
	ACTION COMICS #5	£5350.00
	ACTION COMICS #6	£5350.00
	DETECTIVE COMICS #35	£5350.00
65	BATMAN #11	£5000.00
66	SUPERMAN (1st Series) (ADVENTURES OF SUPERMAN) #3	£4900.00
67	DETECTIVE COMICS #18	£4850.00
	MORE FUN COMICS #101	£4850.00
69	DETECTIVE COMICS #40	£4675.00
70	DETECTIVE COMICS #4	£4500.00
	DETECTIVE COMICS #5	£4500.00
	SUPERBOY #1	£4500.00
73	ACTION COMICS #8	£4350.00
	ACTION COMICS #9	£4350.00
	BATMAN #4	£4350.00
	FLASH COMICS #2	£4350.00
	FLASH COMICS #104	£4350.00
	GREEN LANTERN (1st Series) #2	£4350.00
79	MORE FUN COMICS #9	£4175.00
80	ACTION COMICS #23	£4000.00
	ADVENTURE COMICS #42	£4000.00
	ALL-AMERICAN COMICS #1	£4000.00
	DETECTIVE COMICS #20	£4000.00
	DETECTIVE COMICS #30	£4000.00
	DETECTIVE COMICS #32	£4000.00
	MORE FUN COMICS #7	£4000.00
	MORE FUN COMICS #56	£4000.00
88	MORE FUN COMICS #71	£3875.00
89	ADVENTURE COMICS #44	£3850.00
	DETECTIVE COMICS #36	£3850.00
91	DETECTIVE COMICS #37	£3800.00
92	SUPERMAN (1st Series) (ADVENTURES OF SUPERMAN) #4	£3750.00
93	BATMAN #16	£3675.00
	MORE FUN COMICS #8	£3675.00
	SHOWCASE #9	£3675.00
96	FLASH (1st Series) #105	£3600.00
97	DETECTIVE COMICS #10	£3500.00
	DETECTIVE COMICS #39	£3500.00
	DETECTIVE COMICS #225	£3500.00
	MORE FUN COMICS #51	£3500.00

Top 100 U.S. DC Comics

Rank	Title	Value
1	ACTION COMICS #1	$170000.00
2	DETECTIVE COMICS #27	$160000.00
3	SUPERMAN (1st Series) (ADVENTURES OF SUPERMAN) #1	$120000.00
4	DETECTIVE COMICS #1	$80000.00
5	BATMAN #1	$67500.00
6	ALL-AMERICAN COMICS #16	$62000.00
7	MORE FUN COMICS #1	$60000.00
8	MORE FUN COMICS #52	$56000.00
9	FLASH COMICS #1	$52500.00
10	MORE FUN COMICS #53	$40000.00
11	DETECTIVE COMICS #33	$36000.00
12	ALL-STAR COMICS #3	$35000.00
13	ADVENTURE COMICS #40	$35000.00
14	DETECTIVE COMICS #38	$32500.00
15	ALL-STAR COMICS #8	$30000.00
	MORE FUN COMICS #6	$30000.00
17	GREEN LANTERN (1st Series) #1	$29000.00
18	MORE FUN COMICS #2	$28000.00
	NEW YORK WORLD'S FAIR #1	$28000.00
	SHOWCASE #4	$28000.00
21	SENSATION COMICS #1	$27500.00
22	DETECTIVE COMICS #29	$26000.00
	DETECTIVE COMICS #31	$26000.00
24	ACTION COMICS #2	$25000.00
25	ADVENTURE COMICS #48	$22500.00
26	ADVENTURE COMICS #1	$20000.00
	WONDER WOMAN #1	$20000.00
28	DETECTIVE COMICS #2	$17500.00
29	DETECTIVE COMICS #28	$17500.00
30	NEW YORK WORLD'S FAIR #2	$15500.00
31	ADVENTURE COMICS #73	$15000.00
	NEW BOOK OF COMICS #1	$15000.00
	SHOWCASE #8	$15000.00
34	WORLD'S FINEST COMICS (1st Series) #1	$14500.00
35	ALL-AMERICAN COMICS #19	$14000.00
	MORE FUN COMICS #3	$14000.00
	MORE FUN COMICS #4	$14000.00
	MORE FUN COMICS #5	$14000.00
	MORE FUN COMICS #73	$14000.00
40	ALL-AMERICAN COMICS #17	$13750.00
41	MORE FUN COMICS #55	$13600.00
42	ACTION COMICS #3	$13500.00
43	ADVENTURE COMICS #61	$12500.00
	ALL-FLASH #1	$12500.00
	ALL-STAR COMICS #1	$12500.00
	DETECTIVE COMICS #3	$12500.00
47	ADVENTURE COMICS #72	$12000.00
	BATMAN #2	$12000.00
	MORE FUN COMICS #14	$12000.00
50	SUPERMAN (1st Series) (ADVENTURES OF SUPERMAN) #2	$11000.00
51	ACTION COMICS #7	$10500.00
52	NEW BOOK OF COMICS #2	$10000.00
53	MORE FUN COMICS #54	$9750.00
54	ALL-AMERICAN COMICS #25	$9250.00
55	ACTION COMICS #10	$9000.00
	ADVENTURE COMICS #2	$9000.00
	ALL-AMERICAN COMICS #18	$9000.00
	COMIC CAVALCADE #1	$9000.00
	DETECTIVE COMICS #8	$9000.00
60	BATMAN #3	$8250.00
61	ACTION COMICS #4	$8000.00
	ACTION COMICS #5	$8000.00
	ACTION COMICS #6	$8000.00
	DETECTIVE COMICS #35	$8000.00
65	BATMAN #11	$7500.00
66	SUPERMAN (1st Series) (ADVENTURES OF SUPERMAN) #3	$7350.00
67	MORE FUN COMICS #18	$7250.00
	DETECTIVE COMICS #101	$7250.00
69	DETECTIVE COMICS #40	$7000.00
70	DETECTIVE COMICS #4	$6750.00
	DETECTIVE COMICS #5	$6750.00
	SUPERBOY #1	$6750.00
73	ACTION COMICS #8	$6500.00
	ACTION COMICS #9	$6500.00
	BATMAN #4	$6500.00
	FLASH COMICS #2	$6500.00
	FLASH COMICS #104	$6500.00
	GREEN LANTERN (1st Series) #2	$6500.00
79	MORE FUN COMICS #9	$6250.00
80	ACTION COMICS #23	$6000.00
	ADVENTURE COMICS #42	$6000.00
	ALL-AMERICAN COMICS #1	$6000.00
	DETECTIVE COMICS #20	$6000.00
	DETECTIVE COMICS #30	$6000.00
	DETECTIVE COMICS #32	$6000.00
	FLASH (1st Series) #105	$6000.00
	MORE FUN COMICS #7	$6000.00
	MORE FUN COMICS #56	$6000.00
89	MORE FUN COMICS #71	$5800.00
90	ADVENTURE COMICS #44	$5750.00
	DETECTIVE COMICS #36	$5750.00
92	DETECTIVE COMICS #37	$5700.00
93	SUPERMAN (1st Series) (ADVENTURES OF SUPERMAN) #4	$5600.00
94	BATMAN #16	$5500.00
	MORE FUN COMICS #8	$5500.00
	SHOWCASE #9	$5500.00
97	BRAVE AND THE BOLD, THE #28	$5250.00
	DETECTIVE COMICS #39	$5250.00
	DETECTIVE COMICS #225	$5250.00
	MORE FUN COMICS #51	$5250.00

Top 100 U.K. Marvel Comics

Rank	Title	Price
1	MARVEL COMICS #1	£65000.00
2	CAPTAIN AMERICA COMICS #1	£41675.00
3	HUMAN TORCH (1st Series) #2	£16000.00
	MARVEL COMICS #2	£16000.00
	SUB-MARINER (1st) COMICS #1	£16000.00
6	AMAZING FANTASY #15	£15000.00
7	MARVEL COMICS #9	£13350.00
8	AMAZING SPIDERMAN, THE #1	£12000.00
9	FANTASTIC FOUR #1	£11000.00
10	MARVEL COMICS #5	£10000.00
11	CAPTAIN AMERICA COMICS #22	£8500.00
12	CAPTAIN AMERICA COMICS #2	£7675.00
13	INCREDIBLE HULK (1st Series) #1	£7000.00
14	MARVEL COMICS #3	£6675.00
15	CAPTAIN AMERICA COMICS #3	£6350.00
16	MARVEL COMICS #8	£6000.00
17	MARVEL COMICS #4	£5350.00
18	MARVEL COMICS #10	£4175.00
19	MARVEL COMICS #6	£3675.00
	MARVEL COMICS #7	£3675.00
21	CAPTAIN AMERICA COMICS #4	£3500.00
	CAPTAIN AMERICA COMICS #7	£3500.00
23	CAPTAIN AMERICA COMICS #5	£3350.00
	SUB-MARINER (1st) COMICS #2	£3350.00
25	X-MEN, THE UNCANNY #1	£3250.00
26	HUMAN TORCH (1st Series) #3	£3170.00
27	CAPTAIN AMERICA COMICS #6	£3000.00
28	JOURNEY INTO MYSTERY #83	£2950.00
29	HUMAN TORCH (1st Series) #5	£2750.00
30	MARVEL COMICS #13	£2675.00
31	TALES OF SUSPENSE (1st Series) #39	£2600.00
32	CAPTAIN AMERICA COMICS #8	£2550.00
	CAPTAIN AMERICA COMICS #9	£2550.00
	CAPTAIN AMERICA COMICS #10	£2550.00
35	HUMAN TORCH (1st Series) #4	£2500.00
	TALES TO ASTONISH (1st Series) #27	£2500.00
37	CAPTAIN AMERICA COMICS #16	£2350.00
	MARVEL COMICS #12	£2350.00
39	CAPTAIN AMERICA COMICS #74	£2175.00
40	CAPTAIN AMERICA COMICS #11	£2150.00
	FANTASTIC FOUR #2	£2150.00
	SUB-MARINER (1st) COMICS #3	£2150.00
43	CAPTAIN AMERICA COMICS #12	£2000.00
	CAPTAIN AMERICA COMICS #13	£2000.00
45	HUMAN TORCH (1st Series) #5	£1950.00
46	HUMAN TORCH (1st Series) #8	£1875.00
	MARVEL COMICS #11	£1875.00
	SUB-MARINER (1st) COMICS #4	£1875.00
49	CAPTAIN AMERICA COMICS #14	£1850.00
	CAPTAIN AMERICA COMICS #15	£1850.00
51	FANTASTIC FOUR #5	£1750.00
	INCREDIBLE HULK (1st Series) #2	£1750.00
	JOURNEY INTO MYSTERY #1	£1750.00
54	AMAZING SPIDERMAN, THE #2	£1700.00
55	FANTASTIC FOUR #4	£1650.00
56	CAPTAIN AMERICA COMICS #17	£1600.00
	CAPTAIN AMERICA COMICS #59	£1600.00
58	HUMAN TORCH (1st Series) #10	£1575.00
	STRANGE TALES (1st Series) #1	£1575.00
60	AVENGERS #1	£1500.00
	CAPTAIN AMERICA COMICS #36	£1500.00
	MARVEL COMICS #92	£1500.00
63	MARVEL COMICS #17	£1475.00
64	DAREDEVIL #1	£1400.00
65	FANTASTIC FOUR #3	£1350.00
	MARVEL COMICS #14	£1350.00
	MARVEL COMICS #15	£1350.00
	MARVEL COMICS #16	£1350.00
	MARVEL COMICS #19	£1350.00
70	HUMAN TORCH (1st Series) #7	£1300.00
	MARVEL COMICS #20	£1300.00
72	CAPTAIN AMERICA COMICS #20	£1275.00
	SUB-MARINER (1st) COMICS #5	£1275.00
74	CAPTAIN AMERICA COMICS #18	£1250.00
	CAPTAIN AMERICA COMICS #19	£1250.00
76	CAPTAIN AMERICA COMICS #61	£1200.00
	INCREDIBLE HULK (1st Series) #6	£1200.00
78	CAPTAIN AMERICA COMICS #21	£1175.00
	CAPTAIN AMERICA COMICS #22	£1175.00
	CAPTAIN AMERICA COMICS #23	£1175.00
	CAPTAIN AMERICA COMICS #24	£1175.00
	CAPTAIN AMERICA COMICS #25	£1175.00
	HUMAN TORCH (1st Series) #6	£1175.00
	HUMAN TORCH (1st Series) #9	£1175.00
	MARVEL COMICS #21	£1175.00
	MARVEL COMICS #82	£1175.00
87	AMAZING SPIDERMAN, THE #3	£1150.00
	CAPTAIN AMERICA COMICS #26	£1150.00
	CAPTAIN AMERICA COMICS #27	£1150.00
	CAPTAIN AMERICA COMICS #28	£1150.00
	CAPTAIN AMERICA COMICS #29	£1150.00
	CAPTAIN AMERICA COMICS #30	£1150.00
	MARVEL COMICS #18	£1150.00
94	SUB-MARINER (1st) COMICS #6	£1075.00
	SUB-MARINER (1st) COMICS #7	£1075.00
	SUB-MARINER (1st) COMICS #8	£1075.00
	SUB-MARINER (1st) COMICS #9	£1075.00
	SUB-MARINER (1st) COMICS #10	£1075.00
99	TALES TO ASTONISH (1st Series) #1	£1025.00
100	MARVEL COMICS #25	£1000.00

Top 100 U.S. Marvel Comics

Rank	Title	Price
1	MARVEL COMICS #1	$97500.00
2	CAPTAIN AMERICA COMICS #1	$62500.00
3	AMAZING FANTASY #15	$30000.00
4	MARVEL COMICS #2	$24000.00
	SUB-MARINER (1st) COMICS #1	$24000.00
6	HUMAN TORCH (1st Series) #2	$23000.00
7	AMAZING SPIDERMAN, THE #1	$22000.00
8	FANTASTIC FOUR #1	$21000.00
9	MARVEL COMICS #9	$20000.00
10	CAPTAIN AMERICA COMICS #22	$16000.00
11	MARVEL COMICS #5	$15000.00
12	CAPTAIN AMERICA COMICS #2	$11500.00
	INCREDIBLE HULK (1st Series) #1	$11500.00
14	MARVEL COMICS #3	$10000.00
15	CAPTAIN AMERICA COMICS #3	$9500.00
16	MARVEL COMICS #8	$9000.00
17	MARVEL COMICS #4	$8000.00
18	MARVEL COMICS #10	$6250.00
19	X-MEN, THE UNCANNY #1	$5750.00
20	MARVEL COMICS #6	$5500.00
	MARVEL COMICS #7	$5500.00
22	CAPTAIN AMERICA COMICS #4	$5250.00
	CAPTAIN AMERICA COMICS #7	$5250.00
24	CAPTAIN AMERICA COMICS #5	$5000.00
	SUB-MARINER (1st) COMICS #2	$5000.00
26	HUMAN TORCH (1st Series) #3	$4750.00
27	JOURNEY INTO MYSTERY #83	$4600.00
28	CAPTAIN AMERICA COMICS #6	$4500.00
29	HUMAN TORCH (1st Series) #5	$4100.00
30	MARVEL COMICS #13	$4000.00
	TALES OF SUSPENSE (1st Series) #39	$4000.00
32	FANTASTIC FOUR #2	$3850.00
33	CAPTAIN AMERICA COMICS #8	$3800.00
	CAPTAIN AMERICA COMICS #9	$3800.00
	CAPTAIN AMERICA COMICS #10	$3800.00
36	HUMAN TORCH (1st Series) #4	$3750.00
37	CAPTAIN AMERICA COMICS #16	$3500.00
	MARVEL COMICS #12	$3500.00
	TALES TO ASTONISH (1st Series) #27	$3500.00
40	CAPTAIN AMERICA COMICS #74	$3250.00
41	CAPTAIN AMERICA COMICS #11	$3200.00
	FANTASTIC FOUR #5	$3200.00
	INCREDIBLE HULK (1st Series) #2	$3200.00
	SUB-MARINER (1st) COMICS #3	$3200.00
45	AMAZING SPIDERMAN, THE #2	$3000.00
	CAPTAIN AMERICA COMICS #12	$3000.00
	CAPTAIN AMERICA COMICS #13	$3000.00
48	FANTASTIC FOUR #4	$2950.00
49	HUMAN TORCH (1st Series) #5	$2900.00
50	HUMAN TORCH (1st Series) #8	$2800.00
	MARVEL COMICS #11	$2800.00
	SUB-MARINER (1st) COMICS #4	$2800.00
53	CAPTAIN AMERICA COMICS #14	$2750.00
	CAPTAIN AMERICA COMICS #15	$2750.00
55	AVENGERS #1	$2500.00
	FANTASTIC FOUR #3	$2500.00
	JOURNEY INTO MYSTERY #1	$2500.00
58	CAPTAIN AMERICA COMICS #17	$2400.00
	CAPTAIN AMERICA COMICS #59	$2400.00
60	HUMAN TORCH (1st Series) #10	$2350.00
	STRANGE TALES (1st Series) #1	$2350.00
62	CAPTAIN AMERICA COMICS #36	$2250.00
	MARVEL COMICS #92	$2250.00
64	MARVEL COMICS #17	$2200.00
65	INCREDIBLE HULK (1st Series) #6	$2100.00
66	AMAZING SPIDERMAN, THE #3	$2000.00
	DAREDEVIL #1	$2000.00
	MARVEL COMICS #14	$2000.00
	MARVEL COMICS #15	$2000.00
	MARVEL COMICS #16	$2000.00
	MARVEL COMICS #19	$2000.00
72	HUMAN TORCH (1st Series) #7	$1950.00
	MARVEL COMICS #20	$1950.00
74	FANTASTIC FOUR #6	$1925.00
75	CAPTAIN AMERICA COMICS #20	$1900.00
	SUB-MARINER (1st) COMICS #5	$1900.00
77	CAPTAIN AMERICA COMICS #18	$1850.00
	CAPTAIN AMERICA COMICS #19	$1850.00
79	CAPTAIN AMERICA COMICS #61	$1800.00
80	CAPTAIN AMERICA COMICS #21	$1750.00
	CAPTAIN AMERICA COMICS #22	$1750.00
	CAPTAIN AMERICA COMICS #23	$1750.00
	CAPTAIN AMERICA COMICS #24	$1750.00
	CAPTAIN AMERICA COMICS #25	$1750.00
	HUMAN TORCH (1st Series) #6	$1750.00
	HUMAN TORCH (1st Series) #9	$1750.00
	MARVEL COMICS #21	$1750.00
	MARVEL COMICS #82	$1750.00
89	CAPTAIN AMERICA COMICS #26	$1700.00
	CAPTAIN AMERICA COMICS #27	$1700.00
	CAPTAIN AMERICA COMICS #28	$1700.00
	CAPTAIN AMERICA COMICS #29	$1700.00
	CAPTAIN AMERICA COMICS #30	$1700.00
	MARVEL COMICS #18	$1700.00
95	X-MEN, THE UNCANNY #2	$1675.00
96	AMAZING SPIDERMAN, THE #4	$1600.00
	INCREDIBLE HULK (1st Series) #3	$1600.00
	SUB-MARINER (1st) COMICS #9	$1600.00
	SUB-MARINER (1st) COMICS #10	$1600.00
	TALES TO ASTONISH (1st Series) #35	$1600.00

Top 100 U.K. Independent Comics

Rank	Comic	Price
1	WHIZ COMICS #1	£42750.00
2	CAPTAIN MARVEL ADVENTURES #0	£20000.00
3	WALT DISNEY'S COMICS AND STORIES #1	£13300.00
4	RED RAVEN COMICS #1	£8000.00
5	ARCHIE COMICS #1	£7000.00
6	FOUR COLOR (Series I) #16	£6930.00
7	FOUR COLOR (Series I) #4	£5775.00
8	FOUR COLOR (Series II) #9	£5500.00
9	WALT DISNEY'S COMICS AND STORIES #2	£4650.00
10	MASTER COMICS #1	£4500.00
11	FOUR COLOR (Series II) #29	£4350.00
12	FOUR COLOR (Series I) #1	£4000.00
	POLICE COMICS #1	£4000.00
14	MAD MAGAZINE #1	£3670.00
15	WHIZ COMICS #25	£3650.00
16	CAPTAIN MARVEL JR. #1	£3350.00
17	WHIZ COMICS #2	£2950.00
18	MASTER COMICS #21	£2800.00
	VAULT OF HORROR #12	£2800.00
20	MASTER COMICS #22	£2400.00
21	CAPTAIN MARVEL ADVENTURES #2	£2275.00
22	WALT DISNEY'S COMICS AND STORIES #31	£2175.00
23	ARCHIE COMICS #2	£1750.00
24	WHIZ COMICS #3	£1600.00
25	WALT DISNEY'S COMICS AND STORIES #3	£1500.00
26	POLICE COMICS #2	£1475.00
27	CAPTAIN MARVEL ADVENTURES #3	£1375.00
28	MASTER COMICS #7	£1350.00
	MASTER COMICS #23	£1350.00
30	WHIZ COMICS #4	£1325.00
31	ARCHIE COMICS #3	£1300.00
32	MASTER COMICS #11	£1250.00
33	POLICE COMICS #11	£1200.00
	WEIRD SCIENCE (1st Series) #1	£1200.00
35	EERIE #1	£1175.00
	HAUNT OF FEAR #1	£1175.00
37	FOUR COLOR (Series II) #62	£1075.00
	WHIZ COMICS #5	£1075.00
39	FOUR COLOR (Series I) #17	£1015.00
40	CAPTAIN MARVEL JR. #2	£1000.00
	MASTER COMICS #2	£1000.00
	POLICE COMICS #8	£1000.00
	WALT DISNEY'S COMICS AND STORIES #4	£1000.00
	WEIRD FANTASY (1st Series) #1	£1000.00
45	CAPTAIN MARVEL ADVENTURES #18	£950.00
	POLICE COMICS #3	£950.00
	POLICE COMICS #4	£950.00
	RICHIE RICH #1	£950.00
	WEIRD SCIENCE-FANTASY (1st Series) ANNUAL #1	£950.00
50	ARCHIE ANNUAL #1	£935.00
	MASTER COMICS #13	£935.00
52	CAPTAIN MARVEL ADVENTURES #4	£900.00
	MARY MARVEL COMICS #1	£900.00
	WALT DISNEY'S COMICS AND STORIES #32	£900.00
	WHIZ COMICS #6	£900.00
	WHIZ COMICS #7	£900.00
	WHIZ COMICS #8	£900.00
	WHIZ COMICS #9	£900.00
	WHIZ COMICS #10	£900.00
60	ARCHIE'S GIRLS BETTY AND VERONICA #1	£850.00
	POLICE COMICS #5	£850.00
62	FOUR COLOR (Series I) #13	£840.00
	FOUR COLOR (Series II) #108	£840.00
64	ADVENTURES INTO THE UNKNOWN #1	£800.00
	CRIME SUSPENSTORIES #1	£800.00
	MARVEL FAMILY, THE #1	£800.00
	MASTER COMICS #3	£800.00
	MASTER COMICS #4	£800.00
	MASTER COMICS #5	£800.00
	MASTER COMICS #6	£800.00
71	POLICE COMICS #6	£750.00
	POLICE COMICS #7	£750.00
73	MAD MAGAZINE #2	£735.00
	MAD MAGAZINE #5	£735.00
75	WALT DISNEY'S COMICS AND STORIES #5	£720.00
76	ARCHIE COMICS #4	£700.00
	ARCHIE COMICS #5	£700.00
	ARCHIE COMICS #6	£700.00
	FOUR COLOR (Series I) #2	£700.00
	FOUR COLOR (Series I) #6	£700.00
	FOUR COLOR (Series II) #79	£700.00
	FOUR COLOR (Series II) #386	£700.00
	MASTER COMICS #8	£700.00
	POLICE COMICS #9	£700.00
	POLICE COMICS #10	£700.00
	POLICE COMICS #12	£700.00
	POLICE COMICS #13	£700.00
88	FORBIDDEN WORLDS (1st Series) #1	£675.00
89	WALT DISNEY'S COMICS AND STORIES #33	£670.00
90	FOUR COLOR (Series II) #38	£653.00
	FOUR COLOR (Series II) #48	£653.00
92	ARCHIE'S PAL JUGHEAD #1	£650.00
	CAPTAIN MARVEL ADVENTURES #5	£650.00
	TALES FROM THE CRYPT #20	£650.00
	WEIRD SCIENCE-FANTASY (1st Series) ANNUAL #2	£650.00
	WHIZ COMICS #15	£650.00
	WHIZ COMICS #16	£650.00
	WHIZ COMICS #17	£650.00
	WHIZ COMICS #18	£650.00
100	MASTER COMICS #12	£635.00

Top 100 U.S. Independent Comics

Rank	Title	Value
1	WHIZ COMICS #1	$64000.00
2	CAPTAIN MARVEL ADVENTURES #0	$30000.00
3	WALT DISNEY'S COMICS AND STORIES #1	$20000.00
4	RED RAVEN COMICS #1	$12500.00
5	ARCHIE COMICS #1	$10500.00
6	FOUR COLOR (Series I) #16	$9900.00
7	FOUR COLOR (Series I) #4	$8500.00
8	FOUR COLOR (Series II) #9	$7500.00
9	WALT DISNEY'S COMICS AND STORIES #2	$7000.00
10	FOUR COLOR (Series II) #29	$6500.00
	MASTER COMICS #1	$6500.00
12	FOUR COLOR (Series I) #1	$6000.00
	POLICE COMICS #1	$6000.00
14	MAD MAGAZINE #1	$5500.00
	WHIZ COMICS #25	$5500.00
16	CAPTAIN MARVEL JR. #1	$5000.00
17	WHIZ COMICS #2	$4400.00
18	MASTER COMICS #21	$4200.00
	VAULT OF HORROR #12	$4200.00
20	MASTER COMICS #22	$3600.00
21	CAPTAIN MARVEL ADVENTURES #2	$3400.00
22	WALT DISNEY'S COMICS AND STORIES #31	$3250.00
23	ARCHIE COMICS #2	$2500.00
24	WHIZ COMICS #3	$2400.00
25	WALT DISNEY'S COMICS AND STORIES #3	$2250.00
26	POLICE COMICS #2	$2200.00
27	CAPTAIN MARVEL ADVENTURES #3	$2050.00
28	MASTER COMICS #7	$2000.00
	MASTER COMICS #23	$2000.00
	WHIZ COMICS #4	$2000.00
31	ARCHIE COMICS #3	$1950.00
32	MASTER COMICS #11	$1850.00
33	WEIRD SCIENCE (1st Series) #1	$1800.00
34	EERIE #1	$1750.00
	HAUNT OF FEAR #1	$1750.00
	POLICE COMICS #11	$1750.00
37	FOUR COLOR (Series II) #62	$1610.00
38	WHIZ COMICS #5	$1600.00
39	FOUR COLOR (Series I) #17	$1505.00
40	CAPTAIN MARVEL JR. #2	$1500.00
	MASTER COMICS #2	$1500.00
	POLICE COMICS #8	$1500.00
	WALT DISNEY'S COMICS AND STORIES #4	$1500.00
	WEIRD FANTASY (1st Series) #1	$1500.00
45	ARCHIE ANNUAL #1	$1400.00
	CAPTAIN MARVEL ADVENTURES #18	$1400.00
	MASTER COMICS #13	$1400.00
	POLICE COMICS #3	$1400.00
	POLICE COMICS #4	$1400.00
	WEIRD SCIENCE-FANTASY (1st Series) ANNUAL #1	$1400.00
51	CAPTAIN MARVEL ADVENTURES #4	$1350.00
	MARY MARVEL COMICS #1	$1350.00
	RICHIE RICH #1	$1350.00
	WALT DISNEY'S COMICS AND STORIES #32	$1350.00
	WHIZ COMICS #6	$1350.00
	WHIZ COMICS #7	$1350.00
	WHIZ COMICS #8	$1350.00
	WHIZ COMICS #9	$1350.00
	WHIZ COMICS #10	$1350.00
60	FOUR COLOR (Series I) #13	$1260.00
	FOUR COLOR (Series II) #108	$1260.00
62	POLICE COMICS #5	$1250.00
63	ADVENTURES INTO THE UNKNOWN #1	$1200.00
	ARCHIE'S GIRLS BETTY AND VERONICA #1	$1200.00
	CRIME SUSPENSTORIES #1	$1200.00
	MARVEL FAMILY, THE #1	$1200.00
	MASTER COMICS #3	$1200.00
	MASTER COMICS #4	$1200.00
	MASTER COMICS #5	$1200.00
	MASTER COMICS #6	$1200.00
71	POLICE COMICS #6	$1125.00
	POLICE COMICS #7	$1125.00
73	MAD MAGAZINE #2	$1100.00
	MAD MAGAZINE #5	$1100.00
75	WALT DISNEY'S COMICS AND STORIES #5	$1075.00
76	FOUR COLOR (Series I) #2	$1050.00
	FOUR COLOR (Series I) #6	$1050.00
	FOUR COLOR (Series II) #79	$1050.00
	FOUR COLOR (Series II) #386	$1050.00
	MASTER COMICS #8	$1050.00
	POLICE COMICS #9	$1050.00
	POLICE COMICS #10	$1050.00
	POLICE COMICS #12	$1050.00
	POLICE COMICS #13	$1050.00
85	ARCHIE COMICS #4	$1000.00
	ARCHIE COMICS #5	$1000.00
	ARCHIE COMICS #6	$1000.00
	FORBIDDEN WORLDS (1st Series) #1	$1000.00
	WALT DISNEY'S COMICS AND STORIES #33	$1000.00
90	FOUR COLOR (Series II) #38	$980.00
	FOUR COLOR (Series II) #48	$980.00
92	CAPTAIN MARVEL ADVENTURES #5	$975.00
	TALES FROM THE CRYPT #20	$975.00
	WHIZ COMICS #15	$975.00
	WHIZ COMICS #16	$975.00
	WHIZ COMICS #17	$975.00
	WHIZ COMICS #18	$975.00
98	MASTER COMICS #12	$950.00
	WEIRD SCIENCE-FANTASY (1st Series) ANNUAL #2	$950.00
100	TARZAN #1	$925.00

Top 100 U.K. DC Titles

Rank	Title	Value
1	DETECTIVE COMICS	£495125.10
2	MORE FUN COMICS	£339460.00
3	ACTION COMICS	£281259.80
4	ADVENTURE COMICS	£266093.75
5	SUPERMAN (1st Series) (ADVENTURES OF SUPERMAN)	£162448.75
6	BATMAN	£148220.20
7	ALL-AMERICAN COMICS	£136130.00
8	FLASH COMICS	£118260.00
9	ALL-STAR COMICS	£111475.00
10	SHOWCASE	£67321.10
11	WORLD'S FINEST COMICS (1st Series)	£53909.50
12	GREEN LANTERN (1st Series)	£53220.00
13	SENSATION COMICS	£51205.00
14	WONDER WOMAN	£44233.50
15	NEW YORK WORLD'S FAIR	£29000.00
16	COMIC CAVALCADE	£25405.00
17	STRANGE ADVENTURES	£24302.50
18	ALL-FLASH	£23980.00
19	SUPERBOY	£21216.50
20	BRAVE AND THE BOLD, THE	£19772.60
21	MYSTERY IN SPACE	£18748.00
22	OUR ARMY AT WAR	£16923.00
23	NEW BOOK OF COMICS	£16675.00
24	HOUSE OF MYSTERY	£13647.75
25	FLASH (1st Series)	£11575.75
26	STAR-SPANGLED WAR STORIES	£11453.00
27	LEADING COMICS	£10912.50
28	JIMMY OLSEN, SUPERMAN'S PAL	£10589.50
29	TALES OF THE UNEXPECTED	£10007.50
30	ALL-AMERICAN MEN OF WAR	£8742.50
31	MY GREATEST ADVENTURE	£8402.50
32	SUGAR AND SPIKE	£7525.75
33	JUSTICE LEAGUE OF AMERICA	£7100.25
34	BOB HOPE, THE ADVENTURES OF	£7057.50
35	LOIS LANE, SUPERMAN'S GIRLFRIEND	£6977.75
36	GREEN LANTERN (2nd Series)	£6801.00
37	CHALLENGERS OF THE UNKNOWN	£6473.25
38	HOUSE OF SECRETS	£6183.50
39	OUR FIGHTING FORCES	£5594.50
40	REAL FACT COMICS	£4630.00
41	G.I. COMBAT	£3987.50
42	BLACKHAWK	£3691.00
43	GIRL'S LOVE STORIES	£3684.00
44	REX THE WONDER DOG	£3675.00
45	GIRL'S ROMANCES	£3535.00
46	ALL-AMERICAN WESTERN	£3295.00
47	ALL-STAR WESTERN	£3120.00
48	BIG TOWN	£2970.00
49	CONGO BILL	£2555.00
50	SERGEANT BILKO	£2445.00
51	DANGER TRAIL	£2330.00
52	FALLING IN LOVE	£2282.00
53	HEART THROBS	£2065.00
54	FLIPPITY AND FLOP	£1790.00
55	RIP HUNTER TIME MASTER	£1790.00
56	EIGHTY PAGE GIANT MAGAZINE	£1725.00
57	SEA DEVILS	£1665.00
58	FRONTIER FIGHTERS	£1545.00
59	ATOM, THE	£1507.00
60	SUPERMAN (1st Series) ANNUAL	£1505.50
61	CHARLIE CHAN, THE NEW ADVENTURES OF	£1500.00
62	MANY LOVES OF DOBIE GILLIS	£1400.00
63	JERRY LEWIS, THE ADVENTURES OF	£1324.50
64	AQUAMAN	£1323.00
65	SECRET HEARTS	£1164.00
66	ROBIN HOOD TALES	£1160.00
67	HAWKMAN	£1062.50
68	DOOM PATROL	£990.50
69	SGT. BILKO'S PVT. DOBERMAN	£985.00
70	TOMAHAWK	£948.00
71	METAL MEN	£940.50
72	PAT BOONE	£880.00
73	BATMAN ANNUAL	£871.50
74	BATMAN 3-D	£800.00
75	TEEN TITANS	£766.00
76	FOX AND THE CROW	£712.00
77	YOUNG ROMANCE COMICS	£499.00
78	YOUNG LOVE	£442.00
79	TV SCREEN CARTOONS	£380.00
80	SANDMAN (2nd Series)	£379.00
81	UNEXPECTED, THE	£346.50
82	SWAMP THING (2nd Series)	£306.25
83	SECRET ORIGINS (1st Series)	£300.00
	WESTERN COMICS	£300.00
85	METAMORPHO	£282.50
86	SPECTRE, THE	£280.00
87	SGT. ROCK	£269.00
88	PHANTOM STRANGER	£268.50
89	JONAH HEX	£258.50
90	HELLBLAZER	£239.00
91	FLASH (1st Series) ANNUAL	£225.00
92	TARZAN	£211.00
93	WITCHING HOUR	£200.75
94	WEIRD WAR TALES	£199.00
95	SUPERMAN (2nd Series)	£196.50
96	LOIS LANE ANNUAL, SUPERMAN'S GIRLFRIEND	£185.00
97	SWING WITH SCOOTER	£183.50
98	PLASTIC MAN	£178.50
99	DATE WITH JUDY, A	£172.50
100	FLASH (2nd Series)	£168.50

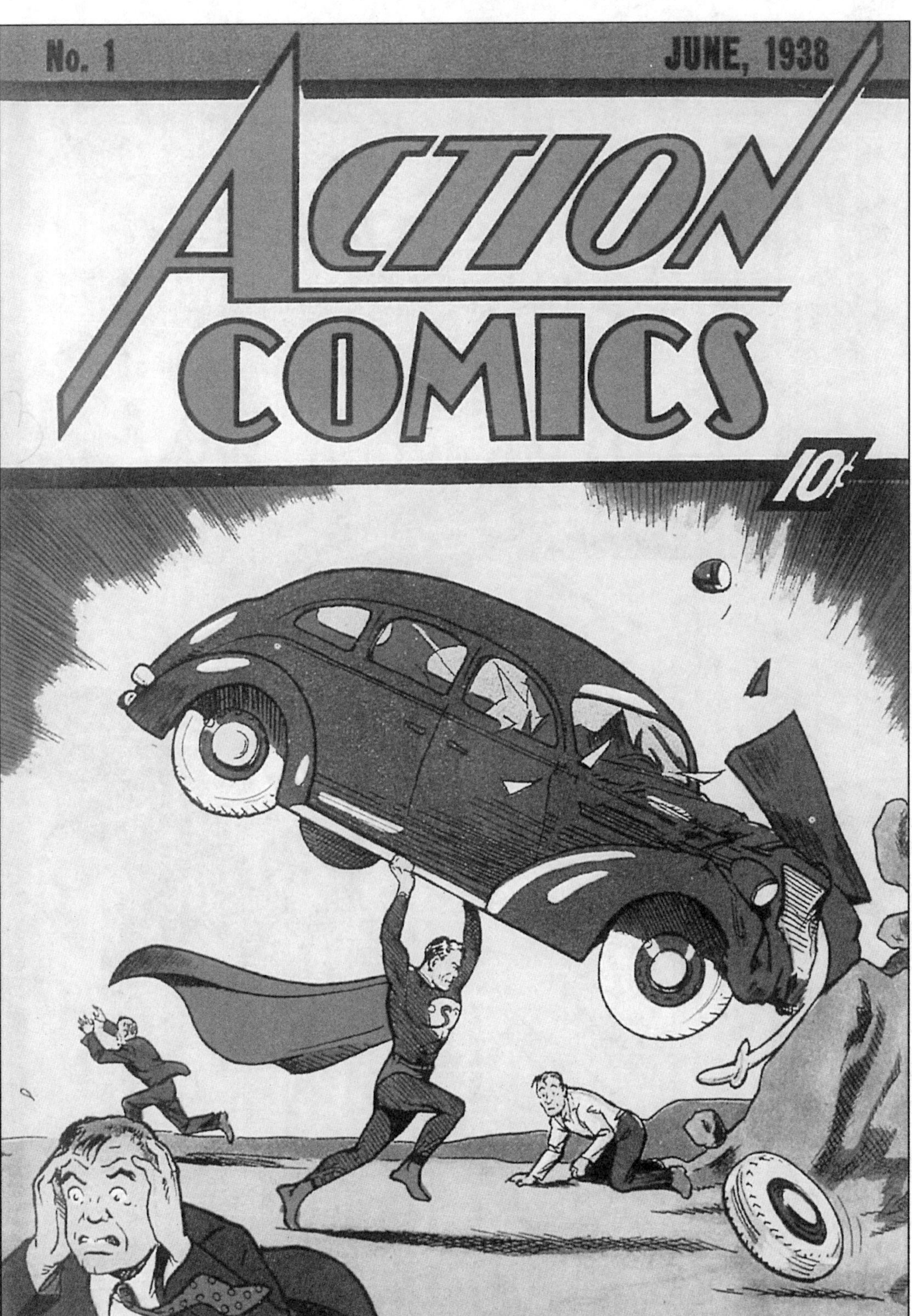

ACTION COMICS #1 (JUNE 1938) – ARGUABLY THE MOST IMPORTANT COMIC BOOK EVER PUBLISHED AS MOST SUPER-HEROES ADOPTED SOME OF THE ELEMENTS ESTABLISHED BY SUPERMAN. NOW THE MOST VALUABLE COMIC BOOK IN THE WORLD, THERE ARE REPORTS OF A COPY BEING OFFERED AT A QUARTER OF A MILLION DOLLARS.

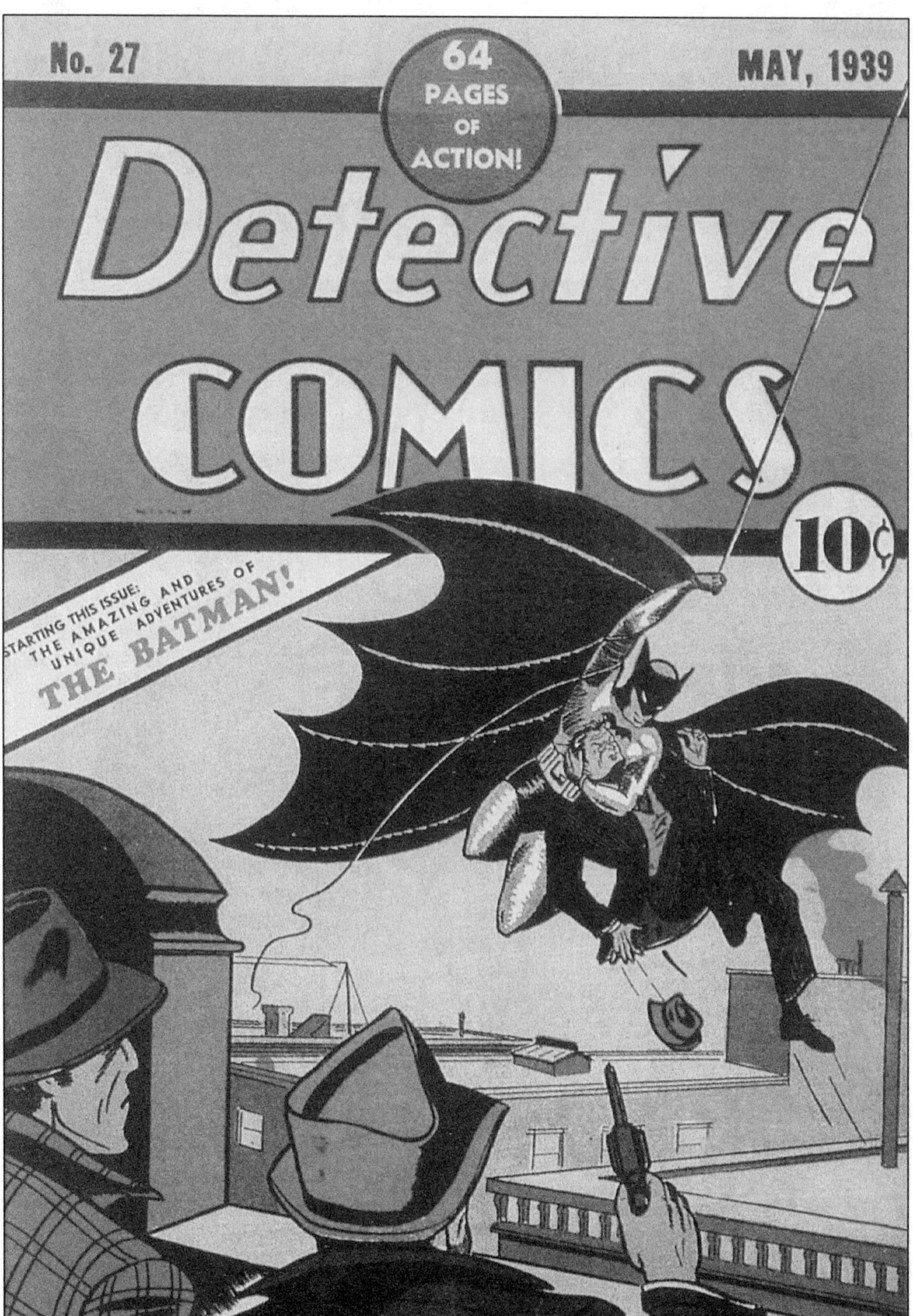

DETECTIVE COMICS #27 (MAY 1939) – PUSHED INTO SECOND PLACE BY ACTION COMICS #1 AS THE MOST VALUABLE COMIC BOOK, A TREND THAT MAY NOW CONTINUE FOR A FEW YEARS.

Top 100 U.S. DC Titles

Rank	Title	Value
1	DETECTIVE COMICS	$745061.25
2	MORE FUN COMICS	$507625.00
3	ACTION COMICS	$421429.75
4	ADVENTURE COMICS	$397241.25
5	SUPERMAN (1st Series) (ADVENTURES OF SUPERMAN)	$244612.00
6	BATMAN	$224836.00
7	ALL-AMERICAN COMICS	$202050.00
8	FLASH COMICS	$176650.00
9	ALL-STAR COMICS	$167350.00
10	SHOWCASE	$103216.25
11	WORLD'S FINEST COMICS (1st Series)	$81509.50
12	GREEN LANTERN (1st Series)	$79675.00
13	SENSATION COMICS	$76575.00
14	WONDER WOMAN	$66074.00
15	NEW YORK WORLD'S FAIR	$43500.00
16	STRANGE ADVENTURES	$39389.00
17	COMIC CAVALCADE	$37970.00
18	ALL-FLASH	$36025.00
19	SUPERBOY	$32940.00
20	BRAVE AND THE BOLD, THE	$30982.25
21	MYSTERY IN SPACE	$29468.00
22	OUR ARMY AT WAR	$28023.50
23	NEW BOOK OF COMICS	$25000.00
24	HOUSE OF MYSTERY	$22994.00
25	FLASH (1st Series)	$22400.50
26	STAR-SPANGLED WAR STORIES	$18080.00
27	JIMMY OLSEN, SUPERMAN'S PAL	$16497.00
28	LEADING COMICS	$16190.00
29	TALES OF THE UNEXPECTED	$15835.00
30	GREEN LANTERN (2nd Series)	$13835.50
31	MY GREATEST ADVENTURE	$13610.00
32	ALL-AMERICAN MEN OF WAR	$13465.00
33	JUSTICE LEAGUE OF AMERICA	$13310.50
34	LOIS LANE, SUPERMAN'S GIRLFRIEND	$13195.00
35	SUGAR AND SPIKE	$12256.25
36	BOB HOPE, THE ADVENTURES OF	$10865.00
37	HOUSE OF SECRETS	$10245.75
38	CHALLENGERS OF THE UNKNOWN	$10157.00
39	OUR FIGHTING FORCES	$9607.50
40	G.I. COMBAT	$8595.00
41	GIRL'S LOVE STORIES	$6935.00
42	GIRL'S ROMANCES	$6872.50
43	REAL FACT COMICS	$6760.00
44	BLACKHAWK	$5984.50
45	REX THE WONDER DOG	$5530.00
46	ALL-AMERICAN WESTERN	$4855.00
47	ALL-STAR WESTERN	$4765.00
48	ATOM, THE	$4490.00
49	BIG TOWN	$4430.00
50	AQUAMAN	$4157.00
51	CONGO BILL	$3810.00
52	HEART THROBS	$3685.00
53	SERGEANT BILKO	$3670.00
54	FALLING IN LOVE	$3653.50
55	DANGER TRAIL	$3450.00
56	EIGHTY PAGE GIANT MAGAZINE	$3040.00
57	METAL MEN	$3015.00
58	FLIPPITY AND FLOP	$2840.00
	RIP HUNTER TIME MASTER	$2840.00
60	SEA DEVILS	$2752.50
61	SUPERMAN (1st Series) ANNUAL	$2586.00
62	JERRY LEWIS, THE ADVENTURES OF	$2460.00
63	HAWKMAN	$2455.00
64	FRONTIER FIGHTERS	$2295.00
65	MANY LOVES OF DOBIE GILLIS	$2260.00
66	CHARLIE CHAN, THE NEW ADVENTURES OF	$2230.00
67	SECRET HEARTS	$2077.00
68	DOOM PATROL	$1985.00
69	BATMAN ANNUAL	$1789.50
70	ROBIN HOOD TALES	$1675.00
71	TOMAHAWK	$1513.50
72	TEEN TITANS	$1511.00
73	SGT. BILKO'S PVT. DOBERMAN	$1415.00
74	PAT BOONE	$1325.00
75	FOX AND THE CROW	$1277.50
76	BATMAN 3-D	$1225.00
77	SANDMAN (2nd Series)	$1001.00
78	YOUNG ROMANCE COMICS	$881.50
79	YOUNG LOVE	$833.50
80	SGT. ROCK	$776.50
81	METAMORPHO	$740.00
82	UNEXPECTED, THE	$665.00
83	SPECTRE, THE	$605.00
84	TV SCREEN CARTOONS	$560.00
85	JONAH HEX	$538.00
86	SECRET ORIGINS (1st Series)	$495.00
87	TARZAN	$471.00
88	SWAMP THING (2nd Series)	$469.75
89	PHANTOM STRANGER	$450.00
90	WESTERN COMICS	$440.00
91	FLASH (1st Series) ANNUAL	$425.00
92	KAMANDI THE LAST BOY ON EARTH	$410.50
93	HELLBLAZER	$391.00
94	PLASTIC MAN	$342.50
95	WEIRD WAR TALES	$337.50
96	SWAMP THING	$335.00
97	SWING WITH SCOOTER	$323.00
98	LOIS LANE ANNUAL, SUPERMAN'S GIRLFRIEND	$310.00
99	DEMON, THE	$307.50
100	MISTER MIRACLE	$306.00

Top 100 U.K. Marvel Titles

1	MARVEL COMICS	£200095.00
2	CAPTAIN AMERICA COMICS	£157592.50
3	HUMAN TORCH (1st Series)	£51295.00
4	SUB-MARINER (1st) COMICS	£49120.00
5	AMAZING SPIDERMAN, THE	£29112.25
6	FANTASTIC FOUR	£28687.75
7	JOURNEY INTO MYSTERY	£20185.00
8	STRANGE TALES (1st Series)	£19469.50
9	AMAZING FANTASY	£15009.50
10	TALES OF SUSPENSE (1st Series)	£13934.50
11	TALES TO ASTONISH (1st Series)	£13792.50
12	INCREDIBLE HULK (1st Series)	£12551.50
13	X-MEN, THE UNCANNY	£10037.50
14	AVENGERS	£6530.25
15	DAREDEVIL	£4832.30
16	RAWHIDE KID	£3250.00
17	SGT. FURY AND HIS HOWLING COMMANDOS	£2613.50
18	AMAZING ADULT FANTASY	£2250.00
19	AMAZING ADVENTURES	£2090.00
20	INCREDIBLE HULK (2nd Series)	£1722.75
21	THOR	£1622.75
22	IRON MAN	£1539.50
23	CAPTAIN AMERICA	£1431.25
24	SILVER SURFER (1st Series)	£1367.50
25	MILLIE THE MODEL	£1332.50
26	CONAN THE BARBARIAN	£1023.50
27	STAR WARS	£999.00
28	FANTASTIC FOUR ANNUAL	£933.50
29	GUNSMOKE WESTERN	£809.50
30	PATSY WALKER	£760.00
31	AMAZING SPIDERMAN, THE ANNUAL	£710.50
32	MARVEL MASTERWORKS	£690.00
33	MARVEL GRAPHIC NOVEL	£674.50
34	MILLIE, MODELLING WITH	£625.00
	STRANGE TALES (1st Series) ANNUAL	£625.00
36	SPECTACULAR SPIDERMAN	£585.75
37	CONAN, SAVAGE SWORD OF	£583.00
38	SUB-MARINER (2nd Series)	£536.00
39	MARVEL TEAM-UP	£503.00
40	KID COLT OUTLAW	£478.50
41	MARVEL TALES	£463.50
42	TWO-GUN KID	£439.00
43	MILLIE THE MODEL ANNUAL	£437.50
44	DEFENDERS	£432.00
45	DOCTOR STRANGE (1st Series)	£396.00
46	CAPTAIN MARVEL	£389.50
47	MARVEL SUPER-HEROES	£382.75
48	TOMB OF DRACULA	£367.50
49	GHOST RIDER	£343.00
50	X-MEN GIANT SIZE	£288.00
51	WOLVERINE	£286.50
52	MARVEL PREMIERE	£284.25
53	MILLIE, A DATE WITH	£280.00
54	SPIDERMAN	£276.25
55	MILLIE, LIFE WITH	£250.00
56	MARVEL COLLECTOR'S ITEM CLASSICS	£247.50
57	PATSY AND HEDY CAREER GIRLS	£246.00
58	MARVEL SPOTLIGHT	£240.50
59	FOOM	£238.50
60	IRON FIST	£234.85
61	X-FACTOR	£229.75
62	WEB OF SPIDERMAN, THE	£218.50
63	WEREWOLF BY NIGHT	£217.50
64	MARVEL COMICS PRESENTS	£217.25
65	MARVEL TWO-IN-ONE	£215.75
66	BATTLE	£215.00
	MILLIE, MAD ABOUT	£215.00
68	GROO THE WANDERER	£207.25
69	MARVEL TALES ANNUAL	£200.00
70	DOCTOR STRANGE (2nd Series)	£187.50
71	MARVEL SUPER SPECIAL	£187.00
	NEW MUTANTS	£187.00
73	MASTER OF KUNG FU	£185.00
74	POWERMAN	£184.75
75	NICK FURY, AGENT OF SHIELD	£184.50
76	WHAT IF...? (1st Series)	£176.50
77	G.I. JOE	£175.75
78	AKIRA	£165.50
79	SGT. FURY ANNUAL	£165.00
80	SILVER SURFER (3rd Series)	£163.75
81	EXCALIBUR	£163.25
82	SAVAGE TALES	£161.00
83	ALPHA FLIGHT	£158.00
84	X-MEN	£155.00
85	CONAN SAGA	£152.50
86	ASTONISHING TALES	£151.50
87	AVENGERS ANNUAL, THE	£147.50
88	AMAZING ADVENTURES (2nd Series)	£145.50
89	X-MEN, THE UNCANNY ANNUAL	£141.50
90	PUNISHER (1st Series)	£140.50
91	MARVEL FEATURE	£137.00
92	CRAZY (2nd Series)	£134.00
93	CLASSIC X-MEN	£132.00
94	FANTASY MASTERPIECES	£130.00
95	GHOST RIDER (2nd Series)	£128.50
96	TEEN-AGE ROMANCE	£125.00
97	PUNISHER WAR JOURNAL	£124.25
98	SPECTACULAR SPIDERMAN, THE	£120.00
99	NOT BRAND ECHH	£117.50
100	MARVEL'S GREATEST COMICS	£116.00

Top 100 U.S. Marvel Titles

Rank	Title	Value
1	MARVEL COMICS	$299665.00
2	CAPTAIN AMERICA COMICS	$238924.00
3	HUMAN TORCH (1st Series)	$75725.00
4	SUB-MARINER (1st) COMICS	$73465.00
5	AMAZING SPIDERMAN, THE	$52444.50
6	FANTASTIC FOUR	$52356.50
7	STRANGE TALES (1st Series)	$31939.50
8	JOURNEY INTO MYSTERY	$30815.00
9	AMAZING FANTASY	$30015.00
10	TALES OF SUSPENSE (1st Series)	$22843.00
11	TALES TO ASTONISH (1st Series)	$22022.50
12	INCREDIBLE HULK (1st Series)	$21177.50
13	X-MEN, THE UNCANNY	$19512.25
14	AVENGERS	$10906.50
15	DAREDEVIL	$7605.25
16	SGT. FURY AND HIS HOWLING COMMANDOS	$5520.00
17	RAWHIDE KID	$5476.00
18	AMAZING ADULT FANTASY	$3600.00
19	AMAZING ADVENTURES	$3310.00
20	INCREDIBLE HULK (2nd Series)	$3063.50
21	THOR	$3025.00
22	IRON MAN	$2679.75
23	STAR WARS	$2660.00
24	CAPTAIN AMERICA	$2477.50
25	MILLIE THE MODEL	$2420.00
26	SILVER SURFER (1st Series)	$2045.00
27	CONAN THE BARBARIAN	$1861.00
28	FANTASTIC FOUR ANNUAL	$1587.00
29	GUNSMOKE WESTERN	$1455.00
30	AMAZING SPIDERMAN, THE ANNUAL	$1330.50
31	PATSY WALKER	$1245.00
32	CONAN, SAVAGE SWORD OF	$1218.25
33	MARVEL MASTERWORKS	$1042.50
34	KID COLT OUTLAW	$1024.50
35	MILLIE, MODELLING WITH	$1017.50
36	SPECTACULAR SPIDERMAN	$1017.25
37	SUB-MARINER (2nd Series)	$1009.00
38	MARVEL GRAPHIC NOVEL	$996.50
39	STRANGE TALES (1st Series) ANNUAL	$925.00
40	TOMB OF DRACULA	$893.50
41	DEFENDERS	$837.00
42	MARVEL TEAM-UP	$812.00
43	MARVEL TALES	$797.25
44	DOCTOR STRANGE (1st Series)	$780.00
45	GHOST RIDER	$741.00
46	MILLIE THE MODEL ANNUAL	$670.00
47	TWO-GUN KID	$667.00
48	MARVEL SUPER-HEROES	$651.50
49	CAPTAIN MARVEL	$626.00
50	MARVEL SPOTLIGHT	$579.50
51	MARVEL COLLECTOR'S ITEM CLASSICS	$575.00
52	WEREWOLF BY NIGHT	$544.50
53	WOLVERINE	$537.50
54	MARVEL PREMIERE	$491.00
55	MILLIE, A DATE WITH	$475.00
56	PATSY AND HEDY CAREER GIRLS	$472.00
57	X-MEN GIANT SIZE	$469.50
58	SPIDERMAN	$432.75
59	MASTER OF KUNG FU	$427.00
60	MILLIE, LIFE WITH	$410.00
61	IRON FIST	$390.75
62	WEB OF SPIDERMAN, THE	$389.50
63	X-FACTOR	$383.50
64	BATTLE	$370.00
65	MARVEL COMICS PRESENTS	$367.00
66	MARVEL TALES ANNUAL	$365.00
67	NEW MUTANTS	$359.00
68	MARVEL TWO-IN-ONE	$357.00
69	POWERMAN	$352.50
70	MARVEL SUPER SPECIAL	$352.00
71	FOOM	$346.50
72	MILLIE, MAD ABOUT	$337.50
73	NICK FURY, AGENT OF SHIELD	$334.00
74	DOCTOR STRANGE (2nd Series)	$330.00
75	AMAZING ADVENTURES (2nd Series)	$325.00
76	ASTONISHING TALES	$315.00
77	SAVAGE TALES	$309.00
78	G.I. JOE	$292.50
	WHAT IF...? (1st Series)	$292.50
80	INVADERS, THE (1st Series)	$284.00
81	SGT. FURY ANNUAL	$275.00
82	NOT BRAND ECHH	$267.50
83	GROO THE WANDERER	$264.50
84	X-MEN	$261.00
85	SILVER SURFER (3rd Series)	$260.50
86	EXCALIBUR	$256.75
87	AVENGERS ANNUAL, THE	$250.00
88	FANTASY MASTERPIECES	$247.50
89	CLASSIC X-MEN	$238.25
90	X-MEN, THE UNCANNY ANNUAL	$237.50
91	CONAN SAGA	$236.75
92	AKIRA	$234.00
93	MARVEL FEATURE	$231.00
94	PUNISHER (1st Series)	$219.75
95	CRAZY (2nd Series)	$218.00
96	ALPHA FLIGHT	$209.50
97	FEAR, ADVENTURE INTO	$204.50
98	CHILI	$202.50
99	GHOST RIDER (2nd Series)	$200.50
100	TEEN-AGE ROMANCE	$200.00

Top 100 U.K. Independent Titles

Rank	Title	Value
1	FOUR COLOR (Series II)	£96637.25
2	WHIZ COMICS	£81070.00
3	WALT DISNEY'S COMICS AND STORIES	£55396.50
4	CAPTAIN MARVEL ADVENTURES	£49620.00
5	MASTER COMICS	£39015.00
6	POLICE COMICS	£33425.00
7	FOUR COLOR (Series I)	£24825.00
8	ARCHIE COMICS	£23862.00
9	CAPTAIN MARVEL JR.	£20185.00
10	MAD MAGAZINE	£16467.50
11	ADVENTURES INTO THE UNKNOWN	£9697.50
12	ARCHIE'S GIRLS BETTY AND VERONICA	£8584.50
13	TARZAN	£8541.00
14	MARVEL FAMILY, THE	£8540.00
15	VAULT OF HORROR	£8070.00
16	RED RAVEN COMICS	£8000.00
17	TALES FROM THE CRYPT	£7125.00
18	FORBIDDEN WORLDS (1st Series)	£6805.00
19	WEIRD SCIENCE (1st Series)	£5885.00
20	ARCHIE'S PAL JUGHEAD	£5878.00
21	HAUNT OF FEAR	£5820.00
22	RICHIE RICH	£5303.75
23	WEIRD FANTASY (1st Series)	£5100.00
24	STRANGE SUSPENSE STORIES	£4975.00
25	CRIME SUSPENSTORIES	£4700.00
26	TUROK SON OF STONE	£4564.00
27	MARY MARVEL COMICS	£4430.00
28	DELL GIANTS	£4137.50
29	EERIE	£4080.00
30	SPACE ADVENTURES	£3882.00
31	LITTLE DOT	£3717.00
32	ARCHIE ANNUAL	£3177.50
33	STAR TREK	£3127.50
34	ARCHIE'S JOKE BOOK MAGAZINE	£2957.50
35	TWO-FISTED TALES	£2895.00
36	SHOCK SUSPENSTORIES (1st Series)	£2780.00
37	ARCHIE'S PALS 'N GALS	£2624.00
38	FAMOUS MONSTERS OF FILMLAND	£2269.50
39	VAMPIRELLA (1st Series)	£2060.50
40	TALES OF THE MYSTERIOUS TRAVELLER	£2017.50
41	MYSTERIES OF UNEXPLORED WORLDS	£2012.50
42	THREE STOOGES, THE	£1792.50
43	FLY, ADVENTURES OF THE	£1737.50
44	UNUSUAL TALES	£1720.00
45	FRONTLINE COMBAT	£1715.00
46	BABY HUEY, THE BABY GIANT	£1651.00
47	WEIRD SCIENCE-FANTASY (1st Series) ANNUAL	£1600.00
48	SPOOKY	£1589.00
49	ARCHIE'S GALS BETTY AND VERONICA ANNUAL	£1535.00
50	CASPER, THE FRIENDLY GHOST	£1432.15
51	OUT OF THIS WORLD	£1392.50
52	BLACK RIDER	£1380.00
53	UNKNOWN WORLDS	£1352.50
54	MAGNUS ROBOT FIGHTER	£1347.00
55	SAD SACK AND THE SARGE	£1310.75
56	ARCHIE'S PAL JUGHEAD ANNUAL	£1280.00
57	JETSONS, THE	£1255.00
58	RIFLEMAN, THE	£1220.00
59	SIX-GUN HEROES	£1182.50
60	CRY FOR DAWN	£1180.00
61	WEIRD SCIENCE-FANTASY (1st Series)	£1150.00
62	DARK SHADOWS	£1141.00
63	MY LITTLE MARGIE	£1087.50
64	BILLY THE KID	£1073.50
65	STRANGE WORLDS	£1065.00
66	SPACE FAMILY ROBINSON	£1027.50
67	ROCKY LANE WESTERN	£1025.00
68	SPACE WAR	£1015.50
69	FLINTSTONES, THE	£999.50
70	ROMANTIC STORY	£970.50
71	LASH LARUE WESTERN	£952.50
72	SAD SACK LAUGH SPECIAL	£944.00
73	CHEYENNE	£920.00
74	CEREBUS THE AARDVARK	£893.00
75	HAVE GUN WILL TRAVEL	£882.50
76	DOCTOR SOLAR, MAN OF THE ATOM	£877.50
77	PHANTOM, THE	£873.50
78	ARCHIE'S MADHOUSE	£856.00
79	KONGA	£792.50
80	TWILIGHT ZONE	£779.50
81	GEN 13 LIMITED EDITION COLLECTOR'S PACK	£765.00
82	EERIE (Magazine)	£726.50
83	INCREDIBLE SCIENCE FICTION	£720.00
84	CHEYENNE KID	£694.50
85	GORGO	£682.50
86	MUNSTERS, THE	£670.00
87	TWO-FISTED ANNUAL	£655.00
88	CREEPY	£636.50
89	WARFRONT	£625.00
90	FIGHTIN' MARINES	£621.00
91	HERBIE	£620.00
92	MAN FROM U.N.C.L.E., THE	£600.00
	WIN A PRIZE COMICS	£600.00
94	FIGHTIN' ARMY	£581.50
95	OUTER SPACE	£560.00
96	DOUBLE LIFE OF PRIVATE STRONG, THE	£550.00
97	I LOVE YOU	£544.00
98	OUTLAWS OF THE WEST	£540.75
99	MONKEES, THE	£537.50
100	WYATT EARP, FRONTIER MARSHAL	£527.50

Top 100 U.S. Independent Titles

Rank	Title	Value
1	FOUR COLOR (Series II)	$143765.50
2	WHIZ COMICS	$121440.00
3	WALT DISNEY'S COMICS AND STORIES	$84175.75
4	CAPTAIN MARVEL ADVENTURES	$74055.00
5	MASTER COMICS	$58085.00
6	POLICE COMICS	$49870.00
7	FOUR COLOR (Series I)	$36531.00
8	ARCHIE COMICS	$35625.50
9	CAPTAIN MARVEL JR.	$30090.00
10	MAD MAGAZINE	$24767.50
11	ADVENTURES INTO THE UNKNOWN	$14825.00
12	ARCHIE'S GIRLS BETTY AND VERONICA	$13145.50
13	TARZAN	$12904.50
14	MARVEL FAMILY, THE	$12785.00
15	RED RAVEN COMICS	$12500.00
16	VAULT OF HORROR	$12060.00
17	TALES FROM THE CRYPT	$10645.00
18	FORBIDDEN WORLDS (1st Series)	$10480.00
19	ARCHIE'S PAL JUGHEAD	$9151.50
20	WEIRD SCIENCE (1st Series)	$8840.00
21	HAUNT OF FEAR	$8655.00
22	RICHIE RICH	$7966.25
23	WEIRD FANTASY (1st Series)	$7650.00
24	STRANGE SUSPENSE STORIES	$7455.00
25	TUROK SON OF STONE	$7162.50
26	CRIME SUSPENSTORIES	$7015.00
27	MARY MARVEL COMICS	$6630.00
28	SPACE ADVENTURES	$6173.00
29	DELL GIANTS	$6130.00
30	EERIE	$6045.00
31	LITTLE DOT	$5498.50
32	STAR TREK	$4680.00
33	ARCHIE ANNUAL	$4660.00
34	ARCHIE'S JOKE BOOK MAGAZINE	$4417.00
35	TWO-FISTED TALES	$4325.00
36	ARCHIE'S PALS 'N GALS	$4166.00
37	SHOCK SUSPENSTORIES (1st Series)	$4125.00
38	VAMPIRELLA (1st Series)	$4025.00
39	FAMOUS MONSTERS OF FILMLAND	$3470.50
40	MYSTERIES OF UNEXPLORED WORLDS	$3050.00
41	TALES OF THE MYSTERIOUS TRAVELLER	$3049.00
42	SPOOKY	$2812.00
43	FLY, ADVENTURES OF THE	$2660.00
44	THREE STOOGES, THE	$2647.50
45	UNUSUAL TALES	$2635.00
46	JETSONS, THE	$2610.00
47	BABY HUEY, THE BABY GIANT	$2553.00
48	FRONTLINE COMBAT	$2545.00
49	CASPER, THE FRIENDLY GHOST	$2526.50
50	WEIRD SCIENCE-FANTASY (1st Series) ANNUAL	$2350.00
51	ARCHIE'S GALS BETTY AND VERONICA ANNUAL	$2200.00
52	UNKNOWN WORLDS	$2177.50
53	MAGNUS ROBOT FIGHTER	$2072.00
54	BLACK RIDER	$2065.00
55	FLINTSTONES, THE	$2062.50
56	OUT OF THIS WORLD	$2060.00
57	DARK SHADOWS	$1987.50
58	SAD SACK AND THE SARGE	$1969.00
59	SIX-GUN HEROES	$1960.00
60	LASH LARUE WESTERN	$1950.00
61	RIFLEMAN, THE	$1915.00
62	CRY FOR DAWN	$1895.00
63	MY LITTLE MARGIE	$1870.00
64	ARCHIE'S PAL JUGHEAD ANNUAL	$1775.00
65	WEIRD SCIENCE-FANTASY (1st Series)	$1725.00
66	CREEPY	$1683.00
67	EERIE (Magazine)	$1633.00
68	SPACE FAMILY ROBINSON	$1615.00
69	ROMANTIC STORY	$1600.00
70	STRANGE WORLDS	$1585.00
71	SPACE WAR	$1580.00
72	ROCKY LANE WESTERN	$1570.00
73	BILLY THE KID	$1563.75
74	PHANTOM, THE	$1535.00
75	KONGA	$1490.00
76	DOCTOR SOLAR, MAN OF THE ATOM	$1450.00
77	CEREBUS THE AARDVARK	$1441.25
78	SAD SACK LAUGH SPECIAL	$1420.00
79	ARCHIE'S MADHOUSE	$1417.00
80	CHEYENNE	$1355.00
81	HAVE GUN WILL TRAVEL	$1305.00
82	FIGHTIN' MARINES	$1293.00
83	GORGO	$1215.00
84	MUNSTERS, THE	$1190.00
85	TWILIGHT ZONE	$1186.00
86	FIGHTIN' ARMY	$1167.50
87	HERBIE	$1165.00
88	MAN FROM U.N.C.L.E., THE	$1162.50
89	GEN 13 LIMITED EDITION COLLECTOR'S PACK	$1150.00
90	INCREDIBLE SCIENCE FICTION	$1070.00
91	CHEYENNE KID	$1060.00
92	WARFRONT	$1015.00
93	TWO-FISTED ANNUAL	$985.00
94	KORAK, SON OF TARZAN (1st Series)	$950.00
95	I LOVE YOU	$939.00
96	OUTLAWS OF THE WEST	$897.50
97	WIN A PRIZE COMICS	$875.00
98	BONE	$870.00
99	L'IL GENIUS	$862.00
100	OUTER SPACE	$830.00

Top 100 U.K. Titles

Rank	Title	Value
1	DETECTIVE COMICS	£495125.10
2	MORE FUN COMICS	£339460.00
3	ACTION COMICS	£281259.80
4	ADVENTURE COMICS	£266093.75
5	MARVEL COMICS	£200095.00
6	SUPERMAN (1st Series) (ADVENTURES OF SUPERMAN)	£162448.75
7	CAPTAIN AMERICA COMICS	£157592.50
8	BATMAN	£148220.20
9	ALL-AMERICAN COMICS	£136130.00
10	FLASH COMICS	£118260.00
11	ALL-STAR COMICS	£111475.00
12	FOUR COLOR (Series II)	£96637.25
13	WHIZ COMICS	£81070.00
14	SHOWCASE	£67321.10
15	WALT DISNEY'S COMICS AND STORIES	£55396.50
16	WORLD'S FINEST COMICS (1st Series)	£53909.50
17	GREEN LANTERN (1st Series)	£53220.00
18	HUMAN TORCH (1st Series)	£51295.00
19	SENSATION COMICS	£51205.00
20	CAPTAIN MARVEL ADVENTURES	£49620.00
21	SUB-MARINER (1st) COMICS	£49120.00
22	PLANET COMICS	£45135.00
23	WONDER WOMAN	£44233.50
24	MASTER COMICS	£39015.00
25	POLICE COMICS	£33425.00
26	AMAZING SPIDERMAN, THE	£29112.25
27	NEW YORK WORLD'S FAIR	£29000.00
28	FANTASTIC FOUR	£28687.75
29	COMIC CAVALCADE	£25405.00
30	FOUR COLOR (Series I)	£24825.00
31	STRANGE ADVENTURES	£24302.50
32	ALL-FLASH	£23980.00
33	ARCHIE COMICS	£23862.00
34	SUPERBOY	£21216.50
35	JOURNEY INTO MYSTERY	£20185.00
36	CAPTAIN MARVEL JR.	£20185.00
37	BRAVE AND THE BOLD, THE	£19772.60
38	STRANGE TALES (1st Series)	£19469.50
39	MYSTERY IN SPACE	£18748.00
40	OUR ARMY AT WAR	£16923.00
41	NEW BOOK OF COMICS	£16675.00
42	MAD MAGAZINE	£16467.50
43	AMAZING FANTASY	£15009.50
44	TALES OF SUSPENSE (1st Series)	£13934.50
45	TALES TO ASTONISH (1st Series)	£13792.50
46	HOUSE OF MYSTERY	£13647.75
47	INCREDIBLE HULK (1st Series)	£12551.50
48	FLASH (1st Series)	£11575.75
49	STAR-SPANGLED WAR STORIES	£11453.00
50	LEADING COMICS	£10912.50
51	JIMMY OLSEN, SUPERMAN'S PAL	£10589.50
52	X-MEN, THE UNCANNY	£10037.50
53	TALES OF THE UNEXPECTED	£10007.50
54	ADVENTURES INTO THE UNKNOWN	£9697.50
55	DANDY COMIC, THE	£9641.35
56	ALL-AMERICAN MEN OF WAR	£8742.50
57	ARCHIE'S GIRLS BETTY AND VERONICA	£8584.50
58	TARZAN	£8541.00
59	MARVEL FAMILY, THE	£8540.00
60	MY GREATEST ADVENTURE	£8402.50
61	VAULT OF HORROR	£8070.00
62	RED RAVEN COMICS	£8000.00
63	SUGAR AND SPIKE	£7525.75
64	TALES FROM THE CRYPT	£7125.00
65	JUSTICE LEAGUE OF AMERICA	£7100.25
66	BOB HOPE, THE ADVENTURES OF	£7057.50
67	LOIS LANE, SUPERMAN'S GIRLFRIEND	£6977.75
68	FORBIDDEN WORLDS (1st Series)	£6805.00
69	GREEN LANTERN (2nd Series)	£6801.00
70	AVENGERS	£6530.25
71	CHALLENGERS OF THE UNKNOWN	£6473.25
72	HOUSE OF SECRETS	£6183.50
73	WEIRD SCIENCE (1st Series)	£5885.00
74	ARCHIE'S PAL JUGHEAD	£5878.00
75	HAUNT OF FEAR	£5820.00
76	OUR FIGHTING FORCES	£5594.50
77	RICHIE RICH	£5303.75
78	WEIRD FANTASY (1st Series)	£5100.00
79	STRANGE SUSPENSE STORIES	£4975.00
80	RUPERT ANNUAL	£4969.00
81	DAREDEVIL	£4832.30
82	CRIME SUSPENSTORIES	£4700.00
83	REAL FACT COMICS	£4630.00
84	DANDY BOOK, THE	£4572.50
85	TUROK SON OF STONE	£4564.00
86	MARY MARVEL COMICS	£4430.00
87	DELL GIANTS	£4137.50
88	EERIE	£4080.00
89	G.I. COMBAT	£3987.50
90	SPACE ADVENTURES	£3882.00
91	LITTLE DOT	£3717.00
92	BLACKHAWK	£3691.00
93	GIRL'S LOVE STORIES	£3684.00
94	REX THE WONDER DOG	£3675.00
95	GIRL'S ROMANCES	£3535.00
96	ALL-AMERICAN WESTERN	£3295.00
97	RAWHIDE KID	£3250.00
98	ARCHIE ANNUAL	£3177.50
99	STAR TREK	£3127.50
100	ALL-STAR WESTERN	£3120.00

Top 100 U.S. Titles

Rank	Title	Value
1	DETECTIVE COMICS	$745061.25
2	MORE FUN COMICS	$507625.00
3	ACTION COMICS	$421429.75
4	ADVENTURE COMICS	$397241.25
5	MARVEL COMICS	$299665.00
6	SUPERMAN (1st Series) (ADVENTURES OF SUPERMAN)	$244612.00
7	CAPTAIN AMERICA COMICS	$238924.00
8	BATMAN	$224836.00
9	ALL-AMERICAN COMICS	$202050.00
10	FLASH COMICS	$176650.00
11	ALL-STAR COMICS	$167350.00
12	FOUR COLOR (Series II)	$143765.50
13	WHIZ COMICS	$121440.00
14	SHOWCASE	$103216.25
15	WALT DISNEY'S COMICS AND STORIES	$84175.75
16	WORLD'S FINEST COMICS (1st Series)	$81509.50
17	GREEN LANTERN (1st Series)	$79675.00
18	SENSATION COMICS	$76575.00
19	HUMAN TORCH (1st Series)	$75725.00
20	CAPTAIN MARVEL ADVENTURES	$74055.00
21	SUB-MARINER (1st) COMICS	$73465.00
22	PLANET COMICS	$66900.00
23	WONDER WOMAN	$66074.00
24	MASTER COMICS	$58085.00
25	AMAZING SPIDERMAN, THE	$52444.50
26	FANTASTIC FOUR	$52356.50
27	POLICE COMICS	$49870.00
28	NEW YORK WORLD'S FAIR	$43500.00
29	STRANGE ADVENTURES	$39389.00
30	COMIC CAVALCADE	$37970.00
31	FOUR COLOR (Series I)	$36531.00
32	ALL-FLASH	$36025.00
33	ARCHIE COMICS	$35625.50
34	SUPERBOY	$32940.00
35	STRANGE TALES (1st Series)	$31939.50
36	BRAVE AND THE BOLD, THE	$30982.25
37	JOURNEY INTO MYSTERY	$30815.00
38	CAPTAIN MARVEL JR.	$30090.00
39	AMAZING FANTASY	$30015.00
40	MYSTERY IN SPACE	$29468.00
41	OUR ARMY AT WAR	$28023.50
42	NEW BOOK OF COMICS	$25000.00
43	MAD MAGAZINE	$24767.50
44	HOUSE OF MYSTERY	$22994.00
45	TALES OF SUSPENSE (1st Series)	$22843.00
46	FLASH (1st Series)	$22400.50
47	TALES TO ASTONISH (1st Series)	$22022.50
48	INCREDIBLE HULK (1st Series)	$21177.50
49	X-MEN, THE UNCANNY	$19512.25
50	STAR-SPANGLED WAR STORIES	$18080.00
51	JIMMY OLSEN, SUPERMAN'S PAL	$16497.00
52	LEADING COMICS	$16190.00
53	TALES OF THE UNEXPECTED	$15835.00
54	ADVENTURES INTO THE UNKNOWN	$14825.00
55	DANDY COMIC, THE	$14462.05
56	GREEN LANTERN (2nd Series)	$13835.50
57	MY GREATEST ADVENTURE	$13610.00
58	ALL-AMERICAN MEN OF WAR	$13465.00
59	JUSTICE LEAGUE OF AMERICA	$13310.50
60	LOIS LANE, SUPERMAN'S GIRLFRIEND	$13195.00
61	ARCHIE'S GIRLS BETTY AND VERONICA	$13145.50
62	TARZAN	$12904.50
63	MARVEL FAMILY, THE	$12785.00
64	RED RAVEN COMICS	$12500.00
65	SUGAR AND SPIKE	$12256.25
66	VAULT OF HORROR	$12060.00
67	AVENGERS	$10906.50
68	BOB HOPE, THE ADVENTURES OF	$10865.00
69	TALES FROM THE CRYPT	$10645.00
70	FORBIDDEN WORLDS (1st Series)	$10480.00
71	HOUSE OF SECRETS	$10245.75
72	CHALLENGERS OF THE UNKNOWN	$10157.00
73	OUR FIGHTING FORCES	$9607.50
74	ARCHIE'S PAL JUGHEAD	$9151.50
75	WEIRD SCIENCE (1st Series)	$8840.00
76	HAUNT OF FEAR	$8655.00
77	G.I. COMBAT	$8595.00
78	RICHIE RICH	$7966.25
79	WEIRD FANTASY (1st Series)	$7650.00
80	DAREDEVIL	$7605.25
81	STRANGE SUSPENSE STORIES	$7455.00
82	RUPERT ANNUAL	$7433.50
83	TUROK SON OF STONE	$7162.50
84	CRIME SUSPENSTORIES	$7015.00
85	GIRL'S LOVE STORIES	$6935.00
86	DANDY BOOK, THE	$6888.25
87	GIRL'S ROMANCES	$6872.50
88	REAL FACT COMICS	$6760.00
89	MARY MARVEL COMICS	$6630.00
90	SPACE ADVENTURES	$6173.00
91	DELL GIANTS	$6130.00
92	EERIE	$6045.00
93	BLACKHAWK	$5984.50
94	REX THE WONDER DOG	$5530.00
95	SGT. FURY AND HIS HOWLING COMMANDOS	$5520.00
96	LITTLE DOT	$5498.50
97	RAWHIDE KID	$5476.00
98	ALL-AMERICAN WESTERN	$4855.00
99	ALL-STAR WESTERN	$4765.00
100	STAR TREK	$4680.00

Top 100 U.K. Comics

Rank	Comic	Price
1	ACTION COMICS #1	£113500.00
2	DETECTIVE COMICS #27	£106675.00
3	SUPERMAN (1st Series) (ADVENTURES OF SUPERMAN) #1	£80000.00
4	MARVEL COMICS #1	£65000.00
5	DETECTIVE COMICS #1	£53500.00
6	BATMAN #1	£45000.00
7	WHIZ COMICS #1	£42750.00
8	ALL-AMERICAN COMICS #16	£42500.00
9	CAPTAIN AMERICA COMICS #1	£41675.00
10	MORE FUN COMICS #1	£40000.00
11	MORE FUN COMICS #52	£37350.00
12	FLASH COMICS #1	£35000.00
13	MORE FUN COMICS #53	£26700.00
14	DETECTIVE COMICS #33	£24000.00
15	ADVENTURE COMICS #40	£23350.00
	ALL-STAR COMICS #3	£23350.00
17	DETECTIVE COMICS #38	£21675.00
18	ALL-STAR COMICS #8	£20000.00
	CAPTAIN MARVEL ADVENTURES #0	£20000.00
	MORE FUN COMICS #6	£20000.00
21	GREEN LANTERN (1st Series) #1	£19350.00
22	NEW YORK WORLD'S FAIR #1	£18750.00
23	SHOWCASE #4	£18700.00
24	MORE FUN COMICS #2	£18675.00
25	SENSATION COMICS #1	£18350.00
26	DETECTIVE COMICS #29	£17350.00
	DETECTIVE COMICS #31	£17350.00
28	ACTION COMICS #2	£16750.00
29	HUMAN TORCH (1st Series) #2	£16000.00
	MARVEL COMICS #2	£16000.00
	SUB-MARINER (1st) COMICS #1	£16000.00
32	ADVENTURE COMICS #48	£15000.00
	AMAZING FANTASY #15	£15000.00
34	ADVENTURE COMICS #1	£13350.00
	MARVEL COMICS #9	£13350.00
	WONDER WOMAN #1	£13350.00
37	WALT DISNEY'S COMICS AND STORIES #1	£13300.00
38	AMAZING SPIDERMAN, THE #1	£12000.00
39	DETECTIVE COMICS #2	£11700.00
40	DETECTIVE COMICS #28	£11675.00
41	FANTASTIC FOUR #1	£11000.00
42	ADVENTURE COMICS #73	£10500.00
43	NEW YORK WORLD'S FAIR #2	£10250.00
44	MARVEL COMICS #5	£10000.00
	NEW BOOK OF COMICS #1	£10000.00
	SHOWCASE #8	£10000.00
47	WORLD'S FINEST COMICS (1st Series) #1	£9700.00
48	MORE FUN COMICS #3	£9350.00
	MORE FUN COMICS #4	£9350.00
	MORE FUN COMICS #5	£9350.00
	MORE FUN COMICS #73	£9350.00
52	ALL-AMERICAN COMICS #17	£9250.00
	ALL-AMERICAN COMICS #19	£9250.00
54	MORE FUN COMICS #55	£9100.00
55	ACTION COMICS #3	£9000.00
56	CAPTAIN AMERICA COMICS #22	£8500.00
57	ADVENTURE COMICS #61	£8350.00
	ALL-STAR COMICS #1	£8350.00
	DETECTIVE COMICS #3	£8350.00
60	ADVENTURE COMICS #72	£8250.00
	ALL-FLASH #1	£8250.00
62	BATMAN #2	£8000.00
	MORE FUN COMICS #14	£8000.00
	RED RAVEN COMICS #1	£8000.00
65	CAPTAIN AMERICA COMICS #2	£7675.00
66	SUPERMAN (1st Series) (ADVENTURES OF SUPERMAN) #2	£7350.00
67	ACTION COMICS #7	£7000.00
	ARCHIE COMICS #1	£7000.00
	INCREDIBLE HULK (1st Series) #1	£7000.00
70	FOUR COLOR (Series I) #16	£6930.00
71	MARVEL COMICS #3	£6675.00
	NEW BOOK OF COMICS #2	£6675.00
73	MORE FUN COMICS #54	£6500.00
	PLANET COMICS #1	£6500.00
75	CAPTAIN AMERICA COMICS #3	£6350.00
76	ALL-AMERICAN COMICS #25	£6250.00
77	ACTION COMICS #10	£6000.00
	ADVENTURE COMICS #2	£6000.00
	ALL-AMERICAN COMICS #18	£6000.00
	COMIC CAVALCADE #1	£6000.00
	DETECTIVE COMICS #8	£6000.00
	MARVEL COMICS #8	£6000.00
83	FOUR COLOR (Series I) #4	£5775.00
84	BATMAN #3	£5500.00
	FOUR COLOR (Series II) #9	£5500.00
86	ACTION COMICS #4	£5350.00
	ACTION COMICS #5	£5350.00
	ACTION COMICS #6	£5350.00
	DETECTIVE COMICS #35	£5350.00
	MARVEL COMICS #4	£5350.00
91	BATMAN #11	£5000.00
92	SUPERMAN (1st Series) (ADVENTURES OF SUPERMAN) #3	£4900.00
93	DETECTIVE COMICS #18	£4850.00
	MORE FUN COMICS #101	£4850.00
95	DETECTIVE COMICS #40	£4675.00
96	WALT DISNEY'S COMICS AND STORIES #2	£4650.00
97	DETECTIVE COMICS #4	£4500.00
	DETECTIVE COMICS #5	£4500.00
	MASTER COMICS #1	£4500.00
	SUPERBOY #1	£4500.00

Top 100 U.S. Comics

Rank	Comic	Value
1	ACTION COMICS #1	$170000.00
2	DETECTIVE COMICS #27	$160000.00
3	SUPERMAN (1st Series) (ADVENTURES OF SUPERMAN) #1	$120000.00
4	MARVEL COMICS #1	$97500.00
5	DETECTIVE COMICS #1	$80000.00
6	BATMAN #1	$67500.00
7	WHIZ COMICS #1	$64000.00
8	CAPTAIN AMERICA COMICS #1	$62500.00
9	ALL-AMERICAN COMICS #16	$62000.00
10	MORE FUN COMICS #1	$60000.00
11	MORE FUN COMICS #52	$56000.00
12	FLASH COMICS #1	$52500.00
13	MORE FUN COMICS #53	$40000.00
14	DETECTIVE COMICS #33	$36000.00
15	ADVENTURE COMICS #40	$35000.00
	ALL-STAR COMICS #3	$35000.00
17	DETECTIVE COMICS #38	$32500.00
18	ALL-STAR COMICS #8	$30000.00
	AMAZING FANTASY #15	$30000.00
	CAPTAIN MARVEL ADVENTURES #0	$30000.00
	MORE FUN COMICS #6	$30000.00
22	GREEN LANTERN (1st Series) #1	$29000.00
23	MORE FUN COMICS #2	$28000.00
	NEW YORK WORLD'S FAIR #1	$28000.00
	SHOWCASE #4	$28000.00
26	SENSATION COMICS #1	$27500.00
27	DETECTIVE COMICS #29	$26000.00
	DETECTIVE COMICS #31	$26000.00
29	ACTION COMICS #2	$25000.00
30	MARVEL COMICS #2	$24000.00
	SUB-MARINER (1st) COMICS #1	$24000.00
32	HUMAN TORCH (1st Series) #2	$23000.00
33	ADVENTURE COMICS #48	$22500.00
34	AMAZING SPIDERMAN, THE #1	$22000.00
35	FANTASTIC FOUR #1	$21000.00
36	ADVENTURE COMICS #1	$20000.00
	MARVEL COMICS #9	$20000.00
	WALT DISNEY'S COMICS AND STORIES #1	$20000.00
	WONDER WOMAN #1	$20000.00
40	DETECTIVE COMICS #2	$17500.00
	DETECTIVE COMICS #28	$17500.00
42	CAPTAIN AMERICA COMICS #22	$16000.00
43	NEW YORK WORLD'S FAIR #2	$15500.00
44	ADVENTURE COMICS #73	$15000.00
	MARVEL COMICS #5	$15000.00
	NEW BOOK OF COMICS #1	$15000.00
	SHOWCASE #8	$15000.00
48	WORLD'S FINEST COMICS (1st Series) #1	$14500.00
49	ALL-AMERICAN COMICS #19	$14000.00
	MORE FUN COMICS #3	$14000.00
	MORE FUN COMICS #4	$14000.00
	MORE FUN COMICS #5	$14000.00
	MORE FUN COMICS #73	$14000.00
54	ALL-AMERICAN COMICS #17	$13750.00
55	MORE FUN COMICS #55	$13600.00
56	ACTION COMICS #3	$13500.00
57	ADVENTURE COMICS #61	$12500.00
	ALL-FLASH #1	$12500.00
	ALL-STAR COMICS #1	$12500.00
	DETECTIVE COMICS #3	$12500.00
	RED RAVEN COMICS #1	$12500.00
62	ADVENTURE COMICS #72	$12000.00
	BATMAN #2	$12000.00
	MORE FUN COMICS #14	$12000.00
65	CAPTAIN AMERICA COMICS #2	$11500.00
	INCREDIBLE HULK (1st Series) #1	$11500.00
67	SUPERMAN (1st Series) (ADVENTURES OF SUPERMAN) #2	$11000.00
68	ACTION COMICS #7	$10500.00
	ARCHIE COMICS #1	$10500.00
70	MARVEL COMICS #3	$10000.00
	NEW BOOK OF COMICS #2	$10000.00
72	FOUR COLOR (Series I) #16	$9900.00
73	MORE FUN COMICS #54	$9750.00
74	CAPTAIN AMERICA COMICS #3	$9500.00
	PLANET COMICS #1	$9500.00
76	ALL-AMERICAN COMICS #25	$9250.00
77	ACTION COMICS #10	$9000.00
	ADVENTURE COMICS #2	$9000.00
	ALL-AMERICAN COMICS #18	$9000.00
	COMIC CAVALCADE #1	$9000.00
	DETECTIVE COMICS #8	$9000.00
	MARVEL COMICS #8	$9000.00
83	FOUR COLOR (Series I) #4	$8500.00
84	BATMAN #3	$8250.00
85	ACTION COMICS #4	$8000.00
	ACTION COMICS #5	$8000.00
	ACTION COMICS #6	$8000.00
	DETECTIVE COMICS #35	$8000.00
	MARVEL COMICS #4	$8000.00
90	BATMAN #11	$7500.00
	FOUR COLOR (Series II) #9	$7500.00
92	SUPERMAN (1st Series) (ADVENTURES OF SUPERMAN) #3	$7350.00
93	DETECTIVE COMICS #18	$7250.00
	MORE FUN COMICS #101	$7250.00
95	DETECTIVE COMICS #40	$7000.00
	WALT DISNEY'S COMICS AND STORIES #2	$7000.00
98	DETECTIVE COMICS #4	$6750.00
	DETECTIVE COMICS #5	$6750.00
	SUPERBOY #1	$6750.00
100	GREEN LANTERN (1st Series) #2	$6500.00

Differential Examples

Percentages quoted below are not hard and fast but at least give some idea of relative differences in value between the US and UK markets

Ms Marvel #18 – 400% greater value in the US Market than in the UK Market (555% last year)

The Man Called Nova #25 – 166% greater value in the UK Market than in the US Market (same as last year)

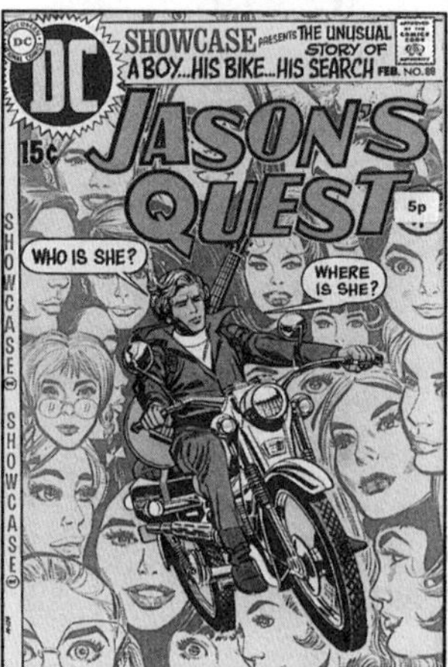

Showcase #88 – 381% greater value in the US Market than in the UK Market (same as last year)

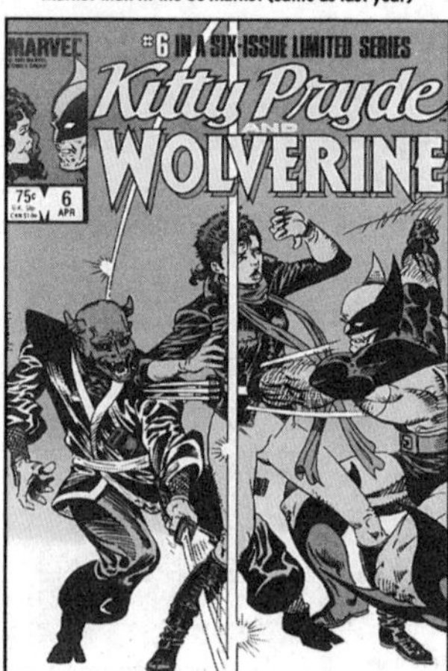

Kitty Pryde & Wolverine #6 – 77% greater value in the UK Market than in the US Market (111% last year)

Machine Man #19 – 200% greater value in the US Market than in the UK Market (400% last year)

Adventure Comics #492 – 111% greater value in the UK Market than in the US Market (133% last year)

TOP 50
Differential DC Comics and ranges £ to $

Below are listed comics valued in pounds sterling on the U.K. market and their equivalent guide value in dollars on the U.S. market. Rather than list simply individual comics when there may be a run of ten or twenty all the same price/percentage, ranges are included.

1	ADVENTURE COMICS #467	£1.50	$10.00	444.44%
2	GREEN LANTERN (2ND SERIES) #116	£4.00	$25.00	416.67%
3	ATOM, THE #41-42, 45	£7.00	$42.50	404.76%
4	METAL MEN #51-56	£2.50	$15.00	400.00%
5	OUR FIGHTING FORCES #171, 175-177	£1.25	$7.50	400.00%
6	SHOWCASE #88-90	£3.50	$20.00	380.95%
7	ATOM, THE #43-44	£7.50	$42.50	377.78%
8	METAL MEN #27	£12.50	$70.00	373.33%
9	SANDMAN (2ND SERIES) #8	£9.00	$50.00	370.37%
10	AQUAMAN #36-40	£10.00	$55.00	366.67%
11	AQUAMAN #48	£6.50	$35.00	358.97%
12	AQUAMAN #33	£15.00	$80.00	355.56%
13	HOUSE OF MYSTERY #301-321	£0.75	$4.00	355.56%
14	ATOM, THE #31-35, 37-38	£9.00	$47.50	351.85%
15	AQUAMAN #41-4, 49	£6.00	$30.00	333.33%
16	ATOM, THE #39-40	£9.00	$45.00	333.33%
17	FLASH (1ST SERIES) #191-195, 197-199, 215	£7.50	$37.50	333.33%
18	FLASH (1ST SERIES) #215	£5.00	$25.00	333.33%
19	GREEN LANTERN (2ND SERIES) #66-69	£8.00	$40.00	333.33%
20	HOUSE OF MYSTERY #281, 283-300	£1.00	$5.00	333.33%
21	METAL MEN #45, 48-50	£3.00	$15.00	333.33%
22	OUR FIGHTING FORCES #163-164, 167-170, 172-174	£1.50	$7.50	333.33%
23	SANDMAN (2ND SERIES) #3	£7.00	$35.00	333.33%
24	SANDMAN (2ND SERIES) #4-5	£6.00	$30.00	333.33%
25	SANDMAN (2ND SERIES) #6-7	£5.00	$25.00	333.33%
26	FLASH (1ST SERIES) #200	£8.00	$37.50	312.50%
27	ADVENTURE COMICS #381	£7.50	$35.00	311.11%
28	METAL MEN #31-41	£7.50	$35.00	311.11%
29	JUSTICE LEAGUE OF AMERICA #56	£10.00	$45.00	300.00%
30	LOIS LANE, SUPERMAN'S GIRLFRIEND #74	£10.00	$45.00	300.00%
31	METAL MEN #21-26, 28-30	£10.00	$45.00	300.00%
32	OUR FIGHTING FORCES #141-150	£2.00	$9.00	300.00%
33	STRANGE ADVENTURES #132	£20.00	$90.00	300.00%
34	AQUAMAN #31-32, 34-35	£12.50	$55.00	293.33%
35	DEMON, THE #6-7, 9-10	£4.00	$17.50	291.67%
36	BATMAN #442	£1.75	$7.50	285.71%
37	DEMON, THE #11-16	£3.50	$15.00	285.71%
38	G.I. COMBAT #148-150	£3.50	$15.00	285.71%
39	JUSTICE LEAGUE OF AMERICA #61-62, 65-66, 68-70	£7.00	$30.00	285.71%
40	METAL MEN #42-44	£3.50	$15.00	285.71%
41	OUR FIGHTING FORCES #165-166, 178-180	£1.75	$7.50	285.71%
42	SANDMAN (2ND SERIES) #11-13	£3.50	$15.00	285.71%
43	AQUAMAN #53-56	£3.00	$12.50	277.78%
44	JUSTICE LEAGUE OF AMERICA	£6.00	$25.00	277.78%
45	SANDMAN (2ND SERIES) #22	£6.00	$25.00	277.78%
46	JUSTICE LEAGUE OF AMERICA #64	£8.00	$32.50	270.83%
47	SANDMAN (2ND SERIES) #2	£10.00	$40.00	266.67%
48	SGT. ROCK #311-312	£2.50	$10.00	266.67%
49	STRANGE ADVENTURES #141, 144, 147	£22.50	$90.00	266.67%
50	SUPERMAN (1ST SERIES) (ADVENTURES OF SUPERMAN) #499	£0.75	$3.00	266.67%

TOP 50 Differential DC Comics and ranges $ to £

Below are listed comics valued in pounds sterling on the U.K market and their equivalent guide value in dollars on the U.S market after conversion. Rather than list simply individual comics when there may be a run of ten or twenty all the same price/percentage, ranges are included.

1	DC COMICS PRESENTS #26	$1.50	£4 00	177.78%
2	DC SUPER-STARS #3	$2.00	£5.00	166.67%
3	ADVENTURE COMICS #491	$3.00	£6.00	133.33%
4	ADVENTURE COMICS#500	$3.00	£6.00	133.33%
5	DC SPECIAL BLUE RIBBON DIGEST#1	$2.50	£5.00	133.33%
6	SUPERBOY #211	$2.50	£5.00	133.33%
7	SUPERBOY #227	$2.00	£3.50	116.67%
8	ADVENTURE COMICS#492-499, 501-503	$3.00	£5.00	111.11%
9	BATMAN PIZZA HUT GIVEAWAY #NN	$3.00	£5.00	111.11 %
10	BATMAN AND THE OUTSIDERS #1	$2 00	£3 00	100.00%
11	DC SUPER-STARS #17	$3.00	£4.50	100.00%
12	LIMITED COLLECTOR'S EDITION #C-51, C-59	$10.00	£15.00	100.00%
13	SUPERBOY #221-226, 230	$2.00	£3.00	100.00%
14	SUPERBOY #212-213, 218	$2.50	£3.50	93.33%
15	ALL-STAR COMICS (2ND SERIES) #61, 65	$1.50	£2.00	88 89%
16	BATMAN AND THE OUTSIDERS #2	$1.50	£2.00	88.89%
17	DC SUPER-STARS #12-14	$1.50	£2.00	88 89%
18	FOUR STAR SPECTACULAR #1	$1.50	£2.00	88.89%
19	ANIMAL MAN #6-10	$2.00	£2.50	83.33%
20	BATMAN, SHADOW OF THE #2-3, 5	$4.00	£5.00	83 33%
21	DC SUPER-STARS #6	$2.00	£2.50	83.33%
22	JUSTICE LEAGUE OF AMERICA #150	$4 00	£5.00	83.33%
23	SUPER-TEAM FAMILY #2	$2.00	£2.50	83.33%
24	SUPERBOY #232, 235	$2.00	£2.50	83.33%
25	SWAMP THING (2ND SERIES) #15	$2 00	£2 50	83.33%
26	BATMAN FAMILY#19-20	$5.00	£6.00	80.00%
27	DC SPECIAL BLUE RIBBON DIGEST #2-5	$2 50	£3 00	80.00%
28	SUPERBOY #198-199, 202, 205	$5 00	£6.00	80.00%
29	SUPERBOY #219-220	$2.50	£3.00	80.00%
30	JOKER, THE #9	$6.00	£7.00	77.78%
31	SUPERMAN FAMILY#182	$3.00	£3.50	77.78%
32	BATMAN #180	$65.00	£75.00	76.92%
33	ANIMANIACS #19	$1.75	£2.00	76.19%
34	JUSTICE LEAGUE OF AMERICA #123-124	$3.50	£4.00	76.19%
35	JUSTICE LEAGUE OF AMERICA #143, 145	$4.00	£4.50	75.00%
36	BATMAN FAMILY#7-8, 11-13	$5.00	£5.50	73.33%
37	SUPERBOY #208	$5 00	£5.50	73.33%
38	WITCHING HOUR #26	$2.50	£2.75	73.33%
39	BATMAN FAMILY#5	$6.00	£6.50	72.22%
40	LEGION OF SUPER-HEROES (1 ST SERIES) #294	$2 50	£2 50	66 67%
41	LEGION OF SUPER-HEROES (1ST SERIES) #285-287	$2.00	£2.00	66.67%
42	SUPERMAN FAMILY#194	$3.00	£3.00	66.67%
43	SWAMP THING (2ND SERIES) #26-27	$5.00	£5.00	66.67%
44	SWAMP THING(2NDSERIES)#11-14, 16-19	$2.00	£2.00	66.67%
45	VIGILANTE, THE #50	$1.50	£1.50	66.67%
46	WHO'S WHO #2	$1.25	£1.25	66.67%
47	WITCHING HOUR #15-20	$3.00	£3.00	66.67%
48	WITCHING HOUR #21-30	$2.50	£2.50	66.67%
49	WITCHING HOUR #31-40	$2.00	£2.00	66.67%
50	WONDER WOMAN #247	$2.00	£2.00	66.67%

TOP 50 Differential Marvel Comics and ranges £ to $

Below are listed comics valued in pounds sterling on the U.K. market and their equivalent guide value in dollars on the U.S. market after conversion. Rather than list simply individual comics when there may be a run of ten or twenty all the same price/percentage, ranges are included.

1	MS. MARVEL #17	£1.50	$10.00	444.44%
2	X-MEN, THE UNCANNY #244	£3.00	$20.00	444.44%
3	MARVEL SPOTLIGHT #8	£7.00	$45.00	428.57%
4	MS. MARVEL #18	£2.50	$15.00	400.00%
5	MARVEL SPOTLIGHT #9-11	£7.00	$40.00	380.95%
6	HOWARD THE DUCK #13	£2.50	$12.50	333.33%
7	MS. MARVEL #16	£2.00	$10.00	333.33%
8	POWERMAN #78, 84	£4.00	$20.00	333.33%
9	SPECTACULAR SPIDERMAN #147	£3.50	$17.50	333.33%
10	WEB OF SPIDERMAN, THE #48	£3.00	$15.00	333.33%
11	AMAZING SPIDERMAN, THE #326-327	£1.50	$7.00	311.11%
12	NEW MUTANTS #87	£6.00	$28.00	311.11%
13	WEREWOLF BY NIGHT #33	£7.50	$35.00	311.11%
14	X-MEN, THE UNCANNY #283	£3.00	$14.00	311.11%
15	MARVEL SPOTLIGHT #7	£10.00	$45.00	300.00%
16	POWERMAN #66	£10.00	$45.00	300.00%
17	X-MEN, THE UNCANNY #248	£5.00	$22.50	300.00%
18	AMAZING SPIDERMAN, THE #315-317	£4.00	$17.50	291.67%
19	STAR WARS #61-80	£4.00	$17.50	291.67%
20	STAR WARS #81-99	£3.50	$15.00	285.71%
21	X-MEN, THE UNCANNY #98-99	£14.00	$60.00	285.71%
22	STAR WARS #100	£6.00	$25.00	277.78%
23	X-MEN, THE UNCANNY #100	£16.00	$65.00	270.83%
24	AMAZING SPIDERMAN, THE #312	£5.00	$20.00	266.67%
25	AMAZING SPIDERMAN, THE #344	£2.50	$10.00	266.67%
26	AMAZING SPIDERMAN, THE #359	£1.50	$6.00	266.67%
27	AMAZING SPIDERMAN, THE #360	£2.00	$8.00	266.67%
28	HOWARD THE DUCK #12	£2.50	$10.00	266.67%
29	HUMAN FLY #2	£0.75	$3.00	266.67%
30	X-MEN, THE UNCANNY (30¢ COVER) #98-99	£15.00	$60.00	266.67%
31	X-MEN, THE UNCANNY #139	£7.50	$30.00	266.67%
32	X-MEN, THE UNCANNY #216-218, 220-221	£1.50	$6.00	266.67%
33	X-MEN, THE UNCANNY #240	£2.00	$8.00	266.67%
34	AMAZING SPIDERMAN, THE #200	£8.00	$30.00	250.00%
35	AMAZING SPIDERMAN, THE #245	£4.00	$15.00	250.00%
36	GODZILLA #2	£2.00	$7.50	250.00%
37	X-MEN, THE UNCANNY #222	£4.00	$15.00	250.00%
38	CHAMPIONS, THE #11-12	£3.50	$12.50	238.10%
39	STAR WARS #50	£7.00	$25.00	238.10%
40	TOMB OF DRACULA #23-28	£3.50	$12.50	238.10%
41	WEREWOLF BY NIGHT #20	£3.50	$12.50	238.10%
42	X-MEN, THE UNCANNY #101	£14.00	$50.00	238.10%
43	AMAZING SPIDERMAN, THE #252	£10.00	$35.00	233.33%
44	AMAZING SPIDERMAN, THE #300	£20.00	$70.00	233.33%
45	AMAZING SPIDERMAN, THE #386-387	£1.00	$3.50	233.33%
46	AMAZING SPIDERMAN, THE ANNUAL #26	£2.00	$7.00	233.33%
47	HUMAN FLY #1	£1.00	$3.50	233.33%
48	INCREDIBLE HULK (2ND SERIES) #340	£10.00	$35.00	233.33%
49	STAR WARS #51-60	£5.00	$17.50	233.33%
50	X-MEN, THE UNCANNY #131-132, 134-136	£5.00	$17.50	233.33%

TOP 50 Differential Marvel Comics and ranges $ to £

Below are listed comics valued in pounds sterling on the U.K. market and their equivalent guide value in dollars on the U.S. market after conversion. Rather than list simply individual comics when there may be a run of ten or twenty all the same price/percentage, ranges are included.

1	NOVA #25	$2.00	£5.00	166.67%
2	EPIC ILLUSTRATED #34	$2.50	£6.00	160.00%
3	AVENGERS #183	$3.00	£6.00	133.33%
4	BLACK DRAGON, THE #1	$1.50	£2.50	111.11%
5	NICK FURY, AGENT OF SHIELD #17-18	$3.00	£5.00	111.11%
6	GROO THE WANDERER #7	$4.00	£6.50	108.33%
7	EPIC ILLUSTRATED #26, 29, 33	$2.50	£4.00	106.67%
8	DAREDEVIL #161	$10.00	£15.00	100.00%
9	DRACULA LIVES! #2	$5.00	£7.50	100.00%
10	GROO THE WANDERER #6	$4.00	£6.00	100.00%
11	KULL AND THE BARBARIANS #3	$2.00	£3.00	100.00%
12	MARVEL GRAPHIC NOVEL #1 2ND PRINTING	$5.00	£7.50	100.00%
13	MARVEL GRAPHIC NOVEL #39 2ND PRINTING	$6.00	£9.00	100.00%
14	NICK FURY, AGENT OF SHIELD #16	$3.00	£4.50	100.00%
15	EPIC ILLUSTRATED #15	$2.50	£3.50	93.33%
16	HAWKEYE #2	$1.50	£2.00	88.89%
17	MARVEL SPOTLIGHT (2ND SERIES) #8	$1.50	£2.00	88.89%
18	POWERMAN #122-124	$1.50	£2.00	88.89%
19	ALPHA FLIGHT #1	$2.00	£2.50	83.33%
20	AVENGERS #302	$2.00	£2.50	83.33%
21	BIZARRE ADVENTURES #25-26, 29	$2.00	£2.50	83.33%
22	DAREDEVIL #169	$10.00	£12.50	83.33%
23	EPIC ILLUSTRATED #1	$4.00	£5.00	83.33%
24	FANTASTIC FOUR 2099 #1	$2.00	£2.50	83 33%
25	G.L. JOE SPECIAL TREASURY EDITION #NN	$4.00	£5.00	83.33%
26	GENERATION X COLLECTOR'S PREVIEW #1	$2.00	£2.50	83.33%
27	GROO THE WANDERER #2	$6.00	£7.50	83.33%
28	INCREDIBLE HULK (2ND SERIES) #153	$6.00	£7.50	83.33%
29	KID COLT OUTLAW #200	$2.00	£2.50	83.33%
30	MARVEL TRIPLE ACTION GIANT SIZE #1	$4.00	£5.00	83.33%
31	WEST COAST AVENGERS, THE #3	$2.00	£2.50	83.33%
32	X-MEN AT THE STATE FAIR OF TEXAS	$20.00	£25.00	83.33%
33	AKIRA #25	$5.00	£6.00	80.00%
34	CAPTAIN AMERICA ANNUAL #4	$5.00	£6.00	80 00%
35	EPIC ILLUSTRATED #11, 16, 27-28, 30-32	$2.50	£3.00	80 00%
36	GROO THE WANDERER #3, 5	$5 00	£6.00	80.00%
37	POWERMAN #125	$2.50	£3.00	80.00%
38	REN & STIMPY #1	$5 00	£6.00	80.00%
39	WEST COAST AVENGERS #1	$2.50	£3.00	80.00%
40	ALPHA FLIGHT #11-12	$1.50	£1.75	77 78%
41	AVENGERS #200	$3.00	£3.50	77.78%
42	DAREDEVIL #252	$3.00	£3.50	77.78%
43	DEATH'S HEAD #10	$1.50	£1.75	77.78%
44	KITTY PRYDE AND WOLVERINE #6	$3.00	£3.50	77.78%
45	MAN-THING #6-7	$3.00	£3.50	77.78%
46	MARVEL TRIPLE ACTION GIANT SIZE #2	$3.50	£4.00	76.19%
47	INCREDIBLE HULK VS. VENOM #1	$4.00	£4.50	75.00%
48	INDEPENDENCE DAY #0 (BLACK COVER VARIANT EDITION)	$5.00	£5 00	66.67%
49	WESTERN TEAM-UP #1	$3.00	£3.00	66.67%
50	X-MEN SURVIVAL GUIDE TO THE MANSION #1	$7.50	£7.50	66.67%

TOP 50 Differential Independent Comics and ranges £ to $

Below are listed comics valued in pounds sterling on the U.K. market and their equivalent guide value in dollars on the U.S. market after conversion. Rather than list simply individual comics when there may be a run of ten or twenty all the same price/percentage, ranges are included. For Independent Comics read all publishers other than Marvel and DC.

1	CEREBUS BI-WEEKLY #20	£3.00	$25.00	555.56%
2	WALT DISNEY'S COMICS AND STORIES #513	£1.50	$12.50	555.56%
3	DONALD DUCK #248-249, 251	£1.25	$9.00	480.00%
4	CEREBUS BI-WEEKLY #17	£1.50	$10.00	444.44%
5	FROM THE DARKNESS #1-4	£1.50	$10.00	444.44%
6	GRAPHIQUE MUSIQUE #1	£3.00	$20.00	444.44%
7	WALT DISNEY'S COMICS AND STORIES #416-429, 512	£2.00	$12.50	416.67%
8	DONALD DUCK #247	£1.50	$9.00	400.00%
9	MILK AND CHEESE SPECIAL #1	£10.00	$60.00	400.00%
10	WALT DISNEY'S COMICS AND STORIES #523	£1.25	$7.50	400.00%
11	CADILLACS AND DINOSAURS: THE WILD ONES #1	£1.50	$7.50	333.33%
12	DONALD DUCK #266-277, 279-280	£1.00	$5.00	333.33%
13	GRAPHIQUE MUSIQUE #2-3	£3.00	$15.00	333.33%
14	MIGHTY SAMSON #32	£1.50	$7.50	333.33%
15	MILK AND CHEESE'S OTHER #1	£5.00	$25.00	333.33%
16	MUNDEN'S BAR ANNUAL #2	£4.00	$20.00	333.33%
17	WALT DISNEY'S COMICS AND STORIES #511	£4.00	$20.00	333.33%
18	WALT DISNEY'S COMICS AND STORIES #514-516, 520	£1.50	$7.50	333.33%
19	DONALD DUCK #250	£2.50	$12.00	320.00%
20	SIMPSONS COMICS #29	£0.50	$2.25	300.00%
21	DRAG-STRIP HOTRODDERS #11-16	£4.00	$17.50	291.67%
22	MILK AND CHEESE'S THIRD NUMBER ONE #1	£4.00	$17.50	291.67%
23	HATE #3	£3.50	$15.00	285.71%
24	VAMPIRELLA (1ST SERIES) #101-112	£7.00	$30.00	285.71%
25	DONALD DUCK #246	£3.00	$12.50	277.78%
26	JIM (1ST SERIES) #1	£3.00	$12.50	277.78%
27	WALT DISNEY'S COMICS AND STORIES #401-415	£3.00	$12.50	277.78%
28	CADILLACS AND DINOSAURS: THE WILD ONES #2-3	£1.50	$6.00	266.67%
29	CEREBUS THE AARDVARK #0 (GOLD EDITION)	£5.00	$20.00	266.67%
30	CHARLTON PREMIERE (2ND SERIES) #1	£2.50	$10.00	266.67%
31	DONALD DUCK #252-256, 258-265, 278	£1.25	$5.00	266.67%
32	DONALD DUCK #281-284	£1.00	$4.00	266.67%
33	EERIE (MAGAZINE) #66-80	£2.00	$8.00	266.67%
34	JIM (1ST SERIES) #2	£2.50	$10.00	266.67%
35	MICKEY DONALD, WALT DISNEY'S #1	£1.00	$4.00	266.67%
36	MICKEY MOUSE #219	£1.00	$4.00	266.67%
37	WALT DISNEY'S COMICS AND STORIES #430, 433, 437-438, 441, 444-445	£1.50	$6.00	266.67%
38	WALT DISNEY'S COMICS AND STORIES #446-510	£1.25	$5.00	266.67%
39	CHARLTON PREMIERE (2ND SERIES) #2	£2.00	$7.50	250.00%
40	HATE #1	£6.00	$22.50	250.00%
41	HATE #2	£4.00	$15.00	250.00%
42	JIM (1ST SERIES) #3-4	£2.00	$7.50	250.00%
43	WALT DISNEY'S COMICS AND STORIES #431-432, 434-436, 439-440, 442-443	£2.00	$7.50	250.00%
44	FRANKENSTEIN #3-4	£3.50	$12.50	238.10%
45	WALT DISNEY'S COMICS AND STORIES #380-400	£3.50	$12.50	238.10%
46	CAVEWOMAN #5-6	£10.00	$35.00	233.33%
47	DRAG-STRIP HOTRODDERS #6-10	£5.00	$17.50	233.33%
48	PINK PANTHER, THE #61-74, 77-87	£1.00	$3.50	233.33%
49	ROMAN HOLIDAYS, THE #3-4	£3.50	$12.00	228.57%
50	PINK PANTHER, THE #31-60	£1.50	$5.00	222.22%

TOP 50 Differential Independent Comics and ranges $ to £

Below are listed comics valued in pounds sterling on the U.K market and their equivalent guide value in dollars on the U.S market. Rather than list simply individual comics when there may be a run of ten or twenty all the same price/percentage, ranges are included. For Independent Comics read all publishers other than Marvel and DC.

1	FAMOUS MONSTERS OF FILMLAND #56	$15.00	£25.00	111.11%
2	QUANTUM LEAP #1	$7.50	£12.50	111.11%
3	DEATHBLOW #5	$2.50	£4.00	106.67%
4	QUANTUM LEAP #4-5	$2.50	£4.00	106.67%
5	QUANTUM LEAP TIME AND SPACE SPECIAL #1	$2.50	£4.00	106.67%
6	SUPREME #30	$2.50	£4.00	106.67%
7	ANYTHING GOES #2, 5	$2.00	£3.00	100.00%
8	BLUE BEETLE (1ST SERIES) #1, 3 (REPRINT)	$1.00	£1.50	100.00%
9	CAPTAIN ATOM #83-85 (MODERN COMICS REPRINT)	$1.00	£1.50	100.00%
10	CHEYENNE KID #87, 89 (MODERN COMICS REPRINT)	$1.00	£1.50	100.00%
11	DR. SPEKTOR, THE OCCULT FILES OF #9 (MODERN COMICS REPRINT)	$1.00	£1.50	100.00%
12	FAMOUS MONSTERS OF FILMLAND #95	$10.00	£15.00	100.00%
13	HOUSE OF YANG #1, 3 (REPRINT)	$1.00	£1.50	100.00%
14	MIRACLEMAN #12	$2.00	£3.00	100.00%
15	QUANTUM LEAP #2	$5.00	£7.50	100.00%
16	TERMINATOR: THE BURNING EARTH #2	$2.00	£3.00	100.00%
17	GRIFTER/SHI HARDBOUND COLLECTOR'S EDITION # (SIGNED & NUMBERED)	$45.00	£65.00	96.30%
18	QUANTUM LEAP #3	$3.50	£5.00	95.24%
19	MR. MONSTER (1ST SERIES) #3	$2.50	£3.50	93.33%
20	QUANTUM LEAP #6-10	$2.50	£3.50	93.33%
21	TERMINATOR: THE BURNING EARTH #1	$2.50	£3.50	93.33%
22	ANYTHING GOES #1	$3.00	£4.00	88.89%
23	BLOOD SWORD #2-3	$1.50	£2 00	88.89%
24	BLOOD SWORD DYNASTY #2-5	$1.50	£2.00	88.89%
25	DOOMSDAY PLUS ONE #7	$1.50	£2.00	88.89%
26	DRUNKEN FIST #2-5	$1.50	£2.00	88.89%
27	EMERGENCY #1	$3.00	£4.00	88.89%
28	FORCE OF BUDDHA'S PALM #2-5	$1.50	£2.00	88.89%
29	RAMM #1	$3.00	£4.00	88.89%
30	SATANIKA #4	$3.00	£4.00	88.89%
31	AMERICAN FLAGG! #19	$2.00	£2.50	83.33%
32	BLOOD SWORD #1	$2.00	£2.50	83.33%
33	DARKCHYLDE #2 (VARIANT COVER EDITION)	$4.00	£5.00	83.33%
34	DOOMSDAY PLUS ONE #3	$4.00	£5.00	83.33%
35	EMERGENCY #2-4	$2 00	£2 50	83.33%
36	GRENDEL: DEVIL'S VAGARY	$20.00	£2 50	83.33%
37	LADY DEATH: THE CRUCIBLE # 1/2	$10.00	£12.50	83.33%
38	QUANTUM LEAP: SECOND CHILDHOOD #1-3	$2.00	£2.50	83.33%
39	TERMINATOR: THE BURNING EARTH #3-5	$2.00	£2.50	83.33%
40	BADGER #1	$2.50	£3.00	80.00%
41	DARKCHYLDE #1 (AMERICAN ENTERTAINMENT EDITION)	$5.00	£6.00	80.00%
42	DARKCHYLDE #1 (COMICON EDITION)	$5.00	£6.00	80.00%
43	DARKCHYLDE #1 ("PROBLEM CHILD" EDITION)	$5.00	£6.00	80.00%
44	DARKCHYLDE #1 (VARIANT COVER EDITION)	$5.00	£6.00	80.00%
45	PITT #4	$2.50	£3.00	80.00%
46	QUANTUM LEAP #1 (SPECIAL EDITION REPRINT)	$2.50	£3.00	80.00%
47	MIRACLEMAN 3D SPECIAL #1 (NON 3D VERSION)	$3.00	£3.50	77.78%
48	FAMOUS MONSTERS OF FILMLAND #140-142	$3.50	£4.00	76.19%
49	CEREBUS THE AARDVARK #105	$2.25	£2.50	74.07%
50	ELEVEN OR ONE #1 (2ND PRINTING)	$3.00	£3.00	66.67%

TOP 50 Differential Comics and ranges £ to $

Below are listed comics valued in pounds sterling on the U.K. market and their equivalent guide value in dollars on the U.S. market. Rather than list simply individual comics when there may be a run of ten or twenty all the same price/percentage, ranges are included.

1	CEREBUS BI-WEEKLY #20	£3.00	$25.00	555.56%
2	WALT DISNEY'S COMICS AND STORIES #513	£1.50	$12.50	555.56%
3	DONALD DUCK #248-249, 251	£1.25	$9.00	480.00%
4	ADVENTURE COMICS #467	£1.50	$10.00	444.44%
5	CEREBUS BI-WEEKLY #17	£1.50	$10.00	444.44%
6	FROM THE DARKNESS #1-4	£1.50	$10.00	444.44%
7	GRAPHIQUE MUSIQUE #1	£3.00	$20.00	444.44%
8	MS. MARVEL #17	£1.50	$10.00	444.44%
9	X-MEN, THE UNCANNY #244	£3.00	$20.00	444.44%
10	MARVEL SPOTLIGHT #8	£7.00	$45.00	428.57%
11	GREEN LANTERN (2ND SERIES) #116	£4.00	$25.00	416.67%
12	WALT DISNEY'S COMICS AND STORIES #416-429, 512	£2.00	$12.50	416.67%
13	ATOM, THE #41-42, 45	£7.00	$42.50	404.76%
14	DONALD DUCK #247	£1.50	$9.00	400.00%
15	METAL MEN #51-56	£2.50	$15.00	400.00%
16	MILK AND CHEESE SPECIAL #1	£10.00	$60.00	400.00%
17	MS. MARVEL #18	£2.50	$15.00	400.00%
18	OUR FIGHTING FORCES #171, 175-177	£1.25	$7.50	400.00%
19	WALT DISNEY'S COMICS AND STORIES #523	£1.25	$7.50	400.00%
20	MARVEL SPOTLIGHT #9-11	£7.00	$40.00	380.95%
21	SHOWCASE #88-90	£3.50	$20.00	380.95%
22	ATOM, THE #43-44	£7.50	$42.50	377.78%
23	METAL MEN #27	£12.50	$70.00	373.33%
24	SANDMAN (2ND SERIES) #8	£9.00	$50.00	370.37%
25	AQUAMAN #36-40	£10.00	$55.00	366.67%
26	AQUAMAN #48	£6.50	$35.00	358.97%
27	AQUAMAN #33	£15.00	$80.00	355.56%
28	HOUSE OF MYSTERY #301-321	£0.75	$4.00	355.56%
29	ATOM, THE #31-35, 37-38	£9.00	$47.50	351.85%
30	AQUAMAN #41-4, 49	£6.00	$30.00	333.33%
31	ATOM, THE #39-40	£9.00	$45.00	333.33%
32	CADILLACS AND DINOSAURS: THE WILD ONES #1	£1.50	$7.50	333.33%
33	DONALD DUCK #266-277, 279-280	£1.00	$5.00	333.33%
34	FLASH (1ST SERIES) #191-195, 197-199, 215	£7.50	$37.50	333.33%
35	FLASH (1ST SERIES) #215	£5.00	$25.00	333.33%
36	GRAPHIQUE MUSIQUE #2-3	£3.00	$15.00	333.33%
37	GREEN LANTERN (2ND SERIES) #66-69	£8.00	$40.00	333.33%
38	HOUSE OF MYSTERY #281, 283-300	£1.00	$5.00	333.33%
39	HOWARD THE DUCK #13	£2.50	$12.50	333.33%
40	METAL MEN #45, 48-50	£3.00	$15.00	333.33%
41	MIGHTY SAMSON #32	£1.50	$7.50	333.33%
42	MILK AND CHEESE'S OTHER #1	£5.00	$25.00	333.33%
43	MS. MARVEL #16	£2.00	$10.00	333.33%
44	MUNDEN'S BAR ANNUAL #2	£4.00	$20.00	333.33%
45	OUR FIGHTING FORCES #163-164, 167-170, 172-174	£1.50	$7.50	333.33%
46	POWERMAN #78, 84	£4.00	$20.00	333.33%
47	SANDMAN (2ND SERIES) #3	£7.00	$35.00	333.33%
48	SANDMAN (2ND SERIES) #4-5	£6.00	$30.00	333.33%
49	SANDMAN (2ND SERIES) #6-7	£5.00	$25.00	333.33%
50	SPECTACULAR SPIDERMAN #147	£3.50	$17.50	333.33%

TOP 50 Differential Comics and ranges $ to £

Below are listed comics valued in pounds sterling on the U.K. market and their equivalent guide value in dollars on the U.S. market. Rather than list simply individual comics when there may be a run of ten or twenty all the same price/percentage, ranges are included.

1	DC COMICS PRESENTS #26	$1.50	£4 00	177.78%
2	DC SUPER-STARS #3	$2.00	£5.00	166.67%
3	NOVA #25	$2.00	£5.00	166.67%
4	EPIC ILLUSTRATED #34	$2.50	£6.00	160.00%
5	ADVENTURE COMICS #491	$3.00	£6.00	133.33%
6	ADVENTURE COMICS #500	$3.00	£6.00	133.33%
7	AVENGERS #183	$3.00	£6.00	133.33%
8	DC SPECIAL BLUE RIBBON DIGEST #1	$2.50	£5.00	133.33%
9	SUPERBOY #211	$2.50	£5.00	133.33%
10	SUPERBOY #227	$2.00	£3.50	116.67%
11	ADVENTURE COMICS #492-499, 501-503	$3.00	£5.00	111.11%
12	BATMAN PIZZA HUT GIVEAWAY	$3.00	£5.00	111.11%
13	BLACK DRAGON, THE #1	$1.50	£2.50	111.11%
14	FAMOUS MONSTERS OF FILMLAND #56	$15.00	£25.00	111.11%
15	NICK FURY, AGENT OF SHIELD #17-18	$3.00	£5.00	111.11%
16	QUANTUM LEAP #1	$7.50	£12.50	111.11%
17	GROO THE WANDERER #7	$4.00	£6.50	108.33%
18	DEATHBLOW #5	$2.50	£4.00	106.67%
19	EPIC ILLUSTRATED #26, 29, 33	$2.50	£4.00	106.67%
20	QUANTUM LEAP #4-5	$2.50	£4.00	106.67%
21	QUANTUM LEAP TIME AND SPACE SPECIAL #1	$2.50	£4.00	106.67%
22	SUPREME #30	$2.50	£4.00	106.67%
23	ANYTHING GOES #2, 5	$2.00	£3.00	100.00%
24	BATMAN AND THE OUTSIDERS #1	$2.00	£3 00	100.00%
25	BLUE BEETLE (1ST SERIES) #1, 3 (REPRINT)	$1.00	£1.50	100.00%
26	CAPTAIN ATOM #83-85 (MODERN COMICS REPRINT)	$1.00	£1.50	100.00%
27	CHEYENNE KID #87, 89 (MODERN COMICS REPRINT)	$1.00	£1.50	100.00%
28	DAREDEVIL #161	$10.00	£15.00	100.00%
29	DC SUPER-STARS #17	$3.00	£4.50	100.00%
30	DR. SPEKTOR, THE OCCULT FILES OF #9 (MODERN COMICS REPRINT)	$1.00	£1.50	100.00%
31	DRACULA LIVES! #2	$5.00	£7.50	100.00%
32	FAMOUS MONSTERS OF FILMLAND #95	$10.00	£15.00	100.00%
33	GROO THE WANDERER #6	$4.00	£6.00	100.00%
34	HOUSE OF YANG #1, 3 (REPRINT)	$1.00	£1.50	100.00%
35	KULL AND THE BARBARIANS #3	$2.00	£3.00	100.00%
36	LIMITED COLLECTOR'S EDITION #C-51, C-59	$10.00	£15.00	100.00%
37	MARVEL GRAPHIC NOVEL #1 (2ND PRINTING)	$5.00	£7.50	100.00%
38	MARVELGRAPHICNOVEL #39 (2ND PRINTING)	$6.00	£9.00	100.00%
39	MIRACLEMAN #12	$2.00	£3.00	100.00%
40	NICK FURY,AGENT OF SHIELD #16	$3.00	£4.50	100.00%
41	QUANTUM LEAP #2	$5.00	£7.50	100.00%
42	SUPERBOY #221-226, 230	$2.00	£3.00	100.00%
43	TERMINATOR: THE BURNING EARTH #2	$2.00	£3.00	100.00%
44	GRIFTER/SHI HARDBOUND COLLECTOR'S EDITION (SIGNED & NUMBERED)	$45.00	£65.00	96.30%
45	QUANTUM LEAP #3	$3.50	£5.00	95.24%
46	EPIC ILLUSTRATED#15	$2.50	£3.50	93.33%
47	MR. MONSTER (1ST SERIES) #3	$2.50	£3.50	93.33%
48	QUANTUM LEAP #6-10	$2.50	£3.50	93.33%
49	SUPERBOY #212-213, 218	$2.50	£3.50	93.33%
50	TERMINATOR: THE BURNING EARTH #1	$2.50	£3.50	93.33%

Selected Further Reading

Below is a list of reference works on comics for general reading. It is by no means exhaustive but gives some idea of the material available.

REFERENCE

THE BRITISH COMIC CATALOGUE
by Denis Gifford (Mansell 1975).

CANUCK COMICS
edited by John Bell (Matrix Books 1986): guide to Canadian comics, with price guide.

THE CHILDREN'S ANNUAL: A HISTORY AND COLLECTOR'S GUIDE
by Alan Clark (Boxtree 1988): the story of British annuals, with selected price guide.

THE COMIC BOOK
by Paul Sassienie (Ebury Press. 1994): Excellent.

THE COMIC BOOK IN AMERICA
by Mike Benton (Taylor Publishing. USA. 1989): chronological history of comics, publishers and genres.

COMIX: A HISTORY OF COMIC BOOKS IN AMERICA
by Les Daniels (Wildwood House 1971,1973): the history of American comics, with selected reprints.

THE COMPLETE CATALOGUE OF BRITISH COMICS
by Denis Gifford (Webb & Bower 1985). With (an out of date) Price Guide

THE DANDY MONSTER INDEX
Vol 1 & 2 by Ray Moore (BCW 1985)

DC COMICS: Sixty Years of the World's Favourite Comic Book Heroes
by Les Daniels (Virgin Books. 1995): an indispensable overview of DC comics with many excellent illustrations

ENCYCLOPAEDIA OF COMIC CHARACTERS
by Denis Gifford (Longman 1987): alphabetical listing of 1200 British characters.

THE GREAT COMIC BOOK HEROES
by Jules Feiffer (Penguin Press 1965, 1967): a short history of the Golden Age American heroes, with selected reprints.

HAPPY DAYS: A CENTURY OF COMICS
by Denis Gifford (Jupiter 1975): a guide to British comics.

HORROR COMICS: THE ILLUSTRATED HISTORY
by Mike Benton (Taylor Publishing 1991): an overview of the horror comic genre from the 1940's to present.

THE HOTSPUR - A CATALOGUE: 1933 to 1959
by D.J. Adley & W.O.G. Lofts (Cadwallender).

IDENTIFICATION GUIDE TO THE UNDATED D.C.THOMSON & JOHN LENG CHILDREN'S ANNUALS 1921-1965
by D.J. Adley & W.O.G. Lofts (Cadwallender 1982): cover descriptions and dates of 300+ annuals.

THE INTERNATIONAL BOOK OF COMICS
by Denis Gifford (W.H. Smith 1984): an introduction to comics, heavily illustrated.

AN INTRODUCTION TO CANADIAN COMIC BOOKS
by Dan Threaker (Aurora 1986): short history of Canadian-published comics, with price guide.

THE LYLE PRICE GUIDE TO PRINTED COLLECTIBLES
(Lyle 1984).

THE MAGIC INDEX
by Ray Moore (BCW 1988).

MARVEL: FIVE FABULOUS DECADES
by Les Daniels (Virgin Books. 1991): excellent overview of Marvel's out-put over the years, lavishly illustrated.

NOSTALGIA ABOUT COMICS
by Phil Clarke and Mike Higgs (Pegasus Publishing): a look at British albums and comics of the 1940s and 1950s. Also Australian, Canadian and some American material.

THE OFFICIAL COMIC BOOK PRICE GUIDE
by Robert M. Overstreet (House of Collectibles, annually): comprehensive listing of all American comic books from 1900-present, with American prices. The industry standard in America for many years now.

OVERSTREET'S FAN
by Robert M. Overstreet & Michael Renegar (Gemstone Publishing): monthly supplement to the above that replaced Overstreet's Comic Book Marketplace. The last issue will be issue #24.

THE OFFICIAL UNDERGROUND AND NEWAVE COMIX PRICE GUIDE
by Jay Kennedy (Boatner Norton 1982): history of the Undergrounds, with price guide.

THE PENGUIN BOOK OF COMICS
by George Perry & Alan Aldridge (Penguin 1967, revised 1971): offers an overview of British and American comic books and newspaper strips. Soon to be re-issued by Paul Gravett?

THE ROVER INDEX
by Colin Morgan (Cadwallender).

SCIENCE FICTION COMICS: THE ILLUSTRATED HISTORY
by Mike Benton (Taylor Publishing. 1992): an overview of sci-fi comics from the 1920's to date. Illustrated.

A SMITHSONIAN BOOK OF COMIC-BOOK COMICS
edited by Michael Barrier & Martin Williams (Smithsonian Institution Press/Harry N. Abrams Inc. 1981): selected history and reprints.

STAP ME! THE BRITISH NEWSPAPER STRIP
by Denis Gifford (Shire 1971).

THE STERANKO HISTORY OF COMICS Vol 1 & 2
(Supergraphics 1970, 1972): comprehensive history of the early days of American comics.

SUPER-HERO COMICS OF THE GOLDEN AGE:THE ILLUSTRATED HISTORY
by Mike Benton (Taylor Publishing, 1992): an overview of the Golden Age period of American comics from the 1930s to 1950s. Illustrated.

SUPER-HERO COMICS OF THE SILVER AGE: THE ILLUSTRATED HISTORY
by Mike Benton (Taylor Publishing. 1991): an overview of the Silver Age period of American comics from mid 1950 to mid 1960. Illustrated.

TWO DECADES OF COMICS: A REVIEW
by David Cutler, Frank Plowright, Adrian Snowdon, Steve Whitaker & Hassan Yusuf (Slings & Arrows 1981).

VICTORIAN COMICS
by Denis Gifford (Allen & Unwin 1976).

THE WORLD ENCYCLOPAEDIA OF COMICS
edited by Maurice Horn (Chelsea House, New English Library 1976): massive work listing comic-book and newspaper strip characters, creators and publications.

Note: some of these publications may now be out of print and only available from specialist shops and libraries.

ABOUT COMIC ART AND ARTISTS

THE ART OF JACK DAVIS
by Hank Harrison (Stabur 1987).

THE BEST OF EAGLE
edited by Marcus Morris (Michael Joseph/Edbury Press 1977): short history and selected reprints.

CARL BARKS AND THE ART OF THE COMIC BOOK
by Michael Barrier (M. Lilien 1981).

COMICS AND SEQUENTIAL ART
by Will Eisner (Poorhouse/Eclipse 1985,1986, 1987): detailed guide to the execution and interpretation of comic art. Seminal work and essential reading.

A VERY FUNNY BUSINESS
by Leo Baxendale (Duckworth 1978).

THE COMIC ART OF REG PARLETT
by Alan Clark & David Ashford (Golden Fun 1986).

THE COMIC ART OF ROY WILSON
by Alan Clark & David Ashford (Midas 1983).

THE MAN WHO DREW TOMORROW
by Alistair Crompton (Who Dares 1985): the story of Frank Hampson's work on Dan Dare.

SUPERMAN AT FIFTY: THE PERSISTENCE OF A LEGEND
edited by Dennis Dooley and Gary Engle (Octavia Press 1987).

TIMEVIEW: THE COMPLETE DR. WHO ILLUSTRATIONS OF FRANK BELLAMY
(Who Dares 1985).

Note: some of these publications may now be out of print and only available at specialist shops and libraries.

BRITISH MAGAZINES AND NEWSPAPERS

ARK
(Titan bi-monthly): British and American comics interviews and articles. Now available as back-issues only.

BRITISH COMICS WORLD
(Alan & David Coates): British comics articles. Back issues now.

COMIC COLLECTOR
(Aceville Publications, monthly): news and features magazine on American and British comics with retailer ads. Re-titled Comics World before its cancellation in 1995. Real shame. Back issues only.

COMICS INTERNATIONAL
(Dez Skinn, monthly): trade journal/newspaper plus reviews of British and American comics. Comic shop and news-stand distribution. Still going strong.

COMICS SPECULATOR NEWS
(Jaspal S. Dale, monthly): trade journal that tended towards the speculator market as the title implies. Back issues only now.

ESCAPE
(Titan, bi-monthly): articles and reviews of mainly British and European comics and media, plus comics material. Now available as back issues only.

FANTASY ADVERTISER
(30th Century, quarterly): British and American comics information, news, reviews and articles. Available as back issues only.

GOLDEN FUN
(Alan & Laurel Clark): Golden Age British comics articles. Back issues only.

SPEAKEASY
(Acme Press, monthly): British and American comics information, news, reviews and articles. Amalgamated into a new magazine called BLAST. Cancelled so both are available as back issues only.

AMERICAN

ADVANCE COMICS
(Capital Distributors, monthly): A fully comprehensive listing of up and coming comics, merchandise, posters, books, portfolios, games and toys with descriptions and reviews. Available as back issues only now.

AMAZING HEROES
(Fantagraphics, bi-weekly): news, reviews and articles on mainly American comics.

AMAZING HEROES PREVIEW SPECIAL
(Fantagraphics, semi-annually): special oversized editions of the above, listing the majority of coming American comics.

COMICS BUYER'S GUIDE
(Krause Publications, weekly): News and articles on mainly new and coming American comics. Essential reading.

COMIC BUYER'S GUIDE PRICE GUIDE
(Krause Publications, quarterly): Price guide update with some features/articles geared towards the speculator market.

COMICS INTERVIEW
(Fictioneer, monthly): interviews with American comic creators.

THE COMICS JOURNAL
(Fantagraphics, monthly): Articles, news and criticism of American and foreign comics.

COMIC VALUES MONTHLY
(Attic Books Ltd, monthly): Price guide update with better-than-average Independents listing. Back issues now.

PREVIEWS
(Diamond Distributors, monthly): A fully comprehensive listing of up and coming comics, merchandise, posters, books, portfolios, games and toys with reviews and descriptions.

WIZARD: THE GUIDE TO COMICS
(Wizard Press Ltd, monthly): Glossy covered price guide update with design-oriented articles and features that have surprising breadth. Least comprehensive comics listing but includes cards and toys. Very good on "hot" artists and with Jon Warren's influence, pricing is very sensible now.

BATMAN #1

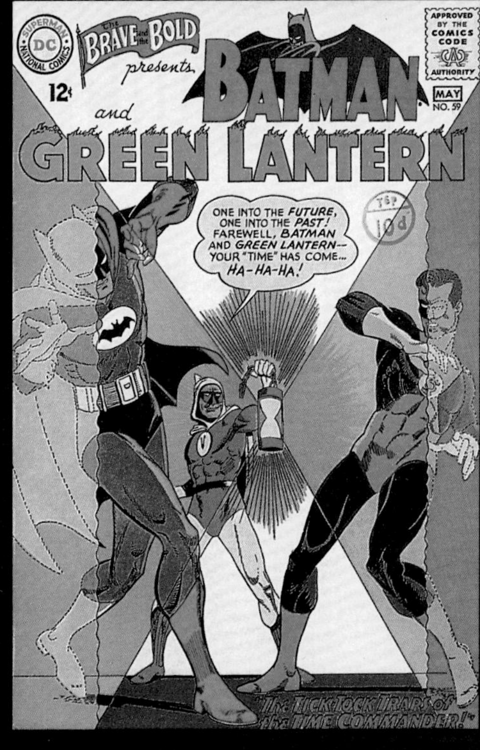

THE BRAVE AND THE BOLD #59

DETECTIVE COMICS #233

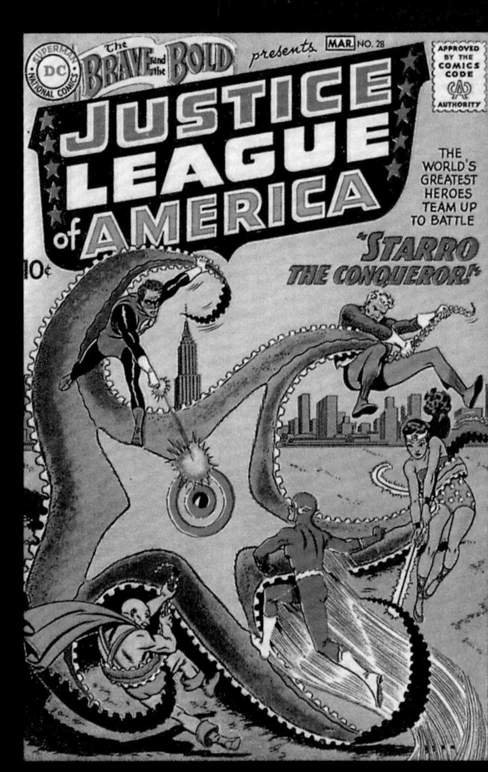

JUSTICE LEAGUE OF AMERICA #28

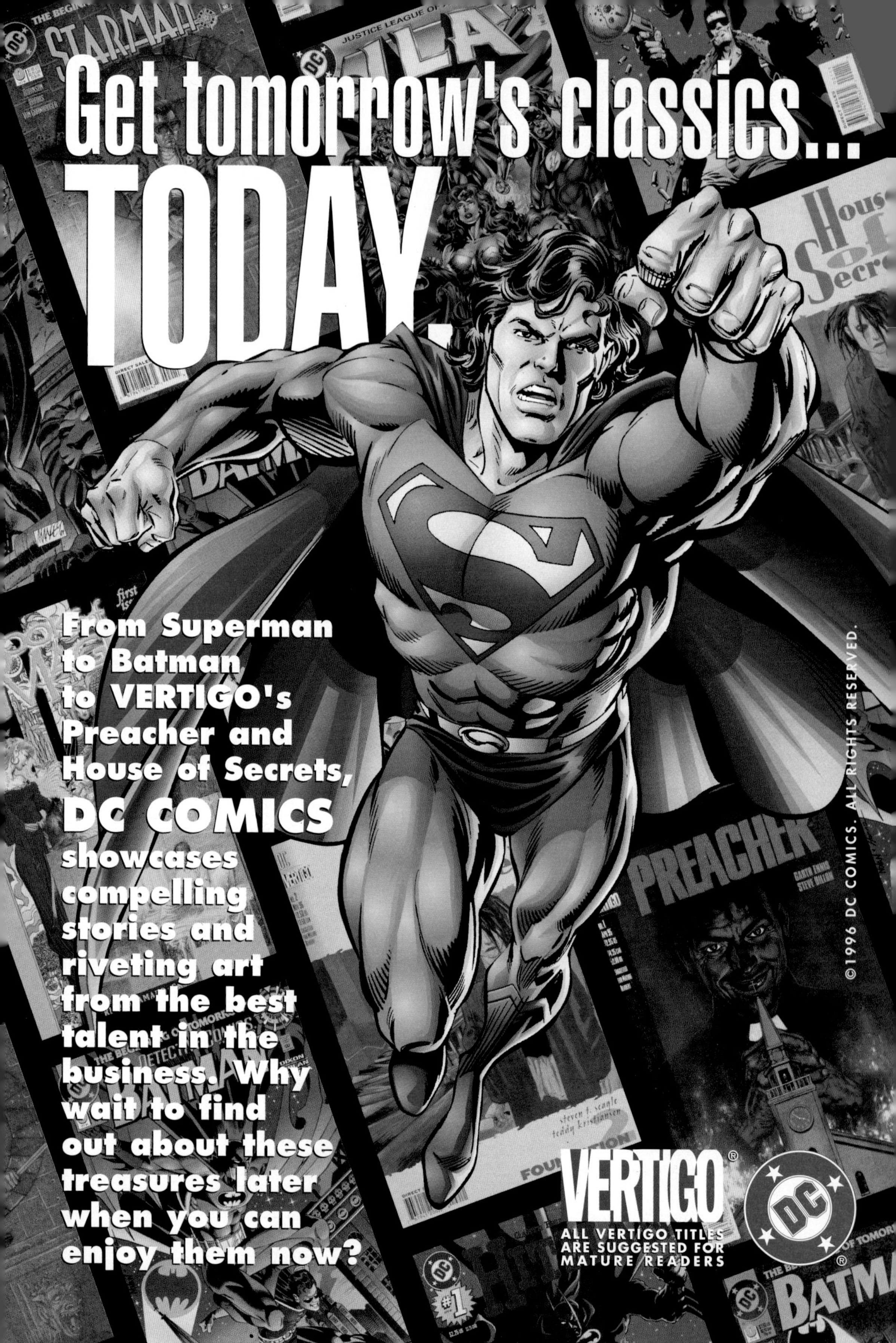

Get tomorrow's classics...
TODAY.
From Superman to Batman to VERTIGO's Preacher and House of Secrets, DC COMICS showcases compelling stories and riveting art from the best talent in the business. Why wait to find out about these treasures later when you can enjoy them now?
VERTIGO®
ALL VERTIGO TITLES ARE SUGGESTED FOR MATURE READERS
DC®
©1996 DC COMICS. ALL RIGHTS RESERVED.

DETECTIVE COMICS #168

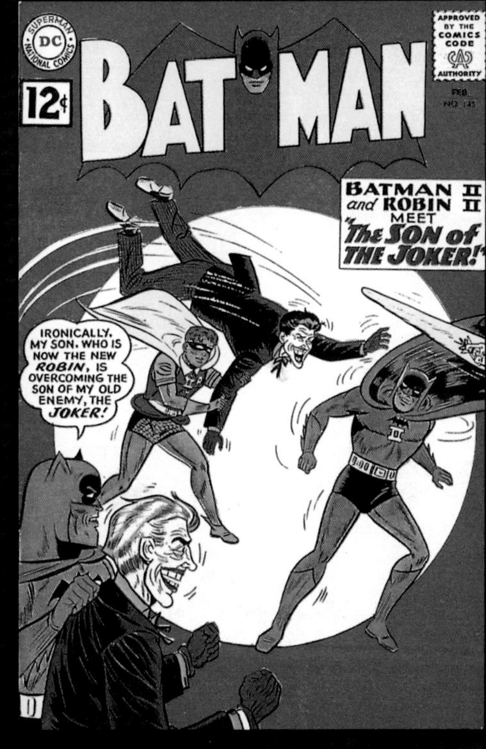

BATMAN #145

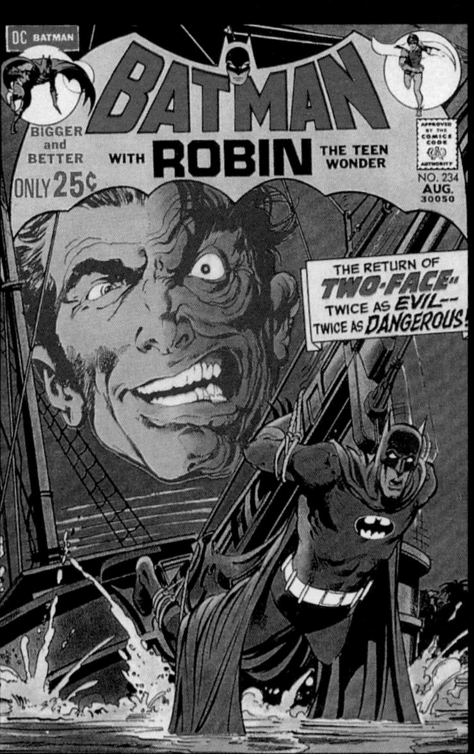

BATMAN #234

WORLD'S FINEST COMICS #71

THE VERY BES
BATM
FROM TITAN B

Batman: The Killing Joke
ISBN 1 85286 082 0

Batman: The Dark Knight Returns – Tenth Anniversary Edition
(Hardcover) ISBN 1 85286 788 4 – (Softcover) ISBN 1 85286 798 1

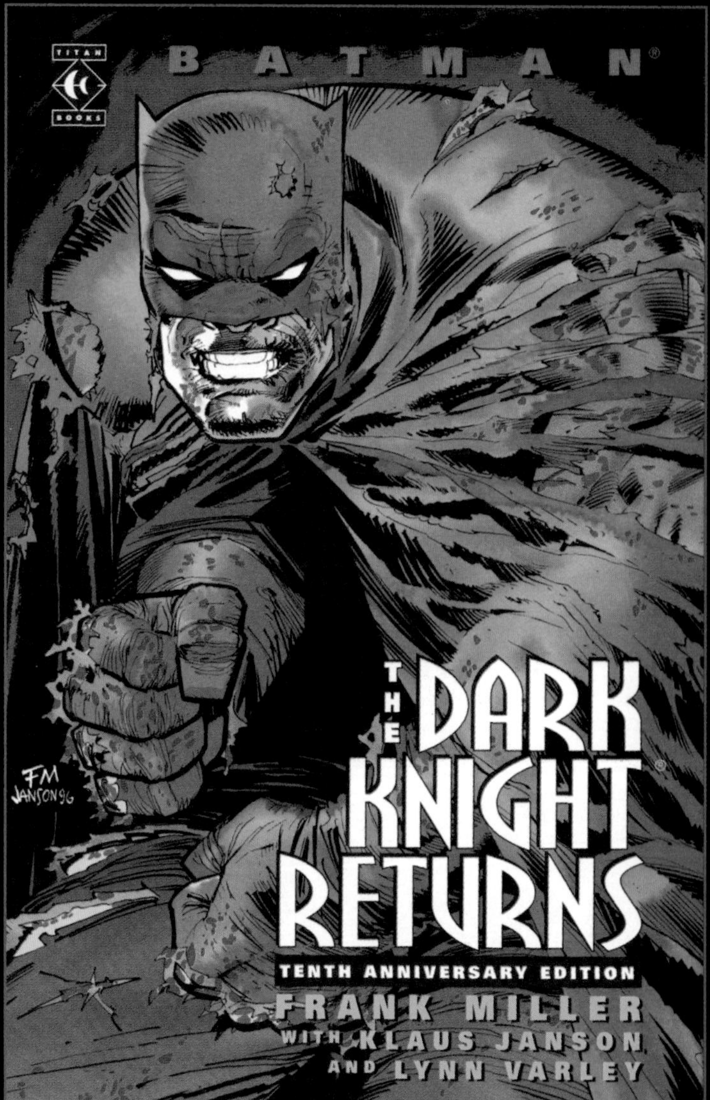

Batman: Arkham Asylum
ISBN 1 85286 280 7

Batman: Haunted Knight
ISBN 1 85286 739 6

T OF

AN

OOKS!

All Titan Books' graphic novels are available through most good bookshops or direct from Titan Books' mail order service. For a free graphic novels catalogue or to order, telephone **01536 763 631** or contact Titan Books Mail Order, PO Box 54, Desborough, Northants., NN14 2UH, quoting reference CBPG97.

Batman: Legacy – ISBN 1 85286 791 4

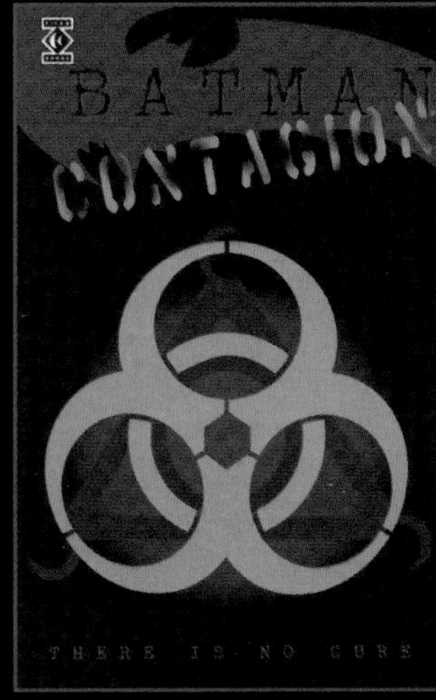

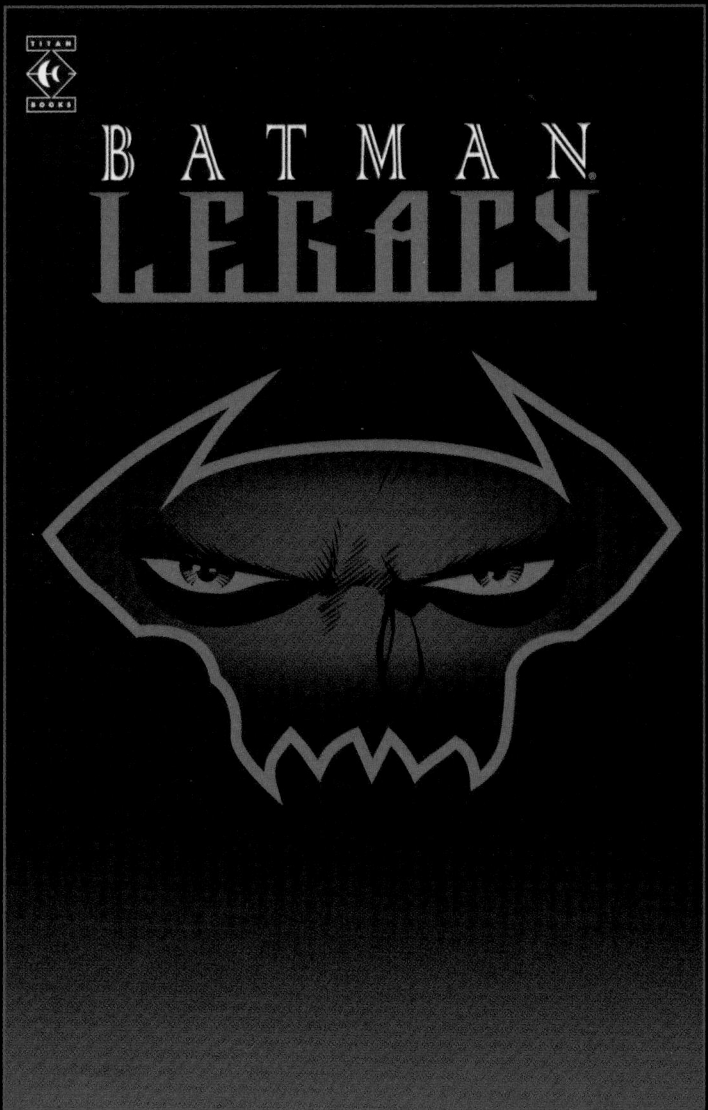

Batman: Contagion
ISBN 1 85286 732 9

Batman: Knightfall Pt. 1
ISBN 1 85286 515 6

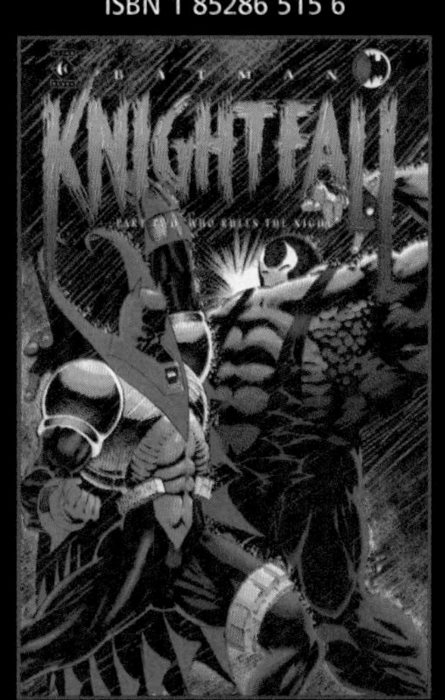

Batman: Knightfall Pt. 2
ISBN 1 85286 516 4

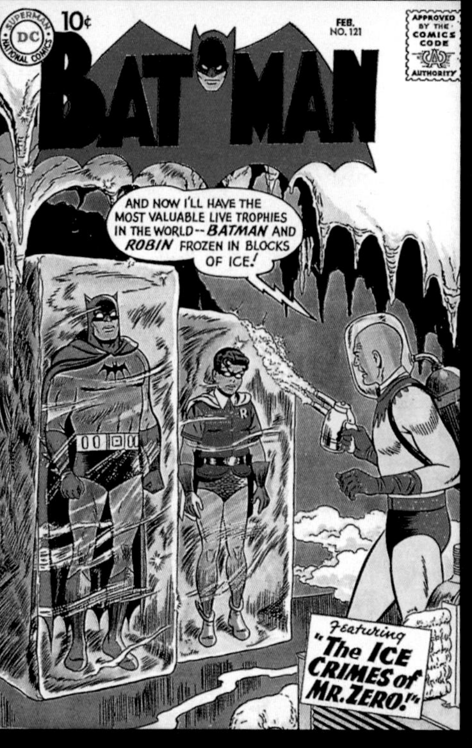

BATMAN #121

DETECTIVE COMICS #33

DETECTIVE COMICS #225

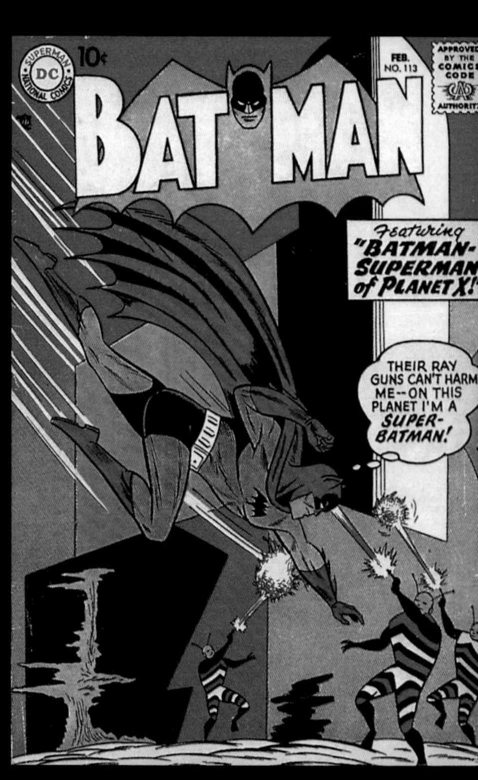

BATMAN #113

BATMAN #79

52 BIG PAGES
NO.76
MAY JUNE
10¢
SUPERMAN
DOUBLE-FEATURE!
BATMAN, THE WORLD'S GREATEST DETECTIVE, JOINS FORCES WITH THE MAN OF STEEL TO BECOME... "The MIGHTIEST TEAM ON EARTH!"
LOIS IN DANGER! THIS IS A JOB FOR SUPERMAN!
NO, THIS IS A JOB FOR BATMAN!

SUPERMAN #76

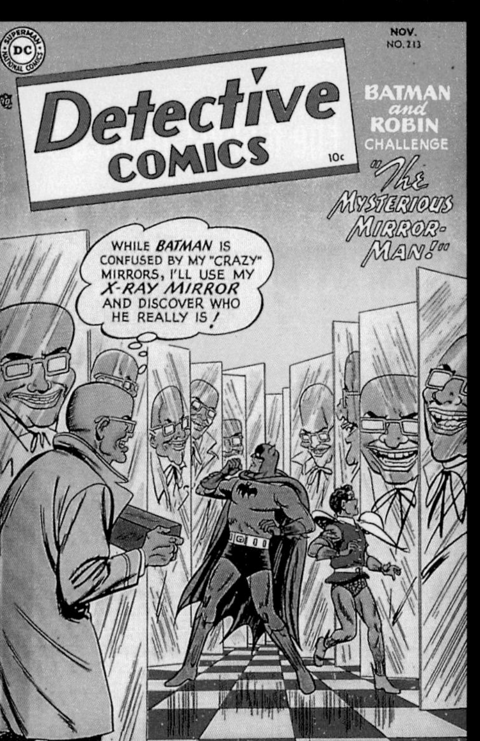

DETECTIVE COMICS #213

DETECTIVE COMICS #31

THE TRADING CARD GUIDE

Original foundation by BARRIE RONESS with ROB BARROW & The Fantasy Domain Trading Card Company
Further notes by RON HALL of First Choice cards

We have expanded a number of entries with a view to a more complete listing in future editions. Any additional information may be sent to the editorial address. We are also pleased to list selected sets from Merlin Publishing Ltd, the UK's only large-scale indigenous producer of trading cards.

PLEASE NOTE THAT "COMPLETE SET" AND ITS VALUE REFERS TO THE SET OF CARDS NOT INCLUDING ANY SPECIALS

ADDAMS FAMILY

PRODUCER:	TOPPS U.S.
ISSUE YEAR:	1991
CARD SET:	99 CARDS
SPECIAL CARDS:	11 STICKERS
COMPLETE SET:	£12.00
SINGLE CARDS:	10p - 15p
SINGLE SPECIAL CARDS:	20p

Important Notes: These sets broke badly from their boxes. In many cases more than one box of cards was required to complete a set.

ADVANCE COMICS PROMOTIONAL HOLOGRAM

Venom: £3.00
Issued free with Advance Comics magazine Spring 1992
DIAMOND U.S. PREVIEWS
Uncut promo sheet: £3.00
Issued free with Diamond Previews magazine

ADVENTURES OF BATMAN & ROBIN

PRODUCER:	SKYBOX
ISSUE YEAR:	1995
CARD SET:	90 CARDS
SPECIAL CARDS:	3 CARD DARK KNIGHT SET 9 CARD FOIL SET 12 CARD POP UP SET
COMPLETE SET:	£8.00
SINGLE CARDS:	10p

AKIRA MASTER SET

PRODUCER:	CORNERSTONE
ISSUE YEAR:	1994
CARD SET:	100 CARDS
SPECIAL CARDS:	3 CHROMIUM CARDS, 1 PRISM (1 PER CASE)
COMPLETE SET:	£15.00
SINGLE CARDS:	15p
SINGLE SPECIAL CARDS (Chromium):	£4.00
SINGLE SPECIAL CARDS (Prism):	£20.00

ALADDIN

PRODUCER:	SKYBOX
ISSUE YEAR:	1993
CARD SET:	90 CARDS
SPECIAL CARDS:	3 SPECTRA CARDS
COMPLETE SET:	£8.00
SINGLE CARDS:	10p
SINGLE SPECIAL CARDS:	£5.00

ALF I

PRODUCER:	TOPPS U.S.
ISSUE YEAR:	1987
CARD SET:	69 CARDS
SPECIAL CARDS:	18 STICKERS
COMPLETE SET:	£8.00
SINGLE CARDS:	10p-15p
SINGLE SPECIAL CARDS:	20p

Important Notes: There are two different trading card sets, both of which are based on the hit American television series about a friendly alien.

ALF II

PRODUCER:	TOPPS U.S.
ISSUE YEAR:	1988
CARD SET:	66 CARDS
SPECIAL CARDS:	18 STICKERS
COMPLETE SET:	£6.00
SINGLE CARDS:	5p - 10p
SINGLE SPECIAL CARDS:	15p

Important Notes: See also Alf series I

ALIEN I

PRODUCER:	TOPPS U.S.
ISSUE YEAR:	1979
CARD SET:	84 CARDS
SPECIAL CARDS:	22 STICKERS
COMPLETE SET (without stickers):	£20.00

Animal Mystic #68

COMPLETE SET (with stickers):	£45.00
SINGLE CARDS:	25p
SINGLE SPECIAL CARDS:	£1.00

Important Notes: Upon release of the Dark Horse Alien 3 trading card set, demand for the original set has risen making this set now even harder to locate. The complete set with stickers is very rare.

ALIEN 3

PRODUCER:	STAR PICS
ISSUE YEAR:	1992
CARD SET:	80 CARDS
SPECIAL CARDS:	8 DARK HORSE COMICS CARDS
COMPLETE SET:	£8.00
SINGLE CARDS:	10p
SINGLE SPECIAL CARDS:	15p

Important Notes: Widely sold throughout U.K. specialist comic shops, prices vary on this particular set.

ALIEN NATION

PRODUCER:	FTCC
ISSUE YEAR:	1990
CARD SET:	60 CARDS
SPECIAL CARDS:	No special cards
COMPLETE SET:	£15.00
SINGLE CARDS:	25p

ALIENS/PREDATOR UNIVERSE

PRODUCER:	TOPPS U.S.
ISSUE YEAR:	1995
CARD SET:	72 CARDS
SUB-SET CARDS:	15
SPECIAL CARDS:	6 CHASE CARDS
COMPLETE SET:	£8.00
SINGLE CARDS:	15p
SUB-SET CARD:	£1.00
SINGLE SPECIAL CARDS:	£5.00

Important Notes: The sub-set cards are numbered A1-A15 and should be included when considering the actual complete set

AMALGAM

PRODUCER:	FLEER/SKYBOX
ISSUE YEAR:	1996
CARD SET:	90 CARDS
POWER BLAST CARD:	£2.50
CANVAS CARD:	£2.50
HOLOPIX CARD:	£7.00
COMPLETE SET:	£12.00
SINGLE CARDS:	20p

AMERICAN GLADIATORS

PRODUCER:	TOPPS U.S.
ISSUE YEAR:	1992
CARD SET:	88 CARDS
SPECIAL CARDS:	11 STICKERS
COMPLETE SET:	£7.00
SINGLE CARDS:	5p - 15p

AN AMERICAN TAIL I

PRODUCER:	TOPPS U.S.
ISSUE YEAR:	1991
CARD SET:	150 CARDS
SPECIAL CARDS:	5 HOLOGRAMS
COMPLETE SET:	£15.00
SINGLE CARDS:	10p
SINGLE SPECIAL CARDS:	£6.00

Important Notes: Scarce set, rarely seen in the U.K.

ANIMAL MYSTIC

PRODUCER:	COMIC IMAGES
ISSUE YEAR:	1996
CARD SET:	90 CARDS
SPECIAL CARDS: 6 GLOW CARDS:	£5.00 each
3 SUB-SET CARDS:	£7.00 each
1 BOXCARD:	£3.00
1 AUTOGRAPH CARD:	£25.00?
COMPLETE SET:	£10.00
SINGLE CARDS:	15p

ANIMANIACS

PRODUCER:	TOPPS
ISSUE YEAR:	1995
CARD SET:	72 CARDS
SPECIAL CARDS: VINYL MINI-CEL:	£10.00
12 FOIL STICKERS:	£1.50 each
COMPLETE SET:	£10.00
SINGLE CARD:	15p

ARCHIE COMIC CARDS

PRODUCER:	SKYBOX
ISSUE YEAR:	1992
CARD SET:	120 CARDS
SPECIAL CARDS:	5 HOLOGRAMS
COMPLETE SET:	£30.00
CARD SET ONLY:	£12.00
SINGLE CARDS:	10p
SINGLE SPECIAL CARDS:	£4.00

Important Notes: Generally unavailable in the U.K. This set will be difficult to locate due to its limited collector U.K. following.

ARTHUR ADAMS

PRODUCER:	COMIC IMAGES
ISSUE YEAR:	1989
CARD SET:	45 CARDS
SPECIAL CARDS:	No special cards
COMPLETE SET:	£10.00
SINGLE CARDS:	15p

A-TEAM

PRODUCER:	TOPPS U.S.
ISSUE YEAR:	1983
CARD SET:	66 CARDS
SPECIAL CARDS:	12 STICKERS
COMPLETE SET:	£8.00
SINGLE CARDS:	10p
SINGLE SPECIAL CARDS:	25p

Important Notes: Never sold on general distribution in England

AVENGELYNE

PRODUCER:	WILDSTORM
ISSUE YEAR:	1996
CARD SET:	99 CARDS
SPECIAL CARDS:	

9 PHOTO EMBOSSED CHASE CARDS: £5.00 each
9 GLOW CHASE CARDS: £4.00 each
COMPLETE SET: £20.00
SINGLE SET: 30p

AVENGELYNE 2

PRODUCER: WILDSTORM
ISSUE YEAR: 1996
CARD SET: 100 CARDS
SPECIAL CARDS: MORPH CARD: £10.00
CHASE CARD: £10.00
COMPLETE SET: £25.00
SINGLE CARDS: 30p

AVENGERS (BLACK + WHITE)

PRODUCER: TOPPS U.S.
ISSUE YEAR: 1992
CARD SET: 81 CARDS
COMPLETE SET: £20.00
SINGLE CARDS: 25p

AVENGERS (COLOUR)

PRODUCER: TOPPS U.S.
ISSUE YEAR: 1993
CARD SET: 100 CARDS
COMPLETE SET: £15.00
SINGLE CARDS: 15p

AVENGERS RETURN

PRODUCER: CORNERSTONE
ISSUE YEAR: 1995
CARD SET: 81 CARDS
SPECIAL CARDS:
1 PREMIERE CARD: £1.50
1 AUTOGRAPHED CARD (Patrick Macnee): £45.00
COMPLETE SET: £8.00
SINGLE CARDS: 10p - 15p

BABY

PRODUCER: TOPPS U.S.
ISSUE YEAR: 1984
CARD SET: 66 CARDS
CARD SET 11 STICKERS
COMPLETE SET: £5.00
SINGLE CARDS: 15p

BABYLON 5

PRODUCER: FLEER
ISSUE YEAR: 1995
CARD SET: 120 CARDS
SPECIAL CARDS: 8 CARD HOLOGRAM SET (Single Holo Cards up to £25.00 each)
8 CARD SPACE GALLERY SET (Single Gallery Cards up to £3.00 each)
8 CARD PRISMATIC SET (Single Holofoil Cards up to £5.00 each)
COMPLETE SET: £40.00
SINGLE CARDS: 30p - 35p

BABYLON 5 SERIES 2

PRODUCER: SKYBOX
ISSUE YEAR: 1996
CARD SET: 60 CARDS
SPECIAL CARDS:
50 CARD TRIVIA SET: £25.00
10 CARD POSTER SET: £25.00
10 CARD CREATORS GOLD EMBOSSED: £3.00 - £5.00 each
2 CARD LAZER CUT: £10.00-£15.00 each
1 AUTOGRAPH CARD: £75-£150 approximately
COMPLETE SET: £8.00
SINGLE CARDS: 15p

Important Notes: Character cards tend to fetch more

BACK TO THE FUTURE II MOVIE

PRODUCER: TOPPS U.S.
ISSUE YEAR: 1989
CARD SET: 88 CARDS
SPECIAL CARDS: 11 STICKERS
COMPLETE SET: £12.00
SINGLE CARDS: 10p - 15p
SINGLE SPECIAL CARDS: 20p

BARBIE

PRODUCER: MATTELL TOY COMPANY
ISSUE YEAR: 1990
CARD SET: 300 CARDS
SPECIAL CARDS: No special cards

Babylon 5 (Series 2) #12

COMPLETE SET: £20.00
SINGLE CARDS: 10p

BARBIE 2

PRODUCER: MATTELL TOY COMPANY
ISSUE YEAR: 1991
CARD SET: 300 CARDS
SPECIAL CARDS: No special cards
COMPLETE SET: £20.00
SINGLE CARDS: 20p

BARB WIRE

PRODUCER: TOPPS
ISSUE YEAR: 1996
CARD SET: 90 CARDS
SPECIAL CARDS:
EMBOSSED CARD: £1.00
LASER-CUT CARD: £8.00
COMPLETE SET: £8.00
SINGLE CARDS: 10p

BATMAN AND ROBIN ACTION PACKS

PRODUCER: FLEER/SKYBOX
ISSUE YEAR: 1996
ARKHAM ESCAPE CARD: £1.00
ARKHAM ESCAPE SET (12): £10.00
POP-OUT CARD: £1.00
POP-OUT SET (12): £10.00
PUZZLE CARD: £1.00
PUZZLE SET (6): £5.00
COLOURING CARD: £.75
COLOURING SET (6): £3.00
GUM PIECES SET (4): £1.00

BATMAN ANIMATED

PRODUCER: TOPPS U.S.
ISSUE YEAR: 1993
CARD SET: 100 CARDS
SPECIAL CARDS: 6 CARD CEL SET
COMPLETE SET: £63.00
CARD SET ONLY: £15.00
CEL CARDS £8.00
SINGLE CARDS: 15p

BATMAN ANIMATED II

PRODUCER: TOPPS U.S.
ISSUE YEAR: 1994
CARD SET: 90 CARDS
SPECIAL CARDS: 4 CARD CEL SET
COMPLETE SET: £47.00
CARD SET ONLY £15.00
SINGLE CARDS: 15p
CEL CARDS £8.00

BATMAN FOREVER FLEER ULTRA

PRODUCER: FLEER
ISSUE YEAR: 1995
CARD SET: 120 CARDS
SPECIAL CARDS: 10 ANIMACTION CARDS
COMPLETE SET: £15.00
SINGLE CARDS: 10p - 15p
SPECIAL SINGLE CARDS: £2.50
HOLOGRAM SET (36): £35.00

BATMAN FOREVER METAL

PRODUCER: FLEER
ISSUE YEAR: 1995
CARD SET: 100 CARDS
SPECIAL CARDS: 8 MOVIE PREVIEW CARDS
COMPLETE SET: £25.00
SINGLE CARDS: 25p
HOLOGRAM SET (4): £30.00

BATMAN MASTER SERIES

PRODUCER: SKYBOX
ISSUE YEAR: 1996
CARD SET: 90 CARDS
ARTIST PROOF CARD: £1.50
MASTER VILLAINS: £3.00
SPECTRA-ETCH CARD: £4.00
CHROMIUM CARD: £10.00
CLEAR CHROMIUM CARD: £10.00
COMPLETE SET: £15.00
SINGLE CARDS: 15p

BATMAN MOVIE SERIES I (U.S.)

PRODUCER: TOPPS U.S.
ISSUE YEAR: 1989
CARD SET: 132
SPECIAL CARDS: 22 STICKERS
COMPLETE SET: £12.00
SINGLE CARDS: 15p
SINGLE SPECIAL CARDS: 50p

Important Notes: There is a smaller British set available which are virtually identical, except in size.

BATMAN MOVIE SERIES II (U.S.)

PRODUCER: TOPPS U.S.
ISSUE YEAR: 1989
CARD SET: 132
SPECIAL CARDS: 22 STICKERS
COMPLETE SET: £12.00
SINGLE CARDS: 15p
SINGLE SPECIAL CARDS: 50p

Important Notes: There was not a British set of this set produced by Topps.

BATMAN MOVIE I U.K.

PRODUCER: TOPPS U.K.
ISSUE YEAR: 1989
CARD SET: 132
SPECIAL CARDS: 22 STICKERS
COMPLETE SET: £6.00
SINGLE CARDS: 10p
SINGLE SPECIAL CARDS: 25p

Important Notes: There was a slightly larger Topps U.S. set produced. Please see revelant section for further information.

BATMAN MOVIE DELUXE I U.S.

PRODUCER: TOPPS U.S.
ISSUE YEAR: 1989
CARD SET: 132 CARDS
SPECIAL CARDS: 22 STICKERS
COMPLETE FACTORY SET: £15.00

BATMAN MOVIE DELUXE II U.S.

PRODUCER: TOPPS U.S.
ISSUE YEAR: 1989
CARD SET: 132
SPECIAL CARDS: 22 STICKERS
COMPLETE FACTORY SET: £12.00

BATMAN RETURNS

PRODUCER: TOPPS U.S.
ISSUE YEAR: 1992
CARD SET: 88 CARDS
SPECIAL CARDS: 10 STADIUM CLUB CARDS
COMPLETE SET: £9.00
SINGLE CARDS: 10p
SINGLE SPECIAL CARDS: 25p

Important Notes: Stadium club card sub set cards are all lettered A-J (Complete Subset £3.00)

BATMAN RETURNS STADIUM CLUB EDITION

PRODUCER: TOPPS U.S.
ISSUE YEAR: 1992
CARD SET: 100 CARDS
COMPLETE SET: £15.00
SINGLE CARDS: 20p

Important Notes: This second set of Batman Returns cards were produced with a very high quality gloss finish with gold embossed Batman Returns logo on each card.

BATMAN RETURNS CANADIAN

PRODUCER: ZELLER
ISSUE YEAR: 1992
CARD SET: 24 CARDS

SPECIAL CARDS: No special cards
COMPLETE SET: £4.00
SINGLE CARDS: 25p

BATMAN, SAGA OF THE DARK KNIGHT

PRODUCER: SKYBOX
ISSUE YEAR: 1994
CARD SET: 100 CARDS
SPECIAL CARDS:
5 SPECTRA ETCH FOIL CARDS £8 EACH
SKYDISC -(Rare) £50.00
SKYDISC C.D. RETAILER GIVEAWAY £80.00
COMPLETE SET: £55.00
CARD SET ONLY: £10.00
SINGLE CARDS: 10p

BATTLE CARDS - UK EDITION

PRODUCER: MERLIN PUBLISHING LTD
ISSUE YEAR: 1993
CARD SET: 150
COMPLETE SET: £20.00
SINGLE CARDS: 15p
SPECIAL CARDS: TREASURE CARDS

Important Notes: A special card #150 Emperor of Vangoria was only obtainable from the publisher by solving a special quest on the other cards.

BATTLE CARDS - US EDITION

PRODUCER: MERLIN PUBLISHING LTD
ISSUE YEAR: 1994
CARD SET: 140
COMPLETE SET: £20.00
SINGLE CARDS: 15p
SPECIAL CARDS: TREASURE CARDS

Important Notes: A special card #140 Emperor of Vangor was only obtainable from the publisher in the US by solving all the quests.

BATTLESTAR GALACTICA

PRODUCER: TOPPS U.S.
ISSUE YEAR: 1978
CARD SET: 132 CARDS
SPECIAL CARDS: 22 STICKERS
COMPLETE SET: £25.00
SINGLE CARDS: 20p
SPECIAL SINGLE CARDS: 75p

Important Notes: This set may gain in popularity in the U.K. with the TV series showing on the Sci-Fi Channel

BAYWATCH

PRODUCER: SPORTS TIME
ISSUE YEAR: 1995
CARD SET: 100 CARDS
SPECIAL CARDS:
RAINBOW CARD: £2.00
PLATINUM CARD: £3.00
PHONE CARD: £10.00
AUTOGRAPH CARD: £25.00
COMPLETE SET: £10.00
SINGLE CARDS: 10p - 15p

BEATLES COLLECTION

PRODUCER: RIVER GROUP
ISSUE YEAR: 1993
CARD SET: 220 CARDS
COMPLETE SET: £35.00
SINGLE CARDS: 15p
SPECIAL CARDS:
8 SILVER CHASE CARDS: £2.00 each
10 GOLD CHASE CARDS: £8.00 each

BEAUTY AND THE BEAST

PRODUCER: SKYBOX
ISSUE YEAR: 1992
CARD SET: 75 CARDS
SPECIAL CARDS: 20 ACTIVITY CARDS
COMPLETE SET: £12.00
SINGLE CARDS: 15p
SINGLE SPECIAL CARDS: 25p

Important Notes: Following the success of the movie and subsequent video in the U.K., this card set picked up in popularity.

BEAVIS & BUTT-HEAD

PRODUCER: FLEER ULTRA
ISSUE YEAR: 1994
CARD SET: 150 CARDS
COMPLETE SET: £18.00
SPECIAL CARDS: 10 SCRATCH 'N' SNIFF SET
SINGLE CARDS: 15p
SPECIAL SINGLE CARDS: £1.00

BENCHWARMERS

PRODUCER: BENCHWARMER
ISSUE YEAR: 1992
CARD SET: 120 CARDS
COMPLETE SET: £20.00
SINGLE CARDS: 15p

BENCHWARMERS MAIL IN PRISM SET

PRODUCER: BENCHWARMER
ISSUE YEAR: 1992
CARD SET: 4 CARDS
SPECIAL CARDS: No special cards
COMPLETE SET: £15.00
SINGLE CARDS: N/A

BERNI WRIGHTSON

PRODUCER: FPG
ISSUE YEAR: 1993
CARD SET: 135 CARDS
SPECIAL CARDS: 3 HOLOGRAMS: £5.00 each
COMPLETE SET: £20.00
SINGLE CARDS: 15p

BERNIE WRIGHTSON: MORE MACABRE

PRODUCER: FPG
ISSUE YEAR: 1994
CARD SET: 90 CARDS
SPECIAL CARDS:
METALLIC STORM CARD: £6.00
AUTOGRAPH CARD (50): £35.00
COMPLETE SET: £8.00
SINGLE CARDS: 10p

BEVERLEY HILLBILLIES

PRODUCER: ECLIPSE
ISSUE YEAR: 1993
CARD SET: 110 CARDS
SPECIAL CARDS:
BLACK/GOLD FOIL CARD: £4.00
COMPLETE SET: £8.00
SINGLE CARDS: 10p

BEVERLY HILLS 90210

PRODUCER: TOPPS U.S.
ISSUE YEAR: 1992
CARD SET: 88 CARDS
SPECIAL CARDS: 11 STICKERS
COMPLETE SET: £8.00
SINGLE CARDS: 10p
SINGLE SPECIAL CARDS: 25p

Important Notes: Scarce in the U.K.

BILL AND TED'S EXCELLENT COLLECTOR CARDS

PRODUCER: MERLIN PUBLISHING LTD
ISSUE YEAR: 1993
CARD SET: 128
COMPLETE SET: £15.00
SINGLE CARDS: 5p

Important Notes: Photography provided by the film studio meant that this series was similar to the US published Pro-Set Bill and Ted series. Certain key cards were changed when the UK edition was produced.

BILL AND TED'S MOST ATYPICAL ADVENTURE

PRODUCER: PRO SET
ISSUE YEAR: 1991
CARD SET: 100 CARDS
SPECIAL CARDS: No special cards issued
COMPLETE SET: £8.00
SINGLE CARDS: 10p

Important Notes: The Bill & Ted movie success, led to the now infamous production ideas on which Wayne's World was based.

BINGO THE DOG MOVIE

PRODUCER: PACIFIC

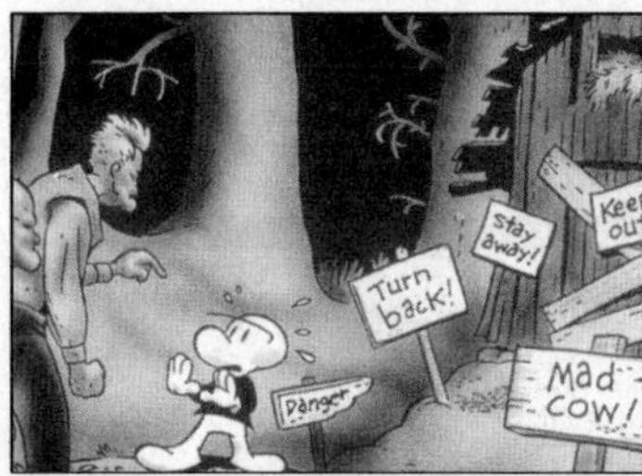

Bone #69

ISSUE YEAR: 1991
CARD SET: 110 CARDS
SPECIAL CARDS: No special cards
COMPLETE SET: £5.00
SINGLE CARDS: 10p

BLACK HOLE

PRODUCER: TOPPS U.S.
ISSUE YEAR: 1979
CARD SET: 88 CARDS
SPECIAL CARDS: 22 STICKERS
COMPLETE SET: £15.00
SINGLE CARDS: 15p - 20p
SINGLE SPECIAL CARDS: 30p

Important Notes: Based on the Disney movie of the same name

BLOOM COUNTY

PRODUCER: KROME PRODUCTIONS
ISSUE YEAR: 1995
CARD SET: 100 CARDS
SPECIAL CARDS:100 STICKERS: 20p each
HOLOCHROME CARD: £6.00
COMPLETE SET: £15.00
SINGLE CARDS: 15p

BLUE CHIPS (SHAQUILLE O'NEAL MOVIE)

PRODUCER: SKYBOX
ISSUE YEAR: 1994
CARD SET: 90 CARDS
SPECIAL CARDS: 5 FOIL CARDS
CARD SET: £15.00
SINGLE CARDS: 15p
SINGLE SPECIAL CARDS: £5.00-£10.00 EACH

BOB EGGLETON

PRODUCER: FPG
ISSUE YEAR: 1995
CARD SET: 90 CARDS
SPECIAL CARDS:
METALLIC STORM CARD: £6.00
AUTOGRAPH CARD (1000): £25.00
COMPLETE SET: £8.00
SINGLE CARDS: 10p

BOB MARLEY, LEGEND OF

PRODUCER: ISLAND VIBES
ISSUE YEAR: 1996
CARD SET: 51 CARDS
SPECIAL CARDS:
GOLDEN SIGNATURE CARD: £1.50
EMBOSSED CARD: £5.00
ETCHED FOIL CARD: £5.00
KEN KELLY FANTASY CARD: £5.00
FOIL FRAMED EMBOSSED CARD: £8.00
BOB MARLEY MEDALLION: £8.00
COMPLETE SET: £10.00
SINGLE CARDS: 25p

BOND CROSSOVER VOL. 1

PRODUCER: INKWORKS
ISSUE YEAR: 1996
CARD SET: 100 CARDS
SPECIAL CARDS:
1 GOLD EMBOSSED BOND £25.00
9 FOIL BOND GIRLS £5.00 each
6 FOIL POSTERS £8.00 each
COMPLETE SET: £15.00
SINGLE CARDS: 15p

BONE

PRODUCER: COMIC IMAGES
ISSUE YEAR: 1994
CARD SET: 90 CARDS
SPECIAL CARDS: 6 FOIL CARDS
COMPLETE SET: £9.00
SINGLE CARDS: 10p
SPECIAL SINGLE CARDS: £5.00

BONE ALL CHROMIUM SERIES

PRODUCER: COMIC IMAGES
CARD SET: 90 CARDS
SPECIAL CARDS: 6 MAGNACHROME CARDS
COMPLETE SET: £15.00
SINGLE CARDS: 15p
SPECIAL SINGLE CARDS: £5.00

BONE: DRAGONSLAYER

PRODUCER: COMIC IMAGES
ISSUE YEAR: 1996
CARD SET: 90 CARDS
SPECIAL CARDS:
CHROME COVERS CARD: £6.00

VILLAINS SUB-SET (3):	£25.00 the set
AUTOGRAPH CARD (500):	£40.00
BOXCARD:	£1.50
COMPLETE SET:	£10.00
SINGLE CARDS:	15p

BORIS I

PRODUCER:	COMIC IMAGES
ISSUE YEAR:	1991
CARD SET:	90 CARDS
SPECIAL CARDS:	No special cards
COMPLETE SET:	£13.00
SINGLE CARDS:	15p

BORIS II

PRODUCER:	COMIC IMAGES
ISSUE YEAR:	1992
CARD SET:	90 CARDS
SPECIAL CARDS:	6 PRISM CARDS
COMPLETE SET:	£45.00
CARD SET ONLY	£10.00
SINGLE CARDS:	10p
SINGLE SPECIAL CARDS:	£7.00

BORIS III, ALL PRISM

PRODUCER:	COMIC IMAGES
ISSUE YEAR:	1993
CARD SET:	90 CARDS
SPECIAL CARDS:	6 CHROMIUM CARDS
COMPLETE SET:	£80.00
CARD SET ONLY	£15.00
SINGLE CARDS:	15p
SINGLE SPECIAL CARDS:	£10.00 EACH

BORIS IV

PRODUCER:	COMIC IMAGES
ISSUE YEAR:	1994
CARD SET:	90 CARDS
SPECIAL CARDS:	6 FOIL CHASE CARDS
COMPLETE SET:	£7.50
SINGLE CARDS:	10p
SINGLE SPECIAL CARDS:	£5.00

BORIS, BEST OF (All Chrome Set)

PRODUCER:	COMIC IMAGES
ISSUE YEAR:	1995
CARD SET:	90 CARDS
SPECIAL CARDS:	6 OMNICHROME CARDS
COMPLETE SET:	£20.00
SINGLE CARDS:	20p
SINGLE SPECIAL CARDS:	£6.00

BORIS WITH JULIE

PRODUCER:	COMIC IMAGES
ISSUE YEAR:	1996
CARD SET:	90 CARDS
SPECIAL CARDS:	
MAGNACHROME CARD:	£6.00
HOLOCHROME CARD:	£6.00
AUTOGRAPH CARD (BORIS):	£35.00
AUTOGRAPH CARD (JULIE):	£35.00
UNICORNS SUB-SET (3):	£40.00 the set
MAGNACHROME BOX BONUS:	£4.00
COMPLETE SET:	£15.00
SINGLE CARDS:	20p

BUCK ROGERS IN THE 25TH CENTURY

PRODUCER:	TOPPS U.S.
ISSUE YEAR:	1979
CARD SET:	88 CARDS
SPECIAL CARDS:	22 STICKERS
COMPLETE SET:	£17.50
SINGLE CARDS:	20p
SINGLE SPECIAL CARDS:	30p

CALENDAR GIRLS - GIL ELVGREN

PRODUCER:	COMIC IMAGES
ISSUE YEAR:	1993
CARD SET:	90 CARDS
SPECIAL CARDS:	6 CHASE CARDS (3 Spectra and 3 Chrome at up to £25.00 each)
COMPLETE SET:	£65.00
SINGLE CARDS:	15p

Important Notes: a set that is becoming increasingly scarce

CALENDAR GIRLS - GIL ELVGREN II

PRODUCER:	COMIC IMAGES
ISSUE YEAR:	1994
CARD SET:	90 CARDS
SPECIAL CARDS:	6 CHASE CARDS
COMPLETE SET:	£12.00
SINGLE CARDS:	15p

DC Comics Cards #1

SINGLE SPECIAL CARDS:	£5.00

CAMPBELL'S COLLECTION, THE

PRODUCER:	COLLECT-A-CARD
ISSUE YEAR:	1995
CARD SET:	72 CARDS
SPECIAL CARDS:	
FOIL ETCHED CARD:	£8.00
DYNAMIC-TEXTURED CARD:	£5.00
SOUPER STICKERS:	£1.25
PRE-PAID PHONE CARDS:	£10.00
COMPLETE SET:	£6.00
SINGLE CARDS:	5p - 10P

CAPTAIN AMERICA 50TH ANNIVERSARY

PRODUCER:	COMIC IMAGES
ISSUE YEAR:	1990
CARD SET:	45 CARDS
SPECIAL CARDS:	No special cards
COMPLETE SET:	£12.00
SINGLE CARDS:	25p

CASPER ULTRA

PRODUCER:	FLEER
CARD SET:	119 CARDS
SPECIAL CARDS:	15 PRISMATIC FOIL CARDS
COMPLETE SET:	£15.00
SINGLE CARDS:	10p - 15p
SPECIAL SINGLE CARDS:	£1.00

Important Notes: the odd number of the set arises from the fact that numbers #13 and #77 were not printed for legal reasons and a Promo card was withdrawn. A duplicate #12 replaced the original #13 and a duplicate #69 replaced the original #77

CHARLES VESS

PRODUCER:	FPG
ISSUE YEAR:	1995
CARD SET:	90 CARDS
SPECIAL CARDS:	
METALLIC STORM CARD:	£6.00
AUTOGRAPH CARD (1000):	£35.00
COMPLETE SET:	£8.00
SINGLE CARDS:	15p

CHARLIE'S ANGELS SERIES I

PRODUCER:	TOPPS U.S.
ISSUE YEAR:	1977
CARD SET:	55
SPECIAL CARDS:	11 STICKERS
COMPLETE SET:	£40.00
SINGLE CARD:	60p - 75p
SPECIAL SINGLE CARD:	£2.00

CHARLIE'S ANGELS SERIES II

PRODUCER:	TOPPS U.S.
ISSUE YEAR:	1977
CARD SET:	66 CARDS
SPECIAL CARDS:	11 STICKERS
COMPLETE SET:	£30.00
SINGLE CARDS:	40p - 50p
SPECIAL SINGLE CARDS:	75p

CHARLIE'S ANGELS SERIES III

PRODUCER:	TOPPS U.S.
ISSUE YEAR:	1978
CARD SET:	66 CARDS
SPECIAL CARDS:	11 STICKERS
COMPLETE SET:	£30.00
SINGLE CARDS:	40p - 50p
SPECIAL SINGLE CARDS:	75p

CHARLIE'S ANGELS SERIES IV

PRODUCER:	TOPPS U.S.
ISSUE YEAR:	1978
CARD SET:	66 CARDS
SPECIAL CARDS:	11 STICKERS
COMPLETE SET:	£20.00
SINGLE CARDS:	30p
SPECIAL SINGLE CARDS:	60p

CHRIS ACHILLEOS I

PRODUCER:	FPG
ISSUE YEAR:	1992
CARD SET:	90 CARDS
SPECIAL CARDS:	
90 SILVER FOIL:	£2.50 each
90 GOLD FOIL:	£4.00 each
AUTOGRAPH CARD (1000):	£35.00
COMPLETE SET:	£8.00
SINGLE CARDS:	15p

CHRIS ACHILLEOS II

PRODUCER:	FPG
ISSUE YEAR:	1994
CARD SET:	90 CARDS
SPECIAL CARDS:	
METALLIC STORM CARD:	£6.00
AUTOGRAPH CARD (1000):	£35.00
COMPLETE SET:	£8.00
SINGLE CARDS:	15p

CINDERELLA

PRODUCER:	SKYBOX
ISSUE YEAR:	1995
CARD SET:	90 CARDS
SPECIAL CARDS:	5 FOIL CARD SET 2 TRANSFORMATION CARD SET
COMPLETE SET:	£9.00
SINGLE CARDS:	10p

CIVIL WAR: THE ART OF MORT KUNSTLER

PRODUCER:	COMIC IMAGES
ISSUE YEAR:	1996
CARD SET:	90 CARDS
SPECIAL CARDS:	
CHROMIUM GENERLS:	£6.00
BATTLE SUB-SET CARDS (3):	£25.00 the set
AUTOGRAPH CARD (500):	£35.00
0 BOX CARD:	£3.00
COMPLETE SET:	£8.00
SINGLE CARDS:	15p

CLOSE ENCOUNTERS OF THE THIRD KIND

PRODUCER:	TOPPS U.S.
ISSUE YEAR:	1978
CARD SET:	66 CARDS
SPECIAL CARDS:	11 STICKERS
COMPLETE SET:	£12.00
SINGLE CARDS:	20p
SINGLE SPECIAL CARDS:	30p

CLYDE CALDWEL

PRODUCER:	FPG
ISSUE YEAR:	1995
CARD SET:	90 CARDS
SPECIAL CARDS:	
METALLIC STORM CARD:	£6.00
AUTOGRAPG CAR (1000):	£30.00
COMPLETE SET:	£8.00
SINGLE CARDS:	15p

COMICS' GREATEST WORLD

PRODUCER:	TOPPS U.S.
ISSUE YEAR:	1994
CARD SET:	100 CARDS
SPECIAL CARDS:	6 MATRIX CARDS
COMPLETE SET:	£10.00
SINGLE CARDS:	10p
SPECIAL SINGLE CARDS:	£2.50

CONAN COLLECTORS CARDS

PRODUCER:	COMIC IMAGES
ISSUE YEAR:	1993
CARD SET (Chromium):	90 CARDS

CARD SET (Holochrome): 90 CARDS
SPECIAL CARDS: 10 COLOUR VARIATIONS FOR EACH SET
PRISM CARDS: 6
COMPLETE SET (Chromium): £25.00
COMPLETE SET (Holochrome): ?
SINGLE CARDS (Chromium): 25p
SINGLE CARDS (Holochrome): ?
SPECIAL SINGLE CARDS: £10.00

Important Notes: there is one holochrome card per box

CONAN II (CHROMIUM)

PRODUCER: COMIC IMAGES
ISSUE YEAR: 1994
CARD SET: 90 CARDS
SPECIAL CARDS: 6 GALAXY PRISM CARDS
COMPLETE SET: £20.00
SINGLE CARDS: 20p
SPECIAL SINGLE CARDS: £4.00

CONAN III - ALL CHROMIUM

PRODUCER: COMIC IMAGES
ISSUE YEAR: 1995
CARD SET: 90 CARDS
SPECIAL CARDS:
MAGNACHROME CARDS: £5.00
3 CARD SUB-SET: £20.00
MEDALLION CARDS: £15.00
HOLOCHROME CARD: £6.00
COMPLETE SET: £15.00
SINGLE CARDS: 20p

CONAN THE MARVEL YEARS

PRODUCER: COMIC IMAGES
ISSUE YEAR: 1995
CARDS SET: 90 CARDS
SPECIAL CARDS:
KING CONAN CHASE CARD: £6.00
CONAN THE SAVAGE SUB-SET (3): £20.00 the set
HOLOCHROME CARD: £6.00
SIMON BISLEY AUTOGRAPH CARD (500): £40.00
COMPLETE SET: £17.50
SINGLE CARDS: 20p

CREATORS ALTERNATE UNIVERSE

PRODUCER: DYNAMIC ENTERTAINMENT
ISSUE YEAR: 1996
CARD SET: 90 CARDS
SPECIAL CARDS: AUTOGRAPH CARDS (87): £20.00 each
LANCE BLAST-OFF PHONE CARD: £20.00
COMPLETE SET: £8.00
SINGLE CARDS: 15p

CREATORS MASTER SERIES

PRODUCER: FLEER/SKYBOX
ISSUE YEAR: 1995
CARD SET: 90 CARDS
SPECIAL CARDS:
5 SPECTRA-ETCH CARD (B-1 TO B-5): £5.00
EMBOSSED SPECTRA SKYBOX CARD (SB1): £20.00
COMPLETE SET: £12.00
SINGLE CARDS: 15p

CROW, THE

PRODUCER: KITCHEN SINK
ISSUE YEAR: 1994
CARD SET: 100 CARDS
SPECIAL CARDS:
10 CROW VISION CARDS: £5.00 each
COMPLETE SET: £12.00
SINGLE CARDS: 15p

Important Note: the special cards are becoming very scarce in the U.K.

CROW, CITY OF ANGELS

PRODUCER: KITCHEN SINK
ISSUE YEAR: 1996
CARD SET: 90 CARDS
SPECIAL CARDS: 10 EMBOSSED CARDS: £2.00 each
6 CROW-MIUM CARDS: £7.00 each
ULTRA CHASE CARD: £35.00
5 PROMOS: WIZARD (1), NSU (2), COMBO (3), ADVANCE COMICS (4 + 5): £2.00 each
COMPLETE SET: £8.00
SINGLE CARDS: 15p

CYBERFORCE

PRODUCER: TOPPS
ISSUE YEAR: 1995
CARD SET: 72 CARDS
SPECIAL CARDS:
18 CYBER OPTICS CARD SET: £4.00
3 CLEARZONE CARDS: £10.00 each
6 MATRIX CARD: £6.00 each
COMPLETE SET: £15.00
SINGLE CARDS: 20p

CYBERFORCE SUMMER

PRODUCER: INTREPID
ISSUE YEAR: 1996
CARD SET: 90 CARDS
SPECIAL CARDS:
FOIL CARD: £5.00
PUZZLE CARD: £5.00
ACETATE FOIL CARD: £10.00
COMPLETE SET: £17.50
SINGLE CARDS: 20p

DARRELL SWEET

PRODUCER: FPG
ISSUE YEAR: 1994
CARD SET: 90 CARDS
SPECIAL CARDS:
METALLIC STORM CARD: £7.00
AUTOGRAPH CARD (1000): £35.00
COMPLETE SET: £6.00
SINGLE CARDS: 5p - 10p

DAVID CHERRY

PRODUCER: FPG
ISSUE YEAR: 1995
CARD SET: 90 CARDS
SPECIAL CARDS:
METALLIC STORM CARD: £5.00
AUTOGRAPH CARD (1000): £30.00
COMPLETE SET: £8.00
SINGLE CARDS: 15p

DAVID MATTINGLY

PRODUCER: FPG
ISSUE YEAR: 1995
CARD SET: 90 CARDS
SPECIAL CARDS:
METALLIC STORM CARD: £5.00
AUTOGRAPH CARD (1000): £30.00
COMPLETE SET: £8.00
SINGLE CARDS: 15p

DAWN AND BEYOND

PRODUCER: COMIC IMAGES
ISSUE YEAR: 1995
CARD SET: 90 CARDS
SPECIAL CARDS: 6 CARD UNCUT SHEET
6 MAGNACHROME CARD SET
3 RARE ART CARD SET
COMPLETE SET: £10.00
SINGLE CARDS: 10p

DC BLOODLINES

PRODUCER: SKYBOX
ISSUE YEAR: 1993
CARD SET: 81 CARDS
SPECIAL CARDS: 4 SUPERMAN EMBOSSED CARD SET
SUPERMAN REDEMPTIONAL CARD
COMPLETE SET: £5.00
SINGLE CARDS: 5p

DC COSMIC CARDS I

PRODUCER: IMPEL
ISSUE YEAR: 1992
CARD SET: 180 CARDS
SPECIAL CARDS: 10 HOLOGRAM CARDS
COMPLETE SET: £25.00
SINGLE CARDS: 15p
SINGLE SPECIAL CARDS: £3.00

DC COSMIC TEAMS

PRODUCER: SKYBOX
ISSUE YEAR: 1993
CARD SET: 120 CARDS
SPECIAL CARDS: 6 HOLOGRAM CARDS
COMPLETE SET: £12.00
SINGLE CARDS: 10p
SINGLE SPECIAL CARDS: £4.00

Important Notes: As there are certain cards that are more difficult to get than others, a complete set is more difficult to put together than one would expect

DC LEGENDS '95 POWER-CHROME

PRODUCER: SKYBOX
ISSUE YEAR: 1995
CARD SET: 150 CARDS
SPECIAL CARDS:
HARD HITTER CARD: £2.00
BATTKEZOE CARD: £7.00
LEGACY CARD: £10.00
COMLETE SET: £25.00
SINGLE CARDS: 15p

DC MASTER SERIES

PRODUCER: SKYBOX
ISSUE YEAR: 1994
CARD SET: 90 CARDS
SPECIAL CARDS:
SUPERMAN SKYDISC: £50.00
4 FOIL CARDS: £6.00 each
5 SPECTRA-FOIL CARD: £10.00 each
COMPLETE SET: £10.00
SINGLE CARDS: 10p

DC MILESTONE MEDIA

PRODUCER: SKYBOX
ISSUE YEAR: 1993
CARD SET: 100 CARDS
SPECIAL CARDS:
2 FOIL-EMBOSSED CARDS: £3.00 each
COMPLETE SET: £4.00
SINGLE CARDS: 5p

DC VERTIGO

PRODUCER: SKYBOX
ISSUE YEAR: 1995
CARD SET: 90 CARDS
SPECIAL CARDS:
DEATH SKYDISC: £60.00
6 GOLD FOIL CARDS: £10.00 each
COMPLETE SET: £9.00
SINGLE CARDS: 15p

DC VERSUS MARVEL

PRODUCER: FLEER/SKYBOX
ISSUE YEAR: 1995
CARD SET: 100 CARDS
SPECIAL CARDS:
HOLO FX CARD: £4.00
IMPACT CARD: £4.00
MIRAGE CARD: £30.00
COMPLETE SET: £12.00
SINGLE CARDS: 15p

DC VILLAINS

PRODUCER: FLEER/SKYBOX
ISSUE YEAR: 1995
CARD SET: 90 CARDS
SPECIAL CARDS:
SKYMOTION REDEMPTION CARD: £40.00
3 FOIL EMBOSSED CARDS SET: £30.00
9 SPECTRA-ETCH CARD SET: £30.00
COMPLETE SET: £10.00
SINGLE CARDS: 15p

DARK CRYSTAL

PRODUCER: DONRUSS
ISSUE YEAR: 1982
CARD SET: 78 CARDS
SPECIAL CARDS: No special cards
COMPLETE SET: £9.00
SINGLE CARDS: 20p

DEATHMATE

PRODUCER: UPPER DECK
ISSUE YEAR: 1993
CARD SET: 110 CARDS
SPECIAL CARDS: 18 (Gold Foil Embossed, 9 Foil)
COMPLETE SET: £5.00
SINGLE CARDS: 5p
SPECIAL SINGLE CARDS
(Gold Embossed): £2.00
(Foil): £5.00

DEATHWATCH 2000

PRODUCER: CLASSIC/CONTINUITY
ISSUE YEAR: 1993
CARD SET: 100 CARDS
SPECIAL CARDS:
7 HYBRID CARDS: £5.00 each
COMPLETE SET: £10.00
SINGLE CARDS: 10p
SPECIAL SINGLE CARDS: £6.00

DESERT STORM I

PRODUCER: TOPPS U.S.
ISSUE YEAR: 1991
CARD SET: 88 CARDS
SPECIAL CARDS: 22 STICKERS: £1.00 each
COMPLETE SET: £10.00
SINGLE CARDS: 5p-10p
SINGLE SPECIAL CARDS: 15p

DESERT STORM I DELUXE EDITION

PRODUCER: TOPPS U.S.
ISSUE YEAR: 1991
CARD SET: 88 CARDS
SPECIAL CARDS: 22 STICKERS: £1.00 each
COMPLETE FACTORY SET: £13.00

DESERT STORM II - VICTORY

PRODUCER: TOPPS U.S.
ISSUE YEAR: 1991
CARD SET: 66 CARDS
SPECIAL CARDS: 11 STICKERS: £1.00 each
COMPLETE SET: £5.00
SINGLE CARDS: 5p
SINGLE SPECIAL CARDS: 15p

DESERT STORM III - HOMECOMING

PRODUCER: TOPPS U.S.
ISSUE YEAR: 1991
CARD SET: 66 CARDS
SPECIAL CARDS: 11 STICKERS: £1.00 each
COMPLETE SET: £5.00
SINGLE CARDS: 5p
SINGLE SPECIAL CARDS: 15p

DINOSAURS, TV SERIES

PRODUCER: PRO SET
ISSUE YEAR: 1992
CARD SET: 65 CARDS
COMPLETE SET: £6.00
SINGLE CARDS: 10p

DINOSAURS ATTACK

PRODUCER: TOPPS U.S.
ISSUE YEAR: 1988
CARD SET: 55 CARDS
SPECIAL CARDS: 11 STICKERS: 50p each
COMPLETE SET: £8.00
SINGLE CARDS: 20p
Important Notes: This set was a send up of the Mars Attacks! series, famous for its gory artwork

DISNEY PREMIUM

PRODUCER: SKYBOX
ISSUE YEAR: 1995
CARD SET: 80 CARDS
SPECIAL CARDS:
2 HOLOBOSSED CARDS: £7.50 each
9 SILVERSCREEN CARD SET £15.00
COMPLETE SET: £17.50
SINGLE CARDS: 20p

DISNEY SERIES I

PRODUCER: IMPEL
ISSUE YEAR: 1991
CARD SET: 200 CARDS
SPECIAL CARDS:
2 HOLOGRAMS: £20.00 each
COMPLETE SET: £55.00
CARD SET ONLY £15.00
SINGLE CARDS: 10p
Important Notes: The two holograms in this set are very scarce. They are the first double sided holograms to be produced for a trading card set.

DON MAITZ FANTASY ART

PRODUCER: FPG
ISSUE YEAR: 1994
CARD SET: 90 CARDS
SPECIAL CARDS:
METALLIC STORM CARDS: £7.00
AUTOGRAPH CARD (1000): £35.00
COMPLETE SET: £8.00
SINGLE CARDS: 15p

DON MAITZ II

PRODUCER: FPG
ISSUE YEAR: 1996
CARD SET: 90 CARDS
SPECIAL CARDS:
METALLIC STORM CARD: £6.00
COMPLETE SET: £8.00
SINGLE CARDS: 15p

DOUBLE IMPACT

PRODUCER: COMIC IMAGES
ISSUE YEAR: 1996
CARD SET: 90 CARDS
SPECIAL CARDS:
6 FOIL CHASE CARDS £5.00 each
3 CARD BULLSHOTS SUB-SET £7.00
1 BOXCARD £3.00
HOLOCHROME CARDS ??
COMPLETE SET: £16.00
SINGLE CARDS: 20p

DRACULA MOVIE

PRODUCER: TOPPS
ISSUE YEAR: 1992
CARD SET: 100 CARDS
SPECIAL CARDS: No special cards
COMPLETE SET: £15.00
SINGLE CARDS: 15p
Important Note: This is increasingly becoming a very difficult set to obtain

DRAGONHEART

PRODUCER: TOPPS
ISSUE YEAR: 1996
CARD SET: 72 CARDS
SPECIAL CARDS:
DRACOFOIL CARD: £5.00
COMPLETE SET: £10.00
SINGLE CARDS: 15p

DR. WHO SERIES I

PRODUCER: CORNERSTONE
ISSUE YEAR: 1994
CARD SET: 110 CARDS
SPECIAL CARDS: 7 DOCTOR'S FOIL CARDS
COMPLETE SET: £17.50
FACTORY SET (with Dalek Prism card): £20.00
GOLD FACTORY SET
(with 7 Prism cards and 1 gold ink autographed card): £50.00?
SINGLE CARDS: 15p - 20p
SINGLE SPECIAL CARDS: £8.00.
CARD #2 £15.00 (Rare in the U.K.)

DR. WHO SERIES II

PRODUCER: CORNERSTONE
ISSUE YEAR: 1995
CARD SET: 110 CARDS
SPECIAL CARDS: 6 FOIL CHASE CARDS
COMPLETE SET: £12.50
FACTORY SET: £30.00
SINGLE CARDS: 15p
SPECIAL SINGLE CARDS: £5.00
Important Notes: The Factory Set was UV COATED and came with a Davros foil card #7. This set without the card would be about £20.00. The numbering starts at #111.

DR. WHO SERIES III

PRODUCER: CORNERSTONE
ISSUE YEAR: 1995
CARD SET: 100 CARDS
SPECIAL CARDS:
COMPANION'S PREMIERE CARD: £1.50
DOCTOR FOIL CARD: £6.00
AUTOGRAPH CARDS (5): £40.00
MASTER FOIL CARD: £7.00
COMPLETE SET: £15.00
SINGLE CARDS: 20p

DR. WHO SERIES IV

PRODUCER: CORNERSTONE
ISSUE YEAR: 1996
CARD SET: 100 CARDS
SPECIAL CARDS:
7 FOIL DOCTORS £5.00 each
VARIOUS AUTOGRAPH CARDS £25.00 each
COMPLETE SET: £15.00
SINGLE CARDS: 15p
Important Notes: there is an 8th Doctor Card in Factory Set at £12.00 to £15.00

EASTER HOLIDAY CARDS

PRODUCER: FLEER
ISSUE YEAR: 1995
CARD SET: 42 CARDS
SPECIAL CARDS: 42 STICKERS: 25p
GOLDEN MEMORIES CARD: £3.00
COMPLETE SET: £5.00
SINGLE CARDS: 10p

ELVIRA

PRODUCER: COMIC IMAGES
ISSUE YEAR: 1996
CARD SET: 75 CARDS
SPECIAL CARDS:
6 CHROME CHASE CARDS £5.00 each
1 AUTOGRAPH CARD?
COMPLETE SET: £9.00
SINGLE CARDS: 15p

EMPIRE STRIKES BACK SERIES I

PRODUCER: TOPPS U.S.
ISSUE YEAR: 1980
CARD SET: 132 CARDS
SPECIAL CARDS: 33 STICKERS
COMPLETE SET: £40.00
SINGLE CARDS: 30p
SPECIAL SINGLE CARDS: £1.00

EMPIRE STRIKES BACK SERIES II

PRODUCER: TOPPS U.S.
ISSUE YEAR: 1980
CARD SET: 132 CARDS
SPECIAL CARDS: 33 STICKERS
COMPLETE SET: £30.00
SINGLE CARDS: 25p
SPECIAL SINGLE CARDS: £1.00

EMPIRE STRIKES BACK SERIES III

PRODUCER: TOPPS U.S.
ISSUE YEAR: 1980
CARDS SET: 88 CARDS
SPECIAL CARDS: 22 STICKERS
COMPLETE SET: £25.00
SINGLE CARDS: 25p
SPECIAL SINGLE CARDS: 70p

EMPIRE STRIKES BACK WIDEVISION

PRODUCER: TOPPS U.S.
ISSUE YEAR: 1995
CARD SET: 144 CARDS
SPECIAL CARDS: 7 PROMO CARDS
COMPLETE SET: £20.00
SINGLE CARDS: 15p
SPECIAL SINGLE CARDS: £8.50 each
Important Notes: The Promo Cards were numbered from #0 to #6 and were available in different magazines such as Combo and Wizard. Card #5 seems much scarcer and would be valued at about £10.00

E.T. THE EXTRA TERRESTRIAL MOVIE

PRODUCER: TOPPS U.S.
ISSUE YEAR: 1982
CARD SET: 87 CARDS
SPECIAL CARDS: 12 STICKERS
COMPLETE SET: £15.00
SINGLE CARDS: 20p
SINGLE SPECIAL CARDS: 40p

EVIL ERNIE

PRODUCER: KROME PRODUCTIONS
ISSUE YEAR: 1994
CARD SET: 100 CARDS
SPECIAL CARDS: 6 KROME CARDS
COMPLETE SET: £12.50
FACTORY SET: 55 CARDS (all chrome)
COMPLETE FACTORY SET: £40.00
SINGLE CARDS: 15p
SPECIAL SINGLE CARDS: £6.00
SIGNED KROME CARD: £20.00
SIGNED & NUMBERED KROME CARD: £30.00
Important Notes: There were two signed Krome cards per case and one signed and numbered Krome card per case

EVIL ERNIE CHROMIUM

PRODUCER: KROME PRODUCTIONS
ISSUE YEAR: 1995
CARD SET: 100 CARDS
SPECIAL CARDS: 5 SUPER PREMIUM CARDS
COMPLETE SET: £20.00
SINGLE CARDS: 20p
SPECIAL SINGLE CARDS: £6.00
Important Notes: Special cards signed by Brian Pulido and Steven Hughes are about £40 each

FAMOUS COMICBOOK CREATORS

PRODUCER: ECLIPSE
ISSUE YEAR: 1992
CARD SET: 110 CARDS
SPECIAL CARDS: No special cards
COMPLETE SET: £15.00

FIRST CHOICE
FIRST CHOICE
TRADING CARDS
11 Keith Avenue
Liverpool L4 5SL
SEND FOR NEW
MAIL ORDER LIST
Orders taken on
single cards upwards
CALL NOW FOR DETAILS!
TEL: 0976 285087
Captain
Jean-Luc Picard
STAR TREK
THE NEXT GENERATION
62
LAST LICKS
CARL HUBBELL—THE MEAL TICKET
PSYLOCKE
X-MEN
BILL96

SINGLE CARDS: 10p

FIEVEL GOES WEST
PRODUCER: IMPEL
ISSUE YEAR: 1991
CARD SET: 150 CARDS
SPECIAL CARDS: 5 HOLOGRAM CARDS
COMPLETE SET: £20.00
CARD SET ONLY £10.00
SINGLE CARDS: 10p
SINGLE SPECIAL CARDS: £3.00

FLAIR MARVEL
PRODUCER: FLEER
ISSUE YEAR: 1994
CARD SET: 150 CARDS
SPECIAL CARDS:
18 POWER BLASTS CARD SET £50.00
COMPLETE SET: £30.00
SINGLE CARDS: 20p
SINGLE SPECIAL CARDS: £3.00-£4.50

FLINTSTONES MOVIE CARDS
PRODUCER: TOPPS U.S.
ISSUE YEAR: 1994
CARD SET: 88 CARDS
SPECIAL CARDS: 11 STICKERS
COMPLETE SET: £8.00
SINGLE CARDS: 10p
SPECIAL SINGLE CARDS: 75p
Important Notes: Factory Sets were heavily remaindered in the U.S.

FREE WILLY 2
PRODUCER: SKYBOX
ISSUE YEAR: 1995
CARD SET: 90 CARDS
SPECIAL CARDS:
9 SPECTRA CARDS: £2.50 each
COMPLETE SET: £10.00
SINGLE CARDS: 10p
Important Notes: Two holograms are available at approximately £10.00 each

FRIGHTENERS, THE
PRODUCER: DART FLIPCARDS
ISSUE YEAR: 1996
CARD SET: 72 CARDS
SPECIAL CARDS:
GOLD FOIL CARD: £8.00
BIG BOY CARD: £6.00
COMPLETE SET: £17.50
SINGLE CARDS: 25p

FRIGHT FLICKS
PRODUCER: TOPPS U.S.
ISSUE YEAR: 1988
CARD SET: 90 CARDS
SPECIAL CARDS: 11 STICKERS
COMPLETE SET: £15.00
SINGLE CARDS: 15p - 20p
SINGLE SPECIAL CARDS: 20p
Important Notes: The sticker set is hard to find and the cards and stickers would be valued at around £15.00

FRAZETTA
PRODUCER: COMIC IMAGES
ISSUE YEAR: 1991
CARD SET: 90 CARDS
SPECIAL CARDS: No special cards
COMPLETE SET: £10.00
SINGLE CARDS: 15p

FRAZETTA II
PRODUCER: COMIC IMAGES
ISSUE YEAR: 1993
CARD SET: 90 CARDS
SPECIAL CARDS: 3 SPECTROSCOPE/3 CHROME
COMPLETE SET: £9.00
SINGLE CARDS: 10p
SPECIAL SINGLE CARDS: £5.00

GARFIELD THE CAT
PRODUCER: SKYBOX
ISSUE YEAR: 1992
CARD SET: 100 CARDS
SPECIAL CARDS: 9 TATTOOS, 5 HOLOGRAMS
COMPLETE SET: £35.00
SINGLE CARDS: 10p
SINGLE SPECIAL CARDS:
TATTOOS 50p,
HOLOGRAMS £5.00
Important Notes: Very scarce in the U.K.

Gen 13 #86

GEN 13
PRODUCER: WILDSTORM
ISSUE YEAR: 1995
CARD SET: 107 CARDS
SPECIAL CARDS:
SINGLE REFRACTOR CARD £6.00
9 GLOW-IN-THE-DARK CARD SET £58.00
9 GEN-ACTIVE CARD SET 70.00
COMPLETE SET: £25.00
SINGLE CARDS: 20p - 25p
SINGLE SPECIAL CARDS: £6.00-£15.00

GHOSTBUSTERS II MOVIE
PRODUCER: TOPPS U.S.
ISSUE YEAR: 1989
CARD SET: 88 cards
SPECIAL CARDS: 11 stickers
COMPLETE SET: £6.00
SINGLE CARDS: 10p
SINGLE SPECIAL CARDS: 25p
Important Notes: There were no trading cards produced for the first Ghostbusters movie.

GHOST RIDER I
PRODUCER: COMIC IMAGES
ISSUE YEAR: 1990
CARD SET: 45 CARDS
SPECIAL CARDS: No special cards
COMPLETE SET: £8.00
SINGLE CARDS: 25p
Important Notes: This first set of Ghost Rider trading cards was only produced in limited quantities.

GHOST RIDER II
PRODUCER: COMIC IMAGES
ISSUE YEAR: 1992
CARD SET: 80 CARDS
SPECIAL CARDS: 10 GLOW IN THE DARK CARDS
COMPLETE SET: £7.00
SINGLE CARDS: 10p
SINGLE SPECIAL CARDS: 30p
Important Notes: There was one glow in dark special card contained within each packet of Ghost Rider II trading cards, so they are not scarce.

G.I.JOE
PRODUCER: IMPEL
ISSUE YEAR: 1991
CARD SET: 200 CARDS
SPECIAL CARDS: No special cards
COMPLETE SET: £15.00
SINGLE CARDS: 10p

GLADIATORS
PRODUCER: MERLIN PUBLISHING LTD
ISSUE YEAR: 1993
CARD SET: 32
COMPLETE SET: £5.00
SINGLE CARDS: 5p
Important Notes: These cards were sold as a sub-set of the 1993 sticker collection and were never available separately.

GOLDEN AGE OF COMICS CHROMIUM
PRODUCER: COMIC IMAGES
ISSUE YEAR: 1995
CARD SET: 90
SPECIAL CARDS:
3 MAGNACHROME ART SET £15.00
6 MAGNACHROME COVER SET £25.00
6 MINI PROMO SHEET CARD SET £10.00
MEDALLION CARD £13.00
SIGNED CARD £25.00
COMPLETE SET: £18.00
SINGLE CARDS: 20p

GOLDENEYE
PRODUCER: GRAFFITTI.
ISSUE YEAR: 1995
CARD SET: 90 CARDS
SPECIAL CARDS: 3 PUZZLE SET £18.00
6 GADGETS SET: £18.00
9 BOND COMPOSITE SET: £18.00
COMPLETE SET: £12.00
SINGLE CARDS: 15p

GOONIES
PRODUCER: TOPPS U.S.
ISSUE YEAR: 1986
CARD SET: 86 CARDS
SPECIAL CARDS: 22 STICKERS
COMPLETE SET: £7.00
SINGLE CARDS: 10p
SINGLE SPECIAL CARDS: 25p

GREMLINS I MOVIE
PRODUCER: TOPPS
ISSUE YEAR: 1984
CARD SET: 82 CARDS
SPECIAL CARDS: 11 STICKERS
COMPLETE SET: £12.00
SINGLE CARDS: 15p
SINGLE SPECIAL CARDS: 25p

GREMLINS II MOVIE
PRODUCER: TOPPS
ISSUE YEAR: 1992
CARD SET: 88 CARDS
SPECIAL CARDS: 11 STICKERS
COMPLETE SET: £6.00
SINGLE CARDS: 10p
SINGLE SPECIAL CARDS: 20p

GROO
PRODUCER: WILDSTORM
ISSUE YEAR: 1996
CARD SET: 153 CARDS
SPECIAL CARDS:
CHROMIUM CARD: £10.00
AUTOGRAPH CARD: £40.00
COMPLETE SET: £50.00
SINGLE CARDS: 30p - 40p
Important Notes: A very difficult set to find in the U.K. with prices much higher than in the U.S.

GROWING PAINS (US TV SERIES)
PRODUCER: TOPPS US
ISSUE YEAR: 1988
CARD SET: 66
COMPLETE SET: £4.00
SINGLE ACRDS: 10p
SPECIAL CARDS: 11 STICKERS
SINGLE SPECIAL CARDS: 15p

HAMMER HORROR
PRODUCER: CORNERSTONE
ISSUE YEAR: 1995
CARD SET: 81 CARDS
SPECIAL CARDS:
TRYP-TYCH CARD: £4.00
COMPLETE SET: £15.00
SINGLE CARDS: 20p

HARRY AND THE HENDERSONS MOVIE
PRODUCER: TOPPS U.S.
ISSUE YEAR: 1987
CARD SET: 77 CARDS
SPECIAL CARDS: 22 STICKERS
COMPLETE SET: £6.00
SINGLE CARDS: 10p
SINGLE SPECIAL CARDS: 15p

HEAVY METAL, ART OF
PRODUCER: COMIC IMAGES
ISSUE YEAR: 1995
CARD SET: 90 CARDS

SPECIAL CARDS:
CHROMIUM CARD: £6.00
BLACK MAGIC SUB-SET (3): £35.00 the set
MEDALLION CARD: £15.00
COMPLETE SET: £7.00
SINGLE CARDS: 15p

HEAVY METAL MOVIE AND MORE

PRODUCER: COMIC IMAGES
ISSUE YEAR: 1996
CARD SET: 90 CARDS
SPECIAL CARDS:
6 CHROMIUM CARDS: £5.00 each
CALENDAR SUB-SET (3): £30.00 the set
MAGNACHROME BOX BONUS: £4.00
PROMO CARD: £1.50
COMPLETE SET: £8.00
SINGLE CARDS: 15p

HELLRAISER (FIRST 3 MOVIES)

PRODUCER: ECLIPSE
ISSUE YEAR: 1992
CARD SET: 110 CARDS
SPECIAL CARDS: 2 SILVER HOLOGRAMS/ 2 GOLD HOLOGRAMS (Pinhead and Cube)
COMPLETE SET: £40.00
CARD SET ONLY £10.00
SINGLE CARDS: 10p
SINGLE SPECIAL CARDS: £20.00

Important Notes: Gold holograms were given to retailers with cases of cards, the silver were randomly inserted

HILDEBRANDT I

PRODUCER: COMIC IMAGES
ISSUE YEAR: 1992
CARD SET: 90 CARDS
SPECIAL CARDS: 6 CHROME CHASE CARDS
COMPLETE SET: £10.00
SINGLE CARDS: 10p
SINGLE SPECIAL CARDS: £5.00

HILDEBRANDT II

PRODUCER: COMIC IMAGES
ISSUE YEAR: 1993
CARD SET: 90 CARDS
COMPLETE SET: £9.00
SINGLE CARDS: 10p

HILDEBRANDT BROS.

PRODUCER: COMIC IMAGES
ISSUE YEAR: 1994
CARD SET: 90 CARDS
SPECIAL CARDS: 6 FOIL EMBOSSED CHROME
COMPLETE SET: £9.00
SINGLE CARDS: 10p
SPECIAL SINGLE CARDS: £4.00

HILDEBRANDT CHROME

PRODUCER: COMIC IMAGES
ISSUE YEAR: 1995
CARDS SET: 90 CARDS
SPECIAL CARDS: 6 FOIL EMBOSSED CHROME
COMPLETE SET: £20.00
SINGLE CARDS: 20p
SPECIAL SINGLE CARDS: £4.00

HOME ALONE 2 - LOST IN NEW YORK MOVIE

PRODUCER: TOPPS U.S.
ISSUE YEAR: 1992
CARD SET: 66 CARDS
SPECIAL CARDS: 11 STICKERS
COMPLETE SET: £8.00
SINGLE CARDS: 15p
SINGLE SPECIAL CARDS: 25p

HOOK MOVIE

PRODUCER: TOPPS U.S.
ISSUE YEAR: 1991
CARD SET: 99 CARDS
SPECIAL CARDS: 11 STICKERS
COMPLETE SET: £9.00
SINGLE CARDS: 10p - 20p
SINGLE SPECIAL CARDS: 25p

Important Notes: These sets broke badly from their boxes. In many cases more than one box of cards was required to complete a set.

HOWARD THE DUCK MOVIE

PRODUCER: TOPPS
ISSUE YEAR: 1986
CARD SET: 77 CARDS
SPECIAL CARDS: 22 STICKERS
COMPLETE SET: £10.00
SINGLE CARDS: 10p
SINGLE SPECIAL CARDS: 20p

HUNCHBACK OF NOTRE DAME

PRODUCER: FLEER/SKYBOX
ISSUE YEAR: 1996
CARD SET: 101 CARDS
SPECIAL CARDS: IRON-ON: £2.00
3D MOTION CARD: £12.00
JESTERS CHALLENGE CARDS (35): £10.00
COMPLETE SET: £15.00
SINGLE CARDS: 15p - 20p

IMAGE UNIVERSE

PRODUCER: TOPPS
ISSUE YEAR: 1995
CARD SET: 90 CARDS
SPECIAL CARDS:6 CLEAR ZONE SET £24.00
6 "I" HOLOCHROME SET £24.00
6 "D" HOLOCHROME SET £24.00
COMPLETE SET: £30.00
SINGLE CARDS: 35p

IMAGES OF SHADOWHAWK

PRODUCER: IMAGE
ISSUE YEAR: 1994
CARD SET: 100 CARDS
SPECIAL CARDS: 7 FOIL CARDS
COMPLETE SET: £10.00
SINGLE CARDS: 10p
SPECIAL SINGLE CARDS: £4.00

INCREDIBLE HULK

PRODUCER: COMIC IMAGES
ISSUE YEAR: 1991
CARD SET: 90 CARDS
SPECIAL CARDS: No special cards
COMPLETE SET: £12.00
SINGLE CARDS: 10p

Important Notes: See also other set produced by Topps.

INCREDIBLE HULK TV PILOT MOVIE

PRODUCER: TOPPS U.S.
ISSUE YEAR: 1979
CARD SET: 88 CARDS
SPECIAL CARDS: 22 STICKERS
COMPLETE SET: £15.00
SINGLE CARDS: 20p
SINGLE SPECIAL CARDS: 30p

Important Notes: There was also a set produced by Comic Images in 1991.

INDEPENDENCE DAY

PRODUCER: TOPPS
ISSUE YEAR: 1996
CARD SET: 72 CARDS
SPECIAL CARDS:
HOLOFOIL CARD: £7.50
COMPLETE SET: £10.00
SINGLE CARDS: 10p

INDIANA JONES AND THE TEMPLE OF DOOM MOVIE

PRODUCER: TOPPS U.S.
ISSUE YEAR: 1984
CARD SET: 88 CARDS
SPECIAL CARDS: 11 STICKERS
COMPLETE SET: £10.00
SINGLE CARDS: 15p
SINGLE SPECIAL CARDS: 20p

INSIDE COMICS (RARE ISSUE)

PRODUCER: DOUBLE BARREL PRODUCTIONS
ISSUE YEAR: 1992
CARD SET: 3 CARDS
SPECIAL CARDS: No special cards
COMPLETE SET: £6.00
SINGLE CARDS: £2.00

Important Notes: Card One: WildC.A.T.S. by Jim Lee; Card Two: Youngblood by Rob Liefeld; Card Three: Spawn by Todd McFarlane. This set of three cards was originally intended as a giveaway with Inside Comics #3. The magazine was cancelled and the cards withdrawn after Image Comics issued a writ, claiming that the cards were produced without the correct licensing agreement. The magazines with their cards are now believed to have been destroyed, but a limited numberof sets came over to the U.K.

JACK KIRBY, THE COMIC ART TRIBUTE TO JOE SIMON AND

PRODUCER: 21ST CENTURY
ISSUE YEAR: 1995
CARD SET: 50 CARDS
SPECIAL CARDS: 5 K INSERT CARDS
COMPLETE SET: £8.00
SINGLE CARDS: 15p
SPECIAL SINGLE CARDS: £3.00

JACK KIRBY'S UNPUBLISHED ARCHIVES

PRODUCER: COMIC IMAGES
ISSUE YEAR: 1994
CARD SET: 90 CARDS
SPECIAL CARDS: 6 CHROMIUM CARDS
COMPLETE SET: £9.00
SINGLE CARDS: 10p
SINGLE SPECIAL CARDS: £4.00

JAMES BOND

PRODUCER: ECLIPSE
ISSUE YEAR: 1993
CARD SET: 110 CARDS (gold border)
SPECIAL CARDS: 2 HOLOGRAMS
COMPLETE SET: £15.00
SINGLE CARDS: 15p
SINGLE SPECIAL CARDS: £8.00

Important Notes: Boxes withdrawn from U.K. sale because Eclipse, only had production rights for th U.S. and Canada.

JAMES BOND II

PRODUCER: ECLIPSE
ISSUE YEAR: 1994
CARD SET: 110 CARDS
SPECIAL CARDS: 6 BOND GIRL CHASE CARDS
COMPLETE SET: £15.00
SINGLE CARDS: 15p
SINGLE SPECIAL CARDS: £4.00

Important Notes: same set as before but with silver border

JAWS II

PRODUCER: TOPPS U.S.
ISSUE YEAR: 1978
CARD SET: 59 CARDS
SPECIAL CARDS: 11 STICKERS
COMPLETE SET: £7.00
SINGLE CARDS: 10p
SINGLE SPECIAL CARDS: 20p

JAWS 3D

PRODUCER: TOPPS U.S.
ISSUE YEAR: 1983
CARD SET: 44 CARDS
SPECIAL CARDS: No special cards
COMPLETE SET: £5.00
SINGLE CARDS: 10p

J.C. LEYENDECKER

PRODUCER: 21st CENTURY ARCHIVES
ISSUE YEAR: 1995
CARD SET: 50 CARDS
COMPLETE SET: £8.00
SINGLE CARDS: 15p

JEFF EASLEY

PRODUCER: FPG
ISSUE YEAR: 1995
CARD SET: 90 CARDS
SPECIAL CARDS:
METALLIC STORM CARD: £5.00
AUTOGRAPH CARD (1000): £35.00
COMPLETE SET: £6.00
SINGLE CARDS: 5p - 10p

JEFFREY JONES

PRODUCER: FPG
ISSUE YEAR: 1993
CARD SET: 90 CARDS
SPECIAL CARDS:
3 HOLOGRAM CHASE CARDS: £5.00 each
COMPLETE SET: £6.00
SINGLE CARDS: 10p

JEFFREY JONES II

PRODUCER: FPG
ISSUE YEAR: 1996
CARD SET: 90 CARDS
SPECIAL CARDS: CANVAS CARD: £5.00
AUTOGRAPH CARD (1000): £35.00
COMPLETE SET: £6.00
SINGLE CARDS: 10p

JIM STERANKO

PRODUCER: FPG
ISSUE YEAR: 1995
CARD SET: 72 CARDS
SPECIAL CARDS:

SUPERGIRL METALLIC CARD:	£5.00
AUTOGRAPH CARD (1000):	£35.00
COMPLETE SET:	£10.00
SINGLE CARDS:	15p

JIM WARHOLA

PRODUCER:	FPG
ISSUE YEAR:	1995
CARD SET:	90 CARDS
SPECIAL CARDS:	
METALLIC STORM CARD:	£6.00
AUTOGRAPH CARD (1000):	£35.00
COMPLETE SET:	£7.50
SINGLE CARDS:	15p

JIM WARREN - BEYOND BIZARRE

PRODUCER:	COMIC IMAGES
ISSUE YEAR:	1993
CARD SET:	90 CARDS
SPECIAL CARDS:	3 SPECTRA/3 OPTI-PRISM CARDS
COMPLETE SET:	£9.00
SINGLE CARDS:	10p
SINGLE SPECIAL CARDS:	£5.00

JIM WARREN II - MORE BEYOND BIZARRE

PRODUCER:	COMIC IMAGES
ISSUE YEAR:	1994
CARD SET:	90 CARDS
SPECIAL CARDS:	6 PRISM CARDS
COMPLETE SET:	£9.00
SINGLE CARDS:	10p
SINGLE SPECIAL CARDS:	£5.00

JOE JUSKO'S EDGAR RICE BURROUGHS I

PRODUCER:	FPG
ISSUE YEAR:	1994
CARDS SET:	60 CARDS
SPECIAL CARDS:	6 METALLIC STORM CARDS
COMPLETE SET:	£15.00
SINGLE CARDS:	25p
SINGLE SPECIAL CARDS:	£5.00

JOE JUSKO'S EDGAR RICE BURROUGHS II

PRODUCER:	FPG
ISSUE YEAR:	1995
CARD SET:	60 CARDS
SPECIAL CARDS:	6 METALLIC STORM CARDS
COMPLETE SET:	£15.00
SINGLE CARDS:	25p
SINGLE SPECIAL CARDS:	£5.00

JOHN BERKEY - SPACE ART

PRODUCER:	COMIC IMAGES
ISSUE YEAR:	1994
CARD SET:	90 CARDS
SPECIAL CARDS:	5 METAL STORM CHASE CARDS
CARD SET	£7.00
SINGLE CARDS:	10p
SINGLE SPECIAL CARDS:	£6.00

JOHN BERKEY SERIES II

PRODUCER:	FPG
ISSUE YEAR:	1996
CARD SET:	90 CARDS
SPECIAL CARDS:METALLIC CARD:	£5.00
COMPLETE SET:	£7.00
SINGLE CARDS:	10p

JOSEPH MICHAEL LINSNER

PRODUCER:	COMIC IMAGES
ISSUE YEAR:	1995
CARD SET:	90 CARDS
SPECIAL CARDS:CHROMIUM CARD:	£ 6.00
AUTOGRAPH CARD (500):	£40.00
DAWN SUB-SET (3):	£45.00 the set
MEDALLION CARD:	£25.00
COMPLETE SET:	£15.00
SINGLE CARDS:	15p - 20p

JUDGE DREDD

PRODUCER:	EDGE
ISSUE YEAR:	1995
CARD SET:	90 CARDS
SPECIAL CARDS: 3 MOVIE CARD SET	£7.00
4 DEATH DIMENSION 1 CARD SET	£30.00
4 DEATH DIMENSION 2 CARD SET	£30.00
9 SLEEP CARD SET	£10.00
13 LEGENDS CARD SET	£30.00
COMPLETE SET:	£6.00

Judge Dredd Prog 02

SINGLE CARDS:	10p

JULIE BELL

PRODUCER:	CARDZ
ISSUE YEAR:	1994
CARD SET:	46 CARDS
SPECIAL CARDS:	
10 TEKCHROME CARDS:	£2.00 each
COMPLETE SET:	£10.00
SINGLE CARDS:	20p

JURASSIC PARK

PRODUCER:	TOPPS U.S.
ISSUE YEAR:	1993
CARD SET:	88 CARDS
SPECIAL CARDS:	11 STICKERS
COMPLETE SET:	£10.00
SINGLE CARDS:	10p
SINGLE SPECIAL CARDS:	20p

JURASSIC PARK II

PRODUCER:	TOPPS U.S.
ISSUE YEAR:	1993
CARD SET:	88 CARDS
SPECIAL CARDS:	11 STICKERS
COMPLETE SET:	£12.00
SINGLE CARDS:	10p
SINGLE SPECIAL CARDS:	20p

JURASSIC PARK GOLD

PRODUCER:	TOOPS U.S.
ISSUE YEAR:	1993
CARD SET:	88 CARDS
SPECIAL CARDS:	10 ART CARDS
COMPLETE SET:	£15.00
SINGLE CARDS:	20p
SINGLE SPECIAL CARDS:	50p

KEITH PARKINSON - FANTASY ART]

PRODUCER:	FPG
ISSUE YEAR:	1994
CARD SET:	90 CARDS
SPECIAL CARDS:	5 METALLIC STORM CARDS
COMPLETE SET:	£12.00
SINGLE CARDS:	10p
SINGLE SPECIAL CARDS:	£6.00

KEN BARR - THE BEAST WITHIN

PRODUCER:	COMIC IMAGES
ISSUE YEAR:	1994
CARD SET:	90 CARDS
SPECIAL CARDS:	6 FOIL EMBOSSED CHASE CARDS
COMPLETE SET:	£8.00
SINGLE CARDS:	15p
SINGLE SPECIAL CARDS:	£4.50

KEN KELLY

PRODUCER:	FPG
ISSUE YEAR:	1993
CARD SET:	90 CARDS
SPECIAL CARDS:	3 HOLOGRAMS
CARD SET:	£12.00
SINGLE CARDS:	15p
SINGLE SPECIAL CARDS:	£6.00

KEN KELLY 2

PRODUCER:	FPG
ISSUE YEAR:	1994
CARD SET:	90 CARDS
SPECIAL CARDS:	
5 METALLIC STORM CARDS:	£5.00 each
AUTOGRAPH CARD:	£35.00
COMPLETE SET:	£8.00
SINGLE CARDS:	15p

KING KONG

PRODUCER:	TOPPS U.S.
ISSUE YEAR:	1976
CARD SET:	55 CARDS
SPECIAL CARDS:	11 STICKERS
COMPLETE SET:	£20.00
SINGLE CARDS:	40p
SINGLE SPECIAL CARDS:	£1.50

KING KONG II

PRODUCER:	ECLIPSE
ISSUE YEAR:	1993
CARD SET:	110 CARDS
SPECIAL CARD:	1 EMBOSSED
COMPLETE SET:	£10.00
SINGLE CARD:	10p
SINLGE SPECIAL CARD:	£10.00

KNIGHT RIDER

PRODUCER:	DONRUSS
ISSUE YEAR:	1983
CARD SET:	55 CARDS
SPECIAL CARDS:	No special cards
COMPLETE SET:	£5.00
SINGLE CARDS:	15p

LADY DEATH I

PRODUCER:	KROME PRODUCTIONS
ISSUE YEAR:	1994
CARD SET:	90 CARDS
SPECIAL CARDS:	5 HOLOGRAM CARDS
COMPLETE SET:	£25.00
SINGLE CARD:	25p
SINGLE SPECIAL CARD:	£7.50

Note: This is becoming an increasingly difficult set to obtain

LADY DEATH SERIES 2

PRODUCER:	KROME PRODUCTIONS
ISSUE YEAR:	1995
CARD SET:	100 CARDS
SPECIAL CARDS:	
3 TRYPTIC CARD SET	£18.00
5 CHROMIUM CARD SET	£18.00
MYSTERY CARD	£10.00
PULIDO/HUGHES SIGNED CARD	£25.00
CHROMIUM (7"x9") CARD	£15.00
FULL CHROMIUM STICKER SET(100)	£55.00
COMPLETE SET:	£15.00
SINGLE CARD:	15p - 20p

LARRY ELMORE

PRODUCER:	FPG
ISSUE YEAR:	1994
CARD SET:	90 CARDS
SPECIAL CARDS:	
METALLIC STORM CARDS:	£5.00
AUTOGRAPH CARD (1000):	£35.00
COMPLETE SET:	£10.00
SINGLE CARDS:	15p

LION KING

PRODUCER:	SKY BOX
ISSUE YEAR:	1994
CARD SET:	90 CARDS
SPECIAL CARDS:	9 EMBOSSED FOIL CARDS
OTHER SPECIAL CARDS:	5 POP-UP CARDS
COMPLETE SET:	£10.00
SINGLE CARDS:	10p
SINGLE SPECIAL CARDS:	£6.00
OTHER SINGLE SPECIAL CARDS:	£3.00
FACTORY SET IN TIN:	£40.00

LION KING II

PRODUCER:	SKYBOX
ISSUE YEAR:	1994
CARD SET:	80 CARDS
SPECIAL CARDS:	9 THERMOGRAPH CARDS
COMPLETE SET:	£10.00
SINGLE CARDS:	10p
SINGLE SPECIAL CARDS:	£4.00

Important Notes: Other Special Cards include 5 Pop-Up cards at £3.00 each and 2 Foil-Border Art cards at £15,00 each. Numbering runs from #91-170

LITTLE MERMAID - FACTORY SET

PRODUCER: PRO SET
ISSUE YEAR: 1993
CARD SET: 127 CARDS
SPECIAL CARDS: VARIOUS NOVELTY ITEMS
COMPLETE SET: £17.50

Important Notes: Novelty items consist of 15 stand up cards, 15 colour in cards, 6 character sponges and 7 static sticks.

LOIS & CLARK

PRODUCER: SKYBOX
ISSUE YEAR: 1995
CARD SET: 90 CARDS
SPECIAL CARDS: 6 HOLO-CHIP FOIL/ 9 DIFFUSER FOIL CARDS
COMPLETE SET: £10.00
SINGLE CARDS: 10p
SINGLE SPECIAL CARDS: £5.00

LUIS ROYO

PRODUCER: COMIC IMAGES
ISSUE YEAR: 1993
CARD SET: 90 CARDS
SPECIAL CARDS: 6 PRISM CARDS
COMPLETE SET: £8.00
SINGLE CARDS: 10p
SINGLE SPECIAL CARDS: £5.00

LUIS ROYO II

PRODUCER: COMIC IMAGES
ISSUE YEAR: 1994
CARD SET: 90 CARDS
SPECIAL CARDS: 6 PRISM CARDS
COMPLETE SET: £8.00
SINGLE CARDS: 10p
SINGLE SPECIAL CARDS: £5.00

LUIS ROYO CHROMIUM, THE BEST OF

PRODUCER: COMIC IMAGES
ISSUE YEAR: 1995
CARD SET: 90 CARDS (all chrome)
SPECIAL CARDS: 6 MAGNACHROME CARDS
COMPLETE SET: £20.00
SINGLE CARDS: 25p
SINGLE SPECIAL CARDS: £5.00

MAD MAGAZINE I

PRODUCER: LIME ROCK
ISSUE YEAR: 1992
CARD SET: 50 CARDS
SPECIAL CARDS: 1 HOLOGRAM
COMPLETE SET: £15.00
CARD SET ONLY £5.00
SINGLE CARDS: 15p
SINGLE SPECIAL CARDS: £10.00

MAD MAGAZINE II

PRODUCER: LIME ROCK
ISSUE YEAR: 1992
CARD SET: 50 CARDS
SPECIAL CARDS: 1 Hologram
COMPLETE SET: £15.00
CARD SET ONLY £5.00
SINGLE CARDS: 15p
SINGLE SPECIAL CARDS: £10.00

MAGNUM P.I.

PRODUCER: DONRUSS
ISSUE YEAR: 1983
CARD SET: 66 CARDS
SPECIAL CARDS: No special cards
COMPLETE SET: 15.00
SINGLE CARDS: 15p

Important Notes: Based on the US television series

MARILYN MONROE

PRODUCER: SPORTS TIME CARD COMPANY
ISSUE YEAR: 1993
CARD SET: 100 CARDS
SPECIAL CARDS: 10 CHROMIUM CARDS
COMPLETE SET: £15.00
SINGLE CARDS: 15p
SINGLE SPECIAL CARDS: £6.00

Important Notes: There was also a Diamond Redemption Card (1 per case) which is rare in the U.K. and valued at approximately £250.00 when redeemed

MARILYN MONROE II

PRODUCER: SPORTS TIME CARD COMPANY

Mard Attacks! #58

ISSUE YEAR: 1995
CARD SET: 100 CARDS
SPECIAL CARDS:
10 HOLOCHROME CARDS: £5.00 each
COMPLETE SET: £15.00
SINGLE CARDS: 15p

Note: There is a special Ruby Redemption Card which is rare in the U.K. and valued at approximately £150.00 when redeemed

MARS ATTACKS!

PRODUCER: TOPPS U.S.
ISSUE YEAR: 1994
CARD SET: 100 CARDS
SPECIAL CARDS:
4 MATRIX CARDS: £6.00 each
COMPLETE SET: £25.00
SINGLE CARDS: 25p

MARVEL 1ST ISSUE COVERS I

PRODUCER: FTCC
ISSUE YEAR: 1984
CARD SET: 60 CARDS
SPECIAL CARDS: No special cards
COMPLETE SET: £18.00
SINGLE CARDS: 25p

MARVEL 1ST ISSUE COVERS II

PRODUCER: COMIC IMAGES
ISSUE YEAR: 1991
CARD SET: 90 CARDS
CARD SET: £10.00
SINGLE CARDS: 15p

MARVEL FLAIR ANNUAL '95

PRODUCER: FLEER
ISSUE YEAR: 1995
CARD SET: 100 CARDS
SPECIAL CARDS: 3 DUOBLAST/9 POWER BLAST/ 9 HOLOBLAST CARDS
COMPLETE SET: £30.00
SINGLE CARDS: 25p
SINGLE SPECIAL CARDS: £4.00 (Duoblast), £2.00 (Powerblast), £4.00 (Holoblast)

Important Notes: Printed on extra thick stock

Marvel Universe III #36

MARVEL FLAIR UNIVERSE DELUXE

PRODUCER: FLEER
ISSUE YEAR: 1994
CARD SET: 150 CARDS
SPECIAL CARDS: 18 POWERBLAST CARDS
COMPLETE SET: £35.00
SINGLE CARDS: 25p
SINGLE SPECIAL CARDS: £6.00

Important Notes: Printed on extra thick stock

MARVEL MASTERPIECES I

PRODUCER: SKYBOX
ISSUE YEAR: 1992
CARD SET: 100 CARDS
SPECIAL CARDS: 5 SPECTRA-ETCH CARDS
COMPLETE SET: £40.00
CARD SET ONLY £18.00
SINGLE CARDS: 15p
SINGLE SPECIAL CARDS: £10.00

Important Notes: There were 5 Limited Cards available only in the Factory Set. Prices on these vary from £15.00 to £25.00

MARVEL MASTERPIECES II

PRODUCER: SKYBOX
ISSUE YEAR: 1993
CARD SET: 90 CARDS
SPECIAL CARDS: 8 DYNA-ETCH FOIL CARDS
COMPLETE SET: £60.00
CARD SET ONLY £15.00
SINGLE CARDS: 15p
SINGLE SPECIAL CARDS: £5.00

MARVEL MASTERPIECES III

PRODUCER: SKYBOX
ISSUE YEAR: 1994
CARD SET: 150 CARDS
SPECIAL CARDS: 9 POWERBLAST CARDS/ 10 HOLOFOIL CARDS
COMPLETE SET: £15.00
SINGLE CARDS: 10p

Important Notes: Powerblast Cards at £3.00 each, Holoblast Cards at £2.00 each. There are also 150 Parallel Signature cards at about 50p each.

MARVEL MASTERPIECES IV

PRODUCER: SKYBOX
ISSUE YEAR: 1995
CARD SET: 150 CARDS
SPECIAL CARDS: 9 HOLOFOIL CARDS
COMPLETE SET: £20.00
SINGLE CARDS: 15p
SINGLE SPECIAL CARDS: £6.00

Important Notes: There are 2 Lenticular chase cards which are very rare in the U.K. priced at about £50.00 each. There are also 150 Parallel Signature Cards at about 50p each and 22 Canvas chase cards at about £2.00 each.

MARVEL MASTERPIECES

PRODUCER: FLEER
ISSUE YEAR: 1995
CARD SET: 150 CARDS
FULL E-MOTION SET (150) £65.00
SPECIAL CARDS:
2 MIRAGE CARD SET £40.00
8 HOLOFLASH CARD SET £30.00
24 CANVAS CARD SET £25.00
COMPLETE SET: £20.00
SINGLE CARDS: 15p

MARVEL METAL

PRODUCER: FLEER
ISSUE YEAR: 1995
CARD SET: 100 CARDS
SPECIAL CARDS: 18 GOLD BLASTER/ 18 SILVER BLASTER
COMPLETE SET: £20.00
SINGLE CARDS: 25p
SINGLE SPECIAL CARDS £2-£3 (Gold), £1-£2 (Silver)

MARVEL TRADING CARD TREATS

PRODUCER: IMPEL
ISSUE YEAR: 1992
CARD SET: 36 CARD SET
COMPLETE SET: £6.00
SINGLE CARDS: 20p

MARVEL UNIVERSE I

PRODUCER: IMPEL
ISSUE YEAR: 1990
CARD SET: 162 CARDS
SPECIAL CARDS: 5 HOLOGRAM
COMPLETE SET: £85.00

CARD SET ONLY £25.00
SINGLE CARDS: 15p - 20p
SINGLE SPECIAL CARDS: £12.00
FACTORY TIN COLLECTORS SET £150.00

MARVEL UNIVERSE II
PRODUCER: IMPEL
ISSUE YEAR: 1991
CARD SET: 162 CARDS
SPECIAL CARDS: 5 HOLOGRAM CARDS
COMPLETE SET: £50.00
CARD SET ONLY £18.00
SINGLE CARDS: 20p
SINGLE SPECIAL CARDS: £7.00
Important Notes: Factory Tin Collectors set £85.00

MARVEL UNIVERSE III
PRODUCER: SKYBOX
ISSUE YEAR: 1992
CARD SET: 200 CARDS
SPECIAL CARDS: 5 HOLOGRAM CARDS
COMPLETE SET: £30.00
CARD SET ONLY £12.50
SINGLE CARDS: 10p
SINGLE SPECIAL CARDS: £4.00
Important Notes: Factory Tin Collectors set £60.00

MARVEL UNIVERSE IV
PRODUCER: SKYBOX
ISSUE YEAR: 1993
CARD SET: 180 CARDS
SPECIAL CARDS: 9 FOIL CARDS + H-IV HOLOGRAM CARD
COMPLETE SET: £60.00
CARD SET ONLY £10.00
SINGLE CARDS: 10p
SINGLE SPECIAL CARDS: £4.00
SPIDEY/VENOM HOLOGRAM: £35.00

MASTERS OF FANTASY
PRODUCER: FPG
ISSUE YEAR: 1996
CARD SET: 90 CARDS
SPECIAL CARDS:
GOLD METALLIC CARD: £6.00
COMPLETE SET: £20.00
SINGLE CARDS: 20p - 25p

MASTERS OF JAPANIMATION
PRODUCER: COMIC IMAGES
ISSUE YEAR: 1996
CARD SET: 90 CARDS
SPECIAL CARDS:
UROTSUKIDOJI OVA CHROMIUM: £4.00
MIGHTY WARRIOR SUB-SET (3): £30.00 the set
AUTOGRAPH CARD: £30.00
MAGNACHROME BOX CARD: £3.00
COMPLETE SET: £6.00
SINGLE CARDS: 5p - 10p

MELTING POT CHROMIUM
PRODUCER: COMIC IMAGES
ISSUE YEAR: 1993
CARD SET: 100 CARDS
SPECIAL CARDS: No Special cards
COMPLETE SET: £25.00
SINGLE CARDS: 25p

MICHAEL JACKSON
PRODUCER: TOPPS U.S.
ISSUE YEAR: 1984
CARD SET: 33 CARDS
SPECIAL CARDS: 33 STICKERS
COMPLETE SET: £5.00
SINGLE CARDS: 15p
SINGLE SPECIAL CARDS: 50p

MICHAEL KALUTA
PRODUCER: FPG
ISSUE YEAR: 1994
CARD SET: 90 CARDS
SPECIAL CARDS:
METALLIC STORM CARD: £5.00
AUTOGRAPH CARD (1000): £35.00
COMPLETE SET: £7.00
SINGLE CARDS: 10p

MICHAEL KALUTA SERIES II
PRODUCER: FPG
ISSUE YEAR: 1995
CARD SET: 90 CARDS
SPECIAL CARDS:
METALLIC STORM CARD: £5.00
AUTOGRAPH CARD (1000): £35.00
COMPLETE SET: £6.00
SINGLE CARDS: 10p

MICHAEL WHELAN - ADVENTURES IN FANTASY
PRODUCER: COMIC IMAGES
ISSUE YEAR: 1993
CARD SET: 90 CARDS
SPECIAL CARDS: 3 SPECTRA/3 OPTI-PRISM CARDS
COMPLETE SET: £8.00
SINGLE CARDS: 10p
SINGLE SPECIAL CARDS: £5.00

MICHAEL WHELAN II
PRODUCER: COMIC IMAGES
ISSUE YEAR: 1994
CARD SET: 90 CARDS
SPECIAL CARDS: 6 CHASE CARDS
COMPLETE SET: £8.00
SINGLE CARDS: 10p
SINGLE SPECIAL CARDS: £5.00

MIKE PLOOG
PRODUCER: FPG
ISSUE YEAR: 1994
CARD SET: 90 CARDS
SPECIAL CARDS:
5 METALLIC STORM CARDS: £5.00 each
AUTOGRAPH CARD (1000): £35.00
COMPLETE SET: £10.00
SINGLE CARDS: 15p

MIKE ZECK
PRODUCER: COMIC IMAGES
ISSUE YEAR: 1991
CARD SET: 45 CARD SET
SPECIAL CARDS: No special cards
COMPLETE SET: £9.00
SINGLE CARDS: 20p

MINNIE AND ME
PRODUCER: IMPEL
ISSUE YEAR: 1991
CARD SET: 160 CARDS
SPECIAL CARDS: No special cards
COMPLETE SET: £10.00
SINGLE CARDS: 10p

MOEBIUS
PRODUCER: COMIC IMAGES
ISSUE YEAR: 1993
CARD SET: 90 CARDS
SPECIAL CARDS: 6 CHROMIUM CARDS
COMPLETE SET: £9.00
SINGLE CARDS: 10p
SINGLE SPECIAL CARDS: £5.00

MONKEES
PRODUCER: CORNERSTONE
ISSUE YEAR: 1995
CARD SET: 90 CARDS
SPECIAL CARDS:
FOIL-STAMPED CARD: £3.00
AUTOGRAPH CARD: £35.00
COMPLETE SET: £10.00
SINGLE CARDS: 15p

MONTY PYTHON AND THE HOLY GRAIL
PRODUCER: CORNERSTONE
ISSUE YEAR: 1995
CARD SET: 72 CARDS
SPECIAL CARDS:
KNIGHT CARDS (K-1 TO K6): £4.00 each
HOLY GRAIL CARD (HG): £10.00
COMPLETE SET: £12.00
SINGLE CARDS: 15p

MONTY PYTHON'S FLYING CIRCUS
PRODUCER: CORNERSTONE
ISSUE YEAR: 1995
CARD SET: 108 CARDS
SPECIAL CARDS: 4 FOIL CARDS
COMPLETE SET: £18.00
SINGLE CARDS: 10p
SINGLE SPECIAL CARDS: £6.00
Important Notes: there was also a Real Scratch and Listen card, rare in the U.K. and valued at approximately £40.00. The Fake Scratch and Listen Card was part of the normal set

MOONRAKER MOVIE
PRODUCER: TOPPS U.S.
ISSUE YEAR: 1979
CARD SET: 99 CARDS
SPECIAL CARDS: 22 STICKERS
COMPLETE SET: £25.00
SINGLE CARDS: 25p
SINGLE SPECIAL CARDS: 50p

MORK AND MINDY TV
PRODUCER: TOPPS U.S.
ISSUE YEAR: 1978
CARD SET: 99 CARDS
SPECIAL CARDS: 22 STICKERS
COMPLETE SET: £10.00
SINGLE CARDS: 15p
SINGLE SPECIAL CARDS: 30p

MORTAL KOMBAT
PRODUCER: CLASSIC
ISSUE YEAR: 1994
CARD SET: 100 CARDS
SPECIAL CARDS: 5 CHASE CARDS
COMPLETE SET: £10.00
SINGLE CARDS: 10p
SINGLE SPECIAL CARDS: £2.00

MUNSTER DELUXE
PRODUCER: DART FLIPCARDS
ISSUE YEAR: 1994?
CARD SET: 90 CARDS
SPECIAL CARDS: GOLD FOIL CARD: £5.00
DIE-CUT CARD: £10.00
COMPLETE SET: £15.00
SINGLE CARDS: 20p

NEW KIDS ON THE BLOCK
PRODUCER: TOPPS U.S.
ISSUE YEAR: 1989
CARD SET: 90 CARDS
SPECIAL CARDS: 11 STICKERS
COMPLETE SET: £6.00
SINGLE CARDS: 10p
SINGLE SPECIAL CARDS: 30p

NIGHTMARE BEFORE CHRISTMAS
PRODUCER: SKYBOX
ISSUE YEAR: 1993
CARD SET: 90 CARDS
SPECIAL CARDS: 4 SPECTRA CARDS
COMPLETE SET: £10.00
SINGLE CARDS: 10p
SINGLE SPECIAL CARDS: £4.00
Important Notes: based on Tim Burton film

NIGHTMARE ON ELM STREET FACTORY SET
PRODUCER: IMPEL
ISSUE YEAR: 1991
CARD SET: 118 CARDS
SPECIAL CARDS: 2 HOLOGRAM CARDS
COMPLETE SET: £25.00

NORMAN ROCKWELL
PRODUCER: COMIC IMAGES
ISSUE YEAR: 1993
CARD SET: 90 CARDS
SPECIAL CARDS: 6 WOODGRAIN CHASE CARDS
COMPLETE SET: £7.00
SINGLE CARDS: 10p
SINGLE SPECIAL CARDS: £5.00

NORMAN ROCKWELL II
PRODUCER: COMICS IMAGES
ISSUE YEAR: 1995
CARD SET: 90 CARDS
SPECIAL CARDS: 6 SANTA CHROME CHASE CARDS
COMPLETE SET: £8.00
SINGLE CARDS: 10p
SINGLE SPECIAL CARDS: £6.00

OLIVIA I
PRODUCER: COMIC IMAGES
ISSUE YEAR: 1992
CARD SET: 90 CARDS
SPECIAL CARDS: 6 PRISM CARDS
COMPLETE SET: £40.00
CARD SET ONLY £17.50
SINGLE CARDS: 20p
SINGLE SPECIAL CARDS: £8.00

OLIVIA II ALL PRISM SET
PRODUCER: COMIC IMAGES
ISSUE YEAR: 1993
CARD SET: 72 PRISM CARDS
SPECIAL CARDS: 6 CHROMIUM CARDS

COMPLETE SET: £20.00
SINGLE CARDS: 25p
SINGLE SPECIAL CARDS: £8.00-£10.00

OLIVIA III - LADIES, LEATHER & LACE

PRODUCER: COMIC IMAGES
ISSUE YEAR: 1994
CARD SET: 90 CARDS
SPECIAL CARDS: 6 CHROMIUM CARDS
COMPLETE SET: £40.00
CARD SET ONLY £7.50
SINGLE CARDS: 15p
SINGLE SPECIAL CARDS: £8.00

OLIVIA CHROME, BEST OF

PRODUCER: COMIC IMAGES
ISSUE YEAR: 1994
CARD SET: 90 CARDS
SPECIAL CARDS: 6 OMNICHROME CARDS
COMPLETE SET: £20.00
SINGLE CARDS: 25p
SINGLE SPECIAL CARDS: £6.00

OLIVIA OMNICHROME

PRODUCER: COMIC IMAGES
ISSUE YEAR: 1996
CARD SET: 90 CARDS
SPECIAL CARDS: 6 CLEAR CELS: £7.00 each
3 SUB-SET CARDS: £8.00 each
1 BOXCARD: £3.00
AUTOGRAPH CARDS: £25.00-£40.00 each
COMPLETE SET: £18.00
SINGLE CARDS: 25p

OLIVIA SENSUALITY CHROME II

PRODUCER: COMIC IMAGES
ISSUE YEAR: 1995
CARD SET: 90 CARDS
SPECIAL CARDS: 6 FOIL EMBOSSED CARDS
COMPLETE SET: £16-£20
SINGLE CARDS: 25p
SINGLE SPECIAL CARDS: £8.00

OUTBURST: DC FIREPOWER

PRODUCER: FLEER/SKYBOX
ISSUE YEAR: 1996
CARD SET: 80 EMBOSSED CARDS
SPECIAL CARDS:
MAXIMUM FIREPOWER CARD: £1.50
HOLOBURST CARD: £6.00
COMPLETE SET: £15.00
SINGLE CARDS: 15p

PAUL CHADWICK

PRODUCER: FPG
ISSUE YEAR: 1995
CARD SET: 90 CARDS
SPECIAL CARDS:
METALLIC STORM CARD: £5.00
AUTOGRAPH CARD (1000): £35.00
COMPLETE SET: £7.00
SINGLE CARDS: 15p

PHANTOM, THE

PRODUCER: COMIC IMAGES
ISSUE YEAR: 1995
CARD SET: 90 CARDS
SPECIAL CARDS: 6 CHROMIUM CARDS
COMPLETE SET: £5.00
SINGLE CARDS: 5p - 10p
SINGLE SPECIAL CARDS: £4.00

PHANTOM, THE

PRODUCER: INKWORKS
ISSUE YEAR: 1996
CARD SET: 90 CARDS
SPECIAL CARDS: 9 EMBOSSED CARDS
COMPLETE SET: £10.00
SINGLE CARDS: 10p
SINGLE SPECIAL CARDS: £4.00

PINOCCHIO

PRODUCER: INKWORKS
ISSUE YEAR: 1996
CARD SET: 90 CARDS
SPECIAL CARDS: PUZZLE CARD: £2.00
FOILWORKS CARD: £10.00
LENTICULAR CARD: £17.50
GAME-WINNER CARD: £12.50
COMPLETE SET: £8.00
SINGLE CARDS: 15p

PITT

PRODUCER: INTREPID

Phantom (1996) #20

ISSUE YEAR: 1995
CARD SET: 100 CARDS
SPECIAL CARDS:
ASHCAN CHARACTER CARD: £1.50
ASHCAN COVER CARD: £1.50
HOLOFORGE CARD: £6.00
SILICONITE CARD: £10.00
MEGAMOTION CARD: £20.00
COMPLETE SET: £17.50
SINGLE CARDS: 20p

PLANET OF THE APES

PRODUCER: TOPPS U.S.
ISSUE YEAR: 1975
CARD SET: 66 CARDS
SPECIAL CARDS: NO SPECIAL CARDS
COMPLETE SET: £40.00
SINGLE CARDS: 70p

POISON ELVES

PRODUCER: COMIC IMAGES
ISSUE YEAR: 1996
CARD SET: 75 CARDS
SPECIAL CARDS: 6 CHROME CARDS: £5.00 each
3 SUB-SET CARDS: £7.00 each
1 BOXCARD: £3.00
COMPLETE SET: £9.00
SINGLE CARDS: 15p

PORTFOLIO 92 - SWIMSUITS

PRODUCER: PORTFOLIO
ISSUE YEAR: 1992
CARD SET: 50 CARDS
SPECIAL CARDS:
COMPLETE SET: £5.00
SINGLE CARDS: 10p

PORTFOLIO 93 - SWIMSUITS

PRODUCER: PORTFOLIO
ISSUE YEAR: 1993
CARD SET: 50 CARDS
SPECIAL CARDS: BONUS CARDS 101-108
CARD SET: £5.00
SINGLE CARDS: 10p
SPECIAL SINGLE CARDS: £5.00

Important Notes: Cards Numbered 51-100 see Portfolio 92 for cards #1-50

PRO CHEERLEADERS

PRODUCER: LIME ROCK
ISSUE YEAR: 1992
CARD SET: 41 CARDS
SPECIAL CARDS: No Special Cards
COMPLETE SET: £4.00
SINGLE CARDS: 10p

PRO CHEERLEADERS II

PRODUCER: LIME ROCK
ISSUE YEAR: 1992
CARD SET: 150 CARDS
SPECIAL CARDS: No Special Cards

COMPLETE SET: £15.00
SINGLE CARDS: 10p

PUNISHER I

PRODUCER: COMIC IMAGES
ISSUE YEAR: 1988
CARD SET: 50 CARDS
SPECIAL CARDS: No special cards
COMPETE SET £12.00
SINGLE CARDS: 20p

PUNISHER II

PRODUCER: COMIC IMAGES
ISSUE YEAR: 1992
CARD SET: 90 CARDS
SPECIAL CARDS: 3 PRISM & 3 SCRATCH N' SNIFF
COMPLETE SET: £25.00
CARD SET ONLY £ 5.00
SINGLE CARDS: 10p
SINGLE SPECIAL CARDS: Prism cards £4.00,
SCRATCH N' SNIFF CARDS: £3.00

Important Notes: When buying separate Scratch n' sniff cards, look carefully for damaged surface scratch marks. Imperfect cards are worth 50%-75% less than guide price.

RAIDERS OF THE LOST ARK

PRODUCER: TOPPS U.S.
ISSUE YEAR: 1981
CARD SET: 88 CARDS
SPECIAL CARDS: No special cards
COMPLETE SET: £15.00
SINGLE CARDS: 15p

RAMBO - FIRST BLOOD II MOVIE

PRODUCER: TOPPS
ISSUE YEAR: 1985
CARD SET: 66 CARDS
SPECIAL CARDS: 11 STICKERS
COMPLETE SET: £10.00
SINGLE CARDS: 10p
SINGLE SPECIAL CARDS: 20p

RAZOR

PRODUCER: KROME PRODUCTIONS
ISSUE YEAR: 1996
CARD SET: 90 CARDS
SPECIAL CARDS:
HOLOCHROME CARD: £6.00
SUPER CHASE CARD: £10.00
EVERETTE HARTSOE
AUTOGRAPH CARD (500): £35.00
COMPLETE SET: £17.50
SINGLE CARDS: 25p

REN AND STIMPY I

PRODUCER: TOPPS
ISSUE YEAR: 1994
CARD SET: 50 CARDS
SPECIAL CARDS:
50 PRISMATIC STICKERS: £25.00 the set
CHEESY CHASE CARD: £5.00
COMPLETE SET: £15.00
SINGLE CARDS: 15p

REN AND STIMPY II

PRODUCER: DYNAMIC MARKETING
ISSUE YEAR: 1995
CARD SET: 110 CARDS
SPECIAL CARDS: KITTY GLITTER CARD: £5.00
CHROME CARD SET (10): £20.00
COMPLETE SET: £15.00
SINGLE CARDS: 15p

RETURN OF THE JEDI I - MOVIE

PRODUCER: TOPPS U.S.
ISSUE YEAR: 1983
CARD SET: 132 CARDS
SPECIAL CARDS: 33 STICKERS
COMPLETE SET: £25.00
COMPLETE SET (with stickers): £40.00
SINGLE CARDS: 15p
SINGLE SPECIAL CARDS: 25p

RETURN OF THE JEDI II - MOVIE

PRODUCER: TOPPS U.S.
ISSUE YEAR: 1982
CARD SET: 88 CARDS
SPECIAL CARDS: 22 STICKERS
COMPLETE SET: £20.00
COMPLETE SET (with stickers): £35.00
SINGLE CARDS: 15p

SINGLE SPECIAL CARDS: 25p

RETURN OF THE JEDI WIDEVISION

PRODUCER: TOPPS
ISSUE YEAR: 1995
CARD SET: 144 CARDS
SPECIAL CARDS:
TOPPS FINEST CHROMIUM CARD: £10.00
3-D CARD: £25.00
MINI-POSTER £5.00
COMPLETE SET: £15.00
SINGLE CARDS: 15p

RICHARD CORBEN

PRODUCER: COMIC IMAGES
ISSUE YEAR: 1994
CARD SET: 90 CARDS
SPECIAL CARDS: PRISM CARD: £4.00
COMPLETE SET: £7.00
SINGLE CARDS: 15p

RICHARD HESCOX

PRODUCER: FPG
ISSUE YEAR: 1994
SPECIAL CARDS:
METALLIC STORM CARD: £6.00
AUTOGRAPH CARD (1000): £30.00
COMPLETE SET: £10.00
SINGLE CARDS: 15p

ROBH RUPPEL

PRODUCER: FPG
ISSUE YEAR: 1996
CARD SET: 90 CARDS
SPECIAL CARDS: METALLIC CARD: £5.00
AUTOGRAPH CARD (1000): £35.00
COMPLETE SET: £7.00
SINGLE CARDS: 15p

ROBIN HOOD, PRINCE OF THIEVES MOVIE

PRODUCER: TOPPS U.S.
ISSUE YEAR: 1991
CARD SET: 55 CARDS
SPECIAL CARDS: 9 STICKERS
COMPLETE SET: £5.00
SINGLE CARDS: 10p
SINGLE SPECIAL CARDS: 15p

ROBIN HOOD, PRINCE OF THIEVES MOVIE

PRODUCER: TOPPS U.S.
ISSUE YEAR: 1991
CARD SET: 88 CARDS
SPECIAL CARDS: 9 STICKERS
COMPLETE SET: £10.00
SINGLE CARDS: 15p
SINGLE SPECIAL CARDS: 30p

Important Notes: Based on the movie of the same name starring Kevin Costner. Rare Set (based on the above set and is called the Mistake Set in the U.S.)

ROBOT CARNIVAL

PRODUCER: CORNERSTONE
ISSUE YEAR: 1994
CARD SET: 82 CARDS
SPECIAL CARDS: FOIL CARD: £5.00
COMPLETE SET: £10.00
SINGLE CARDS: 15p

ROBOCOP II MOVIE

PRODUCER: TOPPS U.S.
ISSUE YEAR: 1990
CARD SET: 88 CARDS
SPECIAL CARDS: 11 STICKERS
COMPLETE SET: £5.00
SINGLE CARDS: 10p
SINGLE SPECIAL CARDS: 25p

ROCKETEER MOVIE

PRODUCER: TOPPS U.S.
ISSUE YEAR: 1991
CARD SET: 99 CARDS
SPECIAL CARDS: 11 STICKERS
COMPLETE SET: £7.00
SINGLE CARDS: 15p
SINGLE SPECIAL CARDS: 30p

Important Notes: A very high quality and highly desirable set of trading cards and stickers.

ROCKY II MOVIE

PRODUCER: TOPPS U.S.
ISSUE YEAR: 1979
CARD SET: 99 CARDS
SPECIAL CARDS: 11 STICKERS

Spiderman Premium #5

COMPLETE SET: £10.00
SINGLE CARDS: 15p
SINGLE SPECIAL CARDS: 25p

ROCKY IV MOVIE

PRODUCER: TOPPS U.S.
ISSUE YEAR: 1985
CARD SET: 66 CARDS
SPECIAL CARDS: 11 STICKERS
COMPLETE SET: £7.00
SINGLE CARDS: 15p
SINGLE SPECIAL CARDS: 25p

ROCKY HORROR PICTURE SHOW MOVIE

PRODUCER: FTCC
ISSUE YEAR: 1980
CARD SET: 60 CARDS
SPECIAL CARDS: No special cards
COMPLETE SET: £12.00
SINGLE CARDS: 25p

ROCKY HORROR PICTURE SHOW II

PRODUCER: COMIC IMAGES
ISSUE YEAR: 1995
CARD SET: 90 CARDS
SPECIAL CARDS: 6 CHROME CHASE CARDS
COMPLETE SET: £8.00
SINGLE CARDS: 10p
SINGLE SPECIAL CARDS: £5.00

ROGER DEAN

PRODUCER: FPG
ISSUE YEAR: 1993
CARD SET: 90 CARDS
SPECIAL CARDS: 5 METALLIC STORM CARDS
COMPLETE SET £10.00
SINGLE CARDS: 15p
SINGLE SPECIAL CARDS: £5.00

ROGER RABBIT MOVIE, WHO FRAMED

PRODUCER: TOPPS U.S.
ISSUE YEAR: 1990
CARD SET: 132 CARDS
SPECIAL CARDS: 22 STICKERS
COMPLETE SET: £12.00
SINGLE CARDS: 10p
SINGLE SPECIAL CARDS: 25p

RON MILLER'S FIREBRANDS

PRODUCER: COMIC IMAGES
ISSUE YEAR: 1994
CARD SET: 90 CARDS
SPECIAL CARDS: 6 GALAXY PRISM CARDS
COMPLETE SET: £9.00
SINGLE CARDS: 10p
SINGLE SPECIAL CARDS: £5.00

ROWENA

PRODUCER: FPG
ISSUE YEAR: 1993
CARD SET: 90 CARDS
SPECIAL CARDS: 3 HOLOGRAMS
COMPLETE SET £10.00
SINGLE CARDS: 15p

SINGLE SPECIAL CARDS: £5.00

SALVADOR DALI ALL CHROMIUM

PRODUCER: COMIC IMAGES
ISSUE YEAR: 1995
CARD SET: 90 CARDS
SPECIAL CARDS:
MAGNACHROME CARD (HORSEPLAY): £5.00
3 CARD PRECIOUS TIME: £20.00
MEDALLION CARD: £15.00
HOLOCHROME CARD: £5.00
24K GOLD SIGNATURE CARD: £30.00
COMPLETE SET: £15.00
SINGLE CARDS: 15p

SANDMAN

PRODUCER: SKYBOX
ISSUE YEAR: 1994
CARD SET: 90 CARDS
SPECIAL CARDS: 7 ENDLESS GALLERY BONUS CARDS
COMPLETE SET: £90.00
CARD SET ONLY £20.00
SINGLE CARDS: 15p
SINGLE SPECIAL CARDS: £15.00

Important Notes: Morpheus Hologram would be about £40.00

SANJULIAN COLLECTION

PRODUCER: FPG
ISSUE YEAR: 1994
CARD SET: 90 CARDS
SPECIAL CARDS: 5 METALLIC STORM CARDS
COMPLETE SET £10.00
SINGLE CARDS: 15p
SINGLE SPECIAL CARDS: £5.00

SAVAGE DRAGON

PRODUCER: COMIC IMAGES
ISSUE YEAR: 1992
CARD SET: 90 CARDS
SPECIAL CARDS: 6 PRISM CARDS
COMPLETE SET: £30.00
CARD SET ONLY £5.00
SINGLE CARDS: 10p
SINGLE SPECIAL CARDS: £4.00

Important Notes: Generally the quality of the Image series trading cards are quite poor and only the prism cards are impressive to view.

SEAQUEST DSV

PRODUCER: SKYBOX
ISSUE YEAR: 1994
CARD SET: 100 CARDS
SPECIAL ACRDS: 4 FOIL CARDS
COMPLETE SET: £10.00
SINGLE CARDS: 10p
SINGLE SPECIAL CARDS: £5.00

SHADOW HAWK

PRODUCER: COMIC IMAGES
ISSUE YEAR: 1992
CARD SET: 90 CARDS
SPECIAL CARDS: 6 PRISM CARDS
COMPLETE SET: £5.00
SINGLE CARDS: 5p - 10p
SINGLE SPECIAL CARDS: £5.00

SHI

PRODUCER: COMIC IMAGES
ISSUE YEAR: 1995
CARD SET: 90 CARDS
SPECIAL CARDS:
3 MAGNACHROME CARD SET £22.00
6 MAGNACHROME CARD SET £30.00
6 CARD UNCUT SHEET £10.00
COMPLETE SET ALL-CHROMIUM: £18.00
SINGLE CARDS: 25p

SHI 2

PRODUCER: COMIC IMAGES
ISSUE YEAR: 1996
CARD SET: 90 CARDS
SPECIAL CARDS: 6 CLEAR CELS: £7.00 each
3 SUB-SET CELS: £8.00 each
1 BOXCARD: £3.00
HOLOCHROME CARD (1 PER BOX): ?
COMPLETE SET: £17.50
SINGLE CARDS: 25p

SILVER SURFER ALL PRISM SERIES

PRODUCER: COMIC IMAGES

ISSUE YEAR:	1992
CARD SET:	72 ALL PRISM SET
SPECIAL CARDS:	No special cards
COMPLETE SET:	£20.00
SINGLE CARDS:	30p

SIMPSONS

PRODUCER:	TOPPS
ISSUE YEAR:	1990
CARD SET:	88 CARDS
SPECIAL CARDS:	22 STICKERS
COMPLETE SET:	£12.00
SINGLE CARDS:	10p
SINGLE SPECIAL CARDS:	20p

SIMPSONS

PRODUCER:	SKYBOX
ISSUE YEAR:	1994
CARD SET:	70 CARDS
SPECIAL CARDS:	4 GLOW IN THE DARK CARDS
COMPLETE SET:	£10.00
SINGLE CARDS:	15p
SINGLE SPECIAL CARDS:	£6.00

SIMPSONS II

PRODUCER:	SKYBOX
ISSUE YEAR:	1994
CARD SET:	80 CARDS
SPECIAL CARDS:	
ART CARDS (A-1 to A-4):	£25.00
DISAPPEARING INK CARDS: (D-1 to D-4):	£10.00
WIGGLE CARDS (W-1 to W-9):	£3.00
SMELL-O-RAMA CARDS:	£1.50
COMPLETE SET:	£8.00
SINGLE CARDS:	15p

SNOW WHITE AND THE SEVEN DWARFS

PRODUCER:	SKYBOX
ISSUE YEAR:	1993
CARD SET:	90 CARDS
SPECIAL CARDS:	4 SPECTRA CARDS
COMPLETE SET:	£10.00
SINGLE CARDS:	10p
SINGLE SPECIAL CARDS:	£3.00

SNOW WHITE AND THE SEVEN DWARFS II

PRODUCER:	SKYBOX
ISSUE YEAR:	1994
CARD SET:	90 CARDS
SPECIAL CARDS:	4 FOIL EMBOSSED CARDS
COMPLETE SET:	£10.00
SINGLE CARDS:	10p
SINGLE SPECIAL CARDS:	£5.00

SONIC THE HEDGEHOG

PRODUCER:	TOPPS U.S.
ISSUE YEAR:	1993
CARD SET:	33 CARDS
SPECIAL CARDS:	33 STICKERS
COMPLETE SET	£5.00
SINGLE CARDS:	15p

SORAYAMA - SEXY ROBOTS

PRODUCER:	COMIC IMAGES
ISSUE YEAR:	1993
CARD SET:	90 CARDS
SPECIAL CARDS:	6 CHROMIUM CARDS
COMPLETE SET	£15.00
SINGLE CARDS:	20p
SINGLE SPECIAL CARDS:	£4.00

SORAYAMA II - CHROMIUM CREATURES

PRODUCER:	COMIC IMAGES
ISSUE YEAR:	1994
CARD SET:	100 CARDS
SPECIAL CARDS:	6 FOIL CARDS
COMPLETE SET	£25.00
SINGLE CARDS:	25p
SINGLE SPECIAL CARDS:	£5.00

SPAWN

PRODUCER:	WILDSTORM
ISSUE YEAR:	1995
CARD SET:	150 CARDS
SPECIAL CARDS:	12 PAINTED/6 TODD TOY CARDS
COMPLETE SET	£15.00
SINGLE CARD:	10p
SINGLE SPECIAL CARDS:	£3.00

SPIDERMAN FLEER ULTRA

PRODUCER:	FLEER
ISSUE YEAR:	1995
CARD SET:	150 CARDS
SPECIAL CARDS:	10 CLEARZONE CHASE/ 9 GOLD WEB CHASE/ 9 MONSTER CHASE CARDS
COMPLETE SET:	£18.00
SINGLE CARDS:	15p
SINGLE SPECIAL CARDS:	£5.00 (Clearzone), £3.00 (Gold Web and Monster)
GOLD SIGNATURE CARD SET:	£75.00
GOLD SIGNATURE SINGLE CARD:	50p

SPIDERMAN PREMIUM

PRODUCER:	FLEER/SKYBOX
ISSUE YEAR:	1996
CARD SET:	100 CARDS
SPECIAL CARDS: CANVAS CARD:	£3.00
HOLOMOTION CARD:	£10.00
COMPLETE SET:	£15.00
SINGLE CARDS:	15p - 20p

SPIDERMAN, 30TH ANNIVERSARY

PRODUCER:	COMIC IMAGES
ISSUE YEAR:	1992
CARD SET:	90 CARDS
SPECIAL CARDS:	6 PRISM CARDS
COMPLETE SET:	£35.00
CARD SET ONLY	£ 5.00
SINGLE CARDS:	10p
SINGLE SPECIAL CARDS:	£6.00

SPIDERMAN, TODD MCFARLANE

PRODUCER:	COMIC IMAGES
ISSUE YEAR:	1992
CARD SET:	90 CARDS
SPECIAL CARDS:	6 PRISM CARDS
CARD SET ONLY	£9.00
SINGLE CARDS:	15p
SINGLE SPECIAL CARDS:	£10.00

SPIDERMAN

PRODUCER:	FLEER/MARVEL CARDS
ISSUE YEAR:	1994
CARD SET:	150 CARDS
SPECIAL CARDS:	4 HOLOGRAM CARDS & 12 ANIMATION CARDS
COMPLETE SET:	£80.00
CARD SET ONLY	£18.00
SINGLE CARDS:	15p
SINGLE HOLOGRAM CARDS:	£8.00
SINGLE ANIMATION CARDS:	£4.00

STARLOG COVERS COLLECTION

PRODUCER:	TOPPS
ISSUE YEAR:	1993
CARD SET:	100 CARDS
SPECIAL CARDS:	4 + 1 HOLO?
COMPLETE SET	£25.00
SINGLE CARDS:	15p

STAR TREK

PRODUCER:	TOPPS U.S.
ISSUE YEAR:	1976
CARD SET:	88 CARDS
COMPLETE SET:	£150.00
SPECIAL CARDS:	22 STICKERS
SINGLE CARD:	£2.00
SINGLE SPECIAL CARDS:	£3.50

STAR TREK

PRODUCER:	TOPPS U.S.
ISSUE YEAR:	1979
CARD SET:	88 CARDS
COMPLETE SET:	£35.00
SPECIAL CARDS:	22 STICKERS
SINGLE CARDS:	50p
SINGLE SPECIAL CARDS:	£1.00

STAR TREK II

PRODUCER:	FTCC
ISSUE YEAR:	1983
CARD SET:	30 CARDS
COMPLETE SET:	£40.00
SINGLE CARDS:	£1.50

Important Notes: Scarce set in the U.K.

STAR TREK III

PRODUCER:	FTCC
ISSUE YEAR:	1985
CARD SET:	80 CARDS
COMPLETE SET:	£35.00
SINGLE CARDS:	50p

STAR TREK IV

PRODUVER:	FTCC
ISSUE YEAR:	1987
CARD SET:	60 CARDS
SPECIAL CARDS:	No Special Cards
COMPLETE SET:	£25.00
SINGLE CARDS:	40p

STAR TREK COLLECTORS TIN

PRODUCER:	IMPEL
ISSUE YEAR:	1992
CARD SET:	312 CARDS
SPECIAL CARDS:	4 HOLOGRAMS
COMPLETE FACTORY SET:	£75.00

Important Notes: Released in limited quantities, with no British retailer being allowed to order more than two tins.

STAR TREK - DEEP SPACE NINE

PRODUCER:	SKYBOX
ISSUE YEAR:	1994
CARD SET:	100 CARDS
SPECIAL CARDS:	5 SPECTRA CARDS
COMPLETE SET:	£15.00
SINGLE CARDS:	15p
SINGLE SPECIAL CARDS:	£6.00

STAR TREK GENERATIONS CINEMA CARDS

PRODUCER:	SKYBOX
ISSUE YEAR:	1995
CARD SET:	72 CARDS
SPECIAL CARDS:	3 SPECTRA (Captains), 3 FOIL (Villains)
COMPLETE SET:	£15.00
SINGLE CARDS:	15p
SINGLE SPECIAL CARDS:	£7.50

Important Notes: There was a SkyMotion card available to US collectors through a wrapper offer. Rare in the U.K. and valued at approximately £50.00

STAR TREK - MASTERWORKS

PRODUCER:	SKYBOX
ISSUE YEAR:	1993
CARD SET:	90 CARDS
SPECIAL CARDS:	5 SPECTRA ETCH CARDS
CARD SET	£12.00
SINGLE CARDS:	15p
SINGLE SPECIAL CARDS	£6.00

STAR TREK - MASTERWORKS II

PRODUCER:	SKYBOX
ISSUE YEAR:	1994
CARD SET:	90 CARDS
SPECIAL CARDS:	9 FOIL EMBOSSED (3 with artist signature)
COMPLETE SET:	£10.00
SINGLE CARDS:	15p
SINGLE SPECIAL CARDS:	£4.00

STAR TREK, 25TH ANNIVERSARY I

PRODUCER:	IMPEL
ISSUE YEAR:	1991
CARD SET:	160 CARDS
SPECIAL CARDS:	2 HOLOGRAM CARDS
COMPLETE SET:	£45.00
SINGLE CARDS:	10p
SINGLE SPECIAL CARDS:	£10.00

Important Notes: Large quantities of these holograms have recently appeared on the market and the price has halved within the last year. The price has also depreciated due to Impel's release of the Collectors Tin.

Note also that odd number cards feature Star Trek and even number cards feature Next Generation

STAR TREK, 25TH ANNIVERSARY II

PRODUCER:	IMPEL
ISSUE YEAR:	1991
CARD SET:	150 CARDS
SPECIAL CARDS:	2 HOLOGRAMS
COMPLETE SET:	£45.00
SINGLE CARDS:	10p
SINGLE SPECIAL CARDS:	£10.00

Important Notes: See Series One for important information on Star Trek 25th Anniversary holograms

STAR TREK 30th PHASE 1

PRODUCER:	FLEER/SKYBOX
ISSUE YEAR:	1995
CARD SET:	100 CARDS
SPECIAL CARDS:	
FOIL-STAMPED TECH CARD:	£5.00
DIE-CUT TECHNOLOGY CARD:	£10.00
GOLD PLAQUE SHIP CARD:	£25.00
SURVEY CAR:	£1.50
SKYMOTION CARD:	up to £50.00
COMPLETE SET:	£12.00
SINGLE CARDS:	15p

STAR TREK 30th PHASE 2

PRODUCER: FLEER/SKYBOX
ISSUE YEAR: 1996
CARD SET: 100 CARDS
SPECIAL CARDS:
DOPPLEGANGER CARD: £6.00
DUAL-IMAGE LENTICULAR CARD: £15.00
SKYMOTION CARD: up to £50.00
SURVEY CARD: £1.50
COMPLETE SET: £10.00
SINGLE CARDS: 15p

STAR TREK 30TH PHASE 3

PRODUCER: FLEER/SKYBOX
ISSUE YEAR: 1996
CARD SET: 100 CARDS
SPECIAL CARDS: 9 BLUEPRINT: £1.00-£2.00 each
3 MOTION CARDS: £15.00 each
1 SKYMOTION CARD: up to £50.00
9 FOIL CARDS: £5.00 each
SURVEY CARD: £2.00
6 GAMING CARDS: £1.00 each
COMPLETE SET: £15.00
SINGLE CARDS: 15p

STAR TREK, THE NEXT GENERATION

PRODUCER: IMPEL
ISSUE YEAR: 1992
CARD SET: 120 CARDS, 5 LANGUAGE CARDS
SPECIAL CARDS: 4 HOLOGRAMS, 1 "MAIL-IN" HOLO
COMPLETE SET: £60.00
SINGLE CARDS: 10p
LANGUAGE CARDS £2.00
SINGLE SPECIAL CARDS: £5.00,
"MAIL-IN" HOLO £20.00

Important Notes: The special "mail-in" hologram was only available to American collectors by post

STAR TREK, THE NEXT GENERATION, BEHIND THE SCENES

PRODUCER: SKYBOX
ISSUE YEAR: 1993
CARD SET: 39 CARDS
SPECIAL CARDS: No special cards
COMPETE FACTORY SET: £12.00

STAR TREK, THE NEXT GENERATION, THE MAKING OF

PRODUCER: SKYBOX
ISSUE YEAR: 1994
CARD SET: 100 CARDS
COMPLETE SET: £30.00
SINLE CARDS: 30p

Important Notes: The same set of 100 cards was available in a Gold Edition (set value approximately £50.00) and a Platinum Edition (set value approximately £70.00)

STAR TREK, THE NEXT GENERATION SEASON I

PRODUCER: SKYBOX
ISSUE YEAR: 1994
CARD SET: 108 CARDS
COMPLETE SET: £20.00
SPECIAL CARDS: 6 FOIL EMBOSSED/ 2 HOLOGRAMS (very scarce in the U.K.)
SINGLE CARDS: 15p
SINGLE SPECIAL CARDS: £6.00 (Foil), £50.00 (Hologram)

Important Notes: This series is getting harder to obtain in the U.K.

STAR TREK, THE NEXT GENERATION SEASON II

PRODUCER: SKYBOX
ISSUE YEAR: 1995
CARD SET: 96 CARDS
SPECIAL CARDS: 6 FOIL EMBOSSED/ 2 HOLOGRAMS
COMPLETE SET: £10.00
SINGLE CARDS: 10p - 15p
SINGLE SPECIAL CARDS: £6.00 (Foil), £50.00 (Hologram)

Important Notes: Number on cards continues from #109-#204

STAR TREK, THE NEXT GENERATION SEASON III

PRODUCER: SKYBOX
ISSUE YEAR: 1995
CARD SET: 106 CARDS
SPECIAL CARDS: 6 FOIL EMBOSSED/ 2 HOLOGRAMS
COMPLETE SET: £10.00
SINGLE CARDS: 10p

Star Wars Galaxy Promo Card

SINGLE SPECIAL CARDS: £6.00 (Foil), £50.00 (Hologram)

Important Notes: Numbering on cards continues #205-#310. Note also that each of the above three sets contains a Survey Card which varies greatly in price in the U.K. but in fact is scarcer than the embossed cards

STAR TREK VOYAGER

PRODUCER: SKYBOX
ISSUE YEAR: 1995
CARD SET: 101 CARDS
SPECIAL CARDS: 9 SPECTRA CARDS
COMPLETE SET: £15.00
SINGLE CARDS: 15p
SINGLE SPECIAL CARDS: £4.00

STAR TREK VOYAGER SERIES 2

PRODUCER: FLEER/SKYBOX
ISSUE YEAR: 1995
CARD SET W/TATTOO: 90 CARDS
SPECIAL CARDS: 6 RECIPE CARDS £15.00
9 SPECTRA FOIL CARD SET £40.00
SKYMOTION: CAPT. JANEWAY £35.00
SUPERSIZE SKYMOTION JANEMOTION £30.00
COLLECTORS' ALBUM £10.00
COMPLETE SET: £7.00
SINGLE CARDS: 10p

STAR WARS

PRODUCER: TOPPS
ISSUE YEAR 1977-78
CARD SET 1: 66 CARDS/11 STICKERS
COMPLETE SET: £60.00
SINGLE CARDS: £1.00
CARD SET 2: 66 CARDS/11 STICKERS
COMPLETE SET: £50.00
SINGLE CARDS: 90p
CARD SET 3: 66 CARDS/11 STICKERS
COMPLETE SET: £50.00
SINGLE CARDS: 90p
CARD SET 4: 66 CARDS/11 STICKERS
COMPLETE SET: £45.00
SINGLE CARDS: 80p
CARD SET 5: 66 CARDS/11 STICKERS
COMPLETE SET: £45.00
SINGLE CARDS: 80p

STAR WARS FINEST

PRODUCER: TOPPS
ISSUE YEAR: 1996
CARD SET: 90 CARDS
SPECIAL CARDS: MATRIX CARD: £6.00
EMBOSSED CARD: £6.00
SHADOWS OF EMPIRE PROMO CARD: £3.00
MATRIX REDEMPTION CARD: £25.00
REFRACTOR CARD: £6.00
COMPLETE SET: £30.00
SINGLE CARDS: 40p

STAR WARS GALAXY

PRODUCER: SKYBOX
ISSUE YEAR: 1993
CARD SET: 140 CARDS
SPECIAL CARDS: 6 FOIL CARDS
CARD SET £25.00
SINGLE CARDS: 15p - 20p
SINGLE SPECIAL CARDS £8.00

STAR WARS GALAXY II

PRODUCER: TOPPS U.S.
ISSUE YEAR: 1994
CARD SET: 135 CARDS
SPECIAL CARDS: 6 FOIL ETCHED CARDS
COMPLETE SET: £15.00
SINGLE CARDS: 15p
SINGLE SPECIAL CARDS: £6.00
FACTORY SET: £50.00

Important Notes: The factory set consists of 135 foil-stamped cards, 6 foil-etched cards, 3-D hologram, WideVision and Preview cards

STAR WARS GALAXY III

PRODUCER: TOPPS
ISSUE YEAR: 1995
CARD SET: 90 CARDS
SPECIAL CARDS:
12 LUCAS ART CARDS: £1.50 each
FOIL-ETCHED CARD: £4.00
CLEARZONE CARD: £6.00
90 FIRST DAY CARDs: £1.50 each
COMPLETE SET: £15.00
SINGLE CARDS: 15p - 20p

STAR WARS WIDEVISION

PRODUCER: TOPPS U.S.
IISUE YEAR: 1995
CARD SET: 120 CARDS
SPECIAL CARDS: 10 CHASE CARDS
COMPLETE SET: £40.00
SINGLE CARDS: 30p - 40p
SINGLE SPECIAL CARDS: £12.50 each

STARS OF BOLLYWOOD (ASIAN CINEMA)

PRODUCER: MERLIN PUBLISHING LTD
ISSUE YEAR: 1993
CARD SET: 144
COMPLETE SET: £20.00
SINGLE CARDS: 5p

STRANGERS IN PARADISE

PRODUCER: COMIC IMAGES
ISSUE YEAR: 1996
CARD SET: 90 CARDS
SPECIAL CARDS: 6 CHROME CARDS: £5.00 each
3 SUB-SET CARDS: £7.00 each
1 BOXCARD: £3.00
COMPLETE SET: £8.00
SINGLE CARDS: 15p

STREET FIGHTER

PRODUCER: UPPER DECK
ISSUE YEAR: 1995
CARD SET: 90 CARDS
SPECIAL CARDS: 10 FX CARDS
COMPLETE SET: £10.00
SINGLE CARDS: 10p
SINGLE SPECIAL CARDS: £5.00

STREET FIGHTER II

PRODUCER: TOPPS U.S.
ISSUE YEAR: 1993
CARD SET: 88 CARDS
SPECIAL CARDS: 11 STICKERS/4 HOLOFOIL CARDS
COMPLETE SET: £8.00
SINGLE CARDS: 10p
SINGLE SPECIAL CARDS: £1.00 (Stickers), £4.00 (Holofoil)

SUPERGIRL MOVIE

PRODUCER: TOPPS
ISSUE YEAR: 1985
CARD SET: 44 STICKERS
COMPLETE SET: £3.00
SINGLE CARDS: 15p

SUPERMAN: THE MOVIE

PRODUCER: TOPPS U.S.
ISSUE YEAR: 1978
CARD SET: 77 CARDS
SPECIAL CARDS: 6 REGULAR STICKERS/ 6 FOIL STICKERS
COMPLETE SET: £10.00
SINGLE CARDS: 15p

SINGLE SPECIAL CARDS: 50p (regular), £2.00 (foil)

SUPERMAN II MOVIE

PRODUCER: TOPPS U.S.
ISSUE YEAR: 1981
CARD SET: 88 CARDS
SPECIAL CARDS: 22 STICKERS
COMPLETE SET: £12.00
SINGLE CARDS: 15p
SINGLE SPECIAL CARDS: 25p

SUPERMAN III MOVIE

PRODUCER: TOPPS U.S.
ISSUE YEAR: 1983
CARD SET: 99 CARDS
SPECIAL CARDS: 22 STICKERS
COMPLETE SET: £9.00
SINGLE CARDS: 15p
SINGLE SPECIAL CARDS: 20P

SUPERMAN: DOOMSDAY

PRODUCER: SKYBOX
ISSUE YEAR: 1992
CARD SET: 100 CARDS
CARD SET ONLY: £18.00
SPECIAL CARDS:
4 SPECTRA CARDS/2 FOIL CARDS
COMPLETE SET: £100.00
SINGLE CARDS: 15p
SINGLE SPECIAL CARDS: £15.00
FOIL CARDS £12.50

SUPERMAN HOLO SERIES

PRODUCER: FLEER/SKYBOX
ISSUE YEAR: 1996
CARD SET: 50 HOLOGRAMS
SPECIAL CARDS:
PARALLEL GOLD HOLOGRAM SET: £30.00
PARALLEL GOLD HOLOACTION: £4.00
HOLO CEL: £12.00
COMPLETE SET: £20.00
SINGLE HOLOGRAMS: 50p each

SUPERMAN: THE MAN OF STEEL COLLECTORS EDITION

PRODUCER: SKYBOX
ISSUE YEAR: 1994
CARD SET: 90 CARDS
SPECIAL CARDS: 6 SPECTRA-ETCHED CARDS
COMPLETE SET: £10.00
SINGLE CARDS: 10p
SINGLE SPECIAL CARDS: £4.00

SUPERMAN: THE MAN OF STEEL PREMIUM EDITION

PRODUCER: SKYBOX
ISSUE YEAR: 1994
CARD SET: 90 CARDS
SPECIAL CARDS: 4 SILVER/4 GOLD
COMPLETE SET: £25.00
SINGLE CARDS: 25p
SINGLE SPECIAL CARDS: £20.00 (Silver), £35.00 (Gold)

SUPER MARIO BROS.

PRODUCER: SKYBOX
ISSUE YEAR: 1993
CARD SET: 100 CARDS
SPECIAL CARDS: 3 HOLOGRAMS
CARD SET £10.00
SINGLE CARDS: 10p
SINGLE SPECIAL CARDS £10.00

TANK GIRL

PRODUCER: COMIC IMAGES
ISSUE YEAR: 1995
CARD SET: 90 CARDS
SPECIAL CARDS: 6 MAGNACHROME CARDS
COMPLETE SET: £9.00
SINGLE CARDS: 10p
SINGLE SPECIAL CARDS: £4.00

TEENAGE MUTANT NINJA TURTLES TV 1

PRODUCER: TOPPS
ISSUE YEAR: 1989
CARD SET: 88 CARDS
SPECIAL CARDS: 11 STICKERS
COMPLETE SET: £12.00
SINGLE CARDS: 15p
SINGLE SPECIAL CARDS: 25p

TEENAGE MUTANT NINJA TURTLES TV II

PRODUCER: TOPPS U.S.
ISSUE YEAR: 1989
CARD SET: 88 CARDS
SPECIAL CARDS: 11 STICKERS
COMPLETE SET: £10.00
SINGLE CARDS: 10p
SINGLE SPECIAL CARDS: 20p

TEENAGE MUTANT NINJA TURTLES MOVIE I

PRODUCER: TOPPS U.S.
ISSUE YEAR: 1990
CARD SET: 132 CARDS
SPECIAL CARDS: 11 STICKERS
COMPLETE SET: £12.00
SINGLE CARDS: 10p
SINGLE SPECIAL CARDS: 25p

TEENAGE MUTANT NINJA TURTLES SECRET OF THE OOZE, MOVIE 2

PRODUCER: TOPPS U.S.
ISSUE YEAR: 1990
CARD SET: 99 CARDS
SPECIAL CARDS: 11 STICKERS
COMPLETE SET: £12.00
SINGLE CARDS: 10p
SINGLE SPECIAL CARDS: 25p

TEK WORLD

PRODUCER: CARDZ
ISSUE YEAR: 1994
CARD SET: 100 CARDS
SPECIAL CARDS: 4 TEKCHROME CARDS
COMPLETE SET: £15.00
SINGLE CARDS: 15p
SINGLE SPECIAL CARDS: £6.00

TERMINATOR 2

PRODUCER: IMPEL
ISSUE YEAR: 1991
CARD SET: 140 CARDS
SPECIAL CARDS: No special cards
COMPLETE SET: £15.00
SINGLE CARDS: 10p - 20p
Important Notes: See also Impel factory set and Topps set

TERMINATOR 2 - FACTORY SET

PRODUCER: IMPEL
ISSUE YEAR: 1992
CARD SET: 141 CARDS
SPECIAL CARDS: 1 HOLOGRAM CARD
COMPLETE SET: £30.00
Important Notes: Sold only as a complete set. Look for sets missing the hologram

T2 (TERMINATOR 2)

PRODUCER: TOPPS
ISSUE YEAR: 1991
CARD SET: 44 ALL STICKER SET
SPECIAL CARDS: No special cards
COMPLETE SET: £4.00
SINGLE CARDS: 10p

THE MAXX

PRODUCER: TOPPS U.S.
ISSUE YEAR: 1994
CARD SET: 100 CARDS
SPECIAL CARDS: 7 FOIL CARDS:
COMPLETE SET: £10.00
SINGLE CARDS: 10p
SINGLE SPECIAL CARDS: £4.00

THUNDERBIRDS ARE GO

PRODUCER: PRO SET U.K.
ISSUE YEAR: 1992
CARD SET: 100 CARD SET
SPECIAL CARDS: No special cards
COMPLETE SET: £12.00
SINGLE CARDS: 10p

TIM HILDERBRANDT'S FLIGHTS OF FANTASY

PRODUCER: COMIC IMAGES
ISSUE YEAR: 1994
CARD SET: 90 CARDS
SPECIAL CARDS: 6 CHASE CARDS
COMPLETE SET: £7.00
SINGLE CARDS: 15p
SINGLE SPECIAL CARDS: £4.00

TOM & JERRY

PRODUCER: CARDZ
ISSUE YEAR: 1994
CARD SET: 60 CARDS
SPECIAL CARDS: 3 HOLOGRAMS
COMPLETE SET: £6.00
SINGLE CARDS: 10p
SINGLE SPECIAL CARDS: £5.00

TOM KIDD

PRODUCER: FPG
ISSUE YEAR: 1995
CARD SET: 90 CARDS
SPECIAL CARDS:
METALLIC STORM CARDS: £4.00
AUTOGRAPH CARD (1000): £30.00
COMPLETE SET: £6.00
SINGLE CARDS: 5p - 10p

TOON WORLD

PRODUCER: UPPER DECK
ISSUE YEAR: 1993
CARD SET: 90 CARDS
SPECIAL CARDS: 5 HOLOGRAMS AND 5 INSERT CARDS
COMPLETE SET: £13.00
CARD SET ONLY: £ 5.00
SINGLE CARDS: 5p - 10p

TOY STORY

PRODUCER: FLEER/SKYBOX
ISSUE YEAR: 1995
CARD SET: 90 CARDS
SPECIAL CARDS:
2 3-D LENTICULAR CARD SET £20.00
9 FOIL EMBOSSED CARD SET: £40.00
COMPLETE SET: £10.00
SINGLE CARDS: 15p

TOTAL RECALL - FACTORY SET

PRODUCER: PACIFIC
ISSUE YEAR: 1990
CARD SET: 110 CARDS
SPECIAL CARDS: VARIOUS NOVELTY ITEMS
COMPLETE SET: £15.00

TOXIC CRUSADERS - RARE TEST ISSUE

PRODUCER: TOPPS
ISSUE YEAR: 1992
CARD SET: 88 CARDS
SPECIAL CARDS: 8 HOLOGRAMS
COMPLETE SET £12.50
SINGLE CARDS: 15p
SINGLE SPECIAL CARDS: £2.50

TOXIC HIGH SCHOOL

PRODUCER: TOPPS
ISSUE YEAR: 1992
CARD SET: 88 STICKERS
SPECIAL CARDS: No special cards
COMPLETE SET: £4.00
SINGLE CARDS: 5p

TRANSFORMERS

PRODUCER: HASBRO
ISSUE YEAR: 1985
CARD SET: 192 CARDS
SPECIAL CARDS: 24 STICKERS
COMPLETE SET: £30.00
SINGLE CARDS: 15p
SINGLE SPECIAL CARDS: 25p

TRON MOVIE

PRODUCER: DONRUSS
ISSUE YEAR: 1982
CARD SET: 66 CARDS
SPECIAL CARDS: 8 STICKERS
COMPLETE SET: £10.00
SINGLE CARDS: 20p
SINGLE SPECIAL CARDS: 50p

UJENA - SWIMWEAR ILLUSTRATED GIRLS

PRODUCER: COMIC IMAGES
ISSUE YEAR: 1993
CARD SET: 90 CARDS
SPECIAL CARDS: 6 CHASE CARDS
COMPLETE SET: £8.50
SINGLE CARDS: 10p
SINGLE SPECIAL CARDS: £5.00

UJENA II

PRODUCER: COMIC IMAGES
ISSUE YEAR: 1994
CARD SET: 90 CARDS
SPECIAL CARDS: 6 EMBOSSED CHASE CARDS
COMPLETE SET: £9.00
SINGLE CARDS: 10p
SINGLE SPECIAL CARDS: £4.00

ULTRA X-MEN

PRODUCER: FLEER ULTRA
ISSUE YEAR: 1994
CARD SET: 150 CARDS

SPECIAL CARDS:
6 FATAL ATTRACTIONS CARD SET £25.00
6 GREATEST BATTLES CARD SET: £25.00
9 PORTRAITS CARD SET: £22.50
6 RED-FOIL BONUS CARD SET: £22.50
6 SILVER X-OVERS: £40.00
5 ULTRAPRINTS: £8.00
COMPLETE SET: £20.00
SINGLE CARDS: 15p

ULTRA X-MEN SERIES 2

PRODUCER: FLEER ULTRA
ISSUE YEAR: 1994
CARD SET: 150 CARDS
SPECIAL CARDS:
10 SINISTER OBSERVATIONS CHROMIUM CARD SET £45.00
9 HUNTERS AND STALKERS CARD SET £15.00
10 SUSPENDED ANIMATION CARD SET £20.00
COMPLETE SET: £12.00
SINGLE CARDS: 10p

ULTRAVERSE I

PRODUCER: SKYBOX
ISSUE YEAR: 1993
CARD SET: 100 CARDS
SPECIAL CARDS: 9 ROOKIE/ 4 ULTIMATE ROOKIE CARDS
COMPLETE SET: £10.00
SINGLE CARDS: 10p
SINGLE SPECIAL CARDS: £1.50 (Rookie), £2.50 (Ultimate)

ULTRAVERSE 2

PRODUCER: SKYBOX
ISSUE YEAR: 1994
CARD SET: 90 CARDS
SPECIAL CARDS: 9 BONUS CARDS
COMPLETE SET: £40.00
CARD SET ONLY £10.00
SINGLE CARDS: 10p
SINGLE SPECIAL CARDS £5.00

ULTRAVERSE MASTER SERIES

PRODUCER: SKYBOX
ISSUE YEAR: 1994
CARD SET: 90 CARDS
SPECIAL CARDS: 8 FOIL CARDS
COMPLETE SET: £15.00
SINGLE CARDS: 15p
SINGLE SPECIAL CARDS: £5.00

UNCANNY X MEN COVERS I

PRODUCER: COMIC IMAGES
ISSUE YEAR: 1990
CARD SET: 90 CARD SET
SPECIAL CARDS: No special cards
COMPLETE SET: £12.00
SINGLE CARDS: 15p

UNCANNY X MEN COVERS II

PRODUCER: COMIC IMAGES
ISSUE YEAR: 1991
CARD SET: 45 CARDS
SPECIAL CARDS: No special cards
COMPLETE SET: £9.00
SINGLE CARDS: 15p

UNITY

PRODUCER: COMIC IMAGES
ISSUE YEAR: 1992
CARD SET: 90 CARDS
SPECIAL CARDS: 6 CHROMIUM CARDS
COMPLETE SET: £40.00
CARD SET ONLY £ 7.50
SINGLE CARDS: 15p
SINGLE SPECIAL CARDS: £6.00
Important Notes: PROMO CHROMIUM CARD: £7.50

UNIVERSAL MONSTERS

PRODUCER: TOPPS U.S.
ISSUE YEAR: 1994
CARD SET: 100 CARDS
SPECIAL CARDS: 10 MONSTERCHROME/ 4 HORRORGLOW
COMPLETE SET: £15.00
SINGLE CARDS: 15p
SINGLE SPECIAL CARDS: £5.00 (Monsterchrome), £15.00 (Horrorglow)

VAMPIRELLA

PRODUCER: TOPPS U.S.
ISSUE YEAR: 1995
CARD SET: 90 CARDS (Red Foil)
SPECIAL CARDS: 6 HORRORGLOW CARDS
COMPLETE SET: £15.00
SINGLE CARDS: 15p
SINGLE SPECIAL CARDS: £6.00
Important Notes: A Gold Foil set of the 100 cards was available and is valued at approximately £75.00

VAMPIRELLA GALLERY

PRODUCER: TOPPS
ISSUE YEAR: 1995
CARD SET: 72 CARDS
SPECIAL CARDS: HOLOGRAM: £35.00
CHROME CARD: £6.00
72 PARALLEL GOLD CARDS: £1.00 each
COMPLETE SET: £15.00
SINGLE CARDS: 25p

WATERWORLD

PRODUCER: FLEER
ISSUE YEAR: 1995
CARD SET: 150 CARDS
SPECIAL CARDS:
DOUBLE FOIL CARD: £2.00
PRISMATIC FOIL CARD: £2.00
HOLOGRAM CARD: £2.00
COMPLETE SET: £15.00
SINGLE CARDS: 10p

WAYNE BARLOWE, THE ALIEN WORLD OF

PRODUCER: COMIC IMAGES
ISSUE YEAR: 1994
CARD SET: 90 CARDS
SPECIAL CARDS: 6 PRISM CARDS
COMPLETE SET: £8.00
SINGLE CARDS: 10p
SINGLE SPECIAL CARDS: £4.00

WCW WRESTLNG - YELLOW BORDER

PRODUCER: IMPEL
ISSUE YEAR: 1991
CARD SET: 160 CARDS
SPECIAL CARDS: No special cards
COMPLETE SET: £6.00
SINGLE CARDS: 10p

WCW WRESTLING - BLACK BORDER

PRODUCER: IMPEL
ISSUE YEAR: 1991
CARD SET: 110 CARDS
SPECIAL CARDS: No special cards
COMPLETE SET: £9.00
SINGLE CARDS: 15p

WILDC.A.T.S

PRODUCER: TOPPS U.S.
ISSUE YEAR: 1993
CARD SET: 100 CARDS
SPECIAL CARDS: 6 PRISM CARDS
CARD SET: £12.50
SINGLE CARDS: 15p
SINGLE SPECIAL CARDS £15.00

WILDC.A.T.S. ANIMATED

PRODUCER: WILDSTORM
ISSUE YEAR: 1995
CARD SET: 135 CARDS
SPECIAL CARDS: 9 ANIMATION CEL/ 9 FOIL ETCHED CARDS
COMPLETE SET: £17.00
SINGLE CARDS: 15p
SINGLE SPECIAL CARDS: £3.00

WILDC.A.T.S. CHROMIUM

PRODUCER: IMAGE
ISSUE YEAR: 1994
CARD SET: 96 CARDS
SPECIAL CARDS: 5 CHROME CAP SET £30.00
6 DOUBLE-SIDED CARD SET £20.00
12 PAINTED CARD SET £50.00
COMPLETE SET: £14.00
SINGLE CARDS: 15p

WILDSTORM

PRODUCER: WILDSTORM
ISSUE YEAR: 1994
CARD SET: 100 (Chromium) CARDS
SPECIAL CARDS: 9 HOLOCHROME CARDS
COMPLETE SET: £30.00
SINGLE CARDS: 30p
SINGLE SPECIAL CARDS: £6.00

WILDSTORM ARCHIVES

PRODUCER: WILDSTORM
ISSUE YEAR: 1995
CARD SET: 99 (Chromium) CARDS
SPECIAL CARDS: 11 GEN 13 HOLO-FOIL CARDS
COMPLETE SET: £20.00
SINGLE CARDS: 20p
SINGLE SPECIAL CARDS: £5.00

WILDSTORM GALLERY

PRODUCER: WILDSTORM
ISSUE YEAR: 1995
CARD SET: 126 CARDS
SPECIAL CARDS: 12 FAMOUS BATTLE/ 6 WILD STORM CHARACTER CARDS
COMPLETE SET: £20.00
SINGLE CARDS: 15p
SINGLE SPECIAL CARDS: £2.00 (Battles), £5.00 (Characters)

WILLIAM STOUT

PRODUCER: COMIC IMAGES
ISSUE YEAR: 1993
CARD SET: 90 CARDS
CARD SET: £8.00
SINGLE CARDS: 10p

WILLIAM STOUT II

PRODUCER: COMIC IMAGES
ISSUE YEAR: 1994
CARD SET: 90 CARDS
SPECIAL CARDS: 6 CHROME CHASE CARDS
COMPLETE SET: £7.50
SINGLE CARDS: 10p
SINGLE SPECIAL CARDS: £6.00

WIZARD. THE GUIDE TO COMICS PROMOTIONAL GIVEAWAY CARDS

PRODUCER: WIZARD
ISSUE YEAR: 1992
CARD SET: ON-GOING SERIES

CARD NO/DESCRIPTION		VALUE
#0	Youngblood (Prism border) Issued Wizard #11	£ 3.50
#1	Spawn (Prism border) Issued Wizard #12	£ 3.50
#1	gold*	£ 5.00
#2	Shadowhawk (Prism border) Issued Wizard #13	£ 3.50
#2	gold*	£ 5.00
#3	Savage Dragon (Prism border) Issued Wizard #14	£ 3.50
#3	gold*	£ 5.00
#4	Savage Dragon, Youngblood, Cyberforce, WildC.A.T.S. (Prism border) Issued Wizard #15	£ 3.50
#4	gold*	£ 5.00
#5	Spawn, Wetworks, Shadowhawk (Prism border) Issued Wizard #16	£ 3.50
#5	gold*	£ 5.00
#6	Cyberforce (Prism border) Issued Wizard #17	£ 3.50
#6	gold*	£ 5.00
#7	Jim Lee's WildC.A.T.S. (Prism border) Issued Wizard #18	£ 3.50
#7	gold*	£ 5.00
#8	Wetworks (Prism border) Issued Wizard #19	£ 3.50
nn	The Spirit by Will Eisner Issued with 100 Most Collectible Comics	£ 2.00

** sealed in plastic cases*

WOLVERINE: FROM THEN 'TIL NOW I

PRODUCER: COMIC IMAGES
ISSUE YEAR: 1988
CARD SET: 45 CARDS
SPECIAL CARDS: No special cards
COMPLETE SET: £12.00
SINGLE CARDS: 25p
Important Notes: Card #50 is scarcer in the U.K. than the rest and sells for about £2.00

WOLVERINE: FROM THEN 'TIL NOW II

PRODUCER: COMIC IMAGES
ISSUE YEAR: 1992
CARD SET: 90 CARDS
SPECIAL CARDS: 6 PRISM CARDS
COMPLETE SET: £40.00
SINGLE CARDS: 10p
SINGLE SPECIAL CARDS: £7.00

WWF BLACK SERIES - ENGLISH

PRODUCER: MERLIN PUBLISHING LTD
ISSUE YEAR: 1992
CARD SET: 150
COMPLETE SET: £20.00

SINGLE CARDS: 15p

Important Notes: The English language version of this series was only distributed in blister packs of 25 cards each through a limited number of retailers - WH Smith, John Menzies, Woolworth, Toys 'R Us.

WWF BLACK SERIES - GERMAN

PRODUCER: MERLIN PUBLISHING LTD
ISSUE YEAR: 1992
CARD SET: 150
COMPLETE SET: £25.00
SINGLE CARDS: 20p

WWF BLACK SERIES - ITALIAN

PRODUCER: MERLIN PUBLISHING LTD
ISSUE YEAR: 1992
CARD SET: 150
COMPLETE SET: £25.00
SINGLE CARDS: 20p

WWF "BRET HART" SERIES

PRODUCER: MERLIN PUBLISHING LTD
ISSUE YEAR: 1993
CARD SET: 92
COMPLETE SET: £30.00
SINGLE CARDS: 20p

Important Notes: German language only

WWF CLASSIC SERIES

PRODUCER: MERLIN PUBLISHING LTD
ISSUE YEAR: 1991
CARD SET: 150
COMPLETE SET: £20.00
SINGLE CARDS: 15p

Important Notes: First ever European WWF series. Produced as a co-edition from material originated by Classic cards in USA.

WWF GOLD SERIES PARTS 1 & 2

PRODUCER MERLIN PUBLISHING LTD
ISSUE YEAR: 1992
CARD SET: 96 + 96
COMPLETE SET: £30.00
SINGLE CARDS: 20p

Important Notes: The series was split into two parts to allow part publication prior to SummerSlam '92, a live event which filled Wembley Stadium with 85,000 fans. Part 2 contained some photographs of action from SummerSlam.

WWF WRESTLEMANIA III

PRODUCER: TOPPS U.S.
ISSUE YEAR: 1987
CARD SET: 75 CARDS
SPECIAL CARDS: 22 STICKERS
COMPLETE SET: £7.00
SINGLE CARDS: 10p
SINGLE SPECIAL CARDS: 15p

X-CUTIONERS SONG

PRODUCER: MARVEL/IMPEL
ISSUE YEAR: 1992
CARD SET: 12 CARDS
SPECIAL CARDS: No special cards
COMPLETE SET: £8.00
SINGLE CARDS: 50p

All cards issued free with the following comic books:

Card 1	X MEN #294	XAVIER
Card 2	X FACTOR #84	CALIBAN
Card 3	X MEN #14	APOCALYPSE
Card 4	X FORCE #16	CABLE
Card 5	X MEN #295	WOLVERINE/BISHOP
Card 6	X FACTOR #85	HAVOK/POLARIS
Card 7	X MEN #15	MUTANT LIBERATION
Card 8	X FORCE #17	MR SINISTER
Card 9	X MEN 296	JEAN GREY/CYCLOPS
Card 10	X FACTOR #86	MOONBOY
Card 11	X MEN #16	ARCHANGEL
Card 12	X FORCE #18	STRYFE/CABLE

X-FILES

PRODUCER: TOPPS
ISSUE YEAR: 1995
CARD SET: 72 CARDS
SPECIAL CARDS:
4 TOPPS FINEST CARD SET £40.00
6 COMIC COVER CARD SET: £60.00
DELUXE BINDER W/INSERT CARD: £9.00
COMPLETE SET: £15.00
SINGLE CARDS: 20p

X-FILES SERIES 2

PRODUCER: TOPPS
ISSUE YEAR: 1996
CARD SET: 72 CARDS

Ultra X-Men #6

SPECIAL CARDS: 72 FOIL
PARALLEL VERSION CARDS: £1.00 each
ETCHED-FOIL CARD: £6.00
HOLOGRAM CARD: £8.00
COMPLETE SET: £10.00
SINGLE CARDS: 15p

X-FILES SERIES 3

PRODUCER: TOPPS
ISSUE YEAR: 1996
CARD SET: 72 CARDS
SPECIAL CARDS: 6 FOIL CARDS: £5.00 each
2 HOLOGRAM CARDS: £5.00 each
2 HOLOCHROME CARDS: £4.00 each
COMPLETE SET: £8.00 - £10.00
SINGLE CARDS: 15p

Important Notes: Character cards are about three times the size of normal cards

X FORCE

PRODUCER: COMIC IMAGES
ISSUE YEAR: 1991
CARD SET: 90 CARDS
SPECIAL CARDS: No special cards
COMPLETE SET: £8.00
SINGLE CARDS: 10p

X FORCE MINI SET

PRODUCER: MARVEL/COMIC IMAGES
ISSUE YEAR: 1991
CARD SET: 5 CARDS
SPECIAL CARDS: No special cards
COMPLETE SET: £3.00
SINGLE CARDS: 50p, Cable card £1.00

Important Notes: These cards were issued within copies of X Force comic #1 1st printing

X MEN - JIM LEE

PRODUCER: COMIC IMAGES
ISSUE YEAR: 1991
CARD SET: 90 CARDS
COMPLETE SET: £8.00
SINGLE CARDS: 10p

X MEN - JIM LEE

PRODUCER: IMPEL
ISSUE YEAR: 1992
CARD SET: 100 CARDS
SPECIAL CARDS: 5 HOLOGRAMS
COMPLETE SET: £30.00
CARD SET ONLY: £12.50
SINGLE CARDS: 15p - 35p
SINGLE SPECIAL CARDS: H1, H2-£5.00; H3, H4-£4.00

X-MEN '95

PRODUCER: FLEER ULTRA
CARD SET: 150 CARDS
SPECIAL CARDS: 9 POWERBLAST/10 CHROMIUM
COMPLETE SET: £17.50
SINGLE CARDS: 15p
SINGLE SPECIAL CARDS: £2.00 (Powerblast), £5.00 (Chromium)

X-MEN '96

PRODUCER: FLEER
ISSUE YEAR: 1996
CARD SET: 100 CARDS
SPECIAL CARDS: 9 HOLOFOIL: £9.00
1 MORPH CARD/1 MIRAGE CARD/
1 MOTION CARD: £15.00-£20.00 each
COMPLETE SET: £17.50
SINGLE CARDS: 20p

X MEN, PREMIERE SERIES

PRODUCER: FLEER ULTRA
ISSUE YEAR: 1994
CARD SET: 150 CARDS
SPECIAL CARDS: 6 FATAL ATTRACTIONS CARDS AND 9 PORTRAITS CARDS
COMPLETE SET: £90.00
CARD SET ONLY £20.00
SINGLE CARDS: 10p - 30p
SINGLE FATAL CARDS: £6.00
SINGLE PORTRAITS CARDS: £4.00

X MEN II

PRODUCER: SKYBOX
ISSUE YEAR: 1993
CARD SET: 100 CARDS
SPECIAL CARDS: 3 COLOUR HOLOGRAMS, 9 FOIL STAMPED CARDS AND 1 H-X 3D WOLVERINE HOLOGRAM
COMPLETE SET: £80.00
CARD SET ONLY £12.00
SINGLE CARDS: 10p - 20p
COLOUR HOLOGRAMS: £8.00
FOIL STAMPED CARDS: £2.00
WOLVERINE H-X HOLOGRAM: £30.00
TIN SET: £40.00

X MEN ULTRA PRINTS

PRODUCER: FLEER
ISSUE YEAR: 1994
CARD SET: 5 PRINTS
SPECIAL CARDS: SEE ABOVE
COMPLETE SET: £10.00
SINGLE CARDS: N/A

Important Notes: One set of X Men Ultra prints were included free in each full case of Fleer Card boxes.

YO! RAPS - MTV

PRODUCER: PRO SET U.S.
ISSUE YEAR: 1992
CARD SET: 150 CARDS
SPECIAL CARDS: No special cards
COMPLETE SET: £7.00
SINGLE CARDS: 10p

YOUNGBLOOD

PRODUCER: COMIC IMAGES
ISSUE YEAR: 1992
CARD SET: 90 CARDS
SPECIAL CARDS: 6 PRISM CARDS
COMPLETE SET: £30.00
CARD SET ONLY: £5.00
SINGLE CARDS: 10p
SINGLE SPECIAL CARDS: £5.00

Important Notes: Image's first set of trading cards were produced on rather poor quality card and were simply pictures taken straight out of its comic book appearances. Prism cards are quite impressive

YOUNGBLOOD MASTER SERIES

PRODUCER: SKYBOX
ISSUE YEAR: 1995
CARD SET: 90 CARDS
SPECIAL CARDS: 9 STICKERS
COMPLETE SET: £10.00
SINGLE CARDS: 10p
SINGLE SPECIAL CARDS: £1.00

YOUNG INDIANA JONES CHRONICLES

PRODUCER: PRO-SET
ISSUE YEAR: 1992
CARD SET: 114 CARDS
COMPLETE SET: £15.00
SINGLE CARDS: 10p

Important Notes: The set breakdown is as follows: 95 TV Cards, 8 Hidden Treasure Crads, 10 3-D Cards and 1 Viewer Card.

BUBBLE GUM CARDS

with grateful thanks to RON HALL of First Choice Trading Cards for the extended information
First Choice Trading Cards 11 Keith Avenue Liverpool L4 5FL Tel (0831) 765 811).

INTRODUCTION

Bubble Gum cards are usually manufactured in 2 sizes 88mm x 63mm and 80mm x 55mm. The most prolific company in the 1960's was American and British Chewing Gum Ltd (A & BC GUM), owned by Topps Gum Inc., USA. Broadly speaking, US equivalent sets copyrighted Topps have a higher value. Other gum card companies included: Anglo Chewing Gum Ltd, Bubbles Inc. Chewing Gum (a subsidiary of A & BC Gum), Donruss (USA), Monty Gum (a Dutch company mainly active in the 1970's) and Somportex Ltd UK.

Sweet cigarette cards are normally, as tobacco cards, manufactured to the regimental size of 35mm x 65mm. An example of an exception to this rule is (Fireball) XL5 by Como. Companies that have issued popular sets include Barratt & Co. Ltd, Cadet Sweets, Como Confectionery Products Ltd and Primrose Confectionery Co. Ltd. A point to mention is that in this politically correct age, "Sweet Cigarettes" is now not allowed to be used as product terminology. On the occasions a product appears now, they are called "Candy Sticks".

Some sets, in particular A & BC Gum cards, vary in "finishing" ie. matt or shiny fronts. In normal circumstances this is of no consequence to collectors as differences are slight. However some sets do have obvious differences to their backs with strong distinction on colour. This is more important so colour matching sets are the order of the day!

Most card sets were/are manufactured in 2 separate sheets. Uncut sheets can command high prices although they are generally not in great demand. Cards that have been cut off-centre eg. wide border at the top of the card and picture pushed to the bottom edge of the card can detract from the price. Any card that has the picture incomplete with an adjacent card illustration showing is of very low value (note the difference to printing errors on comic books which can have a much higher value sometimes).

A first and foremost…you read it here! Also included here is a Price Guide to individual wrappers and packets that the cards were sold in. Bubble gum cards were usually sold in "wax packs" (an average of 6-8 in a packet) and a pack could be opened without damaging the wrapper. However, Somportex for example did issue most card sets in paper wrappers that were sealed at the edges so the packet had to be torn to remove that cards. A mint wrapper would therefore have to be an unopened pack! This would command a price 2-4 times that stated.

Sweet cigarette packets contained 1 card. Today's packets have the card printed on the box itself - no comment!

A few sets had an album exclusively produced. Prices stated for these is for Mint and Unused. The value of an exclusive album with the card set stuck down can vary widely depending on desirability of the set, the neatness of the sticking and personal choice. Cards that have been adhered to anything else or show clear signs of having once been, are of low value. It should be noted that card dealers usually charge double for Mint end numbers eg. Champions #1 and #45 at £4.00 each. This is because a large number of cards collected would be kept in number order with the end numbers being handled constantly and usually the cards were held together with an elastic band thus putting a strain on the edges.

Finally, the years stated are, where available, copyright dated on the card or packaging. Values for cards and sets are for those graded in EXCELLENT condition or NEAR MINT condition, that is, cards without any creases, dents, marks or rounded corners, nearly perfect in every way.

While some sets (Stingray (Cadet Sweets) or UFO (Barratt) turn up in MINT condition fairly regularly, most of the sets listed below (and particularly the older ones) can command more than the listed price should they be found in genuine MINT condition.

ADDAMS FAMILY

PRODUCER: DONRUSS
ISSUE YEAR: 1964
CARD SET: 66
COMPLETE SET: £250.00
SINGLE CARDS: £3.50
WRAPPER: £35.00

Important Notes: With the success of the Addams Family movies, this rare set is now sought after. Issued in USA only. Fronts are black and white photos and backs are photo composites.

BATMAN (Pink Back, Fan Club Panel)

PRODUCER: A & BC GUM
ISSUE YEAR: 1966
CARD SET: 55
COMPLETE SET: £80.00
SINGLE CARDS: £1.50
WRAPPER: £25.00

BATMAN (Pink Back, no Fan Club Panel)

PRODUCER: A & BC GUM
ISSUE YEAR: 1966
CARD SET: 55
COMPLETE SET: £55.00
SINGLE CARDS: £1.00
WRAPPER: £25.00

BATMAN A SET

PRODUCER: A & BC GUM
ISSUE YEAR: 1966
CARD SET: 44
COMPLETE SET: £55.00
SINGLE CARDS: £1.25
WRAPPER: £25.00

Important Notes: the letter A appears after the number on the back which, like the B set, makes up a larger jigsaw picture of Batman, Robin and other characters.

BATMAN B SET

PRODUCER: A & BC GUM
ISSUE YEAR: 1966
CARD SET: 44
COMPLETE SET: £110.00
SINGLE CARDS: £2.50
WRAPPER: £25.00

Important Notes: This B set is much scarcer than the A set. Backs also make up a larger picture composite.

BATMAN (Black Back)

PRODUCER: A & BC GUM
ISSUE YEAR: 1966
CARD SET: 38
COMPLETE SET: £75.00
SINGLE CARDS: £2.00

Important Notes: A secret decoder was included in each packet, used to decipher the Riddlers Riddles on the back. These are very rare and can fetch £10-£12 each for an excellent condition example. The fronts show colour photos fron the 1966 feature film.

BATMAN (Black Back, Dutch)

PRODUCER: A & BC GUM
ISSUE YEAR: 1966
CARD SET: 38
COMPLETE SET: £115.00
SINGLE CARDS: £3.00

Important Notes: As with the above, the cards featured scenes from the feature film. Backs of cards different to UK issue (different Riddler drawing, no Decoder message).

BATMAN (Number on front)

PRODUCER: A & BC GUM
ISSUE YEAR: 1966
CARD SET: 55
COMPLETE SET: £110.00
SINGLE CARDS: £2.00
WRAPPER: £30.00

Important Notes: These cards show scenes from the Batman TV series and the Batman 1966 movie including the famous rubber shark and anti-Bat shark repellent! Backs comprise of separate picture composites. The printing on this set often shows colour imperfections. Note also a BATMAN ALBUM which could house any of the above Batman sets, valued at about £40.00 in Near Mint unused condition.

BATTLE

PRODUCER: A & BC GUM
ISSUE YEAR: 1966
CARD SET: 73
COMPLETE SET: £75.00
SINGLE CARDS: £1.00
WRAPPER: £20.00

Important Notes: As with the Civil War News set, these were particularly violent and occasionally brutal cards and are highly collectible. This set had a check card which listed all the numbers of the set and they are often filled in or ticked off. Unmarked check cards are very scarce and would add £10 to the value of the set. There are two variations of the check cardas #32, 39, 42 and 44 were eventually withdrawn owing to excessive torture and violence. There are 2 variations of backs, the common being dark brown borders, the scarcer being light brown. Backs contain Headline Reports.

Note also:
MILITARY EMBLEMS. Set of 24 stickers (card size), one available in each packet.
COMPLETE SET: £60.00

BATTLE OF BRITAIN

PRODUCER: A & BC GUM
ISSUE YEAR: 1969
CARD SET: 66
COMPLETE SET: £82.50
SINGLE CARDS: £1.25
WRAPPER: £20.00

Important Notes: fronts show colour photos from the 1969 film. Backs contain Daily Mirror newspaper reports from 1940.

BEATLES (Black & white)

PRODUCER: A & BC GUM
ISSUE YEAR: 1964
CARD SET: 60
COMPLETE SET: £150.00
SINGLE CARDS: £2.50
WRAPPER: £35.00

Important Notes: black and white photos with individual signatiures. Although this set was produced in large quantitles, mint sets are not common.

BEATLES (2nd Series)

PRODUCER: A & BC GUM
ISSUE YEAR: 1965
CARD SET: 45
COMPLETE SET: £225.00
SINGLE CARDS: £5.00
WRAPPER: £45.00

Important Notes: This set carried on the numbering from the 1st Series as card numbers 61-105.

BEATLES (Colour)

PRODUCER: A & BC GUM
ISSUE YEAR: 1965
CARD SET: 40
COMPLETE SET: £200.00
SINGLE CARDS: £5.00
WRAPPER: £45.00

Important Notes: new series of colour photographs. Odds are not to be confused with the Top Pop Stars set of 50 from 1964 which includes 1-22 of The Beatles which state "in a series of 50 photos".

BEATLES (Yellow Submarine)

PRODUCER: ANGLO CONFECTIONERY LTD
ISSUE YEAR: 1968
CARD SET: 66
COMPLETE SET: £420.00
SINGLE CARDS: £6.25
WRAPPER: £60.00

Important Notes: Picture back composite. A very rare and collectible cult set, particularly as it was unissued in the USA.

BEATLES (Yellow Submarine)

PRODUCER: PRIMROSE CONFECTIONERY LTD
ISSUE YEAR: 1968
CARDS SET: 50
COMPLETE SET: £115.00
SINGLE CARDS: £2.25
PACKET: £35.00

Important Notes: sweet cigarettes set. Variation on the above gum card set, backs of cards containing a storyline.

CAPTAIN SCARLET & THE MYSTERONS

PRODUCER: ANGLO CONFECTIONERY LTD
ISSUE YEAR: 1967
CARD SET: 66
COMPLETE SET: £115.00
SINGLE CARDS: £1.75
WRAPPER: £20.00

Important Notes: This set is becoming more and more collectible with the current screening of the TV series. The cards are a mixture of scenes from the series and line drawings. The backs of the cards made up a giant collage picture of all the characters and machines. This composite picture could be obtained as a poster made of card via mail order. It is very rare and valued at £70.00.

CAPTAIN SCARLET

PRODUCER: BARRATT & CO. LTD
ISSUE YEAR: 1967
CARD SET: 50
COMPLETE SET: £55.00
SINGLE CARDS: £1.10
PACKET: £15.00

Important Notes: a sweet cigarette set which is rising rapidly in price.

CAPTAIN SCARLET

PRODUCER: EDWARD SHARP & SONS
ISSUE YEAR: 1970
CARD SET: 20
COMPLETE SET: £75.00
SINGLE CARDS: £3.75

Important Notes: Re-issue of the character photos taken from the Barratt set. Also include 5 vehicle cards which are drawings which are not so sharp unlike the producer! 3 sides of the card are serrated as these were given out separately from the toffee. Although a scarce set, it is for completists only.

CHAMPIONS

PRODUCER: A & BC GUM
ISSUE YEAR: 1969
CARD SET: 45
COMPLETE SET: £90.00
SINGLE CARDS: £2.00
WRAPPER: £25.00

Important Notes: These cards show colour photos from the TV series. The female star Alexander Bastedo adds to the desirability of this set. As with the Batman Black Backs, each pack had a secret decoder in order to answer the general knowledge questions on the back. Slightly different, these are harder to find and in top shape can fetch £20 or add £20 to the value of the set.

CIVIL WAR NEWS

PRODUCER: A & BC GUM
ISSUE YEAR: 1965
CARD SET: 88
COMPLETE SET: £110.00
SINGLE CARDS: £1.25
WRAPPER: £20.00

Important Notes: As these cards were particularly gory, they were banned in some parts of the UK.
The backs contain headline reports from 1861 –1865. One of 15 Civil War Bank notes were also available in certain packets and these fetch £3.00 each. The denominations were as follows: 2 x $1.00, 2 x $2.00, 2 x $5.00, 2 x $10.00, 2 x $20.00, 2 x $50.00, 1 x $100.00, 1 x $500.00 and 1 x $1,000.00.

CLIFF RICHARD

PRODUCER: LEAF SALES CONFECTIONERY LTD
ISSUE YEAR: 1960
CARD SET: £50.00
COMPLETE SET: £115.00
SINGLE CARDS: £2.25
PACKET: No price available

Important Notes: Black and white photos. Company and copyright not stated on the cards.

COMIC BOOK FOLDEES

PRODUCER: A & BC GUM
ISSUE YEAR: 1968
CARD SET: 43
COMPLETE SET: £65.00
SINGLE CARDS: £1.50
WRAPPER: £25.00

Important Notes: Originally produced as a 44 issue set, one featuring the Queen was banned but it occasionally turns up. This one fetches up to £20. They were not cards as such but two comedy pictures and one DC Super-hero and each outer picture folded in half with the third to form weird and wonderful combinations. Near Mint condition would mean that they would have to be unfolded and completely flat. Also, the original display box tends to turn up with reasonable frequency, some think after a quantity warehouse find.

COMBAT

PRODUCER: SELMUR
ISSUE YEAR: 1963
CARD SET: 66
COMPLETE SET: £100.00
SINGLE CARDS: £1.50
WRAPPER: £20.00

Important Notes: Black and white photos from TV series. Issued in the USA only. A 2nd series in the same year was also produced.

DANGER MAN, JOHN DRAKE

PRODUCER: SOMPORTEX LTD
ISSUE YEAR: 1966
CARD SET: 72
COMPLETE SET: £180.00
SINGLE CARDS: £2.50
WRAPPER: £20.00

Important Notes: A very scarce set with scenes from the TV series starring Patrick McGoohan. Black and white.

DOCTOR WHO ADVENTURE

PRODUCER: T. WALL & SON
ISSUE YEAR: 1966
CARD SET: 36
COMPLETE SET: £65.00
SINGLE CARDS: £1.75
WRAPPER (Ice lolly): £65.00
ALBUM: £75.00

Important Notes: Colour art. This set was being produced at the time of Patrick Troughton taking over from William Hartnell in the TV series. The drawings of Hartnell on the front were changed at the last minute but the backs with Hartnell headers are unchanged!

DOCTOR WHO AND THE DALEKS

PRODUCER: CADET SWEETS
ISSUE YEAR: 1965
CARD SET: 50
COMPLETE SET: £125.00
SINGLE CARDS: £2.50
PACKET: £45.00

Important Notes: Although this set does not depict William Hartnell but rather a non-descript grey-haired character, the superb artwork which is compatible with the subject makes this set very desirable so expect a steady increase.

DOCTOR WHO AND THE DALEKS

PRODUCER: GOODIES LTD
ISSUE YEAR: 1968
CARD SET: 50
COMPLETE SET: £200.00
SINGLE CARDS: £4.00
PACKET: No price available.

Important Notes: Much scarcer re-issue set of the Cadet Sweets series.

DOCTOR WHO

PRODUCER: WEETABIX
ISSUE YEAR: 1977
CARD SET: 24
COMPLETE SET £48.00
SINGLE CARDS: £1.50
SOURCE: issued inside the cereal packets

Important Notes: Double-sided: colour photographs/ art.

DOCTOR WHO, THE AMAZING WORLD OF

PRODUCER: TYPHOO TEA
ISSUE UEAR: 1976
CARD SET: 12
COMPLETE SET: 24
SINGLE CARDS: £2.00

Important Notes: Colour photo portraits of Doctor Who and assorted villains. The cards were hexagonal! Reprint imitations have been known.

ELVIS PRESLEY

PRODUCER: A & BC GUM
ISSUE YEAR: 1959
CARD SET: 66
COMPLETE SET: £630.00
SINGLE CARDS: £9.50
WRAPPER: £100.00

Important Notes: Hand coloured photographs.

FIREBALL XL5

PRODUCER: COMO CONFECTIONERY PRODUCTS LTD
ISSUE YEAR: 1964
CARD SET: 26
COMPLETE SET: £260.00
SINGLE CARDS: £10.00
PACKET: £35.00

Important Notes: Square cards measuring 65mm x 65mm. The cards were titled simply "XL5" while the packets were fully titled "Fireball XL5".

FIREBALL XL5

PRODUCER: COMO CONFECTIONERY PRODUCTS LTD
ISSUE YEAR: 1965
CARDS SET: 26
COMPLETE SET: £290.00
SINGLE CARDS: £11.00
ALBUM: £100.00

Important Notes: Very scarce, especially as a set. The numbering continued from the 1st series as #27-52. The format size is the same as the above. XL5 was not a big seller as the cards were issued after the initial screening of the TV series thus all the XL5 cards are very scarce. Note also: a smaller card of the above two series was issued in bags of "dolly mixture" type sweets. They are very scarce and single cards and sets would be valued at approximately 10%-15% more than the sweet cigarette prices.

GIRL FROM U.N.C.L.E., THE

PRODUCER: A & BC GUM
ISSUE YEAR: 1967
CARD SET: 25
COMPLETE SET: £50.00
SINGLE CARDS: £2.00
WRAPPER: £25.00

Important Notes: colour photos. Titled cards (un-numbered)

GREEN HORNET

PRODUCER: DONRUSS
ISSUE YEAR: 1966
CARD SET: 44
COMPLETE SET: £132.00
SINGLE CARDS: £3.00
WRAPPER: £45.00

Important Notes: Colour photos. Issued in USA only.

HIGH CHAPARRAL, THE

PRODUCER: A & BC GUM
ISSUE YEAR: 1969
CARD SET: 36
COMPLETE SET: £30.00
SINGLE CARDS: 85p
WRAPPER: £15.00

Important Notes: Colour photos. Composite picture backs.

HUCK FINN

PRODUCER: A & BC GUM
ISSUE YEAR: 1969
CARD SET: 55
COMPLETE SET: £25.00
SINGLE CARDS: 45p
WRAPPER: £15.00

Important Notes: Colour photos/art. 2 different copyrights stated: ILAMI 1968 and 1968 HANNA-BARBERA PRODUCTIONS INC.

JAMES BOND (Film Scene Series)

PRODUCER: SOMPORTEX LTD
ISSUE YEAR: 1965
CARD SET: 60
COMPLETE SET: £150.00
SINGLE CARDS: £2.50
WRAPPER: £25.00

Important Notes: Black and white photos depicting mainly scantily clad females!

JAMES BOND (Thunderball)

PRODUCER: SOMPORTEX LTD
ISSUE YEAR: 1967
CARD SET: 72
COMPLETE SET: £75.00
SINGLE CARDS: £1.00
WRAPPER (Paper): £25.00

Important Notes: These cards feature black & white scenes from the 4th Bond film Thunderball. There are five numbers that were issued with two different photos including numbers 15, 24 and 51. Number 24 was withdrawn as it depicted Bond about to punch a girl but it is not too difficult to obtain.

JAMES BOND, THE EXCITING WORLD OF

PRODUCER: SOMPORTEX LTD
ISSUE YEAR: 1966
CARD SET: 50
COMPLETE SET: £137.50
SINGLE CARDS: £2.75
WRAPPER: £35.00

Important Notes: Black and white photos.

Batman (Number on Front Series) #10

Captain Scarlet #64

James Bond (Thunderball) #14

JAMES BOND - YOU ONLY LIVE TWICE

PRODUCER: SOMPORTEX LTD
ISSUE YEAR: 1969
SLIDE SET: 26
COMPLETE SET £210.00
SLIDE STRIP: £8.00
WRAPPER (Paper) £18.00

Important Notes: Not cards but small colour film slides joined in strips of three individually numbered #1-72. Individual mounts were available by sending away a postal order for 1 shilling (5p) and Special Agent 007 Viewers by sending a postal order for 3 shillings and sixpence (17.5p). In order to mount and view the slides, the strips of three had to be cut. The price quoted is for un-cut strips.

JAMES BOND - THE NEW JAMES BOND 007: O.H.M.S.S.

PRODUCER: ANGLO CONFECTIONERY LTD
ISSUE YEAR: 1969
CARD SET: 56
COMPLETE SET: £170.00
SINGLE CARDS: £3.00
WRAPPER: £30.00

Important Notes: Unlike previous the Somportex sets featuring Sean Connery, this series featutres George Lazenby (and Diana Rigg).

JOE 90

PRODUCER: ANGLO CONFECTIONERY LTD
ISSUE YEAR: 1968
CARD SET: 66
COMPLETE SET: £115.00
SINGLE CARDS: £1.75
WRAPPER: £20.00

Important Notes: Colour photos/art. A scarce set that may rise in value as the TV series is now being repeated on cable/satellite. The composite picture on the backs of the cards like the Captain Scarlet set by Anglo could be purchased as a poster made of card and is similarly valued at £70.00.

JOE 90

PRODUCER: PRIMROSE CONFECTIONERY LTD
ISSUE YEAR: 1968
CARD SET: 50
COMPLETE SET: £45.00
SINGLE CARDS: 90p
PACKET: £20.00

Important Notes: Sets produced on paper-thin card are much more common than the standard thickness cards. These inferior sets were probably produced after the initial release.

KUNG FU

PRODUCER: A & BC GUM
ISSUE YEAR: 1974
CARD SET: £60.00
COMPLETE SET: £33.00
SINGLE CARDS: 55p
WRAPPER: £6.00

Important Notes: Colour photos of David Carradine series which may experience renewed interest with the updated new TV series in USA about to air in the U.K.. Nos. 1-44 have two different composite pictures: Picture A and Picture B. Other backs have the history of Kung Fu, references to the TV series and diagrams on the art of Kung Fu which state: "CAUTION: Do not use Caine's combat techniques without professional training".

LAND OF THE GIANTS

PRODUCER: A & BC GUM
ISSUE YEAR: 1969
CARD SET: 55
COMPLETE SET: £165.00
SINGLE CARDS: £3.00
WRAPPER: £25.00

Important Notes: A scarce set that has risen in value owing to the recent screening of the TV series on cable/satellite. The check card is often marked or ticked and an unmarked one is vakued more highly. The backs depict a small cartoon strip and a small composite picture.

LEGEND OF CUSTER, THE

PRODUCER: A & BC GUM
ISSUE YEAR: 1965
CARD SET: 54
COMPLETE SET: £40.00
SINGLE CARDS: 75p
WRAPPER: £12.00

Important Notes: Colour photos from TV series. The first 22 backs have spaces for colour, drawn Indian Chief Stamps, one included in each pack. Set of 22 unused stamps: £60.00.

MAN FROM U.N.C.L.E., THE (see U.N.C.L.E.)

PRODUCER: A & BC GUM
ISSUE YEAR: 1966
CARD SET: 55
COMPLETE SET: £55.00
SINGLE CARDS: £1.00
WRAPPER: £20.00

Important Notes: This set features black & white scenes and publicity stills from the series, "signed" by Robert Vaughan and David McCallum on the front. Composite picture backs. These cards were produced on 2 different types of card: one was more yellowy, giving an "aged" look and one was white, giving a "fresher" look. The yellower cards would be valued as a set at about £40.00.

MARS ATTACKS

PRODUCER: BUBBLES INC
ISSUE YEAR: 1965
CARD SET: 55
COMPLETE SET: £825.00
SINGLE CARDS: £15.00
WRAPPER: £175.00
REPRINT SET (copyright TOPPS): £30.00

Important Notes: A very rare set and infamous in the 1960s for being particularly gory and consequently banned. The check card is often filled in. An untouched one would make the complete set worth in the region of £850.00.

MONKEES, THE

PRODUCER: A & BC GUM
ISSUE YEAR: 1967
CARD SET: 55
COMPLETE SET: £50.00
SINGLE CARDS: £.90
WRAPPER: £20.00

Important Notes: A particularly cult set based on the TV series. There is a colour set with different photographs available though with no discernible difference in price. Both sets have composite picture backs.

MONKEES HIT SONGS, THE

PRODUCER: A & BC GUM
ISSUE YEAR: 1967
CARD SET: 30
COMPLTETE SET: £37.50
SINGLE CARDS: £1.25
WRAPPER: £25.00

Important Notes: Colour photographs.Each card back has the lyrics to a Monkees song. Also stated on the back, including #27-30, is "Collect all 26"!

MONKEES, THE (1st Series)

PRODUCER: GOODIES LTD
ISSUE YEAR: 1967
CARD SET: 25
COMPLETE SET: £19.00
SINGLE CARDS: 75p
PACKET: £25.00

Important Notes: Black and white photos.

MONKEES, THE (2nd Series)

PRODUCER: GOODIES LTD
IISUE YEAR: 1968
CARD SET: 25
COMPLETE SET: £62.50
SINGLE CARDS: £2.50
PACKET: £25.00

Important Notes: A scarcer set of black and white photos.

MUNSTERS, THE

PRODUCER: DONRUSS
ISSUE YEAR: 1964
CARD SET: 72
COMPLETE SET: £215.00
SINGLE CARDS: £3.00
WRAPPER: £35.00

Important Notes: Comey captions below photgraphs from the TV series.

OUTER LIMITS, THE

PRODUCER: A & BC GUM
ISSUE YEAR: 1966
CARD SET: 50
COMPLETE SET: £125.00
SINGLE CARDS: £2.50
WRAPPER: £50.00

Important Notes: Based on the TV series, these feature weird and wonderful schlock horror monsters.

PARTRIDGE FAMILY, THE

PRODUCER: A & BC GUM
ISSUE YEAR: 1971
CARD SET: 55
COMPLETE SET: £22.00
SINGLE CARDS: 40p
WRAPPER: £8.00

Important Notes: Colour photos with composite picture backs.

PLANET OF THE APES

PRODUCER: A & BC GUM
ISSUE YEAR: 1968
CARD SET: 44
COMPLETE SET: £82.50
SINGLE CARDS: £1.50
WRAPPER: £20.00

Important Notes: Colour photos from first film. Backs contain storyline.

PLANET OF THE APES

PRODUCER: TOPPS
ISSUE YEAR: 1974
CARD SET: 66
COMPLETE SET: £33.00
SINGLE CARDS: 50p
WRAPPER: £8.00

Important Notes: Colour photos from TV series (recently shown on cable/satellite TV). Backs contain story and separate composite pictures.

ROBIN HOOD – A BOMBSHELL FOR THE SHERRIFF

PRODUCER: MASTER VENDING CO.
ISSUE YEAR: 1959
CARD SET: 25
COMPLETE SET: £22.50
SINGLE CARDS: 90p
WRAPPER: £15.00

Important Notes: Colour art. 2 different backs: dark grey and beige.

ROLLING STONES

PRODUCER: A & BC GUM
ISSUE YEAR: 1965
CARD SET: 40
COMPLETE SET: £250.00
SINGLE CARDS: £6.00
WRAPPER: £45.00

Important Notes: Colour photos. Unissued in USA. Backs state: "..in a series of 40 photos". This therefore should not be confused with TOP POP STARS series of 40 as there are no Stones cards in that particular set.

QUICK DRAW McGRAW

PRODUCER: PRIMROSE CONFECTIONERY LTD
ISSUE YEAR: 1965
CARD SET (Q1): 50
COMPLETE SET: £15.00
SINGLE CARDS: 30p
PACKET: £12.00
ALBUM: £40.00

Important Notes: Based on Hanna Barbera cartoon.

THE SAINT

PRODUCER: SOMPORTEX LTD
ISSUE YEAR: 1967
CARD SET: 72
COMPLETE SET: £220.00
SINGLE CARDS: £3.00
WRAPPER (Paper): £25.00

Important Notes: One of the rarest 60s gum card sets. Black and white photos.

SEA HUNT, T.V's

PRODUCER: BARRATT & CO. LTD
ISSUE YEAR: 1961
CARD SET: 35
COMPLETE SET: £65.00
SINGLE CARDS: £1.80
PACKET: £12.00
ALBUM: £20.00

Important Notes: Colour art of TV series.

SECRET SERVICE

PRODUCER: BARRATT & CO. LTD
ISSSUE YEAR: 1970
CARD SET: 50
COMPLETE SET: £45.00
SINGLE CARDS: 90p
PACKET: £25.00

Important Notes: Colour photos from Gerry Anderson puppet/live action TV series. Rarely seen on television, a screening would do much to popularise this set.

SPACE 1999

PRODUCER: BASSETT
ISSUE YEAR: 1975
CARD SET: 50
COMPLETE SET: £30.00
SINGLE CARDS: 40p
CARD NO. 42: £10.00
PACKET: £12.00

Important Notes: Card No. 42 was given a low distribution owing to the fact that it displayed face disfigurement. It was eventually withdrawn. Set without #42: £25.00

SPACE 1999

PRODUCER: LYONS MAID
ISSUE YEAR: 1975
CARD SET: 25
COMPLETE SET: £37.50
SINGLE CARDS: £1.50
WRAPPER (Ice lolly): £20.00

Important Notes: Colour art.

SPACE 1999

PRODUCER: DONRUSS
ISSUE YEAR: 1976
CARD SET: 66
COMPLETE SET: £36.00
SINGLE CARDS: 55p
WRAPPER: £4.00

Important Notes: Colour photos with picture composite backs.

SPACE ALPHA 1999

PRODUCER: MONTY GUM (Dutch)
ISSUE YEAR: 1976
CARD SET: 64
COMPLETE SET: £20.00
SINGLE CARDS: 30p
WRAPPER: £8.00

Important Notes: Small gum cards with colour photos dominated by title.

SPACE COSMO 1999

PRODUCER: MONTY GUM (Dutch)
ISSUE YEAR: 1976
CARD SET: 64
COMPLETE SET: £20.00
SINGLE CARDS: 30p
WRAPPER: £8.00

Important Notes: Same format as "Alpha" set.

SPACE 1999

PRODUCER: SUNICREST (New Zealand)
ISSUE YEAR: 1974
CARD SET: 50
COMPLETE SET: £87.50
SINGLE CARDS: £1.75

Important Notes: Issued in Australia/New Zealand only from bread packets.

STAR TREK

PRODUCER: A & BC GUM
ISSUE YEAR: 1969
CARD SET: 55
COMPLETE SET: £330.00
SINGLE CARDS: £6.00
WRAPPER: £35.00

Important Notes: Scenes from the TV series make this a particularly popular set, especially with all the recent Star Trek sets to come out in the wake of the 30th Anniversary.

STAR TREK

PRODUCER: LYONS MAID
ISSUE YEAR: 1979
CARD SET: 25
COMPLETE SET: £65.00
SINGLE CARDS: £2.50
WRAPPER (Ice lolly): £15.00
CHART (folded): £10.00

Important Notes: Colour photos from first Star Trek film.

STAR TREK

PRODUCER: WEETABIX
ISSUE YEAR: 1979
CARD SET: 18
COMPLETE SET: £36.00

Important Notes: Double-sided: colour photos from the first film with art. Came in the cereal packet. 3 x 6 cards to a strip. £12.00 per strip. Separated cards at 50p each.

STINGRAY

PRODUCER: CADET SWEETS
ISSUE YEAR: 1964
CARD SET: 50
COMPLETE SET: £30.00
SINGLE CARDS: 60p
PACKET: £15.00
ALBUM: £85.00

Important Notes: Colour art though many feel the drawings are only average.

SUPERCAR (1st Series)

PRODUCER: COMO CONFECTIONERY PRODUCTS LTD
ISSUE YEAR: 1962
CARD SET: 25
COMPLETE SET: £87.50
SINGLE CARDS: £3.50
PACKET: £40.00

Important Notes: Colour photos and art - some combined.

SUPERCAR (2nd Series)

PRODUCER: COMO CONFECTIONERY PRODUCTS LTD
ISSUE YEAR: 1962
CARD SET: 25
COMPLETE SET: £62.50
SINGLE CARDS: £2.50

Important Notes: Colour art only, numbered 26-50.

SUPERMAN IN THE JUNGLE

PRODUCER: A & BC GUM
ISSUE YEAR: 1968
CARD SET: 66
COMPLETE SET: £82.50
SINGLE CARDS: £1.25
WRAPPER: £30.00

Important Notes: Selected packs contained jig-saw pieces. There were 16 in all and made up a picture of Superman wrestling with a lion. These pieces are very rare and fetch up to £3.00 each.

TARZAN

PRODUCER: ANGLO CONFECTIONERY LTD
ISSUE YEAR: 1966
CARD SET: 66
COMPLETE SET: £33.00
SINGLE CARDS: £0.50
WRAPPER: £20.00

Important Notes: Cards 15 & 16 are unusually scarce. Don't know why! The artwork is fairly primitive, based on the Ron Ely TV series. Backs make up a single composite picture of Tarzan and family.

THUNDERBIRDS (Black & white)

PRODUCER: SOMPORTEX LTD
ISSUE YEAR: 1966
CARD SET: 72
COMPLETE SET: £165.00
SINGLE CARDS: £2.25
WRAPPER: £20.00

Important Notes: Card size 88mm x 63mm. Black and white photos, composite picture backs. Although not scarce, this set rarely turns up in truly mint condition.

THUNDERBIRDS (Black and White)

PRODUCER: SOMPORTEX LTD
ISSUE YEAR: 1966
CARD SET: 72
COMPLETE SET: £180.00
SINGLE CARDS: £2.50
WRAPPER: £30.00

Important Notes: Same series as above but card size is 76mm x 57mm (varying) and photos are grainy (dot matrix).

THUNDERBIRDS (Colour)

PRODUCER: SOMPORTEX LTD
ISSUE YEAR: 1967
CARD SET: 73 (strange number?!)
COMPLETE SET: £200.00
SINGLE CARDS: £2.75
WRAPPER: £25.00

Important Notes: These cards were slightly smaller than the black & white set. They are sometimes assumed to have been trimmed when directly compared.

THUNDERBIRDS

PRODUCER: BARRATT & CO. LTD
ISSUE YEAR: 1965
CARD SET: 50
COMPLETE SET: £125.00
SINGLE CARDS: £2.50
PACKET: £20.00

Important Notes: Colour art.

THUNDERBIRDS

PRODUCER: BARRATT & CO. LTD
ISSUE YEAR: 1966
CARD SET: 50
COMPLETE SET: £45.00
SINGLE CARDS: 90p
PACKET: £20.00
ALBUM: £90.00

Important Notes: Colour photos. Although not as scarce, this set should increase more in line with the first series owing to popularity and the fact the set shows scenes from the TV series. Time will tell.

TOP POP STARS

PRODUCER: A & BC GUM
ISSUE YEAR: 1964
CARD SET: 50
COMPLETE SET: £125.00
SINGLE CARDS: BEATLES: £2.75
OTHERS: £2.25
WRAPPER: £35.00

Important Notes: Colour photos. Most cards have colour print errors (out of sync.)

TOP POP STARS

PRODUCER: A & BC GUM
ISSUE YEAR: 40
COMPLETE SET: £100.00
SINGLE CARDS: £2.50
WRAPPER: £40.00

Important Notes: Colour photos. Different to the above. A scarce set.

TV WESTERNS

PRODUCER: A & BC GUM
ISSUE YEAR: 1958
CARD SET: 56
COMPLETE SET: £84.00
SINGLE CARDS: £1.50
WRAPPER: £45.00

Important Notes: Colour photos. Most have colour print imperfections. Stars featured include Robert Horton, Dale Robertson, John Payne (not Wayne!), Steve McQueen etc. The are two different backs: light grey and dark grey.

U.F.O.

PRODUCER: ANGLO CONFECTIONERY LTD
ISSUE YEAR: 1970
CARD SET: 64
COMPLETE SET: £50.00
SINGLE CARDS: £0.75
WRAPPER: £25.00

Important Notes: These cards are a mixture of scenes from the Gerry Anderson TV series and line drawings. The backs make up a large collage picture of U.F.O. characters and machines. As with Captain Scarlet and Joe 90, this picture could be purchased as a poster made of card via mail order offer. It is scarcer/more sought after and would be valued at £125.00.

U.F.O.

PRODUCER: BARRATT & CO. LTD
ISSUE YEAR: 1970
CARD SET: 70
COMPLETE SET: £45.00
SINGLE CARDS: 65p
PACKET: £15.00

Important Notes: Colour photographs.

U.F.O.

PRODUCER: BASSETT
ISSUE YEAR: 1975
CARD SET: 70
COMPLETE SET: £14.00
SINGLE CARDS: 20p
PACKET: £15.00

Important Notes: Re-issue of Barratt set. Not usually sold in odds as there are a quantity of mint sets in circulation.

U.N.C.L.E.

PRODUCER: CADET SWEETS
ISSUE YEAR: 1966
CARD SET: 50
COMPLETE SET: £50.00
SINGLE CARDS: 90p
PACKET: £18.00

Important Notes: Colour photos. There is also a colour art set by the same company and same number of cards. Card Set: £112.50, Single Cards: £2.25.

VOYAGE TO THE BOTTOM OF THE SEA

PRODUCER: DONRUSS
ISSUE YEAR: 1964
CARD SET: 66
COMPLETE SET: £100.00
SINGLE CARDS: £1.25
WRAPPER: £25.00

Important Notes: Black and white photos with blue backs. There is a reprint set with black and white backs. The photos are of poor quality.

WAR BULLETIN

PRODUCER: P.C.G.C.
ISSUE YEAR: 1965
CARD SET: 88
COMPLETE SET: £110.00
SINGLE CARDS: £1.25
WRAPPER: £35.00

Important Notes: Black and white action photographs from World War 2. Backs contain war headlines.

YOGI BEAR, T.V's

PRODUCER: BARRATT & CO. LTD
ISSUE YEAR: 1968
CARD SET: 35
COMPLETE SET: £70.00
SINGLE CARDS: £2.00
PACKET: £15.00

Important Notes: Black/yellow/white drawings, including Huckleberry Hound.

ZORRO

PRODUCER: TOPPS
ISSUE YEAR: 1958
CARD SET: 88
COMPLETE SET: £220.00
SINGLE CARDS: £2.50
WRAPPER: £65.00

Important Notes: Issued in the USA. There is also a Canadian set with photos produced with different backs.

A & BC GUM UNIVERSAL ALBUMS:

Blue/Grey: £6.00
Red/Orange: £12.00

These can house up to 96 cards. The spaces have slots so adhesive is not used. There is also a Red/Grey version, housing 80 cards at £5.00.

BARRATT/GOODIES LTD UNIVERSAL ALBUMS

These can house up to 80 cards and would be valued in Near Mint at £5.00.

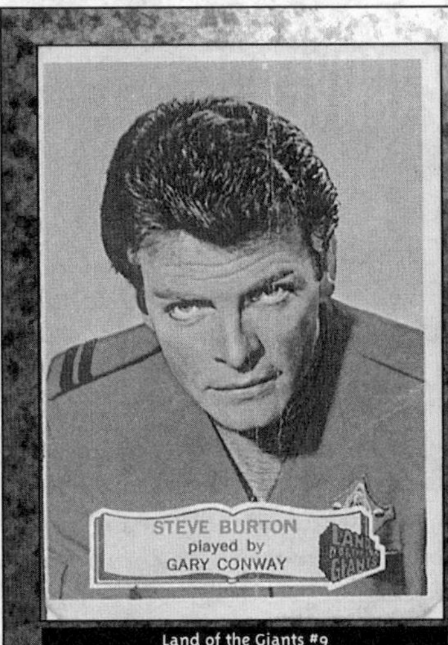

Land of the Giants #9

Kung Fu #51

Outer Limits #38

American Comics

THE HISTORICAL AGES OF COMIC BOOKS

With the wide variety of comics available, this Guide has a listing that is necessarily selective in its starting points as collecting markets determine the viability of exactly what to spend time according values to. Throughout the American comics section, reference is made to titles and comics outside the listing scope of this book for the time being, particularly those comics of the Golden Age which has a vastly greater functioning market in America than in this country. It is hoped that in the not too distant future a complete main title Golden Age listing will be possible. For a more complete listing of Golden Age material, we recommend the Overstreet Guide currently in its 27th year.

AS WITH MOST OTHER HISTORICAL LEISURE INTEREST HOBBIES, comic book collecting has its own set of generally accepted ages that separate different groups of comics to give some sort of historical perspective. British comics are generally referred to in time spans governed by actual dates and/or decades which need little explanation of the actual terms involved. Victorian, Edwardian, Twenties, Pre-War,War, Post-War, Fifties, Sixties, Seventies, Eighties and Nineties mean what they say though it is hoped to explore what exactly appeared when in a future article, as there are certain periods which are more complex than others. But American comic books have their own set of distinctive terms and phrases which are used in preference to simply naming the decade.

THESE HISTORICAL AGES ARE BY NO MEANS SET IN STONE AND INDEED VERY OFTEN OVERLAP.

Significant dates prior to the establishment of the American comic book are as follows:

1876 – Humorous story and political cartoon magazines "Puck" and "Judge" appear.

1895 – The Yellow Kid by R.F. Outcault appeared as a regular cartoon in the New York Sunday World and The Sunday Journal, reprinted as a collection of strips in 1897.

1911 – The Chicago American newspaper issues a number of books containing reprints of Sunday newspaper cartoon characters such as Mutt and Jeff. The print run was about 50,000.

1929 – The Dell Publishing Company issues a newspaper size collection of comic and cartoon strips called "The Funnies", reprinting material from what was affectionately known as The Funny Pages being a specific section inside the Sunday papers of the 1920s. "The Funnies" ran for 13 issues and most of the strips were four-colour rather than black and white or red on white.

1933 – Small, squat, hardcover books appeared called Big Little Books featuring characters from The Funny Pages newspaper sections and more significantly from film and film serials such as Tarzan and Flash Gordon. The format consisted of a full page of text next to a full page illustration alternating throughout the entire book.

At this point the established terms of American comic book collecting come into play.

Thus for the purposes of easy classification, the history and evolution of American comic books from 1933 on may be broken down into these ages:

1933-1937 THE PRE GOLDEN AGE

Sometimes referred to as the "antediluvian" era, it dates from the first recognisable comic book, **Funnies on Parade**. This was given away as a sales or radio premium. **Famous Funnies #1** was the first comic book to be sold on the news-stands in the early part of 1934. It sold for 10 cents and had 100 pages of strips, puzzles and games. Only by issue #7 did it make money for the Dell Publishing Company and thus the comic book industry had begun. This age is characterised by non-costumed heroes, usually police, secret agents and adventurers towards the latter half of the age with funny animals and slapstick characters in the earlier part. 1935 saw a number of other company's and products come to prominence: King Comics produced by King Features, Tip Top Comics by United Features and Popular Comics by M.C. Gaines to name three of the most influential. 1936/37 saw the rise of Centaur Comics which produced Funny Picture Stories and Detective Picture Stories. The publishing group went on to produce much super-hero material in the 1940s as Quality Comics.

One publisher in particular went on to become the most well established.

In February 1935, **New Fun #1** was produced by Donenfield and Co. in a format measuring 10" x 12", larger than the more standard format that the company went on to produce in comics like NEW FUN, MORE FUN, ADVENTURE and DETECTIVE COMICS, the latter from which the renamed National Periodical Publications took their modern initials DC Comics that today publish two of the most well-known comic book characters, Superman and Batman. Most of these comics are very scarce and very rare in the U.K. and very rare worldwide in anything approaching high grade condition. It is thought that less than 1% of comics published in this age remain today in any condition.

The rarest published comics are thought to be **New Fun #2** (March 1935) which was the 2nd DC comic published and **New (Adventure) Comics #7** (February 1937) also from DC. There may be fewer 6 copies in existence though these figures are difficult to verify. The most valuable comic from this period is **Detective Comics #1** and its current U.S and estimated U.K. value may be checked on the Top 50 Rarest Comics table elsewhere in this book.

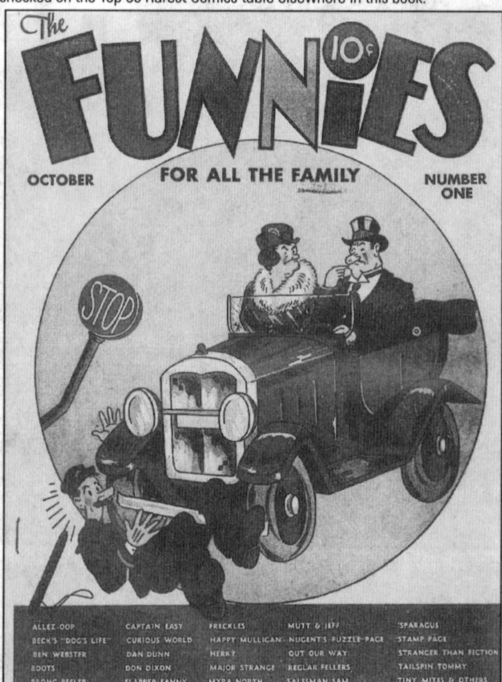

The Funnies #1

1938-1945 THE GOLDEN AGE

Traditionally dating from **Action Comics #1** which saw the first appearance of the archetypal costumed hero Superman and coinciding with the end of the Second World War, this was the age of the most famous costumed superheroes of today. Batman (1939), Sub-Mariner (1939), Human Torch (1939),

Wonder Woman (1940), Flash (1940), Robin (1940), Green Lantern (1940), Captain Marvel (1940), The Spirit (1940) and Captain America (1941) all came to prominence during this period along with a host of successful and unsuccessful imitators. Some of these early comics may have come over to this country with the establishment of the G.I.s and U.S.A.F. bases but they were not generally distributed and available. They are prized among collectors today as the most valuable items in terms of financial worth and historical significance. The two most valuable would be **Action Comics #1** from June 1938 and **Detective Comics #27** from May 1939 featuring the first appearance of Batman. A copy of Detective #27 sold in 1994 for $135,000 (or £90,000 depending on which side of the Atlantic you stand) and though relatively high grade, it was by no means the best copy available. There is the Mile High or Edgar Church copy of Action Comics #1 that, if it ever came onto the market, would command in excess of $200,000. Superman #1 came out in the summer of 1939 and reprinted the first four Superman stories from Action Comics #1-4 in this one volume with some extra introductory pages. It is a comic that is thought to have been shipped over to the British mainland in an effort to test the viability of the market as there seems to be more copies of this comic in British collectors' hands than other significant late 1930s comics. The massive paper drives of 1941 and particularly 1942 in America destroyed millions of comic books for the War Effort and comics dated before this time are generally in much scarcer supply than all others.

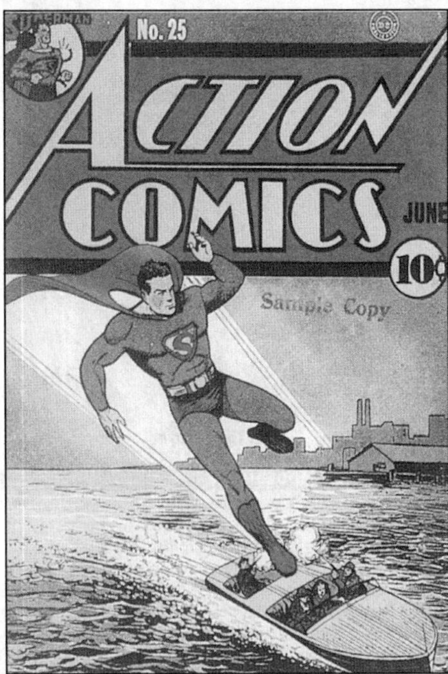

Action Comics #25

1946-1949 THE LATE GOLDEN AGE

This period saw the beginning of a decline in the popularity of the super-hero and the establishment of a much wider variety of genres from movie and television comics to crime, horror and mystery titles. For example, 1947 saw Timely (later to become Atlas then Marvel) introduce its first crime comic called JUSTICE which prided itself on the fact that the stories were based on fact while 1948 saw TWO GUN KID from the same publisher as the first all Western comic. The exception to this variation from the super-hero genre was the phenomenally successful story of Fawcett's CAPTAIN MARVEL which saw sales recorded in the millions per month rather than the hundred thousands. Encouraged by this and the steady sales of SUPERMAN at around the one million mark per month, **Superboy #1** was published in 1949 though the same year saw SUBMARINER COMICS falter with #32 and the great MARVEL MYSTERY COMICS end with #92 to become MARVEL TALES.

1950-1954 THE PRE SILVER AGE

More comic titles were published at the beginning of this period than at any other time (estimated to be a staggering 74 million individual copies per month at its height) though in one sense these years are often thought of by some as "The Dark Ages" of comics as paper quality and paper rationing meant slimmer comics which do survive today in the best of condition but in much smaller relative percentages. For sheer depth in diversity, this period is unparalleled. One comics' historian has noted that there were over 50 horror titles per month published between 1951 and 1954. While genre comics flourished, superheroes like Sub-Mariner and Captain America finally saw the sunset. The rise of the horror comic and in particular the line published by EC Comics lead to a series of Congressional Hearings in 1954 which sought to prove a direct correlation between comics and rising juvenile delinquency. The net result was the establishment of The Comics Code Authority in 1955 to which all comics were morally obliged to subject themselves. In many cases this established a generally safe formulaic approach to story and character. A notable exception are the "monster" comics like Journey into Mystery, Strange Tales, Tales of Suspense and Tales to Astonish with the bold art styles of Steve Ditko and Jack Kirby to name but two. Concerns with a post nuclear age, global divide and faltering exploration of space became characterised in the mid and late 1950s by an array of fantastic monsters with names and story titles to match the best B-movie cliches: "Groot, The Monster from Planet X", "Fin Fang Foom" and "Gigantus, The Monster That Walked Like A Man".

1955-1965 THE SILVER AGE

The Silver Age relates to the Golden Age in that this period saw the re-launch of a number of costumed heroes in an up-dated form. Traditionally dating from **Detective Comics #225** (Nov 1955) which introduced the first significant new hero The Manhunter from Mars for some years (since Captain Comet in **Strange Adventures #9** in June 1951), it has since become more widely associated with **Showcase #4** which introduced a new realisation (though essentially a revival) of The Flash. The mid point of this age saw a panoply of successful remodellings from a new Green Lantern in **Showcase #22** (Sep/Oct 1959) through Aquaman in **Showcase #30** (Feb 1961), Hawkman in **Brave and the Bold #34** (Mar 1961) to Atom in **Showcase #34** (October 1961). More significantly however was the appearance of **Fantastic Four #1** in November 1961 which ushered in what has become known as "The Marvel Age" which saw the rapid introduction of Spiderman, Hulk, a re-discovered Sub-Mariner and Captain America and, not ashamed of besprinkling their epithets, the"mighty" Thor. For many collectors in this country, this sub-age is the most revered and fondly remembered, particularly because most Marvel comics were officially distributed in this country and continued to be distributed in generally good supply. Thus complete sets were possible from first issues and fan involvement meant that there was more scope for having one's name mentioned or even a full letter to the Editor in print (look for the many letters submitted by U.K. though U.S. born radio DJ Paul Gambaccini when he was a young fan in Fantastic Four #7 for example). The Silver Age will continue to expand as it includes comics that are roughly 25 years old or more.

Showcase #22

1966-1969 THE LATE SILVER AGE

This period is gradually being swallowed up by the advance of the Silver Age. Some collectors and dealers already accept the Silver Age as lasting right up to 1969, particularly in America. However, what characterises and makes this small period unique is a flourish of re-launched characters in their own titles, particularly from Marvel Comics. **Hulk #102** (April 1968) continued the numbering from the anthology title TALES TO ASTONISH while **Captain America #100** (April 1968) continued from TALES OF SUSPENSE. **Iron Man #1** shortly followed in May 1968 and perhaps the most important mainstream publishing event came in August 1968 with **Silver Surfer #1**. At DC Comics there was a short-lived attempt to cash in on the energy of the hip and groovy youth with TEEN BEAT in December 1967 and BROTHER POWER, THE GEEK in October 1968. A chequered design ("go-go checks") found its way along the top edge of DC comic titles from February 1966 to July 1967 that sought to identify the company with a zappier image as well as being a marketing aid to find the comics more easily in the news-stand racks. Perhaps the most significant example of colourful camp came with the Batman television series that lasted three seasons from 1966 to 1969. Well remembered are those famous fight-scenes with pop-art word sound-effects splattered across the screen which found their way into the comic.

Nick Fury #1

1970-1979 THE SEVENTIES

This period is now becoming recognised in its own right as it is now twenty years removed and had a particular feel about it. In some cases that meant change with a re-vamp for Superman who had remained largely unchanged for over three decades. Clark Kent became a television reporter and that gruesome green chunk of rock called kryptonite transmuted to harmless lead. Supergirl got a wide variety of less than flattering costumes and Jack Kirby established his own unique art style in his "Fourth World" series including NEW GODS, FOREVER PEOPLE and giving Superman's pal Jimmy Olsen a few things to think about. Marvel Comics introduced Giant Size comics and multi-cross over annuals, some interesting characters like Killraven and Howard the Duck and hard, calculated market manipulation with endless reprint titles. For the first time, significant amounts of Marvel and a few DC comics were Non Distributed in the U.K. at the time of publication, leading to price differentials and new business opportunities for U.K. dealers. An air of uncertainty as to where comics were going lead (partly) to the DC Implosion of 1978 in which titles were cut back or cancelled after a period of steady exploration and the unquestioned establishment of Marvel as market leaders. Characters such as Deathlok and Wolverine, Ghost Rider and Punisher were all established in this period without any huge effect at the time but once re-introduced to modern audiences in new forms and formats, they enjoyed something of a renaissance through to the mid 1990s. In the current market, even these once extremely popular characters are subject to intense scrutiny for story quality and can easily become out of favour virtually overnight. This age is also referred to by some (mostly American dealers/collectors rather than U.K. ones) as "The Bronze Age" and traditionally it takes as its starting point the comic **Green Lantern #76** which featured new dynamic art by Neal Adams and a more down-to-earth and human story-line by Denny O'Neill. Quite when this Bronze Age is supposed to finish is unclear, so much so that the term "Lead Age of Comics" has been known to crop up on U.D. dealer lists which is perhaps the jaundiced view by some older dealers and collectors on today's output of material. The Bronze Age may be established more fully in time but for now the use of the actual decades will suffice.

Indeed The Seventies may well prove to be an important era of character-rediscovery and potential financial investment as prices are still within most people's reach as Golden and Silver Age prices continue to soar.

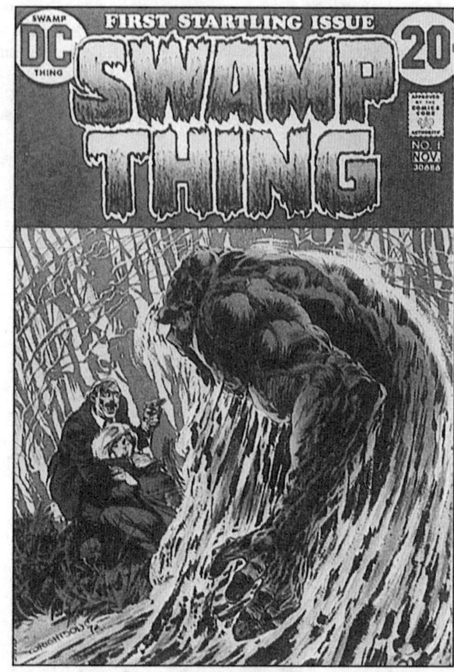

Swamp Thing (1st) #1

1980-PRESENT THE MODERN AGE

Never before has the medium of comic books gained so much widespread exposure through film and television. Films like Batman, Dick Tracy, The Teenage Mutant Ninja Turtles and Judge Dredd have grossed hundreds of millions of dollars at the box office in the last 15 years and plagued youth market pockets with their merchandising. Television has yet to find its own comic book hero but Star Trek - Voyager, Deep Space Nine, Babylon 5 and Sliders may at least herald a new wave. There are something like 150 comic and cartoon characters under developmental consideration so the staple diet of screen entertainment for the next few years is not hard to fathom. Comic companies have been at once bold and bland in their efforts to cash in on such media awareness. The Independent Explosion in the early 80s saw hundreds of small presses spring up to produce some interesting material, champion creator rights and artist royalty payments but sadly the duopoly of Marvel and DC has all but re-established itself as cold hard economics count in the world of comics. The graphic novel became an accepted art form and concomitant catchword to be pilloried. While the age may be characterised by new formats/high-production value packages, media exposure as to the literacy and ultimate worth of comics has seen the inevitable backlash. Somewhere along the line someone forgot to mention that comics are still at root an escapist form of entertainment foremost with skillfully rendered art and fine story-telling making the most of the genre that for many still has its best potential to be realised. In spite of a world-wide market recession at the start of this decade, the future looks very bright for comics. More titles than ever before are being published with new experiments in story, art and subject. British artists and writers are held in the highest esteem on both sides of the Atlantic which is something that cannot be said of many industries in this country. Back issue collecting has never been more popular and record prices are being realised for comics in the best condition possible. Already several comics have passed the $100,000 mark with a copy of Superman #1 selling in the summer of 1996 for $175,000. But the real pleasure of the hobby is in the constant reading enjoyment and stimulus for thought that comics can bring, whether reading the latest in socio-political observations or fondly remembering a tale from one's childhood. After over 60 years of the American comic (and well over a hundred of the English variety), the genre is only now being recognised as something more than "kid's stuff".

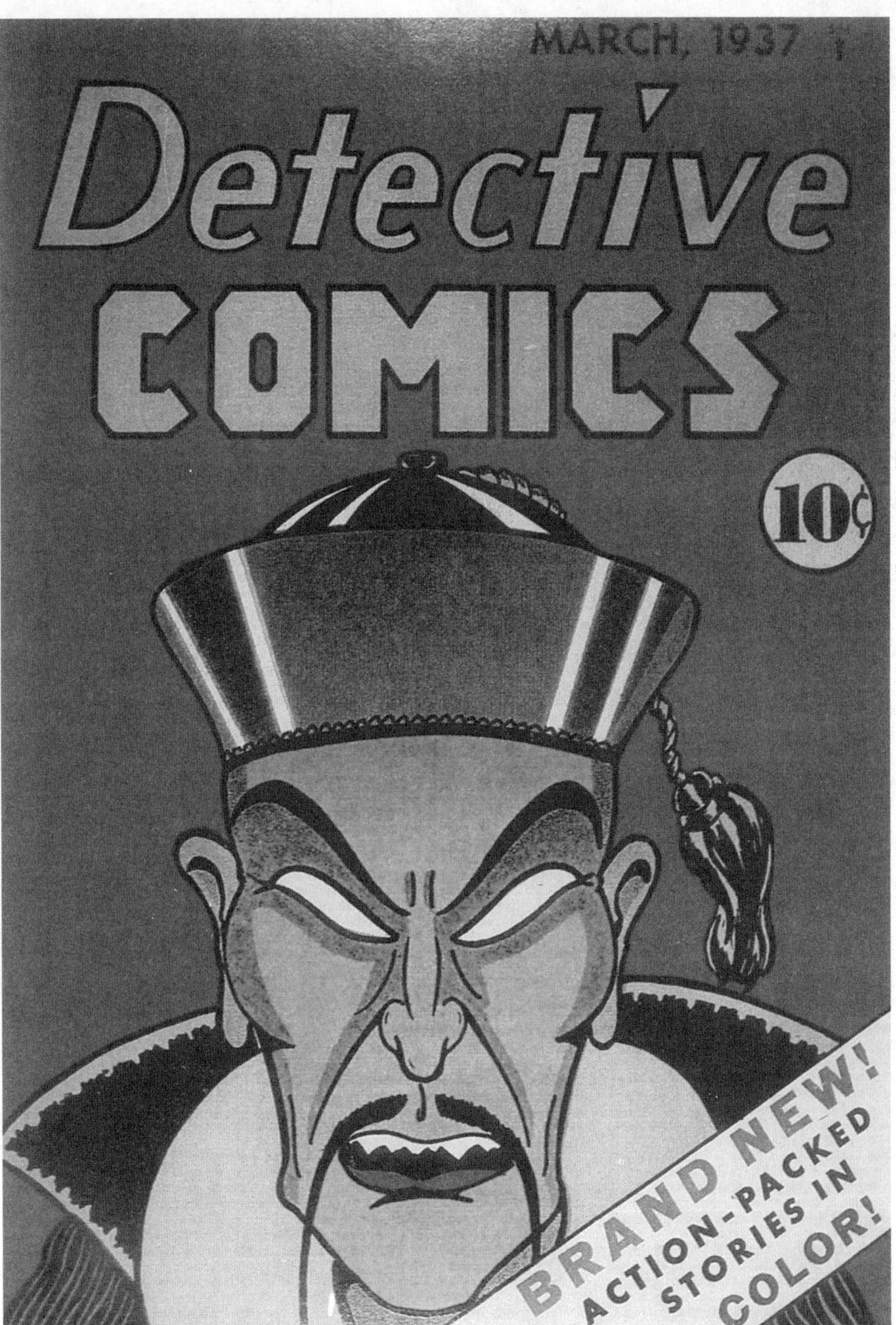

Detective Comics #1 – the *first* successful anthology *of* detectives and policemen, this was the comic that gave DC its initials

INTRODUCTION TO D.C. COMICS

D.C. comics have been published and distributed in America since February 1935 with **New Fun Comics Number #1**. For many years, the company was known as National Periodical Publications until it changed simply to D.C. at the beginning of 1977, the letters traditionally taken from the long running (since 1937) Batman title, Detective Comics. The Golden Age that saw the appearance of the main characters Superman in **Action Comics #1** in June 1938 and Batman in **Detective Comics #27**, May 1939, technically runs up to 1955 but the high point which saw the great plethora of costumed heroes ran from 1938 to 1942. What is known as the Silver Age runs from about January 1955 up to about 1965, in which a second age of costume heroes began more officially with an updated version of The Flash in **Showcase #4**, cover dated Sept/Oct 1956. There are many who cite the Martian Manhunter in **Detective #225**, November 1955, as the first significant costumed hero within the correct dates (some affectionately remember and would claim for Captain Comet from **Strange Adventures #9**, June 1951). In any event, many characters from the 1940s were updated and revamped by the then Editor, Julius Schwartz, like Hawkman, Atom and Green Lantern. D.C. Silver Age comics are in great demand in the current market, especially 10 cents cover-priced issues and especially in high grade.

In 1955, the Comics Code Authority was formed in response to Dr. Frederick Wertham's book "The Seduction of the Innocent" that decried the moral and sexual downslide of some comics that were available at the time; most notably the horror and mystery titles from E.C. (or Educational Comics) and its many, usually inferior, imitators. Although Code approval is not compulsory, most DC comics are still submitted for approval by the C.C.A. in order to ensure the widest distribution. Some comics have been submitted i the past but failed to gain Code acceptance; where applicable and of importance, this has been noted in the Guide. The introduction of the C.A.A. is another indication of the start of D.C.'s Silver Age.

Official distribution of D.C. comics in the U.K. began in very early 1960 with cover-dated issues November 1959, although there was some extremely limited distribution of romance and funny titles and the occasional super-hero title before this date. D.C. comics in the 1960s and 1970s were distributed through Thorpe and Porter who ink-stamped the front cover with their price. As they were not imported on a sale or return basis, any excess copies were further shipped abroad, resulting in an intrinsic scarcity of early 1960's DC's in this country. DC's (and especially Marvels) often came across on ships as ballast, so many issues have emerged as being water-damaged in some way; the varying degrees of damage greatly and proportionately devaluing a comic.

As they had remained unchallenged since the late 1930's, D.C. tended to rest on its laurels in spite of producing some excellent super-heroes stories and science fiction art up to the late 1950s. When Marvel Comics appeared in November 1961, with **Fantastic Four #1**, their rapid success meant that for the first time in 25 years, D.C. could no longer rest on its laurels. They did seem, however, to be quite content with their position and in January 1962, did what seemed to be the unthinkable of putting the cover price up from 10 cents to 12, compounded by a letter of apology in their comics explaining rising paper costs. However, top D.C. titles continued to out-sell Marvel comics throughout the 1960s with Superman reaching sales of 800,000 and Batman at one point close on a million.

In May 1964, Batman and Detective Comics were revamped with a new look at art by Carmine Infantino and stories that did not pit the Caped Crusader against pink or green aliens. Batman reached new heights of popularity with the screening of the networked T.V. show in 1966 and another sign of the swinging Sixties was the appearance of the "Go Go Checks" at the top edge of the covers. This collectable quirk appeared from February 1966 to July 1967, but the story and art content of some D.C titles were at an all time low.

June 1969 saw another cover price rise to 15 cents and in January 1971, Superman had his first update in over thirty years. All Kryptonite was turned to harmless lead and Clark Kent became a T.V. news reporter and anchorman rather than the Daily Planet's ace newshound. Superman also lost about a third of his powers as it was felt that he was getting too omnipotent, but he gradually returned to normal without anybody noticing throughout the 1970's. In August 1971, the cover price went to 25 cents and the pages from 32 to 48. D.C. reprinted much classic 40's and 50's material in this expansion but it only lasted until June 1972 when comics reverted to normal page count but were up to 20 cents. "All New Stories Best in Comics", it said.

D.C. giants had always been popular since the first Superman Annual in 1960. Thereafter, annuals and 80 page giants featuring mainly reprints of the Superman and Batman family of stories, appeared with increasing frequency. As they were thicker comics, fewer were sent over to the U.K. in the regular packets, so they are generally scarcer. Very often the spines are crinkled owing to the way the glue dried, so perfectly flat and therefore near mint or mint copies are very rare. D.C. comics of the 1960s are generally of a higher quality than comparative Marvel comics in the paper stock they used, although it may be noticed that Marvel comics often retain the whiteness of their pages better and particularly their cover gloss owing to the composition of the papers used. Marvel comics from about 1964 onwards are in generally greater supply than D.C.'s. Media coverage in America meant that dealers went around buying up vast stocks for a ready-made back issue market and it was also noticed that Marvel comic readers tended to save their comics more as stories and often referred back to previous incidents and characters, so there was more of an idea of a set of comics. Indeed, sets were more possible to collect as the numbers were not so astronomically high as D.C. titles seemed to be.

In 1973, a comic fan and dealer, Theo Holstein, paid $1,800 for a good copy of **Action Comics #1** and as news spread across America over the next year, the emergence of rare comics and the upward spiral of the sums they commanded began. The publication in 1970 of the Overstreet Comic Book Price Guide and its rapid acceptance as a monitor of market values contributed to public awareness of the potential value of comic books. The 1973 Overstreet mint price for **Action Comics #1** jumped from $1,000 to $2,800 in 1974. Such a percentage rise would be unthinkable today. D.C. reprinted a number of" Famous First Editions" facsimiles in an oversized format which further popularised the appeal of the top comics like **Action #1**, **Detective #27**, **Sensation #1**, **Whiz #2**, **Batman #1**, **Wonder Woman #1**, **All Star #3** and **Flash Comics #1**. In that same year, D.C.'s went up to 25 cents and in August 1975, the unprecedented collaboration between Marvel and D.C. brought M.G.M.'s Marvelous Wizard of Oz. There followed in 1976, the confrontation between Superman and Spiderman which was the same year that Jenette Kahn was appointed Publisher after having edited such magazine as "Smash" and "Dyna Mite". D.C. were, however, steadily declining in the face of the unstoppable, untoppable Marvel. Just as there had been a set-back to expansion in 1971, in 1978 came the "D.C. Implosion". Warner Brothers Communications who had taken over D.C. drastically cut back the number of monthly titles by 40% in an effort to halt declining sales. After only three months, the new 50 cents/44 pages format was cut back to 32 pages for 40 cents and most of the newer titles were cancelled. Among the casualties were All Star Comics, Black Lightning, Kamandi, Firestorm, Steel, the relaunched Showcase and The Witching Hour. New comics like The Vixen and The Deserter never saw print at all. The official reason was a revamped distribution process which sold larger quantities of proven sellers rather than risk and bombard the retailers with newer unknown titles. Marvel were at their strongest, still holding out on a 35 cent cover price and Spiderman being a runaway best-seller with the revamped X-Men not far behind.

In 1980/81, the advent of "Direct Sale" comics revolutionised the whole structure. Some comics were distributed only to specialist shops and the publishers who got their orders direct from the Direct Sale distributor were able to print a more exact number of the copies they needed with no unprofitable over-print runs. As more comic shops open, so the Direct Sale market expands. However, In 1981, increased paper costs and the fuel crisis forced the cover price of DC comics to 60 cents but in November of that year, D.C. followed the lead from the Independent comics group, Pacific, and offered royalty payments to artists and writers on the basis of sales (back dated to July). Marvel were soon to follow suit. D.C. underwent a steady period of growth with quality products like George Perez's New Teen Titans and Crisis on Infinite Earths which simplified and re-defined the D.C. Universe. They celebrated their 50th year in 1985 by introducing a "Superman for the 80's" in a six part mini-series called The Man of Steel, by the British-born John Byrne. Wonder Woman was similarly updated by George Perez.

In 1986 there occurred a piece of comics and publishing history with Frank Miller's apocryphal Batman tale, The Dark Knight Returns, which set new standards of excellence in story and art and introduced comics to a far wider range of people than ever before. It remained on the New York Times Best Seller list for 38 weeks. With Alan Moore's revitalised Swamp Thing, Howard Chaykin and Bill Seinkiewicz on The Shadow, and Alan Moore and Dave Gibbons on The Watchmen, D.C. went on to regain the lead of the comic market share from Marvel in early 1988 for the first time in more than 10 years but this was very much in terms of revenue earned rather than volume sold and it only lasted for a couple of months.

In 1987, D.C. announced a labelling policy which would display "For Mature Readers Only" on comics that were deemed to be unsuitable for universal readership. Many artists and writers felt this to be a judgement constraint akin to censorship and their disagreements became resignations, most notably Alan Moore and Frank Miller. While labelling still occurs, all other disagreements seem to have been ironed out.

The dating of comic books has long been the system of advance where the cover date is three months ahead of sale. This was thought to give a comic a longer shelf-life in comic shops and in newsagents. Towards the end of 1988, D.C. announced that they would suspend cover-dating for three months from October to December and either simply put "Winter", "Holiday" or nothing at all. Then in January 1989, the cover date would match the real date at which it was on sale. It was felt that this would be less confusing and more in keeping with other magazines available on the shelf, so that people would know it was "this month's".

1989 was also remarkable for the unprecedented media and cultural phenomenon surrounding the long-awaited release of the Batman movie starring Michael Keaton and Jack Nicholson. Shattering all previous box-office records the film has taken over $300 million worldwide to date. Although something of a backlash necessarily developed, this was almost entirely against the merchandising over-kill. The values of Batman and Batman-related comic books sky-rocketed. It seems that the Chinese menagerie has been added to with what has become "The Year of the Bat".

The end of the decade saw the continuation of quality products like Batman, The Cult, The Killing Joke and The Prisoner and other comics like Invasion, Black Orchid, Catwoman, Gotham by Gaslight, Hawkworld and the Arkham Asylum hardcover graphic novel. D.C.'s policy of revamped titles, high quality formats and mass-market trade paperbacks seemed designed less to wrest the existing market-share lead from Marvel Comics than to attract a larger market from outside the usual comics readership.

The Batman boom dissipated during 1990 as was seen by the luke-warm reception given to Batman: Digital Justice which boasted a new era of computer-generated graphics and a colour palette of over sixteen million combinations. Traditional comics are best it seems. Interest was kept alive by the new Robin, Tim Drake and his own mini-series and Batman celebrated his 600th appearance in **Detective Comics #627** featuring a painted cover by Norm Breyfogle based on the original back in 1939. Flash celebrated his fiftieth year in 1990 with a number of specials including a hardcover collection of "The Greatest Flash Stories Ever Told". Coupled with the success of the Flash TV series on CBS-Fox in America, **Showcase #4** featuring the first appearance of the Silver Age Flash consolidated its position as the most valuable Silver Age comic. Superman titles generally received a new injection of interest with Lois Lane finally getting her man after 52 years of courtship while Superman's arch foe, Lex Luthor, "died" in a plane crash, re-emerged as an Australian, died of kryptomite poisoning and has lately made a remarkable recovery!

For the start of 1991, comeback seemed to be the operative word with the return of the cult duo Angel and the Ape, the 1st super team in comics The Justice Society of America, the Challengers of the Unknown and a little-known Golden Age character called Kid Eternity given the Grant Morrison writing treatment though this and Bryan Talbot's The Nazz suffered from production delays which plagued DC even more towards the end of 1991. A follow up to the successful Green Lantern: Emerald Dawn mini-series epitomised DC's attempts to launch a two-pronged attack of commercially successful projects and more specialised high-quality packages on the runaway success that Marvel Comics have enjoyed in recent times. However, DC slumped at one point in the latter half of 1991 to a market share of less than 20% while Marvel peaked at 68% largely through the marketing success of X-Men and other mutant titles. DC's answers to all of this was another Robin mini-series in more permutations than one could imagine and the release of a line of comics based on old Archie Comics heroes like The Web, The Jaguar, The Fly and The Shield. It was greeted with cynicism from the retailers and little enthusiasm from the fans. The line was cancelled in 1992.

The last couple of years have seen mixed fortunes of the company off-set with the occasional flashes of brilliance. Much hope was pinned on their being a repeat of the Batmania of 1989 with the release of the second film in 1991 but back-issue and current issue sales barely blipped. The absolute nadir for DC Comics came with the news in 1992 of their market share falling to an all-time low of 18%, in third place behind Marvel Comics and the new young upstart Valiant - new and forbidding territory for the giant publisher knocking 58 years old at the time.

The flashes of brilliance have been there more increasingly however. Some would say the most cynical of marketing ploys but others would argue one of the most successful for DC was the Death of Superman which recorded sales of 4 million for the issue of Superman #75. True to comic book fashion, he's back but it all showed that he was missed. More creatively, DC collected their horror and mystery titles under the generic banner of Vertigo with its own look and promotional push. Given that Swamp Thing, Hellblazer, Sandman, Shade and Animal Man feature some of the best in (British!) writing and drawing talent, it is a very strong base from which to launch spin-offs and one-shots which they have duly done.

DC had a good year in 1993 with the interest in Superman and Batman surprisingly catapulting these characters into some of the top-selling comics slots. In 1993/94 DC increasingly took the lead in innovative ideas with re-vamps for Superman and Batman followed by one for Green Lantern in issue #50 of his 2nd series. The 1994 mini-series Zero Hour tidied up many inconsistencies and loose ends much in the same way as Crisis on Infinite Earths did and has supposedly established one consistent timeline for the company. No doubt there will be another revision in ten years time.

1995 saw the release of Batman Forever which critics hated but audiences loved. Judge Dredd did not fare so well at the box office and DC cancelled both their Judge Dredd titles. And fans everywhere mourned the horrific accident that befell Superman actor Christopher Reeve that left him paralysed from the neck down. An ironic mirroring of the Death of Clark Kent storyline that ran for a while throughout the Superman titles. At the end of the year, **DC Vs. Marvel #1** appeared, pitting selected heroes from one company against another in fights that fans could vote on the outcome. Such inter-company co-operation was extended by a series of Amalgam Comics featuring amalgamated DC and Marvel characters like Spider-Boy and Dr. Strange-Fate.

DC COMICS MARKET REPORT

This Market Report for DC comics examines the last twelve months or so of activity, looking particularly at value trends and reasons for increased or decreased collector interest. It is very generalized and regional variations should be taken into account. For titles and comics not mentioned, one may assume relatively stable values and collector interest not significantly differing from the last Guide.

ACTION COMICS

The listing starts from issue #1 to include those classic Golden Age comics and information. Though the market is small in the U.K. for these earlier comics owing to their generally being over the £500 mark, it is growing slowly as the fashion is often to possess at least one comic from Superman's hey-day of the 1930s and 1940s though of necessity in lower grade condition. Calculating values for these issues in the U.K. becomes virtually instinctive as copies of really early Action Comics are rarely offered for sale in the British market but if someone wanted to invest in them, they couldn't go far wrong with unrestored mid to high grades. It has been increasingly noticed at comic marts that lower grade copies of comics over 40 years old are popular sellers. Just out of curiosity it is well worth spending a hundred pounds for a fair to good (but make sure it's complete!) copy of an Action Comic in the teens just to see the very genesis of Superman as a character and the development of his powers like the first example of X-Ray vision in issue #18.

There is also an editorial struggle with assigning scarcity values to these early issues. In theory any copy of Action Comics before issue #100 is at least scarce in the U.K. with the early issues being very rare as the number of copies in the British market of issues #1-10 could be counted on the fingers of one hand. Rather than put "scarce in the U.K." on every issue, we have taken it as read that most people understand and accept that most early Golden Age comics are not often seen in the U.K. and indeed their demand is very limited.

Action Comics #1 assumes its place as the most valuable comic ahead of **Detective Comics #27**. This is a trend that I would see to continue now. Even though Detective #27 is harder to find, it cannot be argued any other way than Action Comics #1 being the most important and influential comic ever published. I can foresee Action Comics #1 far out-stripping any other comic to become the first quarter of a million dollar book in the very near future. The values listed for both comics are very conservative. The 3rd most high grade copy of Action Comics #1 was offered in 1996 for $160,000.

A more marked increase on #242 again by £100 in Near Mint compared to a comparatively small increase on issue #252 which surprised us. With the current interest in the Supergirl character and the relative scarcity of #252, this is definitely an issue to watch. There have been increases on early Legion appearances (not around in high grade) and increases as ever on the 80pg giants (#334, #347 and #360 in particular) and annuals which are generally snapped up as good reading value for those that like early '60s reprints.

Issues to watch out for in the 70s are those 48 pagers that suddenly happened right across most DC titles in 1971. Issues #403-413 are becoming increasingly hard to find. Also issue #432 as the first Silver Age Toyman. Highly rated in some parts of America. Time will tell here, particularly as The Toyman of late has been revealed as much more of a psychopath rather than a funny little man. Issue #484 where the Earth-2 Superman weds in the light of the recent nuptials between Clark and Lois and #583, the very excellent "Last Superman Story" by Alan Moore, are issues in demand.

Action Comics Weekly continues to occupy the bargain bins and will probably do so forever more. While interest in the Death of Superman and Reign of the Supermen issues stabilized owing to the Trade paperback versions becoming available (and rattling good reads they are too), Superman as a character has surprised many dealers in the U.K. by sustaining sales in the last couple of years. One reason for this may be the "Lois & Clark" Superman TV series screened on a more prime time Saturday evening slot in the U.K. and also that there are now five Superman titles continuing to interweave their soap opera-like storylines very successfully.

It remains to be seen how the new-look, new-power Superman will fare. Many commentators believe that it is yet another marketing gimmick and that it is not possible or even wise to play around with the familiar look and product recognition base of Superman and his costume. But at least it got comics on the national news on both sides of the Atlantic and any publicity for comics can't be a bad thing.

ADVENTURE COMICS

The listing starts from #1 when it was known as New Comics to give more information on these rare Golden Age issues. In some cases they are so rare that existing copies in any condition worldwide can be counted in tens. While there is a very small (if any) market in the U.K. as yet for this material, in low grades it is quite possible to purchase some of these antediluvian comics, to see how it all began. Interesting to think that New Comics #1 was the first ever comic published by DC. Could they have had any inkling what it would lead to? Early issues are beginning to be offered in the U.K. market and it will be interesting to see if they actually disappear from the walls at recent marts. Other early Golden Age classics include the first Sandman in #40, the first Hourman in #48, the first Starman in #61 and some great Simon and Kirby Golden Age Sandman material from #72-91: crying out for reprinting (DC take note...).

A hundred pound increase in Near Mint on Krypto's first appearance in issue #210 is merely guess work. To my knowledge, no issues have been sold in the U.K. as demand for an item like this is very specialised (me, Ian Holmes and Ian Faris? And we've got copies anyway!). The same rate of increase on the first appearance of the Legion in #247 but now that this issue is beyond the reach of most collectors in high grade (if you can find one!), the market interest for such a book in the U.K. necessarily shrinks. Time was it was the issue to get but it seems when this and other issues like it reach that £1,000+ barrier, the interest may still be there but sales are fewer and fewer. But it is worth noting that this comic is rarely seen in the U.K., it's light cover is prone to marking and I've seen quite a few water-stained copies which suggests a batch were damaged in this way a long time ago at the warehouse stage. An under-rated comic in my opinion. The Legion was one of the most successful teams in comic history after all and the first obviously mainstream teen group.

So what's the first Silver Age appearance of Green Arrow? A tricky one as Green Arrow was a back-up strip right through the Fifties and so the September 1956 issue (#228) is technically the first Silver Age appearance as it co-incides with Showcase #4 but that is very unsatisfactory. Perhaps it should be issue #256 that recounts the origin of Green Arrow. American price guides seem to hold to the opinion that such a retelling of the origin makes issue #260 the first Silver Age Aquaman. But that Aquaman looks the same Aquaman to me as in issue #259 (#260 is so over-rated!). Perhaps the first Silver Age Green Arrow appearance is as late as the September 1969 issue of Brave and the Bold (#85) where Green Arrow sports a new costume, goatee beard and irascible attitude. Answers on a post-card please...

The Legion issues from #300-380 are still in steady demand and a high grade run of these issues is becoming very difficult to put together. Many low grades have been reported sold as the stories are still a fun read. The John Forte artwork issues are significantly preferred to the Jim Mooney ones. Check out the art-style differences and how well John Forte delineated and distinguished each character. Issue #381 is a very difficult issue to find, featuring the first of the Supergirl-starring series. It has risen from £4.00 to £7.50 in Near Mint and that is nothing compared to the $35.00 that can be commanded in America! Issues #412, #414, #415, #420 and #421 have long ago been picked up by those who can't afford the original Animal appearances and they are a part of the general Silver Age Animal malaise so values are stagnant. The killers to find are those last Digest size issues - numbers #491 to #503. Drives completists wild. Others of interest are The Spectre issues #431-440, gaining in popularity on the back of the Spectre series by Tom Mandrake. They both evoke the "avenging spirit" of the character in the 1940s. Other issues of note are the 68 page issues #459-465, under-valued in the U.K. market. #462 features the death of the Golden Age Batman, surely a very significant issue (all personal bias aside...)

ALL AMERICAN COMICS/ALL FLASH/ ALL STAR COMICS

The market in the U.K. for these Golden Age titles is quite small but issues can be picked up in average grades comparatively cheaply just to see what they are all about. For about forty to fifty pounds you could have a comic that is nearly 50 years old. All Star Comics have some great covers and lots of heroes for your money. Highly recommend issue #5 with the first Hawkgirl and for my money the first DC costumed heroine (and a lovely black cover to boot!) or issue #36 with Superman and Batman together in the same story for the first time, ahead of their long run in World's Finest.

ALL STAR WESTERN

Worth mentioning for the first and early Jonah Hex stories. #10 is very hard to come by in any grade and has become something of a minor key issue.

1993 NM Price: £15.00 1994 NM Price: £30.00
1996 NM Price: £50.00 1997 NM Price: £65.00

In America, copies have been regularly offered at $125 and $150. All Star Western #1-9 don't turn up in the U.K. that often either and they have some excellent Al Williamson art and feature Pow-Wow Smith, Billy the Kid and El Diablo.

ANIMAL MAN

Animal Man underwent a period of revitalization under the Vertigo banner of titles with excellent scripting begun by Jamie Delano and experienced something of a comeback to fan popularity of yore. But now that the series has been cancelled, early issues (#1-10) are hardly in demand though the excellent Trade paperback reprints these and is a great read with a fab Brian Bolland cover. Amazing to think that issue #1 was once a £15 comic in the U.K. £3.00 or £4.00 now if you're lucky.

AQUAMAN

Back-issues sales of the 1960's issues are still very slow in the U.K. market though the latest series (how many times have DC tried to launch this character?) has finally proved to be a winner with its "no more Mr. Nice Guy" approach. Now past 30 issues, this latest series looks like the one to stay. About time.

Still can't understand why the prices of the Silver Age material in America seem to be, if not ablaze, then at least very healthily warm, particularly on early issues. Time was when every other Overstreet Fan Magazine had them coloured in red. Why? Love to know who's buying them over there. Get this for a differential. Aquaman #12 at $75 would be translated back to £50. No way! The listed value of £20 is even a little on the high side in my opinion. Aquaman #1 is still a reasonable key issue and tough to find in high grade. Issues #50-52 are sought after by Neal Adams completists even though the artwork is on the Deadman back-up strip. For the best in Aquaman entertainment, check out the back-up stories in early 1960's Adventure Comics. Octopi with boxing gloves, swordfish cutting through chains and Aquaman launching himself into the fray on a whale-spout. Great stuff.

ATOM

Still attractive as a set to complete for some collectors but like Aquaman not as popular here in the U.K. as he seems to be in America. General back issue buyers in the U.K. are just not interested in The Atom. Funny how it too goes up in value in one monthly Update magazine or other to the point of ridicule. Issue #1 is still a reasonable DC Silver Age first issue, particularly with the comic exceeding the 30 years old barrier but we have decided to drop the value in the U.K. market while pushing up slightly the U.S. listed value. This is a reflection of the growing disparity between U.K. and U.S. prices on key Silver Age. Issues #29 and #36 continue to be more highly valued in the States than in the U.K. but they are getting noticeably harder to find though once again we have decided to drop the Near Mint value of issue #29 as a reflection of its demand status. The Atom & Hawkman issues of #39-45 are a little harder to find as print runs were lower. They also have some nice moody covers by Joe Kubert.

BATMAN

Although still regarded as DC's most popular character, Batman has never quite attained the dizzy heights it did in the summer of 1989 when the first movie opened in a blaze of publicity. In recent times, Batman has a mixed reception from fans in the U.K. The Knightfall issues of Batman and Detective seem to be in demand once more. The "breaking" of Batman issue #497 slackened in demand as the issue seems very common at marts and conventions in the U.K. now. Back issues are still raided from comic-shop bins, particularly any issues before #300. Even those in the 300's are in shorter supply than they were. Either way, 1997 should prove to be an interesting year for the Dark Knight Detective as he teams up with Daredevil amongst others and a fourth Batman film with Poison Ivy and Mr. Freeze will be released this June. It will interesting to see how George Clooney takes on the character and how he makes it different. Hopefully there will be a little of Michael Keaton's madness and Val Kilmer's square jaw.

The listing starts from #1 to give more information on some of these classic issues featuring some of the most classic Golden Age comics of all (perhaps more if that little personal bias comes into play here...). Low grade copies of these issues are excellent value for reading and enjoying the artwork of Bob Kane, Jerry Robinson, George Roussos, Dick Sprang and Charles Paris. As a general rule, this Guide has adopted a parity between the values of Golden Age Batman issues in the U.K. and the U.S. though in theory earlier issues of Batman, in common with virtually all Golden Age comics, are harder to get in the U.K. than in the U.S. Though they may be harder to obtain, the size of the market for them in the U.K. must be taken into account. #100 has taken another in value to become a serious back issue.

1993 NM Price: £690.00 1994 NM Price: £875.00
1996 NM Price: £1,100 1997 NM Price: £1,400.00

It is very tough to find in high grade. Unfortunately this also makes even a Good condition copy list at over the hundred pound mark and for my money this is too much. Blame it on those Americans again! #155 featuring the first Silver Age appearance of the Penguin has crept up slightly, a little more than the rate from 1995 to 1996.

1993 NM Price: £120.00 1994 NM Price: £140.00
1996 NM Price: £150.00 1997 NM price: £170.00

The U.S. listed value of $325 converts back to nearly £220 which gives you some idea of the growing gap in the markets. #171 featuring the first Silver Age Riddler has remained static at £200 Near Mint price as it has proved to be a fairly common book with many copies in lower grades appearing on Mart walls. Admittedly, the pink cover colour is prone to fading so very high grade copies are hard to come by. For this reason it still sky-rockets in the States. The dollar listing is $425 which is about £280. Historically however it is the 3rd ever appearance of this major Batman villain, made popular by Frank Gorshin on the Batman TV series. With Jim Carrey playing The Riddler in Batman Forever, much was done to popularise the character but prices only really rose in America on this comic so that the differential between values in the U.K. and U.S markets is increasing. Perhaps the answer is to increase the Good/Fine/Near Mint ratios drastically to reflect the possibility of a Near Mint copy coming on the British market and someone being prepared to pay near the £300 mark for it. More answers on a postcard please...

The 80pg giants continue to be hard to find in high grade (#176 and #198 in particular) and with their reprints going back to the 1940's, they are excellent reading material. #200 is another very common issue in some areas of the U.K. It has always been much sought after in America as many collectors traditionally start their runs at anniversary numbers. #200 sports a fine Neal Adams collage cover but the story and artwork (not by Adams) are less than breath-taking and the Near Mint value has stuck in the last year at £75 with the American listing at $160 or just over £100. In its favour there are cameo appearances from The Joker and The Penguin and the first page from Detective #27 is reprinted. #213 is becoming a minor classic with so many excellent key reprints. £25 for a high grade copy is an under-value in my opinion. #234 features the first modern appearance of Two Face as delineated by Neal Adams - amazing to think that such a major character never appeared right throughout the Silver Age. It is, however, an issue that turns up regularly on mart walls and £35 is a reflection of how this issue has been dragged up by the American market that considers it worth $100 or thereabouts. In old English guineas that's over £60. #238 has become sought after as a giant issue with a dark cover that shows all the wear and tear. The 1st Doom Patrol reprint also helps. The 100 pagers from #254 to 261 continue to fly out of dealers boxes though #260 seems way higher in value on the American market ($35 to £12.50). The run from #270 to #290 generally is as hard as ever to find and there are some excellent multi-part stories in amongst that run.

Year One and Ten Nights of the Beast continue to drop in value and Death in the Family has dropped quite considerably in demand. There are still a lot of copies in circulation from this period of Batman and unless the fourth film catches fire, supplies should meet demand. Watch out for #181 with the first appearance of Poison Ivy. And I guess #121 with Mr. Zero.

The current Batman storyline has had some fun with contagious diseases and Deadmen in Mexico but the style of the character is becoming more and more Bat-Demon with Kelley Jones delighting in how many yards of fabric he can get into the cape and have many teeth he can get into the Cheshire Cat-like grin. With pervading interest in all things mysterious and supernatural, it was inevitable that the Batman character would go the same X-Filesy sort of way but I hope that the fact that Batman is mortal and psychologically screwed up is not lost in favour of Bat-Demons with increased powers.

One other footnote: Catwoman appearances will continue to be watched with interest as speculators wonder if the Catwoman film (if it's ever made!) will do anything like what it did for the Batman character.

BATMAN ANNUAL

Earlier issues elude in high grade. #1 in particular is becoming something of a major key issue, very hard to find in high grade with its darker cover. Lower grades always sell (Batman in various bizarre forms and roles - the Zebra Batman a particular favourite of mine). Try finding any of these issues in shop back-issue bins or on the walls at marts and conventions.

BATMAN CHRONICLES

Not necessarily a hot back issue but worth drawing attention to as a new title which supports the main Batman titles and provides writers and artists with one-shot opportunities. Issue #5 with more details of what happened to Barbara Gordon after The Joker blew her abdomen away in Batman: The Killing Joke is a good example of what this series has to offer. Check it out.

BATMAN FAMILY

One of the more impossible sets to put together from recent times. Those that want one are continually frustrated. Keep looking. Values are steady in the U.K. market and still very reasonable on the U.S. market. The differential between the two is still quite high with "for-dollar-write-pound" prices. Slight drop on issue #17 as The Huntress is in something of a limbo with no current series.

BATMAN: LEGENDS OF THE DARK KNIGHT

One of DC's continued best-sellers. The "Venom" story from #16-20 is a particular favourite making #16 and #17 tough to find in the U.K. The Destroyer story was well received at the time as it crossed into the Batman and Detective titles. The Prey and Gothic storylines from earlier issues continue to be sought after. "Mask" by Bryan Talbot was well received and sold well. #50 with its stunning Brian Bolland cover is still sought after. Other general issues, particularly the earlier issues, have fallen slightly in price from Guide #7 with issue #1 dropping from £4.50 to £3.50 as a general Near Mint price. The Garth Ennis scripted issues #91 to #93 are ones to watch.

BATMAN: SWORD OF AZRAEL

This mini-series remains static in value in the U.K. after dropping in the years 1995 to 1996 with prices almost double in the U.S. The stunning Joe Quesada artwork and covers are probably the only reason why this title does not slide more than it has. Production values on the current Azrael series continue to be high and its recent involvement in the Contagion storyline has brought in new readers.

BATMAN: SON OF THE DEMON

The hardback graphic novel from 1987 has become sought after in the U.K. with average prices at around £30 though I have seen a copy at a recent mart at £50 (though whether it sold or not I don't know).

BATMAN: THE DARK KNIGHT RETURNS

The mini-series that started it all for Batman in 1986. It has reached a point of stasis as a back-issue seller as Batman: The Cult did in 1991 (and that is now a relatively poor seller). It was thought at the time that these two series would continue to sky-rocket but only goes to show how dangerous it is to predict prices in the world of comics. Far better to reflect prices in a Guide. The value on #1 has fallen dramatically in the U.K. over the last couple of years. £30-£35 at one time, now about half that at £15 to £16. For those that have never read it or are hard-core Marvel-ites, this is one to pick up and read if only to love it or loathe it. DC Comics have released a very handsome slip-case set with a sketch book and a Press Book with lots of articles surrounding the hype at the time ten years ago.

BATMAN: VENGEANCE OF BANE

Once a £15 comic in the U.K., the demand has slackened off a little and the £10 listing that we have given it seems more reasonable.

BATMAN VS. PREDATOR

A reasonable back-issue market has developed for this title but only really worth a mention for its marketing from DC and Dark Horse, the script by Dave Gibbons (who continues to grow in stature as a writer) and art by the Kuberts. The Prestige and Standard formats of each number smack a little of the Big Companies Game but none the less no harm done to the Batman character. One complaint however was the very dark reproduction in the Prestige Format issues, making it difficult to read. No change in prices.

BEST OF DC DIGEST

Worth mentioning as issues of these, let alone sets, just do not turn up. Or if they do they are not in any great shape as their Digest size makes them more difficult to store so they tend to get squeezed into book-shelves or get buried in dealers' boxes. Excellent reading value and some nice early Silver Age reprints. Not everyone's cup of tea owing to their smaller size but a title to watch. By the way, I'm still looking for a #57!

BLACKHAWK

A title much more highly rated in the U.S. market than in the U.K. market. Early issues in high grade are very hard to find in the U.K. though the customer base for them is very small. Sixties issues in low grade sell quite well as do issues around #230. These issues with the Blackhawks as super-heroes have achieved something of a cult status for epitomizing the era. The area where prices have fallen dramatically is around issues #160 with Near Mint price cuts of £5 and £10.

BRAVE AND THE BOLD

A big increase for #28 in 1995 to 1996 as it assumes it's rightful place as one of the main DC key issues but for the 1997 Guide we have decided to keep it static. This sells very well in poor and fair grades just for the sake of having one but high grade sales are few and far between at the moment and this Guide must reflect sales in the U.K. Up another $500 in the U.S. #29 and #30 are deservedly recognised as minor key issues. #25 is as rare in the U.K. as it ever was and is impossible to find in any grade (has Brian Bolland still got his? Want it!). Issues before this occasionally appear on mart walls in the U.K. and in spite of great Kubert art, there is little interest in Robin Hood, Viking Prince or Silent Knight. It would take a blood and guts, slice 'em dice 'em mini-series featuring all three of these characters to stir the interest. One of the big movers of recent times has been #34, the first Silver Age Hawkman.

1993 NM Price: £510.00
1994 NM Price: £1,050.00
1996 NM Price: £1,200.00

While we have nudged up the U.S market price to $1,800, we felt that this comic is just so fantastically expensive that demand in the U.K. for a Near Mint issue, if indeed one could be found, was just not there. So we have decided to drop the U.K. market price from £1,200 to £1,100. This is not to say that the comic is becoming worthless. But it is to say that there is a disparity between the U.K. and U.S. market prices on some comics and this one is a very good example as the issue is much more highly regarded in the U.S. Perhaps the visit of Joe Kubert to this year's UKCAC will heighten awareness of this comic and its place in comics' history.

The other Hawkman appearances in #35, #36, #42-44 have risen nicely in value in the U.S. but prices remain static in the U.K. Indeed we have dropped that value of #35 slightly. #54 continues to rise in the U.S. as it is proving hard to find though more research is being done on its scarcity in the U.K. As such we have frozen the value for this year. Those other issues from #55 to #59 are also undervalued in many people's opinion. Especially mine. But I have not let my own preferences get too much the better of me and values on #55 and #56 have been frozen with small increases on other issues in that run. Oh, the responsibility of it all! The Neal Adams issues from #79 to #86 have picked up in interest but we have dropped the prices on #80-82 a little. The 100 page issues from #112-117 are always missing from back-issue boxes which must tell you something. We have kept the prices static and as always adopt a wait and see policy rather than be accused of forcing prices up. Generally these 100 page DC comics can go for up to £6 or £7, particularly if they are perfectly square cut and don't have wrinkled or crushed spines. Later issues from #150 onwards are in plentiful supply apart from #191 which annoys completists. #197 is a very popular issue too wherein Earth 2 (Golden Age) Batman marries Catwoman.

CAPTAIN ATOM

A slight decrease in interest in the U.K. market reflected in the title value decreasing from £38.25 in 1996 to £30.00 in 1997.

CATWOMAN

The first few issues are always in demand with prices in the U.K. market holding steady at around £3.50 for issue #1, £2.00 for #2 and £1.50 on #3. Nice to see a heroine title do well.

CHALLENGERS OF THE UNKNOWN

Back issues of this title have remained very static. Shame. It seems that the earlier issues are just not wanted by the U.K. collector, even in half price sales. Only issues #1 and #2 have seen increases owing to their age and scarcity. Low grade copies of these early issues do tend to sell but they don't exactly fly off the wall. The Swamp Thing appearances in #82-87 again picked up as they are harder to find than ever. And the late reprint issues that ran the early Showcase appearances in all their glory are far cheaper than the originals and sport some nice Joe Kubert covers! Check them out. We'll see how the newest series pans out (currently on #3 at the time of writing).

CRISIS ON INFINITE EARTHS

A check-list has been included for those after the cross-over issues. It still remains DC's most successful mini-series. Having said that we have dropped the prices on issues #1 and #2 as they are turning up more regularly. Amazing that there hasn't been a trade paperback version which would be of great benefit to those that missed it first time around. The Zero Hour mini-series of 1994 was not exactly regarded by many as "Crisis II" and it remains to see how long it will be before there is a "Crisis III"

DC 100 PAGE SUPER SPECTACULAR

A very sought after run of 100 page giants. Never seen a complete set. Title value has gone from £48.50 to £66.50 which tells you something. #14 and #20 are the most popular with their excellent Golden Age Batman reprints but has anyone ever seen #5? Send it to me now!

DC SPECIAL

A much under-rated title that put together some nice classic collections for those who don't know a lot about where DC is coming from but would like to get a taste. Only 29 issues but it covers everything from super-hero to humour, horror to medieval. Reasonable parity of prices between the U.S. and U.K. markets. Notable exceptions are the last two issues which are scarce in the U.K.

DC SUPERSTARS

Another of those 70's sets which rarely show up on dealers' lists in the U.K. The title value has gone from £35 in 1996 to £42.50 for this Guide. Small increases maybe but nevertheless this title is on the up. #3 with The Legion of Super-Heroes is probably the hardest to find.

DEMON

The Kirby series from the 1970s continues to be sought after but prices in the U.K. market have been frozen across the board. Increases on the U.S. listings but we feel that the British market can't take these prices and a gap is starting to develop. Great covers - a fab monster in issue #2 (check it out - Fin Fang Foom's cousin?). The 16 issues are difficult to put together as a run in a hurry. The Lobo cross-overs in the 2nd series are about the only thing worth mentioning, cancelled in 1995.

DETECTIVE COMICS

The 2nd string Batman title has been extended back into the mists of time to #1 and includes of course the classic comics Detective #27-38 that would need a mortgage to buy. There is a small market for the very early issues of this title in the U.K. though copies sold are usually low grade. Nice to see a restored copy of #1 sell for £15,000 after an abortive attempt to sell it through the New York Sotheby's catalogue. I hear there were some absolute horror stories regarding the management of that sale, allegedly. A small cachet of early issues was discovered in the U.K. about four years ago by Bruce Paley of Skinny Melinks down in South London though some had missing pages. As with early issues of Action and Adventure Comics, we are assuming that most collectors realise that these issues are all at least scarce in the U.K. and most of them rare rather than putting as such against every entry and adding about 30 pages to the total page count of the book!

Still interesting is #168 with the first origin of The Joker though he had already been around for a dozen years or so and this issue has picked up in value with some recorded sales in the U.S. and two in the U.K. quite unusually. Detective #225 saw a very healthy increase in value in the last year - it really is tough to find in high grade with its bright yellow cover and its been helped by some interest in the Martian Manhunter and his role in Justice League Task Force. An increase of £500 on the U.K. market price does seem high (£3,000 to £3,500 in Near Mint) especially when there is no mention of the Martian Manhunter on the cover. But it does have a place in comics' history as for some it is the start of the Silver Age and its date of 1955 is a convenient one. #233 saw a smaller increase (from £700 to £785 in Near Mint) though it is thought to be much scarcer than #225.

Issues around #235-239 are virtually never seen in the U.K. #235 in particular is extremely hard to find and the £400 Near Mint value is probably very conservative believe it or not. I have been looking for a very high grade copy for over 20 years and I know of virtually every one that is ever offered. Talk about anal-retentive!

#327 is fast becoming a minor key issue at around £50 in the U.K. Try and find one with a bright white cover. #387 is sought after for its cover and reprinting the first Batman appearance in Detective #27 (May 1939). It is regularly missing from collections bought in. Slight increase on #400 from £27.50 to £30.00 with Man-Bat in the current storyline and the excellent Man-Bat series from John Bolton. A character worthy of his own series. The Marshall Rogers issues in the #470's remain static though their classic renditions of Batman and particularly the Joker are well worth the view if you're not familiar. The new Robin appearances in #524, #525 and #535 are down slightly. #599 and #600 remain static as there seem to be a lot of copies hoarded by collectors. #627 with its tribute to #27 remains an attractive issue but in good supply therefore no price change. The conclusion to The Destroyer story proved very popular. Covers on issues #654-660 by Sam Kieth have been real eye-catchers but some fans may feel disappointed that such artwork is not carried on once the book is opened.

#691's new Spellbinder was quite a hit with some fans, cashing in on the fad for "hot babes". Hot babes continue with Poison Ivy in #693/694. Classic villains are back with The Riddler and the Cluemaster and a multi-part Joker story is on the way.

DOOM PATROL

Fortunes were revived for this title for a time under the Vertigo banner and scripting by Rachel Pollack but back-issue sales seem to have fallen off dramatically as the title was cancelled in early 1995. Back issues from #19 are static in terms of demand, in spite of the stunning Simon Bisley covers and for the Grant Morrison scripts that remain as thought-provoking as ever. #19 has fallen from £6 in 1996 to £3.50 in this Guide and even that seems quite high to me.

The original series has not fared too well with hardly any increases at all in the Good and Fine grades and copies sticking on Mart walls, even at 50% off. Only strict Near Mint copies are in demand. Seems that no-one is really that interested in the likes of Arnold Drake's bizarre scripts or the Bruno Premiani artwork. #121 continues its something of a cult status book. Readers, it's up to you. You decide if the Doom Patrol lives or dies. Well, the readers decided alright as that was the last issue! The only real activity has been the trade in Erik Larsen issues (#6-15) of the 2nd series because they remain cheap and they are in plentiful supply.

ECLIPSO

His first appearances in House of Secrets have slight demand though still tough to find in high grade. No interest in own series. Prices exactly the same as last year.

EIGHTY PAGE GIANT

This series has shown more interest as people realise what excellent reprints are to be found in there at a fraction of the cost of the originals. Having said that, the phenomenal interest in this title in the States keeps forcing up the price. This Guide is reflecting the availability and consequent static nature of prices in Good and Fine grades. The title value in pounds has not changed though the dollar title value is up by nearly $400. For those that want very high grade copies, reasonable parity of U.S. and U.K. prices comes into play. Of particular interest are #4 with the early Flash reprints, #8 for the origin stories and #14/#15 for their scarcity. #7 is still classified as rare in the U.K. as it does not seem to turn up in any grade.

FAMOUS FIRST EDITION

Love 'em. Tabloid size replicas of early DC super-key issues. Very hard to find in Near Mint and though the Action Comics #1 has been listed at £15, in reality £25 to £30 for a true Near Mint copy is what you would have to shell out. Believe me I've been looking for long enough and that's what I had to pay!

FLASH

Demand for this title has slackened off considerably in spite of being one of the biggest success stories as far as Silver Age DC back-issues go in recent years. All the early issues are in demand in the U.K. but really only in low grades. Flash #105 is proving to be one of the top DC key issues but again only really in top, top grade:

1993 NM Price: £1,350.00 1994 NM Price: £1,995.00
1996 NM Price: £2,900 1997 NM Price: £3,600.00

In lower grades, this is a difficult sell in the U.K. as a Good copy lists at £300 (a small increase on last year in spite of the massive increase at the top end. A ratio adjustment was inevitable). A big jump also for #110, especially in America to a massive $1,500! A mere skip for #123 and no change in the U.K. for #175 for the second year running. Though hard to find, it is well over-priced in the U.K. The 80pg giants are much in demand for their reprints, indeed all the early issues can be found in reprint somewhere (see the Reprint Index). The 2nd series continues to sell, particularly the later issues with the introduction of Impulse, the Terminal Velocity and Dead Heat storylines and generally Mark Waid's writing. Nice tribute to the original cover on issue #123 of the new series.

G.I. COMBAT

Issue #138 is of interest with the first appearance of The Losers. The main interest in this title of late has been the run from #75 to #109 of grey-tone or painted covers. Very sexy in a glossy Mylar protective sleeve.

GREEN LANTERN

#1 saw a healthy increase from £1,400 to £1,950 from Guides #6 to #7 but we have decided to keep this value static. Still very tough to find in unrestored NM. Early issues have been generally static and #40 still remains a mystery. It is highly regarded in America and priced as such but according to observations and Questionnaires in this country it would be valued at around half current American prices. Indeed in the Guide we have priced it at less than half the U.S. value ($500 to £150 - big difference!). #45 has been forced up to £40 by the American average price of $125 or over £80 in conversion, #59 has gone up a little but #116 has gone down from £5 to £4. #76 still seems to be undervalued for its historical importance and its package as a very attractive comic book. £100 for a true Near Mint copy seems very reasonable to me. Emerald Dawn I and II remain static. The Golden Age Green Lantern market seems very slow in the U.K. This Guide has adopted a parity of pricing between U.S. and U.K. prices though in theory Golden Age issues are harder to get in the U.K. and should be more expensive.

HAWKMAN

Early issues continue to rise steadily in the U.S. but that is only refected in the U.K. in the highest grades on the earliest issues. Issue #1 has seen a significant rise from £275.00 to £350.00. A copy sold in a postal auction in 1996 for £400. Good and Fine prices have gone down substantially in the U.K. as there seems to be a plentiful supply in most comic shops, at marts and on dealers' lists. Funny how all grades keep going up in American guides (see Aquaman and Atom!).

HEART THROBS

Mentioning these only as part of the DC Romance titles which are an under-collected genre in the U.K. Perhaps not to everyone's taste but they do have some great story titles, some nice grey-tone covers and their rarity drives DC completists wild (like me! Send me all your copies now).

HELLBLAZER

Always worth a mention as one of DC's fan-favourites. Early issues are still in demand though prices in the U.K. have remained static from the last Guide. Garth Ennis successfully took up the reigns of Jamie Delano and kept this title right on track along with Sean Phillips excellent art. There are stories that make you laugh out loud. Excellent. Nice Al Davison art in #101. It is seen very much as a companion title to Sandman and collectors of one usually collect the other. Though as Sandman has been cancelled it will be interesting to see how Hellblazer fares on its own. Gets from me the "Title/character most worthy of Film Treatment" award.

HITMAN

Big hit title in recent times and back issues still sought after. Issue #1 at around £5 nationwide. Prices will probably remain fairly static from now on.

HOUSE OF MYSTERY

There has been a marked swing away from the earlier horror/mystery issues which have fallen in value. They are still hard to find in high grade though and low grade copies are an excellent read. #143 has risen in value slightly from £150 to £160 in Near Mint and small rises for #178 and #179. Some lovely moody covers around here by Neal Adams.

HOUSE OF SECRETS

Very early issues collected for their Jack Kirby art. The Eclipso run from #61 to #80 has its collectors, #61 rising from £75 to £85 in Near Mint. #92 continues to defy best efforts to find it in NM and interest in it has surged as sales have been reported consistently over the psychological £200 barrier.

1993 NM Price: £95.00 1994 NM Price: £160.00
1996 NM Price: £250.00 1997 NM Price: £300.00

A good seller in low grade too but very hard to sell in mid grade. May have to adjust the ratio next year to a 1:3:12.

IMPULSE

A fan favourite on both sides of the Atlantic. Supplies seem to be reaching the fairly plentiful in the U.K. as #1 went up to £5.00 and slipped back to about half that in the last Guide. We've tweaked it up another 50p to £3.50. A fun read.

INFINITY INC.

#49 and #50 may be ones to watch with the appearance of Lyta that ties into the modern Sandman title. Otherwise this title is a cheap read and of great interest if you want a taste of Golden Age heroes and their off-spring.

INVISIBLES

Another Vertigo success story and the Britpack show the way in comics yet again. Issue #1 of the first series goes for around £2.00 and a 2nd series has just started sporting very nice Brian Bolland covers, still the best cover artist in the business.

JERRY LEWIS

Good oddball stuff with some Neal Adams art to boot. Issues #101-105 sought after. A title to watch.

JIMMY OLSEN

Does #1 exist in high grade outside the U.S? A genuinely hard book to find in any grade. A title that appeals to thirty-somethings only these days. Probably true in the U.S. as well. Current collectors have no interest in Superman signal watches (prizes for anyone who can remember the sound it made?) and hoax stories involving kryptonite. Legion collectors pick up Legion appearances, the 80 page giants are as hard to find as in any other title and most interest lies in issues #133-135 with the first appearances of Darkseid.

Issue #1 - 1996 NM Price: £2,500 1997 NM Price: £3,000

JONAH HEX

This 92 issue series has come on leaps and bounds in the U.K. in the last couple of years. Hard to believe that a #1 can fetch up to £30.00. More Price Guide prizes on offer here - can you find the issue with my (poetic but embarrassing) letter in it? Although prices have risen in the U.S. we have frozen prices in the U.K. market just to see how sales and interest are maintained. Don't want to do anything silly in a price guide now do we?

JUSTICE LEAGUE

#3 test cover has slipped again in interest. Hard to believe that this was once a £100 comic. £17.50 now if you're lucky as we've listed it but in truth I would be surprised if anyone would pay more than £10. A personal opinion. How unlike the Firestorm #61 test cover which is incredibly hard to find! The Justice League family of titles have slipped badly in the past couple of years to the point where Justice League Europe and Justice League Quarterly were cancelled whereas in 1992/3 interest was very high. The alternative Justice League storyline of recent times where they broke people's arms and kicked in heads got great fan reaction. Recent storylines like Aftershocks, Judgement Day and Way of the Warrior did their best to involve other characters in cross-over opportunities. But the series finally fell at #113 in mid 1996. The relaunched JLA has caused some interest with the first issue seen at £2.50 at recent marts.

JUSTICE LEAGUE OF AMERICA

#1 has been dropped in value slightly for the U.K. market. A very tough decision but one that reflects the level of sales. We have kept the dollar price static. #2 has remained static. As for #3 with its black cover, this issue is notoriously hard to find in any decent shape. Reluctantly we have frozen this issue as well, just to see how the new JLA may kick-start back issue sales on this title as the two Leagues are more similar that they have been in recent years. Small jump for #9 as well for #21 and #22 though in this latter case, the dollar price is rising faster. There are just so many mid grade copies of #21 and #22 on the British market. Issue #39 is still in demand with its excellent reprints though the value remains static for now. Issues from #60-100 are getting scarcer in the U.K., particularly the Neal Adams cover issues in the #80s and #90s. The 100 pagers (#110-116) are always missing from back-issue boxes and always seem to sell, more so than, say, the Brave and Bold 100 page issues. #122-150 continue to drive JLA completists mad. Were more than just a few copies of #150 ever printed? This title is a steady back issue seller from about #50 onwards and gains new fans all the time.

KAMANDI

Still an under-rated title in the U.K. It's just not to everyone's taste. Not the easiest of sets to complete but possible as prices remain static. Growing U.S/U.K. differential. #1 at $45 or £30. About £15 in the U.K. at the moment. A few shades of Jack Kirby at his Fourth World best. We'll see if DC's new Fourth World title makes any difference to Kamandi this year.

KOBRA

Only seven issues but surprisingly in demand. Jack Kirby's swan-song at DC.

L.E.G.I.O.N.

Lobo's presence used to ensure that this book sold consistently though this seems to be a particularly regional creature - hot seller in some areas of the U.K., distinctly cool in others. Cancelled in late 1994 and back issue sales have suffered accordingly.

LEGION OF SUPER-HEROES

Throughout the history of the Legion of Super-Heroes, each incarnation has brought re-vamps and change but there is more than the feeling that the huge popularity gained by the first 25 issues of the 2nd series in the mid 1980s has never been regained since. The Quiet Darkness storyline towards the end of 1991 did something to improve the ratings. The destruction of the planet Earth went down very well which gave rise to a popular spin-off The Legionnaires - the spirit of the Legion as they first were back in the very early 1960s, all about 14 years old and ready to take on the world. But though this title remains a decent seller, there just does not seem to be the interest in team books that there once was. Time will tell just how the back-to-basics approach of very young teen heroes will perform in the marketplace. Back-issue prices in the current Legion series have dropped to a general £1.00/£1.25 mark.

LIMITED COLLECTORS' EDITION

More tabloids as with Famous First Edition. A nice 70's set of varying quality from the sublime of Tarzan reprints by Joe Kubert to the ridiculous of Rudolph the Red Nosed Reindeer.

LOBO"

Still one of DC's most popular characters. The first mini-series continues to sell but supplies seem adequate for demand. Prices have dropped slightly from Guide #7.

Subsequent mini-series have done quite well and Lobo guest-appearances in other titles are a useful stand-by to halt flagging sales in lesser titles so that says something of the character's overall status in the DC universe. His first appearance in Omega Men #3 still hasn't taken off as any sort of key issue however (no matter how hard you try Darryl!)

LOIS LANE

As with Jimmy Olsen, #1 is very hard to find in high grade though does turn up in the U.K. in lower grades fairly regularly. #1 has risen from £1,650 to £1,750 but if a true Near Mint copy became available I know several people who would pay two or three times that, including myself! As with Jimmy Olsen, only a certain section of collectors bother with this title. Stories about Lois tricking Superman into revealing his identity belong to a different era. #70 is still quite big news in America, not so much in the U.K. and that is reflected in the price difference ($275 plays £90 - work it out!). One or two issues in the early '70s are sought after for Darkseid appearances and the last few issue can be quite scarce in the U.K. for completists.

METAL MEN/METAMORPHO

"Very static as back issues and reaching the stage of U.K. prices being half that of U.S. values" is what we said last year. No change.

MISTER MIRACLE

The latest series was sadly cancelled after only 7 issues. There is something of the Conan Syndrome here: no matter how many times they try to re-launch the title, the buying public fail to respond. The original Jack Kirby series still continues to attract fans keen to collect The Fourth World of Kirby despite having no current series to keep the interest going. New Gods, the latest series also having been cancelled after only 15 issues, has generally suffered a downturn in interest. The original series from the early 1970's has been less affected and it does remain the most popular Fourth World series.

MORE FUN COMICS

A monster of a title, many a classic has passed through its numbers. First appearances of the Spectre, Dr. Fate and Aquaman but demand is strictly limited to those that can afford them. Later issues in lower grades are fairly common and worth picking up. Issue #101 is slowing down in popularity. The very first few issues are very popular in America but sales are unheard of in the U.K. Will that ever change? About time more American dealers took a chance and came over to the U.K. with some interesting material at realistic prices. They may be pleasantly surprised.

MY GREATEST ADVENTURE

Some lovely covers on early issues. Notable for #80 being the first appearance of Doom Patrol. Hard to find in high grade with its black cover but in general these Doom Patrol issues are slow sellers and almost non-existent as far as sales go in middle grades.

MYSTERY IN SPACE

Much under-rated in the U.K. All that lovely Infantino artwork and some lovely covers on issues between #53 and about #90. No wonder they are starting to appear on dealers' lists. Issue #75 continues to elude British collectors and #55 with its grey-tone cover is a genuine rarity in the U.K. #53 is sought after but only in lower grades as far as we can tell.

Issue #53 - 1996 NM Price : £900.00
1997 NM Price: £1,000.00

THE NEW TITANS

Like the Legion of Super-Heroes, this is one of those titles that enjoyed a high profile and popularity in the mid 1980's but saw years of decline and final cancellation in early 1996. The New Titans title was helped in 1990 with the Batman/Tim Drake Robin cross-over and again in 1991 with Deathstroke appearances, his relationship with Jericho, a death here and there and a line-up change. The Titans Sell Out storyline was quite well received at the time. Back issues will probably remain static for some time to come. Time will tell what effect the latest Teen Titans title (launched in October 1996) will have.

NEW YORK WORLD'S FAIR

Unbelievably hard to find but to devoted Golden Age collectors covet these comics like very few others. The Guide can only adopt reasonable parity between U.S. and U.K. values. Theoretically it would be much harder for a U.K. collector to find and buy one of these issues without going to America himself/herself. Very low grade copies would sell in the U.K. with some regularity if they could be supplied. Noted for the only appearance of Superman with blond hair and the fist published appearance of the Golden Age Sandman.

OMEGA MEN

The first Lobo appearances seem to be very static in the U.K. marketplace and this is refected in the downward turn in the listed value from last year's £6.00 down to £3.50. Seems odd that Lobo is a major character in the DC universe and yet his 1st appearance commands nothing like the attention and value that it should. Maybe because it isn't really like the Lobo that the character has evolved into.

OUR ARMY AT WAR/OUR FIGHTING FORCES

The war comic genre is generally under-rated in the U.K. which is a shame as there are some lovely grey-tone covers and some great Russ Heath and Joe Kubert art to be sampled. The market on these is very U.S. driven and the U.K. Guide can only reflect the constantly rising prices in the U.S. with a conversion back-to-pounds-less-a-bit. The same can be said for All American Men of War, G.I. Combat and Star Spangled War Stories. Our Army at War #81 is big in the States. I can think of maybe two people over here that would be interested/could afford £1,000 or thereabouts for a Near Mint copy. An example of the difference of the size and nature of the respective U.K. and U.S. markets.

PHANTOM STRANGER

A title to watch. One of those that occupied bargain bins for years, now try even finding them. Noted for a long run of excellent Neal Adams covers. Phantom Stranger is one of those characters that has a bit of the gothic horror and the gumshoe detective and with the right creative team (Gary Frank recently expressed an interest in it to me. Or was it Charlie Adlard?), the title could be another winner from Vertigo.

PREACHER

One of the hottest (how I detest that word!) series around. Preacher caught everyone by surprise last year on both sides of the Atlantic. Prices are generally more here in the U.K. but it won't be long before the dollar price goes up and beyond. Well done Garth Ennis and Steve Dillon. Price on #1 about the £17.50 mark at the time of writing (£7.50 last year!). For crackingly good reads, check out the Preacher Specials Saint of Killers and Arseface.

RAY

Issues of the first mini-series featuring Joe Quesada still sell. Shame he didn't do more of them. The on-going series was cancelled with issue #28 and may have effectively killed off any back issue interest in the character.

SANDMAN

What is there to say that hasn't been already? Still DC's most popular series and award-winner (worth re-iterating that #19 won an international award for Best Short Story, significantly without there having to be a special category because it's a comic) is still a good read. Some over-criticize in the fan press, some over-intellectualize but it still demonstrates some of the best qualities about comics. The release of the trade paperbacks collecting the first 69 issues (ie. virtually all of them) has proved very popular over the last few years. #8 is still in demand as the first appearance of Death and the variant issue has been recorded as selling consistently in America for over $150 with a few recorded sales in this country at £100. Not sure sure that this will continue as the market for any kind of premium or special variant issue is virtually dead now. The Season of Mists storyline beginning in #21/#22 excited some interest in 1991 while the more recent Game of You and Brief Lives storylines continue the excellence. Issue #69, the conclusion of "The Kindly Ones", is one to watch where Sandman/Morpheus dies. The storyline of "The Wake" provoked much interest. And then they cancelled the title at issue #75 and I don't have a reason for living. At least some sort of monthly fix can be found in the spin-off series, The Dreaming.

RIP HUNTER, TIME MASTER

Consistently steady price rises on this title though it must be said that this is one of those US dealer driven titles - anyone who wants to collect this attractive short series but wants high grade would have to rely on American sources. Low grade issues of this title sell well.

SECRET ORIGINS ANNUAL

Big book in high grade now. We have kept the prices on Good and Fine grades static as that is probably a true reflection in the U.K. market but the issue is quite hard find in any grade.

1996 NM price: £250.00 1997 NM Price: £300.00

SEEKERS INTO THE MYSTERY

Just when this title was being noticed by fans here in the U.K., it was cancelled with issue #15. This has probably killed any back-issue interest but it is still a title worth picking up for a thought-provoking read.

SENSATION COMICS

We mentioned this title in the DC Market Overview last year only because we were so gob-smacked to hear about the phenomenal price rises in the States at the time. Can a second-string title really double in price from one year to the next? Is #1 in particular that sought after? Not here in the U.K. And this is our constant problem. The U.K. Guide has to adopt some sort of parity on these issues as someone wishing to buy could reasonably be expected to pay at least the going U.S. rate and probably more without dealers' discounts if you go over to America yourself. And with dealers' profit margins taken into consideration if you rely on a U.K. dealer bringing something back for you, as a collector you are caught both ways.

SHADE

Another British affair. This title began with a bang and promptly fizzled out in 1990. 1991 saw a steady improvement and the painted covers by Jamie Hewlett were well received. Improvement continued and steadied with the storyline of Shade the Changing Woman and then the Birth Pains storyline under the Vertigo banner by scripter Garth Ennis so finally people were beginning to pick it up along with their Sandmans and Hellblazers. Interest continued as the title reached its 50th issue but in the last year it has proved static so much so that back issue prices on early issues have fallen. Good read though. I'll always champion the reading of comics. There is no interest it seems in the original late 1970's series featuring Steve Ditko artwork. Perhaps because the characters are completely different. Maybe for that reason alone, it is worth picking them up for comparison.

SHAZAM!

A 70s title that is starting to be in demand again on the strength of the current Power of Shazam series. This original series is twenty years old and is an entertaining read. The 100 page issues #12-17 are increasingly hard to find.

SHOWCASE

The title that requires a mortgage to acquire is rapidly seeing the same steps needed for single issues. It seems a pity that this title is pricing itself out of the reach of almost all collectors on both sides of the Atlantic. There are very few people in the U.K. right now saying to themselves "Right, I'm going to start collecting a set of Showcase". There are probably not many more saying "Well, I'll forget the first 20 or so". Showcase #4 widened the gap with its nearest rivals in the "most valuable" stakes.

1993 NM Price: £6,000.00 1994 NM Price: £9,000.00
1996 NM Price: £17,500 1997 NM Price: £18,700.00

Price variations on this comic are huge. Several high grade issues have sold in America in the last two years at up to $30,000 and one sold for a staggering $29,000 cash alone! One was very recently offered at $50,000 in an auction system of buying. As incredible as it may seem, a relatively conservative value has been chosen for this British guide but bear in mind that this is one of those comics that genuinely sell for multiples of guide in high grades. Showcase #8 went much the same way:

1993 NM Price: £1,950.00 1994 NM Price: £4,000.00
1996 NM Price: £9750.00 1997 NM Price: £10,000.00

It is very hard to find in Fine or above let alone Very Fine or better. As Showcase #4 rises, this 2nd appearance of Flash must also. #13 and #14 continue to climb (#14 is definitely harder to find). #15 took another jump. Space Ranger may not be a major character (a Space Ranger series is still apparently on its way) but it is a notoriously hard issue to find, particularly with its black cover that usually hides someone's attempts at colour-touching with a felt tip pen. Other issues with significant value increases: #17, #22, #27, #34, #37, #45, #55, #59, #60-#62. And the whole set will put you back about 67 grand. Bargain. A series crying out for careful reprinting.

Showcase '93 was a nice idea but executed pretty poorly apart from issues #7 and #8. Showcase '94-'96 looked a lot better. The two Supergirl issues from Showcase '95 are asked for on the strength of the latest Supergirl series.

SPECTRE

This 3rd series has really caught on with many people. Back issue prices are still very reasonable but supplies of the first few numbers are drying up. We have kept the prices the same as last year on these first few issues but we can foresee rises in the Update. The first series has always been popular in the States and has dragged that British market price along with it, not to parity levels but bubbling just under. #1 with its black cover is hard to find in high grade.

STAR TREK: THE NEXT GENERATION

Now that the series is regularly shown on satellite TV in the U.K., the comic book is bound to be a good, consistent seller. Star Trek in general is faring well after the media attention of the 30th anniversary last year and the Star Trek: First Contact film. There is a healthy back-issue market for all DC, Marvel and Gold Key Star Trek series though the prices on the early Gold key series are getting beyond the reach of most U.K. collectors.

STARMAN

This new series is really getting into its stride and back issue prices on the first few issues are climbing. £3.50 for #1 is listed in this Guide but £5 and more is not uncommon on dealers' lists. Have a read if you are not familiar.

STRANGE ADVENTURES

The Animal Man issues (#180, #184, #190, #195, #201) are well dead. #117 (1st Atomic Knights) seems a more interesting book though its appeal is for the dedicated few. Excellent reading value as quirky sci-fi was one area that DC excelled in and didn't always rely on fabulous monsters that threatened the Earth etc. Some nice art by Gil Kane and Carmine Infantino too. The Deadman run from #205 to #216 with Neal Adams art in most has enjoyed a slight price increase at the front end, static city for the rest of the run for the last two years. The last few issues from #227 to #231 are excellent reading value with great Silver Age reprints.

SUPERBOY

Issue #100 was always a biggie in the States and the British equivalent price inevitably gets dragged up with the US dollar increases. This year we have frozen the U.K. price while the dollar value climbs as an indication of how over-priced we think the book is! Silver Age collectors in the U.K. still like #86 and #89 and for my money #147 is a hard comic to find with its new Legion origin story. Interest remains in the increasingly difficult issues #197-#202 (Legion). All the 80pg giants with their value-for-money reprints are hard to find in back-issue boxes. Late Golden Age issues (ie. the first 20 or so) have a minority following but then they don't exactly turn up in cartloads.

SUPER DC GIANT

A title to watch. Try finding #17. Great reprints throughout the series.

SUPER FRIENDS

Something of a cult follows this title. Very cheap (when you can find them) and a must for DC completists. Price increases on the first few issues from last year.

SUPERGIRL

The latest series with Gary Frank art caught on very quickly with issue #1 rising to about £5.00 at marts. The interest may wain a little now that Gary is off the book (at the time of writing this) so we have listed #1 at £3.50. After so many attempts to launch this character with her own ongoing series, it would be a shame to see it cancelled before it was really given a chance. Watch this space...

SUPERMAN

The listing starts from #1 to take in some of those early classics. Even though the Golden Age market is relatively small in the U.K., Superman comics always sell, particularly in lower grades. Get a load, if you can, of such classic covers as #14 and #24. Note also undervalued keys like #61 and #76. #100 is as hard to find in any grade as ever. Back-issue sales on the 1960's material is steady: once again the 80pg giants are snapped up and some becoming noticeably scarcer (#193 and #202 for example). Issue #200 is one that doesn't seem to turn up and it is 30 years old! #233 is an undervalued issue as all Kryptonite is turned to harmless lead. Fab Neal Adams cover. Issues from about #290 to #300 are very hard to find in the U.K. Issues in the 300's and 400's are in good supply but still don't stay long in back issue bins as they are still relatively cheap. As with Action Comics, interest in the Death and Rebirth issues of Superman is steady and sales of the current issues are healthy with storylines such as The Death of Clark Kent and The Trial of Superman still holding the attention. Latest storylines have been a marketing person's dream with the marriage of Superman to Lois Lane after nearly 60 years and most recently the new look Superman, new costume, new powers, new gimmick. The Wise Old Ones say that this storyline will be resolved in the summer annuals so that the familiar costume is back for the merchandising people to begin the run into the Superman: Reborn film for 1998. And for Superman's 60th anniversary next year, will we see a super-baby now that Superman is mortal (for the time being) and can presumably make babies without making too much of a mess of Lois Lane's parts...?

SWAMP THING

Sadly cancelled after 171 issues. Now that Alan Moore is back in the frame scripting super-hero stuff over at Image, there is renewed interest in the Alan Moore issues starting at #20. There is interest in the first series too. Some excellent Bernie Wrightson art and Len Wein scripts. £35 for a Near Mint #1 is not unreasonable. The last five issue of this original series are hard to find in the U.K.

TARZAN

Worth a mention as this 70s series has some excellent Joe Kubert artwork, much of it was Non-Distributed at the newsagents in the U.K. and the 100 page issues are becoming scarcer.

WEIRD WESTERN TALES

Jonah Hex appearances in #12 and #13 are especially sought after in the U.K. as is the rest of the series up to #38 before Jonah Hex graduated on to his own series. We have kept prices static in order to monitor the progress of this title as a back-issue seller. It was not so long ago that this was a bargain box title.

WITCHING HOUR

This long-standing mystery title is being picked up in the U.K. for the Wrightson and Neal Adams art in the early issues and are good reading value for money. #3, #5, #8 and #13 are the issues to watch out for.

WONDER WOMAN

Listing is from #1 on the first series to take in some of those early classics though there is some increased interest from last year in these very early issues in the U.K. Mid Golden Age issues in low to mid grades sell. Issue #105 has caused much excitement in the US with the powers that be behind the Overstreet Guide in particular hyping it up above and beyond. Impossible to say what the outcome and eventual listed value will be. Unfortunately the knock-on effect for U.K. collectors can only be immediate increases if they want a copy. Issues around #200 are much in demand as are the 100 page issues #211 and #214. The Animal Man appearances in #267/268 have long died in interest. War of the Gods, which was centred very much around the second series but to no great acclaim, did nothing as back issues shortly after the time and still haven't. The Brian Bolland covers on recent issues were up to his usual excellent standard. The title enjoyed a new lease of life with artwork by Mike Deodato but sadly his tenure was short-lived. Issues #85 and #90 are still in demand. Much was expected of John Byrne taking over the reins but fan reaction has been mixed and fans are still waiting.

WORLD'S FINEST

Listing starts at #1 to include the very scarce and rare issues with cardboard covers that obviously hardly ever turn up in great shape. Unfortunately the demand for early issues of this title is quite low in the U.K. and looks set to remain so. The absurdity of the stories remain the chief delight of this title. How else could you team the world's mightiest hero with a mere mortal man (even if it was Batman?). By using a healthy dose of magic and monsters, role reversal and powerlessness. Silver Age issues in general are quite sought after and there is that very tough-to-find late Golden Age/early Silver Age range from about #65-85. The 80pg and 100pg giants seem to be the best sellers along with #198/#199's Superman/Flash race part 3. #71 is still an undervalued issue and under-rated for its historical importance of being the first of regular Superman/Batman stories. The run of 80 page issues from #244 to #252 are becoming harder to find, particularly the first few. Nice Neal Adams covers too.

ZERO HOUR

The mini-series that removed the 25th and 30th Centuries from DC continuity but didn't set the back-issue world alight. #4 is slightly harder to find in the U.K. as the series caught many shops and dealers on the hop. The time-line chart is quite groovy but incomprehensible to a sad old Silver Age freak like me.

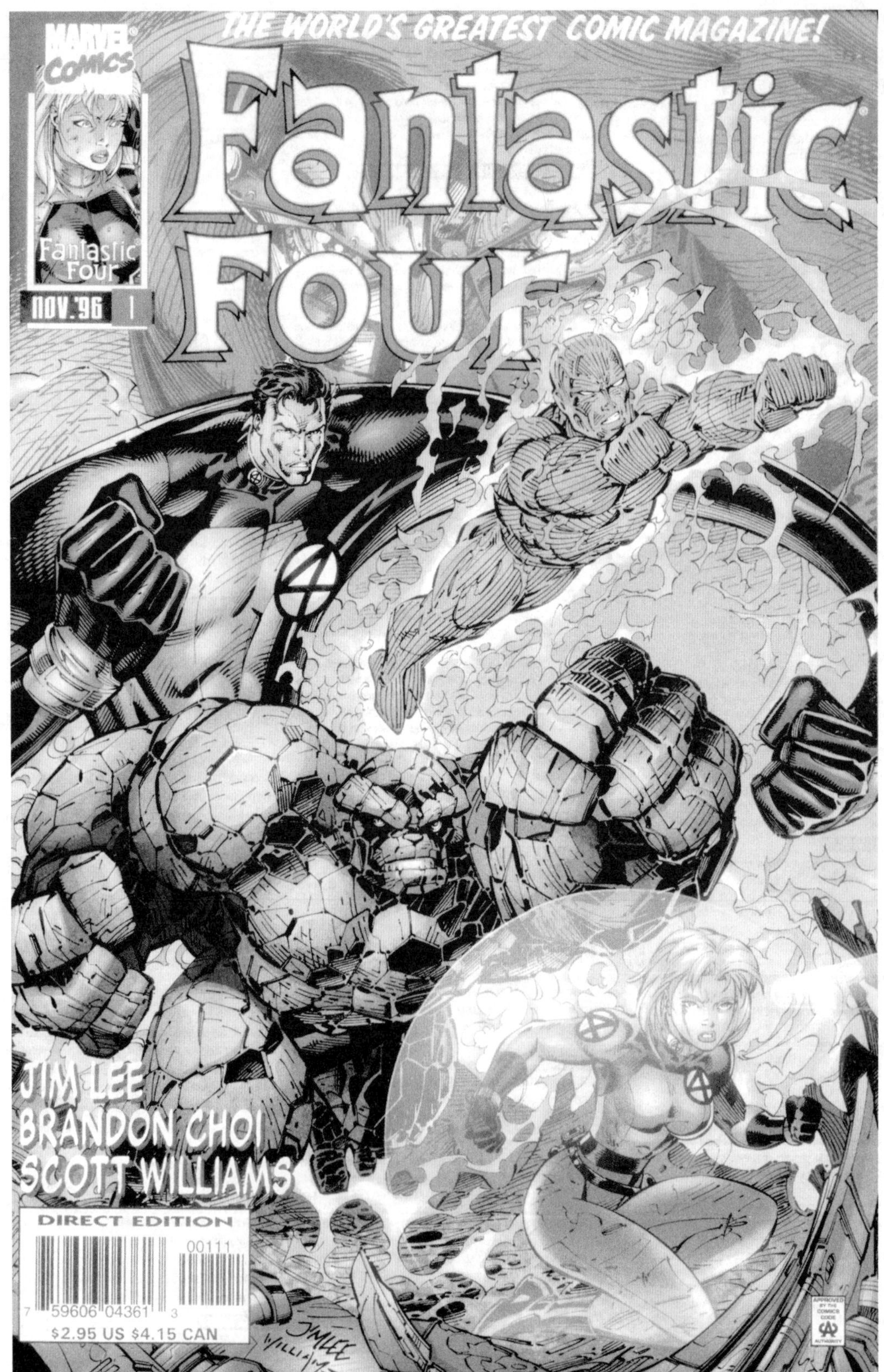

Fantastic Four #1 (2nd) – the flagship Marvel title relaunched under the Image Comics banner with origins and characters updated for the 90s

INTRODUCTION TO MARVEL COMICS

Marvel Comics (also known as Timely Comics in the 1940s and Atlas Comics in the 1950s) have been published and distributed in America since 1939. Official distribution in the U.K. began in July 1960, although there may have been sporadic trial distribution before this date. The first years of the original Marvel Bullpen fronted by Stan Lee, Jack Kirby, Steve Ditko and Dick Ayers produced Fantastic Four in November 1961, followed by The Incredible Hulk in May 1962 and Spiderman in **Amazing Fantasy #15** in August 1962, Sgt. Fury in May 1963, The Mighty Thor in August, The Avengers and The X-Men in September and Daredevil in April 1964. It was an impressive and enduring output.

The Marvel style was very much more dynamic than that of the more well established but by that time somewhat staid-in-some-areas D.C. Their heroes were younger and created a new kind of rapport with their readers. Heroes like the impetuous Human Torch, the misunderstood Hulk and the has-trouble-with-the-girls-gets-bullied-at-college Spiderman. The Marvel universe was very much more integrated from the start with characters crossing over into each other's territories and every permutation of team-up. This was very different from the D.C. Universe of more hermetically sealed characters and stories. Also, the use of a tight stable of artists and Stan Lee writing virtually everything made the feel and look of the Marvel Universe more coherent. Marvel very much led the way with the potential of team books like The Avengers, X-Men and Fantastic Four and later The Champions, The Defenders, Alpha Flight, Squadron Supreme, The New Mutants and Power Pack, although ironically,

D.C. Comics had the first super-hero team of all in the Justice Society of America. Marvel also gave a kind of value for money by having composite books - The Hulk and Giant Man in Tales to Astonish and Captain America and Iron Man in Tales of Suspense.

Perhaps where Marvel scored most of all was with the different kind of intimacy between creators and public. "Smiling" Stan Lee used his editorials and letters pages to add to the Marvel bandwagon and soon True Believers earned their "No Prizes" for spotting mistakes in stories, enrolled in the Merry Marching Marvel Society, became Quite Nuff Sayers if their letters got printed and read their own fanzine FOOM (Friends of Ol' Marvel). No wonder Stan Lee was smiling.

In the D.C. manner, Marvel went in for revivals. In **Avengers #4**, January 1964, Captain America was revived from being frozen in a block of ice, his first appearance since the heyday of the 1940s and his slide into oblivion in the early 1950s. The Sub-Mariner had also been found wandering about as a down-and-out in the pages of The Fantastic Four and thus the origins of Marvel comics found their way to the forefront of their second age. While team-ups and confrontations abounded with the much heralded punch-ups between The Thing and The Hulk, the disadvantage of the Marvel formula was that it became well tried too quickly. When two heroes met it seemed the only way to fight a villain was to fight it out with each other first. Mountains moved, fights became more preposterous and the Marvel style gloried in their majesty. Jack Kirby's four-square style did much to enhance splash-page spectacle in the early to mid 1960s.

Much more so than D.C., Marvel were quick to reprint even relatively recent material in King Size Annuals and anthologies like Marvel Collector's Item Classics and Marvel Tales. British reprints like Fantastic and Terrific and later the Mighty World of Marvel did much to popularize the early Marvel style in the U.K. Reprinting reached its peak in the mid 1970s and one expected to see new titles like Marvel Old Reprints Again and Marvel Marvel Marvel.

More recently, Marvel have reprinted the first 10 or 20 of their main line titles in coffee table format Marvel Masterworks. With such marketing and their zappier in-house style, Marvel have earned their place as the market leaders, virtually uninterrupted, for the last 10 years.

Marvel suffered from a patchy distribution network in this country and it was often easier to get DC comics at the newsagents, particularly in the North and Scotland. In the early part of 1964, however, a dock strike at the major ports of the U.K. meant that for two months, Marvels were strictly limited in distribution and across the whole line cover-dated November and December 1964, these issues are either SCARCE or RARE as noted in this guide (for more information on this, see the Comparison Between the U.S. and U.K. Markets article)

This situation may also have been aggravated by a change over of contracts for distribution. A bold experiment to expand to 52 pages across the range of titles in October and November 1971, lead to a limited distribution as less copies of these thicker issues came over in the regular size packets.

The experiment was a short-lived one. It may be noticed that many of these comics are ink-stained along the edges. This occurred when batches marked for return were splattered with ink, sometimes very heavily. Comics like **Conan the Barbarian #11** are extremely hard to find without such staining.

This practice continued well into the 1970s and ink stained comics must be considered damaged by at least a full grade.

Another defect peculiar to Marvel comics is that of "Marvel Chipping". Many early Marvels suffer from little chips out of the right hand side of the cover, particularly **X-Men #1, Spiderman #2, Hulk #3, and Fantastic Four #4**. This can vary from tiny surface cracks to major raggedness. The reason for this is, according to legend, one of the then Editors of the Marvel Bullpen would not invest in a new sharp guillotine machine. When bundles of comics were cut and trimmed in post-production, the top copies were strained under the blunt blade and suffered the chipping damage. Whether this story is true or not, the defect is a serious one and would detract from the value of a comic by at least a full grade if noticeable, 2 full grades at least if the damage is heavy (see the Defects Chart for more information).

In August 1968, there debuted a character that more than any other captured the spirit of the times – The Silver Surfer. With his incredible powers first seen in the pages of the Fantastic Four as the herald of an almighty power called Galactus, his later stranding on Earth, suffering and penance, many believe this to be Stan Lee's personal vision of Jesus Christ, Son of the Father. Appropriately enough, the character returned to preach to a new generation when his adventures were reprinted in a second series of Fantasy Masterpieces beginning in December 1979 and born again under the auspices of Steve Englehart and Marshall Rogers in July 1987.

In October 1970, Marvel introduced Robert. E. Howard's Conan the Barbarian under the pencils of Barry Smith. Although nearly cancelled, the character grew to achieve early cult status. The Barbarian was first tried out in April 1970 in **Chamber of Darkness #4**, an example of Marvel showcasing a character before trying an on-going series which was much more of a D.C. tradition.

The mid to late 1970s were the biggest crisis for Marvel when many of the lesser titles were cancelled like, Amazing Adventures, Astonishing Tales, Skull the Slayer, Doc Savage, Marvel Chillers, Tomb of Darkness and most horror/fantasy reprint titles. This was followed hard on the heels of the collapse of the quarterly Giant Size issues that were introduced in May 1974 in the Fantastic Four title. It was a case of too much too soon as fans had to buy to keep up. Rising paper costs affected all companies including D.C. who also cancelled many new titles like Justice Inc., The Stalker, Kong and Claw, leading to their "Implosion" of 1978. From August 1974 to mid 1980, Marvel comics in this country were denoted by the banner "Marvel All Colour Comics" at the top of the cover instead of "Marvel Comics Group", resulting in a confusion over British reprints. The confusion was added to as Marvel had four different price/number codes on the top left of the cover. The diamond shape with the number on the left and the cents price on the right denotes copies for direct sale/no return to American comic shops. The diamond shape with the cents price on the left, pence price on the right and number underneath, denotes copies for direct sale/no return to overseas (i.e U.K.) comic shops. The square shape with the cents price on the left and the number on the right is for the American news-stands and the square shape with pence price right and number left is for overseas and U.K. newsagents. There is no evidence to suggest that any one is a reprint of another. All comics were produced at the same time on the same machine on the same paper. It is possible that the overseas issues were produced towards the end of the print run with the usual substitution of pricing/code plates. This lasted until September 1982 when Marvel then rationalised their systems.

May 1979 saw **Daredevil #158** which brought artist and then writer, Frank Miller to the fore. His run on Daredevil until issue #191 and a second stint from #227 to #233 brought new heights and maturity of story and art working as an organic whole. March 1982 saw the first slick format regular comic book Marvel Fanfare whose higher production values and presentation lead to the current trend of D.C.'s New and Deluxe format and Marvel's on-going Epic Line. Marvel took the opportunity to combine the new slick process with reprints to produce in 1983 the Special Editions of Avengers and X-Men, Moon Knight and Micronauts to name but a few. These were high quality reprints and in some ways the pre-cursor to the now ubiquitous and it seems obligatory Trade Paperback. The early Eighties saw an expansion of the mini and maxi series with further permutations of team-ups and spin-offs to reach the plethora of X-Men progeny from Kitty Pryde/Wolverine and Iceman to Excalibur and the X-Babies. Coupled with this was the advent of the Direct Sales market which saw the unprecedented sale of 400,000 copies of **Dazzler #1** in May 1981 which was bettered still by Marvel Super Heroes Secret Wars in May 1984.

To celebrate their 25th anniversary in 1986, Marvel created a line of titles called New Universe which were all set in a Universe separate from the regular Marvel titles. With the exception of Star Brand and D.P. 7 they were not well received and the line all but disappeared in the first year with only sporadic appearances scheduled for the future. Another marketing ploy from Marvel was to produce their top three titles Spiderman, G.I.Joe and the X-Men twice monthly during the summer of 1988, summer being the peak sales period. Thus the cover dates would read "early" or "late" whatever the month.

In the same way that Walt Simonson breathed new life into (what had become a flagging title) **Thor #337**, Todd McFarlane similarly invigorated the traditionally slow-selling title Hulk, with issue #330. McFarlane's depiction of Spiderman has also proved to be very popular and his recent departure from that title will ensure their collectibility. The end of the decade saw the mutant titles like Excalibur, illustrated by British artists Alan Davis and Paul Neary proving to be extremely successful as other recent developments including a new-style Captain America, on-going titles for Wolverine and She-Hulk, constant line-up changes for the Avengers and the Fantastic Four and the return of the anthology title with Solo Avengers and **Marvel Comics Presents. Spectacular Spiderman #158** had Spiderman acquire "cosmic powers" from another Marvel character Captain Universe which met with much fan interest and the fact that The Punisher, Wolverine and Sabretooth, three of Marvel's ostensibly most violent characters also proving to be the most popular, is an interesting indicator of fashion, particularly with Sabretooth meeting a suitably bloody demise most recently. Probably the appeal of Marvel comics has always been their intricate continuity and it is probably because of this that they have dominated the recent back-issue market for so many years. The inter-locking structure of the main group of titles, the proven loyalty of Marvel readers and the company's traditional alacrity to take advantage of current buying trends are all indications of Marvel's strong customer-base; there seems no reason to believe that Marvel back-issue sales shouldn't continue to make up a healthy percentage of every dealer's business though this may fluctuate from time to time. Big sellers in the cross-story stakes have been Lifeform, Atlantis Attacks, Acts of Vengeance, Inferno and Spidey's Totally Tiny Adventure all of which are detailed in the Guide. Another was the very popular X-Tinction Agenda storyline sought to resolve some of the loose plot threads and unnecessary complications that had built up in the X-Men and other mutant titles over the last two years. The arrival of artist Jim Lee has consolidated the X-Men's position as the biggest selling monthly comic.

The biggest selling individual comic of 1990 was the phenomenon of the latest Spiderman series from writer/artist Todd McFarlane. The first issue in its many variations sold over 2.5 million copies with a special Platinum version of 10,000 copies for retailers only. At best it is a carefully executed marketing ploy and at worst it is a speculator's nightmare. A printing error made an unspecified number of the first edition have a blue instead of green Lizard character on three pages. Isolated copies sold at premium prices all over the U.K. at the time. Printing mistakes have happened throughout comics history but a special importance has been attached to this particular issue. Collectors have been told that others may exist in their sealed bags but to open one in the hope of a gold mine reduces the value of that sealed-bag copy. Collectors have been told that these bags may not be acid-free and in an air-sealed environment the comic may deteriorate faster than a regular unbagged copy. Little mention is made of story content and art as the debate raged. While individuals are free to choose how much value and importance they place on this particular comic, the overall situation saw the uglier side of the industry come to the fore.

As 1991 developed, Marvel continued to consolidate their market-share lead with the promotion of the new Ghost Rider appearing in just about every other title, the new intelligent green Hulk with fine draughtsmanship by Dale Keown to match, a new detailed origin for Wolverine in a 13 part serial called "Weapon X", the New Mutants disbanding to form "X-Force" later on in the year, which itself became a record in volume sales. The new X-Men title was launched in 5 cover variations and a staggering 8 million copies printed. Speculators who stocked up with case-fulls for a rainy day may have a long time to wait. Through this extended marketing push Marvel gained an unprecedented 68% share of the market towards the latter half of 1991. No wonder Marvel's Editor-in-Chief Tom DeFalco claimed that 1991 was The Year of the Mutant.

In the early 1990s, Marvel have seen their fortunes rise to the dizzy heights of an unprecedented 68% market share followed by a falling off in sales in the face of the up and coming Independent companies Image and Valiant. Marvel had much to celebrate and use to their advantage with 30th anniversaries being achieved by all of their major characters who started in the years 1961-1963. The X-Men was perhaps the most widely publicised and marketed milestone. Where Marvel experienced some back-lash however has been in the realm of "gimmick" covers. There was a time when if a title reaches double figures it's a cause for celebration and so the answer was to slap a foil cover on it. Or a holo-grafix one or an embossed one or a hologram one or a mirror finish one. As these are more expensive to produce so they cost more to the collector who has to let lesser titles go by the by as money can only stretch so far. The situation was not helped by Marvel's compulsive drive to produce as many new titles as they possibly can making it a nightmare for retailers who order blind three months ahead and fans who face the dilemma of missing certain regular titles to pick up the specials and the mini-series.

Marvel launched their 2099 Universe in 1992 with Doom, Spiderman, Punisher and Ravage and contrary to popular expectation, it wasn't another New Universe. But sales on the entire line have continued to slip with Ravage 2099 being the worst. Whereas once Marvel were credited as "The House of Ideas" it now seems that they observe more from the sidelines to see what DC will do next, learn from any mistakes and then bring out their own version. A good example of this would be DC's Death of Superman storyline followed more recently by Marvel's plans to kill off Mr. Fantastic of the Fantastic Four. Or not. Mr. Fantastic and Dr. Doom duly returned. 1994 saw the demise of Marvel UK which many found sad but others rejoiced. A case of too much similar product was blamed.

In recent times, Marvel have sought to catch fan attention with The Age of Apocalypse storyline where all the X-titles were put on hiatus for new titles to appear - a nightmare for anyone writing Price Guides! Fans were mixed in their reaction to the news that Peter Parker as Spiderman has in fact been a clone for the last five years and the real Spiderman is in fact Ben Reilly. It didn't last. In issue **#75 of Spiderman**, the one true Spiderman returned and he who in fact the clone, Ben Reilly, died. The last year or so has seen major upheavals for Marvel Comics. Firstly, in a bid to make the company more profitable and to please their shareholders, major characters like the Fantastic Four, Iron Man and Captain America were farmed out on license to the Image Comics group under the direction of Rob Liefeld. Marvel meanwhile had also gone into direct distribution of their product through Heroes World. Marvel also acquired Malibu Comics and their Ultraverse characters and many creative staff were lost in a reorganisation and streamlining. Malibu was effectively closed down and most characters have had their series cancelled after a brief re-launch. Then on December 27th 1996, Marvel went Chapter 11 and filed for bankruptcy. In truth this is no more than a paper exercise to give the company breathing space while a buyer is sought and statements have had to be made to reassure retailers and public alike on both sides of the Atlantic. And Marvel also went back to Diamond Distributors, ending their Heroes World operation and any exclusivity deals. Time will tell as to how solid Marvel's creativity is and what they can do to dominate as they did so strongly at the start of the decade.

MARVEL COMICS MARKET REPORT

This Market Report for Marvel comics examines the last twelve months or so of activity, looking particularly at value trends and reasons for increased or decreased collector interest. It is very generalized and as such, regional variations should be taken into account. This is also purely a comparison with Guide #6 prices by way of on-going information. For titles and comics not mentioned one may assume relatively stable values and collector interest not significantly differing from last time. See the Market Reports from selected dealers around the country for more information.

AKIRA

Finished in fits and starts in February 1996. Still a title in demand but not helped by the uncertainty of the publication of the last few issues - interest is easily lost on a title if there is a sudden and extended delay in the shipping of issues. And these last issues were expensive at a $6.95 cover price. Early numbers still hold their values and the series as a whole has only dropped marginally. The title value has gone down from£168 in Guide #7 to £165.50 in this guide. Not as popular in the U.K. as it used to be.

ALPHA FLIGHT

This title has dropped in value considerably in the last year. Compare a title value in Guide #7 of £190.50 with this Guide's £158.00. That should tell you something! Not that any one issue has fallen very dramatically. It's 50p off here and £1 off there. It all adds up. Issue #51 (1st Jim Lee) for example has some demand but has dropped in value from£3.50 to £3.00. Issue #106 having been hyped as the first homosexuality in comics (unbelievably - goes to show how hermetically sealed comics can occasionally be from real life and current concerns) has now dropped from a high in the U.K. of about £5.00 to half that last year and the value has remained static. #33 has dropped from £3 to £2.

AMAZING ADVENTURES

An excellent 70's series with a variety of heroes and art styles. The title value had crept up from £134.00 to £145.50 for this Guide. Issue #11 has leapt in value from £7.50 to £12.50 as the first in a series starring The Beast from the X-Men. So many of these Non-Distributed issues were ink-stained or water-damaged when they came over to the U.K. and high grade copies are genuinely scarce.

AMAZING FANTASY

It's been on then off, off and on again. News of director Jim "Terminator" Cameron's live-action Spiderman film has experienced about five and a half years of frustration and rumour but seems to have done nothing to dampen the enthusiasm of fans and collectors for this title. The first appearance of arguably Marvel's most famous character has once again gained incredibly in value, thanks largely to the hype in the States of the White Mountain copy selling for $39,100 (or 26 grand in real money!) in 1995. There is a noticeably good supply of Amazing Fantasy #15's around in the U.K. but very few in very high grade and even fewer in an unrestored state. Beware browning pages, even if the exterior looks glossy. A common fault. Must be something to do with the original paper composition. Beware also copies with amateur brown felt tip touching in around the top of the cover!

1993 NM Price: £4,250.00 1994 NM Price: £8,100.00
1996 NM Price: £14,000 1997 NM Price: £15,000

A realistic U.K. price is a difficult one to determine. We have increased the U.S. general market value to $30,000 or £20,000 in conversion but we feel that that is too high for the British market. But if one had the money to spend on a true Near Mint unrestored cents copy, expect anything up to $50,000! We prefer to be conservative and restate the case that this book is a Guide only, not values carved in stone. U.S. dealers and collectors should take note of the fact that pence copies of this comic are exactly the same as the cents copy version apart from printed cover price and the cover month being removed. It could be regarded as a rare cover variant!

AMAZING SPIDERMAN

Listing Spiderman under "Amazing Spiderman". Grudgingly. After all, why not "M" for Mighty Thor? I bow to our American cousins on this one. McFarlane Mania isn't what it used to be on issues #298-#315. Prices in the U.K. have generally dropped on these. #300 in particular has established itself as a minor key book but with a big difference in prices between the dollar and the pound ($70 and £20). Carnage and Venom appearances continue to be in some demand but not quite at the pitch they were (#361 falls from £6 to £5). The general consensus of opinion seemed to be at mid 1996 that this Spiderman-clone-thing had made the title into a kind of "X-Men at its most complicated" and there were reports of fans dropping the title in droves. The resolution of the Clone Saga has brought stability back to the title and much audience relief. The fact remains that should the Spiderman film ever get off the ground, the general audience are going to be more familiar with Peter Parker and the traditional costume, very valuable from a merchandising point of view. The Spiderman 2nd Series continues with healthy sales. The various permutations of issue #1, bagged and un-bagged, signed and unsigned, continue to sell but as they were produced in such vast quantities and as collectors bought and saved multiple copies, long term investment value is very long term indeed. The phenomenon of the Platinum Spiderman edition seems to be dying a death (remember the Dark Knight Returns Signed/Limited Edition in 1986 - selling for £700 at one point and today can be picked up for around £200). All those who want copies have got copies and one more often sees a copy held up for auction with proceeds going to charitable causes which is no bad thing. All this is not to say that the Platinum Spiderman is worthless: it has settled on an average price at the moment and may see some movement if Spiderman hype surrounds a new film. But rather than play the predictive game, better to enjoy the comic as a high production value package of a very successful comic. The only other Spiderman variant worth mentioning is the "Blue Lizard" phenomenon of 1990 (an unknown quantity of the silver ink/black cover editions of #1 which had a blue rather than green coloured Lizard character in a number of panels) which waned rather in 1992 and 1993 and though copies still change hands today at whatever the purchaser is prepared to pay should he or she so desire one, there is still no firm proof as to exact numbers of this comic that is essentially a printing error (and how many of those have there been throughout comics' history?) Amazing Spiderman back-issues of great interest are those from #100-#150 or so. Some very tough issues to find and some important changes for the Spiderman character though some of these issues are prone to volatile changes. #101 and #102 are prime examples of a once hot character (Morbius) peaking and now remaining static, even if they are difficult to find in high grade. #129 was very static for a time, picked up slightly in 1996 and has now slumped again to around £160. This is mainly due to the general disinterest in The Punisher character. There seem to be a lot of copies around but not many in strict NM. Many copies have a few millimetres of white area on the left of cover ("white spine") where the copy has been mis-cut slightly. Perfectly square-cut covers are difficult to find. The U.K. Guide remains cautious on this comic. It is still after all a minor key issue and regarded by many new to collecting as one of their "Silver Age" super-keys. #149 sky-rocketed but now seems to have settled down at the £50.00 mark in the U.K. Hobgoblin appearances seem to be big news in American price guides but not in the U.K. #238 at $65 in the States translates to around £43 - no way! We have suggested a U.K. market value of £22.50. Issue #400 white cover variant edition remains static at £12.50. The early Spiderman annuals are creeping up in value though #4 and #5 have slipped slightly in the U.K. market.

ASTONISHING TALES

As little a while ago as 1992 it was all Deathlok and Astonishing Tales #25. It still seems to be such a case over in America with their Guides, if not going crazy on the price, values are still holding. But over here in the U.K., Deathlok may as well be dead. Copies just do not seem to be shifting. Copies are in plentiful supply, particularly in lower grades. Perhaps yet another mini-series is needed to kick-start this title. Or not.

1993 NM Price: £25.00 1994 NM Price: £22.50
1996 NM Price: £20.00 1997 NM Price: £15.00

While the title value may have slipped from £172.50 in Guide #7 to £151.50 in this Guide, there are some other bits and pieces in the series of interest from Dr. Doom solo stories to Ka-Zar and Spiderman cross- overs. But this title does not have the variety of Amazing Adventures.

AVENGERS

1996 saw the cancellation of The Avengers as a Marvel title after 33 years with issue #402. It has since been farmed out to Image Comics as part of the Heroes Reborn scheme. Time will tell if that was a good move or not but early fan reaction after 6 issues at the time of writing has been mixed to say the least. As 1993 was the 30th anniversary year of The Avengers, there was a welcome turn-around in the fortunes of this title, against the then general backlash towards team books. #360's bronze-foil cover was a real eye-catcher followed by all-silver #363 and all-gold #366. #1 has crept up £50 to £1,500 though this is still seems fairly low relative to the other Marvel #1's as high grade copies of Avengers #1 are surprisingly common in both the U.S. and the U.K. Issues #3 and #5 with their darker covers have become increasingly harder to obtain in higher grades. There's new interest in #57/58 and #93 is still in demand and harder than ever to find without any label damage in the top left hand corner. Indeed the main collector interest seems to be for issues between #50 and #100 as these rarely appear on dealers lists. Issues from #121 to #150 also have a following as they were Non-Distributed in the U.K. at the time (mid 1970's) and are hard to obtain in top grade. Also, #183, #204 and #205 seem noticeably scarcer in the general circulation in the U.K. The only issues of note most recently are #401 and #402 which seem slightly harder to get than they should be. Prices on Avengers annuals remain fairly static though #7 has held steady at a £12.50 suggestion.

BATTLESTAR GALACTICA

Comparing the title values of £17.95 in Guide #7 and £27.00 in this Guide should tell you there is increased interest in this series, possibly with repeated showings on cable television. And the fact that this series is now over fifteen years old.

BEAVIS & BUTT-HEAD

A palpable hit, owing much to its screening on late night satellite TV in the U.K. Shame it was cancelled with #28 in mid 1996. Find the first issue if you can. U.K. prices are keeping up with U.S. prices and #1 would see around £2.50, a slight drop on last year owing to cancellation.

BIZARRE ADVENTURES

No change in the title values from last year to this but Bizarre Adventures may be one to watch. All sorts of interesting characters and a variety of artists. #27 is as popular as ever with various artists doing their thing on the X-Men.

BLACK DRAGON

A much under-rated mini-series with stunning artwork by John Bolton. Over 10 years old now and excellent reading value at about £2 per issue.

BLACK PANTHER

A slight increase across the board on this short series. Jack Kirby art though a little loose and free-flowing with some wild stories.

CAPTAIN AMERICA

Cancelled in mid 1996 after 28 years as a title. Part of the Heroes Reborn package farmed out to Image Comics and much like The Avengers, the early fan reaction was not overwhelmingly enthusiastic to start with but the situation has improved to such an extent that #1 is in demand at marts and conventions and can't be found. Watch this space. After a fairly stable couple of years for the good Captain though there was much interest in the Operation Rebirth story courtesy of that man Mark Waid (see Impulse in the DC Market Report). Issues #445-448 are still in demand at around £2.50 to £3.00 and this is an increase on the suggested values in Guide #7. #100 has stabilised in value after a slight drop in 1996 - very common in lower grades and while an absolute top grade copy is hard to find, high grade copies do seem to turn up in the U.K. #101-110 are static in the U.K. #117 is still a tough issue to find too - very annoying for completists one would imagine. The Mike Zeck and Ron Lim issues used to be reasonably sought after but not now. #241 has slumped from £20.00 in Guide #6 to £14.00 in Guide #7 to a lowly £8 in this one. To think how popular this issue once was! Captain America Annual #8 was another high demand issue in the U.K. but this has slumped from around £10 in Guide #7 to around the £7.50 mark or less. The Golden Age title has something of a following here in the U.K. but the days of owning a Good copy of even the cheapest issue of the run for under £50.00 may be over. And as for issues #76 to #78 - forget it! Ballistic over in the States and suggested values here are merely informed guess-work. In reality you may have to pay twice the price suggested here. If you can find the slipcase set of Captain America The Classic Years that reprints issues #1-10, grab it and enjoy.

CAPTAIN MARVEL

No longer regarded as one of those seemingly junk titles from the 1970's with gains in U.K. Guides #6 and #7, there has been a slight drop in the overall title value from £394.50 to £389.50 in this Guide but in the scheme of things, that is negligible. It's still attractive as a run, not impossible to put together at 62 issues but increasingly harder. Interest in this title is mixed however, and that is reflected in the static nature of #1 for the second year running and yet price rises on some earlier issues which do not seem to be around. The 2nd appearance of Thanos in #26 and indeed the other Starlin art issues have seen slight drops or no change (#26 down from £17.50 to £15.00). The new Captain Marvel series was cancelled after only 6 issues which was a great disappointment and thus has done little to fuel interest in back issues. We'll see what the ever newer series featuring the classic Captain Marvel will do (#1 just out as I write this).

CHAMPIONS

No change in values for this popular little series. Issue #17 is as hard to obtain as ever.

CLASSIC X-MEN

Slight change in overall value from £130 to £132 for the title. Very static for the past year though at least selling steadily and not experiencing massive falls as in Alpha Flight and X-Factor.

CONAN THE BARBARIAN

It was sad to see this title cancelled after nearly 24 years in 1993. A re-launch as Conan the Adventurer stuttered to a halt after 14 issues. Another re-launch as Conan in August 1995 also failed after only 11 issues. Just what is the problem with this character? In this age of hi-tech mutants, maybe barbarians have had their day. Early issues still sell well and #1 in top shape a price of £200 has not been unknown in the U.K. We have chosen to increase the listed Near Mint value from £140 in Guide #7 to £175 for this Guide. Other early issues remain static but for my money, the Barry Smith issues represent a very nice run of art and story content and at least with prices so static, collectors can enjoy and read which is no bad thing. The annuals are up in value with #1 rising to £6. The Giant Sizes are similarly up by a fraction.

CREATURES ON THE LOOSE

Up quite nicely from Guide #7's title value of £54.25 to the current £63.25. An interesting mix of sci-fi and sword and sorcery characters and George Perez' first work in comics. Can't be bad.

DAREDEVIL

Still one of the most undervalued titles of the early Marvel output. People forget that #1 only came out 7 months after X-Men #1; 1964 is well over 30 years ago! Daredevil #1 in NM is very hard to find. The cover should be pure white and not the off-white/yellowing that often occurs. The Near Mint value on issue #1 has remained static which personally I find extraordinary but one must bow to the market in the U.K.

1995 NM Price: £1,200.00 1996 NM Price: £1,400.00
1997 NM Price: £1,400.00

The U.S. dollar value has crept up to the psychological $2,000 mark in our opinion though Overstreet values it less and always has done. This has forced us to keep the U.K. price static and it may well remain so next year. This is one of the few comics that I feel is very under-valued. I have seen a perfect copy of Daredevil #1 sell for $4,000 at the San Diego convention. Other early issues of note: #4 which still maintains its "rare in the U.K." status though copies do seem to be surfacing at marts so status will be monitored, #7 (still hard to find in high grade with that dark blue cover), #81 and particularly #82 definitely very scarce in the U.K. (particularly in high grade), the Miller issues from #158 showing a static status for #158 and no change for the rest of the run. #227-#230 experienced slight decreases and the first appearance of Typhoid Mary in #254 has dropped from £6.50 to £5. #257 has dropped slightly from £7.50 to £7. #319 was the shot in the arm that the title needed at the time and this issue peaked in the U.K. at about £10.00 in Guide #6, slipped back to the £7.50 mark with Guide #7 and now £5.00 with this Guide. That whole story arc has dropped slightly mostly because supply seems to have met demand. Recent celebrations surrounding the 350th issue suggest that the title is quite strong and the new creative team of Karl Kesel and Cary Nord have had positive fan reaction. The Daredevil annuals have crept up in value across the board and though we have suggested a £9 Guide price for #3, it is very hard to come by in perfect shape and we noted a copy that sold at a mart in 1996 for £15.

DARKHAWK

One of the genuine surprises of 1992/93, this title crashed last Guide. While issues #1-5 are generally not around in either the U.K. or the U.S., everyone who wants them seems to have them. Issue #1 was at £6.00 in U.K. Guide #6 and now struggles to £1.25. Now that the series has been cancelled, back-issue sales will be affected to the point of this title appearing more and more in the 50p bins at marts.

DEADPOOL

The most recent series has caused some interest with issue #1 much sought after at the moment. The two previous mini-series may be ones to watch.

DEFENDERS

With issue #1 25 years old (is it possible?) and with those appearances of the Silver Surfer in the early numbers, this title has maintained interest and the title value has increased from £427 in Guide #7 to £432 in this Guide. Not a huge increase of course but at least it demonstrates the stability of the title. The Thor vs. Hulk #10 is a genuinely very scarce book in the U.K. and continues to defy many collections though the price seems to have reached a peak of an average of £27.50 in Near Mint for the time being. Either that or there are so few sales that information is hard to come by. The Guardians of the Galaxy appearances that were once snapped up along with Son of Satan appearances between #92 and #109 in times past are no longer. Giant Size issues are static. The return of The (Secret) Defenders promised much but failed to deliver. The title was cancelled in March 1995.

DEVIL DINOSAUR

A classic of a title! If you like 70's nonsense. Jack Kirby at his most wacky, the title value has gone up from last year's £11.25 to £15.50.

DOCTOR STRANGE

Absolutely no change on the first series with the British values as they do tend to turn up in the U.K. and in high grade quite frequently. The title value for the American prices has risen by $50. The second series rose by all of a pound in Guide #7 and by just over a pound for this Guide so that must say something. U.S. values are up by about $40. Prices on the early issues of the third series have dropped (for example #1 from £2 down to £1.50) though his new "hippie" look at issue #76 went down well with a lot of fans at the time. Scripts by Warren Ellis and J.M. DeMatteis helped to keep this title alive but it was finally cancelled with issue #90. The character is in that comic book limbo without a series.

DOCTOR WHO

"With renewed interest in the character and a highly collectible series (of reprints admittedly) that are 10 years old, watch this space..." was what was said last year. Nothing happened.

DREADSTAR

Some notable decreases on issues #1-26 from Marvel with last year's title value at £40.25 now at £33. Still a popular seller and presumably even more so at these new lower rates.

EPIC ILLUSTRATED

While there have been no price increases on this title for the second year running, it is one to watch out for. A highly collectible set with some great art (Paul Gulacy, Neal Adams, John Bolton, Barry Windsor-Smith, John Byrne etc.) and some great stories (featuring Silver Surfer, Galactus and Dreadstar etc.). Good reading value if you can find them at marts and conventions. Forget the gimmicks. Forget the fads and fashions. Read!

EWOKS

Not a title one would have considered a couple of years ago as anything more than kids' stuff but Star Wars completists have pushed these comics up from 50p each last year to about £1.00 this. Any more room for increases?

EXCALIBUR

The title that dropped in value generally by about 10% from Guide #6 to #7 has risen back by about 5% for this Guide pointing to a plentiful supply of issues in the U.K. marketplace but also a sustained interest. Mutant Genesis issues are still popular but no change in prices.

FANTASTIC FOUR

Big increases on early issues thanks to ever-spiralling rises in American guides.

1995 NM Price: £6,200.00 1996 NM Price: £9,000.00
1997 NM Price: £11,000.00

Having said that it will be noticed that prices on Good and Fine issues have been kept fairly static as this is a true reflection of the U.K. marketplace. Average grades are just not selling at the moment. How long this trend will last is hard to say. People seem to snap up very low grade copies to complete their runs and one or two who can afford it are prepared to pay for top quality. F.F. #48 is not unknown at $1,000 in the States. The rise in price by £50 from Guide #7 values has taken this reluctantly into account but the ceiling on this issue in the U.K. must have been reached. As far as other earlier issues go, there is less interest in #66 and #67 as the first appearances of "Him", later Warlock, though it's still hard to believe that people will pay such big money for basically a non-appearance. This is purely as a result of hype in America and too much regarding of America price guides. One hopes that fans and collectors will get wise to this. The U.K. Guide has had to follow U.S. prices to a certain extent but refuses to consider parity and indeed has kept the British values unchanged from last year. If you want a Near Mint cents copy of these issues, be prepared to pay silly money. #80 seems finally to have lost its traditional rare/scarce status in the U.K. - so many have been brought over to this country from the States by dealers that it generally shows up in collections now. #100 is still as hard as ever to find for those completists and though dollar prices seem to keep rising, even less- than-dollar/pound-translation of £40 for this issue does seem a lot of money even though this value is unchanged from last year. The John Byrne issues (ranging between #209 and #293) are picking up in sales again after a lull. Current storylines ran to completion with issue #415 before the Fantastic Four joined Avengers, Captain America and Iron Man as part of the Image Experiment. Reed Richards and Dr. Doom weren't dead after all (surprise, surprise!) and love triangles abound in the new series as much as ever before. Fans were tiring of increasingly higher percentages of issues being taken up with flashbacks, re-caps and the-story-so-far stuff. At least with the Image incarnation, there is a chance to start afresh and slightly re-write the history books (Wyatt Wingfoot as a baddie for example). Produced in such vast quantities, even the variant covers came tumbling down in price from £5 to about £3.50. Those of you who bought 100 copies of the first issue regular format should know better by now.

FEAR, ADVENTURE INTO

One of the biggest 1970's titles of recent times with the Morbius appearances has plummeted in interest in the last 2 years. While #20 is genuinely hard to find in high grade on both sides of the Atlantic with its black-bordered cover, even in the States the price has dropped from around $50 to about half that or less.

1994 NM Price: £10.00 1995 NM Price: £15.00
1996 NM Price: £12.00 1997 NM Price: £10.00

The problem in the U.K. is that lots of copies turn up with some sort of inking stains on them, usually along the top edge in blue. All part of the same batch marked for return all those years ago. So one could expect to pay more than the Guide price stated for a genuinely Near Mint copy, especially as only cents copies are available. A decent read but forget words like "investment" or "speculation".

FRANKENSTEIN

After a year of being completely static both in the U.S. and U.K., this title is experiencing something of a resurgence in interest. Title values have gone up from $94/£64 to $129/£76.25 which in the current climate is a substantial increase. The Mike Ploog art captures the mood of the subject quite well and there is something of a collectors' challenge to put a set together.

GHOST RIDER (1970s)

Prices on the early issues have inched up slightly against expectation (hey, I only crunch the raw data!) in the U.K. and #1 is still quite hard to find in top grades. Formerly one of the hottest of the '70s Marvel series that everyone wanted to collect, it is experiencing a slight comeback but that may just be due to the number of sales recorded and the extreme diversity of prices noted. The current series initially did much to hype its predecessor and elevated it to a status it perhaps didn't deserve. This was borne out by the fact that people begun to realise that the two Ghost Rider characters were different and separate and sales did begin to wane. Interest was temporarily renewed thanks largely to a few obscure panels showing Daimon Hellstrom (otherwise Son of Satan) getting dressed! But now that the Son of Satan has long cooled off as a character, these first few issues have little to commend them to back-issue collectors. As ever, the genuine scarcity of the last few issues (#72-81 in particular) when the title was on its last legs makes this a difficult set to complete and may sustain collector interest and the fact that the second series is still going, again against expectations in the light of other Marvel titles being cancelled.

GHOST RIDER (NEW)

Speaking of the second series, big drop in value on issue #1 from £6 to £4. The early issues almost halved in value from the Guide #6 to #7. And they have near enough done the same this time. Scary. The status as one of, if not the, hottest Marvel characters around at one time experienced a distinct resurgence of interest with the Rise of the Midnight Sons storyline, #28 being particularly in demand. The inclusion of other magic/horror-related characters like Morbius and Dr. Strange helped the situation. But this resurgence of interest was not sustained. The 20th anniversary issue #25 with its pop-up centre-spread is more or less back to cover price. The recent inclusion of guest-stars like Valkyrie, Howard the Duck and Devil Dinosaur has helped keep the title alive. The future looks uncertain. But at least the title is still here.

GODZILLA

One of those 70s gems that often get over-looked by collectors but judging by the increased title value from Guide #7 from £18.25 to £34.50, this is a title that does not often turn up and may be one to watch with a big budget Godzilla movie on the drawing board.

GROO

Early issues of this title are always in demand with #1 at a very healthy £10.00 although this has dropped a little from last year's £12.50. Prices in the U.K. are static as they rose so fast in the early 1990's. With no current series, this title will probably remain static but for retailers it will always sell and for fans it's nothing short of a great read.

GUARDIANS OF THE GALAXY

Early issues of this title are generally not around in the U.K. and some very great price variations have been noticed at comic marts. Prices on early issues have slipped again however with #1 down from £4 to £2.50 as an average. There is no interest in issues #17-19 as there once was. Now that the title has been cancelled it would seem that back-issue sales are going to slip further as fan interest wanes.

HULK, THE INCREDIBLE

Prices on the first series are getting well out of most people's reach on both sides of the Atlantic, particularly looking at American guides (but we don't do that, do we?). The all Steve Dikto issue #6 finally (and reluctantly) reaches the £1,000 barrier in the U.K. but if one does a direct translation from the American guides, one would be looking at over £1,400! Is this book so superior to #3, #4 and #5? The time has come now that these issues are lovely to look at but are difficult to sell now that they all top the £700.00 mark. Delighted to be proved wrong, however. Issue #181 is a comic on every Wants List as it doesn't seem to be around in NM shape. So the U.K. Guide has reflected this with a jump from £220 last year to £250 this, just under the conversion equivalent of the U.S. $400. The Warlock issues from #176 to #178 have taken a drop in suggested value by a pound. #200 is down a fraction from £8 to £7.50. But the run from #211 onwards for 50 or so issues is up in value. These are consistently good sellers and in our opinion are worth putting up by 50p. #330 is down from £7 to £6, #340 static at £10 and #367 is down from £6 to £5. The 30th anniversary issue #393 still sells well and the 2nd print grey cover seems to be harder to find in some areas of the U.K. #400 sported a dazzling holo-grafix cover and the great Dale Keown passed on from the book. Britain's own Gary Frank took on the unenviable task of following in his foot-steps for a while and with recent Mike Deodato Jnr. art, the title is still a firm fan favourite. The incarnation of The Hulk in the new Image universe is a question of back to basics. The character is disproportionately huge, barbaric and long haired. Just how the target audience want him.

INHUMANS

Popular set to collect of only 12 issues though down slightly from last year from a title value of £31.00 to £29.50. Not a huge drop but another sign of a general downward pricing trend for many titles in this Guide.

INVADERS

Slight increases in price for this title. Always quite highly valued in America, sets of these do not often turn up in the U.K. as #1, #2 and #41 are getting harder to find. Title value up from £81 last year to £105.50 this.

IRON FIST

Increases on last year's title value from £199.85 to £234.85 - significant. As we all know it's a highly attractive 1970's set with only 15 issues, all Byrne art and all Non-Distributed in the U.K. Though issues have been brought over by dealers over the years it is still not the easiest set to complete, some claiming that #2 is impossible to find. #14 and the first appearance of Sabretooth was the Marvel back-issue for the greater part of the last three years. It is still tough to find in Very Fine+ or better.

1995 NM Price: £50.00 1996 NM Price: £70.00
1997 NM Price: £85.00

You often see copies on marts walls for £50 to £60 but they are never the Near Mint as claimed (believe me, I've looked!) I have only seen one copy that I would call Near Mint so check carefully and don't overpay.

IRON MAN

It was 30th anniversary time for this character in 1993 and with Tony Stark being cryogenically frozen and brought back to life, with zappy new armour and Iron Man's struggles with The Avengers, it's been a decent couple of years for old Tin Head. Fans and collectors often talk about how great Armour Wars was but what about the 200 or so issues before that? Tons to look at with many odd issues to look out for. #101 with Frankenstein is often over-looked, a Thanos appearance in #88, Tony Stark's alcohol struggle in #123-128, the great Barry Smith origin issue #47, some Jim Starlin art, John Romita Jnr's 1st work -all fab stuff. Demand for the fabled issue #55 has slackened off to the point of itself being cryogenically frozen.

1995 NM Price: £40.00 1996 NM Price: £30.00
1997 NM Price: £25.00

There is slightly more demand for the 20 cents version (rather than the British 6p one) but it is nowhere near the key issue it used to be.

JOURNEY INTO MYSTERY

A mention for back issues of this late, great title. Catch Jack (still The King) Kirby at his quintessential best from #100-125. And issues #83 to #99 are not easy to come by in high grade, especially #84 with its dark brown cover. #112 is becoming a tough one to find but the size of the market after it is equally tough to estimate.

LUKE CAGE

The first 16 issues of this 1970s title are still hard to find being Non Distributed in the U.K. and #1 with its black-border cover is still very hard to find in anything approaching high grade. Historically an interesting title as one of the major black superheroes (not too many of those around). Note that prices are unchanged from the last U.K. Guide reflecting its static status.

MARVEL COMICS

A mention for this Golden Age title if only to say that U.K. prices have to be calculated on the basis of U.S. guide values. The market in the U.K. for this title is small but could grow if more lower grade copies were brought over for people to try. Check out those fabulous Alex Schomburg war covers.

MARVEL CLASSICS COMICS

A mention for this much under-rated set. Great reading for those who haven't tunnelled through several feet of college and university reading lists (I remember having to "do Dickens in a week"!). Issues #9 and #20 have decent Dracula and Frankenstein adaptations and a complete set is hard to come by.

MARVEL PREMIERE

One of the most attractive sets to collect for character and artist variation. #1 and #2 have Warlock-as-superhero for the first time, #3 sees the start of the Dr. Strange run by Barry Smith and Frank Brunner, #15 has the first Iron Fist (continuing to rise in value) and later issues have a variety of characters (Ant-Man, Man-Wolf) and a variety of artists (Chaykin, Byrne, Perez). Many issues are Non Distributed in the U.K. which makes collecting all 61 not the easiest task in the world. Last year we thought that there might have been some movement on #57-60 the Dr. Who issues given the publicity surrounding the film with Paul McGann. No effect whatsoever...

MARVEL SPOTLIGHT

This title is very similar to Marvel Premiere as it introduced Werewolf By Night in #2, Ghost Rider in #5 (increasingly hard to find in top shape with its black cover) and a wide variety of characters in later issues (Son of Satan, Spiderwoman, Deathlok, Moon Knight, Sub-Mariner). The Ghost Rider run from #5 to #11 is hard to find without ink-staining along one or more edges. Prices are generally static and in one or two instances, issue #12 for example, have halved in value. Some good reading value here though. The overall title value has fallen from £261 last year to £240.50 for this Guide.

MARVEL TALES

A series that represents remarkably good value as far as classic reprints go (and the same also applies to Marvel Collectors Item Classics). #1 may be beyond many people's pockets but later issues, particularly in low grade, provide the opportunity to read the very early issues of Spiderman, Fantastic Four, Tales to Astonish and Journey Into Mystery. Issues in the 100's reprint many classics like Spiderman #1 and Amazing Fantasy #15 and issues in the 200's reprint many 70's classics like Marvel Team Up #4. Some new covers by Todd McFarlane (#223 to #239) make for attractive packaging. This series deserves more attention, particularly as prices have fallen slightly so now's the time to buy.

MARVEL TEAM UP

With early issues now reaching 25 years old, this series is coming into its own more and more. The first 23 issues are Non Distributed in the U.K. and feature most main Marvel characters teaming with Spiderman. They are all becoming harder to find in NM. Later issues with John Byrne art are still asked for and the greater part of the series is in enough supply to be very affordable and thus collectible. #1 with its black-border cover is as notoriously hard as ever to find in very high grade but we have kept the listed value the same as last year.

1993 NM Price: £35.00 1994 NM Price: £45.00
1996 NM Price: £50.00 1997 NM Price: £50.00

Issue #150 has also remained static in price in the U.K.

MARVELS

Hailed as the best mini-series that Marvel (or perhaps anyone) has ever produced. A cracking read. A short-term goldmine but issues are in plentiful supply so don't over-pay. £4-£5 for #1. Plans are afoot for Marvels II. Can't wait. Meanwhile a hardcover collection produced in association with Graphitti is an essential addition to your bookshelf.

MASTER OF KUNG FU

Absolutely no changes in price from the last Guide though this title remains a popular seller. Most issues before #50 have the fluid lines of Paul Gulacy's artwork and are well worth the £2 and £3, much less if you only want reading copies.

MOON KNIGHT

Prices on the Stephen Platt issues are steady in both the U.S and U.K. Not much interest in other Moon Knight back issues as the last series was cancelled in early 1994. Title value drop from £85.75 to £75.50.

MS. MARVEL

Worth mentioning for issue #18. £2.50 in the U.K., $15.00 in the U.S. Go Figure.

NAMOR

With the cancellation of this title after 62 issues, Namor finds himself in comic book limbo to a certain extent although the character has been nicely re-invented in the pages of Fantastic Four courtesy of the Image group of creators but his title s otherwise dead. The label of "hot" artist is becoming increasingly more volatile. Jae Lee is seemingly not held in as high regard as of yore, at least in association with this character and consequently #26 has taken another tumble from £4 to £3 to £2 in the two years. Overall title value is down slightly from £65.50 to £61.75.

NEW MUTANTS

A title that was all the rage at the start of the '90s but now seems to have died somewhere along the line. Interest in #87 is very low now.

1993 NM Price: £25.00 1994 NM Price: £15.00
1996 NM Price: £7.50 1997 NM Price: £6.00

Issues in the 90s seem to be steady in demand with 1st appearances of Deadpool and Feral and the 1st print of #100 is still popular but the title as a whole has lost about 11%.

NEW WARRIORS

Launched in 1990 this title was initially under-ordered by dealers, gained a fan-following after a year or so and thus early issues went up in value. This trend has now reversed with #1 slipping down from a U.K. Guide #6 value of £12.50 to £7.50 last year to £5.00 now. Storylines involving the Scarlet Spider helped this title for a time but it was finally cancelled at issue #75 cover dated September 1996.

NICK FURY

Brave of Marvel to kill off a character that's been around for over 30 years. It will be interesting to see what effect that will have on back issues of all Fury's various series. Probably negative.

NOVA

A title that did little to excite when it appeared from 1976 to 1979 but at only 25 issues and fuelled by the success of his appearances in New Warriors, this became an attractive title in the early 1990s. Completists have been known to go mad trying to find that elusive last issue which has been given a "very scarce in the U.K." status pending more information. The new on-going series started well with a (yet another!) gimmick cover but was cancelled after only 18 issues. Prices have remained absolutely static on the first series with a title value of £42.

POWERMAN

The Luke Cage - Hero for Hire title quickly metamorphosed into Powerman, added Iron Fist and has now produced a title of some collector interest. This was also helped by the appearances of Sabretooth in issues #66, #78 and #84. The appearance in #78 is, though highly suspect, most probably Sabretooth. For those that don't know/don't care (delete where applicable), there is one panel that shows a claw like Sabretooth's appearing from under a cloak and otherwise the mystery character wears a sack over his head. There is no mention by the name of Sabretooth but rather as "The Slasher". Prices are static. The last few issues of the run are the hardest to find and a completists nightmare though again prices are static.

PUNISHER

This once the hottest of all Marvel characters experienced an all-time low in 1995 when the long-running title was cancelled after 104 issues. Demand for the first series of 5 issues has slackened off to the point where the title value is about half the U.K. Guide #6 listing. The character achieved some notoriety by killing off Nick Fury and has been re-launched once more. Time will tell.

REN & STIMPY

Like Beavis & Butt Head, a cult favourite cartoon but like so many cults, this title is experiencing violent ups and downs. Issue #1 rose from £7.50 in U.K. Guide #6 to £12.50 in #7 but has plummeted back down to £6.00 for this Guide. Heh Heh...Heh Heh..

SGT. FURY

Worth a mention to say that early issues are not around and #1 is rarely offered for sale in the U.K. It's a Marvel #1 that always gets over-looked. Surprising to think that it came out before Daredevil! A Near Mint #1 still seems very reasonable at £570 (£450 last time) but the size of the market in the U.K. that wants one must be taken into consideration. U.S. prices seem to value this key issue more at around $950 or £633 at a rough conversion.

SILVER SURFER

As much a cult character as ever he was, the Silver Surfer continued to enjoy much success in the early 1990s. The first series remains much in demand, helped by the publication of the excellent Marvel Masterworks edition of reprinting #1-18. A pleasure to read. #4 over-took #1 in value for its rarity status around 1993 but now the situation has reversed and #1 has assumed precedence over #4 in importance and value. The John Byrne one-shot series remains in high demand though there are copies about in the U.K. so prices have remained largely unchanged. The Moebius two-issue mini-series has risen slightly in value. Also watch out for the one-shot graphic novel The Ultimate Cosmic Experience. An all-new Stan Lee/Jack Kirby book which is very hard to find, let alone in high grade. £100.00 has been seen at recent marts. It has been noted that a number of mis-print copies f the current series #50 came over to this country in varying degrees of the silver foil flaking off. Most look rather ugly and soiled but ones that have a pure-white Surfer and logo look very attractive indeed and the few that have sold have gone for a wide variety of prices. It remains to be seen how many there are of this curious mis-print and indeed how to judge an accurate market value in the U.K. Note that U.S. price guides make no mention of it.

SPIDEY SUPER STORIES

One to watch, I kid you not. Not around, a set is impossible and some interesting villains appear to appeal to completists. And cheap.

STAR TREK

A very tough to put together 18 issue series that increased from £36 last year to £44.50 for this Guide. Prizes for guessing what that tells you...

STAR WARS

Definitely a title to watch. It's all Star Wars this year with the release of the upgraded effects trilogy in March/April/May 1997 and the next trilogy (parts I-III) are expected to shoot beginning this year. All of this makes this once under-rated title very attractive indeed. And for completists there's all the Dark Horse stuff and the British Marvel weeklies. The first 6 issues adapt the first film then #7 onwards brings all new stories with an adaptation of Empire Strikes Back in issues #39-44. The title value has jumped massively from £650 in the last Guide to £999 in this. Issue #107 (the last) is a monster of a comic to find in the U.K. and a £40.00 price tag takes some getting used to if you were lucky enough to pick it up at cover price when it came out.

STRANGE TALES

Issues to watch as ever are #110, #114, #115 and #135. #135 does not seem to be around in NM and the death of Nick Fury may add to its appeal. The Warlock issues #178-181 have been static in value for the last two years as they seem to be around in the U.K. in plentiful supply. Beware of these so called "prototype" issues that seem to be a big favourite of American guides. I prefer to qualify all these prototypes with the word possible as some are so far removed from the characters they are supposed to be a prototype of that it's laughable. Issue #84 is a case in point.

SUB-MARINER

Completely static to the point where not a single price has changed.

TALES OF SUSPENSE

Beware "prototype" issues again here. Issues #16 and #32 are the ones to watch. #16's "Iron Man" is actually a criminal trapped inside a robot forever and #32's Dr. Strange is 15th century, evil and grotesque looking. Not even a passing resemblance in any way to Dr. Strange! Issues between #57 and #66 continue to grow in desirability and are genuinely hard to find in top grades. Price rises for #57-59. As a general rule of thumb in the U.K. market, later issues of Tales of Suspense do not turn up in higher grades any more whereas comparative issues of Tales to Astonish do. Prices are generally static though. #39 is in demand but very common in lower grades. True NM copies are impossible to find but demand in the U.K. seems to be low. Pre super-hero issues are not often offered for sale which is a pity as there is some lovely artwork and great covers. Low grade copies would sell well in the U.K. if some enterprising dealer from the States brought them over.

TALES TO ASTONISH

Just as with Strange Tales #101 and #110, Astonish #35 is more sought after than #27. The first Ant Man in costume is deemed more important than a man-in-an-ant-hill fantasy type story though #27 remains the hardest early Marvel key issue to get in very high grade with Hulk #1 a close second. Astonish #57 is much sought after on both sides of the Atlantic as an early Spiderman appearance (1964), there's some interest in #59 as a battle issue, #60 as hard-to-find-in-high-grade and #61 as the first Ditko Hulk since Hulk #6 back in March 1963. Issues #92 and #93 are must-haves for all Silver Surfer fans being his 4th and 5th appearances. As commented above, later issues of this title do seem to turn up in higher grades and are very common in lower grades in the U.K. As a title, prices are up by about 12% across the board.

THANOS QUEST

Dropped from £5 each to £4 as an average price around the country but still sought after.

THOR

Cancelled with issue #502 after thirty years. The title then continued on as Journey into Mystery, focusing more on the family of gods that populate Asgard. Otherwise the short run from #491-#494 is still attracting some interest. Nice Mike Deodato artwork and crisp Warren Ellis writing that at the time injected new enthusiasm for this title. Though prices are static, older back issue interest continues to focus on #134 with the 1st High Evolutionary (still at £30), #158 for origin facts and a great cover (still at £30), #165 (still £30) and #166 (still £27.50) in which "Him" appears, not yet called Warlock and issues in the #220's with Galactus and Firelord. #193 remains tough to find in high grade and like Avengers #93, Fantastic Four #116 and Daredevil #81 can suffer from label damage in the top left-hand corner. #126 is said by many to be under-rated as it is technically the first issue of Thor as a title (up from £70 in the last Guide to £75 in this). The Simonson issues beginning with #337 have enjoyed a new lease of interest as a rattling good read and more attention has been focused on the first and much under-rated Simonson run from #259-271.

TOMB OF DRACULA

Tomb of Dracula does very well as one of the best 1970's titles with its moody Gene Colan artwork and Marv Wolfman scripts. #1-6 are increasingly hard to find in top shape though #10 with Blade the Vampire Slayer hasn't taken off as well as some thought it might. We shall see what the film with Wesley Snipes does for it as a back issue. #18 and #50 are worth looking out for and the last issue (#70) is always one to defeat the completists. Check out the availability Dracula Giant Sizes as well and be surprised at their scarcity in the U.K. The whole title value is up slightly on last year from £349.00 to £367.50.

WARLOCK

This character gained a huge following in the early 1990s and this short-lived series that ran 15 issues between 1972 and 1976 became much sought after. The "Thanos factor", with appearances in #9,#10,#11 and #15, did much to fuel prices though these have showed yet more signs of slowing down drastically, certainly falling behind American excesses. Issues #10 and #11 have slumped in price in the U.K. #10 is down from £12.50 in the last Guide to £7.50 in this and #11 fell from £10.00 to £7.00. Overall the title has fallen by about 15%.

WEB OF SPIDERMAN

Worth mentioning as it is was cancelled in late 1995. The value of #1 has remained static at £8.00 and early issues generally static though they remain in some demand. #29 and #30 have slipped down in listed value from £7.00 and £6.00 respectively to £4.50 each. #48 is $15.00 in the States, about £3.00 over here in the U.K. (ie. 3 times less).

WEREWOLF BY NIGHT

And yet another example of bargain bins of yester-year now wall books of many a comic shop. Not quite in the same league as Dracula or Frankenstein but still an attractive set at 43 issues, some common as dirt, others ND and very scarce in the U.K. This title does not seem to have suffered as much as other horror titles in falling back issue sales and the title value was up by about £30 from U.K. Guide #6 to #7 and it seems to have done the same again this year.

WHAT IF

The first series is 20 years old incredibly and is one to watch. The early issues are becoming harder to find in the U.K. and the title value as a whole is up by about 20% or so.

WHERE CREATURES ROAM/ WHERE MONSTERS DWELL

I just love these 70s monster reprint titles and they are incredibly hard to find in high grade and cents copies. Far too cheap in my opinion but then I'm probably one of about two people seriously collecting them (the other one is Peter Jacques. Hello Peter).

WOLVERINE

Still as popular as ever, early issues of his main title are difficult to keep in constant stock. #50 still seems to be in plentiful supply (speculators beware) and Sabretooth keeps cropping up to fuel fan interest. Interest in the Charleston Chew Bar Wolverine give-away comic with Sam Kieth cover and art featured has remained static at £6.00. The Limited series seems to be in as much demand as ever before with the title value rising from £38.50 to £47.50 this year.

X-FACTOR

Early issues of X-Factor were holding in value from Guide #6 to #7 but now they are slipping. #1 is down slightly. #24 is static. #40 is down from £3.00 to £2.00. #60 is static. As a general rule, this title seems to be the poorest seller of the X-titles.

X-FORCE

As a more than abundant supply of copies abound, the first issue will almost definitely remain static for some time. The preference for the issue #1 with the Cable trading card and thus selling for more in the U.K. marketplace no longer applies.

X-MEN

Still number one in just about every category, the X-Men just cannot be ignored as far as volume sales go. Looking back through the 1990s, 1991 was a great year with an incredible 8 million copies supposedly printed of the first issue with its five cover variations, dealers ordered heavily and some sold out, some got stung. There is no doubt that there will be enough copies to supply demand for some considerable time to come. The first issue was well distributed to the U.K. newsagents though they suffer from a large and ugly bar-code label stuck on the front cover which is very difficult to remove (not advised!). It is not yet fully established whether all distributed copies have these labels but it is thought highly likely. 1992 was also a good year for the X-Men with the build-up to #300 and the 30th anniversary celebrations neatly falling into place. Gimmick covers again but quite tastefully done on #300. As far as earlier back issues go on the X-Men title, #1 is deservedly over the psychological £3,000 barrier as #94 and Giant Size #1 are likewise over the £250 barrier. These two are very important milestones as far as back issues go. #94 is as difficult as ever to find in Near Mint with that dark/black cover showing the tiniest crease. The Neal Adams issues from #56-#63 and #65 have shown a lot of increased interest. #201 with the first appearance of Cyclops' son Nathan (who becomes Cable) has slackened off in demand but that does not mean it turns up with any more frequency. Prices have dropped on this from about £7.50 to £6.00. #248 with the first Jim Lee art on X-Men was in huge demand but slackened off as there seems to be a reasonable supply. £7.00 in U.K. Guide #6, £5.00 for the last two years. #268 is still in reasonable demand for its striking cover as are all Jim Lee and Whilce Portacio art issues. The return of Magneto, the marriage of Scott and Jean and the most recent Age of Apocalypse and the Onslaught storylines have kept interest in this title reasonably high. There is still the general fan complaint that the sub-plots are still too complicated and new fans have trouble just getting into the title though Marvel seem to be addressing this situation. Ones to watch out for though are #150-200, always in demand and supply could be exhausted to dangerous levels in the U.K. soon. Issues in the #210-250 range seem fairly common in the U.K. and issues #212 and #213 have remained static but expect falls in price. They are everywhere.

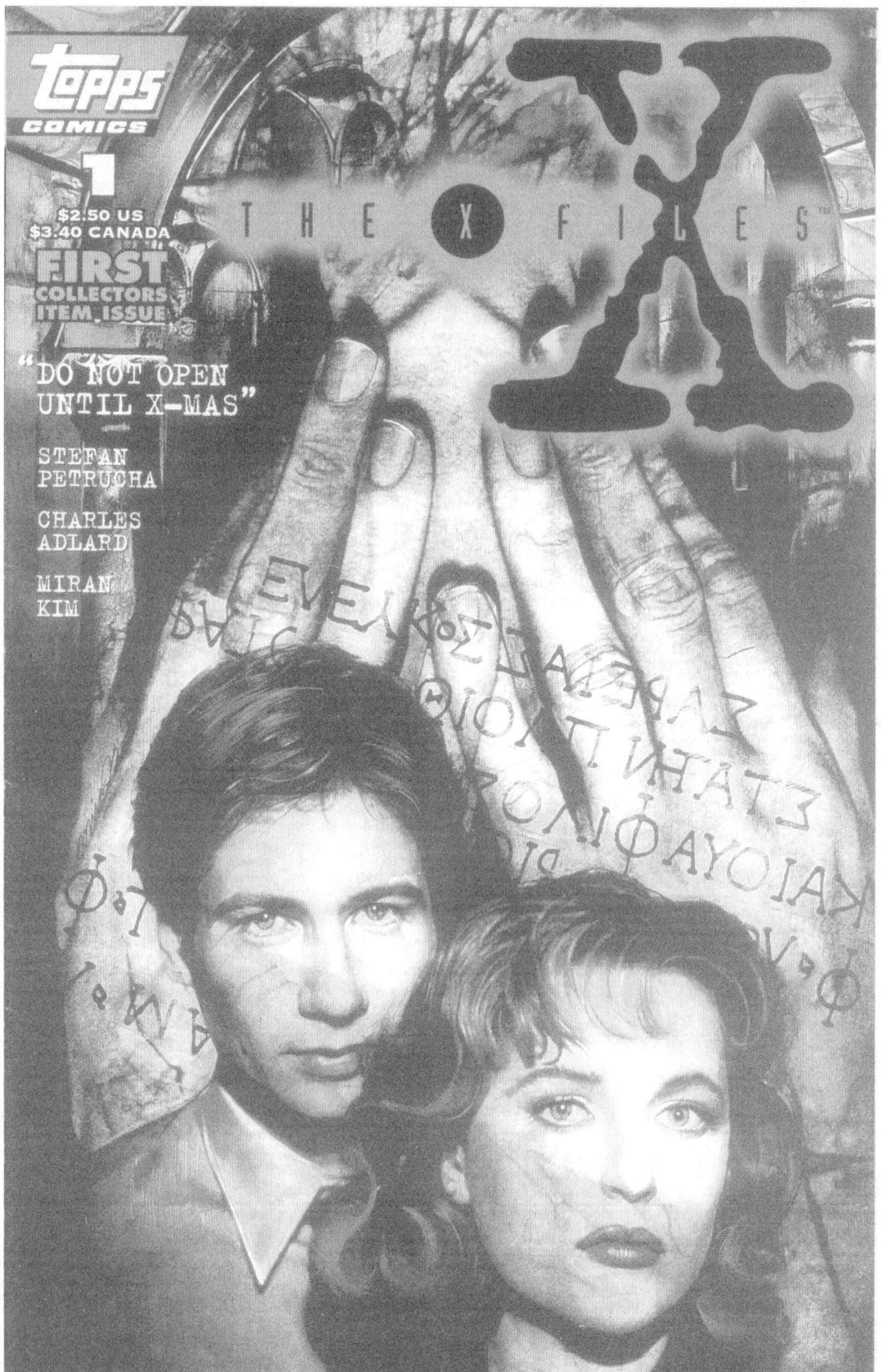

X-Files #1 – the most successful Independent comic of recent times based on the equally successful television series.

INTRODUCTION TO THE INDEPENDENTS
(Independence Daze!!) by Rick Appleby

Firstly, I would like to take a moment to thank everyone who responded to my article in last years guide titled "Variety – is the Spice of life", I'm glad that you all enjoyed it. This year Duncan has invited me to do a short article on the independent comics' scene.

"Independent comics" was as a term used to refer to the smaller comic publishing houses that were not owned or had any ties to the big two companies at the time (Marvel and D.C). A good example would be **Teenage Mutant Ninja Turtles, Fish Police** and of course **Cerebus**.

These days the term is a lot looser, with the label "creator owned" prefered. This is due to a number of factors, principally the recognition by the major publishing houses of the growing popularity of the small press, declining sales and a greater recognition of the role of the artist/ writer/ creator. For example, Image now has the excellent **Strangers in Paradise**, **Leave it to Chance** and of course Kurt Busiek's **Astro City**. Greater creator freedom is also being demonstrated at D.C with the Vertigo Imprint of which **Preacher** is a good example.

However, whilst some of the independents have moved over to the "majors", others have elected to stay as they are. This has had mixed blessings. Some titles have managed to maintain some sort of regular schedule, but others (e.g. **Agony Acres**) have lost their way a bit. The net result of this is that the reader quickly loses interest and loyalty in the title. Quite often the delays could be for reasons totally beyond the creators or publishers control, but on the other hand, some creators are guilty on the non-appearance of their book when they spend a good proportion of their time at the major conventions producing variant covers for such. This may make good commercial sense for the conventions, but the long term effect is only to alienate the regular reader who can't get his/her regular "fix". Such titles to suffer from this syndrome include **Shi, Creed, Double Impact** and **Razor**. The golden rule is quite simple, if the book isn't on the shelves – it won't sell!!

Recently, there has been much focus has been on the small press and independents. British creators (Martin Shipp and Gary Spencer Millidge) have both enjoyed good reviews on **Six Degrees** and **Strangehaven** respectively, the latter now on second prints of the early issues. **Memory Man** is also starting to get some deserved attention. On the other side of the Atlantic, **Scud, the Disposable Assassin** is drawing fans attention (the imminent release of the computer game no doubt helping) and **Stray Bullets** continues to attract rave reviews. **Johnny the Homicidal Maniac, Cerebus, Dawn** and **Darkchylde** are other titles that we are frequently asked for. **Poisen Elves** remains something of a cult, with early issues published by Mulehide press being expensive and sought after.

For the speculator, the independent comics' scene presents a great opportunity. Both this and last year's guide will show the oftimes phenomenal price rises on first and subsequent prints on certain books. This is because of the extremely low print runs, sometimes 2000 copies or less. **Bone #1** first print and the **Strangers in Paradise** (Antarctic Press) #1 through #3 (mini-series) are classic examples to be found. At the last UKCAC we sold a **Strangers in Paradise #3** (mini-series 1st print) at £65.00 at was told that this was too cheap!

Every month a close inspection of Previews will detail in some form or another some books that may be the potential **Bone** of tomorrow, but beware – many dealers' stockrooms are littered with books like this. Can you really afford to speculate on 40+ copies of Polka-dot-Turkey Man, Pink Pyjamas or whatever the latest titles to be tipped are?

Speaking of tips, what are mine for the future. Ha! If I knew, I wouldn't be writing this article! Perhaps the easiest way to answer this question is by saying that those titles that have moved to the bigger publishers have undoubtedly enjoyed the added exposure that this brings. The rumour wagon has it that **Strangers in Paradise** doubled its print run for Volume III (Homage) to only 25000 for #1!! Whilst Volume I of this title is beyond most peoples reach, demand for Volume II (Abstract Studios) is increasing as a result. Recent trade paperback reprints continue to make an easy entry point for readers as more and more people see what an excellent book this is.

On a final note, it would be remiss of me not to mention the shop, Page 45 in Nottingham. The guys up there have done an excellent job of stocking probably the fullest range of titles that come under this banner and I strongly recommend that you give them a visit or contact them for advice or help on a particular title.

Strangers In Paradise (2nd) #3

Preacher #2

Strangehaven #1

DC • MARVEL • INDEPENDENT COMICS

Points to Remember

- THIS BOOK IS ONLY A GUIDE AND SHOULD BE TREATED AS ONLY A GUIDE.
- COMICS SHOULD BE VERY STRICTLY GRADED, EVEN UNDER-GRADED, TO ENSURE CORRECT VALUATION.
- WHEN GRADING A COMIC, THE WHOLE COMIC MUST BE GRADED, NOT JUST THE COVER. START FROM THE INSIDE AND WORK OUT.
- MINT CONDITION MEANS MINT CONDITION. IT IS A VERY RARE GRADE.
- PRICES OF COMICS ARE CALCULATED AND SET AT TIME OF GOING TO PRESS ONLY. PLEASE ALLOW FOR A PERCENTAGE INCREASE AT LEAST IN LINE WITH INFLATION THROUGHOUT THE YEAR. THIS PERCENTAGE MAY BE MUCH HIGHER FOR OLDER, SCARCER OR IMPORTANT ISSUES.
- PRICES MAY VARY WIDELY ON VERY HIGH GRADE OR VERY "HOT" COMIC BOOKS.
- THE PRICING STRUCTURE FOR THE AMERICAN COMICS SECTION IS IN A NUMBER OF DIFFERENT RATIOS RANGING FROM 1:3:5 UP TO 1:3:16 IN EXCEPTIONAL CIRCUMSTANCES (USUALLY MAJOR KEY ISSUES). PLEASE REFER TO THE DIFFERENT PERCENTAGE CHARTS AT THE BOTTOM OF EACH PAGE FOR FURTHER CLARIFICATION.
- SOME DEALERS AND SOME COLLECTORS MAKE A DISTINCTION BETWEEN CENTS AND PENCE COPIES THOUGH THIS IS MAINLY ON RARE OR "KEY" ISSUES. IT IS AN INDIVIDUAL CHOICE.
- SOME COMICS, PARTICULARLY RARE AND "KEY" ISSUES, MAY FETCH PREMIUM PRICES IN HIGH GRADE CONDITION, THAT IS, VERY FINE PLUS OR BETTER. THESE MAY BE CALCULATED IN MULTIPLES OF GUIDE (1.25, 1.5, 2.0 TIMES GUIDE - SEE RELEVANT SECTION IN THE INTRODUCTION). FOR THOSE NEW TO COLLECTING, IT IS ADVISED TO SEEK PROFESSIONAL OPINIONS.
- ON COMICS FROM THE LAST 5 YEARS OR SO, THE NEAR MINT PRICE MAY BE TAKEN AS THE MINT PRICE.
- SCARCE, RARE AND VERY RARE HAVE BEEN USED SPARINGLY. THEY MUST NOT BE OVER-USED OR USED CASUALLY.
- THIS BOOK MUST AT ALL TIMES BE USED WITH COMMON SENSE AND FLEXIBILITY OF INTERPRETATION WITH REGARD TO PRICES.

A

	$Good	$Fine	$N.Mint	£Good	£Fine	£N.Mint
A PLUS						
Megaton Publications; 1 1977-5 1978						
1-5 ND 68pgs, sci-fi anthology	*$0.25*	*$0.75*	*$1.25*	£0.15	£0.45	£0.75
Title Value:	*$1.25*	*$3.75*	*$6.25*	£0.75	£2.25	£3.75
Note: quarterly frequency						
A-1						
Marvel Comics Group/Epic,MS; 1 Dec 1992-4 Mar 1993						
(see British section)						
1 ND 48pgs, squarebound, anthology featuring work by P. Craig Russell and Scott Hampton, Fabry cover	*$1.00*	*$3.00*	*$5.00*	£0.60	£1.80	£3.00
2 ND 48pgs, squarebound, anthology featuring work by George Pratt and Roger Langridge, Hunt Emerson cover	*$1.00*	*$3.00*	*$5.00*	£0.60	£1.80	£3.00
3 ND 48pgs, squarebound, anthology featuring work by Kent Williams, Dave Dorman, cover by Simon Bisley	*$1.00*	*$3.00*	*$5.00*	£0.60	£1.80	£3.00
4 ND 48pgs, squarebound, anthology featuring work by Jamie Hewlett and Colin McNeil	*$1.00*	*$3.00*	*$5.00*	£0.60	£1.80	£3.00
Title Value:	*$4.00*	*$12.00*	*$20.00*	£2.40	£7.20	£12.00
A-TEAM, THE						
Marvel Comics Group,MS TV; 1 Mar 1984-3 May 1984						
1-3 ND	*$0.15*	*$0.45*	*$0.75*	£0.10	£0.30	£0.50
Title Value:	*$0.45*	*$1.35*	*$2.25*	£0.30	£0.90	£1.50
A-V IN 3-D						
Aardvark-Vanaheim,OS; 1 Dec 1984						
1 ND scarce in the U.K. Cerebus, Flaming Carrot, Ms.Tree, Journey, Neil the Horse, Normalman appear; with bound-in 3-D glasses (25% less if without glasses)	*$1.50*	*$4.50*	*$7.50*	£1.00	£3.00	£5.00
Title Value:	*$1.50*	*$4.50*	*$7.50*	£1.00	£3.00	£5.00
A.R.M						
Adventure,MS; 1 Sep 1990-3 Dec 1990						
1-3 ND based on story by Larry Niven	*$0.40*	*$1.20*	*$2.00*	£0.25	£0.75	£1.25
Title Value:	*$1.20*	*$3.60*	*$6.00*	£0.75	£2.25	£3.75
ABOMINATIONS						
Marvel Comics Group,MS; 1 Dec 1996-3 Feb 1997						
1-3 ND Angel Medina art; continues plotlines from Hulk: Future Imperfect	*$0.30*	*$0.90*	*$1.50*	£0.20	£0.60	£1.00
Title Value:	*$0.90*	*$2.70*	*$4.50*	£0.60	£1.80	£3.00
ABRAHAM STONE						
Marvel Comics Group,MS; 1 Jul 1995-2 Aug 1995						
1-2 ND 48pgs, Joe Kubert script and art	*$1.40*	*$4.20*	*$7.00*	£0.90	£2.70	£4.50
Title Value:	*$2.80*	*$8.40*	*$14.00*	£1.80	£5.40	£9.00
Note: originally presented in graphic novel format by Malibu Comics						
ABSOLUTE VERTIGO						
DC Comics,OS; nn Mar 1995						
1 ND promotional sampler previewing Vertigo titles with an original 6pg Invisibles story, plus a preview of Preacher (1st appearance)	*$3.00*	*$9.00*	*$15.00*	£1.50	£4.50	£7.50
Title Value:	*$3.00*	*$9.00*	*$15.00*	£1.50	£4.50	£7.50
ABSOLUTE ZERO						
Antarctic Press; 1 1995-6 1996						
1-4 ND 40pgs, anthology; black and white	*$0.70*	*$2.10*	*$3.50*	£0.50	£1.50	£2.50
5 ND anthology: black and white	*$0.60*	*$1.80*	*$3.00*	£0.40	£1.20	£2.00
6 ND anthology; black and white	*$0.60*	*$1.80*	*$3.00*	£0.40	£1.20	£2.00
Title Value:	*$4.00*	*$12.00*	*$20.00*	£2.80	£8.40	£14.00
ABYSS, THE						
Dark Horse; 1,2 1989						
1 ND Mike Kaluta art begins, colour	*$0.60*	*$1.80*	*$3.00*	£0.40	£1.20	£2.00
2 ND scarce in the U.K.	*$0.60*	*$1.80*	*$3.00*	£0.40	£1.20	£2.00
Title Value:	*$1.20*	*$3.60*	*$6.00*	£0.80	£2.40	£4.00
Trade paperback				1.20	3.60	6.00
Note: all adaptations of film						
AC ANNUAL						
AC Comics; 1 1991-4 1994						
1 ND 64pgs	*$0.70*	*$2.10*	*$3.50*	£0.50	£1.50	£2.50
2 ND 64pgs, Femforce	*$0.70*	*$2.10*	*$3.50*	£0.50	£1.50	£2.50
3 ND 48pgs	*$0.70*	*$2.10*	*$3.50*	£0.50	£1.50	£2.50
4 ND 48pgs, Femforce X-over	*$0.70*	*$2.10*	*$3.50*	£0.50	£1.50	£2.50
Title Value:	*$2.80*	*$8.40*	*$14.00*	£2.00	£6.00	£10.00
ACCIDENT MAN						
Dark Horse,MS; 1 May 1993-3 Aug 1993						
1-3 ND Howard Chaykin covers	*$0.50*	*$1.50*	*$2.50*	£0.30	£0.90	£1.50
Title Value:	*$1.50*	*$4.50*	*$7.50*	£0.90	£2.70	£4.50
ACE COMICS PRESENTS						
Ace; 1 May 1987-4 1987						
1 ND Jack Cole reprints	*$0.30*	*$0.90*	*$1.50*	£0.20	£0.60	£1.00
2 ND Jack Bradbury reprints	*$0.30*	*$0.90*	*$1.50*	£0.20	£0.60	£1.00
3-4 ND Lou Fine reprints	*$0.30*	*$0.90*	*$1.50*	£0.20	£0.60	£1.00
Title Value:	*$1.20*	*$3.60*	*$6.00*	£0.80	£2.40	£4.00
ACES						
(see British section)						
ACES HIGH						
Gladstone; nn 1990						
nn ND Hardcover, reprints E.C's Aces High #1-5	*$3.00*	*$9.00*	*$15.00*	£2.00	£6.00	£10.00
Title Value:	*$3.00*	*$9.00*	*$15.00*	£2.00	£6.00	£10.00
ACHILLES STORM						
Aja Blu Comix; 1 Oct 1990; 2 Feb 1992						
1-2 ND Sandra Chang script, Mark Beachum art; black and white	*$0.30*	*$0.90*	*$1.50*	£0.20	£0.60	£1.00
Title Value:	*$0.60*	*$1.80*	*$3.00*	£0.40	£1.20	£2.00
ACK THE BARBARIAN						
Innovation,OS; 1 1991						
1 ND b&w	*$0.40*	*$1.20*	*$2.00*	£0.25	£0.75	£1.25
Title Value:	*$0.40*	*$1.20*	*$2.00*	£0.25	£0.75	£1.25
ACTION COMICS						
DC Comics; 0 Oct 1994; 1 Jun 1938-642 Mar 1989; 643 Jul 1989-present						
(Becomes Action Comics Weekly #601-642)						
0 (Oct 1994) Zero Hour X-over, origin retold; continued from Adventures of Superman #0	*$0.40*	*$1.20*	*$2.00*	£0.25	£0.75	£1.25
1 origin and 1st appearance Superman, 1st appearance Lois Lane and Zatara the Magician; arguably the most important comic ever published; probably no more than 100 extant copies	*$17000.00*	*$51000.00*	*$170000.00*	£11300.00	£34000.00	£113500.00
[Prices may vary widely on this comic]						
2	*$2750.00*	*$8300.00*	*$25000.00*	£1850.00	£5500.00	£16750.00
3 cover used in black and white as comic called "Action Funnies" to secure the "Action Comics" title and logo design						

Action Comics #16

Action Comics #56

Action Comics #57

	$Good	$Fine	$N.Mint	£Good	£Fine	£N.Mint
	$1500.00	$4500.00	$13500.00	£1000.00	£3000.00	£9000.00
4-5	$880.00	$2650.00	$8000.00	£590.00	£1775.00	£5350.00
6 1st appearance Jimmy Olsen (as office boy - see Superman #13)	$1000.00	$3000.00	$8000.00	£660.00	£2000.00	£5350.00
7 2nd ever Superman cover	$1300.00	$3900.00	$10500.00	£870.00	£2600.00	£7000.00
8 (Jan 1939)	$810.00	$2425.00	$6500.00	£540.00	£1625.00	£4350.00
9	$810.00	$2425.00	$6500.00	£540.00	£1625.00	£4350.00
10 3rd ever Superman cover	$1125.00	$3350.00	$9000.00	£750.00	£2250.00	£6000.00
[please note that the above are approximate values only as copies very rarely come onto the UK market]						
11	$405.00	$1200.00	$3250.00	£270.00	£810.00	£2175.00
12 classic science-fiction cover featuring Zatara and a rocketship blasted from a cannon; Detective Comics #27 advertised inside	$400.00	$1200.00	$3200.00	£265.00	£800.00	£2150.00
13 4th ever Superman cover	$650.00	$1950.00	$5250.00	£435.00	£1300.00	£3500.00
14	$375.00	$1125.00	$3000.00	£250.00	£750.00	£2000.00
15 5th ever Superman cover	$560.00	$1675.00	$4500.00	£375.00	£1125.00	£3000.00
16	$280.00	$840.00	$2250.00	£185.00	£560.00	£1500.00
17 6th ever Superman cover	$435.00	$1300.00	$3500.00	£290.00	£880.00	£2350.00
18 last non-Superman cover, 1st mention of X-Ray vision	$300.00	$900.00	$2400.00	£200.00	£600.00	£1600.00
19 1st regular Superman cover	$405.00	$1200.00	$3250.00	£270.00	£810.00	£2175.00
20 (Jan 1940), 1st mention of "The Daily Star" (later "The Daily Planet")	$375.00	$1125.00	$3000.00	£250.00	£750.00	£2000.00
21	$300.00	$900.00	$2400.00	£200.00	£600.00	£1600.00
22	$225.00	$670.00	$1800.00	£150.00	£450.00	£1200.00
23 1st appearance Lex Luthor (red hair, not bald), 1st Black Pirate, 1st mention of The Daily Planet newspaper	$750.00	$2250.00	$6000.00	£500.00	£1500.00	£4000.00
24-25	$215.00	$650.00	$1750.00	£145.00	£440.00	£1175.00
26-28	$185.00	$560.00	$1500.00	£125.00	£375.00	£1000.00
29 1st appearance of Lois Lane on cover; the cover was also used in a black and white version for "World's Best Comics" ash-can (see Top 50 Rarest Comics section)	$250.00	$750.00	$2000.00	£165.00	£500.00	£1350.00
30	$185.00	$560.00	$1500.00	£125.00	£375.00	£1000.00
31	$115.00	$355.00	$950.00	£77.50	£235.00	£635.00
32 (Jan 1941)	$115.00	$355.00	$950.00	£77.50	£235.00	£635.00
33 origin Mr. America	$130.00	$390.00	$1050.00	£87.50	£260.00	£700.00
34-35	$105.00	$315.00	$850.00	£70.00	£215.00	£575.00
36 robot cover	$105.00	$315.00	$850.00	£70.00	£215.00	£575.00
37 origin Congo Bill	$105.00	$315.00	$850.00	£70.00	£215.00	£575.00
38-39	$105.00	$315.00	$850.00	£70.00	£215.00	£575.00
40 1st appearance Star Spangled Kid	$105.00	$315.00	$850.00	£70.00	£215.00	£575.00
41	$100.00	$300.00	$800.00	£65.00	£200.00	£535.00
42 origin and 1st appearance Vigilante; Lex Luthor appears	$150.00	$450.00	$1200.00	£100.00	£300.00	£800.00
43	$100.00	$300.00	$800.00	£65.00	£200.00	£535.00
44 (Jan 1942)	$100.00	$300.00	$800.00	£65.00	£200.00	£535.00
45-46	$100.00	$300.00	$800.00	£65.00	£200.00	£535.00
47 1st Lex Luthor (bald) cover in title; Luthor acquires super-powers for the 1st time (see Superman #17) with the aid of the Powerstone (see also Superman #252)	$140.00	$430.00	$1150.00	£95.00	£290.00	£775.00
48-50	$100.00	$300.00	$800.00	£65.00	£200.00	£535.00
51 1st appearance The Prankster	$100.00	$305.00	$825.00	£67.50	£205.00	£550.00
52 1st Americommandoes (Fatman and Mr. America), classic cover	$105.00	$315.00	$850.00	£70.00	£210.00	£570.00
53-55	$67.50	$205.00	$550.00	£46.00	£135.00	£370.00
56 (Jan 1943)	$67.50	$205.00	$550.00	£46.00	£135.00	£370.00
57 Prankster cover	$67.50	$205.00	$550.00	£46.00	£135.00	£370.00
58 "You Can Slap A Jap" patriotic war cover	$67.50	$205.00	$550.00	£46.00	£135.00	£370.00
59	$67.50	$205.00	$550.00	£46.00	£135.00	£370.00
60 1st appearance Lois Lane as Superwoman (see Superman #45)	$67.50	$205.00	$550.00	£46.00	£135.00	£370.00
61-63	$62.50	$185.00	$500.00	£42.00	£125.00	£335.00
64 1st appearance The Toyman, 1st Toyman cover	$75.00	$225.00	$600.00	£50.00	£150.00	£400.00
65-67	$62.50	$185.00	$500.00	£42.00	£125.00	£335.00
68 (Jan 1944)	$62.50	$185.00	$500.00	£42.00	£125.00	£335.00
69 Prankster cover and story	$62.50	$185.00	$500.00	£42.00	£125.00	£335.00
70	$62.50	$185.00	$500.00	£42.00	£125.00	£335.00
71-76	$44.00	$130.00	$350.00	£29.00	£87.50	£235.00
77 Prankster cover and story	$44.00	$130.00	$350.00	£29.00	£87.50	£235.00
78-79	$44.00	$130.00	$350.00	£29.00	£87.50	£235.00
80 (Jan 1945), 2nd appearance Mr. Myxyztplk (see Superman #30), 1st cover appearance	$90.00	$270.00	$725.00	£60.00	£180.00	£485.00
80 U.S. Navy Edition, scarce in the U.S, very scarce in the U.K. - giveaway issue with the banner "Special Edition - US Navy" across the top of cover	$100.00	$300.00	$800.00	£65.00	£200.00	£535.00
81	$57.50	$175.00	$475.00	£40.00	£120.00	£320.00
81 U.S. Navy Edition, very scarce in the U.K., scarce in the U.S. - giveaway issue with "Special Edition - US Navy" banner across the top of cover	$65.00	$195.00	$525.00	£44.00	£130.00	£350.00
82	$57.50	$175.00	$475.00	£40.00	£120.00	£320.00
83 1st appearance Hocus and Pocus	$57.50	$175.00	$475.00	£40.00	£120.00	£320.00
84-87	$57.50	$175.00	$475.00	£40.00	£120.00	£320.00
88 Hocus and Pocus appear	$57.50	$175.00	$475.00	£40.00	£120.00	£320.00
89-90	$57.50	$175.00	$475.00	£40.00	£120.00	£320.00
91	$55.00	$165.00	$450.00	£38.00	£110.00	£300.00
92 (Jan 1946)	$55.00	$165.00	$450.00	£38.00	£110.00	£300.00
93-94	$55.00	$165.00	$450.00	£38.00	£110.00	£300.00
95 Prankster cover and story	$55.00	$165.00	$450.00	£38.00	£110.00	£300.00
96	$55.00	$165.00	$450.00	£38.00	£110.00	£300.00
97 Hocus and Pocus appear	$55.00	$165.00	$450.00	£38.00	£110.00	£300.00
98	$55.00	$165.00	$450.00	£38.00	£110.00	£300.00
99 1st smaller logo on cover	$55.00	$165.00	$450.00	£38.00	£110.00	£300.00
100	$115.00	$345.00	$925.00	£77.50	£230.00	£620.00
[Issues before #100 are generally at least scarce in the U.K.]						
101 nuclear explosion cover; cover-dated October 1946 and out on the news-stands therefore almost exactly a year after Hiroshima (deliberate anniversary?)	$175.00	$530.00	$1250.00	£115.00	£355.00	£835.00
102 Mr. Mxyztplk cover and story (the "t" and "p" were reversed in spelling in the Silver Age)	$62.50	$190.00	$450.00	£43.00	£125.00	£300.00
103	$62.50	$190.00	$450.00	£43.00	£125.00	£300.00
104 (Jan 1947), Prankster cover and story	$62.50	$190.00	$450.00	£43.00	£125.00	£300.00
105 Christmas cover	$62.50	$190.00	$450.00	£43.00	£125.00	£300.00
106-108	$60.00	$180.00	$425.00	£41.00	£120.00	£285.00
109 Prankster cover and story	$62.50	$190.00	$450.00	£43.00	£125.00	£300.00
110-111	$60.00	$180.00	$425.00	£41.00	£120.00	£285.00
112 Mr. Mxyztplk cover and story	$62.50	$190.00	$450.00	£43.00	£125.00	£300.00
113-115	$60.00	$180.00	$425.00	£41.00	£120.00	£285.00
116 (Jan 1948)	$60.00	$180.00	$425.00	£41.00	£120.00	£285.00
117 Christmas cover	$62.50	$190.00	$450.00	£43.00	£125.00	£300.00
118-120	$60.00	$180.00	$425.00	£41.00	£120.00	£285.00
121 Superman vs. Atlas	$55.00	$170.00	$400.00	£39.00	£115.00	£270.00
122-126	$55.00	$170.00	$400.00	£39.00	£115.00	£270.00
127 Tommy Tomorrow feature begins, Vigilante by Kubert	$67.50	$200.00	$475.00	£46.00	£135.00	£320.00
128 (Jan 1949)	$55.00	$170.00	$400.00	£39.00	£115.00	£270.00
129-130	$55.00	$170.00	$400.00	£39.00	£115.00	£270.00
131 Lex Luthor cover and story	$60.00	$180.00	$425.00	£41.00	£120.00	£285.00
132-137	$55.00	$170.00	$400.00	£39.00	£115.00	£270.00
138 nuclear bomb-carrying "flying wing" aeroplane cover	$60.00	$180.00	$425.00	£41.00	£120.00	£285.00
139	$55.00	$170.00	$400.00	£39.00	£115.00	£270.00
140 (Jan 1950)	$55.00	$170.00	$400.00	£39.00	£115.00	£270.00
141 Lex Luthor cover and story	$55.00	$170.00	$400.00	£39.00	£115.00	£270.00
142-145	$52.50	$160.00	$375.00	£36.00	£105.00	£250.00
146 cover based on Action Comics #20	$52.50	$160.00	$375.00	£36.00	£105.00	£250.00
147-150	$52.50	$160.00	$375.00	£36.00	£105.00	£250.00
151 Luthor, Prankster, Mr. Mxyztplk appear	$52.50	$160.00	$375.00	£36.00	£105.00	£250.00
152 (Jan 1951)	$52.50	$160.00	$375.00	£36.00	£105.00	£250.00
153-155	$52.50	$160.00	$375.00	£36.00	£105.00	£250.00
156 Lois Lane as The Girl of Steel; the blonde wig makes this a much more direct Supergirl try-out than the brunette in Superman #123	$52.50	$160.00	$375.00	£36.00	£105.00	£250.00
157	$52.50	$160.00	$375.00	£36.00	£105.00	£250.00
158 Superman's origin retold	$135.00	$405.00	$950.00	£90.00	£270.00	£635.00
159-160	$52.50	$160.00	$375.00	£36.00	£105.00	£250.00
161-163	$43.00	$125.00	$300.00	£29.00	£85.00	£200.00
164 (Jan 1952)	$43.00	$125.00	$300.00	£29.00	£85.00	£200.00
165-175	$43.00	$125.00	$300.00	£29.00	£85.00	£200.00
176 (Jan 1953)	$43.00	$125.00	$300.00	£29.00	£85.00	£200.00
177-180	$43.00	$125.00	$300.00	£29.00	£85.00	£200.00
181	$41.00	$120.00	$290.00	£28.00	£82.50	£195.00
182 The Return of Planet Krypton story	$41.00	$120.00	$290.00	£28.00	£82.50	£195.00
183-187	$41.00	$120.00	$290.00	£28.00	£82.50	£195.00
188 (Jan 1954)	$41.00	$120.00	$290.00	£28.00	£82.50	£195.00
189-193	$41.00	$120.00	$290.00	£28.00	£82.50	£195.00
194 Return of the Foes from Krypton (see Superman #65)	$41.00	$120.00	$290.00	£28.00	£82.50	£195.00
195-199	$41.00	$120.00	$290.00	£28.00	£82.50	£195.00
200 very scarce in the U.K., scarce in the U.S.	$46.00	$135.00	$325.00	£31.00	£92.50	£220.00

	$Good	$Fine	$N.Mint	£Good	£Fine	£N.Mint
201-210 very scarce in the U.K., scarce in the U.S.						
	$34.00	$100.00	$240.00	£23.50	£70.00	£165.00
211	$34.00	$100.00	$235.00	£22.00	£65.00	£155.00
212 (Jan 1956), 1956 Superman calendar included						
	$34.00	$100.00	$235.00	£22.00	£65.00	£155.00
213-217	$34.00	$100.00	$235.00	£22.00	£65.00	£155.00
218 Super-Ape from Krypton (pre Titano)						
	$34.00	$100.00	$235.00	£22.00	£65.00	£155.00
219-220	$34.00	$100.00	$235.00	£22.00	£65.00	£155.00
221-222	$29.00	$85.00	$200.00	£19.00	£57.50	£135.00
223 scarce in the U.K. Jor-El as "Superman" on Krypton						
	$29.00	$85.00	$200.00	£20.00	£60.00	£140.00
224 (Jan 1957) 1st appearance Golden Gorilla						
	$29.00	$85.00	$200.00	£19.00	£57.50	£135.00
225-230	$29.00	$85.00	$200.00	£19.00	£57.50	£135.00
231	$27.00	$80.00	$190.00	£17.50	£52.50	£125.00
232 1st Curt Swan cover						
	$27.00	$80.00	$190.00	£17.50	£52.50	£125.00
233-234	$27.00	$80.00	$190.00	£17.50	£52.50	£125.00
235 scarce in the U.K.						
	$27.00	$80.00	$190.00	£20.00	£60.00	£140.00
236 scarce in the U.K. (Jan 1958)						
	$27.00	$80.00	$190.00	£20.00	£60.00	£140.00
237 scarce in the U.K.						
	$27.00	$80.00	$190.00	£20.00	£60.00	£140.00
238-240	$27.00	$80.00	$190.00	£17.50	£52.50	£125.00
241 Batman appears						
	$24.00	$72.50	$170.00	£16.00	£49.00	£115.00
242 origin and 1st appearance Brainiac, 1st mention of bottle-city of Kandor						
	$125.00	$380.00	$1150.00	£82.50	£250.00	£750.00
[Rare in high grade - Very Fine+ or better]						
243-247	$22.00	$65.00	$155.00	£15.00	£45.00	£105.00
248 (Jan 1959), 1st appearance Congorilla (see #224)						
	$22.00	$65.00	$155.00	£15.00	£45.00	£105.00
249-250	$22.00	$65.00	$155.00	£15.00	£45.00	£105.00
251 last Tommy Tomorrow						
	$20.00	$60.00	$140.00	£14.00	£43.00	£100.00
252 less common in the U.K. origin and 1st appearance Supergirl, Metallo appears						
	$160.00	$485.00	$1300.00	£105.00	£325.00	£875.00
252 Silver Age Classic, ND (Mar 1992) reprints original issue featuring the origin and first appearance of Supergirl						
	$0.25	$0.75	$1.25	£0.15	£0.45	£0.80
253 2nd appearance Supergirl						
	$50.00	$150.00	$350.00	£31.00	£92.50	£220.00
254 Bizarro and Superman 1st meeting						
	$35.00	$105.00	$245.00	£22.50	£67.50	£160.00
255 1st appearance Bizarro Lois and making of Bizarro World						
	$25.00	$75.00	$175.00	£17.00	£50.00	£120.00
256	$15.00	$45.00	$105.00	£10.00	£30.00	£70.00
257 copies known with distribution stamps						
	$15.00	$45.00	$105.00	£10.00	£30.00	£70.00
1st official distribution in the U.K						
258-259	$15.00	$45.00	$105.00	£10.00	£30.00	£70.00
260 (Jan 1960)	$15.00	$45.00	$105.00	£10.00	£30.00	£70.00
261 1st appearance X-Kryptonite, origin Streaky the Super-Cat						
	$16.00	$49.00	$115.00	£10.50	£32.00	£75.00
262	$12.50	$39.00	$90.00	£8.50	£26.00	£60.00
263 origin of the Bizarro World; Superman becomes a Bizarro						
	$12.50	$39.00	$90.00	£8.50	£26.00	£60.00
264 Superman as Bizarro						
	$12.50	$39.00	$90.00	£8.50	£26.00	£60.00
265-266	$12.50	$39.00	$90.00	£8.50	£26.00	£60.00
267 3rd appearance of Legion (Superboy story); 1st Invisible Kid, Chameleon Boy, Colossal Boy						
	$46.00	$135.00	$370.00	£30.00	£90.00	£240.00
268-270	$12.50	$39.00	$90.00	£8.50	£26.00	£60.00
271	$10.50	$32.00	$75.00	£7.00	£21.00	£50.00
272 (Jan 1961)	$10.50	$32.00	$75.00	£7.00	£21.00	£50.00
273-275	$10.50	$32.00	$75.00	£7.00	£21.00	£50.00
276 6th appearance of Legion (Supergirl story); 1st Brainiac 5, Bouncing Boy, Sun Boy, Shrinking Violet, Triplicate Girl, Phantom Girl						
	$21.50	$65.00	$175.00	£14.00	£43.00	£115.00
277-281	$10.50	$32.00	$75.00	£7.00	£21.00	£50.00
282 last 10 cents issue						
	$10.50	$32.00	$75.00	£7.00	£21.00	£50.00
283 Legion of Super-Villains appear; 1st 12 cents issue						
	$10.50	$32.00	$75.00	£7.00	£21.00	£50.00
284 (Jan 1962), Mon-El appearance						
	$10.50	$32.00	$75.00	£7.00	£21.00	£50.00
285 12th appearance of Legion; Supergirl's existence revealed to the world						
	$10.50	$32.00	$75.00	£7.00	£21.00	£50.00
286 Legion of Super-Villains appear						
	$7.75	$23.50	$55.00	£5.00	£15.00	£35.00
287 15th appearance of Legion (Supergirl story)						
	$7.75	$23.50	$55.00	£5.00	£15.00	£35.00
288 Mon-El appearance						
	$7.75	$23.50	$55.00	£5.00	£15.00	£35.00
289 17th appearance of Legion, as adults (Supergirl story)						
	$7.75	$23.50	$55.00	£5.00	£15.00	£35.00
290 18th appearance of Legion, 3 panels (Supergirl story)						
	$7.75	$23.50	$55.00	£5.00	£15.00	£35.00
291-292	$6.25	$19.00	$45.00	£3.55	£10.50	£25.00
293 origin Comet, the Super-Horse						
	$12.00	$36.00	$85.00	£6.25	£19.00	£45.00
294-295	$6.25	$19.00	$45.00	£3.55	£10.50	£25.00
296 (Jan 1963)	$6.25	$19.00	$45.00	£3.55	£10.50	£25.00
297-299	$6.25	$19.00	$45.00	£3.55	£10.50	£25.00
300 classic cover - "Superman Under a Red Sun"						
	$7.75	$23.50	$55.00	£5.00	£15.00	£35.00
301-303	$4.25	$12.50	$30.00	£2.50	£7.50	£17.50
304 1st appearance Black Flame						
	$4.25	$12.50	$30.00	£2.50	£7.50	£17.50
305-307	$4.25	$12.50	$30.00	£2.50	£7.50	£17.50
308 (Jan 1964)	$4.25	$12.50	$30.00	£2.50	£7.50	£17.50
309 Batman and Legion appear						
	$4.25	$12.50	$30.00	£2.50	£7.50	£17.50
310 1st appearance Jewel Kryptonite						
	$4.25	$12.50	$30.00	£2.50	£7.50	£17.50
311-312	$3.55	$10.50	$25.00	£1.75	£5.25	£12.50
313 Batman appears; Lena Thorul learns she's Luthor's sister						
	$3.55	$10.50	$25.00	£1.75	£5.25	£12.50
314 Justice League of America X-over (Flash, Aquaman, Batman and Green Lantern)						
	$3.55	$10.50	$25.00	£1.75	£5.25	£12.50
315-319	$3.55	$10.50	$25.00	£1.75	£5.25	£12.50
320 (Jan 1965)	$3.55	$10.50	$25.00	£1.75	£5.25	£12.50
321-330	$2.85	$8.50	$20.00	£1.40	£4.25	£10.00
331 last Silver Age issue cover-dated Dec 1965						
	$2.85	$8.50	$20.00	£1.10	£3.40	£8.00
332 (Jan 1966)	$2.85	$8.50	$20.00	£1.10	£3.40	£8.00
333	$2.85	$8.50	$20.00	£1.10	£3.40	£8.00
334 scarce in the U.K. 80pgs, Giant G-20, reprints Supergirl origin from #252 and 3rd Legion from #267						
	$5.00	$15.00	$40.00	£3.10	£9.25	£25.00
335-339	$2.85	$8.50	$20.00	£1.10	£3.40	£8.00
340 1st appearance Parasite						
	$3.55	$10.50	$25.00	£1.75	£5.25	£12.50
341-344	$2.10	$6.25	$15.00	£1.00	£3.00	£7.00
345 (Jan 1967)	$2.10	$6.25	$15.00	£1.00	£3.00	£7.00
346	$2.10	$6.25	$15.00	£1.00	£3.00	£7.00
347 scarce in the U.K. 80pgs, Giant G-33						
	$3.55	$10.50	$25.00	£2.50	£7.50	£17.50
348-350	$2.10	$6.25	$15.00	£1.00	£3.00	£7.00
351 Captain Marvel inspired "Zha-Vam" story						
	$2.10	$6.25	$15.00	£0.85	£2.55	£6.00
352-357	$2.10	$6.25	$15.00	£0.85	£2.55	£6.00
358 (Jan 1968), Neal Adams cover						
	$2.10	$6.25	$15.00	£0.85	£2.55	£6.00
359 Neal Adams cover						
	$2.10	$6.25	$15.00	£0.85	£2.55	£6.00
360 scarce in the U.K. 80pgs, Giant G-45, full length Supergirl story from back-up reprints						
	$3.55	$10.50	$25.00	£2.50	£7.50	£17.50
361-365	$1.40	$4.25	$10.00	£0.70	£2.10	£5.00
366 Justice League of America appears						
	$1.40	$4.25	$10.00	£0.70	£2.10	£5.00
367 Neal Adams cover						
	$1.40	$4.25	$10.00	£0.70	£2.10	£5.00
368-369	$1.40	$4.25	$10.00	£0.70	£2.10	£5.00
370 Neal Adams cover						
	$1.40	$4.25	$10.00	£0.70	£2.10	£5.00
371 (Jan 1969), Neal Adams cover						
	$1.40	$4.25	$10.00	£0.70	£2.10	£5.00
372 Neal Adams cover						
	$1.40	$4.25	$10.00	£0.70	£2.10	£5.00
373 68pgs, Giant G-57						
	$3.55	$10.50	$25.00	£1.75	£5.25	£12.50
374 Neal Adams cover						
	$1.40	$4.25	$10.00	£0.70	£2.10	£5.00
375-376	$1.40	$4.25	$10.00	£0.70	£2.10	£5.00
377-383 Legion back-up						
	$1.40	$4.25	$10.00	£0.70	£2.10	£5.00
384 (Jan 1970), Legion back-up						
	$1.30	$4.00	$8.00	£0.80	£2.50	£5.00
385-390 Legion back-up						
	$1.30	$4.00	$8.00	£0.80	£2.50	£5.00
391 Legion back-up						
	$1.30	$4.00	$8.00	£0.65	£2.00	£4.00
392 Legion back-up						
	$1.30	$4.00	$8.00	£0.65	£2.00	£4.00
393-395	$1.30	$4.00	$8.00	£0.55	£1.75	£3.50
396 (Jan 1971)	$1.30	$4.00	$8.00	£0.55	£1.75	£3.50
397	$1.30	$4.00	$8.00	£0.55	£1.75	£3.50
398-400 Neal Adams cover						
	$1.30	$4.00	$8.00	£0.55	£1.75	£3.50
401	$1.30	$4.00	$8.00	£0.55	£1.75	£3.50
402 Neal Adams cover						
	$1.30	$4.00	$8.00	£0.55	£1.75	£3.50
403-407 48pgs	$1.30	$4.00	$8.00	£0.65	£2.00	£4.00
408 48pgs, (Jan 1972)						
	$1.30	$4.00	$8.00	£0.65	£2.00	£4.00
409-410 48pgs	$1.30	$4.00	$8.00	£0.65	£2.00	£4.00
411 48pgs, Eclipso origin reprinted						
	$1.30	$4.00	$8.00	£0.65	£2.00	£4.00
412 48pgs	$1.30	$4.00	$8.00	£0.65	£2.00	£4.00
413 48pgs, Metamorpho begins, ends #418						
	$1.30	$4.00	$8.00	£0.65	£2.00	£4.00
414 scarce in the U.K.						

	$Good	$Fine	$N.Mint	£Good	£Fine	£N.Mint
	$1.30	$4.00	$8.00	£0.65	£2.00	£4.00
415-418	$1.30	$4.00	$8.00	£0.50	£1.50	£3.00
419 scarce in the U.K. photo cover						
	$1.30	$4.00	$8.00	£0.55	£1.75	£3.50
420 (Jan 1973)	$1.30	$4.00	$8.00	£0.50	£1.50	£3.00
421 Green Arrow begins						
	$1.30	$4.00	$8.00	£0.40	£1.25	£2.50
422-424	$1.30	$4.00	$8.00	£0.40	£1.25	£2.50
425 Neal Adams art, Atom back-up begins						
	$2.50	$7.50	$15.00	£1.00	£3.00	£6.00
426-430	$1.15	$3.50	$7.00	£0.30	£1.00	£2.00
431 (Jan 1974)	$1.15	$3.50	$7.00	£0.30	£1.00	£2.00
432 1st appearance Silver Age Toyman						
	$1.15	$3.50	$7.00	£0.30	£1.00	£2.00
433-436	$1.15	$3.50	$7.00	£0.30	£1.00	£2.00
437 LD in the U.K. 100pgs, reprints Sea Devils #1						
	$2.00	$6.00	$12.00	£0.65	£2.00	£4.00
438-439	$1.15	$3.50	$7.00	£0.30	£1.00	£2.00
440 1st Mike Grell Green Arrow						
	$1.00	$3.00	$6.00	£0.55	£1.75	£3.50
441 Grell Green Arrow						
	$0.80	$2.50	$5.00	£0.40	£1.25	£2.50
442	$0.65	$2.00	$4.00	£0.30	£1.00	£2.00
443 LD in the U.K. 100pgs, (Jan 1975), Justice League appears						
	$2.00	$6.00	$12.00	£0.65	£2.00	£4.00
444-448	$0.65	$2.00	$4.00	£0.30	£1.00	£2.00
449 LD in the U.K. 68pgs						
	$0.65	$2.00	$4.00	£0.50	£1.50	£3.00
450	$0.65	$2.00	$4.00	£0.30	£1.00	£2.00
451-454 scarce in the U.K.						
	$0.65	$2.00	$4.00	£0.40	£1.25	£2.50
455 (Jan 1976)	$0.65	$2.00	$4.00	£0.30	£1.00	£2.00
456-457	$0.65	$2.00	$4.00	£0.30	£1.00	£2.00
458 last Green Arrow back-up						
	$0.65	$2.00	$4.00	£0.30	£1.00	£2.00
459 scarce in the U.K.						
	$0.65	$2.00	$4.00	£0.40	£1.25	£2.50
460	$0.65	$2.00	$4.00	£0.30	£1.00	£2.00
461 ND	$0.55	$1.75	$3.50	£0.50	£1.50	£3.00
462-465 scarce in the U.K.						
	$0.55	$1.75	$3.50	£0.30	£1.00	£2.00
466 scarce in the U.K. Neal Adams cover						
	$0.55	$1.75	$3.50	£0.30	£1.00	£2.00
467 scarce in the U.K. (Jan 1977)						
	$0.55	$1.75	$3.50	£0.30	£1.00	£2.00
468 scarce in the U.K. Neal Adams cover						
	$0.55	$1.75	$3.50	£0.30	£1.00	£2.00
469-472 scarce in the U.K.						
	$0.55	$1.75	$3.50	£0.30	£1.00	£2.00
473 scarce in the U.K. Neal Adams cover						
	$0.55	$1.75	$3.50	£0.30	£1.00	£2.00
474-478 scarce in the U.K.						
	$0.55	$1.75	$3.50	£0.30	£1.00	£2.00
479 scarce in the U.K. (Jan 1978)						
	$0.55	$1.75	$3.50	£0.30	£1.00	£2.00
480	$0.55	$1.75	$3.50	£0.25	£0.75	£1.50
481 1st Supermobile						
	$0.55	$1.75	$3.50	£0.25	£0.75	£1.50
482-483	$0.55	$1.75	$3.50	£0.25	£0.75	£1.50
484 40th anniversary, Earth-2 Superman weds						
	$0.55	$1.75	$3.50	£0.30	£1.00	£2.00
485 Neal Adams cover						
	$0.55	$1.75	$3.50	£0.25	£0.75	£1.50
486	$0.55	$1.75	$3.50	£0.25	£0.75	£1.50
487 scarce in the U.K. 44pgs, origin Atom retold						
	$0.55	$1.75	$3.50	£0.40	£1.25	£2.50
488-489 ND	$0.55	$1.75	$3.50	£0.40	£1.25	£2.50
490	$0.55	$1.75	$3.50	£0.25	£0.75	£1.50
491 (Jan 1979)	$0.55	$1.75	$3.50	£0.25	£0.75	£1.50
492-499	$0.55	$1.75	$3.50	£0.25	£0.75	£1.50
500 ND 68pgs, Superman's life story						
	$0.80	$2.50	$5.00	£0.50	£1.50	£3.00
501-502	$0.40	$1.20	$2.00	£0.25	£0.75	£1.25
503 (Jan 1980)	$0.40	$1.20	$2.00	£0.25	£0.75	£1.25
504-508	$0.40	$1.20	$2.00	£0.25	£0.75	£1.25
509 58pgs, Jim Starlin art on 28pg Superman insert "The Computer That Saved Metropolis" (later issued as a giveaway)						
	$0.40	$1.20	$2.00	£0.30	£0.90	£1.50
510-514	$0.40	$1.20	$2.00	£0.25	£0.75	£1.25
515 (Jan 1981)	$0.40	$1.20	$2.00	£0.25	£0.75	£1.25
516-520	$0.40	$1.20	$2.00	£0.25	£0.75	£1.25
521 1st appearance The Vixen						
	$0.40	$1.20	$2.00	£0.25	£0.75	£1.25
522 Teen Titans cameo						
	$0.40	$1.20	$2.00	£0.25	£0.75	£1.25
523-526	$0.40	$1.20	$2.00	£0.25	£0.75	£1.25
527 (Jan 1982), 1st appearance Lord Satanis						
	$0.40	$1.20	$2.00	£0.25	£0.75	£1.25
528	$0.40	$1.20	$2.00	£0.25	£0.75	£1.25
529 George Perez cover						
	$0.40	$1.20	$2.00	£0.25	£0.75	£1.25
530-534	$0.40	$1.20	$2.00	£0.25	£0.75	£1.25

	$Good	$Fine	$N.Mint	£Good	£Fine	£N.Mint
535-536 Omega Men appear						
	$0.40	$1.20	$2.00	£0.25	£0.75	£1.25
537-538	$0.40	$1.20	$2.00	£0.25	£0.75	£1.25
539 (Jan 1983), Keith Giffen cover						
	$0.40	$1.20	$2.00	£0.25	£0.75	£1.25
540-543	$0.40	$1.20	$2.00	£0.25	£0.75	£1.25
544 LD in the U.K. 68pgs, 45th anniversary, origins new Brainiac and Luthor						
	$0.50	$1.50	$2.50	£0.50	£1.50	£2.50
545	$0.40	$1.20	$2.00	£0.25	£0.75	£1.25
546 Justice League of America, Teen Titans X-over						
	$0.40	$1.20	$2.00	£0.25	£0.75	£1.25
547	$0.40	$1.20	$2.00	£0.25	£0.75	£1.25
548 Jewel Kryptonite returns (see #310)						
	$0.40	$1.20	$2.00	£0.25	£0.75	£1.25
549-550	$0.40	$1.20	$2.00	£0.25	£0.75	£1.25
551 (Jan 1984)	$0.40	$1.20	$2.00	£0.25	£0.75	£1.25
552-553 Animal Man story/cover						
	$0.80	$2.40	$4.00	£0.30	£0.90	£1.50
554-559	$0.40	$1.20	$2.00	£0.25	£0.75	£1.25
560 Keith Giffen Ambush Bug						
	$0.40	$1.20	$2.00	£0.25	£0.75	£1.25
561-562	$0.40	$1.20	$2.00	£0.25	£0.75	£1.25
563 (Jan 1985), Ambush Bug						
	$0.40	$1.20	$2.00	£0.25	£0.75	£1.25
564	$0.40	$1.20	$2.00	£0.25	£0.75	£1.25
565 Ambush Bug						
	$0.40	$1.20	$2.00	£0.25	£0.75	£1.25
566-574	$0.40	$1.20	$2.00	£0.25	£0.75	£1.25
575 (Jan 1986)	$0.40	$1.20	$2.00	£0.25	£0.75	£1.25
576-578	$0.40	$1.20	$2.00	£0.25	£0.75	£1.25
579 unofficial Asterix X-over, Giffen art						
	$0.40	$1.20	$2.00	£0.25	£0.75	£1.25
580-582	$0.40	$1.20	$2.00	£0.25	£0.75	£1.25
583 "Last Superman story" (see Superman #423), Alan Moore script						
	$1.60	$4.80	$8.00	£0.50	£1.50	£2.50
584 (Jan 1987), New Teen Titans appear, John Byrne art begins						
	$0.40	$1.20	$2.00	£0.25	£0.75	£1.25
585 Phantom Stranger appears, John Byrne art						
	$0.30	$0.90	$1.50	£0.20	£0.60	£1.00
586 New Gods appear, John Byrne art						
	$0.30	$0.90	$1.50	£0.20	£0.60	£1.00
587 The Demon appears, John Byrne art						
	$0.30	$0.90	$1.50	£0.20	£0.60	£1.00
588 Hawkman appears, John Byrne art						
	$0.30	$0.90	$1.50	£0.20	£0.60	£1.00
589 Green Lantern Corps appear, John Byrne art						
	$0.30	$0.90	$1.50	£0.20	£0.60	£1.00
590 Metal Men appear, John Byrne art						
	$0.30	$0.90	$1.50	£0.20	£0.60	£1.00
591 Superboy, Legion of Super-Heroes appears; Superboy's existence explained Post-Crisis (see Legion (2nd Series) #37/38, Superman (2nd Series) #8), John Byrne art						
	$0.30	$0.90	$1.50	£0.25	£0.75	£1.25
592 Big Barda appears, John Byrne art						
	$0.30	$0.90	$1.50	£0.20	£0.60	£1.00
593 Mister Miracle appears, John Byrne art						
	$0.30	$0.90	$1.50	£0.20	£0.60	£1.00
594 Booster Gold appears, John Byrne art						
	$0.30	$0.90	$1.50	£0.20	£0.60	£1.00
595 Martian Manhunter appears, John Byrne art						
	$0.30	$0.90	$1.50	£0.20	£0.60	£1.00
596 (Jan 1988), The Spectre appears; unofficial Millennium X-over, John Byrne art						
	$0.30	$0.90	$1.50	£0.20	£0.60	£1.00
597 Lois Lane & Lana Lang appear, John Byrne art						
	$0.30	$0.90	$1.50	£0.20	£0.60	£1.00
598 1st appearance of Checkmate, John Byrne art						
	$0.30	$0.90	$1.50	£0.20	£0.60	£1.00
599 Metal Men appear, John Byrne art						
	$0.30	$0.90	$1.50	£0.20	£0.60	£1.00
600 LD in the U.K. 80pgs, Giant, Golden anniversary issue; Wonder Woman and Darkseid appear; John Byrne, George Perez, Curt Swan & Mike Mignola art featured						
	$1.00	$3.00	$5.00	£0.50	£1.50	£2.50
601 48pgs, Blackhawk, Deadman, Secret Six, Green Lantern, Superman, Wild Dog begin (5/6 features rotate around a Superman strip until #642)						
	$0.35	$1.05	$1.75	£0.15	£0.45	£0.75
602-608 48pgs	$0.35	$1.05	$1.75	£0.15	£0.45	£0.75
609 48pgs, Brian Bolland cover						
	$0.35	$1.05	$1.75	£0.15	£0.45	£0.75
610 48pgs	$0.35	$1.05	$1.75	£0.15	£0.45	£0.75
611-614 48pgs, Catwoman appears						
	$0.35	$1.05	$1.75	£0.15	£0.45	£0.75
615-625 48pgs	$0.35	$1.05	$1.75	£0.10	£0.35	£0.60
626 48pgs, Paul Chadwick cover						
	$0.35	$1.05	$1.75	£0.10	£0.35	£0.60
627 48pgs, Gil Kane cover						
	$0.35	$1.05	$1.75	£0.10	£0.35	£0.60
628 48pgs, (Jan 1989)						
	$0.35	$1.05	$1.75	£0.10	£0.35	£0.60
629-633 48pgs	$0.35	$1.05	$1.75	£0.10	£0.35	£0.60
634 48pgs, (Jan 1989)						
	$0.35	$1.05	$1.75	£0.10	£0.35	£0.60
635 48pgs, X-over story; Green Lantern, Superman, Black Canary, Blackhawk & Batman appear						
	$0.35	$1.05	$1.75	£0.15	£0.45	£0.75

	$Good	$Fine	$N.Mint	£Good	£Fine	£N.Mint
636 48pgs, 1st appearance of new Phantom Lady, Demon begins written by Alan Grant (ends #641)	***$0.35***	***$1.05***	***$1.75***	**£0.15**	**£0.45**	**£0.75**
637 48pgs	***$0.35***	***$1.05***	***$1.75***	**£0.15**	**£0.45**	**£0.75**
638 48pgs, Jack Kirby cover (Demon)	***$0.35***	***$1.05***	***$1.75***	**£0.15**	**£0.45**	**£0.75**
639 48pgs, Bolland cover	***$0.35***	***$1.05***	***$1.75***	**£0.15**	**£0.45**	**£0.75**
640 48pgs	***$0.35***	***$1.05***	***$1.75***	**£0.15**	**£0.45**	**£0.75**
641 48pgs, Superman cover based on Action Comics #13	***$0.35***	***$1.05***	***$1.75***	**£0.15**	**£0.45**	**£0.75**
642 48pgs, full length story, featuring art by Bob Kane/Steve Ditko/Curt Swan/Infantino/Nowlan	***$0.35***	***$1.05***	***$1.75***	**£0.15**	**£0.45**	**£0.75**
643 cover based on Superman #1, George Perez art	***$0.25***	***$0.75***	***$1.25***	**£0.15**	**£0.45**	**£0.75**
644 George Perez art	***$0.25***	***$0.75***	***$1.25***	**£0.15**	**£0.45**	**£0.75**
645 1st appearence of Maxima, George Perez art	***$0.25***	***$0.75***	***$1.25***	**£0.15**	**£0.45**	**£0.75**
646 Giffen art	***$0.25***	***$0.75***	***$1.25***	**£0.15**	**£0.45**	**£0.75**
647-648 Brainiac Trilogy, George Perez art	***$0.25***	***$0.75***	***$1.25***	**£0.15**	**£0.45**	**£0.75**
649 (Jan 1990), Brainiac Trilogy, George Perez art	***$0.25***	***$0.75***	***$1.25***	**£0.15**	**£0.45**	**£0.75**
650 48pgs, features Jerry Ordway, Curt Swan, George Perez art; Justice League International appear; Lobo cameo	***$0.30***	***$0.90***	***$1.50***	**£0.25**	**£0.75**	**£1.25**
651 George Perez lay-out art	***$0.25***	***$0.75***	***$1.25***	**£0.15**	**£0.45**	**£0.75**
652 X-over with Superman #42/Adventures of Superman #465; George Perez lay-out art	***$0.25***	***$0.75***	***$1.25***	**£0.15**	**£0.45**	**£0.75**
653	***$0.25***	***$0.75***	***$1.25***	**£0.15**	**£0.45**	**£0.75**
654 continues from Superman #44/Adventures of Superman #467; Batman appears, George Perez cover	***$0.25***	***$0.75***	***$1.25***	**£0.15**	**£0.45**	**£0.75**
655 free 8 page insert	***$0.25***	***$0.75***	***$1.25***	**£0.15**	**£0.45**	**£0.75**
656 X-over with Superman #47/Adventures of Superman #470	***$0.25***	***$0.75***	***$1.25***	**£0.15**	**£0.45**	**£0.75**
657 Toyman appears	***$0.25***	***$0.75***	***$1.25***	**£0.15**	**£0.45**	**£0.75**
658 The Sinbad Contract part 3	***$0.25***	***$0.75***	***$1.25***	**£0.15**	**£0.45**	**£0.75**
659 Krisis of the Krimson Kryptonite part 3, X-over Superman #50	***$0.25***	***$0.75***	***$1.25***	**£0.15**	**£0.45**	**£0.75**
660 Lex Luthor "dies"	***$0.25***	***$0.75***	***$1.25***	**£0.15**	**£0.45**	**£0.75**
661 (Jan 1991), Plastic Man appears	***$0.25***	***$0.75***	***$1.25***	**£0.15**	**£0.45**	**£0.75**
662 Superman's identity revealed to Lois Lane, story continued in Superman #53	***$0.90***	***$2.70***	***$4.50***	**£0.25**	**£0.75**	**£1.25**
663 Time and Time Again part 2, continues in Superman #54	***$0.25***	***$0.75***	***$1.25***	**£0.15**	**£0.45**	**£0.75**
664 Time and Time Again part 5	***$0.25***	***$0.75***	***$1.25***	**£0.15**	**£0.45**	**£0.75**
665 LD in the U.K.	***$0.25***	***$0.75***	***$1.25***	**£0.20**	**£0.60**	**£1.00**
666 LD in the U.K. The Red Glass Trilogy part 3	***$0.25***	***$0.75***	***$1.25***	**£0.20**	**£0.60**	**£1.00**
667 48pgs, Revenge of the Krypton Man part 4	***$0.25***	***$0.75***	***$1.25***	**£0.15**	**£0.45**	**£0.75**
668-669	***$0.25***	***$0.75***	***$1.25***	**£0.15**	**£0.45**	**£0.75**
670 Armageddon: 2001 tie-in	***$0.25***	***$0.75***	***$1.25***	**£0.15**	**£0.45**	**£0.75**
671 Blackout part 2	***$0.25***	***$0.75***	***$1.25***	**£0.15**	**£0.45**	**£0.75**
672	***$0.25***	***$0.75***	***$1.25***	**£0.15**	**£0.45**	**£0.75**
673 (Jan 1992)	***$0.25***	***$0.75***	***$1.25***	**£0.15**	**£0.45**	**£0.75**
674 Supergirl (Matrix) returns	***$0.25***	***$0.75***	***$1.25***	**£0.15**	**£0.45**	**£0.75**
675 Panic in the Sky part 4	***$0.25***	***$0.75***	***$1.25***	**£0.15**	**£0.45**	**£0.75**
676 Art Thibert cover	***$0.25***	***$0.75***	***$1.25***	**£0.15**	**£0.45**	**£0.75**
677 Superman vs. Supergirl, Art Thibert cover	***$0.25***	***$0.75***	***$1.25***	**£0.15**	**£0.45**	**£0.75**
678 Art Thibert cover	***$0.25***	***$0.75***	***$1.25***	**£0.15**	**£0.45**	**£0.75**
679 $1.25 cover begins, Art Thibert cover	***$0.25***	***$0.75***	***$1.25***	**£0.15**	**£0.45**	**£0.75**
680 The Blaze/Satanus War part 2, continued in Superman Man of Steel #15, Art Thibert cover	***$0.25***	***$0.75***	***$1.25***	**£0.15**	**£0.45**	**£0.75**
681 Art Thibert cover	***$0.25***	***$0.75***	***$1.25***	**£0.15**	**£0.45**	**£0.75**
682	***$0.25***	***$0.75***	***$1.25***	**£0.15**	**£0.45**	**£0.75**
683 Robin appears and Doomsday cameo	***$0.90***	***$2.70***	***$4.50***	**£0.25**	**£0.75**	**£1.25**
683 2nd/3rd printing	***$0.25***	***$0.75***	***$1.25***	**£0.20**	**£0.60**	**£1.00**
684 Superman: Doomsday part 4, continued in Superman: Man of Steel #19	***$0.90***	***$2.70***	***$4.50***	**£0.30**	**£0.90**	**£1.50**
685 (Jan 1993), Funeral for a Friend part 2, continued in Superman: Man of Steel #20; cover showing Supergirl smashing car overhead is based on Action Comics #1 - nice touch	***$0.40***	***$1.20***	***$2.00***	**£0.25**	**£0.75**	**£1.25**
685 2nd printing, (II in number/date box)	***$0.30***	***$0.90***	***$1.50***	**£0.20**	**£0.60**	**£1.00**
685 3rd printing	***$0.25***	***$0.75***	***$1.25***	**£0.15**	**£0.45**	**£0.75**
686 Funeral for a Friend part 6, continued in Superman: Man of Steel #21	***$0.40***	***$1.20***	***$2.00***	**£0.20**	**£0.60**	**£1.00**
687 Reign of the Supermen part 1	***$0.30***	***$0.90***	***$1.50***	**£0.25**	**£0.75**	**£1.25**
687 Collectors Edition, ND : Reign of the Supermen part 1, die-cut outer cover and bound-in mini-poster	***$0.40***	***$1.20***	***$2.00***	**£0.30**	**£0.90**	**£1.50**
687 Dynamic Forces Edition, ND - signed by Stern and Guice; 10,000 copies	***$3.00***	***$9.00***	***$15.00***	**£1.50**	**£4.50**	**£7.50**
688 Reign of the Supermen part 5	***$0.30***	***$0.90***	***$1.50***	**£0.20**	**£0.60**	**£1.00**
689 Reign of the Supermen part 9	***$0.30***	***$0.90***	***$1.50***	**£0.20**	**£0.60**	**£1.00**
690 Reign of the Supermen part 13, continued in Superman: The Man of Steel #25	***$0.30***	***$0.90***	***$1.50***	**£0.20**	**£0.60**	**£1.00**
691 Reign of the Supermen part 17, continued in Superman: The Man of Steel #26	***$0.30***	***$0.90***	***$1.50***	**£0.20**	**£0.60**	**£1.00**
692-693	***$0.30***	***$0.90***	***$1.50***	**£0.20**	**£0.60**	**£1.00**
694 continued from Superman #507, continued in Superman: The Man of Steel #29	***$0.30***	***$0.90***	***$1.50***	**£0.20**	**£0.60**	**£1.00**
695 (Jan 1994), Lobo cameo	***$0.30***	***$0.90***	***$1.50***	**£0.20**	**£0.60**	**£1.00**
695 Collectors Edition, ND - silver foil embossed cover	***$0.50***	***$1.50***	***$2.50***	**£0.30**	**£0.90**	**£1.50**
696	***$0.30***	***$0.90***	***$1.50***	**£0.20**	**£0.60**	**£1.00**
697 Bizarro appears, continued in Superman: The Man of Steel #32	***$0.30***	***$0.90***	***$1.50***	**£0.20**	**£0.60**	**£1.00**
698-699	***$0.30***	***$0.90***	***$1.50***	**£0.20**	**£0.60**	**£1.00**
700 64pgs, The Fall of Metropolis story; Lex Luthor revealed as a villain						

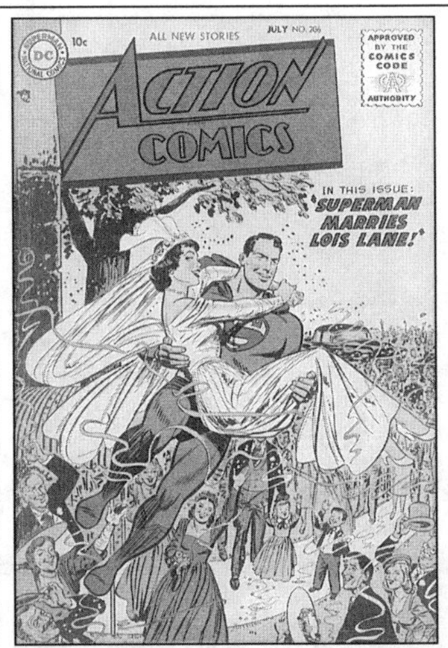

Action Comics #206

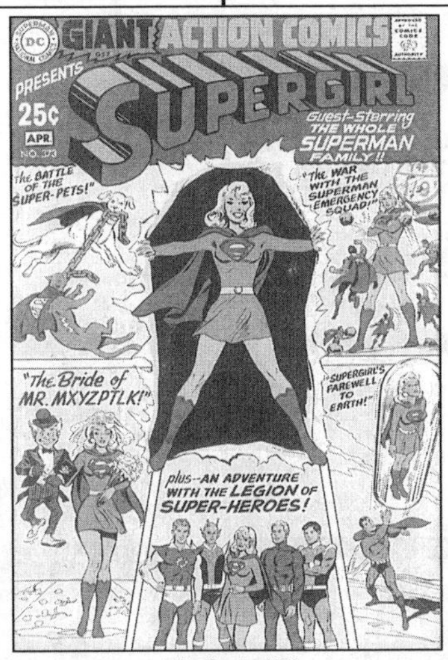

Action Comics #373

Adventure Comics #41

	$Good	$Fine	$N.Mint	£Good	£Fine	£N.Mint
	$0.60	$1.80	$3.00	£0.40	£1.20	£2.00
701 Fall of Metropolis concludes						
	$0.30	$0.90	$1.50	£0.20	£0.60	£1.00
702 David Michelinie scripts begin						
	$0.30	$0.90	$1.50	£0.20	£0.60	£1.00
703 Zero Hour X-over						
	$0.30	$0.90	$1.50	£0.20	£0.60	£1.00
704 Outsiders appear						
	$0.30	$0.90	$1.50	£0.20	£0.60	£1.00
705	$0.30	$0.90	$1.50	£0.20	£0.60	£1.00
706 (Jan 1995)	$0.30	$0.90	$1.50	£0.20	£0.60	£1.00
707	$0.30	$0.90	$1.50	£0.20	£0.60	£1.00
708 Mister Miracle appears						
	$0.30	$0.90	$1.50	£0.20	£0.60	£1.00
709 Guy Gardner appears, story continues in Guy Gardner #30						
	$0.30	$0.90	$1.50	£0.20	£0.60	£1.00
710 The Death of Clark Kent part 3, continued in Superman: The Man of Steel #45; upgraded coated paper stock (Miraweb Format) begins						
	$0.40	$1.20	$2.00	£0.25	£0.75	£1.25
711 The Death of Clark Kent part 7 (conclusion)						
	$0.40	$1.20	$2.00	£0.25	£0.75	£1.25
712-713	$0.40	$1.20	$2.00	£0.25	£0.75	£1.25
714 Joker appears	$0.40	$1.20	$2.00	£0.25	£0.75	£1.25
715 the new parasite appears						
	$0.40	$1.20	$2.00	£0.25	£0.75	£1.25
716 The Trial of Superman, continued in Superman: The Man of Steel #51						
	$0.40	$1.20	$2.00	£0.25	£0.75	£1.25
717 (Jan 1996), The Trial of Superman, continued in Superman: The Man of Steel #52						
	$0.40	$1.20	$2.00	£0.25	£0.75	£1.25
718	$0.40	$1.20	$2.00	£0.25	£0.75	£1.25
719 Batman guest-stars						
	$0.40	$1.20	$2.00	£0.25	£0.75	£1.25
720 Lois Lane breaks off her engagement to Clark Kent						
	$0.50	$1.50	$2.50	£0.30	£0.90	£1.50
721 Mr. Mxyzptlk appears (cameo)						
	$0.40	$1.20	$2.00	£0.25	£0.75	£1.25
722	$0.40	$1.20	$2.00	£0.25	£0.75	£1.25
723 Brainiac appears						
	$0.40	$1.20	$2.00	£0.25	£0.75	£1.25
724-726	$0.40	$1.20	$2.00	£0.25	£0.75	£1.25
727 Final Night tie-in						
	$0.40	$1.20	$2.00	£0.25	£0.75	£1.25
728-731 ND	$0.40	$1.20	$2.00	£0.25	£0.75	£1.25
Title Value:	$48400.75	$145234.70	$421429.75	£32316.35	£96875.10	£281259.80

NEW FEATURES

Air Wave in 488, 511, 512, 525, 526, 534, 535. Air Wave/ Atom in 513, 514, 524, 533. Air Wave/Aquaman in 527. Atom in 425, 427, 430, 433, 435, 438, 439, 442, 447, 448, 453, 454, 487, 489, 515, 516, 522, 523, 531, 532. Atom/Aquaman in 521, 530. Aquaman in 517-520, 528, 529, 536-540. Black Canary in 609-614, 624-635. Blackhawk in 601-608, 615-622, 628-635. Catwoman in 611-614. Clark Kent in 459, 464, 469, 471, 474, 477. Congorilla in 258-261. Deadman in 601-612, 618-621, 623-626, 642 Demon in 636-641. Green Arrow in 421, 424, 426, 431, 434, 436, 440, 441. Green Arrow/Black Canary in 428, 444-446, 450-452, 456-458. Green Lantern in 601-635, 642. Hero Hotline in 637-641. Jimmy Olsen in 599. Krypto in 462, 467. Legion of Super-Heroes in 378-387, 389-392. Lex Luthor in 486. Lori Lemaris in 475. Metamorpho in 413-418. Morgan Edge in 468. Mr Mxyzptlk in 460. Nightwing in 613-617, 627-631. Night-Wing/Speedy in 618, 632-635. Perry White in 461. Phantom Lady in 636-641. Phantom Stranger in 610, 613, 614, 617, 623, 631-635. Secret Six in 601-612 619-630. Shazam in 623-626. Speedy in 636-641. Starman in 622. Steve Lombard in 465, 472. Supergirl in 252-333, 335-346, 348-359, 361-372, 374-376. Superman in 1-333, 335-346, 348-359, 361-372, 374-483, 486-642; Earth-2 Superman in 484. Wild Dog in 601-609, 615-622, 636-641.

REPRINT FEATURES

Aquaman, Vigilante in 405. Atom in 408. Atom, Aquaman in 404. Atom/Flash in 406, 407. Atom, Green Arrow in 449. Eclipso in 411-413. Legion of Super-Heroes in 377, 388. Supergirl in 334. Adam Strange, Doll Man, Sea Devils in 443. Sea Devils, Matt Savage, Hawkman, Adam Strange, Black Pirate in 443. Supergirl, Superman in 347. Supergirl, Superman/Supergirl in 360. Superboy, Vigilante in 403. Superman in 485. Teen Titans in 409, 410.

ACTION COMICS ANNUAL

DC Comics; 1 Aug 1987-present

	$Good	$Fine	$N.Mint	£Good	£Fine	£N.Mint
1 LD in the U.K. Art Adams art; Batman co-stars						
	$1.20	$3.60	$6.00	£0.40	£1.20	£2.00
2 64pgs, squarebound, ties in with Superman #32; Curt Swan, Mike Mignola, Jerry Ordway, George Perez art						
	$0.50	$1.50	$2.50	£0.30	£0.90	£1.50
3 64pgs, squarebound, Armageddon: 2001 tie-in						
	$0.50	$1.50	$2.50	£0.30	£0.90	£1.50
4 64pgs, squarebound,Eclipso: The Darkness Within tie-in, Justice League appears; Joe Quesada cover						
	$0.50	$1.50	$2.50	£0.30	£0.90	£1.50
5 64pgs, squarebound, Bloodlines (Wave Two) part 11, 1st appearance Loose Cannon, continued in Legion of Super-Heroes Annual #4						
	$0.50	$1.50	$2.50	£0.30	£0.90	£1.50
6 ND 64pgs, Elseworlds story; John Byrne script and art						
	$0.60	$1.80	$3.00	£0.40	£1.20	£2.00
7 ND 56pgs, Year One story; Superman's first space adventure; David Michelinie script, Darick Robertson and Brad Vancata art						
	$0.80	$2.40	$4.00	£0.50	£1.50	£2.50
8 ND 48pgs, Legends of the Death Earth story, Bizarro appears						
	$0.60	$1.80	$3.00	£0.40	£1.20	£2.00
Title Value:	$5.20	$15.60	$26.00	£2.90	£8.70	£14.50

ACTION COMICS NUMBER ONE

DC Comics; nn 1976

	$Good	$Fine	$N.Mint	£Good	£Fine	£N.Mint
nn ND 16pgs, reprint of the first Superman story (Action Comics #1, June 1939), paper cover; inside front cover is a pin-up by original artist Joe Shuster though this is not to be found in the original comic						
	$0.40	$1.25	$2.50	£0.25	£0.75	£1.50
Title Value:	$0.40	$1.25	$2.50	£0.25	£0.75	£1.50

ACTION COMICS NUMBER ONE (2ND SERIES)

DC Comics; nn Jun 1988

	$Good	$Fine	$N.Mint	£Good	£Fine	£N.Mint
nn ND 16pgs, reprint of the first Superman story (Action Comics #1, June 1938), glossy cover; celebrates Superman's 50th anniversary. The cover is not an exact reprint of the original						
	$0.25	$0.75	$1.25	£0.15	£0.45	£0.75
Title Value:	$0.25	$0.75	$1.25	£0.15	£0.45	£0.75

ACTION GIRL

Slave Labor Graphics; 1 Oct 1994-present

	$Good	$Fine	$N.Mint	£Good	£Fine	£N.Mint
1 ND b&w	$0.50	$1.50	$2.50	£0.30	£0.90	£1.50
1 2nd printing, ND (Feb 1996)						
	$0.50	$1.50	$2.50	£0.30	£0.90	£1.50
2 ND b&w	$0.50	$1.50	$2.50	£0.30	£0.90	£1.50
2 2nd printing, ND (Feb 1996)						
	$0.50	$1.50	$2.50	£0.30	£0.90	£1.50
3 ND b&w	$0.50	$1.50	$2.50	£0.30	£0.90	£1.50
3 2nd printing, ND (Feb 1996)						
	$0.50	$1.50	$2.50	£0.30	£0.90	£1.50
4-8 ND b&w	$0.50	$1.50	$2.50	£0.30	£0.90	£1.50
Title Value:	$5.50	$16.50	$27.50	£3.30	£9.90	£16.50

ACTS OF VENGEANCE

Marvel Comics Group; 1990

Marvel cross-over series running throughout the issues listed in order below. Those in bold type are "core" titles, others are simply related.

Avengers Spotlight .... **#26**
Amazing Spiderman .... #326
Avengers .... **#311**
Incredible Hulk .... #363
Iron Man .... **#250**
Thor .... **#411**
Fantastic Four .... **#334**
Damage Control II .... **#1**
Doctor Strange (3rd Series) .... #11
Marc Spector: Moon Knight .... #8
Spectacular Spiderman .... #158
Punisher War Journal .... #12
Avengers West Coast .... **#53**
Captain America .... **#365**
Uncanny X-Men .... #256
Web of Spiderman .... #59
Daredevil .... #275
Avengers Spotlight .... **#27**
Quasar .... **#5**
Amazing Spiderman .... #327
Alpha Flight .... #79
New Mutants .... #84
Wolverine .... #19
Avengers .... **#312**
Punisher .... #28
Iron Man .... **#251**
Thor .... **#412**
Fantastic Four .... **#335**
Damage Control II .... **#2**
Mutant Misadventures of Cloak & Dagger .... #9
Marc Spector: Moon Knight .... #9
Punisher War Journal .... #13
Spectacular Spiderman .... #159
X-Factor .... #49
Doctor Strange (3rd Series) .... #12
Avengers West Coast .... **#54**
Captain America .... **#366**
Daredevil .... #276
Uncanny X-Men .... #257
Web of Spiderman .... #60
Avengers Spotlight .... **#28**
Quasar .... **#6**
Amazing Spiderman .... #328
Alpha Flight .... #80
New Mutants .... #85
Wolverine .... #20
Avengers .... **#313**
Power Pack .... #53
Punisher .... #29
Iron Man .... **#252**
Fantastic Four .... **#336**
Damage Control II .... **#3**
Doctor Strange (3rd Series) .... #13
Marc Spector: Moon Knight .... #10
Spectacular Spiderman .... #160
Thor .... #413
X-Factor .... #50
Avengers West Coast .... **#55**
Captain America .... **#367**
Web of Spiderman .... #61
Uncanny X-Men .... #258
Damage Control II .... **#4**
What The -?! (parody) .... #6
Avengers Spotlight (Epilogue) .... **#29**

ADAM & EVE A.D.

BAM Productions; 1 Sep 1985-8 1986

	$Good	$Fine	$N.Mint	£Good	£Fine	£N.Mint
1-2 ND Jerry Ordway covers; black and white begins						
	$0.30	$0.90	$1.50	£0.20	£0.60	£1.00
3-8 ND	$0.30	$0.90	$1.50	£0.20	£0.60	£1.00

	$Good	$Fine	$N.Mint	£Good	£Fine	£N.Mint
Title Value:	***$2.40***	***$7.20***	***$12.00***	**£1.60**	**£4.80**	**£8.00**

ADAM STRANGE

DC Comics,MS; 1 Mar 1990-3 May 1990
(see Brave and the Bold, DC Presents, Mystery in Space, Showcase)

	$Good	$Fine	$N.Mint	£Good	£Fine	£N.Mint
1-3 ND 48pgs	***$0.80***	***$2.40***	***$4.00***	**£0.40**	**£1.20**	**£2.00**
Title Value:	***$2.40***	***$7.20***	***$12.00***	**£1.20**	**£3.60**	**£6.00**

ADAM-12

Gold Key; 1 Dec 1973-10 Feb 1976

	$Good	$Fine	$N.Mint	£Good	£Fine	£N.Mint
1 scarce, distributed in the U.K. photo cover	***$8.50***	***$26.00***	***$60.00***	**£2.85**	**£8.50**	**£20.00**
2-10 scarce, distributed in the U.K.	***$3.55***	***$10.50***	***$25.00***	**£1.05**	**£3.20**	**£7.50**
Title Value:	***$40.45***	***$120.50***	***$285.00***	**£12.30**	**£37.30**	**£87.50**

ADDAMS FAMILY

Gold Key; 1 Oct 1974-3 Apr 1975

	$Good	$Fine	$N.Mint	£Good	£Fine	£N.Mint
1 scarce, distributed in the U.K. based on cartoon show	***$10.00***	***$30.00***	***$70.00***	**£4.25**	**£12.50**	**£30.00**
2-3 scarce, distributed in the U.K. based on cartoon show	***$4.25***	***$12.50***	***$30.00***	**£1.40**	**£4.25**	**£10.00**
Title Value:	***$18.50***	***$55.00***	***$130.00***	**£7.05**	**£21.00**	**£50.00**

ADOLESCENT RADIOACTIVE BLACKBELT HAMSTERS

Eclipse; 1 1986-9 Feb 1988
(see Clint,Laffin' Gas, Target Airboy)

	$Good	$Fine	$N.Mint	£Good	£Fine	£N.Mint
1 ND scarce in the U.K. red/black cover	***$0.60***	***$1.80***	***$3.00***	**£0.40**	**£1.20**	**£2.00**
1 2nd printing, ND pink/black cover	***$0.50***	***$1.50***	***$2.50***	**£0.30**	**£0.90**	**£1.50**
2-5 ND	***$0.50***	***$1.50***	***$2.50***	**£0.30**	**£0.90**	**£1.50**
6-9 ND	***$0.40***	***$1.20***	***$2.00***	**£0.25**	**£0.75**	**£1.25**
Title Value:	***$4.70***	***$14.10***	***$23.50***	**£2.90**	**£8.70**	**£14.50**
Limited Edition (Oct 1990), reprints 3 early tales.						
Signed and numbered Hardcover				£3.50	£10.50	£17.50
America The Beautiful Trade paperback				£1.10	£3.30	£5.50

ADOLESCENT RADIOACTIVE BLACKBELT HAMSTERS IN 3-D

Eclipse; 1 Jul 1986-4 Dec 1986

	$Good	$Fine	$N.Mint	£Good	£Fine	£N.Mint
1 ND all with bound-in 3-D glasses (25% less if without glasses)	***$0.40***	***$1.20***	***$2.00***	**£0.25**	**£0.75**	**£1.25**
1 Non 3-D Edition ND scarce in the U.K.	***$0.60***	***$1.80***	***$3.00***	**£0.40**	**£1.20**	**£2.00**
2 ND	***$0.40***	***$1.20***	***$2.00***	**£0.25**	**£0.75**	**£1.25**
2 Non 3-D Edition ND	***$0.50***	***$1.50***	***$2.50***	**£0.30**	**£0.90**	**£1.50**
3 ND (Eclipse 3-D Series #13)	***$0.40***	***$1.20***	***$2.00***	**£0.25**	**£0.75**	**£1.25**
3 Non 3-D Edition ND	***$0.50***	***$1.50***	***$2.50***	**£0.30**	**£0.90**	**£1.50**
4 ND (Eclipse 3-D series #14)	***$0.40***	***$1.20***	***$2.00***	**£0.25**	**£0.75**	**£1.25**
4 Non 3-D Edition ND	$0.50	$1.50	$2.50	**£0.30**	**£0.90**	**£1.50**
Title Value:	***$3.70***	***$11.10***	***$18.50***	**£2.30**	**£6.90**	**£11.50**
...Massacre The Japanese Invasion (1989)				£0.30	£0.90	£1.50

ADVANCED DUNGEONS AND DRAGONS

DC Comics, Game; 1 Dec 1988-36 Dec 1991

	$Good	$Fine	$N.Mint	£Good	£Fine	£N.Mint
1 ND based on the Advanced Dungeons and Dragons Role Playing Game	***$1.00***	***$3.00***	***$5.00***	**£0.60**	**£1.80**	**£3.00**
2 ND	***$0.60***	***$1.80***	***$3.00***	**£0.40**	**£1.20**	**£2.00**
3-5 ND	***$0.50***	***$1.50***	***$2.50***	**£0.30**	**£0.90**	**£1.50**
6-11 ND	***$0.40***	***$1.20***	***$2.00***	**£0.25**	**£0.75**	**£1.25**
12-18 ND	***$0.30***	***$0.90***	***$1.50***	**£0.20**	**£0.60**	**£1.00**
19-22 ND Lunatics story	***$0.30***	***$0.90***	***$1.50***	**£0.20**	**£0.60**	**£1.00**
23 ND	***$0.30***	***$0.90***	***$1.50***	**£0.20**	**£0.60**	**£1.00**
24-26 ND Scavengers story	***$0.30***	***$0.90***	***$1.50***	**£0.20**	**£0.60**	**£1.00**
27-36 ND	***$0.30***	***$0.90***	***$1.50***	**£0.20**	**£0.60**	**£1.00**
Title Value:	***$13.00***	***$39.00***	***$65.00***	**£8.40**	**£25.20**	**£42.00**

Note: New Format

ADVANCED DUNGEONS AND DRAGONS ANNUAL

DC Comics; 1 Sep 1990

	$Good	$Fine	$N.Mint	£Good	£Fine	£N.Mint
1 ND 64pgs	***$0.50***	***$1.50***	***$2.50***	**£0.30**	**£0.90**	**£1.50**
Title Value:	***$0.50***	***$1.50***	***$2.50***	**£0.30**	**£0.90**	**£1.50**

ADVENTURE COMICS

National Periodical Publications/DC Comics; 1 Dec 1935-11 Dec 1936; 12 Jan 1937-31 Oct 1938; 32 Nov 1938-490 Feb 1982; 491 Sep 1982-503 Sep 1983
(Formerly New Comics #1-11, becomes New Adventure Comics #12-32)
(Becomes Adventure Comics Presents Dial H For Hero #479-490)

	$Good	$Fine	$N.Mint	£Good	£Fine	£N.Mint
1 very rare in the U.K. 80pgs, probably less than 50 extant copies, the 1st comic ever published by DC (then known as National Periodical Publications)	***$2200.00***	***$6600.00***	***$20000.00***	**£1475.00**	**£4450.00**	**£13350.00**
2 very rare in the U.K. 80pgs, (Jan 1936), almost certainly less than 50 extant copies, could be as few as 10	***$1125.00***	***$3350.00***	***$9000.00***	**£750.00**	**£2250.00**	**£6000.00**
3-5 rare in the U.K. 80pgs	***$550.00***	***$1650.00***	***$4400.00***	**£365.00**	**£1100.00**	**£2950.00**
6-10 rare in the U.K.	***$500.00***	***$1500.00***	***$4000.00***	**£330.00**	**£1000.00**	**£2675.00**
11 rare in the U.K. last New Comics title	***$500.00***	***$1500.00***	***$4000.00***	**£330.00**	**£1000.00**	**£2675.00**

(please note that the above are approximate values as far as the British market is concerned as copies very rarely become available. Also note that the Near Mint values are theoretical projections only in the event of any true Near Mint copies being discovered)

	$Good	$Fine	$N.Mint	£Good	£Fine	£N.Mint
12 rare in the U.K. (Jan 1937) titled New Adventure Comics for 1st time; contenets shift away from purely funny animal and naughty kids material	***$560.00***	***$1675.00***	***$4500.00***	**£375.00**	**£1125.00**	**£3000.00**
13 very rare in the U.K. probably no more than 25 extant copies (see Top 50 Rarest section)	***$530.00***	***$1575.00***	***$4250.00***	**£355.00**	**£1050.00**	**£2850.00**
14 rare in the U.K.	***$500.00***	***$1500.00***	***$4000.00***	**£330.00**	**£1000.00**	**£2675.00**
15 rare in the U.K. 1st time the more familiar "Adventure" logo appears	***$400.00***	***$1200.00***	***$3200.00***	**£265.00**	**£800.00**	**£2150.00**
16-17 rare in the U.K.	***$400.00***	***$1200.00***	***$3200.00***	**£265.00**	**£800.00**	**£2150.00**
18 rare in the U.K. (Jan 1938)	***$400.00***	***$1200.00***	***$3200.00***	**£265.00**	**£800.00**	**£2150.00**
19-20 rare in the U.K.	***$400.00***	***$1200.00***	***$3200.00***	**£265.00**	**£800.00**	**£2150.00**
21-22 very scarce in the U.K.	***$335.00***	***$1000.00***	***$2700.00***	**£225.00**	**£670.00**	**£1800.00**
23 very scarce in the U.K. 1st "Adventure" theme cover; begins a line of classic covers of man vs. beast or the elements	***$300.00***	***$900.00***	***$2400.00***	**£200.00**	**£600.00**	**£1600.00**
24-26 very scarce in the U.K.	***$300.00***	***$900.00***	***$2400.00***	**£200.00**	**£600.00**	**£1600.00**
27 rare in the U.K. carries advertisment for Action Comics #1 (1st Superman)	***$300.00***	***$900.00***	***$2400.00***	**£200.00**	**£600.00**	**£1600.00**
28-30 very scarce in the U.K.	***$300.00***	***$900.00***	***$2400.00***	**£200.00**	**£600.00**	**£1600.00**
31 very scarce in the U.K. last New Adventure Comics	***$300.00***	***$900.00***	***$2400.00***	**£200.00**	**£600.00**	**£1600.00**
32 very scarce in the U.K. title becomes simply Adventure Comics for 1st time	***$375.00***	***$1125.00***	***$3000.00***	**£250.00**	**£750.00**	**£2000.00**
33 very scarce in the U.K.	***$185.00***	***$560.00***	***$1500.00***	**£125.00**	**£375.00**	**£1000.00**
34 very scarce in the U.K. (Jan 1939)	***$185.00***	***$560.00***	***$1500.00***	**£125.00**	**£375.00**	**£1000.00**
35-36 very scarce in the U.K.	***$185.00***	***$560.00***	***$1500.00***	**£125.00**	**£375.00**	**£1000.00**
37 very scarce in the U.K. cover used for Double Action Comics #2	***$185.00***	***$560.00***	***$1500.00***	**£125.00**	**£375.00**	**£1000.00**
38 very scarce in the U.K.	***$185.00***	***$560.00***	***$1500.00***	**£125.00**	**£375.00**	**£1000.00**
39 very scarce in the U.K.	***$180.00***	***$540.00***	***$1450.00***	**£120.00**	**£365.00**	**£975.00**
40 very rare in the U.K. Sandman series begins, probably less than 50 extant copies	***$3500.00***	***$10500.00***	***$35000.00***	**£2325.00**	**£7000.00**	**£23350.00**
[Rare in high grade - Very Fine+ or better]						
41 very scarce in the U.K. 2nd appearance Sandman	***$530.00***	***$1575.00***	***$4250.00***	**£355.00**	**£1050.00**	**£2850.00**
42 very scarce in the U.K. 3rd appearance Sandman, Sandman cover	***$750.00***	***$2250.00***	***$6000.00***	**£500.00**	**£1500.00**	**£4000.00**
43 very scarce in the U.K.	***$340.00***	***$1025.00***	***$2750.00***	**£230.00**	**£690.00**	**£1850.00**
44 very scarce in the U.K. Sandman cover	***$710.00***	***$2150.00***	***$5750.00***	**£480.00**	**£1425.00**	**£3850.00**
45 very scarce in the U.K.	***$325.00***	***$970.00***	***$2600.00***	**£215.00**	**£650.00**	**£1750.00**
46 very scarce in the U.K. (Jan 1940), Sandman cover	***$465.00***	***$1400.00***	***$3750.00***	**£310.00**	**£930.00**	**£2500.00**
47 very scarce in the U.K. Sandman cover	***$465.00***	***$1400.00***	***$3750.00***	**£310.00**	**£930.00**	**£2500.00**
48 rare in the U.K. origin and 1st appearance of Hourman, Hourman cover	***$2250.00***	***$6700.00***	***$22500.00***	**£1500.00**	**£4500.00**	**£15000.00**
[Scarce in high grade - Very Fine+ or better]						
49 scarce in the U.K. 2nd appearance Hourman	***$250.00***	***$750.00***	***$2000.00***	**£165.00**	**£500.00**	**£1350.00**
50 scarce in the U.K. 3rd appearance Hourman, Hourman cover	***$225.00***	***$670.00***	***$1800.00***	**£150.00**	**£450.00**	**£1200.00**
51 Sandman cover	***$325.00***	***$970.00***	***$2600.00***	**£215.00**	**£650.00**	**£1750.00**
52-57 Hourman cover	***$190.00***	***$580.00***	***$1550.00***	**£130.00**	**£390.00**	**£1050.00**
58 (Jan 1941), Hourman cover	***$190.00***	***$580.00***	***$1550.00***	**£130.00**	**£390.00**	**£1050.00**
59 Hourman cover	***$190.00***	***$580.00***	***$1550.00***	**£130.00**	**£390.00**	**£1050.00**
60 Sandman cover	***$300.00***	***$900.00***	***$2400.00***	**£200.00**	**£600.00**	**£1600.00**
61 very scarce in the U.K. origin and 1st appearance Starman, classic cover	***$1250.00***	***$3750.00***	***$12500.00***	**£830.00**	**£2500.00**	**£8350.00**
62 2nd appearance Starman	***$215.00***	***$650.00***	***$1750.00***	**£145.00**	**£440.00**	**£1175.00**
63 3rd appearance Starman	***$180.00***	***$540.00***	***$1450.00***	**£120.00**	**£365.00**	**£975.00**
64-65	***$165.00***	***$500.00***	***$1350.00***	**£110.00**	**£335.00**	**£900.00**
66 origin and 1st appearance The Shining Knight	***$210.00***	***$630.00***	***$1700.00***	**£140.00**	**£430.00**	**£1150.00**
67-68	***$165.00***	***$500.00***	***$1350.00***	**£110.00**	**£335.00**	**£900.00**
69 1st appearance Sandy, new Sandman costume	***$175.00***	***$520.00***	***$1400.00***	**£115.00**	**£350.00**	**£940.00**
70 (Jan 1942)	***$160.00***	***$485.00***	***$1300.00***	**£105.00**	**£325.00**	**£870.00**
71 1st Miracle Ray machine used by Hourman	***$145.00***	***$440.00***	***$1175.00***	**£97.50**	**£290.00**	**£785.00**
72 very scarce in the U.K. 1st Sandman by Joe Simon and Jack Kirby	***$1200.00***	***$3600.00***	***$12000.00***	**£820.00**	**£2475.00**	**£8250.00**
73 rare in the U.K. origin Manhunter by Joe Simon and Jack Kirby, classic cover						

Issue	$Good	$Fine	$N.Mint	£Good	£Fine	£N.Mint
	$1500.00	$4500.00	$15000.00	£1050.00	£3150.00	£10500.00
74 2nd Manhunter by Joe Simon and Jack Kirby	$190.00	$580.00	$1550.00	£130.00	£390.00	£1050.00
75	$190.00	$580.00	$1550.00	£130.00	£390.00	£1050.00
76 scarce in the U.K.	$190.00	$580.00	$1550.00	£135.00	£410.00	£1100.00
77-78	$190.00	$580.00	$1550.00	£130.00	£390.00	£1050.00
79 classic cover, Manhunter stalks Nazi Raiders	$190.00	$580.00	$1550.00	£130.00	£390.00	£1050.00
80 last Manhunter by Joe Simon and Jack Kirby	$190.00	$580.00	$1550.00	£130.00	£390.00	£1050.00
81	$115.00	$355.00	$950.00	£77.50	£235.00	£635.00
82 (Jan 1943)	$115.00	$355.00	$950.00	£77.50	£235.00	£635.00
83-86	$115.00	$355.00	$950.00	£77.50	£235.00	£635.00
87 scarce in the U.K.	$115.00	$355.00	$950.00	£82.50	£245.00	£660.00
88	$115.00	$355.00	$950.00	£77.50	£235.00	£635.00
89 (Dec/Jan 1944)	$115.00	$355.00	$950.00	£77.50	£235.00	£635.00
90	$115.00	$355.00	$950.00	£77.50	£235.00	£635.00
91 last Sandman by Joe Simon and Jack Kirby	$95.00	$290.00	$775.00	£65.00	£195.00	£520.00
92-93	$92.50	$280.00	$750.00	£62.50	£185.00	£500.00
94 scarce in the U.K.	$92.50	$280.00	$750.00	£65.00	£200.00	£535.00
95 (Dec/Jan 1945)	$92.50	$280.00	$750.00	£62.50	£185.00	£500.00
96-99	$92.50	$280.00	$750.00	£62.50	£185.00	£500.00
100	$130.00	$390.00	$1050.00	£87.50	£260.00	£700.00
[Issues before #100 are generally at least scarce in the U.K.]						
101 (Dec/Jan 1946)	$105.00	$315.00	$740.00	£70.00	£210.00	£495.00
102 last Sandman and Starman, last Sandman cover	$105.00	$315.00	$740.00	£70.00	£210.00	£495.00
103 scarce in the U.K. 1st small logo, Superboy covers and stories begin	$275.00	$830.00	$2500.00	£185.00	£550.00	£1675.00
[Scarce in high grade - Very Fine+ or better]						
104 2nd Superboy in title	$115.00	$350.00	$825.00	£77.50	£235.00	£550.00
105-110	$77.50	$235.00	$550.00	£52.50	£155.00	£370.00
111	$70.00	$210.00	$500.00	£48.00	£140.00	£335.00
112 (Jan 1947)	$70.00	$210.00	$500.00	£48.00	£140.00	£335.00
113 Christmas cover	$70.00	$210.00	$500.00	£48.00	£140.00	£335.00
114-120	$70.00	$210.00	$500.00	£48.00	£140.00	£335.00
121-123	$67.50	$200.00	$475.00	£46.00	£135.00	£320.00
124 (Jan 1948)	$67.50	$200.00	$475.00	£46.00	£135.00	£320.00
125-126	$67.50	$200.00	$475.00	£46.00	£135.00	£320.00
127	$70.00	$210.00	$500.00	£48.00	£140.00	£335.00
128 1st time Superboy meets a young Lois Lane - classic story	$75.00	$225.00	$525.00	£50.00	£150.00	£350.00
129-130	$67.50	$200.00	$475.00	£46.00	£135.00	£320.00
131	$55.00	$165.00	$390.00	£37.00	£110.00	£260.00
132 "The Aquagirl" appears in Aquaman back-up story	$55.00	$165.00	$390.00	£37.00	£110.00	£260.00
133-135	$55.00	$165.00	$390.00	£37.00	£110.00	£260.00
136 (Jan 1949)	$55.00	$165.00	$390.00	£37.00	£110.00	£260.00
137-141	$55.00	$165.00	$390.00	£37.00	£110.00	£260.00
142	$62.50	$190.00	$450.00	£43.00	£125.00	£300.00
143-147	$52.50	$160.00	$380.00	£36.00	£105.00	£255.00
148 (Jan 1950)	$52.50	$160.00	$380.00	£36.00	£105.00	£255.00
149	$52.50	$160.00	$380.00	£36.00	£105.00	£255.00
150-151 Shining Knight, Frank Frazetta art	$60.00	$180.00	$425.00	£41.00	£120.00	£285.00
152	$46.00	$135.00	$325.00	£31.00	£92.50	£220.00
153 Shining Knight, Frank Frazetta art	$60.00	$180.00	$425.00	£41.00	£120.00	£285.00
154	$46.00	$135.00	$325.00	£31.00	£92.50	£220.00
155 Shining Knight, Frank Frazetta art	$60.00	$180.00	$425.00	£41.00	£120.00	£285.00
156	$46.00	$135.00	$325.00	£31.00	£92.50	£220.00
157 Shining Knight, Frank Frazetta art	$60.00	$180.00	$425.00	£41.00	£120.00	£285.00
158	$46.00	$135.00	$325.00	£31.00	£92.50	£220.00
159 Shining Knight, Frank Frazetta art, origin Johnny Quick	$60.00	$180.00	$425.00	£41.00	£120.00	£285.00
160 (Jan 1951)	$46.00	$135.00	$325.00	£31.00	£92.50	£220.00
161 Shining Knight, Frank Frazetta art	$57.50	$175.00	$410.00	£39.00	£115.00	£275.00
162	$45.00	$135.00	$315.00	£30.00	£90.00	£210.00
163 Shining Knight, Frank Frazetta art	$57.50	$175.00	$410.00	£39.00	£115.00	£275.00
164-166	$45.00	$135.00	$315.00	£30.00	£90.00	£210.00
167 Lana Lang: Super-Girl story	$50.00	$150.00	$350.00	£34.00	£100.00	£235.00
168 last 52pg issue	$43.00	$125.00	$300.00	£29.00	£85.00	£200.00
169-170	$43.00	$125.00	$300.00	£29.00	£85.00	£200.00
171	$41.00	$120.00	$290.00	£28.00	£82.50	£195.00
172 (Jan 1952)	$41.00	$120.00	$290.00	£28.00	£82.50	£195.00
173-180	$41.00	$120.00	$290.00	£28.00	£82.50	£195.00
181-183	$40.00	$120.00	$280.00	£27.00	£80.00	£187.50
184 (Jan 1953)	$40.00	$120.00	$280.00	£27.00	£80.00	£187.50
185-188	$40.00	$120.00	$280.00	£27.00	£80.00	£187.50
189 Lana Lang as The Girl of Steel	$45.00	$135.00	$315.00	£30.00	£90.00	£210.00
190-195	$39.00	$115.00	$275.00	£26.00	£77.50	£185.00
196 (Jan 1954)	$39.00	$115.00	$275.00	£26.00	£77.50	£185.00
197-198	$39.00	$115.00	$275.00	£26.00	£77.50	£185.00
199 Superboy meets Superlad	$43.00	$125.00	$300.00	£29.00	£85.00	£200.00
200 scarce in the U.K.	$60.00	$180.00	$425.00	£43.00	£125.00	£300.00
201-207	$40.00	$120.00	$280.00	£26.00	£77.50	£185.00
208 (Jan 1955)	$40.00	$120.00	$280.00	£26.00	£77.50	£185.00
209	$40.00	$120.00	$280.00	£26.00	£77.50	£185.00
210 very scarce in the U.K. 1st appearance of Krypto the Wonder dog	$225.00	$670.00	$2700.00	£150.00	£460.00	£1850.00
[Scarce in high grade - Very Fine+ or better]						
211 young Lois Lane appears	$32.00	$95.00	$225.00	£21.00	£62.50	£150.00
212-213	$32.00	$95.00	$225.00	£21.00	£62.50	£150.00
214 2nd appearance Krypto	$50.00	$150.00	$350.00	£37.00	£110.00	£260.00
215-216	$32.00	$95.00	$225.00	£21.00	£62.50	£150.00
217-218 classic two part story; Jor-El and Lara return for Superboy	$32.00	$95.00	$225.00	£21.00	£62.50	£150.00
219	$32.00	$95.00	$225.00	£21.00	£62.50	£150.00
220 (Jan 1956), 3rd appearance Krypto	$36.00	$105.00	$250.00	£23.50	£70.00	£165.00
221-230	$28.00	$82.50	$195.00	£18.50	£55.00	£130.00
231	$26.00	$77.50	$185.00	£17.50	£52.50	£125.00
232 (Jan 1957)	$26.00	$77.50	$185.00	£17.50	£52.50	£125.00
233-234	$26.00	$77.50	$185.00	£17.50	£52.50	£125.00
235-236 scarce in the U.K.	$26.00	$77.50	$185.00	£20.00	£60.00	£140.00
237 1st (and only) appearance The Intergalactic Vigilante Squadron, a possible Legion of Super-Heroes protoytpe	$26.00	$77.50	$185.00	£17.50	£52.50	£125.00
238-243	$26.00	$77.50	$185.00	£17.50	£52.50	£125.00
244 (Jan 1958)	$25.00	$75.00	$175.00	£17.50	£52.50	£125.00
245	$25.00	$75.00	$175.00	£17.50	£52.50	£125.00
246 scarce in the U.K.	$25.00	$75.00	$175.00	£20.00	£60.00	£140.00
247 1st appearance of Legion of Super Heroes (Superboy story), Green Arrow by Jack Kirby	$425.00	$1275.00	$4250.00	£275.00	£820.00	£2750.00
[Prices may vary widely on this comic]						
247 Silver Age Classic, ND (Mar 1992) reprints original issue featuring the origin and 1st appearance of the Legion of Super-Heroes	$0.25	$0.75	$1.25	£0.15	£0.45	£0.75
248 scarce in the U.K.	$21.00	$62.50	$150.00	£15.50	£47.00	£110.00
249	$21.00	$62.50	$150.00	£14.00	£43.00	£100.00
250 Jack Kirby art on Green arrow	$21.00	$62.50	$150.00	£14.00	£43.00	£100.00
251 Jack Kirby art on Green Arrow, 1st appearance Superboy robot	$21.00	$62.50	$150.00	£14.00	£43.00	£100.00
252 Jack Kirby art on Green Arrow, 1st mention of Red Kryptonite	$21.00	$62.50	$150.00	£14.00	£43.00	£100.00
253 Jack Kirby art on Green Arrow, Superboy meets Robin	$30.00	$90.00	$210.00	£20.00	£60.00	£140.00
254 Jack Kirby art on Green Arrow	$21.00	$62.50	$150.00	£14.00	£43.00	£100.00
255 Jack Kirby art on Green Arrow, 1st Red Kryptonite effect	$21.00	$62.50	$150.00	£14.00	£43.00	£100.00
256 (Jan 1959), Jack Kirby art, origin Green Arrow retold (1st time since Golden Age)	$62.50	$190.00	$575.00	£36.00	£105.00	£325.00
257	$19.00	$57.50	$135.00	£12.50	£39.00	£90.00
258 Superboy meets young Green Arrow	$19.00	$57.50	$135.00	£12.50	£39.00	£90.00
259 part origin Krypto	$19.00	$57.50	$135.00	£12.50	£39.00	£90.00
260 origin and 1st Silver Age appearance of Aquaman (see Showcase #30)	$65.00	$200.00	$600.00	£39.00	£115.00	£350.00
261 young Lois Lane appears	$15.00	$45.00	$105.00	£10.00	£30.00	£70.00
262-264	$15.00	$45.00	$105.00	£10.00	£30.00	£70.00
265 1st appearance Superman robot	$15.00	$45.00	$105.00	£10.00	£30.00	£70.00
1st official distribution in the U.K						
266 1st appearance prototype Aquagirl (see Aquaman #33)	$15.00	$45.00	$105.00	£10.00	£30.00	£70.00
267 2nd appearance of Legion of Super-Heroes (Superboy story)	$82.50	$250.00	$750.00	£52.50	£155.00	£475.00
268 (Jan 1960)	$15.00	$45.00	$105.00	£10.00	£30.00	£70.00
269 1st appearance Aqualad	$30.00	$90.00	$210.00	£20.00	£60.00	£140.00
270	$15.00	$45.00	$105.00	£10.00	£30.00	£70.00
271 1st Silver Age appearance Lex Luthor, origin retold	$30.00	$90.00	$210.00	£20.00	£60.00	£140.00
272-274	$13.50	$41.00	$95.00	£8.50	£26.00	£60.00
275 Superman/Batman team origin retold	$25.00	$75.00	$175.00	£15.50	£47.00	£110.00

Issue	$Good	$Fine	$N.Mint	£Good	£Fine	£N.Mint
276-278	$13.50	$41.00	$95.00	£8.50	£26.00	£60.00
279 1st appearance White Kryptonite	$13.50	$41.00	$95.00	£8.50	£26.00	£60.00
280 (Jan 1961), Superboy meets young Lori Lemaris	$13.50	$41.00	$95.00	£8.50	£26.00	£60.00
281	$13.50	$41.00	$95.00	£8.50	£26.00	£60.00
282 5th appearance of Legion (Superboy story), origin and 1st appearance Star Boy	$21.00	$62.50	$150.00	£14.00	£43.00	£100.00
283 1st appearance of the Phantom Zone	$22.50	$67.50	$160.00	£14.00	£43.00	£100.00
284	$13.50	$41.00	$95.00	£8.50	£26.00	£60.00
285 Bizarro World series begins, classic cover (series ends #299)	$17.50	$52.50	$125.00	£10.50	£32.00	£75.00
286 1st appearance Bizarro Mr. Mxyzptlk	$15.00	$45.00	$105.00	£10.00	£30.00	£70.00
287-288	$12.50	$39.00	$90.00	£7.75	£23.50	£55.00
289 8th appearance of Legion (one panel, as statuettes only thus highly debateable as an official appearance)	$12.50	$39.00	$90.00	£10.00	£30.00	£70.00
290 9th appearance of Legion (Superboy story), 1st appearance Sunboy	$21.00	$62.50	$150.00	£14.00	£43.00	£100.00
291	$8.50	$26.00	$60.00	£5.00	£15.00	£35.00
292 (Jan 1962)	$8.50	$26.00	$60.00	£5.00	£15.00	£35.00
293 14th appearance of Legion (Superboy story), 1st Legion of Super-Pets	$13.50	$41.00	$95.00	£8.50	£26.00	£60.00
294 Bizarro Marilyn Monroe and President Kennedy; classic cover	$15.00	$45.00	$105.00	£7.00	£21.00	£50.00
295-298	$8.50	$26.00	$60.00	£5.00	£15.00	£35.00
299 1st Gold Kryptonite (more significant than White or Blue as it removes super-powers permanently)	$9.25	$28.00	$65.00	£5.50	£17.00	£40.00
300 1st of Legion series, ends #380	$46.00	$135.00	$365.00	£28.00	£82.50	£225.00
301 origin Bouncing Boy	$17.00	$50.00	$120.00	£10.50	£32.00	£75.00
302-303	$11.00	$34.00	$80.00	£7.00	£21.00	£50.00
304 (Jan 1963), death of Lightning Lad (returns #312)	$11.00	$34.00	$80.00	£7.00	£21.00	£50.00
305 Mon-El cured from lead poisoning	$11.00	$34.00	$80.00	£7.00	£21.00	£50.00
306 1st appearance Legion of Substitute Heroes	$9.25	$28.00	$65.00	£5.50	£17.00	£40.00
307 1st appearance Element Lad	$9.25	$28.00	$65.00	£5.50	£17.00	£40.00
308 1st appearance Lightning Lass	$9.25	$28.00	$65.00	£5.50	£17.00	£40.00
309-310	$9.25	$28.00	$65.00	£5.00	£15.00	£35.00
311-315	$7.00	$21.00	$50.00	£4.25	£12.50	£30.00
316 (Jan 1964)	$7.00	$21.00	$50.00	£3.90	£11.50	£27.50
317 1st appearance Dream Girl; Lightning Lass becomes Light Lass	$7.00	$21.00	$50.00	£4.25	£12.50	£30.00
318-320	$7.00	$21.00	$50.00	£3.90	£11.50	£27.50
321 1st appearance Time Trapper (see Crisis on Infinite Earths)	$7.00	$21.00	$50.00	£3.55	£10.50	£25.00
322-324	$5.50	$17.00	$40.00	£2.85	£8.50	£20.00
325 Lex Luthor appears	$5.50	$17.00	$40.00	£2.85	£8.50	£20.00
326	$5.50	$17.00	$40.00	£2.85	£8.50	£20.00
327 1st appearance Timber Wolf (initially called Lone Wolf)	$5.50	$17.00	$40.00	£3.20	£9.50	£22.50
328 (Jan 1965)	$5.50	$17.00	$40.00	£2.85	£8.50	£20.00
329 1st Bizarro Legion	$5.50	$17.00	$40.00	£2.85	£8.50	£20.00
330	$5.50	$17.00	$40.00	£2.85	£8.50	£20.00
331-335	$5.00	$15.00	$35.00	£2.50	£7.50	£17.50
336-339	$5.00	$15.00	$35.00	£2.10	£6.25	£15.00
340 (Jan 1966)	$5.00	$15.00	$35.00	£2.10	£6.25	£15.00
341 Triplicate Girl becomes Duo Damsel (1st appearance)	$4.25	$12.50	$30.00	£2.50	£7.50	£17.50
342-345	$2.85	$8.50	$20.00	£1.75	£5.25	£12.50
346 1st appearance Princess Projectra, Nemesis Kid, Karate Kid, Ferro Lad	$3.55	$10.50	$25.00	£2.10	£6.25	£15.00
347	$2.85	$8.50	$20.00	£1.75	£5.25	£12.50
348 origin Sunboy	$2.85	$8.50	$20.00	£1.75	£5.25	£12.50
349-350	$2.85	$8.50	$20.00	£1.75	£5.25	£12.50
351	$2.10	$6.25	$15.00	£1.25	£3.85	£9.00
352 (Jan 1967), classic Sun-Eater story begins	$2.10	$6.25	$15.00	£1.25	£3.85	£9.00
353 Ferro Lad dies destroying Sun-Eater	$2.85	$8.50	$20.00	£1.75	£5.25	£12.50
354-360	$2.10	$6.25	$15.00	£1.25	£3.85	£9.00
361-363	$1.70	$5.00	$12.00	£0.85	£2.55	£6.00
364 (Jan 1968)	$1.70	$5.00	$12.00	£0.85	£2.55	£6.00
365	$1.70	$5.00	$12.00	£0.85	£2.55	£6.00
366 1st appearance Shadow Lass	$1.70	$5.00	$12.00	£1.00	£3.00	£7.00
367-374	$1.70	$5.00	$12.00	£0.85	£2.55	£6.00
375 1st appearance Quantum Queen and The Wanderers	$1.40	$4.25	$10.00	£1.00	£3.00	£7.00
376 (Jan 1969)	$1.40	$4.25	$10.00	£0.85	£2.55	£6.00
377-379	$1.40	$4.25	$10.00	£0.85	£2.55	£6.00
380 last of Legion series - moves to back-ups in Action Comics; text feature on Detective Comics #27	$1.40	$4.25	$10.00	£0.85	£2.55	£6.00
381 Supergirl series begins (continued from Action Comics #376; series ends #424)	$5.00	$15.00	$35.00	£1.05	£3.20	£7.50
382-383 Neal Adams cover	$0.85	$2.55	$6.00	£0.40	£1.25	£3.00
384-387	$0.85	$2.55	$6.00	£0.40	£1.25	£3.00
388 (Jan 1970)	$1.00	$3.00	$6.00	£0.50	£1.50	£3.00
389	$1.00	$3.00	$6.00	£0.50	£1.50	£3.00
390 68pgs, Giant G-69, all romance issue	$2.90	$8.75	$17.50	£1.15	£3.50	£7.00
391-396	$1.00	$3.00	$6.00	£0.50	£1.50	£3.00
397 Supergirl's new costume	$1.00	$3.00	$6.00	£0.50	£1.50	£3.00
398-400 scarce in the U.K.	$1.00	$3.00	$6.00	£0.50	£1.50	£3.00
401 (Jan 1971)	$0.80	$2.50	$5.00	£0.30	£1.00	£2.00
402	$0.80	$2.50	$5.00	£0.30	£1.00	£2.00
403 68pgs, Giant G-81, all Legion reprints including classic death/rebirth Lightning Lad	$2.50	$7.50	$15.00	£1.15	£3.50	£7.00
404-408	$0.80	$2.50	$5.00	£0.30	£1.00	£2.00
409-411 48pgs	$0.80	$2.50	$5.00	£0.40	£1.25	£2.50
412 48pgs, reprints origin Animal Man from Strange Adventures #180	$0.65	$2.00	$4.00	£0.40	£1.25	£2.50
413 48pgs	$0.65	$2.00	$4.00	£0.25	£0.85	£1.75
414 48pgs, (Jan 1972), 2nd Animal Man reprint from Strange Adventures #184	$0.65	$2.00	$4.00	£0.35	£1.10	£2.25
415 48pgs, 1st Animal Man in costume reprint from Strange Adventures #190	$0.65	$2.00	$4.00	£0.35	£1.10	£2.25
416 100pgs, DC-100pg Super Spectacular #10	$0.65	$2.00	$4.00	£0.40	£1.25	£2.50
417 48pgs, Frazetta reprint	$0.50	$1.50	$3.00	£0.25	£0.85	£1.75

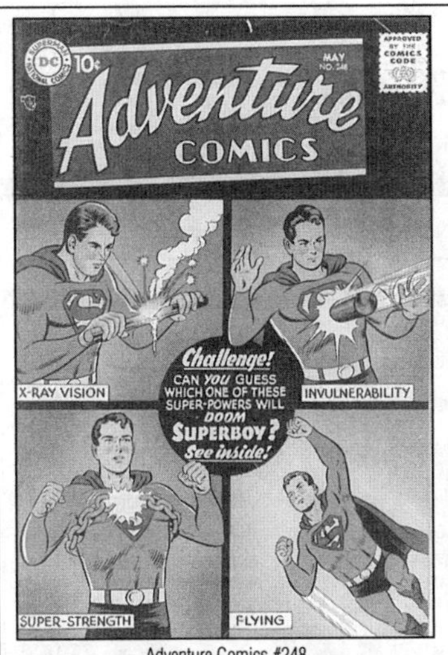

Adventure Comics #248

Adventure Comics #381

Adventure Comics #459

Issue	$Good	$Fine	$N.Mint	£Good	£Fine	£N.Mint
418-419 48pgs	$0.50	$1.50	$3.00	£0.25	£0.85	£1.75
420 48pgs, Animal Man reprint from Strange Adventures #195	$0.50	$1.50	$3.00	£0.25	£0.85	£1.75
421 scarce in the U.K. Animal Man reprint from Strange Adventures #201	$0.50	$1.50	$3.00	£0.30	£1.00	£2.00
422	$0.30	$1.00	$2.00	£0.25	£0.75	£1.50
423 Justice League of America appear	$0.30	$1.00	$2.00	£0.30	£1.00	£2.00
424 scarce in the U.K.	$0.30	$1.00	$2.00	£0.25	£0.85	£1.75
425 (Jan 1973), Alex Toth, Gil Kane art, Kaluta cover; title becomes mystery orientated	$0.30	$1.00	$2.00	£0.25	£0.75	£1.50
426-427	$0.30	$1.00	$2.00	£0.25	£0.75	£1.50
428 1st appearance Black Orchid	$2.05	$6.25	$12.50	£1.00	£3.00	£6.00
429 2nd appearance Black Orchid	$1.15	$3.50	$7.00	£0.55	£1.75	£3.50
430 3rd appearance Black Orchid	$1.15	$3.50	$7.00	£0.55	£1.75	£3.50
431 (Feb 1974), Spectre series begins by Fleischer and Aparo (reprinted in Wrath of the Spectre); a return to the Golden Age avenging spirit	$1.25	$3.75	$7.50	£0.55	£1.75	£3.50
432	$0.50	$1.50	$3.00	£0.30	£1.00	£2.00
433 Spectre, cover titled "Weird Adventure Comics" (ends #437)	$0.50	$1.50	$3.00	£0.25	£0.85	£1.75
434 Spectre	$0.50	$1.50	$3.00	£0.25	£0.85	£1.75
435 Spectre, Mike Grell's 1st pro work on back-up Aquaman story	$0.50	$1.50	$3.00	£0.30	£1.00	£2.00
436 Spectre	$0.50	$1.50	$3.00	£0.25	£0.85	£1.75
437 (Feb 1975), Spectre	$0.50	$1.50	$3.00	£0.25	£0.85	£1.75
438 Spectre; Shining Knight back-up by Chaykin	$0.50	$1.50	$3.00	£0.25	£0.85	£1.75
439 Spectre	$0.50	$1.50	$3.00	£0.25	£0.85	£1.75
440 Spectre, origin retold	$0.50	$1.50	$3.00	£0.25	£0.85	£1.75
441 1st of Aquaman series	$0.30	$1.00	$2.00	£0.25	£0.75	£1.50
442	$0.30	$1.00	$2.00	£0.20	£0.60	£1.25
443 (Feb 1976)	$0.30	$1.00	$2.00	£0.20	£0.60	£1.25
444-445	$0.30	$1.00	$2.00	£0.20	£0.60	£1.25
446-448 scarce in the U.K.	$0.30	$1.00	$2.00	£0.25	£0.75	£1.50
449 scarce in the U.K. (Jan 1977)	$0.30	$1.00	$2.00	£0.25	£0.75	£1.50
450 scarce in the U.K.	$0.30	$1.00	$2.00	£0.25	£0.75	£1.50
451-452	$0.30	$1.00	$2.00	£0.20	£0.60	£1.25
453 Batgirl appears	$0.30	$1.00	$2.00	£0.20	£0.60	£1.25
454	$0.30	$1.00	$2.00	£0.20	£0.60	£1.25
455 (Jan 1978)	$0.30	$1.00	$2.00	£0.20	£0.60	£1.25
456	$0.30	$1.00	$2.00	£0.20	£0.60	£1.25
457-458 Eclipso appears	$0.30	$1.00	$2.00	£0.20	£0.60	£1.25
459-460 scarce in the U.K. 68pgs, Darkseid, New Gods appear; story continued from New Gods #19	$1.25	$3.75	$7.50	£0.40	£1.25	£2.50
461 ND 68pgs, (Jan 1979)	$0.80	$2.50	$5.00	£0.30	£1.00	£2.00
462 ND very scarce in the U.K. 68pgs, Earth-2 Batman dies	$1.25	$3.75	$7.50	£0.80	£2.50	£5.00
463-464 scarce in the U.K. 68pgs	$0.30	$1.00	$2.00	£0.25	£0.75	£1.50
465 ND 68pgs	$0.30	$1.00	$2.00	£0.30	£1.00	£2.00
466 scarce in the U.K. 68pgs	$0.30	$1.00	$2.00	£0.25	£0.75	£1.50
467 ND (Jan 1980), Starman appears (an 80s version by Steve Ditko; see First Issue Special #12)	$2.00	$6.00	$10.00	£0.30	£0.90	£1.50
468-472 ND	$0.40	$1.20	$2.00	£0.25	£0.75	£1.25
473-474	$0.30	$0.90	$1.50	£0.20	£0.60	£1.00
475 Bolland cover	$0.30	$0.90	$1.50	£0.20	£0.60	£1.00
476-478	$0.30	$0.90	$1.50	£0.20	£0.60	£1.00
479 (Mar 1981), Dial H for Hero begins	$0.30	$0.90	$1.50	£0.20	£0.60	£1.00
480-483	$0.30	$0.90	$1.50	£0.20	£0.60	£1.00
484-486 George Perez cover	$0.30	$0.90	$1.50	£0.20	£0.60	£1.00
487-488	$0.30	$0.90	$1.50	£0.20	£0.60	£1.00
489 (Jan 1982)	$0.30	$0.90	$1.50	£0.20	£0.60	£1.00
490 George Perez cover	$0.30	$0.90	$1.50	£0.20	£0.60	£1.00
491 very scarce in the U.K. 1st of digest size (all 100pgs), reprints Adventure #247 and #267	$0.60	$1.80	$3.00	£1.20	£3.60	£6.00
492 scarce in the U.K.	$0.60	$1.80	$3.00	£1.00	£3.00	£5.00
493 scarce in the U.K. new origin story Challengers of the Unknown	$0.60	$1.80	$3.00	£1.00	£3.00	£5.00
494 scarce in the U.K.	$0.60	$1.80	$3.00	£1.00	£3.00	£5.00
495 scarce in the U.K. (Jan 1983), Neal Adams reprint, Toth art	$0.60	$1.80	$3.00	£1.00	£3.00	£5.00
496 scarce in the U.K. Neal Adams reprint, Toth, Cockrum art	$0.60	$1.80	$3.00	£1.00	£3.00	£5.00
497 scarce in the U.K. Neal Adams reprint, Toth art	$0.60	$1.80	$3.00	£1.00	£3.00	£5.00
498 scarce in the U.K. Neal Adams reprint	$0.60	$1.80	$3.00	£1.00	£3.00	£5.00
499 scarce in the U.K.	$0.60	$1.80	$3.00	£1.00	£3.00	£5.00
500 very scarce in the U.K. 144pgs	$0.60	$1.80	$3.00	£1.20	£3.60	£6.00
501 scarce in the U.K.	$0.60	$1.80	$3.00	£1.00	£3.00	£5.00
502-503 scarce in the U.K. Morrow reprints	$0.60	$1.80	$3.00	£1.00	£3.00	£5.00
Title Value:	$47421.30	$142440.40	$397241.25	£31734.75	£95240.30	£266093.75

ARTISTS

Ditko in 467-478. Nasser in 466. Nino in 425-427, 429, 432, 433.

NEW FEATURES

Adventurer's Club in 426, 427, 430. Aquaman in 260-280, 282, 284, 435-437, 441-452, 460-466, 475-478. Aqualad in 453-455. Bizarro World in 285-299. Black Canary in 399, 418, 419. Black Orchid in 428-430. Captain Fear in 425-427, 429, 432, 433. Capt. Marvel in 49, 492, 499. Capt.Marvel/Mary Marvel in 498. Capt. Marvel Jr. in 496. Challengers of the Unknown in 493-497. Congorilla in 270-281, 283. Creeper in 445-447. Deadman in 459-466. Dr Mid-Nite in 418. Dr.13 in 428. Eclipso in 457, 458. Elongated Man in 459. Flash in 459-466. Green Arrow in 266-269. Green Lantern in 459, 460. Justice Society in 461-466. Legion of Super-Heroes in 300-380. Martian Manhunter in 449-451. New Gods in 459, 460. Plastic Man in 467-478, 498, 499. Seven Soldiers of Victory in 438-443. Starman in 467-478. Superboy in 103-315, 453-458. Supergirl in 381-389, 391-402, 404-415, 417-424. Tracy Thompson in 410, 402. Vigilante in 417, 422, 426, 427. Wonder Woman in 459-464. Zatanna in 413-415, 419, 421.

REPRINT FEATURES

Animal Man in 412, 414, 415, 420, 421. Aqualad in 494. Aquaman in 491-493, 495-499, 501-503. Black Canary in 491, 492. Capt. Marvel in 493-495, 497-499, 501, 502. Enchantress in 417, 419. Guardian/Newsboy Legion in 503. Hawkman in 413. Jimmy Olsen/Legion in 500, 503. Johnny Thunder in 416. Legion of Super-Heroes in 403, 409-411, 491-497, 498 (Bouncing Boy origin), 499-503. Merry, Phantom Lady in 416. Phantom Stranger in 418, 419. Plastic Man in 498, 499, 501-503. The Ray in 501. Robotman in 413. Sandman by Simon & Kirby in 491, 492, 495, 496, 499. Shining Knight in 417. Spectre in 491-499, 501, 502. Superboy in 317-338, 340-345, 356, 356. Superboy/Mon-El in 491. Supergirl in 390, 398, 416. Superman in 339, 420. Wonder Woman in 416. Zatanna in 493, 502, 503.

ADVENTURERS

Aircel/Adventure; 1 Aug 1986-10 1987

Issue	$Good	$Fine	$N.Mint	£Good	£Fine	£N.Mint
0 ND origin issue (July 1988)	$0.60	$1.80	$3.00	£0.40	£1.20	£2.00
1 ND light blue cover	$1.00	$3.00	$5.00	£0.60	£1.80	£3.00
1 2nd printing, ND dark blue cover, 1st Elf-Warrior	$0.50	$1.50	$2.50	£0.30	£0.90	£1.50
1 Limited Edition, ND - skeleton cover	$1.50	$4.50	$7.50	£1.00	£3.00	£5.00
2 ND	$0.50	$1.50	$2.50	£0.30	£0.90	£1.50
3 ND 1st Adventure Comics issue	$0.50	$1.50	$2.50	£0.30	£0.90	£1.50
4-10 ND	$0.40	$1.20	$2.00	£0.25	£0.75	£1.25
Title Value:	$7.40	$22.20	$37.00	£4.65	£13.95	£23.25

ADVENTURERS BOOK 2

Adventure; 1 1987-9 1989

Issue	$Good	$Fine	$N.Mint	£Good	£Fine	£N.Mint
1 ND regular edition	$0.50	$1.50	$2.50	£0.30	£0.90	£1.50
1 Limited Edition ND	$0.55	$1.65	$2.75	£0.35	£1.05	£1.75
2-9 ND	$0.40	$1.20	$2.00	£0.25	£0.75	£1.25
Title Value:	$4.25	$12.75	$21.25	£2.65	£7.95	£13.25

ADVENTURERS BOOK 3

Adventure; 1 Oct 1989-6 1990

Issue	$Good	$Fine	$N.Mint	£Good	£Fine	£N.Mint
1 ND regular edition	$0.50	$1.50	$2.50	£0.30	£0.90	£1.50
1 Limited Edition ND	$0.55	$1.65	$2.75	£0.35	£1.05	£1.75
2-6 ND	$0.40	$1.20	$2.00	£0.25	£0.75	£1.25
Title Value:	$3.05	$9.15	$15.25	£1.90	£5.70	£9.50
Trade Paperback (B&W)				£1.00	£3.00	£5.00
Adventurers Graphic Novel Three Pack (May 199)1 - The Chaos Gate/The Halls of Anubis/The Ways of the Worm				£1.40	£4.20	£7.00

ADVENTURES IN THE MYSTWOOD

Blackthorne; 1 1986

Issue	$Good	$Fine	$N.Mint	£Good	£Fine	£N.Mint
1 ND Williams art	$0.30	$0.90	$1.50	£0.20	£0.60	£1.00
Title Value:	$0.30	$0.90	$1.50	£0.20	£0.60	£1.00
Trade Paperback (B&W)				£1.00	£3.00	£5.00

ADVENTURES INTO THE UNKNOWN

ACG; 1 Autumn 1948-174 Aug 1967

Issue	$Good	$Fine	$N.Mint	£Good	£Fine	£N.Mint
1 ND scarce in the U.K. adaptation of gothic novel Castle of Otranto; Fred Guardineer art featured	$150.00	$450.00	$1200.00	£100.00	£300.00	£800.00
2 ND scarce in the U.K.	$70.00	$215.00	$575.00	£48.00	£140.00	£385.00
3 ND scarce in the U.K.	$75.00	$225.00	$600.00	£50.00	£150.00	£400.00
4-5 ND scarce in the U.K.	$37.00	$110.00	$260.00	£25.00	£75.00	£175.00
6-10 ND scarce in the U.K.	$29.00	$85.00	$200.00	£19.00	£57.50	£135.00
11-20 ND	$22.50	$67.50	$160.00	£15.50	£47.00	£110.00
21-30 ND	$20.00	$60.00	$140.00	£13.50	£41.00	£95.00
31-50 ND	$15.50	$47.00	$110.00	£10.50	£32.00	£75.00
51-58 ND scarce in the U.K. 3-D cover and story	$34.00	$100.00	$240.00	£22.50	£67.50	£160.00

	$Good	$Fine	$N.Mint	£Good	£Fine	£N.Mint
59 ND scarce in the U.K. 3-D story	$27.00	$80.00	$190.00	£18.50	£55.00	£130.00
60-61 ND	$10.50	$32.00	$75.00	£7.00	£21.00	£50.00
62-70 ND	$7.00	$21.00	$50.00	£5.00	£15.00	£35.00
71-90 ND	$5.00	$15.00	$35.00	£3.55	£10.50	£25.00
91 ND Williamson art	$4.25	$12.50	$30.00	£2.85	£8.50	£20.00
92-95 ND	$4.25	$12.50	$30.00	£2.85	£8.50	£20.00
96 ND Williamson art	$4.25	$12.50	$30.00	£2.85	£8.50	£20.00
97-99 ND	$4.25	$12.50	$30.00	£2.85	£8.50	£20.00
100 ND scarce in the U.K.	$5.50	$17.00	$40.00	£3.90	£11.50	£27.50
101-106 ND	$4.25	$12.50	$30.00	£2.85	£8.50	£20.00
107 ND Williamson art	$4.25	$12.50	$30.00	£2.85	£8.50	£20.00
108-110 ND	$4.25	$12.50	$30.00	£2.85	£8.50	£20.00
1st official distribution in the U.K.						
111-115	$4.25	$12.50	$30.00	£2.50	£7.50	£17.50
116 Williamson art	$4.25	$12.50	$30.00	£2.50	£7.50	£17.50
117	$4.25	$12.50	$30.00	£2.50	£7.50	£17.50
118 painted cover	$4.25	$12.50	$30.00	£2.50	£7.50	£17.50
119-127	$4.25	$12.50	$30.00	£2.50	£7.50	£17.50
128 Williamson reprint	$4.25	$12.50	$30.00	£2.50	£7.50	£17.50
129-130	$4.25	$12.50	$30.00	£2.50	£7.50	£17.50
131-153	$3.55	$10.50	$25.00	£1.40	£4.25	£10.00
154 1st appearance/origin Nemesis	$4.25	$12.50	$30.00	£2.50	£7.50	£17.50
155-167	$3.55	$10.50	$25.00	£1.40	£4.25	£10.00
168 Steve Ditko art	$4.25	$12.50	$30.00	£2.50	£7.50	£17.50
169-174	$3.55	$10.50	$25.00	£1.40	£4.25	£10.00
Title Value:	$2060.85	$6153.50	$14825.00	£1343.35	£4046.00	£9697.50

ADVENTURES INTO THE UNKNOWN (2ND SERIES)

A Plus Comics; 1 Oct 1990-5 1991

	$Good	$Fine	$N.Mint	£Good	£Fine	£N.Mint
1 ND 48pgs, Frank Frazetta cover; reprints of ACG series begin	$0.50	$1.50	$2.50	£0.30	£0.90	£1.50
2 ND 48pgs, Williamson, Steve Ditko, Mike Zeck art, Frank Frazetta cover	$0.50	$1.50	$2.50	£0.30	£0.90	£1.50
3 ND 48pgs, Williamson, Wood art	$0.50	$1.50	$2.50	£0.30	£0.90	£1.50
4-5 ND 48pgs	$0.50	$1.50	$2.50	£0.30	£0.90	£1.50
Title Value:	$2.50	$7.50	$12.50	£1.50	£4.50	£7.50

Note: bi-monthly.
Note also: issue #1 was re-released in April 1996 in limited quantities at $2.50 cover price.

	$Good	$Fine	$N.Mint	£Good	£Fine	£N.Mint
Halloween Special (Nov 1991) ND 48pgs				£0.30	£0.90	£1.50

ADVENTURES OF BARON MUNCHAUSEN

Now Comics,MS; 1 Jul 1989-4 Oct 1989

	$Good	$Fine	$N.Mint	£Good	£Fine	£N.Mint
1-4 ND movie adaptation in colour	$0.40	$1.20	$2.00	£0.25	£0.75	£1.25
Title Value:	$1.60	$4.80	$8.00	£1.00	£3.00	£5.00

ADVENTURES OF BOB HOPE

(see Bob Hope)

ADVENTURES OF CAPT JACK

(see Captain Jack)

ADVENTURES OF CAPTAIN NEMO, THE

Rip Off Press,MS; 1 Jun 1992-3 Aug 1992

	$Good	$Fine	$N.Mint	£Good	£Fine	£N.Mint
1-3 ND	$0.50	$1.50	$2.50	£0.30	£0.90	£1.50
Title Value:	$1.50	$4.50	$7.50	£0.90	£2.70	£4.50

ADVENTURES OF CHUK, THE

White Wolf/Avatar; 1 Jul 1986-3 1987 (#3 published by Avatar)
(becomes Chuk the Barbaric with #3)

	$Good	$Fine	$N.Mint	£Good	£Fine	£N.Mint
1-2 ND	$0.25	$0.75	$1.25	£0.15	£0.45	£0.75
3 ND scarce in the U.K.	$0.25	$0.75	$1.25	£0.20	£0.60	£1.00
Title Value:	$0.75	$2.25	$3.75	£0.50	£1.50	£2.50

ADVENTURES OF CYCLOPS & PHOENIX, THE

Marvel Comics Group,MS; 1 May 1994-4 Aug 1994

	$Good	$Fine	$N.Mint	£Good	£Fine	£N.Mint
1 Scott Lobdell script begins	$0.90	$2.70	$4.50	£0.60	£1.80	£3.00
2-4	$0.80	$2.40	$4.00	£0.50	£1.50	£2.50
Title Value:	$3.30	$9.90	$16.50	£2.10	£6.30	£10.50

ADVENTURES OF CYCLOPS & PHOENIX, THE FURTHER

Marvel Comics Group,MS; 1 Jun 1996-4 Sep 1996

	$Good	$Fine	$N.Mint	£Good	£Fine	£N.Mint
1-4 ND Peter Milligan script, John Paul Leon and Klaus Janson art	$0.40	$1.20	$2.00	£0.25	£0.75	£1.25
Title Value:	$1.60	$4.80	$8.00	£1.00	£3.00	£5.00

ADVENTURES OF JERRY LEWIS

(see Jerry Lewis)

ADVENTURES OF JUNGLE JIM, THE

Avalon Communications; 1 Feb 1996

	$Good	$Fine	$N.Mint	£Good	£Fine	£N.Mint
1 ND reprints; cover by Wally Wood and Steve Ditko	$0.50	$1.50	$2.50	£0.30	£0.90	£1.50
Title Value:	$0.50	$1.50	$2.50	£0.30	£0.90	£1.50

ADVENTURES OF LUTHER ARKWRIGHT

(see British section and Luther Arkwright)

ADVENTURES OF MR.PYRIDINE

Fantagraphics,Magazine OS; nn Dec 1988

	$Good	$Fine	$N.Mint	£Good	£Fine	£N.Mint
nn ND Singh art	$0.50	$1.50	$2.50	£0.30	£0.90	£1.50
Title Value:	$0.50	$1.50	$2.50	£0.30	£0.90	£1.50

ADVENTURES OF SUPERMAN

(see Superman #424 onwards)

ADVENTURES OF THE OUTSIDERS

(see Batman and the Outsiders)

ADVENTURES ON THE PLANET OF THE APES

Marvel Comics Group, Film; 1 Oct 1975-11 Dec 1976

	$Good	$Fine	$N.Mint	£Good	£Fine	£N.Mint
1 ND Jim Starlin cover	$1.00	$3.00	$6.00	£0.30	£1.00	£2.00
2-3 ND	$0.50	$1.50	$3.00	£0.25	£0.75	£1.50
4-11 ND	$0.30	$1.00	$2.00	£0.20	£0.60	£1.25
Title Value:	$4.40	$14.00	$28.00	£2.40	£7.30	£15.00

AESOP'S FABLES

Fantagraphics; 1 Feb 1991-3 1991

	$Good	$Fine	$N.Mint	£Good	£Fine	£N.Mint
1-3 ND	$0.40	$1.20	$2.00	£0.25	£0.75	£1.25
Title Value:	$1.20	$3.60	$6.00	£0.75	£2.25	£3.75

AFTER DARK

Millennium,OS; nn Mar 1995

	$Good	$Fine	$N.Mint	£Good	£Fine	£N.Mint
nn ND horror anthology; black and white	$0.60	$1.80	$3.00	£0.40	£1.20	£2.00
Title Value:	$0.60	$1.80	$3.00	£0.40	£1.20	£2.00

AGAINST BLACKSHARD: 3-D

Sirius; 1 Aug 1986

	$Good	$Fine	$N.Mint	£Good	£Fine	£N.Mint
1 ND Scott Hampton inks	$0.50	$1.50	$2.50	£0.30	£0.90	£1.50
Title Value:	$0.50	$1.50	$2.50	£0.30	£0.90	£1.50

AGE OF HEROES, THE

Halloween Comics; 1 1996-present

	$Good	$Fine	$N.Mint	£Good	£Fine	£N.Mint
1-2 ND James Hudnall script, John Ridgway art begins; black and white	$0.60	$1.80	$3.00	£0.40	£1.20	£2.00
Title Value:	$1.20	$3.60	$6.00	£0.80	£2.40	£4.00

AGE OF REPTILES

Dark Horse,MS; 1 Nov 1993-4 Feb 1994

	$Good	$Fine	$N.Mint	£Good	£Fine	£N.Mint
1-4 ND Ricardo Delgado script and art	$0.50	$1.50	$2.50	£0.30	£0.90	£1.50
Title Value:	$2.00	$6.00	$10.00	£1.20	£3.60	£6.00

Age of Reptiles: Tribal Warfare (Jan 1996)

	$Good	$Fine	$N.Mint	£Good	£Fine	£N.Mint
Trade paperback reprints mini-series, Ray Harryhausen introduction				£2.00	£6.00	£10.00

AGE OF REPTILES: THE HUNT

Dark Horse,MS; 1 May 1996-5 Sep 1996

	$Good	$Fine	$N.Mint	£Good	£Fine	£N.Mint
1-5 ND Ricardo Delgado script and art	$0.60	$1.80	$3.00	£0.40	£1.20	£2.00
Title Value:	$3.00	$9.00	$15.00	£2.00	£6.00	£10.00

AGENT LIBERTY SPECIAL

DC Comics,OS; 1 Jan 1992
(see Superman [2nd Series] #60)

	$Good	$Fine	$N.Mint	£Good	£Fine	£N.Mint
1 48pgs	$0.40	$1.20	$2.00	£0.25	£0.75	£1.25
Title Value:	$0.40	$1.20	$2.00	£0.25	£0.75	£1.25

AGENT UNKNOWN

Renegade; 1 Oct 1987-3 Feb 1988

	$Good	$Fine	$N.Mint	£Good	£Fine	£N.Mint
1-3 ND Dell Barras art	$0.40	$1.20	$2.00	£0.25	£0.75	£1.25
Title Value:	$1.20	$3.60	$6.00	£0.75	£2.25	£3.75

AGENTS OF LAW

Dark Horse; 1 Mar 1995-6 Aug 1995

	$Good	$Fine	$N.Mint	£Good	£Fine	£N.Mint
1-6 ND Keith Giffen co-script; spin off from Comics Greatest World	$0.40	$1.20	$2.00	£0.25	£0.75	£1.25
Title Value:	$2.40	$7.20	$12.00	£1.50	£4.50	£7.50

AIDS AWARENESS

Chaos City Comics,OS; 1 Dec 1993

	$Good	$Fine	$N.Mint	£Good	£Fine	£N.Mint
1 ND features art by Dave Gibbons, Liam Sharp, Bryan Hitch, John Higgins, Kev O'Neill with Simon Bisley painted cover; black and white, printed on heavy stock paper	$0.60	$1.80	$3.00	£0.40	£1.20	£2.00
1 Limited Edition ND	$1.00	$3.00	$5.00	£0.70	£2.10	£3.50
Title Value:	$1.60	$4.80	$8.00	£1.10	£3.30	£5.50

AIR RAIDERS

Marvel Comics Group, Toy; 1 Jan 1988-5 Mar 1988

	$Good	$Fine	$N.Mint	£Good	£Fine	£N.Mint
1-5	$0.15	$0.45	$0.75	£0.10	£0.30	£0.50
Title Value:	$0.75	$2.25	$3.75	£0.50	£1.50	£2.50

AIRBOY

Eclipse; 1 Jul 1986-50 Oct 1989
(see Airfighters, Airmaidens, Target: Airboy)

	$Good	$Fine	$N.Mint	£Good	£Fine	£N.Mint
1 20pgs, bi-weekly, 50¢ cover	$0.50	$1.50	$2.50	£0.30	£0.90	£1.50
2	$0.40	$1.20	$2.00	£0.25	£0.75	£1.25
3 The Heap begins (looks very much like Marvel's Man-Thing)	$0.40	$1.20	$2.00	£0.25	£0.75	£1.25
4	$0.40	$1.20	$2.00	£0.25	£0.75	£1.25
5 rare in the U.K. Dave Stevens cover, re-intro Valkyrie	$0.40	$1.20	$2.00	£0.30	£0.90	£1.50
6	$0.40	$1.20	$2.00	£0.25	£0.75	£1.25
7 Gulacy cover	$0.40	$1.20	$2.00	£0.25	£0.75	£1.25
8	$0.40	$1.20	$2.00	£0.25	£0.75	£1.25
9 Skywolf begins	$0.40	$1.20	$2.00	£0.25	£0.75	£1.25
10	$0.40	$1.20	$2.00	£0.25	£0.75	£1.25
11 origin Airboy retold	$0.40	$1.20	$2.00	£0.25	£0.75	£1.25
12 Dave Dorman cover	$0.40	$1.20	$2.00	£0.25	£0.75	£1.25
13-16	$0.40	$1.20	$2.00	£0.25	£0.75	£1.25
17 Steacy painted cover	$0.40	$1.20	$2.00	£0.25	£0.75	£1.25

	$Good	$Fine	$N.Mint	£Good	£Fine	£N.Mint
18-23	$0.40	$1.20	$2.00	£0.25	£0.75	£1.25
24 The Heap returns	$0.40	$1.20	$2.00	£0.25	£0.75	£1.25
25-27	$0.40	$1.20	$2.00	£0.25	£0.75	£1.25
28 Mr. Monster vs. The Heap back-up story	$0.40	$1.20	$2.00	£0.25	£0.75	£1.25
29-32	$0.40	$1.20	$2.00	£0.25	£0.75	£1.25
33 painted Steacy cover	$0.40	$1.20	$2.00	£0.25	£0.75	£1.25
34 1st monthly issue	$0.40	$1.20	$2.00	£0.25	£0.75	£1.25
35-45	$0.40	$1.20	$2.00	£0.25	£0.75	£1.25
46-49 Airboy Diary story	$0.40	$1.20	$2.00	£0.25	£0.75	£1.25
50 48pgs, DS squarebound, Joe Kubert cover, Andy and Adam Kubert art	$0.60	$1.80	$3.00	£0.40	£1.20	£2.00
Title Value:	$20.30	$60.90	$101.50	£12.75	£38.25	£63.75

Note: all Non-Distributed on the news-stands in the U.K.

AIRBOY AND MR.MONSTER SPECIAL

Eclipse,OS; 1 Aug 1987

	$Good	$Fine	$N.Mint	£Good	£Fine	£N.Mint
1 ND Michael T. Gilbert script/art	$0.50	$1.50	$2.50	£0.30	£0.90	£1.50
Title Value:	$0.50	$1.50	$2.50	£0.30	£0.90	£1.50

AIRBOY MEETS PROWLER

Eclipse,OS; 1 Dec 1987

	$Good	$Fine	$N.Mint	£Good	£Fine	£N.Mint
1 ND	$0.50	$1.50	$2.50	£0.30	£0.90	£1.50
Title Value:	$0.50	$1.50	$2.50	£0.30	£0.90	£1.50

AIRBOY VERSUS THE AIR MAIDENS

Eclipse,OS; 1 Jul 1988

	$Good	$Fine	$N.Mint	£Good	£Fine	£N.Mint
1 ND	$0.50	$1.50	$2.50	£0.30	£0.90	£1.50
Title Value:	$0.50	$1.50	$2.50	£0.30	£0.90	£1.50

AIRFIGHTERS CLASSICS

Eclipse; 1 Nov 1987-6 May 1989

	$Good	$Fine	$N.Mint	£Good	£Fine	£N.Mint
1 ND 64pgs, squarebound, classic contraversial Japanese fighter pilot cover reprinted, black and white	$0.80	$2.40	$4.00	£0.50	£1.50	£2.50
2-6 ND 64pgs, squarebound, Golden Age Airboy reprints, black and white	$0.80	$2.40	$4.00	£0.50	£1.50	£2.50
Title Value:	$4.80	$14.40	$24.00	£3.00	£9.00	£15.00

Note: all bookshelf format. Issue #1 reprints Airfighters #2 originally published by Hillman Periodicals from Nov 1942 on. Issues #2-6 reprints original issues #3-7.

AIRFIGHTERS MEET SGT.STRIKE

Eclipse,OS; 1 Jan 1988

	$Good	$Fine	$N.Mint	£Good	£Fine	£N.Mint
1 ND Tom Lyle cover and art (colour), card stock covers	$0.40	$1.20	$2.00	£0.25	£0.75	£1.25
Title Value:	$0.40	$1.20	$2.00	£0.25	£0.75	£1.25

AIRMAIDENS SPECIAL

Eclipse,OS; 1 Aug 1987

	$Good	$Fine	$N.Mint	£Good	£Fine	£N.Mint
1 ND Airboy tie-in, Larry Elmore cover and art; colour	$0.40	$1.20	$2.00	£0.25	£0.75	£1.25
Title Value:	$0.40	$1.20	$2.00	£0.25	£0.75	£1.25

AIRMAN

Malibu,OS; 1 Mar 1993

	$Good	$Fine	$N.Mint	£Good	£Fine	£N.Mint
1 ND Protectors spin-off	$0.40	$1.20	$2.00	£0.25	£0.75	£1.25
Title Value:	$0.40	$1.20	$2.00	£0.25	£0.75	£1.25

AIRTIGHT GARAGE, THE

Marvel Comics Group/Epic,MS; 1 Jul 1993-4 Oct 1993

	$Good	$Fine	$N.Mint	£Good	£Fine	£N.Mint
1 ND reprint of Moebius Graphic Novel #3 begins	$0.40	$1.20	$2.00	£0.25	£0.75	£1.25
2-4 ND	$0.40	$1.20	$2.00	£0.25	£0.75	£1.25
Title Value:	$1.60	$4.80	$8.00	£1.00	£3.00	£5.00

AIRWAVES

Caliber Press; 1 Apr 1991-6 1991

	$Good	$Fine	$N.Mint	£Good	£Fine	£N.Mint
1-6 ND	$0.40	$1.20	$2.00	£0.25	£0.75	£1.25
Title Value:	$2.40	$7.20	$12.00	£1.50	£4.50	£7.50

AKIKO

Sirius Entertainment; 1 Mar 1996-present

	$Good	$Fine	$N.Mint	£Good	£Fine	£N.Mint
1-5 ND 24pgs, Mark Crilley script and art; black and white	$0.50	$1.50	$2.50	£0.30	£0.90	£1.50
Title Value:	$2.50	$7.50	$12.50	£1.50	£4.50	£7.50

AKIRA

Marvel Comics Group/Epic; 1 Nov 1988-33 1992; 34 Oct 1995-38 Feb 1996

	$Good	$Fine	$N.Mint	£Good	£Fine	£N.Mint
1 ND scarce in the U.K. 64pgs	$3.60	$10.50	$18.00	£1.50	£4.50	£7.50
1 2nd printing ND	$0.90	$2.70	$4.50	£0.60	£1.80	£3.00
2 ND 64pgs	$1.50	$4.50	$7.50	£1.00	£3.00	£5.00
2 2nd printing ND	$0.80	$2.40	$4.00	£0.50	£1.50	£2.50
3 ND very scarce in the U.K. 64pgs	$1.50	$4.50	$7.50	£1.50	£4.50	£7.50
4 ND scarce in the U.K. 64pgs	$1.50	$4.50	$7.50	£1.40	£4.20	£7.00
5 ND scarce in the U.K. 64pgs	$1.50	$4.50	$7.50	£1.30	£3.90	£6.50
6-10 ND 64pgs	$1.20	$3.60	$6.00	£1.00	£3.00	£5.00
11-15 ND 64pgs	$1.20	$3.60	$6.00	£0.80	£2.40	£4.00
16-24 ND 64pgs	$1.00	$3.00	$5.00	£0.70	£2.10	£3.50
25 ND scarce in the U.K. 64pgs	$1.00	$3.00	$5.00	£1.20	£3.60	£6.00
26-30 ND 64pgs	$0.90	$2.70	$4.50	£0.60	£1.80	£3.00
31-33 ND 64pgs	$0.80	$2.40	$4.00	£0.50	£1.50	£2.50
34-35 ND 64pgs	$1.20	$3.60	$6.00	£0.80	£2.40	£4.00
36-38 ND 64pgs	$1.40	$4.20	$7.00	£0.90	£2.70	£4.50
Title Value:	$46.80	$140.10	$234.00	£33.10	£99.30	£165.50

Note: Bookshelf Format. Japanese post-holocaust story, translation by Mary Jo Duffy. Mature Readers.
Note also: last five issues very delayed in frequency.

	£Good	£Fine	£N.Mint
Trade paperback 1 (May 1991), reprints issues #1-3	£2.25	£6.75	£11.25
Trade paperback 2 (Aug 1991), reprints issues #4-6	£2.00	£6.00	£10.00
Trade paperback 3 (Jan 1992), reprints issues #7-9	£2.00	£6.00	£10.00
Trade paperback 4 (May 1992), reprints issues #10-12	£2.00	£6.00	£10.00
Trade paperback 5 (Jul 1992), reprints issues #13-15	£2.00	£6.00	£10.00
Trade paperback 6 (Sep 1992), reprints issues #16-18	£2.00	£6.00	£10.00
Trade paperback 7 (Feb 1993), reprints issues #19-21	£2.00	£6.00	£10.00
Trade paperback 8 (May 1993), reprints issues #22-24	£2.00	£6.00	£10.00
Trade paperback 9 (Aug 1993), reprints issues #25-27	£2.00	£6.00	£10.00
Trade paperback 10 (Nov 1993), reprints issues #28-30	£2.00	£6.00	£10.00

ALADDIN

Marvel Comics Group; 1 Oct 1994-12 Sep 1995

	$Good	$Fine	$N.Mint	£Good	£Fine	£N.Mint
1-12 ND new adventures	$0.30	$0.90	$1.50	£0.20	£0.60	£1.00
Title Value:	$3.60	$10.80	$18.00	£2.40	£7.20	£12.00

	£Good	£Fine	£N.Mint
Aladdin Volume 1 (Jun 1995) Trade paperback, reprints issues #1-4	£1.30	£3.90	£6.50

ALARMING ADVENTURES

Harvey; 1 Oct 1962-3 Feb 1963

	$Good	$Fine	$N.Mint	£Good	£Fine	£N.Mint
1 rare although distributed in the U.K. Crandall/Williamson art	$8.25	$25.00	$50.00	£5.00	£15.00	£30.00
2-3 rare although distributed in the U.K. Crandall/Williamson art	$5.75	$17.50	$35.00	£3.30	£10.00	£20.00
Title Value:	$19.75	$60.00	$120.00	£11.60	£35.00	£70.00

ALBEDO

Thoughts and Images; 0 Apr 1985-15 1989

	$Good	$Fine	$N.Mint	£Good	£Fine	£N.Mint
0 1st printing, blue cover	$2.50	$7.50	$12.50	£1.50	£4.50	£7.50
0 2nd printing, blue cover, "Second printing" on cover and price removed	$1.50	$4.50	$7.50	£1.00	£3.00	£5.00
0 3rd printing, blue cover; "Third printing" on cover and new address in indicia	$0.60	$1.80	$3.00	£0.40	£1.20	£2.00
0 4th printing	$0.50	$1.50	$2.50	£0.30	£0.90	£1.50
1 dark red cover, 1st appearance Usagi Yojimbo	$2.00	$6.00	$10.00	£1.50	£4.50	£7.50
1 Red Cover Variant	$2.00	$6.00	$10.00	£1.50	£4.50	£7.50
2	$1.50	$4.50	$7.50	£1.00	£3.00	£5.00
3	$0.90	$2.70	$4.50	£0.60	£1.80	£3.00
4-8	$0.60	$1.80	$3.00	£0.40	£1.20	£2.00
9-15	$0.40	$1.20	$2.00	£0.25	£0.75	£1.25
Title Value:	$17.30	$51.90	$86.50	£11.55	£34.65	£57.75

Note: all Non-Distributed on the news-stands in the U.K.

ALBEDO COLOR SPECIAL

Antarctic Press,OS; 1 Sep 1993

	$Good	$Fine	$N.Mint	£Good	£Fine	£N.Mint
1 ND Steve Gallacci's first story for Albedo re-done in colour	$0.60	$1.80	$3.00	£0.40	£1.20	£2.00
Title Value:	$0.60	$1.80	$3.00	£0.40	£1.20	£2.00

ALBEDO VOLUME 2

Antarctic Press; 1 Aug 1991-10 1993

	$Good	$Fine	$N.Mint	£Good	£Fine	£N.Mint
1 ND	$0.50	$1.50	$2.50	£0.30	£0.90	£1.50
1 2nd printing ND	$0.50	$1.50	$2.50	£0.30	£0.90	£1.50
2-10 ND	$0.50	$1.50	$2.50	£0.30	£0.90	£1.50
Title Value:	$5.50	$16.50	$27.50	£3.30	£9.90	£16.50

ALBEDO VOLUME 3

Antarctic Press; 1 Feb 1994-3 Apr 1994

	$Good	$Fine	$N.Mint	£Good	£Fine	£N.Mint
1-4 ND Steve Gallacci script and art	$0.60	$1.80	$3.00	£0.40	£1.20	£2.00
Title Value:	$2.40	$7.20	$12.00	£1.60	£4.80	£8.00

ALEX

Fantagraphics; 1 Mar 1994-2 1994

	$Good	$Fine	$N.Mint	£Good	£Fine	£N.Mint
1-2 ND Mark Kalesniko script and art; black and white	$0.40	$1.20	$2.00	£0.25	£0.75	£1.25
Title Value:	$0.80	$2.40	$4.00	£0.50	£1.50	£2.50

ALF

Marvel Comics Group, TV; 1 Mar 1988-50 Feb 1992

	$Good	$Fine	$N.Mint	£Good	£Fine	£N.Mint
1 ND	$0.20	$0.60	$1.00	£0.15	£0.45	£0.75
1 2nd printing ND	$0.20	$0.60	$1.00	£0.15	£0.45	£0.75
2-10 ND	$0.20	$0.60	$1.00	£0.15	£0.45	£0.75
11-28 ND	$0.15	$0.45	$0.75	£0.10	£0.35	£0.60
29 ND mock 3-D cover	$0.15	$0.45	$0.75	£0.10	£0.35	£0.60
30-49 ND	$0.15	$0.45	$0.75	£0.10	£0.35	£0.60
50 ND DS	$0.20	$0.60	$1.00	£0.15	£0.45	£0.75
Title Value:	$8.25	$24.75	$41.25	£5.70	£19.05	£32.40

ALF ANNUAL

Marvel Comics Group, TV; 1 1988-3 1990

	$Good	$Fine	$N.Mint	£Good	£Fine	£N.Mint
1-2 ND	$0.25	$0.75	$1.25	£0.15	£0.45	£0.75
3 ND New Age Melmutant Abstract Turtles appear	$0.25	$0.75	$1.25	£0.15	£0.45	£0.75
Title Value:	$0.75	$2.25	$3.75	£0.45	£1.35	£2.25

ALF HOLIDAY SPECIAL

Marvel Comics Group,OS; 1 Jul 1988

	$Good	$Fine	$N.Mint	£Good	£Fine	£N.Mint
1 ND 64pgs, squarebound, Wolverine appears	$0.30	$0.90	$1.50	£0.20	£0.60	£1.00
Title Value:	$0.30	$0.90	$1.50	£0.20	£0.60	£1.00

ALF SPECIAL EDITION

Marvel Comics Group,OS; 1 Aug 1990

	$Good	$Fine	$N.Mint	£Good	£Fine	£N.Mint
1 reprints Alf #1-#3, photo cover from #1	$0.50	$1.50	$2.50	£0.30	£0.90	£1.50

	$Good	$Fine	$N.Mint	£Good	£Fine	£N.Mint
Title Value:	*$0.50*	*$1.50*	*$2.50*	£0.30	£0.90	£1.50
Note: Bookshelf Format						
ALF SPRING SPECIAL						
Marvel Comics Group,OS; 1 Feb 1989						
1 ND 64pgs, squarebound						
	$0.40	*$1.20*	*$2.00*	£0.25	£0.75	£1.25
Title Value:	*$0.40*	*$1.20*	*$2.00*	£0.25	£0.75	£1.25
ALFRED HITCHCOCK'S PSYCHO						
Innovation,MS; 1 Nov 1991-3 Aug 1992						
1-3 ND	*$0.40*	*$1.20*	*$2.00*	£0.25	£0.75	£1.25
Title Value:	*$1.20*	*$3.60*	*$6.00*	£0.75	£2.25	£3.75
ALI BABA: SCOURGE OF THE DESERT						
Caliber Press,OS; 1 Jan 1993						
1 ND cover layouts by Dave Sim, finishes by Dale Keown						
	$0.50	*$1.50*	*$2.50*	£0.30	£0.90	£1.50
1 Limited Edition Signed, ND - metallic logo, 3,000 copies						
	$0.90	*$2.70*	*$4.50*	£0.60	£1.80	£3.00
1 Signed, Limited Edition, ND - metallic logo, 3,000 copies						
	$0.90	*$2.70*	*$4.50*	£0.60	£1.80	£3.00
Title Value:	*$2.30*	*$6.90*	*$11.50*	£1.50	£4.50	£7.50
ALI-BABA: THETA'S REVENGE						
Caliber Press,OS; 1 Sep 1993						
1 ND	*$0.50*	*$1.50*	*$2.50*	£0.30	£0.90	£1.50
Title Value:	*$0.50*	*$1.50*	*$2.50*	£0.30	£0.90	£1.50
ALIAS: STORMFRONT						
Now Comics; 1,2 1990						
1-2 ND Jeff Starling art						
	$0.40	*$1.20*	*$2.00*	£0.25	£0.75	£1.25
Title Value:	*$0.80*	*$2.40*	*$4.00*	£0.50	£1.50	£2.50
ALICE COOPER: LAST TEMPTATION OF ALICE						
Marvel Comics Group,MS; 1 Aug 1994-3 Nov 1994						
1-3 ND Neil Gaiman script, Michael Zulli art, Dave McKean covers						
	$0.90	*$2.70*	*$4.50*	£0.60	£1.80	£3.00
Title Value:	*$2.70*	*$8.10*	*$13.50*	£1.80	£5.40	£9.00
Alice Cooper: The Complete Last Temptation (May 1995)						
Trade paperback reprints mini-series with Dave McKean cover				£2.00	£6.00	£10.00
ALICE IN WONDERLAND						
Gold Key/Movie Comics,OS Movie; 10144-503 Mar 1965						
10144-503 scarce in the U.K. part reprint from Four Color #331						
	$4.25	*$12.50*	*$30.00*	£2.85	£8.50	£20.00
Title Value:	*$4.25*	*$12.50*	*$30.00*	£2.85	£8.50	£20.00
ALIEN						
Avon Books,OS; nn Sep 1979						
nn ND scarce in the U.K. 100pgs, softcover; Dan O'Bannon screenplay illustrated with several hundred movie stills						
	$22.00	*$65.00*	*$110.00*	£15.00	£45.00	£75.00
Title Value:	*$22.00*	*$65.00*	*$110.00*	£15.00	£45.00	£75.00
ALIEN 3 MOVIE						
Dark Horse,MS; 1 Aug 1992-3 Sep 1992						
1-3 ND adaptation of film, Arthur Suydam covers, bi-weekly						
	$0.50	*$1.50*	*$2.50*	£0.30	£0.90	£1.50
Title Value:	*$1.50*	*$4.50*	*$7.50*	£0.90	£2.70	£4.50
Alien 3 Movie Special - U.K. Edition (Feb 1993)						
magazine, 44pgs, behind-the-scenes material				£0.35	£1.05	£1.75
ALIEN ENCOUNTERS						
Eclipse; 1 Jun 1985-14 Aug 1987						
1-7 ND	*$0.50*	*$1.50*	*$2.50*	£0.30	£0.90	£1.50
8 ND Marilyn Monroe cover						
	$0.50	*$1.50*	*$2.50*	£0.30	£0.90	£1.50
9-13 ND	*$0.50*	*$1.50*	*$2.50*	£0.30	£0.90	£1.50
14 ND John Ridgway art, John Bolton cover						
	$0.50	*$1.50*	*$2.50*	£0.30	£0.90	£1.50

	$Good	$Fine	$N.Mint	£Good	£Fine	£N.Mint
Title Value:	*$7.00*	*$21.00*	*$35.00*	£4.20	£12.60	£21.00
ALIEN FIRE						
Kitchen Sink; 1 Jan 1987-3 Jul 1987						
1-3 ND	*$0.40*	*$1.20*	*$2.00*	£0.25	£0.75	£1.25
Title Value:	*$1.20*	*$3.60*	*$6.00*	£0.75	£2.25	£3.75
Alien Fire: Pass in Thunder (May 1995)						
64pgs, new novella plus reprint of two-part story						
from Dark Horse Presents; black and white				£0.90	£2.70	£4.50
ALIEN FIRE: PASS IN THUNDER						
Kitchen Sink,OS; 1 Aug 1993						
1 ND reprints Alien Fire stories from Dark Horse Presents with extra art pages						
	$0.80	*$2.40*	*$4.00*	£0.50	£1.50	£2.50
Title Value:	*$0.80*	*$2.40*	*$4.00*	£0.50	£1.50	£2.50
Note: originally announced as a mini-series						
ALIEN LEGION						
Marvel Comics Group/Epic; 1 Apr 1984-20 Sep 1987						
(see Marvel Graphic Novel)						
1 ND DS	*$0.60*	*$1.80*	*$3.00*	£0.40	£1.20	£2.00
2-5 ND	*$0.50*	*$1.50*	*$2.50*	£0.30	£0.90	£1.50
6-8 ND Portacio inks						
	$0.50	*$1.50*	*$2.50*	£0.30	£0.90	£1.50
9-20 ND	*$0.50*	*$1.50*	*$2.50*	£0.30	£0.90	£1.50
Title Value:	*$10.10*	*$30.30*	*$50.50*	£6.10	£18.30	£30.50
Note: all high quality paper.						
Alien Legion: Slaughter-World (Nov 1991)						
Trade paperback reprints #1,7-11				£1.10	£3.30	£5.50
ALIEN LEGION (2ND SERIES)						
Marvel Comics Group/Epic; 1 Aug 1987-18 Aug 1990						
1 ND	*$0.50*	*$1.50*	*$2.50*	£0.30	£0.90	£1.50
2-18 ND	*$0.40*	*$1.20*	*$2.00*	£0.25	£0.75	£1.25
Title Value:	*$7.30*	*$21.90*	*$36.50*	£4.55	£13.65	£22.75
Note: Mature Readers.						
ALIEN LEGION: BINARY DEEP						
Marvel Comics Group/Epic,OS; 1 Nov 1993						
1 ND 48pgs, Chuck Dixon and Quigue Alcatena; bound-in trading card						
	$0.60	*$1.80*	*$3.00*	£0.40	£1.20	£2.00
Title Value:	*$0.60*	*$1.80*	*$3.00*	£0.40	£1.20	£2.00
ALIEN LEGION: ON THE EDGE						
Marvel Comics Group/Epic,MS; 1 Jan 1991-3 Mar 1991						
1-3 ND 48pgs	*$0.70*	*$2.10*	*$3.50*	£0.50	£1.50	£2.50
Title Value:	*$2.10*	*$6.30*	*$10.50*	£1.50	£4.50	£7.50
Note: Bookshelf Format						
ALIEN LEGION: ONE PLANET AT A TIME						
Marvel Comics Group/Epic,MS; 1 Jul 1993-3 Sep 1993						
1-3 ND	*$0.90*	*$2.70*	*$4.50*	£0.60	£1.80	£3.00
Title Value:	*$2.70*	*$8.10*	*$13.50*	£1.80	£5.40	£9.00
ALIEN LEGION: TENANTS OF HELL						
Marvel Comics Group/Epic,MS; 1 Sep 1991-2 Oct 1991						
1 ND continues on from On The Edge story						
	$0.90	*$2.70*	*$4.50*	£0.60	£1.80	£3.00
2 ND	*$0.90*	*$2.70*	*$4.50*	£0.60	£1.80	£3.00
Title Value:	*$1.80*	*$5.40*	*$9.00*	£1.20	£3.60	£6.00
ALIEN NATION						
DC Comics, Film; 1 Dec 1988						
1 58pgs, squarebound						
	$0.30	*$0.90*	*$1.50*	£0.20	£0.60	£1.00
Title Value:	*$0.30*	*$0.90*	*$1.50*	£0.20	£0.60	£1.00
ALIEN NATION: A BREED APART						
Adventure,MS; 1 1990-4 Apr 1991						
1-4 ND	*$0.40*	*$1.20*	*$2.00*	£0.25	£0.75	£1.25
Title Value:	*$1.60*	*$4.80*	*$8.00*	£1.00	£3.00	£5.00

Albedo #0 (1st print)

Alien Encounters #7

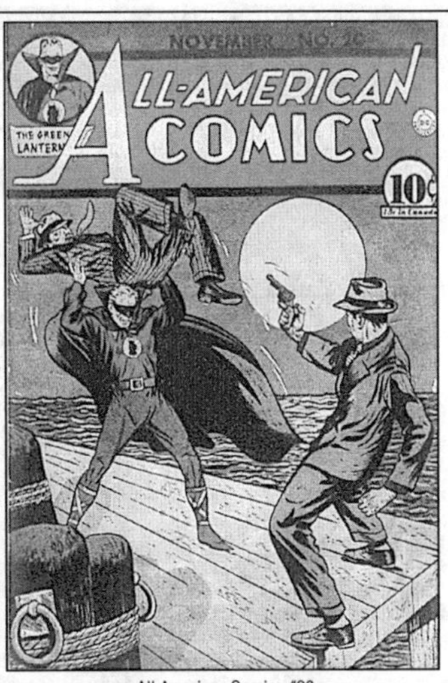

All American Comics #20

ALIEN NATION: PUBLIC ENEMY

Adventure,MS; 1 Feb 1992-4 May 1992

	$Good	$Fine	$N.Mint	£Good	£Fine	£N.Mint
1-4 ND	*$0.40*	*$1.20*	*$2.00*	£0.25	£0.75	£1.25
Title Value:	*$1.60*	*$4.80*	*$8.00*	£1.00	£3.00	£5.00

ALIEN NATION: THE FIRSTCOMERS

Adventure,MS; 1 Jul 1991-4 Oct 1991

	$Good	$Fine	$N.Mint	£Good	£Fine	£N.Mint
1-4 ND	*$0.40*	*$1.20*	*$2.00*	£0.25	£0.75	£1.25
Title Value:	*$1.60*	*$4.80*	*$8.00*	£1.00	£3.00	£5.00

ALIEN NATION: THE LOST EPISODE

Adventure,OS; 1 Aug 1992

	$Good	$Fine	$N.Mint	£Good	£Fine	£N.Mint
1 ND 48pgs, ties up plot-lines left when TV series was cancelled, photo cover	*$0.70*	*$2.10*	*$3.50*	£0.50	£1.50	£2.50
Title Value:	*$0.70*	*$2.10*	*$3.50*	£0.50	£1.50	£2.50

ALIEN NATION: THE SKIN TRADE

Adventure,MS; 1 May 1991-4 Aug 1991

	$Good	$Fine	$N.Mint	£Good	£Fine	£N.Mint
1-4 ND	*$0.40*	*$1.20*	*$2.00*	£0.25	£0.75	£1.25
Title Value:	*$1.60*	*$4.80*	*$8.00*	£1.00	£3.00	£5.00

ALIEN NATION: THE SPARTANS

Adventure,MS; 1 Sep 1990-4 Dec 1990

	$Good	$Fine	$N.Mint	£Good	£Fine	£N.Mint
1 ND cover available in 4 different colours	*$0.40*	*$1.20*	*$2.00*	£0.25	£0.75	£1.25
1 2nd printing ND	*$0.40*	*$1.20*	*$2.00*	£0.25	£0.75	£1.25
1 Limited Edition, ND (Sep 1990) - 5,000 copies exclusive to Diamond Distributors with gold embossed logo on card-stock cover: limited number on top left of cover	*$1.00*	*$3.00*	*$5.00*	£0.60	£1.80	£3.00
2-4 ND	*$0.40*	*$1.20*	*$2.00*	£0.25	£0.75	£1.25
Title Value:	*$3.00*	*$9.00*	*$15.00*	£1.85	£5.55	£9.25
Special Edition (of #1), runs in conjunction with regular series with additional art and embossed logo, 40pgs				£0.60	£1.80	£3.00
Trade Paperback (Sep 1991), reprints mini-series				£1.00	£3.00	£5.00

ALIEN WORLDS

Pacific/Eclipse; 1 Dec 1982-9 Jan 1985

(see Three Dimensional Alien Worlds)

	$Good	$Fine	$N.Mint	£Good	£Fine	£N.Mint
1 Al Williamson, Tim Conrad and Val Mayerik art featured	*$0.60*	*$1.80*	*$3.00*	£0.40	£1.20	£2.00
2 Aurora by Dave Stevens; Bruce Jones, Ken Steacy art; Stevens cover	*$0.60*	*$1.80*	*$3.00*	£0.40	£1.20	£2.00
3 Scott Hampton, Tom Yeates, Ken Steacy art; Bill Stout cover	*$0.60*	*$1.80*	*$3.00*	£0.40	£1.20	£2.00
4 Dave Stevens, Jeff Jones, Ken Steacy, Bo Hampton art; Stevens cover	*$0.60*	*$1.80*	*$3.00*	£0.40	£1.20	£2.00
5 John Bolton, Ken Steacy, Adolpho Buylla, Tom Yeates art; Bolton cover	*$0.60*	*$1.80*	*$3.00*	£0.40	£1.20	£2.00
6 Brunner/Mignola, Roy Krenkel, Arthur Suydam art; Brunner cover	*$0.60*	*$1.80*	*$3.00*	£0.40	£1.20	£2.00
7 Richard Corben, Brent Anderson, Gray Morrow, George Perez art; Corben cover	*$0.60*	*$1.80*	*$3.00*	£0.40	£1.20	£2.00
8 Al Williamson, Ken Steacy, Paul Rivoche art	*$0.60*	*$1.80*	*$3.00*	£0.40	£1.20	£2.00
9 Bo Hampton, Frank Brunner art; John Bolton cover	*$0.60*	*$1.80*	*$3.00*	£0.40	£1.20	£2.00
Title Value:	*$5.40*	*$16.20*	*$27.00*	£3.60	£10.80	£18.00

Note: all Non-Distributed on the news-stands in the U.K.
Note also: publication delays between issues #7-9.

ALIEN WORLDS (2ND SERIES)

Blackthorne; nn 1986

	$Good	$Fine	$N.Mint	£Good	£Fine	£N.Mint
nn ND scarce in the U.K. Book 1 Hardcover: Williamson, Conrad, Jones, George Perez, Bo Hampton, Yeates, Brent Anderson, Barry Windsor Smith, John Bolton reprints	*$3.00*	*$9.00*	*$15.00*	£2.00	£6.00	£10.00
nn ND Book 1 Softcover	*$1.50*	*$4.50*	*$7.50*	£1.00	£3.00	£5.00
Title Value:	*$4.50*	*$11.50*	*$22.50*	£3.00	£9.00	£15.00

ALIEN WORLDS GRAPHIC NOVEL

Eclipse; nn May 1988

(Eclipse Graphic Novel #22)

	$Good	$Fine	$N.Mint	£Good	£Fine	£N.Mint
nn ND Bruce Jones script, Reese, Shanower, Yeates, Wray art	*$0.90*	*$2.70*	*$4.50*	£0.60	£1.80	£3.00
Title Value:	*$0.90*	*$2.70*	*$4.50*	£0.60	£1.80	£3.00

Note: Bookshelf Format

ALIENS

Dark Horse,MS Film; 1 May 1988-6 1989

(see Dark Horse Presents #24)

	$Good	$Fine	$N.Mint	£Good	£Fine	£N.Mint
1 Mark Nelson art begins	*$4.50*	*$13.50*	*$22.50*	£3.00	£9.00	£15.00
1 2nd printing, new art inside cover	*$1.00*	*$3.00*	*$5.00*	£0.60	£1.80	£3.00
1 3rd printing	*$1.00*	*$3.00*	*$5.00*	£0.60	£1.80	£3.00
1 4th printing	*$0.80*	*$2.40*	*$4.00*	£0.50	£1.50	£2.50
1 5th printing	*$0.60*	*$1.80*	*$3.00*	£0.40	£1.20	£2.00
2	*$2.50*	*$7.50*	*$12.50*	£1.50	£4.50	£7.50
2 2nd printing	*$0.80*	*$2.40*	*$4.00*	£0.50	£1.50	£2.50
2 3rd printing	*$0.60*	*$1.80*	*$3.00*	£0.40	£1.20	£2.00
2 4th printing	*$0.50*	*$1.50*	*$2.50*	£0.30	£0.90	£1.50
3	*$1.50*	*$4.50*	*$7.50*	£1.00	£3.00	£5.00
3 2nd printing	*$0.60*	*$1.80*	*$3.00*	£0.40	£1.20	£2.00
3 3rd printing	*$0.50*	*$1.50*	*$2.50*	£0.30	£0.90	£1.50
4	*$1.20*	*$3.60*	*$6.00*	£0.80	£2.40	£4.00
4 2nd printing	*$0.60*	*$1.80*	*$3.00*	£0.40	£1.20	£2.00
4 3rd printing	*$0.50*	*$1.50*	*$2.50*	£0.30	£0.90	£1.50
5 scarce in the U.K.	*$1.20*	*$3.60*	*$6.00*	£1.00	£3.00	£5.00
5 2nd printing	*$0.60*	*$1.80*	*$3.00*	£0.40	£1.20	£2.00
5 3rd printing	*$0.50*	*$1.50*	*$2.50*	£0.30	£0.90	£1.50
6	*$1.00*	*$3.00*	*$5.00*	£0.70	£2.10	£3.50
Title Value:	*$20.50*	*$61.50*	*$102.50*	£13.40	£40.20	£67.00
Book 1, Trade paperback, reprints #1-6 plus story from Dark Horse Presents #24				£1.50	£4.50	£7.50
(2nd print - Oct 1991)				£1.40	£4.20	£7.00
Book 1, Hardcover (Apr 1990), reprints #1-6				£3.50	£10.50	£17.50
Signed and Numbered Edition, Hardcover (1,000 copies)				£6.00	£18.00	£30.00
Book 1 3rd printing (Apr 1996)				£1.80	£5.40	£9.00

Note: all Non-Distributed on the news-stands in the U.K.

ALIENS II

Dark Horse,MS Film; 1 Aug 1989-4 May 1990

	$Good	$Fine	$N.Mint	£Good	£Fine	£N.Mint
1 colour art begins	*$1.20*	*$3.60*	*$6.00*	£0.80	£2.40	£4.00
1 2nd printing	*$0.70*	*$2.10*	*$3.50*	£0.50	£1.50	£2.50
2	*$0.80*	*$2.40*	*$4.00*	£0.50	£1.50	£2.50
2 2nd printing	*$0.50*	*$1.50*	*$2.50*	£0.30	£0.90	£1.50
3	*$0.80*	*$2.40*	*$4.00*	£0.50	£1.50	£2.50
3 2nd printing	*$0.50*	*$1.50*	*$2.50*	£0.30	£0.90	£1.50
4	*$0.80*	*$2.40*	*$4.00*	£0.50	£1.50	£2.50
Title Value:	*$5.30*	*$15.90*	*$26.50*	£3.40	£10.20	£17.00
Aliens II Collection (Oct 1990) Trade paperback ND reprints the above series (3 printings)				£1.60	£4.80	£8.00
Signed, Limited Edition Hardcover (2,500 copies) ND signed and numbered, reprints #1-4				£6.00	£18.00	£30.00
Aliens: Nightmare Asylum (1996) Titan Books Trade paperback collects mini-series with new John Bolton cover				£2.00	£6.00	£10.00

Note: all Non-Distributed on the news-stands in the U.K.

ALIENS VS. PREDATOR

Dark Horse,MS; 0 Jul 1990; 1 Jun 1990-4 Dec 1990

	$Good	$Fine	$N.Mint	£Good	£Fine	£N.Mint
0 ND (Jul 1990), collects Dark Horse Presents #34-#36, new Mignola cover	*$2.00*	*$6.00*	*$10.00*	£0.80	£2.40	£4.00
1 ND story continues from Dark Horse Presents #34-#36 in colour, has similar art on front/back covers	*$1.50*	*$4.50*	*$7.50*	£0.80	£2.40	£4.00
1 2nd printing, ND has "Give Me Liberty" ad on back cover	*$0.50*	*$1.50*	*$2.50*	£0.30	£0.90	£1.50
2 ND	*$0.80*	*$2.40*	*$4.00*	£0.50	£1.50	£2.50
3 ND extra pages of story/art	*$0.80*	*$2.40*	*$4.00*	£0.50	£1.50	£2.50
4 ND	*$0.80*	*$2.40*	*$4.00*	£0.50	£1.50	£2.50
Title Value:	*$6.40*	*$19.20*	*$32.00*	£3.40	£10.20	£17.00
Aliens Vs. Predator Collection (Feb 1992) reprints Aliens Vs. Predator mini-series plus prequel stories from Dark Horse Presents #34-#36, all colour				£2.60	£7.80	£13.00
(2nd printing - Feb 1993, 3rd print - Aug 1994)				£2.50	£7.50	£12.50
Aliens Vs. Predator Hardcover Edition (Feb 1993) custom hardcover binding & slipcase; 1,000 copies				£10.00	£30.00	£50.00

Note: bi-monthly

ALIENS VS. PREDATOR: BOOTY SPECIAL

Dark Horse,OS; nn Jan 1996

	$Good	$Fine	$N.Mint	£Good	£Fine	£N.Mint
nn ND collects the 2pg installments orginally shown in Previews magazine	*$0.50*	*$1.50*	*$2.50*	£0.30	£0.90	£1.50
Title Value:	*$0.50*	*$1.50*	*$2.50*	£0.30	£0.90	£1.50

ALIENS VS. PREDATOR: DUEL

Dark Horse,MS; 1 Mar 1995-2 Apr 1995

	$Good	$Fine	$N.Mint	£Good	£Fine	£N.Mint
1-2 ND Javier Saltares and Jimmy Palmiotti art	*$0.50*	*$1.50*	*$2.50*	£0.30	£0.90	£1.50
Title Value:	*$1.00*	*$3.00*	*$5.00*	£0.60	£1.80	£3.00

ALIENS VS. PREDATOR: THE DEADLIEST OF THE SPECIES

Dark Horse,MS; 1 Jul 1993-12 Jul 1995

	$Good	$Fine	$N.Mint	£Good	£Fine	£N.Mint
1 ND Chris Claremont script, Guice and Beatty art begins; painted covers by John Bolton	*$0.60*	*$1.80*	*$3.00*	£0.35	£1.05	£1.75
1 Limited Edition, ND (Jul 1993) - silver foil embossed cover	*$3.00*	*$9.00*	*$15.00*	£1.50	£4.50	£7.50
2-12 ND	*$0.50*	*$1.50*	*$2.50*	£0.30	£0.90	£1.50
Title Value:	*$9.10*	*$27.30*	*$45.50*	£5.15	£15.45	£25.75

ALIENS VS. PREDATOR: WAR

Dark Horse,OS; 1 Apr 1995

	$Good	$Fine	$N.Mint	£Good	£Fine	£N.Mint
1 ND collects story from Dark Horse Insider #1-14 with additional art, cover by Richard Corben	*$0.50*	*$1.50*	*$2.50*	£0.30	£0.90	£1.50
Title Value:	*$0.50*	*$1.50*	*$2.50*	£0.30	£0.90	£1.50

ALIENS VS. PREDATOR: WAR (LIMITED SERIES)

Dark Horse,MS; 1 May 1995-4 Aug 1995

	$Good	$Fine	$N.Mint	£Good	£Fine	£N.Mint
1-4 ND Richard Corben covers	*$0.50*	*$1.50*	*$2.50*	£0.30	£0.90	£1.50
Title Value:	*$2.00*	*$6.00*	*$10.00*	£1.20	£3.60	£6.00

ALIENS, THE (CAPTAIN JOHNER AND...)

(see Captain Johner and the Aliens)

ALIENS: BERSERKER

Dark Horse,MS; 1 Jan 1995-4 Apr 1995

	$Good	$Fine	$N.Mint	£Good	£Fine	£N.Mint
1-4 ND John Wagner script	*$0.50*	*$1.50*	*$2.50*	£0.30	£0.90	£1.50
Title Value:	*$2.00*	*$6.00*	*$10.00*	£1.20	£3.60	£6.00

ALIENS: COLONIAL MARINES

Dark Horse,MS; 1 Jan 1993-10 Jun 1994

	$Good	$Fine	$N.Mint	£Good	£Fine	£N.Mint
1 ND painted covers by Robert Mentor begin	*$0.50*	*$1.50*	*$2.50*	£0.30	£0.90	£1.50
2-10 ND	*$0.50*	*$1.50*	*$2.50*	£0.30	£0.90	£1.50
Title Value:	*$5.00*	*$15.00*	*$25.00*	£3.00	£9.00	£15.00

ALIENS: EARTH ANGEL

Dark Horse,OS; 1 Aug 1994

	$Good	$Fine	$N.Mint	£Good	£Fine	£N.Mint
1 ND collects together the John Byrne strip from Previews magazine, new John Byrne cover	*$0.60*	*$1.80*	*$3.00*	£0.40	£1.20	£2.00

SOME INDEPENDENT COMICS MAY NOT HAVE APPEARED ALTHOUGH THEY WERE ADVERTISED AND SOLICITED.

	$Good	$Fine	$N.Mint	£Good	£Fine	£N.Mint
Title Value:	*$0.60*	*$1.80*	*$3.00*	£0.40	£1.20	£2.00
Aliens: Earth Angel Deluxe Hardcover Edition (Aug 1994) 24pg story plus 8pg interview with John Byrne; 1,000 copies randomly signed				£2.50	£7.50	£12.50

ALIENS: EARTH WAR

Dark Horse,MS; 1 Jun 1990-4 Oct 1990

	$Good	$Fine	$N.Mint	£Good	£Fine	£N.Mint
1 ND Sam Kieth art begins and John Bolton painted covers begin	*$1.20*	*$3.60*	*$6.00*	£0.70	£2.10	£3.50
1 2nd printing, ND has "Give Me Liberty" ad on back cover	*$0.50*	*$1.50*	*$2.50*	£0.30	£0.90	£1.50
2-3 ND	*$0.80*	*$2.40*	*$4.00*	£0.50	£1.50	£2.50
4 ND extra pages of story/art	*$0.80*	*$2.40*	*$4.00*	£0.50	£1.50	£2.50
Title Value:	*$4.10*	*$12.30*	*$20.50*	£2.50	£7.50	£12.50

Note: bi-monthly, colour interior art

	$Good	$Fine	$N.Mint	£Good	£Fine	£N.Mint
Earth War Collection (Sep 1991), reprints mini-series, cover painting by John Bolton				£1.60	£4.80	£8.00
Earth War Collection - Limited Edition (Feb 1992), new dust-jacket illustration by John Bolton, signed by Sam Kieth (2,000 copies)				£8.00	£24.00	£40.00

ALIENS: GENOCIDE

Dark Horse,MS; 1 Jan 1992-4 Apr 1992

	$Good	$Fine	$N.Mint	£Good	£Fine	£N.Mint
1 ND Arthur Suydam covers begin	*$0.50*	*$1.50*	*$2.50*	£0.30	£0.90	£1.50
2-3 ND	*$0.50*	*$1.50*	*$2.50*	£0.30	£0.90	£1.50
4 ND mini-poster of cover without text included	*$0.50*	*$1.50*	*$2.50*	£0.30	£0.90	£1.50
Title Value:	*$2.00*	*$6.00*	*$10.00*	£1.20	£3.60	£6.00
Aliens: Genocide Softcover Collection (Jan 1993) 112pgs, reprints issues #1-4				£1.70	£5.10	£8.50

ALIENS: HIVE

Dark Horse,MS; 1 Apr 1992-4 Jul 1992

	$Good	$Fine	$N.Mint	£Good	£Fine	£N.Mint
1-4 ND Kelley Jones art	*$0.50*	*$1.50*	*$2.50*	£0.30	£0.90	£1.50
Title Value:	*$2.00*	*$6.00*	*$10.00*	£1.20	£3.60	£6.00
Aliens: Hive Softcover Collection (Apr 1993) reprints issues #1-#4, painted cover by Dave Dorman				£1.75	£5.25	£8.75
Aliens: Hive Trade Paperback (Aug 1994) as above with new painted cover by Dave Dorman				£1.75	£5.25	£8.75

ALIENS: LABYRINTH

Dark Horse,MS; 1 Sep 1993-4 Jan 1994

	$Good	$Fine	$N.Mint	£Good	£Fine	£N.Mint
1-4 ND Jim Woodring & Kilian Plunkett	*$0.50*	*$1.50*	*$2.50*	£0.30	£0.90	£1.50
Title Value:	*$2.00*	*$6.00*	*$10.00*	£1.20	£3.60	£6.00
Aliens: Labyrinth (Jun 1995) Trade paperback reprints mini-series with new Kilian Plunkett cover				£2.40	£7.20	£12.00

ALIENS: MONDO HEAT

Dark Horse,OS; nn Feb 1996

	$Good	$Fine	$N.Mint	£Good	£Fine	£N.Mint
nn ND Herk Mondo from Aliens: Mondo Pest returns	*$0.50*	*$1.50*	*$2.50*	£0.30	£0.90	£1.50
Title Value:	*$0.50*	*$1.50*	*$2.50*	£0.30	£0.90	£1.50

ALIENS: MONDO PEST

Dark Horse,OS; 1 Mar 1995

	$Good	$Fine	$N.Mint	£Good	£Fine	£N.Mint
1 ND reprints stories from Dark Horse Comics #22-24 plus sketches	*$0.60*	*$1.80*	*$3.00*	£0.40	£1.20	£2.00
Title Value:	*$0.60*	*$1.80*	*$3.00*	£0.40	£1.20	£2.00

ALIENS: MUSIC OF THE SPEARS

Dark Horse,MS; 1 Jan 1994-4 Apr 1994

	$Good	$Fine	$N.Mint	£Good	£Fine	£N.Mint
1-4 ND Williamson, Hamilton and Bradstreet	*$0.50*	*$1.50*	*$2.50*	£0.30	£0.90	£1.50
Title Value:	*$2.00*	*$6.00*	*$10.00*	£1.20	£3.60	£6.00

ALIENS: NEWT'S TALE

Dark Horse,MS; 1 Jul 1992-2 Aug 1992

	$Good	$Fine	$N.Mint	£Good	£Fine	£N.Mint
1-2 ND John Bolton covers	*$0.90*	*$2.70*	*$4.50*	£0.60	£1.80	£3.00
Title Value:	*$1.80*	*$5.40*	*$9.00*	£1.20	£3.60	£6.00

ALIENS: ROGUE

Dark Horse,MS; 1 Apr 1993-4 Aug 1993

	$Good	$Fine	$N.Mint	£Good	£Fine	£N.Mint
1-4 ND	*$0.50*	*$1.50*	*$2.50*	£0.30	£0.90	£1.50
Title Value:	*$2.00*	*$6.00*	*$10.00*	£1.20	£3.60	£6.00
Aliens: Rogue (Aug 1994) Trade paperback reprints mini-series, painted cover by Nelson				£2.00	£6.00	£10.00

ALIENS: SACRIFICE

Dark Horse,OS; 1 May 1993

	$Good	$Fine	$N.Mint	£Good	£Fine	£N.Mint
1 ND 48pgs, squarebound, collects material originally published in U.K. Aliens title; Peter Milligan script, Paul Johnson art	*$0.90*	*$2.70*	*$4.50*	£0.60	£1.80	£3.00
Title Value:	*$0.90*	*$2.70*	*$4.50*	£0.60	£1.80	£3.00

ALIENS: SALVATION

Dark Horse,OS; 1 Nov 1993

	$Good	$Fine	$N.Mint	£Good	£Fine	£N.Mint
1 ND 48pgs, Dave Gibbons script, Mignola and Nowlan art	*$1.00*	*$3.00*	*$5.00*	£0.70	£2.10	£3.50
Title Value:	*$1.00*	*$3.00*	*$5.00*	£0.70	£2.10	£3.50

ALIENS: STRONGHOLD

Dark Horse,MS; 1 May 1994-4 Aug 1994

	$Good	$Fine	$N.Mint	£Good	£Fine	£N.Mint
1-4 ND	*$0.50*	*$1.50*	*$2.50*	£0.30	£0.90	£1.50
Title Value:	*$2.00*	*$6.00*	*$10.00*	£1.20	£3.60	£6.00
Aliens: Stronghold (Jun 1996) collects mini-series with new wraparound cover by Duncan Fegrado				£2.00	£6.00	£10.00

ALIENS: THE ILLUSTRATED STORY

Heavy Metal; nn 1979

	$Good	$Fine	$N.Mint	£Good	£Fine	£N.Mint
nn ND 56pgs, scarce in the U.K., Archie Goodwin script, Walt Simonson art	*$5.50*	*$16.50*	*$27.50*	£3.50	£10.50	£17.50
nn U.K. Edition , published by Futura (1979)	*$4.00*	*$12.00*	*$20.00*	£2.50	£7.50	£12.50
Title Value:	*$9.50*	*$30.50*	*$47.50*	£6.00	£18.00	£30.00

ALIENS: TRIBES HARDCOVER GRAPHIC NOVEL

Dark Horse,OS; nn Jan 1992

	$Good	$Fine	$N.Mint	£Good	£Fine	£N.Mint
1 ND Steve Bissette script, Dave Dorman art	*$4.50*	*$13.50*	*$22.50*	£3.00	£9.00	£15.00
Title Value:	*$4.50*	*$13.50*	*$22.50*	£3.00	£9.00	£15.00
Aliens: Tribes Softcover Graphic Novel (Apr 1993) softcover version of the above, Dave Dorman cover				£1.50	£4.50	£7.50

ALL-AMERICAN COMICS

National Periodical Publications; 1 Apr 1939-102 Oct 1948

(becomes All American Western #103-#126 then All American Men of War #127 onwards)

	$Good	$Fine	$N.Mint	£Good	£Fine	£N.Mint
1 anthology of "funnies" such as Scribbly and Mutt & Jeff begin plus adventure strips like Hop Harrigan	*$750.00*	*$2250.00*	*$6000.00*	£500.00	£1500.00	£4000.00
2	*$210.00*	*$640.00*	*$1500.00*	£140.00	£425.00	£1000.00
3-5	*$160.00*	*$490.00*	*$1150.00*	£110.00	£330.00	£770.00
6-7	*$135.00*	*$405.00*	*$950.00*	£90.00	£270.00	£635.00
8 Gary Concord the Ultra-Man begins	*$170.00*	*$510.00*	*$1375.00*	£115.00	£345.00	£920.00
9	*$115.00*	*$350.00*	*$825.00*	£77.50	£235.00	£550.00
10 Christmas cover	*$115.00*	*$350.00*	*$825.00*	£77.50	£235.00	£550.00
11-15 very scarce in the U.K.	*$110.00*	*$340.00*	*$800.00*	£75.00	£225.00	£535.00
16 very rare in the U.K., rare in the U.S. origin and 1st appearance Golden Age Green Lantern; estimated 40 extant copies in any condition; created/drawn by Martin Nodell, inspired by Aladdin's Lamp	*$5100.00*	*$15500.00*	*$62000.00*	£3500.00	£10600.00	£42500.00
[Rare in high grade - Very Fine+ or better] **[Prices may vary widely on this comic]**						
17 rare in the U.K, scarce in the U.S. 2nd appearance Green Lantern	*$1700.00*	*$5100.00*	*$13750.00*	£1150.00	£3450.00	£9250.00
[Very scarce in high grade - Very Fine+ or better]						
18 3rd appearance Green Lantern	*$1125.00*	*$3350.00*	*$9000.00*	£750.00	£2250.00	£6000.00
19 origin and 1st appearance Golden Age Atom, last Ultra Man	*$1750.00*	*$5200.00*	*$14000.00*	£1150.00	£3450.00	£9250.00
20 scarce in the U.K. 1st appearance Golden Age Red Tornado (Ma Hunkle), DC's first costumed heroine (see All Star Comics #5), part origin Green Lantern	*$540.00*	*$1625.00*	*$3800.00*	£360.00	£1075.00	£2550.00
21-23	*$285.00*	*$850.00*	*$2000.00*	£190.00	£570.00	£1350.00
24 origin Sargon the Sorcerer and Dr. Mid-Nite in illustrated text	*$350.00*	*$1050.00*	*$2450.00*	£235.00	£700.00	£1650.00
25 origin and 1st appearance Dr. Mid-Nite	*$1025.00*	*$3050.00*	*$9250.00*	£690.00	£2075.00	£6250.00
26 origin and 1st story appearance Sargon the Sorcerer	*$425.00*	*$1275.00*	*$3000.00*	£285.00	£850.00	£2000.00
27 1st appearance Doiby Dickles as Green Lantern's comic partner	*$425.00*	*$1275.00*	*$3000.00*	£285.00	£850.00	£2000.00
28-30	*$160.00*	*$480.00*	*$1125.00*	£105.00	£320.00	£750.00
31-40	*$130.00*	*$395.00*	*$930.00*	£87.50	£265.00	£625.00
41-46	*$110.00*	*$330.00*	*$775.00*	£75.00	£225.00	£525.00
47 non-Green Lantern cover (Hop Harrigan)	*$110.00*	*$330.00*	*$775.00*	£75.00	£225.00	£525.00
48-50	*$110.00*	*$330.00*	*$775.00*	£75.00	£225.00	£525.00
51	*$77.50*	*$235.00*	*$550.00*	£50.00	£150.00	£350.00
52 intro The Silhouette	*$77.50*	*$235.00*	*$550.00*	£50.00	£150.00	£350.00
53-60	*$77.50*	*$235.00*	*$550.00*	£50.00	£150.00	£350.00
61 origin and 1st appearance Solomon Grundy	*$500.00*	*$1500.00*	*$4000.00*	£330.00	£1000.00	£2675.00
62-69	*$87.50*	*$265.00*	*$625.00*	£60.00	£180.00	£420.00
70 Kubert art	*$87.50*	*$265.00*	*$625.00*	£60.00	£180.00	£420.00
71-76	*$80.00*	*$245.00*	*$575.00*	£55.00	£165.00	£385.00
77 non-Green Lantern cover (Hop Harrigan)	*$80.00*	*$245.00*	*$575.00*	£55.00	£165.00	£385.00
78	*$80.00*	*$245.00*	*$575.00*	£55.00	£165.00	£385.00
79 non-Green Lantern cover (Mutt & Jeff)	*$80.00*	*$245.00*	*$575.00*	£55.00	£165.00	£385.00
80-82	*$80.00*	*$245.00*	*$575.00*	£55.00	£165.00	£385.00
83 non-Green Lantern cover (Mutt & Jeff)	*$80.00*	*$245.00*	*$575.00*	£55.00	£165.00	£385.00
84-88	*$80.00*	*$245.00*	*$575.00*	£55.00	£165.00	£385.00
89 origin and 1st appearance of The Harlequin	*$110.00*	*$330.00*	*$775.00*	£72.50	£220.00	£520.00
90 origin and 1st appearance The Icicle	*$77.50*	*$235.00*	*$550.00*	£52.50	£155.00	£370.00
91-95	*$77.50*	*$235.00*	*$550.00*	£52.50	£155.00	£370.00
96 Alex Toth cover and art featured	*$77.50*	*$235.00*	*$550.00*	£52.50	£155.00	£370.00
97 Alex Toth cover	*$77.50*	*$235.00*	*$550.00*	£52.50	£155.00	£370.00
98 Alex Toth cover and art featured	*$77.50*	*$235.00*	*$550.00*	£52.50	£155.00	£370.00
99 Alex Toth cover and art featured, last Green Lantern cover	*$77.50*	*$235.00*	*$550.00*	£52.50	£155.00	£370.00
100 scarce in the U.K. 1st appearance Johnny Thunder (Western character) by Alex Toth, Toth cover	*$190.00*	*$570.00*	*$1350.00*	£125.00	£385.00	£900.00
101 scarce in the U.K. Alex Toth cover and art	*$125.00*	*$385.00*	*$900.00*	£85.00	£255.00	£600.00
102 very scarce in the U.K. Alex Toth cover and art						

	$Good	$Fine	$N.Mint	£Good	£Fine	£N.Mint
	$210.00	*$640.00*	*$1500.00*	£140.00	£425.00	£1000.00
Title Value:	*$23747.50*	*$71665.00*	*$202050.00*	£16017.50	£48190.00	£136130.00

Note: though not officially distributed in the U.K., some copies **may** have come over through American G.I's or U.S. relatives of U.K. citizens

ALL-AMERICAN MEN OF WAR

National Periodical Publications; 1 (#128) Oct/Nov 1952-117 Oct 1966
(see All American Western)

Issue	$Good	$Fine	$N.Mint	£Good	£Fine	£N.Mint
1 Krigstein art; numbered #128 on cover which is a continuation of All American Western title	*$60.00*	*$180.00*	*$425.00*	£41.00	£120.00	£285.00
2-3 no number on cover, Krigstein art	*$52.50*	*$160.00*	*$375.00*	£36.00	£105.00	£250.00
4 no number on cover	*$52.50*	*$160.00*	*$375.00*	£36.00	£105.00	£250.00
5 1st time a number appears on the cover	*$52.50*	*$160.00*	*$375.00*	£36.00	£105.00	£250.00
6-10	*$37.00*	*$110.00*	*$260.00*	£25.00	£75.00	£175.00
11-18	*$34.00*	*$100.00*	*$235.00*	£22.50	£67.50	£160.00
19-28	*$22.50*	*$67.50*	*$160.00*	£15.50	£47.00	£110.00
29-30 Wood art	*$26.00*	*$77.50*	*$185.00*	£17.50	£52.50	£125.00
31	*$20.00*	*$60.00*	*$140.00*	£13.50	£41.00	£95.00
32 Wood art	*$26.00*	*$77.50*	*$185.00*	£17.50	£52.50	£125.00
33-40	*$20.00*	*$60.00*	*$140.00*	£13.50	£41.00	£95.00
41-50	*$16.00*	*$49.00*	*$115.00*	£11.00	£33.00	£77.50
51-66	*$12.50*	*$39.00*	*$90.00*	£7.75	£23.50	£55.00
67 1st appearance of Gunner & Sarge	*$28.00*	*$82.50*	*$220.00*	£17.50	£52.50	£140.00
68-70	*$12.00*	*$36.00*	*$85.00*	£7.00	£21.00	£50.00
71-75	*$8.50*	*$26.00*	*$60.00*	£4.60	£13.50	£32.50
1st official distribution in the U.K.						
76-80 scarce in the U.K.	*$8.50*	*$26.00*	*$60.00*	£4.60	£13.50	£32.50
81 scarce in the U.K.	*$7.00*	*$21.00*	*$50.00*	£4.25	£12.50	£30.00
82 scarce in the U.K. 1st appearance of Johnny Cloud	*$12.00*	*$36.00*	*$85.00*	£6.25	£19.00	£45.00
83-88 scarce in the U.K.	*$7.00*	*$21.00*	*$50.00*	£4.25	£12.50	£30.00
89-99	*$5.00*	*$15.00*	*$35.00*	£2.55	£7.50	£18.00
100	*$5.00*	*$15.00*	*$35.00*	£2.85	£8.50	£20.00
101-117	*$3.55*	*$10.50*	*$25.00*	£1.90	£5.75	£13.50
Title Value:	*$1900.35*	*$5723.50*	*$13465.00*	£1236.70	£3703.25	£8742.50

NEW FEATURES

Balloon Buster in 112-114, 116. Johnny Cloud in 82-111, 115, 117.

ALL-AMERICAN WESTERN

National Periodical Publications; 103 Nov 1948-127 Aug/Sep 1952
(formerly All-American Comics #1-#102; becomes All American Men of War #127 onwards)

Issue	$Good	$Fine	$N.Mint	£Good	£Fine	£N.Mint
103 Johnny Thunder by Alex Toth continues from All-American Comics	*$57.50*	*$175.00*	*$475.00*	£40.00	£120.00	£320.00
104 Kubert art featured	*$36.00*	*$105.00*	*$250.00*	£24.00	£72.50	£170.00
105 Kubert art featured	*$31.00*	*$90.00*	*$215.00*	£20.50	£60.00	£145.00
106	*$22.50*	*$67.50*	*$160.00*	£15.50	£47.00	£110.00
107 Kubert art featured	*$31.00*	*$90.00*	*$215.00*	£20.50	£60.00	£145.00
108-110	*$22.50*	*$67.50*	*$160.00*	£15.50	£47.00	£110.00
111 Kubert art	*$25.00*	*$75.00*	*$175.00*	£17.00	£50.00	£120.00
112	*$22.50*	*$67.50*	*$160.00*	£15.50	£47.00	£110.00
113 1st appearance Swift Deer	*$29.00*	*$85.00*	*$200.00*	£19.00	£57.50	£135.00
114-116 Kubert art	*$25.00*	*$75.00*	*$175.00*	£17.00	£50.00	£120.00
117-120	*$17.50*	*$52.50*	*$125.00*	£12.00	£36.00	£85.00
121 Kubert art	*$17.50*	*$52.50*	*$125.00*	£12.00	£36.00	£85.00
122-126	*$17.50*	*$52.50*	*$125.00*	£12.00	£36.00	£85.00
127 cover title changes to "All American Men of War"	*$105.00*	*$320.00*	*$750.00*	£70.00	£210.00	£500.00
Title Value:	*$677.00*	*$2027.50*	*$4855.00*	£459.50	£1375.00	£3295.00

Note: all Non-Distributed on the news-stands in the U.K.

ALL-FLASH

National Periodical Publications; 1 Summer 1941-32 Dec/Jan 1947/1948

Issue	$Good	$Fine	$N.Mint	£Good	£Fine	£N.Mint
1 origin of the Golden Age Flash retold	*$1375.00*	*$4150.00*	*$12500.00*	£910.00	£2750.00	£8250.00
[Scarce in high grade - Very Fine+ or better]						
2	*$390.00*	*$1175.00*	*$2750.00*	£260.00	£790.00	£1850.00
3-4	*$185.00*	*$550.00*	*$1300.00*	£120.00	£370.00	£870.00
5	*$130.00*	*$395.00*	*$925.00*	£87.50	£265.00	£620.00
6-10	*$115.00*	*$350.00*	*$825.00*	£77.50	£235.00	£550.00
11-13	*$95.00*	*$285.00*	*$675.00*	£62.50	£190.00	£450.00
14 Golden Age Green Lantern appears	*$115.00*	*$350.00*	*$825.00*	£77.50	£235.00	£550.00
15-20	*$87.50*	*$265.00*	*$625.00*	£60.00	£180.00	£420.00
21-31	*$75.00*	*$225.00*	*$525.00*	£50.00	£150.00	£350.00
32 very scarce in the U.K., scarce in the U.S. origin and 1st appearance of The Fiddler	*$105.00*	*$320.00*	*$750.00*	£70.00	£210.00	£500.00
Title Value:	*$4695.00*	*$14160.00*	*$36025.00*	£3130.00	£9465.00	£23980.00

Note: issues #1-#5 titled "All Flash Quarterly". Bi-monthly thereafter.
Note also: though not officially distributed on the news-stands in the U.K., some copies **may** have come over through American G.I's or U.S. relatives of U.K. citizens

ALL-NEW COLLECTOR'S EDITION

DC Comics,Tabloid; C-53 Jan 1978 - C-56, C-58, C-60, C-62 1979
(see Famous First Edition, Limited Collector's Edition)

Issue	$Good	$Fine	$N.Mint	£Good	£Fine	£N.Mint
C-53, ND 72pgs, Rudolph the Red-Nosed Reindeer	*$0.50*	*$1.50*	*$3.00*	£0.40	£1.25	£2.50
C-54, ND 72pgs, Superman vs. Wonder Woman	*$1.00*	*$3.00*	*$6.00*	£0.80	£2.50	£5.00
C-55, ND 72pgs, Superboy & The Legion of Super-Heroes	*$1.25*	*$3.75*	*$7.50*	£1.25	£3.75	£7.50
C-56, ND 72pgs, Superman vs. Muhammed Ali	*$1.25*	*$3.75*	*$7.50*	£1.25	£3.75	£7.50
C-58, ND 72pgs, Superman vs. Shazam	*$1.00*	*$3.00*	*$6.00*	£0.80	£2.50	£5.00
C-60, ND 64pgs, Rudolph the Red-Nosed Reindeer	*$0.50*	*$1.50*	*$3.00*	£0.40	£1.25	£2.50
C-62, distributed in the U.K. 64pgs, Superman: The Movie	*$0.50*	*$1.50*	*$3.00*	£0.40	£1.25	£2.50
Title Value:	*$6.00*	*$18.00*	*$36.00*	£5.30	£16.25	£32.50

Note: owing to their size, original mail packaging and problems with display, truly near mint copies are very scarce in both the U.S and the U.K.

ALL-OUT WAR

DC Comics; 1 Sep/Oct 1979-6 Jul/Aug 1980

Issue	$Good	$Fine	$N.Mint	£Good	£Fine	£N.Mint
1 ND 68pgs	*$0.40*	*$1.25*	*$2.50*	£0.25	£0.75	£1.50
2-6 ND 68pgs	*$0.30*	*$1.00*	*$2.00*	£0.20	£0.60	£1.25
Title Value:	*$1.90*	*$6.25*	*$12.50*	£1.25	£3.75	£7.75

FEATURES

Viking Commando in all, plus various war stories.

ALL-STAR ARCHIVES

DC Comics; 1 Jul 1992-2 1993

Issue	$Good	$Fine	$N.Mint	£Good	£Fine	£N.Mint
1 ND 272pgs, reprints All Star Comics #3-#6 featuring the first cases of the Justice Society of America	*$10.00*	*$30.00*	*$50.00*	£6.50	£19.50	£32.50
2 ND 256pgs, reprints All Star Comics #7-#10	*$9.00*	*$27.00*	*$45.00*	£6.00	£18.00	£30.00
Title Value:	*$19.00*	*$57.00*	*$95.00*	£12.50	£37.50	£62.50

ALL-STAR COMICS

National Periodical Publications; 1 Summer 1940-57 Feb/Mar 1951

Issue	$Good	$Fine	$N.Mint	£Good	£Fine	£N.Mint
1 The Flash, Hourman, Hawkman, Spectre, Sandman begin	*$1375.00*	*$4150.00*	*$12500.00*	£920.00	£2750.00	£8350.00
2 Green Lantern feature begins	*$650.00*	*$1950.00*	*$5250.00*	£435.00	£1300.00	£3500.00
3 scarce in the U.K. origin and 1st appearance Justice Society of America (see Famous First Edition F-7); historically important as the 1st major super-team	*$2900.00*	*$8700.00*	*$35000.00*	£1925.00	£5800.00	£23350.00
[Prices may vary widely on this comic]						
4	*$710.00*	*$2125.00*	*$5000.00*	£445.00	£1325.00	£3125.00
5 1st appearance Hawkgirl, DC's first costumed super-heroine (see All-American Comics #20)	*$670.00*	*$2025.00*	*$4750.00*	£450.00	£1350.00	£3175.00
6 Johnny Thunder joins Justice Society of America	*$390.00*	*$1175.00*	*$2750.00*	£260.00	£790.00	£1850.00
7 Superman, Batman cameo appearance	*$460.00*	*$1375.00*	*$3250.00*	£310.00	£930.00	£2175.00
8 origin and 1st appearance Wonder Woman (8pg origin added to comic)	*$3000.00*	*$9000.00*	*$30000.00*	£2000.00	£6000.00	£20000.00
9-10	*$355.00*	*$1050.00*	*$2500.00*	£225.00	£670.00	£1575.00
11-12	*$340.00*	*$1025.00*	*$2400.00*	£225.00	£680.00	£1600.00
13-14	*$325.00*	*$980.00*	*$2300.00*	£220.00	£660.00	£1550.00
15 1st appearance and origin Brain Wave	*$325.00*	*$980.00*	*$2300.00*	£220.00	£660.00	£1550.00
16-20	*$235.00*	*$710.00*	*$1675.00*	£160.00	£480.00	£1125.00
21	*$210.00*	*$640.00*	*$1500.00*	£140.00	£425.00	£1000.00
22 classic flag cover	*$210.00*	*$640.00*	*$1500.00*	£140.00	£425.00	£1000.00
23 1st appearance and origin Psycho Pirate	*$210.00*	*$640.00*	*$1500.00*	£140.00	£425.00	£1000.00
24	*$220.00*	*$660.00*	*$1550.00*	£150.00	£450.00	£1050.00
25	*$175.00*	*$530.00*	*$1250.00*	£120.00	£360.00	£850.00
26 robot cover	*$175.00*	*$530.00*	*$1250.00*	£120.00	£360.00	£850.00
27	*$175.00*	*$530.00*	*$1250.00*	£120.00	£360.00	£850.00
28-32	*$160.00*	*$480.00*	*$1125.00*	£105.00	£320.00	£750.00
33 Solomon Grundy appears	*$310.00*	*$930.00*	*$2500.00*	£205.00	£620.00	£1675.00
34-35	*$135.00*	*$415.00*	*$975.00*	£92.50	£275.00	£650.00
36 Superman and Batman appear, 1st time they appear together in the same story (pre World's Finest Adventures from #71 onwards)	*$325.00*	*$970.00*	*$2600.00*	£215.00	£650.00	£1750.00
37 origin Injustice Society	*$195.00*	*$580.00*	*$1375.00*	£130.00	£390.00	£920.00
38 Black Canary appears; classic Alex Toth cover	*$210.00*	*$640.00*	*$1500.00*	£140.00	£425.00	£1000.00
39-40	*$135.00*	*$405.00*	*$950.00*	£90.00	£270.00	£635.00
41 Black Canary joins Justice Society of America	*$140.00*	*$425.00*	*$1000.00*	£95.00	£285.00	£675.00
42 new costumes for Hawkman and Atom, cover concept used for Justice League of America #6	*$135.00*	*$405.00*	*$950.00*	£90.00	£270.00	£635.00
43 cover concept used for Brave and the Bold #29	*$135.00*	*$405.00*	*$950.00*	£90.00	£270.00	£635.00
44-49	*$135.00*	*$405.00*	*$950.00*	£90.00	£270.00	£635.00
50 part Frank Frazetta art	*$160.00*	*$480.00*	*$1125.00*	£105.00	£320.00	£750.00
51-56	*$130.00*	*$395.00*	*$925.00*	£87.50	£265.00	£620.00
57 very scarce in the U.K. part Kubert art	*$175.00*	*$530.00*	*$1250.00*	£115.00	£355.00	£835.00
Title Value:	*$19785.00*	*$59515.00*	*$167350.00*	£13175.00	£39615.00	£111475.00

Note: none of these comics were officially distributed into the U.K. but some **may** have come over during the War Years with American G.I's that were stationed here or through American relatives of U.K. residents.

VERY GENERAL PERCENTAGE CONVERSION CHART WHICH MAY BE USED TO CALCULATE LOW AND INBETWEEN GRADES:

ALL-STAR COMICS (2ND SERIES)

DC Comics; 58 Jan/Feb 1976-74 Sep/Oct 1978

(numbering continues from Golden Age All Star Comics)

Issue	$Good	$Fine	$N.Mint	£Good	£Fine	£N.Mint
58 Flash, Hawkman, Dr.Mid-Nite, Robin, Green Lantern, Dr.Fate, Wildcat, Star-Spangled Kid (Justice Society of America characters); 1st appearance Power Girl, Wood art	$0.50	$1.50	$3.00	£0.40	£1.25	£2.50
59 ND Wood art	$0.30	$1.00	$2.00	£0.30	£1.00	£2.00
60 Wood art	$0.30	$1.00	$2.00	£0.25	£0.75	£1.50
61 ND Wood art	$0.25	$0.75	$1.50	£0.30	£1.00	£2.00
62 scarce in the U.K.	$0.25	$0.75	$1.50	£0.25	£0.75	£1.50
63 Wood art	$0.25	$0.75	$1.50	£0.25	£0.75	£1.50
64 scarce in the U.K.	$0.25	$0.75	$1.50	£0.25	£0.75	£1.50
65 ND Wood art	$0.25	$0.75	$1.50	£0.30	£1.00	£2.00
66 scarce in the U.K.	$0.25	$0.75	$1.50	£0.25	£0.75	£1.50
67-69 Wood art	$0.25	$0.75	$1.50	£0.20	£0.60	£1.25
70 scarce in the U.K.	$0.25	$0.75	$1.50	£0.25	£0.75	£1.50
71-73 Wood art	$0.25	$0.75	$1.50	£0.20	£0.60	£1.25
74 scarce in the U.K. 44pgs	$0.30	$1.00	$2.00	£0.30	£1.00	£2.00
Title Value:	$4.65	$14.25	$28.50	£4.30	£13.35	£27.00

FEATURES

Justice Society of America and Super Squad in all. (See DC Special 29 & Adventure Comics #461-466)

ALL-STAR INDEX, THE

ICG/Eclipse; 1 Feb 1987

Issue	$Good	$Fine	$N.Mint	£Good	£Fine	£N.Mint
1 ND scarce in the U.K. information and colour cover repros All Star Comics #1-4 and DC Special #29 plus detailed character indexes	$0.80	$2.40	$4.00	£0.50	£1.50	£2.50
Title Value:	$0.80	$2.40	$4.00	£0.50	£1.50	£2.50

ALL-STAR SQUADRON

DC Comics; 1 Sep 1981-67 Mar 1987

(see Justice League of America #193)

Issue	$Good	$Fine	$N.Mint	£Good	£Fine	£N.Mint
1 original Dr.Mid-Nite, Atom, Plastic Man Hawkman, Johnny Quick, Liberty Belle, Shining Knight begin; origin Robotman retold	$0.30	$0.90	$1.50	£0.20	£0.60	£1.00
2	$0.25	$0.75	$1.25	£0.15	£0.45	£0.75
3 Solomon Grundy appears	$0.25	$0.75	$1.25	£0.15	£0.45	£0.75
4 Justice Society of America appears	$0.25	$0.75	$1.25	£0.15	£0.45	£0.75
5 1st new Firebrand	$0.25	$0.75	$1.25	£0.15	£0.45	£0.75
6-11	$0.25	$0.75	$1.25	£0.15	£0.45	£0.75
12 Golden Age Hawkman origin retold	$0.20	$0.60	$1.00	£0.15	£0.45	£0.75
13-14	$0.20	$0.60	$1.00	£0.15	£0.45	£0.75
15 Masters of the Universe insert, Justice League of America/Justice Society of America appear	$0.20	$0.60	$1.00	£0.15	£0.45	£0.75
16-20	$0.20	$0.60	$1.00	£0.15	£0.45	£0.75
21-22	$0.15	$0.45	$0.75	£0.10	£0.35	£0.60
23 origin Amazing-Man	$0.15	$0.45	$0.75	£0.10	£0.35	£0.60
24 Golden Age Batman and Robin appear	$0.15	$0.45	$0.75	£0.10	£0.35	£0.60
25 1st appearance Infinity Inc.	$0.30	$0.90	$1.50	£0.20	£0.60	£1.00
26 origin Infinity Inc., Golden Age Batman and Robin appear, ties in with Annual #2	$0.15	$0.45	$0.75	£0.15	£0.45	£0.75
27-28 Justice Society of America appears	$0.15	$0.45	$0.75	£0.10	£0.35	£0.60
29 Seven Soldiers of Victory appear	$0.15	$0.45	$0.75	£0.10	£0.35	£0.60
30 Justice Society of America appears	$0.15	$0.45	$0.75	£0.10	£0.35	£0.60
31 Freedom Fighters (Earth-X) origin begins, Golden Age Batman appears	$0.15	$0.45	$0.75	£0.10	£0.35	£0.60
32-34 Freedom Fighters appear	$0.15	$0.45	$0.75	£0.10	£0.35	£0.60
35 Freedom Fighters origin concludes, death of Red Bee, Batman appears (1 panel)	$0.15	$0.45	$0.75	£0.10	£0.35	£0.60
36-37 Shazam appears	$0.15	$0.45	$0.75	£0.10	£0.35	£0.60
38-40	$0.15	$0.45	$0.75	£0.10	£0.35	£0.60
41 origin Starman	$0.15	$0.45	$0.75	£0.10	£0.35	£0.60
42-46	$0.15	$0.45	$0.75	£0.10	£0.35	£0.60
47 origin Dr.Fate, early Todd McFarlane pencils	$0.60	$1.80	$3.00	£0.30	£0.90	£1.50
48 Shining Knight and Blackhawk appear	$0.15	$0.45	$0.75	£0.10	£0.35	£0.60
49 Dr. Occult returns (after nearly 50 years!)	$0.15	$0.45	$0.75	£0.10	£0.35	£0.60
50 DS, Crisis X-over	$0.30	$0.90	$1.50	£0.20	£0.60	£1.00
51 Crisis X-over	$0.25	$0.75	$1.25	£0.15	£0.45	£0.75
52 Crisis X-over, Shazam appears	$0.25	$0.75	$1.25	£0.15	£0.45	£0.75
53-55 Crisis X-over	$0.25	$0.75	$1.25	£0.15	£0.45	£0.75
56 Crisis X-over, Seven Soldiers of Victory appear	$0.25	$0.75	$1.25	£0.15	£0.45	£0.75
57 Atom, Starman and Wonder Woman spotlighted	$0.15	$0.45	$0.75	£0.10	£0.35	£0.60
58-59	$0.15	$0.45	$0.75	£0.10	£0.35	£0.60
60 unofficial Crisis X-over, Justice Sociiety of America appear	$0.15	$0.45	$0.75	£0.10	£0.35	£0.60
61 origin Liberty Belle	$0.15	$0.45	$0.75	£0.10	£0.35	£0.60
62 origin Shining Knight	$0.15	$0.45	$0.75	£0.10	£0.35	£0.60
63 origin Robotman	$0.15	$0.45	$0.75	£0.10	£0.35	£0.60
64 Wayne Boring (Golden and Silver Age Superman artist) pencils	$0.15	$0.45	$0.75	£0.10	£0.35	£0.60
65 origin Johnny Quick	$0.15	$0.45	$0.75	£0.10	£0.35	£0.60
66 origin Tarantula	$0.15	$0.45	$0.75	£0.10	£0.35	£0.60
67 Justice Society of America's 1st case	$0.15	$0.45	$0.75	£0.10	£0.35	£0.60
Title Value:	$13.00	$39.00	$64.75	£8.50	£27.35	£46.20

Note: JSA appears in 15, 19, 27, 28, 30, 36, 37, 51, 60, 67. Seven Soldiers of Victory appear in 29, 56.

ARTISTS

Jerry Ordway inks in 1-14. Pencils in 23-26. Art in 19-22. Ordway covers 19-26, 29-31, 33-39, 41, 60. Joe Kubert covers 2,7-18.

ALL-STAR SQUADRON ANNUAL

DC Comics; 1 Nov 1982-3 Sep 1984

Issue	$Good	$Fine	$N.Mint	£Good	£Fine	£N.Mint
1 Golden Age Atom, Guardian, Wildcat origins retold	$0.30	$0.90	$1.50	£0.20	£0.60	£1.00
2 Infinity Inc. X-over, Jerry Ordway cover and art						

All Star Comics #22

All Star Western #1

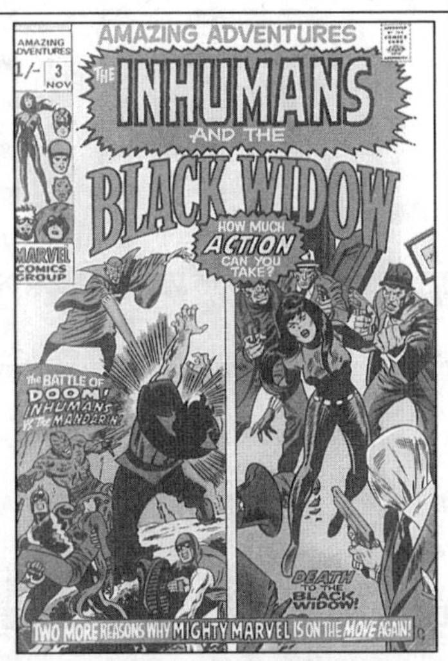

Amazing Adventures (2nd series) #3

Issue	$Good	$Fine	$N.Mint	£Good	£Fine	£N.Mint
	$0.30	$0.90	$1.50	£0.20	£0.60	£1.00
3 Batman and Justice Society of America appear	$0.30	$0.90	$1.50	£0.20	£0.60	£1.00
Title Value:	$0.90	$2.70	$4.50	£0.60	£1.80	£3.00

ALL-STAR WESTERN

National Periodical Publications; 58 Apr/May 1951-119 Jun/Jul 1961
(formerly All Star Comics #1-57)

Issue	$Good	$Fine	$N.Mint	£Good	£Fine	£N.Mint
58 Strong Bow Indian Warrior and Trigger Twins begin	$41.00	$120.00	$325.00	£28.00	£82.50	£220.00
59	$22.50	$67.50	$160.00	£15.50	£47.00	£110.00
60 Infantino cover	$22.50	$67.50	$160.00	£15.50	£47.00	£110.00
61-64 Toth art	$17.50	$52.50	$125.00	£12.00	£36.00	£85.00
65 Infantino cover	$17.50	$52.50	$125.00	£12.00	£36.00	£85.00
66	$17.50	$52.50	$125.00	£12.00	£36.00	£85.00
67 Johnny Thunder by Gil Kane	$22.50	$67.50	$160.00	£15.50	£47.00	£110.00
68-81	$10.50	$32.00	$75.00	£7.00	£21.00	£50.00
82-98	$9.25	$28.00	$65.00	£5.50	£17.00	£40.00
99 Frazetta art (reprint)	$10.00	$30.00	$70.00	£6.00	£18.00	£42.50
100	$10.00	$30.00	$70.00	£6.25	£19.00	£45.00
101-107	$6.25	$19.00	$45.00	£3.90	£11.50	£27.50
108 origin Johnny Thunder	$17.50	$52.50	$125.00	£11.00	£34.00	£80.00
109	$5.50	$17.00	$40.00	£3.90	£11.50	£27.50
1st official distribution in the U.K.						
110-116 rare in the U.K.	$5.50	$17.00	$40.00	£3.90	£11.50	£27.50
117 rare in the U.K. origin of Super-Chief	$10.50	$32.00	$75.00	£6.25	£19.00	£45.00
118-119 rare in the U.K.	$5.50	$17.00	$40.00	£3.90	£11.50	£27.50
Title Value:	$664.50	$2009.00	$4765.00	£433.80	£1308.00	£3120.00

ALL-STAR WESTERN (2ND SERIES)

DC Comics; 1 Aug/Sep 1970-11 Apr/May 1972

Issue	$Good	$Fine	$N.Mint	£Good	£Fine	£N.Mint
1 reprints (Pow Wow Smith)	$2.00	$6.00	$12.00	£0.65	£2.00	£4.00
2 scarce in the U.K. 1st El Diablo, 1st Outlaw, Williamson inks	$0.80	$2.50	$5.00	£0.40	£1.25	£2.50
3 origin El Diablo	$0.80	$2.50	$5.00	£0.30	£1.00	£2.00
4-8	$0.80	$2.50	$5.00	£0.25	£0.75	£1.50
9 52pgs, Frazetta reprint	$0.80	$2.50	$5.00	£0.30	£1.00	£2.00
10 52pgs, 1st appearance Jonah Hex	$17.50	$52.50	$125.00	£9.25	£28.00	£65.00
11 2nd appearance Jonah Hex	$9.25	$28.00	$65.00	£3.55	£10.50	£25.00
Title Value:	$35.15	$106.50	$242.00	£15.70	£47.50	£108.00

FEATURES
Billy the Kid in 6-8. El Diablo in 2-5,7,10,11. Jonah Hex in 10,11. Outlaw in 2-8.
REPRINT FEATURES
Bat Lash in 9-11. Buffalo Bill in 7-9. Davy Crockett in 7,8. Pow-Wow Smith in 1,8,9,11.

ALLEGRA

Image; 1 Aug 1996-present

Issue	$Good	$Fine	$N.Mint	£Good	£Fine	£N.Mint
1 ND Steven Seagle script, Scott Clark and Chris Carlson art begins	$0.50	$1.50	$2.50	£0.30	£0.90	£1.50
2-3 ND	$0.50	$1.50	$2.50	£0.30	£0.90	£1.50
Title Value:	$1.50	$4.50	$7.50	£0.90	£2.70	£4.50

ALLIANCE, THE

Image; 1 Aug 1995-3 Dec 1995

Issue	$Good	$Fine	$N.Mint	£Good	£Fine	£N.Mint
1 ND Jim Valentino script/art	$0.50	$1.50	$2.50	£0.30	£0.90	£1.50
1 Variant Cover Edition ND	$0.50	$1.50	$2.50	£0.30	£0.90	£1.50
2 ND Jim Valentino script/art	$0.50	$1.50	$2.50	£0.30	£0.90	£1.50
2 Variant Cover Edition ND	$0.50	$1.50	$2.50	£0.30	£0.90	£1.50
3 ND Jim Valentino script/art	$0.50	$1.50	$2.50	£0.30	£0.90	£1.50
3 Variant Cover Edition ND	$0.50	$1.50	$2.50	£0.30	£0.90	£1.50
Title Value:	$3.00	$9.00	$15.00	£1.80	£5.40	£9.00

ALLIANCES – A MAGIC: THE GATHERING SPECIAL EDITION

Acclaim Comics,OS; nn Oct 1996

Issue	$Good	$Fine	$N.Mint	£Good	£Fine	£N.Mint
nn ND, 64pgs	$1.20	$3.60	$6.00	£0.80	£2.40	£4.00
Title Value:	$1.20	$3.60	$6.00	£0.80	£2.40	£4.00

ALLIES, THE

Image; 1 Oct 1995-3 Dec 1995

Issue	$Good	$Fine	$N.Mint	£Good	£Fine	£N.Mint
1 ND Diehard, Glory, Roman, Superpatriot and Battlestone begin; Len Wein script, Fabian Ribiero art	$0.50	$1.50	$2.50	£0.30	£0.90	£1.50
2-3 ND	$0.50	$1.50	$2.50	£0.30	£0.90	£1.50
Title Value:	$1.50	$4.50	$7.50	£0.90	£2.70	£4.50

ALMURIC GRAPHIC NOVEL

Dark Horse,OS; nn Aug 1991

Issue	$Good	$Fine	$N.Mint	£Good	£Fine	£N.Mint
nn ND reprints from Marvel's Epic Illustrated; Roy Thomas script, Tim Conrad art	$1.80	$5.25	$9.00	£1.20	£3.60	£6.00
Title Value:	$1.80	$5.25	$9.00	£1.20	£3.60	£6.00

ALONE IN THE SHADE SPECIAL

Alchemy Studios; 1 1990

Issue	$Good	$Fine	$N.Mint	£Good	£Fine	£N.Mint
1 ND b&w	$0.25	$0.75	$1.25	£0.15	£0.45	£0.75
Title Value:	$0.25	$0.75	$1.25	£0.15	£0.45	£0.75

ALPHA CENTURION SPECIAL

DC Comics,OS; 1 Sep 1996

Issue	$Good	$Fine	$N.Mint	£Good	£Fine	£N.Mint
1 ND 48pgs, Stuart Immonen cover and art	$0.60	$1.80	$3.00	£0.40	£1.20	£2.00
Title Value:	$0.60	$1.80	$3.00	£0.40	£1.20	£2.00

ALPHA FLIGHT

Marvel Comics Group; 1 Aug 1983-130 Mar 1994
(see X-Men #120, X-Men vs Alpha Flight)

Issue	$Good	$Fine	$N.Mint	£Good	£Fine	£N.Mint
1 ND 52pgs, John Byrne art begins	$0.40	$1.20	$2.00	£0.50	£1.50	£2.50
2 origin Marrina and Alpha Flight, John Byrne art	$0.30	$0.90	$1.50	£0.30	£0.90	£1.50
3 origin Marrina and Alpha Flight continued, Sub-Mariner and Sue Richards guest-star, John Byrne art	$0.30	$0.90	$1.50	£0.30	£0.90	£1.50
4-5 John Byrne art	$0.30	$0.90	$1.50	£0.30	£0.90	£1.50
6 Dr. Strange guest-stars, John Byrne art	$0.30	$0.90	$1.50	£0.30	£0.90	£1.50
7-8 John Byrne art	$0.30	$0.90	$1.50	£0.30	£0.90	£1.50
9 origin Sasquatch, Wolverine guest-stars, John Byrne art	$0.30	$0.90	$1.50	£0.30	£0.90	£1.50
10 John Byrne art	$0.30	$0.90	$1.50	£0.30	£0.90	£1.50
11 LD in the U.K. origin Sasquatch concluded, John Byrne art	$0.30	$0.90	$1.50	£0.35	£1.05	£1.75
12 DS Guardian dies, John Byrne art	$0.30	$0.90	$1.50	£0.35	£1.05	£1.75
13 Wolverine appears, John Byrne art	$0.40	$1.20	$2.00	£0.35	£1.05	£1.75
14 Sub-Mariner appears, John Byrne art	$0.30	$0.90	$1.50	£0.30	£0.90	£1.50
15 LD in the U.K. Sub-Mariner vs. Marrina, John Byrne art	$0.30	$0.90	$1.50	£0.30	£0.90	£1.50
16 Sub-Mariner appears, Wolverine appears (1pg), John Byrne art	$0.30	$0.90	$1.50	£0.30	£0.90	£1.50
17 Wolverine and X-Men appear, John Byrne art	$0.40	$1.20	$2.00	£0.35	£1.05	£1.75
18-22 John Byrne art	$0.30	$0.90	$1.50	£0.25	£0.75	£1.25
23 LD in the U.K. Sasquatch battles Sasquatch, John Byrne art	$0.30	$0.90	$1.50	£0.30	£0.90	£1.50
24 DS John Byrne art	$0.30	$0.90	$1.50	£0.30	£0.90	£1.50
25-27 John Byrne art	$0.30	$0.90	$1.50	£0.25	£0.75	£1.25
28 Secret Wars II X-over, Hulk appears, last John Byrne art	$0.30	$0.90	$1.50	£0.25	£0.75	£1.25
29 LD in the U.K. Alpha Flight vs. Hulk	$0.30	$0.90	$1.50	£0.30	£0.90	£1.50
30 LD in the U.K.	$0.30	$0.90	$1.50	£0.30	£0.90	£1.50
31 LD in the U.K.	$0.25	$0.75	$1.25	£0.25	£0.75	£1.25
32 LD in the U.K. 1st appearance new Vindicator	$0.25	$0.75	$1.25	£0.25	£0.75	£1.25
33 LD in the U.K. Wolverine/X-Men appear	$0.50	$1.50	$2.50	£0.40	£1.20	£2.00
34 Wolverine/X-Men appear; 1st full appearance of Lady Deathstroke, part origin Wolverine's claws and adamantium skeleton	$0.50	$1.50	$2.50	£0.40	£1.20	£2.00
35 Wolverine appears	$0.25	$0.75	$1.25	£0.25	£0.75	£1.25
36 Avengers and Dr. Strange appear	$0.25	$0.75	$1.25	£0.20	£0.60	£1.00
37	$0.25	$0.75	$1.25	£0.20	£0.60	£1.00
38 Sub-Mariner appears	$0.25	$0.75	$1.25	£0.20	£0.60	£1.00
39 Sub-Mariner and Avengers appear, Whilce Portacio inks	$0.25	$0.75	$1.25	£0.20	£0.60	£1.00
40	$0.25	$0.75	$1.25	£0.20	£0.60	£1.00
41	$0.20	$0.60	$1.00	£0.15	£0.45	£0.75
42 Whilce Portacio inks	$0.20	$0.60	$1.00	£0.15	£0.45	£0.75
43 Sentinels appear	$0.20	$0.60	$1.00	£0.15	£0.45	£0.75
44-46	$0.20	$0.60	$1.00	£0.15	£0.45	£0.75
47-49 LD in the U.K.	$0.20	$0.60	$1.00	£0.20	£0.60	£1.00
50 DS Whilce Portacio co-artist	$0.30	$0.90	$1.50	£0.25	£0.75	£1.25
51 Jim Lee art (his 1st on a mutant comic), Whilce Portacio inks	$1.00	$3.00	$5.00	£0.60	£1.80	£3.00
52 ND scarce in the U.K. Wolverine appears	$0.80	$2.40	$4.00	£0.50	£1.50	£2.50
53 ND scarce in the U.K. Wolverine appears, Jim Lee art	$0.80	$2.40	$4.00	£0.60	£1.80	£3.00
54 ND Whilce Portacio inks	$0.30	$0.90	$1.50	£0.25	£0.75	£1.25
55-60 ND Jim Lee art	$0.30	$0.90	$1.50	£0.25	£0.75	£1.25
61 ND paper stock changes to a more glossy format, Jim Lee art	$0.30	$0.90	$1.50	£0.20	£0.60	£1.00
62 ND Jim Lee art	$0.30	$0.90	$1.50	£0.20	£0.60	£1.00
63 ND	$0.30	$0.90	$1.50	£0.20	£0.60	£1.00
64 ND Jim Lee art	$0.30	$0.90	$1.50	£0.20	£0.60	£1.00

TRADE PAPERBACKS, GRAPHIC NOVELS AND OTHER COLLECTIONS ARE PRICED IN POUNDS STERLING ONLY. CONVERT AT 1.5 FOR DOLLARS.

Issue	$Good	$Fine	$N.Mint	£Good	£Fine	£N.Mint
65-73 ND	$0.30	$0.90	$1.50	£0.20	£0.60	£1.00
74 ND Spiderman appears: Wolverine in last panel	$0.30	$0.90	$1.50	£0.20	£0.60	£1.00
75 ND 48pgs, Wolverine appears	$0.30	$0.90	$1.50	£0.20	£0.60	£1.00
76-78 ND	$0.30	$0.90	$1.50	£0.20	£0.60	£1.00
79-80 ND Acts of Vengeance tie-in	$0.30	$0.90	$1.50	£0.20	£0.60	£1.00
81-82 ND Quest for Northstar	$0.30	$0.90	$1.50	£0.20	£0.60	£1.00
83-86 ND	$0.30	$0.90	$1.50	£0.20	£0.60	£1.00
87-90 ND Building Blocks story; new direction for title, Wolverine appears	$0.50	$1.50	$2.50	£0.25	£0.75	£1.25
91-92 ND	$0.30	$0.90	$1.50	£0.20	£0.60	£1.00
93-94 ND Fantastic Four appear	$0.30	$0.90	$1.50	£0.20	£0.60	£1.00
95 ND line-up changes	$0.30	$0.90	$1.50	£0.20	£0.60	£1.00
96 ND Michael Golden cover	$0.30	$0.90	$1.50	£0.20	£0.60	£1.00
97-99 ND The Final Option story	$0.30	$0.90	$1.50	£0.20	£0.60	£1.00
100 ND DS The Final Option concludes, Avengers and Galactus appear	$0.40	$1.20	$2.00	£0.25	£0.75	£1.25
101 ND Dr. Strange and Avengers appear	$0.30	$0.90	$1.50	£0.20	£0.60	£1.00
102-103 ND	$0.30	$0.90	$1.50	£0.20	£0.60	£1.00
104 ND new costumes	$0.30	$0.90	$1.50	£0.20	£0.60	£1.00
105 ND	$0.30	$0.90	$1.50	£0.20	£0.60	£1.00
106 ND Northstar declares his homosexuality (see Flash [2nd Series] #53)	$0.70	$2.10	$3.50	£0.50	£1.50	£2.50
106 2nd printing ND	$0.30	$0.90	$1.50	£0.25	£0.75	£1.25
107 ND X-Factor appear	$0.30	$0.90	$1.50	£0.20	£0.60	£1.00
108-109 ND	$0.30	$0.90	$1.50	£0.20	£0.60	£1.00
110-112 ND Infinity War X-over	$0.30	$0.90	$1.50	£0.20	£0.60	£1.00
113 ND Infinity War aftermath	$0.30	$0.90	$1.50	£0.20	£0.60	£1.00
114 ND	$0.30	$0.90	$1.50	£0.20	£0.60	£1.00
115 ND 1st appearance of Wyre	$0.30	$0.90	$1.50	£0.20	£0.60	£1.00
116-119 ND	$0.30	$0.90	$1.50	£0.20	£0.60	£1.00
120 ND pre-bagged 10th anniversary issue; 11"x17" poster	$0.40	$1.20	$2.00	£0.25	£0.75	£1.25
121 ND Spiderman guest-stars, Wolverine cameo	$0.30	$0.90	$1.50	£0.20	£0.60	£1.00
122-126 ND Infinity Crusade X-over	$0.30	$0.90	$1.50	£0.20	£0.60	£1.00
127 ND Infinity Crusade epilogue	$0.30	$0.90	$1.50	£0.20	£0.60	£1.00
128-129 ND	$0.30	$0.90	$1.50	£0.20	£0.60	£1.00
130 ND 48pgs, leads into Northstar mini-series	$0.40	$1.20	$2.00	£0.25	£0.75	£1.25
Title Value:	$41.90	$125.70	$209.50	£31.60	£94.80	£158.00

ALPHA FLIGHT ANNUAL

Marvel Comics Group; 1 Sep 1986-2 Dec 1987

Issue	$Good	$Fine	$N.Mint	£Good	£Fine	£N.Mint
1-2 ND	$0.40	$1.20	$2.00	£0.25	£0.75	£1.25
Title Value:	$0.80	$2.40	$4.00	£0.50	£1.50	£2.50

ALPHA FLIGHT SPECIAL

Marvel Comics Group,MS; 1 Jul 1991-4 Oct 1991

Issue	$Good	$Fine	$N.Mint	£Good	£Fine	£N.Mint
1-4 ND	$0.30	$0.90	$1.50	£0.25	£0.75	£1.25
Title Value:	$1.20	$3.60	$6.00	£1.00	£3.00	£5.00

Note: reprints Alpha Flight #97-100, one per issue with altered logo, as a market-tester to establish viability of returning title to news-stand distribution

ALPHA FLIGHT SPECIAL (2ND SERIES)

Marvel Comics Group,OS; 1 Jun 1992

Issue	$Good	$Fine	$N.Mint	£Good	£Fine	£N.Mint
1 ND 48pgs, origin Alpha Flight	$0.40	$1.20	$2.00	£0.30	£0.90	£1.50
Title Value:	$0.40	$1.20	$2.00	£0.30	£0.90	£1.50

ALPHA ILLUSTRATED

Alpha Productions; 1 1991

Issue	$Good	$Fine	$N.Mint	£Good	£Fine	£N.Mint
1 ND 48pgs, black and white anthology	$0.60	$1.80	$3.00	£0.40	£1.20	£2.00
Title Value:	$0.60	$1.80	$3.00	£0.40	£1.20	£2.00

ALPHA WAVE

Darkline Comics; 1 1987

Issue	$Good	$Fine	$N.Mint	£Good	£Fine	£N.Mint
1 ND colour	$0.40	$1.20	$2.00	£0.25	£0.75	£1.25
Title Value:	$0.40	$1.20	$2.00	£0.25	£0.75	£1.25

ALTER EGO

First,MS; 1 May 1986-4 Nov 1986

Issue	$Good	$Fine	$N.Mint	£Good	£Fine	£N.Mint
1-4 ND Roy Thomas script, Ron Harris art; colour	$0.40	$1.20	$2.00	£0.25	£0.75	£1.25
Title Value:	$1.60	$4.80	$8.00	£1.00	£3.00	£5.00

ALTERNIVERSE VISIONS: THE X-MEN TRADE PAPERBACK

Marvel Comics Group,OS; nn Jun 1996

Issue	$Good	$Fine	$N.Mint	£Good	£Fine	£N.Mint
nn ND collection of What If reprints featuring X-Men	$3.20	$9.50	$16.00	£2.00	£6.00	£10.00
Title Value:	$3.20	$9.50	$16.00	£2.00	£6.00	£10.00

AMALGAM AGE OF COMICS: THE DC COMICS COLLECTION

DC Comics,OS; nn Nov 1996

Issue	$Good	$Fine	$N.Mint	£Good	£Fine	£N.Mint
nn ND 160pgs, collects the six DC Amalgam one-shots; Legends of the Dark Claw, Super-Soldier, Amazon, JLX, Assassins and Dr. Strangefate	$2.60	$7.75	$13.00	£1.70	£5.00	£8.50
Title Value:	$2.60	$7.75	$13.00	£1.70	£5.00	£8.50

AMALGAM AGE OF COMICS: THE MARVEL COMICS COLLECTION

Marvel Comics Group,OS; nn Nov 1996

Issue	$Good	$Fine	$N.Mint	£Good	£Fine	£N.Mint
nn ND collects the six Marvel Amalgam one-shots; Spider-Boy, Magneto & The Magnetic Men, Bullets & Bracelets, Speed Demon, Bruce Wayne Agent of Shield and X-Patrol	$2.60	$7.75	$13.00	£1.70	£5.00	£8.50
Title Value:	$2.60	$7.75	$13.00	£1.70	£5.00	£8.50

AMAZING ADULT FANTASY

Marvel Comics Group; 7 Dec 1961-14 Jul 1962

(formerly Amazing Adventures, becomes Amazing Fantasy)

Issue	$Good	$Fine	$N.Mint	£Good	£Fine	£N.Mint
7	$87.50	$265.00	$625.00	£52.50	£160.00	£375.00
8 last 10 cents issue	$70.00	$210.00	$500.00	£43.00	£125.00	£300.00
9-13	$55.00	$170.00	$400.00	£37.00	£110.00	£260.00
14 "The Boy Who Could Fly" - the first mutant story in the Marvel Universe?	$67.50	$200.00	$475.00	£39.00	£115.00	£275.00
Title Value:	$500.00	$1525.00	$3600.00	£319.50	£950.00	£2250.00

Note: all have Ditko art throughout. Ditko covers #7-13

AMAZING ADVENTURES

Marvel Comics Group; 1 Jun 1961-6 Nov 1961

(becomes Amazing Adult Fantasy)

Issue	$Good	$Fine	$N.Mint	£Good	£Fine	£N.Mint
1 origin Dr. Droom (1st Marvel Age Super-Hero); see Weird Wonder Tales #19	$130.00	$400.00	$1200.00	£87.50	£265.00	£800.00
2 Dr. Droom	$60.00	$180.00	$480.00	£38.00	£110.00	£300.00
3-4 Dr. Droom	$50.00	$150.00	$410.00	£31.00	£92.50	£250.00
5 no Dr. Droom	$50.00	$150.00	$400.00	£30.00	£90.00	£240.00
6 Dr. Droom	$50.00	$150.00	$410.00	£31.00	£92.50	£250.00
Title Value:	$390.00	$1180.00	$3310.00	£248.50	£742.50	£2090.00

Note: Ditko, Kirby art 1-6. Kirby covers 1-6.

AMAZING ADVENTURES (2ND SERIES)

Marvel Comics Group; 1 Aug 1970-39 Aug 1976

Issue	$Good	$Fine	$N.Mint	£Good	£Fine	£N.Mint
1 ND Inhumans/Black Widow begin	$5.75	$17.50	$35.00	£1.65	£5.00	£10.00
2 ND Fantastic Four appear in Inhumans story	$1.65	$5.00	$10.00	£0.80	£2.50	£5.00
3-4	$1.65	$5.00	$10.00	£0.55	£1.75	£3.50
5-7 Neal Adams art	$1.65	$5.00	$10.00	£0.90	£2.75	£5.50
8 last Black Widow; Avengers appear in Inhumans story; Thor vs. Black Bolt, Neal Adams art	$1.65	$5.00	$10.00	£0.90	£2.75	£5.50
9 very scarce in the U.K. Magneto vs. Inhumans	$1.65	$5.00	$10.00	£1.00	£3.00	£6.00
10 scarce in the U.K. X-over Avengers #95, Magneto vs. Inhumans	$1.65	$5.00	$10.00	£0.80	£2.50	£5.00
11 scarce in the U.K. Beast series begins, X-Men appear	$5.75	$17.50	$35.00	£2.05	£6.25	£12.50
12 scarce in the U.K.	$1.30	$4.00	$8.00	£0.80	£2.50	£5.00
13 scarce in the U.K. Brotherhood of Evil Mutants appear	$1.30	$4.00	$8.00	£0.80	£2.50	£5.00
14 scarce in the U.K. Iron Man appears	$1.30	$4.00	$8.00	£0.80	£2.50	£5.00
15 scarce in the U.K. Angel appears	$1.30	$4.00	$8.00	£0.80	£2.50	£5.00
16 scarce in the U.K. Beast battles Juggernaut; Spiderman and Avengers appear on cover only	$1.30	$4.00	$8.00	£0.80	£2.50	£5.00
17 scarce in the U.K. cover and 2pgs Jim Starlin art, rest edited reprint of X-Men #49, #53; origin Beast, X-Men and Magneto appear	$1.30	$4.00	$8.00	£0.80	£2.50	£5.00
18 1st War of the Worlds/Killraven, Neal Adams and Howard Chaykin art	$1.65	$5.00	$10.00	£1.00	£3.00	£6.00
19 Howard Chaykin art	$1.00	$3.00	$6.00	£0.50	£1.50	£3.00
20	$1.00	$3.00	$6.00	£0.40	£1.25	£2.50
21-22	$0.80	$2.50	$5.00	£0.30	£1.00	£2.00
23-25 ND	$0.80	$2.50	$5.00	£0.50	£1.50	£3.00
26-30	$0.80	$2.50	$5.00	£0.30	£1.00	£2.00
31-34	$0.80	$2.50	$5.00	£0.25	£0.75	£1.50
35 Keith Giffen art (his first in comics?)	$0.80	$2.50	$5.00	£0.25	£0.75	£1.50
36-37	$0.80	$2.50	$5.00	£0.25	£0.75	£1.50
38 Man-Thing, Iron Man, Dr. Strange cameos, U.S. President Gerald Ford appears, Keith Giffen art	$0.80	$2.50	$5.00	£0.25	£0.75	£1.50
39 Keith Giffen inks	$0.80	$2.50	$5.00	£0.25	£0.75	£1.50
Title Value:	$53.00	$162.50	$325.00	£23.55	£72.75	£145.50

Note: issues 11-17 very often have ink-staining along one or more edges.

ARTISTS

Kirby in 1-4. Ploog in 12. P.Craig Russell in 33, 39. Adams covers 6-8

FEATURES

Inhumans in 1-10. Black Widow in 1-8. Beast in 11-17 (17 part reprint). War of the Worlds (Killraven) in 18-28; Killraven 29-39.

AMAZING ADVENTURES (3RD SERIES)

Marvel Comics Group; 1 Dec 1979-14 Jan 1981

Issue	$Good	$Fine	$N.Mint	£Good	£Fine	£N.Mint
1 ND reprints first half of X-Men #1	$1.00	$3.00	$5.00	£0.70	£2.10	£3.50
2 ND reprints second half of X-Men #1						

	$Good	$Fine	$N.Mint	£Good	£Fine	£N.Mint
	$0.80	$2.40	$4.00	£0.50	£1.50	£2.50
3-4 ND reprints X-Men #2	$0.60	$1.80	$3.00	£0.40	£1.20	£2.00
5 ND reprints X-Men #3	$0.60	$1.80	$3.00	£0.40	£1.20	£2.00
6 ND reprints X-Men #3	$0.50	$1.50	$2.50	£0.30	£0.90	£1.50
7-8 ND reprints X-Men #4	$0.50	$1.50	$2.50	£0.30	£0.90	£1.50
9 ND reprints X-Men #5, Steranko back-up reprint	$0.50	$1.50	$2.50	£0.30	£0.90	£1.50
10 ND reprints X-Men #5	$0.50	$1.50	$2.50	£0.30	£0.90	£1.50
11-12 ND reprints X-Men #6	$0.50	$1.50	$2.50	£0.30	£0.90	£1.50
13 ND reprints X-Men #7	$0.50	$1.50	$2.50	£0.30	£0.90	£1.50
14 ND reprints X-Men #8	$0.50	$1.50	$2.50	£0.30	£0.90	£1.50
Title Value:	$8.10	$24.30	$40.50	£5.10	£15.30	£25.50

Note: issues 1-12 have reprinted back-up features. Selected issues re-draw the original X-Men covers from 1-8. These are noted as follows in brackets: 1(1), 4(2), 5(3), 7(4), 10(5), 12(6), 13(7), 14(8).

AMAZING ADVENTURES (4TH SERIES)

Marvel Comics Group,OS; 1 Jul 1988

	$Good	$Fine	$N.Mint	£Good	£Fine	£N.Mint
1 ND 64pgs, squarebound, art by Mayerik, Golden and Ridgway	$0.80	$2.40	$4.00	£0.50	£1.50	£2.50
Title Value:	$0.80	$2.40	$4.00	£0.50	£1.50	£2.50

AMAZING COMICS PREMIERES

Amazing Publishing; 1 1987-5 Aug 1987

	$Good	$Fine	$N.Mint	£Good	£Fine	£N.Mint
1 ND Ninja Bots; black and white begins	$0.30	$0.90	$1.50	£0.20	£0.60	£1.00
2 ND Untouchabots	$0.30	$0.90	$1.50	£0.20	£0.60	£1.00
3 ND Shadowalker and the Ghost Chasers	$0.30	$0.90	$1.50	£0.20	£0.60	£1.00
4 ND The Great American Murder Bar; 10pgs Sam Kieth art, Sam Kieth cover	$0.40	$1.20	$2.00	£0.25	£0.75	£1.25
5 ND Friends; 5pgs Ron Lim art, Ron Lim cover art; 1st appearance of Legends of the Stargrazers	$0.30	$0.90	$1.50	£0.20	£0.60	£1.00
Title Value:	$1.60	$4.80	$8.00	£1.05	£3.15	£5.25

AMAZING CYNICALMAN

Eclipse,OS; 1 Jun 1987

	$Good	$Fine	$N.Mint	£Good	£Fine	£N.Mint
1 ND Matt Feazell art	$0.30	$0.90	$1.50	£0.20	£0.60	£1.00
Title Value:	$0.30	$0.90	$1.50	£0.20	£0.60	£1.00

AMAZING FANTASY

Marvel Comics Group; 15 Aug 1962; 16 Dec 1995-18 Mar 1996

(formerly Amazing Adult Fantasy)

	$Good	$Fine	$N.Mint	£Good	£Fine	£N.Mint
15 origin and 1st appearance of Spiderman by Stan Lee and Steve Ditko, Jack Kirby/Steve Ditko cover (alternative cover version can be found in Spiderman index no.1)	$1750.00	$5200.00	$30000.00	£880.00	£2600.00	£15000.00
[Prices may vary widely on this comic] **[Very scarce in high grade - Very Fine+ or better]**						
15 Marvel Milestone Edition, ND (Mar 1992), reprints original issue with ads, silver border around cover	$0.60	$1.80	$3.00	£0.40	£1.20	£2.00
16 ND Kurt Busiek script, Paul Lee painted art; Spiderman's adventures days after his origin; UV coated cover	$0.80	$2.40	$4.00	£0.50	£1.50	£2.50
17-18 ND Kurt Busiek script, Paul Lee painted art; UV coated cover	$0.80	$2.40	$4.00	£0.50	£1.50	£2.50
Title Value:	$1753.00	$5209.00	$30015.00	£881.90	£2605.70	£15009.50

AMAZING HIGH ADVENTURE

Marvel Comics Group; 1 Aug 1984-5 Dec 1986

	$Good	$Fine	$N.Mint	£Good	£Fine	£N.Mint
1 ND Severin art	$0.50	$1.50	$2.50	£0.30	£0.90	£1.50
2 ND Paul Smith art, Williamson inks	$0.50	$1.50	$2.50	£0.30	£0.90	£1.50
3 ND Mike Mignola art	$0.50	$1.50	$2.50	£0.30	£0.90	£1.50
4 ND John Bolton art	$0.50	$1.50	$2.50	£0.30	£0.90	£1.50
5 ND scarce in the U.K. Bissette and Ridgway art, Bolton cover	$0.50	$1.50	$2.50	£0.30	£0.90	£1.50
Title Value:	$2.50	$7.50	$12.50	£1.50	£4.50	£7.50

Note: all Baxter paper.

AMAZING SCARLET SPIDER

Marvel Comics Group; 1 Nov 1995-2 Jan 1996

	$Good	$Fine	$N.Mint	£Good	£Fine	£N.Mint
1 ND J.M. DeMatteis script, Mark Bagley and Larry Mahlstedt art, continued in Scarlet Spider #1; metallic ink cover	$0.40	$1.20	$2.00	£0.25	£0.75	£1.25
2 ND continued in Scarlet Spider #2	$0.40	$1.20	$2.00	£0.25	£0.75	£1.25
Title Value:	$0.80	$2.40	$4.00	£0.50	£1.50	£2.50

AMAZING SPIDERMAN '96

Marvel Comics Group,OS; nn Oct 1996

	$Good	$Fine	$N.Mint	£Good	£Fine	£N.Mint
nn ND 64pgs, Kraven the Hunter appears	$0.60	$1.80	$3.00	£0.40	£1.20	£2.00
Title Value:	$0.60	$1.80	$3.00	£0.40	£1.20	£2.00

AMAZING SPIDERMAN COLLECTION

Marvel Comics Group,MS; 1 May 1995-4 Aug 1995

	$Good	$Fine	$N.Mint	£Good	£Fine	£N.Mint
1-4 ND reprints the set of Fleer Spiderman '93 trading cards	$0.60	$1.80	$3.00	£0.40	£1.20	£2.00
Title Value:	$2.40	$7.20	$12.00	£1.60	£4.80	£8.00

AMAZING SPIDERMAN SUPER SIZE SPECIAL

Marvel Comics Group; 1 Jun 1995

	$Good	$Fine	$N.Mint	£Good	£Fine	£N.Mint
1 ND 64pgs, Planet of Symbiotes part 1, continued in Spiderman Super Size Special; Dave Hoover art	$0.80	$2.40	$4.00	£0.50	£1.50	£2.50
Title Value:	$0.80	$2.40	$4.00	£0.50	£1.50	£2.50

AMAZING SPIDERMAN, THE

Marvel Comics Group; 1 Mar 1963-406 Oct 1995; 407 Jan 1996-present

(see Amazing Fantasy, Deadly Foes of.., Marvel Fanfare, Marvel Graphic Novel, Marvel Special Edition, Marvel Tales, Marvel Team Up, Marvel Treasury Edition, Official Index to.., Sensational Spiderman, Spectacular Spiderman, Spiderman Digest, Spiderman vs. Wolverine, Spidey Super Stories, Superman vs. Spiderman, Web of Spiderman)

	$Good	$Fine	$N.Mint	£Good	£Fine	£N.Mint
1 retells origin, Fantastic Four appear, intro J. Jonah Jameson, The Chameleon, Steve Ditko art begins (ends #38); Jack Kirby cover	$1450.00	$4400.00	$22000.00	£800.00	£2400.00	£12000.00
[Prices may vary widely on this comic]						
1 Marvel Milestone Edition, ND (Dec 1992), reprints original issue with ads	$0.50	$1.50	$2.50	£0.30	£0.90	£1.50
1 Reprint, ND very scarce in the U.K. (1966)	$25.00	$75.00	$175.00	£14.00	£43.00	£100.00
1 Reprint with Golden Record, ND very rare in the U.K to form complete sealed package	$38.00	$110.00	$300.00	£21.50	£65.00	£175.00
2 1st appearance Vulture, 1st appearance The Tinkerer	$300.00	$900.00	$3000.00	£170.00	£510.00	£1700.00
3 1st appearance Dr. Octopus, Human Torch cameo	$220.00	$660.00	$2000.00	£125.00	£380.00	£1150.00
3 Marvel Milestone Edition, ND (Mar 1995) - metallic ink cover	$0.60	$1.80	$3.00	£0.40	£1.20	£2.00
4 less common in the U.K. 1st appearance Betty Brant and Liz Allen, origin and 1st appearance The Sandman	$175.00	$530.00	$1600.00	£100.00	£300.00	£900.00
5 Dr. Doom appears (1st encounter with Spiderman)	$155.00	$465.00	$1400.00	£90.00	£275.00	£825.00
6 1st appearance The Lizard	$125.00	$380.00	$1150.00	£77.50	£230.00	£700.00
7 2nd appearance The Vulture	$87.50	$265.00	$800.00	£52.50	£155.00	£475.00
8 scarce in the U.K. (Jan 1964), Fantastic Four X-over (in back-up story)	$87.50	$265.00	$800.00	£57.50	£175.00	£525.00
9 origin and 1st appearance Electro	$92.50	$280.00	$850.00	£60.00	£180.00	£550.00
10 1st appearance Big Man and the Enforcers	$82.50	$250.00	$750.00	£50.00	£150.00	£450.00
11 2nd appearance Dr. Octopus	$70.00	$210.00	$500.00	£43.00	£125.00	£300.00
12 3rd appearance Dr. Octopus; Spiderman unmasked by Dr. Octopus	$70.00	$210.00	$500.00	£43.00	£125.00	£300.00
13 1st appearance Mysterio	$80.00	$245.00	$575.00	£50.00	£150.00	£350.00
14 1st appearance of the original Green Goblin (Norman Osborn), Hulk appears	$155.00	$465.00	$1400.00	£85.00	£255.00	£775.00
15 origin and 1st appearance Kraven the Hunter, 1st mention Mary Jane Watson though unseen	$70.00	$210.00	$500.00	£39.00	£115.00	£275.00
16 Daredevil vs. Spiderman (see Daredevil #16/17), 4th ever appearance of Daredevil (in original costume)	$50.00	$150.00	$350.00	£29.00	£85.00	£200.00
17 less common in the U.K. 2nd appearance Green Goblin	$75.00	$225.00	$525.00	£46.00	£135.00	£325.00
18 rare in the U.K. Fantastic Four appear, 1st appearance Ned Leeds (later Hobgoblin), Green Goblin cameo (3 panels thus 3rd ever appearance)	$50.00	$150.00	$350.00	£32.00	£95.00	£225.00
19 rare in the U.K. Human Torch appears, 1st appearance Scorpion (not in costume)	$43.00	$125.00	$300.00	£29.00	£85.00	£200.00
20 very scarce in the U.K., scarce in the U.S. (Jan 1965), origin and 1st appearance The Scorpion	$46.00	$135.00	$325.00	£29.00	£85.00	£200.00
21 2nd appearance The Beetle (see Strange Tales #123)	$32.00	$95.00	$225.00	£20.00	£60.00	£140.00
22 1st appearance Princess Python	$32.00	$95.00	$225.00	£20.00	£60.00	£140.00
23 4th appearance Green Goblin	$43.00	$125.00	$300.00	£25.00	£75.00	£175.00
24 2nd appearance Mysterio, Sandman and Vulture cameos	$27.00	$80.00	$190.00	£15.50	£47.00	£110.00
25 1st Mary Jane Watson? cameo only, face unseen..., 1st appearance Spider-Slayer	$34.00	$100.00	$235.00	£17.50	£52.50	£125.00
26 1st appearance Crimemaster, 5th appearance Green Goblin	$32.00	$95.00	$225.00	£18.50	£55.00	£130.00
27 Green Goblin cover and story	$31.00	$90.00	$215.00	£16.00	£49.00	£115.00
28 origin and 1st appearance Molten Man; Peter Parker graduates	$41.00	$120.00	$325.00	£25.00	£75.00	£200.00
[Very scarce in high grade - Very Fine+ or better]						
29 scarce in the U.K. 2nd appearance Scorpion	$21.00	$62.50	$150.00	£13.50	£41.00	£95.00
30 1st appearance The Cat (not to be confused with Tigra who was previously called The Cat)	$21.00	$62.50	$150.00	£12.50	£39.00	£90.00
31 less common in the U.K. 1st Harry Osborn (later 2nd Green Goblin), 1st appearance Gwen Stacy and Professor Warren; last Silver Age issue indicia-dated Dec 1965	$20.00	$60.00	$140.00	£12.00	£36.00	£85.00
32 (Jan 1966)	$20.00	$60.00	$140.00	£10.50	£32.00	£75.00
33 classic interior sequence considered by many as among Steve Ditko's finest work on Spiderman	$20.00	$60.00	$140.00	£10.50	£32.00	£75.00
34 3rd appearance Kraven	$20.00	$60.00	$140.00	£10.50	£32.00	£75.00
35 2nd appearance Molten Man	$20.00	$60.00	$140.00	£10.50	£32.00	£75.00
36 1st appearance The Looter						

Issue	$Good	$Fine	$N.Mint	£Good	£Fine	£N.Mint
	$20.00	$60.00	$140.00	£10.50	£32.00	£75.00
37 Norman Osborn character introduced: not yet known that he's Green Goblin	$20.00	$60.00	$140.00	£10.50	£32.00	£75.00
38 last Steve Ditko art, 2nd Mary Jane Watson? (cameo), face unseen again...	$20.00	$60.00	$140.00	£10.50	£32.00	£75.00
39 Green Goblin appears and reveals he's Norman Osborn, 1st John Romita Snr. art, classic cover	$29.00	$85.00	$200.00	£15.50	£47.00	£110.00
40 Green Goblin appears, origin told for 1st time	$36.00	$105.00	$285.00	£20.00	£60.00	£160.00
41 less common in the U.K. 1st appearance The Rhino	$19.00	$57.50	$135.00	£10.50	£32.00	£75.00
42 scarce in the U.K. 3rd Mary Jane Watson? (cameo), face fully shown in one panel (last)	$17.50	$52.50	$125.00	£10.00	£30.00	£70.00
43 scarce in the U.K. 1st full appearance Mary Jane Watson, 2nd appearance Rhino	$12.50	$39.00	$90.00	£7.75	£23.50	£55.00
44 less common in the U.K. (Jan 1967), 2nd appearance Lizard	$12.50	$39.00	$90.00	£7.00	£21.00	£50.00
45 3rd appearance Lizard	$12.50	$39.00	$90.00	£6.25	£19.00	£45.00
46 1st appearance The Shocker	$12.50	$39.00	$90.00	£6.25	£19.00	£45.00
47 Kraven appears	$12.50	$39.00	$90.00	£6.25	£19.00	£45.00
48-49 Vulture appears	$12.50	$39.00	$90.00	£6.25	£19.00	£45.00
50 scarce in the U.K. 1st appearance Kingpin, origin retold, classic cover	$47.00	$140.00	$375.00	£28.00	£82.50	£225.00
51 2nd appearance Kingpin	$19.00	$57.50	$135.00	£8.50	£26.00	£60.00
52 1st appearance Joe Robertson	$10.00	$30.00	$70.00	£5.00	£15.00	£35.00
53-55 Dr. Octopus appears	$10.00	$30.00	$70.00	£5.00	£15.00	£35.00
56 (Jan 1968), 1st appearance Captain George Stacy (Gwen Stacy's father), Dr. Octopus appears	$10.00	$30.00	$70.00	£5.00	£15.00	£35.00
57-58 Ka-Zar appears	$10.00	$30.00	$70.00	£5.00	£15.00	£35.00
59-60	$10.00	$30.00	$70.00	£5.00	£15.00	£35.00
61-62	$7.00	$21.00	$50.00	£3.90	£11.50	£27.50
63 Green Goblin cameo	$7.00	$21.00	$50.00	£3.90	£11.50	£27.50
64-67	$7.00	$21.00	$50.00	£3.90	£11.50	£27.50
68 (Jan 1969), Kingpin appears	$7.00	$21.00	$50.00	£3.90	£11.50	£27.50
69-70 Kingpin appears	$7.00	$21.00	$50.00	£3.90	£11.50	£27.50
71	$7.00	$21.00	$50.00	£3.55	£10.50	£25.00
72 2nd appearance Shocker	$7.00	$21.00	$50.00	£3.55	£10.50	£25.00
73	$7.00	$21.00	$50.00	£3.55	£10.50	£25.00
74 last 12 cents issue	$7.00	$21.00	$50.00	£3.55	£10.50	£25.00
75-76	$6.25	$19.00	$45.00	£2.85	£8.50	£20.00
77 Human Torch appears	$6.25	$19.00	$45.00	£2.85	£8.50	£20.00
78 1st appearance The Prowler	$6.25	$19.00	$45.00	£2.85	£8.50	£20.00
79	$6.25	$19.00	$45.00	£2.85	£8.50	£20.00
80 (Jan 1970)	$6.25	$19.00	$45.00	£2.85	£8.50	£20.00
81 1st appearance Kangaroo	$6.25	$19.00	$45.00	£2.85	£8.50	£20.00
82	$6.25	$19.00	$45.00	£2.85	£8.50	£20.00
83 1st appearance Schemer	$6.25	$19.00	$45.00	£2.85	£8.50	£20.00
84-85	$6.25	$19.00	$45.00	£2.85	£8.50	£20.00
86 Black Widow appears	$6.25	$19.00	$45.00	£2.50	£7.50	£17.50
87	$6.25	$19.00	$45.00	£2.50	£7.50	£17.50
88-89 Dr. Octopus appears	$6.25	$19.00	$45.00	£2.50	£7.50	£17.50
90 less common in the U.K. Captain Stacy dies, Dr. Octopus appears	$6.75	$20.00	$47.50	£3.20	£9.50	£22.50
91	$6.25	$19.00	$45.00	£2.50	£7.50	£17.50
92 (Jan 1971), Iceman appears	$6.25	$19.00	$45.00	£2.50	£7.50	£17.50
93	$6.25	$19.00	$45.00	£2.50	£7.50	£17.50
94 scarce in the U.K. origin retold	$9.25	$28.00	$65.00	£4.25	£12.50	£30.00
95 scarce in the U.K.	$6.25	$19.00	$45.00	£3.20	£9.50	£22.50
96-98 scarce in the U.K. non Code-approved drugs story, Green Goblin appears	$11.00	$34.00	$80.00	£4.25	£12.50	£30.00
99	$6.25	$19.00	$45.00	£2.50	£7.50	£17.50
100 scarce in the U.K. anniversary issue and retrospective (Dr. Octopus, Green Goblin and Kingpin in dream sequence), Spiderman with six arms	$25.00	$75.00	$200.00	£11.50	£36.00	£95.00
101 scarce in the U.K. 1st appearance Morbius the Living Vampire, Lizard appears; last 15 cents issue	$23.50	$70.00	$165.00	£12.00	£36.00	£85.00
101 Marvel Milestone Edition, ND (Sep 1992) - silver metallic ink cover; released to tie in with Morbius #1 (same cover date month)	$0.40	$1.20	$2.00	£0.25	£0.75	£1.25
102 scarce in the U.K. 52pgs, origin and 2nd appearance Morbius (spelt incorrectly on cover as "Moribus"), Lizard appears	$16.00	$49.00	$115.00	£10.50	£32.00	£75.00
103 scarce in the U.K. Ka-Zar and Kraven appear; Gil Kane cover	$4.15	$12.50	$25.00	£2.50	£7.50	£15.00
104 scarce in the U.K. (Jan 1972), Ka-Zar and Kraven appear; Gil Kane cover	$4.15	$12.50	$25.00	£2.50	£7.50	£15.00
105-108 scarce in the U.K.	$4.15	$12.50	$25.00	£2.50	£7.50	£15.00
109 scarce in the U.K. Dr. Strange appears	$4.15	$12.50	$25.00	£2.50	£7.50	£15.00
110 scarce in the U.K. 1st appearance The Gibbon	$4.15	$12.50	$25.00	£2.50	£7.50	£15.00
111 scarce in the U.K.	$4.15	$12.50	$25.00	£2.50	£7.50	£15.00
112 scarce in the U.K. Dr. Octopus appears	$4.15	$12.50	$25.00	£2.50	£7.50	£15.00
113 scarce in the U.K. 1st appearance Hammerhead, Dr. Octopus appears; part Starlin art	$4.15	$12.50	$25.00	£2.50	£7.50	£15.00
114 scarce in the U.K. Dr. Octopus appears; part Starlin art	$4.15	$12.50	$25.00	£2.50	£7.50	£15.00
115 Dr. Octopus appears	$4.15	$12.50	$25.00	£2.05	£6.25	£12.50
116 (Jan 1973)	$4.15	$12.50	$25.00	£2.05	£6.25	£12.50
117-118 scarce in the U.K.	$4.15	$12.50	$25.00	£2.50	£7.50	£15.00
119-120 scarce in the U.K. Spiderman vs. Hulk	$6.50	$20.00	$40.00	£3.30	£10.00	£20.00
121 ND Gwen Stacy dies (murdered by The Green Goblin)(Note: this was the first issue of this title to be officially Non Distributed in the U.K.)	$17.50	$52.50	$125.00	£11.00	£34.00	£80.00
122 ND Green Goblin (Norman Osborn) dies	$20.00	$60.00	$140.00	£12.00	£36.00	£85.00
123 ND Luke Cage appears	$4.15	$12.50	$25.00	£2.50	£7.50	£15.00
124 ND 1st appearance Man-Wolf (J. Jonah Jameson's son)	$4.15	$12.50	$25.00	£2.50	£7.50	£15.00
125 ND 2nd appearance Man-Wolf	$4.15	$12.50	$25.00	£2.05	£6.25	£12.50
126 ND	$4.15	$12.50	$25.00	£2.05	£6.25	£12.50
127 ND Vulture returns	$4.15	$12.50	$25.00	£2.05	£6.25	£12.50
128 ND (Jan 1974), Vulture returns	$4.15	$12.50	$25.00	£2.05	£6.25	£12.50
129 ND 1st appearance Punisher, 1st appearance The Jackal	$36.00	$105.00	$250.00	£22.50	£67.50	£160.00
129 Marvel Milestone Edition, ND (Nov 1992)	$0.50	$1.50	$2.50	£0.30	£0.90	£1.50
130-131 ND Dr. Octopus appears	$2.90	$8.75	$17.50	£1.65	£5.00	£10.00
132-133 ND	$2.90	$8.75	$17.50	£1.65	£5.00	£10.00
134 ND scarce in the U.K. Punisher cameo, 1st appearance Tarantula	$3.30	$10.00	$20.00	£2.50	£7.50	£15.00
135 ND 2nd full appearance Punisher	$10.00	$30.00	$60.00	£5.75	£17.50	£35.00
136 ND 1st appearance Green Goblin II (Harry Osborn)	$6.50	$20.00	$40.00	£2.90	£8.75	£17.50
137 ND Green Goblin II appears (full story and cover)	$6.50	$20.00	$40.00	£2.05	£6.25	£12.50
138-139 ND	$2.90	$8.75	$17.50	£1.65	£5.00	£10.00
140 ND (Jan 1975)	$2.90	$8.75	$17.50	£1.65	£5.00	£10.00
141 ND Morbius and Green Goblin cameos in dream sequence; 1st appearance Mysterio II	$2.90	$8.75	$17.50	£1.65	£5.00	£10.00
142 ND Gwen Stacy clone cameo	$4.15	$12.50	$25.00	£2.05	£6.25	£12.50
143 ND Gwen Stacy clone cameo; 1st appearance Cyclone	$4.15	$12.50	$25.00	£2.05	£6.25	£12.50
144 ND 1st full appearance Gwen Stacy clone	$4.15	$12.50	$25.00	£2.05	£6.25	£12.50
145-146 ND Gwen Stacy clone	$3.30	$10.00	$20.00	£1.65	£5.00	£10.00
147 ND Spiderman learns of Gwen Stacy clone	$3.30	$10.00	$20.00	£1.65	£5.00	£10.00
148 ND The Jackal revealed as Professor Warren	$4.55	$13.50	$27.50	£2.90	£8.75	£17.50
149 ND 1st appearance Spiderman clone, origin Jackal	$10.50	$32.00	$75.00	£7.00	£21.00	£50.00
149 Marvel Milestone Edition, ND (Nov 1994) - silver border cover	$0.60	$1.80	$3.00	£0.40	£1.20	£2.00
150 ND Spiderman clone appears	$8.25	$25.00	$50.00	£5.75	£17.50	£35.00
150 Marvel Milestone Edition, ND (1995) - silver border cover	$0.60	$1.80	$3.00	£0.40	£1.20	£2.00
151 ND Spiderman clone appears	$5.75	$17.50	$35.00	£3.30	£10.00	£20.00
152 ND (Jan 1976)	$2.50	$7.50	$15.00	£1.30	£4.00	£8.00
153-154 ND	$2.50	$7.50	$15.00	£1.30	£4.00	£8.00
155-156 ND	$2.50	$7.50	$15.00	£1.15	£3.50	£7.00
157-159 ND Dr. Octopus appears	$2.50	$7.50	$15.00	£1.15	£3.50	£7.00
160 ND	$2.50	$7.50	$15.00	£1.15	£3.50	£7.00
161 ND Nightcrawler appears, Punisher, Wolverine, Colossus cameos; Jigsaw appears though hidden	$2.05	$6.25	$12.50	£1.15	£3.50	£7.00

Issue	$Good	$Fine	$N.Mint	£Good	£Fine	£N.Mint
162 ND Punisher, Nightcrawler appear, 1st full appearance Jigsaw	$2.50	$7.50	$15.00	£1.30	£4.00	£8.00
163 ND	$1.50	$4.50	$9.00	£0.80	£2.50	£5.00
164 ND (Jan 1977)	$1.50	$4.50	$9.00	£0.80	£2.50	£5.00
165-166 ND	$1.50	$4.50	$9.00	£0.80	£2.50	£5.00
167 ND 1st appearance Barton Hamilton (later Green Goblin III in #176)	$1.50	$4.50	$9.00	£0.80	£2.50	£5.00
168-170 ND	$1.50	$4.50	$9.00	£0.80	£2.50	£5.00
171 ND Nova appears, X-over Nova #12	$1.50	$4.50	$9.00	£0.80	£2.50	£5.00
172-173 ND	$1.50	$4.50	$9.00	£0.80	£2.50	£5.00
174-175 ND Punisher appears	$2.50	$7.50	$15.00	£1.30	£4.00	£8.00
176 ND (Jan 1978), 1st appearance Green Goblin III (Barton Hamilton)	$2.90	$8.75	$17.50	£1.15	£3.50	£7.00
177-179 ND Green Goblin III appears	$2.90	$8.75	$17.50	£1.15	£3.50	£7.00
180 ND Green Goblin II & III appear	$2.90	$8.75	$17.50	£1.15	£3.50	£7.00
181 ND origin retold	$1.50	$4.50	$9.00	£0.80	£2.50	£5.00
182-184 ND	$1.50	$4.50	$9.00	£0.80	£2.50	£5.00
185 ND Peter Parker's graduation (1st graduation in #28!)	$1.50	$4.50	$9.00	£0.80	£2.50	£5.00
186 ND	$1.50	$4.50	$9.00	£0.80	£2.50	£5.00
187 ND Jim Starlin art, Captain America appears	$1.50	$4.50	$9.00	£0.80	£2.50	£5.00
188 ND (Jan 1979)	$1.50	$4.50	$9.00	£0.80	£2.50	£5.00
189-190 ND Man-Wolf appears, John Byrne art	$1.50	$4.50	$9.00	£0.80	£2.50	£5.00
191-193 ND	$1.30	$4.00	$8.00	£0.65	£2.00	£4.00
194 ND 1st appearance Black Cat	$3.00	$9.00	$18.00	£1.25	£3.75	£7.50
195-199 ND	$1.30	$4.00	$8.00	£0.65	£2.00	£4.00
200 ND (Jan 1980), DS, origin retold, return of the burglar that killed Peter Parker's uncle in Amazing Fantasy #15	$5.00	$15.00	$30.00	£1.30	£4.00	£8.00
201-202 ND Punisher appears	$2.05	$6.25	$12.50	£1.25	£3.75	£7.50
203 ND 2nd appearance Dazzler	$1.30	$4.00	$8.00	£0.65	£2.00	£4.00
204-205 ND Black Cat appears	$1.30	$4.00	$8.00	£0.65	£2.00	£4.00
206 ND John Byrne art	$1.30	$4.00	$8.00	£0.65	£2.00	£4.00
207-208 ND	$1.30	$4.00	$8.00	£0.65	£2.00	£4.00
209 ND 1st appearance Calypso	$2.00	$6.00	$12.00	£0.80	£2.50	£5.00
210 ND	$1.30	$4.00	$8.00	£0.65	£2.00	£4.00
211 ND Sub-Mariner appears	$1.30	$4.00	$8.00	£0.65	£2.00	£4.00
212 ND (Jan 1981), 1st appearance Hydroman	$1.30	$4.00	$8.00	£0.65	£2.00	£4.00
213 ND	$1.30	$4.00	$8.00	£0.65	£2.00	£4.00
214 ND Sub-Mariner appears	$1.30	$4.00	$8.00	£0.65	£2.00	£4.00
215 Sub-Mariner X-over/origin	$1.30	$4.00	$8.00	£0.55	£1.75	£3.50
216-218	$1.30	$4.00	$8.00	£0.55	£1.75	£3.50
219 Frank Miller cover	$1.30	$4.00	$8.00	£0.55	£1.75	£3.50
220 Moon Knight appears	$1.30	$4.00	$8.00	£0.55	£1.75	£3.50
221-223	$1.15	$3.50	$7.00	£0.50	£1.50	£3.00
224 (Jan 1982)	$1.15	$3.50	$7.00	£0.50	£1.50	£3.00
225 Foolkiller appears	$1.15	$3.50	$7.00	£0.50	£1.50	£3.00
226-227 Black Cat appears	$1.15	$3.50	$7.00	£0.50	£1.50	£3.00
228 LD in the U.K.	$1.15	$3.50	$7.00	£0.50	£1.60	£3.25
229-231 LD in the U.K. Juggernaut appears	$1.15	$3.50	$7.00	£0.50	£1.60	£3.25
232-233 LD in the U.K.	$1.15	$3.50	$7.00	£0.50	£1.60	£3.25
234 LD in the U.K. free insert - Marvel Guide to Collecting Comics	$1.15	$3.50	$7.00	£0.50	£1.60	£3.25
234 as above but without insert	$1.00	$3.00	$5.00	£0.50	£1.50	£2.50
235 LD in the U.K. Walt Simonson cover	$1.15	$3.50	$7.00	£0.50	£1.50	£3.00
236 LD in the U.K. (Jan 1983)	$1.15	$3.50	$7.00	£0.50	£1.50	£3.00
237 LD in the U.K.	$1.15	$3.50	$7.00	£0.50	£1.50	£3.00
238 LD in the U.K. 1st appearance Hobgoblin (Ned Leeds), issue includes free stick-on skin tattoos	$10.50	$33.00	$65.00	£3.75	£11.00	£22.50
238 as above but without tattoos	$5.00	$15.00	$30.00	£2.50	£7.50	£15.00
239 LD in the U.K. 2nd appearance Hobgoblin	$5.75	$17.50	$35.00	£2.05	£6.25	£12.50
240-242 LD in the U.K.	$1.15	$3.50	$7.00	£0.50	£1.50	£3.00
243 LD in the U.K. return of Mary Jane Watson	$1.15	$3.50	$7.00	£0.50	£1.50	£3.00

Issue	$Good	$Fine	$N.Mint	£Good	£Fine	£N.Mint
244 LD in the U.K. Hobgoblin appears (cameo)	$1.65	$5.00	$10.00	£0.55	£1.75	£3.50
245 LD in the U.K. "Hobgoblin" (Lefty Donovan) vs. Spiderman	$2.50	$7.50	$15.00	£0.65	£2.00	£4.00
246 LD in the U.K. Avengers and Fantastic Four cameos	$1.15	$3.50	$7.00	£0.50	£1.50	£3.00
247 LD in the U.K.	$1.15	$3.50	$7.00	£0.50	£1.50	£3.00
248 LD in the U.K. (Jan 1984)	$1.15	$3.50	$7.00	£0.50	£1.50	£3.00
249-251 LD in the U.K. Hobgoblin vs. Spiderman	$2.05	$6.25	$12.50	£0.65	£2.00	£4.00
252 LD in the U.K. 1st appearance (alien) black costume which later transforms into Venom (see Secret Wars I and Marvel Team Up #141)	$5.00	$15.00	$35.00	£1.40	£4.25	£10.00
253 LD in the U.K. 1st appearance Rose	$1.30	$4.00	$8.00	£0.55	£1.75	£3.50
254 LD in the U.K. Jack O'Lantern appears	$1.15	$3.50	$7.00	£0.40	£1.25	£2.50
255 LD in the U.K. 1st appearance Black Fox; Red Ghost appears	$0.80	$2.50	$5.00	£0.40	£1.25	£2.50
256 LD in the U.K. 1st appearance Puma	$0.80	$2.50	$5.00	£0.40	£1.25	£2.50
257 LD in the U.K. Hobgoblin cameo; Hobgoblin costume discovered to be alive	$1.25	$3.75	$7.50	£0.50	£1.50	£3.00
258 LD in the U.K. Hobgoblin cameo, Fantastic Four appear	$1.65	$5.00	$10.00	£0.50	£1.50	£3.00
259 LD in the U.K. Hobgoblin appears, old costume returns alternating with black costume, Fantastic Four appear; origin of Mary Jane Watson told	$2.50	$7.50	$15.00	£0.75	£2.25	£4.50
260 (Jan 1985), Hobgoblin appears	$1.65	$5.00	$10.00	£0.65	£2.00	£4.00
261 Hobgoblin appears	$1.65	$5.00	$10.00	£0.65	£2.00	£4.00
262 photo cover	$1.15	$3.50	$7.00	£0.40	£1.25	£2.50
263-264	$1.00	$3.00	$6.00	£0.30	£1.00	£2.00
265 1st appearance Silver Sable	$1.15	$3.50	$7.00	£0.50	£1.50	£3.00
265 2nd printing, ND (Jun 1992) - metallic ink cover	$0.40	$1.20	$2.00	£0.25	£0.75	£1.25
266 Peter David's 1st published script for Marvel though the script for Spectacular Spiderman #103 was commissioned earlier	$0.80	$2.50	$5.00	£0.30	£1.00	£2.00
267 Human Torch appears	$0.80	$2.50	$5.00	£0.30	£1.00	£2.00
268 Secret Wars X-over, John Byrne cover	$0.80	$2.50	$5.00	£0.30	£1.00	£2.00
269 LD in the U.K. Firelord appears	$0.80	$2.50	$5.00	£0.35	£1.10	£2.25
270 LD in the U.K. Avengers appear	$0.80	$2.50	$5.00	£0.35	£1.10	£2.25
271	$0.80	$2.50	$5.00	£0.30	£1.00	£2.00
272 (Jan 1986)	$0.80	$2.50	$5.00	£0.30	£1.00	£2.00
273 LD in the U.K. Secret Wars X-over; alien black costume appears	$0.80	$2.50	$5.00	£0.35	£1.10	£2.25
274 Secret Wars X-over, Zarathos (The Spirit of Vengeance) appears	$0.80	$2.50	$5.00	£0.30	£1.00	£2.00
275 LD in the U.K. DS, Hobgoblin appears, Spiderman origin reprinted (Steve Ditko art)	$2.05	$6.25	$12.50	£0.65	£2.00	£4.00
276 LD in the U.K. Hobgoblin appears	$1.50	$4.50	$9.00	£0.50	£1.50	£3.00
277 Daredevil, Kingpin appear, Charles Vess art	$0.80	$2.50	$5.00	£0.30	£1.00	£2.00
278 Hobgoblin appears on last page	$0.80	$2.50	$5.00	£0.30	£1.00	£2.00
279 Silver Sable vs. Jack O' Lantern	$0.80	$2.50	$5.00	£0.30	£1.00	£2.00
280 Silver Sable appears	$0.80	$2.50	$5.00	£0.30	£1.00	£2.00
281 Hobgoblin vs. Jack O'Lantern, Silver Sable appears	$1.65	$5.00	$10.00	£0.50	£1.50	£3.00
282 LD in the U.K. X-Factor appear	$0.80	$2.50	$5.00	£0.40	£1.25	£2.50
283 LD in the U.K. Hobgoblin appears	$1.15	$3.50	$7.00	£0.40	£1.25	£2.50
284 (Jan 1987), Punisher cameo, Hobgoblin appears, Daredevil appears, Gang War story begins	$1.25	$3.75	$7.50	£0.55	£1.75	£3.50
285 Punisher, Hobgoblin appear, Zeck art	$1.65	$5.00	$10.00	£0.75	£2.25	£4.50
286 Hobgoblin cameo	$1.00	$3.00	$6.00	£0.40	£1.25	£2.50
287 Spiderman vs. Daredevil, Hobgoblin cameo, Falcon appears; 1st Erik Larsen art on Spiderman	$1.00	$3.00	$6.00	£0.50	£1.50	£3.00
288 LD in the U.K. Gang War ends, Hobgoblin appears, Punisher appears (2 panels), Black Cat and Daredevil appear	$1.30	$4.00	$8.00	£0.50	£1.50	£3.00
289 DS, Hobgoblin's identity revealed, X-over with Web of Spiderman #30, death Ned Leeds (original Hobgoblin), Philip Macendale (Jack O'Lantern) becomes Hobgoblin II, Wolverine cameo	$3.30	$10.00	$20.00	£1.00	£3.00	£6.00
290 LD in the U.K. Peter Parker proposes to Mary J. Watson	$0.80	$2.50	$5.00	£0.30	£1.00	£2.00
291-292 LD in the U.K.	$0.80	$2.50	$5.00	£0.30	£1.00	£2.00

Issue	$Good	$Fine	$N.Mint	£Good	£Fine	£N.Mint
293 Kraven Saga, Zeck art	$1.25	$3.75	$7.50	£0.55	£1.75	£3.50
294 Kraven Saga, Zeck art	$1.25	$3.75	$7.50	£0.50	£1.50	£3.00
295 LD in the U.K. Sienkiewicz cover	$1.00	$3.00	$6.00	£0.30	£1.00	£2.00
296 LD in the U.K. (Jan 1988)	$1.00	$3.00	$6.00	£0.30	£1.00	£2.00
297 LD in the U.K.	$1.00	$3.00	$6.00	£0.30	£1.00	£2.00
298 LD in the U.K. 1st Todd McFarlane art, 1st Venom without costume (cameo)	$5.25	$16.00	$32.50	£2.05	£6.25	£12.50
299 LD in the U.K. Todd McFarlane art, 1st appearance Venom (cameo)	$3.75	$11.00	$22.50	£1.30	£4.00	£8.00
300 LD in the U.K. DS, Todd McFarlane art, Spiderman fully returns to old costume, 1st full appearance Venom, Thing appears; 25th anniversary issue	$11.50	$35.00	$70.00	£3.30	£10.00	£20.00
301-302 LD in the U.K. Todd McFarlane art, Silver Sable appears	$2.50	$7.50	$15.00	£0.80	£2.50	£5.00
303 LD in the U.K. Todd McFarlane art, Silver Sable and Sandman appear	$2.05	$6.25	$12.50	£0.80	£2.50	£5.00
304-305 Todd McFarlane art; bi-weekly	$1.50	$4.50	$9.00	£0.65	£2.00	£4.00
306 Todd McFarlane art, Black Cat appears; bi-weekly - cover based on Action Comics #1	$1.50	$4.50	$9.00	£0.65	£2.00	£4.00
307 Todd McFarlane art, origin Chameleon retold; bi-weekly	$1.50	$4.50	$9.00	£0.65	£2.00	£4.00
308-309 Todd McFarlane art; bi-weekly	$1.50	$4.50	$9.00	£0.65	£2.00	£4.00
310 Todd McFarlane art	$1.50	$4.50	$9.00	£0.65	£2.00	£4.00
311 (Jan 1989), Todd McFarlane art, Mysterio appears, Inferno tie-in	$1.50	$4.50	$9.00	£0.55	£1.75	£3.50
312 LD in the U.K. Todd McFarlane art, Hobgoblin II vs. Green Goblin II, Inferno tie-in	$3.30	$10.00	$20.00	£0.80	£2.50	£5.00
313 Todd McFarlane art, Lizard appears, Inferno tie-in	$1.50	$4.50	$9.00	£0.55	£1.75	£3.50
314 Todd McFarlane art	$1.50	$4.50	$9.00	£0.55	£1.75	£3.50
315-316 Todd McFarlane art, Venom appears	$2.90	$8.75	$17.50	£0.65	£2.00	£4.00
317 Todd McFarlane art, Thing appears, Venom appears	$2.90	$8.75	$17.50	£0.65	£2.00	£4.00
318 Todd McFarlane art	$1.30	$4.00	$8.00	£0.50	£1.50	£3.00
319 Todd McFarlane art; bi-weekly	$1.30	$4.00	$8.00	£0.50	£1.50	£3.00
320-321 Silver Sable appears, Todd McFarlane art; bi-weekly	$1.30	$4.00	$8.00	£0.50	£1.50	£3.00
322 Silver Sable appears, Sabretooth appears (unidentified), Todd McFarlane art; bi-weekly	$1.15	$3.50	$7.00	£0.50	£1.50	£3.00
323 Silver Sable appears, Todd McFarlane art	$1.15	$3.50	$7.00	£0.50	£1.50	£3.00
324 LD in the U.K. Sabretooth appears; Silver Sable appears, Erik Larsen art, Todd McFarlane cover, Acts of Vengeance tie-in	$1.65	$5.00	$10.00	£0.65	£2.00	£4.00
325 Silver Sable appears, Todd McFarlane art	$1.15	$3.50	$7.00	£0.50	£1.50	£3.00
326 Acts of Vengeance tie-in	$1.15	$3.50	$7.00	£0.25	£0.75	£1.50
327 Acts of Vengeance tie-in, Erik Larsen art, Magneto appears, Cosmic Spiderman (see Spectacular Spiderman #158)	$1.15	$3.50	$7.00	£0.25	£0.75	£1.50
328 LD in the U.K. (Jan 1990), Acts of Vengeance tie-in, last Todd McFarlane art, Hulk vs. Cosmic Spiderman (apparently stronger than Hulk)	$1.65	$5.00	$10.00	£0.65	£2.00	£4.00
329 Erik Larsen art run begins, Acts of Vengeance tie-in, Cosmic Spiderman	$0.80	$2.50	$5.00	£0.25	£0.75	£1.50
330 Punisher appears (continued in Punisher War Journal #14), Larsen art	$0.65	$2.00	$4.00	£0.25	£0.75	£1.50
331 Punisher appears (continued in Punisher War Journal #15), Larsen art	$0.65	$2.00	$4.00	£0.25	£0.75	£1.50
332-333 Venom appears, Larsen art	$1.00	$3.00	$6.00	£0.25	£0.85	£1.75
334-336 Sinister Six, Larsen art	$0.50	$1.50	$3.00	£0.20	£0.60	£1.25
337 Sinister Six, Hobgoblin appears, Larsen art	$0.50	$1.50	$3.00	£0.20	£0.60	£1.25
338 Sinister Six, Larsen art; Hobgoblin appears	$0.50	$1.50	$3.00	£0.20	£0.60	£1.25
339 Sinister Six, Larsen art	$0.50	$1.50	$3.00	£0.20	£0.60	£1.25
340-342 Larsen art	$0.50	$1.50	$3.00	£0.20	£0.60	£1.25
343 (Jan 1991), Larsen art, 1st appearance Cardiac (cameo)	$0.50	$1.50	$3.00	£0.20	£0.60	£1.25
344 LD in the U.K. 1st full appearance Cardiac, 1st appearance (cameo) Cletus Kasady (later Carnage), Larsen art	$1.65	$5.00	$10.00	£0.40	£1.25	£2.50
345 LD in the U.K. Venom appears, 1st full appearance Cletus Kasady, Larsen art	$1.65	$5.00	$10.00	£0.80	£2.50	£5.00
346 ND scarce in the U.K. Venom appears, Larsen art	$1.30	$4.00	$8.00	£0.55	£1.75	£3.50
347 ND Venom appears, Larsen art	$1.30	$4.00	$8.00	£0.40	£1.25	£2.50
348 ND The Avengers guest-star, Larsen art	$0.50	$1.50	$3.00	£0.20	£0.60	£1.25
349 ND Black Fox appears, Larsen art	$0.50	$1.50	$3.00	£0.20	£0.60	£1.25
350 ND DS Black Fox appears, last Larsen art, origin retold; pin-up gallery included	$0.55	$1.75	$3.50	£0.30	£1.00	£2.00
351 ND Mark Bagley art begins, Nova appears	$0.50	$1.50	$2.50	£0.25	£0.75	£1.25
352 ND New Warriors appear, Mark Bagley art	$0.50	$1.50	$2.50	£0.25	£0.75	£1.25
353 ND Round Robin part 1, Darkhawk, Punisher appear, Mark Bagley art, bi-weekly issue	$0.50	$1.50	$2.50	£0.25	£0.75	£1.25
354 ND Round Robin story, Darkhawk, Punisher, Nova appear, Mark Bagley art, bi-weekly issue	$0.50	$1.50	$2.50	£0.25	£0.75	£1.25
355 ND Round Robin story, Darkhawk, Puisher, Nova, Moon Knight appear, Mark Bagley art, bi-weekly issue	$0.50	$1.50	$2.50	£0.25	£0.75	£1.25
356 ND Round Robin story, Daredevil, Punisher, Moon Knight, Nova appear, Mark Bagley art, bi-weekly issue	$0.50	$1.50	$2.50	£0.25	£0.75	£1.25
357 ND (Jan 1992), Round Robin story, Punisher, Darkhawk, Moon Knight appear, Mark Bagley art, bi-weekly issue	$0.50	$1.50	$2.50	£0.25	£0.75	£1.25
358 ND Round Robin story concludes, Punisher, Darkhawk, Moon Knight, Nova, Night Thrasher appear, Mark Bagley art, gatefold cover, bi-weekly issue	$0.50	$1.50	$2.50	£0.25	£0.75	£1.25
359 ND $1.25 cover begins, Cardiac appears, Carnage cameo	$1.20	$3.60	$6.00	£0.30	£0.90	£1.50
360 ND fuller appearance of Carnage, Cardiac appears	$1.60	$4.80	$8.00	£0.40	£1.20	£2.00
361 ND 1st full appearance of Carnage	$3.00	$9.00	$15.00	£1.00	£3.00	£5.00
361 2nd printing, ND silver ink cover	$0.40	$1.20	$2.00	£0.25	£0.75	£1.25
362 ND Carnage, Venom and Human Torch appear	$2.00	$6.00	$10.00	£0.70	£2.10	£3.50
362 2nd printing, ND silver ink cover	$0.30	$0.90	$1.50	£0.20	£0.60	£1.00
363 ND Spiderman and Venom vs. Carnage, Mr. Fantastic and Human Torch appear	$1.60	$4.80	$8.00	£0.70	£2.10	£3.50
364 ND	$0.40	$1.20	$2.00	£0.25	£0.75	£1.25
365 ND 80pgs, 30th anniversary issue, origin retold, silver hologram cover, previews Spider 2099 (1st appearance), poster by John Romita Jnr, contributions from Stan Lee and Steve Ditko	$1.20	$3.60	$6.00	£0.60	£1.80	£3.00
365 2nd printing, ND gold hologram cover	$0.80	$2.40	$4.00	£0.50	£1.50	£2.50
366-367 ND Red Skull appears	$0.30	$0.90	$1.50	£0.20	£0.60	£1.00
368-370 ND Invasion of the Spider Slayers, bi-weekly	$0.30	$0.90	$1.50	£0.20	£0.60	£1.00
371 ND Invasion of the Spider Slayers, bi-weekly	$0.30	$0.90	$1.50	£0.15	£0.45	£0.75
372 ND (Jan 1993), Invasion of the Spider Slayers, bi-weekly	$0.30	$0.90	$1.50	£0.15	£0.45	£0.75
373 ND Invasion of the Spider Slayers, bi-weekly; Venom back-up story	$0.30	$0.90	$1.50	£0.15	£0.45	£0.75
374 ND Venom appears	$0.30	$0.90	$1.50	£0.15	£0.45	£0.75
375 ND 64pgs, 30th anniversary issue, holo-grafix metallic ink cover, Spiderman vs. Venom	$1.20	$3.60	$6.00	£0.50	£1.50	£2.50
376-377 ND Cardiac appears	$0.30	$0.90	$1.50	£0.15	£0.45	£0.75
378 ND Maximum Carnage part 3, continued in Spiderman #35	$0.30	$0.90	$1.50	£0.15	£0.45	£0.75
379 ND Maximum Carnage part 7, continued in Spiderman #36	$0.30	$0.90	$1.50	£0.15	£0.45	£0.75
380 ND Maximum Carnage part 11 continued in Spiderman #37	$0.30	$0.90	$1.50	£0.15	£0.45	£0.75
381-382 ND Hulk guest-stars, Doc Samson appears	$0.30	$0.90	$1.50	£0.15	£0.45	£0.75
383-384 ND	$0.30	$0.90	$1.50	£0.15	£0.45	£0.75
385 ND (Jan 1994)	$0.30	$0.90	$1.50	£0.15	£0.45	£0.75
386 ND Lifetheft story	$0.70	$2.10	$3.50	£0.20	£0.60	£1.00
387 ND Lifetheft story, reveals his identitly to parents	$0.70	$2.10	$3.50	£0.20	£0.60	£1.00
388 ND 64pgs, Collector's Edition with red foil cover; Lifetheft story; the true fate of Spiderman's parents revealed	$0.60	$1.80	$3.00	£0.40	£1.20	£2.00
388 Newstand Edition, ND 64pgs, - without cover enhancement; Lifetheft story; the true fate of Spiderman's parents revealed	$0.50	$1.50	$2.50	£0.30	£0.90	£1.50
389 ND Pursuit part 4 (conclusion); Spiderman vs. Chameleon; with free Spiderman's Amazing Powers card sheet	$0.30	$0.90	$1.50	£0.20	£0.60	£1.00
390 ND Shriek and Carrion appear	$0.30	$0.90	$1.50	£0.20	£0.60	£1.00
390 Collectors Edition, ND : pre-bagged with 16pg preview and animation cel from Spiderman TV series; metallic ink cover	$0.60	$1.80	$3.00	£0.40	£1.20	£2.00
391 ND	$0.30	$0.90	$1.50	£0.20	£0.60	£1.00
392 ND cover based on issue #50 (a classic!)						

	$Good	$Fine	$N.Mint	£Good	£Fine	£N.Mint
	$0.30	***$0.90***	***$1.50***	**£0.20**	**£0.60**	**£1.00**
393 ND	***$0.30***	***$0.90***	***$1.50***	**£0.20**	**£0.60**	**£1.00**
394 ND Power and Responsibility part 2						
	$0.40	***$1.20***	***$2.00***	**£0.20**	**£0.60**	**£1.00**
394 Collectors Edition, ND 48pgs, : Power and Responsibility part 2, foil stamped cover; incorporates 16pg flip-book with second foil stamped cover; continued in Spiderman (2nd) #51						
	$0.80	***$2.40***	***$4.00***	**£0.40**	**£1.20**	**£2.00**
395 ND Puma appears						
	$0.30	***$0.90***	***$1.50***	**£0.20**	**£0.60**	**£1.00**
396 ND Spiderman and Daredevil vs. The Vulture and The Owl (see Spectacular Spiderman #219)						
	$0.30	***$0.90***	***$1.50***	**£0.20**	**£0.60**	**£1.00**
397 ND (Jan 1995), Web of Death part 1, continued in Spectacular Spiderman #220; Dr. Octopus appears						
	$0.50	***$1.50***	***$2.50***	**£0.30**	**£0.90**	**£1.50**
398 ND Web of Death part 3, continued in Spectacular Spiderman #221; Dr. Octopus appears						
	$0.30	***$0.90***	***$1.50***	**£0.20**	**£0.60**	**£1.00**
399 ND The Jackal appears						
	$0.30	***$0.90***	***$1.50***	**£0.20**	**£0.60**	**£1.00**
400 ND 64pgs, the death of Aunt May						
	$0.60	***$1.80***	***$3.00***	**£0.40**	**£1.20**	**£2.00**
400 Enhanced Edition, ND 64pgs, - die-cut multi-level debossed cover						
	$1.20	***$3.60***	***$6.00***	**£0.60**	**£1.80**	**£3.00**
400 White Cover Variant Edition ND						
	$3.50	***$10.50***	***$17.50***	**£2.50**	**£7.50**	**£12.50**
401 ND The Mark of Kaine part 2, continued in Spiderman [2nd Series] #58						
	$0.30	***$0.90***	***$1.50***	**£0.20**	**£0.60**	**£1.00**
402 ND continued in Spiderman [2nd Series] #59						
	$0.30	***$0.90***	***$1.50***	**£0.20**	**£0.60**	**£1.00**
403 ND The Trial of Peter Parker part 2, continued in Spiderman [2nd series] #60; Carnage appears						
	$0.30	***$0.90***	***$1.50***	**£0.20**	**£0.60**	**£1.00**
404 ND Maximum Clonage part 3, continued in Spiderman [2nd Series] #61; Spiderman vs. The Scarlet Spider						
	$0.30	***$0.90***	***$1.50***	**£0.20**	**£0.60**	**£1.00**
405 ND Exiled part 2, continued in Spiderman [2nd Series] #62						
	$0.30	***$0.90***	***$1.50***	**£0.20**	**£0.60**	**£1.00**
406 ND The Great Responsibility part 1, continued in Spiderman [2nd Series] #63; 1st new Dr. Octopus; Angel Medina guest art						
	$0.30	***$0.90***	***$1.50***	**£0.20**	**£0.60**	**£1.00**
407 ND The Return of Spiderman part 2, Spiderman vs. Sandman, Human Torch appears; continued Spiderman #64						
	$0.30	***$0.90***	***$1.50***	**£0.20**	**£0.60**	**£1.00**
408 ND Media Blizzard part 2, continued in Spiderman #65						
	$0.30	***$0.90***	***$1.50***	**£0.20**	**£0.60**	**£1.00**
409 ND The Return of Kaine part 3, continued in Spiderman #66						
	$0.30	***$0.90***	***$1.50***	**£0.20**	**£0.60**	**£1.00**
410 ND Web of Carnage part 2, continued in Spiderman #67; Carnage appears						
	$0.30	***$0.90***	***$1.50***	**£0.20**	**£0.60**	**£1.00**
411 ND Blood Brothers part 2, continued in Spiderman #68						
	$0.30	***$0.90***	***$1.50***	**£0.20**	**£0.60**	**£1.00**
412 ND Blood Brothers part 6 (conclusion)						
	$0.30	***$0.90***	***$1.50***	**£0.20**	**£0.60**	**£1.00**
413 ND Mysterio appears						
	$0.30	***$0.90***	***$1.50***	**£0.20**	**£0.60**	**£1.00**
414 ND	***$0.30***	***$0.90***	***$1.50***	**£0.20**	**£0.60**	**£1.00**
415 ND Onslaught tie-in						
	$0.30	***$0.90***	***$1.50***	**£0.20**	**£0.60**	**£1.00**
416 ND with bound-in Overpower cards						
	$0.30	***$0.90***	***$1.50***	**£0.20**	**£0.60**	**£1.00**
417 ND	***$0.30***	***$0.90***	***$1.50***	**£0.20**	**£0.60**	**£1.00**
418 ND Revelations part 3, concluded in Spiderman #75						
	$0.30	***$0.90***	***$1.50***	**£0.20**	**£0.60**	**£1.00**
419 ND intro The Black Tarantula						
	$0.30	***$0.90***	***$1.50***	**£0.20**	**£0.60**	**£1.00**
420 ND X-Man appears, continued in X-Man #24						
	$0.30	***$0.90***	***$1.50***	**£0.20**	**£0.60**	**£1.00**
421 ND	***$0.40***	***$1.20***	***$2.00***	**£0.25**	**£0.75**	**£1.25**
Title Value:	***$5354.55***	***$16137.85***	***$52444.50***	**£2977.05**	**£8940.15**	**£29112.25**

	£Good	£Fine	£N.Mint
Sensational Spiderman (1988)			
Trade paperback ND reprints Annual #14, #15 (Miller art) plus issue #8 back-up featuring Human Torch (Ditko art)	£0.80	£2.40	£4.00
Spiderman Hardcover (Jun 1989)			
ND reprints 6 part Kraven Saga, Mike Zeck art	£2.40	£7.20	£12.00
Alien Costume			
Trade paperback ND reprints issues #252-259	£1.60	£4.80	£8.00
(2nd printing - Aug 1990)	£1.50	£4.50	£7.50
(3rd printing - Dec 1992)	£1.50	£4.50	£7.50
Nothing Can Stop The Juggernaut (Sep 1989)			
Trade paperback [Headlined: The Sensational Spiderman] ND reprints issues #229,#230	£0.50	£1.50	£2.50
(2nd printing - Oct 1990)	£0.45	£1.35	£2.25
Spiderman vs. Venom			
Trade paperback ND reprints issues #298 & #299 as 1 pagers plus #300, #315-317	£1.00	£3.00	£5.00
Spiderman: Kraven's Last Hunt (Sep 1990)			
Trade paperback ND reprints Kraven Saga, Mike Zeck art	£1.00	£3.00	£5.00
(2nd printing - Dec 1992)	£0.80	£2.40	£4.00
The Death of Jean DeWolff			
Trade paperback ND 96pgs, reprints 4 part story	£1.00	£3.00	£5.00
Spiderman's Wedding (Nov 1991)			
Trade paperback ND reprints lead-up to wedding plus syndicated newspaper material	£1.50	£4.50	£7.50
Spiderman: Assassination Plot			
Trade paperback (Jul 1992) ND reprints Amazing Spiderman #320-325	£2.00	£6.00	£10.00
(2nd print - Jun 1993)	£1.90	£5.70	£9.50
Spiderman: The Cosmic Adventures			
Trade paperback (Mar 1993) ND 196pgs, reprints Spectacular Spiderman #158-#160, Web of Spiderman #59-#61, Amazing Spiderman #327-#329, Ron Lim cover	£2.50	£7.50	£12.50
Spiderman: Venom Returns (May 1993)			
Trade paperback ND reprints Amazing Spiderman #331-333, #344-347	£1.60	£4.80	£8.00
Spiderman: Origin of Hobgoblin (Jul 1993)			
Trade paperback ND reprints Amazing Spiderman #238, 239, 244, 245, 249-251	£1.80	£5.40	£9.00
Spiderman: Carnage (Aug 1993)			
Trade paperback ND reprints Amazing Spiderman #361-363	£0.90	£2.70	£4.50
The Complete Frank Miller Spiderman (Jun 1994)			
Hardback with embossed dust-wrapped ND reprints Annual #14,15 plus Marvel Team Up #100, Annual #4 and Spectacular Spiderman #27 and 28	£4.00	£12.00	£20.00
Spiderman: Round Robin (Jul 1994)			
Trade paperback ND reprints	£2.00	£6.00	£10.00
Spiderman: Maximum Carnage (Oct 1994)			
Trade paperback ND 336pgs, reprints Maximum Carnage storyline	£3.30	£9.90	£16.50
Spiderman: Return of the Sinister Six (Nov 1994)			
Trade paperback ND reprints Spiderman #334-339	£2.00	£6.00	£10.00
Very Best of Spiderman (Dec 1994)			
Trade paperback ND 176pgs, classic reprints	£2.00	£6.00	£10.00
Spiderman: Revenge of the Sinister Six (Jan 1995)			
Trade paperback ND reprints Spiderman #18-23 with Erik Larsen art	£2.00	£6.00	£10.00
Spiderman: Invasion of the Spider-Slayers (Apr 1995)			
Trade paperback ND 144pgs, reprints issues #368-373	£2.00	£6.00	£10.00

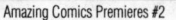

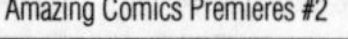
Amazing Comics Premieres #2

American Freak #1

Amazing Spiderman Annual #8

$Good $Fine $N.Mint £Good £Fine £N.Mint

Spiderman: Carnage (Apr 1995)
80pgs Bookshelf Edition, reprints issues #361-363 £0.90 £2.70 £4.50
Spiderman: Clone Genesis (Aug 1995)
Trade paperback
ND reprints the Clone Saga from Spiderman #141-151 £2.30 £6.90 £11.50
Spiderman vs. Dr. Doom (Sep 1995)
ND reprints Amazing Spiderman #349/350 with new cover £0.90 £2.70 £4.50
Spiderman vs. Green Goblin (Oct 1995)
Trade paperback ND reprints classic encounters £2.00 £6.00 £10.00
Spiderman Premiere (Nov 1995)
ND boxed set of Web of Spiderman #117, Spiderman #51, Amazing Spiderman #394, Spectacular Spiderman #217 that make up the "Power and Responsibility" story £1.50 £4.50 £7.50
Spiderman & The X-Men Team Up (Apr 1996)
Trade paperback ND 176pgs, reprints classic team-ups £2.20 £6.60 £11.00
Spiderman's Greatest Team-Ups (Aug 1996)
ND 176pgs, reprints classic team-ups inc. Marvel Team-Up #100 £2.20 £6.60 £11.00
Spiderman: The Lost Years (Oct 1996)
Trade paperback
ND reprints mini-series, new cover by John Romita Jnr. £1.30 £3.90 £6.50
Spiderman's Strangest Adventures (Dec 1996)
Trade paperback
ND 176pgs, collects selected stories like Amazing Spiderman #101 £2.30 £6.90 £11.50
The Greatest Spiderman & Daredevil Team-Ups (Feb 1997)
Trade paperback ND 176pgs, collects selected stories including Amazing Spiderman #16 and Spectacular Spiderman #27 £2.30 £6.90 £11.50
The Essential Spiderman (Feb 1996)
Trade paperback ND 528pgs, collects Amazing Fantasy #15, Spiderman #1-20 and Annual #1 on newsprint £1.70 £5.10 £8.50

AMAZING SPIDERMAN, THE ANNUAL

Marvel Comics Group; 1 1964-9 1973; 10 Jun 1976-present
1 scarce in the U.K. 72pgs, origin retold, 1st appearance Sinister Six; Steve Ditko art
$57.50 $175.00 $525.00 **£33.00 £100.00 £300.00**
[Scarce in high grade - Very Fine+ or better]
2 72pgs, Dr. Strange appears; reprints from issues #1,#2 and #5; Steve Ditko art
$31.00 $92.50 $250.00 **£18.50 £55.00 £150.00**
3 72pgs, Avengers vs. Hulk
$16.50 $50.00 $100.00 **£8.25 £25.00 £50.00**
4 72pgs, Spiderman vs. Human Torch (new 40pg story)
$15.00 $45.00 $90.00 **£5.75 £17.50 £35.00**
5 72pgs, Peter Parker's parents appear, Red Skull appears (see 30th anniversay issues of Spiderman), Fantastic Four appear
$14.00 $43.00 $85.00 **£6.50 £20.00 £40.00**
6 68pgs, Sinister Six appear (story reprinted from Annual #1)
$5.75 $17.50 $35.00 **£2.90 £8.75 £17.50**
7 68pgs, reprints Spiderman #1, #6 (Lizard)
$5.25 $16.00 $32.50 **£2.50 £7.50 £15.00**
8 ND scarce in the U.K. 68pgs
$5.25 $16.00 $32.50 **£2.50 £7.50 £15.00**
9 ND very scarce in the U.K. 52pgs, reprints edited version of story from Spectacular Spiderman Magazine #2 with Green Goblin (hard to find without inking stains around edges)
$5.25 $16.00 $32.50 **£3.30 £10.00 £20.00**
10 ND scarce in the U.K. 52pgs
$1.65 $5.00 $10.00 **£1.15 £3.50 £7.00**
11 ND 52pgs, John Romita Jnr. art (very early - 1st?)
$1.30 $4.00 $8.00 **£0.80 £2.50 £5.00**
12 ND 52pgs, John Byrne cover
$1.30 $4.00 $8.00 **£0.65 £2.00 £4.00**
13 ND 52pgs, John Byrne art
$1.30 $4.00 $8.00 **£0.80 £2.50 £5.00**
14 ND 52pgs, Frank Miller art (Ditkoesque Dr. Strange)
$1.80 $5.25 $9.00 **£1.00 £3.00 £5.00**
15 ND 52pgs, Frank Miller art, Dr. Octopus/Punisher appear
$3.00 $9.00 $15.00 **£1.30 £3.90 £6.50**
16 ND 52pgs, 1st appearance new Captain Marvel (female)
$1.40 $4.20 $7.00 **£0.60 £1.80 £3.00**
17-19 ND ***$1.40 $4.20 $7.00*** **£0.50 £1.50 £2.50**
20 scarce in the U.K. 1st appearance Iron Man of 2020
$1.40 $4.20 $7.00 **£0.60 £1.80 £3.00**
21 ND costume cover, Peter Parker, Mary Jane wed
$1.80 $5.25 $9.00 **£0.60 £1.80 £3.00**
21 plain clothes cover, ND Peter Parker, Mary Jane wed
$1.80 $5.25 $9.00 **£0.60 £1.80 £3.00**
22 ND 64pgs, squarebound, Evolutionary War, Ron Lim art on back-up
$1.20 $3.60 $6.00 **£0.40 £1.20 £2.00**
23 ND squarebound, Atlantis Attacks part 4, She-Hulk appears, Rob Liefeld art
$0.80 $2.40 $4.00 **£0.50 £1.50 £2.50**
24 ND squarebound, Spiderman's Totally Tiny Adventure part 1, continues in Spectacular Spiderman Annual #10, Sandman back-up by Mike Zeck
$0.80 $2.40 $4.00 **£0.40 £1.20 £2.00**
25 ND The Vibranium Vendetta part 1, continued in Spectacular Spiderman Annual #11; 1st solo Venom story
$2.00 $6.00 $10.00 **£0.70 £2.10 £3.50**
26 ND The Hero Killers part 1, New Warriors and Venom appear, continued in Spectacular Spiderman Annual #12
$1.40 $4.20 $7.00 **£0.40 £1.20 £2.00**
27 ND pre-bagged with trading card; Tom Lyle art
$0.60 $1.80 $3.00 **£0.40 £1.20 £2.00**
28 ND Spiderman vs. Carnage
$0.60 $1.80 $3.00 **£0.40 £1.20 £2.00**
Title Value: *$183.85 $555.95 $1330.50* £96.00 £289.95 £710.50
Note: #3-8 titled "Special. #9 titled "King Size". #1-3 have back-up reprints. #6-8, 12 are all reprint.
Note also that Annual 1 & 2 occasionally turn up with blank back and inside covers (see Fantastic Four Annuals #1-3, Sgt. Fury Annual #1, Strange Tales Annual #2). These were originally subscription copies sent over to this country as left-overs. They are very scarce and with their white back covers they show soiling and wear that much more easily. They are very rare in near mint condition.

AMAZING WORLD OF DC COMICS, THE

DC Comics; 1 Jul/Aug 1974-17 Apr 1978
1 ND 48pgs, Joe Kubert interview, unpublished Jack Kirby story
$1.25 $3.75 $7.50 **£0.80 £2.50 £5.00**
2 ND 48pgs, Fifties issue
$1.25 $3.75 $7.50 **£0.75 £2.25 £4.50**
3 ND 48pgs, Julius Schwartz issue, unpublished Golden Age Green Lantern story
$1.25 $3.75 $7.50 **£0.75 £2.25 £4.50**
4 ND 48pgs, Batman issue, Jerry Robinson interview
$1.25 $3.75 $7.50 **£0.80 £2.50 £5.00**
5 ND 48pgs, Sheldon Mayer/Golden Age issue
$1.00 $3.00 $6.00 **£0.65 £2.00 £4.00**
6 ND 48pgs ***$1.00 $3.00 $6.00*** **£0.65 £2.00 £4.00**
7 ND 48pgs, Superman issue, Mort Weisinger/Curt Swan interviews
$1.25 $3.75 $7.50 **£0.80 £2.50 £5.00**
8 ND 48pgs, Carmine Infantino issue
$1.00 $3.00 $6.00 **£0.65 £2.00 £4.00**
9 ND 48pgs, Legion of Super-Heroes issue, Legion check-list
$1.25 $3.75 $7.50 **£0.80 £2.50 £5.00**
10 ND 48pgs, feature on Showcase title
$1.00 $3.00 $6.00 **£0.65 £2.00 £4.00**
11 ND 48pgs, Super-Villain issue
$1.00 $3.00 $6.00 **£0.65 £2.00 £4.00**
12 ND 48pgs, Sci-Fi issue, Mike Grell feature
$1.00 $3.00 $6.00 **£0.65 £2.00 £4.00**
13 ND 48pgs, Humour issue, Wonder Woman feature
$1.00 $3.00 $6.00 **£0.65 £2.00 £4.00**
14 ND 48pgs, Justice League of America issue
$1.50 $4.50 $9.00 **£1.00 £3.00 £6.00**
15 ND 48pgs, Wonder Woman issue
$1.00 $3.00 $6.00 **£0.65 £2.00 £4.00**
16 ND 48pgs, Golden Age issue, Silver Age comics feature
$1.00 $3.00 $6.00 **£0.65 £2.00 £4.00**
17 ND 48pgs, Shazam issue
$1.00 $3.00 $6.00 **£0.65 £2.00 £4.00**
Title Value: *$19.00 $57.00 $114.00* £12.20 £37.50 £75.00
Note: magazine format professional "fanzine" published by DC Comics. Each issue carries check-list/covers of Dc comics to be published that month.

AMAZON

DC Comics/Amalgam,OS; 1 May 1996
1 ND a DC/Marvel amalgamation of Wonder Woman and Storm; John Byrne script, John Byrne and Terry Austin art
$0.50 $1.50 $2.50 **£0.40 £1.20 £2.00**
Title Value: *$0.50 $1.50 $2.50* £0.40 £1.20 £2.00

AMAZON WARRIORS

AC Comics,OS; 1 1989
1 ND b&w ***$0.50 $1.50 $2.50*** **£0.30 £0.90 £1.50**
Title Value: *$0.50 $1.50 $2.50* £0.30 £0.90 £1.50

AMAZON WOMAN

Fantaco,MS; 1 Feb 1996-4 May 1996
1-4 ND Tom Simonton script and art; black and white
$0.60 $1.80 $3.00 **£0.40 £1.20 £2.00**
Title Value: *$2.40 $7.20 $12.00* £1.60 £4.80 £8.00

AMAZON, THE

Comico,MS; 1 Mar 1989-3 May 1989
1-3 ND Tim Sale art, colour
$0.40 $1.20 $2.00 **£0.25 £0.75 £1.25**
Title Value: *$1.20 $3.60 $6.00* £0.75 £2.25 £3.75

AMBER: THE GUNS OF AVALON

DC Comics,MS; 1 Oct 1996-3 Dec 1996
1-3 ND 48pgs, adaptation of Roger Zelazny novel
$1.40 $4.20 $7.00 **£0.90 £2.70 £4.50**
Title Value: *$4.20 $12.60 $21.00* £2.70 £8.10 £13.50

AMBUSH BUG

DC Comics,MS; 1 Jun 1985-4 Sep 1985
1-4 Keith Giffen art ***$0.25 $0.75 $1.25*** **£0.15 £0.45 £0.75**
Title Value: *$1.00 $3.00 $5.00* £0.60 £1.80 £3.00

AMBUSH BUG NOTHING SPECIAL

DC Comics,OS; 1 Sep 1992
1 64pgs, Lobo, Death, Sandman, Aquaman appear
$0.40 $1.20 $2.00 **£0.25 £0.75 £1.25**
Title Value: *$0.40 $1.20 $2.00* £0.25 £0.75 £1.25

AMBUSH BUG STOCKING STUFFER

DC Comics,OS; nn Feb 1986
nn 48pgs, Giffen art; Joker cameo
$0.25 $0.75 $1.25 **£0.15 £0.45 £0.75**
Title Value: *$0.25 $0.75 $1.25* £0.15 £0.45 £0.75

AMBUSH BUG, SON OF

DC Comics,MS; 1 Jul 1986-6 Dec 1986
1-6 Giffen art ***$0.15 $0.45 $0.75*** **£0.10 £0.35 £0.60**
Title Value: *$0.90 $2.70 $4.50* £0.60 £2.10 £3.60

AMERICA VERSUS THE JUSTICE SOCIETY

DC Comics,MS; 1 Jan 1985-4 Apr 1985
1-4 ND 48pgs ***$0.30 $0.90 $1.50*** **£0.20 £0.60 £1.00**
Title Value: *$1.20 $3.60 $6.00* £0.80 £2.40 £4.00

AMERICA'S BEST TV COMICS

ABC; nn 1967
nn ND scarce in the U.K. 64pgs, squarebound; promotion for cartoon show, reprints F.F. #19, Spiderman #51
$11.00 $34.00 $80.00 **£7.00 £21.00 £50.00**

	$Good	$Fine	$N.Mint	£Good	£Fine	£N.Mint
Title Value:	$11.00	$34.00	$80.00	£7.00	£21.00	£50.00
AMERICAN FLAGG!						
First; 1 Oct 1983-50 Mar 1988						
1 ND Chaykin story/art begins, ends #26	$1.00	$3.00	$5.00	£0.60	£1.80	£3.00
2-3 ND	$0.70	$2.10	$3.50	£0.50	£1.50	£2.50
4-5 ND	$0.60	$1.80	$3.00	£0.40	£1.20	£2.00
6-10 ND	$0.50	$1.50	$2.50	£0.30	£0.90	£1.50
11-18 ND	$0.40	$1.20	$2.00	£0.25	£0.75	£1.25
19 ND scarce in the U.K.	$0.40	$1.20	$2.00	£0.50	£1.50	£2.50
20 ND	$0.40	$1.20	$2.00	£0.25	£0.75	£1.25
21-25 ND Alan Moore back-up	$0.50	$1.50	$2.50	£0.30	£0.90	£1.50
26 ND Alan Moore back-up, last Chaykin art	$0.50	$1.50	$2.50	£0.30	£0.90	£1.50
27 ND Alan Moore script, Don Lomax art	$0.50	$1.50	$2.50	£0.30	£0.90	£1.50
28-30 ND Staton art	$0.40	$1.20	$2.00	£0.25	£0.75	£1.25
31-45 ND Badger art	$0.40	$1.20	$2.00	£0.25	£0.75	£1.25
46 ND retrospective/apology issue	$0.50	$1.50	$2.50	£0.30	£0.90	£1.50
47-49 ND Paul Smith art	$0.50	$1.50	$2.50	£0.30	£0.90	£1.50
50 ND Howard Chaykin art	$0.50	$1.50	$2.50	£0.30	£0.90	£1.50
Title Value:	$23.30	$69.90	$116.50	£14.75	£44.25	£73.75
Hard Times: Trade paperback, reprints #1-3, plus new material				1.50	4.50	7.50
Southern Comfort: Trade paperback, reprints #4-6, plus new material				1.50	4.50	7.50
AMERICAN FLAGG! (2ND SERIES)						
First,MS; 1 May 1988-12 Apr 1989						
1 ND Chaykin story/breakdowns/part art begins	$0.50	$1.50	$2.50	£0.30	£0.90	£1.50
2-12 ND	$0.40	$1.20	$2.00	£0.25	£0.75	£1.25
Title Value:	$4.90	$14.70	$24.50	£3.05	£9.15	£15.25
AMERICAN FLAGG! SPECIAL						
First,OS; 1 Nov 1986						
1 ND 1st Time Squared	$0.50	$1.50	$2.50	£0.30	£0.90	£1.50
Title Value:	$0.50	$1.50	$2.50	£0.30	£0.90	£1.50
AMERICAN FREAK: A TALE OF THE UN-MEN						
DC Comics/Vertigo,MS; 1 Feb 1994-5 Jun 1994						
1-5 Dave Louapre script, Vince Locke art	$0.40	$1.20	$2.00	£0.25	£0.75	£1.25
Title Value:	$2.00	$6.00	$10.00	£1.25	£3.75	£6.25
AMERICAN SPLENDOUR SPECIAL: A STEP OUT OF THE NEST						
Dark Horse,OS; 1 Aug 1994						
1 ND Harvey Pekar script; comic sized version of American Splendour book	$0.60	$1.80	$3.00	£0.40	£1.20	£2.00
Title Value:	$0.60	$1.80	$3.00	£0.40	£1.20	£2.00
AMERICAN SPLENDOUR: COMIC-CON COMICS						
Dark Horse,OS; 1 Aug 1996						
1 ND Harvey Pekar script; black and white	$0.60	$1.80	$3.00	£0.40	£1.20	£2.00
Title Value:	$0.60	$1.80	$3.00	£0.40	£1.20	£2.00
AMERICAN SPLENDOUR: WINDFALL						
Dark Horse,MS; 1 Sep 1995-2 Oct 1995						
1-2 ND 40pgs, Harvey Pekar script; black and white	$0.80	$2.40	$4.00	£0.50	£1.50	£2.50
Title Value:	$1.60	$4.80	$8.00	£1.00	£3.00	£5.00
AMERICAN, THE						
Dark Horse; 1 Aug 1987-8 1989						
1 ND scarce in the U.K. Mark Veheiden script/Chris Warner art begins	$1.00	$3.00	$5.00	£0.70	£2.10	£3.50
2 ND scarce in the U.K.	$0.80	$2.40	$4.00	£0.50	£1.50	£2.50
3 ND	$0.60	$1.80	$3.00	£0.40	£1.20	£2.00
4-5 ND	$0.50	$1.50	$2.50	£0.30	£0.90	£1.50
6-8 ND	$0.40	$1.20	$2.00	£0.25	£0.75	£1.25
Title Value:	$4.60	$13.80	$23.00	£2.95	£8.85	£14.75
Book 1, reprints #1-4				£0.80	£2.40	£4.00
Special (Jul 1990), story continues from issue 8, colour				£0.30	£0.90	£1.50
AMERICAN: LOST IN AMERICA, THE						
Dark Horse,MS; 1 Jul 1992-4 Dec 1992						
1 ND Dave Dorman cover	$0.50	$1.50	$2.50	£0.30	£0.90	£1.50
2-3 ND	$0.50	$1.50	$2.50	£0.30	£0.90	£1.50
4 ND Mike Mignola cover	$0.50	$1.50	$2.50	£0.30	£0.90	£1.50
Title Value:	$2.00	$6.00	$10.00	£1.20	£3.60	£6.00
AMERICOMICS						
AC Comics; 1 Apr 1983-6 Mar 1984						
1 ND intro The Shade, Captain Freedom; George Perez cover	$0.40	$1.20	$2.00	£0.25	£0.75	£1.25
2 ND intro Messenger (Ordway art - 13pgs) Shade appears; Jerry Ordway cover	$0.40	$1.20	$2.00	£0.25	£0.75	£1.25
3 ND Blue Beetle returns; Shade appears	$0.40	$1.20	$2.00	£0.25	£0.75	£1.25
4 ND 1st colour issue, origin Shade, Dragonfly; Jerry Ordway cover	$0.40	$1.20	$2.00	£0.25	£0.75	£1.25
5 ND intro Commando D, Captain Freedom appears	$0.40	$1.20	$2.00	£0.25	£0.75	£1.25
6 ND origin Scarlet Scorpion; Steve Lightle and Jerry Ordway cover	$0.40	$1.20	$2.00	£0.25	£0.75	£1.25
Title Value:	$2.40	$7.20	$12.00	£1.50	£4.50	£7.50
AMERICOMICS SPECIAL						
AC Comics; 1 Aug 1983						
1 ND Blue Beetle, Question, Nightshade, Captain Atom (Sentinels of Justice)	$0.40	$1.20	$2.00	£0.25	£0.75	£1.25
Title Value:	$0.40	$1.20	$2.00	£0.25	£0.75	£1.25
AMETHYST						
DC Comics; 1 Jan 1985-16 Aug 1986						
1-12	$0.15	$0.45	$0.75	£0.10	£0.35	£0.60
13 Crisis X-over	$0.25	$0.75	$1.25	£0.15	£0.45	£0.75
14-16	$0.15	$0.45	$0.75	£0.10	£0.35	£0.60
Title Value:	$2.50	$7.50	$12.50	£1.65	£5.70	£9.75
AMETHYST (LIMITED SERIES)						
DC Comics,MS; 1 Nov 1987-4 Feb 1988						
1-4	$0.15	$0.45	$0.75	£0.10	£0.35	£0.60
Title Value:	$0.60	$1.80	$3.00	£0.40	£1.40	£2.40
Note: New Format						
AMETHYST ANNUAL						
DC Comics; 1 Sep 1984						
1 48pgs	$0.25	$0.75	$1.25	£0.15	£0.45	£0.75
Title Value:	$0.25	$0.75	$1.25	£0.15	£0.45	£0.75
AMETHYST SPECIAL						
DC Comics,OS; nn Sep 1986						
nn Giffen plot	$0.25	$0.75	$1.25	£0.15	£0.45	£0.75
Title Value:	$0.25	$0.75	$1.25	£0.15	£0.45	£0.75
AMETHYST, PRINCESS OF GEMWORLD						
DC Comics,MS; 1 May 1983-12 May 1984						
1 60c cover	$0.15	$0.45	$0.75	£0.10	£0.35	£0.60
1 35 cents cover, ND very scarce in the U.K., scarce in the U.S. (distributed to certain U.S. states only)	$0.40	$1.20	$2.00	£0.30	£0.90	£1.50
2	$0.15	$0.45	$0.75	£0.10	£0.35	£0.60
2 35 cents cover, ND scarce in the U.K. , as above	$0.60	$1.80	$3.00	£0.40	£1.20	£2.00
3-4	$0.15	$0.45	$0.75	£0.10	£0.35	£0.60
5-12 George Perez co-cover artist	$0.15	$0.45	$0.75	£0.10	£0.35	£0.60
Title Value:	$2.80	$8.40	$14.00	£1.90	£6.30	£10.70
AMUSING STORIES						
Renegade; 1 Mar 1986-3 1986						
1-3 ND	$0.30	$0.90	$1.50	£0.20	£0.60	£1.00
Title Value:	$0.90	$2.70	$4.50	£0.60	£1.80	£3.00
AMY PAPUDA						
Northstar,MS; 1 1990-4 1991						
1-4 ND Michael Pearlstein script/art, black and white	$0.50	$1.50	$2.50	£0.30	£0.90	£1.50
Title Value:	$2.00	$6.00	$10.00	£1.20	£3.60	£6.00
Amy Papuda Collection (May 1993) collects mini-series plus Amy Papuda Returns				£1.20	£3.60	£6.00
AMY PAPUDA, THE RETURN OF						
Northstar,OS; 1 Dec 1992						
1 ND	$0.50	$1.50	$2.50	£0.30	£0.90	£1.50
Title Value:	$0.50	$1.50	$2.50	£0.30	£0.90	£1.50
AN AMERICAN TAIL II						
Marvel Comics Group,MS; 1 Jan 1992-3 Feb 1992						
1-3 ND adaptation of Don Bluth animated film, bi-weekly	$0.25	$0.75	$1.25	£0.15	£0.45	£0.75
Title Value:	$0.75	$2.25	$3.75	£0.45	£1.35	£2.25
ANDREW VACHSS' UNDERGROUND						
Dark Horse,MS; 1 Nov 1993-4 Feb 1994						
1-4 ND 48pgs, anthology	$0.70	$2.10	$3.50	£0.50	£1.50	£2.50
Title Value:	$2.80	$8.40	$14.00	£2.00	£6.00	£10.00
ANDROMEDA						
Andromeda; Andromeda/Silver Snail; 1 1977-7 1979						
1-6 ND colour cover	$0.50	$1.50	$2.50	£0.30	£0.90	£1.50
7 ND scarce in the U.K. colour cover	$0.50	$1.50	$2.50	£0.35	£1.05	£1.75
Title Value:	$3.50	$10.50	$17.50	£2.15	£6.45	£10.75
ANGEL AND THE APE						
National Periodical Publications; 1 Nov/Dec 1968-7 Nov/Dec 1969						
(see Showcase #77) (becomes Meet Angel with issue #7)						
1	$3.55	$10.50	$25.00	£2.10	£6.25	£15.00
2-6 Wood inks	$2.10	$6.25	$15.00	£1.10	£3.40	£8.00
7 ND title becomes "Meet Angel", Wood art	$1.40	$4.25	$10.00	£0.85	£2.55	£6.00
Title Value:	$15.45	$46.00	$110.00	£8.45	£25.80	£61.00
ANGEL AND THE APE (2ND SERIES)						
DC Comics,MS; 1 Mar 1990-4 Jun 1991						
1	$0.15	$0.45	$0.75	£0.10	£0.35	£0.60
2 Guy Gardner, Dumb Bunny appear	$0.15	$0.45	$0.75	£0.10	£0.35	£0.60
3-4 Inferior Five appear	$0.15	$0.45	$0.75	£0.10	£0.35	£0.60
Title Value:	$0.60	$1.80	$3.00	£0.40	£1.40	£2.40

ANGEL LOVE
DC Comics,MS; 1 Aug 1986-8 Mar 1987

Issue	$Good	$Fine	$N.Mint	£Good	£Fine	£N.Mint
1-8 Barbara Slate script/art	$0.15	$0.45	$0.75	£0.10	£0.35	£0.60
Title Value:	$1.20	$3.60	$6.00	£0.80	£2.80	£4.80

ANGEL LOVE SPECIAL
DC Comics; 1 Apr 1987

Issue	$Good	$Fine	$N.Mint	£Good	£Fine	£N.Mint
1 48pgs, Barbara Slate script/art	$0.15	$0.45	$0.75	£0.10	£0.35	£0.60
Title Value:	$0.15	$0.45	$0.75	£0.10	£0.35	£0.60

ANGEL OF DEATH
Innovation,MS; 1 Jan 1991-4 Apr 1991

Issue	$Good	$Fine	$N.Mint	£Good	£Fine	£N.Mint
1-4 ND b&w	$0.50	$1.50	$2.50	£0.30	£0.90	£1.50
Title Value:	$2.00	$6.00	$10.00	£1.20	£3.60	£6.00

ANGELA
Image,MS; nn Jan 1995; 1 Dec 1994-3 Feb 1995

Issue	$Good	$Fine	$N.Mint	£Good	£Fine	£N.Mint
nn Pirate Angela ND Pennington cover art; issued with every 25 copies of Spawn #32 ordered	$6.00	$18.00	$30.00	£2.40	£7.00	£12.00
nn Pirate Spawn ND Pennington cover art, Angela and Spawn featured on cover; issued with box of Ultra-Pro mylar sleeves, contains story originaly presented in issue above	$5.00	$15.00	$25.00	£2.40	£7.00	£12.00
1 ND Spawn appears, Neil Gaiman script, Greg Capullo art	$2.00	$6.00	$10.00	£1.00	£3.00	£5.00
2 ND Spawn appears, Neil Gaiman script, Greg Capullo art	$2.00	$6.00	$10.00	£1.20	£3.60	£6.00
3 ND Spawn appears, Neil Gaiman script, Greg Capullo art	$1.60	$4.80	$8.00	£1.00	£3.00	£5.00
Title Value:	$16.60	$49.80	$83.00	£8.00	£23.60	£40.00
Angela (Nov 1995) Trade paperback reprints mini-series, new cover by Greg Capullo				£1.30	£3.90	£6.50

ANGELA/GLORY: RAGE OF ANGELS
Image,OS; 1 Mar 1996

Issue	$Good	$Fine	$N.Mint	£Good	£Fine	£N.Mint
1 ND Rob Liefeld and Robert Napton script, Roger Cruz art; Darkchylde preview flip book	$0.60	$1.80	$3.00	£0.50	£1.50	£2.50
Title Value:	$0.60	$1.80	$3.00	£0.50	£1.50	£2.50

ANGELS OF DESTRUCTION
Marvel Comics Group/Malibu Comics,OS; 1 Oct 1996

Issue	$Good	$Fine	$N.Mint	£Good	£Fine	£N.Mint
1 ND 48pgs, Topaz, Amber and Shuriken from the Ultraverse appear; Hajime Sorayama cover	$0.50	$1.50	$2.50	£0.30	£0.90	£1.50
1 Signed Edition, ND signed by Hajime Sorayama, limited to 500 copies	$3.00	$9.00	$15.00	£2.00	£6.00	£10.00
Title Value:	$3.50	$10.50	$17.50	£2.30	£6.90	£11.50

ANGRY CHRIST TRADE PAPERBACK
Sirius Entertainment,OS; nn Feb 1996

Issue	$Good	$Fine	$N.Mint	£Good	£Fine	£N.Mint
nn ND 144pgs, collects stories from Cry For Dawn between Autumn 1988 and Summer 1994, Joseph Michael Linsner art; black and white	$3.00	$9.00	$15.00	£2.00	£6.00	£10.00
Title Value:	$3.00	$9.00	$15.00	£2.00	£6.00	£10.00

ANGRY SHADOWS
Innovation; 1 1989

Issue	$Good	$Fine	$N.Mint	£Good	£Fine	£N.Mint
1 ND 48pgs, squarebound, black and white horror anthology, John Bolton cover	$0.90	$2.70	$4.50	£0.60	£1.80	£3.00
Title Value:	$0.90	$2.70	$4.50	£0.60	£1.80	£3.00

ANIMA
DC Comics; 0 Oct 1994; 1 Mar 1994-15 May 1995

Issue	$Good	$Fine	$N.Mint	£Good	£Fine	£N.Mint
0 (Oct 1994) Zero Hour X-over, origin revealed	$0.40	$1.20	$2.00	£0.25	£0.75	£1.25
1 spin-off from Bloodbath storyline from 1993 DC annuals	$0.30	$0.90	$1.50	£0.20	£0.60	£1.00
2-6	$0.30	$0.90	$1.50	£0.20	£0.60	£1.00
7 Zero Hour X-over	$0.30	$0.90	$1.50	£0.20	£0.60	£1.00
8-9	$0.30	$0.90	$1.50	£0.20	£0.60	£1.00
10 Superboy appears	$0.30	$0.90	$1.50	£0.20	£0.60	£1.00
11	$0.30	$0.90	$1.50	£0.20	£0.60	£1.00
12-13 Hawkman appears	$0.30	$0.90	$1.50	£0.20	£0.60	£1.00
14-15	$0.30	$0.90	$1.50	£0.20	£0.60	£1.00
Title Value:	$4.90	$14.70	$24.50	£3.25	£9.75	£16.25

ANIMAL CONFIDENTIAL
Dark Horse,OS; 1 Jul 1992

Issue	$Good	$Fine	$N.Mint	£Good	£Fine	£N.Mint
1 ND anthology of parody pulp animal stories	$0.50	$1.50	$2.50	£0.30	£0.90	£1.50
Title Value:	$0.50	$1.50	$2.50	£0.30	£0.90	£1.50

ANIMAL MAN
DC Comics/Vertigo; 1 Sep 1988-89 Nov 1995

Issue	$Good	$Fine	$N.Mint	£Good	£Fine	£N.Mint
1 Grant Morrison scripts, Bolland covers begin	$1.20	$3.60	$6.00	£0.80	£2.40	£4.00
2	$0.60	$1.80	$3.00	£0.60	£1.80	£3.00
3-4	$0.50	$1.50	$2.50	£0.50	£1.50	£2.50
5 "Wile E.Coyote" story	$0.50	$1.50	$2.50	£0.50	£1.50	£2.50
6 Invasion X-over	$0.40	$1.20	$2.00	£0.50	£1.50	£2.50
7-8	$0.40	$1.20	$2.00	£0.50	£1.50	£2.50
9 new Mirror Master appears	$0.40	$1.20	$2.00	£0.50	£1.50	£2.50
10	$0.40	$1.20	$2.00	£0.50	£1.50	£2.50
11 co-stars The Vixen	$0.40	$1.20	$2.00	£0.40	£1.20	£2.00
12-15	$0.40	$1.20	$2.00	£0.40	£1.20	£2.00
16 Justice League Europe appears	$0.35	$1.05	$1.75	£0.30	£0.90	£1.50
17-23	$0.35	$1.05	$1.75	£0.30	£0.90	£1.50
24 Arkham Asylum featured	$0.35	$1.05	$1.75	£0.30	£0.90	£1.50
25	$0.35	$1.05	$1.75	£0.30	£0.90	£1.50
26	$0.35	$1.05	$1.75	£0.25	£0.75	£1.25
27 Pete Milligan scripts begin	$0.35	$1.05	$1.75	£0.25	£0.75	£1.25
28-32	$0.35	$1.05	$1.75	£0.25	£0.75	£1.25
33 Tom Veitch scripts and Steve Dillon art begins	$0.35	$1.05	$1.75	£0.25	£0.75	£1.25
34-39	$0.35	$1.05	$1.75	£0.25	£0.75	£1.25
40 War of the Gods X-over	$0.35	$1.05	$1.75	£0.25	£0.75	£1.25
41-43	$0.35	$1.05	$1.75	£0.25	£0.75	£1.25
44 The Vixen appears	$0.35	$1.05	$1.75	£0.25	£0.75	£1.25
45-46	$0.35	$1.05	$1.75	£0.25	£0.75	£1.25
47 B'wana Beast appears	$0.35	$1.05	$1.75	£0.25	£0.75	£1.25
48-49	$0.35	$1.05	$1.75	£0.25	£0.75	£1.25
50 48pgs, last Tom Veitch script	$0.60	$1.80	$3.00	£0.40	£1.20	£2.00
51 Jamie Delano scripts begin, new direction for title	$0.35	$1.05	$1.75	£0.25	£0.75	£1.25
52-56	$0.35	$1.05	$1.75	£0.25	£0.75	£1.25
57 Recreation part 1, 1st issue under "Vertigo" banner	$0.35	$1.05	$1.75	£0.25	£0.75	£1.25
58-59 John Higgins art	$0.35	$1.05	$1.75	£0.25	£0.75	£1.25
60 John Higgins art, $1.95 cover price begin	$0.35	$1.05	$1.75	£0.25	£0.75	£1.25
61-66	$0.35	$1.05	$1.75	£0.25	£0.75	£1.25
67 ties in with Animal Man Annual #1	$0.35	$1.05	$1.75	£0.25	£0.75	£1.25
68-78	$0.35	$1.05	$1.75	£0.25	£0.75	£1.25
79 last Jamie Delano script	$0.35	$1.05	$1.75	£0.25	£0.75	£1.25
80-88	$0.35	$1.05	$1.75	£0.25	£0.75	£1.25
89	$0.45	$1.35	$2.25	£0.30	£0.90	£1.50
Title Value:	$33.55	$100.65	$167.75	£26.60	£79.80	£133.00

Note: New Format

Issue	$Good	$Fine	$N.Mint	£Good	£Fine	£N.Mint
Trade paperback (Sep 1991), reprints issues #1-9 with covers; intro by Grant Morrison, new painted cover by Brian Bolland				£2.40	£7.20	£12.00

ANIMAL MAN ANNUAL
DC Comics/Vertigo; 1 Dec 1993

Issue	$Good	$Fine	$N.Mint	£Good	£Fine	£N.Mint
1 The Children's Crusade part 3, continued in Swamp Thing Annual #7; Brian Bolland cover	$0.60	$1.80	$3.00	£0.40	£1.20	£2.00
Title Value:	$0.60	$1.80	$3.00	£0.40	£1.20	£2.00

ANIMAL MYSTIC
CFD Productions; 1 1993-4 1995

Issue	$Good	$Fine	$N.Mint	£Good	£Fine	£N.Mint
1 ND	$12.00	$36.00	$60.00	£7.00	£21.00	£35.00
1 2nd printing ND	$1.60	$4.80	$8.00	£1.00	£3.00	£5.00
1 Variant Cover Signed & Numbered, ND; contains 8 new pages plus pin-ups	$20.00	$60.00	$100.00	£11.00	£33.00	£55.00
2 ND 1st appearance of Klor	$13.00	$39.00	$65.00	£7.00	£21.00	£35.00
2 2nd printing, ND new cover art	$1.60	$4.80	$8.00	£0.80	£2.40	£4.00
3 ND	$5.00	$15.00	$25.00	£3.00	£9.00	£15.00
3 2nd printing ND	$1.60	$4.80	$8.00	£0.80	£2.40	£4.00
4 ND DS, contains poster insert	$2.00	$6.00	$10.00	£1.20	£3.60	£6.00
Title Value:	$56.80	$170.40	$284.00	£31.80	£95.40	£159.00

ANIMAL MYSTIC: WATER WARS
Sirius,MS; 1 Jul 1996-present

Issue	$Good	$Fine	$N.Mint	£Good	£Fine	£N.Mint
1-3 ND 24pgs	$0.60	$1.80	$3.00	£0.40	£1.20	£2.00
Title Value:	$1.80	$5.40	$9.00	£1.20	£3.60	£6.00

ANIMAL MYSTIC: WIZARD ACE EDITION
Sirius/Wizard,OS; nn 1996

Issue	$Good	$Fine	$N.Mint	£Good	£Fine	£N.Mint
nn ND black and white with card-stock cover and wraparound acetate overlay cover; numbered Wizard Ace Edition #7	$3.00	$9.00	$15.00	£2.00	£6.00	£10.00
Title Value:	$3.00	$9.00	$15.00	£2.00	£6.00	£10.00

ANIMANIACS
DC Comics; 1 May 1995-present

Issue	$Good	$Fine	$N.Mint	£Good	£Fine	£N.Mint
1-18 ND based on cartoon show	$0.30	$0.90	$1.50	£0.20	£0.60	£1.00
19 ND based on cartoon show; X-Files parody	$0.35	$1.05	$1.75	£0.40	£1.20	£2.00
20-24 ND based on cartoon show	$0.30	$0.90	$1.50	£0.20	£0.60	£1.00
Title Value:	$7.25	$21.75	$36.25	£5.00	£15.00	£25.00

ANIMANIACS: A CHRISTMAS SPECIAL
DC Comics,OS; 1 Jan 1995

Issue	$Good	$Fine	$N.Mint	£Good	£Fine	£N.Mint
1	$0.30	$0.90	$1.50	£0.20	£0.60	£1.00
Title Value:	$0.30	$0.90	$1.50	£0.20	£0.60	£1.00

ANIMAX
Marvel Comics Group/Star, Toy; 1 Dec 1986-4 Jun 1987

Issue	$Good	$Fine	$N.Mint	£Good	£Fine	£N.Mint
1-4	$0.15	$0.45	$0.75	£0.10	£0.30	£0.50
Title Value:	$0.60	$1.80	$3.00	£0.40	£1.20	£2.00

	$Good	$Fine	$N.Mint	£Good	£Fine	£N.Mint
ANNEX						
Marvel Comics Group,MS; 1 Aug 1994-4 Nov 1994						
1-4 spin-off from Amazing Spiderman Annual #27						
	$0.30	$0.90	$1.50	£0.20	£0.60	£1.00
Title Value:	$1.20	$3.60	$6.00	£0.80	£2.40	£4.00
ANNIE						
Marvel Comics Group,MS Film; 1 Oct 1982-2 Nov 1982						
1-2 ND	$0.15	$0.45	$0.75	£0.10	£0.35	£0.60
Title Value:	$0.30	$0.90	$1.50	£0.20	£0.70	£1.20
ANNIE (2ND SERIES)						
Marvel Comics Group,Tabloid OS; 1 Oct 1982						
1 ND reprints mini-series						
	$0.30	$0.90	$1.50	£0.20	£0.60	£1.00
Title Value:	$0.30	$0.90	$1.50	£0.20	£0.60	£1.00
ANT BOY						
Steeldragon Press; 1 1987-2 1987						
1 ND Matt Feazell story and art						
	$0.40	$1.20	$2.00	£0.25	£0.75	£1.25
1 2nd printing ND	$0.30	$0.90	$1.50	£0.20	£0.60	£1.00
2 ND	$0.40	$1.20	$2.00	£0.25	£0.75	£1.25
Title Value:	$1.10	$3.30	$5.50	£0.70	£2.10	£3.50
ANTHRO						
National Periodical Publications; 1 Jul/Aug 1968-6 Jul/Aug 1969						
(see Showcase #74)						
1	$5.50	$17.00	$40.00	£3.55	£10.50	£25.00
2	$3.55	$10.50	$25.00	£1.75	£5.25	£12.50
3-5	$3.55	$10.50	$25.00	£1.40	£4.25	£10.00
6 Wood cover/inks	$3.55	$10.50	$25.00	£1.40	£4.25	£10.00
Title Value:	$23.25	$69.50	$165.00	£10.90	£32.75	£77.50
ANTI-HITLER COMICS						
New England Comics; 1 Aug 1992						
1 ND reprints Golden Age stories						
	$0.50	$1.50	$2.50	£0.30	£0.90	£1.50
Title Value:	$0.50	$1.50	$2.50	£0.30	£0.90	£1.50
ANTIQUITIES WAR ON THE WORLD OF MAGIC: THE GATHERING						
Acclaim Comics/Armada,MS; 1 Nov 1995-4 Feb 1996						
1 ND George Pratt painted cover						
	$0.50	$1.50	$2.50	£0.30	£0.90	£1.50
2-4 ND	$0.50	$1.50	$2.50	£0.30	£0.90	£1.50
Title Value:	$2.00	$6.00	$10.00	£1.20	£3.60	£6.00
ANXIETY TIMES						
Eclipse; 1 Aug 1992						
1 ND 48pgs, anthology of tales featuring work by Gilbert Hernandez, Don McGregor, Gene Colan						
	$0.90	$2.70	$4.50	£0.60	£1.80	£3.00
Title Value:	$0.90	$2.70	$4.50	£0.60	£1.80	£3.00
ANYTHING GOES						
Fantagraphics,MS; 1 Oct 1986-6 Oct 1987						
1 ND Flaming Carrot in colour by Burden (4pgs); Gilbert Hernandez (4pgs), Gil Kane (4pgs), Toth (1pg), Gil Kane cover						
	$0.60	$1.80	$3.00	£0.80	£2.40	£4.00
2 ND "Pictopia" by Alan Moore, Fujitaki, Spiegelman, J.Hernandez (4pgs), Simpson, Kirby pin-ups (4), Frank Miller cover						
	$0.40	$1.20	$2.00	£0.60	£1.80	£3.00
3 ND Cerebus text story by Sim (3pgs), Spiegelman, Clowes, Cruise art, Neal Adams Cerebus cover						
	$0.40	$1.20	$2.00	£0.40	£1.20	£2.00
4 ND Gilbert Hernandez art on Heart Break Soup, Popeye by Segar, Orphan Annie by Gray, Journey by Messner-Loebs, Peter Bagge story, Perez cover						
	$0.40	$1.20	$2.00	£0.40	£1.20	£2.00
5 ND Turtles cover and story by Eastman & Laird, Journey by Messner-Loebs, Crumb, Sutton, Lomax art, Orphan Annie reprints by Gray						
	$0.40	$1.20	$2.00	£0.60	£1.80	£3.00

	$Good	$Fine	$N.Mint	£Good	£Fine	£N.Mint
6 ND Keif Llama by Howarth, Eddie Campbell, Phill Elliott, Mark Martin, Sutton art, Stan Sakai cover						
	$0.40	$1.20	$2.00	£0.40	£1.20	£2.00
Title Value:	$2.60	$7.80	$13.00	£3.20	£9.60	£16.00
APACHE DICK						
Eternity,MS; 1 Feb 1990-4 May 1990						
1-4 ND b&w	$0.30	$0.90	$1.50	£0.20	£0.60	£1.00
Title Value:	$1.20	$3.60	$6.00	£0.80	£2.40	£4.00
Graphic Novel (1991), reprints #1-4				£1.30	£3.90	£6.50
APE CITY						
Adventure,MS; 1 Aug 1990-4 Nov 1990						
1-4 ND	$0.40	$1.20	$2.00	£0.25	£0.75	£1.25
Title Value:	$1.60	$4.80	$8.00	£1.00	£3.00	£5.00
Note: based on Planet of the Apes						
APE NATION						
Adventure,MS; 1 Feb 1991-4 Jun 1991						
1 ND	$0.40	$1.20	$2.00	£0.25	£0.75	£1.25
1 Limited Edition, ND (Feb 1991) - 8,000 copies exclusive to Diamond Distributors with silver embossed logo and card-stock cover: limited number in top right of cover						
	$1.00	$3.00	$5.00	£0.70	£2.10	£3.50
2-4 ND	$0.40	$1.20	$2.00	£0.25	£0.75	£1.25
Title Value:	$2.60	$7.80	$13.00	£1.70	£5.10	£8.50
Special Edition (8,000 copies)				£1.00	£3.00	£5.00
Special Edition (5,000 copies, foil embossed cover by Peter Hsu				£0.80	£2.40	£4.00
APE WORLD						
Comax Productions; 1 Aug 1991						
1 ND Butch Burcham script/art						
	$0.45	$1.35	$2.25	£0.30	£0.90	£1.50
1 Signed & Numbered Edition, ND as above, limited to 1500 copies						
	$0.60	$1.80	$3.00	£0.40	£1.20	£2.00
Title Value:	$1.05	$3.15	$5.25	£0.70	£2.10	£3.50
APOCALYPSE STRIKE FILES, THE						
Marvel Comics Group,OS; 1 Apr 1995						
1 ND additional information tied into "The Age of Apocalypse" storyline (see X-Planations title header)						
	$0.60	$1.80	$3.00	£0.40	£1.20	£2.00
Title Value:	$0.60	$1.80	$3.00	£0.40	£1.20	£2.00
APPARITION						
Caliber Press; 1 Jan 1996						
1-3 ND b&w	$0.60	$1.80	$3.00	£0.40	£1.20	£2.00
Title Value:	$1.80	$5.40	$9.00	£1.20	£3.60	£6.00
APPARITION: ABANDONED, THE						
Caliber Press,OS; 1 Apr 1995						
1 ND 48pgs, spin-off from the Negative Burn anthology; black and white						
	$0.80	$2.40	$4.00	£0.50	£1.50	£2.50
Title Value:	$0.80	$2.40	$4.00	£0.50	£1.50	£2.50
APPLESEED						
Eclipse; 1 Sep 1988-5 Jan 1989						
1 ND scarce in the U.K. serialisation of Japanese Graphic Novel begins						
	$2.50	$7.50	$12.50	£1.50	£4.50	£7.50
2 ND	$1.50	$4.50	$7.50	£1.00	£3.00	£5.00
3 ND	$1.00	$3.00	$5.00	£0.80	£2.40	£4.00
4-5 ND	$1.00	$3.00	$5.00	£0.60	£1.80	£3.00
Title Value:	$7.00	$21.00	$35.00	£4.50	£13.50	£22.50
Trade paperback: The Promethean Challenge						
reprints #1-5				£1.50	£4.50	£7.50
2nd print (Nov 1991)				£1.40	£4.20	£7.00
APPLESEED BOOK 2						
Eclipse,MS; 1 Feb 1989-5 Jun 1989						
1 ND Art Adams cover						
	$0.60	$1.80	$3.00	£0.60	£1.80	£3.00
2-5 ND Art Adams cover						
	$0.60	$1.80	$3.00	£0.50	£1.50	£2.50

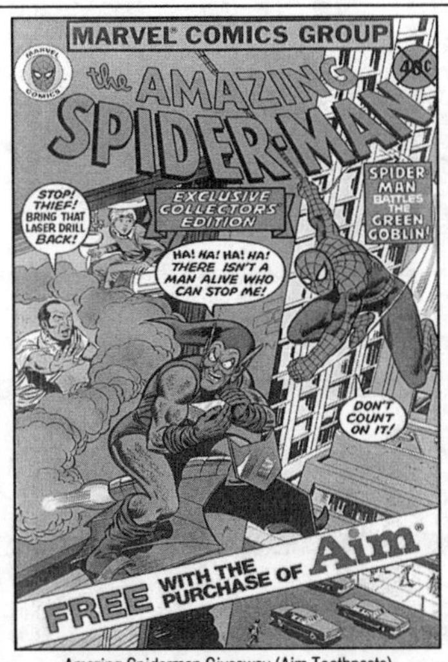

Amazing Spiderman Giveaway (Aim Toothpaste)

Anthro #2

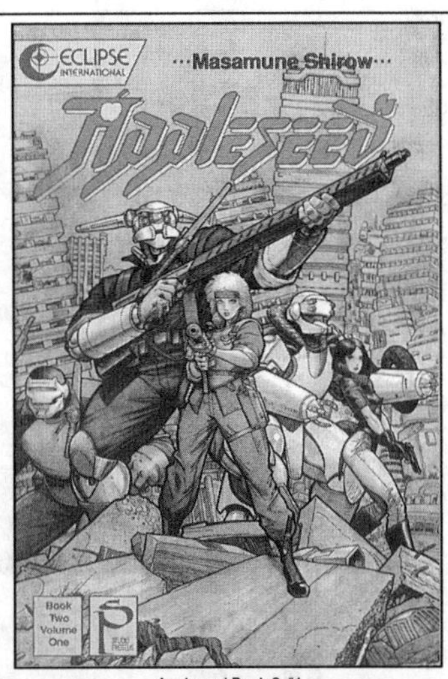

Appleseed Book 2 #1

	$Good	$Fine	$N.Mint	£Good	£Fine	£N.Mint
Title Value:	**$3.00**	**$9.00**	**$15.00**	**£2.60**	**£7.80**	**£13.00**
Trade paperback: Prometheus Unbound, reprints #1-5				£1.50	£4.50	£7.50
Hardcover (Apr 1991)				£5.00	£15.00	£25.00
Limited Edition Hardcover, 300 signed by Masamune Shirow (May 1991)				£10.00	£30.00	£50.00

APPLESEED BOOK 3

Eclipse,MS; 1-5 1991

	$Good	$Fine	$N.Mint	£Good	£Fine	£N.Mint
1-5 ND	$0.60	$1.80	$3.00	£0.50	£1.50	£2.50
Title Value:	$3.00	$9.00	$15.00	£2.50	£7.50	£12.50
Trade paperback: The Scales of Prometheus (Aug 1991), reprints #1-5				£1.70	£5.10	£8.50
Hardcover (Aug 1991)				£5.00	£15.00	£25.00
Deluxe Hardcover (Aug 1991)				£7.00	£21.00	£35.00
Limited Edition Hardcover (Aug 1995)				£11.00	£33.00	£55.00

APPLESEED BOOK 4

Eclipse,MS; 1 Feb 1991-2 Mar 1991

	$Good	$Fine	$N.Mint	£Good	£Fine	£N.Mint
1-2 ND 64pgs	$0.60	$1.80	$3.00	£0.40	£1.20	£2.00
Title Value:	$1.20	$3.60	$6.00	£0.80	£2.40	£4.00
Appleseed Book 4 Collection (Mar 1993) reprints mini-series, now published by Dark Horse Comics				£1.60	£4.80	£8.00

APPLESEED DATABOOK

Dark Horse,MS; 1 Mar 1994-2 Apr 1994

	$Good	$Fine	$N.Mint	£Good	£Fine	£N.Mint
1-2 ND 48pgs	$0.60	$1.80	$3.00	£0.40	£1.20	£2.00
Title Value:	$1.20	$3.60	$6.00	£0.80	£2.40	£4.00
Appleseed Databook (Aug 1995) Trade paperback collects issues #1,2 with wraparound cover by Masamune Shirow				£1.70	£5.10	£8.50

AQUAMAN

National Periodical Publications/DC Comics; 1 Jan/Feb 1962-56 Mar/Apr 1971; 57 Aug/Sep 1977-63 Aug/Sep 1978

(see Action, Adventure, Aquaman Special, Brave and the Bold, DC Comics Presents, DC Comics Presents, DC Special, Detective, Five-Star Super-Hero Spectacular, Secret Origins, Showcase, Super DC Giant, Super-Team Family, World's Finest)

	$Good	$Fine	$N.Mint	£Good	£Fine	£N.Mint
1 1st appearance Quisp	$60.00	$180.00	$600.00	£30.00	£90.00	£300.00
2	$29.00	$85.00	$260.00	£11.00	£33.00	£100.00
3	$18.50	$55.00	$150.00	£8.75	£26.00	£70.00
4-5	$17.50	$52.50	$140.00	£6.75	£20.50	£55.00
6-8	$11.00	$34.00	$90.00	£3.75	£11.00	£30.00
9 Sea Devils appear	$11.00	$34.00	$90.00	£3.75	£11.00	£30.00
10	$11.00	$34.00	$90.00	£3.75	£11.00	£30.00
11 1st appearance Mera	$9.25	$28.00	$75.00	£3.10	£9.25	£25.00
12-17	$9.25	$28.00	$75.00	£2.50	£7.50	£20.00
18 Aquaman & Mera wed, Justice League of America cameo	$9.25	$28.00	$75.00	£2.50	£7.50	£20.00
19-20	$9.25	$28.00	$75.00	£2.50	£7.50	£20.00
21-22	$8.50	$26.00	$60.00	£2.10	£6.25	£15.00
23 birth of Aquababy	$8.50	$26.00	$60.00	£2.10	£6.25	£15.00
24-28	$8.50	$26.00	$60.00	£2.10	£6.25	£15.00
29 1st appearance Ocean Master	$8.50	$26.00	$60.00	£2.10	£6.25	£15.00
30 Batman appears	$8.50	$26.00	$60.00	£2.10	£6.25	£15.00
31-32	$7.75	$23.50	$55.00	£1.75	£5.25	£12.50
33 1st appearance Aquagirl (later killed in Crisis); see Adventure Comics #266	$11.00	$34.00	$80.00	£2.10	£6.25	£15.00
34	$7.75	$23.50	$55.00	£1.75	£5.25	£12.50
35 1st appearance Black Manta	$7.75	$23.50	$55.00	£1.75	£5.25	£12.50
36-40	$7.75	$23.50	$55.00	£1.40	£4.25	£10.00
41-47	$4.25	$12.50	$30.00	£0.85	£2.55	£6.00
48 reprints origin	$5.00	$15.00	$35.00	£0.90	£2.75	£6.50
49	$4.25	$12.50	$30.00	£0.85	£2.55	£6.00
50 Neal Adams art on Deadman	$6.25	$19.00	$45.00	£1.75	£5.25	£12.50
51 scarce in the U.K. Neal Adams art on Deadman	$5.50	$17.00	$40.00	£2.10	£6.25	£15.00
52 Neal Adams art on Deadman	$5.50	$17.00	$40.00	£1.75	£5.25	£12.50
53-55	$1.75	$5.25	$12.50	£0.40	£1.25	£3.00
56 series cancelled; continues as back-up in Adventure #434-437, #441-452 before returning to continue numbering	$1.75	$5.25	$12.50	£0.40	£1.25	£3.00
57 Aquababy dies	$1.00	$3.00	$6.00	£0.40	£1.25	£2.50
58 origin retold	$1.00	$3.00	$6.00	£0.40	£1.25	£2.50
59-60	$1.00	$3.00	$6.00	£0.40	£1.25	£2.50
61 Batman and Green Lantern appear	$1.00	$3.00	$6.00	£0.40	£1.25	£2.50
62-63	$1.00	$3.00	$6.00	£0.30	£1.00	£2.00
Title Value:	$526.00	$1590.50	$4157.00	£162.20	£485.90	£1323.00

FEATURES

Aquaman solo in 26,41,42,47,50-52,54,56. Aquaman/Aqualad in 1-25, 27-40,43-46,48,49,53,56. Aquagirl in 56. Deadman (linked to Aquaman) in 50-52. Mera in 58-60.

AQUAMAN (1ST LIMITED SERIES)

DC Comics,MS; 1 Feb 1986-4 May 1986

	$Good	$Fine	$N.Mint	£Good	£Fine	£N.Mint
1 scarce in the U.K. Neal Pozner script, Craig Hamilton art, new costume	$0.70	$2.10	$3.50	£0.30	£0.90	£1.50
2-4 Neal Pozner script, Craig Hamilton art	$0.50	$1.50	$2.50	£0.20	£0.60	£1.00
Title Value:	$2.20	$6.60	$11.00	£0.90	£2.70	£4.50

AQUAMAN (2ND LIMITED SERIES)

DC Comics,MS; 1 Jun 1989-5 Oct 1989

	$Good	$Fine	$N.Mint	£Good	£Fine	£N.Mint
1-5	$0.30	$0.90	$1.50	£0.20	£0.60	£1.00
Title Value:	$1.50	$4.50	$7.50	£1.00	£3.00	£5.00

AQUAMAN (2ND SERIES)

DC Comics; 1 Dec 1991-13 Dec 1992

	$Good	$Fine	$N.Mint	£Good	£Fine	£N.Mint
1 Martian Manhunter, Blue Beetle appear	$0.30	$0.90	$1.50	£0.20	£0.60	£1.00
2-4	$0.25	$0.75	$1.25	£0.15	£0.45	£0.75
5 New Titans and Martian Manhunter appear	$0.25	$0.75	$1.25	£0.15	£0.45	£0.75
6	$0.25	$0.75	$1.25	£0.15	£0.45	£0.75
7 Justice League appear	$0.25	$0.75	$1.25	£0.15	£0.45	£0.75
8 Batman guest-stars	$0.25	$0.75	$1.25	£0.15	£0.45	£0.75
9-10 Eco-Wars story, Sea Devils appear	$0.25	$0.75	$1.25	£0.15	£0.45	£0.75
11 dinosaur cover	$0.25	$0.75	$1.25	£0.15	£0.45	£0.75
12-13	$0.25	$0.75	$1.25	£0.15	£0.45	£0.75
Title Value:	$3.30	$9.90	$16.50	£2.00	£6.00	£10.00
ND Aquaman Multi-Pack 1 (Dec 1992), pre-bagged with header card containg issues 1-3 (#1 is 2nd print) with four stickers				£0.35	£1.05	£1.75
ND Aquaman Multi-Pack 2 (Dec 1992), pre-bagged with header card containing issues 4-6 with same four illustrated stickers				£0.35	£1.05	£1.75

AQUAMAN (3RD SERIES)

DC Comics; 0 Oct 1994; 1 Aug 1994-present

(see Tempest)

	$Good	$Fine	$N.Mint	£Good	£Fine	£N.Mint
0 (Oct 1994) Zero Hour, new facts about origin	$0.90	$2.70	$4.50	£0.40	£1.20	£2.00
1 Peter David script begins	$1.00	$3.00	$5.00	£0.50	£1.50	£2.50
2 Aquaman loses hand	$1.00	$3.00	$5.00	£0.40	£1.20	£2.00
3 LD in the U.K. Aquaman vs. Superboy, new costume; Aqualad and Dolphin appear	$0.80	$2.40	$4.00	£0.40	£1.20	£2.00
4 Aquaman vs. Lobo	$0.60	$1.80	$3.00	£0.30	£0.90	£1.50
5 new costume	$0.60	$1.80	$3.00	£0.30	£0.90	£1.50
6 Aquaman finds a new son	$0.40	$1.20	$2.00	£0.25	£0.75	£1.25
7	$0.40	$1.20	$2.00	£0.25	£0.75	£1.25
8 Aqualad meets Aquaman's wizard father, Atlan	$0.40	$1.20	$2.00	£0.25	£0.75	£1.25
9	$0.40	$1.20	$2.00	£0.25	£0.75	£1.25
10 Green Lantern guest-stars	$0.40	$1.20	$2.00	£0.25	£0.75	£1.25
11	$0.40	$1.20	$2.00	£0.25	£0.75	£1.25
12 Dolphin vs. Mera	$0.40	$1.20	$2.00	£0.25	£0.75	£1.25
13	$0.40	$1.20	$2.00	£0.25	£0.75	£1.25
14 Underworld Unleashed tie-in	$0.40	$1.20	$2.00	£0.25	£0.75	£1.25
15 Walt Simonson cover	$0.40	$1.20	$2.00	£0.25	£0.75	£1.25
16-17 Justice League guest-stars	$0.40	$1.20	$2.00	£0.25	£0.75	£1.25
18 origin retold Dolphin	$0.40	$1.20	$2.00	£0.25	£0.75	£1.25
19	$0.40	$1.20	$2.00	£0.25	£0.75	£1.25
20 Aquaman vs. Ocean Master, Garth (formerly Aqualad) demonstrates his new powers	$0.40	$1.20	$2.00	£0.25	£0.75	£1.25
21-22	$0.35	$1.05	$1.75	£0.25	£0.75	£1.25
23-24 Power Girl, The Sea Devils and Arion appear	$0.35	$1.05	$1.75	£0.25	£0.75	£1.25
25	$0.35	$1.05	$1.75	£0.25	£0.75	£1.25
26 Final Night tie-in	$0.35	$1.05	$1.75	£0.25	£0.75	£1.25
27 ND	$0.35	$1.05	$1.75	£0.25	£0.75	£1.25
28 ND Martian Manhunter appears	$0.35	$1.05	$1.75	£0.25	£0.75	£1.25
29 ND Black Manta appears	$0.35	$1.05	$1.75	£0.25	£0.75	£1.25
30 ND	$0.35	$1.05	$1.75	£0.25	£0.75	£1.25
Title Value:	$14.40	$43.20	$72.00	£8.55	£25.65	£42.75

AQUAMAN (3RD SERIES) ANNUAL

DC Comics; 1 Jul 1995-present

	$Good	$Fine	$N.Mint	£Good	£Fine	£N.Mint
1 56pgs, Year One, Superman and Wonder Woman guest-star	$0.80	$2.40	$4.00	£0.50	£1.50	£2.50
2 48pgs, Legends of the Dead Earth story	$0.60	$1.80	$3.00	£0.40	£1.20	£2.00
Title Value:	$1.40	$4.20	$7.00	£0.90	£2.70	£4.50

AQUAMAN SPECIAL

DC Comics,OS; 1 1988

	$Good	$Fine	$N.Mint	£Good	£Fine	£N.Mint
1 George Freeman art	$0.30	$0.90	$1.50	£0.20	£0.60	£1.00
Title Value:	$0.30	$0.90	$1.50	£0.20	£0.60	£1.00

AQUAMAN SPECIAL, LEGEND OF

DC Comics,OS; 1 Jun 1989

Issue	$Good	$Fine	$N.Mint	£Good	£Fine	£N.Mint
1 48pgs, Keith Giffen layouts	$0.40	$1.20	$2.00	£0.25	£0.75	£1.25
Title Value:	$0.40	$1.20	$2.00	£0.25	£0.75	£1.25

AQUAMAN: TIME & TIDE

DC Comics,MS; 1 Dec 1993-4 Mar 1994

Issue	$Good	$Fine	$N.Mint	£Good	£Fine	£N.Mint
1 Peter David script begins, Aquaman: Year One-type story; The Flash (Barry Allen) appears	$0.50	$1.50	$2.50	£0.35	£1.05	£1.75
2-3 Aquaman's origin continues	$0.40	$1.20	$2.00	£0.30	£0.90	£1.50
4 Ocean Master's origin; appearances by Mera, Aqualad, Tula and Aquababy	$0.40	$1.20	$2.00	£0.30	£0.90	£1.50
Title Value:	$1.70	$5.10	$8.50	£1.25	£3.75	£6.25

Aquaman: Time & Tide (Mar 1996)

	£Good	£Fine	£N.Mint
Trade paperback reprints mini-series, new cover by Kirk Jarvinen	£1.30	£3.90	£6.50

ARAK, SON OF THUNDER

DC Comics; 1 Sep 1981-50 Nov 1985

(see Warlord #48)

Issue	$Good	$Fine	$N.Mint	£Good	£Fine	£N.Mint
1 origin Arak, 1st appearance Angelica	$0.15	$0.45	$0.75	£0.10	£0.35	£0.60
2	$0.15	$0.45	$0.75	£0.10	£0.30	£0.50
3 intro Valda	$0.15	$0.45	$0.75	£0.10	£0.30	£0.50
4-7	$0.15	$0.45	$0.75	£0.10	£0.30	£0.50
8-11 Viking Prince	$0.15	$0.45	$0.75	£0.10	£0.30	£0.50
12-23	$0.15	$0.45	$0.75	£0.10	£0.30	£0.50
24 DS	$0.20	$0.60	$1.00	£0.10	£0.35	£0.60
25-49	$0.15	$0.45	$0.75	£0.10	£0.30	£0.50
50 DS	$0.20	$0.60	$1.00	£0.10	£0.35	£0.60
Title Value:	$7.60	$22.80	$38.00	£5.00	£15.15	£25.30

ARAK, SON OF THUNDER ANNUAL

DC Comics; 1 Oct 1984

Issue	$Good	$Fine	$N.Mint	£Good	£Fine	£N.Mint
1 48pgs	$0.25	$0.75	$1.25	£0.15	£0.45	£0.75
Title Value:	$0.25	$0.75	$1.25	£0.15	£0.45	£0.75

ARCANA ANNUAL

DC Comics/Vertigo,OS; 1 Feb 1994

Issue	$Good	$Fine	$N.Mint	£Good	£Fine	£N.Mint
1 ND 64pgs, Children's Crusade part 6, concluded in Children's Crusade #2	$0.80	$2.40	$4.00	£0.50	£1.50	£2.50
Title Value:	$0.80	$2.40	$4.00	£0.50	£1.50	£2.50

ARCANE COMIX

Arcane/Eclipse; 1 Dec 1987-5 1990

Issue	$Good	$Fine	$N.Mint	£Good	£Fine	£N.Mint
1 128pgs, "Bad Moon"	$0.70	$2.10	$3.50	£0.50	£1.50	£2.50
2 224pgs, "Fly In My Eye", part Clive Barker text Bissette, Talbot, Howarth, McKeever, SMS, Bolton art	$1.00	$3.00	$5.00	£1.00	£3.00	£5.00
3 "Saturday Mourning"	$1.00	$3.00	$5.00	£1.00	£3.00	£5.00
4 "Daughters of Fly in My Eye"	$1.00	$3.00	$5.00	£1.00	£3.00	£5.00
5 128pgs, "Fly In My Eye Exposed", Clive Barker cover	$1.20	$3.60	$6.00	£1.20	£3.60	£6.00
Title Value:	$4.90	$14.70	$24.50	£4.70	£14.10	£23.50

Note: all Non-Distributed on the news-stands in the U.K.

ARCHANGEL

Marvel Comics Group,OS; 1 Feb 1996

Issue	$Good	$Fine	$N.Mint	£Good	£Fine	£N.Mint
1 ND Peter Milligan script, Steve Lightle art	$0.50	$1.50	$2.50	£0.30	£0.90	£1.50
Title Value:	$0.50	$1.50	$2.50	£0.30	£0.90	£1.50

ARCHANGELS: THE SAGA

Eternal Publishing,MS; 1 Mar 1996-3 May 1996

Issue	$Good	$Fine	$N.Mint	£Good	£Fine	£N.Mint
1-3 ND Patrick Scott script	$0.50	$1.50	$2.50	£0.30	£0.90	£1.50
Title Value:	$1.50	$4.50	$7.50	£0.90	£2.70	£4.50

ARCHER & ARMSTRONG

Valiant; 0 Jul 1992-26 Sep 1994

Issue	$Good	$Fine	$N.Mint	£Good	£Fine	£N.Mint
0 Barry Windsor-Smith art begins, 1st appearance Archer & Armstrong	$0.50	$1.50	$2.50	£0.30	£0.90	£1.50
0 Gold Edition, embossed cover	$1.50	$4.50	$7.50	£1.00	£3.00	£5.00
1 Unity: Chapter 3, Eternal Warrior appears	$0.60	$1.80	$3.00	£0.40	£1.20	£2.00
2 Unity: Chapter 11, 2nd appearance Turok, Walt Simonson cover	$0.50	$1.50	$2.50	£0.30	£0.90	£1.50
3-7	$0.40	$1.20	$2.00	£0.25	£0.75	£1.25
8 48pgs, Archer & Armstrong and Eternal Warrior as The Three Musketeers, 1st appearance of Ivar (note: single issue shared with Eternal Warrior #8)	$0.70	$2.10	$3.50	£0.40	£1.20	£2.00
9	$0.40	$1.20	$2.00	£0.25	£0.75	£1.25
10 Solar guest-stars, Ivar appears	$0.40	$1.20	$2.00	£0.25	£0.75	£1.25
11-12	$0.40	$1.20	$2.00	£0.25	£0.75	£1.25
13-14 Mike Baron script	$0.40	$1.20	$2.00	£0.25	£0.75	£1.25
15	$0.40	$1.20	$2.00	£0.25	£0.75	£1.25
16-20	$0.40	$1.20	$2.00	£0.20	£0.60	£1.00
21 with free Upper Deck card bound-in at centre-fold	$0.40	$1.20	$2.00	£0.20	£0.60	£1.00
22-24	$0.40	$1.20	$2.00	£0.20	£0.60	£1.00
25 continued in Eternal Warrior #25	$0.40	$1.20	$2.00	£0.20	£0.60	£1.00
26 Chaos Effect tie-in; shared issue with Eternal Warrior #26 (see #8 for similar idea)						
	$0.40	$1.20	$2.00	£0.25	£0.75	£1.25
Title Value:	$13.00	$39.00	$65.00	£7.65	£22.95	£38.25

Note: all Non-Distributed at the news-stands in the U.K.

ARCHIE ANNUAL

Archie Comics; 1 1950-26 1975

Issue	$Good	$Fine	$N.Mint	£Good	£Fine	£N.Mint
1 very scarce in the U.K., scarce in the U.S.	$175.00	$520.00	$1400.00	£115.00	£350.00	£935.00
2 scarce in the U.K.	$90.00	$270.00	$725.00	£62.50	£185.00	£500.00
3 scarce in the U.K.	$57.50	$175.00	$475.00	£41.00	£120.00	£325.00
4-5 scarce in the U.K.	$38.00	$110.00	$300.00	£28.00	£82.50	£225.00
6-10	$25.00	$75.00	$175.00	£17.50	£52.50	£125.00
1st official distribution in the U.K.						
11-15	$10.50	$32.00	$75.00	£6.25	£19.00	£45.00
16-20	$4.25	$12.50	$30.00	£2.50	£7.50	£17.50
21-26	$1.65	$5.00	$10.00	£0.80	£2.50	£5.00
Title Value:	$607.15	$1812.50	$4660.00	£410.55	£1230.00	£3177.50

ARCHIE COMICS

Archie Comics; 1 Winter 1942-present

Issue	$Good	$Fine	$N.Mint	£Good	£Fine	£N.Mint
1 very scarce in the U.K., scarce in the U.S. Archie Andrews, Veronica and Jughead begin	$1150.00	$3500.00	$10500.00	£770.00	£2325.00	£7000.00
2 scarce in the U.K.	$275.00	$830.00	$2500.00	£190.00	£580.00	£1750.00
3 very scarce in the U.K. and U.S.	$240.00	$730.00	$1950.00	£160.00	£485.00	£1300.00
4-6 scarce in the U.K.	$125.00	$375.00	$1000.00	£87.50	£260.00	£700.00
7-10 scarce in the U.K.	$80.00	$240.00	$650.00	£57.50	£175.00	£475.00
11-20	$55.00	$165.00	$450.00	£38.00	£110.00	£300.00
21-30	$38.00	$110.00	$300.00	£25.00	£75.00	£200.00
31-40	$20.00	$60.00	$160.00	£13.50	£41.00	£110.00
41-50	$14.00	$43.00	$115.00	£9.25	£28.00	£75.00
51-70	$9.25	$28.00	$75.00	£6.25	£18.50	£50.00
71-80	$5.50	$16.50	$45.00	£3.75	£11.00	£30.00
81-99	$5.00	$15.00	$40.00	£3.10	£9.25	£25.00
100	$6.75	$20.50	$55.00	£4.35	£13.00	£35.00
101-104	$3.10	$9.25	$25.00	£1.85	£5.50	£15.00
1st official distribution in the U.K.						
105-120	$3.55	$10.50	$25.00	£2.10	£6.25	£15.00
121-130	$3.55	$10.50	$25.00	£1.75	£5.25	£12.50
131-150	$2.10	$6.25	$15.00	£1.20	£3.60	£8.50
151-200	$1.25	$3.75	$7.50	£0.65	£2.00	£4.00
201-250	$0.80	$2.50	$5.00	£0.40	£1.25	£2.50
251-300	$0.60	$1.80	$3.00	£0.30	£0.90	£1.50
301-452	$0.30	$0.90	$1.50	£0.20	£0.60	£1.00
Title Value:	$4296.55	$12929.80	$35618.00	£2876.15	£8623.95	£23857.00

ARCHIE'S GALS BETTY AND VERONICA ANNUAL

Archie Comics; 1 1953-8 1960

Issue	$Good	$Fine	$N.Mint	£Good	£Fine	£N.Mint
1 scarce in the U.K.	$100.00	$300.00	$700.00	£70.00	£210.00	£500.00
2	$43.00	$125.00	$300.00	£32.00	£95.00	£225.00
3-5	$36.00	$105.00	$250.00	£24.00	£72.50	£170.00
6-8	$21.00	$62.50	$150.00	£14.00	£43.00	£100.00
Title Value:	$314.00	$927.50	$2200.00	£216.00	£651.50	£1535.00

ARCHIE'S GIRLS BETTY AND VERONICA

Archie Comics; 1 1950-347 Apr 1987

Issue	$Good	$Fine	$N.Mint	£Good	£Fine	£N.Mint
1 scarce in the U.K.	$150.00	$450.00	$1200.00	£105.00	£315.00	£850.00
2 scarce in the U.K.	$75.00	$225.00	$600.00	£55.00	£165.00	£450.00
3-5 scarce in the U.K.	$44.00	$130.00	$350.00	£31.00	£92.50	£250.00
6-10	$36.00	$105.00	$250.00	£25.00	£75.00	£175.00
11-25	$26.00	$75.00	$180.00	£17.50	£52.50	£125.00
26-46	$17.00	$50.00	$120.00	£11.00	£34.00	£80.00
1st official distribution in the U.K.						
47-50	$17.00	$50.00	$120.00	£11.00	£34.00	£80.00
51-75	$8.25	$25.00	$50.00	£4.15	£12.50	£25.00
76-100	$5.00	$15.00	$30.00	£2.90	£8.75	£17.50
101-150	$2.50	$7.50	$15.00	£1.30	£4.00	£8.00
151-200	$1.20	$3.60	$6.00	£0.60	£1.80	£3.00
201-250	$0.60	$1.80	$3.00	£0.30	£0.90	£1.50
251-347	$0.30	$0.90	$1.50	£0.20	£0.60	£1.00
Title Value:	$1927.35	$5697.30	$13145.50	£1221.15	£3694.45	£8584.50

ARCHIE'S JOKE BOOK MAGAZINE

Archie Comics; 1 1953-3 Summer 1954; 15 Autumn 1954-288 Dec 1982

Issue	$Good	$Fine	$N.Mint	£Good	£Fine	£N.Mint
1 very scarce in the U.K.	$67.50	$200.00	$475.00	£47.00	£140.00	£330.00
2 scarce in the U.K.	$39.00	$115.00	$275.00	£26.00	£77.50	£185.00
3 scarce in the U.K.	$26.00	$77.50	$185.00	£17.50	£52.50	£125.00
[Note: no issues #4-14]						
15-17 Katy Keene appears	$18.50	$55.00	$130.00	£12.50	£38.00	£87.50
18-20	$18.50	$55.00	$130.00	£12.50	£38.00	£87.50
21-30	$13.00	$40.00	$80.00	£8.75	£26.00	£52.50
31-40	$8.25	$25.00	$50.00	£5.25	£16.00	£32.50
41 scarce in the U.K. Neal Adams 1st professional comic book art (Jul 1959), 1 page - hard to tell which one!						

	$Good	$Fine	$N.Mint	£Good	£Fine	£N.Mint
	$20.50	$62.50	$125.00	£13.50	£41.00	£82.50
42-43	$8.25	$25.00	$50.00	£5.25	£16.00	£32.50
44 Neal Adams art (3rd ever?)	$10.50	$33.00	$65.00	£7.75	£23.50	£47.50
45-47 Neal Adams art (1/2pgs)	$10.00	$30.00	$60.00	£6.50	£20.00	£40.00
48 Neal Adams art (4pgs)	$10.50	$33.00	$65.00	£7.75	£23.50	£47.50
49-50	$3.30	$10.00	$20.00	£2.25	£6.75	£13.50
51-60	$3.15	$9.50	$19.00	£2.05	£6.25	£12.50
61-80	$1.80	$5.50	$11.00	£1.20	£3.60	£7.25
81-100	$0.80	$2.50	$5.00	£0.50	£1.60	£3.25
101-150	$0.40	$1.25	$2.50	£0.25	£0.85	£1.75
151-200	$0.35	$1.05	$1.75	£0.25	£0.75	£1.25
201-280	$0.25	$0.75	$1.25	£0.15	£0.45	£0.75
281-288	$0.30	$0.90	$1.50	£0.20	£0.60	£1.00
Title Value:	$694.00	$2098.20	$4417.00	£462.10	£1398.80	£2957.50

Note: most issues after Nov 1959 distributed on the news-stands in the U.K. but became more irregular in the late 1970s/early '80s.

ARCHIE'S MADHOUSE

Archie Comics; 1 Sep 1959-66 Feb 1969

1 distributed in the U.K.
(Note that this issue was distributed ahead of the official U.K. distribution cover date of November 1959)

	$Good	$Fine	$N.Mint	£Good	£Fine	£N.Mint
1	$32.00	$95.00	$225.00	£22.50	£67.50	£160.00
2	$17.50	$52.50	$125.00	£12.00	£36.00	£85.00
3-5	$10.50	$32.00	$75.00	£7.00	£21.00	£50.00
6-10	$7.00	$21.00	$50.00	£4.25	£12.50	£30.00
11-21	$2.85	$8.50	$20.00	£1.40	£4.25	£10.00
22 scarce in the U.K. 1st appearance Sabrina	$14.00	$43.00	$100.00	£9.25	£28.00	£65.00
23-50	$1.30	$4.00	$8.00	£0.65	£2.00	£4.00
51-66	$0.50	$1.50	$3.00	£0.25	£0.75	£1.50
Title Value:	$205.75	$621.00	$1417.00	£123.60	£371.75	£856.00

ARCHIE'S MADHOUSE ANNUAL

Archie Comics; 1 1962-6 1969

	$Good	$Fine	$N.Mint	£Good	£Fine	£N.Mint
1 scarce in the U.K.	$10.00	$30.00	$70.00	£7.00	£21.00	£50.00
2	$5.00	$15.00	$35.00	£3.20	£9.50	£22.50
3-6	$2.10	$6.25	$15.00	£1.10	£3.40	£8.00
Title Value:	$23.40	$70.00	$165.00	£14.60	£44.10	£104.50

Note: all distributed in the U.K.

ARCHIE'S PAL JUGHEAD

Archie Comics; 1 1949-352 Jun 1987

	$Good	$Fine	$N.Mint	£Good	£Fine	£N.Mint
1 scarce in the U.K.	$110.00	$335.00	$900.00	£80.00	£240.00	£650.00
2 scarce in the U.K.	$55.00	$165.00	$450.00	£41.00	£120.00	£325.00
3-5 scarce in the U.K.	$40.00	$120.00	$280.00	£29.00	£85.00	£200.00
6-10	$27.00	$80.00	$190.00	£19.00	£57.50	£135.00
11-25	$17.50	$52.50	$125.00	£12.00	£36.00	£85.00
26-50	$7.00	$21.00	$50.00	£4.25	£12.50	£30.00
51-52	$7.00	$21.00	$50.00	£3.20	£9.50	£22.50
1st official distribution in the U.K.						
53-75	$5.00	$15.00	$35.00	£2.85	£8.50	£20.00
76-78	$3.20	$9.50	$22.50	£1.75	£5.25	£12.50
79 Creature From The Black Lagoon cover	$4.25	$12.50	$30.00	£2.10	£6.25	£15.00
80-100	$3.20	$9.50	$22.50	£1.75	£5.25	£12.50
101-126	$2.05	$6.25	$12.50	£1.15	£3.50	£7.00
127 titled becomes Jughead	$2.85	$8.50	$20.00	£1.75	£5.25	£12.50
128-150	$2.05	$6.25	$12.50	£1.15	£3.50	£7.00
151-200	$1.25	$3.75	$7.50	£0.65	£2.00	£4.00
201-250	$0.80	$2.40	$4.00	£0.40	£1.20	£2.00
251-352	$0.40	$1.20	$2.00	£0.25	£0.75	£1.25
Title Value:	$1314.15	$3944.65	$9151.50	£841.40	£2515.00	£5878.00

ARCHIE'S PAL JUGHEAD ANNUAL

Archie Comics; 1 1953-8 1960

	$Good	$Fine	$N.Mint	£Good	£Fine	£N.Mint
1 scarce in the U.K.	$62.50	$185.00	$500.00	£44.00	£130.00	£350.00
2 scarce in the U.K.	$43.00	$125.00	$300.00	£32.00	£95.00	£225.00
3-5 scarce in the U.K.	$29.00	$85.00	$200.00	£21.00	£62.50	£150.00
6-8	$17.50	$52.50	$125.00	£12.00	£36.00	£85.00
Title Value:	$245.00	$722.50	$1775.00	£175.00	£520.50	£1280.00

ARCHIE'S PALS 'N GALS

Archie Comics; 1 1952-224 Sep 1991

	$Good	$Fine	$N.Mint	£Good	£Fine	£N.Mint
1 very scarce in the U.K., scarce in the U.S.	$75.00	$225.00	$600.00	£55.00	£165.00	£450.00
2 scarce in the U.K.	$46.00	$135.00	$325.00	£32.00	£95.00	£225.00
3-5	$32.00	$95.00	$225.00	£21.00	£62.50	£150.00
6-7	$17.50	$52.50	$125.00	£12.00	£36.00	£85.00
8 some issues distributed in the U.K. - stamped "1/3" (1 shilling and threepence)	$17.50	$52.50	$125.00	£12.00	£36.00	£85.00
9 some issues distributed in the U.K. - stamped "1/3" (one shilling and threepence)	$17.50	$52.50	$125.00	£12.00	£36.00	£85.00
10	$17.50	$52.50	$125.00	£11.00	£34.00	£80.00
1st official distribution in th U.K.						
11-16	$8.50	$26.00	$60.00	£5.25	£16.00	£37.50

	$Good	$Fine	$N.Mint	£Good	£Fine	£N.Mint
17-20	$7.00	$21.00	$50.00	£4.25	£12.50	£30.00
21-40	$3.90	$11.50	$27.50	£2.10	£6.25	£15.00
41-75	$1.70	$5.00	$12.00	£0.85	£2.55	£6.00
76-100	$1.00	$3.00	$6.00	£0.50	£1.50	£3.00
101-150	$0.50	$1.50	$3.00	£0.25	£0.75	£1.50
151-224	$0.30	$0.90	$1.50	£0.20	£0.60	£1.00
Title Value:	$593.20	$1769.10	$4166.00	£369.05	£1105.15	£2624.00

ARCHIE'S SUPER HERO COMICS DIGEST MAGAZINE

Archie Comics,Digest; 2 Aug 1979

(previously Archie's Super-Hero Special)

	$Good	$Fine	$N.Mint	£Good	£Fine	£N.Mint
2 148pgs, previously unpublished Neal Adams Black Hood story; limited distribution in the U.K.	$0.90	$2.70	$4.50	£0.60	£1.80	£3.00
Title Value:	$0.90	$2.70	$4.50	£0.60	£1.80	£3.00

ARCHIE'S SUPER-HERO SPECIAL

Archie Comics,Digest; 1 1978

(becomes Archie's Super Hero Comic Digest Magazine)

	$Good	$Fine	$N.Mint	£Good	£Fine	£N.Mint
1 148pgs, Joe Simon and Jack Kirby art; all reprints: Fly, Black Hood, Web, Jaguar appear; limited distribution in the U.K.	$0.50	$1.50	$3.00	£0.30	£1.00	£2.00
Title Value:	$0.50	$1.50	$3.00	£0.30	£1.00	£2.00

ARCHIE'S SUPERTEENS

Archie Comics; 1 Aug 1994-2 1994

	$Good	$Fine	$N.Mint	£Good	£Fine	£N.Mint
1 ND 48pgs, Archie returns as Pureheart the Powerful, Jughead as Captain Hero, Betty as Superteen and Reggie as Evilheart; Elliot S! Maggin script, Joe Staton art	$0.40	$1.20	$2.00	£0.25	£0.75	£1.25
2 ND	$0.40	$1.20	$2.00	£0.25	£0.75	£1.25
Title Value:	$0.80	$2.40	$4.00	£0.50	£1.50	£2.50

AREA 88

Eclipse/Viz; 1 1987-42 May 1989

	$Good	$Fine	$N.Mint	£Good	£Fine	£N.Mint
1 Kaoru Shintani script/art (translated Japanese reprint) begins; black and white	$0.50	$1.50	$2.50	£0.30	£0.90	£1.50
1 2nd printing	$0.40	$1.20	$2.00	£0.25	£0.75	£1.25
2	$0.40	$1.20	$2.00	£0.25	£0.75	£1.25
2 2nd printing	$0.30	$0.90	$1.50	£0.20	£0.60	£1.00
3	$0.40	$1.20	$2.00	£0.25	£0.75	£1.25
4-36	$0.30	$0.90	$1.50	£0.20	£0.60	£1.00
37 1st Viz Comics issue, photo-cover	$0.40	$1.20	$2.00	£0.25	£0.75	£1.25
38-42	$0.30	$0.90	$1.50	£0.20	£0.60	£1.00
Title Value:	$13.80	$41.40	$69.00	£9.10	£27.30	£45.50

Note: all Non-Distributed on the news-stands in the U.K.

	$Good	$Fine	$N.Mint	£Good	£Fine	£N.Mint
Graphic Novel 1 (Apr 1991), 200pgs, reprints				£1.40	£4.20	£7.00
Graphic Novel 2 (Jun 1991), 200pgs, reprints				£1.40	£4.20	£7.00

ARGONAUTS

Eternity; 1 1991-5 1992?

	$Good	$Fine	$N.Mint	£Good	£Fine	£N.Mint
1-5 ND	$0.25	$0.75	$1.25	£0.15	£0.45	£0.75
Title Value:	$1.25	$3.75	$6.25	£0.75	£2.25	£3.75

ARGONAUTS: SYSTEM CRASH, THE

Alpha Productions,MS; 1 Jan 1994

	$Good	$Fine	$N.Mint	£Good	£Fine	£N.Mint
1 ND	$0.40	$1.20	$2.00	£0.25	£0.75	£1.25
Title Value:	$0.40	$1.20	$2.00	£0.25	£0.75	£1.25

Note: solicited and advertised as a mini series but cancelled after one issue

ARGOSY, THE

Caliber Press,OS; 1 Dec 1991

	$Good	$Fine	$N.Mint	£Good	£Fine	£N.Mint
1 ND reprints from Dark Horse Presents	$0.40	$1.20	$2.00	£0.25	£0.75	£1.25
Title Value:	$0.40	$1.20	$2.00	£0.25	£0.75	£1.25

ARGUS

DC Comics,MS; 1 Apr 1995-6 Oct 1995

	$Good	$Fine	$N.Mint	£Good	£Fine	£N.Mint
1-6 spin-off from The Flash series	$0.35	$1.05	$1.75	£0.20	£0.60	£1.00
Title Value:	$2.10	$6.30	$10.50	£1.20	£3.60	£6.00

ARIANE AND BLUEBEARD

Eclipse,OS; nn 1989

	$Good	$Fine	$N.Mint	£Good	£Fine	£N.Mint
nn ND squarebound, P. Craig Russell cover and art	$0.40	$1.20	$2.00	£0.25	£0.75	£1.25

Note: based on opera by Maeterlinck

ARIK KHAN

Silver Snail; 1 1977-3 1979

	$Good	$Fine	$N.Mint	£Good	£Fine	£N.Mint
1-3 ND	$0.30	$0.90	$1.50	£0.20	£0.60	£1.00
Title Value:	$0.90	$2.70	$4.50	£0.60	£1.80	£3.00

ARIK KHAN (2ND SERIES)

A Plus Comics; 1 Jul 1991-3 1991

	$Good	$Fine	$N.Mint	£Good	£Fine	£N.Mint
1-3 ND 48pgs	$0.50	$1.50	$2.50	£0.30	£0.90	£1.50
Title Value:	$1.50	$4.50	$7.50	£0.90	£2.70	£4.50

ARION, LORD OF ATLANTIS

DC Comics; 1 Nov 1982-35 Sep 1985

	$Good	$Fine	$N.Mint	£Good	£Fine	£N.Mint
1	$0.15	$0.45	$0.75	£0.10	£0.35	£0.60
2-35	$0.15	$0.45	$0.75	£0.10	£0.30	£0.50
Title Value:	$5.25	$15.75	$26.25	£3.50	£10.55	£17.60

ARION, LORD OF ATLANTIS SPECIAL

DC Comics; 1 1985

	$Good	$Fine	$N.Mint	£Good	£Fine	£N.Mint
1	$0.25	$0.75	$1.25	£0.15	£0.45	£0.75
Title Value:	$0.25	$0.75	$1.25	£0.15	£0.45	£0.75

ARION, THE IMMORTAL

DC Comics,MS; 1 Jul 1992-6 Dec 1992

	$Good	$Fine	$N.Mint	£Good	£Fine	£N.Mint
1-5	$0.25	$0.75	$1.25	£0.15	£0.45	£0.75
6 Power Girl guest stars	$0.25	$0.75	$1.25	£0.15	£0.45	£0.75
Title Value:	$1.50	$4.50	$7.50	£0.90	£2.70	£4.50

ARISTOCRATIC X-TRATERRESTRIAL TIME-TRAVELLING THIEVES

Fictioneer; 1 Aug 1986; 1 Feb 1987-12 1988

SOME INDEPENDENT COMICS MAY NOT HAVE APPEARED ALTHOUGH THEY WERE ADVERTISED AND SOLICITED.

(becomes X-Thieves)

Issue	$Good	$Fine	$N.Mint	£Good	£Fine	£N.Mint
1 ND one shot issue; black and white	*$0.40*	*$1.20*	*$2.00*	£0.25	£0.75	£1.25
1 2nd printing, ND as above	*$0.30*	*$0.90*	*$1.50*	£0.20	£0.60	£1.00
1 regular series begins, ND; black and white	*$0.35*	*$1.05*	*$1.75*	£0.25	£0.75	£1.25
2-12 ND	*$0.30*	*$0.90*	*$1.50*	£0.20	£0.60	£1.00
Title Value:	*$4.35*	*$13.05*	*$21.75*	£2.90	£8.70	£14.50

ARMAGEDDON 2001

Cross-over series running throughout the DC summer 1991 annuals and tied into a limited series of the same name. The order of the story is as follows:

1) Armageddon 2001 1
2) Superman Annual 3
3) Batman Annual 15
4) Justice League America Annual 5
5) Hawk and Dove Annual 2
6) Hawkworld Annual 2
7) Flash Annual 4
8) Action Comics Annual 3
9) Legion '91 Annual 2
10) New Titans Annual 7
11) Adventures of Superman Annual 3
12) Detective Comics Annual 4
13) Justice League Europe Annual 2
14) Armageddon 2001 2

ARMAGEDDON 2001 (LIMITED SERIES)

DC Comics,MS; 1 May 1991-2 Oct 1991

Issue	$Good	$Fine	$N.Mint	£Good	£Fine	£N.Mint
1 64pgs, multi cross-over series, most major DC characters appear, 1st appearance Waverider	*$0.50*	*$1.50*	*$2.50*	£0.30	£0.90	£1.50
1 2nd printing, "II" in box on cover	*$0.40*	*$1.20*	*$2.00*	£0.25	£0.75	£1.25
1 3rd printing	*$0.40*	*$1.20*	*$2.00*	£0.25	£0.75	£1.25
2 64pgs	*$0.40*	*$1.20*	*$2.00*	£0.25	£0.75	£1.25
Title Value:	*$1.70*	*$5.10*	*$8.50*	£1.05	£3.15	£5.25

ARMAGEDDON: INFERNO

DC Comics,MS; 1 Apr 1992-4 Jul 1992

Issue	$Good	$Fine	$N.Mint	£Good	£Fine	£N.Mint
1 Batman, Creeper, Spectre appear	*$0.20*	*$0.60*	*$1.00*	£0.15	£0.45	£0.75
2 Superman, Flash, Lobo, Wonder Woman, Hawkman appear	*$0.20*	*$0.60*	*$1.00*	£0.15	£0.45	£0.75
3-4 Justice Society of America appears	*$0.20*	*$0.60*	*$1.00*	£0.15	£0.45	£0.75
Title Value:	*$0.80*	*$2.40*	*$4.00*	£0.60	£1.80	£3.00

ARMAGEDDON: THE ALIEN AGENDA

DC Comics,MS; 1 Nov 1991-4 Feb 1992

Issue	$Good	$Fine	$N.Mint	£Good	£Fine	£N.Mint
1 sequel to Armageddon: 2001, Jerry Ordway art	*$0.20*	*$0.60*	*$1.00*	£0.15	£0.45	£0.75
2 Nasser art	*$0.20*	*$0.60*	*$1.00*	£0.15	£0.45	£0.75
3 Weiss art	*$0.20*	*$0.60*	*$1.00*	£0.15	£0.45	£0.75
4 George Perez art	*$0.20*	*$0.60*	*$1.00*	£0.15	£0.45	£0.75
Title Value:	*$0.80*	*$2.40*	*$4.00*	£0.60	£1.80	£3.00

ARMED & DANGEROUS

Acclaim Comics/Armada,MS; 1 Apr 1996-4 Jul 1996

Issue	$Good	$Fine	$N.Mint	£Good	£Fine	£N.Mint
1 ND Bob Hall script and art; black and white	*$0.60*	*$1.80*	*$3.00*	£0.40	£1.20	£2.00
2-4 ND Bob Hall script and art; balck and white	*$0.60*	*$1.80*	*$3.00*	£0.40	£1.20	£2.00
Title Value:	*$2.40*	*$7.20*	*$12.00*	£1.60	£4.80	£8.00
Armed & Dangerous (Nov 1996) Trade paperback ND 104pgs, collects issues #1-4				£1.20	£3.60	£6.00

ARMED & DANGEROUS SPECIAL

Acclaim Comics,OS; 1 Aug 1996

Issue	$Good	$Fine	$N.Mint	£Good	£Fine	£N.Mint
1 ND script and art by Bob Hall; black and white	*$0.60*	*$1.80*	*$3.00*	£0.40	£1.20	£2.00
Title Value:	*$0.60*	*$1.80*	*$3.00*	£0.40	£1.20	£2.00

ARMED & DANGEROUS: HELL'S SLAUGHTERHOUSE

Acclaim Comics,MS; 1 Oct 1996-4 Jan 1997

Issue	$Good	$Fine	$N.Mint	£Good	£Fine	£N.Mint
1-4 ND Bob Hall script and art; black and white	*$0.60*	*$1.80*	*$3.00*	£0.40	£1.20	£2.00
Title Value:	*$2.40*	*$7.20*	*$12.00*	£1.60	£4.80	£8.00

ARMOR

Continuity; 1 Sep 1985; 1 1987-14 1991

Issue	$Good	$Fine	$N.Mint	£Good	£Fine	£N.Mint
1 Neal Adams, Grindberg, Murray art; silver logo on Neal Adams cover; indicia reads "Revengers featuring Armor and Silver Streak"	*$0.40*	*$1.20*	*$2.00*	£0.25	£0.75	£1.25
1 Red Cover Variant, Neal Adams, Grindberg, Murray art; red logo on Neal Adams cover	*$0.40*	*$1.20*	*$2.00*	£0.25	£0.75	£1.25
2 Neal Adams cover; intro The Silver Streak	*$0.40*	*$1.20*	*$2.00*	£0.25	£0.75	£1.25
3-5 Neal Adams cover	*$0.40*	*$1.20*	*$2.00*	£0.25	£0.75	£1.25
6-10 Neal Adams cover	*$0.30*	*$0.90*	*$1.50*	£0.20	£0.60	£1.00
11-12 Son of Sacraman story	*$0.30*	*$0.90*	*$1.50*	£0.20	£0.60	£1.00
13 Son of Sacraman story, Neal Adams cover	*$0.30*	*$0.90*	*$1.50*	£0.20	£0.60	£1.00
14 Son of Sacraman story	*$0.30*	*$0.90*	*$1.50*	£0.20	£0.60	£1.00
Title Value:	*$5.10*	*$15.30*	*$25.50*	£3.30	£9.90	£16.50

Note: irregularly published and Non-Distributed on the news-stands in the U.K.

ARMOR (2ND SERIES)

Continuity; 1 Apr 1993-6 1994

Issue	$Good	$Fine	$N.Mint	£Good	£Fine	£N.Mint
1 Deathwatch 2000 part 3; pre-bagged with 2 trading cards, Mike Golden silver embossed cover	*$0.40*	*$1.20*	*$2.00*	£0.25	£0.75	£1.25
2 Deathwatch 2000 part 9; pre-bagged with trading card	*$0.40*	*$1.20*	*$2.00*	£0.25	£0.75	£1.25
3 Deathwatch 2000 part 15; pre-bagged with trading card; Tyvek indestructible cover	*$0.40*	*$1.20*	*$2.00*	£0.25	£0.75	£1.25
4 Rise of Magic X-over, embossed parchment cover	*$0.40*	*$1.20*	*$2.00*	£0.25	£0.75	£1.25
5-6 Rise of Magic X-over, Michael Golden parchment cover	*$0.40*	*$1.20*	*$2.00*	£0.25	£0.75	£1.25
Title Value:	*$2.40*	*$7.20*	*$12.00*	£1.50	£4.50	£7.50

Note: all Non-Distributed on the news-stands in the U.K.

ARMORINES

Valiant; 1 Jul 1994-12 Jun 1995

Issue	$Good	$Fine	$N.Mint	£Good	£Fine	£N.Mint
1	*$0.40*	*$1.20*	*$2.00*	£0.25	£0.75	£1.25
1 Valiant Validated Signature Series, (Jun 1994), signed by at least one creator; 5,300 copies with certificate and Mylar sleeve	*$1.50*	*$4.50*	*$7.50*	£1.00	£3.00	£5.00
2-4	*$0.40*	*$1.20*	*$2.00*	£0.20	£0.60	£1.00
5 Chaos Effect tie-in	*$0.40*	*$1.20*	*$2.00*	£0.20	£0.60	£1.00
6-12	*$0.40*	*$1.20*	*$2.00*	£0.20	£0.60	£1.00
Title Value:	*$6.30*	*$18.90*	*$31.50*	£3.45	£10.35	£17.25

Note: all Non-Distributed on the news-stands in the U.K.

ARMORINES YEARBOOK

Valiant,OS; 1 Jun 1995

Issue	$Good	$Fine	$N.Mint	£Good	£Fine	£N.Mint
1 ND intro Linhoff	*$0.40*	*$1.20*	*$2.00*	£0.25	£0.75	£1.25
Title Value:	*$0.40*	*$1.20*	*$2.00*	£0.25	£0.75	£1.25

Aquaman (1st) #23

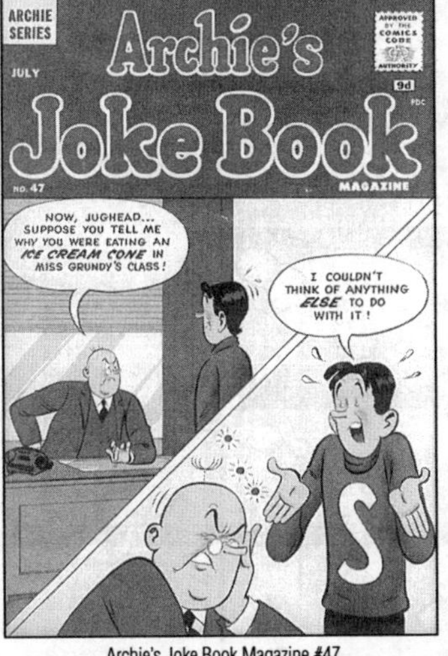

Archie's Joke Book Magazine #47

Archie's Madhouse #17

ARMY AT WAR

DC Comics; 1 Oct/Nov 1978
(see also Our Army at War)

Issue	$Good	$Fine	$N.Mint	£Good	£Fine	£N.Mint
1 ND 44pgs, Kubert cover	*$0.50*	*$1.50*	*$3.00*	£0.30	£1.00	£2.00
Title Value:	*$0.50*	*$1.50*	*$3.00*	£0.30	£1.00	£2.00

ARMY ATTACK (1ST SERIES)

Charlton; 1 Jul 1964-4 Feb 1965

Issue	$Good	$Fine	$N.Mint	£Good	£Fine	£N.Mint
1 distributed in the U.K.	*$2.85*	*$8.50*	*$20.00*	£1.40	£4.25	£10.00
2-4 distributed in the U.K.	*$1.70*	*$5.00*	*$12.00*	£1.00	£3.00	£7.00
Title Value:	*$7.95*	*$23.50*	*$56.00*	£4.40	£13.25	£31.00

ARMY ATTACK (2ND SERIES)

Charlton; 38 Jul 1965-47 Feb 1967
(formerly US Air Force Comics #1-37)

Issue	$Good	$Fine	$N.Mint	£Good	£Fine	£N.Mint
38-40 distributed in the U.K.	*$1.40*	*$4.25*	*$10.00*	£0.85	£2.55	£6.00
41-47 distributed in the U.K.	*$1.40*	*$4.25*	*$10.00*	£0.70	£2.10	£5.00
Title Value:	*$14.00*	*$42.50*	*$100.00*	£7.45	£22.35	£53.00

ARMY SURPLUS COMICS

(see Cutey Bunny)

ARMY WAR HEROES

Charlton; 1 Dec 1963-38 Jun 1970

Issue	$Good	$Fine	$N.Mint	£Good	£Fine	£N.Mint
1 distributed in the U.K.	*$2.85*	*$8.50*	*$20.00*	£1.70	£5.00	£12.00
2-10 distributed in the U.K.	*$1.40*	*$4.25*	*$10.00*	£0.85	£2.55	£6.00
11-20 distributed in the U.K.	*$1.10*	*$3.40*	*$8.00*	£0.70	£2.10	£5.00
21 distributed in the U.K.	*$1.00*	*$3.00*	*$7.00*	£0.60	£1.90	£4.50
22 1st appearance Iron Corporal; distributed in the U.K.	*$1.00*	*$3.00*	*$7.00*	£0.60	£1.90	£4.50
23-30 distributed in the U.K.	*$1.00*	*$3.00*	*$7.00*	£0.60	£1.90	£4.50
31-38 distributed in the U.K.	*$1.15*	*$3.50*	*$7.00*	£0.65	£2.00	£4.00
Title Value:	*$45.65*	*$138.75*	*$306.00*	£27.55	£83.95	£193.00

AROUND THE WORLD UNDER THE SEA

Dell/Movie Classics,OS Movie; 12-030-612 Dec 1966

Issue	$Good	$Fine	$N.Mint	£Good	£Fine	£N.Mint
12-030-212 distributed in the U.K. film adaptation	*$4.25*	*$12.50*	*$30.00*	£2.10	£6.25	£15.00
Title Value:	*$4.25*	*$12.50*	*$30.00*	£2.10	£6.25	£15.00

ARRGH!

Marvel Comics Group; 1 Dec 1974-5 Sep 1975

Issue	$Good	$Fine	$N.Mint	£Good	£Fine	£N.Mint
1-2 ND scarce in the U.K.	*$0.65*	*$2.00*	*$4.00*	£0.40	£1.25	£2.50
3-5 ND scarce in the U.K.	*$0.50*	*$1.50*	*$3.00*	£0.30	£1.00	£2.00
Title Value:	*$2.80*	*$8.50*	*$16.00*	£1.70	£5.50	£11.00

Note: all satire material.

ARROW, THE

Malibu,OS; 1 Oct 1992

Issue	$Good	$Fine	$N.Mint	£Good	£Fine	£N.Mint
1 ND Protectors spin-off, Protectors guest star; Lee Moder pencils, colour	*$0.30*	*$0.90*	*$1.50*	£0.20	£0.60	£1.00
Title Value:	*$0.30*	*$0.90*	*$1.50*	£0.20	£0.60	£1.00

ARSENAL SPECIAL

DC Comics,OS; 1 Jun 1996

Issue	$Good	$Fine	$N.Mint	£Good	£Fine	£N.Mint
1 ND 48pgs, C.J. Henderson script, William Rosado and Prentis Rollins art	*$0.60*	*$1.80*	*$3.00*	£0.40	£1.20	£2.00
Title Value:	*$0.60*	*$1.80*	*$3.00*	£0.40	£1.20	£2.00

ART OF ERIK LARSEN

Image,OS; nn Feb 1995

Issue	$Good	$Fine	$N.Mint	£Good	£Fine	£N.Mint
nn ND 48pgs, information and artwork and even helpful hints!	*$0.90*	*$2.70*	*$4.50*	£0.60	£1.80	£3.00
Title Value:	*$0.90*	*$2.70*	*$4.50*	£0.60	£1.80	£3.00

ART OF HOMAGE STUDIOS, THE

Image,OS; 1 Dec 1993

Issue	$Good	$Fine	$N.Mint	£Good	£Fine	£N.Mint
1 ND 48pgs, squarebound; pin-ups, art and sketches by Lee, Silvestri, Williams and Portacio amongst others	*$0.90*	*$2.70*	*$4.50*	£0.60	£1.80	£3.00
Title Value:	*$0.90*	*$2.70*	*$4.50*	£0.60	£1.80	£3.00

ART OF JOHN ROMITA SNR., THE

Marvel Comics Group,OS; nn Feb 1997

Issue	$Good	$Fine	$N.Mint	£Good	£Fine	£N.Mint
nn ND selected artwork including his first for Marvel in 1951	*$7.00*	*$21.00*	*$35.00*	£5.00	£15.00	£25.00
nn Signed Hardcover Edition ND limited to 500 copies	*$10.00*	*$30.00*	*$50.00*	£7.00	£21.00	£35.00
Title Value:	*$17.00*	*$51.00*	*$85.00*	£12.00	£36.00	£60.00

ARTEMIS: REQUIEM

DC Comics,MS; 1 Jun 1996-6 Nov 1996

Issue	$Good	$Fine	$N.Mint	£Good	£Fine	£N.Mint
1-2 ND Wonder Woman appears	*$0.35*	*$1.05*	*$1.75*	£0.25	£0.75	£1.25
3-6 ND	*$0.35*	*$1.05*	*$1.75*	£0.25	£0.75	£1.25
Title Value:	*$2.10*	*$6.30*	*$10.50*	£1.50	£4.50	£7.50

ARZACH

Dark Horse,OS; nn Feb 1996

Issue	$Good	$Fine	$N.Mint	£Good	£Fine	£N.Mint
nn ND 80pgs, Trade paperback reprinting work by Moebius	*$1.40*	*$4.20*	*$7.00*	£0.90	£2.70	£4.50
Title Value:	*$1.40*	*$4.20*	*$7.00*	£0.90	£2.70	£4.50

ASH

Event Comics; 0 May 1996; 1 Nov 1994-6 1996

Issue	$Good	$Fine	$N.Mint	£Good	£Fine	£N.Mint
0 "Future" cover, ND (May 1996), foil logo	*$0.80*	*$2.40*	*$4.00*	£0.50	£1.50	£2.50
0 "Future" cover Blue Foil Logo, ND (May 1996), limited to 1,000 copies	*$2.40*	*$7.00*	*$12.00*	£1.20	£3.60	£6.00
0 "Future" cover Gold Hologram Logo, ND (May 1996), limited to 1,000 copies	*$4.00*	*$12.00*	*$20.00*	£2.40	£7.00	£12.00
0 "Future" cover Red prism Logo, ND (May 1996), limited to 250 copies	*$7.00*	*$21.00*	*$35.00*	£4.00	£12.00	£20.00
0 "Future" cover SIlver Prism Logo, ND (May 1996), limited to 500 copies	*$5.00*	*$15.00*	*$25.00*	£3.00	£9.00	£15.00
0 "Present" cover, ND (May 1996), foil logo	*$0.80*	*$2.40*	*$4.00*	£0.50	£1.50	£2.50
0 "Present" cover Blue Foil Logo, ND (May 1996), limited to 1,000 copies	*$2.40*	*$7.00*	*$12.00*	£1.20	£3.60	£6.00
0 "Present" cover Gold Hologram Logo, ND (May 1996), limited to 1,000 copies	*$4.00*	*$12.00*	*$20.00*	£2.40	£7.00	£12.00
0 "Present" cover Red Prism Logo, ND (May 1996), limited to 250 copies	*$7.00*	*$21.00*	*$35.00*	£4.00	£12.00	£20.00
0 "Present" cover Silver Prism Logo, ND (May 1996), limited to 500 copies	*$5.00*	*$15.00*	*$25.00*	£3.00	£9.00	£15.00
1 ND Joe Quesada and Jimmy Palmiotti story and art; pin-up by Barry Smith	*$2.50*	*$7.50*	*$12.50*	£1.40	£4.20	£7.00
Connoisseur's Kit, ND (May 1995) - signed and numbered #1 with certificate and lithograph, all pre-bagged	*$5.00*	*$15.00*	*$25.00*	£3.00	£9.00	£15.00
2 ND Joe Quesada and Jimmy Palmiotti story and art; pin-up by Mike Mignola	*$2.00*	*$6.00*	*$10.00*	£1.40	£4.20	£7.00
3 ND Joe Quesada and Jimmy Palmiotti story and art	*$1.20*	*$3.60*	*$6.00*	£0.80	£2.40	£4.00
4 ND Joe Quesada and Jimmy Palmiotti story and art	*$1.20*	*$3.60*	*$6.00*	£0.60	£1.80	£3.00
4 Fahrenheit Edition - Gold, ND limited to 2,000 copies	*$4.00*	*$12.00*	*$20.00*	£2.50	£7.50	£12.50
4 Fahrenheit Edition - Red, ND limited to 1,000 copies	*$5.00*	*$15.00*	*$25.00*	£3.00	£9.00	£15.00
4 Fahrenheit Edition - White, ND limited to 500 copies	*$6.00*	*$18.00*	*$30.00*	£4.00	£12.00	£20.00
5 ND Joe Quesada and Jimmy Palmiotti story and art	*$0.70*	*$2.10*	*$3.50*	£0.40	£1.20	£2.00
5 Fahrenheit Edition - Gold, ND limited to 2,000 copies	*$2.50*	*$7.50*	*$12.50*	£1.50	£4.50	£7.50
5 Fahrenheit Edition - Red, ND limited to 1,000 copies	*$3.00*	*$9.00*	*$15.00*	£2.00	£6.00	£10.00
5 Fahrenheit Edition - White, ND limited to 500 copies	*$3.50*	*$10.50*	*$17.50*	£2.50	£7.50	£12.50
5 Variant Cover Edition, ND by The Brothers Hildebrandt	*$1.00*	*$3.00*	*$5.00*	£0.50	£1.50	£2.50
6 ND Joe Quesada and Jimmy Palmiotti story and art	*$0.70*	*$2.10*	*$3.50*	£0.40	£1.20	£2.00
6 Fahrenheit Edition - Gold, ND limited to 2,000 copies	*$2.50*	*$7.50*	*$12.50*	£1.50	£4.50	£7.50
6 Fahrenheit Edition - Red, ND limited to 1,000 copies	*$3.00*	*$9.00*	*$15.00*	£2.00	£6.00	£10.00
6 Fahrenheit Edition - White, ND limited to 500 copies	*$3.50*	*$10.50*	*$17.50*	£2.50	£7.50	£12.50
6 Variant Cover Edition, ND by Mark Texeira	*$1.00*	*$3.00*	*$5.00*	£0.50	£1.50	£2.50
Title Value:	*$86.70*	*$259.70*	*$433.50*	£52.70	£157.70	£263.50
Ash Volume One (Dec 1995) Trade paperback ND collects issues #1-5				£2.00	£6.00	£10.00

ASH: THE FIRE WITHIN

Event Comics; 1 Sep 1996-present

Issue	$Good	$Fine	$N.Mint	£Good	£Fine	£N.Mint
0 Ashcan Edition, ND 12pgs, signed by Joe Quesada and Jimmy Palmiotti, limited to 500 copies; black and white	*$5.00*	*$15.00*	*$25.00*	£3.00	£9.00	£15.00
1-2 ND follows on from Ash #0; Joe Quesada and Jimmy Palmiotti	*$0.60*	*$1.80*	*$3.00*	£0.40	£1.20	£2.00
Title Value:	*$6.20*	*$18.60*	*$31.00*	£3.80	£11.40	£19.00

ASH: WIZARD ACE EDITION

Event Comics,OS; 1 1996

Issue	$Good	$Fine	$N.Mint	£Good	£Fine	£N.Mint
1 ND card-stock cover with acetate overlay outer cover; Joe Quesada and Jimmy Palmiotti; numbered Wizard Ace Edition #8	*$2.50*	*$7.50*	*$12.50*	£1.50	£4.50	£7.50
Title Value:	*$2.50*	*$7.50*	*$12.50*	£1.50	£4.50	£7.50

ASHES

Caliber Press,MS; 1 Sep 1990-6 May 1991

Issue	$Good	$Fine	$N.Mint	£Good	£Fine	£N.Mint
1-6 ND 48pgs, horror anthology by John Bergin	*$0.50*	*$1.50*	*$2.50*	£0.30	£0.90	£1.50
Title Value:	*$3.00*	*$9.00*	*$15.00*	£1.80	£5.40	£9.00

Note: issue 4 has #3 in indicia.

ASRIAL VERSUS CHEETAH

Antarctic Press,MS; 1 Jan 1996-2 Feb 1996

Issue	$Good	$Fine	$N.Mint	£Good	£Fine	£N.Mint
1-2 ND features characters from Gold Digger and Ninja High School; Fred Perry script and art	*$0.60*	*$1.80*	*$3.00*	£0.40	£1.20	£2.00
Title Value:	*$1.20*	*$3.60*	*$6.00*	£0.80	£2.40	£4.00

ASSASSIN

TSR; 1 1990-4 1991

Issue	$Good	$Fine	$N.Mint	£Good	£Fine	£N.Mint
1-4 distributed in the U.K.	*$0.40*	*$1.20*	*$2.00*	£0.25	£0.75	£1.25
Title Value:	*$1.60*	*$4.80*	*$8.00*	£1.00	£3.00	£5.00

ASSASSIN FORCE

Greater Mercury Comics; 1 Feb 1992-2 Mar 1992

Issue	$Good	$Fine	$N.Mint	£Good	£Fine	£N.Mint
1 regular team story begins with seven different cover versions/origin story extras; Maxwell Faraday cover and origin story	$0.35	$1.05	$1.75	£0.25	£0.75	£1.25
1 Crimson Cougar cover, origin story	$0.35	$1.05	$1.75	£0.25	£0.75	£1.25
1 Death Hawk cover, origin story	$0.35	$1.05	$1.75	£0.25	£0.75	£1.25
1 Death Lord cover, origin story	$0.35	$1.05	$1.75	£0.25	£0.75	£1.25
1 Grips cover, origin story	$0.35	$1.05	$1.75	£0.25	£0.75	£1.25
1 Sting/Ray cover, origin story	$0.35	$1.05	$1.75	£0.25	£0.75	£1.25
1 Vengeance cover, origin story	$0.35	$1.05	$1.75	£0.25	£0.75	£1.25
2	$0.35	$1.05	$1.75	£0.25	£0.75	£1.25
Title Value:	$2.80	$8.40	$14.00	£2.00	£6.00	£10.00

Note: cover colours for variants are: Dark Blue, Green, Grey, Light Blue, Orange, Red and Yellow.
All Non-Distributed on the news-stands in the U.K.

ASSASSINETTE

Pocket Change Comics; 1 1995-10 Apr 1996

Issue	$Good	$Fine	$N.Mint	£Good	£Fine	£N.Mint
1-8 ND Bob Dixon script, Ed Ball art; black and white	$0.50	$1.50	$2.50	£0.30	£0.90	£1.50
9-10 ND Bob Dixon script, Blalock and Anderson art; black and white	$0.50	$1.50	$2.50	£0.30	£0.90	£1.50
Title Value:	$5.00	$15.00	$25.00	£3.00	£9.00	£15.00

ASSASSINETTE: HARDCORE

Pocket Change Comics,MS; 1 Jun 1995-2 Aug 1995

Issue	$Good	$Fine	$N.Mint	£Good	£Fine	£N.Mint
1-2 ND Bob Dixon script, Scott Shriver art; black and white	$0.50	$1.50	$2.50	£0.30	£0.90	£1.50
Title Value:	$1.00	$3.00	$5.00	£0.60	£1.80	£3.00

ASSASSINS

DC Comics/Amalgam,OS; 1 May 1996

Issue	$Good	$Fine	$N.Mint	£Good	£Fine	£N.Mint
1 ND a DC/Marvel amalgamation of Catwoman and Daredevil as a new team; D.G. Chichester script, Scott McDaniel and Derek Fisher art	$0.50	$1.50	$2.50	£0.40	£1.20	£2.00
Title Value:	$0.50	$1.50	$2.50	£0.40	£1.20	£2.00

ASSASSINS INC.

Silverline Comics; 1-4 1987

Issue	$Good	$Fine	$N.Mint	£Good	£Fine	£N.Mint
1-4 ND Rich Buckler inks	$0.25	$0.75	$1.25	£0.15	£0.45	£0.75
Title Value:	$1.00	$3.00	$5.00	£0.60	£1.80	£3.00

ASSAULT ON ARMOR CITY

Marvel Comics Group; 1992

Cross-over storyline that ran throughout the following issues:
Darkhawk Annual #1, **Avengers West Coast Annual #7** and **Iron Man Annual #13**.

ASTER

Entity Comics; 0 May 1995; 1 Oct 1994-4 Feb 1995

Issue	$Good	$Fine	$N.Mint	£Good	£Fine	£N.Mint
0 ND origin told, George Perez cover	$0.70	$2.10	$3.50	£0.40	£1.20	£2.00
1 ND foil-stamped cover by Jae lee	$0.80	$2.40	$4.00	£0.50	£1.50	£2.50
1 2nd printing, ND (Mar 1995)	$0.60	$1.80	$3.00	£0.40	£1.20	£2.00
1 Ashcan Signed & Numbered Edition, ND (May 1995) - in protective case with certificate; 500 copies	$3.00	$9.00	$15.00	£2.00	£6.00	£10.00
1 Signed & Numbered Edition, ND (May 1995) - in protective case with certificate; limited to 500 copies	$2.50	$7.50	$12.50	£1.50	£4.50	£7.50
2-3 ND foil-stamped cover by Joe Quesada	$0.60	$1.80	$3.00	£0.40	£1.20	£2.00
3 Variant Cover Edition ND	$1.20	$3.60	$6.00	£0.50	£1.50	£2.50
4 ND foil-stamped cover by Joe Quesada	$0.60	$1.80	$3.00	£0.40	£1.20	£2.00
Title Value:	$10.60	$31.80	$53.00	£6.50	£19.50	£32.50
Aster (May 1995) Trade paperback ND reprints issues #1-4 with pin-ups by Jae Lee, Joe Quesada and others				£1.70	£5.10	£8.50

ASTER: THE LAST CELESTIAL KNIGHT

Entity Comics; 1 Jul 1995-2 1995

Issue	$Good	$Fine	$N.Mint	£Good	£Fine	£N.Mint
1 ND Narcisco and Ronaldo Roxas script and art; chromium covers	$0.80	$2.40	$4.00	£0.50	£1.50	£2.50
1 Clear Chromium Edition, ND (Mar 1996), pre-bagged with certificate; limited to 600 copies	$1.80	$5.25	$9.00	£1.00	£3.00	£5.00
1 Holo Chromium Edition, ND (Mar 1996), pre-bagged with certificate; limited to 400 copies	$3.00	$9.00	$15.00	£2.00	£6.00	£10.00
2 ND	$0.60	$1.80	$3.00	£0.40	£1.20	£2.00
Title Value:	$6.20	$18.45	$31.00	£3.90	£11.70	£19.50
Aster vs. The Harriers: Kingdom Come (Jan 1996) Trade paperback ND collects mini-series				£1.30	£3.90	£8.50

ASTONISHING TALES

Marvel Comics Group; 1 Aug 1970-36 Jul 1976
(see Ka-Zar, X-Men #10)

Issue	$Good	$Fine	$N.Mint	£Good	£Fine	£N.Mint
1 ND Ka-Zar and Dr. Doom in separate stories begin (Ka-Zar vs. Kraven), part Jack Kirby art, Wood inks	$5.00	$15.00	$30.00	£2.50	£7.50	£15.00
2 Ka-Zar vs. Kraven, Jack Kirby art, Wally Wood inks	$1.65	$5.00	$10.00	£1.00	£3.00	£6.00
3-4 part Barry Windsor Smith art	$2.50	$7.50	$15.00	£1.00	£3.00	£6.00
5 Dr. Doom vs. Red Skull, part Barry Windsor Smith art	$2.50	$7.50	$15.00	£1.00	£3.00	£6.00
6 Black Panther appears, part Barry Windsor Smith art	$2.50	$7.50	$15.00	£1.00	£3.00	£6.00
7 Black Panther appears	$1.65	$5.00	$10.00	£0.55	£1.75	£3.50
8 ND 48pgs, squarebound, last Dr. Doom story and cover credit	$1.65	$5.00	$10.00	£0.80	£2.50	£5.00
9 features Lorna the Jungle Girl reprint (1950s), Gill Kane cover	$0.55	$1.75	$3.50	£0.40	£1.25	£2.50
10 features Lorna the Jungle Girl reprint (1950s), Gill Kane cover, part Barry Smith art	$1.00	$3.00	$6.00	£0.65	£2.00	£4.00
11 origin Ka-Zar and Zabu, Gill Kane cover	$1.00	$3.00	$6.00	£0.50	£1.50	£3.00
12 origin Man-Thing retold, Neal Adams art	$1.25	$3.75	$7.50	£0.80	£2.50	£5.00
13 Man-Thing vs. Ka-Zar	$0.50	$1.50	$3.00	£0.30	£1.00	£2.00
14-15 Gil Kane cover	$0.40	$1.25	$2.50	£0.25	£0.75	£1.50
16	$0.40	$1.25	$2.50	£0.25	£0.75	£1.50
17 Nick Fury appears	$0.40	$1.25	$2.50	£0.25	£0.75	£1.50
18 Nick Fury appears, X-over Amazing Spiderman #104, Gil Kane cover	$0.40	$1.25	$2.50	£0.25	£0.75	£1.50
19-20 Nick Fury appears	$0.40	$1.25	$2.50	£0.25	£0.75	£1.50
21 1st appearance of It! the Colossus, Steve Ditko back-up reprint	$0.40	$1.25	$2.50	£0.25	£0.75	£1.50
22-23	$0.40	$1.25	$2.50	£0.25	£0.75	£1.50
24 ND It! vs. Fin Fang Foom	$0.40	$1.25	$2.50	£0.25	£0.75	£1.50
25 1st appearance of Deathlok, George Perez' 1st professional artwork (last two pages only - see Creatures on the Loose #33)	$5.25	$16.00	$32.50	£2.50	£7.50	£15.00
26 2nd appearance Deathlok	$2.05	$6.25	$12.50	£1.00	£3.00	£6.00
27-28 LD in the U.K. Deathlok	$1.65	$5.00	$10.00	£0.80	£2.50	£5.00
29 Guardians of the Galaxy: 1st appearance reprinted from Marvel Super-Heroes #18, no Deathlok	$2.05	$6.25	$12.50	£0.80	£2.50	£5.00
30 Deathlok	$1.65	$5.00	$10.00	£0.80	£2.50	£5.00
31 Deathlok, Wrightson cover	$1.50	$4.50	$9.00	£0.65	£2.00	£4.00
32-36 Deathlok	$1.50	$4.50	$9.00	£0.65	£2.00	£4.00
Title Value:	$51.95	$157.25	$315.00	£24.85	£75.75	£151.50

ARTISTS
Wood art 1-4.
FEATURES
Ka-Zar in 1-20. Dr.Doom in 1-8. Man Thing in 12, 13. It! in 21-24. Deathlok in 25-28, 30-36.
REPRINT FEATURES
The Watcher in 31.

ASTRO BOY

Gold Key,OS TV; 1 Aug 1965

Issue	$Good	$Fine	$N.Mint	£Good	£Fine	£N.Mint
1 scarce in the U.S, very scarce in the U.K.	$44.00	$130.00	$350.00	£29.00	£87.50	£235.00
Title Value:	$44.00	$130.00	$350.00	£29.00	£87.50	£235.00

ASTRO BOY, THE ORIGINAL

Now Comics, TV; 1 Sep 1987-20 1989

Issue	$Good	$Fine	$N.Mint	£Good	£Fine	£N.Mint
1 ND Ken Steacy cover/art begins	$0.60	$1.80	$3.00	£0.40	£1.20	£2.00
2-3 ND	$0.50	$1.50	$2.50	£0.30	£0.90	£1.50
4-20 ND	$0.40	$1.20	$2.00	£0.25	£0.75	£1.25
Title Value:	$8.40	$25.20	$39.50	£5.25	£15.75	£26.25

ASTRO CITY

Image; 1 Aug 1995-6 Jan 1996

Issue	$Good	$Fine	$N.Mint	£Good	£Fine	£N.Mint
1 ND Kurt Busiek script, Brent Anderson art; Alex Ross cover and poster at centrefold	$1.20	$3.60	$6.00	£0.50	£1.50	£2.50
2 ND	$0.80	$2.40	$4.00	£0.40	£1.20	£2.00
3-6 ND	$0.50	$1.50	$2.50	£0.30	£0.90	£1.50
Title Value:	$4.00	$12.00	$20.00	£2.10	£6.30	£10.50

ASTRO CITY, KURT BUSIEK'S

Homage Comics; 1 Sep 1996-present

Issue	$Good	$Fine	$N.Mint	£Good	£Fine	£N.Mint
1-4 ND Kurt Busiek script, Brent Anderson and William Blyberg art, Alex Ross painted cover	$0.50	$1.50	$2.50	£0.30	£0.90	£1.50
Title Value:	$2.00	$6.00	$10.00	£1.20	£3.60	£6.00

ASTROBOYS WAVE WARRIORS

Herbie Fletcher Productions; 1 1987

Issue	$Good	$Fine	$N.Mint	£Good	£Fine	£N.Mint
1 ND colour	$0.15	$0.45	$0.75	£0.10	£0.35	£0.60
Title Value:	$0.15	$0.45	$0.75	£0.10	£0.35	£0.60

ASYLUM

New Comics Group; 1 Jun 1989-4 1990

Issue	$Good	$Fine	$N.Mint	£Good	£Fine	£N.Mint
1 ND Wrightson cover, Alex Nino/Jon B. Bright art	$0.30	$0.90	$1.50	£0.20	£0.60	£1.00
2-4 ND	$0.30	$0.90	$1.50	£0.20	£0.60	£1.00
Title Value:	$1.20	$3.60	$6.00	£0.80	£2.40	£4.00

ASYLUM

Millennium; 1 Sep 1993-3 1994

Issue	$Good	$Fine	$N.Mint	£Good	£Fine	£N.Mint
1-2 ND	$0.40	$1.20	$2.00	£0.25	£0.75	£1.25
3 ND 48pgs	$0.50	$1.50	$2.50	£0.50	£1.50	£2.50
Title Value:	$1.30	$3.90	$6.50	£1.00	£3.00	£5.00

Note; issues #4-6 were advertised and solicited but never came out.
The Best of Asylum Volume 1 (Jun 1994)

Issue	$Good	$Fine	$N.Mint	£Good	£Fine	£N.Mint
ND John Bolton, Neil Gaiman, P. Craig Russell work featured				£1.00	£3.00	£5.00
The Best of Asylum Volume 2 (Jul 1994)						
ND John Bolton work featured				£1.00	£3.00	£5.00

ASYLUM

Maximum Comic Press; 1 Dec 1995-present

Issue	$Good	$Fine	$N.Mint	£Good	£Fine	£N.Mint
1 ND Rob Liefeld, Stephen Platt, Arthur Adams creative team begins	$0.60	$1.80	$3.00	£0.40	£1.20	£2.00
2 ND 1st appearance of Deathkiss by Mike Deodato	$0.60	$1.80	$3.00	£0.40	£1.20	£2.00
3-5 ND	$0.60	$1.80	$3.00	£0.40	£1.20	£2.00
6 ND Six Million Dollar Man and Bionic Woman appear	$0.60	$1.80	$3.00	£0.40	£1.20	£2.00
7-8 ND	$0.60	$1.80	$3.00	£0.40	£1.20	£2.00
9 ND Kid Supreme appears	$0.60	$1.80	$3.00	£0.40	£1.20	£2.00
10-11 ND	$0.60	$1.80	$3.00	£0.40	£1.20	£2.00
Title Value:	$6.60	$19.80	$33.00	£4.40	£13.20	£22.00

ATARI FORCE

DC Comics; 1 Jan 1984-20 May 1985

(see Teen Titans #27)

Issue	$Good	$Fine	$N.Mint	£Good	£Fine	£N.Mint
1 1st appearance Dart, Tempest, Babe, Packrat, Morphea; Garcia Lopez art	$0.15	$0.45	$0.75	£0.10	£0.35	£0.60
2-12 Garcia Lopez art	$0.15	$0.45	$0.75	£0.10	£0.30	£0.50
13 Keith Giffen back-up story	$0.15	$0.45	$0.75	£0.10	£0.30	£0.50
14-20	$0.15	$0.45	$0.75	£0.10	£0.30	£0.50
Title Value:	$3.00	$9.00	$15.00	£2.00	£6.05	£10.10

ATARI FORCE SPECIAL

DC Comics; 1 Apr 1986

Issue	$Good	$Fine	$N.Mint	£Good	£Fine	£N.Mint
1 ND Rogers art	$0.25	$0.75	$1.25	£0.15	£0.45	£0.75
Title Value:	$0.25	$0.75	$1.25	£0.15	£0.45	£0.75

ATLANTIS ATTACKS

Marvel Comics Group; 1989

Cross-over storyline that ran throughout the following issues:
Silver Surfer Annual #2, Iron Man Annual #10, Uncanny X-Men Annual #13, Amazing Spiderman Annual #23, Punisher Annual #2, Spectacular Spiderman Annual #9, Daredevil Annual #9, Avengers Annual #18, New Mutants Annual #9 X-Factor Annual #4, Web of Spiderman Annual #5, West Coast Avengers Annual #4, Thor Annual #14, Fantastic Four Annual #22. What If [2nd Series] #25 was also included in the cross-over.

ATLANTIS CHRONICLES

DC Comics,MS; 1 Mar 1990-7 Sep 1990

Issue	$Good	$Fine	$N.Mint	£Good	£Fine	£N.Mint
1-7 Peter David script	$0.50	$1.50	$2.50	£0.30	£0.90	£1.50
Title Value:	$3.50	$10.50	$17.50	£2.10	£6.30	£10.50

Note: all 48pgs, Deluxe Format

ATLAS

Dark Horse,MS; 1 Feb 1994-4 Aug 1994

Issue	$Good	$Fine	$N.Mint	£Good	£Fine	£N.Mint
1-4 ND Bruce Zick script and art	$0.50	$1.50	$2.50	£0.30	£0.90	£1.50
Title Value:	$2.00	$6.00	$10.00	£1.20	£3.60	£6.00

ATOM ANT

Gold Key,OS TV; 1 Jan 1966

Issue	$Good	$Fine	$N.Mint	£Good	£Fine	£N.Mint
1 very scarce in the U.K.	$34.00	$100.00	$240.00	£22.50	£67.50	£160.00
Title Value:	$34.00	$100.00	$240.00	£22.50	£67.50	£160.00

ATOM SPECIAL, SWORD OF THE

DC Comics; 1 Jul 1984-3 Jun 1988

Issue	$Good	$Fine	$N.Mint	£Good	£Fine	£N.Mint
1-2 48pgs, Gil Kane cover and art	$0.25	$0.75	$1.25	£0.15	£0.45	£0.75
3 48pgs	$0.25	$0.75	$1.25	£0.15	£0.45	£0.75
Title Value:	$0.75	$2.25	$3.75	£0.45	£1.35	£2.25

ATOM SPECIAL, THE

DC Comics; 1 May 1993; 2 Jan 1995

Issue	$Good	$Fine	$N.Mint	£Good	£Fine	£N.Mint
1 64pgs, squarebound, Steve Dillon art	$0.50	$1.50	$2.50	£0.30	£0.90	£1.50
2 64pgs, Atom re-discovers himself and his powers	$0.60	$1.80	$3.00	£0.40	£1.20	£2.00
Title Value:	$1.10	$3.30	$5.50	£0.70	£2.10	£3.50

ATOM THE CAT

A Plus Comics; 1 Aug 1991

Issue	$Good	$Fine	$N.Mint	£Good	£Fine	£N.Mint
1 ND	$0.40	$1.20	$2.00	£0.25	£0.75	£1.25
Title Value:	$0.40	$1.20	$2.00	£0.25	£0.75	£1.25

ATOM, POWER OF THE

DC Comics; 1 Aug 1988-18 Nov 1989

Issue	$Good	$Fine	$N.Mint	£Good	£Fine	£N.Mint
1	$0.25	$0.75	$1.25	£0.15	£0.45	£0.75
2-5	$0.15	$0.45	$0.75	£0.10	£0.35	£0.60
6 John Byrne pencils	$0.15	$0.45	$0.75	£0.10	£0.35	£0.60
7-8 Invasion X-over	$0.15	$0.45	$0.75	£0.10	£0.35	£0.60
9 Justice League International appear	$0.15	$0.45	$0.75	£0.10	£0.35	£0.60
10-18	$0.15	$0.45	$0.75	£0.10	£0.35	£0.60
Title Value:	$2.80	$8.40	$14.00	£1.85	£6.40	£10.95

ATOM, SWORD OF THE

DC Comics,MS; 1 Sep 1983-4 Dec 1983

Issue	$Good	$Fine	$N.Mint	£Good	£Fine	£N.Mint
1-4 Gil Kane art	$0.15	$0.45	$0.75	£0.10	£0.35	£0.60
Title Value:	$0.60	$1.80	$3.00	£0.40	£1.40	£2.40

ATOM, THE

National Periodical Publications; 1 Jun/Jul 1962-45 Oct/Nov 1969

(see Action,Brave and the Bold,DC Comics Presents,Detective, Five-Star Super-Hero Spectacular,Power of the Atom,Showcase, Super-Team Family,World's Finest) (title becomes Atom and Hawkman with issue #39)

Issue	$Good	$Fine	$N.Mint	£Good	£Fine	£N.Mint
1 1st appearance Jason Woodrue (Plant Master)	$95.00	$290.00	$775.00	£50.00	£150.00	£400.00
2	$41.00	$120.00	$325.00	£16.50	£50.00	£135.00
3 1st Time Pool story, origin and 1st appearance Chronos	$28.00	$82.50	$225.00	£11.00	£34.00	£90.00
4-5	$18.50	$55.00	$150.00	£6.75	£20.50	£55.00
6	$15.50	$47.00	$125.00	£5.00	£15.00	£40.00
7 1st Atom and Hawkman team-up (pre Hawkman #1)	$29.00	$85.00	$260.00	£11.00	£33.00	£100.00
8 Dr. Light, Justice League of America X-over	$15.50	$47.00	$125.00	£5.00	£15.00	£40.00
9-10	$15.50	$47.00	$125.00	£5.00	£15.00	£40.00
11-15	$11.00	$34.00	$90.00	£3.10	£9.25	£25.00
16-18	$8.75	$26.00	$70.00	£2.50	£7.50	£20.00
19 2nd appearance Zatanna (see Hawkman #4)	$8.75	$26.00	$70.00	£2.50	£7.50	£20.00
20	$8.75	$26.00	$70.00	£2.50	£7.50	£20.00
21-28	$7.00	$21.00	$50.00	£1.75	£5.25	£12.50
29 1st solo Silver Age appearance Golden Age Atom	$18.50	$55.00	$150.00	£5.00	£15.00	£40.00
30	$7.00	$21.00	$50.00	£1.75	£5.25	£12.50
31 Hawkman X-over	$6.75	$20.00	$47.50	£1.25	£3.85	£9.00
32-35	$6.75	$20.00	$47.50	£1.25	£3.85	£9.00
36 Golden Age Atom appears	$8.75	$26.00	$70.00	£2.15	£6.50	£17.50
37 1st appearance Major Mynah	$6.75	$20.00	$47.50	£1.25	£3.85	£9.00
38	$6.75	$20.00	$47.50	£1.25	£3.85	£9.00
39 title becomes Atom and Hawkman	$6.25	$19.00	$45.00	£1.25	£3.85	£9.00
40	$6.25	$19.00	$45.00	£1.25	£3.85	£9.00
41-42	$6.00	$18.00	$42.50	£1.00	£3.00	£7.00
43 1st appearance Gentleman Ghost	$6.00	$18.00	$42.50	£1.05	£3.20	£7.50
44 origin retold	$6.00	$18.00	$42.50	£1.05	£3.20	£7.50
45	$6.00	$18.00	$42.50	£1.00	£3.00	£7.00
Title Value:	$570.75	$1713.50	$4490.00	£189.25	£570.55	£1507.00

FEATURES

Atom solo, Hawkman solo in 40,41,43,44. Atom and Hawkman in 39,42,45.

ATOMIC AGE

Marvel Comics Group/Epic,MS; 1 Jan 1991-4 Apr 1991

Issue	$Good	$Fine	$N.Mint	£Good	£Fine	£N.Mint
1-4 ND 48pgs	$0.80	$2.40	$4.00	£0.50	£1.50	£2.50
Title Value:	$3.20	$9.60	$16.00	£2.00	£6.00	£10.00

Note: Bookshelf Format

ATOMIC BUNNY

Charlton; 12 Aug 1958-19 Dec 1959

(previously Atomic Rabbit)

Issue	$Good	$Fine	$N.Mint	£Good	£Fine	£N.Mint
12 distributed in the U.K.	$9.25	$28.00	$65.00	£5.50	£17.00	£40.00
13-19 distributed in the U.K.	$5.00	$15.00	$35.00	£3.20	£9.50	£22.50
Title Value:	$44.25	$133.00	$310.00	£27.90	£83.50	£197.50

ATOMIC CLONES

Comico; 1 1990-5 1991

Issue	$Good	$Fine	$N.Mint	£Good	£Fine	£N.Mint
1-5 ND	$0.40	$1.20	$2.00	£0.25	£0.75	£1.25
Title Value:	$2.00	$6.00	$10.00	£1.25	£3.75	£6.25

ATOMIC MAN COMICS

Blackthorne; 1 Dec 1986-3 1987

Issue	$Good	$Fine	$N.Mint	£Good	£Fine	£N.Mint
1-3 ND Bonivert art	$0.30	$0.90	$1.50	£0.20	£0.60	£1.00
Title Value:	$0.90	$2.70	$4.50	£0.60	£1.80	£3.00

ATOMIC MOUSE

A Plus Comics; 1 Feb 1991-2 1991

Issue	$Good	$Fine	$N.Mint	£Good	£Fine	£N.Mint
1-2 ND reprints from 1950s/60s	$0.40	$1.20	$2.00	£0.25	£0.75	£1.25
Title Value:	$0.80	$2.40	$4.00	£0.50	£1.50	£2.50

ATOMIC RABBIT

Charlton; 1 Aug 1955-11 Mar 1958

(becomes Atomic Bunny)

Issue	$Good	$Fine	$N.Mint	£Good	£Fine	£N.Mint
1 scarce in the U.K. 1st appearance Atomic Rabbit	$17.00	$50.00	$120.00	£10.50	£32.00	£75.00
2 scarce in the U.K.	$8.50	$26.00	$60.00	£5.00	£15.00	£35.00
3 scarce in the U.K.	$5.50	$17.00	$40.00	£4.25	£12.50	£30.00
4-10	$5.50	$17.00	$40.00	£3.55	£10.50	£25.00
11 scarce in the U.K. giant	$8.50	$26.00	$60.00	£5.00	£15.00	£35.00
Title Value:	$78.00	$238.00	$560.00	£49.60	£148.00	£350.00

Note: the last two issues have been recorded with distribution stamps ie. distributed in the U.K.

ATOMIK ANGELS

Crusade Comics,MS; 1 May 1996-4 Aug 1996

Issue	$Good	$Fine	$N.Mint	£Good	£Fine	£N.Mint
nn Intrep-Edition ND giveaway at launch party; black and white	$2.00	$6.00	$10.00	£1.50	£4.50	£7.50
1 ND Freefall appears	$0.60	$1.80	$3.00	£0.40	£1.20	£2.00
1 Gold Foil Bimota Edition, ND (May 1996); available as a giveaway at the 1996 San Diego Comicon	$2.00	$6.00	$10.00	£1.50	£4.50	£7.50
2-4 ND	$0.60	$1.80	$3.00	£0.40	£1.20	£2.00
Title Value:	$6.40	$19.20	$32.00	£4.60	£13.80	£23.00

ATTACK

Charlton; 1 Sep 1971-48 Oct 1984

Issue	$Good	$Fine	$N.Mint	£Good	£Fine	£N.Mint
1 distributed in the U.K.	$0.50	$1.50	$3.00	£0.30	£1.00	£2.00
2-5 distributed in the U.K.	$0.40	$1.25	$2.50	£0.25	£0.75	£1.50
6-30 distributed in the U.K.	$0.30	$1.00	$2.00	£0.20	£0.60	£1.25
31-47 distributed in the U.K.	$0.30	$0.90	$1.50	£0.20	£0.60	£1.00
48 reprint; limited distributed in the U.K.	$0.30	$0.90	$1.50	£0.20	£0.60	£1.00
Title Value:	$15.00	$47.70	$90.00	£9.90	£29.80	£57.25

ATTACK OF THE MUTANT MONSTERS

A Plus Comics; 1 May 1991-2 1991

Issue	$Good	$Fine	$N.Mint	£Good	£Fine	£N.Mint
1 ND 48pgs, Steve Ditko monster reprints	$0.40	$1.20	$2.00	£0.25	£0.75	£1.25
2 ND 48pgs, Reptisaurus reprints	$0.40	$1.20	$2.00	£0.25	£0.75	£1.25
Title Value:	$0.80	$2.40	$4.00	£0.50	£1.50	£2.50

AUGIE DOGGIE

Gold Key; 1 Oct 1963

Issue	$Good	$Fine	$N.Mint	£Good	£Fine	£N.Mint
1 rare although distributed in the U.K. based on Hanna-Barbera cartoon	$19.00	$57.50	$135.00	£11.00	£34.00	£80.00
Title Value:	$19.00	$57.50	$135.00	£11.00	£34.00	£80.00

AUTUMN

Caliber Press; 1 Oct 1995-3 Dec 1995

Issue	$Good	$Fine	$N.Mint	£Good	£Fine	£N.Mint
1-3 ND b&w	$0.60	$1.80	$3.00	£0.40	£1.20	£2.00
Title Value:	$1.80	$5.40	$9.00	£1.20	£3.60	£6.00

AVALON

Comico,MS; 1 Nov 1993-2 1994

Issue	$Good	$Fine	$N.Mint	£Good	£Fine	£N.Mint
1 ND	$0.40	$1.20	$2.00	£0.25	£0.75	£1.25
1 Deluxe Edition, ND emerald foil logo	$0.60	$1.80	$3.00	£0.40	£1.20	£2.00
2 ND	$0.40	$1.20	$2.00	£0.25	£0.75	£1.25
2 Deluxe Edition, ND ruby foil logo	$0.60	$1.80	$3.00	£0.40	£1.20	£2.00
Title Value:	$2.00	$6.00	$10.00	£1.30	£3.90	£6.50

AVANT GUARD

Day One Comics; 1 Mar 1994

Issue	$Good	$Fine	$N.Mint	£Good	£Fine	£N.Mint
1 ND Stephen Conley script and art; black and white	$0.50	$1.50	$2.50	£0.30	£0.90	£1.50
Title Value:	$0.50	$1.50	$2.50	£0.30	£0.90	£1.50

AVATAR COMICS

DC Comics,MS; 1 Dec 1990-3 Apr 1991

Issue	$Good	$Fine	$N.Mint	£Good	£Fine	£N.Mint
1-3 96pgs	$0.60	$1.80	$3.00	£0.40	£1.20	£2.00
Title Value:	$1.80	$5.40	$9.00	£1.20	£3.60	£6.00

Note: based on TSR role-playing games. Issued every six weeks

Note also that these issues are prone to crinkly spines owing to the production process

AVENGEBLADE

Maximum Comic Press; 1 Jul 1996-present

Issue	$Good	$Fine	$N.Mint	£Good	£Fine	£N.Mint
1 ND Robert Napton script; parody of Avengelyne and all that big bad girl stuff	$0.60	$1.80	$3.00	£0.50	£1.50	£2.50
2 ND	$0.60	$1.80	$3.00	£0.40	£1.20	£2.00
Title Value:	$1.20	$3.60	$6.00	£0.90	£2.70	£4.50

AVENGELYNE

Maximum Comic Press; 1 May 1995-3 Aug 1995

Issue	$Good	$Fine	$N.Mint	£Good	£Fine	£N.Mint
½ ND produced in conjunction with Wizard Comics; issued in a Wizard protective Mylar with certificate of authenticity	$2.50	$7.50	$12.50	£1.50	£4.50	£7.50
½ Platinum Edition, ND; as above	$4.50	$13.50	$22.50	£3.00	£9.00	£15.00
0 Ashcan Edition, ND 8.5" x 5.5" Blue card cover, featuring the same cover as Avengelyne #1	$2.50	$7.50	$12.50	£1.50	£4.50	£7.50
1 Gold Edition ND	$5.00	$15.00	$25.00	£3.00	£9.00	£15.00
1 Holochrome Edition, ND wraparound cover, photo certificate of authenticity	$5.00	$15.00	$25.00	£1.50	£4.50	£7.50
1 Newstand Edition, ND Cathy Christian photo cover	$1.00	$3.00	$5.00	£1.00	£3.00	£5.00
1 Version A, ND Direct Marker Edition with wraparound chromium cover, Cathy Christian photo insert standing with spear	$1.50	$4.50	$7.50	£0.80	£2.40	£4.00
1 Version B, ND Direct Marker Edition with wraparound chromium cover, Cathy Christian photo insert kneeling with sword	$1.50	$4.50	$7.50	£0.80	£2.40	£4.00
1 Version C, ND Direct Market Edition with wraparound chromium cover, Cathy Christian photo insert folded arms	$1.50	$4.50	$7.50	£0.80	£2.40	£4.00
1 Version D, ND Direct Marker Edition with wraparound chromium cover, Cathy Christian photo insert standing with sword	$1.50	$4.50	$7.50	£0.80	£2.40	£4.00
2 ND polybagged with trading card	$0.80	$2.40	$4.00	£0.70	£2.10	£3.50
3 ND	$0.80	$2.40	$4.00	£0.70	£2.10	£3.50
3 Variant Cover Edition, ND Arthur Adams cover art	$1.50	$4.50	$7.50	£1.00	£3.00	£5.00
Title Value:	$29.60	$88.80	$148.00	£17.10	£51.30	£85.50

Avengelyne (Dec 1995)

Issue	$Good	$Fine	$N.Mint	£Good	£Fine	£N.Mint
Trade paperback collects 3 issue mini-series				£1.30	£3.90	£6.50

AVENGELYNE (2ND SERIES)

Maximum Comic Press; 0 Oct 1996; 1 Apr 1996-present

Issue	$Good	$Fine	$N.Mint	£Good	£Fine	£N.Mint
0 ND Rob Liefeld and Robert Napton script, Andy Park and John Stinsman art	$0.60	$1.80	$3.00	£0.40	£1.20	£2.00
1 ND Devlin guest-stars	$0.80	$2.40	$4.00	£0.40	£1.20	£2.00
1 Variant Cover Edition, ND photo cover	$0.80	$2.40	$4.00	£0.50	£1.50	£2.50
2 ND	$0.60	$1.80	$3.00	£0.40	£1.20	£2.00
2 Variant Cover Edition, ND photo cover	$0.80	$2.40	$4.00	£0.50	£1.50	£2.50
3 ND	$0.60	$1.80	$3.00	£0.40	£1.20	£2.00
4 ND guest-stars Cybrid	$0.60	$1.80	$3.00	£0.40	£1.20	£2.00
5 ND Cybrid appears	$0.60	$1.80	$3.00	£0.40	£1.20	£2.00
6 ND guest-stars Divinity	$0.60	$1.80	$3.00	£0.40	£1.20	£2.00
7 ND	$0.60	$1.80	$3.00	£0.40	£1.20	£2.00
Title Value:	$6.60	$19.80	$33.00	£4.20	£12.60	£21.00

AVENGELYNE BIBLE

Maximum Comic Press,OS; 1 Oct 1996

Issue	$Good	$Fine	$N.Mint	£Good	£Fine	£N.Mint
1 ND character profiles and information	$0.70	$2.10	$3.50	£0.50	£1.50	£2.50
Title Value:	$0.70	$2.10	$3.50	£0.50	£1.50	£2.50

AVENGELYNE SWIMSUIT EDITION

Maximum Comic Press,OS; 1 Aug 1995

Issue	$Good	$Fine	$N.Mint	£Good	£Fine	£N.Mint
1 ND photographs of Cathy Christian and pin-ups by Rob Liefeld, Mike Deodato, Dan Fraga and others; four cover variations available	$0.70	$2.10	$3.50	£0.50	£1.50	£2.50
1 2nd printing, ND (Feb 1996) new cover	$0.70	$2.10	$3.50	£0.50	£1.50	£2.50
Title Value:	$1.40	$4.20	$7.00	£1.00	£3.00	£5.00

Ash #4

Astonishing Tales #10

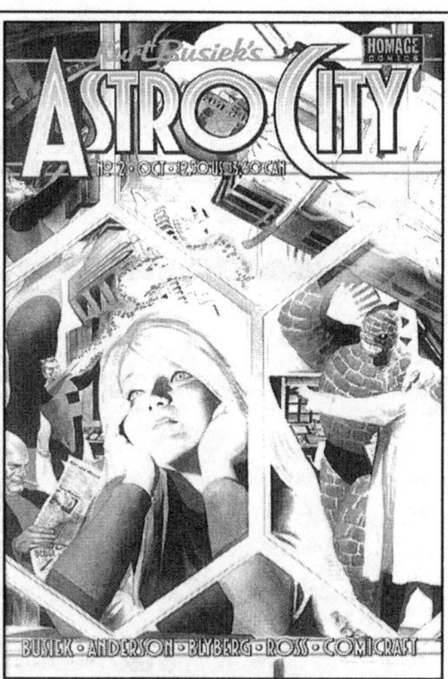

Astro City, Kurt Busiek's #2

AVENGELYNE/GLORY

	$Good	$Fine	$N.Mint	£Good	£Fine	£N.Mint
Maximum Comic Press,OS; 1 Sep 1995						
1 ND Robert Napton script, Rob Liefeld art; wraparound chromium cover						
	$0.90	*$2.70*	*$4.50*	£0.60	£1.80	£3.00
1 Variant Cover Edition, ND Glory on the left hand side of cover back to back with Avengelyne						
	$1.00	*$3.00*	*$5.00*	£0.70	£2.10	£3.50
Title Value:	*$1.90*	*$5.70*	*$9.50*	£1.30	£3.90	£6.50
Avengelyne/Glory Signed Limited Edition Boxed Set (Dec 1995)						
ND set contains both chromium covers and variants and a special new fifth cover ink edition; box signed by Rob Liefeld and John Stinsman				£6.50	£19.50	£32.50

AVENGELYNE/GLORY SWIMSUIT BOOK

	$Good	$Fine	$N.Mint	£Good	£Fine	£N.Mint
Maximum Comic Press,OS; nn May 1996						
nn ND pin-ups of the yummy Glory and Avengelyne						
	$0.60	*$1.80*	*$3.00*	£0.40	£1.20	£2.00
Title Value:	*$0.60*	*$1.80*	*$3.00*	£0.40	£1.20	£2.00

AVENGELYNE/GLORY: THE GODYSSEY

	$Good	$Fine	$N.Mint	£Good	£Fine	£N.Mint
Image,OS; 1 Sep 1996						
1 ND Robert Napton script, Ed Benes and Norm Rapmund art						
	$0.60	*$1.80*	*$3.00*	£0.40	£1.20	£2.00
1 Variant Cover Edition, ND photo cover featuring Avengelyne and Glory models						
	$1.20	*$3.60*	*$6.00*	£0.80	£2.40	£4.00
Title Value:	*$1.80*	*$5.40*	*$9.00*	£1.20	£3.60	£6.00

AVENGELYNE/PROPHET

	$Good	$Fine	$N.Mint	£Good	£Fine	£N.Mint
Maximum Comic Press,OS; 1 May 1996						
1 Cover A, ND Rob Liefeld and Robert Napton script, Rob Liefeld and Jonathan Sibal art; Liefeld cover of characters in head-shots						
	$0.60	*$1.80*	*$3.00*	£0.40	£1.20	£2.00
1 Cover B, ND Rob Liefeld cover of characters in full length						
	$0.60	*$1.80*	*$3.00*	£0.40	£1.20	£2.00
Title Value:	*$1.20*	*$3.60*	*$6.00*	£0.80	£2.40	£4.00

AVENGELYNE/PROPHET HARDCOVER GRAPHIC NOVEL

	$Good	$Fine	$N.Mint	£Good	£Fine	£N.Mint
Image,OS; nn Dec 1995						
nn ND Rob Liefeld script, Stephen Platt and Mike Deodato art						
	$5.00	*$15.00*	*$25.00*	£3.50	£10.50	£17.50
Title Value:	*$5.00*	*$15.00*	*$25.00*	£3.50	£10.50	£17.50
Signed and Numbered Edition (Dec 1995)						
ND limited to 500 copies, signed by Liefeld				£10.00	£30.00	£50.00
Signed and Numbered (Dec 1995)						
ND limited to 500 copies, signed by Platt				£10.00	£30.00	£50.00

AVENGELYNE: ARMAGEDDON

	$Good	$Fine	$N.Mint	£Good	£Fine	£N.Mint
Maximum Comic Press,MS; 1 Dec 1996-3 Feb 1997						
1 ND Robert Napton script, Scott Clark and Norm Rapmund art						
	$0.60	*$1.80*	*$3.00*	£0.40	£1.20	£2.00
1 Variant Cover Edition, ND white background on cover						
	$2.00	*$6.00*	*$10.00*	£1.00	£3.00	£5.00
2-3 ND Robert Napton script, Scott Clark and Norm Rapmund art						
	$0.60	*$1.80*	*$3.00*	£0.40	£1.20	£2.00
Title Value:	*$3.80*	*$11.40*	*$19.00*	£2.20	£6.60	£11.00

AVENGELYNE: DEADLY SINS

	$Good	$Fine	$N.Mint	£Good	£Fine	£N.Mint
Maximum Comic Press,MS; 1 Feb 1996-3 Apr 1996						
1 Line Art Cover, ND Robert Napton script, John Stinsman and Marlo Alquiza art						
	$0.60	*$1.80*	*$3.00*	£0.40	£1.20	£2.00
1 Photo Cover ND	*$0.60*	*$1.80*	*$3.00*	£0.40	£1.20	£2.00
2-3 ND	*$0.60*	*$1.80*	*$3.00*	£0.40	£1.20	£2.00
Title Value:	*$2.40*	*$7.20*	*$12.00*	£1.60	£4.80	£8.00
Note: says February 1995 in indicia						

AVENGELYNE: POWER

	$Good	$Fine	$N.Mint	£Good	£Fine	£N.Mint
Maximum Comic Press; 1 Oct 1995-3 Dec 1995						
1 ND Rob Liefeld/Robert Napton script, John Stinsman art						
	$0.50	*$1.50*	*$2.50*	£0.30	£0.90	£1.50
2 ND	*$0.50*	*$1.50*	*$2.50*	£0.30	£0.90	£1.50
2 Variant Cover Edition, ND photo variant cover of Cathy Christian						
	$0.60	*$1.80*	*$3.00*	£0.40	£1.20	£2.00
3 Cover A ND	*$0.50*	*$1.50*	*$2.50*	£0.30	£0.90	£1.50
3 Cover B, ND photo cover variant - holding mini-crossbow						
	$0.50	*$1.50*	*$2.50*	£0.30	£0.90	£1.50
3 Cover C, ND photo cover variant - holding sword aloft						
	$0.50	*$1.50*	*$2.50*	£0.30	£0.90	£1.50
Title Value:	*$3.10*	*$9.30*	*$15.50*	£1.90	£5.70	£9.50
Avengelyne: Power (May 1996)						
Trade paperback collects mini-series, new painted cover and new pages				£1.30	£3.90	£6.50

AVENGER, THE

	$Good	$Fine	$N.Mint	£Good	£Fine	£N.Mint
I.W. Comics; 9 1964						
9 scarce, distributed in the U.K. 50s reprints						
	$3.75	*$11.00*	*$22.50*	£2.05	£6.25	£12.50
Title Value:	*$3.75*	*$11.00*	*$22.50*	£2.05	£6.25	£12.50

AVENGERS

	$Good	$Fine	$N.Mint	£Good	£Fine	£N.Mint
Marvel Comics Group; 1 Sep 1963-402 Sep 1996						
1 origin and 1st appearance of The Avengers (Thor, Iron Man, Ant-Man, Hulk, Wasp), Loki appears						
	$275.00	*$830.00*	*$2500.00*	£165.00	£500.00	£1500.00
1 Marvel Milestone Edition, ND (Sep 1993), reprints issue #1						
	$0.60	*$1.80*	*$3.00*	£0.40	£1.20	£2.00
2 1st appearance of Avengers Mansion and Space Phantom; Hulk leaves temporarily						
	$82.50	*$250.00*	*$675.00*	£50.00	£150.00	£400.00
3 scarce in the U.K. Sub-Mariner appears (teams with the Hulk against the Avengers); Spiderman appears; X-Men appear (joint 3rd appearance along with Tales of Suspense #49 and X-Men #3, all cover-dated Jan. 1964)						
	$60.00	*$180.00*	*$425.00*	£41.00	£120.00	£285.00
[Scarce in high grade - Very Fine+ or better]						
4 Captain America first revived (1st Silver Age appearance), joins Avengers; storyline continues in Fantastic Four #26; 1st Silver Age appearance Baron Zemo I						
	$165.00	*$500.00*	*$1500.00*	£70.00	£215.00	£650.00
4 Marvel Milestone Edition, ND (Mar 1995), metallic ink cover						
	$0.60	*$1.80*	*$3.00*	£0.40	£1.20	£2.00
4 Reprint, ND scarce in the U.K. (1966)						
	$17.50	*$52.50*	*$125.00*	£10.50	£32.00	£75.00
4 Reprint with Golden Record, ND very rare in the U.K to form complete sealed package						
	$29.00	*$85.00*	*$200.00*	£17.50	£52.50	£125.00
5 less common in the U.K. Hulk leaves team for good						
	$36.00	*$105.00*	*$250.00*	£21.00	£62.50	£150.00
6 less common in the U.K. 1st appearance of Baron Zemo teamed with The Masters of Evil						
	$26.00	*$77.50*	*$185.00*	£17.50	£52.50	£125.00
7	*$26.00*	*$75.00*	*$180.00*	£16.00	£49.00	£115.00
8 1st appearance of Kang the Conqueror						
	$26.00	*$75.00*	*$180.00*	£16.00	£49.00	£115.00
9 very rare in the U.K. 1st appearance of Wonder Man (dies - see #131)						
	$28.00	*$82.50*	*$195.00*	£21.00	£62.50	£150.00
10 scarce in the U.K. 1st appearance of Immortus, 3rd Crime Circus, Hercules appears						
	$23.50	*$70.00*	*$165.00*	£15.50	£47.00	£110.00
11 scarce in the U.K. Spiderman appears (origin briefly retold)						
	$27.00	*$80.00*	*$190.00*	£16.00	£49.00	£115.00
12 Avengers vs. The Mole Man						
	$15.50	*$47.00*	*$110.00*	£10.50	£32.00	£75.00
13 Avengers vs. Count Nefaria						
	$15.50	*$47.00*	*$110.00*	£10.50	£32.00	£75.00
14	*$15.50*	*$47.00*	*$110.00*	£10.50	£32.00	£75.00
15 death of Baron Zemo I						
	$15.50	*$47.00*	*$110.00*	£10.50	£32.00	£75.00
16 1st main line-up change: Hawkeye, Scarlet Witch, Quicksilver, Captain America (Thor, Giant Man, Wasp and Iron Man leave)						
	$17.00	*$50.00*	*$120.00*	£10.50	£32.00	£75.00
16 Marvel Milestone Edition, ND (Oct 1993), reprints issue #16						
	$0.60	*$1.80*	*$3.00*	£0.40	£1.20	£2.00
17-18	*$11.00*	*$34.00*	*$80.00*	£7.00	£21.00	£50.00
19 1st appearance of Swordsman, origin Hawkeye						
	$11.00	*$34.00*	*$80.00*	£7.00	£21.00	£50.00
20 Wood inks	*$7.75*	*$23.50*	*$55.00*	£5.00	£15.00	£35.00
21 Wood inks, 1st appearance original Powerman						
	$7.75	*$23.50*	*$55.00*	£5.00	£15.00	£35.00
22 Wood inks	*$7.75*	*$23.50*	*$55.00*	£5.00	£15.00	£35.00
23 last Silver Age issue, indicia-dated December 1965						
	$5.50	*$17.00*	*$40.00*	£4.00	£12.00	£28.00
24	*$5.50*	*$17.00*	*$40.00*	£4.00	£12.00	£28.00
25 Dr. Doom vs. Avengers, Fantastic Four appear						
	$5.50	*$17.00*	*$40.00*	£4.00	£12.00	£28.00
26-27	*$5.50*	*$17.00*	*$40.00*	£4.00	£12.00	£28.00
28 Giant-Man becomes Goliath						
	$5.50	*$17.00*	*$40.00*	£4.00	£12.00	£28.00
29-30	*$5.50*	*$17.00*	*$40.00*	£4.00	£12.00	£28.00
31-32	*$4.25*	*$12.50*	*$30.00*	£2.50	£7.50	£17.50
33-34 scarce in the U.K.						
	$4.25	*$12.50*	*$30.00*	£2.70	£8.00	£19.00
35 Goliath's power altered (height set)						
	$4.25	*$12.50*	*$30.00*	£2.50	£7.50	£17.50
36-37	*$4.25*	*$12.50*	*$30.00*	£2.50	£7.50	£17.50
38 Hercules joins	*$4.25*	*$12.50*	*$30.00*	£2.50	£7.50	£17.50
39	*$4.25*	*$12.50*	*$30.00*	£2.50	£7.50	£17.50
40 Sub-Mariner appears						
	$4.25	*$12.50*	*$30.00*	£2.50	£7.50	£17.50
41-42	*$3.20*	*$9.50*	*$22.50*	£2.00	£6.00	£14.00
43 1st appearance Red Guardian						
	$3.20	*$9.50*	*$22.50*	£2.00	£6.00	£14.00
44-46	*$3.20*	*$9.50*	*$22.50*	£2.00	£6.00	£14.00
47 Magneto appears						
	$3.55	*$10.50*	*$25.00*	£2.10	£6.25	£15.00
48 1st appearance new Black Knight, Magneto appears						
	$3.55	*$10.50*	*$25.00*	£2.50	£7.50	£17.50
49 Magneto appears						
	$3.55	*$10.50*	*$25.00*	£2.10	£6.25	£15.00
50	*$3.20*	*$9.50*	*$22.50*	£2.00	£6.00	£14.00
51 Thor and Iron Man appear, Goliath's powers restored (variable height)						
	$3.75	*$11.00*	*$22.50*	£2.00	£6.00	£12.00
52	*$3.75*	*$11.00*	*$22.50*	£2.00	£6.00	£12.00
53 less common in the U.K. Avengers vs. original X-Men; story continues from X-Men #45						
	$5.75	*$17.50*	*$35.00*	£3.30	£10.00	£20.00
54 1st appearance of new Masters of Evil						
	$3.75	*$11.00*	*$22.50*	£2.00	£6.00	£12.00
55-56	*$3.75*	*$11.00*	*$22.50*	£2.00	£6.00	£12.00
57 1st appearance The Vision						
	$11.00	*$34.00*	*$80.00*	£5.50	£17.00	£40.00
58 rare in the U.K. origin Vision						
	$7.75	*$23.50*	*$55.00*	£4.25	£12.50	£30.00
59 scarce in the U.K. 1st appearance Yellowjacket						
	$3.75	*$11.00*	*$22.50*	£2.30	£7.00	£14.00
60 scarce in the U.K. Yellowjacket and Wasp's wedding						
	$3.75	*$11.00*	*$22.50*	£2.30	£7.00	£14.00
61 scarce in the U.K. Dr. Strange appears						
	$3.75	*$11.00*	*$22.50*	£2.00	£6.00	£12.00
62 scarce in the U.K.						
	$3.75	*$11.00*	*$22.50*	£2.00	£6.00	£12.00
63 1st appearance new Goliath (Hawkeye)						
	$3.75	*$11.00*	*$22.50*	£1.80	£5.50	£11.00

SOME INDEPENDENT COMICS MAY NOT HAVE APPEARED ALTHOUGH THEY WERE ADVERTISED AND SOLICITED.

	$Good	$Fine	$N.Mint	£Good	£Fine	£N.Mint
64-65	$3.75	$11.00	$22.50	£1.80	£5.50	£11.00
66-67 Barry Smith art	$3.75	$11.00	$22.50	£2.30	£7.00	£14.00
68	$2.50	$7.50	$15.00	£1.65	£5.00	£10.00
69 1st Justice League of America inspired Squadron Sinister (later Squadron Supreme), 1st appearance Nighthawk	$2.50	$7.50	$15.00	£2.00	£6.00	£12.00
70 scarce in the U.K.	$2.50	$7.50	$15.00	£2.00	£6.00	£12.00
71 scarce in the U.K. 1st modern teaming of Golden Age Captain America, Human Torch & Sub-Mariner (later The Invaders), Black Knight appears	$3.30	$10.00	$20.00	£2.30	£7.00	£14.00
72-79	$2.50	$7.50	$15.00	£1.50	£4.50	£9.00
80 1st appearance Red Wolf and Lobo (not to be confused with DC's Lobo!)	$2.50	$7.50	$15.00	£1.50	£4.50	£9.00
81	$2.50	$7.50	$15.00	£1.50	£4.50	£9.00
82 Daredevil appears	$2.50	$7.50	$15.00	£1.50	£4.50	£9.00
83 scarce in the U.K. 1st appearance Valkyrie (Enchantress disguised), intro The Liberators	$2.50	$7.50	$15.00	£1.55	£4.75	£9.50
84 scarce in the U.K.	$2.50	$7.50	$15.00	£1.55	£4.75	£9.50
85-86	$2.50	$7.50	$15.00	£1.50	£4.50	£9.00
87 Black Panther's origin retold	$5.00	$15.00	$30.00	£2.50	£7.50	£15.00
88 Hulk and Professor X appear; story continues in Hulk #140	$2.50	$7.50	$15.00	£1.55	£4.75	£9.50
89 scarce in the U.K. Captain Marvel appears	$2.50	$7.50	$15.00	£1.65	£5.00	£10.00
90 scarce in the U.K.	$2.50	$7.50	$15.00	£1.65	£5.00	£10.00
91 scarce in the U.K. Captain Marvel appears	$2.50	$7.50	$15.00	£1.65	£5.00	£10.00
92 scarce in the U.K. Neal Adams cover	$2.50	$7.50	$15.00	£1.65	£5.00	£10.00
93 scarce in the U.K. 52pgs, , Neal Adams art, Kree-Skrull War begins, Fantastic Four appear	$8.50	$26.00	$60.00	£5.50	£17.00	£40.00
94 very scarce in the U.K. Neal Adams art	$5.75	$17.50	$35.00	£4.15	£12.50	£25.00
95-96 scarce in the U.K. Neal Adams art	$5.75	$17.50	$35.00	£3.65	£11.00	£22.00
97 scarce in the U.K. Gil Kane cover, Golden Age Captain America, Blazing Skull, Sub-Mariner, Human Torch, Patriot, Fin, Angel, Vision cameos, Kree/Skrull War ends	$4.15	$12.50	$25.00	£2.50	£7.50	£15.00
98 scarce in the U.K. Barry Smith art, Goliath reverts back to Hawkeye	$5.75	$17.50	$35.00	£2.90	£8.75	£17.50
99 scarce in the U.K. Barry Smith art	$5.75	$17.50	$35.00	£2.90	£8.75	£17.50
100 very scarce in the U.K. Barry Smith art; features everyone who had been an Avenger up to that point	$10.50	$32.00	$85.00	£5.50	£16.50	£45.00
101-106 scarce in the U.K.	$1.65	$5.00	$10.00	£1.30	£4.00	£8.00
107 scarce in the U.K. Jim Starlin art	$2.00	$6.00	$12.00	£1.40	£4.25	£8.50
108-109	$1.65	$5.00	$10.00	£1.15	£3.50	£7.00
110 original X-Men and Magneto appear, ties into Daredevil #99	$4.15	$12.50	$25.00	£1.65	£5.00	£10.00
111 original X-Men and Magneto appear, Daredevil and Black Widow guest-star; ties into Hulk #172 and Daredevil #100	$4.15	$12.50	$25.00	£1.65	£5.00	£10.00
112 1st appearance Mantis	$2.50	$7.50	$15.00	£1.50	£4.50	£9.00
113-114	$1.30	$4.00	$8.00	£1.05	£3.25	£6.50
115 story continues in Defenders #8	$1.65	$5.00	$10.00	£1.25	£3.75	£7.50
116 Silver Surfer appears (vs. Vision), ties into Defenders #9	$1.65	$5.00	$10.00	£1.25	£3.75	£7.50
117 Silver Surfer and Sub-Mariner appear, ties into Defenders #10	$1.65	$5.00	$10.00	£1.25	£3.75	£7.50
118 Silver Surfer and original Defenders appear, cameos of many Marvel heroes	$1.65	$5.00	$10.00	£1.25	£3.75	£7.50
119-120	$1.30	$4.00	$8.00	£1.05	£3.25	£6.50
121-122 ND	$1.30	$4.00	$8.00	£1.15	£3.50	£7.00
123 ND origin Mantis	$1.30	$4.00	$8.00	£1.15	£3.50	£7.00
124 ND	$1.30	$4.00	$8.00	£1.15	£3.50	£7.00
125 ND Thanos cover and cameo	$2.00	$6.00	$12.00	£1.30	£4.00	£8.00
126 ND	$1.30	$4.00	$8.00	£1.05	£3.25	£6.50
127 ND Fantastic Four and the Inhumans appear	$1.30	$4.00	$8.00	£1.05	£3.25	£6.50
128 ND Fantastic Four appear	$1.30	$4.00	$8.00	£1.05	£3.25	£6.50
129-130 ND	$1.30	$4.00	$8.00	£1.05	£3.25	£6.50
131 ND scarce in the U.K. 2nd appearance Wonderman (raised from the dead); Legion of the Dead appear (inc. Frankenstein and original Human Torch)	$1.30	$4.00	$8.00	£1.25	£3.75	£7.50
132 ND 3rd appearance of Wonderman, Legion of the Dead appear (inc. Frankenstein and original Human Torch)	$1.15	$3.50	$7.00	£1.05	£3.25	£6.50
133 ND	$1.15	$3.50	$7.00	£0.90	£2.75	£5.50
134-135 ND scarce in the U.K. "true" origin Vision	$1.30	$4.00	$8.00	£1.00	£3.00	£6.00
136 ND all reprint (Amazing Adventures #12 featuring Beast vs. Iron Man)	$1.15	$3.50	$7.00	£0.90	£2.75	£5.50
137 ND Beast joins	$1.15	$3.50	$7.00	£0.90	£2.75	£5.50
138-140 ND	$1.15	$3.50	$7.00	£0.90	£2.75	£5.50
141-143 ND	$1.00	$3.00	$6.00	£0.80	£2.50	£5.00
144 ND 1st appearance of Hellcat (formerly The Cat)	$1.15	$3.50	$7.00	£1.00	£3.00	£6.00
145-147 ND	$1.00	$3.00	$6.00	£0.80	£2.50	£5.00
148 ND Squadron Supreme appears	$1.00	$3.00	$6.00	£0.80	£2.50	£5.00
149 ND	$1.00	$3.00	$6.00	£0.80	£2.50	£5.00
150 ND anniversary special; new line-up debated in re-cap of Avengers history: Yellowjacket, Scarlet Witch, Wasp, Captain America, Beast, Vision, Iron Man; part Perez and Kirby art	$1.00	$3.00	$6.00	£0.80	£2.50	£5.00
151 ND new line-up takes effect, Wonderman returns, George Perez art, Jack Kirby cover	$0.80	$2.50	$5.00	£0.75	£2.25	£4.50
152 ND Jack Kirby cover, Wonderman appears	$0.80	$2.50	$5.00	£0.75	£2.25	£4.50
153 Jack Kirby cover	$0.80	$2.50	$5.00	£0.55	£1.75	£3.50
154-155 George Perez art, Jack Kirby cover	$0.80	$2.50	$5.00	£0.55	£1.75	£3.50
156-158 Jack Kirby cover	$0.80	$2.50	$5.00	£0.55	£1.75	£3.50
159	$0.80	$2.50	$5.00	£0.55	£1.75	£3.50
160 George Perez art	$0.80	$2.50	$5.00	£0.55	£1.75	£3.50
161-162 George Perez art	$0.80	$2.50	$5.00	£0.50	£1.50	£3.00
163 Iceman with The Champions appear (no Ghost Rider however)	$0.80	$2.50	$5.00	£0.50	£1.50	£3.00
164-166 John Byrne art	$1.00	$3.00	$6.00	£0.55	£1.75	£3.50
167-168 LD in the U.K. George Perez art, Guardians of the Galaxy appear	$0.80	$2.50	$5.00	£0.55	£1.75	£3.50
169	$0.80	$2.50	$5.00	£0.40	£1.25	£2.50
170 George Perez art	$0.80	$2.50	$5.00	£0.40	£1.25	£2.50
171 scarce in the U.K. George Perez art	$0.65	$2.00	$4.00	£0.45	£1.35	£2.75
172 scarce in the U.K.	$0.65	$2.00	$4.00	£0.45	£1.35	£2.75
173 scarce in the U.K. Korvac Saga begins, Guardians of the Galaxy appear	$0.65	$2.00	$4.00	£0.45	£1.35	£2.75
174-176 scarce in the U.K. Korvac Saga, Guardians of the Galaxy appear	$0.65	$2.00	$4.00	£0.45	£1.35	£2.75
177 scarce in the U.K. Korvac Saga epilogue, Guardians of the Galaxy appear	$0.65	$2.00	$4.00	£0.45	£1.35	£2.75
178-180	$0.65	$2.00	$4.00	£0.40	£1.25	£2.50
181 John Byrne art, new line-up: Captain America, Scarlet Witch, Beast, Vision, Iron Man, Wasp, Falcon; Guardians of the Galaxy appear	$0.50	$1.50	$3.00	£0.50	£1.50	£3.00
182 John Byrne art	$0.50	$1.50	$3.00	£0.30	£1.00	£2.00
183 ND scarce in the U.K. John Byrne art, Ms. Marvel appears	$0.50	$1.50	$3.00	£1.00	£3.00	£6.00
184 John Byrne art, Ms. Marvel joins team	$0.50	$1.50	$3.00	£0.30	£1.00	£2.00
185 John Byrne art, origin Quicksilver and Scarlet Witch	$0.50	$1.50	$3.00	£0.30	£1.00	£2.00
186-187 LD in the U.K. John Byrne art	$0.50	$1.50	$3.00	£0.50	£1.50	£3.00
188 John Byrne art, Inhumans appear, ties into Avengers Annual #9	$0.50	$1.50	$3.00	£0.30	£1.00	£2.00
189 John Byrne art	$0.50	$1.50	$3.00	£0.30	£1.00	£2.00
190 John Byrne art, Daredevil appears	$0.50	$1.50	$3.00	£0.30	£1.00	£2.00
191 John Byrne art	$0.50	$1.50	$2.50	£0.30	£0.90	£1.50
192	$0.50	$1.50	$2.50	£0.30	£0.90	£1.50
193 Frank Miller cover	$0.50	$1.50	$2.50	£0.30	£0.90	£1.50
194-196 George Perez art	$0.50	$1.50	$2.50	£0.30	£0.90	£1.50
197	$0.50	$1.50	$2.50	£0.30	£0.90	£1.50
198-199 George Perez art	$0.50	$1.50	$2.50	£0.30	£0.90	£1.50
200 ND DS George Perez art, anniversary issue	$0.60	$1.80	$3.00	£0.70	£2.10	£3.50
201-202 George Perez art	$0.50	$1.50	$2.50	£0.30	£0.90	£1.50
203	$0.50	$1.50	$2.50	£0.30	£0.90	£1.50
204-205 ND	$0.50	$1.50	$2.50	£0.40	£1.20	£2.00
206 Human Torch appears	$0.50	$1.50	$2.50	£0.30	£0.90	£1.50
207-210	$0.50	$1.50	$2.50	£0.30	£0.90	£1.50
211 new line-up: Captain America, Wasp, Tigra, Iron Man, Thor, Yellowjacket; Angel/Iceman (with Champions), Moonknight cameos	$0.50	$1.50	$2.50	£0.30	£0.90	£1.50

Issue	$Good	$Fine	$N.Mint	£Good	£Fine	£N.Mint
212-213	*$0.50*	*$1.50*	*$2.50*	£0.30	£0.90	£1.50
214 Ghost Rider and Angel appear	*$0.50*	*$1.50*	*$2.50*	£0.30	£0.90	£1.50
215-216 Silver Surfer appears	*$0.60*	*$1.80*	*$3.00*	£0.40	£1.20	£2.00
217-218	*$0.50*	*$1.50*	*$2.50*	£0.30	£0.90	£1.50
219-220 Drax the Destroyer appears	*$0.50*	*$1.50*	*$2.50*	£0.30	£0.90	£1.50
221 Frank Miller cover, She-Hulk joins, Hawkeye returns, Spiderman appears	*$0.50*	*$1.50*	*$2.50*	£0.25	£0.75	£1.25
222-224	*$0.50*	*$1.50*	*$2.50*	£0.25	£0.75	£1.25
225 very LD Black Knight returns	*$0.50*	*$1.50*	*$2.50*	£0.40	£1.20	£2.00
226 LD in the U.K.	*$0.50*	*$1.50*	*$2.50*	£0.40	£1.20	£2.00
227 LD in the U.K. new (female) Captain Marvel joins, Ant-Man/Giant-Man/Goliath/Yellowjacket, Wasp origins retold	*$0.50*	*$1.50*	*$2.50*	£0.40	£1.20	£2.00
228-230 LD in the U.K.	*$0.50*	*$1.50*	*$2.50*	£0.40	£1.20	£2.00
231 LD in the U.K. Nick Fury appears	*$0.50*	*$1.50*	*$2.50*	£0.40	£1.20	£2.00
232 LD in the U.K. Starfox joins	*$0.50*	*$1.50*	*$2.50*	£0.40	£1.20	£2.00
233 LD in the U.K. John Byrne art, Fantastic Four appear	*$0.50*	*$1.50*	*$2.50*	£0.40	£1.20	£2.00
234 LD in the U.K. origin Quicksilver and Scarlet Witch, X-Men and Dr. Strange appear; continues from Fantastic Four #256	*$0.50*	*$1.50*	*$2.50*	£0.35	£1.05	£1.75
235 LD in the U.K.	*$0.50*	*$1.50*	*$2.50*	£0.35	£1.05	£1.75
236 LD in the U.K. Spiderman appears	*$0.50*	*$1.50*	*$2.50*	£0.35	£1.05	£1.75
237 very LD Spiderman appears	*$0.50*	*$1.50*	*$2.50*	£0.40	£1.20	£2.00
238 LD in the U.K.	*$0.50*	*$1.50*	*$2.50*	£0.35	£1.05	£1.75
239 LD in the U.K. David Letterman parody	*$0.50*	*$1.50*	*$2.50*	£0.35	£1.05	£1.75
240 LD in the U.K. return of Spiderwoman, Dr. Strange appears	*$0.50*	*$1.50*	*$2.50*	£0.35	£1.05	£1.75
241-245 LD in the U.K.	*$0.50*	*$1.50*	*$2.50*	£0.30	£0.90	£1.50
246-249 LD in the U.K. Eternals appear	*$0.50*	*$1.50*	*$2.50*	£0.30	£0.90	£1.50
250 DS, Avengers West Coast X-over	*$0.60*	*$1.80*	*$3.00*	£0.40	£1.20	£2.00
251 Paladin appears	*$0.50*	*$1.50*	*$2.50*	£0.25	£0.75	£1.25
252-255	*$0.50*	*$1.50*	*$2.50*	£0.25	£0.75	£1.25
256-257 Ka-Zar appears	*$0.50*	*$1.50*	*$2.50*	£0.25	£0.75	£1.25
258 Spiderman appears (in black costume), Ka-Zar appears	*$0.50*	*$1.50*	*$2.50*	£0.25	£0.75	£1.25
259	*$0.50*	*$1.50*	*$2.50*	£0.25	£0.75	£1.25
260 LD in the U.K. Secret Wars II X-over, Fantastic Four appear	*$0.50*	*$1.50*	*$2.50*	£0.30	£0.90	£1.50
261 Secret Wars II X-over	*$0.50*	*$1.50*	*$2.50*	£0.25	£0.75	£1.25
262 Hercules battles Sub-Mariner	*$0.50*	*$1.50*	*$2.50*	£0.25	£0.75	£1.25
263 LD in the U.K. 1st X-Factor story (see Fantastic Four #286 for continuation); Jean Grey coccoon found	*$1.00*	*$3.00*	*$5.00*	£0.50	£1.50	£2.50
264 1st appearance Yellowjacket II	*$0.50*	*$1.50*	*$2.50*	£0.25	£0.75	£1.25
265 Secret Wars II X-over	*$0.50*	*$1.50*	*$2.50*	£0.25	£0.75	£1.25
266 Secret Wars II X-over (epilogue), Silver Surfer appears	*$0.50*	*$1.50*	*$2.50*	£0.25	£0.75	£1.25
267 Hulk, Storm and Colossus appear	*$0.50*	*$1.50*	*$2.50*	£0.25	£0.75	£1.25
268 John Byrne cover	*$0.50*	*$1.50*	*$2.50*	£0.25	£0.75	£1.25
269-270	*$0.50*	*$1.50*	*$2.50*	£0.25	£0.75	£1.25
271 Paladin appears	*$0.50*	*$1.50*	*$2.50*	£0.20	£0.60	£1.00
272 Alpha Flight appears	*$0.50*	*$1.50*	*$2.50*	£0.20	£0.60	£1.00
273 LD in the U.K.	*$0.50*	*$1.50*	*$2.50*	£0.25	£0.75	£1.25
274-286	*$0.50*	*$1.50*	*$2.50*	£0.20	£0.60	£1.00
287 Machine Man appears	*$0.50*	*$1.50*	*$2.50*	£0.20	£0.60	£1.00
288-290	*$0.50*	*$1.50*	*$2.50*	£0.20	£0.60	£1.00
291-297 Simonson script	*$0.50*	*$1.50*	*$2.50*	£0.20	£0.60	£1.00
298 Inferno X-over, Simonson script	*$0.50*	*$1.50*	*$2.50*	£0.20	£0.60	£1.00
299 Inferno X-over, Simonson script, Mr. Fantastic appears	*$0.50*	*$1.50*	*$2.50*	£0.20	£0.60	£1.00
300 LD in the U.K. 64pgs, Walt Simonson art in bck up story, Inferno, new line-up: Thor, Invisible Woman, The Captain, Mr. Fantastic, Gilgamesh: Simonson script , squarebound (many copies, 25%? with crinkled spines)	*$0.80*	*$2.40*	*$4.00*	£0.40	£1.20	£2.00
301 Nova appears	*$0.40*	*$1.20*	*$2.00*	£0.20	£0.60	£1.00
302 very LD re-intro Quasar, Nova appears	*$0.40*	*$1.20*	*$2.00*	£0.50	£1.50	£2.50
303 Fantastic Four, Quasar, Firelord, West Coast Avengers and Nova appear	*$0.40*	*$1.20*	*$2.00*	£0.20	£0.60	£1.00
304	*$0.40*	*$1.20*	*$2.00*	£0.20	£0.60	£1.00
305 everybody who was an Avenger appears, John Byrne scripts begin (ends #317)	*$0.40*	*$1.20*	*$2.00*	£0.20	£0.60	£1.00
306-310	*$0.40*	*$1.20*	*$2.00*	£0.20	£0.60	£1.00
311-312 LD in the U.K. Acts of Vengeance tie-in	*$0.40*	*$1.20*	*$2.00*	£0.30	£0.90	£1.50
313 Acts of Vengeance tie-in	*$0.40*	*$1.20*	*$2.00*	£0.20	£0.60	£1.00
314-318 Spiderman considers joining storyline	*$0.40*	*$1.20*	*$2.00*	£0.15	£0.45	£0.75
319-324 The Crossing Line story	*$0.40*	*$1.20*	*$2.00*	£0.15	£0.45	£0.75
325 intro the Skull, Byrne cover	*$0.40*	*$1.20*	*$2.00*	£0.15	£0.45	£0.75
326 new line up, 1st appearance Rage	*$0.60*	*$1.80*	*$3.00*	£0.25	£0.75	£1.25
327 story based on Avengers #1, Rage appears	*$0.40*	*$1.20*	*$2.00*	£0.15	£0.45	£0.75
328 origin Rage	*$0.50*	*$1.50*	*$2.50*	£0.20	£0.60	£1.00
329	*$0.40*	*$1.20*	*$2.00*	£0.15	£0.45	£0.75
330 line up change	*$0.40*	*$1.20*	*$2.00*	£0.15	£0.45	£0.75
331-333	*$0.30*	*$0.90*	*$1.50*	£0.15	£0.45	£0.75
334-339 bi-weekly issue, Collection Obsession story	*$0.30*	*$0.90*	*$1.50*	£0.15	£0.45	£0.75
340-342 New Warriors guest star	*$0.30*	*$0.90*	*$1.50*	£0.15	£0.45	£0.75
343	*$0.30*	*$0.90*	*$1.50*	£0.15	£0.45	£0.75
344 $1.25 cover begins	*$0.30*	*$0.90*	*$1.50*	£0.15	£0.45	£0.75
345 Galactic Storm part 5	*$0.30*	*$0.90*	*$1.50*	£0.15	£0.45	£0.75
346 Galactic Storm part 12	*$0.30*	*$0.90*	*$1.50*	£0.15	£0.45	£0.75
347 DS Galactic Storm part 19 (conclusion)	*$0.40*	*$1.20*	*$2.00*	£0.25	£0.75	£1.25
348	*$0.30*	*$0.90*	*$1.50*	£0.15	£0.45	£0.75
349 Rage appears	*$0.30*	*$0.90*	*$1.50*	£0.15	£0.45	£0.75
350 64pgs, Cyclops and Professor X appear, reprints of past Avengers covers, gatefold cover	*$0.50*	*$1.50*	*$2.50*	£0.30	£0.90	£1.50
351-353 bi-weekly	*$0.30*	*$0.90*	*$1.50*	£0.15	£0.45	£0.75
354-355	*$0.30*	*$0.90*	*$1.50*	£0.15	£0.45	£0.75
356 Black Panther appears	*$0.30*	*$0.90*	*$1.50*	£0.15	£0.45	£0.75
357-359	*$0.30*	*$0.90*	*$1.50*	£0.15	£0.45	£0.75
360 30th anniversary issue, embossed all-bronze foil cover	*$1.00*	*$3.00*	*$5.00*	£0.40	£1.20	£2.00
361-362	*$0.30*	*$0.90*	*$1.50*	£0.20	£0.60	£1.00
363 48pgs, embossed all-silver foil cover 30th anniversary celebration issue	*$0.60*	*$1.80*	*$3.00*	£0.40	£1.20	£2.00
364 Giant-Man returns to the Avengers	*$0.30*	*$0.90*	*$1.50*	£0.20	£0.60	£1.00
365	*$0.30*	*$0.90*	*$1.50*	£0.20	£0.60	£1.00
366 64pgs, squarebound, embossed all-gold foil cover 30th anniversary actual issue (by date)	*$0.80*	*$2.40*	*$4.00*	£0.50	£1.50	£2.50
367	*$0.30*	*$0.90*	*$1.50*	£0.20	£0.60	£1.00
368 Bloodties part 1, continued in X-Men #26	*$0.30*	*$0.90*	*$1.50*	£0.30	£0.90	£1.50
369 48pgs, platinum foil embossed cover, Bloodties part 5 (conclusion)	*$0.60*	*$1.80*	*$3.00*	£0.40	£1.20	£2.00
370-373	*$0.30*	*$0.90*	*$1.50*	£0.20	£0.60	£1.00
374 with free Spiderman vs. Venom card sheet	*$0.30*	*$0.90*	*$1.50*	£0.20	£0.60	£1.00
375 48pgs, Thunderstrike returns	*$0.40*	*$1.20*	*$2.00*	£0.25	£0.75	£1.25
375 Collectors Edition, 48pgs, Thunderstrike returns; bound-in poster	*$0.50*	*$1.50*	*$2.50*	£0.30	£0.90	£1.50
376 Black Panther appears	*$0.30*	*$0.90*	*$1.50*	£0.20	£0.60	£1.00
377	*$0.30*	*$0.90*	*$1.50*	£0.20	£0.60	£1.00
378 Magneto and High Evolutionary appear	*$0.30*	*$0.90*	*$1.50*	£0.20	£0.60	£1.00
379-384	*$0.30*	*$0.90*	*$1.50*	£0.20	£0.60	£1.00
385 ties into Captain America #438	*$0.30*	*$0.90*	*$1.50*	£0.20	£0.60	£1.00
386 ties into Captain America #439	*$0.30*	*$0.90*	*$1.50*	£0.20	£0.60	£1.00
387 Taking AIM part 2, continued in Captain America #441	*$0.30*	*$0.90*	*$1.50*	£0.20	£0.60	£1.00
388 Taking AIM part 4 (conclusion)	*$0.30*	*$0.90*	*$1.50*	£0.20	£0.60	£1.00
389	*$0.30*	*$0.90*	*$1.50*	£0.20	£0.60	£1.00
390 Avengers: The Crossing prelude and lead into Avengers/Ultraforce team-up, Mike Deodato art	*$0.30*	*$0.90*	*$1.50*	£0.20	£0.60	£1.00
391-394 Avengers: The Crossing tie-in, Mike Deodato art	*$0.30*	*$0.90*	*$1.50*	£0.20	£0.60	£1.00
395 Avengers: Timeslide	*$0.30*	*$0.90*	*$1.50*	£0.20	£0.60	£1.00

Issue	$Good	$Fine	$N.Mint	£Good	£Fine	£N.Mint
396 The First Sign part 4 (conclusion from Iron Man #326)	*$0.30*	*$0.90*	*$1.50*	£0.20	£0.60	£1.00
397 continued from Incredible Hulk #440	*$0.30*	*$0.90*	*$1.50*	£0.20	£0.60	£1.00
398 Mark Waid scripts begin	*$0.30*	*$0.90*	*$1.50*	£0.20	£0.60	£1.00
399	*$0.30*	*$0.90*	*$1.50*	£0.20	£0.60	£1.00
400 48pgs, Onslaught tie-in, wraparound cover by Mike Wieringo	*$0.50*	*$1.50*	*$2.50*	£0.30	£0.90	£1.50
401 Onslaught tie-in	*$0.30*	*$0.90*	*$1.50*	£0.20	£0.60	£1.00
402 Onslaught tie-in, continued in Onslaught: Marvel Universe	*$0.30*	*$0.90*	*$1.50*	£0.20	£0.60	£1.00
Title Value:	***$1467.50***	***$4410.90***	***$10906.50***	**£884.55**	**£2673.80**	**£6530.25**

Greatest Battles of the Avengers (Oct 1993)
Trade paperback

	£Good	£Fine	£N.Mint
reprints issues #54,55, 79,160 plus Annuals #7,10	£2.00	£6.00	£10.00

Avengers Anniversary Cover Set (Jan 1994)

	£Good	£Fine	£N.Mint
collects the four foil cover issues Avengers #360, 363, 366 and 369	£2.70	£8.10	£13.50

Avengers: Yesterday Quest (Oct 1994)

	£Good	£Fine	£N.Mint
Trade paperback reprints issues #181,182 and #185-187	£0.90	£2.70	£4.50

ARTISTS
Paul Neary art in 292-329. Paul Neary covers 293, 294, 298-307, 309-312, 315, 319. John Byrne covers 239, 247-254, 290, 308, 313. Mike Zeck covers 224, 258, 259, 261-270, 272, 273, 275, 276, 278-289, 321, 323-326, 332,334,337.

AVENGERS (2ND SERIES)

Marvel Comics Group; 1 Nov 1996-present

Issue	$Good	$Fine	$N.Mint	£Good	£Fine	£N.Mint
1 ND 48pgs, Rob Liefeld and Jim Valentino script, Rob Liefeld and Chap Yaep art; origin of The Avengers re-told; Rob Liefeld cover art	*$0.60*	*$1.80*	*$3.00*	£0.40	£1.20	£2.00
1 Gold Stamped Signature Edition, ND 48pgs, (Jan 1997) pre-bagged with certificate featuring 22 carat gold stamped signatures of Rob Liefeld, Jim Valentino and Chap Yaep; 5,000 copies	*$5.00*	*$15.00*	*$25.00*	£3.50	£10.50	£17.50
1 Variant Cover Edition, ND 48pgs, Chap Yaep cover art	*$1.00*	*$3.00*	*$5.00*	£0.80	£2.40	£4.00
2-3 ND Kang the Conqueror appears	*$0.40*	*$1.20*	*$2.00*	£0.25	£0.75	£1.25
4-5 ND Avengers vs. The Incredible Hulk	*$0.40*	*$1.20*	*$2.00*	£0.25	£0.75	£1.25
Title Value:	***$8.20***	***$24.60***	***$41.00***	**£5.70**	**£17.10**	**£28.50**

AVENGERS ANNIVERSARY MAGAZINE

Marvel Comics Group,OS; 1 Nov 1993

Issue	$Good	$Fine	$N.Mint	£Good	£Fine	£N.Mint
1 ND 48pgs, features and articles on The Avengers; 8.5" x 11"	*$0.90*	*$2.70*	*$4.50*	£0.60	£1.80	£3.00
Title Value:	***$0.90***	***$2.70***	***$4.50***	**£0.60**	**£1.80**	**£3.00**

AVENGERS ANNUAL, THE

Marvel Comics Group; 1 Sep 1967-5 1972; 6 1976-23 1994

Issue	$Good	$Fine	$N.Mint	£Good	£Fine	£N.Mint
1 68pgs, all new 40pg story; original Avengers team-up with current team of the time, Sub-Mariner and Nick Fury appear	*$7.75*	*$23.50*	*$55.00*	£5.00	£15.00	£35.00
2 68pgs, all new story; original Avengers vs. new Avengers, Dr. Strange cameo	*$4.25*	*$12.50*	*$30.00*	£2.50	£7.50	£17.50
3 scarce in the U.K. 68pgs, reprints #4 (1st Silver Age Captain America) plus three new stories by Jack Kirby	*$4.25*	*$12.50*	*$30.00*	£2.50	£7.50	£17.50
4 scarce in the U.K. 68pgs, reprints issues #5,6	*$2.05*	*$6.25*	*$12.50*	£1.50	£4.50	£9.00
5 ND very scarce in the U.K. 52pgs, (often ink-stained), Spiderman appears (reprint of #11)	*$2.05*	*$6.25*	*$12.50*	£1.50	£4.50	£9.00
6 ND 52pgs, George Perez art	*$1.50*	*$4.50*	*$7.50*	£0.90	£2.70	£4.50
7 ND 52pgs, Jim Starlin cover & art, Captain Marvel and Thanos appear, death of Warlock; story continues in Marvel Two-In-One Annual #2	*$4.50*	*$13.50*	*$22.50*	£2.50	£7.50	£12.50
8 ND scarce in the U.K. 52pgs, Dr. Strange with Ms. Marvel and Thundra appear, George Perez art	*$1.00*	*$3.00*	*$5.00*	£0.80	£2.40	£4.00
9 ND scarce in the U.K. 52pgs	*$1.00*	*$3.00*	*$5.00*	£0.80	£2.40	£4.00
10 ND 52pgs, Golden art, 1st appearance Rogue, 1st appearance Madelyn Prior (see X-Men #168), Spiderman appears, X-Men cameo	*$5.00*	*$15.00*	*$25.00*	£1.50	£4.50	£7.50
11 ND 52pgs, Silver Surfer appears; Avengers vs. Defenders	*$0.80*	*$2.40*	*$4.00*	£0.60	£1.80	£3.00
12 ND 52pgs, Guice art, Inhumans appear	*$0.80*	*$2.40*	*$4.00*	£0.40	£1.20	£2.00
13 ND Hulk appears, Ditko pencils, John Byrne inks	*$0.80*	*$2.40*	*$4.00*	£0.40	£1.20	£2.00
14 ND Fantastic Four appears, John Byrne and Kyle Baker art	*$0.80*	*$2.40*	*$4.00*	£0.40	£1.20	£2.00
15 ND Freedom Force, Ditko and Janson art; ties into West Coast Avengers Annual #1	*$0.80*	*$2.40*	*$4.00*	£0.40	£1.20	£2.00
16 ND Avengers vs. Legion of the Dead inc. Captain Marvel and Drax, Silver Surfer and Green Goblin appear, Marshall Rogers art	*$0.80*	*$2.40*	*$4.00*	£0.40	£1.20	£2.00
17 ND 64pgs, Evolutionary War	*$0.60*	*$1.80*	*$3.00*	£0.40	£1.20	£2.00
18 ND Atlantis Attacks part 8	*$0.60*	*$1.80*	*$3.00*	£0.40	£1.20	£2.00
19 ND Terminus Factor part 5 (see Captain America/Thor/Iron Man/West Coast Avengers Annuals)	*$0.60*	*$1.80*	*$3.00*	£0.40	£1.20	£2.00
20 ND Subterranean Odyssey part 1 (continued in Hulk Annual #17)	*$0.60*	*$1.80*	*$3.00*	£0.40	£1.20	£2.00
21 ND 64pgs, Citizen Kang part 4 (conclusion), Fantastic Four appear	*$0.60*	*$1.80*	*$3.00*	£0.40	£1.20	£2.00
22 ND 64pgs, pre-bagged with trading card introducing Bloodwraith	*$0.60*	*$1.80*	*$3.00*	£0.40	£1.20	£2.00
23 ND 64pgs, Hercules appears	*$0.60*	*$1.80*	*$3.00*	£0.40	£1.20	£2.00
Title Value:	***$42.35***	***$127.00***	***$250.00***	**£24.90**	**£74.70**	**£147.50**

Note: 1, 2 have back-up reprints; 3-5 all reprint. 1-6 called King Size Special, 7-18 called Annuals.

AVENGERS DOUBLE FEATURE

Marvel Comics Group,MS; 1 Oct 1994-4 Jan 1995

Issue	$Good	$Fine	$N.Mint	£Good	£Fine	£N.Mint
1 ND 48pgs, flip-book format; features Avengers #379 plus Giant Man #1; George Perez 1st script for Marvel	*$0.50*	*$1.50*	*$2.50*	£0.30	£0.90	£1.50
2 ND 48pgs, flip-book format; Avengers #380 plus Giant Man back-up story	*$0.50*	*$1.50*	*$2.50*	£0.30	£0.90	£1.50
3 ND 48pgs, flip-book format; Avengers #381 plus Giant Man back-up story	*$0.50*	*$1.50*	*$2.50*	£0.30	£0.90	£1.50
4 ND 48pgs, flip-book format; Avengers #382 plus Giant Man back-up story	*$0.50*	*$1.50*	*$2.50*	£0.30	£0.90	£1.50
Title Value:	***$2.00***	***$6.00***	***$10.00***	**£1.20**	**£3.60**	**£6.00**

AVENGERS GIANT SIZE

Marvel Comics Group; 1 Aug 1974-5 Dec 1975

Issue	$Good	$Fine	$N.Mint	£Good	£Fine	£N.Mint
1 ND scarce in the U.K. 68pgs, All Winner's Squad appear; Rich Buckler's Kirbyesque art	*$2.05*	*$6.25*	*$12.50*	£1.25	£3.75	£7.50
2 ND scarce in the U.K. 68pgs, Kang and Rama-Tut appear	*$1.65*	*$5.00*	*$10.00*	£1.15	£3.50	£7.00
3 ND rare in the U.K. 68pgs	*$1.65*	*$5.00*	*$10.00*	£1.30	£4.00	£8.00
4 ND rare in the U.K. 68pgs, wedding of Scarlet Witch and Vision	*$1.65*	*$5.00*	*$10.00*	£1.15	£3.50	£7.00
5 ND 68pgs, all reprint (Avengers King Size Special #1)	*$1.30*	*$4.00*	*$8.00*	£1.00	£3.00	£6.00

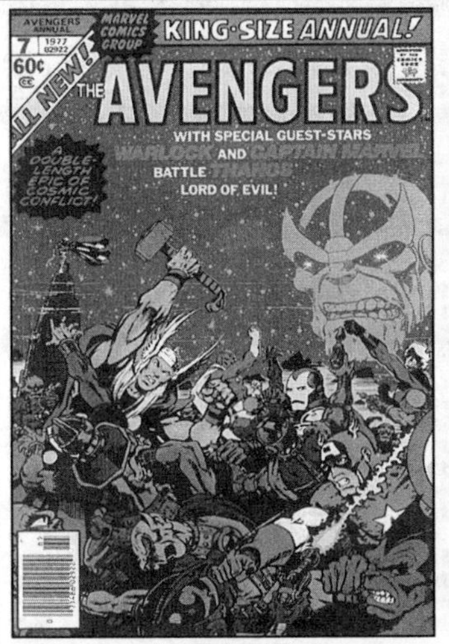

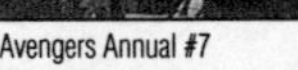
Avengers Annual #7

Avengelyne/Warrior Nun Areala #1

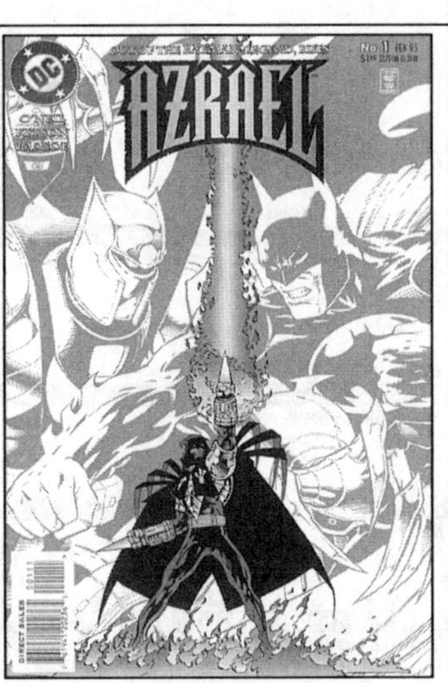

Azrael #1

	$Good	$Fine	$N.Mint	£Good	£Fine	£N.Mint
Title Value:	$8.30	$25.25	$50.50	£5.85	£17.75	£35.50

AVENGERS LOG

Marvel Comics Group,OS; 1 Feb 1994

	$Good	$Fine	$N.Mint	£Good	£Fine	£N.Mint
1 ND 48pgs, reference index from Avengers #1 to present; George Perez cover						
	$0.40	$1.20	$2.00	£0.25	£0.75	£1.25
Title Value:	$0.40	$1.20	$2.00	£0.25	£0.75	£1.25

AVENGERS STRIKE FILE

Marvel Comics Group,OS; 1 Jan 1994

	$Good	$Fine	$N.Mint	£Good	£Fine	£N.Mint
1 ND Avengers pin-ups plus operation: Galactic Storm re-told						
	$0.30	$0.90	$1.50	£0.20	£0.60	£1.00
Title Value:	$0.30	$0.90	$1.50	£0.20	£0.60	£1.00

AVENGERS UNPLUGGED

Marvel Comics Group; 1 Oct 1995-6 Mar 1996

	$Good	$Fine	$N.Mint	£Good	£Fine	£N.Mint
1 ND new stories begin, cover priced at 99 cents						
	$0.20	$0.60	$1.00	£0.15	£0.45	£0.75
2-3 ND	$0.20	$0.60	$1.00	£0.15	£0.45	£0.75
4 ND Absorbing Man and Titania marry						
	$0.20	$0.60	$1.00	£0.15	£0.45	£0.75
5 ND Captain Marvel (Monica Rambeau) vs. Captain Marvel (Genis Marvell)						
	$0.20	$0.60	$1.00	£0.15	£0.45	£0.75
6 ND	$0.20	$0.60	$1.00	£0.15	£0.45	£0.75
Title Value:	$1.20	$3.60	$6.00	£0.90	£2.70	£4.50

Note: originally announced as Avengers Unleashed

AVENGERS, OFFICIAL INDEX TO

Marvel Comics Group,MS; 1 Oct 1994-6 Mar 1995

	$Good	$Fine	$N.Mint	£Good	£Fine	£N.Mint
1 ND information and cover repros of issues #1-62						
	$0.40	$1.20	$2.00	£0.25	£0.75	£1.25
2 ND information and cover repros of issues #63-121						
	$0.40	$1.20	$2.00	£0.25	£0.75	£1.25
3 ND information and cover repros of issues #122-180						
	$0.40	$1.20	$2.00	£0.25	£0.75	£1.25
4 ND information and cover repros of issues #181-240						
	$0.40	$1.20	$2.00	£0.25	£0.75	£1.25
5 ND information and cover repros of issues #241-299						
	$0.40	$1.20	$2.00	£0.25	£0.75	£1.25
6 ND information and cover repros of issues #300-360						
	$0.40	$1.20	$2.00	£0.25	£0.75	£1.25
Title Value:	$2.40	$7.20	$12.00	£1.50	£4.50	£7.50

AVENGERS, THE

Gold Key, TV; 1 Nov 1968

	$Good	$Fine	$N.Mint	£Good	£Fine	£N.Mint
1 rare although distributed in the U.K. features Steed and Mrs. Peel from the TV series, photo cover titled "John Steed and Emma Peel"						
	$36.00	$105.00	$250.00	£21.00	£62.50	£150.00
Title Value:	$36.00	$105.00	$250.00	£21.00	£62.50	£150.00

AVENGERS, THE OFFICIAL MARVEL INDEX TO

Marvel Comics Group,MS; 1 Jun 1987-7 Aug 1988

	$Good	$Fine	$N.Mint	£Good	£Fine	£N.Mint
1 ND 48pgs, squarebound; information and colour cover reproductions Avengers #1-#23						
	$0.50	$1.50	$2.50	£0.30	£0.90	£1.50
2 ND 48pgs, squarebound; information and colour cover reproductions Avengers #24-#45, Annual #1, cover and splash page by Mark Texeira						
	$0.50	$1.50	$2.50	£0.30	£0.90	£1.50
3 ND 48pgs, squarebound; information and colour cover reproductions Avengers #46-#66, Annual #2, Marvel Super-Heroes #17						
	$0.50	$1.50	$2.50	£0.30	£0.90	£1.50
4 ND 48pgs, squarebound; information and colour cover reproductions Avengers #67-#87, Annual #3-#5, Ka-Zar (1st Series) #1						
	$0.50	$1.50	$2.50	£0.30	£0.90	£1.50
5 ND 48pgs, squarebound; information and colour cover reproductions Avengers #88-#108 Annual #3-#5, Avengers Special Edition #1,#2						
	$0.50	$1.50	$2.50	£0.30	£0.90	£1.50
6 ND 48pgs, squarebound; information and colour cover reproductions Avengers #109-#126, Avengers Giant Size #1, Defenders #8-#11, Jim Valentino cover and splash page pencils						
	$0.50	$1.50	$2.50	£0.30	£0.90	£1.50
7 NC 48pgs, squarebound; information and colour cover reproductions Avengers #127-#145, Avengers Giant Size #2-#5						
	$0.50	$1.50	$2.50	£0.30	£0.90	£1.50
Title Value:	$3.50	$10.50	$17.50	£2.10	£6.30	£10.50

AVENGERS/DEFENDERS WAR

Marvel Comics Group; 1973

Cross-over storyline that ran throughout the following issues: **Avengers #115**, **Defenders #9**, **Avengers #116**, **Defenders #10**, **Avengers #117** , **Defenders #11**, **Avengers #118**.

AVENGERS/ULTRAFORCE

Marvel Comics Group/Malibu Ultraverse,OS; 1 Oct 1995

(see Ultraforce/Avengers)

	$Good	$Fine	$N.Mint	£Good	£Fine	£N.Mint
1 ND 48pgs, Loki vs. The Avengers and Ultraforce; Glenn Herdling and Angel Medina art, wraparound cover by George Perez with silver foil logo						
	$0.80	$2.40	$4.00	£0.50	£1.50	£2.50
Title Value:	$0.80	$2.40	$4.00	£0.50	£1.50	£2.50

AVENGERS: THE CROSSING

Marvel Comics Group,OS; nn Sep 1995

	$Good	$Fine	$N.Mint	£Good	£Fine	£N.Mint
nn ND Mike Deodato art, chromium cover; tie-in with Avengers #390						
	$1.00	$3.00	$5.00	£0.60	£1.80	£3.00
Title Value:	$1.00	$3.00	$5.00	£0.60	£1.80	£3.00

AVENGERS: THE LEGEND

Marvel Comics Group,OS; nn Oct 1996

	$Good	$Fine	$N.Mint	£Good	£Fine	£N.Mint
nn ND 48pgs, facts and figures, character profiles and timelines about The Avengers						
	$0.80	$2.40	$4.00	£0.50	£1.50	£2.50
Title Value:	$0.80	$2.40	$4.00	£0.50	£1.50	£2.50

AVENGERS: THE TERMINATRIX OBJECTIVE

Marvel Comics Group,MS; 1 Sep 1993-4 Dec 1993

	$Good	$Fine	$N.Mint	£Good	£Fine	£N.Mint
1 ND sequel to "Citizen Kang" begins; holo-grafix starfield foil pattern cover.						
	$0.35	$1.05	$1.75	£0.25	£0.75	£1.25
2-4 ND	$0.25	$0.75	$1.25	£0.15	£0.45	£0.75
Title Value:	$1.10	$3.30	$5.50	£0.70	£2.10	£3.50

AVENGERS: TIMESLIDE

Marvel Comics Group,OS; 1 Feb 1995

	$Good	$Fine	$N.Mint	£Good	£Fine	£N.Mint
1 ND 48pgs, metallic chrome cover, continued in Force Works #20						
	$1.00	$3.00	$5.00	£0.60	£1.80	£3.00
Title Value:	$1.00	$3.00	$5.00	£0.60	£1.80	£3.00

AVENGING WORLD

Bruce Hershenson,OS; 1 1973

	$Good	$Fine	$N.Mint	£Good	£Fine	£N.Mint
1 ND 32pgs, black and white; Steve Ditko art and cover; the second in an intended series of quartlerly magazines, Mr. A #1 being the first						
	$0.75	$2.25	$4.50	£0.50	£1.50	£3.00
Title Value:	$0.75	$2.25	$4.50	£0.50	£1.50	£3.00

AVENUE X

Innovation,MS; 1 Oct 1992

	$Good	$Fine	$N.Mint	£Good	£Fine	£N.Mint
1 ND b&w	$0.40	$1.20	$2.00	£0.25	£0.75	£1.25
Title Value:	$0.40	$1.20	$2.00	£0.25	£0.75	£1.25

Note: cancelled mini-series

AXA

First American (Eclipse); 1 1983-9 1988

	$Good	$Fine	$N.Mint	£Good	£Fine	£N.Mint
1-8 ND complete newspaper strip reprints						
	$1.00	$3.00	$5.00	£0.70	£2.10	£3.50
9 ND includes unfinished strip "The Betrayal"						
	$1.00	$3.00	$5.00	£0.70	£2.10	£3.50
Title Value:	$9.00	$27.00	$45.00	£6.30	£18.90	£31.50

AXA (2ND SERIES)

Eclipse; 1 Apr 1987-2 Jun 1987

	$Good	$Fine	$N.Mint	£Good	£Fine	£N.Mint
1-2 ND new Romero art						
	$0.50	$1.50	$2.50	£0.30	£0.90	£1.50
Title Value:	$1.00	$3.00	$5.00	£0.60	£1.80	£3.00

AXED FILES, THE

Entity Comics,OS; 1 Aug 1995

	$Good	$Fine	$N.Mint	£Good	£Fine	£N.Mint
1 ND parody of X-Files; black and white						
	$0.50	$1.50	$2.50	£0.30	£0.90	£1.50
1 Encore Edition, ND (Dec 1995), new cover, new 4pg story						
	$0.50	$1.50	$2.50	£0.30	£0.90	£1.50
Title Value:	$1.00	$3.00	$5.00	£0.60	£1.80	£3.00

AXEL PRESSBUTTON

Eclipse/Quality; 1 Nov 1984-6 Sep 1985

(see Laser Eraser)

	$Good	$Fine	$N.Mint	£Good	£Fine	£N.Mint
1 Steve Dillon art, Brian Bolland cover; 4pgs Bolland art in Zirk back-up story						
	$0.40	$1.20	$2.00	£0.25	£0.75	£1.25
2 Steve Dillon art, Alan Moore script and Garry Leach art on "Cold War, Cold Warrior", 2pg Gibbons back-up (classic time-loop tale), Dave Gibbons cover						
	$0.40	$1.20	$2.00	£0.25	£0.75	£1.25
3 Steve Dillon art, John Ridgway and Cam Kennedy back-ups, Alan Davis cover						
	$0.40	$1.20	$2.00	£0.25	£0.75	£1.25
4 Steve Dillon art, Garry Leach and Cam Kennedy back-ups, Austin painted cover						
	$0.40	$1.20	$2.00	£0.25	£0.75	£1.25
5 Alan Davis cover and art, Hunt Emerson back-up						
	$0.40	$1.20	$2.00	£0.25	£0.75	£1.25
6 Steve Dillon art throughout, Austin painted cover						
	$0.40	$1.20	$2.00	£0.25	£0.75	£1.25
Title Value:	$2.40	$7.20	$12.00	£1.50	£4.50	£7.50

Note: made up entirely from Warrior Magazine reprints. Some limited distribution on the news-stands in the U.K. of issues #2-6

AXIS ALPHA

Axis Comics,OS; nn Feb 1994

	$Good	$Fine	$N.Mint	£Good	£Fine	£N.Mint
nn ND 30pgs, 1st appearances of Dethgrip, Beasties, W, Shelter plus a prequel to Tribe #1; Larry Stroman cover and art featured						
	$0.40	$1.20	$2.00	£0.25	£0.75	£1.25
Title Value:	$0.40	$1.20	$2.00	£0.25	£0.75	£1.25

AXIS BETA

Axis Comics,OS; nn Apr 1994

	$Good	$Fine	$N.Mint	£Good	£Fine	£N.Mint
nn ND continuation of Axis Alpha; 1st appearances Quantum 5, Marcus Arena, Power, Night Avenger						
	$0.40	$1.20	$2.00	£0.25	£0.75	£1.25
Title Value:	$0.40	$1.20	$2.00	£0.25	£0.75	£1.25

AXIS SOURCE BOOK

Axis Comics,OS; 1 Jun 1994

	$Good	$Fine	$N.Mint	£Good	£Fine	£N.Mint
1 ND information about all Axis characters						
	$0.40	$1.20	$2.00	£0.25	£0.75	£1.25
Title Value:	$0.40	$1.20	$2.00	£0.25	£0.75	£1.25

AZ

Comico; 1 Feb 1983-2 1984

(see Primer)

	$Good	$Fine	$N.Mint	£Good	£Fine	£N.Mint
1-2 ND	$0.50	$1.50	$2.50	£0.30	£0.90	£1.50
Title Value:	$1.00	$3.00	$5.00	£0.60	£1.80	£3.00

AZRAEL

DC Comics; 1 Feb 1995-present

	$Good	$Fine	$N.Mint	£Good	£Fine	£N.Mint
1 Denny O'Neil script and Barry Kitson pencils begin						
	$1.40	$4.20	$7.00	£0.50	£1.50	£2.50
2	$0.80	$2.40	$4.00	£0.40	£1.20	£2.00
3	$0.60	$1.80	$3.00	£0.30	£0.90	£1.50
4	$0.40	$1.20	$2.00	£0.25	£0.75	£1.25
5 upgraded coated paper stock (Miraweb Format) begins						
	$0.40	$1.20	$2.00	£0.25	£0.75	£1.25
6 Ra's Al Ghul appears						
	$0.40	$1.20	$2.00	£0.25	£0.75	£1.25
7-9	$0.40	$1.20	$2.00	£0.25	£0.75	£1.25
10 Underworld Unleashed tie-in; Batman, Robin and Lady Shiva ppear						
	$0.40	$1.20	$2.00	£0.25	£0.75	£1.25
11 Batman guest-stars						

TRADE PAPERBACKS, GRAPHIC NOVELS AND OTHER COLLECTIONS ARE PRICED IN POUNDS STERLING ONLY. CONVERT AT 1.5 FOR DOLLARS.

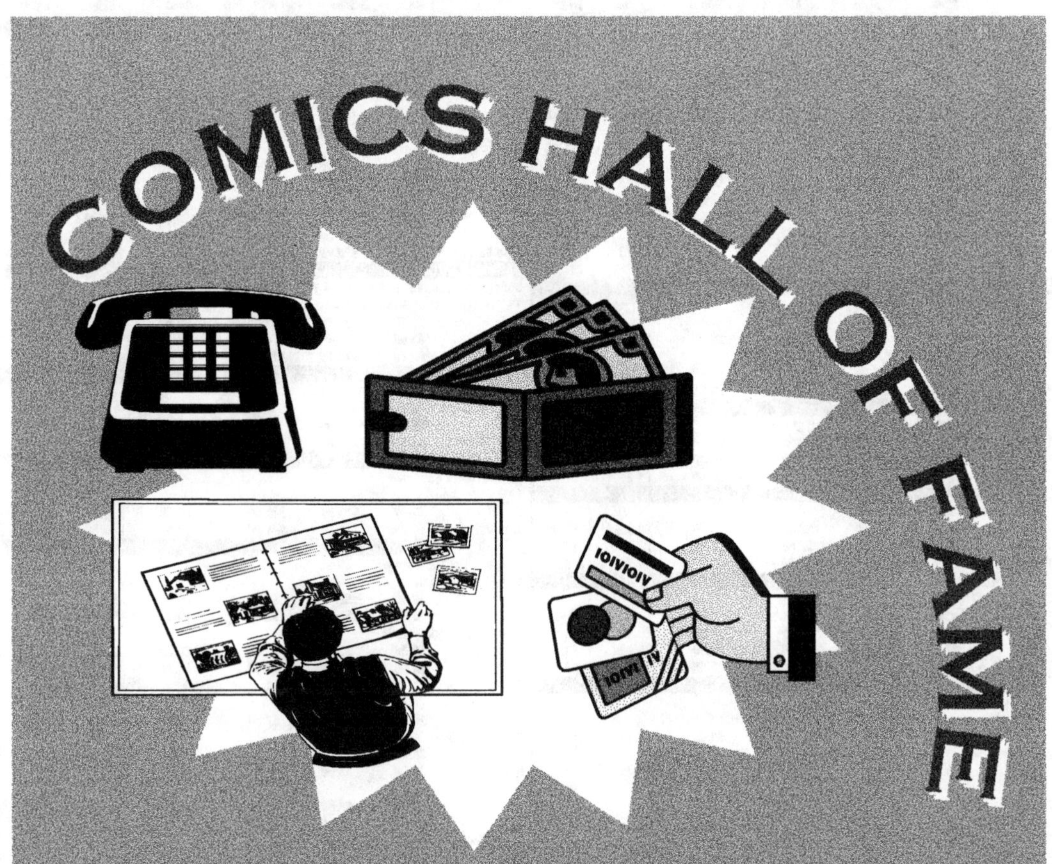
COMICS HALL OF FAME

Issue	$Good	$Fine	$N.Mint	£Good	£Fine	£N.Mint
	$0.40	*$1.20*	*$2.00*	£0.25	£0.75	£1.25
12	*$0.40*	*$1.20*	*$2.00*	£0.25	£0.75	£1.25
13 Demon Time story	*$0.40*	*$1.20*	*$2.00*	£0.25	£0.75	£1.25
14 Demon Time story, bi-monthly	*$0.40*	*$1.20*	*$2.00*	£0.25	£0.75	£1.25
15 Contagion part 5, continued in Batman #529	*$0.40*	*$1.20*	*$2.00*	£0.25	£0.75	£1.25
16 Contagion part 10, continued in Robin #28	*$0.40*	*$1.20*	*$2.00*	£0.25	£0.75	£1.25
17-20	*$0.40*	*$1.20*	*$2.00*	£0.25	£0.75	£1.25
21-23 Angel in Hiding story	*$0.40*	*$1.20*	*$2.00*	£0.25	£0.75	£1.25
24-28 ND	*$0.40*	*$1.20*	*$2.00*	£0.25	£0.75	£1.25
Title Value:	*$12.80*	*$38.40*	*$64.00*	£7.45	£22.35	£37.25

AZRAEL ANNUAL

DC Comics; 1 Oct 1995-present

Issue	$Good	$Fine	$N.Mint	£Good	£Fine	£N.Mint
1 ND 56pgs, Year One, Denny O'Neil script, Barry Kitson art	*$0.60*	*$1.80*	*$3.00*	£0.40	£1.20	£2.00
2 ND Legends of the Dead Earth story	*$0.60*	*$1.80*	*$3.00*	£0.40	£1.20	£2.00
Title Value:	*$1.20*	*$3.60*	*$6.00*	£0.80	£2.40	£4.00

AZRAEL PLUS #1

DC Comics,OS; 1 Dec 1996

Issue	$Good	$Fine	$N.Mint	£Good	£Fine	£N.Mint
1 ND 48pgs, Denny O'Neill script, Vince Giarrano art, Barry Kitson cover; The Question appears	*$0.60*	*$1.80*	*$3.00*	£0.40	£1.20	£2.00
Title Value:	*$0.60*	*$1.80*	*$3.00*	£0.40	£1.20	£2.00

AZTEC ACE

Eclipse; 1 Mar 1984-15 Sep 1985

Issue	$Good	$Fine	$N.Mint	£Good	£Fine	£N.Mint
1-3 ND 52pgs	*$0.50*	*$1.50*	*$2.50*	£0.30	£0.90	£1.50
4-15 ND	*$0.40*	*$1.20*	*$2.00*	£0.25	£0.75	£1.25
Title Value:	*$6.30*	*$18.90*	*$30.50*	£3.90	£11.70	£19.50

AZTEC ACE (2ND SERIES)

Eclipse; 1 Jul 1992-2 1992?

Issue	$Good	$Fine	$N.Mint	£Good	£Fine	£N.Mint
1 ND Doug Moench script begins	*$0.50*	*$1.50*	*$2.50*	£0.30	£0.90	£1.50
2 ND	*$0.50*	*$1.50*	*$2.50*	£0.30	£0.90	£1.50
Title Value:	*$1.00*	*$3.00*	*$5.00*	£0.60	£1.80	£3.00

AZTEK: THE ULTIMATE MAN

DC Comics; 1 Aug 1996-present

Issue	$Good	$Fine	$N.Mint	£Good	£Fine	£N.Mint
1 ND Grant Morrison and Mark Millar script, Steven Harris and Keith Champagne art	*$0.35*	*$1.05*	*$1.75*	£0.25	£0.75	£1.25
2 ND Green Lantern guest-stars	*$0.35*	*$1.05*	*$1.75*	£0.25	£0.75	£1.25
3-6 ND	*$0.35*	*$1.05*	*$1.75*	£0.25	£0.75	£1.25
7 ND Batman and The Joker appear	*$0.35*	*$1.05*	*$1.75*	£0.25	£0.75	£1.25
8-9 ND	*$0.35*	*$1.05*	*$1.75*	£0.25	£0.75	£1.25
Title Value:	*$3.15*	*$9.45*	*$15.75*	£2.25	£6.75	£11.25

B

B.E.A.S.T.I.E.S.

Axis Comics; 1 Apr 1994

Issue	$Good	$Fine	$N.Mint	£Good	£Fine	£N.Mint
1 ND Javier Saltares script and art	*$0.40*	*$1.20*	*$2.00*	£0.25	£0.75	£1.25
Title Value:	*$0.40*	*$1.20*	*$2.00*	£0.25	£0.75	£1.25

Note: issue 2 advertised and solicited but doubtful if it ever came out

BABE

Dark Horse/Legend,MS; 1 Jul 1994-4 Oct 1994

Issue	$Good	$Fine	$N.Mint	£Good	£Fine	£N.Mint
1-4 ND John Byrne scipt, art and covers	*$0.50*	*$1.50*	*$2.50*	£0.30	£0.90	£1.50
Title Value:	*$2.00*	*$6.00*	*$10.00*	£1.20	£3.60	£6.00

BABE 2

Dark Horse,MS; 1 Feb 1995-2 Mar 1995

Issue	$Good	$Fine	$N.Mint	£Good	£Fine	£N.Mint
1-2 ND John Byrne script and art	*$0.50*	*$1.50*	*$2.50*	£0.30	£0.90	£1.50
Title Value:	*$1.00*	*$3.00*	*$5.00*	£0.60	£1.80	£3.00

BABES OF BROADWAY

Broadway Comics,OS; 1 May 1996

Issue	$Good	$Fine	$N.Mint	£Good	£Fine	£N.Mint
1 ND pin-ups by Alan Davis, Mike Kaluta and others	*$0.60*	*$1.80*	*$3.00*	£0.40	£1.20	£2.00
Title Value:	*$0.60*	*$1.80*	*$3.00*	£0.40	£1.20	£2.00

BABY HUEY, THE BABY GIANT

Harvey; 1 Sep 1956-103 1991?

Issue	$Good	$Fine	$N.Mint	£Good	£Fine	£N.Mint
1	*$57.50*	*$175.00*	*$350.00*	£39.00	£115.00	£235.00
2	*$33.00*	*$97.50*	*$195.00*	£21.50	£65.00	£130.00
3	*$20.00*	*$60.00*	*$120.00*	£13.00	£40.00	£80.00
4-5	*$15.00*	*$45.00*	*$90.00*	£10.00	£30.00	£60.00
6-10	*$7.50*	*$22.50*	*$45.00*	£5.00	£15.00	£30.00
11-20	*$5.75*	*$17.50*	*$35.00*	£4.00	£12.00	£24.00
21-40	*$4.15*	*$12.50*	*$25.00*	£2.65	£8.00	£16.00
41-60	*$2.40*	*$7.00*	*$12.00*	£1.50	£4.50	£7.50
61-79	*$1.80*	*$5.25*	*$9.00*	£1.00	£3.00	£5.00
80-95 giant	*$2.40*	*$7.00*	*$12.00*	£1.40	£4.20	£7.00
96-97 giant	*$1.80*	*$5.25*	*$9.00*	£1.10	£3.30	£5.50
98-99	*$0.60*	*$1.80*	*$3.00*	£0.40	£1.20	£2.00
100-103	*$0.30*	*$0.90*	*$1.50*	£0.20	£0.60	£1.00
Title Value:	*$445.10*	*$1329.45*	*$2553.00*	£286.70	£860.60	£1651.00

Note: while no official distribution date in known, it is thought that most issues after about 1958/59 were distributed in the U.K.

BABYLON 5

DC Comics, TV; 1 Jan 1995-11 Dec 1995

Issue	$Good	$Fine	$N.Mint	£Good	£Fine	£N.Mint
1 Mike Kaluta painted cover	*$1.50*	*$4.50*	*$7.50*	£1.00	£3.00	£5.00
2	*$1.00*	*$3.00*	*$5.00*	£0.80	£2.40	£4.00
3	*$0.80*	*$2.40*	*$4.00*	£0.60	£1.80	£3.00
4	*$0.80*	*$2.40*	*$4.00*	£0.40	£1.20	£2.00
5 upgraded paper format begins	*$0.80*	*$2.40*	*$4.00*	£0.40	£1.20	£2.00
6-8	*$0.50*	*$1.50*	*$2.50*	£0.30	£0.90	£1.50
9-10 David Gerrold script	*$0.50*	*$1.50*	*$2.50*	£0.30	£0.90	£1.50
11	*$0.50*	*$1.50*	*$2.50*	£0.30	£0.90	£1.50
Title Value:	*$7.90*	*$23.70*	*$39.50*	£5.00	£15.00	£25.00

BABYLON CRUSH

Boneyard Press,MS; 1 May 1995-6 1995 ?

Issue	$Good	$Fine	$N.Mint	£Good	£Fine	£N.Mint
1 ND Hart Fisher script, Thomas Derenick and Joseph Eiden art begins; black and white	*$0.60*	*$1.80*	*$3.00*	£0.40	£1.20	£2.00
2-6 ND	*$0.60*	*$1.80*	*$3.00*	£0.40	£1.20	£2.00
Title Value:	*$3.60*	*$10.80*	*$18.00*	£2.40	£7.20	£12.00

BACCHUS COLOR SPECIAL

Dark Horse,OS; 1 Apr 1995

Issue	$Good	$Fine	$N.Mint	£Good	£Fine	£N.Mint
1 ND Eddy Campbell and Terry Kristiansen	*$0.60*	*$1.80*	*$3.00*	£0.40	£1.20	£2.00
Title Value:	*$0.60*	*$1.80*	*$3.00*	£0.40	£1.20	£2.00

BACK DOWN THE LINE HARDCOVER

Eclipse,OS; 1 Sep 1991

Issue	$Good	$Fine	$N.Mint	£Good	£Fine	£N.Mint
1 ND 48pgs, John Bolton early stories	*$5.00*	*$15.00*	*$25.00*	£3.50	£10.50	£17.50
Title Value:	*$5.00*	*$15.00*	*$25.00*	£3.50	£10.50	£17.50

BACKLASH

Image; 1 Oct 1994-present

Issue	$Good	$Fine	$N.Mint	£Good	£Fine	£N.Mint
1 ND Ty Templeton art	*$0.80*	*$2.40*	*$4.00*	£0.40	£1.20	£2.00
2-5 ND	*$0.60*	*$1.80*	*$3.00*	£0.30	£0.90	£1.50
6 ND WetWorks guest-star	*$0.50*	*$1.50*	*$2.50*	£0.30	£0.90	£1.50
7 ND	*$0.50*	*$1.50*	*$2.50*	£0.30	£0.90	£1.50
8 Collectors Edition, ND Wildstorm Rising part 8, continued in Stormwatch #22; with two foil-bagged painted trading cards. Cover by Barry Windsor-Smith	*$0.50*	*$1.50*	*$2.50*	£0.30	£0.90	£1.50
8 Newstand Edition, ND without trading cards	*$0.40*	*$1.20*	*$2.00*	£0.25	£0.75	£1.25
9 ND	*$0.50*	*$1.50*	*$2.50*	£0.30	£0.90	£1.50
10 ND 1st appearance Crimson	*$0.50*	*$1.50*	*$2.50*	£0.30	£0.90	£1.50
11 ND	*$0.50*	*$1.50*	*$2.50*	£0.30	£0.90	£1.50
12 ND $2.95 cover	*$0.60*	*$1.80*	*$3.00*	£0.40	£1.20	£2.00
13 ND	*$0.45*	*$1.35*	*$2.25*	£0.30	£0.90	£1.50
14 ND Deathblow appears	*$0.50*	*$1.50*	*$2.50*	£0.30	£0.90	£1.50
15 ND	*$0.50*	*$1.50*	*$2.50*	£0.30	£0.90	£1.50
16 ND Grifter guest-stars	*$0.50*	*$1.50*	*$2.50*	£0.30	£0.90	£1.50
17-18 ND	*$0.50*	*$1.50*	*$2.50*	£0.30	£0.90	£1.50
19 ND Fire From Heaven part 2, continued in Gen 13 #10	*$0.50*	*$1.50*	*$2.50*	£0.30	£0.90	£1.50
20 ND Fire From Heaven part 10, continued in Wetworks #17	*$0.50*	*$1.50*	*$2.50*	£0.30	£0.90	£1.50
21-24 ND	*$0.50*	*$1.50*	*$2.50*	£0.30	£0.90	£1.50
25 ND 56pgs	*$0.80*	*$2.40*	*$4.00*	£0.50	£1.50	£2.50
26,27 ND	*$0.50*	*$1.50*	*$2.50*	£0.30	£0.90	£1.50
Title Value:	*$14.95*	*$44.85*	*$73.25*	£8.75	£26.25	£43.75

BACKLASH/SPIDERMAN

Image,MS; 1 Sep 1996-2 Oct 1996

Issue	$Good	$Fine	$N.Mint	£Good	£Fine	£N.Mint
1-2 ND Sean Ruffer and Brett Botth script, Brett Booth and Tom McWeeney art; Venom appears	*$0.50*	*$1.50*	*$2.50*	£0.30	£0.90	£1.50
Title Value:	*$1.00*	*$3.00*	*$5.00*	£0.60	£1.80	£3.00

BAD EGGS

Acclaim Comics,MS; 1 Jun 1996-4 Sep 1996

Issue	$Good	$Fine	$N.Mint	£Good	£Fine	£N.Mint
1-4 ND Bob Layton script, Don Perlin and Gonzalo Mayo art	*$0.60*	*$1.80*	*$3.00*	£0.40	£1.20	£2.00
Title Value:	*$2.40*	*$7.20*	*$12.00*	£1.60	£4.80	£8.00

BAD EGGS (2ND SERIES)

Acclaim Comics,MS; 1 Oct 1996-4 Jan 1997

Issue	$Good	$Fine	$N.Mint	£Good	£Fine	£N.Mint
1-4 ND Bob Layton script, Don Perlin and Gonzalo Mayo art	*$0.60*	*$1.80*	*$3.00*	£0.40	£1.20	£2.00
Title Value:	*$2.40*	*$7.20*	*$12.00*	£1.60	£4.80	£8.00

BAD GIRLS OF BLACKOUT

Blackout Comics; 0 Apr 1995

Issue	$Good	$Fine	$N.Mint	£Good	£Fine	£N.Mint
0 ND Extreme Violet, Lady Vampre, Ms. Cyanide and Ice appear; Outbreed 999 also appears	*$0.80*	*$2.40*	*$4.00*	£0.50	£1.50	£2.50
Title Value:	*$0.80*	*$2.40*	*$4.00*	£0.50	£1.50	£2.50

BAD GIRLS OF BLACKOUT: HARI KARI, LADY VAMPRE & VIOLET ANNUAL

Blackout Comics; 1 Oct 1995

Issue	$Good	$Fine	$N.Mint	£Good	£Fine	£N.Mint
1 ND Guy Dorian art	*$0.70*	*$2.10*	*$3.50*	£0.50	£1.50	£2.50
Title Value:	*$0.70*	*$2.10*	*$3.50*	£0.50	£1.50	£2.50

BAD GIRLS OF BLACKOUT: VIOLET, LADY VAMPRE, MS. CYANIDE & ICE

Blackout Comics,OS; 1 Jun 1995

Issue	$Good	$Fine	$N.Mint	£Good	£Fine	£N.Mint
1 ND Dell Barras and Jake Jacobsen art	*$0.60*	*$1.80*	*$3.00*	£0.40	£1.20	£2.00

SOME INDEPENDENT COMICS MAY NOT HAVE APPEARED ALTHOUGH THEY WERE ADVERTISED AND SOLICITED.

	$Good	$Fine	$N.Mint	£Good	£Fine	£N.Mint
Title Value:	$0.60	$1.80	$3.00	£0.40	£1.20	£2.00
BAD NEWS						
Fantagraphics; 1 1988-3 Oct 1988						
1-3 ND 48pgs, oversized	$0.60	$1.80	$3.00	£0.40	£1.20	£2.00
Title Value:	$1.80	$5.40	$9.00	£1.20	£3.60	£6.00
BADAXE						
Adventure,MS; 1 Oct 1989-3 Dec 1989						
1-3 ND b&w	$0.50	$1.50	$2.50	£0.30	£0.90	£1.50
Title Value:	$1.50	$4.50	$7.50	£0.90	£2.70	£4.50
BADE BIKER & ORSON						
Mirage Studios; 1 Sep 1986-5 1987						
1-5 ND	$0.30	$0.90	$1.50	£0.20	£0.60	£1.00
Title Value:	$1.50	$4.50	$7.50	£1.00	£3.00	£5.00
Collection, reprints #1-4 plus 14 new pages				£1.30	£3.90	£6.50
BADGER						
Capital/First; 1 Oct 1983-70 Feb 1991						
(see Coyote #14 [Marvel])						
1 Jeff Butler art	$0.50	$1.50	$2.50	£0.60	£1.80	£3.00
2-4 Butler art	$0.40	$1.20	$2.00	£0.40	£1.20	£2.00
5 1st First issue, Bill Reinhold art	$0.40	$1.20	$2.00	£0.40	£1.20	£2.00
6-16	$0.30	$0.90	$1.50	£0.30	£0.90	£1.50
17 Butler art	$0.30	$0.90	$1.50	£0.30	£0.90	£1.50
18-22	$0.30	$0.90	$1.50	£0.30	£0.90	£1.50
23 Beckam art	$0.30	$0.90	$1.50	£0.30	£0.90	£1.50
24-39	$0.30	$0.90	$1.50	£0.30	£0.90	£1.50
40-49 Ron Lim art	$0.30	$0.90	$1.50	£0.30	£0.90	£1.50
50 48pgs, prestige issue with die-cut cover, Jeff Butler and Mark E. Nelson art, Ron Lim art	$0.70	$2.10	$3.50	£0.50	£1.50	£2.50
51 Ron Lim art	$0.30	$0.90	$1.50	£0.30	£0.90	£1.50
52-54 Tim Vigil art	$0.30	$0.90	$1.50	£0.30	£0.90	£1.50
55	$0.30	$0.90	$1.50	£0.30	£0.90	£1.50
56-67	$0.30	$0.90	$1.50	£0.25	£0.75	£1.25
68 George Freeman guest pencils	$0.30	$0.90	$1.50	£0.25	£0.75	£1.25
69-70	$0.30	$0.90	$1.50	£0.25	£0.75	£1.25
Title Value:	$22.00	$66.00	$110.00	£21.15	£63.45	£105.75
Note: all Non-Distributed on the news-stands in the U.K.						
BADGER GOES BERSERK						
First,MS; 1 Sep 1989-4 Dec 1989						
1 script by Mike Baron, variety of artist pgs/panels throughout the 4 issues inc. John Beatty, John Butler Paul Chadwick, Denys Cowan, Steve Epting, J.Geldhof,Flint Henry, Malcolm Jones III, Mark Nelson	$0.50	$1.50	$2.50	£0.30	£0.90	£1.50
2-4 script by Mike Baron, variety of artist pgs/panels throughout the 4 issues inc. John Beatty, John Butler, Paul Chadwick, Denys Cowan, Steve Epting, J.Geldhof, Flint Henry, Malcolm Jones III, MarkNelson	$0.50	$1.50	$2.50	£0.30	£0.90	£1.50
Title Value:	$2.00	$6.00	$10.00	£1.20	£3.60	£6.00
Note: all Non-Distributed on the news-stands in the U.K.						
BADGER: BEDLAM						
First,OS; 1 Mar 1991						
1 ND 48pgs, squarebound, Baron and Butler	$1.00	$3.00	$5.00	£0.60	£1.80	£3.00
Title Value:	$1.00	$3.00	$5.00	£0.60	£1.80	£3.00
BADGER: SHATTERED MIRROR						
Dark Horse,MS; 1 Jul 1994-4 Oct 1994						
1-4 ND Mike Baron script, Jill Thompson art	$0.50	$1.50	$2.50	£0.30	£0.90	£1.50
Title Value:	$2.00	$6.00	$10.00	£1.20	£3.60	£6.00
BADGER: ZEN POP FUNNY ANIMAL VERSION						
Dark Horse,MS; 1 Jul 1994-2 Aug 1994						

	$Good	$Fine	$N.Mint	£Good	£Fine	£N.Mint
1-2 ND Mike Baron script, Steve Butler and Val Mayerik art	$0.50	$1.50	$2.50	£0.30	£0.90	£1.50
Title Value:	$1.00	$3.00	$5.00	£0.60	£1.80	£3.00
BADLANDS						
Vortex,OS; 1 1990						
1 black and white	$0.50	$1.50	$2.50	£0.30	£0.90	£1.50
Title Value:	$0.50	$1.50	$2.50	£0.30	£0.90	£1.50
BADLANDS (2ND SERIES)						
Dark Horse; 1 Sep 1991-6 Feb 1992						
1-6 ND Kennedy assassination story	$0.50	$1.50	$2.50	£0.30	£0.90	£1.50
Title Value:	$3.00	$9.00	$15.00	£1.80	£5.40	£9.00
Note: Vortex series suddenly cancelled and rights picked up by Dark Horse						
Badlands Softcover Collection (May 1993)						
reprints mini-series, intro by Frank Miller				£1.65	£4.95	£8.25
BADROCK						
Image; 1 Mar 1995-2 1995 ?						
1 Cover A, ND Rob Liefeld script, Eric Stephenson art; inked by Todd McFarlane	$0.40	$1.20	$2.00	£0.25	£0.75	£1.25
1 Cover B, ND Rob Liefeld script, Eric Stephenson art; inked by Stephen Platt	$0.40	$1.20	$2.00	£0.25	£0.75	£1.25
1 Cover C, ND Rob Liefeld script, Eric Stephenson art; inked by Dan Fraga	$0.40	$1.20	$2.00	£0.25	£0.75	£1.25
2 ND guest-starring Savage Dragon	$0.40	$1.20	$2.00	£0.25	£0.75	£1.25
Title Value:	$1.60	$4.80	$8.00	£1.00	£3.00	£5.00
BADROCK AND COMPANY						
Image,MS; 1 Sep 1994-6 Feb 1995						
1-5 ND Keith Giffen script, Todd Nauck art	$0.50	$1.50	$2.50	£0.30	£0.90	£1.50
6 ND Keith Giffen script, Todd Nauck art; Shadowhawk guest-stars	$0.50	$1.50	$2.50	£0.30	£0.90	£1.50
Title Value:	$3.00	$9.00	$15.00	£1.80	£5.40	£9.00
BADROCK ANNUAL						
Image; 1 Sep 1995						
1 ND Tom and Mary Bierbaum script, Todd Nauck art	$0.60	$1.80	$3.00	£0.40	£1.20	£2.00
Title Value:	$0.60	$1.80	$3.00	£0.40	£1.20	£2.00
BADROCK/WOLVERINE						
Image Comics/Marvel Comics Group,OS; 1 Jun 1996						
1 ND 48pgs, squarebound, Jim Valentino script, Chap Yaep and Jonathan Sibal art	$1.00	$3.00	$5.00	£0.65	£1.95	£3.25
1 Comicon Edition ND, limited to 1,000 copies; available at the 1996 San Diego Comicon	$1.50	$4.50	$7.50	£1.00	£3.00	£5.00
Title Value:	$2.50	$7.50	$12.50	£1.65	£4.95	£8.25
BAKER STREET						
Caliber Press; 1 1989-10 1992						
1 ND	$0.50	$1.50	$2.50	£0.30	£0.90	£1.50
2-10 ND	$0.40	$1.20	$2.00	£0.25	£0.75	£1.25
Title Value:	$4.10	$12.30	$20.50	£2.55	£7.65	£12.75
Honour Among Punks (Aug 1990)						
Trade paperback reprints #1-5 (softcover)				£1.70	£5.10	£8.50
Hardcover (500 copies), signed by Gary Reed and Guy Davis				£4.00	£12.00	£20.00
BAKER STREET GRAPHITTI						
Caliber Press,OS; 1 Nov 1991						
1 ND includes reprints from Caliber Presents	$0.50	$1.50	$2.50	£0.30	£0.90	£1.50
Title Value:	$0.50	$1.50	$2.50	£0.30	£0.90	£1.50
BALANCE OF POWER						
Mu Press,MS; 1 May 1990-6 Mar 1991						
1-6 ND ND Paula Shoudy script, Mike Raabe art; black and white						

Badger #1

Barbie Fashion #1

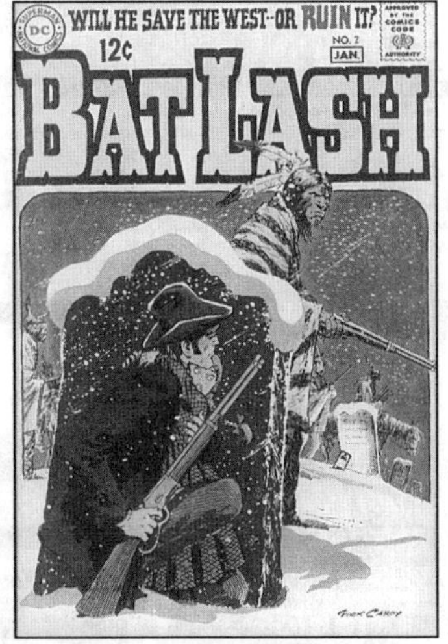

Batlash #2

	$Good	$Fine	$N.Mint	£Good	£Fine	£N.Mint
	$0.30	*$0.90*	*$1.50*	£0.20	£0.60	£1.00
Title Value:	*$1.80*	*$5.40*	*$9.00*	£1.20	£3.60	£6.00

BALDER THE BRAVE
Marvel Comics Group,MS; 1 Nov 1985-4 Feb 1986

1-4 ND Simonson script, Sal Buscema art

	$Good	$Fine	$N.Mint	£Good	£Fine	£N.Mint
	$0.25	*$0.75*	*$1.25*	£0.15	£0.45	£0.75
Title Value:	*$1.00*	*$3.00*	*$5.00*	£0.60	£1.80	£3.00

BALLISTIC
Image; 1 Sep 1995-3 Dec 1995

	$Good	$Fine	$N.Mint	£Good	£Fine	£N.Mint
1 ND Brian Haberlin script, Michael Turner art; Wetworks appear	*$0.70*	*$2.10*	*$3.50*	£0.30	£0.90	£1.50
2 ND Wetworks appear	*$0.60*	*$1.80*	*$3.00*	£0.30	£0.90	£1.50
3 ND	*$0.60*	*$1.80*	*$3.00*	£0.30	£0.90	£1.50
Title Value:	*$1.90*	*$5.70*	*$9.50*	£0.90	£2.70	£4.50

BALLISTIC ACTION!
Image,OS; nn Apr 1996

	$Good	$Fine	$N.Mint	£Good	£Fine	£N.Mint
nn ND anthology; Marc Silvestri cover	*$0.60*	*$1.80*	*$3.00*	£0.40	£1.20	£2.00
Title Value:	*$0.60*	*$1.80*	*$3.00*	£0.40	£1.20	£2.00

BALLISTIC IMAGERY
Image; 1 Nov 1995

	$Good	$Fine	$N.Mint	£Good	£Fine	£N.Mint
1 ND anthology series begins; Hell Cop, Heavy Space and True Tales of Cyberforce	*$0.50*	*$1.50*	*$2.50*	£0.30	£0.90	£1.50
Title Value:	*$0.50*	*$1.50*	*$2.50*	£0.30	£0.90	£1.50

BANANA SPLITS, THE
Gold Key; 1 Jun 1969-8 Oct 1971

	$Good	$Fine	$N.Mint	£Good	£Fine	£N.Mint
1 rare although distributed in the U.K. based on TV series; photo cover	*$7.00*	*$21.00*	*$50.00*	£4.25	£12.50	£30.00
2-8 scarce, distributed in the U.K.	*$3.90*	*$11.50*	*$27.50*	£1.75	£5.25	£12.50
Title Value:	*$34.30*	*$101.50*	*$242.50*	£16.50	£49.25	£117.50

BANDY MAN, THE
Caliber Press; 1 1996

	$Good	$Fine	$N.Mint	£Good	£Fine	£N.Mint
1 ND Stefan Petrucha script, Jill Thompson and Charles Adlard art; black and white	*$0.60*	*$1.80*	*$3.00*	£0.40	£1.20	£2.00
Title Value:	*$0.60*	*$1.80*	*$3.00*	£0.40	£1.20	£2.00

BAOH
Viz Communications,MS; 1 Feb 1990-8 Sep 1990

	$Good	$Fine	$N.Mint	£Good	£Fine	£N.Mint
1 ND 48pgs, squarebound, Japanese reprint material in black and white, art by Hirohiko Araki	*$0.60*	*$1.80*	*$3.00*	£0.40	£1.20	£2.00
2-8 ND 48pgs, squarebound, Japanese reprint material in black and white, art by Hirohiko Araki	*$0.50*	*$1.50*	*$2.50*	£0.30	£0.90	£1.50
Title Value:	*$4.10*	*$12.30*	*$20.50*	£2.50	£7.50	£12.50
Baoh Graphic Novel Vol. 1 (May 1995) reprints mini-series				£2.00	£6.00	£10.00
Baoh Graphic Novel Vol. 2 (Jul 1995) reprints mini-series				£2.00	£6.00	£10.00

BAR SINISTER
Valiant/Windjammer; 1 Jun 1995-4 Sep 1995

	$Good	$Fine	$N.Mint	£Good	£Fine	£N.Mint
1 ND Mike Grell script and cover, storyline continued from Shaman's Tears #4	*$0.50*	*$1.50*	*$2.50*	£0.30	£0.90	£1.50
2-4 ND Mike Grell script and cover	*$0.50*	*$1.50*	*$2.50*	£0.30	£0.90	£1.50
Title Value:	*$2.00*	*$6.00*	*$10.00*	£1.20	£3.60	£6.00

BARABBAS
Slave Labor; 1 Aug 1986-4 May 1987

	$Good	$Fine	$N.Mint	£Good	£Fine	£N.Mint
1-4 ND b&w	*$0.25*	*$0.75*	*$1.25*	£0.15	£0.45	£0.75
Title Value:	*$1.00*	*$3.00*	*$5.00*	£0.60	£1.80	£3.00

BARB WIRE
Dark Horse; 1 Apr 1994-9 Feb 1995

	$Good	$Fine	$N.Mint	£Good	£Fine	£N.Mint
1 ND Arcudi, Moder and Parks creative team begins; spin-off from Comics Greatest World series	*$1.00*	*$3.00*	*$5.00*	£0.50	£1.50	£2.50
2-3 ND	*$0.80*	*$2.40*	*$4.00*	£0.40	£1.20	£2.00
4-9 ND	*$0.60*	*$1.80*	*$3.00*	£0.30	£0.90	£1.50
Title Value:	*$6.20*	*$18.60*	*$28.50*	£3.10	£9.30	£15.50
Barb Wire (Jan 1996) Trade paperback ND 96pgs, reprints series				£1.20	£3.60	£6.00

BARB WIRE MOVIE MAGAZINE SPECIAL
Dark Horse,OS; nn Mar 1996

	$Good	$Fine	$N.Mint	£Good	£Fine	£N.Mint
nn ND 48pgs, adaptation of film with Pamela Anderson plus behind-the-scenes photos	*$0.70*	*$2.10*	*$3.50*	£0.50	£1.50	£2.50
Title Value:	*$0.70*	*$2.10*	*$3.50*	£0.50	£1.50	£2.50

BARB WIRE MOVIE SPECIAL
Dark Horse,OS; nn Mar 1996

	$Good	$Fine	$N.Mint	£Good	£Fine	£N.Mint
nn ND 48pgs, adaptation of film with Pamela Anderson	*$0.80*	*$2.40*	*$4.00*	£0.50	£1.50	£2.50
Title Value:	*$0.80*	*$2.40*	*$4.00*	£0.50	£1.50	£2.50

BARB WIRE: ACE OF SPADES
Dark Horse,MS; 1 May 1996-4 Aug 1996

	$Good	$Fine	$N.Mint	£Good	£Fine	£N.Mint
1 ND Chris Warner script, Tim Bradstreet and Chris Chaloner art; Barb Wire looking a lot more like Pamela Anderson!	*$0.60*	*$1.80*	*$3.00*	£0.40	£1.20	£2.00
2-4 ND	*$0.60*	*$1.80*	*$3.00*	£0.40	£1.20	£2.00
Title Value:	*$2.40*	*$7.20*	*$12.00*	£1.60	£4.80	£8.00

BARBARIANS
Atlas; 1 Jun 1975

(see Ironjaw)

BARBARIC TALES
Pyramid Comics; 1 1986

	$Good	$Fine	$N.Mint	£Good	£Fine	£N.Mint
1 ND b&w	*$0.30*	*$0.90*	*$1.50*	£0.20	£0.60	£1.00
Title Value:	*$0.30*	*$0.90*	*$1.50*	£0.20	£0.60	£1.00

BARBI TWINS ADVENTURES, THE
Topps,OS; 1 Mar 1995

	$Good	$Fine	$N.Mint	£Good	£Fine	£N.Mint
1 ND the adventures of Shane and Sia Barbi - jolly nice girls	*$0.50*	*$1.50*	*$2.50*	£0.30	£0.90	£1.50
1 Signed & Numbered Edition, ND signed by Steve Fastner and Rich Larson	*$3.00*	*$9.00*	*$15.00*	£1.50	£4.50	£7.50
Title Value:	*$3.50*	*$10.50*	*$17.50*	£1.80	£5.40	£9.00

BARBIE
Marvel Comics Group; 1 Jan 1991-63 Mar 1996

	$Good	$Fine	$N.Mint	£Good	£Fine	£N.Mint
1 ND pre-bagged with free "credit card"	*$0.15*	*$0.45*	*$0.75*	£0.10	£0.35	£0.60
2-39 ND	*$0.15*	*$0.45*	*$0.75*	£0.10	£0.30	£0.50
40 ND Trina Robbins and Mary Wilshire	*$0.15*	*$0.45*	*$0.75*	£0.10	£0.30	£0.50
41 ND Trina Robbins	*$0.15*	*$0.45*	*$0.75*	£0.10	£0.30	£0.50
42-49 ND	*$0.15*	*$0.45*	*$0.75*	£0.10	£0.30	£0.50
50 ND 48pgs	*$0.25*	*$0.75*	*$1.25*	£0.10	£0.35	£0.60
51-63 ND	*$0.20*	*$0.60*	*$1.00*	£0.10	£0.30	£0.50
Title Value:	*$10.20*	*$30.60*	*$52.50*	£6.30	£19.00	£31.70
Barbie Trade paperback (Jul 1992), reprints most popular stories from the first year of Barbie and Barbie Fashion				£1.00	£3.00	£5.00

BARBIE FASHION
Marvel Comics Group; 1 Jan 1991-55 Jul 1995

	$Good	$Fine	$N.Mint	£Good	£Fine	£N.Mint
1 ND pre-bagged with Barbie door-hanger	*$0.15*	*$0.45*	*$0.75*	£0.10	£0.35	£0.60
2-49 ND	*$0.15*	*$0.45*	*$0.75*	£0.10	£0.30	£0.50
50 ND 48pgs	*$0.20*	*$0.60*	*$1.00*	£0.10	£0.35	£0.60
51-55 ND	*$0.15*	*$0.45*	*$0.75*	£0.10	£0.30	£0.50
Title Value:	*$8.30*	*$24.90*	*$41.50*	£5.50	£16.60	£27.70

BAREFOOTZ - THE COMIC BOOK STORIES
Renegade; 1 Mar 1986

	$Good	$Fine	$N.Mint	£Good	£Fine	£N.Mint
1 ND Howard Cruse art; reprints	*$0.30*	*$0.90*	*$1.50*	£0.20	£0.60	£1.00
Title Value:	*$0.30*	*$0.90*	*$1.50*	£0.20	£0.60	£1.00

BARON WEIRWULF'S HAUNTED LIBRARY
(see Haunted)

BARRY WINDSOR-SMITH: STORYTELLER
Dark Horse,Oversized; 1 Oct 1996-present

	$Good	$Fine	$N.Mint	£Good	£Fine	£N.Mint
1 ND 40pgs, features Freebooters, The Paradox Man and Young Gods; Barry Windsor-Smith art	*$1.00*	*$3.00*	*$5.00*	£0.70	£2.10	£3.50
2-5 ND 40pgs	*$1.00*	*$3.00*	*$5.00*	£0.70	£2.10	£3.50
Title Value:	*$5.00*	*$15.00*	*$25.00*	£3.50	£10.50	£17.50

BART SIMPSON'S TREEHOUSE OF HORROR
Bongo Comics; 1 Oct 1995-2 1995 ?

	$Good	$Fine	$N.Mint	£Good	£Fine	£N.Mint
1 ND 48pgs	*$0.60*	*$1.80*	*$3.00*	£0.40	£1.20	£2.00
2 ND	*$0.50*	*$1.50*	*$2.50*	£0.30	£0.90	£1.50
Title Value:	*$1.10*	*$3.30*	*$5.50*	£0.70	£2.10	£3.50

BARTMAN
Bongo Comics; 1 Dec 1993-3 Feb 1994; 4 May 1995-6 1995 ?

	$Good	$Fine	$N.Mint	£Good	£Fine	£N.Mint
1 ND silver foil cover, pull-out poster	*$0.70*	*$2.10*	*$3.50*	£0.50	£1.50	£2.50
1 Newstand Edition, ND without poster insert	*$0.50*	*$1.50*	*$2.50*	£0.40	£1.20	£2.00
2-6 ND	*$0.50*	*$1.50*	*$2.50*	£0.30	£0.90	£1.50
Title Value:	*$3.70*	*$11.10*	*$18.50*	£2.40	£7.20	£12.00

BASIL WOLVERTON'S FANTASTIC FABLES
Dark Horse; 1 Oct 1993-2 Dec 1993

	$Good	$Fine	$N.Mint	£Good	£Fine	£N.Mint
1-2 ND	*$0.50*	*$1.50*	*$2.50*	£0.30	£0.90	£1.50
Title Value:	*$1.00*	*$3.00*	*$5.00*	£0.60	£1.80	£3.00

BASIL WOLVERTON'S GATEWAY TO HORROR
Dark Horse; 1 Jun 1988

	$Good	$Fine	$N.Mint	£Good	£Fine	£N.Mint
1 ND Bissette cover, black and white sci-fi and horror reprints	*$0.50*	*$1.50*	*$2.50*	£0.30	£0.90	£1.50
Title Value:	*$0.50*	*$1.50*	*$2.50*	£0.30	£0.90	£1.50

BASIL WOLVERTON'S PLANET OF TERROR
Dark Horse; 1 Oct 1987

	$Good	$Fine	$N.Mint	£Good	£Fine	£N.Mint
1 ND Alan Moore cover art	*$0.50*	*$1.50*	*$2.50*	£0.30	£0.90	£1.50
Title Value:	*$0.50*	*$1.50*	*$2.50*	£0.30	£0.90	£1.50

BASIL WOLVERTON'S SPACE FUNNIES
Robert Brosch/Archival Photography; 1 Nov 1990-2 1991

	$Good	$Fine	$N.Mint	£Good	£Fine	£N.Mint
1 ND reprints Spacehawk/Space Patrol in colour from 1940s "Target Comics"	*$0.90*	*$2.70*	*$4.50*	£0.60	£1.80	£3.00
2 ND	*$0.90*	*$2.70*	*$4.50*	£0.60	£1.80	£3.00
Title Value:	*$1.80*	*$5.40*	*$9.00*	£1.20	£3.60	£6.00

BAT LASH
National Periodical Publications; 1 Oct/Nov 1968-7 Oct/Nov 1969

(see Jonah Hex, Jonah Hex Spectacular, Showcase #76, Weird Western Tales)

	$Good	$Fine	$N.Mint	£Good	£Fine	£N.Mint
1 2nd appearance of Bat Lash (see showcase #76)	*$2.90*	*$8.75*	*$17.50*	£1.65	£5.00	£10.00
2	*$2.50*	*$7.50*	*$12.50*	£1.20	£3.60	£6.00
3-7	*$2.00*	*$6.00*	*$10.00*	£1.00	£3.00	£5.00
Title Value:	*$15.40*	*$46.25*	*$80.00*	£7.85	£23.60	£41.00

BAT MASTERSON
Dell; (Four Color #1013) 1 Oct 1959-9 Nov 1961/Jan 1962

	$Good	$Fine	$N.Mint	£Good	£Fine	£N.Mint
1 scarce though distributed in the U.K. Four Color #1013; Gene Barry photo covers begin	*$15.50*	*$47.00*	*$125.00*	£9.25	£28.00	£75.00
2-3 scarce though distributed in the U.K.	*$10.00*	*$30.00*	*$80.00*	£6.25	£18.50	£50.00
4-9 scarce though distributed in the U.K.	*$8.75*	*$26.00*	*$70.00*	£5.00	£15.00	£40.00
Title Value:	*$88.00*	*$263.00*	*$705.00*	£51.75	£155.00	£415.00

Note: all Limited Distribution on the news-stands in the U.K.

VERY GENERAL PERCENTAGE CONVERSION CHART WHICH MAY BE USED TO CALCULATE LOW AND INBETWEEN GRADES:

	$Good	$Fine	$N.Mint	£Good	£Fine	£N.Mint

BAT, THE

Apple Comics,OS; 1 1990

1 ND *$0.60* *$1.80* *$3.00* £0.40 £1.20 £2.00

Title Value: *$0.60* *$1.80* *$3.00* £0.40 £1.20 £2.00

Note: based on 1930s pulp hero, a direct antecedent of Batman

BAT, THE (2ND SERIES)

Adventure,OS; 1 Aug 1992

1 ND adaptation of Mary Roberts Rinehart 1926 play that influenced the creation of Batman
$0.40 *$1.20* *$2.00* £0.25 £0.75 £1.25

Title Value: *$0.40* *$1.20* *$2.00* £0.25 £0.75 £1.25

BATGIRL SPECIAL

DC Comics,OS; 1 Mar 1988

1 48pgs, Barry Kitson art
$0.70 *$2.10* *$3.50* £0.50 £1.50 £2.50

Title Value: *$0.70* *$2.10* *$3.50* £0.50 £1.50 £2.50

BATMAN

National Periodical Publications/DC Comics; 0 Oct 1994; 1 Spring 1940-present

(see Arkham Asylum, Batman: The Cult, Batman Family, Batman: The Son of the Demon, Batman 3D, Best of DC, Brave and the Bold, The Dark Knight Returns, DC Special, Detective, Dynamic Classics, Eighty Page Giant, Famous First Edition, Gotham by Gaslight, Greatest Batman Stories Ever Told, The Killing Joke, Legends of the Dark Knight, Limited Collector's Edition, One Hundred Page Super-Spectacular, Batman and the Outsiders, Saga of Ra's Al Ghul, Shadow of the Batman, Untold Legend of the Batman)

0 (Oct 1994) Zero Hour X-over, origin retold; continued in Batman: Shadow of the Bat #31
$0.20 *$0.60* *$1.00* £0.15 £0.45 £0.75

1 (Spring 1940), 1st appearance The Joker and The Cat (later Catwoman), 2 page origin from Detective Comics #33 reprinted; around 300 copies extant in any condition
$5600.00 *$16800.00* *$67500.00* £3750.00 £11200.00 £45000.00
[Prices may vary widely on this comic]

2 scarce in the U.S, very scarce in the U.K. 2nd appearance of The Joker and Catwoman (though she's out of costume)
$1500.00 *$4500.00* *$12000.00* £1000.00 £3000.00 £8000.00

3 scarce in the U.S, very scarce in the U.K. 1st appearance Catwoman in costume (and her 3rd ever appearance. 1st ever villainess in costume?)
$1025.00 *$3050.00* *$8250.00* £680.00 £2050.00 £5500.00

4 5th ever appearance of The Joker (see Detective Comics #45)
$810.00 *$2425.00* *$6500.00* £540.00 £1625.00 £4350.00

5 (Spring 1941), 1st appearance of the Batmobile classic with bat-head front
$620.00 *$1875.00* *$5000.00* £415.00 £1250.00 £3350.00

6-7 *$530.00* *$1575.00* *$4250.00* £355.00 £1050.00 £2850.00

8 (Dec/Jan 1942), classic infinity cover effect
$435.00 *$1300.00* *$3500.00* £290.00 £880.00 £2350.00

9 classic cover that was repeated in reverse on Batman #16
$375.00 *$1125.00* *$3000.00* £250.00 £750.00 £2000.00

10 Catwoman appears
$375.00 *$1125.00* *$3000.00* £250.00 £750.00 £2000.00

11 classic Joker cover with playing card background; Penguin appears for 1st time in title
$750.00 *$2250.00* *$7500.00* £500.00 £1500.00 £5000.00

12 *$280.00* *$840.00* *$2250.00* £185.00 £560.00 £1500.00

13 Superman's co-creator Jerry Siegel appears in one of the Batman stories
$340.00 *$1025.00* *$2750.00* £230.00 £690.00 £1850.00

14 (Dec/Jan 1943), 1st Penguin cover and story in title
$300.00 *$900.00* *$2400.00* £200.00 £600.00 £1600.00

15 Catwoman appears
$280.00 *$840.00* *$2250.00* £185.00 £560.00 £1500.00

16 1st appearance of Alfred the Butler (fat rather than skinny as later Alfred came to be)
$610.00 *$1825.00* *$5500.00* £405.00 £1225.00 £3675.00

17 classic patriotic cover; Batman and Robin on American Eagle (see Superman #14); Penguin appears
$185.00 *$560.00* *$1500.00* £125.00 £375.00 £1000.00

18 Hirohito, Mussolini and Hitler on cover
$250.00 *$750.00* *$2000.00* £165.00 £500.00 £1350.00

19 *$185.00* *$560.00* *$1500.00* £125.00 £375.00 £1000.00

20 (Dec/Jan 1944), classic Batmobile cover
$200.00 *$600.00* *$1600.00* £130.00 £400.00 £1075.00

21 Penguin appears; Alfred becomes skinny (for no apparent reason! Lousy editing?)
$140.00 *$420.00* *$1125.00* £92.50 £280.00 £750.00

22 Alfred begins solo story series (much like Lois Lane in Superman); Catwoman appears
$140.00 *$420.00* *$1125.00* £92.50 £280.00 £750.00

23 classic Joker cover and story
$215.00 *$650.00* *$1750.00* £145.00 £440.00 £1175.00
[Very scarce in high grade - Very Fine+ or better]

24 1st Batman and Robin sent back through time by Professor Carter Nichols (the first of about 30 occasions)
$140.00 *$420.00* *$1125.00* £92.50 £280.00 £750.00

25 Joker and Penguin team (reprinted in Wanted #2); 1st DC "super-villain team-up" (see Fantastic Four #6)
$200.00 *$600.00* *$1600.00* £130.00 £400.00 £1075.00

26 (Dec/Jan 1945)
$140.00 *$420.00* *$1125.00* £92.50 £280.00 £750.00

27 classic Christmas cover; Penguin appears
$180.00 *$540.00* *$1450.00* £120.00 £365.00 £975.00

28-30 *$140.00* *$420.00* *$1125.00* £92.50 £280.00 £750.00

31 infinity cover effect (see Batman #8)
$105.00 *$315.00* *$850.00* £70.00 £215.00 £575.00

32 (Dec/Jan 1946), origin of Robin recapped
$105.00 *$315.00* *$850.00* £70.00 £215.00 £575.00

33 Christmas cover
$125.00 *$375.00* *$1000.00* £82.50 £250.00 £675.00

34 *$105.00* *$315.00* *$850.00* £70.00 £215.00 £575.00

35 Catwoman appears
$105.00 *$315.00* *$850.00* £70.00 £215.00 £575.00

36 Penguin appears
$105.00 *$315.00* *$850.00* £70.00 £215.00 £575.00

37 Joker cover and story
$130.00 *$390.00* *$1050.00* £87.50 £260.00 £700.00

38 (Dec/Jan 1947), Penguin cover and story
$100.00 *$300.00* *$800.00* £65.00 £200.00 £535.00

39 Catwoman story
$105.00 *$315.00* *$850.00* £70.00 £215.00 £575.00

40 Joker cover and story
$130.00 *$390.00* *$1050.00* £87.50 £260.00 £700.00

41 "Batman, Interplanetary Policeman" - 1st sci-fi Batman story (a theme which was to become dominant in the 1950s); Penguin appears
$87.50 *$260.00* *$700.00* £57.50 £175.00 £475.00

42 2nd Catwoman cover (1st in Batman title - see Detective Comics #122), Catwoman story
$95.00 *$290.00* *$775.00* £65.00 £195.00 £520.00

43 Penguin cover and story
$95.00 *$290.00* *$775.00* £65.00 £195.00 £520.00

44 (Dec/Jan 1948), Joker cover and story
$125.00 *$380.00* *$1025.00* £85.00 £255.00 £685.00

45 1st appearance Vicki Vale, Christmas cover
$80.00 *$240.00* *$650.00* £52.50 £160.00 £435.00

46 *$80.00* *$240.00* *$650.00* £52.50 £160.00 £435.00

47 classic origin of Batman, more detailed than Detective Comics #33
$330.00 *$1000.00* *$3000.00* £220.00 £660.00 £2000.00

48 classic 1000 Secrets of the Batcave
$100.00 *$300.00* *$800.00* £65.00 £200.00 £535.00

49 1st appearance The Mad Hatter (see Detective Comics #230), 2nd appearance Vicki Vale, Joker cover and story
$165.00 *$500.00* *$1350.00* £110.00 £335.00 £900.00

50 (Dec/Jan 1949), Two Face returns
$90.00 *$270.00* *$725.00* £60.00 £180.00 £485.00

51 *$75.00* *$225.00* *$600.00* £50.00 £150.00 £400.00

52 Joker cover and story
$92.50 *$280.00* *$750.00* £62.50 £185.00 £500.00

53 Joker appears *$82.50* *$250.00* *$675.00* £55.00 £165.00 £450.00

54 *$75.00* *$225.00* *$600.00* £50.00 £150.00 £400.00

55 Joker cover and story
$92.50 *$280.00* *$750.00* £62.50 £185.00 £500.00

56 (Dec/Jan 1950)
$75.00 *$225.00* *$600.00* £50.00 £150.00 £400.00

57 calendar for 1950 at centrefold (often missing!)
$75.00 *$225.00* *$600.00* £50.00 £150.00 £400.00

58 Penguin cover and story
$85.00 *$255.00* *$690.00* £57.50 £170.00 £460.00

59 classic "Batman in the Future" story and cover; 1st appearance Deadshot (not to be confused with later DC hero)
$75.00 *$225.00* *$600.00* £50.00 £150.00 £400.00

60 Joker appears
$82.50 *$250.00* *$675.00* £55.00 £165.00 £450.00

61 origin Bat-Plane II
$82.50 *$250.00* *$675.00* £55.00 £165.00 £450.00

62 (Dec/Jan 1951), origin Catwoman, Catwoman cover and story
$105.00 *$315.00* *$850.00* £70.00 £215.00 £575.00

63 origin and 1st appearance Killer Moth; Joker appears
$65.00 *$200.00* *$535.00* £45.00 £135.00 £360.00

64 *$52.50* *$155.00* *$425.00* £36.00 £105.00 £285.00

65 Catwoman cover and story
$55.00 *$165.00* *$450.00* £38.00 £110.00 £300.00

66 Joker cover and story
$75.00 *$225.00* *$600.00* £50.00 £150.00 £400.00

67 *$52.50* *$155.00* *$425.00* £36.00 £105.00 £285.00

68 (Dec/Jan 1952), classic Two Face story
$62.50 *$185.00* *$500.00* £42.00 £125.00 £335.00

69 Catwoman cover and story
$55.00 *$165.00* *$450.00* £38.00 £110.00 £300.00

70-71 *$52.50* *$155.00* *$425.00* £36.00 £105.00 £285.00

72 last 52pg issue
$52.50 *$155.00* *$425.00* £36.00 £105.00 £285.00

73 Joker cover and story
$60.00 *$180.00* *$485.00* £41.00 £120.00 £325.00

74 (Dec/Jan 1953), Joker story
$52.50 *$155.00* *$425.00* £36.00 £105.00 £285.00

75-77 *$52.50* *$155.00* *$425.00* £36.00 £105.00 £285.00

78 Roh Kar, The Manhunter From Mars character/story (pre J'onn J'onzz in Detective #225)
$77.50 *$230.00* *$620.00* £50.00 £155.00 £415.00

79 Vicki Vale appears
$52.50 *$155.00* *$425.00* £36.00 £105.00 £285.00

80 (Dec/Jan 1954), Joker appears
$65.00 *$195.00* *$525.00* £44.00 £130.00 £350.00

81 Two Face cover and story
$60.00 *$180.00* *$490.00* £41.00 £120.00 £330.00

82 flying Batman (see Detective Comics #153)
$57.50 *$175.00* *$475.00* £40.00 £120.00 £320.00

83 *$57.50* *$175.00* *$475.00* £40.00 £120.00 £320.00

84 Catwoman cover and story
$62.50 *$185.00* *$500.00* £42.00 £125.00 £335.00

85 *$57.50* *$170.00* *$465.00* £39.00 £115.00 £310.00

86 1st Bat-Submarine
$57.50 *$170.00* *$465.00* £39.00 £115.00 £310.00

87-88 *$57.50* *$170.00* *$465.00* £39.00 £115.00 £310.00

89 (Feb 1955), 1st Aunt Agatha (later became Aunt Harriet for the 1960s Batman TV series)
$57.50 *$170.00* *$465.00* £39.00 £115.00 £310.00

90 scarce in the U.K. 1st Code-approved issue
$48.00 *$140.00* *$385.00* £33.00 £97.50 £260.00

91 very scarce in the U.K.
$48.00 *$140.00* *$385.00* £33.00 £97.50 £260.00

Issue	$Good	$Fine	$N.Mint	£Good	£Fine	£N.Mint
92 very scarce in the U.K. 1st Bat-Hound						
	$57.50	*$175.00*	*$475.00*	£40.00	£120.00	£320.00
93-96 very scarce in the U.K.						
	$47.00	*$140.00*	*$375.00*	£31.00	£92.50	£250.00
97 very scarce in the U.K. (Feb 1956), return of Bat-Hound (2nd appearance)						
	$47.00	*$140.00*	*$375.00*	£31.00	£92.50	£250.00
98 very scarce in the U.K.						
	$47.00	*$140.00*	*$375.00*	£31.00	£92.50	£250.00
99 very scarce in the U.K. Penguin story, on cover as statuette						
	$47.00	*$140.00*	*$375.00*	£31.00	£92.50	£250.00
100 scarce in the U.K. cover features reproductions of six early issues (#1, #23, #25, #47, #48, #61)						
	$175.00	*$520.00*	*$2100.00*	£115.00	£350.00	£1400.00
[Very scarce in high grade - Very Fine+ or better]						
101-104	*$47.00*	*$140.00*	*$375.00*	£31.00	£92.50	£250.00
105 (Feb 1957), 2nd appearance of Batwoman and 1st Batwoman in Batman title (see Detective Comics #233)						
	$52.50	*$160.00*	*$480.00*	£36.00	£105.00	£320.00
106-109	*$47.00*	*$140.00*	*$375.00*	£31.00	£92.50	£250.00
110 1st appearance of The Joker in Silver Age						
	$46.00	*$135.00*	*$370.00*	£31.00	£92.50	£250.00
111-112	*$40.00*	*$120.00*	*$320.00*	£27.00	£80.00	£215.00
113 (Feb 1958), 1st science-fiction type story of Batman-on-strange-worlds, the theme to dominate for the next 6 years						
	$40.00	*$120.00*	*$320.00*	£27.00	£80.00	£215.00
114-115	*$40.00*	*$120.00*	*$320.00*	£27.00	£80.00	£215.00
116-120	*$38.00*	*$110.00*	*$300.00*	£25.00	£75.00	£200.00
121 (Feb 1959)	*$25.00*	*$75.00*	*$200.00*	£16.50	£50.00	£135.00
122 marriage of Batman and Batwoman story						
	$25.00	*$75.00*	*$200.00*	£16.50	£50.00	£135.00
123 Joker story	*$28.00*	*$82.50*	*$225.00*	£18.50	£55.00	£150.00
124-125	*$25.00*	*$75.00*	*$200.00*	£16.00	£49.00	£130.00
126 Batwoman/Batman/Robin team-up						
	$25.00	*$75.00*	*$200.00*	£16.50	£50.00	£135.00
127 Joker story, Superman cameo, "Thor" appears (note Marvel character!); copies known with distribution (pence) stamp						
	$23.50	*$70.00*	*$190.00*	£15.00	£45.00	£120.00
1st official distribution in the U.K.						
128	*$23.50*	*$70.00*	*$190.00*	£14.00	£43.00	£115.00
129 (Feb 1960), origin Robin retold						
	$28.00	*$82.50*	*$225.00*	£15.00	£45.00	£120.00
130	*$23.50*	*$70.00*	*$190.00*	£14.00	£43.00	£115.00
131 1st Batman and Robin II; 1st imaginary Batman story?						
	$21.00	*$62.50*	*$170.00*	£12.50	£38.00	£100.00
132	*$21.00*	*$62.50*	*$170.00*	£10.50	£32.00	£85.00
133 3rd appearance Bat-Mite						
	$21.00	*$62.50*	*$170.00*	£11.00	£34.00	£90.00
134	*$21.00*	*$62.50*	*$170.00*	£10.50	£32.00	£85.00
135 scarce in the U.K.						
	$21.00	*$62.50*	*$170.00*	£11.00	£34.00	£90.00
136 Joker cover and story						
	$23.00	*$67.50*	*$185.00*	£14.00	£43.00	£115.00
137 scarce in the U.K. (Feb 1961)						
	$21.00	*$62.50*	*$170.00*	£11.00	£34.00	£90.00
138	*$21.00*	*$62.50*	*$170.00*	£10.00	£30.00	£80.00
139 1st appearance original Batgirl						
	$21.00	*$62.50*	*$170.00*	£10.50	£32.00	£85.00
140 Joker story, Superman cameo						
	$18.50	*$55.00*	*$150.00*	£10.50	£32.00	£85.00
141-142	*$20.00*	*$60.00*	*$160.00*	£10.00	£30.00	£80.00
143 last 10 cents issue						
	$20.00	*$60.00*	*$160.00*	£10.00	£30.00	£80.00
144 Joker story, Bat-Mite meets original Batgirl						
	$18.50	*$55.00*	*$150.00*	£10.50	£32.00	£85.00
145 (Feb 1962), Joker cover and story ("Son of the Joker" - only appearance?)						
	$21.50	*$65.00*	*$175.00*	£10.50	£32.00	£85.00
146 Bat-Mite appears						
	$15.50	*$47.00*	*$125.00*	£7.50	£22.50	£60.00
147	*$15.50*	*$47.00*	*$125.00*	£7.50	£22.50	£60.00
148 Joker cover and story						
	$21.50	*$65.00*	*$175.00*	£10.00	£30.00	£80.00
149-150	*$15.50*	*$47.00*	*$125.00*	£7.50	£22.50	£60.00
151-152	*$15.00*	*$45.00*	*$105.00*	£6.75	£20.00	£47.50
153 (Feb 1963), 1st 3-part full length story (features Batwoman and original Batgirl)						
	$15.00	*$45.00*	*$105.00*	£6.75	£20.00	£47.50
154	*$15.00*	*$45.00*	*$105.00*	£6.75	£20.00	£47.50
155 1st Silver Age appearance of The Penguin (last seen in issue #99)						
	$36.00	*$105.00*	*$325.00*	£18.50	£55.00	£170.00
156-158	*$12.50*	*$39.00*	*$90.00*	£6.25	£19.00	£45.00
159 Joker cover and story, original Bat-Girl appears; back-up story featuring Bruce Wayne Jnr.						
	$14.00	*$43.00*	*$100.00*	£7.75	£23.50	£55.00
160	*$12.50*	*$39.00*	*$90.00*	£6.25	£19.00	£45.00
161	*$12.00*	*$36.00*	*$85.00*	£5.50	£17.00	£40.00
162 (Feb 1964)	*$12.00*	*$36.00*	*$85.00*	£5.50	£17.00	£40.00
163 Joker cover and story; last appearance original Bat-girl						
	$14.00	*$43.00*	*$100.00*	£7.00	£21.00	£50.00
164 new-look Batman, new Batmobile (see Detective Comics #327)						
	$12.00	*$36.00*	*$85.00*	£5.50	£17.00	£40.00
165	*$12.00*	*$36.00*	*$85.00*	£5.50	£17.00	£40.00
166-168	*$11.00*	*$34.00*	*$80.00*	£5.00	£15.00	£35.00
169 (Feb 1965), Penguin cover and story						
	$19.00	*$57.50*	*$135.00*	£6.25	£19.00	£45.00
170	*$11.00*	*$34.00*	*$80.00*	£5.00	£15.00	£35.00
171 1st Silver Age appearance of The Riddler (1st since Dec. 1948 in Detective Comics #142 making this his 3rd ever appearance)						
	$52.50	*$155.00*	*$425.00*	£25.00	£75.00	£200.00
172-175	*$8.50*	*$26.00*	*$60.00*	£3.55	£10.50	£25.00
176 scarce in the U.K. 80pgs, Giant G-17, Joker cover and story, Catwoman story; last Silver Age issue (indica-dated Dec 1965)						
	$8.75	*$26.00*	*$70.00*	£3.75	£11.00	£30.00
177	*$8.50*	*$26.00*	*$60.00*	£3.55	£10.50	£25.00
178 (Feb 1966)	*$8.50*	*$26.00*	*$60.00*	£3.55	£10.50	£25.00
179 rare in the U.K, scarce in the U.S. (see note at end of title entry) 2nd appearance Silver Age Riddler						
	$16.50	*$50.00*	*$135.00*	£12.50	£38.00	£100.00
180 rare in the U.K, scarce in the U.S. (see note at end of title entry)						
	$8.00	*$24.00*	*$65.00*	£9.25	£28.00	£75.00
181 1st appearance of Poison Ivy, centre-spread pin-up poster of Batman and Robin (often missing!)						
	$11.00	*$34.00*	*$80.00*	£5.00	£15.00	£35.00
182 80pgs, Giant G-24, Joker cover and story						
	$10.00	*$30.00*	*$70.00*	£4.25	£12.50	£30.00
183 2nd appearance of Poison Ivy						
	$9.25	*$28.00*	*$65.00*	£4.25	£12.50	£30.00
184	*$8.50*	*$26.00*	*$60.00*	£3.55	£10.50	£25.00
185 80pgs, Giant G-27, all Robin reprints including the classic "Robin Dies At Dawn"						
	$8.50	*$26.00*	*$60.00*	£3.55	£10.50	£25.00
186 Joker cover and story						
	$6.25	*$19.00*	*$45.00*	£2.85	£8.50	£20.00
187 80pgs, (Jan 1967), Giant G-30, Joker cover and story						
	$8.75	*$27.00*	*$62.50*	£3.90	£11.50	£27.50
188	*$5.00*	*$15.00*	*$35.00*	£2.50	£7.50	£17.50
189 1st appearance Silver Age Scarecrow						
	$11.00	*$34.00*	*$80.00*	£3.55	£10.50	£25.00
190 Penguin cover and story						
	$6.25	*$19.00*	*$45.00*	£2.85	£8.50	£20.00
191-192	*$5.00*	*$15.00*	*$35.00*	£2.10	£6.25	£15.00
193 80pgs, Giant G-37, reprints "bizarre action roles" including "The Flying Batman"						
	$7.00	*$21.00*	*$50.00*	£3.20	£9.50	£22.50
194-196	*$5.00*	*$15.00*	*$35.00*	£1.75	£5.25	£12.50
197 1st Silver Age appearance of Catwoman in Batman title (see Lois Lane #70); 4th overall						
	$10.00	*$30.00*	*$70.00*	£4.25	£12.50	£30.00
198 80pgs, (Feb 1968), Giant G-43, reprints origin from Batman #47 (1948), Joker cover and story, Penguin and Catwoman reprints and cover appearances						
	$11.50	*$35.00*	*$82.50*	£5.25	£16.00	£37.50
199	*$5.00*	*$15.00*	*$35.00*	£1.75	£5.25	£12.50
200 retells origin, Joker on cover by Neal Adams; Joker and Penguin appear, reprints 1st page from Detective Comics #27 and also re-tells Robin's origin						
	$22.50	*$67.50*	*$160.00*	£10.50	£32.00	£75.00
201 Joker, Penguin and Catwoman cameos						
	$3.85	*$11.50*	*$27.00*	£1.75	£5.25	£12.50
202	*$2.55*	*$7.50*	*$18.00*	£1.10	£3.40	£8.00
203 80pgs, Giant G-49, "Secrets of the Bat-Cave", Neal Adams cover						
	$5.00	*$15.00*	*$35.00*	£2.50	£7.50	£17.50
204-207	*$2.55*	*$7.50*	*$18.00*	£1.10	£3.40	£8.00
208 80pgs, (Feb 1969), Giant G-55; new origin Batman by Gil Kane (see note below)						
	$5.00	*$15.00*	*$35.00*	£2.85	£8.50	£20.00
209-210	*$2.55*	*$7.50*	*$18.00*	£1.10	£3.40	£8.00
211	*$2.55*	*$7.50*	*$18.00*	£1.05	£3.20	£7.50
212 last 12 cents issue						
	$2.55	*$7.50*	*$18.00*	£1.05	£3.20	£7.50
213 68pgs, Giant G-61, origin Alfred (from Batman #16), Robin (from Detective #38), Joker (from Detective #168), Clayface II (Detective #298)						
	$8.50	*$26.00*	*$60.00*	£3.55	£10.50	£25.00
214-216	*$2.55*	*$7.50*	*$18.00*	£1.05	£3.20	£7.50
217 Robin leaves, Bat-Cave closed down, Neal Adams cover						
	$2.55	*$7.50*	*$18.00*	£1.05	£3.20	£7.50
218 68pgs, (Feb 1970), Giant G-67; reprints 1944 syndicated newspaper story, Neal Adams cover						
	$5.75	*$17.50*	*$35.00*	£2.90	£8.75	£17.50
219 Neal Adams art; solo Batman without Robin begins in title (temporary)						
	$5.25	*$16.00*	*$32.50*	£2.50	£7.50	£15.00
220 Neal Adams cover						
	$2.50	*$7.50*	*$15.00*	£1.25	£3.75	£7.50
221	*$2.50*	*$7.50*	*$15.00*	£1.05	£3.25	£6.50
222 scarce in the U.K. "Beatles" cover and story, Robin appears						
	$5.75	*$17.50*	*$35.00*	£2.50	£7.50	£15.00
223 68pgs, Giant G-73, Neal Adams cover						
	$4.15	*$12.50*	*$25.00*	£2.05	£6.25	£12.50
224-225 Neal Adans covers						
	$2.50	*$7.50*	*$15.00*	£1.05	£3.25	£6.50
226-227	*$2.50*	*$7.50*	*$15.00*	£0.90	£2.75	£5.50
228 68pgs, (Feb 1971), Giant G-79						
	$4.15	*$12.50*	*$25.00*	£1.65	£5.00	£10.00
229	*$2.50*	*$7.50*	*$15.00*	£0.90	£2.75	£5.50
230 Neal Adams cover						
	$2.50	*$7.50*	*$15.00*	£0.90	£2.75	£5.50
231	*$2.50*	*$7.50*	*$15.00*	£0.90	£2.75	£5.50
232 Neal Adams art, 1st appearance Ra's Al Ghul, Robin appears						
	$11.00	*$34.00*	*$80.00*	£5.00	£15.00	£35.00
233 68pgs, Giant G-85						
	$4.15	*$12.50*	*$25.00*	£1.50	£4.50	£9.00
234 52pgs, Neal Adams art, 1st modern appearance (not Silver Age!) Two Face						
	$18.50	*$55.00*	*$130.00*	£5.50	£17.00	£40.00
235-236 52pgs	*$2.00*	*$6.00*	*$12.00*	£1.00	£3.00	£6.00
237 52pgs, Neal Adams art, back-up reprint of Detective Comics #37, Robin appears						
	$6.50	*$20.00*	*$40.00*	£2.50	£7.50	£15.00
238 scarce in the U.K. 100pgs, (Jan 1972), DC-100pg Super Spectacular #8; reprints My Greatest Adventure #80 (1st Doom Patrol), Neal Adams cover						

	$Good	$Fine	$N.Mint	£Good	£Fine	£N.Mint
	$2.90	$8.75	$17.50	£2.00	£6.00	£12.00
239 52pgs	$2.00	$6.00	$12.00	£1.00	£3.00	£6.00
240 scarce in the U.K. 52pgs, Neal Adams cover	$2.00	$6.00	$12.00	£1.05	£3.25	£6.50
241-242 scarce in the U.K. 52pgs	$2.00	$6.00	$12.00	£1.05	£3.25	£6.50
243 Neal Adams art, classic Ra's Al Ghul story, Robin appears	$4.15	$12.50	$25.00	£2.50	£7.50	£15.00
244-245 Neal Adams art, classic Ra's Al Ghul story	$4.15	$12.50	$25.00	£2.50	£7.50	£15.00
246 scarce in the U.K. Robin appears	$2.00	$6.00	$12.00	£1.15	£3.50	£7.00
247 (Feb 1973), Robin appears	$2.00	$6.00	$12.00	£1.00	£3.00	£6.00
248-249	$2.00	$6.00	$12.00	£0.90	£2.75	£5.50
250	$2.00	$6.00	$12.00	£1.00	£3.00	£6.00
251 Neal Adams art, classic Joker rendition, first appearance in title since issue issue #201	$7.75	$23.50	$47.50	£3.75	£11.00	£22.50
252	$2.00	$6.00	$12.00	£0.80	£2.50	£5.00
253 Batman/Shadow team-up	$2.00	$6.00	$12.00	£1.00	£3.00	£6.00
254 100pgs, (Feb 1974)	$2.90	$8.75	$17.50	£1.50	£4.50	£9.00
255 100pgs, Neal Adams art	$4.15	$12.50	$25.00	£2.05	£6.25	£12.50
256 100pgs	$2.90	$8.75	$17.50	£1.50	£4.50	£9.00
257 100pgs, Joker reprint	$2.90	$8.75	$17.50	£1.50	£4.50	£9.00
258-259 100pgs	$2.90	$8.75	$17.50	£1.50	£4.50	£9.00
260 100pgs, (Feb 1975), Joker cover and new story, Catwoman and Penguin reprints	$5.75	$17.50	$35.00	£2.05	£6.25	£12.50
261 100pgs	$2.90	$8.75	$17.50	£1.30	£4.00	£8.00
262 scarce in the U.K. 68pgs	$1.65	$5.00	$10.00	£1.00	£3.00	£6.00
263-264	$1.65	$5.00	$10.00	£0.65	£2.00	£4.00
265 Wrightson part-inks	$1.65	$5.00	$10.00	£0.75	£2.25	£4.50
266	$1.65	$5.00	$10.00	£0.65	£2.00	£4.00
267 scarce in the U.K.	$1.65	$5.00	$10.00	£0.75	£2.25	£4.50
268	$1.65	$5.00	$10.00	£0.65	£2.00	£4.00
269-270 scarce in the U.K.	$1.65	$5.00	$10.00	£0.75	£2.25	£4.50
271 (Jan 1976)	$1.50	$4.50	$9.00	£0.65	£2.00	£4.00
272-276	$1.50	$4.50	$9.00	£0.65	£2.00	£4.00
277-282 scarce in the U.K.	$1.50	$4.50	$9.00	£0.75	£2.25	£4.50
283 scarce in the U.K. (Jan 1977)	$1.30	$4.00	$8.00	£0.75	£2.25	£4.50
284 scarce in the U.K.	$1.30	$4.00	$8.00	£0.75	£2.25	£4.50
285 ND scarce in the U.K.	$1.30	$4.00	$8.00	£1.00	£3.00	£6.00
286 scarce in the U.K. Joker cover and story	$2.00	$6.00	$12.00	£0.80	£2.50	£5.00
287-290 scarce in the U.K. Grell art	$1.30	$4.00	$8.00	£0.75	£2.25	£4.50
291 Joker and Catwoman appear	$2.00	$6.00	$12.00	£0.80	£2.50	£5.00
292	$1.30	$4.00	$8.00	£0.65	£2.00	£4.00
293 Lex Luthor and Superman appear	$1.30	$4.00	$8.00	£0.65	£2.00	£4.00
294 Joker cover and story	$2.00	$6.00	$12.00	£0.80	£2.50	£5.00
295 scarce in the U.K. (Jan 1978), Michael Golden art	$1.30	$4.00	$8.00	£0.65	£2.00	£4.00
296-299	$1.30	$4.00	$8.00	£0.65	£2.00	£4.00
300 48pgs	$2.00	$6.00	$12.00	£1.05	£3.25	£6.50
301-302	$1.65	$5.00	$10.00	£0.55	£1.75	£3.50
303 ND 44pgs, Golden art	$1.65	$5.00	$10.00	£1.05	£3.25	£6.50
304-305 ND 44pgs	$1.65	$5.00	$10.00	£0.80	£2.50	£5.00
306	$1.65	$5.00	$10.00	£0.55	£1.75	£3.50
307 (Jan 1979)	$1.65	$5.00	$10.00	£0.55	£1.75	£3.50
308-310	$1.65	$5.00	$10.00	£0.55	£1.75	£3.50
311 Batgirl guest stars	$1.65	$5.00	$10.00	£0.55	£1.75	£3.50
312-317	$1.65	$5.00	$10.00	£0.55	£1.75	£3.50
318 1st appearance Firebug	$1.65	$5.00	$10.00	£0.55	£1.75	£3.50
319 (Jan 1980)	$2.00	$6.00	$10.00	£0.70	£2.10	£3.50
320	$2.00	$6.00	$10.00	£0.70	£2.10	£3.50
321 Joker cover and story, Walt Simonson art	$2.40	$7.00	$12.00	£1.10	£3.30	£5.50
322	$2.00	$6.00	$10.00	£0.70	£2.10	£3.50
323-324 Catwoman appears	$2.00	$6.00	$10.00	£0.80	£2.40	£4.00
325-326	$2.00	$6.00	$10.00	£0.70	£2.10	£3.50
327 Arkham Asylum	$2.00	$6.00	$10.00	£0.70	£2.10	£3.50
328-330	$2.00	$6.00	$10.00	£0.70	£2.10	£3.50
331 (Jan 1981)	$2.00	$6.00	$10.00	£0.70	£2.10	£3.50
332-335 Catwoman story	$2.00	$6.00	$10.00	£0.80	£2.40	£4.00
336-338	$2.00	$6.00	$10.00	£0.70	£2.10	£3.50
339 scarce in the U.K. Vicki Vale returns	$2.00	$6.00	$10.00	£0.80	£2.40	£4.00
340 Gene Colan art	$2.00	$6.00	$10.00	£0.70	£2.10	£3.50
341-342	$2.00	$6.00	$10.00	£0.70	£2.10	£3.50
343 (Jan 1982)	$2.00	$6.00	$10.00	£0.70	£2.10	£3.50
344-352	$2.00	$6.00	$10.00	£0.70	£2.10	£3.50
353 Joker cover/story, free 16pg insert "Masters of the Universe"	$2.40	$7.00	$12.00	£1.10	£3.30	£5.50
354	$1.60	$4.80	$8.00	£0.70	£2.10	£3.50
355 (Jan 1983), Catwoman appears	$1.60	$4.80	$8.00	£0.75	£2.25	£3.75
356	$1.60	$4.80	$8.00	£0.70	£2.10	£3.50
357 1st appearance Jason Todd (later the new Robin); see Detective #524 (2nd appearance)	$1.80	$5.25	$9.00	£0.90	£2.70	£4.50
358	$1.60	$4.80	$8.00	£0.70	£2.10	£3.50
359 Joker cover and story	$2.40	$7.00	$12.00	£0.90	£2.70	£4.50
360	$1.60	$4.80	$8.00	£0.70	£2.10	£3.50
361 Man Bat appears	$1.60	$4.80	$8.00	£0.70	£2.10	£3.50
362 Riddler appears	$1.60	$4.80	$8.00	£0.70	£2.10	£3.50
363-365	$1.60	$4.80	$8.00	£0.60	£1.80	£3.00
366 1st new Robin in costume, Joker cover and story	$3.50	$10.50	$17.50	£2.00	£6.00	£10.00
367 (Jan 1984)	$1.60	$4.80	$8.00	£0.60	£1.80	£3.00

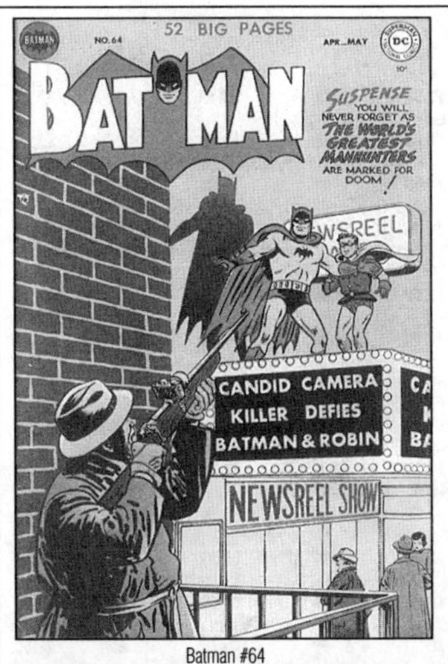

Batman #64

Batman #82

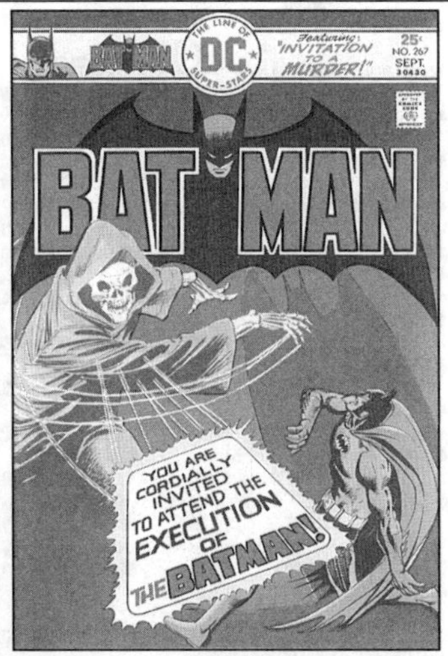

Batman #267

	$Good	$Fine	$N.Mint	£Good	£Fine	£N.Mint
368 1st official introduction of Jason Todd as new Robin (see Detective #535)	$2.00	$6.00	$10.00	£1.60	£4.80	£8.00
369-373	$1.60	$4.80	$8.00	£0.60	£1.80	£3.00
374 Penguin appears	$1.00	$3.00	$5.00	£0.60	£1.80	£3.00
375-378	$1.00	$3.00	$5.00	£0.60	£1.80	£3.00
379 (Jan 1985)	$1.00	$3.00	$5.00	£0.60	£1.80	£3.00
380-381	$1.00	$3.00	$5.00	£0.60	£1.80	£3.00
382 Catwoman appears and "dies"	$0.80	$2.40	$4.00	£0.70	£2.10	£3.50
383-387	$0.80	$2.40	$4.00	£0.60	£1.80	£3.00
388 Mirror Master and Captain Boomerang appear	$0.80	$2.40	$4.00	£0.60	£1.80	£3.00
389-390	$0.80	$2.40	$4.00	£0.60	£1.80	£3.00
391 (Jan 1986)	$0.80	$2.40	$4.00	£0.60	£1.80	£3.00
392	$0.80	$2.40	$4.00	£0.60	£1.80	£3.00
393-394 Gulacy art	$0.80	$2.40	$4.00	£0.60	£1.80	£3.00
395-399	$0.80	$2.40	$4.00	£0.60	£1.80	£3.00
400 64pgs, "Dark Knight" special, intro by Stephen King, Bolland, Sienkiewicz, Art Adams, George Perez art, 1pg John Byrne	$3.50	$10.50	$17.50	£2.00	£6.00	£10.00
401 Legends X-over (1st), John Byrne cover	$0.70	$2.10	$3.50	£0.50	£1.50	£2.50
402 Jim Starlin art, 1st Batman's "long ears", very popular look in the 1990s	$0.70	$2.10	$3.50	£0.50	£1.50	£2.50
403 (Jan 1987)	$0.70	$2.10	$3.50	£0.50	£1.50	£2.50
404 Batman Year One by Frank Miller begins; 1st appearance modern Catwoman (as Selina Kyle only)	$2.60	$7.75	$13.00	£1.00	£3.00	£5.00
405 Batman Year One	$1.20	$3.60	$6.00	£0.70	£2.10	£3.50
406 Batman Year One, 1st appearance modern Catwoman in costume	$1.40	$4.20	$7.00	£0.90	£2.70	£4.50
407 Batman Year One	$1.20	$3.60	$6.00	£0.65	£1.95	£3.25
408 new origin Jason Todd (Robin II) begins	$0.90	$2.70	$4.50	£0.60	£1.80	£3.00
409-410 new origin Jason Todd (Robin II) continued	$0.90	$2.70	$4.50	£0.50	£1.50	£2.50
411-413	$0.60	$1.80	$3.00	£0.35	£1.05	£1.75
414 Jim Starlin script	$0.60	$1.80	$3.00	£0.35	£1.05	£1.75
415 (Jan 1988), Jim Starlin script, Millennium X-over	$0.60	$1.80	$3.00	£0.35	£1.05	£1.75
416 Jim Starlin script	$0.60	$1.80	$3.00	£0.35	£1.05	£1.75
417 LD in the U.K. Ten Nights of the Beast, Jim Starlin script, Mike Zeck cover	$1.80	$5.25	$9.00	£1.20	£3.60	£6.00
418 Ten Nights of the Beast, Jim Starlin script, Mike Zeck cover	$1.80	$5.25	$9.00	£0.80	£2.40	£4.00
419-420 Ten Nights of the Beast, Jim Starlin script, Mike Zeck cover	$1.80	$5.25	$9.00	£0.75	£2.25	£3.75
421-422 Jim Starlin script	$0.60	$1.80	$3.00	£0.30	£0.90	£1.50
423 Jim Starlin script, Todd McFarlane cover	$0.60	$1.80	$3.00	£0.30	£0.90	£1.50
423 2nd printing	$0.25	$0.75	$1.25	£0.15	£0.45	£0.75
423 3rd printing	$0.15	$0.45	$0.75	£0.10	£0.35	£0.60
424 Jim Starlin script	$0.60	$1.80	$3.00	£0.30	£0.90	£1.50
424 2nd printing	$0.25	$0.75	$1.25	£0.15	£0.45	£0.75
425 Jim Starlin script	$0.60	$1.80	$3.00	£0.30	£0.90	£1.50
426 A Death in the Family begins	$1.20	$3.60	$6.00	£0.90	£2.70	£4.50
427 DS, regular edition	$1.00	$3.00	$5.00	£0.80	£2.40	£4.00
427 Phone Number Edition, DS (phone number inside cover)	$1.00	$3.00	$5.00	£0.80	£2.40	£4.00
428 (Jan 1989), death of Robin II (Jason Todd)	$1.00	$3.00	$5.00	£0.70	£2.10	£3.50
429 Death in the Family ends, Superman appears, Joker cover	$0.80	$2.40	$4.00	£0.50	£1.50	£2.50
430-432	$0.40	$1.20	$2.00	£0.25	£0.75	£1.25
433-435 Many Deaths of Batman, John Byrne script	$0.40	$1.20	$2.00	£0.25	£0.75	£1.25
436 Year 3 part 1, blue DC logo; 1st appearance Timothy Drake	$0.80	$2.40	$4.00	£0.45	£1.35	£2.25
436 2nd printing, green DC logo	$0.25	$0.75	$1.25	£0.15	£0.45	£0.75
437-438 Year 3 parts 2,3	$0.40	$1.20	$2.00	£0.25	£0.75	£1.25
439 Year 3 part 4, George Perez cover	$0.40	$1.20	$2.00	£0.25	£0.75	£1.25
440 A Lonely Place of Dying, X-over with New Teen Titans #60, #61; George Perez cover	$0.40	$1.20	$2.00	£0.25	£0.75	£1.25
441 A Lonely Place of Dying continues, George Perez cover	$0.40	$1.20	$2.00	£0.25	£0.75	£1.25
442 last part A Lonely Place of Dying, 1st appearance Tim Drake in new Robin costume (see #457); George Perez cover	$1.50	$4.50	$7.50	£0.35	£1.05	£1.75
443 (Jan 1990), free 16pg insert	$0.30	$0.90	$1.50	£0.20	£0.60	£1.00
444	$0.30	$0.90	$1.50	£0.20	£0.60	£1.00
445-447 Bolland covers	$0.30	$0.90	$1.50	£0.20	£0.60	£1.00
448-449 bi-weekly X-over with Detective #615, Penguin appears	$0.30	$0.90	$1.50	£0.20	£0.60	£1.00
450-451 bi-weekly X-over with Detective #617, The Joker appears	$0.30	$0.90	$1.50	£0.20	£0.60	£1.00
452-454 Riddler story by Pete Milligan	$0.30	$0.90	$1.50	£0.20	£0.60	£1.00
455-456 Identity Crisis story; Scarecrow appears	$0.30	$0.90	$1.50	£0.20	£0.60	£1.00
457 Identity Crisis part 3; Tim Drake becomes the new Robin (III), Scarecrow appears (Note: the direct sales edition has "000" instead of "457" in indicia at the bottom of the 1st page)	$1.40	$4.20	$7.00	£0.50	£1.50	£2.50
457 2nd printing, (Jan 1991)	$0.15	$0.45	$0.75	£0.10	£0.35	£0.60
458-459 Sarah Essen (from Batman: Year One) appears	$0.30	$0.90	$1.50	£0.20	£0.60	£1.00
460-461 Sister in Arms story, Catwoman appears	$0.35	$1.05	$1.75	£0.20	£0.60	£1.00
462-463	$0.30	$0.90	$1.50	£0.20	£0.60	£1.00
464-466 bi-weekly	$0.30	$0.90	$1.50	£0.20	£0.60	£1.00
467-469 The Shadow Box, sequel to Robin mini-series, Louise Simonson script, bi-weekly	$0.30	$0.90	$1.50	£0.20	£0.60	£1.00
470 War of the Gods X-over	$0.30	$0.90	$1.50	£0.20	£0.60	£1.00
471	$0.25	$0.75	$1.25	£0.15	£0.45	£0.75
472 The Idiot Root part 1, X-over with Detective #639	$0.25	$0.75	$1.25	£0.15	£0.45	£0.75
473 (Jan 1992), The Idiot Root part 3, X-over with Detective #440	$0.25	$0.75	$1.25	£0.15	£0.45	£0.75
474 Destroyer part 1, continued in Legends of the Dark Knight #27	$0.25	$0.75	$1.25	£0.15	£0.45	£0.75
475 X-over with Detective Comics #642	$0.25	$0.75	$1.25	£0.15	£0.45	£0.75
476 Batman "reveals" identity to Vicki Vale	$0.25	$0.75	$1.25	£0.15	£0.45	£0.75
477 A Gotham Tale story, bi-weekly issue, photo cover, $1.25 cover begins	$0.25	$0.75	$1.25	£0.15	£0.45	£0.75
478 A Gotham Tale story, bi-weekly issue, photo cover	$0.25	$0.75	$1.25	£0.15	£0.45	£0.75
479-480 bi-weekly	$0.25	$0.75	$1.25	£0.15	£0.45	£0.75
481-482 Messenger of Zeus story, bi-weekly	$0.25	$0.75	$1.25	£0.15	£0.45	£0.75
483 The Ballad of Crash story	$0.25	$0.75	$1.25	£0.15	£0.45	£0.75
484	$0.25	$0.75	$1.25	£0.15	£0.45	£0.75
485 Mike Golden cover	$0.25	$0.75	$1.25	£0.15	£0.45	£0.75
486-487	$0.25	$0.75	$1.25	£0.15	£0.45	£0.75
488 (Jan 1993), continued from Batman: Sword of Azrael #4, Travis Charest cover	$1.60	$4.80	$8.00	£0.70	£2.10	£3.50
489 Azrael dons Batman costume for 1st time; Travis Charest cover	$1.60	$4.80	$8.00	£0.70	£2.10	£3.50
490 Bane and Azrael appear; Riddler appears, Travis Charest cover	$1.40	$4.20	$7.00	£0.60	£1.80	£3.00
491 Joker cover and story; Azrael and Bane appear, Knightfall prequel	$1.00	$3.00	$5.00	£0.50	£1.50	£2.50
492 Knightfall part 1, bi-weekly; continued in Detective Comics #659	$0.90	$2.70	$4.50	£0.45	£1.35	£2.25
492 2nd printing	$0.30	$0.90	$1.50	£0.20	£0.60	£1.00
492 Platinum Edition, ND made available by DC at the Capital City Distribution Sales Conference; enlarged "492" no date no price and platinum coloured logo background	$2.00	$6.00	$10.00	£1.20	£3.60	£6.00
493 Knightfall part 3, bi-weekly; continued in Detective Comics #660	$0.60	$1.80	$3.00	£0.40	£1.20	£2.00
494 Knightfall part 5, bi-weekly; continued in Detective Comics #661; Joker appears	$0.60	$1.80	$3.00	£0.30	£0.90	£1.50
495 Knightfall part 7, bi-weekly; continued in Detective Comics #662; Bane and Joker cameos	$0.60	$1.80	$3.00	£0.30	£0.90	£1.50
496 Knightfall part 9, bi-weekly; continued in Detective Comics #663; Joker and bane appear	$0.60	$1.80	$3.00	£0.25	£0.75	£1.25
497 Knightfall part 11, bi-weekly; continued in Detective Comics #664; protective outer half cover, Batman vs. Bane - "the breaking of Batman"	$1.20	$3.60	$6.00	£0.50	£1.50	£2.50
497 2nd printing, no outer cover	$0.30	$0.90	$1.50	£0.20	£0.60	£1.00
497 Newstand Edition, as 1st printing but without outer cover	$0.40	$1.20	$2.00	£0.20	£0.60	£1.00
498 Knightfall part 15; continued in Detective Comics #665; Bane and Catwoman appear	$0.40	$1.20	$2.00	£0.25	£0.75	£1.25
499 Knightfall part 17; continued in Detective Comics #666, Kelley Jones cover; Bane appears	$0.40	$1.20	$2.00	£0.25	£0.75	£1.25
500 64pgs, Knightfall part 19; Azrael takes over as Batman with new costume, cover by Kelley Jones	$0.50	$1.50	$2.50	£0.30	£0.90	£1.50
500 Collectors Edition, ND 64pgs, die-cut outer cover with foil enhancement by Joe Quesada	$1.00	$3.00	$5.00	£0.50	£1.50	£2.50
501 Knightquest: The Crusade part 3, continued in Batman: Shadow of the Bat #20, Kelley Jones cover	$0.30	$0.90	$1.50	£0.20	£0.60	£1.00
502 Knightquest: The Crusade part 6, continued in Detective Comics #669; Kelley Jones cover	$0.30	$0.90	$1.50	£0.20	£0.60	£1.00

	$Good	$Fine	$N.Mint	£Good	£Fine	£N.Mint
503 (Jan 1994), Knightquest: The Crusade story, Kelley Jones cover; continued in Catwoman #6						
	$0.30	***$0.90***	***$1.50***	**£0.20**	**£0.60**	**£1.00**
504 Knightquest: The Crusade story, Kelley Jones cover; continued in Catwoman #7						
	$0.30	***$0.90***	***$1.50***	**£0.20**	**£0.60**	**£1.00**
505 Knightquest: The Crusade story, Kelley Jones cover; continued in Batman: Shadow of the Bat #26						
	$0.30	***$0.90***	***$1.50***	**£0.20**	**£0.60**	**£1.00**
506-507 Knightquest: The Crusade story, Ballistic appears; Kelley Jones cover						
	$0.30	***$0.90***	***$1.50***	**£0.20**	**£0.60**	**£1.00**
508 Knightquest: The Crusade story conclusion; continued in Batman: Shadow of the Bat #28, Kelley Jones cover						
	$0.30	***$0.90***	***$1.50***	**£0.20**	**£0.60**	**£1.00**
509 48pgs, Knightsend part 1, continued in Batman: Shadow of the Bat #29						
	$0.55	***$1.65***	***$2.75***	**£0.30**	**£0.90**	**£1.50**
510 Knightsend part 7, continued in Batman: Shadow of the Bat #30; Kelley Jones cover						
	$0.30	***$0.90***	***$1.50***	**£0.20**	**£0.60**	**£1.00**
511 Zero Hour X-over						
	$0.30	***$0.90***	***$1.50***	**£0.20**	**£0.60**	**£1.00**
512 Dick Grayson as Batman vs. Killer Croc						
	$0.30	***$0.90***	***$1.50***	**£0.20**	**£0.60**	**£1.00**
513 Dick Grayson as Batman vs. Two-Face						
	$0.30	***$0.90***	***$1.50***	**£0.20**	**£0.60**	**£1.00**
514 (Jan 1995)	***$0.30***	***$0.90***	***$1.50***	**£0.20**	**£0.60**	**£1.00**
515 The Troika part 1, continued in Batman: Shadow of the Bat #35						
	$0.30	***$0.90***	***$1.50***	**£0.20**	**£0.60**	**£1.00**
515 Collectors Edition, ND embossed black cover						
	$0.45	***$1.35***	***$2.25***	**£0.30**	**£0.90**	**£1.50**
516-518	***$0.30***	***$0.90***	***$1.50***	**£0.20**	**£0.60**	**£1.00**
519 upgraded coated paper stock (Miraweb Format) begins						
	$0.40	***$1.20***	***$2.00***	**£0.25**	**£0.75**	**£1.25**
520-521	***$0.40***	***$1.20***	***$2.00***	**£0.25**	**£0.75**	**£1.25**
522 Swamp Thing appears						
	$0.40	***$1.20***	***$2.00***	**£0.25**	**£0.75**	**£1.25**
523-524	***$0.40***	***$1.20***	***$2.00***	**£0.25**	**£0.75**	**£1.25**
525 Underworld Unleashed tie-in, Mr. Freeze appears						
	$0.40	***$1.20***	***$2.00***	**£0.25**	**£0.75**	**£1.25**
526 (Jan 1996)	***$0.40***	***$1.20***	***$2.00***	**£0.25**	**£0.75**	**£1.25**
527 Two-Face appears						
	$0.40	***$1.20***	***$2.00***	**£0.25**	**£0.75**	**£1.25**
528 Two-Face appears						
	$0.40	***$1.20***	***$2.00***	**£0.25**	**£0.75**	**£1.25**
529 Contagion part 6, continued in Batman: Shadow of the Bat #49						
	$0.40	***$1.20***	***$2.00***	**£0.25**	**£0.75**	**£1.25**
530 The Aztec Connection part 1, Deadman appears						
	$0.40	***$1.20***	***$2.00***	**£0.25**	**£0.75**	**£1.25**
530 Collectors Edition, ND glow-in-the-dark cardstock cover						
	$0.50	***$1.50***	***$2.50***	**£0.30**	**£0.90**	**£1.50**
531	***$0.40***	***$1.20***	***$2.00***	**£0.25**	**£0.75**	**£1.25**
531 Collectors Edition, ND glow-in-the-dark cardstock cover						
	$0.50	***$1.50***	***$2.50***	**£0.30**	**£0.90**	**£1.50**
532 ND	***$0.50***	***$1.50***	***$2.50***	**£0.30**	**£0.90**	**£1.50**
532 Collectors Edition, ND glow-in-the-dark cardstock cover						
	$0.50	***$1.50***	***$2.50***	**£0.30**	**£0.90**	**£1.50**
533 ND Legacy Prelude 2, continued in Detective Comics #700						
	$0.50	***$1.50***	***$2.50***	**£0.30**	**£0.90**	**£1.50**
534 ND Legacy part 5, continued in Detective Comics #701						
	$0.50	***$1.50***	***$2.50***	**£0.30**	**£0.90**	**£1.50**
535 ND 48pgs	***$0.60***	***$1.80***	***$3.00***	**£0.40**	**£1.20**	**£2.00**
535 Collectors Edition, ND 48pgs, die-cut gatefold cover						
	$0.80	***$2.40***	***$4.00***	**£0.50**	**£1.50**	**£2.50**
536 ND Final Night tie-in, Man-Bat appears						
	$0.40	***$1.20***	***$2.00***	**£0.25**	**£0.75**	**£1.25**
537-538 ND Man-Bat appears						
	$0.40	***$1.20***	***$2.00***	**£0.25**	**£0.75**	**£1.25**
539 ND 1st appearance The Undertaker						
	$0.40	***$1.20***	***$2.00***	**£0.25**	**£0.75**	**£1.25**
540 ND The Spectre guest-stars						
	$0.40	***$1.20***	***$2.00***	**£0.25**	**£0.75**	**£1.25**
Title Value:	***$24959.00***	***$74811.05***	***$224836.00***	**£16381.95**	**£49167.80**	**£148220.20**

Note: Joker covers - 100, 200. Joker covers and stories - 136, 145, 148, 159, 163, 176, 181, 182, 183, 184, 185, 186, 187, 193, 198, 251, 260, 286, 291, 294, 321, 353, 359, 366, 429, 450, 451. Joker stories - 110, 123, 127, 140, 144, 152, 201.

FEATURES

Atom (previously unpublished GA story) in 238. Batman/Commissioner Gordon in 328, 331. Bruce Wayne in 304. Catwoman solo in 332. Robin solo in 227, 229-231, 234-236, 239-242, 244, 245, 248-250, 252, 254, 337-339, 341-343. Tales of Gotham City in 334. Unsolved Cases of the Batman in 303, 305, 306.

REPRINT FEATURES

Batman/Robin in 176, 182, 185, 187, 193, 198, 203, 208, 213, 218, 223, 228, 233-242, 254-262. Alfred in 255, 257, 260. Doom Patrol, Plastic Man, Sargon the Sorcerer, Aquaman, Legion in 238.

	£Good	£Fine	£N.Mint
Challenge of the Man-Bat (May 1989)			
Trade Paperback ND black and white reprints of Detective Comics issues #395, #397, #400, #402. Neal Adams art	£1.00	£3.00	£5.00
Vow from the Grave (1989) Trade Paperback			
Titan Edition reprints of classic Neal Adams art; b&w	£1.00	£3.00	£5.00
The Demon Awakes (1989) Trade Paperback			
Titan Edition Neal Adams reprints; black and white	£1.00	£3.00	£5.00
The Joker's Revenge (1990) Trade Paperback			
Titan Edition Neal Adams reprints; black and white. Great foreword!	£1.00	£3.00	£5.00
The Frightened City (1990) Trade Paperback			
Titan Edition Neal Adams reprints; black and white. Even greater foreword!	£1.00	£3.00	£5.00
Red Water, Crimson Death (1990) Trade Paperback			
Titan Edition Neal Adams reprints; black and white. The best foreword of them all!	£1.00	£3.00	£5.00
Batman: A Death in the Family (1988)			
Trade paperback ND 144pgs, reprints #425-428	£1.00	£3.00	£5.00
(**Note:** 5 prints available - story title colour in red/purple/green/yellow/orange; 2nd-5th prints at 80% of above)			
Batman: Year One (1988)			
Hardcover, with dustjacket ND reprints #404-407 with corrections	£2.00	£6.00	£10.00
Batman: Year One (1988)			
Softcover, as above, Titan (UK)/DC Edition	£1.00	£3.00	£5.00
2nd/3rd prints DC Edition (1988)	£0.90	£2.70	£4.50
Batman: Year Two (Jan 1990)			
Trade paperback ND reprints Detective #575-578, 104pgs McFarlane/Davis/Neary art	£1.00	£3.00	£5.00
Batman: A Lonely Place of Dying (Sep 1990)			
Trade paperback ND reprints Batman #440-442, New Titans #60, #61, new cover by George Perez	£0.50	£1.50	£2.50
Batman: Tales of the Demon (Sep 1991)			
Trade paperback ND reprints Ra's Al Ghul mini-series, Detective #485, #489, #490, DC Special Series #15	£2.50	£7.50	£12.50
The Many Deaths of Batman (Apr 1992)			
Trade paperback ND reprints Batman #433-435 by John Byrne. John Byrne cover	£0.50	£1.50	£2.50
Batman: Blind Justice (Apr 1992)			
Trade paperback ND reprints Detective Comics #598-600, new intro by Sam Hamm	£0.90	£2.70	£4.50
Batman: Night Cries (Apr 1993)			
Trade paperback, ND Scott Hampton art and painted cover	£1.60	£4.80	£8.00
Multi-Pack (1990)			
ND three issues from #397-399 or #414-416, pre-bagged with illustrated header card	£0.30	£0.90	£1.50
Batman: Sword of Azrael (Aug 1993)			
Trade paperback ND reprints four issue mini-series, new cover by Joe Quesada and Kevin Nowlan	£1.30	£3.90	£6.50
Batman: Venom (Oct 1993)			
Trade paperback ND reprints Batman: Legends of the Dark Knight #16-20, new embossed painted cover by Russell Braun	£1.30	£3.90	£6.50
Batman: Knightfall Vol 1 (Mar 1994)			
Trade paperback ND reprints Batman #491-497, Detective #659-663; Kelley Jones cover	£1.70	£5.10	£8.50
Batman: Knightfall Vol 2 (Mar 1994)			
Trade paperback ND reprints Batman #498,500,Detective #664-666, Showcase '93 #7&8, Batman: Shadow of the Bat #16-18	£1.70	£5.10	£8.50
Batman: Ten Nights of the Beast (Aug 1994)			
Trade paperback ND reprints issues #417-420, new painted cover by Mike Zeck	£0.80	£2.40	£4.00
Knightsend (Jun 1995)			
Trade paperback ND reprints Batman #509/510, Batman: Shadow of the Bat #29/30, Detective Comics #676/677, Batman: Legends of the Dark Knight #62/63, Catwoman #12, Robin #8 and 17pgs of Robin #9	£2.00	£6.00	£10.00
Batman: Featuring The Riddler & Two-Face (Aug 1995)			
Trade paperback ND 192pgs, classic collection of reprints from Golden Age to present	£1.70	£5.10	£8.50
Batman Collector's Set (May 1996)			
ND pack featuring Batman #520, Batman: Shadow of the Bat #38,40-41, Detective Comics #683 and Annual #8 plus trading card	£2.00	£6.00	£10.00
Batman: Contagion (Sep 1996)			
Trade paperback ND reprints Contagion storyline	£1.70	£5.10	£8.50
Batman: Haunted Knight (Nov 1996)			
ND collects three Halloween specials "Fears", "Madness" and "Ghosts"	£1.70	£5.10	£8.50
Batman: Legacy (Mar 1997)			
Trade paperback ND reprints Batman: Shadow of the Bat #53,54, Batman #533,534, Detective Comics #700,701, Catwoman #36, Robin #32, 33	£2.40	£7.20	£12.00

Note: The front cover of #208 often bears ink marks, the result of inferior printing inks detaching from the back covers when the copies were originally stacked. Superman #207 and New Teen Titans 4 often suffer the same defacement. Perfect mint copies are scarce.

Note also: A large percentage of the print-runs of #179 and #180 were distributed to American cinemas to promote the Batman film, and many were destroyed resulting in today's rarity.

BATMAN 3-D

National Periodical Publications,Magazine; nn 1953, nn 1966

	$Good	$Fine	$N.Mint	£Good	£Fine	£N.Mint
nn (1953) ND rare in the U.K. with bound in 3-D glasses (deduct 25% if without glasses); Batman and Tommy Tomorrow reprints						
	$100.00	***$305.00***	***$925.00***	**£65.00**	**£200.00**	**£600.00**
nn (1966) scarce in the U.K. reprints the above, with bound-in 3-D glasses (deduct 25% if without glasses)						
	$38.00	***$110.00***	***$300.00***	**£25.00**	**£75.00**	**£200.00**
Title Value:	***$138.00***	***$415.00***	***$1225.00***	**£90.00**	**£275.00**	**£800.00**

Note: if 3-D glasses are detached deduct 15%, if missing deduct 25%

BATMAN 3-D GRAPHIC ALBUM

DC Comics,OS; nn Dec 1990

	$Good	$Fine	$N.Mint	£Good	£Fine	£N.Mint
nn ND 80pgs, John Byrne art, Penguin, Joker, Two Face, Riddler appear plus 3-D pin-ups featuring work by Art Adams, Dave Gibbons. Reprint from 1953 3-D comic included. With glasses						
	$1.50	***$4.50***	***$7.50***	**£1.00**	**£3.00**	**£5.00**
Title Value:	***$1.50***	***$4.50***	***$7.50***	**£1.00**	**£3.00**	**£5.00**

BATMAN ADVENTURES

DC Comics; 1 Nov 1992-36 Oct 1995

	$Good	$Fine	$N.Mint	£Good	£Fine	£N.Mint
1 based on US animated series, Ty Templeton art begins, bi-weekly						
	$1.00	***$3.00***	***$5.00***	**£0.60**	**£1.80**	**£3.00**
2	***$0.80***	***$2.40***	***$4.00***	**£0.40**	**£1.20**	**£2.00**

	$Good	$Fine	$N.Mint	£Good	£Fine	£N.Mint
3 Joker story and cover	$0.60	$1.80	$3.00	£0.30	£0.90	£1.50
4-5	$0.60	$1.80	$3.00	£0.30	£0.90	£1.50
6	$0.50	$1.50	$2.50	£0.25	£0.75	£1.25
7 pre-bagged with Batman vs. Man-Bat trading card	$1.60	$4.80	$8.00	£0.50	£1.50	£2.50
8-10	$0.50	$1.50	$2.50	£0.25	£0.75	£1.25
11-17	$0.40	$1.20	$2.00	£0.20	£0.60	£1.00
18 Batgirl appears	$0.40	$1.20	$2.00	£0.20	£0.60	£1.00
19-21	$0.40	$1.20	$2.00	£0.20	£0.60	£1.00
22 Two Face appears	$0.40	$1.20	$2.00	£0.20	£0.60	£1.00
23-24	$0.40	$1.20	$2.00	£0.20	£0.60	£1.00
25 48pgs, Superman guest-stars	$0.60	$1.80	$3.00	£0.30	£0.90	£1.50
26 Robin and Batgirl team-up	$0.40	$1.20	$2.00	£0.20	£0.60	£1.00
27-28	$0.40	$1.20	$2.00	£0.20	£0.60	£1.00
29 Talia returns	$0.40	$1.20	$2.00	£0.20	£0.60	£1.00
30	$0.40	$1.20	$2.00	£0.20	£0.60	£1.00
31 Alan Grant script	$0.40	$1.20	$2.00	£0.20	£0.60	£1.00
32-33	$0.40	$1.20	$2.00	£0.20	£0.60	£1.00
34-36 Catwoman appears	$0.35	$1.05	$1.75	£0.20	£0.60	£1.00
Title Value:	$17.65	$52.95	$88.00	£8.70	£26.10	£43.50

Batman: The Collected Adventures (Jan 1994)

Trade paperback reprints #1-6 with new wraparound cover				£0.80	£2.50	£4.00

Batman: The Collected Adventures (Jul 1994)

Trade paperback reprints #7-12 with new painted cover				£0.80	£2.50	£4.00

BATMAN ADVENTURES ANNUAL, THE

DC Comics; 1 Nov 1994-2 1995

	$Good	$Fine	$N.Mint	£Good	£Fine	£N.Mint
1 64pgs, Joker appears; Matt Wagner art featured	$0.80	$2.40	$4.00	£0.50	£1.50	£2.50
2 56pgs, Batman vs. Demon; Ra's Al Ghul appears	$0.80	$2.40	$4.00	£0.50	£1.50	£2.50
Title Value:	$1.60	$4.80	$8.00	£1.00	£3.00	£5.00

BATMAN ADVENTURES HOLIDAY SPECIAL, THE

DC Comics,OS; 1 Feb 1995

	$Good	$Fine	$N.Mint	£Good	£Fine	£N.Mint
1 ND 48pgs, Bruce Timm cover and art	$0.60	$1.80	$3.00	£0.40	£1.20	£2.00
Title Value:	$0.60	$1.80	$3.00	£0.40	£1.20	£2.00

BATMAN ADVENTURES, THE - MAD LOVE

DC Comics,OS; 1 Feb 1994; 1 Sep 1995

	$Good	$Fine	$N.Mint	£Good	£Fine	£N.Mint
1 64pgs, squarebound, origin of Harley Quinn	$0.80	$2.40	$4.00	£0.50	£1.50	£2.50
1 Prestige Format, ND 64pgs, with new painted cover by Bruce Timm	$1.00	$3.00	$5.00	£0.70	£2.10	£3.50
Title Value:	$1.80	$5.40	$9.00	£1.20	£3.60	£6.00

BATMAN AND OTHER DC CLASSICS

DC Comics,OS; nn Jan 1990

	$Good	$Fine	$N.Mint	£Good	£Fine	£N.Mint
nn ND giveaway advertising material from DC Trade paperbacks; reprints the origin of Batman from Batman #47 (1948)	$0.30	$0.90	$1.50	£0.20	£0.60	£1.00
Title Value:	$0.30	$0.90	$1.50	£0.20	£0.60	£1.00

BATMAN AND ROBIN ADVENTURES, THE

DC Comics; 1 Nov 1995-present

	$Good	$Fine	$N.Mint	£Good	£Fine	£N.Mint
1 based on US animated series, Two-Face appears	$0.35	$1.05	$1.75	£0.25	£0.75	£1.25
2 Two-Face appears	$0.35	$1.05	$1.75	£0.25	£0.75	£1.25
3 Riddler appears	$0.35	$1.05	$1.75	£0.25	£0.75	£1.25
4 Penguin appears	$0.35	$1.05	$1.75	£0.25	£0.75	£1.25
5 The Joker appears	$0.35	$1.05	$1.75	£0.25	£0.75	£1.25
6-9	$0.35	$1.05	$1.75	£0.25	£0.75	£1.25
10 Ra's Al Ghul appears	$0.35	$1.05	$1.75	£0.25	£0.75	£1.25
11	$0.35	$1.05	$1.75	£0.25	£0.75	£1.25
12 Bane appears	$0.35	$1.05	$1.75	£0.25	£0.75	£1.25
13 ND The Scarecrow appears	$0.35	$1.05	$1.75	£0.25	£0.75	£1.25
14 ND	$0.35	$1.05	$1.75	£0.25	£0.75	£1.25
15 ND Deadman appears	$0.35	$1.05	$1.75	£0.25	£0.75	£1.25
16 ND Catwoman and Catman appear	$0.35	$1.05	$1.75	£0.25	£0.75	£1.25
Title Value:	$5.60	$16.80	$28.00	£4.00	£12.00	£20.00

BATMAN AND ROBIN ADVENTURES ANNUAL

DC Comics; 1 Nov 1996-present

	$Good	$Fine	$N.Mint	£Good	£Fine	£N.Mint
1 ND	$0.60	$1.80	$3.00	£0.40	£1.20	£2.00
Title Value:	$0.60	$1.80	$3.00	£0.40	£1.20	£2.00

BATMAN AND THE OUTSIDERS

DC Comics; 1 Aug 1983-46 Jun 1987

(see Outsiders) (becomes Adventures of the Outsiders with issue #33)

	$Good	$Fine	$N.Mint	£Good	£Fine	£N.Mint
1 scarce in the U.K. Batman, Black Lightning, Katana, Halo, Geo-Force, Metamorpho begin	$0.40	$1.20	$2.00	£0.60	£1.80	£3.00
2 scarce in the U.K.	$0.30	$0.90	$1.50	£0.40	£1.20	£2.00
3-4	$0.30	$0.90	$1.50	£0.30	£0.90	£1.50
5 New Teen Titans X-over, Mando (higher quality) paper begins	$0.30	$0.90	$1.50	£0.30	£0.90	£1.50
6-10	$0.25	$0.75	$1.25	£0.20	£0.60	£1.00
11	$0.20	$0.60	$1.00	£0.15	£0.45	£0.75
12 origin Katana	$0.20	$0.60	$1.00	£0.15	£0.45	£0.75
13-21	$0.20	$0.60	$1.00	£0.15	£0.45	£0.75
22-32 Alan Davis art	$0.25	$0.75	$1.25	£0.20	£0.60	£1.00
33 Alan Davis art, title becomes Adventures of the Outsiders	$0.25	$0.75	$1.25	£0.20	£0.60	£1.00
34-36 Alan Davis and Paul Neary art	$0.25	$0.75	$1.25	£0.20	£0.60	£1.00
37-38	$0.20	$0.60	$1.00	£0.15	£0.45	£0.75
39 reprints from The Outsiders #1 onwards begin	$0.20	$0.60	$1.00	£0.15	£0.45	£0.75
40-46	$0.20	$0.60	$1.00	£0.15	£0.45	£0.75
Title Value:	$10.80	$32.40	$54.00	£9.05	£27.15	£45.25

BATMAN AND THE OUTSIDERS ANNUAL

DC Comics; 1 Sep 1984-2 Sep 1985

	$Good	$Fine	$N.Mint	£Good	£Fine	£N.Mint
1 Frank Miller/Jim Aparo cover	$0.30	$0.90	$1.50	£0.20	£0.60	£1.00
2 Metamorpho and Sapphire Stagg wed	$0.30	$0.90	$1.50	£0.20	£0.60	£1.00
Title Value:	$0.60	$1.80	$3.00	£0.40	£1.20	£2.00

BATMAN ANNUAL

National Periodical Publications; 1 Sep/Oct 1961-7 Jul 1964; 8 Oct 1982-present

	$Good	$Fine	$N.Mint	£Good	£Fine	£N.Mint
1 80pgs, classic reprints featuring re-telling of origin plus origin of The Bat-Cave from Detective #205	$67.50	$205.00	$620.00	£36.00	£105.00	£325.00
[Scarce in high grade - Very Fine+ or better]						
2 80pgs, classic reprints including 1st Bat-Marine from Batman #86, The Super Batman from #113; Batman calendar and back cover pin-up	$33.00	$100.00	$300.00	£15.50	£47.00	£140.00
3 80pgs, Joker cover/story, reprints include 1st Mad Hatter from Detective #230, 1st Mirror Man from Detective #213 and Two Face from Batman #68	$36.00	$105.00	$325.00	£15.50	£47.00	£140.00
4 80pgs, reprints include 1st Bat-Woman from Detective #233 and The First Batman from Detective #235	$15.50	$47.00	$140.00	£7.75	£23.00	£70.00
5 80pgs, "Strange Lives" reprints including Batman #110, #118, #119 and World's Finest #109; covers of Batman #1 and Detective #27 on the back	$15.50	$47.00	$140.00	£7.75	£23.00	£70.00
6 scarce in the U.K. 80pgs, reprints include Batman #91, #94 and Detective #255	$12.00	$37.00	$110.00	£5.50	£16.50	£50.00
7 80pgs, reprints include 1st Bat-Mite from Detective #267 and 1st original Bat-Girl from Batman #139	$11.50	$35.00	$105.00	£4.70	£14.00	£42.50
8	$0.90	$2.70	$4.50	£0.60	£1.80	£3.00
9 Nino/Paul Smith art, painted cover, high quality paper	$0.70	$2.10	$3.50	£0.60	£1.80	£3.00
10	$0.70	$2.10	$3.50	£0.60	£1.80	£3.00
11 Alan Moore story, John Byrne cover	$1.00	$3.00	$5.00	£0.80	£2.40	£4.00
12 Mike Baron story	$0.70	$2.10	$3.50	£0.50	£1.50	£2.50
13 LD in the U.K. 64pgs, squarebound, George Pratt pencils, Gray Morrow inks	$0.90	$2.70	$4.50	£0.60	£1.80	£3.00
14 follows on from Year One, Harvey Dent appears with origin Two-Face retold; Neal Adams cover	$0.80	$2.40	$4.00	£0.50	£1.50	£2.50
15 64pgs, Armageddon: 2001 tie-in, Joker/Catwoman/Anarky appear	$0.80	$2.40	$4.00	£0.50	£1.50	£2.50
15 2nd printing, Feb 1992	$0.50	$1.50	$2.50	£0.30	£0.90	£1.50
16 64pgs, Eclipso: The Darkness Within tie-in, Joker cover and story, Sam Kieth cover	$0.50	$1.50	$2.50	£0.30	£0.90	£1.50
17 64pgs, Bloodlines part 8, 1st appearance Decimator, continued in Justice League International Annual #4	$0.50	$1.50	$2.50	£0.30	£0.90	£1.50
18 64pgs, Elseworlds story by Doug Moench	$0.50	$1.50	$2.50	£0.30	£0.90	£1.50
19 56pgs, Year One, Batman vs. Scarecrow and origins told of both	$0.80	$2.40	$4.00	£0.50	£1.50	£2.50
20 Legends of the Dead Earth tie-in	$0.60	$1.80	$3.00	£0.40	£1.20	£2.00
Title Value:	$200.90	$605.70	$1789.50	£99.50	£295.90	£871.50

Note: Many 80pg Giants and Annuals from the early '60s, and in particular Batman Annual #1-7, have crinkled covers at the spine, (particularly #2) caused by uneven drying of the glue. Perfectly flat (and therefore Near Mint or Mint) copies are rare.

BATMAN ARCHIVES

DC Comics; nn Oct 1990; nn Jul 1991; nn 1992

(see Superman Archives)

	$Good	$Fine	$N.Mint	£Good	£Fine	£N.Mint
nn (1990) ND 306pgs, Hardcover; reprints Detective Comics #27-50 by Bob Kane and Jerry Robinson plus covers and ads	$7.50	$22.50	$37.50	£5.00	£15.00	£25.00
nn (1991) ND 288pgs, Hardcover; reprints Detective Comics #51-70 by Bob Kane and Jerry Robinson plus covers and ads	$7.50	$22.50	$37.50	£5.00	£15.00	£25.00
nn (1992) ND 224pgs, Hardcover; reprints Detective Comics #71-86 by Bob Kane and Jerry Robinson plus covers and ads	$7.50	$22.50	$37.50	£5.00	£15.00	£25.00
Title Value:	$22.50	$67.50	$112.50	£15.00	£45.00	£75.00

BATMAN BOOK AND RECORD SET

Power Records; PR-27, PR-30 1974

	$Good	$Fine	$N.Mint	£Good	£Fine	£N.Mint
PR-27 scarce in the U.K. features The Joker in a 20pg booklet with 45 rpm record	$2.05	$6.25	$12.50	£1.25	£3.75	£7.50
PR-30 scarce in the U.K. features Man-Bat in a 20pg booklet with 45 rpm record	$1.50	$4.50	$9.00	£1.00	£3.00	£6.00
Title Value:	$3.55	$10.75	$21.50	£2.25	£6.75	£13.50

VERY GENERAL PERCENTAGE CONVERSION CHART WHICH MAY BE USED TO CALCULATE LOW AND INBETWEEN GRADES:

BATMAN CHRONICLES, THE
DC Comics; 1 Summer 1995-present

Issue	$Good	$Fine	$N.Mint	£Good	£Fine	£N.Mint
1 ND 48pgs, three stories each issue; Huntress and Anarky appear, work by Alan Grant, Doug Moench and Bill Sienkiewicz (art and cover inks) feature	$0.60	$1.80	$3.00	£0.40	£1.20	£2.00
2 ND 48pgs, continued from Batman: Shadow of the Bat #42	$0.60	$1.80	$3.00	£0.40	£1.20	£2.00
3 ND The Riddler and Killer Croc appear; Brian Bolland cover	$0.60	$1.80	$3.00	£0.40	£1.20	£2.00
4 ND 48pgs, Hitman appears (lead into Hitman #1); Contagion storyline tie-in	$0.60	$1.80	$3.00	£0.40	£1.20	£2.00
5 ND origin Barbara Gordon as Oracle told in more detail; featured art includes Brian Stelfreeze and Howard Chaykin	$0.60	$1.80	$3.00	£0.40	£1.20	£2.00
6 ND features Curt Swan art (one of his last?) and cover by Mike Kaluta	$0.60	$1.80	$3.00	£0.40	£1.20	£2.00
7 ND Superman and the original Green Arrow appear in separate stories	$0.60	$1.80	$3.00	£0.40	£1.20	£2.00
Title Value:	$4.20	$12.60	$21.00	£2.80	£8.40	£14.00

Note: quarterly frequency and rotating creative teams

BATMAN COLLECTION, THE
DC Comics; nn Jul 1992; Vol 2 Aug 1992

Issue	$Good	$Fine	$N.Mint	£Good	£Fine	£N.Mint
nn Special Slipcase Set featuring Trade paperbacks Batman: The Dark Knight Returns, Batman: Year One, Batman: Arkham Asylum and Catwoman: Her Sister's Keeper; all latest printings as of date	$6.00	$18.00	$30.00	£4.00	£12.00	£20.00
2 (Volume 2), Special Slipcase Set featuring Trade paperbacks The Greatest Batman Stories Ever Told, Batman: The Cult and Batman: Gotham By Gaslight	$5.00	$15.00	$25.00	£3.50	£10.50	£17.50
Title Value:	$11.00	$33.00	$55.00	£7.50	£22.50	£37.50

BATMAN FAMILY
DC Comics; 1 Sep/Oct 1975-20 Oct/Nov 1978

(see Detective #481-483)

Issue	$Good	$Fine	$N.Mint	£Good	£Fine	£N.Mint
1 scarce in the U.K. 68pgs, Neal Adams reprint	$1.65	$5.00	$10.00	£1.25	£3.75	£7.50
2-4 68pgs	$1.00	$3.00	$6.00	£1.00	£3.00	£6.00
5 ND 52pgs	$1.00	$3.00	$6.00	£1.05	£3.25	£6.50
6 ND 52pgs, Joker appears	$1.05	$3.25	$6.50	£1.05	£3.25	£6.50
7 scarce in the U.K. 52pgs	$0.80	$2.50	$5.00	£0.90	£2.75	£5.50
8 scarce in the U.K. 52pgs, Catwoman cover	$0.80	$2.50	$5.00	£0.90	£2.75	£5.50
9 52pgs, 1st appearance Penguin's, Riddler's and Scarcecrow's daughters	$0.80	$2.50	$5.00	£0.80	£2.50	£5.00
10 52pgs	$0.80	$2.50	$5.00	£0.65	£2.00	£4.00
11 scarce in the U.K. 52pgs, Rogers art; 1st Commissioner Gordon and Alfred team-up	$0.80	$2.50	$5.00	£0.90	£2.75	£5.50
12-13 scarce in the U.K. 52pgs, Rogers art	$0.80	$2.50	$5.00	£0.90	£2.75	£5.50
14 scarce in the U.K. 52pgs	$0.80	$2.50	$5.00	£0.80	£2.50	£5.00
15 scarce in the U.K. 52pgs, Golden art	$0.80	$2.50	$5.00	£0.80	£2.50	£5.00
16 52pgs, Golden art	$0.80	$2.50	$5.00	£0.65	£2.00	£4.00
17 scarce in the U.K. 80pgs, Demon appears, Huntress arrives on Earth 1 from Earth 2, Golden art on Man-Bat	$0.80	$2.50	$5.00	£0.80	£2.50	£5.00
18 scarce in the U.K. 80pgs, Huntress, Staton and Golden art	$0.80	$2.50	$5.00	£0.80	£2.50	£5.00
19-20 ND scarce in the U.K. 80pgs, Huntress, Staton and Golden art	$0.80	$2.50	$5.00	£1.00	£3.00	£6.00
Title Value:	$17.90	$55.25	$110.50	£18.15	£55.50	£111.00

BATMAN FOREVER MOVIE ADAPTATION
DC Comics,OS Film; 1 Aug 1995

Issue	$Good	$Fine	$N.Mint	£Good	£Fine	£N.Mint
1 ND 64pgs, Prestige Edition, Denny O'Neil script, Michael Dutkiewicz art, painted cover by John Hanley	$1.00	$3.00	$5.00	£0.70	£2.10	£3.50
1 Newstand Edition, 64pgs, , as above with alternate cover by Michael Dutkiewicz	$0.70	$2.10	$3.50	£0.50	£1.50	£2.50
Title Value:	$1.70	$5.10	$8.50	£1.20	£3.60	£6.00

BATMAN GALLERY, THE
DC Comics,OS; 1 Sep 1992

Issue	$Good	$Fine	$N.Mint	£Good	£Fine	£N.Mint
1 ND collection of poster and promotional material by Frank Miller, McKean, Bolton, Todd McFarlane, Mazzucchelli, Mike Zeck etc; Joe Quesada cover	$0.50	$1.50	$2.50	£0.30	£0.90	£1.50
Title Value:	$0.50	$1.50	$2.50	£0.30	£0.90	£1.50

BATMAN GCPD
DC Comics,MS; 1 Aug 1996-4 Nov 1996

Issue	$Good	$Fine	$N.Mint	£Good	£Fine	£N.Mint
1-4 ND Chuck Dixon script, Jim Aparo and Bill Sienkiewicz art	$0.45	$1.35	$2.25	£0.30	£0.90	£1.50
Title Value:	$1.80	$5.40	$9.00	£1.20	£3.60	£6.00

BATMAN PIZZA HUT GIVEAWAY
DC Comics/Pizza Hut; nn 1977

(see Superman, Wonder Woman)

Issue	$Good	$Fine	$N.Mint	£Good	£Fine	£N.Mint
nn ND scarce in the U.K. Batman #122 and #123 reprinted in their entirety only different ads and Pizza Hut banner on cover. Cover colour differs from original on #123	$0.50	$1.50	$3.00	£0.80	£2.50	£5.00
Title Value:	$0.50	$1.50	$3.00	£0.80	£2.50	£5.00

BATMAN PLUS #1
DC Comics,OS; 1 Feb 1997

Issue	$Good	$Fine	$N.Mint	£Good	£Fine	£N.Mint
1 ND 48pgs, Batman and Arsenal team up	$0.60	$1.80	$3.00	£0.40	£1.20	£2.00
Title Value:	$0.60	$1.80	$3.00	£0.40	£1.20	£2.00

BATMAN RETURNS MOVIE ADAPTATION
DC Comics; 1 Aug 1992

Issue	$Good	$Fine	$N.Mint	£Good	£Fine	£N.Mint
1 Newstand Edition 64pgs	$0.60	$1.80	$3.00	£0.40	£1.20	£2.00
1 Prestige Format, ND 64pgs, , adaptation of Batman film sequel	$1.00	$3.00	$5.00	£0.70	£2.10	£3.50
Title Value:	$1.60	$4.80	$8.00	£1.10	£3.30	£5.50

BATMAN SPECIAL
DC Comics,OS; 1 Jun 1984

Issue	$Good	$Fine	$N.Mint	£Good	£Fine	£N.Mint
1 48pgs, Mike Golden art	$1.00	$3.00	$5.00	£0.70	£2.10	£3.50
Title Value:	$1.00	$3.00	$5.00	£0.70	£2.10	£3.50

BATMAN SPECTACULAR
DC Comics; 15 Summer 1978

(DC Special Series #15)

Issue	$Good	$Fine	$N.Mint	£Good	£Fine	£N.Mint
15 ND scarce in the U.K. 68pgs, Rogers, Nasser, Golden art	$1.50	$4.50	$9.00	£1.00	£3.00	£6.00
Title Value:	$1.50	$4.50	$9.00	£1.00	£3.00	£6.00

BATMAN VS THE INCREDIBLE HULK
DC/Marvel Co-production,OS Tabloid; nn Autumn 1981

(DC Special Series #27)

Issue	$Good	$Fine	$N.Mint	£Good	£Fine	£N.Mint
nn ND 68pgs, Garcia Lopez art; Joker appears	$1.25	$3.75	$7.50	£1.00	£3.00	£6.00
Title Value:	$1.25	$3.75	$7.50	£1.00	£3.00	£6.00
(May 1996), ND 64pgs, reprints tabloid in comic form with gold metallic border around cover				£0.50	£1.50	£2.50

BATMAN VS. PREDATOR
DC Comics,MS; 1 Jan 1992-3 Mar 1992

Issue	$Good	$Fine	$N.Mint	£Good	£Fine	£N.Mint
1 script by Dave Gibbons, art by Andy and Adam Kubert, cover by Chris Warner	$0.50	$1.50	$2.50	£0.30	£0.90	£1.50

Batman Adventures #1

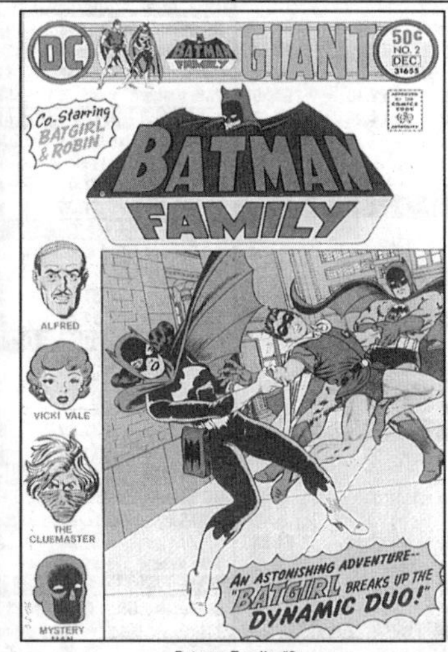

Batman Family #2

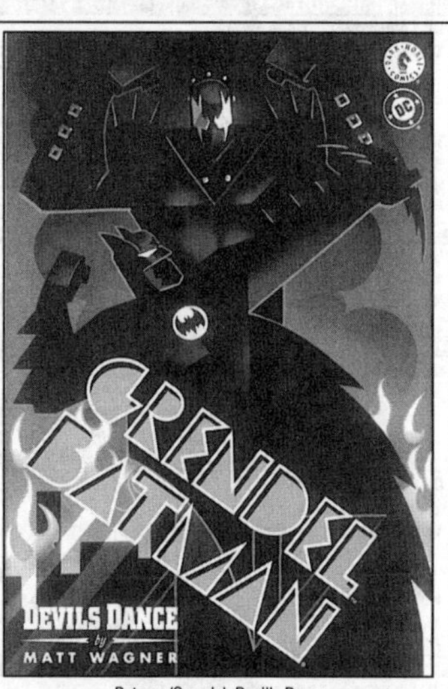

Batman/Grendel; Devil's Dance

	$Good	$Fine	$N.Mint	£Good	£Fine	£N.Mint
1 Prestige Format, ND; as above but painted cover by Arthur Suydam and uncut sheet of eight trading cards	$1.00	$3.00	$5.00	£0.70	£2.10	£3.50
2 script by Dave Gibbons, art by Andy and Adam Kubert, cover by Chris Warner	$0.40	$1.20	$2.00	£0.25	£0.75	£1.25
2 Prestige Format, ND; as above but painted cover by Arthur Suydam and 16 pin-up pages	$1.00	$3.00	$5.00	£0.70	£2.10	£3.50
3 script by Dave Gibbons, art by Andy and Adam Kubert, cover by Chris Warner	$0.40	$1.20	$2.00	£0.25	£0.75	£1.25
3 Prestige Format, ND; as above but painted cover by Arthur Suydam and eight trading cards	$1.00	$3.00	$5.00	£0.70	£2.10	£3.50
Title Value:	$4.30	$12.90	$21.50	£2.90	£8.70	£14.50
Trade paperback (Feb 1993) 128pgs, reprints mini-series with new introduction and new wraparound cover by Dave Gibbons				£0.75	£2.25	£3.75

BATMAN VS. PREDATOR II: BLOODMATCH

DC Comics,MS; 1 Dec 1994-4 Mar 1995

	$Good	$Fine	$N.Mint	£Good	£Fine	£N.Mint
1-4 ND Doug Moench script, Paul Gulacy and Terry Austin art	$0.50	$1.50	$2.50	£0.30	£0.90	£1.50
Title Value:	$2.00	$6.00	$10.00	£1.20	£3.60	£6.00

Note: this mini-series is co-published by DC and Dark Horse Comics

	$Good	$Fine	$N.Mint	£Good	£Fine	£N.Mint
Batman Vs. Predator II: Bloodmatch (Dec 1995) Trade paperback reprints mini-series with new Simon Bisley cover				£0.90	£2.70	£4.50

BATMAN, SHADOW OF THE

DC Comics,MS; 1 Dec 1985-5 Apr 1986

	$Good	$Fine	$N.Mint	£Good	£Fine	£N.Mint
1 very scarce in the U.K. Rogers reprints	$1.20	$3.60	$6.00	£1.20	£3.60	£6.00
2-3 very scarce in the U.K. Rogers reprints	$0.80	$2.40	$4.00	£1.00	£3.00	£5.00
4 very scarce in the U.K. Rogers reprints, classic Joker	$1.00	$3.00	$5.00	£1.00	£3.00	£5.00
5 very scarce in the U.K. Rogers reprints	$0.80	$2.40	$4.00	£1.00	£3.00	£5.00
Title Value:	$4.60	$13.80	$23.00	£5.20	£15.60	£26.00

Note: reprints classic Detective #471-478 by Englehart/Rogers/Austin. New cover art on each issue.

BATMAN/CAPTAIN AMERICA

DC Comics/Marvel Comics Group/Elseworlds,OS; 1 Feb 1997

	$Good	$Fine	$N.Mint	£Good	£Fine	£N.Mint
1 ND 64pgs, John Byrne script and art	$1.20	$3.60	$6.00	£0.80	£2.40	£4.00
Title Value:	$1.20	$3.60	$6.00	£0.80	£2.40	£4.00

BATMAN/DEADMAN HARDCOVER GRAPHIC NOVEL

DC Comics,OS; nn Feb 1997

	$Good	$Fine	$N.Mint	£Good	£Fine	£N.Mint
nn ND 96pgs, James Robinson script, painted art and cover by John Estes	$5.00	$15.00	$25.00	£3.00	£9.00	£15.00
Title Value:	$5.00	$15.00	$25.00	£3.00	£9.00	£15.00

BATMAN/DEMON

DC Comics,OS; 1 Aug 1996

	$Good	$Fine	$N.Mint	£Good	£Fine	£N.Mint
1 ND 48pgs, Alan Grant script, David Roach art	$1.00	$3.00	$5.00	£0.70	£2.10	£3.50
Title Value:	$1.00	$3.00	$5.00	£0.70	£2.10	£3.50

BATMAN/DRACULA: RED RAIN GRAPHIC NOVEL

DC Comics,OS; nn Jan 1992

	$Good	$Fine	$N.Mint	£Good	£Fine	£N.Mint
nn Hardcover ND scarce in the U.K. 96pgs, Doug Moench script and Kelley Jones art	$8.00	$24.00	$40.00	£5.00	£15.00	£25.00
nn Softcover ND new cover by Kelley Jones	$2.00	$6.00	$10.00	£1.30	£3.90	£6.50
Title Value:	$10.00	$30.00	$50.00	£6.30	£18.90	£31.50

BATMAN/GREEN ARROW: THE POISON TOMORROW

DC Comics,OS; 1 Nov 1992

	$Good	$Fine	$N.Mint	£Good	£Fine	£N.Mint
1 ND 64pgs, Poison Ivy and Black Canary appear	$1.00	$3.00	$5.00	£0.70	£2.10	£3.50
Title Value:	$1.00	$3.00	$5.00	£0.70	£2.10	£3.50

BATMAN/GRENDEL

DC Comics,MS; 1,2 Aug 1993

	$Good	$Fine	$N.Mint	£Good	£Fine	£N.Mint
1 ND 48pgs, squarebound, Matt Wagner script and art; sub-titled "Devil's Riddle", bi-weekly	$1.00	$3.00	$5.00	£0.70	£2.10	£3.50
2 ND 48pgs, squarebound, Matt Wagner script and art; sub-titled "Devil's Masque", bi-weekly	$1.00	$3.00	$5.00	£0.70	£2.10	£3.50
Title Value:	$2.00	$6.00	$10.00	£1.40	£4.20	£7.00
Batman/Grendel Comico Edition (Apr 1996) ND both issues of the original series, each with signed certificate; 100 copies of each only				£6.50	£19.50	£32.50

BATMAN/GRENDEL II: DEVIL'S BONES

Dark Horse,MS; 1 Jun 1996-2 Jul 1996

	$Good	$Fine	$N.Mint	£Good	£Fine	£N.Mint
1-2 ND Matt Wagner script and art	$1.00	$3.00	$5.00	£0.70	£2.10	£3.50
Title Value:	$2.00	$6.00	$10.00	£1.40	£4.20	£7.00

BATMAN/HOUDINI: THE DEVIL'S WORKSHOP

DC Comics/Elseworlds,OS; 1 Oct 1993

	$Good	$Fine	$N.Mint	£Good	£Fine	£N.Mint
1 ND 64pgs, squarebound; Howard Chaykin and John Francis Moore script, Mark Chiarello art	$1.00	$3.00	$5.00	£0.70	£2.10	£3.50
Title Value:	$1.00	$3.00	$5.00	£0.70	£2.10	£3.50

BATMAN/JUDGE DREDD: JUDGEMENT ON GOTHAM

DC Comics,OS; 1 Dec 1991

(see British section)

	$Good	$Fine	$N.Mint	£Good	£Fine	£N.Mint
1 ND 64pgs, story by Alan Grant and John Wagner, art by Simon Bisley, Judge Anderson and The Scarecrow appear	$1.20	$3.60	$6.00	£0.80	£2.40	£4.00
1 2nd printing, ND Aug 1992	$1.00	$3.00	$5.00	£0.70	£2.10	£3.50
Title Value:	$2.20	$6.60	$11.00	£1.50	£4.50	£7.50

BATMAN/JUDGE DREDD: THE ULTIMATE RIDDLE

DC Comics,OS; 1 Sep 1995

	$Good	$Fine	$N.Mint	£Good	£Fine	£N.Mint
1 ND 48pgs, Alan Grant script, Carl Critchlow and Dermot Power art; Critchlow painted cover	$1.00	$3.00	$5.00	£0.70	£2.10	£3.50
Title Value:	$1.00	$3.00	$5.00	£0.70	£2.10	£3.50

BATMAN/JUDGE DREDD: VENDETTA IN GOTHAM

DC Comics,OS; 1 Dec 1993

	$Good	$Fine	$N.Mint	£Good	£Fine	£N.Mint
1 ND 48pgs, squarebound; Alan Grant/John Wagner script, Cam Kennedy art, Mike Mignola cover	$1.00	$3.00	$5.00	£0.70	£2.10	£3.50
Title Value:	$1.00	$3.00	$5.00	£0.70	£2.10	£3.50

BATMAN/PUNISHER: LAKE OF FIRE

DC Comics,OS; 1 Aug 1994

	$Good	$Fine	$N.Mint	£Good	£Fine	£N.Mint
1 ND 48pgs, squarebound, Barry Kitson cover and art	$0.60	$1.80	$3.00	£0.40	£1.20	£2.00
Title Value:	$0.60	$1.80	$3.00	£0.40	£1.20	£2.00

BATMAN/SPAWN: WAR DEVIL

DC Comics,OS; 1 May 1994

	$Good	$Fine	$N.Mint	£Good	£Fine	£N.Mint
1 ND 48pgs, Doug Moench, Chuck Dixon and Alan Grant script, Klaus Janson art	$1.00	$3.00	$5.00	£0.70	£2.10	£3.50
Title Value:	$1.00	$3.00	$5.00	£0.70	£2.10	£3.50

BATMAN: ARKHAM ASYLUM

DC Comics; nn Nov 1989

	$Good	$Fine	$N.Mint	£Good	£Fine	£N.Mint
1 DC Hardcover, ND; Grant Morrison script, Dave McKean painted art and cover	$4.50	$13.50	$22.50	£3.00	£9.00	£15.00
2 Titan Hardcover, ND; Grant Morrison script, Dave McKean painted art and cover	$4.00	$12.00	$20.00	£2.50	£7.50	£12.50
Title Value:	$8.50	$25.50	$42.50	£5.50	£16.50	£27.50

Note: there were some production problems on the DC copy which resulted in defective bindings causing loose pages.

	$Good	$Fine	$N.Mint	£Good	£Fine	£N.Mint
Softcover (May 1990) new painted cover by Dave McKean				£1.80	£5.40	£9.00

BATMAN: BIRTH OF THE DEMON

DC Comics,OS; nn Jan 1993

	$Good	$Fine	$N.Mint	£Good	£Fine	£N.Mint
nn Hardcover ND scarce in the U.K. 112pgs, origin of Ra'S Al Ghul; Denny O'Neill script, Norm Breyfogle art	$4.00	$12.00	$20.00	£3.00	£9.00	£15.00
nn Softcover ND (Sep 1993)	$2.40	$7.00	$12.00	£1.60	£4.80	£8.00
Title Value:	$6.40	$19.00	$32.00	£4.60	£13.80	£23.00

BATMAN: BLACK AND WHITE

DC Comics,MS; 1 Jun 1996-4 Sep 1996

	$Good	$Fine	$N.Mint	£Good	£Fine	£N.Mint
1 ND 48pgs, selection of stories featuring art by Joe Kubert, Howard Chaykin and Ted McKeever; Jim Lee cover; black and white	$0.80	$2.40	$4.00	£0.70	£2.10	£3.50
2 ND 48pgs, features work by Neil Gaiman and Simon Bisley, Richard Corben and Kent Williams; Frank Miller cover; black and white	$0.60	$1.80	$3.00	£0.50	£1.50	£2.50
3 ND features work by Bill Sienkiewicz, Matt Wagner and Klaus Janson, Barry Windsor-Smith cover; black and white	$0.60	$1.80	$3.00	£0.40	£1.20	£2.00
4 ND features work by Brian Bolland, Katsuhiro Otomo, Kevin Nowlan and Brian Stelfreeze, Alex Toth cover; black and white	$0.60	$1.80	$3.00	£0.40	£1.20	£2.00
Title Value:	$2.60	$7.80	$13.00	£2.00	£6.00	£10.00

BATMAN: BLACKGATE

DC Comics,OS; 1 Jan 1997

	$Good	$Fine	$N.Mint	£Good	£Fine	£N.Mint
1 ND Joe Staton and James Hodgkins art	$0.80	$2.40	$4.00	£0.50	£1.50	£2.50
Title Value:	$0.80	$2.40	$4.00	£0.50	£1.50	£2.50

BATMAN: BLOODSTORM

DC Comics/Elseworlds,OS; nn Jan 1995

	$Good	$Fine	$N.Mint	£Good	£Fine	£N.Mint
1 ND 96pgs, hardcover; Doug Moench script, Kelley Jones and John Beatty art	$4.50	$13.50	$22.50	£3.00	£9.00	£15.00
Title Value:	$4.50	$13.50	$22.50	£3.00	£9.00	£15.00
Batman: Bloodstorm (Jul 1995) Softcover version of the above with cover by Kelley Jones				£1.70	£5.10	£8.50

BATMAN: BRIDE OF THE DEMON

DC Comics,OS; nn Jan 1991

	$Good	$Fine	$N.Mint	£Good	£Fine	£N.Mint
nn ND 96pgs, Hardcover sequel to Son of the Demon; Barr and Grindberg	$4.00	$12.00	$20.00	£2.50	£7.50	£12.50
Title Value:	$4.00	$12.00	$20.00	£2.50	£7.50	£12.50

BATMAN: BROTHERHOOD OF THE BAT

DC Comics/Elseworlds,OS; 1 Nov 1995

	$Good	$Fine	$N.Mint	£Good	£Fine	£N.Mint
1 ND Doug Moench script with a variety of Batman artists in a story centred around different costume designs	$1.00	$3.00	$5.00	£0.65	£1.95	£3.25
Title Value:	$1.00	$3.00	$5.00	£0.65	£1.95	£3.25

BATMAN: CASTLE OF THE BAT

DC Comics,OS; 1 Dec 1994

	$Good	$Fine	$N.Mint	£Good	£Fine	£N.Mint
1 ND 64pgs, Bo Hampton art	$1.00	$3.00	$5.00	£0.70	£2.10	£3.50
Title Value:	$1.00	$3.00	$5.00	£0.70	£2.10	£3.50

BATMAN: CATWOMAN DEFIANT

DC Comics,OS; 1 Jul 1992

	$Good	$Fine	$N.Mint	£Good	£Fine	£N.Mint
1 ND 48pgs, foil finish logo, cover painted by Brian Stelfreeze which inter-locks with cover of Batman: Penguin Triumphant	$1.00	$3.00	$5.00	£0.70	£2.10	£3.50
Title Value:	$1.00	$3.00	$5.00	£0.70	£2.10	£3.50

BATMAN: DARK ALLEGIANCES

DC Comics/Elseworlds,OS; 1 Feb 1996

	$Good	$Fine	$N.Mint	£Good	£Fine	£N.Mint
1 ND 64pgs, Howard Chaykin script and art	$1.20	$3.60	$6.00	£0.80	£2.40	£4.00
Title Value:	$1.20	$3.60	$6.00	£0.80	£2.40	£4.00

BATMAN: DARK JOKER – THE WILD

DC Comics,OS; 1 Dec 1993; 1 Sep 1994

	$Good	$Fine	$N.Mint	£Good	£Fine	£N.Mint
1 Hardcover, 96pgs, with holographic foil enhanced dust-jacket	$5.00	$15.00	$25.00	£3.50	£10.50	£17.50

	$Good	$Fine	$N.Mint	£Good	£Fine	£N.Mint
1 Softcover, 96pgs, (Sep 1994)	*$2.00*	*$6.00*	*$10.00*	£1.30	£3.90	£6.50
Title Value:	*$7.00*	*$21.00*	*$35.00*	£4.80	£14.40	£24.00

BATMAN: DARK KNIGHT ARCHIVES

DC Comics; 1 Jul 1992; 2 Apr 1995

	$Good	$Fine	$N.Mint	£Good	£Fine	£N.Mint
1 reprints Batman #1-4 featuring the first appearances of The Joker and Catwoman	*$7.50*	*$22.50*	*$37.50*	£5.00	£15.00	£25.00
2 reprints Batman #5-8	*$12.00*	*$36.00*	*$60.00*	£8.00	£24.00	£40.00
Title Value:	*$19.50*	*$58.50*	*$97.50*	£13.00	£39.00	£65.00

BATMAN: DARK KNIGHT GALLERY

DC Comics,OS; 1 Jan 1996

	$Good	$Fine	$N.Mint	£Good	£Fine	£N.Mint
1 ND pin-ups by Klaus Jansen, Bill Sienkiewicz, Barry Kitson and others	*$0.70*	*$2.10*	*$3.50*	£0.50	£1.50	£2.50
Title Value:	*$0.70*	*$2.10*	*$3.50*	£0.50	£1.50	£2.50

BATMAN: DEATH OF INNOCENTS

DC Comics,OS; 1 Dec 1996

	$Good	$Fine	$N.Mint	£Good	£Fine	£N.Mint
1 ND 64pgs, Denny O'Neill script, Joe Staton and Bill Sienkiewicz art	*$0.80*	*$2.40*	*$4.00*	£0.50	£1.50	£2.50
Title Value:	*$0.80*	*$2.40*	*$4.00*	£0.50	£1.50	£2.50

BATMAN: DIGITAL JUSTICE

DC Comics,OS; nn 1990

	$Good	$Fine	$N.Mint	£Good	£Fine	£N.Mint
nn ND Hardcover 110pgs; computer-generated art by Pepe Moreno	*$5.00*	*$15.00*	*$25.00*	£2.00	£6.00	£10.00
Title Value:	*$5.00*	*$15.00*	*$25.00*	£2.00	£6.00	£10.00

BATMAN: FULL CIRCLE

DC Comics,OS; 1 Jul 1991

	$Good	$Fine	$N.Mint	£Good	£Fine	£N.Mint
1 ND 64pgs, Alan Davis art	*$1.00*	*$3.00*	*$5.00*	£0.70	£2.10	£3.50
Title Value:	*$1.00*	*$3.00*	*$5.00*	£0.70	£2.10	£3.50

BATMAN: GHOSTS- LEGEND OF THE DARK KNIGHT HALLOWEEN SPECIAL

DC Comics,OS; 1 Dec 1995

	$Good	$Fine	$N.Mint	£Good	£Fine	£N.Mint
1 ND 48pgs, Jeph Loeb script, Tim Sale art	*$1.00*	*$3.00*	*$5.00*	£0.70	£2.10	£3.50
Title Value:	*$1.00*	*$3.00*	*$5.00*	£0.70	£2.10	£3.50

BATMAN: GORDON'S LAW

DC Comics,MS; 1 Dec 1996-4 Mar 1997

	$Good	$Fine	$N.Mint	£Good	£Fine	£N.Mint
1-4 ND Chuck Dixon script, Klaus Janson art; stars Commissoner Gordon	*$0.40*	*$1.20*	*$2.00*	£0.25	£0.75	£1.25
Title Value:	*$1.60*	*$4.80*	*$8.00*	£1.00	£3.00	£5.00

BATMAN: GOTHAM BY GASLIGHT

DC Comics,OS; 1 Jan 1990

	$Good	$Fine	$N.Mint	£Good	£Fine	£N.Mint
1 ND Mike Mignola, P.Craig Russell art; Batman meets Jack the Ripper in non-continuity story in "Elseworlds" series	*$0.90*	*$2.70*	*$4.50*	£0.60	£1.80	£3.00
1 Titan Books Edition	*$0.80*	*$2.40*	*$4.00*	£0.50	£1.50	£2.50
Title Value:	*$1.70*	*$5.10*	*$8.50*	£1.10	£3.30	£5.50

BATMAN: GOTHAM NIGHTS

DC Comics,MS; 1 Mar 1992-4 Jun 1992

	$Good	$Fine	$N.Mint	£Good	£Fine	£N.Mint
1-4 Anton Furst's designs from Batman film used throughout	*$0.25*	*$0.75*	*$1.25*	£0.15	£0.45	£0.75
Title Value:	*$1.00*	*$3.00*	*$5.00*	£0.60	£1.80	£3.00

BATMAN: GOTHAM NIGHTS II

DC Comics,MS; 1 Mar 1995-4 Jun 1995

	$Good	$Fine	$N.Mint	£Good	£Fine	£N.Mint
1-4	*$0.40*	*$1.20*	*$2.00*	£0.25	£0.75	£1.25
Title Value:	*$1.60*	*$4.80*	*$8.00*	£1.00	£3.00	£5.00

BATMAN: GREATEST STORIES EVER TOLD

DC Comics; nn May 1990; Vol 2 Jul 1992

	$Good	$Fine	$N.Mint	£Good	£Fine	£N.Mint
nn Hardcover 1st printing ND; classic reprints including Batman #1, #47, #156 and Detective Comics #31, #32, #211 and #500	*$9.00*	*$27.00*	*$45.00*	£5.00	£15.00	£25.00
nn Hardcover 2nd printing ND (Aug 1990)	*$7.00*	*$21.00*	*$35.00*	£4.00	£12.00	£20.00
2 Softcover, ND; classic reprints including Batman #1 (1st Catwoman) and Detective Comics #58 (1st Penguin)	*$3.00*	*$9.00*	*$15.00*	£2.00	£6.00	£10.00
Title Value:	*$22.00*	*$66.00*	*$110.00*	£13.00	£39.00	£65.00

BATMAN: IN DARKEST KNIGHT

DC Comics/Elseworlds,OS; 1 Feb 1994

	$Good	$Fine	$N.Mint	£Good	£Fine	£N.Mint
1 ND 48pgs, squarebound, Mike Barr script and Jerry Bingham art, embossed logo	*$1.00*	*$3.00*	*$5.00*	£0.70	£2.10	£3.50
Title Value:	*$1.00*	*$3.00*	*$5.00*	£0.70	£2.10	£3.50

BATMAN: JAZZ

DC Comics,MS; 1 Apr 1995-3 Jun 1995

	$Good	$Fine	$N.Mint	£Good	£Fine	£N.Mint
1-3 ND Gerard Jones script, Mark Badger art	*$0.50*	*$1.50*	*$2.50*	£0.30	£0.90	£1.50
Title Value:	*$1.50*	*$4.50*	*$7.50*	£0.90	£2.70	£4.50

BATMAN: KELLOG'S AND POPTARTS GIVEAWAYS

Kellogs/National Periodical Publications; nn 1966

	$Good	$Fine	$N.Mint	£Good	£Fine	£N.Mint
nn ND rare in the U.K. 6 different small size comics (3" x 5.5")	*$4.25*	*$12.50*	*$30.00*	£3.55	£10.50	£25.00
Title Value:	*$4.25*	*$12.50*	*$30.00*	£3.55	£10.50	£25.00

Titles are as follows:

The Case of Batman II, The Catwoman's Catnapping Caper, The Joker's Happy Victims, The Mad Hatter's Hat Crimes, The Man in the Iron Mask, The Penguin's Fowl Play

BATMAN: KNIGHT GALLERY

DC Comics,OS; 1 Oct 1995

	$Good	$Fine	$N.Mint	£Good	£Fine	£N.Mint
1 ND designs for Batman costume by Neal Adams, Norm Breyfogle, Jim Aparo, George Perez and others	*$0.80*	*$2.40*	*$4.00*	£0.50	£1.50	£2.50
Title Value:	*$0.80*	*$2.40*	*$4.00*	£0.50	£1.50	£2.50

BATMAN: KNIGHTFALL

Multi-part storyline that leads to the breaking of Batman by the villain Bane and the introduction of the new Batman of Jean Paul Valley, formerly known as Azrael. The parts are as follows: **Part 1** - Batman #492; **Part 2** - Detective Comics #659; **Part 3** - Batman #493; **Part 4** - Detective Comics #660; **Part 5** - Batman #494; **Part 6** - Detective Comics #661; **Part 7** - Batman #495; **Part 8** - Detective Comics #662; **Part 9** - Batman #496; **Part 10** - Detective Comics #663; **Part 11** - Batman #497; **Part 12** - Detective Comics #664; **Part 13** - Showcase '93 #7 **Part 14** - Showcase '93 #8; **Part 15** - Batman #498; **Part 16** - Detective Comics #665; **Part 17** - Batman #499; **Part 18** - Detecive Comics #666; **Part 19** - Batman #500

BATMAN: LEGENDS OF THE DARK KNIGHT

DC Comics; 0 Oct 1994; 1 Nov 1989-present

	$Good	$Fine	$N.Mint	£Good	£Fine	£N.Mint
0 (Oct 1994) Zero Hour X-over, exploring the psyche of Batman	*$0.40*	*$1.20*	*$2.00*	£0.25	£0.75	£1.25
1 LD in the U.K. George Pratt cover, available in four different colour variations (see note below)	*$1.00*	*$3.00*	*$5.00*	£0.70	£2.10	£3.50
2 George Pratt cover	*$0.60*	*$1.80*	*$3.00*	£0.40	£1.20	£2.00
3-4 George Pratt covers	*$0.50*	*$1.50*	*$2.50*	£0.30	£0.90	£1.50
5 George Pratt cover	*$0.50*	*$1.50*	*$2.50*	£0.30	£0.90	£1.50
6 Grant Morrison story "Gothic" begins	*$0.60*	*$1.80*	*$3.00*	£0.40	£1.20	£2.00
7-10 Gothic	*$0.50*	*$1.50*	*$2.50*	£0.30	£0.90	£1.50
11-15 Prey by Moench, art by Gulacy/Austin	*$0.50*	*$1.50*	*$2.50*	£0.30	£0.90	£1.50
16 LD in the U.K. Venom by O'Neill, art by Von Eeden/Garcia Lopez	*$0.90*	*$2.70*	*$4.50*	£0.60	£1.80	£3.00
17 LD in the U.K. Venom by O'Neill, art by Von Eeden/Garcia Lopez	*$0.60*	*$1.80*	*$3.00*	£0.40	£1.20	£2.00
18-20 Venom by O'Neil, art by Von Eeden/Garcia Lopez	*$0.50*	*$1.50*	*$2.50*	£0.30	£0.90	£1.50
21-23 Faith	*$0.40*	*$1.20*	*$2.00*	£0.25	£0.75	£1.25
24-26 Flyer by Howard Chaykin and Gil Kane	*$0.40*	*$1.20*	*$2.00*	£0.25	£0.75	£1.25
27 Destroyer part 2, continued in Detective Comics #641	*$0.40*	*$1.20*	*$2.00*	£0.25	£0.75	£1.25
28 Faces part 1, Matt Wagner script and art begins	*$0.40*	*$1.20*	*$2.00*	£0.25	£0.75	£1.25
29-30 Faces	*$0.40*	*$1.20*	*$2.00*	£0.25	£0.75	£1.25
31 Brent Anderson art, bi-weekly	*$0.40*	*$1.20*	*$2.00*	£0.25	£0.75	£1.25
32-34 Blades, bi-weekly	*$0.40*	*$1.20*	*$2.00*	£0.25	£0.75	£1.25
35 Destiny story, Viking Prince appears, Bo Hampton cover/art, bi-weekly	*$0.40*	*$1.20*	*$2.00*	£0.25	£0.75	£1.25
36 Destiny story, Viking Prince appears, Bo Hampton cover/art	*$0.40*	*$1.20*	*$2.00*	£0.25	£0.75	£1.25
37	*$0.40*	*$1.20*	*$2.00*	£0.25	£0.75	£1.25
38 Bat-Mite returns	*$0.40*	*$1.20*	*$2.00*	£0.25	£0.75	£1.25
39-40 Mask story, Bryan Talbot script and art	*$0.40*	*$1.20*	*$2.00*	£0.25	£0.75	£1.25
41 previews Scarlett series	*$0.40*	*$1.20*	*$2.00*	£0.25	£0.75	£1.25
42-43 Hothouse story, Poison Ivy appears	*$0.40*	*$1.20*	*$2.00*	£0.25	£0.75	£1.25
44-45	*$0.40*	*$1.20*	*$2.00*	£0.25	£0.75	£1.25
46 Russ Heath art	*$0.40*	*$1.20*	*$2.00*	£0.25	£0.75	£1.25
47 Catwoman vs. Catman, Russ Heath art	*$0.40*	*$1.20*	*$2.00*	£0.25	£0.75	£1.25
48-49 Russ Heath art, bi-weekly	*$0.40*	*$1.20*	*$2.00*	£0.25	£0.75	£1.25
50 64pgs, the 1st case of Batman vs. The Joker, holo-grafix foil cover, pin-up gallery	*$0.80*	*$2.40*	*$4.00*	£0.50	£1.50	£2.50
51	*$0.40*	*$1.20*	*$2.00*	£0.25	£0.75	£1.25
52-53 Tao by Alan Grant and Arthur Ranson	*$0.40*	*$1.20*	*$2.00*	£0.25	£0.75	£1.25
54 Mike Mignola art	*$0.40*	*$1.20*	*$2.00*	£0.25	£0.75	£1.25
55-57 Mike McMahon art	*$0.40*	*$1.20*	*$2.00*	£0.25	£0.75	£1.25
58 John Higgins cover and art	*$0.40*	*$1.20*	*$2.00*	£0.25	£0.75	£1.25
59-60 Quarry story	*$0.40*	*$1.20*	*$2.00*	£0.25	£0.75	£1.25
61 Quarry story, continued in Robin #7	*$0.40*	*$1.20*	*$2.00*	£0.25	£0.75	£1.25
62 Knightsend part 4, continued in Robin #8; Mignola cover	*$0.40*	*$1.20*	*$2.00*	£0.25	£0.75	£1.25
63 Knightsend part 10 (conclusion), continued in Robin #9	*$0.40*	*$1.20*	*$2.00*	£0.25	£0.75	£1.25
64 Jamie Delano and Chris Bachalo one-off story	*$0.40*	*$1.20*	*$2.00*	£0.25	£0.75	£1.25
65-68 Joker appears	*$0.40*	*$1.20*	*$2.00*	£0.25	£0.75	£1.25
69-70 Mike Zeck art	*$0.40*	*$1.20*	*$2.00*	£0.25	£0.75	£1.25
71-73 Werewolf story, John Watkiss painted cover	*$0.40*	*$1.20*	*$2.00*	£0.25	£0.75	£1.25
74-75 Ted McKeever cover and art	*$0.40*	*$1.20*	*$2.00*	£0.25	£0.75	£1.25
76-78 Scott Hampton script and art	*$0.40*	*$1.20*	*$2.00*	£0.25	£0.75	£1.25
79 Mark Millar script, Steve Yeowell and Dick Giordano art	*$0.40*	*$1.20*	*$2.00*	£0.25	£0.75	£1.25

	$Good	$Fine	$N.Mint	£Good	£Fine	£N.Mint
80-85	$0.40	$1.20	$2.00	£0.25	£0.75	£1.25
86-88 Conspiracy story						
	$0.40	$1.20	$2.00	£0.25	£0.75	£1.25
89-90 ND Clayface appears						
	$0.40	$1.20	$2.00	£0.25	£0.75	£1.25
91-93 ND Garth Ennis script, Will Simpson art						
	$0.40	$1.20	$2.00	£0.25	£0.75	£1.25
Title Value:	$41.20	$123.60	$206.00	£25.75	£77.25	£128.75

Note: series designed to contain 5 issue stories by a variety of artists and writers, harder-hitting but no Mature Readers label. Four different protective covers produced for #1: blue/orange/yellow/pink. The blue cover seems to be the most popular.

	£Good	£Fine	£N.Mint
Batman: Gothic (Jul 1992)			
Trade paperback, reprints issues #6-10, new cover by Klaus Janson	£1.40	£4.20	£7.00
Batman: Prey (Dec 1992)			
Trade paperback, reprints issues #11-15, new cover by Paul Gulacy	£1.50	£4.50	£7.50
Batman: Shaman (Feb 1993)			
Trade paperback, reprints issues #1-5, new painted cover by George Pratt	£1.50	£4.50	£7.50
Batman: The Collected Legends of the Dark Knight (Apr 1994)			
Trade paperback, reprints issues #32-34, #38 and #42,43	£1.70	£5.10	£8.50
Batman: Faces (Aug 1995)			
Trade paperback reprints issues #28-30, Matt Wagner painted cover	£1.30	£3.90	£6.50
Batman: Legends of the Dark Knight (Jun 1996)			
Trade paperback reprints issues #39,40,50,52-54 with new page by Bryan Talbot	£2.00	£6.00	£10.00

BATMAN: LEGENDS OF THE DARK KNIGHT ANNUAL

DC Comics; 1 Dec 1991-present

	$Good	$Fine	$N.Mint	£Good	£Fine	£N.Mint
1 64pgs, Joker, Two Face, Penguin appear, Mignola cover						
	$0.80	$2.40	$4.00	£0.50	£1.50	£2.50
2 64pgs	$0.80	$2.40	$4.00	£0.50	£1.50	£2.50
3 64pgs, Bloodlines (Wave Two) part 21, 1st appearance Cardinal Sin and Samaritan, continued in Team Titans Annual #1						
	$0.70	$2.10	$3.50	£0.45	£1.35	£2.25
4 64pgs, Elseworlds						
	$0.70	$2.10	$3.50	£0.45	£1.35	£2.25
5 64pgs, Year One, origin of Man-Bat featured						
	$0.80	$2.40	$4.00	£0.50	£1.50	£2.50
6 48pgs, Legends of the Dead Earth story						
	$0.60	$1.80	$3.00	£0.40	£1.20	£2.00
Title Value:	$4.40	$13.20	$22.00	£2.80	£8.40	£14.00

BATMAN: LEGENDS OF THE DARK KNIGHT HALLOWEEN SPECIAL

DC Comics,OS; 1 Dec 1993

	$Good	$Fine	$N.Mint	£Good	£Fine	£N.Mint
1 ND 48pgs, squarebound; Tim Sale art, embossed cover						
	$1.20	$3.60	$6.00	£0.80	£2.40	£4.00
Title Value:	$1.20	$3.60	$6.00	£0.80	£2.40	£4.00

BATMAN: MADNESS

DC Comics,OS; 1 Nov 1994

	$Good	$Fine	$N.Mint	£Good	£Fine	£N.Mint
1 ND 48pgs, Jeph Loeb and Tim Sale; follow up Halloween Special						
	$0.90	$2.70	$4.50	£0.60	£1.80	£3.00
Title Value:	$0.90	$2.70	$4.50	£0.60	£1.80	£3.00

BATMAN: MAN-BAT

DC Comics/Elseworlds,MS; 1 Oct 1995-3 Dec 1995

	$Good	$Fine	$N.Mint	£Good	£Fine	£N.Mint
1-3 ND 48pgs, Jamie Delano script, John Bolton painted art						
	$1.00	$3.00	$5.00	£0.70	£2.10	£3.50
Title Value:	$3.00	$9.00	$15.00	£2.10	£6.30	£10.50

BATMAN: MASK OF THE PHANTASM

DC Comics,OS; 1 Feb 1994

	$Good	$Fine	$N.Mint	£Good	£Fine	£N.Mint
1 64pgs, squarebound; adaptation of the Twentieth Century Fox Batman animated film						
	$1.00	$3.00	$5.00	£0.70	£2.10	£3.50
Title Value:	$1.00	$3.00	$5.00	£0.70	£2.10	£3.50

BATMAN: MASQUE

DC Comics/Elseworlds; nn Mar 1997

	$Good	$Fine	$N.Mint	£Good	£Fine	£N.Mint
nn ND 64pgs, Mike Grell script and art						
	$1.20	$3.60	$6.00	£0.80	£2.40	£4.00
Title Value:	$1.20	$3.60	$6.00	£0.80	£2.40	£4.00

BATMAN: MASTER OF THE FUTURE

DC Comics/Elseworlds,OS; 1 Jan 1992

	$Good	$Fine	$N.Mint	£Good	£Fine	£N.Mint
1 ND 48pgs	$1.00	$3.00	$5.00	£0.70	£2.10	£3.50
Title Value:	$1.00	$3.00	$5.00	£0.70	£2.10	£3.50

BATMAN: MITEFALL

DC Comics,OS; 1 Mar 1995

	$Good	$Fine	$N.Mint	£Good	£Fine	£N.Mint
1 ND 48pgs, Alan Grant script, Kev O'Neill art						
	$1.00	$3.00	$5.00	£0.70	£2.10	£3.50
Title Value:	$1.00	$3.00	$5.00	£0.70	£2.10	£3.50

BATMAN: MOVIE ADAPTATION

DC Comics; nn Aug 1989

	$Good	$Fine	$N.Mint	£Good	£Fine	£N.Mint
nn Prestige Format ND; Denny O'Neill script, Jerry Ordway art						
	$0.75	$2.25	$3.75	£0.50	£1.50	£2.50
nn Standard Format ND; Denny O'Neill script, Jerry Ordway art						
	$0.50	$1.50	$2.50	£0.35	£1.05	£1.75
Title Value:	$1.25	$3.75	$6.25	£0.85	£2.55	£4.25

BATMAN: PENGUIN TRIUMPHANT

DC Comics,OS; 1 Jul 1992

	$Good	$Fine	$N.Mint	£Good	£Fine	£N.Mint
1 ND 48pgs, foil finish logo, cover painted by Brian Stelfreeze which interlocks with cover of Batman: Catwoman Defiant						
	$1.00	$3.00	$5.00	£0.70	£2.10	£3.50
Title Value:	$1.00	$3.00	$5.00	£0.70	£2.10	£3.50

BATMAN: RIDDLER - THE RIDDLE FACTORY

DC Comics,OS; nn Aug 1995

	$Good	$Fine	$N.Mint	£Good	£Fine	£N.Mint
nn ND 48pgs, Matt Wagner script, Dave Taylor art, painted cover by Brian Stelfreeze						
	$1.00	$3.00	$5.00	£0.70	£2.10	£3.50
Title Value:	$1.00	$3.00	$5.00	£0.70	£2.10	£3.50

BATMAN: RUN RIDDLER RUN

DC Comics,MS; 1 Jun 1992-3 Aug 1992

	$Good	$Fine	$N.Mint	£Good	£Fine	£N.Mint
1-3 ND 48pgs, Batman vs. Riddler by Gerard Jones and Mark Badger						
	$1.00	$3.00	$5.00	£0.70	£2.10	£3.50
Title Value:	$3.00	$9.00	$15.00	£2.10	£6.30	£10.50

BATMAN: SCAR OF THE BAT

DC Comics,OS; 1 Mar 1996

	$Good	$Fine	$N.Mint	£Good	£Fine	£N.Mint
1 ND Max Allan Collins script, Eduardo Barreto art						
	$1.00	$3.00	$5.00	£0.70	£2.10	£3.50
Title Value:	$1.00	$3.00	$5.00	£0.70	£2.10	£3.50

BATMAN: SEDUCTION OF THE GUN

DC Comics,OS; 1 Feb 1993

	$Good	$Fine	$N.Mint	£Good	£Fine	£N.Mint
1 ND 64pgs, deals with gun-control issue						
	$0.50	$1.50	$2.50	£0.30	£0.90	£1.50
Title Value:	$0.50	$1.50	$2.50	£0.30	£0.90	£1.50

BATMAN: SHADOW OF THE BAT

DC Comics; 0 Oct 1994; 1 Jul 1992-present

	$Good	$Fine	$N.Mint	£Good	£Fine	£N.Mint
0 (Oct 1994) Zero Hour X-over, origin retold; continued from Batman #0						
	$0.50	$1.50	$2.50	£0.30	£0.90	£1.50
1 Alan Grant script begins, painted covers by Brian Stelfreeze begin, bi-weekly						
	$0.50	$1.50	$2.50	£0.30	£0.90	£1.50
1 Collectors Edition, ND , pre-bagged, features a pull-out poster, a pop-up and blueprint plans of Arham Asylum and a book-mark						
	$0.80	$2.40	$4.00	£0.50	£1.50	£2.50
2 bi-weekly	$0.40	$1.20	$2.00	£0.25	£0.75	£1.25
3-4 Nightwing appears, bi-weekly						
	$0.40	$1.20	$2.00	£0.25	£0.75	£1.25
5 Black Spider appears						
	$0.40	$1.20	$2.00	£0.25	£0.75	£1.25
6 Catwoman appears						
	$0.40	$1.20	$2.00	£0.25	£0.75	£1.25
7 The Misfits story begins, intro Chancer						
	$0.40	$1.20	$2.00	£0.25	£0.75	£1.25
8 The Misfits story, Brian Stelfreeze cover; $1.75 cover begins						
	$0.40	$1.20	$2.00	£0.25	£0.75	£1.25
9 The Misfits story, Brian Stelfreeze cover						
	$0.40	$1.20	$2.00	£0.25	£0.75	£1.25
10 Brian Stelfreeze cover						
	$0.40	$1.20	$2.00	£0.25	£0.75	£1.25
11-13 Brian Stelfreeze cover						
	$0.30	$0.90	$1.50	£0.20	£0.60	£1.00
14-15 Gotham Freaks story						
	$0.30	$0.90	$1.50	£0.20	£0.60	£1.00
16-18 The God of Fear, Brian Stelfreeze cover, bi-weekly						
	$0.30	$0.90	$1.50	£0.20	£0.60	£1.00
19 Knightquest: The Crusade part 2, continued in Batman #501; Brian Stelfreeze cover						
	$0.30	$0.90	$1.50	£0.20	£0.60	£1.00
20 Knightquest: The Crusade part 4, continued in Detective Comics #668; Brian Stelfreeze cover						
	$0.30	$0.90	$1.50	£0.20	£0.60	£1.00
21-24 Knightquest: The Crusade, Brian Stelfreeze cover						
	$0.30	$0.90	$1.50	£0.20	£0.60	£1.00
25 Knightquest: The Crusade, Brian Stelfreeze cover; Joe Public appears						
	$0.30	$0.90	$1.50	£0.20	£0.60	£1.00
26-27 Knightquest: The Crusade, Brian Stelfreeze cover						
	$0.30	$0.90	$1.50	£0.20	£0.60	£1.00
28 Knightquest: The Crusade, Brian Stelfreeze cover; continued in Detective Comics #675						
	$0.30	$0.90	$1.50	£0.20	£0.60	£1.00
29 48pgs, Knightsend part 2, continued in Detective Comics #676						
	$0.40	$1.20	$2.00	£0.25	£0.75	£1.25
30 Knightsend part 8, continued in Detective Comics #677						
	$0.40	$1.20	$2.00	£0.25	£0.75	£1.25
31 Zero Hour X-over						
	$0.40	$1.20	$2.00	£0.25	£0.75	£1.25
32-33 Two Face appears						
	$0.40	$1.20	$2.00	£0.25	£0.75	£1.25
34	$0.40	$1.20	$2.00	£0.25	£0.75	£1.25
35 The Troika part 2, continued in Detective Comics #682						
	$0.40	$1.20	$2.00	£0.25	£0.75	£1.25
35 Collectors Edition, ND , embossed black cover						
	$0.60	$1.80	$3.00	£0.40	£1.20	£2.00
36 Black Canary appears						
	$0.40	$1.20	$2.00	£0.25	£0.75	£1.25
37	$0.40	$1.20	$2.00	£0.25	£0.75	£1.25
38 The Joker appears						
	$0.40	$1.20	$2.00	£0.25	£0.75	£1.25
39 upgraded coated paper stock (Miraweb Format) begins						
	$0.40	$1.20	$2.00	£0.25	£0.75	£1.25
40-41	$0.40	$1.20	$2.00	£0.25	£0.75	£1.25
42 continued in Batman Chronicles #2						
	$0.40	$1.20	$2.00	£0.25	£0.75	£1.25
43 The Secret of the Universe part 1, continued in Catwoman #26; painted cover by Brian Stelfreeze						
	$0.40	$1.20	$2.00	£0.25	£0.75	£1.25
44 The Secret of the Universe part 3, continued from Catwoman #26; painted cover by Brian Stelfreeze						
	$0.40	$1.20	$2.00	£0.25	£0.75	£1.25
45-47	$0.40	$1.20	$2.00	£0.25	£0.75	£1.25
48 Contagion part 1, continued in Detective Comics #695						
	$0.50	$1.50	$2.50	£0.30	£0.90	£1.50
49 Contagion part 7, continued in Detective Comics #696						
	$0.40	$1.20	$2.00	£0.25	£0.75	£1.25
50 features all villains that have appeared in this title so far						

	$Good	$Fine	$N.Mint	£Good	£Fine	£N.Mint
	$0.40	$1.20	$2.00	£0.25	£0.75	£1.25
51-52	$0.40	$1.20	$2.00	£0.25	£0.75	£1.25
53 Legacy Prelude 1, continued in Batman #533						
	$0.40	$1.20	$2.00	£0.25	£0.75	£1.25
54 Legacy part 4, continued in Robin #32						
	$0.40	$1.20	$2.00	£0.25	£0.75	£1.25
55-57	$0.40	$1.20	$2.00	£0.25	£0.75	£1.25
58 ND Poison Ivy appears						
	$0.40	$1.20	$2.00	£0.25	£0.75	£1.25
59-60 ND	$0.40	$1.20	$2.00	£0.25	£0.75	£1.25
Title Value:	$24.30	$72.90	$121.50	£15.40	£46.20	£77.00
Batman: The Last Arkham (Jan 1996)						
Trade paperback reprints issues #1-4, new Brian Stelfreeze cover				£1.70	£5.10	£8.50

BATMAN: SHADOW OF THE BAT ANNUAL

DC Comics; 1 Jul 1993-present

	$Good	$Fine	$N.Mint	£Good	£Fine	£N.Mint
1 64pgs, Bloodlines part 3, 1st appearance Joe Public, continued in Flash Annual #6						
	$0.80	$2.40	$4.00	£0.50	£1.50	£2.50
2 64pgs, Elseworlds story; Alan Grant script						
	$0.80	$2.40	$4.00	£0.50	£1.50	£2.50
3 56pgs, Year One; Poison Ivy appears, painted cover by Brian Stelfreeze						
	$0.80	$2.40	$4.00	£0.50	£1.50	£2.50
4 48pgs, Legends of the Dead Earth story						
	$0.60	$1.80	$3.00	£0.40	£1.20	£2.00
Title Value:	$3.00	$9.00	$15.00	£1.90	£5.70	£9.50

BATMAN: SON OF THE DEMON

DC Comics,OS; nn Sep 1987

(see Batman: Bride of the Demon)

	$Good	$Fine	$N.Mint	£Good	£Fine	£N.Mint
nn Hardcover ND scarce in the U.K. 80pgs, with dust-jacket						
	$10.00	$30.00	$50.00	£6.00	£18.00	£30.00
nn Softcover ND 80pgs, new cover art						
	$2.40	$7.00	$12.00	£1.50	£4.50	£7.50
Title Value:	$12.40	$37.00	$62.00	£7.50	£22.50	£37.50

Note: 1700 hardback copies were signed by writer and artist. These would be valued at approximately 30% more than the hardback price above

BATMAN: SWORD OF AZRAEL

DC Comics,MS; 1 Oct 1992-4 Jan 1993

	$Good	$Fine	$N.Mint	£Good	£Fine	£N.Mint
1 Joe Queseda cover and art begins, wraparound three-part gatefold cover						
	$2.00	$6.00	$10.00	£1.00	£3.00	£5.00
2	$1.60	$4.80	$8.00	£0.90	£2.70	£4.50
3	$1.40	$4.20	$7.00	£0.80	£2.40	£4.00
4 continued in Batman #488						
	$1.40	$4.20	$7.00	£0.80	£2.40	£4.00
Title Value:	$6.40	$19.20	$32.00	£3.50	£10.50	£17.50

BATMAN: THE ANIMATED MOVIE

DC Comics,OS; 1 Feb 1994

	$Good	$Fine	$N.Mint	£Good	£Fine	£N.Mint
1 64pgs, squarebound, adaptation of animated film "The Mask of the Phantasm"						
	$0.60	$1.80	$3.00	£0.40	£1.20	£2.00
1 Prestige Format, 64pgs, - squarebound, adaptation of animated film "The Mask of the Phantasm", painted cover	$1.00	$3.00	$5.00	£0.70	£2.10	£3.50
Title Value:	$1.60	$4.80	$8.00	£1.10	£3.30	£5.50

BATMAN: THE BLUE, THE GREY AND THE BAT

DC Comics/Elseworlds,OS; 1 Jan 1993

	$Good	$Fine	$N.Mint	£Good	£Fine	£N.Mint
1 ND 64pgs, story set during the American Civil War, parchment-style covers						
	$1.00	$3.00	$5.00	£0.70	£2.10	£3.50
Title Value:	$1.00	$3.00	$5.00	£0.70	£2.10	£3.50

BATMAN: THE CULT

DC Comics,MS; 1 Sep 1988-4 Dec 1988

	$Good	$Fine	$N.Mint	£Good	£Fine	£N.Mint
1 ND 2nd DC embossed cover; Jim Starlin script, Bernie Wrightson art begins						
	$1.40	$4.20	$7.00	£1.00	£3.00	£5.00
2 ND scarce in the U.K.						
	$1.00	$3.00	$5.00	£1.00	£3.00	£5.00
3 ND	$1.00	$3.00	$5.00	£0.80	£2.40	£4.00
4 ND some pages bound out of sequence						
	$0.80	$2.40	$4.00	£0.80	£2.40	£4.00
Title Value:	$4.20	$12.60	$21.00	£3.60	£10.80	£18.00

Note: 48pgs, Dark Knight format, UV (glossy) coated.

	£Good	£Fine	£N.Mint
Trade paperback (Mar 1991), new cover painting by Berni Wrightson	£1.40	£4.20	£7.00

BATMAN: THE DAILIES

DC Comics; 1 Jan 1991-3 1991

(see Batman: The Sunday Classics)

	$Good	$Fine	$N.Mint	£Good	£Fine	£N.Mint
1 reprints daily newspaper strips from 25/10/43 to 28/10/44 plus features						
	$1.80	$5.25	$9.00	£1.20	£3.60	£6.00
2 reprints daily newspaper strips from 30/10/44 to 24/11/45 plus features						
	$1.80	$5.25	$9.00	£1.20	£3.60	£6.00
3 reprints daily newpaper strips from 26/11/45 to 2/11/46 plus features						
	$1.80	$5.25	$9.00	£1.20	£3.60	£6.00
Title Value:	$5.40	$15.75	$27.00	£3.60	£10.80	£18.00
Limited Hardcover Edition (Feb 1992), all three volumes collected into a slipcase				£7.50	£22.50	£37.50
Batman: The Dailies 1943-1946 Hardcover Signed & Numbered (Feb 1995) signed by the five surviving Batman creators				£20.00	£60.00	£100.00

BATMAN: THE DARK KNIGHT RETURNS

DC Comics,MS; 1 Mar 1986-4 1986

	$Good	$Fine	$N.Mint	£Good	£Fine	£N.Mint
1 ND Frank Miller story/art begins						
	$4.00	$12.00	$20.00	£3.20	£9.50	£16.00
1 2nd printing ND	$1.00	$3.00	$5.00	£0.80	£2.40	£4.00
1 3rd printing ND	$0.80	$2.40	$4.00	£0.60	£1.80	£3.00
2 ND Carrie Kelly (female) becomes new Robin						
	$3.00	$9.00	$15.00	£1.60	£4.80	£8.00
2 2nd printing, ND (see note below)						
	$0.80	$2.40	$4.00	£0.60	£1.80	£3.00
2 3rd printing ND	$0.60	$1.80	$3.00	£0.50	£1.50	£2.50
3 ND death of The Joker						
	$1.40	$4.20	$7.00	£1.00	£3.00	£5.00
3 2nd printing ND	$0.60	$1.80	$3.00	£0.50	£1.50	£2.50
4 ND Alfred dies	$1.40	$4.20	$7.00	£0.80	£2.40	£4.00
Title Value:	$13.60	$40.80	$68.00	£9.60	£28.70	£48.00
Hardcover (1986), with dustjacket, ND signed & numbered (4,000 copies)				£30.00	£90.00	£150.00
Hardcover (1986), with dustjacket, ND Trade Edition				£6.00	£18.00	£30.00
Trade paperback, Warner Books Edition, ND scarce in the U.K., reprints #1-4 with corrections				£1.80	£5.40	£9.00
Trade paperback, as above, DC Edition ND				£1.75	£5.25	£8.75
Trade paperback, as above, Titan (UK) Edition, Alan Moore intro (7 printings available)				£1.60	£4.80	£8.00
Batman: The Dark Knight Returns 10th Anniversary Edition (Dec 1996) ND 224pgs with new sketches, art and text. The set also includes a Dark Knight returns Sketchbook, a bound copy of the script for issue #1 and a bound collection of press clippings about the original series				£13.00	£39.00	£65.00
Batman: The Dark Knight Returns 10th Anniversary Hardcover (Dec 1996) ND 224pgs with new art and sketches				£6.00	£18.00	£30.00

Note: due to a printer's error, the indicia of issue 2 has no mention of first and second prints; however, they can be identified as follows: Issue 2 (1st print) has a slight grey "ghosting" around the ears of the bat-shadow on the inside front cover; this had been corrected for the second print, which is noticeably crisper. The 3rd print of issue 2 is clearly marked as such.

BATMAN: THE HOLY TERROR

DC Comics/Elseworlds,OS; 1 Oct 1991

	$Good	$Fine	$N.Mint	£Good	£Fine	£N.Mint
1 ND 48pgs, 1st "Elseworlds Series" where major characters have alternative adventures						
	$1.00	$3.00	$5.00	£0.70	£2.10	£3.50
Title Value:	$1.00	$3.00	$5.00	£0.70	£2.10	£3.50

Batman; Legends of the Dark Knight #50

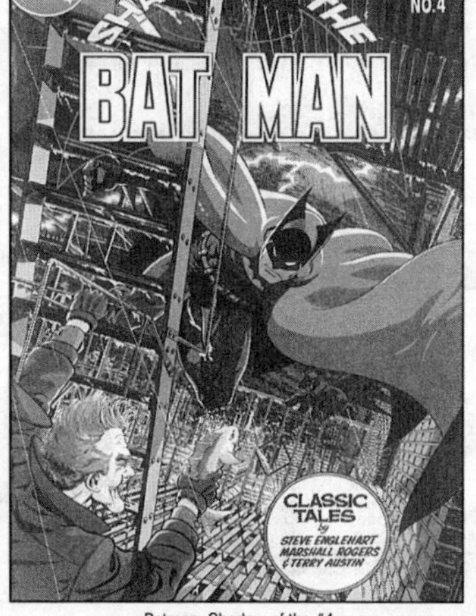

Batman, Shadow of the #4

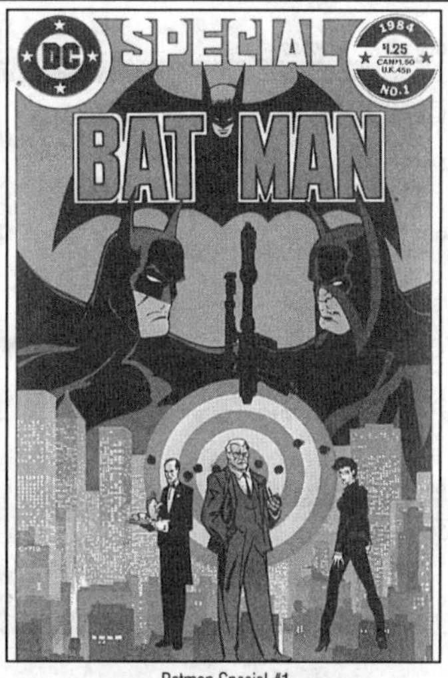

Batman Special #1

BATMAN: THE KILLING JOKE

DC Comics,OS; nn 1988

Issue	$Good	$Fine	$N.Mint	£Good	£Fine	£N.Mint
nn ND 48pgs, 1st DC embossed logo (green), more details concerning the origin of the Joker; Alan Moore script, Brian Bolland art	*$1.60*	*$4.80*	*$8.00*	£1.20	£3.60	£6.00
nn 2nd printing ND 48pgs, (green logo)	*$1.00*	*$3.00*	*$5.00*	£0.80	£2.40	£4.00
nn 3rd printing ND 48pgs, (green logo)	*$0.90*	*$2.70*	*$4.50*	£0.60	£1.80	£3.00
nn 4th printing ND 48pgs, (green logo)	*$0.80*	*$2.40*	*$4.00*	£0.60	£1.80	£3.00
nn 5th printing ND 48pgs, (blue logo)	*$0.60*	*$1.80*	*$3.00*	£0.50	£1.50	£2.50
nn 6th printing ND 48pgs, (pink logo)	*$0.60*	*$1.80*	*$3.00*	£0.50	£1.50	£2.50
nn 7th printing ND 48pgs, (light green logo)	*$0.60*	*$1.80*	*$3.00*	£0.50	£1.50	£2.50
nn 8th printing ND 48pgs, (silver logo)	*$0.60*	*$1.80*	*$3.00*	£0.50	£1.50	£2.50
nn Titan Edition (U.K) 48pgs, (green logo)	*$0.60*	*$1.80*	*$3.00*	£0.50	£1.50	£2.50
nn Titan Edition (U.K.) 2nd printing 48pgs, (pink logo)	*$0.60*	*$1.80*	*$3.00*	£0.40	£1.20	£2.00
Title Value:	*$7.90*	*$23.70*	*$39.50*	£6.10	£18.30	£30.50

Note: Prestige Format, UV (glossy) coated cover.

BATMAN: THE LAST ANGEL

DC Comics,OS; 1 Nov 1994

Issue	$Good	$Fine	$N.Mint	£Good	£Fine	£N.Mint
1 ND 96pgs, squarebound, Catwoman and The Joker appear; Eric Lustbader script, Lee Moder and Scott Hanna art	*$2.40*	*$7.00*	*$12.00*	£1.60	£4.80	£8.00
Title Value:	*$2.40*	*$7.00*	*$12.00*	£1.60	£4.80	£8.00

BATMAN: THE LONG HALLOWEEN

DC Comics,MS; 1 Dec 1996-present

Issue	$Good	$Fine	$N.Mint	£Good	£Fine	£N.Mint
1 ND 48pgs, Jeph Loeb script and Tim Sale covers and art begins	*$1.00*	*$3.00*	*$5.00*	£0.70	£2.10	£3.50
2 ND	*$0.60*	*$1.80*	*$3.00*	£0.40	£1.20	£2.00
3 ND The Joker appears	*$0.60*	*$1.80*	*$3.00*	£0.40	£1.20	£2.00
4-5 ND	*$0.60*	*$1.80*	*$3.00*	£0.40	£1.20	£2.00
Title Value:	*$3.40*	*$10.20*	*$17.00*	£2.30	£6.90	£11.50

BATMAN: THE SUNDAY CLASSICS

DC Comics; nn 1994

(see Batman: The Dailes)

Issue	$Good	$Fine	$N.Mint	£Good	£Fine	£N.Mint
nn ND 208pgs, reprints Sunday paper strips from 1943-1946	*$5.00*	*$15.00*	*$25.00*	£3.50	£10.50	£17.50
Title Value:	*$5.00*	*$15.00*	*$25.00*	£3.50	£10.50	£17.50
Batman: The Sunday Classics 1943-1946 Hardcover Signed & Numbered (Feb 1995), 208pgs, signed and numbered by the five surviving Batman creators				£20.00	£60.00	£100.00

BATMAN: THE ULTIMATE EVIL

DC Comics,MS; 1 Dec 1995-2 Jan 1996

Issue	$Good	$Fine	$N.Mint	£Good	£Fine	£N.Mint
1-2 ND 48pgs, adaptation of Andrew Vachss' novel; Denys Cowan and Prentis Rollins art	*$1.20*	*$3.60*	*$6.00*	£0.80	£2.40	£4.00
Title Value:	*$2.40*	*$7.20*	*$12.00*	£1.60	£4.80	£8.00

BATMAN: TWO-FACE - CRIME AND PUNISHMENT

DC Comics,OS; nn Aug 1995

Issue	$Good	$Fine	$N.Mint	£Good	£Fine	£N.Mint
nn ND 48pgs, J.M. DeMatteis script, Scott McDaniel art painted cover by Brian Stelfreeze	*$1.00*	*$3.00*	*$5.00*	£0.70	£2.10	£3.50
Title Value:	*$1.00*	*$3.00*	*$5.00*	£0.70	£2.10	£3.50

BATMAN: TWO-FACE STRIKES TWICE

DC Comics,MS; 1 Dec 1993-2 Jan 1994

Issue	$Good	$Fine	$N.Mint	£Good	£Fine	£N.Mint
1-2 ND 48pgs, flip-book format with Golden Age story with cover by Dick Sprang and Modern Age story with cover by Daerrick Gross	*$1.00*	*$3.00*	*$5.00*	£0.70	£2.10	£3.50
Title Value:	*$2.00*	*$6.00*	*$10.00*	£1.40	£4.20	£7.00

BATMAN: UNTOLD LEGEND OF THE

DC Comics,MS; 1 Jul 1980-3 Sep 1980

Issue	$Good	$Fine	$N.Mint	£Good	£Fine	£N.Mint
1 Joker on cover, John Byrne art	*$1.00*	*$3.00*	*$5.00*	£0.80	£2.40	£4.00
2 scarce in the U.K.	*$0.80*	*$2.40*	*$4.00*	£0.70	£2.10	£3.50
3	*$0.70*	*$2.10*	*$3.50*	£0.60	£1.80	£3.00
Title Value:	*$2.50*	*$7.50*	*$12.50*	£2.10	£6.30	£10.50
MPI Audio Edition (1980), same issues with stiffer card covers, featuring Golden and Silver Age Batman covers inside. Each issue came with a 30 minute audio cassette of that part of the story. Smaller than standard comic size. ND				£1.00	£3.00	£5.00

BATMAN: VENGEANCE OF BANE

DC Comics,OS; 1 Jan 1993

Issue	$Good	$Fine	$N.Mint	£Good	£Fine	£N.Mint
1 ND 64pgs, 1st appearance of Bane; ties in with "Venom" story from Batman: Legends of the Dark Knight	*$3.20*	*$9.50*	*$16.00*	£2.00	£6.00	£10.00
1 2nd printing ND 64pgs	*$1.00*	*$3.00*	*$5.00*	£0.50	£1.50	£2.50
Title Value:	*$4.20*	*$12.50*	*$21.00*	£2.50	£7.50	£12.50

BATMAN: VENGEANCE OF BANE II - THE REDEMPTION

DC Comics,OS; 1 Oct 1995

Issue	$Good	$Fine	$N.Mint	£Good	£Fine	£N.Mint
1 ND Graham Nolan and Eduardo Barreto art	*$0.80*	*$2.40*	*$4.00*	£0.50	£1.50	£2.50
Title Value:	*$0.80*	*$2.40*	*$4.00*	£0.50	£1.50	£2.50

BATPAC SPECIAL

National Periodical Publications; B-6 Jun 1966

Issue	$Good	$Fine	$N.Mint	£Good	£Fine	£N.Mint
6 rare in the U.K. Batman #181, JLA #45, Metal Men #20, World's Finest #158 in sealed plastic bag attached to illustrated header card; priced 47 cents	*$10.50*	*$32.00*	*$75.00*	£7.00	£21.00	£50.00
Title Value:	*$10.50*	*$32.00*	*$75.00*	£7.00	£21.00	£50.00

Note: not distributed on U.K. news-stands

BATS, CATS AND CADILLACS

Now Comics; 1 1990-6 1991

Issue	$Good	$Fine	$N.Mint	£Good	£Fine	£N.Mint
1-6 ND	*$0.30*	*$0.90*	*$1.50*	£0.20	£0.60	£1.00
Title Value:	*$1.80*	*$5.40*	*$9.00*	£1.20	£3.60	£6.00

BATS, CATS AND CADILLACS ANNUAL

Innovation; 1 May 1991

Issue	$Good	$Fine	$N.Mint	£Good	£Fine	£N.Mint
1 ND 48pgs	*$0.60*	*$1.80*	*$3.00*	£0.40	£1.20	£2.00
Title Value:	*$0.60*	*$1.80*	*$3.00*	£0.40	£1.20	£2.00

BATTLE

Atlas/Marvel Comics Group; 63 Nov 1959-70 Jun 1960

(Atlas Comics company title 1-62)

Issue	$Good	$Fine	$N.Mint	£Good	£Fine	£N.Mint
63 ND scarce in the U.K. Steve Ditko art	*$7.00*	*$21.00*	*$50.00*	£4.25	£12.50	£30.00
64 ND scarce in the U.K. Jack Kirby art	*$7.00*	*$21.00*	*$50.00*	£4.25	£12.50	£30.00
65-66 ND scarce in the U.K. Jack Kirby art	*$6.25*	*$19.00*	*$45.00*	£3.55	£10.50	£25.00
67 ND scarce in the U.K. part Jack Kirby art	*$5.50*	*$17.00*	*$40.00*	£3.20	£9.50	£22.50
68 ND scarce in the U.K. part Jack Kirby and Steve Ditko art	*$5.50*	*$17.00*	*$40.00*	£3.20	£9.50	£22.50
69 ND scarce in the U.K. Jack Kirby art	*$6.25*	*$19.00*	*$45.00*	£3.55	£10.50	£25.00
70 rare in the U.K. Jack Kirby and Steve Ditko art	*$7.75*	*$23.50*	*$55.00*	£5.00	£15.00	£35.00
Title Value:	*$51.50*	*$156.50*	*$370.00*	£30.55	£90.50	£215.00

Note: all Ditko, Kirby art throughout.

BATTLE ANGEL ALITA

Viz Communications,MS; 1 Sep 1992-9 May 1993

Issue	$Good	$Fine	$N.Mint	£Good	£Fine	£N.Mint
1-9 ND Yukito Kishiro; black and white	*$0.55*	*$1.65*	*$2.75*	£0.35	£1.05	£1.75
Title Value:	*$4.95*	*$14.85*	*$24.75*	£3.15	£9.45	£15.75
Battle Angel Alita Vol 1 (1994) 208pgs, reprints of series begin; black and white				£2.00	£6.00	£10.00
Battle Angel Alita Vol 2: Tears of an Angel (Oct 1994) 208pgs, reprints of series continue; black and white				£2.00	£6.00	£10.00

BATTLE ANGEL ALITA BOOK 2

Viz Communications,MS; 1 Jun 1993-7 Dec 1993

Issue	$Good	$Fine	$N.Mint	£Good	£Fine	£N.Mint
1-7 ND Yukito Kishiro; black and white	*$0.55*	*$1.65*	*$2.75*	£0.35	£1.05	£1.75
Title Value:	*$3.85*	*$11.55*	*$19.25*	£2.45	£7.35	£12.25

BATTLE ANGEL ALITA BOOK 3

Viz Communications,MS; 1 Jan 1994-13 Jan 1995

Issue	$Good	$Fine	$N.Mint	£Good	£Fine	£N.Mint
1-13 ND Yukito Kishiro; black and white	*$0.55*	*$1.65*	*$2.75*	£0.35	£1.05	£1.75
Title Value:	*$7.15*	*$21.45*	*$35.75*	£4.55	£13.65	£22.75

BATTLE ANGEL ALITA PART 4

Viz Communications,MS; 1 Dec 1994-7 Jun 1995

Issue	$Good	$Fine	$N.Mint	£Good	£Fine	£N.Mint
1-7 ND Yukito Kishiro; black and white	*$0.55*	*$1.65*	*$2.75*	£0.35	£1.05	£1.75
Title Value:	*$3.85*	*$11.55*	*$19.25*	£2.45	£7.35	£12.25
Battle Angel Alita: Angel of Victory (Aug 1995) Trade paperback reprints mini-series				£2.10	£6.30	£10.50

BATTLE ANGEL ALITA PART 5

Viz Communications,MS; 1 Jul 1995-7 Jan 1996

Issue	$Good	$Fine	$N.Mint	£Good	£Fine	£N.Mint
1-7 ND Yukito Kishiro script and art; black and white	*$0.55*	*$1.65*	*$2.75*	£0.35	£1.05	£1.75
Title Value:	*$3.05*	*$11.55*	*$19.25*	£2.45	£7.35	£12.25

BATTLE ANGEL ALITA: KILLING ANGEL

Viz Communications,OS; nn Jun 1995

Issue	$Good	$Fine	$N.Mint	£Good	£Fine	£N.Mint
nn ND 184pgs, Yukito Kishiro script and art; 5" x 7"	*$3.00*	*$9.00*	*$15.00*	£2.00	£6.00	£10.00
Title Value:	*$3.00*	*$9.00*	*$15.00*	£2.00	£6.00	£10.00

BATTLE ARMOR

Eternity; 1 1988-4 1988

Issue	$Good	$Fine	$N.Mint	£Good	£Fine	£N.Mint
1-4 ND game tie-in	*$0.40*	*$1.20*	*$2.00*	£0.25	£0.75	£1.25
Title Value:	*$1.60*	*$4.80*	*$8.00*	£1.00	£3.00	£5.00

BATTLE CLASSICS

DC Comics; 1 Sep/Oct 1978

Issue	$Good	$Fine	$N.Mint	£Good	£Fine	£N.Mint
1 ND 44pgs	*$0.50*	*$1.50*	*$3.00*	£0.25	£0.75	£1.50
Title Value:	*$0.50*	*$1.50*	*$3.00*	£0.25	£0.75	£1.50

Note: was intended as an on-going series (see Dynamic Classics) Johnny Cloud/Sgt. Rock story

REPRINT FEATURES

Johnny Cloud/Sgt. Rock story

BATTLE FOR A THREE-DIMENSIONAL WORLD

3-D Cosmic,OS; 1 1982

Issue	$Good	$Fine	$N.Mint	£Good	£Fine	£N.Mint
1 ND Ray Zone script, Jack Kirby art plus photos; back cover features 1st full-colour 3-D in comics; with 3-D glasses (25% less if without glasses)	*$0.60*	*$1.80*	*$3.00*	£0.40	£1.20	£2.00
Title Value:	*$0.60*	*$1.80*	*$3.00*	£0.40	£1.20	£2.00

Note: 1st 1980s 3-D comic.

BATTLE GROUP PEIPER

Tome Press; 1 1991

Issue	$Good	$Fine	$N.Mint	£Good	£Fine	£N.Mint
1 ND black and white	*$0.30*	*$0.90*	*$1.50*	£0.15	£0.45	£0.75
Title Value:	*$0.30*	*$0.90*	*$1.50*	£0.15	£0.45	£0.75

BATTLE OF THE PLANETS

Gold Key/Whitman, TV; 1 Jun 1979-10 Dec 1980

Issue	$Good	$Fine	$N.Mint	£Good	£Fine	£N.Mint
1 scarce in the U.K.	$0.50	$1.50	$3.00	£0.30	£1.00	£2.00
2-5	$0.30	$1.00	$2.00	£0.20	£0.60	£1.25
6-10	$0.25	$0.75	$1.50	£0.15	£0.50	£1.00
Title Value:	$2.95	$9.25	$18.50	£1.85	£5.90	£12.00

Note: there was Limited Distribution of this title on U.K. new-stands

BATTLE STORIES

Super Comics; 10-12, 15-18 1963-1964

Issue	$Good	$Fine	$N.Mint	£Good	£Fine	£N.Mint
10-12 1950s war reprints begin	$0.55	$1.70	$4.00	£0.25	£0.85	£2.00
15-18 1950s war reprints	$0.40	$1.25	$3.00	£0.20	£0.60	£1.50
Title Value:	$3.25	$10.10	$24.00	£1.55	£4.95	£12.00

BATTLE TO THE DEATH

Eternity; 1 Sep 1987-2 Nov 1987

Issue	$Good	$Fine	$N.Mint	£Good	£Fine	£N.Mint
1-2 ND black and white	$0.30	$0.90	$1.50	£0.15	£0.45	£0.75
Title Value:	$0.60	$1.80	$3.00	£0.30	£0.90	£1.50

BATTLEFORCE

Blackthorne; 1 Oct 1988-2 1988

Issue	$Good	$Fine	$N.Mint	£Good	£Fine	£N.Mint
1-2 ND	$0.30	$0.90	$1.50	£0.20	£0.60	£1.00
Title Value:	$0.60	$1.80	$3.00	£0.40	£1.20	£2.00

BATTLESTAR GALACTICA

Marvel Comics Group, TV; 1 Mar 1979-23 Jan 1981

(see also Marvel Super Special #8)

Issue	$Good	$Fine	$N.Mint	£Good	£Fine	£N.Mint
1 ND	$0.65	$2.00	$4.00	£0.25	£0.75	£1.50
2-3	$0.50	$1.50	$3.00	£0.20	£0.60	£1.25
4-5 ND Walt Simonson art	$0.50	$1.50	$3.00	£0.20	£0.60	£1.25
6-9 ND	$0.50	$1.50	$3.00	£0.20	£0.60	£1.25
10 ND Barreto art	$0.50	$1.50	$3.00	£0.20	£0.60	£1.25
11-13 ND Walt Simonson art	$0.50	$1.50	$3.00	£0.20	£0.60	£1.25
14 ND	$0.50	$1.50	$3.00	£0.20	£0.60	£1.25
15 ND Walt Simonson art	$0.50	$1.50	$3.00	£0.20	£0.60	£1.25
16-20 ND Walt Simonson art	$0.50	$1.50	$3.00	£0.15	£0.50	£1.00
21 ND Brent Anderson art	$0.50	$1.50	$3.00	£0.15	£0.50	£1.00
22 ND Walt Simonson cover	$0.50	$1.50	$3.00	£0.15	£0.50	£1.00
23 ND Walt Simonson cover and art	$0.50	$1.50	$3.00	£0.15	£0.50	£1.00
Title Value:	$11.65	$35.00	$70.00	£4.25	£13.15	£27.00

BATTLESTAR GALACTICA

Maximum Comic Press,MS; 1 Jul 1995-4 Dec 1995

Issue	$Good	$Fine	$N.Mint	£Good	£Fine	£N.Mint
1-4 ND continuing adventures from the TV series	$0.50	$1.50	$2.50	£0.30	£0.90	£1.50
Title Value:	$2.00	$6.00	$10.00	£1.20	£3.60	£6.00
Battlestar Galactica (Dec 1995 Trade paperback ND collects mini-series				£1.70	£5.10	£8.50

BATTLESTAR GALACTICA: APOLLO'S JOURNEY

Maximum Comic Press; 1 May 1996-3 Jul 1996

Issue	$Good	$Fine	$N.Mint	£Good	£Fine	£N.Mint
1-3 ND Richard Hatch script, Hector Gomez art	$0.60	$1.80	$3.00	£0.40	£1.20	£2.00
Title Value:	$1.80	$5.40	$9.00	£1.20	£3.60	£6.00

BATTLESTAR GALACTICA: JOURNEY'S END

Maximum Comic Press,MS; 1 Aug 1996-4 Nov 1996

Issue	$Good	$Fine	$N.Mint	£Good	£Fine	£N.Mint
1-4 ND Robert Napton script, Hector Gomez art	$0.60	$1.80	$3.00	£0.40	£1.20	£2.00
Title Value:	$2.40	$7.20	$12.00	£1.60	£4.80	£8.00

BATTLESTAR GALACTICA: STARBUCK

Maximum Comic Press,MS; 1 Dec 1995-3 Feb 1996

Issue	$Good	$Fine	$N.Mint	£Good	£Fine	£N.Mint
1-3 ND Rob Liefeld script, Robert Napton and Hector Gomez art	$0.60	$1.80	$3.00	£0.40	£1.20	£2.00
Title Value:	$1.80	$5.40	$9.00	£1.20	£3.60	£6.00

BATTLESTAR GALACTICA: THE ENEMY WITHIN

Maximum Comic Press; 1 Nov 1995-3 Jan 1996

Issue	$Good	$Fine	$N.Mint	£Good	£Fine	£N.Mint
1 ND Rob Liefeld story, Robert Knapton script, Hector Gomez and Rene Micheletti art	$0.50	$1.50	$2.50	£0.30	£0.90	£1.50
2-3 ND	$0.50	$1.50	$2.50	£0.30	£0.90	£1.50
Title Value:	$1.50	$4.50	$7.50	£0.90	£2.70	£4.50
Battlestar Galacica: The Enemy Within (May 1996) Trade paperback ND collects mini-series with new pages and new cover				£1.30	£3.90	£6.50

BATTLESTONE

Image,MS; 1 Nov 1994-2 Dec 1994

Issue	$Good	$Fine	$N.Mint	£Good	£Fine	£N.Mint
1-2 ND Youngblood spin-off	$0.50	$1.50	$2.50	£0.30	£0.90	£1.50
Title Value:	$1.00	$3.00	$5.00	£0.60	£1.80	£3.00

BATTLETECH

Blackthorne; 1 Aug 1987-12 1988

Issue	$Good	$Fine	$N.Mint	£Good	£Fine	£N.Mint
1 ND	$0.40	$1.20	$2.00	£0.25	£0.75	£1.25
1 3-D issue ND	$0.50	$1.50	$2.50	£0.30	£0.90	£1.50
2 ND	$0.40	$1.20	$2.00	£0.25	£0.75	£1.25
2 3-D issue ND	$0.50	$1.50	$2.50	£0.30	£0.90	£1.50
3-12 ND	$0.40	$1.20	$2.00	£0.25	£0.75	£1.25
Title Value:	$5.80	$17.40	$29.00	£3.60	£10.80	£18.00
Annual 1				£0.50	£1.50	£2.50

Note: first six issues in black and white

BATTLETECH: FALL OUT

Malibu; 0 Feb 1995; 1 Dec 1994-4 Mar 1995

Issue	$Good	$Fine	$N.Mint	£Good	£Fine	£N.Mint
0 ND three stories plus guide to Battletech universe	$0.40	$1.20	$2.00	£0.25	£0.75	£1.25
1 ND based on video game	$0.40	$1.20	$2.00	£0.25	£0.75	£1.25
1 Foil Logo Edition, ND (Dec 1994)	$0.60	$1.80	$3.00	£0.40	£1.20	£2.00
1 Hologram Cover Edition, ND (Dec 1994)	$0.60	$1.80	$3.00	£0.40	£1.20	£2.00
2-4 ND based on video game	$0.40	$1.20	$2.00	£0.25	£0.75	£1.25
Title Value:	$3.20	$9.60	$16.00	£2.05	£6.15	£10.25

BATTRON

New England Comics; 1 Oct 1992-3 1993

Issue	$Good	$Fine	$N.Mint	£Good	£Fine	£N.Mint
1-3 ND	$0.40	$1.20	$2.00	£0.25	£0.75	£1.25
Title Value:	$1.20	$3.60	$6.00	£0.75	£2.25	£3.75

BAYWATCH THE MAGAZINE

Acclaim Comics; 1 Apr 1996-present

Issue	$Good	$Fine	$N.Mint	£Good	£Fine	£N.Mint
1-7 ND 64pgs, photos and features	$1.00	$3.00	$5.00	£0.70	£2.10	£3.50
Title Value:	$7.00	$21.00	$35.00	£4.90	£14.70	£24.50

BEACH PARTY

Eternity,OS; 1 Aug 1989

Issue	$Good	$Fine	$N.Mint	£Good	£Fine	£N.Mint
1 ND Dale Keown cover	$0.40	$1.20	$2.00	£0.25	£0.75	£1.25
Title Value:	$0.40	$1.20	$2.00	£0.25	£0.75	£1.25

BEAST WARRIORS OF SHAOLIN

Pied Piper Comics; 1 Jul 1987-5 1988

Issue	$Good	$Fine	$N.Mint	£Good	£Fine	£N.Mint
1-5 ND Glen Johnson art	$0.20	$0.60	$1.00	£0.15	£0.45	£0.75
Title Value:	$1.00	$3.00	$5.00	£0.75	£2.25	£3.75

BEATLES LIFE STORY, THE

Dell; 1 Sep/Nov 1964

Issue	$Good	$Fine	$N.Mint	£Good	£Fine	£N.Mint
1 very scarce in the U.K., scarce in the U.S. Giant; colour pin-ups and photos	$57.50	$175.00	$525.00	£39.00	£115.00	£350.00
Title Value:	$57.50	$175.00	$525.00	£39.00	£115.00	£350.00

BEAUTIFUL STORIES FOR UGLY CHILDREN

DC Comics/Piranha Press; 1 1989-30 1994

Issue	$Good	$Fine	$N.Mint	£Good	£Fine	£N.Mint
1-10 ND 40pgs	$0.40	$1.20	$2.00	£0.30	£0.90	£1.50
11-18 ND 40pgs	$0.35	$1.05	$1.75	£0.25	£0.75	£1.25
19 ND 112pgs, quarterly format begins	$1.00	$3.00	$5.00	£0.70	£2.10	£3.50
20 ND 112pgs, What If This Were Heaven, Wouldn't That Be Hell?	$1.50	$4.50	$7.50	£1.00	£3.00	£5.00
21 ND Dances With Cows	$0.35	$1.05	$1.75	£0.25	£0.75	£1.25
22 ND Prince: Alter Ego, promo for Prince album Diamonds and Pearls	$0.35	$1.05	$1.75	£0.25	£0.75	£1.25
23 ND Tiny Writhing Slimy Thing	$0.35	$1.05	$1.75	£0.25	£0.75	£1.25
24 ND I Am Paul's Dog	$0.35	$1.05	$1.75	£0.25	£0.75	£1.25
25 ND A Legion of Ogs	$0.35	$1.05	$1.75	£0.25	£0.75	£1.25
26 ND Dead, Like Me	$0.35	$1.05	$1.75	£0.25	£0.75	£1.25
27 ND The No-Wax Killing Floor	$0.35	$1.05	$1.75	£0.25	£0.75	£1.25
28 ND The Guilty Orphan	$0.35	$1.05	$1.75	£0.25	£0.75	£1.25
29 ND Gravity Sucks	$0.35	$1.05	$1.75	£0.25	£0.75	£1.25
30 ND The Dream is Dead	$0.35	$1.05	$1.75	£0.25	£0.75	£1.25
Title Value:	$12.80	$38.40	$64.00	£9.20	£27.60	£46.00

Note: 1-18 all black and white art by Dave Louapre and Dan Sweetman

BEAUTY & THE BEAST - MINI SERIES

Disney,MS; 1 Sep 1992-2 Oct 1992

Issue	$Good	$Fine	$N.Mint	£Good	£Fine	£N.Mint
1-2 ND prequel to animated feature film	$0.30	$0.90	$1.50	£0.20	£0.60	£1.00
Title Value:	$0.60	$1.80	$3.00	£0.40	£1.20	£2.00

BEAUTY AND THE BEAST

First; 1 May 1989-3 1990

Issue	$Good	$Fine	$N.Mint	£Good	£Fine	£N.Mint
1 ND 48pgs, squarebound, script/art by Wendy Pini, based on TV series (blue and red cover logos available)	$1.00	$3.00	$5.00	£0.70	£2.10	£3.50
2 ND 48pgs, squarebound, script/art by Wendy Pini	$1.00	$3.00	$5.00	£0.70	£2.10	£3.50
3 ND 56pgs, Barb Rausch art	$1.00	$3.00	$5.00	£0.70	£2.10	£3.50
Title Value:	$3.00	$9.00	$15.00	£2.10	£6.30	£10.50

Note: embossed covers on all

BEAUTY AND THE BEAST

Marvel Comics Group; 1 Sep 1994-13 Sep 1995

Issue	$Good	$Fine	$N.Mint	£Good	£Fine	£N.Mint
1-13 ND new adventures	$0.30	$0.90	$1.50	£0.20	£0.60	£1.00
Title Value:	$3.90	$11.70	$19.50	£2.60	£7.80	£13.00
Beauty & The Beast (May 1995) Trade paperback reprints first four issues				£1.30	£3.90	£6.50

BEAUTY AND THE BEAST

Innovation; 1 Mar 1993-9 1993

Issue	$Good	$Fine	$N.Mint	£Good	£Fine	£N.Mint
1 ND	$0.50	$1.50	$2.50	£0.30	£0.90	£1.50

	$Good	$Fine	$N.Mint	£Good	£Fine	£N.Mint
1 Special Edition, ND - pre-bagged with poster						
	$0.80	$2.40	$4.00	£0.50	£1.50	£2.50
2-9 ND	$0.50	$1.50	$2.50	£0.30	£0.90	£1.50
Title Value:	$5.30	$15.90	$26.50	£3.20	£9.60	£16.00

BEAUTY AND THE BEAST MOVIE ADAPTATION

Disney,OS; 1 Dec 1991

	$Good	$Fine	$N.Mint	£Good	£Fine	£N.Mint
1 Newstand Edition ND						
	$0.50	$1.50	$2.50	£0.30	£0.90	£1.50
1 Prestige Format ND						
	$1.00	$3.00	$5.00	£0.70	£2.10	£3.50
Title Value:	$1.50	$4.50	$7.50	£1.00	£3.00	£5.00

BEAUTY AND THE BEAST, THE

Marvel Comics Group,MS; 1 Jan 1985-4 Apr 1985

	$Good	$Fine	$N.Mint	£Good	£Fine	£N.Mint
1 ND Dazzler/Beast appear, Dr. Doom cameo, Bill Sienkiewicz cover						
	$0.50	$1.50	$2.50	£0.30	£0.90	£1.50
2-4 ND Dazzler/Beast appear, Dr. Doom cameo, Bill Sienkiewicz cover						
	$0.40	$1.20	$2.00	£0.25	£0.75	£1.25
Title Value:	$1.70	$5.10	$8.50	£1.05	£3.15	£5.25

BEAVIS & BUTT-HEAD

Marvel Comics Group; 1 Mar 1994-28 Jun 1996

	$Good	$Fine	$N.Mint	£Good	£Fine	£N.Mint
1 ND Mike Lackey and Rick Parker creative team begin						
	$0.60	$1.80	$3.00	£0.40	£1.20	£2.00
2-3 ND	$0.50	$1.50	$2.50	£0.30	£0.90	£1.50
4-28 ND	$0.40	$1.20	$2.00	£0.25	£0.75	£1.25
Title Value:	$11.60	$34.80	$58.00	£7.25	£21.75	£36.25
Beavis & Butt-Head Greatest Hits (Aug 1994)						
Trade paperback ND, reprints issues #1-4, 96pgs				£1.70	£5.10	£8.50
Beavis & Butt-Head: Trashcan Edition (Jan 1995)						
Trade paperback ND, reprints issues #5-8, 96pgs				£1.70	£5.10	£8.50
Beavis & Butt-Head: Holidazed and Confused (Jun 1995)						
Trade paperback ND, collection of holiday stories				£1.70	£5.10	£8.50
Beavis & Butt-Head: Wanted (Jan 1996)						
Trade paperback ND reprints issues #9,13,15,16				£1.70	£5.10	£8.50

BECK & CAUL

Caliber Press; 1 1994-6 1995

	$Good	$Fine	$N.Mint	£Good	£Fine	£N.Mint
1-6 ND black and white						
	$0.50	$1.50	$2.50	£0.30	£0.90	£1.50
Title Value:	$3.00	$9.00	$15.00	£1.80	£5.40	£9.00
Beck & Caul Special (Aug 1994)						
reprints issues #1 & 2 plus short story from U.N. Flies #1				£0.65	£1.95	£3.25

BECK AND CAUL ANNUAL

Caliber Press; 1 May 1995

	$Good	$Fine	$N.Mint	£Good	£Fine	£N.Mint
1 ND 48pgs, black and white						
	$0.80	$2.40	$4.00	£0.50	£1.50	£2.50
Title Value:	$0.80	$2.40	$4.00	£0.50	£1.50	£2.50

BEDLAM

Eclipse,MS; 1 Sep 1985-2 Oct 1985

	$Good	$Fine	$N.Mint	£Good	£Fine	£N.Mint
1-2 ND Bisette/Veitch reprints						
	$0.50	$1.50	$2.50	£0.30	£0.90	£1.50
Title Value:	$1.00	$3.00	$5.00	£0.60	£1.80	£3.00

BEETLE BAILEY

King Comics; 54 Aug 1966-65 Dec 1967; Charlton; 67 Feb 1969-119 Nov 1976; Gold Key; 120 Apr 1978-132 Apr 1980

	$Good	$Fine	$N.Mint	£Good	£Fine	£N.Mint
54	$0.40	$1.25	$3.00	£0.25	£0.85	£2.00
55-75	$0.35	$1.05	$2.50	£0.20	£0.60	£1.50
76-120	$0.30	$1.00	$2.00	£0.20	£0.60	£1.25
121-132	$0.25	$0.75	$1.50	£0.15	£0.50	£1.00
Title Value:	$24.25	$77.30	$163.50	£15.25	£46.45	£101.75

BENEATH THE PLANET OF THE APES

Gold Key/Movie Comics,OS Movie; 30044-012 Dec 1970

	$Good	$Fine	$N.Mint	£Good	£Fine	£N.Mint
30044-012 rare although distributed in the U.K., with pull-out Ape Protest poster (25% less without poster)						
	$5.50	$17.00	$40.00	£3.90	£11.50	£27.50
Title value:	$5.50	$17.00	$40.00	£3.90	£11.50	£27.50

Note: published under Gold Key series Movie Comics

BENEATH THE PLANET OF THE APES GRAPHIC ALBUM

Adventure,OS; 1 Apr 1991

	$Good	$Fine	$N.Mint	£Good	£Fine	£N.Mint
1 ND 164pgs, reprints 1970s Marvel series plus unseen photos from film						
	$1.50	$4.50	$7.50	£1.00	£3.00	£5.00
Title Value:	$1.50	$4.50	$7.50	£1.00	£3.00	£5.00

BEOWULF

DC Comics; 1 Apr/May 1975-6 Feb/Mar 1976

	$Good	$Fine	$N.Mint	£Good	£Fine	£N.Mint
1	$0.30	$1.00	$2.00	£0.25	£0.75	£1.50
2-3	$0.30	$1.00	$2.00	£0.20	£0.60	£1.25
4 scarce in the U.K.	$0.30	$1.00	$2.00	£0.25	£0.75	£1.50
5	$0.30	$1.00	$2.00	£0.20	£0.60	£1.25
6 scarce in the U.K.	$0.30	$1.00	$2.00	£0.25	£0.75	£1.50
Title Value:	$1.80	$6.00	$12.00	£1.35	£4.05	£8.25

BEOWULF

First; nn 1976

	$Good	$Fine	$N.Mint	£Good	£Fine	£N.Mint
nn ND Graphic Novel (the first one the company produced); Jerry Bingham art						
	$1.00	$3.00	$6.00	£0.65	£2.00	£4.00
Title Value:	$1.00	$3.00	$6.00	£0.65	£2.00	£4.00

BERNI WRIGHTSON, MASTER OF THE MACABRE

Pacific/Eclipse; 1 Jul 1983-5 Nov 1984

	$Good	$Fine	$N.Mint	£Good	£Fine	£N.Mint
1 ND classic Edgar Allan Poe adaptation of The Black Cat, reprint; all Berni Wrightson covers						
	$0.40	$1.20	$2.00	£0.30	£0.90	£1.50
2-4 ND all reprint	$0.40	$1.20	$2.00	£0.30	£0.90	£1.50
5 ND Eclipse issue, reprints						
	$0.40	$1.20	$2.00	£0.30	£0.90	£1.50
Title Value:	$2.00	$6.00	$10.00	£1.50	£4.50	£7.50

BERZERKER

Gauntlet Comics,MS; 1 Feb 1993-6 1994

	$Good	$Fine	$N.Mint	£Good	£Fine	£N.Mint
1-6 ND Angel Medina art, black and white						
	$0.40	$1.20	$2.00	£0.30	£0.90	£1.50
Title Value:	$2.40	$7.20	$12.00	£1.80	£5.40	£9.00

BERZERKERS

Image,MS; 1 Aug 1995-3 Oct 1995

	$Good	$Fine	$N.Mint	£Good	£Fine	£N.Mint
1 ND Beau Smith script, Dan Fraga art						
	$0.50	$1.50	$2.50	£0.30	£0.90	£1.50
1 Variant Cover Edition, ND Joe Quesada/Jimmy Palmiotti cover art						
	$0.60	$1.80	$3.00	£0.40	£1.20	£2.00
2-3 ND Beau Smith script, Dan Fraga art						
	$0.50	$1.50	$2.50	£0.30	£0.90	£1.50
Title Value:	$2.10	$6.30	$10.50	£1.30	£3.90	£6.50

BEST OF DC, THE

DC Comics,Digest; 1 Sep/Oct 1979-71 Dec 1985

	$Good	$Fine	$N.Mint	£Good	£Fine	£N.Mint
1 ND Superman	$0.50	$1.50	$3.00	£0.40	£1.25	£2.50
2 ND Batman, celebrates 40th anniversary with reprints including Batman #7 and #251 (Neal Adams)						
	$0.50	$1.50	$3.00	£0.40	£1.25	£2.50
3 ND Super Friends, Garcia Lopez painted cover						
	$0.35	$1.10	$2.25	£0.30	£1.00	£2.00
4 ND Rudolph the Red Nosed Reindeer						
	$0.30	$1.00	$2.00	£0.25	£0.75	£1.50
5 ND 132pgs, Year's Best Comic Stories 1979						
	$0.35	$1.10	$2.25	£0.30	£1.00	£2.00
6 ND Superman, mostly 1960s reprints						
	$0.30	$1.00	$2.00	£0.25	£0.75	£1.50
7 ND Superboy, mostly 1960s reprints						
	$0.30	$1.00	$2.00	£0.25	£0.75	£1.50
8 ND Superman	$0.30	$1.00	$2.00	£0.25	£0.75	£1.50
9 ND Batman	$0.30	$1.00	$2.00	£0.25	£0.75	£1.50
10 ND Secret Origins of Super-Villains						
	$0.30	$1.00	$2.00	£0.25	£0.75	£1.50
11 ND 132pgs, Year's Best Comic Stories 1980						
	$0.35	$1.10	$2.25	£0.30	£1.00	£2.00
12 ND Superman	$0.30	$1.00	$2.00	£0.25	£0.75	£1.50
13 ND DC Comics Presents (Superman team up)						
	$0.30	$1.00	$2.00	£0.25	£0.75	£1.50
14 ND Batman's Villains, Marshall Rogers reprint and Neal Adams reprint from Batman #234 (1st modern age Two Face)						
	$0.35	$1.10	$2.25	£0.30	£1.00	£2.00
15 ND Superboy, mostly 1960s reprints						
	$0.30	$1.00	$2.00	£0.25	£0.75	£1.50
16 ND Superman, anniversary reprints inc. origin of Superman from Superman #53						
	$0.35	$1.10	$2.25	£0.30	£1.00	£2.00
17 ND Supergirl	$0.30	$1.00	$2.00	£0.25	£0.75	£1.50
18 ND New Teen Titans, new story which was later reprinted in Tales of the Teen Titans #59						
	$0.50	$1.50	$3.00	£0.40	£1.25	£2.50
19 ND Superman, reprints classic Superman Red and Superman Blue						
	$0.30	$1.00	$2.00	£0.25	£0.75	£1.50
20 ND World's Finest Comics (Superman and Batman)						
	$0.30	$1.00	$2.00	£0.25	£0.75	£1.50
21 ND Justice Society of America, featuring Golden Age reprint						
	$0.35	$1.10	$2.25	£0.30	£1.00	£2.00
22 ND Christmas with the Super-Heroes, features unpublished Sandman story by Jack Kirby (18pgs)						
	$0.50	$1.50	$3.00	£0.40	£1.25	£2.50
23 ND 148pgs, Year's Best Comic Stories 1981						
	$0.35	$1.10	$2.25	£0.30	£1.00	£2.00
24 ND Legion of Super-Heroes, new story featured						
	$0.50	$1.50	$3.00	£0.40	£1.25	£2.50
25 ND Superman, featuring kid pals						
	$0.30	$1.00	$2.00	£0.25	£0.75	£1.50
26 ND Brave and the Bold (Batman team up plus Robin Hood, Suicide Squad, Viking Prince, Silent Knight abd Cave Carson)						
	$0.30	$1.00	$2.00	£0.25	£0.75	£1.50
27 ND Superman vs. Luthor						
	$0.30	$1.00	$2.00	£0.25	£0.75	£1.50
28 ND Binky's Summer Fun						
	$0.25	$0.75	$1.50	£0.20	£0.60	£1.25
29 ND Sugar and Spike						
	$0.30	$1.00	$2.00	£0.25	£0.75	£1.50
30 ND Detective Comics						
	$0.35	$1.10	$2.25	£0.30	£1.00	£2.00
31 ND Justice League of America, special initiation issue						
	$0.25	$0.75	$1.50	£0.20	£0.60	£1.25
32 ND Superman	$0.30	$1.00	$2.00	£0.25	£0.75	£1.50
33 ND Legion of Super-Heroes						
	$0.35	$1.10	$2.25	£0.30	£1.00	£2.00
34 ND Metal Men, reprints Showcase #37-40; has #497 on cover (intended for Adveture Comics?)						
	$0.35	$1.10	$2.25	£0.30	£1.00	£2.00
35 ND 148pgs, Year's Best Comic Stories 1982						
	$0.35	$1.10	$2.25	£0.30	£1.00	£2.00
36 ND Superman vs. Kryptonite						
	$0.30	$1.00	$2.00	£0.25	£0.75	£1.50
37 ND Funny Stuff	$0.20	$0.60	$1.25	£0.15	£0.50	£1.00
38 ND Superman: The Supernatural, features some 40s and 50s reprints						
	$0.30	$1.00	$2.00	£0.25	£0.75	£1.50
39 ND Binky and His Buddies						
	$0.25	$0.75	$1.50	£0.20	£0.60	£1.25
40 ND Superman: The Fabulous World of Krypton						
	$0.30	$1.00	$2.00	£0.25	£0.75	£1.50
41 ND Sugar and Spike						
	$0.25	$0.75	$1.50	£0.20	£0.60	£1.25
42 ND Superman vs. Aliens, 1950s/1960s classic reprints						

	$Good	$Fine	$N.Mint	£Good	£Fine	£N.Mint
	$0.25	**$0.75**	**$1.50**	£0.20	£0.60	£1.25
43 ND Funny Stuff	**$0.25**	**$0.75**	**$1.50**	£0.20	£0.60	£1.25
44 ND Legion of Super-Heroes (reprints Adventure Comics #319-323)						
	$0.35	**$1.10**	**$2.25**	£0.30	£1.00	£2.00
45 ND Binky and His Buddies						
	$0.20	**$0.60**	**$1.25**	£0.15	£0.50	£1.00
46 ND Jimmy Olsen, reprints Jimmy Olsen #1 and #2						
	$0.30	**$1.00**	**$2.00**	£0.25	£0.75	£1.50
47 ND Sugar and Spike						
	$0.30	**$1.00**	**$2.00**	£0.25	£0.75	£1.50
48 ND Superman Team Up Action						
	$0.30	**$1.00**	**$2.00**	£0.25	£0.75	£1.50
49 ND Funny Stuff	**$0.20**	**$0.60**	**$1.25**	£0.15	£0.50	£1.00
50 ND Year's Best Superman Stories						
	$0.35	**$1.10**	**$2.25**	£0.30	£1.00	£2.00
51 ND Batman Family, Neal Adams, Marshall Rogers reprints						
	$0.50	**$1.50**	**$3.00**	£0.40	£1.25	£2.50
52 ND 148pgs, Year's Best Comic Stories 1983						
	$0.35	**$1.10**	**$2.25**	£0.30	£1.00	£2.00
53 ND Binky and His Buddies						
	$0.20	**$0.60**	**$1.25**	£0.15	£0.50	£1.00
54 ND Superman Battles Weird Villains						
	$0.30	**$1.00**	**$2.00**	£0.25	£0.75	£1.50
55 ND Funny Stuff	**$0.20**	**$0.60**	**$1.25**	£0.15	£0.50	£1.00
56 ND Superman vs. More Aliens						
	$0.25	**$0.75**	**$1.50**	£0.20	£0.60	£1.25
57 ND	**$0.25**	**$0.75**	**$1.50**	£0.20	£0.60	£1.25
58 ND Super Jrs. Holiday Special						
	$0.25	**$0.75**	**$1.50**	£0.20	£0.60	£1.25
59 ND Superman Sagas						
	$0.30	**$1.00**	**$2.00**	£0.25	£0.75	£1.50
60 ND Plop!	**$0.30**	**$1.00**	**$2.00**	£0.25	£0.75	£1.50
61 ND 148pgs, Year's Best Comic Stories 1984 inc. Swamp Thing #21 (Alan Moore)						
	$0.35	**$1.10**	**$2.25**	£0.30	£1.00	£2.00
62 ND Year's Best Batman Stories						
	$0.35	**$1.10**	**$2.25**	£0.30	£1.00	£2.00
63 ND Plop!	**$0.30**	**$1.00**	**$2.00**	£0.25	£0.75	£1.50
64 ND Legion of Super-Heroes (reprints Adventure Comics #330-334)						
	$0.25	**$0.75**	**$1.50**	£0.20	£0.60	£1.25
65 ND Sugar and Spike						
	$0.25	**$0.75**	**$1.50**	£0.20	£0.60	£1.25
66 ND Superman Team Up Action						
	$0.25	**$0.75**	**$1.50**	£0.20	£0.60	£1.25
67 ND Legion of Super-Heroes						
	$0.35	**$1.10**	**$2.25**	£0.30	£1.00	£2.00
68 ND Sugar and Spike Halloween Special						
	$0.25	**$0.75**	**$1.50**	£0.20	£0.60	£1.25
69 ND Year's Best Team Stories						
	$0.30	**$1.00**	**$2.00**	£0.25	£0.75	£1.50
70 ND Binky's Buddies						
	$0.20	**$0.60**	**$1.25**	£0.15	£0.50	£1.00
71 ND 148pgs, Year's Best Comic Stories 1985 inc. Swamp Thing #34						
	$0.35	**$1.10**	**$2.25**	£0.30	£1.00	£2.00
Title Value:	**$22.15**	**$70.15**	**$141.50**	£18.30	£57.30	£115.25

Note: unless otherwise stated, issues are 100pgs.

ARTISTS

Adams reprints in 2,14,16,18,25,26. Rogers reprints in 14. Kirby in 22 (previously unpublished Sandman 7). Perez in 24.

FEATURES

Batman in 10. Legion of Super-Heroes in 24 (with 16pgs of new costumes). Teen Titans in 18. Sandman in 22. One page origins of various villains in 14.

REPRINT FEATURES

(other than featured character) Aquaman in 10. Batman in 5,11,22,23. Batman/Deadman in 26. Captain Marvel Crimson Avenger in 23. Captain Marvel Jnr. in 22. Cave Carson, Robin Hood, Silent Knight, Suicide Squad, Viking Prince Superman/Sgt. Rock in 5. Flash in 10. Green Arrow, Green Lantern in 10. Green Lantern Corps, New Teen Titans in 23. Hawkman in 10. Jimmy Olsen in 6,16. Jonah Hex in 5,11,23. JLA in 3. Legion in 11. Lois Lane in 6,19. Robin in 22. Sgt. Rock in 11,23. Starman/Black Canary in 21. Superman in 5,10,11,13,23. Superman/Aquaman in 13. Superman/Batgirl, Superman/Batman, Superman/Green Arrow, Superman/ Lantern, Superman/Supergirl in 13. Superman/Batman in 19,20. Superman/Deadman in 11. Superman/Dr. Fate in 20. Teen Titans in 3,18,22.

BEST OF MARVEL '96

Marvel Comics Group,OS; nn Jan 1997

	$Good	$Fine	$N.Mint	£Good	£Fine	£N.Mint
nn ND 224pgs, Wolverine and Elektra, Spiderman, Onslaught, Captain America appear						
	$3.80	**$11.00**	**$19.00**	£2.70	£8.00	£13.50
Title Value:	**$3.80**	**$11.00**	**$19.00**	£2.70	£8.00	£13.50

BEST OF MARVEL 1994

Marvel Comics Group,OS; nn Dec 1994

	$Good	$Fine	$N.Mint	£Good	£Fine	£N.Mint
nn ND Trade paperback. Ten reprints from 1994 featuring X-Men, X-Factor, Spiderman, Thunderstrike and others						
	$2.50	**$7.50**	**$12.50**	£1.70	£5.00	£8.50
Title Value:	**$2.50**	**$7.50**	**$12.50**	£1.70	£5.00	£8.50

BEST OF MARVEL 1995

Marvel Comics Group,OS; nn Jan 1996

	$Good	$Fine	$N.Mint	£Good	£Fine	£N.Mint
nn ND 224pgs, Trade paperback. Reprints iclude Generation X #5,6, Amazing Spiderman #400, Spiderman #57, Spectacular Spiderman #223, Hulk #345 among others						
	$4.00	**$12.00**	**$20.00**	£2.70	£8.00	£13.50
Title Value:	**$4.00**	**$12.00**	**$20.00**	£2.70	£8.00	£13.50

BEST OF SORCERY, THE

Millennium,MS; 1 Dec 1992

	$Good	$Fine	$N.Mint	£Good	£Fine	£N.Mint
1 ND 48pgs, reprints begin from Red Circle's Sorcery and Madhouse featuring work by Chaykin, Williamson, Morrow and Toth; new John Bolton cover						
	$0.40	**$1.20**	**$2.00**	£0.25	£0.75	£1.25
Title Value:	**$0.40**	**$1.20**	**$2.00**	£0.25	£0.75	£1.25

BEST OF THE BRAVE AND THE BOLD

DC Comics,MS; 1 Oct 1988-6 Mar 1989

	$Good	$Fine	$N.Mint	£Good	£Fine	£N.Mint
1-6 ND Neal Adams reprints						
	$0.40	**$1.20**	**$2.00**	£0.30	£0.90	£1.50
Title Value:	**$2.40**	**$7.20**	**$12.00**	£1.80	£5.40	£9.00

REPRINT FEATURES

Batman/Aquaman (from Brave & Bold 82) in 3; Batman/Creeper (from Brave & Bold 80) in 4; Batman/ Flash (from B&B 81) in 2; Batman/Green Arrow (from Brave & Bold 85) in 1; Batman/House of Mystery (from B&B 93 in 5; Batman/Teen Titans (from B&B 83) in 6. Golden Gladiator in 3-5. Robin Hood in 2-6. Silent Knight (from B&B 1) in 1. Viking Prince in 1-6.

BETTIE PAGE COMICS

Dark Horse,OS; 1 Mar 1996

	$Good	$Fine	$N.Mint	£Good	£Fine	£N.Mint
1 ND features work by Dave Stevens and Bret Blevins amongst others in three separate stories						
	$0.60	**$1.80**	**$3.00**	£0.40	£1.20	£2.00
Title Value:	**$0.60**	**$1.80**	**$3.00**	£0.40	£1.20	£2.00

BETTY BEING BAD

Eros Comix,OS; 1 Feb 1991

	$Good	$Fine	$N.Mint	£Good	£Fine	£N.Mint
1 ND rare in the U.K. photo's of the 1950s pin-up Betty Page						
	$0.80	**$2.40**	**$4.00**	£0.50	£1.50	£2.50
Title Value:	**$0.80**	**$2.40**	**$4.00**	£0.50	£1.50	£2.50

BETTY BOOP IN 3-D

Blackthorne; (3-D Series #11) Nov 1986

	$Good	$Fine	$N.Mint	£Good	£Fine	£N.Mint
1 ND 1934 reprints by Bud Counihan; with bound-in 3-D glasses (25% less if without glasses)						
	$0.50	**$1.50**	**$2.50**	£0.30	£0.90	£1.50
Title Value:	**$0.50**	**$1.50**	**$2.50**	£0.30	£0.90	£1.50

Note: see also Little Nemo in Slumberland as this is also numbered Blackthorne 3-D Series #11 in the indicia

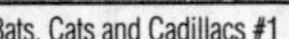
Bats, Cats and Cadillacs #1

Battle Stories #15

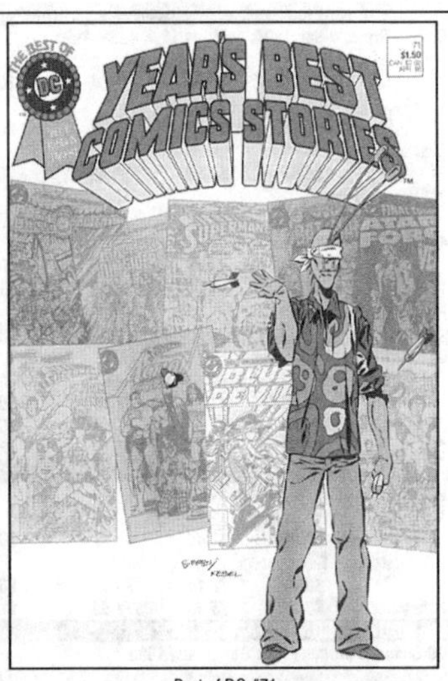

Best of DC #71

BETTY BOOP'S BIG BREAK

First,OS; 1 Oct 1990

Issue	$Good	$Fine	$N.Mint	£Good	£Fine	£N.Mint
1 ND 48pgs, squarebound	$1.00	$3.00	$5.00	£0.70	£2.10	£3.50
Title Value:	$1.00	$3.00	$5.00	£0.70	£2.10	£3.50

BETTY PAGE 3-D COMICS

The 3-D Zone,OS; 1 Apr 1991

Issue	$Good	$Fine	$N.Mint	£Good	£Fine	£N.Mint
1 ND with glasses (25% less if without glasses); oversize issue (8"x10")	$0.80	$2.40	$4.00	£0.50	£1.50	£2.50
Title Value:	$0.80	$2.40	$4.00	£0.50	£1.50	£2.50

BETTY PAGE 3-D PICTURE BOOK, THE

The 3-D Zone,OS; 1 1989

Issue	$Good	$Fine	$N.Mint	£Good	£Fine	£N.Mint
1 ND scarce in the U.K. topless photos of Betty Page, with bound-in 3-D glasses (25% less if without glasses); intro by Dave Stevens	$1.20	$3.60	$6.00	£0.80	£2.40	£4.00
Title Value:	$1.20	$3.60	$6.00	£0.80	£2.40	£4.00

BETTY PAGE CAPTURED JUNGLE GIRL 3-D

The 3-D Zone,OS; 1 1990

Issue	$Good	$Fine	$N.Mint	£Good	£Fine	£N.Mint
1 ND scarce in the U.K. bondage pin-ups of Betty Page, with bound-in (excuse pun) 3-D glasses (25% less if without glasses)	$0.90	$2.70	$4.50	£0.60	£1.80	£3.00
Title Value:	$0.90	$2.70	$4.50	£0.60	£1.80	£3.00

BEWARE!

Marvel Comics Group; 1 Mar 1973-8 May 1974

(becomes Tomb of Darkness)

Issue	$Good	$Fine	$N.Mint	£Good	£Fine	£N.Mint
1 ND scarce in the U.K. horror reprints from the 1950s/early 1960s begin	$0.75	$2.25	$4.50	£0.55	£1.75	£3.50
2-3 ND scarce in the U.K.	$0.65	$2.00	$4.00	£0.50	£1.50	£3.00
4 ND scarce in the U.K. Gil Kane cover	$0.55	$1.75	$3.50	£0.40	£1.25	£2.50
5-8 ND scarce in the U.K.	$0.55	$1.75	$3.50	£0.40	£1.25	£2.50
Title Value:	$4.80	$15.00	$30.00	£3.55	£11.00	£22.00

BEWARE! THE CLAWS OF THE CAT

(see Cat...)

BEWARE THE CREEPER

(see Creeper)

BEWITCHED

Dell,TV; 1 Apr/Jun 1965-11 Oct 1967; 12 Oct 1968-13 Jan 1969; 14 Oct 1969

Issue	$Good	$Fine	$N.Mint	£Good	£Fine	£N.Mint
1 scarce in the U.K. photo cover	$21.00	$62.50	$150.00	£14.00	£43.00	£100.00
2 scarce in the U.K. no photo cover	$10.50	$32.00	$75.00	£7.00	£21.00	£50.00
3-11 photo cover	$7.00	$21.00	$50.00	£4.60	£13.50	£32.50
12-13 photo cover	$5.00	$15.00	$35.00	£3.20	£9.50	£22.50
14 no photo cover	$5.00	$15.00	$35.00	£3.20	£9.50	£22.50
Title Value:	$109.50	$328.50	$780.00	£72.00	£214.00	£510.00

BEYOND THE GRAVE

Charlton; 1 Jul 1975-6 Jun 1976; 7 Jan 1983-17 Oct 1984

Issue	$Good	$Fine	$N.Mint	£Good	£Fine	£N.Mint
1 distributed in the U.K.	$0.30	$1.00	$2.00	£0.20	£0.60	£1.25
2-5 distributed in the U.K.	$0.25	$0.75	$1.50	£0.15	£0.50	£1.00
6-17 distributed in the U.K.	$0.20	$0.60	$1.25	£0.10	£0.35	£0.75
Title Value:	$3.70	$11.20	$23.00	£2.00	£6.80	£14.25

BIFF THUNDERSAUR

Innovation,OS; 1 1991

Issue	$Good	$Fine	$N.Mint	£Good	£Fine	£N.Mint
1 ND black and white	$0.40	$1.20	$2.00	£0.25	£0.75	£1.25
Title Value:	$0.40	$1.20	$2.00	£0.25	£0.75	£1.25

BIG BANG COMICS

Caliber Press; 0 Sep 1994; 1 Spring 1994-4 Mar 1996

Issue	$Good	$Fine	$N.Mint	£Good	£Fine	£N.Mint
0 ND 16pgs, information and timeline on Big Bang characters	$0.20	$0.60	$1.00	£0.15	£0.45	£0.75
1 ND 64pgs, Sheldon Moldoff cover; 1940s period feel	$0.60	$1.80	$3.00	£0.40	£1.20	£2.00
2 ND Curt Swan and Murphy Anderson cover	$0.50	$1.50	$2.50	£0.30	£0.90	£1.50
3 ND Silver Age issue	$0.40	$1.20	$2.00	£0.25	£0.75	£1.25
4 ND The Free Agents appear	$0.40	$1.20	$2.00	£0.25	£0.75	£1.25
Title Value:	$2.10	$6.30	$10.50	£1.35	£4.05	£6.75

Note: Golden Age homage/parody

BIG BANG COMICS (2ND SERIES)

Image; 1 May 1996-present

Issue	$Good	$Fine	$N.Mint	£Good	£Fine	£N.Mint
1 ND Silver Age style stories and art featuring heroes such as Ultiman and Thunder Girl	$0.50	$1.50	$2.50	£0.30	£0.90	£1.50
2-7 ND	$0.50	$1.50	$2.50	£0.30	£0.90	£1.50
Title Value:	$3.50	$10.50	$17.50	£2.10	£6.30	£10.50

BIG BLACK KISS

Vortex,MS; 1 Sep 1989-3 Nov 1989

Issue	$Good	$Fine	$N.Mint	£Good	£Fine	£N.Mint
1 ND reprints of Black Kiss begin	$0.80	$2.40	$4.00	£0.50	£1.50	£2.50
2-3 ND reprints of Black Kiss begin	$0.70	$2.10	$3.50	£0.45	£1.35	£2.25
Title Value:	$2.20	$6.60	$11.00	£1.40	£4.20	£7.00

BIG BOOK OF CONSPIRACIES, THE

DC Comics/Paradox Press,OS; nn Aug 1995

Issue	$Good	$Fine	$N.Mint	£Good	£Fine	£N.Mint
nn ND 224pgs, Doug Moench script with art by Rick Geary, Kev O'Neill, Brett Ewins, Bryan Talbot and others	$2.50	$7.50	$12.50	£1.50	£4.50	£7.50
Title Value:	$2.50	$7.50	$12.50	£1.50	£4.50	£7.50

BIG BOOK OF DEATH, THE

DC Comics/Paradox Press,OS; nn Jun 1995

Issue	$Good	$Fine	$N.Mint	£Good	£Fine	£N.Mint
nn ND 224pgs, squarebound, everything you wanted to know about death; black and white	$2.50	$7.50	$12.50	£1.50	£4.50	£7.50
Title Value:	$2.50	$7.50	$12.50	£1.50	£4.50	£7.50

BIG BOOK OF FREAKS, THE

DC Comics/Paradox Press,OS; nn Apr 1996

Issue	$Good	$Fine	$N.Mint	£Good	£Fine	£N.Mint
nn ND 224pgs, Gahan Wilson script	$3.00	$9.00	$15.00	£2.00	£6.00	£10.00
Title Value:	$3.00	$9.00	$15.00	£2.00	£6.00	£10.00

BIG BOOK OF HOAXES, THE

DC Comics/Paradox Press,OS; nn Nov 1996

Issue	$Good	$Fine	$N.Mint	£Good	£Fine	£N.Mint
nn ND 192pgs, a history of great lies and falsehoods; features Hunt Emerson art	$3.00	$9.00	$15.00	£2.00	£6.00	£10.00
Title Value:	$3.00	$9.00	$15.00	£2.00	£6.00	£10.00

BIG BOOK OF LITTLE CRIMINALS, THE

DC Comics,OS; nn Jun 1996

Issue	$Good	$Fine	$N.Mint	£Good	£Fine	£N.Mint
nn ND 192pgs, black and white	$3.00	$9.00	$15.00	£2.00	£6.00	£10.00
Title Value:	$3.00	$9.00	$15.00	£2.00	£6.00	£10.00

BIG BOOK OF LOSERS, THE

DC Comics/Paradox Press,OS; nn Mar 1997

Issue	$Good	$Fine	$N.Mint	£Good	£Fine	£N.Mint
nn ND 192pgs, Rick Geary and Charlie Adlard art feature	$3.00	$9.00	$15.00	£2.00	£6.00	£10.00
Title Value:	$3.00	$9.00	$15.00	£2.00	£6.00	£10.00

BIG BOOK OF THUGS, THE

DC Comics/Paradox Press,OS; nn Dec 1996

Issue	$Good	$Fine	$N.Mint	£Good	£Fine	£N.Mint
nn ND, 192pgs	$3.00	$9.00	$15.00	£2.00	£6.00	£10.00
Title Value:	$3.00	$9.00	$15.00	£2.00	£6.00	£10.00

BIG BOOK OF URBAN LEGENDS, THE

DC Comics/Paradox Press; nn Jan 1995

Issue	$Good	$Fine	$N.Mint	£Good	£Fine	£N.Mint
nn ND 224pgs, contributions from Art Adams, Terry Austin, Mike Mignola among others	$2.50	$7.50	$12.50	£1.50	£4.50	£7.50
Title Value:	$2.50	$7.50	$12.50	£1.50	£4.50	£7.50

BIG BOOK OF WEIRDOS, THE

DC Comics/Paradox Press,OS; nn Mar 1995

Issue	$Good	$Fine	$N.Mint	£Good	£Fine	£N.Mint
nn ND 224pgs, contributors include Joe Staton and Mike Zeck; black and white	$2.50	$7.50	$12.50	£1.50	£4.50	£7.50
Title Value:	$2.50	$7.50	$12.50	£1.50	£4.50	£7.50

BIG BRUISERS

Image,OS; 1 Jul 1996

Issue	$Good	$Fine	$N.Mint	£Good	£Fine	£N.Mint
1 ND 40pgs, Badrock, Maul and Impact appear	$0.70	$2.10	$3.50	£0.50	£1.50	£2.50
Title Value:	$0.70	$2.10	$3.50	£0.50	£1.50	£2.50

BIG GUY & RUSTY THE BOY ROBOT, THE

Dark Horse,MS; 1 Jul 1995-2 Aug 1995

Issue	$Good	$Fine	$N.Mint	£Good	£Fine	£N.Mint
1 ND Frank Miller script, Geoff Darrow art, cover by Darrow, Olivia and Lynn Varley; 9" x 12.5" format	$1.00	$3.00	$5.00	£0.70	£2.10	£3.50
2 ND Frank Miller script, Geoff Darrow art, cover by Geoff Darrow and Lynn Varley; 9" x 12.5" format	$1.00	$3.00	$5.00	£0.70	£2.10	£3.50
Title Value:	$2.00	$6.00	$10.00	£1.40	£4.20	£7.00

BIG NUMBERS

(see British section)

BIG PRIZE, THE

Eternity; 1 May 1988-2 Sep 1988

Issue	$Good	$Fine	$N.Mint	£Good	£Fine	£N.Mint
1-2 ND	$0.40	$1.20	$2.00	£0.25	£0.75	£1.25
Title Value:	$0.80	$2.40	$4.00	£0.50	£1.50	£2.50

BIG TOWN

National Periodical Publications; 1 Jan 1951-50 Mar/Apr 1958

Issue	$Good	$Fine	$N.Mint	£Good	£Fine	£N.Mint
1 scarce in the U.K. Dan Barry art begins	$57.50	$175.00	$475.00	£41.00	£120.00	£325.00
2 scarce in the U.K.	$36.00	$105.00	$250.00	£25.00	£75.00	£175.00
3-5 scarce in the U.K.	$21.00	$62.50	$150.00	£14.00	£43.00	£100.00
6-10 scarce in the U.K.	$19.00	$57.50	$135.00	£12.50	£39.00	£90.00
11-20	$12.50	$39.00	$90.00	£8.50	£26.00	£60.00
21-31	$10.50	$32.00	$75.00	£7.00	£21.00	£50.00
32-50	$6.25	$19.00	$45.00	£4.25	£12.50	£30.00
Title Value:	$610.75	$1858.00	$4430.00	£413.25	£1247.50	£2970.00

BIKER MICE FROM MARS

Marvel Comics Group, TV; 1 Nov 1993-6 Apr 1994

Issue	$Good	$Fine	$N.Mint	£Good	£Fine	£N.Mint
1 adaptation of animated TV film	$0.25	$0.75	$1.25	£0.15	£0.45	£0.75
2-6	$0.25	$0.75	$1.25	£0.15	£0.45	£0.75
Title Value:	$1.50	$4.50	$7.50	£0.90	£2.70	£4.50

BILL & TED II MOVIE ADAPTATION

Marvel Comics Group,OS; 1 Sep 1991

Issue	$Good	$Fine	$N.Mint	£Good	£Fine	£N.Mint
1 adaptation of film, news-stand edition	$0.40	$1.20	$2.00	£0.25	£0.75	£1.25
1 Direct Market Edition, ND - adaptation of film, bookshelf format	$0.90	$2.70	$4.50	£0.60	£1.80	£3.00
Title Value:	$1.30	$3.90	$6.50	£0.85	£2.55	£4.25

BILL & TED'S EXCELLENT COMIC BOOK

Marvel Comics Group; 1 Dec 1991-12 Nov 1992

Issue	$Good	$Fine	$N.Mint	£Good	£Fine	£N.Mint
1 based on film	$0.15	$0.45	$0.75	£0.10	£0.35	£0.60
2	$0.15	$0.45	$0.75	£0.10	£0.35	£0.60
3 $1.25 cover begins	$0.15	$0.45	$0.75	£0.10	£0.35	£0.60

	$Good	$Fine	$N.Mint	£Good	£Fine	£N.Mint
4-12	*$0.15*	*$0.45*	*$0.75*	£0.10	£0.35	£0.60
Title Value:	*$1.80*	*$5.40*	*$9.00*	£1.20	£4.20	£7.20

BILL 99

Dark Horse,MS; 1 Nov 1991-4 Feb 1992

	$Good	$Fine	$N.Mint	£Good	£Fine	£N.Mint
1-4 ND 48pgs	*$0.60*	*$1.80*	*$3.00*	£0.40	£1.20	£2.00
Title Value:	*$2.40*	*$7.20*	*$12.00*	£1.60	£4.80	£8.00

BILL BLACK'S FUN COMICS

Paragon/AC Comics; 1 Dec 1982-4 Mar 1983

	$Good	$Fine	$N.Mint	£Good	£Fine	£N.Mint
1 ND oversize, intro Captain Paragon	*$0.40*	*$1.20*	*$2.00*	£0.25	£0.75	£1.25
2 ND oversize, Commando D	*$0.40*	*$1.20*	*$2.00*	£0.25	£0.75	£1.25
3 ND oversize, Captain Paragon, Nightveil	*$0.40*	*$1.20*	*$2.00*	£0.25	£0.75	£1.25
4 ND 1st Colour, 1st Americomics issue, Phantom Lady becomes Nightfall	*$0.40*	*$1.20*	*$2.00*	£0.25	£0.75	£1.25
Title Value:	*$1.60*	*$4.80*	*$8.00*	£1.00	£3.00	£5.00

BILL THE GALACTIC HERO

Topps,MS; 1 Jul 1994-3 Sep 1994

	$Good	$Fine	$N.Mint	£Good	£Fine	£N.Mint
1-3 ND 48pgs, adaptation of Harry Harrison characters	*$1.00*	*$3.00*	*$5.00*	£0.70	£2.10	£3.50
Title Value:	*$3.00*	*$9.00*	*$15.00*	£2.10	£6.30	£10.50

BILLY NGUYEN

Caliber Press,MS; 1 Feb 1991-2 May 1991

	$Good	$Fine	$N.Mint	£Good	£Fine	£N.Mint
1-2 ND	*$0.40*	*$1.20*	*$2.00*	£0.25	£0.75	£1.25
Title Value:	*$0.80*	*$2.40*	*$4.00*	£0.50	£1.50	£2.50

Compilation Novel, reprints early adventures published by Attitude Zone Comics £6.75

BILLY THE KID

Charlton; 9 Nov 1957-153 Mar 1983

(#1-8 called The Masked Raider)

	$Good	$Fine	$N.Mint	£Good	£Fine	£N.Mint
9	*$8.50*	*$26.00*	*$60.00*	£5.50	£17.00	£40.00
10	*$5.75*	*$17.50*	*$35.00*	£4.15	£12.50	£25.00
11 origin	*$6.50*	*$20.00*	*$40.00*	£4.55	£13.50	£27.50
12	*$5.75*	*$17.50*	*$35.00*	£4.15	£12.50	£25.00
13 Williamson art	*$7.50*	*$22.50*	*$45.00*	£5.00	£15.00	£30.00
14	*$5.75*	*$17.50*	*$35.00*	£4.15	£12.50	£25.00
15 part Williamson art	*$7.50*	*$22.50*	*$45.00*	£5.00	£15.00	£30.00
16 part Williamson art	*$6.50*	*$20.00*	*$40.00*	£4.55	£13.50	£27.50
17-19	*$5.75*	*$17.50*	*$35.00*	£4.15	£12.50	£25.00
20-25	*$6.50*	*$20.00*	*$40.00*	£4.55	£13.50	£27.50
26-30	*$6.50*	*$20.00*	*$40.00*	£3.30	£10.00	£20.00
31-40	*$3.30*	*$10.00*	*$20.00*	£2.50	£7.50	£15.00
41-60	*$2.00*	*$6.00*	*$12.00*	£1.30	£4.00	£8.00
61-80	*$1.00*	*$3.00*	*$6.00*	£0.65	£2.00	£4.00
81-99	*$0.50*	*$1.50*	*$3.00*	£0.30	£1.00	£2.00
100	*$0.75*	*$2.25*	*$4.50*	£0.50	£1.50	£3.00
101-125	*$0.35*	*$1.10*	*$2.25*	£0.25	£0.75	£1.50
126-153	*$0.40*	*$1.20*	*$2.00*	£0.25	£0.75	£1.25
Title Value:	*$265.70*	*$807.85*	*$1563.75*	£176.75	£535.25	£1073.50

BINKY

National Periodical Publications; 61 Jun/Jul 1968-81 Oct/Nov 1971; 82 1977

(see Super DC Giant, Showcase) (previous issues ND)

	$Good	$Fine	$N.Mint	£Good	£Fine	£N.Mint
61-71 titled Leave It To Binky	*$1.40*	*$4.25*	*$10.00*	£0.85	£2.55	£6.00
72-81 title becomes Binky	*$1.00*	*$3.00*	*$6.00*	£0.50	£1.50	£3.00
82	*$0.40*	*$1.25*	*$2.50*	£0.25	£0.75	£1.50
Title Value:	*$25.80*	*$78.00*	*$172.50*	£14.60	£43.80	£97.50

BINKY'S BUDDIES

National Periodical Publications; 1 Jan/Feb 1969-12 Nov/Dec 1970

	$Good	$Fine	$N.Mint	£Good	£Fine	£N.Mint
1 scarce in the U.K.	*$1.30*	*$4.00*	*$8.00*	£0.80	£2.50	£5.00
2-12 scarce in the U.K.	*$0.80*	*$2.50*	*$5.00*	£0.50	£1.50	£3.00
Title Value:	*$10.10*	*$31.50*	*$63.00*	£6.30	£19.00	£38.00

BIO-BOOSTER ARMOR GUYVER

Viz Communications,MS; 1 Dec 1993-12 Nov 1994

	$Good	$Fine	$N.Mint	£Good	£Fine	£N.Mint
1-12 ND Yoshiki Takaya; black and white	*$0.45*	*$1.35*	*$2.25*	£0.30	£0.90	£1.50
Title Value:	*$5.40*	*$16.20*	*$27.00*	£3.60	£10.80	£18.00
Bio-Booster Armor Guyver Graphic Novel (Apr 1995) collects issues #1-6 retelling origin				£2.00	£6.00	£10.00

BIO-BOOSTER ARMOR GUYVER PART 2

Viz Communications,MS; 1 Oct 1994-6 Mar 1995

	$Good	$Fine	$N.Mint	£Good	£Fine	£N.Mint
1-6 ND Yoshiki Takaya; black and white	*$0.45*	*$1.35*	*$2.25*	£0.30	£0.90	£1.50
Title Value:	*$2.70*	*$8.10*	*$13.50*	£1.80	£5.40	£9.00
Bio-Booster Armor Guyver: Revenge of Chronos (Jun 1995) Trade paperback reprints issues #1-6				£2.10	£6.30	£10.50

BIO-BOOSTER ARMOR GUYVER PART 3

Viz Communications,MS; 1 Apr 1995-7 Oct 1995

	$Good	$Fine	$N.Mint	£Good	£Fine	£N.Mint
1-7 ND Yoshiki Takaya script and art; black and white	*$0.45*	*$1.35*	*$2.25*	£0.30	£0.90	£1.50
Title Value:	*$3.15*	*$9.45*	*$15.75*	£2.10	£6.30	£10.50

BIO-BOOSTER ARMOR GUYVER PART 4

Viz Communications,MS; 1 Nov 1995-6 Apr 1996

	$Good	$Fine	$N.Mint	£Good	£Fine	£N.Mint
1-6 ND Yoshiki Takaya script and art; black and white	*$0.55*	*$1.65*	*$2.75*	£0.35	£1.05	£1.75
Title Value:	*$3.30*	*$9.90*	*$16.50*	£2.10	£6.30	£10.50

BIONEERS

Mirage/Next Comics; 1 Aug 1994-3 1994

	$Good	$Fine	$N.Mint	£Good	£Fine	£N.Mint
1-2 ND A.C. Farley script and art	*$0.50*	*$1.50*	*$2.50*	£0.30	£0.90	£1.50
3 ND A.C. Farley script and art; with two bound-in trading cards	*$0.50*	*$1.50*	*$2.50*	£0.30	£0.90	£1.50
Title Value:	*$1.50*	*$4.50*	*$7.50*	£0.90	£2.70	£4.50

BIONIC WOMAN, THE ALL NEW

Charlton, TV; 1 Oct 1977-5 Jun 1978

	$Good	$Fine	$N.Mint	£Good	£Fine	£N.Mint
1 distributed in the U.K.	*$0.55*	*$1.75*	*$3.50*	£0.40	£1.25	£2.50
2-5 distributed in the U.K.	*$0.50*	*$1.50*	*$3.00*	£0.30	£1.00	£2.00
Title Value:	*$2.55*	*$7.75*	*$15.50*	£1.60	£5.25	£10.50

BIRDLAND

Eros Comix,MS; 1 Oct 1990-3 Apr 1991

	$Good	$Fine	$N.Mint	£Good	£Fine	£N.Mint
1 ND scarce in the U.K. features Bang Bang and Inez from Love and Rockets, Gilbert Hernandez art; adult material	*$1.50*	*$4.50*	*$7.50*	£0.90	£2.70	£4.50
2-3 ND scarce in the U.K. features Bang Bang and Inez from Love and Rockets, Gilbert Hernandez art; adult material	*$0.90*	*$2.70*	*$4.50*	£0.60	£1.80	£3.00
Title Value:	*$3.30*	*$9.90*	*$16.50*	£2.10	£6.30	£10.50

Note: issues delayed and also made scarce owing to cutoms seizure

BIRDS OF PREY: MANHUNT

DC Comics,MS; 1 Sep 1996-4 Dec 1996

	$Good	$Fine	$N.Mint	£Good	£Fine	£N.Mint
1 ND Black Canary, Oracle, Catwoman and Huntress appear; Chuck Dixon script, Gary Frank covers	*$0.40*	*$1.20*	*$2.00*	£0.30	£0.90	£1.50
2-4 ND	*$0.40*	*$1.20*	*$2.00*	£0.25	£0.75	£1.25
Title Value:	*$1.60*	*$4.80*	*$8.00*	£1.05	£3.15	£5.25

BIRTH RITE

(see British Section)

BISHOP

Marvel Comics Group,MS; 1 Dec 1994-4 Mar 1995

	$Good	$Fine	$N.Mint	£Good	£Fine	£N.Mint
1-4 foil stamped cover	*$0.60*	*$1.80*	*$3.00*	£0.40	£1.20	£2.00
Title Value:	*$2.40*	*$7.20*	*$12.00*	£1.60	£4.80	£8.00
Bishop Mini Masterpiece (Nov 1995) boxed set of issues #1-4, ND				£1.50	£4.50	£7.50
Bishop: Mountjoy Crisis (Mar 1996) Trade paperback ND collects mini-series				£1.70	£5.10	£8.50

BIZARRE 3-D ZONE

Blackthorne; (3-D Series #5) 1 Jul 1986

	$Good	$Fine	$N.Mint	£Good	£Fine	£N.Mint
1 ND Spain, Strand, Pound, Stout, Scott Shaw, Sekowsky, Robert Williams art, with 3-D glasses (25% less without glasses)	*$0.50*	*$1.50*	*$2.50*	£0.30	£0.90	£1.50
Title Value:	*$0.50*	*$1.50*	*$2.50*	£0.30	£0.90	£1.50

BIZARRE ADVENTURES

Marvel Comics Group,Magazine; 25 Mar 1981-34 Feb 1983

(formerly Marvel Preview)

	$Good	$Fine	$N.Mint	£Good	£Fine	£N.Mint
25 ND Lethal Ladies; Rogers/Gulacy/Golden art	*$0.40*	*$1.20*	*$2.00*	£0.50	£1.50	£2.50
26 ND Kull; Bolton art	*$0.40*	*$1.20*	*$2.00*	£0.50	£1.50	£2.50
27 ND X-Men; Phoenix, Iceman, Nightcrawler; John Buscema art on Phoenix story, George Perez art on Iceman story, Dave Cockrum art on Nightcrawler story	*$0.80*	*$2.40*	*$4.00*	£0.70	£2.10	£3.50
28 ND Unlikely Heroes; Miller's Elektra, Neal Adams, Golden art	*$0.80*	*$2.40*	*$4.00*	£0.70	£2.10	£3.50
29 ND Horror; 1st appearance Greenberg the Vampire, Walt Simonson art	*$0.40*	*$1.20*	*$2.00*	£0.50	£1.50	£2.50
30 ND Paradox	*$0.40*	*$1.20*	*$2.00*	£0.30	£0.90	£1.50
31 ND Violence issue; Frank Miller, John Byrne art	*$0.50*	*$1.50*	*$2.50*	£0.30	£0.90	£1.50
32 ND scarce in the U.K. Gods (inc. Thor); Bolton art	*$0.40*	*$1.20*	*$2.00*	£0.40	£1.20	£2.00
33 ND Horror stories	*$0.40*	*$1.20*	*$2.00*	£0.30	£0.90	£1.50
34 ND Son of Santa; Howard the Duck by Paul Smith	*$0.40*	*$1.20*	*$2.00*	£0.30	£0.90	£1.50
Title Value:	*$4.90*	*$14.70*	*$24.50*	£4.50	£13.50	£22.50

Note: #34 in comic and magazine format.

BLACK AND WHITE

Image,MS; 1 Oct 1994-3 Dec 1994

	$Good	$Fine	$N.Mint	£Good	£Fine	£N.Mint
1-3 ND Art Thibert art	*$0.40*	*$1.20*	*$2.00*	£0.25	£0.75	£1.25
Title Value:	*$1.20*	*$3.60*	*$6.00*	£0.75	£2.25	£3.75

BLACK AND WHITE (2ND SERIES)

Image; 1 Feb 1996-4 1996 ?

	$Good	$Fine	$N.Mint	£Good	£Fine	£N.Mint
1-4 ND Art Thibert art	*$0.50*	*$1.50*	*$2.50*	£0.30	£0.90	£1.50
Title Value:	*$2.00*	*$6.00*	*$10.00*	£1.20	£3.60	£6.00

BLACK ANVIL

Image,MS; 1 Jan 1996-2 1996 ?

	$Good	$Fine	$N.Mint	£Good	£Fine	£N.Mint
1-2 ND Len Wein script, Frank Gomez art	*$0.50*	*$1.50*	*$2.50*	£0.30	£0.90	£1.50
Title Value:	*$1.00*	*$3.00*	*$5.00*	£0.60	£1.80	£3.00

BLACK AXE

Marvel UK; 1 Apr 1993-10 Jan 1994

	$Good	$Fine	$N.Mint	£Good	£Fine	£N.Mint
1 Simon Jowett script, Death's Head II appears, cover pencils by John Romita Jnr.	*$0.30*	*$0.90*	*$1.50*	£0.15	£0.45	£0.75
2-3 Death's Head II appears						

	$Good	$Fine	$N.Mint	£Good	£Fine	£N.Mint
	$0.30	$0.90	$1.50	£0.15	£0.45	£0.75
4 Liam Sharp cover	$0.30	$0.90	$1.50	£0.15	£0.45	£0.75
5 1st appearance Afrikaa, Black Panther appears						
	$0.30	$0.90	$1.50	£0.15	£0.45	£0.75
6-7 Black Panther appears						
	$0.30	$0.90	$1.50	£0.15	£0.45	£0.75
8 Liam Sharp cover	$0.30	$0.90	$1.50	£0.15	£0.45	£0.75
9-10	$0.30	$0.90	$1.50	£0.15	£0.45	£0.75
Title Value:	$3.00	$9.00	$15.00	£1.50	£4.50	£7.50

BLACK CANARY

DC Comics,MS; 1 Nov 1991-4 Feb 1992

	$Good	$Fine	$N.Mint	£Good	£Fine	£N.Mint
1-4 Trevor Von Eeden art						
	$0.30	$0.90	$1.50	£0.20	£0.60	£1.00
Title Value:	$1.20	$3.60	$6.00	£0.80	£2.40	£4.00

BLACK CANARY (2ND SERIES)

DC Comics; 1 Jan 1993-12 Dec 1993

	$Good	$Fine	$N.Mint	£Good	£Fine	£N.Mint
1-5	$0.25	$0.75	$1.25	£0.15	£0.45	£0.75
6 leads into Green Arrow #75						
	$0.25	$0.75	$1.25	£0.15	£0.45	£0.75
7-10	$0.25	$0.75	$1.25	£0.15	£0.45	£0.75
11 Nightwing and Huntress appear						
	$0.25	$0.75	$1.25	£0.15	£0.45	£0.75
12	$0.25	$0.75	$1.25	£0.15	£0.45	£0.75
Title Value:	$3.00	$9.00	$15.00	£1.80	£5.40	£9.00

BLACK CANARY/ORACLE: BIRDS OF PREY

DC Comics,OS; 1 Jan 1996

	$Good	$Fine	$N.Mint	£Good	£Fine	£N.Mint
1 ND 48pgs, Chuck Dixon script, Gary Frank and John Dell art						
	$1.00	$3.00	$5.00	£0.60	£1.80	£3.00
Title Value:	$1.00	$3.00	$5.00	£0.60	£1.80	£3.00

BLACK CAT

Harvey; 63 Oct 1962-65 Apr 1963

	$Good	$Fine	$N.Mint	£Good	£Fine	£N.Mint
63-65 scarce though distributed in the U.K. giant size, all reprint						
	$12.50	$39.00	$90.00	£8.50	£26.00	£60.00
Title Value:	$37.50	$117.00	$270.00	£25.50	£78.00	£180.00

BLACK CAT, ALFRED HARVEY'S

Lorne Harvey Publications/Recollections,MS; 1 Aug 1995-2 Oct 1995

	$Good	$Fine	$N.Mint	£Good	£Fine	£N.Mint
1 ND 52pgs, new costume and new origin by Mark Evanier and Murphy Anderson plus Lee Elias reprint; cover by the Brothers Hildebrandt						
	$0.70	$2.10	$3.50	£0.50	£1.50	£2.50
2 ND origin continues plus the origin of Ms. Fortune						
	$0.70	$2.10	$3.50	£0.50	£1.50	£2.50
Title Value:	$1.40	$4.20	$7.00	£1.00	£3.00	£5.00

BLACK CAT, FELICIA HARDY

Marvel Comics Group,MS; 1 Jul 1994-4 Oct 1994

	$Good	$Fine	$N.Mint	£Good	£Fine	£N.Mint
1-2 Spiderman appears						
	$0.25	$0.75	$1.25	£0.15	£0.45	£0.75
3-4 Spiderman and Cardiac appear						
	$0.25	$0.75	$1.25	£0.15	£0.45	£0.75
Title Value:	$1.00	$3.00	$5.00	£0.60	£1.80	£3.00

BLACK CAT, THE ORIGINAL

Recollections; 1 Sep 1988-2 1988; Lorne-Harvey; 3 1990-11 1992

	$Good	$Fine	$N.Mint	£Good	£Fine	£N.Mint
1 ND Lee Elias/Joe Kubert reprints begin						
	$0.30	$0.90	$1.50	£0.20	£0.60	£1.00
2-11 ND	$0.30	$0.90	$1.50	£0.20	£0.60	£1.00
Title Value:	$3.30	$9.90	$16.50	£2.20	£6.60	£11.00

BLACK COMMANDO: DARK DYNAMO

AC Comics; 1 Jan 1993

	$Good	$Fine	$N.Mint	£Good	£Fine	£N.Mint
1 ND Thunder Agents tie-in; flash-back sequence by Wally Wood						
	$0.40	$1.20	$2.00	£0.25	£0.75	£1.25
Title Value:	$0.40	$1.20	$2.00	£0.25	£0.75	£1.25

BLACK CONDOR, THE

DC Comics; 1 Jun 1992-12 May 1993

	$Good	$Fine	$N.Mint	£Good	£Fine	£N.Mint
1-8	$0.25	$0.75	$1.25	£0.15	£0.45	£0.75
9-10 The Ray appears						
	$0.25	$0.75	$1.25	£0.15	£0.45	£0.75
11 origin	$0.25	$0.75	$1.25	£0.15	£0.45	£0.75
12 Batman appears	$0.25	$0.75	$1.25	£0.15	£0.45	£0.75
Title Value:	$3.00	$9.00	$15.00	£1.80	£5.40	£9.00

BLACK CROSS SPECIAL

Dark Horse,OS; 1 Jan 1988

	$Good	$Fine	$N.Mint	£Good	£Fine	£N.Mint
1 ND Dark Horse Presents reprints						
	$0.90	$2.70	$4.50	£0.60	£1.80	£3.00
Title Value:	$0.90	$2.70	$4.50	£0.60	£1.80	£3.00

BLACK DIAMOND

Americomics, Film; 1 May 1983-5 Apr 1984

(see Colt Special)

	$Good	$Fine	$N.Mint	£Good	£Fine	£N.Mint
1 ND Sybil Danning photos/features						
	$0.40	$1.20	$2.00	£0.25	£0.75	£1.25
2-4 ND Colt backups, Gulacy covers						
	$0.40	$1.20	$2.00	£0.25	£0.75	£1.25
5 ND Colt backup, Gulacy cover, Sybil Danning/"V" feature						
	$0.40	$1.20	$2.00	£0.25	£0.75	£1.25
Title Value:	$2.00	$6.00	$10.00	£1.25	£3.75	£6.25

BLACK DOMINION

Anubis Press; 1 Jul 1993

	$Good	$Fine	$N.Mint	£Good	£Fine	£N.Mint
1 ND black and white						
	$0.40	$1.20	$2.00	£0.25	£0.75	£1.25
Title Value:	$0.40	$1.20	$2.00	£0.25	£0.75	£1.25

BLACK DRAGON, THE

Marvel Comics Group/Epic,MS; 1 May 1985-6 Oct 1985

	$Good	$Fine	$N.Mint	£Good	£Fine	£N.Mint
1 ND scarce in the U.K. Claremont scripts, Bolton art begins						
	$0.30	$0.90	$1.50	£0.50	£1.50	£2.50
2-6 ND Bolton art	$0.30	$0.90	$1.50	£0.30	£0.90	£1.50
Title Value:	$1.80	$5.40	$9.00	£2.00	£6.00	£10.00

The Black Dragon (Sep 1994) Trade paperback

	$Good	$Fine	$N.Mint	£Good	£Fine	£N.Mint
reprints mini-series with new painted cover by John Bolton				£2.00	£6.00	£10.00

Note: this edition published by Dark Horse Comics and re-solicited with new painted cover in March 1996

BLACK ENCHANTRESS

Heroic Publishing; 1 Jan 1995-2 1995

	$Good	$Fine	$N.Mint	£Good	£Fine	£N.Mint
1 ND origin told	$0.40	$1.20	$2.00	£0.25	£0.75	£1.25
2 ND	$0.40	$1.20	$2.00	£0.25	£0.75	£1.25
Title Value:	$0.80	$2.40	$4.00	£0.50	£1.50	£2.50

BLACK FLAG

Image; 1 Jun 1994

	$Good	$Fine	$N.Mint	£Good	£Fine	£N.Mint
1 ND black and white						
	$0.40	$1.20	$2.00	£0.25	£0.75	£1.25
Title Value:	$0.40	$1.20	$2.00	£0.25	£0.75	£1.25

BLACK FLAG (2ND SERIES)

Maximum Comic Press; 0 Jul 1995; 1 Jan 1995-6 1995 ?

	$Good	$Fine	$N.Mint	£Good	£Fine	£N.Mint
0 ND Dan Fraga script and part art						
	$0.50	$1.50	$2.50	£0.30	£0.90	£1.50
1 ND Dan Fraga script, Eric Stephenson art; gatefold cover						
	$0.50	$1.50	$2.50	£0.30	£0.90	£1.50
2 ND	$0.50	$1.50	$2.50	£0.30	£0.90	£1.50
2 Variant Cover Edition, ND Stephen Platt/Dan Fraga cover art, Black Flag solo on cover						
	$0.60	$1.80	$3.00	£0.40	£1.20	£2.00
3-4 ND	$0.50	$1.50	$2.50	£0.30	£0.90	£1.50
4 Variant Cover Edition, ND same as regular issue but with white background						
	$0.50	$1.50	$2.50	£0.30	£0.90	£1.50
5-6 ND	$0.50	$1.50	$2.50	£0.30	£0.90	£1.50
Title Value:	$4.60	$13.80	$23.00	£2.80	£8.40	£14.00

BLACK FLAG PREVIEW EDITION

Image,OS; 1 Jun 1994

	$Good	$Fine	$N.Mint	£Good	£Fine	£N.Mint
1 ND previews series, black and white; 100,000 copies						
	$0.40	$1.20	$2.00	£0.25	£0.75	£1.25
Title Value:	$0.40	$1.20	$2.00	£0.25	£0.75	£1.25

BLACK FURY

Charlton; 1 May 1955-57 Mar/Apr 1966

	$Good	$Fine	$N.Mint	£Good	£Fine	£N.Mint
1	$5.00	$15.00	$40.00	£3.40	£10.00	£27.50
2	$2.85	$8.50	$20.00	£1.70	£5.00	£12.00
3-5	$2.10	$6.25	$15.00	£1.40	£4.25	£10.00
6-10	$1.70	$5.00	$12.00	£1.10	£3.40	£8.00
11-15	$1.25	$3.85	$9.00	£0.85	£2.55	£6.00
16-18 Steve Ditko art						
	$5.50	$17.00	$40.00	£3.90	£11.50	£27.50
19-20	$1.00	$3.00	$7.00	£0.60	£1.90	£4.50
21-30	$1.05	$3.20	$7.50	£0.70	£2.10	£5.00
31-57	$0.55	$1.70	$4.00	£0.35	£1.05	£2.50
Title Value:	$72.75	$221.40	$527.00	£48.40	£145.15	£348.50

Note: Limited Distribution in the U.K. after 1959.

BLACK GOLIATH

Marvel Comics Group; 1 Feb 1976-5 Nov 1976

(see Powerman #24)

	$Good	$Fine	$N.Mint	£Good	£Fine	£N.Mint
1	$0.65	$2.00	$4.00	£0.30	£1.00	£2.00
2	$0.50	$1.50	$3.00	£0.25	£0.75	£1.50
3	$0.50	$1.50	$3.00	£0.20	£0.60	£1.25
4 Black Goliath vs. Stiltman, Jack Kirby cover						
	$0.50	$1.50	$3.00	£0.20	£0.60	£1.25
5	$0.50	$1.50	$3.00	£0.20	£0.60	£1.25
Title Value:	$2.65	$8.00	$16.00	£1.15	£3.55	£7.25

Note: #2-5 Claremont script

BLACK HOLE

Kitchen Sink,OS; 1 Mar 1995

	$Good	$Fine	$N.Mint	£Good	£Fine	£N.Mint
1 ND Charles Burns script and art						
	$0.80	$2.40	$4.00	£0.50	£1.50	£2.50
Title Value:	$0.80	$2.40	$4.00	£0.50	£1.50	£2.50

BLACK HOLE, THE

Whitman, Film; 1 Mar 1980-3 Jul 1980

	$Good	$Fine	$N.Mint	£Good	£Fine	£N.Mint
1-2 adaptation of Walt Disney film, photo cover						
	$0.30	$0.90	$1.50	£0.20	£0.60	£1.00
3 titled "Beyond The Black Hole"; new adventures, photo cover						
	$0.30	$0.90	$1.50	£0.20	£0.60	£1.00
Title Value:	$0.90	$2.70	$4.50	£0.60	£1.80	£3.00

Note: Limited Distribution in the U.K.

BLACK HOOD

Red Circle; 1 Jan 1983-3 Oct 1983

	$Good	$Fine	$N.Mint	£Good	£Fine	£N.Mint
1 ND Gray Morrow and Doug Wildey art, Alex Toth cover						
	$0.30	$0.90	$1.50	£0.20	£0.60	£1.00
2 ND Alex Toth art on The Fox back-up, Alex Toth cover						
	$0.30	$0.90	$1.50	£0.20	£0.60	£1.00
3 ND Gray Morrow art on The Fox back-up, Alex Toth cover						
	$0.30	$0.90	$1.50	£0.20	£0.60	£1.00
Title Value:	$0.90	$2.70	$4.50	£0.60	£1.80	£3.00

BLACK HOOD

DC Comics/Impact; 1 Dec 1991-12 Dec 1992

	$Good	$Fine	$N.Mint	£Good	£Fine	£N.Mint
1-12	$0.15	$0.45	$0.75	£0.10	£0.35	£0.60
Title Value:	$1.80	$5.40	$9.00	£1.20	£4.20	£7.20

BLACK HOOD ANNUAL

DC Comics/Impact; 1 Jun 1992

	$Good	$Fine	$N.Mint	£Good	£Fine	£N.Mint
1 64pgs, Earthquest part 6 (see other Impact annuals), includes trading card						
	$0.30	$0.90	$1.50	£0.20	£0.60	£1.00
Title Value:	$0.30	$0.90	$1.50	£0.20	£0.60	£1.00

VERY GENERAL PERCENTAGE CONVERSION CHART WHICH MAY BE USED TO CALCULATE LOW AND INBETWEEN GRADES:

BLACK KISS

Vortex,MS; 1 Jun 1988-12 Jul 1989
(see Big Black Kiss)

	$Good	$Fine	$N.Mint	£Good	£Fine	£N.Mint
1 Chaykin story/art begins, 2-colour cover	$1.20	$3.60	$6.00	£0.80	£2.40	£4.00
1 2nd printing	$0.60	$1.80	$3.00	£0.40	£1.20	£2.00
1 3rd printing	$0.40	$1.20	$2.00	£0.25	£0.75	£1.25
2	$0.90	$2.70	$4.50	£0.60	£1.80	£3.00
2 2nd printing	$0.60	$1.80	$3.00	£0.40	£1.20	£2.00
3	$0.75	$2.25	$3.75	£0.50	£1.50	£2.50
3 2nd printing	$0.40	$1.20	$2.00	£0.25	£0.75	£1.25
4	$0.60	$1.80	$3.00	£0.40	£1.20	£2.00
4 2nd printing	$0.40	$1.20	$2.00	£0.25	£0.75	£1.25
5 1st full-colour cover	$0.60	$1.80	$3.00	£0.40	£1.20	£2.00
6-12	$0.60	$1.80	$3.00	£0.40	£1.20	£2.00
Title Value:	$10.65	$31.95	$53.25	£7.05	£21.15	£35.25

Note: all Non-Distributed on the news-stands in the U.K. All pre-bagged. At the time, there were fears about the plastic being low grade/acidic so most were torn off (and also to enjoy the content!). Intact pre-bagged issues are very scarce

Thick Black Kiss (Sep 1993)

	$Good	$Fine	$N.Mint	£Good	£Fine	£N.Mint
138pgs, softcover; collects 12 part series				£1.20	£3.60	£6.00

BLACK KNIGHT

Marvel Comics Group,MS; 1 Jun 1990-4 Sep 1990
(see Avengers, Avengers Spotlight)

	$Good	$Fine	$N.Mint	£Good	£Fine	£N.Mint
1 ND	$0.30	$0.90	$1.50	£0.20	£0.60	£1.00
2 ND Captain Britain appears	$0.30	$0.90	$1.50	£0.20	£0.60	£1.00
3-4 ND Dr. Strange appears	$0.30	$0.90	$1.50	£0.20	£0.60	£1.00
Title Value:	$1.20	$3.60	$6.00	£0.80	£2.40	£4.00

BLACK KNIGHT

Super Comics; 11 1963

	$Good	$Fine	$N.Mint	£Good	£Fine	£N.Mint
11 scarce, distributed in the U.K. All reprints	$2.50	$7.50	$17.50	£1.75	£5.25	£12.50
Title Value:	$2.50	$7.50	$17.50	£1.75	£5.25	£12.50

BLACK KNIGHT: EXODUS

Marvel Comics Group,OS; nn Dec 1996

	$Good	$Fine	$N.Mint	£Good	£Fine	£N.Mint
nn ND 48pgs, Black Knight and Sersi appear, origin of Exodus	$0.50	$1.50	$2.50	£0.30	£0.90	£1.50
Title Value:	$0.50	$1.50	$2.50	£0.30	£0.90	£1.50

BLACK LAMB, THE

DC Comics/Helix,MS; 1 Nov 1996-6 Apr 1996

	$Good	$Fine	$N.Mint	£Good	£Fine	£N.Mint
1-6 ND Tim Truman script and art	$0.50	$1.50	$2.50	£0.30	£0.90	£1.50
Title Value:	$3.00	$9.00	$15.00	£1.80	£5.40	£9.00

BLACK LIGHTNING

DC Comics; 1 Apr 1977-11 Sep/Oct 1978
(see DC Comics Presents, Detective, World's Finest)

	$Good	$Fine	$N.Mint	£Good	£Fine	£N.Mint
1 scarce in the U.K. Von Eeden art	$0.65	$2.00	$4.00	£0.30	£1.00	£2.00
2-3 Von Eeden art	$0.50	$1.50	$3.00	£0.25	£0.75	£1.50
4-5 Von Eeden art, Superman appears	$0.50	$1.50	$3.00	£0.25	£0.75	£1.50
6-10 Von Eeden art	$0.30	$1.00	$2.00	£0.20	£0.60	£1.25
11 44pgs, The Ray appears	$0.40	$1.25	$2.50	£0.25	£0.75	£1.50
Title Value:	$4.55	$14.25	$28.50	£2.55	£7.75	£15.75

BLACK LIGHTNING (2ND SERIES)

DC Comics; 1 Feb 1995-13 Feb 1996

	$Good	$Fine	$N.Mint	£Good	£Fine	£N.Mint
1 Tony Isabella script begins	$0.40	$1.20	$2.00	£0.25	£0.75	£1.25
2-4	$0.40	$1.20	$2.00	£0.25	£0.75	£1.25
5	$0.45	$1.35	$2.25	£0.30	£0.90	£1.50
6-8 Gangbuster guest-stars	$0.45	$1.35	$2.25	£0.30	£0.90	£1.50
9-11	$0.45	$1.35	$2.25	£0.30	£0.90	£1.50
12-13 Batman appears	$0.45	$1.35	$2.25	£0.30	£0.90	£1.50
Title Value:	$5.65	$16.95	$28.25	£3.70	£11.10	£18.50

BLACK MAGIC

Crestwood Publishing; Vol 7 #3 Jul/Aug 1960-Vol 8 #5 Nov/Dec 1961
(prevoius issues ND)

	$Good	$Fine	$N.Mint	£Good	£Fine	£N.Mint
Vol 7 #3 distributed in the U.K.	$6.25	$19.00	$45.00	£4.25	£12.50	£30.00
Vol 7 #4 distributed in the U.K.	$5.25	$16.00	$37.50	£3.55	£10.50	£25.00
Vol 7 #5 distributed in the U.K.	$5.25	$16.00	$37.50	£3.55	£10.50	£25.00
Vol 7 #6 distributed in the U.K.	$5.25	$16.00	$37.50	£3.55	£10.50	£25.00
Vol 8 #1 distributed in the U.K.	$5.25	$16.00	$37.50	£3.55	£10.50	£25.00
Vol 8 #2, distributed in the U.K. Steve Ditko art	$7.00	$21.00	$50.00	£4.60	£13.50	£32.50
Vol 8 #3 distributed in the U.K.	$6.25	$19.00	$45.00	£4.60	£13.50	£32.50
Vol 8 #4 distributed in the U.K.	$5.25	$16.00	$37.50	£3.55	£10.50	£25.00
Vol 8 #5 distributed in the U.K.	$6.25	$19.00	$45.00	£4.60	£13.50	£32.50
Title Value:	$52.00	$158.00	$372.50	£35.80	£105.50	£252.50

BLACK MAGIC

DC Comics; 1 Oct/Nov 1973-9 Apr/May 1975

	$Good	$Fine	$N.Mint	£Good	£Fine	£N.Mint
1 Simon & Jack Kirby pre-code horror reprints begin	$0.65	$2.00	$4.00	£0.30	£1.00	£2.00
2-3	$0.50	$1.50	$3.00	£0.25	£0.75	£1.50
4-9	$0.50	$1.50	$3.00	£0.20	£0.60	£1.25
Title Value:	$4.65	$14.00	$28.00	£2.00	£6.10	£12.50

BLACK MASK

DC Comics,MS; 1 Nov 1993-3 Jan 1994

	$Good	$Fine	$N.Mint	£Good	£Fine	£N.Mint
1-3 ND 48pgs, squarebound, Brian Augustyn and Jim Baikie	$0.80	$2.40	$4.00	£0.50	£1.50	£2.50
Title Value:	$2.40	$7.20	$12.00	£1.50	£4.50	£7.50

BLACK MIST: ANGUISH OF THE MIST GRAPHIC NOVEL

Caliber Press,OS; nn Apr 1995

	$Good	$Fine	$N.Mint	£Good	£Fine	£N.Mint
nn ND Negative Burn anthology spin-off	$2.50	$7.50	$12.50	£1.50	£4.50	£7.50
Title Value:	$2.50	$7.50	$12.50	£1.50	£4.50	£7.50

BLACK OPS

Image,MS; 1 Jan 1996-5 May 1996 ?

	$Good	$Fine	$N.Mint	£Good	£Fine	£N.Mint
1-3 ND Dan Norton and Shon Bury script, Dan Norton and Sandra Hope art	$0.50	$1.50	$2.50	£0.30	£0.90	£1.50
4-5 ND Shon Bury and Dan Norton script, Dan Norton and Sandra Hope art	$0.50	$1.50	$2.50	£0.30	£0.90	£1.50
Title Value:	$2.50	$7.50	$12.50	£1.50	£4.50	£7.50

BLACK ORCHID

DC Comics,MS; 1 Nov 1988-3 Jan 1989
(see Adventure #428)

	$Good	$Fine	$N.Mint	£Good	£Fine	£N.Mint
1 ND Neil Gaiman script, Dave McKean painted art begins	$1.20	$3.60	$6.00	£0.60	£1.80	£3.00
2 ND Arkham Asylum						

Beware! #7

Bionic Woman #2

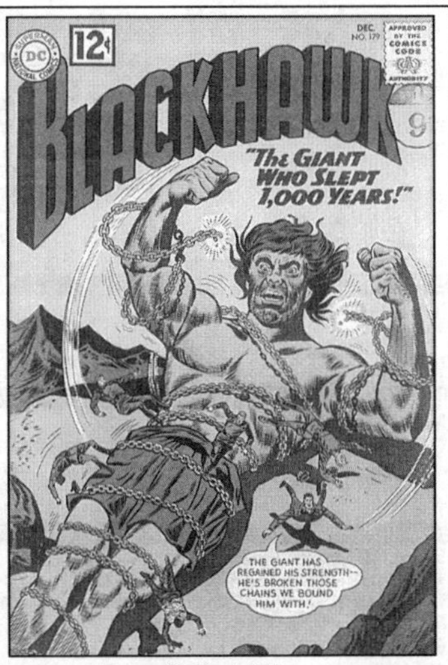

Blackhawk #179

	$Good	$Fine	$N.Mint	£Good	£Fine	£N.Mint
	$1.20	$3.60	$6.00	£0.60	£1.80	£3.00
3 ND	$1.20	$3.60	$6.00	£0.60	£1.80	£3.00
Title Value:	$3.60	$10.80	$18.00	£1.80	£5.40	£9.00

Note: 48pg Dark Knight format, UV glossy coated, squarebound

				£Good	£Fine	£N.Mint
Trade paperback (Aug 1991), 160pgs reprints mini-series with new Dave McKean cover				£2.50	£7.50	£12.50

BLACK ORCHID (2ND SERIES)

DC Comics/Vertigo; 1 Sep 1993-22 Jun 1995

	$Good	$Fine	$N.Mint	£Good	£Fine	£N.Mint
1 Dave McKean painted covers begin	$0.40	$1.20	$2.00	£0.25	£0.75	£1.25
1 Platinum Edition ND	$2.50	$7.50	$12.50	£1.50	£4.50	£7.50
2-16	$0.40	$1.20	$2.00	£0.25	£0.75	£1.25
17-22 Twisted Season story	$0.40	$1.20	$2.00	£0.25	£0.75	£1.25
Title Value:	$11.30	$33.90	$56.50	£7.00	£21.00	£35.00

BLACK ORCHID ANNUAL

DC Comics/Vertigo; 1 Dec 1993

	$Good	$Fine	$N.Mint	£Good	£Fine	£N.Mint
1 64pgs, Children's Crusade part 2, continued in Animal Man Annual #1	$0.80	$2.40	$4.00	£0.50	£1.50	£2.50
Title Value:	$0.80	$2.40	$4.00	£0.50	£1.50	£2.50

BLACK PANTHER, THE

Marvel Comics Group; 1 Jan 1977-15 May 1979

(see also Jungle Action)

	$Good	$Fine	$N.Mint	£Good	£Fine	£N.Mint
1 1st appearance King Solomon's frog (!), Jack Kirby art	$1.30	$4.00	$8.00	£0.50	£1.50	£3.00
2 ND Jack Kirby art	$0.80	$2.50	$5.00	£0.40	£1.25	£2.50
3-6 ND Jack Kirby art	$0.55	$1.75	$3.50	£0.30	£1.00	£2.00
7-12 Jack Kirby art	$0.40	$1.25	$2.50	£0.25	£0.75	£1.50
13 Bingham/Day art	$0.30	$1.00	$2.00	£0.20	£0.60	£1.25
14 Bingham/Day art, Avengers appear	$0.30	$1.00	$2.00	£0.20	£0.60	£1.25
15 scarce in the U.K. Bingham/Day art, Avengers appear	$0.30	$1.00	$2.00	£0.25	£0.75	£1.50
Title Value:	$7.60	$24.00	$47.50	£4.25	£13.20	£26.50

BLACK PANTHER, THE (LIMITED SERIES)

Marvel Comics Group,MS; 1 Jul 1988-4 Oct 1988

	$Good	$Fine	$N.Mint	£Good	£Fine	£N.Mint
1-4 ND Cowan art	$0.30	$0.90	$1.50	£0.20	£0.60	£1.00
Title Value:	$1.20	$3.60	$6.00	£0.80	£2.40	£4.00

BLACK PANTHER: PANTHER'S PREY

Marvel Comics Group,MS; 1 May 1991-4 Aug 1991

	$Good	$Fine	$N.Mint	£Good	£Fine	£N.Mint
1-4 ND 48pgs	$0.60	$1.80	$3.00	£0.40	£1.20	£2.00
Title Value:	$2.40	$7.20	$12.00	£1.60	£4.80	£8.00

Note: Bookshelf Format. Originally solicited for Oct 1990 but series delayed

BLACK PEARL, THE

Dark Horse,MS; 1 Sep 1996-5 Jan 1997

	$Good	$Fine	$N.Mint	£Good	£Fine	£N.Mint
1-5 ND Mark Hamill and Eric Johnson script, H.M. Baker and Bruce Patterson art	$0.60	$1.80	$3.00	£0.40	£1.20	£2.00
Title Value:	$3.00	$9.00	$15.00	£2.00	£6.00	£10.00

BLACK PHANTOM

AC Comics; 1 1989-3 1990

	$Good	$Fine	$N.Mint	£Good	£Fine	£N.Mint
1-3 ND new colour stories by Bill Black plus black and white reprints featuring Black Phantom and Red Mask	$0.40	$1.20	$2.00	£0.25	£0.75	£1.25
Title Value:	$1.20	$3.60	$6.00	£0.75	£2.25	£3.75

BLACK RIDER

Atlas Comics; 8 Mar 1950-27 Mar 1955

(previously Western Winners #1-7)

	$Good	$Fine	$N.Mint	£Good	£Fine	£N.Mint
8 ND scarce in the U.K.	$35.00	$105.00	$280.00	£23.00	£67.50	£185.00
9 ND 48pgs	$20.00	$60.00	$140.00	£13.50	£41.00	£95.00
10 ND 48pgs, origin retold	$22.50	$67.50	$160.00	£15.50	£47.00	£110.00
11-14 ND 48pgs	$15.00	$45.00	$105.00	£10.00	£30.00	£70.00
15-18 ND	$12.50	$39.00	$90.00	£8.50	£26.00	£60.00
19-20 ND Two Gun Kid story	$12.50	$39.00	$90.00	£8.50	£26.00	£60.00
21-22 ND	$10.50	$32.00	$75.00	£7.00	£21.00	£50.00
23 ND Two Gun Kid story	$10.50	$32.00	$75.00	£7.00	£21.00	£50.00
24-25 ND	$10.50	$32.00	$75.00	£7.00	£21.00	£50.00
26-27 ND Kid Colt story	$10.50	$32.00	$75.00	£7.00	£21.00	£50.00
Title Value:	$286.00	$870.50	$2065.00	£192.00	£578.50	£1380.00

BLACK SCORPION

Special Studio; 1 Apr 1991

	$Good	$Fine	$N.Mint	£Good	£Fine	£N.Mint
1 ND black and white	$0.40	$1.20	$2.00	£0.25	£0.75	£1.25
Title Value:	$0.40	$1.20	$2.00	£0.25	£0.75	£1.25

BLACK SEPTEMBER: INFINITY

Marvel Comics Group,OS; nn Nov 1995

	$Good	$Fine	$N.Mint	£Good	£Fine	£N.Mint
nn ND Dan Danko and Roland Mann script, Steve Butler and M.C. Wyman art; follow on from Ultraforce/Avengers and how the Marvel Universe and Malibu Ultraverse will merge	$0.60	$1.80	$3.00	£0.40	£1.20	£2.00
Title Value:	$0.60	$1.80	$3.00	£0.40	£1.20	£2.00

BLACK TERROR

Eclipse,MS; 1 Oct 1989-3 1990

	$Good	$Fine	$N.Mint	£Good	£Fine	£N.Mint
1-3 ND 48pgs	$0.80	$2.40	$4.00	£0.50	£1.50	£2.50
Title Value:	$2.40	$7.20	$12.00	£1.50	£4.50	£7.50

Note: squarebound, painted art by Daniel Brereton

				£Good	£Fine	£N.Mint
Graphic Album Softcover (Dec 1991) reprints 3 issue mini-series				£1.90	£5.70	£9.50
Graphic Album Hardcover Deluxe (Dec 1991) reprints mini-series, signed and numbered				£5.00	£15.00	£25.00

BLACK THUNDER

Breeze Comics; 1 1991

	$Good	$Fine	$N.Mint	£Good	£Fine	£N.Mint
1 ND black and white	$0.30	$0.90	$1.50	£0.20	£0.60	£1.00
Title Value:	$0.30	$0.90	$1.50	£0.20	£0.60	£1.00

BLACK ZEPPELIN, GENE DAY'S

Renegade; 1 Apr 1985-5 1986

	$Good	$Fine	$N.Mint	£Good	£Fine	£N.Mint
1 ND scarce in the U.K. Gene/Dan Day art	$0.30	$0.90	$1.50	£0.25	£0.75	£1.25
2-5 ND Gene/Dan Day art	$0.30	$0.90	$1.50	£0.20	£0.60	£1.00
Title Value:	$1.50	$4.50	$7.50	£1.05	£3.15	£5.25

BLACK-BOW

Artline Studios; 1 Mar 1991

	$Good	$Fine	$N.Mint	£Good	£Fine	£N.Mint
1 ND black and white	$0.30	$0.90	$1.50	£0.20	£0.60	£1.00
Title Value:	$0.30	$0.90	$1.50	£0.20	£0.60	£1.00

BLACKBALL COMICS

Blackball Comics; 1 Mar 1994

	$Good	$Fine	$N.Mint	£Good	£Fine	£N.Mint
1 ND 48pgs, Kev O'Neill and Keith Giffen art	$0.30	$0.90	$1.50	£0.20	£0.60	£1.00
Title Value:	$0.30	$0.90	$1.50	£0.20	£0.60	£1.00

Note: issues #2-4 were advertised and solicited but never came out.

BLACKBALL COMICS SPECIAL

Blackball Comics,OS; 1 Aug 1994

	$Good	$Fine	$N.Mint	£Good	£Fine	£N.Mint
1 ND Mark Wheatley, Bill Wray and Keith Giffen work featured	$0.50	$1.50	$2.50	£0.30	£0.90	£1.50
Title Value:	$0.50	$1.50	$2.50	£0.30	£0.90	£1.50

BLACKHAWK

National Periodical Publications/DC Comics; 108 Jan 1957-243 Oct/Nov 1968; 244 Jan/Feb 1976-250 Jan/Feb 1977; 251 Oct 1982-273 Nov 1984

(see also Brave and the Bold #167)

(previously published as Uncle Sam #1-8. #9-107 published by Quality Comics)

	$Good	$Fine	$N.Mint	£Good	£Fine	£N.Mint
108 1st DC issue	$52.50	$155.00	$425.00	£34.00	£100.00	£275.00
109	$29.00	$85.00	$200.00	£19.00	£57.50	£135.00
110-117	$20.00	$60.00	$140.00	£13.50	£41.00	£95.00
118 Frazetta reprint	$21.00	$62.50	$150.00	£14.00	£43.00	£100.00
119-130	$12.50	$39.00	$90.00	£8.50	£26.00	£60.00
131-132	$10.00	$30.00	$70.00	£6.25	£19.00	£45.00
133 1st appearance Lady Blackhawk	$10.00	$30.00	$70.00	£6.25	£19.00	£45.00
1st official distribution in the U.K.						
134-138	$10.00	$30.00	$70.00	£6.25	£19.00	£45.00
139 Lady Blackhawk returns	$10.00	$30.00	$70.00	£6.25	£19.00	£45.00
140	$10.00	$30.00	$70.00	£6.25	£19.00	£45.00
141-142	$7.75	$23.50	$55.00	£4.25	£12.50	£30.00
143 dinosaur cover	$7.75	$23.50	$55.00	£4.25	£12.50	£30.00
144-150	$7.75	$23.50	$55.00	£4.25	£12.50	£30.00
151 Lady Blackhawk with super powers (like a Supergirl-in-uniform!)	$6.25	$19.00	$45.00	£3.55	£10.50	£25.00
152-160	$6.25	$19.00	$45.00	£3.55	£10.50	£25.00
161-163	$5.00	$15.00	$35.00	£2.85	£8.50	£20.00
164 origin retold	$6.25	$19.00	$45.00	£2.85	£8.50	£20.00
165	$5.00	$15.00	$35.00	£2.85	£8.50	£20.00
166 last 10 cents issue	$5.00	$15.00	$35.00	£2.85	£8.50	£20.00
167-180	$3.90	$11.50	$27.50	£2.10	£6.25	£15.00
181-190	$2.10	$6.25	$15.00	£1.20	£3.60	£8.50
191-196	$1.75	$5.25	$12.50	£1.05	£3.20	£7.50
197 "new look" begins with new uniforms and change of direction for title	$1.75	$5.25	$12.50	£1.05	£3.20	£7.50
198 origins of these "new" Blackhawks retold	$2.10	$6.25	$15.00	£1.20	£3.60	£8.50
199	$1.75	$5.25	$12.50	£1.05	£3.20	£7.50
200 scarce in the U.K.	$2.10	$6.25	$15.00	£1.20	£3.60	£8.50
201-202	$1.75	$5.25	$12.50	£0.85	£2.55	£6.00
203 origin Chop-Chop	$1.75	$5.25	$12.50	£0.85	£2.55	£6.00
204-210	$1.75	$5.25	$12.50	£0.85	£2.55	£6.00
211-227	$1.05	$3.20	$7.50	£0.50	£1.50	£3.50
228 Superman, Batman, Green Lantern, Flash cameos	$1.05	$3.20	$7.50	£0.50	£1.50	£3.50
229	$1.05	$3.20	$7.50	£0.50	£1.50	£3.50
230 Blackhawks become super-heroes; The Leaper, The Golden Centurion, Dr. Hands, The Listener, M'Sieu Machine, The Weapons Master	$1.05	$3.20	$7.50	£0.50	£1.50	£3.50
231-241	$1.05	$3.20	$7.50	£0.50	£1.50	£3.50
242 original costumes return	$1.05	$3.20	$7.50	£0.50	£1.50	£3.50
243	$1.05	$3.20	$7.50	£0.50	£1.50	£3.50
244-249	$0.50	$1.50	$2.50	£0.30	£0.90	£1.50
250 Chuck dies	$0.50	$1.50	$2.50	£0.30	£0.90	£1.50
251 origin retold	$0.30	$0.90	$1.50	£0.20	£0.60	£1.00
252-256	$0.30	$0.90	$1.50	£0.20	£0.60	£1.00
257 Chaykin cover	$0.30	$0.90	$1.50	£0.20	£0.60	£1.00

Issue	$Good	$Fine	$N.Mint	£Good	£Fine	£N.Mint
258 Blackhawk Island destroyed, Chaykin "Iwo Jima" cover	$0.30	$0.90	$1.50	£0.20	£0.60	£1.00
259-260 Chaykin cover	$0.30	$0.90	$1.50	£0.20	£0.60	£1.00
261	$0.30	$0.90	$1.50	£0.20	£0.60	£1.00
262 Chaykin cover	$0.30	$0.90	$1.50	£0.20	£0.60	£1.00
263-273	$0.30	$0.90	$1.50	£0.20	£0.60	£1.00
Title Value:	$840.10	$2536.80	$5984.50	£518.50	£1562.90	£3691.00

BLACKHAWK (2ND SERIES)
DC Comics; 1 Apr 1989-16 Aug 1990

Issue	$Good	$Fine	$N.Mint	£Good	£Fine	£N.Mint
1-6	$0.25	$0.75	$1.25	£0.15	£0.45	£0.75
7 DS	$0.30	$0.90	$1.50	£0.20	£0.60	£1.00
8-16	$0.25	$0.75	$1.25	£0.15	£0.45	£0.75
Title Value:	$4.05	$12.15	$20.25	£2.45	£7.35	£12.25

Note: Mature Readers, New Format

BLACKHAWK (LIMITED SERIES)
DC Comics,MS; 1 Mar 1988-3 May 1988

Issue	$Good	$Fine	$N.Mint	£Good	£Fine	£N.Mint
1-3 ND 48pgs, Chaykin art	$0.60	$1.80	$3.00	£0.40	£1.20	£2.00
Title Value:	$1.80	$5.40	$9.00	£1.20	£3.60	£6.00

Note: Prestige Format

BLACKHAWK ANNUAL
DC Comics; 1 Jun 1989

Issue	$Good	$Fine	$N.Mint	£Good	£Fine	£N.Mint
1	$0.40	$1.20	$2.00	£0.25	£0.75	£1.25
Title Value:	$0.40	$1.20	$2.00	£0.25	£0.75	£1.25

Note: Mature Readers, New Format

BLACKHAWK SPECIAL
DC Comics,OS; 1 Dec 1992

Issue	$Good	$Fine	$N.Mint	£Good	£Fine	£N.Mint
1 64pgs	$0.60	$1.80	$3.00	£0.40	£1.20	£2.00
Title Value:	$0.60	$1.80	$3.00	£0.40	£1.20	£2.00

BLACKMASK
Eastern; 1 1988-6 1990

Issue	$Good	$Fine	$N.Mint	£Good	£Fine	£N.Mint
1-6 ND 48pgs, original Korean art	$0.30	$0.90	$1.50	£0.20	£0.60	£1.00
Title Value:	$1.80	$5.40	$9.00	£1.20	£3.60	£6.00

BLACKMOON
US Comics; 1 1985-2 1986

Issue	$Good	$Fine	$N.Mint	£Good	£Fine	£N.Mint
1-2 ND black and white	$0.15	$0.45	$0.75	£0.10	£0.35	£0.60
Title Value:	$0.30	$0.90	$1.50	£0.20	£0.70	£1.20

BLACKTHORNE 3-IN-1
Blackthorne; 1 Dec 1986-2 Feb 1987

Issue	$Good	$Fine	$N.Mint	£Good	£Fine	£N.Mint
1-2 ND Axis & Pandor, Starlight Squad, Merlinrealm	$0.30	$0.90	$1.50	£0.20	£0.60	£1.00
Title Value:	$0.60	$1.80	$3.00	£0.40	£1.20	£2.00

BLACKWATCH
Heroic Comics; 1 Sep 1993

Issue	$Good	$Fine	$N.Mint	£Good	£Fine	£N.Mint
1 ND Daerick Gross script/art begins	$0.60	$1.80	$3.00	£0.40	£1.20	£2.00
Title Value:	$0.60	$1.80	$3.00	£0.40	£1.20	£2.00

BLACKWULF
Marvel Comics Group; 1 Jun 1994-10 Mar 1995

Issue	$Good	$Fine	$N.Mint	£Good	£Fine	£N.Mint
1 Angel Medina pencils begin, foil embossed cover	$0.30	$0.90	$1.50	£0.20	£0.60	£1.00
2-3	$0.30	$0.90	$1.50	£0.20	£0.60	£1.00
4 Giant Man guest-stars	$0.30	$0.90	$1.50	£0.20	£0.60	£1.00
5-8	$0.30	$0.90	$1.50	£0.20	£0.60	£1.00
9 Daredevil guest-stars	$0.30	$0.90	$1.50	£0.20	£0.60	£1.00
10	$0.30	$0.90	$1.50	£0.20	£0.60	£1.00
Title Value:	$3.00	$9.00	$15.00	£2.00	£6.00	£10.00

BLADE OF SHURIKEN
Eternity; 1 1987-8 1988

Issue	$Good	$Fine	$N.Mint	£Good	£Fine	£N.Mint
1-8 ND	$0.35	$1.05	$1.75	£0.25	£0.75	£1.25
Title Value:	$2.80	$8.40	$14.00	£2.00	£6.00	£10.00

BLADE THE IMMORTAL
Dark Horse; 1 Jul 1996-3 Sep 1996

Issue	$Good	$Fine	$N.Mint	£Good	£Fine	£N.Mint
1-3 ND 40pgs, Hiroaki Samura script and art; black and white	$0.60	$1.80	$3.00	£0.40	£1.20	£2.00
Title Value:	$1.80	$5.40	$9.00	£1.20	£3.60	£6.00

BLADE: THE VAMPIRE HUNTER
Marvel Comics Group; 1 Jul 1994-11 May 1995

Issue	$Good	$Fine	$N.Mint	£Good	£Fine	£N.Mint
1 foil stamped cover	$0.50	$1.50	$2.50	£0.30	£0.90	£1.50
2-3 Blade vs. Dracula	$0.40	$1.20	$2.00	£0.25	£0.75	£1.25
4-9	$0.40	$1.20	$2.00	£0.25	£0.75	£1.25
10-11 Dracula appears	$0.40	$1.20	$2.00	£0.25	£0.75	£1.25
Title Value:	$4.50	$13.50	$22.50	£2.80	£8.40	£14.00

BLADERUNNER
Marvel Comics Group,MS Film; 1 Oct 1982-2 Nov 1982

Issue	$Good	$Fine	$N.Mint	£Good	£Fine	£N.Mint
1-2 ND Al Williamson art	$0.30	$0.90	$1.50	£0.20	£0.60	£1.00
Title Value:	$0.60	$1.80	$3.00	£0.40	£1.20	£2.00

Note: movie adaptation, reprinted from Marvel Super Special 22, Williamson art.

BLADESMAN UNDERSEA
Blue Comet Press,OS; 1 1994

Issue	$Good	$Fine	$N.Mint	£Good	£Fine	£N.Mint
1 ND pre-bagged with trading card	$0.70	$2.10	$3.50	£0.50	£1.50	£2.50
Title Value:	$0.70	$2.10	$3.50	£0.50	£1.50	£2.50

BLANCHE GOES TO HOLLYWOOD
Dark Horse,OS; 1 Oct 1993

Issue	$Good	$Fine	$N.Mint	£Good	£Fine	£N.Mint
1 ND Rick Geary script and art	$0.40	$1.20	$2.00	£0.25	£0.75	£1.25
Title Value:	$0.40	$1.20	$2.00	£0.25	£0.75	£1.25

BLANCHE GOES TO NEW YORK
Dark Horse,OS; 1 Nov 1992

Issue	$Good	$Fine	$N.Mint	£Good	£Fine	£N.Mint
1 ND	$0.40	$1.20	$2.00	£0.25	£0.75	£1.25
Title Value:	$0.40	$1.20	$2.00	£0.25	£0.75	£1.25

BLANDMAN
Eclipse,OS; 1 Jul 1992

Issue	$Good	$Fine	$N.Mint	£Good	£Fine	£N.Mint
1 ND parody of Sandman, black and white	$0.50	$1.50	$2.50	£0.30	£0.90	£1.50
Title Value:	$0.50	$1.50	$2.50	£0.30	£0.90	£1.50

BLAST-OFF
Harvey; 1 Oct 1965
(Three Rocketeers)

Issue	$Good	$Fine	$N.Mint	£Good	£Fine	£N.Mint
1 ND rare in the U.K. Jack Kirby, Williamson, Crandall art	$4.25	$12.50	$30.00	£2.85	£8.50	£20.00
Title Value:	$4.25	$12.50	$30.00	£2.85	£8.50	£20.00

BLASTERS SPECIAL
DC Comics,OS; 1 May 1989

Issue	$Good	$Fine	$N.Mint	£Good	£Fine	£N.Mint
1 48pgs	$0.25	$0.75	$1.25	£0.15	£0.45	£0.75
Title Value:	$0.25	$0.75	$1.25	£0.15	£0.45	£0.75

Note: Invasion spin-off

BLAZE
Marvel Comics Group,MS; 1 Dec 1993-4 Mar 1994

Issue	$Good	$Fine	$N.Mint	£Good	£Fine	£N.Mint
1 John Blaze (the former Ghost Rider) stars	$0.40	$1.20	$2.00	£0.25	£0.75	£1.25
2-4	$0.40	$1.20	$2.00	£0.25	£0.75	£1.25
Title Value:	$1.60	$4.80	$8.00	£1.00	£3.00	£5.00

BLAZE (2ND SERIES)
Marvel Comics Group; 1 Aug 1994-12 Jul 1995

Issue	$Good	$Fine	$N.Mint	£Good	£Fine	£N.Mint
1 foil stamped cover	$0.50	$1.50	$2.50	£0.30	£0.90	£1.50
2	$0.40	$1.20	$2.00	£0.25	£0.75	£1.25
3 X-Force appear	$0.40	$1.20	$2.00	£0.25	£0.75	£1.25
4	$0.40	$1.20	$2.00	£0.25	£0.75	£1.25
5-6 Warpath of X-Force appears	$0.40	$1.20	$2.00	£0.25	£0.75	£1.25
7-10	$0.40	$1.20	$2.00	£0.25	£0.75	£1.25
11 Punisher appears	$0.40	$1.20	$2.00	£0.25	£0.75	£1.25
12	$0.40	$1.20	$2.00	£0.25	£0.75	£1.25
Title Value:	$4.90	$14.70	$24.50	£3.05	£9.15	£15.25

BLAZING BATTLE TALES (FEATURING SGT. HAWK)
Atlas; 1 Jul 1975

Issue	$Good	$Fine	$N.Mint	£Good	£Fine	£N.Mint
1 distributed in the U.K. Frank Thorne cover	$0.15	$0.50	$1.00	£0.10	£0.30	£0.60
Title Value:	$0.15	$0.50	$1.00	£0.10	£0.30	£0.60

BLAZING COMBAT
Warren,Magazine; 1 Oct 1965-4 Jul 1966

Issue	$Good	$Fine	$N.Mint	£Good	£Fine	£N.Mint
1 scarce, distributed in the U.K.	$16.00	$49.00	$115.00	£10.50	£32.00	£75.00
2 distributed in the U.K.	$4.25	$12.50	$30.00	£2.85	£8.50	£20.00
3-4 ND	$2.85	$8.50	$20.00	£1.75	£5.25	£12.50
Title Value:	$25.95	$78.50	$185.00	£16.85	£51.00	£120.00

Note: all have Crandall, Wood, Williamson art; Frazetta covers

BLAZING COMBAT WW I & II
Apple Comics,MS; 1 Oct 1993-2 Nov 1993

Issue	$Good	$Fine	$N.Mint	£Good	£Fine	£N.Mint
1-2 ND Wally Wood and Alex Toth reprints	$0.80	$2.40	$4.00	£0.50	£1.50	£2.50
Title Value:	$1.60	$4.80	$8.00	£1.00	£3.00	£5.00

BLIP AND THE C.C.A.D.S.
Amazing Comics; 1 1987

Issue	$Good	$Fine	$N.Mint	£Good	£Fine	£N.Mint
1 ND	$0.25	$0.75	$1.25	£0.15	£0.45	£0.75
Title Value:	$0.25	$0.75	$1.25	£0.15	£0.45	£0.75

BLITZ
Night Wynd,MS; 1 May 1992-4 Aug 1992

Issue	$Good	$Fine	$N.Mint	£Good	£Fine	£N.Mint
1-4 ND Barry Blair script and art; black and white	$0.50	$1.50	$2.50	£0.30	£0.90	£1.50
Title Value:	$2.00	$6.00	$10.00	£1.20	£3.60	£6.00

BLITZKRIEG
DC Comics; 1 Jan/Feb 1976-5 Sep/Oct 1976

Issue	$Good	$Fine	$N.Mint	£Good	£Fine	£N.Mint
1 Joe Kubert cover art	$0.50	$1.50	$3.00	£0.30	£1.00	£2.00
2-5 ND	$0.40	$1.25	$2.50	£0.20	£0.60	£1.25
Title Value:	$2.10	$6.50	$13.00	£1.10	£3.40	£7.00

FEATURES
WWII stories as seen through the enemy's eyes.

BLONDIE, CHIC YOUNG'S
King Comics; 164 Aug 1966-175 Dec 1967; Charlton; 177 Feb 1969-222 Nov 1976

Issue	$Good	$Fine	$N.Mint	£Good	£Fine	£N.Mint
164-167	$1.40	$4.25	$10.00	£0.90	£2.75	£6.50
168-175	$0.70	$2.10	$5.00	£0.50	£1.50	£3.50
177-200	$0.55	$1.70	$4.00	£0.35	£1.05	£2.50
201-222	$0.50	$1.50	$3.00	£0.30	£1.00	£2.00
Title Value:	$35.40	$107.60	$242.00	£22.60	£70.20	£158.00

Note: all Limited Distribution in the U.K.

BLOOD & ROSES ADVENTURES
Knight Press; 1 Apr 1995-4 1995

1 ND Bob Hickey script, picks up storyline from Sky Comics series; black and white

	$Good	$Fine	$N.Mint	£Good	£Fine	£N.Mint
	$0.60	$1.80	$3.00	£0.40	£1.20	£2.00
2 ND black and white						
	$0.60	$1.80	$3.00	£0.40	£1.20	£2.00
3-4 ND	$0.60	$1.80	$3.00	£0.40	£1.20	£2.00
Title Value:	$2.40	$7.20	$12.00	£1.60	£4.80	£8.00

BLOOD & ROSES SPECIAL

Knight Press,OS; 1 Mar 1996

	$Good	$Fine	$N.Mint	£Good	£Fine	£N.Mint
1 ND ties up plot lines from Sky Comics' series						
	$0.60	$1.80	$3.00	£0.40	£1.20	£2.00
Title Value:	$0.60	$1.80	$3.00	£0.40	£1.20	£2.00

Note: originally solicited as Blood & Roses: the End of Infinity

BLOOD & ROSES: FUTURE PAST TENSE

Sky Comics; 1 Dec 1993-2 Mar 1994

	$Good	$Fine	$N.Mint	£Good	£Fine	£N.Mint
1 ND	$0.40	$1.20	$2.00	£0.25	£0.75	£1.25
Title Value:	$0.40	$1.20	$2.00	£0.25	£0.75	£1.25

BLOOD & ROSES: SEARCH FOR THE TIME STONE

Sky Comics; 0 Jul 1994; 1 Feb 1994; 2 Nov 1994

	$Good	$Fine	$N.Mint	£Good	£Fine	£N.Mint
0 ND Leif Jones script and art						
	$0.40	$1.20	$2.00	£0.25	£0.75	£1.25
1 ND Bob Hickey script, Gene Gonzales art; painted cover by Daerick Gross						
	$0.40	$1.20	$2.00	£0.25	£0.75	£1.25
2 ND	$0.40	$1.20	$2.00	£0.25	£0.75	£1.25
Title Value:	$1.20	$3.60	$6.00	£0.75	£2.25	£3.75
Blood & Roses (Feb 1995)						
Trade paperback reprints mini-series plus new pin-ups				£1.70	£5.10	£8.50

Note: Trade paperback published by Knight Press

BLOOD & SHADOWS

DC Comics/Vertigo,MS; 1 Mar 1996-4 Jun 1996

	$Good	$Fine	$N.Mint	£Good	£Fine	£N.Mint
1-4 ND 48pgs, Joe R. Lansdale script, Mark Nelson art						
	$1.20	$3.60	$6.00	£0.80	£2.40	£4.00
Title Value:	$4.80	$14.40	$24.00	£3.20	£9.60	£16.00

BLOOD 'N GUTS

Aircel,MS; 1 Nov 1990-3 Jan 1991

	$Good	$Fine	$N.Mint	£Good	£Fine	£N.Mint
1-3 ND Barry Blair script and art; black and white						
	$0.40	$1.20	$2.00	£0.25	£0.75	£1.25
Title Value:	$1.20	$3.60	$6.00	£0.75	£2.25	£3.75

BLOOD AND THUNDER

Marvel Comics Group; 1993

Cross-over storyline throughout the following issues:
Thor #468, **Silver Surfer #86**, **Warlock Chronicles #6**, **Warlock & The Infinity Watch #23**, **Thor #469**, **Silver Surfer #87**, **Warlock Chronicles #7**, **Warlock & The Infinity Watch #24**, **Thor #470**, **Silver Surfer #88**, **Warlock Chronicles #8**, **Warlock & The Infinity Watch #25**, **Thor #471**.

BLOOD FEAST

Eternity,OS; 1 Feb 1991

	$Good	$Fine	$N.Mint	£Good	£Fine	£N.Mint
1 ND film adaptation, graphic photo cover						
	$0.40	$1.20	$2.00	£0.25	£0.75	£1.25
Title Value:	$0.40	$1.20	$2.00	£0.25	£0.75	£1.25

BLOOD GOTHIC

Fantaco,MS; 1 Feb 1995-2 Mar 1995

	$Good	$Fine	$N.Mint	£Good	£Fine	£N.Mint
1-2 ND Dave Stephenson script and art; black and white						
	$0.80	$2.40	$4.00	£0.50	£1.50	£2.50
Title Value:	$1.60	$4.80	$8.00	£1.00	£3.00	£5.00

BLOOD HUNTER

Brainstorm Comics; 1 Oct 1996-present

	$Good	$Fine	$N.Mint	£Good	£Fine	£N.Mint
1 ND Kirk Lindo script, David Brewer and Eman Torre art; black and white						
	$0.60	$1.80	$3.00	£0.40	£1.20	£2.00
Title Value:	$0.60	$1.80	$3.00	£0.40	£1.20	£2.00

BLOOD IS THE HARVEST

Eclipse/FX Comix,MS; 1 Jul 1992-4 Oct 1992

	$Good	$Fine	$N.Mint	£Good	£Fine	£N.Mint
1 ND based on film; bound-in FX scratchcard; black and white begins						
	$0.30	$0.90	$1.50	£0.25	£0.75	£1.25
2-4 ND based on film						
	$0.30	$0.90	$1.50	£0.25	£0.75	£1.25
Title Value:	$1.20	$3.60	$6.00	£1.00	£3.00	£5.00

BLOOD JUNKIES ON CAPITOL HILL

Eternity,MS; 1 Aug 1992-2 Nov 1992

	$Good	$Fine	$N.Mint	£Good	£Fine	£N.Mint
1-2 ND black and white						
	$0.30	$0.90	$1.50	£0.20	£0.60	£1.00
Title Value:	$0.60	$1.80	$3.00	£0.40	£1.20	£2.00

BLOOD LINES

Aircel/Vortex; 1 Jun 1987-7 Mar 1988

	$Good	$Fine	$N.Mint	£Good	£Fine	£N.Mint
1-2 ND	$0.40	$1.20	$2.00	£0.25	£0.75	£1.25
3 ND 1st Vortex issue						
	$0.40	$1.20	$2.00	£0.25	£0.75	£1.25
4-7 ND	$0.40	$1.20	$2.00	£0.25	£0.75	£1.25
Title Value:	$2.80	$8.40	$14.00	£1.75	£5.25	£8.75

BLOOD OF DRACULA

Apple Comics; 1 Nov 1987-18 1990?

	$Good	$Fine	$N.Mint	£Good	£Fine	£N.Mint
1-14 ND	$0.30	$0.90	$1.50	£0.20	£0.60	£1.00
15 ND with flexidisc						
	$0.30	$0.90	$1.50	£0.20	£0.60	£1.00
16-18 ND	$0.30	$0.90	$1.50	£0.20	£0.60	£1.00
Title Value:	$5.40	$16.20	$27.00	£3.60	£10.80	£18.00

BLOOD OF THE APES, THE

Adventure,MS; 1 Jan 1992-4 Apr 1992

	$Good	$Fine	$N.Mint	£Good	£Fine	£N.Mint
1-4 ND	$0.40	$1.20	$2.00	£0.25	£0.75	£1.25
Title Value:	$1.60	$4.80	$8.00	£1.00	£3.00	£5.00

BLOOD OF THE INNOCENT

Warp,MS; 1-4 Jul 1986

	$Good	$Fine	$N.Mint	£Good	£Fine	£N.Mint
1-4 ND	$0.40	$1.20	$2.00	£0.25	£0.75	£1.25
Title Value:	$1.60	$4.80	$8.00	£1.00	£3.00	£5.00

BLOOD PACK

DC Comics,MS; 1 Mar 1995-4 Jun 1995

	$Good	$Fine	$N.Mint	£Good	£Fine	£N.Mint
1 Sparx, Geist, Nightblade, Razorsharp and Loria begin as a team						
	$0.30	$0.90	$1.50	£0.20	£0.60	£1.00
2 Superboy guest-stars						
	$0.30	$0.90	$1.50	£0.20	£0.60	£1.00
3-4	$0.30	$0.90	$1.50	£0.20	£0.60	£1.00
Title Value:	$1.20	$3.60	$6.00	£0.80	£2.40	£4.00

BLOOD REIGN SAGA

London Night Studios; 1 Jun 1996

	$Good	$Fine	$N.Mint	£Good	£Fine	£N.Mint
1 ND Tim Tyler cover; black and white						
	$0.60	$1.80	$3.00	£0.40	£1.20	£2.00
Title Value:	$0.60	$1.80	$3.00	£0.40	£1.20	£2.00

BLOOD SWORD

Jademan; 1 Aug 1988-56 Mar 1993

	$Good	$Fine	$N.Mint	£Good	£Fine	£N.Mint
1 ND 64pgs	$0.40	$1.20	$2.00	£0.50	£1.50	£2.50
2-3 ND 64pgs	$0.30	$0.90	$1.50	£0.40	£1.20	£2.00
4-10 ND 64pgs	$0.30	$0.90	$1.50	£0.30	£0.90	£1.50
11-20 ND 64pgs	$0.30	$0.90	$1.50	£0.25	£0.75	£1.25
21-40 ND 64pgs	$0.30	$0.90	$1.50	£0.20	£0.60	£1.00
41-56 ND 64pgs	$0.25	$0.75	$1.25	£0.15	£0.45	£0.75
Title Value:	$16.10	$48.30	$80.50	£12.30	£36.90	£61.50
Collectors Album 1,2 scarce in the U.K.				£1.20	£3.60	£6.00

Note: Japanese material

BLOOD SWORD DYNASTY

Jademan; 1 1989-43 Mar 1993

	$Good	$Fine	$N.Mint	£Good	£Fine	£N.Mint
1 ND	$0.50	$1.50	$2.50	£0.50	£1.50	£2.50
2-5 ND	$0.30	$0.90	$1.50	£0.40	£1.20	£2.00
6-10 ND	$0.30	$0.90	$1.50	£0.30	£0.90	£1.50
11-20 ND	$0.30	$0.90	$1.50	£0.25	£0.75	£1.25
21-30 ND	$0.30	$0.90	$1.50	£0.20	£0.60	£1.00
31-43 ND	$0.25	$0.75	$1.25	£0.15	£0.45	£0.75
Title Value:	$12.45	$37.35	$62.25	£10.05	£30.15	£50.25

Note: 36pgs, Japanese material

BLOOD SYNDICATE

DC Comics/Milestone; 1 Apr 1993-35 Feb 1995

	$Good	$Fine	$N.Mint	£Good	£Fine	£N.Mint
1	$0.40	$1.20	$2.00	£0.25	£0.75	£1.25
1 Direct Market Edition, ND - pre-bagged with poster, profile, trading card and jig-saw puzzle pieces						
	$0.60	$1.80	$3.00	£0.40	£1.20	£2.00
2-9	$0.30	$0.90	$1.50	£0.20	£0.60	£1.00
10 48pgs, spot varnished cover by Walt Simonson						
	$0.50	$1.50	$2.50	£0.30	£0.90	£1.50
11-14	$0.30	$0.90	$1.50	£0.20	£0.60	£1.00
15 John Byrne cover						
	$0.30	$0.90	$1.50	£0.20	£0.60	£1.00
16 Worlds Collide X-over, continued in Worlds Collide #1						
	$0.30	$0.90	$1.50	£0.20	£0.60	£1.00
17 Worlds Collide X-over, continued in Static #14						
	$0.30	$0.90	$1.50	£0.20	£0.60	£1.00
18-24	$0.30	$0.90	$1.50	£0.20	£0.60	£1.00
25 48pgs	$0.50	$1.50	$2.50	£0.30	£0.90	£1.50
26-28	$0.40	$1.20	$2.00	£0.25	£0.75	£1.25
29 special 99 cents issue						
	$0.20	$0.60	$1.00	£0.10	£0.35	£0.60
30-31	$0.40	$1.20	$2.00	£0.25	£0.75	£1.25
32 cover by Howard Chaykin						
	$0.40	$1.20	$2.00	£0.25	£0.75	£1.25
33 special price of 99 cents						
	$0.20	$0.60	$1.00	£0.10	£0.35	£0.60
34	$0.50	$1.50	$2.50	£0.30	£0.90	£1.50
35	$0.70	$2.10	$3.50	£0.50	£1.50	£2.50
Title Value:	$12.60	$37.80	$63.00	£8.15	£24.55	£40.95

BLOOD WING

Eternity; 1 Jan 1988-5 1988

	$Good	$Fine	$N.Mint	£Good	£Fine	£N.Mint
1-5 ND	$0.40	$1.20	$2.00	£0.25	£0.75	£1.25
Title Value:	$2.00	$6.00	$10.00	£1.25	£3.75	£6.25

BLOOD: A TALE

Marvel Comics Group/Epic,MS; 1 Feb 1988-4 May 1988

	$Good	$Fine	$N.Mint	£Good	£Fine	£N.Mint
1 ND scarce in the U.K. Kent Williams art						
	$1.00	$3.00	$5.00	£0.70	£2.10	£3.50
2-4 ND Williams art						
	$0.60	$1.80	$3.00	£0.40	£1.20	£2.00
Title Value:	$2.80	$8.40	$14.00	£1.90	£5.70	£9.50

Note: Bookshelf Format, Mature Readers;

	$Good	$Fine	$N.Mint	£Good	£Fine	£N.Mint
Trade paperback (1989). Reprints #1-4				£1.80	£5.40	£9.00
(2nd print Dec 1990)				£1.75	£5.25	£8.75

BLOOD: A TALE (2ND SERIES)

DC Comics,MS; 1 Nov 1996-4 Feb 1997

	$Good	$Fine	$N.Mint	£Good	£Fine	£N.Mint
1-4 ND reprinting original series from Marvel/Epic with new painted covers by Kent Williams						
	$0.60	$1.80	$3.00	£0.40	£1.20	£2.00
Title Value:	$2.40	$7.20	$12.00	£1.60	£4.80	£8.00

BLOODBATH

DC Comics,MS; 1 Early Dec 1993-2 Late Dec 1993

	$Good	$Fine	$N.Mint	£Good	£Fine	£N.Mint
1-2 64pgs, conclusion to the Bloodlines story, Superman appears						
	$0.50	$1.50	$2.50	£0.30	£0.90	£1.50
Title Value:	$1.00	$3.00	$5.00	£0.60	£1.80	£3.00

BLOODBROTHERS

Eternity; 1 Oct 1988-4 Jan 1989

	$Good	$Fine	$N.Mint	£Good	£Fine	£N.Mint
1-4 ND	$0.40	$1.20	$2.00	£0.25	£0.75	£1.25
Title Value:	$1.60	$4.80	$8.00	£1.00	£3.00	£5.00

BLOODCHILDE

Millennium; 1 1995-4 1995

	$Good	$Fine	$N.Mint	£Good	£Fine	£N.Mint
1-4 ND Faye Perozich script from a Neil Gaiman story						
	$0.60	*$1.80*	*$3.00*	£0.40	£1.20	£2.00
Title Value:	*$2.40*	*$7.20*	*$12.00*	£1.60	£4.80	£8.00

Note; issues #0 and #5 were advertised and solicited but never came out.

BLOODFIRE

Lightning Comics; 0 Jun 1994; 1 Aug 1993-12 1994

	$Good	$Fine	$N.Mint	£Good	£Fine	£N.Mint
0 ND (Jun 1994) origin Brian Reace						
	$0.60	*$1.80*	*$3.00*	£0.40	£1.20	£2.00
1 ND foil-stamped cover						
	$0.80	*$2.40*	*$4.00*	£0.55	£1.65	£2.75
1 Platinum Edition ND	*$1.60*	*$4.80*	*$8.00*	£1.00	£3.00	£5.00
1 Signed & Numbered Edition, ND (Oct 1994), pre-bagged with certificate; 1,000 copies						
	$2.50	*$7.50*	*$12.50*	£1.50	£4.50	£7.50
2 ND origin Bloodfire						
	$0.60	*$1.80*	*$3.00*	£0.40	£1.20	£2.00
3 ND 1st appearances of Dreadwolf, Perg and Judgement Day						
	$0.60	*$1.80*	*$3.00*	£0.40	£1.20	£2.00
3 Signed & Numbered Edition, ND (Feb 1995) - pre-bagged, limited to 4,000 copies						
	$1.50	*$4.50*	*$7.50*	£1.00	£3.00	£5.00
4 ND	*$0.60*	*$1.80*	*$3.00*	£0.40	£1.20	£2.00
5 ND pre-bagged with trading card						
	$0.60	*$1.80*	*$3.00*	£0.40	£1.20	£2.00
6-12 ND	*$0.60*	*$1.80*	*$3.00*	£0.40	£1.20	£2.00
Title Value:	*$13.60*	*$40.80*	*$68.00*	£8.85	£26.55	£44.25

BLOODFIRE/HELLINA

Lightning Comics; 1 Aug 1995

	$Good	$Fine	$N.Mint	£Good	£Fine	£N.Mint
1 ND	*$0.60*	*$1.80*	*$3.00*	£0.40	£1.20	£2.00
1 Nude Edition, ND polybagged, Mike Deodato cover art						
	$2.00	*$6.00*	*$10.00*	£1.20	£3.60	£6.00
1 Platinum Edition, ND Trenk Kaniuga cover art, signed by J. Zyskowski with certificate of authenticity						
	$2.00	*$6.00*	*$10.00*	£1.20	£3.60	£6.00
1 Variant Cover Edition, ND Trent Kaniuga cover art						
	$0.70	*$2.10*	*$3.50*	£0.50	£1.50	£2.50
Title Value:	*$5.30*	*$15.90*	*$26.50*	£3.30	£9.90	£16.50

BLOODLINES

The cross over story for the 1993 DC Annuals that introduces one new super- hero in each or as DC put it "introducing new blood into the DC Universe". The parts of the story are as follows: **Part 1** - Lobo Annual #1; **Part 2** - Superman: The Man of Steel Annual #2; **Part 3** - Batman: Shadow of the Bat Annual #1; **Part 4** - Flash Annual #6 **Part 5** - New Titans Annual #9; **Part 6** - Superman (2nd) Annual #5 **Part 7** - Green Lantern Annual #2; **Part 8** - Batman Annual #17; **Part 9** - Justice League International Annual #5; **Part 10** - Robin Annual #2; **Part 11** - Action Comics Annual #5; **Part 12** - Legion of Super-Heroes Annual #4 **Part 13** - Green Arrow Annual #6; **Part 14** - Detective Comics Annual #6 **Part 15** - Justice League America Annual #7; **Part 16** - Superman (1st) Annual #5; **Part 17** - Hawkman Annual #1; **Part 18** - Deathstroke the Terminator Annual #2; **Part 19** - Eclipso Annual #1; **Part 20** - Demon Annual #2; **Part 21** - Batman: Legends of the Dark Knight Annual #3; **Part 22** - Team Titans Annual #1; **Part 23** - Legion '93 Annual #4. Concluded in Bloodbath #1, #2

BLOODLINES: A TALE FROM THE HEART OF AFRICA

Marvel Comics Group/Epic,OS; 1 Oct 1992

	$Good	$Fine	$N.Mint	£Good	£Fine	£N.Mint
1 ND 48pgs, sequel to Temporary Natives, Brian Stelfreeze cover						
	$1.00	*$3.00*	*$5.00*	£0.70	£2.10	£3.50
Title Value:	*$1.00*	*$3.00*	*$5.00*	£0.70	£2.10	£3.50

BLOODLUST

Slave Labor,MS; 1 Dec 1990-2 1991

	$Good	$Fine	$N.Mint	£Good	£Fine	£N.Mint
1-2 ND black and white						
	$0.30	*$0.90*	*$1.50*	£0.20	£0.60	£1.00
Title Value:	*$0.60*	*$1.80*	*$3.00*	£0.40	£1.20	£2.00

BLOODPOOL

Image,MS; 1 Aug 1995-4 Nov 1995

	$Good	$Fine	$N.Mint	£Good	£Fine	£N.Mint
1-4 ND Jo Duffy script, Pat Lee art						
	$0.50	*$1.50*	*$2.50*	£0.30	£0.90	£1.50
Title Value:	*$2.00*	*$6.00*	*$10.00*	£1.20	£3.60	£6.00
Bloodpool (Apr 1996)						
Trade paperback ND collects four issue mini-series				£1.70	£5.10	£8.50

BLOODPOOL (2ND SERIES)

Image; 1 Feb 1996-present

	$Good	$Fine	$N.Mint	£Good	£Fine	£N.Mint
1-3 ND Jo Duffy script, Pat Lee art						
	$0.50	*$1.50*	*$2.50*	£0.30	£0.90	£1.50
Title Value:	*$1.50*	*$4.50*	*$7.50*	£0.90	£2.70	£4.50

BLOODPOOL SPECIAL

Image,OS; 1 Mar 1996

	$Good	$Fine	$N.Mint	£Good	£Fine	£N.Mint
1 ND Jo Duffy script, Patrick Lee art						
	$0.50	*$1.50*	*$2.50*	£0.30	£0.90	£1.50
Title Value:	*$0.50*	*$1.50*	*$2.50*	£0.30	£0.90	£1.50

BLOODRUSH

Marvel Comics Group,OS; 1 Dec 1993

	$Good	$Fine	$N.Mint	£Good	£Fine	£N.Mint
1 contains four-card uncut sheet						
	$0.40	*$1.20*	*$2.00*	£0.25	£0.75	£1.25
Title Value:	*$0.40*	*$1.20*	*$2.00*	£0.25	£0.75	£1.25

BLOODSCENT

Comico,OS; 1 Oct 1988

	$Good	$Fine	$N.Mint	£Good	£Fine	£N.Mint
1 ND Gene Colan art (colour)						
	$0.40	*$1.20*	*$2.00*	£0.25	£0.75	£1.25
Title Value:	*$0.40*	*$1.20*	*$2.00*	£0.25	£0.75	£1.25

BLOODSEED

Marvel UK/Frontier,MS; 1 Sep 1993-3 Nov 1993

	$Good	$Fine	$N.Mint	£Good	£Fine	£N.Mint
1 Paul Neary script, Liam Sharp art begins; gold-ink enhanced background on cover						
	$0.40	*$1.20*	*$2.00*	£0.25	£0.75	£1.25
2-3 gold ink enhanced cover						
	$0.40	*$1.20*	*$2.00*	£0.25	£0.75	£1.25
Title Value:	*$1.20*	*$3.60*	*$6.00*	£0.75	£2.25	£3.75

BLOODSHOT

Valiant/Acclaim Comics; 1 Jan 1993-51 Aug 1996

	$Good	$Fine	$N.Mint	£Good	£Fine	£N.Mint
0 ND (Mar 1994) - Chromium wrap around cover; Kevin Van Hook art with Dick Giordano inks						
	$0.60	*$1.80*	*$3.00*	£0.30	£0.90	£1.50
0 Gold Edition ND	*$1.50*	*$4.50*	*$7.50*	£0.80	£2.40	£4.00
0 Valiant Validated Signature Series, ND (Jun 1994), signed by Kevin Van Horn and Dick Giordano; 5,300 copies with certificate and Mylar sleeve						
	$1.80	*$5.25*	*$9.00*	£1.00	£3.00	£5.00
1 ND Barry Smith cover, fold-out poster, chromium metallic cover						
	$0.60	*$1.80*	*$3.00*	£0.40	£1.20	£2.00
2-3 ND	*$0.40*	*$1.20*	*$2.00*	£0.25	£0.75	£1.25
4 ND Eternal Warrior cameo						
	$0.40	*$1.20*	*$2.00*	£0.25	£0.75	£1.25
5 ND Rai Guest-stars						
	$0.40	*$1.20*	*$2.00*	£0.25	£0.75	£1.25
6 ND 1st appearance of Ninjak (cameo)						
	$0.50	*$1.50*	*$2.50*	£0.35	£1.05	£1.75
7 ND 1st full appearance of Ninjak						
	$0.45	*$1.35*	*$2.25*	£0.30	£0.90	£1.50
8 ND The Coming of the Darque Age story; prelude to Secret Weapons #1						
	$0.40	*$1.20*	*$2.00*	£0.25	£0.75	£1.25
9-10 ND	*$0.40*	*$1.20*	*$2.00*	£0.25	£0.75	£1.25
11 ND Empirical Dynasty part 2, continued from Secret Weapons #3						
	$0.40	*$1.20*	*$2.00*	£0.25	£0.75	£1.25
12-19 ND	*$0.40*	*$1.20*	*$2.00*	£0.25	£0.75	£1.25
20 ND Chaos Effect tie-in						
	$0.40	*$1.20*	*$2.00*	£0.25	£0.75	£1.25
21-23 ND	*$0.40*	*$1.20*	*$2.00*	£0.25	£0.75	£1.25
24 ND Geomancer appears						
	$0.40	*$1.20*	*$2.00*	£0.25	£0.75	£1.25
25-26 ND	*$0.40*	*$1.20*	*$2.00*	£0.25	£0.75	£1.25
27-28 ND Bloodshot Rampage story						

Black Magic #2

Blitzkrieg #1

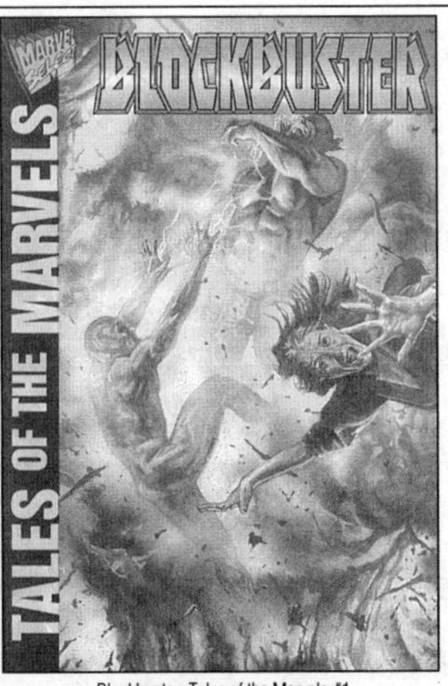

Blockbuster: Tales of the Marvels #1

	$Good	$Fine	$N.Mint	£Good	£Fine	£N.Mint
	$0.40	*$1.20*	*$2.00*	£0.25	£0.75	£1.25
29 ND Bloodshot Rampage story; Ninjak appears	*$0.40*	*$1.20*	*$2.00*	£0.25	£0.75	£1.25
30 ND 1st Acclaim Comics issue; Norm Breyfogle art begins; bi-weekly	*$0.40*	*$1.20*	*$2.00*	£0.25	£0.75	£1.25
31-39 ND bi-weekly	*$0.40*	*$1.20*	*$2.00*	£0.25	£0.75	£1.25
40 ND Jackson Guice art; bi-weekly	*$0.50*	*$1.50*	*$2.50*	£0.30	£0.90	£1.50
41 ND Paul Gulacy art; bi-weekly	*$0.50*	*$1.50*	*$2.50*	£0.30	£0.90	£1.50
42-45 ND bi-weekly	*$0.50*	*$1.50*	*$2.50*	£0.30	£0.90	£1.50
46 ND	*$0.50*	*$1.50*	*$2.50*	£0.30	£0.90	£1.50
47-48 ND Dan Abnett co-script; bi-weekly	*$0.50*	*$1.50*	*$2.50*	£0.30	£0.90	£1.50
49-51 ND	*$0.50*	*$1.50*	*$2.50*	£0.30	£0.90	£1.50
Title Value:	*$25.85*	*$77.40*	*$129.25*	£15.75	£47.25	£78.75

BLOODSHOT YEARBOOK

Valiant; 1 Jul 1994; 2 Apr 1995

	$Good	$Fine	$N.Mint	£Good	£Fine	£N.Mint
1 ND Kevin van Hook script, Michael Bair art	*$0.50*	*$1.50*	*$2.50*	£0.35	£1.05	£1.75
2 ND Mike Grell script, Tommy Lee Edwards art	*$0.50*	*$1.50*	*$2.50*	£0.35	£1.05	£1.75
Title Value:	*$1.00*	*$3.00*	*$5.00*	£0.70	£2.10	£3.50

BLOODSHOT: LAST STAND

Valiant/Acclaim Comics,OS; 1 Nov 1995

	$Good	$Fine	$N.Mint	£Good	£Fine	£N.Mint
1 ND 48pgs, Mike Zeck art	*$1.20*	*$3.60*	*$6.00*	£0.80	£2.40	£4.00
Title Value:	*$1.20*	*$3.60*	*$6.00*	£0.80	£2.40	£4.00

BLOODSTRIKE

Image; 1 Apr 1993-22 May 1994; 25 May 1994

	$Good	$Fine	$N.Mint	£Good	£Fine	£N.Mint
1 Rob Liefeld plot/layouts, Dan Fraga pencils and Danny Miki inks begin	*$0.60*	*$1.80*	*$3.00*	£0.40	£1.20	£2.00
2-7	*$0.50*	*$1.50*	*$2.50*	£0.30	£0.90	£1.50
8 Chapel joins the team	*$0.50*	*$1.50*	*$2.50*	£0.30	£0.90	£1.50
9	*$0.50*	*$1.50*	*$2.50*	£0.30	£0.90	£1.50
10 Extreme Prejudice part 7, with coupon	*$0.50*	*$1.50*	*$2.50*	£0.30	£0.90	£1.50
11 Savage Dragon appears	*$0.50*	*$1.50*	*$2.50*	£0.30	£0.90	£1.50
12 team disbands temporarily	*$0.50*	*$1.50*	*$2.50*	£0.30	£0.90	£1.50
13-14	*$0.50*	*$1.50*	*$2.50*	£0.30	£0.90	£1.50
15 War Games storyline, X-over with Prophet #8	*$0.50*	*$1.50*	*$2.50*	£0.30	£0.90	£1.50
16 War Games storyline, Prophet appears	*$0.50*	*$1.50*	*$2.50*	£0.30	£0.90	£1.50
17	*$0.50*	*$1.50*	*$2.50*	£0.30	£0.90	£1.50
18 Extreme Sacrifice part 2, continued in Brigade #16; pre-bagged with trading card	*$0.50*	*$1.50*	*$2.50*	£0.30	£0.90	£1.50
19	*$0.50*	*$1.50*	*$2.50*	£0.30	£0.90	£1.50
20 Lily and Bailout join team	*$0.50*	*$1.50*	*$2.50*	£0.30	£0.90	£1.50
21-22	*$0.50*	*$1.50*	*$2.50*	£0.30	£0.90	£1.50
25 cover-dated May 1994; issued in between issues #10 and 11 as part of "Images of Tomorrow", showing what the 25th issues of titles will look/read like	*$0.50*	*$1.50*	*$2.50*	£0.30	£0.90	£1.50
Title Value:	*$11.60*	*$34.80*	*$58.00*	£7.00	£21.00	£35.00

Note: all Non-Distributed on the news-stands in the U.K.

	$Good	$Fine	$N.Mint	£Good	£Fine	£N.Mint
Blood Brothers (Aug 1994) Trade paperback reprints the Extreme prejudice storyline including early issues of Bloodstrike				£1.70	£5.10	£8.50

BLOODSTRIKE: ASSASSIN

Image; 0 Oct 1995; 1 Jun 1995-3 Aug 1995 ?

	$Good	$Fine	$N.Mint	£Good	£Fine	£N.Mint
0 ND Robert Napton script, Karl Altstaetter art	*$0.50*	*$1.50*	*$2.50*	£0.30	£0.90	£1.50
1 ND Robert Napton script, Karl Alstaetter art begins	*$0.50*	*$1.50*	*$2.50*	£0.30	£0.90	£1.50
2-3 ND	*$0.50*	*$1.50*	*$2.50*	£0.30	£0.90	£1.50
Title Value:	*$2.00*	*$6.00*	*$10.00*	£1.20	£3.60	£6.00

BLOODTHIRST: THE NIGHTFALL CONSPIRACY

Alpha Productions,MS; 1 Jul 1994-2 Aug 1994

	$Good	$Fine	$N.Mint	£Good	£Fine	£N.Mint
1-2 ND black and white	*$0.50*	*$1.50*	*$2.50*	£0.30	£0.90	£1.50
Title Value:	*$1.00*	*$3.00*	*$5.00*	£0.60	£1.80	£3.00

BLOODTIES

Marvel Comics Group; 1993

Cross-over storyline running throughout the following issues:
Avengers #368, **X-Men #26**, **Avengers #369**, **Avengers West Coast #101**, **Uncanny X-Men #307**.

BLOODWULF

Image,MS; 1 Feb 1995-4 May 1995

	$Good	$Fine	$N.Mint	£Good	£Fine	£N.Mint
1-4 ND Andy Mangels script, Daerick Gross art	*$0.50*	*$1.50*	*$2.50*	£0.30	£0.90	£1.50
Title Value:	*$2.00*	*$6.00*	*$10.00*	£1.20	£3.60	£6.00

BLOODWULF SPECIAL

Image,OS; 1 Aug 1995

	$Good	$Fine	$N.Mint	£Good	£Fine	£N.Mint
1 ND	*$0.50*	*$1.50*	*$2.50*	£0.30	£0.90	£1.50
Title Value:	*$0.50*	*$1.50*	*$2.50*	£0.30	£0.90	£1.50

BLOODY MARY

DC Comics/Helix,MS; 1 Oct 1996-4 Jan 1997

	$Good	$Fine	$N.Mint	£Good	£Fine	£N.Mint
1-4 ND Garth Ennis script, Carlos Ezquerra art	*$0.45*	*$1.35*	*$2.25*	£0.30	£0.90	£1.50
Title Value:	*$1.80*	*$5.40*	*$9.00*	£1.20	£3.60	£6.00

BLUE BEETLE

DC Comics; 1 Jun 1986-24 May 1988

	$Good	$Fine	$N.Mint	£Good	£Fine	£N.Mint
1 origin retold	*$0.20*	*$0.60*	*$1.00*	£0.15	£0.45	£0.75
2-4	*$0.20*	*$0.60*	*$1.00*	£0.15	£0.45	£0.75
5-7 The Question X-over	*$0.20*	*$0.60*	*$1.00*	£0.15	£0.45	£0.75
8	*$0.20*	*$0.60*	*$1.00*	£0.15	£0.45	£0.75
9-10 Legends X-over	*$0.20*	*$0.60*	*$1.00*	£0.15	£0.45	£0.75
11-13 Titans X-over	*$0.15*	*$0.45*	*$0.75*	£0.10	£0.35	£0.60
14-17	*$0.15*	*$0.45*	*$0.75*	£0.10	£0.35	£0.60
18 original Blue Beetle appears	*$0.15*	*$0.45*	*$0.75*	£0.10	£0.35	£0.60
19	*$0.15*	*$0.45*	*$0.75*	£0.10	£0.35	£0.60
20-21 Millennium X-over	*$0.15*	*$0.45*	*$0.75*	£0.10	£0.35	£0.60
22-24	*$0.15*	*$0.45*	*$0.75*	£0.10	£0.35	£0.60
Title Value:	*$4.10*	*$12.30*	*$20.50*	£2.90	£9.40	£15.90

BLUE BEETLE (1ST SERIES)

Charlton; 1 Jun 1964-5 Mar/Apr 1965

	$Good	$Fine	$N.Mint	£Good	£Fine	£N.Mint
1 distributed in the U.K. 1st Silver Age appearance of the Blue Beetle (Dan Garrett), origin retold	*$7.75*	*$23.50*	*$55.00*	£4.25	£12.50	£30.00
1 reprint, ND scarce in the U.K. (1977) Modern Comics reprint, 35 cents cover	*$0.20*	*$0.60*	*$1.00*	£0.30	£0.90	£1.50
2-3 distributed in the U.K.	*$5.50*	*$17.00*	*$40.00*	£2.50	£7.50	£17.50
3 reprint, ND scarce in the U.K. (1977) Modern Comics reprint, 35 cents cover	*$0.20*	*$0.60*	*$1.00*	£0.30	£0.90	£1.50
4-5 distributed in the U.K.	*$5.50*	*$17.00*	*$40.00*	£2.50	£7.50	£17.50
Title Value:	*$30.15*	*$92.70*	*$217.00*	£14.85	£44.30	£103.00

BLUE BEETLE (2ND SERIES)

Charlton; 50 Jul 1965-54 Feb/Mar 1966

(previously Unusual Tales #1-49, becomes Ghostly Tales #55-169)

	$Good	$Fine	$N.Mint	£Good	£Fine	£N.Mint
50-54 distributed in the U.K.	*$5.50*	*$17.00*	*$40.00*	£2.50	£7.50	£17.50
Title Value:	*$27.50*	*$85.00*	*$200.00*	£12.50	£37.50	£87.50

BLUE BEETLE (3RD SERIES)

Charlton; 1 Jun 1967-5 Oct 1968

	$Good	$Fine	$N.Mint	£Good	£Fine	£N.Mint
1 distributed in the U.K. Question begins; Steve Ditko art	*$11.00*	*$34.00*	*$80.00*	£5.50	£17.00	£40.00
2 distributed in the U.K. origin Blue Beetle (Ted Kord - see Captain Atom [Charlton] #83); Steve Ditko art	*$5.00*	*$15.00*	*$35.00*	£2.10	£6.25	£15.00
3-5 distributed in the U.K. Steve Ditko art	*$3.90*	*$11.50*	*$27.50*	£1.75	£5.25	£12.50
Title Value:	*$27.70*	*$83.50*	*$197.50*	£12.85	£39.00	£92.50

BLUE DEVIL

DC Comics; 1 Jun 1984-31 Dec 1986

	$Good	$Fine	$N.Mint	£Good	£Fine	£N.Mint
1	*$0.15*	*$0.45*	*$0.75*	£0.10	£0.35	£0.60
2	*$0.15*	*$0.45*	*$0.75*	£0.10	£0.30	£0.50
3 Blue Devil vs. Metallo, Superman appears	*$0.15*	*$0.45*	*$0.75*	£0.10	£0.30	£0.50
4 origin Nebiros	*$0.15*	*$0.45*	*$0.75*	£0.10	£0.30	£0.50
5	*$0.15*	*$0.45*	*$0.75*	£0.10	£0.30	£0.50
6 Flash Force 2000 insert	*$0.15*	*$0.45*	*$0.75*	£0.10	£0.30	£0.50
7 Gil Kane art	*$0.15*	*$0.45*	*$0.75*	£0.10	£0.30	£0.50
8-9 Blue Devil vs. The Trickster	*$0.15*	*$0.45*	*$0.75*	£0.10	£0.30	£0.50
10-12	*$0.15*	*$0.45*	*$0.75*	£0.10	£0.30	£0.50
13 Green Lantern and Zatanna appear	*$0.15*	*$0.45*	*$0.75*	£0.10	£0.30	£0.50
14 Detective Comics #38 cover parody (Kid Devil instead of Robin bursting through the hoop)	*$0.15*	*$0.45*	*$0.75*	£0.10	£0.30	£0.50
15-16	*$0.15*	*$0.45*	*$0.75*	£0.10	£0.30	£0.50
17-18 Crisis X-over	*$0.15*	*$0.45*	*$0.75*	£0.10	£0.30	£0.50
19 Robin appears	*$0.15*	*$0.45*	*$0.75*	£0.10	£0.30	£0.50
20-22	*$0.15*	*$0.45*	*$0.75*	£0.10	£0.30	£0.50
23 Blue Devil vs. Firestorm	*$0.15*	*$0.45*	*$0.75*	£0.10	£0.30	£0.50
24-29	*$0.15*	*$0.45*	*$0.75*	£0.10	£0.30	£0.50
30 DS Flash's Rogue's Gallery appear	*$0.15*	*$0.45*	*$0.75*	£0.10	£0.35	£0.60
31 DS	*$0.15*	*$0.45*	*$0.75*	£0.10	£0.35	£0.60
Title Value:	*$4.65*	*$13.95*	*$23.25*	£3.10	£9.45	£15.80

BLUE DEVIL ANNUAL

DC Comics; 1 Nov 1985

	$Good	$Fine	$N.Mint	£Good	£Fine	£N.Mint
1 Black Orchid, Creeper, Demon, Man-Bat, Madame Xanadu, Phantom Stranger appear, Bollandesque pin-up re-done from Superman #400	*$0.20*	*$0.60*	*$1.00*	£0.15	£0.45	£0.75
Title Value:	*$0.20*	*$0.60*	*$1.00*	£0.15	£0.45	£0.75

BLUE LILY, THE

Dark Horse,MS; 1 Mar 1993-2 Apr 1993

1-2 ND 48pgs, Angus McKie script and art

VERY GENERAL PERCENTAGE CONVERSION CHART WHICH MAY BE USED TO CALCULATE LOW AND INBETWEEN GRADES:

	$Good	$Fine	$N.Mint	£Good	£Fine	£N.Mint
	$0.60	$1.80	$3.00	£0.40	£1.20	£2.00
Title Value:	$1.20	$3.60	$6.00	£0.80	£2.40	£4.00

Note: originally planned as a four issue mini-series but was cancelledby Dark Horse after 2 issues as the creator apparently failed to meet deadlines.

BLUE RIBBON COMICS
Red Circle (Archie); 1 Oct 1983-14 Dec 1985

	$Good	$Fine	$N.Mint	£Good	£Fine	£N.Mint
1 reprints Adventures of the Fly #1 by Jack Kirby	$0.20	$0.60	$1.00	£0.15	£0.45	£0.75
2 Mr. Justice by Trevor Von Eeden/Alex Nino	$0.15	$0.45	$0.75	£0.10	£0.35	£0.60
3 Steel Sterling	$0.15	$0.45	$0.75	£0.10	£0.35	£0.60
4 Fly by Von Eeden/Buckler	$0.15	$0.45	$0.75	£0.10	£0.35	£0.60
5 Shield (reprints, including origin by Joe Simon & Jack Kirby from Double Life of Private Strong), new Jack Kirby/Buckler cover	$0.15	$0.45	$0.75	£0.10	£0.35	£0.60
6-7 The Fox	$0.15	$0.45	$0.75	£0.10	£0.35	£0.60
8 Black Hood by Morrow, Williamson, Neal Adams reprint	$0.15	$0.45	$0.75	£0.10	£0.35	£0.60
9 Agents of Atlantis, Adamsesque art	$0.15	$0.45	$0.75	£0.10	£0.35	£0.60
10 The Fly (50s reprints)	$0.15	$0.45	$0.75	£0.10	£0.35	£0.60
11	$0.15	$0.45	$0.75	£0.10	£0.35	£0.60
12 ThunderAgents	$0.15	$0.45	$0.75	£0.10	£0.35	£0.60
13 Thunderbunny	$0.15	$0.45	$0.75	£0.10	£0.35	£0.60
14 Web and Jaguar	$0.15	$0.45	$0.75	£0.10	£0.35	£0.60
Title Value:	$2.15	$6.45	$10.75	£1.45	£5.00	£8.55

Note: all Non-Distributed on the news-stands in the U.K.

BLUEBERRY
Marvel Comics Group/Epic Graphic Novel; 1 1989-8 1992

(see Moebius)

	$Good	$Fine	$N.Mint	£Good	£Fine	£N.Mint
1 ND 96pgs, Chihuahua Pearl, Charlier script, Moebius art begins	$1.80	$5.25	$9.00	£1.20	£3.60	£6.00
2 ND 120pgs, Ballad for a Coffin Graphic Novel	$1.80	$5.25	$9.00	£1.20	£3.60	£6.00
3 ND 96pgs, Angel Face	$1.80	$5.25	$9.00	£1.20	£3.60	£6.00
4 ND 96pgs, The Ghost Tribe	$1.80	$5.25	$9.00	£1.20	£3.60	£6.00
5 ND 96pgs, End of the Trail	$1.50	$4.50	$7.50	£1.00	£3.00	£5.00
6 ND 48pgs, The Iron Horse	$1.50	$4.50	$7.50	£1.00	£3.00	£5.00
7 ND 48pgs, Steel Finger	$1.50	$4.50	$7.50	£1.00	£3.00	£5.00
8 ND 48pgs, General Golden Mane	$2.50	$7.50	$12.50	£1.50	£4.50	£7.50
Title Value:	$14.20	$42.00	$71.00	£9.30	£27.90	£46.50

Note: script by J.M. Lofficier, art by Moebius. Titan Editions of 1,2 available

BOB HOPE, THE ADVENTURES OF
National Periodical Publications; 1 Feb/Mar 1950-109 Feb/Mar 1968

	$Good	$Fine	$N.Mint	£Good	£Fine	£N.Mint
1	$155.00	$465.00	$1250.00	£105.00	£315.00	£850.00
2	$70.00	$215.00	$575.00	£48.00	£140.00	£385.00
3-4	$45.00	$135.00	$360.00	£30.00	£90.00	£240.00
5-10	$39.00	$115.00	$310.00	£26.00	£77.50	£210.00
11-20	$24.00	$72.50	$170.00	£16.00	£49.00	£115.00
21-31	$15.00	$45.00	$105.00	£10.00	£30.00	£70.00
32-40	$13.50	$41.00	$95.00	£9.25	£28.00	£65.00
41-48	$10.50	$32.00	$75.00	£7.00	£21.00	£50.00
1st official distribution in the U.K.						
49-50	$10.50	$32.00	$75.00	£7.00	£21.00	£50.00
51-60	$7.00	$21.00	$50.00	£4.25	£12.50	£30.00
61-70	$6.25	$19.00	$45.00	£3.55	£10.50	£25.00
71-93	$3.55	$10.50	$25.00	£1.75	£5.25	£12.50
94 Aquaman appears	$4.25	$12.50	$30.00	£2.10	£6.25	£15.00
95-96	$3.55	$10.50	$25.00	£1.75	£5.25	£12.50
97 Batman and Robin X-over, Joker's Health Club story	$5.00	$15.00	$35.00	£2.85	£8.50	£20.00
98-105	$3.55	$10.50	$25.00	£1.75	£5.25	£12.50
106-109 scarce in the U.K. Neal Adams art	$5.50	$17.00	$40.00	£2.85	£8.50	£20.00
Title Value:	$1461.40	$4391.00	$10865.00	£944.35	£2834.00	£7057.50

Note: early issues at least scarce in the U.K.

BOB MARLEY: TALE OF THE TUFF GONG BOOK
Marvel Comics Group,MS; 1 Oct 1994-3 Dec 1994

	$Good	$Fine	$N.Mint	£Good	£Fine	£N.Mint
1-3 ND 48pgs, Gene Colan art	$1.00	$3.00	$5.00	£0.70	£2.10	£3.50
Title Value:	$3.00	$9.00	$15.00	£2.10	£6.30	£10.50

BOB, THE GALACTIC BUM
DC Comics,MS; 1 Feb 1995-4 Jun 1995

	$Good	$Fine	$N.Mint	£Good	£Fine	£N.Mint
1-4 Alan Grant and John Wagner script, Carlos Ezquerra art	$0.40	$1.20	$2.00	£0.25	£0.75	£1.25
Title Value:	$1.60	$4.80	$8.00	£1.00	£3.00	£5.00

BODY BAGS
Dark Horse,MS; 1 Sep 1996-4 Dec 1996

	$Good	$Fine	$N.Mint	£Good	£Fine	£N.Mint
1-4 ND Jason Pearson script and art	$0.60	$1.80	$3.00	£0.40	£1.20	£2.00
Title Value:	$2.40	$7.20	$12.00	£1.60	£4.80	£8.00

BODY COUNT
Aircel,MS; 1 Dec 1989-4 Apr 1990

	$Good	$Fine	$N.Mint	£Good	£Fine	£N.Mint
1-4 ND Barry Blair script/lay-outs, Dave Cooper finishes	$0.50	$1.50	$2.50	£0.30	£0.90	£1.50
Title Value:	$2.00	$6.00	$10.00	£1.20	£3.60	£6.00

BODY COUNT
Marvel UK,OS; 1 Oct 1993

	$Good	$Fine	$N.Mint	£Good	£Fine	£N.Mint
1 ND Marvel U.K. arist and writer information and listings; originally given away for free	$0.30	$0.90	$1.50	£0.20	£0.60	£1.00
Title Value:	$0.30	$0.90	$1.50	£0.20	£0.60	£1.00

BODY COUNT
Image,MS; 1 Apr 1996-5 Aug 1996 ?

	$Good	$Fine	$N.Mint	£Good	£Fine	£N.Mint
1-5 ND Kevin Eastman script, Simon Bisley covers and art	$0.50	$1.50	$2.50	£0.30	£0.90	£1.50
Title Value:	$2.50	$7.50	$12.50	£1.50	£4.50	£7.50

BODY GUARD
Aircel,MS; 1 Nov 1990-3 Jan 1991

	$Good	$Fine	$N.Mint	£Good	£Fine	£N.Mint
1-3 ND reprints from Australian Penthouse	$0.50	$1.50	$2.50	£0.30	£0.90	£1.50
Title Value:	$1.50	$4.50	$7.50	£0.90	£2.70	£4.50

BOLD ADVENTURE
Pacific; 1 Nov 1983-3 Jun 1984

	$Good	$Fine	$N.Mint	£Good	£Fine	£N.Mint
1 ND Time Force begins	$0.15	$0.45	$0.75	£0.10	£0.35	£0.60
2 ND Alex Nino art	$0.15	$0.45	$0.75	£0.10	£0.35	£0.60
3 ND Mike Kaluta cover	$0.15	$0.45	$0.75	£0.10	£0.35	£0.60
Title Value:	$0.45	$1.35	$2.25	£0.30	£1.05	£1.80

BOLT & STARFORCE SIX
AC Comics; 1 Mar 1984

(see Starforce Six Special)

	$Good	$Fine	$N.Mint	£Good	£Fine	£N.Mint
1 ND	$0.30	$0.90	$1.50	£0.20	£0.60	£1.00
Title Value:	$0.30	$0.90	$1.50	£0.20	£0.60	£1.00

BOLT SPECIAL
AC Comics; 1 1984

	$Good	$Fine	$N.Mint	£Good	£Fine	£N.Mint
1 ND 52pgs, black and white	$0.30	$0.90	$1.50	£0.20	£0.60	£1.00
Title Value:	$0.30	$0.90	$1.50	£0.20	£0.60	£1.00

BOMARC
Night Wynd,MS; 1 Sep 1992-5 Jan 1993

	$Good	$Fine	$N.Mint	£Good	£Fine	£N.Mint
1-5 ND Ken Branch script/art	$0.40	$1.20	$2.00	£0.25	£0.75	£1.25
Title Value:	$2.00	$6.00	$10.00	£1.25	£3.75	£6.25

BOMBA, THE JUNGLE BOY
National Periodical Publications, TV; 1 Sep/Oct 1967-7 Sep/Oct 1968

	$Good	$Fine	$N.Mint	£Good	£Fine	£N.Mint
1 1st appearance Bomba; Infantino/Anderson cover	$2.50	$7.50	$17.50	£1.75	£5.25	£12.50
2-7	$1.40	$4.25	$10.00	£0.85	£2.55	£6.00
Title Value:	$10.90	$33.00	$77.50	£6.85	£20.55	£48.50

BOMBAST
Topps,OS; 1 Apr 1993

	$Good	$Fine	$N.Mint	£Good	£Fine	£N.Mint
1 ND pre-bagged with coupon #3 for Secret City Saga #0 plus Bombast chrome trading card; Savage Dragon appears; Jack Kirby cover	$0.40	$1.20	$2.00	£0.20	£0.60	£1.00
1 without coupon/card ND	$0.20	$0.60	$1.00	£0.15	£0.45	£0.75
Title Value:	$0.60	$1.80	$3.00	£0.35	£1.05	£1.75

BONE
Cartoon Books/Image Comics; 1 1992-present

	$Good	$Fine	$N.Mint	£Good	£Fine	£N.Mint
1 ND Jeff Smith script/art begins; black and white	$50.00	$150.00	$250.00	£30.00	£90.00	£150.00
1 2nd printing ND	$5.00	$15.00	$25.00	£3.00	£9.00	£15.00
1 3rd printing ND	$1.50	$4.50	$7.50	£1.00	£3.00	£5.00
1 4th printing ND	$0.90	$2.70	$4.50	£0.60	£1.80	£3.00
1 5th printing ND	$0.60	$1.80	$3.00	£0.40	£1.20	£2.00
1 6th - 10th printing ND	$0.60	$1.80	$3.00	£0.40	£1.20	£2.00
2 ND	$28.00	$82.50	$140.00	£16.00	£48.00	£80.00
2 2nd printing ND	$0.90	$2.70	$4.50	£0.60	£1.80	£3.00
2 3rd - 7th printing ND	$0.60	$1.80	$3.00	£0.40	£1.20	£2.00
3 ND	$20.00	$60.00	$100.00	£12.00	£36.00	£60.00
3 2nd printing ND	$0.90	$2.70	$4.50	£0.60	£1.80	£3.00
3 3rd printing ND	$0.60	$1.80	$3.00	£0.40	£1.20	£2.00
3 4th - 7th printing ND	$0.55	$1.65	$2.75	£0.35	£1.05	£1.75
4 ND	$10.00	$30.00	$50.00	£6.00	£18.00	£30.00
4 2nd printing ND	$0.90	$2.70	$4.50	£0.60	£1.80	£3.00
4 3rd - 6th printing ND	$0.55	$1.65	$2.75	£0.35	£1.05	£1.75
5 ND	$9.00	$27.00	$45.00	£5.00	£15.00	£25.00
6 ND	$8.00	$24.00	$40.00	£4.00	£12.00	£20.00
7 ND	$7.00	$21.00	$35.00	£3.50	£10.50	£17.50
8 ND	$6.00	$18.00	$30.00	£3.00	£9.00	£15.00
9-10 ND	$2.40	$7.00	$12.00	£1.20	£3.60	£6.00
11-13 ND	$0.80	$2.40	$4.00	£0.50	£1.50	£2.50
13½ ND Wizard send-away promotion, with certificate	$3.00	$9.00	$15.00	£2.00	£6.00	£10.00
13½ Gold Edition, ND Wizard send away promotion, with certificate	$5.00	$15.00	$25.00	£2.50	£7.50	£12.50
14-20 ND	$0.60	$1.80	$3.00	£0.40	£1.20	£2.00
21 ND 1st Image Comics issue	$0.60	$1.80	$3.00	£0.40	£1.20	£2.00
22-25 ND	$0.60	$1.80	$3.00	£0.40	£1.20	£2.00

	$Good	$Fine	$N.Mint	£Good	£Fine	£N.Mint
Title Value:	**$174.00**	**$520.10**	**$870.00**	**£101.40**	**£304.20**	**£507.00**
The Complete Bone Adventures: Out From Boneville (Aug 1993)						
ND reprints issues #1-6, foreword by Will Eisner				£1.75	£5.25	£8.25
Holiday Special (1993)						
ND, 16pgs, larger size format; free with Hero Illustrated				£0.25	£0.75	£1.25
The Complete Bone Adventures Vol. 2: The Great Cow Race (Jul 1994)						
ND reprints issues #7-12, foreword by Neil Gaiman				£1.70	£5.10	£8.50
The Complete Bone Adventures Vol. 3: Eye of the Storm (Aug 1995)						
ND reprints issues #13-18, foreword by Frank Miller				£1.70	£5.10	£8.50
The Complete Bone Adventures : Eyes of the Storm (1996)						
ND Hardcover with five new pages of art				£3.30	£9.90	£16.50

BONE (2ND SERIES)

Image; 1 Nov 1995-12 Nov 1996

	$Good	$Fine	$N.Mint	£Good	£Fine	£N.Mint
1 ND reprint of #1 celebrating Image Comics taking over the title	$0.60	$1.80	$3.00	£0.40	£1.20	£2.00
2 ND reprints begin from issue #2 of original series with new covers	$0.60	$1.80	$3.00	£0.40	£1.20	£2.00
3-12 ND	$0.60	$1.80	$3.00	£0.40	£1.20	£2.00
Title Value:	**$7.20**	**$21.60**	**$36.00**	**£4.80**	**£14.40**	**£24.00**
Bone Volume One: Out From Boneville Hardcover (Jul 1995)						
ND new hardcover format collecting issues #1-6 with dust-jacket				£3.00	£9.00	£15.00
Bone Volume Two: The Great Cow Race Hardcover (Jan 1996)						
ND new format hardcover collecting issues #7-11 with dust-jacket				£3.00	£9.00	£15.00

BONE SAW

Tundra,OS; 1 1992

	$Good	$Fine	$N.Mint	£Good	£Fine	£N.Mint
1 ND horror anthology featuring John Bergin art, black and white and colour	$3.00	$9.00	$15.00	£2.00	£6.00	£10.00
Title Value:	**$3.00**	**$9.00**	**$15.00**	**£2.00**	**£6.00**	**£10.00**

BONE SOURCEBOOK

Image,OS; 1 Sep 1995

	$Good	$Fine	$N.Mint	£Good	£Fine	£N.Mint
1 ND black and white giveaway to celebrate Bone joining Image	$0.25	$0.75	$1.25	£0.15	£0.45	£0.75
Title Value:	**$0.25**	**$0.75**	**$1.25**	**£0.15**	**£0.45**	**£0.75**

BONES

Malibu; 1 Aug 1987-4 Nov 1987

	$Good	$Fine	$N.Mint	£Good	£Fine	£N.Mint
1-4 ND	$0.20	$0.60	$1.00	£0.15	£0.45	£0.75
Title Value:	**$0.80**	**$2.40**	**$4.00**	**£0.60**	**£1.80**	**£3.00**

BOOF

Image; 1 Jul 1994-6 Dec 1994

	$Good	$Fine	$N.Mint	£Good	£Fine	£N.Mint
1-6 ND John Cleary art	$0.30	$0.90	$1.50	£0.20	£0.60	£1.00
Title Value:	**$1.80**	**$5.40**	**$9.00**	**£1.20**	**£3.60**	**£6.00**

BOOF AND THE BRUISE CREW

Image; 1 Jul 1994-6 Dec 1994

	$Good	$Fine	$N.Mint	£Good	£Fine	£N.Mint
1-6 ND Tim Harkins art	$0.30	$0.90	$1.50	£0.20	£0.60	£1.00
Title Value:	**$1.80**	**$5.40**	**$9.00**	**£1.20**	**£3.60**	**£6.00**

BOOK OF FATE, THE

DC Comics; 1 Feb 1997-present

	$Good	$Fine	$N.Mint	£Good	£Fine	£N.Mint
1-2 ND Keith Giffen script, Ron Wagner and Bill Reinhold art	$0.45	$1.35	$2.25	£0.30	£0.90	£1.50
Title Value:	**$0.90**	**$2.70**	**$4.50**	**£0.60**	**£1.80**	**£3.00**

BOOK OF NIGHT, CHARLES VESS'

Dark Horse; 1 Jul 1987-3 Oct 1987

	$Good	$Fine	$N.Mint	£Good	£Fine	£N.Mint
1-3 ND Charles Vess art	$0.50	$1.50	$2.50	£0.30	£0.90	£1.50
Title Value:	**$1.50**	**$4.50**	**$7.50**	**£0.90**	**£2.70**	**£4.50**
Book of Night Softcover (Nov 1991), reprints mini-series				£1.40	£4.20	£7.00
Book of Night Hardcover (Nov 1991), slipcase with foil stamping, signed and numbered (500 copies)				£7.00	£21.00	£35.00

BOOK OF THE DEAD

Marvel Comics Group,MS; 1 Dec 1993-4 Mar 1994

	$Good	$Fine	$N.Mint	£Good	£Fine	£N.Mint
1 ND 48pgs, Man-Thing and Frankenstein reprints begin	$0.30	$0.90	$1.50	£0.20	£0.60	£1.00
2 ND 48pgs, Adventure Into Fear #10 reprinted (1st Man-Thing)	$0.30	$0.90	$1.50	£0.20	£0.60	£1.00
3-4 ND 48pgs	$0.30	$0.90	$1.50	£0.20	£0.60	£1.00
Title Value:	**$1.20**	**$3.60**	**$6.00**	**£0.80**	**£2.40**	**£4.00**

BOOKS OF MAGIC

DC Comics,MS; 1 Dec 1990-4 Apr 1991

	$Good	$Fine	$N.Mint	£Good	£Fine	£N.Mint
1 ND Phantom Stranger/Arion/Zatara/Sargon/Spectre/Dr. Fate/Deadman/Zatanna/Mister E appear in this series	$2.50	$7.50	$12.50	£0.80	£2.40	£4.00
2 ND John Constantine appears	$2.00	$6.00	$10.00	£0.70	£2.10	£3.50
3 ND scarce in the U.K. Sandman appears	$1.60	$4.80	$8.00	£0.80	£2.40	£4.00
4 ND Death appears	$1.80	$5.25	$9.00	£0.80	£2.40	£4.00
Title Value:	**$7.90**	**$23.55**	**$39.50**	**£3.10**	**£9.30**	**£15.50**

Note: painted art by John Bolton, Charles Vess, Scott Hampton and Paul Johnson in #1-4 respectively; script by Neil Gaiman in all. Prestige Format

	$Good	$Fine	$N.Mint	£Good	£Fine	£N.Mint
Trade paperback (Mar 1993) 200pgs, reprints mini-series, foil-enhanced cover and new introduction by Roger Zelazny				£2.50	£7.50	£12.50

BOOKS OF MAGIC ANNUAL, THE

DC Comics; 1 Feb 1997-present

	$Good	$Fine	$N.Mint	£Good	£Fine	£N.Mint
1 ND 48pgs, Mark Buckingham art	$0.80	$2.40	$4.00	£0.50	£1.50	£2.50
Title Value:	**$0.80**	**$2.40**	**$4.00**	**£0.50**	**£1.50**	**£2.50**

BOOKS OF MAGIC, THE

DC Comics/Vertigo; 1 May 1994-present

	$Good	$Fine	$N.Mint	£Good	£Fine	£N.Mint
1 John Reiber script, Gary Amaro art; painted cover by Charles Vess	$1.00	$3.00	$5.00	£0.40	£1.20	£2.00
1 Platinum Edition ND	$3.00	$9.00	$15.00	£1.20	£3.60	£6.00
2-3	$0.80	$2.40	$4.00	£0.30	£0.90	£1.50
4 Death appears	$1.00	$3.00	$5.00	£0.30	£0.90	£1.50
5-12	$0.60	$1.80	$3.00	£0.30	£0.90	£1.50
13 upgraded paper format begins	$0.50	$1.50	$2.50	£0.30	£0.90	£1.50
14-27	$0.50	$1.50	$2.50	£0.30	£0.90	£1.50
28-30 painted cover by Mike Kaluta	$0.50	$1.50	$2.50	£0.30	£0.90	£1.50
31-35 ND	$0.50	$1.50	$2.50	£0.30	£0.90	£1.50
Title Value:	**$22.90**	**$68.70**	**$113.50**	**£11.80**	**£35.40**	**£59.00**
The Books of Magic: Bindings (Mar 1995)						
Trade paperback reprints issues #1-4				£1.70	£5.10	£8.50
Books of Magic: Summonings (Jun 1996)						
reprints issues #5-13 plus story from Vertigo Rave #1				£2.30	£6.90	£11.50

BOOKS OF THE FAERIE

DC Comics,MS; 1 Mar 1997-present

	$Good	$Fine	$N.Mint	£Good	£Fine	£N.Mint
1-2 ND Bronwyn Carlton script, Peter Gross art; features Titania and Oberon	$0.50	$1.50	$2.50	£0.30	£0.90	£1.50
Title Value:	**$1.00**	**$3.00**	**$5.00**	**£0.60**	**£1.80**	**£3.00**

BOOKS OF THE OPRESSOR

Northstar; 1 Apr 1993

	$Good	$Fine	$N.Mint	£Good	£Fine	£N.Mint
1 ND features David and Dan Day and Andrew Pepoy art; black and white	$0.40	$1.20	$2.00	£0.20	£0.60	£1.00
Title Value:	**$0.40**	**$1.20**	**$2.00**	**£0.20**	**£0.60**	**£1.00**

BOOSTER GOLD

DC Comics; 1 Feb 1986-25 Feb 1988

(see Adventures of Superman, Justice League)

	$Good	$Fine	$N.Mint	£Good	£Fine	£N.Mint
1 Superman appears	$0.15	$0.45	$0.75	£0.10	£0.35	£0.60
2-5	$0.15	$0.45	$0.75	£0.10	£0.30	£0.50
6 origin	$0.15	$0.45	$0.75	£0.10	£0.30	£0.50
7	$0.15	$0.45	$0.75	£0.10	£0.30	£0.50
8 Legion of Super-heroes appear	$0.15	$0.45	$0.75	£0.10	£0.30	£0.50
9-21	$0.15	$0.45	$0.75	£0.10	£0.30	£0.50
22 Justice League International appear	$0.15	$0.45	$0.75	£0.10	£0.30	£0.50
23	$0.15	$0.45	$0.75	£0.10	£0.30	£0.50
24-25 Millennium X-over	$0.15	$0.45	$0.75	£0.10	£0.30	£0.50
Title Value:	**$3.75**	**$11.25**	**$18.75**	**£2.50**	**£7.55**	**£12.60**

BORDER WORLDS

Kitchen Sink; 1 Jul 1986-7 Aug 1987

	$Good	$Fine	$N.Mint	£Good	£Fine	£N.Mint
1-6 ND Don Simpson story/art	$0.35	$1.05	$1.75	£0.25	£0.75	£1.25
7 ND Don Simpson story/art; with printing error	$0.35	$1.05	$1.75	£0.25	£0.75	£1.25
7 2nd Printing, ND Don Simpson story/art; "Corrected Edition" on cover	$0.35	$1.05	$1.75	£0.25	£0.75	£1.25
Title Value:	**$2.80**	**$8.40**	**$14.00**	**£2.00**	**£6.00**	**£10.00**

BORDER WORLDS: MAROONED

Kitchen Sink,OS; 1 1990

	$Good	$Fine	$N.Mint	£Good	£Fine	£N.Mint
1 ND Don Simpson script/art	$0.35	$1.05	$1.75	£0.25	£0.75	£1.25
Title Value:	**$0.35**	**$1.05**	**$1.75**	**£0.25**	**£0.75**	**£1.25**

BORDERGUARD

Eternity; 1 Nov 1987-2 Mar 1988

	$Good	$Fine	$N.Mint	£Good	£Fine	£N.Mint
1-2 ND	$0.20	$0.60	$1.00	£0.15	£0.45	£0.75
Title Value:	**$0.40**	**$1.20**	**$2.00**	**£0.30**	**£0.90**	**£1.50**

BORIS ADVENTURE MAGAZINE

Nicotat; 1 Aug 1988

	$Good	$Fine	$N.Mint	£Good	£Fine	£N.Mint
1 ND Rocketeer parody cover	$0.50	$1.50	$2.50	£0.30	£0.90	£1.50
Title Value:	**$0.50**	**$1.50**	**$2.50**	**£0.30**	**£0.90**	**£1.50**

BORIS KARLOFF TALES OF MYSTERY

Gold Key; 3 Apr 1963-97 Feb 1980

(previously Boris Karloff Thriller)

	$Good	$Fine	$N.Mint	£Good	£Fine	£N.Mint
3	$3.55	$10.50	$25.00	£2.10	£6.25	£15.00
4-8	$3.20	$9.50	$22.50	£2.00	£6.00	£14.00
9 Wally Wood art	$3.55	$10.50	$25.00	£2.10	£6.25	£15.00
10	$2.85	$8.50	$20.00	£2.00	£6.00	£14.00
11 Williamson art	$3.55	$10.50	$25.00	£2.10	£6.25	£15.00
12-14	$2.10	$6.25	$15.00	£1.40	£4.25	£10.00
15 Crandall, Evans art	$2.10	$6.25	$15.00	£1.40	£4.25	£10.00
16-20	$2.10	$6.25	$15.00	£1.40	£4.25	£10.00
21 Jeff Jones art	$2.55	$7.50	$18.00	£1.70	£5.00	£12.00
22	$1.40	$4.25	$10.00	£0.90	£2.75	£6.50
23 reprint	$1.40	$4.25	$10.00	£0.90	£2.75	£6.50
24-30	$1.40	$4.25	$10.00	£0.90	£2.75	£6.50
31-50	$1.15	$3.50	$7.00	£0.75	£2.25	£4.50
51-70	$1.00	$3.00	$5.00	£0.60	£1.80	£3.00
71-97	$0.50	$1.50	$2.50	£0.35	£1.05	£1.75
Title Value:	**$120.05**	**$360.00**	**$758.00**	**£77.15**	**£232.10**	**£486.75**

Note: all Limited Distribution on the news-stands in the U.K.

BORIS KARLOFF THRILLER

Gold Key; 1 Oct 1962-2 Jan 1963

(becomes Boris Karloff Tales of Mystery)

1 scarce, very limited distributed in the U.K. 80pgs

	$Good	$Fine	$N.Mint	£Good	£Fine	£N.Mint
	$7.75	$23.50	$55.00	£4.25	£12.50	£30.00
2 scarce, very limited distributed in the U.K. 80pgs						
	$4.25	$12.50	$30.00	£2.85	£8.50	£20.00
Title Value:	$12.00	$36.00	$85.00	£7.10	£21.00	£50.00

BORIS THE BEAR

Nicotat/Dark Horse; 1 1986-24 1989; 25 1990-37 1993 ?

	$Good	$Fine	$N.Mint	£Good	£Fine	£N.Mint
1	$0.60	$1.80	$3.00	£0.40	£1.20	£2.00
1 2nd printing	$0.50	$1.50	$2.50	£0.30	£0.90	£1.50
2 scarce in the U.K.						
	$0.50	$1.50	$2.50	£0.30	£0.90	£1.50
3 Secret Wars parody						
	$0.50	$1.50	$2.50	£0.30	£0.90	£1.50
4 origin, "Man of Steel" parody, 2 covers exist						
	$0.50	$1.50	$2.50	£0.30	£0.90	£1.50
5 Swamp Thing parody						
	$0.50	$1.50	$2.50	£0.30	£0.90	£1.50
6 Batman parody (Bat-Bear)						
	$0.40	$1.20	$2.00	£0.25	£0.75	£1.25
7 Elfquest parody	$0.40	$1.20	$2.00	£0.25	£0.75	£1.25
8 DS	$0.50	$1.50	$2.50	£0.30	£0.90	£1.50
9-12	$0.40	$1.20	$2.00	£0.25	£0.75	£1.25
13 1st Nicotat issue, Punisher parody						
	$0.40	$1.20	$2.00	£0.25	£0.75	£1.25
14-24	$0.40	$1.20	$2.00	£0.25	£0.75	£1.25
25 Southern Squadron appears						
	$0.40	$1.20	$2.00	£0.25	£0.75	£1.25
26-33	$0.30	$0.90	$1.50	£0.20	£0.60	£1.00
34-37 The Return of Blackbear						
	$0.30	$0.90	$1.50	£0.20	£0.60	£1.00
Title Value:	$14.80	$44.40	$74.00	£9.35	£28.05	£46.75

Note: all Non-Distributed on the news-stands in the U.K.

BORIS THE BEAR INSTANT COLOR CLASSICS

Dark Horse; 1 Jul 1987-7 1988

	$Good	$Fine	$N.Mint	£Good	£Fine	£N.Mint
1-7 ND reprints from Boris the Bear, in colour						
	$0.40	$1.20	$2.00	£0.25	£0.75	£1.25
Title Value:	$2.80	$8.40	$14.00	£1.75	£5.25	£8.75

BORN TO BE WILD

Eclipse,OS; 1 Dec 1991

	$Good	$Fine	$N.Mint	£Good	£Fine	£N.Mint
1 ND 72pgs, features work by Neil Gaiman, Grant Morrison, Moebius, Starlin, David Lloyd, Todd McFarlane and others for animal charities						
	$1.50	$4.50	$7.50	£1.00	£3.00	£5.00
Title Value:	$1.50	$4.50	$7.50	£1.00	£3.00	£5.00

BORN TO KILL

Aircel; 1 May 1991-2 1991

	$Good	$Fine	$N.Mint	£Good	£Fine	£N.Mint
1-2 ND black and white						
	$0.40	$1.20	$2.00	£0.25	£0.75	£1.25
Title Value:	$0.80	$2.40	$4.00	£0.50	£1.50	£2.50

BOSTON BOMBERS, THE

Caliber Press,MS; 1 Nov 1990-6 Sep 1991

	$Good	$Fine	$N.Mint	£Good	£Fine	£N.Mint
1-6 ND	$0.30	$0.90	$1.50	£0.20	£0.60	£1.00
Title Value:	$1.80	$5.40	$9.00	£1.20	£3.60	£6.00

BOUNTY

Caliber Press; 1 Aug 1991-3 Oct 1991

	$Good	$Fine	$N.Mint	£Good	£Fine	£N.Mint
1-3 ND	$0.30	$0.90	$1.50	£0.20	£0.60	£1.00
Title Value:	$0.90	$2.70	$4.50	£0.60	£1.80	£3.00

BOY AND HIS BOT

Now Comics; 1 Jan 1987

	$Good	$Fine	$N.Mint	£Good	£Fine	£N.Mint
1 ND	$0.30	$0.90	$1.50	£0.20	£0.60	£1.00
Title Value:	$0.30	$0.90	$1.50	£0.20	£0.60	£1.00

BOY COMMANDOS

DC Comics; 1 Sep/Oct 1973-2 Nov/Dec 1973

	$Good	$Fine	$N.Mint	£Good	£Fine	£N.Mint
1 Golden Age Joe Simon & Jack Kirby reprints from Boy Commandoes #1 and Detective Comics #66						
	$0.80	$2.50	$5.00	£0.40	£1.25	£2.50
2 Golden Age Joe Simon & Jack Kirby reprints						
	$0.65	$2.00	$4.00	£0.30	£1.00	£2.00
Title Value:	$1.45	$4.50	$9.00	£0.70	£2.25	£4.50

BOZO THE CLOWN IN 3-D

Blackthorne; (3-D Series #24) 1 Autumn 1987

	$Good	$Fine	$N.Mint	£Good	£Fine	£N.Mint
1 ND with bound-in 3-D glasses (25% less if without glasses)						
	$0.40	$1.20	$2.00	£0.25	£0.75	£1.25
Title Value:	$0.40	$1.20	$2.00	£0.25	£0.75	£1.25

BOZZ CHRONICLES, THE

Marvel Comics Group/Epic; 1 Dec 1985-6 May 1986

	$Good	$Fine	$N.Mint	£Good	£Fine	£N.Mint
1-6 ND	$0.40	$1.20	$2.00	£0.25	£0.75	£1.25
Title Value:	$2.40	$7.20	$12.00	£1.50	£4.50	£7.50

Note: all high-quality paper.

BRAIN BOY

Dell; 1 Apr/Jun 1962-6 Sep/Nov 1963

	$Good	$Fine	$N.Mint	£Good	£Fine	£N.Mint
1 scarce, distributed in the U.K.						
	$19.00	$57.50	$135.00	£11.00	£34.00	£80.00
2-6 distributed in the U.K.						
	$10.50	$32.00	$75.00	£5.50	£17.00	£40.00
Title Value:	$71.50	$217.50	$510.00	£38.50	£119.00	£280.00

BRAINBANX

DC Comics/Helix,MS; 1 Mar 1997-present

	$Good	$Fine	$N.Mint	£Good	£Fine	£N.Mint
1-2 ND Elaine Lee script, Temujin cover and art						
	$0.50	$1.50	$2.50	£0.30	£0.90	£1.50
Title Value:	$1.00	$3.00	$5.00	£0.60	£1.80	£3.00

BRAM STOKER'S BURIAL OF THE RATS

Cosmic Comics; 1 Apr 1995-3 1995

	$Good	$Fine	$N.Mint	£Good	£Fine	£N.Mint
1-3 ND Jerry Prosser script, Val Mayerik art; based on film						
	$0.40	$1.20	$2.00	£0.25	£0.75	£1.25
Title Value:	$1.20	$3.60	$6.00	£0.75	£2.25	£3.75

BRASS

Image; 1 Aug 1996-present

	$Good	$Fine	$N.Mint	£Good	£Fine	£N.Mint
1 ND Richard Bennett script and art						
	$0.50	$1.50	$2.50	£0.30	£0.90	£1.50
2 ND	$0.50	$1.50	$2.50	£0.30	£0.90	£1.50
Title Value:	$1.00	$3.00	$5.00	£0.60	£1.80	£3.00

BRATPACK

Tundra Publishing,MS; 1 Aug 1990-5 1991

	$Good	$Fine	$N.Mint	£Good	£Fine	£N.Mint
1 ND Rick Veitch story/art						
	$0.60	$1.80	$3.00	£0.40	£1.20	£2.00
1 2nd printing ND	$0.45	$1.35	$2.25	£0.30	£0.90	£1.50
2-5 ND	$0.50	$1.50	$2.50	£0.35	£1.05	£1.75
Title Value:	$3.05	$9.15	$15.25	£2.10	£6.30	£10.50

Note: bi-monthly

BRATS BIZARRE

Marvel Comics Group/Epic,MS; 1 May 1994-4 Aug 1994

	$Good	$Fine	$N.Mint	£Good	£Fine	£N.Mint
1-4 ND Pat Mills and Tony Skinner script						
	$0.30	$0.90	$1.50	£0.20	£0.60	£1.00
Title Value:	$1.20	$3.60	$6.00	£0.80	£2.40	£4.00

BRAVE AND THE BOLD SPECIAL, THE

DC Comics; 8 1978

(DC Special Series #8)

	$Good	$Fine	$N.Mint	£Good	£Fine	£N.Mint
8 ND 52pgs, features Batman and Sgt. Rock, Deadman and Sherlock Holmes						
	$0.75	$2.25	$4.50	£0.55	£1.75	£3.50
Title Value:	$0.75	$2.25	$4.50	£0.55	£1.75	£3.50

BRAVE AND THE BOLD, THE

National Periodical Publications/DC Comics; 1 Aug/Sep 1955-200 Jul 1983

(see Best of the Brave and the Bold, Super DC Giant 16)

1 Viking Prince by Kubert, Golden Gladiator and Silent Knight all begin

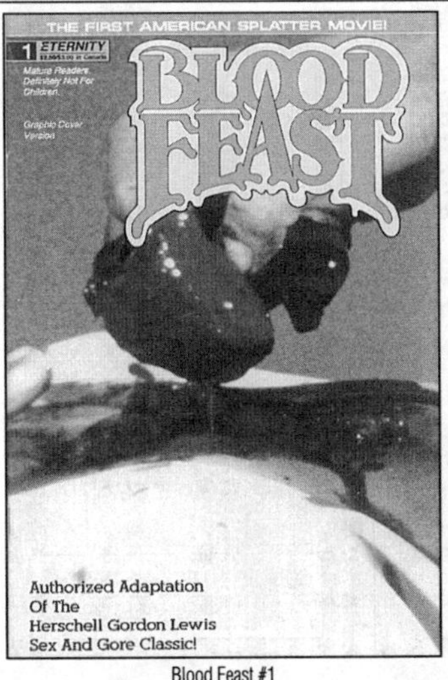

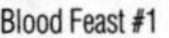
Blood Feast #1

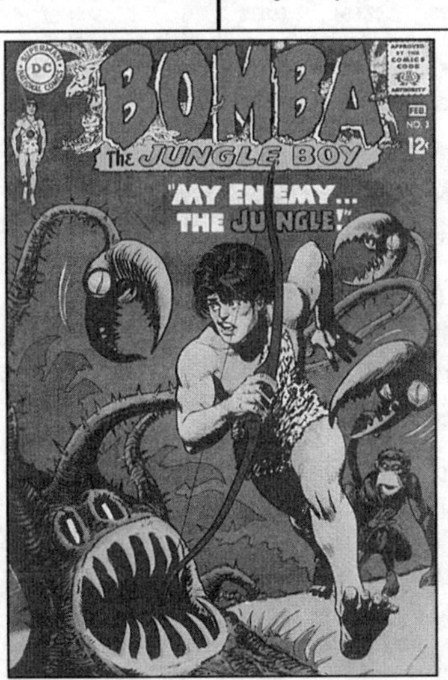

Bomba #3

Brave and the Bold #27

Issue	$Good	$Fine	$N.Mint	£Good	£Fine	£N.Mint
	$270.00	$810.00	$2700.00	£185.00	£550.00	£1850.00
2	$120.00	$365.00	$1100.00	£82.50	£250.00	£750.00
3-4	$65.00	$200.00	$600.00	£44.00	£130.00	£400.00
5 Robin Hood begins	$65.00	$200.00	$600.00	£44.00	£130.00	£400.00
6 no Viking Prince	$50.00	$150.00	$400.00	£33.00	£97.50	£260.00
7-10	$50.00	$150.00	$400.00	£33.00	£97.50	£260.00
11-21	$38.00	$110.00	$300.00	£25.00	£75.00	£200.00
22 last Silent Knight	$38.00	$110.00	$300.00	£25.00	£75.00	£200.00
23 origin Viking Prince by Kubert; 1st small logo	$50.00	$150.00	$400.00	£34.00	£100.00	£275.00
24	$38.00	$110.00	$300.00	£25.00	£75.00	£200.00
25 rare in the U.K. 1st appearance of Suicide Squad	$41.00	$120.00	$325.00	£28.00	£82.50	£225.00
1st official distribution in the U.K.						
26 very scarce in the U.K. Suicide Squad	$38.00	$110.00	$300.00	£25.00	£75.00	£200.00
27 scarce in the U.K. Suicide Squad	$36.00	$105.00	$290.00	£23.50	£70.00	£190.00
28 1st appearance Justice League of America, origin and 1st appearance Snapper Carr	$435.00	$1300.00	$5250.00	£280.00	£850.00	£3400.00
[Scarce in high grade - Very Fine+ or better]						
28 Silver Age Classic, ND (Mar 1992)	$0.25	$0.75	$1.25	£0.15	£0.50	£0.85
29 2nd appearance Justice League of America	$225.00	$670.00	$2250.00	£140.00	£420.00	£1400.00
30 scarce in the U.K. 3rd appearance of Justice League of America, 1st appearance of Amazo	$190.00	$570.00	$1900.00	£140.00	£420.00	£1400.00
[Scarce in high grade - Very Fine+ or better]						
31 1st appearance Cave Carson	$38.00	$110.00	$300.00	£23.50	£70.00	£190.00
32 rare in the U.K. 2nd appearance of Cave Carson	$25.00	$75.00	$200.00	£15.00	£45.00	£120.00
33 3rd appearance Cave Carson	$25.00	$75.00	$200.00	£13.50	£41.00	£110.00
34 origin and 1st appearance Silver Age Hawkman by Kubert; classic cover	$180.00	$540.00	$1800.00	£110.00	£330.00	£1100.00
[Scarce in high grade - Very Fine+ or better]						
35 2nd appearance Silver Age Hawkman by Kubert	$62.50	$185.00	$500.00	£41.00	£120.00	£325.00
36 3rd appearance Silver Age Hawkman by Kubert	$52.50	$155.00	$425.00	£34.00	£100.00	£275.00
37 Suicide Squad	$33.00	$97.50	$260.00	£21.50	£65.00	£175.00
38-39 Suicide Squad	$28.00	$82.50	$225.00	£17.50	£52.50	£140.00
40-41 Cave Carson	$19.00	$57.50	$155.00	£11.00	£34.00	£90.00
42 Hawkman by Kubert	$38.00	$110.00	$300.00	£23.50	£70.00	£190.00
43 Hawkman origin retold by Kubert	$39.00	$115.00	$350.00	£25.00	£75.00	£225.00
44 Hawkman by Kubert, painted cover	$31.00	$90.00	$245.00	£18.50	£55.00	£150.00
45-49 Strange Sports	$9.25	$28.00	$65.00	£5.00	£15.00	£35.00
50 1st team-up issue, Green Arrow and Manhunter from Mars	$18.50	$55.00	$170.00	£11.00	£33.00	£100.00
51 Aquaman and Hawkman (pre-dates Hawkman #1)	$28.00	$82.50	$250.00	£9.25	£28.00	£85.00
52 scarce in the U.K. Sgt. Rock & 3 Battle Aces; Kubert art	$14.00	$43.00	$115.00	£8.00	£24.00	£65.00
53 Atom and Flash, art by Alex Toth	$9.25	$28.00	$65.00	£5.00	£15.00	£35.00
54 Kid Flash, Robin and Aqualad; 1st "Teen Titans"	$36.00	$105.00	$255.00	£21.00	£62.50	£150.00
55 Metal Men and Atom	$7.00	$21.00	$50.00	£3.55	£10.50	£25.00
56 Flash and Manhunter from Mars	$7.75	$23.50	$55.00	£3.55	£10.50	£25.00
57 1st appearance Metamorpho	$20.50	$60.00	$145.00	£10.00	£30.00	£70.00
58 2nd appearance Metamorpho	$10.00	$30.00	$70.00	£5.00	£15.00	£35.00
59 Batman team-ups begin; Green Lantern	$14.00	$43.00	$100.00	£7.00	£21.00	£50.00
60 Teen Titans (first time title used: see Showcase #59)	$11.00	$34.00	$80.00	£7.00	£21.00	£50.00
61 Starman and Black Canary, 1pg text origins of both	$15.00	$45.00	$105.00	£4.60	£13.50	£32.50
62 Starman and Black Canary; 1st Silver Age Wildcat	$15.00	$45.00	$105.00	£4.60	£13.50	£32.50
63 Supergirl and Wonder Woman; last Silver Age issue cover-dated January but indicia-dated December 1965/January 1966	$5.25	$16.00	$37.50	£2.50	£7.50	£17.50
64 2nd Batman team-up, with and versus Eclipso	$7.75	$23.50	$55.00	£4.60	£13.50	£32.50
65 Flash and Doom Patrol	$2.50	$7.50	$17.50	£1.40	£4.25	£10.00
66 Metamorpho and Metal Men	$2.50	$7.50	$17.50	£1.40	£4.25	£10.00
67 Batman and Flash by Infantino	$5.25	$16.00	$37.50	£3.20	£9.50	£22.50
68 Batman (as Bat-Hulk) and Metamorpho; Joker, Riddler and Penguin appear	$8.00	$24.50	$57.50	£4.25	£12.50	£30.00
69 Batman and Green Lantern	$3.90	$11.50	$27.50	£2.10	£6.25	£15.00
70 Batman and Hawkman	$3.90	$11.50	$27.50	£2.10	£6.25	£15.00
71 Batman and Green Arrow	$3.90	$11.50	$27.50	£1.75	£5.25	£12.50
72 Flash and Spectre; pre dates Spectre #1	$3.90	$11.50	$27.50	£1.75	£5.25	£12.50
73 Aquaman and Atom	$3.20	$9.50	$22.50	£1.40	£4.25	£10.00
74 Batman and Metal Men; regular Batman team-ups begin (end #200)	$3.20	$9.50	$22.50	£1.75	£5.25	£12.50
75 Spectre	$3.90	$11.50	$27.50	£1.40	£4.25	£10.00
76 Plastic Man	$3.20	$9.50	$22.50	£1.40	£4.25	£10.00
77 Atom	$3.20	$9.50	$22.50	£1.40	£4.25	£10.00
78 Wonder Woman, Batgirl	$3.20	$9.50	$22.50	£1.40	£4.25	£10.00
79 Neal Adams art, Deadman; the first issue of a classic run	$6.25	$19.00	$45.00	£2.85	£8.50	£20.00
80 Neal Adams art, Creeper appears	$5.25	$16.00	$37.50	£2.10	£6.25	£15.00
81 Neal Adams art, Flash appears	$5.25	$16.00	$37.50	£2.10	£6.25	£15.00
82 Neal Adams art, Aquaman appears	$5.25	$16.00	$37.50	£2.10	£6.25	£15.00
83 Neal Adams art, Teen Titans appears	$6.25	$19.00	$45.00	£2.85	£8.50	£20.00
84 Neal Adams art, Sgt. Rock appears	$5.25	$16.00	$37.50	£2.10	£6.25	£15.00
85 Neal Adams art, Green Arrow appears (1st "new look" Green Arrow with new costume and goatee beard)	$5.25	$16.00	$37.50	£2.10	£6.25	£15.00
86 Neal Adams art, Deadman appears	$5.25	$16.00	$37.50	£2.10	£6.25	£15.00
87 (Dec/Jan 1970) Wonder Woman	$2.85	$8.50	$20.00	£1.40	£4.25	£10.00
88 Wildcat	$3.30	$10.00	$20.00	£1.65	£5.00	£10.00
89 Phantom Stranger	$3.30	$10.00	$20.00	£1.65	£5.00	£10.00
90 Adam Strange	$3.30	$10.00	$20.00	£1.65	£5.00	£10.00
91 Black Canary	$3.30	$10.00	$20.00	£1.65	£5.00	£10.00
92 Bat Squad	$3.30	$10.00	$20.00	£1.65	£5.00	£10.00
93 Neal Adams art, House of Mystery	$5.25	$16.00	$32.50	£2.50	£7.50	£15.00
94 Teen Titans	$2.50	$7.50	$15.00	£1.25	£3.75	£7.50
95 Plastic Man	$2.05	$6.25	$12.50	£1.15	£3.50	£7.00
96 Sgt. Rock	$2.05	$6.25	$12.50	£1.15	£3.50	£7.00
97 52pgs, Wildcat; Deadman origin	$2.05	$6.25	$12.50	£1.15	£3.50	£7.00
98 52pgs, Phantom Stranger	$2.05	$6.25	$12.50	£1.15	£3.50	£7.00
99 52pgs, Flash	$2.05	$6.25	$12.50	£1.15	£3.50	£7.00
100 52pgs, Neal Adams art on Deadman reprints, Green Lantern, Green Arrow, Black Canary and Robin appear	$5.25	$16.00	$32.50	£1.65	£5.00	£10.00
101 52pgs, Metamorpho	$1.25	$3.75	$7.50	£0.65	£2.00	£4.00
102 Neal Adams art, Teen Titans appear	$1.65	$5.00	$10.00	£0.80	£2.50	£5.00
103 Metal Men	$1.15	$3.50	$7.00	£0.55	£1.75	£3.50
104 Deadman	$1.15	$3.50	$7.00	£0.55	£1.75	£3.50
105 Wonder Woman	$1.15	$3.50	$7.00	£0.55	£1.75	£3.50
106 Green Arrow	$1.15	$3.50	$7.00	£0.55	£1.75	£3.50
107 Black Canary	$1.15	$3.50	$7.00	£0.55	£1.75	£3.50
108 Sgt. Rock	$1.15	$3.50	$7.00	£0.55	£1.75	£3.50
109 Demon	$1.15	$3.50	$7.00	£0.55	£1.75	£3.50
110 Wildcat	$1.15	$3.50	$7.00	£0.55	£1.75	£3.50
111 The Joker	$1.80	$5.50	$11.00	£1.00	£3.00	£6.00
112 100pgs, Mister Miracle; reprints Brave and the Bold #15, #51, #58	$1.30	$4.00	$8.00	£0.80	£2.50	£5.00
113 100pgs, Metal Men; reprints Brave and the Bold #34 (1st Silver Age Hawkman)	$1.30	$4.00	$8.00	£0.80	£2.50	£5.00
114 100pgs, Aquaman; reprints Brave and the Bold #50	$1.30	$4.00	$8.00	£0.80	£2.50	£5.00
115 100pgs, Atom; reprints Showcase #55	$1.30	$4.00	$8.00	£0.80	£2.50	£5.00
116 100pgs, Spectre; reprints Brave and the Bold #2, #78, Teen Titans #16	$1.30	$4.00	$8.00	£0.80	£2.50	£5.00
117 100pgs, Sgt.Rock; reprints Brave and the Bold #24, Secret Six #1	$1.30	$4.00	$8.00	£0.80	£2.50	£5.00
118 Wildcat and The Joker	$2.05	$6.25	$12.50	£1.15	£3.50	£7.00
119 Man-Bat	$0.80	$2.50	$5.00	£0.40	£1.25	£2.50
120 scarce in the U.K. 68pgs, Kamandi The Last Boy On Earth	$0.80	$2.50	$5.00	£0.55	£1.75	£3.50
121 scarce in the U.K. Metal Men	$0.80	$2.50	$5.00	£0.50	£1.50	£3.00
122 scarce in the U.K. Swamp Thing						

Issue	$Good	$Fine	$N.Mint	£Good	£Fine	£N.Mint
	$0.80	*$2.50*	*$5.00*	£0.50	£1.50	£3.00
123 Plastic Man and Metamorpho	*$0.80*	*$2.50*	*$5.00*	£0.40	£1.25	£2.50
124 Sgt. Rock	*$0.80*	*$2.50*	*$5.00*	£0.40	£1.25	£2.50
125 scarce in the U.K. Flash	*$0.80*	*$2.50*	*$5.00*	£0.45	£1.35	£2.75
126 scarce in the U.K. Aquaman	*$0.80*	*$2.50*	*$5.00*	£0.45	£1.35	£2.75
127 Wildcat	*$0.80*	*$2.50*	*$5.00*	£0.40	£1.25	£2.50
128 scarce in the U.K. Mister Miracle	*$0.80*	*$2.50*	*$5.00*	£0.45	£1.35	£2.75
129 ND Green Arrow, Joker and Two Face appear	*$2.05*	*$6.25*	*$12.50*	£1.15	£3.50	£7.00
130 Two-Face, Joker, Green Arrow and Atom	*$2.05*	*$6.25*	*$12.50*	£1.00	£3.00	£6.00
131 scarce in the U.K. Wonder Woman; Catwoman appears	*$1.65*	*$5.00*	*$10.00*	£0.40	£1.25	£2.50
132 scarce in the U.K. Richard Dragon Kung Fu Fighter	*$0.65*	*$2.00*	*$4.00*	£0.40	£1.25	£2.50
133 scarce in the U.K. Deadman	*$0.65*	*$2.00*	*$4.00*	£0.40	£1.25	£2.50
134 Green Lantern	*$0.65*	*$2.00*	*$4.00*	£0.30	£1.00	£2.00
135 Metal Men	*$0.65*	*$2.00*	*$4.00*	£0.30	£1.00	£2.00
136 Green Arrow and Metal Men	*$0.65*	*$2.00*	*$4.00*	£0.30	£1.00	£2.00
137 Demon	*$0.65*	*$2.00*	*$4.00*	£0.30	£1.00	£2.00
138 Mister Miracle	*$0.65*	*$2.00*	*$4.00*	£0.30	£1.00	£2.00
139 scarce in the U.K. Hawkman	*$0.65*	*$2.00*	*$4.00*	£0.35	£1.10	£2.25
140 Wonder Woman	*$0.65*	*$2.00*	*$4.00*	£0.30	£1.00	£2.00
141 Black Canary; Joker appears	*$2.05*	*$6.25*	*$12.50*	£0.80	£2.50	£5.00
142 Aquaman	*$0.55*	*$1.75*	*$3.50*	£0.25	£0.75	£1.50
143 scarce in the U.K. 44pgs, Creeper	*$0.55*	*$1.75*	*$3.50*	£0.30	£1.00	£2.00
144 scarce in the U.K. 44pgs, Green Arrow	*$0.55*	*$1.75*	*$3.50*	£0.30	£1.00	£2.00
145 Phantom Stranger	*$0.55*	*$1.75*	*$3.50*	£0.25	£0.75	£1.50
146 Unknown Soldier	*$0.55*	*$1.75*	*$3.50*	£0.25	£0.75	£1.50
147 Supergirl	*$0.55*	*$1.75*	*$3.50*	£0.25	£0.75	£1.50
148 Plastic Man	*$0.55*	*$1.75*	*$3.50*	£0.25	£0.75	£1.50
149 Teen Titans	*$0.55*	*$1.75*	*$3.50*	£0.25	£0.75	£1.50
150 Superman	*$0.55*	*$1.75*	*$3.50*	£0.25	£0.75	£1.50
151 Flash	*$0.55*	*$1.75*	*$3.50*	£0.25	£0.75	£1.50
152 Atom	*$0.55*	*$1.75*	*$3.50*	£0.25	£0.75	£1.50
153 Red Tornado	*$0.55*	*$1.75*	*$3.50*	£0.25	£0.75	£1.50
154 Metamorpho	*$0.55*	*$1.75*	*$3.50*	£0.25	£0.75	£1.50
155 Green Lantern	*$0.55*	*$1.75*	*$3.50*	£0.25	£0.75	£1.50
156 Dr. Fate	*$0.55*	*$1.75*	*$3.50*	£0.25	£0.75	£1.50
157 Kamandi	*$0.55*	*$1.75*	*$3.50*	£0.25	£0.75	£1.50
158 (Jan 1980) Wonder Woman	*$0.55*	*$1.75*	*$3.50*	£0.25	£0.75	£1.50
159 R'As Al Ghul	*$0.55*	*$1.75*	*$3.50*	£0.25	£0.75	£1.50
160 Supergirl	*$0.55*	*$1.75*	*$3.50*	£0.25	£0.75	£1.50
161 Adam Strange	*$0.55*	*$1.75*	*$3.50*	£0.25	£0.75	£1.50
162 Sgt. Rock	*$0.55*	*$1.75*	*$3.50*	£0.25	£0.75	£1.50
163 Black Lightning	*$0.55*	*$1.75*	*$3.50*	£0.25	£0.75	£1.50
164 Hawkman	*$0.55*	*$1.75*	*$3.50*	£0.25	£0.75	£1.50
165 Man-Bat	*$0.55*	*$1.75*	*$3.50*	£0.25	£0.75	£1.50
166 Black Canary; Penguin appears	*$0.55*	*$1.75*	*$3.50*	£0.25	£0.75	£1.50
167 Blackhawk	*$0.55*	*$1.75*	*$3.50*	£0.25	£0.75	£1.50
168 Green Arrow	*$0.55*	*$1.75*	*$3.50*	£0.25	£0.75	£1.50
169 Zatanna	*$0.55*	*$1.75*	*$3.50*	£0.25	£0.75	£1.50
170 Nemesis	*$0.55*	*$1.75*	*$3.50*	£0.25	£0.75	£1.50
171 Scalphunter	*$0.55*	*$1.75*	*$3.50*	£0.20	£0.60	£1.25
172 Firestorm	*$0.55*	*$1.75*	*$3.50*	£0.20	£0.60	£1.25
173 Guardians of the Universe	*$0.55*	*$1.75*	*$3.50*	£0.20	£0.60	£1.25
174 Green Lantern	*$0.55*	*$1.75*	*$3.50*	£0.20	£0.60	£1.25
175 Lois Lane	*$0.55*	*$1.75*	*$3.50*	£0.20	£0.60	£1.25
176 Swamp Thing, Kaluta cover	*$0.55*	*$1.75*	*$3.50*	£0.20	£0.60	£1.25
177 Elongated Man	*$0.55*	*$1.75*	*$3.50*	£0.20	£0.60	£1.25
178 Creeper	*$0.55*	*$1.75*	*$3.50*	£0.20	£0.60	£1.25
179 Legion of Super-Heroes	*$0.55*	*$1.75*	*$3.50*	£0.20	£0.60	£1.25
180 The Spectre	*$0.55*	*$1.75*	*$3.50*	£0.20	£0.60	£1.25
181 Hawk and the Dove	*$0.50*	*$1.50*	*$3.00*	£0.20	£0.60	£1.25
182 Earth-2 Robin	*$0.55*	*$1.75*	*$3.50*	£0.20	£0.60	£1.25
183 Riddler	*$0.50*	*$1.50*	*$3.00*	£0.20	£0.60	£1.25
184 Huntress	*$0.50*	*$1.50*	*$3.00*	£0.20	£0.60	£1.25
185 Green Arrow	*$0.50*	*$1.50*	*$3.00*	£0.20	£0.60	£1.25
186 Hawkman	*$0.50*	*$1.50*	*$3.00*	£0.20	£0.60	£1.25
187 Metal Men	*$0.50*	*$1.50*	*$3.00*	£0.20	£0.60	£1.25
188-189 Rose and the Thorn	*$0.50*	*$1.50*	*$3.00*	£0.20	£0.60	£1.25
190 Adam Strange	*$0.50*	*$1.50*	*$3.00*	£0.20	£0.60	£1.25
191 LD in the U.K. Joker	*$1.60*	*$4.80*	*$8.00*	£0.50	£1.50	£2.50
192 Superboy	*$0.50*	*$1.50*	*$3.00*	£0.20	£0.60	£1.25
193 Nemesis	*$0.50*	*$1.50*	*$3.00*	£0.20	£0.60	£1.25
194 Flash	*$0.50*	*$1.50*	*$3.00*	£0.20	£0.60	£1.25
195 "I" Vampire	*$0.50*	*$1.50*	*$3.00*	£0.20	£0.60	£1.25
196 Ragman	*$0.50*	*$1.50*	*$3.00*	£0.20	£0.60	£1.25
197 Catwoman, Staton art; Earth-2 Batman marries Catwoman	*$0.55*	*$1.75*	*$3.50*	£0.25	£0.75	£1.50
198 Karate Kid	*$0.50*	*$1.50*	*$3.00*	£0.20	£0.60	£1.25
199 Spectre	*$0.50*	*$1.50*	*$3.00*	£0.20	£0.60	£1.25
200 68pgs, Earth-1 and Earth-2 Batman team, Gibbons art; 1st appearance Batman & the Outsiders (preview)	*$1.30*	*$4.00*	*$8.00*	£0.75	£2.25	£4.50
Title Value:	*$3446.70*	*$10275.30*	*$30982.25*	£2177.95	£6522.10	£19772.60

Note: Joker covers and stories-68, 111, 118, 129, 130, 141, 191. **Note also** that Neal Adams finished the artwork for issue 102 when Jim Aparo fell ill.

BRAVE AND THE BOLD, THE (2ND SERIES)

DC Comics,MS; 1 Dec 1991-6 Jun 1992

Issue	$Good	$Fine	$N.Mint	£Good	£Fine	£N.Mint
1 Green Arrow, Black Canary, Butcher and The Question feature, Mike Grell covers begin	*$0.30*	*$0.90*	*$1.50*	£0.20	£0.60	£1.00
2-6	*$0.30*	*$0.90*	*$1.50*	£0.20	£0.60	£1.00
Title Value:	*$1.80*	*$5.40*	*$9.00*	£1.20	£3.60	£6.00

BRAVESTARR IN 3-D

Blackthorne; (3-D Series #27,#40); 1 Autumn 1987-2 Apr 1988

Issue	$Good	$Fine	$N.Mint	£Good	£Fine	£N.Mint
1-2 ND with bound-in 3-D glasses (25% less if without glasses)	*$0.40*	*$1.20*	*$2.00*	£0.25	£0.75	£1.25
Title Value:	*$0.80*	*$2.40*	*$4.00*	£0.50	£1.50	£2.50

BRAVURA

Hero Illustrated; ½ Feb 1994

Issue	$Good	$Fine	$N.Mint	£Good	£Fine	£N.Mint
½ ND presented free with Hero Illustrated #9; previews Bravura titles	*$0.25*	*$0.75*	*$1.25*	£0.15	£0.45	£0.75
Title Value:	*$0.25*	*$0.75*	*$1.25*	£0.15	£0.45	£0.75

BREAK THE CHAIN

Marvel Comics Group; 1 Aug 1994

Issue	$Good	$Fine	$N.Mint	£Good	£Fine	£N.Mint
1 ND pre-bagged with audio cassette	*$1.00*	*$3.00*	*$5.00*	£0.70	£2.10	£3.50
Title Value:	*$1.00*	*$3.00*	*$5.00*	£0.70	£2.10	£3.50

BREAK-THRU

Malibu Ultraverse; 1 Dec 1993-2 Jan 1994

Issue	$Good	$Fine	$N.Mint	£Good	£Fine	£N.Mint
1 ND continued directly from Exiles #4, George Perez cover and art	*$0.40*	*$1.20*	*$2.00*	£0.25	£0.75	£1.25
2 ND George Perez cover and art	*$0.40*	*$1.20*	*$2.00*	£0.25	£0.75	£1.25
Title Value:	*$0.80*	*$2.40*	*$4.00*	£0.50	£1.50	£2.50

BREATHTAKER

DC Comics,MS; 1 Sep 1990-4 Dec 1990

Issue	$Good	$Fine	$N.Mint	£Good	£Fine	£N.Mint
1-4 ND 48pgs	*$0.60*	*$1.80*	*$3.00*	£0.40	£1.20	£2.00
Title Value:	*$2.40*	*$7.20*	*$12.00*	£1.60	£4.80	£8.00

Note: Prestige Format, Mature Readers

Issue	£Good	£Fine	£N.Mint
Breathtaker (Jun 1994) Trade paperback reprints mini-series, new introduction by Neil Gaiman	£2.00	£6.00	£10.00

BREED

Malibu Bravura,MS; 1 Jan 1994-6 Jun 1994

Issue	$Good	$Fine	$N.Mint	£Good	£Fine	£N.Mint
1 ND Jim Starlin script and art begins	*$0.60*	*$1.80*	*$3.00*	£0.40	£1.20	£2.00
1 Newstand Edition, ND - pre-bagged but with alternative cover	*$0.60*	*$1.80*	*$3.00*	£0.40	£1.20	£2.00
2-6 ND	*$0.50*	*$1.50*	*$2.50*	£0.30	£0.90	£1.50
Title Value:	*$3.70*	*$11.10*	*$18.50*	£2.30	£6.90	£11.50

Note: all Non-Distributed on the news-stands in the U.K.

Issue	£Good	£Fine	£N.Mint
Breed Collection Softcover (Sep 1994) Trade paperback reprints mini-series, digitally re-mastered. Bagged	£1.70	£5.10	£8.50
Breed Collection Softcover Limited Signed Edition (Sep 1994) as above, signed by Jim Starlin. 500 copies	£4.00	£12.00	£20.00

BREED II: THE BOOK OF REVELATIONS

Malibu Bravura,MS; 1 Nov 1994-6 Apr 1995

Issue	$Good	$Fine	$N.Mint	£Good	£Fine	£N.Mint
1 ND 40pgs, Jim Starlin script and art	*$0.50*	*$1.50*	*$2.50*	£0.35	£1.05	£1.75
1 Gold Foil Edition, ND (Mar 1995)	*$1.50*	*$4.50*	*$7.50*	£1.00	£3.00	£5.00
2-6 ND 40pgs, Jim Starlin script and art	*$0.50*	*$1.50*	*$2.50*	£0.30	£0.90	£1.50
Title Value:	*$4.50*	*$13.50*	*$22.50*	£2.85	£8.55	£14.25

BRENDA STARR, REPORTER

Charlton; 13 Jun 1955-15 Oct 1955

Issue	$Good	$Fine	$N.Mint	£Good	£Fine	£N.Mint
13-15 ND scarce in the U.K.	*$34.00*	*$100.00*	*$235.00*	£21.00	£62.50	£150.00
Title Value:	*$102.00*	*$300.00*	*$705.00*	£63.00	£187.50	£450.00

BRENDA STARR, REPORTER (2ND SERIES)

Blackthorne; 1 Apr 1986

Issue	$Good	$Fine	$N.Mint	£Good	£Fine	£N.Mint
1 ND 72pgs, squarebound	*$0.50*	*$1.50*	*$2.50*	£0.30	£0.90	£1.50
Title Value:	*$0.50*	*$1.50*	*$2.50*	£0.30	£0.90	£1.50

BRIAN BOLLAND'S BLACK BOOK

Eclipse/Quality,OS; 1 Jul 1985

Issue	$Good	$Fine	$N.Mint	£Good	£Fine	£N.Mint
1 ND reprints left-over inventory from House of Hammer magazine (packaged by then Quality editor Dez Skinn)	*$0.60*	*$1.80*	*$3.00*	£0.40	£1.20	£2.00
Title Value:	*$0.60*	*$1.80*	*$3.00*	£0.40	£1.20	£2.00

BRIGADE

Image,MS; 1 Aug 1992-4 Apr 1993

Issue	$Good	$Fine	$N.Mint	£Good	£Fine	£N.Mint
1 Rob Liefeld script and cover art, includes two trading cards						
	$0.80	$2.40	$4.00	£0.50	£1.50	£2.50
1 Gold Edition	$1.50	$4.50	$7.50	£1.00	£3.00	£5.00
1 Gold Signed Edition, , signed by Rob Liefeld						
	$2.50	$7.50	$12.50	£1.50	£4.50	£7.50
2 contains Image #0 coupon 4						
	$0.60	$1.80	$3.00	£0.40	£1.20	£2.00
2 wiithout coupon	$0.50	$1.50	$2.50	£0.30	£0.90	£1.50
3 with 2 trading cards						
	$0.50	$1.50	$2.50	£0.30	£0.90	£1.50
4	$0.50	$1.50	$2.50	£0.30	£0.90	£1.50
Title Value:	$6.90	$20.70	$34.50	£4.30	£12.90	£21.50

Note: all Non-Distributed on the news-stands in the U.K.

BRIGADE (2ND SERIES)

Image; 0 Sep 1993; 1 May 1993-25 May 1994

Issue	$Good	$Fine	$N.Mint	£Good	£Fine	£N.Mint
0 ND (Sep 1993) Jeff Matsuda and Norm Rapmund art						
	$0.40	$1.20	$2.00	£0.25	£0.75	£1.25
1 ND Rob Liefeld script, Marat Mychaels and Norm Rapmund art begin; gatefold cover						
	$0.50	$1.50	$2.50	£0.30	£0.90	£1.50
2 ND silver foil embossed cover						
	$0.50	$1.50	$2.50	£0.30	£0.90	£1.50
3 ND	$0.40	$1.20	$2.00	£0.25	£0.75	£1.25
4 ND new facts about Seahawk's and Coldsnap's origins						
	$0.40	$1.20	$2.00	£0.25	£0.75	£1.25
5-7 ND	$0.40	$1.20	$2.00	£0.25	£0.75	£1.25
8 ND Extreme Prejudice part 2						
	$0.40	$1.20	$2.00	£0.25	£0.75	£1.25
9 ND Extreme Prejudice part 6, with coupon						
	$0.40	$1.20	$2.00	£0.25	£0.75	£1.25
10 ND Extreme Prejudice Aftermath						
	$0.40	$1.20	$2.00	£0.25	£0.75	£1.25
11 ND Brigade vs. WildC.A.T.S..						
	$0.40	$1.20	$2.00	£0.25	£0.75	£1.25
12-13 ND	$0.40	$1.20	$2.00	£0.25	£0.75	£1.25
14-15 ND ties into issue #25						
	$0.40	$1.20	$2.00	£0.25	£0.75	£1.25
16 ND Extreme Sacrifice part 3, continued in Newmen #10; pre-bagged with trading card						
	$0.50	$1.50	$2.50	£0.30	£0.90	£1.50
17-19 ND	$0.50	$1.50	$2.50	£0.30	£0.90	£1.50
20 ND Alien Cult Saga concludes						
	$0.50	$1.50	$2.50	£0.30	£0.90	£1.50
20 Variant Cover Edition, ND - Joe Quesada/Jimmy Palmiotti cover art						
	$0.80	$2.40	$4.00	£0.50	£1.50	£2.50
21 ND	$0.50	$1.50	$2.50	£0.30	£0.90	£1.50
22 ND Supreme Apocalypse part 4, continued in Supreme #30						
	$0.50	$1.50	$2.50	£0.30	£0.90	£1.50
23-24 ND	$0.50	$1.50	$2.50	£0.30	£0.90	£1.50
25 ND cover-dated May 1994, issued between issues #9 and 10 as part of "Images of Tomorrow" previewing what the 25th issue will read/look like						
	$0.40	$1.20	$2.00	£0.25	£0.75	£1.25
Title Value:	$112.30	$36.90	$61.50	£7.55	£22.65	£37.75

BRIGADE SOURCEBOOK

Image; 1 Aug 1994

Issue	$Good	$Fine	$N.Mint	£Good	£Fine	£N.Mint
1 ND information and statistics about Brigade characters						
	$0.50	$1.50	$2.50	£0.30	£0.90	£1.50
Title Value:	$0.50	$1.50	$2.50	£0.30	£0.90	£1.50

BRINKE OF DESTRUCTION

High-Top Comics,MS; 1 Dec 1995-2 1996 ?

Issue	$Good	$Fine	$N.Mint	£Good	£Fine	£N.Mint
1-2 ND the return of scream queen Brinke Stevens						
	$0.60	$1.80	$3.00	£0.40	£1.20	£2.00
Title Value:	$1.20	$3.60	$6.00	£0.80	£2.40	£4.00

BRINKE OF ETERNITY

Chaos Comics,MS; 1 Apr 1994-3 Jun 1994

Issue	$Good	$Fine	$N.Mint	£Good	£Fine	£N.Mint
1-3 ND scream queen Brinke Stevens appears						
	$0.50	$1.50	$2.50	£0.30	£0.90	£1.50
Title Value:	$1.50	$4.50	$7.50	£0.90	£2.70	£4.50

BRONX

Eternity,MS; 1 Sep 1991-3 Nov 1991

Issue	$Good	$Fine	$N.Mint	£Good	£Fine	£N.Mint
1-3 ND	$0.40	$1.20	$2.00	£0.25	£0.75	£1.25
Title Value:	$1.20	$3.60	$6.00	£0.75	£2.25	£3.75

BROOKLYN DREAMS

DC Comics/Paradox Press,MS; 1 Jan 1995-4 Apr 1995

Issue	$Good	$Fine	$N.Mint	£Good	£Fine	£N.Mint
1-4 ND 96pgs, black and white; unusual 5" x 8" size						
	$0.90	$2.70	$4.50	£0.60	£1.80	£3.00
Title Value:	$3.60	$10.80	$18.00	£2.40	£7.20	£12.00

BROTHER BILLY, THE PAIN FROM THE PLAINS

Marvel Comics Group,Magazine OS; 1 1979

Issue	$Good	$Fine	$N.Mint	£Good	£Fine	£N.Mint
1 ND Jimmy Carter satire						
	$0.40	$1.25	$2.50	£0.25	£0.75	£1.50
Title Value:	$0.40	$1.25	$2.50	£0.25	£0.75	£1.50

BROTHER MAN: DICTATOR OF DISCIPLINE

Big City Comics; 1 1990-9 Sep 1993

Issue	$Good	$Fine	$N.Mint	£Good	£Fine	£N.Mint
1 ND David & Guy Sim script and art; black and white; outsize comics						
	$0.40	$1.20	$2.00	£0.30	£0.90	£1.50
1 2nd/3rd printings ND	$0.40	$1.20	$2.00	£0.25	£0.75	£1.25
2 ND	$0.40	$1.20	$2.00	£0.25	£0.75	£1.25
2 2nd printing ND	$0.40	$1.20	$2.00	£0.25	£0.75	£1.25
3-9 ND	$0.40	$1.20	$2.00	£0.25	£0.75	£1.25
Title Value:	$4.40	$13.20	$22.00	£2.80	£8.40	£14.00

BROTHER POWER, THE GEEK

(see Geek)

BROTHERS OF THE SPEAR

Gold Key; 1 Jun 1972-17 Feb 1976; Whitman; 18 May 1982

Issue	$Good	$Fine	$N.Mint	£Good	£Fine	£N.Mint
1 scarce in the U.K. Dan-El and Natongo stories continue from Tarzan back-up; Jesse Santos art begins (ends #12)						
	$3.30	$10.00	$20.00	£2.05	£6.25	£12.50
2 painted covers begin						
	$1.65	$5.00	$10.00	£1.00	£3.00	£6.00
3	$1.00	$3.00	$6.00	£0.55	£1.75	£3.50
4-10	$0.80	$2.50	$5.00	£0.50	£1.50	£3.00
11	$0.50	$1.50	$3.00	£0.30	£1.00	£2.00
12 line drawn cover, reprints #1						
	$0.50	$1.50	$3.00	£0.30	£1.00	£2.00
13 Dan Spiegle art begins (ends #17)						
	$0.50	$1.50	$3.00	£0.30	£1.00	£2.00
14-16	$0.50	$1.50	$3.00	£0.30	£1.00	£2.00
17 last painted cover						
	$0.50	$1.50	$3.00	£0.30	£1.00	£2.00
18 scarce in the U.K. reprints #2, line-drawn cover						
	$0.80	$2.40	$4.00	£0.50	£1.50	£2.50
Title Value:	$15.85	$48.40	$96.00	£9.70	£30.00	£59.50

Note: all Limited Distribution on the news-stands in the U.K.

BRU-HED

Schism Comics,MS; 1 1995-4 Jan 1996

Issue	$Good	$Fine	$N.Mint	£Good	£Fine	£N.Mint
1-4 ND Mike Pascale script and art with Dave Sonnett; black and white						
	$0.50	$1.50	$2.50	£0.30	£0.90	£1.50
Title Value:	$2.00	$6.00	$10.00	£1.20	£3.60	£6.00

BRUCE JONES' OUTER EDGE

Innovation,OS; 1 Nov 1992

Issue	$Good	$Fine	$N.Mint	£Good	£Fine	£N.Mint
1 ND four sci-fi stories						
	$0.40	$1.20	$2.00	£0.25	£0.75	£1.25
Title Value:	$0.40	$1.20	$2.00	£0.25	£0.75	£1.25

BRUCE JONES' RAZOR EDGE

Innovation,OS; 1 Dec 1992

Issue	$Good	$Fine	$N.Mint	£Good	£Fine	£N.Mint
1 ND four horror stories						
	$0.40	$1.20	$2.00	£0.25	£0.75	£1.25
Title Value:	$0.40	$1.20	$2.00	£0.25	£0.75	£1.25

BRUCE LEE

Malibu,MS; 1 Jul 1994-6 Dec 1994

Issue	$Good	$Fine	$N.Mint	£Good	£Fine	£N.Mint
1-6 Mike Baron script and Val Mayerik art						
	$0.50	$1.50	$2.50	£0.30	£0.90	£1.50
Title Value:	$3.00	$9.00	$15.00	£1.80	£5.40	£9.00

Note: all Non-Distributed on the newstands in the U.K.

BRUCE WAYNE: AGENT OF SHIELD

Marvel Comics Group/Amalgam,OS; 1 Apr 1996

Issue	$Good	$Fine	$N.Mint	£Good	£Fine	£N.Mint
1 ND a Marvel/DC amalgamation of Bruce (Batman) Wayne and Nick Fury, Agent of Shield; Chuck Dixon script, Cary Nord art						
	$0.50	$1.50	$2.50	£0.40	£1.20	£2.00
Title Value:	$0.50	$1.50	$2.50	£0.40	£1.20	£2.00

BRUTE & BABE MONUMENT SET

Ominous Press; 1 Jul 1994

Issue	$Good	$Fine	$N.Mint	£Good	£Fine	£N.Mint
1 ND 16pg unstapled comic forming a single splash page included in a clear plastic slipcase; Bart Sears script, Andy Smith art						
	$0.80	$2.40	$4.00	£0.50	£1.50	£2.50
Title Value:	$0.80	$2.40	$4.00	£0.50	£1.50	£2.50

Note: issue #2 advertised & solicited but was probably never released

BRUTE & BABE: CHAKALL, SHE-SLAVE FROM BEYOND

Ominous Press,MS; 1 Dec 1994

Issue	$Good	$Fine	$N.Mint	£Good	£Fine	£N.Mint
1 ND Bart Sears script						
	$0.40	$1.20	$2.00	£0.25	£0.75	£1.25
Title Value:	$0.40	$1.20	$2.00	£0.25	£0.75	£1.25

BRUTE & BABE: INFINITY

Ominous Press,OS; nn Oct 1994

Issue	$Good	$Fine	$N.Mint	£Good	£Fine	£N.Mint
nn ND Bart Sears script, Andy Smith art						
	$0.40	$1.20	$2.00	£0.25	£0.75	£1.25
Title Value:	$0.40	$1.20	$2.00	£0.25	£0.75	£1.25

BRUTE & BABE: MAEL'S RAGE

Ominous Press,OS; 1 Aug 1994

Issue	$Good	$Fine	$N.Mint	£Good	£Fine	£N.Mint
1 ND story continued from Monument Set 1						
	$0.40	$1.20	$2.00	£0.25	£0.75	£1.25
Title Value:	$0.40	$1.20	$2.00	£0.25	£0.75	£1.25

BRUTE & BABE: OMEN

Ominous Press,OS; nn Sep 1994

Issue	$Good	$Fine	$N.Mint	£Good	£Fine	£N.Mint
nn ND Bart Sears script, Mark Pennington art						
	$0.40	$1.20	$2.00	£0.25	£0.75	£1.25
Title Value:	$0.40	$1.20	$2.00	£0.25	£0.75	£1.25

BRUTE FORCE

Marvel Comics Group,MS; 1 Aug 1990-4 Nov 1990

Issue	$Good	$Fine	$N.Mint	£Good	£Fine	£N.Mint
1-4	$0.15	$0.45	$0.75	£0.10	£0.30	£0.50
Title Value:	$0.60	$1.80	$3.00	£0.40	£1.20	£2.00

Note: eco-theme comic

BRUTE, THE

Atlas; 1 Feb 1975-3 Jun 1975

Issue	$Good	$Fine	$N.Mint	£Good	£Fine	£N.Mint
1-2 distributed in the U.K. Mike Sekowsky art						
	$0.20	$0.60	$1.25	£0.10	£0.35	£0.75
3 distributed in the U.K.						
	$0.20	$0.60	$1.25	£0.10	£0.35	£0.75
Title Value:	$0.60	$1.80	$3.75	£0.30	£1.05	£2.25

BUBBLEGUM CRISIS: GRAND MAL

Dark Horse,MS; 1 Mar 1994-4 Jun 1994

1-4 ND Adam Warren script and art

	$Good	$Fine	$N.Mint	£Good	£Fine	£N.Mint
	$0.50	$1.50	$2.50	£0.30	£0.90	£1.50
Title Value:	$2.00	$6.00	$10.00	£1.20	£3.60	£6.00
Bubblegum Crisis: Grand Mal (Aug 1995)						
Trade paperback collects issues #1-4				£2.00	£6.00	£10.00
BUCCANEER						
I.W. Comics; 1,8 1963; 12 1964						
1 distributed in the U.K. Captain Daring, Black Roger, Eric Falcon reprints, Crandall art	$3.55	$10.50	$25.00	£1.75	£5.25	£12.50
8-12 distributed in the U.K. reprints	$2.85	$8.50	$20.00	£1.40	£4.25	£10.00
Title Value:	$9.25	$27.50	$65.00	£4.55	£13.75	£32.50
BUCK ROGERS						
Gold Key/Whitman; 1 Oct 1964; 2 Aug 1979-6 Feb 1980; Whitman; 7 Aug 1980-16 1982						
1 rare although distributed in the U.K.	$6.25	$19.00	$45.00	£3.90	£11.50	£27.50
2 LD in the U.K. film adaptation; Frank Bolle and Al McWilliams art; painted cover	$0.65	$2.00	$4.00	£0.30	£1.00	£2.00
3-4 LD in the U.K. film adaptation; Frank Bolle and Al McWilliams art; painted cover	$0.40	$1.25	$2.50	£0.25	£0.75	£1.50
5 LD in the U.K. new stories begin, Al McWilliams art and painted covers begin	$0.40	$1.25	$2.50	£0.25	£0.75	£1.50
6 LD in the U.K.	$0.40	$1.25	$2.50	£0.25	£0.75	£1.50
7 LD in the U.K. 1st Whitman issue	$0.50	$1.50	$2.50	£0.30	£0.90	£1.50
8-9 LD in the U.K.	$0.50	$1.50	$2.50	£0.30	£0.90	£1.50
10 LD in the U.K.	$0.40	$1.20	$2.00	£0.25	£0.75	£1.25
11 LD in the U.K. J.M. DeMatteis script	$0.40	$1.20	$2.00	£0.25	£0.75	£1.25
12 LD in the U.K. Mike Roy art begins	$0.40	$1.20	$2.00	£0.25	£0.75	£1.25
13 LD in the U.K. last painted cover	$0.40	$1.20	$2.00	£0.25	£0.75	£1.25
14 LD in the U.K. line-drawn covers begin	$0.40	$1.20	$2.00	£0.25	£0.75	£1.25
15-16 LD in the U.K.	$0.40	$1.20	$2.00	£0.25	£0.75	£1.25
Title Value:	$12.80	$38.90	$80.50	£7.85	£23.45	£48.75
BUCK ROGERS (2ND SERIES)						
TSR; 1 1990-12 1991?						
1-12 ND	$0.50	$1.50	$2.50	£0.30	£0.90	£1.50
Title Value:	$6.00	$18.00	$30.00	£3.60	£10.80	£18.00
BUCKAROO BANZAI						
Marvel Comics Group,MS Film; 1 Dec 1984-2 Feb 1985						
1-2 Mark Texeira cover and pencil art	$0.15	$0.45	$0.75	£0.10	£0.30	£0.50
Title Value:	$0.30	$0.90	$1.50	£0.20	£0.60	£1.00
Note: reprints Marvel Super Special #33						
BUCKY O'HARE (1ST SERIES)						
Continuity; 1 1988						
1 ND reprints series from Echoes of Future Past #1-6	$0.80	$2.40	$4.00	£0.50	£1.50	£2.50
Title Value:	$0.80	$2.40	$4.00	£0.50	£1.50	£2.50
Deluxe Hardcover Edition (1988), 52pgs, reprints the above				£5.00	£15.00	£25.00
BUCKY O'HARE (2ND SERIES)						
Continuity; 1 Jan 1991-6 1992						
1-6 ND	$0.40	$1.20	$2.00	£0.25	£0.75	£1.25
Title Value:	$2.40	$7.20	$12.00	£1.50	£4.50	£7.50
BUCKY O'HARE (3RD SERIES)						
Continuity; 1 Aug 1993						
1 ND 48pgs, Neal Adams cover with green flock on figure of Bucky	$0.60	$1.80	$3.00	£0.40	£1.20	£2.00

	$Good	$Fine	$N.Mint	£Good	£Fine	£N.Mint
Title Value:	$0.60	$1.80	$3.00	£0.40	£1.20	£2.00
BUG						
Planet X Productions,OS; 1 1986						
1 ND Tony Basilicato script/art; black and white	$0.30	$0.90	$1.50	£0.20	£0.60	£1.00
Title Value:	$0.30	$0.90	$1.50	£0.20	£0.60	£1.00
BUG!						
Marvel Comics Group,OS; nn Mar 1997						
nn ND 48pgs, spin-off from Cable	$0.60	$1.80	$3.00	£0.40	£1.20	£2.00
Title Value:	$0.60	$1.80	$3.00	£0.40	£1.20	£2.00
BUGS BUNNY						
DC Comics,MS; 1 Jun 1990-3 Sep 1990						
1-3 ND	$0.15	$0.45	$0.75	£0.10	£0.35	£0.60
Title Value:	$0.45	$1.35	$2.25	£0.30	£1.05	£1.80
Multi-pack (Dec 1990), pre-bagged set of #1-3 with illustrated header card, ND				£0.30	£0.90	£1.50
BULLET CROW, FOWL OF FORTUNE						
Eclipse,MS; 1 Feb 1987-2 Apr 1987						
1-2 ND	$0.25	$0.75	$1.25	£0.15	£0.45	£0.75
Title Value:	$0.50	$1.50	$2.50	£0.30	£0.90	£1.50
Note: based on role-playing game						
BULLETS & BRACELETS						
Marvel Comics Group/Amalgam,OS; 1 Apr 1996						
1 ND a Marvel/DC amalgamation of Punisher and Wonder Woman team-up; John Ostrander script, Gary Frank and Cam Smith art	$0.50	$1.50	$2.50	£0.40	£1.20	£2.00
Title Value:	$0.50	$1.50	$2.50	£0.40	£1.20	£2.00
BULLWINKLE AND ROCKY						
Marvel Comics Group/Star; 1 Jun 1988-9 Mar 1989						
1-9 less common in the U.K. Dave Manak scripts	$0.15	$0.45	$0.75	£0.10	£0.30	£0.50
Title Value:	$1.35	$4.05	$6.75	£0.90	£2.70	£4.50
Trade paperback (Mar 1992), selected reprints from issues #1-9				£0.65	£1.95	£3.25
BULLWINKLE AND ROCKY IN 3-D						
Blackthorne; (3-D Series #18) 1 Mar 1987						
1 ND with bound-in 3-D glasses (25% less if without glasses)	$0.40	$1.20	$2.00	£0.25	£0.75	£1.25
Title Value:	$0.40	$1.20	$2.00	£0.25	£0.75	£1.25
BULLWINKLE FOR PRESIDENT IN 3-D						
Blackthorne; (3-D Series #50) 1 Autumn 1988						
1 ND with bound-in 3-D glasses (25% less if without glasses)	$0.40	$1.20	$2.00	£0.25	£0.75	£1.25
Title Value:	$0.40	$1.20	$2.00	£0.25	£0.75	£1.25
BULWARK						
Millennium; 1 Jul 1995						
1 ND Brian Main script and art; black and white	$0.60	$1.80	$3.00	£0.40	£1.20	£2.00
Title Value:	$0.60	$1.80	$3.00	£0.40	£1.20	£2.00
BURIED TERROR						
New England Comics; 1 Jan 1995-2 1995						
1-2 ND horror reprints; black and white	$0.40	$1.20	$2.00	£0.25	£0.75	£1.25
Title Value:	$0.80	$2.40	$4.00	£0.50	£1.50	£2.50
BURIED TREASURE						
Caliber Press; 1 Apr 1990-5 Dec 1990						
(previously published by Pure Imagination)						
1 ND Joe Simon/Jack Kirby, Williamson, Toth, Kubert	$0.40	$1.20	$2.00	£0.25	£0.75	£1.25
2 ND Jack Kirby, Kubert, Wally Wood	$0.40	$1.20	$2.00	£0.25	£0.75	£1.25

Brave and the Bold #52

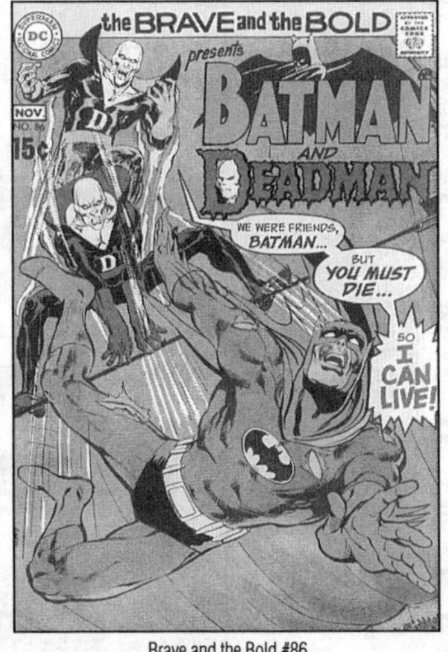

Brave and the Bold #86

Bravura #½

	$Good	$Fine	$N.Mint	£Good	£Fine	£N.Mint
3 ND Wally Wood, Frank Frazetta	$0.40	$1.20	$2.00	£0.25	£0.75	£1.25
4 ND all Frazetta issue	$0.40	$1.20	$2.00	£0.25	£0.75	£1.25
5 ND Joe Simon/Jack Kirby, Toth, Jack Cole, Jerry Robinson	$0.40	$1.20	$2.00	£0.25	£0.75	£1.25
Title Value:	$2.00	$6.00	$10.00	£1.25	£3.75	£6.25

Note: all reprint featuring classic art-work of the 1940s/1950s

BUSHIDO

Eternity; 1 1988-6 1989

	$Good	$Fine	$N.Mint	£Good	£Fine	£N.Mint
1-6 ND	$0.40	$1.20	$2.00	£0.25	£0.75	£1.25
Title Value:	$2.40	$7.20	$12.00	£1.50	£4.50	£7.50

BUSHIDO BLADE OF ZATOICHI WALRUS

Solson Publications; 1,2 1986

	$Good	$Fine	$N.Mint	£Good	£Fine	£N.Mint
1-2 ND	$0.40	$1.20	$2.00	£0.25	£0.75	£1.25
Title Value:	$0.80	$2.40	$4.00	£0.50	£1.50	£2.50

BUTCHER, THE

DC Comics,MS; 1 May 1990-5 Sep 1990

	$Good	$Fine	$N.Mint	£Good	£Fine	£N.Mint
1-5	$0.25	$0.75	$1.25	£0.15	£0.45	£0.75
Title Value:	$1.25	$3.75	$6.25	£0.75	£2.25	£3.75

Note: Mature Readers, New Format

C

CABINET OF DR. CALIGARI, THE

Monster Comics,MS; 1 Jun 1992-3 Oct 1992

	$Good	$Fine	$N.Mint	£Good	£Fine	£N.Mint
1-3 ND 24pgs, painted art	$0.40	$1.20	$2.00	£0.25	£0.75	£1.25
Title Value:	$1.20	$3.60	$6.00	£0.75	£2.25	£3.75

CABLE

Marvel Comics Group,MS; 1 Oct 1992-2 Nov 1992

	$Good	$Fine	$N.Mint	£Good	£Fine	£N.Mint
1 ND Cable vs. Stryfe, John Romita Jnr. art begins	$0.60	$1.80	$3.00	£0.35	£1.05	£1.75
2 ND sequel to X-Cutioner's Song (see X-Force #18)	$0.50	$1.50	$2.50	£0.30	£0.90	£1.50
Title Value:	$1.10	$3.30	$5.50	£0.65	£1.95	£3.25
Cable Trade paperback (Sep 1992)						
176pgs, reprints New Mutants #87-94				£2.20	£6.60	£11.00
(2nd print - Apr 1993)				£2.00	£6.00	£10.00

CABLE & X-FORCE

Marvel Comics Group,OS; Dec 1995; Oct 1996

	$Good	$Fine	$N.Mint	£Good	£Fine	£N.Mint
nn 1995, ND 48pgs, Mark Waid and Jeph Loeb script, Matt Ryan art; Impossible Man appears	$0.80	$2.40	$4.00	£0.50	£1.50	£2.50
nn 1996, ND 64pgs, John Francis Moore script, Luke Ross and Rob Hunter art	$0.60	$1.80	$3.00	£0.40	£1.20	£2.00
Title Value:	$1.40	$4.20	$7.00	£0.90	£2.70	£4.50

CABLE (2ND SERIES)

Marvel Comics Group; 1 May 1993-20 Feb 1995; 21 Jul 1995-present

(becomes X-Man for the Age of Apocalypse storyline)

	$Good	$Fine	$N.Mint	£Good	£Fine	£N.Mint
1 ND Art Thibert art begins	$0.80	$2.40	$4.00	£0.50	£1.50	£2.50
1 Signed & Numbered Edition, ND (Jun 1993) - signed by Art Thibert; 3,000 copies	$2.50	$7.50	$12.50	£1.50	£4.50	£7.50
2-5 ND	$0.40	$1.20	$2.00	£0.30	£0.90	£1.50
6-7 ND	$0.40	$1.20	$2.00	£0.25	£0.75	£1.25
8 ND Cyclops, Jean Grey and Professor X appear	$0.40	$1.20	$2.00	£0.25	£0.75	£1.25
9 ND	$0.40	$1.20	$2.00	£0.25	£0.75	£1.25
10 ND Nightcrawler and Kitty Pryde appear	$0.40	$1.20	$2.00	£0.25	£0.75	£1.25
11 ND with free Spiderman and his Deadly Foes card sheet	$0.40	$1.20	$2.00	£0.25	£0.75	£1.25
12-15 ND	$0.40	$1.20	$2.00	£0.25	£0.75	£1.25
16 ND ties into the formation of Generation X	$0.60	$1.80	$3.00	£0.40	£1.20	£2.00
16 Deluxe Edition, ND - foil stamped cover; ties into the formation of Generation X	$1.20	$3.60	$6.00	£0.80	£2.40	£4.00
17 ND	$0.30	$0.90	$1.50	£0.20	£0.60	£1.00
17 Deluxe Edition, ND - printed on glossy stock paper	$0.40	$1.20	$2.00	£0.25	£0.75	£1.25
18 ND	$0.30	$0.90	$1.50	£0.20	£0.60	£1.00
18 Deluxe Edition, ND - printed on glossy stock paper	$0.40	$1.20	$2.00	£0.25	£0.75	£1.25
19 ND	$0.30	$0.90	$1.50	£0.20	£0.60	£1.00
19 Deluxe Edition, ND - printed on glossy stock paper	$0.40	$1.20	$2.00	£0.25	£0.75	£1.25
20 ND	$0.30	$0.90	$1.50	£0.20	£0.60	£1.00
20 Deluxe Edition, ND - printed on glossy stock paper plus bound-in Fleer trading card; see X-Man #1	$0.40	$1.20	$2.00	£0.25	£0.75	£1.25
21 ND continued from X-Men: Prime; Jeph Loeb script, Ian Churchill art	$0.40	$1.20	$2.00	£0.25	£0.75	£1.25
22-24 ND	$0.40	$1.20	$2.00	£0.25	£0.75	£1.25
25 ND 48pgs, prismatic foil cover	$0.80	$2.40	$4.00	£0.50	£1.50	£2.50
26-29 ND	$0.40	$1.20	$2.00	£0.25	£0.75	£1.25
30-31 ND Nate vs. Cable, continued in X-Man #14	$0.40	$1.20	$2.00	£0.25	£0.75	£1.25
32 ND	$0.40	$1.20	$2.00	£0.25	£0.75	£1.25
33 ND 40pgs, Onslaught tie-in	$0.40	$1.20	$2.00	£0.25	£0.75	£1.25
34 ND 40pgs, Onslaught tie-in; continued in Incredible Hulk #444	$0.40	$1.20	$2.00	£0.25	£0.75	£1.25
35 ND Onslaught tie-in	$0.40	$1.20	$2.00	£0.25	£0.75	£1.25
36 ND with bound-in Overpower cards	$0.40	$1.20	$2.00	£0.25	£0.75	£1.25
37-40 ND	$0.40	$1.20	$2.00	£0.25	£0.75	£1.25
41 ND Bishop guest-stars	$0.40	$1.20	$2.00	£0.25	£0.75	£1.25
Title Value:	$22.30	$66.90	$111.50	£14.20	£42.60	£71.00

CADILLACS AND DINOSAURS

Marvel Comics Group/Epic,MS; 1 Nov 1990-6 Apr 1991

	$Good	$Fine	$N.Mint	£Good	£Fine	£N.Mint
1 ND reprints of Mark Schultz's Xenozoic Tales begins	$0.50	$1.50	$2.50	£0.30	£0.90	£1.50
2-6 ND	$0.50	$1.50	$2.50	£0.30	£0.90	£1.50
Title Value:	$3.00	$9.00	$15.00	£1.80	£5.40	£9.00

Note: all new covers by Mark Schultz

CADILLACS AND DINOSAURS (2ND SERIES)

Topps,MS; 1 Feb 1994-3 Apr 1994

	$Good	$Fine	$N.Mint	£Good	£Fine	£N.Mint
1 ND Roy Thomas script and Dick Giordano art begin	$0.50	$1.50	$2.50	£0.30	£0.90	£1.50
1 Collectors Edition, ND , foil embossed logo on card-stock cover	$0.60	$1.80	$3.00	£0.40	£1.20	£2.00
2-3 ND	$0.50	$1.50	$2.50	£0.30	£0.90	£1.50
Title Value:	$2.10	$6.30	$10.50	£1.30	£3.90	£6.50

CADILLACS AND DINOSAURS: MAN-EATER

Topps,MS; 1 Jun 1994-3 Aug 1994

	$Good	$Fine	$N.Mint	£Good	£Fine	£N.Mint
1 ND Roy Thomas script, Claude St. Aubin art	$0.40	$1.20	$2.00	£0.25	£0.75	£1.25
1 Collectors Edition, ND - with Sam Kieth cover	$0.40	$1.20	$2.00	£0.25	£0.75	£1.25
2 ND Roy Thomas script, Claude St. Aubin art	$0.40	$1.20	$2.00	£0.25	£0.75	£1.25
2 Collectors Edition, ND - with Sam Kieth cover	$0.40	$1.20	$2.00	£0.25	£0.75	£1.25
3 ND Roy Thomas script, Claude St. Aubin art	$0.40	$1.20	$2.00	£0.25	£0.75	£1.25
3 Collectors Edition, ND - with Sam Kieth cover	$0.40	$1.20	$2.00	£0.25	£0.75	£1.25
Title Value:	$2.40	$7.20	$12.00	£1.50	£4.50	£7.50

CADILLACS AND DINOSAURS: THE WILD ONES

Topps,MS; 1 Sep 1994-3 Nov 1994

	$Good	$Fine	$N.Mint	£Good	£Fine	£N.Mint
1-3 ND Roy Thomas script, Esteban Maroto art, Joseph Michael Linsner cover art	$1.50	$4.50	$7.50	£0.30	£0.90	£1.50
Title Value:	$4.50	$13.50	$19.50	£0.90	£2.70	£4.50

CAGE

Marvel Comics Group; 1 Apr 1992-20 Nov 1993

(see Luke Cage Hero for Hire, Powerman and Iron Fist, Punisher #60)

	$Good	$Fine	$N.Mint	£Good	£Fine	£N.Mint
1 ND originally advertised as having an acetate cover overlay which never appeared owing to production problems	$0.25	$0.75	$1.25	£0.20	£0.60	£1.00
2 ND	$0.25	$0.75	$1.25	£0.15	£0.45	£0.75
3-4 ND Punisher guest stars	$0.25	$0.75	$1.25	£0.15	£0.45	£0.75
5-8 ND	$0.25	$0.75	$1.25	£0.15	£0.45	£0.75
9-10 ND Cage vs. Rhino; Hulk appears	$0.25	$0.75	$1.25	£0.15	£0.45	£0.75
11 ND	$0.25	$0.75	$1.25	£0.15	£0.45	£0.75
12 ND DS Cage (Powerman) vs. Iron Fist	$0.25	$0.75	$1.25	£0.20	£0.60	£1.00
13-14 ND	$0.25	$0.75	$1.25	£0.15	£0.45	£0.75
15 ND Silver Sable appears; X-over with Silver Sable #13	$0.25	$0.75	$1.25	£0.15	£0.45	£0.75
16 ND Silver Sable appears; X-over with Silver Sable #14	$0.25	$0.75	$1.25	£0.15	£0.45	£0.75
17 Infinity Crusade tie-in	$0.25	$0.75	$1.25	£0.15	£0.45	£0.75
18-19 The Dark story	$0.25	$0.75	$1.25	£0.15	£0.45	£0.75
20 Fantastic Four appear	$0.25	$0.75	$1.25	£0.15	£0.45	£0.75
Title Value:	$5.00	$15.00	$25.00	£3.10	£9.30	£15.50

CAGES

Tundra Publishing,Magazine MS; 1 Feb 1991-8 1992

	$Good	$Fine	$N.Mint	£Good	£Fine	£N.Mint
1 ND 48pgs, Dave McKean black and white art	$1.60	$4.80	$8.00	£0.60	£1.80	£3.00
2-8 ND 48pgs, Dave McKean black and white art	$1.20	$3.60	$6.00	£0.50	£1.50	£2.50
Title Value:	$10.00	$30.00	$38.00	£4.10	£12.30	£20.50

Note: bi-monthly

CAIN

Harris Comics; 1 Jul 1993-4 1993

	$Good	$Fine	$N.Mint	£Good	£Fine	£N.Mint
1-4 ND	$0.50	$1.50	$2.50	£0.30	£0.90	£1.50
Title Value:	$2.00	$6.00	$10.00	£1.20	£3.60	£6.00

CAIN'S HUNDRED

Dell,TV; nn May/Jul 1962-2 Sep/Nov 1962

	$Good	$Fine	$N.Mint	£Good	£Fine	£N.Mint
01-094-207 scarce in the U.K. based on TV series starring Mark Richman; photo cover	$2.50	$7.50	$17.50	£1.40	£4.25	£10.00
2 scarce in the U.K. photo cover	$1.40	$4.25	$10.00	£0.70	£2.10	£5.00
Title Value:	$3.90	$11.75	$27.50	£2.10	£6.35	£15.00

CALIBER CHRISTMAS, A

Caliber Press,OS; 1 Dec 1989

Issue	$Good	$Fine	$N.Mint	£Good	£Fine	£N.Mint
1 ND 64pgs, squarebound; new anthology featuring Aniverse, Baker Street, Crow, Deadworld, Frost, Fugitive, Gideon's, The Realm, Street Shadows; black and white	$3.00	$9.00	$15.00	£1.50	£4.50	£7.50
Title Value:	$3.00	$9.00	$15.00	£1.50	£4.50	£7.50

CALIBER PRESENTS
Caliber Press; 1 Jun 1989-24 1992

Issue	$Good	$Fine	$N.Mint	£Good	£Fine	£N.Mint
1 1st appearance of The Crow	$18.00	$52.50	$90.00	£9.00	£27.00	£45.00
2 Deadworld cover and story (see Realm #4)	$1.00	$3.00	$5.00	£0.50	£1.50	£2.50
3-5	$0.50	$1.50	$2.50	£0.30	£0.90	£1.50
6-7 Tim Vigil art featured	$0.50	$1.50	$2.50	£0.30	£0.90	£1.50
8 Deadworld cover and story (see Realm #4)	$0.50	$1.50	$2.50	£0.30	£0.90	£1.50
9 Baker Street cover and story	$0.50	$1.50	$2.50	£0.30	£0.90	£1.50
10 Realm cover and story	$0.50	$1.50	$2.50	£0.30	£0.90	£1.50
11-14	$0.40	$1.20	$2.00	£0.25	£0.75	£1.25
15 64pgs, previews final issue of The Crow	$4.00	$12.00	$20.00	£1.50	£4.50	£7.50
16 64pgs	$0.50	$1.50	$2.50	£0.30	£0.90	£1.50
17 64pgs, new Deadworld story	$0.50	$1.50	$2.50	£0.30	£0.90	£1.50
18-24 64pgs	$0.50	$1.50	$2.50	£0.30	£0.90	£1.50
Title Value:	$33.10	$97.80	$165.50	£17.10	£51.30	£85.50

Note: anthology series. 1-14 are all 48pgs and Non-Distributed on the news-stands in the U.K.

CALIBER SPOTLIGHT SPECIAL
Caliber Press,OS; 1 May 1995

Issue	$Good	$Fine	$N.Mint	£Good	£Fine	£N.Mint
1 ND 64pgs, new stories featuring Kabuki, Oz and Kilroy	$0.60	$1.80	$3.00	£0.40	£1.20	£2.00
Title Value:	$0.60	$1.80	$3.00	£0.40	£1.20	£2.00

CALIBRATIONS
Caliber Press,OS; 1 1992

Issue	$Good	$Fine	$N.Mint	£Good	£Fine	£N.Mint
1 ND 48pgs, Baker Street, Airwaves, Fringe, Deadworld included; originally announced as "Caliber Summer Special"; black and white	$0.80	$2.40	$4.00	£0.50	£1.50	£2.50
Title Value:	$0.80	$2.40	$4.00	£0.50	£1.50	£2.50

CALIBRATIONS (2ND SERIES)
Caliber Press; 1 Jun 1996-present

Issue	$Good	$Fine	$N.Mint	£Good	£Fine	£N.Mint
1 ND 16pgs, Warren Ellis story featured	$0.20	$0.60	$1.00	£0.15	£0.45	£0.75
2-3 ND	$0.20	$0.60	$1.00	£0.15	£0.45	£0.75
Title Value:	$0.60	$1.80	$3.00	£0.45	£1.35	£2.25

CALIFORNIA GIRLS
Eclipse; 1 Jun 1987-8 May 1988

Issue	$Good	$Fine	$N.Mint	£Good	£Fine	£N.Mint
1-8 ND Trina Robbins script and art	$0.30	$0.90	$1.50	£0.20	£0.60	£1.00
Title Value:	$2.40	$7.20	$12.00	£1.60	£4.80	£8.00

CALIFORNIA RAISINS IN 3-D, THE
Blackthorne; (3-D Series #31,#44,#46,#63); 1 Dec 1987-4 1988

Issue	$Good	$Fine	$N.Mint	£Good	£Fine	£N.Mint
1 ND inside front and back covers are printed upside-down on most copies with the indicia for Blackthorne 3-D Series #32 (not #31); all with 3-D glasses (25% less if without glasses)	$0.40	$1.20	$2.00	£0.25	£0.75	£1.25
2-4 ND	$0.40	$1.20	$2.00	£0.25	£0.75	£1.25
Title Value:	$1.60	$4.80	$8.00	£1.00	£3.00	£5.00

CALIGARI 2050
Monster Comics; 1 Jul 1992

Issue	$Good	$Fine	$N.Mint	£Good	£Fine	£N.Mint
1 ND	$0.30	$0.90	$1.50	£0.20	£0.60	£1.00
Title Value:	$0.30	$0.90	$1.50	£0.20	£0.60	£1.00

Note: announced as a mini-series and then cancelled after one issue

CAMELOT 3000
DC Comics,MS; 1 Dec 1982-12 Apr 1985

Issue	$Good	$Fine	$N.Mint	£Good	£Fine	£N.Mint
1 ND Brian Bolland art begins	$0.50	$1.50	$2.50	£0.40	£1.20	£2.00
2-3 ND	$0.50	$1.50	$2.50	£0.35	£1.05	£1.75
4 ND	$0.50	$1.50	$2.50	£0.30	£0.90	£1.50
5 ND 1st appearance Knights of New Camelot	$0.50	$1.50	$2.50	£0.30	£0.90	£1.50
6-11 ND	$0.50	$1.50	$2.50	£0.30	£0.90	£1.50
12 ND scarce in the U.K.	$0.80	$2.40	$4.00	£0.50	£1.50	£2.50
Title Value:	$6.30	$18.90	$31.50	£4.00	£12.00	£20.00

Note: there was a long delay between issues 11 and 12 due to production problems

				£Good	£Fine	£N.Mint
Trade paperback (Titan UK Edition/DC Edition)				£1.40	£4.20	£7.00

CAMELOT ETERNAL
Caliber Press; 1 1990-8 1991

Issue	$Good	$Fine	$N.Mint	£Good	£Fine	£N.Mint
1-8 ND	$0.30	$0.90	$1.50	£0.20	£0.60	£1.00
Title Value:	$2.40	$7.20	$12.00	£1.60	£4.80	£8.00

CAMP CANDY
Marvel Comics Group, Film; 1 May 1990-7 Nov 1990

Issue	$Good	$Fine	$N.Mint	£Good	£Fine	£N.Mint
1-7 ND	$0.15	$0.45	$0.75	£0.10	£0.30	£0.50
Title Value:	$1.05	$3.15	$5.25	£0.70	£2.10	£3.50

Note: based on cartoon TV series

CANNON
Heroes Inc; 1 1969-4 1971

Issue	$Good	$Fine	$N.Mint	£Good	£Fine	£N.Mint
1 ND scarce in the U.K. Steve Ditko, Wally Wood art; reprints begin	$3.75	$11.00	$22.50	£2.50	£7.50	£15.00
2-4 ND scarce in the U.K.	$3.30	$10.00	$20.00	£2.05	£6.25	£12.50
Title Value:	$13.65	$41.00	$82.50	£8.65	£26.25	£52.50

CANNON (2ND SERIES)
Eros Comix,MS; 1 Feb 1991-8 Sep 1991

Issue	$Good	$Fine	$N.Mint	£Good	£Fine	£N.Mint
1-8 ND reprints from newspaper strips by Wally Wood	$0.40	$1.20	$2.00	£0.25	£0.75	£1.25
Title Value:	$3.20	$9.60	$16.00	£2.00	£6.00	£10.00

Note: contains nudity and sexual situations

CAP'N QUICK & A FOOZLE
Eclipse; 1 Jul 1984-3 Aug 1985
(see Eclipse Magazine)

Issue	$Good	$Fine	$N.Mint	£Good	£Fine	£N.Mint
1-2 ND Rogers art	$0.30	$0.90	$1.50	£0.20	£0.60	£1.00
3 ND titled "Foozle", Rogers art	$0.30	$0.90	$1.50	£0.20	£0.60	£1.00
Title Value:	$0.90	$2.70	$4.50	£0.60	£1.80	£3.00

CAPTAIN 3-D
Harvey,OS; 1 Dec 1953

Issue	$Good	$Fine	$N.Mint	£Good	£Fine	£N.Mint
1 ND scarce in the U.K. features Jack Kirby and Steve Ditko artwork, with bound-in 3-D glasses (25% less without glasses); this is thought to be Steve Ditko's 2nd ever work in comics	$10.00	$30.00	$70.00	£7.00	£21.00	£50.00
Title Value:	$10.00	$30.00	$70.00	£7.00	£21.00	£50.00

CAPTAIN ACTION
National Periodical Publications; 1 Oct/Nov 1968-5 Jun/Jul 1969

Issue	$Good	$Fine	$N.Mint	£Good	£Fine	£N.Mint
1 origin, Wally Wood inks; Superman appears on the cover	$11.00	$34.00	$80.00	£5.50	£17.00	£40.00
2-3 Wally Wood inks	$7.00	$21.00	$50.00	£3.20	£9.50	£22.50
4	$5.50	$17.00	$40.00	£2.55	£7.50	£18.00
5 Wally Wood inks	$7.00	$21.00	$50.00	£3.20	£9.50	£22.50
Title Value:	$37.50	$114.00	$270.00	£17.65	£53.00	£125.50
Captain Action and Action Boy (1967), Ideal Toy Giveaway, ND rare in the U.K.				£5.00	£15.00	£25.00

CAPTAIN AMERICA
Marvel Comics Group; 100 Apr 1968-454 Aug 1996
(see also Avengers #4, The Invaders, Marvel Double Feature, Marvel Fanfare, Marvel Super Action, Marvel Super Heroes, Marvel Team Up, Marvel Treasury, Edition)(formerly Tales of Suspense up to #99)

Issue	$Good	$Fine	$N.Mint	£Good	£Fine	£N.Mint
100 flashbacks of revival with Avengers, Black Panther appears; Jack Kirby art	$46.00	$135.00	$325.00	£29.00	£85.00	£200.00
101 scarce in the U.K. Jack Kirby art	$12.00	$36.00	$85.00	£7.00	£21.00	£50.00
102 very scarce in the U.K. Jack Kirby art	$6.75	$20.00	$47.50	£5.00	£15.00	£35.00
103-105 Jack Kirby art	$6.75	$20.00	$47.50	£4.25	£12.50	£30.00
106-108 Jack Kirby art	$6.25	$19.00	$45.00	£4.00	£12.00	£28.00
109 (Jan 1969), origin retold, Jack Kirby art	$10.00	$30.00	$70.00	£5.00	£15.00	£35.00
110 Captain America battles Hulk, Jim Steranko art	$9.50	$29.00	$67.50	£5.00	£15.00	£35.00
111 classic cover, Jim Steranko art	$9.50	$29.00	$67.50	£5.00	£15.00	£35.00
112 less common in the U.K. Iron Man recounts Captain America's origin and life story, Jack Kirby art	$4.25	$12.50	$30.00	£2.55	£7.50	£18.00
113 ND scarce in the U.K. Steranko art, classic cover	$9.50	$29.00	$67.50	£5.50	£17.00	£40.00
114 scarce in the U.K. Avengers and Nick Fury appear	$3.55	$10.50	$25.00	£2.00	£6.00	£14.00
115 ND Cosmic Cube appears	$3.55	$10.50	$25.00	£2.10	£6.25	£15.00
116 ND Avengers appear	$3.55	$10.50	$25.00	£2.10	£6.25	£15.00
117 very scarce in the U.K. 1st appearance Falcon	$5.00	$15.00	$35.00	£4.25	£12.50	£30.00
118-120	$3.55	$10.50	$25.00	£1.75	£5.25	£12.50
121 (Jan 1970), retells origin	$2.05	$6.25	$12.50	£1.25	£3.75	£7.50
122-126	$2.05	$6.25	$12.50	£1.25	£3.75	£7.50
127 Nick Fury appears	$2.05	$6.25	$12.50	£1.25	£3.75	£7.50
128	$2.05	$6.25	$12.50	£1.25	£3.75	£7.50
129 Red Skull appears	$2.05	$6.25	$12.50	£1.25	£3.75	£7.50
130 Hulk appears	$2.05	$6.25	$12.50	£1.25	£3.75	£7.50
131 Bucky re-appears	$2.00	$6.00	$12.00	£1.00	£3.00	£6.00
132 scarce in the U.K.	$2.00	$6.00	$12.00	£1.15	£3.50	£7.00
133 scarce in the U.K. (Jan 1971), origin Modok	$2.00	$6.00	$12.00	£1.15	£3.50	£7.00
134 scarce in the U.K. Falcon shares title on cover	$2.00	$6.00	$12.00	£1.15	£3.50	£7.00
135-136 scarce in the U.K.	$2.00	$6.00	$12.00	£1.15	£3.50	£7.00
137-138 scarce in the U.K. Spiderman appears	$2.00	$6.00	$12.00	£1.25	£3.75	£7.50
139 scarce in the U.K.	$2.00	$6.00	$12.00	£1.15	£3.50	£7.00
140-142 ND	$2.00	$6.00	$12.00	£1.00	£3.00	£6.00
143 ND 52pgs	$1.30	$4.00	$8.00	£1.05	£3.25	£6.50
144 ND Gray Morrow back-up	$1.30	$4.00	$8.00	£1.00	£3.00	£6.00
145 ND (Jan 1972)	$1.30	$4.00	$8.00	£1.00	£3.00	£6.00
146-150 ND	$1.30	$4.00	$8.00	£1.00	£3.00	£6.00

Issue	$Good	$Fine	$N.Mint	£Good	£Fine	£N.Mint
151-152 ND	$1.25	$3.75	$7.50	£0.80	£2.50	£5.00
153 ND 1st appearance (cameo) Jack Monroe (later Nomad II)	$1.30	$4.00	$8.00	£1.00	£3.00	£6.00
154 ND 1st full appearance Jack Monroe, Avengers appear	$1.30	$4.00	$8.00	£1.00	£3.00	£6.00
155 ND "secret origin" Captain America, origin Jack Monroe	$1.25	$3.75	$7.50	£0.80	£2.50	£5.00
156 ND Captain America vs. Captain America	$1.25	$3.75	$7.50	£0.80	£2.50	£5.00
157 ND (Jan 1973)	$1.25	$3.75	$7.50	£0.80	£2.50	£5.00
158 ND Captain America gains super-strength (temporarily)	$1.25	$3.75	$7.50	£0.80	£2.50	£5.00
159 1st display of super-strength	$1.25	$3.75	$7.50	£0.55	£1.75	£3.50
160 scarce in the U.K. 1st appearance of Solarr	$1.25	$3.75	$7.50	£0.65	£2.00	£4.00
161-163	$1.25	$3.75	$7.50	£0.55	£1.75	£3.50
164 Jim Starlin colours	$1.25	$3.75	$7.50	£0.55	£1.75	£3.50
165-167	$1.25	$3.75	$7.50	£0.50	£1.50	£3.00
168 1st appearance of Baron Zemo II	$1.25	$3.75	$7.50	£0.50	£1.50	£3.00
169 (Jan 1974), Black Panther appears (and meets Falcon for 1st time)	$1.25	$3.75	$7.50	£0.50	£1.50	£3.00
170 Black Panther appears	$1.25	$3.75	$7.50	£0.50	£1.50	£3.00
171 Black Panther and Iron Man appear; new Falcon costume, Falcon "flies"	$1.25	$3.75	$7.50	£0.50	£1.50	£3.00
172-175 ND old X-Men appear	$2.65	$8.00	$16.00	£1.05	£3.25	£6.50
176 history of Captain America retold; Thor, Iron Man and Vision appear	$1.25	$3.75	$7.50	£0.50	£1.50	£3.00
177 Beast appears	$1.25	$3.75	$7.50	£0.50	£1.50	£3.00
178	$1.25	$3.75	$7.50	£0.50	£1.50	£3.00
179 Hawkeye appears	$1.25	$3.75	$7.50	£0.50	£1.50	£3.00
180 1st appearance Steve Rogers as Nomad I, Hawkeye appears	$1.30	$4.00	$8.00	£0.55	£1.75	£3.50
181 (Jan 1975), Nomad appears, origin new Captain America, Sub-Mariner appears	$1.25	$3.75	$7.50	£0.50	£1.50	£3.00
182 Nomad appears	$0.80	$2.50	$5.00	£0.30	£1.00	£2.00
183 death of new Captain America, Nomad (Steve Rogers) returns to being Captain America, Beast cameo	$1.05	$3.25	$6.50	£0.50	£1.50	£3.00
184-185	$0.80	$2.50	$5.00	£0.30	£1.00	£2.00
186 origin Falcon	$0.80	$2.50	$5.00	£0.30	£1.00	£2.00
187-190	$0.80	$2.50	$5.00	£0.30	£1.00	£2.00
191 Ghost Rider appears (2pgs)	$0.65	$2.00	$4.00	£0.25	£0.85	£1.75
192	$0.65	$2.00	$4.00	£0.25	£0.85	£1.75
193 (Jan 1976), Jack Kirby art, his return to drawing Captain America	$0.65	$2.00	$4.00	£0.25	£0.85	£1.75
194-200 Jack Kirby art	$0.65	$2.00	$4.00	£0.25	£0.85	£1.75
201-204 Jack Kirby art	$0.50	$1.50	$3.00	£0.25	£0.75	£1.50
205 (Jan 1977), Jack Kirby art	$0.50	$1.50	$3.00	£0.25	£0.75	£1.50
206-214 Jack Kirby art	$0.50	$1.50	$3.00	£0.25	£0.75	£1.50
215 origin retold, Invaders and original Avengers appear	$0.50	$1.50	$3.00	£0.25	£0.75	£1.50
216 reprints Strange Tales #114 (1st appearance of Captain America since Golden Age, actually The Acrobat disguised), Captain America battles Human Torch	$0.50	$1.50	$3.00	£0.25	£0.75	£1.50
217 (Jan 1978), Iron Man appears	$0.50	$1.50	$3.00	£0.25	£0.75	£1.50
218 origin retold; secret history of Steve Rogers begins (ends #225)	$0.50	$1.50	$3.00	£0.25	£0.75	£1.50
219	$0.50	$1.50	$3.00	£0.25	£0.75	£1.50
220 Falcon back-up story	$0.50	$1.50	$3.00	£0.25	£0.75	£1.50
221 Rick Jones back-up story	$0.50	$1.50	$3.00	£0.20	£0.60	£1.25
222-223	$0.50	$1.50	$3.00	£0.20	£0.60	£1.25
224 1st Mike Zeck art on Captain America	$0.50	$1.50	$3.00	£0.20	£0.60	£1.25
225-228	$0.50	$1.50	$3.00	£0.20	£0.60	£1.25
229 (Jan 1979), Quasar appears	$0.50	$1.50	$3.00	£0.200	£0.60	£1.25
230 Quasar and Hulk appear	$0.50	$1.50	$3.00	£0.20	£0.60	£1.25
231 Hulk appears	$0.50	$1.50	$3.00	£0.20	£0.60	£1.25
232-233	$0.50	$1.50	$3.00	£0.20	£0.60	£1.25
234-236 Daredevil appears	$0.50	$1.50	$3.00	£0.20	£0.60	£1.25
237-240	$0.50	$1.50	$3.00	£0.20	£0.60	£1.25
241 (Jan 1980), Punisher appears, Frank Miller cover	$2.90	$8.75	$17.50	£1.30	£4.00	£8.00
242	$0.60	$1.80	$3.00	£0.25	£0.75	£1.25
243 George Perez cover art	$0.60	$1.80	$3.00	£0.25	£0.75	£1.25
244-245 Frank Miller cover art	$0.60	$1.80	$3.00	£0.25	£0.75	£1.25
246 George Perez cover art	$0.60	$1.80	$3.00	£0.25	£0.75	£1.25
247-252 John Byrne art	$0.70	$2.10	$3.50	£0.40	£1.20	£2.00
253 (Jan 1981), John Byrne art	$0.70	$2.10	$3.50	£0.40	£1.20	£2.00
254 ND John Byrne art	$0.70	$2.10	$3.50	£0.50	£1.50	£2.50
255 ND John Byrne art, anniversary issue	$0.70	$2.10	$3.50	£0.60	£1.80	£3.00
256	$0.40	$1.20	$2.00	£0.25	£0.75	£1.25
257 Hulk appears	$0.40	$1.20	$2.00	£0.25	£0.75	£1.25
258-259 Mike Zeck art	$0.40	$1.20	$2.00	£0.25	£0.75	£1.25
260	$0.40	$1.20	$2.00	£0.25	£0.75	£1.25
261-263 Mike Zeck art	$0.40	$1.20	$2.00	£0.25	£0.75	£1.25
264 Mike Zeck art; X-Men appear in dream sequence	$0.40	$1.20	$2.00	£0.25	£0.75	£1.25
265 (Jan 1982), Spiderman appears, Mike Zeck art	$0.40	$1.20	$2.00	£0.25	£0.75	£1.25
266 Spiderman appears, Mike Zeck art	$0.40	$1.20	$2.00	£0.25	£0.75	£1.25
267 1st appearance Everyman, Mike Zeck art	$0.40	$1.20	$2.00	£0.25	£0.75	£1.25
268 Mike Zeck art; ties into Defenders #104, #106	$0.40	$1.20	$2.00	£0.25	£0.75	£1.25
269 Mike Zeck art, 1st appearance Team America	$0.40	$1.20	$2.00	£0.25	£0.75	£1.25
270 Mike Zeck art	$0.40	$1.20	$2.00	£0.25	£0.75	£1.25
271	$0.40	$1.20	$2.00	£0.25	£0.75	£1.25
272-276 Mike Zeck art	$0.40	$1.20	$2.00	£0.25	£0.75	£1.25
277 (Jan 1983), Mike Zeck art	$0.40	$1.20	$2.00	£0.25	£0.75	£1.25
278 Mike Zeck art	$0.40	$1.20	$2.00	£0.25	£0.75	£1.25
279 LD in the U.K. Mike Zeck art, Iron Man appears	$0.40	$1.20	$2.00	£0.30	£0.90	£1.50
280 LD in the U.K. Mike Zeck art	$0.40	$1.20	$2.00	£0.30	£0.90	£1.50
281 LD in the U.K. Mike Zeck art, Spiderwoman and Bucky appear	$0.40	$1.20	$2.00	£0.30	£0.90	£1.50
282 LD in the U.K. 1st appearance Nomad II (Jack Monroe), Spiderwoman appears, Mike Zeck art	$0.90	$2.70	$4.50	£0.50	£1.50	£2.50
282 2nd printing, ND (1992) - silver ink cover	$0.40	$1.20	$2.00	£0.25	£0.75	£1.25
283 LD in the U.K. 2nd appearance Nomad II, Mike Zeck art	$0.80	$2.40	$4.00	£0.35	£1.05	£1.75
284 Nomad appears	$0.40	$1.20	$2.00	£0.25	£0.75	£1.25
285	$0.40	$1.20	$2.00	£0.25	£0.75	£1.25
286-288 LD in the U.K. Deathlok appears, Zeck art	$0.40	$1.20	$2.00	£0.30	£0.90	£1.50
289 (Jan 1984), Deathlok cameo, Mike Zeck art	$0.40	$1.20	$2.00	£0.25	£0.75	£1.25
290-291 LD in the U.K. John Byrne cover, Nomad appears	$0.40	$1.20	$2.00	£0.30	£0.90	£1.50
292-296 Nomad appears	$0.40	$1.20	$2.00	£0.25	£0.75	£1.25
297 LD in the U.K.	$0.40	$1.20	$2.00	£0.30	£0.90	£1.50
298 LD in the U.K. origin Red Skull retold	$0.40	$1.20	$2.00	£0.35	£1.05	£1.75
299 LD in the U.K.	$0.40	$1.20	$2.00	£0.30	£0.90	£1.50
300 LD in the U.K. Captain America vs. The Red Skull	$0.60	$1.80	$3.00	£0.40	£1.20	£2.00
301 LD in the U.K. (Jan 1985), Avengers and Nomad appear	$0.40	$1.20	$2.00	£0.30	£0.90	£1.50
302-304 LD in the U.K.	$0.40	$1.20	$2.00	£0.25	£0.75	£1.25
305 LD in the U.K. Captain Britain appears	$0.40	$1.20	$2.00	£0.25	£0.75	£1.25
306 LD in the U.K. Captain Britain by Paul Neary	$0.40	$1.20	$2.00	£0.40	£1.20	£2.00
307 Captain Britain by Paul Neary, Nomad appears	$0.40	$1.20	$2.00	£0.30	£0.90	£1.50
308 Secret Wars X-over	$0.40	$1.20	$2.00	£0.25	£0.75	£1.25
309 Nomad appears	$0.40	$1.20	$2.00	£0.25	£0.75	£1.25
310	$0.40	$1.20	$2.00	£0.25	£0.75	£1.25
311	$0.40	$1.20	$2.00	£0.20	£0.60	£1.00
312 LD in the U.K.	$0.40	$1.20	$2.00	£0.25	£0.75	£1.25
313 LD in the U.K. (Jan 1986)	$0.40	$1.20	$2.00	£0.25	£0.75	£1.25
314-320 LD in the U.K.	$0.40	$1.20	$2.00	£0.25	£0.75	£1.25
321-322	$0.40	$1.20	$2.00	£0.20	£0.60	£1.00
323 1st appearance new Super Patriot	$0.60	$1.80	$3.00	£0.30	£0.90	£1.50

SOME INDEPENDENT COMICS MAY NOT HAVE APPEARED ALTHOUGH THEY WERE ADVERTISED AND SOLICITED.

	$Good	$Fine	$N.Mint	£Good	£Fine	£N.Mint
324	$0.40	$1.20	$2.00	£0.20	£0.60	£1.00
325 (Jan 1987), Nomad appears						
	$0.40	$1.20	$2.00	£0.20	£0.60	£1.00
326	$0.40	$1.20	$2.00	£0.20	£0.60	£1.00
327 LD in the U.K.	$0.50	$1.50	$2.50	£0.25	£0.75	£1.25
328 LD in the U.K. origin and 1st appearance D. Man						
	$0.50	$1.50	$2.50	£0.30	£0.90	£1.50
329-331 LD in the U.K.						
	$0.40	$1.20	$2.00	£0.25	£0.75	£1.25
332 LD in the U.K. Captain America resigns						
	$0.60	$1.80	$3.00	£0.30	£0.90	£1.50
333 very LD new Super Patriot becomes new Captain America						
	$0.60	$1.80	$3.00	£0.30	£0.90	£1.50
334 1st appearance new Bucky						
	$0.80	$2.40	$4.00	£0.30	£0.90	£1.50
335 LD in the U.K.	$0.80	$2.40	$4.00	£0.40	£1.20	£2.00
336	$0.80	$2.40	$4.00	£0.30	£0.90	£1.50
337 LD in the U.K. (Jan 1988), cover based on classic Avengers #4, return of Steve Rogers						
	$0.80	$2.40	$4.00	£0.40	£1.20	£2.00
338 LD in the U.K.	$0.80	$2.40	$4.00	£0.40	£1.20	£2.00
339 Fall of Mutants, ties into Iron Man #238						
	$0.80	$2.40	$4.00	£0.30	£0.90	£1.50
340	$0.80	$2.40	$4.00	£0.30	£0.90	£1.50
341 LD in the U.K. Captain America battles Iron Man						
	$0.40	$1.20	$2.00	£0.35	£1.05	£1.75
342-343	$0.30	$0.90	$1.50	£0.25	£0.75	£1.25
344 DS	$0.50	$1.50	$2.50	£0.30	£0.90	£1.50
345	$0.30	$0.90	$1.50	£0.25	£0.75	£1.25
346 Freedom Force	$0.30	$0.90	$1.50	£0.25	£0.75	£1.25
347-348	$0.30	$0.90	$1.50	£0.25	£0.75	£1.25
349 (Jan 1989)	$0.30	$0.90	$1.50	£0.25	£0.75	£1.25
350 LD in the U.K. 64pgs, squarebound, origin Red Skull, John Byrne art (most copies have spine crinkling); return of Steve Rogers to original Captain America						
	$0.80	$2.40	$4.00	£0.40	£1.20	£2.00
351-356	$0.30	$0.90	$1.50	£0.20	£0.60	£1.00
357 LD in the U.K. Captain America and Diamondback in separate stories, Bloodstone story begins, bi-weekly						
	$0.30	$0.90	$1.50	£0.25	£0.75	£1.25
358-360 Bloodstone story, bi-weekly issue						
	$0.30	$0.90	$1.50	£0.20	£0.60	£1.00
361-362 Bloodstone story, bi-weekly issue						
	$0.30	$0.90	$1.50	£0.15	£0.45	£0.75
363 Bloodstone story concludes						
	$0.30	$0.90	$1.50	£0.15	£0.45	£0.75
364	$0.30	$0.90	$1.50	£0.15	£0.45	£0.75
365 Acts of Vengeance tie-in, Captain America battles Sub-Mariner						
	$0.30	$0.90	$1.50	£0.15	£0.45	£0.75
366 (Jan 1990), Acts of Vengeance tie-in, 1st Ron Lim art on Captain America						
	$0.30	$0.90	$1.50	£0.15	£0.45	£0.75
367 Acts of Vengeance tie-in, Magneto appears, no Lim art						
	$0.30	$0.90	$1.50	£0.15	£0.45	£0.75
368-371 Ron Lim art						
	$0.30	$0.90	$1.50	£0.15	£0.45	£0.75
372-377 Streets of Poison story, bi-weekly issue, Ron Lim art						
	$0.30	$0.90	$1.50	£0.15	£0.45	£0.75
378 Ron Lim art	$0.30	$0.90	$1.50	£0.15	£0.45	£0.75
379 Quasar appears, Ron Lim art						
	$0.30	$0.90	$1.50	£0.15	£0.45	£0.75
380 Ron Lim art	$0.30	$0.90	$1.50	£0.15	£0.45	£0.75
381 (Jan 1991), Ron Lim art						
	$0.30	$0.90	$1.50	£0.15	£0.45	£0.75
382 Ron Lim art	$0.30	$0.90	$1.50	£0.15	£0.45	£0.75
383 LD in the U.K. 64pgs, 50th anniversary issue, Ron Lim art, Jim Lee cover						
	$0.70	$2.10	$3.50	£0.40	£1.20	£2.00
384 Ron Lim art	$0.30	$0.90	$1.50	£0.15	£0.45	£0.75
385-386 West Coast Avengers appear, Ron Lim art						
	$0.30	$0.90	$1.50	£0.15	£0.45	£0.75
387-392 Superia Stratagem story, bi-weekly issue						
	$0.30	$0.90	$1.50	£0.15	£0.45	£0.75
393	$0.30	$0.90	$1.50	£0.15	£0.45	£0.75
394-395 Heart of the Viper story, Red Skull appears						
	$0.30	$0.90	$1.50	£0.15	£0.45	£0.75
396 (Jan 1992), Heart of the Viper story, Red Skull appears						
	$0.30	$0.90	$1.50	£0.15	£0.45	£0.75
397 Heart of the Viper story, Red Skull appears, $1.25 cover						
	$0.30	$0.90	$1.50	£0.15	£0.45	£0.75
398 Galactic Storm part 1						
	$0.30	$0.90	$1.50	£0.15	£0.45	£0.75
399 Galactic Storm part 8						
	$0.30	$0.90	$1.50	£0.15	£0.45	£0.75
400 LD in the U.K. 96pgs, Galactic Storm part 15, reprints Avengers #4, gatefold cover						
	$0.60	$1.80	$3.00	£0.40	£1.20	£2.00
401 Galactic Storm: Aftermath						
	$0.25	$0.75	$1.25	£0.15	£0.45	£0.75
402-406 The Man & The Wolf story, Wolverine appears, bi-weekly						
	$0.25	$0.75	$1.25	£0.15	£0.45	£0.75
407 The Man & The Wolf (conclusion), Captain America vs. Cable, Wolverine appears, bi-weekly						
	$0.25	$0.75	$1.25	£0.15	£0.45	£0.75
408 Falcon, Red Skull appear						
	$0.25	$0.75	$1.25	£0.15	£0.45	£0.75
409	$0.25	$0.75	$1.25	£0.15	£0.45	£0.75
410 Falcon appears						
	$0.25	$0.75	$1.25	£0.15	£0.45	£0.75
411 (Jan 1993), Falcon becomes Captain America's partner again						
	$0.25	$0.75	$1.25	£0.15	£0.45	£0.75
412-413 Master of Kung Fu appears						
	$0.25	$0.75	$1.25	£0.15	£0.45	£0.75
414-417 Ka-Zar and Black Panther appear						
	$0.25	$0.75	$1.25	£0.15	£0.45	£0.75
418 Daredevil appears						
	$0.25	$0.75	$1.25	£0.15	£0.45	£0.75
419 Silver Sable appers						
	$0.25	$0.75	$1.25	£0.15	£0.45	£0.75
420	$0.25	$0.75	$1.25	£0.15	£0.45	£0.75
420 pre-bagged, ND with Dirt Magazine and sticker						
	$0.60	$1.80	$3.00	£0.40	£1.20	£2.00
421	$0.25	$0.75	$1.25	£0.15	£0.45	£0.75
422 (Jan 1994)	$0.25	$0.75	$1.25	£0.15	£0.45	£0.75
423-424	$0.25	$0.75	$1.25	£0.15	£0.45	£0.75
425 48pgs, Fighting Chance story begins (ends #436)						
	$0.40	$1.20	$2.00	£0.25	£0.75	£1.25
425 Collectors Edition, ND , multi-level foil embossed cover						
	$0.60	$1.80	$3.00	£0.40	£1.20	£2.00
426	$0.30	$0.90	$1.50	£0.20	£0.60	£1.00
427 with free Spiderman vs. Venom card sheet						
	$0.30	$0.90	$1.50	£0.20	£0.60	£1.00
428-434	$0.30	$0.90	$1.50	£0.20	£0.60	£1.00
435 (Jan 1995)	$0.30	$0.90	$1.50	£0.20	£0.60	£1.00
436 Fighting Chance part 12 (conclusion)						
	$0.30	$0.90	$1.50	£0.20	£0.60	£1.00
437 Iron Man and Giant Man appear						
	$0.30	$0.90	$1.50	£0.20	£0.60	£1.00
438 Captain America dons a new exo-skeleton armour, Iron Man and Nick Fury appear						

Buried Treasure #2

Captain Action #5

Captain America #175

Issue	$Good	$Fine	$N.Mint	£Good	£Fine	£N.Mint
	$0.30	$0.90	$1.50	£0.20	£0.60	£1.00
439	$0.30	$0.90	$1.50	£0.20	£0.60	£1.00
440 Taking AIM part 1, continued in Avengers #387						
	$0.30	$0.90	$1.50	£0.20	£0.60	£1.00
441 Taking AIM part 3, continued in Avengers #388						
	$0.30	$0.90	$1.50	£0.20	£0.60	£1.00
442-443	$0.30	$0.90	$1.50	£0.20	£0.60	£1.00
444 Mark Waid script						
	$1.20	$3.60	$6.00	£0.80	£2.40	£4.00
445 Operation Rebirth story, Red Skull and the Cosmic Cube appear; Mark Waid script						
	$0.80	$2.40	$4.00	£0.60	£1.80	£3.00
446 Operation Rebirth story, Red Skull and the Cosmic Cube appear; Mark Waid script						
	$0.70	$2.10	$3.50	£0.50	£1.50	£2.50
447 (Jan 1996), Operation Rebirth story, Red Skull and the Cosmic Cube appear; Mark Waid script						
	$0.70	$2.10	$3.50	£0.50	£1.50	£2.50
448 48pgs, Operation Rebirth concludes, Red Skull and Cosmic Cube appear; metallic fifth ink cover; Mark Waid script						
	$0.90	$2.70	$4.50	£0.50	£1.50	£2.50
449 The First Sign part 1; Captain America, Thor and Iron Man return to the Avengers; continued in Thor #496; Mark Waid script						
	$0.60	$1.80	$3.00	£0.40	£1.20	£2.00
450 Steve Rogers on cover in a Clark Kent/Superman pose (opening his shirt to reveal his costume)						
	$0.30	$0.90	$1.50	£0.25	£0.75	£1.25
450 Alternate Cover Edition, - issued on a 1 for 1 basis, features Captain America on the cover in full costume with the sub-title "Ex-Patriot"						
	$0.30	$0.90	$1.50	£0.25	£0.75	£1.25
451 new costume and new identity for Captain America						
	$0.30	$0.90	$1.50	£0.25	£0.75	£1.25
452	$0.30	$0.90	$1.50	£0.25	£0.75	£1.25
453 Man Without A Country part 4 (conclusion)						
	$0.30	$0.90	$1.50	£0.25	£0.75	£1.25
454	$0.30	$0.90	$1.50	£0.25	£0.75	£1.25
Title Value:	$396.65	$1190.80	$2477.50	£228.05	£685.35	£1431.25

Captain America: War & Remembrance (Oct 1990)

	£Good	£Fine	£N.Mint
Trade paperback			
ND reprints issues #247-255 with John Byrne art	£1.40	£4.20	£7.00
2nd print - Mar 1995	£1.70	£5.10	£8.50

Captain America: The Bloodstone Hunt (Aug 1993)

	£Good	£Fine	£N.Mint
Trade paperback			
ND reprints issues #357-364, foil embossed cover	£1.90	£5.70	£9.50

Captain America: Deathlok Lives (Dec 1993)

	£Good	£Fine	£N.Mint
Trade paperback ND reprints issues #286-288	£0.65	£1.95	£3.25

Captain America: Streets of Poison (Aug 1994)

	£Good	£Fine	£N.Mint
Trade paperback ND reprints issues #372-377	£2.00	£6.00	£10.00

Captain America: Operation Rebirth (Sep 1996)

	£Good	£Fine	£N.Mint
Trade paperback ND 112pgs, collects classic storyline	£1.30	£3.90	£6.50

Note: Captain America becomes Nomad in #180, becomes Captain America America again in #183. Bucky becomes Nomad in #282. Titled "Captain America and the Falcon" #134-223. #216 is all reprint.

ARTISTS

Mike Zeck art in 258,259,261-270,272-283,288,289.

CAPTAIN AMERICA (2ND SERIES)

Marvel Comics Group; 1 Jul 1996; 1 Nov 1996-present

Issue	$Good	$Fine	$N.Mint	£Good	£Fine	£N.Mint
1 ND 48pgs, Rob Liefeld cover and art						
	$0.60	$1.80	$3.00	£0.40	£1.20	£2.00
1 Comicon Edition, ND (Jul 1996), Rob Liefeld cover and art; limited to 3,000 copies, released at the 1996 San Diego Comicon						
	$1.50	$4.50	$7.50	£1.50	£4.50	£7.50
1 Gold Stamped Signature Edition, ND (Jan 1997) pre-bagged with certificate featuring 22 carat gold stamped signatures from Jeph Loeb and Rob Liefeld; 5,000 copies						
	$5.00	$15.00	$25.00	£3.50	£10.50	£17.50
1 Variant Cover Edition, ND Captain America leaping forward						
	$1.00	$3.00	$5.00	£0.80	£2.40	£4.00
2 ND Red Skull and The Falcon appear						
	$0.40	$1.20	$2.00	£0.25	£0.75	£1.25
3 ND The Incredible Hulk guest-stars						
	$0.40	$1.20	$2.00	£0.25	£0.75	£1.25
4 ND Namor the Sub-Mariner guest-stars						
	$0.40	$1.20	$2.00	£0.25	£0.75	£1.25
5-6 ND	$0.40	$1.20	$2.00	£0.25	£0.75	£1.25
Title Value:	$10.10	$30.30	$50.50	£7.45	£22.35	£37.25

CAPTAIN AMERICA AND THE FALCON BOOK AND RECORD SET

Power Records; PR-12 1974

Issue	$Good	$Fine	$N.Mint	£Good	£Fine	£N.Mint
PR-12 ND scarce in the U.K., 20pg booklet with 45 rpm record						
	$1.25	$3.75	$7.50	£0.80	£2.50	£5.00
Title Value:	$1.25	$3.75	$7.50	£0.80	£2.50	£5.00

Note: the item would be valued 50% less without record

CAPTAIN AMERICA ANNUAL

Marvel Comics Group; 1 Jan 1971-7 1983; 8 Sep 1986-13 1994

Issue	$Good	$Fine	$N.Mint	£Good	£Fine	£N.Mint
1 68pgs, all reprint, origin retold						
	$3.30	$10.00	$20.00	£1.65	£5.00	£10.00
2 ND scarce in the U.K. 68pgs, all reprint						
	$2.50	$7.50	$15.00	£1.30	£4.00	£8.00
3 ND 52pgs, Jack Kirby art						
	$1.25	$3.75	$7.50	£0.55	£1.75	£3.50
4 ND very scarce in the U.K. 52pgs, Captain America vs. Magneto; Jack Kirby cover and art						
	$0.80	$2.50	$5.00	£1.00	£3.00	£6.00
5 ND 52pgs	$0.50	$1.50	$3.00	£0.30	£1.00	£2.00
6 ND 52pgs, Invaders appear						
	$0.60	$1.80	$3.00	£0.40	£1.20	£2.00
7 ND 52pgs, Cosmic Cube story						
	$0.60	$1.80	$3.00	£0.40	£1.20	£2.00
8 ND Wolverine appears, Mike Zeck art						
	$4.50	$13.50	$22.50	£1.50	£4.50	£7.50
9 ND The Terminus Factor part 1, Nomad appears, continues in Iron Man Annual #11						
	$0.80	$2.40	$4.00	£0.30	£0.90	£1.50
10 ND Von Strucker Gambit, story concludes from Daredevil Annual #7/Punisher Annual #4						
	$0.50	$1.50	$2.50	£0.30	£0.90	£1.50
11 ND Citizen Kang part 1, Gilgamesh appears, continued in Thor Annual #17						
	$0.50	$1.50	$2.50	£0.30	£0.90	£1.50
12 ND 64pgs, pre-bagged with trading card introducing The Battling Bantam						
	$0.50	$1.50	$2.50	£0.40	£1.20	£2.00
13 ND 64pgs, Captain America vs. Red Skull						
	$0.60	$1.80	$3.00	£0.40	£1.20	£2.00
Title Value:	$16.95	$51.05	$93.50	£8.80	£26.75	£49.50

Note: King Size Special 1-2, Annual 3 on.

CAPTAIN AMERICA ASHCAN

Marvel Comics Group; nn Mar 1995

Issue	$Good	$Fine	$N.Mint	£Good	£Fine	£N.Mint
nn ND 16pgs, previews the storylines and changes for Captain America in 1995						
	$0.15	$0.45	$0.75	£0.10	£0.30	£0.50
Title Value:	$0.15	$0.45	$0.75	£0.10	£0.30	£0.50

CAPTAIN AMERICA COLLECTORS PREVIEW

Marvel Comics Group,OS; 1 Mar 1995

Issue	$Good	$Fine	$N.Mint	£Good	£Fine	£N.Mint
1 ND 48pgs, previews storylines plus articles and features						
	$0.40	$1.20	$2.00	£0.25	£0.75	£1.25
Title Value:	$0.40	$1.20	$2.00	£0.25	£0.75	£1.25

CAPTAIN AMERICA COMICS

Timely/Atlas/Marvel; 1 Mar 1941-75 Feb 1950; 76 May 1954-78 Sep 1954

Issue	$Good	$Fine	$N.Mint	£Good	£Fine	£N.Mint
1 origin and 1st appearance Captain America and Bucky by Joe Simon and Jack Kirby						
	$6200.00	$18700.00	$62500.00	£4150.00	£12500.00	£41675.00
1 Marvel Milestone Edition, ND 48pgs, (Mar 1995) - metallic ink cover						
	$0.80	$2.40	$4.00	£0.50	£1.50	£2.50
2	$1275.00	$3800.00	$11500.00	£850.00	£2550.00	£7675.00
3 1st ever text work by Stan Lee and his first job as Assistant Editor						
	$1050.00	$3150.00	$9500.00	£700.00	£2100.00	£6350.00
4	$580.00	$1750.00	$5250.00	£385.00	£1150.00	£3500.00
5	$550.00	$1650.00	$5000.00	£370.00	£1100.00	£3350.00
6	$500.00	$1500.00	$4500.00	£330.00	£1000.00	£3000.00
7 Red Skull appears						
	$580.00	$1750.00	$5250.00	£385.00	£1150.00	£3500.00
8-9	$420.00	$1250.00	$3800.00	£280.00	£850.00	£2550.00
10 (Jan 1942), last issue by Simon and Kirby						
	$420.00	$1250.00	$3800.00	£280.00	£850.00	£2550.00
11	$400.00	$1200.00	$3200.00	£265.00	£800.00	£2150.00
12-13	$375.00	$1125.00	$3000.00	£250.00	£750.00	£2000.00
14-15	$340.00	$1025.00	$2750.00	£230.00	£690.00	£1850.00
16 classic Captain America vs. Red Skull, Red Skull on cover						
	$435.00	$1300.00	$3500.00	£290.00	£880.00	£2350.00
17	$300.00	$900.00	$2400.00	£200.00	£600.00	£1600.00
18	$230.00	$690.00	$1850.00	£155.00	£465.00	£1250.00
19 Human Torch back-up begins						
	$230.00	$690.00	$1850.00	£155.00	£465.00	£1250.00
20 Sub-Mariner appears						
	$235.00	$710.00	$1900.00	£155.00	£475.00	£1275.00
21	$215.00	$650.00	$1750.00	£145.00	£440.00	£1175.00
22 (Jan 1943)	$215.00	$650.00	$1750.00	£145.00	£440.00	£1175.00
22 Canadian Issue, very rare in the U.K., rare in the U.S. 128pgs, same cover as #22 but with contents of Marvel Mystery #33 and Captain America #18						
	$1600.00	$4800.00	$16000.00	£850.00	£2550.00	£8500.00
23-25	$215.00	$650.00	$1750.00	£145.00	£440.00	£1175.00
26	$210.00	$630.00	$1700.00	£140.00	£430.00	£1150.00
27 last 68pg issue						
	$210.00	$630.00	$1700.00	£140.00	£430.00	£1150.00
28-30	$210.00	$630.00	$1700.00	£140.00	£430.00	£1150.00
31-33	$180.00	$540.00	$1450.00	£120.00	£365.00	£975.00
34 (Jan 1944)	$180.00	$540.00	$1450.00	£120.00	£365.00	£975.00
35	$180.00	$540.00	$1450.00	£120.00	£365.00	£975.00
36 Hitler on cover - the classic confrontation						
	$280.00	$840.00	$2250.00	£185.00	£560.00	£1500.00
37 Red Skull appears						
	$185.00	$560.00	$1500.00	£125.00	£375.00	£1000.00
38-40	$175.00	$520.00	$1400.00	£115.00	£355.00	£950.00
41-43	$155.00	$465.00	$1250.00	£100.00	£310.00	£835.00
44 (Jan 1945)	$155.00	$465.00	$1250.00	£100.00	£310.00	£835.00
45-47	$155.00	$465.00	$1250.00	£100.00	£310.00	£835.00
48-51	$150.00	$450.00	$1200.00	£100.00	£300.00	£800.00
52 (Jan 1946)	$150.00	$450.00	$1200.00	£100.00	£300.00	£800.00
53-58	$150.00	$450.00	$1200.00	£100.00	£300.00	£800.00
59 origin retold	$300.00	$900.00	$2400.00	£200.00	£600.00	£1600.00
60 (Jan 1947)	$150.00	$450.00	$1200.00	£100.00	£300.00	£800.00
61 Red Skull cover and story						
	$225.00	$670.00	$1800.00	£150.00	£450.00	£1200.00
62-64	$155.00	$465.00	$1250.00	£100.00	£310.00	£835.00
65 (Jan 1948)	$155.00	$465.00	$1250.00	£100.00	£310.00	£835.00
66 scarce in the U.K. Golden Girl appears, origin Golden Girl						
	$165.00	$495.00	$1320.00	£110.00	£330.00	£880.00
67 Golden Girl appears						
	$155.00	$465.00	$1250.00	£100.00	£310.00	£835.00
68 Sub-Mariner appears						
	$155.00	$465.00	$1250.00	£100.00	£310.00	£835.00
69 Human Torch appears						
	$155.00	$465.00	$1250.00	£100.00	£310.00	£835.00
70 Sub-Mariner appears						
	$155.00	$465.00	$1250.00	£100.00	£310.00	£835.00
71	$150.00	$450.00	$1200.00	£100.00	£300.00	£800.00

	$Good	$Fine	$N.Mint	£Good	£Fine	£N.Mint
72 (Jan 1949)	$150.00	$450.00	$1200.00	£100.00	£300.00	£800.00
73	$150.00	$450.00	$1200.00	£100.00	£300.00	£800.00
74 very scarce in the U.K. titled "Captain America's Weird Tales", classic Red Skull cover	$405.00	$1200.00	$3250.00	£270.00	£810.00	£2175.00
75 very scarce in the U.K. (Feb 1950), titled "Captain America's Weird Tales"	$155.00	$465.00	$1250.00	£100.00	£310.00	£835.00
76 scarce in the U.K. (May 1954), Human Torch and Toro appear, classic cover headline begins: "Captain America...Commie Smasher!"	$105.00	$315.00	$850.00	£70.00	£215.00	£575.00
77 scarce in the U.K. Human Torch and Toro appear	$105.00	$315.00	$850.00	£70.00	£215.00	£575.00
78 scarce in the U.K. Human Torch and Toro appear	$110.00	$335.00	$900.00	£75.00	£225.00	£600.00
Title Value:	$27015.80	$81122.40	$238924.00	£17765.50	£53696.50	£157592.50

Note: though not officially distributed on the news-stands in the U.K. copies are thought to have come over with American G.I's or through US relatives of UK citizens. A copy of #50 has been recorded with a 9 (old) pence stamp on the cover

CAPTAIN AMERICA GIANT SIZE

Marvel Comics Group; 1 Dec 1975

	$Good	$Fine	$N.Mint	£Good	£Fine	£N.Mint
1 ND scarce in the U.K. 68pgs, all reprint	$2.00	$6.00	$12.00	£1.00	£3.00	£6.00
Title Value:	$2.00	$6.00	$12.00	£1.00	£3.00	£6.00

CAPTAIN AMERICA GOES TO WAR AGAINST DRUGS

Marvel Comics Group; nn Dec 1990

	$Good	$Fine	$N.Mint	£Good	£Fine	£N.Mint
nn ND script by Peter David highlighting drugs problem among kids; promotional giveaway	$0.30	$0.90	$1.50	£0.20	£0.60	£1.00
Title Value:	$0.30	$0.90	$1.50	£0.20	£0.60	£1.00

CAPTAIN AMERICA MOVIE ADAPTATION

Marvel Comics Group,OS; 1 May 1992

	$Good	$Fine	$N.Mint	£Good	£Fine	£N.Mint
1 ND 48pgs, Stan Lee script; printed on special coated stock paper	$0.50	$1.50	$2.50	£0.30	£0.90	£1.50
Title Value:	$0.50	$1.50	$2.50	£0.30	£0.90	£1.50

Note: originally scheduled for 1991 release but held over and re-formatted as the film was not distributed and went straight to video.

CAPTAIN AMERICA SPECIAL EDITION

Marvel Comics Group; 1 Feb 1984-2 Mar 1984

	$Good	$Fine	$N.Mint	£Good	£Fine	£N.Mint
1 ND reprints Captain America #110, #111	$0.60	$1.80	$3.00	£0.40	£1.20	£2.00
2 ND reprints Captain America #113	$0.60	$1.80	$3.00	£0.40	£1.20	£2.00
Title Value:	$1.20	$3.60	$6.00	£0.80	£2.40	£4.00

Note: all Jim Steranko reprints on Baxter paper.

CAPTAIN AMERICA, THE ADVENTURES OF

Marvel Comics Group,MS; 1 Sep 1991-4 Dec 1991

	$Good	$Fine	$N.Mint	£Good	£Fine	£N.Mint
1 ND Year One origin type story, Kevin Maguire art with Terry Austin inks on all; full embossed cover figure and title	$1.00	$3.00	$5.00	£0.70	£2.10	£3.50
2 ND meeting with Bucky, Kevin Maguire art	$1.00	$3.00	$5.00	£0.70	£2.10	£3.50
3 ND Kevin Maguire art	$1.00	$3.00	$5.00	£0.70	£2.10	£3.50
4 ND Steve Carr/Kevin West art	$1.00	$3.00	$5.00	£0.70	£2.10	£3.50
Title Value:	$4.00	$12.00	$20.00	£2.80	£8.40	£14.00

CAPTAIN AMERICA: DRUG WARS

Marvel Comics Group,OS; nn Apr 1994

	$Good	$Fine	$N.Mint	£Good	£Fine	£N.Mint
nn ND New Warriors guest-star	$0.40	$1.20	$2.00	£0.25	£0.75	£1.25
Title Value:	$0.40	$1.20	$2.00	£0.25	£0.75	£1.25

CAPTAIN AMERICA: THE CLASSIC YEARS

Marvel Comics Group; nn Dec 1990

	$Good	$Fine	$N.Mint	£Good	£Fine	£N.Mint
nn Hardcover ND scarce in the U.K. 2 volume set reprinting original 1940s Joe Simon & Jack Kirby issues #1-10 in slipcase	$12.00	$36.00	$60.00	£9.00	£27.00	£45.00
Title Value:	$12.00	$36.00	$60.00	£9.00	£27.00	£45.00

CAPTAIN AMERICA: THE LEGEND

Marvel Comics Group,OS; 1 Sep 1996

	$Good	$Fine	$N.Mint	£Good	£Fine	£N.Mint
1 ND 48pgs, retells the life and times of Captain America	$0.80	$2.40	$4.00	£0.50	£1.50	£2.50
Title Value:	$0.80	$2.40	$4.00	£0.50	£1.50	£2.50

CAPTAIN AMERICA: THE MEDUSA EFFECT

Marvel Comics Group,OS; 1 Mar 1994

	$Good	$Fine	$N.Mint	£Good	£Fine	£N.Mint
1 ND 64pgs, Golden Age Captain America and Bucky vs. Baron Zemo	$0.60	$1.80	$3.00	£0.40	£1.20	£2.00
Title Value:	$0.60	$1.80	$3.00	£0.40	£1.20	£2.00

CAPTAIN ATOM

Charlton; 78 Dec 1965-89 Dec 1967

(previously Strange Suspense Stories)

	$Good	$Fine	$N.Mint	£Good	£Fine	£N.Mint
78 ND Steve Ditko art	$10.00	$30.00	$70.00	£5.50	£17.00	£40.00
79 ND Steve Ditko art	$6.25	$19.00	$45.00	£4.25	£12.50	£30.00
80-82 distributed in the U.K. Steve Ditko art	$6.25	$19.00	$45.00	£3.55	£10.50	£25.00
83 distributed in the U.K. 1st appearance Ted Kord (2nd Blue Beetle, see Blue Beetle [3rd Series] #2); Steve Ditko art	$5.50	$17.00	$40.00	£3.20	£9.50	£22.50
83 Modern Comics Reprint, (1977)	$0.15	$0.50	$1.00	£0.25	£0.75	£1.50
84 distributed in the U.K. Blue Beetle appears, Steve Ditko art	$5.50	$17.00	$40.00	£3.20	£9.50	£22.50
84 Modern Comics Reprint, (1977)	$0.15	$0.50	$1.00	£0.25	£0.75	£1.50
85 distributed in the U.K. Blue Beetle appears, Steve Ditko art	$5.50	$17.00	$40.00	£3.20	£9.50	£22.50
85 Modern Comics Reprint, (1977)	$0.15	$0.50	$1.00	£0.25	£0.75	£1.50
86-87 distributed in the U.K. Blue Beetle appears, Steve Ditko art	$5.50	$17.00	$40.00	£3.20	£9.50	£22.50
88-89 distributed in the U.K. Nightshade appears, Steve Ditko art	$5.50	$17.00	$40.00	£3.20	£9.50	£22.50
Title Value:	$73.95	$226.50	$533.00	£43.55	£129.75	£307.00

Note: stories intended for issue #90 appeared in Charlton Bullseye #1,2

CAPTAIN ATOM (2ND SERIES)

DC Comics; 1 Mar 1987-57 Sep 1991

	$Good	$Fine	$N.Mint	£Good	£Fine	£N.Mint
1 44pgs, origin, 1st DC appearance, new costume; Pat Broderick art begins (ends #27)	$0.20	$0.60	$1.00	£0.15	£0.45	£0.75
2-4	$0.15	$0.45	$0.75	£0.10	£0.35	£0.60
5 Captain Atom vs. Firestorm	$0.15	$0.45	$0.75	£0.10	£0.35	£0.60
6-10	$0.15	$0.45	$0.75	£0.10	£0.35	£0.60
11 Millennium X-over	$0.15	$0.45	$0.75	£0.10	£0.30	£0.50
12-13	$0.15	$0.45	$0.75	£0.10	£0.30	£0.50
14 Nightshade guest-stars	$0.15	$0.45	$0.75	£0.10	£0.30	£0.50
15 Captain Atom vs. Major Force	$0.15	$0.45	$0.75	£0.10	£0.30	£0.50
16 Justice League X-over	$0.15	$0.45	$0.75	£0.10	£0.30	£0.50
17 Swamp Thing appears	$0.15	$0.45	$0.75	£0.10	£0.30	£0.50
18-19	$0.15	$0.45	$0.75	£0.10	£0.30	£0.50
20 Blue Beetle appears	$0.15	$0.45	$0.75	£0.10	£0.30	£0.50
21-23	$0.15	$0.45	$0.75	£0.10	£0.30	£0.50
24-25 Invasion X-over	$0.15	$0.45	$0.75	£0.10	£0.30	£0.50
26-28 Captain Atom File story; Blue Beetle, Mister Miracle, Booster Gold appear - leads into "true" origin	$0.15	$0.45	$0.75	£0.10	£0.30	£0.50
29	$0.15	$0.45	$0.75	£0.10	£0.30	£0.50
30 Janus Directive tie-in, Captain Atom vs. Black Manta	$0.15	$0.45	$0.75	£0.10	£0.30	£0.50
31-32	$0.15	$0.45	$0.75	£0.10	£0.30	£0.50
33 Batman appears; cover in style of classic 60s Batman/Robin pin-up	$0.15	$0.45	$0.75	£0.10	£0.30	£0.50
34-41	$0.15	$0.45	$0.75	£0.10	£0.30	£0.50
42 Death appears	$0.20	$0.60	$1.00	£0.15	£0.45	£0.75
43-45	$0.15	$0.45	$0.75	£0.10	£0.30	£0.50
46-47 Superman guest-stars	$0.15	$0.45	$0.75	£0.10	£0.30	£0.50
48 Red Tornado appears	$0.15	$0.45	$0.75	£0.10	£0.30	£0.50
49	$0.15	$0.45	$0.75	£0.10	£0.30	£0.50
50 48pgs	$0.15	$0.45	$0.75	£0.10	£0.35	£0.60
51-52	$0.15	$0.45	$0.75	£0.10	£0.30	£0.50
53 Aquaman appears	$0.15	$0.45	$0.75	£0.10	£0.30	£0.50
54-57	$0.15	$0.45	$0.75	£0.10	£0.30	£0.50
Title Value:	$8.65	$25.95	$43.25	£5.80	£17.90	£30.00

CAPTAIN ATOM ANNUAL

DC Comics; 1 1987-2 1988

	$Good	$Fine	$N.Mint	£Good	£Fine	£N.Mint
1-2 48pgs	$0.30	$0.90	$1.50	£0.20	£0.60	£1.00
Title Value:	$0.60	$1.80	$3.00	£0.40	£1.20	£2.00

CAPTAIN BRITAIN

Marvel UK; nn Nov 1988

(see Excalibur)

Trade Paperback

	£Good	£Fine	£N.Mint
196pgs, reprints British issues of Captain Britain #1-14, Mighty World of Marvel #14-16; Alan Davis art	£1.25	£3.75	£6.25
(2nd print, 1990)	£1.00	£3.00	£5.00
(3rd print. Oct 1991)	£1.85	£5.55	£9.25

CAPTAIN CANUCK

Comely/CKR; 1 Jul 1975-4 Jul 1977; 4 Jul/Aug 1979-14 Mar/Apr 1981

	$Good	$Fine	$N.Mint	£Good	£Fine	£N.Mint
1 1st appearance Captain Canuck	$0.50	$1.50	$3.00	£0.30	£1.00	£2.00
2-3	$0.40	$1.25	$2.50	£0.25	£0.75	£1.50
4 1st printing, rare in the U.K. 300 copies signed and numbered, with certificate	$2.05	$6.25	$12.50	£0.80	£2.50	£5.00
4 2nd printing, extremely rare in the U.K., very rare in the U.S.; 15 copies, orange card cover, none known in the UK at time of going to press	$4.15	$12.50	$25.00	£1.65	£5.00	£10.00
4 3rd printing	$0.25	$0.75	$1.50	£0.15	£0.50	£1.00
5 origin	$0.25	$0.75	$1.50	£0.15	£0.50	£1.00
6-14	$0.20	$0.60	$1.25	£0.10	£0.35	£0.75
Title Value:	$9.80	$29.65	$59.75	£4.45	£14.15	£28.75

Note: all Non-Distributed on the news-stands in the U.K.

CAPTAIN CANUCK FIRST SUMMER SPECIAL

CKR; 1 Jul/Sep 1980

	$Good	$Fine	$N.Mint	£Good	£Fine	£N.Mint
1 ND 64pgs, Gene Day, Dave Sim pin-ups & biographies	$0.60	$1.80	$3.00	£0.40	£1.20	£2.00
Title Value:	$0.60	$1.80	$3.00	£0.40	£1.20	£2.00

CAPTAIN CARROT AND HIS AMAZING ZOO CREW

DC Comics; 1 Mar 1982-20 Nov 1983

	$Good	$Fine	$N.Mint	£Good	£Fine	£N.Mint
(see New Teen Titans #16, Oz-Wonderland War)						
1 Superman appears	$0.15	$0.45	$0.75	£0.10	£0.35	£0.60
2-11	$0.15	$0.45	$0.75	£0.10	£0.30	£0.50
12 Art Adams pin-up (his first published comic work)	$0.15	$0.45	$0.75	£0.10	£0.30	£0.50
13-19	$0.15	$0.45	$0.75	£0.10	£0.30	£0.50
20 Changeling appears	$0.15	$0.45	$0.75	£0.10	£0.30	£0.50
Title Value:	$3.00	$9.00	$15.00	£2.00	£6.05	£10.10

CAPTAIN CONFEDERACY

Steeldragon Press; 1 1986-12 1987

	$Good	$Fine	$N.Mint	£Good	£Fine	£N.Mint
1 ND Ant Boy back-up by Matt Feazell; black and white	$0.35	$1.05	$1.75	£0.25	£0.75	£1.25
2-12 ND Ant Boy back-up by Matt Feazell; black and white	$0.30	$0.90	$1.50	£0.20	£0.60	£1.00
Title Value:	$3.65	$10.95	$18.25	£2.45	£7.35	£12.25

CAPTAIN CONFEDERACY SPECIAL

Steeldragon Press; 1 1986-3 1987

	$Good	$Fine	$N.Mint	£Good	£Fine	£N.Mint
1 ND	$0.40	$1.20	$2.00	£0.25	£0.75	£1.25
2-3 ND	$0.30	$0.90	$1.50	£0.20	£0.60	£1.00
Title Value:	$1.00	$3.00	$5.00	£0.65	£1.95	£3.25

CAPTAIN CONFERACY

Marvel Comics Group/Epic,MS; 1 Nov 1991-4 Feb 1992

	$Good	$Fine	$N.Mint	£Good	£Fine	£N.Mint
1 ND computer-generated colours begin	$0.30	$0.90	$1.50	£0.20	£0.60	£1.00
2-4 ND	$0.30	$0.90	$1.50	£0.20	£0.60	£1.00
Title Value:	$1.20	$3.60	$6.00	£0.80	£2.40	£4.00

CAPTAIN EO 3-D

Eclipse, Film; (3-D Special 18) 1 Jul 1987

	$Good	$Fine	$N.Mint	£Good	£Fine	£N.Mint
1 ND adapts Michael Jackson film, Tom Yeates art, painted cover; glasses included (25% less without glasses)	$0.60	$1.80	$3.00	£0.40	£1.20	£2.00
1 Souvenir Edition, ND , treasury size	$1.20	$3.60	$6.00	£0.80	£2.40	£4.00
Title Value:	$1.80	$5.40	$9.00	£1.20	£3.60	£6.00

CAPTAIN GALLANT

Charlton, TV; 1 1955; 2 Jan 1956-4 Sep 1956

	$Good	$Fine	$N.Mint	£Good	£Fine	£N.Mint
1 ND Buster Crabbe photo feature; Don Heck art	$8.00	$24.00	$65.00	£4.35	£13.00	£35.00
2-4 ND	$6.75	$20.50	$55.00	£3.40	£10.00	£27.50
Title Value:	$28.25	$85.50	$230.00	£14.55	£43.00	£117.50

CAPTAIN GLORY

Topps,OS; 1 Apr 1993

	$Good	$Fine	$N.Mint	£Good	£Fine	£N.Mint
1 ND pre-bagged with coupon #2 for Secret City Saga #0 with chrome trading card; Steve Ditko art and Jack Kirby cover	$0.40	$1.20	$2.00	£0.25	£0.75	£1.25
1 without coupon/card ND	$0.20	$0.60	$1.00	£0.15	£0.45	£0.75
Title Value:	$0.60	$1.80	$3.00	£0.40	£1.20	£2.00

CAPTAIN HARLOCK

Eternity; 1 Oct 1989-13 Oct 1990

	$Good	$Fine	$N.Mint	£Good	£Fine	£N.Mint
1-13 ND	$0.35	$1.05	$1.75	£0.25	£0.75	£1.25
Title Value:	$4.55	$13.65	$22.75	£3.25	£9.75	£16.25

CAPTAIN HARLOCK CHRISTMAS SPECIAL

Eternity,OS; 1 Feb 1992

	$Good	$Fine	$N.Mint	£Good	£Fine	£N.Mint
1 ND	$0.50	$1.50	$2.50	£0.30	£0.90	£1.50
Title Value:	$0.50	$1.50	$2.50	£0.30	£0.90	£1.50

CAPTAIN HARLOCK: DEATHSHADOW RISING

Eternity,MS; 1 Jul 1991-6 Dec 1991

	$Good	$Fine	$N.Mint	£Good	£Fine	£N.Mint
1-6 ND	$0.35	$1.05	$1.75	£0.25	£0.75	£1.25
Title Value:	$2.10	$6.30	$10.50	£1.50	£4.50	£7.50

CAPTAIN HARLOCK: FALL OF THE EMPIRE

Eternity,MS; 1 Oct 1992-4 Dec 1992

	$Good	$Fine	$N.Mint	£Good	£Fine	£N.Mint
1-4 ND	$0.35	$1.05	$1.75	£0.25	£0.75	£1.25
Title Value:	$1.40	$4.20	$7.00	£1.00	£3.00	£5.00

CAPTAIN HARLOCK: THE MACHINE PEOPLE

Eternity; 1 Jul 1993-4 Oct 1993

	$Good	$Fine	$N.Mint	£Good	£Fine	£N.Mint
1-4 ND	$0.35	$1.05	$1.75	£0.25	£0.75	£1.25
Title Value:	$1.40	$4.20	$7.00	£1.00	£3.00	£5.00

CAPTAIN JACK, THE ADVENTURES OF

Fantagraphics; 1 Jun 1986-12 1987

	$Good	$Fine	$N.Mint	£Good	£Fine	£N.Mint
1-12 ND DS, black and white	$0.35	$1.05	$1.75	£0.25	£0.75	£1.25
Title Value:	$4.20	$12.60	$21.00	£3.00	£9.00	£15.00

CAPTAIN JOHNER AND THE ALIENS

Gold Key/Whitman; 1 Sep/Dec 1967; Whitman; 2 May 1982

(see Captain Johner)

	$Good	$Fine	$N.Mint	£Good	£Fine	£N.Mint
1 scarce though distributed in the U.K. reprints back-up from Magnus Robot Fighter #1,3,4,6-10 by Russ Manning	$2.50	$7.50	$17.50	£1.75	£5.25	£12.50
2 LD in the U.K. reprints Magnus Robot Fighter #1 by Russ Manning	$1.00	$3.00	$5.00	£1.00	£3.00	£5.00
Title Value:	$3.50	$10.50	$22.50	£2.75	£8.25	£17.50

Note: reprints from Magnus, Robot Fighter with Russ Manning art

CAPTAIN JOHNER AND THE ALIENS, THE ORIGINAL

Valiant/Western Publishing; 1 Apr 1995-2 May 1995

	$Good	$Fine	$N.Mint	£Good	£Fine	£N.Mint
1-2 ND reprints from original back-up stories in Gold Key's Magnus Robot Fighter	$0.60	$1.80	$3.00	£0.40	£1.20	£2.00
Title Value:	$1.20	$3.60	$6.00	£0.80	£2.40	£4.00

CAPTAIN JUSTICE

Marvel Comics Group,MS TV; 1 Mar 1988-2 Apr 1988

	$Good	$Fine	$N.Mint	£Good	£Fine	£N.Mint
1-2	$0.15	$0.45	$0.75	£0.10	£0.30	£0.50
Title Value:	$0.30	$0.90	$1.50	£0.20	£0.60	£1.00

CAPTAIN MARVEL

(see Adventure, DC Comics Presents, Justice League of America, Shazam!, World's Finest)

CAPTAIN MARVEL

Marvel Comics Group; 1 May 1968-19 Dec 1969; 20 Jun 1970-21 Aug 1970; 22 Sep 1972-62 May 1979

(see Marvel Graphic Novel, Marvel Spotlight, Marvel Super Heroes #12)

	$Good	$Fine	$N.Mint	£Good	£Fine	£N.Mint
1	$14.00	$43.00	$100.00	£9.25	£28.00	£65.00
2 Captain Marvel battles Super Skrull	$5.50	$17.00	$40.00	£3.20	£9.50	£22.50
3 Super Skrull appears	$4.25	$12.50	$30.00	£2.50	£7.50	£17.50
4 Captain Marvel battles Sub-Mariner	$3.55	$10.50	$25.00	£2.10	£6.25	£15.00
5	$2.85	$8.50	$20.00	£1.75	£5.25	£12.50
6	$2.10	$6.25	$15.00	£1.40	£4.25	£10.00
7-10	$2.10	$6.25	$15.00	£1.05	£3.20	£7.50
11-13	$1.40	$4.25	$10.00	£0.85	£2.55	£6.00
14 Iron Man appears	$1.40	$4.25	$10.00	£0.85	£2.55	£6.00
15	$1.40	$4.25	$10.00	£0.85	£2.55	£6.00
16	$1.10	$3.40	$8.00	£0.75	£2.35	£5.50
17 new costume; Captain America, Bucky appear	$1.10	$3.40	$8.00	£0.75	£2.35	£5.50
18-19	$1.10	$3.40	$8.00	£0.75	£2.35	£5.50
20 LD in the U.K.	$1.50	$4.50	$9.00	£1.00	£3.00	£6.00
21 Captain Marvel vs. Hulk; Gil Kane art	$1.30	$4.00	$8.00	£0.90	£2.75	£5.50
22 ND scarce in the U.K. Wayne Boring art, Gil Kane cover	$1.30	$4.00	$8.00	£1.00	£3.00	£6.00
23-24 ND scarce in the U.K. Wayne Boring art	$1.30	$4.00	$8.00	£1.00	£3.00	£6.00
25 scarce in the U.K. 1st Jim Starlin cover and art, Thanos cameo, battles many old foes inc. Hulk and Sub-Mariner	$3.30	$10.00	$20.00	£2.05	£6.25	£12.50
26 scarce in the U.K. Jim Starlin art, Captain Marvel battles Thing; 2nd full appearance of Thanos, 1st Thanos cover	$4.15	$12.50	$25.00	£2.50	£7.50	£15.00
27 Jim Starlin art, Captain Marvel batttles Super Skrull, 3rd appearance of Thanos, 1st Eros & Mentor	$3.30	$10.00	$20.00	£2.05	£6.25	£12.50
28 Jim Starlin art, part script. Avengers appear. Thanos battles Drax the Destroyer, Thanos on cover	$2.50	$7.50	$15.00	£1.65	£5.00	£10.00
29 Jim Starlin art/script, Captain Marvel gets Cosmic Powers	$1.65	$5.00	$10.00	£1.15	£3.50	£7.00
30 Jim Starlin art, Thanos in 4 panels, Captain Marvel's 1st use of Cosmic Power, Avengers appear	$1.65	$5.00	$10.00	£1.15	£3.50	£7.00
31 ND classic Jim Starlin art and Thanos War. Drax and Avengers appear	$2.05	$6.25	$12.50	£1.25	£3.75	£7.50
32 ND classic Jim Starlin art, Thanos War. Drax and Avengers appear	$2.05	$6.25	$12.50	£1.25	£3.75	£7.50
33 ND scarce in the U.K. 1st origin Thanos, Captain Marvel vs. Thanos, Jim Starlin art	$3.75	$11.00	$22.50	£2.50	£7.50	£15.00
34 last full Jim Starlin art, Avengers appear	$1.00	$3.00	$6.00	£0.65	£2.00	£4.00
35	$0.30	$1.00	$2.00	£0.20	£0.60	£1.25
36 Starlin art (3pgs), reprints 1st Captain Marvel story from Marvel Super-Heroes #12	$0.65	$2.00	$4.00	£0.40	£1.25	£2.50
37-38	$0.30	$1.00	$2.00	£0.20	£0.60	£1.25
39 origin The Watcher retold	$0.30	$1.00	$2.00	£0.20	£0.60	£1.25
40	$0.30	$1.00	$2.00	£0.20	£0.60	£1.25
41 Wrightson part inks, P. Craig Russell part inks	$0.30	$1.00	$2.00	£0.20	£0.60	£1.25
42 Drax the Destroyer appears	$0.30	$1.00	$2.00	£0.20	£0.60	£1.25
43 Wrightson part inks, Captain Marvel battles Drax	$0.30	$1.00	$2.00	£0.20	£0.60	£1.25
44 Drax appears	$0.30	$1.00	$2.00	£0.20	£0.60	£1.25
45-46	$0.30	$1.00	$2.00	£0.20	£0.60	£1.25
47 Human Torch appears	$0.30	$1.00	$2.00	£0.20	£0.60	£1.25
48	$0.30	$1.00	$2.00	£0.20	£0.60	£1.25
49 ND part Jim Starlin art	$0.30	$1.00	$2.00	£0.25	£0.75	£1.50
50 ND Captain Marvel and the Avengers battles the Super Adaptoid	$0.30	$1.00	$2.00	£0.25	£0.75	£1.50
51 ND Avengers appear	$0.30	$1.00	$2.00	£0.25	£0.75	£1.50
52 ND	$0.30	$1.00	$2.00	£0.25	£0.75	£1.50
53 Inhumans appear	$0.30	$1.00	$2.00	£0.20	£0.60	£1.25
54 Wonder Man appears	$0.30	$1.00	$2.00	£0.20	£0.60	£1.25
55-56 Broderick art	$0.30	$1.00	$2.00	£0.20	£0.60	£1.25
57 Captain Marvel battles Thor, Thanos appearance in flashback	$0.55	$1.75	$3.50	£0.25	£0.75	£1.50
58 Broderick art, Drax returns	$0.30	$1.00	$2.00	£0.20	£0.60	£1.25
59-62 Broderick art, Drax appears	$0.30	$1.00	$2.00	£0.20	£0.60	£1.25
Title Value:	$93.15	$284.35	$626.00	£58.80	£177.65	£389.50

	$Good	$Fine	$N.Mint	£Good	£Fine	£N.Mint
Trade Paperback (Dec 1990), reprints Iron Man #55, Marvel Feature #12, Captain Marvel #25-34, Avengers Annual #7 Marvel Two-in-One Annual #2				£1.40	£4.20	£7.00

CAPTAIN MARVEL

MF; 1 Jun 1966-4 Nov 1966
(becomes Captain Marvel Presents the Terrible 5)

	$Good	$Fine	$N.Mint	£Good	£Fine	£N.Mint
1 LD in the U.K. giant, origin told	*$2.50*	*$7.50*	*$17.50*	£1.75	£5.25	£12.50
2 LD in the U.K. giant	*$1.25*	*$3.85*	*$9.00*	£0.85	£2.55	£6.00
3 LD in the U.K. giant (titled ...Fights The Bat)	*$1.40*	*$4.25*	*$10.00*	£1.00	£3.00	£7.00
4 LD in the U.K. giant	*$1.25*	*$3.85*	*$9.00*	£0.85	£2.55	£6.00
Title Value:	*$6.40*	*$19.45*	*$45.50*	£4.45	£13.35	£31.50

CAPTAIN MARVEL (2ND SERIES)

Marvel Comics Group; 1 Dec 1995-6 May 1996

	$Good	$Fine	$N.Mint	£Good	£Fine	£N.Mint
1 ND Fabian Nicieza script, Ed Benes art on the son of Mar-vell; foil-stamped cover	*$0.60*	*$1.80*	*$3.00*	£0.40	£1.20	£2.00
2-6 ND	*$0.40*	*$1.20*	*$2.00*	£0.25	£0.75	£1.25
Title Value:	*$2.60*	*$7.80*	*$13.00*	£1.65	£4.95	£8.25

CAPTAIN MARVEL ADVENTURES

Fawcett; nn Spring 1941-150 Nov 1953
(see Whiz Comics)

	$Good	$Fine	$N.Mint	£Good	£Fine	£N.Mint
nn scarce in the U.K. (#1), Jack Kirby cover and art	*$3000.00*	*$9000.00*	*$30000.00*	£2000.00	£6000.00	£20000.00
2 Jack Kirby cover and art	*$425.00*	*$1275.00*	*$3400.00*	£280.00	£850.00	£2275.00
3 Jack Kirby cover and art	*$255.00*	*$760.00*	*$2050.00*	£170.00	£510.00	£1375.00
4 Jack Kirby cover and art	*$165.00*	*$500.00*	*$1350.00*	£110.00	£335.00	£900.00
5	*$120.00*	*$365.00*	*$975.00*	£80.00	£240.00	£650.00
6-10	*$100.00*	*$300.00*	*$800.00*	£65.00	£200.00	£535.00
11-15	*$90.00*	*$270.00*	*$725.00*	£60.00	£180.00	£485.00
16	*$67.50*	*$205.00*	*$550.00*	£47.00	£140.00	£375.00
17 painted cover - "Captain Marvel Smacks the Axis"	*$67.50*	*$205.00*	*$550.00*	£47.00	£140.00	£375.00
18 1st appearance Mary Marvel, painted cover	*$175.00*	*$520.00*	*$1400.00*	£115.00	£355.00	£950.00
19 Christmas cover	*$65.00*	*$195.00*	*$525.00*	£44.00	£130.00	£350.00
20	*$65.00*	*$195.00*	*$525.00*	£44.00	£130.00	£350.00
21	*$62.50*	*$185.00*	*$500.00*	£42.00	£125.00	£335.00
22 1st appearance Mr. Mind	*$80.00*	*$240.00*	*$650.00*	£52.50	£160.00	£435.00
23-25	*$55.00*	*$165.00*	*$450.00*	£38.00	£110.00	£300.00
26 patriotic flag cover	*$50.00*	*$150.00*	*$350.00*	£34.00	£100.00	£235.00
27-30	*$50.00*	*$150.00*	*$350.00*	£34.00	£100.00	£235.00
31-35	*$48.00*	*$140.00*	*$335.00*	£32.00	£95.00	£225.00
36-40	*$39.00*	*$115.00*	*$275.00*	£26.00	£77.50	£185.00
41	*$32.00*	*$95.00*	*$225.00*	£21.00	£62.50	£150.00
42 Christmas cover	*$32.00*	*$95.00*	*$225.00*	£21.00	£62.50	£150.00
43-50	*$32.00*	*$95.00*	*$225.00*	£21.00	£62.50	£150.00
51-53	*$25.00*	*$75.00*	*$175.00*	£17.00	£50.00	£120.00
54 68pgs	*$25.00*	*$75.00*	*$175.00*	£17.00	£50.00	£120.00
55-60	*$25.00*	*$75.00*	*$175.00*	£17.00	£50.00	£120.00
61 The Cult of the Curse story begins (ends #66)	*$29.00*	*$85.00*	*$200.00*	£19.00	£57.50	£135.00
62-65	*$25.00*	*$75.00*	*$175.00*	£17.00	£50.00	£120.00
66 famous Atomic War story	*$25.00*	*$75.00*	*$175.00*	£17.00	£50.00	£120.00
67-71	*$25.00*	*$75.00*	*$175.00*	£17.00	£50.00	£120.00
72 "Flash" cover (running in mid-air with speed-lines behind him)	*$25.00*	*$75.00*	*$175.00*	£17.00	£50.00	£120.00
73-77	*$25.00*	*$75.00*	*$175.00*	£17.00	£50.00	£120.00
78 1st appearance Mr. Atom (robot), origin Mr. Tawney	*$28.00*	*$82.50*	*$195.00*	£18.50	£55.00	£130.00
79	*$25.00*	*$75.00*	*$175.00*	£17.00	£50.00	£120.00
80 origin Captain Marvel re-told	*$45.00*	*$135.00*	*$315.00*	£30.00	£90.00	£210.00
81-84	*$21.00*	*$62.50*	*$150.00*	£14.00	£43.00	£100.00
85	*$25.00*	*$75.00*	*$175.00*	£17.00	£50.00	£120.00
86-90	*$21.00*	*$62.50*	*$150.00*	£14.00	£43.00	£100.00
91-99	*$20.00*	*$60.00*	*$140.00*	£13.50	£41.00	£95.00
100 origin re-told	*$43.00*	*$125.00*	*$300.00*	£29.00	£85.00	£200.00
101-120	*$20.00*	*$60.00*	*$140.00*	£13.50	£41.00	£95.00
121 origin re-told	*$27.00*	*$80.00*	*$190.00*	£18.50	£55.00	£130.00
122-137	*$20.00*	*$60.00*	*$140.00*	£13.50	£41.00	£95.00
138 flying saucer paranoia story	*$21.00*	*$62.50*	*$150.00*	£14.00	£43.00	£100.00
139-149	*$18.50*	*$55.00*	*$130.00*	£12.00	£36.00	£85.00
150 scarce in the U.S, very scarce in the U.K.	*$32.00*	*$95.00*	*$225.00*	£21.00	£62.50	£150.00
Title Value:	*$8885.00*	*$26597.50*	*$74055.00*	£5932.00	£17808.50	£49620.00

Note: though not officially distributed on the news-stands in the U.K. many copies were sent over in bundles as ballast on ships. There have been hundreds of instances of copies with British pence stamps on the cover

CAPTAIN MARVEL GIANT SIZE

Marvel Comics Group; 1 Dec 1975

	$Good	$Fine	$N.Mint	£Good	£Fine	£N.Mint
1 ND scarce in the U.K. 68pgs, all reprint from Captain Marvel #19, #20 and #21 (Captain Marvel vs. Hulk), all Gil Kane art	*$1.50*	*$4.50*	*$9.00*	£1.00	£3.00	£6.00
Title Value:	*$1.50*	*$4.50*	*$9.00*	£1.00	£3.00	£6.00

CAPTAIN MARVEL JR.

Fawcett; 1 Nov 1942-119 Jun 1953

	$Good	$Fine	$N.Mint	£Good	£Fine	£N.Mint
1 origin of Captain Marvel Jnr. retold	*$550.00*	*$1650.00*	*$5000.00*	£370.00	£1100.00	£3350.00
2 Captain Marvel Jnr. meets Captain Nippon (politically correct or what!)	*$185.00*	*$560.00*	*$1500.00*	£125.00	£375.00	£1000.00
3	*$100.00*	*$300.00*	*$800.00*	£65.00	£200.00	£535.00
4 classic "shell-burst" cover	*$110.00*	*$335.00*	*$900.00*	£75.00	£225.00	£600.00
5	*$92.50*	*$280.00*	*$750.00*	£62.50	£185.00	£500.00
6-8	*$65.00*	*$195.00*	*$525.00*	£44.00	£130.00	£350.00
9 patriotic flag cover	*$65.00*	*$195.00*	*$525.00*	£44.00	£130.00	£350.00
10 Adolf Hitler on cover	*$65.00*	*$195.00*	*$525.00*	£44.00	£130.00	£350.00
11-13	*$52.50*	*$155.00*	*$425.00*	£36.00	£105.00	£285.00
14 Christmas cover	*$52.50*	*$155.00*	*$425.00*	£36.00	£105.00	£285.00
15-20	*$52.50*	*$155.00*	*$425.00*	£36.00	£105.00	£285.00
21-24	*$39.00*	*$115.00*	*$315.00*	£26.00	£77.50	£210.00
25 patriotic flag cover	*$39.00*	*$115.00*	*$315.00*	£26.00	£77.50	£210.00
26-27	*$39.00*	*$115.00*	*$315.00*	£26.00	£77.50	£210.00
28 Captain Marvel Jnr. vs. Sivana	*$39.00*	*$115.00*	*$315.00*	£26.00	£77.50	£210.00
29-30	*$39.00*	*$115.00*	*$315.00*	£26.00	£77.50	£210.00

Captain America Comics #10

Captain Carrot #3

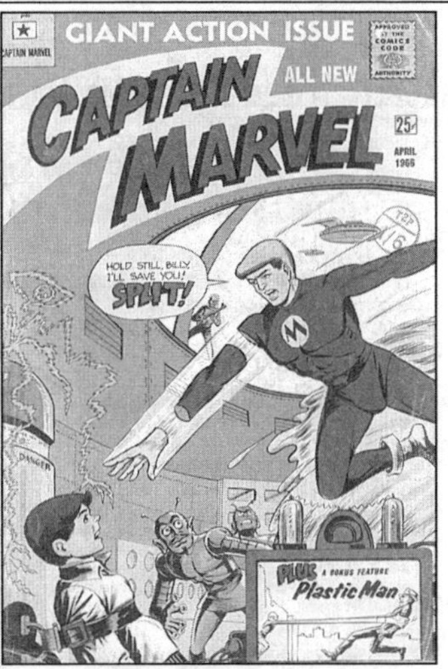

Captain Marvel (MF) #1

	$Good	$Fine	$N.Mint	£Good	£Fine	£N.Mint
31-33	$21.50	$65.00	$175.00	£15.00	£45.00	£120.00
35 Captain Marvel Jnr. vs. Sivana; issue has #35 on cover, #34 inside	$21.50	$65.00	$175.00	£15.00	£45.00	£120.00
36-40	$21.50	$65.00	$175.00	£15.00	£45.00	£120.00
41-75	$20.00	$60.00	$140.00	£13.50	£41.00	£95.00
76-99	$15.00	$45.00	$105.00	£10.00	£30.00	£70.00
100 Captain MArvel Jnr. vs. Sivana Jnr.	$17.50	$52.50	$125.00	£12.00	£36.00	£85.00
101-119	$15.00	$45.00	$105.00	£10.00	£30.00	£70.00
Title Value:	$3833.50	$11472.50	$30090.00	£2587.00	£7726.00	£20185.00

CAPTAIN MARVEL PRESENTS THE TERRIBLE 5

MF; 1 Aug 1966; 5 Sep 1967
(previously Captain Marvel)

	$Good	$Fine	$N.Mint	£Good	£Fine	£N.Mint
1 distributed in the U.K. giant	$2.10	$6.25	$15.00	£1.40	£4.25	£10.00
5 distributed in the U.K. giant	$1.25	$3.85	$9.00	£0.85	£2.55	£6.00
Title Value:	$3.35	$10.10	$24.00	£2.25	£6.80	£16.00

CAPTAIN MARVEL SPECIAL

Marvel Comics Group,OS; 1 Nov 1989

	$Good	$Fine	$N.Mint	£Good	£Fine	£N.Mint
1 ND 48pgs, new career and new powers for female version	$0.40	$1.20	$2.00	£0.25	£0.75	£1.25
Title Value:	$0.40	$1.20	$2.00	£0.25	£0.75	£1.25

CAPTAIN MARVEL, DEATH OF

Marvel Comics Group,OS; nn Oct 1994

	$Good	$Fine	$N.Mint	£Good	£Fine	£N.Mint
nn ND 64pgs, reprints the first Marvel Graphic Novel with new cover by Jim Starlin	$1.50	$4.50	$7.50	£1.00	£3.00	£5.00
Title Value:	$1.50	$4.50	$7.50	£1.00	£3.00	£5.00

CAPTAIN MARVEL, THE LIFE OF

Marvel Comics Group,MS; 1 Aug 1985-5 Dec 1985
(see Captain Marvel)

	$Good	$Fine	$N.Mint	£Good	£Fine	£N.Mint
1 ND Jim Starlin reprints from Captain Marvel begin, Baxter paper	$0.60	$1.80	$3.00	£0.40	£1.20	£2.00
2-5 ND	$0.60	$1.80	$3.00	£0.40	£1.20	£2.00
Title Value:	$3.00	$9.00	$15.00	£2.00	£6.00	£10.00
The Life of Captain Marvel (Dec 1995) Trade paperback 224pgs, collects 5 issue mini-series				£2.00	£6.00	£10.00

CAPTAIN MARVEL: SPEAKING WITHOUT CONCERN

Marvel Comics Group,OS; nn Feb 1994

	$Good	$Fine	$N.Mint	£Good	£Fine	£N.Mint
nn ND 48pgs, female Captain Marvel story about racism	$0.40	$1.20	$2.00	£0.25	£0.75	£1.25
Title Value:	$0.40	$1.20	$2.00	£0.25	£0.75	£1.25

CAPTAIN NAUTICUS AND THE OCEAN FORCE

Entity Comics/National Maritime Center; 1 Oct 1994-3 1995

	$Good	$Fine	$N.Mint	£Good	£Fine	£N.Mint
1-3 ND Bill Maus script and art	$0.60	$1.80	$3.00	£0.40	£1.20	£2.00
Title Value:	$1.80	$5.40	$9.00	£1.20	£3.60	£6.00

CAPTAIN PARAGON

AC Comics,MS; 1 Dec 1983-4 Jun 1984
(see Americomics, Bill Black's Fun Comics)

	$Good	$Fine	$N.Mint	£Good	£Fine	£N.Mint
1-4 ND	$0.30	$0.90	$1.50	£0.20	£0.60	£1.00
Title Value:	$1.20	$3.60	$6.00	£0.80	£2.40	£4.00

CAPTAIN PARAGON & THE SENTINELS OF JUSTICE

AC Comics; 1 Apr 1985-6 1986
(becomes Sentinels of Justice)

	$Good	$Fine	$N.Mint	£Good	£Fine	£N.Mint
1-6 ND	$0.35	$1.05	$1.75	£0.25	£0.75	£1.25
Title Value:	$2.10	$6.30	$10.50	£1.50	£4.50	£7.50

CAPTAIN PLANET

Marvel Comics Group,MS; 1 Oct 1991-12 Oct 1992

	$Good	$Fine	$N.Mint	£Good	£Fine	£N.Mint
1 based on U.S. animated series	$0.15	$0.45	$0.75	£0.10	£0.35	£0.60
2-4	$0.15	$0.45	$0.75	£0.10	£0.35	£0.60
5 $1.25 cover begins	$0.15	$0.45	$0.75	£0.10	£0.35	£0.60
6-12	$0.15	$0.45	$0.75	£0.10	£0.35	£0.60
Title Value:	$1.80	$5.40	$9.00	£1.20	£4.20	£7.20

CAPTAIN POWER (AND THE SOLDIERS OF THE FUTURE)

Continuity; 1 Aug 1988-2 Jan 1989

	$Good	$Fine	$N.Mint	£Good	£Fine	£N.Mint
1-2 ND Neal Adams pencils, co-plot and cover	$0.35	$1.05	$1.75	£0.25	£0.75	£1.25
Title Value:	$0.70	$2.10	$3.50	£0.50	£1.50	£2.50

CAPTAIN SATAN

Millennium; 1 Jul 1994-2 1994

	$Good	$Fine	$N.Mint	£Good	£Fine	£N.Mint
1 ND Steven Seagle script, Sean Shaw art	$0.60	$1.80	$3.00	£0.40	£1.20	£2.00
1 Collectors Edition, ND with Matt Wagner cover	$0.80	$2.40	$4.00	£0.50	£1.50	£2.50
2 ND	$0.60	$1.80	$3.00	£0.40	£1.20	£2.00
Title Value:	$2.00	$6.00	$10.00	£1.30	£3.90	£6.50

CAPTAIN SAVAGE AND HIS LEATHERNECK RAIDERS

Marvel Comics Group; 1 Jan 1968-19 Mar 1970
(see Sgt. Fury #10)

	$Good	$Fine	$N.Mint	£Good	£Fine	£N.Mint
1 Sgt. Fury cameo	$1.75	$5.25	$12.50	£1.05	£3.20	£7.50
2-3	$1.05	$3.20	$7.50	£0.50	£1.50	£3.50
4 origin of Hydra	$1.05	$3.20	$7.50	£0.50	£1.50	£3.50
5-6	$1.05	$3.20	$7.50	£0.50	£1.50	£3.50
7 Ben Grimm appears	$1.05	$3.20	$7.50	£0.50	£1.50	£3.50
8-10 scarce in the U.K.	$1.05	$3.20	$7.50	£0.50	£1.50	£3.50
11 Sgt. Fury appears	$0.85	$2.55	$6.00	£0.35	£1.05	£2.50
12-19	$0.85	$2.55	$6.00	£0.35	£1.05	£2.50
Title Value:	$18.85	$57.00	$134.00	£8.70	£26.15	£61.50

CAPTAIN STORM

National Periodical Publications; 1 May/Jun 1964-18 Mar/Apr 1967
(see G.I. Combat, Losers Special, Unknown Soldier)

	$Good	$Fine	$N.Mint	£Good	£Fine	£N.Mint
1	$3.55	$10.50	$25.00	£1.75	£5.25	£12.50
2	$2.10	$6.25	$15.00	£1.05	£3.20	£7.50
3 Kubert art	$2.10	$6.25	$15.00	£1.05	£3.20	£7.50
4-5	$2.10	$6.25	$15.00	£1.05	£3.20	£7.50
6 Kubert art	$2.10	$6.25	$15.00	£1.05	£3.20	£7.50
7-10	$2.10	$6.25	$15.00	£1.05	£3.20	£7.50
11	$1.75	$5.25	$12.50	£0.85	£2.55	£6.00
12 Kubert cover art	$1.75	$5.25	$12.50	£0.85	£2.55	£6.00
13 Kubert art	$1.75	$5.25	$12.50	£0.85	£2.55	£6.00
14-17	$1.75	$5.25	$12.50	£0.85	£2.55	£6.00
18 scarce in the U.K.	$1.75	$5.25	$12.50	£1.00	£3.00	£7.00
Title Value:	$36.45	$108.75	$260.00	£18.15	£54.90	£129.00

CAPTAIN THUNDER

Hero; 1 Aug 1992-3 Mar 1993

	$Good	$Fine	$N.Mint	£Good	£Fine	£N.Mint
1-3 ND Roy and Dann Thomas script	$0.40	$1.20	$2.00	£0.25	£0.75	£1.25
Title Value:	$1.20	$3.60	$6.00	£0.75	£2.25	£3.75

CAPTAIN THUNDER & BLUE BOLT

Hero; 1 Sep 1987-12 1988

	$Good	$Fine	$N.Mint	£Good	£Fine	£N.Mint
1-12 ND	$0.40	$1.20	$2.00	£0.25	£0.75	£1.25
Title Value:	$4.80	$14.40	$24.00	£3.00	£9.00	£15.00
The Complete Captain Thunder (Mar 1993) reprints 12 issue mini-series plus #1 & 2 of 2nd series				£3.00	£9.00	£15.00

CAPTAIN THUNDER (2ND SERIES)

Heroic Publishing; 1 Jan 1995

	$Good	$Fine	$N.Mint	£Good	£Fine	£N.Mint
1 ND original stories of Captain Thunder and Blue Bolt reprinted	$0.40	$1.20	$2.00	£0.25	£0.75	£1.25
Title Value:	$0.40	$1.20	$2.00	£0.25	£0.75	£1.25

CAPTAIN VENTURE AND THE LAND BENEATH THE SEA

Gold Key; 1 Oct 1968-2 Oct 1969

	$Good	$Fine	$N.Mint	£Good	£Fine	£N.Mint
1 LD in the U.K. Space Family Robinson reprint	$5.00	$15.00	$35.00	£3.20	£9.50	£22.50
2 LD in the U.K.	$4.25	$12.50	$30.00	£2.85	£8.50	£20.00
Title Value:	$9.25	$27.50	$65.00	£6.05	£18.00	£42.50

CAPTAIN VICTORY AND THE GALACTIC RANGERS

Pacific; 1 Nov 1981-13 Nov 1983

	$Good	$Fine	$N.Mint	£Good	£Fine	£N.Mint
1-2 ND Jack Kirby art	$0.25	$0.75	$1.25	£0.15	£0.45	£0.75
3 ND Ms. Mystic back-up, Neal Adams art	$0.30	$0.90	$1.50	£0.20	£0.60	£1.00
4-5 ND Jack Kirby art	$0.25	$0.75	$1.25	£0.15	£0.45	£0.75
6 ND Jack Kirby art, Missing Man by Steve Ditko	$0.25	$0.75	$1.25	£0.15	£0.45	£0.75
7-10 ND Jack Kirby art	$0.25	$0.75	$1.25	£0.15	£0.45	£0.75
11 ND origin, Jack Kirby, Conrad art	$0.25	$0.75	$1.25	£0.15	£0.45	£0.75
12-13 ND Jack Kirby art	$0.25	$0.75	$1.25	£0.15	£0.45	£0.75
Title Value:	$3.30	$9.90	$16.50	£2.00	£6.00	£10.00

CAPTAIN VICTORY SPECIAL

Pacific; 1 Oct 1983

	$Good	$Fine	$N.Mint	£Good	£Fine	£N.Mint
1 ND Jack Kirby cover and art	$0.25	$0.75	$1.25	£0.15	£0.45	£0.75
Title Value:	$0.25	$0.75	$1.25	£0.15	£0.45	£0.75

CAR WARRIORS

Marvel Comics Group/Epic,MS; 1 Jun 1991-4 Sep 1991

	$Good	$Fine	$N.Mint	£Good	£Fine	£N.Mint
1-4 ND	$0.40	$1.20	$2.00	£0.25	£0.75	£1.25
Title Value:	$1.60	$4.80	$8.00	£1.00	£3.00	£5.00

CARAVAN KIDD

Dark Horse; 1 Jul 1992-10 Apr 1993

	$Good	$Fine	$N.Mint	£Good	£Fine	£N.Mint
1 ND Johji Manabe script/art begins	$0.50	$1.50	$2.50	£0.30	£0.90	£1.50
2-10 ND	$0.50	$1.50	$2.50	£0.30	£0.90	£1.50
Title Value:	$5.00	$15.00	$25.00	£3.00	£9.00	£15.00

CARAVAN KIDD HOLIDAY SPECIAL

Dark Horse,OS; 1 Nov 1993

	$Good	$Fine	$N.Mint	£Good	£Fine	£N.Mint
1 ND Johji Manabe script and art, black and white	$0.50	$1.50	$2.50	£0.30	£0.90	£1.50
Title Value:	$0.50	$1.50	$2.50	£0.30	£0.90	£1.50

CARAVAN KIDD PART 2

Dark Horse,MS; 1 May 1993-10 Apr 1994

	$Good	$Fine	$N.Mint	£Good	£Fine	£N.Mint
1-10 ND black and white	$0.50	$1.50	$2.50	£0.30	£0.90	£1.50
Title Value:	$5.00	$15.00	$25.00	£3.00	£9.00	£15.00

CARAVAN KIDD PART 3

Dark Horse,MS; 1 May 1994-8 Dec 1994

	$Good	$Fine	$N.Mint	£Good	£Fine	£N.Mint
1-6 ND black and white	$0.50	$1.50	$2.50	£0.30	£0.90	£1.50
7 ND 48pgs, black and white	$0.60	$1.80	$3.00	£0.40	£1.20	£2.00
8 ND black and white	$0.50	$1.50	$2.50	£0.30	£0.90	£1.50
Title Value:	$4.10	$12.30	$20.50	£2.50	£7.50	£12.50

CARAVAN KIDD VALENTINE'S DAY SPECIAL
Dark Horse,OS; 1 Feb 1994

Issue	$Good	$Fine	$N.Mint	£Good	£Fine	£N.Mint
1 ND Johji Manabe script and art, black and white	$0.50	$1.50	$2.50	£0.30	£0.90	£1.50
Title Value:	$0.50	$1.50	$2.50	£0.30	£0.90	£1.50

CARE BEARS
Marvel Comics Group/Star, TV; 1 Nov 1985-20 Jan 1990

Issue	$Good	$Fine	$N.Mint	£Good	£Fine	£N.Mint
1-20 less common in the U.K.	$0.15	$0.45	$0.75	£0.10	£0.30	£0.50
Title Value:	$3.00	$9.00	$15.00	£2.00	£6.00	£10.00

CARNAGE
Eternity; 1,2 1987

Issue	$Good	$Fine	$N.Mint	£Good	£Fine	£N.Mint
1-2 ND	$0.40	$1.20	$2.00	£0.25	£0.75	£1.25
Title Value:	$0.80	$2.40	$4.00	£0.50	£1.50	£2.50

CARNAGE: IT'S A WONDERFUL LIFE
Marvel Comics Group,OS; nn Oct 1996

Issue	$Good	$Fine	$N.Mint	£Good	£Fine	£N.Mint
nn ND David Quinn script, Kyle Hotz art	$0.50	$1.50	$2.50	£0.30	£0.90	£1.50
Title Value:	$0.50	$1.50	$2.50	£0.30	£0.90	£1.50

CARNAGE: MINDBOMB
Marvel Comics Group,OS; 1 Feb 1996

Issue	$Good	$Fine	$N.Mint	£Good	£Fine	£N.Mint
1 ND Warren Ellis script, Kyle Hotz art; foil stamped cover	$0.60	$1.80	$3.00	£0.40	£1.20	£2.00
Title Value:	$0.60	$1.80	$3.00	£0.40	£1.20	£2.00

CARNIVAL OF SOULS
Malibu,OS; 1 Sep 1991

Issue	$Good	$Fine	$N.Mint	£Good	£Fine	£N.Mint
1 ND 48pgs, squarebound, black and white horror anthology	$0.90	$2.70	$4.50	£0.60	£1.80	£3.00
Title Value:	$0.90	$2.70	$4.50	£0.60	£1.80	£3.00

CASES OF SHERLOCK HOLMES
Renegade/Northstar; 1 May 1986-24 1990 ?

Issue	$Good	$Fine	$N.Mint	£Good	£Fine	£N.Mint
1 ND Dan Day art begins	$0.40	$1.20	$2.00	£0.25	£0.75	£1.25
2-24 ND	$0.40	$1.20	$2.00	£0.25	£0.75	£1.25
Title Value:	$9.60	$28.80	$48.00	£6.00	£18.00	£30.00
Vol I Collection Trade paperback, reprints issues #1-5				£1.00	£3.00	£5.00
Vol II Collection Trade paperback, reprints issues #6-9				£1.00	£3.00	£5.00

Note: all adaptations of Sir Arthur Conan Doyle stories

CASEY JONES & RAPHAEL
Mirage Studios; 1 Oct 1994-5 1995

Issue	$Good	$Fine	$N.Mint	£Good	£Fine	£N.Mint
1-5 ND Kevin Eastman script, Simon Bisley art	$0.50	$1.50	$2.50	£0.30	£0.90	£1.50
Title Value:	$2.50	$7.50	$12.50	£1.50	£4.50	£7.50

CASPER
Marvel Comics Group; 1 Apr 1996-3 Jun 1996

Issue	$Good	$Fine	$N.Mint	£Good	£Fine	£N.Mint
1-3 ND based on Saturday morning US TV cartoon	$0.30	$0.90	$1.50	£0.20	£0.60	£1.00
Title Value:	$0.90	$2.70	$4.50	£0.60	£1.80	£3.00

CASPER, THE FRIENDLY GHOST
Harvey; 1 Aug 1958-224 Oct 1982; 225 Oct 1986-253 1989

Issue	$Good	$Fine	$N.Mint	£Good	£Fine	£N.Mint
1 scarce in the U.K.	$32.00	$95.00	$225.00	£21.00	£62.50	£150.00
2 scarce in the U.K.	$15.00	$45.00	$105.00	£10.00	£30.00	£70.00
3-5 scarce in the U.K.	$8.50	$26.00	$60.00	£5.50	£17.00	£40.00
6-10	$7.00	$21.00	$50.00	£4.60	£13.50	£32.50
11-20	$5.00	$15.00	$35.00	£3.20	£9.50	£22.50
21-30	$2.85	$8.50	$20.00	£1.75	£5.25	£12.50
31-50	$1.75	$5.25	$12.50	£1.05	£3.20	£7.50
51-100	$1.30	$4.00	$8.00	£0.65	£2.00	£4.00
101-125	$1.00	$3.00	$6.00	£0.40	£1.25	£2.50
126-159	$1.00	$3.00	$6.00	£0.30	£1.00	£2.00
160-163 giants	$1.50	$4.50	$7.50	£0.60	£1.80	£3.00
164-175	$0.50	$1.50	$2.50	£0.30	£0.90	£1.50
176-200	$0.50	$1.50	$2.50	£0.25	£0.75	£1.25
201-210	$0.40	$1.20	$2.00	£0.20	£0.60	£1.00
211-224	$0.40	$1.20	$2.00	£0.15	£0.45	£0.75
225-253	$0.40	$1.20	$2.00	£0.10	£0.35	£0.60
Title Value:	$390.70	$1177.10	$2526.50	£212.95	£646.95	£1432.15

Note: most issues distributed on the news-stands in the U.K. though more irregularly after #225

CASUAL HEROES
Image,MS; 1 Jan 1996-5 May 1996 ?

Issue	$Good	$Fine	$N.Mint	£Good	£Fine	£N.Mint
1-5 ND Kevin McCarthy script and art with John Strangeland; Steve Rude covers	$0.50	$1.50	$2.50	£0.30	£0.90	£1.50
Title Value:	$2.50	$7.50	$12.50	£1.50	£4.50	£7.50

CAT AND MOUSE
Aircel; 1 Mar 1990-18 Nov 1991

Issue	$Good	$Fine	$N.Mint	£Good	£Fine	£N.Mint
1 ND 48pgs, squarebound; black and white begins	$0.40	$1.20	$2.00	£0.25	£0.75	£1.25
2-18 ND	$0.40	$1.20	$2.00	£0.25	£0.75	£1.25
Title Value:	$7.20	$21.60	$36.00	£4.50	£13.50	£22.50
Collection 1, reprints #1-4				£1.00	£3.00	£5.00
Hardcover, reprints early issues				£2.50	£7.50	£12.50
Collection 2, reprints #5-8				£1.00	£3.00	£5.00
Tooth and Nail Trade paperback (Jan 1993) reprints issues #9-12				£0.75	£2.25	£3.75

CAT CLAW
Eternity; 1 Sep 1990-9 May 1991

Issue	$Good	$Fine	$N.Mint	£Good	£Fine	£N.Mint
1 ND black and white begins	$0.50	$1.50	$2.50	£0.30	£0.90	£1.50
1 2nd printing ND	$0.40	$1.20	$2.00	£0.25	£0.75	£1.25
2 ND	$0.50	$1.50	$2.50	£0.30	£0.90	£1.50
3 ND pre-bagged (25% less if non-bagged)	$0.50	$1.50	$2.50	£0.40	£1.20	£2.00
4-5 ND	$0.50	$1.50	$2.50	£0.30	£0.90	£1.50
6-9 ND	$0.40	$1.20	$2.00	£0.25	£0.75	£1.25
Title Value:	$4.50	$13.50	$22.50	£2.85	£8.55	£14.25
Graphic Album (Aug 1991)				£1.00	£3.00	£5.00

CAT TALES
Eternity,OS; 1 May 1989

Issue	$Good	$Fine	$N.Mint	£Good	£Fine	£N.Mint
1 ND Felix the Cat in 3-D	$0.50	$1.50	$2.50	£0.30	£0.90	£1.50
Title Value:	$0.50	$1.50	$2.50	£0.30	£0.90	£1.50

CAT, BEWARE! THE CLAWS OF THE
Marvel Comics Group; 1 Nov 1972-4 Jun 1973

Issue	$Good	$Fine	$N.Mint	£Good	£Fine	£N.Mint
1 ND origin and 1st appearance The Cat (later becomes Tigra), Severin/Wood art	$2.90	$8.75	$17.50	£1.25	£3.75	£7.50
2 ND Severin inks, The Owl appears	$1.50	$4.50	$9.00	£0.80	£2.50	£5.00
3 ND Bill Everett inks	$1.50	$4.50	$9.00	£0.80	£2.50	£5.00
4 ND Jim Starlin art, part reprint from X-Men #57, Weiss inks	$1.50	$4.50	$9.00	£0.80	£2.50	£5.00
Title Value:	$7.40	$22.25	$44.50	£3.65	£11.25	£22.50

CATALYST: AGENTS OF CHANGE
Dark Horse/Comics Greatest World; 1 Feb 1994-7 Sep 1994

Issue	$Good	$Fine	$N.Mint	£Good	£Fine	£N.Mint
1-7 ND spin-off from Comics' Greatest World series	$0.40	$1.20	$2.00	£0.25	£0.75	£1.25
Title Value:	$2.80	$8.40	$14.00	£1.75	£5.25	£8.75

CATFIGHT
Lightning Comics/Insomnia Press,OS; 1 Jun 1995

Issue	$Good	$Fine	$N.Mint	£Good	£Fine	£N.Mint
1 ND Hellina appears	$0.70	$2.10	$3.50	£0.40	£1.20	£2.00
1 Gold Edition, ND (Jun 1995)	$1.20	$3.60	$6.00	£0.50	£1.50	£2.50
1 Signed & Numbered Edition, ND (May 1995) - pre-bagged in mylar, signed by Steven Zyskowski; limited to 1,500 copies	$1.00	$3.00	$5.00	£0.70	£2.10	£3.50
Title Value:	$2.90	$8.70	$14.50	£1.60	£4.80	£8.00

CATFIGHT: DREAM INTO ACTION
Lightning Comics,OS; 1 Mar 1996

Issue	$Good	$Fine	$N.Mint	£Good	£Fine	£N.Mint
1 ND guest-starring Creed; black and white	$0.55	$1.65	$2.75	£0.35	£1.05	£1.75
1 Commemorative Edition, ND pre-bagged with platinum metallic ink cover with certificate	$1.20	$3.60	$6.00	£0.80	£2.40	£4.00
1 Nude Cover A, ND art by Paul Abrams and Gary Barnes	$2.00	$6.00	$10.00	£1.30	£3.90	£6.50
1 Nude Cover B, ND art by John Cleary	$2.00	$6.00	$10.00	£1.30	£3.90	£6.50
Title Value:	$5.75	$17.25	$28.75	£3.75	£11.25	£18.75

CATFIGHT: DREAM WARRIOR
Lightning Comics,OS; 1 Jun 1995

Issue	$Good	$Fine	$N.Mint	£Good	£Fine	£N.Mint
1 ND Steven Zyskowski script; black and white	$0.60	$1.80	$3.00	£0.35	£1.05	£1.75
1 Variant Cover Edition, ND limited to 25% of the print run	$0.90	$2.70	$4.50	£0.60	£1.80	£3.00
Title Value:	$1.50	$4.50	$7.50	£0.95	£2.85	£4.75

CATMAN ASHCAN EDITION
AC Comics; nn Apr 1995; 2 Feb 1996

Issue	$Good	$Fine	$N.Mint	£Good	£Fine	£N.Mint
nn ND black and white, cover by L.B. Cole; 2,000 copies	$1.00	$3.00	$5.00	£0.70	£2.10	£3.50
2 ND available in bagged and un-bagged editions	$1.20	$3.60	$6.00	£0.90	£2.70	£4.50
Title Value:	$2.20	$6.60	$11.00	£1.60	£4.80	£8.00

CATSEYE AGENCY
Rip Off Press; 1 Jul 1992

Issue	$Good	$Fine	$N.Mint	£Good	£Fine	£N.Mint
1 ND	$0.40	$1.20	$2.00	£0.25	£0.75	£1.25
Title Value:	$0.40	$1.20	$2.00	£0.25	£0.75	£1.25

CATWOMAN
DC Comics,MS; 1 Mar 1989-4 June 1989

(see Batman, Brave and Bold, Detective Comics, Lois Lane, Showcase 94)

Issue	$Good	$Fine	$N.Mint	£Good	£Fine	£N.Mint
1-2	$1.80	$5.25	$9.00	£0.80	£2.40	£4.00
3-4 Batman appears	$1.00	$3.00	$5.00	£0.50	£1.50	£2.50
Title Value:	$5.60	$16.50	$25.50	£2.60	£7.80	£13.00

Note: alternative perspective to Batman Year One (#404-407)

Issue	$Good	$Fine	$N.Mint	£Good	£Fine	£N.Mint
Trade paperback (Jul 1991), reprints mini-series with new cover painting by Brian Stelfreeze				£1.10	£3.30	£5.50

CATWOMAN (2ND SERIES)
DC Comics; 0 Oct 1994; 1 Aug 1993-present

Issue	$Good	$Fine	$N.Mint	£Good	£Fine	£N.Mint
0 (Oct 1994) Zero Hour X-over, origin retold	$0.50	$1.50	$2.50	£0.30	£0.90	£1.50
1 embossed cover; spin-off from the "Knightfall" story in Batman	$1.20	$3.60	$6.00	£0.70	£2.10	£3.50
2	$0.70	$2.10	$3.50	£0.40	£1.20	£2.00
3	$0.60	$1.80	$3.00	£0.30	£0.90	£1.50
4-5	$0.40	$1.20	$2.00	£0.25	£0.75	£1.25
6 Knightquest: The Crusade, continued from Batman #503	$0.50	$1.50	$2.50	£0.25	£0.75	£1.25
7 Knightquest: The Crusade, continued from Batman #505	$0.40	$1.20	$2.00	£0.25	£0.75	£1.25
8-11	$0.40	$1.20	$2.00	£0.25	£0.75	£1.25

Issue	$Good	$Fine	$N.Mint	£Good	£Fine	£N.Mint
12 Knightsend part 6, continued in Batman #510	$0.40	$1.20	$2.00	£0.25	£0.75	£1.25
13 Knightsend: Aftermath part 2 (of 2)	$0.40	$1.20	$2.00	£0.25	£0.75	£1.25
14 Zero Hour X-over	$0.40	$1.20	$2.00	£0.25	£0.75	£1.25
15 new direction for title	$0.40	$1.20	$2.00	£0.25	£0.75	£1.25
16-24	$0.40	$1.20	$2.00	£0.25	£0.75	£1.25
25 48pgs	$0.60	$1.80	$3.00	£0.40	£1.20	£2.00
26 The Secret of the Universe, continued in Batman: Shadow of the Bat #44	$0.40	$1.20	$2.00	£0.25	£0.75	£1.25
27 Underworld Unleashed tie-in, Gorilla Grodd appears	$0.40	$1.20	$2.00	£0.25	£0.75	£1.25
28	$0.40	$1.20	$2.00	£0.25	£0.75	£1.25
29 Penguin appears	$0.40	$1.20	$2.00	£0.25	£0.75	£1.25
30 bi-monthly	$0.40	$1.20	$2.00	£0.25	£0.75	£1.25
31 Contagion part 4, continued in Azrael #15	$0.40	$1.20	$2.00	£0.25	£0.75	£1.25
32 Contagion part 9, continued in Azrael #16	$0.40	$1.20	$2.00	£0.25	£0.75	£1.25
33-35 Catwoman vs. Hellhound	$0.40	$1.20	$2.00	£0.25	£0.75	£1.25
36 Legacy part 2, continued in Robin #32	$0.40	$1.20	$2.00	£0.25	£0.75	£1.25
37	$0.40	$1.20	$2.00	£0.25	£0.75	£1.25
38-40 ND Catwoman: Year Two	$0.40	$1.20	$2.00	£0.25	£0.75	£1.25
41 ND	$0.40	$1.20	$2.00	£0.25	£0.75	£1.25
42 ND 1st appearance Cybercat	$0.40	$1.20	$2.00	£0.25	£0.75	£1.25
43 ND	$0.40	$1.20	$2.00	£0.25	£0.75	£1.25
Title Value:	$19.30	$57.90	$96.50	£11.85	£35.55	£59.25
Catwoman: The Catfile (May 1996) Trade paperback reprints issues #15-19				£1.30	£3.90	£6.50

CATWOMAN ANNUAL

DC Comics; 1 May 1994-present

Issue	$Good	$Fine	$N.Mint	£Good	£Fine	£N.Mint
1 64pgs, Elseworlds story	$0.60	$1.80	$3.00	£0.40	£1.20	£2.00
2 56pgs, Year One, origin retold	$0.80	$2.40	$4.00	£0.50	£1.50	£2.50
3 Legends of the Dead Earth tie-in; Joker and Riddler appear as detectives	$0.60	$1.80	$3.00	£0.40	£1.20	£2.00
Title Value:	$2.00	$6.00	$10.00	£1.30	£3.90	£6.50

CATWOMAN/VAMPIRELLA: THE FURIES

DC Comics/Harris Comics,OS; 1 Feb 1997

Issue	$Good	$Fine	$N.Mint	£Good	£Fine	£N.Mint
1 ND 48pgs, Chuck Dixon scipt, Jim Balent and Ray McCarthy art; cover by Jim Balent and Jimmy Palmiotti	$1.00	$3.00	$5.00	£0.70	£2.10	£3.50
Title Value:	$1.00	$3.00	$5.00	£0.70	£2.10	£3.50

CAULDRON

Real Comics; 1 Oct 1995-3 1996 ?

Issue	$Good	$Fine	$N.Mint	£Good	£Fine	£N.Mint
1 ND Steve Brown script and art	$0.60	$1.80	$3.00	£0.40	£1.20	£2.00
1 Variant Cover Edition, ND by Glenn Fabry (20% of print run)	$0.60	$1.80	$3.00	£0.40	£1.20	£2.00
2-3 ND	$0.60	$1.80	$3.00	£0.40	£1.20	£2.00
Title Value:	$2.40	$7.20	$12.00	£1.60	£4.80	£8.00

CAVE GIRL

AC Comics; 1 1988

Issue	$Good	$Fine	$N.Mint	£Good	£Fine	£N.Mint
1 Bob Powell reprints	$0.60	$1.80	$3.00	£0.30	£0.90	£1.50
Title Value:	$0.60	$1.80	$3.00	£0.30	£0.90	£1.50

CAVE KIDS

Gold Key; 1 Feb 1963-16 Mar 1967

Issue	$Good	$Fine	$N.Mint	£Good	£Fine	£N.Mint
1 scarce in the U.K. based on Hanna-Barbera cartoon	$5.50	$17.00	$40.00	£2.85	£8.50	£20.00
2-5	$2.90	$8.75	$17.50	£1.25	£3.75	£7.50
6-16	$2.05	$6.25	$12.50	£0.80	£2.50	£5.00
Title Value:	$39.65	$120.75	$247.50	£16.65	£51.00	£105.00

Note: Pebbles and Bamm Bamm appear in #7,10,12. Quarterly frequency

CAVEWOMAN

Basement Comics; 1 1994-6 1994

Issue	$Good	$Fine	$N.Mint	£Good	£Fine	£N.Mint
1 ND Budd Root script and art begins; black and white	$15.00	$45.00	$75.00	£7.00	£21.00	£35.00
1 2nd printing, ND (Mar 1995)	$1.00	$3.00	$5.00	£0.60	£1.80	£3.00
2 ND black and white	$11.00	$33.00	$55.00	£4.00	£12.00	£20.00
3 ND black and white	$8.00	$24.00	$40.00	£3.00	£9.00	£15.00
4 ND black and white	$7.00	$21.00	$35.00	£2.50	£7.50	£12.50
5-6 ND black and white	$7.00	$21.00	$35.00	£2.00	£6.00	£10.00
Title Value:	$56.00	$168.00	$280.00	£21.10	£63.30	£105.50

CAVEWOMAN: RAIN

Caliber Press,MS; 1 Mar 1996-present

Issue	$Good	$Fine	$N.Mint	£Good	£Fine	£N.Mint
1 ND Budd Root script and art; black and white	$1.20	$3.60	$6.00	£0.60	£1.80	£3.00
2-5 ND Budd Root script and art; black and white	$0.70	$2.10	$3.50	£0.40	£1.20	£2.00

Issue	$Good	$Fine	$N.Mint	£Good	£Fine	£N.Mint
Title Value:	$4.00	$12.00	$20.00	£2.20	£6.60	£11.00

CECIL KUNKLE

Renegade; 1 May 1986

Issue	$Good	$Fine	$N.Mint	£Good	£Fine	£N.Mint
1 ND	$0.30	$0.90	$1.50	£0.20	£0.60	£1.00
Title Value:	$0.30	$0.90	$1.50	£0.20	£0.60	£1.00

CECIL KUNKLE (2ND SERIES)

Darkline/Renegade; 1 1987-2 1988

Issue	$Good	$Fine	$N.Mint	£Good	£Fine	£N.Mint
1-2 ND	$0.30	$0.90	$1.50	£0.20	£0.60	£1.00
Title Value:	$0.60	$1.80	$3.00	£0.40	£1.20	£2.00

CECIL KUNKLE CHRISTMAS SPECIAL

Renegade; 1 1988

Issue	$Good	$Fine	$N.Mint	£Good	£Fine	£N.Mint
1 ND	$0.40	$1.20	$2.00	£0.25	£0.75	£1.25
Title Value:	$0.40	$1.20	$2.00	£0.25	£0.75	£1.25

CELESTIAL MECHANICS

Innovation; 1 Nov 1990

Issue	$Good	$Fine	$N.Mint	£Good	£Fine	£N.Mint
1 ND	$0.40	$1.20	$2.00	£0.25	£0.75	£1.25
Title Value:	$0.40	$1.20	$2.00	£0.25	£0.75	£1.25

CELESTINE

Image; 1 May 1996-2 Jun 1996

Issue	$Good	$Fine	$N.Mint	£Good	£Fine	£N.Mint
1 ND Warren Ellis script, Patrick Lee and Al Vey art	$0.50	$1.50	$2.50	£0.30	£0.90	£1.50
2 ND	$0.50	$1.50	$2.50	£0.30	£0.90	£1.50
Title Value:	$1.00	$3.00	$5.00	£0.60	£1.80	£3.00

CENOTAPH: CYBER-GODDESS

Northstar; 1 Jan 1995

Issue	$Good	$Fine	$N.Mint	£Good	£Fine	£N.Mint
1 ND Tony Akins script and art; black and white	$0.80	$2.40	$4.00	£0.50	£1.50	£2.50
1 Signed & Numbered Edition, ND , pre-bagged with gold foil cover; 2,500 copies	$2.00	$6.00	$10.00	£1.30	£3.90	£6.50
Title Value:	$2.80	$8.40	$14.00	£1.80	£5.40	£9.00

CENTRIFUGAL BUMBLE-PUPPY

Fantagraphics,Magazine; 1 Sep 1987-8 1988

Issue	$Good	$Fine	$N.Mint	£Good	£Fine	£N.Mint
1-8 ND	$0.50	$1.50	$2.50	£0.30	£0.90	£1.50
Title Value:	$4.00	$12.00	$20.00	£2.40	£7.20	£12.00

CENTURIONS

DC Comics,MS Toy; 1 Jun 1987-4 Sep 1987

Issue	$Good	$Fine	$N.Mint	£Good	£Fine	£N.Mint
1-4 scarce in the U.K.	$0.15	$0.45	$0.75	£0.10	£0.30	£0.50
Title Value:	$0.60	$1.80	$3.00	£0.40	£1.20	£2.00

CENTURY: DISTANT SONS

Marvel Comics Group,OS; 1 Feb 1996

Issue	$Good	$Fine	$N.Mint	£Good	£Fine	£N.Mint
1 ND 48pgs, Dan Abnett/Andy Lanning script, Jim Calafiore and Peter Palmiotti art; wraparounf fifth ink cover	$0.60	$1.80	$3.00	£0.40	£1.20	£2.00
Title Value:	$0.60	$1.80	$3.00	£0.40	£1.20	£2.00

CEREBUS BI-WEEKLY

Aardvark-Vanaheim; 1 Dec 1988-25 May 1989

Issue	$Good	$Fine	$N.Mint	£Good	£Fine	£N.Mint
1 ND reprints Cerebus the Aardvark #1	$0.30	$0.90	$1.50	£0.25	£0.75	£1.25
2 ND reprints issue #2	$0.30	$0.90	$1.50	£0.25	£0.75	£1.25
3-16 ND	$0.30	$0.90	$1.50	£0.25	£0.75	£1.25
17 ND 1st appearance of the Hepcats	$2.00	$6.00	$10.00	£0.30	£0.90	£1.50
18-19 ND	$0.30	$0.90	$1.50	£0.25	£0.75	£1.25
20 ND 1st appearance of Milk & Cheese	$2.00	$6.00	$10.00	£0.30	£0.90	£1.50
21-25 ND	$0.30	$0.90	$1.50	£0.25	£0.75	£1.25
Title Value:	$10.90	$32.70	$54.50	£6.35	£19.05	£31.75

Note: there was an un-numbered issue published after #25 which reprinted the two stories set in continuity in Swords of Cerebus #4. It would be valued at approximately ú1.50 ($2.25) at the time of going to press

CEREBUS HIGH SOCIETY

Aardvark-Vanaheim; 1 Jun 1989-25 Jun 1991

(continues from Cerebus Bi-Weekly)

Issue	$Good	$Fine	$N.Mint	£Good	£Fine	£N.Mint
1 ND reprints Cerebus #26	$0.30	$0.90	$1.50	£0.25	£0.75	£1.25
2 ND reprints Cerebus #27	$0.30	$0.90	$1.50	£0.25	£0.75	£1.25
3-24 ND	$0.30	$0.90	$1.50	£0.25	£0.75	£1.25
25 ND reprints issue #50	$0.30	$0.90	$1.50	£0.25	£0.75	£1.25
Title Value:	$7.50	$22.50	$37.50	£6.25	£18.75	£31.25
Trade Paperback (Apr 1991), reprints #26-50				£3.00	£9.00	£15.00

CEREBUS JAM

Aardvark-Vanaheim; 1 Apr 1985

Issue	$Good	$Fine	$N.Mint	£Good	£Fine	£N.Mint
1 ND Eisner, Anderson, Scott/Bo Hampton, Austin art, Sienkiewicz cover	$1.00	$3.00	$5.00	£0.70	£2.10	£3.50
Title Value:	$1.00	$3.00	$5.00	£0.70	£2.10	£3.50

CEREBUS THE AARDVARK

Aardvark-Vanaheim; 0 Jun 1993; 1 Dec 1977-present

(see A-V in 3-D,Cerebus Jam)

Issue	$Good	$Fine	$N.Mint	£Good	£Fine	£N.Mint
0 1st printing, (Jun 1993) pre-bagged with gold ink logo and Cerebus hologram trading card; Mothers and Daughters storyline from #151-200 reprinted	$1.20	$3.60	$6.00	£0.80	£2.40	£4.00
0 2nd printing, (Jun 1993) - Mothers and Daughters storyline from #151-200 reprinted	$0.60	$1.80	$3.00	£0.40	£1.20	£2.00
0 Gold Edition ND	$4.00	$12.00	$20.00	£1.00	£3.00	£5.00
1 [counterfeit, see note below]	$42.00	$125.00	$250.00	£25.00	£75.00	£150.00
2	$13.00	$40.00	$80.00	£8.25	£25.00	£50.00
3 1st Red Sophia	$10.50	$33.00	$65.00	£5.75	£17.50	£35.00

	$Good	$Fine	$N.Mint	£Good	£Fine	£N.Mint
4 1st Elric of Melvinbone						
	$6.50	$20.00	$40.00	£4.15	£12.50	£25.00
5-6	$5.75	$17.50	$35.00	£3.75	£11.00	£22.50
7-10	$4.55	$13.50	$27.50	£2.90	£8.75	£17.50
11 origin Captain Cockroach						
	$4.55	$13.50	$27.50	£2.90	£8.75	£17.50
12	$3.30	$10.00	$20.00	£2.05	£6.25	£12.50
13-15	$2.05	$6.25	$12.50	£1.25	£3.75	£7.50
16-20	$1.50	$4.50	$9.00	£1.00	£3.00	£6.00
21 scarce in the U.K.						
	$5.75	$17.50	$35.00	£3.30	£10.00	£20.00
22 scarce in the U.K. Captain Cockroach and Bunky						
	$2.05	$6.25	$12.50	£1.15	£3.50	£7.00
23-24	$1.25	$3.75	$7.50	£0.75	£2.25	£4.50
25	$1.25	$3.75	$7.50	£0.65	£2.00	£4.00
26 High Society begins						
	$1.25	$3.75	$7.50	£0.65	£2.00	£4.00
27-30	$1.25	$3.75	$7.50	£0.65	£2.00	£4.00
31 Moonroach origin						
	$1.50	$4.50	$9.00	£1.00	£3.00	£6.00
32-40	$0.80	$2.50	$5.00	£0.50	£1.50	£3.00
41-50	$0.65	$2.00	$4.00	£0.40	£1.25	£2.50
51 Interlude	$2.00	$6.00	$10.00	£1.00	£3.00	£5.00
52 Church & State I begins						
	$0.90	$2.70	$4.50	£0.60	£1.80	£3.00
53 Wolveroach cameo (1st appearance)						
	$1.50	$4.50	$7.50	£1.00	£3.00	£5.00
54 1st Wolveroach full story						
	$1.50	$4.50	$7.50	£1.00	£3.00	£5.00
55-56 Wolveroach	$1.20	$3.60	$6.00	£0.80	£2.40	£4.00
57-60	$0.80	$2.40	$4.00	£0.50	£1.50	£2.50
61-62 Flaming Carrot back-up						
	$1.00	$3.00	$5.00	£0.70	£2.10	£3.50
63-73	$0.80	$2.40	$4.00	£0.50	£1.50	£2.50
74 scarce in the U.K.						
	$0.80	$2.40	$4.00	£0.80	£2.40	£4.00
75	$0.80	$2.40	$4.00	£0.50	£1.50	£2.50
76-80	$0.60	$1.80	$3.00	£0.40	£1.20	£2.00
81 Church & State II begins						
	$0.70	$2.10	$3.50	£0.50	£1.50	£2.50
82-84	$0.60	$1.80	$3.00	£0.40	£1.20	£2.00
85-99	$0.50	$1.50	$2.50	£0.30	£0.90	£1.50
100	$0.60	$1.80	$3.00	£0.40	£1.20	£2.00
101-103	$0.45	$1.35	$2.25	£0.30	£0.90	£1.50
104 Flaming Carrot appears						
	$0.70	$2.10	$3.50	£0.50	£1.50	£2.50
105 scarce in the U.K.						
	$0.45	$1.35	$2.25	£0.50	£1.50	£2.50
106-111	$0.45	$1.35	$2.25	£0.30	£0.90	£1.50
112-113 double issue, interlude						
	$0.70	$2.10	$3.50	£0.45	£1.35	£2.25
114 Jaka's story begins						
	$0.60	$1.80	$3.00	£0.40	£1.20	£2.00
115-136	$0.45	$1.35	$2.25	£0.30	£0.90	£1.50
137-138 Jaka's Story Epilogues						
	$0.45	$1.35	$2.25	£0.30	£0.90	£1.50
139 Melmoth Zero						
	$0.45	$1.35	$2.25	£0.30	£0.90	£1.50
140 Melmoth story begins (ends #149)						
	$0.45	$1.35	$2.25	£0.30	£0.90	£1.50
141-149	$0.45	$1.35	$2.25	£0.30	£0.90	£1.50
150 Melmoth storyline epilogue						
	$0.45	$1.35	$2.25	£0.30	£0.90	£1.50
151 Mothers & Daughters story begins						
	$0.60	$1.80	$3.00	£0.40	£1.20	£2.00
151 2nd printing, (Jun 1992)						
	$0.45	$1.35	$2.25	£0.30	£0.90	£1.50
151 3rd printing	$0.45	$1.35	$2.25	£0.30	£0.90	£1.50
152	$0.45	$1.35	$2.25	£0.30	£0.90	£1.50
152 2nd printing, (Jul 1992)						
	$0.45	$1.35	$2.25	£0.30	£0.90	£1.50
153	$0.45	$1.35	$2.25	£0.30	£0.90	£1.50
153 2nd printing, (Aug 1992)						
	$0.45	$1.35	$2.25	£0.30	£0.90	£1.50
154-162	$0.45	$1.35	$2.25	£0.30	£0.90	£1.50
163 Mothers & Daughters Book 2 - Women story begins						
	$0.60	$1.80	$3.00	£0.40	£1.20	£2.00
163 2nd printing, (Aug 1993)						
	$0.45	$1.35	$2.25	£0.30	£0.90	£1.50
164	$0.45	$1.35	$2.25	£0.30	£0.90	£1.50
164 2nd printing, (Aug 1993)						
	$0.45	$1.35	$2.25	£0.30	£0.90	£1.50
165 Dave McKean parody cover						
	$0.45	$1.35	$2.25	£0.30	£0.90	£1.50
165 2nd printing, (Aug 1993)						
	$0.45	$1.35	$2.25	£0.30	£0.90	£1.50
166-173	$0.45	$1.35	$2.25	£0.30	£0.90	£1.50
174 Mothers & Daughters Book Two: Women conclusion						
	$0.45	$1.35	$2.25	£0.30	£0.90	£1.50
175 Mothers & Daughters Book Three begins						
	$0.45	$1.35	$2.25	£0.30	£0.90	£1.50
176-185	$0.45	$1.35	$2.25	£0.30	£0.90	£1.50
186 Mothers & Daughters Book Three concludes						
	$0.45	$1.35	$2.25	£0.30	£0.90	£1.50
187-199	$0.45	$1.35	$2.25	£0.30	£0.90	£1.50
200 Guys storyline begins						
	$0.45	$1.35	$2.25	£0.30	£0.90	£1.50
201-212	$0.45	$1.35	$2.25	£0.30	£0.90	£1.50
Title Value:	$254.25	$766.65	$1436.75	£158.20	£475.95	£890.00

Note: all Non-Distributed on the news-stands in the U.K.

Trade Paperback collections:

	£Good	£Fine	£N.Mint
Cerebus Book One			
ND reprints #1-25	£3.50	£10.50	£17.50
ND (2nd printing - 1991)	£3.00	£9.00	£15.00
Cerebus Book Two: High Society			
ND reprints #26-50	£3.50	£10.50	£17.50
Cerebus Book Three: Church & State 1			
ND reprints #52-80	£4.00	£12.00	£20.00
Cerebus Book Four: Church & State II			
ND reprints #81-111:			
1st print, Limited Edition, 435 copies, signed	£10.00	£30.00	£50.00
2nd print	£4.00	£12.00	£20.00
Swords of Cerebus:			
Vol 1 ND reprints #1-4 plus new story	£1.25	£3.75	£6.25
Vol 1 ND 2nd/3rd/4th print	£1.00	£3.00	£5.00
Vol 2 ND reprints #5-8 plus new story	£1.00	£3.00	£5.00
Vol 2 ND 2nd/3rd print	£0.90	£2.70	£4.50
Vol 3 ND (1st,2nd) reprints #9-12 plus new story	£1.00	£3.00	£5.00
Vol 4 ND (1st,2nd) reprints #13-16 plus 2 new stories	£1.00	£3.00	£5.00
Vol 5 ND (1st,2nd) reprints #17-20 plus new story	£1.00	£3.00	£5.00
Vol 6 ND reprints #21-25 plus new story; contains supplement insert	£1.00	£3.00	£5.00
Cerebus Book Five: Jaka's Story			

Cat, Beware! The Claws of the #4

Catwoman (2nd) #1

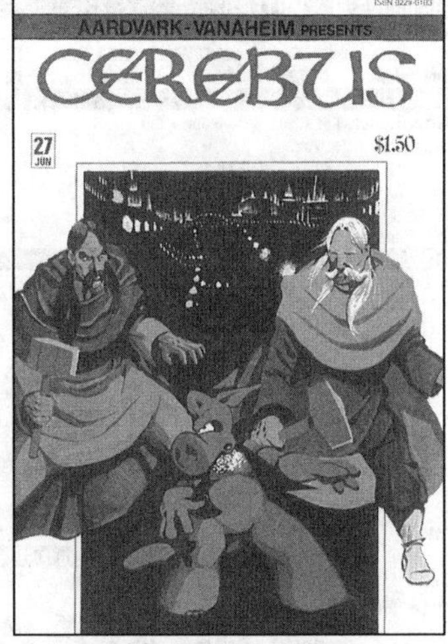

Cerebus the Aardvark #27

	$Good	$Fine	$N.Mint	£Good	£Fine	£N.Mint
Trade paperback (Nov 1992) ND reprints issues #114-136				£3.00	£9.00	£15.00
Cerebus Book Six: Melmoth						
Trade paperback (Feb 1993) ND reprints issues #139-150				£2.00	£6.00	£10.00
Cerebus Book Seven: Mothers & Daughters Vol. I - Flight						
Trade paperback (Jun 1993) ND reprints issues #151-200.						
1st prints signed and numbered by Dave Sim and Gerhard				£3.00	£9.00	£15.00
ND 2nd prints, unsigned				£2.40	£7.20	£12.00
Cerebus Book Eight: Mothers & Daughters Vol. II - Women (May 1994)						
Trade paperback ND reprints issues #163-174.						
1st prints signed and numbered by Dave Sim and Gerhard				£3.25	£9.75	£16.25
ND 2nd prints, unsigned				£2.40	£7.20	£12.00
Cerebus Book Nine: Mothers & Daughters Vol. III - Reads (Apr 1995)						
Trade paperback ND reprints issues #175-186.						
1st prints signed and numbered by Dave Sim and Gerhard				£3.25	£9.75	£16.25
ND 2nd prints, unsigned (Apr 1995)				£2.40	£7.20	£12.00
Cerebus Book 10: Minds (Jun 1996)						
Trade paperback						
ND reprints issues #187-200, signed and numbered				£3.30	£9.90	£16.50
ND 2nd printing, unsigned				£2.40	£7.20	£12.00
Cerebus World Tour Book '95 (Feb 1995)						
ND reprints back-up and supplementary stories						
from Swords of Cerebus				£0.40	£1.20	£2.00

Note: counterfeit copies of #1 exist. The inside covers of the counterfeit copies have a glossy black finish, whereas the genuine copies have a matt black inside cover and the black background on the counterfeit front cover appears flecked with white. **The Guide does not give a value and thereby promote forgery.**

CEREBUS: CHURCH AND STATE

Aardvark-Vanaheim; 1 Apr 1991-30 Jun 1992

(continues from Cerebus High Society)

	$Good	$Fine	$N.Mint	£Good	£Fine	£N.Mint
1 reprints Cerebus #51, bi-weekly begins	$0.40	$1.20	$2.00	£0.25	£0.75	£1.25
2 reprints Cerebus #52 etc	$0.35	$1.05	$1.75	£0.25	£0.75	£1.25
3-30	$0.35	$1.05	$1.75	£0.25	£0.75	£1.25
Title Value:	$10.55	$31.65	$52.75	£7.50	£22.50	£37.50

CHAIN GANG WAR

DC Comics; 1 Jul 1993-12 Jun 1994

	$Good	$Fine	$N.Mint	£Good	£Fine	£N.Mint
1 Alan Grant and John Wagner script begins	$0.35	$1.05	$1.75	£0.25	£0.75	£1.25
1 Platinum Edition, ND - silver embossed logo and chain design on left of cover	$1.00	$3.00	$5.00	£0.60	£1.80	£3.00
2-6	$0.35	$1.05	$1.75	£0.25	£0.75	£1.25
7 Gary Erskine guest art	$0.35	$1.05	$1.75	£0.25	£0.75	£1.25
8-9	$0.35	$1.05	$1.75	£0.25	£0.75	£1.25
10 Deathstroke the Terminator appears	$0.35	$1.05	$1.75	£0.25	£0.75	£1.25
11 Batman appears	$0.35	$1.05	$1.75	£0.25	£0.75	£1.25
12	$0.35	$1.05	$1.75	£0.25	£0.75	£1.25
Title Value:	$5.20	$15.60	$26.00	£3.60	£10.80	£18.00

CHAIN UNTAMED

ACG; 1 Apr 1996

	$Good	$Fine	$N.Mint	£Good	£Fine	£N.Mint
1 ND features unpublished Jeff Jones story; black and white	$0.50	$1.50	$2.50	£0.30	£0.90	£1.50
Title Value:	$0.50	$1.50	$2.50	£0.30	£0.90	£1.50

CHAINGANG

Northstar; 1 Apr 1990-2 1990

	$Good	$Fine	$N.Mint	£Good	£Fine	£N.Mint
1 ND scarce in the U.K. "Night City" back-ups by Mark Nelson begin	$2.50	$7.50	$12.50	£1.50	£4.50	£7.50
2 ND scarce in the U.K. part Tim Vigil, part Mark Nelson art	$1.50	$4.50	$7.50	£1.00	£3.00	£5.00
Title Value:	$4.00	$12.00	$20.00	£2.50	£7.50	£12.50

CHAINGANG, REX MILLER'S

Northstar; 1 May 1992

	$Good	$Fine	$N.Mint	£Good	£Fine	£N.Mint
1 ND	$0.50	$1.50	$2.50	£0.30	£0.90	£1.50
Title Value:	$0.50	$1.50	$2.50	£0.30	£0.90	£1.50

CHAINS OF CHAOS

Harris Comics,MS; 1 Nov 1994-3 Jan 1995

	$Good	$Fine	$N.Mint	£Good	£Fine	£N.Mint
1 ND Vampirella appears	$0.70	$2.10	$3.50	£0.50	£1.50	£2.50
2-3 ND Vampirella appears	$0.60	$1.80	$3.00	£0.40	£1.20	£2.00
Title Value:	$1.90	$5.70	$9.50	£1.30	£3.90	£6.50

CHALLENGERS OF THE UNKNOWN

DC Comics; 1 Apr/May 1958-77 Dec/Jan 1970/71; 78 Feb 1973-80 Jun/Jul 1973; 81 Jun/Jul 1977-87 Jun/Jul 1978

(see Secret Origins, Showcase, Super DC Giant, Super-Team Family)

	$Good	$Fine	$N.Mint	£Good	£Fine	£N.Mint
1 Jack Kirby/Stein art	$200.00	$600.00	$2000.00	£135.00	£405.00	£1350.00
2 Jack Kirby/Stein art	$95.00	$290.00	$775.00	£62.50	£185.00	£500.00
3 Jack Kirby/Stein art	$80.00	$240.00	$650.00	£48.00	£140.00	£385.00
4-8 Jack Kirby/Wood art	$65.00	$195.00	$525.00	£41.00	£120.00	£325.00
9-10	$33.00	$97.50	$260.00	£20.00	£60.00	£160.00
1st official distribution in the U.K.						
11-13	$25.00	$75.00	$175.00	£17.00	£50.00	£120.00
14 origin Multi-Man	$25.00	$75.00	$175.00	£17.00	£50.00	£120.00
15	$25.00	$75.00	$175.00	£17.00	£50.00	£120.00
16-17	$20.50	$60.00	$145.00	£13.50	£41.00	£95.00
18 intro Cosmo, Challengers' space-pet	$20.50	$60.00	$145.00	£13.50	£41.00	£95.00
19-20	$20.50	$60.00	$145.00	£13.50	£41.00	£95.00
21	$20.50	$60.00	$145.00	£12.00	£36.00	£85.00
22 last 10 cents issue	$20.50	$60.00	$145.00	£12.00	£36.00	£85.00
23-30	$11.00	$34.00	$80.00	£7.75	£23.50	£55.00
31 origin retold	$12.00	$36.00	$85.00	£8.00	£24.50	£57.50
32-40	$5.50	$17.00	$40.00	£3.55	£10.50	£25.00
41-42	$2.85	$8.50	$20.00	£1.75	£5.25	£12.50
43 new look begins	$2.85	$8.50	$20.00	£1.75	£5.25	£12.50
44-45	$2.85	$8.50	$20.00	£1.75	£5.25	£12.50
46 last Silver Age issue indicia dated November 1965	$2.85	$8.50	$20.00	£1.75	£5.25	£12.50
47	$2.85	$8.50	$20.00	£1.60	£4.90	£11.50
48 Doom Patrol appears	$2.85	$8.50	$20.00	£1.60	£4.90	£11.50
49 intro Challenger Corps	$2.85	$8.50	$20.00	£1.60	£4.90	£11.50
50	$2.85	$8.50	$20.00	£1.60	£4.90	£11.50
51 Sea Devils X-over	$2.85	$8.50	$20.00	£1.60	£4.90	£11.50
52-54	$2.85	$8.50	$20.00	£1.60	£4.90	£11.50
55 Red Ryan dies	$2.85	$8.50	$20.00	£1.60	£4.90	£11.50
56-59	$2.85	$8.50	$20.00	£1.60	£4.90	£11.50
60 Red Ryan returns	$2.85	$8.50	$20.00	£1.60	£4.90	£11.50
61-62	$1.40	$4.25	$10.00	£0.55	£1.70	£4.00
63 scarce in the U.K.	$1.40	$4.25	$10.00	£0.65	£2.00	£4.75
64 origin retold (reprints #1); Joe Kubert cover, Jack Kirby art	$1.40	$4.25	$10.00	£0.55	£1.70	£4.00
65 origin retold (reprints #1), Jack Kirby art	$1.40	$4.25	$10.00	£0.55	£1.70	£4.00
66 Joe Kubert cover	$1.40	$4.25	$10.00	£0.55	£1.70	£4.00
67 Neal Adams cover	$1.40	$4.25	$10.00	£0.55	£1.70	£4.00
68	$1.40	$4.25	$10.00	£0.55	£1.70	£4.00
69 intro Corinna Stark	$1.40	$4.25	$10.00	£0.55	£1.70	£4.00
70 new costumes, Neal Adams cover	$1.40	$4.25	$10.00	£0.55	£1.70	£4.00
71	$1.00	$3.00	$7.00	£0.50	£1.50	£3.50
72 Neal Adams cover	$1.00	$3.00	$7.00	£0.50	£1.50	£3.50
73	$1.00	$3.00	$7.00	£0.50	£1.50	£3.50
74 Deadman by George Tuska and Neal Adams, also 1pg Wrightson art, Neal Adams cover	$2.85	$8.50	$20.00	£1.05	£3.20	£7.50
75 reprints Showcase #7	$1.00	$3.00	$7.00	£0.40	£1.25	£3.00
76 reprints stories from issues #2 and #3; Joe Kubert cover	$1.00	$3.00	$7.00	£0.40	£1.25	£3.00
77 reprints Showcase #12	$1.00	$3.00	$7.00	£0.40	£1.25	£3.00
78 scarce in the U.K. reprints stories from issues #6 and #7	$0.80	$2.50	$5.00	£0.40	£1.25	£2.50
79 scarce in the U.K. reprints stories from issues #1 and #2; Joe Kubert cover	$0.80	$2.50	$5.00	£0.40	£1.25	£2.50
80 scarce in the U.K. reprints Showcase #11	$0.80	$2.50	$5.00	£0.40	£1.25	£2.50
81 scarce in the U.K. Nasser art, Neal Adams cover inks	$0.80	$2.50	$5.00	£0.40	£1.25	£2.50
82 Swamp Thing X-over, Nasser art	$0.80	$2.50	$5.00	£0.30	£1.00	£2.00
83 Swamp Thing X-over	$0.80	$2.50	$5.00	£0.30	£1.00	£2.00
84-85 Swamp Thing and Deadman X-over	$0.80	$2.50	$5.00	£0.30	£1.00	£2.00
86 Swamp Thing and Deadman X-over, Keith Giffen art	$0.80	$2.50	$5.00	£0.30	£1.00	£2.00
87 Swamp Thing and Deadman X-over	$0.80	$2.50	$5.00	£0.30	£1.00	£2.00
Title Value:	$1271.85	$3820.00	$10157.00	£814.60	£2423.85	£6473.25

CHALLENGERS OF THE UNKNOWN (2ND SERIES)

DC Comics,MS; 1 Mar 1991-8 Oct 1991

	$Good	$Fine	$N.Mint	£Good	£Fine	£N.Mint
1 Brian Bolland cover	$0.30	$0.90	$1.50	£0.20	£0.60	£1.00
2-6	$0.30	$0.90	$1.50	£0.20	£0.60	£1.00
7 Art Adams cover	$0.30	$0.90	$1.50	£0.20	£0.60	£1.00
8	$0.30	$0.90	$1.50	£0.20	£0.60	£1.00
Title Value:	$2.40	$7.20	$12.00	£1.60	£4.80	£8.00

CHALLENGERS OF THE UNKNOWN (3RD SERIES)

DC Comics; 1 Feb 1997-present

	$Good	$Fine	$N.Mint	£Good	£Fine	£N.Mint
1 ND Steven Grant script, John Paul Leon and Shawn Martinborough art begins	$0.45	$1.35	$2.25	£0.30	£0.90	£1.50
2-3 ND	$0.45	$1.35	$2.25	£0.30	£0.90	£1.50
Title Value:	$1.35	$4.05	$6.75	£0.90	£2.70	£4.50

CHAMBER OF CHILLS

Marvel Comics Group; 1 Nov 1972-25 Nov 1976

Issue	$Good	$Fine	$N.Mint	£Good	£Fine	£N.Mint
1 ND P. Craig Russell/Russ Heath art	*$1.15*	*$3.50*	*$7.00*	£0.55	£1.75	£3.50
2-4 ND Brunner art	*$0.65*	*$2.00*	*$4.00*	£0.40	£1.25	£2.50
5 ND	*$0.40*	*$1.25*	*$2.50*	£0.30	£1.00	£2.00
6-18 ND	*$0.40*	*$1.25*	*$2.50*	£0.25	£0.75	£1.50
19-20	*$0.40*	*$1.25*	*$2.50*	£0.20	£0.60	£1.25
21 ND	*$0.40*	*$1.25*	*$2.50*	£0.25	£0.75	£1.50
22	*$0.40*	*$1.25*	*$2.50*	£0.20	£0.60	£1.25
23-24 ND	*$0.40*	*$1.25*	*$2.50*	£0.25	£0.75	£1.50
25	*$0.40*	*$1.25*	*$2.50*	£0.20	£0.60	£1.25
Title Value:	*$11.50*	*$35.75*	*$70.50*	£6.85	£20.90	£42.00

FEATURES

Brak the Barbarian in 2, 3. 8 is all 1950s horror reprints.

CHAMBER OF DARKNESS

Marvel Comics Group; 1 Oct 1969-8 Dec 1970

(becomes Monsters on the Prowl)

Issue	$Good	$Fine	$N.Mint	£Good	£Fine	£N.Mint
1 Buscema art	*$5.00*	*$15.00*	*$35.00*	£3.20	£9.50	£22.50
2 Neal Adams co-script	*$2.50*	*$7.50*	*$15.00*	£1.25	£3.75	£7.50
3 ND Barry Smith art (7pgs)	*$2.50*	*$7.50*	*$15.00*	£1.30	£4.00	£8.00
4 ND Barry Smith art on Conan "try out", reprinted in Conan #16	*$5.75*	*$17.50*	*$35.00*	£3.30	£10.00	£20.00
5 ND Jack Kirby script and art (6pgs)	*$1.00*	*$3.00*	*$6.00*	£0.50	£1.50	£3.00
6 Steve Ditko reprint	*$1.00*	*$3.00*	*$6.00*	£0.40	£1.25	£2.50
7 Bernie Wrightson art (1st Marvel work), self-cameo on first and last page	*$1.65*	*$5.00*	*$10.00*	£1.00	£3.00	£6.00
8 Wrightson cover, Bill Everett inks	*$0.80*	*$2.50*	*$5.00*	£0.40	£1.25	£2.50
Title Value:	*$20.20*	*$61.00*	*$127.00*	£11.35	£34.25	£72.00

ARTISTS

Kirby in 4, 5.

FEATURES

All issues have new fantasy/horror stories, except reprints in 6 (one story), 7 (two stories), 8 (three stories)

CHAMBER OF DARKNESS SPECIAL

Marvel Comics Group; 1 Jan 1972

Issue	$Good	$Fine	$N.Mint	£Good	£Fine	£N.Mint
1 ND scarce in the U.K. 52pgs, all reprints	*$1.15*	*$3.50*	*$7.00*	£0.55	£1.75	£3.50
Title Value:	*$1.15*	*$3.50*	*$7.00*	£0.55	£1.75	£3.50

CHAMPION SPORTS

DC Comics; 1 Oct/Nov 1973-3 Feb/Mar 1974

Issue	$Good	$Fine	$N.Mint	£Good	£Fine	£N.Mint
1	*$0.50*	*$1.50*	*$3.00*	£0.25	£0.75	£1.50
2-3	*$0.30*	*$1.00*	*$2.00*	£0.20	£0.60	£1.25
Title Value:	*$1.10*	*$3.50*	*$7.00*	£0.65	£1.95	£4.00

CHAMPIONS

Eclipse, Game; 1 Jun 1986-6 Feb 1987

Issue	$Good	$Fine	$N.Mint	£Good	£Fine	£N.Mint
1 ND Carol Lay art, colour; based on role playing game and includes character stats	*$0.30*	*$0.90*	*$1.50*	£0.20	£0.60	£1.00
2-6 ND Chris Marrinan art, with stats	*$0.30*	*$0.90*	*$1.50*	£0.20	£0.60	£1.00
Title Value:	*$1.80*	*$5.40*	*$9.00*	£1.20	£3.60	£6.00

CHAMPIONS (2ND SERIES)

Hero, Game; 1 Sep 1987-15 1990

Issue	$Good	$Fine	$N.Mint	£Good	£Fine	£N.Mint
1-2 ND	*$0.35*	*$1.05*	*$1.75*	£0.25	£0.75	£1.25
3 ND Flare vs. Champions	*$0.35*	*$1.05*	*$1.75*	£0.25	£0.75	£1.25
4 ND intro Icicle	*$0.35*	*$1.05*	*$1.75*	£0.25	£0.75	£1.25
5-7 ND	*$0.35*	*$1.05*	*$1.75*	£0.25	£0.75	£1.25
8 ND origin Foxbat	*$0.35*	*$1.05*	*$1.75*	£0.25	£0.75	£1.25
9-15 ND	*$0.35*	*$1.05*	*$1.75*	£0.25	£0.75	£1.25
Title Value:	*$5.25*	*$15.75*	*$26.25*	£3.75	£11.25	£18.75

CHAMPIONS ADVENTURES

Heroic Publishing; 1 Feb 1994-3 1994

Issue	$Good	$Fine	$N.Mint	£Good	£Fine	£N.Mint
1-3 ND 44pgs	*$0.60*	*$1.80*	*$3.00*	£0.40	£1.20	£2.00
Title Value:	*$1.80*	*$5.40*	*$9.00*	£1.20	£3.60	£6.00

CHAMPIONS ANNUAL

Hero; 1 1988-2 1989

Issue	$Good	$Fine	$N.Mint	£Good	£Fine	£N.Mint
1-2 ND	*$0.60*	*$1.80*	*$3.00*	£0.40	£1.20	£2.00
Title Value:	*$1.20*	*$3.60*	*$6.00*	£0.80	£2.40	£4.00

CHAMPIONS CLASSICS

Hero; 1 Jan 1992-5 May 1992

Issue	$Good	$Fine	$N.Mint	£Good	£Fine	£N.Mint
1 ND 20pgs, new and reprint material begins, George Perez cover	*$0.25*	*$0.75*	*$1.25*	£0.15	£0.45	£0.75
2-5 ND 20pgs	*$0.25*	*$0.75*	*$1.25*	£0.15	£0.45	£0.75
Title Value:	*$1.25*	*$3.75*	*$6.25*	£0.75	£2.25	£3.75

CHAMPIONS, THE

Marvel Comics Group; 1 Oct 1975-17 Jan 1978

Issue	$Good	$Fine	$N.Mint	£Good	£Fine	£N.Mint
1 Angel, Black Widow, Ghost Rider, Ice Man, Hercules begin (Note: as with many of these mid '70s Marvels, the British pence version has "Marvel All-Colour Comics" at the top)	*$2.90*	*$8.75*	*$17.50*	£1.00	£3.00	£6.00
2	*$1.65*	*$5.00*	*$10.00*	£0.55	£1.75	£3.50
3-10	*$1.65*	*$5.00*	*$10.00*	£0.50	£1.50	£3.00
11-12 Black Goliath appears, John Byrne art	*$2.05*	*$6.25*	*$12.50*	£0.55	£1.75	£3.50
13 ND Black Goliath appears, John Byrne art	*$2.05*	*$6.25*	*$12.50*	£0.65	£2.00	£4.00
14-15 ND John Byrne art	*$2.05*	*$6.25*	*$12.50*	£0.65	£2.00	£4.00
16 ND Magneto and Beast appear	*$2.05*	*$6.25*	*$12.50*	£0.65	£2.00	£4.00
17 ND very scarce in the U.K. Hulk appears, John Byrne inks	*$2.05*	*$6.25*	*$12.50*	£1.25	£3.75	£7.50
Title Value:	*$32.10*	*$97.50*	*$195.00*	£10.50	£32.00	£64.00

Note: Ghost Rider on cover of 1-4,7,8,10,14,16,17.

CHAOS BIBLE

Chaos Comics,OS; nn Oct 1995

Issue	$Good	$Fine	$N.Mint	£Good	£Fine	£N.Mint
nn ND, 40pgs	*$0.70*	*$2.10*	*$3.50*	£0.50	£1.50	£2.50
Title Value:	*$0.70*	*$2.10*	*$3.50*	£0.50	£1.50	£2.50

CHAOS EFFECT EPILOGUE

Valiant,MS; 1,2 Jan 1995

Issue	$Good	$Fine	$N.Mint	£Good	£Fine	£N.Mint
1-2 ND Kevin van Hook script, Louis Small Jnr. art	*$0.30*	*$0.90*	*$1.50*	£0.20	£0.60	£1.00
Title Value:	*$0.60*	*$1.80*	*$3.00*	£0.40	£1.20	£2.00

CHAOS EFFECT INDEX, THE

Valiant; 1994

Cross-over storyline running throughout the following issues:

Chaos Effect Alpha, Shadowman #29, Dr. Mirage #1, Turok #16, Secrets of the Valiant Universe #2, Bloodshot #20, Secret Weapons #13, Ninjak #8, Archer & Armstrong/Eternal Warrior #26, Harbinger #34, Armorines #5, X-O Manowar #33, H.A.R.D. Corps #23, Solar #38, Psi-Lords #3, Rai #26, Magnus #41, Chaos Effect Omega, Chaos Effect Epilogue #1, Chaos Effect Epilogue #2.

CHAOS EFFECT, THE

Valiant,MS; 1,2 Oct 1994

Issue	$Good	$Fine	$N.Mint	£Good	£Fine	£N.Mint
1 ND 16pgs, The Chaos Effect - Alpha. Promotional giveaway featuring a preview of The Visitor with free trading card checklist	*$0.30*	*$0.90*	*$1.50*	£0.20	£0.60	£1.00
2 ND The Chaos Effect - Omega. Conclusion to the 18 part cross-over story. Timewalker preview	*$0.30*	*$0.90*	*$1.50*	£0.20	£0.60	£1.00
Title Value:	*$0.60*	*$1.80*	*$3.00*	£0.40	£1.20	£2.00

CHAOS QUARTERLY

Chaos Comics; 1 Sep 1995-present

Issue	$Good	$Fine	$N.Mint	£Good	£Fine	£N.Mint
1 ND 48pgs, Lady Death by Pulido and Hughes plus Purgatori, Bedlam and Cremator stories; cover by Julie Bell	*$1.00*	*$3.00*	*$5.00*	£0.70	£2.10	£3.50
1 Signed & Numbered Edition, ND (Apr 1996), pre-bagged with certificate; limited to 7,500 copies	*$4.00*	*$12.00*	*$20.00*	£2.50	£7.50	£12.50
2 ND 48pgs, Lady Demon, Robo-Evil, Cremator and Bad Girls feature	*$1.00*	*$3.00*	*$5.00*	£0.70	£2.10	£3.50
3 ND 40pgs	*$0.80*	*$2.40*	*$4.00*	£0.50	£1.50	£2.50
Title Value:	*$6.80*	*$20.40*	*$34.00*	£4.40	£13.20	£22.00

CHAPEL

Image,MS; 1 Feb 1995-2 Mar 1995

Issue	$Good	$Fine	$N.Mint	£Good	£Fine	£N.Mint
1 ND Tom Tenney art	*$0.50*	*$1.50*	*$2.50*	£0.30	£0.90	£1.50
1 Variant Cover Edition, ND Jimmy Palmiotti cover	*$1.00*	*$3.00*	*$5.00*	£0.60	£1.80	£3.00
2 ND Tom Tenney art	*$0.50*	*$1.50*	*$2.50*	£0.30	£0.90	£1.50
Title Value:	*$2.00*	*$6.00*	*$10.00*	£1.20	£3.60	£6.00

CHAPEL (2ND SERIES)

Image; 1 Aug 1995-present

Issue	$Good	$Fine	$N.Mint	£Good	£Fine	£N.Mint
1 ND Brian Witten script, Calvin Irving art	*$0.50*	*$1.50*	*$2.50*	£0.30	£0.90	£1.50
1 Variant Cover Edition, ND Joe Quesada/Jimmy Palmiotti cover art	*$0.80*	*$2.40*	*$4.00*	£0.50	£1.50	£2.50
2-3 ND Brian Witten script, Calvin Irving art	*$0.50*	*$1.50*	*$2.50*	£0.30	£0.90	£1.50
4 ND Extreme Babewatch tie-in; Brian Witten script, Calvin Irving art	*$0.50*	*$1.50*	*$2.50*	£0.30	£0.90	£1.50
5-6 ND Hell on Earth story, Spawn appears	*$0.50*	*$1.50*	*$2.50*	£0.30	£0.90	£1.50
7 ND Shadowhunt part 2, continued in Youngblood #7	*$0.50*	*$1.50*	*$2.50*	£0.30	£0.90	£1.50
Title Value:	*$4.30*	*$12.90*	*$21.50*	£2.60	£7.80	£13.00

CHARLEMAGNE

Defiant; 0 Feb 1994; 1 Mar 1994-5 Jul 1994

Issue	$Good	$Fine	$N.Mint	£Good	£Fine	£N.Mint
0 ND (Feb 1994) - presented free with Hero Illustrated #9	*$0.30*	*$0.90*	*$1.50*	£0.20	£0.60	£1.00
1 ND 48pgs, Jim Shooter plot; Adam Pollina and Mike Witherby art	*$0.30*	*$0.90*	*$1.50*	£0.20	£0.60	£1.00
2-5 ND	*$0.30*	*$0.90*	*$1.50*	£0.20	£0.60	£1.00
Title Value:	*$1.80*	*$5.40*	*$9.00*	£1.20	£3.60	£6.00

Note: issues #6-8 were advertised and solicited but never appeared

CHARLIE CHAN, THE NEW ADVENTURES OF

National Periodical Publications; 1 May/Jun 1958-5 Feb/Mar 1949; Charlton; 6 Jun 1955-9 Mar 1956

Issue	$Good	$Fine	$N.Mint	£Good	£Fine	£N.Mint
1 rare in the U.K.	*$70.00*	*$210.00*	*$500.00*	£48.00	£140.00	£335.00
2 very scarce in the U.K.	*$50.00*	*$150.00*	*$350.00*	£34.00	£100.00	£235.00
3 very scarce in the U.K.	*$46.00*	*$135.00*	*$325.00*	£31.00	£92.50	£220.00
4 very scarce in the U.K.	*$43.00*	*$125.00*	*$300.00*	£29.00	£85.00	£200.00
5 very scarce in the U.K.	*$32.00*	*$95.00*	*$225.00*	£21.00	£62.50	£150.00
6 very scarce in the U.K.	*$29.00*	*$85.00*	*$200.00*	£19.00	£57.50	£135.00
7-9 scarce in the U.K.	*$15.50*	*$47.00*	*$110.00*	£10.50	£32.00	£75.00
Title Value:	*$316.50*	*$941.00*	*$2230.00*	£213.50	£633.50	£1500.00

CHARLTON BULLSEYE, THE

Charlton,Magazine; 1 1975-5 1976

Issue	$Good	$Fine	$N.Mint	£Good	£Fine	£N.Mint
1 scarce in the U.K. newszine devoted to Charlton material; Captain Atom by John Byrne and Steve Ditko; all black and white with card cover	*$2.50*	*$7.50*	*$15.00*	£1.25	£3.75	£7.50
2 scarce in the U.K. Captain Atom by John Byrne and Steve Ditko; black and white with colour cover by Joe Staton	*$2.05*	*$6.25*	*$12.50*	£1.00	£3.00	£6.00
3 Kung-Fu issue	*$1.50*	*$4.50*	*$9.00*	£0.75	£2.25	£4.50
4 Doomsday + 1 by John Byrne	*$2.00*	*$6.00*	*$12.00*	£0.90	£2.75	£5.50
5 Doomsday + 1 by John Byrne, The Question by Alex Toth; Toth front cover and Neal Adams back cover art	*$2.50*	*$7.50*	*$15.00*	£1.15	£3.50	£7.00
Title Value:	***$10.55***	***$31.75***	***$63.50***	**£5.05**	**£15.25**	**£30.50**

Note: all Non-Distributed on the news-stands in the U.K.

CHARLTON BULLSEYE, THE (2ND SERIES)

Charlton; 1 Jun 1981-10 Dec 1982

Issue	$Good	$Fine	$N.Mint	£Good	£Fine	£N.Mint
1 Blue Beetle and The Question team-up	*$0.50*	*$1.50*	*$2.50*	£0.30	£0.90	£1.50
2 Cap'n Catnip, 1st Neil the Horse	*$0.30*	*$0.90*	*$1.50*	£0.25	£0.75	£1.25
3 science fiction stories	*$0.30*	*$0.90*	*$1.50*	£0.20	£0.60	£1.00
4 The Vanguards	*$0.30*	*$0.90*	*$1.50*	£0.20	£0.60	£1.00
5 Warhund	*$0.30*	*$0.90*	*$1.50*	£0.20	£0.60	£1.00
6 Thunderbunny	*$0.30*	*$0.90*	*$1.50*	£0.20	£0.60	£1.00
7 Captain Atom	*$0.30*	*$0.90*	*$1.50*	£0.25	£0.75	£1.25
8 mystery stories	*$0.30*	*$0.90*	*$1.50*	£0.20	£0.60	£1.00
9 Bludd the Ultimate Barbarian	*$0.30*	*$0.90*	*$1.50*	£0.20	£0.60	£1.00
10 Thunderbunny	*$0.30*	*$0.90*	*$1.50*	£0.20	£0.60	£1.00
Title Value:	***$3.20***	***$9.60***	***$16.00***	**£2.20**	**£6.60**	**£11.00**

Note: all Limited Distribution on the new-stands in the U.K.

CHARLTON CLASSICS

Charlton; 1 Apr 1980-9 Aug 1981

Issue	$Good	$Fine	$N.Mint	£Good	£Fine	£N.Mint
1-9 distributed in the U.K. reprints	*$0.30*	*$0.90*	*$1.50*	£0.20	£0.60	£1.00
Title Value:	***$2.70***	***$8.10***	***$13.50***	**£1.80**	**£5.40**	**£9.00**

CHARLTON PREMIERE (2ND SERIES)

Charlton; 1 Sep 1967-4 May 1968

Issue	$Good	$Fine	$N.Mint	£Good	£Fine	£N.Mint
1 Trio - 1st appearance of The Shape, Tyro Team and The Spookman in separate stories	*$1.40*	*$4.25*	*$10.00*	£0.35	£1.05	£2.50
2 Children of Doom	*$1.05*	*$3.20*	*$7.50*	£0.25	£0.85	£2.00
3 scarce in the U.K. Sinestro Boy Fiend	*$1.05*	*$3.20*	*$7.50*	£0.35	£1.05	£2.50
4 scarce in the U.K. Unlikely Tales	*$1.05*	*$3.20*	*$7.50*	£0.35	£1.05	£2.50
Title Value:	***$4.55***	***$13.85***	***$32.50***	**£1.30**	**£4.00**	**£9.50**

CHASER PLATOON

Aircel,MS; 1 Feb 1991-6 Jul 1991

Issue	$Good	$Fine	$N.Mint	£Good	£Fine	£N.Mint
1-6 ND black and white	*$0.35*	*$1.05*	*$1.75*	£0.25	£0.75	£1.25
Title Value:	***$2.10***	***$6.30***	***$10.50***	**£1.50**	**£4.50**	**£7.50**

CHASSIS

Millennium; 1 Jun 1996

Issue	$Good	$Fine	$N.Mint	£Good	£Fine	£N.Mint
1 ND Darryl Taylor and William O'Neill script and art begins	*$0.60*	*$1.80*	*$3.00*	£0.40	£1.20	£2.00
Title Value:	***$0.60***	***$1.80***	***$3.00***	**£0.40**	**£1.20**	**£2.00**

CHECKMATE

DC Comics; 1 Apr 1988-33 Dec 1990

(see Action #598)

Issue	$Good	$Fine	$N.Mint	£Good	£Fine	£N.Mint
1	*$0.20*	*$0.60*	*$1.00*	£0.10	£0.35	£0.60
2 Gil Kane cover	*$0.20*	*$0.60*	*$1.00*	£0.10	£0.35	£0.60
3 part Rob Liefeld cover	*$0.20*	*$0.60*	*$1.00*	£0.10	£0.35	£0.60
4 Gil Kane cover	*$0.20*	*$0.60*	*$1.00*	£0.10	£0.35	£0.60
5	*$0.20*	*$0.60*	*$1.00*	£0.10	£0.35	£0.60
6 Gil Kane cover	*$0.20*	*$0.60*	*$1.00*	£0.10	£0.35	£0.60
7 Art Thibert cover	*$0.20*	*$0.60*	*$1.00*	£0.10	£0.35	£0.60
8 Gil Kane cover	*$0.20*	*$0.60*	*$1.00*	£0.10	£0.35	£0.60
9 Art Thibert cover	*$0.20*	*$0.60*	*$1.00*	£0.10	£0.35	£0.60
10 Gil Kane cover	*$0.20*	*$0.60*	*$1.00*	£0.10	£0.35	£0.60
11 Invasion X-over, Gil Kane cover	*$0.20*	*$0.60*	*$1.00*	£0.10	£0.35	£0.60
12 Invasion X-over, Art Thibert cover	*$0.20*	*$0.60*	*$1.00*	£0.10	£0.35	£0.60
13-14	*$0.20*	*$0.60*	*$1.00*	£0.10	£0.35	£0.60
15 The Janus Directive, X-over Suicide Squad #27	*$0.20*	*$0.60*	*$1.00*	£0.10	£0.35	£0.60
16 The Janus Directive, X-over Suicide Squad #28, Gil Kane cover	*$0.20*	*$0.60*	*$1.00*	£0.10	£0.35	£0.60
17-18 Janus Directive tie-in, Gil Kane cover	*$0.20*	*$0.60*	*$1.00*	£0.10	£0.35	£0.60
19-33	*$0.20*	*$0.60*	*$1.00*	£0.10	£0.35	£0.60
Title Value:	***$6.60***	***$19.80***	***$33.00***	**£3.30**	**£11.55**	**£19.80**

CHEQUE MATE, THE

Fantagraphics,OS; 1 May 1992

Issue	$Good	$Fine	$N.Mint	£Good	£Fine	£N.Mint
1 ND reprints early and rare work of Eddie Campbell	*$0.70*	*$2.10*	*$3.50*	£0.45	£1.35	£2.25
Title Value:	***$0.70***	***$2.10***	***$3.50***	**£0.45**	**£1.35**	**£2.25**

CHEVAL NOIR

Dark Horse; 1 Feb 1989-50 Jan 1994

Issue	$Good	$Fine	$N.Mint	£Good	£Fine	£N.Mint
1 Loan Sloane by Phillipe Druillet, Fever in Urbicand by Schusten, Fred and Bob by Cailleteau and Vatine, Adele and the Beast by Tardi, Angel Fusion by Hiroyuki Kato, Rork by Andreas. Dave Stevens cover	*$1.00*	*$3.00*	*$5.00*	£0.70	£2.10	£3.50
2 Lone Sloane/Fever/Adele continue plus Oscar Hellion by John Bolton, The Auction by Cossu and Jamsin Poison by Leo Duranon	*$0.90*	*$2.70*	*$4.50*	£0.60	£1.80	£3.00
3 Lone Sloane/Fever/Adele continue plus Dark Horse by Brian Bolland, The Eyeball Kid by Eddie Campbell/Ed Hillyer, Geoff- The Man by Geoff Darrow God is Love by Bolland. Rick Geary illustrations pg 1,3	*$0.80*	*$2.40*	*$4.00*	£0.50	£1.50	£2.50
4 Lone Sloane/Fever/Adele plus The Promise by John Bolton/Steve Moore, painted cover John Bolton	*$0.80*	*$2.40*	*$4.00*	£0.50	£1.50	£2.50
5 Lone Sloane/Fever plus Eddie Campbell, Geary, Bolland, The Demon of the Eiffel Tower by Tardi, cover by Moebius	*$0.80*	*$2.40*	*$4.00*	£0.50	£1.50	£2.50
6 Sunstroke by Kaluta, Tardi, Bolland, Geary	*$0.80*	*$2.40*	*$4.00*	£0.50	£1.50	£2.50
7 Cailleteau/Vatine, Bolland, Geary, Eddie Campbell, Jacques Tardi, cover by Dave Stevens	*$0.80*	*$2.40*	*$4.00*	£0.50	£1.50	£2.50
8 80pgs, Demon of Eiffel Tower by Tardi, Fun by Brian Bolland, Cailleteau/Vatine/Druillet art featured	*$0.90*	*$2.70*	*$4.50*	£0.60	£1.80	£3.00
9 80pgs, The Tower by Schuiten and Peeters plus Bolland, Druillet, Eddie Campbell, Rick Geary, a fold-out Geof Darrow poster. Cover by Moebius	*$0.90*	*$2.70*	*$4.50*	£0.60	£1.80	£3.00
10 Jacques Tardi's "The Roach Killer" begins plus Druillet, Cailleteau and Vatine and article on the art of H.R. Giger	*$0.80*	*$2.40*	*$4.00*	£0.50	£1.50	£2.50
11 80pgs, features art by Jacques Tardi, Druillet, Rick Geary, Geof Darrow	*$0.90*	*$2.70*	*$4.50*	£0.60	£1.80	£3.00
12 64pgs, Jacques Tardi, Druillet, cover by Mignola	*$0.80*	*$2.40*	*$4.00*	£0.50	£1.50	£2.50
13 80pgs, Tardi, Bolland, Geary, cover by Paul Chadwick	*$0.90*	*$2.70*	*$4.50*	£0.60	£1.80	£3.00
14 72pgs, Tardi, Bolland, Darrow, Geary	*$0.80*	*$2.40*	*$4.00*	£0.50	£1.50	£2.50
15 80pgs, Jacques Tardi's Mad Scientist begins plus Bolland. Cailleteau and Vatine, Geary	*$0.90*	*$2.70*	*$4.50*	£0.60	£1.80	£3.00
16 64pgs, Tardi, Bolland, Darrow, Geary	*$0.80*	*$2.40*	*$4.00*	£0.50	£1.50	£2.50
17 80pgs, Eddie Campbell, Tardi, Bolland, Darrow, Geary	*$0.90*	*$2.70*	*$4.50*	£0.60	£1.80	£3.00
18 64pgs, Eddie Campbell, Tardi, Bolland, Darrow, Geary	*$0.80*	*$2.40*	*$4.00*	£0.50	£1.50	£2.50
19 64pgs, Tardi's "The Mummies On Parade" begins, Bolland, Darrow, Geary	*$0.80*	*$2.40*	*$4.00*	£0.50	£1.50	£2.50
20 80pgs, Angriest Dog in the World by David Lynch begins, John Bolton cover	*$0.90*	*$2.70*	*$4.50*	£0.60	£1.80	£3.00
21 64pgs, Chris Warner cover	*$1.00*	*$3.00*	*$5.00*	£0.70	£2.10	£3.50
22 64pgs, The Great Power of the Chninkel concludes	*$0.90*	*$2.70*	*$4.50*	£0.60	£1.80	£3.00
23 64pgs, The Forever War Book Three concludes	*$0.80*	*$2.40*	*$4.00*	£0.50	£1.50	£2.50
24 64pgs, Izo the Man Cleaver by Masahi Tanaka begins, Adieu Brindavoine by Tardi begins, Arthur Suydam cover	*$1.00*	*$3.00*	*$5.00*	£0.70	£2.10	£3.50
25 64pgs, Matt Wagner cover painting	*$0.80*	*$2.40*	*$4.00*	£0.50	£1.50	£2.50
26 64pgs, The Man From Ciguri by Moebius begins, cover painting by Moebius	*$0.80*	*$2.40*	*$4.00*	£0.50	£1.50	£2.50
27 32pgs, cover painting by Kelley Jones	*$0.60*	*$1.80*	*$3.00*	£0.40	£1.20	£2.00
28 32pgs, The Flower and The Rifle by Tardi begins	*$0.60*	*$1.80*	*$3.00*	£0.40	£1.20	£2.00
29-30 32pgs	*$0.60*	*$1.80*	*$3.00*	£0.40	£1.20	£2.00
31 32pgs, cover painting by Steve Pugh	*$0.60*	*$1.80*	*$3.00*	£0.40	£1.20	£2.00
32 32pgs, Sabotage by Daniel Torres begins, cover painting by Dave Gibbons	*$0.60*	*$1.80*	*$3.00*	£0.40	£1.20	£2.00
33-35 32pgs	*$0.60*	*$1.80*	*$3.00*	£0.40	£1.20	£2.00
36 32pgs, painted cover by Tom Sutton	*$0.60*	*$1.80*	*$3.00*	£0.40	£1.20	£2.00
37 32pgs, painted cover by Olivier Vatine	*$0.60*	*$1.80*	*$3.00*	£0.40	£1.20	£2.00
38-39 32pgs	*$0.60*	*$1.80*	*$3.00*	£0.40	£1.20	£2.00
40 32pgs, Dave Mazzucchelli painted cover	*$0.60*	*$1.80*	*$3.00*	£0.40	£1.20	£2.00
41-45 32pgs	*$0.60*	*$1.80*	*$3.00*	£0.40	£1.20	£2.00
46 32pgs, Moebius cover	*$0.60*	*$1.80*	*$3.00*	£0.40	£1.20	£2.00
47-48 32pgs	*$0.60*	*$1.80*	*$3.00*	£0.40	£1.20	£2.00
49 32pgs, John Bolton painted cover	*$0.60*	*$1.80*	*$3.00*	£0.40	£1.20	£2.00
50 48pgs	*$0.80*	*$2.40*	*$4.00*	£0.50	£1.50	£2.50
Title Value:	***$36.90***	***$110.70***	***$184.50***	**£24.20**	**£72.60**	**£121.00**

Note: all Non-Distributed on the news-stands in the U.K.

Note: owing to bad printing, many copies of issue #1 were returned

CHEYENNE

Dell; (Four Color #734) 1 Oct 1956-25 Dec 1961/Jan 1962

Issue	$Good	$Fine	$N.Mint	£Good	£Fine	£N.Mint
1 (Four Color #734) photo cover Clint Walker	*$25.00*	*$75.00*	*$175.00*	£17.00	£50.00	£120.00

	$Good	$Fine	$N.Mint	£Good	£Fine	£N.Mint
2 (Four Color #772) photo cover Clint Walker	$11.00	$34.00	$80.00	£7.75	£23.50	£55.00
3 (Four Color #803) photo cover Clint Walker	$10.50	$32.00	$75.00	£7.00	£21.00	£50.00
4-9 Clint Walker photo cover	$7.00	$21.00	$50.00	£5.00	£15.00	£35.00
10	$7.00	$21.00	$50.00	£5.00	£15.00	£35.00
11-12	$6.25	$19.00	$45.00	£4.25	£12.50	£30.00
13 Clint Walker photo covers return (ends #25)	$6.25	$19.00	$45.00	£4.25	£12.50	£30.00
14-25	$6.25	$19.00	$45.00	£4.25	£12.50	£30.00
Title Value:	$189.25	$573.00	$1355.00	£130.50	£387.00	£920.00

Note: limited distribution in the U.K. after 1959

CHEYENNE KID

Charlton; 8 Jul 1957-99 Nov 1973
(previously Wild Frontier #1-7)

	$Good	$Fine	$N.Mint	£Good	£Fine	£N.Mint
8 scarce in the U.K.	$5.50	$17.00	$40.00	£3.90	£11.50	£27.50
9	$3.55	$10.50	$25.00	£2.50	£7.50	£17.50
10 Williamson art, Steve Ditko cover	$8.50	$26.00	$60.00	£5.50	£17.00	£40.00
11-12 Williamson art	$10.00	$30.00	$70.00	£6.75	£20.00	£47.50
13-14 part Williamson art	$5.50	$17.00	$40.00	£3.90	£11.50	£27.50
15-17	$3.55	$10.50	$25.00	£2.50	£7.50	£17.50
18 part Williamson art	$3.55	$10.50	$25.00	£2.50	£7.50	£17.50
19-22	$3.55	$10.50	$25.00	£2.50	£7.50	£17.50
23	$1.75	$5.25	$12.50	£1.10	£3.40	£8.00
24-25	$3.55	$10.50	$25.00	£2.10	£6.25	£15.00
26	$2.55	$7.50	$18.00	£1.70	£5.00	£12.00
27-29	$1.75	$5.25	$12.50	£1.10	£3.40	£8.00
30	$2.55	$7.50	$18.00	£1.70	£5.00	£12.00
31-60	$1.05	$3.20	$7.50	£0.60	£1.90	£4.50
61-75	$1.00	$3.00	$5.00	£0.60	£1.80	£3.00
76-80	$0.80	$2.40	$4.00	£0.50	£1.50	£2.50
81-87	$0.60	$1.80	$3.00	£0.40	£1.20	£2.00
87 Modern Comics Reprint, LD in the U.K. (1978)	$0.20	$0.60	$1.00	£0.30	£0.90	£1.50
88-89	$0.60	$1.80	$3.00	£0.40	£1.20	£2.00
89 Modern Comics Reprint, LD in the U.K. (1978)	$0.20	$0.60	$1.00	£0.30	£0.90	£1.50
90-99	$0.60	$1.80	$3.00	£0.40	£1.20	£2.00
Title Value:	$158.45	$476.90	$1060.00	£102.90	£311.20	£694.50

Note: most issues distributed in the U.K. after 1959

CHEYENNE KID (2ND SERIES)

A Plus Comics; 1 Jan 1992

	$Good	$Fine	$N.Mint	£Good	£Fine	£N.Mint
1 ND reprints from original series	$0.40	$1.20	$2.00	£0.25	£0.75	£1.25
Title Value:	$0.40	$1.20	$2.00	£0.25	£0.75	£1.25

CHIAROSCURO: THE PRIVATE LIVES OF LEONARDO DA VINCI

DC Comics/Vertigo,MS; 1 Jul 1995-10 Apr 1996

	$Good	$Fine	$N.Mint	£Good	£Fine	£N.Mint
1-10 ND Dave Rawson script, Chas Truog art	$0.60	$1.80	$3.00	£0.40	£1.20	£2.00
Title Value:	$6.00	$18.00	$30.00	£4.00	£12.00	£20.00

CHILD'S PLAY 2

Innovation,MS Film; 1 Nov 1991-3 Jan 1991

	$Good	$Fine	$N.Mint	£Good	£Fine	£N.Mint
1-3 ND film adaptation; colour	$0.50	$1.50	$2.50	£0.30	£0.90	£1.50
Title Value:	$1.50	$4.50	$7.50	£0.90	£2.70	£4.50
Trade Paperback (1991) 68pgs, squarebound, film adaptation in full				£0.90	£2.70	£4.50

CHILD'S PLAY 3

Innovation, Film; 1 Oct 1991-3 Nov 1991

	$Good	$Fine	$N.Mint	£Good	£Fine	£N.Mint
1-3 ND film adaptation	$0.50	$1.50	$2.50	£0.30	£0.90	£1.50
Title Value:	$1.50	$4.50	$7.50	£0.90	£2.70	£4.50
Graphic Novel (Jan 1992), reprints mini-series				£0.90	£2.70	£4.50

CHILD'S PLAY: THE SERIES

Innovation; 1 May 1991-5 Jan 1992

	$Good	$Fine	$N.Mint	£Good	£Fine	£N.Mint
1-5 ND	$0.40	$1.20	$2.00	£0.25	£0.75	£1.25
Title Value:	$2.00	$6.00	$10.00	£1.25	£3.75	£6.25

CHILDREN OF FIRE

Fantagor; 1-3 1988

	$Good	$Fine	$N.Mint	£Good	£Fine	£N.Mint
1 ND scarce in the U.K. Corben art begins	$0.80	$2.40	$4.00	£0.50	£1.50	£2.50
2 ND scarce in the U.K. includes redrawn reprint from Promethian Enterprises #3	$0.80	$2.40	$4.00	£0.50	£1.50	£2.50
3 ND scarce in the U.K. includes reprint from Fantagor #3	$0.80	$2.40	$4.00	£0.50	£1.50	£2.50
Title Value:	$2.40	$7.20	$12.00	£1.50	£4.50	£7.50

Note: last series in "Corben-color".

CHILDREN OF THE NIGHT

Night Wynd,MS; 1 Sep 1992-4 Dec 1992

	$Good	$Fine	$N.Mint	£Good	£Fine	£N.Mint
1-4 ND Barry Blair and Jimmy Palmiotti script/art; black and white	$0.50	$1.50	$2.50	£0.30	£0.90	£1.50
Title Value:	$2.00	$6.00	$10.00	£1.20	£3.60	£6.00

CHILDREN OF THE VOYAGER

Marvel UK/Frontier,MS; 1 Sep 1993-4 Dec 1993

	$Good	$Fine	$N.Mint	£Good	£Fine	£N.Mint
1 Nick Abadzis and Paul Johnson begin; embossed, glow-in-the-dark cover	$0.40	$1.20	$2.00	£0.25	£0.75	£1.25
2-4	$0.40	$1.20	$2.00	£0.25	£0.75	£1.25
Title Value:	$1.60	$4.80	$8.00	£1.00	£3.00	£5.00

CHILDREN'S CRUSADE, THE

DC Comics/Vertigo,MS; 1 Dec 1993-2 Jan 1994

	$Good	$Fine	$N.Mint	£Good	£Fine	£N.Mint
1 64pgs, Neil Gaiman and Chris Bachalo	$0.80	$2.40	$4.00	£0.50	£1.50	£2.50
2 64pgs, Neil Gaiman; painted cover by John Totleben	$0.80	$2.40	$4.00	£0.50	£1.50	£2.50
Title Value:	$1.60	$4.80	$8.00	£1.00	£3.00	£5.00

CHILI

Marvel Comics Group; 1 May 1969-17 Sep 1970; 18 Aug 1972-26 Dec 1973

	$Good	$Fine	$N.Mint	£Good	£Fine	£N.Mint
1 ND scarce in the U.K.	$3.20	$9.50	$22.50	£1.75	£5.25	£12.50
2 ND scarce in the U.K.	$2.05	$6.25	$12.50	£1.05	£3.25	£6.50
3-5 ND scarce in the U.K.	$1.65	$5.00	$10.00	£0.80	£2.50	£5.00
6-10 ND	$1.30	$4.00	$8.00	£0.65	£2.00	£4.00
11-17 ND	$1.25	$3.75	$7.50	£0.50	£1.50	£3.00
18-26 ND	$0.80	$2.50	$5.00	£0.30	£1.00	£2.00
Title Value:	$32.65	$99.50	$202.50	£14.65	£45.50	£93.00

CHILI ANNUAL

Marvel Comics Group; 1 Dec 1971

	$Good	$Fine	$N.Mint	£Good	£Fine	£N.Mint
1 ND very scarce in the U.K.	$2.00	$6.00	$12.00	£1.05	£3.25	£6.50
Title Value:	$2.00	$6.00	$12.00	£1.05	£3.25	£6.50

CHILLER

Marvel Comics Group/Epic,MS; 1 Nov 1993-2 Dec 1993

	$Good	$Fine	$N.Mint	£Good	£Fine	£N.Mint
1-2 ND James Hudnall and John Ridgway	$1.50	$4.50	$7.50	£1.00	£3.00	£5.00

Challengers of the Unknown #78

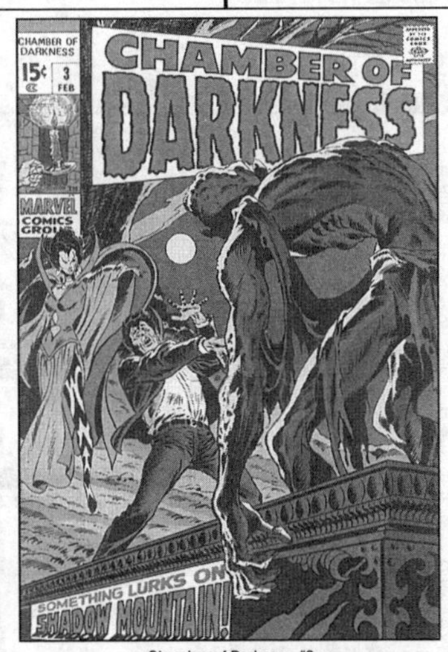

Chamber of Darkness #3

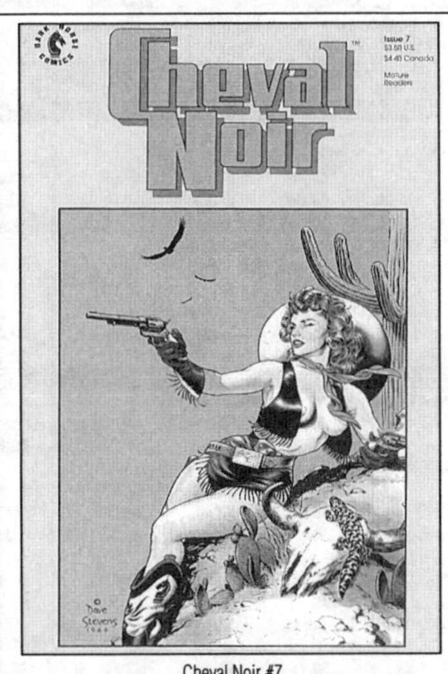

Cheval Noir #7

	$Good	$Fine	$N.Mint	£Good	£Fine	£N.Mint
Title Value:	*$3.00*	*$9.00*	*$15.00*	£2.00	£6.00	£10.00

CHILLERS GIANT SIZE

Marvel Comics Group; 1 Jun 1974
(becomes Dracula Giant Size)

	$Good	$Fine	$N.Mint	£Good	£Fine	£N.Mint
1 ND 52pgs, 1st appearance Lilith (daughter of Dracula); Gene Colan art	*$1.25*	*$3.75*	*$7.50*	£1.00	£3.00	£6.00
Title Value:	*$1.25*	*$3.75*	*$7.50*	£1.00	£3.00	£6.00

CHILLERS GIANT SIZE (2ND SERIES)

Marvel Comics Group; 1 Feb 1975-3 Aug 1975

	$Good	$Fine	$N.Mint	£Good	£Fine	£N.Mint
1 ND scarce in the U.K. 68pgs, Dave Gibbons art featured	*$1.00*	*$3.00*	*$6.00*	£0.65	£2.00	£4.00
2-3 ND 68pgs, all reprint, Wrightson/Smith reprint	*$0.55*	*$1.75*	*$3.50*	£0.55	£1.75	£3.50
Title Value:	*$2.10*	*$6.50*	*$13.00*	£1.75	£5.50	£11.00

CHILLING ADVENTURES IN SORCERY

Red Circle; 1 Sep 1972-5 Feb 1974
(becomes Red Circle Sorcery)

	$Good	$Fine	$N.Mint	£Good	£Fine	£N.Mint
1 distributed in the U.K. Sabrina appears	*$1.00*	*$3.00*	*$6.00*	£0.30	£1.00	£2.00
2 distributed in the U.K. Sabrina appears	*$0.40*	*$1.25*	*$2.50*	£0.20	£0.60	£1.25
3-5 distributed in the U.K. Gray Morrow art	*$0.40*	*$1.25*	*$2.50*	£0.20	£0.60	£1.25
Title Value:	*$2.60*	*$8.00*	*$16.00*	£1.10	£3.40	£7.00

CHINA & JAZZ: CODENAME DOUBLE IMPACT

High Impact Studios; 1 1996

	$Good	$Fine	$N.Mint	£Good	£Fine	£N.Mint
1 ND Matthew Roberts and Jude Millien art begins; black and white	*$0.60*	*$1.80*	*$3.00*	£0.40	£1.20	£2.00
1 Nude Edition ND	*$2.00*	*$6.00*	*$10.00*	£1.20	£3.60	£6.00
Title Value:	*$2.60*	*$7.80*	*$13.00*	£1.60	£4.80	£8.00

CHINA SEA

Night Wynd,MS; 1 Dec 1991-4 Mar 1992

	$Good	$Fine	$N.Mint	£Good	£Fine	£N.Mint
1-4 ND Barry Blair script and art; black and white	*$0.50*	*$1.50*	*$2.50*	£0.30	£0.90	£1.50
Title Value:	*$2.00*	*$6.00*	*$10.00*	£1.20	£3.60	£6.00

CHIP 'N DALE RESCUE RANGERS

Disney; 1 May 1990-20 Dec 1991

	$Good	$Fine	$N.Mint	£Good	£Fine	£N.Mint
1-20 ND	*$0.30*	*$0.90*	*$1.50*	£0.20	£0.60	£1.00
Title Value:	*$6.00*	*$18.00*	*$30.00*	£4.00	£12.00	£20.00

CHIPS & VANILLA

Kitchen Sink,OS; 1 Jun 1988

	$Good	$Fine	$N.Mint	£Good	£Fine	£N.Mint
1 ND Doug Potter script and art	*$0.40*	*$1.20*	*$2.00*	£0.25	£0.75	£1.25
Title Value:	*$0.40*	*$1.20*	*$2.00*	£0.25	£0.75	£1.25

CHITTY CHITTY BANG BANG

Gold Key/Movie Comics,OS Movie; 30038-902 Feb 1969

	$Good	$Fine	$N.Mint	£Good	£Fine	£N.Mint
30038-902 distributed in the U.K. with giant pull-out poster; photo cover	*$7.00*	*$21.00*	*$50.00*	£4.25	£12.50	£30.00
Title Value:	*$7.00*	*$21.00*	*$50.00*	£4.25	£12.50	£30.00

CHOLLY AND FLYTRAP, NEW ADVENTURES OF

Marvel Comics Group/Epic,MS; 1 Dec 1990-3 Feb 1991

	$Good	$Fine	$N.Mint	£Good	£Fine	£N.Mint
1-3 ND characters from Epic Illustrated, Arthur Suydam script/art	*$0.70*	*$2.10*	*$3.50*	£0.50	£1.50	£2.50
Title Value:	*$2.10*	*$6.30*	*$10.50*	£1.50	£4.50	£7.50
Note: Bookshelf Format						
Graphic Novel: The Original Adventures of... (May 1991), reprints above series in colour				£1.10	£3.30	£5.50

CHOSEN

Click! Comics; 1 Jul 1995-2 1995

	$Good	$Fine	$N.Mint	£Good	£Fine	£N.Mint
1-2 ND	*$0.50*	*$1.50*	*$2.50*	£0.30	£0.90	£1.50
Title Value:	*$1.00*	*$3.00*	*$5.00*	£0.60	£1.80	£3.00

CHRISTIAN

Maximum Comic Press,MS; 1 Mar 1996-3 May 1996

	$Good	$Fine	$N.Mint	£Good	£Fine	£N.Mint
1-3 ND Rob Liefeld script, Pop Mhan art	*$0.50*	*$1.50*	*$2.50*	£0.30	£0.90	£1.50
Title Value:	*$1.50*	*$4.50*	*$7.50*	£0.90	£2.70	£4.50

CHRISTMAS WITH SUPERSWINE

Fantagraphics,OS; 1 Feb 1989

	$Good	$Fine	$N.Mint	£Good	£Fine	£N.Mint
1 ND Gary Fields art; black and white	*$0.40*	*$1.20*	*$2.00*	£0.25	£0.75	£1.25
Title Value:	*$0.40*	*$1.20*	*$2.00*	£0.25	£0.75	£1.25

CHRISTMAS WITH THE SUPER-HEROES

DC Comics; 1 Dec 1988; 2 Dec 1989

	$Good	$Fine	$N.Mint	£Good	£Fine	£N.Mint
1 ND 100pgs, reprints Frank Miller Batman, John Byrne cover art	*$0.70*	*$2.10*	*$3.50*	£0.35	£1.05	£1.75
2 ND 100pgs, squarebound, features Batman fable-story by Gibbons, art on Superman by Chadwick	*$0.70*	*$2.10*	*$3.50*	£0.35	£1.05	£1.75
Title Value:	*$1.40*	*$4.20*	*$7.00*	£0.70	£2.10	£3.50

CHROMA-TICK SPECIAL EDITION, THE

New England Press; 1 Apr 1992-11 1993

	$Good	$Fine	$N.Mint	£Good	£Fine	£N.Mint
1 ND 40pgs, reprints begin of Tick series in colour; with 4 bound-in trading cards at centrefold	*$1.00*	*$3.00*	*$5.00*	£0.50	£1.50	£2.50
2 ND 40pgs, with 4 bound-in trading cards at centrefold	*$0.80*	*$2.40*	*$4.00*	£0.50	£1.50	£2.50
3 ND	*$0.80*	*$2.40*	*$4.00*	£0.50	£1.50	£2.50
4 ND issue available with 3 different outer covers predicting the outcome of the 1992 Presidential Election - collect 'em all!	*$0.70*	*$2.10*	*$3.50*	£0.45	£1.35	£2.25
5 ND	*$0.70*	*$2.10*	*$3.50*	£0.45	£1.35	£2.25
6 ND bound-in trading card	*$0.70*	*$2.10*	*$3.50*	£0.45	£1.35	£2.25
7-11 ND	*$0.70*	*$2.10*	*$3.50*	£0.45	£1.35	£2.25
Title Value:	*$8.20*	*$24.60*	*$41.00*	£5.10	£15.30	£25.50

CHROME

Hot; 1 Oct 1986-3 Mar 1987

	$Good	$Fine	$N.Mint	£Good	£Fine	£N.Mint
1 ND Peter Gillis script, Kelly Jones art begins	*$0.40*	*$1.20*	*$2.00*	£0.25	£0.75	£1.25
2 ND (1 on indica)	*$0.40*	*$1.20*	*$2.00*	£0.25	£0.75	£1.25
3 ND	*$0.40*	*$1.20*	*$2.00*	£0.25	£0.75	£1.25
Title Value:	*$1.20*	*$3.60*	*$6.00*	£0.75	£2.25	£3.75

CHROMIUM MAN, THE

Triumphant Comics; 0 Apr 1994; 1 Jan 1993-15 1994

	$Good	$Fine	$N.Mint	£Good	£Fine	£N.Mint
0 ND (Apr 1994)	*$0.30*	*$0.90*	*$1.50*	£0.20	£0.60	£1.00
0 Blue Logo Edition, ND (Oct 1994) - pre-bagged with backing board; 2,000 copies	*$0.70*	*$2.10*	*$3.50*	£0.50	£1.50	£2.50
0 Signed Edition, ND (Aug 1994), pre-bagged with backing board	*$0.60*	*$1.80*	*$3.00*	£0.40	£1.20	£2.00
1 ND Ash Can Edition	*$0.30*	*$0.90*	*$1.50*	£0.20	£0.60	£1.00
2 ND	*$0.30*	*$0.90*	*$1.50*	£0.20	£0.60	£1.00
2 Signed Edition, ND - with mini-poster photo-print; pre-bagged with backing board	*$0.60*	*$1.80*	*$3.00*	£0.40	£1.20	£2.00
3 ND	*$0.30*	*$0.90*	*$1.50*	£0.20	£0.60	£1.00
4 ND Unleashed X-over	*$0.30*	*$0.90*	*$1.50*	£0.20	£0.60	£1.00
5-10 ND	*$0.30*	*$0.90*	*$1.50*	£0.20	£0.60	£1.00
11 ND dual issue with Prince Vandal #8 (Note: there is only one comic between the two titles)	*$0.30*	*$0.90*	*$1.50*	£0.20	£0.60	£1.00
11 Signed Edition, ND (Oct 1994) - pre-bagged with mini-poster photo-print and backing board	*$0.60*	*$1.80*	*$3.00*	£0.40	£1.20	£2.00
12 ND dual issue with Prince Vandal #9 (Note: there is only one comic between the two titles)	*$0.30*	*$0.90*	*$1.50*	£0.20	£0.60	£1.00
13-15 ND	*$0.30*	*$0.90*	*$1.50*	£0.20	£0.60	£1.00
Title Value:	*$7.30*	*$21.90*	*$36.50*	£4.90	£14.70	£24.50

CHROMIUM MAN: VIOLENT PAST

Triumphant Comics,MS; 1,2 Jan 1994

	$Good	$Fine	$N.Mint	£Good	£Fine	£N.Mint
1 ND	*$0.40*	*$1.20*	*$2.00*	£0.25	£0.75	£1.25
1 Signed Edition, ND - with mini-poster photo-print; pre-bagged with backing board	*$0.70*	*$2.10*	*$3.50*	£0.50	£1.50	£2.50
2 ND	*$0.40*	*$1.20*	*$2.00*	£0.25	£0.75	£1.25
2 Signed Edition, ND - with mini-poster photo-print; pre-bagged with backing board	*$0.70*	*$2.10*	*$3.50*	£0.50	£1.50	£2.50
Title Value:	*$2.20*	*$6.60*	*$11.00*	£1.50	£4.50	£7.50

CHRONIC IDIOCY

Caliber Press,MS; 1 Nov 1991-3 Jan 1992

	$Good	$Fine	$N.Mint	£Good	£Fine	£N.Mint
1-3 ND	*$0.50*	*$1.50*	*$2.50*	£0.30	£0.90	£1.50
Title Value:	*$1.50*	*$4.50*	*$7.50*	£0.90	£2.70	£4.50

CHRONICLES OF CORUM

First; 1 Jan 1987-12 Nov 1988
(see Corum)

	$Good	$Fine	$N.Mint	£Good	£Fine	£N.Mint
1 ND Knight of the Swords begins, Mignola covers and art begins	*$0.40*	*$1.20*	*$2.00*	£0.25	£0.75	£1.25
2-4 ND	*$0.40*	*$1.20*	*$2.00*	£0.25	£0.75	£1.25
5 ND Queen of the Swords begins	*$0.40*	*$1.20*	*$2.00*	£0.25	£0.75	£1.25
6 ND last Mignola cover and art	*$0.40*	*$1.20*	*$2.00*	£0.25	£0.75	£1.25
7-8 ND Jackson Guice and Kelly Jones cover and art	*$0.40*	*$1.20*	*$2.00*	£0.25	£0.75	£1.25
9 ND King of the Swords begins, Ken Hooper and Kelly Jones cover and art	*$0.40*	*$1.20*	*$2.00*	£0.25	£0.75	£1.25
10 ND Ken Hooper and Kelly Jones cover and art	*$0.40*	*$1.20*	*$2.00*	£0.25	£0.75	£1.25
11 ND Ken Hooper and Kelly Jones art, Mignola cover	*$0.40*	*$1.20*	*$2.00*	£0.25	£0.75	£1.25
12 ND Jill Thompson and Kelly Jones art, Mignola cover	*$0.40*	*$1.20*	*$2.00*	£0.25	£0.75	£1.25
Title Value:	*$4.80*	*$14.40*	*$24.00*	£3.00	£9.00	£15.00

CHRONICLES OF PANDA KHAN

Apple/Abacus Press; 1 Feb 1987-2 Jul 1987
(becomes Panda Khan)

	$Good	$Fine	$N.Mint	£Good	£Fine	£N.Mint
1-2 ND	*$0.40*	*$1.20*	*$2.00*	£0.25	£0.75	£1.25
Title Value:	*$0.80*	*$2.40*	*$4.00*	£0.50	£1.50	£2.50

CHRONICLES OF PANDA KHAN BOOK 2

Abacus Press; 1 1990-4 1991?

	$Good	$Fine	$N.Mint	£Good	£Fine	£N.Mint
1-4 ND titled Panda Khan	*$0.40*	*$1.20*	*$2.00*	£0.25	£0.75	£1.25
Title Value:	*$1.60*	*$4.80*	*$8.00*	£1.00	£3.00	£5.00
Special (Aug 1990), 48pgs; ties up plot lines; Bryan Talbot art featured				£0.35	£1.05	£1.75

CHRONOWAR

Dark Horse,MS; 1 Aug 1996-9 Apr 1997

	$Good	$Fine	$N.Mint	£Good	£Fine	£N.Mint
1-9 ND black and white	*$0.60*	*$1.80*	*$3.00*	£0.40	£1.20	£2.00
Title Value:	*$5.40*	*$16.20*	*$27.00*	£3.60	£10.80	£18.00

CHUCK NORRIS

Marvel Comics Group/Star; 1 Jan 1987-5 Sep 1987

	$Good	$Fine	$N.Mint	£Good	£Fine	£N.Mint
1-5 ND	*$0.15*	*$0.45*	*$0.75*	£0.10	£0.35	£0.60
Title Value:	*$0.75*	*$2.25*	*$3.75*	£0.50	£1.75	£3.00

CINDER AND ASHE

DC Comics,MS; 1 May 1988-4 Aug 1988

	$Good	$Fine	$N.Mint	£Good	£Fine	£N.Mint
1-4 ND Garcia Lopez art	*$0.50*	*$1.50*	*$2.50*	£0.30	£0.90	£1.50
Title Value:	*$2.00*	*$6.00*	*$10.00*	£1.20	£3.60	£6.00

CITIZEN KANG

Marvel Comics Group; 1992

Cross-over storyline that ran throughout the following issues: **Captain America Annual #11**, **Thor Annual #17**, **Fantastic Four Annual #25**, **Avengers Annual #21**.

CITY KNIGHTS

Acclaim Comics/Windjammer,MS; 1 Jun 1995-3 Aug 1995

	$Good	$Fine	$N.Mint	£Good	£Fine	£N.Mint
1-3 ND Jeff Gomez script, Val Mayerik art						
	$0.45	*$1.35*	*$2.25*	£0.30	£0.90	£1.50
Title Value:	*$1.35*	*$4.05*	*$6.75*	£0.90	£2.70	£4.50

CITYSCAPE

NC Venture; 1 Jun 1990-2 1990

	$Good	$Fine	$N.Mint	£Good	£Fine	£N.Mint
1 ND card-stock cover; black and white						
	$0.40	*$1.20*	*$2.00*	£0.25	£0.75	£1.25
2 ND black and white						
	$0.40	*$1.20*	*$2.00*	£0.25	£0.75	£1.25
Title Value:	*$0.80*	*$2.40*	*$4.00*	£0.50	£1.50	£2.50

CIVIL WAR TALES

ACG,MS; 1 Jul 1995-3 Sep 1995

	$Good	$Fine	$N.Mint	£Good	£Fine	£N.Mint
1-3 ND features story and art by Sam Glanzman						
	$0.50	*$1.50*	*$2.50*	£0.30	£0.90	£1.50
Title Value:	*$1.50*	*$4.50*	*$7.50*	£0.90	£2.70	£4.50

CIVIL WAR TALES (2ND SERIES)

Avalon Communications; 1 Jan 1996-2 1996?

	$Good	$Fine	$N.Mint	£Good	£Fine	£N.Mint
1-2 ND reprints from ACG						
	$0.55	*$1.65*	*$2.75*	£0.35	£1.05	£1.75
Title Value:	*$1.10*	*$3.30*	*$5.50*	£0.70	£2.10	£3.50

CIVIL WAR, THE

Eclipse; 1,2 Jun 1993

	$Good	$Fine	$N.Mint	£Good	£Fine	£N.Mint
1 ND 96pgs, Richard Rockwell and Fred Fredericks painted art, Earl Norem painted cover						
	$2.40	*$7.00*	*$12.00*	£1.50	£4.50	£7.50
2 ND 96pgs, Angelo Torres and George Woodbridge painted art, Earl Norem painted cover						
	$2.40	*$7.00*	*$12.00*	£1.50	£4.50	£7.50
Title Value:	*$4.80*	*$14.00*	*$24.00*	£3.00	£9.00	£15.00

CLAIRE VOYANTE

Lightning Comics; 1 May 1996

	$Good	$Fine	$N.Mint	£Good	£Fine	£N.Mint
1 ND 48pgs, guest stars Hellina						
	$0.70	*$2.10*	*$3.50*	£0.50	£1.50	£2.50
1 Commemorative Edition, ND 48pgs, pre-bagged with certificate; dimensional platinum metallic ink cover (!)						
	$1.20	*$3.60*	*$6.00*	£0.70	£2.10	£3.50
1 Nude Version A, ND 48pgs, pre-bagged with certificate; Claire looking at herself in a mirror						
	$2.00	*$6.00*	*$10.00*	£1.30	£3.90	£6.50
1 Nude Version B, ND pre-bagged with certificate; Claire dressing with lover asleep						
	$2.00	*$6.00*	*$10.00*	£1.30	£3.90	£6.50
Title Value:	*$5.90*	*$17.70*	*$29.50*	£3.80	£11.40	£19.00

CLANDESTINE

Marvel Comics Group; 1 Oct 1994-12 Sep 1995

	$Good	$Fine	$N.Mint	£Good	£Fine	£N.Mint
1 Alan Davis script and art, inks by Mark Farmer; foil stamped cover						
	$0.60	*$1.80*	*$3.00*	£0.40	£1.20	£2.00
2-5	*$0.50*	*$1.50*	*$2.50*	£0.30	£0.90	£1.50
6-7 Spiderman guest-stars						
	$0.50	*$1.50*	*$2.50*	£0.30	£0.90	£1.50
8 Dr. Strange and The Invaders guest-star; last Alan Davis art						
	$0.50	*$1.50*	*$2.50*	£0.30	£0.90	£1.50
9	*$0.50*	*$1.50*	*$2.50*	£0.30	£0.90	£1.50
10 Britanic appears						
	$0.50	*$1.50*	*$2.50*	£0.30	£0.90	£1.50
11-12	*$0.50*	*$1.50*	*$2.50*	£0.30	£0.90	£1.50
Title Value:	*$6.10*	*$18.30*	*$30.50*	£3.70	£11.10	£18.50

Note: issues #12 and #13 were advertised and solicited but never appeared.

CLANDESTINE PREVIEW

Marvel Comics Group,OS; nn Oct 1994

	$Good	$Fine	$N.Mint	£Good	£Fine	£N.Mint
nn ND previews Clandestine series and spotlights Alan Davis' work for Marvel						
	$0.50	*$1.50*	*$2.50*	£0.30	£0.90	£1.50
Title Value:	*$0.50*	*$1.50*	*$2.50*	£0.30	£0.90	£1.50

CLASH

DC Comics,MS; 1 Nov 1991-3 Jan 1992

	$Good	$Fine	$N.Mint	£Good	£Fine	£N.Mint
1-3 ND Tom Veitch script, Adam Kubert art						
	$0.90	*$2.70*	*$4.50*	£0.60	£1.80	£3.00
Title Value:	*$2.70*	*$8.10*	*$13.50*	£1.80	£5.40	£9.00

CLASSIC GIRLS

Eternity; 1 Feb 1991-4 May 1991

	$Good	$Fine	$N.Mint	£Good	£Fine	£N.Mint
1 ND reprints Trouble With Girls #1 etc. New Paul Gulacy cover						
	$0.40	*$1.20*	*$2.00*	£0.25	£0.75	£1.25
2-4 ND	*$0.40*	*$1.20*	*$2.00*	£0.25	£0.75	£1.25
Title Value:	*$1.60*	*$4.80*	*$8.00*	£1.00	£3.00	£5.00

CLASSIC STAR WARS

Dark Horse; 1 Sep 1992-20 May 1994

	$Good	$Fine	$N.Mint	£Good	£Fine	£N.Mint
1 ND reprints of 1980s US newspaper strip begins by Goodwin and Williamson; new Williamson covers						
	$0.80	*$2.40*	*$4.00*	£0.50	£1.50	£2.50
2-20 ND	*$0.60*	*$1.80*	*$3.00*	£0.30	£0.90	£1.50
Title Value:	*$12.20*	*$36.60*	*$52.00*	£6.20	£18.60	£31.00
Classic Star Wars Volume 1 (1995)						
Trade paperback reprints issues #1-7, new Al Williamson cover				£2.20	£6.60	£11.00
Classic Star Wars Volume 2 (Jun 1995)						
Trade paperback reprints issues #8-14, new Al Williamson cover				£2.20	£6.60	£11.00
Classic Star Wars: Star Wars Trilogy Boxed Set (Oct 1995)						
collects the three Star Wars films adaptations in slip-case				£4.00	£12.00	£20.00

CLASSIC STAR WARS: A NEW HOPE

Dark Horse,MS; 1 Jun 1994-2 Jul 1994

	$Good	$Fine	$N.Mint	£Good	£Fine	£N.Mint
1-2 ND reprints film adaptation from the first issues of Star Wars, newly recoloured, covers by Adam Hughes						
	$0.80	*$2.40*	*$4.00*	£0.50	£1.50	£2.50
Title Value:	*$1.60*	*$4.80*	*$8.00*	£1.00	£3.00	£5.00
Classic Star Wars: A New Hope (Oct 1995)						
Trade paperback collects mini-series				£1.30	£3.90	£6.50

CLASSIC STAR WARS: DEVILWORLDS

Dark Horse,MS; 1 Aug 1996-2 Sep 1996

	$Good	$Fine	$N.Mint	£Good	£Fine	£N.Mint
1-2 ND Marvel U.K. reprints featuring Alan Davis art						
	$0.50	*$1.50*	*$2.50*	£0.30	£0.90	£1.50
Title Value:	*$1.00*	*$3.00*	*$5.00*	£0.60	£1.80	£3.00

CLASSIC STAR WARS: RETURN OF THE JEDI

Dark Horse,MS; 1 Oct 1994-2 Nov 1994

	$Good	$Fine	$N.Mint	£Good	£Fine	£N.Mint
1-2 ND film adaptation reprinted from Marvel's comic series; pre-bagged with trading acrd						
	$0.80	*$2.40*	*$4.00*	£0.50	£1.50	£2.50
Title Value:	*$1.60*	*$4.80*	*$8.00*	£1.00	£3.00	£5.00
Classic Star Wars: Return of the Jedi (Oct 1995)						
Trade paperback collects mini-series				£1.30	£3.90	£6.50

CLASSIC STAR WARS: THE EARLY ADVENTURES

Dark Horse,MS; 1 Aug 1994-9 Apr 1995

	$Good	$Fine	$N.Mint	£Good	£Fine	£N.Mint
1-9 ND Russ Manning strip reformatted and coloured						
	$0.50	*$1.50*	*$2.50*	£0.30	£0.90	£1.50
Title Value:	*$4.50*	*$13.50*	*$22.50*	£2.70	£8.10	£13.50

CLASSIC STAR WARS: THE EMPIRE STRIKES BACK

Dark Horse,MS; 1 Aug 1994-2 Sep 1994

	$Good	$Fine	$N.Mint	£Good	£Fine	£N.Mint
1-2 ND reprints film adaptation from Marvel Star Wars comic with new Al Williamson covers						
	$0.80	*$2.40*	*$4.00*	£0.50	£1.50	£2.50
Title Value:	*$1.60*	*$4.80*	*$8.00*	£1.00	£3.00	£5.00
Classic Star Wars: The Empire Strikes Back (Oct 1995)						
Trade paperback collects mini-series				£1.30	£3.90	£6.50

CLASSIC STAR WARS: THE VANDELHEIM MISSION

Dark Horse,OS; 1 Mar 1995

	$Good	$Fine	$N.Mint	£Good	£Fine	£N.Mint
1 ND reprinted from newspaper strip by Archie Goodwin and Al Williamson						
	$0.50	*$1.50*	*$2.50*	£0.30	£0.90	£1.50
Title Value:	*$0.50*	*$1.50*	*$2.50*	£0.30	£0.90	£1.50

CLASSIC X-MEN

Marvel Comics Group; 1 Sep 1986-110 Sep 1995

	$Good	$Fine	$N.Mint	£Good	£Fine	£N.Mint
1 LD in the U.K. reprints Giant Size #1, additional back up material with John Bolton art begins						
	$1.50	*$4.50*	*$7.50*	£0.80	£2.40	£4.00
2 LD in the U.K. reprints X-Men #94, John Bolton art						
	$1.00	*$3.00*	*$5.00*	£0.60	£1.80	£3.00
3 LD in the U.K. reprints X-Men #95, John Bolton art						
	$0.80	*$2.40*	*$4.00*	£0.50	£1.50	£2.50
4-9 ND John Bolton art						
	$0.80	*$2.40*	*$4.00*	£0.40	£1.20	£2.00
10 ND Wolverine stalked by Sabretooth, John Bolton art						
	$1.20	*$3.60*	*$6.00*	£0.50	£1.50	£2.50
11 ND John Bolton art						
	$0.70	*$2.10*	*$3.50*	£0.35	£1.05	£1.75
12 ND more facts about Magneto's origin						
	$0.70	*$2.10*	*$3.50*	£0.35	£1.05	£1.75
13-15 ND John Bolton art						
	$0.70	*$2.10*	*$3.50*	£0.35	£1.05	£1.75
16 ND John Bolton art						
	$0.70	*$2.10*	*$3.50*	£0.30	£0.90	£1.50
17 ND Wolverine cover, John Bolton art						
	$0.70	*$2.10*	*$3.50*	£0.30	£0.90	£1.50
18 ND John Bolton art						
	$0.70	*$2.10*	*$3.50*	£0.30	£0.90	£1.50
19 ND John Bolton art; Magneto's Vengeance story						
	$0.70	*$2.10*	*$3.50*	£0.40	£1.20	£2.00
20-25 ND John Bolton art						
	$0.70	*$2.10*	*$3.50*	£0.30	£0.90	£1.50
26 Wolverine cover, John Bolton art; reprints X-Men #120						
	$0.60	*$1.80*	*$3.00*	£0.30	£0.90	£1.50
27 ND reprints #121, John Bolton art						
	$0.60	*$1.80*	*$3.00*	£0.30	£0.90	£1.50
28 ND John Bolton art						
	$0.60	*$1.80*	*$3.00*	£0.30	£0.90	£1.50
29 ND no John Bolton art in back up material						
	$0.60	*$1.80*	*$3.00*	£0.30	£0.90	£1.50
30 ND John Bolton art						
	$0.60	*$1.80*	*$3.00*	£0.30	£0.90	£1.50
31-35 ND John Bolton art						
	$0.50	*$1.50*	*$2.50*	£0.25	£0.75	£1.25
36-38 ND	*$0.50*	*$1.50*	*$2.50*	£0.25	£0.75	£1.25
39 ND Jim Lee art in back up; 2nd Jim Lee work on X-Men (see X-Men #248)						
	$1.20	*$3.60*	*$6.00*	£0.40	£1.20	£2.00
40-42 ND	*$0.40*	*$1.20*	*$2.00*	£0.25	£0.75	£1.25
43 ND DS reprints X-Men #137 Death of Phoenix						
	$0.40	*$1.20*	*$2.00*	£0.25	£0.75	£1.25
44 ND reprints X-Men #138, new Rogue story by Nocenti and Barta (last new material in title)						
	$0.40	*$1.20*	*$2.00*	£0.25	£0.75	£1.25
45 ND	*$0.40*	*$1.20*	*$2.00*	£0.25	£0.75	£1.25
46 ND title becomes "X-Men Classic"						
	$0.40	*$1.20*	*$2.00*	£0.25	£0.75	£1.25
47 ND last Byrne reprint						
	$0.40	*$1.20*	*$2.00*	£0.25	£0.75	£1.25
48-50 ND	*$0.40*	*$1.20*	*$2.00*	£0.25	£0.75	£1.25
51-53 ND	*$0.30*	*$0.90*	*$1.50*	£0.20	£0.60	£1.00
54 ND DS	*$0.30*	*$0.90*	*$1.50*	£0.20	£0.60	£1.00
55-60 ND	*$0.30*	*$0.90*	*$1.50*	£0.20	£0.60	£1.00
61-65 ND	*$0.25*	*$0.75*	*$1.25*	£0.15	£0.45	£0.75
66 ND Mike Mignola cover						
	$0.25	*$0.75*	*$1.25*	£0.15	£0.45	£0.75
67 ND	*$0.25*	*$0.75*	*$1.25*	£0.15	£0.45	£0.75

Issue	$Good	$Fine	$N.Mint	£Good	£Fine	£N.Mint
68-69 ND Mike Mignola cover	*$0.25*	*$0.75*	*$1.25*	£0.15	£0.45	£0.75
70 ND DS, reprints X-Men #166, Mike Mignola cover	*$0.25*	*$0.75*	*$1.25*	£0.15	£0.45	£0.75
71-89 ND	*$0.25*	*$0.75*	*$1.25*	£0.15	£0.45	£0.75
90 ND 48pgs, Bart Sears cover	*$0.30*	*$0.90*	*$1.50*	£0.20	£0.60	£1.00
91-92 ND Bart Sears cover	*$0.25*	*$0.75*	*$1.25*	£0.15	£0.45	£0.75
93-100 ND	*$0.25*	*$0.75*	*$1.25*	£0.15	£0.45	£0.75
101-103 ND	*$0.30*	*$0.90*	*$1.50*	£0.20	£0.60	£1.00
104 ND 48pgs, reprints X-Men #200	*$0.40*	*$1.20*	*$2.00*	£0.25	£0.75	£1.25
105-108 ND	*$0.30*	*$0.90*	*$1.50*	£0.20	£0.60	£1.00
109 ND reprints X-Men #205 with new Jae Lee cover	*$0.30*	*$0.90*	*$1.50*	£0.20	£0.60	£1.00
110 ND reprints X-Men 206	*$0.30*	*$0.90*	*$1.50*	£0.20	£0.60	£1.00
Title Value:	*$48.55*	*$145.65*	*$238.25*	£26.40	£79.20	£132.00

Note: chronologically reprints new X-Men stories with new back-up material by Claremont, Nocenti & Bolton (Bolton not in issues #29, #36-39)

CLASSICS ILLUSTRATED

Berkley/First Publishing; 1 Feb 1990-27 Jun 1991

Issue	$Good	$Fine	$N.Mint	£Good	£Fine	£N.Mint
1 ND The Raven and Other Poems, Graham Wilson art	*$0.80*	*$2.40*	*$4.00*	£0.50	£1.50	£2.50
2 ND Great Expectations, Rick Geary art	*$0.80*	*$2.40*	*$4.00*	£0.50	£1.50	£2.50
3 ND Through The Looking Glass, Kyle Baker art	*$0.80*	*$2.40*	*$4.00*	£0.50	£1.50	£2.50
4 ND Moby Dick, Bill Sienkiewicz art	*$0.90*	*$2.70*	*$4.50*	£0.60	£1.80	£3.00
5 ND Hamlet, Tom Mandrake art	*$0.80*	*$2.40*	*$4.00*	£0.50	£1.50	£2.50
6 ND The Scarlet Letter, layouts by P. Craig Russell	*$0.80*	*$2.40*	*$4.00*	£0.50	£1.50	£2.50
7 ND The Count of Monte Cristo, Dan Spiegle art	*$0.80*	*$2.40*	*$4.00*	£0.50	£1.50	£2.50
8 ND Dr. Jekyll and Mr. Hyde, John K. Snyder III art	*$0.80*	*$2.40*	*$4.00*	£0.50	£1.50	£2.50
9 ND The Adventures of Tom Sawyer, Michael Ploog art	*$0.80*	*$2.40*	*$4.00*	£0.50	£1.50	£2.50
10 ND The Call of the Wild, Ricardo Villagran art	*$0.80*	*$2.40*	*$4.00*	£0.50	£1.50	£2.50
11 ND Rip Van Winkle, Jeffrey Busch art	*$0.80*	*$2.40*	*$4.00*	£0.50	£1.50	£2.50
12 ND The Island of Dr. Moreau, Eric Vincent art	*$0.80*	*$2.40*	*$4.00*	£0.50	£1.50	£2.50
13 ND Wuthering Heights, Rick Geary art	*$0.80*	*$2.40*	*$4.00*	£0.50	£1.50	£2.50
14 ND Fall of the House of Usher, P. Craig Russell art	*$0.80*	*$2.40*	*$4.00*	£0.50	£1.50	£2.50
15 ND The Gift of the Magi	*$0.80*	*$2.40*	*$4.00*	£0.50	£1.50	£2.50
16 ND A Christmas Carol, Joe Staton art	*$0.80*	*$2.40*	*$4.00*	£0.50	£1.50	£2.50
17 ND Treasure Island, Pat Boyette art	*$0.80*	*$2.40*	*$4.00*	£0.50	£1.50	£2.50
18 ND Devil's Dictionary, Graham Wilson art	*$0.80*	*$2.40*	*$4.00*	£0.50	£1.50	£2.50
19 ND Secret Agent, John K. Snyder III art	*$0.80*	*$2.40*	*$4.00*	£0.50	£1.50	£2.50
20 ND Invisible Man, Rick Geary art	*$0.80*	*$2.40*	*$4.00*	£0.50	£1.50	£2.50
21 ND Cyrano de Bergerac	*$0.80*	*$2.40*	*$4.00*	£0.50	£1.50	£2.50
22 ND The Jungle Books	*$0.80*	*$2.40*	*$4.00*	£0.50	£1.50	£2.50
23 ND Robinson Crusoe, Pat Boyette	*$0.80*	*$2.40*	*$4.00*	£0.50	£1.50	£2.50
24 ND Rime of the Ancient Mariner, Dean Motter	*$0.80*	*$2.40*	*$4.00*	£0.50	£1.50	£2.50
25 ND Ivanhoe	*$0.80*	*$2.40*	*$4.00*	£0.50	£1.50	£2.50
26 ND Aesop's Fables	*$0.80*	*$2.40*	*$4.00*	£0.50	£1.50	£2.50
27 ND The Jungle	*$0.80*	*$2.40*	*$4.00*	£0.50	£1.50	£2.50
Title Value:	*$21.70*	*$65.10*	*$108.50*	£13.60	£40.80	£68.00

Note: all 48pgs, squarebound

Note also: issues **#28-35** were advertised but never appeared owing to the collapse of the project. The intended titles were: **#28** Kidnapped; **#29** Around the World in 80 Days; **#30** The Red Badge of Courage; **#31** 20,000 Leagues Under the Sea; **#32** Candide; **#33** Hunchback of Notre Dame; **#34** Last of the Mohicans; **#35** The Sea Wolf. **#31** and **#34** were taken over by Dark Horse Comics to become Dark Horse Classics (see entry)

CLAW THE UNCONQUERED

DC Comics; 1 May/Jun 1975-9 Sep/Oct 1976; 10 Apr/May 1978-12 Aug/Sep 1978

(see Warlord)

Issue	$Good	$Fine	$N.Mint	£Good	£Fine	£N.Mint
1	*$0.50*	*$1.50*	*$3.00*	£0.25	£0.75	£1.50
2-9	*$0.30*	*$1.00*	*$2.00*	£0.20	£0.60	£1.25
10-12 Kubert cover art	*$0.30*	*$1.00*	*$2.00*	£0.20	£0.60	£1.25
Title Value:	*$3.80*	*$12.50*	*$25.00*	£2.45	£7.35	£15.25

CLINT

Eclipse; 1 Sep 1986-2 Jan 1987

(see Adolescent Radioactive Black Belt Hamsters)

Issue	$Good	$Fine	$N.Mint	£Good	£Fine	£N.Mint
1 ND Dark Knight parody - "Clint, The Hamster Triumphant"; Mike Drigenberg inks	*$0.40*	*$1.20*	*$2.00*	£0.25	£0.75	£1.25
2 ND Apocalypse Now parody; Mike Drigenberg inks	*$0.40*	*$1.20*	*$2.00*	£0.25	£0.75	£1.25
Title Value:	*$0.80*	*$2.40*	*$4.00*	£0.50	£1.50	£2.50

CLIVE BARKER'S TAPPING THE VEIN

Eclipse; 1 May 1990-5 1991

Issue	$Good	$Fine	$N.Mint	£Good	£Fine	£N.Mint
1 ND Scott Hampton, P. Craig Russell art, John Bolton cover	*$1.50*	*$4.50*	*$7.50*	£1.00	£3.00	£5.00
1 2nd printing ND	*$1.00*	*$3.00*	*$5.00*	£0.70	£2.10	£3.50
2 ND Klaus Janson, John Bolton art, Scott Hampton cover	*$1.20*	*$3.60*	*$6.00*	£0.80	£2.40	£4.00
2 2nd printing ND	*$1.00*	*$3.00*	*$5.00*	£0.70	£2.10	£3.50
3 ND Denys Cowan, Bo Hampton art, Dave McKean cover	*$1.20*	*$3.60*	*$6.00*	£0.80	£2.40	£4.00
3 2nd printing ND	*$1.00*	*$3.00*	*$5.00*	£0.70	£2.10	£3.50
4 ND Jim Pearson/Alan Okamato, Stan Woch art, die-cut outer cover	*$1.20*	*$3.60*	*$6.00*	£0.80	£2.40	£4.00
4 2nd printing ND	*$1.00*	*$3.00*	*$5.00*	£0.70	£2.10	£3.50
5 ND Tim Conrad art featured	*$1.20*	*$3.60*	*$6.00*	£0.80	£2.40	£4.00
Title Value:	*$10.30*	*$30.90*	*$51.50*	£7.00	£21.00	£35.00

Note: adapts Books of Blood stories, all 64pgs, painted art.
Titan versions (cover dated Sep-Oct 1990) of #1-4 available at cover price.

Folio Edition 1 (May 1991), reprints #1,2 with foil-embossed	£Good	£Fine	£N.Mint
painted cover by Simon Bisley Softcover	£1.85	£5.55	£9.25
Hardcover	£4.50	£13.50	£22.50

CLOAK AND DAGGER

Marvel Comics Group; 1 Jul 1985-11 Jan 1987

(see also Marvel Fanfare, Marvel Graphic Novel, Strange Tales 2nd Series)

Issue	$Good	$Fine	$N.Mint	£Good	£Fine	£N.Mint
1-2 ND	*$0.40*	*$1.20*	*$2.00*	£0.25	£0.75	£1.25
3 ND Spiderman appears	*$0.40*	*$1.20*	*$2.00*	£0.25	£0.75	£1.25
4 ND Secret Wars II X-over	*$0.40*	*$1.20*	*$2.00*	£0.25	£0.75	£1.25
5-7 ND	*$0.40*	*$1.20*	*$2.00*	£0.25	£0.75	£1.25
8 ND Mike Mignola art	*$0.40*	*$1.20*	*$2.00*	£0.25	£0.75	£1.25
9 ND Art Adams art	*$0.40*	*$1.20*	*$2.00*	£0.25	£0.75	£1.25
10 ND	*$0.40*	*$1.20*	*$2.00*	£0.25	£0.75	£1.25
11 ND DS Larry Stroman art	*$0.40*	*$1.20*	*$2.00*	£0.30	£0.90	£1.50
Title Value:	*$4.40*	*$13.20*	*$22.00*	£2.80	£8.40	£14.00

CLOAK AND DAGGER (LIMITED SERIES)

Marvel Comics Group,MS; 1 Oct 1983-4 Jan 1984

Issue	$Good	$Fine	$N.Mint	£Good	£Fine	£N.Mint
1-3 ND	*$0.40*	*$1.20*	*$2.00*	£0.25	£0.75	£1.25
4 ND scarce in the U.K.	*$0.40*	*$1.20*	*$2.00*	£0.30	£0.90	£1.50
Title Value:	*$1.60*	*$4.80*	*$8.00*	£1.05	£3.15	£5.25

CLOAK AND DAGGER, THE MUTANT MISADVENTURES OF

Marvel Comics Group; 1 Nov 1988-19 Aug 1991

Issue	$Good	$Fine	$N.Mint	£Good	£Fine	£N.Mint
1 ND X-Factor appear	*$0.40*	*$1.20*	*$2.00*	£0.25	£0.75	£1.25
2-3 ND	*$0.40*	*$1.20*	*$2.00*	£0.25	£0.75	£1.25
4 ND New Mutants appear, Inferno X-over	*$0.40*	*$1.20*	*$2.00*	£0.25	£0.75	£1.25
5-7 ND	*$0.40*	*$1.20*	*$2.00*	£0.25	£0.75	£1.25
8 ND Acts of Vengeance tie-in	*$0.40*	*$1.20*	*$2.00*	£0.25	£0.75	£1.25
9 ND DS Acts of Vengeance tie-in, Avengers appear	*$0.40*	*$1.20*	*$2.00*	£0.25	£0.75	£1.25
10-11 ND	*$0.40*	*$1.20*	*$2.00*	£0.25	£0.75	£1.25
12-13 ND Dr. Doom appears	*$0.40*	*$1.20*	*$2.00*	£0.25	£0.75	£1.25
14 ND new direction; Steve Gerber scripts begin	*$0.40*	*$1.20*	*$2.00*	£0.25	£0.75	£1.25
15 ND	*$0.40*	*$1.20*	*$2.00*	£0.25	£0.75	£1.25
16 ND Spiderman appears	*$0.40*	*$1.20*	*$2.00*	£0.25	£0.75	£1.25
17-18 ND Ghost Rider/Spiderman appear	*$0.40*	*$1.20*	*$2.00*	£0.25	£0.75	£1.25
19 ND "true" origin	*$0.40*	*$1.20*	*$2.00*	£0.25	£0.75	£1.25
Title Value:	*$7.60*	*$22.80*	*$38.00*	£4.75	£14.25	£23.75

Note: bi-monthly

CLONEZONE SPECIAL

Dark Horse; 1 1989

Issue	$Good	$Fine	$N.Mint	£Good	£Fine	£N.Mint
1 ND Mike Baron script	*$0.30*	*$0.90*	*$1.50*	£0.20	£0.60	£1.00
Title Value:	*$0.30*	*$0.90*	*$1.50*	£0.20	£0.60	£1.00

COBALT 60

Tundra; 1 1992

Issue	$Good	$Fine	$N.Mint	£Good	£Fine	£N.Mint
1 ND 48pgs, Mark Bode carries on the unfinished work of Vaughn Bode after his death in 1975	*$0.90*	*$2.70*	*$4.50*	£0.60	£1.80	£3.00
Title Value:	*$0.90*	*$2.70*	*$4.50*	£0.60	£1.80	£3.00

COBALT BLUE

Power Comics; 1 Jan 1977

Issue	$Good	$Fine	$N.Mint	£Good	£Fine	£N.Mint
1 ND black and white	*$0.30*	*$0.90*	*$1.50*	£0.20	£0.60	£1.00
Title Value:	*$0.30*	*$0.90*	*$1.50*	£0.20	£0.60	£1.00

	$Good	$Fine	$N.Mint	£Good	£Fine	£N.Mint
COBALT BLUE (2ND SERIES)						
Innovation; 1 Sep 1989-2 Oct 1989						
1-2 ND Mike Gustovich script/art	$0.40	$1.20	$2.00	£0.25	£0.75	£1.25
Title Value:	$0.80	$2.40	$4.00	£0.50	£1.50	£2.50
COBRA						
Viz Communications,MS; 1 Apr 1990-12 Mar 1991						
1-12 ND	$0.60	$1.80	$3.00	£0.40	£1.20	£2.00
Title Value:	$7.20	$21.60	$36.00	£4.80	£14.40	£24.00
CODA						
Coda Publishing; 1 Aug 1986-4 Mar 1987						
1-4 ND	$0.30	$0.90	$1.50	£0.20	£0.60	£1.00
Title Value:	$1.20	$3.60	$6.00	£0.80	£2.40	£4.00
CODE OF HONOUR						
Marvel Comics Group,MS; 1 Feb 1997-present						
1 ND 48pgs, Chuck Dixon script, Tristan Shane painted art	$1.20	$3.60	$6.00	£0.80	£2.40	£4.00
2 ND Chuck Dixon script, Terese Neilsen painted art	$1.20	$3.60	$6.00	£0.80	£2.40	£4.00
Title Value:	$2.40	$7.20	$12.00	£1.60	£4.80	£8.00
CODENAME SPITFIRE						
Marvel Comics Group/New Universe; 10 Jul 1987-12 Oct 1987						
(formerly Spitfire and the Troubleshooters)						
10-12	$0.15	$0.45	$0.75	£0.10	£0.30	£0.50
Title Value:	$0.45	$1.35	$2.25	£0.30	£0.90	£1.50
CODENAME: DANGER						
Lodestone; 1 Aug 1985-4 1986						
1-4 ND colour	$0.30	$0.90	$1.50	£0.20	£0.60	£1.00
Title Value:	$1.20	$3.60	$6.00	£0.80	£2.40	£4.00
CODENAME: FIREARM						
Malibu Ultraverse/Marvel Comics Group,MS; 0 Aug 1995-5 Oct 1995						
0 ND 40pgs, Marv Wolfman and David Quinn script, Gabriel Gecko art, covers by George Perez; bi-weekly	$0.60	$1.80	$3.00	£0.40	£1.20	£2.00
1-5 ND 40pgs, Marv Wolfman and David Quinn script, Gabriel Gecko art, covers by George Perez; bi-weekly	$0.50	$1.50	$2.50	£0.30	£0.90	£1.50
Title Value:	$3.10	$9.30	$15.50	£1.90	£5.70	£9.50
CODENAME: STRYKEFORCE						
Image; 0 May 1995; 1 Jan 1994-14 Jun 1995						
0 (May 1995) origin told	$0.40	$1.20	$2.00	£0.25	£0.75	£1.25
1 Marc Silvestri script, Brandon Peterson art begins	$0.40	$1.20	$2.00	£0.25	£0.75	£1.25
1 Blue Edition ND	$4.00	$12.00	$20.00	£2.00	£6.00	£10.00
1 Gold Edition ND	$2.00	$6.00	$10.00	£1.50	£4.50	£7.50
2-3	$0.40	$1.20	$2.00	£0.25	£0.75	£1.25
4-5 Stormwatch guest-stars	$0.40	$1.20	$2.00	£0.25	£0.75	£1.25
6 Stormwatch guest-stars, Kill Razor dies	$0.40	$1.20	$2.00	£0.25	£0.75	£1.25
7-12	$0.40	$1.20	$2.00	£0.25	£0.75	£1.25
13-14	$0.45	$1.35	$2.25	£0.30	£0.90	£1.50
Title Value:	$12.10	$36.30	$60.50	£7.35	£22.05	£36.75
Note: all Non-Distributed on the news-stands in the U.K.						
Codename: Strykeforce (Mar 1995)						
Trade paperback reprints issues #1-4, cover by Brandon Peterson				£1.30	£3.90	£6.50
COFFIN BLOOD						
Monster Comics; 1 Jul 1992						
1 ND 48pgs, horror anthology	$0.50	$1.50	$2.50	£0.30	£0.90	£1.50
Title Value:	$0.50	$1.50	$2.50	£0.30	£0.90	£1.50

	$Good	$Fine	$N.Mint	£Good	£Fine	£N.Mint
COLD BLOODED						
Northstar; 1 May 1993- 5 1994						
1 32pgs, centre-fold poster by Kelley Jones	$0.60	$1.80	$3.00	£0.40	£1.20	£2.00
1 Collectors Edition, 48pgs, , centre-fold poster by Jim O'Barr and embossed cover by Kelley Jones; Kyle Hotz black and white art	$0.90	$2.70	$4.50	£0.60	£1.80	£3.00
2 32pgs	$0.60	$1.80	$3.00	£0.40	£1.20	£2.00
2 Collectors Edition, , silver foil embossed cover	$0.90	$2.70	$4.50	£0.60	£1.80	£3.00
3 32pgs	$0.60	$1.80	$3.00	£0.40	£1.20	£2.00
3 Collectors Edition, , silver foil embossed cover	$0.90	$2.70	$4.50	£0.60	£1.80	£3.00
4 32pgs	$0.60	$1.80	$3.00	£0.40	£1.20	£2.00
4 Collectors Edition, , silver foil embossed cover	$0.90	$2.70	$4.50	£0.60	£1.80	£3.00
5 32pgs	$0.60	$1.80	$3.00	£0.40	£1.20	£2.00
5 Collectors Edition, , silver foil embossed cover	$0.90	$2.70	$4.50	£0.60	£1.80	£3.00
Title Value:	$7.50	$22.50	$37.50	£5.00	£15.00	£25.00
Note: all Non-Distributed on the news-stands in the U.K.						
Cold-Blooded (Mar 1995)						
Trade paperback reprints issues #1-5				£1.30	£3.90	£6.50
COLD-BLOODED CHAMELEON COMMANDOS						
Blackthorne; 1 Jun 1986-6 1987						
1-6 ND	$0.30	$0.90	$1.50	£0.20	£0.60	£1.00
Title Value:	$1.80	$5.40	$9.00	£1.20	£3.60	£6.00
COLD-BLOODED: THE SLAYER						
Northstar; 1 Feb 1995						
1 ND 40pgs, Vincent Proce art; black and white	$0.60	$1.80	$3.00	£0.40	£1.20	£2.00
1 Signed & Numbered Edition, ND (Feb 1995) - pre-bagged with gold foil cover; 2,500 copies	$1.00	$3.00	$5.00	£0.70	£2.10	£3.50
Title Value:	$1.60	$4.80	$8.00	£1.10	£3.30	£5.50
COLORS IN BLACK						
Dark Horse; 1 Mar 1995-4 Jun 1995						
1-4 ND anthology in association with Spike Lee	$0.60	$1.80	$3.00	£0.40	£1.20	£2.00
Title Value:	$2.40	$7.20	$12.00	£1.60	£4.80	£8.00
COLOSSUS: GOD'S COUNTRY						
Marvel Comics Group,OS; 1 Oct 1994						
1 ND 64pgs, squarebound, Ann Nocenti script, P. Craig Russell art	$1.20	$3.60	$6.00	£0.80	£2.40	£4.00
Title Value:	$1.20	$3.60	$6.00	£0.80	£2.40	£4.00
COLOUR OF MAGIC						
Innovation,MS; 1 Feb 1991-4 Sep 1991						
1-4 ND adaptation of Terry Pratchett's "Discworld"	$0.50	$1.50	$2.50	£0.30	£0.90	£1.50
Title Value:	$2.00	$6.00	$10.00	£1.20	£3.60	£6.00
COLT SPECIAL						
AC Comics; 1 1985						
(see Black Diamond)						
1 ND scarce in the U.K. 52pgs	$0.50	$1.50	$2.50	£0.30	£0.90	£1.50
Title Value:	$0.50	$1.50	$2.50	£0.30	£0.90	£1.50
COLUMBUS						
Dark Horse,OS; 1 Oct 1992						
1 ND	$0.50	$1.50	$2.50	£0.30	£0.90	£1.50
Title Value:	$0.50	$1.50	$2.50	£0.30	£0.90	£1.50
COMBAT						
Image,MS; 1 Jan 1996-2 Feb 1996						

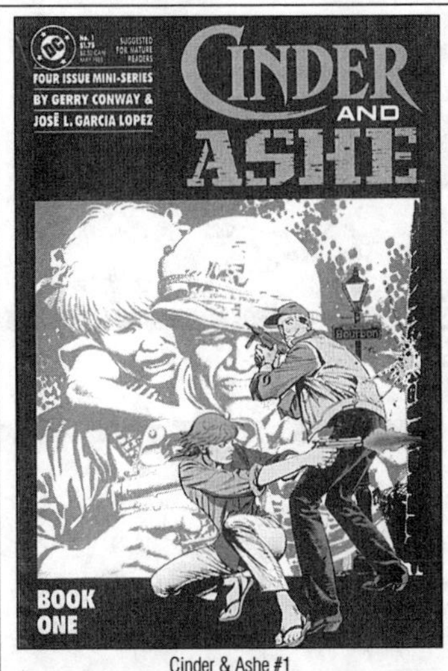

Cinder & Ashe #1

Classic X-Men #1

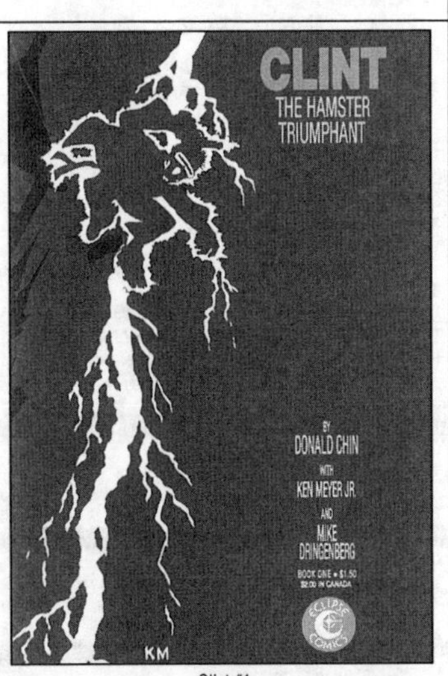

Clint #1

	$Good	$Fine	$N.Mint	£Good	£Fine	£N.Mint
1-2 ND Brian Witten and Cyrus Voris script, Mark Pajarillo art						
	$0.50	*$1.50*	*$2.50*	£0.30	£0.90	£1.50
Title Value:	*$1.00*	*$3.00*	*$5.00*	£0.60	£1.80	£3.00

COMBAT KELLY AND THE DEADLY DOZEN

Marvel Comics Group; 1 Jun 1972-9 Oct 1973

	$Good	$Fine	$N.Mint	£Good	£Fine	£N.Mint
1 ND 1st appearance Combat Kelly						
	$1.15	*$3.50*	*$7.00*	£0.50	£1.50	£3.00
2-9 ND	*$0.40*	*$1.25*	*$2.50*	£0.25	£0.75	£1.50
Title Value:	*$4.35*	*$13.50*	*$27.00*	£2.50	£7.50	£15.00

FEATURES

All new war stories; all characters killed off in the last issue

COMET

DC Comics/Impact; 1 Jul 1991-18 Dec 1992

	$Good	$Fine	$N.Mint	£Good	£Fine	£N.Mint
1-9	*$0.15*	*$0.45*	*$0.75*	£0.10	£0.35	£0.60
10 continued from The Fly #8						
	$0.15	*$0.45*	*$0.75*	£0.10	£0.35	£0.60
11 previews Crusaders #1 (see Jaguar #9), includes trading cards						
	$0.15	*$0.45*	*$0.75*	£0.10	£0.35	£0.60
12-18	*$0.15*	*$0.45*	*$0.75*	£0.10	£0.35	£0.60
Title Value:	*$2.70*	*$8.10*	*$13.50*	£1.80	£6.30	£10.80

COMET ANNUAL, THE

DC Comics/Impact; 1 Jun 1992

	$Good	$Fine	$N.Mint	£Good	£Fine	£N.Mint
1 64pgs, ties into Crusaders #1 (see Jaguar #9), includes trading cards						
	$0.30	*$0.90*	*$1.50*	£0.20	£0.60	£1.00
Title Value:	*$0.30*	*$0.90*	*$1.50*	£0.20	£0.60	£1.00

COMET MAN, THE

Marvel Comics Group,MS; 1 Feb 1987-6 Jul 1987

	$Good	$Fine	$N.Mint	£Good	£Fine	£N.Mint
1-2 ND	*$0.30*	*$0.90*	*$1.50*	£0.20	£0.60	£1.00
3 ND Hulk appears	*$0.30*	*$0.90*	*$1.50*	£0.20	£0.60	£1.00
4-5 ND Fantastic Four appear						
	$0.30	*$0.90*	*$1.50*	£0.20	£0.60	£1.00
6 ND	*$0.30*	*$0.90*	*$1.50*	£0.20	£0.60	£1.00
Title Value:	*$1.80*	*$5.40*	*$9.00*	£1.20	£3.60	£6.00

Note: Sienkiewicz covers on all. Created and written by Billy Mumy/Miguel Ferrer

COMET, THE

Red Circle (Archie); 1 Oct 1983-2 Dec 1983

(un-finished 6 issue series)

	$Good	$Fine	$N.Mint	£Good	£Fine	£N.Mint
1-2 Carmine Infantino pencils, Alex Nino inks; limited distribution in the U.K.						
	$0.40	*$1.20*	*$2.00*	£0.25	£0.75	£1.25
Title Value:	*$0.80*	*$2.40*	*$4.00*	£0.50	£1.50	£2.50

COMIC CAVALCADE

National Periodical Publications; 1 Winter 1942-63 Jun/Jul 1954

	$Good	$Fine	$N.Mint	£Good	£Fine	£N.Mint
1 scarce in the U.K. The Flash, Wonder Woman, Green Lantern (cover features) and Wildcat and Black Pirate features begin						
	$1000.00	*$3000.00*	*$9000.00*	£660.00	£2000.00	£6000.00
2 Mutt & Jeff begin (replacing Black Pirate)						
	$225.00	*$670.00*	*$1800.00*	£150.00	£450.00	£1200.00
3 Hop Harrigan and Sargon the Sorceror begin						
	$165.00	*$500.00*	*$1350.00*	£110.00	£335.00	£900.00
4	*$135.00*	*$410.00*	*$1100.00*	£90.00	£275.00	£735.00
5 Christmas cover						
	$135.00	*$410.00*	*$1100.00*	£90.00	£275.00	£735.00
6-10	*$105.00*	*$315.00*	*$850.00*	£70.00	£210.00	£570.00
11-12	*$92.50*	*$280.00*	*$750.00*	£62.50	£185.00	£500.00
13 Solomon Grundy appears; Christmas cover						
	$150.00	*$450.00*	*$1200.00*	£100.00	£300.00	£800.00
14-18	*$92.50*	*$280.00*	*$750.00*	£62.50	£185.00	£500.00
19 Christmas cover						
	$92.50	*$280.00*	*$750.00*	£62.50	£185.00	£500.00
20	*$92.50*	*$280.00*	*$750.00*	£62.50	£185.00	£500.00
21-23	*$87.50*	*$260.00*	*$700.00*	£57.50	£175.00	£470.00
24 Solomon Grundy battles Green Lantern						
	$100.00	*$300.00*	*$800.00*	£65.00	£200.00	£535.00
25-28 scarce in the U.K.						
	$67.50	*$205.00*	*$550.00*	£46.00	£135.00	£370.00
29 Flash, Wonder Woman and Green Lantern features end; an indication of the decline of the super-hero genre after the War						
	$75.00	*$225.00*	*$600.00*	£50.00	£150.00	£400.00
30 1st appearance The Fox & The Crow; title becomes "Funny Animal" orientated						
	$47.00	*$140.00*	*$375.00*	£31.00	£92.50	£250.00
31-35	*$22.50*	*$67.50*	*$180.00*	£15.00	£45.00	£120.00
36-49	*$16.50*	*$50.00*	*$135.00*	£11.00	£34.00	£90.00
50-62 scarce in the U.S, very scarce in the U.K.						
	$21.50	*$65.00*	*$175.00*	£15.00	£45.00	£120.00
63 rare in the U.S., very rare in the U.K.						
	$35.00	*$105.00*	*$280.00*	£23.50	£70.00	£190.00
Title Value:	*$4580.00*	*$13787.50*	*$37970.00*	£3062.50	£9213.50	£25405.00

Note: in common with all Golden Age comics, these were not officially distributed on the news-stands in the U.K. but some issues may have found their way over as ballast on ships or through serving personnel/relatives during the war.

COMICO BLACK BOOK

Comico,OS; 1 1987

	$Good	$Fine	$N.Mint	£Good	£Fine	£N.Mint
1 ND 5th anniversary retrospective						
	$0.40	*$1.20*	*$2.00*	£0.25	£0.75	£1.25
Title Value:	*$0.40*	*$1.20*	*$2.00*	£0.25	£0.75	£1.25

COMICO CHRISTMAS SPECIAL

Comico,OS; 1 1988

	$Good	$Fine	$N.Mint	£Good	£Fine	£N.Mint
1 ND 40pgs, Mireault, Willingham/Warner, Steve Rude/Williamson art, Dave Stevens cover						
	$0.50	*$1.50*	*$2.50*	£0.30	£0.90	£1.50
Title Value:	*$0.50*	*$1.50*	*$2.50*	£0.30	£0.90	£1.50

COMICO COLLECTION

Comico,OS; nn Oct 1987

(see Grendel: Devil's Vagary)

	$Good	$Fine	$N.Mint	£Good	£Fine	£N.Mint
nn rare, Slipcase containing poster, 10 Comico back issues (contents vary) and all-new 16pg 2-colour comic (Grendel - Devil's Vagary)				£15.00	£45.00	£75.00

Note: originally available shrink-wrapped. The item would be valued at approximately 10% more if unopened. Non-Distributed on the news-stands in the U.K.

COMICO ILLUSTRATED

Comico,OS; 1 Jul 1992

	$Good	$Fine	$N.Mint	£Good	£Fine	£N.Mint
1 ND anthology, black and white						
	$0.40	*$1.20*	*$2.00*	£0.25	£0.75	£1.25
Title Value:	*$0.40*	*$1.20*	*$2.00*	£0.25	£0.75	£1.25

COMICO PRIMER

(see Primer)

COMICS' GREATEST WORLD: ARCADIA

Dark Horse,MS; 1-4 Jun 1993

	$Good	$Fine	$N.Mint	£Good	£Fine	£N.Mint
1 ND (Week 1) X (see Dark Horse Comics #8); Chris Warner pencils, Frank Miller cover						
	$0.40	*$1.20*	*$2.00*	£0.25	£0.75	£1.25
1 Press Proof Edition, ND approx. 1,500 copies, black and white						
	$2.40	*$7.00*	*$12.00*	£1.30	£3.90	£6.50
1 Silver Edition, ND all silver foil cover, available only through Diamond Distributors						
	$2.00	*$6.00*	*$10.00*	£1.00	£3.00	£5.00
2 ND (Week 2) Pit Bulls						
	$0.30	*$0.90*	*$1.50*	£0.20	£0.60	£1.00
3 ND (Week 3) 1st appearance Ghost; Adam Hughes pencils, Dave Dorman cover						
	$1.20	*$3.60*	*$6.00*	£0.50	£1.50	£2.50
4 ND (Week 4) Monster						
	$0.30	*$0.90*	*$1.50*	£0.20	£0.60	£1.00
nn Limited Collected Edition, ND Arcadia Week 1-4; silver foil logo						
	$1.50	*$4.50*	*$7.50*	£1.00	£3.00	£5.00
Title Value:	*$8.10*	*$24.10*	*$40.50*	£4.45	£13.35	£22.25

Note: a continuing story, each issue 16pgs with card-stock glossy covers

COMICS' GREATEST WORLD: GOLDEN CITY

Dark Horse,MS; 1-4 Jul 1993

	$Good	$Fine	$N.Mint	£Good	£Fine	£N.Mint
1 ND (Week 1) Rebel; Jerry Ordway cover						
	$0.30	*$0.90*	*$1.50*	£0.20	£0.60	£1.00
1 Gold Edition, ND all gold foil cover, available only through Diamond Distributors						
	$1.50	*$4.50*	*$7.50*	£1.00	£3.00	£5.00
2 ND (Week 2) Mecha						
	$0.30	*$0.90*	*$1.50*	£0.20	£0.60	£1.00
3 ND (Week 3) Titan; Walt Simonson cover						
	$0.30	*$0.90*	*$1.50*	£0.20	£0.60	£1.00
4 ND (Week 4) Catalyst: Agents of Change; George Perez cover						
	$0.30	*$0.90*	*$1.50*	£0.20	£0.60	£1.00
nn Limited Collected Edition, ND Golden City Week 1-4; gold foil logo						
	$1.50	*$4.50*	*$7.50*	£1.00	£3.00	£5.00
Title Value:	*$4.20*	*$12.60*	*$21.00*	£2.80	£8.40	£14.00

COMICS' GREATEST WORLD: STEEL HARBOR

Dark Horse,MS; 1-4 Aug 1993

	$Good	$Fine	$N.Mint	£Good	£Fine	£N.Mint
1 ND (Week 1) 1st appearance of Barb Wire; Paul Gulacy pencils and cover						
	$1.00	*$3.00*	*$5.00*	£0.40	£1.20	£2.00
1 Silver Edition, ND all silver foil cover; available only through Diamond Distributors						
	$1.50	*$4.50*	*$7.50*	£1.00	£3.00	£5.00
2 ND (Week 2) The Machine; Mike Mignola cover						
	$0.30	*$0.90*	*$1.50*	£0.20	£0.60	£1.00
3 ND (Week 3) Wolf Gang						
	$0.30	*$0.90*	*$1.50*	£0.20	£0.60	£1.00
4 ND (Week 4) Motorhead						
	$0.30	*$0.90*	*$1.50*	£0.20	£0.60	£1.00
nn Limited Collected Edition, ND Steel Harbor Week 1-4; red foil logo						
	$1.50	*$4.50*	*$7.50*	£1.00	£3.00	£5.00
Title Value:	*$4.90*	*$14.70*	*$24.50*	£3.00	£9.00	£15.00

COMICS' GREATEST WORLD: THE VORTEX

Dark Horse,MS; 1-4 Sep 1993

	$Good	$Fine	$N.Mint	£Good	£Fine	£N.Mint
1 ND (Week 1) Division 13						
	$0.30	*$0.90*	*$1.50*	£0.20	£0.60	£1.00
1 Gold Edition, ND all gold foil cover; available only through Diamond Distributors						
	$1.50	*$4.50*	*$7.50*	£1.00	£3.00	£5.00
2 ND (Week 2) Hero Zero; Eric Shanower art						
	$0.30	*$0.90*	*$1.50*	£0.20	£0.60	£1.00
3 ND (Week 3) King Tiger						
	$0.30	*$0.90*	*$1.50*	£0.20	£0.60	£1.00
4 ND (Week 4) Vortex; Bob McLeod art						
	$0.30	*$0.90*	*$1.50*	£0.20	£0.60	£1.00
nn Limited Collected Edition, ND Vortex Week 1-4; blue foil logo						
	$1.50	*$4.50*	*$7.50*	£1.00	£3.00	£5.00
Title Value:	*$4.20*	*$12.60*	*$21.00*	£2.80	£8.40	£14.00

COMICS' GREATEST WORLD: WILL TO POWER

Dark Horse,MS; 1 Jun 1994-12 Aug 1994

	$Good	$Fine	$N.Mint	£Good	£Fine	£N.Mint
1-12 ND Jerry Prosser script, Mike Manley art, bart Sears covers; weekly issues						
	$0.25	*$0.75*	*$1.25*	£0.15	£0.45	£0.75
Title Value:	*$3.00*	*$9.00*	*$15.00*	£1.80	£5.40	£9.00

COMIX BOOK

Marvel Comics Group,Magazine; 1 Oct 1974-3 Mar 1975; 4,5 1976

	$Good	$Fine	$N.Mint	£Good	£Fine	£N.Mint
1 ND Wolverton art (1pg)						
	$0.80	*$2.50*	*$5.00*	£0.55	£1.75	£3.50
2-3 ND scarce in the U.K.						
	$0.65	*$2.00*	*$4.00*	£0.40	£1.25	£2.50
4-5 scarce in the U.K.						
	$0.50	*$1.50*	*$3.00*	£0.30	£1.00	£2.00
Title Value:	*$3.10*	*$9.50*	*$19.00*	£1.95	£6.25	£12.50

Note: Marvel's experimental underground-style comic; issues 4, 5 published by Krupp Comics Works in 1976. Stan Lee had invited Denis Kitchen to produce an underground comic that would not tarnish

SOME INDEPENDENT COMICS MAY NOT HAVE APPEARED ALTHOUGH THEY WERE ADVERTISED AND SOLICITED.

Marvel's clean-cut image. A short-lived but vital project.

COMIX INTERNATIONAL

Warren; 1 Jul 1974-5 Spring 1977

Issue	$Good	$Fine	$N.Mint	£Good	£Fine	£N.Mint
1 ND rare in the U.K.						
	$5.00	$15.00	$30.00	£2.50	£7.50	£15.00
2 ND	$2.50	$7.50	$15.00	£1.30	£4.00	£8.00
3-5 ND	$1.50	$4.50	$9.00	£0.65	£2.00	£4.00
Title Value:	$12.00	$36.00	$72.00	£5.75	£17.50	£35.00

COMIX ZONE

Marvel Comics Group; 1 Jan 1996-4 Apr 1996 ?

Issue	$Good	$Fine	$N.Mint	£Good	£Fine	£N.Mint
1-4 ND based on Sega video game						
	$0.50	$1.50	$2.50	£0.30	£0.90	£1.50
Title Value:	$2.00	$6.00	$10.00	£1.20	£3.60	£6.00

COMMAND REVIEW

Thoughts and Images; 1 Jul 1986-3 1987

Issue	$Good	$Fine	$N.Mint	£Good	£Fine	£N.Mint
1 ND reprints Albedo #1-4						
	$0.60	$1.80	$3.00	£0.40	£1.20	£2.00
2 ND reprints Albedo #5-8						
	$0.60	$1.80	$3.00	£0.40	£1.20	£2.00
3 ND reprints Albedo #9-12						
	$0.60	$1.80	$3.00	£0.40	£1.20	£2.00
Title Value:	$1.80	$5.40	$9.00	£1.20	£3.60	£6.00

COMMAND REVIEW (2ND SERIES)

Antarctic Press; 4 Jan 1994

Issue	$Good	$Fine	$N.Mint	£Good	£Fine	£N.Mint
4 ND collects Albedo #14 and Albedo Vol. 2 #1 & 2; UV-coated cover						
	$0.90	$2.70	$4.50	£0.60	£1.80	£3.00
Title Value:	$0.90	$2.70	$4.50	£0.60	£1.80	£3.00

COMPANY X

Triumphant Comics; 1 Jun 1994-5 1994

Issue	$Good	$Fine	$N.Mint	£Good	£Fine	£N.Mint
1-2 ND John Riley script, Bill Knapp art						
	$0.40	$1.20	$2.00	£0.25	£0.75	£1.25
3 ND dual issue with Doctor Chaos #10 (Note: there is only one issue between the two titles)						
	$0.40	$1.20	$2.00	£0.25	£0.75	£1.25
4 ND dual issue with Doctor Chaos #11 (Note: there is only one issue between the two titles)						
	$0.40	$1.20	$2.00	£0.25	£0.75	£1.25
5 ND	$0.40	$1.20	$2.00	£0.25	£0.75	£1.25
Title Value:	$2.00	$6.00	$10.00	£1.25	£3.75	£6.25

CONAN

Marvel Comics Group; 1 Aug 1995-11 Jun 1996

Issue	$Good	$Fine	$N.Mint	£Good	£Fine	£N.Mint
1 ND Larry Hama script, Barry Crain art begins						
	$0.60	$1.80	$3.00	£0.40	£1.20	£2.00
2-3 ND	$0.60	$1.80	$3.00	£0.40	£1.20	£2.00
4 ND Conan/Rune Prologue						
	$0.60	$1.80	$3.00	£0.40	£1.20	£2.00
5-7 ND	$0.60	$1.80	$3.00	£0.40	£1.20	£2.00
8 ND Godkiller story						
	$0.60	$1.80	$3.00	£0.40	£1.20	£2.00
9-11 ND	$0.60	$1.80	$3.00	£0.40	£1.20	£2.00
Title Value:	$6.60	$19.80	$33.00	£4.40	£13.20	£22.00

CONAN CLASSIC

Marvel Comics Group; 1 Jun 1994-11 Apr 1995

Issue	$Good	$Fine	$N.Mint	£Good	£Fine	£N.Mint
1 ND reprints begin from Conan the Barbarian #1						
	$0.30	$0.90	$1.50	£0.20	£0.60	£1.00
2-11 ND	$0.30	$0.90	$1.50	£0.20	£0.60	£1.00
Title Value:	$3.30	$9.90	$16.50	£2.20	£6.60	£11.00

CONAN SAGA

Marvel Comics Group,Magazine; 1 Apr 1987-98 May 1995

Issue	$Good	$Fine	$N.Mint	£Good	£Fine	£N.Mint
1 ND reprints begin from Conan the Barbarian #1 by Barry Windsor-Smith, three stories per issue with original covers; black and white						
	$0.80	$2.40	$4.00	£0.80	£2.40	£4.00
2 ND	$0.60	$1.80	$3.00	£0.60	£1.80	£3.00
3 ND	$0.50	$1.50	$2.50	£0.40	£1.20	£2.00
4-30 ND	$0.50	$1.50	$2.50	£0.30	£0.90	£1.50
31 ND Neal Adams reprint						
	$0.50	$1.50	$2.50	£0.30	£0.90	£1.50
32-36 ND	$0.50	$1.50	$2.50	£0.30	£0.90	£1.50
37-41 ND The Amra Saga						
	$0.50	$1.50	$2.50	£0.30	£0.90	£1.50
42-49 ND	$0.50	$1.50	$2.50	£0.30	£0.90	£1.50
50 ND reprints "Queen of the Black Coast" from Conan #57/58						
	$0.50	$1.50	$2.50	£0.30	£0.90	£1.50
51-52 ND "The Ballad of Belit" reprinted						
	$0.45	$1.35	$2.25	£0.30	£0.90	£1.50
53-74 ND	$0.45	$1.35	$2.25	£0.30	£0.90	£1.50
75 ND pre-bagged with Conan Handbook Comic						
	$0.80	$2.40	$4.00	£0.50	£1.50	£2.50
76-98 ND	$0.45	$1.35	$2.25	£0.30	£0.90	£1.50
Title Value:	$47.35	$142.05	$236.75	£30.50	£91.50	£152.50

CONAN SPECIAL EDITION

Marvel Comics Group,OS; 1 1983

Issue	$Good	$Fine	$N.Mint	£Good	£Fine	£N.Mint
1 ND reprints "Red Nails" by Barry Smith, in colour						
	$1.50	$4.50	$7.50	£1.00	£3.00	£5.00
Title Value:	$1.50	$4.50	$7.50	£1.00	£3.00	£5.00

Note: high-quality paper.

CONAN THE ADVENTURER

Marvel Comics Group; 1 Jun 1994-14 Jul 1995

Issue	$Good	$Fine	$N.Mint	£Good	£Fine	£N.Mint
1 ND Roy Thomas script and Rafael Kayanan art begins; the adventures of the young Conan						
	$0.60	$1.80	$3.00	£0.40	£1.20	£2.00
2-14 ND	$0.30	$0.90	$1.50	£0.20	£0.60	£1.00
Title Value:	$4.50	$13.50	$22.50	£3.00	£9.00	£15.00

CONAN THE BARBARIAN

Marvel Comics Group; 1 Oct 1970-275 Dec 1993

(see Chamber of Darkness #4, Conan Saga, Conan the Barbarian, Conan the King, Conan Universe, King Conan, Marvel Treasury Edition, Marvel Graphic Novel, Red Sonja, Savage Sword of Conan, Savage Tales)

Issue	$Good	$Fine	$N.Mint	£Good	£Fine	£N.Mint
1 LD scarce in the U.K. origin and 1st appearance Conan by Barry Smith, King Kull appears in flashback (1st cameo appearance - see Creatures on the Loose #10)						
	$36.00	$105.00	$250.00	£25.00	£75.00	£175.00
2-3 ND scarce in the U.K.						
	$16.50	$50.00	$100.00	£10.00	£30.00	£60.00
4	$10.50	$33.00	$65.00	£5.00	£15.00	£30.00
5	$10.50	$33.00	$65.00	£4.55	£13.50	£27.50
6	$7.50	$22.50	$45.00	£3.75	£11.00	£22.50
7 ND	$7.50	$22.50	$45.00	£4.15	£12.50	£25.00
8 ND scarce in the U.K.						
	$7.50	$22.50	$45.00	£4.55	£13.50	£27.50
9 ND	$7.50	$22.50	$45.00	£4.15	£12.50	£25.00
10 ND 52pgs, 4th appearance Kull (in back-up story)						
	$9.00	$28.00	$55.00	£4.55	£13.50	£27.50
11 scarce in the U.K. 52pgs, (most copies ink-stained in some way)						
	$9.00	$28.00	$55.00	£4.15	£12.50	£25.00
12 scarce in the U.K. part Gil Kane art						
	$5.00	$15.00	$30.00	£2.50	£7.50	£15.00
13 scarce in the U.K.						
	$5.00	$15.00	$30.00	£2.50	£7.50	£15.00
14 scarce in the U.K. 1st appearance Elric						
	$7.50	$22.50	$45.00	£4.15	£12.50	£25.00
15 scarce in the U.K. 2nd appearance Elric						
	$7.50	$22.50	$45.00	£3.75	£11.00	£22.50
16 scarce in the U.K. reprints Savage Tales #1 in colour						
	$4.55	$13.50	$27.50	£3.00	£9.00	£18.00
17-18 part Gil Kane art						
	$2.00	$6.00	$12.00	£2.00	£6.00	£12.00
19-20	$4.55	$13.50	$27.50	£1.80	£5.50	£11.00
21 scarce in the U.K. (award winner)						
	$4.15	$12.50	$25.00	£1.50	£4.50	£9.00
22 reprints issue #1						
	$4.15	$12.50	$25.00	£1.30	£4.00	£8.00
23 1st appearance Red Sonja						
	$5.75	$17.50	$35.00	£2.90	£8.75	£17.50
24 last Smith art, 2nd appearance Red Sonja (in a full story)						
	$5.00	$15.00	$30.00	£2.05	£6.25	£12.50
25 1st John Buscema art						
	$2.05	$6.25	$12.50	£1.25	£3.75	£7.50
26 2nd John Buscema art						
	$1.25	$3.75	$7.50	£0.80	£2.50	£5.00
27-30	$1.25	$3.75	$7.50	£0.55	£1.75	£3.50
31-35	$0.80	$2.50	$5.00	£0.50	£1.50	£3.00
36 ND	$0.80	$2.50	$5.00	£0.65	£2.00	£4.00
37 ND Neal Adams art						
	$1.25	$3.75	$7.50	£0.80	£2.50	£5.00
38-40 ND	$0.80	$2.50	$5.00	£0.65	£2.00	£4.00
41-43	$0.50	$1.50	$3.00	£0.30	£1.00	£2.00
44-45 Neal Adams inks						
	$0.50	$1.50	$3.00	£0.35	£1.10	£2.25
46-48	$0.50	$1.50	$3.00	£0.30	£1.00	£2.00
49 Neal Adams inks						
	$0.50	$1.50	$3.00	£0.35	£1.10	£2.25
50	$0.50	$1.50	$3.00	£0.25	£0.85	£1.75
51-53	$0.50	$1.50	$3.00	£0.25	£0.75	£1.50
54-56 ND	$0.50	$1.50	$3.00	£0.30	£1.00	£2.00
57	$0.50	$1.50	$3.00	£0.25	£0.75	£1.50
58 2nd appearance Belit (see Giant Size Conan #1); Note: this is her first appearance chronologically in the Conan universe						
	$0.80	$2.50	$5.00	£0.25	£0.85	£1.75
59 origin Belit	$0.50	$1.50	$3.00	£0.25	£0.75	£1.50
60-63	$0.50	$1.50	$3.00	£0.20	£0.60	£1.25
64 Jim Starlin art on reprint from Savage Sword of Conan						
	$0.40	$1.25	$2.50	£0.25	£0.75	£1.50
65-81	$0.30	$1.00	$2.00	£0.20	£0.60	£1.25
82-99 ND	$0.30	$1.00	$2.00	£0.25	£0.75	£1.50
100 ND 52pgs, death of Belit						
	$0.65	$2.00	$4.00	£0.30	£1.00	£2.00
101-114 ND	$0.40	$1.20	$2.00	£0.25	£0.75	£1.25
115 ND 52pgs	$0.50	$1.50	$2.50	£0.30	£0.90	£1.50
116 ND Neal Adams inks						
	$0.40	$1.20	$2.00	£0.25	£0.75	£1.25
117-120 ND	$0.40	$1.20	$2.00	£0.25	£0.75	£1.25
121-138	$0.40	$1.20	$2.00	£0.20	£0.60	£1.00
139-149 LD in the U.K.						
	$0.40	$1.20	$2.00	£0.25	£0.75	£1.25
150-162	$0.40	$1.20	$2.00	£0.20	£0.60	£1.00
163 Charles Vess inks						
	$0.30	$0.90	$1.50	£0.20	£0.60	£1.00
164-193	$0.30	$0.90	$1.50	£0.20	£0.60	£1.00
194 ND scarce in the U.K.						
	$0.30	$0.90	$1.50	£0.30	£0.90	£1.50
195-199 ND	$0.30	$0.90	$1.50	£0.25	£0.75	£1.25
200 ND 48pgs	$0.60	$1.80	$3.00	£0.40	£1.20	£2.00
201-215 ND	$0.30	$0.90	$1.50	£0.20	£0.60	£1.00
216 ND scarce in the U.K.						
	$0.30	$0.90	$1.50	£0.25	£0.75	£1.25
217-227 ND	$0.30	$0.90	$1.50	£0.20	£0.60	£1.00
228-231	$0.30	$0.90	$1.50	£0.15	£0.45	£0.75
232 Ron Lim art begins, new direction that explores Conan, "Conan Year 1"						

Issue	$Good	$Fine	$N.Mint	£Good	£Fine	£N.Mint
	$0.30	*$0.90*	*$1.50*	£0.15	£0.45	£0.75
233-236 Ron Lim art	*$0.30*	*$0.90*	*$1.50*	£0.15	£0.45	£0.75
237-249	*$0.30*	*$0.90*	*$1.50*	£0.15	£0.45	£0.75
250 DS	*$0.60*	*$1.80*	*$3.00*	£0.25	£0.75	£1.25
251-252	*$0.30*	*$0.90*	*$1.50*	£0.15	£0.45	£0.75
253 $1.25 cover begins	*$0.30*	*$0.90*	*$1.50*	£0.15	£0.45	£0.75
254-274	*$0.30*	*$0.90*	*$1.50*	£0.15	£0.45	£0.75
275 64pgs	*$0.60*	*$1.80*	*$3.00*	£0.25	£0.75	£1.25
Title Value:	*$299.50*	*$906.10*	*$1861.00*	£171.00	£514.85	£1023.50

Note: 64, 78, 87 are reprint.

ARTISTS

Barry Smith in 1-16, 19-24. Ploog in 57. Wood back-up reprint in 47. Gil Kane in 17, 18, 127-134.

CONAN THE BARBARIAN ANNUAL

Marvel Comics Group; 1 Sep 1973; 2 Jun 1976-5 Dec 1979; 6 Nov 1981-12 1987

Issue	$Good	$Fine	$N.Mint	£Good	£Fine	£N.Mint
1 ND 52pgs, all Barry Smith reprints (issues #2 and #4)	*$2.00*	*$6.00*	*$12.00*	£1.00	£3.00	£6.00
2 ND 52pgs	*$1.00*	*$3.00*	*$6.00*	£0.55	£1.75	£3.50
3 ND 52pgs, Neal Adams inks	*$0.80*	*$2.50*	*$5.00*	£0.50	£1.50	£3.00
4 ND 52pgs	*$0.55*	*$1.75*	*$3.50*	£0.40	£1.25	£2.50
5 ND 52pgs	*$0.50*	*$1.50*	*$3.00*	£0.30	£1.00	£2.00
6 ND 52pgs	*$0.40*	*$1.20*	*$2.00*	£0.30	£0.90	£1.50
7-12 ND 52pgs	*$0.30*	*$0.90*	*$1.50*	£0.20	£0.60	£1.00
Title Value:	*$7.05*	*$21.35*	*$40.50*	£4.25	£13.00	£24.50

CONAN THE BARBARIAN BOOK AND RECORD SET

Power Records; PR-31 1974

Issue	$Good	$Fine	$N.Mint	£Good	£Fine	£N.Mint
PR-31 scarce in the U.K., 20 pg bookley with 45 rpm record	*$1.25*	*$3.75*	*$7.50*	£0.80	£2.50	£5.00
Title Value:	*$1.25*	*$3.75*	*$7.50*	£0.80	£2.50	£5.00

Note: item would be valued 50% less without record

CONAN THE BARBARIAN GIANT SIZE

Marvel Comics Group; 1 Sep 1974-5 1975

Issue	$Good	$Fine	$N.Mint	£Good	£Fine	£N.Mint
1 ND 68pgs, 1st appearance Belit (see Conan #58); this is her first appearance in Marvel publication terms though the story is set years after her death	*$1.30*	*$4.00*	*$8.00*	£0.80	£2.50	£5.00
2 ND 68pgs	*$1.00*	*$3.00*	*$6.00*	£0.65	£2.00	£4.00
3-4 ND 68pgs	*$0.80*	*$2.50*	*$5.00*	£0.55	£1.75	£3.50
5 ND 68pgs, Jack Kirby cover	*$0.80*	*$2.50*	*$5.00*	£0.55	£1.75	£3.50
Title Value:	*$4.70*	*$14.50*	*$29.00*	£3.10	£9.75	£19.50

CONAN THE BARBARIAN MOVIE SPECIAL

Marvel Comics Group,MS; 1 Oct 1982-2 Nov 1982

Issue	$Good	$Fine	$N.Mint	£Good	£Fine	£N.Mint
1-2 ND	*$0.30*	*$0.90*	*$1.50*	£0.20	£0.60	£1.00
Title Value:	*$0.60*	*$1.80*	*$3.00*	£0.40	£1.20	£2.00

Note: adapts film

CONAN THE DESTROYER MOVIE SPECIAL

Marvel Comics Group,MS; 1 Jan 1985-2 Mar 1985

Issue	$Good	$Fine	$N.Mint	£Good	£Fine	£N.Mint
1-2 ND	*$0.30*	*$0.90*	*$1.50*	£0.20	£0.60	£1.00
Title Value:	*$0.60*	*$1.80*	*$3.00*	£0.40	£1.20	£2.00

CONAN THE KING

(see King Conan)

CONAN THE SAVAGE

Marvel Comics Group,Magazine; 1 Aug 1995-10 May 1996

Issue	$Good	$Fine	$N.Mint	£Good	£Fine	£N.Mint
1 ND Simon Bisley cover; black and white	*$0.60*	*$1.80*	*$3.00*	£0.40	£1.20	£2.00
2-3 ND black and white	*$0.60*	*$1.80*	*$3.00*	£0.40	£1.20	£2.00
4 ND Conan/Rune tie-in, set years after the Conan/Rune first encounter; black and white	*$0.60*	*$1.80*	*$3.00*	£0.40	£1.20	£2.00
5 ND Mike Baron script, Val Mayerik art; black and white	*$0.60*	*$1.80*	*$3.00*	£0.40	£1.20	£2.00
6 ND cover by Brothers Hildebrandt; black and white	*$0.60*	*$1.80*	*$3.00*	£0.40	£1.20	£2.00
7-10 ND black and white	*$0.60*	*$1.80*	*$3.00*	£0.40	£1.20	£2.00
Title Value:	*$6.00*	*$18.00*	*$30.00*	£4.00	£12.00	£20.00

CONAN UNIVERSE

Marvel Comics Group,OS; 1 1990

Issue	$Good	$Fine	$N.Mint	£Good	£Fine	£N.Mint
1 ND guide to characters in Conan series; Kaluta wraparound cover	*$0.50*	*$1.50*	*$2.50*	£0.30	£0.90	£1.50
Title Value:	*$0.50*	*$1.50*	*$2.50*	£0.30	£0.90	£1.50

CONAN, SAVAGE SWORD OF

Marvel Comics Group,Magazine; 1 Aug 1974-235 Jul 1995

Issue	$Good	$Fine	$N.Mint	£Good	£Fine	£N.Mint
1 part Neal Adams art, Barry Smith reprint, origin Blackmark by Gil Kane, Red Sonja (3rd appearance)	*$12.00*	*$36.00*	*$85.00*	£5.50	£17.00	£40.00
2 Neal Adams inks, Chaykin art	*$6.25*	*$18.50*	*$37.50*	£3.30	£10.00	£20.00
3 Barry Smith art	*$3.75*	*$11.00*	*$22.50*	£2.50	£7.50	£15.00
4 Neal Adams/Gil Kane art, Corben reprints	*$2.90*	*$8.75*	*$17.50*	£1.80	£5.50	£11.00
5 Jim Starlin art	*$2.05*	*$6.25*	*$12.50*	£1.30	£4.00	£8.00
6 Nino art	*$2.00*	*$6.00*	*$12.00*	£1.05	£3.25	£6.50
7-10	*$2.00*	*$6.00*	*$12.00*	£1.05	£3.25	£6.50
11-13	*$1.65*	*$5.00*	*$10.00*	£0.80	£2.50	£5.00
14 Neal Adams art	*$2.00*	*$6.00*	*$12.00*	£1.00	£3.00	£6.00
15	*$1.65*	*$5.00*	*$10.00*	£0.75	£2.25	£4.50
16 Barry Smith/Tim Conrad art	*$1.65*	*$5.00*	*$10.00*	£0.75	£2.25	£4.50
17 Tim Conrad art	*$1.65*	*$5.00*	*$10.00*	£0.75	£2.25	£4.50
18-21	*$1.65*	*$5.00*	*$10.00*	£0.75	£2.25	£4.50
22-29	*$1.50*	*$4.50*	*$9.00*	£0.55	£1.75	£3.50
30 ND Brunner art	*$1.50*	*$4.50*	*$9.00*	£0.55	£1.75	£3.50
31-40 ND	*$1.30*	*$4.00*	*$8.00*	£0.50	£1.50	£3.00
41-59 ND	*$1.15*	*$3.50*	*$7.00*	£0.40	£1.25	£2.50
60 ND Neal Adams story-boards for film	*$1.20*	*$3.60*	*$6.00*	£0.50	£1.50	£2.50
61-80 ND	*$1.20*	*$3.60*	*$6.00*	£0.50	£1.50	£2.50
81-82 ND	*$1.00*	*$3.00*	*$5.00*	£0.40	£1.20	£2.00
83 ND reprints Red Sonja by Neal Adams from issue 1	*$1.00*	*$3.00*	*$5.00*	£0.40	£1.20	£2.00
84-100 ND	*$1.00*	*$3.00*	*$5.00*	£0.40	£1.20	£2.00
101-177 ND	*$0.80*	*$2.40*	*$4.00*	£0.30	£0.90	£1.50
178 ND 54pgs, story featuring dinosaurs	*$0.45*	*$1.35*	*$2.25*	£0.30	£0.90	£1.50
179-189 ND	*$0.45*	*$1.35*	*$2.25*	£0.30	£0.90	£1.50
190 ND Skull on the Seas part 1, classic creative team of Thomas, Buscema and DeZuniga reunited	*$0.45*	*$1.35*	*$2.25*	£0.30	£0.90	£1.50
191 ND Skull on the Seaes	*$0.45*	*$1.35*	*$2.25*	£0.30	£0.90	£1.50
192-193 ND Skull on the Seas	*$0.45*	*$1.35*	*$2.25*	£0.30	£0.90	£1.50
194-195 ND	*$0.45*	*$1.35*	*$2.25*	£0.30	£0.90	£1.50
196 ND Valeria appears	*$0.45*	*$1.35*	*$2.25*	£0.30	£0.90	£1.50
197-201 ND	*$0.45*	*$1.35*	*$2.25*	£0.30	£0.90	£1.50
202-205 ND The City of Magicians story	*$0.45*	*$1.35*	*$2.25*	£0.30	£0.90	£1.50
206 ND	*$0.45*	*$1.35*	*$2.25*	£0.30	£0.90	£1.50
207-210 ND Conan and the Spider God	*$0.45*	*$1.35*	*$2.25*	£0.30	£0.90	£1.50
211-221 ND	*$0.45*	*$1.35*	*$2.25*	£0.30	£0.90	£1.50
222 ND features John Buscema's pencilled version of Conan the Barbarian #1	*$0.45*	*$1.35*	*$2.25*	£0.30	£0.90	£1.50
223-224 ND	*$0.45*	*$1.35*	*$2.25*	£0.30	£0.90	£1.50
225 ND John Buscema art	*$0.45*	*$1.35*	*$2.25*	£0.30	£0.90	£1.50
226 ND	*$0.45*	*$1.35*	*$2.25*	£0.30	£0.90	£1.50
227 ND John Buscema art	*$0.45*	*$1.35*	*$2.25*	£0.30	£0.90	£1.50
228 ND	*$0.45*	*$1.35*	*$2.25*	£0.30	£0.90	£1.50
229-233 ND Red Sonja and King Kull appear	*$0.45*	*$1.35*	*$2.25*	£0.30	£0.90	£1.50
234-235 ND	*$0.45*	*$1.35*	*$2.25*	£0.30	£0.90	£1.50
Title Value:	*$236.70*	*$712.20*	*$1218.25*	£104.85	£318.00	£583.00

CONAN, SAVAGE SWORD OF ANNUAL

Marvel Comics Group; 1 1975

Issue	$Good	$Fine	$N.Mint	£Good	£Fine	£N.Mint
1 ND 88pgs, squarebound, all reprint featuring Barry Smith art	*$1.30*	*$4.00*	*$8.00*	£1.00	£3.00	£6.00
Title Value:	*$1.30*	*$4.00*	*$8.00*	£1.00	£3.00	£6.00

CONAN/RUNE

Marvel Comics Group/Malibu Ultraverse,OS; 1 Nov 1995

Issue	$Good	$Fine	$N.Mint	£Good	£Fine	£N.Mint
1 ND Barry Windsor-Smith cover, script and art	*$0.60*	*$1.80*	*$3.00*	£0.40	£1.20	£2.00
Title Value:	*$0.60*	*$1.80*	*$3.00*	£0.40	£1.20	£2.00

CONCRETE

Dark Horse; 1 Mar 1987-10 1989

(see Dark Horse Presents)

Issue	$Good	$Fine	$N.Mint	£Good	£Fine	£N.Mint
1 ND Paul Chadwick story/art begins; black and white	*$3.00*	*$9.00*	*$15.00*	£1.80	£5.25	£9.00
1 2nd printing ND	*$0.80*	*$2.40*	*$4.00*	£0.50	£1.50	£2.50
2 ND scarce in the U.K.	*$1.20*	*$3.60*	*$6.00*	£1.00	£3.00	£5.00
3 ND origin	*$1.00*	*$3.00*	*$5.00*	£0.80	£2.40	£4.00
4-5 ND	*$1.00*	*$3.00*	*$5.00*	£0.70	£2.10	£3.50
6-10 ND	*$0.80*	*$2.40*	*$4.00*	£0.60	£1.80	£3.00
Title Value:	*$12.00*	*$36.00*	*$60.25*	£8.50	£25.35	£42.50
Colour Special 1 (new story and reprint of first 2 adventures from Dark Horse Presents, all colour)				£0.70	£2.10	£3.50
Concrete: Land and Sea (1989), reprints #1,2 with new material				£0.70	£2.10	£3.50
Concrete: A New Life (1989), reprints #3,4				£0.55	£1.65	£2.75
Concrete: Earth Day Special, features a wordless S/F tale by Moebius, 4pg Charles Vess story				£0.60	£1.80	£3.00
Concrete: Odd Jobs (Jul 1990), reprints and new material, 48pgs squarebound				£0.50	£1.50	£2.50
Concrete: Complete Short Stories 1986-1989, r eprints Dark Horse Presents material				£1.80	£5.40	£9.00
(2nd printing - Apr 1993)				£1.75	£5.25	£8.75
Hardcover (May 1991 - 2000 copies)				£5.00	£15.00	£25.00
The Complete Concrete (Aug 1994 Trade paperback 320pgs, reprints all 10 issues, black and white				£3.40	£10.20	£17.00
Concrete: The Complete Short Stories 1990-1995 (Dec 1995) Trade paperback reprints with new cover by Paul Chadwick				£2.00	£6.00	£10.00

CONCRETE: ELECTICA

Dark Horse,MS; 1 Apr 1993-2 May 1993

Issue	$Good	$Fine	$N.Mint	£Good	£Fine	£N.Mint
1-2 Paul Chadwick script/art	*$0.60*	*$1.80*	*$3.00*	£0.40	£1.20	£2.00
Title Value:	*$1.20*	*$3.60*	*$6.00*	£0.80	£2.40	£4.00

CONCRETE: FRAGILE CREATURE

Dark Horse,MS; 1 Jun 1991-4 Jun 1992

1-4 ND Paul and Elizabeth Chadwick

	$Good	$Fine	$N.Mint	£Good	£Fine	£N.Mint
	$0.40	$1.20	$2.00	£0.25	£0.75	£1.25
Title Value:	$1.60	$4.80	$8.00	£1.00	£3.00	£5.00

Note: issues printed on "environmentally-friendly" recycled paper

Concrete: Fragile Creature (Jul 1994)

	£Good	£Fine	£N.Mint
Trade paperback reprints mini-series plus essay by Paul Chadwick	£2.00	£6.00	£10.00

CONCRETE: KILLER SMILE

Dark Horse/Legend,MS; 1 Jul 1994-4 Oct 1994

1-4 ND Paul Chadwick script, art and painted covers

	$Good	$Fine	$N.Mint	£Good	£Fine	£N.Mint
	$0.60	$1.80	$3.00	£0.40	£1.20	£2.00
Title Value:	$2.40	$7.20	$12.00	£1.60	£4.80	£8.00

Concrete: Killer Smile (Sep 1995)

	£Good	£Fine	£N.Mint
Trade paperback reprints mini-series with new Paul Chadwick cover	£2.30	£6.90	£11.50

CONCRETE: THINK LIKE A MOUNTAIN

Dark Horse,MS; 1 Mar 1996-6 Aug 1996

1-6 ND Paul Chadwick script and art; Geof Darrow covers

	$Good	$Fine	$N.Mint	£Good	£Fine	£N.Mint
	$0.60	$1.80	$3.00	£0.40	£1.20	£2.00
Title Value:	$3.60	$10.80	$18.00	£2.40	£7.20	£12.00

CONDOM-MAN

Aaaahh!! Comics; 1 Jun 1994; 2 Jul 1995

	$Good	$Fine	$N.Mint	£Good	£Fine	£N.Mint
1 ND 20pgs, signed by the creator (Chris Swafford); black and white	$0.70	$2.10	$3.50	£0.50	£1.50	£2.50
2-5 ND 24pgs, black and white	$0.70	$2.10	$3.50	£0.50	£1.50	£2.50
Title Value:	$3.50	$10.50	$17.50	£2.50	£7.50	£12.50

CONDORMAN

Whitman; 1 Oct 1981-3 Jan 1982

	$Good	$Fine	$N.Mint	£Good	£Fine	£N.Mint
1-2 scarce in the U.K. adaptation of Walt Disney film with Michael Crawford; photo cover	$0.50	$1.50	$2.50	£0.40	£1.20	£2.00
3 new story; photo cover	$0.50	$1.50	$2.50	£0.30	£0.90	£1.50
Title Value:	$1.50	$4.50	$7.50	£1.10	£3.30	£5.50

Note: limited distribution on the news-stands in the U.K.

CONEHEADS

Marvel Comics Group,MS; 1 Jun 1994-4 Sep 1994

	$Good	$Fine	$N.Mint	£Good	£Fine	£N.Mint
1-4 ND based on cult film and Saturday Night Live tv sketch	$0.30	$0.90	$1.50	£0.20	£0.60	£1.00
Title Value:	$1.20	$3.60	$6.00	£0.80	£2.40	£4.00

CONFESSIONS OF THE LOVELORN

ACG; 109 Nov 1959-114 Jun/Jul 1960

(previous issues ND)

	$Good	$Fine	$N.Mint	£Good	£Fine	£N.Mint
109-114 distributed in the U.K.	$2.85	$8.50	$20.00	£1.40	£4.25	£10.00
Title Value:	$17.10	$51.00	$120.00	£8.40	£25.50	£60.00

CONGO BILL

National Periodical Publications; 1 Aug/Sep 1954-7 Aug/Sep 1955

	$Good	$Fine	$N.Mint	£Good	£Fine	£N.Mint
1 very rare in the U.K.	$87.50	$260.00	$700.00	£57.50	£175.00	£470.00
2 very rare in the U.K.	$70.00	$210.00	$560.00	£47.00	£140.00	£375.00
3-6 very rare in the U.K.	$62.50	$185.00	$500.00	£42.00	£125.00	£335.00
7 very rare in the U.K.	$67.50	$205.00	$550.00	£46.00	£135.00	£370.00
Title Value:	$475.00	$1415.00	$3810.00	£318.50	£950.00	£2555.00

CONGORILLA

DC Comics,MS; 1 Nov 1992-4 Feb 1993

	$Good	$Fine	$N.Mint	£Good	£Fine	£N.Mint
1 Brian Bolland cover	$0.25	$0.75	$1.25	£0.15	£0.45	£0.75
2-4	$0.25	$0.75	$1.25	£0.15	£0.45	£0.75
Title Value:	$1.00	$3.00	$5.00	£0.60	£1.80	£3.00

CONQUEROR OF THE BARREN EARTH

DC Comics,MS; 1 Feb 1985-4 May 1985

(see Warlord)

	$Good	$Fine	$N.Mint	£Good	£Fine	£N.Mint
1-4 Ron Randall art	$0.15	$0.45	$0.75	£0.10	£0.35	£0.60
Title Value:	$0.60	$1.80	$3.00	£0.40	£1.40	£2.40

CONSTRUCT

Caliber Press,MS; 1 Jun 1996-6 1997

	$Good	$Fine	$N.Mint	£Good	£Fine	£N.Mint
1-6 ND 48pgs, black and white	$0.60	$1.80	$3.00	£0.40	£1.20	£2.00
Title Value:	$3.60	$10.80	$18.00	£2.40	£7.20	£12.00

Note: originally solicited by Mirage Studios, that series never came out.

CONTEMPORARY BIO-GRAPHICS

Revolutionary Comics; 1 Dec 1991

	$Good	$Fine	$N.Mint	£Good	£Fine	£N.Mint
1 ND Stan Lee	$0.50	$1.50	$2.50	£0.30	£0.90	£1.50
Title Value:	$0.50	$1.50	$2.50	£0.30	£0.90	£1.50

CONTINUM

Continum,OS; 1 Oct 1988

	$Good	$Fine	$N.Mint	£Good	£Fine	£N.Mint
1 ND 1st appearance Dawn (in advert for Cry For Dawn #1) and 1st appearance The Dark; featured art by Scott Hanna and Dan Panosian plus 4pg story and art by Linsner (1st published work?); black and white	$22.50	$67.50	$135.00	£13.00	£40.00	£80.00
Title Value:	$22.50	$67.50	$135.00	£13.00	£40.00	£80.00

CONTRACTORS

Eclipse; 1 Jun 1987

	$Good	$Fine	$N.Mint	£Good	£Fine	£N.Mint
1 ND Ken Macklin script and art; black and white	$0.40	$1.20	$2.00	£0.25	£0.75	£1.25
Title Value:	$0.40	$1.20	$2.00	£0.25	£0.75	£1.25

CONVOCATIONS - A MAGIC: THE GATHERING GALLERY

Acclaim Comics/Armada,OS; 1 Jan 1996

	$Good	$Fine	$N.Mint	£Good	£Fine	£N.Mint
1 ND pin-ups by Charles Vess, Mike Kaluta, Alex Maleev and others	$0.50	$1.50	$2.50	£0.30	£0.90	£1.50
Title Value:	$0.50	$1.50	$2.50	£0.30	£0.90	£1.50

COOL WORLD

DC Comics,MS; 1 May 1992-4 Jul 1992

	$Good	$Fine	$N.Mint	£Good	£Fine	£N.Mint
1-2 ND based on animated film, bi-weekly	$0.25	$0.75	$1.25	£0.15	£0.45	£0.75
3-4 ND based on animated film	$0.25	$0.75	$1.25	£0.15	£0.45	£0.75
Title Value:	$1.00	$3.00	$5.00	£0.60	£1.80	£3.00

COOL WORLD MOVIE ADAPTATION

DC Comics,OS; 1 Aug 1992

	$Good	$Fine	$N.Mint	£Good	£Fine	£N.Mint
1 ND 64pgs, adapts animated film	$0.50	$1.50	$2.50	£0.30	£0.90	£1.50
Title Value:	$0.50	$1.50	$2.50	£0.30	£0.90	£1.50

COPS

DC Comics,MS Toy; 1 Aug 1988-15 Oct 1989

	$Good	$Fine	$N.Mint	£Good	£Fine	£N.Mint
1 LD in the U.K. DS	$0.15	$0.45	$0.75	£0.10	£0.30	£0.50
2-15 ND	$0.15	$0.45	$0.75	£0.10	£0.30	£0.50
Title Value:	$2.25	$6.75	$11.25	£1.50	£4.50	£7.50

COPS: THE JOB

Marvel Comics Group,MS; 1 Jun 1992-4 Sep 1992

	$Good	$Fine	$N.Mint	£Good	£Fine	£N.Mint
1-4 Michael Golden covers	$0.15	$0.45	$0.75	£0.10	£0.35	£0.60
Title Value:	$0.60	$1.80	$3.00	£0.40	£1.40	£2.40

CORBEN SPECIAL

Pacific,OS; 1 May 1984

	$Good	$Fine	$N.Mint	£Good	£Fine	£N.Mint
1 ND House of Usher, Richard Corben art	$0.50	$1.50	$2.50	£0.30	£0.90	£1.50
Title Value:	$0.50	$1.50	$2.50	£0.30	£0.90	£1.50

CORBO

Sword in Stone; 1 Feb 1987

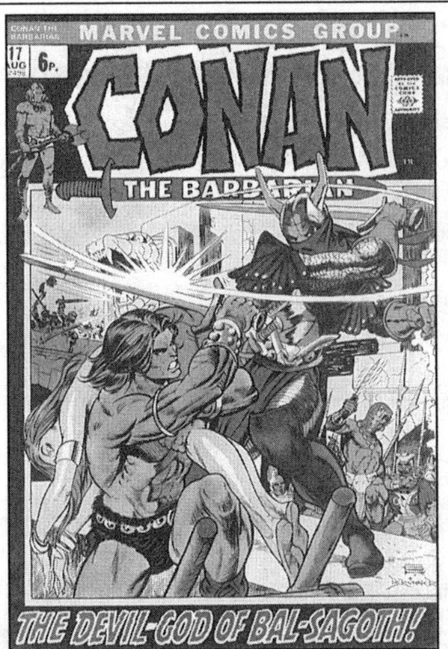

Conan the Barbarian #17

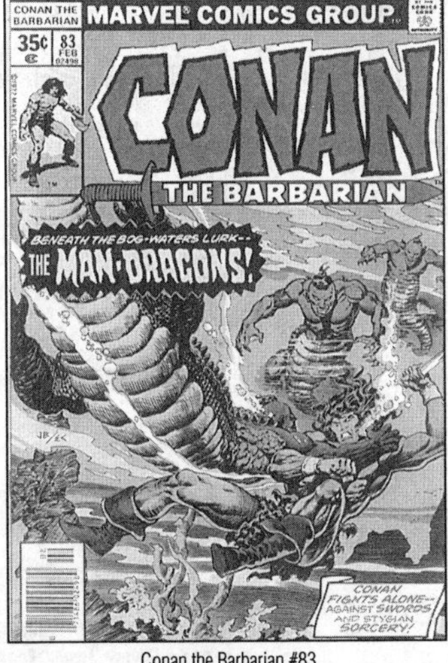

Conan the Barbarian #83

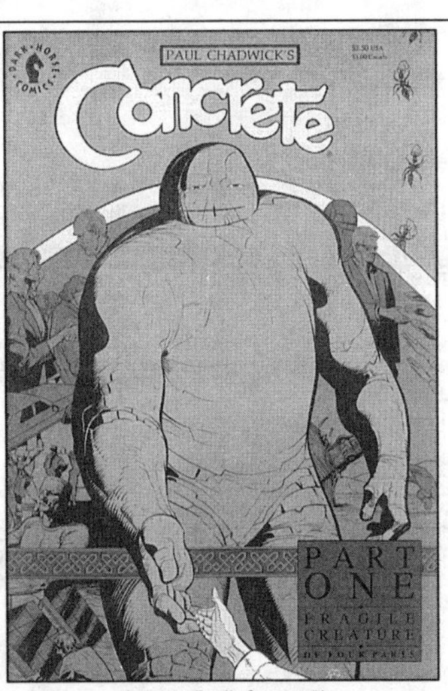

Concrete: Fragile Creature #1

	$Good	$Fine	$N.Mint	£Good	£Fine	£N.Mint
1 ND Mike Kaluta cover art						
	$0.25	*$0.75*	*$1.25*	£0.15	£0.45	£0.75
Title Value:	*$0.25*	*$0.75*	*$1.25*	£0.15	£0.45	£0.75

CORMAC MAC ART

Dark Horse,MS; 1 Mar 1990-4 Jun 1990

	$Good	$Fine	$N.Mint	£Good	£Fine	£N.Mint
1-3 ND	*$0.40*	*$1.20*	*$2.00*	£0.25	£0.75	£1.25
4 ND John Bolton cover art						
	$0.40	*$1.20*	*$2.00*	£0.25	£0.75	£1.25
Title Value:	*$1.60*	*$4.80*	*$8.00*	£1.00	£3.00	£5.00

CORUM: THE BULL AND THE SPEAR

First,MS; 1 Jan 1989-4 Jul 1989

(see Chronicles of Corum)

	$Good	$Fine	$N.Mint	£Good	£Fine	£N.Mint
1-4 ND Jill Thompson art begins; Mike Mignola covers						
	$0.40	*$1.20*	*$2.00*	£0.25	£0.75	£1.25
Title Value:	*$1.60*	*$4.80*	*$8.00*	£1.00	£3.00	£5.00

COSMIC BOOK, THE

Ace,OS; 1 Dec 1986

	$Good	$Fine	$N.Mint	£Good	£Fine	£N.Mint
1 ND 40pgs, Wally Wood (2pgs) and Alex Toth art, Pat Boyette cover						
	$0.30	*$0.90*	*$1.50*	£0.20	£0.60	£1.00
Title Value:	*$0.30*	*$0.90*	*$1.50*	£0.20	£0.60	£1.00

COSMIC BOY

DC Comics,MS; 1 Dec 1986-4 Mar 1987

(see Adventure Comics, Legion of Super-Heroes)

	$Good	$Fine	$N.Mint	£Good	£Fine	£N.Mint
1-4 Legends tie-in, Giffen art						
	$0.25	*$0.75*	*$1.25*	£0.15	£0.45	£0.75
Title Value:	*$1.00*	*$3.00*	*$5.00*	£0.60	£1.80	£3.00

COSMIC HEROES

Eternity; 1 Oct 1988-11 Dec 1989

	$Good	$Fine	$N.Mint	£Good	£Fine	£N.Mint
1 ND 48pgs, squarebound begins; 1930s Buck Rogers reprints by Phil Nowlan/Dick Calkins; all black and white						
	$0.40	*$1.20*	*$2.00*	£0.25	£0.75	£1.25
2-6 ND Buck Rogers						
	$0.40	*$1.20*	*$2.00*	£0.25	£0.75	£1.25
7-11 ND	*$0.40*	*$1.20*	*$2.00*	£0.25	£0.75	£1.25
Title Value:	*$4.40*	*$13.20*	*$22.00*	£2.75	£8.25	£13.75

COSMIC ODYSSEY

DC Comics,MS; 1 Dec 1988-4 Mar 1989

	$Good	$Fine	$N.Mint	£Good	£Fine	£N.Mint
1 ND 48pgs, features New Gods, Superman, Batman, Starfire, Martian Manhunter, Green Lantern (John Stewart)						
	$0.80	*$2.40*	*$4.00*	£0.50	£1.50	£2.50
2-4 ND 48pgs	*$0.80*	*$2.40*	*$4.00*	£0.50	£1.50	£2.50
Title Value:	*$3.20*	*$9.60*	*$16.00*	£2.00	£6.00	£10.00

Note: all Prestige Format, squarebound

	$Good	$Fine	$N.Mint	£Good	£Fine	£N.Mint
Trade paperback (Aug 1992), reprints issues #1-4, painted cover by Mike Mignola				£2.50	£7.50	£12.50

COSMIC POWERS

Marvel Comics Group,MS; 1 Mar 1994-6 Aug 1994

	$Good	$Fine	$N.Mint	£Good	£Fine	£N.Mint
1 ND 48pgs, Thanos appears; Ron Lim art						
	$0.50	*$1.50*	*$2.50*	£0.30	£0.90	£1.50
2 ND 48pgs, Thanos and Terrax appear; Moore art						
	$0.50	*$1.50*	*$2.50*	£0.30	£0.90	£1.50
3 ND 48pgs, Thanos and Terrax with Jack of Hearts and Ganymede; Ron Lim cover						
	$0.50	*$1.50*	*$2.50*	£0.30	£0.90	£1.50
4 ND 48pgs, Legacy appears						
	$0.50	*$1.50*	*$2.50*	£0.30	£0.90	£1.50
5 ND 48pgs, Thanos appears						
	$0.50	*$1.50*	*$2.50*	£0.30	£0.90	£1.50
6 ND 48pgs, Thanos, Galactus and Terrax appear						
	$0.50	*$1.50*	*$2.50*	£0.30	£0.90	£1.50
Title Value:	*$3.00*	*$9.00*	*$15.00*	£1.80	£5.40	£9.00

COSMIC POWERS UNLIMITED

Marvel Comics Group; 1 May 1995-5 1996

	$Good	$Fine	$N.Mint	£Good	£Fine	£N.Mint
1 ND 64pgs, Silver Surfer vs. Thanos, Death and Captain Marvel back-up						
	$0.80	*$2.40*	*$4.00*	£0.50	£1.50	£2.50
2 ND 64pgs, Silver Surfer vs. Cosmic Enclave, Jack of Hearts back-up						
	$0.80	*$2.40*	*$4.00*	£0.50	£1.50	£2.50
3 ND 64pgs, Silver Surfer and Jack of Hearts						
	$0.80	*$2.40*	*$4.00*	£0.50	£1.50	£2.50
4 ND continued from Star Masters #3						
	$0.80	*$2.40*	*$4.00*	£0.50	£1.50	£2.50
5 ND Captain Universe returns						
	$0.80	*$2.40*	*$4.00*	£0.50	£1.50	£2.50
Title Value:	*$4.00*	*$12.00*	*$20.00*	£2.50	£7.50	£12.50

Note: quarterly frequency

COTTON CANDY AUTOPSY, A

DC Comics/Piranha Press; nn 1991

	$Good	$Fine	$N.Mint	£Good	£Fine	£N.Mint
nn ND Trade paperback, reprints Beautiful Stories for Ugly Children #1,13 plus new Sweetman/Louapre story						
	$2.40	*$7.00*	*$12.00*	£1.60	£4.80	£8.00
Title Value:	*$2.40*	*$7.00*	*$12.00*	£1.60	£4.80	£8.00

COUGAR, THE

Atlas; 1 Apr 1975-2 Jun 1975

	$Good	$Fine	$N.Mint	£Good	£Fine	£N.Mint
1-2 distributed in the U.K. Frank Springer art						
	$0.25	*$0.75*	*$1.25*	£0.15	£0.45	£0.75
Title Value:	*$0.50*	*$1.50*	*$2.50*	£0.30	£0.90	£1.50

COUNT DUCKULA

Marvel Comics Group; 1 Feb 1989-15 Jan 1991

	$Good	$Fine	$N.Mint	£Good	£Fine	£N.Mint
1-15 ND	*$0.15*	*$0.45*	*$0.75*	£0.10	£0.35	£0.60
Title Value:	*$2.25*	*$6.75*	*$11.25*	£1.50	£5.25	£9.00

COUTOO

Dark Horse,OS; 1 Apr 1994

	$Good	$Fine	$N.Mint	£Good	£Fine	£N.Mint
1 ND French strip collected from reprints in Cheval Noir						
	$0.70	*$2.10*	*$3.50*	£0.50	£1.50	£2.50
Title Value:	*$0.70*	*$2.10*	*$3.50*	£0.50	£1.50	£2.50

COWABUNGA COMICS

Mirage Studios,OS; nn Mar 1991

	$Good	$Fine	$N.Mint	£Good	£Fine	£N.Mint
nn ND 16pgs, features pin-ups and unpublished art of the Turtles by Eastman and Laird and others; card stock covers and painted cover						
	$0.50	*$1.50*	*$2.50*	£0.30	£0.90	£1.50
Title Value:	*$0.50*	*$1.50*	*$2.50*	£0.30	£0.90	£1.50

COYOTE

Marvel Comics Group/Epic; 1 Jun 1983-16 Mar 1986

	$Good	$Fine	$N.Mint	£Good	£Fine	£N.Mint
1 ND origin	*$0.30*	*$0.90*	*$1.50*	£0.20	£0.60	£1.00
2 ND origin concludes						
	$0.30	*$0.90*	*$1.50*	£0.20	£0.60	£1.00
3-10 ND	*$0.30*	*$0.90*	*$1.50*	£0.20	£0.60	£1.00
11 ND McFarlane art back up (Slash) - his first professional work						
	$0.35	*$1.05*	*$1.75*	£0.25	£0.75	£1.25
12-13 ND McFarlane art back up						
	$0.35	*$1.05*	*$1.75*	£0.25	£0.75	£1.25
14 ND Badger X-over, McFarlane art back up						
	$0.35	*$1.05*	*$1.75*	£0.25	£0.75	£1.25
15-16 ND	*$0.30*	*$0.90*	*$1.50*	£0.20	£0.60	£1.00
Title Value:	*$5.00*	*$15.00*	*$25.00*	£3.40	£10.20	£17.00

Note: all Baxter paper.

CRASH RYAN

Marvel Comics Group/Epic,MS; 1 Oct 1984-4 Jan 1985

	$Good	$Fine	$N.Mint	£Good	£Fine	£N.Mint
1-4 ND	*$0.25*	*$0.75*	*$1.25*	£0.15	£0.45	£0.75
Title Value:	*$1.00*	*$3.00*	*$5.00*	£0.60	£1.80	£3.00

Note: all the above on Baxter paper

CRAZY

Marvel Comics Group; 1 Feb 1973-3 Jun 1973

	$Good	$Fine	$N.Mint	£Good	£Fine	£N.Mint
1 ND features X-Men, Avengers, Spiderman parodies						
	$1.00	*$3.00*	*$6.00*	£0.40	£1.25	£2.50
2 ND Fantastic Four and Spiderman romance issue parodies						
	$0.65	*$2.00*	*$4.00*	£0.30	£1.00	£2.00
3 ND Fantastic Four and Superman origin parodies						
	$0.65	*$2.00*	*$4.00*	£0.30	£1.00	£2.00
Title Value:	*$2.30*	*$7.00*	*$14.00*	£1.00	£3.25	£6.50

Note: all reprints from Not Brand Echh.

ARTISTS

Eisner in 9-16. Ploog in 1, 4, 7.

CRAZY (2ND SERIES)

Marvel Comics Group,Magazine; 1 Oct 1973-94 Mar 1983

	$Good	$Fine	$N.Mint	£Good	£Fine	£N.Mint
1 ND	*$0.80*	*$2.50*	*$5.00*	£0.30	£1.00	£2.00
2 ND Neal Adams art						
	$0.65	*$2.00*	*$4.00*	£0.30	£1.00	£2.00
3-10 ND	*$0.50*	*$1.50*	*$3.00*	£0.25	£0.75	£1.50
11-21 ND scarce in the U.K.						
	$0.40	*$1.25*	*$2.50*	£0.25	£0.85	£1.75
22-50 ND	*$0.40*	*$1.25*	*$2.50*	£0.25	£0.75	£1.50
51-81 ND	*$0.40*	*$1.20*	*$2.00*	£0.25	£0.75	£1.25
82 ND Rogers art	*$0.50*	*$1.50*	*$2.50*	£0.30	£0.90	£1.50
83-87 ND	*$0.40*	*$1.20*	*$2.00*	£0.25	£0.75	£1.25
88 ND contains re-lettered version of Death of Phoenix from X-Men 137, Byrne art						
	$0.40	*$1.20*	*$2.00*	£0.25	£0.75	£1.25
89-94 ND	*$0.40*	*$1.20*	*$2.00*	£0.25	£0.75	£1.25
Title Value:	*$39.15*	*$119.60*	*$218.00*	£23.65	£72.25	£134.00

CRAZY SUMMER SPECIAL

Marvel Comics Group,Magazine; 1 Summer 1975

	$Good	$Fine	$N.Mint	£Good	£Fine	£N.Mint
1 ND 100pgs, Neal Adams reprint						
	$0.80	*$2.50*	*$5.00*	£0.50	£1.50	£3.00
Title Value:	*$0.80*	*$2.50*	*$5.00*	£0.50	£1.50	£3.00

CRAZYMAN

Continuity; 1 Nov 1991-2 1992

	$Good	$Fine	$N.Mint	£Good	£Fine	£N.Mint
1 ND	*$0.40*	*$1.20*	*$2.00*	£0.25	£0.75	£1.25
2 ND Neal Adams pencils and Brian Bolland inks on cover						
	$0.40	*$1.20*	*$2.00*	£0.25	£0.75	£1.25
Title Value:	*$0.80*	*$2.40*	*$4.00*	£0.50	£1.50	£2.50

CRAZYMAN (2ND SERIES)

Continuity; 1 May 1993-7 1994

	$Good	$Fine	$N.Mint	£Good	£Fine	£N.Mint
1-3 ND	*$0.35*	*$1.05*	*$1.75*	£0.25	£0.75	£1.25
4 ND parchment embossed cover						
	$0.35	*$1.05*	*$1.75*	£0.25	£0.75	£1.25
5-7 ND	*$0.35*	*$1.05*	*$1.75*	£0.25	£0.75	£1.25
Title Value:	*$2.45*	*$7.35*	*$12.25*	£1.75	£5.25	£8.75

CREATURE, THE

Dell/Movie Classics,OS Movie; 12-142-302 Dec 1962/Feb 1963; 12-142-410 Oct 1964

	$Good	$Fine	$N.Mint	£Good	£Fine	£N.Mint
12-142-302 distributed in the U.K.						
	$6.25	*$19.00*	*$45.00*	£2.85	£8.50	£20.00
12-142-410 distributed in the U.K.						
	$3.55	*$10.50*	*$25.00*	£1.75	£5.25	£12.50
Title Value:	*$9.80*	*$29.50*	*$70.00*	£4.60	£13.75	£32.50

CREATURES GIANT SIZE

Marvel Comics Group; 1 Jul 1974

(becomes Werewolf Giant Size)

	$Good	$Fine	$N.Mint	£Good	£Fine	£N.Mint
1 ND 52pgs, Werewolf, Tigra appear; secret origin of Tigra						
	$1.05	*$3.25*	*$6.50*	£0.80	£2.50	£5.00
Title Value:	*$1.05*	*$3.25*	*$6.50*	£0.80	£2.50	£5.00

CREATURES OF THE ID

Caliber Press,OS; 1 1990

	$Good	$Fine	$N.Mint	£Good	£Fine	£N.Mint
1 ND features Bernie Mireault art; black and white						
	$0.40	*$1.20*	*$2.00*	£0.25	£0.75	£1.25
Title Value:	*$0.40*	*$1.20*	*$2.00*	£0.25	£0.75	£1.25

CREATURES ON THE LOOSE

Marvel Comics Group; 10 Mar 1971-37 Sep 1975

	$Good	$Fine	$N.Mint	£Good	£Fine	£N.Mint
(formerly Tower of Shadows)						
10 scarce in the U.K. 1st appearance King Kull, Wrightson art	$4.65	$14.00	$28.00	£2.50	£7.50	£15.00
11	$0.80	$2.50	$5.00	£0.40	£1.25	£2.50
12 ND Wrightson cover	$0.80	$2.50	$5.00	£0.40	£1.25	£2.50
13-15 ND	$0.80	$2.50	$5.00	£0.40	£1.25	£2.50
16 ND 1st appearance Gullivar Jones, Warrior of Mars, Gil Kane art	$1.00	$3.00	$6.00	£0.50	£1.50	£3.00
17-19 ND Gullivar Jones	$0.65	$2.00	$4.00	£0.30	£1.00	£2.00
20 ND Gullivar Jones, Gray Morrow art	$0.65	$2.00	$4.00	£0.30	£1.00	£2.00
21 ND Gullivar Jones, Gray Morrow art	$0.50	$1.50	$3.00	£0.25	£0.75	£1.50
22 ND 1st appearance Thongor (Conanesque character), Steranko cover	$0.50	$1.50	$3.00	£0.25	£0.75	£1.50
23-29 ND Thongor appears	$0.50	$1.50	$3.00	£0.25	£0.75	£1.50
30 ND 1st of Man-Wolf series	$0.50	$1.50	$3.00	£0.25	£0.85	£1.75
31 LD in the U.K. Man-Wolf	$0.40	$1.25	$2.50	£0.25	£0.85	£1.75
32 Man-Wolf	$0.40	$1.25	$2.50	£0.20	£0.60	£1.25
33 George Perez' 1st full professional artwork in comics (see Astonishing Tales #25), Man-Wolf	$0.40	$1.25	$2.50	£0.25	£0.75	£1.50
34-37 Man-Wolf, George Perez art	$0.40	$1.25	$2.50	£0.20	£0.60	£1.25
Title Value:	$20.05	$61.25	$122.50	£10.20	£31.45	£63.25

ARTISTS

Morrow in 20, 21. Perez in 33-37. Steranko covers 20-22.

FEATURES

King Kull in 10. 50s/60s fantasy reprints in 10-15. Gullivar Jones in 16-21. Thongor in 22-29. Man-Wolf in 30-37.

CREED

Hall of Heroes; 1 Dec 1994-2 Jan 1995

	$Good	$Fine	$N.Mint	£Good	£Fine	£N.Mint
1 ND scarce in the U.K, scarce in the U.S. 7000 print run	$7.00	$21.00	$35.00	£5.00	£15.00	£25.00
2 ND scarce in the U.K, scarce in the U.S. 3500 print run	$7.00	$21.00	$35.00	£5.00	£15.00	£25.00
Title Value:	$14.00	$42.00	$70.00	£10.00	£30.00	£50.00

CREED (2ND SERIES)

Lightning Comics,OS; 1 Jul 1995

	$Good	$Fine	$N.Mint	£Good	£Fine	£N.Mint
1 ND 48pgs, Trent Kaniuga script; reprints 2 issue Hall of Heroes comics, black and white	$1.20	$3.60	$6.00	£0.80	£2.40	£4.00
1 Gold Edition, ND 48pgs, Trent Kaniuga script; pre-bagged with certificate	$3.00	$9.00	$15.00	£1.50	£4.50	£7.50
Title Value:	$4.20	$12.60	$21.00	£2.30	£6.90	£11.50

CREED (3RD SERIES)

Lightning Comics; 1 Sep 1995-present

	$Good	$Fine	$N.Mint	£Good	£Fine	£N.Mint
1 ND Trent Kaniuga script, Steven Zyskowski art	$1.20	$3.60	$6.00	£0.80	£2.40	£4.00
1 Commemorative Edition, ND (Sep 1995) - pre-bagged with signed (Steven Zyskowski) certificate of authenticity; limited to 3,000 copies with metallic ink cover	$3.20	$9.50	$16.00	£2.00	£6.00	£10.00
1 Gold Edition, ND polybagged with certificate of authenticity	$1.20	$3.60	$6.00	£0.80	£2.40	£4.00
1 Variant Cover Edition, ND Creed swinging from a branch	$1.50	$4.50	$7.50	£1.00	£3.00	£5.00
1 Variant Cover Signed & Numbered Edition, ND (Oct 1995) - signed by Trent Kaniuga, issued in a protective Mylar with certificate of authenticity, limited to 1,500 copies	$2.40	$7.00	$12.00	£2.00	£6.00	£10.00
2 ND	$0.80	$2.40	$4.00	£0.50	£1.50	£2.50
2 Variant Cover - Metallic Ink Edition, ND pre-bagged with signed and numbered certificate	$2.00	$6.00	$10.00	£1.30	£3.90	£6.50
2 Variant Cover Edition, ND "Butt Naked" cover	$0.80	$2.40	$4.00	£0.50	£1.50	£2.50
3 ND pre-bagged with chromium trading card	$0.60	$1.80	$3.00	£0.40	£1.20	£2.00
3 Commorative Edition, ND pre-bagged with certificate; dimensional platinum metallic ink cover	$2.00	$6.00	$10.00	£1.30	£3.90	£6.50
Title Value:	$15.70	$46.80	$78.50	£10.60	£31.80	£53.00

CREED/TEENAGE MUTANT NINJA TURTLES

Lightning Comics,OS; 1 May 1996

	$Good	$Fine	$N.Mint	£Good	£Fine	£N.Mint
1 ND Trent Kaniuga script and art	$0.60	$1.80	$3.00	£0.40	£1.20	£2.00
1 Autographed Edition, ND pre-bagged in Mylar sleeve with certificate; limited to 2,500 copies	$2.00	$6.00	$10.00	£1.30	£3.90	£6.50
1 Platinum Edition, ND pre-bagged with certificate of authenticity	$2.00	$6.00	$10.00	£1.30	£3.90	£6.50
1 Variant Cover Edition, ND cover by Trent Kaniuga	$0.60	$1.80	$3.00	£0.40	£1.20	£2.00
Title Value:	$5.20	$15.60	$26.00	£3.40	£10.20	£17.00

CREED: CRANIAL DISORDER

Lightning Comics; 1 Oct 1996

	$Good	$Fine	$N.Mint	£Good	£Fine	£N.Mint
1 ND Trent Kaniuga script and art	$0.60	$1.80	$3.00	£0.40	£1.20	£2.00
1 Platinum Edition ND	$1.20	$3.60	$6.00	£0.80	£2.40	£4.00
Title Value:	$1.80	$5.40	$9.00	£1.20	£3.60	£6.00

CREEPER, BEWARE THE

National Periodical Publications; 1 May/Jun 1968-6 Mar/Apr 1969

(see Brave and the Bold, First Issue Special, Showcase #73, Super-Team Family, World's Finest)

	$Good	$Fine	$N.Mint	£Good	£Fine	£N.Mint
1 Steve Ditko art	$10.00	$30.00	$70.00	£5.00	£15.00	£35.00
2-5 Steve Ditko art	$6.25	$19.00	$45.00	£2.50	£7.50	£17.50
6 part Steve Ditko art	$6.25	$19.00	$45.00	£2.50	£7.50	£17.50
Title Value:	$41.25	$125.00	$295.00	£17.50	£52.50	£122.50

CREEPSVILLE

Go-Go Comics,OS; 1 1991

	$Good	$Fine	$N.Mint	£Good	£Fine	£N.Mint
1 ND black and white humour anthology, bound-in set of 6 trading cards	$0.60	$1.80	$3.00	£0.40	£1.20	£2.00
Title Value:	$0.60	$1.80	$3.00	£0.40	£1.20	£2.00

CREEPY

Warren; 1 no date (1964)-146 1985

	$Good	$Fine	$N.Mint	£Good	£Fine	£N.Mint
1 distributed in the U.K.	$12.00	$36.00	$85.00	£5.50	£17.00	£40.00
2 distributed in the U.K.	$6.25	$19.00	$45.00	£2.85	£8.50	£20.00
3 distributed in the U.K.	$4.25	$12.50	$30.00	£2.10	£6.25	£15.00
4 distributed in the U.K.	$3.55	$10.50	$25.00	£1.40	£4.25	£10.00
5-8 distributed in the U.K.	$2.85	$8.50	$20.00	£1.25	£3.85	£9.00
9 Wrightson's first published work (one panel), distributed	$2.85	$8.50	$20.00	£1.40	£4.25	£10.00
10-13 distributed in the U.K.	$2.85	$8.50	$20.00	£1.05	£3.20	£7.50
14 distributed in the U.K.	$3.55	$10.50	$25.00	£1.25	£3.85	£9.00
15-50 distributed in the U.K.	$2.10	$6.25	$15.00	£0.70	£2.10	£5.00
51-61	$1.65	$5.00	$10.00	£0.65	£2.00	£4.00
62-63 Wrightson art	$1.65	$5.00	$10.00	£0.65	£2.00	£4.00
64-70	$1.65	$5.00	$10.00	£0.65	£2.00	£4.00
71-100 distributed in the U.K.	$1.50	$4.50	$9.00	£0.50	£1.50	£3.00
101-112	$1.60	$4.80	$8.00	£0.50	£1.50	£2.50
113 Bernie Wrightson art	$2.40	$7.00	$12.00	£0.80	£2.40	£4.00
114-146	$1.60	$4.80	$8.00	£0.50	£1.50	£2.50
Title Value:	$283.25	$848.00	$1683.00	£100.20	£302.80	£636.50

CREEPY (2ND SERIES)

Harris Publications/Dark Horse,MS; 1 May 1992-4 Aug 1992

	$Good	$Fine	$N.Mint	£Good	£Fine	£N.Mint
1-4 ND 48pgs, squarebound, all new anthology begins, Peter David scripts featured	$0.80	$2.40	$4.00	£0.50	£1.50	£2.50
Title Value:	$3.20	$9.60	$16.00	£2.00	£6.00	£10.00

CREEPY ANNUAL

Warren; 1968-1971

	$Good	$Fine	$N.Mint	£Good	£Fine	£N.Mint
1968 reprints; distributed in the U.K.	$1.75	$5.25	$12.50	£1.00	£3.00	£7.00
1969-1971 Neal Adams reprints; distributed in the U.K.	$1.75	$5.25	$12.50	£1.00	£3.00	£7.00
Title Value:	$7.00	$21.00	$50.00	£4.00	£12.00	£28.00

CREEPY FEARBOOK

Harris Comics,OS; 1 Feb 1993

	$Good	$Fine	$N.Mint	£Good	£Fine	£N.Mint
1 ND 44pgs, Dan Brereton "Vampirella" cover; Peter David and Art Adams work featured	$0.80	$2.40	$4.00	£0.50	£1.50	£2.50
Title Value:	$0.80	$2.40	$4.00	£0.50	£1.50	£2.50

CREEPY THINGS

Charlton; 1 Jul 1975-6 Jun 1976

	$Good	$Fine	$N.Mint	£Good	£Fine	£N.Mint
1 distributed in the U.K. painted cover	$0.25	$0.75	$1.50	£0.20	£0.60	£1.25
2 distributed in the U.K.	$0.25	$0.75	$1.50	£0.15	£0.50	£1.00
3 distributed in the U.K. Steve Ditko art	$0.25	$0.75	$1.50	£0.15	£0.50	£1.00
4 distributed in the U.K.	$0.25	$0.75	$1.50	£0.15	£0.50	£1.00
5 distributed in the U.K. Steve Ditko art	$0.25	$0.75	$1.50	£0.15	£0.50	£1.00
6 distributed in the U.K.	$0.25	$0.75	$1.50	£0.15	£0.50	£1.00
Title Value:	$1.50	$4.50	$9.00	£0.95	£3.10	£6.25

CREEPY TRADE PAPERBACK

Dark Horse,OS; 1 Oct 1991

	$Good	$Fine	$N.Mint	£Good	£Fine	£N.Mint
1 ND 112pgs, features reprints by Frazetta, Toth, Adams, Crandall, Williamson, Steve Ditko and others	$2.10	$6.25	$10.50	£1.40	£4.20	£7.00
Title Value:	$2.10	$6.25	$10.50	£1.40	£4.20	£7.00

CRIME CLASSICS

Eternity; 1 Sep 1988-13 1989

	$Good	$Fine	$N.Mint	£Good	£Fine	£N.Mint
1-13 ND Shadow newspaper strip reprints	$0.40	$1.20	$2.00	£0.25	£0.75	£1.25
Title Value:	$5.20	$15.60	$26.00	£3.25	£9.75	£16.25

CRIME SUSPENSTORIES

E.C. Comics; 1 Oct/Nov 1950-27 Mar 1955

	$Good	$Fine	$N.Mint	£Good	£Fine	£N.Mint
1 Wally Wood art (Note: copies of #1 exist with Vault of Horror #15 on inside front cover, blacked out and with #1 printed over it)	$150.00	$450.00	$1200.00	£100.00	£300.00	£800.00
2 Jack Kamen art	$110.00	$335.00	$900.00	£75.00	£225.00	£600.00
3 Wally Wood art, Johnny Craig cover and art	$39.00	$115.00	$315.00	£26.00	£77.50	£210.00
4 Ingels art	$39.00	$115.00	$315.00	£26.00	£77.50	£210.00

	$Good	$Fine	$N.Mint	£Good	£Fine	£N.Mint
5 Jack Kamen art	$39.00	$115.00	$315.00	£26.00	£77.50	£210.00
6 Jack Davis art	$31.00	$92.50	$250.00	£21.00	£62.50	£170.00
7-10	$31.00	$92.50	$250.00	£21.00	£62.50	£170.00
11-12	$26.00	$75.00	$180.00	£17.00	£50.00	£120.00
13 Al Williamson art	$30.00	$90.00	$210.00	£20.00	£60.00	£140.00
14-15	$26.00	$75.00	$180.00	£17.00	£50.00	£120.00
16 Al Williamson art, Johnny Craig cover and art	$30.00	$90.00	$210.00	£20.00	£60.00	£140.00
17 Frazetta and Williamson art, Johnny Craig cover and art	$32.00	$95.00	$225.00	£21.00	£62.50	£150.00
18 Johnny Craig cover and art	$21.00	$62.50	$150.00	£14.00	£43.00	£100.00
19 Johnny Craig art	$21.00	$62.50	$150.00	£14.00	£43.00	£100.00
20 Johnny Craig cover and art; famous "hanging noose" cover	$30.00	$90.00	$210.00	£20.00	£60.00	£140.00
21 Crandall art, Johnny Craig cover and art	$15.00	$45.00	$105.00	£10.00	£30.00	£70.00
22 Johnny Craig cover	$22.50	$67.50	$160.00	£15.50	£47.00	£110.00
23 Jack Kamen art	$22.50	$67.50	$160.00	£15.50	£47.00	£110.00
24 Krigstein art	$15.00	$45.00	$105.00	£10.00	£30.00	£70.00
25-27 Jack Kamen cover and art	$15.00	$45.00	$105.00	£10.00	£30.00	£70.00
Title Value:	$920.00	$2742.50	$7015.00	£616.00	£1842.50	£4700.00

Note: all Non-Distributed on the news-stands in the U.K.

CRIME SUSPENSTORIES (2ND SERIES)

Russ Cochran/EC Comics; 1 Nov 1992-present

	$Good	$Fine	$N.Mint	£Good	£Fine	£N.Mint
1 ND reprints begin from original 1950s EC series with exact cover and interior reproduction	$0.30	$0.90	$1.50	£0.20	£0.60	£1.00
2-13 ND	$0.30	$0.90	$1.50	£0.20	£0.60	£1.00
14-15 ND	$0.40	$1.20	$2.00	£0.25	£0.75	£1.25
16 ND	$0.50	$1.50	$2.50	£0.30	£0.90	£1.50
Title Value:	$5.20	$15.60	$26.00	£3.40	£10.20	£17.00
Crime Suspenstories Annual #1 (Oct 1994)						
ND reprints issues #1-5 with covers				£1.20	£3.60	£6.00
Crime Suspenstories Annual 2 (1995)						
ND reprints issues =6-10 with covers				£1.20	£3.60	£6.00
Crime Suspenstories Annual 3 (Jun 1996)						
ND reprints issues #11-15 with covers				£1.20	£3.60	£6.00

CRIMEBUSTER

AC Comics; 0 Apr 1995

	$Good	$Fine	$N.Mint	£Good	£Fine	£N.Mint
0 ND 40pgs, flip-book format with issue #1 of Crimebuster Classics included; spin-off from Fem Force; b&w	$0.60	$1.80	$3.00	£0.40	£1.20	£2.00
Title Value:	$0.60	$1.80	$3.00	£0.40	£1.20	£2.00

CRIMSON AVENGER, THE

DC Comics,MS; 1 Jun 1988-4 Sep 1988

(see Secret Origins)

	$Good	$Fine	$N.Mint	£Good	£Fine	£N.Mint
1 Greg Brooks art	$0.15	$0.45	$0.75	£0.10	£0.35	£0.60
2 Greg Brookes art	$0.15	$0.45	$0.75	£0.10	£0.35	£0.60
3-4 Greg Brooks art	$0.15	$0.45	$0.75	£0.10	£0.35	£0.60
Title Value:	$0.60	$1.80	$3.00	£0.40	£1.40	£2.40

CRIMSON COUGAR

Greater Mercury Comics; 1 Dec 1990

	$Good	$Fine	$N.Mint	£Good	£Fine	£N.Mint
1 ND b&w	$0.40	$1.20	$2.00	£0.25	£0.75	£1.25
Title Value:	$0.40	$1.20	$2.00	£0.25	£0.75	£1.25

CRISIS ON INFINITE EARTHS

Cross-over series that re-shaped the continuity problems of the DC Universe that had accrued over four decades. The number of different planet Earths each with their own heroes started with the story in Flash #123 that saw the Silver Age Flash (Barry Allen) meet his Golden Age Flash counter-part (Jay Garrick). Thereafter, the Golden Age heroes were said to exist on Earth II. Further complications followed introducing other groups of heroes and complicated plot-lines. This series resolved to combine all the various Earths into one and a number of heroes died as a result. It was seen at the time as a great clearing-out process by DC and represents a water-shed in their history. The core mini-series had (appropriately) an almost infinite number of cross-overs listed below in alphabetical rather than chronological order.

1) All Star Squadron 50
2) All Star Squadron 51
3) All Star Squadron 52
4) All Star Squadron 53
5) All Star Squadron 54
6) All Star Squadron 55
7) All Star Squadron 56
8) All Star Squadron 60 - Unofficial X-over
9) Amethyst (1986 series) 13
10) Blue Devil 17
11) Blue Devil 18
12) DC Comics Presents 78
13) DC Comics Presents 86
14) DC Comics Presents 87
15) DC Comics Presents 88
16) DC Comics Presents 94 - post Crisis epilogue
17) DC Comics Presents 95 - unofficial X-over
18) Detective Comics 558 - unofficial X-over
19) Fury of Firestorm 41
20) Fury of Firestorm 42
21) Green Lantern 194
22) Green Lantern 195
23) Green Lantern 196 - unofficial X-over
24) Green Lantern 198
25) Infinity Inc. 18
26) Infinity Inc. 19
27) Infinity Inc. 20
28) Infinity Inc. 21
29) Infinity Inc. 22
30) Infinity Inc. 23
31) Infinity Inc. 24
32) Infinity Inc. 25 - unofficial X-over
33) Infinity Inc. Annual 1
34) Justice League of America 244
35) Justice League of America 245
36) Justice League of America Annual 3
37) Legion of Super-Heroes (2nd Series) 16 - unofficial X-over
38) Legion of Super-Heroes 18
39) Losers Special 1 - Crisis first appears
40) New Teen Titans (2nd Series) 13
41) New Teen Titans (2nd Series) 14
42) Omega Men 31
43) Omega Men 33 - unofficial X-over
44) Superman 413 - unofficial X-over
45) Superman 414
46) Superman 415
47) Swamp Thing (2nd Series) 44 - unofficial X-over
48) Swamp Thing (2nd series) 46
49) Wonder Woman 327
50) Wonder Woman 328
51) Wonder Woman 329

Note: an unofficial cross-over means that the Crisis storyline is referred to in the comic but it is not emblazoned as such on the cover.

CRISIS ON INFINITE EARTHS (LIMITED SERIES)

DC Comics,MS; 1 Apr 1985-12 Mar 1986

	$Good	$Fine	$N.Mint	£Good	£Fine	£N.Mint
1 LD in the U.K. George Perez art	$1.00	$3.00	$5.00	£0.80	£2.40	£4.00
2 LD in the U.K. Joker appers; George Perez art	$0.60	$1.80	$3.00	£0.60	£1.80	£3.00
3 death of Kid Psycho and Nighthawk (Western); George Perez art	$0.50	$1.50	$2.50	£0.40	£1.20	£2.00
4 death of The Monitor, 1st appearance new Dr. Light; George Perez art	$0.50	$1.50	$2.50	£0.40	£1.20	£2.00
5 1st appearance Anti-Monitor; George Perez art	$0.50	$1.50	$2.50	£0.40	£1.20	£2.00
6 1st appearance the new Wildcat; George Perez art	$0.50	$1.50	$2.50	£0.40	£1.20	£2.00
7 LD in the U.K. DS death of Supergirl; George Perez art	$1.00	$3.00	$5.00	£0.60	£1.80	£3.00
8 death of Flash (Barry Allen); George Perez art	$1.00	$3.00	$5.00	£0.60	£1.80	£3.00
9 death of Earth 2 Luthor; Joker appears; George Perez art	$0.50	$1.50	$2.50	£0.40	£1.20	£2.00
10 The Molder cameo (only other appearance Flash #253, actually Elongated Man disguised); George Perez art	$0.50	$1.50	$2.50	£0.40	£1.20	£2.00
11 George Perez art	$0.50	$1.50	$2.50	£0.40	£1.20	£2.00
12 LD in the U.K. DS Dove, Kole, Lori Lemaris, Sunburst, Golden Age Robin, Golden Age Huntress die, 1st appearance new Flash (Wally West); George Perez art	$1.00	$3.00	$5.00	£0.60	£1.80	£3.00
Title Value:	$8.10	$24.30	$40.50	£6.00	£18.00	£30.00

CRISIS ON INFINITE EARTHS - THE EARTH INDEX

Over the years, DC had built up a very complex set of universes and thus very complex continuity problems which was the main reason for having their "clearout". Prior to the events of the mini-series, the known Earths of the DC Universe are as follows:

Earth 1 - where the DC super-heroes and characters from the Silver Age onwards are based. All stories unless otherwise stated from cover date September 1956 (ie. Showcase #4) take place on Earth 1.

Earth 2 - where the DC super-heroes and characters from the Golden Age to just before the beginning of the Silver Age are based. All stories from cover date June 1938 (ie. Action Comics #1) to about 1955/56 take place on Earth 2.

Earth 3 - very similar in make-up to Earth 1 but the only super-powered beings are in The Crime Syndicate of America (Ultraman, Super Woman, Johnny Quick, Owl Man and Power Ring). Alexander Luthor is the only (short-lived) super-hero and his son, Alex Luthor, escaped to Earth 1.

Earth 4 - inhabited by the Charlton Comics characters. These are Captain Atom, Blue Beetle, Nightshade, Thunderbolt, Son of Vulcan, Peacemaker and The Question.

Earth 5 - to my knowledge, an Earth 5 has never been mentioned.

Earth 6 - inhabited by a super-powered family comprising Lord Volt, Lady Quark and their daughter Princess Fern.

Earth S - inhabited by the Shazam family of characters. These are principally Captain Marvel, Mary Marvel, Captain Marvel Junior.

Earth X - a world where the Second World War lasted 40 years and becomes the home of The Freedom Fighters (The Ray, Black Condor, Phantom Lady, Uncle Sam, Human Bomb and Doll Man - all Golden Age heroes.

Earth Quality - a world that also has Freedom Fighter counter-parts plus Kid Eternity, The Spirit, Lady Luck and Mr. Mystic.

Earth B - a world created by DC editorial staff to allow for the many inconsistencies in Brave and the Bold and World's Finest stories. It is named after "The 3 B's": eitor Murray Bolintoff and writers Bob Haney and E. Nelson Bridwell. The mini-series DC Challenge takes place here.

Earth C - inhabited by DC's "funny animals" such as Captain Carrot and co.

Earth C Minus - a world discovered by Captain Carrot in his civillian identity of cartoonist Rodney Rabbit where living versions of the cartoon characters he created announced they were from.

Earth Prime - the "real" world where super-heroes only exist as comic book characters.

CRITICAL ERROR

Dark Horse,OS; 1 Oct 1992

	$Good	$Fine	$N.Mint	£Good	£Fine	£N.Mint
1 ND early John Byrne black and white story in full colour	$0.50	$1.50	$2.50	£0.30	£0.90	£1.50
Title Value:	$0.50	$1.50	$2.50	£0.30	£0.90	£1.50

CRITICAL MASS

Marvel Comics Group/Epic,MS; 1 Jan 1989-7 Jul 1990

	$Good	$Fine	$N.Mint	£Good	£Fine	£N.Mint
1 ND Janson/Sienkiewicz/Kev O'Neill/Gray Morrow art	$0.90	$2.70	$4.50	£0.60	£1.80	£3.00
2 ND Kev O'Neill/Kyle Baker/Mark Texiera art featured	$0.80	$2.40	$4.00	£0.55	£1.65	£2.75
3 ND Ron Randall/Gray Morrow/John Ridgway/Denys Cowan/Kent Williams art	$0.80	$2.40	$4.00	£0.55	£1.65	£2.75
4 ND features John Ridgway, Jim Lee art	$0.80	$2.40	$4.00	£0.55	£1.65	£2.75
5 ND features John Ridgway art	$0.80	$2.40	$4.00	£0.55	£1.65	£2.75
6 ND features Gray Morrow art	$0.80	$2.40	$4.00	£0.55	£1.65	£2.75
7 ND 80pgs, The Shadowline Saga concludes	$0.80	$2.40	$4.00	£0.55	£1.65	£2.75
Title Value:	$5.70	$17.10	$28.50	£3.90	£11.70	£19.50

Note: issues #1-6 are squarebound 64 pgs

FEATURES

Dr. Zero in 1, 2 Powerline in 1, 3 St. George in 2, 3

CRITTERS

Fantagraphics; 1 Jun 1986-50 Mar 1990

	$Good	$Fine	$N.Mint	£Good	£Fine	£N.Mint
1 giant, Usagi Yojimbo and Cutey Bunny appear; black and white	$0.60	$1.80	$3.00	£0.60	£1.80	£3.00
1 2nd printing, (Sep 1991)	$0.45	$1.35	$2.25	£0.30	£0.90	£1.50
2	$0.40	$1.20	$2.00	£0.35	£1.05	£1.75
3 Usagi Yojimbo appears	$0.40	$1.20	$2.00	£0.35	£1.05	£1.75
4-9	$0.40	$1.20	$2.00	£0.35	£1.05	£1.75
10 Usagi Yojimbo appears	$0.40	$1.20	$2.00	£0.35	£1.05	£1.75
11 68pgs, Christmas Special, Usagi Yojimbo appears	$0.40	$1.20	$2.00	£0.30	£0.90	£1.50
12-13	$0.40	$1.20	$2.00	£0.30	£0.90	£1.50
14 Usagi Yojimbo appears	$0.40	$1.20	$2.00	£0.30	£0.90	£1.50
15-21	$0.40	$1.20	$2.00	£0.30	£0.90	£1.50
22 Watchmen parody; two different covers rumoured to exist	$0.40	$1.20	$2.00	£0.30	£0.90	£1.50
23 64pgs, flexi-disc included, Alan Moore's Sinister Ducks story (text- 2pgs), 1pg Sam Kieth art, (without disc = 25% less)	$0.70	$2.10	$3.50	£0.50	£1.50	£2.50
24-30	$0.40	$1.20	$2.00	£0.30	£0.90	£1.50
31-37	$0.35	$1.05	$1.75	£0.25	£0.75	£1.25
38 48pgs, Usagi Yojimbo appears	$0.35	$1.05	$1.75	£0.25	£0.75	£1.25
39-49	$0.35	$1.05	$1.75	£0.25	£0.75	£1.25
50 80pgs, Neil the Horse, Sam and Max, Usagi Yojimbo among others	$0.70	$2.10	$3.50	£0.50	£1.50	£2.50
Title Value:	$20.30	$60.90	$101.50	£15.50	£46.50	£77.50

Note: all Non-Distributed on the news-stands in the U.K.

CRITTERS SPECIAL

Fantagraphics; 1 1988

	$Good	$Fine	$N.Mint	£Good	£Fine	£N.Mint
1 ND Nilson Groundthumper reprints by Stan Sakai	$0.50	$1.50	$2.50	£0.30	£0.90	£1.50
Title Value:	$0.50	$1.50	$2.50	£0.30	£0.90	£1.50

CROMWELL STONE

Dark Horse,OS; 1 Apr 1992

	$Good	$Fine	$N.Mint	£Good	£Fine	£N.Mint
1 ND	$0.70	$2.10	$3.50	£0.50	£1.50	£2.50
Title Value:	$0.70	$2.10	$3.50	£0.50	£1.50	£2.50

CRONA

Dagger Enterprises; 1 Aug 1994-2 1994

	$Good	$Fine	$N.Mint	£Good	£Fine	£N.Mint
1 ND Bart Sears cover	$0.50	$1.50	$2.50	£0.30	£0.90	£1.50
2 ND	$0.50	$1.50	$2.50	£0.30	£0.90	£1.50
Title Value:	$1.00	$3.00	$5.00	£0.60	£1.80	£3.00

CROSS

Dark Horse,MS; 0 Oct 1995-6 Mar 1996

	$Good	$Fine	$N.Mint	£Good	£Fine	£N.Mint
0 ND Andrew Vachss story, Geoff Darrow covers	$0.50	$1.50	$2.50	£0.30	£0.90	£1.50
1 ND Andrew Vachss story, Geof Darrow covers	$0.50	$1.50	$2.50	£0.30	£0.90	£1.50
2-6 ND Andrew Vachss story, Geof Darrow covers	$0.60	$1.80	$3.00	£0.40	£1.20	£2.00
Title Value:	$4.00	$12.00	$20.00	£2.60	£7.80	£13.00

CROSSFIRE

Eclipse; 1 May 1984-26 Feb 1988

	$Good	$Fine	$N.Mint	£Good	£Fine	£N.Mint
1 ND Mark Evanier script and Dan Spiegle art begin; colour issues begin	$0.40	$1.20	$2.00	£0.25	£0.75	£1.25
2-16 ND	$0.40	$1.20	$2.00	£0.25	£0.75	£1.25
17 ND last colour issue	$0.40	$1.20	$2.00	£0.25	£0.75	£1.25
18-26 ND	$0.40	$1.20	$2.00	£0.25	£0.75	£1.25
Title Value:	$10.40	$31.20	$52.00	£6.50	£19.50	£32.50

CROSSFIRE & RAINBOW

Eclipse,MS; 1 Jun 1986-4 Sep 1986

	$Good	$Fine	$N.Mint	£Good	£Fine	£N.Mint
1 ND Jerry Ordway cover	$0.30	$0.90	$1.50	£0.20	£0.60	£1.00
2-3 ND	$0.30	$0.90	$1.50	£0.20	£0.60	£1.00
4 ND Dave Stevens cover	$0.30	$0.90	$1.50	£0.20	£0.60	£1.00
Title Value:	$1.20	$3.60	$6.00	£0.80	£2.40	£4.00

CROSSING, THE

Marvel Comics Group; 1995

Cross-over storyline that ran throughout the following issues:

Avengers #390 (Prelude), Iron Man #320, Avengers: The Crossing #1, Avengers #391, Iron Man #321, Force Works #16, Avengers #392, Iron Man #322, Force Works #17, Avengers #393, Iron Man #323, Force Works #18, Avengers #394, Iron Man #324, Force Works #19.

CROSSOVER CLASSICS: THE MARVEL/DC COLLECTION

Marvel Comics Group/DC Comics,OS; 1 Jan 1992

	$Good	$Fine	$N.Mint	£Good	£Fine	£N.Mint
1 ND 320pgs, reprints Superman vs. Spiderman (1976), Batman vs. Hulk (1981) and Teen Titans vs. The X-Men (1982)	$3.75	$11.00	$18.75	£2.50	£7.50	£12.50
1 2nd printing, ND (Apr 1993)	$3.30	$9.75	$16.50	£2.20	£6.50	£11.00
Title Value:	$7.05	$20.75	$35.25	£4.70	£14.00	£23.50

CROSSROADS

First,MS; 1 Jul 1988-5 Nov 1988

	$Good	$Fine	$N.Mint	£Good	£Fine	£N.Mint
1 ND Whisper/Sable by S. Grant/C. Martin	$0.80	$2.40	$4.00	£0.50	£1.50	£2.50
1 2nd printing ND	$0.55	$1.65	$2.75	£0.35	£1.05	£1.75
2 ND Sable/Badger by Baron/Medina/Whigham	$0.70	$2.10	$3.50	£0.40	£1.20	£2.00
3 ND Badger/Luther Ironheart by Salick/Staton	$0.70	$2.10	$3.50	£0.40	£1.20	£2.00
4 ND Grimjack/Judah Maccabee by Salick/McMannus	$0.70	$2.10	$3.50	£0.40	£1.20	£2.00
5 ND Grimjack/Dreadstar/Nexus by Baron/McDonnell	$0.70	$2.10	$3.50	£0.40	£1.20	£2.00
Title Value:	$4.15	$12.45	$20.75	£2.45	£7.35	£12.25

Note: all Bookshelf Format; Steve Rude painted covers on all

CROW OF THE BEAR CLAW

Blackthorne; 1 Sep 1986-6 Jul 1987

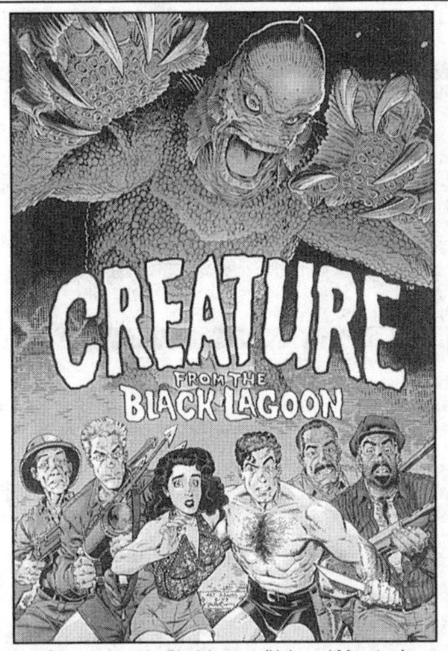

Creature from the Black Lagoon (Universal Monsters)

Creatures on the Loose #24

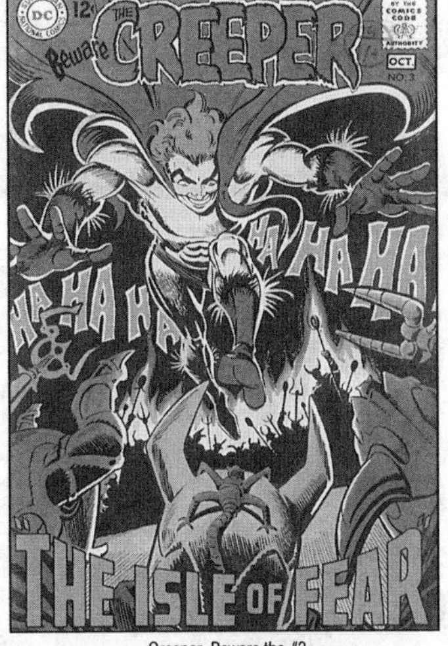

Creeper, Beware the #3

	$Good	$Fine	$N.Mint	£Good	£Fine	£N.Mint
1-6 ND	$0.40	$1.20	$2.00	£0.25	£0.75	£1.25
Title Value:	$2.40	$7.20	$12.00	£1.50	£4.50	£7.50

CROW, THE

Caliber Press,MS; 1 Feb 1989-4 Dec 1990

	$Good	$Fine	$N.Mint	£Good	£Fine	£N.Mint
1 ND	$13.00	$40.00	$80.00	£7.50	£22.50	£45.00
1 2nd printing, ND (Oct 1989)	$1.50	$4.50	$7.50	£1.00	£3.00	£5.00
1 3rd printing ND	$0.90	$2.70	$4.50	£0.60	£1.80	£3.00
2 ND	$10.00	$30.00	$50.00	£5.00	£15.00	£25.00
2 2nd printing, ND (Dec 1989)	$0.70	$2.10	$3.50	£0.50	£1.50	£2.50
2 3rd printing ND	$0.45	$1.35	$2.25	£0.30	£0.90	£1.50
3 ND limited print run	$11.00	$33.00	$55.00	£5.00	£15.00	£25.00
3 2nd printing, ND (Jun 1990)	$0.70	$2.10	$3.50	£0.50	£1.50	£2.50
4 ND	$8.00	$24.00	$40.00	£4.00	£12.00	£20.00
Title Value:	$46.25	$139.75	$246.25	£24.40	£73.20	£129.50

CROW, THE (2ND SERIES)

Tundra; 1-3 1992

	$Good	$Fine	$N.Mint	£Good	£Fine	£N.Mint
1 ND 64pgs, reprints Crow #1,2 with new covers	$2.40	$7.00	$12.00	£1.20	£3.60	£6.00
2-3 ND	$2.40	$7.00	$12.00	£1.20	£3.60	£6.00
Title Value:	$7.20	$21.00	$36.00	£3.60	£10.80	£18.00

CROW: CITY OF ANGELS, THE

Kitchen Sink,MS; 1 Jul 1996-3 Sep 1996

	$Good	$Fine	$N.Mint	£Good	£Fine	£N.Mint
1 Cover A, ND based on film	$0.60	$1.80	$3.00	£0.40	£1.20	£2.00
1 Cover B, ND photo cover; based on film	$0.60	$1.80	$3.00	£0.40	£1.20	£2.00
2 Cover A, ND based on film	$0.60	$1.80	$3.00	£0.40	£1.20	£2.00
2 Cover B, ND photo cover; based on film	$0.60	$1.80	$3.00	£0.40	£1.20	£2.00
3 Cover A, ND based on film	$0.60	$1.80	$3.00	£0.40	£1.20	£2.00
3 Cover B, ND photo cover; based on film	$0.60	$1.80	$3.00	£0.40	£1.20	£2.00
Title Value:	$3.60	$10.80	$18.00	£2.40	£7.20	£12.00

CROW: DEAD TIME

Kitchen Sink,MS; 1-3 1996

	$Good	$Fine	$N.Mint	£Good	£Fine	£N.Mint
1-3 ND	$0.60	$1.80	$3.00	£0.40	£1.20	£2.00
Title Value:	$1.80	$5.40	$9.00	£1.20	£3.60	£6.00

CROW: FLESH & BLOOD

Kitchen Sink,MS; 1-3 1996

	$Good	$Fine	$N.Mint	£Good	£Fine	£N.Mint
1-3 ND	$0.60	$1.80	$3.00	£0.40	£1.20	£2.00
Title Value:	$1.80	$5.40	$9.00	£1.20	£3.60	£6.00

CROW: WILD JUSTICE

Kitchen Sink,OS; 1 Oct 1996

	$Good	$Fine	$N.Mint	£Good	£Fine	£N.Mint
1 ND Jerry Prosser script, Charlie Adlard art; black and white	$0.50	$1.50	$2.50	£0.30	£0.90	£1.50
Title Value:	$0.50	$1.50	$2.50	£0.30	£0.90	£1.50

CRUCIBLE

DC Comics/Impact,MS; 1 Feb 1993-6 Jul 1993

	$Good	$Fine	$N.Mint	£Good	£Fine	£N.Mint
1 ND Shield, Black Hood and The Comet appear, special cover price of 99 cents; Joe Quesada art featured	$0.15	$0.45	$0.75	£0.10	£0.35	£0.60
2-6 ND Joe Quesada art featured	$0.15	$0.45	$0.75	£0.10	£0.35	£0.60
Title Value:	$0.90	$2.70	$4.50	£0.60	£2.10	£3.60

CRUSADERS

Guild Publications,Magazine; 1 Aug 1982

(becomes Southern Knights)

	$Good	$Fine	$N.Mint	£Good	£Fine	£N.Mint
1 ND very scarce in the U.K. black and white	$3.80	$11.00	$19.00	£2.50	£7.50	£12.50
Title Value:	$3.80	$11.00	$19.00	£2.50	£7.50	£12.50

CRUSADERS, THE

DC Comics/Impact; 1 May 1992-8 Dec 1992

	$Good	$Fine	$N.Mint	£Good	£Fine	£N.Mint
1 The Fly, Jaguar, Fireball, Comet and The Web begin as team, includes trading cards	$0.15	$0.45	$0.75	£0.10	£0.35	£0.60
2-8	$0.15	$0.45	$0.75	£0.10	£0.35	£0.60
Title Value:	$1.20	$3.60	$6.00	£0.80	£2.80	£4.80

CRUSH, THE

Image,MS; 1 Mar 1996-5 Jul 1996

	$Good	$Fine	$N.Mint	£Good	£Fine	£N.Mint
1 ND Mike Baron script, N. Steven Harris and Reggie Jones art begin	$0.50	$1.50	$2.50	£0.30	£0.90	£1.50
2-5 ND	$0.50	$1.50	$2.50	£0.30	£0.90	£1.50
Title Value:	$2.50	$7.50	$12.50	£1.50	£4.50	£7.50

CRY FOR DAWN

Cry For Dawn; 1 Spring 1989-9 1992

	$Good	$Fine	$N.Mint	£Good	£Fine	£N.Mint
1 ND Joseph Michael Linsner cover and art, black and white	$46.00	$135.00	$275.00	£25.00	£75.00	£150.00
		[Prices may vary widely on this comic]				
1 2nd printing, ND (1989/1990)	$23.00	$70.00	$140.00	£14.00	£43.00	£85.00
1 3rd printing ND	$15.00	$45.00	$90.00	£9.00	£28.00	£55.00
2 ND Joseph Michael Linsner cover art and interior (8 pages), black and white	$25.00	$75.00	$150.00	£15.50	£48.00	£95.00
2 2nd printing ND	$10.00	$30.00	$60.00	£5.75	£17.50	£35.00
3 ND	$15.50	$48.00	$95.00	£10.00	£30.00	£60.00
4 ND	$12.50	$38.00	$75.00	£7.50	£22.50	£45.00
4 Signed & Numbered Edition ND	$21.50	$65.00	$130.00	£14.00	£43.00	£85.00
5 ND	$10.00	$30.00	$60.00	£5.75	£17.50	£35.00
5 2nd printing, ND (Aug 1993)	$5.75	$17.50	$35.00	£3.30	£10.00	£20.00
5 Signed & Numbered Edition ND	$25.00	$75.00	$150.00	£17.50	£52.50	£105.00
6 ND	$10.00	$30.00	$60.00	£5.75	£17.50	£35.00
6 Signed & Numbered Edition ND	$18.00	$55.00	$110.00	£12.50	£38.00	£75.00
7 ND	$8.25	$25.00	$50.00	£5.00	£15.00	£30.00
7 Signed & Numbered Edition ND	$17.50	$52.50	$105.00	£11.50	£35.00	£70.00
8 ND	$8.25	$25.00	$50.00	£5.00	£15.00	£30.00
8 Signed & Numbered Edition ND	$17.50	$52.50	$105.00	£11.50	£35.00	£70.00
9 ND Joseph Michael Linsner cover art and interior (20 pages), black and white	$8.25	$25.00	$50.00	£5.00	£15.00	£30.00
9 Signed & Numbered Edition ND	$21.00	$62.50	$105.00	£14.00	£42.00	£70.00
Title Value:	$318.00	$956.00	$1895.00	£197.55	£599.50	£1180.00

Note: issue #11 published as Subtle Violence #1

CRYING FREEMAN

Viz Communications; 1 1989-8 Jul 1990

	$Good	$Fine	$N.Mint	£Good	£Fine	£N.Mint
1 ND DS	$0.80	$2.40	$4.00	£0.50	£1.50	£2.50
2-8 ND	$0.80	$2.40	$4.00	£0.50	£1.50	£2.50
Title Value:	$6.40	$19.20	$32.00	£4.00	£12.00	£20.00
Crying Freeman: Portrait of a Killer						
Part 1, reprints issues #1-4				£2.00	£6.00	£10.00
Part 2, reprints issues #5-8				£2.00	£6.00	£10.00
Crying Freeman Perfect Collection: Portrait of a Killer (Aug 1995) 456pgs, collects volumes 1 and 2				£2.70	£8.10	£13.50
Crying Freeman Perfect Collection: Shades of Death (Dec 1995) 292pgs				£2.70	£8.10	£13.50

Note: Manga series by Ikegami (Mai) and Koike (Lone Wolf); contains violence and nudity

CRYING FREEMAN (2ND SERIES)

Viz Communications; 1 Oct 1990-9 1991

	$Good	$Fine	$N.Mint	£Good	£Fine	£N.Mint
1-9 ND	$0.80	$2.40	$4.00	£0.50	£1.50	£2.50
Title Value:	$7.20	$21.60	$36.00	£4.50	£13.50	£22.50

CRYING FREEMAN (3RD SERIES)

Viz Communications,MS; 1 Jul 1991-10 Apr 1992

	$Good	$Fine	$N.Mint	£Good	£Fine	£N.Mint
1-10 ND 40pgs	$0.90	$2.70	$4.50	£0.60	£1.80	£3.00
Title Value:	$9.00	$27.00	$45.00	£6.00	£18.00	£30.00
Crying Freeman: A Taste of Revenge Part 1 (Jan 1993) 184pgs, reprints #1-5				£2.00	£6.00	£10.00
Crying Freeman: A Taste of Revenge Part 2 (Mar 1993) 184pgs, reprints #6-10				£2.00	£6.00	£10.00
Crying Freeman: A Taste of Revenge Perfect Collection (Sep 1995) collects part 1 and part 2				£2.70	£8.10	£13.50

CRYING FREEMAN (4TH SERIES)

Viz Communications,MS; 1 May 1992-8 Jan 1993

	$Good	$Fine	$N.Mint	£Good	£Fine	£N.Mint
1-8 ND 40pgs	$0.90	$2.70	$4.50	£0.60	£1.80	£3.00
Title Value:	$7.20	$21.60	$36.00	£4.80	£14.40	£24.00

CRYING FREEMAN (5TH SERIES)

Viz Communications,MS; 1 Feb 1993-11 Dec 1993

	$Good	$Fine	$N.Mint	£Good	£Fine	£N.Mint
1-11 ND Rumiko Takahashi; black and white	$0.55	$1.65	$2.75	£0.35	£1.05	£1.75
Title Value:	$6.05	$18.15	$30.25	£3.85	£11.55	£19.25
Crying Freeman: Journey to Freedom (Sep 1994) 168pgs, reprints first half of series				£2.00	£6.00	£10.00
Crying Freeman: Journey to Fredom (Nov 1994) 168pgs, reprints second half of series				£2.00	£6.00	£10.00

CRYPT

Image,MS; 1 Aug 1995-2 Sep 1995

	$Good	$Fine	$N.Mint	£Good	£Fine	£N.Mint
1-2 ND Robert Napton script, John Fang art	$0.50	$1.50	$2.50	£0.30	£0.90	£1.50
Title Value:	$1.00	$3.00	$5.00	£0.60	£1.80	£3.00

CRYPT OF DAWN

Sirius Entertainment; 1 Oct 1996

	$Good	$Fine	$N.Mint	£Good	£Fine	£N.Mint
1 ND anthology featuring Joseph Michael Linsner script and art; card-stock cover, black and white	$0.60	$1.80	$3.00	£0.40	£1.20	£2.00
Title Value:	$0.60	$1.80	$3.00	£0.40	£1.20	£2.00

CRYPT OF SHADOWS

Marvel Comics Group; 1 Jan 1973-21 Nov 1975

	$Good	$Fine	$N.Mint	£Good	£Fine	£N.Mint
1 ND horror reprints begin	$1.00	$3.00	$6.00	£0.40	£1.25	£2.50
2-3 ND	$0.65	$2.00	$4.00	£0.30	£1.00	£2.00
4-21 ND	$0.50	$1.50	$3.00	£0.25	£0.75	£1.50
Title Value:	$11.30	$34.00	$62.50	£5.50	£16.75	£33.50

CRYSTAR CRYSTAL WARRIOR, SAGA OF

Marvel Comics Group; 1 May 1983-11 Jan/Feb 1985

	$Good	$Fine	$N.Mint	£Good	£Fine	£N.Mint
1-2 ND	$0.25	$0.75	$1.25	£0.15	£0.45	£0.75
3 ND Doctor Strange appears, Golden cover	$0.25	$0.75	$1.25	£0.15	£0.45	£0.75
4-5 ND Golden cover	$0.25	$0.75	$1.25	£0.15	£0.45	£0.75
6 ND Nightcrawler appears, Golden cover	$0.25	$0.75	$1.25	£0.15	£0.45	£0.75
7-8 ND Golden cover	$0.25	$0.75	$1.25	£0.15	£0.45	£0.75
9-10 ND	$0.25	$0.75	$1.25	£0.15	£0.45	£0.75
11 DS, Alpha Flight X-over	$0.25	$0.75	$1.25	£0.15	£0.45	£0.75
Title Value:	$2.75	$8.25	$13.75	£1.65	£4.95	£8.25

Note: only issues 1-7 have full title on cover. Painted covers on issues 1,4-7,9-11.

CUD COMICS

Fantagraphics; 1 Aug 1992-8 Dec 1994

	$Good	$Fine	$N.Mint	£Good	£Fine	£N.Mint
1 ND Terry LaBan script and art; black and white begins	$0.60	$1.80	$3.00	£0.40	£1.20	£2.00
2-8 ND Terry LaBan script and art	$0.60	$1.80	$3.00	£0.40	£1.20	£2.00
Title Value:	$4.80	$14.40	$24.00	£3.20	£9.60	£16.00

CUD COMICS (2ND SERIES)

Dark Horse,MS; 1 Nov 1995-4 Feb 1996

	$Good	$Fine	$N.Mint	£Good	£Fine	£N.Mint
1-4 ND Terry LaBan script and art; black and white	$0.60	$1.80	$3.00	£0.40	£1.20	£2.00
Title Value:	$2.40	$7.20	$12.00	£1.60	£4.80	£8.00

CUDA

Rebel Studios; 1 Jun 1995

	$Good	$Fine	$N.Mint	£Good	£Fine	£N.Mint
1 ND 16pgs, Tim Vigil and Adam McDaniel; black and white	$0.40	$1.20	$2.00	£0.25	£0.75	£1.25
Title Value:	$0.40	$1.20	$2.00	£0.25	£0.75	£1.25

CURSE OF THE MOLEMEN

Kitchen Sink,OS; 1 Oct 1991

	$Good	$Fine	$N.Mint	£Good	£Fine	£N.Mint
1 ND reprints Charles Burns' story from Raw in colour	$1.00	$3.00	$5.00	£0.70	£2.10	£3.50
Title Value:	$1.00	$3.00	$5.00	£0.70	£2.10	£3.50

CURSE OF THE WEIRD

Marvel Comics Group,MS; 1 Dec 1993-4 Mar 1994

	$Good	$Fine	$N.Mint	£Good	£Fine	£N.Mint
1 pre super-hero reprints by Steve Ditko, Basil Wolverton and Bill Everett; Ditko cover	$0.25	$0.75	$1.25	£0.15	£0.45	£0.75
2 Steve Ditko cover	$0.25	$0.75	$1.25	£0.15	£0.45	£0.75
3 Wolverton, Heath and Kubert reprints	$0.25	$0.75	$1.25	£0.15	£0.45	£0.75
4 Bill Everett reprint plus Steve Ditko's 1st work for Marvel	$0.25	$0.75	$1.25	£0.15	£0.45	£0.75
Title Value:	$1.00	$3.00	$5.00	£0.60	£1.80	£3.00

CUTEY BUNNY, ARMY SURPLUS COMICS FEATURING

Army Surplus/Eclipse; 1 1982-7 1986

	$Good	$Fine	$N.Mint	£Good	£Fine	£N.Mint
1-4 ND	$0.50	$1.50	$2.50	£0.30	£0.90	£1.50
5 ND X-Men parody	$0.50	$1.50	$2.50	£0.30	£0.90	£1.50
6-7 ND	$0.50	$1.50	$2.50	£0.30	£0.90	£1.50
Title Value:	$3.50	$10.50	$17.50	£2.10	£6.30	£10.50

CUTTING EDGE

Marvel Comics Group,OS; 1 Dec 1995

	$Good	$Fine	$N.Mint	£Good	£Fine	£N.Mint
1 ND 48pgs, Ghosts of the Future tie-in, Hulk appears	$0.60	$1.80	$3.00	£0.40	£1.20	£2.00
Title Value:	$0.60	$1.80	$3.00	£0.40	£1.20	£2.00

CYBER 7

Eclipse; 1 Mar 1989-7 Sep 1989

	$Good	$Fine	$N.Mint	£Good	£Fine	£N.Mint
1-7 ND script and art by Shuto Itahishi; black and white	$0.40	$1.20	$2.00	£0.25	£0.75	£1.25
Title Value:	$2.80	$8.40	$14.00	£1.75	£5.25	£8.75

CYBER 7 BOOK TWO

Eclipse; 1 Oct 1989-10 Jul 1990

	$Good	$Fine	$N.Mint	£Good	£Fine	£N.Mint
1-10 ND script and art by Shuto Itahishi; black and white	$0.35	$1.05	$1.75	£0.25	£0.75	£1.25
Title Value:	$3.50	$10.50	$17.50	£2.50	£7.50	£12.50

CYBER CITY: PART 1

CPM Comics,MS; 1,2 Sep 1995

	$Good	$Fine	$N.Mint	£Good	£Fine	£N.Mint
1-2 ND 24pgs, Tim Eldred script with Studio Go!	$0.60	$1.80	$3.00	£0.40	£1.20	£2.00
Title Value:	$1.20	$3.60	$6.00	£0.80	£2.40	£4.00

CYBER CITY: PART 2

CPM Comics,MS; 1 Oct 1995-2 Nov 1995

	$Good	$Fine	$N.Mint	£Good	£Fine	£N.Mint
1-2 ND 24pgs, Tim Eldred script and Go! Studios art	$0.60	$1.80	$3.00	£0.40	£1.20	£2.00
Title Value:	$1.20	$3.60	$6.00	£0.80	£2.40	£4.00

CYBER CITY: PART 3

CPM Comics,MS; 1 Dec 1995-2 Jan 1996

	$Good	$Fine	$N.Mint	£Good	£Fine	£N.Mint
1-2 ND	$0.60	$1.80	$3.00	£0.40	£1.20	£2.00
Title Value:	$1.20	$3.60	$6.00	£0.80	£2.40	£4.00

CYBERELLA

DC Comics/Helix; 1 Sep 1996-present

	$Good	$Fine	$N.Mint	£Good	£Fine	£N.Mint
1 ND Howard Chaykin script and art	$0.45	$1.35	$2.25	£0.30	£0.90	£1.50
2-6 ND Howard Chaykin script, Don Cameron art	$0.45	$1.35	$2.25	£0.30	£0.90	£1.50
7 ND	$0.50	$1.50	$2.50	£0.30	£0.90	£1.50
Title Value:	$3.20	$9.60	$16.25	£2.10	£6.30	£10.50

CYBERFORCE

Image; 0 Sep 1993; Malibu/Image; 1 Oct 1992-4 Jul 1993

	$Good	$Fine	$N.Mint	£Good	£Fine	£N.Mint
0 (Sep 1993) Walt Simonson script and art	$0.50	$1.50	$2.50	£0.30	£0.90	£1.50
1 Marc Silvestri script/art begins; contains Image #0 coupon 3	$0.90	$2.70	$4.50	£0.60	£1.80	£3.00
1 Ashcan Edition, - 8.5" x 5.5" yellow card cover, black and white interior, limited to 5,500 copies (numbered in silver bottom right of cover, each signed in silver ink on cover by Marc Silvestri)	$2.00	$6.00	$10.00	£1.20	£3.60	£6.00
1 without coupon	$0.50	$1.50	$2.50	£0.30	£0.90	£1.50
2	$0.60	$1.80	$3.00	£0.40	£1.20	£2.00
2 Ashcan Edition, - 8.5" x 5.5" yellow card cover, black and white interior, limited to 5,000 copies (numbered in silver bottom right of cover, each signed in silver ink on cover by Marc Silvestri)	$2.00	$6.00	$10.00	£1.20	£3.60	£6.00
3 Bedrock of Youngblood appears	$0.50	$1.50	$2.50	£0.30	£0.90	£1.50
4 silver embossed logo	$0.50	$1.50	$2.50	£0.30	£0.90	£1.50
Title Value:	$7.50	$22.50	$37.50	£4.60	£13.80	£23.00

Note; all Non-Distributed on the news-stands in the U.K.

	$Good	$Fine	$N.Mint	£Good	£Fine	£N.Mint
Cyberforce: The Tin Men of War (Dec 1993) Trade paperback reprints issues #1-4 plus pin-ups; holografix foil embossed				£2.00	£6.00	£10.00

CYBERFORCE (2ND SERIES)

Image; 1 Nov 1993-present

	$Good	$Fine	$N.Mint	£Good	£Fine	£N.Mint
1 ND Marc Silvestri plot and pencils begin	$0.50	$1.50	$2.50	£0.30	£0.90	£1.50
1 Gold Edition ND	$2.50	$7.50	$12.50	£1.50	£4.50	£7.50
1 Reprint Edition, ND (Mar 1996)	$0.20	$0.60	$1.00	£0.15	£0.45	£0.75
2 ND	$0.40	$1.20	$2.00	£0.25	£0.75	£1.25
2 Silver Edition ND	$2.50	$7.50	$12.50	£1.50	£4.50	£7.50
3 ND	$0.40	$1.20	$2.00	£0.25	£0.75	£1.25
3 Gold Edition ND	$2.50	$7.50	$12.50	£1.50	£4.50	£7.50
4-7 ND	$0.40	$1.20	$2.00	£0.25	£0.75	£1.25
8 ND Image X Month tie-in	$0.40	$1.20	$2.00	£0.25	£0.75	£1.25
9 ND Chris Claremont script begins; cover painting by Joe Chiodo	$0.40	$1.20	$2.00	£0.25	£0.75	£1.25
10-12 ND	$0.40	$1.20	$2.00	£0.25	£0.75	£1.25
13-15 ND	$0.45	$1.35	$2.25	£0.30	£0.90	£1.50
16 ND Ripclaw origin	$0.45	$1.35	$2.25	£0.30	£0.90	£1.50
17-22 ND	$0.45	$1.35	$2.25	£0.30	£0.90	£1.50
23-24 ND bi-weekly	$0.50	$1.50	$2.50	£0.30	£0.90	£1.50
25 ND 48pgs, foil enhanced cover	$0.80	$2.40	$4.00	£0.50	£1.50	£2.50
26 ND	$0.50	$1.50	$2.50	£0.30	£0.90	£1.50
27 ND guest-stars Ash, cover by Dave Finch and Joe Weems	$0.50	$1.50	$2.50	£0.30	£0.90	£1.50
27 Variant Cover Edition, ND guest-stars Ash; cover by Joe Quesada and Jimmy Palmiotti, limited to 20% of the print run	$0.80	$2.40	$4.00	£0.60	£1.80	£3.00
28 ND guest-starring Gabriel (from Ash)	$0.50	$1.50	$2.50	£0.30	£0.90	£1.50
29-31 ND	$0.50	$1.50	$2.50	£0.30	£0.90	£1.50
Title Value:	$22.70	$68.10	$114.50	£14.20	£42.60	£71.00
Cyberforce: Assault with a Deadly Woman (Apr 1995) Trade paperback ND collects first story arc				£1.30	£3.90	£6.50

CYBERFORCE ANNUAL

Image; 1 Feb 1995-present

	$Good	$Fine	$N.Mint	£Good	£Fine	£N.Mint
1 ND Velocity falls into a coma	$0.50	$1.50	$2.50	£0.30	£0.90	£1.50
2 ND	$0.60	$1.80	$3.00	£0.40	£1.20	£2.00
Title Value:	$1.10	$3.30	$5.50	£0.70	£2.10	£3.50

CYBERFORCE ORIGINS

Image; 1 Jan 1995-3 1995

	$Good	$Fine	$N.Mint	£Good	£Fine	£N.Mint
1 ND origin Cyblade	$0.50	$1.50	$2.50	£0.30	£0.90	£1.50
1 Reprint Edition, ND (Mar 1996)	$0.20	$0.60	$1.00	£0.15	£0.45	£0.75
1 Reprint Variant Cover Edition, ND produced exclusively by E.T.M.; new cover by Bill Tucci	$0.60	$1.80	$3.00	£0.40	£1.20	£2.00
2 ND origin Stryker	$0.50	$1.50	$2.50	£0.30	£0.90	£1.50
3 ND origin Impact; Marc Silvestri script, Randy Queen art	$0.50	$1.50	$2.50	£0.30	£0.90	£1.50
Title Value:	$2.30	$6.90	$11.50	£1.45	£4.35	£7.25

CYBERFORCE UNIVERSE SOURCEBOOK

Image; 1 Aug 1994-present

	$Good	$Fine	$N.Mint	£Good	£Fine	£N.Mint
1-3 ND information and statistics on Cyberforce characters	$0.50	$1.50	$2.50	£0.30	£0.90	£1.50
Title Value:	$1.50	$4.50	$7.50	£0.90	£2.70	£4.50

CYBERFORCE/CODENAME STRYKEFORCE - OPPOSING FORCES

Image,MS; 1 Sep 1995-2 Oct 1995

	$Good	$Fine	$N.Mint	£Good	£Fine	£N.Mint
1-2 ND Marc Silvestri and Steve Gerber script	$0.50	$1.50	$2.50	£0.30	£0.90	£1.50
Title Value:	$1.00	$3.00	$5.00	£0.60	£1.80	£3.00

CYBERFROG

Harris Comics; 1 Feb 1996-4 1996

	$Good	$Fine	$N.Mint	£Good	£Fine	£N.Mint
1 ND Walt Simonson cover	$0.60	$1.80	$3.00	£0.40	£1.20	£2.00
1 Signed & Numbered Edition, ND (Mar 1996), pre-bagged with certificate; 750 copies	$5.00	$15.00	$25.00	£3.00	£9.00	£15.00
1 Ultra Violet Edition, ND pre-bagged with signed and numbered certificate; 150 copies	$10.00	$30.00	$50.00	£6.00	£18.00	£30.00
2-4 ND	$0.60	$1.80	$3.00	£0.40	£1.20	£2.00
Title Value:	$17.40	$52.20	$87.00	£10.60	£31.80	£53.00

CYBERFROG: RESERVOIR FROG

Harris Comics,MS; 1 Sep 1996-2 Oct 1996

	$Good	$Fine	$N.Mint	£Good	£Fine	£N.Mint
1-2 ND	$0.60	$1.80	$3.00	£0.40	£1.20	£2.00
Title Value:	$1.20	$3.60	$6.00	£0.80	£2.40	£4.00

CYBERHOOD

Entity Comics; 0 Oct 1995

	$Good	$Fine	$N.Mint	£Good	£Fine	£N.Mint
0 ND Bill Maus script and art	$0.50	$1.50	$2.50	£0.30	£0.90	£1.50
0 Interactive Videogame Edition, ND (Oct 1995), pre-bagged with floppy disk	$1.40	$4.20	$7.00	£0.95	£2.85	£4.75
Title Value:	$1.90	$5.70	$9.50	£1.25	£3.75	£6.25

CYBERNARY

Image,MS; 1 Nov 1995-5 Mar 1996

	$Good	$Fine	$N.Mint	£Good	£Fine	£N.Mint
1 ND Steve Gerber script, Jeff Rebner and Richard Friend art begins						
	$0.50	*$1.50*	*$2.50*	£0.30	£0.90	£1.50
2-5 ND	*$0.50*	*$1.50*	*$2.50*	£0.30	£0.90	£1.50
Title Value:	*$2.50*	*$7.50*	*$12.50*	£1.50	£4.50	£7.50

CYBERPUNK

Innovative Corp; 1 Sep 1989-2 1989

	$Good	$Fine	$N.Mint	£Good	£Fine	£N.Mint
1-2 ND	*$0.40*	*$1.20*	*$2.00*	£0.25	£0.75	£1.25
Title Value:	*$0.80*	*$2.40*	*$4.00*	£0.50	£1.50	£2.50
Graphic Novel 1 (1990)						
reprints issues #1,2, squarebound with new material				£0.80	£2.40	£4.00

CYBERPUNK (2ND SERIES)

Innovation; 1 Nov 1990-2 Dec 1990

	$Good	$Fine	$N.Mint	£Good	£Fine	£N.Mint
1-2 ND painted art by Doug Talalla						
	$0.50	*$1.50*	*$2.50*	£0.30	£0.90	£1.50
Title Value:	*$1.00*	*$3.00*	*$5.00*	£0.60	£1.80	£3.00
Graphic Novel 2, reprints issues #1,2				£0.80	£2.40	£4.00

CYBERPUNK: THE SERAPHIM FILES

Innovation,MS; 1 Sep 1990-2 Nov 1990

	$Good	$Fine	$N.Mint	£Good	£Fine	£N.Mint
1-2 ND	*$0.50*	*$1.50*	*$2.50*	£0.30	£0.90	£1.50
Title Value:	*$1.00*	*$3.00*	*$5.00*	£0.60	£1.80	£3.00

CYBERPUNK: THE SERAPHIM PROJECT GRAPHIC NOVEL

Innovation; nn 1991

	$Good	$Fine	$N.Mint	£Good	£Fine	£N.Mint
nn ND reprints 1st Seraphim story plus mini-series, painted cover by Doug Talalla (no number on cover)						
	$1.40	*$4.20*	*$7.00*	£0.90	£2.70	£4.50
Title Value:	*$1.40*	*$4.20*	*$7.00*	£0.90	£2.70	£4.50

CYBERPUNX

Image; 1 Feb 1996-present

	$Good	$Fine	$N.Mint	£Good	£Fine	£N.Mint
1-3 ND Rob Liefeld script and art						
	$0.50	*$1.50*	*$2.50*	£0.30	£0.90	£1.50
Title Value:	*$1.50*	*$4.50*	*$7.50*	£0.90	£2.70	£4.50

CYBERRAD

Continuity; 1 Mar 1991-7 Dec 1991

	$Good	$Fine	$N.Mint	£Good	£Fine	£N.Mint
1 Neal Adams lay-outs; 1st appearance Cyberrad						
	$0.35	*$1.05*	*$1.75*	£0.25	£0.75	£1.25
2-4 Neal Adams lay-outs						
	$0.35	*$1.05*	*$1.75*	£0.25	£0.75	£1.25
5 Neal Adams lay-outs; glow-in-the-dark cover						
	$0.35	*$1.05*	*$1.75*	£0.25	£0.75	£1.25
6 Neal Adams lay-outs; pull-out poster						
	$0.35	*$1.05*	*$1.75*	£0.25	£0.75	£1.25
7 Neal Adams lay-outs; "see-thru" cel overlay cover						
	$0.35	*$1.05*	*$1.75*	£0.25	£0.75	£1.25
Title Value:	*$2.45*	*$7.35*	*$12.25*	£1.75	£5.25	£8.75

Note: all Non-Distributed on the news-stands in the U.K.

CYBERRAD (2ND SERIES)

Continuity; 1 Nov 1992-2 Aug 1993

	$Good	$Fine	$N.Mint	£Good	£Fine	£N.Mint
1 die-cut hologram cover, Neal Adams layouts and sketches						
	$0.35	*$1.05*	*$1.75*	£0.30	£0.90	£1.50
1 Limited Edition, - silver foil logo						
	$1.00	*$3.00*	*$5.00*	£0.60	£1.80	£3.00
1 Newstand Edition, (no holgram, no sketches)						
	$0.35	*$1.05*	*$1.75*	£0.25	£0.75	£1.25
2 Neal Adams layouts; acetate cel overlay cover						
	$0.35	*$1.05*	*$1.75*	£0.30	£0.90	£1.50
Title Value:	*$2.05*	*$6.15*	*$10.25*	£1.45	£4.35	£7.25

Note: all Non-Distributed on the news-stands in the U.K.

CYBERRAD (3RD SERIES)

Continuity; 1 Apr 1993-2 1993

	$Good	$Fine	$N.Mint	£Good	£Fine	£N.Mint
1 Deathwatch 2000 part 7, pre-bagged with 2 trading cards, Neal Adams cover						
	$0.35	*$1.05*	*$1.75*	£0.25	£0.75	£1.25
1 unbagged/without cards						
	$0.30	*$0.90*	*$1.50*	£0.20	£0.60	£1.00
2 Deathwatch 2000, pre-bagged with trading cards						
	$0.35	*$1.05*	*$1.75*	£0.25	£0.75	£1.25
2 unbagged/without cards						
	$0.30	*$0.90*	*$1.50*	£0.20	£0.60	£1.00
Title Value:	*$1.30*	*$3.90*	*$6.50*	£0.90	£2.70	£4.50

Note: all Non-Distributed on the news-stands in the U.K.

CYBERSPACE 3000

Marvel UK; 1 Jul 1993-7 Jan 1994

	$Good	$Fine	$N.Mint	£Good	£Fine	£N.Mint
1 Galactus appears, glow-in-the-dark cover by Liam Sharp						
	$0.30	*$0.90*	*$1.50*	£0.20	£0.60	£1.00
2 Galactus appears	*$0.30*	*$0.90*	*$1.50*	£0.20	£0.60	£1.00
3-5 Galactus and Silver Surfer appear						
	$0.30	*$0.90*	*$1.50*	£0.20	£0.60	£1.00
6 Warlock appears; gold ink enhanced cover						
	$0.30	*$0.90*	*$1.50*	£0.20	£0.60	£1.00
7	*$0.30*	*$0.90*	*$1.50*	£0.20	£0.60	£1.00
Title Value:	*$2.10*	*$6.30*	*$10.50*	£1.40	£4.20	£7.00

CYBERSUIT ARKADYNE

Janus Publications; 1 Mar 1992-6 Aug 1992

	$Good	$Fine	$N.Mint	£Good	£Fine	£N.Mint
1-6 ND b&w	*$0.30*	*$0.90*	*$1.50*	£0.20	£0.60	£1.00
Title Value:	*$1.80*	*$5.40*	*$9.00*	£1.20	£3.60	£6.00

CYBLADE/SHI SPECIAL - THE BATTLE FOR INDEPENDENTS

Image,OS; 1 Sep 1995

	$Good	$Fine	$N.Mint	£Good	£Fine	£N.Mint
1 ND 1st appearance Witchblade; co-wriiten and co-pencilled by Marc Silvestri and William Tucci; cover by Marc Silvestri						
	$2.00	*$6.00*	*$10.00*	£0.80	£2.40	£4.00
1 San Diego Preview Edition, ND Marc Silvestri cover art, distributed at the San Diego comic convention; marked "Special Preview Teaser" along top of comic, black and white						
	$3.00	*$9.00*	*$15.00*	£2.00	£6.00	£10.00
1 Variant Cover Edition, ND Cyblade & Shi faces shown only; Bill Tucci cover art						
	$2.50	*$7.50*	*$12.50*	£1.30	£3.90	£6.50
Title Value:	*$7.50*	*$22.50*	*$37.50*	£4.10	£12.30	£20.50
Cyblade/Shi Limited Edition Boxed Set A (Dec 1995)						
collects all 4 variants in slipcase plus new fifth cover edition; signed by Marc Silvestri and William Tucci				£8.00	£24.00	£40.00
Cyblade/Shi Limited Edition Boxed Set B (Dec 1995)						
collects all 4 variants in slipcase plus new fifth cover edition; signed by Marc Silvestri				£6.50	£19.50	£32.50
Cyblade/Shi Limited Edition Boxed Set C (Dec 1995)						
collects all 4 variants in slipcase plus new fifth cover edition				£4.50	£13.50	£22.50

CYBRID

Maximum Comic Press; 1 Jul 1995

	$Good	$Fine	$N.Mint	£Good	£Fine	£N.Mint
1 ND Rob Liefeld plot and cover, Sam Liu and Danny Miki art						
	$0.60	*$1.80*	*$3.00*	£0.40	£1.20	£2.00
Title Value:	*$0.60*	*$1.80*	*$3.00*	£0.40	£1.20	£2.00

CYCLOPS: RETRIBUTION

Marvel Comics Group,OS; 1 Jan 1995

	$Good	$Fine	$N.Mint	£Good	£Fine	£N.Mint
1 ND 64pgs, reprints from Marvel Comics Presents with Ron Lim art						
	$1.00	*$3.00*	*$5.00*	£0.70	£2.10	£3.50
Title Value:	*$1.00*	*$3.00*	*$5.00*	£0.70	£2.10	£3.50

CYCOPS

Comics Interview,MS; 1-3 Summer 1988

	$Good	$Fine	$N.Mint	£Good	£Fine	£N.Mint
1-3 ND	*$0.40*	*$1.20*	*$2.00*	£0.25	£0.75	£1.25
Title Value:	*$1.20*	*$3.60*	*$6.00*	£0.75	£2.25	£3.75
Trade Paperback, reprints #1-3				£1.20	£3.60	£6.00

CYNDER

Immortelle Studios,MS; 1 Apr 1995-3 1995

	$Good	$Fine	$N.Mint	£Good	£Fine	£N.Mint
1 ND David and Michael Hernandez script and art, Cynder centrefold by Rob Liefeld; black and white						
	$0.50	*$1.50*	*$2.50*	£0.30	£0.90	£1.50
2-3 ND David and Michael Hernandez script and art; centrefold by William Tucci; black and white						
	$0.50	*$1.50*	*$2.50*	£0.30	£0.90	£1.50
Title Value:	*$1.50*	*$4.50*	*$7.50*	£0.90	£2.70	£4.50

CYNDER ANNUAL

Immortelle Studios; 1 Apr 1996

	$Good	$Fine	$N.Mint	£Good	£Fine	£N.Mint
1 ND	*$0.60*	*$1.80*	*$3.00*	£0.40	£1.20	£2.00
Title Value:	*$0.60*	*$1.80*	*$3.00*	£0.40	£1.20	£2.00

CYNDER/NIRA X: RIFTS

Immortelle Comics,MS; 1 Feb 1996-present

	$Good	$Fine	$N.Mint	£Good	£Fine	£N.Mint
1 ND David and Michael Hernandez						
	$0.60	*$1.80*	*$3.00*	£0.40	£1.20	£2.00
Title Value:	*$0.60*	*$1.80*	*$3.00*	£0.40	£1.20	£2.00

D

DADAVILLE

Caliber Press,OS; 1 Nov 1991

	$Good	$Fine	$N.Mint	£Good	£Fine	£N.Mint
1 ND	*$0.40*	*$1.20*	*$2.00*	£0.25	£0.75	£1.25
Title Value:	*$0.40*	*$1.20*	*$2.00*	£0.25	£0.75	£1.25

DAEMON MASK

Amazing Comics; 1 1987

	$Good	$Fine	$N.Mint	£Good	£Fine	£N.Mint
1 ND b&w	*$0.30*	*$0.90*	*$1.50*	£0.20	£0.60	£1.00
Title Value:	*$0.30*	*$0.90*	*$1.50*	£0.20	£0.60	£1.00

DAEMON'S BLOOD

Greater Mercury Comics; 1 Dec 1990-3 1991

	$Good	$Fine	$N.Mint	£Good	£Fine	£N.Mint
1-3 ND b&w	*$0.25*	*$0.75*	*$1.25*	£0.15	£0.45	£0.75
Title Value:	*$0.75*	*$2.25*	*$3.75*	£0.45	£1.35	£2.25

DAGAR THE INVINCIBLE

Gold Key; 1 Oct 1972-18 Dec 1976; Whitman; 19 Apr 1982

(sub-titled Tales of Sword and Sorcery)

	$Good	$Fine	$N.Mint	£Good	£Fine	£N.Mint
1 scarce in the U.K. origin and 1st appearance Dagar; painted covers begin						
	$2.50	*$7.50*	*$15.00*	£1.50	£4.50	£9.00
2 16pg Kenner catalogue insert						
	$1.30	*$4.00*	*$8.00*	£0.80	£2.50	£5.00
3 vampire issue	*$1.15*	*$3.50*	*$7.00*	£0.65	£2.00	£4.00
4-5	*$1.15*	*$3.50*	*$7.00*	£0.65	£2.00	£4.00
6 16pg Kenner catalogue insert						
	$1.00	*$3.00*	*$6.00*	£0.50	£1.50	£3.00
7 slight logo change (this issue only)						
	$0.80	*$2.50*	*$5.00*	£0.40	£1.25	£2.50
8-10	*$0.80*	*$2.50*	*$5.00*	£0.40	£1.25	£2.50
11-13	*$0.50*	*$1.50*	*$3.00*	£0.30	£1.00	£2.00
14 origin briefly retold (Dagar witnessing his own origin as an intangible)						
	$0.50	*$1.50*	*$3.00*	£0.30	£1.00	£2.00
15-17	*$0.50*	*$1.50*	*$3.00*	£0.30	£1.00	£2.00
18 last painted cover						
	$0.50	*$1.50*	*$3.00*	£0.30	£1.00	£2.00
19 scarce in the U.K. line-drawn cover						
	$0.50	*$1.50*	*$2.50*	£0.35	£1.05	£1.75
Title Value:	*$15.95*	*$48.50*	*$96.50*	£9.10	£28.55	£56.75

Note: some issues distributed in the news-stands in the U.K.

DAI KAMIKAZE!

Now Comics; 1 Jun 1987-12 Aug 1988

	$Good	$Fine	$N.Mint	£Good	£Fine	£N.Mint
1 ND 1st appearance Speed Racer; says July 1987 in indicia						
	$0.30	*$0.90*	*$1.50*	£0.20	£0.60	£1.00
1 2nd printing ND	*$0.25*	*$0.75*	*$1.25*	£0.15	£0.45	£0.75
2-12 ND	*$0.30*	*$0.90*	*$1.50*	£0.20	£0.60	£1.00
Title Value:	*$3.85*	*$11.55*	*$19.25*	£2.55	£7.65	£12.75

DAIKAZU VS. GUGURON

Ground Zero Comics,MS; 1 Sep 1991-3 Dec 1991

	$Good	$Fine	$N.Mint	£Good	£Fine	£N.Mint
1-3 ND	*$0.30*	*$0.90*	*$1.50*	£0.20	£0.60	£1.00
Title Value:	*$0.90*	*$2.70*	*$4.50*	£0.60	£1.80	£3.00

DAILY BUGLE

Marvel Comics Group,MS; 1 Dec 1996-3 Feb 1997

	$Good	$Fine	$N.Mint	£Good	£Fine	£N.Mint
1-3 ND Paul Grist script, Karl Kerschel and Greg Adams art; black and white	*$0.40*	*$1.20*	*$2.00*	£0.25	£0.75	£1.25
Title Value:	*$1.20*	*$3.60*	*$6.00*	£0.75	£2.25	£3.75

DAILY PLANET INVASION EDITION

DC Comics,Tabloid OS; nn Nov 1988

	$Good	$Fine	$N.Mint	£Good	£Fine	£N.Mint
nn ND scarce in the U.K. 16pgs, Invasion tie-in, newspaper articles and reports format	*$0.40*	*$1.20*	*$2.00*	£0.30	£0.90	£1.50
Title Value:	*$0.40*	*$1.20*	*$2.00*	£0.30	£0.90	£1.50

DAKOTA NORTH

Marvel Comics Group; 1 Oct 1986-5 Feb 1987

	$Good	$Fine	$N.Mint	£Good	£Fine	£N.Mint
1-5 ND	*$0.15*	*$0.45*	*$0.75*	£0.10	£0.35	£0.60
Title Value:	*$0.75*	*$2.25*	*$3.75*	£0.50	£1.75	£3.00

DALGODA

Fantagraphics; 1 Aug 1984-8 Feb 1986

	$Good	$Fine	$N.Mint	£Good	£Fine	£N.Mint
1 ND DS Fujitaki art, Kevin Nowlan back-up	*$0.40*	*$1.20*	*$2.00*	£0.25	£0.75	£1.25
2-6 ND Fujitaki art, Kevin Nowlan back-up	*$0.40*	*$1.20*	*$2.00*	£0.25	£0.75	£1.25
7 ND Fujitaki art, Journey back-up story by Loebs	*$0.40*	*$1.20*	*$2.00*	£0.25	£0.75	£1.25
8 ND Fujitaki art, Bojeffries back-up story by Moore and Parkhouse	*$0.40*	*$1.20*	*$2.00*	£0.25	£0.75	£1.25
Title Value:	*$3.20*	*$9.60*	*$16.00*	£2.00	£6.00	£10.00

DALGODA: FLESH AND BONES

Fantagraphics,MS; 1-4 1986

	$Good	$Fine	$N.Mint	£Good	£Fine	£N.Mint
1-4 ND Dalgoda by Fujitaki, Bojefries by Alan Moore and Steve Parkhouse	*$0.30*	*$0.90*	*$1.50*	£0.20	£0.60	£1.00
Title Value:	*$1.20*	*$3.60*	*$6.00*	£0.80	£2.40	£4.00

DAMAGE

DC Comics; 0 Oct 1994; 1 Apr 1994-20 Jan 1996

	$Good	$Fine	$N.Mint	£Good	£Fine	£N.Mint
0 (Oct 1994) Zero Hour X-over, origins revealed	*$0.35*	*$1.05*	*$1.75*	£0.25	£0.75	£1.25
1 Bill Marimon and Tom McWeeny art	*$0.35*	*$1.05*	*$1.75*	£0.25	£0.75	£1.25
2-4	*$0.35*	*$1.05*	*$1.75*	£0.25	£0.75	£1.25
5 New Titans appear	*$0.35*	*$1.05*	*$1.75*	£0.25	£0.75	£1.25
6 X-over New Titans #114; $1.95 cover begins	*$0.40*	*$1.20*	*$2.00*	£0.25	£0.75	£1.25
7-8	*$0.40*	*$1.20*	*$2.00*	£0.25	£0.75	£1.25
9 Damage vs. Dr. Polaris	*$0.40*	*$1.20*	*$2.00*	£0.25	£0.75	£1.25
10-11	*$0.40*	*$1.20*	*$2.00*	£0.25	£0.75	£1.25
12 photo cover	*$0.40*	*$1.20*	*$2.00*	£0.25	£0.75	£1.25
13 New Titans appear; $2.25 cover begin	*$0.45*	*$1.35*	*$2.25*	£0.30	£0.90	£1.50
14 The Ray appears; X-over with Justice League Task Force #25	*$0.45*	*$1.35*	*$2.25*	£0.30	£0.90	£1.50
15	*$0.45*	*$1.35*	*$2.25*	£0.30	£0.90	£1.50
16 The Siege of Zi Charam part 4, continued in New Titans #125; Green Lantern appears	*$0.45*	*$1.35*	*$2.25*	£0.30	£0.90	£1.50
17	*$0.45*	*$1.35*	*$2.25*	£0.30	£0.90	£1.50
18-19 Underworld Unleashed tie-in	*$0.45*	*$1.35*	*$2.25*	£0.30	£0.90	£1.50
20	*$0.45*	*$1.35*	*$2.25*	£0.30	£0.90	£1.50
Title Value:	*$8.50*	*$25.50*	*$42.50*	£5.65	£16.95	£28.25

DAMAGE CONTROL

Marvel Comics Group,MS; 1 May 1989-4 Aug 1989

	$Good	$Fine	$N.Mint	£Good	£Fine	£N.Mint
1 ND Spiderman appears	*$0.25*	*$0.75*	*$1.25*	£0.15	£0.45	£0.75
2 ND Dr. Doom appears	*$0.25*	*$0.75*	*$1.25*	£0.15	£0.45	£0.75
3 ND Iron Man appears	*$0.25*	*$0.75*	*$1.25*	£0.15	£0.45	£0.75
4 ND X-Men appear, Wolverine on cover; Inferno tie-in	*$0.25*	*$0.75*	*$1.25*	£0.15	£0.45	£0.75
Title Value:	*$1.00*	*$3.00*	*$5.00*	£0.60	£1.80	£3.00
Trade paperback (Jun 1991), reprints above				£0.55	£1.65	£2.75

DAMAGE CONTROL II

Marvel Comics Group,MS; 1 Dec 1989-4 Feb 1990

	$Good	$Fine	$N.Mint	£Good	£Fine	£N.Mint
1 ND Acts of Vengeance tie-in, features Captain America, Falcon and Thor	*$0.25*	*$0.75*	*$1.25*	£0.15	£0.45	£0.75
2 ND Acts of Vengeance, Punisher and Dr. Doom appear	*$0.25*	*$0.75*	*$1.25*	£0.15	£0.45	£0.75
3 ND Acts of Vengeance tie-in, She-Hulk and original Avengers appear	*$0.25*	*$0.75*	*$1.25*	£0.15	£0.45	£0.75
4 ND Acts of Vengeance tie-in, Shield, Captain America, Thor and Punisher appear	*$0.25*	*$0.75*	*$1.25*	£0.15	£0.45	£0.75
Title Value:	*$1.00*	*$3.00*	*$5.00*	£0.60	£1.80	£3.00

DAMAGE CONTROL III

Marvel Comics Group,MS; 1 Jun 1991-4 Sep 1991

	$Good	$Fine	$N.Mint	£Good	£Fine	£N.Mint
1 ND Spiderman appears	*$0.25*	*$0.75*	*$1.25*	£0.15	£0.45	£0.75
2 ND Hulk, New Warriors appear	*$0.25*	*$0.75*	*$1.25*	£0.15	£0.45	£0.75
3 ND West Coast Avengers, Wonder Man, Silver Surfer appear	*$0.25*	*$0.75*	*$1.25*	£0.15	£0.45	£0.75
4 ND Silver Surfer appears plus most other Marvel characters	*$0.25*	*$0.75*	*$1.25*	£0.15	£0.45	£0.75
Title Value:	*$1.00*	*$3.00*	*$5.00*	£0.60	£1.80	£3.00

DAN TURNER: HOMICIDE HUNCH

Eternity,OS; 1 Sep 1991

	$Good	$Fine	$N.Mint	£Good	£Fine	£N.Mint
1 ND	*$0.30*	*$0.90*	*$1.50*	£0.20	£0.60	£1.00
Title Value:	*$0.30*	*$0.90*	*$1.50*	£0.20	£0.60	£1.00

DAN TURNER: THE STAR CHAMBER

Eternity,OS; 1 Nov 1991

	$Good	$Fine	$N.Mint	£Good	£Fine	£N.Mint
1 ND	*$0.30*	*$0.90*	*$1.50*	£0.20	£0.60	£1.00
Title Value:	*$0.30*	*$0.90*	*$1.50*	£0.20	£0.60	£1.00

DANCES WITH DEMONS

Marvel UK/Frontier; 1 Sep 1993-4 Dec 1993

	$Good	$Fine	$N.Mint	£Good	£Fine	£N.Mint
1 Simon Jowett & Charlie Adlard; foil embossed cover	*$0.30*	*$0.90*	*$1.50*	£0.20	£0.60	£1.00
2-4	*$0.30*	*$0.90*	*$1.50*	£0.20	£0.60	£1.00
Title Value:	*$1.20*	*$3.60*	*$6.00*	£0.80	£2.40	£4.00

DANGER

I.W. Super; 10-12, 15-18 1963-1964

	$Good	$Fine	$N.Mint	£Good	£Fine	£N.Mint
10-12 scarce, distributed in the U.K.	*$1.40*	*$4.25*	*$10.00*	£0.55	£1.70	£4.00
15-18 scarce, distributed in the U.K.	*$1.25*	*$3.85*	*$9.00*	£0.50	£1.50	£3.50
Title Value:	*$9.20*	*$28.15*	*$66.00*	£3.65	£11.10	£26.00

Note: all reprints featuring such strips as Spy Cases, Jonny Danger and Yankee Girl

DANGER COMIX

Danger Graphix; 1 Nov 1990

	$Good	$Fine	$N.Mint	£Good	£Fine	£N.Mint
1 ND b&w	*$0.30*	*$0.90*	*$1.50*	£0.20	£0.60	£1.00
Title Value:	*$0.30*	*$0.90*	*$1.50*	£0.20	£0.60	£1.00

DANGER IS OUR BUSINESS

I.W. Comics;9 1964

	$Good	$Fine	$N.Mint	£Good	£Fine	£N.Mint
9 distributed in the U.K. Williams and Frazetta reprints	*$9.25*	*$28.00*	*$65.00*	£6.25	£19.00	£45.00

Crypt of Dawn #1

Crystar, Crystal Warrior #6

Dagar the Invincible #3

	$Good	$Fine	$N.Mint	£Good	£Fine	£N.Mint
Title Value:	*$9.25*	*$28.00*	*$65.00*	£6.25	£19.00	£45.00

DANGER MAN

Dell, TV; 1231 Sep/Nov 1961

	$Good	$Fine	$N.Mint	£Good	£Fine	£N.Mint
1231 scarce, distributed in the U.K.						
	$15.00	*$45.00*	*$105.00*	£10.00	£30.00	£70.00
Title Value:	*$15.00*	*$45.00*	*$105.00*	£10.00	£30.00	£70.00

DANGER TRAIL

National Periodical Publications; 1 Jul/Aug 1950-5 Mar/Apr 1951

	$Good	$Fine	$N.Mint	£Good	£Fine	£N.Mint
1 very scarce in the U.K. King Faraday begins, Alex Toth art						
	$100.00	*$305.00*	*$825.00*	£67.50	£205.00	£550.00
2 very scarce in the U.K. Alex Toth art						
	$77.50	*$230.00*	*$625.00*	£52.50	£155.00	£425.00
3 very rare in the U.K. Alex Toth art; a leading US dealer/historian believes there to be no more than 10 extant copies						
	$125.00	*$375.00*	*$1000.00*	£82.50	£250.00	£675.00
4 scarce in the U.K. Alex Toth art						
	$62.50	*$185.00*	*$500.00*	£43.00	£125.00	£340.00
5 scarce in the U.K. Johnny Peril, logo change; Alex Toth art						
	$62.50	*$185.00*	*$500.00*	£43.00	£125.00	£340.00
Title Value:	*$427.50*	*$1280.00*	*$3450.00*	£288.50	£860.00	£2330.00

DANGER TRAIL (2ND SERIES)

DC Comics; 1 Apr 1993-4 Jul 1993

	$Good	$Fine	$N.Mint	£Good	£Fine	£N.Mint
1 King Faraday begins, Infantino pencils begin; Paul Gulacy covers begin						
	$0.25	*$0.75*	*$1.25*	£0.15	£0.45	£0.75
2-4 Kobra appears	*$0.25*	*$0.75*	*$1.25*	£0.15	£0.45	£0.75
Title Value:	*$1.00*	*$3.00*	*$5.00*	£0.60	£1.80	£3.00

DANGER UNLIMITED

Dark Horse/Legend,MS; 1 Feb 1994-4 May 1994

	$Good	$Fine	$N.Mint	£Good	£Fine	£N.Mint
1-4 ND John Byrne script and art						
	$0.40	*$1.20*	*$2.00*	£0.25	£0.75	£1.25
Title Value:	*$1.60*	*$4.80*	*$8.00*	£1.00	£3.00	£5.00
Danger Unlimited (Mar 1995) Trade paperback collects mini-series plus story from San Diego Comicon Comics #2 plus a new last page and new cover by John Byrne				£2.00	£6.00	£10.00
Danger Unlimited Limited Edition Hardcover (Jul 1995) foil-stamped cover with dust-jacket; 1,000 copies				£8.00	£24.00	£40.00

DANGEROUS TIMES

Evolution Comics; 1 Jan 1991-4 1991

	$Good	$Fine	$N.Mint	£Good	£Fine	£N.Mint
1 ND Mike Kaluta art						
	$0.30	*$0.90*	*$1.50*	£0.20	£0.60	£1.00
1 2nd printing ND	*$0.25*	*$0.75*	*$1.25*	£0.15	£0.45	£0.75
2 ND Murphy Anderson cover						
	$0.30	*$0.90*	*$1.50*	£0.20	£0.60	£1.00
2 2nd printing ND	*$0.25*	*$0.75*	*$1.25*	£0.15	£0.45	£0.75
3 ND Marshall Rogers cover						
	$0.30	*$0.90*	*$1.50*	£0.20	£0.60	£1.00
3 2nd printing ND	*$0.25*	*$0.75*	*$1.25*	£0.15	£0.45	£0.75
4 ND George Perez cover						
	$0.30	*$0.90*	*$1.50*	£0.20	£0.60	£1.00
Title Value:	*$1.95*	*$5.85*	*$9.75*	£1.25	£3.75	£6.25

DANSE

Blackthorne; 1 1987

	$Good	$Fine	$N.Mint	£Good	£Fine	£N.Mint
1 ND	*$0.30*	*$0.90*	*$1.50*	£0.20	£0.60	£1.00
Title Value:	*$0.30*	*$0.90*	*$1.50*	£0.20	£0.60	£1.00

DARE

Monster Comics,MS; 1 Dec 1991-4 Aug 1992

	$Good	$Fine	$N.Mint	£Good	£Fine	£N.Mint
1-4 ND reprints of Dan Dare by Grant Morrison and Rian Hughes from Revolver magazine in U.K.						
	$0.30	*$0.90*	*$1.50*	£0.20	£0.60	£1.00
Title Value:	*$1.20*	*$3.60*	*$6.00*	£0.80	£2.40	£4.00

DAREDEVIL

Marvel Comics Group; 1 Apr 1964-present

(see Marvel Adventure, Fantastic Four, Marvel Graphic Novel, Marvel Team Up, Marvel Two-in-One, Spiderman) (...and the Black Widow #92-107)

	$Good	$Fine	$N.Mint	£Good	£Fine	£N.Mint
1 origin and 1st appearance Daredevil, Bill Everett cover and art						
	$200.00	*$600.00*	*$2000.00*	£140.00	£420.00	£1400.00
[Scarce in high grade - Very Fine+ or better]						
2 scarce in the U.K. Thing appears, Fantastic Four cameo, 2nd appearance Electro (see Amazing Spiderman #9)						
	$67.50	*$205.00*	*$550.00*	£44.00	£130.00	£350.00
[Very scarce in high grade - Very Fine+ or better]						
3 scarce in the U.K. origin and 1st appearance The Owl						
	$44.00	*$130.00*	*$350.00*	£28.00	£82.50	£225.00
4 rare in the U.K. 1st appearance of The Purple Man						
	$41.00	*$120.00*	*$325.00*	£28.00	£82.50	£225.00
5 Wood art	*$28.00*	*$82.50*	*$225.00*	£16.50	£50.00	£135.00
6 (Feb 1965), Wood art						
	$20.00	*$60.00*	*$160.00*	£12.50	£38.00	£100.00
7 new red costume, Sub-Mariner battles Daredevil						
	$31.00	*$92.50*	*$250.00*	£16.50	£50.00	£135.00
[Scarce in high grade - Very Fine+ or better]						
8 Wood art, origin and 1st appearance Stiltman						
	$20.00	*$60.00*	*$160.00*	£12.50	£38.00	£100.00
9-10 Wood art	*$20.00*	*$60.00*	*$160.00*	£12.50	£38.00	£100.00
11 Wood inks; last Silver Age issue indicia-dated December 1965						
	$10.50	*$32.00*	*$85.00*	£6.25	£18.50	£50.00
12 (Jan 1966), John Romita's 1st 1960s work at Marvel, Ka-Zar appears						
	$10.50	*$32.00*	*$85.00*	£6.25	£18.50	£50.00
13 Jack Kirby art, part Ka-Zar origin						
	$10.50	*$32.00*	*$85.00*	£6.25	£18.50	£50.00
14 Ka-Zar appears						
	$10.50	*$32.00*	*$85.00*	£6.25	£18.50	£50.00
15	*$10.50*	*$32.00*	*$85.00*	£6.25	£18.50	£50.00
16 scarce in the U.K. Spiderman X-over; John Romita Snr's 1st art on Spiderman (pre Amazing Spiderman #39)						
	$11.50	*$36.00*	*$95.00*	£7.50	£22.50	£60.00
17 Spiderman X-over						
	$11.00	*$34.00*	*$90.00*	£6.75	£20.50	£55.00
18 origin and 1st appearance The Gladiator (not to be confused with the Shiar Imperial Guard of the same name)						
	$7.50	*$22.50*	*$60.00*	£4.35	£13.00	£35.00
19-20	*$7.50*	*$22.50*	*$60.00*	£4.35	£13.00	£35.00
21-23 scarce in the U.K.						
	$5.50	*$17.00*	*$40.00*	£3.20	£9.50	£22.50
24 (Jan 1967)	*$5.50*	*$17.00*	*$40.00*	£3.20	£9.50	£22.50
25-26	*$5.50*	*$17.00*	*$40.00*	£3.20	£9.50	£22.50
27 Spiderman appears						
	$6.25	*$19.00*	*$45.00*	£3.55	£10.50	£25.00
28-29	*$5.50*	*$17.00*	*$40.00*	£3.20	£9.50	£22.50
30 Thor appears	*$5.50*	*$17.00*	*$40.00*	£3.20	£9.50	£22.50
31-34	*$3.90*	*$11.50*	*$27.50*	£2.50	£7.50	£17.50
35 scarce in the U.K.						
	$3.90	*$11.50*	*$27.50*	£2.85	£8.50	£20.00
36 (Jan 1968), Fantastic Four appear						
	$3.90	*$11.50*	*$27.50*	£2.50	£7.50	£17.50
37 Dr. Doom appears, Galactus appears (1 panel); Doom rides Surfer's board! Cool.						
	$3.90	*$11.50*	*$27.50*	£2.50	£7.50	£17.50
38 Dr. Doom appears, X-over with Fantastic Four #73						
	$3.90	*$11.50*	*$27.50*	£2.50	£7.50	£17.50
39 1st appearance Exterminator (later becomes Deathstalker)						
	$3.90	*$11.50*	*$27.50*	£2.50	£7.50	£17.50
40	*$3.90*	*$11.50*	*$27.50*	£2.50	£7.50	£17.50
41 death of Mike Murdock (Daredevil's "brother")						
	$2.85	*$8.50*	*$20.00*	£1.70	£5.00	£12.00
42 1st appearance The Jester (note DC's The Joker!)						
	$2.85	*$8.50*	*$20.00*	£1.70	£5.00	£12.00
43 Captain America vs Daredevil; Jack Kirby cover						
	$2.85	*$8.50*	*$20.00*	£1.70	£5.00	£12.00
44 scarce in the U.K.						
	$2.85	*$8.50*	*$20.00*	£1.85	£5.50	£13.00
45 scarce in the U.K. photo cover						
	$2.85	*$8.50*	*$20.00*	£1.85	£5.50	£13.00
46 scarce in the U.K.						
	$2.85	*$8.50*	*$20.00*	£1.85	£5.50	£13.00
47	*$2.85*	*$8.50*	*$20.00*	£1.70	£5.00	£12.00
48 (Jan 1969)	*$2.85*	*$8.50*	*$20.00*	£1.70	£5.00	£12.00
49	*$2.85*	*$8.50*	*$20.00*	£1.70	£5.00	£12.00
50-51 Barry Smith art						
	$3.55	*$10.50*	*$25.00*	£2.10	£6.25	£15.00
52 Barry Smith art, Black Panther appears						
	$3.55	*$10.50*	*$25.00*	£2.10	£6.25	£15.00
53 origin retold, classic cover						
	$3.55	*$10.50*	*$25.00*	£2.10	£6.25	£15.00
54 scarce in the U.K. Spiderman appears						
	$1.75	*$5.25*	*$12.50*	£1.40	£4.25	£10.00
55	*$1.70*	*$5.00*	*$12.00*	£1.00	£3.00	£7.00
56 1st appearance Death's Head (not to be confused with Marvel U.K. character)						
	$1.70	*$5.00*	*$12.00*	£1.00	£3.00	£7.00
57 Daredevil reveals I.D. to Karen Page						
	$1.70	*$5.00*	*$12.00*	£1.00	£3.00	£7.00
58-59	*$1.70*	*$5.00*	*$12.00*	£1.00	£3.00	£7.00
60 (Jan 1970)	*$1.70*	*$5.00*	*$12.00*	£1.00	£3.00	£7.00
61	*$1.65*	*$5.00*	*$10.00*	£1.00	£3.00	£6.00
62 1st appearance Nighthawk						
	$1.65	*$5.00*	*$10.00*	£1.00	£3.00	£6.00
63-68	*$1.65*	*$5.00*	*$10.00*	£1.00	£3.00	£6.00
69 Black Panther appears						
	$1.65	*$5.00*	*$10.00*	£1.00	£3.00	£6.00
70-71	*$1.65*	*$5.00*	*$10.00*	£1.00	£3.00	£6.00
72 scarce in the U.K. (Jan 1971)						
	$1.65	*$5.00*	*$10.00*	£1.05	£3.25	£6.50
73 Iron Man appears						
	$1.65	*$5.00*	*$10.00*	£1.00	£3.00	£6.00
74-76	*$1.65*	*$5.00*	*$10.00*	£1.00	£3.00	£6.00
77 scarce in the U.K. Sub-Mariner and Spiderman appear; classic three-way battle issue						
	$1.65	*$5.00*	*$10.00*	£1.05	£3.25	£6.50
78-80 scarce in the U.K.						
	$1.65	*$5.00*	*$10.00*	£1.05	£3.25	£6.50
81 52pgs, scarce in the U.K., 1st Black Widow in title; Black Widow becomes Daredevil's partner and lover						
	$2.00	*$6.00*	*$12.00*	£1.15	£3.50	£7.00
82 very scarce in the U.K.						
	$1.65	*$5.00*	*$10.00*	£1.15	£3.50	£7.00
83 scarce in the U.K. (Jan 1972), Smith layouts						
	$1.65	*$5.00*	*$10.00*	£1.05	£3.25	£6.50
84-89 scarce in the U.K.						
	$1.65	*$5.00*	*$10.00*	£1.00	£3.00	£6.00
90-91 scarce in the U.K.						
	$1.50	*$4.50*	*$9.00*	£0.90	£2.75	£5.50
92 scarce in the U.K. Black Widow shares title (till #124)						
	$1.50	*$4.50*	*$9.00*	£0.90	£2.75	£5.50
93-94 scarce in the U.K.						
	$1.50	*$4.50*	*$9.00*	£0.90	£2.75	£5.50
95 scarce in the U.K. (Jan 1973)						
	$1.50	*$4.50*	*$9.00*	£0.90	£2.75	£5.50
96-98	*$1.50*	*$4.50*	*$9.00*	£0.75	£2.25	£4.50
99 Hawkeye appears						
	$1.50	*$4.50*	*$9.00*	£0.75	£2.25	£4.50
100 scarce in the U.K. origin retold						
	$4.65	*$14.00*	*$28.00*	£2.15	£6.50	£13.00

	$Good	$Fine	$N.Mint	£Good	£Fine	£N.Mint
101-102	$1.25	$3.75	$7.50	£0.65	£2.00	£4.00
103 Spiderman appears	$1.25	$3.75	$7.50	£0.75	£2.25	£4.50
104 Kraven appears	$1.25	$3.75	$7.50	£0.65	£2.00	£4.00
105 Jim Starlin art (5pgs), origin of Moondragon; Thanos cameo	$1.65	$5.00	$10.00	£0.80	£2.50	£5.00
106 Moondragon appears	$1.25	$3.75	$7.50	£0.65	£2.00	£4.00
107 (Jan 1974), Jim Starlin cover, Captain Marvel and Moondragon appear, Thanos cameo; last Black Widow co-title on cover	$1.25	$3.75	$7.50	£0.65	£2.00	£4.00
108 Gulacy inks	$1.25	$3.75	$7.50	£0.60	£1.85	£3.75
109 ND	$1.25	$3.75	$7.50	£0.80	£2.50	£5.00
110 ND Thing cameo (X-over with Marvel Two-in-One #3)	$1.25	$3.75	$7.50	£0.80	£2.50	£5.00
111 ND	$1.25	$3.75	$7.50	£0.80	£2.50	£5.00
112	$1.25	$3.75	$7.50	£0.50	£1.50	£3.00
113 1st appearance Deathstalker (cameo)	$1.25	$3.75	$7.50	£0.50	£1.50	£3.00
114 1st full appearance Deathstalker, Man-Thing appears	$1.30	$4.00	$8.00	£0.65	£2.00	£4.00
115-116	$1.25	$3.75	$7.50	£0.50	£1.50	£3.00
117 (Jan 1975)	$1.25	$3.75	$7.50	£0.50	£1.50	£3.00
118-119	$1.25	$3.75	$7.50	£0.50	£1.50	£3.00
120 1st appearance El Jaguar	$1.25	$3.75	$7.50	£0.50	£1.50	£3.00
121	$0.80	$2.50	$5.00	£0.40	£1.25	£2.50
122 last Black Widow joint character illustration on cover	$0.80	$2.50	$5.00	£0.40	£1.25	£2.50
123	$0.80	$2.50	$5.00	£0.40	£1.25	£2.50
124 1st appearance Copperhead, last Black Widow co-title appearance	$0.80	$2.50	$5.00	£0.40	£1.25	£2.50
125-128	$0.80	$2.50	$5.00	£0.40	£1.25	£2.50
129 (Jan 1976)	$0.80	$2.50	$5.00	£0.40	£1.25	£2.50
130	$0.80	$2.50	$5.00	£0.40	£1.25	£2.50
131 scarce in the U.K. 2nd appearance/origin Bullseye, (see Nick Fury, Agent of Shield #15)	$4.30	$13.00	$26.00	£1.65	£5.00	£10.00
132 3rd appearance Bullseye	$1.25	$3.75	$7.50	£0.80	£2.50	£5.00
133 Uri Geller appears	$0.80	$2.50	$5.00	£0.35	£1.10	£2.25
134-137	$0.80	$2.50	$5.00	£0.35	£1.10	£2.25
138 Ghost Rider appears (X-over with Ghost Rider #20), Death's Head appears, Byrne art	$1.65	$5.00	$10.00	£1.00	£3.00	£6.00
139-140 LD in the U.K.	$0.80	$2.50	$5.00	£0.40	£1.25	£2.50
141 LD in the U.K. (Jan 1977)	$0.80	$2.50	$5.00	£0.40	£1.25	£2.50
142 LD in the U.K. Nova cameo (2 panels)	$0.80	$2.50	$5.00	£0.40	£1.25	£2.50
143-147 LD in the U.K.	$0.80	$2.50	$5.00	£0.40	£1.25	£2.50
148 LD in the U.K. (30 and 35 cent issues exist)	$0.80	$2.50	$5.00	£0.40	£1.25	£2.50
149 LD in the U.K.	$0.80	$2.50	$5.00	£0.40	£1.25	£2.50
150 ND scarce in the U.K. (Jan 1978), 1st appearance Paladin	$0.80	$2.50	$5.00	£0.80	£2.50	£5.00
151 Daredevil reveals I.D. to Heather Glenn	$0.80	$2.50	$5.00	£0.30	£1.00	£2.00
152 2nd appearance Paladin	$0.80	$2.50	$5.00	£0.30	£1.00	£2.00
153-154	$0.80	$2.50	$5.00	£0.30	£1.00	£2.00
155 LD in the U.K. Avengers, Hercules and Black Widow appear	$0.80	$2.50	$5.00	£0.40	£1.25	£2.50
156 LD in the U.K. (Jan 1979), Avengers appear	$0.80	$2.50	$5.00	£0.40	£1.25	£2.50
157 LD in the U.K. Avengers appear	$0.80	$2.50	$5.00	£0.40	£1.25	£2.50
158 Frank Miller art begins, origin and death of Deathstalker	$7.00	$21.00	$42.00	£3.30	£10.00	£20.00
159 Frank Miller art	$3.30	$10.00	$20.00	£2.05	£6.25	£12.50
160 Frank Miller art	$1.65	$5.00	$10.00	£1.65	£5.00	£10.00
161 ND rare in the U.K. Frank Miller art	$1.65	$5.00	$10.00	£2.50	£7.50	£15.00
162 ND (Jan 1980), Steve Ditko art	$0.65	$2.00	$4.00	£0.50	£1.50	£3.00
163 Hulk battles Daredevil, Frank Miller art	$1.65	$5.00	$10.00	£1.25	£3.75	£7.50
164 origin retold, Avengers appear, Frank Miller art	$1.65	$5.00	$10.00	£1.15	£3.50	£7.00
165-167 Frank Miller art	$1.25	$3.75	$7.50	£1.00	£3.00	£6.00
168 (Jan 1981), 1st appearance Elektra, Frank Miller art	$5.00	$15.00	$30.00	£2.50	£7.50	£15.00
169 ND Elektra appears, Frank Miller art	$1.65	$5.00	$10.00	£2.05	£6.25	£12.50
170-172 LD in the U.K. Frank Miller art	$1.50	$4.50	$7.50	£0.90	£2.70	£4.50
173	$1.00	$3.00	$5.00	£0.60	£1.80	£3.00

	$Good	$Fine	$N.Mint	£Good	£Fine	£N.Mint
174-177 Elektra appears, Frank Miller art	$1.00	$3.00	$5.00	£0.70	£2.10	£3.50
178 (Jan 1982), Elektra appears, Powerman and Iron Fist appear, Frank Miller art	$0.80	$2.40	$4.00	£0.70	£2.10	£3.50
179-180 Elektra appears, Frank Miller art	$0.80	$2.40	$4.00	£0.70	£2.10	£3.50
181 DS, death of Elektra, Punisher and Bullseye appear, Frank Miller art	$1.60	$4.80	$8.00	£1.00	£3.00	£5.00
182 Punisher cameo, Frank Miller art	$1.60	$4.80	$8.00	£0.90	£2.70	£4.50
183-184 Punisher cameo, Frank Miller art	$1.60	$4.80	$8.00	£1.00	£3.00	£5.00
185-186 Frank Miller credited as the story-teller only	$0.70	$2.10	$3.50	£0.50	£1.50	£2.50
187 new Black Widow appears, Frank Miller story-teller only, Elektra's ressurrection begins	$0.70	$2.10	$3.50	£0.50	£1.50	£2.50
188-189 Frank Miller credited as the story-teller only	$0.70	$2.10	$3.50	£0.50	£1.50	£2.50
190 (Jan 1983), DS, Elektra saga ends, partial origin Elektra	$0.70	$2.10	$3.50	£0.60	£1.80	£3.00
191 last Frank Miller Daredevil	$0.70	$2.10	$3.50	£0.40	£1.20	£2.00
192-195	$0.50	$1.50	$2.50	£0.30	£0.90	£1.50
196 Wolverine appears	$1.80	$5.25	$9.00	£0.80	£2.40	£4.00
197-199	$0.50	$1.50	$2.50	£0.30	£0.90	£1.50
200 Bullseye appears, John Byrne cover	$0.50	$1.50	$2.50	£0.40	£1.20	£2.00
201	$0.50	$1.50	$2.50	£0.30	£0.90	£1.50
202 (Jan 1984)	$0.50	$1.50	$2.50	£0.30	£0.90	£1.50
203-205	$0.50	$1.50	$2.50	£0.30	£0.90	£1.50
206 1st Mazzuchelli art	$0.50	$1.50	$2.50	£0.30	£0.90	£1.50
207	$0.50	$1.50	$2.50	£0.30	£0.90	£1.50
208 Harlan Ellison script	$0.50	$1.50	$2.50	£0.30	£0.90	£1.50
209-213	$0.50	$1.50	$2.50	£0.30	£0.90	£1.50
214 (Jan 1985)	$0.40	$1.20	$2.00	£0.30	£0.90	£1.50
215-216	$0.40	$1.20	$2.00	£0.30	£0.90	£1.50
217 Barry Windsor-Smith cover	$0.40	$1.20	$2.00	£0.30	£0.90	£1.50
218 LD in the U.K.	$0.40	$1.20	$2.00	£0.40	£1.20	£2.00
219 Frank Miller story	$0.40	$1.20	$2.00	£0.40	£1.20	£2.00
220-222 LD in the U.K.	$0.40	$1.20	$2.00	£0.35	£1.05	£1.75
223 LD in the U.K. Secret Wars X-over	$0.40	$1.20	$2.00	£0.35	£1.05	£1.75
224-225 LD in the U.K.	$0.40	$1.20	$2.00	£0.35	£1.05	£1.75
226 LD in the U.K. (Jan 1986), Frank Miller plot	$0.50	$1.50	$2.50	£0.50	£1.50	£2.50
227 LD in the U.K. Frank Miller story only	$0.80	$2.40	$4.00	£0.70	£2.10	£3.50
228 Frank Miller	$0.60	$1.80	$3.00	£0.40	£1.20	£2.00
229 very LD Frank Miller	$0.60	$1.80	$3.00	£0.50	£1.50	£2.50
230-233 Frank Miller	$0.60	$1.80	$3.00	£0.40	£1.20	£2.00
234-235 Steve Ditko art	$0.40	$1.20	$2.00	£0.25	£0.75	£1.25
236 Barry Smith art, Nocenti scripts begin	$0.40	$1.20	$2.00	£0.30	£0.90	£1.50
237	$0.40	$1.20	$2.00	£0.25	£0.75	£1.25
238 LD in the U.K. (Jan 1987), Mutant Massacre, Sabretooth X-over, Art Adams art	$1.50	$4.50	$7.50	£0.60	£1.80	£3.00
239-240	$0.40	$1.20	$2.00	£0.25	£0.75	£1.25
241 Todd McFarlane art, Mike Zeck cover	$0.60	$1.80	$3.00	£0.40	£1.20	£2.00
242-246	$0.40	$1.20	$2.00	£0.25	£0.75	£1.25
247 Keith Giffen art	$0.40	$1.20	$2.00	£0.25	£0.75	£1.25
248-249 LD in the U.K. Wolverine appears, Williamson inks	$1.00	$3.00	$5.00	£0.50	£1.50	£2.50
250 LD in the U.K. (Jan 1988)	$0.40	$1.20	$2.00	£0.40	£1.20	£2.00
251 LD in the U.K.	$0.40	$1.20	$2.00	£0.40	£1.20	£2.00
252 LD in the U.K. DS, Fall of the Mutants	$0.60	$1.80	$3.00	£0.70	£2.10	£3.50
253 LD in the U.K.	$0.40	$1.20	$2.00	£0.40	£1.20	£2.00
254 LD in the U.K. origin and 1st appearance Typhoid Mary	$2.00	$6.00	$10.00	£1.00	£3.00	£5.00
255 2nd appearance of Typhoid Mary	$1.00	$3.00	$5.00	£0.50	£1.50	£2.50
256 3rd appearance of Typhoid Mary	$0.80	$2.40	$4.00	£0.40	£1.20	£2.00
257 X-over with Punisher #10	$1.60	$4.80	$8.00	£1.40	£4.20	£7.00
258 Ron Lim art	$0.40	$1.20	$2.00	£0.35	£1.05	£1.75
259 LD in the U.K. Typhoid Mary appears	$0.50	$1.50	$2.50	£0.35	£1.05	£1.75
260 DS Typhoid Mary, Kingpin appear	$0.50	$1.50	$2.50	£0.35	£1.05	£1.75

Issue	$Good	$Fine	$N.Mint	£Good	£Fine	£N.Mint
261 LD in the U.K. Human Torch/Typhoid Mary	$0.40	$1.20	$2.00	£0.30	£0.90	£1.50
262 (Jan 1989), Inferno tie-in	$0.30	$0.90	$1.50	£0.15	£0.45	£0.75
263 Inferno tie-in	$0.30	$0.90	$1.50	£0.15	£0.45	£0.75
264	$0.30	$0.90	$1.50	£0.15	£0.45	£0.75
265 Inferno tie-in	$0.30	$0.90	$1.50	£0.15	£0.45	£0.75
266-268	$0.30	$0.90	$1.50	£0.15	£0.45	£0.75
269 LD in the U.K. Blob/Pyro battle Daredevil	$0.30	$0.90	$1.50	£0.20	£0.60	£1.00
270 Spiderman co-stars, 1st appearance Black Heart	$0.30	$0.90	$1.50	£0.15	£0.45	£0.75
271	$0.30	$0.90	$1.50	£0.15	£0.45	£0.75
272 Inhumans appear, 1st appearance Shotgun	$0.30	$0.90	$1.50	£0.15	£0.45	£0.75
273-274 Inhumans appear	$0.30	$0.90	$1.50	£0.15	£0.45	£0.75
275 Acts of Vengeance tie-in	$0.30	$0.90	$1.50	£0.15	£0.45	£0.75
276 (Jan 1990), Acts of Vengeance tie-in	$0.30	$0.90	$1.50	£0.15	£0.45	£0.75
277-280	$0.30	$0.90	$1.50	£0.15	£0.45	£0.75
281 Silver Surfer appears (cameo)	$0.30	$0.90	$1.50	£0.15	£0.45	£0.75
282 Silver Surfer appears	$0.30	$0.90	$1.50	£0.15	£0.45	£0.75
283 Captain America appears	$0.30	$0.90	$1.50	£0.15	£0.45	£0.75
284-286	$0.30	$0.90	$1.50	£0.15	£0.45	£0.75
287 Bullseye as Daredevil	$0.30	$0.90	$1.50	£0.15	£0.45	£0.75
288 (Jan 1991), Bullseye as Daredevil	$0.30	$0.90	$1.50	£0.15	£0.45	£0.75
289 Bullseye as Daredevil	$0.30	$0.90	$1.50	£0.15	£0.45	£0.75
290	$0.30	$0.90	$1.50	£0.15	£0.45	£0.75
291 last Nocenti script	$0.30	$0.90	$1.50	£0.15	£0.45	£0.75
292-293 Punisher guest-stars	$0.30	$0.90	$1.50	£0.15	£0.45	£0.75
294	$0.30	$0.90	$1.50	£0.15	£0.45	£0.75
295 Ghost Rider guest-stars	$0.30	$0.90	$1.50	£0.15	£0.45	£0.75
296	$0.30	$0.90	$1.50	£0.15	£0.45	£0.75
297 Last Rites (Fall of the Kingpin) part 1, Typhoid Mary appears	$0.30	$0.90	$1.50	£0.15	£0.45	£0.75
298 Last Rites part 2, Nick Fury guest stars	$0.30	$0.90	$1.50	£0.15	£0.45	£0.75
299 Last Rites part 3	$0.30	$0.90	$1.50	£0.15	£0.45	£0.75
300 (Jan 1992), DS Last Rites part 4; "red spot varnish" cover was solicited but it only came out as vaguely fluorescent	$0.40	$1.20	$2.00	£0.25	£0.75	£1.25
301 $1.25 cover begins	$0.30	$0.90	$1.50	£0.15	£0.45	£0.75
302-304	$0.30	$0.90	$1.50	£0.15	£0.45	£0.75
305-306 Spiderman appears	$0.30	$0.90	$1.50	£0.15	£0.45	£0.75
307 Dead Man's Hand part 1, Punisher and Nomad appear, continues in Nomad #4	$0.30	$0.90	$1.50	£0.15	£0.45	£0.75
308 Dead Man's Hand part 4, Punisher and Tombstone appear	$0.30	$0.90	$1.50	£0.15	£0.45	£0.75
309 Dead Man's Hand part 7, Punisher and Nomad appear	$0.30	$0.90	$1.50	£0.15	£0.45	£0.75
310-311 Calypso appears	$0.30	$0.90	$1.50	£0.15	£0.45	£0.75
312 (Jan 1993)	$0.30	$0.90	$1.50	£0.15	£0.45	£0.75
313-314	$0.30	$0.90	$1.50	£0.15	£0.45	£0.75
315 1st appearance Shock	$0.30	$0.90	$1.50	£0.15	£0.45	£0.75
316 ties into Daredevil #304	$0.30	$0.90	$1.50	£0.15	£0.45	£0.75
317-318	$0.30	$0.90	$1.50	£0.15	£0.45	£0.75
319 ND Fall From Grace prologue, Silver Sable appears	$1.00	$3.00	$5.00	£1.00	£3.00	£5.00
319 2nd printing, ND (Jan 1994), cover colours reversed	$0.25	$0.75	$1.25	£0.15	£0.45	£0.80
320 ND Fall From Grace story, Silver Sable appears	$1.00	$3.00	$5.00	£1.00	£3.00	£5.00
321 ND - Fall From Grace story	$0.40	$1.20	$2.00	£0.30	£0.90	£1.50
321 Collectors Edition, ND Fall From Grace story; glow in the dark cover	$0.80	$2.40	$4.00	£0.50	£1.50	£2.50
322 ND Fall From Grace story	$0.70	$2.10	$3.50	£0.40	£1.20	£2.00
323 ND Fall From Grace story, painted cover	$0.40	$1.20	$2.00	£0.25	£0.75	£1.25
324 ND (Jan 1994), Fall From Grace story, Morbius and Elektra appear	$0.40	$1.20	$2.00	£0.25	£0.75	£1.25
325 ND 48pgs, Fall From Grace story, Morbius and Elekta appear; bound-in poster at centre-fold	$0.50	$1.50	$2.50	£0.30	£0.90	£1.50
326 ND Tree of Knowledge story begins (ends #330)	$0.30	$0.90	$1.50	£0.20	£0.60	£1.00
327	$0.30	$0.90	$1.50	£0.20	£0.60	£1.00
328 with free Spiderman's Amazing Powers card sheet	$0.30	$0.90	$1.50	£0.20	£0.60	£1.00
329-330 Gambit guest-stars	$0.30	$0.90	$1.50	£0.20	£0.60	£1.00
331 Captain America appears	$0.30	$0.90	$1.50	£0.20	£0.60	£1.00
332 Captain America and Gambit appear	$0.30	$0.90	$1.50	£0.20	£0.60	£1.00
333-335	$0.30	$0.90	$1.50	£0.20	£0.60	£1.00
336 (Jan 1995)	$0.30	$0.90	$1.50	£0.20	£0.60	£1.00
337 Blackwulf and Kingpin appear	$0.30	$0.90	$1.50	£0.20	£0.60	£1.00
338-339	$0.30	$0.90	$1.50	£0.20	£0.60	£1.00
340-342 Kingpin appears	$0.30	$0.90	$1.50	£0.20	£0.60	£1.00
343	$0.30	$0.90	$1.50	£0.20	£0.60	£1.00
344 Over The Edge tie-in, J.M. DeMatteis script and Ron Wagner art begin	$0.40	$1.20	$2.00	£0.25	£0.75	£1.25
345-347	$0.40	$1.20	$2.00	£0.25	£0.75	£1.25
348 (Jan 1996)	$0.40	$1.20	$2.00	£0.25	£0.75	£1.25
349	$0.40	$1.20	$2.00	£0.25	£0.75	£1.25
350 48pgs	$0.60	$1.80	$3.00	£0.40	£1.20	£2.00
350 Collectors Edition, ND 48pgs, fifth ink aqueous coated cover	$0.70	$2.10	$3.50	£0.50	£1.50	£2.50
351 beginning new life with original costume, Karen Page and Foggy Nelson...	$0.40	$1.20	$2.00	£0.25	£0.75	£1.25
352 Daredevil engineers the return of his alter-ego Matt Murdock	$0.40	$1.20	$2.00	£0.25	£0.75	£1.25
353 new creative team of Karl Kesel and Cary Nord	$0.40	$1.20	$2.00	£0.25	£0.75	£1.25
354 Spiderman guest-stars	$0.30	$0.90	$1.50	£0.25	£0.75	£1.25
355-357	$0.30	$0.90	$1.50	£0.25	£0.75	£1.25
358	$0.30	$0.90	$1.50	£0.20	£0.60	£1.00
359-360 Daredevil vs. The Absorbing Man	$0.30	$0.90	$1.50	£0.20	£0.60	£1.00
361 Black Widow guest-stars	$0.30	$0.90	$1.50	£0.20	£0.60	£1.00
362	$0.40	$1.20	$2.00	£0.25	£0.75	£1.25
Title Value:	$990.05	$2977.15	$7605.25	£624.00	£1871.15	£4832.30
Note: Al Williamson inks #248-267						
Daredevil and Punisher: Child's Play Trade paperback						
ND reprints #182-184				£1.10	£3.30	£5.50
ND (2nd print - May 1991)				£1.00	£3.00	£5.00
Daredevil: Born Again Trade paperback						
ND reprints #226-229				£1.25	£3.75	£6.25
ND (2nd print. Nov 1989)				£1.20	£3.60	£6.00
Daredevil: Love and War Trade paperback						
ND reprints #230-233				£1.25	£3.75	£6.25
ND (2nd print. Dec 1989)				£1.20	£3.60	£6.00
Daredevil: Marked For Death (May 1990) Trade paperback						
ND reprints #159-161,163,164				£1.40	£4.20	£7.00
Daredevil: Gang War (May 1992) Trade paperback						
ND reprints #169-172, 180				£1.40	£4.20	£7.00
Daredevil: Fall of the Kingpin (Apr 1993) Trade paperback						
ND reprints #297-#300				£1.65	£4.95	£8.25
Daredevil: Fall From Grace (Nov 1994) Trade paperback						
ND reprints issues #319-325 plus 12 new pages				£2.60	£7.80	£13.00
Marvel Limited: Daredevil, Man Without Fear Trade paperback						
ND 192pgs, reprints mini-series				£2.60	£7.80	£13.00
Daredevil: Man Without Fear (Dec 1994) Treade paperback						
ND reprints mini-series in softcover format				£2.00	£6.00	£10.00
Daredevil Megahit (Nov 1995)						
ND boxed set of Daredevil: Man Without Fear mini-series, with limited quantities				£2.00	£6.00	£10.00
Daredevil Mini-Masterpiece (Nov 1995)						
ND boxed set of Daredevil #319-325 (#319 2nd print), with limited quantities				£1.40	£4.20	£7.00

DAREDEVIL ANNUAL

Marvel Comics Group; 1 Sep 1967;2 Feb 1971-3 Jan 1972;4 Oct 1976;4 Sep 1989-present

Issue	$Good	$Fine	$N.Mint	£Good	£Fine	£N.Mint
1 68pgs, all new stories; Daredevil vs. The Emissaries of Evil	$5.75	$17.50	$35.00	£3.75	£11.00	£22.50
2 ND scarce in the U.K. 52pgs, reprints issues #10, #11	$2.50	$7.50	$15.00	£1.30	£4.00	£8.00
3 ND very scarce in the U.K. 52pgs, reprints Daredevil #16, #17 featuring Spiderman	$2.50	$7.50	$15.00	£1.50	£4.50	£9.00
4 ND 52pgs, all new material; Black Panther and Sub-Mariner appear	$1.00	$3.00	$6.00	£0.55	£1.75	£3.50
4 2nd #4, ND 52pgs, : squarebound, Atlantis Attacks tie-in, Jim Lee and Whilce Portacio; accidentally mis-numbered by Marvel	$0.60	$1.80	$3.00	£0.40	£1.20	£2.00
6 ND 64pgs, Lifeform part 2, continues in Hulk Annual #16	$0.50	$1.50	$2.50	£0.30	£0.90	£1.50
7 ND 64pgs, story continues in Punisher Annual #4	$0.50	$1.50	$2.50	£0.30	£0.90	£1.50
8 ND 64pgs, The System Bytes part 2, Deathlok appears, continued in Wonderman Annual #1	$0.45	$1.35	$2.25	£0.30	£0.90	£1.50
9 ND 64pgs, pre-bagged with trading card introducing Devourer	$0.60	$1.80	$3.00	£0.40	£1.20	£2.00
10 ND 64pgs, Master of Kung Fu and Black Widow appear						

	$Good	$Fine	$N.Mint	£Good	£Fine	£N.Mint
	$0.60	$1.80	$3.00	£0.40	£1.20	£2.00
Title Value:	$15.00	$45.25	$87.25	£9.20	£27.55	£53.50
Note: Marvel mistakenly issued a 2nd Annual 4, not realising they had already done so in 1976. There is no Annual 5.						
DAREDEVIL GIANT SIZE						
Marvel Comics Group; 1 1975						
1 ND very scarce in the U.K. 68pgs, reprints Daredevil King Size Annual #1						
	$1.65	$5.00	$10.00	£1.15	£3.50	£7.00
Title Value:	$1.65	$5.00	$10.00	£1.15	£3.50	£7.00
DAREDEVIL/BATMAN						
Marvel Comics Group/DC Comics,OS; nn Mar 1997						
nn ND 48pgs, Mr. Hyde and Two-Face appear; D.G. Chichester script, Scott McDaniel art						
	$1.20	$3.60	$6.00	£0.80	£2.40	£4.00
Title Value:	$1.20	$3.60	$6.00	£0.80	£2.40	£4.00
DAREDEVIL/SHI						
Marvel Comics Group/Crusade Comics,OS; nn Feb 1997						
nn ND Jamal Igle and Al Williamson art						
	$0.30	$0.90	$1.50	£0.20	£0.60	£1.00
Title Value:	$0.30	$0.90	$1.50	£0.20	£0.60	£1.00
DAREDEVIL: MAN WITHOUT FEAR						
Marvel Comics Group,MS; 1 Oct 1993-5 Feb 1994						
1 ND Frank Miller script, John Romita Jnr. pencils begin; red foil embossed card-stock cover						
	$0.80	$2.40	$4.00	£0.50	£1.50	£2.50
2 ND scarce in the U.K. Matt Murdock's first meeting with Elektra; foil etched cover						
	$0.70	$2.10	$3.50	£0.50	£1.50	£2.50
3 ND Daredevil's origin explored in more detail						
	$0.70	$2.10	$3.50	£0.50	£1.50	£2.50
4-5 ND red foil embossed cover						
	$0.70	$2.10	$3.50	£0.50	£1.50	£2.50
Title Value:	$3.60	$10.80	$18.00	£2.50	£7.50	£12.50
DARERAT/TADPOLE						
Mighty Pumpkin; nn Feb 1987						
(see Gnatrat, Happy Birthdat Gnatrat)						
nn ND scarce in the U.K. Daredevil/Elektra/Frank Miller parody by Mark Martin						
	$0.60	$1.80	$3.00	£0.40	£1.20	£2.00
Title Value:	$0.60	$1.80	$3.00	£0.40	£1.20	£2.00
DARING ADVENTURES						
I.W. Super;8-12,15-18 1963-1964						
8 scarce in the U.K. reprints Fight Comics #53						
	$5.50	$17.00	$40.00	£2.85	£8.50	£20.00
9 scarce in the U.K. all reprint						
	$5.00	$15.00	$35.00	£2.85	£8.50	£20.00
10-11 scarce in the U.K. all reprint						
	$2.85	$8.50	$20.00	£1.75	£5.25	£12.50
12 scarce in the U.K. Phantom Lady reprints						
	$15.00	$45.00	$105.00	£7.75	£23.50	£55.00
15 scarce in the U.K. Hooded Menace reprint						
	$8.50	$26.00	$60.00	£4.25	£12.50	£30.00
16 scarce in the U.K. all reprint						
	$2.50	$7.50	$17.50	£1.40	£4.25	£10.00
17 scarce in the U.K. all reprint featuring Mac Raboy art						
	$4.60	$13.50	$32.50	£2.10	£6.25	£15.00
18 scarce in the U.K. all reprint featuring the origin of Atlas						
	$3.55	$10.50	$25.00	£1.75	£5.25	£12.50
Title Value:	$50.35	$151.50	$355.00	£26.45	£79.25	£187.50
DARING NEW ADVENTURES OF SUPERGIRL						
(see Supergirl)						
DARK ASSASSIN						
Greater Mercury Comics; 1 Aug 1989-6 1992?						
1 ND Kris Silver script, Richard Carter art; black and white						
	$0.30	$0.90	$1.50	£0.20	£0.60	£1.00

	$Good	$Fine	$N.Mint	£Good	£Fine	£N.Mint
2-6 ND b&w	$0.30	$0.90	$1.50	£0.20	£0.60	£1.00
Title Value:	$1.80	$5.40	$9.00	£1.20	£3.60	£6.00
DARK CRYSTAL, THE						
Marvel Comics Group,MS Film; 1 Apr 1983-2 May 1983						
1-2 ND adapts film	$0.15	$0.45	$0.75	£0.10	£0.35	£0.60
Title Value:	$0.30	$0.90	$1.50	£0.20	£0.70	£1.20
DARK DESTINY						
Alpha Productions; 1 Oct 1994						
1 ND black and white; Paul Pelletier cover						
	$0.80	$2.40	$4.00	£0.50	£1.50	£2.50
Title Value:	$0.80	$2.40	$4.00	£0.50	£1.50	£2.50
DARK DOMINION						
Defiant; 1 Oct 1993-10 Jul 1994						
1 ND Len Wein script begins						
	$0.30	$0.90	$1.50	£0.20	£0.60	£1.00
2-10 ND	$0.30	$0.90	$1.50	£0.20	£0.60	£1.00
Title Value:	$3.00	$9.00	$15.00	£2.00	£6.00	£10.00
Note: issues #11-13 were advertised and solicited but never appeared						
Dark Dominion #0 Special Edition (Aug 1994) Trade paperback						
ND new Joe James art, Jim Shooter's original script; 10,000 copies				£2.70	£8.10	£13.50
DARK FANTASY						
Apple Comics; 1 May 1992						
1 ND Kevin Schnaper script/art, horror/fantasy anthology (3 stories); black and white						
	$0.30	$0.90	$1.50	£0.20	£0.60	£1.00
Title Value:	$0.30	$0.90	$1.50	£0.20	£0.60	£1.00
DARK GUARD						
Marvel UK; 1 Oct 1993-3 Dec 1993						
1 Dan Abnett script and Carlos Pacheco art begin; features Death's Head II, Motormouth, Killpower and Dark Angel; card stock cover with silver foil logo						
	$0.30	$0.90	$1.50	£0.20	£0.60	£1.00
2-3	$0.25	$0.75	$1.25	£0.15	£0.45	£0.75
Title Value:	$0.80	$2.40	$4.00	£0.50	£1.50	£2.50
DARK HORSE CLASSICS						
Dark Horse; 1 Jul 1992-2 1992						
1 ND 48pgs, Last of the Mohicans						
	$0.80	$2.40	$4.00	£0.50	£1.50	£2.50
2 ND 48pgs, 20,000 Leagues Under The Sea						
	$0.80	$2.40	$4.00	£0.50	£1.50	£2.50
Title Value:	$1.60	$4.80	$8.00	£1.00	£3.00	£5.00
DARK HORSE CLASSICS - PREDATOR: JUNGLE TALES						
Dark Horse,OS; nn May 1996						
nn ND 40pgs, collects stories from Dark Horse Comics #1,2,10-12						
	$0.60	$1.80	$3.00	£0.40	£1.20	£2.00
Title Value:	$0.60	$1.80	$3.00	£0.40	£1.20	£2.00
DARK HORSE COMICS						
Dark Horse; 1 Aug 1992-25 Sep 1994						
1 anthology of new stories featuring Predator, Robocop plus Renegade by Claremont and Time Cop by Verheiden, double gatefold cover by Dave Dorman						
	$0.50	$1.50	$2.50	£0.30	£0.90	£1.50
2	$0.50	$1.50	$2.50	£0.30	£0.90	£1.50
3 Aliens: Horror Show by Sarah Byam and David Roach begins, David Roach cover						
	$0.50	$1.50	$2.50	£0.30	£0.90	£1.50
4-5	$0.50	$1.50	$2.50	£0.30	£0.90	£1.50
6 Robocop by Steven Grant and Bruce Patterson begins						
	$0.50	$1.50	$2.50	£0.30	£0.90	£1.50
7 Star Wars: Tales of the Jedi by Tom Veitch begins (1st)						
	$1.00	$3.00	$5.00	£0.50	£1.50	£2.50
8 Star Wars, RoboCop: Invasions, James Bond and 1st appearance X						
	$1.50	$4.50	$7.50	£0.50	£1.50	£2.50
9 Star Wars, RoboCop: Invasions, James Bond, 2nd appearance of X						
	$0.80	$2.40	$4.00	£0.40	£1.20	£2.00

Danger #16

Daredevil #111

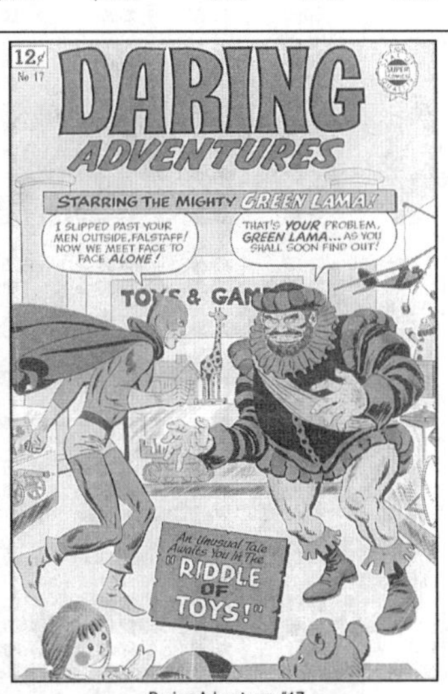

Daring Adventures #17

Issue	$Good	$Fine	$N.Mint	£Good	£Fine	£N.Mint
10 Predator, Godzilla, James Bond, X	$0.80	$2.40	$4.00	£0.30	£0.90	£1.50
11 Predator, Godzilla, James Bond, Aliens: Taste; Art Adams cover	$0.50	$1.50	$2.50	£0.30	£0.90	£1.50
12 Aliens/Predator special	$0.50	$1.50	$2.50	£0.30	£0.90	£1.50
13 Aliens, Predator, Thing from Another World	$0.50	$1.50	$2.50	£0.30	£0.90	£1.50
14 The Mark	$0.50	$1.50	$2.50	£0.30	£0.90	£1.50
15 The Mark, Aliens: Cargo	$0.50	$1.50	$2.50	£0.30	£0.90	£1.50
16 Predator: The Hunted City	$0.50	$1.50	$2.50	£0.30	£0.90	£1.50
17-18 Aliens, Star Wars: Droids, Predator	$0.50	$1.50	$2.50	£0.30	£0.90	£1.50
19-20 Predator	$0.50	$1.50	$2.50	£0.30	£0.90	£1.50
21 Mecha, Predator	$0.50	$1.50	$2.50	£0.30	£0.90	£1.50
22 Aliens, Mecha	$0.50	$1.50	$2.50	£0.30	£0.90	£1.50
23-24 Aliens, The Machine	$0.50	$1.50	$2.50	£0.30	£0.90	£1.50
25 James Bond by Doug Moench and Russ Heath, Aliens vs. Predator; Russ Heath cover	$0.50	$1.50	$2.50	£0.30	£0.90	£1.50
Title Value:	$14.60	$43.80	$73.00	£8.00	£24.00	£40.00

Note: all Non-Distributed on the news-stands in the U.K.

DARK HORSE DOWNUNDER

Dark Horse; 1 May 1994-3 Jul 1994

Issue	$Good	$Fine	$N.Mint	£Good	£Fine	£N.Mint
1 ND features Eddie Campbell script and art; anthology, black and white	$0.50	$1.50	$2.50	£0.30	£0.90	£1.50
2-3 ND features by Australian creative teams continue	$0.50	$1.50	$2.50	£0.30	£0.90	£1.50
Title Value:	$1.50	$4.50	$7.50	£0.90	£2.70	£4.50

DARK HORSE FUTURES

Dark Horse; 1989-1994

Issue	$Good	$Fine	$N.Mint	£Good	£Fine	£N.Mint
1989-1990 ND promotional giveaway	$0.30	$0.90	$1.50	£0.20	£0.60	£1.00
1991 ND promotional giveaway featuring an Aliens mini-poster by Dave Dorman	$0.30	$0.90	$1.50	£0.20	£0.60	£1.00
1992-1994 ND promotional giveaway	$0.30	$0.90	$1.50	£0.20	£0.60	£1.00
Title Value:	$1.80	$5.40	$9.00	£1.20	£3.60	£6.00

DARK HORSE INSIDER

Dark Horse; 1 Dec 1991-49 Dec 1995

Issue	$Good	$Fine	$N.Mint	£Good	£Fine	£N.Mint
1 ND promotional material begins plus Aliens vs. Predator story (ends #14)	$0.15	$0.45	$0.75	£0.10	£0.30	£0.50
2-49 ND	$0.15	$0.45	$0.75	£0.10	£0.30	£0.50
Title Value:	$7.35	$22.05	$36.75	£4.90	£14.70	£24.50

DARK HORSE PRESENTS

Dark Horse; 1 Jul 1986-present

Issue	$Good	$Fine	$N.Mint	£Good	£Fine	£N.Mint
1 ND 1st appearance Concrete by Chadwick, Black Cross	$3.20	$9.50	$16.00	£1.30	£3.90	£6.50
1 2nd printing, ND (Oct 1992) - silver border around cover	$0.60	$1.80	$3.00	£0.40	£1.20	£2.00
1 3rd printing, ND (1993)	$0.60	$1.80	$3.00	£0.40	£1.20	£2.00
1 Wizard Ace Edition, ND (1996) reprints Dark Horse Presents #1 to honour the company's 10th anniversary; wraparound acetate overlay; Wizard Ace Edition #6	$2.50	$7.50	$12.50	£1.50	£4.50	£7.50
2 ND Concrete	$1.40	$4.20	$7.00	£0.80	£2.40	£4.00
3 ND Concrete, Boris the Bear	$1.20	$3.60	$6.00	£0.80	£2.40	£4.00
4 ND 1st Trekker, Concrete	$1.00	$3.00	$5.00	£0.60	£1.80	£3.00
5 ND Concrete, Gulacy cover	$1.00	$3.00	$5.00	£0.60	£1.80	£3.00
6 ND Concrete	$0.60	$1.80	$3.00	£0.40	£1.20	£2.00
7 ND	$0.60	$1.80	$3.00	£0.40	£1.20	£2.00
8 ND Concrete	$0.60	$1.80	$3.00	£0.40	£1.20	£2.00
9 ND	$0.60	$1.80	$3.00	£0.40	£1.20	£2.00
10 ND 1st appearance of Masque (later becomes Mask), Concrete	$1.50	$4.50	$7.50	£0.50	£1.50	£2.50
11 ND Masque	$1.00	$3.00	$5.00	£0.40	£1.20	£2.00
12 ND Concrete, Masque	$1.00	$3.00	$5.00	£0.40	£1.20	£2.00
13 ND Masque	$1.00	$3.00	$5.00	£0.40	£1.20	£2.00
14 ND Masque, Mr. Monster	$1.00	$3.00	$5.00	£0.40	£1.20	£2.00
nn on cover, ND Masque	$1.00	$3.00	$5.00	£0.40	£1.20	£2.00
16 ND Concrete, Masque	$1.00	$3.00	$5.00	£0.40	£1.20	£2.00
17 ND full length Roachmill story	$0.40	$1.20	$2.00	£0.30	£0.90	£1.50
18-19 ND Masque	$1.00	$3.00	$5.00	£0.40	£1.20	£2.00
20 ND 64pgs, (Annual), Concrete, Flaming Carrot, Masque; many were produced with crinkled spines owing to the way the glue dried	$1.20	$3.60	$6.00	£0.50	£1.50	£2.50
21 ND Masque, Trekker	$1.00	$3.00	$5.00	£0.40	£1.20	£2.00
22 ND Trekker	$0.40	$1.20	$2.00	£0.30	£0.90	£1.50
23 ND	$0.40	$1.20	$2.00	£0.30	£0.90	£1.50
24 ND 1st appearance Aliens; Mark A. Nelson plot/art, Mark Verheiden text	$4.50	$13.50	$22.50	£2.00	£6.00	£10.00
25-27 ND	$0.50	$1.50	$2.50	£0.30	£0.90	£1.50
28 ND DS, Concrete, Roachmill	$0.60	$1.80	$3.00	£0.50	£1.50	£2.50
29-31 ND	$0.50	$1.50	$2.50	£0.30	£0.90	£1.50
32 ND 64pgs, (Annual), Concrete, American	$0.90	$2.70	$4.50	£0.60	£1.80	£3.00
33 ND 40pgs	$0.50	$1.50	$2.50	£0.30	£0.90	£1.50
34 ND Aliens story that builds to Aliens vs. Predator	$1.20	$3.60	$6.00	£0.80	£2.40	£4.00
35 ND Predator story that builds to Aliens vs. Predator	$1.20	$3.60	$6.00	£0.80	£2.40	£4.00
36 ND Aliens vs. Predator (1st - predates Aliens vs. Predator mini-series), painted cover with black surround	$1.40	$4.20	$7.00	£1.00	£3.00	£5.00
36 Line Draw Cover Edition, ND Aliens vs. Predator (1st - predates Aliens vs. Predator mini-series), blue and mauve background cover	$1.40	$4.20	$7.00	£1.00	£3.00	£5.00
37-39 ND	$0.50	$1.50	$2.50	£0.30	£0.90	£1.50
40 ND 48pgs, Trekker, Bacchus	$0.60	$1.80	$3.00	£0.40	£1.20	£2.00
41 ND	$0.50	$1.50	$2.50	£0.30	£0.90	£1.50
42-43 ND Aliens	$0.70	$2.10	$3.50	£0.40	£1.20	£2.00
44 ND Crash Ryan returns	$0.40	$1.20	$2.00	£0.30	£0.90	£1.50
45 ND	$0.40	$1.20	$2.00	£0.30	£0.90	£1.50
46 ND Predator	$0.40	$1.20	$2.00	£0.30	£0.90	£1.50
47-49 ND	$0.40	$1.20	$2.00	£0.30	£0.90	£1.50
50 ND George Perez art featured	$0.40	$1.20	$2.00	£0.30	£0.90	£1.50
51 ND Sin City by Frank Miller continues from 5th Anniversary Special (1st appearance in title)	$0.60	$1.80	$3.00	£0.40	£1.20	£2.00
52 ND Eddie Campbell cover	$0.60	$1.80	$3.00	£0.40	£1.20	£2.00
53 ND Frank Miller cover	$0.60	$1.80	$3.00	£0.40	£1.20	£2.00
54 ND previews John Byrne's Next Men (1st appearance)	$1.30	$3.90	$6.50	£0.80	£2.40	£4.00
55 ND previews John Byrne's Next Men, Frank Miller cover	$1.10	$3.30	$5.50	£0.70	£2.10	£3.50
56 ND 64pgs, Next Men, Sin City continues, cover based on DC's famous Superman Annual #7	$0.90	$2.70	$4.50	£0.60	£1.80	£3.00
57 ND 48pgs, Next Men concludes, cover by John Byrne and Frank Miller based on Marvel's Daredevil #1	$0.80	$2.40	$4.00	£0.50	£1.50	£2.50
58 ND	$0.45	$1.35	$2.25	£0.30	£0.90	£1.50
59-60 ND 20pgs Sin City by Frank Miller, cover by Frank Miller and Lynn Varley	$0.45	$1.35	$2.25	£0.30	£0.90	£1.50
61 ND Sin City by Frank Miller, cover by Frank Miller and Lynn Varley	$0.45	$1.35	$2.25	£0.30	£0.90	£1.50
62 ND full length Sin City conclusion by Frank Miller, cover by Frank Miller and Lynn Varley	$0.45	$1.35	$2.25	£0.30	£0.90	£1.50
63 ND Moebius story and cover	$0.45	$1.35	$2.25	£0.30	£0.90	£1.50
64 ND Matt Wagner story and cover	$0.45	$1.35	$2.25	£0.30	£0.90	£1.50
65 ND inter-active do-it-yourself-story	$0.45	$1.35	$2.25	£0.30	£0.90	£1.50
66 ND Concrete by Chadwick returns	$0.45	$1.35	$2.25	£0.30	£0.90	£1.50
67 ND 64pgs, squarebound, Predator mini-series begins that previews Predator: Race War	$0.60	$1.80	$3.00	£0.40	£1.20	£2.00
68-69 ND Predator: Race War continues	$0.45	$1.35	$2.25	£0.30	£0.90	£1.50
70 ND Madwoman of the Sacred Heart begins by Moebius, Moebius cover	$0.45	$1.35	$2.25	£0.30	£0.90	£1.50
71 ND Madwoman of the Sacred Heart	$0.45	$1.35	$2.25	£0.30	£0.90	£1.50
72-74 ND Madwoman of the Sacred Heart, Eudaemon	$0.45	$1.35	$2.25	£0.30	£0.90	£1.50
75-76 ND Madwoman of the Sacred Heart	$0.45	$1.35	$2.25	£0.30	£0.90	£1.50
77 ND Hermes vs. The Eyeball Kid by Eddie Campbell begins	$0.45	$1.35	$2.25	£0.30	£0.90	£1.50
78 ND painted cover by Charles Vess	$0.45	$1.35	$2.25	£0.30	£0.90	£1.50
79 ND The Shadow Empires	$0.45	$1.35	$2.25	£0.30	£0.90	£1.50
80 ND The Shadow Empires, Monkeyman and O'Brien by Arthur Adams; Arthur Adams cover	$0.45	$1.35	$2.25	£0.30	£0.90	£1.50
81 ND The Shadow Empires, Buoy 77 by F. Solano Lopez	$0.45	$1.35	$2.25	£0.30	£0.90	£1.50
82 ND Eddie Campbell cover	$0.45	$1.35	$2.25	£0.30	£0.90	£1.50
83 ND David Lloyd cover (and featured art)	$0.45	$1.35	$2.25	£0.30	£0.90	£1.50
84 ND Solano Lopez and Eddie Campbell stories conclude, Bryan Talbot art featured	$0.45	$1.35	$2.25	£0.30	£0.90	£1.50
85-86 ND	$0.50	$1.50	$2.50	£0.30	£0.90	£1.50
87 ND features Paul Chadwick and Rick Geary work	$0.50	$1.50	$2.50	£0.30	£0.90	£1.50
88-91 ND Hellboy by Mike Mignola	$0.50	$1.50	$2.50	£0.30	£0.90	£1.50
92 ND Shannon Wheeler's Too Much Coffee Man, Rick Geary strip	$0.70	$2.10	$3.50	£0.30	£0.90	£1.50

	$Good	$Fine	$N.Mint	£Good	£Fine	£N.Mint
93 ND Shannon Wheeler's Too Much Coffee Man	*$0.60*	*$1.80*	*$3.00*	£0.30	£0.90	£1.50
94-95 ND Shannon Wheeler's Too Much Coffee Man, Eddie Campbell's Eyeball Kid	*$0.60*	*$1.80*	*$3.00*	£0.30	£0.90	£1.50
96-98 ND Eyeball Kid	*$0.50*	*$1.50*	*$2.50*	£0.30	£0.90	£1.50
99 ND Eyeball Kid, also features work by Harvey Pekar and Jamie Delano	*$0.50*	*$1.50*	*$2.50*	£0.30	£0.90	£1.50
100 weekly issue #1, ND Frank Miller and Lynn Varley dinosaur cover, Dave Stevens back cover; 1st in a weekly mini-series of 5 issues	*$0.50*	*$1.50*	*$2.50*	£0.30	£0.90	£1.50
100 weekly issue #2, ND; Hell Boy cover by Bernie Wrightson, Hellboy's origin by Mike Mignola, Alec by Eddie Campbell	*$0.50*	*$1.50*	*$2.50*	£0.30	£0.90	£1.50
100 weekly issue #3, ND; Concrete cover by Paul Chadwick and Lynn Varley, features Concrete	*$0.50*	*$1.50*	*$2.50*	£0.30	£0.90	£1.50
100 weekly issue #4, ND; Dave Gibbons cover and story featuring Martha Washington, Black Cross by Chris Warner, Bird Dog by Ed Brubaker	*$0.50*	*$1.50*	*$2.50*	£0.30	£0.90	£1.50
100 weekly issue #5, ND; Mike Allred wraparound cover and features work by Jeff Smith, Evan Dorkin and Art Adams	*$0.50*	*$1.50*	*$2.50*	£0.30	£0.90	£1.50
101 ND Aliens by Ron Marz and Bernie Wrightson, work by Paul Pope and Harvey Pekar, painted back cover by John Bolton	*$0.50*	*$1.50*	*$2.50*	£0.30	£0.90	£1.50
102 ND Aliens by Ron Marz and Bernie Wrightson, work by Paul Pope and Harvey Pekar; cover by Bernie Wrightson	*$0.50*	*$1.50*	*$2.50*	£0.30	£0.90	£1.50
103 ND work by Paul Pope and Stan Shaw; cover by Stan Shaw	*$0.50*	*$1.50*	*$2.50*	£0.30	£0.90	£1.50
104-105 ND	*$0.60*	*$1.80*	*$3.00*	£0.40	£1.20	£2.00
106 ND Big Blown Baby by Robert Loren Fleming and Bill Wray	*$0.60*	*$1.80*	*$3.00*	£0.40	£1.20	£2.00
107 ND Rusty Razorclam by Mike Mignola and Steve Purcell; Mike Mignola cover	*$0.60*	*$1.80*	*$3.00*	£0.40	£1.20	£2.00
108-116 ND	*$0.60*	*$1.80*	*$3.00*	£0.40	£1.20	£2.00
Title Value:	*$86.30*	*$258.80*	*$431.50*	£50.90	£152.70	£254.50

Note: Concrete stories in 1-6,8,10,12,14,16,18,20,22,28,32.

Sin City Softcover Collection (Jan 1993)

				£Good	£Fine	£N.Mint
ND 208pgs, reprints from Dark Horse Presents on re-cycled paper				£2.00	£6.00	£10.00
ND 2nd printing (Mar 1993), ND 3rd printing (1994)				£1.80	£5.40	£9.00

DARK HORSE PRESENTS FIFTH ANNIVERSARY SPECIAL

Dark Horse,OS; 1 Oct 1991

	$Good	$Fine	$N.Mint	£Good	£Fine	£N.Mint
1 ND 112pgs, features work by Miller, Gibbons, Bisley, Chadwick, Wagner, Janson; 1st chapter Frank Miller's "Sin City"	*$2.00*	*$6.00*	*$10.00*	£1.20	£3.60	£6.00
Title Value:	*$2.00*	*$6.00*	*$10.00*	£1.20	£3.60	£6.00

DARK HORSE PRESENTS, BEST OF

Dark Horse; 1 1989-3 1991

	$Good	$Fine	$N.Mint	£Good	£Fine	£N.Mint
1 ND 128pgs, reprints selected stories from Dark Horse Presents #1-20; Concrete by Chadwick, Mr. Monster by Gilbert plus Rick Geary, Geoff Darrow, Rich Rice and others	*$1.50*	*$4.50*	*$7.50*	£1.00	£3.00	£5.00
2 ND 112pgs, reprints selected stories from Dark Horse Presents #21-30 featuring Paul Chadwick, Rick Geary	*$1.50*	*$4.50*	*$7.50*	£1.00	£3.00	£5.00
3 ND 144pgs, reprints selected stories from Dark Horse Presents #31-50 featuring Matt Wagner, Eddie Campbell, Rick Geary	*$2.50*	*$7.50*	*$12.50*	£1.50	£4.50	£7.50
Title Value:	*$5.50*	*$16.50*	*$27.50*	£3.50	£10.50	£17.50

DARK HORSE PRESENTS: ALIENS

Dark Horse,OS; 1 May 1992

	$Good	$Fine	$N.Mint	£Good	£Fine	£N.Mint
1 ND reprints black and white Aliens stories from Dark Horse Presents #24, #42, #43, 5th Anniversary Special and #56. New cover by Simon Bisley	*$0.90*	*$2.70*	*$4.50*	£0.60	£1.80	£3.00
1 Platinum Edition, ND - contents as above	*$1.50*	*$4.50*	*$7.50*	£0.80	£2.40	£4.00
Title Value:	*$2.40*	*$7.20*	*$12.00*	£1.40	£4.20	£7.00

DARK MANSION OF FORBIDDEN LOVE, THE

DC Comics; 1 Sep/Oct 1971-4 Mar/Apr 1972

(becomes Forbidden Tales of the Dark Mansion)

	$Good	$Fine	$N.Mint	£Good	£Fine	£N.Mint
1 LD in the U.K. 52pgs	*$3.30*	*$10.00*	*$20.00*	£0.80	£2.50	£5.00
2 ND 52pgs	*$2.05*	*$6.25*	*$12.50*	£0.55	£1.75	£3.50
3-4 ND 52pgs	*$1.65*	*$5.00*	*$10.00*	£0.50	£1.50	£3.00
Title Value:	*$8.65*	*$26.25*	*$52.50*	£2.35	£7.25	£14.50

FEATURES

Gothic romance, mystery stories

DARK ONE'S THIRD EYE

Sirius Entertainment,OS; nn Apr 1996

	$Good	$Fine	$N.Mint	£Good	£Fine	£N.Mint
nn ND 48pgs, collection of pin-ups by Dark One	*$1.00*	*$3.00*	*$5.00*	£0.70	£2.10	£3.50
Title Value:	*$1.00*	*$3.00*	*$5.00*	£0.70	£2.10	£3.50

DARK PASSION

Hero,MS; 1 Dec 1992-2 1993

	$Good	$Fine	$N.Mint	£Good	£Fine	£N.Mint
1-2 ND	*$0.40*	*$1.20*	*$2.00*	£0.25	£0.75	£1.25
Title Value:	*$0.80*	*$2.40*	*$4.00*	£0.50	£1.50	£2.50

DARK SHADOWS

Gold Key; 1 Mar 1969-35 Feb 1976

	$Good	$Fine	$N.Mint	£Good	£Fine	£N.Mint
1 with poster; painted and photo covers begin (to #30)	*$40.00*	*$120.00*	*$240.00*	£25.00	£75.00	£150.00
1 without poster	*$14.00*	*$43.00*	*$85.00*	£7.75	£23.50	£47.50
2	*$14.00*	*$43.00*	*$85.00*	£8.25	£25.00	£50.00
3 with poster	*$18.00*	*$55.00*	*$110.00*	£11.50	£35.00	£70.00
3 without poster	*$10.00*	*$30.00*	*$60.00*	£6.25	£18.50	£37.50
4-6	*$11.50*	*$35.00*	*$70.00*	£7.25	£22.00	£44.00
7 last photo cover	*$11.50*	*$35.00*	*$70.00*	£7.25	£22.00	£44.00
8-10	*$9.00*	*$28.00*	*$55.00*	£5.25	£16.00	£32.50
11-20	*$7.50*	*$22.50*	*$45.00*	£4.15	£12.50	£25.00
21-29	*$5.75*	*$17.50*	*$35.00*	£2.90	£8.75	£17.50
30 last painted cover	*$5.75*	*$17.50*	*$35.00*	£2.90	£8.75	£17.50
31 line drawn covers begin (to #35)	*$5.25*	*$16.00*	*$32.50*	£2.90	£8.75	£17.50
32-35	*$5.25*	*$16.00*	*$32.50*	£2.90	£8.75	£17.50
Title Value:	*$327.75*	*$995.00*	*$1987.50*	£188.50	£569.25	£1141.00

Note: most issues distributed on the news-stands in the U.K.

Dark Shadows: Old Friends (Sep 1993)

				£Good	£Fine	£N.Mint
Trade paperback reprints series with 16pgs of designs and paintings				£1.30	£3.90	£6.50

DARK SHADOWS BOOK 1

Innovation; 1 May 1992-4 Feb 1993

	$Good	$Fine	$N.Mint	£Good	£Fine	£N.Mint
1-4 ND based on US TV series	*$0.50*	*$1.50*	*$2.50*	£0.30	£0.90	£1.50
Title Value:	*$2.00*	*$6.00*	*$10.00*	£1.20	£3.60	£6.00

DARK SHADOWS BOOK 2

Innovation; 1 Apr 1993-4 Aug 1993

	$Good	$Fine	$N.Mint	£Good	£Fine	£N.Mint
1-4 ND Maggie Thompson script	*$0.50*	*$1.50*	*$2.50*	£0.30	£0.90	£1.50
Title Value:	*$2.00*	*$6.00*	*$10.00*	£1.20	£3.60	£6.00

DARK SHADOWS BOOK 3

Innovation; 1 Nov 1993

	$Good	$Fine	$N.Mint	£Good	£Fine	£N.Mint
1 ND Felipe Echevarria painted art	*$0.50*	*$1.50*	*$2.50*	£0.30	£0.90	£1.50
Title Value:	*$0.50*	*$1.50*	*$2.50*	£0.30	£0.90	£1.50

Note: originally intended as a four part mini-series, only issue #1 came out with the demise of Innovation as a company.

DARK STAR

Rebel Studios; 1 Aug 1991

	$Good	$Fine	$N.Mint	£Good	£Fine	£N.Mint
1 ND Kirbyesque art and Japanese animation	*$0.40*	*$1.20*	*$2.00*	£0.25	£0.75	£1.25
Title Value:	*$0.40*	*$1.20*	*$2.00*	£0.25	£0.75	£1.25

DARK WOLF

Malibu; 1 Jul 1987-4 Oct 1987

	$Good	$Fine	$N.Mint	£Good	£Fine	£N.Mint
1-4 ND Butch Burcham art; black and white	*$0.40*	*$1.20*	*$2.00*	£0.25	£0.75	£1.25
Title Value:	*$1.60*	*$4.80*	*$8.00*	£1.00	£3.00	£5.00

DARK WOLF (2ND SERIES)

Eternity; 1 Feb 1988-4 May 1988

	$Good	$Fine	$N.Mint	£Good	£Fine	£N.Mint
1-4 ND Butch Burcham art; black and white	*$0.40*	*$1.20*	*$2.00*	£0.25	£0.75	£1.25
Title Value:	*$1.60*	*$4.80*	*$8.00*	£1.00	£3.00	£5.00

The Dark Wolf Collection (1988)

				£Good	£Fine	£N.Mint
reprints issues #1-4, new Butch Burcham cover and intro by Archie Goodwin				£1.00	£3.00	£5.00

DARK WOLF (3RD SERIES)

Comax Productions; 1 1991

	$Good	$Fine	$N.Mint	£Good	£Fine	£N.Mint
1 ND Butch Burcham script/art, black and white; Halloween special	*$0.30*	*$0.90*	*$1.50*	£0.20	£0.60	£1.00
Title Value:	*$0.30*	*$0.90*	*$1.50*	£0.20	£0.60	£1.00

DARK WORLD #1: VAMPIRES

Millennium,OS; 1 Dec 1994

	$Good	$Fine	$N.Mint	£Good	£Fine	£N.Mint
1 ND Jae Lee, Colleen Doran, Daerick Gross art featured	*$0.60*	*$1.80*	*$3.00*	£0.40	£1.20	£2.00
Title Value:	*$0.60*	*$1.80*	*$3.00*	£0.40	£1.20	£2.00

DARK, THE

Continuum Comics; 1 Sep 1991-4 1992

	$Good	$Fine	$N.Mint	£Good	£Fine	£N.Mint
1 ND quarterly frequency begins, Larry Stroman part pencils, black and white	*$0.50*	*$1.50*	*$2.50*	£0.30	£0.90	£1.50
2-4 ND	*$0.40*	*$1.20*	*$2.00*	£0.25	£0.75	£1.25
Title Value:	*$1.70*	*$5.10*	*$8.50*	£1.05	£3.15	£5.25

DARK, THE (2ND SERIES)

Continuum Comics; 1 Jun 1993-7 1994

	$Good	$Fine	$N.Mint	£Good	£Fine	£N.Mint
1 ND red non-foil cover	*$0.40*	*$1.20*	*$2.00*	£0.25	£0.75	£1.25
1 2nd printing, ND blue foil enhanced cover	*$0.40*	*$1.20*	*$2.00*	£0.25	£0.75	£1.25
1 Collectors Edition, ND - part George Perez art and cover; foil enhanced card stock cover	*$0.50*	*$1.50*	*$2.50*	£0.30	£0.90	£1.50
2 ND part George Perez art and cover; foil enhanced card stock cover	*$0.40*	*$1.20*	*$2.00*	£0.25	£0.75	£1.25
2 2nd printing, ND (Mar 1994), new foil enhanced cover	*$0.40*	*$1.20*	*$2.00*	£0.25	£0.75	£1.25
3-5 ND part George Perez art and cover; foil enhanced card stock cover	*$0.40*	*$1.20*	*$2.00*	£0.25	£0.75	£1.25
6-7 ND part Perez cover; foil enhanced card stock cover	*$0.40*	*$1.20*	*$2.00*	£0.25	£0.75	£1.25
Title Value:	*$4.10*	*$12.30*	*$20.50*	£2.55	£7.65	£12.75

DARK, THE (3RD SERIES)

August House; 1 Jan 1995-5 1995

	$Good	$Fine	$N.Mint	£Good	£Fine	£N.Mint
1 ND 40pgs, foil enhanced cardstock cover, part art George Perez; bound-in Foodang character card by Bart Sears	*$0.50*	*$1.50*	*$2.50*	£0.30	£0.90	£1.50
1 Signed & Numbered Edition, ND (Jun 1995) - foil cover; 1,000 copies with certificate	*$0.80*	*$2.40*	*$4.00*	£0.50	£1.50	£2.50
2 ND foil-enhanced cover by Mike Zeck	*$0.50*	*$1.50*	*$2.50*	£0.30	£0.90	£1.50
3 ND foil-enhanced cover by Todd Lidstone and Mike Hoff	*$0.50*	*$1.50*	*$2.50*	£0.30	£0.90	£1.50

Issue	$Good	$Fine	$N.Mint	£Good	£Fine	£N.Mint
4 ND painted cover by John Rheaume						
	$0.50	*$1.50*	*$2.50*	£0.30	£0.90	£1.50
5 ND	*$0.50*	*$1.50*	*$2.50*	£0.30	£0.90	£1.50
Title Value:	*$3.30*	*$9.90*	*$16.50*	£2.00	£6.00	£10.00

Note: the contents of issue #1 were originally published in part as The Dark #7 by Continuum Comics. New pages have been added throughout the story

DARKCHYLDE

Maximum Comic Press; 1 Jul 1996-present

Issue	$Good	$Fine	$N.Mint	£Good	£Fine	£N.Mint
1 ND Randy Queen script and art begins						
	$0.90	*$2.70*	*$4.50*	£0.60	£1.80	£3.00
1 "Problem Child" Edition ND						
	$1.00	*$3.00*	*$5.00*	£1.20	£3.60	£6.00
1 American Entertainment Edition, ND wraparound cover						
	$1.00	*$3.00*	*$5.00*	£1.20	£3.60	£6.00
1 Comicon Edition, ND released at the 1996 San Diego Comicon; cover identical to the variant edition but with "Special Comicon Edition" also on cover						
	$1.00	*$3.00*	*$5.00*	£1.20	£3.60	£6.00
1 Variant Cover Edition ND						
	$1.00	*$3.00*	*$5.00*	£1.20	£3.60	£6.00
2 ND	*$0.60*	*$1.80*	*$3.00*	£0.40	£1.20	£2.00
2 Variant Cover Edition ND						
	$0.80	*$2.40*	*$4.00*	£1.00	£3.00	£5.00
3 ND	*$0.60*	*$1.80*	*$3.00*	£0.40	£1.20	£2.00
3 Variant Cover Edition, ND cover by Drew, limited to 25% of the print run						
	$0.80	*$2.40*	*$4.00*	£0.70	£2.10	£3.50
Title Value:	*$7.70*	*$23.10*	*$38.50*	£7.90	£23.70	£39.50

DARKER IMAGE

Image,OS; 1 Mar 1993

Issue	$Good	$Fine	$N.Mint	£Good	£Fine	£N.Mint
1 ND 24pgs, anthology of try-out characters; Bloodwulf by Liefeld, The Maxx by Sam Kieth and Deathblow by Jim Lee; pre-bagged with The Maxx trading card						
	$0.50	*$1.50*	*$2.50*	£0.30	£0.90	£1.50
1 Gold Edition, ND - pre-bagged						
	$3.00	*$9.00*	*$15.00*	£1.50	£4.50	£7.50
1 Platinum Edition, ND, embossed silver logo; available for every 100 copies of regular issue ordered						
	$2.50	*$7.50*	*$12.50*	£1.50	£4.50	£7.50
Title Value:	*$6.00*	*$18.00*	*$30.00*	£3.30	£9.90	£16.50

Note: originally solicited as a 4 part mini series

DARKEWOOD

Aircel,MS; 1-5 1988

Issue	$Good	$Fine	$N.Mint	£Good	£Fine	£N.Mint
1-5 ND	*$0.30*	*$0.90*	*$1.50*	£0.20	£0.60	£1.00
Title Value:	*$1.50*	*$4.50*	*$7.50*	£1.00	£3.00	£5.00

DARKHAWK

Marvel Comics Group; 1 Mar 1991-50 Apr 1995

Issue	$Good	$Fine	$N.Mint	£Good	£Fine	£N.Mint
1 ND origin and 1st appearance Darkhawk						
	$0.40	*$1.20*	*$2.00*	£0.25	£0.75	£1.25
2-3 ND Spiderman and Hobgoblin appear						
	$0.40	*$1.20*	*$2.00*	£0.20	£0.60	£1.00
4-5 ND	*$0.30*	*$0.90*	*$1.50*	£0.20	£0.60	£1.00
6 ND Captain America/Daredevil appear						
	$0.30	*$0.90*	*$1.50*	£0.20	£0.60	£1.00
7-8 ND	*$0.30*	*$0.90*	*$1.50*	£0.20	£0.60	£1.00
9 ND Punisher appears						
	$0.30	*$0.90*	*$1.50*	£0.20	£0.60	£1.00
10 ND	*$0.30*	*$0.90*	*$1.50*	£0.20	£0.60	£1.00
11 ND	*$0.25*	*$0.75*	*$1.25*	£0.15	£0.45	£0.75
12 ND Tombstone appears						
	$0.25	*$0.75*	*$1.25*	£0.15	£0.45	£0.75
13-14 ND Darkhawk vs. Venom						
	$0.40	*$1.20*	*$2.00*	£0.15	£0.45	£0.75
15-18 ND	*$0.25*	*$0.75*	*$1.25*	£0.15	£0.45	£0.75
19 ND Spiderman appears						
	$0.25	*$0.75*	*$1.25*	£0.15	£0.45	£0.75
20 ND Darkhawk vs. Brotherhood of Evil Mutants, Spiderman, Sleepwalker appear; continued in Sleepwalker #17						
	$0.25	*$0.75*	*$1.25*	£0.15	£0.45	£0.75
21 ND Return To Forever story begins that reveals Darkhawk's true origin						
	$0.25	*$0.75*	*$1.25*	£0.15	£0.45	£0.75
22 Ghost Rider guest-stars						
	$0.25	*$0.75*	*$1.25*	£0.15	£0.45	£0.75
23-24	*$0.25*	*$0.75*	*$1.25*	£0.15	£0.45	£0.75
25 DS anniversary issue, holo-grafix foil cover, double-gatefold poster of covers #21-24						
	$0.40	*$1.20*	*$2.00*	£0.25	£0.75	£1.25
26 New Warriors appear						
	$0.25	*$0.75*	*$1.25*	£0.15	£0.45	£0.75
27	*$0.25*	*$0.75*	*$1.25*	£0.15	£0.45	£0.75
28-29 New Warriors appear						
	$0.25	*$0.75*	*$1.25*	£0.15	£0.45	£0.75
30 Infinity Crusade tie-in						
	$0.25	*$0.75*	*$1.25*	£0.15	£0.45	£0.75
31 Infinity Crusade tie-in, X-Men appear						
	$0.25	*$0.75*	*$1.25*	£0.15	£0.45	£0.75
32-34	*$0.25*	*$0.75*	*$1.25*	£0.15	£0.45	£0.75
35-37 Venom guest-stars						
	$0.25	*$0.75*	*$1.25*	£0.15	£0.45	£0.75
38 Amulet Quest story begins; new costume and new powers						
	$0.25	*$0.75*	*$1.25*	£0.15	£0.45	£0.75
39 with free Spiderman vs. Venom card sheet						
	$0.25	*$0.75*	*$1.25*	£0.15	£0.45	£0.75
40-41	*$0.25*	*$0.75*	*$1.25*	£0.15	£0.45	£0.75
42 Darkhawk reveals identity to parents						
	$0.25	*$0.75*	*$1.25*	£0.15	£0.45	£0.75
43-46	*$0.25*	*$0.75*	*$1.25*	£0.15	£0.45	£0.75
47 ties into Spiderman: Friends & Enemies #1						
	$0.25	*$0.75*	*$1.25*	£0.15	£0.45	£0.75
48-49	*$0.25*	*$0.75*	*$1.25*	£0.15	£0.45	£0.75
50 48pgs, metallic ink cover						
	$0.30	*$0.90*	*$1.50*	£0.20	£0.60	£1.00
Title Value:	*$13.80*	*$41.40*	*$69.00*	£8.20	£24.60	£41.00

DARKHAWK ANNUAL

Marvel Comics Group; 1 Jul 1992-3 1994

Issue	$Good	$Fine	$N.Mint	£Good	£Fine	£N.Mint
1 ND Assault On Armor City part 1, Iron Man appears, continued in West Coast Avengers Annual #7						
	$0.40	*$1.20*	*$2.00*	£0.25	£0.75	£1.25
2 ND 64pgs, pre-bagged with trading card introducing Dreamkiller						
	$0.40	*$1.20*	*$2.00*	£0.25	£0.75	£1.25
3 ND 64pgs	*$0.40*	*$1.20*	*$2.00*	£0.25	£0.75	£1.25
Title Value:	*$1.20*	*$3.60*	*$6.00*	£0.75	£2.25	£3.75

DARKHOLD

Marvel Comics Group; 1 Oct 1992-16 Jan 1994

Issue	$Good	$Fine	$N.Mint	£Good	£Fine	£N.Mint
1 ND DS Rise of the Midnight Sons part 4, pre-bagged with poster by Andy and Adam Kubert						
	$0.40	*$1.20*	*$2.00*	£0.25	£0.75	£1.25
2 ND	*$0.30*	*$0.90*	*$1.50*	£0.20	£0.60	£1.00
3 ND Scarlet Witch cameo; Modred the Mystic returns						
	$0.30	*$0.90*	*$1.50*	£0.20	£0.60	£1.00
4 ND Sabretooth appears						
	$0.30	*$0.90*	*$1.50*	£0.20	£0.60	£1.00
5 ND Ghost Rider and Punisher appear						
	$0.30	*$0.90*	*$1.50*	£0.20	£0.60	£1.00
6 ND Modred the Mystic vs. Dr. Strange						
	$0.30	*$0.90*	*$1.50*	£0.20	£0.60	£1.00
7-10 ND	*$0.30*	*$0.90*	*$1.50*	£0.20	£0.60	£1.00
11 ND Midnight Massacre part 3, gold-ink black parchment outer cover						
	$0.30	*$0.90*	*$1.50*	£0.20	£0.60	£1.00
12-14 ND	*$0.30*	*$0.90*	*$1.50*	£0.20	£0.60	£1.00
15 ND Siege of Darkness part 4; Ghost Rider appears						
	$0.30	*$0.90*	*$1.50*	£0.20	£0.60	£1.00
16 ND Siege of Darkness part 12; spot varnish cover						
	$0.30	*$0.90*	*$1.50*	£0.20	£0.60	£1.00
Title Value:	*$4.90*	*$14.70*	*$24.50*	£3.25	£9.75	£16.25

DARKLON THE MYSTIC

Pacific; 1 Nov 1983

Issue	$Good	$Fine	$N.Mint	£Good	£Fine	£N.Mint
1 ND DS, Jim Starlin art, reprint						
	$0.40	*$1.20*	*$2.00*	£0.25	£0.75	£1.25
Title Value:	*$0.40*	*$1.20*	*$2.00*	£0.25	£0.75	£1.25

DARKMAN

Marvel Comics Group,MS; 1 Apr 1993-6 Sep 1993

Issue	$Good	$Fine	$N.Mint	£Good	£Fine	£N.Mint
1 48pgs, card-stock covers begin						
	$0.40	*$1.20*	*$2.00*	£0.25	£0.75	£1.25
2-6	*$0.40*	*$1.20*	*$2.00*	£0.25	£0.75	£1.25
Title Value:	*$2.40*	*$7.20*	*$12.00*	£1.50	£4.50	£7.50

DARKMAN MOVIE MAGAZINE

Marvel Comics Group,OS; 1 Sep 1990

Issue	$Good	$Fine	$N.Mint	£Good	£Fine	£N.Mint
1 ND 64pgs, black and white adaptation of film						
	$0.40	*$1.20*	*$2.00*	£0.25	£0.75	£1.25
Title Value:	*$0.40*	*$1.20*	*$2.00*	£0.25	£0.75	£1.25

DARKMAN MOVIE MAGAZINE COMIC

Marvel Comics Group,MS; 1 Oct 1990-3 Dec 1990

Issue	$Good	$Fine	$N.Mint	£Good	£Fine	£N.Mint
1-3 ND comics version of the above						
	$0.15	*$0.45*	*$0.75*	£0.10	£0.35	£0.60
Title Value:	*$0.45*	*$1.35*	*$2.25*	£0.30	£1.05	£1.80

DARKNESS, THE

Top Cow Comics; nn 1996; 1 Dec 1996-present

Issue	$Good	$Fine	$N.Mint	£Good	£Fine	£N.Mint
nn ND 20pgs, special preview edition; Garth Ennis script, Marc Silvestri art						
	$3.00	*$9.00*	*$15.00*	£2.50	£7.50	£12.50
1 ND Garth Ennis script and Marc Silvestri art begins						
	$0.60	*$1.80*	*$3.00*	£0.40	£1.20	£2.00
1 Variant Cover Edition, ND black cover						
	$1.40	*$4.20*	*$7.00*	£1.40	£4.20	£7.00
2 ND	*$0.60*	*$1.80*	*$3.00*	£0.40	£1.20	£2.00
Title Value:	*$5.60*	*$16.80*	*$28.00*	£4.70	£14.10	£23.50

DARKSEID VS. GALACTUS: THE HUNGER

DC Comics/Marvel Comics Group,OS; 1 Oct 1995

Issue	$Good	$Fine	$N.Mint	£Good	£Fine	£N.Mint
1 ND John Byrne script and art, Darkseid, Galactus and Silver Surfer appear						
	$1.00	*$3.00*	*$5.00*	£0.70	£2.10	£3.50
Title Value:	*$1.00*	*$3.00*	*$5.00*	£0.70	£2.10	£3.50

DARKSIDE

Maximum Comic Press,OS; 1 Oct 1996

Issue	$Good	$Fine	$N.Mint	£Good	£Fine	£N.Mint
1 ND Rob Liefeld/Robert Napton script, Mark Pajarillo art						
	$0.60	*$1.80*	*$3.00*	£0.40	£1.20	£2.00
Title Value:	*$0.60*	*$1.80*	*$3.00*	£0.40	£1.20	£2.00

DARKSIDE

Darkline Publications; 1 1987

Issue	$Good	$Fine	$N.Mint	£Good	£Fine	£N.Mint
1 ND b&w	*$0.30*	*$0.90*	*$1.50*	£0.10	£0.30	£0.50
Title Value:	*$0.30*	*$0.90*	*$1.50*	£0.10	£0.30	£0.50

DARKSTAR II

Rebel Studios; 1 Aug 1993-2 1993

Issue	$Good	$Fine	$N.Mint	£Good	£Fine	£N.Mint
1-2 ND	*$0.50*	*$1.50*	*$2.50*	£0.30	£0.90	£1.50
Title Value:	*$1.00*	*$3.00*	*$5.00*	£0.60	£1.80	£3.00

DARKSTARS, THE

DC Comics; 0 Oct 1994; 1 Oct 1992-38 Jan 1996

Issue	$Good	$Fine	$N.Mint	£Good	£Fine	£N.Mint
0 (Oct 1994) Zero Hour X-over, history of Darkstars revealed						
	$0.40	*$1.20*	*$2.00*	£0.25	£0.75	£1.25
1 Larry Stroman art begins, Travis Charest cover						
	$0.40	*$1.20*	*$2.00*	£0.25	£0.75	£1.25
2-3 Travis Charest cover						
	$0.30	*$0.90*	*$1.50*	£0.20	£0.60	£1.00

	$Good	$Fine	$N.Mint	£Good	£Fine	£N.Mint
4 1st Travis Charest art on Darkstars						
	$0.30	*$0.90*	*$1.50*	£0.20	£0.60	£1.00
5-6 Hawkman and Hawkwoman appear, Travis Charest art						
	$0.30	*$0.90*	*$1.50*	£0.20	£0.60	£1.00
7 Travis Charest art						
	$0.30	*$0.90*	*$1.50*	£0.20	£0.60	£1.00
8	*$0.30*	*$0.90*	*$1.50*	£0.20	£0.60	£1.00
9 Travis Charest art						
	$0.30	*$0.90*	*$1.50*	£0.20	£0.60	£1.00
10	*$0.30*	*$0.90*	*$1.50*	£0.20	£0.60	£1.00
11 Trinity part 4, Travis Charest art						
	$0.30	*$0.90*	*$1.50*	£0.20	£0.60	£1.00
12 X-over with DC Universe: Trinity #2						
	$0.30	*$0.90*	*$1.50*	£0.20	£0.60	£1.00
13 Travis Charest cover						
	$0.30	*$0.90*	*$1.50*	£0.20	£0.60	£1.00
14-17	*$0.30*	*$0.90*	*$1.50*	£0.20	£0.60	£1.00
18 Flash appears	*$0.30*	*$0.90*	*$1.50*	£0.20	£0.60	£1.00
19 Flash appears; Alan Davis and Mark Farmer cover						
	$0.30	*$0.90*	*$1.50*	£0.20	£0.60	£1.00
20 Flash appears	*$0.30*	*$0.90*	*$1.50*	£0.20	£0.60	£1.00
21 prelude to Zero Hour						
	$0.30	*$0.90*	*$1.50*	£0.20	£0.60	£1.00
22 $1.95 cover begin; prelude to Zero Hour						
	$0.40	*$1.20*	*$2.00*	£0.25	£0.75	£1.25
23 prelude to Zero Hour						
	$0.40	*$1.20*	*$2.00*	£0.25	£0.75	£1.25
24 Zero Hour X-over						
	$0.40	*$1.20*	*$2.00*	£0.25	£0.75	£1.25
25 John Stewart takes command of The Darkstars						
	$0.40	*$1.20*	*$2.00*	£0.25	£0.75	£1.25
26-29	*$0.40*	*$1.20*	*$2.00*	£0.25	£0.75	£1.25
30 Green Lantern appears						
	$0.40	*$1.20*	*$2.00*	£0.25	£0.75	£1.25
31 $2.25 cover begin						
	$0.45	*$1.35*	*$2.25*	£0.25	£0.75	£1.25
32 The Crimelord/Syndicate War part 3, continued in New Titans #122; Supergirl, New Titans and Deathstroke guest-star						
	$0.45	*$1.35*	*$2.25*	£0.25	£0.75	£1.25
33	*$0.45*	*$1.35*	*$2.25*	£0.25	£0.75	£1.25
34 The Siege of Zi Charam part 3, continued in Damage #16						
	$0.45	*$1.35*	*$2.25*	£0.25	£0.75	£1.25
35-36 Flash guest-stars						
	$0.45	*$1.35*	*$2.25*	£0.25	£0.75	£1.25
37 story continued from Guy Gardner #35						
	$0.45	*$1.35*	*$2.25*	£0.25	£0.75	£1.25
38	*$0.45*	*$1.35*	*$2.25*	£0.25	£0.75	£1.25
Title Value:	***$14.00***	***$42.00***	***$70.00***	**£8.75**	**£26.25**	**£43.75**

DARKWING DUCK

Disney,MS; 1 Oct 1991-4 Jan 1992

	$Good	$Fine	$N.Mint	£Good	£Fine	£N.Mint
1-4 ND	*$0.30*	*$0.90*	*$1.50*	£0.20	£0.60	£1.00
Title Value:	***$1.20***	***$3.60***	***$6.00***	**£0.80**	**£2.40**	**£4.00**

DART

Image,MS; 1 Feb 1996-3 Apr 1996

	$Good	$Fine	$N.Mint	£Good	£Fine	£N.Mint
1-2 ND Bruce Love and Julie Ditrich script, Jozef Szekeres art						
	$0.50	*$1.50*	*$2.50*	£0.30	£0.90	£1.50
3 ND Bruce Love and Julie Ditrich script, Josef Szekeres art						
	$0.50	*$1.50*	*$2.50*	£0.30	£0.90	£1.50
Title Value:	***$1.50***	***$4.50***	***$7.50***	**£0.90**	**£2.70**	**£4.50**

DATE WITH DEBBI

National Periodical Publications; 1 Jan/Feb 1969-17 Sep/Oct 1971; 18 Oct/Nov 1972

	$Good	$Fine	$N.Mint	£Good	£Fine	£N.Mint
1 scarce in the U.K.	*$2.10*	*$6.25*	*$15.00*	£1.25	£3.85	£9.00
2	*$1.25*	*$3.85*	*$9.00*	£0.75	£2.35	£5.50
3-5	*$1.05*	*$3.20*	*$7.50*	£0.55	£1.70	£4.00
6-18	*$0.85*	*$2.55*	*$6.00*	£0.40	£1.25	£3.00
Title Value:	***$17.55***	***$52.85***	***$124.50***	**£8.85**	**£27.55**	**£65.50**

DATE WITH JUDY, A

National Periodical Publications;67 Oct/Nov 1959-79 Oct/Nov 1960

(previous issues #1-66 ND)

	$Good	$Fine	$N.Mint	£Good	£Fine	£N.Mint
67-70	*$3.55*	*$10.50*	*$25.00*	£2.10	£6.25	£15.00
71-79	*$2.85*	*$8.50*	*$20.00*	£1.75	£5.25	£12.50
Title Value:	***$39.85***	***$118.50***	***$280.00***	**£24.15**	**£72.25**	**£172.50**

DAUGHTERS OF TIME

The Three-D Zone,OS; 1 Nov 1991

	$Good	$Fine	$N.Mint	£Good	£Fine	£N.Mint
1 ND Steve Ditko, Kurt Schaffenberger cover, with glasses						
	$0.60	*$1.80*	*$3.00*	£0.40	£1.20	£2.00
Title Value:	***$0.60***	***$1.80***	***$3.00***	**£0.40**	**£1.20**	**£2.00**

DAWN

Sirius Entertainment,MS; ½ 1996; 1 Jul 1995-4 1996

	$Good	$Fine	$N.Mint	£Good	£Fine	£N.Mint
½ ND 24pgs, Joseph Michael Linsner script and layouts, Tom Artis pencils and inks; produced in conjunction with Wizard #59, with certificate						
	$3.00	*$9.00*	*$15.00*	£2.50	£7.50	£12.50
½ Gold Edition, ND Gold logo						
	$5.00	*$15.00*	*$25.00*	£3.00	£9.00	£15.00
1 ND Joseph Michael Linsner art and script						
	$1.80	*$5.25*	*$9.00*	£0.80	£2.40	£4.00
1 "Black Light" edition ND						
	$6.50	*$19.50*	*$32.50*	£4.00	£12.00	£20.00
1 "Look Sharp" edition ND						
	$8.00	*$24.00*	*$40.00*	£5.00	£15.00	£25.00
1 "White Trash" edition ND						
	$7.50	*$22.50*	*$37.50*	£4.50	£13.50	£22.50
2 ND	*$1.20*	*$3.60*	*$6.00*	£0.60	£1.80	£3.00
2 Japanese Edition, ND Dawn on cover holding severed head aloft with Dawn written in Japanese along top of comic						
	$6.00	*$18.00*	*$30.00*	£3.00	£9.00	£15.00
3 ND	*$1.00*	*$3.00*	*$5.00*	£0.50	£1.50	£2.50
3 Variant Cover Edition, ND limited to 1,500 copies						
	$6.00	*$18.00*	*$30.00*	£3.00	£9.00	£15.00
4 ND	*$1.00*	*$3.00*	*$5.00*	£0.50	£1.50	£2.50
Title Value:	***$47.00***	***$140.85***	***$235.00***	**£27.40**	**£82.20**	**£137.00**

DAYS OF DARKNESS

Apple Comics,MS; 1 Mar 1992-4 Sep 1992

	$Good	$Fine	$N.Mint	£Good	£Fine	£N.Mint
1-4 ND chronicle of events leading to Pearl Harbour						
	$0.50	*$1.50*	*$2.50*	£0.30	£0.90	£1.50
Title Value:	***$2.00***	***$6.00***	***$10.00***	**£1.20**	**£3.60**	**£6.00**

DAYS OF FUTURE PRESENT

Marvel Comics Group; 1990

Cross-over storyline that ran throughout the following issues:
Fantastic Four Annual #23, X-Factor Annual #5, New Mutants Annual #6, X-Men Annual 14.

DAZZLER, THE

Marvel Comics Group; 1 Mar 1981-42 Mar 1986

(see Marvel Graphic Novel, X-Men #130)

	$Good	$Fine	$N.Mint	£Good	£Fine	£N.Mint
1 ND X-Men, Spiderman and Avengers appear						
	$0.50	*$1.50*	*$2.50*	£0.30	£0.90	£1.50
2 X-Men, Spiderman and Fantastic Four appear						
	$0.40	*$1.20*	*$2.00*	£0.25	£0.75	£1.25
3-4 Dr. Doom and Fantastic Four appear						
	$0.30	*$0.90*	*$1.50*	£0.20	£0.60	£1.00
5 intro Blue Shield	*$0.30*	*$0.90*	*$1.50*	£0.20	£0.60	£1.00
6-7 Hulk appears	*$0.30*	*$0.90*	*$1.50*	£0.20	£0.60	£1.00
8	*$0.30*	*$0.90*	*$1.50*	£0.20	£0.60	£1.00

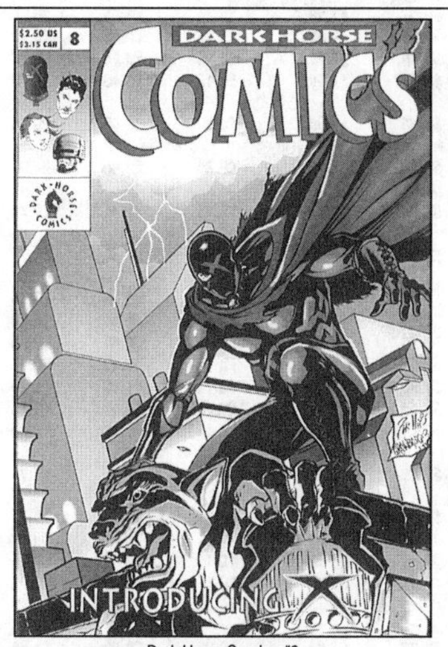

Dark Horse Comics #8

Dark Horse Presents #57

Darkstars #1

Issue	$Good	$Fine	$N.Mint	£Good	£Fine	£N.Mint
9 Quasar appears, Sienkiewicz cover	*$0.30*	*$0.90*	*$1.50*	£0.20	£0.60	£1.00
10 Galactus appears	*$0.30*	*$0.90*	*$1.50*	£0.20	£0.60	£1.00
11 Galactus appears	*$0.25*	*$0.75*	*$1.25*	£0.15	£0.45	£0.75
12-13	*$0.25*	*$0.75*	*$1.25*	£0.15	£0.45	£0.75
14 She-Hulk appears	*$0.25*	*$0.75*	*$1.25*	£0.15	£0.45	£0.75
15 Spiderwoman appears, Sienkiewicz cover	*$0.25*	*$0.75*	*$1.25*	£0.15	£0.45	£0.75
16 Sienkiewicz cover	*$0.25*	*$0.75*	*$1.25*	£0.15	£0.45	£0.75
17 Angel appears	*$0.25*	*$0.75*	*$1.25*	£0.15	£0.45	£0.75
18 Fantastic Four appear, Angel cameo, Sienkiewicz cover	*$0.25*	*$0.75*	*$1.25*	£0.15	£0.45	£0.75
19 Black Bolt appears, Fantastic Four and Angel cameos	*$0.25*	*$0.75*	*$1.25*	£0.15	£0.45	£0.75
20 Angel cameo	*$0.25*	*$0.75*	*$1.25*	£0.15	£0.45	£0.75
21 DS, photo cover, Angel, Avengers, Fantastic Four and Spiderman cameos	*$0.25*	*$0.75*	*$1.25*	£0.15	£0.45	£0.75
22 LD in the U.K. Rogue and Angel appear	*$0.50*	*$1.50*	*$2.50*	£0.30	£0.90	£1.50
23 Rogue and Angel appear, Luke Cage and Iron Fist appear	*$0.25*	*$0.75*	*$1.25*	£0.15	£0.45	£0.75
24 Powerman and Iron Fist appear, Rogue and Angel appear	*$0.25*	*$0.75*	*$1.25*	£0.15	£0.45	£0.75
25	*$0.25*	*$0.75*	*$1.25*	£0.15	£0.45	£0.75
26 LD in the U.K.	*$0.25*	*$0.75*	*$1.25*	£0.20	£0.60	£1.00
27 LD in the U.K. Sienkiewicz run of covers begin, Angel appears	*$0.50*	*$1.50*	*$2.50*	£0.20	£0.60	£1.00
28 LD in the U.K. Rogue appears	*$0.50*	*$1.50*	*$2.50*	£0.20	£0.60	£1.00
29-31	*$0.25*	*$0.75*	*$1.25*	£0.15	£0.45	£0.75
32 Inhumans appear	*$0.25*	*$0.75*	*$1.25*	£0.15	£0.45	£0.75
33-34	*$0.25*	*$0.75*	*$1.25*	£0.15	£0.45	£0.75
35 last Sienkiewicz cover	*$0.25*	*$0.75*	*$1.25*	£0.15	£0.45	£0.75
36 Byrne cover	*$0.25*	*$0.75*	*$1.25*	£0.15	£0.45	£0.75
37	*$0.25*	*$0.75*	*$1.25*	£0.15	£0.45	£0.75
38 very scarce in the U.K. X-Men appear, Paul Chadwick art	*$0.80*	*$2.40*	*$4.00*	£0.30	£0.90	£1.50
39 ND Chadwick art	*$0.25*	*$0.75*	*$1.25*	£0.20	£0.60	£1.00
40 ND Secret Wars II, Chadwick art	*$0.25*	*$0.75*	*$1.25*	£0.20	£0.60	£1.00
41 ND Chadwick art	*$0.25*	*$0.75*	*$1.25*	£0.20	£0.60	£1.00
42 ND scarce in the U.K. Beast appears, Chadwick art	*$0.30*	*$0.90*	*$1.50*	£0.30	£0.90	£1.50
Title Value:	*$12.65*	*$37.95*	*$63.25*	£7.70	£23.10	£38.50

DC 100-PAGE SUPER SPECTACULAR

DC Comics;4 1971-13 Jun 1972; 14 Feb 1973-22 Nov 1973

(No issues #1-3. Becomes 100-Page Super Spectacular #14-22)

Issue	$Good	$Fine	$N.Mint	£Good	£Fine	£N.Mint
4 scarce in the U.K. Weird Mystery Tales; Wrightson art (1pg) and cover	*$2.00*	*$6.00*	*$12.00*	£1.00	£3.00	£6.00
5 ND scarce in the U.K, scarce in the U.S. Love Stories	*$2.50*	*$7.50*	*$15.00*	£1.05	£3.25	£6.50
6 World's Greatest Super-Heroes, reprints Justice League of America #21 (1st Justice Society of America appearance in Silver Age); Neal Adams cover	*$2.00*	*$6.00*	*$12.00*	£1.00	£3.00	£6.00
14 Batman; reprints classic two-part Batman vs. The Mad Monk story from Detective Comics #31 and #32 and Atom's origin from Showcase #34	*$2.50*	*$7.50*	*$15.00*	£1.15	£3.50	£7.00
15 Superboy; reprints Detective Comics #65 the 2nd Boy Commandoes by Joe Simon and Jack Kirby	*$1.25*	*$3.75*	*$7.50*	£0.80	£2.50	£5.00
16 Sgt. Rock; features Haunted Tank, Johnny Cloud and Mlle. Marie reprints	*$1.25*	*$3.75*	*$7.50*	£0.80	£2.50	£5.00
17 Justice League of America; reprints Golden Age Sandman from Adventure Comics #66	*$1.25*	*$3.75*	*$7.50*	£0.80	£2.50	£5.00
18 Superman; reprints classic "Superman Red and Superman Blue" from Superman #166	*$1.25*	*$3.75*	*$7.50*	£0.80	£2.50	£5.00
19 ND Tarzan; Russ Manning newspaper strip reprints	*$1.25*	*$3.75*	*$7.50*	£0.90	£2.75	£5.50
20 Batman; reprints 1st appearance of Two-Face from Detective Comics #66 and #68	*$1.25*	*$3.75*	*$7.50*	£0.90	£2.75	£5.50
21 Superboy; reprints 1st appearance Teen Titans from Brave and the Bold #54	*$1.25*	*$3.75*	*$7.50*	£0.80	£2.50	£5.00
22 Flash; Golden Age Flash reprint from All Flash #13	*$1.25*	*$3.75*	*$7.50*	£0.80	£2.50	£5.00
Title Value:	*$19.00*	*$57.00*	*$114.00*	£10.80	£33.25	£66.50

Note: Numbers 7 to 13 are listed under the individual titles in which they appeared: 7 (Superman #245), 8 (Batman #238), 9 (Our Army at War #242), 10 (Adventure Comics #416), 11 (Flash #214), 12 (Superboy #185), 13 (Superman #252).

ARTISTS

Neal Adams wraparound cover on 6. Part Wrightson art in 4. Wood inks in 5.

FEATURES

Spectre, Johnny Quick, Vigilante, Wildcat, Hawkman, JLA, JSA in 6. Johnny Peril, Phantom Stranger in 4.

REPRINT FEATURES

Aquaman, Dial H for Hero in 15. Atom in 14. Batman in 14, 20. Black Canary in 20. Blackhawk in 14, 20. Boy Commandoes, Hawk and Dove in 15. Captain Storm in 16. Captain Triumph, Hourman, Superman, TNT and Dan the Dynamite in 18. Dollman, Wildcat, Wonder Woman in 14. Dr. Mid-Nite in 20. Elongated Man in 22. Flash, GA Flash, Johnny Quick in 22. Flash, Kid Flash, Robin, Aqualad in 21. Gunner & Sarge, Haunted Tank, Johnny Cloud, Mlle. Marie, Sgt. Rock in 16. JLA, Spectre, Johnny Quick, Vigilante, Wildcat, Hawkman in 6. JLA/JSA in 17. Kid Eternity/LSH in 21. Mystery stories, including Phantom Stranger in 4. Sandman in 15,17. Spectre, Starman in 20.Superboy in 15, 21. Tarzan (Russ Manning newspaper reprints) in 19. Wildcat in 20.

DC CHALLENGE

DC Comics,MS; 1 Nov 1985-12 Oct 1986

Issue	$Good	$Fine	$N.Mint	£Good	£Fine	£N.Mint
1-4 ND	*$0.15*	*$0.45*	*$0.75*	£0.10	£0.30	£0.50
5 ND features Dave Gibbons art	*$0.15*	*$0.45*	*$0.75*	£0.10	£0.30	£0.50
6 ND	*$0.15*	*$0.45*	*$0.75*	£0.10	£0.30	£0.50
7-8 ND Joker appears	*$0.15*	*$0.45*	*$0.75*	£0.10	£0.30	£0.50
9-11 ND	*$0.15*	*$0.45*	*$0.75*	£0.10	£0.30	£0.50
12 ND DS Darkseid appears	*$0.15*	*$0.45*	*$0.75*	£0.10	£0.35	£0.60
Title Value:	*$1.80*	*$5.40*	*$9.00*	£1.20	£3.65	£6.10

Note: all 32pgs; round-robin series, wherein different creative teams continue the previous issue's storyline.

FEATURES/ARTISTS

(Note: main characters only) ***1*** *Superman, Batman, Wonder Woman by Evanier / Colan / Bob Smith;* ***2*** *Superman, Batman, Jonah Hex by Wein / Patton / DeCarlo;* ***3*** *Viking Prince, Hawkman, Aquaman by Moench / Infantino / Bob Smith;* ***4*** *Superman, Zatanna, Detective Chimp by Levitz / Kane / Janson;* ***5*** *Dr.Fate, Captain Marvel, Adam Strange by Mike Barr / Dave Gibbons / Farmer;* ***6*** *Silent Knight, Batman, Adam Strange by Maggin / Jurgens / Malstedt;* ***7*** *Blackhawk, Plastic Man, Deadman, Batman, Joker by Kupperberg / Staton / Mitchell;* ***8*** *Batman, Joker, Blackhawk, New Gods by Conway / Hoberg / Giordano;* ***9*** *Superman, New Teen Titans, Guardians of Oa, Wonder Woman, Batman, Adam Strange by Roy Thomas / Don Heck;* ***10*** *Superman, Deadman, Hawkman, Vigilante, A.Strange by Miskin / Swan / Austin;* ***11*** *Dr. Fate, Superman, Batman by Wolfman / Bates / Giffen / Hunt;* ***12*** *Superman, Batman, Deadman, Dr. Fate & others by various.*

DC COMIC COLLECTION

DC Comics; 1 Jul 1989-2 1989

Issue	$Good	$Fine	$N.Mint	£Good	£Fine	£N.Mint
1 very LD bound collection of selected DC comics - some inc. Batman #417 Ten Nights of the Beast part 1	*$1.20*	*$3.60*	*$6.00*	£0.80	£2.40	£4.00
2 very LD bound collection of selected DC comics	*$0.80*	*$2.40*	*$4.00*	£0.60	£1.80	£3.00
Title Value:	*$2.00*	*$6.00*	*$10.00*	£1.40	£4.20	£7.00

DC COMICS PRESENTS

DC Comics; 1 Jul/Aug 1978-97 Sep 1986

(see Best of DC #13)

[Note: Superman appears in every issue, teamed with the character(s) listed.]

Issue	$Good	$Fine	$N.Mint	£Good	£Fine	£N.Mint
1 Flash	*$0.30*	*$1.00*	*$2.00*	£0.20	£0.60	£1.25
2 ND Flash	*$0.25*	*$0.75*	*$1.50*	£0.25	£0.75	£1.50
3 ND 44pgs, Adam Strange	*$0.25*	*$0.75*	*$1.50*	£0.25	£0.75	£1.50
4 Metal Men	*$0.25*	*$0.75*	*$1.50*	£0.15	£0.50	£1.00
5 Aquaman	*$0.25*	*$0.75*	*$1.50*	£0.15	£0.50	£1.00
6 Green Lantern	*$0.25*	*$0.75*	*$1.50*	£0.15	£0.50	£1.00
7 Red Tornado	*$0.25*	*$0.75*	*$1.50*	£0.15	£0.50	£1.00
8 Swamp Thing	*$0.25*	*$0.75*	*$1.50*	£0.15	£0.50	£1.00
9 Wonder Woman	*$0.25*	*$0.75*	*$1.50*	£0.15	£0.50	£1.00
10 Sgt. Rock	*$0.25*	*$0.75*	*$1.50*	£0.15	£0.50	£1.00
11 Hawkman	*$0.30*	*$0.90*	*$1.50*	£0.15	£0.45	£0.75
12 Mister Miracle	*$0.30*	*$0.90*	*$1.50*	£0.15	£0.45	£0.75
13 Legion of Super-Heroes	*$0.30*	*$0.90*	*$1.50*	£0.15	£0.45	£0.75
14 Superboy	*$0.30*	*$0.90*	*$1.50*	£0.15	£0.45	£0.75
15 Atom	*$0.30*	*$0.90*	*$1.50*	£0.15	£0.45	£0.75
16 Black Lightning	*$0.30*	*$0.90*	*$1.50*	£0.15	£0.45	£0.75
17 Firestorm	*$0.30*	*$0.90*	*$1.50*	£0.15	£0.45	£0.75
18 Zatanna	*$0.30*	*$0.90*	*$1.50*	£0.15	£0.45	£0.75
19 Batgirl	*$0.30*	*$0.90*	*$1.50*	£0.15	£0.45	£0.75
20 Green Arrow	*$0.30*	*$0.90*	*$1.50*	£0.15	£0.45	£0.75
21 Elongated Man	*$0.30*	*$0.90*	*$1.50*	£0.15	£0.45	£0.75
22 Captain Comet	*$0.30*	*$0.90*	*$1.50*	£0.15	£0.45	£0.75
23 Dr. Fate	*$0.30*	*$0.90*	*$1.50*	£0.15	£0.45	£0.75
24 Deadman	*$0.30*	*$0.90*	*$1.50*	£0.15	£0.45	£0.75
25 Phantom Stranger	*$0.30*	*$0.90*	*$1.50*	£0.15	£0.45	£0.75
26 52pgs, Green Lantern; 1st appearance New Teen Titans in insert; Jim Starlin art, George Perez art	*$0.30*	*$0.90*	*$1.50*	£0.80	£2.40	£4.00
27 Jim Starlin art, Manhunter from Mars	*$0.30*	*$0.90*	*$1.50*	£0.15	£0.45	£0.75
28 Jim Starlin art, Supergirl	*$0.30*	*$0.90*	*$1.50*	£0.15	£0.45	£0.75
29 Jim Starlin art, Spectre	*$0.30*	*$0.90*	*$1.50*	£0.15	£0.45	£0.75
30 Black Canary	*$0.30*	*$0.90*	*$1.50*	£0.15	£0.45	£0.75
31 Robin	*$0.30*	*$0.90*	*$1.50*	£0.15	£0.45	£0.75
32 Wonder Woman	*$0.30*	*$0.90*	*$1.50*	£0.15	£0.45	£0.75
33 Shazam	*$0.30*	*$0.90*	*$1.50*	£0.15	£0.45	£0.75
34 Shazam Family	*$0.30*	*$0.90*	*$1.50*	£0.15	£0.45	£0.75
35 Man-Bat	*$0.30*	*$0.90*	*$1.50*	£0.15	£0.45	£0.75
36 Jim Starlin art, Starman	*$0.30*	*$0.90*	*$1.50*	£0.15	£0.45	£0.75
37 Jim Starlin art, Hawkgirl	*$0.30*	*$0.90*	*$1.50*	£0.15	£0.45	£0.75
38 George Perez cover, Flash	*$0.30*	*$0.90*	*$1.50*	£0.15	£0.45	£0.75
39 Plastic Man	*$0.30*	*$0.90*	*$1.50*	£0.15	£0.45	£0.75
40 Metamorpho	*$0.30*	*$0.90*	*$1.50*	£0.15	£0.45	£0.75
41 52pgs, The Joker; Wonder Woman insert, 1st new costume	*$0.60*	*$1.80*	*$3.00*	£0.30	£0.90	£1.50

Issue	$Good	$Fine	$N.Mint	£Good	£Fine	£N.Mint
42 Unknown Soldier	$0.30	$0.90	$1.50	£0.15	£0.45	£0.75
43 Legion of Super-Heroes	$0.30	$0.90	$1.50	£0.15	£0.45	£0.75
44 Dial H For Hero	$0.30	$0.90	$1.50	£0.15	£0.45	£0.75
45 Firestorm	$0.30	$0.90	$1.50	£0.15	£0.45	£0.75
46 The Global Guardians	$0.30	$0.90	$1.50	£0.15	£0.45	£0.75
47 Masters of the Universe	$0.30	$0.90	$1.50	£0.15	£0.45	£0.75
48 Aquaman	$0.30	$0.90	$1.50	£0.15	£0.45	£0.75
49 Shazam	$0.30	$0.90	$1.50	£0.15	£0.45	£0.75
50 Clark Kent; 2pg pin-up of 65 previous co-stars	$0.30	$0.90	$1.50	£0.15	£0.45	£0.75
51 Atom; 16pg Masters of the Universe insert	$0.30	$0.90	$1.50	£0.15	£0.45	£0.75
52 New Doom Patrol; 1st appearance Ambush Bug, cameos of Judge Dredd, Cerebus, Skywise from Elfquest, Giffen art	$0.50	$1.50	$2.50	£0.30	£0.90	£1.50
53 The House of Mystery; 16pg Atari Force insert	$0.30	$0.90	$1.50	£0.15	£0.45	£0.75
54 Green Arrow	$0.30	$0.90	$1.50	£0.15	£0.45	£0.75
55 Airwave; Superboy and original Airwave cameo	$0.30	$0.90	$1.50	£0.15	£0.45	£0.75
56 Power Girl	$0.30	$0.90	$1.50	£0.15	£0.45	£0.75
57 The Atomic Knights	$0.30	$0.90	$1.50	£0.15	£0.45	£0.75
58 Robin, Elongated Man	$0.30	$0.90	$1.50	£0.15	£0.45	£0.75
59 Legion of Substitute-Heroes, Ambush Bug appears, Giffen art	$0.30	$0.90	$1.50	£0.15	£0.45	£0.75
60 Guardians of the Universe	$0.30	$0.90	$1.50	£0.15	£0.45	£0.75
61 George Perez art, Omac	$0.30	$0.90	$1.50	£0.15	£0.45	£0.75
62 Freedom Fighters	$0.30	$0.90	$1.50	£0.15	£0.45	£0.75
63 Amethyst	$0.30	$0.90	$1.50	£0.15	£0.45	£0.75
64 Kamandi	$0.30	$0.90	$1.50	£0.15	£0.45	£0.75
65 Gray Morrow art, Madame Xanadu	$0.30	$0.90	$1.50	£0.15	£0.45	£0.75
66 Joe Kubert art, Demon	$0.30	$0.90	$1.50	£0.15	£0.45	£0.75
67 Curt Swan and Murphy Anderson art, Santa Claus	$0.30	$0.90	$1.50	£0.15	£0.45	£0.75
68 The Vixen	$0.30	$0.90	$1.50	£0.15	£0.45	£0.75
69 Blackhawk	$0.30	$0.90	$1.50	£0.15	£0.45	£0.75
70 Metal Men	$0.30	$0.90	$1.50	£0.15	£0.45	£0.75
71 Bizarro	$0.30	$0.90	$1.50	£0.15	£0.45	£0.75
72 Phantom Stranger; Joker appears	$0.50	$1.50	$2.50	£0.25	£0.75	£1.25
73 Flash, Infantino art	$0.30	$0.90	$1.50	£0.15	£0.45	£0.75
74 Hawkman	$0.30	$0.90	$1.50	£0.15	£0.45	£0.75
75 Arion	$0.30	$0.90	$1.50	£0.15	£0.45	£0.75
76 Wonder Woman	$0.30	$0.90	$1.50	£0.15	£0.45	£0.75
77 The Forgotten Heroes; Dolphin, Animal Man, Congo Bill, Rick Flagg, Rip Hunter, Cave Carson	$0.50	$1.50	$2.50	£0.30	£0.90	£1.50
78 The Forgotten Villains; Ultivac, Atom Master, Krakow, Mr. Poseidon, Enchantress, Faceless Hunter; Space Cabby, Animal Man appear, unofficial Crisis X-over	$0.50	$1.50	$2.50	£0.25	£0.75	£1.25
79 Clark Kent	$0.30	$0.90	$1.50	£0.15	£0.45	£0.75
80 Legion of Super-Heroes	$0.30	$0.90	$1.50	£0.15	£0.45	£0.75
81 Giffen art, Ambush Bug	$0.30	$0.90	$1.50	£0.15	£0.45	£0.75
82 Garcia Lopez art, Adam Strange	$0.30	$0.90	$1.50	£0.15	£0.45	£0.75
83 Batman and the Outsiders	$0.30	$0.90	$1.50	£0.15	£0.45	£0.75
84 Jack Kirby and Toth art, Challengers of the Unknown	$0.30	$0.90	$1.50	£0.15	£0.45	£0.75
85 Swamp Thing, Alan Moore story	$0.50	$1.50	$2.50	£0.25	£0.75	£1.25
86 Supergirl; Crisis X-over	$0.30	$0.90	$1.50	£0.15	£0.45	£0.75
87 Superboy; Crisis X-over, Superman's existence explored	$0.30	$0.90	$1.50	£0.15	£0.45	£0.75
88 Giffen art, Creeper; Crisis X-over	$0.30	$0.90	$1.50	£0.15	£0.45	£0.75
89 Omega Men	$0.30	$0.90	$1.50	£0.15	£0.45	£0.75
90 Firestorm and Captain Atom	$0.30	$0.90	$1.50	£0.15	£0.45	£0.75
91 Captain Comet	$0.30	$0.90	$1.50	£0.15	£0.45	£0.75
92 Vigilante	$0.30	$0.90	$1.50	£0.15	£0.45	£0.75
93 The Elastic Four (Elongated Man, Plastic Man, Elastic Lad, Malleable Man)	$0.30	$0.90	$1.50	£0.15	£0.45	£0.75
94 George Perez cover, Harbinger, Lady Quark, Pariah; post-Crisis issue	$0.30	$0.90	$1.50	£0.15	£0.45	£0.75
95 Hawkman, unofficial Crisis X-over	$0.30	$0.90	$1.50	£0.15	£0.45	£0.75
96 Blue Devil	$0.30	$0.90	$1.50	£0.15	£0.45	£0.75
97 DS, Phantom Zone Villains: Jax-Ur, Dr. Xadu, Faora, General Zod	$0.30	$0.90	$1.50	£0.20	£0.60	£1.00
Title Value:	$29.95	$89.95	$152.50	£16.25	£49.10	£83.75

FEATURES

As above, plus: Air Wave in 40. Earth-2 Atom in 305. Congorilla in 27. Crimson Avenger in 38. Dr.Mid-Nite in 29. Hourman in 25. Johnny Thunder in 28. Mark Merlin, Prince Ra-Man in 32. Rex the Wonder Dog in 35. Richard Dragon in 39. Rip Hunter in 37. Robotman in 31. Sandman in 42. Sargon the Sorcerer in 26. Star Hawkins in 33.

DC COMICS PRESENTS ANNUAL

DC Comics; 1 Sep 1982-4 Oct 1985

Issue	$Good	$Fine	$N.Mint	£Good	£Fine	£N.Mint
1 ND scarce in the U.K. 52pgs, co-stars Golden Age Superman	$0.40	$1.20	$2.00	£0.30	£0.90	£1.50
2 52pgs, Pollard art, 1st appearance Superwoman	$0.40	$1.20	$2.00	£0.25	£0.75	£1.25
3 52pgs, Gill Kane art, co-stars Shazam; intro Captain Thunder	$0.40	$1.20	$2.00	£0.25	£0.75	£1.25
4 52pgs, Barreto art, co-stars Superwoman	$0.40	$1.20	$2.00	£0.25	£0.75	£1.25
Title Value:	$1.60	$4.80	$8.00	£1.05	£3.15	£5.25

DC FOCUS

DC Comics,OS; 1 Summer 1987

Issue	$Good	$Fine	$N.Mint	£Good	£Fine	£N.Mint
1 ND Giveaway checklist and features promotional comic	$0.15	$0.45	$0.75	£0.10	£0.30	£0.50
Title Value:	$0.15	$0.45	$0.75	£0.10	£0.30	£0.50

DC GRAPHIC NOVEL

DC Comics; 1 Nov 1983-7 1986

Issue	$Good	$Fine	$N.Mint	£Good	£Fine	£N.Mint
1 ND Star Raiders; Garcia Lopez art	$1.20	$3.60	$6.00	£0.80	£2.40	£4.00
2 ND Warlords (not from Warlord series)	$1.00	$3.00	$5.00	£0.70	£2.10	£3.50
3 ND The Medusa Chain	$1.00	$3.00	$5.00	£0.70	£2.10	£3.50
4 ND very scarce in the U.K. The Hunger Dogs; Jack Kirby art	$2.40	$7.00	$12.00	£1.60	£4.80	£8.00
5 ND Me and Joe Priest	$1.20	$3.60	$6.00	£0.80	£2.40	£4.00
6 ND Metalzoic (later serialized in British comic 2000AD); Kevin O'Neill art	$1.50	$4.50	$7.50	£1.00	£3.00	£5.00
7 ND Space Clusters; Alex Nino art	$1.00	$3.00	$5.00	£0.70	£2.10	£3.50
Title Value:	$9.30	$27.70	$46.50	£6.30	£18.90	£31.50

Note: all are 68pgs.

DC SAMPLER

DC Comics; 1 Apr 1984-3 Oct 1984

(see DC Spotlight)

Issue	$Good	$Fine	$N.Mint	£Good	£Fine	£N.Mint
1-3 ND 32pgs	$0.15	$0.45	$0.75	£0.10	£0.30	£0.50
Title Value:	$0.45	$1.35	$2.25	£0.30	£0.90	£1.50

Note: contains news, features on current DC titles. No. 3 has "published monthly" in indicia but it was never to be.

DC SCIENCE FICTION GRAPHIC NOVEL

DC Comics; 1 1985-7 1987

Issue	$Good	$Fine	$N.Mint	£Good	£Fine	£N.Mint
1 ND Keith Giffen art, Hell on Earth by Robert Bloch	$1.00	$3.00	$5.00	£0.70	£2.10	£3.50
2 ND Nightwings by Robert Silverberg	$1.00	$3.00	$5.00	£0.70	£2.10	£3.50
3 ND Frost and Fire by Ray Bradbury	$1.00	$3.00	$5.00	£0.70	£2.10	£3.50
4 ND Merchants of Venus by Frederik Pohl	$1.00	$3.00	$5.00	£0.70	£2.10	£3.50
5 ND Rogers art, Demon with a Glass Hand by Harlan Ellison	$1.20	$3.60	$6.00	£0.80	£2.40	£4.00
6 ND The Magic Goes Away by Larry Niven	$1.00	$3.00	$5.00	£0.70	£2.10	£3.50
7 ND Sandkings by George R.R. Martin	$1.00	$3.00	$5.00	£0.70	£2.10	£3.50
Title Value:	$7.20	$21.60	$36.00	£5.00	£15.00	£25.00

Note: adaptations of popular sci-fi books

DC SNEAK PREVIEWS

DC Comics; 1 1991

Issue	$Good	$Fine	$N.Mint	£Good	£Fine	£N.Mint
1 ND 16pgs, promotional giveaway featuring Justice Society of America and Green Lantern: Emerald Dawn II	$0.25	$0.75	$1.25	£0.15	£0.45	£0.75
Title Value:	$0.25	$0.75	$1.25	£0.15	£0.45	£0.75

DC SPECIAL

National Periodical Publications/DC Comics; 1 Oct/Dec 1968-15 Nov/Dec 1971; 16 Spring 1975-29 Aug/Sep 1977

Issue	$Good	$Fine	$N.Mint	£Good	£Fine	£N.Mint
1 68pgs, all Carmine Infantino art	$1.75	$5.25	$12.50	£1.10	£3.40	£8.00
2 scarce in the U.K. 68pgs, Teen Favourites (Binky)	$1.25	$3.85	$9.00	£0.70	£2.10	£5.00
3 very scarce in the U.K. 68pgs, all-Heroines issue; features an un-published Golden Age Wonder Woman story and reprints Green Lantern #16 (1st modern Star Sapphire)	$1.05	$3.20	$7.50	£1.05	£3.20	£7.50
4 68pgs, Mystery Tales	$1.05	$3.20	$7.50	£0.40	£1.25	£3.00
5 68pgs, all Kubert issue (cover and art)	$1.05	$3.20	$7.50	£0.50	£1.50	£3.50
6 68pgs, Wild Frontier	$1.05	$3.20	$7.50	£0.40	£1.25	£3.00
7 68pgs, Strange Sports	$1.05	$3.20	$7.50	£0.40	£1.25	£3.00

	$Good	$Fine	$N.Mint	£Good	£Fine	£N.Mint
8 68pgs, Wanted: The World's Most Dangerous Villains, Joker story/featured on cover	***$1.05***	***$3.20***	***$7.50***	**£0.55**	**£1.70**	**£4.00**
9 68pgs, Strange Sports	***$1.05***	***$3.20***	***$7.50***	**£0.40**	**£1.25**	**£3.00**
10 68pgs, Stop! In the Name of the Law	***$1.25***	***$3.75***	***$7.50***	**£0.50**	**£1.50**	**£3.00**
11 68pgs, The Monsters are Here	***$1.00***	***$3.00***	***$7.00***	**£0.35**	**£1.05**	**£2.50**
12 68pgs, Viking Prince, Kubert reprints	***$1.00***	***$3.00***	***$7.00***	**£0.40**	**£1.25**	**£3.00**
13 68pgs, Strange Sports	***$1.15***	***$3.50***	***$7.00***	**£0.40**	**£1.25**	**£2.50**
14 52pgs, Wanted: The World's Most Dangerous Villains	***$1.00***	***$3.00***	***$7.00***	**£0.40**	**£1.25**	**£3.00**
15 52pgs, Plastic Man, all Jack Cole reprints, including origin from Police Comics #1	***$1.00***	***$3.00***	***$7.00***	**£0.40**	**£1.25**	**£3.00**
16 Super-Heroes vs. Super-Gorillas (see Super-Heroes Battle Super Gorillas)	***$0.80***	***$2.50***	***$5.00***	**£0.40**	**£1.25**	**£2.50**
17 Green Lantern	***$0.80***	***$2.50***	***$5.00***	**£0.40**	**£1.25**	**£2.50**
18 Earth Shaking Disasters	***$0.80***	***$2.50***	***$5.00***	**£0.40**	**£1.25**	**£2.50**
19 ND War Against the Giants	***$0.80***	***$2.50***	***$5.00***	**£0.40**	**£1.25**	**£2.50**
20 Green Lantern	***$0.80***	***$2.50***	***$5.00***	**£0.40**	**£1.25**	**£2.50**
21 ND Super-Heroes War against the Monsters	***$0.80***	***$2.50***	***$5.00***	**£0.30**	**£1.00**	**£2.00**
22-25 Three Musketeers & Robin Hood	***$0.80***	***$2.50***	***$5.00***	**£0.30**	**£1.00**	**£2.00**
26 scarce in the U.K. Enemy Ace; Kubert cover and all art	***$0.80***	***$2.50***	***$5.00***	**£0.50**	**£1.50**	**£3.00**
27 scarce in the U.K. Dinosaurs at Large, all new Captain Comet/Tommy Tomorrow appear; Justice League of America cameo	***$0.80***	***$2.50***	***$5.00***	**£0.50**	**£1.50**	**£3.00**
28 scarce in the U.K. Earth Shattering Disasters, all new Batman/Aquaman/Legion stories	***$0.80***	***$2.50***	***$5.00***	**£0.80**	**£2.50**	**£5.00**
29 scarce in the U.K. Untold Origin of the Justice Society of America, Neal Adams cover	***$0.80***	***$2.50***	***$5.00***	**£0.80**	**£2.50**	**£5.00**
Title Value:	***$27.95***	***$85.75***	***$186.50***	**£14.05**	**£43.70**	**£95.50**

Note: issues 1-13, 16-21 are 68pgs; 14, 15, 22-29 are 52pgs.

FEATURES

All issues are reprint apart from the following new features: Aquaman/Batman in 28. Black Canary in 3 (previously unpublished GA story). Captain Comet in 27. Justice Society of America in 29. Legion of Super-Heroes in 28. Three Musketeers in 22-25.

REPRINT FEATURES

Adam Strange in 1. Batman in 1, 14, 16. Buffalo Bill, Davy Crockett, Daniel Boone, Kit Carson, Pow-Wow Smith, Tomahawk in 6. Captain Marvel in 18. Detective Chimp in 1. Enemy Ace in 26. Flash in 1, 8, 14, 16. Golden Gladiator, Silent Knight in 12. Green Lantern in 3, 8, 14, 16. Hawkman in 5, 8. Marvel Family in 21. Plastic Man in 15. Robin Hood in 12, 22-25. Sgt.Rock in 5. Strange Sports in 1, 7, 9, 13. Supergirl in 3. Superman in 14, 16, 18, 19, 21. Superman/Batman in 8. Viking Prince in 5, 12, 24, 25. War That Time Forgot in 21. Wonder Woman in 3, 16, 19.

DC SPECIAL BLUE RIBBON DIGEST

DC Comics,Digest; 1 Mar/Apr 1980-24 Aug 1982

	$Good	$Fine	$N.Mint	£Good	£Fine	£N.Mint
1 ND scarce in the U.K. Legion of Super-Heroes; reprints Adventure Comics #247 (1st appearance)	***$0.50***	***$1.50***	***$2.50***	**£1.00**	**£3.00**	**£5.00**
2 ND scarce in the U.K. Flash	***$0.50***	***$1.50***	***$2.50***	**£0.60**	**£1.80**	**£3.00**
3 ND scarce in the U.K. Justice Society of America	***$0.50***	***$1.50***	***$2.50***	**£0.60**	**£1.80**	**£3.00**
4 ND scarce in the U.K. Green Lantern	***$0.50***	***$1.50***	***$2.50***	**£0.60**	**£1.80**	**£3.00**
5 ND scarce in the U.K. Secret Origins of Super-Heroes	***$0.50***	***$1.50***	***$2.50***	**£0.60**	**£1.80**	**£3.00**
6 ND Ghosts	***$0.50***	***$1.50***	***$2.50***	**£0.50**	**£1.50**	**£2.50**
7 ND Sgt.Rock's Prize Battle Tales	***$0.50***	***$1.50***	***$2.50***	**£0.50**	**£1.50**	**£2.50**
8 ND Legion of Super-Heroes	***$0.50***	***$1.50***	***$2.50***	**£0.50**	**£1.50**	**£2.50**
9 ND Secret Origins of Super-Heroes	***$0.50***	***$1.50***	***$2.50***	**£0.50**	**£1.50**	**£2.50**
10 ND Warlord	***$0.50***	***$1.50***	***$2.50***	**£0.50**	**£1.50**	**£2.50**
11 ND Justice League of America	***$0.50***	***$1.50***	***$2.50***	**£0.50**	**£1.50**	**£2.50**
12 ND Haunted Tank	***$0.50***	***$1.50***	***$2.50***	**£0.50**	**£1.50**	**£2.50**
13 ND Strange Sports Stories	***$0.50***	***$1.50***	***$2.50***	**£0.50**	**£1.50**	**£2.50**
14 ND UFO Invaders	***$0.50***	***$1.50***	***$2.50***	**£0.50**	**£1.50**	**£2.50**
15 ND Secret Origins of Super-Villains	***$0.50***	***$1.50***	***$2.50***	**£0.50**	**£1.50**	**£2.50**
16 ND Green Lantern, all Neal Adams reprints	***$0.50***	***$1.50***	***$2.50***	**£0.50**	**£1.50**	**£2.50**
17 ND Ghosts	***$0.50***	***$1.50***	***$2.50***	**£0.50**	**£1.50**	**£2.50**
18 ND Sgt. Rock	***$0.50***	***$1.50***	***$2.50***	**£0.50**	**£1.50**	**£2.50**
19 ND Doom Patrol	***$0.50***	***$1.50***	***$2.50***	**£0.50**	**£1.50**	**£2.50**
20 ND Dark Mansion of Forbidden Love	***$0.50***	***$1.50***	***$2.50***	**£0.50**	**£1.50**	**£2.50**
21 ND Our Army at War	***$0.50***	***$1.50***	***$2.50***	**£0.50**	**£1.50**	**£2.50**
22 ND Secret Origins of Super-Heroes	***$0.50***	***$1.50***	***$2.50***	**£0.50**	**£1.50**	**£2.50**
23 ND Green Arrow	***$0.50***	***$1.50***	***$2.50***	**£0.50**	**£1.50**	**£2.50**
24 ND House of Mystery	***$0.50***	***$1.50***	***$2.50***	**£0.50**	**£1.50**	**£2.50**
Title Value:	***$12.00***	***$36.00***	***$60.00***	**£12.90**	**£38.70**	**£64.50**

DC SPECIAL SERIES

DC Comics; 1 1977-27 Fall 1981

Note: All ND in the U.K.

See listings under individual titles, as follows: **1** Five Star Super-Hero Spectacular; **2**, **14**, **17**, **20** Original Swamp Thing Saga; **3** Sgt.Rock Special; **4** Unexpected Special; **5** Superman Spectacular; **6** Secret Society of Super-Villains Special; **7** Ghosts Special; **8** Brave and the Bold Special; **9** Wonder Woman Spectacular; **10** Secret Origins of Super-Heroes Special; **11** Flash Spectacular; **12** Secrets of Haunted House Special; **13** Sgt. Rock Spectacular; **15** Batman Spectacular; **16** Jonah Hex Spectacular; **18** Sgt. Rock's Prize Battle Tales; **19** Secret Origins of Super-Heroes; **21** Super-Star Holiday Special; **22** G.I.Combat; **23** World's Finest Comics Digest; **24** The Flash Digest; **25** Superman II, The Adventure Continues; **26** Superman and His Incredible Fortress of Solitude; **27** Batman vs. The Incredible Hulk. **Note**: Numbers **18**, **19**, **23**, **24** are digest size; numbers **25**, **26**, **27** are tabloid size.

DC SPOTLIGHT

DC Comics,OS; 1 1985

(50th anniversary special giveaway)

	$Good	$Fine	$N.Mint	£Good	£Fine	£N.Mint
1 ND 32pgs, Garcia Lopez cover	***$0.15***	***$0.45***	***$0.75***	**£0.10**	**£0.30**	**£0.50**
Title Value:	***$0.15***	***$0.45***	***$0.75***	**£0.10**	**£0.30**	**£0.50**

Note: contains features on the year's DC projects, including Crisis; 1st published appearance of the Watchmen (1 panel).

DC SUPER-STARS

DC Comics; 1 Mar 1976-18 Jan/Feb 1978

	$Good	$Fine	$N.Mint	£Good	£Fine	£N.Mint
1 Teen Titans	***$1.00***	***$3.00***	***$6.00***	**£0.50**	**£1.50**	**£3.00**
2 scarce in the U.K. Super Stars of Space	***$0.30***	***$1.00***	***$2.00***	**£0.30**	**£1.00**	**£2.00**
3 ND scarce in the U.K. Legion of Super-Heroes	***$0.30***	***$1.00***	***$2.00***	**£0.80**	**£2.50**	**£5.00**
4 Super Stars of Space	***$0.30***	***$1.00***	***$2.00***	**£0.30**	**£1.00**	**£2.00**
5 Flash	***$0.30***	***$1.00***	***$2.00***	**£0.30**	**£1.00**	**£2.00**
6 scarce in the U.K. Super Stars of Space	***$0.30***	***$1.00***	***$2.00***	**£0.40**	**£1.25**	**£2.50**
7 Aquaman	***$0.30***	***$1.00***	***$2.00***	**£0.30**	**£1.00**	**£2.00**
8 Super Stars of Space, reprints 1st Space Ranger from Showcase #15	***$0.65***	***$2.00***	***$4.00***	**£0.30**	**£1.00**	**£2.00**
9 Man Behind the Gun	***$0.30***	***$1.00***	***$2.00***	**£0.25**	**£0.75**	**£1.50**
10 scarce in the U.K. Strange Sports Stories featuring Superman, Batman, Luthor and Joker in new lead story	***$0.80***	***$2.50***	***$5.00***	**£0.50**	**£1.50**	**£3.00**
11 Magic	***$0.25***	***$0.75***	***$1.50***	**£0.25**	**£0.75**	**£1.50**
12 scarce in the U.K. Superboy	***$0.25***	***$0.75***	***$1.50***	**£0.30**	**£1.00**	**£2.00**
13 scarce in the U.K. Sergio Aragones art	***$0.25***	***$0.75***	***$1.50***	**£0.30**	**£1.00**	**£2.00**
14 scarce in the U.K. Secret Origins of Super-Villains, new origins of Gorilla Grodd, Two Face, Dr. Light	***$0.25***	***$0.75***	***$1.50***	**£0.30**	**£1.00**	**£2.00**
15 scarce in the U.K. Sgt. Rock, Unknown Soldier	***$0.30***	***$1.00***	***$2.00***	**£0.30**	**£1.00**	**£2.00**
16 ND 1st appearance Star Hunters	***$0.30***	***$1.00***	***$2.00***	**£0.30**	**£1.00**	**£2.00**
17 ND Secret Origins of Super-Heroes, 1st appearance Huntress, origins Legion/Green Arrow retold	***$0.50***	***$1.50***	***$3.00***	**£0.75**	**£2.25**	**£4.50**
18 Deadman, Phantom Stranger	***$0.30***	***$1.00***	***$2.00***	**£0.25**	**£0.75**	**£1.50**
Title Value:	***$6.95***	***$22.00***	***$44.00***	**£6.70**	**£21.25**	**£42.50**

Note: 1, 2 are 68pgs; 3-18 are 52pgs.

FEATURES

Deadman/Phantom Stranger in 18. Dr.Light, Super-Gorilla Grodd/Green Lantern, Two-Face in 14. GA Flash story re-done in 5. Green Arrow, Huntress, Legion in 17. Sergio Aragones cartoons in 13. Sgt.Rock/Unknown Soldier in 15. Star Hunters in 16. Superboy in 12. Super Heroes vs Super-Villains in 10.

REPRINT FEATURES

Adam Strange in 2, 4, 6, 8. Aqualad, Aquaman in 7. Atomic Knights, Knights of the Galaxy in 2. Captain Comet in 4, 6. Flash in 5, 11; Kid Flash in 5. Green Lantern in 10. Legion in 3. Nighthawk in 9. Space Cabby, Tommy Tomorrow in 6. Space Ranger in 4, 8. Star Rovers in 8. Teen Titans in 1. Zatanna in 11.

DC UNIVERSE HOLIDAY BASH

DC Comics,OS; 1 Jan 1997

	$Good	$Fine	$N.Mint	£Good	£Fine	£N.Mint
1 ND 64pgs, Superman, Batman, Flash, Green Lantern, Catwoman and The New Gods in Christmas stories	***$0.80***	***$2.40***	***$4.00***	**£0.50**	**£1.50**	**£2.50**
Title Value:	***$0.80***	***$2.40***	***$4.00***	**£0.50**	**£1.50**	**£2.50**

DC UNIVERSE: TRINITY

DC Comics,MS; 1 Aug 1993-2 Sep 1993

	$Good	$Fine	$N.Mint	£Good	£Fine	£N.Mint
1-2 ND 48pgs, squarebound, holo-grafix foil cover; Legion '93, Green Lantern Corps and Darkstars begin; features art by Kitson and Charest	***$0.50***	***$1.50***	***$2.50***	**£0.30**	**£0.90**	**£1.50**
Title Value:	***$1.00***	***$3.00***	***$5.00***	**£0.60**	**£1.80**	**£3.00**

DC VERSUS MARVEL

DC Comics/Marvel Comics Group,MS; 1 Jan 1996;4 Apr 1996

(see Marvel versus DC)

	$Good	$Fine	$N.Mint	£Good	£Fine	£N.Mint
1 ND Ron Marz script begins, Dan Jurgens/ Claudio Castellini pencils, Josef Rubenstein/Paul Neary inks; most DC and Marvel major characters appear; card-stock cover	***$1.20***	***$3.60***	***$6.00***	**£0.80**	**£2.40**	**£4.00**
1 2nd printing ND	***$0.70***	***$2.10***	***$3.50***	**£0.50**	**£1.50**	**£2.50**
4 ND Peter David script, Dan Jurgens and Paul Neary art	***$1.00***	***$3.00***	***$5.00***	**£0.60**	**£1.80**	**£3.00**
Title Value:	***$2.90***	***$8.70***	***$14.50***	**£1.90**	**£5.70**	**£9.50**

DC versus Marvel (Oct 1996) Trade paperback

				£Good	£Fine	£N.Mint
ND 192pgs, collects mini-series plus Dr. Strangefate #1				£1.70	£5.10	£8.50

DC/MARVEL: ALL ACCESS

DC Comics/Marvel Comics Group,MS; 1 Dec 1996-4 Feb 1997

1-4 ND 48pgs, Ron Marz script, Jackson Guice and Josef Rubenstein art; most DC and Marvel characters

TRADE PAPERBACKS, GRAPHIC NOVELS AND OTHER COLLECTIONS ARE PRICED IN POUNDS STERLING ONLY. CONVERT AT 1.5 FOR DOLLARS.

	$Good	$Fine	$N.Mint	£Good	£Fine	£N.Mint
appear; bi-weekly	$0.60	$1.80	$3.00	£0.40	£1.20	£2.00
Title Value:	$2.40	$7.20	$12.00	£1.60	£4.80	£8.00

DEAD BOYS
London Night Studios,MS; 1 Sep 1996-3 Nov 1996

	$Good	$Fine	$N.Mint	£Good	£Fine	£N.Mint
1-3 ND Everette Hartsoe script, Stephen Sandoval art; black and white	$0.60	$1.80	$3.00	£0.40	£1.20	£2.00
Title Value:	$1.80	$5.40	$9.00	£1.20	£3.60	£6.00

DEAD CLOWN
Malibu; 1 Oct 1993-2 1993

	$Good	$Fine	$N.Mint	£Good	£Fine	£N.Mint
1-2 ND Chris Ulm script, Joel Thomas pencils	$0.30	$0.90	$1.50	£0.20	£0.60	£1.00
Title Value:	$0.60	$1.80	$3.00	£0.40	£1.20	£2.00

DEAD CREW
Fathom Press,OS; 1 Jun 1992

	$Good	$Fine	$N.Mint	£Good	£Fine	£N.Mint
1 ND Tim Tyler script and art, limited to 1,500 copies; black and white	$0.30	$0.90	$1.50	£0.20	£0.60	£1.00
Title Value:	$0.30	$0.90	$1.50	£0.20	£0.60	£1.00

DEAD HEAT, THE
All American Comics; 1 1990

	$Good	$Fine	$N.Mint	£Good	£Fine	£N.Mint
1 ND	$0.30	$0.90	$1.50	£0.20	£0.60	£1.00
Title Value:	$0.30	$0.90	$1.50	£0.20	£0.60	£1.00

DEAD IN THE WEST
Dark Horse,MS; 1 Oct 1993-2 Jan 1994

	$Good	$Fine	$N.Mint	£Good	£Fine	£N.Mint
1-2 ND 48pgs, painted cover by Tim Truman	$0.80	$2.40	$4.00	£0.50	£1.50	£2.50
Title Value:	$1.60	$4.80	$8.00	£1.00	£3.00	£5.00

DEAD OF NIGHT
Marvel Comics Group; 1 Dec 1973-11 Sep 1975

	$Good	$Fine	$N.Mint	£Good	£Fine	£N.Mint
1 ND	$0.80	$2.50	$5.00	£0.40	£1.25	£2.50
2-3 ND	$0.50	$1.50	$3.00	£0.30	£1.00	£2.00
4 ND Werewolf issue	$0.50	$1.50	$3.00	£0.30	£1.00	£2.00
5 ND	$0.50	$1.50	$3.00	£0.30	£1.00	£2.00
6 ND Jack the Ripper appears	$0.30	$1.00	$2.00	£0.25	£0.75	£1.50
7-9 ND	$0.30	$1.00	$2.00	£0.25	£0.75	£1.50
10 LD in the U.K. Kirby/Ditko reprints	$0.30	$1.00	$2.00	£0.25	£0.75	£1.50
11 ND 1st appearance Scarecrow (note DC villain of the same name)	$0.30	$1.00	$2.00	£0.25	£0.75	£1.50
Title Value:	$4.60	$14.50	$29.00	£3.10	£9.75	£19.50

DEAD WALKERS
Aircel,MS; 1 Jan 1991-4 Apr 1991

	$Good	$Fine	$N.Mint	£Good	£Fine	£N.Mint
1-4 ND b&w	$0.40	$1.20	$2.00	£0.25	£0.75	£1.25
Title Value:	$1.60	$4.80	$8.00	£1.00	£3.00	£5.00

DEADBEATS
Claypool Comics; 1 Jun 1993-present

	$Good	$Fine	$N.Mint	£Good	£Fine	£N.Mint
1-18 ND b&w	$0.50	$1.50	$2.50	£0.30	£0.90	£1.50
19 ND	$0.50	$1.50	$2.50	£0.30	£0.90	£1.50
Title Value:	$9.50	$28.50	$47.50	£5.70	£17.10	£28.50

DEADFACE
(see British section)

DEADFACE: DOING THE ISLANDS WITH BACCHUS
Dark Horse,MS; 1 Jul 1991-3 Sep 1991

	$Good	$Fine	$N.Mint	£Good	£Fine	£N.Mint
1-3 ND 48pgs, Eddie Campbell script and art	$0.50	$1.50	$2.50	£0.30	£0.90	£1.50
Title Value:	$1.50	$4.50	$7.50	£0.90	£2.70	£4.50

DEADFACE: EARTH, AIR, FIRE & WATER
Dark Horse,MS; 1 Aug 1992-4 Dec 1992

	$Good	$Fine	$N.Mint	£Good	£Fine	£N.Mint
1-4 ND Eddie Campbell script and art	$0.50	$1.50	$2.50	£0.30	£0.90	£1.50
Title Value:	$2.00	$6.00	$10.00	£1.20	£3.60	£6.00

DEADLINE U.S.A.
Dark Horse; 1 Nov 1991-3 Jan 1992

	$Good	$Fine	$N.Mint	£Good	£Fine	£N.Mint
1-3 ND 96pgs, features work from British Deadline magazine	$1.50	$4.50	$7.50	£1.00	£3.00	£5.00
Title Value:	$4.50	$13.50	$22.50	£3.00	£9.00	£15.00

DEADLINE USA (2ND SERIES)
Dark Horse; 1 Jun 1992-8 1993

	$Good	$Fine	$N.Mint	£Good	£Fine	£N.Mint
1 ND 48pgs, reprints from UK's Deadline magazine plus new US material	$0.80	$2.40	$4.00	£0.50	£1.50	£2.50
2-8 ND 48pgs	$0.80	$2.40	$4.00	£0.50	£1.50	£2.50
Title Value:	$6.40	$19.20	$32.00	£4.00	£12.00	£20.00

DEADLY DUO
Image; 1 Nov 1994-3 Jan 1995

	$Good	$Fine	$N.Mint	£Good	£Fine	£N.Mint
1 ND Erik Larsen script, spoofing superheroes	$0.50	$1.50	$2.50	£0.30	£0.90	£1.50
2 ND Pitt guest-stars	$0.50	$1.50	$2.50	£0.30	£0.90	£1.50
3 ND Roman from Brigade appears	$0.50	$1.50	$2.50	£0.30	£0.90	£1.50
Title Value:	$1.50	$4.50	$7.50	£0.90	£2.70	£4.50

DEADLY DUO II
Image; 1 Jun 1995-4 Oct 1995

	$Good	$Fine	$N.Mint	£Good	£Fine	£N.Mint
1 ND Erik Larsen script, John Cleary art; Spawn appears	$0.50	$1.50	$2.50	£0.30	£0.90	£1.50
2 ND Freak Force appear	$0.50	$1.50	$2.50	£0.30	£0.90	£1.50
3 ND	$0.50	$1.50	$2.50	£0.30	£0.90	£1.50
4 ND Riptide appears	$0.50	$1.50	$2.50	£0.30	£0.90	£1.50
Title Value:	$2.00	$6.00	$10.00	£1.20	£3.60	£6.00

DEADLY HANDS OF KUNG-FU
Marvel Comics Group,Magazine; 1 Apr 1974-33 Feb 1977

	$Good	$Fine	$N.Mint	£Good	£Fine	£N.Mint
1 ND origin Shang-Chi (3rd ever appearance), Bruce Lee photo pin-up; Jim Starlin art	$0.80	$2.50	$5.00	£0.40	£1.25	£2.50
2 ND Jim Starlin reprint	$0.50	$1.50	$3.00	£0.30	£1.00	£2.00
3 ND Gulacy art	$0.50	$1.50	$3.00	£0.30	£1.00	£2.00
4 ND Bruce Lee cover, 8 page biography on Bruce Lee	$0.50	$1.50	$3.00	£0.30	£1.00	£2.00
5 ND	$0.50	$1.50	$3.00	£0.30	£1.00	£2.00
6-7 George Perez art	$0.40	$1.25	$2.50	£0.30	£1.00	£2.00
8 scarce in the U.K. George Perez art	$0.40	$1.25	$2.50	£0.40	£1.25	£2.50
9-11	$0.40	$1.25	$2.50	£0.30	£1.00	£2.00
12 James Bond feature, George Perez art	$0.50	$1.50	$3.00	£0.40	£1.25	£2.50
13-14	$0.40	$1.25	$2.50	£0.30	£1.00	£2.00
15 squarebound, Annual #1 (Summer 1975), Englehart script, Jim Starlin/Paul Gulacy art, Man Thing appears	$0.40	$1.25	$2.50	£0.40	£1.25	£2.50
16-17	$0.40	$1.25	$2.50	£0.30	£1.00	£2.00
18 Broderick/Austin art	$0.40	$1.25	$2.50	£0.30	£1.00	£2.00
19 George Perez art, Jim Starlin pin-up	$0.40	$1.25	$2.50	£0.30	£1.00	£2.00
20 origin White Tiger, George Perez art	$0.40	$1.25	$2.50	£0.30	£1.00	£2.00
21 George Perez art	$0.40	$1.25	$2.50	£0.25	£0.75	£1.50

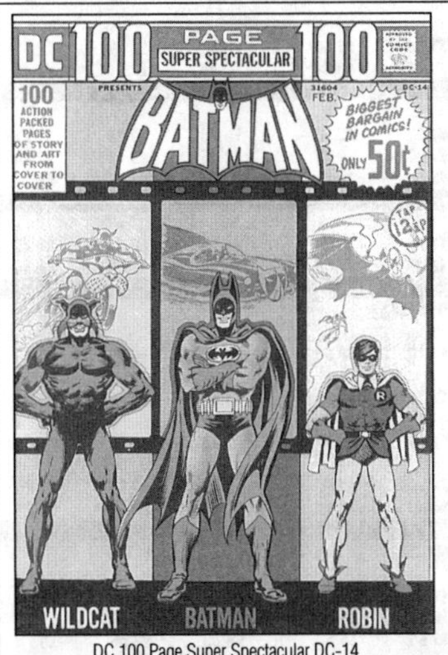

DC 100 Page Super Spectacular DC-14

DC Special #8

DC Versus Marvel #1

Issue	$Good	$Fine	$N.Mint	£Good	£Fine	£N.Mint
22	$0.40	$1.25	$2.50	£0.25	£0.75	£1.50
23 Jack of Hearts appears, Gil Kane art	$0.40	$1.25	$2.50	£0.25	£0.75	£1.50
24 Keith Giffen art	$0.40	$1.25	$2.50	£0.25	£0.75	£1.50
25 Broderick art	$0.40	$1.25	$2.50	£0.25	£0.75	£1.50
26-27	$0.40	$1.25	$2.50	£0.25	£0.75	£1.50
28 full length Bruce Lee life story, Joe Staton art	$0.40	$1.25	$2.50	£0.25	£0.75	£1.50
29 origin Jack of Hearts	$0.40	$1.25	$2.50	£0.25	£0.75	£1.50
30 Jack of Hearts appears, George Perez art	$0.40	$1.25	$2.50	£0.25	£0.75	£1.50
31 Jack of Hearts appears, Joe Staton art	$0.40	$1.25	$2.50	£0.25	£0.75	£1.50
32-33 scarce in the U.K. Marshall Rogers art	$0.65	$2.00	$4.00	£0.40	£1.25	£2.50
Title Value:	$14.60	$45.25	$90.50	£9.95	£31.75	£63.50
Special Album Edition Summer 1974 (sub-titled Deadliest Hands of Kung-Fu) 80pgs featuring Neal Adams inks on Iron Fist, very scarce in the U.K.				£0.75	£2.25	£3.75

Note: Neal Adams painted covers on 1, 2-4, 11, 12, 14, 17. Some others feature covers by Earl Norem.

DEADMAN

DC Comics,MS; 1 May 1985-7 Nov 1985

Issue	$Good	$Fine	$N.Mint	£Good	£Fine	£N.Mint
1 ND Carmine Infantino, Neal Adams reprints	$0.50	$1.50	$2.50	£0.30	£0.90	£1.50
2-7 ND Neal Adams reprints	$0.50	$1.50	$2.50	£0.30	£0.90	£1.50
Title Value:	$3.50	$10.50	$17.50	£2.10	£6.30	£10.50

Note: reprints Strange Adventures #206-216, Brave & Bold #79.

DEADMAN (LIMITED SERIES)

DC Comics,MS; 1 Mar 1986-4 Jun 1986

Issue	$Good	$Fine	$N.Mint	£Good	£Fine	£N.Mint
1 LD in the U.K. Garcia Lopez art begins	$0.30	$0.90	$1.50	£0.20	£0.60	£1.00
2-3	$0.25	$0.75	$1.25	£0.15	£0.45	£0.75
4 John Byrne cover	$0.25	$0.75	$1.25	£0.15	£0.45	£0.75
Title Value:	$1.05	$3.15	$5.25	£0.65	£1.95	£3.25

DEADMAN: EXORCISM

DC Comics,MS; 1 Dec 1992-2 Jan 1993

Issue	$Good	$Fine	$N.Mint	£Good	£Fine	£N.Mint
1-2 ND 48pgs, Mike Baron script, Kelly Jones art	$0.90	$2.70	$4.50	£0.60	£1.80	£3.00
Title Value:	$1.80	$5.40	$9.00	£1.20	£3.60	£6.00
Deadman: Lost Souls (May 1995) Trade paperback reprints Love & Death and Exorcism mini-series				£2.70	£8.10	£13.50

DEADMAN: LOVE AFTER DEATH

DC Comics,MS; 1 Dec 1989-2 Jan 1990

Issue	$Good	$Fine	$N.Mint	£Good	£Fine	£N.Mint
1-2 ND 48pgs, Mike Baron story, Kelly Jones art squarebound	$0.80	$2.40	$4.00	£0.50	£1.50	£2.50
Title Value:	$1.60	$4.80	$8.00	£1.00	£3.00	£5.00

DEADPOOL

Marvel Comics Group,MS; 1 Aug 1993-4 Nov 1993

Issue	$Good	$Fine	$N.Mint	£Good	£Fine	£N.Mint
1 ND embossed Deadpool figure and recessed logo with metallic ink on cover	$0.60	$1.80	$3.00	£0.40	£1.20	£2.00
2-4 ND	$0.50	$1.50	$2.50	£0.30	£0.90	£1.50
Title Value:	$2.10	$6.30	$10.50	£1.30	£3.90	£6.50

DEADPOOL (2ND SERIES)

Marvel Comics Group,MS; 1 Aug 1994-4 Nov 1994

Issue	$Good	$Fine	$N.Mint	£Good	£Fine	£N.Mint
1 ND	$1.00	$3.00	$5.00	£0.60	£1.80	£3.00
2-4 ND	$0.60	$1.80	$3.00	£0.40	£1.20	£2.00
Title Value:	$2.80	$8.40	$14.00	£1.80	£5.40	£9.00
X-Men Premiere (Dec 1995) boxed set collecting issues #1-4, ND				£1.10	£3.30	£5.50
Deadpool: Circle Chase (Jan 1997) Trade paperback ND 96pgs, collects issues #1-4				£1.70	£5.10	£8.50

DEADPOOL (3RD SERIES)

Marvel Comics Group; 1 Jan 1997-present

Issue	$Good	$Fine	$N.Mint	£Good	£Fine	£N.Mint
1 ND Joe Jelly script, Ed McGuiness and Nathan Massengill art begins	$0.60	$1.80	$3.00	£0.40	£1.20	£2.00
2 ND	$0.40	$1.20	$2.00	£0.25	£0.75	£1.25
3 ND Siryn appears	$0.40	$1.20	$2.00	£0.25	£0.75	£1.25
Title Value:	$1.40	$4.20	$7.00	£0.90	£2.70	£4.50

DEADSHOT

DC Comics,MS; 1 Nov 1988-4 Feb 1989

(see Suicide Squad)

Issue	$Good	$Fine	$N.Mint	£Good	£Fine	£N.Mint
1 Batman appears	$0.20	$0.60	$1.00	£0.10	£0.30	£0.50
2-4	$0.20	$0.60	$1.00	£0.10	£0.30	£0.50
Title Value:	$0.80	$2.40	$4.00	£0.40	£1.20	£2.00

DEADTALES: A BODY

Caliber Press,OS; 1 Dec 1991

Issue	$Good	$Fine	$N.Mint	£Good	£Fine	£N.Mint
1 ND reprints from Deadworld #10-13	$0.50	$1.50	$2.50	£0.30	£0.90	£1.50
Title Value:	$0.50	$1.50	$2.50	£0.30	£0.90	£1.50

DEADTIME STORIES

Now Comics,OS; 1 Nov 1987

Issue	$Good	$Fine	$N.Mint	£Good	£Fine	£N.Mint
1 ND Bissette, Breyfogle art, Mike Mignola, Jim Starlin, Art Adams, Gulacy, Walt Simonson, Jones illustrations	$0.50	$1.50	$2.50	£0.30	£0.90	£1.50
Title Value:	$0.50	$1.50	$2.50	£0.30	£0.90	£1.50

DEADWORLD

Arrow; 1 Nov 1987-26 Nov 1992 (Caliber 11 on)

Issue	$Good	$Fine	$N.Mint	£Good	£Fine	£N.Mint
1 ND	$0.60	$1.80	$3.00	£0.40	£1.20	£2.00
2 ND very scarce in the U.K.	$0.50	$1.50	$2.50	£0.50	£1.50	£2.50
3 ND scarce in the U.K.	$0.50	$1.50	$2.50	£0.40	£1.20	£2.00
4-5 ND scarce in the U.K.	$0.40	$1.20	$2.00	£0.35	£1.05	£1.75
6-15 ND	$0.40	$1.20	$2.00	£0.30	£0.90	£1.50
16-25 ND	$0.30	$0.90	$1.50	£0.25	£0.75	£1.25
26 ND	$0.60	$1.80	$3.00	£0.40	£1.20	£2.00
Title Value:	$10.00	$30.00	$47.50	£7.90	£23.70	£39.50

Note: issues #5-26 are published with 2 cover versions, "graphic" or "tame"; prices are the same for either.

Issue	$Good	$Fine	$N.Mint	£Good	£Fine	£N.Mint
Trade paperback: Deadworld Book 1, reprints issues #1-7				£1.50	£4.50	£7.50
Trade paperback: Deadworld Book 2, reprints issues #8-16				£1.50	£4.50	£7.50

DEADWORLD (2ND SERIES)

Caliber Press; 1 May 1993-15 1995?

Issue	$Good	$Fine	$N.Mint	£Good	£Fine	£N.Mint
1 ND b&w begins	$0.60	$1.80	$3.00	£0.40	£1.20	£2.00
1 Limited Edition, ND - red foil enhanced cover	$1.20	$3.60	$6.00	£0.80	£2.40	£4.00
2 ND	$0.60	$1.80	$3.00	£0.40	£1.20	£2.00
2 Limited Edition, ND - signed, pre-bagged with poster	$1.20	$3.60	$6.00	£0.80	£2.40	£4.00
3-4 ND	$0.60	$1.80	$3.00	£0.40	£1.20	£2.00
5 ND die-cut cover	$0.60	$1.80	$3.00	£0.40	£1.20	£2.00
5 Collectors Set, ND - pre-bagged with a copy of issue #1 and trading card	$1.20	$3.60	$6.00	£0.80	£2.40	£4.00
6-9 ND	$0.60	$1.80	$3.00	£0.40	£1.20	£2.00
10-15 ND Death Call story	$0.60	$1.80	$3.00	£0.40	£1.20	£2.00
Title Value:	$12.60	$37.80	$63.00	£8.40	£25.20	£42.00

DEADWORLD ARCHIVES

Caliber Press; 1 Jan 1993-4 Apr 1993

Issue	$Good	$Fine	$N.Mint	£Good	£Fine	£N.Mint
1 ND reprints from Deadworld series begin; solid black cover with red droplets	$0.50	$1.50	$2.50	£0.30	£0.90	£1.50
2-4 ND	$0.50	$1.50	$2.50	£0.30	£0.90	£1.50
Title Value:	$2.00	$6.00	$10.00	£1.20	£3.60	£6.00

DEADWORLD: BITS AND PIECES

Caliber Press,OS; 1 Oct 1991

Issue	$Good	$Fine	$N.Mint	£Good	£Fine	£N.Mint
1 ND reprints from Caliber Presents #2 and #8 being the first Deadworld story	$0.50	$1.50	$2.50	£0.30	£0.90	£1.50
Title Value:	$0.50	$1.50	$2.50	£0.30	£0.90	£1.50

DEADWORLD: TO KILL A KING

Caliber Press,MS; 1 1992-3 Aug 1993

Issue	$Good	$Fine	$N.Mint	£Good	£Fine	£N.Mint
1 ND	$0.60	$1.80	$3.00	£0.40	£1.20	£2.00
1 Limited Edition ND	$1.20	$3.60	$6.00	£0.80	£2.40	£4.00
2 ND	$0.60	$1.80	$3.00	£0.40	£1.20	£2.00
2 Limited Edition ND	$1.20	$3.60	$6.00	£0.80	£2.40	£4.00
3 ND	$0.60	$1.80	$3.00	£0.40	£1.20	£2.00
Title Value:	$4.20	$12.60	$21.00	£2.80	£8.40	£14.00

DEATH DEALER

Verotik; 1 Jul 1995-2 1996

Issue	$Good	$Fine	$N.Mint	£Good	£Fine	£N.Mint
1 ND 48pgs, squarebound; Glenn Danzig script, Simon Bisley art and covers by Frank Frazetta begin	$1.50	$4.50	$7.50	£1.00	£3.00	£5.00
1 2nd printing ND	$1.20	$3.60	$6.00	£0.80	£2.40	£4.00
2 ND 64pgs	$1.40	$4.20	$7.00	£0.90	£2.70	£4.50
Title Value:	$4.10	$12.30	$20.50	£2.70	£8.10	£13.50

DEATH DUTY

Marvel UK; 1 Dec 1993

Issue	$Good	$Fine	$N.Mint	£Good	£Fine	£N.Mint
1 contains four-card uncut sheet	$0.30	$0.90	$1.50	£0.20	£0.60	£1.00
Title Value:	$0.30	$0.90	$1.50	£0.20	£0.60	£1.00

DEATH GALLERY

DC Comics,OS; 1 Jan 1994

Issue	$Good	$Fine	$N.Mint	£Good	£Fine	£N.Mint
1 ND pin-ups of Death by Arthur Adams, Brian Bolland, Dave Gibbons plus Mike Kaluta, Dave McKean, Joe Quesada, Brian Talbot, Charles Vess and lots of others	$0.60	$1.80	$3.00	£0.40	£1.20	£2.00
Title Value:	$0.60	$1.80	$3.00	£0.40	£1.20	£2.00

DEATH HAWK

Adventure; 1 May 1988-3 Nov 1988

Issue	$Good	$Fine	$N.Mint	£Good	£Fine	£N.Mint
1 ND Hughes art	$0.40	$1.20	$2.00	£0.25	£0.75	£1.25
2-3 ND	$0.40	$1.20	$2.00	£0.25	£0.75	£1.25
Title Value:	$1.20	$3.60	$6.00	£0.75	£2.25	£3.75

DEATH HUNT

Eternity; 1,2 1987

Issue	$Good	$Fine	$N.Mint	£Good	£Fine	£N.Mint
1-2 ND	$0.40	$1.20	$2.00	£0.25	£0.75	£1.25
Title Value:	$0.80	$2.40	$4.00	£0.50	£1.50	£2.50

DEATH III

Marvel UK,MS; 1 Sep 1993-4 Dec 1993

Issue	$Good	$Fine	$N.Mint	£Good	£Fine	£N.Mint
1 foil embossed cover	$0.40	$1.20	$2.00	£0.30	£0.90	£1.50
2 Death's Head II appears with Ghost Rider, Kingpin, Thing, Dr. Octopus and Iron Man	$0.40	$1.20	$2.00	£0.25	£0.75	£1.25
3 Death's Head II appears with Hulk, Storm, Cable and Thing	$0.40	$1.20	$2.00	£0.25	£0.75	£1.25
4 Death's Head II appears	$0.40	$1.20	$2.00	£0.25	£0.75	£1.25
Title Value:	$1.60	$4.80	$8.00	£1.05	£3.15	£5.25

DEATH METAL VS. GENETIX

Marvel UK,MS; 1 Dec 1993-4 Mar 1994

Issue	$Good	$Fine	$N.Mint	£Good	£Fine	£N.Mint
1 pre-bagged with 2 trading cards	$0.40	$1.20	$2.00	£0.25	£0.75	£1.25
2-4	$0.30	$0.90	$1.50	£0.20	£0.60	£1.00
Title Value:	$1.30	$3.90	$6.50	£0.85	£2.55	£4.25

DEATH RACE 2020

Cosmic Comics; 1 Apr 1995-8 Aug 1996

Issue	$Good	$Fine	$N.Mint	£Good	£Fine	£N.Mint
1-3 ND Pat Mills script, Tony Skinner and Kev O'Neill art; based on Roger Corman's film Deathrace 2000; bi-monthly	$0.50	$1.50	$2.50	£0.30	£0.90	£1.50
4 ND Pat Mills script, Kev O'Neill and Tony Skinner art; based on Roger Corman's film Death Race 2000	$0.50	$1.50	$2.50	£0.30	£0.90	£1.50
5-8 ND Pat Mills and Tony Skinner script	$0.50	$1.50	$2.50	£0.30	£0.90	£1.50
Title Value:	$4.00	$12.00	$20.00	£2.40	£7.20	£12.00

DEATH RACE 2021

Cosmic Comics; 1 Jan 1996-2 1996

Issue	$Good	$Fine	$N.Mint	£Good	£Fine	£N.Mint
1-2 ND Pat Mills script	$0.50	$1.50	$2.50	£0.30	£0.90	£1.50
Title Value:	$1.00	$3.00	$5.00	£0.60	£1.80	£3.00

DEATH RATTLE

Kitchen Sink; 1 Oct 1985-18 Sep 1988

(previous series Underground-type comic)

Issue	$Good	$Fine	$N.Mint	£Good	£Fine	£N.Mint
1 ND Richard Corben cover, colour begins	$0.40	$1.20	$2.00	£0.25	£0.75	£1.25
2-4 ND	$0.40	$1.20	$2.00	£0.25	£0.75	£1.25
5 ND last colour issue	$0.40	$1.20	$2.00	£0.25	£0.75	£1.25
6-7 ND	$0.40	$1.20	$2.00	£0.25	£0.75	£1.25
8 ND Xenozoic Tales preview	$0.40	$1.20	$2.00	£0.25	£0.75	£1.25
9 ND	$0.40	$1.20	$2.00	£0.25	£0.75	£1.25
10 ND Charles Burns cover	$0.40	$1.20	$2.00	£0.25	£0.75	£1.25
11 ND photo cover	$0.40	$1.20	$2.00	£0.25	£0.75	£1.25
12-17 ND	$0.40	$1.20	$2.00	£0.25	£0.75	£1.25
18 ND 44pgs, Frank Miller cover	$0.40	$1.20	$2.00	£0.30	£0.90	£1.50
Title Value:	$7.20	$21.60	$36.00	£4.55	£13.65	£22.75

DEATH RATTLE (2ND SERIES)

Kitchen Sink; 1 Oct 1995

Issue	$Good	$Fine	$N.Mint	£Good	£Fine	£N.Mint
1 ND Mark Schultz cover and lead story	$0.60	$1.80	$3.00	£0.40	£1.20	£2.00
Title Value:	$0.60	$1.80	$3.00	£0.40	£1.20	£2.00

DEATH TALKS ABOUT LIFE

DC Comics,OS; nn 1993

Issue	$Good	$Fine	$N.Mint	£Good	£Fine	£N.Mint
nn ND 8pgs, promotional giveaway with Death talking about AIDS; Neil Gaiman script, Dave McKean art	$0.15	$0.45	$0.75	£0.10	£0.30	£0.50
Title Value:	$0.15	$0.45	$0.75	£0.10	£0.30	£0.50

DEATH'S HEAD

Crystal; 1 Dec 1987-2 Feb 1988

Issue	$Good	$Fine	$N.Mint	£Good	£Fine	£N.Mint
1-2 ND black and white (note: no relation to Marvel character!)	$0.40	$1.20	$2.00	£0.25	£0.75	£1.25
Title Value:	$0.80	$2.40	$4.00	£0.50	£1.50	£2.50

DEATH'S HEAD

Marvel Comics Group; 1 Mar 1989-10 Dec 1989

(see Marvel Graphic Novel)

Issue	$Good	$Fine	$N.Mint	£Good	£Fine	£N.Mint
1	$0.60	$1.80	$3.00	£0.60	£1.80	£3.00
2	$0.50	$1.50	$2.50	£0.50	£1.50	£2.50
3	$0.40	$1.20	$2.00	£0.40	£1.20	£2.00
4-7	$0.30	$0.90	$1.50	£0.30	£0.90	£1.50
8 Dr. Who appears	$0.30	$0.90	$1.50	£0.30	£0.90	£1.50
9 Simonson cover	$0.30	$0.90	$1.50	£0.30	£0.90	£1.50
10 less common in the U.K.	$0.30	$0.90	$1.50	£0.35	£1.05	£1.75
Title Value:	$3.60	$10.80	$18.00	£3.65	£10.95	£18.25
Trade paperback (1991), reprints				£1.25	£3.75	£6.25

DEATH'S HEAD II

Marvel Comics Group,MS; 1 Mar 1992-4 Jun 1992

Issue	$Good	$Fine	$N.Mint	£Good	£Fine	£N.Mint
1 Dan Abnett script begins, Liam Sharp art; origin Death's Head II	$0.60	$1.80	$3.00	£0.40	£1.20	£2.00
1 2nd printing, silver ink cover	$0.40	$1.20	$2.00	£0.25	£0.75	£1.25
2 Fantastic Four appear	$0.50	$1.50	$2.50	£0.30	£0.90	£1.50
2 2nd printing, silver ink cover	$0.40	$1.20	$2.00	£0.25	£0.75	£1.25
3 less common in the U.K. 1st appearance Tuck, origin Charnel	$0.50	$1.50	$2.50	£0.30	£0.90	£1.50
4 alternate future Spiderman, Punisher, Daredevil, She-Hulk and Wolverine appear	$0.50	$1.50	$2.50	£0.30	£0.90	£1.50
Title Value:	$2.90	$8.70	$14.50	£1.80	£5.40	£9.00
Treat Pedigree Collection (1992) Issues #1-4 (all 1st prints) sealed in plastic display case; 50,000 units with gold seal on outside, ND				£2.50	£7.50	£12.50

DEATH'S HEAD II (2ND SERIES)

Marvel UK; 1 Dec 1992-16 Mar 1994

Issue	$Good	$Fine	$N.Mint	£Good	£Fine	£N.Mint
1 X-Men appear, Liam Sharp art begins	$0.40	$1.20	$2.00	£0.30	£0.90	£1.50
2 Lotus FX story begins (ends #4); Wolverine appears	$0.40	$1.20	$2.00	£0.25	£0.75	£1.25
3 1st appearance Raptor	$0.40	$1.20	$2.00	£0.25	£0.75	£1.25
4 X-Men appear	$0.40	$1.20	$2.00	£0.25	£0.75	£1.25
5 MyS-TECH Wars X-over, Warheads appear, Dell Barras art	$0.40	$1.20	$2.00	£0.25	£0.75	£1.25
6 $1.95 cover begins; Simon Coleby art begins	$0.40	$1.20	$2.00	£0.25	£0.75	£1.25
7 Liam Sharp cover only	$0.40	$1.20	$2.00	£0.25	£0.75	£1.25
8 Liam Sharp cover only; Anthony Williams art	$0.40	$1.20	$2.00	£0.25	£0.75	£1.25
9	$0.40	$1.20	$2.00	£0.25	£0.75	£1.25
10 The Origin of Death's Head II; Dougie Braithewaite art	$0.40	$1.20	$2.00	£0.25	£0.75	£1.25
11-13	$0.30	$0.90	$1.50	£0.20	£0.60	£1.00
14 metallic blue foil cover with flip-side 8pg Death's Head Gold #0 prologue; Sal Larocca art	$0.40	$1.20	$2.00	£0.30	£0.90	£1.50
15-16	$0.30	$0.90	$1.50	£0.20	£0.60	£1.00
Title Value:	$5.90	$17.70	$29.50	£3.85	£11.55	£19.25

Note: #5 not reprinted in Overkill

Issue	$Good	$Fine	$N.Mint	£Good	£Fine	£N.Mint
Death's Head II Gold #0 (Jan 1994) Liam Sharp story and pencils				£0.45	£1.35	£2.25

DEATH'S HEAD II/DIE CUT

Marvel UK,MS; 1 Aug 1993-2 Sep 1993

Issue	$Good	$Fine	$N.Mint	£Good	£Fine	£N.Mint
1 foil embossed logo on cover	$0.40	$1.20	$2.00	£0.25	£0.75	£1.25
2 Liam Sharp cover	$0.30	$0.90	$1.50	£0.20	£0.60	£1.00
Title Value:	$0.70	$2.10	$3.50	£0.45	£1.35	£2.25

DEATH'S HEAD II/KILLPOWER: BATTLETIDE

Marvel UK,MS; 1 Dec 1992-4 Mar 1993

Issue	$Good	$Fine	$N.Mint	£Good	£Fine	£N.Mint
1 Wolverine, Captain America and Hulk appear	$0.40	$1.20	$2.00	£0.25	£0.75	£1.25
2 Wolverine, Dark Angel, Hercules appear	$0.30	$0.90	$1.50	£0.20	£0.60	£1.00
3 Wolverine, Hercules, Psylocke, Dark Angel appear	$0.30	$0.90	$1.50	£0.20	£0.60	£1.00
4 Wolverine, Psylocke, Dark Angel appear	$0.30	$0.90	$1.50	£0.20	£0.60	£1.00
Title Value:	$1.30	$3.90	$6.50	£0.85	£2.55	£4.25

DEATH'S HEAD II/KILLPOWER: BATTLETIDE II

Marvel UK,MS; 1 Aug 1993-4 Nov 1993

Issue	$Good	$Fine	$N.Mint	£Good	£Fine	£N.Mint
1-4 Hulk appears	$0.30	$0.90	$1.50	£0.20	£0.60	£1.00
Title Value:	$1.20	$3.60	$6.00	£0.80	£2.40	£4.00

DEATH'S HEAD, THE INCOMPLETE

Marvel UK,MS; 1 Jan 1993-12 Dec 1993

Issue	$Good	$Fine	$N.Mint	£Good	£Fine	£N.Mint
1 DS reprints begin from original Marvel UK series Dr. Who Monthly with new linking art, die-cut cover	$0.40	$1.20	$2.00	£0.25	£0.75	£1.25
2-4	$0.30	$0.90	$1.50	£0.20	£0.60	£1.00
5 Dr. Who appears	$0.30	$0.90	$1.50	£0.20	£0.60	£1.00
6-11	$0.30	$0.90	$1.50	£0.20	£0.60	£1.00
12 48pgs	$0.40	$1.20	$2.00	£0.25	£0.75	£1.25
Title Value:	$3.80	$11.40	$19.00	£2.50	£7.50	£12.50

Note: contains new linking material by Dan Abnett and Simon Coleby

DEATH: THE HIGH COST OF LIVING

DC Comics/Vertigo,MS; 1 Mar 1993-3 May 1993

(see Sandman [2nd Series])

Issue	$Good	$Fine	$N.Mint	£Good	£Fine	£N.Mint
1 features Sandman's sister Death, scripts by Neil Gaiman, pencils by Chris Bachalo, inks by Mark Buckingham, covers by Dave McKean	$1.60	$4.80	$8.00	£0.50	£1.50	£2.50
1 Platinum Edition ND	$6.00	$18.00	$30.00	£3.00	£9.00	£15.00
1 Signed & Numered Edition, ND (Jun 1993) - 7,500 copies, signed by Chris Bachalo with certificate of authenticity	$3.00	$9.00	$15.00	£2.00	£6.00	£10.00
2 less common in the U.K.	$1.60	$4.80	$8.00	£0.60	£1.80	£3.00
3	$1.00	$3.00	$5.00	£0.50	£1.50	£2.50
Title Value:	$13.20	$39.60	$66.00	£6.60	£19.80	£33.00
Death: The High Cost Of Living (Jan 1994) Hardcover Edition with dust-jacket				£2.70	£8.10	£13.50

DEATH: THE TIME OF YOUR LIFE

DC Comics/Vertigo,MS; 1 Apr 1996-3 Jun 1996

Issue	$Good	$Fine	$N.Mint	£Good	£Fine	£N.Mint
1 ND Neil Gaiman script, Chris Bachalo and Mark Buckingham art	$0.80	$2.40	$4.00	£0.50	£1.50	£2.50
2-3 ND Neil Gaiman script, Chris Bachalo and Mark Buckingham art	$0.60	$1.80	$3.00	£0.40	£1.20	£2.00
Title Value:	$2.00	$6.00	$10.00	£1.30	£3.90	£6.50

DEATHBLOW

Image; 0 Aug 1996; 1 May 1993-29 Aug 1996

Issue	$Good	$Fine	$N.Mint	£Good	£Fine	£N.Mint
0 ND Deathblow story from Darker Image #1 completed	$0.60	$1.80	$3.00	£0.40	£1.20	£2.00
1 ND Jim Lee and Brandon Choi story begins with Jim Lee art plus Cybernary back-up featuring Steve Gerber script and Nick Manabat art	$0.60	$1.80	$3.00	£0.35	£1.05	£1.75
2 ND detachable Deathblow poster included	$0.50	$1.50	$2.50	£0.30	£0.90	£1.50
3 ND less common	$0.80	$2.40	$4.00	£0.30	£0.90	£1.50
4 ND Tim Sale art	$0.50	$1.50	$2.50	£0.30	£0.90	£1.50
5 ND Tim Sale art	$0.50	$1.50	$2.50	£0.80	£2.40	£4.00
5 Variant Cover Edition, ND cover forms larger picture when combined with variant covers of Gen 13 #5, Kindred #3, Stormwatch #10, Team 7 #1, Union #0, Wetworks #2, WildC.A.T.S #11	$2.00	$6.00	$10.00	£1.40	£4.20	£7.00
6-13 ND Tim Sale art	$0.40	$1.20	$2.00	£0.30	£0.90	£1.50
14 ND Johnny Savoy from WetWorks appears, Tim Sale art	$0.50	$1.50	$2.50	£0.30	£0.90	£1.50
15 ND Tim Sale art	$0.50	$1.50	$2.50	£0.30	£0.90	£1.50

16 ND Wildstorm Rising part 6, continued in Wetworks #8; with two foil-bagged painted trading cards.

	$Good	$Fine	$N.Mint	£Good	£Fine	£N.Mint
Cover by Barry Windor-Smith						
	$0.50	$1.50	$2.50	£0.30	£0.90	£1.50
16 Newstand Edition, ND without trading cards						
	$0.40	$1.20	$2.00	£0.25	£0.75	£1.25
17-19 ND	$0.50	$1.50	$2.50	£0.30	£0.90	£1.50
20 ND Gen 13 appear						
	$0.50	$1.50	$2.50	£0.30	£0.90	£1.50
21 ND Brothers in Arms part 2, guest starring Gen 13						
	$0.50	$1.50	$2.50	£0.30	£0.90	£1.50
22 ND Brothers in Arms part 3, guest starring Dane from Wetworks						
	$0.50	$1.50	$2.50	£0.30	£0.90	£1.50
23 ND Brothers in Arms part 4, guest starring Backlash						
	$0.50	$1.50	$2.50	£0.30	£0.90	£1.50
24-25 ND Grifter guest-stars						
	$0.50	$1.50	$2.50	£0.30	£0.90	£1.50
26 ND leads into Fire From Heaven #1						
	$0.50	$1.50	$2.50	£0.30	£0.90	£1.50
27 ND Fire From Heaven part 8, continued in Gen 13 #11						
	$0.50	$1.50	$2.50	£0.30	£0.90	£1.50
28 ND Fire From Heaven part 15, continued in Sword of Damocles #2						
	$0.50	$1.50	$2.50	£0.30	£0.90	£1.50
29 ND	$0.50	$1.50	$2.50	£0.30	£0.90	£1.50
Title Value:	$17.10	$51.30	$87.00	£11.30	£33.90	£56.50
Deathblow (Sep 1995) Trade paperback						
ND reprints The Black Angel Saga				£2.70	£8.10	£13.50

DEATHBLOW/WOLVERINE

Image,MS; 1 Sep 1996-2 Oct 1996

	$Good	$Fine	$N.Mint	£Good	£Fine	£N.Mint
1-2 ND Aron Weisenfeld script, Richard and Monica Bennett art						
	$0.50	$1.50	$2.50	£0.30	£0.90	£1.50
Title Value:	$1.00	$3.00	$5.00	£0.60	£1.80	£3.00

DEATHLOK

Marvel Comics Group; 1 Jul 1991-34 Apr 1994

(see Astonishing Tales)

	$Good	$Fine	$N.Mint	£Good	£Fine	£N.Mint
1 ND story continues from mini-series						
	$0.30	$0.90	$1.50	£0.30	£0.90	£1.50
2 ND The Cybernet Saga part 1, Dr. Doom appears						
	$0.30	$0.90	$1.50	£0.25	£0.75	£1.25
3 ND The Cybernet Saga, Deathlok vs. Dr. Doom						
	$0.30	$0.90	$1.50	£0.25	£0.75	£1.25
4 ND The Cybernet Saga, X-Men, Fantastic Four, Vision appear						
	$0.30	$0.90	$1.50	£0.25	£0.75	£1.25
5 ND The Cybernet Saga, X-Men, Fantastic Four appear						
	$0.30	$0.90	$1.50	£0.25	£0.75	£1.25
6 ND Deathlok vs. Punisher						
	$0.30	$0.90	$1.50	£0.20	£0.60	£1.00
6 Signed & Numbered Edition, ND - Punisher appears, signed by artist Denys Cowan (5,000 copies)						
	$0.80	$2.40	$4.00	£0.50	£1.50	£2.50
7 ND Punisher appears						
	$0.30	$0.90	$1.50	£0.20	£0.60	£1.00
8 ND	$0.30	$0.90	$1.50	£0.20	£0.60	£1.00
9-10 ND Ghost Rider appears						
	$0.30	$0.90	$1.50	£0.20	£0.60	£1.00
11 ND	$0.25	$0.75	$1.25	£0.15	£0.45	£0.75
12 ND Biohazard Agenda part 1, Nick Fury appears						
	$0.25	$0.75	$1.25	£0.15	£0.45	£0.75
13-15 ND Biohazard Agenda						
	$0.25	$0.75	$1.25	£0.15	£0.45	£0.75
16 ND Infinity War X-over						
	$0.25	$0.75	$1.25	£0.15	£0.45	£0.75
17 ND Cyberwar story begins						
	$0.25	$0.75	$1.25	£0.15	£0.45	£0.75
18-19 ND Cyberwar story, Silver Sable appears						
	$0.25	$0.75	$1.25	£0.15	£0.45	£0.75
20 ND Cyberwar story						
	$0.25	$0.75	$1.25	£0.15	£0.45	£0.75
21 ND Cyberwar story, Nick Fury appears						
	$0.25	$0.75	$1.25	£0.15	£0.45	£0.75
22-24 ND Black Panther appears						
	$0.25	$0.75	$1.25	£0.15	£0.45	£0.75
25 ND 48pgs, Black Panther appears, holo-grafix foil cover						
	$0.40	$1.20	$2.00	£0.25	£0.75	£1.25
26 ND Hobgoblin appears; new direction for title						
	$0.25	$0.75	$1.25	£0.15	£0.45	£0.75
27 ND	$0.25	$0.75	$1.25	£0.15	£0.45	£0.75
28-29 ND Infinity Crusade X-over						
	$0.25	$0.75	$1.25	£0.15	£0.45	£0.75
30 ND the original Deathlok returns						
	$0.25	$0.75	$1.25	£0.15	£0.45	£0.75
31-34 ND	$0.25	$0.75	$1.25	£0.15	£0.45	£0.75
Title Value:	$9.95	$29.85	$49.75	£6.50	£19.50	£32.50

Note: Bookshelf Format

DEATHLOK (LIMITED SERIES)

Marvel Comics Group,MS; 1 Jul 1990-4 Oct 1990

	$Good	$Fine	$N.Mint	£Good	£Fine	£N.Mint
1 ND 48pgs, squarebound card cover format begins						
	$0.80	$2.40	$4.00	£0.50	£1.50	£2.50
2 ND 48pgs	$0.80	$2.40	$4.00	£0.50	£1.50	£2.50
3-4 ND 48pgs, Nick Fury appears						
	$0.80	$2.40	$4.00	£0.50	£1.50	£2.50
Title Value:	$3.20	$9.60	$16.00	£2.00	£6.00	£10.00

DEATHLOK ANNUAL

Marvel Comics Group; 1 Aug 1992-2 1993

	$Good	$Fine	$N.Mint	£Good	£Fine	£N.Mint
1 ND Timestream story						
	$0.40	$1.20	$2.00	£0.25	£0.75	£1.25
2 ND 64pgs, pre-bagged with trading card, 1st appearance The Tracer						
	$0.40	$1.20	$2.00	£0.25	£0.75	£1.25
Title Value:	$0.80	$2.40	$4.00	£0.50	£1.50	£2.50

DEATHLOK SPECIAL

Marvel Comics Group,MS; 1 May 1991-4 Jun 1991

	$Good	$Fine	$N.Mint	£Good	£Fine	£N.Mint
1-4 ND 48pgs, reprints mini-series, issued bi-weekly						
	$0.40	$1.20	$2.00	£0.25	£0.75	£1.25
Title Value:	$1.60	$4.80	$8.00	£1.00	£3.00	£5.00

DEATHMARK

Lightning Comics; 1 Dec 1994

	$Good	$Fine	$N.Mint	£Good	£Fine	£N.Mint
1 ND Steven Zyskowski script						
	$0.50	$1.50	$2.50	£0.30	£0.90	£1.50
Title Value:	$0.50	$1.50	$2.50	£0.30	£0.90	£1.50

DEATHMATE

Valiant/Image,MS; 1 Sep 1993-6 Feb 1994

	$Good	$Fine	$N.Mint	£Good	£Fine	£N.Mint
1 Prologue, ND Solar meets Void, card stock cover by Jim Lee and Bob Layton; silver border						
	$0.50	$1.50	$2.50	£0.30	£0.90	£1.50
1 Prologue: Gold Edition ND						
	$1.00	$3.00	$5.00	£0.70	£2.10	£3.50
1 Prologue: Pink Ediition, ND available with Ultra-Pro comic sleeves, one per box						
	$0.80	$2.40	$4.00	£0.50	£1.50	£2.50
2 Blue, ND 48pgs, squarebound; includes Chapter 1 (Magnus/Battlestone), Chapter 2 (Livewire/Stronghold/Striker/Impact),Chapter 3 (Harbinger/Brigade), Chapter 4 (Solar/Supreme)						
	$0.80	$2.40	$4.00	£0.50	£1.50	£2.50
2 Blue: Gold Edition ND 48pgs						
	$1.00	$3.00	$5.00	£0.90	£2.70	£4.50
3 Yellow, ND 48pgs, squarebound; includes Chapter 1 (Ivar/Armstrong), Chapter 2 (H.A.R.D.C.A.T.S.), Chapter 3 (Ninjak/Zealot), Chapter 4 (Shadowman/Grifter)						
	$0.80	$2.40	$4.00	£0.50	£1.50	£2.50
3 Yellow: Gold Edition ND 48pgs						
	$1.00	$3.00	$5.00	£0.90	£2.70	£4.50
4 Black, ND 48pgs, squarebound; Wildc.a.t.s/Hard Corps; 1st app. Gen 13						
	$1.50	$4.50	$7.50	£0.70	£2.10	£3.50
4 Black: Gold Edition ND 48pgs						
	$3.50	$10.50	$17.50	£1.20	£3.60	£6.00
5 Red, ND 48pgs, squarebound; Youngblood/Eternal Warrior						
	$0.80	$2.40	$4.00	£0.50	£1.50	£2.50
5 Red: Gold Edition ND 48pgs						
	$1.00	$3.00	$5.00	£0.90	£2.70	£4.50
6 Epilogue, ND silver foil cover; Solar, Supreme, Master D'Arque, Dr. Eclipse						
	$0.50	$1.50	$2.50	£0.30	£0.90	£1.50
6 Epilogue: Gold Edition ND						
	$1.00	$3.00	$5.00	£0.70	£2.10	£3.50
Title Value:	$14.20	$42.60	$71.00	£8.60	£25.80	£43.00

DEATHSTROKE THE TERMINATOR

DC Comics; 1 Aug 1991-60 Jun 1996

	$Good	$Fine	$N.Mint	£Good	£Fine	£N.Mint
0 (Oct 1994) Zero Hour X-over; title changes here to Deathstroke the Hunted (effective in title as of #41)						
	$0.40	$1.20	$2.00	£0.25	£0.75	£1.25
1 Mike Zeck covers begin						
	$0.80	$2.40	$4.00	£0.40	£1.20	£2.00
1 2nd printing, (1992) - gold ink cover						
	$0.30	$0.90	$1.50	£0.20	£0.60	£1.00
2-3	$0.60	$1.80	$3.00	£0.30	£0.90	£1.50
4-5	$0.40	$1.20	$2.00	£0.25	£0.75	£1.25
6 Batman appears (cameo)						
	$0.40	$1.20	$2.00	£0.25	£0.75	£1.25
7 Batman appears	$0.40	$1.20	$2.00	£0.25	£0.75	£1.25
8	$0.40	$1.20	$2.00	£0.25	£0.75	£1.25
9 Batman appears	$0.40	$1.20	$2.00	£0.25	£0.75	£1.25
10 Guns and Roses part 1, 1st appearance new Vigilante (female)						
	$0.40	$1.20	$2.00	£0.25	£0.75	£1.25
11 Guns and Roses part 2						
	$0.30	$0.90	$1.50	£0.20	£0.60	£1.00
12	$0.30	$0.90	$1.50	£0.20	£0.60	£1.00
13 Superman, Aquaman, Green Lantern, Flash appear, continued from Superman #68						
	$0.30	$0.90	$1.50	£0.20	£0.60	£1.00
14 Total Chaos part 1, continued in New Titans #90						
	$0.30	$0.90	$1.50	£0.20	£0.60	£1.00
15 Total Chaos part 4, continued in New Titans #91						
	$0.30	$0.90	$1.50	£0.20	£0.60	£1.00
16 Total Chaos part 7, continued in New Titans #92						
	$0.30	$0.90	$1.50	£0.20	£0.60	£1.00
17 Titans Sell-Out part 2, new costume						
	$0.30	$0.90	$1.50	£0.20	£0.60	£1.00
18	$0.30	$0.90	$1.50	£0.20	£0.60	£1.00
19 new Speedy appears, nuclear explosion cover						
	$0.30	$0.90	$1.50	£0.20	£0.60	£1.00
20-21	$0.30	$0.90	$1.50	£0.20	£0.60	£1.00
22-25 bi-weekly	$0.30	$0.90	$1.50	£0.20	£0.60	£1.00
26	$0.30	$0.90	$1.50	£0.20	£0.60	£1.00
27 Deathstroke's World Tour part 1 (of 8)						
	$0.30	$0.90	$1.50	£0.20	£0.60	£1.00
28	$0.30	$0.90	$1.50	£0.20	£0.60	£1.00
29 continued in Deathstroke Annual #2						
	$0.30	$0.90	$1.50	£0.20	£0.60	£1.00
30-32	$0.30	$0.90	$1.50	£0.20	£0.60	£1.00
33 Vigilante guest-stars						
	$0.30	$0.90	$1.50	£0.20	£0.60	£1.00
34 change of direction for title, promising a new and grittier Deathstroke..						
	$0.30	$0.90	$1.50	£0.20	£0.60	£1.00
35-37	$0.30	$0.90	$1.50	£0.20	£0.60	£1.00

	$Good	$Fine	$N.Mint	£Good	£Fine	£N.Mint
38 $1.95 cover begin						
	$0.40	*$1.20*	*$2.00*	£0.25	£0.75	£1.25
39-40	*$0.40*	*$1.20*	*$2.00*	£0.25	£0.75	£1.25
41 title changes to Deathstroke the Hunted (see issue #0)						
	$0.40	*$1.20*	*$2.00*	£0.25	£0.75	£1.25
42 Guy Gardner appears						
	$0.40	*$1.20*	*$2.00*	£0.25	£0.75	£1.25
43 Deathstroke vs. Hawkman						
	$0.40	*$1.20*	*$2.00*	£0.25	£0.75	£1.25
44	*$0.40*	*$1.20*	*$2.00*	£0.25	£0.75	£1.25
45 The New Titans guest-star						
	$0.40	*$1.20*	*$2.00*	£0.25	£0.75	£1.25
46 the title now becomes simply "Deathstroke"						
	$0.40	*$1.20*	*$2.00*	£0.25	£0.75	£1.25
47 1st appearance the new Vigilante (female)						
	$0.40	*$1.20*	*$2.00*	£0.25	£0.75	£1.25
48 The Crimelord/Syndicate War, New Titans guest-star; continued in New Titans #122						
	$0.40	*$1.20*	*$2.00*	£0.25	£0.75	£1.25
49 The Crimelord/Syndicate War, New Titans guest-star; continued from Darkstars #32						
	$0.40	*$1.20*	*$2.00*	£0.25	£0.75	£1.25
50 48pgs, guest-starring New Titans, Outsiders, Hawkman, Steel and Deadshot; continued in Deathstroke Annual #4						
	$0.80	*$2.40*	*$4.00*	£0.50	£1.50	£2.50
51-52 Deathstroke of the future vs. Hawkman						
	$0.45	*$1.35*	*$2.25*	£0.30	£0.90	£1.50
53-57	*$0.45*	*$1.35*	*$2.25*	£0.30	£0.90	£1.50
58 The Joker appears						
	$0.45	*$1.35*	*$2.25*	£0.30	£0.90	£1.50
59-60	*$0.45*	*$1.35*	*$2.25*	£0.30	£0.90	£1.50
Title Value:	*$23.70*	*$71.10*	*$118.00*	£15.10	£45.30	£75.50

Note: spin-off from New Teen Titans

Deathstroke The Terminator: Full Cycle (1993)

	$Good	$Fine	$N.Mint	£Good	£Fine	£N.Mint
Trade paperback reprints New Titans #70, Deathstroke #1-5; new cover and cover gallery by Mike Zeck				£1.60	£4.80	£8.00

DEATHSTROKE THE TERMINATOR ANNUAL

DC Comics; 1 Sep 1992-4 1995

	$Good	$Fine	$N.Mint	£Good	£Fine	£N.Mint
1 64pgs, Eclipso: The Darkness Within tie-in, Nightwing appears						
	$0.60	*$1.80*	*$3.00*	£0.40	£1.20	£2.00
2 64pgs, Bloodlines (Wave Two) part 18, 1st appearance Gunfire, continued in Eclipso Annual #1						
	$0.60	*$1.80*	*$3.00*	£0.40	£1.20	£2.00
3 64pgs, Elseworlds						
	$0.60	*$1.80*	*$3.00*	£0.40	£1.20	£2.00
4 56pgs, Year One, continued from Deathstroke #50						
	$0.80	*$2.40*	*$4.00*	£0.50	£1.50	£2.50
Title Value:	*$2.60*	*$7.80*	*$13.00*	£1.70	£5.10	£8.50

DEATHWATCH 2000

Continuity Comics re-launch (yet again!) with a 20 part series. Parts 1 & 2 were only available as send-away items with part 3 as the first distributed to the normal outlets. The parts (to date) are as follows: **Part 1** - Megalith (3rd Series) #0, **Part 2** - Hybrids (2nd Series) #0, **Part 3** - Armor (2nd Series) #1, **Part 4** - Hybrids (2nd Series) #1, **Part 5** - Megalith (3rd Series) #1, **Part 6** - Urth 4 (2nd Series) #1, **Part 7** - Cyberrad (3rd Series) #1, **Part 8** - Ms. Mystic (3rd Series) #1

DEATHWISH

DC Comics/Milestone,MS; 1 Dec 1994-4 Mar 1995

	$Good	$Fine	$N.Mint	£Good	£Fine	£N.Mint
1-4 ND	*$0.50*	*$1.50*	*$2.50*	£0.30	£0.90	£1.50
Title Value:	*$2.00*	*$6.00*	*$10.00*	£1.20	£3.60	£6.00

DEATHWORLD

Adventure,MS; 1 Nov 1990-4 Feb 1991

	$Good	$Fine	$N.Mint	£Good	£Fine	£N.Mint
1-4 ND John Holland script based on Harry Harrison novel, Marcello Campos art; black and white						
	$0.40	*$1.20*	*$2.00*	£0.25	£0.75	£1.25
Title Value:	*$1.60*	*$4.80*	*$8.00*	£1.00	£3.00	£5.00

DEATHWORLD BOOK 2

Adventure,MS; 1 Apr 1991-4 Jul 1991

	$Good	$Fine	$N.Mint	£Good	£Fine	£N.Mint
1-4 ND	*$0.40*	*$1.20*	*$2.00*	£0.25	£0.75	£1.25
Title Value:	*$1.60*	*$4.80*	*$8.00*	£1.00	£3.00	£5.00

DEATHWORLD BOOK 3

Adventure,MS; 1 Sep 1991-4 Dec 1991

	$Good	$Fine	$N.Mint	£Good	£Fine	£N.Mint
1-4 ND	*$0.40*	*$1.20*	*$2.00*	£0.25	£0.75	£1.25
Title Value:	*$1.60*	*$4.80*	*$8.00*	£1.00	£3.00	£5.00

DEBBI'S DATES

National Periodical Publications; 1 Apr/May 1969-11 Dec/Jan 1970/71

	$Good	$Fine	$N.Mint	£Good	£Fine	£N.Mint
1	*$2.00*	*$6.00*	*$14.00*	£0.90	£2.75	£6.50
2-3	*$1.00*	*$3.00*	*$7.00*	£0.50	£1.50	£3.50
4 Neal Adams text illustration						
	$1.10	*$3.40*	*$8.00*	£0.70	£2.10	£5.00
5	*$1.00*	*$3.00*	*$7.00*	£0.40	£1.25	£3.00
6 Superman cameo appearance						
	$1.30	*$4.00*	*$8.00*	£0.55	£1.75	£3.50
7-11	*$1.15*	*$3.50*	*$7.00*	£0.50	£1.50	£3.00
Title Value:	*$13.15*	*$39.90*	*$86.00*	£6.05	£18.35	£40.00

DECADE OF DARK HORSE, A

Dark Horse,MS; 1 Jul 1996-4 Oct 1996

	$Good	$Fine	$N.Mint	£Good	£Fine	£N.Mint
1-4 ND new stories featuring Sin City, Grendel and Predator plus a history of Dark Horse and other information						
	$0.60	*$1.80*	*$3.00*	£0.40	£1.20	£2.00
Title Value:	*$2.40*	*$7.20*	*$12.00*	£1.60	£4.80	£8.00

DEEP DIMENSION OF HORROR

AC Comics; 1 Sep 1994

	$Good	$Fine	$N.Mint	£Good	£Fine	£N.Mint
1 ND horror anthology, Bill Black cover; black and white						
	$0.60	*$1.80*	*$3.00*	£0.40	£1.20	£2.00
Title Value:	*$0.60*	*$1.80*	*$3.00*	£0.40	£1.20	£2.00

DEEP, THE

Marvel Comics Group,OS Film; 1 Nov 1977

	$Good	$Fine	$N.Mint	£Good	£Fine	£N.Mint
1 ND 52pgs, adapts film						
	$0.40	*$1.25*	*$2.50*	£0.25	£0.75	£1.50
Title Value:	*$0.40*	*$1.25*	*$2.50*	£0.25	£0.75	£1.50

DEFCON 4

Image,MS; 1 Feb 1996-4 May 1996

	$Good	$Fine	$N.Mint	£Good	£Fine	£N.Mint
½ ND 16pgs, available with Overstreet's Fan						
	$2.50	*$7.50*	*$12.50*	£2.50	£7.50	£12.50
½ Gold Edition, ND limited to 1,000 copies						
	$3.00	*$9.00*	*$15.00*	£2.00	£6.00	£10.00
1 Cover A, ND - cover by Matt Broome and Edwin Rosell						
	$0.80	*$2.40*	*$4.00*	£0.50	£1.50	£2.50
1 Cover B, ND - cover by Michael Golden						
	$0.80	*$2.40*	*$4.00*	£0.50	£1.50	£2.50
1 Cover C, ND - cover by Jim Lee and Troy Hubbs						
	$4.00	*$12.00*	*$20.00*	£1.20	£3.60	£6.00
1 Cover D, ND - cover by Humberto Ramos and Alex Garner						
	$0.80	*$2.40*	*$4.00*	£0.50	£1.50	£2.50
2-4 ND	*$0.50*	*$1.50*	*$2.50*	£0.30	£0.90	£1.50
Title Value:	*$13.40*	*$40.20*	*$67.00*	£8.10	£24.30	£40.50

DEFENDERS

Marvel Comics Group; 1 Aug 1972-152 Feb 1986

(see Marvel Feature,Marvel Treasury Edition, Sub-Mariner #34,35)

	$Good	$Fine	$N.Mint	£Good	£Fine	£N.Mint
1 ND Hulk, Dr Strange, Sub-Mariner begin						
	$10.00	*$30.00*	*$70.00*	£6.25	£19.00	£45.00
2 ND Silver Surfer appears						
	$5.75	*$17.50*	*$35.00*	£3.30	£10.00	£20.00
3 ND Silver Surfer appears						
	$4.15	*$12.50*	*$25.00*	£2.50	£7.50	£15.00
4-5	*$4.15*	*$12.50*	*$25.00*	£2.05	£6.25	£12.50
6 Silver Surfer appears						

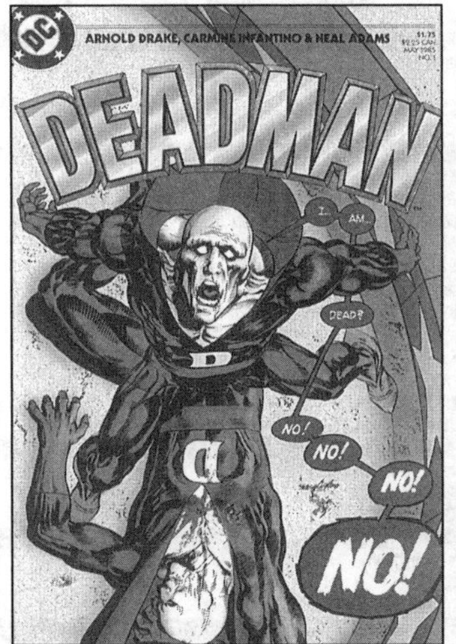

Deadman #1

Deadworld #5

Death's Head #10

Issue	$Good	$Fine	$N.Mint	£Good	£Fine	£N.Mint
	$2.90	$8.75	$17.50	£1.80	£5.50	£11.00
7 Silver Surfer and Hawkeye appear						
	$2.90	$8.75	$17.50	£1.80	£5.50	£11.00
8 ND Surfer appears, story continues from Avengers #115						
	$2.90	$8.75	$17.50	£2.05	£6.25	£12.50
9 Iron Man appears, Silver Surfer appears (6 panels)						
	$2.90	$8.75	$17.50	£1.80	£5.50	£11.00
10 ND scarce in the U.K. Avengers, Silver Surfer appear, Thor vs Hulk						
	$6.50	$19.50	$32.50	£5.50	£16.50	£27.50
11 Silver Surfer and Avengers appear						
	$1.65	$5.00	$10.00	£0.90	£2.75	£5.50
12	$1.65	$5.00	$10.00	£0.90	£2.75	£5.50
13 ND	$1.65	$5.00	$10.00	£1.00	£3.00	£6.00
14 ND Sub-Mariner leaves, Nighthawk joins						
	$1.65	$5.00	$10.00	£1.00	£3.00	£6.00
15-16 Professor X, Magneto and The Brotherhood of Evil Mutants appear						
	$3.00	$9.00	$18.00	£1.15	£3.50	£7.00
17 Luke Cage appears						
	$1.25	$3.75	$7.50	£0.65	£2.00	£4.00
18-19	$1.25	$3.75	$7.50	£0.65	£2.00	£4.00
20 The Thing appears						
	$1.25	$3.75	$7.50	£0.65	£2.00	£4.00
21-23	$1.00	$3.00	$6.00	£0.50	£1.50	£3.00
24 Son of Satan, Yellowjacket and Daredevil appear						
	$1.00	$3.00	$6.00	£0.50	£1.50	£3.00
25 Powerman, Son of Satan, Yellowjacket and Daredevil appear						
	$1.00	$3.00	$6.00	£0.50	£1.50	£3.00
26 Guardians of the Galaxy appear						
	$1.30	$4.00	$8.00	£0.55	£1.75	£3.50
27 Guardians of the Galaxy appear; Starhawk cameo						
	$1.30	$4.00	$8.00	£0.55	£1.75	£3.50
28 1st full appearance Starhawk, Guardians of the Galaxy appear						
	$1.30	$4.00	$8.00	£0.55	£1.75	£3.50
29 Guardians of the Galaxy appear						
	$1.30	$4.00	$8.00	£0.55	£1.75	£3.50
30-35	$0.80	$2.50	$5.00	£0.40	£1.25	£2.50
36	$0.80	$2.50	$5.00	£0.35	£1.10	£2.25
37 Luke Cage appears						
	$0.80	$2.50	$5.00	£0.35	£1.10	£2.25
38-40	$0.80	$2.50	$5.00	£0.35	£1.10	£2.25
41	$0.75	$2.25	$4.50	£0.30	£1.00	£2.00
42 1st Giffen art on title (ends #54)						
	$0.75	$2.25	$4.50	£0.30	£1.00	£2.00
43-46	$0.75	$2.25	$4.50	£0.30	£1.00	£2.00
47 Moon Knight, Wonderman appear						
	$0.75	$2.25	$4.50	£0.30	£1.00	£2.00
48-50 Moon Knight appears						
	$0.75	$2.25	$4.50	£0.30	£1.00	£2.00
51 Moon Knight appears, George Perez cover						
	$0.65	$2.00	$4.00	£0.25	£0.85	£1.75
52 Giffen art	$0.65	$2.00	$4.00	£0.25	£0.85	£1.75
53 Golden art and part Giffen art; Red Guardian re-born						
	$0.65	$2.00	$4.00	£0.25	£0.85	£1.75
54 Golden art, some Giffen art, George Perez cover						
	$0.65	$2.00	$4.00	£0.25	£0.85	£1.75
55 ND origin Red Guardian						
	$0.65	$2.00	$4.00	£0.25	£0.85	£1.75
56 ND	$0.65	$2.00	$4.00	£0.25	£0.85	£1.75
57 ND Ms. Marvel appears						
	$0.65	$2.00	$4.00	£0.25	£0.85	£1.75
58 ND 1st appearance Devil-Slayer (John Buscema's "Demon-Slayer" taken from Atlas to Marvel)						
	$0.65	$2.00	$4.00	£0.25	£0.85	£1.75
59-60 ND	$0.65	$2.00	$4.00	£0.25	£0.85	£1.75
61 ND Spiderman appears						
	$0.55	$1.75	$3.50	£0.25	£0.75	£1.50
62 ND Havok, Polaris appear (Angel on cover but not inside), Nova, Black Goliath, Hercules and Paladin appear						
	$0.55	$1.75	$3.50	£0.25	£0.75	£1.50
63 ND Havok, Polaris, Nova, Paladin, Black Goliath, Iron Man and Hercules appear						
	$0.55	$1.75	$3.50	£0.25	£0.75	£1.50
64 ND Nova, Hercules, Captain Marvel, Paladin, Black Goliath, Jack of Hearts, Havok and Iron Fist appear						
	$0.55	$1.75	$3.50	£0.25	£0.75	£1.50
65-72 ND	$0.55	$1.75	$3.50	£0.25	£0.75	£1.50
73 Foolkiller appearance (1 panel)						
	$0.50	$1.50	$3.00	£0.25	£0.75	£1.50
74 Foolkiller appears						
	$0.50	$1.50	$3.00	£0.25	£0.75	£1.50
75 Foolkiller appears; Omega the Unknown appears, resolving plot-lines from his own title						
	$0.50	$1.50	$3.00	£0.25	£0.75	£1.50
76 Omega the Unknown						
	$0.60	$1.80	$3.00	£0.25	£0.75	£1.25
77 origin Omega the Unknown						
	$0.60	$1.80	$3.00	£0.25	£0.75	£1.25
78 the return of the original Defenders						
	$0.60	$1.80	$3.00	£0.25	£0.75	£1.25
79-88	$0.60	$1.80	$3.00	£0.25	£0.75	£1.25
89-91 Daredevil appears						
	$0.50	$1.50	$2.50	£0.25	£0.75	£1.25
92 ND Son of Satan returns						
	$0.50	$1.50	$2.50	£0.30	£0.90	£1.50
93 ND Son of Satan appears						
	$0.50	$1.50	$2.50	£0.30	£0.90	£1.50
94 Son of Satan appears						
	$0.50	$1.50	$2.50	£0.25	£0.75	£1.25
95 Dracula and Son of Satan appear						
	$0.50	$1.50	$2.50	£0.25	£0.75	£1.25
96 Ghost Rider and Son of Satan appear						
	$0.50	$1.50	$2.50	£0.25	£0.75	£1.25
97 Son of Satan and Man-Thing appear						
	$0.50	$1.50	$2.50	£0.25	£0.75	£1.25
98 Son of Satan appears						
	$0.50	$1.50	$2.50	£0.25	£0.75	£1.25
99 Silver Sufer, Hulk, Sub-Mariner and Son of Satan appear						
	$0.50	$1.50	$2.50	£0.25	£0.75	£1.25
100 52pgs, Silver Sufer, Hulk and Sub-Mariner and Son of Satan appear						
	$0.50	$1.50	$2.50	£0.30	£0.90	£1.50
101 Silver Surfer appears; Son of Satan appears (cameo)						
	$0.50	$1.50	$2.50	£0.20	£0.60	£1.00
102-104	$0.50	$1.50	$2.50	£0.20	£0.60	£1.00
105 Son of Satan appears, Beast and Mr. Fantastic appear						
	$0.50	$1.50	$2.50	£0.20	£0.60	£1.00
106 death of Nighthawk; Son of Satan, Beast, Daredevil and Captain America appear						
	$0.50	$1.50	$2.50	£0.20	£0.60	£1.00
107 Silver Surfer, Son of Satan, Beast, Daredevil and Captain America appear						
	$0.50	$1.50	$2.50	£0.20	£0.60	£1.00
108-109 Son of Satan, Beast and Spiderman appear						
	$0.50	$1.50	$2.50	£0.20	£0.60	£1.00
110-111	$0.50	$1.50	$2.50	£0.20	£0.60	£1.00
112 Silver Surfer, Squadron Supreme appear						
	$0.50	$1.50	$2.50	£0.20	£0.60	£1.00
113 Silver Surfer, Squadron Supreme and Son of Satan appear						
	$0.50	$1.50	$2.50	£0.20	£0.60	£1.00
114 Silver Surfer, Squadron Supreme appear						
	$0.50	$1.50	$2.50	£0.20	£0.60	£1.00
115-116 Son of Satan appears						
	$0.50	$1.50	$2.50	£0.20	£0.60	£1.00
117	$0.50	$1.50	$2.50	£0.20	£0.60	£1.00
118 Son of Satan appears						
	$0.50	$1.50	$2.50	£0.20	£0.60	£1.00
119	$0.50	$1.50	$2.50	£0.20	£0.60	£1.00
120-121 Son of Satan appears						
	$0.50	$1.50	$2.50	£0.20	£0.60	£1.00
122 Son of Satan appears, Silver Surfer guest-stars						
	$0.50	$1.50	$2.50	£0.20	£0.60	£1.00
123-124 Silver Surfer appears						
	$0.50	$1.50	$2.50	£0.20	£0.60	£1.00
125 DS 1st new Defenders; Hell Cat and Son of Satan wed, Silver Surfer appears						
	$0.60	$1.80	$3.00	£0.30	£0.90	£1.50
126-127 Mike Zeck cover						
	$0.50	$1.50	$2.50	£0.20	£0.60	£1.00
128	$0.50	$1.50	$2.50	£0.20	£0.60	£1.00
129 New Mutants appear						
	$0.50	$1.50	$2.50	£0.20	£0.60	£1.00
130 Mike Zeck art	$0.50	$1.50	$2.50	£0.20	£0.60	£1.00
131 Sienkiewicz cover						
	$0.50	$1.50	$2.50	£0.20	£0.60	£1.00
132-134	$0.50	$1.50	$2.50	£0.20	£0.60	£1.00
135-136 Sienkiewicz cover						
	$0.50	$1.50	$2.50	£0.20	£0.60	£1.00
137-149	$0.50	$1.50	$2.50	£0.20	£0.60	£1.00
150 DS Captain America appears						
	$0.60	$1.80	$3.00	£0.30	£0.90	£1.50
151	$0.50	$1.50	$2.50	£0.20	£0.60	£1.00
152 DS scarce, Secret Wars tie-in, X-over with X-Factor						
	$0.60	$1.80	$3.00	£0.35	£1.05	£1.75
Title Value:	$145.10	$439.30	$837.00	£73.05	£223.45	£432.00

Note: title "New Defenders" #125-152

DEFENDERS ANNUAL

Marvel Comics Group; 1 Nov 1976

Issue	$Good	$Fine	$N.Mint	£Good	£Fine	£N.Mint
1 ND 52pgs, Luke Cage appears						
	$0.75	$2.25	$4.50	£0.50	£1.50	£3.00
Title Value:	$0.75	$2.25	$4.50	£0.50	£1.50	£3.00

DEFENDERS GIANT SIZE

Marvel Comics Group; 1 Jul 1974-5 Jul 1975

Issue	$Good	$Fine	$N.Mint	£Good	£Fine	£N.Mint
1 ND 68pgs, Everett Sub-Mariner, Kirby Hulk, Kirby Surfer reprints, 9pgs new Starlin art						
	$2.00	$6.00	$12.00	£1.30	£4.00	£8.00
2 ND 68pgs, Son of Satan appears						
	$1.50	$4.50	$9.00	£1.00	£3.00	£6.00
3 ND scarce in the U.K. 68pgs, Daredevil appears, Starlin lay-outs, Silver Surfer appears						
	$1.25	$3.75	$7.50	£0.80	£2.50	£5.00
4 ND 68pgs, Squadron Supreme appears						
	$1.25	$3.75	$7.50	£0.80	£2.50	£5.00
5 ND 68pgs, Guardians of the Galaxy appear						
	$1.25	$3.75	$7.50	£0.80	£2.50	£5.00
Title Value:	$7.25	$21.75	$43.50	£4.70	£14.50	£29.00

DEFENDERS OF DYNATRON CITY

Marvel Comics Group,MS Game; 1 Feb 1992-6 Jul 1992

Issue	$Good	$Fine	$N.Mint	£Good	£Fine	£N.Mint
1-6	$0.15	$0.45	$0.75	£0.10	£0.30	£0.50
Title Value:	$0.90	$2.70	$4.50	£0.60	£1.80	£3.00

DEFENDERS OF THE EARTH

Marvel Comics Group/Star, TV; 1 Jan 1987-5 Sep 1987

Issue	$Good	$Fine	$N.Mint	£Good	£Fine	£N.Mint
1-5 ND	$0.15	$0.45	$0.75	£0.10	£0.30	£0.50
Title Value:	$0.75	$2.25	$3.75	£0.50	£1.50	£2.50

DEFENSELESS DEAD, THE

Adventure,MS; 1 Feb 1991-3 Apr 1991

Issue	$Good	$Fine	$N.Mint	£Good	£Fine	£N.Mint
1-3 ND adaptation of Larry Niven novel; black and white	$0.35	$1.05	$1.75	£0.25	£0.75	£1.25
Title Value:	$1.05	$3.15	$5.25	£0.75	£2.25	£3.75

DEFIANT ANNIVERSARY TRADE PAPERBACK

Defiant,OS; nn Sep 1994

Issue	$Good	$Fine	$N.Mint	£Good	£Fine	£N.Mint
nn ND 96pgs, reprints Dark Dominion, Charlemagne, Plasm, Glory and Grimmax #0 issues	$0.70	$2.10	$3.50	£0.50	£1.50	£2.50
Title Value:	$0.70	$2.10	$3.50	£0.50	£1.50	£2.50

DEFIANT GENESIS

Defiant,OS; 1 Oct 1993

Issue	$Good	$Fine	$N.Mint	£Good	£Fine	£N.Mint
1 ND 16pgs	$0.30	$0.90	$1.50	£0.20	£0.60	£1.00
1 Published Version, ND (Feb 1994) 16pgs, with updated text; re-titled The Origin of the Defiant Universe	$0.25	$0.75	$1.25	£0.15	£0.45	£0.75
Title Value:	$0.55	$1.65	$2.75	£0.35	£1.05	£1.75

DELIRIUM

Metro Comics; 1,2 1987

Issue	$Good	$Fine	$N.Mint	£Good	£Fine	£N.Mint
1 ND	$0.40	$1.20	$2.00	£0.25	£0.75	£1.25
2 ND Keith Giffen art	$0.40	$1.20	$2.00	£0.25	£0.75	£1.25
Title Value:	$0.80	$2.40	$4.00	£0.50	£1.50	£2.50

DELL GIANTS

Dell;21 Sep 1959-55 Sep 1961

Issue	$Good	$Fine	$N.Mint	£Good	£Fine	£N.Mint
21 80pgs, (Sep 1959) M.G.M's Tom & Jerry Picnic Time	$16.50	$50.00	$200.00	£11.00	£34.00	£135.00
22 80pgs, (Oct 1959) Huey, Dewey & Louie Back to School	$11.50	$35.00	$140.00	£7.75	£23.50	£95.00
23 80pgs, (Oct 1959) Marge's Little Lulu & Tubby Halloween Fun	$12.50	$38.00	$150.00	£8.25	£25.00	£100.00
24 80pgs, (Nov 1959) Woody Woodpecker's Family Fun	$11.50	$35.00	$140.00	£7.75	£23.50	£95.00
25 80pgs, (Nov 1959) Tarzan's Jungle World; Jesse Marsh art	$14.50	$44.00	$175.00	£10.00	£30.00	£120.00
26 80pgs, (Dec 1959) Christmas Parade; Carl Barks art	$29.00	$87.50	$350.00	£20.00	£60.00	£240.00
27 80pgs, (Jan 1960) Man in Space; reprints Four Color #716, #866 and #954	$16.50	$50.00	$200.00	£11.00	£34.00	£135.00
28 80pgs, (Feb 1960) Bugs Bunny's Winter Fun	$14.50	$44.00	$175.00	£10.00	£30.00	£120.00
29 80pgs, (Apr 1960) Marge's Little Lulu & Tubby in Hawaii	$13.00	$40.00	$160.00	£9.00	£28.00	£110.00
30 80pgs, (Jun 1960) Disneyland U.S.A.	$11.50	$35.00	$140.00	£7.75	£23.50	£95.00
31 80pgs, (Jul 1960) Huckleberry Hound's Summer Fun	$18.50	$55.00	$225.00	£12.50	£38.00	£150.00
32 80pgs, (Aug 1960) Bugs Bunny's Beach Party	$10.00	$31.00	$125.00	£7.00	£21.00	£85.00
33 80pgs, (Sep 1960) Daisy Duck & Uncle Scrooge's Picnic Time	$12.50	$38.00	$150.00	£8.25	£25.00	£100.00
34 80pgs, (Aug 1960) Nany & Sluggo's Summer Camp	$10.00	$31.00	$125.00	£7.00	£21.00	£85.00
35 80pgs, (Oct 1960) Huey, Dewey & Louie Go Back to School	$14.50	$44.00	$175.00	£10.00	£30.00	£120.00
36 80pgs, (Oct 1960) Marge's Little Lulu & Witch Hazel's Halloween Fun	$14.50	$44.00	$175.00	£10.00	£30.00	£120.00
37 80pgs, (Nov 1960) Tarzan, King of the Jungle; Jesse Marsh art	$14.50	$44.00	$175.00	£10.00	£30.00	£120.00
38 80pgs, (Nov 1960) Uncle Donald and His Nephews Family Fun	$18.50	$55.00	$225.00	£12.50	£38.00	£150.00
39 80pgs, (Dec 1960) Walt Disney's Merry Christmas	$18.50	$55.00	$225.00	£12.50	£38.00	£150.00
40 80pgs, (Dec 1960) Woody Woodpecker Christmas Parade	$10.00	$31.00	$125.00	£7.00	£21.00	£85.00
41 80pgs, ((Dec 1960) Yogi Bear's Winter Sports	$18.50	$55.00	$225.00	£12.50	£38.00	£150.00
42 80pgs, (Apr 1961) Marge's Little Lulu & Tubby in Australia	$14.50	$44.00	$175.00	£10.00	£30.00	£120.00
43 80pgs, (May 1961) Mighty Mouse in Outer Space	$29.00	$87.50	$350.00	£19.50	£57.50	£235.00
44 80pgs, (Jul 1961) Around The World with Huckleberry & His Friends	$18.50	$55.00	$225.00	£12.50	£38.00	£150.00
45 80pgs, (Aug 1961) Nany & Sluggo's Summer Camp	$8.75	$26.00	$105.00	£5.75	£17.50	£70.00
46 80pgs, (Aug 1961) Bugs Bunny's Beach Party	$8.75	$26.00	$105.00	£5.75	£17.50	£70.00
47 80pgs, (Aug 1961) Mickey & Donald in Vacationland	$12.50	$38.00	$150.00	£8.25	£25.00	£100.00
48 80pgs, (Jul 1961) The Flintstones (#1)	$25.00	$75.00	$300.00	£16.50	£50.00	£200.00
49 80pgs, (Sep 1961) Huey, Dewey & Louie Back to School	$12.50	$38.00	$150.00	£8.25	£25.00	£100.00
50 80pgs, (Marge's Little Lulu & Witch hazel Trick 'n Treat	$14.50	$44.00	$175.00	£10.00	£30.00	£120.00
51 80pgs, (Nov 1961) Tarzan, King of the Jungle; Jesse Marsh art	$10.00	$31.00	$125.00	£7.00	£21.00	£85.00
52 80pgs, (Nov 1961) Uncle Donald & His Nephews Dude Ranch	$10.00	$30.00	$120.00	£6.50	£20.00	£80.00
53 80pgs, (Dec 1961) Donald Duck Merry Christmas	$10.00	$30.00	$120.00	£6.50	£20.00	£80.00
54 80pgs, (Dec 1961) Woody Woodpecker's Christmas Party	$8.25	$25.00	$100.00	£5.50	£16.50	£67.50
55 scarce in the U.K. 80pgs, (1961) Daisy Duck & Uncle Scrooge Showboat	$12.50	$38.00	$150.00	£8.25	£25.00	£100.00
Title Value:	$505.75	$1529.00	$6130.00	£342.00	£1034.50	£4137.50

Note: all distributed in the U.K.

DEMOLITION MAN

DC Comics,MS; 1 Nov 1993-4 Feb 1994

Issue	$Good	$Fine	$N.Mint	£Good	£Fine	£N.Mint
1-4 based on Sylvester Stallone film	$0.25	$0.75	$1.25	£0.15	£0.45	£0.75
Title Value:	$1.00	$3.00	$5.00	£0.60	£1.80	£3.00

DEMON BLADE

New Comics Group; 1 1989

Issue	$Good	$Fine	$N.Mint	£Good	£Fine	£N.Mint
1 ND Alex Nino art; black and white	$0.30	$0.90	$1.50	£0.20	£0.60	£1.00
Title Value:	$0.30	$0.90	$1.50	£0.20	£0.60	£1.00

DEMON DREAMS

Pacific,MS; 1 Feb 1984-2 May 1984

Issue	$Good	$Fine	$N.Mint	£Good	£Fine	£N.Mint
1-2 ND Arthur Suydam reprints; colour	$0.30	$0.90	$1.50	£0.20	£0.60	£1.00
Title Value:	$0.60	$1.80	$3.00	£0.40	£1.20	£2.00

DEMON DREAMS OF DOCTOR DREW

AC Comics; 1 Oct 1994

Issue	$Good	$Fine	$N.Mint	£Good	£Fine	£N.Mint
1 ND Jerry Grandenetti reprints (in Will Eisner-esque style)	$0.30	$0.90	$1.50	£0.20	£0.60	£1.00
Title Value:	$0.30	$0.90	$1.50	£0.20	£0.60	£1.00

DEMON GUN

Crusade Comics; 1 Jun 1996-2 Jul 1996; 3 Jan 1997

Issue	$Good	$Fine	$N.Mint	£Good	£Fine	£N.Mint
1 ND Gary Cohn script, Barry Orkin art begins; black and white	$0.60	$1.80	$3.00	£0.40	£1.20	£2.00
2-3 ND	$0.60	$1.80	$3.00	£0.40	£1.20	£2.00
Title Value:	$1.80	$5.40	$9.00	£1.20	£3.60	£6.00

DEMON HUNTER

Atlas; 1 Sep 1975

Issue	$Good	$Fine	$N.Mint	£Good	£Fine	£N.Mint
1 Rich Buckler art; distributed in the U.K.	$0.20	$0.60	$1.25	£0.10	£0.35	£0.75
Title Value:	$0.20	$0.60	$1.25	£0.10	£0.35	£0.75

DEMON HUNTER (2ND SERIES)

Aircel; 1 Mar 1989-4 1989

Issue	$Good	$Fine	$N.Mint	£Good	£Fine	£N.Mint
1-4 ND	$0.30	$0.90	$1.50	£0.20	£0.60	£1.00
Title Value:	$1.20	$3.60	$6.00	£0.80	£2.40	£4.00

DEMON WARRIOR, THE

Eastern; 1 Aug 1987-14 1988

Issue	$Good	$Fine	$N.Mint	£Good	£Fine	£N.Mint
1 ND Jae hak Lee script and art (1st professional work by Jae Lee?); black and white	$0.30	$0.90	$1.50	£0.20	£0.60	£1.00
2 ND black and white; some copies have indicia information for #1 on the inside	$0.30	$0.90	$1.50	£0.20	£0.60	£1.00
3-14 ND b&w	$0.30	$0.90	$1.50	£0.20	£0.60	£1.00
Title Value:	$4.20	$12.60	$21.00	£2.80	£8.40	£14.00

DEMON'S TAILS

Adventure,MS; 1 Mar 1993-4 Jun 1993

Issue	$Good	$Fine	$N.Mint	£Good	£Fine	£N.Mint
1-4 ND	$0.30	$0.90	$1.50	£0.20	£0.60	£1.00
Title Value:	$1.20	$3.60	$6.00	£0.80	£2.40	£4.00

DEMON, THE

National Periodical Publications; 1 Aug/Sep 1972-16 Jan 1974

(see Brave and the Bold, Detective #482-485))

Issue	$Good	$Fine	$N.Mint	£Good	£Fine	£N.Mint
1 ND origin and 1st appearance The Demon by Jack Kirby	$5.50	$17.00	$40.00	£2.85	£8.50	£20.00
2 scarce in the U.K.	$3.75	$11.00	$22.50	£1.65	£5.00	£10.00
3 scarce in the U.K.	$3.75	$11.00	$22.50	£1.30	£4.00	£8.00
4-5	$3.75	$11.00	$22.50	£1.15	£3.50	£7.00
6-7	$2.90	$8.75	$17.50	£0.65	£2.00	£4.00
8 scarce in the U.K.	$2.90	$8.75	$17.50	£0.75	£2.25	£4.50
9-10	$2.90	$8.75	$17.50	£0.65	£2.00	£4.00
11-14	$2.50	$7.50	$15.00	£0.55	£1.75	£3.50
15 some words missing from front cover word balloon	$2.50	$7.50	$15.00	£0.55	£1.75	£3.50
16	$2.50	$7.50	$15.00	£0.55	£1.75	£3.50
Title Value:	$50.00	$149.75	$307.50	£14.75	£45.25	£93.50

Note: Jack Kirby art in all.

DEMON, THE (2ND SERIES)

DC Comics; 0 Oct 1994; 1 Jul 1990-58 May 1995

Issue	$Good	$Fine	$N.Mint	£Good	£Fine	£N.Mint
0 (Oct 1994) Zero Hour X-over, origin retold	$0.40	$1.20	$2.00	£0.25	£0.75	£1.25
1	$0.50	$1.50	$2.50	£0.40	£1.20	£2.00
2	$0.40	$1.20	$2.00	£0.25	£0.75	£1.25
3 Batman appears	$0.40	$1.20	$2.00	£0.25	£0.75	£1.25
4-7	$0.40	$1.20	$2.00	£0.25	£0.75	£1.25
8 Batman/Arkham Asylum appear	$0.40	$1.20	$2.00	£0.25	£0.75	£1.25
9-10	$0.40	$1.20	$2.00	£0.25	£0.75	£1.25
11 Lobo appears, Apokalypse Now story	$0.40	$1.20	$2.00	£0.25	£0.75	£1.25
12 Demon vs. Lobo, Apokalypse Now story	$0.40	$1.20	$2.00	£0.25	£0.75	£1.25
13-15 Lobo appears, Apokalypse Now story	$0.40	$1.20	$2.00	£0.25	£0.75	£1.25
16	$0.40	$1.20	$2.00	£0.25	£0.75	£1.25
17 War of the Gods X-over	$0.40	$1.20	$2.00	£0.25	£0.75	£1.25
18	$0.40	$1.20	$2.00	£0.25	£0.75	£1.25
19 40pgs, secret origin The Demon, Demon and Lobo mini-poster	$0.50	$1.50	$2.50	£0.30	£0.90	£1.50
20	$0.40	$1.20	$2.00	£0.25	£0.75	£1.25
21 Lobo appears	$0.40	$1.20	$2.00	£0.25	£0.75	£1.25
22 Matt Wagner script/art						

Issue	$Good	$Fine	$N.Mint	£Good	£Fine	£N.Mint
	$0.40	$1.20	$2.00	£0.25	£0.75	£1.25
23 Return of the Howler part 1, Robin appears	$0.40	$1.20	$2.00	£0.25	£0.75	£1.25
24 Return of the Howler part 2, Batman and Robin appear	$0.40	$1.20	$2.00	£0.25	£0.75	£1.25
25	$0.40	$1.20	$2.00	£0.25	£0.75	£1.25
26 Political Asylum story	$0.40	$1.20	$2.00	£0.25	£0.75	£1.25
27 Political Asylum story, Superman appears	$0.40	$1.20	$2.00	£0.25	£0.75	£1.25
28-29 Political Asylum story, Superman vs. Demon	$0.40	$1.20	$2.00	£0.25	£0.75	£1.25
30	$0.40	$1.20	$2.00	£0.25	£0.75	£1.25
31 Lobo appears	$0.40	$1.20	$2.00	£0.25	£0.75	£1.25
32 Lobo and Wonder Woman appear	$0.40	$1.20	$2.00	£0.25	£0.75	£1.25
33 Lobo appears	$0.40	$1.20	$2.00	£0.25	£0.75	£1.25
34-37 The Eternity Quest, Lobo appears	$0.40	$1.20	$2.00	£0.25	£0.75	£1.25
38 Lobo appears	$0.40	$1.20	$2.00	£0.25	£0.75	£1.25
39	$0.40	$1.20	$2.00	£0.25	£0.75	£1.25
40 Garth Ennis and John McCrea creative team begins	$0.40	$1.20	$2.00	£0.25	£0.75	£1.25
41 guest-written and drawn by Kevin Altieri of the Fox Batman animated TV series	$0.40	$1.20	$2.00	£0.25	£0.75	£1.25
42 Ennis and McCrea return	$0.40	$1.20	$2.00	£0.25	£0.75	£1.25
43 Hitman appears	$2.00	$6.00	$10.00	£1.20	£3.60	£6.00
44 Hitman appears	$1.50	$4.50	$7.50	£1.00	£3.00	£5.00
45 Hitman appears	$1.20	$3.60	$6.00	£0.80	£2.40	£4.00
46-48 Haunted Tank appears	$0.40	$1.20	$2.00	£0.25	£0.75	£1.25
49	$0.40	$1.20	$2.00	£0.25	£0.75	£1.25
50 48pgs	$0.50	$1.50	$2.50	£0.30	£0.90	£1.50
51	$0.40	$1.20	$2.00	£0.25	£0.75	£1.25
52-54 Hitman appears	$0.80	$2.40	$4.00	£0.40	£1.20	£2.00
55-58	$0.40	$1.20	$2.00	£0.25	£0.75	£1.25
Title Value:	$28.60	$85.80	$143.00	£17.70	£53.10	£88.50

Note: New Format, script by Alan Grant

DEMON, THE (2ND SERIES) ANNUAL

DC Comics; 1 Aug 1992-2 1993

Issue	$Good	$Fine	$N.Mint	£Good	£Fine	£N.Mint
1 64pgs, Eclipso: The Darkness Within tie-in	$0.60	$1.80	$3.00	£0.40	£1.20	£2.00
2 64pgs, Bloodlines (Wave Two) part 20, 1st appearance Hitman, continued in Batman: Legends of the Dark Knight Annual #3	$2.50	$7.50	$12.50	£1.60	£4.80	£8.00
Title Value:	$3.10	$9.30	$15.50	£2.00	£6.00	£10.00

DEMON, THE (LIMITED SERIES)

DC Comics,MS; 1 Jan 1987-4 Apr 1987

Issue	$Good	$Fine	$N.Mint	£Good	£Fine	£N.Mint
1	$0.30	$0.90	$1.50	£0.20	£0.60	£1.00
2 "4 of 4" on cover	$0.30	$0.90	$1.50	£0.20	£0.60	£1.00
3-4	$0.30	$0.90	$1.50	£0.20	£0.60	£1.00
Title Value:	$1.20	$3.60	$6.00	£0.80	£2.40	£4.00

Note: Matt Wagner script/art in all.

DEMONGATE

Sirius; 1 May 1996-present

Issue	$Good	$Fine	$N.Mint	£Good	£Fine	£N.Mint
1-5 ND Bao Lin Hum script and Colin Chan art; black and white	$0.50	$1.50	$2.50	£0.30	£0.90	£1.50
6 ND	$0.50	$1.50	$2.50	£0.30	£0.90	£1.50
Title Value:	$3.00	$9.00	$15.00	£1.80	£5.40	£9.00

DEMONIC TOYS

Eternity,MS; 1 Jan 1992-4 May 1992

Issue	$Good	$Fine	$N.Mint	£Good	£Fine	£N.Mint
1-4 ND	$0.35	$1.05	$1.75	£0.25	£0.75	£1.25
Title Value:	$1.40	$4.20	$7.00	£1.00	£3.00	£5.00

DEMONIQUE

London Night Studios,MS; 1 Nov 1994-4 Apr 1995

Issue	$Good	$Fine	$N.Mint	£Good	£Fine	£N.Mint
1-4 ND Skye Owens script and art; black and white	$0.50	$1.50	$2.50	£0.30	£0.90	£1.50
Title Value:	$2.00	$6.00	$10.00	£1.20	£3.60	£6.00

DEMONIQUE (2ND SERIES)

London Night Studios; 0 Aug 1996-present

Issue	$Good	$Fine	$N.Mint	£Good	£Fine	£N.Mint
0 ND Sky Owens co-script and art	$0.60	$1.80	$3.00	£0.40	£1.20	£2.00
1 ND script and art by Sky Owens	$0.60	$1.80	$3.00	£0.40	£1.20	£2.00
1 Limited Nude Edition ND	$2.00	$6.00	$10.00	£1.00	£3.00	£5.00
Title Value:	$3.20	$9.60	$16.00	£1.80	£5.40	£9.00

DEN

Fantagor; 1 1988-10 1989

Issue	$Good	$Fine	$N.Mint	£Good	£Fine	£N.Mint
1-10 ND Richard Corben story and art	$0.60	$1.80	$3.00	£0.40	£1.20	£2.00
Title Value:	$6.00	$18.00	$30.00	£4.00	£12.00	£20.00
Den 1: Neverwhere (Sep 1991), selected reprints, 112pgs softcover				£1.90	£5.70	£9.50

DENIZENS OF DEEP CITY

Kitchen Sink; 1 Dec 1988-9 May 1990

Issue	$Good	$Fine	$N.Mint	£Good	£Fine	£N.Mint
1-9 ND Doug Potter script and art, black and white; bi-monthly frequency	$0.60	$1.80	$3.00	£0.40	£1.20	£2.00
Title Value:	$5.40	$16.20	$27.00	£3.60	£10.80	£18.00

DENNIS THE MENACE

Marvel Comics Group; 1 Nov 1981-13 Nov 1982

Issue	$Good	$Fine	$N.Mint	£Good	£Fine	£N.Mint
1-13 ND	$0.15	$0.45	$0.75	£0.10	£0.30	£0.50
Title Value:	$1.95	$5.85	$9.75	£1.30	£3.90	£6.50

DER COUNTESS

Avalon Communications,MS; 1 Feb 1996-2 Mar 1996

Issue	$Good	$Fine	$N.Mint	£Good	£Fine	£N.Mint
1-2 ND reprints from Charlton Comics	$0.55	$1.65	$2.75	£0.35	£1.05	£1.75
Title Value:	$1.10	$3.30	$5.50	£0.70	£2.10	£3.50

DESCENDING ANGELS

Millennium; 1 Apr 1995

Issue	$Good	$Fine	$N.Mint	£Good	£Fine	£N.Mint
1 ND b&w	$0.60	$1.80	$3.00	£0.40	£1.20	£2.00
Title Value:	$0.60	$1.80	$3.00	£0.40	£1.20	£2.00

Note: a second issue was advertised and solicited but never came out.

DESERT PEACH, THE

Mu Press; 1 Nov 1989-14 1991

Issue	$Good	$Fine	$N.Mint	£Good	£Fine	£N.Mint
1-14 ND b&w	$0.30	$0.90	$1.50	£0.20	£0.60	£1.00
Title Value:	$4.20	$12.60	$21.00	£2.80	£8.40	£14.00

DESERT STORM JOURNAL

Apple Comics; 1 Jul 1991-7 1992

Issue	$Good	$Fine	$N.Mint	£Good	£Fine	£N.Mint
1-7 ND Don Lomax script and art	$0.30	$0.90	$1.50	£0.20	£0.60	£1.00
Title Value:	$2.10	$6.30	$10.50	£1.40	£4.20	£7.00

DESERT STREAMS

DC Comics/Piranha Press,OS; 1 1989

Issue	$Good	$Fine	$N.Mint	£Good	£Fine	£N.Mint
1 ND 104pgs, half-size trade paperback format (8" x 5"), Alison Marek script/art	$0.90	$2.70	$4.50	£0.60	£1.80	£3.00
Title Value:	$0.90	$2.70	$4.50	£0.60	£1.80	£3.00

DESTROY!

Eclipse,Tabloid; nn 1986

Issue	$Good	$Fine	$N.Mint	£Good	£Fine	£N.Mint
nn ND Scott McLeod script and art	$1.50	$4.50	$7.50	£1.00	£3.00	£5.00
Title Value:	$1.50	$4.50	$7.50	£1.00	£3.00	£5.00

DESTROY! IN THREE-D

Eclipse;(3-D Special 17) 1 Mar 1987

Issue	$Good	$Fine	$N.Mint	£Good	£Fine	£N.Mint
1 ND Scott McLeod script/art 3-D version; glasses included (less 25% without)	$0.50	$1.50	$2.50	£0.30	£0.90	£1.50
Title Value:	$0.50	$1.50	$2.50	£0.30	£0.90	£1.50

DESTROYER

Marvel Comics Group,Magazine; 1 Dec 1989-10 Jun 1990

Issue	$Good	$Fine	$N.Mint	£Good	£Fine	£N.Mint
1-5 ND	$0.30	$0.90	$1.50	£0.20	£0.60	£1.00
6 ND Infantino art	$0.30	$0.90	$1.50	£0.20	£0.60	£1.00
7-10 ND	$0.30	$0.90	$1.50	£0.20	£0.60	£1.00
Title Value:	$3.00	$9.00	$15.00	£2.00	£6.00	£10.00
Trade Paperback (Dec 1991), reprints selected stories in colour for first time				£1.10	£3.30	£5.50

DESTROYER (2ND SERIES)

Marvel Comics Group,OS; 1 Mar 1991

Issue	$Good	$Fine	$N.Mint	£Good	£Fine	£N.Mint
1 ND Lee Weeks art and painted cover	$0.30	$0.90	$1.50	£0.20	£0.60	£1.00
Title Value:	$0.30	$0.90	$1.50	£0.20	£0.60	£1.00

DESTROYER DUCK

Eclipse; 1 Feb 1982-7 1984

Issue	$Good	$Fine	$N.Mint	£Good	£Fine	£N.Mint
1 ND 1st appearance of Groo in back-up story; Jack Kirby art	$1.00	$3.00	$5.00	£1.00	£3.00	£5.00
2-3 ND Jack Kirby art	$0.50	$1.50	$2.50	£0.30	£0.90	£1.50
4-6 ND	$0.40	$1.20	$2.00	£0.25	£0.75	£1.25
7 ND Frank Miller cover	$0.40	$1.20	$2.00	£0.25	£0.75	£1.25
Title Value:	$3.60	$10.80	$18.00	£2.60	£7.80	£13.00

DESTROYER, THE

Valiant; 0 Apr 1995

Issue	$Good	$Fine	$N.Mint	£Good	£Fine	£N.Mint
0 ND spin-off from Solar, Man of the Atom; Mike Manley art	$0.40	$1.20	$2.00	£0.25	£0.75	£1.25
Title Value:	$0.40	$1.20	$2.00	£0.25	£0.75	£1.25

DESTROYER: TERROR, THE

Marvel Comics Group,MS; 1 Dec 1991-4 Mar 1992

Issue	$Good	$Fine	$N.Mint	£Good	£Fine	£N.Mint
1	$0.30	$0.90	$1.50	£0.20	£0.60	£1.00
2-4 Simonson cover	$0.30	$0.90	$1.50	£0.20	£0.60	£1.00
Title Value:	$1.20	$3.60	$6.00	£0.80	£2.40	£4.00

DESTRUCTOR, THE

Atlas; 1 Feb 1975-4 Aug 1975

Issue	$Good	$Fine	$N.Mint	£Good	£Fine	£N.Mint
1-2 Steve Ditko, Wally Wood art; distributed in the U.K.	$0.20	$0.60	$1.25	£0.10	£0.35	£0.75
3 Steve Ditko art; distributed in the U.K.	$0.20	$0.60	$1.25	£0.10	£0.35	£0.75
4 Steve Ditko, Al Milgrom art; distributed in the U.K.	$0.20	$0.60	$1.25	£0.10	£0.35	£0.75
Title Value:	$0.80	$2.40	$5.00	£0.40	£1.40	£3.00

DETECTIVE COMICS

National Periodical Publications/DC Comics; 0 Oct 1994; 1 Mar 1937-present

(see Batman, Best of DC, Famous First Edition C-28)

Issue	$Good	$Fine	$N.Mint	£Good	£Fine	£N.Mint
0 (Oct 1994) Zero Hour X-over, origin retold	$0.40	$1.20	$2.00	£0.25	£0.75	£1.25
1 very rare in the U.K., rare in the U.S. about 30 or less extant copies, classic "Chinaman" cover by Vincent Sullivan; historically important as the first successful anthology of detectives & policemen	$8000.00	$24000.00	$80000.00	£5300.00	£16000.00	£53500.00

[Extremely Rare in high grade - Very Fine or better]

[Prices may vary widely on this comic]

2 rare in the U.S., very rare in the U.K. fewer than 30 extant copies

	$Good	$Fine	$N.Mint	£Good	£Fine	£N.Mint
	$1925.00	$5800.00	$17500.00	£1300.00	£3900.00	£11700.00
3 rare in the U.S., very rare in the U.K. fewer than 20 extant copies						
	$1375.00	$4150.00	$12500.00	£920.00	£2750.00	£8350.00
4-5 very scarce in the U.S. rare in the U.K.						
	$840.00	$2500.00	$6750.00	£560.00	£1675.00	£4500.00
6-7 scarce in the U.S, very scarce in the U.K.						
	$650.00	$1950.00	$5250.00	£435.00	£1300.00	£3500.00
8 scarce in the U.S, very scarce in the U.K. classic Mister Chang cover						
	$1125.00	$3350.00	$9000.00	£750.00	£2250.00	£6000.00
9-10 scarce in the U.K.						
	$650.00	$1950.00	$5250.00	£435.00	£1300.00	£3500.00
[please note that the above are approximate values only, as copies very rarely come onto the UK market.]						
[Note also that the first three issues have been given theoretical values for Near Mint]						
11 scarce in the U.S, very scarce in the U.K. (Jan 1938)						
	$500.00	$1500.00	$4000.00	£330.00	£1000.00	£2675.00
12-14	$500.00	$1500.00	$4000.00	£330.00	£1000.00	£2675.00
15 1pg advertisement for Action Comics #1						
	$500.00	$1500.00	$4000.00	£330.00	£1000.00	£2675.00
16-17	$500.00	$1500.00	$4000.00	£330.00	£1000.00	£2675.00
18 scarce in the U.S, very scarce in the U.K. classic Fu Manchu cover						
	$900.00	$2700.00	$7250.00	£600.00	£1800.00	£4850.00
19	$500.00	$1500.00	$4000.00	£330.00	£1000.00	£2675.00
20 scarce in the U.S, very scarce in the U.K. 1st appearance The Crimson Avenger						
	$750.00	$2250.00	$6000.00	£500.00	£1500.00	£4000.00
21	$405.00	$1200.00	$3250.00	£270.00	£810.00	£2175.00
22 only Crimson Avenger cover						
	$500.00	$1500.00	$4000.00	£330.00	£1000.00	£2675.00
23 (Jan 1939)	$400.00	$1200.00	$3200.00	£265.00	£800.00	£2150.00
24-25 very scarce in the U.S. rare in the U.K.						
	$400.00	$1200.00	$3200.00	£265.00	£800.00	£2150.00
26 advertises "The Bat-Man" coming next issue						
	$375.00	$1125.00	$3000.00	£250.00	£750.00	£2000.00
27 1st appearance of The Bat-Man, 1st Commissioner Gordon, scarcer than Action Comics #1 at about 65 extant copies and arguably as important in publishing history						
	$13300.00	$40000.00	$160000.00	£8800.00	£26600.00	£106675.00
[Prices may vary widely on this comic]						
27 Oreo Cookies Giveaway Edition, ND rare in the U.K. 14pgs, (1984), paper cover - reprints lead storiies from Detective Comics #27 (origin Batman), #38 (origin Robin) and Batman #1 (origin Joker)						
	$3.75	$11.00	$22.50	£2.50	£7.50	£15.00
28 2nd appearance of Batman, non Batman cover						
	$2175.00	$6500.00	$17500.00	£1450.00	£4350.00	£11675.00
29 3rd appearance of Batman, Dr. Death story, (2nd ever Batman cover)						
	$2850.00	$8600.00	$26000.00	£1925.00	£5700.00	£17350.00
30 Dr. Death story part 2						
	$750.00	$2250.00	$6000.00	£500.00	£1500.00	£4000.00
31 1st appearance Julie Madison (Batman's first girlfriend), 1st use of Bat-Gyro and Batarang, the classic Batman cover						
	$2600.00	$7800.00	$26000.00	£1725.00	£5200.00	£17350.00
32 very scarce in the U.K. and U.S. classic opening page						
	$750.00	$2250.00	$6000.00	£500.00	£1500.00	£4000.00
33 1st details of the origin of Batman (there was no origin in #27); Batman-wearing-gun-holster cover						
	$3600.00	$10800.00	$36000.00	£2400.00	£7200.00	£24000.00
34 2nd Crimson Avenger cover						
	$560.00	$1675.00	$4500.00	£375.00	£1125.00	£3000.00
35 (Jan 1940) regular Batman covers begin; long "bat-ears" and classic hypodermic needle cover						
	$1000.00	$3000.00	$8000.00	£660.00	£2000.00	£5350.00
36 scarce in both US and UK origin and 1st appearance Hugo Strange; 1st finned gauntlets on Batman costume						
	$710.00	$2150.00	$5750.00	£480.00	£1425.00	£3850.00
37	$710.00	$2125.00	$5700.00	£475.00	£1425.00	£3800.00
38 origin and 1st appearance Robin the Boy Wonder						
	$3250.00	$9700.00	$32500.00	£2150.00	£6500.00	£21675.00
39	$650.00	$1950.00	$5250.00	£435.00	£1300.00	£3500.00
40 origin and 1st appearance Clayface I (Basil Karlo), 1st Joker cover (face re-coloured clay-brown to denote Clayface, probably last minute, as Joker story originally intended here was used in Batman #1						
	$770.00	$2325.00	$7000.00	£510.00	£1550.00	£4675.00
41 1st solo Robin story						
	$375.00	$1125.00	$3000.00	£250.00	£750.00	£2000.00
42-44	$225.00	$670.00	$1800.00	£150.00	£450.00	£1200.00
45 1st Joker story in Detective Comics						
	$385.00	$1150.00	$3100.00	£255.00	£770.00	£2075.00
46	$210.00	$630.00	$1700.00	£140.00	£430.00	£1150.00
47 (Jan 1941)	$210.00	$630.00	$1700.00	£140.00	£430.00	£1150.00
48 1st mention of Batmobile (see Batman #5), 1st mention of Gotham City						
	$210.00	$630.00	$1700.00	£140.00	£430.00	£1150.00
49-50	$210.00	$630.00	$1700.00	£140.00	£430.00	£1150.00
51	$140.00	$420.00	$1125.00	£92.50	£280.00	£750.00
52 opium den cover						
	$140.00	$420.00	$1125.00	£92.50	£280.00	£750.00
53-57	$140.00	$420.00	$1125.00	£92.50	£280.00	£750.00
58 1st appearance The Penguin						
	$385.00	$1150.00	$3500.00	£260.00	£780.00	£2350.00
59 (Jan 1942) 2nd appearance The Penguin						
	$165.00	$495.00	$1325.00	£110.00	£330.00	£885.00
60 1st appearance Air Wave						
	$165.00	$495.00	$1325.00	£110.00	£330.00	£885.00
61	$140.00	$420.00	$1125.00	£92.50	£280.00	£750.00
62 Joker cover and story by Jerry Robinson						
	$230.00	$690.00	$1850.00	£155.00	£465.00	£1250.00
63	$140.00	$420.00	$1125.00	£92.50	£280.00	£750.00
64 origin and 1st appearance Boy Commandos by Joe Simon and Jack Kirby						
	$400.00	$1200.00	$3600.00	£265.00	£800.00	£2400.00
65 classic Boy Commandos cover by Simon and Kirby						
	$310.00	$930.00	$2500.00	£205.00	£620.00	£1675.00
66 origin and 1st appearance Two Face						
	$315.00	$950.00	$2850.00	£210.00	£630.00	£1900.00
67 1st Penguin cover						
	$215.00	$650.00	$1750.00	£145.00	£435.00	£1170.00
68 Two Face cover and story (continued from #66)						
	$175.00	$520.00	$1400.00	£115.00	£350.00	£935.00
69 Joker cover and story, classic Joker holding Colt .45's by Jerry Robinson						
	$155.00	$465.00	$1250.00	£100.00	£310.00	£835.00
70 classic montage cover by Jerry Robinson						
	$115.00	$345.00	$925.00	£77.50	£230.00	£620.00
71 (Jan 1943) Joker cover and story; classic "calendar" cover by Jerry Robinson						
	$125.00	$380.00	$1025.00	£85.00	£255.00	£685.00
72	$105.00	$315.00	$850.00	£70.00	£210.00	£570.00
73 Scarecrow cover(1st) and story						
	$130.00	$390.00	$1050.00	£87.50	£260.00	£700.00
74 1st appearance Tweedledum and Tweedledee						
	$100.00	$305.00	$825.00	£67.50	£205.00	£550.00
75	$100.00	$305.00	$825.00	£67.50	£205.00	£550.00
76 Joe Simon and Jack Kirby art, Joker cover and story						
	$165.00	$500.00	$1350.00	£110.00	£335.00	£900.00
77-79	$110.00	$335.00	$900.00	£75.00	£225.00	£600.00
80 Two Face appears						
	$115.00	$355.00	$950.00	£77.50	£235.00	£635.00
81 1st appearance The Cavalier						
	$92.50	$280.00	$750.00	£62.50	£185.00	£500.00
82	$92.50	$280.00	$750.00	£62.50	£185.00	£500.00
83 (Jan 1944) 1st appearance of the more familiar "skinny" Alfred (see cover Batman #22 for 1st cover appearance in this style)						

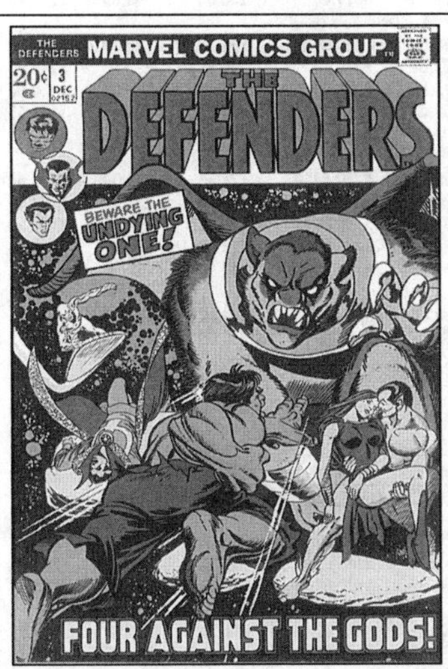

Defenders #3

Demon (1st) #4

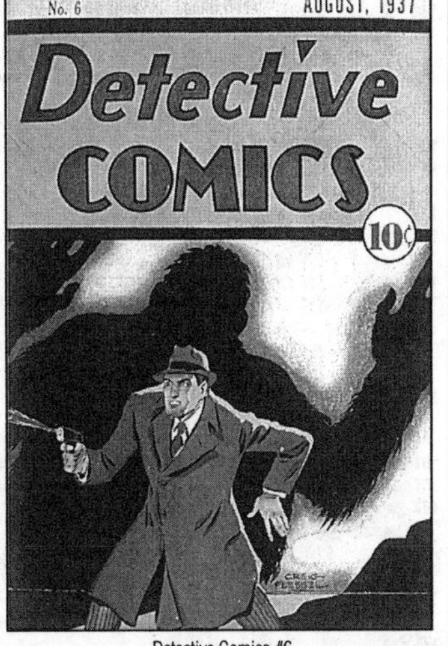

Detective Comics #6

Issue	$Good	$Fine	$N.Mint	£Good	£Fine	£N.Mint
	$100.00	*$300.00*	*$800.00*	£65.00	£200.00	£535.00
84	*$92.50*	*$280.00*	*$750.00*	£62.50	£185.00	£500.00
85 Joker cover and story						
	$110.00	*$335.00*	*$900.00*	£75.00	£225.00	£600.00
86-90	*$92.50*	*$280.00*	*$750.00*	£62.50	£185.00	£500.00
91 Joker cover and story						
	$105.00	*$315.00*	*$850.00*	£70.00	£210.00	£570.00
92-94	*$77.50*	*$230.00*	*$625.00*	£52.50	£155.00	£420.00
95 (Jan 1945)	*$77.50*	*$230.00*	*$625.00*	£52.50	£155.00	£420.00
96 Alfred's surname known to be "Beagle" which became "Pennyworth" in later years						
	$77.50	*$230.00*	*$625.00*	£52.50	£155.00	£420.00
97-98	*$77.50*	*$230.00*	*$625.00*	£52.50	£155.00	£420.00
99 Penguin cover						
	$110.00	*$335.00*	*$900.00*	£75.00	£225.00	£600.00
100	*$120.00*	*$365.00*	*$975.00*	£80.00	£240.00	£650.00
[Note: issues before #100 generally scarce in the U.K.]						
101	*$77.50*	*$230.00*	*$625.00*	£52.50	£155.00	£420.00
102 Joker cover and story						
	$100.00	*$305.00*	*$825.00*	£67.50	£205.00	£550.00
103-106	*$77.50*	*$230.00*	*$625.00*	£52.50	£155.00	£420.00
107 (Jan 1946)	*$77.50*	*$230.00*	*$625.00*	£52.50	£155.00	£420.00
108 1st appearance of the Bat-Plane, classic bat-symbol and bat-plane cover						
	$77.50	*$230.00*	*$625.00*	£52.50	£155.00	£420.00
109 Joker cover and story						
	$100.00	*$300.00*	*$800.00*	£65.00	£200.00	£535.00
110-113	*$75.00*	*$225.00*	*$600.00*	£50.00	£150.00	£400.00
114 Joker cover and story, 1st smaller cover logo						
	$95.00	*$290.00*	*$775.00*	£65.00	£195.00	£520.00
115-117	*$75.00*	*$225.00*	*$600.00*	£50.00	£150.00	£400.00
118 Joker cover and story						
	$95.00	*$290.00*	*$775.00*	£65.00	£195.00	£520.00
119 (Jan 1947)	*$75.00*	*$225.00*	*$600.00*	£50.00	£150.00	£400.00
120 Penguin cover (predominantly white and prone to foxing and/or dust shadows)						
	$175.00	*$520.00*	*$1400.00*	£115.00	£350.00	£935.00
121	*$75.00*	*$225.00*	*$600.00*	£50.00	£150.00	£400.00
122 1st Catwoman cover in Detective title						
	$125.00	*$375.00*	*$1000.00*	£82.50	£250.00	£675.00
123	*$75.00*	*$225.00*	*$600.00*	£50.00	£150.00	£400.00
124 Joker cover and story						
	$92.50	*$280.00*	*$750.00*	£62.50	£185.00	£500.00
125	*$75.00*	*$225.00*	*$600.00*	£50.00	£150.00	£400.00
126 Penguin cover						
	$95.00	*$290.00*	*$775.00*	£65.00	£195.00	£520.00
127	*$75.00*	*$225.00*	*$600.00*	£50.00	£150.00	£400.00
128 Joker cover and story						
	$90.00	*$270.00*	*$725.00*	£60.00	£180.00	£485.00
129-130	*$75.00*	*$225.00*	*$600.00*	£50.00	£150.00	£400.00
131 (Jan 1948)	*$62.50*	*$185.00*	*$500.00*	£42.00	£125.00	£335.00
132-134	*$62.50*	*$185.00*	*$500.00*	£42.00	£125.00	£335.00
135 Batman meets Frankenstein						
	$62.50	*$185.00*	*$500.00*	£42.00	£125.00	£335.00
136	*$62.50*	*$185.00*	*$500.00*	£42.00	£125.00	£335.00
137 Joker cover and story						
	$75.00	*$225.00*	*$600.00*	£50.00	£150.00	£400.00
138 origin Robotman (though he 1st appeared in Star Spangled Comics #7)						
	$110.00	*$335.00*	*$900.00*	£75.00	£225.00	£600.00
139	*$62.50*	*$185.00*	*$500.00*	£42.00	£125.00	£335.00
140 scarce in both US and UK 1st appearance The Riddler, Riddler cover						
	$440.00	*$1325.00*	*$4000.00*	£295.00	£890.00	£2675.00
141	*$67.50*	*$205.00*	*$550.00*	£46.00	£135.00	£370.00
142 2nd Riddler, Riddler cover						
	$110.00	*$335.00*	*$900.00*	£75.00	£225.00	£600.00
143 (Jan 1949)	*$67.50*	*$205.00*	*$550.00*	£46.00	£135.00	£370.00
144-146	*$67.50*	*$205.00*	*$550.00*	£46.00	£135.00	£370.00
147 1st appearance Tiger Shark (note Marvel villain!)						
	$67.50	*$205.00*	*$550.00*	£46.00	£135.00	£370.00
148	*$67.50*	*$205.00*	*$550.00*	£46.00	£135.00	£370.00
149 Joker cover and story						
	$82.50	*$250.00*	*$675.00*	£55.00	£165.00	£450.00
150	*$67.50*	*$205.00*	*$550.00*	£46.00	£135.00	£370.00
151 origin and 1st appearance Pow-Wow Smith						
	$75.00	*$225.00*	*$600.00*	£50.00	£150.00	£400.00
152	*$60.00*	*$180.00*	*$485.00*	£41.00	£120.00	£325.00
153 1st appearance Roy Ramond, TV Detective; also The Flying Batman (see Batman #82)						
	$70.00	*$210.00*	*$560.00*	£47.00	£140.00	£375.00
154	*$60.00*	*$180.00*	*$485.00*	£41.00	£120.00	£325.00
155 (Jan 1950)	*$60.00*	*$180.00*	*$485.00*	£41.00	£120.00	£325.00
156 new Batmobile with bubble canopy and bat-wing fin on top						
	$85.00	*$255.00*	*$680.00*	£55.00	£170.00	£455.00
157	*$60.00*	*$180.00*	*$485.00*	£41.00	£120.00	£325.00
158 Joker face on cover						
	$60.00	*$180.00*	*$485.00*	£41.00	£120.00	£325.00
159-160	*$60.00*	*$180.00*	*$485.00*	£41.00	£120.00	£325.00
161-166	*$70.00*	*$215.00*	*$575.00*	£48.00	£140.00	£385.00
167 (Jan 1951)	*$70.00*	*$215.00*	*$575.00*	£48.00	£140.00	£385.00
168 scarce in the U.S, very scarce in the U.K. 1st origin The Joker ("The Man in the Red Hood") since his first appearance in Batman #1 in 1940, classic cover						
	$330.00	*$1000.00*	*$3000.00*	£220.00	£660.00	£2000.00
[Very rare in high grade - Very Fine+ or better]						
169-170 scarce in both US and UK						
	$70.00	*$215.00*	*$575.00*	£48.00	£140.00	£385.00
171 Penguin cover						
	$55.00	*$165.00*	*$450.00*	£38.00	£110.00	£300.00
172-175	*$55.00*	*$165.00*	*$450.00*	£38.00	£110.00	£300.00
176 last 52pg issue						
	$55.00	*$165.00*	*$450.00*	£38.00	£110.00	£300.00
177-178	*$55.00*	*$165.00*	*$450.00*	£38.00	£110.00	£300.00
179 (Jan 1952)	*$55.00*	*$165.00*	*$450.00*	£38.00	£110.00	£300.00
180 Joker cover and story						
	$60.00	*$180.00*	*$480.00*	£40.00	£120.00	£320.00
181-185	*$52.50*	*$155.00*	*$425.00*	£36.00	£105.00	£285.00
186 The Flying Batcave (see Detective #317)						
	$52.50	*$155.00*	*$425.00*	£36.00	£105.00	£285.00
187 Two Face appears						
	$55.00	*$165.00*	*$440.00*	£37.00	£110.00	£295.00
188-189	*$52.50*	*$155.00*	*$425.00*	£36.00	£105.00	£285.00
190 origin retold	*$75.00*	*$225.00*	*$600.00*	£50.00	£150.00	£400.00
191 (Jan 1953)	*$50.00*	*$150.00*	*$400.00*	£34.00	£100.00	£270.00
192	*$50.00*	*$150.00*	*$400.00*	£34.00	£100.00	£270.00
193 Joker cover and story						
	$55.00	*$165.00*	*$450.00*	£38.00	£110.00	£300.00
194-199	*$50.00*	*$150.00*	*$400.00*	£34.00	£100.00	£270.00
200 scarce in the U.K.						
	$67.50	*$205.00*	*$550.00*	£46.00	£135.00	£370.00
201-202	*$55.00*	*$170.00*	*$400.00*	£39.00	£115.00	£270.00
203 (Jan 1954) Catwoman cover						
	$62.50	*$190.00*	*$450.00*	£43.00	£125.00	£300.00
204	*$55.00*	*$170.00*	*$400.00*	£39.00	£115.00	£270.00
205 origin Batcave						
	$75.00	*$230.00*	*$540.00*	£50.00	£150.00	£360.00
206-210	*$55.00*	*$170.00*	*$400.00*	£39.00	£115.00	£270.00
211 Catwoman cover						
	$60.00	*$185.00*	*$435.00*	£41.00	£120.00	£290.00
212	*$52.50*	*$160.00*	*$380.00*	£36.00	£105.00	£255.00
213 origin and 1st appearance Mirror Man (note the later Flash villain Mirror Master)						
	$70.00	*$210.00*	*$500.00*	£48.00	£140.00	£335.00
214	*$52.50*	*$160.00*	*$380.00*	£36.00	£105.00	£255.00
215 (Jan 1955)	*$52.50*	*$160.00*	*$380.00*	£36.00	£105.00	£255.00
216	*$52.50*	*$160.00*	*$380.00*	£36.00	£105.00	£255.00
217-224	*$50.00*	*$150.00*	*$350.00*	£34.00	£100.00	£235.00
225 origin and 1st appearance John Jones the Martian Manhunter, the first recognised new Silver Age super-hero (The Flash, though more important, was a revival)						
	$435.00	*$1300.00*	*$5250.00*	£290.00	£870.00	£3500.00
225 Silver Age Classic, ND (Mar 1992)						
	$0.25	*$0.75*	*$1.25*	£0.15	£0.45	£0.80
226 2nd appearance Martian Manhunter, origin continued						
	$150.00	*$450.00*	*$1350.00*	£100.00	£300.00	£900.00
227 (Jan 1956) 3rd appearance Martian Manhunter						
	$62.50	*$190.00*	*$450.00*	£43.00	£125.00	£300.00
228-229	*$62.50*	*$190.00*	*$450.00*	£43.00	£125.00	£300.00
230 1st appearance Silver Age Mad Hatter (see Batman #49)						
	$70.00	*$210.00*	*$500.00*	£48.00	£140.00	£335.00
231 origin Martian Manhunter retold in brief						
	$46.00	*$135.00*	*$325.00*	£31.00	£92.50	£220.00
232	*$44.00*	*$130.00*	*$310.00*	£30.00	£90.00	£210.00
233 origin and 1st appearance Batwoman						
	$145.00	*$440.00*	*$1175.00*	£97.50	£290.00	£785.00
234	*$44.00*	*$130.00*	*$310.00*	£30.00	£90.00	£210.00
235 scarce in the U.K. origin partly retold; Bruce Wayne's father Thomas wears a bat-costume to a fancy dress party and prevents a robbery; influences Bruce on choice of name/costume						
	$75.00	*$225.00*	*$600.00*	£50.00	£150.00	£400.00
236 Martian Manhunter contacts Mars						
	$49.00	*$145.00*	*$345.00*	£33.00	£97.50	£230.00
237-238	*$44.00*	*$130.00*	*$310.00*	£30.00	£90.00	£210.00
239 scarce in the U.K. (Jan 1957) painted (grey-tone) cover						
	$46.00	*$135.00*	*$325.00*	£31.00	£92.50	£220.00
240	*$44.00*	*$130.00*	*$310.00*	£30.00	£90.00	£210.00
241-250	*$39.00*	*$115.00*	*$270.00*	£26.00	£75.00	£180.00
251 (Jan 1958)	*$36.00*	*$105.00*	*$250.00*	£23.50	£70.00	£167.50
252-254	*$36.00*	*$105.00*	*$250.00*	£23.50	£70.00	£167.50
255 "Dinasaur" mis-spelling on cover						
	$36.00	*$105.00*	*$250.00*	£23.50	£70.00	£167.50
256-260	*$36.00*	*$105.00*	*$250.00*	£23.50	£70.00	£167.50
261-262	*$27.00*	*$80.00*	*$190.00*	£18.00	£52.50	£127.50
263 (Jan 1959)	*$27.00*	*$80.00*	*$190.00*	£18.00	£52.50	£127.50
264	*$27.00*	*$80.00*	*$190.00*	£18.00	£52.50	£127.50
265 Batman's origin retold						
	$43.00	*$125.00*	*$300.00*	£29.00	£85.00	£200.00
266	*$27.00*	*$80.00*	*$190.00*	£18.00	£52.50	£127.50
267 origin and 1st appearance Bat-Mite						
	$39.00	*$115.00*	*$270.00*	£26.00	£75.00	£180.00
268-270	*$27.00*	*$80.00*	*$190.00*	£18.00	£52.50	£127.50
271 Martian Manhunter origin retold						
	$27.00	*$80.00*	*$190.00*	£18.00	£52.50	£127.50
272	*$20.00*	*$60.00*	*$140.00*	£13.50	£41.00	£95.00
1st official distribution in the U.K.						
273 Jonn Jonzz reveals identity						
	$20.00	*$60.00*	*$140.00*	£12.00	£36.00	£85.00
274	*$20.00*	*$60.00*	*$140.00*	£12.00	£36.00	£85.00
275 (Jan 1960)	*$20.00*	*$60.00*	*$140.00*	£12.00	£36.00	£85.00
276 2nd appearance Bat-Mite						
	$21.00	*$62.50*	*$150.00*	£12.50	£39.00	£90.00
277-279	*$20.00*	*$60.00*	*$140.00*	£12.00	£36.00	£85.00
280	*$20.00*	*$60.00*	*$140.00*	£13.50	£41.00	£95.00

Issue	$Good	$Fine	$N.Mint	£Good	£Fine	£N.Mint
281-286	$17.00	$50.00	$120.00	£10.00	£30.00	£70.00
287 (Jan 1961) origin Martian Manhunter retold	$17.00	$50.00	$120.00	£10.00	£30.00	£70.00
288-292	$17.00	$50.00	$120.00	£10.00	£30.00	£70.00
293-296	$16.00	$49.00	$115.00	£7.75	£23.50	£55.00
297 last 10¢ issue	$16.00	$49.00	$115.00	£7.75	£23.50	£55.00
298 1st appearance Clayface II (Matt Hagen)	$30.00	$90.00	$240.00	£15.50	£47.00	£125.00
299 (Jan 1962)	$16.00	$49.00	$115.00	£7.75	£23.50	£55.00
300	$16.00	$49.00	$115.00	£8.50	£26.00	£60.00
301 Martian Manhunter returns to Mars	$12.50	$39.00	$90.00	£5.50	£17.00	£40.00
302-309	$10.50	$32.00	$75.00	£4.25	£12.50	£30.00
310 scarce in the U.K.	$10.50	$32.00	$75.00	£4.55	£13.50	£32.00
311 (Jan 1963)	$10.50	$32.00	$75.00	£3.90	£11.50	£27.50
312-316	$10.50	$32.00	$75.00	£3.90	£11.50	£27.50
317 flying Batcave	$10.50	$32.00	$75.00	£3.90	£11.50	£27.50
318-320	$10.50	$32.00	$75.00	£3.90	£11.50	£27.50
321	$10.50	$32.00	$75.00	£3.55	£10.50	£25.00
322 1st original Batgirl in title	$10.50	$32.00	$75.00	£3.55	£10.50	£25.00
323 (Jan 1964)	$10.50	$32.00	$75.00	£3.55	£10.50	£25.00
324-326	$10.50	$32.00	$75.00	£3.55	£10.50	£25.00
327 new look Batman costume, 1st official Silver Age Batman (according to DC - debateable however); 1st Elongated Man series	$17.50	$52.50	$125.00	£7.00	£21.00	£50.00
327 Silver Age Classic, ND (Mar 1992)	$0.25	$0.75	$1.25	£0.15	£0.45	£0.80
328 Alfred "dies" (later returns as The Outsider in #340)	$15.00	$45.00	$105.00	£5.50	£17.00	£40.00
329-330	$10.50	$32.00	$75.00	£3.55	£10.50	£25.00
331	$7.75	$23.50	$55.00	£2.85	£8.50	£20.00
332 Joker cover and story	$9.50	$29.00	$68.00	£3.40	£10.00	£24.00
333-334	$7.75	$23.50	$55.00	£2.85	£8.50	£20.00
335 (Jan 1965)	$7.75	$23.50	$55.00	£2.85	£8.50	£20.00
336-339	$7.75	$23.50	$55.00	£2.85	£8.50	£20.00
340 The Outsider appears	$8.50	$26.00	$60.00	£3.20	£9.50	£22.50
341 Joker cover and story	$9.25	$28.00	$65.00	£3.55	£10.50	£25.00
342	$7.75	$23.50	$55.00	£2.85	£8.50	£20.00
343 Elongated Man appears	$7.75	$23.50	$55.00	£2.85	£8.50	£20.00
344	$7.75	$23.50	$55.00	£2.85	£8.50	£20.00
345 1st appearance Block Buster	$7.75	$23.50	$55.00	£2.85	£8.50	£20.00
346 last Silver Age issue indicia dated December 1965	$7.75	$23.50	$55.00	£2.85	£8.50	£20.00
347 (Jan 1966) Earth II Batman appears, Justice League of America cameo	$7.75	$23.50	$55.00	£2.85	£8.50	£20.00
348-349 Kubert cover	$7.75	$23.50	$55.00	£2.85	£8.50	£20.00
350	$7.75	$23.50	$55.00	£2.85	£8.50	£20.00
351	$7.75	$23.50	$55.00	£2.50	£7.50	£17.50
352 pin-up poster at centre-fold (often missing!)	$7.75	$23.50	$55.00	£2.50	£7.50	£17.50
353 Batman vs. Weather Wizard, Flash appears on cover	$7.75	$23.50	$55.00	£2.50	£7.50	£17.50
354-355	$7.75	$23.50	$55.00	£2.50	£7.50	£17.50
356 Alfred returns from his period as The Outsider	$7.75	$23.50	$55.00	£2.50	£7.50	£17.50
357	$7.75	$23.50	$55.00	£2.50	£7.50	£17.50
358 1st appearance Spellbinder	$7.75	$23.50	$55.00	£2.50	£7.50	£17.50
359 (Jan 1967) origin and 1st appearance new Batgirl (prompted by TV Show)	$13.50	$41.00	$95.00	£5.00	£15.00	£35.00
360-364	$7.75	$23.50	$55.00	£2.10	£6.25	£15.00
365 Joker cover and story	$9.25	$28.00	$65.00	£2.55	£7.50	£18.00
366-368	$7.75	$23.50	$55.00	£2.10	£6.25	£15.00
369 Neal Adams art on Elongated Man back-up story, Catwoman appears (cameo) - 3rd Silver Age appearance	$10.00	$30.00	$70.00	£4.60	£13.50	£32.50
370	$7.75	$23.50	$55.00	£2.10	£6.25	£15.00
371 (Jan 1968) new Batmobile modelled on TV show version	$7.75	$23.50	$55.00	£2.50	£7.50	£17.50
372-376	$6.25	$19.00	$45.00	£2.10	£6.25	£15.00
377 Riddler appears	$6.25	$19.00	$45.00	£2.10	£6.25	£15.00
378-380	$6.25	$19.00	$45.00	£2.10	£6.25	£15.00
381-382	$6.25	$19.00	$45.00	£1.75	£5.25	£12.50
383 (Jan 1969)	$6.25	$19.00	$45.00	£1.75	£5.25	£12.50
384	$6.25	$19.00	$45.00	£1.75	£5.25	£12.50
385 Neal Adams cover	$6.25	$19.00	$45.00	£1.75	£5.25	£12.50
386	$6.25	$19.00	$45.00	£1.75	£5.25	£12.50
387 scarce in the U.K. 30th anniversary; reprints 1st Batman story in Detective #27 (May 1939), Joker and Penguin on cover	$10.50	$32.00	$75.00	£4.25	£12.50	£30.00
388 Joker cover and story; last 12 cents issue	$8.25	$24.50	$58.00	£2.10	£6.25	£15.00
389-390	$6.25	$19.00	$45.00	£1.75	£5.25	£12.50
391 Neal Adams cover	$3.55	$10.50	$25.00	£1.40	£4.25	£10.00
392-394	$3.55	$10.50	$25.00	£1.40	£4.25	£10.00
395 (Jan 1970) Neal Adams art	$5.00	$15.00	$30.00	£2.50	£7.50	£15.00
396	$4.15	$12.50	$25.00	£1.65	£5.00	£10.00
397 Neal Adams art	$5.00	$15.00	$30.00	£2.50	£7.50	£15.00
398	$4.15	$12.50	$25.00	£1.50	£4.50	£9.00
399 Neal Adams cover	$4.15	$12.50	$25.00	£1.50	£4.50	£9.00
400 Neal Adams art; 1st appearance Man-Bat	$12.50	$38.00	$75.00	£5.00	£15.00	£30.00
401	$3.30	$10.00	$20.00	£1.30	£4.00	£8.00
402 2nd appearance Man-Bat; Neal Adams art	$5.00	$15.00	$30.00	£2.50	£7.50	£15.00
403 Neal Adams cover	$2.50	$7.50	$15.00	£1.25	£3.75	£7.50
404 Neal Adams art	$5.00	$15.00	$30.00	£2.50	£7.50	£15.00
405-406	$2.50	$7.50	$15.00	£1.25	£3.75	£7.50
407 (Jan 1971) Neal Adams art	$5.00	$15.00	$30.00	£2.50	£7.50	£15.00
408 Neal Adams art	$5.00	$15.00	$30.00	£2.50	£7.50	£15.00
409	$2.50	$7.50	$15.00	£1.25	£3.75	£7.50
410 Neal Adams art	$5.00	$15.00	$30.00	£2.50	£7.50	£15.00
411-413 Neal Adams covers	$2.50	$7.50	$15.00	£1.15	£3.50	£7.00
414-417 scarce in the U.K. 52pgs	$2.50	$7.50	$15.00	£1.30	£4.00	£8.00
418 scarce in the U.K. 52pgs, Creeper appears	$2.50	$7.50	$15.00	£1.30	£4.00	£8.00
419 scarce in the U.K. 52pgs, (Jan 1972)	$2.50	$7.50	$15.00	£1.30	£4.00	£8.00
420 scarce in the U.K. 52pgs	$2.50	$7.50	$15.00	£1.30	£4.00	£8.00
421-424 scarce in the U.K. 52pgs	$2.05	$6.25	$12.50	£1.25	£3.75	£7.50
425-427	$2.05	$6.25	$12.50	£1.00	£3.00	£6.00
428 ND	$2.05	$6.25	$12.50	£1.25	£3.75	£7.50
429-430	$2.05	$6.25	$12.50	£0.80	£2.50	£5.00
431 (Jan 1973)	$2.05	$6.25	$12.50	£0.80	£2.50	£5.00
432-433	$2.05	$6.25	$12.50	£0.80	£2.50	£5.00
434-436 scarce in the U.K.	$2.05	$6.25	$12.50	£1.00	£3.00	£6.00
437 scarce in the U.K. 1st modern Manhunter, Walt Simonson art (ends 443)	$2.90	$8.75	$17.50	£1.40	£4.25	£8.50
438 100pgs, (Jan 1974)	$4.15	$12.50	$25.00	£1.30	£4.00	£8.00
439 100pgs, origin briefly retold, Adamsesque art by Vin and Sal Amendola	$4.15	$12.50	$25.00	£1.50	£4.50	£9.00
440 100pgs	$4.15	$12.50	$25.00	£1.30	£4.00	£8.00
441 100pgs, Chaykin art on Batman	$4.15	$12.50	$25.00	£1.30	£4.00	£8.00
442 100pgs, Toth art on Batman	$4.15	$12.50	$25.00	£1.30	£4.00	£8.00
443 100pgs, death of Manhunter; origin Creeper retold	$4.15	$12.50	$25.00	£1.50	£4.50	£9.00
444 100pgs, (Jan 1975)	$4.15	$12.50	$25.00	£1.25	£3.75	£7.50
445 100pgs	$4.15	$12.50	$25.00	£1.25	£3.75	£7.50
446	$1.65	$5.00	$10.00	£0.65	£2.00	£4.00
447 Creeper appears	$1.65	$5.00	$10.00	£0.65	£2.00	£4.00
448 Batman and The Creeper team up	$1.65	$5.00	$10.00	£0.65	£2.00	£4.00
449 scarce in the U.K.	$1.65	$5.00	$10.00	£0.75	£2.25	£4.50
450 scarce in the U.K. Walt Simonson art	$1.65	$5.00	$10.00	£0.80	£2.50	£5.00
451-454 scarce in the U.K.	$1.65	$5.00	$10.00	£0.75	£2.25	£4.50
455 (Jan 1976)	$1.65	$5.00	$10.00	£0.65	£2.00	£4.00
456	$1.65	$5.00	$10.00	£0.65	£2.00	£4.00
457 origin updated	$1.65	$5.00	$10.00	£0.75	£2.25	£4.50
458	$1.65	$5.00	$10.00	£0.65	£2.00	£4.00
459 Batman and Catwoman vs. Green Arrow and Black Canary, Bolland cover	$1.65	$5.00	$10.00	£0.75	£2.25	£4.50
460	$1.65	$5.00	$10.00	£0.65	£2.00	£4.00
461 ND	$1.25	$3.75	$7.50	£0.80	£2.50	£5.00
462 scarce in the U.K.	$1.25	$3.75	$7.50	£0.65	£2.00	£4.00
463 ND	$1.25	$3.75	$7.50	£0.80	£2.50	£5.00
464-465 scarce in the U.K.	$1.25	$3.75	$7.50	£0.75	£2.25	£4.50
466 ND Marshall Rogers art on Green Arrow	$2.50	$7.50	$15.00	£1.15	£3.50	£7.00

	$Good	$Fine	$N.Mint	£Good	£Fine	£N.Mint
467 scarce in the U.K. (Jan 1977) Marshall Rogers art on Hawkman	***$2.50***	***$7.50***	***$15.00***	£1.00	£3.00	£6.00
468 scarce in the U.K. 1st Marshall Rogers art on Batman	***$2.50***	***$7.50***	***$15.00***	£1.30	£4.00	£8.00
469-470 scarce in the U.K. Walt Simonson art	***$1.25***	***$3.75***	***$7.50***	£0.75	£2.25	£4.50
471 scarce in the U.K. Marshall Rogers art on Batman	***$2.50***	***$7.50***	***$15.00***	£1.30	£4.00	£8.00
472 very scarce in the U.K. Marshall Rogers art on Batma; classic cover	***$2.50***	***$7.50***	***$15.00***	£2.50	£7.50	£15.00
473-474 scarce in the U.K. Marshall Rogers art on Batman	***$2.50***	***$7.50***	***$15.00***	£1.30	£4.00	£8.00
475 (Feb 1978) classic Marshall Rogers art on Batman and Joker	***$4.15***	***$12.50***	***$25.00***	£2.05	£6.25	£12.50
476 Marshall Rogers art on Batman and Joker	***$4.15***	***$12.50***	***$25.00***	£1.65	£5.00	£10.00
477 3pgs Rogers art; Neal Adams reprint	***$3.00***	***$9.00***	***$18.00***	£1.15	£3.50	£7.00
478 Marshall Rogers art on Batman, 1st appearance Clayface III	***$2.50***	***$7.50***	***$15.00***	£1.30	£4.00	£8.00
479 ND 44pgs, Marshall Rogers art on Batman	***$2.50***	***$7.50***	***$15.00***	£1.30	£4.00	£8.00
480 ND 44pgs	***$1.25***	***$3.75***	***$7.50***	£1.05	£3.25	£6.50
481 ND 68pgs, Jim Starlin, Marshall Rogers art	***$2.00***	***$6.00***	***$12.00***	£1.25	£3.75	£7.50
482 ND 68pgs, (Feb 1979) Jim Starlin, Marshall Rogers and Michael Golden art	***$1.30***	***$4.00***	***$8.00***	£1.25	£3.75	£7.50
483 ND 68pgs, 40th anniversary issue; origin Batman retold	***$1.65***	***$5.00***	***$10.00***	£0.80	£2.50	£5.00
484-487 ND 68pgs	***$1.00***	***$3.00***	***$6.00***	£0.65	£2.00	£4.00
488 ND 68pgs, (Feb 1980)	***$1.20***	***$3.60***	***$6.00***	£0.80	£2.40	£4.00
489-490 ND 68pgs	***$1.20***	***$3.60***	***$6.00***	£0.80	£2.40	£4.00
491-495 ND 68pgs	***$1.20***	***$3.60***	***$6.00***	£0.75	£2.25	£3.75
496-497	***$1.20***	***$3.60***	***$6.00***	£0.60	£1.80	£3.00
498 (Jan 1981)	***$1.20***	***$3.60***	***$6.00***	£0.60	£1.80	£3.00
499	***$1.20***	***$3.60***	***$6.00***	£0.60	£1.80	£3.00
500 ND 80pgs, Deadman X-over	***$2.50***	***$7.50***	***$12.50***	£1.20	£3.60	£6.00
501-503	***$0.85***	***$2.55***	***$4.25***	£0.55	£1.65	£2.75
504 Joker cover and story	***$1.00***	***$3.00***	***$5.00***	£0.70	£2.10	£3.50
505-509	***$0.85***	***$2.55***	***$4.25***	£0.55	£1.65	£2.75
510 (Jan 1982)	***$0.85***	***$2.55***	***$4.25***	£0.55	£1.65	£2.75
511	***$0.85***	***$2.55***	***$4.25***	£0.55	£1.65	£2.75
512 45th anniversary issue	***$0.85***	***$2.55***	***$4.25***	£0.55	£1.65	£2.75
513-521	***$0.85***	***$2.55***	***$4.25***	£0.55	£1.65	£2.75
522 (Jan 1983)	***$0.85***	***$2.55***	***$4.25***	£0.55	£1.65	£2.75
523	***$0.85***	***$2.55***	***$4.25***	£0.55	£1.65	£2.75
524 2nd appearance Jason Todd (cameo; see Batman #357)	***$0.85***	***$2.55***	***$4.25***	£0.60	£1.80	£3.00
525 3rd appearance Jason Todd	***$0.85***	***$2.55***	***$4.25***	£0.60	£1.80	£3.00
526 68pgs, Batman's 500th appearance in title, Joker cover and story	***$4.00***	***$12.00***	***$20.00***	£1.00	£3.00	£5.00
527-531	***$0.80***	***$2.40***	***$4.00***	£0.50	£1.50	£2.50
532 Joker appears	***$1.00***	***$3.00***	***$5.00***	£0.70	£2.10	£3.50
533	***$0.80***	***$2.40***	***$4.00***	£0.50	£1.50	£2.50
534 (Jan 1984)	***$0.80***	***$2.40***	***$4.00***	£0.50	£1.50	£2.50
535 intro new Robin (Jason Todd; see Batman #368)	***$0.90***	***$2.70***	***$4.50***	£0.60	£1.80	£3.00
536-545	***$0.80***	***$2.40***	***$4.00***	£0.50	£1.50	£2.50
546 (Jan 1985)	***$0.80***	***$2.40***	***$4.00***	£0.50	£1.50	£2.50
547-550	***$0.80***	***$2.40***	***$4.00***	£0.50	£1.50	£2.50
551-553	***$0.70***	***$2.10***	***$3.50***	£0.45	£1.35	£2.25
554 1st appearance new Black Canary	***$0.80***	***$2.40***	***$4.00***	£0.50	£1.50	£2.50
555-557	***$0.70***	***$2.10***	***$3.50***	£0.45	£1.35	£2.25
558 (Jan 1986) unofficial Crisis X-over	***$0.70***	***$2.10***	***$3.50***	£0.45	£1.35	£2.25
559 LD in the U.K. Catwoman appears	***$0.70***	***$2.10***	***$3.50***	£0.55	£1.65	£2.75
560 LD in the U.K.	***$0.70***	***$2.10***	***$3.50***	£0.50	£1.50	£2.50
561-566	***$0.70***	***$2.10***	***$3.50***	£0.45	£1.35	£2.25
567 Harlan Ellison story	***$0.70***	***$2.10***	***$3.50***	£0.45	£1.35	£2.25
568 Legends X-over, Janson art	***$0.70***	***$2.10***	***$3.50***	£0.45	£1.35	£2.25
569 Alan Davis/Paul Neary Joker rendition	***$1.10***	***$3.30***	***$5.50***	£0.70	£2.10	£3.50
570 (Jan 1987) Alan Davis/Paul Neary Joker rendition	***$1.10***	***$3.30***	***$5.50***	£0.70	£2.10	£3.50
571 Alan Davis/Paul Neary art	***$1.10***	***$3.30***	***$5.50***	£0.70	£2.10	£3.50
572 DS, 50th anniversary, Sherlock Holmes appears, Alan Davis art	***$1.20***	***$3.60***	***$6.00***	£0.80	£2.40	£4.00
573-574 Alan Davis/Paul Neary art	***$1.00***	***$3.00***	***$5.00***	£0.70	£2.10	£3.50
575 LD in the U.K. Davis/Neary art, Batman Year Two	***$2.00***	***$6.00***	***$10.00***	£1.30	£3.90	£6.50
576-578 Todd McFarlane art, Year Two	***$1.60***	***$4.80***	***$8.00***	£0.80	£2.40	£4.00
579 Breyfogle art	***$0.55***	***$1.65***	***$2.75***	£0.35	£1.05	£1.75
580-581 Jim Baikie art	***$0.55***	***$1.65***	***$2.75***	£0.35	£1.05	£1.75
582 (Jan 1988) Breyfogle art, Millennium X-over	***$0.55***	***$1.65***	***$2.75***	£0.35	£1.05	£1.75
583 Breyfogle art, Alan Grant/John Wagner scripts begin	***$0.55***	***$1.65***	***$2.75***	£0.35	£1.05	£1.75
584-585	***$0.55***	***$1.65***	***$2.75***	£0.35	£1.05	£1.75
586-594	***$0.45***	***$1.35***	***$2.25***	£0.30	£0.90	£1.50
595 (Jan 1989) Invasion X-over	***$0.45***	***$1.35***	***$2.25***	£0.30	£0.90	£1.50
596-597	***$0.45***	***$1.35***	***$2.25***	£0.30	£0.90	£1.50
598 LD in the U.K. giant squarebound, Part I Blind Justice, script by Sam Hamm (writer of Batman film), art by Cowans	***$1.50***	***$4.50***	***$7.50***	£1.00	£3.00	£5.00
599 Part II Blind Justice, script by Sam Hamm	***$0.80***	***$2.40***	***$4.00***	£0.50	£1.50	£2.50
600 LD in the U.K. 80pgs, squarebound, Sam Hamm script Part III Blind Justice	***$0.90***	***$2.70***	***$4.50***	£0.60	£1.80	£3.00
601	***$0.40***	***$1.20***	***$2.00***	£0.25	£0.75	£1.25
602-603 The Demon appears	***$0.40***	***$1.20***	***$2.00***	£0.25	£0.75	£1.25
604 Mud Pack story continues from Secret Origins 44; bi-weekly issue; mini-poster with painted art by Norm Breyfogle	***$0.40***	***$1.20***	***$2.00***	£0.25	£0.75	£1.25
605-606 Mud Pack story continues; bi-weekly issue	***$0.40***	***$1.20***	***$2.00***	£0.25	£0.75	£1.25
607 Mud Pack story continues; bi-weekly issue; mini-poster with painted art by Norm Breyfogle	***$0.40***	***$1.20***	***$2.00***	£0.25	£0.75	£1.25
608-609	***$0.40***	***$1.20***	***$2.00***	£0.25	£0.75	£1.25
610 (Jan 1990)	***$0.30***	***$0.90***	***$1.50***	£0.20	£0.60	£1.00
611-614	***$0.30***	***$0.90***	***$1.50***	£0.20	£0.60	£1.00
615 X-over with Batman 448/449	***$0.30***	***$0.90***	***$1.50***	£0.20	£0.60	£1.00
616-617 bi-weekly issue	***$0.30***	***$0.90***	***$1.50***	£0.20	£0.60	£1.00
618 bi-weekly issue, Joker cameo (1 panel)	***$0.30***	***$0.90***	***$1.50***	£0.20	£0.60	£1.00
619 bi-weekly issue	***$0.30***	***$0.90***	***$1.50***	£0.20	£0.60	£1.00
620	***$0.30***	***$0.90***	***$1.50***	£0.20	£0.60	£1.00
621	***$0.25***	***$0.75***	***$1.25***	£0.15	£0.45	£0.75
622-624 The Demon Within story, covers by Dick Sprang, Mike McKone/Flint Henry art	***$0.25***	***$0.75***	***$1.25***	£0.15	£0.45	£0.75
625 (Jan 1991)	***$0.25***	***$0.75***	***$1.25***	£0.15	£0.45	£0.75
626 Sarah Essen from Year: One appears	***$0.25***	***$0.75***	***$1.25***	£0.15	£0.45	£0.75
627 80pgs, 600th appearance of Batman in title, first story from Detective Comics#27 reprinted, and re-worked by a variety of artists/writers, cover painting by Breyfogle based on Detective Comics #27	***$0.60***	***$1.80***	***$3.00***	£0.40	£1.20	£2.00
628-630	***$0.25***	***$0.75***	***$1.25***	£0.15	£0.45	£0.75
631-634 bi-weekly issues	***$0.25***	***$0.75***	***$1.25***	£0.15	£0.45	£0.75
635-636 bi-weekly issues, Arkham Asylum story by Louise Simonson	***$0.25***	***$0.75***	***$1.25***	£0.15	£0.45	£0.75
637-638	***$0.25***	***$0.75***	***$1.25***	£0.15	£0.45	£0.75
639 The Idiot Root part 2, continues in Batman #473	***$0.25***	***$0.75***	***$1.25***	£0.15	£0.45	£0.75
640 (Jan 1992) The Idiot Root part 4 (conclusion)	***$0.25***	***$0.75***	***$1.25***	£0.15	£0.45	£0.75
641 Destroyer part 3 (conclusion)	***$0.25***	***$0.75***	***$1.25***	£0.15	£0.45	£0.75
642 X-over with Batman #476, Batman reveals identity to Vicki Vale	***$0.25***	***$0.75***	***$1.25***	£0.15	£0.45	£0.75
643	***$0.25***	***$0.75***	***$1.25***	£0.15	£0.45	£0.75
644-646 Electric City story	***$0.25***	***$0.75***	***$1.25***	£0.15	£0.45	£0.75
647-649 Return of the Cluemaster, bi-weekly	***$0.25***	***$0.75***	***$1.25***	£0.15	£0.45	£0.75
650-651 bi-weekly	***$0.25***	***$0.75***	***$1.25***	£0.15	£0.45	£0.75
652 Graham Nolan art, Travis Charest cover; prelude to Robin III mini-series, Huntress appears (origin retold), bi-weekly,	***$0.25***	***$0.75***	***$1.25***	£0.15	£0.45	£0.75
653 Travis Charest cover, Huntress appears	***$0.25***	***$0.75***	***$1.25***	£0.15	£0.45	£0.75
654 Sam Kieth cover	***$0.25***	***$0.75***	***$1.25***	£0.15	£0.45	£0.75
655 (Jan 1993) Sam Kieth cover	***$0.25***	***$0.75***	***$1.25***	£0.15	£0.45	£0.75
656-657 Sam Kieth cover	***$0.25***	***$0.75***	***$1.25***	£0.15	£0.45	£0.75
658 bi-weekly, Sam Kieth cover, Knightfall prequel	***$0.30***	***$0.90***	***$1.50***	£0.20	£0.60	£1.00
659 Knightfall part 2, continued in Batman #493; bi-weekly, Sam Kieth cover	***$0.60***	***$1.80***	***$3.00***	£0.40	£1.20	£2.00
660 Knightfall part 4, continued in Batman #494; bi-weekly, Sam Kieth cover featuring Bane	***$0.60***	***$1.80***	***$3.00***	£0.30	£0.90	£1.50
661 Knightfall part 6, continued in Batman #495; bi-weekly; Joker and Riddler cameos	***$0.50***	***$1.50***	***$2.50***	£0.30	£0.90	£1.50
662 Knightfall part 8, continued in Batman #496; bi-weekly; Riddler appears	***$0.50***	***$1.50***	***$2.50***	£0.25	£0.75	£1.25

Issue	$Good	$Fine	$N.Mint	£Good	£Fine	£N.Mint
663 Knightfall part 10, continued in Batman #497; bi-weekly	***$0.50***	***$1.50***	***$2.50***	**£0.25**	**£0.75**	**£1.25**
664 Knightfall part 12, continued in Showcase '93 #7; bi-weekly; Bane and Joker appear	***$0.50***	***$1.50***	***$2.50***	**£0.25**	**£0.75**	**£1.25**
665 Knightfall part 16, continued in Batman: Shadow of the Bat #16; bi-weekly	***$0.40***	***$1.20***	***$2.00***	**£0.25**	**£0.75**	**£1.25**
666 Knightfall part 18, continued in Batman #500	***$0.40***	***$1.20***	***$2.00***	**£0.25**	**£0.75**	**£1.25**
667 Knightquest: The Crusade part 1, continued in Batman: Shadow of the Bat #19; Kelley Jones cover	***$0.40***	***$1.20***	***$2.00***	**£0.25**	**£0.75**	**£1.25**
668 Knightquest: The Crusade part 5, continued in Batman #502; Kelley Jones cover; leads into Robin #1	***$0.25***	***$0.75***	***$1.25***	**£0.15**	**£0.45**	**£0.75**
669 Knightquest: The Crusade part 7, Kelley Jones cover	***$0.25***	***$0.75***	***$1.25***	**£0.15**	**£0.45**	**£0.75**
670 (Jan 1994) Knightquest: The Crusade story, Kelley Jones cover	***$0.25***	***$0.75***	***$1.25***	**£0.15**	**£0.45**	**£0.75**
671 Knightquest: The Crusade story, Kelley Jones cover; Joker appears (in a pony-tail - excellent)	***$0.25***	***$0.75***	***$1.25***	**£0.15**	**£0.45**	**£0.75**
672-673 Knightquest: The Crusade story, Kelley Jones cover; Joker appears	***$0.25***	***$0.75***	***$1.25***	**£0.15**	**£0.45**	**£0.75**
674 Knightquest: The Crusade story, Kelley Jones cover	***$0.25***	***$0.75***	***$1.25***	**£0.15**	**£0.45**	**£0.75**
675 Knightquest: The Crusade story the conclusion, continued in Robin #7; Kelley Jones cover	***$0.25***	***$0.75***	***$1.25***	**£0.15**	**£0.45**	**£0.75**
675 Collectors Edition, ND embossed blue and gold foil cover	***$0.60***	***$1.80***	***$3.00***	**£0.40**	**£1.20**	**£2.00**
676 48pgs, Knightsend part 3, continued in Batman: Legends of the Dark Knight #62	***$0.50***	***$1.50***	***$2.50***	**£0.30**	**£0.90**	**£1.50**
677 Knightsend part 9, continued in Batman: Legends of the Dark Knight #63	***$0.30***	***$0.90***	***$1.50***	**£0.20**	**£0.60**	**£1.00**
678 Zero Hour X-over	***$0.30***	***$0.90***	***$1.50***	**£0.20**	**£0.60**	**£1.00**
679	***$0.30***	***$0.90***	***$1.50***	**£0.20**	**£0.60**	**£1.00**
680 Dick Grayson as Batman vs. Two Face	***$0.30***	***$0.90***	***$1.50***	**£0.20**	**£0.60**	**£1.00**
681 (Jan 1995)	***$0.30***	***$0.90***	***$1.50***	**£0.20**	**£0.60**	**£1.00**
682 The Troika part 3, concluded in Robin #14	***$0.30***	***$0.90***	***$1.50***	**£0.20**	**£0.60**	**£1.00**
682 Collectors Edition, ND embossed black cover	***$0.50***	***$1.50***	***$2.50***	**£0.30**	**£0.90**	**£1.50**
683-684 The Penguin appears	***$0.30***	***$0.90***	***$1.50***	**£0.20**	**£0.60**	**£1.00**
685	***$0.30***	***$0.90***	***$1.50***	**£0.20**	**£0.60**	**£1.00**
686 Batman vs. King Snake and Lynx; upgraded coated paper stock (Miraweb Format) begins	***$0.40***	***$1.20***	***$2.00***	**£0.25**	**£0.75**	**£1.25**
687-690	***$0.40***	***$1.20***	***$2.00***	**£0.25**	**£0.75**	**£1.25**
691 Underworld Unleashed tie-in; death of Spellbinder and intro new Spellbinder	***$0.40***	***$1.20***	***$2.00***	**£0.25**	**£0.75**	**£1.25**
692 Underworld Unleashed tie-in, Spellbinder appears	***$0.40***	***$1.20***	***$2.00***	**£0.25**	**£0.75**	**£1.25**
693 (Jan 1996) Poison Ivy appears	***$0.40***	***$1.20***	***$2.00***	**£0.25**	**£0.75**	**£1.25**
694 Poison Ivy appears	***$0.40***	***$1.20***	***$2.00***	**£0.25**	**£0.75**	**£1.25**
695 Contagion part 2, continued in Robin #27	***$0.40***	***$1.20***	***$2.00***	**£0.25**	**£0.75**	**£1.25**
696 Contagion part 8, continued in Catwoman #32	***$0.40***	***$1.20***	***$2.00***	**£0.25**	**£0.75**	**£1.25**
697	***$0.40***	***$1.20***	***$2.00***	**£0.25**	**£0.75**	**£1.25**
698-699 Two-Face appears; bi-monthly	***$0.40***	***$1.20***	***$2.00***	**£0.25**	**£0.75**	**£1.25**
700 Legacy part 1, Ra's Al Ghul appears; continued in Catwoman #36	***$0.60***	***$1.80***	***$3.00***	**£0.40**	**£1.20**	**£2.00**
700 Collectors Edition, ND card-stock portfolio cover	***$1.00***	***$3.00***	***$5.00***	**£0.65**	**£1.95**	**£3.25**
701 ND Legacy part 6, continued in Robin #33	***$0.40***	***$1.20***	***$2.00***	**£0.25**	**£0.75**	**£1.25**
702 ND Legacy epilogue	***$0.40***	***$1.20***	***$2.00***	**£0.25**	**£0.75**	**£1.25**
703 ND Final Night tie-in	***$0.40***	***$1.20***	***$2.00***	**£0.25**	**£0.75**	**£1.25**
704 ND	***$0.40***	***$1.20***	***$2.00***	**£0.25**	**£0.75**	**£1.25**
705 ND (Jan 1997) The Riddler and The Cluemaster appear	***$0.40***	***$1.20***	***$2.00***	**£0.25**	**£0.75**	**£1.25**
706 ND	***$0.40***	***$1.20***	***$2.00***	**£0.25**	**£0.75**	**£1.25**
707 ND Riddler and Cluemaster appear	***$0.40***	***$1.20***	***$2.00***	**£0.25**	**£0.75**	**£1.25**
Title Value:	***$81004.00***	***$243196.70***	***$745061.25***	**£53660.20**	**£161147.40**	**£495125.10**

Note: Joker cover: 387 Joker cover and stories: 332, 341, 365, 388, 475, 476, 504, 526, 532, 566, 569, 570

ARTISTS

Ditko in 483-485, 487. Golden in 482. Rogers in 466-468, 471-479, 481.

FEATURES

Alfred in 486, 489. Atom in 432, 463, 489. Aquaman in 293-300. Batgirl in 384, 385, 388, 389, 392, 393, 396, 397, 404-424, 481-488, 490-499, 501, 502, 505, 506, 508-510, 512-517. Batman in 27-date; Unsolved Cases of the Batman in 484. Batman/Deadman in 500. Black Canary in 464. Black Lightning in 490, 491, 494, 495. Bat-Mite in 482. Demon in 482-485. Dr. Phosphorus in 469. Elongated Man in 327-383, 426, 430, 436, 444, 449, 453, 456, 457, 462, 465, 488, 500. Green Arrow in 466. Hawkman in 428, 434, 446, 452, 454, 455, 467, 479, 480, 500. Human Target in 483, 484, 486, 493. Jason Bard in 425, 427, 429, 431, 433, 435. Man-Bat in 458, 459, 481, 485, 492. Manhunter in 437-442; Manhunter/Batman in 443. Martian Manhunter in 273-326. Odd Man in 487. Robin solo in 386, 390, 391, 394, 398, 399, 402, 403, 445, 447, 450, 451, 481-488, 490-495; Robin/Batgirl in 400, 401, 489. Roy Raymond in 273-292, 487. Slam Bradley in 500. Tales of Gotham City in 488-495, 504, 507 (featuring Red Tornado in 493). Tim Trench, Private Detective in 460, 461.

REPRINT FEATURES

Alfred in 417, 421. Atom in 438, 439. Batman in 387, 438, 440-443. Black Canary, Guardian in 442. Doll Man, Manhunter in 440. Dr.Fate in 439, 442. Dr.Mid-Nite in 445. Elongated Man in 439, 442, 444, 445. Green Lantern in 438; GA Green Lantern in 440, 443. Hawkman in 438-440, 442. Ibis, The Spider, Eclipso, Kid Eternity in 439, 444. Plastic Man in 441. Rex the Wonder Dog in 416. Robin in 438, 440, 442-444. Roy Raymond in 419, 444, 445. Sierra Smith in 418, 444. Spectre, Creeper (origin) in 443. Star Hawkins in 444, 445.

DETECTIVE COMICS ANNUAL

DC Comics; 1 Aug 1988-present

Issue	$Good	$Fine	$N.Mint	£Good	£Fine	£N.Mint
1 48pgs, ties in with Green Arrow Annual #1, Question Annual #1, Janson art	***$1.00***	***$3.00***	***$5.00***	**£0.70**	**£2.10**	**£3.50**
2 64pgs, squarebound, Bolland cover	***$0.80***	***$2.40***	***$4.00***	**£0.40**	**£1.20**	**£2.00**
3 64pgs, Archie Goodwin script	***$0.50***	***$1.50***	***$2.50***	**£0.30**	**£0.90**	**£1.50**
4 64pgs, Armageddon: 2001 tie-in	***$0.50***	***$1.50***	***$2.50***	**£0.30**	**£0.90**	**£1.50**
5 64pgs, Sam Kieth cover art,Eclipso: The Darkness Within tie-in	***$0.50***	***$1.50***	***$2.50***	**£0.30**	**£0.90**	**£1.50**
6 64pgs, Bloodlines (Wave Two) part 14, 1st appearance Geist, continued in Justice League America Annual #7	***$0.50***	***$1.50***	***$2.50***	**£0.30**	**£0.90**	**£1.50**
7 64pgs, Elseworlds story; Chuck Dixon script, Alcatena art; "Joker" appears	***$0.55***	***$1.65***	***$2.75***	**£0.35**	**£1.05**	**£1.75**
8 64pgs, Year One, origin of the Riddler retold	***$0.80***	***$2.40***	***$4.00***	**£0.50**	**£1.50**	**£2.50**
9 ND 48pgs, Legends of the Dead Earth story	***$0.60***	***$1.80***	***$3.00***	**£0.40**	**£1.20**	**£2.00**
Title Value:	***$5.75***	***$17.25***	***$28.75***	**£3.55**	**£10.65**	**£17.75**

DETECTIVES INC.

Eclipse,MS; 1,2 Apr 1985

1-2 ND reprints graphic novel in colour

Detective Comics #186

Detective Comics #375

Detective Comics #439

	$Good	$Fine	$N.Mint	£Good	£Fine	£N.Mint
	$0.50	$1.50	$2.50	£0.30	£0.90	£1.50
Title Value:	$1.00	$3.00	$5.00	£0.60	£1.80	£3.00
DETECTIVES INC: A TERROR OF DREAMS						
Eclipse,MS; 1 Oct 1987-3 Dec 1987						
1-3 ND Gene Colan art, printed in sepia and black						
	$0.40	$1.20	$2.00	£0.25	£0.75	£1.25
Title Value:	$1.20	$3.60	$6.00	£0.75	£2.25	£3.75
DETECTIVES, THE						
Alpha Productions,OS; 1 Apr 1993						
1 ND 48pgs, squarebound, new anthology featuring Maze Agency and Mike Mauser among others; Adam Hughes cover						
	$0.60	$1.80	$3.00	£0.40	£1.20	£2.00
1 Gold Edition, ND (Sep 1993); signed by one or more of the creators (inc. Mike Barr, Paul Petellier, Cuti, Staton, Beatty); gold foil logo						
	$1.20	$3.60	$6.00	£0.80	£2.40	£4.00
Title Value:	$1.80	$5.40	$9.00	£1.20	£3.60	£6.00
DETENTION COMICS						
DC Comics,OS; 1 Oct 1996						
1 ND 64pgs, Robin, Superboy and Warrior appear in separate stories						
	$0.70	$2.10	$3.50	£0.50	£1.50	£2.50
Title Value:	$0.70	$2.10	$3.50	£0.50	£1.50	£2.50
DETHGRIP						
Immortal Comics; 1 Sep 1994-4 1995						
1-2 ND Beau Smith script, Jim Callahan and Tim Dzon art						
	$0.40	$1.20	$2.00	£0.25	£0.75	£1.25
3-4 ND	$0.40	$1.20	$2.00	£0.25	£0.75	£1.25
Title Value:	$1.60	$4.80	$8.00	£1.00	£3.00	£5.00
Note: originally solicited by Axis Comics for Mar 1994 cover date						
DETONATOR						
Chaos Comics,MS; 1 Dec 1994-2 Jan 1995						
1-2 ND Brian Pulido script, Steven Hughes art						
	$0.60	$1.80	$3.00	£0.40	£1.20	£2.00
Title Value:	$1.20	$3.60	$6.00	£0.80	£2.40	£4.00
DEVIANTS RAVE						
Image,OS; nn Jul 1996						
nn ND interviews and sketches on Deviants						
	$0.35	$1.05	$1.75	£0.25	£0.75	£1.25
Title Value:	$0.35	$1.05	$1.75	£0.25	£0.75	£1.25
DEVIL CHEF						
Dark Horse,OS; nn Jul 1994						
nn ND Jack Pollock script/art; black and white						
	$0.50	$1.50	$2.50	£0.30	£0.90	£1.50
Title Value:	$0.50	$1.50	$2.50	£0.30	£0.90	£1.50
DEVIL DINOSAUR						
Marvel Comics Group; 1 Apr 1978-9 Dec 1978						
1 ND Jack Kirby art	$1.00	$3.00	$6.00	£0.40	£1.25	£2.50
2-3 ND Jack Kirby art						
	$0.65	$2.00	$4.00	£0.30	£1.00	£2.00
4-9 ND Jack Kirby art						
	$0.55	$1.75	$3.50	£0.25	£0.75	£1.50
Title Value:	$5.60	$17.50	$35.00	£2.50	£7.75	£15.50
DEVILINA						
Atlas Seaboard,Magazine; 1 Jan 1975-2 May 1975						
1 distributed in the U.K. origin and 1st appearance Devilina						
	$0.80	$2.50	$5.00	£0.50	£1.50	£3.00
2 distributed in the U.K. though scarce Ric Estrada and Frank Thorne art featured						
	$0.50	$1.50	$3.00	£0.50	£1.50	£3.00
Title Value:	$1.30	$4.00	$8.00	£1.00	£3.00	£6.00
DEVILMAN						
Verotik; 1 Jun 1995-present						
1 ND Go Nagai script and art begins						
	$0.70	$2.10	$3.50	£0.50	£1.50	£2.50
2-3 ND	$0.60	$1.80	$3.00	£0.40	£1.20	£2.00
Title Value:	$1.90	$5.70	$9.50	£1.30	£3.90	£6.50
DEVLIN						
Maximum Comic Press,MS; 1 Apr 1996-3 Jun 1996 ?						
1 ND Avengelyne guest-stars; Robert Napton script, Andy Park, Ching Lau and Sean Parsons art						
	$0.50	$1.50	$2.50	£0.30	£0.90	£1.50
2-3 ND	$0.50	$1.50	$2.50	£0.30	£0.90	£1.50
Title Value:	$1.50	$4.50	$7.50	£0.90	£2.70	£4.50
DHAMPIRE: STILLBORN						
DC Comics,OS; 1 Nov 1996						
1 ND 64pgs, Nancy Collins script, painted art by Paul Lee						
	$1.20	$3.60	$6.00	£0.70	£2.10	£3.50
Title Value:	$1.20	$3.60	$6.00	£0.70	£2.10	£3.50
DICK TRACY						
Harvey; 141 Aug 1960-145 Apr 1961						
141-142 rare in the U.K. giant						
	$7.00	$21.00	$50.00	£4.25	£12.50	£30.00
143 very scarce in the U.K. giant						
	$7.00	$21.00	$50.00	£3.90	£11.50	£27.50
144-145 rare in the U.K. giant						
	$7.00	$21.00	$50.00	£4.25	£12.50	£30.00
Title Value:	$35.00	$105.00	$250.00	£20.90	£61.50	£147.50
Note: all reprints, Prestige Format and all distributed on the news-stands in the U.K.						
DICK TRACY ALBUM, THE ORIGINAL						
Gladstone; 1 Sep 1990-6 1991						
1 ND 48pgs, Mumbles appears						
	$1.00	$3.00	$5.00	£0.60	£1.80	£3.00
2 ND 48pgs, origin of two-way wrist radio						
	$1.00	$3.00	$5.00	£0.60	£1.80	£3.00
3-6 ND 48pgs	$1.00	$3.00	$5.00	£0.60	£1.80	£3.00

	$Good	$Fine	$N.Mint	£Good	£Fine	£N.Mint
Title Value:	$6.00	$18.00	$30.00	£3.60	£10.80	£18.00
Note: bi-monthly						
DICK TRACY IN 3-D						
Blackthorne;(3-D Series #8) 1 Jul 1986						
1 ND reprints by Chester Gould; with bound-1n 3-D glasses (25% less if without)						
	$0.50	$1.50	$2.50	£0.30	£0.90	£1.50
Title Value:	$0.50	$1.50	$2.50	£0.30	£0.90	£1.50
DICK TRACY MAGAZINE						
Gladstone; 1 Aug 1991-2 1991						
1-2 ND 48pgs	$0.80	$2.40	$4.00	£0.50	£1.50	£2.50
Title Value:	$1.60	$4.80	$8.00	£1.00	£3.00	£5.00
DICK TRACY MONTHLY/WEEKLY						
Blackthorne; 1 Jun 1986-108 1992						
1 ND 72pgs, squarebound begins (ends #25)						
	$0.50	$1.50	$2.50	£0.30	£0.90	£1.50
2-25 ND	$0.40	$1.20	$2.00	£0.25	£0.75	£1.25
26 ND becomes Dick Tracy Weekly						
	$0.40	$1.20	$2.00	£0.25	£0.75	£1.25
27-96 ND	$0.40	$1.20	$2.00	£0.25	£0.75	£1.25
97 ND Moon Maid appears						
	$0.40	$1.20	$2.00	£0.25	£0.75	£1.25
98-99 ND	$0.40	$1.20	$2.00	£0.25	£0.75	£1.25
100 ND DS	$0.45	$1.35	$2.25	£0.30	£0.90	£1.50
101-108 ND	$0.40	$1.20	$2.00	£0.25	£0.75	£1.25
Title Value:	$43.35	$130.05	$216.75	£27.10	£81.30	£135.50
Special 1 (Jan 1988)				£0.45	£1.35	£2.25
Special 2,3				£0.40	£1.20	£2.00
DICK TRACY MOVIE ADAPTATION						
Disney,OS; nn Oct 1990						
nn ND 64pgs, regular edition of Prestige Format series (Big City Blues #3)						
	$0.50	$1.50	$2.50	£0.30	£0.90	£1.50
Title Value:	$0.50	$1.50	$2.50	£0.30	£0.90	£1.50
DICK TRACY, THE ORIGINAL						
Gladstone; 1 Jul 1990-5 1991						
1 ND 64pgs, Dick Tracy vs. Mrs. Prune-Face						
	$0.40	$1.20	$2.00	£0.25	£0.75	£1.25
2 ND 64pgs, "Influence" story						
	$0.40	$1.20	$2.00	£0.25	£0.75	£1.25
3 ND 64pgs, "The Extortioner" story						
	$0.40	$1.20	$2.00	£0.25	£0.75	£1.25
4-5 ND 64pgs	$0.40	$1.20	$2.00	£0.25	£0.75	£1.25
Title Value:	$2.00	$6.00	$10.00	£1.25	£3.75	£6.25
Note: bi-monthly						
DICK TRACY: BIG CITY BLUES						
Disney,MS; 1 Apr 1990-3 Jun 1990						
1 ND 48pgs, Kyle Baker art begins						
	$0.70	$2.10	$3.50	£0.50	£1.50	£2.50
2 ND 64pgs, Tracy vs. The Underworld						
	$1.00	$3.00	$5.00	£0.70	£2.10	£3.50
3 ND 64pgs, Len Wein/Kyle Baker adaptation of Warren Beatty film (never legally imported into the U.K. though few issues found their way through)						
	$1.00	$3.00	$5.00	£0.70	£2.10	£3.50
Title Value:	$2.70	$8.10	$13.50	£1.90	£5.70	£9.50
True Hearts and Tommy Guns (Oct 1990)						
Trade paperback reprints the above (never legally imported into the U.K. though a few issues found their way through)				£1.50	£4.50	£7.50
Note: issue #3 and Trade paperback only legally available as Fleetway reprints						
DICK TRACY: THE UNPRINTED STORIES						
Blackthorne; 1 Sep 1987-4 1988						
1-3 ND	$0.60	$1.80	$3.00	£0.40	£1.20	£2.00
4 ND Flat-Top Junior appears						
	$0.60	$1.80	$3.00	£0.40	£1.20	£2.00
Title Value:	$2.40	$7.20	$12.00	£1.60	£4.80	£8.00
DIE-CUT						
Marvel UK; 1 Nov 1993-2 Dec 1993						
1 Beast appears; die-cut cover						
	$0.30	$0.90	$1.50	£0.20	£0.60	£1.00
2 X-Beast appears	$0.30	$0.90	$1.50	£0.20	£0.60	£1.00
Title Value:	$0.60	$1.80	$3.00	£0.40	£1.20	£2.00
DIE-CUT VS. G-FORCE						
Marvel UK,MS; 1 Nov 1993-2 Dec 1993						
1 Liam Sharp cover						
	$0.30	$0.90	$1.50	£0.20	£0.60	£1.00
2 gold foil enhanced cover						
	$0.30	$0.90	$1.50	£0.20	£0.60	£1.00
Title Value:	$0.60	$1.80	$3.00	£0.40	£1.20	£2.00
DIGITEK						
Marvel UK,MS; 1 Dec 1992-4 Mar 1993						
(see Overkill in British section)						
1 origin Digitek, Dermot Power art						
	$0.25	$0.75	$1.25	£0.15	£0.45	£0.75
2-3 Deathlok appears						
	$0.25	$0.75	$1.25	£0.15	£0.45	£0.75
4	$0.25	$0.75	$1.25	£0.15	£0.45	£0.75
Title Value:	$1.00	$3.00	$5.00	£0.60	£1.80	£3.00
DILLINGER						
Rip Off Press,OS; 1 1991						
1 ND b&w	$0.50	$1.50	$2.50	£0.30	£0.90	£1.50
Title Value:	$0.50	$1.50	$2.50	£0.30	£0.90	£1.50
DINO ISLAND						
Mirage Studios,MS; 1 Feb 1993-2 Mar 1993						
1-2 ND	$0.50	$1.50	$2.50	£0.30	£0.90	£1.50

	$Good	$Fine	$N.Mint	£Good	£Fine	£N.Mint
Title Value:	***$1.00***	***$3.00***	***$5.00***	**£0.60**	**£1.80**	**£3.00**

DINO RIDERS

Marvel Comics Group, Toy; 1 Feb 1989-5 Jun 1989

	$Good	$Fine	$N.Mint	£Good	£Fine	£N.Mint
1-5 ND	***$0.15***	***$0.45***	***$0.75***	**£0.10**	**£0.30**	**£0.50**
Title Value:	***$0.75***	***$2.25***	***$3.75***	**£0.50**	**£1.50**	**£2.50**

DINO, THE ALL-NEW FLINTSTONES STARRING

Charlton; 1 Aug 1973-20 Jan 1977

	$Good	$Fine	$N.Mint	£Good	£Fine	£N.Mint
1 distributed in the U.K.	***$1.15***	***$3.50***	***$7.00***	**£0.50**	**£1.50**	**£3.00**
2 distributed in the U.K.	***$0.65***	***$2.00***	***$4.00***	**£0.30**	**£1.00**	**£2.00**
3-10 distributed in the U.K.	***$0.65***	***$2.00***	***$4.00***	**£0.25**	**£0.75**	**£1.50**
11-20 distributed in the U.K.	***$0.50***	***$1.50***	***$3.00***	**£0.20**	**£0.60**	**£1.25**
Title Value:	***$12.00***	***$36.50***	***$73.00***	**£4.80**	**£14.50**	**£29.50**

DINOSAUR BOP

Monster Comics,MS; 1 Aug 1991-2 Oct 1991

	$Good	$Fine	$N.Mint	£Good	£Fine	£N.Mint
1-2 ND Jim Arnon's Kirbyesque art	***$0.40***	***$1.20***	***$2.00***	**£0.25**	**£0.75**	**£1.25**
Title Value:	***$0.80***	***$2.40***	***$4.00***	**£0.50**	**£1.50**	**£2.50**

Note: originally intended as a four issue mini-seies, issues #3 and #4 were advertised and solicited but never came out.

DINOSAUR REX

Upshot Graphics/Fantagraphics,MS; 1-3 1987

	$Good	$Fine	$N.Mint	£Good	£Fine	£N.Mint
1 ND colour; Henry Mayo art; Dennis Fujitaki art on The Dragons of Summer back-up	***$0.40***	***$1.20***	***$2.00***	**£0.25**	**£0.75**	**£1.25**
2-3 ND b&w	***$0.40***	***$1.20***	***$2.00***	**£0.25**	**£0.75**	**£1.25**
Title Value:	***$1.20***	***$3.60***	***$6.00***	**£0.75**	**£2.25**	**£3.75**

DINOSAURS ATTACK!

Eclipse,MS; 1 Feb 1992-3 Apr 1992

	$Good	$Fine	$N.Mint	£Good	£Fine	£N.Mint
1-3 ND 48pgs, based on series of gum cards	***$0.60***	***$1.80***	***$3.00***	**£0.40**	**£1.20**	**£2.00**
Title Value:	***$1.80***	***$5.40***	***$9.00***	**£1.20**	**£3.60**	**£6.00**

DINOSAURS FOR HIRE

Eternity; 1 Mar 1988-9 1989

	$Good	$Fine	$N.Mint	£Good	£Fine	£N.Mint
1 ND	***$0.35***	***$1.05***	***$1.75***	**£0.25**	**£0.75**	**£1.25**
1 2nd printing ND	***$0.35***	***$1.05***	***$1.75***	**£0.25**	**£0.75**	**£1.25**
2-9 ND	***$0.35***	***$1.05***	***$1.75***	**£0.25**	**£0.75**	**£1.25**
Title Value:	***$3.50***	***$10.50***	***$17.50***	**£2.50**	**£7.50**	**£12.50**
Fall Classic				£0.30	£0.90	£1.50
Guns 'N Lizards				£0.70	£2.10	£3.50
Dinosaurs For Hire 3-D				£0.35	£1.05	£1.75

DINOSAURS FOR HIRE (2ND SERIES)

Malibu; 1 Feb 1993-13 Feb 1994

	$Good	$Fine	$N.Mint	£Good	£Fine	£N.Mint
1 ND	***$0.30***	***$0.90***	***$1.50***	**£0.20**	**£0.60**	**£1.00**
1 Ashcan Edition, ND - 16pgs, black and white interior, normal comic size (unusually), signed on cover by Tom Mason; banner stating "Distributed exclusively by Great Eastern Conventions January 22-24 1993"	***$0.80***	***$2.40***	***$4.00***	**£0.50**	**£1.50**	**£2.50**
2-5 ND	***$0.30***	***$0.90***	***$1.50***	**£0.20**	**£0.60**	**£1.00**
6 ND Jurassic Park parody	***$0.30***	***$0.90***	***$1.50***	**£0.20**	**£0.60**	**£1.00**
7 ND	***$0.30***	***$0.90***	***$1.50***	**£0.20**	**£0.60**	**£1.00**
8 ND Genesis Tie-In; pre-bagged with free Sky-Cap (some bags have two)	***$0.30***	***$0.90***	***$1.50***	**£0.20**	**£0.60**	**£1.00**
9-13 ND Genesis Tie-In	***$0.30***	***$0.90***	***$1.50***	**£0.20**	**£0.60**	**£1.00**
Title Value:	***$4.70***	***$14.10***	***$23.50***	**£3.10**	**£9.30**	**£15.50**

DINOSAURS: A CELEBRATION

Marvel Comics Group/Epic,MS; 1-4 Dec 1992

	$Good	$Fine	$N.Mint	£Good	£Fine	£N.Mint
1 ND 48pgs, Terrible Claws and Tyrants, Kevin Walker cover	***$0.60***	***$1.80***	***$3.00***	**£0.40**	**£1.20**	**£2.00**
2 ND 48pgs, Egg Stealers and Earth Shakers, John Bolton cover	***$0.60***	***$1.80***	***$3.00***	**£0.40**	**£1.20**	**£2.00**
3 ND 48pgs, Boneheads and Duckbills, Garry Leach cover	***$0.60***	***$1.80***	***$3.00***	**£0.40**	**£1.20**	**£2.00**
4 ND 48pgs, Horns and Heavy Armour, Richard Dolan cover	***$0.60***	***$1.80***	***$3.00***	**£0.40**	**£1.20**	**£2.00**
Title Value:	***$2.40***	***$7.20***	***$12.00***	**£1.60**	**£4.80**	**£8.00**

DIRTY PAIR

Eclipse,MS; 1 Dec 1988-4 Mar 1989

	$Good	$Fine	$N.Mint	£Good	£Fine	£N.Mint
1-4 ND	***$1.20***	***$3.60***	***$6.00***	**£0.50**	**£1.50**	**£2.50**
Title Value:	***$4.80***	***$14.40***	***$18.00***	**£2.00**	**£6.00**	**£10.00**
Dirty Pair: Bio-Hazards (1990), reprints mini-series				£1.10	£3.30	£5.50
2nd print (Nov 1991)				£1.00	£3.00	£5.00

DIRTY PAIR ANIME COMICS

Viz Communications,MS; 1 Sep 1994-5 Jan 1995

	$Good	$Fine	$N.Mint	£Good	£Fine	£N.Mint
1-5 ND 48pgs, adapted from scripts and cels from the animated series; colour	***$1.00***	***$3.00***	***$5.00***	**£0.70**	**£2.10**	**£3.50**
Title Value:	***$5.00***	***$15.00***	***$25.00***	**£3.50**	**£10.50**	**£17.50**

DIRTY PAIR II

Eclipse,MS; 1 Oct 1989-4 Jan 1990

	$Good	$Fine	$N.Mint	£Good	£Fine	£N.Mint
1 ND	***$0.80***	***$2.40***	***$4.00***	**£0.40**	**£1.20**	**£2.00**
2-4 ND	***$0.60***	***$1.80***	***$3.00***	**£0.30**	**£0.90**	**£1.50**
Title Value:	***$2.60***	***$7.80***	***$12.00***	**£1.30**	**£3.90**	**£6.50**
Dirty Pair II: Dangerous Acquaintances (Sep 1991), reprints mini-series, softcover				£1.40	£4.20	£7.00
Hardcover (Oct 1991)				£4.00	£12.00	£20.00
Signed, numbered hardcover				£5.00	£15.00	£25.00

DIRTY PAIR III: A PLAGUE OF ANGELS

Eclipse,MS; 1 Jul 1990-5 Sep 1991

	$Good	$Fine	$N.Mint	£Good	£Fine	£N.Mint
1-5 ND	***$0.40***	***$1.20***	***$2.00***	**£0.25**	**£0.75**	**£1.25**
Title Value:	***$2.00***	***$6.00***	***$10.00***	**£1.25**	**£3.75**	**£6.25**
The Dirty Pair Book Three: A Plague of Angels (1994) Trade paperback reprints mini-series; black and white				£1.70	£5.10	£8.50

Note: this edition published by Dark Horse Comics

DIRTY PAIR: FATAL BUT NOT SERIOUS

Dark Horse,MS; 1 Jul 1995-5 Nov 1995

	$Good	$Fine	$N.Mint	£Good	£Fine	£N.Mint
1-5 ND Adam Warren script and art	***$0.60***	***$1.80***	***$3.00***	**£0.40**	**£1.20**	**£2.00**
Title Value:	***$3.00***	***$9.00***	***$15.00***	**£2.00**	**£6.00**	**£10.00**
Dirty pair: Fatal But Not Serious (Jul 1996) Trade paperback ND collects issues #1-5				£2.00	£6.00	£10.00

DIRTY PAIR: SIM HELL

Dark Horse,MS; 1 May 1993-4 Aug 1993

	$Good	$Fine	$N.Mint	£Good	£Fine	£N.Mint
1-4 ND Adam Warren script/art	***$0.50***	***$1.50***	***$2.50***	**£0.30**	**£0.90**	**£1.50**
Title Value:	***$2.00***	***$6.00***	***$10.00***	**£1.20**	**£3.60**	**£6.00**
The Dirty Pair: Sim Hell (Nov 1994) Trade paperback reprints mini-series, painted cover by Adam Warren				£1.70	£5.10	£8.50

DIRTY PICTURES

Aircel; 1 Apr 1991

	$Good	$Fine	$N.Mint	£Good	£Fine	£N.Mint
1 ND black and white illustrations from "spicy" 1930s pulp fiction	***$0.40***	***$1.20***	***$2.00***	**£0.25**	**£0.75**	**£1.25**
Title Value:	***$0.40***	***$1.20***	***$2.00***	**£0.25**	**£0.75**	**£1.25**

DIRTY PLOTTE

Drawn and Quarterly; 1 1990-9 1995 ?

	$Good	$Fine	$N.Mint	£Good	£Fine	£N.Mint
1 ND Julie Doucet script and art begins; black and white	***$0.80***	***$2.40***	***$4.00***	**£0.60**	**£1.80**	**£3.00**
2-4 ND	***$0.60***	***$1.80***	***$3.00***	**£0.40**	**£1.20**	**£2.00**
4 2nd printing, ND (Jan 1995)	***$0.45***	***$1.35***	***$2.25***	**£0.30**	**£0.90**	**£1.50**
5-9 ND	***$0.60***	***$1.80***	***$3.00***	**£0.40**	**£1.20**	**£2.00**
Title Value:	***$6.05***	***$18.15***	***$30.25***	**£4.10**	**£12.30**	**£20.50**

DISHMAN, THE MUNDANE ADVENTURES OF

McLeod; 1 Aug 1985-3 Aug 1986;Eclipse; 1 Sep 1988

	$Good	$Fine	$N.Mint	£Good	£Fine	£N.Mint
1 ND mini-comic (500 copies)	***$0.30***	***$0.90***	***$1.50***	**£0.20**	**£0.60**	**£1.00**
1 2nd printing ND	***$0.15***	***$0.45***	***$0.75***	**£0.10**	**£0.35**	**£0.60**
1 3rd printing ND	***$0.15***	***$0.45***	***$0.75***	**£0.10**	**£0.30**	**£0.50**
2 ND mini-comic (1000 copies)	***$0.30***	***$0.90***	***$1.50***	**£0.20**	**£0.60**	**£1.00**
2 2nd printing ND	***$0.15***	***$0.45***	***$0.75***	**£0.10**	**£0.30**	**£0.50**
3 ND full size comic, reprints #1,2	***$0.30***	***$0.90***	***$1.50***	**£0.20**	**£0.60**	**£1.00**
Title Value:	***$1.35***	***$4.05***	***$6.75***	**£0.90**	**£2.75**	**£4.60**

DISNEY AFTERNOON

Marvel Comics Group; 1 Nov 1994-10 Sep 1995

	$Good	$Fine	$N.Mint	£Good	£Fine	£N.Mint
1-10 ND	***$0.30***	***$0.90***	***$1.50***	**£0.20**	**£0.60**	**£1.00**
Title Value:	***$3.00***	***$9.00***	***$15.00***	**£2.00**	**£6.00**	**£10.00**

DISNEY COMIC ALBUM

Gladstone/Disney; 1 Jul 1990-8 1991

	$Good	$Fine	$N.Mint	£Good	£Fine	£N.Mint
1 ND Donald Duck/Gyro Gearloose	***$0.30***	***$0.90***	***$1.50***	**£0.20**	**£0.60**	**£1.00**
2 ND Uncle Scrooge	***$0.30***	***$0.90***	***$1.50***	**£0.20**	**£0.60**	**£1.00**
3 ND 64pgs, Donald Duck	***$0.70***	***$2.10***	***$3.50***	**£0.50**	**£1.50**	**£2.50**
4 ND 64pgs, Mickey Mouse/Phantom Blot	***$0.70***	***$2.10***	***$3.50***	**£0.50**	**£1.50**	**£2.50**
5 ND 64pgs, Chip 'N Dale, all new stories	***$0.70***	***$2.10***	***$3.50***	**£0.50**	**£1.50**	**£2.50**
6 ND 64pgs, Uncle Scrooge	***$0.70***	***$2.10***	***$3.50***	**£0.50**	**£1.50**	**£2.50**
7 ND 64pgs, Donald Duck	***$0.70***	***$2.10***	***$3.50***	**£0.50**	**£1.50**	**£2.50**
8 ND 64pgs, Super-Goof	***$0.70***	***$2.10***	***$3.50***	**£0.50**	**£1.50**	**£2.50**
Title Value:	***$4.80***	***$14.40***	***$24.00***	**£3.40**	**£10.20**	**£17.00**
Special (Oct 1990): Super Goof Adventures, all reprint, 64pgs				£0.90	£2.70	£4.50

Note: Carl Barks/Floyd Gottfredson reprints packaged by Gladstone for Disney, bi-weekly

DISNEY COMIC HITS

Marvel Comics Group; 1 Oct 1995-present ?

	$Good	$Fine	$N.Mint	£Good	£Fine	£N.Mint
1 ND Aladdin	***$0.30***	***$0.90***	***$1.50***	**£0.20**	**£0.60**	**£1.00**
2 ND Lion King: Stories from the Prideland	***$0.30***	***$0.90***	***$1.50***	**£0.20**	**£0.60**	**£1.00**
3 ND Pocahontas	***$0.30***	***$0.90***	***$1.50***	**£0.20**	**£0.60**	**£1.00**
4 ND 48pgs, Disney's Toy Story movie adaptation	***$0.30***	***$0.90***	***$1.50***	**£0.20**	**£0.60**	**£1.00**
5 ND Pocahontas	***$0.45***	***$1.35***	***$2.25***	**£0.30**	**£0.90**	**£1.50**
6 ND Toy Story	***$0.45***	***$1.35***	***$2.25***	**£0.30**	**£0.90**	**£1.50**
7-8 ND Timon and Pumbaa from The Lion King	***$0.45***	***$1.35***	***$2.25***	**£0.30**	**£0.90**	**£1.50**
9 ND Timon and Pumbaa from The Lion King plus Pocahontas, Toy Story and Aladdin	***$0.45***	***$1.35***	***$2.25***	**£0.30**	**£0.90**	**£1.50**
10 ND The Hunchback of Notre Dame (film adaptation); bi-weekly	***$0.50***	***$1.50***	***$2.50***	**£0.30**	**£0.90**	**£1.50**
11 ND three stories from The Hunchback of Notre Dame; bi-weekly	***$0.30***	***$0.90***	***$1.50***	**£0.20**	**£0.60**	**£1.00**
12 ND Aladdin and the King of Thieves	***$0.30***	***$0.90***	***$1.50***	**£0.20**	**£0.60**	**£1.00**
13 ND Timon, Pumbaa, Woody and Buzz Lightyear	***$0.30***	***$0.90***	***$1.50***	**£0.20**	**£0.60**	**£1.00**
14 ND Woody and Buzz Lightyear						

	$Good	$Fine	$N.Mint	£Good	£Fine	£N.Mint
	$0.30	$0.90	$1.50	£0.20	£0.60	£1.00
15 ND three stories from the live-action 101 Dalmatians	$0.30	$0.90	$1.50	£0.20	£0.60	£1.00
16 ND adaptation of live-action 101 Dalmatians movie	$0.30	$0.90	$1.50	£0.20	£0.60	£1.00
17 ND Mickey Mouse	$0.30	$0.90	$1.50	£0.20	£0.60	£1.00
18 ND Mouse in the House	$0.30	$0.90	$1.50	£0.20	£0.60	£1.00
Title Value:	$6.35	$19.05	$31.75	£4.20	£12.60	£21.00

Note: originally announced as Disney Presents

DISNEY COMICS FIRST ISSUE COLLECTORS EDITION

Disney,OS; nn 1991

	$Good	$Fine	$N.Mint	£Good	£Fine	£N.Mint
nn ND scarce in the U.K. set of six of the all-new Disney comics boxed with certificate	$7.50	$22.50	$37.50	£5.00	£15.00	£25.00
Title Value:	$7.50	$22.50	$37.50	£5.00	£15.00	£25.00

DISNEY COMICS IN 3-D

Disney,OS; 1 May 1992

	$Good	$Fine	$N.Mint	£Good	£Fine	£N.Mint
1 ND 48pgs, Barks, van Horn and Rosa art, with 3-D glasses (25% less without glasses)	$0.50	$1.50	$2.50	£0.30	£0.90	£1.50
Title Value:	$0.50	$1.50	$2.50	£0.30	£0.90	£1.50

DISNEY HOLIDAY PARADE

Disney; 1 Jan 1991-2 1991

	$Good	$Fine	$N.Mint	£Good	£Fine	£N.Mint
1 ND 64pgs	$0.50	$1.50	$2.50	£0.30	£0.90	£1.50
2 ND 64pgs, Christmas stories	$0.50	$1.50	$2.50	£0.30	£0.90	£1.50
Title Value:	$1.00	$3.00	$5.00	£0.60	£1.80	£3.00

DISNEY'S HUNCHBACK OF NOTRE DAME

Marvel Comics Group,OS; nn Aug 1996

	$Good	$Fine	$N.Mint	£Good	£Fine	£N.Mint
nn ND 48pgs, adaptation of film	$1.00	$3.00	$5.00	£0.70	£2.10	£3.50
Title Value:	$1.00	$3.00	$5.00	£0.70	£2.10	£3.50

DISNEY'S POCAHONTAS MOVIE ADAPTATION

Marvel Comics Group,OS; 1 Aug 1995

	$Good	$Fine	$N.Mint	£Good	£Fine	£N.Mint
1 ND 48pgs, adaptation of Disney film, Dan Spiegle art	$1.00	$3.00	$5.00	£0.70	£2.10	£3.50
Title Value:	$1.00	$3.00	$5.00	£0.70	£2.10	£3.50

DISNEY'S TOY STORY

Marvel Comics Group,OS; 1 Jan 1996

	$Good	$Fine	$N.Mint	£Good	£Fine	£N.Mint
1 ND adaptation of Disney film	$1.00	$3.00	$5.00	£0.70	£2.10	£3.50
Title Value:	$1.00	$3.00	$5.00	£0.70	£2.10	£3.50

DISNEYLAND BIRTHDAY PARTY

Gladstone; 1 1985

	$Good	$Fine	$N.Mint	£Good	£Fine	£N.Mint
1 ND 20pgs Carl Barks art	$1.00	$3.00	$5.00	£0.70	£2.10	£3.50
Title Value:	$1.00	$3.00	$5.00	£0.70	£2.10	£3.50

DISTANT SOIL, A

Warp Graphics,Magazine; 1 Dec 1983-10 1985

	$Good	$Fine	$N.Mint	£Good	£Fine	£N.Mint
1 ND Panda Khan appears	$2.00	$6.00	$10.00	£0.70	£2.10	£3.50
2-3 ND	$1.20	$3.60	$6.00	£0.50	£1.50	£2.50
4-9 ND	$0.80	$2.40	$4.00	£0.40	£1.20	£2.00
10 ND	$0.50	$1.50	$2.50	£0.30	£0.90	£1.50
Title Value:	$9.70	$29.10	$48.50	£4.40	£13.20	£22.00
Graphic Novel 1				£0.75	£2.25	£3.75
Graphic Album 2: Knights of the Angel				£1.50	£4.50	£7.50

Note: In October 1994, Aria Press offered the remaining copies of this Graphic Album that they had obtained from the publisher The Donning Company at $12.95

DISTANT SOIL, A (2ND SERIES)

Aria Press; 1 Aug 1991-16 1996;Image; 15 Jul 1996-present

	$Good	$Fine	$N.Mint	£Good	£Fine	£N.Mint
1 ND Colleen Doran script/art begins; black and white reprints	$1.00	$3.00	$5.00	£0.50	£1.50	£2.50
1 2nd printing, ND (Sep 1991)	$0.30	$0.90	$1.50	£0.20	£0.60	£1.00
1 3rd printing ND	$0.30	$0.90	$1.50	£0.20	£0.60	£1.00
1 4th printing, ND (Sep 1995)	$0.30	$0.90	$1.50	£0.20	£0.60	£1.00
2 ND	$0.70	$2.10	$3.50	£0.40	£1.20	£2.00
2 2nd printing ND	$0.30	$0.90	$1.50	£0.20	£0.60	£1.00
3 ND	$0.50	$1.50	$2.50	£0.30	£0.90	£1.50
3 2nd printing, ND (Jan 1994)	$0.30	$0.90	$1.50	£0.20	£0.60	£1.00
4 ND	$0.50	$1.50	$2.50	£0.30	£0.90	£1.50
4 2nd printing, ND (Apr 1995)	$0.30	$0.90	$1.50	£0.20	£0.60	£1.00
5-11 ND	$0.40	$1.20	$2.00	£0.25	£0.75	£1.25
12 ND all new material begins	$0.40	$1.20	$2.00	£0.25	£0.75	£1.25
13-16 ND	$0.60	$1.80	$3.00	£0.40	£1.20	£2.00
Title Value:	$10.10	$30.30	$50.50	£6.30	£18.90	£31.50
A Distant Soil Starter Pack (Jan 1994) ND, set of the first three issues plus limited edition print				£0.80	£2.40	£4.00
Deluxe Edition (Jan 1994) ND, as above with another signed print and signed certificate				£3.00	£9.00	£15.00
A Distant Soil: Immigrant's Song Deluxe Graphic Novel (Oct 1995) ND, reprints issues #1,2, pre-bagged with colour print and certificate				£2.00	£6.00	£10.00
A Distant Soil: Knights of the Angel Deluxe Graphic Novel (Dec 1994) ND, reprints issues #3-11, pre-bagged with colour print and certificate				£2.70	£8.10	£13.50

DISTANT THUNDER

ACG; 1 Apr 1996

	$Good	$Fine	$N.Mint	£Good	£Fine	£N.Mint
1 ND Sam Glanzman reprints from Charlton Comics	$0.55	$1.65	$2.75	£0.35	£1.05	£1.75
Title Value:	$0.55	$1.65	$2.75	£0.35	£1.05	£1.75

DITKO'S WORLD

Renegade; 1 May 1986-3 Jul 1986

(see Frisky Frolics Annual, Murder, Revolver)

	$Good	$Fine	$N.Mint	£Good	£Fine	£N.Mint
1-3 ND	$0.40	$1.20	$2.00	£0.25	£0.75	£1.25
Title Value:	$1.20	$3.60	$6.00	£0.75	£2.25	£3.75

DIVA'S

Caliber Press; 1 Feb 1992-2 Mar 1992

	$Good	$Fine	$N.Mint	£Good	£Fine	£N.Mint
1-2 ND	$0.40	$1.20	$2.00	£0.25	£0.75	£1.25
Title Value:	$0.80	$2.40	$4.00	£0.50	£1.50	£2.50

DIVISION 13

Dark Horse/Comics Greatest World,MS; 1 Aug 1994-4 Nov 1994

	$Good	$Fine	$N.Mint	£Good	£Fine	£N.Mint
1 ND spin-off from Comics' Greatest World series; Art Adams cover	$0.50	$1.50	$2.50	£0.30	£0.90	£1.50
2-4 ND	$0.50	$1.50	$2.50	£0.30	£0.90	£1.50
Title Value:	$2.00	$6.00	$10.00	£1.20	£3.60	£6.00

DJANGO & ANGEL

Caliber Press; 1 Jun 1990-5 1990

	$Good	$Fine	$N.Mint	£Good	£Fine	£N.Mint
1 ND Donne Avenell script and Florenci Clave art; black and white	$0.30	$0.90	$1.50	£0.20	£0.60	£1.00
2-5 ND	$0.30	$0.90	$1.50	£0.20	£0.60	£1.00
Title Value:	$1.50	$4.50	$7.50	£1.00	£3.00	£5.00

DNAGENTS

Eclipse; 1 Mar 1983-24 Jul 1985

	$Good	$Fine	$N.Mint	£Good	£Fine	£N.Mint
1-17 ND	$0.30	$0.90	$1.50	£0.20	£0.60	£1.00
18 ND infinity cover	$0.30	$0.90	$1.50	£0.20	£0.60	£1.00
19-23 ND	$0.30	$0.90	$1.50	£0.20	£0.60	£1.00
24 ND guest art by Dan Spiegle, Dave Stevens cover; story continues in Crossfire #14	$0.30	$0.90	$1.50	£0.20	£0.60	£1.00
Title Value:	$7.20	$21.60	$36.00	£4.80	£14.40	£24.00

DNAGENTS, THE NEW

Eclipse; 1 Oct 1985-17 Mar 1987

	$Good	$Fine	$N.Mint	£Good	£Fine	£N.Mint
1 ND Mark Evanier script begins, colour	$0.30	$0.90	$1.50	£0.20	£0.60	£1.00
2-8 ND	$0.30	$0.90	$1.50	£0.20	£0.60	£1.00
9 ND 1st appearance New Wave team (preview)	$0.30	$0.90	$1.50	£0.20	£0.60	£1.00
10 ND Airboy preview, continues in Airboy #1; Jerry Ordway cover	$0.30	$0.90	$1.50	£0.20	£0.60	£1.00
11 ND Summer Fun issue	$0.30	$0.90	$1.50	£0.20	£0.60	£1.00
12 ND	$0.30	$0.90	$1.50	£0.20	£0.60	£1.00
13-15 ND Erik Larsen cover and art	$0.40	$1.20	$2.00	£0.25	£0.75	£1.25
16 ND Erik Larsen art, Erik Larsen and Jerry Ordway cover	$0.40	$1.20	$2.00	£0.25	£0.75	£1.25
17 ND Erik Larsen cover and art	$0.40	$1.20	$2.00	£0.25	£0.75	£1.25
Title Value:	$5.60	$16.80	$28.00	£3.65	£10.95	£18.25

DOC SAMSON

Marvel Comics Group,MS; 1 Jan 1996-4 Apr 1996

	$Good	$Fine	$N.Mint	£Good	£Fine	£N.Mint
1-2 ND She-Hulk appears, Ken Lashley art	$0.40	$1.20	$2.00	£0.25	£0.75	£1.25
3 ND Punisher appears, Ken Lashley art	$0.40	$1.20	$2.00	£0.25	£0.75	£1.25
4 ND Polaris guest-stars; Ken Lashley art	$0.40	$1.20	$2.00	£0.25	£0.75	£1.25
Title Value:	$1.60	$4.80	$8.00	£1.00	£3.00	£5.00

DOC SAVAGE

DC Comics; 1 Nov 1988-24 Sep 1990

	$Good	$Fine	$N.Mint	£Good	£Fine	£N.Mint
1-16 ND	$0.25	$0.75	$1.25	£0.15	£0.45	£0.75
17-18 ND X-over with Shadow Strikes 5, 6	$0.25	$0.75	$1.25	£0.15	£0.45	£0.75
19-24 ND	$0.25	$0.75	$1.25	£0.15	£0.45	£0.75
Title Value:	$6.00	$18.00	$30.00	£3.60	£10.80	£18.00

Note: Deluxe Format, Baxter paper.

DOC SAVAGE

Gold Key; 1 Nov 1966

	$Good	$Fine	$N.Mint	£Good	£Fine	£N.Mint
1 very scarce in the U.K. though distributed on the newstands	$11.00	$34.00	$80.00	£7.75	£23.50	£55.00
Title Value:	$11.00	$34.00	$80.00	£7.75	£23.50	£55.00

DOC SAVAGE

Marvel Comics Group; 1 Nov 1972-8 Jan 1974

(see DC series)

	$Good	$Fine	$N.Mint	£Good	£Fine	£N.Mint
1 ND	$1.65	$5.00	$10.00	£0.65	£2.00	£4.00
2-3 ND Steranko covers	$1.00	$3.00	$6.00	£0.40	£1.25	£2.50
4-5 ND	$1.00	$3.00	$6.00	£0.40	£1.25	£2.50
6-8 ND	$0.80	$2.50	$5.00	£0.30	£1.00	£2.00
Title Value:	$8.05	$24.50	$49.00	£3.15	£10.00	£20.00

Note: Pulp novels adapted as follows: **1, 2** The Man of Bronze; **3, 4** Death in Silver; **5, 6** The Monsters; **7, 8** Brand of the Werewolf. Tom Palmer inks throughout.

DOC SAVAGE (LIMITED SERIES)

DC Comics,MS; 1 Jul 1987-4 Oct 1987

	$Good	$Fine	$N.Mint	£Good	£Fine	£N.Mint
1-4 Adam & Andy Kubert art	$0.30	$0.90	$1.50	£0.20	£0.60	£1.00
Title Value:	$1.20	$3.60	$6.00	£0.80	£2.40	£4.00

DOC SAVAGE (MAGAZINE SERIES)

Marvel Comics Group,Magazine; 1 Aug 1975-8 Apr 1977

	$Good	$Fine	$N.Mint	£Good	£Fine	£N.Mint
1 ND Doug Moench scripts and Tony DeZuniga art begins, painted covers by Ken Barr; cover from film poster	$1.00	$3.00	$6.00	£0.40	£1.25	£2.50

VERY GENERAL PERCENTAGE CONVERSION CHART WHICH MAY BE USED TO CALCULATE LOW AND INBETWEEN GRADES:

	$Good	$Fine	$N.Mint	£Good	£Fine	£N.Mint
2 interview with Ron Ely and Doc Savage movie	*$0.55*	*$1.75*	*$3.50*	£0.30	£1.00	£2.00
3-8	*$0.55*	*$1.75*	*$3.50*	£0.30	£1.00	£2.00
Title Value:	*$4.85*	*$15.25*	*$30.50*	£2.50	£8.25	£16.50

DOC SAVAGE ANNUAL

DC Comics; 1 Jun 1989

	$Good	$Fine	$N.Mint	£Good	£Fine	£N.Mint
1 ND 48pgs	*$0.60*	*$1.80*	*$3.00*	£0.40	£1.20	£2.00
Title Value:	*$0.60*	*$1.80*	*$3.00*	£0.40	£1.20	£2.00

DOC SAVAGE GIANT SIZE

Marvel Comics Group; 1 1975

	$Good	$Fine	$N.Mint	£Good	£Fine	£N.Mint
1 ND 68pgs, reprints issues #1, #2	*$1.30*	*$4.00*	*$8.00*	£0.80	£2.50	£5.00
Title Value:	*$1.30*	*$4.00*	*$8.00*	£0.80	£2.50	£5.00

DOC SAVAGE: CURSE OF THE FIRE GOD

Dark Horse,MS; 1 Sep 1995-4 Dec 1995

	$Good	$Fine	$N.Mint	£Good	£Fine	£N.Mint
1-4 ND Steve Vance script, Pat Broderick art	*$0.60*	*$1.80*	*$3.00*	£0.40	£1.20	£2.00
Title Value:	*$2.40*	*$7.20*	*$12.00*	£1.60	£4.80	£8.00

DOC SAVAGE: DOOM DYNASTY

Millennium,MS; 1 May 1992-2 Jun 1992

	$Good	$Fine	$N.Mint	£Good	£Fine	£N.Mint
1-2 ND Brian Stelfreeze cover	*$0.50*	*$1.50*	*$2.50*	£0.30	£0.90	£1.50
Title Value:	*$1.00*	*$3.00*	*$5.00*	£0.60	£1.80	£3.00

DOC SAVAGE: MAN OF BRONZE

Millennium,MS; 1 Dec 1991-4 Mar 1992

	$Good	$Fine	$N.Mint	£Good	£Fine	£N.Mint
1 ND Brian Stelfreeze cover	*$0.50*	*$1.50*	*$2.50*	£0.30	£0.90	£1.50
2-4 ND	*$0.50*	*$1.50*	*$2.50*	£0.30	£0.90	£1.50
Title Value:	*$2.00*	*$6.00*	*$10.00*	£1.20	£3.60	£6.00

DOC SAVAGE: REPEL

Millennium,MS; 1 Dec 1992-2 Jan 1993

	$Good	$Fine	$N.Mint	£Good	£Fine	£N.Mint
1-2 ND	*$0.50*	*$1.50*	*$2.50*	£0.30	£0.90	£1.50
Title Value:	*$1.00*	*$3.00*	*$5.00*	£0.60	£1.80	£3.00

DOC SAVAGE: THE DEVIL'S THOUGHTS

Millennium,MS; 1 Aug 1992-3 Oct 1992

	$Good	$Fine	$N.Mint	£Good	£Fine	£N.Mint
1-3 ND	*$0.50*	*$1.50*	*$2.50*	£0.30	£0.90	£1.50
Title Value:	*$1.50*	*$4.50*	*$7.50*	£0.90	£2.70	£4.50

DOC SAVAGE: THE MANUAL OF BRONZE

Millennium,OS; 1 Aug 1992

	$Good	$Fine	$N.Mint	£Good	£Fine	£N.Mint
1 ND features art by Tim Truman and Adam Hughes, cover by Brian Stelfreeze	*$0.50*	*$1.50*	*$2.50*	£0.30	£0.90	£1.50
Title Value:	*$0.50*	*$1.50*	*$2.50*	£0.30	£0.90	£1.50

DOCTOR CHAOS

Triumphant Comics; 0 Jun 1994; 1 Nov 1993-12 Oct 1994

	$Good	$Fine	$N.Mint	£Good	£Fine	£N.Mint
0 ND origin of Doctor Chaos	*$0.30*	*$0.90*	*$1.50*	£0.20	£0.60	£1.00
0 Signed Edition, ND (Oct 1994) - pre-bagged with mini-poster photo-print and backing board	*$0.60*	*$1.80*	*$3.00*	£0.40	£1.20	£2.00
1 ND serially numbered at top of cover; Unleashed X-over	*$0.30*	*$0.90*	*$1.50*	£0.20	£0.60	£1.00
2-3 ND	*$0.30*	*$0.90*	*$1.50*	£0.20	£0.60	£1.00
3 Signed Edition, ND with mini-poster photo-print; pre-bagged with backing board	*$0.60*	*$1.80*	*$3.00*	£0.40	£1.20	£2.00
4 ND	*$0.30*	*$0.90*	*$1.50*	£0.20	£0.60	£1.00
4 Signed & Numbered Edition, ND - signed by Adam Post and Eric Shefferman with Doctor Chaos mini-print. 18,000 print run	*$0.60*	*$1.80*	*$3.00*	£0.40	£1.20	£2.00
5-9 ND	*$0.30*	*$0.90*	*$1.50*	£0.20	£0.60	£1.00
10 ND dual issue with Company X #3 (Note: there is only one issue between the two titles)	*$0.30*	*$0.90*	*$1.50*	£0.20	£0.60	£1.00
11 ND dual issue with Company X #4 (Note: there is only one issue between the two titles)	*$0.30*	*$0.90*	*$1.50*	£0.20	£0.60	£1.00
12 ND	*$0.30*	*$0.90*	*$1.50*	£0.20	£0.60	£1.00
Title Value:	*$5.70*	*$17.10*	*$28.50*	£3.80	£11.40	£19.00

DOCTOR FATE

DC Comics; 1 Winter 1988-41 Jun 1992

	$Good	$Fine	$N.Mint	£Good	£Fine	£N.Mint
1 "Return Of Dr.Fate" on cover	*$0.25*	*$0.75*	*$1.25*	£0.15	£0.45	£0.75
2-14	*$0.25*	*$0.75*	*$1.25*	£0.15	£0.45	£0.75
15 Justice League International appears	*$0.25*	*$0.75*	*$1.25*	£0.15	£0.45	£0.75
16-18	*$0.25*	*$0.75*	*$1.25*	£0.15	£0.45	£0.75
19-20 guest stars Phantom Stranger	*$0.25*	*$0.75*	*$1.25*	£0.15	£0.45	£0.75
21-24	*$0.25*	*$0.75*	*$1.25*	£0.15	£0.45	£0.75
25 1st appearance of new female Doctor Fate; new direction/creative team	*$0.25*	*$0.75*	*$1.25*	£0.15	£0.45	£0.75
26-31	*$0.25*	*$0.75*	*$1.25*	£0.15	£0.45	£0.75
32-33 War of the Gods tie-in	*$0.25*	*$0.75*	*$1.25*	£0.15	£0.45	£0.75
34-39	*$0.25*	*$0.75*	*$1.25*	£0.15	£0.45	£0.75
40 Wonder Woman appears	*$0.25*	*$0.75*	*$1.25*	£0.15	£0.45	£0.75
41	*$0.25*	*$0.75*	*$1.25*	£0.15	£0.45	£0.75
Title Value:	*$10.25*	*$30.75*	*$51.25*	£6.15	£18.45	£30.75

Note: New Format

DOCTOR FATE (LIMITED SERIES)

DC Comics,MS; 1 Jul 1987-4 Oct 1987

	$Good	$Fine	$N.Mint	£Good	£Fine	£N.Mint
1-4 Keith Giffen art	*$0.40*	*$1.20*	*$2.00*	£0.25	£0.75	£1.25
Title Value:	*$1.60*	*$4.80*	*$8.00*	£1.00	£3.00	£5.00

DOCTOR FATE ANNUAL

DC Comics; 1 Sep 1989

	$Good	$Fine	$N.Mint	£Good	£Fine	£N.Mint
1 ND	*$0.40*	*$1.20*	*$2.00*	£0.25	£0.75	£1.25
Title Value:	*$0.40*	*$1.20*	*$2.00*	£0.25	£0.75	£1.25

DOCTOR FATE, THE IMMORTAL

DC Comics,MS; 1 Jan 1985-3 Mar 1985

	$Good	$Fine	$N.Mint	£Good	£Fine	£N.Mint
1 Walt Simonson reprint from First Issue Special #9 plus Golden Age reprint, also included Dr. Fate by Staton	*$0.30*	*$0.90*	*$1.50*	£0.20	£0.60	£1.00
2 Giffen part reprint	*$0.30*	*$0.90*	*$1.50*	£0.20	£0.60	£1.00
3 reprints	*$0.30*	*$0.90*	*$1.50*	£0.20	£0.60	£1.00
Title Value:	*$0.90*	*$2.70*	*$4.50*	£0.60	£1.80	£3.00

Note: issues 2 and 3 reprint back-up stories from Flash #306-#313

DOCTOR GIGGLES

Dark Horse,MS; 1,2 Dec 1992

	$Good	$Fine	$N.Mint	£Good	£Fine	£N.Mint
1-2 ND adaptation of horror film	*$0.50*	*$1.50*	*$2.50*	£0.30	£0.90	£1.50
Title Value:	*$1.00*	*$3.00*	*$5.00*	£0.60	£1.80	£3.00

DOCTOR GORPON

Eternity,MS; 1 Aug 1991-3 Oct 1991

	$Good	$Fine	$N.Mint	£Good	£Fine	£N.Mint
1-3 ND	*$0.40*	*$1.20*	*$2.00*	£0.25	£0.75	£1.25
Title Value:	*$1.20*	*$3.60*	*$6.00*	£0.75	£2.25	£3.75

DOCTOR MIRAGE, THE SECOND LIFE OF

Valiant; 1 Nov 1993-19 Jun 1995

	$Good	$Fine	$N.Mint	£Good	£Fine	£N.Mint
1 ND Master D'Arque appears; Bernard Chang art begins	*$0.30*	*$0.90*	*$1.50*	£0.20	£0.60	£1.00
1 Gold Edition, ND, no price on cover, gold ink logo	*$0.80*	*$2.40*	*$4.00*	£0.40	£1.20	£2.00
2-3 ND Master D'Arque appears	*$0.30*	*$0.90*	*$1.50*	£0.20	£0.60	£1.00
4-6 ND	*$0.30*	*$0.90*	*$1.50*	£0.20	£0.60	£1.00
7 ND with free Upper Deck trading card	*$0.30*	*$0.90*	*$1.50*	£0.20	£0.60	£1.00

Doc Savage Giant Size #1

Doctor Gorpon #1

Doctor Strangefate #1

	$Good	$Fine	$N.Mint	£Good	£Fine	£N.Mint
8-10 ND	$0.30	$0.90	$1.50	£0.20	£0.60	£1.00
11 ND Chaos Effect tie-in	$0.30	$0.90	$1.50	£0.20	£0.60	£1.00
12-19 ND	$0.30	$0.90	$1.50	£0.20	£0.60	£1.00
Title Value:	$6.50	$19.50	$32.50	£4.20	£12.60	£21.00

DOCTOR OCCULT (VERTIGO VISIONS)

DC Comics/Vertigo,OS; 1 Jul 1994

	$Good	$Fine	$N.Mint	£Good	£Fine	£N.Mint
1 ND 64pgs	$0.80	$2.40	$4.00	£0.50	£1.50	£2.50
Title Value:	$0.80	$2.40	$4.00	£0.50	£1.50	£2.50

DOCTOR SOLAR MAN OF THE ATOM, THE ORIGINAL

Valiant/Western Publishing; 1 Apr 1995-3 Jun 1995

	$Good	$Fine	$N.Mint	£Good	£Fine	£N.Mint
1 ND reprints from the Gold Key series begin; Paul Smith cover	$0.50	$1.50	$2.50	£0.30	£0.90	£1.50
2-3 ND reprints from the Gold Key series begin; Dave Ross cover	$0.50	$1.50	$2.50	£0.30	£0.90	£1.50
Title Value:	$1.50	$4.50	$7.50	£0.90	£2.70	£4.50

DOCTOR SOLAR, MAN OF THE ATOM

Gold Key; 1 Oct 1962-27 Apr 1969;Whitman;28 Apr 1981-31 1982

	$Good	$Fine	$N.Mint	£Good	£Fine	£N.Mint
1 distributed in the U.K.	$46.00	$135.00	$320.00	£30.00	£90.00	£210.00
2 distributed in the U.K.	$15.00	$45.00	$105.00	£10.00	£30.00	£70.00
3-5 distributed in the U.K.	$10.00	$30.00	$70.00	£6.25	£19.00	£45.00
6-10 distributed in the U.K.	$6.25	$19.00	$45.00	£3.55	£10.50	£25.00
11-14 distributed in the U.K.	$5.00	$15.00	$35.00	£2.85	£8.50	£20.00
15 distributed in the U.K.	$7.00	$21.00	$50.00	£3.90	£11.50	£27.50
16-20 distributed in the U.K.	$5.00	$15.00	$35.00	£2.85	£8.50	£20.00
21-27 distributed in the U.K.	$3.55	$10.50	$25.00	£2.10	£6.25	£15.00
28 scarce in the U.K. line drawn covers and new logo begins; Solar by Roger McKenzie and Frank Bolle begins	$2.50	$7.50	$12.50	£1.20	£3.60	£6.00
29 scarce in the U.K. Magnus Robot Fighter back-up and his origin re-told	$2.50	$7.50	$12.50	£1.20	£3.60	£6.00
30 scarce in the U.K. Magnus Robot Fighter back-up	$2.50	$7.50	$12.50	£1.20	£3.60	£6.00
31 very scarce in the U.K. Magnus Robot Fighter back-up	$2.50	$7.50	$12.50	£1.40	£4.20	£7.00
Title Value:	$209.10	$624.50	$1450.00	£125.75	£376.25	£877.50

Note: painted covers #1-27 and also back cover pin-ups without cover logo

DOCTOR STRANGE (1ST SERIES)

Marvel Comics Group; 169 Jun 1968-183 Nov 1969

(formerly Strange Tales) (see Marvel Fanfare, Marvel Graphic Novel, Marvel Premiere, Marvel Treasury Edition, Strange Tales 2nd Series)

	$Good	$Fine	$N.Mint	£Good	£Fine	£N.Mint
169 origin retold	$20.00	$60.00	$140.00	£11.00	£34.00	£80.00
170-175	$8.50	$26.00	$60.00	£3.55	£10.50	£25.00
176	$6.25	$19.00	$45.00	£2.85	£8.50	£20.00
177 new costume	$6.25	$19.00	$45.00	£2.85	£8.50	£20.00
178	$5.50	$17.00	$40.00	£2.85	£8.50	£20.00
179 very LD all reprint from Spiderman Annual #2, Ditko art	$5.50	$17.00	$40.00	£3.10	£9.25	£22.00
180 scarce in the U.K. part photo cover	$5.50	$17.00	$40.00	£3.10	£9.25	£22.00
181 ND	$5.50	$17.00	$40.00	£3.10	£9.25	£22.00
182 scarce in the U.K. Dr. Strange vs. Juggernaut	$5.50	$17.00	$40.00	£2.85	£8.50	£20.00
183 scarce in the U.K.	$5.50	$17.00	$40.00	£2.85	£8.50	£20.00
Title Value:	$116.50	$356.00	$780.00	£55.85	£167.25	£396.00

DOCTOR STRANGE (2ND SERIES)

Marvel Comics Group; 1 Jun 1974-81 Feb 1987

	$Good	$Fine	$N.Mint	£Good	£Fine	£N.Mint
1 ND scarce in the U.K. Brunner art	$5.75	$17.50	$35.00	£2.90	£8.75	£17.50
2 ND Defenders appear, Brunner art	$2.90	$8.75	$17.50	£1.65	£5.00	£10.00
3 ND 2pgs Brunner art, rest reprint	$1.65	$5.00	$10.00	£1.05	£3.25	£6.50
4-5 Brunner art	$1.65	$5.00	$10.00	£0.80	£2.50	£5.00
6-10	$1.25	$3.75	$7.50	£0.65	£2.00	£4.00
11-12	$0.80	$2.50	$5.00	£0.50	£1.50	£3.00
13 Gene Colan art	$0.80	$2.50	$5.00	£0.50	£1.50	£3.00
14 Dracula appears	$0.80	$2.50	$5.00	£0.55	£1.75	£3.50
15-16	$0.80	$2.50	$5.00	£0.40	£1.25	£2.50
17 Gene Colan art	$0.80	$2.50	$5.00	£0.40	£1.25	£2.50
18-20	$0.80	$2.50	$5.00	£0.40	£1.25	£2.50
21 reprints origin from Strange Tales #169	$0.65	$2.00	$4.00	£0.30	£1.00	£2.00
22 ND scarce in the U.K. Brunner cover	$0.65	$2.00	$4.00	£0.40	£1.25	£2.50
23-24 ND Jim Starlin art	$0.65	$2.00	$4.00	£0.40	£1.25	£2.50
25 ND	$0.65	$2.00	$4.00	£0.40	£1.25	£2.50
26 Jim Starlin art	$0.65	$2.00	$4.00	£0.30	£1.00	£2.00
27-30	$0.65	$2.00	$4.00	£0.30	£1.00	£2.00
31-45	$0.60	$1.80	$3.00	£0.30	£0.90	£1.50
46 LD in the U.K. Golden art	$0.50	$1.50	$2.50	£0.25	£0.75	£1.25
47 LD in the U.K.	$0.50	$1.50	$2.50	£0.25	£0.75	£1.25
48-50 LD in the U.K. Rogers art	$0.50	$1.50	$2.50	£0.30	£0.90	£1.50
51-53 ND Rogers art	$0.40	$1.20	$2.00	£0.25	£0.75	£1.25
54 LD in the U.K. Paul Smith art	$0.50	$1.50	$2.50	£0.30	£0.90	£1.50
55 LD in the U.K. Golden art	$0.40	$1.20	$2.00	£0.25	£0.75	£1.25
56 LD in the U.K. origin retold, Paul Smith art	$0.50	$1.50	$2.50	£0.30	£0.90	£1.50
57-61 LD in the U.K.	$0.40	$1.20	$2.00	£0.25	£0.75	£1.25
62 LD in the U.K. Dracula appears, death of all vampires	$0.40	$1.20	$2.00	£0.30	£0.90	£1.50
63-64 LD in the U.K.	$0.40	$1.20	$2.00	£0.25	£0.75	£1.25
65-66 LD in the U.K. Paul Smith art	$0.45	$1.35	$2.25	£0.30	£0.90	£1.50
67 LD in the U.K.	$0.40	$1.20	$2.00	£0.25	£0.75	£1.25
68-73 LD in the U.K. Paul Smith art	$0.45	$1.35	$2.25	£0.30	£0.90	£1.50
74 LD in the U.K. Secret Wars X-over	$0.40	$1.20	$2.00	£0.30	£0.90	£1.50
75-77 ND	$0.40	$1.20	$2.00	£0.30	£0.90	£1.50
78 ND scarce in the U.K. Cloak and Dagger appear	$0.40	$1.20	$2.00	£0.40	£1.20	£2.00
79-80 ND	$0.40	$1.20	$2.00	£0.30	£0.90	£1.50
81 ND scarce in the U.K.	$0.40	$1.20	$2.00	£0.40	£1.20	£2.00
Title Value:	$58.85	$178.50	$330.00	£33.10	£101.15	£187.50

DOCTOR STRANGE (3RD SERIES)

Marvel Comics Group; 1 Oct 1988-90 Jun 1996

	$Good	$Fine	$N.Mint	£Good	£Fine	£N.Mint
1 ND	$0.50	$1.50	$2.50	£0.30	£0.90	£1.50
2-3 ND	$0.40	$1.20	$2.00	£0.25	£0.75	£1.25
4-5 ND New Defenders appear	$0.40	$1.20	$2.00	£0.25	£0.75	£1.25
6 ND 1st appearance Dread (Mephisto's daughter)	$0.40	$1.20	$2.00	£0.25	£0.75	£1.25
7-8 ND	$0.40	$1.20	$2.00	£0.25	£0.75	£1.25
9 ND scarce in the U.K. History of Vampires begins	$0.40	$1.20	$2.00	£0.25	£0.75	£1.25
10 ND Morbius returns (cover and story)	$0.40	$1.20	$2.00	£0.25	£0.75	£1.25
11-13 ND Acts of Vengeance tie-in	$0.60	$1.80	$3.00	£0.25	£0.75	£1.25
14 ND Vampiric Verses story; Morbius appears	$0.40	$1.20	$2.00	£0.25	£0.75	£1.25
15 ND Vampiric Verses story; Morbius appears	$0.60	$1.80	$3.00	£0.30	£0.90	£1.50
16-18 ND Vampiric Verses story; Morbius appears	$0.40	$1.20	$2.00	£0.25	£0.75	£1.25
19 ND	$0.40	$1.20	$2.00	£0.25	£0.75	£1.25
20 ND Morbius appears, Gene Colan art	$0.40	$1.20	$2.00	£0.25	£0.75	£1.25
21-24 ND The Dark Wars	$0.40	$1.20	$2.00	£0.25	£0.75	£1.25
25 ND Ron Lim art	$0.40	$1.20	$2.00	£0.25	£0.75	£1.25
26-27 ND Werewolf By Night appears	$0.40	$1.20	$2.00	£0.25	£0.75	£1.25
28 ND Ghost Rider appears, X-over from Ghost Rider #12	$0.60	$1.80	$3.00	£0.30	£0.90	£1.50
29-30 ND	$0.40	$1.20	$2.00	£0.25	£0.75	£1.25
31 ND Infinity Gauntlet tie-in, Silver Surfer appears	$0.30	$0.90	$1.50	£0.20	£0.60	£1.00
32-34 ND Infinity Gauntlet tie-in	$0.30	$0.90	$1.50	£0.20	£0.60	£1.00
35 ND Infinity Gauntlet tie-in, guest stars Hulk, Thor, Dr. Doom, Firelord, Drax vs. Thanos	$0.30	$0.90	$1.50	£0.20	£0.60	£1.00
36 ND Infinity Gauntlet tie-in, Warlock appears	$0.30	$0.90	$1.50	£0.20	£0.60	£1.00
37 ND	$0.30	$0.90	$1.50	£0.20	£0.60	£1.00
38-40 ND The Fear Lords Epic	$0.30	$0.90	$1.50	£0.20	£0.60	£1.00
41 ND Wolverine appears	$0.30	$0.90	$1.50	£0.20	£0.60	£1.00
42 ND Infinity War X-over (1st), Galactus appears	$0.30	$0.90	$1.50	£0.20	£0.60	£1.00
43-45 ND Infinity War X-over, Galactus appears	$0.30	$0.90	$1.50	£0.20	£0.60	£1.00
46 ND Infinity War X-over, Scarlet Witch appears	$0.30	$0.90	$1.50	£0.20	£0.60	£1.00
47 ND Infinity War X-over	$0.30	$0.90	$1.50	£0.20	£0.60	£1.00
48-49 ND	$0.30	$0.90	$1.50	£0.20	£0.60	£1.00
50 ND Hulk, Ghost Rider and Silver Surfer appear (leads in to Secret Defenders #1), holo-grafix cover	$0.60	$1.80	$3.00	£0.40	£1.20	£2.00
51 ND	$0.30	$0.90	$1.50	£0.20	£0.60	£1.00
52 ND X-over with Morbius #9	$0.30	$0.90	$1.50	£0.20	£0.60	£1.00
53 ND new direction for title	$0.30	$0.90	$1.50	£0.20	£0.60	£1.00
54-56 ND Infinity Crusade X-over						

TRADE PAPERBACKS, GRAPHIC NOVELS AND OTHER COLLECTIONS ARE PRICED IN POUNDS STERLING ONLY. CONVERT AT 1.5 FOR DOLLARS.

	$Good	$Fine	$N.Mint	£Good	£Fine	£N.Mint
	$0.30	$0.90	$1.50	£0.20	£0.60	£1.00
57-59 ND	$0.30	$0.90	$1.50	£0.20	£0.60	£1.00
60 ND Siege of Darkness part 7; neon ink/spot varnish cover						
	$0.40	$1.20	$2.00	£0.25	£0.75	£1.25
61 ND Siege of Darkness part 15; neon ink/spot varnish cover						
	$0.40	$1.20	$2.00	£0.25	£0.75	£1.25
62-63 ND Morbius appears						
	$0.30	$0.90	$1.50	£0.20	£0.60	£1.00
64 ND Mark Buckingham cover						
	$0.30	$0.90	$1.50	£0.20	£0.60	£1.00
65 ND Mark Buckingham cover; with free Spiderman vs. Venom card sheet						
	$0.30	$0.90	$1.50	£0.20	£0.60	£1.00
66 ND continued in Dr. Strange Annual #4						
	$0.30	$0.90	$1.50	£0.20	£0.60	£1.00
67 ND Clea returns	$0.30	$0.90	$1.50	£0.20	£0.60	£1.00
68 ND	$0.30	$0.90	$1.50	£0.20	£0.60	£1.00
69 ND Polaris appears						
	$0.30	$0.90	$1.50	£0.20	£0.60	£1.00
70-71 ND Hulk guest-stars						
	$0.30	$0.90	$1.50	£0.20	£0.60	£1.00
72-74 ND Last Rites story, metallic ink cover						
	$0.40	$1.20	$2.00	£0.25	£0.75	£1.25
75 ND 48pgs, Last Rites (conclusion)						
	$0.50	$1.50	$2.50	£0.30	£0.90	£1.50
75 Collectors Edition, ND - prismatic-foil stamped cover						
	$0.80	$2.40	$4.00	£0.50	£1.50	£2.50
76 ND new look/new costume begins						
	$0.40	$1.20	$2.00	£0.25	£0.75	£1.25
77-79 ND	$0.40	$1.20	$2.00	£0.25	£0.75	£1.25
80 ND Warren Ellis script, Mark Buckingham and Kev Sutherland art begin						
	$0.40	$1.20	$2.00	£0.25	£0.75	£1.25
81 ND Over The Edge tie-in, Punisher, Ghost Rider and Nick Fury appear						
	$0.40	$1.20	$2.00	£0.25	£0.75	£1.25
82-83 ND	$0.40	$1.20	$2.00	£0.25	£0.75	£1.25
84 ND J.M. DeMatteis scripts with Mark Buckingham and Kev Sutherland art begins						
	$0.40	$1.20	$2.00	£0.25	£0.75	£1.25
85-87 ND	$0.40	$1.20	$2.00	£0.25	£0.75	£1.25
88-89 ND Dr. Strange vs. Wong; bi-monthly						
	$0.40	$1.20	$2.00	£0.25	£0.75	£1.25
90 ND	$0.40	$1.20	$2.00	£0.25	£0.75	£1.25
Title Value:	$34.40	$103.20	$170.00	£21.45	£64.35	£107.25

Note: issue #50 has been recorded with a normal non-holo grafix cover and a recorded sale of **£10.00**: an unknown and obviously very limited quantity slipped through the full production process.

DOCTOR STRANGE ANNUAL

Marvel Comics Group; 1 1976;2 Jun 1992-4 1994

	$Good	$Fine	$N.Mint	£Good	£Fine	£N.Mint
1 ND 52pgs, P. Craig Russell art						
	$0.90	$2.70	$4.50	£0.60	£1.80	£3.00
2 ND 64pgs, Return of the Defenders part 4 (conclusion)						
	$0.50	$1.50	$2.50	£0.30	£0.90	£1.50
3 ND 64pgs, pre-bagged with trading card introducing Killiam						
	$0.50	$1.50	$2.50	£0.30	£0.90	£1.50
4 ND 64pgs, Mark Buckingham cover						
	$0.50	$1.50	$2.50	£0.30	£0.90	£1.50
Title Value:	$2.40	$7.20	$12.00	£1.50	£4.50	£7.50

DOCTOR STRANGE ASHCAN

Marvel Comics Group,OS; nn Apr 1995

	$Good	$Fine	$N.Mint	£Good	£Fine	£N.Mint
1 ND 16pgs, black and white; previews changes and new costume in the current issue of the 3rd series						
	$0.15	$0.45	$0.75	£0.10	£0.30	£0.50
Title Value:	$0.15	$0.45	$0.75	£0.10	£0.30	£0.50

DOCTOR STRANGE CLASSICS

Marvel Comics Group; 1 Mar 1984-4 Jun 1984

	$Good	$Fine	$N.Mint	£Good	£Fine	£N.Mint
1-4 ND Steve Ditko reprint						
	$0.40	$1.20	$2.00	£0.25	£0.75	£1.25
Title Value:	$1.60	$4.80	$8.00	£1.00	£3.00	£5.00

DOCTOR STRANGE GIANT SIZE

Marvel Comics Group; 1 Nov 1975

	$Good	$Fine	$N.Mint	£Good	£Fine	£N.Mint
1 ND scarce in the U.K. 68pgs, all reprint						
	$1.25	$3.75	$7.50	£0.80	£2.50	£5.00
Title Value:	$1.25	$3.75	$7.50	£0.80	£2.50	£5.00

DOCTOR STRANGE SPECIAL EDITION

Marvel Comics Group; 1 Feb 1983

	$Good	$Fine	$N.Mint	£Good	£Fine	£N.Mint
1 ND features Silver Dagger, reprints Dr. Strange #1, #2, #4, #5 & Strange Tales #127, Wrightson cover						
	$0.60	$1.80	$3.00	£0.40	£1.20	£2.00
Title Value:	$0.60	$1.80	$3.00	£0.40	£1.20	£2.00

Note: high-quality paper.

DOCTOR STRANGE/GHOST RIDER SPECIAL

Marvel Comics Group,OS; 1 Apr 1991

	$Good	$Fine	$N.Mint	£Good	£Fine	£N.Mint
1 ND market-tester reprint of Doctor Strange #28 with new logo						
	$0.50	$1.50	$2.50	£0.30	£0.90	£1.50
Title Value:	$0.50	$1.50	$2.50	£0.30	£0.90	£1.50

DOCTOR STRANGEFATE

DC Comics/Amalgam,OS; 1 May 1996

	$Good	$Fine	$N.Mint	£Good	£Fine	£N.Mint
1 ND a DC/Marvel amalgamation of Dr. Fate and Dr. Strange; Ron Marz script, Jose Luis Garcia-Lopez and Kevin Nowlan art						
	$0.50	$1.50	$2.50	£0.40	£1.20	£2.00
Title Value:	$0.50	$1.50	$2.50	£0.40	£1.20	£2.00

DOCTOR WHO

Marvel Comics Group; 1 Oct 1984-23 Aug 1986

(see also Marvel Premiere #57-60)

	$Good	$Fine	$N.Mint	£Good	£Fine	£N.Mint
1 ND Dave Gibbons art begins (reprints)						
	$0.30	$0.90	$1.50	£0.20	£0.60	£1.00
2-8 ND	$0.30	$0.90	$1.50	£0.20	£0.60	£1.00
9 ND scarce in the U.K.						
	$0.30	$0.90	$1.50	£0.25	£0.75	£1.25
10-23 ND	$0.30	$0.90	$1.50	£0.20	£0.60	£1.00
Title Value:	$6.90	$20.70	$34.50	£4.65	£13.95	£23.25

Note: all reprints from British Doctor Who Magazine, Dave Gibbons art.

DOCTOR ZERO

Marvel Comics Group/Epic; 1 Apr 1988-8 Jun 1989

	$Good	$Fine	$N.Mint	£Good	£Fine	£N.Mint
1-3 ND Cowan/Sienkiewicz art						
	$0.30	$0.90	$1.50	£0.20	£0.60	£1.00
4 ND	$0.30	$0.90	$1.50	£0.20	£0.60	£1.00
5 ND DS, Brett Ewins/Steve Dillon art						
	$0.30	$0.90	$1.50	£0.20	£0.60	£1.00
6-8 ND	$0.30	$0.90	$1.50	£0.20	£0.60	£1.00
Title Value:	$2.40	$7.20	$12.00	£1.60	£4.80	£8.00

DODEKAIN

Antarctic Press,MS; 1 Nov 1994-8 Jun 1995

	$Good	$Fine	$N.Mint	£Good	£Fine	£N.Mint
1-8 ND Masajuki Fujiwara script and art; black and white						
	$0.50	$1.50	$2.50	£0.30	£0.90	£1.50
Title Value:	$4.00	$12.00	$20.00	£2.40	£7.20	£12.00

DOG

Rebel Studios; 1 Aug 1991

	$Good	$Fine	$N.Mint	£Good	£Fine	£N.Mint
1 ND Joe Vigil script/art						
	$0.50	$1.50	$2.50	£0.30	£0.90	£1.50
Title Value:	$0.50	$1.50	$2.50	£0.30	£0.90	£1.50

DOG BOY

Fantagraphics; 1 Mar 1987-10 1988

	$Good	$Fine	$N.Mint	£Good	£Fine	£N.Mint
1-10 ND Steve Lafler script/art; black and white						
	$0.40	$1.20	$2.00	£0.25	£0.75	£1.25
Title Value:	$4.00	$12.00	$20.00	£2.50	£7.50	£12.50

DOG MOON

DC Comics/Vertigo,OS; nn Apr 1996

	$Good	$Fine	$N.Mint	£Good	£Fine	£N.Mint
nn ND 64pgs, Robert Hunter script, Tim Truman painted art						
	$1.40	$4.20	$7.00	£0.90	£2.70	£4.50
Title Value:	$1.40	$4.20	$7.00	£0.90	£2.70	£4.50

DOGS O WAR

Crusade Comics; 1 Jun 1996-present

	$Good	$Fine	$N.Mint	£Good	£Fine	£N.Mint
1 ND Mark Masztal art						
	$0.60	$1.80	$3.00	£0.40	£1.20	£2.00
2 ND	$0.60	$1.80	$3.00	£0.40	£1.20	£2.00
Title Value:	$1.20	$3.60	$6.00	£0.80	£2.40	£4.00

DOGS OF WAR

Defiant; 1 Apr 1994-5 Aug 1994

	$Good	$Fine	$N.Mint	£Good	£Fine	£N.Mint
1-4 ND	$0.30	$0.90	$1.50	£0.20	£0.60	£1.00
5 ND Schism X-over	$0.30	$0.90	$1.50	£0.20	£0.60	£1.00
Title Value:	$1.50	$4.50	$7.50	£1.00	£3.00	£5.00

Note: issues #6-8 were advertised and solicited but never appeared

DOLL

Rip Off Press; 1 1989-8 1991?

	$Good	$Fine	$N.Mint	£Good	£Fine	£N.Mint
1 ND Guy Colwell script/art begins; black and white						
	$0.80	$2.40	$4.00	£0.50	£1.50	£2.50
1 2nd printing ND	$0.50	$1.50	$2.50	£0.30	£0.90	£1.50
2 ND	$0.60	$1.80	$3.00	£0.40	£1.20	£2.00
2 2nd printing ND	$0.50	$1.50	$2.50	£0.30	£0.90	£1.50
3-8 ND	$0.50	$1.50	$2.50	£0.30	£0.90	£1.50
Title Value:	$5.40	$16.20	$27.00	£3.30	£9.90	£16.50
Trade Paperback, reprints #1-3				£1.20	£3.60	£6.00

DOLL MAN

I.W. Super; 11,15,17 1963-1964

	$Good	$Fine	$N.Mint	£Good	£Fine	£N.Mint
11,15,17 scarce though distributed in the U.K. reprint						
	$3.55	$10.50	$25.00	£1.75	£5.25	£12.50
Title Value:	$10.65	$31.50	$75.00	£5.25	£15.75	£37.50

DOLLMAN

Eternity,MS; 1 Nov 1991-4 Feb 1991

	$Good	$Fine	$N.Mint	£Good	£Fine	£N.Mint
1 ND based on US film (not released in UK); great covers!						
	$0.50	$1.50	$2.50	£0.30	£0.90	£1.50
2-4 ND	$0.50	$1.50	$2.50	£0.30	£0.90	£1.50
Title Value:	$2.00	$6.00	$10.00	£1.20	£3.60	£6.00

DOMINION

Eclipse,MS; 1 Dec 1989-6 Jul 1990

	$Good	$Fine	$N.Mint	£Good	£Fine	£N.Mint
1-6 ND	$0.30	$0.90	$1.50	£0.20	£0.60	£1.00
Title Value:	$1.80	$5.40	$9.00	£1.20	£3.60	£6.00

DOMINION SPECIAL

Dark Horse,OS; 1 Mar 1994

	$Good	$Fine	$N.Mint	£Good	£Fine	£N.Mint
1 ND bw	$0.50	$1.50	$2.50	£0.30	£0.90	£1.50
Title Value:	$0.50	$1.50	$2.50	£0.30	£0.90	£1.50

DOMINION: CONFLICT 1 - NO MORE NOISE

Dark Horse,MS; 1 Mar 1996-6 Aug 1996

	$Good	$Fine	$N.Mint	£Good	£Fine	£N.Mint
1-6 ND Masamune Shirow script and art; black and white						
	$0.60	$1.80	$3.00	£0.40	£1.20	£2.00
Title Value:	$3.60	$10.80	$18.00	£2.40	£7.20	£12.00

DOMINIQUE

Caliber Press; 1 Jul 1994

	$Good	$Fine	$N.Mint	£Good	£Fine	£N.Mint
1 ND spin-off character from Dark Horse Presents						
	$0.60	$1.80	$3.00	£0.40	£1.20	£2.00
Title Value:	$0.60	$1.80	$3.00	£0.40	£1.20	£2.00

DOMINIQUE: KILLZONE

Caliber Press; 1 Apr 1995

	$Good	$Fine	$N.Mint	£Good	£Fine	£N.Mint
1 ND Negative Burn anthology spin-off; black and white						
	$0.60	$1.80	$3.00	£0.40	£1.20	£2.00
Title Value:	$0.60	$1.80	$3.00	£0.40	£1.20	£2.00

DOMINIQUE: PROTECT & SERVE

Caliber Press,OS; 1 1995

	$Good	$Fine	$N.Mint	£Good	£Fine	£N.Mint
1 ND	$0.60	$1.80	$3.00	£0.40	£1.20	£2.00
Title Value:	$0.60	$1.80	$3.00	£0.40	£1.20	£2.00
DOMINIQUE: WHITE KNUCKLE DRIVE						
Caliber Press,OS; 1 1994						
1 ND	$0.60	$1.80	$3.00	£0.40	£1.20	£2.00
Title Value:	$0.60	$1.80	$3.00	£0.40	£1.20	£2.00
DOMINO						
Marvel Comics Group,MS; 1 Jan 1997-3 Mar 1997						
1-3 ND Ben Raab script, David Perrin art	$0.40	$1.20	$2.00	£0.25	£0.75	£1.25
Title Value:	$1.20	$3.60	$6.00	£0.75	£2.25	£3.75
DOMINO CHANCE						
Chance Ent.; 1 May/Jun 1982-9 May 1985						
1 ND	$0.30	$0.90	$1.50	£0.20	£0.60	£1.00
1 2nd printing, ND (May 1985)	$0.25	$0.75	$1.25	£0.15	£0.45	£0.75
2-6 ND	$0.30	$0.90	$1.50	£0.20	£0.60	£1.00
7 ND 1st appearance Gizmo	$0.30	$0.90	$1.50	£0.20	£0.60	£1.00
8 ND 1st full Gizmo story	$0.30	$0.90	$1.50	£0.20	£0.60	£1.00
9 ND	$0.30	$0.90	$1.50	£0.20	£0.60	£1.00
Title Value:	$2.95	$8.85	$14.75	£1.95	£5.85	£9.75
DOMINO CHANCE: ROACH EXTRAORDINAIRE						
Amazing Comics; 1-3 1987						
1-3 ND	$0.40	$1.20	$2.00	£0.25	£0.75	£1.25
Title Value:	$1.20	$3.60	$6.00	£0.75	£2.25	£3.75
DOMU: A CHILD'S DREAMS						
Dark Horse,MS; 1 Mar 1995-3 May 1995						
1-3 ND Katsuhiro Otomo script and art	$1.20	$3.60	$6.00	£0.80	£2.40	£4.00
Title Value:	$3.60	$10.80	$18.00	£2.40	£7.20	£12.00
Domu: A Child's Dream (Jan 1996)						
Trade paperback ND 240pgs, reprints mini-series				£2.40	£7.20	£12.00
DON SIMPSON'S BIZARRE HEROES						
Fiasco Comics; 00 Dec 1995; 0 Dec 1994; 1 Jul 1994-15 1995						
00 ND	$0.60	$1.80	$3.00	£0.40	£1.20	£2.00
0 ND (Dec 1994)	$0.60	$1.80	$3.00	£0.40	£1.20	£2.00
1 ND features Megaton Man; black and white begins	$0.60	$1.80	$3.00	£0.40	£1.20	£2.00
2-6 ND	$0.60	$1.80	$3.00	£0.40	£1.20	£2.00
7 ND page count now down from 32 to 24 pages but printed on heavier stock paper	$0.60	$1.80	$3.00	£0.40	£1.20	£2.00
8 ND	$0.60	$1.80	$3.00	£0.40	£1.20	£2.00
9 ND Yarn Man returns	$0.60	$1.80	$3.00	£0.40	£1.20	£2.00
10 ND	$0.60	$1.80	$3.00	£0.40	£1.20	£2.00
11 ND The Search for Megaton Man story	$0.60	$1.80	$3.00	£0.40	£1.20	£2.00
12-15 ND	$0.60	$1.80	$3.00	£0.40	£1.20	£2.00
Title Value:	$10.20	$30.60	$51.00	£6.80	£20.40	£34.00
Bizarre Heroes: The Apocalypse Affiliation (May 1995)						
Trade paperback reprints issues #1-4 with Larry Marder intro				£1.70	£5.10	£8.50
DONALD AND MICKEY						
Gladstone/Disney; 1 Aug 1992-30 1995 ?						
1-30 ND	$0.30	$0.90	$1.50	£0.20	£0.60	£1.00
Title Value:	$9.00	$27.00	$45.00	£6.00	£18.00	£30.00
DONALD DUCK						
Gladstone;246 Oct 1986-279 1989;Gladstone/Disney;280 Aug 1993-present						
(see Donald Duck Adventures, Christmas Parade, Gladstone Album Series, Walt Disney's Comics)						
(previously published by Whitman)						
246 scarce in the U.K. 1st Gladstone issue, 75c	$2.50	$7.50	$12.50	£0.60	£1.80	£3.00
247 scarce in the U.K.	$1.80	$5.25	$9.00	£0.30	£0.90	£1.50
248-249	$1.80	$5.25	$9.00	£0.25	£0.75	£1.25
250 64pgs, reprints 1st Carl Barks Donald Duck	$2.40	$7.00	$12.00	£0.50	£1.50	£2.50
251 reprints 1945 Firestone giveaway	$1.80	$5.25	$9.00	£0.25	£0.75	£1.25
252 1st 95¢ issue	$1.00	$3.00	$5.00	£0.25	£0.75	£1.25
253	$1.00	$3.00	$5.00	£0.25	£0.75	£1.25
254 scarce in the U.K. reprints Old California	$1.00	$3.00	$5.00	£0.25	£0.75	£1.25
255-256	$1.00	$3.00	$5.00	£0.25	£0.75	£1.25
257 52pgs, Summer Special	$1.00	$3.00	$5.00	£0.30	£0.90	£1.50
258-263	$1.00	$3.00	$5.00	£0.25	£0.75	£1.25
264 feature on various Donald Duck artists	$1.00	$3.00	$5.00	£0.25	£0.75	£1.25
265	$1.00	$3.00	$5.00	£0.25	£0.75	£1.25
266-277	$1.00	$3.00	$5.00	£0.20	£0.60	£1.00
278 68pgs	$1.00	$3.00	$5.00	£0.25	£0.75	£1.25
279	$1.00	$3.00	$5.00	£0.20	£0.60	£1.00
280 Carl Barks and Al Taliaferro reprints	$1.00	$3.00	$5.00	£0.20	£0.60	£1.00
281-285	$0.80	$2.40	$4.00	£0.20	£0.60	£1.00
286 64pgs, 60th anniversary tribute	$0.60	$1.80	$3.00	£0.40	£1.20	£2.00
287-291	$0.40	$1.20	$2.00	£0.20	£0.60	£1.00
292-294	$0.40	$1.20	$2.00	£0.25	£0.75	£1.25
295-298	$0.30	$0.90	$1.50	£0.20	£0.60	£1.00

	$Good	$Fine	$N.Mint	£Good	£Fine	£N.Mint
Title Value:	$50.10	$149.50	$248.50	£12.70	£38.10	£63.50
Note: all Non-Distributed on the news-stands in the U.K.						
DONALD DUCK ADVENTURES						
Gladstone; 1 Nov 1987-20 Apr 1990;21 Aug 1993-present						
1-7 ND	$0.40	$1.20	$2.00	£0.25	£0.75	£1.25
8 ND Crocodile Collector by Don Rosa	$0.40	$1.20	$2.00	£0.25	£0.75	£1.25
9 ND	$0.40	$1.20	$2.00	£0.25	£0.75	£1.25
10 ND classic Barks cover	$0.40	$1.20	$2.00	£0.25	£0.75	£1.25
11 ND	$0.25	$0.75	$1.25	£0.15	£0.45	£0.75
12 ND DS Don Rosa story/art, Barks poster	$0.40	$1.20	$2.00	£0.25	£0.75	£1.25
13-20 ND	$0.30	$0.90	$1.50	£0.20	£0.60	£1.00
21 ND Carl Barks reprint; title now re-published by Gladstone	$0.30	$0.90	$1.50	£0.20	£0.60	£1.00
22-29 ND Carl Barks reprint	$0.30	$0.90	$1.50	£0.20	£0.60	£1.00
30 ND 64pgs, Carl Barks reprint	$0.60	$1.80	$3.00	£0.40	£1.20	£2.00
31-32 ND	$0.30	$0.90	$1.50	£0.20	£0.60	£1.00
33-35 ND 64pgs	$0.60	$1.80	$3.00	£0.40	£1.20	£2.00
36-37 ND	$0.30	$0.90	$1.50	£0.20	£0.60	£1.00
38 ND full length William van Horn issue, the first for Gladstone since 1990	$0.30	$0.90	$1.50	£0.20	£0.60	£1.00
Title Value:	$13.65	$40.95	$68.25	£8.90	£26.70	£44.50
Note: Barks art in all						
DONALD DUCK ADVENTURES (2ND SERIES)						
Disney; 1 Jun 1990-38 Jun 1993;Gladstone/Hamilton 39 May 1996-present						
1 ND Don Rosa cover/art	$0.30	$0.90	$1.50	£0.20	£0.60	£1.00
2 ND William van Horn art begins, Carl Barks reprint	$0.30	$0.90	$1.50	£0.20	£0.60	£1.00
3 ND Carl Barks reprint	$0.30	$0.90	$1.50	£0.20	£0.60	£1.00
4-20 ND	$0.30	$0.90	$1.50	£0.20	£0.60	£1.00
21 ND Barks reprints	$0.30	$0.90	$1.50	£0.20	£0.60	£1.00
22 ND	$0.30	$0.90	$1.50	£0.20	£0.60	£1.00
23 ND Barks reprints	$0.30	$0.90	$1.50	£0.20	£0.60	£1.00
24-25 ND	$0.30	$0.90	$1.50	£0.20	£0.60	£1.00
26 ND reprints "Race to the South Seas" from a 1948 giveaway by Carl Barks	$0.30	$0.90	$1.50	£0.20	£0.60	£1.00
27-29 ND Carl Barks reprints	$0.30	$0.90	$1.50	£0.20	£0.60	£1.00
30-39 ND	$0.30	$0.90	$1.50	£0.20	£0.60	£1.00
Title Value:	$11.70	$35.10	$58.50	£7.80	£23.40	£39.00
DONALD DUCK AND MICKEY MOUSE						
Gladstone/Disney; 1 Jun 1995-present						
1 ND new material plus Carl Barks reprints begin	$0.30	$0.90	$1.50	£0.20	£0.60	£1.00
2-7 ND	$0.30	$0.90	$1.50	£0.20	£0.60	£1.00
Title Value:	$2.10	$6.30	$10.50	£1.40	£4.20	£7.00
DONALD DUCK DIGEST						
Gladstone; 1 Oct 1986-5 1987						
1-5 ND	$0.30	$0.90	$1.50	£0.20	£0.60	£1.00
Title Value:	$1.50	$4.50	$7.50	£1.00	£3.00	£5.00
DONATELLO						
Mirage Studios; 1 Aug 1985						
(see Teenage Mutant Ninja Turtles)						
1 ND Jack Kirby tribute, Stan Sakai pin-up	$1.00	$3.00	$5.00	£0.70	£2.10	£3.50
Title Value:	$1.00	$3.00	$5.00	£0.70	£2.10	£3.50
DONNA MIA						
Dark Fantasy,MS; 1-2 1996						
1 ND Mike Kaluta cover	$0.80	$2.40	$4.00	£0.50	£1.50	£2.50
1 Collectors Edition, ND Mike Kaluta cover; red foil logo	$1.00	$3.00	$5.00	£0.70	£2.10	£3.50
2 ND Mike Kaluta cover	$0.80	$2.40	$4.00	£0.50	£1.50	£2.50
2 Collectors Edition, ND Mike Kaluta cover; red foil logo	$1.00	$3.00	$5.00	£0.70	£2.10	£3.50
Title Value:	$3.60	$10.80	$18.00	£2.40	£7.20	£12.00
DOOM 2099						
Marvel Comics Group; 1 Jan 1993-44 Aug 1996						
1 ND metallic foil (silver) stamped cover; Dr. Doom arrives in the year 2099	$0.30	$0.90	$1.50	£0.20	£0.60	£1.00
2-5 ND	$0.25	$0.75	$1.25	£0.15	£0.45	£0.75
6 ND virtual reality Hulk appears	$0.25	$0.75	$1.25	£0.15	£0.45	£0.75
7 ND	$0.25	$0.75	$1.25	£0.15	£0.45	£0.75
8 ND Ravage 2099 cameo	$0.25	$0.75	$1.25	£0.15	£0.45	£0.75
9 ND	$0.25	$0.75	$1.25	£0.15	£0.45	£0.75
10-12 ND covers fit together	$0.25	$0.75	$1.25	£0.15	£0.45	£0.75
13 ND	$0.25	$0.75	$1.25	£0.15	£0.45	£0.75
14 ND Dr. Doom vs. Loki	$0.25	$0.75	$1.25	£0.15	£0.45	£0.75
15-16 ND	$0.25	$0.75	$1.25	£0.15	£0.45	£0.75

	$Good	$Fine	$N.Mint	£Good	£Fine	£N.Mint
17 ND with free Spiderman and his Deadly Foes card sheet	$0.25	$0.75	$1.25	£0.15	£0.45	£0.75
18-24 ND	$0.25	$0.75	$1.25	£0.15	£0.45	£0.75
25 ND new armour	$0.40	$1.20	$2.00	£0.25	£0.75	£1.25
25 Collectors Edition, ND - foil-stamped multi-level embossed cover	$0.60	$1.80	$3.00	£0.40	£1.20	£2.00
26-28 ND	$0.30	$0.90	$1.50	£0.20	£0.60	£1.00
29 ND Doom invades America; upgraded paper stock begins	$0.40	$1.20	$2.00	£0.25	£0.75	£1.25
29 Collectors Edition, ND - Doom invades America; clear chromium cover and upgraded paper	$0.80	$2.40	$4.00	£0.50	£1.50	£2.50
30-31 ND	$0.40	$1.20	$2.00	£0.25	£0.75	£1.25
32-35 ND One Nation Under Doom	$0.40	$1.20	$2.00	£0.25	£0.75	£1.25
36 ND continued from 2099 Apocalypse, guest-starring X-Men 2099; continued in X-Men 2099 #27	$0.40	$1.20	$2.00	£0.25	£0.75	£1.25
37 ND guest-starring X-Men 2099; continued in X-Men 2099 #28 and 2099 Genesis	$0.40	$1.20	$2.00	£0.25	£0.75	£1.25
38 ND continued in X-Men 2099 #29	$0.40	$1.20	$2.00	£0.25	£0.75	£1.25
39 ND X-Nation tie-in, continued in X-Men 2099 #30	$0.40	$1.20	$2.00	£0.25	£0.75	£1.25
40 ND Rage Against Time storyline	$0.40	$1.20	$2.00	£0.25	£0.75	£1.25
41 ND Rage Against Time storyline; Dr. Doom vs. Daredevil	$0.40	$1.20	$2.00	£0.25	£0.75	£1.25
42 ND Rage Against Time storyline; ties into Fantastic Four #413	$0.40	$1.20	$2.00	£0.25	£0.75	£1.25
43 ND Rage Against Time storyline concludes	$0.40	$1.20	$2.00	£0.25	£0.75	£1.25
44 ND	$0.40	$1.20	$2.00	£0.25	£0.75	£1.25
Title Value:	$15.15	$45.45	$75.75	£9.40	£28.20	£47.00

DOOM FORCE SPECIAL

DC Comics,OS; 1 Jul 1992

	$Good	$Fine	$N.Mint	£Good	£Fine	£N.Mint
1 64pgs, Grant Morrison script, parody of Marvel Comics themes and styles	$0.40	$1.20	$2.00	£0.25	£0.75	£1.25
Title Value:	$0.40	$1.20	$2.00	£0.25	£0.75	£1.25

DOOM PATROL

National Periodical Publications;86 Mar 1964-121 Sep/Oct 1968; 122 Feb 1973-124 Jun/Jul 1973

(see Brave and the Bold, DC Special Blue Ribbon Digest 19, Showcase #94-96)
(previously My Greatest Adventure)

	$Good	$Fine	$N.Mint	£Good	£Fine	£N.Mint
86 scarce in the U.K. 1pg origin	$12.00	$37.00	$110.00	£6.50	£20.00	£60.00
87	$10.00	$30.00	$80.00	£5.00	£15.00	£40.00
88 origin the Chief	$10.50	$32.00	$85.00	£5.50	£16.50	£45.00
89-90	$10.00	$30.00	$80.00	£5.00	£15.00	£40.00
91 intro Mento	$9.25	$28.00	$75.00	£5.50	£16.50	£45.00
92-98	$9.25	$28.00	$75.00	£4.35	£13.00	£35.00
99 1st appearance Beast Boy later becomes Changeling in New Teen Titans	$9.25	$28.00	$75.00	£4.35	£13.00	£35.00
100 origin Beast Boy; last Silver Age issue cover-dated December 1965	$10.00	$30.00	$80.00	£5.00	£15.00	£40.00
101	$5.00	$15.00	$40.00	£2.50	£7.50	£20.00
102 Challengers of the Unknown X-over	$5.00	$15.00	$40.00	£2.50	£7.50	£20.00
103-105	$5.00	$15.00	$40.00	£2.50	£7.50	£20.00
106 origin Negative Man	$5.00	$15.00	$40.00	£2.50	£7.50	£20.00
107-110	$5.00	$15.00	$40.00	£2.50	£7.50	£20.00
111-120	$3.75	$11.00	$30.00	£1.85	£5.50	£15.00
121 very scarce in the U.K. Doom Patrol dies	$10.00	$30.00	$80.00	£5.00	£15.00	£40.00
122 scarce in the U.K. reprint	$0.80	$2.50	$5.00	£0.55	£1.75	£3.50
123 scarce in the U.K. reprint; Negative Man appears on cover without face bandages	$0.80	$2.50	$5.00	£0.55	£1.75	£3.50
124 scarce in the U.K. reprint	$0.80	$2.50	$5.00	£0.55	£1.75	£3.50
Title Value:	$245.65	$738.50	$1985.00	£122.45	£367.25	£990.50

FEATURES

Beast Boy in 112-115. Elasti-Girl in 89. Private World of Negative Man in 106, 107, 109, 111. Robotman in 87, 100, 101, 105.

DOOM PATROL (2ND SERIES)

DC Comics; 1 Oct 1987-87 Feb 1995

	$Good	$Fine	$N.Mint	£Good	£Fine	£N.Mint
1	$0.30	$0.90	$1.50	£0.20	£0.60	£1.00
2-5	$0.25	$0.75	$1.25	£0.15	£0.45	£0.75
6-8 Erik Larsen art	$0.25	$0.75	$1.25	£0.15	£0.45	£0.75
9 Eric Larsen art, extra 16pg Doom Patrol story insert	$0.25	$0.75	$1.25	£0.15	£0.45	£0.75
10-15 Erik Larsen art	$0.25	$0.75	$1.25	£0.15	£0.45	£0.75
16	$0.25	$0.75	$1.25	£0.15	£0.45	£0.75
17 Invasion X-over, Aquaman, Aqualad, Sea Devils appear	$0.25	$0.75	$1.25	£0.15	£0.45	£0.75
18 Invasion X-over	$0.25	$0.75	$1.25	£0.15	£0.45	£0.75
19 1st Grant Morrison story; Crawling From The Wreckage part 1 (ends #22)	$1.40	$4.20	$7.00	£0.70	£2.10	£3.50
20	$0.80	$2.40	$4.00	£0.50	£1.50	£2.50
21-28	$0.60	$1.80	$3.00	£0.40	£1.20	£2.00
29 Simon Bisley covers begin, Superman and Justice League of America appear	$0.60	$1.80	$3.00	£0.40	£1.20	£2.00
30	$0.60	$1.80	$3.00	£0.40	£1.20	£2.00
31-38	$0.40	$1.20	$2.00	£0.30	£0.90	£1.50
39 preview of new series World Without End	$0.40	$1.20	$2.00	£0.30	£0.90	£1.50
40	$0.40	$1.20	$2.00	£0.30	£0.90	£1.50
41-44	$0.40	$1.20	$2.00	£0.25	£0.75	£1.25
45 Brendan McCarthy art	$0.40	$1.20	$2.00	£0.25	£0.75	£1.25
46	$0.40	$1.20	$2.00	£0.25	£0.75	£1.25
47 $1.75 covers begin	$0.40	$1.20	$2.00	£0.25	£0.75	£1.25
48-49	$0.40	$1.20	$2.00	£0.25	£0.75	£1.25
50 DS pin-ups by Bisley, Bolland and others	$0.50	$1.50	$2.50	£0.30	£0.90	£1.50
51-52	$0.40	$1.20	$2.00	£0.25	£0.75	£1.25
53 Phantom Stranger, Hellblazer, Mister E appear	$0.40	$1.20	$2.00	£0.25	£0.75	£1.25
54 photo cover	$0.40	$1.20	$2.00	£0.25	£0.75	£1.25
55-56	$0.40	$1.20	$2.00	£0.25	£0.75	£1.25
57 48pgs, true history of the Doom Patrol	$0.40	$1.20	$2.00	£0.25	£0.75	£1.25
58-62	$0.40	$1.20	$2.00	£0.25	£0.75	£1.25
63 last Grant Morrison script, last Simon Bisley cover	$0.40	$1.20	$2.00	£0.25	£0.75	£1.25
64 1st issue scripted by Rachel Pollack, Brian Bolland covers begin, 1st issue under "Vertigo" banner	$0.40	$1.20	$2.00	£0.25	£0.75	£1.25
65	$0.40	$1.20	$2.00	£0.25	£0.75	£1.25
66 $1.95 cover begins	$0.40	$1.20	$2.00	£0.25	£0.75	£1.25

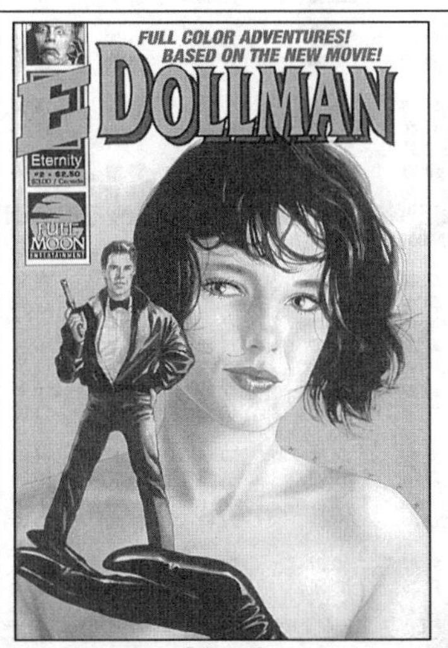

Dollman #2

Doom Patrol (1st) #92

Doom 2099 #2

Issue	$Good	$Fine	$N.Mint	£Good	£Fine	£N.Mint
67 30th anniversary appearance of The Doom Patrol	$0.40	$1.20	$2.00	£0.25	£0.75	£1.25
68	$0.40	$1.20	$2.00	£0.25	£0.75	£1.25
69 John Higgins art	$0.40	$1.20	$2.00	£0.25	£0.75	£1.25
70-74	$0.40	$1.20	$2.00	£0.25	£0.75	£1.25
75-76 The Teiresias Wars story	$0.40	$1.20	$2.00	£0.25	£0.75	£1.25
77-78 The Teiresias Wars story; cover by Brian Bolland	$0.40	$1.20	$2.00	£0.25	£0.75	£1.25
79-87	$0.40	$1.20	$2.00	£0.25	£0.75	£1.25
Title Value:	$35.65	$106.95	$178.25	£22.75	£68.25	£113.75

Note: Direct sale from issue 19 as New Format. For Mature Readers from #37.

Doom Patrol: Crawling From The Wreckage (Aug 1992)

Issue	$Good	$Fine	$N.Mint	£Good	£Fine	£N.Mint
Trade paperback, reprints issues 19-25, painted cover by Simon Bisley				£2.50	£7.50	£12.50

DOOM PATROL AND SUICIDE SQUAD SPECIAL

DC Comics,OS; 1 1988

Issue	$Good	$Fine	$N.Mint	£Good	£Fine	£N.Mint
1 48pgs, Erik Larsen art	$0.40	$1.20	$2.00	£0.25	£0.75	£1.25
Title Value:	$0.40	$1.20	$2.00	£0.25	£0.75	£1.25

DOOM PATROL ANNUAL

DC Comics; 1 Nov 1988-2 1989

Issue	$Good	$Fine	$N.Mint	£Good	£Fine	£N.Mint
1 48pgs	$0.40	$1.20	$2.00	£0.25	£0.75	£1.25
2 48pgs, The Children's Crusade part 5	$0.60	$1.80	$3.00	£0.30	£0.90	£1.50
Title Value:	$1.00	$3.00	$5.00	£0.55	£1.65	£2.75

DOOM'S IV

Image; 1 Jul 1994-4 Oct 1994

Issue	$Good	$Fine	$N.Mint	£Good	£Fine	£N.Mint
½ ND Marc Pacella cover art, produced in conjunction with Wizard Comics; issued in a Wizard protective Mylar with certificate of authenticity	$1.50	$4.50	$7.50	£1.00	£3.00	£5.00
1 ND Rob Liefeld script, Mark Pacella art begin	$0.50	$1.50	$2.50	£0.30	£0.90	£1.50
1 Variant Cover Edition, ND part of four interlocking covers by Rob Liefeld, limited to 25% of the print run	$0.70	$2.10	$3.50	£0.40	£1.20	£2.00
2 ND	$0.50	$1.50	$2.50	£0.30	£0.90	£1.50
2 Variant Cover Edition, ND part of 4 interlocking covers by Rob Liefeld, limited to 25% of the print run	$0.70	$2.10	$3.50	£0.40	£1.20	£2.00
3-4 ND	$0.50	$1.50	$2.50	£0.30	£0.90	£1.50
Title Value:	$4.90	$14.70	$24.50	£3.00	£9.00	£15.00

DOOM'S IV SOURCEBOOK

Image; 1 Nov 1994

Issue	$Good	$Fine	$N.Mint	£Good	£Fine	£N.Mint
1 ND information and statistics about the characters	$0.50	$1.50	$2.50	£0.30	£0.90	£1.50
Title Value:	$0.50	$1.50	$2.50	£0.30	£0.90	£1.50

DOOMSDAY ANNUAL

DC Comics; 1 Dec 1995

Issue	$Good	$Fine	$N.Mint	£Good	£Fine	£N.Mint
1 ND 56pgs, Year One; four stories including origin before meeting Superman; Darkseid and the Green Lantern Corps appear	$0.80	$2.40	$4.00	£0.50	£1.50	£2.50
Title Value:	$0.80	$2.40	$4.00	£0.50	£1.50	£2.50

DOOMSDAY PLUS ONE

Charlton; 1 Jul 1975-6 May 1976;7 Jun 1978-12 May 1979

Issue	$Good	$Fine	$N.Mint	£Good	£Fine	£N.Mint
1 distributed in the U.K. John Byrne art	$1.25	$3.75	$7.50	£0.80	£2.50	£5.00
2 distributed in the U.K. John Byrne art	$0.80	$2.50	$5.00	£0.65	£2.00	£4.00
3 distributed in the U.K. John Byrne art	$0.65	$2.00	$4.00	£0.80	£2.50	£5.00
4 distributed in the U.K. John Byrne art	$0.65	$2.00	$4.00	£0.65	£2.00	£4.00
5 distributed in the U.K. John Byrne, Steve Ditko art	$0.65	$2.00	$4.00	£0.65	£2.00	£4.00
6 distributed in the U.K. John Byrne art	$0.65	$2.00	$4.00	£0.55	£1.75	£3.50
7 distributed in the U.K. reprints #1,2,4-6	$0.25	$0.75	$1.50	£0.30	£1.00	£2.00
8-12 distributed in the U.K. reprints #1,2,4-6	$0.25	$0.75	$1.50	£0.25	£0.75	£1.50
Title Value:	$6.15	$18.75	$37.50	£5.65	£17.50	£35.00

DOOMSDAY SQUAD

Fantagraphics; 1 Aug 1986-7 Jun 1987

Issue	$Good	$Fine	$N.Mint	£Good	£Fine	£N.Mint
1 ND John Byrne reprints from Doomsday + 1 begin, Dalgoda back-up, new Byrne cover	$0.50	$1.50	$2.50	£0.30	£0.90	£1.50
2 ND Lloyd Llewellyn back-up, new John Byrne cover	$0.50	$1.50	$2.50	£0.30	£0.90	£1.50
3 ND Usagi Yojimbo back-up, Gil Kane cover	$0.50	$1.50	$2.50	£0.30	£0.90	£1.50
4 ND Miracle Squad back-up, new Neal Adams cover	$0.50	$1.50	$2.50	£0.30	£0.90	£1.50
5 ND Captain Jack back-up, Gil Kane cover	$0.50	$1.50	$2.50	£0.30	£0.90	£1.50
6 ND Keif Llama back-up, Gil Kane cover	$0.50	$1.50	$2.50	£0.30	£0.90	£1.50
7 ND scarce in the U.K.	$0.50	$1.50	$2.50	£0.40	£1.20	£2.00
Title Value:	$3.50	$10.50	$17.50	£2.20	£6.60	£11.00

Note: all Non-Distributed on the news-stands in the U.K.

DOORWAY TO NIGHTMARE

DC Comics; 1 Jan/Feb 1978-5 Sep/Oct 1978

(see Books of Magic, Madame Xanadu, the Unexpected)

Issue	$Good	$Fine	$N.Mint	£Good	£Fine	£N.Mint
1	$0.65	$2.00	$4.00	£0.30	£1.00	£2.00
2-4	$0.30	$1.00	$2.00	£0.25	£0.75	£1.50
5 ND 44pgs	$0.40	$1.25	$2.50	£0.30	£1.00	£2.00
Title Value:	$1.95	$6.25	$12.50	£1.35	£4.25	£8.50

FEATURES

Madame Xanadu in all issues.

DOUBLE DARE ADVENTURES

Harvey; 1 Dec 1966-2 Mar 1967

Issue	$Good	$Fine	$N.Mint	£Good	£Fine	£N.Mint
1 rare although distributed in the U.K. giant, Jack Kirby art featured	$5.50	$17.00	$40.00	£3.55	£10.50	£25.00
2 scarce though distributed in the U.K. Williamson/Crandall reprint	$4.25	$12.50	$30.00	£2.50	£7.50	£17.50
Title Value:	$9.75	$29.50	$70.00	£6.05	£18.00	£42.50

DOUBLE DRAGON

Marvel Comics Group,MS; 1 Jul 1991-6 Dec 1991

Issue	$Good	$Fine	$N.Mint	£Good	£Fine	£N.Mint
1-6 ND	$0.15	$0.45	$0.75	£0.10	£0.35	£0.60
Title Value:	$0.90	$2.70	$4.50	£0.60	£2.10	£3.60

Note: based on Nintendo video game

DOUBLE EDGE

Night Wynd,MS; 1 Mar 1994-4 Jun 1994

Issue	$Good	$Fine	$N.Mint	£Good	£Fine	£N.Mint
1-4 ND Dwayne J. Ferguson script and art; black and white	$0.35	$1.05	$1.75	£0.25	£0.75	£1.25
Title Value:	$1.40	$4.20	$7.00	£1.00	£3.00	£5.00

DOUBLE EDGE: ALPHA

Marvel Comics Group,OS; 1 Sep 1995

Issue	$Good	$Fine	$N.Mint	£Good	£Fine	£N.Mint
1 ND 48pgs, Over The Edge story arc begins as The Punisher must kill Nick Fury; Larry Hama script, Kerry Gammill and Tom Palmer art; concluded in Double Edge: Omega	$1.00	$3.00	$5.00	£0.70	£2.10	£3.50
Title Value:	$1.00	$3.00	$5.00	£0.70	£2.10	£3.50

DOUBLE EDGE: OMEGA

Marvel Comics Group,OS; 1 Oct 1995

Issue	$Good	$Fine	$N.Mint	£Good	£Fine	£N.Mint
1 ND 48pgs, Over The Edge tie-in; Daredevil, Doc Sampson, Ghost Rider, Nick Fury and Punisher appear; chromium cover by Joe Quesada and Jimmy Palmiotti; Nick Fury dies at the Punisher's hand	$1.00	$3.00	$5.00	£0.70	£2.10	£3.50
Title Value:	$1.00	$3.00	$5.00	£0.70	£2.10	£3.50

DOUBLE IMPACT

High Impact Studios; 1 Mar 1995-8 May 1996

Issue	$Good	$Fine	$N.Mint	£Good	£Fine	£N.Mint
0 San Diego '95 Edition, ND pre-bagged with a silver front outer cover; produced and distributed at the San Diego comic convention, limited to 5,000 copies	$8.00	$24.00	$40.00	£5.00	£15.00	£25.00
0 San Diego '96 Edition, ND includes nude pictures of Mrs. Carrelero, limited to 1,000 copies	$3.00	$9.00	$15.00	£2.00	£6.00	£10.00
0 San Diego '96 Nude Signed Edition, ND with those naked pictures again, signed by husband Ricky (lucky, lucky b......)	$5.00	$15.00	$25.00	£3.00	£9.00	£15.00
1 ND Ricky Carralero art and script; chromium wraparound cover	$1.50	$4.50	$7.50	£0.70	£2.10	£3.50
1 Prismatic Cover Edition ND	$6.00	$18.00	$30.00	£2.50	£7.50	£12.50
2 ND Ricky Carralero script and art, colour with 8 pages of black and white gallery pin-ups	$0.80	$2.40	$4.00	£0.60	£1.80	£3.00
2 Nude Edition, ND pre-bagged with a black sealed outer cover, limited to 5,000 copies	$4.00	$12.00	$20.00	£2.50	£7.50	£12.50
3 ND Ricky Carralero script and art; black and white	$0.80	$2.40	$4.00	£0.60	£1.80	£3.00
3 "Blondage" Edition, ND pre-bagged with certificate and signed; limited to 5,000 copies	$4.00	$12.00	$20.00	£2.50	£7.50	£12.50
4 ND	$0.60	$1.80	$3.00	£0.40	£1.20	£2.00
4 "Bad Boy Arizona" Edition, ND pre-bagged with certificate and signed; limited to 3,000 copies	$4.00	$12.00	$20.00	£2.50	£7.50	£12.50
5 ND	$0.60	$1.80	$3.00	£0.40	£1.20	£2.00
5 Variant Cover Edition, ND - limited to 600 copies - available to retailers for every 50 copies of the regular issue ordered; white nude cover with gatefold back cover	$4.00	$12.00	$20.00	£2.50	£7.50	£12.50
6 Cover A: China ND	$0.60	$1.80	$3.00	£0.40	£1.20	£2.00
6 Cover B: Jazz ND	$0.60	$1.80	$3.00	£0.40	£1.20	£2.00
6 Cover C: Blondage ND	$1.20	$3.60	$6.00	£0.70	£2.10	£3.50
7-8 ND	$0.60	$1.80	$3.00	£0.40	£1.20	£2.00
8 Variant Cover Edition, ND cover by Ricky Carrelero	$1.80	$5.25	$9.00	£1.20	£3.60	£6.00
Title Value:	$47.70	$142.95	$238.50	£28.70	£86.10	£143.50

DOUBLE IMPACT (2ND SERIES)

High Impact Studios; 1 1996-present

Issue	$Good	$Fine	$N.Mint	£Good	£Fine	£N.Mint
1 ND wraparound chromium cover	$0.80	$2.40	$4.00	£0.50	£1.50	£2.50
1 Nude Edition ND	$2.00	$6.00	$10.00	£1.00	£3.00	£5.00
1 Nude Edition - Gold, ND, gold foil logo	$2.00	$6.00	$10.00	£1.20	£3.60	£6.00
1 Nude Edition Signed, ND $14.95 cover	$3.00	$9.00	$15.00	£2.00	£6.00	£10.00
2 ND	$0.60	$1.80	$3.00	£0.40	£1.20	£2.00
2 Chromium Edition ND	$1.20	$3.60	$6.00	£0.80	£2.40	£4.00
2 Nude Edition ND	$2.00	$6.00	$10.00	£1.30	£3.90	£6.50
2 Nude Edition Signed ND	$4.00	$12.00	$20.00	£2.60	£7.80	£13.00
3 "All That Jazz" cover	$0.60	$1.80	$3.00	£0.40	£1.20	£2.00
3 Nikki Blaze cover	$0.60	$1.80	$3.00	£0.40	£1.20	£2.00
Title Value:	$16.80	$50.40	$84.00	£10.60	£31.80	£53.00

DOUBLE IMPACT LINGERIE SPECIAL

High Impact Studios,OS; 1 1996

Issue	$Good	$Fine	$N.Mint	£Good	£Fine	£N.Mint
1 ND	*$0.60*	*$1.80*	*$3.00*	£0.40	£1.20	£2.00
Title Value:	*$0.60*	*$1.80*	*$3.00*	£0.40	£1.20	£2.00

DOUBLE IMPACT/HELLINA

High Impact Studios,OS; 1 Mar 1996

(see Hellina/Double Impact)

Issue	$Good	$Fine	$N.Mint	£Good	£Fine	£N.Mint
1 ND Ricky Carrelero art	*$0.60*	*$1.80*	*$3.00*	£0.40	£1.20	£2.00
1 Nude Edition, ND Ricky Carrelero art	*$2.00*	*$6.00*	*$10.00*	£1.00	£3.00	£5.00
1 Nude Edition - Gold ND	*$2.00*	*$6.00*	*$10.00*	£1.20	£3.60	£6.00
1 Nude Edition - Signed, ND - by Ricky Carrelero	*$3.00*	*$9.00*	*$15.00*	£2.00	£6.00	£10.00
Title Value:	*$7.60*	*$22.80*	*$38.00*	£4.60	£13.80	£23.00

DOUBLE IMPACT/LETHAL STRIKE: DOUBLE STRYKE

Issue	$Good	$Fine	$N.Mint	£Good	£Fine	£N.Mint
nn ND Matthew Roberts and Jude Millien art; black and white	*$0.60*	*$1.80*	*$3.00*	£0.40	£1.20	£2.00
Title Value:	*$0.60*	*$1.80*	*$3.00*	£0.40	£1.20	£2.00

DOUBLE LIFE OF PRIVATE STRONG, THE

Archie; 1 Jun 1959-2 Aug 1959

Issue	$Good	$Fine	$N.Mint	£Good	£Fine	£N.Mint
1 rare although distributed in the U.K. origin The Shield, 1st appearance The Fly (Archie's 1st Silver Age Superhero), Joe Simon and Jack Kirby art	*$75.00*	*$225.00*	*$525.00*	£50.00	£150.00	£350.00
2 scarce though distributed in the U.K. Fly appears, Joe Simon and Jack Kirby art	*$43.00*	*$125.00*	*$300.00*	£29.00	£85.00	£200.00
Title Value:	*$118.00*	*$350.00*	*$825.00*	£79.00	£235.00	£550.00

DP 7

Marvel Comics Group/New Universe; 1 Nov 1986-32 Jun 1989

Issue	$Good	$Fine	$N.Mint	£Good	£Fine	£N.Mint
1-29 ND	*$0.15*	*$0.45*	*$0.75*	£0.10	£0.35	£0.60
30 ND intro Capt Manhattan	*$0.15*	*$0.45*	*$0.75*	£0.10	£0.35	£0.60
31-32 ND	*$0.15*	*$0.45*	*$0.75*	£0.10	£0.35	£0.60
Title Value:	*$4.80*	*$14.40*	*$24.00*	£3.20	£11.20	£19.20

DP 7 ANNUAL

Marvel Comics Group/New Universe; 1 Nov 1987

Issue	$Good	$Fine	$N.Mint	£Good	£Fine	£N.Mint
1 ND intro The Witness	*$0.25*	*$0.75*	*$1.25*	£0.15	£0.45	£0.75
Title Value:	*$0.25*	*$0.75*	*$1.25*	£0.15	£0.45	£0.75

DR. BOOGIE

Media Arts Publishing; 1 1987

Issue	$Good	$Fine	$N.Mint	£Good	£Fine	£N.Mint
1 ND cover inks by Nicola Cuti	*$0.40*	*$1.20*	*$2.00*	£0.25	£0.75	£1.25
Title Value:	*$0.40*	*$1.20*	*$2.00*	£0.25	£0.75	£1.25

DR. FU MANCHU

I.W. Comics; 1 1964

Issue	$Good	$Fine	$N.Mint	£Good	£Fine	£N.Mint
1 rare although distributed in the U.K. Wally Wood art, all reprint	*$9.25*	*$28.00*	*$65.00*	£5.00	£15.00	£35.00
Title Value:	*$9.25*	*$28.00*	*$65.00*	£5.00	£15.00	£35.00

DR. GRAVES' THE DEAD FILES

Avalon Communications; 1 Feb 1996

Issue	$Good	$Fine	$N.Mint	£Good	£Fine	£N.Mint
1 ND reprints from Charlton Comics	*$0.55*	*$1.65*	*$2.75*	£0.35	£1.05	£1.75
Title Value:	*$0.55*	*$1.65*	*$2.75*	£0.35	£1.05	£1.75

DR. GRAVES, ADVENTURES OF

A Plus Comics; 1 May 1991-2 1991

Issue	$Good	$Fine	$N.Mint	£Good	£Fine	£N.Mint
1 ND 48pgs, Charlton Comics character revived	*$0.40*	*$1.20*	*$2.00*	£0.25	£0.75	£1.25
2 ND 48pgs	*$0.40*	*$1.20*	*$2.00*	£0.25	£0.75	£1.25
Title Value:	*$0.80*	*$2.40*	*$4.00*	£0.50	£1.50	£2.50

DR. GRAVES, THE MANY GHOSTS OF

Charlton; 1 May 1967-65 Apr 1978;66 Jun 1981-75 Jan 1986

Issue	$Good	$Fine	$N.Mint	£Good	£Fine	£N.Mint
1 scarce in the U.K.	*$2.00*	*$6.00*	*$12.00*	£1.00	£3.00	£6.00
2 scarce in the U.K.	*$1.00*	*$3.00*	*$6.00*	£0.50	£1.50	£3.00
3 scarce in the U.K.	*$0.80*	*$2.50*	*$5.00*	£0.30	£1.00	£2.00
4-44	*$0.80*	*$2.50*	*$5.00*	£0.25	£0.75	£1.50
45 1st pro work by Don Newton	*$0.50*	*$1.50*	*$3.00*	£0.25	£0.75	£1.50
46-50	*$0.40*	*$1.25*	*$2.50*	£0.25	£0.75	£1.50
51-65	*$0.30*	*$1.00*	*$2.00*	£0.20	£0.60	£1.25
66 reprints begin	*$0.30*	*$0.90*	*$1.50*	£0.20	£0.60	£1.00
67-75	*$0.30*	*$0.90*	*$1.50*	£0.20	£0.60	£1.00
Title Value:	*$46.60*	*$145.75*	*$218.50*	£18.55	£55.75	£110.25

Note: most issues distributed on the news-stands in the U.K.

DR. RADIUM, MAN OF SCIENCE

Slave Labor,MS; 1 Oct 1992-3 Jan 1995

Issue	$Good	$Fine	$N.Mint	£Good	£Fine	£N.Mint
1-3 ND b&w	*$0.30*	*$0.90*	*$1.50*	£0.20	£0.60	£1.00
Title Value:	*$0.90*	*$2.70*	*$4.50*	£0.60	£1.80	£3.00

DR. SPEKTOR, THE OCCULT FILES OF

Gold Key; 1 Apr 1973-24 Feb 1977;Whitman: 25 May 1982

Issue	$Good	$Fine	$N.Mint	£Good	£Fine	£N.Mint
1 scarce in the U.K. 1st appearance Dr. Adam Spektor and Lakota; painted covers begin	*$1.65*	*$5.00*	*$10.00*	£1.00	£3.00	£6.00
2	*$1.00*	*$3.00*	*$6.00*	£0.55	£1.75	£3.50
3	*$0.75*	*$2.25*	*$4.50*	£0.50	£1.50	£3.00
4	*$0.75*	*$2.25*	*$4.50*	£0.40	£1.25	£2.50
5 16pg Kenner Catalogue insert	*$0.75*	*$2.25*	*$4.50*	£0.40	£1.25	£2.50
6-9	*$0.50*	*$1.50*	*$3.00*	£0.30	£1.00	£2.00
9 Modern Comics Reprint, scarce in the U.K. (1977)	*$0.20*	*$0.60*	*$1.00*	£0.30	£0.90	£1.50
10	*$0.50*	*$1.50*	*$3.00*	£0.30	£1.00	£2.00
11 Dr. Spektor becomes a werewolf; 16pg Kenner Catalogue insert	*$0.40*	*$1.25*	*$2.50*	£0.30	£1.00	£2.00
12 Werewolf vs. Frankenstein	*$0.40*	*$1.25*	*$2.50*	£0.30	£1.00	£2.00
13	*$0.40*	*$1.25*	*$2.50*	£0.25	£0.75	£1.50
14 Dr. Solar Man of the Atom appears	*$1.15*	*$3.50*	*$7.00*	£0.65	£2.00	£4.00
15-24	*$0.40*	*$1.25*	*$2.50*	£0.25	£0.75	£1.50
25 scarce in the U.K. reprint; line drawn cover	*$0.50*	*$1.50*	*$2.50*	£0.40	£1.20	£2.00
Title Value:	*$14.45*	*$44.10*	*$87.50*	£9.05	£28.10	£55.50

Note: most issues distributed in the newstands in the U.K.

DR. STRANGE VS. DRACULA

Marvel Comics Group,OS; 1 Mar 1994

Issue	$Good	$Fine	$N.Mint	£Good	£Fine	£N.Mint
1 ND 48pgs, reprints Tomb of Dracula #44 and Dr. Strange (2nd Series) #14; Kyle Baker cover	*$0.40*	*$1.20*	*$2.00*	£0.25	£0.75	£1.25
Title Value:	*$0.40*	*$1.20*	*$2.00*	£0.25	£0.75	£1.25

DR. WEIRD

Caliber Press; 1 Oct 1994

Issue	$Good	$Fine	$N.Mint	£Good	£Fine	£N.Mint
1 ND Frank Brunner cover; black and white	*$0.45*	*$1.35*	*$2.25*	£0.30	£0.90	£1.50
Title Value:	*$0.45*	*$1.35*	*$2.25*	£0.30	£0.90	£1.50

DR. WEIRD SPECIAL

Caliber Press,OS; 1 Feb 1994

Issue	$Good	$Fine	$N.Mint	£Good	£Fine	£N.Mint
1 ND 64pgs, reprints Jim Starlin material	*$0.90*	*$2.70*	*$4.50*	£0.60	£1.80	£3.00
Title Value:	*$0.90*	*$2.70*	*$4.50*	£0.60	£1.80	£3.00

DR. WHO AND THE DALEKS

Dell/Movie Classics,OS Movie; 12-190-612 Dec 1966

Issue	$Good	$Fine	$N.Mint	£Good	£Fine	£N.Mint
12-190-612 rare although distributed in the U.K. adapts film; Peter Cushing photo cover; 1st U.S. appearance	*$15.00*	*$45.00*	*$105.00*	£9.25	£28.00	£65.00
Title Value:	*$15.00*	*$45.00*	*$105.00*	£9.25	£28.00	£65.00

DR. WONDER

Old Town Publishing; 1 Jul 1996-4 1996 ?

Issue	$Good	$Fine	$N.Mint	£Good	£Fine	£N.Mint
1-4 ND b&w	*$0.60*	*$1.80*	*$3.00*	£0.40	£1.20	£2.00
Title Value:	*$2.40*	*$7.20*	*$12.00*	£1.60	£4.80	£8.00

DRACULA

Dell; 12-231-212 1962;2 Nov 1966-4 Mar 1967;6 Jul 1972-8 Jul 1973

Issue	$Good	$Fine	$N.Mint	£Good	£Fine	£N.Mint
12-231-212 rare in the U.K. (Movie Classics #1) adapts film	*$5.00*	*$15.00*	*$35.00*	£2.10	£6.25	£15.00
2 origin of Dracula-as-super hero	*$2.10*	*$6.25*	*$15.00*	£1.05	£3.20	£7.50
3-4 scarce in the U.K.	*$1.40*	*$4.25*	*$10.00*	£0.55	£1.70	£4.00
6 scarce in the U.K. reprints #2	*$1.25*	*$3.75*	*$7.50*	£0.65	£2.00	£4.00
7-8 reprints #3,4	*$0.80*	*$2.50*	*$5.00*	£0.50	£1.50	£3.00
Title Value:	*$12.75*	*$38.50*	*$87.50*	£5.90	£17.85	£40.50

Note: all distributed on the news-stands in the U.K.

DRACULA (2ND SERIES)

Eternity,MS; 1 Dec 1989-4 May 1990

Issue	$Good	$Fine	$N.Mint	£Good	£Fine	£N.Mint
1 ND b&w begins	*$0.40*	*$1.20*	*$2.00*	£0.25	£0.75	£1.25
1 2nd printing ND	*$0.30*	*$0.90*	*$1.50*	£0.20	£0.60	£1.00
2-4 ND	*$0.40*	*$1.20*	*$2.00*	£0.25	£0.75	£1.25
Title Value:	*$1.90*	*$5.70*	*$9.50*	£1.20	£3.60	£6.00

DRACULA (3RD SERIES)

Topps,MS; 1 Dec 1992-4 Mar 1993

Issue	$Good	$Fine	$N.Mint	£Good	£Fine	£N.Mint
1 ND pre-bagged, adaptation of Francis Ford Coppola film, with four trading cards, Mike Mignola cover and art	*$0.50*	*$1.50*	*$2.50*	£0.30	£0.90	£1.50
1 2nd printing, ND (printed on poly-bag)	*$0.40*	*$1.20*	*$2.00*	£0.25	£0.75	£1.25
1 Red Premium Edition, ND, red embossed logo	*$2.00*	*$6.00*	*$10.00*	£1.20	£3.60	£6.00
2-4 ND pre-bagged, adaptation of Francis Ford Coppola film, with four trading cards, Mike Mignola cover and art	*$0.50*	*$1.50*	*$2.50*	£0.30	£0.90	£1.50
Title Value:	*$4.40*	*$13.20*	*$22.00*	£2.65	£7.95	£13.25
Bram Stoker's Dracula Graphic Album (Feb 1994) reprints mini-series, new wraparound cover with crimson foil enhancement. Foreword by Francis Ford Coppola				£1.80	£5.40	£9.00

DRACULA BOOK AND RECORD SET

Power Records;PR-15 1974

Issue	$Good	$Fine	$N.Mint	£Good	£Fine	£N.Mint
PR-15, scarce in the U.K. 20pg booklet with 45 rpm record	*$1.25*	*$3.75*	*$7.50*	£0.80	£2.50	£5.00
Title Value:	*$1.25*	*$3.75*	*$7.50*	£0.80	£2.50	£5.00

Note: the item would be valued at approximately 50% without record

DRACULA CHRONICLES

Topps,MS; 1 Apr 1995-3 Jun 1995

Issue	$Good	$Fine	$N.Mint	£Good	£Fine	£N.Mint
1-3 ND Roy Thomas script, Esteban Maroto art	*$0.40*	*$1.20*	*$2.00*	£0.25	£0.75	£1.25
Title Value:	*$1.20*	*$3.60*	*$6.00*	£0.75	£2.25	£3.75

DRACULA GIANT SIZE

Marvel Comics Group;2 Sep 1974-5 Jun 1975

(formerly Chillers Giant Size)

Issue	$Good	$Fine	$N.Mint	£Good	£Fine	£N.Mint
2 ND 68pgs	*$1.25*	*$3.75*	*$7.50*	£0.90	£2.75	£5.50
3-4 ND 68pgs	*$1.00*	*$3.00*	*$6.00*	£0.80	£2.50	£5.00
5 ND 68pgs, 1st John Byrne art at Marvel	*$1.25*	*$3.75*	*$7.50*	£1.00	£3.00	£6.00
Title Value:	*$4.50*	*$13.50*	*$27.00*	£3.50	£10.75	£21.50

DRACULA IN HELL

Apple Comics,MS; 1 Jul 1991

Issue	$Good	$Fine	$N.Mint	£Good	£Fine	£N.Mint
1 ND Tim Vigil cover	*$0.40*	*$1.20*	*$2.00*	£0.25	£0.75	£1.25
Title Value:	*$0.40*	*$1.20*	*$2.00*	£0.25	£0.75	£1.25

Note: originally solicited as a mini series

DRACULA LIVES ANNUAL

Marvel Comics Group,Magazine; 1 Summer 1975

	$Good	$Fine	$N.Mint	£Good	£Fine	£N.Mint
1 ND	*$0.55*	*$1.75*	*$3.50*	£0.50	£1.50	£3.00
Title Value:	*$0.55*	*$1.75*	*$3.50*	£0.50	£1.50	£3.00

Note: all reprint, includes Adams art.

DRACULA LIVES!

Marvel Comics Group,Magazine; 1 1973-13 Jul 1975

	$Good	$Fine	$N.Mint	£Good	£Fine	£N.Mint
1 ND	*$1.25*	*$3.75*	*$7.50*	£0.80	£2.50	£5.00
2 ND scarce in the U.K. Neal Adams art, origin of Dracula	*$0.80*	*$2.50*	*$5.00*	£1.25	£3.75	£7.50
3 ND Neal Adams inks	*$0.80*	*$2.50*	*$5.00*	£0.50	£1.50	£3.00
4 scarce in the U.K.	*$0.65*	*$2.00*	*$4.00*	£0.40	£1.25	£2.50
5-13	*$0.50*	*$1.50*	*$3.00*	£0.30	£1.00	£2.00
Title Value:	*$8.00*	*$24.25*	*$47.00*	£5.65	£18.00	£36.00

DRACULA THE IMPALER

Comax Productions; 1 1991

	$Good	$Fine	$N.Mint	£Good	£Fine	£N.Mint
1 ND Butch Burcham script/art, black and white	*$0.30*	*$0.90*	*$1.50*	£0.20	£0.60	£1.00
Title Value:	*$0.30*	*$0.90*	*$1.50*	£0.20	£0.60	£1.00

DRACULA VERSUS ZORRO

Topps,MS; 1 Oct 1993-2 Nov 1993

	$Good	$Fine	$N.Mint	£Good	£Fine	£N.Mint
1 ND black cover with red foil logo and red metallic ink	*$0.50*	*$1.50*	*$2.50*	£0.30	£0.90	£1.50
2 ND pre-bagged with Zorro #0 included	*$0.50*	*$1.50*	*$2.50*	£0.30	£0.90	£1.50
Title Value:	*$1.00*	*$3.00*	*$5.00*	£0.60	£1.80	£3.00
Dracula vs. Zorro (Apr 1994) Trade paperback reprints mini-series with new wraparound cover by Tom Yeates				£0.80	£2.40	£4.00

DRACULA, BIG BAD BLOOD OF

Apple Comics,MS; 1 Oct 1991-2 Nov 1991

	$Good	$Fine	$N.Mint	£Good	£Fine	£N.Mint
1-2 ND	*$0.40*	*$1.20*	*$2.00*	£0.25	£0.75	£1.25
Title Value:	*$0.80*	*$2.40*	*$4.00*	£0.50	£1.50	£2.50

DRACULA, REQUIEM FOR

Marvel Comics Group,OS; 1 Feb 1993

	$Good	$Fine	$N.Mint	£Good	£Fine	£N.Mint
1 ND reprints Tomb of Dracula #69-#70	*$0.40*	*$1.20*	*$2.00*	£0.25	£0.75	£1.25
Title Value:	*$0.40*	*$1.20*	*$2.00*	£0.25	£0.75	£1.25

DRACULA, THE COLLECTOR'S

Millennium,MS; 1 Dec 1993-2 Jan 1994

	$Good	$Fine	$N.Mint	£Good	£Fine	£N.Mint
1-2 ND 48pgs, anthology featuring John Bolton among others	*$0.60*	*$1.80*	*$3.00*	£0.40	£1.20	£2.00
Title Value:	*$1.20*	*$3.60*	*$6.00*	£0.80	£2.40	£4.00

DRACULA, THE GHOSTS OF

Eternity,MS; 1 Sep 1991-5 Jan 1992

	$Good	$Fine	$N.Mint	£Good	£Fine	£N.Mint
1-5 ND	*$0.40*	*$1.20*	*$2.00*	£0.25	£0.75	£1.25
Title Value:	*$2.00*	*$6.00*	*$10.00*	£1.25	£3.75	£6.25

DRACULA, THE SAVAGE RETURN OF

Marvel Comics Group,OS; 1 Jan 1993

	$Good	$Fine	$N.Mint	£Good	£Fine	£N.Mint
1 ND 48pgs, reprints Tomb of Dracula #1,#2	*$0.40*	*$1.20*	*$2.00*	£0.25	£0.75	£1.25
Title Value:	*$0.40*	*$1.20*	*$2.00*	£0.25	£0.75	£1.25

DRACULA, THE WEDDING OF

Marvel Comics Group,OS; 1 Jan 1993

	$Good	$Fine	$N.Mint	£Good	£Fine	£N.Mint
1 ND 48pgs, reprints Tomb of Dracula #30, #45-#46	*$0.40*	*$1.20*	*$2.00*	£0.25	£0.75	£1.25
Title Value:	*$0.40*	*$1.20*	*$2.00*	£0.25	£0.75	£1.25

DRACULA: RETURN OF THE IMPALER

Slave Labor; 1 Sep 1993-3 1993;4 Oct 1994

	$Good	$Fine	$N.Mint	£Good	£Fine	£N.Mint
1-4 ND b&w	*$0.40*	*$1.20*	*$2.00*	£0.25	£0.75	£1.25
Title Value:	*$1.60*	*$4.80*	*$8.00*	£1.00	£3.00	£5.00

DRACULA: THE SUICIDE CLUB

Adventure,MS; 1 Oct 1991-4 Jan 1993

	$Good	$Fine	$N.Mint	£Good	£Fine	£N.Mint
1-4 ND	*$0.40*	*$1.20*	*$2.00*	£0.25	£0.75	£1.25
Title Value:	*$1.60*	*$4.80*	*$8.00*	£1.00	£3.00	£5.00

DRACULA: VLAD THE IMPALER

Topps,MS; 1 Feb 1993-3 Apr 1993

	$Good	$Fine	$N.Mint	£Good	£Fine	£N.Mint
1 ND pre-bagged with 3 trading cards, Roy Thomas script, Esteban Marato art	*$0.50*	*$1.50*	*$2.50*	£0.30	£0.90	£1.50
1 Red Premium Edition, ND, foil embossed logo	*$2.00*	*$6.00*	*$10.00*	£1.20	£3.60	£6.00
2-3 ND pre-bagged with 3 trading cards, Roy Thomas script, Esteban Marato art	*$0.50*	*$1.50*	*$2.50*	£0.30	£0.90	£1.50
Title Value:	*$3.50*	*$10.50*	*$17.50*	£2.10	£6.30	£10.50

DRAFT, THE

New Universe,OS; 1 Jun 1988

(see also The Pitt, The War)

	$Good	$Fine	$N.Mint	£Good	£Fine	£N.Mint
1 ND part Kyle Baker art, Klaus Jansen inks	*$0.60*	*$1.80*	*$3.00*	£0.40	£1.20	£2.00
Title Value:	*$0.60*	*$1.80*	*$3.00*	£0.40	£1.20	£2.00

Note: Bookshelf Format.

DRAG-STRIP HOTRODDERS

Charlton; 1 Summer 1963;2 Jan 1965-16 Jul 1967

	$Good	$Fine	$N.Mint	£Good	£Fine	£N.Mint
1 scarce, distributed in the U.K.	*$5.00*	*$15.00*	*$35.00*	£2.10	£6.25	£15.00
2 distributed in the U.K.	*$3.55*	*$10.50*	*$25.00*	£1.40	£4.25	£10.00
3-5 distributed in the U.K.	*$2.85*	*$8.50*	*$20.00*	£1.05	£3.20	£7.50
6-10 distributed in the U.K.	*$2.50*	*$7.50*	*$17.50*	£0.70	£2.10	£5.00
11-16 distributed in the U.K.	*$2.50*	*$7.50*	*$17.50*	£0.55	£1.70	£4.00
Title Value:	*$44.60*	*$133.50*	*$312.50*	£13.45	£40.80	£96.50

DRAGON

Comics Interview,MS; 1-3 1988

	$Good	$Fine	$N.Mint	£Good	£Fine	£N.Mint
1-3 ND	*$0.40*	*$1.20*	*$2.00*	£0.25	£0.75	£1.25
Title Value:	*$1.20*	*$3.60*	*$6.00*	£0.75	£2.25	£3.75

DRAGON FLUX

Antarctic Press,MS; 1 Feb 1996-2 Mar 1996

	$Good	$Fine	$N.Mint	£Good	£Fine	£N.Mint
1 ND Tyrone Ford script and art; black and white	*$0.60*	*$1.80*	*$3.00*	£0.40	£1.20	£2.00
2 ND	*$0.60*	*$1.80*	*$3.00*	£0.40	£1.20	£2.00
Title Value:	*$1.20*	*$3.60*	*$6.00*	£0.80	£2.40	£4.00

DRAGON LINES

Marvel Comics Group/Epic,MS; 1 May 1993-4 Aug 1993

	$Good	$Fine	$N.Mint	£Good	£Fine	£N.Mint
1 ND Ron Lim pencils begin; embossed cover	*$0.40*	*$1.20*	*$2.00*	£0.25	£0.75	£1.25
2-4 ND	*$0.40*	*$1.20*	*$2.00*	£0.25	£0.75	£1.25
Title Value:	*$1.60*	*$4.80*	*$8.00*	£1.00	£3.00	£5.00

DRAGON LINES: WAY OF THE WARRIOR

Marvel Comics Group/Epic,MS; 1 Nov 1993-2 Dec 1993

	$Good	$Fine	$N.Mint	£Good	£Fine	£N.Mint
1-2 ND Ron Lim pencils; bound-in trading card	*$0.40*	*$1.20*	*$2.00*	£0.25	£0.75	£1.25
Title Value:	*$0.80*	*$2.40*	*$4.00*	£0.50	£1.50	£2.50

DRAGON PEARL & JADE

CFD Productions; 1 Apr 1996

	$Good	$Fine	$N.Mint	£Good	£Fine	£N.Mint
1 ND b&w	*$0.40*	*$1.20*	*$2.00*	£0.25	£0.75	£1.25
Title Value:	*$0.40*	*$1.20*	*$2.00*	£0.25	£0.75	£1.25

DRAGON STRIKE

Marvel Comics Group,OS; 1 Feb 1994

	$Good	$Fine	$N.Mint	£Good	£Fine	£N.Mint
1 ND adaptation of TSR game	*$0.25*	*$0.75*	*$1.25*	£0.15	£0.45	£0.75
Title Value:	*$0.25*	*$0.75*	*$1.25*	£0.15	£0.45	£0.75

DRAGON'S CLAWS

Marvel Comics Group; 1 Oct 1988-10 Jul 1989

(see Transformers in British section)

	$Good	$Fine	$N.Mint	£Good	£Fine	£N.Mint
1 Simon Furman script, Geoff Senior art	*$0.30*	*$0.90*	*$1.50*	£0.20	£0.60	£1.00
2	*$0.30*	*$0.90*	*$1.50*	£0.20	£0.60	£1.00
3 1st cameo appearance Death's Head in mainstream Marvel Universe (on back cover one page strip)	*$0.40*	*$1.20*	*$2.00*	£0.25	£0.75	£1.25
4 Death's Head on back page advertisement announcing appearance next issue	*$0.30*	*$0.90*	*$1.50*	£0.20	£0.60	£1.00
5 1st full appearance of Death's Head in mainstream Marvel Universe (see Transformers #113 in British section)	*$0.70*	*$2.10*	*$3.50*	£0.40	£1.20	£2.00
6-10	*$0.30*	*$0.90*	*$1.50*	£0.20	£0.60	£1.00
Title Value:	*$3.50*	*$10.50*	*$17.50*	£2.25	£6.75	£11.25

DRAGON'S STAR

Caliber Press,MS; 1 Sep 1993-2 1993

	$Good	$Fine	$N.Mint	£Good	£Fine	£N.Mint
1-2 ND b&w	*$0.50*	*$1.50*	*$2.50*	£0.30	£0.90	£1.50
Title Value:	*$1.00*	*$3.00*	*$5.00*	£0.60	£1.80	£3.00

DRAGON, THE

Image,MS; 1 Mar 1996-5 Jul 1996

	$Good	$Fine	$N.Mint	£Good	£Fine	£N.Mint
1 ND reprints Savage Dragon mini-series with additional sketchbook pages	*$0.20*	*$0.60*	*$1.00*	£0.15	£0.45	£0.75
2-5 ND	*$0.20*	*$0.60*	*$1.00*	£0.15	£0.45	£0.75
Title Value:	*$1.00*	*$3.00*	*$5.00*	£0.75	£2.25	£3.75

DRAGON: BLOOD & GUTS

Image,MS; 1 Mar 1995-3 May 1995

	$Good	$Fine	$N.Mint	£Good	£Fine	£N.Mint
1-3 ND Jason Pearson and Karl Story script and art	*$0.50*	*$1.50*	*$2.50*	£0.30	£0.90	£1.50
Title Value:	*$1.50*	*$4.50*	*$7.50*	£0.90	£2.70	£4.50
Dragon: Blood & Guts (Nov 1995) Trade paperback collects mini-series, new cover by Jason Pearson				£1.10	£3.30	£5.50

DRAGONFIRE

Night Wynd,MS; 1 Feb 1992-4 May 1992

	$Good	$Fine	$N.Mint	£Good	£Fine	£N.Mint
1-4 ND Barry Blair script and art; black and white	*$0.35*	*$1.05*	*$1.75*	£0.25	£0.75	£1.25
Title Value:	*$1.40*	*$4.20*	*$7.00*	£1.00	£3.00	£5.00

DRAGONFIRE (2ND SERIES)

Night Wynd,MS; 1 Jun 1992-4 Sep 1992

	$Good	$Fine	$N.Mint	£Good	£Fine	£N.Mint
1-4 ND Barry Blair script and art; black and white	*$0.35*	*$1.05*	*$1.75*	£0.25	£0.75	£1.25
Title Value:	*$1.40*	*$4.20*	*$7.00*	£1.00	£3.00	£5.00

DRAGONFIRE: THE CLASSIFIED FILES

Night Wynd,MS; 1 Jul 1992-4 Oct 1992

	$Good	$Fine	$N.Mint	£Good	£Fine	£N.Mint
1-4 ND Barry Blair script and art; black and white	*$0.35*	*$1.05*	*$1.75*	£0.25	£0.75	£1.25
Title Value:	*$1.40*	*$4.20*	*$7.00*	£1.00	£3.00	£5.00

DRAGONFIRE: THE EARLY YEARS

Night Wynd,MS; 1 Apr 1993-8 Nov 1993

	$Good	$Fine	$N.Mint	£Good	£Fine	£N.Mint
1-8 ND Barry Blair and Dale Keown script and art; black and white	*$0.35*	*$1.05*	*$1.75*	£0.25	£0.75	£1.25
Title Value:	*$2.80*	*$8.40*	*$14.00*	£2.00	£6.00	£10.00

DRAGONFIRE: THE SAMURAI SWORD

Night Wynd,MS; 1 Oct 1993-2 1993

	$Good	$Fine	$N.Mint	£Good	£Fine	£N.Mint
1-2 ND Barry Blair script and art; black and white	*$0.35*	*$1.05*	*$1.75*	£0.25	£0.75	£1.25
Title Value:	*$0.70*	*$2.10*	*$3.50*	£0.50	£1.50	£2.50

DRAGONFIRE: UFO WARS

Night Wynd,MS; 1 Nov 1992-4 Mar 1993

	$Good	$Fine	$N.Mint	£Good	£Fine	£N.Mint
1-4 ND Barry Blair script and art; black and white	*$0.35*	*$1.05*	*$1.75*	£0.25	£0.75	£1.25

	$Good	$Fine	$N.Mint	£Good	£Fine	£N.Mint
Title Value:	$1.40	$4.20	$7.00	£1.00	£3.00	£5.00
DRAGONFLIGHT						
Eclipse,MS; 1 Feb 1991-3 Aug 1991						
1-3 ND 48pgs, adaptation Anne McCaffrey's book by Brynne Stephans, art by Lela Dowling and Cynthia Martin	$0.70	$2.10	$3.50	£0.50	£1.50	£2.50
Title Value:	$2.10	$6.30	$10.50	£1.50	£4.50	£7.50
Dragonflight Collection (Feb 1993)						
Softcover, reprints mini-series				£1.85	£5.55	£9.25
Hardcover, reprints mini-series				£4.20	£12.60	£21.00
DRAGONFLY						
AC Comics; 1 1986-8 1987						
(see Americomics, Fem Force)						
1-8 ND	$0.40	$1.20	$2.00	£0.25	£0.75	£1.25
Title Value:	$3.20	$9.60	$16.00	£2.00	£6.00	£10.00
Cycle of Fire,						
Trade paperback, reworked reprint of issues #1,2 plus new art				£1.20	£3.60	£6.00
DRAGONFORCE						
Aircel; 1 1988-13 1989						
1 ND Dale Keown cover art	$0.70	$2.10	$3.50	£0.30	£0.90	£1.50
2-12 ND Dale Keown cover art	$0.50	$1.50	$2.50	£0.25	£0.75	£1.25
13 ND	$0.40	$1.20	$2.00	£0.25	£0.75	£1.25
Title Value:	$6.60	$19.80	$28.00	£3.30	£9.90	£16.50
DRAGONHEART						
Topps,MS; 1 May 1996-2 Jun 1996						
1 ND adaptation of film; David Anthony Kraft script, Ron Lim art	$0.60	$1.80	$3.00	£0.40	£1.20	£2.00
2 ND 64pgs, adaptation of film; David Anthony Kraft script, Ron Lim art	$1.00	$3.00	$5.00	£0.70	£2.10	£3.50
Title Value:	$1.60	$4.80	$8.00	£1.10	£3.30	£5.50
DRAGONLANCE COMICS						
DC Comics, Game; 1 Dec 1988-34 Sep 1991						
1 based on the DragonLance books by Weis and Hickman	$0.50	$1.50	$2.50	£0.50	£1.50	£2.50
2-5	$0.40	$1.20	$2.00	£0.30	£0.90	£1.50
6-10	$0.30	$0.90	$1.50	£0.25	£0.75	£1.25
11-21	$0.30	$0.90	$1.50	£0.20	£0.60	£1.00
22-25 Taladas story	$0.30	$0.90	$1.50	£0.20	£0.60	£1.00
26-29	$0.30	$0.90	$1.50	£0.20	£0.60	£1.00
30-32 Dwarf War, covers by Mike Kaluta	$0.30	$0.90	$1.50	£0.20	£0.60	£1.00
33-34	$0.30	$0.90	$1.50	£0.20	£0.60	£1.00
Title Value:	$10.80	$32.40	$54.00	£7.75	£23.25	£38.75
DRAGONLANCE COMICS ANNUAL						
DC Comics, Game; 1 Dec 1990						
1 64pgs, painted cover	$0.50	$1.50	$2.50	£0.30	£0.90	£1.50
Title Value:	$0.50	$1.50	$2.50	£0.30	£0.90	£1.50
DRAGONLANCE GRAPHIC NOVEL						
TSR; 1,2 1988;3 1989						
(see DC's Dragonlance)						
1-2 ND Tom Yeates art	$2.00	$6.00	$10.00	£1.20	£3.60	£6.00
3 ND	$2.00	$6.00	$10.00	£1.20	£3.60	£6.00
Title Value:	$6.00	$18.00	$30.00	£3.60	£10.80	£18.00
DRAGONLANCE SAGA GRAPHIC NOVEL						
DC Comics;4 Apr 1990;5 Apr 1991						
4-5 ND 80pgs	$2.00	$6.00	$10.00	£1.20	£3.60	£6.00
Title Value:	$4.00	$12.00	$20.00	£2.40	£7.20	£12.00

	$Good	$Fine	$N.Mint	£Good	£Fine	£N.Mint
Note: first three volumes published by TSR Games						
DRAGONRING						
Aircel; 1-6 1986						
1-6 ND b&w	$0.40	$1.20	$2.00	£0.25	£0.75	£1.25
Title Value:	$2.40	$7.20	$12.00	£1.50	£4.50	£7.50
DRAGONRING (2ND SERIES)						
Aircel; 1 Dec 1987-15 1988						
1-15 ND colour	$0.40	$1.20	$2.00	£0.25	£0.75	£1.25
Title Value:	$6.00	$18.00	$30.00	£3.75	£11.25	£18.75
DRAGONS IN THE MOON						
Aircel,MS; 1 Aug 1990-4 Nov 1990						
1-4 ND	$0.40	$1.20	$2.00	£0.25	£0.75	£1.25
Title Value:	$1.60	$4.80	$8.00	£1.00	£3.00	£5.00
DRAGONSLAYER						
Marvel Comics Group,MS Film; 1 Oct 1981-2 Nov 1981						
1-2 ND	$0.15	$0.45	$0.75	£0.10	£0.35	£0.60
Title Value:	$0.30	$0.90	$1.50	£0.20	£0.70	£1.20
Note: reprints Marvel Super Special #20.						
DRAMA						
Sirius Entertainment,OS; 1 Jun 1994						
1 ND 1st full colour appearance of Dawn, Joseph Michael Linsner art	$5.00	$15.00	$25.00	£2.50	£7.50	£12.50
1 Signed & Numbered Edition, ND - signed by Joseph Michael Linsner; 1,400 copies with fingerprint authenticity	$15.00	$45.00	$75.00	£5.00	£15.00	£25.00
Title Value:	$20.00	$60.00	$100.00	£7.50	£22.50	£37.50
DREADLANDS						
Marvel Comics Group,MS; 1 Jan 1992-4 Apr 1992						
1-4 ND 48pgs	$0.80	$2.40	$4.00	£0.50	£1.50	£2.50
Title Value:	$3.20	$9.60	$16.00	£2.00	£6.00	£10.00
DREADSTAR						
Marvel Comics Group/Epic; 1 Nov 1982-26 Aug 1986						
(see Marvel Graphic Novel) (published by First Comics #27 on)						
1 ND Jim Starlin story/art begins	$0.40	$1.20	$2.00	£0.30	£0.90	£1.50
2-5 ND	$0.30	$0.90	$1.50	£0.25	£0.75	£1.25
6-7 ND Wrightson art	$0.30	$0.90	$1.50	£0.25	£0.75	£1.25
8-15 ND	$0.30	$0.90	$1.50	£0.25	£0.75	£1.25
16 ND scarce in the U.K.	$0.30	$0.90	$1.50	£0.30	£0.90	£1.50
17-26 ND	$0.30	$0.90	$1.50	£0.25	£0.75	£1.25
Title Value:	$7.90	$23.70	$39.50	£6.60	£19.80	£33.00
DREADSTAR (2ND SERIES)						
First;27 Sep 1986-64 Jan 1991						
(previously published by Marvel)						
27-49 ND	$0.30	$0.90	$1.50	£0.25	£0.75	£1.25
50 ND squarebound	$0.40	$1.20	$2.00	£0.30	£0.90	£1.50
51-64 ND	$0.30	$0.90	$1.50	£0.25	£0.75	£1.25
Title Value:	$11.50	$34.50	$57.50	£9.55	£28.65	£47.75
DREADSTAR AND CO.						
Marvel Comics Group/Epic; 1 Jul 1985-6 Dec 1985						
1-6 ND reprints from Dreadstar series	$0.25	$0.75	$1.25	£0.15	£0.45	£0.75
Title Value:	$1.50	$4.50	$7.50	£0.90	£2.70	£4.50
DREADSTAR ANNUAL						
Marvel Comics Group/Epic; 1 Dec 1983						
1 ND reprints "The Price" (see Eclipso Grpahic Album Series)	$0.40	$1.20	$2.00	£0.30	£0.90	£1.50
Title Value:	$0.40	$1.20	$2.00	£0.30	£0.90	£1.50

Doom's IV #1

Doorway to Nightmare #2

Dracula Giant Size #5

DREADSTAR, JIM STARLIN'S

Malibu Bravura,MS; 1 Apr 1994-6 Oct 1994

Issue	$Good	$Fine	$N.Mint	£Good	£Fine	£N.Mint
1-6 ND Peter David script, Ernie Colon art						
	$0.50	*$1.50*	*$2.50*	£0.30	£0.90	£1.50
Title Value:	*$3.00*	*$9.00*	*$15.00*	£1.80	£5.40	£9.00

DREADWOLF

Lightning Comics; 1 Aug 1994

Issue	$Good	$Fine	$N.Mint	£Good	£Fine	£N.Mint
1 ND	*$0.80*	*$2.40*	*$4.00*	£0.50	£1.50	£2.50
1 Ashcan Edition, ND black and white; 4,000 copies						
	$1.50	*$4.50*	*$7.50*	£0.80	£2.40	£4.00
1 Platinum Edition ND						
	$1.00	*$3.00*	*$5.00*	£0.60	£1.80	£3.00
1 Signed & Numbered Edition, ND (Feb 1995) - new metallic ink cover, pre-bagged and limited to 1,000 copies						
	$1.50	*$4.50*	*$7.50*	£0.80	£2.40	£4.00
1 Signed Ashcan Edition, ND (by Joseph Zyskowski), black and white; 1,000 copies						
	$1.60	*$4.80*	*$8.00*	£0.90	£2.70	£4.50
Title Value:	*$6.40*	*$19.20*	*$32.00*	£3.60	£10.80	£18.00

DREADWOLF, CURSE OF THE

Lightning Comics,OS; 1 Sep 1994

Issue	$Good	$Fine	$N.Mint	£Good	£Fine	£N.Mint
1 ND origin Dreadwolf; black and white						
	$0.50	*$1.50*	*$2.50*	£0.30	£0.90	£1.50
Title Value:	*$0.50*	*$1.50*	*$2.50*	£0.30	£0.90	£1.50

DREADWOLF, VENGEANCE OF

Lightning Comics,OS; 1 Feb 1995

Issue	$Good	$Fine	$N.Mint	£Good	£Fine	£N.Mint
1 ND black and white						
	$0.50	*$1.50*	*$2.50*	£0.30	£0.90	£1.50
Title Value:	*$0.50*	*$1.50*	*$2.50*	£0.30	£0.90	£1.50

DREAMER

Kitchen Sink; nn 1986

Issue	$Good	$Fine	$N.Mint	£Good	£Fine	£N.Mint
nn ND Hardback, Will Eisner script and art, semi-auto biographical						
	$3.60	*$10.50*	*$18.00*	£2.40	£7.00	£12.00
Title Value:	*$3.60*	*$10.50*	*$18.00*	£2.40	£7.00	£12.00
Softback Edition				£0.90	£2.70	£4.50

DREAMERY, THE

Eclipse; 1 Dec 1986-14 Feb 1989

Issue	$Good	$Fine	$N.Mint	£Good	£Fine	£N.Mint
1 ND Leila Dowling art begins						
	$0.40	*$1.20*	*$2.00*	£0.25	£0.75	£1.25
2-14 ND	*$0.40*	*$1.20*	*$2.00*	£0.25	£0.75	£1.25
Title Value:	*$5.60*	*$16.80*	*$28.00*	£3.50	£10.50	£17.50

Note: Alice in Wonderland #2-7. All Non-Distributed on the news-stands in the U.K.

DREAMING, THE

DC Comics/Vertigo; 1 Jun 1996-present

Issue	$Good	$Fine	$N.Mint	£Good	£Fine	£N.Mint
1-3 ND Cain and Abel and citizens of The Dreaming appear						
	$0.50	*$1.50*	*$2.50*	£0.30	£0.90	£1.50
4-7 ND Peter Hogan script, Steve Parkhouse art						
	$0.50	*$1.50*	*$2.50*	£0.30	£0.90	£1.50
8 ND Alisa Kwitney script, Michael Zulli art						
	$0.50	*$1.50*	*$2.50*	£0.30	£0.90	£1.50
9-10 ND Bryan Talbot script						
	$0.50	*$1.50*	*$2.50*	£0.30	£0.90	£1.50
Title Value:	*$5.00*	*$15.00*	*$25.00*	£3.00	£9.00	£15.00

DROIDS

Marvel Comics Group/Star, TV; 1 Apr 1986-8 Jun 1987

Issue	$Good	$Fine	$N.Mint	£Good	£Fine	£N.Mint
1 ND R2-D2 and C-3PO from Star Wars begin						
	$0.15	*$0.45*	*$0.75*	£0.30	£0.90	£1.50
2-8 ND	*$0.15*	*$0.45*	*$0.75*	£0.20	£0.60	£1.00
Title Value:	*$1.20*	*$3.60*	*$6.00*	£1.70	£5.10	£8.50

DRONE

Dagger Enterprises; 1 Aug 1994-2 1994

Issue	$Good	$Fine	$N.Mint	£Good	£Fine	£N.Mint
1-2 ND	*$0.40*	*$1.20*	*$2.00*	£0.25	£0.75	£1.25
Title Value:	*$0.80*	*$2.40*	*$4.00*	£0.50	£1.50	£2.50

DROOPY, TEX AVERY'S

Dark Horse,MS; 1 Oct 1995-3 Dec 1995

Issue	$Good	$Fine	$N.Mint	£Good	£Fine	£N.Mint
1-3 ND Bill Morrison painted covers						
	$0.50	*$1.50*	*$2.50*	£0.30	£0.90	£1.50
Title Value:	*$1.50*	*$4.50*	*$7.50*	£0.90	£2.70	£4.50

DRUID

Marvel Comics Group; 1 May 1995-4 Aug 1995

Issue	$Good	$Fine	$N.Mint	£Good	£Fine	£N.Mint
1 Warren Ellis script, Leonardo Manco art; card-stock cover						
	$0.40	*$1.20*	*$2.00*	£0.25	£0.75	£1.25
2-3	*$0.40*	*$1.20*	*$2.00*	£0.25	£0.75	£1.25
4 Daiman Hellstrom appears						
	$0.40	*$1.20*	*$2.00*	£0.25	£0.75	£1.25
Title Value:	*$1.60*	*$4.80*	*$8.00*	£1.00	£3.00	£5.00

DRUNKEN FIST

Jademan; 1 Aug 1988-56 Mar 1993

Issue	$Good	$Fine	$N.Mint	£Good	£Fine	£N.Mint
1 ND	*$0.50*	*$1.50*	*$2.50*	£0.50	£1.50	£2.50
2-5 ND	*$0.30*	*$0.90*	*$1.50*	£0.40	£1.20	£2.00
6-10 ND	*$0.30*	*$0.90*	*$1.50*	£0.30	£0.90	£1.50
11-20 ND	*$0.30*	*$0.90*	*$1.50*	£0.25	£0.75	£1.25
21-30 ND	*$0.30*	*$0.90*	*$1.50*	£0.20	£0.60	£1.00
31-56 ND	*$0.25*	*$0.75*	*$1.25*	£0.15	£0.45	£0.75
Title Value:	*$15.70*	*$47.10*	*$78.50*	£12.00	£36.00	£60.00

Note: all Non-Distributed on the news-stands in the U.K.

DUCK TALES

Gladstone, TV; 1 Oct 1988-13 May 1989

Issue	$Good	$Fine	$N.Mint	£Good	£Fine	£N.Mint
1-2 48pgs, features TV characters, Barks Uncle Scrooge back-up						
	$0.30	*$0.90*	*$1.50*	£0.20	£0.60	£1.00
3 36pgs	*$0.30*	*$0.90*	*$1.50*	£0.20	£0.60	£1.00
4 36pgs, no back-ups						
	$0.30	*$0.90*	*$1.50*	£0.20	£0.60	£1.00
5-13	*$0.30*	*$0.90*	*$1.50*	£0.20	£0.60	£1.00
Title Value:	*$3.90*	*$11.70*	*$19.50*	£2.60	£7.80	£13.00

Note: banned from distribution in the U.K.

Issue	$Good	$Fine	$N.Mint	£Good	£Fine	£N.Mint
Movie Adaptation Graphic Novel (Oct 1990)						
64pgs, Prestige Format				£0.90	£2.70	£4.50

DUCK TALES (2ND SERIES)

Disney; 1 Jun 1990-19 Nov 1991

Issue	$Good	$Fine	$N.Mint	£Good	£Fine	£N.Mint
1-19 ND	*$0.30*	*$0.90*	*$1.50*	£0.20	£0.60	£1.00
Title Value:	*$5.70*	*$17.10*	*$28.50*	£3.80	£11.40	£19.00

DUCKMAN

Topps; 0 Feb 1996; 1 Nov 1994-5 Mar 1995

Issue	$Good	$Fine	$N.Mint	£Good	£Fine	£N.Mint
0 ND reprints black and white Dark Horse one-shot comic; Everett Peck script and art						
	$0.60	*$1.80*	*$3.00*	£0.40	£1.20	£2.00
1 ND based on US animated show, with poster and 3-D cover enhancement						
	$0.40	*$1.20*	*$2.00*	£0.25	£0.75	£1.25
2-5 ND	*$0.40*	*$1.20*	*$2.00*	£0.25	£0.75	£1.25
Title Value:	*$2.60*	*$7.80*	*$13.00*	£1.65	£4.95	£8.25

DUCKMAN: THE MOB FROG SAGA

Topps,MS; 1 Nov 1994-3 Jan 1995

Issue	$Good	$Fine	$N.Mint	£Good	£Fine	£N.Mint
1-3 ND based on US animated show						
	$0.40	*$1.20*	*$2.00*	£0.25	£0.75	£1.25
Title Value:	*$1.20*	*$3.60*	*$6.00*	£0.75	£2.25	£3.75

DUMBO

Dell/Movie Comics,OS Movie; 10090-310 Oct 1963

Issue	$Good	$Fine	$N.Mint	£Good	£Fine	£N.Mint
10090-310 distributed in the U.K. reprints Four Color #668						
	$3.55	*$10.50*	*$25.00*	£1.75	£5.25	£12.50
Title Value:	*$3.55*	*$10.50*	*$25.00*	£1.75	£5.25	£12.50

DUNE

Marvel Comics Group,MS Film; 1 Apr 1985-3 Jun 1985

Issue	$Good	$Fine	$N.Mint	£Good	£Fine	£N.Mint
1-3 ND Sienkiewicz art; reprints Marvel Super Special #3						
	$0.40	*$1.20*	*$2.00*	£0.25	£0.75	£1.25
Title Value:	*$1.20*	*$3.60*	*$6.00*	£0.75	£2.25	£3.75

DUNGEONEERS

Silver Wolf; 1 Sep 1986-4 Dec 1986

Issue	$Good	$Fine	$N.Mint	£Good	£Fine	£N.Mint
1-4 ND b&w	*$0.30*	*$0.90*	*$1.50*	£0.20	£0.60	£1.00
Title Value:	*$1.20*	*$3.60*	*$6.00*	£0.80	£2.40	£4.00

DV8

Image; 1 Aug 1996-present

Issue	$Good	$Fine	$N.Mint	£Good	£Fine	£N.Mint
1 ND Warren Ellis script, Humberto Ramos and Sal Regla art; Humberto Ramos cover						
	$0.50	*$1.50*	*$2.50*	£0.30	£0.90	£1.50
1 "Envy" Cover, ND cover art by Michael Lopez and Edwin Rosell						
	$1.00	*$3.00*	*$5.00*	£0.50	£1.50	£2.50
1 "Gluttony" Cover, ND cover art by Glenn Fabry						
	$1.00	*$3.00*	*$5.00*	£0.50	£1.50	£2.50
1 "Greed" Cover ND						
	$1.00	*$3.00*	*$5.00*	£0.50	£1.50	£2.50
1 "Lust" Cover, ND cover art by Kevin Nowlan						
	$1.00	*$3.00*	*$5.00*	£0.50	£1.50	£2.50
1 "Pride" Cover ND						
	$1.00	*$3.00*	*$5.00*	£0.50	£1.50	£2.50
1 "Sloth" Cover, ND cover art by Jim Lee						
	$1.50	*$4.50*	*$7.50*	£0.70	£2.10	£3.50
1 "Wrath" Cover ND						
	$1.00	*$3.00*	*$5.00*	£0.50	£1.50	£2.50
2-4 ND	*$0.50*	*$1.50*	*$2.50*	£0.30	£0.90	£1.50
Title Value:	*$9.50*	*$28.50*	*$47.50*	£4.90	£14.70	£24.50

DV8 RAVE

Image,OS; 1 Jul 1996

Issue	$Good	$Fine	$N.Mint	£Good	£Fine	£N.Mint
1 ND contains pin-ups and interviews						
	$0.40	*$1.20*	*$2.00*	£0.25	£0.75	£1.25
Title Value:	*$0.40*	*$1.20*	*$2.00*	£0.25	£0.75	£1.25

DYNAMIC CLASSICS

DC Comics; 1 Sep/Oct 1978

Issue	$Good	$Fine	$N.Mint	£Good	£Fine	£N.Mint
1 ND scarce in the U.K. 44pgs, Neal Adams Batman and Walt Simonson Manhunter reprints, origin of Manhunter retold						
	$0.80	*$2.50*	*$5.00*	£0.65	£2.00	£4.00
Title Value:	*$0.80*	*$2.50*	*$5.00*	£0.65	£2.00	£4.00

Note: intended as on-going series (see Battle Classics)

DYNAMO

Tower Comics; 1 Aug 1966-4 Jun 1967

Issue	$Good	$Fine	$N.Mint	£Good	£Fine	£N.Mint
1 rare in the U.K. giant, Wally Wood and Steve Ditko art						
	$5.25	*$16.00*	*$37.50*	£3.55	£10.50	£25.00
2-4 giants, Wood art						
	$3.90	*$11.50*	*$27.50*	£2.10	£6.25	£15.00
Title Value:	*$16.95*	*$50.50*	*$120.00*	£9.85	£29.25	£70.00

Note: all were distributed on the news-stands in the U.K.

DYNAMO JOE

First; 1 May 1986-15 Jan 1988

(see Mars #10-12, First Adventures #1-5, Grimjack #30)

Issue	$Good	$Fine	$N.Mint	£Good	£Fine	£N.Mint
1-15 ND	*$0.30*	*$0.90*	*$1.50*	£0.20	£0.60	£1.00
Title Value:	*$4.50*	*$13.50*	*$22.50*	£3.00	£9.00	£15.00

Note: issues 1-3 marked as 3 issue mini-series

DYNAMO JOE SPECIAL

First,OS; 1 Jan 1987

Issue	$Good	$Fine	$N.Mint	£Good	£Fine	£N.Mint
1 ND reprints Mars #10-12 plus new pages						
	$0.40	*$1.20*	*$2.00*	£0.25	£0.75	£1.25
Title Value:	*$0.40*	*$1.20*	*$2.00*	£0.25	£0.75	£1.25

DYNOMUTT

Marvel Comics Group, TV; 1 Nov 1977-6 Sep 1978

Issue	$Good	$Fine	$N.Mint	£Good	£Fine	£N.Mint
1-6 ND	*$0.10*	*$0.35*	*$0.75*	£0.05	£0.25	£0.50
Title Value:	*$0.60*	*$2.10*	*$4.50*	£0.30	£1.50	£3.00

E

E-MAN

Charlton; 1 Oct 1973-10 Sep 1975

Issue	$Good	$Fine	$N.Mint	£Good	£Fine	£N.Mint
1 Joe Staton art	$2.00	$6.00	$12.00	£1.00	£3.00	£6.00
2-3 Joe Staton, Steve Ditko art	$1.30	$4.00	$8.00	£0.65	£2.00	£4.00
4-5 Joe Staton, Steve Ditko art	$1.15	$3.50	$7.00	£0.55	£1.75	£3.50
6-7 Joe Staton, John Byrne art	$1.00	$3.00	$6.00	£0.55	£1.75	£3.50
8 Joe Staton	$1.00	$3.00	$6.00	£0.55	£1.75	£3.50
9-10 Joe Staton, John Byrne art	$1.00	$3.00	$6.00	£0.55	£1.75	£3.50
Title Value:	$11.90	$36.00	$72.00	£6.15	£19.25	£38.50

Note: all distributed on the news-stands in the U.K.

E-MAN (2ND SERIES)

First; 1 Apr 1983-25 Aug 1985

Issue	$Good	$Fine	$N.Mint	£Good	£Fine	£N.Mint
1 Joe Staton art begins, 1pg John Byrne art	$0.30	$0.90	$1.50	£0.20	£0.60	£1.00
2 Joe Staton art, X-Men parody	$0.30	$0.90	$1.50	£0.20	£0.60	£1.00
3 Joe Staton art, X-Men parody (cover of X-Men #101)	$0.30	$0.90	$1.50	£0.20	£0.60	£1.00
4-10 Joe Staton art	$0.30	$0.90	$1.50	£0.20	£0.60	£1.00
11-25 Joe Staton art	$0.25	$0.75	$1.25	£0.15	£0.45	£0.75
Title Value:	$6.75	$20.25	$33.75	£4.25	£12.75	£21.25

Note: all Non-Distributed on the news-standsin the U.K.

E-MAN (3RD SERIES)

Comico,OS; 1 Sep 1989

Issue	$Good	$Fine	$N.Mint	£Good	£Fine	£N.Mint
1 ND colour, no ads, high quality paper	$0.60	$1.80	$3.00	£0.40	£1.20	£2.00
Title Value:	$0.60	$1.80	$3.00	£0.40	£1.20	£2.00

E-MAN (4TH SERIES)

Comico,MS; 1 Jan 1990-3 Mar 1990

Issue	$Good	$Fine	$N.Mint	£Good	£Fine	£N.Mint
1-3 ND Staton cover/art, colour	$0.50	$1.50	$2.50	£0.30	£0.90	£1.50
Title Value:	$1.50	$4.50	$7.50	£0.90	£2.70	£4.50
E-Man Limited Edition (May 1993) ND issues #1-3 pre-bagged with orange paper wrapper				£0.70	£2.10	£3.50

E-MAN (5TH SERIES)

Alpha Productions; 1 Oct 1993-3 Jan 1994

Issue	$Good	$Fine	$N.Mint	£Good	£Fine	£N.Mint
1 ND Nicola Cuti script and Joe Staton art begins	$0.50	$1.50	$2.50	£0.30	£0.90	£1.50
1 Ashcan, ND - 16pgs, limited to 3,000 copies	$0.80	$2.40	$4.00	£0.50	£1.50	£2.50
2 ND	$0.50	$1.50	$2.50	£0.30	£0.90	£1.50
2 pre-bagged with poster ND	$0.60	$1.80	$3.00	£0.40	£1.20	£2.00
3 ND	$0.50	$1.50	$2.50	£0.30	£0.90	£1.50
3 pre-bagged with poster ND	$0.60	$1.80	$3.00	£0.40	£1.20	£2.00
Title Value:	$3.50	$10.50	$17.50	£2.20	£6.60	£11.00

E-MAN RETURNS

Alpha Productions,OS; 1 Mar 1994

Issue	$Good	$Fine	$N.Mint	£Good	£Fine	£N.Mint
1 ND Nicola Cuti script, Joe Staton art; black and white	$0.50	$1.50	$2.50	£0.30	£0.90	£1.50
Title Value:	$0.50	$1.50	$2.50	£0.30	£0.90	£1.50

E-MAN, THE ORIGINAL

First,MS; 1 Oct 1985-7 Apr 1986

Issue	$Good	$Fine	$N.Mint	£Good	£Fine	£N.Mint
1 ND reprints Charlton series, Michael Mauser back-ups begin	$0.30	$0.90	$1.50	£0.20	£0.60	£1.00
2-7 ND	$0.30	$0.90	$1.50	£0.20	£0.60	£1.00
Title Value:	$2.10	$6.30	$10.50	£1.40	£4.20	£7.00

E-MAN: FUTURE TENSE

Alpha Productions,OS; 1 Mar 1995

Issue	$Good	$Fine	$N.Mint	£Good	£Fine	£N.Mint
1 ND Nicola Cuti script, Joe Staton art; E-Man visits the time of The Morlocks who feature in H.G. Wells "The Time Machine"	$0.50	$1.50	$2.50	£0.30	£0.90	£1.50
Title Value:	$0.50	$1.50	$2.50	£0.30	£0.90	£1.50

E.C. CLASSIC REPRINTS

East Coast; 1 1973-12 1976

Issue	$Good	$Fine	$N.Mint	£Good	£Fine	£N.Mint
1 scarce in the U.K. Crypt of Terror #1	$1.00	$3.00	$6.00	£0.80	£2.50	£5.00
2 Weird Science #15	$0.80	$2.50	$5.00	£0.50	£1.50	£3.00
3 Shock-SuspensStories #12	$0.80	$2.50	$5.00	£0.50	£1.50	£3.00
4 Haunt of Fear #12	$0.80	$2.50	$5.00	£0.50	£1.50	£3.00
5 Weird Fantasy #13	$0.80	$2.50	$5.00	£0.50	£1.50	£3.00
6 Crime-SuspensStories #25	$0.80	$2.50	$5.00	£0.50	£1.50	£3.00
7 scarce in the U.K. Vault of Horror #26	$0.80	$2.50	$5.00	£0.55	£1.75	£3.50
8 Shock-SuspensStories #6	$0.80	$2.50	$5.00	£0.50	£1.50	£3.00
9 Two-Fisted Tales #34	$0.80	$2.50	$5.00	£0.50	£1.50	£3.00
10 Haunt of Fear #23	$0.80	$2.50	$5.00	£0.50	£1.50	£3.00
11 scarce in the U.K. Weird Science #12	$0.80	$2.50	$5.00	£0.55	£1.75	£3.50
12 Shock-SuspensStories #2	$0.80	$2.50	$5.00	£0.50	£1.50	£3.00
Title Value:	$9.80	$30.50	$61.00	£6.40	£19.50	£39.00

Note: all Non-Distributed on the news-stands in the U.K.

E.C. CLASSICS

Russ Cochran; 1 Aug 1985-12 1988

Issue	$Good	$Fine	$N.Mint	£Good	£Fine	£N.Mint
1 ND 56pgs, large format 8" x 11" reprints of classic EC Comics begins; Tales from the Crypt reprints, Jack Davis cover	$1.00	$3.00	$5.00	£0.70	£2.10	£3.50
2 ND Weird Science	$1.00	$3.00	$5.00	£0.70	£2.10	£3.50
3 ND Two Fisted Tales, Kurtzman cover	$1.00	$3.00	$5.00	£0.70	£2.10	£3.50
4 ND Shock Suspenstories, Wally Wood cover	$1.00	$3.00	$5.00	£0.70	£2.10	£3.50
5 ND Weird Fantasy, Feldstein cover	$1.00	$3.00	$5.00	£0.70	£2.10	£3.50
6 ND The Vault of Horror	$1.00	$3.00	$5.00	£0.70	£2.10	£3.50
7 ND Weird Science-Fantasy, Wally Wood cover	$1.00	$3.00	$5.00	£0.70	£2.10	£3.50
8 ND Crime Suspenstories	$1.00	$3.00	$5.00	£0.70	£2.10	£3.50
9 ND The Haunt of Fear	$1.00	$3.00	$5.00	£0.70	£2.10	£3.50
10 ND Panic	$1.00	$3.00	$5.00	£0.70	£2.10	£3.50
11 ND Tales From The Crypt	$1.00	$3.00	$5.00	£0.70	£2.10	£3.50
12 ND Weird Science, Wally Wood cover	$1.00	$3.00	$5.00	£0.70	£2.10	£3.50
Title Value:	$12.00	$36.00	$60.00	£8.40	£25.20	£42.00

EAGLE

Crystal/Apple (#17 on); 1 Sep 1986-26 1991

Issue	$Good	$Fine	$N.Mint	£Good	£Fine	£N.Mint
1-11 ND	$0.30	$0.90	$1.50	£0.20	£0.60	£1.00
12 ND DS, origin issue	$0.30	$0.90	$1.50	£0.20	£0.60	£1.00
13-26 ND	$0.30	$0.90	$1.50	£0.20	£0.60	£1.00
Title Value:	$7.80	$23.40	$39.00	£5.20	£15.60	£26.00

EAGLE: THE DARK MIRROR SAGA

Comic Zone; 1 Apr 1992-4 1992

Issue	$Good	$Fine	$N.Mint	£Good	£Fine	£N.Mint
1-4 ND black and white	$0.30	$0.90	$1.50	£0.20	£0.60	£1.00
Title Value:	$1.20	$3.60	$6.00	£0.80	£2.40	£4.00

EARTH 4

Continuity; 1 Apr 1993-4 1994

Issue	$Good	$Fine	$N.Mint	£Good	£Fine	£N.Mint
1 ND Deathwatch 2000 part 6, embossed cover, pre-bagged with trading card	$0.30	$0.90	$1.50	£0.20	£0.60	£1.00
2 ND Deathwatch 2000, pre-bagged with trading card	$0.30	$0.90	$1.50	£0.20	£0.60	£1.00
3 ND	$0.30	$0.90	$1.50	£0.20	£0.60	£1.00
4 ND Crossbreeds story	$0.30	$0.90	$1.50	£0.20	£0.60	£1.00
Title Value:	$1.20	$3.60	$6.00	£0.80	£2.40	£4.00

EARTHWORM JIM

Marvel Comics Group,MS; 1 Dec 1995-3 Feb 1996

Issue	$Good	$Fine	$N.Mint	£Good	£Fine	£N.Mint
1-3 ND based on video game and cartoon	$0.50	$1.50	$2.50	£0.30	£0.90	£1.50
Title Value:	$1.50	$4.50	$7.50	£0.90	£2.70	£4.50

EASTER STORY, THE

Marvel Comics Group,OS; 1 Jan 1994

Issue	$Good	$Fine	$N.Mint	£Good	£Fine	£N.Mint
1 ND Louise Simonson script about The Resurrection of Christ	$0.40	$1.20	$2.00	£0.25	£0.75	£1.25
Title Value:	$0.40	$1.20	$2.00	£0.25	£0.75	£1.25

EB'NN THE RAVEN

Crowquill/Now; 1 Oct 1985-10 1987

Issue	$Good	$Fine	$N.Mint	£Good	£Fine	£N.Mint
1-9 ND	$0.30	$0.90	$1.50	£0.20	£0.60	£1.00
10 ND colour	$0.30	$0.90	$1.50	£0.20	£0.60	£1.00
Title Value:	$3.00	$9.00	$15.00	£2.00	£6.00	£10.00

ECHO OF FUTURE PAST

Continuity; 1 May 1984-9 Jan 1986

Issue	$Good	$Fine	$N.Mint	£Good	£Fine	£N.Mint
1 48pgs, anthology begins; features Bucky O'Hare by Golden, Frankenstein by Adams, Mudwogs by Suydam	$0.50	$1.50	$2.50	£0.30	£0.90	£1.50
2 48pgs, Arthur Suydam, Neal Adams and Michael Golden art; Arthur Suydam cover	$0.50	$1.50	$2.50	£0.30	£0.90	£1.50
3 48pgs, Arthur Suydam, Neal Adams and Michael Golden art; Michael Golden cover	$0.50	$1.50	$2.50	£0.30	£0.90	£1.50
4 48pgs, Arthur Suydam, Neal Adams and Michael Golden art; Arthur Suydam cover	$0.50	$1.50	$2.50	£0.30	£0.90	£1.50
5 Arthur Suydam, Neal Adams and Michael Golden art featured; part Neal Adams cover	$0.50	$1.50	$2.50	£0.30	£0.90	£1.50
6 48pgs, Michael Golden, Neal Adams and Alex Toth art featured; Michael Golden cover	$0.50	$1.50	$2.50	£0.30	£0.90	£1.50
7 48pgs, part Neal Adams art, Alex Toth art; cover by Neal and Cory Adams	$0.50	$1.50	$2.50	£0.30	£0.90	£1.50
8 48pgs, part Neal Adams art featured	$0.50	$1.50	$2.50	£0.30	£0.90	£1.50
9 48pgs, Neal Adams part art and part cover art						

	$Good	$Fine	$N.Mint	£Good	£Fine	£N.Mint
	$0.50	$1.50	$2.50	£0.30	£0.90	£1.50
Title Value:	$4.50	$13.50	$22.50	£2.70	£8.10	£13.50

Note: all Non-Distributed on the news-stands in the U.K.

ECLIPSE GRAPHIC ALBUM SERIES

Eclipse; 1 Oct 1978-31 1990

	$Good	$Fine	$N.Mint	£Good	£Fine	£N.Mint
1 Sabre (Oct 1978) by Don McGregor, Paul Gulacy art						
	$1.50	$4.50	$7.50	£1.00	£3.00	£5.00
1 2nd printing, (Jan 1979)						
	$1.20	$3.60	$6.00	£0.80	£2.40	£4.00
1 3rd printing	$1.00	$3.00	$5.00	£0.70	£2.10	£3.50
2 Night Music (Nov 1979) by P. Craig Russell						
	$0.90	$2.70	$4.50	£0.60	£1.80	£3.00
3 Detectives Inc: A Remembrance of Threatening Green (May 1980) by Marshall Rogers						
	$1.40	$4.20	$7.00	£0.90	£2.70	£4.50
4 Stewart the Rat (1980), Gene Colan art						
	$1.20	$3.60	$6.00	£0.80	£2.40	£4.00
5 The Price (Oct 1981) by Jim Starlin, features Dreadstar						
	$2.40	$7.00	$12.00	£1.50	£4.50	£7.50
6 I Am Coyote (Nov 1984), Marshall Rogers art						
	$1.20	$3.60	$6.00	£1.00	£3.00	£5.00
7 The Rocketeer (Sep 1985), Dave Stevens art						
	$1.80	$5.25	$9.00	£1.20	£3.60	£6.00
7 2nd printing	$1.40	$4.20	$7.00	£0.90	£2.70	£4.50
7 3rd printing, ND (1991)						
	$1.80	$5.25	$9.00	£1.20	£3.60	£6.00
7 Signed Limited Hardcover Edition scarce in the U.K.						
	$9.00	$27.00	$45.00	£6.00	£18.00	£30.00
8 Zorro in Old California (1986)						
	$1.20	$3.60	$6.00	£0.80	£2.40	£4.00
9 Sacred and the Profane (1986), Ken Steacy art						
	$2.80	$8.25	$14.00	£1.80	£5.25	£9.00
9 Hardcover Edition	$4.50	$13.50	$22.50	£3.00	£9.00	£15.00
10 Somerset Holmes						
	$2.80	$8.25	$14.00	£1.80	£5.25	£9.00
10 Hardcover Edition						
	$4.50	$13.50	$22.50	£3.00	£9.00	£15.00
11 Floyd Farland, Citizen of the Future (1987), Chris Ware story & art						
	$0.80	$2.40	$4.00	£0.40	£1.20	£2.00
12 Silverheels (1987)						
	$1.50	$4.50	$7.50	£1.00	£3.00	£5.00
12 Hardcover Edition	$3.00	$9.00	$15.00	£2.00	£6.00	£10.00
12 Signed Limited Hardcover Edition						
	$4.50	$13.50	$22.50	£3.00	£9.00	£15.00
13 The Sisterhood of Steel (1987)						
	$1.80	$5.25	$9.00	£1.20	£3.60	£6.00
14 Samurai, Son of Death (1987)						
	$0.90	$2.70	$4.50	£0.60	£1.80	£3.00
14 2nd printing	$0.80	$2.40	$4.00	£0.50	£1.50	£2.50
15 Twisted Tales (Nov 1987), Dave Stevens cover						
	$0.80	$2.40	$4.00	£0.50	£1.50	£2.50
16 Airfighter Classics #1						
	$0.90	$2.70	$4.50	£0.60	£1.80	£3.00
17 Valkyrie, Prisoner of the Past (1988), reprints #1-3						
	$1.50	$4.50	$7.50	£1.00	£3.00	£5.00
18 Airfighter Classics #2						
	$0.90	$2.70	$4.50	£0.60	£1.80	£3.00
19 Scout: The Four Monsters (1988), reprints Scout #1-7						
	$3.00	$9.00	$15.00	£2.00	£6.00	£10.00
20 Airfighter Classics #3						
	$0.90	$2.70	$4.50	£0.60	£1.80	£3.00
21 XYR - role playing adventure with a number of possible endings, 48pgs squarebound, black and white						
	$0.80	$2.40	$4.00	£0.50	£1.50	£2.50
22 Alien Worlds #1 (May 1988), Bruce Jones script; Yeates, Reese, Shanover, Wray art						
	$1.00	$3.00	$5.00	£0.60	£1.80	£3.00
23 Airfighter Classics #4						
	$0.90	$2.70	$4.50	£0.60	£1.80	£3.00
24 Heartbreak	$0.90	$2.70	$4.50	£0.60	£1.80	£3.00
25 Zorro Volume #1 by Alex Toth						
	$1.80	$5.25	$9.00	£1.20	£3.60	£6.00
26 Zorro Volume #2 by Alex Toth						
	$1.80	$5.25	$9.00	£1.20	£3.60	£6.00
27 Fast Fiction	$1.05	$3.15	$5.25	£0.70	£2.10	£3.50
28 Miracleman Book 1: A Dream of Flying						
	$1.80	$5.25	$9.00	£1.20	£3.60	£6.00
29 Real Love: The Best of Simon and Kirby Romance Comics (Oct 1988)						
	$2.40	$7.00	$12.00	£1.50	£4.50	£7.50
30 Brought To Light (1988); Alan Moore script, Bill Sienkiewicz art						
	$1.80	$5.25	$9.00	£1.20	£3.60	£6.00
30 Hardcover Edition	$5.00	$15.00	$25.00	£3.50	£10.50	£17.50
31 Pigeons From Hell (Nov 1988) by Robert E. Howard						
	$1.40	$4.20	$7.00	£0.90	£2.70	£4.50
31 Signed Limited Hardcover Edition						
	$5.00	$15.00	$25.00	£3.50	£10.50	£17.50
Title Value:	$87.55	$260.90	$437.75	£58.20	£174.30	£291.00

Note: all Non-Distributed on the news-standsin the U.K.

ECLIPSE MONTHLY

Eclipse; 1 Aug 1983-10 Jul 1984

	$Good	$Fine	$N.Mint	£Good	£Fine	£N.Mint
1-10 ND	$0.30	$0.90	$1.50	£0.20	£0.60	£1.00
Title Value:	$3.00	$9.00	$15.00	£2.00	£6.00	£10.00

ECLIPSO

DC Comics; 1 Nov 1992-18 Apr 1994

(see House of Secrets #61)

	$Good	$Fine	$N.Mint	£Good	£Fine	£N.Mint
1 Eclipso: The Darkness Within spin-off						
	$0.30	$0.90	$1.50	£0.15	£0.45	£0.75
2	$0.25	$0.75	$1.25	£0.15	£0.45	£0.75
3-6 Cave Carson and Creeper appear						
	$0.25	$0.75	$1.25	£0.15	£0.45	£0.75
7 Ted McKeever art						
	$0.25	$0.75	$1.25	£0.15	£0.45	£0.75
8 Ted McKeever art, Sherlock Holmes appears						
	$0.25	$0.75	$1.25	£0.15	£0.45	£0.75
9 Johnny Peril appears						
	$0.25	$0.75	$1.25	£0.15	£0.45	£0.75
10 Darkseid appears						
	$0.25	$0.75	$1.25	£0.15	£0.45	£0.75
11-12 Creeper, Peacemaker, Mark Shaw: Manhunter, the new Wildcat, Dr. Midnight, Commander Steel and Major Victory appear						
	$0.25	$0.75	$1.25	£0.15	£0.45	£0.75
13 deaths of Creeper, Peacemaker, Mark Shaw: Manhunter, the new Wildcat, Dr. Midnight, Commander Steel and Major Victory						
	$0.25	$0.75	$1.25	£0.15	£0.45	£0.75
14-15	$0.25	$0.75	$1.25	£0.15	£0.45	£0.75
16 Green Lantern, Guy Gardner, Hourman, Jade, Obsidian, Green Arrow and Mister Miracle appear						
	$0.25	$0.75	$1.25	£0.15	£0.45	£0.75
17 Martian Manhunter, Wonder Woman, Flash, Bloodwynd, Booster Gold appear						
	$0.25	$0.75	$1.25	£0.15	£0.45	£0.75
18 Spectre vs. Eclipso, Justice League appear						
	$0.25	$0.75	$1.25	£0.15	£0.45	£0.75
Title Value:	$4.55	$13.65	$22.75	£2.70	£8.10	£13.50

ECLIPSO - THE DARKNESS WITHIN CROSSOVERS

Cross-over event for DC summer '92 annuals. A minor villain from the House of Secrets title, he is transformed into an evil god of vengeance and plans to rule the Earth through his puppet soldiers - the heroes that defend the Earth. The story begins in Eclipso: The Darkness Within #1 and ends in number two with the annuals in between. The order is as follows:

Eclipso: The Darkness Within **#1**, Superman: The Man of Steel Annual **#1**, Green Lantern Annual **#1**, Detective Comics Annual **#5**, Superman Annual **#4**, Justice League America Annual **#6**, The Demon Annual **#1**, Green Arrow Annual **#5**, Flash Annual **#5**, Action Comics Annual **#4**, Hawkworld Annual **#3** Robin Annual **#1**, Deathstroke, The Terminator Annual **#1**, New Titans Annual **#8**, Legion '92 Annual **#3**, Justice League Europe Annual **#3**, Wonder Woman Annual **#3**, Batman Annual **#16**, Adventures of Superman Annual **#4**, Eclipso: The Darkness Within **#2**

ECLIPSO ANNUAL

DC Comics; 1 Oct 1993

	$Good	$Fine	$N.Mint	£Good	£Fine	£N.Mint
1 64pgs, Bloodlines (Wave Two) part 19, 1st appearance Prism, continued in Demon Annual #2						
	$0.30	$0.90	$1.50	£0.20	£0.60	£1.00
Title Value:	$0.30	$0.90	$1.50	£0.20	£0.60	£1.00

ECLIPSO: THE DARKNESS WITHIN

DC Comics; 1 Jul 1992-2 Oct 1992

	$Good	$Fine	$N.Mint	£Good	£Fine	£N.Mint
1 ND 64pgs, The Darkness Within begins; Superman, Valor and Creeper appear, lead into summer '92 DC annual x-overs, 3-D plastic purple diamond on cover. Direct Sales edition to comic shops						
	$0.50	$1.50	$2.50	£0.30	£0.90	£1.50
1 Newstand Edition, , without 3-D plastic diamond						
	$0.40	$1.20	$2.00	£0.25	£0.75	£1.25
2 ND 64pgs, The Darkness Within concludes, Hawkman, Aquaman, Blue Devil, Black Canary, Challengers and Suicide Squad appear						
	$0.40	$1.20	$2.00	£0.25	£0.75	£1.25
Title Value:	$1.30	$3.90	$6.50	£0.80	£2.40	£4.00

ECTOKID

Marvel Comics Group/Razorline; 1 Sep 1993-9 May 1994

	$Good	$Fine	$N.Mint	£Good	£Fine	£N.Mint
1 ND prismatic foil cover						
	$0.30	$0.90	$1.50	£0.20	£0.60	£1.00
2-9 ND	$0.30	$0.90	$1.50	£0.20	£0.60	£1.00
Title Value:	$2.70	$8.10	$13.50	£1.80	£5.40	£9.00

ECTOKID UNLEASHED

Marvel Comics Group/Razorline,OS; 1 Oct 1994

	$Good	$Fine	$N.Mint	£Good	£Fine	£N.Mint
1 ND 48pgs	$0.40	$1.20	$2.00	£0.25	£0.75	£1.25
Title Value:	$0.40	$1.20	$2.00	£0.25	£0.75	£1.25

EDDIE CAMPBELL'S ALEC IN: THE DANCE OF LIFEY DEATH

Dark Horse,OS; 1 Jan 1994

	$Good	$Fine	$N.Mint	£Good	£Fine	£N.Mint
1 ND 48pgs, black and white						
	$0.80	$2.40	$4.00	£0.50	£1.50	£2.50
Title Value:	$0.80	$2.40	$4.00	£0.50	£1.50	£2.50

EDDIE CAMPBELL'S BACCHUS

Eddie Campbell Comics; 1 May 1995-present

	$Good	$Fine	$N.Mint	£Good	£Fine	£N.Mint
1 ND reprints early adventures from Deadface with new art revisions plus new naterial						
	$0.60	$1.80	$3.00	£0.40	£1.20	£2.00
2-19 ND	$0.60	$1.80	$3.00	£0.40	£1.20	£2.00
Title Value:	$11.40	$34.20	$57.00	£7.60	£22.80	£38.00
Eddie Campbell's Collected Bacchus Vol. 1 (Dec 1995)						
Trade paperback ND 96pgs, the first 24 chapters collected				£1.30	£3.90	£6.50
Eddie Campbell's Collected Bacchus Vol. 2 (Jun 1996)						
Trade paperback ND 96pgs,				£1.30	£3.90	£6.50

EDDY CURRENT

Mad Dog Graphics; 1 Jul 1987-12 Dec 1988

(see Splat! #3)

	$Good	$Fine	$N.Mint	£Good	£Fine	£N.Mint
1 ND scarce in the U.K.						
	$1.50	$4.50	$7.50	£1.20	£3.60	£6.00
2 ND	$1.20	$3.60	$6.00	£0.80	£2.40	£4.00
3 ND scarce in the U.K.						
	$1.20	$3.60	$6.00	£1.00	£3.00	£5.00
4-5 ND	$1.00	$3.00	$5.00	£0.70	£2.10	£3.50
6-10 ND	$0.80	$2.40	$4.00	£0.50	£1.50	£2.50
11-12 ND	$0.60	$1.80	$3.00	£0.40	£1.20	£2.00
Title Value:	$11.10	$33.30	$55.50	£7.70	£23.10	£38.50

Hardcover Collection (Sep 1991),

VERY GENERAL PERCENTAGE CONVERSION CHART WHICH MAY BE USED TO CALCULATE LOW AND INBETWEEN GRADES:

	$Good	$Fine	$N.Mint	£Good	£Fine	£N.Mint
360pgs with new cover				£3.70	£11.10	£18.50

EDGE

Malibu Bravura,MS; 1 Jul 1994-4 Nov 1994

	$Good	$Fine	$N.Mint	£Good	£Fine	£N.Mint
1-4 ND Gil Kane art	$0.50	$1.50	$2.50	£0.30	£0.90	£1.50
Title Value:	$2.00	$6.00	$10.00	£1.20	£3.60	£6.00

Note: all Non-Distributed on the news-stands in the U.K.

EDGE OF CHAOS

Pacific; 1 Jul 1983-3 Dec 1983

	$Good	$Fine	$N.Mint	£Good	£Fine	£N.Mint
1 ND origin issue, Gray Morrow art; colour begins	$0.20	$0.60	$1.00	£0.15	£0.45	£0.75
2-3 ND Gray Morrrow art	$0.20	$0.60	$1.00	£0.15	£0.45	£0.75
Title Value:	$0.60	$1.80	$3.00	£0.45	£1.35	£2.25

EERIE

Avon Periodicals; 1 Jan 1947; 1 May 1951-17 Aug 1954

	$Good	$Fine	$N.Mint	£Good	£Fine	£N.Mint
1 scarce in the U.K. widely acknowledged to be the first horror anthology comic	$215.00	$650.00	$1750.00	£145.00	£440.00	£1175.00
1 reprint, scarce in the U.K. : reprints original issue #1, classic "ghoul" cover	$55.00	$170.00	$400.00	£39.00	£115.00	£270.00
2 classic Wally Wood bondage cover, Wood art	$65.00	$195.00	$460.00	£44.00	£130.00	£310.00
3 Wally Wood cover and art plus Joe Kubert art	$62.50	$190.00	$450.00	£43.00	£125.00	£300.00
4 Wally Wood cover	$50.00	$155.00	$365.00	£35.00	£105.00	£245.00
5 Wally Wood cover	$50.00	$150.00	$350.00	£34.00	£100.00	£235.00
6	$25.00	$75.00	$175.00	£17.00	£50.00	£120.00
7 Wally Wood vampire cover, Kubert art	$39.00	$115.00	$275.00	£26.00	£77.50	£185.00
8	$25.00	$75.00	$175.00	£17.00	£50.00	£120.00
9 Kubert art	$32.00	$95.00	$225.00	£21.00	£62.50	£150.00
10-11	$25.00	$75.00	$175.00	£17.00	£50.00	£120.00
12 Dracula cover; Dracula story adaptation	$36.00	$105.00	$250.00	£25.00	£75.00	£175.00
13-14	$25.00	$75.00	$175.00	£17.00	£50.00	£120.00
15 reprints part issue #1 with different cover	$19.00	$57.50	$135.00	£12.50	£39.00	£90.00
16 Wally Wood reprint; Mummy cover	$21.00	$62.50	$150.00	£14.00	£43.00	£100.00
17 Wally Wood reprint	$26.00	$77.50	$185.00	£17.50	£52.50	£125.00
Title Value:	$820.50	$2472.50	$6045.00	£558.00	£1664.50	£4080.00

Note; all Non-Distributed on the news-stands in the U.K.

EERIE (MAGAZINE)

Warren,Magazine; 1 Sep 1965;2 Mar 1966-139 Feb 1983

	$Good	$Fine	$N.Mint	£Good	£Fine	£N.Mint
1 very rare, distributed in the U.K. (small size)	$39.00	$115.00	$275.00	£25.00	£75.00	£175.00
1 2nd printing, scarce in the U.K. distinguishable by its un-timmed and therefore un-even edges	$16.50	$50.00	$100.00	£10.50	£33.00	£65.00
2 distributed in the U.K.	$8.25	$25.00	$50.00	£5.00	£15.00	£30.00
3 distributed in the U.K.	$5.75	$17.50	$35.00	£3.30	£10.00	£20.00
4-5 distributed in the U.K.	$4.15	$12.50	$25.00	£2.05	£6.25	£12.50
6-8 distributed in the U.K.	$4.15	$12.50	$25.00	£1.65	£5.00	£10.00
9 scarce, distributed in the U.K. Neal Adams art	$4.15	$12.50	$25.00	£2.05	£6.25	£12.50
10 distributed in the U.K.	$4.15	$12.50	$25.00	£1.65	£5.00	£10.00
11 distributed in the U.K.	$2.50	$7.50	$15.00	£1.15	£3.50	£7.00
12-14 distributed in the U.K.	$2.50	$7.50	$15.00	£1.00	£3.00	£6.00
15 scarce, distributed in the U.K.	$2.50	$7.50	$15.00	£1.15	£3.50	£7.00
16 distributed in the U.K.	$2.50	$7.50	$15.00	£1.00	£3.00	£6.00
17-18 scarce, distributed in the U.K.	$2.50	$7.50	$15.00	£1.15	£3.50	£7.00
19-20 distributed in the U.K.	$2.50	$7.50	$15.00	£1.00	£3.00	£6.00
21-29 distributed in the U.K.	$2.50	$7.50	$15.00	£0.80	£2.50	£5.00
30-33	$2.00	$6.00	$10.00	£0.80	£2.40	£4.00
34 distributed in the U.K.	$2.00	$6.00	$10.00	£0.70	£2.10	£3.50
35-37	$2.00	$6.00	$10.00	£0.80	£2.40	£4.00
38 distributed in the U.K.	$2.00	$6.00	$10.00	£0.70	£2.10	£3.50
39-40	$2.00	$6.00	$10.00	£0.80	£2.40	£4.00
41-53	$1.60	$4.80	$8.00	£0.70	£2.10	£3.50
54-55 Eisner Spirit	$2.00	$6.00	$10.00	£0.80	£2.40	£4.00
56-57	$1.60	$4.80	$8.00	£0.70	£2.10	£3.50
58 Wrightson art	$2.00	$6.00	$10.00	£0.80	£2.40	£4.00
59	$1.60	$4.80	$8.00	£0.70	£2.10	£3.50
60 Wrightson art	$2.00	$6.00	$10.00	£0.80	£2.40	£4.00
61	$1.60	$4.80	$8.00	£0.70	£2.10	£3.50
62 Wrightson art	$1.60	$4.80	$8.00	£0.60	£1.80	£3.00
63-64	$1.60	$4.80	$8.00	£0.70	£2.10	£3.50
65	$1.60	$4.80	$8.00	£0.60	£1.80	£3.00
66-68 distributed in the U.K.	$1.60	$4.80	$8.00	£0.40	£1.20	£2.00
69 distributed in the U.K. Paul Neary art (Hunter story)	$1.60	$4.80	$8.00	£0.40	£1.20	£2.00
70 distributed in the U.K.	$1.60	$4.80	$8.00	£0.40	£1.20	£2.00
71 Paul Neary art featured	$1.60	$4.80	$8.00	£0.40	£1.20	£2.00
72-80	$1.60	$4.80	$8.00	£0.40	£1.20	£2.00
81-139	$1.00	$3.00	$5.00	£0.30	£0.90	£1.50
Title Value:	$292.65	$877.30	$1633.00	£124.35	£376.25	£726.50
Eerie's Greatest Hits (Dec 1994) Softcover collection of classic stories, black and white; Kelley Jones cover. Published by Harris Comics				£1.70	£5.10	£8.50

EERIE ANNUAL

Warren,Magazine; 1-3 1970-1972

	$Good	$Fine	$N.Mint	£Good	£Fine	£N.Mint
1 distributed in the U.K. reprints	$3.00	$9.00	$15.00	£1.40	£4.20	£7.00
2 scarce in the U.K. reprints	$3.00	$9.00	$15.00	£1.60	£4.80	£8.00
3 scarce in the U.K. reprints	$2.40	$7.00	$12.00	£1.50	£4.50	£7.50
Title Value:	$8.40	$25.00	$42.00	£4.50	£13.50	£22.50

EERIE TALES

I.W. Super; 10,11,12,15,18 1963-1964

	$Good	$Fine	$N.Mint	£Good	£Fine	£N.Mint
10-12 distributed in the U.K.	$2.10	$6.25	$15.00	£1.10	£3.40	£8.00

Dreaming, The #1

Dynomutt #1

Eerie Tales (IW) #12

	$Good	$Fine	$N.Mint	£Good	£Fine	£N.Mint
15 distributed in the U.K.						
	$5.00	*$15.00*	*$35.00*	£2.85	£8.50	£20.00
18 distributed in the U.K.						
	$2.10	*$6.25*	*$15.00*	£1.05	£3.20	£7.50
Title Value:	*$13.40*	*$40.00*	*$95.00*	£7.20	£21.90	£51.50

EGYPT

DC Comics/Vertigo,MS; 1 Aug 1995-7 Feb 1996

	$Good	$Fine	$N.Mint	£Good	£Fine	£N.Mint
1-7 ND Peter Milligan script, Glyn Dillon art						
	$0.50	*$1.50*	*$2.50*	£0.30	£0.90	£1.50
Title Value:	*$3.50*	*$10.50*	*$17.50*	£2.10	£6.30	£10.50

EH

ACG; 1 Apr 1996

	$Good	$Fine	$N.Mint	£Good	£Fine	£N.Mint
1 ND reprints from Charlton Comics; black and white						
	$0.50	*$1.50*	*$2.50*	£0.30	£0.90	£1.50
Title Value:	*$0.50*	*$1.50*	*$2.50*	£0.30	£0.90	£1.50

EIGHTBALL

Fantagraphics; 1 Jul 1990-present

	$Good	$Fine	$N.Mint	£Good	£Fine	£N.Mint
1 Dan Clowes story/art, Lloyd Llewellyn featured						
	$2.00	*$6.00*	*$10.00*	£1.30	£3.90	£6.50
1 2nd printing	*$0.55*	*$1.65*	*$2.75*	£0.35	£1.05	£1.75
1 3rd printing	*$0.45*	*$1.35*	*$2.25*	£0.30	£0.90	£1.50
1 4th printing	*$0.40*	*$1.20*	*$2.00*	£0.25	£0.75	£1.25
1 5th printing, (May 1993)						
	$0.40	*$1.20*	*$2.00*	£0.25	£0.75	£1.25
1 6th printing, (Aug 1994)						
	$0.60	*$1.80*	*$3.00*	£0.40	£1.20	£2.00
2	*$1.50*	*$4.50*	*$7.50*	£0.90	£2.70	£4.50
2 2nd printing	*$0.55*	*$1.65*	*$2.75*	£0.35	£1.05	£1.75
2 3rd/4th printing	*$0.50*	*$1.50*	*$2.50*	£0.30	£0.90	£1.50
2 5th printing, (May 1996), $3.95 cover						
	$0.80	*$2.40*	*$4.00*	£0.50	£1.50	£2.50
3	*$1.20*	*$3.60*	*$6.00*	£0.70	£2.10	£3.50
3 2nd printing, (Nov 1991)						
	$0.50	*$1.50*	*$2.50*	£0.30	£0.90	£1.50
3 3rd/4th printing	*$0.50*	*$1.50*	*$2.50*	£0.30	£0.90	£1.50
4	*$1.00*	*$3.00*	*$5.00*	£0.60	£1.80	£3.00
4 2nd printing	*$0.60*	*$1.80*	*$3.00*	£0.40	£1.20	£2.00
4 3rd/4th printing	*$0.50*	*$1.50*	*$2.50*	£0.30	£0.90	£1.50
5	*$1.00*	*$3.00*	*$5.00*	£0.60	£1.80	£3.00
5 2nd printing, (Aug 1992)						
	$0.50	*$1.50*	*$2.50*	£0.30	£0.90	£1.50
6	*$0.80*	*$2.40*	*$4.00*	£0.50	£1.50	£2.50
6 2nd printing, (Sep 1992)						
	$0.50	*$1.50*	*$2.50*	£0.30	£0.90	£1.50
7	*$0.80*	*$2.40*	*$4.00*	£0.40	£1.20	£2.00
7 2nd printing, (Sep 1993)						
	$0.50	*$1.50*	*$2.50*	£0.30	£0.90	£1.50
8	*$0.80*	*$2.40*	*$4.00*	£0.40	£1.20	£2.00
9	*$0.50*	*$1.50*	*$2.50*	£0.35	£1.05	£1.75
10 conclusion "Like A Velvet Glove Cast In Iron"						
	$0.50	*$1.50*	*$2.50*	£0.35	£1.05	£1.75
11 $2.95 cover	*$0.60*	*$1.80*	*$3.00*	£0.40	£1.20	£2.00
12 $2.75 cover	*$0.55*	*$1.65*	*$2.75*	£0.35	£1.05	£1.75
13 $2.95 cover	*$0.60*	*$1.80*	*$3.00*	£0.40	£1.20	£2.00
13 Improved Edition, (Nov 1994) An "improved" edition as the original issue #13 had colour and printing problems; heavier paper stock cover						
	$0.60	*$1.80*	*$3.00*	£0.40	£1.20	£2.00
14 $2.75 cover	*$0.55*	*$1.65*	*$2.75*	£0.35	£1.05	£1.75
15 $2.95 cover	*$0.60*	*$1.80*	*$3.00*	£0.40	£1.20	£2.00
16 $3.95 cover	*$0.80*	*$2.40*	*$4.00*	£0.50	£1.50	£2.50
17 ND	*$0.80*	*$2.40*	*$4.00*	£0.50	£1.50	£2.50
Title Value:	*$23.05*	*$69.15*	*$115.25*	£14.30	£42.90	£71.50

Note: all Non-Distributed on the news-stands in the U.K.

EIGHTY PAGE GIANT MAGAZINE

National Periodical Publications/DC Comics; 1 Aug 1964-15 Oct 1965; 16 Nov 1965-89 Jul 1971

(#57-89 are actually 68pgs)

	$Good	$Fine	$N.Mint	£Good	£Fine	£N.Mint
1 Superman (not to be confused with Superman Annual 1!); originally announced as Superman Annual #9						
	$35.00	*$105.00*	*$425.00*	£20.50	£62.50	£250.00
2 Jimmy Olsen	*$21.50*	*$65.00*	*$260.00*	£12.50	£38.00	£150.00
3 Lois Lane	*$20.00*	*$60.00*	*$200.00*	£11.50	£35.00	£115.00
4 The Flash, reprints Showcase #13 (cover story), #14 (cover story), Flash #105 (cover story), Flash #110 (cover story)						
	$20.00	*$60.00*	*$200.00*	£11.50	£35.00	£115.00
5 Batman, Silver anniversary issue; classic reprints						
	$20.00	*$60.00*	*$200.00*	£9.00	£27.00	£90.00
6 Superman, reprints including 1st Bizarro Lois Lane from Action Comics #255						
	$16.00	*$48.00*	*$160.00*	£9.00	£27.00	£90.00
7 rare in the U.K. Sgt. Rock's Prize Battle Tales						
	$17.50	*$52.50*	*$175.00*	£10.00	£30.00	£100.00
8 Secret Origins, reprints Justice League of America #9, Aquaman (Adventure #260), Robin origin re-told, Atom origin from Showcase #34, Superman #146						
	$36.00	*$105.00*	*$360.00*	£21.00	£62.50	£210.00
9 The Flash, reprints Flash #123						
	$15.00	*$45.00*	*$150.00*	£8.50	£26.00	£85.00
10 Superboy, reprints Adventure #271 (origin Luthor)						
	$15.00	*$45.00*	*$150.00*	£8.50	£26.00	£85.00
11 Superman, reprints Superboy #86 (4th Legion)						
	$15.00	*$45.00*	*$150.00*	£8.50	£26.00	£85.00
12 Batman	*$15.00*	*$45.00*	*$150.00*	£8.50	£26.00	£85.00
13 Jimmy Olsen	*$15.00*	*$45.00*	*$150.00*	£8.50	£26.00	£85.00
14 less common in the U.K. Lois Lane, reprints Superman #127 (1st Lori Lemaris)						
	$15.00	*$45.00*	*$150.00*	£9.00	£27.00	£90.00
15 Superman and Batman (World's Finest), Joker cover and story						
	$16.00	*$48.00*	*$160.00*	£9.00	£27.00	£90.00
Title Value:	*$292.00*	*$873.50*	*$3040.00*	£165.50	£501.00	£1725.00

Note: Many 80pg Giants and Annuals from the early '60s have crinkled covers at the spine, caused by uneven drying of the glue. Perfectly flat (and therefore Mint) copies are very scarce. Numbers 16-93 are included in the numbering of other titles, as follows:

16 Nov 1965-89 Oct/Nov 1971 #16: JLA 39. **#17**: Batman 176. **#18**: Superman 183. **#19**: Our Army at War 164. **#20**: Action 334. **#21**: Flash 160. **#22**: Superboy 129. **#23**: Superman 187. **#24**: Batman 182. **#25**: Jimmy Olsen 95. **#26**: Lois Lane 68. **#27**: Batman 185. **#28**: World's Finest 161. **#29**: JLA 48. **#30**: Batman 187. **#31**: Superman 193. **#32**: Our Army at War 177. **#33**: Action 347. **#34**: Flash 169. **#35**: Superboy 138. **#36**: Superman 198. **#37**: Batman 193. **#38**: Jimmy Olsen 104. **#39**: Lois Lane 77. **#40**: World's Finest 170. **#41**: JLA 58. **#42**: Superman 202. **#43**: Batman 198. **#44**: Our Army at War 190. **#45**: Action 360. **#46**: Flash 178. **#47**: Superboy 147. **#48**: Superman 207. **#49**: Batman 203. **#50**: Jimmy Olsen 113. **#51**: Lois Lane 86. **#52**: World's Finest 179. **#53**: JLA 67. **#54**: Superman 212. **#55**: Batman 208. **#56**: Our Army at War 203. **#57**: Action 373. **#58**: Flash 187. **#59**: Superboy 156. **#60**: Superman 217. **#61**: Batman 213. **#62**: Jimmy Olsen 122. **#63**: Lois Lane 95. **#64** World's Finest 188. **#65**: JLA 76. **#66**: Superman 222. **#67**: Batman 218. **#68**: Our Army at War 216. **#69**: Adventure 390. **#70**: Flash 196. **#71**: Superboy 165. **#72**: Superman 227. **#73**: Batman 223. **#74**: Jimmy Olsen 131. **#75**: Lois Lane 104. **#76**: World's Finest 197. **#77**: JLA 85. **#78**: Superman 232. **#79**: Batman 228. **#80**: Our Army at War 229. **#81**: Adventure 403. **#82**: Flash 205. **#83**: Superboy 174. **#84**: Superman 239. **#85**: Batman 233. **#86**: Jimmy Olsen 140. **#87**: Lois Lane 113. **#88**: World's Finest 206. **#89**: JLA 93.

EL DIABLO

DC Comics; 1 Aug 1989-16 Dec 1990

	$Good	$Fine	$N.Mint	£Good	£Fine	£N.Mint
1-12 ND 48pgs	*$0.25*	*$0.75*	*$1.25*	£0.10	£0.35	£0.60
13-15 The River story						
	$0.25	*$0.75*	*$1.25*	£0.10	£0.35	£0.60
16	*$0.25*	*$0.75*	*$1.25*	£0.10	£0.35	£0.60
Title Value:	*$4.00*	*$12.00*	*$20.00*	£1.60	£5.60	£9.60

Note: New Format

EL DORADO

Dell/Movie Classics,OS,Movie; 12-240-710 Oct 1967

	$Good	$Fine	$N.Mint	£Good	£Fine	£N.Mint
12-240-710 distributed in the U.K. film adaptation; John Wayne photo cover						
	$16.00	*$49.00*	*$115.00*	£10.50	£32.00	£75.00
Title Value:	*$16.00*	*$49.00*	*$115.00*	£10.50	£32.00	£75.00

EL SALVADOR: A HOUSE DIVIDED

Eclipse,OS; 1 1989

	$Good	$Fine	$N.Mint	£Good	£Fine	£N.Mint
1 ND Bill Tulp script/art; black and white						
	$0.30	*$0.90*	*$1.50*	£0.20	£0.60	£1.00
Title Value:	*$0.30*	*$0.90*	*$1.50*	£0.20	£0.60	£1.00

ELECTRIC BALLET

Caliber Press,MS; 1 Feb 1992-3 Apr 1993

	$Good	$Fine	$N.Mint	£Good	£Fine	£N.Mint
1-3 ND	*$0.40*	*$1.20*	*$2.00*	£0.25	£0.75	£1.25
Title Value:	*$1.20*	*$3.60*	*$6.00*	£0.75	£2.25	£3.75

ELECTRIC UNDERTOW

Marvel Comics Group,MS; 1 Dec 1989-5 Apr 1990

	$Good	$Fine	$N.Mint	£Good	£Fine	£N.Mint
1-5 ND 48pgs, squarebound, Mark Bagley pencils						
	$0.70	*$2.10*	*$3.50*	£0.40	£1.20	£2.00
Title Value:	*$3.50*	*$10.50*	*$17.50*	£2.00	£6.00	£10.00

Note: spin-off from Strikeforce: Morituri

ELECTRIC WARRIOR

DC Comics; 1 May 1986-18 Oct 1987

	$Good	$Fine	$N.Mint	£Good	£Fine	£N.Mint
1 ND Jim Baikie art						
	$0.25	*$0.75*	*$1.25*	£0.15	£0.45	£0.75
2-18 ND Jim Baikie art						
	$0.25	*$0.75*	*$1.25*	£0.10	£0.35	£0.60
Title Value:	*$4.50*	*$13.50*	*$22.50*	£1.85	£6.40	£10.95

Note: Baxter paper.

ELEKTRA

Marvel Comics Group; 1 Nov 1996-present

	$Good	$Fine	$N.Mint	£Good	£Fine	£N.Mint
1 ND 40pgs, Peter Milligan script, Mike Deodato Jnr. art						
	$0.40	*$1.20*	*$2.00*	£0.25	£0.75	£1.25
1 Variant Cover Edition, ND 40pgs, Mike Deodato Jnr. cover art; Elektra smashing through window						
	$1.00	*$3.00*	*$5.00*	£0.80	£2.40	£4.00
2 ND Elektra vs. Bullseye						
	$0.40	*$1.20*	*$2.00*	£0.25	£0.75	£1.25
3-5 ND	*$0.40*	*$1.20*	*$2.00*	£0.25	£0.75	£1.25
Title Value:	*$3.00*	*$9.00*	*$15.00*	£2.05	£6.15	£10.25

ELEKTRA LIVES AGAIN

Marvel Comics Group,OS; nn Nov 1996

	$Good	$Fine	$N.Mint	£Good	£Fine	£N.Mint
nn ND 80pgs, reprints the hardcover Marvel Graphic Novel in softcover						
	$1.40	*$4.20*	*$7.00*	£0.90	£2.70	£4.50
Title Value:	*$1.40*	*$4.20*	*$7.00*	£0.90	£2.70	£4.50

ELEKTRA MEGAZINE

Marvel Comics Group,MS; 1,2 Nov 1996

	$Good	$Fine	$N.Mint	£Good	£Fine	£N.Mint
1-2 ND 96pgs, reprints the original history highlights series from 1984						
	$0.80	*$2.40*	*$4.00*	£0.50	£1.50	£2.50
Title Value:	*$1.60*	*$4.80*	*$8.00*	£1.00	£3.00	£5.00

ELEKTRA SAGA, THE

Marvel Comics Group/Epic,MS; 1 Feb 1984-4 Jun 1984

	$Good	$Fine	$N.Mint	£Good	£Fine	£N.Mint
1 ND	*$1.20*	*$3.60*	*$6.00*	£0.80	£2.40	£4.00
2-4 ND	*$1.00*	*$3.00*	*$5.00*	£0.70	£2.10	£3.50
Title Value:	*$4.20*	*$12.60*	*$21.00*	£2.90	£8.70	£14.50

Note: edited reprints of Daredevil 168-190 with new covers, Miller story/art.

				£Good	£Fine	£N.Mint
Trade paperback (Nov 1989) Reprints of above				£2.00	£6.00	£10.00

ELEKTRA/WITCHBLADE

Marvel Comics Group/Top Cow Comics,OS; nn Mar 1997

	$Good	$Fine	$N.Mint	£Good	£Fine	£N.Mint
nn ND Devil's Reign part 6, continued in Elektra/Cyblade; Christina Z script, Mike Turner and D-Tron art						
	$0.60	*$1.80*	*$3.00*	£0.40	£1.20	£2.00
Title Value:	*$0.60*	*$1.80*	*$3.00*	£0.40	£1.20	£2.00

ELEKTRA: ASSASSIN

Marvel Comics Group/Epic,MS; 1 Aug 1986-8 Mar 1987

	$Good	$Fine	$N.Mint	£Good	£Fine	£N.Mint
1 ND	*$1.00*	*$3.00*	*$5.00*	£0.50	£1.50	£2.50
2-8 ND	*$0.80*	*$2.40*	*$4.00*	£0.40	£1.20	£2.00
Title Value:	*$6.60*	*$19.80*	*$27.00*	£3.30	£9.90	£16.50
Trade Paperback, reprints #1-8				£1.25	£3.75	£6.25
Hardcover (2000 copies, signed and numbered. Jul 1989)				£5.00	£15.00	£25.00
Note: Miller story, Sienkiewicz art. Mature Readers.						

ELEKTRA: ROOT OF EVIL

Marvel Comics Group,MS; 1 Mar 1995-4 Jun 1995

	$Good	$Fine	$N.Mint	£Good	£Fine	£N.Mint
1 foil stamped cover	*$0.80*	*$2.40*	*$4.00*	£0.50	£1.50	£2.50
2-4 foil stamped cover	*$0.60*	*$1.80*	*$3.00*	£0.40	£1.20	£2.00
Title Value:	*$2.60*	*$7.80*	*$13.00*	£1.70	£5.10	£8.50

ELEMENTALS

Comico; 1 Jun 1984-29 Sep 1988

(see Justice Machine)

	$Good	$Fine	$N.Mint	£Good	£Fine	£N.Mint
1 ND scarce in the U.K. 1st Comico flat-colour comic	*$1.00*	*$3.00*	*$5.00*	£1.00	£3.00	£5.00
2 ND	*$0.60*	*$1.80*	*$3.00*	£0.60	£1.80	£3.00
3 ND	*$0.50*	*$1.50*	*$2.50*	£0.40	£1.20	£2.00
4 ND	*$0.40*	*$1.20*	*$2.00*	£0.30	£0.90	£1.50
5-10 ND	*$0.40*	*$1.20*	*$2.00*	£0.25	£0.75	£1.25
11-29 ND	*$0.30*	*$0.90*	*$1.50*	£0.20	£0.60	£1.00
Title Value:	*$10.60*	*$31.80*	*$53.00*	£7.60	£22.80	£38.00
The Natural Order Trade paperback, reprints #1-5 plus story from Justice Machine Annual #1				£1.80	£5.40	£9.00
The Natural Order A (Dec 1992) as above with certificate and 11x17 print by Kelley Jones				£1.80	£5.40	£9.00
The Natural Order B (Dec 1992) as above plus rerint of Monolith #1 and Vortex #1 and certificate. 2,000 copies				£2.00	£6.00	£10.00
Trade paperback (Sep 1991), reprints #6-10 with new cover by Bill Willingham				£2.00	£6.00	£10.00

ELEMENTALS OBLIVION WAR SPECIAL

Comico,MS; 1 Jul 1992-2 Aug 1992

	$Good	$Fine	$N.Mint	£Good	£Fine	£N.Mint
1 ND pin-ups, glow in the dark cover by Walt Simonson	*$0.50*	*$1.50*	*$2.50*	£0.30	£0.90	£1.50
1 Deluxe Format, ND - silver embossed cover, 3,000 copies	*$0.90*	*$2.70*	*$4.50*	£0.60	£1.80	£3.00
2 ND includes two trading cards, cover by Walt Simonson	*$0.50*	*$1.50*	*$2.50*	£0.30	£0.90	£1.50
Title Value:	*$1.90*	*$5.70*	*$9.50*	£1.20	£3.60	£6.00

ELEMENTALS SEXY LINGERIE SPECIAL

Comico,OS; 1 Jan 1993

	$Good	$Fine	$N.Mint	£Good	£Fine	£N.Mint
1 ND includes giant pull-out poster	*$1.00*	*$3.00*	*$5.00*	£0.60	£1.80	£3.00
Title Value:	*$1.00*	*$3.00*	*$5.00*	£0.60	£1.80	£3.00

ELEMENTALS SPECIAL

Comico; 1 Mar 1986;2 Jan 1989

	$Good	$Fine	$N.Mint	£Good	£Fine	£N.Mint
1 ND	*$0.30*	*$0.90*	*$1.50*	£0.25	£0.75	£1.25
1 2nd printing, ND (Sep 1991)	*$0.30*	*$0.90*	*$1.50*	£0.20	£0.60	£1.00
2 ND	*$0.30*	*$0.90*	*$1.50*	£0.25	£0.75	£1.25
Title Value:	*$0.90*	*$2.70*	*$4.50*	£0.70	£2.10	£3.50

ELEMENTALS SWIMSUIT SPECTACULAR

Comico,OS; 1 Jun 1996

	$Good	$Fine	$N.Mint	£Good	£Fine	£N.Mint
1 ND	*$0.60*	*$1.80*	*$3.00*	£0.40	£1.20	£2.00
1 Variant Cover Edition, ND no logo on cover	*$0.60*	*$1.80*	*$3.00*	£0.40	£1.20	£2.00
Title Value:	*$1.20*	*$3.60*	*$6.00*	£0.80	£2.40	£4.00

ELEMENTALS VOLUME 2

Comico; 1 Mar 1989-32 1993

	$Good	$Fine	$N.Mint	£Good	£Fine	£N.Mint
1 ND Mike Leeke and Mike Chen art begins	*$0.45*	*$1.35*	*$2.25*	£0.30	£0.90	£1.50
2-15 ND	*$0.40*	*$1.20*	*$2.00*	£0.25	£0.75	£1.25
16 ND 1st appearance Strike Force America	*$0.50*	*$1.50*	*$2.50*	£0.30	£0.90	£1.50
17-24 ND	*$0.30*	*$0.90*	*$1.50*	£0.20	£0.60	£1.00
25 ND wraparound Kelley Jones cover	*$0.40*	*$1.20*	*$2.00*	£0.25	£0.75	£1.25
25 2nd printing, ND (May 1993)	*$0.30*	*$0.90*	*$1.50*	£0.20	£0.60	£1.00
26 ND origin of Strike Force America begins	*$0.30*	*$0.90*	*$1.50*	£0.20	£0.60	£1.00
27 ND	*$0.30*	*$0.90*	*$1.50*	£0.20	£0.60	£1.00
28 ND prism-embossed wraparound cover	*$0.30*	*$0.90*	*$1.50*	£0.20	£0.60	£1.00
29 ND	*$0.30*	*$0.90*	*$1.50*	£0.20	£0.60	£1.00
29 With Giant Poster by Walt Simonson ND	*$0.80*	*$2.40*	*$4.00*	£0.50	£1.50	£2.50
30 ND Oblivion War conclusion	*$0.30*	*$0.90*	*$1.50*	£0.20	£0.60	£1.00
30 Collectors Edition, ND 48pgs, Oblivion War conclusion, 16pg pin-up gallery; foil enhanced logo	*$0.80*	*$2.40*	*$4.00*	£0.50	£1.50	£2.50
31 ND sub-titled Birth of a Nation #0; new direction for title	*$0.30*	*$0.90*	*$1.50*	£0.20	£0.60	£1.00
32 ND	*$0.30*	*$0.90*	*$1.50*	£0.20	£0.60	£1.00
Title Value:	*$13.35*	*$40.05*	*$66.75*	£8.55	£25.65	£42.75

ELEMENTALS VOLUME 3

Comico; 1 Aug 1995-present

	$Good	$Fine	$N.Mint	£Good	£Fine	£N.Mint
1 ND pre-bagged with trading card	*$0.50*	*$1.50*	*$2.50*	£0.30	£0.90	£1.50
1 Signed & Numbered Edition, ND pre-bagged with certificate and print; 500 copies	*$5.00*	*$15.00*	*$25.00*	£3.00	£9.00	£15.00
2-6 ND	*$0.50*	*$1.50*	*$2.50*	£0.30	£0.90	£1.50
Title Value:	*$8.00*	*$24.00*	*$40.00*	£4.80	£14.40	£24.00

ELEMENTALS: BABES

Comico,MS; 1 Aug 1996-3 Oct 1996

	$Good	$Fine	$N.Mint	£Good	£Fine	£N.Mint
1-3 ND photo and comic strip art/pin-ups	*$0.80*	*$2.40*	*$4.00*	£0.50	£1.50	£2.50
Title Value:	*$2.40*	*$7.20*	*$12.00*	£1.50	£4.50	£7.50

ELEMENTALS: GHOST OF A CHANCE GRAPHIC NOVEL

Comico,OS; nn Jul 1995

	$Good	$Fine	$N.Mint	£Good	£Fine	£N.Mint
nn ND 48pgs, Alex Ross painted cover	*$1.20*	*$3.60*	*$6.00*	£0.80	£2.40	£4.00
nn Signed & Numbered Edition ND with certifucate	*$5.00*	*$15.00*	*$25.00*	£3.00	£9.00	£15.00
Title Value:	*$6.20*	*$18.60*	*$31.00*	£3.80	£11.40	£19.00

ELEMENTALS: HOW THE WAR WAS WON

Comico,MS; 1 Jun 1996-4 Sep 1996

	$Good	$Fine	$N.Mint	£Good	£Fine	£N.Mint
1 ND Jack Herman script, Tony Daniels art	*$0.60*	*$1.80*	*$3.00*	£0.40	£1.20	£2.00
1 Variant Cover Edition, ND no logo on cover	*$0.60*	*$1.80*	*$3.00*	£0.40	£1.20	£2.00
2-4 ND Jack Herman script, Tony Daniels art	*$0.60*	*$1.80*	*$3.00*	£0.40	£1.20	£2.00
Title Value:	*$3.00*	*$9.00*	*$15.00*	£2.00	£6.00	£10.00

ELEMENTALS: SEX, LIES, SANS VIDEOTAPE SPECIAL

Comico,OS; 1 Oct 1991

	$Good	$Fine	$N.Mint	£Good	£Fine	£N.Mint
1 ND	*$0.50*	*$1.50*	*$2.50*	£0.30	£0.90	£1.50
Title Value:	*$0.50*	*$1.50*	*$2.50*	£0.30	£0.90	£1.50

ELEMENTALS: THE STRIKE FORCE LEGACY

Comico,OS; 1 Jul 1993

	$Good	$Fine	$N.Mint	£Good	£Fine	£N.Mint
1 ND 64pgs	*$0.60*	*$1.80*	*$3.00*	£0.40	£1.20	£2.00
Title Value:	*$0.60*	*$1.80*	*$3.00*	£0.40	£1.20	£2.00

ELEMENTALS: THE VAMPIRE'S REVENGE

Comico,MS; 1 Jun 1996-4 Sep 1996

	$Good	$Fine	$N.Mint	£Good	£Fine	£N.Mint
1 ND Bill Willingham script, Kelly McQuain art	*$0.60*	*$1.80*	*$3.00*	£0.40	£1.20	£2.00
1 Variant Cover Edition, ND no logo on cover	*$0.60*	*$1.80*	*$3.00*	£0.40	£1.20	£2.00
2-4 ND Bill Willingham script, Kelly McQuain art	*$0.60*	*$1.80*	*$3.00*	£0.40	£1.20	£2.00
Title Value:	*$3.00*	*$9.00*	*$15.00*	£2.00	£6.00	£10.00

ELEVEN ELEVEN

Crusade Comics; 1 Oct 1996-present

	$Good	$Fine	$N.Mint	£Good	£Fine	£N.Mint
1 ND Bernie Wrightson art; black and white	*$0.60*	*$1.80*	*$3.00*	£0.40	£1.20	£2.00
Title Value:	*$0.60*	*$1.80*	*$3.00*	£0.40	£1.20	£2.00

ELEVEN OR ONE

Sirius,OS; 1 Apr 1995

	$Good	$Fine	$N.Mint	£Good	£Fine	£N.Mint
1 ND Joseph Michael Linsner cover and art, reprints Angry Christ Comic in colour	*$3.50*	*$10.50*	*$17.50*	£2.50	£7.50	£12.50
1 2nd printing, ND (Jun 1996)	*$0.60*	*$1.80*	*$3.00*	£0.60	£1.80	£3.00
Title Value:	*$4.10*	*$12.30*	*$20.50*	£3.10	£9.30	£15.50

ELF TREK

Dimension Graphics; 1 Jul 1986-2 Aug 1986

	$Good	$Fine	$N.Mint	£Good	£Fine	£N.Mint
1-2 ND parody of Star Trek, X-Men and Elflord, black and white	*$0.25*	*$0.75*	*$1.25*	£0.15	£0.45	£0.75
Title Value:	*$0.50*	*$1.50*	*$2.50*	£0.30	£0.90	£1.50

ELF-THING

Eclipse,OS; 1 Mar 1987

	$Good	$Fine	$N.Mint	£Good	£Fine	£N.Mint
1 ND Elfquest/Swamp Thing/Hulk parody; black and white	*$0.40*	*$1.20*	*$2.00*	£0.25	£0.75	£1.25
Title Value:	*$0.40*	*$1.20*	*$2.00*	£0.25	£0.75	£1.25

ELF-WARRIOR

Adventure/Quadrant; 1 1987-4 1988

	$Good	$Fine	$N.Mint	£Good	£Fine	£N.Mint
1-4 ND Peter Hsu art	*$0.30*	*$0.90*	*$1.50*	£0.20	£0.60	£1.00
Title Value:	*$1.20*	*$3.60*	*$6.00*	£0.80	£2.40	£4.00

ELFHEIM

Night Wynd,MS; 1 Dec 1991-4 Mar 1992

	$Good	$Fine	$N.Mint	£Good	£Fine	£N.Mint
1-4 ND Barry Blair script and art; black and white	*$0.35*	*$1.05*	*$1.75*	£0.25	£0.75	£1.25
Title Value:	*$1.40*	*$4.20*	*$7.00*	£1.00	£3.00	£5.00

ELFHEIM (2ND SERIES)

Night Wynd,MS; 1 Apr 1992-4 Jul 1992

	$Good	$Fine	$N.Mint	£Good	£Fine	£N.Mint
1-4 ND Barry Blair script and art; black and white	*$0.35*	*$1.05*	*$1.75*	£0.25	£0.75	£1.25
Title Value:	*$1.40*	*$4.20*	*$7.00*	£1.00	£3.00	£5.00

ELFHEIM (3RD SERIES)

Night Wynd,MS; 1 Aug 1992-4 Nov 1992

	$Good	$Fine	$N.Mint	£Good	£Fine	£N.Mint
1-4 ND Barry Blair script and art; black and white	*$0.35*	*$1.05*	*$1.75*	£0.25	£0.75	£1.25
Title Value:	*$1.40*	*$4.20*	*$7.00*	£1.00	£3.00	£5.00

ELFHEIM (4TH SERIES)

Night Wynd,MS; 1 Dec 1992-4 Apr 1993

	$Good	$Fine	$N.Mint	£Good	£Fine	£N.Mint
1-4 ND Barry Blair script and art; black and white	*$0.35*	*$1.05*	*$1.75*	£0.25	£0.75	£1.25
Title Value:	*$1.40*	*$4.20*	*$7.00*	£1.00	£3.00	£5.00

ELFHEIM: DRAGON'S DREAMS

Night Wynd,MS; 1 Jul 1993-4 Aug 1993

1-4 ND Barry Blair script and art; black and white

	$Good	$Fine	$N.Mint	£Good	£Fine	£N.Mint
	$0.35	$1.05	$1.75	£0.25	£0.75	£1.25
Title Value:	$1.40	$4.20	$7.00	£1.00	£3.00	£5.00

ELFHEIM: DRAGON'S EYE

Night Wynd,MS; 1 Sep 1993-4 Feb 1994

	$Good	$Fine	$N.Mint	£Good	£Fine	£N.Mint
1-4 ND Barry Blair script and art; black and white						
	$0.35	$1.05	$1.75	£0.25	£0.75	£1.25
Title Value:	$1.40	$4.20	$7.00	£1.00	£3.00	£5.00

ELFHEIM: SHADE WARS

Night Wynd,MS; 1 Jan 1994-4 Apr 1994

	$Good	$Fine	$N.Mint	£Good	£Fine	£N.Mint
1-4 ND Barry Blair script and art; black and white						
	$0.35	$1.05	$1.75	£0.25	£0.75	£1.25
Title Value:	$1.40	$4.20	$7.00	£1.00	£3.00	£5.00

ELFHEIM: TIME OF THE WOLF

Night Wynd,MS; 1 Oct 1993-3 Dec 1993

	$Good	$Fine	$N.Mint	£Good	£Fine	£N.Mint
1-3 ND Barry Blair script and art						
	$0.35	$1.05	$1.75	£0.25	£0.75	£1.25
Title Value:	$1.05	$3.15	$5.25	£0.75	£2.25	£3.75

ELFLORD (1ST SERIES)

Aircel; 1 1986-6 1986

	$Good	$Fine	$N.Mint	£Good	£Fine	£N.Mint
1 ND Barry Blair pencils begin; black and white						
	$0.80	$2.40	$4.00	£0.60	£1.80	£3.00
1 2nd printing ND	$0.40	$1.20	$2.00	£0.25	£0.75	£1.25
2 ND	$0.50	$1.50	$2.50	£0.40	£1.20	£2.00
2 2nd printing ND	$0.40	$1.20	$2.00	£0.25	£0.75	£1.25
3-6 ND	$0.50	$1.50	$2.50	£0.30	£0.90	£1.50
Title Value:	$4.10	$12.30	$20.50	£2.70	£8.10	£13.50

ELFLORD (2ND SERIES)

Aircel; 1 1987-30 1989

	$Good	$Fine	$N.Mint	£Good	£Fine	£N.Mint
1-10 ND colour	$0.50	$1.50	$2.50	£0.30	£0.90	£1.50
11-20 ND colour	$0.35	$1.05	$1.75	£0.25	£0.75	£1.25
21 ND DS colour	$0.40	$1.20	$2.00	£0.30	£0.90	£1.50
22 ND last colour issue, new characters						
	$0.30	$0.90	$1.50	£0.20	£0.60	£1.00
23-30 ND	$0.30	$0.90	$1.50	£0.20	£0.60	£1.00
Title Value:	$11.60	$34.80	$53.50	£7.60	£22.80	£38.00

ELFLORD (3RD SERIES)

Mad Monkey Press; 1 Apr 1996-present ?

	$Good	$Fine	$N.Mint	£Good	£Fine	£N.Mint
1 ND 64pgs, Barry Blair and Colin Chan creative team begins						
	$1.40	$4.20	$7.00	£0.90	£2.70	£4.50
Title Value:	$1.40	$4.20	$7.00	£0.90	£2.70	£4.50

ELFLORD CHRONICLES

Aircel,MS; 1 Sep 1990-8 1991

	$Good	$Fine	$N.Mint	£Good	£Fine	£N.Mint
1 ND 40pgs, reprints begin, Barry Blair art begins						
	$0.35	$1.05	$1.75	£0.25	£0.75	£1.25
2-8 ND	$0.35	$1.05	$1.75	£0.25	£0.75	£1.25
Title Value:	$2.80	$8.40	$14.00	£2.00	£6.00	£10.00

ELFLORD: DRAGON'S EYE

Night Wynd,MS; 1 Aug 1993-4 Nov 1993

	$Good	$Fine	$N.Mint	£Good	£Fine	£N.Mint
1-4 ND Barry Blair script and art						
	$0.35	$1.05	$1.75	£0.25	£0.75	£1.25
Title Value:	$1.40	$4.20	$7.00	£1.00	£3.00	£5.00

ELFLORD: SHADOW SPELL

Night Wynd,MS; 1 Oct 1993-4 Mar 1994

	$Good	$Fine	$N.Mint	£Good	£Fine	£N.Mint
1-4 ND Barry Blair script and art; black and white						
	$0.35	$1.05	$1.75	£0.25	£0.75	£1.25
Title Value:	$1.40	$4.20	$7.00	£1.00	£3.00	£5.00

ELFLORD: SUMMER'S MAGIC

Night Wynd,MS; 1 Apr 1993-4 Jul 1993

	$Good	$Fine	$N.Mint	£Good	£Fine	£N.Mint
1-4 ND Barry Blair script and art						
	$0.35	$1.05	$1.75	£0.25	£0.75	£1.25
Title Value:	$1.40	$4.20	$7.00	£1.00	£3.00	£5.00

ELFLORD: THE RETURN OF THE KING

Night Wynd,MS; 1 Nov 1992-4 Mar 1993

	$Good	$Fine	$N.Mint	£Good	£Fine	£N.Mint
1-4 ND Barry Blair script and art						
	$0.35	$1.05	$1.75	£0.25	£0.75	£1.25
Title Value:	$1.40	$4.20	$7.00	£1.00	£3.00	£5.00

ELFLORE

Night Wynd,MS; 1 Apr 1992-4 Jul 1992

	$Good	$Fine	$N.Mint	£Good	£Fine	£N.Mint
1-4 ND Barry Blair script and art						
	$0.30	$0.90	$1.50	£0.20	£0.60	£1.00
Title Value:	$1.20	$3.60	$6.00	£0.80	£2.40	£4.00

ELFLORE (2ND SERIES)

Night Wynd,MS; 1 Aug 1992-4 Nov 1992

	$Good	$Fine	$N.Mint	£Good	£Fine	£N.Mint
1-4 ND Barry Blair script and art						
	$0.30	$0.90	$1.50	£0.20	£0.60	£1.00
Title Value:	$1.20	$3.60	$6.00	£0.80	£2.40	£4.00

ELFLORE (3RD SERIES)

Night Wynd,MS; 1 Dec 1992-4 Apr 1993

	$Good	$Fine	$N.Mint	£Good	£Fine	£N.Mint
1-4 ND Barry Blair script and art						
	$0.30	$0.90	$1.50	£0.20	£0.60	£1.00
Title Value:	$1.20	$3.60	$6.00	£0.80	£2.40	£4.00

ELFLORE: FIRE MOUNTAIN

Night Wynd,MS; 1 Jan 1994-4 Apr 1994

	$Good	$Fine	$N.Mint	£Good	£Fine	£N.Mint
1-4 ND Barry Blair script and art; black and white						
	$0.35	$1.05	$1.75	£0.25	£0.75	£1.25
Title Value:	$1.40	$4.20	$7.00	£1.00	£3.00	£5.00

ELFLORE: HIGH SEAS

Night Wynd,MS; 1 Jul 1993-4 Oct 1993

	$Good	$Fine	$N.Mint	£Good	£Fine	£N.Mint
1-4 ND Barry Blair script and art						
	$0.35	$1.05	$1.75	£0.25	£0.75	£1.25
Title Value:	$1.40	$4.20	$7.00	£1.00	£3.00	£5.00

ELFLORE: LAND OF DREAMS

Night Wynd,MS; 1 Sep 1993-3 Nov 1993

	$Good	$Fine	$N.Mint	£Good	£Fine	£N.Mint
1-3 ND Barry Blair script and art						
	$0.35	$1.05	$1.75	£0.25	£0.75	£1.25
Title Value:	$1.05	$3.15	$5.25	£0.75	£2.25	£3.75

ELFQUEST

Warp,Magazine; 1 Apr 1979;2 Aug 1978-21 Feb 1985

(see other Elfquest titles,Fantasy Quarterly)

	$Good	$Fine	$N.Mint	£Good	£Fine	£N.Mint
1 Elfquest story from Fantasy Quarterly #1 reprinted; Wendy Pini story and art						
	$8.00	$24.00	$40.00	£4.00	£12.00	£20.00
1 2nd printing	$3.00	$9.00	$15.00	£1.00	£3.00	£5.00
1 3rd/4th printing, (slightly different cover on 4th print)						
	$0.80	$2.40	$4.00	£0.50	£1.50	£2.50
2	$5.00	$15.00	$25.00	£2.50	£7.50	£12.50
2 2nd/3rd/4th printings						
	$0.50	$1.50	$2.50	£0.30	£0.90	£1.50
3	$5.00	$15.00	$25.00	£2.00	£6.00	£10.00
3 2nd/3rd/4th printings						
	$0.50	$1.50	$2.50	£0.30	£0.90	£1.50
4	$4.00	$12.00	$20.00	£1.50	£4.50	£7.50
4 2nd/3rd/4th printings						
	$0.50	$1.50	$2.50	£0.30	£0.90	£1.50
5	$4.00	$12.00	$20.00	£1.50	£4.50	£7.50
5 2nd/3rd/4th printings						
	$0.50	$1.50	$2.50	£0.30	£0.90	£1.50
6	$2.00	$6.00	$10.00	£1.00	£3.00	£5.00
6 2nd/3rd printings	$0.40	$1.20	$2.00	£0.25	£0.75	£1.25
7	$2.00	$6.00	$10.00	£1.00	£3.00	£5.00
7 2nd/3rd printings	$0.40	$1.20	$2.00	£0.25	£0.75	£1.25
8	$2.00	$6.00	$10.00	£1.00	£3.00	£5.00
8 2nd/3rd printings	$0.40	$1.20	$2.00	£0.25	£0.75	£1.25
9	$2.00	$6.00	$10.00	£1.00	£3.00	£5.00
9 2nd/3rd printings	$0.40	$1.20	$2.00	£0.25	£0.75	£1.25
10-20	$1.20	$3.60	$6.00	£0.80	£2.40	£4.00
21 sketches and background information						
	$1.20	$3.60	$6.00	£0.80	£2.40	£4.00
Title Value:	$55.80	$167.40	$279.00	£28.80	£86.40	£144.00

Note: all Non-Distributed on the news-stands in the U.K.

Note also: the reason that issue #1 is dated later than #2 is that the creators, Richard and Wendy Pini, formed Warp Graphics after their original publisher went into receivership and continued the Fantasy Quarterly story as Elfquest #2. Issue #1, reprinting the first story, came out eight months later, around the time that issue #4 was released.

	£Good	£Fine	£N.Mint
Elfquest Book One: Fire and Flight,			
reprints #1-8 with additional art from the Marvel Epic Comics title	£2.00	£6.00	£10.00
Hardcover Edition (Jul 1993)	£3.00	£9.00	£15.00
Signed, Limited Edition #1-8 in slipcase	£25.00	£75.00	£125.00
Elfquest Book Two, reprints #9-16 plus new art	£2.00	£6.00	£10.00
Elfquest Book Three: Captives of Blue Mountain,			
reprints #17-24 with additional art	£2.00	£6.00	£10.00
Hardcover Edition (1994)	£3.00	£9.00	£15.00
Elfquest Book Four: Quest's End	£2.00	£6.00	£10.00
Elfquest Book Five: The Siege at Blue Mountain	£2.00	£6.00	£10.00
Elfquest Book Six: The Secret of Two-Edge	£2.00	£6.00	£10.00
Elfquest Book Seven: The Cry From Beyond	£2.00	£6.00	£10.00
Elfquest Book Eight: Kings of the Broken Wheel	£2.00	£6.00	£10.00

ELFQUEST (2ND SERIES)

Marvel Comics Group/Epic; 1 Aug 1985-32 Mar 1988

	$Good	$Fine	$N.Mint	£Good	£Fine	£N.Mint
1 ND	$0.60	$1.80	$3.00	£0.40	£1.20	£2.00
2-4	$0.40	$1.20	$2.00	£0.25	£0.75	£1.25
5 ND scarce in the U.K.						
	$0.40	$1.20	$2.00	£0.30	£0.90	£1.50
6	$0.30	$0.90	$1.50	£0.20	£0.60	£1.00
7 ND scarce in the U.K.						
	$0.30	$0.90	$1.50	£0.25	£0.75	£1.25
8-32	$0.30	$0.90	$1.50	£0.20	£0.60	£1.00
Title Value:	$10.30	$30.90	$51.50	£6.90	£20.70	£34.50

ELFQUEST (3RD SERIES)

Warp Graphics; 1 May 1996-present

	$Good	$Fine	$N.Mint	£Good	£Fine	£N.Mint
1 ND 64pgs, four separate stories begin; black and white						
	$1.00	$3.00	$5.00	£0.70	£2.10	£3.50
2-5 ND 64pgs	$1.00	$3.00	$5.00	£0.70	£2.10	£3.50
Title Value:	$5.00	$15.00	$25.00	£3.50	£10.50	£17.50

ELFQUEST GATHERUM

Warp; 1,2 1985

	$Good	$Fine	$N.Mint	£Good	£Fine	£N.Mint
1-2 ND 146pgs, new art						
	$3.00	$9.00	$15.00	£1.60	£4.80	£8.00
Title Value:	$6.00	$18.00	$30.00	£3.20	£9.60	£16.00
The Big Elfquest Gatherum (Nov 1994)						
selection from the two volumes plus new material Hardcover				£2.70	£8.10	£13.50

ELFQUEST: BLOOD OF TEN CHIEFS

Warp Graphics; 1 Sep 1993-20 Sep 1995

	$Good	$Fine	$N.Mint	£Good	£Fine	£N.Mint
1 ND Richard Pini and Janine Johnson						
	$0.40	$1.20	$2.00	£0.25	£0.75	£1.25
2-20 ND	$0.40	$1.20	$2.00	£0.25	£0.75	£1.25
Title Value:	$8.00	$24.00	$40.00	£5.00	£15.00	£25.00

ELFQUEST: JINK

Warp Graphics; 1 Nov 1994-12 Feb 1996

	$Good	$Fine	$N.Mint	£Good	£Fine	£N.Mint
1-12 ND John Ostrander script						
	$0.50	$1.50	$2.50	£0.30	£0.90	£1.50
Title Value:	$6.00	$18.00	$30.00	£3.60	£10.80	£18.00

ELFQUEST: KAHVI

Warp Graphics,MS; 1 Oct 1995-6 Mar 1996

	$Good	$Fine	$N.Mint	£Good	£Fine	£N.Mint
1-6 ND black and white	$0.45	$1.35	$2.25	£0.30	£0.90	£1.50
Title Value:	$2.70	$8.10	$13.50	£1.80	£5.40	£9.00

ELFQUEST: KINGS OF THE BROKEN WHEEL

Warp Graphics; 1 Aug 1990-9 Dec 1991

	$Good	$Fine	$N.Mint	£Good	£Fine	£N.Mint
1 ND	$0.50	$1.50	$2.50	£0.30	£0.90	£1.50
1 2nd printing ND	$0.40	$1.20	$2.00	£0.25	£0.75	£1.25
2-8 ND	$0.40	$1.20	$2.00	£0.25	£0.75	£1.25
9 ND conclusion of first story	$0.40	$1.20	$2.00	£0.25	£0.75	£1.25
Title Value:	$4.10	$12.30	$20.50	£2.55	£7.65	£12.75

Note: bi-monthly, carries on from Siege at Blue Mountain

ELFQUEST: METAMORPHOSIS

Warp Graphics,OS; 1 Apr 1996

	$Good	$Fine	$N.Mint	£Good	£Fine	£N.Mint
1 ND 48pgs, reprints of past titles and previews of forthcoming titles	$0.60	$1.80	$3.00	£0.40	£1.20	£2.00
Title Value:	$0.60	$1.80	$3.00	£0.40	£1.20	£2.00

ELFQUEST: NEW BLOOD

Warp Graphics,MS; 1 Oct 1992-35 Jan 1996

	$Good	$Fine	$N.Mint	£Good	£Fine	£N.Mint
1 ND 64pgs	$0.80	$2.40	$4.00	£0.50	£1.50	£2.50
2-26 ND	$0.40	$1.20	$2.00	£0.25	£0.75	£1.25
27 ND $2.50 cover begins	$0.50	$1.50	$2.50	£0.30	£0.90	£1.50
28-35 ND	$0.50	$1.50	$2.50	£0.30	£0.90	£1.50
Title Value:	$15.30	$45.90	$76.50	£9.45	£28.35	£47.25
Elfquest: New Blood 1993 Summer Special (Sep 1993) 64pgs, new stories				£1.20	£3.60	£6.00
Elfquest: New Blood Collection (1994) Hard cover edition, collects first five issues				£2.40	£7.20	£12.00

ELFQUEST: REBELS

Warp Graphics; 1 Feb 1995-12 Jan 1996

	$Good	$Fine	$N.Mint	£Good	£Fine	£N.Mint
1-12 ND	$0.50	$1.50	$2.50	£0.30	£0.90	£1.50
Title Value:	$6.00	$18.00	$30.00	£3.60	£10.80	£18.00

ELFQUEST: SHARDS

Warp Graphics; 1 Aug 1994-16 Mar 1996

	$Good	$Fine	$N.Mint	£Good	£Fine	£N.Mint
1 ND continues from Elfquest: The Hidden Years	$0.50	$1.50	$2.50	£0.30	£0.90	£1.50
2-9 ND	$0.50	$1.50	$2.50	£0.30	£0.90	£1.50
10 ND X-over Elfquest: The Hidden Years #23	$0.50	$1.50	$2.50	£0.30	£0.90	£1.50
11-16 ND	$0.50	$1.50	$2.50	£0.30	£0.90	£1.50
Title Value:	$8.00	$24.00	$40.00	£4.80	£14.40	£24.00

ELFQUEST: SIEGE AT BLUE MOUNTAIN

Apple Comics,MS; 1 Mar 1987-8 Dec 1988

	$Good	$Fine	$N.Mint	£Good	£Fine	£N.Mint
1 ND Staton/Pini art begins, black and white	$1.00	$3.00	$5.00	£0.60	£1.80	£3.00
1 2nd printing ND	$0.40	$1.20	$2.00	£0.25	£0.75	£1.25
2 ND	$0.60	$1.80	$3.00	£0.30	£0.90	£1.50
2 2nd printing ND	$0.40	$1.20	$2.00	£0.25	£0.75	£1.25
3-5 ND	$0.50	$1.50	$2.50	£0.30	£0.90	£1.50
6-8 ND	$0.40	$1.20	$2.00	£0.25	£0.75	£1.25
Title Value:	$5.10	$15.30	$25.50	£3.05	£9.15	£15.25

ELFQUEST: THE HIDDEN YEARS

Warp Graphics; 1 Jul 1992-29 Mar 1996

	$Good	$Fine	$N.Mint	£Good	£Fine	£N.Mint
1 ND Richard and Wendy Pini	$0.40	$1.20	$2.00	£0.25	£0.75	£1.25
2-9 ND	$0.40	$1.20	$2.00	£0.25	£0.75	£1.25
9 sub-titled issue ½ ND 48pgs; Wendy Pini and John Byrne	$0.60	$1.80	$3.00	£0.40	£1.20	£2.00
10-14 ND	$0.45	$1.35	$2.25	£0.30	£0.90	£1.50
15 ND 48pgs	$0.80	$2.40	$4.00	£0.50	£1.50	£2.50
16-29 ND	$0.45	$1.35	$2.25	£0.30	£0.90	£1.50
Title Value:	$13.55	$40.65	$67.75	£8.85	£26.55	£44.25
Note: all Non-Distributed on the news-stands in the U.K.						
Elfquest: The Hidden Years Hardcover (1993) collects issues #1-5				£2.40	£7.20	£12.00
Elfquest: Hidden Years - Rogue's Challenge Hardcover (Feb 1994) collects issues #6-9 and #9 ½				£2.70	£8.10	£13.50

ELFQUEST: THE REBELS

Warp Graphics; 1 Nov 1994-12 Mar 1996

	$Good	$Fine	$N.Mint	£Good	£Fine	£N.Mint
1-12 ND	$0.50	$1.50	$2.50	£0.30	£0.90	£1.50
Title Value:	$6.00	$18.00	$30.00	£3.60	£10.80	£18.00

ELFQUEST: TWO SPEAR

Warp Graphics,MS; 1 Oct 1995-5 Feb 1996

	$Good	$Fine	$N.Mint	£Good	£Fine	£N.Mint
1-5 ND Barry Blair art; black and white	$0.45	$1.35	$2.25	£0.30	£0.90	£1.50
Title Value:	$2.25	$6.75	$11.25	£1.50	£4.50	£7.50

ELFQUEST: WAVEDANCERS

Warp Graphics,MS; 1 Apr 1994-6 Mar 1996

	$Good	$Fine	$N.Mint	£Good	£Fine	£N.Mint
1-6 ND	$0.45	$1.35	$2.25	£0.30	£0.90	£1.50
Title Value:	$2.70	$8.10	$13.50	£1.80	£5.40	£9.00

ELFQUEST: WAVERIDERS SPECIAL

Warp Graphics,OS; 1 Feb 1996

	$Good	$Fine	$N.Mint	£Good	£Fine	£N.Mint
1 ND Kathryn Bollinger script, Steve Blevins art	$0.60	$1.80	$3.00	£0.40	£1.20	£2.00
Title Value:	$0.60	$1.80	$3.00	£0.40	£1.20	£2.00

ELIMINATOR

Eternity,MS; 1 Jan 1992-3 Mar 1992

	$Good	$Fine	$N.Mint	£Good	£Fine	£N.Mint
1-3 ND	$0.30	$0.90	$1.50	£0.20	£0.60	£1.00
Title Value:	$0.90	$2.70	$4.50	£0.60	£1.80	£3.00

ELIMINATOR

Malibu Ultraverse; 0 Apr 1995; 1 May 1995-3 Jul 1995

	$Good	$Fine	$N.Mint	£Good	£Fine	£N.Mint
0 ND 40pgs, Godwheel spin-off, Mike Zeck cover and art	$0.40	$1.20	$2.00	£0.25	£0.75	£1.25
1 ND Mike Zeck cover and art; The Search for the Missing Infinity Gem story begins	$0.40	$1.20	$2.00	£0.25	£0.75	£1.25
1 Limited Edition, ND (May 1995) - solid black cover, limited to 5,000 copies	$0.60	$1.80	$3.00	£0.40	£1.20	£2.00
2-3 ND The Search for the Missing Infinity Gem, Mike Zeck cover	$0.40	$1.20	$2.00	£0.25	£0.75	£1.25
Title Value:	$2.20	$6.60	$11.00	£1.40	£4.20	£7.00

Note: no connection to 1st series called Eliminator by Eternity Comics

ELIMINATOR SPECIAL

Eternity,OS; 1 Oct 1991

	$Good	$Fine	$N.Mint	£Good	£Fine	£N.Mint
1 ND	$0.50	$1.50	$2.50	£0.30	£0.90	£1.50
Title Value:	$0.50	$1.50	$2.50	£0.30	£0.90	£1.50

ELITE PRESENTS

Elite Comics; 1 Jan 1987

	$Good	$Fine	$N.Mint	£Good	£Fine	£N.Mint
1 ND Night Wolf by Butch Burcham, colour	$0.30	$0.90	$1.50	£0.20	£0.60	£1.00
Title Value:	$0.30	$0.90	$1.50	£0.20	£0.60	£1.00

ELITE WARRIORS

Alchemy Studios,MS; 1 Sep 1991-2 1992

	$Good	$Fine	$N.Mint	£Good	£Fine	£N.Mint
1-2 ND	$0.30	$0.90	$1.50	£0.20	£0.60	£1.00
Title Value:	$0.60	$1.80	$3.00	£0.40	£1.20	£2.00

ELONGATED MAN

DC Comics,MS; 1 Dec 1991-4 Apr 1992

(see Flash [1st Series] #110)

	$Good	$Fine	$N.Mint	£Good	£Fine	£N.Mint
1	$0.15	$0.45	$0.75	£0.10	£0.35	£0.60
2-3 Flash appears	$0.15	$0.45	$0.75	£0.10	£0.35	£0.60
4	$0.15	$0.45	$0.75	£0.10	£0.35	£0.60
Title Value:	$0.60	$1.80	$3.00	£0.40	£1.40	£2.40

Eighty Page Giant #9

Elektra Saga #1

Elementals (1st) #1

	$Good	$Fine	$N.Mint	£Good	£Fine	£N.Mint
ELRIC OF MELNIBONE						
Pacific; 1 Apr 1983-6 Apr 1984						
1 ND P. Craig Russell art begins	*$0.40*	*$1.20*	*$2.00*	£0.30	£0.90	£1.50
2-6 ND	*$0.40*	*$1.20*	*$2.00*	£0.30	£0.90	£1.50
Title Value:	*$2.40*	*$7.20*	*$12.00*	£1.80	£5.40	£9.00
Trade Paperback (First Publishing), reprints #1-6				£2.20	£6.60	£11.00
ELRIC: ONE LIFE						
Topps,OS; 0 Apr 1996						
0 ND Neil Gaiman script, P.Craig Russell art	*$0.60*	*$1.80*	*$3.00*	£0.40	£1.20	£2.00
Title Value:	*$0.60*	*$1.80*	*$3.00*	£0.40	£1.20	£2.00
ELRIC: SAILOR ON THE SEAS OF FATE						
First,MS; 1 Jun 1985-7 Jun 1986						
1 ND scarce in the U.K. Michael T. Gilbert art begins	*$0.40*	*$1.20*	*$2.00*	£0.40	£1.20	£2.00
2 ND scarce in the U.K.	*$0.40*	*$1.20*	*$2.00*	£0.35	£1.05	£1.75
3-7 ND	*$0.40*	*$1.20*	*$2.00*	£0.30	£0.90	£1.50
Title Value:	*$2.80*	*$8.40*	*$14.00*	£2.25	£6.75	£11.25
Trade Paperback, reprints #1-7				£2.20	£6.60	£11.00
ELRIC: THE BANE OF THE BLACK SWORD						
First,MS; 1 Aug 1988-6 Jun 1989						
1-6 ND Mark Pacella art	*$0.35*	*$1.05*	*$1.75*	£0.25	£0.75	£1.25
Title Value:	*$2.10*	*$6.30*	*$10.50*	£1.50	£4.50	£7.50
ELRIC: THE VANISHING TOWER						
First,MS; 1 Aug 1987-6 Jun 1988						
1-6 ND Jan Duursema art	*$0.35*	*$1.05*	*$1.75*	£0.25	£0.75	£1.25
Title Value:	*$2.10*	*$6.30*	*$10.50*	£1.50	£4.50	£7.50
ELRIC: WEIRD OF THE WHITE WOLF						
First,MS; 1 Oct 1986-5 Jun 1987						
1-5 ND Michael T. Gilbert art	*$0.35*	*$1.05*	*$1.75*	£0.25	£0.75	£1.25
Title Value:	*$1.75*	*$5.25*	*$8.75*	£1.25	£3.75	£6.25
ELSEWHERE PRINCE						
Marvel Comics Group/Epic,MS; 1 May 1990-6 Oct 1990						
1-6 ND Moebius/Lofficier/Shanower art/script	*$0.35*	*$1.05*	*$1.75*	£0.25	£0.75	£1.25
Title Value:	*$2.10*	*$6.30*	*$10.50*	£1.50	£4.50	£7.50
ELVEN						
Malibu Ultraverse,MS; 0 Oct 1994; 1 Feb 1995-4 May 1995						
0 ND 48pgs, reprints Ultraverse Premiere material with new Norm Breyfogle sketches	*$0.50*	*$1.50*	*$2.50*	£0.30	£0.90	£1.50
1 ND Prime appears	*$0.40*	*$1.20*	*$2.00*	£0.25	£0.75	£1.25
1 Limited Edition, ND (Feb 1995) - green foil logo	*$0.50*	*$1.50*	*$2.50*	£0.50	£1.50	£2.50
2-4 ND	*$0.40*	*$1.20*	*$2.00*	£0.25	£0.75	£1.25
Title Value:	*$2.60*	*$7.80*	*$13.00*	£1.80	£5.40	£9.00
ELVIRA'S HOUSE OF MYSTERY						
DC Comics; 1 Jan 1986-11 Jan 1987						
(see House of Mystery)						
1 64pgs, Bolland cover, photo back cover	*$0.30*	*$0.90*	*$1.50*	£0.20	£0.60	£1.00
2-5	*$0.25*	*$0.75*	*$1.25*	£0.15	£0.45	£0.75
6 entire issue reads sideways	*$0.25*	*$0.75*	*$1.25*	£0.15	£0.45	£0.75
7 sci-fi issue	*$0.25*	*$0.75*	*$1.25*	£0.15	£0.45	£0.75
8	*$0.25*	*$0.75*	*$1.25*	£0.15	£0.45	£0.75
9 photo cover	*$0.25*	*$0.75*	*$1.25*	£0.15	£0.45	£0.75
10-11	*$0.25*	*$0.75*	*$1.25*	£0.15	£0.45	£0.75
Title Value:	*$2.80*	*$8.40*	*$14.00*	£1.70	£5.10	£8.50
ELVIRA'S HOUSE OF MYSTERY SPECIAL						
DC Comics,OS; 1 Mar 1987						
1 48pgs	*$0.30*	*$0.90*	*$1.50*	£0.20	£0.60	£1.00
Title Value:	*$0.30*	*$0.90*	*$1.50*	£0.20	£0.60	£1.00
Note: cover labelled "Haunted Holidays".						
ELVIRA, MISTRESS OF THE DARK						
Claypool Comics; 1 May 1993-present						
1 ND photo cover	*$0.50*	*$1.50*	*$2.50*	£0.30	£0.90	£1.50
2-15 ND	*$0.50*	*$1.50*	*$2.50*	£0.25	£0.75	£1.25
16-38 ND	*$0.50*	*$1.50*	*$2.50*	£0.30	£0.90	£1.50
39 ND	*$0.60*	*$1.80*	*$3.00*	£0.40	£1.20	£2.00
40-42 ND	*$0.50*	*$1.50*	*$2.50*	£0.30	£0.90	£1.50
Title Value:	*$21.10*	*$63.30*	*$105.50*	£12.00	£36.00	£60.00
EMERALDAS						
Eternity,MS; 1 Jan 1991-4 Apr 1991						
1-4 ND	*$0.30*	*$0.90*	*$1.50*	£0.20	£0.60	£1.00
Title Value:	*$1.20*	*$3.60*	*$6.00*	£0.80	£2.40	£4.00
EMERGENCY						
Charlton,Magazine; 1 Jun 1976-4 Jan 1977						
1 Neal Adams art	*$0.50*	*$1.50*	*$3.00*	£0.65	£2.00	£4.00
2 Neal Adams art	*$0.30*	*$1.00*	*$2.00*	£0.40	£1.25	£2.50
3-4	*$0.30*	*$1.00*	*$2.00*	£0.40	£1.25	£2.50
Title Value:	*$1.40*	*$4.50*	*$9.00*	£1.85	£5.75	£11.50
Note: from TV series Limited Distribution on the news-stands in the U.K.						
EMERGENCY (2ND SERIES)						
Charlton, TV; 1 Jun 1976-4 Dec 1976						
1 ND John Byrne art	*$0.80*	*$2.50*	*$5.00*	£0.55	£1.75	£3.50
2-4 distributed in the U.K.	*$0.50*	*$1.50*	*$3.00*	£0.30	£1.00	£2.00
Title Value:	*$2.30*	*$7.00*	*$14.00*	£1.45	£4.75	£9.50
EMMA DAVENPORT						
Lohman Hills Press; 1 Oct 1995-present						
1-8 ND Gina and Richie Prosch script and art; black and white	*$0.55*	*$1.65*	*$2.75*	£0.35	£1.05	£1.75
Title Value:	*$4.40*	*$13.20*	*$22.00*	£2.80	£8.40	£14.00
EMPIRE						
Eternity; 1 Mar 1988-4 1988						
1-4 ND	*$0.35*	*$1.05*	*$1.75*	£0.25	£0.75	£1.25
Title Value:	*$1.40*	*$4.20*	*$7.00*	£1.00	£3.00	£5.00
EMPIRE LANES						
Northern Lights; 1 Dec 1986-4 Aug 1987						
1-4 ND black and white	*$0.35*	*$1.05*	*$1.75*	£0.25	£0.75	£1.25
Title Value:	*$1.40*	*$4.20*	*$7.00*	£1.00	£3.00	£5.00
Collected (Dec 1989)				£0.40	£1.20	£2.00
EMPIRE LANES (2ND SERIES)						
Comico; 1 Dec 1989						
1 ND 48pgs, squarebound	*$0.40*	*$1.20*	*$2.00*	£0.25	£0.75	£1.25
Title Value:	*$0.40*	*$1.20*	*$2.00*	£0.25	£0.75	£1.25
EMPIRE LANES (ONE SHOT)						
Comico,OS; 1 May 1990						
1 ND 48pgs, squarebound	*$0.40*	*$1.20*	*$2.00*	£0.25	£0.75	£1.25
Title Value:	*$0.40*	*$1.20*	*$2.00*	£0.25	£0.75	£1.25
ENCHANTER						
Eclipse; 1 Apr 1987-3 Aug 1987						
(cancelled 12 issue series)						
1-3 ND	*$0.35*	*$1.05*	*$1.75*	£0.25	£0.75	£1.25
Title Value:	*$1.05*	*$3.15*	*$5.25*	£0.75	£2.25	£3.75
ENDLESS GALLERY, THE						
DC Comics,OS; 1 May 1995						
1 ND pin-ups of Sandman characters by a variety of artists including Capullo, Chaykin and Al Davison	*$0.80*	*$2.40*	*$4.00*	£0.50	£1.50	£2.50
Title Value:	*$0.80*	*$2.40*	*$4.00*	£0.50	£1.50	£2.50
ENEMY						
Dark Horse,MS; 1 May 1994-5 Sep 1994						
1-5 ND Mike Zeck covers	*$0.50*	*$1.50*	*$2.50*	£0.30	£0.90	£1.50
Title Value:	*$2.50*	*$7.50*	*$12.50*	£1.50	£4.50	£7.50
Enemy						
Trade paperback ND120pgs, collects mini-series				£2.00	£6.00	£10.00
ENEMY ACE SPECIAL						
DC Comics,OS; 1 1990						
(see Star Spangled War Stories #138)						
1 LD in the U.K. reprints Our Army At War #151, #153 (1st and 2nd appearances), Joe Kubert cover	*$0.35*	*$1.05*	*$1.75*	£0.25	£0.75	£1.25
Title Value:	*$0.35*	*$1.05*	*$1.75*	£0.25	£0.75	£1.25
ENEMY ACE: WAR IDYLL						
DC Comics; nn Jan 1991						
Hardcover Graphic Novel						
nn Jan 1991 128pgs, George Pratt painted art				£2.40	£7.20	£12.00
Softcover Graphic Novel						
nn Jul 1991 128pgs, George Pratt painted art				£1.80	£5.40	£9.00
Signed, Limited Edition (Nov 1991),						
16 pages of new text/illustrations limited to 2,000 copies				£9.50	£28.50	£47.50
ENIGMA						
DC Comics/Vertigo,MS; 1 Mar 1993-8 Oct 1993						
1 ND Peter Milligan script, Duncan Fegredo art and painted covers	*$0.50*	*$1.50*	*$2.50*	£0.30	£0.90	£1.50
2-8 ND	*$0.50*	*$1.50*	*$2.50*	£0.30	£0.90	£1.50
Title Value:	*$4.00*	*$12.00*	*$20.00*	£2.40	£7.20	£12.00
Enigma (Sep 1995) Trade paperback						
reprints mini-series with new Duncan Fegredo cover				£2.70	£8.10	£13.50
ENTERPRISE LOGS						
Golden Press; 1-4 1976						
1 ND very scarce in the U.K. 233pgs, compilation of Gold Key Star Trek issues #1-8 plus Kirk's psychofile, starship portrait and Scotty's diary	*$6.50*	*$20.00*	*$40.00*	£4.55	£13.50	£27.50
2 ND scarce in the U.K. 224pgs, compilation of Gold Key Star Trek issues #9-17	*$4.15*	*$12.50*	*$25.00*	£2.90	£8.75	£17.50
3 ND scarce in the U.K. 224pgs, compilation of Gold Key Star Trek issues #18-26 plus Spock's psychofile	*$4.15*	*$12.50*	*$25.00*	£2.90	£8.75	£17.50
4 ND scarce in the U.K. 224pgs, compilation of Gold Key Star Trek issues #27,28,30,31,32,34,36 and 38 plus Enterprise history	*$4.15*	*$12.50*	*$25.00*	£2.90	£8.75	£17.50
Title Value:	*$18.95*	*$57.50*	*$115.00*	£13.25	£39.75	£80.00
EO						
Rebel Studios,MS; 1 Jun 1992-2 1992						
1 ND Tim Vigil art, oversized format, wraparound cover	*$2.00*	*$6.00*	*$10.00*	£1.20	£3.60	£6.00
1 2nd printing, ND (Aug 1994)	*$0.60*	*$1.80*	*$3.00*	£0.40	£1.20	£2.00
1 Signed Edition, ND (Aug 1992) - cardstock cover, signed by Tim Vigil, 2,000 copies	*$8.00*	*$24.00*	*$40.00*	£3.50	£10.50	£17.50
2 ND Tim Vigil art	*$1.20*	*$3.60*	*$6.00*	£0.80	£2.40	£4.00
Title Value:	*$11.80*	*$35.40*	*$59.00*	£5.90	£17.70	£29.50
EPIC						
Marvel Comics Group,MS; 1 Jun 1992-4 Sep 1992						

	$Good	$Fine	$N.Mint	£Good	£Fine	£N.Mint
1 ND 48pgs, squarebound, anthology (Nightbreed/Stalkers/Wild Cards/Sleeze Brothers begin), Dave McKean cover	***$0.90***	***$2.70***	***$4.50***	**£0.60**	**£1.80**	**£3.00**
2 ND 48pgs, squarebound, anthology, Dave Dorman cover	***$0.90***	***$2.70***	***$4.50***	**£0.60**	**£1.80**	**£3.00**
3-4 ND 48pgs, squarebound, anthology, Dougie Braithwaite cover	***$0.90***	***$2.70***	***$4.50***	**£0.60**	**£1.80**	**£3.00**
Title Value:	***$3.60***	***$10.80***	***$18.00***	**£2.40**	**£7.20**	**£12.00**

EPIC ILLUSTRATED

Marvel Comics Group,Magazine; 1 Spring 1980-34 Feb 1986

	$Good	$Fine	$N.Mint	£Good	£Fine	£N.Mint
1 ND Silver Surfer story, Buscema art, cover by Frazetta	***$0.80***	***$2.40***	***$4.00***	**£1.00**	**£3.00**	**£5.00**
2 ND Chaykin, Veitch and Bissette art, Corben cover	***$0.60***	***$1.80***	***$3.00***	**£0.50**	**£1.50**	**£2.50**
3 ND Elric, Russell and Golden art, Gulacy cover and art	***$0.60***	***$1.80***	***$3.00***	**£0.50**	**£1.50**	**£2.50**
4 ND Elric, Russell art	***$0.60***	***$1.80***	***$3.00***	**£0.50**	**£1.50**	**£2.50**
5 ND Veitch art	***$0.60***	***$1.80***	***$3.00***	**£0.50**	**£1.50**	**£2.50**
6 ND Bissette and Veitch art, Neal Adams cover	***$0.60***	***$1.80***	***$3.00***	**£0.50**	**£1.50**	**£2.50**
7 ND Neal Adams and John Bolton art, Barry Smith interview and cover	***$0.60***	***$1.80***	***$3.00***	**£0.60**	**£1.80**	**£3.00**
8 ND Suydam and Vess art, Chaykin cover	***$0.60***	***$1.80***	***$3.00***	**£0.50**	**£1.50**	**£2.50**
9 ND	***$0.60***	***$1.80***	***$3.00***	**£0.50**	**£1.50**	**£2.50**
10 ND Bolton cover and art	***$0.60***	***$1.80***	***$3.00***	**£0.50**	**£1.50**	**£2.50**
11 ND scarce in the U.K. Bolton art, Brunner cover	***$0.50***	***$1.50***	***$2.50***	**£0.60**	**£1.80**	**£3.00**
12 ND Wolverton Spacehawk reprint edited and re-coloured, Wolverton articl; John Bolton art	***$0.50***	***$1.50***	***$2.50***	**£0.50**	**£1.50**	**£2.50**
13 ND	***$0.50***	***$1.50***	***$2.50***	**£0.50**	**£1.50**	**£2.50**
14 ND Elric by Russell, Revenge of the Jedi preview, P. Craig Russell cover	***$0.50***	***$1.50***	***$2.50***	**£0.50**	**£1.50**	**£2.50**
15 ND scarce in the U.K. Bolton and Corben art, Boris Vallejo cover and interview, tie-in with Dreadstar #1, Dreadstar by Jim Starlin	***$0.50***	***$1.50***	***$2.50***	**£0.70**	**£2.10**	**£3.50**
16 ND Barry Smith cover/art, Dave Sim art	***$0.50***	***$1.50***	***$2.50***	**£0.60**	**£1.80**	**£3.00**
17 ND Scott Hampton art, Walt Simonson art	***$0.50***	***$1.50***	***$2.50***	**£0.50**	**£1.50**	**£2.50**
18 ND John Bolton cover and art	***$0.50***	***$1.50***	***$2.50***	**£0.50**	**£1.50**	**£2.50**
19 ND Bode, Muth, Smith and Jones art, Steranko cover	***$0.50***	***$1.50***	***$2.50***	**£0.50**	**£1.50**	**£2.50**
20 ND Muth, Williams and Pratt art	***$0.50***	***$1.50***	***$2.50***	**£0.50**	**£1.50**	**£2.50**
21 ND Muth art	***$0.50***	***$1.50***	***$2.50***	**£0.40**	**£1.20**	**£2.00**
22 ND Sienkiewicz art, John Bolton cover	***$0.50***	***$1.50***	***$2.50***	**£0.40**	**£1.20**	**£2.00**
23 ND Bode art, John Bolton cover	***$0.50***	***$1.50***	***$2.50***	**£0.40**	**£1.20**	**£2.00**
24-25 ND	***$0.50***	***$1.50***	***$2.50***	**£0.40**	**£1.20**	**£2.00**
26 ND "The Last Galactus story" by John Byrne begins, ends #34; Dave Sim Cerebus story, Sienkiewicz cover	***$0.50***	***$1.50***	***$2.50***	**£0.80**	**£2.40**	**£4.00**
27 ND Galactus by John Byrne, Groo by Aragones, Bode art	***$0.50***	***$1.50***	***$2.50***	**£0.60**	**£1.80**	**£3.00**
28 ND Cerebus by Sim, Galactus by John Byrne	***$0.50***	***$1.50***	***$2.50***	**£0.60**	**£1.80**	**£3.00**
29 ND scarce in the U.K. Galactus by John Byrne	***$0.50***	***$1.50***	***$2.50***	**£0.80**	**£2.40**	**£4.00**
30 ND Cerebus by Sim, Galactus by John Byrne	***$0.50***	***$1.50***	***$2.50***	**£0.60**	**£1.80**	**£3.00**
31 ND Galactus by John Byrne, John Bolton cover	***$0.50***	***$1.50***	***$2.50***	**£0.60**	**£1.80**	**£3.00**
32 ND Cerebus by Sim, Galactus by John Byrne	***$0.50***	***$1.50***	***$2.50***	**£0.60**	**£1.80**	**£3.00**
33 ND scarce in the U.K. Galactus by John Byrne, Kent Williams art, Totleben cover	***$0.50***	***$1.50***	***$2.50***	**£0.80**	**£2.40**	**£4.00**
34 ND very scarce in the U.K. Alan Moore script, Wrightson, Barry Smith, Sienkiewicz art, Suydam cover	***$0.50***	***$1.50***	***$2.50***	**£1.20**	**£3.60**	**£6.00**
Title Value:	***$18.20***	***$54.60***	***$91.00***	**£19.60**	**£58.80**	**£98.00**

ARTISTS

Bissette in 2,6. Bolton in 7, 10-12, 15, 24, 25, 31. Conrad in 7-9. Potts in 1, 13. P. Craig Russell in 2, 9, 33. Starlin in 1-9, 14, 34. Steacy in 4, 6. Suydam in 1, 8, 10, 13, 14, 34. Veitch in 2, 4-6, 8, 28, 29, 34. Vess in 5, 8-10, 16, 21, 22, 24, 27. Wrightson in 22, 25.

FEATURES

Abraxas by Veitch in 10-17. Almuric by Tim Conrad in 2-5. Elric stories (by P. Craig Russell) in 3, 4, 14. Generation Zero by Pepe Moreno in 17-24. Last Galactus story in 26-34 (all by Byrne). Last of the Dragons by Carl Potts in 15-20. Marada the She-Wolf by Bolton in 10-12, 22, 23. Sacred and Profane by Ken Steacy in 20-25. Weirdworld in 9.

EPIC LITE

Marvel Comics Group,OS; 1 Sep 1991

	$Good	$Fine	$N.Mint	£Good	£Fine	£N.Mint
1 ND anthology of humour stories	***$0.90***	***$2.70***	***$4.50***	**£0.50**	**£1.50**	**£2.50**
Title Value:	***$0.90***	***$2.70***	***$4.50***	**£0.50**	**£1.50**	**£2.50**

EPICURUS THE SAGE

DC Comics/Piranha Press; 1 1990;2 Aug 1991

	$Good	$Fine	$N.Mint	£Good	£Fine	£N.Mint
1 ND	***$2.00***	***$6.00***	***$10.00***	**£1.30**	**£3.90**	**£6.50**
1 2nd printing ND	***$1.80***	***$5.25***	***$9.00***	**£1.20**	**£3.60**	**£6.00**
2 ND 48pgs	***$1.60***	***$4.80***	***$8.00***	**£1.00**	**£3.00**	**£5.00**
Title Value:	***$5.40***	***$16.05***	***$27.00***	**£3.50**	**£10.50**	**£17.50**

EPSILON WAVE, THE

Independent Comics Group; 1 Oct 1985-2 Dec 1985

	$Good	$Fine	$N.Mint	£Good	£Fine	£N.Mint
1-2 ND colour	***$0.25***	***$0.75***	***$1.25***	**£0.15**	**£0.45**	**£0.75**
Title Value:	***$0.50***	***$1.50***	***$2.50***	**£0.30**	**£0.90**	**£1.50**

EQUINOX CHRONICLES

Innovation,MS; 1 Spring 1991-2 Summer 1991

	$Good	$Fine	$N.Mint	£Good	£Fine	£N.Mint
1-2 ND black and white	***$0.35***	***$1.05***	***$1.75***	**£0.25**	**£0.75**	**£1.25**
Title Value:	***$0.70***	***$2.10***	***$3.50***	**£0.50**	**£1.50**	**£2.50**

EQUINOX CHRONICLES SPECIAL EDITION

Gauntlet Comics/Caliber Press; 1 Aug 1993;2 1993

	$Good	$Fine	$N.Mint	£Good	£Fine	£N.Mint
1 ND 64pgs, Blind Faith; reprints previous series	***$0.50***	***$1.50***	***$2.50***	**£0.30**	**£0.90**	**£1.50**
2 ND 64pgs, Circumstantial Saviours; reprints previous series	***$0.50***	***$1.50***	***$2.50***	**£0.30**	**£0.90**	**£1.50**
Title Value:	***$1.00***	***$3.00***	***$5.00***	**£0.60**	**£1.80**	**£3.00**

ERADICATOR

DC Comics,MS; 1 Aug 1996-3 Oct 1996

	$Good	$Fine	$N.Mint	£Good	£Fine	£N.Mint
1 ND Superman spin-off	***$0.35***	***$1.05***	***$1.75***	**£0.25**	**£0.75**	**£1.25**
2-3 ND	***$0.35***	***$1.05***	***$1.75***	**£0.25**	**£0.75**	**£1.25**
Title Value:	***$1.05***	***$3.15***	***$5.25***	**£0.75**	**£2.25**	**£3.75**

ERADICATORS (2ND SERIES)

Greater Mercury Comics; 1 Jul 1990-6 Dec 1990

	$Good	$Fine	$N.Mint	£Good	£Fine	£N.Mint
1-6 ND black and white	***$0.25***	***$0.75***	***$1.25***	**£0.15**	**£0.45**	**£0.75**
Title Value:	***$1.50***	***$4.50***	***$7.50***	**£0.90**	**£2.70**	**£4.50**

ERADICATORS, THE

Silverwolf/Greater Mercury; 1-8 1986?

	$Good	$Fine	$N.Mint	£Good	£Fine	£N.Mint
1 ND Ron Lim 1st pro work in comics	***$0.50***	***$1.50***	***$2.50***	**£0.30**	**£0.90**	**£1.50**
1 2nd printing ND	***$0.40***	***$1.20***	***$2.00***	**£0.25**	**£0.75**	**£1.25**
2 ND	***$0.40***	***$1.20***	***$2.00***	**£0.25**	**£0.75**	**£1.25**
3 ND Tim Vigil art	***$0.40***	***$1.20***	***$2.00***	**£0.25**	**£0.75**	**£1.25**
4-8 ND	***$0.30***	***$0.90***	***$1.50***	**£0.20**	**£0.60**	**£1.00**
Title Value:	***$3.20***	***$9.60***	***$16.00***	**£2.05**	**£6.15**	**£10.25**

EREWHON

Tome Press,OS; 1 1992

	$Good	$Fine	$N.Mint	£Good	£Fine	£N.Mint
1 ND based on book by Samuel Butler, black and white	***$0.60***	***$1.80***	***$3.00***	**£0.40**	**£1.20**	**£2.00**
Title Value:	***$0.60***	***$1.80***	***$3.00***	**£0.40**	**£1.20**	**£2.00**

EROTIC WORLDS OF FRANK THORNE, THE

Eros Comix,MS; 1 Oct 1990-6 1991

	$Good	$Fine	$N.Mint	£Good	£Fine	£N.Mint
1-6 ND adult material; black and white	***$0.50***	***$1.50***	***$2.50***	**£0.30**	**£0.90**	**£1.50**
Title Value:	***$3.00***	***$9.00***	***$15.00***	**£1.80**	**£5.40**	**£9.00**

Note: hot and tame covers of issue 1 available

ERT! NOT AVAILABLE COMICS 1987-1994 GRAPHIC NOVEL

Caliber Press,OS; nn Jul 1995

	$Good	$Fine	$N.Mint	£Good	£Fine	£N.Mint
nn ND 112pgs, collected strips by Matt Feazell; black and white	***$2.60***	***$7.75***	***$13.00***	**£1.70**	**£5.00**	**£8.50**
Title Value:	***$2.60***	***$7.75***	***$13.00***	**£1.70**	**£5.00**	**£8.50**

ESC

Comico; 1 Aug 1996-present

	$Good	$Fine	$N.Mint	£Good	£Fine	£N.Mint
1-2 ND Stefan Petrucha script, Marc Caribe art and Miran Kim covers	***$0.60***	***$1.80***	***$3.00***	**£0.40**	**£1.20**	**£2.00**
Title Value:	***$1.20***	***$3.60***	***$6.00***	**£0.80**	**£2.40**	**£4.00**

ESCAPE FROM THE PLANET OF THE APES GRAPHIC NOVEL

Adventure,OS; 1 Jul 1991

	$Good	$Fine	$N.Mint	£Good	£Fine	£N.Mint
1 ND reprints original material from Marvel Comics published in the 1970s	***$1.50***	***$4.50***	***$7.50***	**£1.00**	**£3.00**	**£5.00**
Title Value:	***$1.50***	***$4.50***	***$7.50***	**£1.00**	**£3.00**	**£5.00**

ESCAPE TO THE STARS

Solson Publications/Visionary; 1 1987-7 1988

	$Good	$Fine	$N.Mint	£Good	£Fine	£N.Mint
1-7 ND Rich Buckler art	***$0.25***	***$0.75***	***$1.25***	**£0.15**	**£0.45**	**£0.75**
Title Value:	***$1.75***	***$5.25***	***$8.75***	**£1.05**	**£3.15**	**£5.25**

ESCAPE TO THE STARS (2ND SERIES)

Visionary; 1,2 1988

	$Good	$Fine	$N.Mint	£Good	£Fine	£N.Mint
1-2 ND	***$0.15***	***$0.45***	***$0.75***	**£0.10**	**£0.35**	**£0.60**
Title Value:	***$0.30***	***$0.90***	***$1.50***	**£0.20**	**£0.70**	**£1.20**

ESCAPE VELOCITY

Escape Velocity Press; 1 1986

	$Good	$Fine	$N.Mint	£Good	£Fine	£N.Mint
1 ND black and white	***$0.25***	***$0.75***	***$1.25***	**£0.15**	**£0.45**	**£0.75**
Title Value:	***$0.25***	***$0.75***	***$1.25***	**£0.15**	**£0.45**	**£0.75**

ESPERS

Eclipse; 1 Jul 1986-5 Apr 1987

(see Interface)

	$Good	$Fine	$N.Mint	£Good	£Fine	£N.Mint
1-4 ND David Lloyd art	***$0.35***	***$1.05***	***$1.75***	**£0.25**	**£0.75**	**£1.25**
5 ND John Burns art	***$0.35***	***$1.05***	***$1.75***	**£0.25**	**£0.75**	**£1.25**
Title Value:	***$1.75***	***$5.25***	***$8.75***	**£1.25**	**£3.75**	**£6.25**

Note: pre-figures Marvel series Interface

Espers (Oct 1990) Trade paperback

	$Good	$Fine	$N.Mint	£Good	£Fine	£N.Mint
ND 128pgs, reprints mini-series				£1.10	£3.30	£5.50

Espers Graphic Novel (Dec 1995)

	$Good	$Fine	$N.Mint	£Good	£Fine	£N.Mint
ND re-published by Caliber Press				£1.70	£5.10	£8.50

ESPERS (2ND SERIES)

Halloween Comics; 1 1996-present

	$Good	$Fine	$N.Mint	£Good	£Fine	£N.Mint
1-4 ND James Hudnall script; black and white						
	$0.60	$1.80	$3.00	£0.40	£1.20	£2.00
Title Value:	$2.40	$7.20	$12.00	£1.60	£4.80	£8.00

ESSENTIAL VERTIGO: SWAMP THING

DC Comics; 1 Nov 1996-present

	$Good	$Fine	$N.Mint	£Good	£Fine	£N.Mint
1 ND 24pgs, reprints begin from Swamp Thing #21 with classic Alan Moore scripts; black and white begins						
	$0.40	$1.20	$2.00	£0.25	£0.75	£1.25
2-6 ND 24pgs	$0.40	$1.20	$2.00	£0.25	£0.75	£1.25
Title Value:	$2.40	$7.20	$12.00	£1.50	£4.50	£7.50

ESSENTIAL VERTIGO: THE SANDMAN

DC Comics; 1 Aug 1996-present

	$Good	$Fine	$N.Mint	£Good	£Fine	£N.Mint
1 ND reprints begin from Sandman #1 - cool!						
	$0.40	$1.20	$2.00	£0.30	£0.90	£1.50
2-3 ND	$0.40	$1.20	$2.00	£0.25	£0.75	£1.25
4 ND The Demon appears						
	$0.40	$1.20	$2.00	£0.25	£0.75	£1.25
5-8 ND	$0.40	$1.20	$2.00	£0.25	£0.75	£1.25
Title Value:	$3.20	$9.60	$16.00	£2.05	£6.15	£10.25

ETC

DC Comics/Piranha Press,MS; 1 1989-5 1989

	$Good	$Fine	$N.Mint	£Good	£Fine	£N.Mint
1-5 ND 48pgs, squarebound; Tim Conrad script, Michael Davis painted art						
	$0.80	$2.40	$4.00	£0.50	£1.50	£2.50
Title Value:	$4.00	$12.00	$20.00	£2.50	£7.50	£12.50

ETERNAL WARRIOR YEARBOOK

Valiant; 1 Dec 1993;2 Mar 1995

	$Good	$Fine	$N.Mint	£Good	£Fine	£N.Mint
1 ND 48pgs, painted art						
	$0.70	$2.10	$3.50	£0.40	£1.20	£2.00
2 ND 48pgs	$0.70	$2.10	$3.50	£0.40	£1.20	£2.00
Title Value:	$1.40	$4.20	$7.00	£0.80	£2.40	£4.00

ETERNAL WARRIOR, THE

Valiant/Acclaim Comics; 1 Aug 1992-50 1996

	$Good	$Fine	$N.Mint	£Good	£Fine	£N.Mint
1 Unity: Chapter 2	$0.70	$2.10	$3.50	£0.40	£1.20	£2.00
1 Gold Edition (embossed), embossed foil logo						
	$1.50	$4.50	$7.50	£1.00	£3.00	£5.00
1 Gold Edition (flat)	$2.50	$7.50	$12.50	£1.50	£4.50	£7.50
2 Unity: Chapter 10, Archer and Sting appear, Walt Simonson cover						
	$0.50	$1.50	$2.50	£0.30	£0.90	£1.50
3	$0.50	$1.50	$2.50	£0.30	£0.90	£1.50
4 joint 1st appearance Bloodshot cameo (see Rai #0)						
	$0.80	$2.40	$4.00	£0.40	£1.20	£2.00
5 1st full appearance Bloodshot						
	$0.60	$1.80	$3.00	£0.40	£1.20	£2.00
6 Barry Windsor-Smith scripts begin						
	$0.50	$1.50	$2.50	£0.30	£0.90	£1.50
7	$0.50	$1.50	$2.50	£0.30	£0.90	£1.50
8 48pgs, special dual-issue with Archer & Armstrong #8 (note: there is only one single issue, not two different ones therefore cross-refer to Archer & Armstrong); 1st appearance Ivar						
	$0.70	$2.10	$3.50	£0.40	£1.20	£2.00
9-10 The Book of the Geomancer story						
	$0.50	$1.50	$2.50	£0.30	£0.90	£1.50
11-15	$0.40	$1.20	$2.00	£0.25	£0.75	£1.25
16 Empirical Dynasty Prologue, continued in Secret Weapons #3						
	$0.40	$1.20	$2.00	£0.25	£0.75	£1.25
17 Master D'Arque appears						
	$0.40	$1.20	$2.00	£0.25	£0.75	£1.25
18 Dr. Mirage cameo						
	$0.40	$1.20	$2.00	£0.25	£0.75	£1.25
19 Dr. Mirage appears						
	$0.40	$1.20	$2.00	£0.25	£0.75	£1.25
20-23	$0.40	$1.20	$2.00	£0.25	£0.75	£1.25
24 features The Immortal Enemy						
	$0.40	$1.20	$2.00	£0.25	£0.75	£1.25
25 continued from Archer & Armstrong #25						
	$0.40	$1.20	$2.00	£0.25	£0.75	£1.25
26 Chaos Effect X-over; flip side Archer & Armstrong #26						
	$0.40	$1.20	$2.00	£0.25	£0.75	£1.25
27-34	$0.40	$1.20	$2.00	£0.25	£0.75	£1.25
35 1st Acclaim Comics issue; Paul Gulacy cover, shipped in a cover wrapper to obscure the graphic cover image; bi-weekly						
	$0.40	$1.20	$2.00	£0.25	£0.75	£1.25
36 Paul Gulacy cover and art; bi-weekly						
	$0.40	$1.20	$2.00	£0.25	£0.75	£1.25
37-42 bi-weekly	$0.40	$1.20	$2.00	£0.25	£0.75	£1.25
43-44 Jackson Guice art; bi-weekly						
	$0.40	$1.20	$2.00	£0.25	£0.75	£1.25
45 bi-weekly	$0.40	$1.20	$2.00	£0.25	£0.75	£1.25
46 bi-weekly	$0.45	$1.35	$2.25	£0.30	£0.90	£1.50
47-50 Jackson Guice art; bi-weekly						
	$0.45	$1.35	$2.25	£0.30	£0.90	£1.50
Title Value:	$26.05	$78.15	$130.25	£16.15	£48.45	£80.75

Note: all Non-Distributed on the news-stands in the U.K.

ETERNAL WARRIOR: FIST AND STEEL

Acclaim Comics,MS; 1,2 Jan 1996

	$Good	$Fine	$N.Mint	£Good	£Fine	£N.Mint
1-2 ND Jerry Prosser script, Hannibal King art; bi-weekly						
	$0.50	$1.50	$2.50	£0.30	£0.90	£1.50
Title Value:	$1.00	$3.00	$5.00	£0.60	£1.80	£3.00

ETERNAL WARRIOR: THE WINGS OF JUSTICE

Valiant/Acclaim Comics,OS; 1 Oct 1995

	$Good	$Fine	$N.Mint	£Good	£Fine	£N.Mint
1 ND Geomancer appears						
	$0.50	$1.50	$2.50	£0.30	£0.90	£1.50
Title Value:	$0.50	$1.50	$2.50	£0.30	£0.90	£1.50

ETERNALS ANNUAL, THE

Marvel Comics Group; 1 Oct 1977

	$Good	$Fine	$N.Mint	£Good	£Fine	£N.Mint
1 ND 52pgs, Jack Kirby art						
	$0.55	$1.75	$3.50	£0.25	£0.85	£1.75
Title Value:	$0.55	$1.75	$3.50	£0.25	£0.85	£1.75

ETERNALS GIANT SIZE SPECTACULAR

Marvel Comics Group,OS; 1 Nov 1991

	$Good	$Fine	$N.Mint	£Good	£Fine	£N.Mint
1 ND 64pgs, squarebound, many copies have crinkled spines; "The Herod Factor" story						
	$0.50	$1.50	$2.50	£0.30	£0.90	£1.50
Title Value:	$0.50	$1.50	$2.50	£0.30	£0.90	£1.50

ETERNALS, THE

Marvel Comics Group; 1 Jul 1976-19 Jan 1978

	$Good	$Fine	$N.Mint	£Good	£Fine	£N.Mint
1 origin	$1.00	$3.00	$6.00	£0.40	£1.25	£2.50
2 1st appearance The Celestials						
	$0.65	$2.00	$4.00	£0.25	£0.85	£1.75
3-13	$0.55	$1.75	$3.50	£0.25	£0.75	£1.50
14-15 Eternals vs. Hulk (cosmic-powered)						
	$0.50	$1.50	$3.00	£0.25	£0.75	£1.50
16-18	$0.50	$1.50	$3.00	£0.25	£0.75	£1.50
19 ND scarce in the U.K.						
	$0.50	$1.50	$3.00	£0.40	£1.25	£2.50
Title Value:	$10.70	$33.25	$62.50	£5.05	£15.35	£30.75

Note: all Jack Kirby art.

ETERNALS, THE (LIMITED SERIES)

Marvel Comics Group,MS; 1 Oct 1985-12 Sep 1986

	$Good	$Fine	$N.Mint	£Good	£Fine	£N.Mint
1 ND DS	$0.40	$1.20	$2.00	£0.25	£0.75	£1.25
2-8 ND	$0.30	$0.90	$1.50	£0.20	£0.60	£1.00
9-11 ND Walt Simonson script						
	$0.30	$0.90	$1.50	£0.20	£0.60	£1.00
12 ND DS Walt Simonson script, West Coast Avengers appear						
	$0.40	$1.20	$2.00	£0.25	£0.75	£1.25
Title Value:	$3.80	$11.40	$19.00	£2.50	£7.50	£12.50

ETERNITY SMITH

Renegade; 1 Sep 1986-5 May 1987

	$Good	$Fine	$N.Mint	£Good	£Fine	£N.Mint
1-5 ND Rick Hoberg art, colour						
	$0.30	$0.90	$1.50	£0.20	£0.60	£1.00
Title Value:	$1.50	$4.50	$7.50	£1.00	£3.00	£5.00

ETERNITY SMITH (2ND SERIES)

Hero; 1 Sep 1987-10 Jun 1988

	$Good	$Fine	$N.Mint	£Good	£Fine	£N.Mint
1-10 ND colour						
	$0.30	$0.90	$1.50	£0.20	£0.60	£1.00
Title Value:	$3.00	$9.00	$15.00	£2.00	£6.00	£10.00
Book 1				£0.90	£2.70	£4.50

ETERNITY SMITH (3RD SERIES)

Heroic Publishing; 1 Dec 1994

	$Good	$Fine	$N.Mint	£Good	£Fine	£N.Mint
1 ND reprints of second series						
	$0.30	$0.90	$1.50	£0.20	£0.60	£1.00
Title Value:	$0.30	$0.90	$1.50	£0.20	£0.60	£1.00

ETERNITY TRIPLE ACTION

Eternity; 1 May 1993-6 1993

	$Good	$Fine	$N.Mint	£Good	£Fine	£N.Mint
1-6 ND anthology title featuring three stories						
	$0.35	$1.05	$1.75	£0.25	£0.75	£1.25
Title Value:	$2.10	$6.30	$10.50	£1.50	£4.50	£7.50

EUDAEMON, THE

Dark Horse; 1 Aug 1993-3 Nov 1993

	$Good	$Fine	$N.Mint	£Good	£Fine	£N.Mint
1-3 ND script and art by Nelson						
	$0.50	$1.50	$2.50	£0.30	£0.90	£1.50
Title Value:	$1.50	$4.50	$7.50	£0.90	£2.70	£4.50

EUREKA!

Eureka; 1 Apr 1988

	$Good	$Fine	$N.Mint	£Good	£Fine	£N.Mint
1 ND Australian material						
	$0.30	$0.90	$1.50	£0.20	£0.60	£1.00
Title Value:	$0.30	$0.90	$1.50	£0.20	£0.60	£1.00

EVANGELINE

Comico; 1 Mar 1984-2 Jun 1984

(see Primer)

	$Good	$Fine	$N.Mint	£Good	£Fine	£N.Mint
1-2 ND	$0.50	$1.50	$2.50	£0.30	£0.90	£1.50
Title Value:	$1.00	$3.00	$5.00	£0.60	£1.80	£3.00

EVANGELINE (2ND SERIES)

First; 1 May 1987-12 Mar 1989

	$Good	$Fine	$N.Mint	£Good	£Fine	£N.Mint
1-12 ND	$0.35	$1.05	$1.75	£0.25	£0.75	£1.25
Title Value:	$4.20	$12.60	$21.00	£3.00	£9.00	£15.00

EVANGELINE SPECIAL

Lodestone; 1 1986

	$Good	$Fine	$N.Mint	£Good	£Fine	£N.Mint
1 ND reprints Comico series in colour						
	$0.50	$1.50	$2.50	£0.30	£0.90	£1.50
Title Value:	$0.50	$1.50	$2.50	£0.30	£0.90	£1.50

EVERYMAN, THE

Marvel Comics Group,OS; 1 Jan 1992

	$Good	$Fine	$N.Mint	£Good	£Fine	£N.Mint
1 ND Bernie Mireault art						
	$0.80	$2.40	$4.00	£0.50	£1.50	£2.50
Title Value:	$0.80	$2.40	$4.00	£0.50	£1.50	£2.50

EVIL DEAD: ARMY OF DARKNESS

Dark Horse,MS; 1 Jul 1992-3 Sep 1992

	$Good	$Fine	$N.Mint	£Good	£Fine	£N.Mint
1-3 ND adaptation of film, John Bolton cover and art						
	$0.50	$1.50	$2.50	£0.30	£0.90	£1.50
Title Value:	$1.50	$4.50	$7.50	£0.90	£2.70	£4.50

EVIL ERNIE

Eternity/Adventure,MS; 0 Dec 1993; 1 Dec 1991-5 Apr 1992

	$Good	$Fine	$N.Mint	£Good	£Fine	£N.Mint
0 ND Mark McKenna art						
	$1.50	$4.50	$7.50	£1.00	£3.00	£5.00
0 Platinum Edition, ND Mark McKenna art; Platinum colour cover						

	$Good	$Fine	$N.Mint	£Good	£Fine	£N.Mint
	$10.00	$30.00	$50.00	£6.00	£18.00	£30.00
1 ND scarce in the U.K. Brian Pulido script, Steven Hughes art begin; 1st appearance Lady Death; approximately 12,000 print run	$25.00	$75.00	$125.00	£11.00	£33.00	£55.00
1 Special Edition, ND scarce in the U.K. (Aug 1992) - reprint plus new 8pg story plus sketches	$12.00	$36.00	$60.00	£6.00	£18.00	£30.00
2 ND scarce in the U.K. Lady Death appears, 1st Lady Death cover; approximately 7,000 print run	$20.00	$60.00	$100.00	£10.00	£30.00	£50.00
3 ND scarce in the U.K. Lady Death appears; approximately 7,000 print run	$14.00	$42.00	$70.00	£7.00	£21.00	£35.00
4 ND scarce in the U.K. Lady Death appears; approximately 8,000 print run	$13.00	$39.00	$65.00	£5.00	£15.00	£25.00
5 ND scarce in the U.K. Lady Death appears; approximately 8,000 print run	$12.00	$36.00	$60.00	£4.50	£13.50	£22.50
Title Value:	$107.50	$322.50	$537.50	£50.50	£151.50	£252.50
Evil Ernie's Graphic Novel (Nov 1992) reprints issues #1-5, new cover by Steven Hughes				£1.40	£4.20	£7.00
Youth Gone Wild: Evil Ernie Trade Paperback (Nov 1994) reprints issues #1-5 plus sketches from issue #1				£1.30	£3.90	£6.50

EVIL ERNIE VS. THE SUPER HEROES

Chaos Comics,OS; 1 Aug 1995

	$Good	$Fine	$N.Mint	£Good	£Fine	£N.Mint
1 ND Brian Pullido script, Justiniano and Jimmy Palmiotti art	$0.80	$2.40	$4.00	£0.60	£1.80	£3.00
1 Limited Edition, ND red foil cover with green Evil Ernie logo, limited to 10,000 copies [Aug 1995]	$5.00	$15.00	$25.00	£3.00	£9.00	£15.00
1 Signed & Numbered Edition, ND (May 1996), pre-bagged with certificate; 1,000 copies	$4.00	$12.00	$20.00	£2.50	£7.50	£12.50
Title Value:	$9.80	$29.40	$49.00	£6.10	£18.30	£30.50

EVIL ERNIE/LADY DEATH

Chaos Comics,OS; nn 1995

	$Good	$Fine	$N.Mint	£Good	£Fine	£N.Mint
nn Ashcan Edition, ND orange card stock cover	$3.00	$9.00	$15.00	£1.50	£4.50	£7.50
Title Value:	$3.00	$9.00	$15.00	£1.50	£4.50	£7.50

EVIL ERNIE: REVENGE

Chaos Comics; 1 Oct 1994-4 Jan 1995

	$Good	$Fine	$N.Mint	£Good	£Fine	£N.Mint
1 ND Brian Pulido script, Steven Hughes art; Lady Death centre-fold	$1.60	$4.80	$8.00	£1.00	£3.00	£5.00
1 Commemorative Edition, ND (Mar 1996), green foil cover, produced in conjunction with Comic Cavalcade; limited to 4,000	$5.00	$15.00	$25.00	£3.00	£9.00	£15.00
1 Commemorative Signed Edition, ND signed by Hughes, Jensen and Pulido, with certificate; limited to 4,000 copies	$6.00	$18.00	$30.00	£4.00	£12.00	£20.00
1 Glow in the Dark Edition, ND limited to 10,000 copies	$9.00	$27.00	$45.00	£5.00	£15.00	£25.00
2 ND Brian Pulido script, Steven Hughes art; Lady Death centre-fold	$1.00	$3.00	$5.00	£0.70	£2.10	£3.50
3-4 ND Brian Pulido script, Steven Hughes art; Lady Death centre-fold	$0.80	$2.40	$4.00	£0.50	£1.50	£2.50
Title Value:	$24.20	$72.60	$121.00	£14.70	£44.10	£73.50
Evil Ernie: The Revenge (Oct 1995) Trade paperback reprints issues #1-4				£1.70	£5.10	£8.50

EVIL ERNIE: STRAIGHT TO HELL

Chaos Comics,MS; 1 Oct 1995-5 Feb 1996

	$Good	$Fine	$N.Mint	£Good	£Fine	£N.Mint
1 ND Brian Pulido script, Justiniano art; coffin-shaped cover by Steven Hughes	$0.80	$2.40	$4.00	£0.50	£1.50	£2.50
1 Special Edition, ND limited to 10,000 copies	$6.00	$18.00	$30.00	£3.50	£10.50	£17.50
2 ND Brian Pulido script, Justiniano art; cover by Steven Hughes	$0.60	$1.80	$3.00	£0.40	£1.20	£2.00
3-5 ND Brian Pulido script, Justiniano art	$0.60	$1.80	$3.00	£0.40	£1.20	£2.00
Title Value:	$9.20	$27.60	$46.00	£5.60	£16.80	£28.00

EVIL ERNIE: STRAIGHT TO HELL ASHCAN

Chaos Comics,OS; nn Sep 1995

	$Good	$Fine	$N.Mint	£Good	£Fine	£N.Mint
nn ND 24pgs, black and white	$0.30	$0.90	$1.50	£0.20	£0.60	£1.00
Title Value:	$0.30	$0.90	$1.50	£0.20	£0.60	£1.00

EVIL ERNIE: THE RESURRECTION

Chaos Comics,MS; 1 Jul 1993-4 Oct 1993

	$Good	$Fine	$N.Mint	£Good	£Fine	£N.Mint
1 ND Joe Quesada cover	$3.00	$9.00	$15.00	£1.50	£4.50	£7.50
1 Ashcan Edition, ND Yellow card stock cover	$8.00	$24.00	$40.00	£4.00	£12.00	£20.00
1 Gold Edition, ND Gold embossed logo	$10.00	$30.00	$50.00	£4.00	£12.00	£20.00
2 ND Chris Bachalo cover	$3.00	$9.00	$15.00	£1.20	£3.60	£6.00
3 ND poster insert by George Perez, Tom Morgan cover	$2.40	$7.00	$12.00	£1.00	£3.00	£5.00
4 ND 40pgs	$2.40	$7.00	$12.00	£1.00	£3.00	£5.00
Title Value:	$28.80	$86.00	$144.00	£12.70	£38.10	£63.50
Evil Ernie: The Ressurrection (Dec 1994) Trade paperback ND reprints mini-series plus pin-ups by Jim Balent, George Perez and others				£2.00	£6.00	£10.00

EVIL ERNIE: YOUTH GONE WILD DIRECTOR'S CUT

Chaos Comics,OS; 1 Sep 1995

	$Good	$Fine	$N.Mint	£Good	£Fine	£N.Mint
1 ND 40pgs, limited to 15,000 copies; black and white interior	$1.00	$3.00	$5.00	£0.70	£2.10	£3.50
Title Value:	$1.00	$3.00	$5.00	£0.70	£2.10	£3.50

EVOLUTIONARY WAR, THE

Marvel Comics Group; 1988

Cross-over storyline that ran throughout the following issues: **Punisher Annual #1**, **X-Factor Annual #3**, **Silver Surfer Annual #1**, **New Mutants Annual #4**, **Fantastic Four Annual #21**, **Amazing Spiderman Annual #22**, **Uncanny X-Men Annual #12**, **Web of Spiderman Annual #4**, **West Coast Avengers Annual #3**, **Spectacular Spiderman Annual #8**, **Avengers Annual #17**. **What If [2nd Series] #1** was also included in the cross-over.

EWOKS

Marvel Comics Group/Star, TV; 1 Jun 1985-15 Sep 1987

	$Good	$Fine	$N.Mint	£Good	£Fine	£N.Mint
1-9	$0.30	$0.90	$1.50	£0.20	£0.60	£1.00
10 Williamson art	$0.30	$0.90	$1.50	£0.20	£0.60	£1.00
11-13	$0.30	$0.90	$1.50	£0.20	£0.60	£1.00
14 DS	$0.30	$0.90	$1.50	£0.20	£0.60	£1.00
15	$0.30	$0.90	$1.50	£0.20	£0.60	£1.00
Title Value:	$4.50	$13.25	$22.50	£3.00	£9.00	£15.00

EX-MUTANTS

Amazing/Eternity; 1 Aug 1986-15 1991

(see New Humans)

	$Good	$Fine	$N.Mint	£Good	£Fine	£N.Mint
1 Ron Lim art and cover	$0.40	$1.20	$2.00	£0.30	£0.90	£1.50
1 2nd printing	$0.40	$1.20	$2.00	£0.25	£0.75	£1.25
2 1st Eternity issue, Ron Lim cover	$0.40	$1.20	$2.00	£0.30	£0.90	£1.50
3 Ron Lim cover	$0.40	$1.20	$2.00	£0.30	£0.90	£1.50
4-15 scarce in the U.K.	$0.40	$1.20	$2.00	£0.30	£0.90	£1.50
Title Value:	$6.40	$19.20	$32.00	£4.75	£14.25	£23.75

Note: all Non-Distributed on the news-stands in the U.K.

				£Good	£Fine	£N.Mint
Annual 1 (Apr 1988)				£0.30	£0.90	£1.50
Trade Paperback 1, reprints #1-3 with new material (2nd/3rd prints also)				£1.00	£3.00	£5.00
Trade paperback 2, all reprint				£1.00	£3.00	£5.00

Elfquest (2nd) #1

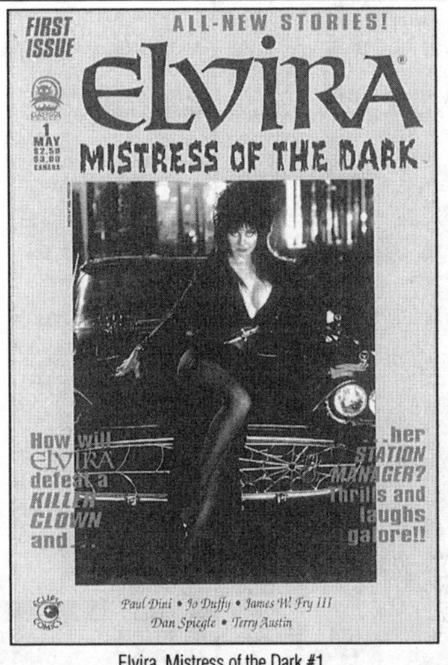

Elvira, Mistress of the Dark #1

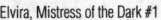

Elvira's House of Mystery #1

EX-MUTANTS (2ND SERIES)

Malibu; 1 Nov 1992-18 Apr 1994

	$Good	$Fine	$N.Mint	£Good	£Fine	£N.Mint
1 ND Paul Pelletier cover and pencils begin, colour						
	$0.40	$1.20	$2.00	£0.25	£0.75	£1.25
1 Collectors Edition, ND, silver foil-graphix cover - 1 copy made available to retailers for every 50 copies of #1 ordered						
	$1.00	$3.00	$5.00	£0.60	£1.80	£3.00
2-10 ND	$0.40	$1.20	$2.00	£0.25	£0.75	£1.25
11 ND Genesis Tie-In; pre-bagged with free Sky-Cap						
	$0.40	$1.20	$2.00	£0.25	£0.75	£1.25
12-16 ND Genesis Tie-In						
	$0.40	$1.20	$2.00	£0.25	£0.75	£1.25
17-18 ND	$0.40	$1.20	$2.00	£0.25	£0.75	£1.25
Title Value:	$8.20	$24.60	$41.00	£5.10	£15.30	£25.50

EX-MUTANTS MICRO SERIES

Pied Piper Comics,OS; 1 1987

	$Good	$Fine	$N.Mint	£Good	£Fine	£N.Mint
1 ND features Erin	$0.40	$1.20	$2.00	£0.25	£0.75	£1.25
Title Value:	$0.40	$1.20	$2.00	£0.25	£0.75	£1.25

EX-MUTANTS PIN-UP BOOK

Eternity; 1 1988

	$Good	$Fine	$N.Mint	£Good	£Fine	£N.Mint
1 ND	$0.40	$1.20	$2.00	£0.25	£0.75	£1.25
Title Value:	$0.40	$1.20	$2.00	£0.25	£0.75	£1.25

EX-MUTANTS SPECIAL EDITION

Amazing/Eternity; 1,2 1987

	$Good	$Fine	$N.Mint	£Good	£Fine	£N.Mint
1 ND	$0.40	$1.20	$2.00	£0.25	£0.75	£1.25
2 ND Winter Special						
	$0.40	$1.20	$2.00	£0.25	£0.75	£1.25
Title Value:	$0.80	$2.40	$4.00	£0.50	£1.50	£2.50

EX-MUTANTS: THE SHATTERED EARTH CHRONICLES

Eternity; 1 Apr 1988-15 1989

	$Good	$Fine	$N.Mint	£Good	£Fine	£N.Mint
1-15 ND	$0.40	$1.20	$2.00	£0.25	£0.75	£1.25
Title Value:	$6.00	$18.00	$30.00	£3.75	£11.25	£18.75

EXCALIBUR

Marvel Comics Group; 1 Oct 1988-86 Feb 1995;87 Jul 1995-present

(see Excalibur Special Edition, Marvel Graphic Novel) (becomes X-Calibre)

	$Good	$Fine	$N.Mint	£Good	£Fine	£N.Mint
1 ND Alan Davis art						
	$1.50	$4.50	$7.50	£0.80	£2.40	£4.00
2-3 ND Alan Davis art						
	$0.80	$2.40	$4.00	£0.60	£1.80	£3.00
4-5 ND Alan Davis art						
	$0.70	$2.10	$3.50	£0.50	£1.50	£2.50
6-7 ND Inferno X-over, Alan Davis art						
	$0.60	$1.80	$3.00	£0.40	£1.20	£2.00
8 ND Ron Lim art	$0.60	$1.80	$3.00	£0.40	£1.20	£2.00
9 ND Alan Davis art						
	$0.60	$1.80	$3.00	£0.40	£1.20	£2.00
10 ND Rogers art	$0.60	$1.80	$3.00	£0.40	£1.20	£2.00
11 ND Rogers art	$0.50	$1.50	$2.50	£0.30	£0.90	£1.50
12-15 ND Alan Davis art						
	$0.50	$1.50	$2.50	£0.30	£0.90	£1.50
16-17 ND Alan Davis art						
	$0.40	$1.20	$2.00	£0.25	£0.75	£1.25
18-19 LD in the U.K.						
	$0.40	$1.20	$2.00	£0.25	£0.75	£1.25
20 LD in the U.K. Ron Lim art						
	$0.40	$1.20	$2.00	£0.25	£0.75	£1.25
21 LD in the U.K.	$0.40	$1.20	$2.00	£0.25	£0.75	£1.25
22 LD in the U.K. Cable appears						
	$0.40	$1.20	$2.00	£0.25	£0.75	£1.25
23 LD in the U.K. Alan Davis art						
	$0.40	$1.20	$2.00	£0.25	£0.75	£1.25
24 LD in the U.K. bi-weekly issue, Alan Davis art						
	$0.40	$1.20	$2.00	£0.25	£0.75	£1.25
25 LD in the U.K. bi-weekly issue, Galactus and Phoenix appear						
	$0.40	$1.20	$2.00	£0.25	£0.75	£1.25
26 LD in the U.K. Ron Lim art, bi-weekly issue						
	$0.40	$1.20	$2.00	£0.25	£0.75	£1.25
27 LD in the U.K. ties in with "Days of Future Past" story and other X-Men events, Barry Windsor-Smith and Bill Sienkiewicz art, bi-weekly issue						
	$0.40	$1.20	$2.00	£0.25	£0.75	£1.25
28 LD in the U.K. bi-weekly issue						
	$0.40	$1.20	$2.00	£0.25	£0.75	£1.25
29 LD in the U.K. last bi-weekly issue						
	$0.40	$1.20	$2.00	£0.25	£0.75	£1.25
30 LD in the U.K.	$0.40	$1.20	$2.00	£0.25	£0.75	£1.25
31 LD in the U.K. X-Men appear						
	$0.45	$1.35	$2.25	£0.30	£0.90	£1.50
32-34 LD in the U.K.						
	$0.40	$1.20	$2.00	£0.25	£0.75	£1.25
35 LD in the U.K. 1st appearance D'Spayre						
	$0.40	$1.20	$2.00	£0.25	£0.75	£1.25
36 LD in the U.K.	$0.40	$1.20	$2.00	£0.25	£0.75	£1.25
37-38 LD in the U.K. Promethium Exchange story, Avengers West Coast guest-star; covers 37-39 form one poster						
	$0.40	$1.20	$2.00	£0.25	£0.75	£1.25
39 LD in the U.K. Promethium Exchange story, Avengers West Coast guest-star; covers 37-39 form one poster, Spiderman appears						
	$0.40	$1.20	$2.00	£0.25	£0.75	£1.25
40 LD in the U.K.	$0.40	$1.20	$2.00	£0.25	£0.75	£1.25
41 LD in the U.K. Mutant Genesis tie-in, Wolverine and Cable appear						
	$0.60	$1.80	$3.00	£0.40	£1.20	£2.00
42 LD in the U.K. Alan Davis art begins, Captain Britain appears, Mutant Genesis tie-in, bi-weekly issue						
	$0.60	$1.80	$3.00	£0.40	£1.20	£2.00
43-45 LD in the U.K. Captain Britain appears, Alan Davis art, bi-weekly issue						
	$0.40	$1.20	$2.00	£0.25	£0.75	£1.25
46 LD in the U.K. bi-weekly issue, Alan Davis art						
	$0.40	$1.20	$2.00	£0.25	£0.75	£1.25
47 LD in the U.K. 1st appearance Cerise, Alan Davis art						
	$0.40	$1.20	$2.00	£0.25	£0.75	£1.25
48-49 LD in the U.K. Alan Davis art						
	$0.40	$1.20	$2.00	£0.25	£0.75	£1.25
50 ND 64pgs, Alan Davis art						
	$0.60	$1.80	$3.00	£0.40	£1.20	£2.00
51 LD in the U.K. Dougie Braithwaite art, new logo						
	$0.40	$1.20	$2.00	£0.25	£0.75	£1.25
52 LD in the U.K. Dougie Braithwaite art						
	$0.40	$1.20	$2.00	£0.25	£0.75	£1.25
53 LD in the U.K.	$0.40	$1.20	$2.00	£0.25	£0.75	£1.25
54-55 LD in the U.K. Alan Davis script/art						
	$0.40	$1.20	$2.00	£0.25	£0.75	£1.25
56 LD in the U.K. Alan Davis script/art, Psylocke appears, bi-weekly						
	$0.40	$1.20	$2.00	£0.25	£0.75	£1.25
57 LD in the U.K. Alan Davis script/art, X-Men appear, bi-weekly						
	$0.40	$1.20	$2.00	£0.25	£0.75	£1.25
58 LD in the U.K. X-Men appear, bi-weekly						
	$0.40	$1.20	$2.00	£0.25	£0.75	£1.25
59 LD in the U.K. bi-weekly, Captain America, Black Panther and Iron Man appear						
	$0.40	$1.20	$2.00	£0.25	£0.75	£1.25
60 LD in the U.K. Alan Davis script/art, Galactus appears						
	$0.40	$1.20	$2.00	£0.25	£0.75	£1.25
61 LD in the U.K. Phoenix returns						
	$0.40	$1.20	$2.00	£0.25	£0.75	£1.25
62-66 LD in the U.K.						
	$0.40	$1.20	$2.00	£0.25	£0.75	£1.25
67 LD in the U.K. last Alan Davis						
	$0.40	$1.20	$2.00	£0.25	£0.75	£1.25
68 LD in the U.K. Scott Lobdell scripts begin; new direction for title, Steve Buccellato art						
	$0.40	$1.20	$2.00	£0.25	£0.75	£1.25
69-70 LD in the U.K.						
	$0.40	$1.20	$2.00	£0.25	£0.75	£1.25
71 LD in the U.K. 48pgs, holo-gram cover; X-Men appear						
	$0.80	$2.40	$4.00	£0.50	£1.50	£2.50
72-74 LD in the U.K.						
	$0.40	$1.20	$2.00	£0.25	£0.75	£1.25
75 LD in the U.K. 48pgs						
	$0.45	$1.35	$2.25	£0.30	£0.90	£1.50
75 Collectors Edition, ND 48pgs, holo-grafix foil cover						
	$1.00	$3.00	$5.00	£0.70	£2.10	£3.50
76 LD in the U.K. continued tie-in fron X-Men Unlimited #4						
	$0.40	$1.20	$2.00	£0.25	£0.75	£1.25
77 LD in the U.K. Captain Britain guest-stars; with free Spiderman vs. Venom card sheet						
	$0.40	$1.20	$2.00	£0.25	£0.75	£1.25
78 LD in the U.K. Wolverine and Kitty Pryde appear						
	$0.40	$1.20	$2.00	£0.25	£0.75	£1.25
79-81 LD in the U.K.						
	$0.40	$1.20	$2.00	£0.25	£0.75	£1.25
82 ND 48pgs	$0.45	$1.35	$2.25	£0.30	£0.90	£1.50
82 Collectors Edition, ND 48pgs, foil stamped cover						
	$0.80	$2.40	$4.00	£0.50	£1.50	£2.50
83 ND	$0.30	$0.90	$1.50	£0.20	£0.60	£1.00
83 Deluxe Edition, ND printed on glossy stock paper						
	$0.40	$1.20	$2.00	£0.25	£0.75	£1.25
84 ND	$0.30	$0.90	$1.50	£0.20	£0.60	£1.00
84 Deluxe Edition, ND printed on glossy stock paper						
	$0.40	$1.20	$2.00	£0.25	£0.75	£1.25
85 ND	$0.30	$0.90	$1.50	£0.20	£0.60	£1.00
85 Deluxe Edition, ND printed on glossy stock paper						
	$0.40	$1.20	$2.00	£0.25	£0.75	£1.25
86 ND	$0.30	$0.90	$1.50	£0.20	£0.60	£1.00
86 Deluxe Edition, ND printed on glossy stock paper plus bound-in Fleer trading card; see X-Calibre #1						
	$0.40	$1.20	$2.00	£0.25	£0.75	£1.25
87 ND continued from X-Men: Prime, leading into X-Men #42; Warren Ellis script, Ken Lashley art						
	$0.40	$1.20	$2.00	£0.25	£0.75	£1.25
88-89 ND	$0.40	$1.20	$2.00	£0.25	£0.75	£1.25
90 ND 48pgs, leads into Starjammers #1						
	$0.60	$1.80	$3.00	£0.40	£1.20	£2.00
91-93 ND	$0.40	$1.20	$2.00	£0.25	£0.75	£1.25
94 ND Karma and Psylocke appear						
	$0.40	$1.20	$2.00	£0.25	£0.75	£1.25
95 ND continued from X-Man #12						
	$0.40	$1.20	$2.00	£0.25	£0.75	£1.25
96-98 ND	$0.40	$1.20	$2.00	£0.25	£0.75	£1.25
99 ND 40pgs, Mountjoy guest-stars						
	$0.40	$1.20	$2.00	£0.25	£0.75	£1.25
100 ND 48pgs, Onslaught tie-in						
	$0.60	$1.80	$3.00	£0.40	£1.20	£2.00
101 ND	$0.40	$1.20	$2.00	£0.25	£0.75	£1.25
102 ND with bound-in Overpower cards						
	$0.40	$1.20	$2.00	£0.25	£0.75	£1.25
103-107 ND	$0.40	$1.20	$2.00	£0.25	£0.75	£1.25
Title Value:	$51.35	$154.05	$256.75	£32.65	£97.95	£163.25

EXCALIBUR ANNUAL

Marvel Comics Group; 1 Sep 1993-present

1 ND 64pgs, pre-bagged with trading card; 1st appearance Khaos

	$Good	$Fine	$N.Mint	£Good	£Fine	£N.Mint
	$0.60	$1.80	$3.00	£0.40	£1.20	£2.00
2 ND 64pgs, X-Men and Psylocke appear	$0.60	$1.80	$3.00	£0.40	£1.20	£2.00
Title Value:	$1.20	$3.60	$6.00	£0.80	£2.40	£4.00

EXCALIBUR SPECIAL
Marvel Comics Group,OS; 1 Jul 1991

	$Good	$Fine	$N.Mint	£Good	£Fine	£N.Mint
1 ND 48pgs, Meggan possessed story	$0.60	$1.80	$3.00	£0.40	£1.20	£2.00
Title Value:	$0.60	$1.80	$3.00	£0.40	£1.20	£2.00

EXCALIBUR SPECIAL EDITION (1ST SERIES)
Marvel Comics Group; nn Apr 1988

	$Good	$Fine	$N.Mint	£Good	£Fine	£N.Mint
nn 1st printing, ND **The Sword is Drawn**; 1st appearance "British" X-Men by Chris Claremont, Alan Davis and Paul Neary	$1.60	$4.80	$8.00	£1.10	£3.30	£5.50
nn 2nd printing, ND (Oct 1989)	$1.00	$3.00	$5.00	£0.90	£2.70	£4.50
nn 3rd printing, ND (Dec 1989)	$0.80	$2.40	$4.00	£0.70	£2.10	£3.50
Title Value:	$3.40	$10.20	$17.00	£2.70	£8.10	£13.50

EXCALIBUR: AIR APPARENT
Marvel Comics Group,OS; 1 Dec 1991

	$Good	$Fine	$N.Mint	£Good	£Fine	£N.Mint
1 ND 48pgs, squarebound, Ron Lim, Eric Larsen art featured	$1.00	$3.00	$5.00	£0.70	£2.10	£3.50
Title Value:	$1.00	$3.00	$5.00	£0.70	£2.10	£3.50

EXCALIBUR: MOJO MAYHEM
Marvel Comics Group,OS; nn Mar 1990

	$Good	$Fine	$N.Mint	£Good	£Fine	£N.Mint
nn ND X-Babies appear; Art Adams art	$0.80	$2.40	$4.00	£0.70	£2.10	£3.50
Title Value:	$0.80	$2.40	$4.00	£0.70	£2.10	£3.50

EXCALIBUR: WILD, WILD LIFE
Marvel Comics Group,OS; 1 Apr 1995

	$Good	$Fine	$N.Mint	£Good	£Fine	£N.Mint
1 ND 64pgs, reprints storyline from Marvel Comics Presents	$1.20	$3.60	$6.00	£0.80	£2.40	£4.00
Title Value:	$1.20	$3.60	$6.00	£0.80	£2.40	£4.00

EXCALIBUR: XX CROSSING SPECIAL
Marvel Comics Group,OS; 1 Jul 1992

	$Good	$Fine	$N.Mint	£Good	£Fine	£N.Mint
1 ND 48pgs, ties into Uncanny X-Men #1, featured art includes Ron Lim and Jackson Guice, Sam Kieth cover	$0.50	$1.50	$2.50	£0.30	£0.90	£1.50
Title Value:	$0.50	$1.50	$2.50	£0.30	£0.90	£1.50

EXILES
Alpha Productions,MS; 1 May 1991-5 Sep 1991

	$Good	$Fine	$N.Mint	£Good	£Fine	£N.Mint
1-5 ND	$0.40	$1.20	$2.00	£0.25	£0.75	£1.25
Title Value:	$2.00	$6.00	$10.00	£1.25	£3.75	£6.25

EXILES
Malibu Ultraverse; 1 Aug 1993-4 Nov 1993

	$Good	$Fine	$N.Mint	£Good	£Fine	£N.Mint
1 ND Steve Gerber script begins	$0.50	$1.50	$2.50	£0.30	£0.90	£1.50
2 ND	$0.40	$1.20	$2.00	£0.25	£0.75	£1.25
3 ND 40pgs, Rune insert	$0.50	$1.50	$2.50	£0.30	£0.90	£1.50
4 ND leads directly into Break Thru #1	$0.40	$1.20	$2.00	£0.25	£0.75	£1.25
Title Value:	$1.80	$5.40	$9.00	£1.10	£3.30	£5.50

EXILES, THE ALL NEW
Marvel Comics Group; 1 Dec 1995-11 Oct 1996

	$Good	$Fine	$N.Mint	£Good	£Fine	£N.Mint
1 ND Terry Kavanagh script, Ken Lashley art; cover by Jeff Matsuda and Steve Moncuse	$0.30	$0.90	$1.50	£0.20	£0.60	£1.00
1 E.T.M. Variant, ND exclusively produced by E.T.M. with a variant cover featuring Juggernaut and Shuriken	$1.00	$3.00	$5.00	£0.70	£2.10	£3.50
1 Variant Cover Edition, ND Jeff Matsuda cover computer painted by Chuck Maiden	$1.00	$3.00	$5.00	£0.70	£2.10	£3.50
1 Variant Cover Signed Edition, ND (Jun 1996), signed by Terry Kavanagh with certificate of authenticity	$2.20	$6.50	$11.00	£1.50	£4.50	£7.50
2 ND flip-book format with Phoenix Ressurrection chapter	$0.30	$0.90	$1.50	£0.20	£0.60	£1.00
3 ND	$0.30	$0.90	$1.50	£0.20	£0.60	£1.00
4 ND Ultraforce guest-stars	$0.30	$0.90	$1.50	£0.20	£0.60	£1.00
5 ND 48pgs, Juggernaut appears; ties into the Uncanny X-Men	$0.50	$1.50	$2.50	£0.30	£0.90	£1.50
6 ND new costumes	$0.50	$1.50	$2.50	£0.30	£0.90	£1.50
7 ND	$0.30	$0.90	$1.50	£0.20	£0.60	£1.00
8 ND intro Maxis	$0.30	$0.90	$1.50	£0.20	£0.60	£1.00
9-10 ND	$0.30	$0.90	$1.50	£0.20	£0.60	£1.00
11 ND Michael Golden cover	$0.30	$0.90	$1.50	£0.20	£0.60	£1.00
Title Value:	$7.90	$23.60	$39.50	£5.30	£15.90	£26.50

EXILES: INFINITY
Marvel Comics Group,OS; nn Nov 1995

	$Good	$Fine	$N.Mint	£Good	£Fine	£N.Mint
nn ND Black September tie-in; introduces The Juggernaut leading a new team	$0.50	$1.50	$2.50	£0.40	£1.20	£2.00
nn Signed & Numbered Edition, ND (Dec 1995); 2,000 copies with certificate	$2.50	$7.50	$12.50	£1.50	£4.50	£7.50
nn Variant Cover Edition, ND 1 copy received for every 5 copies of the regular issue ordered	$0.80	$2.40	$4.00	£0.50	£1.50	£2.50
Title Value:	$3.80	$11.40	$19.00	£2.40	£7.20	£12.00

EXOSQUAD
Topps,MS; 0 Jan 1994-3 Apr 1994

	$Good	$Fine	$N.Mint	£Good	£Fine	£N.Mint
0 ND 16pgs, Len Wein script, Joe Staton art; card-stock cover	$0.30	$0.90	$1.50	£0.20	£0.60	£1.00
1 ND origin told	$0.30	$0.90	$1.50	£0.20	£0.60	£1.00
2 ND	$0.30	$0.90	$1.50	£0.20	£0.60	£1.00
3 ND Michael Golden cover	$0.30	$0.90	$1.50	£0.20	£0.60	£1.00
Title Value:	$1.20	$3.60	$6.00	£0.80	£2.40	£4.00

EXQUISITE CORPSE
Dark Horse,OS; 1 Jul 1990

	$Good	$Fine	$N.Mint	£Good	£Fine	£N.Mint
1 ND black and white, pre-bagged (25% less if un-bagged)	$0.50	$1.50	$2.50	£0.30	£0.90	£1.50
Title Value:	$0.50	$1.50	$2.50	£0.30	£0.90	£1.50

Note: red/yellow/green variants available (logo and Dark Horse emblem on cover) and the issues may be read in any order.

EXTINCT
New England Comics; 1 Feb 1992-2 1992

	$Good	$Fine	$N.Mint	£Good	£Fine	£N.Mint
1-2 ND 64pgs, 1940s and 1950s bizarre reprints	$0.70	$2.10	$3.50	£0.40	£1.20	£2.00
Title Value:	$1.40	$4.20	$7.00	£0.80	£2.40	£4.00

EXTREME 3000 PRELUDE
Image,OS; nn Aug 1995

	$Good	$Fine	$N.Mint	£Good	£Fine	£N.Mint
nn ND Rob Liefeld part script and part art	$0.50	$1.50	$2.50	£0.30	£0.90	£1.50
Title Value:	$0.50	$1.50	$2.50	£0.30	£0.90	£1.50

EXTREME ANTHOLOGY
Image,OS; nn May 1996

	$Good	$Fine	$N.Mint	£Good	£Fine	£N.Mint
nn ND Prophet, Glory and NewMen appear	$0.50	$1.50	$2.50	£0.30	£0.90	£1.50
Title Value:	$0.50	$1.50	$2.50	£0.30	£0.90	£1.50

EXTREME DESTROYER EPILOGUE
Image,OS; 1 Jan 1996

	$Good	$Fine	$N.Mint	£Good	£Fine	£N.Mint
1 ND Extreme Destroyer part 9 (of 9), continued from New Force #1; pre-bagged with trading card; features Rob Liefeld script and art with Mike Deodato and Stephen Platt	$0.50	$1.50	$2.50	£0.30	£0.90	£1.50
Title Value:	$0.50	$1.50	$2.50	£0.30	£0.90	£1.50

EXTREME DESTROYER PROLOGUE
Image,OS; 1 Jan 1996

	$Good	$Fine	$N.Mint	£Good	£Fine	£N.Mint
1 ND Extreme Destroyer part 1, continued in Maximage #2; pre-bagged with trading card; Rob Liefeld script and art with Mike Deodato and Stephen Platt	$0.50	$1.50	$2.50	£0.30	£0.90	£1.50
Title Value:	$0.50	$1.50	$2.50	£0.30	£0.90	£1.50

EXTREME JUSTICE
DC Comics; 0 Jan 1995-18 Jun 1996

	$Good	$Fine	$N.Mint	£Good	£Fine	£N.Mint
0 Zero Hour spin-off. New team formed featuring Captain Atom, Maxima, Blue Beetle, Booster Gold and Amazing Man	$0.40	$1.20	$2.00	£0.25	£0.75	£1.25
1-3	$0.35	$1.05	$1.75	£0.25	£0.75	£1.25
4 Firestorm the Nuclear Man returns	$0.35	$1.05	$1.75	£0.25	£0.75	£1.25
5 Firestorm, Captain Atom and Justice League appear	$0.35	$1.05	$1.75	£0.25	£0.75	£1.25
6 Captain Atom and Booster Gold appear	$0.35	$1.05	$1.75	£0.25	£0.75	£1.25
7-8 Captain Atom, Justice League and Monarch appear	$0.35	$1.05	$1.75	£0.25	£0.75	£1.25
9 Firestorm appears	$0.35	$1.05	$1.75	£0.25	£0.75	£1.25
10-11 Underworld Unleashed tie-in, Star Sapphire appears	$0.35	$1.05	$1.75	£0.25	£0.75	£1.25
12-18	$0.35	$1.05	$1.75	£0.25	£0.75	£1.25
Title Value:	$6.70	$20.10	$33.50	£4.75	£14.25	£23.75

EXTREME PREJUDICE TRADE PAPERBACK
Image,OS; nn May 1996

	$Good	$Fine	$N.Mint	£Good	£Fine	£N.Mint
nn ND 192pgs, collects Extreme Studios first cross-over story	$3.40	$10.00	$17.00	£2.30	£6.75	£11.50
Title Value:	$3.40	$10.00	$17.00	£2.30	£6.75	£11.50

EXTREME SACRIFICE
Image; 1994

Cross-over storyline from Image Comics scripted by Rob Liefeld and forcing changes in the Image Comics universe. The issues are as follows:

Prelude - Extreme Sacrifice Prelude
Part 0 - Youngblood Strikefile #11
Part 1 - Supreme #23
Part 2 - Bloodstrike #18
Part 3 - Brigade #16
Part 4 - Newmen #10
Part 5 - Team Youngblood #17
Part 6 - Prophet #10
Epilogue - Extreme Sacrifice Epilogue

EXTREME SACRIFICE EPILOGUE
Image,OS; 1 Jan 1995

	$Good	$Fine	$N.Mint	£Good	£Fine	£N.Mint
1 ND Extreme Prejudice/Sacrifice storyline concludes, Stephen Platt art featured; pre-bagged with trading card	$0.50	$1.50	$2.50	£0.30	£0.90	£1.50
Title Value:	$0.50	$1.50	$2.50	£0.30	£0.90	£1.50

EXTREME SACRIFICE PRELUDE
Image,OS; 1 Jan 1995

	$Good	$Fine	$N.Mint	£Good	£Fine	£N.Mint
1 ND sequel to Extreme Prejudice X-over story, Stephen Platt art featured; pre-bagged with trading card	$0.50	$1.50	$2.50	£0.30	£0.90	£1.50
Title Value:	$0.50	$1.50	$2.50	£0.30	£0.90	£1.50

EXTREME SACRIFICE TRADE PAPERBACK
Image,OS; nn Jul 1995

	$Good	$Fine	$N.Mint	£Good	£Fine	£N.Mint
nn ND collects parts #0-8 of Extreme Sacrifice storyline	$3.40	$10.00	$17.00	£2.30	£6.75	£11.50
Title Value:	$3.40	$10.00	$17.00	£2.30	£6.75	£11.50

EXTREME STUDIOS TOUR BOOK
Extreme Studios,OS; 1 1993

	$Good	$Fine	$N.Mint	£Good	£Fine	£N.Mint
1 ND biogs, pictures and pin-ups of Rob Liefeld, Brian Murray, Marat Mychaels, Dan Fraga, Danny Miki and others; gold/black embossed logo on black cover - 5,000 copies	*$1.00*	*$3.00*	*$5.00*	£0.50	£1.50	£2.50
1 Gold Edition, ND - as above but with gold logo embossed on gold cover - 1,000 copies	*$2.00*	*$6.00*	*$10.00*	£0.60	£1.80	£3.00
Title Value:	*$3.00*	*$9.00*	*$15.00*	£1.10	£3.30	£5.50

EXTREME SUPER CHRISTMAS SPECIAL
Image,OS; 1 Dec 1994

	$Good	$Fine	$N.Mint	£Good	£Fine	£N.Mint
1 ND stories featuring Youngblood, Prophet and Team Youngblood by Liefeld, Platt and Matsuda	*$0.60*	*$1.80*	*$3.00*	£0.40	£1.20	£2.00
Title Value:	*$0.60*	*$1.80*	*$3.00*	£0.40	£1.20	£2.00

EXTREMELY YOUNGBLOOD
Image,OS; 1 Sep 1996

	$Good	$Fine	$N.Mint	£Good	£Fine	£N.Mint
1 ND 48pgs	*$0.70*	*$2.10*	*$3.50*	£0.50	£1.50	£2.50
Title Value:	*$0.70*	*$2.10*	*$3.50*	£0.50	£1.50	£2.50

EXTREMES OF VIOLET
Blackout Comics,MS; 0 Dec 1994; 1 Feb 1995-2 1995

	$Good	$Fine	$N.Mint	£Good	£Fine	£N.Mint
0 ND wraparound cover	*$0.60*	*$1.80*	*$3.00*	£0.40	£1.20	£2.00
0 Commemorative Edition, ND (Jun 1995) - signed by Dell Barras and Bruce Schoengood in silver ink, large gold sticker on front cover; with certificate, 5000 print run	*$2.00*	*$6.00*	*$10.00*	£1.30	£3.90	£6.50
1-2 ND	*$0.60*	*$1.80*	*$3.00*	£0.40	£1.20	£2.00
Title Value:	*$3.80*	*$11.40*	*$19.00*	£2.50	£7.50	£12.50

Note: originally solicited as Extreme Violet

EXTREMIST, THE
DC Comics/Vertigo,MS; 1 Sep 1993-4 Dec 1993

	$Good	$Fine	$N.Mint	£Good	£Fine	£N.Mint
1 Peter Milligan script, Ted McKeever art begins	*$0.40*	*$1.20*	*$2.00*	£0.25	£0.75	£1.25
1 Platinum Edition ND	*$3.00*	*$9.00*	*$15.00*	£1.50	£4.50	£7.50
2-4	*$0.40*	*$1.20*	*$2.00*	£0.25	£0.75	£1.25
Title Value:	*$4.60*	*$13.80*	*$23.00*	£2.50	£7.50	£12.50

EYEBALL KID
Dark Horse,MS; 1 Apr 1992-3 Jun 1992

	$Good	$Fine	$N.Mint	£Good	£Fine	£N.Mint
1-3 ND reprints Eyeball Kid stories by Eddie Campbell and Ed Hillyer previously published by Harrier	*$0.50*	*$1.50*	*$2.50*	£0.30	£0.90	£1.50
Title Value:	*$1.50*	*$4.50*	*$7.50*	£0.90	£2.70	£4.50

F

F-III BANDIT
Antarctic Press,MS; 1 Jan 1995-10 Jul 1996

	$Good	$Fine	$N.Mint	£Good	£Fine	£N.Mint
1-8 ND Ippongi Bang script and art; black and white	*$0.60*	*$1.80*	*$3.00*	£0.40	£1.20	£2.00
9 ND with trading card	*$0.60*	*$1.80*	*$3.00*	£0.40	£1.20	£2.00
10 ND	*$0.60*	*$1.80*	*$3.00*	£0.40	£1.20	£2.00
Title Value:	*$6.00*	*$18.00*	*$30.00*	£4.00	£12.00	£20.00

FACE
DC Comics/Vertigo,OS; 1 Jan 1995

	$Good	$Fine	$N.Mint	£Good	£Fine	£N.Mint
1 ND 64pgs, Peter Milligan script and Duncan Fegredo art	*$0.90*	*$2.70*	*$4.50*	£0.60	£1.80	£3.00
Title Value:	*$0.90*	*$2.70*	*$4.50*	£0.60	£1.80	£3.00

FACE, WHAT IS THE
Ace; 1 Dec 1986-3 Aug 1987

	$Good	$Fine	$N.Mint	£Good	£Fine	£N.Mint
1-3 ND Steve Ditko art	*$0.40*	*$1.20*	*$2.00*	£0.25	£0.75	£1.25
Title Value:	*$1.20*	*$3.60*	*$6.00*	£0.75	£2.25	£3.75

FACTOR X
Marvel Comics Group; 1 Mar 1995-4 Jun 1995

(title previously called X-Factor)

	$Good	$Fine	$N.Mint	£Good	£Fine	£N.Mint
1 J.F. Moore script, Epting and Milgrom art	*$0.80*	*$2.40*	*$4.00*	£0.50	£1.50	£2.50
2-3 J.F. Moore script, Epting and Milgrom art	*$0.50*	*$1.50*	*$2.50*	£0.30	£0.90	£1.50
4 J.F. Moore script, Epting and Milgrom art; continued in X-Men: Omega	*$0.50*	*$1.50*	*$2.50*	£0.30	£0.90	£1.50
Title Value:	*$2.30*	*$6.90*	*$11.50*	£1.40	£4.20	£7.00
The Ultimate Factor X (Jul 1995) 96pgs, Bookshelf Edition collects issues #1-4 with etched gold cover				£1.20	£3.60	£6.00

FAFHRD & THE GREY MOUSER
Marvel Comics Group/Epic,MS; 1 Dec 1990-4 Mar 1991

	$Good	$Fine	$N.Mint	£Good	£Fine	£N.Mint
1-4 ND 48pgs, Howard Chaykin script, Mike Mignola/Williamson art	*$0.80*	*$2.40*	*$4.00*	£0.50	£1.50	£2.50
Title Value:	*$3.20*	*$9.60*	*$16.00*	£2.00	£6.00	£10.00

Note: Bookshelf Format

FAILED UNIVERSE
Blackthorne,OS; 1 Dec 1986

	$Good	$Fine	$N.Mint	£Good	£Fine	£N.Mint
1 ND New Universe parody (see Marvel Comics); black and white	*$0.40*	*$1.20*	*$2.00*	£0.25	£0.75	£1.25
Title Value:	*$0.40*	*$1.20*	*$2.00*	£0.25	£0.75	£1.25

FALCON
Marvel Comics Group,MS; 1 Nov 1983-4 Feb 1984

	$Good	$Fine	$N.Mint	£Good	£Fine	£N.Mint
1 ND Paul Smith cover/part art	*$0.30*	*$0.90*	*$1.50*	£0.20	£0.60	£1.00
2 ND Paul Smith cover, Sentinels appear	*$0.30*	*$0.90*	*$1.50*	£0.20	£0.60	£1.00
3-4 ND	*$0.30*	*$0.90*	*$1.50*	£0.20	£0.60	£1.00
Title Value:	*$1.20*	*$3.60*	*$6.00*	£0.80	£2.40	£4.00

FALL OF THE MUTANTS, THE
Marvel Comics Group; 1987

Cross-over storyline that ran throughout the following issues:
Uncanny X-Men #225, X-Factor #24, New Mutants #59, Uncanny X-Men #226, X-Factor #25, New Mutants #60, Uncanny X-Men #227, X-Factor #26, New Mutants #61.

FALLEN ANGELS
Marvel Comics Group,MS; 1 Apr 1987-8 Nov 1987

	$Good	$Fine	$N.Mint	£Good	£Fine	£N.Mint
1 ND scarce in the U.K.	*$0.40*	*$1.20*	*$2.00*	£0.30	£0.90	£1.50
2-8 ND	*$0.40*	*$1.20*	*$2.00*	£0.25	£0.75	£1.25
Title Value:	*$3.20*	*$9.60*	*$16.00*	£2.05	£6.15	£10.25

Note: mainly stars New Mutants members.

FALLEN EMPIRES
Acclaim Comics/Armada,MS; 1 Oct 1995-2 Nov 1995

	$Good	$Fine	$N.Mint	£Good	£Fine	£N.Mint
1-2 ND Alexander Maleev art	*$0.50*	*$1.50*	*$2.50*	£0.30	£0.90	£1.50
Title Value:	*$1.00*	*$3.00*	*$5.00*	£0.60	£1.80	£3.00

Note: based on fantasy game Magic: The Gathering by Wizards of the Coast

	$Good	$Fine	$N.Mint	£Good	£Fine	£N.Mint
Fallen Empires - A Magic: The Gathering (Oct 1995) Trade paperback reprints issues #1,2, shrink-wrapped with booster pack				£0.65	£1.95	£3.25

FALLING IN LOVE
National Periodical Publications; 1 Sep/Oct 1955-143 Oct/Nov 1973

	$Good	$Fine	$N.Mint	£Good	£Fine	£N.Mint
1 very scarce in the U.K.	*$39.00*	*$115.00*	*$275.00*	£26.00	£77.50	£185.00
2 very scarce in the U.K.	*$19.00*	*$57.50*	*$135.00*	£12.50	£39.00	£90.00
3-10 scarce in the U.K.	*$10.50*	*$32.00*	*$75.00*	£7.00	£21.00	£50.00
11-20 scarce in the U.K.	*$7.75*	*$23.50*	*$55.00*	£5.00	£15.00	£35.00
21-30 scarce in the U.K.	*$5.50*	*$17.00*	*$40.00*	£3.55	£10.50	£25.00
1st official distribution in the U.K.						
31-39 scarce in the U.K.	*$5.50*	*$17.00*	*$40.00*	£3.55	£10.50	£25.00
40 scarce in the U.K.	*$2.10*	*$6.25*	*$15.00*	£1.25	£3.85	£9.00
41-46 scarce in the U.K.	*$4.15*	*$12.50*	*$25.00*	£2.50	£7.50	£15.00
47 scarce in the U.K. last 10 cents issue	*$4.15*	*$12.50*	*$25.00*	£2.50	£7.50	£15.00
48-60 scarce in the U.K.	*$2.90*	*$8.75*	*$17.50*	£2.05	£6.25	£12.50
61-80	*$2.50*	*$7.50*	*$15.00*	£1.65	£5.00	£10.00
81-90	*$2.05*	*$6.25*	*$12.50*	£1.30	£4.00	£8.00
91-100	*$2.05*	*$6.25*	*$12.50*	£1.25	£3.75	£7.50
101-107	*$1.65*	*$5.00*	*$10.00*	£0.80	£2.50	£5.00
108 Wood art	*$2.30*	*$7.00*	*$14.00*	£1.25	£3.75	£7.50
109-110	*$1.50*	*$4.50*	*$9.00*	£0.75	£2.25	£4.50
111-143	*$1.30*	*$4.00*	*$8.00*	£0.50	£1.50	£3.00
Title Value:	*$543.60*	*$1652.00*	*$3653.50*	£340.70	£1024.35	£2282.00

FALLOUT 3000, MIKE DEODATO'S
Caliber Press,OS; 1 Jun 1996

	$Good	$Fine	$N.Mint	£Good	£Fine	£N.Mint
1 ND Mike Deodato Snr. script, Mike Deodato Jnr. art; black and white. Originally published in Brazil, this was Mike Deodato Jnr's first work	*$0.60*	*$1.80*	*$3.00*	£0.40	£1.20	£2.00
Title Value:	*$0.60*	*$1.80*	*$3.00*	£0.40	£1.20	£2.00

FALLS THE GOTHAM RAIN
Comico,MS; 1 Feb 1992-2 Oct 1992

	$Good	$Fine	$N.Mint	£Good	£Fine	£N.Mint
1-2 ND 48pgs, duo-tone black and white art; reprints graphic novel	*$0.50*	*$1.50*	*$2.50*	£0.30	£0.90	£1.50
Title Value:	*$1.00*	*$3.00*	*$5.00*	£0.60	£1.80	£3.00

FAMILY AFFAIR
Gold Key; 1 Feb 1970-4 Oct 1970

	$Good	$Fine	$N.Mint	£Good	£Fine	£N.Mint
1 scarce distributed in the U.K. based on TV series, photo cover; with pull-out poster	*$6.25*	*$18.50*	*$37.50*	£2.90	£8.75	£17.50
2-4 scarce distributed in the U.K.	*$3.75*	*$11.00*	*$22.50*	£1.65	£5.00	£10.00
Title Value:	*$17.50*	*$51.50*	*$105.00*	£7.85	£23.75	£47.50

FAMILY MAN
DC Comics/Paradox Press,MS; 1 Apr 1995-3 Jul 1995

	$Good	$Fine	$N.Mint	£Good	£Fine	£N.Mint
1-3 ND 96pgs, black and white	*$1.00*	*$3.00*	*$5.00*	£0.70	£2.10	£3.50
Title Value:	*$3.00*	*$9.00*	*$15.00*	£2.10	£6.30	£10.50

FAMOUS FIRST EDITION
DC Comics,Tabloid;C-26 1974-F8 Aug/Sep 1975;C-61 Sep 1978

(see Limited Collectors' Edition and All New Collectors' Edition)

	$Good	$Fine	$N.Mint	£Good	£Fine	£N.Mint
C-26, ND Action Comics #1	*$3.30*	*$10.00*	*$20.00*	£2.50	£7.50	£15.00
C-28, ND Detective Comics #27	*$5.75*	*$17.50*	*$35.00*	£4.15	£12.50	£25.00
C-30, ND Sensation Comics #1	*$2.50*	*$7.50*	*$15.00*	£1.65	£5.00	£10.00
C-61, distributed in the U.K. Superman #1	*$2.50*	*$7.50*	*$15.00*	£1.00	£3.00	£6.00
F-4, ND Whiz Comics #2 (#1); cover not identical to original	*$2.50*	*$7.50*	*$15.00*	£1.25	£3.75	£7.50
F-5, ND Batman #1 (indicia misprinted as F-6 on inside)	*$4.15*	*$12.50*	*$25.00*	£3.30	£10.00	£20.00
F-6, ND Wonder Woman #1	*$2.50*	*$7.50*	*$15.00*	£1.25	£3.75	£7.50
F-7, ND All-Star Comics #3						

VERY GENERAL PERCENTAGE CONVERSION CHART WHICH MAY BE USED TO CALCULATE LOW AND INBETWEEN GRADES:

	$Good	$Fine	$N.Mint	£Good	£Fine	£N.Mint
	$2.50	$7.50	$15.00	£1.65	£5.00	£10.00
F-8, ND Flash Comics #1	$2.50	$7.50	$15.00	£1.65	£5.00	£10.00
Title Value:	$28.20	$85.00	$170.00	£18.40	£55.50	£111.00

Note: **F-6**, **F-7** and **F-8** are all 64pgs and all other issues are 72pgs. All issues are exact but larger reprints of the original comics with new, thicker outer covers.

Hardcover editions with dust-jackets of **C-26**, **C-28** and **C-30** along with **F-4** and **F-6** are known. They are very scarce in the U.K. and prices would be in the £30.00-£40.00 range for all. Some **F-5** Batman #1 copies have no paper cover on the inside though it is not known what proportion of the print run. Owing to their size and consequent problems with mailing and display, perfectly flat, uncreased and therefore near mint copies are generally very scarce in both the U.K. and U.S.

FAMOUS MONSTERS OF FILMLAND

Warren; 1 1962-160 1980

	$Good	$Fine	$N.Mint	£Good	£Fine	£N.Mint
1 scarce in the U.K.	$92.50	$275.00	$650.00	£55.00	£170.00	£400.00
2	$21.00	$62.50	$150.00	£14.00	£43.00	£100.00
3-5	$12.50	$39.00	$90.00	£8.50	£26.00	£60.00
6-10	$10.00	$30.00	$70.00	£6.25	£19.00	£45.00
11-20	$7.75	$23.50	$55.00	£4.25	£12.50	£30.00
21-30	$5.50	$17.00	$40.00	£3.55	£10.50	£25.00
31	$3.55	$10.50	$25.00	£2.10	£6.25	£15.00
32 scarce in the U.K. Munsters	$3.55	$10.50	$25.00	£3.55	£10.50	£25.00
33-35	$3.55	$10.50	$25.00	£2.10	£6.25	£15.00
36-50	$2.10	$6.25	$15.00	£1.40	£4.25	£10.00
51-55	$2.40	$7.00	$12.00	£1.50	£4.50	£7.50
56 very rare in the U.K. Frankenstein cover	$3.00	$9.00	$15.00	£5.00	£15.00	£25.00
57-80	$2.40	$7.00	$12.00	£1.50	£4.50	£7.50
81-88	$2.00	$6.00	$10.00	£1.20	£3.60	£6.00
89 rare in the U.K. Werewolf cover	$2.00	$6.00	$10.00	£1.80	£5.25	£9.00
90-94	$1.50	$4.50	$7.50	£1.00	£3.00	£5.00
95 very rare in the U.K. Dracula	$2.00	$6.00	$10.00	£3.00	£9.00	£15.00
96-113	$1.00	$3.00	$5.00	£0.90	£2.70	£4.50
114 100pgs, special edition on Japanese monsters	$1.50	$4.50	$7.50	£1.00	£3.00	£5.00
115-139	$0.70	$2.10	$3.50	£0.70	£2.10	£3.50
140 scarce in the U.K. Frankenstein cover	$0.70	$2.10	$3.50	£0.80	£2.40	£4.00
141 scarce in the U.K. Close Encounters issue	$0.70	$2.10	$3.50	£0.80	£2.40	£4.00
142 scarce in the U.K. Star Wars issue	$0.70	$2.10	$3.50	£0.80	£2.40	£4.00
143-157	$0.60	$1.80	$3.00	£0.60	£1.80	£3.00
158 1980 Annual Giant Size	$0.70	$2.10	$3.50	£0.70	£2.10	£3.50
159-160	$0.60	$1.80	$3.00	£0.60	£1.80	£3.00
Title Value:	$532.85	$1600.25	$3470.50	£352.60	£1062.80	£2269.50

Note: most issues distributed on the news-stands in the U.K.

FAMOUS MONSTERS OF FILMLAND YEARBOOK

Warren; 1 1963-9 1971

	$Good	$Fine	$N.Mint	£Good	£Fine	£N.Mint
1 (1963)	$7.00	$21.00	$50.00	£5.00	£15.00	£35.00
2 (1964)	$5.00	$15.00	$35.00	£3.55	£10.50	£25.00
3 (1965)	$4.25	$12.50	$30.00	£2.85	£8.50	£20.00
4 (1966)	$3.20	$9.50	$22.50	£2.10	£6.25	£15.00
5 scarce in the U.K. (1967)	$3.20	$9.50	$22.50	£2.10	£6.25	£15.00
6-8 (1968-1971)	$2.50	$7.50	$17.50	£1.70	£5.00	£12.00
9 (1969-1971)	$2.50	$7.50	$17.50	£1.70	£5.00	£12.00

	$Good	$Fine	$N.Mint	£Good	£Fine	£N.Mint
Title Value:	$32.65	$97.50	$230.00	£22.40	£66.50	£158.00

Note: most issues distributed on the news-stands in the U.K.

FANG

Sirius Entertainment,MS; 1 Feb 1995-3 Jun 1995

	$Good	$Fine	$N.Mint	£Good	£Fine	£N.Mint
1-3 ND Kevin J. Taylor script and art	$0.60	$1.80	$3.00	£0.40	£1.20	£2.00
Title Value:	$1.80	$5.40	$9.00	£1.20	£3.60	£6.00

FANG: TESTAMENT

Sirius Entertainment; 1 1996

	$Good	$Fine	$N.Mint	£Good	£Fine	£N.Mint
1 ND Kevin J. Taylor script and art; black and white	$0.60	$1.80	$3.00	£0.40	£1.20	£2.00
Title Value:	$0.60	$1.80	$3.00	£0.40	£1.20	£2.00

FANGORIA

O'Quinn Studios/Starlog Group; 1 1979-present

	$Good	$Fine	$N.Mint	£Good	£Fine	£N.Mint
1	$2.50	$7.50	$15.00	£1.65	£5.00	£10.00
2	$2.00	$6.00	$12.00	£1.25	£3.75	£7.50
3-5	$1.50	$4.50	$9.00	£1.00	£3.00	£6.00
6-10	$1.25	$3.75	$7.50	£0.80	£2.50	£5.00
11-19	$1.40	$4.20	$7.00	£0.90	£2.70	£4.50
20-39	$1.20	$3.60	$6.00	£0.80	£2.40	£4.00
40-55	$0.90	$2.70	$4.50	£0.60	£1.80	£3.00
56-130	$0.80	$2.40	$4.00	£0.50	£1.50	£2.50
131-145	$1.00	$3.00	$5.00	£0.65	£1.95	£3.25
146-149	$1.20	$3.60	$6.00	£0.80	£2.40	£4.00
150	$1.20	$3.60	$6.00	£0.90	£2.70	£4.50
151	$1.20	$3.60	$6.00	£0.80	£2.40	£4.00
Title Value:	$148.45	$445.35	$757.50	£95.75	£287.80	£489.75

Note: distributed on the news-stands in the U.K.

FANGORIA HORROR SPECIAL/SPECTACULAR

O'Quinn Studios/Starlog Group; 1 1985-present

	$Good	$Fine	$N.Mint	£Good	£Fine	£N.Mint
1-10	$0.90	$2.70	$4.50	£0.60	£1.80	£3.00
Title Value:	$9.00	$27.00	$45.00	£6.00	£18.00	£30.00

Note: distrbuted on the news-stands in the U.K.

FANGS OF THE WIDOW

London Night Studios,MS; 1 1995-5 1996;Ground Zero Comics;6 Mar 1996-present

	$Good	$Fine	$N.Mint	£Good	£Fine	£N.Mint
1 ND black and white	$0.60	$1.80	$3.00	£0.40	£1.20	£2.00
1 Platinum Edition ND	$1.00	$3.00	$5.00	£0.60	£1.80	£3.00
2-9 ND black and white	$0.60	$1.80	$3.00	£0.40	£1.20	£2.00
Title Value:	$6.40	$19.20	$32.00	£4.20	£12.60	£21.00

FANTASCI

Warp/Apple; 1 Jun 1986-9 Sep 1988

	$Good	$Fine	$N.Mint	£Good	£Fine	£N.Mint
1-9 ND	$0.40	$1.20	$2.00	£0.25	£0.75	£1.25
Title Value:	$3.60	$10.80	$18.00	£2.25	£6.75	£11.25

FANTASTIC ADVENTURES

I.W. Super; 9,10-12,15-18 1963-1964

	$Good	$Fine	$N.Mint	£Good	£Fine	£N.Mint
9-10 reprints	$2.10	$6.25	$15.00	£1.10	£3.40	£8.00
11 reprints, Wally Wood art	$4.25	$12.50	$30.00	£2.10	£6.25	£15.00
12 reprints	$2.10	$6.25	$15.00	£1.10	£3.40	£8.00
15 reprints "The Gorilla" from Spook #23	$2.10	$6.25	$15.00	£1.10	£3.40	£8.00
16 reprints	$2.10	$6.25	$15.00	£1.10	£3.40	£8.00
17 reprints, Matt Baker art	$3.55	$10.50	$25.00	£1.75	£5.25	£12.50
18 reprints	$1.75	$5.25	$12.50	£1.10	£3.40	£8.00
Title Value:	$20.05	$59.50	$142.50	£10.45	£31.90	£75.50

Note: all distributed in the U.K.

Excalibur #3

Extreme Destroyer Prologue

Falling In Love #37

FANTASTIC ADVENTURES (2ND SERIES)

Ace; 1 1987

Issue	$Good	$Fine	$N.Mint	£Good	£Fine	£N.Mint
1 ND Golden Age reprints	$0.40	$1.20	$2.00	£0.25	£0.75	£1.25
Title Value:	$0.40	$1.20	$2.00	£0.25	£0.75	£1.25

FANTASTIC FABLES

Silverwolf Comics; 1 Feb 1987-2 1987

Issue	$Good	$Fine	$N.Mint	£Good	£Fine	£N.Mint
1-2 ND features Tim Vigil art	$0.40	$1.20	$2.00	£0.25	£0.75	£1.25
Title Value:	$0.80	$2.40	$4.00	£0.50	£1.50	£2.50

FANTASTIC FORCE

Marvel Comics Group; 1 Oct 1994-18 Apr 1996

Issue	$Good	$Fine	$N.Mint	£Good	£Fine	£N.Mint
1 Psi-Lord, Vibraxis, Huntara and Gigantus begin; Black Panther appears; foil stamped cover	$0.50	$1.50	$2.50	£0.30	£0.90	£1.50
2-3	$0.35	$1.05	$1.75	£0.25	£0.75	£1.25
4 Captain America appears	$0.35	$1.05	$1.75	£0.25	£0.75	£1.25
5-6	$0.35	$1.05	$1.75	£0.25	£0.75	£1.25
7 ties into Fantastic Four #400	$0.35	$1.05	$1.75	£0.25	£0.75	£1.25
8-9 Atlantis Rising tie-in	$0.35	$1.05	$1.75	£0.25	£0.75	£1.25
10	$0.35	$1.05	$1.75	£0.25	£0.75	£1.25
11-12 Black Panther appears	$0.35	$1.05	$1.75	£0.25	£0.75	£1.25
13 Black Panther appears and She-Hulk joins the Fantastic Force	$0.35	$1.05	$1.75	£0.25	£0.75	£1.25
14-18	$0.35	$1.05	$1.75	£0.25	£0.75	£1.25
Title Value:	$6.45	$19.35	$32.25	£4.55	£13.65	£22.75

FANTASTIC FOUR

Marvel Comics Group; 1 Nov 1961-416 Sep 1996

(see also Marvel Collector's Item Classics, Marvel's Greatest Comics, Marvel Treasury Edition, Marvel Triple Action, Official Marvel Index to.., What If?)

Issue	$Good	$Fine	$N.Mint	£Good	£Fine	£N.Mint
1 origin/1st appearance Fantastic Four (Mr. Fantastic, Invisible Girl, Human Torch, The Thing), 1st appearance Mole Man; generally regarded as the comic that started "The Marvel Age of Comics"	$1400.00	$4200.00	$21000.00	£730.00	£2200.00	£11000.00
[Prices may vary widely on this comic]						
1 Marvel Milestone Edition, ND (Nov 1991), reprints original issue with ads, silver border around cover	$0.60	$1.80	$3.00	£0.40	£1.20	£2.00
1 Marvel Milestone Edition 2nd printing, ND (Nov 1994), reprints original issue with ads, metallic ink cover	$0.60	$1.80	$3.00	£0.40	£1.20	£2.00
1 Reprint, ND very scarce in the U.K. (1966)	$29.00	$85.00	$200.00	£17.50	£52.50	£125.00
1 Reprint with Golden Record, ND very rare in the U.K to form complete sealed package	$41.00	$120.00	$290.00	£26.00	£77.50	£185.00
2 (Jan 1962), 1st appearance The Skrulls	$385.00	$1150.00	$3850.00	£215.00	£640.00	£2150.00
3 1st appearance costumes, 1st Baxter Building and Fantasti-Car	$250.00	$750.00	$2500.00	£135.00	£405.00	£1350.00
4 Sub-Mariner returns (1st Silver Age appearance)	$295.00	$880.00	$2950.00	£165.00	£495.00	£1650.00
[Scarce in high grade - Very Fine+ or better]						
5 origin and 1st appearance Dr. Doom	$320.00	$960.00	$3200.00	£175.00	£520.00	£1750.00
5 Marvel Milestone Edition, ND (Jan 1993) - silver border around cover	$0.60	$1.80	$3.00	£0.40	£1.20	£2.00
6 2nd appearance Dr. Doom, 2nd Silver Age Sub-Mariner appearance, 1st villain "Marvel Age" team-up; plans for Baxter Building shown	$190.00	$570.00	$1925.00	£90.00	£270.00	£900.00
7 very scarce in the U.K. (previously listed as Rare but more copies are turning up)	$92.50	$280.00	$850.00	£60.00	£180.00	£550.00
[Very scarce in high grade - Very Fine+ or better]						
8 scarce in the U.K. 1st appearance Puppet Master, 1st appearance Alicia Masters	$92.50	$280.00	$850.00	£57.50	£175.00	£525.00
9 3rd Silver Age Sub-Mariner appearance	$92.50	$280.00	$850.00	£55.00	£165.00	£500.00
10 (Jan 1963), 3rd appearance Dr. Doom	$92.50	$280.00	$850.00	£55.00	£165.00	£500.00
11 scarce in the U.K. origin and 1st appearance Impossible Man	$77.50	$230.00	$625.00	£50.00	£150.00	£400.00
12 Hulk appears (1st appearance in another title), 1st confrontation Hulk/Thing (1st ever Marvel X-over along with Amazing Spiderman #1)	$130.00	$400.00	$1200.00	£60.00	£180.00	£550.00
13 1st appearance Red Ghost, 1st appearance The Watcher	$60.00	$185.00	$495.00	£34.00	£100.00	£275.00
14 less common in the U.K. Sub-Mariner appears; Steve Ditko cover?	$38.00	$110.00	$305.00	£23.00	£67.50	£185.00
15 scarce in the U.K. 1st appearance The Mad Thinker and Awesome Android	$38.00	$110.00	$305.00	£28.00	£82.50	£225.00
16 scarce in the U.K. Ant-Man and Dr. Doom appear	$38.00	$110.00	$305.00	£28.00	£82.50	£225.00
17 less common in the U.K. Ant-Man cameo	$38.00	$110.00	$305.00	£25.00	£75.00	£200.00
18 1st appearance Super Skrull	$38.00	$110.00	$305.00	£23.00	£67.50	£185.00
19 1st appearance Rama Tut	$38.00	$110.00	$305.00	£23.00	£67.50	£185.00
20 origin and 1st appearance Molecule Man	$39.00	$115.00	$310.00	£24.00	£72.50	£195.00
21 1st appearance Hate Monger, Nick Fury (CIA, pre-Shield), appears	$29.00	$85.00	$200.00	£17.50	£52.50	£125.00
22 (Jan 1964), Mole Man appears	$21.00	$62.50	$150.00	£14.00	£43.00	£100.00
23 Dr. Doom appears	$21.00	$62.50	$150.00	£14.00	£43.00	£100.00
24 1st appearance The Infant ("Terrible")	$21.00	$62.50	$150.00	£14.00	£43.00	£100.00
25 classic Thing vs Hulk fight; the first of many! Avengers cameoes including Captain America - technically his 2nd Silver Age appearance after Avengers #4	$49.00	$145.00	$390.00	£33.00	£97.50	£260.00
26 Thing vs Hulk, Avengers X-over (1st) - story ties into Avengers #4	$47.00	$140.00	$375.00	£31.00	£92.50	£250.00
27 Sub-Mariner, Dr. Strange X-over (1st)	$22.50	$67.50	$160.00	£14.00	£43.00	£100.00
28 less common in the U.K. X-Men X-over (1st in title)	$36.00	$105.00	$250.00	£19.00	£57.50	£135.00
29 The Watcher appears	$17.50	$52.50	$125.00	£11.00	£34.00	£80.00
30 1st appearance Diablo	$17.50	$52.50	$125.00	£11.00	£34.00	£80.00
31 Avengers cameo; 1st appearance Dr. Franklin Storm, Mole Man appears	$13.50	$41.00	$95.00	£8.50	£26.00	£60.00
32-33 rare in the U.K.	$13.50	$41.00	$95.00	£9.25	£28.00	£65.00
34 scarce in the U.K. (Jan 1965), 1st appearance Gideon	$13.50	$41.00	$95.00	£8.50	£26.00	£60.00
35 1st appearance Dragon Man, Reed and Sue engaged (later married in Annual #3)	$13.50	$41.00	$95.00	£8.50	£26.00	£60.00
36 1st appearance Frightful Four (Medusa, Paste-Pot Pete, Wizard, Sandman) (Note: this is the first appearance of Medusa)	$13.50	$41.00	$95.00	£7.75	£23.50	£55.00
37 Skrulls appear	$13.50	$41.00	$95.00	£7.75	£23.50	£55.00
38 Paste-Pot Pete becomes The Trapster, Frightful Four return	$13.50	$41.00	$95.00	£7.75	£23.50	£55.00
39 Daredevil X-over (a classic - D.D. battles Dr. Doom with powerless F.F.), classic cover	$13.50	$41.00	$95.00	£8.00	£24.50	£57.50
40 Daredevil X-over (a classic - D.D. battles Dr. Doom with powerless F.F.)	$13.50	$41.00	$95.00	£8.00	£24.50	£57.50
41-43 Frightful Four appear; Thing leaves F.F. temporarily	$9.25	$28.00	$65.00	£5.50	£17.00	£40.00
44 1st appearance Gorgon, Madame Medusa from Frightful Four appears	$9.25	$28.00	$65.00	£5.50	£17.00	£40.00
45 1st appearance Inhumans (Madame Medusa plus Crystal, Karnak, Black Bolt [cameo], Triton, Lockjaw); last Silver Age issue indicia-dated December 1965	$9.25	$28.00	$65.00	£5.50	£17.00	£40.00
46 (Jan 1966), 1st full appearance Black Bolt, 1st appearance The Seeker	$9.25	$28.00	$65.00	£5.50	£17.00	£40.00
47 1st appearance Maximus and The Great Refuge	$9.25	$28.00	$65.00	£5.50	£17.00	£40.00
48 1st appearance Silver Surfer (origin in Silver Surfer #1), 1st appearance Galactus (with part origin only)	$100.00	$300.00	$1000.00	£50.00	£150.00	£500.00
49 2nd appearance Silver Surfer and Galactus	$33.00	$97.50	$265.00	£18.50	£55.00	£150.00
50 1st appearance Wyatt Wingfoot, 3rd Silver Surfer (vs. Galactus), classic cover	$32.00	$95.00	$290.00	£19.00	£57.50	£175.00
51 scarce in the U.K.	$7.00	$21.00	$50.00	£4.25	£12.50	£30.00
52 1st appearance Black Panther (in a cape!), Inhumans cameo	$14.00	$43.00	$100.00	£7.00	£21.00	£50.00
53 origin and 2nd appearance Black Panther	$12.00	$36.00	$85.00	£5.25	£16.00	£37.50
54 Black Panther and Inhumans guest-star	$7.00	$21.00	$50.00	£4.25	£12.50	£30.00
55 Silver Surfer battles The Thing	$10.50	$32.00	$75.00	£5.25	£16.00	£37.50
56 very scarce in the U.K. and U.S. Silver Surfer cameo (note: a slightly thinner paper was used on the cover resulting in many copies with spine splits)	$9.25	$28.00	$65.00	£5.25	£16.00	£37.50
57 very scarce in the U.K. Silver Surfer and Dr. Doom appear	$9.25	$28.00	$65.00	£5.25	£16.00	£37.50
58 (Jan 1967), Dr. Doom appear	$9.25	$28.00	$65.00	£5.00	£15.00	£35.00
59 Silver Surfer and Dr. Doom appear; Inhumans appear. Dr. Doom acquires Silver Surfer's board and powers	$9.25	$28.00	$65.00	£5.00	£15.00	£35.00
60 Silver Surfer and Dr. Doom appear	$9.25	$28.00	$65.00	£5.00	£15.00	£35.00
61 Silver Surfer and Dr. Doom appear	$6.25	$19.00	$45.00	£4.25	£12.50	£30.00
62 1st appearance Blastaar	$6.25	$19.00	$45.00	£3.90	£11.50	£27.50
63-65	$6.25	$19.00	$45.00	£3.90	£11.50	£27.50
66 1st appearance Warlock (as "Him"), still in "coccoon", partial origin told	$13.50	$41.00	$95.00	£6.25	£19.00	£45.00
67 2nd appearance "Him", emerges from "coccoon" (two panels only on last page - see Thor #165 for 1st full appearance)	$14.00	$43.00	$100.00	£7.00	£21.00	£50.00
68-69	$6.25	$19.00	$45.00	£2.85	£8.50	£20.00
70 (Jan 1968)	$6.25	$19.00	$45.00	£2.85	£8.50	£20.00
71	$5.00	$15.00	$35.00	£2.55	£7.50	£18.00
72 less common in the U.K. Silver Surfer appears; classic cover	$5.25	$16.00	$37.50	£3.00	£9.00	£21.00
73 Thor, Spider-Man appear; X-over with Daredevil #38	$5.00	$15.00	$35.00	£2.55	£7.50	£18.00

THE WORLD'S GREATEST COMIC BOOK FONTS!
APPROVED BY THE COMICCRAFT AUTHORITY
Spills!
DL205: $49
Thrills!
DL206: $49
Chills!
DL207: $49
AP1: ACTION PACK ALL THREE FONTS FOR ONLY $99! SAVE $50!
BALLOON LETTERING!
BL001: Comicrazy Regular, Italic, Bold Italic & International $395
BL002: ASTRO CITY REGULAR, ITALIC, BOLD ITALIC $129
BL002i WITH A FULL SET OF INTERNATIONAL CHARACTERS $199
BL003: WILDWORDS REGULAR, ITALIC, BOLD ITALIC $129
BL003i WITH INT'L CHARACTERS $199
BL004: SPOOKY TOOTH REGULAR, ITALIC, BOLD ITALIC $39
SOUND EFFECTS!
CLOBBERIN TIME FX101 $59
FX103 Zoinks! $49
PHASES ON STUN FX 102 $49
BRONTO BURGER FX104 $59
CARRY ON SCREAMING! FX105 $59
DISPLAY LETTERING!
DUTCH COURAGE DARK, DRAUGHT, LITE, BLACK&TAN DL201 $149
Adamantium DL202 $59
Incy Wincy Spider DL203 $59
Yuletide Log DL204 $39
CAPTION LETTERING!
CL301: PulpFiction $39
SUBTOTAL: $
SHIPPING & HANDLING: $40.00
TOTAL: $
HERE'S HOW TO ORDER:
1. All orders must allow $40 for shipping and handling.
2. Fill in the boxes above and the information at right.
3. Place your order in an envelope and mail it with your credit card number, check or money order (payable to ACTIVE IMAGES) to:
ACTIVE IMAGES,
430 COLORADO AVE #301,
SANTA MONICA CA 90401 USA
(You can also FAX your order to us at 0101 310 451 9761 or call us at 0101 310 458 9094. Have your credit card ready)
NAME:
MAC PC
ADDRESS:
AMEX
DISC
POSTCODE: COUNTRY:
M/C
PHONE:( ) FAX: ( )
VISA
NAME ON CARD:
CHECK
CARD NUMBER: EXP. DATE: /
SIGNATURE:
All fonts available for MAC or PC
Visit us on the world wide web at: www.comicbookfonts.com

Issue	$Good	$Fine	$N.Mint	£Good	£Fine	£N.Mint
74 Silver Surfer, Galactus appears, 1st different quality paper and covers (less glossy)	*$5.25*	*$16.00*	*$37.50*	£2.85	£8.50	£20.00
75 Silver Surfer, Galactus appear	*$5.25*	*$16.00*	*$37.50*	£2.85	£8.50	£20.00
76-77 Silver Surfer appears	*$5.25*	*$16.00*	*$37.50*	£2.85	£8.50	£20.00
78-80	*$5.00*	*$15.00*	*$35.00*	£2.55	£7.50	£18.00
81 Crystal joins F.F	*$3.55*	*$10.50*	*$25.00*	£2.00	£6.00	£14.00
82 (Jan 1969)	*$3.55*	*$10.50*	*$25.00*	£2.00	£6.00	£14.00
83	*$3.55*	*$10.50*	*$25.00*	£2.00	£6.00	£14.00
84-87 Dr.Doom story inspired by "The Prisoner" TV series	*$3.55*	*$10.50*	*$25.00*	£2.00	£6.00	£14.00
88 scarce in the U.K.	*$3.55*	*$10.50*	*$25.00*	£2.10	£6.25	£15.00
89-93	*$2.85*	*$8.50*	*$20.00*	£1.10	£3.40	£8.00
94 (Jan 1970), 1st appearance Agatha Harkness	*$2.85*	*$8.50*	*$20.00*	£1.10	£3.40	£8.00
95-97	*$2.85*	*$8.50*	*$20.00*	£1.10	£3.40	£8.00
98 Apollo mission story	*$2.85*	*$8.50*	*$20.00*	£1.10	£3.40	£8.00
99	*$2.85*	*$8.50*	*$20.00*	£1.10	£3.40	£8.00
100 very scarce in the U.K. guest-stars nearly every FF foe up to that point (as androids) under the control of the Puppet Master	*$10.00*	*$30.00*	*$70.00*	£5.50	£17.00	£40.00
101	*$2.90*	*$8.75*	*$17.50*	£1.15	£3.50	£7.00
102 Magneto X-over, Sub-Mariner appears; last Jack Kirby issue	*$2.90*	*$8.75*	*$17.50*	£1.15	£3.50	£7.00
103 Magneto X-over, Thing vs. Sub-Mariner	*$2.50*	*$7.50*	*$15.00*	£1.15	£3.50	£7.00
104 Magneto X-over	*$2.50*	*$7.50*	*$15.00*	£1.30	£4.00	£8.00
105	*$2.50*	*$7.50*	*$15.00*	£1.15	£3.50	£7.00
106 (Jan 1971)	*$2.50*	*$7.50*	*$15.00*	£1.15	£3.50	£7.00
107	*$2.50*	*$7.50*	*$15.00*	£1.15	£3.50	£7.00
108 part Jack Kirby art	*$2.50*	*$7.50*	*$15.00*	£1.15	£3.50	£7.00
109	*$2.50*	*$7.50*	*$15.00*	£1.15	£3.50	£7.00
110 (some copies have green misprinting on cover areas that are normally blue and yellow)	*$2.50*	*$7.50*	*$15.00*	£1.15	£3.50	£7.00
111	*$2.05*	*$6.25*	*$12.50*	£1.15	£3.50	£7.00
112 very scarce in the U.K. Hulk vs The Thing	*$9.00*	*$28.00*	*$55.00*	£4.15	£12.50	£25.00
113-115 scarce in the U.K.	*$2.05*	*$6.25*	*$12.50*	£1.25	£3.75	£7.50
116 very scarce in the U.K. 52pgs, origin The Stranger, Dr. Doom appears	*$2.05*	*$6.25*	*$12.50*	£1.30	£4.00	£8.00
117 scarce in the U.K.	*$2.05*	*$6.25*	*$12.50*	£1.15	£3.50	£7.00
118 scarce in the U.K. (Jan 1972)	*$2.05*	*$6.25*	*$12.50*	£1.15	£3.50	£7.00
119-120 scarce in the U.K.	*$2.05*	*$6.25*	*$12.50*	£1.15	£3.50	£7.00
121 very scarce in the U.K. Silver Surfer and Galactus appear, 1st appearance Gabriel (2nd herald of Galactus)	*$2.90*	*$8.75*	*$17.50*	£1.30	£4.00	£8.00
122-123 very scarce in the U.K. Silver Surfer and Galactus appear	*$2.90*	*$8.75*	*$17.50*	£1.30	£4.00	£8.00
124-125 scarce in the U.K.	*$1.65*	*$5.00*	*$10.00*	£1.15	£3.50	£7.00
126 scarce in the U.K. origin re-done from issue #1	*$2.00*	*$6.00*	*$12.00*	£1.15	£3.50	£7.00
127 scarce in the U.K.	*$1.65*	*$5.00*	*$10.00*	£1.15	£3.50	£7.00
128 high-quality colour 4pg centre-fold insert Friends and Foes	*$2.00*	*$6.00*	*$12.00*	£1.00	£3.00	£6.00
128 without insert, as above	*$1.65*	*$5.00*	*$10.00*	£0.90	£2.75	£5.50
129 1st appearance Thundra	*$1.65*	*$5.00*	*$10.00*	£1.00	£3.00	£6.00
130 (Jan 1973), Jim Steranko cover	*$1.65*	*$5.00*	*$10.00*	£1.00	£3.00	£6.00
131 Inhumans appear, Steranko cover	*$1.65*	*$5.00*	*$10.00*	£0.75	£2.25	£4.50
132 Jim Steranko cover	*$1.65*	*$5.00*	*$10.00*	£0.75	£2.25	£4.50
133 Thing vs. Thundra	*$1.65*	*$5.00*	*$10.00*	£0.75	£2.25	£4.50
134-140	*$1.65*	*$5.00*	*$10.00*	£0.75	£2.25	£4.50
141	*$1.50*	*$4.50*	*$9.00*	£0.60	£1.85	£3.75
142 (Jan 1974)	*$1.50*	*$4.50*	*$9.00*	£0.60	£1.85	£3.75
143	*$1.50*	*$4.50*	*$9.00*	£0.60	£1.85	£3.75
144 ND scarce in the U.K.	*$1.50*	*$4.50*	*$9.00*	£1.25	£3.75	£7.50
145-146 ND	*$1.50*	*$4.50*	*$9.00*	£0.75	£2.25	£4.50
147 ND Thing vs. Sub-Mariner	*$1.50*	*$4.50*	*$9.00*	£0.75	£2.25	£4.50
148 ND	*$1.50*	*$4.50*	*$9.00*	£0.75	£2.25	£4.50
149 Sub-Mariner appears	*$1.50*	*$4.50*	*$9.00*	£0.65	£2.00	£4.00
150 Crystal, Quicksilver wed, continues from Avengers #127	*$1.65*	*$5.00*	*$10.00*	£0.75	£2.25	£4.50
151-153	*$1.60*	*$4.80*	*$8.00*	£0.70	£2.10	£3.50
154 (Jan 1975), edited reprint of Strange Tales #127 with 7 new pages	*$1.60*	*$4.80*	*$8.00*	£0.70	£2.10	£3.50
155 Silver Surfer vs. Thing, cover based on #55	*$1.80*	*$5.25*	*$9.00*	£0.80	£2.40	£4.00
156-157 Silver Surfer/Dr. Doom	*$1.80*	*$5.25*	*$9.00*	£0.80	£2.40	£4.00
158	*$1.50*	*$4.50*	*$7.50*	£0.70	£2.10	£3.50
159 Inhumans appear	*$1.50*	*$4.50*	*$7.50*	£0.70	£2.10	£3.50
160	*$1.50*	*$4.50*	*$7.50*	£0.70	£2.10	£3.50
161	*$1.00*	*$3.00*	*$5.00*	£0.50	£1.50	£2.50
162 Thing vs. Thing	*$1.00*	*$3.00*	*$5.00*	£0.50	£1.50	£2.50
163	*$1.00*	*$3.00*	*$5.00*	£0.50	£1.50	£2.50
164 1st George Perez art on F.F., Marvel Boy returns as Crusader	*$1.00*	*$3.00*	*$5.00*	£0.60	£1.80	£3.00
165 George Perez art	*$1.00*	*$3.00*	*$5.00*	£0.50	£1.50	£2.50
166 (Jan 1976), George Perez art, Thing vs. Hulk	*$1.00*	*$3.00*	*$5.00*	£0.50	£1.50	£2.50
167 George Perez art	*$1.00*	*$3.00*	*$5.00*	£0.50	£1.50	£2.50
168-169 Luke Cage appears	*$1.00*	*$3.00*	*$5.00*	£0.50	£1.50	£2.50
170 Thing vs. Luke Cage	*$1.00*	*$3.00*	*$5.00*	£0.50	£1.50	£2.50
171 George Perez art	*$0.80*	*$2.40*	*$4.00*	£0.50	£1.50	£2.50
172 George Perez art, Galactus appears	*$1.00*	*$3.00*	*$5.00*	£0.60	£1.80	£3.00
173-174 Galactus appears	*$1.00*	*$3.00*	*$5.00*	£0.60	£1.80	£3.00
175 High Evolutionary vs. Galactus	*$1.00*	*$3.00*	*$5.00*	£0.60	£1.80	£3.00
176 ND Impossible Man, Marvel Bullpen appear, George Perez art	*$1.00*	*$3.00*	*$5.00*	£0.60	£1.80	£3.00
177 George Perez art	*$1.00*	*$3.00*	*$5.00*	£0.40	£1.20	£2.00
178 (Jan 1977), George Perez art	*$1.00*	*$3.00*	*$5.00*	£0.40	£1.20	£2.00
179	*$1.00*	*$3.00*	*$5.00*	£0.30	£0.90	£1.50
180 reprints issue #101	*$1.00*	*$3.00*	*$5.00*	£0.30	£0.90	£1.50
181-183	*$0.80*	*$2.40*	*$4.00*	£0.30	£0.90	£1.50
184-188 George Perez art	*$0.80*	*$2.40*	*$4.00*	£0.30	£0.90	£1.50
189 reprints part F.F. Annual #4 Human Torch vs. original Human Torch	*$0.80*	*$2.40*	*$4.00*	£0.30	£0.90	£1.50
190 LD in the U.K. (Jan 1978), history of F.F. retold; Silver Surfer and Galactus appear	*$0.80*	*$2.40*	*$4.00*	£0.50	£1.50	£2.50
191-192 George Perez art	*$0.80*	*$2.40*	*$4.00*	£0.30	£0.90	£1.50
193-199 ND	*$0.80*	*$2.40*	*$4.00*	£0.40	£1.20	£2.00
200 ND 52pgs, 17th anniversary, Mr. Fantastic vs. Dr. Doom	*$1.50*	*$4.50*	*$7.50*	£0.70	£2.10	£3.50
201 ND	*$0.60*	*$1.80*	*$3.00*	£0.40	£1.20	£2.00
202 ND (Jan 1979), Iron Man appears	*$0.60*	*$1.80*	*$3.00*	£0.40	£1.20	£2.00
203 ND	*$0.60*	*$1.80*	*$3.00*	£0.40	£1.20	£2.00
204 ND storyline introduces the new Champions (ends #209)	*$0.60*	*$1.80*	*$3.00*	£0.40	£1.20	£2.00
205-206 ND	*$0.60*	*$1.80*	*$3.00*	£0.40	£1.20	£2.00
207 ND Spider-Man vs Torch	*$0.60*	*$1.80*	*$3.00*	£0.40	£1.20	£2.00
208 ND	*$0.60*	*$1.80*	*$3.00*	£0.40	£1.20	£2.00
209 ND 1st appearance Herbie (robot), John Byrne art	*$0.70*	*$2.10*	*$3.50*	£0.60	£1.80	£3.00
210-211 ND Galactus appears, John Byrne art	*$0.60*	*$1.80*	*$3.00*	£0.50	£1.50	£2.50
212 Galactus appears, John Byrne art	*$0.60*	*$1.80*	*$3.00*	£0.40	£1.20	£2.00
213 ND John Byrne art	*$0.60*	*$1.80*	*$3.00*	£0.50	£1.50	£2.50
214 ND (Jan 1980), John Byrne art	*$0.60*	*$1.80*	*$3.00*	£0.50	£1.50	£2.50
215-216 ND John Byrne art	*$0.60*	*$1.80*	*$3.00*	£0.50	£1.50	£2.50
217 ND Dazzler appears, John Byrne art	*$0.60*	*$1.80*	*$3.00*	£0.50	£1.50	£2.50
218 ND Spider-Man appears, John Byrne art; continues from Spectacular Spiderman #42	*$0.60*	*$1.80*	*$3.00*	£0.50	£1.50	£2.50
219 ND Sub-Mariner appears, Sienkiewicz art	*$0.60*	*$1.80*	*$3.00*	£0.50	£1.50	£2.50
220 ND John Byrne art	*$0.60*	*$1.80*	*$3.00*	£0.50	£1.50	£2.50
221 ND John Byrne art	*$0.60*	*$1.80*	*$3.00*	£0.40	£1.20	£2.00
222-224 ND Sienkiewicz art	*$0.60*	*$1.80*	*$3.00*	£0.40	£1.20	£2.00
225 ND Sienkiewicz art, Thor appears	*$0.60*	*$1.80*	*$3.00*	£0.40	£1.20	£2.00
226 ND (Jan 1981), Shogun Warriors storyline completed, Sienkiewicz art						

Issue	$Good	$Fine	$N.Mint	£Good	£Fine	£N.Mint
	$0.60	$1.80	$3.00	£0.40	£1.20	£2.00
227-228 ND Sienkiewicz art						
	$0.60	$1.80	$3.00	£0.40	£1.20	£2.00
229 Sienkiewicz art						
	$0.60	$1.80	$3.00	£0.30	£0.90	£1.50
230 Sienkiewicz art, Avengers appear						
	$0.60	$1.80	$3.00	£0.30	£0.90	£1.50
231 Sienkiewicz art (cover character not Magneto as has been erroneously printed in other guides!)						
	$0.60	$1.80	$3.00	£0.30	£0.90	£1.50
232 John Byrne art begins (ends #293), credited as "Bjorn Heyn", start of new "old" direction, Dr. Strange cameo						
	$0.80	$2.40	$4.00	£0.40	£1.20	£2.00
233-234 John Byrne art						
	$0.70	$2.10	$3.50	£0.30	£0.90	£1.50
235 scarce in the U.K. John Byrne art						
	$0.70	$2.10	$3.50	£0.40	£1.20	£2.00
236 68pgs, Jack Kirby/John Byrne art, 20th anniversary, F.F. #5 re-done						
	$0.70	$2.10	$3.50	£0.30	£0.90	£1.50
237 John Byrne art						
	$0.70	$2.10	$3.50	£0.25	£0.75	£1.25
238 (Jan 1982), John Byrne art						
	$0.70	$2.10	$3.50	£0.25	£0.75	£1.25
239 scarce in the U.K. John Byrne art						
	$0.70	$2.10	$3.50	£0.30	£0.90	£1.50
240 scarce in the U.K. Crystal gives birth, Great Refuge moved to Moon, John Byrne art						
	$0.70	$2.10	$3.50	£0.30	£0.90	£1.50
241 scarce in the U.K. Black Panther appears, John Byrne art						
	$0.60	$1.80	$3.00	£0.30	£0.90	£1.50
242 John Byrne art, Thor, Spiderman, Iron Man and Daredevil appear						
	$0.60	$1.80	$3.00	£0.25	£0.75	£1.25
243 scarce in the U.K. Avengers and Spiderman battle Galactus, Daredevil and Dr. Strange appear, John Byrne art						
	$0.60	$1.80	$3.00	£0.40	£1.20	£2.00
244 John Byrne art, Galactus appears; Frankie Raye becomes new Nova (later Galactus' herald)						
	$0.60	$1.80	$3.00	£0.25	£0.75	£1.25
245-248 John Byrne art						
	$0.60	$1.80	$3.00	£0.25	£0.75	£1.25
249 Gladiator battles F.F., X-Men appear, John Byrne art						
	$0.60	$1.80	$3.00	£0.30	£0.90	£1.50
250 52pgs, (Jan 1983), Spiderman and Avengers battle New X-Men, Captain America and Spiderman (disguised Skrulls referred to as "X-Factor"), John Byrne art						
	$0.80	$2.40	$4.00	£0.40	£1.20	£2.00
251 John Byrne art						
	$0.60	$1.80	$3.00	£0.25	£0.75	£1.25
252 sideways issue, John Byrne art (Note: an unknown number came with free Skin Tattoos - see Amazing Spiderman #238)						
	$0.60	$1.80	$3.00	£0.25	£0.75	£1.25
253-255 John Byrne art						
	$0.60	$1.80	$3.00	£0.25	£0.75	£1.25
256 continues in Thing #2, Avengers #234, John Byrne art						
	$0.60	$1.80	$3.00	£0.25	£0.75	£1.25
257-258 John Byrne art						
	$0.60	$1.80	$3.00	£0.25	£0.75	£1.25
259 Silver Surfer last page, John Byrne art						
	$0.60	$1.80	$3.00	£0.30	£0.90	£1.50
260 Silver Surfer, Alpha Flight X-over, Sub-Mariner appears, John Byrne art						
	$0.60	$1.80	$3.00	£0.30	£0.90	£1.50
261 Silver Surfer and Sub-Mariner appear, John Byrne art						
	$0.60	$1.80	$3.00	£0.30	£0.90	£1.50
262 (Jan 1984), new origin Galactus, John Byrne art						
	$0.60	$1.80	$3.00	£0.30	£0.90	£1.50
263 John Byrne art						
	$0.60	$1.80	$3.00	£0.25	£0.75	£1.25
264 John Byrne art, cover based on F.F. #1						
	$0.60	$1.80	$3.00	£0.25	£0.75	£1.25
265 John Byrne art, She-Hulk joins (temporarily), Avengers appear						
	$0.60	$1.80	$3.00	£0.25	£0.75	£1.25
266-272 John Byrne art						
	$0.60	$1.80	$3.00	£0.25	£0.75	£1.25
273 1st appearance Nathaniel Richards, John Byrne art						
	$0.80	$2.40	$4.00	£0.25	£0.75	£1.25
274 (Jan 1985), John Byrne art, Thing re-joins (continued from Thing #19)						
	$0.60	$1.80	$3.00	£0.25	£0.75	£1.25
275 John Byrne art, She-Hulk appears						
	$0.60	$1.80	$3.00	£0.25	£0.75	£1.25
276-277 Dr. Strange appears, John Byrne art						
	$0.60	$1.80	$3.00	£0.25	£0.75	£1.25
278 origin Dr. Doom retold, John Byrne art						
	$0.60	$1.80	$3.00	£0.25	£0.75	£1.25
279-280 John Byrne art						
	$0.60	$1.80	$3.00	£0.25	£0.75	£1.25
281 John Byrne art, Daredevil appears						
	$0.60	$1.80	$3.00	£0.25	£0.75	£1.25
282 LD in the U.K. Secret Wars II X-over, Power Pack appear, John Byrne art						
	$0.60	$1.80	$3.00	£0.30	£0.90	£1.50
283-284 John Byrne art						
	$0.60	$1.80	$3.00	£0.25	£0.75	£1.25
285 LD in the U.K. Secret Wars II X-over, John Byrne art						
	$0.60	$1.80	$3.00	£0.30	£0.90	£1.50
286 LD in the U.K. (Jan 1986), 2nd X-Factor tie-in (story continued in X-Factor #1), X-Men and Avengers appear, John Byrne art (see Avengers #263)						
	$1.00	$3.00	$5.00	£0.60	£1.80	£3.00
287 LD in the U.K. John Byrne art						
	$0.40	$1.20	$2.00	£0.30	£0.90	£1.50
288 LD in the U.K. Secret Wars II X-over, John Byrne art						
	$0.40	$1.20	$2.00	£0.30	£0.90	£1.50
289-290 Nick Fury appears, John Byrne art						
	$0.40	$1.20	$2.00	£0.25	£0.75	£1.25
291-292 Nick Fury appears, John Byrne art						
	$0.40	$1.20	$2.00	£0.20	£0.60	£1.00
293 last John Byrne art						
	$0.40	$1.20	$2.00	£0.20	£0.60	£1.00
294-295	$0.40	$1.20	$2.00	£0.20	£0.60	£1.00
296 DS, Thing re-joins, Barry Smith art						
	$0.60	$1.80	$3.00	£0.30	£0.90	£1.50
297	$0.40	$1.20	$2.00	£0.20	£0.60	£1.00
298 (Jan 1987)	$0.40	$1.20	$2.00	£0.20	£0.60	£1.00
299	$0.40	$1.20	$2.00	£0.20	£0.60	£1.00
300 Johnny Storm and Alicia Masters marry						
	$0.40	$1.20	$2.00	£0.20	£0.60	£1.00
301-304	$0.40	$1.20	$2.00	£0.20	£0.60	£1.00
305 Thing vs. Human Torch						
	$0.40	$1.20	$2.00	£0.20	£0.60	£1.00
306 line-up change: Mr. Fantastic and Invisible Woman leave						
	$0.40	$1.20	$2.00	£0.20	£0.60	£1.00
307 LD in the U.K. Ms. Marvel appears and joins to make (yet another) new team						
	$0.40	$1.20	$2.00	£0.25	£0.75	£1.25
308-309 LD in the U.K.						
	$0.40	$1.20	$2.00	£0.25	£0.75	£1.25
310 LD in the U.K. (Jan 1988), 1st new shape Thing appears, 1st new Ms. Marvel						
	$0.40	$1.20	$2.00	£0.25	£0.75	£1.25
311 LD in the U.K. Black Panther appears						

Fantastic Four #102

Fantastic Four Annual #9

Fantastic Tales #1

Issue	$Good	$Fine	$N.Mint	£Good	£Fine	£N.Mint
	$0.40	*$1.20*	*$2.00*	£0.25	£0.75	£1.25
312 LD in the U.K. Fall of the Mutants, Black Panther and X-Factor appear	*$0.40*	*$1.20*	*$2.00*	£0.30	£0.90	£1.50
313-314 LD in the U.K.	*$0.40*	*$1.20*	*$2.00*	£0.25	£0.75	£1.25
315 LD in the U.K. Morbius appears	*$0.40*	*$1.20*	*$2.00*	£0.25	£0.75	£1.25
316 LD in the U.K. Ka-Zar appears	*$0.40*	*$1.20*	*$2.00*	£0.25	£0.75	£1.25
317-318 LD in the U.K.	*$0.40*	*$1.20*	*$2.00*	£0.25	£0.75	£1.25
319 LD in the U.K. DS, Dr. Doom vs. The Beyonder	*$0.50*	*$1.50*	*$2.50*	£0.30	£0.90	£1.50
320 LD in the U.K. Thing vs. Grey Hulk	*$0.40*	*$1.20*	*$2.00*	£0.40	£1.20	£2.00
321 She-Hulk vs. She-Thing, Ron Lim art (1st on F.F.)	*$0.40*	*$1.20*	*$2.00*	£0.20	£0.60	£1.00
322 (Jan 1989), Inferno tie-in	*$0.40*	*$1.20*	*$2.00*	£0.20	£0.60	£1.00
323 Inferno tie-in	*$0.40*	*$1.20*	*$2.00*	£0.20	£0.60	£1.00
324-325 Inferno tie-in, Silver Surfer appears	*$0.40*	*$1.20*	*$2.00*	£0.20	£0.60	£1.00
326	*$0.40*	*$1.20*	*$2.00*	£0.20	£0.60	£1.00
327 LD in the U.K. Mr. Fantastic and Invisible Woman return	*$0.40*	*$1.20*	*$2.00*	£0.25	£0.75	£1.25
328-333 LD in the U.K.	*$0.40*	*$1.20*	*$2.00*	£0.25	£0.75	£1.25
334 Acts of Vengeance tie-in, Walt Simonson art	*$0.40*	*$1.20*	*$2.00*	£0.20	£0.60	£1.00
335 Acts of Vengeance tie-in, Walt Simonson story	*$0.40*	*$1.20*	*$2.00*	£0.20	£0.60	£1.00
336 (Jan 1990), Acts of Vengeance tie-in, Ron Lim art, Walt Simonson story	*$0.40*	*$1.20*	*$2.00*	£0.20	£0.60	£1.00
337 Walt Simonson story/art begins, Thor appears	*$0.40*	*$1.20*	*$2.00*	£0.20	£0.60	£1.00
338 Thor and Death's Head appear	*$0.40*	*$1.20*	*$2.00*	£0.20	£0.60	£1.00
339 Thor battles Gladiator	*$0.40*	*$1.20*	*$2.00*	£0.20	£0.60	£1.00
340-341 Thor and Iron Man appear	*$0.40*	*$1.20*	*$2.00*	£0.20	£0.60	£1.00
342-343 LD in the U.K.	*$0.40*	*$1.20*	*$2.00*	£0.25	£0.75	£1.25
344 ND scarce in the U.K.	*$0.40*	*$1.20*	*$2.00*	£0.30	£0.90	£1.50
345-346 ND	*$0.40*	*$1.20*	*$2.00*	£0.25	£0.75	£1.25
347 ND Ghost Rider, Wolverine, Spiderman appear, Art Adams cover/art	*$0.90*	*$2.70*	*$4.50*	£0.50	£1.50	£2.50
347 2nd printing, ND Ghost Rider, Wolverine, Spiderman appear, Art Adams cover/art (gold cover)	*$0.40*	*$1.20*	*$2.00*	£0.40	£1.20	£2.00
348 ND (Jan 1991), Ghost Rider, Wolverine, Spiderman appear, Art Adams cover/art	*$0.60*	*$1.80*	*$3.00*	£0.40	£1.20	£2.00
348 2nd printing, ND Ghost Rider, Wolverine, Spiderman appear, Art Adams cover/art (gold cover)	*$0.40*	*$1.20*	*$2.00*	£0.25	£0.75	£1.25
349 ND Ghost Rider, Wolverine, Spiderman appear (plus Punisher in a few panels), Art Adams art	*$0.60*	*$1.80*	*$3.00*	£0.40	£1.20	£2.00
350 ND DS The Thing returns, Walt Simonson story/art	*$0.50*	*$1.50*	*$2.50*	£0.35	£1.05	£1.75
351-352 LD in the U.K.	*$0.30*	*$0.90*	*$1.50*	£0.20	£0.60	£1.00
353 LD in the U.K. The Avengers guest-star	*$0.30*	*$0.90*	*$1.50*	£0.20	£0.60	£1.00
354 LD in the U.K. last Walt Simonson issue	*$0.30*	*$0.90*	*$1.50*	£0.20	£0.60	£1.00
355 LD in the U.K.	*$0.30*	*$0.90*	*$1.50*	£0.20	£0.60	£1.00
356 ND New Warriors appear, new direction for title	*$0.30*	*$0.90*	*$1.50*	£0.25	£0.75	£1.25
357 ND	*$0.30*	*$0.90*	*$1.50*	£0.25	£0.75	£1.25
358 ND 80pgs, 30th anniversary issue, die-cut card cover, John Byrne pin-up	*$0.50*	*$1.50*	*$2.50*	£0.40	£1.20	£2.00
359 LD in the U.K.	*$0.30*	*$0.90*	*$1.50*	£0.20	£0.60	£1.00
360 LD in the U.K. (Jan 1992)	*$0.30*	*$0.90*	*$1.50*	£0.20	£0.60	£1.00
361 LD in the U.K. $1.25 cover	*$0.30*	*$0.90*	*$1.50*	£0.20	£0.60	£1.00
362-363 LD in the U.K. Spiderman appears	*$0.30*	*$0.90*	*$1.50*	£0.20	£0.60	£1.00
364 LD in the U.K.	*$0.30*	*$0.90*	*$1.50*	£0.20	£0.60	£1.00
365 LD in the U.K. Alpha Flight appear	*$0.30*	*$0.90*	*$1.50*	£0.20	£0.60	£1.00
366-367 Infinity War X-over	*$0.30*	*$0.90*	*$1.50*	£0.20	£0.60	£1.00
368 Infinity War X-over, Hulk appears	*$0.30*	*$0.90*	*$1.50*	£0.20	£0.60	£1.00
369 Infinity War X-over, Thanos appears	*$0.30*	*$0.90*	*$1.50*	£0.20	£0.60	£1.00
370 Infinity War X-over	*$0.30*	*$0.90*	*$1.50*	£0.20	£0.60	£1.00
371 embossed all-white cover showing Torch going super-nova	*$0.70*	*$2.10*	*$3.50*	£0.30	£0.90	£1.50
371 2nd printing, ND all-red embossed cover	*$0.40*	*$1.20*	*$2.00*	£0.30	£0.90	£1.50
372 (Jan 1993), Ms. Marvel and Silver Sable appear	*$0.30*	*$0.90*	*$1.50*	£0.20	£0.60	£1.00
373 Silver Sable appears	*$0.30*	*$0.90*	*$1.50*	£0.20	£0.60	£1.00
374 Spiderman, Ghost Rider, Hulk and Wolverine (The Secret Defenders) vs. Fantastic Four; Dr. Strange and Silver Sable appear	*$0.30*	*$0.90*	*$1.50*	£0.20	£0.60	£1.00
375 LD in the U.K. DS anniversary issue, Ms. Marvel appears, holo-grafix foil cover	*$0.60*	*$1.80*	*$3.00*	£0.40	£1.20	£2.00
376	*$0.30*	*$0.90*	*$1.50*	£0.25	£0.75	£1.25
376 pre-bagged, ND with copy of "Dirt" magazine and audio cassette	*$0.60*	*$1.80*	*$3.00*	£0.40	£1.20	£2.00
377 lead into Fantastic Four Annual #26	*$0.30*	*$0.90*	*$1.50*	£0.20	£0.60	£1.00
378 Spiderman, Daredevil, Silver Surfer appear	*$0.30*	*$0.90*	*$1.50*	£0.20	£0.60	£1.00
379-380	*$0.30*	*$0.90*	*$1.50*	£0.20	£0.60	£1.00
381 Reed Richards and Dr. Doom "die"	*$0.50*	*$1.50*	*$2.50*	£0.30	£0.90	£1.50
382-383	*$0.30*	*$0.90*	*$1.50*	£0.15	£0.45	£0.75
384 (Jan 1994), Ant-Man "joins" the Fantastic Four	*$0.30*	*$0.90*	*$1.50*	£0.15	£0.45	£0.75
385-386 Starblast X-over	*$0.30*	*$0.90*	*$1.50*	£0.15	£0.45	£0.75
387 Nobody Gets Out Alive part 1	*$0.30*	*$0.90*	*$1.50*	£0.20	£0.60	£1.00
387 Collectors Edition, LD in the U.K. die-cut prismatic foil cover	*$0.60*	*$1.80*	*$3.00*	£0.40	£1.20	£2.00
388-389 Nobody Gets Out Alive story	*$0.30*	*$0.90*	*$1.50*	£0.15	£0.45	£0.75
390 Nobody Gets Out Alive story; Black Panther and Silver Surfer appear; cover based on issue #48	*$0.30*	*$0.90*	*$1.50*	£0.15	£0.45	£0.75
391 Nobody Gets Out Alive story; Black Panther begins to assemble Fantastic Force	*$0.30*	*$0.90*	*$1.50*	£0.15	£0.45	£0.75
392 Nobody Gets Out Alive story conclusion; 1st appearance Fantastic Force	*$0.30*	*$0.90*	*$1.50*	£0.15	£0.45	£0.75
393-394	*$0.30*	*$0.90*	*$1.50*	£0.15	£0.45	£0.75
394 Collectors Edition, ND pre-bagged with acetate print from Marvel Action Hour animated TV series	*$0.60*	*$1.80*	*$3.00*	£0.40	£1.20	£2.00
395 Thing vs. Wolverine	*$0.30*	*$0.90*	*$1.50*	£0.20	£0.60	£1.00
396 (Jan 1995)	*$0.30*	*$0.90*	*$1.50*	£0.20	£0.60	£1.00
397-398	*$0.30*	*$0.90*	*$1.50*	£0.20	£0.60	£1.00
398 Collectors Edition, ND prismatic foil-enhanced cover	*$0.60*	*$1.80*	*$3.00*	£0.30	£0.90	£1.50
399	*$0.30*	*$0.90*	*$1.50*	£0.20	£0.60	£1.00
399 Collectors Edition, ND prismatic foil-enhanced cover	*$0.60*	*$1.80*	*$3.00*	£0.30	£0.90	£1.50
400 LD in the U.K. 64pgs, prismatic foil-stamped cover, 10pg preview of Atlantis Rising	*$0.80*	*$2.40*	*$4.00*	£0.50	£1.50	£2.50
401 Atlantis Rising	*$0.30*	*$0.90*	*$1.50*	£0.20	£0.60	£1.00
402 Atlantis Rising; Namor vs. Black Bolt	*$0.30*	*$0.90*	*$1.50*	£0.20	£0.60	£1.00
403	*$0.30*	*$0.90*	*$1.50*	£0.20	£0.60	£1.00
404 Namor the Sub-Mariner appears; bi-weekly	*$0.30*	*$0.90*	*$1.50*	£0.20	£0.60	£1.00
405 Namor the Sub-Mariner joins the Fantastic Four; bi-weekly	*$0.30*	*$0.90*	*$1.50*	£0.20	£0.60	£1.00
406 The return of Dr. Doom...	*$0.30*	*$0.90*	*$1.50*	£0.20	£0.60	£1.00
407 The return of Reed Richards...	*$0.30*	*$0.90*	*$1.50*	£0.20	£0.60	£1.00
408 (Jan 1996)	*$0.30*	*$0.90*	*$1.50*	£0.20	£0.60	£1.00
409-410	*$0.30*	*$0.90*	*$1.50*	£0.20	£0.60	£1.00
411 Black Bolt appears	*$0.30*	*$0.90*	*$1.50*	£0.20	£0.60	£1.00
412 Sub-Mariner, Black Bolt and the Inhumans appear	*$0.30*	*$0.90*	*$1.50*	£0.20	£0.60	£1.00
413 continued from Doom 2099 #42	*$0.30*	*$0.90*	*$1.50*	£0.20	£0.60	£1.00
414 Onslaught tie-in	*$0.30*	*$0.90*	*$1.50*	£0.25	£0.75	£1.25
415 Onslaught tie-in; continued in X-Men #55	*$0.30*	*$0.90*	*$1.50*	£0.25	£0.75	£1.25
416 48pgs, Onslaught tie-in; continued in Onslaught: Marvel Universe	*$0.50*	*$1.50*	*$2.50*	£0.30	£0.90	£1.50
Title Value:	***$5024.30***	***$15057.45***	***$52356.50***	**£2781.40**	**£8350.80**	**£28687.75**

Note: #154, #180, #189 are all reprint.

	£Good	£Fine	£N.Mint
The Trial of Galactus Trade paperback (Oct 1989) reprints edited version of issues #244-262, John Byrne art	£1.25	£3.75	£6.25
2nd print (Nov 1994) new John Byrne cover			
Bookshelf Edition (Mar 1992), reprints issues #347-349	£0.75	£2.25	£3.75
Fantastic Four: Nobody Gets Out Alive (Feb 1995) Trade paperback 144pgs, reprints issues #387-392 plus new material	£2.00	£6.00	£10.00
Greatest Villains of the Fantastic Four (Jun 1995) Trade paperback 144pgs, classic reprints featuring Dr. Doom et al.	£2.00	£6.00	£10.00

ARTISTS

Kirby art in 1-102, 108, 236. Perez art 164-172, 176-178, 184-188, 191, 192. Steranko covers on 130-132. Perez covers on 191, 192, 194-198, 208.

FANTASTIC FOUR (2ND SERIES)

Marvel Comics Group; 1 Nov 1996-present

VERY GENERAL PERCENTAGE CONVERSION CHART WHICH MAY BE USED TO CALCULATE LOW AND INBETWEEN GRADES:

Issue	$Good	$Fine	$N.Mint	£Good	£Fine	£N.Mint
1 ND 48pgs, Jim Lee script, Brandon Choi and Scott Williams art; retells the origin of the Fantastic Four						
	$0.70	*$2.10*	*$3.50*	£0.50	£1.50	£2.50
1 Gold Stamped Signature Edition, ND 48pgs, (Jan 1997) pre-bagged with certificate featuring 22 carat gold stamped signatures of Jim Lee and Brandon Choi; 5,000 copies						
	$5.00	*$15.00*	*$25.00*	£3.50	£10.50	£17.50
1 Signed Edition, ND signed by Jim Lee, limited to 1,500 copies						
	$3.00	*$9.00*	*$15.00*	£2.00	£6.00	£10.00
1 Variant Cover Edition, ND 48pgs, Brett Booth cover						
	$1.00	*$3.00*	*$5.00*	£0.80	£2.40	£4.00
2-3 ND	*$0.40*	*$1.20*	*$2.00*	£0.25	£0.75	£1.25
4 ND Black Panther appears						
	$0.40	*$1.20*	*$2.00*	£0.25	£0.75	£1.25
5 ND Fantastic Four vs. Dr. Doom - nuff said!						
	$0.40	*$1.20*	*$2.00*	£0.25	£0.75	£1.25
Title Value:	*$11.30*	*$33.90*	*$56.50*	£7.80	£23.40	£39.00

FANTASTIC FOUR 2099

Marvel Comics Group; 1 Jan 1996-8 Aug 1996

Issue	$Good	$Fine	$N.Mint	£Good	£Fine	£N.Mint
1 ND Karl Kesel script, Rick Leonardi and Al Williamson art; chromium cover						
	$0.40	*$1.20*	*$2.00*	£0.50	£1.50	£2.50
2-4 ND	*$0.40*	*$1.20*	*$2.00*	£0.25	£0.75	£1.25
5 ND Spiderman 2099 appears						
	$0.40	*$1.20*	*$2.00*	£0.25	£0.75	£1.25
6-8 ND	*$0.40*	*$1.20*	*$2.00*	£0.25	£0.75	£1.25
Title Value:	*$3.20*	*$9.60*	*$15.95*	£2.25	£6.75	£11.25

FANTASTIC FOUR ANNUAL

Marvel Comics Group; 1 1963-9 1971; 10 1973; 11 1976-27 1994

Issue	$Good	$Fine	$N.Mint	£Good	£Fine	£N.Mint
1 origin Fantastic Four retold, reprints 1st part FF #1 and 2nd part Spiderman #1; Sub-Mariner appears (alternative cover in F.F. Index 2), Kirby cover and art						
	$70.00	*$215.00*	*$650.00*	£44.00	£130.00	£400.00
[Scarce in high grade - Very Fine+ or better]						
2 origin Dr. Doom retold from FF #5 plus new Dr. Doom story, Jack Kirby cover and art						
	$47.00	*$140.00*	*$375.00*	£26.00	£77.50	£210.00
3 Reed Richards & Sue Storm wed; X-Men, Avengers, Daredevil and The Watcher appear, Stan Lee & Jack Kirby cameo, reprints part FF #6, #11, Kirby cover and art						
	$25.00	*$75.00*	*$175.00*	£14.00	£43.00	£100.00
4 origin and 1st Silver Age appearance of Golden Age Human Torch, reprints part FF #25, #26, Jack Kirby cover and art						
	$15.50	*$48.00*	*$95.00*	£9.00	£28.00	£55.00
5 intro Psycho Man, Silver Surfer appears (1st solo story); Jack Kirby cover and art, Giacoia inks (not Sinnott as credited)						
	$14.00	*$43.00*	*$100.00*	£8.00	£24.50	£57.50
6 1st appearance Annihilus, Franklin Richards is born, Jack Kirby cover and art						
	$9.00	*$28.00*	*$55.00*	£5.00	£15.00	£30.00
7 reprints part FF #1 (Mole Man), Annual #2 (origin Dr. Doom), Jack Kirby cover and art						
	$4.15	*$12.50*	*$25.00*	£2.05	£6.25	£12.50
8 reprints part Annual #1 (Sub-Mariner story), Jack Kirby art						
	$2.50	*$7.50*	*$15.00*	£1.65	£5.00	£10.00
9 ND scarce in the U.K. reprints part Annual #3, Jack Kirby cover and art						
	$2.50	*$7.50*	*$15.00*	£1.65	£5.00	£10.00
10 ND scarce in the U.K. reprints part Annual #3, #4, Jack Kirby art						
	$2.30	*$7.00*	*$14.00*	£1.50	£4.50	£9.00
11 ND Invaders appear, continues in Marvel Two-In-One Annual #1, Jack Kirby cover						
	$1.20	*$3.60*	*$6.00*	£0.70	£2.10	£3.50
12-13 ND	*$1.20*	*$3.60*	*$6.00*	£0.60	£1.80	£3.00
14 ND George Perez art						
	$1.20	*$3.60*	*$6.00*	£0.60	£1.80	£3.00
15 ND George Perez art						
	$0.80	*$2.40*	*$4.00*	£0.50	£1.50	£2.50
16 ND Steve Ditko art						
	$0.80	*$2.40*	*$4.00*	£0.50	£1.50	£2.50
17 ND John Byrne art						
	$0.80	*$2.40*	*$4.00*	£0.50	£1.50	£2.50
18 ND John Byrne art; ties into X-Men #137, Wolverine appears						
	$0.80	*$2.40*	*$4.00*	£0.50	£1.50	£2.50
19 ND John Byrne art, Avengers appear						
	$0.80	*$2.40*	*$4.00*	£0.50	£1.50	£2.50
20 ND scarce in the U.K.						
	$0.80	*$2.40*	*$4.00*	£0.50	£1.50	£2.50
21 ND Evolutionary War, squarebound						
	$0.80	*$2.40*	*$4.00*	£0.40	£1.20	£2.00
22 ND part 14 (conclusion) Atlantis Attacks						
	$0.50	*$1.50*	*$2.50*	£0.30	£0.90	£1.50
23 ND Days of Future Present story (see X-Factor/ New Mutants/X-Men Annuals)						
	$0.50	*$1.50*	*$2.50*	£0.30	£0.90	£1.50
24 ND story continued in Thor Annual #16						
	$0.50	*$1.50*	*$2.50*	£0.30	£0.90	£1.50
25 ND 64pgs, Citizen Kang part 3, Black Widow, Falcon, Sersi, Hercules, Crystal and Black Knight appear, continued in Avengers Annual #21						
	$0.50	*$1.50*	*$2.50*	£0.30	£0.90	£1.50
26 ND 64pgs, pre-bagged with trading card introducing Black Marvel						
	$0.60	*$1.80*	*$3.00*	£0.40	£1.20	£2.00
27 ND 64pgs	*$0.60*	*$1.80*	*$3.00*	£0.40	£1.20	£2.00
Title Value:	*$205.55*	*$624.30*	*$1587.00*	£120.75	£362.45	£933.50

Note: 4-7 called Specials on cover. 7-10 are all reprint. 1-10 are 72pgs, 11-16 are 52pgs. 21 and 22 are 64pgs.

Note also: Annuals #1-3 occasionally turn up with blank back and inside front and back covers (see also Sgt. Fury Annual #1, Spiderman Annual #2, Strange Tales Annual #2). These were subscription copies sent over to this country as left-overs and are very scarce. With their white back covers which show soiling and wear that much more easily, they are very rare in near mint condition.

FANTASTIC FOUR ASHCAN EDITION

Marvel Comics Group,OS; nn Jun 1995

Issue	$Good	$Fine	$N.Mint	£Good	£Fine	£N.Mint
nn ND 16pgs, retells origin; black and white						
	$0.15	*$0.45*	*$0.75*	£0.10	£0.30	£0.50
Title Value:	*$0.15*	*$0.45*	*$0.75*	£0.10	£0.30	£0.50

FANTASTIC FOUR BOOK AND RECORD SET

Power Records;PR-13 1974

Issue	$Good	$Fine	$N.Mint	£Good	£Fine	£N.Mint
PR-13, scarce in the U.K. 20pgs, based on origin from issue #1 with 45 rpm record						
	$1.25	*$3.75*	*$7.50*	£1.00	£3.00	£6.00
Title Value:	*$1.25*	*$3.75*	*$7.50*	£1.00	£3.00	£6.00

Note: this item would be valued at approximately 50% less without record

FANTASTIC FOUR COLLECTOR'S PREVIEW

Marvel Comics Group,OS; 1 May 1995

Issue	$Good	$Fine	$N.Mint	£Good	£Fine	£N.Mint
1 ND information, articles and interviews on the Fantastic Four; Alan Davis cover						
	$0.50	*$1.50*	*$2.50*	£0.30	£0.90	£1.50
Title Value:	*$0.50*	*$1.50*	*$2.50*	£0.30	£0.90	£1.50

FANTASTIC FOUR GIANT SIZE

Marvel Comics Group;2 Aug 1974-6 Aug 1975

(formerly Super-Stars Giant Size)

Issue	$Good	$Fine	$N.Mint	£Good	£Fine	£N.Mint
2 ND 68pgs	*$2.00*	*$6.00*	*$12.00*	£1.15	£3.50	£7.00
3 ND 68pgs	*$1.65*	*$5.00*	*$10.00*	£1.00	£3.00	£6.00
4 ND 68pgs, Professor X appears, 1st appearance Madrox the Multiplying Man						
	$1.65	*$5.00*	*$10.00*	£1.00	£3.00	£6.00
5-6 ND 68pgs	*$1.65*	*$5.00*	*$10.00*	£1.00	£3.00	£6.00
Title Value:	*$8.60*	*$26.00*	*$52.00*	£5.15	£15.50	£31.00

Note: #2-4 have back-up reprints; #5, #6 are all reprint.

FANTASTIC FOUR ROAST

Marvel Comics Group,OS; 1 May 1982

Issue	$Good	$Fine	$N.Mint	£Good	£Fine	£N.Mint
1 ND celebrates 20th anniversary, John Byrne, Hembeck, Frank Miller, Rogers, Buscema, Golden, Anderson, Sienkiewicz art						
	$0.50	*$1.50*	*$2.50*	£0.30	£0.90	£1.50
Title Value:	*$0.50*	*$1.50*	*$2.50*	£0.30	£0.90	£1.50

FANTASTIC FOUR SPECIAL EDITION

Marvel Comics Group,OS; 1 May 1984

Issue	$Good	$Fine	$N.Mint	£Good	£Fine	£N.Mint
1 ND reprints F.F. Annual #l, John Byrne cover and few pages art						
	$0.60	*$1.80*	*$3.00*	£0.40	£1.20	£2.00
Title Value:	*$0.60*	*$1.80*	*$3.00*	£0.40	£1.20	£2.00

FANTASTIC FOUR UNLIMITED

Marvel Comics Group; 1 Mar 1993-12 Apr 1996

Issue	$Good	$Fine	$N.Mint	£Good	£Fine	£N.Mint
1 ND 64pgs, Black Panther appears						
	$0.80	*$2.40*	*$4.00*	£0.50	£1.50	£2.50
2 ND 64pgs, Black Panther appears, Joe Quesada cover						
	$0.80	*$2.40*	*$4.00*	£0.50	£1.50	£2.50
3 ND 64pgs	*$0.80*	*$2.40*	*$4.00*	£0.50	£1.50	£2.50
4 ND 64pgs, Thing vs. Hulk						
	$0.80	*$2.40*	*$4.00*	£0.50	£1.50	£2.50
5 ND 64pgs, Fantastic Four vs. The Frightful Four						
	$0.80	*$2.40*	*$4.00*	£0.50	£1.50	£2.50
6 ND 64pgs, Fantastic Four vs. Namor the Sub-Mariner						
	$0.80	*$2.40*	*$4.00*	£0.50	£1.50	£2.50
7 ND 64pgs, classic pre-super hero monsters appear						
	$0.80	*$2.40*	*$4.00*	£0.50	£1.50	£2.50
8 ND 64pgs, Dr. Doom appears						
	$0.80	*$2.40*	*$4.00*	£0.50	£1.50	£2.50
9 ND 64pgs, Thor guest-stars						
	$0.80	*$2.40*	*$4.00*	£0.50	£1.50	£2.50
10 ND 64pgs, The Eternals appear						
	$0.80	*$2.40*	*$4.00*	£0.50	£1.50	£2.50
11 ND 64pgs, The Inhumans mutate and Namor the Sub-Mariner appears						
	$0.80	*$2.40*	*$4.00*	£0.50	£1.50	£2.50
12 ND 64pgs, Fantastic Four vs. Hyperstorm						
	$0.80	*$2.40*	*$4.00*	£0.50	£1.50	£2.50
Title Value:	*$9.60*	*$28.80*	*$48.00*	£6.00	£18.00	£30.00

Note: quarterly frequency

FANTASTIC FOUR UNPLUGGED

Marvel Comics Group; 1 Sep 1995-6 Sep 1996

Issue	$Good	$Fine	$N.Mint	£Good	£Fine	£N.Mint
1 ND The Thing stars in his own bi-monthly series; cover priced at a special 99 cents						
	$0.20	*$0.60*	*$1.00*	£0.10	£0.35	£0.65
2 ND	*$0.20*	*$0.60*	*$1.00*	£0.10	£0.35	£0.65
3 ND ties into Fantastic Four #408						
	$0.20	*$0.60*	*$1.00*	£0.10	£0.35	£0.65
4 ND	*$0.20*	*$0.60*	*$1.00*	£0.10	£0.35	£0.65
5 ND Blastaar appears						
	$0.20	*$0.60*	*$1.00*	£0.10	£0.35	£0.65
6 ND	*$0.20*	*$0.60*	*$1.00*	£0.10	£0.35	£0.65
Title Value:	*$1.20*	*$3.60*	*$6.00*	£0.60	£2.10	£3.90

Note: originally announced as Marvel: Fantastic Four

FANTASTIC FOUR VS THE X-MEN

Marvel Comics Group,MS; 1 Feb 1987-4 May 1987

Issue	$Good	$Fine	$N.Mint	£Good	£Fine	£N.Mint
1 ND Jon Bogdanove art begins						
	$0.70	*$2.10*	*$3.50*	£0.30	£0.90	£1.50
2-4 ND	*$0.50*	*$1.50*	*$2.50*	£0.30	£0.90	£1.50
Title Value:	*$2.20*	*$6.60*	*$11.00*	£1.20	£3.60	£6.00

Note: Jon Bogdanove art/Claremont script

Fantastic Four vs. The X-Men (Nov 1994)

Issue	$Good	$Fine	$N.Mint	£Good	£Fine	£N.Mint
reprints mini-series				£2.00	£6.00	£10.00

FANTASTIC FOUR, THE OFFICIAL MARVEL INDEX TO

Marvel Comics Group; 1 Dec 1985-12 Jan 1987

Issue	$Good	$Fine	$N.Mint	£Good	£Fine	£N.Mint
1 ND information and colour cover reproductions Fantastic Four #1-#15, new John Byrne cover; alternative original cover to F.F. #3 on back cover						
	$0.60	*$1.80*	*$3.00*	£0.40	£1.20	£2.00
2 ND information and colour cover reproductions Fantastic Four #16-#30, Annual #1, Sienkiewicz cover; alternative original cover to F.F. Annual #1 on back cover						
	$0.60	*$1.80*	*$3.00*	£0.40	£1.20	£2.00
3 ND information and colour cover reproductions Fantastic Four #31-#45, Annual #2,#3						

$Good $Fine $N.Mint £Good £Fine £N.Mint

$0.60 $1.80 $3.00 £0.40 £1.20 £2.00
4 ND information and colour cover reproductions Fantastic Four #46-#65, Annual #4
$0.60 $1.80 $3.00 £0.40 £1.20 £2.00
5 ND information and colour cover reproductions Fantastic Four #66-#84, Annual #5,#6
$0.60 $1.80 $3.00 £0.40 £1.20 £2.00
6 ND information and colour cover reproductions Fantastic Four #85-#106, Annual #7,#8
$0.60 $1.80 $3.00 £0.40 £1.20 £2.00
7 ND information and colour cover reproductions Fantastic Four #107-#125, Annual #9
$0.60 $1.80 $3.00 £0.40 £1.20 £2.00
8 ND information and colour cover reproductions Fantastic Four #126-#141, Annual #10 and Giant Size Super Stars #1
$0.60 $1.80 $3.00 £0.40 £1.20 £2.00
9 ND information and colour cover reproductions Fantastic Four #142-#160, Annual #10 and Giant Size #2,#3
$0.60 $1.80 $3.00 £0.40 £1.20 £2.00
10 ND information and colour cover reproductions Fantastic Four #161-#176, Annual #11 and Giant Size #4-#6
$0.60 $1.80 $3.00 £0.40 £1.20 £2.00
11 ND information and colour cover reproductions Fantastic Four #177-#198
$0.60 $1.80 $3.00 £0.40 £1.20 £2.00
12 ND information and colour cover reproductions Fantastic Four #199-#214, Annual #12,#13
$0.60 $1.80 $3.00 £0.40 £1.20 £2.00
Title Value: $7.20 $21.60 $36.00 £4.80 £14.40 £24.00
Note: Volume 2 in Official Marvel Index Series of 5.

FANTASTIC FOUR/FORCE ASHCAN
Marvel Comics Group,OS; nn Oct 1994
nn ND 16pgs, reviews origin of FF and Fantastic Force
$0.25 $0.75 $1.25 £0.15 £0.45 £0.75
Title Value: $0.25 $0.75 $1.25 £0.15 £0.45 £0.75

FANTASTIC FOUR: ATLANTIS RISING
Marvel Comics Group,MS; 1 Jun 1995-2 Jul 1995
1-2 ND 48pgs, M.C. Wyman art, The Inhumans appear; acetate outer cover
$0.80 $2.40 $4.00 £0.50 £1.50 £2.50
Title Value: $1.60 $4.80 $8.00 £1.00 £3.00 £5.00

FANTASTIC FOUR: THE LEGEND
Marvel Comics Group,OS; nn Oct 1996
nn ND 48pgs, facts and figures, character profiles and timelines about the Fantastic Four
$0.80 $2.40 $4.00 £0.50 £1.50 £2.50
Title Value: $0.80 $2.40 $4.00 £0.50 £1.50 £2.50

FANTASTIC GIANTS
Charlton;24 Sep 1966
(previously Konga)
24 distributed in the U.K. giant, new and reprint Steve Ditko art; Konga and Gorgo featured
$7.00 $21.00 $50.00 £4.25 £12.50 £30.00
Title Value: $7.00 $21.00 $50.00 £4.25 £12.50 £30.00

FANTASTIC TALES
I.W. Enterprises; 1 1958
1 distributed in the U.K. reprints Avon Periodicals "City of the Living Dead"
$3.55 $10.50 $25.00 £2.10 £6.25 £15.00
Title Value: $3.55 $10.50 $25.00 £2.10 £6.25 £15.00

FANTASTIC VOYAGE
Gold Key/Movie Comics,OS Movie; 10178-702 Feb 1967
10178-702 distributed in the U.K. film adaptation; Wally Wood and Dan Adkins art; photo cover
$7.00 $21.00 $50.00 £4.25 £12.50 £30.00
Title Value: $7.00 $21.00 $50.00 £4.25 £12.50 £30.00

FANTASTIC VOYAGE (2ND SERIES)
Gold Key, Movie; 1 Aug 1969-2 Dec 1969
1 distributed in the U.K. based on TV cartoon rather than Raquel Welch film
$4.25 $12.50 $30.00 £2.10 £6.25 £15.00
2 distributed in the U.K. based on TV cartoon rather than Raquel Welch film
$3.90 $11.50 $27.50 £2.00 £6.00 £14.00
Title Value: $8.15 $24.00 $57.50 £4.10 £12.25 £29.00

FANTASY FEATURES
AC Comics; 1,2 1987
1-2 ND $0.40 $1.20 $2.00 £0.25 £0.75 £1.25
Title Value: $0.80 $2.40 $4.00 £0.50 £1.50 £2.50

FANTASY MASTERPIECES
Marvel Comics Group; 1 Feb 1966-11 Oct 1967
(becomes Marvel Super-Heroes)
1 scarce in the U.K. 60s horror reprints featuring art by Steve Ditko (Amazing Fantasy #10) and Jack Kirby (Journey into Mystery #60)
$5.50 $17.00 $40.00 £3.55 £10.50 £25.00
2 early 60s reprints including 1st appearance Fin Fang Foom from Strange Tales #89
$3.20 $9.50 $22.50 £1.75 £5.25 £12.50
3 72pgs, Captain America 1940s reprints begin
$2.85 $8.50 $20.00 £1.40 £4.25 £10.00
4-6 72pgs, Captain America reprints
$2.85 $8.50 $20.00 £1.40 £4.25 £10.00
7 72pgs, begin Golden Age Sub-Mariner/Torch reprints
$2.85 $8.50 $20.00 £1.40 £4.25 £10.00
8 72pgs, Golden Age Torch vs Sub-Mariner reprint from Marvel Mystery #9
$2.85 $8.50 $20.00 £1.40 £4.25 £10.00
9 72pgs, reprints Golden Age Human Torch origin from Marvel Comics #1
$3.55 $10.50 $25.00 £1.75 £5.25 £12.50
10 72pgs, All Winners Squad reprint
$2.85 $8.50 $20.00 £1.40 £4.25 £10.00
11 72pgs, reprints origins Toro and Black Knight
$2.85 $8.50 $20.00 £1.40 £4.25 £10.00
Title Value: $35.05 $105.00 $247.50 £18.25 £55.00 £130.00

FANTASY MASTERPIECES (2ND SERIES)
Marvel Comics Group; 1 Dec 1979-14 Jan 1981
1 ND 52pgs, squarebound, reprints Silver Surfer #1
$1.00 $3.00 $6.00 £0.80 £2.50 £5.00
2 ND 52pgs, squarebound, reprints Silver Surfer #2
$0.80 $2.40 $4.00 £0.60 £1.80 £3.00
3 ND 52pgs, squarebound, reprints Silver Surfer #3
$0.80 $2.40 $4.00 £0.60 £1.80 £3.00
4 ND 52pgs, squarebound, reprints Silver Surfer #4
$0.80 $2.40 $4.00 £0.70 £2.10 £3.50
5 ND 52pgs, squarebound, reprints Silver Surfer #5
$0.80 $2.40 $4.00 £0.60 £1.80 £3.00
6 ND 52pgs, squarebound, reprints Silver Surfer #6
$0.70 $2.10 $3.50 £0.50 £1.50 £2.50
7 ND 52pgs, squarebound, reprints Silver Surfer #7
$0.70 $2.10 $3.50 £0.50 £1.50 £2.50
8 ND 52pgs, squarebound, reprints Silver Surfer #8 and Warlock from Strange Tales #178
$0.70 $2.10 $3.50 £0.60 £1.80 £3.00
9 ND 52pgs, squarebound, reprints Silver Surfer #9 and Warlock from Strange Tales #179
$0.70 $2.10 $3.50 £0.50 £1.50 £2.50
10 ND 52pgs, squarebound, reprints Silver Surfer #10 and Warlock from Strange Tales #180
$0.70 $2.10 $3.50 £0.50 £1.50 £2.50
11 ND 52pgs, squarebound, reprints Silver Surfer #11 and Warlock from Strange Tales #181
$0.70 $2.10 $3.50 £0.40 £1.20 £2.00
12 ND 52pgs, reprints Silver Surfer #12 and Warlock #9
$0.70 $2.10 $3.50 £0.40 £1.20 £2.00
13 ND 52pgs, reprints Silver Surfer #13 and Warlock #10
$0.70 $2.10 $3.50 £0.50 £1.50 £2.50
14 ND 52pgs, reprints Silver Surfer #14 and Warlock #11 (plus cover repro)
$0.70 $2.10 $3.50 £0.40 £1.20 £2.00
Title Value: $10.50 $31.50 $53.50 £7.60 £22.90 £39.00
Note: all reprint from original Silver Surfer series. Warlock in 8-14 (Starlin art).

FANTASY QUARTERLY
IPS; 1 Spring 1978
1 ND 1st appearance Elfquest, Wendy Pini story/art
$7.50 $22.50 $45.00 £4.55 £13.50 £27.50
Title Value: $7.50 $22.50 $45.00 £4.55 £13.50 £27.50

FAREWELL TO WEAPONS DIRT BAG SPECIAL
Marvel Comics Group,OS; 1 Jun 1992
1 ND pre-bagged, Farewell To Arms comic by Katsuhiro Otomo, "Dirt" magazine, pop music cassette
$0.70 $2.10 $3.50 £0.40 £1.20 £2.00
Title Value: $0.70 $2.10 $3.50 £0.40 £1.20 £2.00

FAREWELL, MOONSHADOW
DC Comics,OS; nn Jan 1997
nn ND 64pgs, J.M. DeMatteis script, Jon J. Muth painted art
$1.60 $4.80 $8.00 £1.00 £3.00 £5.00
Title Value: $1.60 $4.80 $8.00 £1.00 £3.00 £5.00

FASHION IN ACTION SUMMER SPECIAL
Eclipse,OS; 1 Aug 1986
1 ND John K. Snyder III art, Scout spin-off; colour
$0.50 $1.50 $2.50 £0.30 £0.90 £1.50
Title Value: $0.50 $1.50 $2.50 £0.30 £0.90 £1.50

FASHION IN ACTION WINTER SPECIAL
Eclipse,OS; 1 Feb 1987
1 ND John K. Snyder III art, Scout spin-off; colour
$0.50 $1.50 $2.50 £0.30 £0.90 £1.50
Title Value: $0.50 $1.50 $2.50 £0.30 £0.90 £1.50

FAST FORWARD
DC Comics/Piranha Press,MS; 1 Dec 1992-3 1993
1 ND 64pgs, Phobias; anthology featuring Grant Morrison story
$0.90 $2.70 $4.50 £0.60 £1.80 £3.00
2-3 ND 64pgs, anthology
$0.90 $2.70 $4.50 £0.60 £1.80 £3.00
Title Value: $2.70 $8.10 $13.50 £1.80 £5.40 £9.00

FAT NINJA
Silverwolf Comics; 1 Aug 1986-8 1987
1-8 ND black and white
$0.25 $0.75 $1.25 £0.15 £0.45 £0.75
Title Value: $2.00 $6.00 $10.00 £1.20 £3.60 £6.00

FATALE
Broadway Comics; 1 Jan 1996-6 Aug 1996
1 ND $0.80 $2.40 $4.00 £0.50 £1.50 £2.50
2-4 ND $0.50 $1.50 $2.50 £0.30 £0.90 £1.50
5-6 ND $0.60 $1.80 $3.00 £0.40 £1.20 £2.00
Title Value: $3.50 $10.50 $17.50 £2.20 £6.60 £11.00

FATE
DC Comics; 0 Oct 1994; 1 Nov 1994-22 Sep 1996
0 (Oct 1994) Zero Hour X-over, origin
$0.40 $1.20 $2.00 £0.25 £0.75 £1.25
1-4 $0.40 $1.20 $2.00 £0.25 £0.75 £1.25
5 Phantom Stranger and Dr. Occult appear
$0.40 $1.20 $2.00 £0.25 £0.75 £1.25
6-7 $0.40 $1.20 $2.00 £0.25 £0.75 £1.25
8-9 $0.45 $1.35 $2.25 £0.30 £0.90 £1.50
10 Zatanna guest-stars
$0.45 $1.35 $2.25 £0.30 £0.90 £1.50
11-12 $0.45 $1.35 $2.25 £0.30 £0.90 £1.50
13 Underworld Unleashed tie-in
$0.45 $1.35 $2.25 £0.30 £0.90 £1.50
14 Underworld Unleashed tie-in with Sentinel, Deadman and Zatanna
$0.45 $1.35 $2.25 £0.30 £0.90 £1.50
15-19 $0.45 $1.35 $2.25 £0.30 £0.90 £1.50
20-22 Fate vs. Dr. Fate
$0.45 $1.35 $2.25 £0.30 £0.90 £1.50
Title Value: $9.95 $29.85 $49.75 £6.50 £19.50 £32.50

FATHER & SON
Kitchen Sink,MS; 1 Sep 1995-3 1996

	$Good	$Fine	$N.Mint	£Good	£Fine	£N.Mint
1 ND Jeff Nicholson script and art; black and white	$0.50	$1.50	$2.50	£0.30	£0.90	£1.50
2-3 ND	$0.50	$1.50	$2.50	£0.30	£0.90	£1.50
Title Value:	$1.50	$4.50	$7.50	£0.90	£2.70	£4.50

FATHOM

Comico,MS; 1 May 1987-3 Jul 1987

	$Good	$Fine	$N.Mint	£Good	£Fine	£N.Mint
1-3 ND Elementals spin-off	$0.40	$1.20	$2.00	£0.25	£0.75	£1.25
Title Value:	$1.20	$3.60	$6.00	£0.75	£2.25	£3.75
Trade Paperback (Sep 1991), reprints mini-series plus new story, new cover by Bill Willingham				£1.50	£4.50	£7.50

FATHOM (2ND SERIES)

Comico,MS; 1 Nov 1992-3 Jun 1993

	$Good	$Fine	$N.Mint	£Good	£Fine	£N.Mint
1-3 ND colour	$0.40	$1.20	$2.00	£0.25	£0.75	£1.25
Title Value:	$1.20	$3.60	$6.00	£0.75	£2.25	£3.75

FATMAN THE HUMAN FLYING SAUCER

Lightning Comics/Milson Publishing; 1 Apr 1967-3 Aug/Sep 1967

	$Good	$Fine	$N.Mint	£Good	£Fine	£N.Mint
1 origin, script begins by Otto Binder, art begins by C.C. Beck	$7.50	$22.50	$45.00	£4.15	£12.50	£25.00
2	$5.00	$15.00	$30.00	£2.90	£8.75	£17.50
3 very scarce in the U.K., scarce in the U.S.	$8.25	$25.00	$50.00	£5.00	£15.00	£30.00
Title Value:	$20.75	$62.50	$125.00	£12.05	£36.25	£72.50

Note: irregular distribution in the U.K.

FATMAN THE HUMAN FLYING SAUCER (2ND SERIES)

A Plus Comics,MS; 1 Jan 1992-3 1992

	$Good	$Fine	$N.Mint	£Good	£Fine	£N.Mint
1 ND reprints from original series begin, C.C. Beck covers begin	$0.40	$1.20	$2.00	£0.25	£0.75	£1.25
2-3 ND	$0.40	$1.20	$2.00	£0.25	£0.75	£1.25
Title Value:	$1.20	$3.60	$6.00	£0.75	£2.25	£3.75

FAUNA REBELLION, THE

Fantagraphics,MS; 1 Mar 1990-3 May 1990

	$Good	$Fine	$N.Mint	£Good	£Fine	£N.Mint
1-3 ND ecology theme comic	$0.40	$1.20	$2.00	£0.25	£0.75	£1.25
Title Value:	$1.20	$3.60	$6.00	£0.75	£2.25	£3.75

FAUST

Northstar/Rebel Studios,MS; 1 1989-10 1995; 11 1996

	$Good	$Fine	$N.Mint	£Good	£Fine	£N.Mint
1 ND David Quinn and Tim Vigil art begins	$7.50	$22.50	$37.50	£3.00	£9.00	£15.00
1 2nd printing ND	$2.00	$6.00	$10.00	£1.00	£3.00	£5.00
1 3rd printing ND	$0.80	$2.40	$4.00	£0.50	£1.50	£2.50
1 4th printing ND	$0.40	$1.20	$2.00	£0.25	£0.75	£1.25
1 5th printing, ND (Aug 1994)	$0.45	$1.35	$2.25	£0.30	£0.90	£1.50
2 ND	$5.50	$16.50	$27.50	£2.50	£7.50	£12.50
2 2nd printing ND	$0.90	$2.70	$4.50	£0.60	£1.80	£3.00
2 3rd printing ND	$0.60	$1.80	$3.00	£0.40	£1.20	£2.00
2 4th printing ND	$0.50	$1.50	$2.50	£0.30	£0.90	£1.50
3 ND	$3.50	$10.50	$17.50	£1.50	£4.50	£7.50
3 2nd printing ND	$0.50	$1.50	$2.50	£0.50	£1.50	£2.50
3 3rd printing ND	$0.45	$1.35	$2.25	£0.30	£0.90	£1.50
4 ND	$1.50	$4.50	$7.50	£1.00	£3.00	£5.00
4 2nd printing ND	$0.50	$1.50	$2.50	£0.40	£1.20	£2.00
4 3rd printing ND	$0.45	$1.35	$2.25	£0.30	£0.90	£1.50
5 ND	$1.20	$3.60	$6.00	£0.80	£2.40	£4.00
5 2nd printing ND	$0.50	$1.50	$2.50	£0.30	£0.90	£1.50
5 3rd printing, ND (Mar 1996)	$0.50	$1.50	$2.50	£0.30	£0.90	£1.50
6 ND	$1.20	$3.60	$6.00	£0.60	£1.80	£3.00
7 ND scarce in the U.K. 1st Rebel Studios issue	$0.80	$2.40	$4.00	£0.60	£1.80	£3.00
7 2nd printing, ND (May 1993)	$0.50	$1.50	$2.50	£0.30	£0.90	£1.50
8 ND scarce in the U.K.	$0.80	$2.40	$4.00	£0.50	£1.50	£2.50
8 2nd printing, ND (Jun 1993)	$0.50	$1.50	$2.50	£0.30	£0.90	£1.50
9 ND scarce in the U.K.	$0.80	$2.40	$4.00	£0.50	£1.50	£2.50
9 2nd printing, ND (Sep 1993)	$0.50	$1.50	$2.50	£0.30	£0.90	£1.50
9 3rd printing ND	$0.50	$1.50	$2.50	£0.30	£0.90	£1.50
10-11 ND scarce in the U.K.	$0.80	$2.40	$4.00	£0.50	£1.50	£2.50
Title Value:	$34.95	$104.85	$173.75	£18.65	£55.95	£93.25

Note: all Non-Distributed on the news-stands in the U.K.

FAUST (2ND SERIES)

Rebel Studios,MS; 1 Aug 1992-6 Apr 1993

	$Good	$Fine	$N.Mint	£Good	£Fine	£N.Mint
1 ND reprints begin of original series with new covers, corrected art and editorial supplements	$0.60	$1.80	$3.00	£0.40	£1.20	£2.00
1 2nd printing ND	$0.45	$1.35	$2.25	£0.30	£0.90	£1.50
2 ND	$0.50	$1.50	$2.50	£0.30	£0.90	£1.50
2 2nd printing, ND (Aug 1993)	$0.45	$1.35	$2.25	£0.30	£0.90	£1.50
3 ND	$0.50	$1.50	$2.50	£0.30	£0.90	£1.50
3 2nd printing ND	$0.45	$1.35	$2.25	£0.30	£0.90	£1.50
4 ND	$0.50	$1.50	$2.50	£0.30	£0.90	£1.50
4 2nd printing, ND (Oct 1993)	$0.45	$1.35	$2.25	£0.30	£0.90	£1.50
5 ND	$0.50	$1.50	$2.50	£0.30	£0.90	£1.50
5 2nd printing, ND (Oct 1993)	$0.45	$1.35	$2.25	£0.30	£0.90	£1.50
6 ND	$0.50	$1.50	$2.50	£0.30	£0.90	£1.50
6 2nd printing, ND (Nov 1993)	$0.45	$1.35	$2.25	£0.30	£0.90	£1.50
Title Value:	$5.80	$17.40	$29.00	£3.70	£11.10	£18.50

FAZE ONE FAZERS

AC Comics; 1 1986-4 1986

	$Good	$Fine	$N.Mint	£Good	£Fine	£N.Mint
1-4 ND	$0.40	$1.20	$2.00	£0.25	£0.75	£1.25
Title Value:	$1.60	$4.80	$8.00	£1.00	£3.00	£5.00

FAZERS

Dagger Enterprises; 1 Aug 1994

	$Good	$Fine	$N.Mint	£Good	£Fine	£N.Mint
1 ND Vic Bridges script and art	$0.40	$1.20	$2.00	£0.25	£0.75	£1.25
Title Value:	$0.40	$1.20	$2.00	£0.25	£0.75	£1.25

FEAR BOOK

Eclipse,OS; 1 Apr 1986

	$Good	$Fine	$N.Mint	£Good	£Fine	£N.Mint
1 ND Bissette/Veitch art	$0.40	$1.20	$2.00	£0.25	£0.75	£1.25
Title Value:	$0.40	$1.20	$2.00	£0.25	£0.75	£1.25

FEAR, ADVENTURE INTO

Marvel Comics Group; 1 Nov 1970-31 Dec 1975

	$Good	$Fine	$N.Mint	£Good	£Fine	£N.Mint
1 scarce in the U.K. 64pgs, titled "Fear"	$1.65	$5.00	$10.00	£1.25	£3.75	£7.50
2-4 scarce in the U.K. 64pgs	$1.00	$3.00	$6.00	£0.65	£2.00	£4.00
5-9 ND 48pgs	$0.80	$2.50	$5.00	£0.40	£1.25	£2.50
10 ND 1st of Man-Thing series, title becomes "Adventure into Fear", Howard Chaykin and Gray Morrow art	$1.30	$4.00	$8.00	£0.80	£2.50	£5.00
11 ND Neal Adams cover	$0.65	$2.00	$4.00	£0.50	£1.50	£3.00
12 ND Jim Starlin art						

Fantasy Masterpieces #4

Faust #1

Fear #7

Issue	$Good	$Fine	$N.Mint	£Good	£Fine	£N.Mint
	$0.65	*$2.00*	*$4.00*	£0.55	£1.75	£3.50
13 ND	*$0.65*	*$2.00*	*$4.00*	£0.50	£1.50	£3.00
14 ND Val Mayerik art	*$0.65*	*$2.00*	*$4.00*	£0.50	£1.50	£3.00
15-16 ND Val Mayerik art, Brunner cover	*$0.80*	*$2.50*	*$5.00*	£0.50	£1.50	£3.00
17 ND Man-Thing vs. Wundarr, Val Mayerik art, Brunner cover	*$0.65*	*$2.00*	*$4.00*	£0.50	£1.50	£3.00
18 ND Val Mayerik art, Brunner cover	*$0.65*	*$2.00*	*$4.00*	£0.50	£1.50	£3.00
19 ND 1st appearance of Howard the Duck (few panels only), Val Mayerik art, Brunner cover	*$1.65*	*$5.00*	*$10.00*	£0.80	£2.50	£5.00
20 ND Gulacy art, Morbius the Living Vampire series begins, very "Steranko-esque" art; X-Men and Spiderman appear in "flash-back"	*$3.30*	*$10.00*	*$20.00*	£1.65	£5.00	£10.00
21 ND	*$1.65*	*$5.00*	*$10.00*	£0.80	£2.50	£5.00
22 ND	*$1.50*	*$4.50*	*$9.00*	£0.65	£2.00	£4.00
23 P. Craig Russell art	*$1.30*	*$4.00*	*$8.00*	£0.55	£1.75	£3.50
24 Morbius vs. Blade, P. Craig Russell art	*$1.30*	*$4.00*	*$8.00*	£0.55	£1.75	£3.50
25	*$1.30*	*$4.00*	*$8.00*	£0.50	£1.50	£3.00
26-31	*$1.15*	*$3.50*	*$7.00*	£0.40	£1.25	£2.50
Title Value:	*$34.35*	*$105.00*	*$204.50*	£17.95	£55.25	£110.50

Note: Steve Gerber stories 21-24

FEATURES

Early 1960s horror/fantasy reprints in 1-9. Other reprints in 11-14,20-26. Man-Thing in 10-19. Morbius in 20-31.

FEM 5

Entity Comics,MS; 1 Jan 1996-5 May 1996

Issue	$Good	$Fine	$N.Mint	£Good	£Fine	£N.Mint
1 Cover A, ND Shelby Robertson art	*$0.60*	*$1.80*	*$3.00*	£0.40	£1.20	£2.00
1 Cover B, ND Bill Maus and Rob Hunter art	*$0.60*	*$1.80*	*$3.00*	£0.40	£1.20	£2.00
1 Cover C, ND Tatsuya Ishida art	*$0.60*	*$1.80*	*$3.00*	£0.40	£1.20	£2.00
1 Cover D, ND Thad Rhodes art	*$0.60*	*$1.80*	*$3.00*	£0.40	£1.20	£2.00
1 Cover E, ND "mystery artist"	*$0.60*	*$1.80*	*$3.00*	£0.40	£1.20	£2.00
1 Signed & Numbered Edition, ND pre-bagged with certificate; 1,000 copies	*$2.40*	*$7.00*	*$12.00*	£1.60	£4.80	£8.00
2-5 ND	*$0.60*	*$1.80*	*$3.00*	£0.40	£1.20	£2.00
Title Value:	*$7.80*	*$23.20*	*$39.00*	£5.20	£15.60	£26.00

FEM 5: UNTOLD TALES

Entity Comics; 1 Nov 1996-present

Issue	$Good	$Fine	$N.Mint	£Good	£Fine	£N.Mint
1 ND Steve Mateo script, Shelby Robertson and Abraham Madison art; black and white	*$0.55*	*$1.65*	*$2.75*	£0.35	£1.05	£1.75
1 Cover A, ND cover art by John Fang	*$0.55*	*$1.65*	*$2.75*	£0.35	£1.05	£1.75
Title Value:	*$1.10*	*$3.30*	*$5.50*	£0.70	£2.10	£3.50

FEM FANTASTIQUE

AC Comics; 1 Aug 1988

Issue	$Good	$Fine	$N.Mint	£Good	£Fine	£N.Mint
1 ND	*$0.40*	*$1.20*	*$2.00*	£0.25	£0.75	£1.25
Title Value:	*$0.40*	*$1.20*	*$2.00*	£0.25	£0.75	£1.25

FEM FORCE

AC Comics; 1 Apr 1985-present

Issue	$Good	$Fine	$N.Mint	£Good	£Fine	£N.Mint
1 ND rare in the U.K. DS	*$1.00*	*$3.00*	*$5.00*	£0.70	£2.10	£3.50
2 ND	*$0.60*	*$1.80*	*$3.00*	£0.40	£1.20	£2.00
3-5 ND	*$0.50*	*$1.50*	*$2.50*	£0.35	£1.05	£1.75
6-24 ND	*$0.50*	*$1.50*	*$2.50*	£0.30	£0.90	£1.50
25 ND 1st appearance new Ms. Victory	*$0.50*	*$1.50*	*$2.50*	£0.30	£0.90	£1.50
26-27 ND The Devil Below story	*$0.50*	*$1.50*	*$2.50*	£0.30	£0.90	£1.50
28-35 ND	*$0.50*	*$1.50*	*$2.50*	£0.30	£0.90	£1.50
36 ND 48pgs	*$0.60*	*$1.80*	*$3.00*	£0.40	£1.20	£2.00
37 ND The Bulleteer and Golden Age She-Cat appear	*$0.50*	*$1.50*	*$2.50*	£0.30	£0.90	£1.50
38 ND Blue Bulleteer vs. Lady Luger	*$0.50*	*$1.50*	*$2.50*	£0.30	£0.90	£1.50
39-43 ND	*$0.50*	*$1.50*	*$2.50*	£0.30	£0.90	£1.50
44 ND Catman and Kitten preview	*$0.50*	*$1.50*	*$2.50*	£0.30	£0.90	£1.50
45 ND	*$0.50*	*$1.50*	*$2.50*	£0.30	£0.90	£1.50
46-49 ND	*$0.50*	*$1.50*	*$2.50*	£0.35	£1.05	£1.75
50 ND with flexi-disc and wraparound cover	*$0.60*	*$1.80*	*$3.00*	£0.40	£1.20	£2.00
51 ND photo cover	*$0.55*	*$1.65*	*$2.75*	£0.35	£1.05	£1.75
52 ND story continues in Good Girl Art Quarterly #9	*$0.55*	*$1.65*	*$2.75*	£0.35	£1.05	£1.75
53-56 ND	*$0.55*	*$1.65*	*$2.75*	£0.35	£1.05	£1.75
57 ND 1st full colour issue, with trading card	*$0.60*	*$1.80*	*$3.00*	£0.40	£1.20	£2.00
58-63 ND	*$0.55*	*$1.65*	*$2.75*	£0.35	£1.05	£1.75
63 pre-bagged, ND with Rayda trading card	*$0.70*	*$2.10*	*$3.50*	£0.45	£1.35	£2.25
64-67 ND	*$0.55*	*$1.65*	*$2.75*	£0.35	£1.05	£1.75
67 pre-bagged, ND with Brad Gorby print	*$0.70*	*$2.10*	*$3.50*	£0.45	£1.35	£2.25
68 ND	*$0.55*	*$1.65*	*$2.75*	£0.35	£1.05	£1.75
68 pre-bagged, ND with print of Jillian Fontaine	*$0.90*	*$2.70*	*$4.50*	£0.60	£1.80	£3.00
69 ND $2.95 cover begins	*$0.60*	*$1.80*	*$3.00*	£0.40	£1.20	£2.00
69 pre-bagged, ND with Pog	*$0.80*	*$2.40*	*$4.00*	£0.50	£1.50	£2.50
70-72 ND	*$0.60*	*$1.80*	*$3.00*	£0.40	£1.20	£2.00
72 pre-bagged, ND with Sentinels of Justice mini-comic	*$0.80*	*$2.40*	*$4.00*	£0.50	£1.50	£2.50
73 ND	*$0.60*	*$1.80*	*$3.00*	£0.40	£1.20	£2.00
73 pre-bagged, ND with Sentinels of Justice mini-comic	*$0.60*	*$1.80*	*$3.00*	£0.40	£1.20	£2.00
74 ND	*$0.60*	*$1.80*	*$3.00*	£0.40	£1.20	£2.00
74 pre-bagged, ND with signed art print of Fear Force by Mark Heike	*$1.00*	*$3.00*	*$5.00*	£0.65	£1.95	£3.25
75 ND	*$0.60*	*$1.80*	*$3.00*	£0.40	£1.20	£2.00
75 pre-bagged, ND with signed mini-poster art print of the wraparound cover by Brad Gorby	*$1.00*	*$3.00*	*$5.00*	£0.65	£1.95	£3.25
76 ND	*$0.60*	*$1.80*	*$3.00*	£0.40	£1.20	£2.00
76 pre-bagged, ND with Captain Wings #1 mini-comic	*$0.60*	*$1.80*	*$3.00*	£0.40	£1.20	£2.00
77-78 ND	*$0.60*	*$1.80*	*$3.00*	£0.40	£1.20	£2.00
78 pre-bagged, ND with Sentinels of Justice mini-comic	*$1.00*	*$3.00*	*$5.00*	£0.65	£1.95	£3.25
79 ND	*$0.60*	*$1.80*	*$3.00*	£0.40	£1.20	£2.00
79 pre-bagged, ND with Volume 1 of the Fem Force Index	*$1.20*	*$3.60*	*$6.00*	£0.80	£2.40	£4.00
80 ND	*$0.60*	*$1.80*	*$3.00*	£0.40	£1.20	£2.00
80 pre-bagged, ND with Volume 2 of the Fem Force Index	*$1.20*	*$3.60*	*$6.00*	£0.80	£2.40	£4.00
81 ND	*$0.60*	*$1.80*	*$3.00*	£0.40	£1.20	£2.00
81 pre-bagged, ND with art supplement for Vols. 1 & 2 of the Fem Force Index	*$1.20*	*$3.60*	*$6.00*	£0.80	£2.40	£4.00
82 ND	*$0.60*	*$1.80*	*$3.00*	£0.40	£1.20	£2.00
82 pre-bagged, ND with Volume 3 of the Fem Force Index	*$1.20*	*$3.60*	*$6.00*	£0.80	£2.40	£4.00
83 ND	*$0.60*	*$1.80*	*$3.00*	£0.40	£1.20	£2.00
83 pre-bagged, ND with Ms. Victory print by Jackson Guice	*$0.80*	*$2.40*	*$4.00*	£0.50	£1.50	£2.50
84 ND	*$0.60*	*$1.80*	*$3.00*	£0.40	£1.20	£2.00
84 pre-bagged, ND with Volume 4 of the Fem Force Index	*$0.80*	*$2.40*	*$4.00*	£0.50	£1.50	£2.50
85 ND	*$0.60*	*$1.80*	*$3.00*	£0.40	£1.20	£2.00
85 pre-bagged, ND with trading card	*$1.00*	*$3.00*	*$5.00*	£0.65	£1.95	£3.25
86 ND	*$0.60*	*$1.80*	*$3.00*	£0.40	£1.20	£2.00
86 pre-bagged, ND with part 5 of the Fem Force Index	*$1.20*	*$3.60*	*$6.00*	£0.80	£2.40	£4.00
87 ND 10th anniversary edition	*$0.80*	*$2.40*	*$4.00*	£0.50	£1.50	£2.50
87 pre-bagged, ND with special illustrated plate	*$2.00*	*$6.00*	*$10.00*	£1.30	£3.90	£6.50
88 ND	*$0.60*	*$1.80*	*$3.00*	£0.40	£1.20	£2.00
88 pre-bagged, ND with part 6 of the Fem Force Index	*$1.20*	*$3.60*	*$6.00*	£0.80	£2.40	£4.00
89 ND	*$0.60*	*$1.80*	*$3.00*	£0.40	£1.20	£2.00
89 pre-bagged, ND with part 7 of the Fem Force Index	*$1.20*	*$3.60*	*$6.00*	£0.80	£2.40	£4.00
90 ND	*$0.60*	*$1.80*	*$3.00*	£0.40	£1.20	£2.00
90 pre-bagged, ND with part 8 of the Fem Force Index	*$1.20*	*$3.60*	*$6.00*	£0.80	£2.40	£4.00
91 ND	*$0.60*	*$1.80*	*$3.00*	£0.40	£1.20	£2.00
91 pre-bagged, ND with part 9 of the Fem Force Index	*$1.20*	*$3.60*	*$6.00*	£0.80	£2.40	£4.00
92 ND	*$0.60*	*$1.80*	*$3.00*	£0.40	£1.20	£2.00
92 pre-bagged, ND with part 10 of Fem Force Index focusing on issues #71-78	*$1.20*	*$3.60*	*$6.00*	£0.80	£2.40	£4.00
93 ND	*$0.60*	*$1.80*	*$3.00*	£0.40	£1.20	£2.00
93 pre-bagged, ND with Fem Force Index	*$1.20*	*$3.60*	*$6.00*	£0.80	£2.40	£4.00
94 ND	*$0.60*	*$1.80*	*$3.00*	£0.40	£1.20	£2.00
94 pre-bagged, ND with Fem Force Index	*$1.20*	*$3.60*	*$6.00*	£0.80	£2.40	£4.00
95 ND	*$0.60*	*$1.80*	*$3.00*	£0.40	£1.20	£2.00
95 pre-bagged, ND with Fem Force Index	*$1.20*	*$3.60*	*$6.00*	£0.80	£2.40	£4.00
96 ND	*$0.60*	*$1.80*	*$3.00*	£0.40	£1.20	£2.00
96 pre-bagged, ND includes mini manga poster	*$1.20*	*$3.60*	*$6.00*	£0.80	£2.40	£4.00
Title Value:	*$82.25*	*$246.75*	*$411.25*	£53.10	£159.30	£265.50
Femforce: The Capricorn Chronicles (Feb 1994) Trade paperback reprints issues #55-57, signed by ceators and limited to 1,000 copies				£3.20	£9.60	£16.00
Sisters in Sin Graphic Novel (Apr 1995) Brad Gorby art				£1.70	£5.10	£8.50
Signed Edition (Apr 1995)				£2.00	£6.00	£10.00

FEM FORCE FRIGHTBOOK

AC Comics,OS; 1 Dec 1992

Issue	$Good	$Fine	$N.Mint	£Good	£Fine	£N.Mint
1 ND Halloween stories	*$0.50*	*$1.50*	*$2.50*	£0.30	£0.90	£1.50
Title Value:	*$0.50*	*$1.50*	*$2.50*	£0.30	£0.90	£1.50

FEM FORCE IN THE HOUSE OF HORROR

AC Comics; 1 1989

	$Good	$Fine	$N.Mint	£Good	£Fine	£N.Mint
1 ND 36pgs	$0.50	$1.50	$2.50	£0.30	£0.90	£1.50
Title Value:	$0.50	$1.50	$2.50	£0.30	£0.90	£1.50

FEM FORCE PIN-UP PORTFOLIO

AC Comics; 1 1987-5 1989

	$Good	$Fine	$N.Mint	£Good	£Fine	£N.Mint
1 ND various artists inc. Art Adams						
	$0.40	$1.20	$2.00	£0.25	£0.75	£1.25
2-4 ND	$0.40	$1.20	$2.00	£0.25	£0.75	£1.25
5 ND Jerry Ordway cover with Brian Stelfreeze and Jackson Guice art featured						
	$0.40	$1.20	$2.00	£0.25	£0.75	£1.25
Title Value:	$2.00	$6.00	$10.00	£1.25	£3.75	£6.25

FEM FORCE SPECIAL

AC Comics,OS; 1 1987

	$Good	$Fine	$N.Mint	£Good	£Fine	£N.Mint
1 ND 52pgs, 1st Miss Victory						
	$0.40	$1.20	$2.00	£0.25	£0.75	£1.25
Title Value:	$0.40	$1.20	$2.00	£0.25	£0.75	£1.25

FEM FORCE UP CLOSE

AC Comics; 1 Jun 1992-11 1993

	$Good	$Fine	$N.Mint	£Good	£Fine	£N.Mint
1 ND black and white begins						
	$0.60	$1.80	$3.00	£0.40	£1.20	£2.00
2 ND	$0.60	$1.80	$3.00	£0.40	£1.20	£2.00
3 ND Dragonfly	$0.60	$1.80	$3.00	£0.40	£1.20	£2.00
4 ND Ms. Victory; pre-bagged with bumper sticker						
	$0.80	$2.40	$4.00	£0.50	£1.50	£2.50
4 Collectors Edition, ND : She-Cat; pre-bagged with She-Cat trading card						
	$0.80	$2.40	$4.00	£0.50	£1.50	£2.50
5 ND Blue Bulleteer	$0.60	$1.80	$3.00	£0.40	£1.20	£2.00
5 Collectors Edition, ND - pre-bagged with sticker						
	$0.80	$2.40	$4.00	£0.50	£1.50	£2.50
6-11 ND	$0.60	$1.80	$3.00	£0.40	£1.20	£2.00
Title Value:	$8.40	$25.20	$42.00	£5.50	£16.50	£27.50

FEM FORCE, THE UNTOLD ORIGIN OF

AC Comics,OS; 1 1992

	$Good	$Fine	$N.Mint	£Good	£Fine	£N.Mint
1 ND 64pgs, also reprints cover of Fem Force #1						
	$0.90	$2.70	$4.50	£0.60	£1.80	£3.00
Title Value:	$0.90	$2.70	$4.50	£0.60	£1.80	£3.00

FEM FORCE: NIGHT OF THE DEMON SPECIAL

AC Comics,OS; 1 Dec 1990

	$Good	$Fine	$N.Mint	£Good	£Fine	£N.Mint
1 ND 36pgs	$0.50	$1.50	$2.50	£0.30	£0.90	£1.50
Title Value:	$0.50	$1.50	$2.50	£0.30	£0.90	£1.50

FEM FORCE: OUT OF THE ASYLUM SPECIAL

AC Comics,OS; 1 1987

	$Good	$Fine	$N.Mint	£Good	£Fine	£N.Mint
1 ND 52pgs	$0.40	$1.20	$2.00	£0.25	£0.75	£1.25
Title Value:	$0.40	$1.20	$2.00	£0.25	£0.75	£1.25

FEMFORCE BAD GIRL BACKLASH

AC Comics,OS; 1 Nov 1995

	$Good	$Fine	$N.Mint	£Good	£Fine	£N.Mint
1 ND pin-ups with framing sequence by all-girl creative team						
	$1.00	$3.00	$5.00	£0.70	£2.10	£3.50
1 Signed Edition, (Nov 1995) - signed by creators, pre-bagged						
	$1.40	$4.20	$7.00	£0.90	£2.70	£4.50
Title Value:	$2.40	$7.20	$12.00	£1.60	£4.80	£8.00

FEMFORCE TIMELINES

AC Comics,OS; nn Sep 1995

	$Good	$Fine	$N.Mint	£Good	£Fine	£N.Mint
nn ND 10th anniversary illustration of the birth and development of Fem Force; Compact Format						
	$0.60	$1.80	$3.00	£0.40	£1.20	£2.00
Title Value:	$0.60	$1.80	$3.00	£0.40	£1.20	£2.00

FERRET

Malibu,OS; 1 Sep 1992

	$Good	$Fine	$N.Mint	£Good	£Fine	£N.Mint
1 ND Thomas Derenick art						
	$0.40	$1.20	$2.00	£0.25	£0.75	£1.25
Title Value:	$0.40	$1.20	$2.00	£0.25	£0.75	£1.25

FERRET (2ND SERIES)

Malibu; 1 May 1993-10 Feb 1994

	$Good	$Fine	$N.Mint	£Good	£Fine	£N.Mint
1 entire die-cut comic following the outline of Ferret's head						
	$0.40	$1.20	$2.00	£0.25	£0.75	£1.25
2	$0.30	$0.90	$1.50	£0.20	£0.60	£1.00
2 Direct Sales Edition, with pull-out poster						
	$0.35	$1.05	$1.75	£0.25	£0.75	£1.25
3	$0.30	$0.90	$1.50	£0.20	£0.60	£1.00
3 Direct Sales Edition, with pull-out poster						
	$0.35	$1.05	$1.75	£0.25	£0.75	£1.25
4	$0.30	$0.90	$1.50	£0.20	£0.60	£1.00
5 Genesis Tie-In; pre-bagged with free Sky-Cap						
	$0.30	$0.90	$1.50	£0.20	£0.60	£1.00
6-10 Genesis Tie-In						
	$0.30	$0.90	$1.50	£0.20	£0.60	£1.00
Title Value:	$3.80	$11.40	$19.00	£2.55	£7.65	£12.75

Note: all Non-Distributed on the news-stands in the U.K.

FEUD

Marvel Comics Group/Epic,MS; 1 Jul 1993-4 Oct 1993

	$Good	$Fine	$N.Mint	£Good	£Fine	£N.Mint
1 ND Mike Baron script begins, embossed cover with metallic ink						
	$0.40	$1.20	$2.00	£0.25	£0.75	£1.25
2-4 ND	$0.40	$1.20	$2.00	£0.25	£0.75	£1.25
Title Value:	$1.60	$4.80	$8.00	£1.00	£3.00	£5.00

FIFTIES TERROR

Eternity; 1 Oct 1988-6 Apr 1989

	$Good	$Fine	$N.Mint	£Good	£Fine	£N.Mint
1-6 ND pre-Code horror reprints						
	$0.40	$1.20	$2.00	£0.25	£0.75	£1.25
Title Value:	$2.40	$7.20	$12.00	£1.50	£4.50	£7.50

FIFTY WHO MADE DC GREAT

DC Comics,OS; nn 1985

	$Good	$Fine	$N.Mint	£Good	£Fine	£N.Mint
nn ND 56pgs, high quality paper; text and illustrations of 50 people and products that contributed to DC's 50 year history; released as part of the company's 50th anniversary						
	$0.90	$2.70	$4.50	£0.60	£1.80	£3.00
Title Value:	$0.90	$2.70	$4.50	£0.60	£1.80	£3.00

FIGHT THE ENEMY

Tower Comics; 1 Aug 1966-3 Mar 1967

	$Good	$Fine	$N.Mint	£Good	£Fine	£N.Mint
1 scarce distributed in the U.K. Lucky 7 begins						
	$3.55	$10.50	$25.00	£1.75	£5.25	£12.50
2-3 scarce distributed in the U.K. McWilliams art						
	$2.85	$8.50	$20.00	£1.40	£4.25	£10.00
Title Value:	$9.25	$27.50	$65.00	£4.55	£13.75	£32.50

FIGHT-MAN ONE SHOT

Marvel Comics Group,OS; 1 Jun 1993

	$Good	$Fine	$N.Mint	£Good	£Fine	£N.Mint
1 ND Evan Dorkin script and art						
	$0.40	$1.20	$2.00	£0.25	£0.75	£1.25
Title Value:	$0.40	$1.20	$2.00	£0.25	£0.75	£1.25

FIGHTIN' AIR FORCE

Charlton;3 Feb 1956-53 Feb/Mar 1966

	$Good	$Fine	$N.Mint	£Good	£Fine	£N.Mint
3 scarce in the U.K.						
	$5.00	$15.00	$35.00	£2.50	£7.50	£17.50
4-5 scarce in the U.K.						
	$2.85	$8.50	$20.00	£1.40	£4.25	£10.00
6-10	$2.85	$8.50	$20.00	£1.05	£3.20	£7.50
11 64pgs	$3.55	$10.50	$25.00	£1.40	£4.25	£10.00
12 scarce in the U.K. 100pgs, squarebound; 25 cents cover. There are copies known with pence stamps (as indeed for issues #13-21)						
	$4.25	$12.50	$30.00	£1.70	£5.00	£12.00
13-21	$2.50	$7.50	$15.00	£1.00	£3.00	£6.00
1st official distribution in the U.K.						
22-30	$2.50	$7.50	$15.00	£0.90	£2.75	£5.50
31-49	$2.00	$6.00	$12.00	£0.80	£2.50	£5.00
50 1st appearance American Eagle						
	$2.00	$6.00	$12.00	£0.80	£2.50	£5.00
51-53	$1.30	$4.00	$8.00	£0.65	£2.00	£4.00
Title Value:	$121.65	$364.50	$764.00	£48.70	£149.00	£312.50

Note: it is unclear what issues #1 and #2 were known as

FIGHTIN' ARMY

Charlton; 16 Jan 1956-127 Dec 1976; 128 Sep 1977-172 Nov 1984

	$Good	$Fine	$N.Mint	£Good	£Fine	£N.Mint
16 scarce in the U.K.						
	$5.00	$15.00	$35.00	£2.50	£7.50	£17.50
17-19	$2.85	$8.50	$20.00	£1.40	£4.25	£10.00
20 Steve Ditko art	$4.25	$12.50	$30.00	£2.10	£6.25	£15.00
21-23	$2.85	$8.50	$20.00	£1.10	£3.40	£8.00
24 giant	$3.20	$9.50	$22.50	£1.40	£4.25	£10.00
25-30	$3.30	$10.00	$20.00	£1.30	£4.00	£8.00
31-34	$2.50	$7.50	$15.00	£1.00	£3.00	£6.00
1st official distribution in the U.K.						
35-50	$2.50	$7.50	$15.00	£1.00	£3.00	£6.00
51-60	$2.05	$6.25	$12.50	£0.80	£2.50	£5.00
61-70	$1.25	$3.75	$7.50	£0.65	£2.00	£4.00
71-80	$1.20	$3.60	$6.00	£0.70	£2.10	£3.50
81-100	$0.90	$2.70	$4.50	£0.60	£1.80	£3.00
101-120	$0.60	$1.80	$3.00	£0.50	£1.50	£2.50
121-140	$0.50	$1.50	$2.50	£0.40	£1.20	£2.00
141-160	$0.50	$1.50	$2.50	£0.30	£0.90	£1.50
161-172	$0.50	$1.50	$2.50	£0.20	£0.60	£1.00
Title Value:	$200.35	$602.00	$1167.50	£101.20	£306.15	£581.50

Note: issues #1-15 were called Soldier & Marine Comics

FIGHTIN' FIVE, THE

Charlton;28 Jul 1964-41 Jan 1967;42 Oct 1981-49 Dec 1982

(formerly Space War #1-27)

	$Good	$Fine	$N.Mint	£Good	£Fine	£N.Mint
28 scarce in the U.K.						
	$4.25	$12.50	$30.00	£2.10	£6.25	£15.00
29-30	$3.55	$10.50	$25.00	£1.40	£4.25	£10.00
31-39	$2.50	$7.50	$17.50	£1.10	£3.40	£8.00
40 1st appearance Peacemaker						
	$4.25	$12.50	$30.00	£1.75	£5.25	£12.50
41	$2.50	$7.50	$17.50	£1.10	£3.40	£8.00
42 reprints begin	$0.40	$1.20	$2.00	£0.25	£0.75	£1.25
43-49	$0.40	$1.20	$2.00	£0.25	£0.75	£1.25
Title Value:	$43.80	$130.60	$301.00	£19.65	£60.00	£137.50

Note: all distributed on the news-stands in the U.K.

FIGHTIN' MARINES

Charlton; 14 May 1955-132 Nov 1976; 133 Oct 1977-176 Sep 1984

	$Good	$Fine	$N.Mint	£Good	£Fine	£N.Mint
14 scarce in the U.K.						
	$14.00	$43.00	$100.00	£7.00	£21.00	£50.00
15	$5.50	$17.00	$40.00	£2.10	£6.25	£15.00
16	$2.85	$8.50	$20.00	£1.40	£4.25	£10.00
17 Canteen Kate by Matt Baker						
	$10.50	$32.00	$75.00	£4.25	£12.50	£30.00
18-20	$2.85	$8.50	$20.00	£1.40	£4.25	£10.00
21-24	$2.85	$8.50	$20.00	£1.10	£3.40	£8.00
25 giant	$4.25	$12.50	$30.00	£2.10	£6.25	£15.00
26 scarce in the U.K. giant						
	$6.25	$19.00	$45.00	£2.85	£8.50	£20.00
27-30	$2.10	$6.25	$15.00	£1.05	£3.20	£7.50
31-44	$1.75	$5.25	$12.50	£0.90	£2.75	£6.50
1st official distribution in the U.K.						
45-50	$1.75	$5.25	$12.50	£0.90	£2.75	£6.50
51-80	$1.25	$3.75	$7.50	£0.55	£1.75	£3.50
81	$1.25	$3.75	$7.50	£0.50	£1.50	£3.00
82 giant						
	$1.65	$5.00	$10.00	£0.80	£2.50	£5.00
83-100	$1.00	$3.00	$6.00	£0.50	£1.50	£3.00

	$Good	$Fine	$N.Mint	£Good	£Fine	£N.Mint
101-125	$0.65	$2.00	$4.00	£0.30	£1.00	£2.00
126-140	$0.30	$1.00	$2.00	£0.15	£0.50	£1.00
141-176	$0.40	$1.20	$2.00	£0.15	£0.45	£0.75
Title Value:	$200.25	$604.95	$1293.00	£92.45	£285.10	£621.00

Note: previous issues published by St. John (Approved Comics)

Note also: copies from #41 on known with pence stamps as many Charlton titles were distributed in the U.K. before official distribution cover date Novwmber 1959.

FIGHTIN' NAVY

Charlton;74 Jan 1956-125 Apr/May 1966; 126 Aug 1983-133 Oct 1984

	$Good	$Fine	$N.Mint	£Good	£Fine	£N.Mint
74 scarce in the U.K.	$4.60	$13.50	$32.50	£2.50	£7.50	£17.50
75-80	$2.85	$8.50	$20.00	£1.40	£4.25	£10.00
81	$2.10	$6.25	$15.00	£1.05	£3.20	£7.50
82 Sam Glanzman art	$1.75	$5.25	$12.50	£1.05	£3.20	£7.50
83 100pgs, squarebound; some copies known with pence stamps (as well as issues #84-87)	$1.40	$4.25	$10.00	£1.20	£3.60	£8.50
84-87	$1.40	$4.25	$10.00	£0.60	£1.90	£4.50
1st official distribution in the U.K.						
88-99	$1.10	$3.40	$8.00	£0.55	£1.70	£4.00
100	$1.25	$3.85	$9.00	£0.60	£1.90	£4.50
101-110	$1.05	$3.20	$7.50	£0.40	£1.25	£3.00
111-125	$1.05	$3.20	$7.50	£0.35	£1.05	£2.50
126-133	$0.45	$1.35	$2.25	£0.30	£0.90	£1.50
Title Value:	$76.85	$232.70	$540.50	£35.45	£108.35	£251.00

FIGHTING AMERICAN

Harvey; 1 Oct 1966

	$Good	$Fine	$N.Mint	£Good	£Fine	£N.Mint
1 distributed in the U.K. giant; Joe Simon and Jack Kirby reprints, 1pg Neal Adams art	$3.55	$10.50	$25.00	£1.75	£5.25	£12.50
Title Value:	$3.55	$10.50	$25.00	£1.75	£5.25	£12.50

FIGHTING AMERICAN (2ND SERIES)

DC Comics,MS; 1 Feb 1994-6 Jul 1994

	$Good	$Fine	$N.Mint	£Good	£Fine	£N.Mint
1-6 based on the 1950s creation by Joe Simon and Jack Kirby	$0.25	$0.75	$1.25	£0.15	£0.45	£0.75
Title Value:	$1.50	$4.50	$7.50	£0.90	£2.70	£4.50

FIGHTING AMERICAN HARDCOVER

Marvel Comics Group; nn Mar 1990

	$Good	$Fine	$N.Mint	£Good	£Fine	£N.Mint
nn ND Hardcover collection of all 7 issues of the Simon and Kirby Cold War comic book of satire and super-heroes. Recoloured throughout	$3.00	$9.00	$15.00	£2.00	£6.00	£10.00
Title Value:	$3.00	$9.00	$15.00	£2.00	£6.00	£10.00

FINAL CYCLE

Dragon's Teeth,MS; 1 Jul 1987-4 Oct 1987

	$Good	$Fine	$N.Mint	£Good	£Fine	£N.Mint
1-3 ND Cirocco/Amaro art	$0.40	$1.20	$2.00	£0.25	£0.75	£1.25
4 ND Amaro art	$0.40	$1.20	$2.00	£0.25	£0.75	£1.25
Title Value:	$1.60	$4.80	$8.00	£1.00	£3.00	£5.00

FINAL FANTASY

Disney/Hollywood Comics,MS; 1 Jan 1992-2 1992

	$Good	$Fine	$N.Mint	£Good	£Fine	£N.Mint
1-2 ND Mike Mignola cover, based on game	$0.30	$0.90	$1.50	£0.20	£0.60	£1.00
Title Value:	$0.60	$1.80	$3.00	£0.40	£1.20	£2.00

FINAL NIGHT, THE

DC Comics,MS; 1-4 Nov 1996

(see Green Lantern 2nd series)

	$Good	$Fine	$N.Mint	£Good	£Fine	£N.Mint
1-4 ND Karl Kesel script, Stuart Immonen art; weekly	$0.40	$1.20	$2.00	£0.25	£0.75	£1.25
Title Value:	$1.60	$4.80	$8.00	£1.00	£3.00	£5.00
The Final Night Collectors Set (Feb 1997) ND boxed set of the mini-series, Parallax: Emerald Night and Green Lantern #81				£2.00	£6.00	£10.00

FIRE FROM HEAVEN

Image; 1 Mar 1996-2 May 1996

	$Good	$Fine	$N.Mint	£Good	£Fine	£N.Mint
½ ND 24pgs, issued by Wizard, with certificate of authenticity	$2.50	$7.50	$12.50	£1.50	£4.50	£7.50
1 ND 40pgs, Alan Moore script, Ryan Benjamin art; continued in Backlash #19	$0.60	$1.80	$3.00	£0.40	£1.20	£2.00
2 ND story concluded from Sword of Damocles #2; Alan Moore script, Jim Lee art	$0.50	$1.50	$2.50	£0.30	£0.90	£1.50
Title Value:	$3.60	$10.80	$18.00	£2.20	£6.60	£11.00

FIRE TRIPPER

Viz Comics; 1 1989

	$Good	$Fine	$N.Mint	£Good	£Fine	£N.Mint
1 ND 64pgs, squarebound, black and white; script/art by Rumiko Takahashi	$0.60	$1.80	$3.00	£0.40	£1.20	£2.00
Title Value:	$0.60	$1.80	$3.00	£0.40	£1.20	£2.00

FIREARM

Malibu Ultraverse; 0 1994; 1 Sep 1993-18 Feb 1995

(see Codename: Firearm)

	$Good	$Fine	$N.Mint	£Good	£Fine	£N.Mint
0 ND issued with live action video containing 1st part of story (continued in comic)	$3.00	$9.00	$15.00	£3.00	£9.00	£15.00
1 ND Cully Hamner art begins	$0.50	$1.50	$2.50	£0.30	£0.90	£1.50
2 ND 40pgs, Rune insert	$0.50	$1.50	$2.50	£0.30	£0.90	£1.50
3-4 ND	$0.40	$1.20	$2.00	£0.20	£0.60	£1.00
5 ND origins month tie-in	$0.40	$1.20	$2.00	£0.20	£0.60	£1.00
6-10 ND	$0.40	$1.20	$2.00	£0.20	£0.60	£1.00
11 ND flip-book format with Ultraverse Premiere #5	$0.50	$1.50	$2.50	£0.30	£0.90	£1.50
12-14 ND	$0.30	$0.90	$1.50	£0.20	£0.60	£1.00
15 ND tie-in with Freex #15 and Night Man #14	$0.30	$0.90	$1.50	£0.20	£0.60	£1.00
16 ND Howard Chaykin cover	$0.30	$0.90	$1.50	£0.20	£0.60	£1.00
17 ND	$0.30	$0.90	$1.50	£0.20	£0.60	£1.00
18 ND Prime, Nightman and Strangers all appear	$0.30	$0.90	$1.50	£0.20	£0.60	£1.00
Title Value:	$9.80	$29.40	$49.00	£6.90	£20.70	£34.50

FIREBALL XL5

(see Steve Zodiac)

FIREBRAND

DC Comics; 1 Feb 1996-9 Oct 1996

	$Good	$Fine	$N.Mint	£Good	£Fine	£N.Mint
1-9 ND Brian Augustyn script and Sal Velluto art begin	$0.35	$1.05	$1.75	£0.25	£0.75	£1.25
Title Value:	$3.15	$9.45	$15.75	£2.25	£6.75	£11.25

FIREHAIR

I.W. Comics;8 early 1960s

	$Good	$Fine	$N.Mint	£Good	£Fine	£N.Mint
8 scarce, distributed in the U.K. all reprints	$2.85	$8.50	$20.00	£1.40	£4.25	£10.00
Title Value:	$2.85	$8.50	$20.00	£1.40	£4.25	£10.00

FIRESTAR

Marvel Comics Group,MS; 1 Mar 1988-4 Jun 1988

	$Good	$Fine	$N.Mint	£Good	£Fine	£N.Mint
1 ND X-Men and New Mutants appear	$0.60	$1.80	$3.00	£0.25	£0.75	£1.25
2 ND	$0.50	$1.50	$2.50	£0.25	£0.75	£1.25
3 ND Wolverine appears	$0.50	$1.50	$2.50	£0.25	£0.75	£1.25
4 ND	$0.50	$1.50	$2.50	£0.25	£0.75	£1.25
Title Value:	$2.10	$6.30	$10.50	£1.00	£3.00	£5.00

FIRESTORM

DC Comics; 1 Mar 1978-5 Oct/Nov 1978

(see also Brave & the Bold, Captain Atom, DC Presents, Flash)

	$Good	$Fine	$N.Mint	£Good	£Fine	£N.Mint
1 origin, 1st appearance Firestorm	$0.65	$2.00	$4.00	£0.30	£1.00	£2.00
2 origin Multiplex	$0.40	$1.25	$2.50	£0.25	£0.75	£1.50
3 origin Killer Frost	$0.40	$1.25	$2.50	£0.25	£0.75	£1.50
4 1st appearance Hyena (Summer Day)	$0.40	$1.25	$2.50	£0.25	£0.75	£1.50
5 ND 44pgs	$0.40	$1.25	$2.50	£0.25	£0.85	£1.75
Title Value:	$2.25	$7.00	$14.00	£1.30	£4.10	£8.25

FIRESTORM (2ND SERIES)

DC Comics; 1 Jun 1982-100 Aug 1990

(becomes Firestorm the Nuclear Man with issue 50)

	$Good	$Fine	$N.Mint	£Good	£Fine	£N.Mint
1 intro Black Bison, origin briefly retold	$0.40	$1.20	$2.00	£0.25	£0.75	£1.25
2-5	$0.30	$0.90	$1.50	£0.20	£0.60	£1.00
6-16	$0.25	$0.75	$1.25	£0.15	£0.45	£0.75
17 1st appearance Firehawk	$0.30	$0.90	$1.50	£0.15	£0.45	£0.75
18-21	$0.25	$0.75	$1.25	£0.15	£0.45	£0.75
22 origin told	$0.25	$0.75	$1.25	£0.15	£0.45	£0.75
23	$0.25	$0.75	$1.25	£0.15	£0.45	£0.75
24 1st appearance Blue Devil	$0.30	$0.90	$1.50	£0.20	£0.60	£1.00
25-40	$0.25	$0.75	$1.25	£0.15	£0.45	£0.75
41-42 Crisis X-over	$0.20	$0.60	$1.00	£0.15	£0.45	£0.75
43-47	$0.20	$0.60	$1.00	£0.15	£0.45	£0.75
48 1st appearance Moonbow	$0.20	$0.60	$1.00	£0.15	£0.45	£0.75
49	$0.20	$0.60	$1.00	£0.15	£0.45	£0.75
50 48pgs	$0.30	$0.90	$1.50	£0.20	£0.60	£1.00
51-52	$0.20	$0.60	$1.00	£0.15	£0.45	£0.75
53 origin, 1st appearance Silver Shade	$0.20	$0.60	$1.00	£0.15	£0.45	£0.75
54	$0.20	$0.60	$1.00	£0.15	£0.45	£0.75
55-56 Legends X-over	$0.20	$0.60	$1.00	£0.15	£0.45	£0.75
57-60	$0.20	$0.60	$1.00	£0.15	£0.45	£0.75
61 regular cover	$0.20	$0.60	$1.00	£0.15	£0.45	£0.75
61 Test Cover Edition, very scarce in the U.K., scarce in the U.S. (see note below)	$6.00	$18.00	$30.00	£5.00	£15.00	£25.00
62	$0.20	$0.60	$1.00	£0.15	£0.45	£0.75
63 Captain Atom X-over	$0.20	$0.60	$1.00	£0.15	£0.45	£0.75
64 Suicide Squad, Justice League X-over	$0.20	$0.60	$1.00	£0.15	£0.45	£0.75
65 Firestorm merges with Mikhail	$0.20	$0.60	$1.00	£0.15	£0.45	£0.75
66 Green Lantern X-over	$0.20	$0.60	$1.00	£0.15	£0.45	£0.75
67 Millennium X-over; Green Lantern Corps, Justice League of America, Batman and the Outsiders cameo	$0.20	$0.60	$1.00	£0.15	£0.45	£0.75
68 Millennium X-over, Justice League of America cameo, Captain Atom, Green Lantern, Driq, Harbinger appear	$0.20	$0.60	$1.00	£0.15	£0.45	£0.75
69-79	$0.20	$0.60	$1.00	£0.15	£0.45	£0.75
80-81 Invasion X-over	$0.20	$0.60	$1.00	£0.15	£0.45	£0.75
82-84	$0.20	$0.60	$1.00	£0.15	£0.45	£0.75
85 new costume, new identity	$0.20	$0.60	$1.00	£0.15	£0.45	£0.75
86 Janus Directive X-over	$0.20	$0.60	$1.00	£0.15	£0.45	£0.75

VERY GENERAL PERCENTAGE CONVERSION CHART WHICH MAY BE USED TO CALCULATE LOW AND INBETWEEN GRADES:

	$Good	$Fine	$N.Mint	£Good	£Fine	£N.Mint
87-89	*$0.20*	*$0.60*	*$1.00*	£0.15	£0.45	£0.75
90 intro Naiad; Swamp Thing, Red Tornado appear - begin 4 part story	*$0.20*	*$0.60*	*$1.00*	£0.15	£0.45	£0.75
91 Swamp Thing appears	*$0.20*	*$0.60*	*$1.00*	£0.15	£0.45	£0.75
92-93 Elemental war story continues, Red Tornado appears	*$0.20*	*$0.60*	*$1.00*	£0.15	£0.45	£0.75
94-99	*$0.20*	*$0.60*	*$1.00*	£0.15	£0.45	£0.75
100 giant issue with creators Gerry Conway and Al Milgrom presenting a new sequence of early adventures	*$0.50*	*$1.50*	*$2.50*	£0.30	£0.90	£1.50
Title Value:	*$28.85*	*$86.55*	*$141.75*	£20.55	£61.65	£102.75

Note: in a distribution experiment #61 was issued with alternative test-cover in some US states, very rare. It has a white cover as opposed to pink with a circular Superman logo in the top left hand corner (see Justice League International 3).

Note also that the title became simply "Firestorm" in issues #55-58 and from #83 onwards.

FIRESTORM (2ND SERIES) ANNUAL

DC Comics; 1 Nov 1983-5 Oct 1987

(becomes simply Firestorm The Nuclear Man Annual issue #4 onwards)

	$Good	$Fine	$N.Mint	£Good	£Fine	£N.Mint
1-5 48pgs	*$0.30*	*$0.90*	*$1.50*	£0.20	£0.60	£1.00
Title Value:	*$1.50*	*$4.50*	*$7.50*	£1.00	£3.00	£5.00

FIRETEAM

Aircel,MS; 1 Dec 1990-6 May 1991

	$Good	$Fine	$N.Mint	£Good	£Fine	£N.Mint
1-6 ND Don Lomax script and art	*$0.40*	*$1.20*	*$2.00*	£0.25	£0.75	£1.25
Title Value:	*$2.40*	*$7.20*	*$12.00*	£1.50	£4.50	£7.50

FIRST ADVENTURES

First; 1 Dec 1985-5 Apr 1986

	$Good	$Fine	$N.Mint	£Good	£Fine	£N.Mint
1-5 ND Blaze Barlow, Whisper, Dynamo Joe	*$0.30*	*$0.90*	*$1.50*	£0.20	£0.60	£1.00
Title Value:	*$1.50*	*$4.50*	*$7.50*	£1.00	£3.00	£5.00

FIRST FOLIO

Pacific; 1 Mar 1984

	$Good	$Fine	$N.Mint	£Good	£Fine	£N.Mint
1 ND Joe Kubert Art School graduates; Ron Randall, Adam and Andy Kubert	*$0.30*	*$0.90*	*$1.50*	£0.20	£0.60	£1.00
Title Value:	*$0.30*	*$0.90*	*$1.50*	£0.20	£0.60	£1.00

FIRST ISSUE SPECIAL

DC Comics; 1 Apr 1975-13 Apr 1976

	$Good	$Fine	$N.Mint	£Good	£Fine	£N.Mint
1 Atlas; Jack Kirby cover and art	*$0.65*	*$2.00*	*$4.00*	£0.25	£0.75	£1.50
2 Green Team; Joe Simon and Jerry Grandenetti art	*$0.55*	*$1.75*	*$3.50*	£0.20	£0.60	£1.25
3 Metamorpho	*$0.55*	*$1.75*	*$3.50*	£0.20	£0.60	£1.25
4 Lady Cop, mentions venereal disease (unusual for a mainstream comic to do so, let alone in 1975)	*$0.55*	*$1.75*	*$3.50*	£0.20	£0.60	£1.25
5 Manhunter; Jack Kirby cover and art	*$0.55*	*$1.75*	*$3.50*	£0.20	£0.60	£1.25
6 Dingbats; Jack Kirby cover and art	*$0.55*	*$1.75*	*$3.50*	£0.20	£0.60	£1.25
7 Creeper; Steve Ditko cover and art	*$0.55*	*$1.75*	*$3.50*	£0.20	£0.60	£1.25
8 origin and 1st appearance Warlord by Mike Grell; story continues in Warlord #1	*$0.80*	*$2.50*	*$5.00*	£0.65	£2.00	£4.00
9 Dr. Fate; Walt Simonson art, Joe Kubert cover	*$0.55*	*$1.75*	*$3.50*	£0.20	£0.60	£1.25
10 scarce in the U.K. Outsiders	*$0.55*	*$1.75*	*$3.50*	£0.20	£0.60	£1.25
11 scarce in the U.K. Codename: Assassin	*$0.50*	*$1.50*	*$3.00*	£0.20	£0.60	£1.25
12 scarce in the U.K. Starman (a 70s version; see Adventure Comics #467)	*$0.50*	*$1.50*	*$3.00*	£0.20	£0.60	£1.25
13 scarce in the U.K. New Gods; features The Return of the New Gods that pre-dates the title by more than a year; 1st new costume for Orion	*$1.65*	*$5.00*	*$10.00*	£0.50	£1.50	£3.00
Title Value:	*$8.50*	*$26.50*	*$53.00*	£3.40	£10.25	£21.00

FIRST KISS

Charlton; 1 Dec 1957-40 Jan 1965

	$Good	$Fine	$N.Mint	£Good	£Fine	£N.Mint
1 scarce in the U.K.	*$3.55*	*$10.50*	*$25.00*	£2.00	£6.00	£14.00
2-5	*$2.10*	*$6.25*	*$15.00*	£1.00	£3.00	£7.00
6-10	*$1.75*	*$5.25*	*$12.50*	£0.85	£2.55	£6.00
1st official distribution in the U.K.						
11-40	*$0.85*	*$2.55*	*$6.00*	£0.40	£1.25	£3.00
Title Value:	*$46.20*	*$138.25*	*$327.50*	£22.25	£68.25	£162.00

Note: issues distributed in the U.K. around 1958 onwards. It is possible that the title was distributed from issue #1 as an experiment.

FIRST SIX PACK

First; 1 Jul 1987-2 Nov 1987

	$Good	$Fine	$N.Mint	£Good	£Fine	£N.Mint
1 ND 50 cents; American Flagg, Badger, Dynamo Joe, Grim Jack, Jon Sable, Nexus previews in black and white; card stock covers, painted cover by Dave Dorman	*$0.25*	*$0.75*	*$1.25*	£0.15	£0.45	£0.75
2 ND 50 cents; American Flagg, Dreadstar, Jon Sable, Psychoblast, Shatter, Whisper previews in black and white; heavy stock paper cover	*$0.25*	*$0.75*	*$1.25*	£0.15	£0.45	£0.75
Title Value:	*$0.50*	*$1.50*	*$2.50*	£0.30	£0.90	£1.50

FISH POLICE (1ST SERIES)

Fishwrap; 1 Dec 1985-11 Nov 1987

	$Good	$Fine	$N.Mint	£Good	£Fine	£N.Mint
1 ND Steve Moncuse story/art begins, black and white	*$0.40*	*$1.20*	*$2.00*	£0.30	£0.90	£1.50
1 2nd printing, ND (May 1986)	*$0.35*	*$1.05*	*$1.75*	£0.25	£0.75	£1.25
1 3rd printing ND	*$0.30*	*$0.90*	*$1.50*	£0.20	£0.60	£1.00
2 ND	*$0.35*	*$1.05*	*$1.75*	£0.25	£0.75	£1.25
2 2nd printing ND	*$0.30*	*$0.90*	*$1.50*	£0.20	£0.60	£1.00
3-11 ND	*$0.35*	*$1.05*	*$1.75*	£0.25	£0.75	£1.25
Title Value:	*$4.85*	*$14.55*	*$24.25*	£3.45	£10.35	£17.25
Hairballs Graphic Novel (Comico) ND reprints #1-4 incolour, some new art, Harlan Ellison intro				£1.00	£3.00	£5.00
Fish Police Bargain Prepack (Jun 1991) ND issues #18-20 pre-bagged				£0.60	£1.80	£3.00

FISH POLICE (2ND SERIES)

Comico; 0 Apr 1991;5 Apr 1988-17 May 1989;Apple; 18 Aug 1989-26 Oct/Nov 1990

	$Good	$Fine	$N.Mint	£Good	£Fine	£N.Mint
0 ND previously unseen pilot issue from 1985, Art Adams cover (Apr 1991)	*$0.30*	*$0.90*	*$1.50*	£0.20	£0.60	£1.00
5 ND reprints from Fishwrap series begin; issues #1-5 in colour for the first time	*$0.30*	*$0.90*	*$1.50*	£0.20	£0.60	£1.00
6-11 ND	*$0.30*	*$0.90*	*$1.50*	£0.20	£0.60	£1.00
12 ND new material begins, colour	*$0.30*	*$0.90*	*$1.50*	£0.20	£0.60	£1.00
13-17 ND	*$0.30*	*$0.90*	*$1.50*	£0.20	£0.60	£1.00
18 ND 1st Apple issue; reverts to black and white	*$0.30*	*$0.90*	*$1.50*	£0.20	£0.60	£1.00
19-22 ND	*$0.30*	*$0.90*	*$1.50*	£0.20	£0.60	£1.00
23 ND proposed issue #1 lay-outs shown for 1st time	*$0.30*	*$0.90*	*$1.50*	£0.20	£0.60	£1.00
24 ND	*$0.30*	*$0.90*	*$1.50*	£0.20	£0.60	£1.00
25-26 ND bi-weekly	*$0.30*	*$0.90*	*$1.50*	£0.20	£0.60	£1.00
Title Value:	*$6.90*	*$20.70*	*$34.50*	£4.60	£13.80	£23.00

FISH POLICE (3RD SERIES)

Marvel Comics Group,MS; 1 Oct 1992-6 Mar 1993

	$Good	$Fine	$N.Mint	£Good	£Fine	£N.Mint
1 ND reprints original series from Fishwrap in colour	*$0.25*	*$0.75*	*$1.25*	£0.15	£0.45	£0.75
2-6 ND	*$0.25*	*$0.75*	*$1.25*	£0.15	£0.45	£0.75

Fem 5 #1

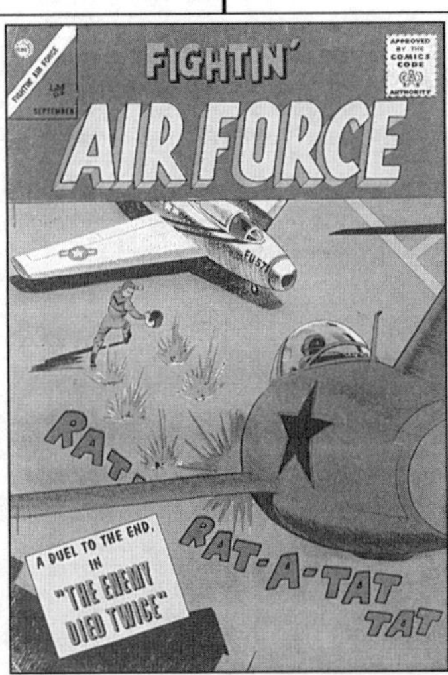

Fightin' Air Force #40

1st Issue Special #10

	$Good	$Fine	$N.Mint	£Good	£Fine	£N.Mint
Title Value:	$1.50	$4.50	$7.50	£0.90	£2.70	£4.50

FISH POLICE SPECIAL
Comico,OS; 1 Jul 1987

	$Good	$Fine	$N.Mint	£Good	£Fine	£N.Mint
1 ND story precedes issue #1	$0.40	$1.20	$2.00	£0.25	£0.75	£1.25
Title Value:	$0.40	$1.20	$2.00	£0.25	£0.75	£1.25

FISH SHTICKS
Apple Comics; 1 Sep 1991-6 1992

	$Good	$Fine	$N.Mint	£Good	£Fine	£N.Mint
1-6 ND return of the Fish Police	$0.30	$0.90	$1.50	£0.20	£0.60	£1.00
Title Value:	$1.80	$5.40	$9.00	£1.20	£3.60	£6.00

FIST OF GOD
Eternity,MS; 1 May 1988-4 1988

	$Good	$Fine	$N.Mint	£Good	£Fine	£N.Mint
1-4 ND	$0.40	$1.20	$2.00	£0.25	£0.75	£1.25
Title Value:	$1.60	$4.80	$8.00	£1.00	£3.00	£5.00

FIST OF THE NORTH STAR
Viz Communications,MS; 1 1989-8 1989

	$Good	$Fine	$N.Mint	£Good	£Fine	£N.Mint
1-8 ND 52pgs, black and white	$0.55	$1.65	$2.75	£0.35	£1.05	£1.75
Title Value:	$4.40	$13.20	$22.00	£2.80	£8.40	£14.00
Fist of the Northstar Graphic Novel (Apr 1995) collects 8 part mini-series				£2.70	£8.10	£13.50

FIST OF THE NORTH STAR PART 2
Viz Communications,MS; 1 Nov 1995-5 Mar 1996

	$Good	$Fine	$N.Mint	£Good	£Fine	£N.Mint
1-5 ND black and white	$0.55	$1.65	$2.75	£0.35	£1.05	£1.75
Title Value:	$2.75	$8.25	$13.75	£1.75	£5.25	£8.75

FIVE-STAR SUPER-HERO SPECTACULAR
DC Comics,OS; nn Sep 1977

(see DC Special Series)

	$Good	$Fine	$N.Mint	£Good	£Fine	£N.Mint
nn ND 80pgs, Batman, Aquaman, Green Lantern, Flash, Atom and Kobra appear; Mike Nasser and Mike Golden art	$0.80	$2.50	$5.00	£0.80	£2.50	£5.00
Title Value:	$0.80	$2.50	$5.00	£0.80	£2.50	£5.00

FLAMING CARROT (1ST SERIES)
Killan Barracks,Magazine; 1 Summer/Autumn 1981

	$Good	$Fine	$N.Mint	£Good	£Fine	£N.Mint
1 ND	$11.50	$35.00	$70.00	£6.50	£20.00	£40.00
Title Value:	$11.50	$35.00	$70.00	£6.50	£20.00	£40.00

FLAMING CARROT (2ND SERIES)
Aardvark/Renegade/Dark Horse; 1 Mar 1984-present

(see Visions)

	$Good	$Fine	$N.Mint	£Good	£Fine	£N.Mint
1 ND Bob Burden script and art; black and white	$9.00	$27.00	$45.00	£4.00	£12.00	£20.00
2 ND Bob Burden script and art; black and white	$5.00	$15.00	$25.00	£2.50	£7.50	£12.50
3 ND Bob Burden script and art; black and white	$3.00	$9.00	$15.00	£1.50	£4.50	£7.50
4-6 ND Bob Burden script and art; black and white	$2.50	$7.50	$12.50	£1.00	£3.00	£5.00
7 ND 1st Renegade issue	$1.40	$4.20	$7.00	£0.70	£2.10	£3.50
8-10 ND	$1.40	$4.20	$7.00	£0.70	£2.10	£3.50
11-12 ND	$1.00	$3.00	$5.00	£0.60	£1.80	£3.00
13-15 ND	$0.60	$1.80	$3.00	£0.40	£1.20	£2.00
16-17 ND	$0.45	$1.35	$2.25	£0.30	£0.90	£1.50
18 ND 1st Dark Horse issue	$0.45	$1.35	$2.25	£0.30	£0.90	£1.50
19-20 ND	$0.45	$1.35	$2.25	£0.30	£0.90	£1.50
21-23 ND	$0.40	$1.20	$2.00	£0.25	£0.75	£1.25
24 ND giant	$0.55	$1.65	$2.75	£0.35	£1.05	£1.75
25-26 ND	$0.40	$1.20	$2.00	£0.25	£0.75	£1.25
27 ND Todd McFarlane cover	$0.40	$1.20	$2.00	£0.25	£0.75	£1.25
28 ND	$0.40	$1.20	$2.00	£0.25	£0.75	£1.25
29 ND $2.50 cover begins	$0.45	$1.35	$2.25	£0.30	£0.90	£1.50
30-31 ND	$0.45	$1.35	$2.25	£0.30	£0.90	£1.50
Title Value:	$40.85	$122.55	$204.25	£20.70	£62.10	£103.50

Note: 25% of the print run of issue 15 appeared as "ash can" copies. There is no price on the cover, the ground on the cover is brown (not grey/green) and there is a contents banner at the top of the cover. While this is obviously scarcer than the regular edition, the Price Guide cannot offer a precise different value at this time though a figure of **£7.50** has been suggested in questionnaires.

FLARE
Hero; 1 Nov 1985-4 1986

(see Champions)

	$Good	$Fine	$N.Mint	£Good	£Fine	£N.Mint
1-4 ND	$0.40	$1.20	$2.00	£0.25	£0.75	£1.25
Title Value:	$1.60	$4.80	$8.00	£1.00	£3.00	£5.00

FLARE (2ND SERIES)
Hero; 1 Nov 1990-17 1993

	$Good	$Fine	$N.Mint	£Good	£Fine	£N.Mint
1-11 ND	$0.60	$1.80	$3.00	£0.40	£1.20	£2.00
12-13 ND 44pgs	$0.70	$2.10	$3.50	£0.45	£1.35	£2.25
14 ND pre-bagged with trading card	$0.70	$2.10	$3.50	£0.45	£1.35	£2.25
15-17 ND 44pgs	$0.60	$1.80	$3.00	£0.40	£1.20	£2.00
Title Value:	$10.50	$31.50	$52.50	£6.95	£20.85	£34.75

FLARE ADVENTURES
Hero; 1 Jan 1992-5 May 1992

	$Good	$Fine	$N.Mint	£Good	£Fine	£N.Mint
1-5 ND 20pgs, new and reprint material	$0.15	$0.45	$0.75	£0.10	£0.35	£0.60
Title Value:	$0.75	$2.25	$3.75	£0.50	£1.75	£3.00

FLARE ADVENTURES (2ND SERIES)
Heroic Publishing; 1 Apr 1994

	$Good	$Fine	$N.Mint	£Good	£Fine	£N.Mint
1 ND ties into Championd Adventures #2	$0.60	$1.80	$3.00	£0.40	£1.20	£2.00
Title Value:	$0.60	$1.80	$3.00	£0.40	£1.20	£2.00

FLARE ADVENTURES/CHAMPION CLASSICS
Hero,MS; 1 Jun 1992-17 1993

	$Good	$Fine	$N.Mint	£Good	£Fine	£N.Mint
1 ND flip-book format combination of the two previously individual titles begins	$0.50	$1.50	$2.50	£0.30	£0.90	£1.50
2-7 ND	$0.50	$1.50	$2.50	£0.30	£0.90	£1.50
8-12 ND $3.95 cover	$0.60	$1.80	$3.00	£0.40	£1.20	£2.00
13 ND $2.95 cover; title becomes "Champions Classics"	$0.60	$1.80	$3.00	£0.40	£1.20	£2.00
14-17 ND	$0.60	$1.80	$3.00	£0.40	£1.20	£2.00
Title Value:	$9.50	$28.50	$47.50	£6.10	£18.30	£30.50

FLARE FIRST EDITION
Innovation; 1 Jun 1991-13 1992

	$Good	$Fine	$N.Mint	£Good	£Fine	£N.Mint
1 ND 96pgs, squarebound, reprints Hero's Flare #1, Mark Beachum cover	$0.90	$2.70	$4.50	£0.60	£1.80	£3.00
2-13 ND	$0.60	$1.80	$3.00	£0.40	£1.20	£2.00
Title Value:	$8.10	$24.30	$40.50	£5.40	£16.20	£27.00
Flare First Edition Presents: Eternity Smith (Nov 1991) 3 original comics bound together with new cover, 6,000 print run				£0.50	£1.50	£2.50

FLARE VS. THE TIGRESS
Hero,MS; 1 Aug 1992-2 Sep 1992

	$Good	$Fine	$N.Mint	£Good	£Fine	£N.Mint
1-2 ND	$0.60	$1.80	$3.00	£0.40	£1.20	£2.00
Title Value:	$1.20	$3.60	$6.00	£0.80	£2.40	£4.00
Flare vs. Tigress Trade paperback (Jan 1993) reprints mini-series				£1.85	£5.55	£9.25

FLASH (1ST SERIES)
National Periodical Publications/DC Comics; 105 Feb/Mar 1959-350 Oct 1985

(numbering continues from Flash Comics [Golden Age])

(see Adventure, Brave and the Bold, DC Comics Presents, DC Special Blue Ribbon Digest, DC Super-Stars, Eighty Page Giant Magazine, Famous First Edition, Five-Star Super-Hero Spectacular, Limited Collector's Edition, One Hundred Page Super Spectacular, Secret Origins, Super-Heroes Battle Super-Gorillas, Super-Team Family, World's Finest)

	$Good	$Fine	$N.Mint	£Good	£Fine	£N.Mint
105 origin Flash retold, 1st appearance Mirror Master	$500.00	$1500.00	$6000.00	£300.00	£900.00	£3600.00
[Very scarce in high grade - Very Fine+ or better]						
106 origin and 1st appearance Gorilla Grodd and Pied Piper	$160.00	$480.00	$1600.00	£90.00	£270.00	£900.00
107 Gorilla Grodd appears	$85.00	$255.00	$850.00	£50.00	£150.00	£500.00
108 Gorilla Grodd appears	$87.50	$260.00	$700.00	£50.00	£150.00	£400.00
1st official distribution in the U.K.						
109 2nd appearance The Mirror Master	$62.50	$185.00	$500.00	£38.00	£110.00	£300.00
110 (Jan 1960) origin and 1st appearance Kid Flash (later new Flash), 1st appearance Weather Wizard	$150.00	$450.00	$1500.00	£75.00	£225.00	£750.00
111 scarce in the U.K. 2nd appearance Kid Flash; Cloud Creatures appear	$47.00	$140.00	$375.00	£25.00	£75.00	£200.00
112 very scarce in the U.K. 1st appearance Elongated Man	$57.50	$175.00	$475.00	£34.00	£100.00	£275.00
113 origin and 1st appearance Trickster	$47.00	$140.00	$375.00	£25.00	£75.00	£200.00
114 Captain Cold appears and origin re-told (see Showcase #8)	$36.00	$105.00	$285.00	£20.00	£60.00	£160.00
115-116	$27.00	$80.00	$215.00	£15.50	£47.00	£125.00
117 origin and 1st appearance Captain Boomerang	$36.00	$105.00	$290.00	£20.00	£60.00	£160.00
118 (Feb 1961)	$27.00	$80.00	$215.00	£15.50	£47.00	£125.00
119-120	$27.00	$80.00	$215.00	£15.50	£47.00	£125.00
121	$21.00	$62.50	$150.00	£10.50	£32.00	£75.00
122 origin and 1st appearance The Top	$21.00	$62.50	$150.00	£12.00	£36.00	£85.00
123 1st Earth 1/Earth 2 story, re-intro Golden Age Flash, classic story and cover; historically important to the shaping of the Silver Age DC Universe	$97.50	$290.00	$975.00	£55.00	£165.00	£550.00
124 last 10 cents issue	$20.00	$60.00	$140.00	£10.50	£32.00	£75.00
125	$17.50	$52.50	$125.00	£9.25	£28.00	£65.00
126 (Feb 1962)	$17.50	$52.50	$125.00	£9.25	£28.00	£65.00
127	$17.50	$52.50	$125.00	£9.25	£28.00	£65.00
128 origin Abra-Kadabra	$17.50	$52.50	$125.00	£9.25	£28.00	£65.00
129 Golden Age Flash on cover, Justice Society of America cameo (first since 1950s)	$38.00	$110.00	$300.00	£18.50	£55.00	£150.00
130	$17.50	$52.50	$125.00	£9.25	£28.00	£65.00
131 Green Lantern co-stars	$17.00	$50.00	$120.00	£8.50	£26.00	£60.00
132-133	$17.00	$50.00	$120.00	£8.50	£26.00	£60.00
134 (Feb 1963) Elongated Man and Flash team, versus Captain Cold	$17.00	$50.00	$120.00	£8.50	£26.00	£60.00
135 Kid Flash appears, his costume is altered	$17.00	$50.00	$120.00	£8.50	£26.00	£60.00
136 1st appearance Dexter Miles, curator of the Flash Museum	$17.00	$50.00	$120.00	£8.50	£26.00	£60.00
137 Golden Age Flash on cover, Justice Society of America cameo and decision to re-form, 1st Silver Age appearance Vandal Savage, 1st full appearance Golden Age Green Lantern	$52.50	$155.00	$425.00	£16.50	£50.00	£135.00
138 Elongated Man and Flash team, versus Pied Piper	$17.00	$50.00	$120.00	£8.50	£26.00	£60.00

Issue	$Good	$Fine	$N.Mint	£Good	£Fine	£N.Mint
139 origin and 1st appearance Professor Zoom/Reverse Flash	$20.50	$60.00	$145.00	£10.50	£32.00	£75.00
140 1st appearance Heat Wave, Captain Cold appears	$17.00	$50.00	$120.00	£8.50	£26.00	£60.00
141 "Paul Gamby" appears, based on American-born/U.K. resident radio broadcaster/author Paul Gambaccini	$13.50	$41.00	$95.00	£5.25	£16.00	£37.50
142 (Feb 1964)	$13.50	$41.00	$95.00	£5.25	£16.00	£37.50
143 co-stars Green Lantern	$13.50	$41.00	$95.00	£5.50	£17.00	£40.00
144-146	$13.50	$41.00	$95.00	£5.25	£16.00	£37.50
147 Reverse Flash appears, cover based on #123	$13.50	$41.00	$95.00	£5.25	£16.00	£37.50
148	$13.50	$41.00	$95.00	£5.25	£16.00	£37.50
149 Kid Flash co-stars	$13.50	$41.00	$95.00	£5.25	£16.00	£37.50
150 (Feb 1965)	$13.50	$41.00	$95.00	£5.25	£16.00	£37.50
151 Golden Age Flash versus The Shade	$17.00	$50.00	$120.00	£5.00	£15.00	£35.00
152-154	$9.25	$28.00	$65.00	£3.55	£10.50	£25.00
155 1st Flash's Rogues Gallery (Pied Piper, Mirror Master, Captain Cold, The Top, Heatwave, Boomerang), Gorilla Grodd appears	$9.25	$28.00	$65.00	£3.55	£10.50	£25.00
156	$9.25	$28.00	$65.00	£3.55	£10.50	£25.00
157 last Silver Age issue, indicia dated December 1965	$9.25	$28.00	$65.00	£3.55	£10.50	£25.00
158 (Feb 1966)	$9.25	$28.00	$65.00	£3.55	£10.50	£25.00
159	$9.25	$28.00	$65.00	£3.55	£10.50	£25.00
160 scarce in the U.K. 80pgs, Giant G-21, reprints #107, Golden Age Flash reprint (Note: black cover makes this scarce in high grade)	$12.00	$36.00	$85.00	£4.25	£12.50	£30.00
161-164	$7.75	$23.50	$55.00	£2.85	£8.50	£20.00
165 Barry Allen marries Iris West	$7.75	$23.50	$55.00	£2.85	£8.50	£20.00
166	$7.75	$23.50	$55.00	£2.85	£8.50	£20.00
167 (Feb 1967) "true" origin The Flash (lightning bolt no accident..?)	$7.75	$23.50	$55.00	£2.85	£8.50	£20.00
168 Green Lantern guest-stars	$7.75	$23.50	$55.00	£3.20	£9.50	£22.50
169 scarce in the U.K. 80pgs, Giant G-34, reprints #129	$11.00	$34.00	$80.00	£3.55	£10.50	£25.00
170 Golden Age Flash appears	$7.75	$23.50	$55.00	£2.85	£8.50	£20.00
171-172	$7.00	$21.00	$50.00	£2.10	£6.25	£15.00
173 Golden Age Flash/Kid Flash appear	$7.00	$21.00	$50.00	£2.10	£6.25	£15.00
174 Infantino art ends, Rogues Gallery return (see Secret Origins #41)	$7.00	$21.00	$50.00	£2.10	£6.25	£15.00
175 scarce in the U.K. 2nd Superman/Flash race, Justice League of America cameo (see Superman #199, World's Finest #198/199)	$18.50	$55.00	$130.00	£6.25	£19.00	£45.00
176 (Feb 1968)	$7.00	$21.00	$50.00	£1.75	£5.25	£12.50
177	$7.00	$21.00	$50.00	£1.75	£5.25	£12.50
178 80pgs, Giant G-46	$8.50	$26.00	$60.00	£2.85	£8.50	£20.00
179-180	$7.00	$21.00	$50.00	£1.75	£5.25	£12.50
181-184	$5.25	$16.00	$37.50	£1.40	£4.25	£10.00
185 (Feb 1969)	$5.25	$16.00	$37.50	£1.40	£4.25	£10.00
186	$5.25	$16.00	$37.50	£1.40	£4.25	£10.00
187 68pgs, Giant G-58	$7.00	$21.00	$50.00	£2.10	£6.25	£15.00
188-190	$5.25	$16.00	$37.50	£1.40	£4.25	£10.00
191-193	$5.25	$16.00	$37.50	£1.05	£3.20	£7.50
194 (Feb 1970) Neal Adams cover	$6.25	$18.50	$37.50	£1.25	£3.75	£7.50
195 Neal Adams cover	$6.25	$18.50	$37.50	£1.25	£3.75	£7.50
196 Giant G-70, reprints #108	$8.25	$25.00	$50.00	£2.05	£6.25	£12.50
197-199	$6.25	$18.50	$37.50	£1.25	£3.75	£7.50
200 scarce in the U.K.	$6.25	$18.50	$37.50	£1.30	£4.00	£8.00
201-202	$3.00	$9.00	$18.00	£0.75	£2.25	£4.50
203 (Feb 1971) Superman cameo	$3.00	$9.00	$18.00	£0.75	£2.25	£4.50
204	$3.00	$9.00	$18.00	£0.75	£2.25	£4.50
205 68pgs, Giant G-82	$5.75	$17.50	$35.00	£1.65	£5.00	£10.00
206-207	$3.00	$9.00	$18.00	£0.75	£2.25	£4.50
208-210 52pgs	$3.00	$9.00	$18.00	£0.80	£2.50	£5.00
211 52pgs, Golden Age Flash origin from issue #104, last of original run	$3.00	$9.00	$18.00	£0.80	£2.50	£5.00
212 52pgs, (Feb 1972)	$3.00	$9.00	$18.00	£0.80	£2.50	£5.00
213 52pgs, reprints #137	$3.00	$9.00	$18.00	£0.80	£2.50	£5.00
214 100pgs, DC-100pg Super Spectacular #11; origin Metal Men from Showcase #37, 1st Golden Age Flash published story	$4.15	$12.50	$25.00	£1.30	£4.00	£8.00
215 52pgs, reprints 2nd Showcase #4 story "The Man Who Broke The Time Barrier"	$4.15	$12.50	$25.00	£0.80	£2.50	£5.00
216 52pgs	$3.00	$9.00	$18.00	£0.75	£2.25	£4.50
217-218 Neal Adams art on Green Lantern/Arrow back-up	$3.30	$10.00	$20.00	£1.30	£4.00	£8.00
219 (Jan 1973) Neal Adams art on Green Lantern/Arrow back-up	$3.30	$10.00	$20.00	£1.30	£4.00	£8.00
220 Green Lantern appears	$3.00	$9.00	$18.00	£0.75	£2.25	£4.50
221 Green Lantern appears	$1.30	$4.00	$8.00	£0.50	£1.50	£3.00
222	$1.30	$4.00	$8.00	£0.50	£1.50	£3.00
223 Neal Adams inks on Green Lantern back-up, Green Lantern teams with Flash (up to #228)	$1.30	$4.00	$8.00	£0.55	£1.75	£3.50
224 scarce in the U.K.	$1.30	$4.00	$8.00	£0.55	£1.75	£3.50
225 (Feb 1974)	$1.30	$4.00	$8.00	£0.50	£1.50	£3.00
226 Neal Adams art	$2.00	$6.00	$12.00	£1.00	£3.00	£6.00
227	$1.30	$4.00	$8.00	£0.50	£1.50	£3.00
228 Cary Bates (scripter) appears	$1.30	$4.00	$8.00	£0.50	£1.50	£3.00
229 100pgs, Golden Age Flash appears	$1.65	$5.00	$10.00	£1.25	£3.75	£7.50
230 Green Lantern appears	$1.30	$4.00	$8.00	£0.50	£1.50	£3.00
231 (Feb 1975) Green Lantern appears	$1.30	$4.00	$8.00	£0.50	£1.50	£3.00
232 100pgs	$1.65	$5.00	$10.00	£1.15	£3.50	£7.00
233-234 Green Lantern appears	$1.00	$3.00	$6.00	£0.40	£1.25	£2.50
235	$1.00	$3.00	$6.00	£0.40	£1.25	£2.50
236 ND	$1.00	$3.00	$6.00	£0.50	£1.50	£3.00
237-238 Green Lantern appears	$1.00	$3.00	$6.00	£0.40	£1.25	£2.50
239 (Feb 1976)	$1.00	$3.00	$6.00	£0.40	£1.25	£2.50
240 Green Lantern appears	$1.00	$3.00	$6.00	£0.40	£1.25	£2.50
241-242 Green Lantern appears	$0.65	$2.00	$4.00	£0.30	£1.00	£2.00
243 LD in the U.K. death of The Top, Green Lantern appears	$0.65	$2.00	$4.00	£0.40	£1.25	£2.50
244 LD in the U.K.	$0.65	$2.00	$4.00	£0.35	£1.10	£2.25
245 LD in the U.K. Green Lantern appears	$0.65	$2.00	$4.00	£0.35	£1.10	£2.25
246 LD in the U.K. (Jan 1977) Green Lantern appears	$0.65	$2.00	$4.00	£0.35	£1.10	£2.25
247-249 LD in the U.K.	$0.65	$2.00	$4.00	£0.35	£1.10	£2.25
250 LD in the U.K. 1st appearance Golden Glider	$0.65	$2.00	$4.00	£0.30	£1.00	£2.00
251-256	$0.55	$1.75	$3.50	£0.25	£0.85	£1.75
257 (Jan 1978)	$0.55	$1.75	$3.50	£0.25	£0.85	£1.75
258-264	$0.55	$1.75	$3.50	£0.25	£0.85	£1.75
265 ND 44pgs	$0.55	$1.75	$3.50	£0.40	£1.25	£2.50
266 ND 44pgs, Kid Flash solo back-up	$0.55	$1.75	$3.50	£0.40	£1.25	£2.50
267 ND 44pgs, origin of the Flash costume retold	$0.55	$1.75	$3.50	£0.40	£1.25	£2.50
268 features Flash Comics #26 as part of plot	$0.55	$1.75	$3.50	£0.25	£0.75	£1.50
269 (Jan 1979)	$0.55	$1.75	$3.50	£0.25	£0.75	£1.50
270-274	$0.55	$1.75	$3.50	£0.25	£0.75	£1.50
275 Green Lantern cameo, Iris Allen dies	$0.55	$1.75	$3.50	£0.25	£0.75	£1.50
276-280	$0.55	$1.75	$3.50	£0.25	£0.75	£1.50
281 (Jan 1980)	$0.55	$1.75	$3.50	£0.25	£0.75	£1.50
282 Green Lantern X-over	$0.55	$1.75	$3.50	£0.25	£0.75	£1.50
283-288	$0.55	$1.75	$3.50	£0.25	£0.75	£1.50
289 Firestorm back-up begins (8pgs) featuring 1st DC art by George Perez	$0.75	$2.25	$4.50	£0.40	£1.25	£2.50
290 George Perez art	$0.55	$1.75	$3.50	£0.25	£0.85	£1.75
291 Flash vs. The Sabertooth (not Marvel character!); George Perez art	$0.50	$1.50	$3.00	£0.25	£0.75	£1.50
292 George Perez art	$0.50	$1.50	$3.00	£0.25	£0.75	£1.50
293 (Jan 1981) Flash and Firestorm team-up; George Perez art	$0.50	$1.50	$3.00	£0.25	£0.75	£1.50
294-295 Jim Starlin art	$0.50	$1.50	$3.00	£0.20	£0.60	£1.25
296 Jim Starlin, Infantino art, Flash vs. Elongated Man	$0.50	$1.50	$3.00	£0.20	£0.60	£1.25
297-299 Infantino, Cowan art	$0.50	$1.50	$3.00	£0.20	£0.60	£1.25
300 ND 52pgs, (no ads), 25th anniversary, Infantino art on Flash's life story	$0.80	$2.50	$5.00	£0.55	£1.75	£3.50
301-302 Infantino, Cowan art	$0.40	$1.25	$2.50	£0.15	£0.50	£1.00
303-304 Infantino art	$0.40	$1.25	$2.50	£0.15	£0.50	£1.00
305 (Jan 1982) Golden Age Flash X-over, Dr. Fate appears	$0.40	$1.25	$2.50	£0.15	£0.50	£1.00
306-308 Dr.Fate back-up by Giffen	$0.40	$1.25	$2.50	£0.20	£0.60	£1.25

Issue	$Good	$Fine	$N.Mint	£Good	£Fine	£N.Mint
309 Dr.Fate back-up by Giffen, origin The Flash retold	$0.40	$1.25	$2.50	£0.20	£0.60	£1.25
310-311 Dr.Fate back-up by Giffen	$0.40	$1.25	$2.50	£0.20	£0.60	£1.25
312 Infantino art, Giffen layouts on Dr. Fate	$0.40	$1.25	$2.50	£0.20	£0.60	£1.25
313 Dr.Fate back-up by Giffen	$0.40	$1.25	$2.50	£0.20	£0.60	£1.25
314-316	$0.40	$1.25	$2.50	£0.15	£0.50	£1.00
317 (Jan 1983)	$0.40	$1.25	$2.50	£0.15	£0.50	£1.00
318 Dave Gibbons art on Creeper back-up (his first for American comics)	$0.40	$1.25	$2.50	£0.20	£0.60	£1.25
319 Dave Gibbons art on Creeper back-up	$0.40	$1.25	$2.50	£0.15	£0.50	£1.00
320-323 Creeper back-up stories	$0.40	$1.25	$2.50	£0.15	£0.50	£1.00
324 scarce in the U.K. Reverse Flash dies	$0.40	$1.25	$2.50	£0.25	£0.85	£1.75
325 Kid Flash back-up	$0.40	$1.25	$2.50	£0.15	£0.50	£1.00
326-328	$0.40	$1.25	$2.50	£0.15	£0.50	£1.00
329 (Jan 1984)	$0.40	$1.25	$2.50	£0.15	£0.50	£1.00
330-339	$0.40	$1.25	$2.50	£0.15	£0.50	£1.00
340 Flash on Trial begins	$0.40	$1.25	$2.50	£0.20	£0.60	£1.25
341 (Jan 1985) Flash on Trial	$0.40	$1.25	$2.50	£0.20	£0.60	£1.25
342-343 Flash on Trial	$0.40	$1.25	$2.50	£0.20	£0.60	£1.25
344 Flash on Trial, origin Kid Flash retold	$0.40	$1.25	$2.50	£0.20	£0.60	£1.25
345-347 Flash on Trial	$0.40	$1.25	$2.50	£0.20	£0.60	£1.25
348-349	$0.40	$1.25	$2.50	£0.15	£0.50	£1.00
350 very LD DS	$1.00	$3.00	$6.00	£0.65	£2.00	£4.00
Title Value:	$2560.55	$7666.25	$22400.50	£1279.35	£3848.60	£11575.75

Note: #340-347 are The Flash on Trial

FEATURES

Dr.Fate in 306-312. Elongated Man solo in 206, 208, 210, 212. Firestorm in 289-292, 294-299, 301-304. Firestorm/Flash in 293. Green Lantern in 220, 221, 223-228, 230, 231, 233, 234, 237, 238, 240-243, 245, 246. Green Lantern/Green Arrow in 217-219. GA Flash in 201. Kid Flash solo in 111, 112, 114, 116, 118, 112, 127, 130, 133, 138, 144, 202, 204, 207, 209, 211, 216, 265, 266.

REPRINT FEATURES

Flash in 160, 169, 178, 187, 196, 205, 208-215, 229, 232. Flash/Green Lantern, Flash/GA Flash in 178. Green Lantern in 229, 232. GA Flash in 160, 205,14, 216, 216, 232. Johnny Quick in 160, 205, 214, 229, 232. Kid Flash in 160, 205, 214, 229, 232. Metal Men in 214. Quicksilver in 214.

FLASH (1ST SERIES) ANNUAL

National Periodical Publications; 1 Nov/Dec 1963

Issue	$Good	$Fine	$N.Mint	£Good	£Fine	£N.Mint
1 80pgs, reprints #106 (Gorilla Grodd), origins Elongated Man (#112), Kid Flash (#110) retold, Showcase #13 (Mr. Element), also 1st Golden Age Star Sapphire from Flash Comics	$43.00	$125.00	$425.00	£22.50	£67.50	£225.00
Title Value:	$43.00	$125.00	$425.00	£22.50	£67.50	£225.00

Note: this comic, in common with many 60s DC annuals, tends to suffer from a crinkled spine effect owing to the way the glue dried in the production process

FLASH (2ND SERIES)

DC Comics; 0 Oct 1994; 1 Jun 1987-present

Issue	$Good	$Fine	$N.Mint	£Good	£Fine	£N.Mint
0 (Oct 1994) Zero Hour X-over, origin retold	$0.50	$1.50	$2.50	£0.30	£0.90	£1.50
1 Wally West as new Flash (see Crisis on Infinite Earths #12)	$1.00	$3.00	$5.00	£0.40	£1.20	£2.00
2-3	$0.70	$2.10	$3.50	£0.30	£0.90	£1.50
4-7	$0.40	$1.20	$2.00	£0.25	£0.75	£1.25
8-9 Millennium X-over	$0.40	$1.20	$2.00	£0.25	£0.75	£1.25
10-11	$0.40	$1.20	$2.00	£0.25	£0.75	£1.25
12 free 16pg Bonus Book (Dr.Light)	$0.40	$1.20	$2.00	£0.25	£0.75	£1.25
13-18	$0.40	$1.20	$2.00	£0.25	£0.75	£1.25
19 free 16pg Bonus Book (Blue Trinity)	$0.40	$1.20	$2.00	£0.25	£0.75	£1.25
20	$0.40	$1.20	$2.00	£0.25	£0.75	£1.25
21 Invasion X-over	$0.40	$1.20	$2.00	£0.25	£0.75	£1.25
22 Invasion X-over, new Manhunter appears	$0.40	$1.20	$2.00	£0.25	£0.75	£1.25
23-27	$0.40	$1.20	$2.00	£0.25	£0.75	£1.25
28 Captain Cold appears	$0.40	$1.20	$2.00	£0.25	£0.75	£1.25
29 new Phantom Lady appears	$0.40	$1.20	$2.00	£0.25	£0.75	£1.25
30-32	$0.40	$1.20	$2.00	£0.25	£0.75	£1.25
33 Joker cover and story	$0.40	$1.20	$2.00	£0.25	£0.75	£1.25
34	$0.40	$1.20	$2.00	£0.25	£0.75	£1.25
35 Elongated Man, Manhunter appear	$0.40	$1.20	$2.00	£0.25	£0.75	£1.25
36-44	$0.40	$1.20	$2.00	£0.25	£0.75	£1.25
45 Gorilla Grodd appears	$0.40	$1.20	$2.00	£0.25	£0.75	£1.25
46-47 The Vixen co-stars	$0.40	$1.20	$2.00	£0.25	£0.75	£1.25
48-49	$0.40	$1.20	$2.00	£0.25	£0.75	£1.25
50 48pgs, Vandal Savage appears	$0.50	$1.50	$2.50	£0.30	£0.90	£1.50
51-52	$0.40	$1.20	$2.00	£0.25	£0.75	£1.25
53 Superman/Jimmy Olsen appear; Pied Piper declares his homosexuality (pre Northstar in Alpha Flight #106)	$0.40	$1.20	$2.00	£0.25	£0.75	£1.25
54-61	$0.40	$1.20	$2.00	£0.25	£0.75	£1.25
62 Flash - Year One: Born To Run part 1, Silver Age Flash (Barry Allen) appears, bi-weekly; 1st Mark Waid on Flash	$1.00	$3.00	$5.00	£0.40	£1.20	£2.00
63 Flash - Year One: Born To Run part 2, Silver Age Flash (Barry Allen) appears, bi-weekly	$0.40	$1.20	$2.00	£0.25	£0.75	£1.25
64 Flash - Year One: Born To Run part 3, Mirror Master appears, bi-weekly	$0.40	$1.20	$2.00	£0.25	£0.75	£1.25
65 Flash - Year One: Born To Run part 4, bi-weekly	$0.40	$1.20	$2.00	£0.25	£0.75	£1.25
66 Flash vs. Aquaman, $1.25 cover begins	$0.40	$1.20	$2.00	£0.25	£0.75	£1.25
67-68	$0.40	$1.20	$2.00	£0.25	£0.75	£1.25
69 Gorilla Warfare part 2, Flash vs. Hector Hammond, continued in Green Lantern [2nd Series] #31	$0.40	$1.20	$2.00	£0.25	£0.75	£1.25
70 Gorilla Warfare part 4 (conclusion)	$0.40	$1.20	$2.00	£0.25	£0.75	£1.25
71-72	$0.40	$1.20	$2.00	£0.25	£0.75	£1.25
73 Golden Age Flash (Jay Garrick) appears	$0.40	$1.20	$2.00	£0.25	£0.75	£1.25
74 Barry Allen (Silver Age Flash) appears	$0.40	$1.20	$2.00	£0.25	£0.75	£1.25
75 Barry Allen (Silver Age Flash) returns	$0.40	$1.20	$2.00	£0.25	£0.75	£1.25
76-78	$0.40	$1.20	$2.00	£0.25	£0.75	£1.25
79 64pgs, Barry Allen vs. Wally West, Green Lantern appears	$0.60	$1.80	$3.00	£0.30	£0.90	£1.50
80 covers begin Alan Davis and Mark Farmer	$0.40	$1.20	$2.00	£0.25	£0.75	£1.25
80 Collectors Edition, ND foil-enhanced cover	$0.45	$1.35	$2.25	£0.30	£0.90	£1.50
81 Nightwing and Starfire appear	$0.40	$1.20	$2.00	£0.25	£0.75	£1.25
82 Alan Davis and Mark Farmer cover	$0.40	$1.20	$2.00	£0.25	£0.75	£1.25
83	$0.40	$1.20	$2.00	£0.25	£0.75	£1.25
84 Barry Kitson pencils, Alan Davis and Mark Farmer cover	$0.40	$1.20	$2.00	£0.25	£0.75	£1.25
85 Alan Davis and Mark Farmer art	$0.40	$1.20	$2.00	£0.25	£0.75	£1.25
86 Argus appears; Alan Davis and Mark Farmer art	$0.40	$1.20	$2.00	£0.25	£0.75	£1.25
87-91 Alan Davis and Mark Farmer cover	$0.40	$1.20	$2.00	£0.25	£0.75	£1.25
92 1st appearance Impulse (cameo), Alan Davis and Mark Farmer cover	$2.00	$6.00	$10.00	£0.80	£2.40	£4.00
93 1st full appearance Impulse	$1.20	$3.60	$6.00	£0.60	£1.80	£3.00
94 Zero Hour X-over	$1.00	$3.00	$5.00	£0.40	£1.20	£2.00
95 Terminal Velocity part 1 (ends #100)	$0.70	$2.10	$3.50	£0.30	£0.90	£1.50
96-99	$0.50	$1.50	$2.50	£0.30	£0.90	£1.50
100 Terminal Velocity concludes; Flash has increased speed powers	$0.50	$1.50	$2.50	£0.30	£0.90	£1.50
100 Collectors Edition, ND holographic foil-enhanced cover	$0.80	$2.40	$4.00	£0.50	£1.50	£2.50
101-104	$0.40	$1.20	$2.00	£0.25	£0.75	£1.25
105 Ron Lim cover and art	$0.40	$1.20	$2.00	£0.25	£0.75	£1.25
106	$0.40	$1.20	$2.00	£0.25	£0.75	£1.25
107 Underworld Unleashed tie-in, Captain Marvel teams up with Flash	$0.40	$1.20	$2.00	£0.25	£0.75	£1.25
108	$0.40	$1.20	$2.00	£0.25	£0.75	£1.25
109 Dead Heat part 2, continued in Impulse #10	$0.40	$1.20	$2.00	£0.25	£0.75	£1.25
110 Dead Heat part 4, continued in Impulse #11	$0.40	$1.20	$2.00	£0.25	£0.75	£1.25
111 Dead Heat part 6 (conclusion), continued from Impulse #11	$0.40	$1.20	$2.00	£0.25	£0.75	£1.25
112-118	$0.40	$1.20	$2.00	£0.25	£0.75	£1.25
119 ND Final Night tie-in; Paul Ryan art begins	$0.35	$1.05	$1.75	£0.25	£0.75	£1.25
120-121 ND Pied Piper appears	$0.35	$1.05	$1.75	£0.25	£0.75	£1.25
122 ND	$0.35	$1.05	$1.75	£0.25	£0.75	£1.25
123 ND cover based on the classic Flash (1st Series) #123	$0.35	$1.05	$1.75	£0.25	£0.75	£1.25
Title Value:	$56.60	$169.80	$281.00	£33.70	£101.10	£168.50
Flash Multi-Pack (Feb 1992), ND contains issues #44 (2nd printing), #51, #52 plus illustrated header card				£0.40	£1.20	£2.00
The Flash: Terminal Velocity (Nov 1995) Trade paperback ND reprints Flash #0 and #95-100 with new cover				£1.70	£5.10	£8.50
The Flash: Terminal Velocity Collector's Set (Apr 1996) ND issues #95-99 plus holographic cover edition of #100 and phonecard				£2.00	£6.00	£10.00

	$Good	$Fine	$N.Mint	£Good	£Fine	£N.Mint
The Flash: The Return of Barry Allen (Aug 1996)						
ND collects issues #74-79				£1.70	£5.10	£8.50

FLASH (2ND SERIES) ANNUAL

DC Comics; 1 Sep 1987-present

	$Good	$Fine	$N.Mint	£Good	£Fine	£N.Mint
1 48pgs, Mike Baron story, Jackson Guice art						
	$0.40	*$1.20*	*$2.00*	£0.25	£0.75	£1.25
2 48pgs	*$0.35*	*$1.05*	*$1.75*	£0.25	£0.75	£1.25
3 48pgs, squarebound, features all three Flashes						
	$0.35	*$1.05*	*$1.75*	£0.25	£0.75	£1.25
4 64pgs, Armageddon: 2001 tie-in						
	$0.40	*$1.20*	*$2.00*	£0.25	£0.75	£1.25
5 64pgs, Eclipso: The Darkness Within tie-in, Travis Charest art						
	$0.45	*$1.35*	*$2.25*	£0.30	£0.90	£1.50
6 64pgs, Bloodlines part 4, 1st appearance Argus, continued in New Titans Annual #9						
	$0.45	*$1.35*	*$2.25*	£0.30	£0.90	£1.50
7 64pgs, Elseworlds story						
	$0.55	*$1.65*	*$2.75*	£0.35	£1.05	£1.75
8 56pgs, Year One, Flash (Wally West's) first mission vs. Hal Jordan Green Lantern						
	$0.80	*$2.40*	*$4.00*	£0.50	£1.50	£2.50
9 48pgs, Legends of the Dead Earth story						
	$0.60	*$1.80*	*$3.00*	£0.40	£1.20	£2.00
Title Value:	*$4.35*	*$13.05*	*$21.75*	£2.85	£8.55	£14.25

FLASH ARCHIVES

DC Comics; 1 Aug 1996

	$Good	$Fine	$N.Mint	£Good	£Fine	£N.Mint
1 ND collects Flash Comics #104, Showcase #4,8,13,14 and Flash #105-108						
	$10.00	*$30.00*	*$50.00*	£6.50	£19.50	£32.50
Title Value:	*$10.00*	*$30.00*	*$50.00*	£6.50	£19.50	£32.50

FLASH COMICS

National Periodical Publications; 1 Jan 1940-104 Feb 1949

	$Good	$Fine	$N.Mint	£Good	£Fine	£N.Mint
1 origin and 1st appearance Golden Age Flash (Jay Garrick), origin and 1st appearance Golden Age Hawkman, probably no more than 100 extant copies in any condition						
	$5200.00	*$15700.00*	*$52500.00*	£3500.00	£10500.00	£35000.00
	[Prices may vary widely on this comic]					
2	*$810.00*	*$2425.00*	*$6500.00*	£540.00	£1625.00	£4350.00
3	*$590.00*	*$1775.00*	*$4750.00*	£395.00	£1175.00	£3175.00
4	*$450.00*	*$1350.00*	*$3600.00*	£300.00	£900.00	£2400.00
5	*$375.00*	*$1125.00*	*$3000.00*	£250.00	£750.00	£2000.00
6 2nd Flash cover						
	$550.00	*$1650.00*	*$4400.00*	£375.00	£1125.00	£3000.00
7 2nd Golden Age Hawkman app. on cover						
	$475.00	*$1425.00*	*$3800.00*	£315.00	£950.00	£2550.00
8-10	*$275.00*	*$820.00*	*$2200.00*	£180.00	£550.00	£1475.00
11-20	*$210.00*	*$640.00*	*$1500.00*	£140.00	£425.00	£1000.00
21-23	*$175.00*	*$530.00*	*$1250.00*	£120.00	£360.00	£850.00
24 Shiera Sanders becomes Golden Age Hawkgirl (see All Star Comics #5), Flash vs. The Spidermen From Mars						
	$250.00	*$750.00*	*$1750.00*	£170.00	£510.00	£1200.00
25-27	*$125.00*	*$385.00*	*$900.00*	£85.00	£255.00	£600.00
28 Hollywood cover						
	$125.00	*$385.00*	*$900.00*	£85.00	£255.00	£600.00
29	*$140.00*	*$425.00*	*$1000.00*	£95.00	£285.00	£675.00
30	*$125.00*	*$385.00*	*$900.00*	£85.00	£255.00	£600.00
31-40	*$105.00*	*$320.00*	*$750.00*	£70.00	£210.00	£500.00
41-50	*$100.00*	*$300.00*	*$700.00*	£67.50	£200.00	£475.00
51-55	*$87.50*	*$265.00*	*$625.00*	£60.00	£180.00	£420.00
56 scarce in the U.K.						
	$87.50	*$265.00*	*$625.00*	£62.50	£190.00	£450.00
57-61	*$87.50*	*$265.00*	*$625.00*	£60.00	£180.00	£420.00
62 Joe Kubert art on Hawkman						
	$110.00	*$340.00*	*$800.00*	£75.00	£225.00	£535.00
63-65 Joe Kubert art on Hawkman						
	$87.50	*$265.00*	*$625.00*	£60.00	£180.00	£420.00
66-70	*$87.50*	*$265.00*	*$625.00*	£60.00	£180.00	£420.00
71-85	*$85.00*	*$255.00*	*$600.00*	£55.00	£170.00	£400.00
86 1st appearance Black Canary (Golden Age)						
	$225.00	*$680.00*	*$1825.00*	£150.00	£450.00	£1200.00
87-88	*$115.00*	*$350.00*	*$825.00*	£77.50	£235.00	£550.00
89 Flash vs. The Thorn						
	$115.00	*$350.00*	*$825.00*	£77.50	£235.00	£550.00
90	*$115.00*	*$350.00*	*$825.00*	£77.50	£235.00	£550.00
91 scarce in the U.K.						
	$135.00	*$405.00*	*$950.00*	£90.00	£270.00	£635.00
92 scarce in the U.K. 1st solo Black Canary story, classic cover						
	$280.00	*$840.00*	*$2250.00*	£185.00	£560.00	£1500.00
93-99 scarce in the U.K.						
	$135.00	*$405.00*	*$950.00*	£90.00	£270.00	£635.00
100 very scarce in the U.K., scarce in the U.S.						
	$325.00	*$980.00*	*$2300.00*	£215.00	£650.00	£1535.00
101 very scarce in the U.K., scarce in the U.S. Flash time travel story						
	$270.00	*$810.00*	*$1900.00*	£180.00	£540.00	£1275.00
102 very scarce in the U.K., scarce in the U.S.						
	$270.00	*$810.00*	*$1900.00*	£180.00	£540.00	£1275.00
103 rare in the U.K, scarce in the U.S.						
	$250.00	*$750.00*	*$1750.00*	£175.00	£520.00	£1225.00
104 rare in the U.K, scarce in the U.S.						
	$810.00	*$2425.00*	*$6500.00*	£540.00	£1625.00	£4350.00
Title Value:	*$21982.50*	*$66335.00*	*$176650.00*	£14737.50	£44365.00	£118260.00

Note: in common with all Golden Age comics, these were not distributed on the news-stands in the U.K. but some may have come over during the war or in the late 1940s as ballast on ships. All issues are generally scarce in the U.K.

FLASH DIGEST, THE

DC Comics,Digest;24 Feb 1981

(DC Special Series 24)

	$Good	$Fine	$N.Mint	£Good	£Fine	£N.Mint
24 ND 68pgs, Flash, Golden Age Flash reprints						
	$0.70	*$2.10*	*$3.50*	£0.50	£1.50	£2.50
Title Value:	*$0.70*	*$2.10*	*$3.50*	£0.50	£1.50	£2.50

FLASH GORDON (1ST SERIES)

Gold Key; 1 Jun 1965

	$Good	$Fine	$N.Mint	£Good	£Fine	£N.Mint
1 rare although distributed in the U.K. all reprint						
	$4.25	*$12.50*	*$30.00*	£2.85	£8.50	£20.00
Title Value:	*$4.25*	*$12.50*	*$30.00*	£2.85	£8.50	£20.00

FLASH GORDON (2ND LIMITED SERIES)

Marvel Comics Group,MS; 1 Jun 1995-2 Jul 1995

	$Good	$Fine	$N.Mint	£Good	£Fine	£N.Mint
1-2 ND Mark Schultz script, Al Williamson art						
	$0.60	*$1.80*	*$3.00*	£0.40	£1.20	£2.00
Title Value:	*$1.20*	*$3.60*	*$6.00*	£0.80	£2.40	£4.00

FLASH GORDON (2ND SERIES)

King Comics; 1 Sep 1966-11 Dec 1967;Charlton; 12 Feb 1969-18 Jan 1970;Gold Key; 19 Nov 1978-27 Jul 1980;Whitman;28 Aug 1980-37 Mar 1982

	$Good	$Fine	$N.Mint	£Good	£Fine	£N.Mint
1 scarce, distributed in the U.K. Williamson art; painted covers begin						
	$5.00	*$15.00*	*$35.00*	£2.85	£8.50	£20.00
2 scarce, distributed in the U.K.						
	$2.85	*$8.50*	*$20.00*	£1.40	£4.25	£10.00
3-5 scarce, distributed in the U.K. Williamson art						
	$2.85	*$8.50*	*$20.00*	£1.40	£4.25	£10.00
6 scarce, distributed in the U.K. Crandall art						
	$2.50	*$7.50*	*$17.50*	£1.40	£4.25	£10.00
7-10 distributed in the U.K.						
	$2.50	*$7.50*	*$17.50*	£1.10	£3.40	£8.00
11 distributed in the U.K.						
	$2.10	*$6.25*	*$15.00*	£1.00	£3.00	£7.00
12 rare in the U.K. Crandall art						

Flash (1st) #135

Flash (1st) #237

Flash Comics #9

Issue	$Good	$Fine	$N.Mint	£Good	£Fine	£N.Mint
	$2.55	$7.50	$18.00	£1.10	£3.40	£8.00
13 rare in the U.K. Jones art	$2.85	$8.50	$20.00	£1.10	£3.40	£8.00
14-17 rare in the U.K.	$1.25	$3.85	$9.00	£0.70	£2.10	£5.00
18 rare in the U.K. Kaluta art	$1.70	$5.00	$12.00	£0.85	£2.55	£6.00
19-25	$0.80	$2.50	$5.00	£0.40	£1.25	£2.50
26-30	$1.00	$3.00	$5.00	£0.40	£1.20	£2.00
31-33 adapts Queen-soundtrack film, Al Williamson art; photo montage cover	$0.50	$1.50	$2.50	£0.50	£1.50	£2.50
34	$0.50	$1.50	$2.50	£0.40	£1.20	£2.00
35-37 line drawn cover	$0.50	$1.50	$2.50	£0.40	£1.20	£2.00
Title Value:	$57.20	$172.15	$381.00	£29.00	£88.15	£194.00

FLASH GORDON (LIMITED SERIES)

DC Comics,MS; 1 Jun 1988-9 Feb 1989

Issue	$Good	$Fine	$N.Mint	£Good	£Fine	£N.Mint
1-9	$0.25	$0.75	$1.25	£0.15	£0.45	£0.75
Title Value:	$2.25	$6.75	$11.25	£1.35	£4.05	£6.75

Note: New Format

FLASH PLUS #1

DC Comics,OS; 1 Jan 1997

Issue	$Good	$Fine	$N.Mint	£Good	£Fine	£N.Mint
1 ND Flash and Nightwing team up	$0.60	$1.80	$3.00	£0.40	£1.20	£2.00
Title Value:	$0.60	$1.80	$3.00	£0.40	£1.20	£2.00

FLASH SPECIAL

DC Comics,OS; 1 Jul 1990

Issue	$Good	$Fine	$N.Mint	£Good	£Fine	£N.Mint
1 80pgs, features all three Flashes, cover by Kubert; story by Mark Waid	$1.00	$3.00	$5.00	£0.60	£1.80	£3.00
Title Value:	$1.00	$3.00	$5.00	£0.60	£1.80	£3.00

Note: celebrates Flash's 50th anniversary

FLASH SPECTACULAR

DC Comics; 11 1978

(DC Special Series 11)

Issue	$Good	$Fine	$N.Mint	£Good	£Fine	£N.Mint
11 ND 80pgs, Flash, Golden Age Flash, Johnny Quick, Kid Flash reprints	$0.90	$2.70	$4.50	£0.60	£1.80	£3.00
Title Value:	$0.90	$2.70	$4.50	£0.60	£1.80	£3.00

FLASH TV SPECIAL

DC Comics,OS; 1 Jul 1991

Issue	$Good	$Fine	$N.Mint	£Good	£Fine	£N.Mint
1 ND 80pgs, based on pilot film of CBS TV series plus pin-up pages	$0.80	$2.40	$4.00	£0.40	£1.20	£2.00
Title Value:	$0.80	$2.40	$4.00	£0.40	£1.20	£2.00

FLASH/GREEN LANTERN: FASTER FRIENDS

DC Comics,MS; 1,2 Feb 1997

Issue	$Good	$Fine	$N.Mint	£Good	£Fine	£N.Mint
1-2 ND 48pgs, Mark Waid script, Val Semeiks and Chip Wallace art; bi-weekly	$1.00	$3.00	$5.00	£0.70	£2.10	£3.50
Title Value:	$2.00	$6.00	$10.00	£1.40	£4.20	£7.00

FLAXEN

Golden Apple Comics/Dark Horse,OS; 1 Sep 1992

Issue	$Good	$Fine	$N.Mint	£Good	£Fine	£N.Mint
1 ND based on life story of Playboy model Suzie Owens, cover painting by Steve Rude	$0.50	$1.50	$2.50	£0.30	£0.90	£1.50
Title Value:	$0.50	$1.50	$2.50	£0.30	£0.90	£1.50

FLAXEN: ALTER EGO

Caliber Press; 1 Mar 1995

Issue	$Good	$Fine	$N.Mint	£Good	£Fine	£N.Mint
1 ND David Mack art and back cover by Adam Hughes	$0.60	$1.80	$3.00	£0.40	£1.20	£2.00
Title Value:	$0.60	$1.80	$3.00	£0.40	£1.20	£2.00

FLEENER

Bongo Comics,OS; 1 May 1996

Issue	$Good	$Fine	$N.Mint	£Good	£Fine	£N.Mint
1 ND Mary Fleener script and art; black and white	$0.60	$1.80	$3.00	£0.40	£1.20	£2.00
Title Value:	$0.60	$1.80	$3.00	£0.40	£1.20	£2.00

FLESH AND BLOOD

Brainstorm Comics; 1 Dec 1995

Issue	$Good	$Fine	$N.Mint	£Good	£Fine	£N.Mint
1 ND adult material; Franco Aureliani script and art	$0.60	$1.80	$3.00	£0.40	£1.20	£2.00
Title Value:	$0.60	$1.80	$3.00	£0.40	£1.20	£2.00

FLESH AND BONES

(see Dalgoda)

FLEX MENTALLO

DC Comics/Vertigo,MS; 1 Jun 1996-4 Sep 1996

Issue	$Good	$Fine	$N.Mint	£Good	£Fine	£N.Mint
1 ND Grant Morrison script, Frank Quitely art	$0.50	$1.50	$2.50	£0.40	£1.20	£2.00
2-4 ND Grant Morrison script, Frank Quitely art	$0.50	$1.50	$2.50	£0.30	£0.90	£1.50
Title Value:	$2.00	$6.00	$10.00	£1.30	£3.90	£6.50

FLINT ARMBUSTER JNR. SPECIAL

Alchemy Studios,OS; 1 1990

Issue	$Good	$Fine	$N.Mint	£Good	£Fine	£N.Mint
1 ND Scot Eaton script/art	$0.50	$1.50	$2.50	£0.30	£0.90	£1.50
Title Value:	$0.50	$1.50	$2.50	£0.30	£0.90	£1.50

FLINTSTONE KIDS, THE

Marvel Comics Group/Star, TV; 1 Aug 1987-12 Apr 1989

Issue	$Good	$Fine	$N.Mint	£Good	£Fine	£N.Mint
1-12	$0.15	$0.45	$0.75	£0.10	£0.30	£0.50
Title Value:	$1.80	$5.40	$9.00	£1.20	£3.60	£6.00

FLINTSTONES AND PEBBLES, THE

Charlton; 1 Nov 1970-50 Feb 1977

Issue	$Good	$Fine	$N.Mint	£Good	£Fine	£N.Mint
1	$6.50	$20.00	$40.00	£3.30	£10.00	£20.00
2	$3.75	$11.00	$22.50	£2.05	£6.25	£12.50
3-10	$2.50	$7.50	$15.00	£1.25	£3.75	£7.50
11-20	$2.05	$6.25	$12.50	£1.00	£3.00	£6.00
21-36	$1.65	$5.00	$10.00	£0.80	£2.50	£5.00
37 John Byrne's 1st professional work (4 text illustrations) (May 1975)	$1.65	$5.00	$10.00	£1.25	£3.75	£7.50
38-41	$1.65	$5.00	$10.00	£0.80	£2.50	£5.00
42 John Byrne art (2pgs)	$1.65	$5.00	$10.00	£1.00	£3.00	£6.00
43-50	$1.65	$5.00	$10.00	£0.80	£2.50	£5.00
Title Value:	$100.25	$303.50	$607.50	£50.00	£153.00	£306.00

Note: most issues distributed in the U.K.

FLINTSTONES IN 3-D, THE

Blackthorne;(3-D Series #19,#22,#36,#42); 1 Apr 1987-4 Feb 1988

Issue	$Good	$Fine	$N.Mint	£Good	£Fine	£N.Mint
1 ND all with bound-in 3-D glasses (25% less if without glasses)	$0.50	$1.50	$2.50	£0.30	£0.90	£1.50
2 ND	$0.50	$1.50	$2.50	£0.30	£0.90	£1.50
3 ND scarce in the U.K.	$0.50	$1.50	$2.50	£0.40	£1.20	£2.00
4 ND	$0.50	$1.50	$2.50	£0.30	£0.90	£1.50
Title Value:	$2.00	$6.00	$10.00	£1.30	£3.90	£6.50

FLINTSTONES, THE

Dell/Gold Key;2 Nov/Dec 1961-60 Sep 1970

Issue	$Good	$Fine	$N.Mint	£Good	£Fine	£N.Mint
2 2nd comic book appearance (see Dell Giant. TV show came out about a year before)	$12.50	$39.00	$90.00	£7.00	£21.00	£50.00
3-6	$9.25	$28.00	$65.00	£5.00	£15.00	£35.00
7 1st Gold Key issue	$9.25	$28.00	$65.00	£5.00	£15.00	£35.00
8-10	$6.25	$19.00	$45.00	£3.40	£10.00	£24.00
11 1st appearance Pebbles	$10.00	$30.00	$70.00	£5.25	£16.00	£37.50
12-15	$5.25	$16.00	$37.50	£2.85	£8.50	£20.00
16 1st appearance Bamm-Bamm	$7.75	$23.50	$55.00	£3.55	£10.50	£25.00
17-20	$5.25	$16.00	$37.50	£2.85	£8.50	£20.00
21-30	$4.25	$12.50	$30.00	£2.10	£6.25	£15.00
31-33	$3.90	$11.50	$27.50	£1.75	£5.25	£12.50
34 1st appearance The Great Gazoo	$5.50	$17.00	$40.00	£2.50	£7.50	£17.50
35-40	$3.90	$11.50	$27.50	£1.75	£5.25	£12.50
41-60	$3.55	$10.50	$25.00	£1.40	£4.25	£10.00
Title Value:	$291.35	$873.00	$2062.50	£141.05	£422.75	£999.50

Note: all distributed on the news-stands in the U.K.

Note also: issue #1 is Dell Giant #48 - see Overtstreet Guide

FLINTSTONES, THE

Marvel Comics Group, TV; 1 Oct 1977-9 Feb 1979

Issue	$Good	$Fine	$N.Mint	£Good	£Fine	£N.Mint
1-9 ND	$0.10	$0.35	$0.75	£0.10	£0.30	£0.60
Title Value:	$0.90	$3.15	$6.75	£0.90	£2.70	£5.40

Note: see also Yogi Bear.

FLIPPER

Gold Key, TV; 1 Apr 1966-3 Nov 1967

Issue	$Good	$Fine	$N.Mint	£Good	£Fine	£N.Mint
1 distributed in the U.K.	$7.00	$21.00	$50.00	£3.90	£11.50	£27.50
2-3 distributed in the U.K.	$5.00	$15.00	$35.00	£2.85	£8.50	£20.00
Title Value:	$17.00	$51.00	$120.00	£9.60	£28.50	£67.50

FLIPPITY AND FLOP

National Periodical Publications; 1 Dec 1951/Jan 1952-46 Aug/Oct 1959;47 Sep 1960

Issue	$Good	$Fine	$N.Mint	£Good	£Fine	£N.Mint
1 very scarce in the U.K.	$26.00	$75.00	$180.00	£17.00	£50.00	£120.00
2 scarce in the U.K.	$15.50	$47.00	$110.00	£10.50	£32.00	£75.00
3-5 scarce in the U.K.	$12.00	$36.00	$85.00	£7.75	£23.50	£55.00
6-10	$10.00	$30.00	$70.00	£6.25	£19.00	£45.00
11-20	$8.50	$26.00	$60.00	£5.50	£17.00	£40.00
21-46	$7.00	$21.00	$50.00	£4.25	£12.50	£30.00
1st official distribution in the U.K.						
47	$6.25	$19.00	$45.00	£3.55	£10.50	£25.00
Title Value:	$400.75	$1205.00	$2840.00	£251.05	£753.00	£1790.00

FLOATERS

Dark Horse,MS; 1 Sep 1993-5 Jan 1994

Issue	$Good	$Fine	$N.Mint	£Good	£Fine	£N.Mint
1-5 ND script by Cinque Lee (Spike's brother)	$0.50	$1.50	$2.50	£0.30	£0.90	£1.50
Title Value:	$2.50	$7.50	$12.50	£1.50	£4.50	£7.50

FLOOD RELIEF

Malibu/American Red Cross,OS; 1 Jan 1994

Issue	$Good	$Fine	$N.Mint	£Good	£Fine	£N.Mint
1 ND special charity comic produced for American Flood Relief agencies; features Ultraverse characters and available only through the mail; no price on cover, 15,000 copies	$0.90	$2.70	$4.50	£0.50	£1.50	£2.50
Title Value:	$0.90	$2.70	$4.50	£0.50	£1.50	£2.50

FLOYD FARLAND, CITIZEN OF THE FUTURE

(see Eclipse Graphic Album series #11)

FLY

DC Comics/Impact; 1 Aug 1991-17 Dec 1992

Issue	$Good	$Fine	$N.Mint	£Good	£Fine	£N.Mint
1-7	$0.15	$0.45	$0.75	£0.10	£0.35	£0.60
8 X-over with The Comet #10	$0.15	$0.45	$0.75	£0.10	£0.35	£0.60
9-17	$0.15	$0.45	$0.75	£0.10	£0.35	£0.60
Title Value:	$2.55	$7.65	$12.75	£1.70	£5.95	£10.20

Note: Archie Comics character acquired by DC. Events fall outside DC Universe continuity

FLY ANNUAL

DC Comics/Impact; 1 Jun 1992

Issue	$Good	$Fine	$N.Mint	£Good	£Fine	£N.Mint
1 64pgs, Earthquest part 5, ties into Crusaders #1 (see other Impact annuals), trading cards included	$0.30	$0.90	$1.50	£0.20	£0.60	£1.00
Title Value:	$0.30	$0.90	$1.50	£0.20	£0.60	£1.00

FLY IN MY EYE

(see Arcane Comix)

FLY MAN

Archie;32 July 1965-39 Sep 1966
(previously Fly; becomes Mighty Comics Presents)

Issue	$Good	$Fine	$N.Mint	£Good	£Fine	£N.Mint
32-33 distributed in the U.K.	$4.60	$13.50	$32.50	£2.50	£7.50	£17.50
34-39 distributed in the U.K.	$3.55	$10.50	$25.00	£1.75	£5.25	£12.50
Title Value:	$30.50	$90.00	$207.50	£15.50	£46.50	£110.00

FLY, ADVENTURES OF THE

Archie; 1 Aug 1959-30 Oct 1964; 31 May 1965
(becomes Fly Man)

Issue	$Good	$Fine	$N.Mint	£Good	£Fine	£N.Mint
1 scarce in the U.K. origin The Fly, Joe Simon and Jack Kirby art	$65.00	$195.00	$525.00	£44.00	£130.00	£350.00
2 rare in the U.K. Jack Kirby and Al Williamson art	$40.00	$120.00	$280.00	£27.00	£80.00	£190.00
3 rare in the U.K. origin retold	$32.00	$95.00	$225.00	£21.00	£62.50	£150.00
4 scarce in the U.K. Neal Adams art (1 panel), 2nd ever published art? (see Archie's Joke Book Magazine #41)	$17.00	$50.00	$120.00	£11.00	£34.00	£80.00
5-10 rare in the U.K.	$12.00	$36.00	$85.00	£8.00	£24.50	£57.50
11-13	$8.50	$26.00	$60.00	£5.50	£17.00	£40.00
14 1st appearance Flygirl	$10.50	$32.00	$75.00	£6.25	£19.00	£45.00
15-20	$7.75	$23.50	$55.00	£5.00	£15.00	£35.00
21-31	$5.25	$16.00	$37.50	£3.20	£9.50	£22.50
Title Value:	$366.25	$1103.00	$2660.00	£238.95	£718.00	£1737.50

Note: all distributed on the news-stands in the U.K.

FLY, THE

Archie (Red Circle); 1 May 1983-9 Oct 1984

Issue	$Good	$Fine	$N.Mint	£Good	£Fine	£N.Mint
1 ND origin Shield, Mr. Justice appears	$0.30	$0.90	$1.50	£0.20	£0.60	£1.00
2 ND Flygirl appears, Steranko cover	$0.30	$0.90	$1.50	£0.20	£0.60	£1.00
3-4 ND Steve Ditko art	$0.30	$0.90	$1.50	£0.20	£0.60	£1.00
5-7 ND	$0.30	$0.90	$1.50	£0.20	£0.60	£1.00
8 ND Steve Ditko cover and art	$0.30	$0.90	$1.50	£0.20	£0.60	£1.00
9 ND	$0.30	$0.90	$1.50	£0.20	£0.60	£1.00
Title Value:	$2.70	$8.10	$13.50	£1.80	£5.40	£9.00

FOODANG

Continuum Comics; 1 Jul 1994

Issue	$Good	$Fine	$N.Mint	£Good	£Fine	£N.Mint
1 ND 40pgs, Michael Duggan script and art; black and white	$0.35	$1.05	$1.75	£0.25	£0.75	£1.25
Title Value:	$0.35	$1.05	$1.75	£0.25	£0.75	£1.25

FOODANG (2ND SERIES)

August House; 1 Jan 1995-4 1995

Issue	$Good	$Fine	$N.Mint	£Good	£Fine	£N.Mint
1 ND 40pgs, Michael Duggan script and art with bound-in The Dark character card by Bart Sears	$0.35	$1.05	$1.75	£0.25	£0.75	£1.25
1 Special Edition, ND (Jun 1995) - foil cover; 1,000 copies with certificate	$0.40	$1.20	$2.00	£0.25	£0.75	£1.25
2 ND foil-enhanced cover by Ben Edlund	$0.35	$1.05	$1.75	£0.25	£0.75	£1.25
3 ND foil-enhanced cover by Michael Duggan and Mike Sagara	$0.35	$1.05	$1.75	£0.25	£0.75	£1.25
4 ND	$0.35	$1.05	$1.75	£0.25	£0.75	£1.25
Title Value:	$1.80	$5.40	$9.00	£1.25	£3.75	£6.25

Note: originally solicited by Continuum Comics six months earlier. The contents were exactly the same but published now in full colour

FOODANG (3RD SERIES)

Entity Comics; 1 May 1996

Issue	$Good	$Fine	$N.Mint	£Good	£Fine	£N.Mint
1 ND 40pgs, reprints original series	$0.60	$1.80	$3.00	£0.40	£1.20	£2.00
1 Balloon Edition, ND 40pgs, pre-bagged with Foodang balloon	£0.50	£1.50	£2.50	$0.70	$2.10	$3.50
Title Value:	$1.30	$3.90	$6.50	£0.90	£2.70	£4.50

FOOLKILLER

Marvel Comics Group,MS; 1 Oct 1990-10 Jul 1991
(see Omega the Unknown)

Issue	$Good	$Fine	$N.Mint	£Good	£Fine	£N.Mint
1-7 ND	$0.30	$0.90	$1.50	£0.20	£0.60	£1.00
8 ND Spiderman appears	$0.30	$0.90	$1.50	£0.20	£0.60	£1.00
9-10 ND	$0.30	$0.90	$1.50	£0.20	£0.60	£1.00
Title Value:	$3.00	$9.00	$15.00	£2.00	£6.00	£10.00

Note: Mature Readers

FOOM

Marvel Comics Group; 1 Feb 1973-22 Autumn 1978
(see Amazing World of DC Comics)

Issue	$Good	$Fine	$N.Mint	£Good	£Fine	£N.Mint
1 ND scarce in the U.K. 30pgs, Fantastic Four index/article; puzzles, games, advance information on Marvel comics begin	$7.50	$22.50	$45.00	£5.00	£15.00	£30.00
1 with original packaging, ND very scarce in the U.K. containing free gifts; Steranko poster, 6 Marvel mini-labels, FOOM members card	$20.00	$60.00	$100.00	£15.00	£45.00	£75.00
2 ND Hulk index/article, Steranko cover	$5.00	$15.00	$30.00	£3.30	£10.00	£20.00
3 ND Spiderman index/article	$3.30	$10.00	$20.00	£2.05	£6.25	£12.50
4 ND	$2.00	$6.00	$12.00	£1.30	£4.00	£8.00
5 ND The Thing featured in article	$1.50	$4.50	$9.00	£1.00	£3.00	£6.00
6 ND	$1.25	$3.75	$7.50	£0.80	£2.50	£5.00
7 ND The Avengers	$1.25	$3.75	$7.50	£0.80	£2.50	£5.00
8 ND Captain America	$1.25	$3.75	$7.50	£0.80	£2.50	£5.00
9 ND Silver Surfer issue	$1.50	$4.50	$9.00	£1.00	£3.00	£6.00
10 ND X-Men issue	$1.50	$4.50	$9.00	£1.00	£3.00	£6.00
11 ND features a returning-to-Marvel Jack Kirby, John Byrne cover and centrefold (wrongly credited as Jack Byrne!)	$1.25	$3.75	$7.50	£0.80	£2.50	£5.00
12 ND The Avengers	$1.25	$3.75	$7.50	£0.80	£2.50	£5.00
13 ND Daredevil	$1.25	$3.75	$7.50	£0.80	£2.50	£5.00
14 ND Conan	$1.25	$3.75	$7.50	£0.80	£2.50	£5.00
15 ND Howard the Duck	$1.25	$3.75	$7.50	£0.80	£2.50	£5.00
16 ND	$1.25	$3.75	$7.50	£0.80	£2.50	£5.00
17 ND Stan Lee interview/profile	$1.25	$3.75	$7.50	£0.80	£2.50	£5.00
18 ND John Romita interview/profile	$1.25	$3.75	$7.50	£0.80	£2.50	£5.00
19 ND Defenders	$1.25	$3.75	$7.50	£0.80	£2.50	£5.00
20 ND Edgar Rice Burroughs/John Carter of Mars/Tarzan	$1.25	$3.75	$7.50	£0.80	£2.50	£5.00
21 ND Sci-Fi/Star Wars issue	$1.25	$3.75	$7.50	£0.80	£2.50	£5.00
22 ND Marvel Heroes on TV	$1.25	$3.75	$7.50	£0.80	£2.50	£5.00
Title Value:	$61.05	$183.25	$346.50	£41.65	£126.75	£238.50

Note: Marvel fanzine; title acronym for Friends Of Old Marvel

FOOT SOLDIERS, THE

Dark Horse,MS; 1 Jan 1996-4 Apr 1994

Issue	$Good	$Fine	$N.Mint	£Good	£Fine	£N.Mint
1 ND Alex Ross painted cover	$0.60	$1.80	$3.00	£0.40	£1.20	£2.00
2 ND Walt Simonson cover	$0.60	$1.80	$3.00	£0.40	£1.20	£2.00
3-4 ND	$0.60	$1.80	$3.00	£0.40	£1.20	£2.00
Title Value:	$2.40	$7.20	$12.00	£1.60	£4.80	£8.00

FOOZLE

(see Cap'n Quick)

FOR LOVERS ONLY

Charlton;60 Aug 1971-87 Nov 1976

Issue	$Good	$Fine	$N.Mint	£Good	£Fine	£N.Mint
60-87	$0.20	$0.60	$1.25	£0.10	£0.35	£0.75
Title Value:	$5.60	$16.80	$35.00	£2.80	£9.80	£21.00

Note: sporadic distribution in the U.K.

FOR YOUR EYES ONLY

Marvel Comics Group, Film; 1,2 1981

Issue	$Good	$Fine	$N.Mint	£Good	£Fine	£N.Mint
1-2 Chaykin art, adapts James Bond film	$0.30	$0.90	$1.50	£0.20	£0.60	£1.00
Title Value:	$0.60	$1.80	$3.00	£0.40	£1.20	£2.00

FORBIDDEN KINGDOM

Eastern; 1 1988-11 1989

Issue	$Good	$Fine	$N.Mint	£Good	£Fine	£N.Mint
1-11 ND	$0.40	$1.20	$2.00	£0.25	£0.75	£1.25
Title Value:	$4.40	$13.20	$22.00	£2.75	£8.25	£13.75

FORBIDDEN PLANET

Innovation,MS; 1 May 1992-4 Oct 1992

Issue	$Good	$Fine	$N.Mint	£Good	£Fine	£N.Mint
1-4 ND adaptation of film	$0.50	$1.50	$2.50	£0.30	£0.90	£1.50
Title Value:	$2.00	$6.00	$10.00	£1.20	£3.60	£6.00

Forbidden Planet: The Saga of the Krell (May 1993)

Issue	$Good	$Fine	$N.Mint	£Good	£Fine	£N.Mint
collects mini-series plus information on film; intro by Leslie Nielsen				£1.20	£3.60	£6.00

FORBIDDEN TALES OF DARK MANSION

DC Comics;5 May/Jun 1972-15 Feb/Mar 1974
(previously Dark Mansion of Forbidden Love)

Issue	$Good	$Fine	$N.Mint	£Good	£Fine	£N.Mint
5 ND 52pgs	$1.00	$3.00	$6.00	£0.40	£1.25	£2.50
6 ND Jack Kirby art	$1.00	$3.00	$6.00	£0.50	£1.50	£3.00
7-15 ND	$0.80	$2.50	$5.00	£0.40	£1.25	£2.50
Title Value:	$9.20	$28.50	$57.00	£4.50	£14.00	£28.00

ARTISTS

Nino in 8, 12, 15. Wood inks in 13.

FORBIDDEN WORLDS (1ST SERIES)

ACG; 1 Jul/Aug 1951-145 Aug 1967

Issue	$Good	$Fine	$N.Mint	£Good	£Fine	£N.Mint
1 scarce in the U.K. 52pgs, Frank Frazetta art featured	$110.00	$330.00	$1000.00	£75.00	£225.00	£675.00
2 scarce in the U.K. 52pgs	$65.00	$195.00	$525.00	£44.00	£130.00	£350.00
3 scarce in the U.K. 52pgs, Al Williamson and Fank Frazetta art	$67.50	$205.00	$550.00	£46.00	£135.00	£370.00
4 scarce in the U.K. 52pgs	$34.00	$100.00	$240.00	£22.50	£67.50	£160.00
5 scarce in the U.K. 52pgs, Williamson/Krenkel art	$55.00	$170.00	$400.00	£39.00	£115.00	£270.00
6 Harrison/Williamson art	$49.00	$145.00	$340.00	£33.00	£97.50	£227.50
7-8	$26.00	$75.00	$180.00	£17.00	£50.00	£120.00
9	$29.00	$85.00	$200.00	£19.00	£57.50	£135.00
10	$25.00	$75.00	$175.00	£16.50	£50.00	£117.50

Issue	$Good	$Fine	$N.Mint	£Good	£Fine	£N.Mint
11-20	$17.50	$52.50	$125.00	£12.00	£36.00	£85.00
21-30	$12.50	$39.00	$90.00	£8.50	£26.00	£60.00
31-34	$11.00	$34.00	$80.00	£7.75	£23.50	£55.00
35 very scarce in the U.K., scarce in the U.S.	$12.50	$39.00	$90.00	£8.50	£26.00	£60.00
36-40	$9.25	$28.00	$65.00	£5.50	£17.00	£40.00
41-70	$7.75	$23.50	$55.00	£5.00	£15.00	£35.00
71-72	$5.50	$17.00	$40.00	£3.55	£10.50	£25.00
73 1st appearance of Herbie by Ogden Whitney	$36.00	$105.00	$250.00	£25.00	£75.00	£175.00
74-83	$5.50	$17.00	$40.00	£3.55	£10.50	£25.00
1st official distribution in the U.K.						
84-90	$5.00	$15.00	$35.00	£3.20	£9.50	£22.50
91-93	$3.90	$11.50	$27.50	£2.10	£6.25	£15.00
94 Herbie appears	$8.50	$26.00	$60.00	£3.55	£10.50	£25.00
95-100	$3.90	$11.50	$27.50	£2.10	£6.25	£15.00
101-109	$3.20	$9.50	$22.50	£1.75	£5.25	£12.50
110 Herbie appears	$5.25	$16.00	$37.50	£2.10	£6.25	£15.00
111-113	$3.20	$9.50	$22.50	£1.75	£5.25	£12.50
114 Herbie appears	$5.00	$15.00	$35.00	£2.10	£6.25	£15.00
115	$3.20	$9.50	$22.50	£1.75	£5.25	£12.50
116 Herbie appears	$5.00	$15.00	$35.00	£2.10	£6.25	£15.00
117-120	$3.20	$9.50	$22.50	£1.75	£5.25	£12.50
121-124	$2.85	$8.50	$20.00	£1.40	£4.25	£10.00
125 1st appearance Magicman	$3.90	$11.50	$27.50	£1.75	£5.25	£12.50
126-130	$2.85	$8.50	$20.00	£1.40	£4.25	£10.00
131-136	$2.85	$8.50	$20.00	£1.25	£3.85	£9.00
137-138 Steve Ditko art	$2.85	$8.50	$20.00	£1.25	£3.85	£9.00
139	$2.85	$8.50	$20.00	£1.25	£3.85	£9.00
140 Steve Ditko art	$2.85	$8.50	$20.00	£1.25	£3.85	£9.00
141-145	$2.10	$6.25	$15.00	£1.05	£3.20	£7.50
Title Value:	$1440.55	$4345.25	$10480.00	£931.60	£2792.75	£6805.00

Note: all distributed on the news-stands in the U.K.

FORBIDDEN WORLDS (2ND SERIES)

A Plus Comics; 1 Jul 1991-3 1991

Issue	$Good	$Fine	$N.Mint	£Good	£Fine	£N.Mint
1 ND 48pgs, two new stories plus Steve Ditko reprint	$0.50	$1.50	$2.50	£0.30	£0.90	£1.50
2 ND 48pgs, reprints 1st Herbie story	$0.50	$1.50	$2.50	£0.30	£0.90	£1.50
3 ND 48pgs, Williamson, Steve Ditko reprints featured	$0.50	$1.50	$2.50	£0.30	£0.90	£1.50
Title Value:	$1.50	$4.50	$7.50	£0.90	£2.70	£4.50

FORCE OF BUDDHA'S PALM

Jademan; 1 Aug 1988-56 Mar 1993

Issue	$Good	$Fine	$N.Mint	£Good	£Fine	£N.Mint
1 ND	$0.50	$1.50	$2.50	£0.50	£1.50	£2.50
2-5 ND	$0.30	$0.90	$1.50	£0.40	£1.20	£2.00
6-10 ND	$0.30	$0.90	$1.50	£0.30	£0.90	£1.50
11-20 ND	$0.30	$0.90	$1.50	£0.25	£0.75	£1.25
21-30 ND	$0.30	$0.90	$1.50	£0.20	£0.60	£1.00
31-56 ND	$0.25	$0.75	$1.25	£0.15	£0.45	£0.75
Title Value:	$15.70	$47.10	$78.50	£12.00	£36.00	£60.00

FORCE WORKS

Marvel Comics Group; 1 Jul 1993-22 Apr 1996

Issue	$Good	$Fine	$N.Mint	£Good	£Fine	£N.Mint
1 48pgs, Abnett & Lanning script, Tenney & Garcia art begins; Iron Man, Scarlet Witch, Spider-Woman, US Agent, Wonder Man and Century begin; pop-up cover	$0.80	$2.40	$4.00	£0.50	£1.50	£2.50
1 Ashcan Edition, ND, 12pgs, black and white	$0.30	$0.90	$1.50	£0.20	£0.60	£1.00
2-5	$0.30	$0.90	$1.50	£0.20	£0.60	£1.00
5 Collectors Edition, ND : pre-bagged with acetate print from Marvel Action Hour TV series; neon ink cover	$0.60	$1.80	$3.00	£0.40	£1.20	£2.00
6 Hands of the Mandarin part 1, continued in War Machine #9	$0.30	$0.90	$1.50	£0.20	£0.60	£1.00
7 Hands of the Mandarin part 4, continued in War Machine #10	$0.30	$0.90	$1.50	£0.20	£0.60	£1.00
8 Quicksilver, Captain America and Hank Pym appear	$0.30	$0.90	$1.50	£0.20	£0.60	£1.00
9-10	$0.30	$0.90	$1.50	£0.20	£0.60	£1.00
11 X-over with War Machine #14	$0.30	$0.90	$1.50	£0.20	£0.60	£1.00
12 48pgs, flip-book format, continued in War Machine #15 and Iron Man #317	$0.50	$1.50	$2.50	£0.30	£0.90	£1.50
13-14 The Avengers guest-star	$0.30	$0.90	$1.50	£0.20	£0.60	£1.00
15	$0.30	$0.90	$1.50	£0.20	£0.60	£1.00
16-17 Avengers: The Crossing tie-in	$0.30	$0.90	$1.50	£0.20	£0.60	£1.00
18 Avengers: The Crossing tie-in; Hawkeye, War Machine and the Avengers appear	$0.30	$0.90	$1.50	£0.20	£0.60	£1.00
19 Avengers: The Crossing tie-in; Hawkeye and the Avengers appear	$0.30	$0.90	$1.50	£0.20	£0.60	£1.00
20 Avengers: Timeslide tie-in	$0.30	$0.90	$1.50	£0.20	£0.60	£1.00
21-22	$0.30	$0.90	$1.50	£0.20	£0.60	£1.00
Title Value:	$8.20	$24.60	$41.00	£5.40	£16.20	£27.00

FORD FAIRLANE

DC Comics,MS Film; 1 May 1990-4 Aug 1990

Issue	$Good	$Fine	$N.Mint	£Good	£Fine	£N.Mint
1-4 based on 20th Century Fox film	$0.25	$0.75	$1.25	£0.10	£0.35	£0.60
Title Value:	$1.00	$3.00	$5.00	£0.40	£1.40	£2.40

Note: New Format

FOREVER PEOPLE

DC Comics; 1 Feb/Mar 1971-11 Oct/Nov 1972

Issue	$Good	$Fine	$N.Mint	£Good	£Fine	£N.Mint
1 Jack Kirby art begins, 1st full appearance Darkseid (see Jimmy Olsen #134 and New Gods #1)	$8.25	$25.00	$50.00	£4.15	£12.50	£25.00
2	$5.75	$17.50	$35.00	£2.50	£7.50	£15.00
3	$5.25	$16.00	$32.50	£1.65	£5.00	£10.00
4-5 52pgs, Joe Simon & Jack Kirby back-up reprints	$5.25	$16.00	$32.50	£1.65	£5.00	£10.00
6-9 52pgs, Joe Simon & Jack Kirby back-up reprints	$2.90	$8.75	$17.50	£1.05	£3.25	£6.50
10 Deadman X-over	$2.90	$8.75	$17.50	£1.05	£3.25	£6.50
11	$2.90	$8.75	$17.50	£1.05	£3.25	£6.50
Title Value:	$47.15	$143.00	$287.50	£17.90	£54.50	£109.00

FOREVER PEOPLE (LIMITED SERIES)

DC Comics,MS; 1 Feb 1988-6 Jul 1988

Issue	$Good	$Fine	$N.Mint	£Good	£Fine	£N.Mint
1-6	$0.25	$0.75	$1.25	£0.15	£0.45	£0.75
Title Value:	$1.50	$4.50	$7.50	£0.90	£2.70	£4.50

Note: Deluxe Format

FORGOTTEN REALMS

DC Comics; 1 Sep 1989-25 Sep 1991

Issue	$Good	$Fine	$N.Mint	£Good	£Fine	£N.Mint
1	$0.40	$1.20	$2.00	£0.40	£1.20	£2.00
2-5	$0.30	$0.90	$1.50	£0.30	£0.90	£1.50
6-15	$0.30	$0.90	$1.50	£0.25	£0.75	£1.25
16-19 Mad Gods and Paladins story	$0.30	$0.90	$1.50	£0.20	£0.60	£1.00
20-25	$0.30	$0.90	$1.50	£0.20	£0.60	£1.00
Title Value:	$7.60	$22.80	$38.00	£6.10	£18.30	£30.50

Note: New Format

FORGOTTEN REALMS ANNUAL

DC Comics; 1 Jan 1991

Issue	$Good	$Fine	$N.Mint	£Good	£Fine	£N.Mint
1 painted cover by Gil Kane	$0.50	$1.50	$2.50	£0.30	£0.90	£1.50
Title Value:	$0.50	$1.50	$2.50	£0.30	£0.90	£1.50

FOUR COLOR (SERIES I)

Dell; 1 Sep 1939-25 1942

Issue	$Good	$Fine	$N.Mint	£Good	£Fine	£N.Mint
1 rare in the U.K. Dick Tracy by Chester Gould; probably no more than 120 copies in any grade in existence	$660.00	$1975.00	$6600.00	£440.00	£1300.00	£4400.00
2 rare in the U.K. Don Winslow of The Navy	$160.00	$490.00	$1150.00	£110.00	£330.00	£770.00
3 scarce in the U.K. Myra North - Special Nurse	$97.50	$295.00	$690.00	£65.00	£195.00	£460.00
4 rare in the U.K. Donald Duck, script and art by Al Taliaferro; classic cover	$930.00	$2750.00	$9300.00	£630.00	£1875.00	£6300.00
5 Smilin' Jack, Mosely art	$80.00	$240.00	$570.00	£55.00	£165.00	£385.00
6 scarce in the U.S, very scarce in the U.K. Dick Tracy by Chester Gould	$160.00	$490.00	$1150.00	£110.00	£330.00	£770.00
7 Gang Busters	$49.00	$145.00	$345.00	£33.00	£97.50	£230.00
8 scarce in the U.K. Dick Tracy by Chester Gould	$92.50	$275.00	$650.00	£65.00	£195.00	£460.00
9 Terry and the Pirates	$80.00	$240.00	$570.00	£55.00	£165.00	£385.00
10 Smilin' Jack	$70.00	$210.00	$500.00	£49.00	£145.00	£345.00
11 Smitty	$49.00	$145.00	$345.00	£33.00	£97.50	£230.00
12 Little Orphan Annie; reprints from newspaper strips	$65.00	$195.00	$460.00	£44.00	£130.00	£305.00
13 Walt Disney's The Reluctant Dragon; plus Donald Duck and Goofy stories	$195.00	$580.00	$1375.00	£130.00	£390.00	£920.00
14 Moon Mullins	$44.00	$130.00	$305.00	£29.00	£85.00	£200.00
15 Tillie the Toiler	$44.00	$130.00	$305.00	£29.00	£85.00	£200.00
16 Mickey Mouse Outwits the Phantom Blot; uncommon in high grade	$1200.00	$3600.00	$10800.00	£840.00	£2500.00	£7600.00
17 Walt Disney's Dumbo the Flying Elephant; plus Donald Duck, Mickey Mouse and Pluto stories	$235.00	$700.00	$1650.00	£155.00	£470.00	£1100.00
18 Jiggs and Maggie	$55.00	$165.00	$385.00	£36.00	£105.00	£250.00
19 Barney Google and Snuffy Smith; the sub-title "Four Color Comic" now appears on the cover	$49.00	$145.00	$345.00	£33.00	£97.50	£230.00
20 Tiny Tim	$38.00	$110.00	$265.00	£25.00	£75.00	£175.00
21 Dick Tracy by Chester Gould	$75.00	$225.00	$530.00	£49.00	£145.00	£345.00
22 Don Winslow of the Navy	$39.00	$115.00	$275.00	£26.00	£75.00	£180.00
23 Gang Busters	$35.00	$105.00	$245.00	£22.50	£67.50	£160.00
24 Captain Easy	$60.00	$180.00	$420.00	£40.00	£120.00	£280.00
25 Popeye	$100.00	$310.00	$730.00	£70.00	£210.00	£500.00
Title Value:	$4662.00	$13945.00	$39960.00	£3173.50	£9450.00	£27180.00

Note: not distributed on the news-stands in the U.K. Generally scarce or very scarce in the U.K.

FOUR COLOR (SERIES II)

Dell; 1 1942-1354 Apr 1962

Issue	$Good	$Fine	$N.Mint	£Good	£Fine	£N.Mint
1 Little Jo; newspaper strip reprints	$60.00	$180.00	$420.00	£40.00	£120.00	£280.00
2 Harold Teen; newspaper strip reprints						

Issue	$Good	$Fine	$N.Mint	£Good	£Fine	£N.Mint
	$33.00	$97.50	$230.00	£21.00	£62.50	£150.00
3 Alley Oop; newspaper strip reprints	$60.00	$180.00	$420.00	£40.00	£120.00	£280.00
4 Smilin' Jack; Mosely art	$60.00	$180.00	$420.00	£40.00	£120.00	£280.00
5 Raggedy Ann and Andy; Mosely art	$60.00	$180.00	$420.00	£40.00	£120.00	£280.00
6 Smitty; newspaper strip reprints	$27.00	$80.00	$190.00	£17.50	£52.50	£125.00
7 Smokey Stover; newspaper strip reprints	$44.00	$130.00	$305.00	£29.00	£87.50	£205.00
8 Tillie the Toiler; newspaper strip reprints	$27.00	$80.00	$190.00	£17.50	£52.50	£125.00
9 Donald Duck Finds Pirate Gold; classic art by Carl Barks and a great cover	$820.00	$2450.00	$8200.00	£600.00	£1800.00	£6000.00
10 Flash Gordon by Alex Raymond	$75.00	$225.00	$530.00	£50.00	£150.00	£355.00
11 Wash Tubbs; newspaper strip reprints	$38.00	$110.00	$265.00	£26.00	£77.50	£185.00
12 Walt Disney's Bambi	$75.00	$225.00	$530.00	£50.00	£150.00	£355.00
13 Mr. District Attorney (later a classic DC title); newspaper strip reprints	$35.00	$105.00	$245.00	£23.50	£70.00	£165.00
14 Smilin' Jack; Mosely art	$46.00	$135.00	$320.00	£31.00	£90.00	£215.00
15 Felix The Cat; Otto Messmer cover and art	$92.50	$275.00	$650.00	£60.00	£185.00	£435.00
16 Porky Pig in "The Secret of the Haunted House"	$100.00	$310.00	$730.00	£70.00	£210.00	£490.00
17 Popeye; Segar art	$80.00	$240.00	$570.00	£55.00	£165.00	£385.00
18 Little Orphan Annie's Junior Commandoes - patriotic flag cover	$49.00	$145.00	$345.00	£33.00	£97.50	£230.00
19 Walt Disney's Thumper meets The Seven Dwarfs	$75.00	$225.00	$530.00	£50.00	£150.00	£355.00
20 Barney Baxter; newspaper strip reprints	$31.00	$90.00	$215.00	£20.00	£60.00	£140.00
21 Oswald the Rabbit; Chester Gould cover and art	$70.00	$210.00	$500.00	£48.00	£140.00	£335.00
22 Tillie the Toiler; newspaper reprints	$21.00	$62.50	$150.00	£14.00	£43.00	£100.00
23 Raggedy Ann and Andy	$46.00	$135.00	$320.00	£31.00	£90.00	£215.00
24 Gang Busters; Crane art	$35.00	$105.00	$245.00	£23.50	£70.00	£165.00
25 Andy Panda; from Walter Lantz cartoon	$75.00	$225.00	$530.00	£50.00	£150.00	£355.00
26 Popeye; Segar art	$80.00	$240.00	$570.00	£55.00	£165.00	£385.00
27 Walt Disney's Mickey Mouse and the Seven Coloured Terror	$120.00	$360.00	$840.00	£80.00	£240.00	£560.00
28 Wash Tubbs; newspaper reprints	$27.00	$80.00	$190.00	£17.50	£52.50	£125.00
29 Donald Duck and The Mummy's Ring; Carl Barks art	$710.00	$2125.00	$7100.00	£475.00	£1425.00	£4750.00
30 Bambi's Children	$80.00	$240.00	$570.00	£55.00	£165.00	£385.00
31 Moon Mullins; newspaper reprints	$23.50	$70.00	$165.00	£16.00	£49.00	£115.00
32 Smitty	$21.00	$62.50	$150.00	£14.00	£43.00	£100.00
33 Bug's Bunny as Public Nuisance No. 1	$80.00	$240.00	$570.00	£55.00	£165.00	£385.00
34 Dick Tracy; Chester Gould art	$60.00	$180.00	$420.00	£40.00	£120.00	£280.00
35 Smokey Stover; newspaper reprints	$21.00	$62.50	$150.00	£14.00	£43.00	£100.00
36 Smilin' Jack; Moseley art	$27.00	$80.00	$190.00	£17.50	£52.50	£125.00
37 Bringing Up Father; newspaper rreprints	$23.50	$70.00	$165.00	£16.00	£49.00	£115.00
38 Roy Rogers; photo cover (great shirt!); 1st ever Western comic	$150.00	$460.00	$1075.00	£100.00	£300.00	£710.00
39 Oswald the Rabbit	$55.00	$165.00	$385.00	£37.00	£110.00	£260.00
40 Barney Google and Snuffy Smith; newspaper reprints	$27.00	$80.00	$190.00	£17.50	£52.50	£125.00
41 Mother Goose and Nursery Rhyme Comics; Walt Kelly art	$31.00	$90.00	$215.00	£20.00	£60.00	£140.00
42 Tiny Tim; newspaper reprints	$23.50	$70.00	$165.00	£16.00	£49.00	£115.00
43 Popeye; newspaper reprints; Segar art	$44.00	$130.00	$305.00	£29.00	£87.50	£205.00
44 Terry and the Pirates; newspaper reprints; Milton Caniff cover and art	$55.00	$165.00	$385.00	£37.00	£110.00	£260.00
45 Raggedy Ann	$35.00	$105.00	$245.00	£23.50	£70.00	£165.00
46 Felix the Cat and The Haunted Castle; Otto Messmer cover and art	$60.00	$180.00	$420.00	£40.00	£120.00	£280.00
47 Gene Autry in The Ghost Mine	$55.00	$165.00	$385.00	£37.00	£110.00	£260.00
48 Porkie Pig of the Mounties; Carl Barks art	$150.00	$460.00	$1075.00	£100.00	£300.00	£710.00
49 Snow White and the Seven Dwarfs	$92.50	$275.00	$650.00	£60.00	£185.00	£435.00
50 Fairy Tale Parade; Walt Kelly art	$35.00	$105.00	$245.00	£23.50	£70.00	£165.00
51 Bugs Bunny Finds The Lost Tresure	$44.00	$130.00	$305.00	£29.00	£87.50	£205.00
52 Little Orphan Annie; strip reprints	$41.00	$120.00	$290.00	£27.00	£80.00	£190.00
53 Wash Tubbs; strip reprints	$21.00	$62.50	$150.00	£14.00	£43.00	£100.00
54 Andy Panda	$44.00	$130.00	$305.00	£29.00	£87.50	£205.00
55 Tillie the Toiler; strip reprints	$17.00	$50.00	$120.00	£11.00	£34.00	£80.00
56 Dick Tracy; Chester Gould cover and art	$44.00	$130.00	$305.00	£29.00	£87.50	£205.00
57 Gene Autry; scarce, "Riders of the Range"	$46.00	$135.00	$320.00	£31.00	£90.00	£215.00
58 Smilin' Jack; Mosely art	$40.00	$120.00	$280.00	£28.00	£82.50	£195.00
59 Mother Goose and Nuresy Rhyme Comics; Walt Kelly cover and art	$23.50	$70.00	$165.00	£16.00	£49.00	£115.00
60 Tiny Folks Funnies	$19.00	$57.50	$135.00	£13.00	£40.00	£92.50
61 Santa Claus Funnies; Walt Kelly cover and art	$29.00	$87.50	$205.00	£19.00	£57.50	£135.00
62 Donald Duck in Frozen Gold; Carl Barks cover and art	$250.00	$750.00	$1750.00	£165.00	£500.00	£1175.00
63 Roy Rogers; photo cover	$60.00	$180.00	$420.00	£40.00	£120.00	£280.00
64 Smokey Stover; strip reprints	$18.50	$55.00	$130.00	£12.50	£38.00	£87.50

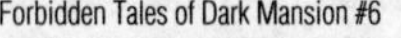
Forbidden Tales of Dark Mansion #6

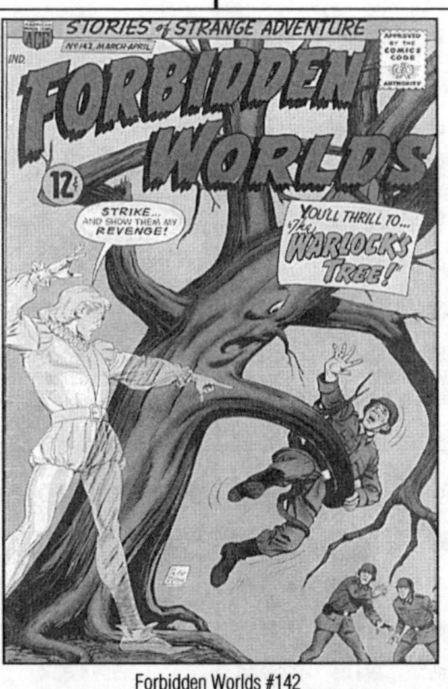

Forbidden Worlds #142

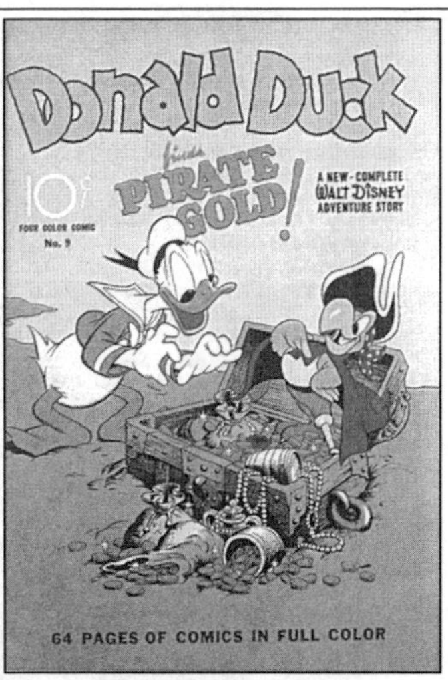

Four Color #9

Issue	$Good	$Fine	$N.Mint	£Good	£Fine	£N.Mint
65 Smitty; strip reprints	$18.50	$55.00	$130.00	£12.50	£38.00	£87.50
66 Gene Autry; Marsh art	$46.00	$135.00	$320.00	£31.00	£90.00	£215.00
67 Oswald the Rabbit	$21.00	$62.50	$150.00	£14.00	£43.00	£100.00
68 Mother Goose and Nursery Rhyme Comics; Walt Kelly cover and art	$21.00	$62.50	$150.00	£14.00	£43.00	£100.00
69 Fairy Tale Parade; Walt Kelly cover and art	$35.00	$105.00	$245.00	£23.50	£70.00	£165.00
70 Popeye and Wimpy; newspaper strip reprints	$35.00	$105.00	$245.00	£23.50	£70.00	£165.00
71 Walt Disney's Three Caballeros; Walt Kelly cover and art	$120.00	$360.00	$840.00	£80.00	£240.00	£560.00
72 Raggedy Ann	$33.00	$97.50	$230.00	£21.00	£62.50	£150.00
73 The Gumps	$16.00	$49.00	$115.00	£10.50	£32.00	£75.00
74 Marge's Little Lulu (1st appearance); J. Stanley cover and art	$135.00	$410.00	$960.00	£90.00	£270.00	£640.00
75 Gene Autrey and the Wildcat; Marsh art	$38.00	$110.00	$265.00	£26.00	£77.50	£185.00
76 Little Orphan Annie; strip reprints	$33.00	$97.50	$230.00	£21.00	£62.50	£150.00
77 Felix the Cat; Otto Messmer cover and art	$49.00	$145.00	$345.00	£33.00	£97.50	£230.00
78 Porky Pig and the Bandit Twins	$31.00	$90.00	$215.00	£20.00	£60.00	£140.00
79 Walt Disney's Mickey Mouse in The Riddle of the Red Hat; Carl Barks cover and art	$160.00	$490.00	$1150.00	£110.00	£330.00	£770.00
80 Smilin' Jack; Mosley art	$21.00	$62.50	$150.00	£14.00	£43.00	£100.00
81 Moon Mullins; strip reprints	$16.00	$49.00	$115.00	£10.50	£32.00	£75.00
82 Lone Ranger; strip reprints	$49.00	$145.00	$345.00	£33.00	£97.50	£230.00
83 Gene Autrey in "Outlaw Trail" (most copies have #84 printed inside)	$38.00	$110.00	$265.00	£26.00	£77.50	£185.00
84 Flash Gordon; Alex Raymond newspaper srtip reprints	$49.00	$145.00	$345.00	£33.00	£97.50	£230.00
85 Andy Panda and The Mad Dog Mystery (most copies have #86 printed inside)	$19.00	$57.50	$135.00	£13.00	£40.00	£92.50
86 Roy Rogers; photo cover (most copies have #87 printed indside)	$44.00	$130.00	$305.00	£29.00	£87.50	£205.00
87 Fairy Tale Parade; Walt Kelly art	$38.00	$110.00	$265.00	£26.00	£77.50	£185.00
88 Bugs Bunny's Great Adventure (most copies have #83 printed inside)	$31.00	$90.00	$215.00	£20.00	£60.00	£140.00
89 Tillie the Toiler; strip reprints	$17.00	$50.00	$120.00	£11.00	£34.00	£80.00
90 Christmas with Mother Goose; Walt Kelly cover and art	$21.00	$62.50	$150.00	£14.00	£43.00	£100.00
91 Santa Claus Funnies; Walt Kelly cover and art	$23.50	$70.00	$165.00	£16.00	£49.00	£115.00
92 Waly Disney's The Wonderful Adventures of Pinocchio, Donald Duck appears; Walt Kelly cover and art	$100.00	$310.00	$730.00	£70.00	£210.00	£490.00
93 Gene Autrey in "The Bandit of Black Rock"; Marsh art	$33.00	$97.50	$230.00	£21.00	£62.50	£150.00
94 Winnie Winkle; strip reprints	$16.00	$49.00	$115.00	£10.50	£32.00	£75.00
95 Roy Rogers Comics; photo cover	$44.00	$130.00	$305.00	£29.00	£87.50	£205.00
96 Dick Tracy; Chester Gould cover and art	$33.00	$97.50	$230.00	£21.00	£62.50	£150.00
97 Marge's Little Lulu; J. Stanley cover and art	$62.50	$190.00	$445.00	£42.00	£125.00	£295.00
98 The Lone Ranger; strip reprints	$38.00	$110.00	$265.00	£26.00	£77.50	£185.00
99 Smitty; strip reprints	$16.00	$49.00	$115.00	£10.50	£32.00	£75.00
100 Gene Autrey Comics; photo cover; Marsh art	$33.00	$97.50	$230.00	£21.00	£62.50	£150.00
101 Terry and The Pirates; Milton Caniff cover and art	$33.00	$97.50	$230.00	£21.00	£62.50	£150.00
102 Oswald the Rabbit; Walt Kelly art (1pg)	$19.00	$57.50	$135.00	£13.00	£40.00	£92.50
103 Easter with Mother Goose; Walt Kelly cover and art	$27.00	$80.00	$190.00	£17.50	£52.50	£125.00
104 Fairy Tale Parade; Walt Kelly cover and art	$27.00	$80.00	$190.00	£17.50	£52.50	£125.00
105 Albert the Alligator and Pogo Possum (1st appearance); Walt Kelly cover and art	$97.50	$295.00	$690.00	£65.00	£195.00	£460.00
106 Tillie the Toiler; newspaper strip reprints	$16.00	$49.00	$115.00	£10.50	£32.00	£75.00
107 Little Orphan Annie; strip reprints	$27.00	$80.00	$190.00	£17.50	£52.50	£125.00
108 Donald Duck in "The Terror of the River"; Carl Barks art	$195.00	$580.00	$1375.00	£130.00	£390.00	£920.00
109 Roy Rogers Comics; photo cover	$33.00	$97.50	$230.00	£21.00	£62.50	£150.00
110 Marge's Little Lulu; Jack Stanley cover and art	$44.00	$130.00	$305.00	£29.00	£87.50	£205.00
111 Captain Easy; Crane art	$19.00	$57.50	$135.00	£13.00	£40.00	£92.50
112 Porky Pig's Adventure in Gopher Gulch	$19.00	$57.50	$135.00	£13.00	£40.00	£92.50
113 Popeye (has #114 on inside indicia)	$19.00	$57.50	$135.00	£13.00	£40.00	£92.50
114 Fairy Tale Parade; Walt Kelly cover and art	$27.00	$80.00	$190.00	£17.50	£52.50	£125.00
115 Marge's Little Lulu; Jack Stanley cover and art	$44.00	$130.00	$305.00	£29.00	£87.50	£205.00
116 Mickey Mouse and The House of Many Mysteries	$33.00	$97.50	$230.00	£21.00	£62.50	£150.00
117 Roy Rogers Comics; photo cover	$23.50	$70.00	$165.00	£16.00	£49.00	£115.00
118 The Lone Ranger; strip reprints	$35.00	$105.00	$245.00	£23.50	£70.00	£165.00
119 Felix the Cat; Otto Messmer cover and art	$44.00	$130.00	$305.00	£29.00	£87.50	£205.00
120 Marge's Little Lulu; Jack Stanley cover and art	$38.00	$110.00	$265.00	£26.00	£77.50	£185.00
121 Fairy Tale Parade	$16.00	$49.00	$115.00	£10.50	£32.00	£75.00
122 Henry (1st appearance - has #121 on inside indicia)	$16.00	$49.00	$115.00	£10.50	£32.00	£75.00
123 Bugs Bunny's Dangerous Venture	$19.00	$57.50	$135.00	£13.00	£40.00	£92.50
124 Roy Rogers Comics; photo cover	$23.50	$70.00	$165.00	£16.00	£49.00	£115.00
125 The Lone Ranger; strip reprints	$27.00	$80.00	$190.00	£17.50	£52.50	£125.00
126 Christmas with Mother Goose; Walt Kelly cover and art	$23.50	$70.00	$165.00	£16.00	£49.00	£115.00
127 Popeye	$19.00	$57.50	$135.00	£13.00	£40.00	£92.50
128 Santa Claus Funnies featuring "A Mouse in the House" by Walt Kelly	$19.00	$57.50	$135.00	£13.00	£40.00	£92.50
129 Walt Disney's Uncle Remus and His Tales of Brer Rabbit (1st appearance)	$49.00	$145.00	$345.00	£33.00	£97.50	£230.00
130 Andy Panda by Walter Lantz	$16.00	$49.00	$115.00	£10.50	£32.00	£75.00
131 Marge's Little Lulu; Jack Stanley cover and art	$38.00	$110.00	$265.00	£26.00	£77.50	£185.00
132 Tillie the Toiler; newspaper reprints	$14.00	$43.00	$100.00	£9.25	£28.00	£65.00
133 Dick Tracy; Chester Gould cover and art	$27.00	$80.00	$190.00	£17.50	£52.50	£125.00
134 Tarzan and the Devil Ogre; Marsh cover and art (has #136 inside)	$80.00	$240.00	$570.00	£55.00	£165.00	£385.00
135 Felix the Cat; Otto Messmer cover and art	$33.00	$97.50	$230.00	£21.00	£62.50	£150.00
136 The Lone Ranger; strip reprints	$27.00	$80.00	$190.00	£17.50	£52.50	£125.00
137 Roy Rogers Comics; photo cover	$23.50	$70.00	$165.00	£16.00	£49.00	£115.00
138 Smitty; strip reprints	$14.00	$43.00	$100.00	£9.25	£28.00	£65.00
139 Marge's Little Lulu; Jack Stanley cover and art	$35.00	$105.00	$245.00	£23.50	£70.00	£165.00
140 Easter with Mother Gosse; Walt Kelly cover and art	$19.00	$57.50	$135.00	£13.00	£40.00	£92.50
141 Mickey Mouse and the Submarine Pirates	$27.00	$80.00	$190.00	£17.50	£52.50	£125.00
142 Bugs Bunny and the Haunted Mountain	$19.00	$57.50	$135.00	£13.00	£40.00	£92.50
143 Oswald the Rabbit and the Prehistoric Egg	$14.00	$43.00	$100.00	£9.25	£28.00	£65.00
144 Roy Rogers Comics; photo cover	$23.50	$70.00	$165.00	£16.00	£49.00	£115.00
145 Popeye (has #134 on inside indicia)	$19.00	$57.50	$135.00	£13.00	£40.00	£92.50
146 Marge's Little Lulu; Jack Stanley cover and art	$35.00	$105.00	$245.00	£23.50	£70.00	£165.00
147 Donald Duck in Volcano Valley; Carl Barks cover and art	$120.00	$360.00	$840.00	£80.00	£240.00	£560.00
148 Albert the Alligator and Pogo Possum; Walt Kelly cover and art	$92.50	$275.00	$650.00	£60.00	£185.00	£435.00
149 Smilin' Jack; strip reprints	$16.00	$49.00	$115.00	£10.50	£32.00	£75.00
150 Tillie the Toiler; strip reprints	$12.50	$39.00	$90.00	£8.50	£26.00	£60.00
151 The Lone Ranger; strip reprints	$23.50	$70.00	$165.00	£16.00	£49.00	£115.00
152 Little Orphan Annie; strip reprints	$19.00	$57.50	$135.00	£13.00	£40.00	£92.50
153 Roy Rogers Comics; photo cover	$19.00	$57.50	$135.00	£13.00	£40.00	£92.50
154 Andy Panda by Walter Lantz	$12.50	$39.00	$90.00	£8.50	£26.00	£60.00
155 Henry	$12.50	$39.00	$90.00	£8.50	£26.00	£60.00
156 Porky Pig and The Phantom	$14.00	$43.00	$100.00	£9.25	£28.00	£65.00
157 Mickey Mouse and the Beanstalk	$33.00	$97.50	$230.00	£21.00	£62.50	£150.00
158 Marge's Little Lulu; Jack Stanley cover and art	$35.00	$105.00	$245.00	£23.50	£70.00	£165.00

#	Title	$Good	$Fine	$N.Mint	£Good	£Fine	£N.Mint
159	Donald Duck and the Ghost of the Grotto; CArl Barks cover and art	$100.00	$310.00	$730.00	£70.00	£210.00	£490.00
160	Roy Rogers Comics; photo cover	$19.00	$57.50	$135.00	£13.00	£40.00	£92.50
161	Tarzan and the Fires of Tohr; Marsh cover and art	$65.00	$195.00	$460.00	£44.00	£130.00	£305.00
162	Felix the Cat; Otto Messmer cover and art	$23.50	$70.00	$165.00	£16.00	£49.00	£115.00
163	Dick Tracy; Chester Gould cover and art	$23.50	$70.00	$165.00	£16.00	£49.00	£115.00
164	Bugs Bunny Finds the Frozen Kingdom	$19.00	$57.50	$135.00	£13.00	£40.00	£92.50
165	Marge's Little Lulu; Jack Stanley cover and art	$35.00	$105.00	$245.00	£23.50	£70.00	£165.00
166	Roy Rogers Comics; photo cover	$19.00	$57.50	$135.00	£13.00	£40.00	£92.50
167	The Lone Ranger; strip reprints	$23.50	$70.00	$165.00	£16.00	£49.00	£115.00
168	Popeye	$19.00	$57.50	$135.00	£13.00	£40.00	£92.50
169	Woody Woodpecker (1st appearance) in The Manhunter From The North	$23.50	$70.00	$165.00	£16.00	£49.00	£115.00
170	Mickey Mouse on Spook's Island	$23.50	$70.00	$165.00	£16.00	£49.00	£115.00
171	Charlie McCarthy and the Twenty Thieves	$23.50	$70.00	$165.00	£16.00	£49.00	£115.00
172	Christmas with Mother Goose; Walt Kelly cover and art	$19.00	$57.50	$135.00	£13.00	£40.00	£92.50
173	Flash Gordon	$17.00	$50.00	$120.00	£11.00	£34.00	£80.00
174	Winnie Winkle; strip reprints	$11.50	$35.00	$82.50	£7.75	£23.50	£55.00
175	Santa Claus Funnies; Walt Kelly cover and art	$19.00	$57.50	$135.00	£13.00	£40.00	£92.50
176	Tillie the Toiler; strip reprints	$11.50	$35.00	$82.50	£7.75	£23.50	£55.00
177	Roy Rogers Comics; photo cover	$20.50	$60.00	$145.00	£13.50	£41.00	£95.00
178	Donald Duck in Christmas on Bear Mountain; Carl Barks cover and art	$125.00	$375.00	$880.00	£85.00	£255.00	£600.00
179	Uncle Wiggily; Walt Kelly cover	$19.00	$57.50	$135.00	£13.00	£40.00	£92.50
180	Ozark Ike; strip reprints	$11.50	$35.00	$82.50	£7.75	£23.50	£55.00
181	Walt Disney's Mickey Mouse in Jungle Magic	$23.50	$70.00	$165.00	£16.00	£49.00	£115.00
182	Porky Pig in Never-Never Land	$12.50	$39.00	$90.00	£8.50	£26.00	£60.00
183	Oswald the Rabbit by Walter Lantz (has #184 in inside indicia)	$11.50	$35.00	$82.50	£7.75	£23.50	£55.00
184	Tillie the Toiler; strip reprints (has #186 in inside indicia)	$12.50	$39.00	$90.00	£8.50	£26.00	£60.00
185	Easter with Mother Goose; Walt Kelly cover and art (has #187 in inside indicia)	$19.00	$57.50	$135.00	£13.00	£40.00	£92.50
186	Walt Disney's Bambi	$27.00	$80.00	$190.00	£17.50	£52.50	£125.00
187	Bugs Bunny and the Dreadful Dragon	$16.00	$49.00	$115.00	£10.50	£32.00	£75.00
188	Woody Woodpecker by Walter Lantz	$19.00	$57.50	$135.00	£13.00	£40.00	£92.50
189	Donald Duck in the Old Castle's Secret; Carl Barks cover and art	$100.00	$310.00	$730.00	£70.00	£210.00	£490.00
190	Flash Gordon	$16.00	$49.00	$115.00	£10.50	£32.00	£75.00
191	Porky Pig to the Rescue	$12.50	$39.00	$90.00	£8.50	£26.00	£60.00
192	The Brownies; Walt Kelly cover and art	$16.00	$49.00	$115.00	£10.50	£32.00	£75.00
193	M.G.M. Presents Tom and Jerry (1st comics appearance - has #192 in inside indicia)	$21.00	$62.50	$150.00	£14.00	£43.00	£100.00
194	Mickey Mouse in The World Under The Sea	$21.00	$62.50	$150.00	£14.00	£43.00	£100.00
195	Tiile the Toiler; strip reprints	$9.50	$29.00	$67.50	£6.50	£19.50	£46.00
196	Charlie McCarthy in The Haunted Hideout	$19.00	$57.50	$135.00	£13.00	£40.00	£92.50
197	Spirit of the Border by Zane Gey	$19.00	$57.50	$135.00	£13.00	£40.00	£92.50
198	Andy Panda	$11.50	$35.00	$82.50	£7.75	£23.50	£55.00
199	Donald Duck in Sheriff of Bullet Valley; Carl Barks cover and art (he appears himself on a wanted poster)	$100.00	$305.00	$720.00	£67.50	£205.00	£480.00
200	Bugs Bunny Super Sleuth	$16.00	$49.00	$115.00	£10.50	£32.00	£75.00
201	Christmas with Mother Goose; Walt Kelly cover and art	$16.00	$49.00	$115.00	£10.50	£32.00	£75.00
202	Woody Woodpecker	$11.50	$35.00	$82.50	£7.75	£23.50	£55.00
203	Donald Duck in The Golden Christmas Tree; Carl Barks cover and art	$80.00	$240.00	$570.00	£55.00	£165.00	£385.00
204	Flash Gordon	$16.00	$49.00	$115.00	£10.50	£32.00	£75.00
205	Santa Claus Funnies; Walt Kelly cover and art	$16.00	$49.00	$115.00	£10.50	£32.00	£75.00
206	Little Orphan Annie; strip reprints	$11.50	$35.00	$82.50	£7.75	£23.50	£55.00
207	King of The Royal Mounted	$23.50	$70.00	$165.00	£16.00	£49.00	£115.00
208	Brer Rabbit Does It Again	$14.00	$43.00	$100.00	£9.25	£28.00	£65.00
209	Harold Teen; strip reprints	$6.50	$19.50	$46.00	£4.25	£12.50	£30.00
210	Tippie and Cap Stubbs	$8.50	$26.00	$60.00	£5.50	£17.00	£40.00
211	Little Beaver	$9.50	$29.00	$67.50	£6.50	£19.50	£46.00
212	Dr. Bobbs	$6.50	$19.50	$46.00	£4.25	£12.50	£30.00
213	Tillie the Toiler; strip reprints	$7.50	$22.50	$52.50	£5.00	£15.00	£36.00
214	Mickey Mouse and His Sky Adventure	$19.00	$57.50	$135.00	£13.00	£40.00	£92.50
215	Sparkle Plenty; Chester Gould cover and art	$12.50	$39.00	$90.00	£8.50	£26.00	£60.00
216	Andy Panda and the Police Pup by Walter Lantz	$8.50	$26.00	$60.00	£5.50	£17.00	£40.00
217	Bugs Bunny in Court Jester	$16.00	$49.00	$115.00	£10.50	£32.00	£75.00
218	Three Little Pigs and the Wonderful Magic Lamp	$21.00	$62.50	$150.00	£14.00	£43.00	£100.00
219	Swee'pea	$11.50	$35.00	$82.50	£7.75	£23.50	£55.00
220	Easter with Mother Goose; Walt Kelly cover and art	$16.00	$49.00	$115.00	£10.50	£32.00	£75.00
221	Uncle Wiggily; part Walt Kelly cover	$12.50	$39.00	$90.00	£8.50	£26.00	£60.00
222	West of the Pecos by Zane Grey	$11.50	$35.00	$82.50	£7.75	£23.50	£55.00
223	Donald Duck in Lost in the Andes; Carl Barks cover and art	$92.50	$275.00	$650.00	£60.00	£185.00	£435.00
224	Little Iodine; Hatlo art	$12.50	$39.00	$90.00	£8.50	£26.00	£60.00
225	Oswald the Rabbit by Walter Lantz	$7.50	$22.50	$52.50	£5.00	£15.00	£36.00
226	Porky Pig and Spoofy the Spook	$9.50	$29.00	$67.50	£6.50	£19.50	£46.00
227	Seven Dwarfs	$12.50	$39.00	$90.00	£8.50	£26.00	£60.00
228	The Mark of Zorro	$33.00	$97.50	$230.00	£20.50	£60.00	£145.00
229	Smokey Stover; strip reprints	$6.50	$19.50	$46.00	£4.25	£12.50	£30.00
230	Sunset Pass by Zane Grey	$9.50	$29.00	$67.50	£6.50	£19.50	£46.00
231	Mickey Mouse and the Rajah's Treasure	$19.00	$57.50	$135.00	£13.00	£40.00	£92.50
232	Woody Woodpecker by Walter Lantz	$9.50	$29.00	$67.50	£6.50	£19.50	£46.00
233	Bugs Bunny Sleepwalking Sleuth	$16.00	$49.00	$115.00	£10.50	£32.00	£75.00
234	Dumbo in Sky Voyage	$14.00	$43.00	$100.00	£9.25	£28.00	£65.00
235	Tiny Tim	$7.50	$22.50	$52.50	£5.00	£15.00	£36.00
236	Hertitage of the Desert by Zane Grey	$9.50	$29.00	$67.50	£6.50	£19.50	£46.00
237	Tillie the Toiler; strip reprints	$7.50	$22.50	$52.50	£5.00	£15.00	£36.00
238	Donald Duck in Hoodoo Voodoo; Carl Barks cover and art	$80.00	$240.00	$570.00	£55.00	£165.00	£385.00
239	Adventure Bound	$7.50	$22.50	$52.50	£5.00	£15.00	£36.00
240	Andy Panda by Walter Lantz	$9.50	$29.00	$67.50	£6.50	£19.50	£46.00
241	Porky Pig, Mighty Hunter	$9.50	$29.00	$67.50	£6.50	£19.50	£46.00
242	Tippie and Cap Stubbs	$6.50	$19.50	$46.00	£4.25	£12.50	£30.00
243	Thumper Follows His Nose	$16.00	$49.00	$115.00	£10.50	£32.00	£75.00
244	The Brownies; Walt Kelly cover and art	$16.00	$49.00	$115.00	£10.50	£32.00	£75.00
245	Dick's Adventures in Dreamland; strip reprints	$7.50	$22.50	$52.50	£5.00	£15.00	£36.00
246	Thunder Mountain by Zane Grey	$6.50	$19.50	$46.00	£4.25	£12.50	£30.00
247	Flash Gordon	$16.00	$49.00	$115.00	£10.50	£32.00	£75.00
248	Mickey Mouse and the Black Sorceror	$19.00	$57.50	$135.00	£13.00	£40.00	£92.50
249	Woody Woodpecker in The Globetrotter	$9.50	$29.00	$67.50	£6.50	£19.50	£46.00
250	Bugs Bunny in Diamond Daze	$16.00	$49.00	$115.00	£10.50	£32.00	£75.00
251	Hubert at Camp Moonbeam	$6.50	$19.50	$46.00	£4.25	£12.50	£30.00
252	Pinocchio	$12.50	$39.00	$90.00	£8.50	£26.00	£60.00
253	Christmas with Mother Goose; Waly Kelly cover and art (has #254 on inside indicia)	$12.50	$39.00	$90.00	£8.50	£26.00	£60.00
254	Santa Claus Funnies; Walt Kelly cover and art plus Albert and Pogo story by Kelly						

#	Title	$Good	$Fine	$N.Mint	£Good	£Fine	£N.Mint
	(has #256 on inside indicia)	*$19.00*	*$57.50*	*$135.00*	£13.00	£40.00	£92.50
255	The Ranger by Zane Grey (has #256 on inside indicia)	*$6.50*	*$19.50*	*$46.00*	£4.25	£12.50	£30.00
256	Donald Duck in Luck of the North; Carl Barks cover and art (has #257 on inside indicia)	*$55.00*	*$165.00*	*$385.00*	£37.00	£110.00	£260.00
257	Little Iodine (has #258 on inside indicia)	*$9.50*	*$29.00*	*$67.50*	£6.50	£19.50	£46.00
258	Andy Panda and the Balloon Race by Walter Lantz	*$9.50*	*$29.00*	*$67.50*	£6.50	£19.50	£46.00
259	Santa and the Angel/Santa at the Zoo	*$7.50*	*$22.50*	*$52.50*	£5.00	£15.00	£36.00
260	Porky Pig Hero of the Wild West	*$9.50*	*$29.00*	*$67.50*	£6.50	£19.50	£46.00
261	Mickey Mouse and the Missing Key	*$19.00*	*$57.50*	*$135.00*	£13.00	£40.00	£92.50
262	Raggedy Ann and Andy	*$7.50*	*$22.50*	*$52.50*	£5.00	£15.00	£36.00
263	Donald Duck in The Land of the Totem Poles; Carl Barks cover and art	*$55.00*	*$165.00*	*$385.00*	£37.00	£110.00	£260.00
264	Woody Woodpecker in The Magic Lantern by Walter Lantz	*$9.50*	*$29.00*	*$67.50*	£6.50	£19.50	£46.00
265	King of the Royal Mounted by Zane Grey; strip reprints	*$11.50*	*$35.00*	*$82.50*	£7.75	£23.50	£55.00
266	Bugs Bunny on The Isle of Hercules	*$11.50*	*$35.00*	*$82.50*	£7.75	£23.50	£55.00
267	Little Beaver	*$6.50*	*$19.50*	*$46.00*	£4.25	£12.50	£30.00
268	Mickey Mouse's Surprise Visitor; Gottfredson art	*$19.00*	*$57.50*	*$135.00*	£13.00	£40.00	£92.50
269	Johnny Mack Brown	*$27.00*	*$80.00*	*$190.00*	£17.50	£52.50	£125.00
270	Drift Fence by Zane Grey	*$6.50*	*$19.50*	*$46.00*	£4.25	£12.50	£30.00
271	Porky Pig in Phantom of the Plains	*$9.50*	*$29.00*	*$67.50*	£6.50	£19.50	£46.00
272	Cinderella	*$16.00*	*$49.00*	*$115.00*	£10.50	£32.00	£75.00
273	Oswald the Rabbit	*$7.50*	*$22.50*	*$52.50*	£5.00	£15.00	£36.00
274	Bugs Bunny, Hare-Brained Reporter	*$11.50*	*$35.00*	*$82.50*	£7.75	£23.50	£55.00
275	Donald Duck in Ancient Persia; Carl Barks cover and art	*$49.00*	*$145.00*	*$345.00*	£33.00	£97.50	£230.00
276	Uncle Wiggily (has #277 on inside indicia)	*$9.50*	*$29.00*	*$67.50*	£6.50	£19.50	£46.00
277	Porky Pig in Desert Adventure	*$9.50*	*$29.00*	*$67.50*	£6.50	£19.50	£46.00
278	Bill Elliott Comics; photo cover	*$16.00*	*$49.00*	*$115.00*	£10.50	£32.00	£75.00
279	Mickey Mouse and Pluto Battle The Giant Ants (has #280 on iside indicia)	*$16.00*	*$49.00*	*$115.00*	£10.50	£32.00	£75.00
280	Andy Panda in The Isle of Mechanical Men by Walter Lantz	*$9.50*	*$29.00*	*$67.50*	£6.50	£19.50	£46.00
281	Bugs Bunny in The Great Circus Mystery	*$11.50*	*$35.00*	*$82.50*	£7.75	£23.50	£55.00
282	Donald Duck and The Pixilated Parrot; Carl Barks cover and story	*$49.00*	*$145.00*	*$345.00*	£33.00	£97.50	£230.00
283	King of the Royal Mounted	*$11.50*	*$35.00*	*$82.50*	£7.75	£23.50	£55.00
284	Porky Pig in The Kingdom of Nowhere	*$9.50*	*$29.00*	*$67.50*	£6.50	£19.50	£46.00
285	Bozo the Clown and his Minikin Circus	*$19.00*	*$57.50*	*$135.00*	£13.00	£40.00	£92.50
286	Mickey Mouse in The Uninvited Guest	*$16.00*	*$49.00*	*$115.00*	£10.50	£32.00	£75.00
287	Gene Autrey's Champion in The Ghost of Black Mountain	*$16.00*	*$49.00*	*$115.00*	£10.50	£32.00	£75.00
288	Woody Woodpecker in Klondike Gold by Walter Lantz	*$9.50*	*$29.00*	*$67.50*	£6.50	£19.50	£46.00
289	Bugs Bunny in Indian Trouble	*$12.50*	*$39.00*	*$90.00*	£8.50	£26.00	£60.00
290	The Chief	*$6.50*	*$19.50*	*$46.00*	£4.25	£12.50	£30.00
291	Donald Duck in The Magic Hourglass; Carl Barks cover and art	*$49.00*	*$145.00*	*$345.00*	£33.00	£97.50	£230.00
292	The Cisco Kid Comics	*$27.00*	*$80.00*	*$190.00*	£17.50	£52.50	£125.00
293	The Brownies; Walt Kelly cover and art	*$16.00*	*$49.00*	*$115.00*	£10.50	£32.00	£75.00
294	Little Beaver	*$6.50*	*$19.50*	*$46.00*	£4.25	£12.50	£30.00
295	Porky Pig in President Porky	*$9.50*	*$29.00*	*$67.50*	£6.50	£19.50	£46.00
296	Mickey Mouse in Private Eye For Hire	*$16.00*	*$49.00*	*$115.00*	£10.50	£32.00	£75.00
297	Andy Panda in The Haunted Inn by Walter Lantz	*$9.50*	*$29.00*	*$67.50*	£6.50	£19.50	£46.00
298	Bugs Bunny in Sheik For A Day	*$11.50*	*$35.00*	*$82.50*	£7.75	£23.50	£55.00
299	Buck Jones and The iron Horse Trail	*$19.00*	*$57.50*	*$135.00*	£13.00	£40.00	£92.50
300	Donald Duck in Big Top Bedlam; Carl Barks cover and art	*$49.00*	*$145.00*	*$345.00*	£33.00	£97.50	£230.00
301	The Mysterious Rider by Zane Grey	*$6.50*	*$19.50*	*$46.00*	£4.25	£12.50	£30.00
302	Santa Claus Funnies	*$5.25*	*$16.00*	*$38.00*	£3.55	£10.50	£25.00
303	Porky Pig in The Land of the Monstrous Flies	*$6.50*	*$19.50*	*$46.00*	£4.25	£12.50	£30.00
304	Mickey Mouse in Tom-Tom Island	*$9.50*	*$29.00*	*$67.50*	£6.50	£19.50	£46.00
305	Woody Woodpecker	*$6.50*	*$19.50*	*$46.00*	£4.25	£12.50	£30.00
306	Raggedy Ann	*$6.50*	*$19.50*	*$46.00*	£4.25	£12.50	£30.00
307	Bugs Bunny in Lumberjack Rabbit	*$9.50*	*$29.00*	*$67.50*	£6.50	£19.50	£46.00
308	Donald Duck in Dangerous Disguise; Carl Bark cover and art	*$44.00*	*$130.00*	*$305.00*	£29.00	£87.50	£205.00
309	Betty Betz' Dollface and Her Gang	*$6.50*	*$19.50*	*$46.00*	£4.25	£12.50	£30.00
310	King of the Royal Mounted	*$9.50*	*$29.00*	*$67.50*	£6.50	£19.50	£46.00
311	Porky Pig in Midget Horses of Hidden Valley	*$6.50*	*$19.50*	*$46.00*	£4.25	£12.50	£30.00
312	Tonto	*$19.00*	*$57.50*	*$135.00*	£13.00	£40.00	£92.50
313	Mickey Mouse in The Mystery of the Double Cross Ranch	*$9.50*	*$29.00*	*$67.50*	£6.50	£19.50	£46.00
314	Ambush by Zane Grey (has #1 on inside indicia)	*$6.50*	*$19.50*	*$46.00*	£4.25	£12.50	£30.00
315	Oswald the Rabbit by Walter Lantz	*$5.25*	*$16.00*	*$38.00*	£3.55	£10.50	£25.00
316	Rex Allen; photo cover, Marsh art	*$21.00*	*$62.50*	*$150.00*	£14.00	£43.00	£100.00
317	Bugs Bunny in Hare Today Gone Tomorrow	*$9.50*	*$29.00*	*$67.50*	£6.50	£19.50	£46.00
318	Donald Duck in No Such Varmint; Carl Barks cover and art	*$44.00*	*$130.00*	*$305.00*	£29.00	£87.50	£205.00
319	Gene Autrey's Champion	*$5.25*	*$16.00*	*$38.00*	£3.55	£10.50	£25.00
320	Uncle Wiggily	*$9.50*	*$29.00*	*$67.50*	£6.50	£19.50	£46.00
321	Little Scouts	*$4.25*	*$12.50*	*$30.00*	£2.85	£8.50	£20.00
322	Porky Pig in Roaring Rockets	*$6.50*	*$19.50*	*$46.00*	£4.25	£12.50	£30.00
323	Susie Q. Smith	*$6.50*	*$19.50*	*$46.00*	£4.25	£12.50	£30.00
324	I Met A Handsome Cowboy	*$9.50*	*$29.00*	*$67.50*	£6.50	£19.50	£46.00
325	Mickey Mouse in The Haunted Castle	*$11.50*	*$35.00*	*$82.50*	£7.75	£23.50	£55.00
326	Andy Panda by Walter Lantz	*$4.25*	*$12.50*	*$30.00*	£2.85	£8.50	£20.00
327	Bugs Bunny and The Rajah's Treasure	*$9.50*	*$29.00*	*$67.50*	£6.50	£19.50	£46.00
328	Donald Duck in Old California; Carl Barks cover and art	*$44.00*	*$130.00*	*$305.00*	£29.00	£87.50	£205.00
329	Roy Roger's Trigger; photo cover	*$16.00*	*$49.00*	*$115.00*	£10.50	£32.00	£75.00
330	Porky Pig Meets The Bristled Bruiser	*$6.50*	*$19.50*	*$46.00*	£4.25	£12.50	£30.00
331	Alice in Wonderland	*$21.00*	*$62.50*	*$150.00*	£14.00	£43.00	£100.00
332	Little Beaver	*$5.25*	*$16.00*	*$38.00*	£3.55	£10.50	£25.00
333	Wilderness Trek by Zane Grey	*$6.50*	*$19.50*	*$46.00*	£4.25	£12.50	£30.00
334	Mickey Mouse and Yukon Gold	*$9.50*	*$29.00*	*$67.50*	£6.50	£19.50	£46.00
335	Francis the Famous Talking Mule	*$11.50*	*$35.00*	*$82.50*	£7.75	£23.50	£55.00
336	Woody Woodpecker by Walter Lantz	*$5.25*	*$16.00*	*$38.00*	£3.55	£10.50	£25.00
337	The Brownies; no Walt Kelly art	*$5.25*	*$16.00*	*$38.00*	£3.55	£10.50	£25.00
338	Bugs Bunny and the Rocking Horse Thieves	*$9.50*	*$29.00*	*$67.50*	£6.50	£19.50	£46.00
339	Donald Duck and The Magic Fountain; no Carl Barks art	*$11.50*	*$35.00*	*$82.50*	£7.75	£23.50	£55.00
340	King of the Royal Mounted	*$9.50*	*$29.00*	*$67.50*	£6.50	£19.50	£46.00
341	Unbirthday Party with Alice in Wonderland	*$21.00*	*$62.50*	*$150.00*	£14.00	£43.00	£100.00
342	Porky Pig in The Lucky Peppermint Mine	*$5.25*	*$16.00*	*$38.00*	£3.55	£10.50	£25.00
343	Mickey Mouse in The Ruby Eye of Homar-Guy-Am	*$9.50*	*$29.00*	*$67.50*	£6.50	£19.50	£46.00
344	Sergeant Preston from Challenge of the Yukon; based on TV show	*$16.00*	*$49.00*	*$115.00*	£10.50	£32.00	£75.00
345	Andy Panda in Scotland Yard by Walter Lantz	*$5.25*	*$16.00*	*$38.00*	£3.55	£10.50	£25.00
346	Hideout by Zane Grey (has #347 on inside indicia)	*$6.50*	*$19.50*	*$46.00*	£4.25	£12.50	£30.00
347	Bugs Bunny the Frigid Hare (has #349 on inside indicia)	*$9.50*	*$29.00*	*$67.50*	£6.50	£19.50	£46.00
348	Donald Duck in The Crocodile Collector; Carl Barks cover only	*$27.00*	*$80.00*	*$190.00*	£17.50	£52.50	£125.00
349	Uncle Wiggily	*$9.50*	*$29.00*	*$67.50*	£6.50	£19.50	£46.00
350	Woody Woodpecker by Walter Lantz	*$5.25*	*$16.00*	*$38.00*	£3.55	£10.50	£25.00

#	Title	$Good	$Fine	$N.Mint	£Good	£Fine	£N.Mint
351	Porky Pig and The Grand Canyon Giant	$5.25	$16.00	$38.00	£3.55	£10.50	£25.00
352	Mickey Mouse in The Mystery of Painted Valley	$9.50	$29.00	$67.50	£6.50	£19.50	£46.00
353	Duck Album; Carl Barks cover only	$11.50	$35.00	$82.50	£7.75	£23.50	£55.00
354	Raggedy Ann and Andy	$6.50	$19.50	$46.00	£4.25	£12.50	£30.00
355	Bugs Bunny Hot Rod Hare	$9.50	$29.00	$67.50	£6.50	£19.50	£46.00
356	Donald Duck in Rags To Riches; Carl Barks cover only	$21.00	$62.50	$150.00	£14.00	£43.00	£100.00
357	Comeback by Zane Grey	$6.50	$19.50	$46.00	£4.25	£12.50	£30.00
358	Andy Panda by Walter Lantz	$5.25	$16.00	$38.00	£3.55	£10.50	£25.00
359	Frosty the Snowman	$9.50	$29.00	$67.50	£6.50	£19.50	£46.00
360	Porky Pig in Tree of Fortune	$5.25	$16.00	$38.00	£3.55	£10.50	£25.00
361	Santa Claus Funnies	$5.25	$16.00	$38.00	£3.55	£10.50	£25.00
362	Mickey Mouse and The Smuggled Diamonds	$9.50	$29.00	$67.50	£6.50	£19.50	£46.00
363	King of the Royal Mounted	$8.00	$24.50	$57.50	£5.50	£16.50	£39.00
364	Woody Woodpecker by Walter Lantz	$5.25	$16.00	$38.00	£3.55	£10.50	£25.00
365	The Brownies; no Walt Kelly art	$5.25	$16.00	$38.00	£3.55	£10.50	£25.00
366	Bugs Bunny in Uncle Buckskin Comes To Town	$9.50	$29.00	$67.50	£6.50	£19.50	£46.00
367	Donald Duck in A Christmas for Shacktown; Carl Barks cover and art	$44.00	$130.00	$305.00	£29.00	£87.50	£205.00
368	Bob Clampett's Beany and Cecil	$33.00	$97.50	$230.00	£21.00	£62.50	£150.00
369	The Lone Ranger's Famous Horse Hi-Yo Silver	$11.50	$35.00	$82.50	£7.75	£23.50	£55.00
370	Porky Pig in Trouble in the Big Trees	$5.25	$16.00	$38.00	£3.55	£10.50	£25.00
371	Mickey Mouse in The Inca Idol Case	$8.00	$24.50	$57.50	£5.50	£16.50	£39.00
372	Riders of the Purple Sage by Zane Grey	$5.25	$16.00	$38.00	£3.55	£10.50	£25.00
373	Sergeant Preston; based on TV show	$8.00	$24.50	$57.50	£5.50	£16.50	£39.00
374	Woody Woodpecker by Walter Lantz	$5.25	$16.00	$38.00	£3.55	£10.50	£25.00
375	John Carter of Mars; Jesse Marsh cover and art; origin John Carter	$33.00	$97.50	$230.00	£21.00	£62.50	£150.00
376	Bugs Bunny in The Magic Sneeze	$9.50	$29.00	$67.50	£6.50	£19.50	£46.00
377	Susie Q. Smith	$5.25	$16.00	$38.00	£3.55	£10.50	£25.00
378	Tom Corbett, Space Cadet (1st appearance in comics); based on TV show; Al McWilliams art	$21.00	$62.50	$150.00	£14.00	£43.00	£100.00
379	Donald Duck in Southern Hospitality; no Carl Barks art	$7.50	$22.50	$52.50	£5.00	£15.00	£36.00
380	Raggedy Ann and Andy (has #378 on inside indicia)	$6.50	$19.50	$46.00	£4.25	£12.50	£30.00
381	Marge's Tubby (1st appearance)	$21.00	$62.50	$150.00	£14.00	£43.00	£100.00
382	Snow White and the Seven Dwarfs	$21.00	$62.50	$150.00	£14.00	£43.00	£100.00
383	Andy Panda by Walter Lantz	$4.25	$12.50	$30.00	£2.85	£8.50	£20.00
384	King of the Royal Mounted (has #383 on inside indicia)	$7.50	$22.50	$52.50	£5.00	£15.00	£36.00
385	Porky Pig in The Isle of Missing Ships	$5.25	$16.00	$38.00	£3.55	£10.50	£25.00
386	Uncle Scrooge in Only a Poor Old Man (1st appearance); Carl Barks cover and art	$160.00	$490.00	$1150.00	£110.00	£330.00	£770.00
387	Mickey Mouse in High Tibet	$8.00	$24.50	$57.50	£5.50	£16.50	£39.00
388	Oswald the Rabbit by Walter Lantz	$5.25	$16.00	$38.00	£3.55	£10.50	£25.00
389	Andy Hardy Comics	$5.25	$16.00	$38.00	£3.55	£10.50	£25.00
390	Woody Woodpecker by Walter Lantz (has #389 on inside indicia)	$5.25	$16.00	$38.00	£3.55	£10.50	£25.00
391	Uncle Wiggily	$7.50	$22.50	$52.50	£5.00	£15.00	£36.00
392	Hi-Yo Silver	$6.50	$19.50	$46.00	£4.25	£12.50	£30.00
393	Bugs Bunny	$9.50	$29.00	$67.50	£6.50	£19.50	£46.00
394	Donald Duck in The Malayalaya; Carl Barks cover only	$21.00	$62.50	$150.00	£14.00	£43.00	£100.00
395	Forlorn River by Zane Grey	$6.50	$19.50	$46.00	£4.25	£12.50	£30.00
396	Tales of the Texas Rangers, photo cover; based on TV show	$16.00	$49.00	$115.00	£10.50	£32.00	£75.00
397	Sergeant Preston of the Yukon; based on TV show	$9.50	$29.00	$67.50	£6.50	£19.50	£46.00
398	The Brownies; no Walt Kelly art	$5.25	$16.00	$38.00	£3.55	£10.50	£25.00
399	Porky Pig in The Lost Gold Mine	$5.25	$16.00	$38.00	£3.55	£10.50	£25.00
400	Tom Corbett, Space Cadet; based on TV show; Al McWilliams art	$19.00	$57.50	$135.00	£13.00	£40.00	£92.50
401	Mickey Mouse and Goofy's Mechanical Wizard	$6.50	$19.50	$46.00	£4.25	£12.50	£30.00
402	Mary Jane and Sniffles	$11.50	$35.00	$82.50	£7.75	£23.50	£55.00
403	L'il Bad Wolf	$12.50	$39.00	$90.00	£8.50	£26.00	£60.00
404	The Range Rider; photo cover	$16.00	$49.00	$115.00	£10.50	£32.00	£75.00
405	Woody Woodpecker by Walter Lantz	$5.25	$16.00	$38.00	£3.55	£10.50	£25.00
406	Tweety and Sylvester	$9.50	$29.00	$67.50	£6.50	£19.50	£46.00
407	Bugs Bunny, Foreign Legion-Hare	$6.50	$19.50	$46.00	£4.25	£12.50	£30.00
408	Donald Duck and The Golden Helmet; Carl Barks cover and art	$38.00	$110.00	$265.00	£26.00	£77.50	£185.00
409	Andy Panda	$4.25	$12.50	$30.00	£2.85	£8.50	£20.00
410	Porky Pig in The Water Wizard	$5.25	$16.00	$38.00	£3.55	£10.50	£25.00
411	Mickey Mouse and The Old Sea Dog	$6.50	$19.50	$46.00	£4.25	£12.50	£30.00
412	Nevada by Zane Grey	$5.25	$16.00	$38.00	£3.55	£10.50	£25.00
413	Robin Hood; photo cover						

Four Color #159

Four Color #178

Four Color #189

#	Title	$Good	$Fine	$N.Mint	£Good	£Fine	£N.Mint
		$16.00	*$49.00*	*$115.00*	£10.50	£32.00	£75.00
414	Bob Clampett's Beany and Cecil	*$23.50*	*$70.00*	*$165.00*	£16.00	£49.00	£115.00
415	Rootie Kazootie	*$12.50*	*$39.00*	*$90.00*	£8.50	£26.00	£60.00
416	Woody Woodpecker by Walter Lantz	*$5.25*	*$16.00*	*$38.00*	£3.55	£10.50	£25.00
417	Double Trouble with Goober	*$4.25*	*$12.50*	*$30.00*	£2.85	£8.50	£20.00
418	Rusty Riley; A Boy, A Horse and A Dog; Godwin art	*$5.25*	*$16.00*	*$38.00*	£3.55	£10.50	£25.00
419	Sergeant Preston	*$9.50*	*$29.00*	*$67.50*	£6.50	£19.50	£46.00
420	Bugs Bunny in The Mysterious Buckaroo	*$6.50*	*$19.50*	*$46.00*	£4.25	£12.50	£30.00
421	Tom Corbett, Space Cadet; Al McWilliams art	*$12.50*	*$39.00*	*$90.00*	£8.50	£26.00	£60.00
422	Donald Duck and The Gilded Man; Carl Barks cover and art	*$38.00*	*$110.00*	*$265.00*	£26.00	£77.50	£185.00
423	Rhubarb, Owner of The Brooklyn Ball Club	*$5.25*	*$16.00*	*$38.00*	£3.55	£10.50	£25.00
424	Flash Gordon - Test Flight in Space	*$9.50*	*$29.00*	*$67.50*	£6.50	£19.50	£46.00
425	The Return of Zorro	*$21.00*	*$62.50*	*$150.00*	£14.00	£43.00	£100.00
426	Porky Pig in The Scallywag Leprechaun	*$5.25*	*$16.00*	*$38.00*	£3.55	£10.50	£25.00
427	Mickey Mouse and The Wonderful Whizzix	*$5.25*	*$16.00*	*$38.00*	£3.55	£10.50	£25.00
428	Uncle Wiggily	*$5.25*	*$16.00*	*$38.00*	£3.55	£10.50	£25.00
429	Pluto in Why Dogs Leave Home	*$16.00*	*$49.00*	*$115.00*	£10.50	£32.00	£75.00
430	Marge's Tubby, The Shadow of a Man-Eater	*$9.50*	*$29.00*	*$67.50*	£6.50	£19.50	£46.00
431	Woody Woodpecker by Walter Lantz	*$4.25*	*$12.50*	*$30.00*	£2.85	£8.50	£20.00
432	Bugs Bunny and The Rabbit Olympics	*$6.50*	*$19.50*	*$46.00*	£4.25	£12.50	£30.00
433	Wildfire by Zane Grey	*$5.25*	*$16.00*	*$38.00*	£3.55	£10.50	£25.00
434	Rin Tin Tin - In Dark Danger	*$27.00*	*$80.00*	*$190.00*	£17.50	£52.50	£125.00
435	Frosty the Snowman	*$4.25*	*$12.50*	*$30.00*	£2.85	£8.50	£20.00
436	The Brownies; no Walt Kelly art	*$4.25*	*$12.50*	*$30.00*	£2.85	£8.50	£20.00
437	John Carter of Mars; Marsh art	*$21.00*	*$62.50*	*$150.00*	£14.00	£43.00	£100.00
438	Annie Oakley	*$19.00*	*$57.50*	*$135.00*	£13.00	£40.00	£92.50
439	Little Hiawatha	*$9.50*	*$29.00*	*$67.50*	£6.50	£19.50	£46.00
440	Black Beauty	*$4.25*	*$12.50*	*$30.00*	£2.85	£8.50	£20.00
441	Fearless Fagan	*$5.25*	*$16.00*	*$38.00*	£3.55	£10.50	£25.00
442	Peter Pan	*$9.50*	*$29.00*	*$67.50*	£6.50	£19.50	£46.00
443	Ben Bowie and his Mountain Men	*$9.50*	*$29.00*	*$67.50*	£6.50	£19.50	£46.00
444	Marge's Tubby	*$9.50*	*$29.00*	*$67.50*	£6.50	£19.50	£46.00
445	Charlie McCarthy	*$6.50*	*$19.50*	*$46.00*	£4.25	£12.50	£30.00
446	Captain Hook and Peter Pan	*$12.50*	*$39.00*	*$90.00*	£8.50	£26.00	£60.00
447	Andy Hardy Comics	*$3.25*	*$9.75*	*$23.00*	£2.10	£6.25	£15.00
448	Bob Clampett's Beany and Cecil	*$23.50*	*$70.00*	*$165.00*	£16.00	£49.00	£115.00
449	Tapan's Burro by Zane Grey	*$5.25*	*$16.00*	*$38.00*	£3.55	£10.50	£25.00
450	Duck Album; Carl Barks cover	*$8.00*	*$24.50*	*$57.50*	£5.50	£16.50	£39.00
451	Rusty Riley; Godwin art	*$5.25*	*$16.00*	*$38.00*	£3.55	£10.50	£25.00
452	Raggedy Ann & Andy	*$5.25*	*$16.00*	*$38.00*	£3.55	£10.50	£25.00
453	Susie Q. Smith	*$3.70*	*$11.00*	*$26.00*	£2.40	£7.25	£17.00
454	Krazy Kat Comics; no George Herriman	*$4.25*	*$12.50*	*$30.00*	£2.85	£8.50	£20.00
455	Johnny Mack Brown Comics	*$6.50*	*$19.50*	*$46.00*	£4.25	£12.50	£30.00
456	Uncle Scrooge Back To The Klondike; Carl Barks cover and art	*$80.00*	*$240.00*	*$570.00*	£55.00	£165.00	£385.00
457	Daffy	*$11.50*	*$35.00*	*$82.50*	£7.75	£23.50	£55.00
458	Oswald the Rabbit	*$3.70*	*$11.00*	*$26.00*	£2.40	£7.25	£17.00
459	Rootie Kazootie	*$9.50*	*$29.00*	*$67.50*	£6.50	£19.50	£46.00
460	Buck Jones	*$6.50*	*$19.50*	*$46.00*	£4.25	£12.50	£30.00
461	Marge's Tubby; Stanley art	*$9.50*	*$29.00*	*$67.50*	£6.50	£19.50	£46.00
462	Little Scouts	*$3.25*	*$9.75*	*$23.00*	£2.10	£6.25	£15.00
463	Petunia	*$4.25*	*$12.50*	*$30.00*	£2.85	£8.50	£20.00
464	Bozo	*$12.50*	*$39.00*	*$90.00*	£8.50	£26.00	£60.00
465	Francis The Famous Talking Mule	*$5.25*	*$16.00*	*$38.00*	£3.55	£10.50	£25.00
466	Rhubarb, the Millionaire Cat	*$3.70*	*$11.00*	*$26.00*	£2.40	£7.25	£17.00
467	Desert Gold by Zane Grey	*$5.25*	*$16.00*	*$38.00*	£3.55	£10.50	£25.00
468	Goofy	*$21.00*	*$62.50*	*$150.00*	£14.00	£43.00	£100.00
469	Beetle Bailey; Walker art	*$12.50*	*$39.00*	*$90.00*	£8.50	£26.00	£60.00
470	Elmer Fudd	*$3.25*	*$9.75*	*$23.00*	£2.10	£6.25	£15.00
471	Double Trouble with Goober	*$2.70*	*$8.00*	*$19.00*	£1.70	£5.00	£12.00
472	Wild Bill Elliott	*$6.50*	*$19.50*	*$46.00*	£4.25	£12.50	£30.00
473	L'il Bad Wolf	*$9.50*	*$29.00*	*$67.50*	£6.50	£19.50	£46.00
474	Mary Jane and Sniffles	*$9.50*	*$29.00*	*$67.50*	£6.50	£19.50	£46.00
475	M.G.M's The Two Mouseketeers	*$8.00*	*$24.50*	*$57.50*	£5.50	£16.50	£39.00
476	Rin Tin Tin	*$10.50*	*$32.00*	*$75.00*	£7.00	£21.00	£50.00
477	Bob Clampett's Beany and Cecil	*$21.00*	*$62.50*	*$150.00*	£14.00	£43.00	£100.00
478	Charlie McCarthy	*$6.50*	*$19.50*	*$46.00*	£4.25	£12.50	£30.00
479	Queen of the West Dale Evans	*$19.00*	*$57.50*	*$135.00*	£13.00	£40.00	£92.50
480	Andy Hardy Comics	*$3.25*	*$9.75*	*$23.00*	£2.10	£6.25	£15.00
481	Annie Oakley and Tagg	*$9.50*	*$29.00*	*$67.50*	£6.50	£19.50	£46.00
482	The Brownies; no Walt Kelly	*$3.70*	*$11.00*	*$26.00*	£2.40	£7.25	£17.00
483	Little Beaver	*$4.25*	*$12.50*	*$30.00*	£2.85	£8.50	£20.00
484	River Feud by Zane Grey	*$5.25*	*$16.00*	*$38.00*	£3.55	£10.50	£25.00
485	The Little People by Walt Scott	*$8.00*	*$24.50*	*$57.50*	£5.50	£16.50	£39.00
486	Rusty Riley; Godwin art	*$4.25*	*$12.50*	*$30.00*	£2.85	£8.50	£20.00
487	Mowgli, the Jungle Book	*$5.25*	*$16.00*	*$38.00*	£3.55	£10.50	£25.00
488	John Carter of Mars; Marsh art	*$21.00*	*$62.50*	*$150.00*	£14.00	£43.00	£100.00
489	Tweety and Sylvester	*$4.25*	*$12.50*	*$30.00*	£2.85	£8.50	£20.00
490	Jungle Jim	*$8.00*	*$24.50*	*$57.50*	£5.50	£16.50	£39.00
491	Silvertip; Kinstler art	*$10.50*	*$32.00*	*$75.00*	£7.00	£21.00	£50.00
492	Duck Album	*$8.00*	*$24.50*	*$57.50*	£5.50	£16.50	£39.00
493	Johnny Mack Brown Comics	*$7.50*	*$22.50*	*$52.50*	£5.00	£15.00	£36.00
494	The Little King	*$10.50*	*$32.00*	*$75.00*	£7.00	£21.00	£50.00
495	Uncle Scrooge; Carl Barks cover and art	*$60.00*	*$180.00*	*$420.00*	£40.00	£120.00	£280.00
496	The Green Hornet	*$38.00*	*$110.00*	*$265.00*	£26.00	£77.50	£185.00
497	The Sword of Zorro	*$19.00*	*$57.50*	*$135.00*	£13.00	£40.00	£92.50
498	Bugs Bunny's Album	*$5.25*	*$16.00*	*$38.00*	£3.55	£10.50	£25.00
499	M.G.M's Spike and Tyke	*$3.25*	*$9.75*	*$23.00*	£2.10	£6.25	£15.00
500	Buck Jones	*$6.50*	*$19.50*	*$46.00*	£4.25	£12.50	£30.00
501	Francis The Talking Mule	*$5.25*	*$16.00*	*$38.00*	£3.55	£10.50	£25.00
502	Rootie Kazootie	*$9.50*	*$29.00*	*$67.50*	£6.50	£19.50	£46.00
503	Uncle Wiggily	*$5.25*	*$16.00*	*$38.00*	£3.55	£10.50	£25.00
504	Krazy Kat	*$4.25*	*$12.50*	*$30.00*	£2.85	£8.50	£20.00
505	The Sword and the Rose; photo cover of Disney film	*$5.25*	*$16.00*	*$38.00*	£3.55	£10.50	£25.00
506	The Little Scouts	*$2.70*	*$8.00*	*$19.00*	£1.70	£5.00	£12.00
507	Oswald the Rabbit	*$3.25*	*$9.75*	*$23.00*	£2.10	£6.25	£15.00
508	Bozo	*$12.50*	*$39.00*	*$90.00*	£8.50	£26.00	£60.00
509	Pluto	*$8.00*	*$24.50*	*$57.50*	£5.50	£16.50	£39.00
510	Son of Black Beauty (has #511 on inside indicia)	*$3.70*	*$11.00*	*$26.00*	£2.40	£7.25	£17.00
511	Outlaw Trail by Zane Grey; Kinstler art	*$5.25*	*$16.00*	*$38.00*	£3.55	£10.50	£25.00
512	Flash Gordon	*$5.25*	*$16.00*	*$38.00*	£3.55	£10.50	£25.00
513	Ben Bowie and his Mountain Men	*$4.25*	*$12.50*	*$30.00*	£2.85	£8.50	£20.00
514	Frosty the Snowman	*$4.25*	*$12.50*	*$30.00*	£2.85	£8.50	£20.00
515	Andy Hardy	*$3.25*	*$9.75*	*$23.00*	£2.10	£6.25	£15.00
516	Double Trouble with Goober	*$3.25*	*$9.75*	*$23.00*	£2.10	£6.25	£15.00

#	Title	$Good	$Fine	$N.Mint	£Good	£Fine	£N.Mint
517	Chip 'n Dale	$11.50	$35.00	$82.50	£7.75	£23.50	£55.00
518	Rivets	$2.70	$8.00	$19.00	£1.70	£5.00	£12.00
519	Steve Canyon; no Milton Caniff art	$9.50	$29.00	$67.50	£6.50	£19.50	£46.00
520	Wild Bill Elliot; photo cover	$6.50	$19.50	$46.00	£4.25	£12.50	£30.00
521	Beetle Bailey	$5.25	$16.00	$38.00	£3.55	£10.50	£25.00
522	The Brownies (has #523 on inside indicia)	$3.70	$11.00	$26.00	£2.40	£7.25	£17.00
523	Rin Tin Tin; photo cover (has #524 on inside indicia)	$11.50	$35.00	$82.50	£7.75	£23.50	£55.00
524	Tweety and Sylvester	$4.25	$12.50	$30.00	£2.85	£8.50	£20.00
525	Santa Claus Funnies	$4.25	$12.50	$30.00	£2.85	£8.50	£20.00
526	Napoleon	$2.70	$8.00	$19.00	£1.70	£5.00	£12.00
527	Charlie McCarthy	$6.50	$19.50	$46.00	£4.25	£12.50	£30.00
528	Queen of the West Dale Evans; photo cover	$10.50	$32.00	$75.00	£7.00	£21.00	£50.00
529	Little Beaver	$4.25	$12.50	$30.00	£2.85	£8.50	£20.00
530	Bob Clampett's Beany and Cecil	$21.00	$62.50	$150.00	£14.00	£43.00	£100.00
531	Duck Album	$7.50	$22.50	$52.50	£5.00	£15.00	£36.00
532	The Rustlers by Zane Grey	$6.50	$19.50	$46.00	£4.25	£12.50	£30.00
533	Raggedy Ann and Andy	$6.50	$19.50	$46.00	£4.25	£12.50	£30.00
534	Western Marshall; Kinstler art	$6.50	$19.50	$46.00	£4.25	£12.50	£30.00
535	I Love Lucy; photo cover	$44.00	$130.00	$305.00	£29.00	£87.50	£205.00
536	Daffy Duck	$5.25	$16.00	$38.00	£3.55	£10.50	£25.00
537	Stormy the Thoroughbred and Pluto	$5.25	$16.00	$38.00	£3.55	£10.50	£25.00
538	The Mask of Zorro; Kinstler art	$21.00	$62.50	$150.00	£14.00	£43.00	£100.00
539	Ben and Me (has #540 on inside indicia)	$4.25	$12.50	$30.00	£2.85	£8.50	£20.00
540	The Knights of the Round Table; photo cover	$8.00	$24.50	$57.50	£5.50	£16.50	£39.00
541	Johnny MAck Brown	$7.50	$22.50	$52.50	£5.00	£15.00	£36.00
542	Super Circus	$7.50	$22.50	$52.50	£5.00	£15.00	£36.00
543	Uncle Wiggily	$7.50	$22.50	$52.50	£5.00	£15.00	£36.00
544	Rob Roy; Russ Manning art; photo cover	$10.50	$32.00	$75.00	£7.00	£21.00	£50.00
545	Pinocchio; part reprint Four Colour #92	$10.50	$32.00	$75.00	£7.00	£21.00	£50.00
546	Buck Jones	$6.50	$19.50	$46.00	£4.25	£12.50	£30.00
547	Francis The Talking Mule	$6.50	$19.50	$46.00	£4.25	£12.50	£30.00
548	Krazy Kat; no Herriman art	$4.25	$12.50	$30.00	£2.85	£8.50	£20.00
549	Oswald the Rabbit by Walter Lantz (has #548 on inside indicia)	$3.25	$9.75	$23.00	£2.10	£6.25	£15.00
550	The Little Scouts	$3.25	$9.75	$23.00	£2.10	£6.25	£15.00
551	Bozo	$12.50	$39.00	$90.00	£8.50	£26.00	£60.00
552	Beetle Bailey; Walker art	$5.25	$16.00	$38.00	£3.55	£10.50	£25.00
553	Susie Q. Smith	$4.25	$12.50	$30.00	£2.85	£8.50	£20.00
554	Rusty Riley; Godwin art, strip reprints	$4.25	$12.50	$30.00	£2.85	£8.50	£20.00
555	Range War by Zane Grey	$5.25	$16.00	$38.00	£3.55	£10.50	£25.00
556	Double Trouble with Goober	$3.25	$9.75	$23.00	£2.10	£6.25	£15.00
557	Ben Bowie and his Mountain Men (has #554 on inside indicia)	$5.25	$16.00	$38.00	£3.55	£10.50	£25.00
558	Elmer Fudd	$3.25	$9.75	$23.00	£2.10	£6.25	£15.00
559	I Love Lucy; photo cover	$33.00	$97.50	$230.00	£21.00	£62.50	£150.00
560	Duck Album	$8.00	$24.50	$57.50	£5.50	£16.50	£39.00
561	Mister Magoo	$11.50	$35.00	$82.50	£7.75	£23.50	£55.00
562	Goofy	$10.50	$32.00	$75.00	£7.00	£21.00	£50.00
563	Rhubarb the Millionaire Cat	$4.25	$12.50	$30.00	£2.85	£8.50	£20.00
564	L'il Bad Wolf	$8.00	$24.50	$57.50	£5.50	£16.50	£39.00
565	Jungle Jim	$4.25	$12.50	$30.00	£2.85	£8.50	£20.00
566	Son of Black Beauty	$4.25	$12.50	$30.00	£2.85	£8.50	£20.00
567	Prince Valiant; Bob Fuji art, photo cover from film	$10.50	$32.00	$75.00	£7.00	£21.00	£50.00
568	Gypsy Colt	$5.25	$16.00	$38.00	£3.55	£10.50	£25.00
569	Priscilla's Pop	$3.70	$11.00	$26.00	£2.40	£7.25	£17.00
570	Bob Clampett's Beany and Cecil	$23.50	$70.00	$165.00	£16.00	£49.00	£115.00
571	Charlie McCarthy	$6.50	$19.50	$46.00	£4.25	£12.50	£30.00
572	Silvertip; Kinstler art	$6.50	$19.50	$46.00	£4.25	£12.50	£30.00
573	Little People by Walt Scoot	$4.25	$12.50	$30.00	£2.85	£8.50	£20.00
574	The Hand of Zorro	$19.00	$57.50	$135.00	£13.00	£40.00	£92.50
575	Annie Oakley; photo cover	$9.50	$29.00	$67.50	£6.50	£19.50	£46.00
576	Angel	$3.25	$9.75	$23.00	£2.10	£6.25	£15.00
577	M.G.M's Spike and Tyke	$3.25	$9.75	$23.00	£2.10	£6.25	£15.00
578	Steve Canyon; no Milton Caniff art	$5.25	$16.00	$38.00	£3.55	£10.50	£25.00
579	Francis The Talking Mule	$5.25	$16.00	$38.00	£3.55	£10.50	£25.00
580	Luke Short and Six Gun Ranch	$5.25	$16.00	$38.00	£3.55	£10.50	£25.00
581	Chip 'n Dale	$5.25	$16.00	$38.00	£3.55	£10.50	£25.00
582	Mowgli, The Jungle Book	$4.25	$12.50	$30.00	£2.85	£8.50	£20.00
583	The Lost Wagon Train by Zane Grey	$5.25	$16.00	$38.00	£3.55	£10.50	£25.00
584	Johnny Mack Brown; photo cover	$7.50	$22.50	$52.50	£5.00	£15.00	£36.00
585	Bugs Bunny's Album	$5.25	$16.00	$38.00	£3.55	£10.50	£25.00
586	Duck Album	$6.50	$19.50	$46.00	£4.25	£12.50	£30.00
587	The Little Scouts	$3.25	$9.75	$23.00	£2.10	£6.25	£15.00
588	King Richard and the Crusades; Matt Baker art, photo cover	$12.50	$39.00	$90.00	£8.50	£26.00	£60.00
589	Buck Jones	$6.50	$19.50	$46.00	£4.25	£12.50	£30.00
590	Hansel and Gretel; photo collage cover	$6.50	$19.50	$46.00	£4.25	£12.50	£30.00
591	Western Marshall; Kinstler art	$6.50	$19.50	$46.00	£4.25	£12.50	£30.00
592	Super Circus	$6.50	$19.50	$46.00	£4.25	£12.50	£30.00
593	Oswald the Rabbit by Walter Lantz	$3.25	$9.75	$23.00	£2.10	£6.25	£15.00
594	Bozo	$12.50	$39.00	$90.00	£8.50	£26.00	£60.00
595	Pluto	$5.25	$16.00	$38.00	£3.55	£10.50	£25.00
596	very scarce in the U.K. Turok, Son of Stone (1st appearance); painted dinosaur cover	$92.50	$275.00	$650.00	£60.00	£180.00	£430.00
597	Little King	$8.00	$24.50	$57.50	£5.50	£16.50	£39.00
598	Captain Davy Jones	$3.70	$11.00	$26.00	£2.40	£7.25	£17.00
599	Ben Bowie and his Mountain Men	$4.25	$12.50	$30.00	£2.85	£8.50	£20.00
600	Daisy Duck's Diary	$7.50	$22.50	$52.50	£5.00	£15.00	£36.00
601	Frosty the Snowman	$4.25	$12.50	$30.00	£2.85	£8.50	£20.00
602	Mister Magoo and Gerald McBoing-Boing	$10.50	$32.00	$75.00	£7.00	£21.00	£50.00
603	M.G.M's The Two Mouseketeers	$5.25	$16.00	$38.00	£3.55	£10.50	£25.00
604	Shadow on the Trail by Zane Grey	$5.25	$16.00	$38.00	£3.55	£10.50	£25.00
605	The Brownies; no Walt Kelly art	$5.25	$16.00	$38.00	£3.55	£10.50	£25.00
606	Sir Lancelot	$9.50	$29.00	$67.50	£6.50	£19.50	£46.00
607	Santa Claus Funnies	$4.25	$12.50	$30.00	£2.85	£8.50	£20.00
608	Silvertip in Valley of Vanishing Men; Kinstler art	$5.25	$16.00	$38.00	£3.55	£10.50	£25.00
609	The Littlest Outlaw (Disney); photo cover	$9.50	$29.00	$67.50	£6.50	£19.50	£46.00
610	Drum Beat; Alan Ladd photo cover	$12.50	$39.00	$90.00	£8.50	£26.00	£60.00
611	Duck Album	$8.00	$24.50	$57.50	£5.50	£16.50	£39.00
612	Little Beaver	$4.25	$12.50	$30.00	£2.85	£8.50	£20.00
613	Western Marshall; Kinstler art	$6.50	$19.50	$46.00	£4.25	£12.50	£30.00
614	20,000 Leagues Under the Sea (Disney); photo cover	$12.50	$39.00	$90.00	£8.50	£26.00	£60.00
615	Daffy Duck	$5.25	$16.00	$38.00	£3.55	£10.50	£25.00
616	To The Last Man by Zane Grey	$5.25	$16.00	$38.00	£3.55	£10.50	£25.00
617	The Quest of Zorro	$16.00	$49.00	$115.00	£10.50	£32.00	£75.00
618	Johnny Mack Brown; photo cover	$6.50	$19.50	$46.00	£4.25	£12.50	£30.00
619	Krazy Kat; no Herriman art	$5.25	$16.00	$38.00	£3.55	£10.50	£25.00
620	Mowgli Jungle Book	$5.25	$16.00	$38.00	£3.55	£10.50	£25.00
621	Francis The Talking Mule	$5.25	$16.00	$38.00	£3.55	£10.50	£25.00
622	Beetle Bailey	$5.25	$16.00	$38.00	£3.55	£10.50	£25.00

No.	Title	$Good	$Fine	$N.Mint	£Good	£Fine	£N.Mint
623	Oswald the Rabbit by Walter Lantz	$3.25	$9.75	$23.00	£2.10	£6.25	£15.00
624	Treasure Island (Disney); photo cover	$12.50	$39.00	$90.00	£8.50	£26.00	£60.00
625	Beaver Valley (Disney); photo cover	$9.50	$29.00	$67.50	£6.50	£19.50	£46.00
626	Ben Bowie and Hs Mountain Men	$5.25	$16.00	$38.00	£3.55	£10.50	£25.00
627	Goofy	$9.50	$29.00	$67.50	£6.50	£19.50	£46.00
628	Elmer Fudd	$3.25	$9.75	$23.00	£2.10	£6.25	£15.00
629	Lady and the Tramp	$7.50	$22.50	$52.50	£5.00	£15.00	£36.00
630	Priscilla's Pop	$3.70	$11.00	$26.00	£2.40	£7.25	£17.00
631	Davy Crockett, Indian Fighter; Fess Parker photo cover	$21.00	$62.50	$150.00	£14.00	£43.00	£100.00
632	Fighting Caravans by Zane Grey	$6.50	$19.50	$46.00	£4.25	£12.50	£30.00
633	Little People by Walt Scott	$6.50	$19.50	$46.00	£4.25	£12.50	£30.00
634	Walt Disney's Lady and the Tramp Album	$6.50	$19.50	$46.00	£4.25	£12.50	£30.00
635	Bob Clampett's Beany and Cecil	$21.00	$62.50	$150.00	£14.00	£43.00	£100.00
636	Chip 'n Dale	$3.25	$9.75	$23.00	£2.10	£6.25	£15.00
637	Silvertip; Kinstler art	$5.25	$16.00	$38.00	£3.55	£10.50	£25.00
638	M.G.M's Spike and Tyke	$3.25	$9.75	$23.00	£2.10	£6.25	£15.00
639	Davy Crockett at the Alamo; Fess Parker photo cover	$21.00	$62.50	$150.00	£14.00	£43.00	£100.00
640	Western Marshall; Kinstler art	$6.50	$19.50	$46.00	£4.25	£12.50	£30.00
641	Steve Canyon by Milton Caniff	$5.25	$16.00	$38.00	£3.55	£10.50	£25.00
642	M.G.M's The Two Mouseketeers	$4.25	$12.50	$30.00	£2.85	£8.50	£20.00
643	Wild Bill Elliot; photo cover	$5.25	$16.00	$38.00	£3.55	£10.50	£25.00
644	Sir Walter Raleigh (from the film "The Virgin Queen"); photo cover	$9.50	$29.00	$67.50	£6.50	£19.50	£46.00
645	Johnny Mack Brown; photo cover	$7.50	$22.50	$52.50	£5.00	£15.00	£36.00
646	Dottie Dripple and Taffy	$4.25	$12.50	$30.00	£2.85	£8.50	£20.00
647	Bugs Bunny Album	$6.50	$19.50	$46.00	£4.25	£12.50	£30.00
648	Tales of the Texas Rangers; photo cover	$7.50	$22.50	$52.50	£5.00	£15.00	£36.00
649	Duck Album	$6.50	$19.50	$46.00	£4.25	£12.50	£30.00
650	Prince Valiant by Bob Fuje	$6.50	$19.50	$46.00	£4.25	£12.50	£30.00
651	King Colt; Kinstler art	$5.25	$16.00	$38.00	£3.55	£10.50	£25.00
652	Buck Jones	$4.25	$12.50	$30.00	£2.85	£8.50	£20.00
653	Smokey Bear	$11.50	$35.00	$82.50	£7.75	£23.50	£55.00
654	Pluto	$5.25	$16.00	$38.00	£3.55	£10.50	£25.00
655	Francis The Talking Mule	$5.25	$16.00	$38.00	£3.55	£10.50	£25.00
656	very scarce in the U.K. Turok, Son of Stone (#2) - see #596	$55.00	$165.00	$385.00	£36.00	£105.00	£255.00
657	Ben Bowie and His Mountain Men	$5.25	$16.00	$38.00	£3.55	£10.50	£25.00
658	Goofy	$9.50	$29.00	$67.50	£6.50	£19.50	£46.00
659	Daisy Duck Diary	$6.50	$19.50	$46.00	£4.25	£12.50	£30.00
660	Little Beaver	$4.25	$12.50	$30.00	£2.85	£8.50	£20.00
661	Frosty the Snowman	$4.25	$12.50	$30.00	£2.85	£8.50	£20.00
662	Zoo Parade (TV)	$6.50	$19.50	$46.00	£4.25	£12.50	£30.00
663	Winky Dink (TV)	$9.50	$29.00	$67.50	£6.50	£19.50	£46.00
664	Davy Crockett in The Great Keelboat Race; Fess Parker photo cover	$21.00	$62.50	$150.00	£14.00	£43.00	£100.00
665	The African Lion (Disney)	$7.50	$22.50	$52.50	£5.00	£15.00	£36.00
666	Santa Claus Funnies	$4.25	$12.50	$30.00	£2.85	£8.50	£20.00
667	Silvertip and the Stolen Stallion; Kinstler art	$5.25	$16.00	$38.00	£3.55	£10.50	£25.00
668	Dumbo (1955)	$10.50	$32.00	$75.00	£7.00	£21.00	£50.00
668	Alternate Cover Edition, Dumbo with different cover (1958)	$5.50	$17.00	$34.00	£3.80	£11.50	£23.00
669	Robin Hood; reprint of #413; photo cover	$6.50	$19.50	$46.00	£4.25	£12.50	£30.00
670	M.G.M's The Mouse Musketeers	$4.25	$12.50	$30.00	£2.85	£8.50	£20.00
671	Davy Crockett and the River Pirates; Fess Parker photo cover; Jesse Marsh art	$21.00	$62.50	$150.00	£14.00	£43.00	£100.00

No.	Title	$Good	$Fine	$N.Mint	£Good	£Fine	£N.Mint
672	Quentin Durward (Robert Taylor film); photo cover	$9.50	$29.00	$67.50	£6.50	£19.50	£46.00
673	Buffalo Bill Junior; photo cover	$9.50	$29.00	$67.50	£6.50	£19.50	£46.00
674	The Little Rascals (TV)	$9.50	$29.00	$67.50	£6.50	£19.50	£46.00
675	Steve Donovan, Western Marshal; Kinstler art; photo cover	$9.50	$29.00	$67.50	£6.50	£19.50	£46.00
676	Will-Yum!	$3.25	$9.75	$23.00	£2.10	£6.25	£15.00
677	The Little King	$7.50	$22.50	$52.50	£5.00	£15.00	£36.00
678	The Last Hunt; photo cover	$8.00	$24.50	$57.50	£5.50	£16.50	£39.00
679	Gunsmoke (TV)	$16.00	$49.00	$115.00	£10.50	£32.00	£75.00
680	Out Our Way with Worry Wart	$3.25	$9.75	$23.00	£2.10	£6.25	£15.00
681	Forever Darling with Lucille Ball	$14.00	$43.00	$100.00	£9.25	£28.00	£65.00
682	When Knighthood was in Flower; reprint of #505, photo cover	$9.50	$29.00	$67.50	£6.50	£19.50	£46.00
683	Hi and Lois	$3.25	$9.75	$23.00	£2.10	£6.25	£15.00
684	Helen of Troy; photo cover, John Buscema art	$16.00	$49.00	$115.00	£10.50	£32.00	£75.00
685	Johnny Mack Brown; photo cover	$8.00	$24.50	$57.50	£5.50	£16.50	£39.00
686	Duck Album	$8.00	$24.50	$57.50	£5.50	£16.50	£39.00
687	Indian Fighter; Kirk Douglas photo cover	$8.00	$24.50	$57.50	£5.50	£16.50	£39.00
688	Alexander the Great; photo cover, John Buscena art	$8.00	$24.50	$57.50	£5.50	£16.50	£39.00
689	Elmer Fudd	$3.25	$9.75	$23.00	£2.10	£6.25	£15.00
690	The Conqueror; John Wayne photo cover	$21.00	$62.50	$150.00	£14.00	£43.00	£100.00
691	Dottie Dripple and Taffy	$3.70	$11.00	$26.00	£2.40	£7.25	£17.00
692	Little People by Walt Scott	$3.70	$11.00	$26.00	£2.40	£7.25	£17.00
693	Song of the South; part reprint #129	$12.50	$39.00	$90.00	£8.50	£26.00	£60.00
694	Super Circus; photo cover	$6.50	$19.50	$46.00	£4.25	£12.50	£30.00
695	Little Beaver	$4.25	$12.50	$30.00	£2.85	£8.50	£20.00
696	Krazy Kat; no Herriman art	$4.25	$12.50	$30.00	£2.85	£8.50	£20.00
697	Oswald the Rabbit by Walter Lantz	$4.25	$12.50	$30.00	£2.85	£8.50	£20.00
698	Francis The Talking Mule	$5.25	$16.00	$38.00	£3.55	£10.50	£25.00
699	Prince Valiant by Bob Fuje	$6.50	$19.50	$46.00	£4.25	£12.50	£30.00
700	Water Birds & Olympic Elk (Disney); photo cover	$9.50	$29.00	$67.50	£6.50	£19.50	£46.00
701	Jiminy Cricket	$9.50	$29.00	$67.50	£6.50	£19.50	£46.00
702	Goofy Success Story	$9.50	$29.00	$67.50	£6.50	£19.50	£46.00
703	Scamp	$12.50	$39.00	$90.00	£8.50	£26.00	£60.00
704	Pricilla's Pop	$3.70	$11.00	$26.00	£2.40	£7.25	£17.00
705	Brave Eagle; photo cover	$7.50	$22.50	$52.50	£5.00	£15.00	£36.00
706	Bongo and Lumpjaw	$5.25	$16.00	$38.00	£3.55	£10.50	£25.00
707	Corky and White Shadow; photo cover	$9.50	$29.00	$67.50	£6.50	£19.50	£46.00
708	Smokey Bear	$5.25	$16.00	$38.00	£3.55	£10.50	£25.00
709	The Searchers; John Wayne photo cover	$38.00	$110.00	$265.00	£26.00	£77.50	£185.00
710	Francis The Talking Mule	$5.25	$16.00	$38.00	£3.55	£10.50	£25.00
711	The Two Mouseketeers	$3.25	$9.75	$23.00	£2.10	£6.25	£15.00
712	The Great Locomotive Chase; photo cover	$9.50	$29.00	$67.50	£6.50	£19.50	£46.00
713	The Animal World (Disney film)	$6.50	$19.50	$46.00	£4.25	£12.50	£30.00
714	Spin and Marty (Disney TV); photo cover	$16.00	$49.00	$115.00	£10.50	£32.00	£75.00
715	Timmy	$4.25	$12.50	$30.00	£2.85	£8.50	£20.00
716	Man In Space (Disney film)	$12.50	$39.00	$90.00	£8.50	£26.00	£60.00
717	Moby Dick; photo cover	$9.50	$29.00	$67.50	£6.50	£19.50	£46.00
718	Dottie Dripple and Daffy	$3.25	$9.75	$23.00	£2.10	£6.25	£15.00
719	Prince Valiant; Bob Fuje art	$7.50	$22.50	$52.50	£5.00	£15.00	£36.00
720	Gunsmoke; photo cover	$9.50	$29.00	$67.50	£6.50	£19.50	£46.00
721	Captain Kangaroo; photo cover	$19.00	$57.50	$135.00	£13.00	£40.00	£92.50

No.	Title	$Good	$Fine	$N.Mint	£Good	£Fine	£N.Mint
722	Johnny Mack Brown; photo cover	$8.00	$24.50	$57.50	£5.50	£16.50	£39.00
723	Santiago; Alan Ladd photo cover; Kinstler art	$16.00	$49.00	$115.00	£10.50	£32.00	£75.00
724	Bugs Bunny Album	$6.50	$19.50	$46.00	£4.25	£12.50	£30.00
725	Elmer Fudd	$3.25	$9.75	$23.00	£2.10	£6.25	£15.00
726	Duck Album	$6.50	$19.50	$46.00	£4.25	£12.50	£30.00
727	The Nature of Things; Jesse Marsh art	$9.50	$29.00	$67.50	£6.50	£19.50	£46.00
728	The Two Mouseketeers	$3.25	$9.75	$23.00	£2.10	£6.25	£15.00
729	Bob, Son of Battle	$3.70	$11.00	$26.00	£2.40	£7.25	£17.00
730	Smokey Stover	$3.70	$11.00	$26.00	£2.40	£7.25	£17.00
731	Silvertip; Kinstler art	$5.25	$16.00	$38.00	£3.55	£10.50	£25.00
732	The Challenge of Zorro	$19.00	$57.50	$135.00	£13.00	£40.00	£92.50
733	Buck Jones	$4.25	$12.50	$30.00	£2.85	£8.50	£20.00
734	Cheyenne; Clint Walker photo cover	$21.00	$62.50	$150.00	£14.00	£43.00	£100.00
735	Crusader Rabbit, scarce	$33.00	$97.50	$230.00	£21.00	£62.50	£150.00
736	Pluto	$6.50	$19.50	$46.00	£4.25	£12.50	£30.00
737	Steve Canyon; Milton Caniff art	$6.50	$19.50	$46.00	£4.25	£12.50	£30.00
738	Westward Ho The Wagons; Fess Parker photo cover	$14.00	$43.00	$100.00	£9.25	£28.00	£65.00
739	Bounty Guns; Drucker art	$5.25	$16.00	$38.00	£3.55	£10.50	£25.00
740	Chilly Willy by Walter Lantz	$5.25	$16.00	$38.00	£3.55	£10.50	£25.00
741	The Fastest Gun Alive; photo cover	$9.50	$29.00	$67.50	£6.50	£19.50	£46.00
742	Buffalo Bill Junior; photo cover	$5.25	$16.00	$38.00	£3.55	£10.50	£25.00
743	Daisy Duck's Diary	$6.50	$19.50	$46.00	£4.25	£12.50	£30.00
744	Little Beaver	$3.70	$11.00	$26.00	£2.40	£7.25	£17.00
745	Francis The Talking Mule	$5.25	$16.00	$38.00	£3.55	£10.50	£25.00
746	Dottie Dripple and Taffy	$3.25	$9.75	$23.00	£2.10	£6.25	£15.00
747	Goofy	$9.50	$29.00	$67.50	£6.50	£19.50	£46.00
748	Frosty the Snowman	$3.70	$11.00	$26.00	£2.40	£7.25	£17.00
749	Secrets of Life; photo cover	$8.00	$24.50	$57.50	£5.50	£16.50	£39.00
750	The Great Cat Family (Disney film)	$8.00	$24.50	$57.50	£5.50	£16.50	£39.00
751	Our Miss Brooks; photo cover	$9.50	$29.00	$67.50	£6.50	£19.50	£46.00
752	Mandrake the Magician	$11.50	$35.00	$82.50	£7.75	£23.50	£55.00
753	Walt Scott's The Little People	$4.25	$12.50	$30.00	£2.85	£8.50	£20.00
754	Smokey The Bear	$5.25	$16.00	$38.00	£3.55	£10.50	£25.00
755	The Littlest Snowman	$5.25	$16.00	$38.00	£3.55	£10.50	£25.00
756	Santa Claus Funnies	$4.25	$12.50	$30.00	£2.85	£8.50	£20.00
757	The Story of Jesse James; photo cover	$11.50	$35.00	$82.50	£7.75	£23.50	£55.00
758	Bear Country (Disney film)	$7.50	$22.50	$52.50	£5.00	£15.00	£36.00
759	Circus Boy; Mickey Dolenz photo cover	$14.00	$43.00	$100.00	£9.25	£28.00	£65.00
760	The Hardy Boys; photo cover	$16.00	$49.00	$115.00	£10.50	£32.00	£75.00
761	Howdy Doody	$11.50	$35.00	$82.50	£7.75	£23.50	£55.00
762	Sharkfighters; photo cover; John Buscema art	$16.00	$49.00	$115.00	£10.50	£32.00	£75.00
763	Grandma Duck's Farm Friends	$9.50	$29.00	$67.50	£6.50	£19.50	£46.00
764	The Two Mouseketeers	$3.25	$9.75	$23.00	£2.10	£6.25	£15.00
765	Will-Yum!	$3.25	$9.75	$23.00	£2.10	£6.25	£15.00
766	Buffalo Bill Junior; photo cover	$5.25	$16.00	$38.00	£3.55	£10.50	£25.00
767	Spin and Marty; photo cover	$10.50	$32.00	$75.00	£7.00	£21.00	£50.00
768	Steve Donovan; photo cover; Kinstler art	$7.50	$22.50	$52.50	£5.00	£15.00	£36.00
769	Gunsmoke	$7.50	$22.50	$52.50	£5.00	£15.00	£36.00
770	Brave Eagle; photo cover	$4.25	$12.50	$30.00	£2.85	£8.50	£20.00
771	Brand of Empire; Drucker art	$5.25	$16.00	$38.00	£3.55	£10.50	£25.00
772	Cheyenne; Clint Walker photo cover	$9.50	$29.00	$67.50	£6.50	£19.50	£46.00
773	The Brave One; photo cover	$6.50	$19.50	$46.00	£4.25	£12.50	£30.00
774	Hi and Lois	$3.25	$9.75	$23.00	£2.10	£6.25	£15.00
775	Sir Lancelot; photo cover; John Buscema art	$11.50	$35.00	$82.50	£7.75	£23.50	£55.00
776	Johnny Mack Brown; photo cover	$7.50	$22.50	$52.50	£5.00	£15.00	£36.00
777	Scamp	$8.00	$24.50	$57.50	£5.50	£16.50	£39.00
778	The Little Rascals	$4.25	$12.50	$30.00	£2.85	£8.50	£20.00
779	The Indian Fighter	$6.50	$19.50	$46.00	£4.25	£12.50	£30.00
780	scarce in the U.K. Captain Kangaroo	$19.00	$57.50	$135.00	£13.00	£40.00	£92.50
781	Fury; photo cover	$11.50	$35.00	$82.50	£7.75	£23.50	£55.00
782	Duck Album	$7.50	$22.50	$52.50	£5.00	£15.00	£36.00
783	Elmer Fudd	$3.25	$9.75	$23.00	£2.10	£6.25	£15.00
784	Around The World in Eighty Days; photo cover	$8.00	$24.50	$57.50	£5.50	£16.50	£39.00
785	Circus Boy; Mickey Dolenz photo cover	$12.50	$39.00	$90.00	£8.50	£26.00	£60.00
786	Cinderella - part reprint #272	$6.50	$19.50	$46.00	£4.25	£12.50	£30.00
787	Little Hiawatha	$6.50	$19.50	$46.00	£4.25	£12.50	£30.00
788	Prince Valiant; Bob Fuje art	$6.50	$19.50	$46.00	£4.25	£12.50	£30.00

Four Color #1061

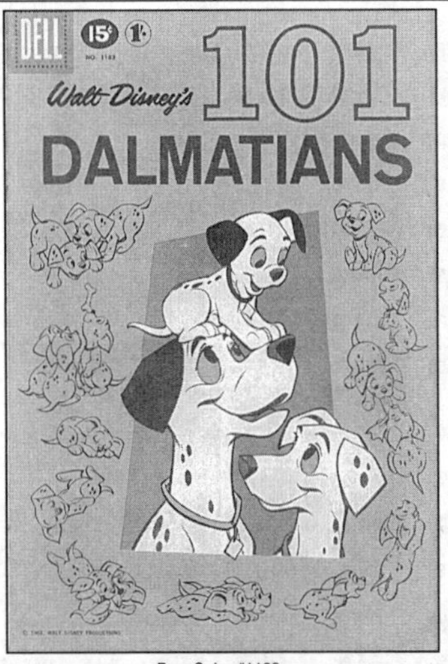

Four Color #1183

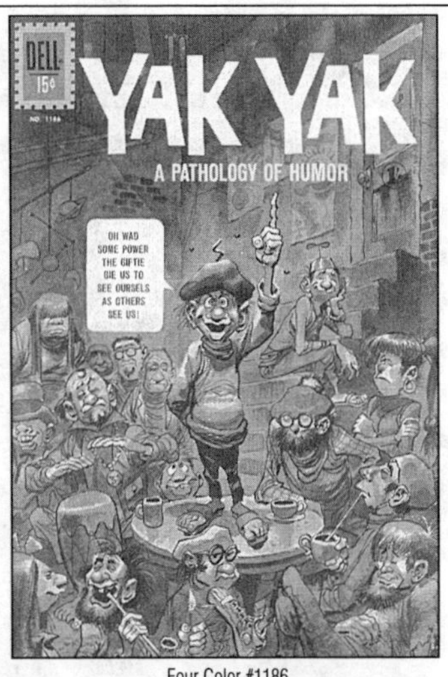

Four Color #1186

No.	Title	$Good	$Fine	$N.Mint	£Good	£Fine	£N.Mint
789	Silvertip; Kinstler art	$5.25	$16.00	$38.00	£3.55	£10.50	£25.00
790	The Wings of Eagles; John Wayne photo cover; Alex Toth art	$21.00	$62.50	$150.00	£14.00	£43.00	£100.00
791	The 77th Bengal Lancers; photo cover	$9.50	$29.00	$67.50	£6.50	£19.50	£46.00
792	Oswald the Rabbit	$3.25	$9.75	$23.00	£2.10	£6.25	£15.00
793	Morty Meekle	$3.70	$11.00	$26.00	£2.40	£7.25	£17.00
794	The Count of Mont Cristo; John Buscema art	$11.50	$35.00	$82.50	£7.75	£23.50	£55.00
795	Jiminy Cricket	$7.50	$22.50	$52.50	£5.00	£15.00	£36.00
796	Madelein & Genevieve	$4.25	$12.50	$30.00	£2.85	£8.50	£20.00
797	Gunsmoke; photo cover	$8.00	$24.50	$57.50	£5.50	£16.50	£39.00
798	Buffalo Bill Junior; photo cover	$6.50	$19.50	$46.00	£4.25	£12.50	£30.00
799	Priscilla's Pop	$3.70	$11.00	$26.00	£2.40	£7.25	£17.00
800	The Buccaneers; photo cover	$8.00	$24.50	$57.50	£5.50	£16.50	£39.00
801	Dottie Dripple and Taffy	$4.30	$13.00	$26.00	£2.80	£8.50	£17.00
802	Goofy	$10.50	$33.00	$65.00	£7.25	£22.00	£44.00
803	Cheyenne; Clint Walker photo cover	$10.50	$33.00	$65.00	£7.25	£22.00	£44.00
804	Steve Canyon; Milton Caniff art	$6.50	$19.50	$39.00	£4.30	£13.00	£26.00
805	Crusader Rabbit	$29.00	$87.50	$175.00	£20.00	£60.00	£120.00
806	Scamp	$9.50	$29.00	$57.50	£6.50	£19.50	£39.00
807	Savage Range; Drucker art	$6.50	$19.50	$39.00	£4.30	£13.00	£26.00
808	Spin and Marty; photo cover; less common	$12.50	$39.00	$77.50	£8.25	£25.00	£50.00
809	Walt Scott's The Little People	$4.30	$13.00	$26.00	£2.80	£8.50	£17.00
810	Francis The Talking Mule	$5.50	$16.50	$33.00	£3.65	£11.00	£22.00
811	Howdy Doody	$12.50	$39.00	$77.50	£8.25	£25.00	£50.00
812	The Big Land; Alan Ladd photo cover	$15.00	$45.00	$90.00	£10.00	£30.00	£60.00
813	Circus Boy; Mickey Dolenz photo cover	$15.00	$45.00	$90.00	£10.00	£30.00	£60.00
814	Covered Wagons, Ho! - Donald Duck and Mickey Mouse	$8.25	$25.00	$50.00	£5.75	£17.50	£35.00
815	Dragoon Wells Massacre; photo cover	$10.50	$33.00	$65.00	£7.25	£22.00	£44.00
816	Brave Eagle; photo cover	$5.50	$16.50	$33.00	£3.65	£11.00	£22.00
817	Little Beaver	$4.30	$13.00	$26.00	£2.80	£8.50	£17.00
818	Smokey the Bear	$6.50	$19.50	$39.00	£4.30	£13.00	£26.00
819	Mickey Mouse in Magicland	$5.50	$16.50	$33.00	£3.65	£11.00	£22.00
820	The Oklahoman; photo cover	$12.50	$39.00	$77.50	£8.25	£25.00	£50.00
821	Wringle Wrangle; Fess Parker photo cover; Jesse Marsh art	$12.50	$39.00	$77.50	£8.25	£25.00	£50.00
822	Paul Revere's Ride, scarce; Alex Toth art	$21.50	$65.00	$130.00	£14.50	£44.00	£87.50
823	Timmy	$4.30	$13.00	$26.00	£2.80	£8.50	£17.00
824	Pride and Passion; Cary Grant and Frank Sinatra photo cover	$12.50	$39.00	$77.50	£8.25	£25.00	£50.00
825	The Little Rascals	$5.50	$16.50	$33.00	£3.65	£11.00	£22.00
826	Spin and Marty and Annette; photo cover	$33.00	$97.50	$195.00	£21.50	£65.00	£130.00
827	Smokey Stover	$4.30	$13.00	$26.00	£2.80	£8.50	£17.00
828	Buffalo Bill Junior; photo cover	$6.50	$19.50	$39.00	£4.30	£13.00	£26.00
829	Tales of the Pony Express; painted cover	$6.50	$19.50	$39.00	£4.30	£13.00	£26.00
830	The Hardy Boys; photo cover	$15.00	$45.00	$90.00	£10.00	£30.00	£60.00
831	No Sleep Till Dawn - The Story of B52 Bombers	$8.25	$25.00	$50.00	£5.75	£17.50	£35.00
832	Lolly and Pepper	$4.30	$13.00	$26.00	£2.80	£8.50	£17.00
833	Scamp	$8.25	$25.00	$50.00	£5.75	£17.50	£35.00
834	Johnny Mack Brown; photo cover	$8.25	$25.00	$50.00	£5.75	£17.50	£35.00
835	Silvertip; Kinstler art	$5.50	$16.50	$33.00	£3.65	£11.00	£22.00
836	Man in Flight; Jesse Marsh art	$11.50	$35.00	$70.00	£8.00	£24.00	£48.00
837	All American Athlete Cotton Woods	$7.50	$23.00	$46.00	£5.00	£15.00	£30.00
838	Bugs Bunny's Life Story Album	$8.25	$25.00	$50.00	£5.75	£17.50	£35.00
839	Vigilantes	$11.50	$35.00	$70.00	£8.00	£24.00	£48.00
840	Duck Album	$8.25	$25.00	$50.00	£5.75	£17.50	£35.00
841	Elmer Fudd	$3.15	$9.50	$19.00	£2.15	£6.50	£13.00
842	The Nature of Things; Jesse Marsh art	$10.50	$33.00	$65.00	£7.25	£22.00	£44.00
843	The First Americans; Jesse Marsh art	$12.50	$39.00	$77.50	£8.25	£25.00	£50.00
844	Gunsmoke; photo cover	$8.25	$25.00	$50.00	£5.75	£17.50	£35.00
845	scarce in the U.K. The Land Unknown; Alex Toth art	$21.50	$65.00	$130.00	£14.50	£44.00	£87.50
846	Gun Glory; photo cover; Alex Toth art	$19.00	$57.50	$115.00	£12.50	£39.00	£77.50
847	Perri (Disney)	$10.50	$33.00	$65.00	£7.25	£22.00	£44.00
848	Marauder's Moon	$7.50	$23.00	$46.00	£5.00	£15.00	£30.00
849	Prince Valiant: Bob Fuje art	$7.50	$23.00	$46.00	£5.00	£15.00	£30.00
850	Buck Jones	$5.50	$16.50	$33.00	£3.65	£11.00	£22.00
851	The Story of Mankind; Vincent Price photo cover; Jesse Marsh art	$10.50	$33.00	$65.00	£7.25	£22.00	£44.00
852	Chilly Willy by Walter Lantz	$4.30	$13.00	$26.00	£2.80	£8.50	£17.00
853	Pluto	$6.50	$19.50	$39.00	£4.30	£13.00	£26.00
854	The Hunchback of Notre Dame; photo cover	$19.00	$57.50	$115.00	£12.50	£39.00	£77.50
855	Broken Arrow; photo cover	$7.50	$23.00	$46.00	£5.00	£15.00	£30.00
856	Buffalo Bill Junior; photo cover	$7.50	$23.00	$46.00	£5.00	£15.00	£30.00
857	The Goofy Adventure Story	$10.50	$33.00	$65.00	£7.25	£22.00	£44.00
858	Daisy Duck's Diary (#859 on inside indicia)	$5.50	$16.50	$33.00	£3.65	£11.00	£22.00
859	Topper and Neil	$5.50	$16.50	$33.00	£3.65	£11.00	£22.00
860	Wyatt Earp; photo cover; Russ Manning art	$19.00	$57.50	$115.00	£12.50	£39.00	£77.50
861	Frosty the Snowman	$4.30	$13.00	$26.00	£2.80	£8.50	£17.00
862	The Truth about Mother Goose	$10.50	$33.00	$65.00	£7.25	£22.00	£44.00
863	Francis The Talking Mule	$5.50	$16.50	$33.00	£3.65	£11.00	£22.00
864	The Littlest Snowman	$5.50	$16.50	$33.00	£3.65	£11.00	£22.00
865	Andy Burnett; photo cover	$19.00	$57.50	$115.00	£12.50	£39.00	£77.50
866	Mars and Beyond	$15.00	$45.00	$90.00	£10.00	£30.00	£60.00
867	Santa Claus Funnies	$4.30	$13.00	$26.00	£2.80	£8.50	£17.00
868	Walt Scott's The Little People	$4.30	$13.00	$26.00	£2.80	£8.50	£17.00
869	Old Yeller (Disney film); photo cover	$10.50	$33.00	$65.00	£7.25	£22.00	£44.00
870	Little Beaver	$4.30	$13.00	$26.00	£2.80	£8.50	£17.00
871	Curly Kayoe	$4.30	$13.00	$26.00	£2.80	£8.50	£17.00
872	Captain Kangaroo; photo cover	$21.50	$65.00	$130.00	£14.50	£44.00	£87.50
873	Grandma Duck's Farm Friends	$10.50	$33.00	$65.00	£7.25	£22.00	£44.00
874	Old Ironsides (Disney)	$10.50	$33.00	$65.00	£7.25	£22.00	£44.00
875	Trumpets West	$6.50	$19.50	$39.00	£4.30	£13.00	£26.00
876	Tales of Wells Fargo; photo cover	$15.00	$45.00	$90.00	£10.00	£30.00	£60.00
877	Frontier Doctor with Rex Allen; photo cover; Alex Toth art	$16.00	$49.00	$97.50	£10.50	£33.00	£65.00
878	Peanuts by Charles Schultz; scarce	$21.50	$65.00	$130.00	£14.50	£44.00	£87.50
879	Brave Eagle; photo cover	$4.30	$13.00	$26.00	£2.80	£8.50	£17.00
880	Steve Donovan; photo cover	$6.50	$19.50	$39.00	£4.30	£13.00	£26.00
881	Captain and the Kids	$5.50	$16.50	$33.00	£3.65	£11.00	£22.00
882	Zorro (Disney); Alex Toth art	$38.00	$115.00	$230.00	£25.00	£75.00	£150.00
883	The Little Rascals	$4.30	$13.00	$26.00	£2.80	£8.50	£17.00
884	Hawkeye and the Last of the Mohicans; photo cover	$10.50	$33.00	$65.00	£7.25	£22.00	£44.00
885	Fury; photo cover	$9.50	$29.00	$57.50	£6.50	£19.50	£39.00
886	Bongo and Lumpjaw	$4.30	$13.00	$26.00	£2.80	£8.50	£17.00
887	The Hardy Boys; photo cover						

VERY GENERAL PERCENTAGE CONVERSION CHART WHICH MAY BE USED TO CALCULATE LOW AND INBETWEEN GRADES:

	$Good	$Fine	$N.Mint	£Good	£Fine	£N.Mint
	$16.00	$49.00	$97.50	£10.50	£33.00	£65.00
888 Elmer Fudd	$4.30	$13.00	$26.00	£2.80	£8.50	£17.00
889 Clint and Mac; photo cover; Alex Toth art	$21.50	$65.00	$130.00	£14.50	£44.00	£87.50
890 Wyatt Earp; photo cover; Russ Manning art	$11.50	$35.00	$70.00	£8.00	£24.00	£48.00
891 Light in the Forest; Fess Parker photo cover	$11.50	$35.00	$70.00	£8.00	£24.00	£48.00
892 Maverick; James Garner photo cover	$24.00	$72.50	$145.00	£15.50	£48.00	£95.00
893 Jim Bowie; photo cover	$7.50	$23.00	$46.00	£5.00	£15.00	£30.00
894 Oswald the Rabbit by Walter Lantz	$4.30	$13.00	$26.00	£2.80	£8.50	£17.00
895 Wagon Train; photo cover	$15.00	$46.00	$92.50	£10.00	£30.00	£60.00
896 The Adventures of Tinker Bell	$11.50	$35.00	$70.00	£8.00	£24.00	£48.00
897 Jiminy Cricket	$7.50	$23.00	$46.00	£5.00	£15.00	£30.00
898 Silvertip; Kinstler art	$7.50	$23.00	$46.00	£5.00	£15.00	£30.00
899 Goofy	$8.25	$25.00	$50.00	£5.75	£17.50	£35.00
900 Prince Valiant; Bob Fuje art	$7.50	$23.00	$46.00	£5.00	£15.00	£30.00
901 Little Hiawatha	$7.50	$23.00	$46.00	£5.00	£15.00	£30.00
902 Will-Yum!	$4.30	$13.00	$26.00	£2.80	£8.50	£17.00
903 Dottie Dripple and Taffy	$4.30	$13.00	$26.00	£2.80	£8.50	£17.00
904 The Indian Fighter	$6.50	$19.50	$39.00	£4.30	£13.00	£26.00
905 Annette; photo cover	$45.00	$135.00	$270.00	£31.00	£92.50	£185.00
906 Francis The Talking Mule	$5.50	$16.50	$33.00	£3.65	£11.00	£22.00
907 Sugarfoot; photo cover	$21.50	$65.00	$130.00	£14.50	£44.00	£87.50
908 Walt Scott's The Little People	$4.30	$13.00	$26.00	£2.80	£8.50	£17.00
909 Smitty and Herby	$4.30	$13.00	$26.00	£2.80	£8.50	£17.00
910 The Vikings; Kirk Douglas photo cover; John Buscema art	$15.00	$45.00	$90.00	£10.00	£30.00	£60.00
911 The Gray Ghost; photo cover; Russ Manning art	$10.50	$33.00	$65.00	£7.25	£22.00	£44.00
912 scarce in the U.K. Leave It To Beaver; photo cover	$29.00	$87.50	$175.00	£19.00	£57.50	£115.00
913 The Left-Handed Gun; Paul Newman photo cover	$16.00	$49.00	$97.50	£10.50	£33.00	£65.00
914 No Time For Sergeants; photo cover; Alex Toth art	$12.50	$39.00	$77.50	£8.25	£25.00	£50.00
915 Casey Jones; photo cover	$8.25	$25.00	$50.00	£5.75	£17.50	£35.00
916 Red Ryder	$4.30	$13.00	$26.00	£2.80	£8.50	£17.00
917 Life of Riley; photo cover	$21.50	$65.00	$130.00	£14.50	£44.00	£87.50
918 Beep Beep, the Road Runner	$12.50	$39.00	$77.50	£8.25	£25.00	£50.00
919 Boots and Saddles; photo cover	$11.50	$35.00	$70.00	£8.00	£24.00	£48.00
920 Zorro; photo cover; Alex Toth art	$24.00	$72.50	$145.00	£15.50	£48.00	£95.00
921 Wyatt Earp; photo cover; Russ Manning art	$10.50	$33.00	$65.00	£7.25	£22.00	£44.00
922 Johnny Mack Brown; photo cover; Russ Manning art	$10.50	$33.00	$65.00	£7.25	£22.00	£44.00
923 Timmy	$4.30	$13.00	$26.00	£2.80	£8.50	£17.00
924 Colt .45; photo cover	$16.00	$49.00	$97.50	£10.50	£33.00	£65.00
925 Last of the Fast Guns; photo cover	$9.50	$29.00	$57.50	£6.50	£19.50	£39.00
926 Peter Pan; reprints #442	$7.50	$23.00	$46.00	£5.00	£15.00	£30.00
927 Top Gun; John Buscema art	$6.50	$19.50	$39.00	£4.30	£13.00	£26.00
928 Sea Hunt; Lloyd Bridges photo cover	$21.50	$65.00	$130.00	£14.50	£44.00	£87.50
929 Brave Eagle; photo cover	$4.30	$13.00	$26.00	£2.80	£8.50	£17.00
930 Maverick; James Garner photo cover	$12.50	$39.00	$77.50	£8.25	£25.00	£50.00
931 Have Gun, Will Travel; photo cover	$19.00	$57.50	$115.00	£12.50	£39.00	£77.50
932 Smokey the Bear	$6.50	$19.50	$39.00	£4.30	£13.00	£26.00
933 Zorro; Alex Toth art	$24.00	$72.50	$145.00	£15.50	£48.00	£95.00
934 Restless Gun; photo cover	$19.00	$57.50	$115.00	£12.50	£39.00	£77.50
935 King of the Royal Mounted	$6.50	$19.50	$39.00	£4.30	£13.00	£26.00
936 The Little Rascals	$4.30	$13.00	$26.00	£2.80	£8.50	£17.00
937 Ruff and Reddy (Hanna-Barbera)	$21.50	$65.00	$130.00	£14.50	£44.00	£87.50
938 Elmer Fudd	$4.30	$13.00	$26.00	£2.80	£8.50	£17.00
939 Steve Canyon, no Caniff art	$6.50	$19.50	$39.00	£4.30	£13.00	£26.00
940 Lolly and Pepper	$4.30	$13.00	$26.00	£2.80	£8.50	£17.00
941 Pluto	$4.30	$13.00	$26.00	£2.80	£8.50	£17.00
942 Tales of the Pony Express	$6.50	$19.50	$39.00	£4.30	£13.00	£26.00
943 White Wilderness	$11.50	$35.00	$70.00	£8.00	£24.00	£48.00
944 The Seventh Voyage of Sinbad; John Buscema art	$21.50	$65.00	$130.00	£14.50	£44.00	£87.50
945 Maverick; James Garner photo cover	$12.50	$39.00	$77.50	£8.25	£25.00	£50.00
946 The Big Country; photo cover	$9.50	$29.00	$57.50	£6.50	£19.50	£39.00
947 Broken Arrow; photo cover	$7.50	$23.00	$46.00	£5.00	£15.00	£30.00
948 Daisy Duck's Diary	$6.50	$19.50	$39.00	£4.30	£13.00	£26.00
949 High Adventure - Lowell Thomas; photo cover; Alex Toth art	$7.50	$23.00	$46.00	£5.00	£15.00	£30.00
950 Frosty the Snowman	$4.30	$13.00	$26.00	£2.80	£8.50	£17.00
951 scarce in the U.K. The Lennon Sisters; photo cover; Alex Toth art	$26.00	$77.50	$155.00	£16.50	£50.00	£100.00
952 Goofy	$7.50	$23.00	$46.00	£5.00	£15.00	£30.00
953 Francis The Talking Mule	$5.50	$16.50	$33.00	£3.65	£11.00	£22.00
954 Man in Space (Disney)	$10.50	$33.00	$65.00	£7.25	£22.00	£44.00
955 Hi and Lois	$4.30	$13.00	$26.00	£2.80	£8.50	£17.00
956 scarce in the U.K. Ricky Nelson; photo cover	$38.00	$115.00	$230.00	£25.00	£75.00	£150.00
957 Buffalo Bee	$12.50	$39.00	$77.50	£8.25	£25.00	£50.00
958 Santa Claus Funnies	$4.30	$13.00	$26.00	£2.80	£8.50	£17.00
959 Christmas Stories; strip reprints	$5.50	$16.50	$33.00	£3.65	£11.00	£22.00
960 Zorro; Alex Toth art	$21.50	$65.00	$130.00	£14.50	£44.00	£87.50
961 Tales of the Texas Rangers; photo cover; Spiegle art	$7.50	$23.00	$46.00	£5.00	£15.00	£30.00
962 Maverick; James Garner photo cover	$12.50	$39.00	$77.50	£8.25	£25.00	£50.00
963 Johnny Mack Brown; photo cover	$8.25	$25.00	$50.00	£5.75	£17.50	£35.00
964 The Hardy Boys; photo cover	$16.00	$49.00	$97.50	£10.50	£33.00	£65.00
965 Grandma Duck's Farm Friends	$7.50	$23.00	$46.00	£5.00	£15.00	£30.00
966 Tonka (Disney); photo cover	$15.00	$45.00	$90.00	£10.00	£30.00	£60.00
967 Chilly Willy by Walter Lantz	$4.30	$13.00	$26.00	£2.80	£8.50	£17.00
968 Tales of Wells Fargo; photo cover	$11.50	$35.00	$70.00	£8.00	£24.00	£48.00
969 Peanuts by Charles Schultz	$15.00	$45.00	$90.00	£10.00	£30.00	£60.00
970 Lawman; photo cover	$16.00	$49.00	$97.50	£10.50	£33.00	£65.00
971 Wagon Train; photo cover	$7.50	$23.00	$46.00	£5.00	£15.00	£30.00
972 Tom Thumb, scarce	$21.50	$65.00	$130.00	£14.50	£44.00	£87.50
973 Sleeping Beauty	$24.00	$72.50	$145.00	£15.50	£48.00	£95.00
974 The Little Rascals	$4.30	$13.00	$26.00	£2.80	£8.50	£17.00
975 Fury; photo cover	$9.50	$29.00	$57.50	£6.50	£19.50	£39.00
976 Zorro; photo cover; Alex Toth art	$21.50	$65.00	$130.00	£14.50	£44.00	£87.50
977 Elmer Fudd	$4.30	$13.00	$26.00	£2.80	£8.50	£17.00
978 Lolly and Pepper	$4.30	$13.00	$26.00	£2.80	£8.50	£17.00
979 Oswald the Rabbit by Walter Lantz	$4.30	$13.00	$26.00	£2.80	£8.50	£17.00
980 Maverick; James Garner photo cover	$12.50	$39.00	$77.50	£8.25	£25.00	£50.00
981 Ruff and Reddy (Hanna-Barbera)	$11.50	$35.00	$70.00	£8.00	£24.00	£48.00
982 The New Adventures of Tinker Bell	$10.50	$33.00	$65.00	£7.25	£22.00	£44.00
983 Have Gun, Will Travel; photo cover	$11.50	$35.00	$70.00	£8.00	£24.00	£48.00
984 Sleeping Beauty's Fairy Godmother	$19.00	$57.50	$115.00	£12.50	£39.00	£77.50

No.	Title	$Good	$Fine	$N.Mint	£Good	£Fine	£N.Mint
985	Shaggy Dog; photo cover	$8.25	$25.00	$50.00	£5.75	£17.50	£35.00
986	Restless Gun; photo cover	$10.50	$33.00	$65.00	£7.25	£22.00	£44.00
987	Goofy	$8.25	$25.00	$50.00	£5.75	£17.50	£35.00
988	Little Hiawatha	$9.50	$29.00	$57.50	£6.50	£19.50	£39.00
989	Jiminy Cricket	$8.25	$25.00	$50.00	£5.75	£17.50	£35.00
990	Huckleberry Hound; Yogi Bear appears	$21.50	$65.00	$130.00	£14.50	£44.00	£87.50
991	Francis The Talking Mule	$4.30	$13.00	$26.00	£2.80	£8.50	£17.00
992	Sugarfoot; photo cover; Alex Toth art	$19.00	$57.50	$115.00	£12.50	£39.00	£77.50
993	Jim Bowie; photo cover	$8.25	$25.00	$50.00	£5.75	£17.50	£35.00
994	Sea Hunt; Lloyd Bridges photo cover; Alex Toth art	$11.50	$35.00	$70.00	£8.00	£24.00	£48.00
995	Donald Duck Album	$8.25	$25.00	$50.00	£5.75	£17.50	£35.00
996	Nevada by Zane Grey	$5.50	$16.50	$33.00	£3.65	£11.00	£22.00
997	Tales of Texas John; photo cover	$11.50	$35.00	$70.00	£8.00	£24.00	£48.00
998	Ricky Nelson; photo cover	$33.00	$97.50	$195.00	£21.50	£65.00	£130.00
999	Leave It To Beaver; photo cover	$26.00	$77.50	$155.00	£16.50	£50.00	£100.00
1000	The Gray Ghost; photo cover	$10.50	$33.00	$65.00	£7.25	£22.00	£44.00
1001	High Adventure - Lowell Thomas; photo cover	$8.25	$25.00	$50.00	£5.75	£17.50	£35.00
1002	Buffalo Bee	$8.25	$25.00	$50.00	£5.75	£17.50	£35.00
1003	Zorro; photo cover; Alex Toth art	$21.50	$65.00	$130.00	£14.50	£44.00	£87.50
1004	Colt .45; photo cover	$11.50	$35.00	$70.00	£8.00	£24.00	£48.00
1005	Maverick; James Garner photo cover	$11.50	$35.00	$70.00	£8.00	£24.00	£48.00
1006	Hercules; John Buscema art	$15.00	$45.00	$90.00	£10.00	£30.00	£60.00
1007	John Paul Jones; Robert Stack photo cover	$7.50	$23.00	$46.00	£5.00	£15.00	£30.00
1008	Beep Beep, The Road Runner	$7.50	$23.00	$46.00	£5.00	£15.00	£30.00
1009	The Rifleman; Chuck Connors photo cover	$28.00	$82.50	$165.00	£18.00	£55.00	£110.00
1010	Grandma Duck's Farm Friends; Carl Barks art	$24.00	$72.50	$145.00	£15.50	£48.00	£95.00
1011	Buckskin; photo cover	$12.50	$39.00	$77.50	£8.25	£25.00	£50.00
1012	Last Train From Gun Hill; photo cover	$12.50	$39.00	$77.50	£8.25	£25.00	£50.00
1013	Bat Masterson; Gene Barry photo cover	$15.00	$46.00	$92.50	£10.00	£30.00	£60.00
1014	The Lennon Sisters; photo cover; Alex Toth art	$24.00	$72.50	$145.00	£15.50	£48.00	£95.00
1015	Peanuts by Charles Schultz	$15.00	$45.00	$90.00	£10.00	£30.00	£60.00
1016	Smokey the Bear Nature Stories	$5.50	$16.50	$33.00	£3.65	£11.00	£22.00
1017	Chilly Willy by Walter Lantz	$4.30	$13.00	$26.00	£2.80	£8.50	£17.00
1018	Rio Bravo; John Wayne and Dean Martin photo cover; Alex Toth art	$29.00	$87.50	$175.00	£19.00	£57.50	£115.00
1019	Wagon Train; photo cover	$7.50	$23.00	$46.00	£5.00	£15.00	£30.00
1020	Jungle Jim; McWilliams art	$4.30	$13.00	$26.00	£2.80	£8.50	£17.00
1021	Tales of Texas Rangers; photo cover	$6.50	$19.50	$39.00	£4.30	£13.00	£26.00
1022	Timmy	$4.30	$13.00	$26.00	£2.80	£8.50	£17.00
1023	Tales of Wells Fargo; photo cover	$11.50	$35.00	$70.00	£8.00	£24.00	£48.00
1024	Darby O'Gill and The Little People; Alex Toth art	$24.00	$72.50	$145.00	£15.50	£48.00	£95.00
1025	Vacation in Disneyland by Barl Barks	$33.00	$97.50	$195.00	£21.50	£65.00	£130.00
1026	Spin and Marty; photo cover	$10.50	$33.00	$65.00	£7.25	£22.00	£44.00
1027	The Texan; photo cover	$10.50	$33.00	$65.00	£7.25	£22.00	£44.00
1028	Rawhide; Clint Eastwood photo cover	$38.00	$115.00	$230.00	£25.00	£75.00	£150.00
1029	Boots and Saddles; photo cover	$7.50	$23.00	$46.00	£5.00	£15.00	£30.00
1030	The Little Rascals	$4.30	$13.00	$26.00	£2.80	£8.50	£17.00
1031	Fury; photo cover	$8.25	$25.00	$50.00	£5.75	£17.50	£35.00
1032	Elmer Fudd	$4.30	$13.00	$26.00	£2.80	£8.50	£17.00
1033	Steve Canyon; not Milton Caniff art; photo cover	$6.50	$19.50	$39.00	£4.30	£13.00	£26.00
1034	Nancy and Sluggo	$4.30	$13.00	$26.00	£2.80	£8.50	£17.00
1035	Lawman; photo cover; Alex Toth art	$8.25	$25.00	$50.00	£5.75	£17.50	£35.00
1036	The Big Circus; photo cover	$8.25	$25.00	$50.00	£5.75	£17.50	£35.00
1037	Zorro; Alex Toth art	$26.00	$77.50	$155.00	£16.50	£50.00	£100.00
1038	Ruff and Reddy (Hanna-Barbera)	$11.50	$35.00	$70.00	£8.00	£24.00	£48.00
1039	Pluto	$4.30	$13.00	$26.00	£2.80	£8.50	£17.00
1040	Quick Draw McGraw (Hanna-Barbera)	$16.00	$49.00	$97.50	£10.50	£33.00	£65.00
1041	Sea Hunt; Lloyd Bridges photo cover; Alex Toth art	$14.00	$43.00	$85.00	£9.00	£28.00	£55.00
1042	The Three Chipmunks	$5.50	$16.50	$33.00	£3.65	£11.00	£22.00
1043	scarce in the U.K. The Three Stooges; photo cover	$29.00	$87.50	$175.00	£19.00	£57.50	£115.00
1044	Have Gun, Will Travel; photo cover	$10.50	$33.00	$65.00	£7.25	£22.00	£44.00
1045	Restless Gun; photo cover	$11.50	$35.00	$70.00	£8.00	£24.00	£48.00
1046	Beep Beep, The Road Runner	$7.50	$23.00	$46.00	£5.00	£15.00	£30.00
1047	Gyro Gearloose	$29.00	$87.50	$175.00	£19.00	£57.50	£115.00
1048	The Horse Soldiers; John Wayne photo cover; Mike Sekowsky art	$29.00	$87.50	$175.00	£19.00	£57.50	£115.00
1049	Don't Give Up The Ship; Jerry Lewis photo cover	$9.50	$29.00	$57.50	£6.50	£19.50	£39.00
1050	Huckleberry Hound (Hanna-Barbera)	$10.50	$33.00	$65.00	£7.25	£22.00	£44.00
1051	Donald in Mathmagicland	$15.00	$45.00	$90.00	£10.00	£30.00	£60.00
	1st official distribution in the U.K.						
1052	Ben Hur; Russ Manning art	$15.00	$45.00	$90.00	£10.00	£30.00	£60.00
1053	Goofy	$8.25	$25.00	$50.00	£5.75	£17.50	£35.00
1054	Huckleberry Hound	$9.50	$29.00	$57.50	£6.50	£19.50	£39.00
1055	Daisy Duck's Diary by Carl Barks	$16.00	$49.00	$97.50	£10.50	£33.00	£65.00
1056	Yellowstone Kelly; Clint Walker photo cover	$8.25	$25.00	$50.00	£5.75	£17.50	£35.00
1057	Mickey Mouse Album	$4.30	$13.00	$26.00	£2.80	£8.50	£17.00
1058	Colt .45; photo cover	$10.50	$33.00	$65.00	£7.25	£22.00	£44.00
1059	Sugarfoot; photo cover	$10.50	$33.00	$65.00	£7.25	£22.00	£44.00
1060	Journey To The Centre of the Earth; Pat Boone photo cover	$21.50	$65.00	$130.00	£14.50	£44.00	£87.50
1061	Buffalo Bee	$9.50	$29.00	$57.50	£6.50	£19.50	£39.00
1062	Christmas Stories; strip reprints	$4.30	$13.00	$26.00	£2.80	£8.50	£17.00
1063	Santa Claus Funnies	$4.30	$13.00	$26.00	£2.80	£8.50	£17.00
1064	Bugs Bunny's Merry Christmas	$6.50	$19.50	$39.00	£4.30	£13.00	£26.00
1065	Frosty the Snowman	$4.30	$13.00	$26.00	£2.80	£8.50	£17.00
1066	77 Sunset Strip; photo cover; Alex Toth art	$21.50	$65.00	$130.00	£14.50	£44.00	£87.50
1067	Yogi Bear (Hanna-Barbera)	$20.50	$62.50	$125.00	£13.00	£40.00	£80.00
1068	Francis The Talking Mule	$4.30	$13.00	$26.00	£2.80	£8.50	£17.00
1069	The FBI Story; James Stewart photo cover	$16.00	$49.00	$97.50	£10.50	£33.00	£65.00
1070	Solomon and Sheba; photo cover; Mike Sekowsky art	$12.50	$39.00	$77.50	£8.25	£25.00	£50.00
1071	The Real McCoys; photo cover; Alex Toth art	$16.00	$49.00	$97.50	£10.50	£33.00	£65.00
1072	Blythe	$7.50	$23.00	$46.00	£5.00	£15.00	£30.00
1073	Grandma Duck's Farm Friends by Carl Barks	$21.50	$65.00	$130.00	£14.50	£44.00	£87.50
1074	Chily Willy by Walter Lantz	$4.30	$13.00	$26.00	£2.80	£8.50	£17.00
1075	Tales of Wells Fargo; photo cover	$11.50	$35.00	$70.00	£8.00	£24.00	£48.00
1076	Johnny Yuma's Journal - The Rebel; photo cover; Mike Sekowsky art	$15.00	$45.00	$90.00	£10.00	£30.00	£60.00
1077	The Deputy; Henry Fonda photo cover; John Buscema art	$21.50	$65.00	$130.00	£14.50	£44.00	£87.50
1078	The Three Stooges; photo cover	$15.00	$45.00	$90.00	£10.00	£30.00	£60.00
1079	The Little Rascals	$4.30	$13.00	$26.00	£2.80	£8.50	£17.00
1080	Fury; photo cover						

TRADE PAPERBACKS, GRAPHIC NOVELS AND OTHER COLLECTIONS ARE PRICED IN POUNDS STERLING ONLY. CONVERT AT 1.5 FOR DOLLARS.

	$Good	$Fine	$N.Mint	£Good	£Fine	£N.Mint
	$9.50	$29.00	$57.50	£6.50	£19.50	£39.00
1081 Elmer Fudd	$4.30	$13.00	$26.00	£2.80	£8.50	£17.00
1082 Spin and Marty; photo cover	$10.50	$33.00	$65.00	£7.25	£22.00	£44.00
1083 Men into Space; photo cover	$10.50	$33.00	$65.00	£7.25	£22.00	£44.00
1084 Speedy Gonzales	$4.30	$13.00	$26.00	£2.80	£8.50	£17.00
1085 The Time Machine; Alex Toth art	$26.00	$77.50	$155.00	£16.50	£50.00	£100.00
1086 Lolly and Pepper	$4.30	$13.00	$26.00	£2.80	£8.50	£17.00
1087 Peter Gunn; photo cover	$12.50	$39.00	$77.50	£8.25	£25.00	£50.00
1088 A Dog of Flanders; photo cover	$7.50	$23.00	$46.00	£5.00	£15.00	£30.00
1089 Restless Gun; photo cover	$10.50	$33.00	$65.00	£7.25	£22.00	£44.00
1090 Francis The Talking Mule	$4.30	$13.00	$26.00	£2.80	£8.50	£17.00
1091 Jack's Diary	$8.25	$25.00	$50.00	£5.75	£17.50	£35.00
1092 Toby Tyler; photo cover	$10.50	$33.00	$65.00	£7.25	£22.00	£44.00
1093 MacKenzie's Raiders; photo cover	$9.50	$29.00	$57.50	£6.50	£19.50	£39.00
1094 Goofy	$7.50	$23.00	$46.00	£5.00	£15.00	£30.00
1095 Gyro Gearloose by Carl Barks	$17.50	$52.50	$105.00	£11.50	£35.00	£70.00
1096 The Texan; Rory Calhoun photo cover	$10.50	$33.00	$65.00	£7.25	£22.00	£44.00
1097 Rawhide; Clint Eastwood photo cover	$24.00	$72.50	$145.00	£15.50	£48.00	£95.00
1098 Sugarfoot; photo cover	$10.50	$33.00	$65.00	£7.25	£22.00	£44.00
1099 Donald Duck Album; Carl Barks cover only	$8.25	$25.00	$50.00	£5.75	£17.50	£35.00
1100 Annette's Life Story; photo cover	$29.00	$87.50	$175.00	£19.00	£57.50	£115.00
1101 Kidnapped; photo cover	$8.25	$25.00	$50.00	£5.75	£17.50	£35.00
1102 Wanted Dead or Alive; Steve McQueen photo cover	$20.50	$62.50	$125.00	£13.00	£40.00	£80.00
1103 Leave It To Beaver; photo cover	$24.00	$72.50	$145.00	£15.50	£48.00	£95.00
1104 Yogi Bear Goes to College (Hanna-Barbera)	$10.50	$33.00	$65.00	£7.25	£22.00	£44.00
1105 Gail Storm; photo cover; Alex Toth art	$21.50	$65.00	$130.00	£14.50	£44.00	£87.50
1106 77 Sunset Strip; photo cover; Alex Toth art	$12.50	$39.00	$77.50	£8.25	£25.00	£50.00
1107 Buckskin; photo cover	$10.50	$33.00	$65.00	£7.25	£22.00	£44.00
1108 The Troubleshooters; photo cover	$8.25	$25.00	$50.00	£5.75	£17.50	£35.00
1109 This Is Your Life Donald Duck; "origin" of Donald Duck	$28.00	$82.50	$165.00	£18.00	£55.00	£110.00
1110 Bonanza, scarce; photo cover	$49.00	$145.00	$295.00	£33.00	£97.50	£195.00
1111 Shotgun Slade; photo cover	$8.25	$25.00	$50.00	£5.75	£17.50	£35.00
1112 Pixie, Dixie and Mr. Jinks (Hanna-Barbera)	$8.25	$25.00	$50.00	£5.75	£17.50	£35.00
1113 Tales of Wells Fargo; photo cover	$10.50	$33.00	$65.00	£7.25	£22.00	£44.00
1114 The Adventures of Huckleberry Finn; photo cover	$7.50	$23.00	$46.00	£5.00	£15.00	£30.00
1115 Ricky Nelson; photo cover; not Russ Manning art	$24.00	$72.50	$145.00	£15.50	£48.00	£95.00
1116 Boots and Saddles; photo cover	$7.50	$23.00	$46.00	£5.00	£15.00	£30.00
1117 The Boy and the Pirates; photo cover	$8.25	$25.00	$50.00	£5.75	£17.50	£35.00
1118 The Sword and the Dragon; photo cover	$10.50	$33.00	$65.00	£7.25	£22.00	£44.00
1119 Smokey the Bear Nature Stories	$4.30	$13.00	$26.00	£2.80	£8.50	£17.00
1120 Dinosaurs! - painted cover	$10.50	$33.00	$65.00	£7.25	£22.00	£44.00
1121 Hercules Unchained; Reed Crandall art	$12.50	$39.00	$77.50	£8.25	£25.00	£50.00
1122 Chilly Willy by Walter Lantz	$4.30	$13.00	$26.00	£2.80	£8.50	£17.00
1123 Tombstone Territory; photo cover	$12.50	$39.00	$77.50	£8.25	£25.00	£50.00
1124 Whirlybirds; photo cover	$12.50	$39.00	$77.50	£8.25	£25.00	£50.00
1125 Laramie; photo cover; Russ Heath art	$12.50	$39.00	$77.50	£8.25	£25.00	£50.00
1126 Sundance; photo cover	$12.50	$39.00	$77.50	£8.25	£25.00	£50.00
1127 The Three Stooges; photo cover	$12.50	$39.00	$77.50	£8.25	£25.00	£50.00
1128 scarce in the U.K. Rocky and His Friends; photo cover	$40.00	$120.00	$240.00	£28.00	£82.50	£165.00
1129 Pollyana; photo cover	$15.00	$45.00	$90.00	£10.00	£30.00	£60.00
1130 The Deputy; Henry Fonda photo cover; John Buscema art	$12.50	$39.00	$77.50	£8.25	£25.00	£50.00
1131 Elmer Fudd	$3.15	$9.50	$19.00	£2.15	£6.50	£13.00
1132 less common in the U.K. Space Mouse by Walter Lantz	$6.50	$19.50	$39.00	£4.30	£13.00	£26.00
1133 Fury; photo cover	$8.25	$25.00	$50.00	£5.75	£17.50	£35.00
1134 The Real McCoys; photo cover; Alex Toth art	$16.00	$49.00	$97.50	£10.50	£33.00	£65.00
1135 The Mouseketeers	$3.15	$9.50	$19.00	£2.15	£6.50	£13.00
1136 Jungle Cat; photo cover	$10.50	$33.00	$65.00	£7.25	£22.00	£44.00
1137 The Little Rascals	$4.30	$13.00	$26.00	£2.80	£8.50	£17.00
1138 Johnny Yuma's Journal - The Rebel; photo cover	$12.50	$39.00	$77.50	£8.25	£25.00	£50.00
1139 Spartacus; Kirk Douglas photo cover; John Buscema art	$21.50	$65.00	$130.00	£14.50	£44.00	£87.50
1140 Donald Duck Album	$9.50	$29.00	$57.50	£6.50	£19.50	£39.00
1141 Huckleberry Hound	$9.50	$29.00	$57.50	£6.50	£19.50	£39.00
1142 Johnny Ringo; photo cover	$10.50	$33.00	$65.00	£7.25	£22.00	£44.00
1143 Pluto	$4.30	$13.00	$26.00	£2.80	£8.50	£17.00

Four Star Spectacular #6

Fragments #1

Francis, Brother of the Universe #1

No.	Title	$Good	$Fine	$N.Mint	£Good	£Fine	£N.Mint
1144	The Story of Ruth; photo cover	$16.00	$49.00	$97.50	£10.50	£33.00	£65.00
1145	The Lost World; photo cover; Gil Kane art	$17.50	$52.50	$105.00	£11.50	£35.00	£70.00
1146	Restless Gun; photo cover	$10.50	$33.00	$65.00	£7.25	£22.00	£44.00
1147	Sugarfoot; photo cover	$10.50	$33.00	$65.00	£7.25	£22.00	£44.00
1148	I Aim At The Stars; photo cover	$8.25	$25.00	$50.00	£5.75	£17.50	£35.00
1149	Goofy	$8.25	$25.00	$50.00	£5.75	£17.50	£35.00
1150	Daisy Duck's Diary by Carl Barks	$16.00	$49.00	$97.50	£10.50	£33.00	£65.00
1151	Mickey Muse Album	$5.50	$16.50	$33.00	£3.65	£11.00	£22.00
1152	Rocky and His Friends	$33.00	$97.50	$195.00	£21.50	£65.00	£130.00
1153	Frosty the Snowman	$4.30	$13.00	$26.00	£2.80	£8.50	£17.00
1154	Santa Claus Funnies	$5.50	$16.50	$33.00	£3.65	£11.00	£22.00
1155	North to Alaska; John Wayne photo cover	$21.50	$65.00	$130.00	£14.50	£44.00	£87.50
1156	Swiss Family Robinson; photo cover	$10.50	$33.00	$65.00	£7.25	£22.00	£44.00
1157	Master of the World	$7.50	$23.00	$46.00	£5.00	£15.00	£30.00
1158	The Three Worlds of Gulliver; photo cover	$7.50	$23.00	$46.00	£5.00	£15.00	£30.00
1159	77 Sunset Strip; photo cover; Alex Toth art	$12.50	$39.00	$77.50	£8.25	£25.00	£50.00
1160	Rawhide; Clint Eastwood photo cover	$21.50	$65.00	$130.00	£14.50	£44.00	£87.50
1161	Grandma Duck's Farm Friends by Carl Barks	$21.50	$65.00	$130.00	£14.50	£44.00	£87.50
1162	Yogi Bear Joins The Marines	$10.50	$33.00	$65.00	£7.25	£22.00	£44.00
1163	Daniel Boone; Jesse Marsh art	$9.50	$29.00	$57.50	£6.50	£19.50	£39.00
1164	Wanted Dead or Alive; Steve McQueen photo cover	$16.00	$49.00	$97.50	£10.50	£33.00	£65.00
1165	Ellery Queen, Detective	$17.50	$52.50	$105.00	£11.50	£35.00	£70.00
1166	Rocky and his Friends	$33.00	$97.50	$195.00	£21.50	£65.00	£130.00
1167	Tales of Wells Fargo; photo cover	$10.50	$33.00	$65.00	£7.25	£22.00	£44.00
1168	The Detectives; Robert Taylor photo cover	$12.50	$39.00	$77.50	£8.25	£25.00	£50.00
1169	The New Adventures of Sherlock Holmes	$24.00	$72.50	$145.00	£15.50	£48.00	£95.00
1170	The Three Stooges; photo cover	$15.00	$45.00	$90.00	£10.00	£30.00	£60.00
1171	Elmer Fudd	$4.30	$13.00	$26.00	£2.80	£8.50	£17.00
1172	Fury; photo cover	$8.25	$25.00	$50.00	£5.75	£17.50	£35.00
1173	The Twilight Zone; Crandall/Evans art	$28.00	$82.50	$165.00	£18.00	£55.00	£110.00
1174	The Little Rascals	$4.30	$13.00	$26.00	£2.80	£8.50	£17.00
1175	The Two Mouseketeers	$4.30	$13.00	$26.00	£2.80	£8.50	£17.00
1176	Dondi; photo cover	$7.50	$23.00	$46.00	£5.00	£15.00	£30.00
1177	Chilly Willy by Walter Lantz	$4.30	$13.00	$26.00	£2.80	£8.50	£17.00
1178	Ten Who Dared; painted cover	$10.50	$33.00	$65.00	£7.25	£22.00	£44.00
1179	Swamp Fox; Leslie Neilsen photo cover	$12.50	$39.00	$77.50	£8.25	£25.00	£50.00
1180	The Danny Thomas Show; Alex Toth art	$28.00	$82.50	$165.00	£18.00	£55.00	£110.00
1181	Texas John; photo cover	$10.50	$33.00	$65.00	£7.25	£22.00	£44.00
1182	Donald Duck Album	$6.50	$19.50	$39.00	£4.30	£13.00	£26.00
1183	101 Dalmatians	$12.50	$39.00	$77.50	£8.25	£25.00	£50.00
1184	Gyro Gearloose	$16.00	$49.00	$97.50	£10.50	£33.00	£65.00
1185	Sweetie Pie	$5.50	$16.50	$33.00	£3.65	£11.00	£22.00
1186	Yak Yak	$11.50	$35.00	$70.00	£8.00	£24.00	£48.00
1187	The Three Stooges; photo cover	$15.00	$45.00	$90.00	£10.00	£30.00	£60.00
1188	Atlantis, The Lost Continent; photo cover	$15.00	$45.00	$90.00	£10.00	£30.00	£60.00
1189	Greyfriars Bobby; photo cover	$10.50	$33.00	$65.00	£7.25	£22.00	£44.00
1190	Donald and The Wheel by Carl Barks (cover only)	$8.25	$25.00	$50.00	£5.75	£17.50	£35.00
1191	Leave It To Beaver; photo cover	$24.00	$72.50	$145.00	£15.50	£48.00	£95.00
1192	Ricky Nelso; photo cover; Russ Manning art	$26.00	$77.50	$155.00	£16.50	£50.00	£100.00
1193	The Real McCoys; photo cover	$12.50	$39.00	$77.50	£8.25	£25.00	£50.00
1194	Pepe	$5.50	$16.50	$33.00	£3.65	£11.00	£22.00
1195	National Velvet; photo cover	$8.25	$25.00	$50.00	£5.75	£17.50	£35.00
1196	Pixie, Dixie and Mr. Jinks	$7.50	$23.00	$46.00	£5.00	£15.00	£30.00
1197	The Astronauts; photo cover	$8.25	$25.00	$50.00	£5.75	£17.50	£35.00
1198	Donald in Mathmagicland; reprints #1051	$8.25	$25.00	$50.00	£5.75	£17.50	£35.00
1199	The Absent Minded Professor; photo cover	$9.50	$29.00	$57.50	£6.50	£19.50	£39.00
1200	Hennesey; photo cover; Gil Kane art	$8.25	$25.00	$50.00	£5.75	£17.50	£35.00
1201	Goofy	$8.25	$25.00	$50.00	£5.75	£17.50	£35.00
1202	Rawhide; Clint Eastwood photo cover	$21.50	$65.00	$130.00	£14.50	£44.00	£87.50
1203	Pinocchio	$8.25	$25.00	$50.00	£5.75	£17.50	£35.00
1204	Scamp	$4.30	$13.00	$26.00	£2.80	£8.50	£17.00
1205	David and Goliath; photo cover	$9.50	$29.00	$57.50	£6.50	£19.50	£39.00
1206	Lolly and Pepper	$3.15	$9.50	$19.00	£2.15	£6.50	£13.00
1207	Johnny Yuma's Journal - The Rebel; photo cover; Mike Sekowsky art	$12.50	$39.00	$77.50	£8.25	£25.00	£50.00
1208	Rocky and his Friends	$33.00	$97.50	$195.00	£21.50	£65.00	£130.00
1209	Sugarfoot	$10.50	$33.00	$65.00	£7.25	£22.00	£44.00
1210	The Parent Trap	$16.00	$49.00	$97.50	£10.50	£33.00	£65.00
1211	77 Sunset Strip; photo cover; Russ Manning art	$12.50	$39.00	$77.50	£8.25	£25.00	£50.00
1212	Chilly Willy by Walter Lantz	$3.15	$9.50	$19.00	£2.15	£6.50	£13.00
1213	Mysterious Island; photo cover	$11.50	$35.00	$70.00	£8.00	£24.00	£48.00
1214	Smokey the Bear	$5.50	$16.50	$33.00	£3.65	£11.00	£22.00
1215	Tales of Wells Fargo; photo cover	$10.50	$33.00	$65.00	£7.25	£22.00	£44.00
1216	Whirlybirds; photo cover	$10.50	$33.00	$65.00	£7.25	£22.00	£44.00
1218	Fury; photo cover	$9.50	$29.00	$57.50	£6.50	£19.50	£39.00
1219	The Detectives; Robert Taylor and Adam West photo cover	$11.50	$35.00	$70.00	£8.00	£24.00	£48.00
1220	Gunslinger; photo cover	$10.50	$33.00	$65.00	£7.25	£22.00	£44.00
1221	Bonanza; photo cover	$28.00	$82.50	$165.00	£18.00	£55.00	£110.00
1222	Elmer Fudd	$3.15	$9.50	$19.00	£2.15	£6.50	£13.00
1223	Laramie; photo cover; Gil Kane art	$8.25	$25.00	$50.00	£5.75	£17.50	£35.00
1224	The Little Rascals	$4.30	$13.00	$26.00	£2.80	£8.50	£17.00
1225	The Deputy; Henry Fonda photo cover	$12.50	$39.00	$77.50	£8.25	£25.00	£50.00
1226	Nikki, Wild Dog of the North; photo cover	$9.50	$29.00	$57.50	£6.50	£19.50	£39.00
1227	Morgan the Pirate; photo cover	$12.50	$39.00	$77.50	£8.25	£25.00	£50.00
1229	Thief of Bagdad; photo cover; George Evans art	$15.00	$45.00	$90.00	£10.00	£30.00	£60.00
1230	scarce in the U.K. Voyage to the Bottom of the Sea; part photo cover	$12.00	$36.00	$72.50	£8.00	£24.50	£49.00
1231	Danger Man; Patrick McGoohan photo cover	$12.00	$36.00	$72.50	£8.00	£24.50	£49.00
1232	On the Double	$6.50	$19.50	$39.00	£4.30	£13.00	£26.00
1233	Tammy Tell Me True	$8.25	$25.00	$50.00	£5.75	£17.50	£35.00
1234	The Phantom Planet	$8.25	$25.00	$50.00	£5.75	£17.50	£35.00
1235	Mister Magoo	$6.50	$19.50	$39.00	£4.30	£13.00	£26.00
1236	King of Kings; photo cover	$10.50	$33.00	$65.00	£7.25	£22.00	£44.00
1237	The Untouchables; photo cover	$21.50	$65.00	$130.00	£14.50	£44.00	£87.50
1238	Deputy Dawg	$16.00	$49.00	$97.50	£10.50	£33.00	£65.00
1239	Donald Duck Album; Carl Barks cover	$10.50	$33.00	$65.00	£7.25	£22.00	£44.00
1240	The Detectives; Robert Taylor photo cover	$10.50	$33.00	$65.00	£7.25	£22.00	£44.00
1241	Sweetie Pie	$4.30	$13.00	$26.00	£2.80	£8.50	£17.00
1242	scarce in the U.K. King Leonard	$21.50	$65.00	$130.00	£14.50	£44.00	£87.50
1243	Ellery Queen, Detective						

	$Good	$Fine	$N.Mint	£Good	£Fine	£N.Mint
	$10.50	*$33.00*	*$65.00*	£7.25	£22.00	£44.00
1244 Space Mouse by Walter Lantz	*$6.50*	*$19.50*	*$39.00*	£4.30	£13.00	£26.00
1245 The New Adventures of Sherlock Holmes	*$24.00*	*$72.50*	*$145.00*	£15.50	£48.00	£95.00
1246 Mickey Mouse Album	*$5.50*	*$16.50*	*$33.00*	£3.65	£11.00	£22.00
1247 Daisy Duck's Diary	*$5.50*	*$16.50*	*$33.00*	£3.65	£11.00	£22.00
1248 Pluto	*$5.50*	*$16.50*	*$33.00*	£3.65	£11.00	£22.00
1249 The Danny Thomas Show; photo cover; Russ Manning art	*$24.00*	*$72.50*	*$145.00*	£15.50	£48.00	£95.00
1250 The Four Horsemen of the Apocalypse; photo cover	*$8.25*	*$25.00*	*$50.00*	£5.75	£17.50	£35.00
1251 Everything's Ducky	*$7.50*	*$23.00*	*$46.00*	£5.00	£15.00	£30.00
1252 The Andy Griffith Show	*$38.00*	*$115.00*	*$230.00*	£25.00	£75.00	£150.00
1253 very scarce, limited distribution in the U.K. Space Man	*$10.50*	*$33.00*	*$65.00*	£7.25	£22.00	£44.00
1254 Diver Dan; photo cover	*$8.25*	*$25.00*	*$50.00*	£5.75	£17.50	£35.00
1255 The Wonders of Aladdin	*$8.25*	*$25.00*	*$50.00*	£5.75	£17.50	£35.00
1256 Kona, Monarch of Monster Isle; Sam Glanzman art	*$8.25*	*$25.00*	*$50.00*	£5.75	£17.50	£35.00
1257 Car 54, Where Are You?; photo cover	*$10.50*	*$33.00*	*$65.00*	£7.25	£22.00	£44.00
1258 The Frogmen; George Evans art	*$11.50*	*$35.00*	*$70.00*	£8.00	£24.00	£48.00
1259 El Cid; Charlton Heston photo cover	*$8.25*	*$25.00*	*$50.00*	£5.75	£17.50	£35.00
1260 The Horsemasters; photo cover	*$16.00*	*$49.00*	*$97.50*	£10.50	£33.00	£65.00
1261 Rawhide; Clint Eastwood photo cover	*$21.50*	*$65.00*	*$130.00*	£14.50	£44.00	£87.50
1262 Johnny Yuma's Journal - The Rebel; photo cover	*$12.50*	*$39.00*	*$77.50*	£8.25	£25.00	£50.00
1263 77 Sunset Strip; photo cover; Russ Manning art	*$12.50*	*$39.00*	*$77.50*	£8.25	£25.00	£50.00
1264 Pixie, Dixie and Mr. Jinks	*$7.50*	*$23.00*	*$46.00*	£5.00	£15.00	£30.00
1265 The Real McCoys; photo cover	*$12.50*	*$39.00*	*$77.50*	£8.25	£25.00	£50.00
1266 Spike and Tyke	*$3.15*	*$9.50*	*$19.00*	£2.15	£6.50	£13.00
1267 Gyro Gearloose, some Barks art	*$10.50*	*$33.00*	*$65.00*	£7.25	£22.00	£44.00
1268 Oswald the Rabbit by Walter Lantz	*$3.15*	*$9.50*	*$19.00*	£2.15	£6.50	£13.00
1269 Rawhide; Clint Eastwood photo cover	*$21.50*	*$65.00*	*$130.00*	£14.50	£44.00	£87.50
1270 Bullwinkle and Rocky	*$28.00*	*$82.50*	*$165.00*	£18.00	£55.00	£110.00
1271 Yogi Bear Birthday Party	*$7.50*	*$23.00*	*$46.00*	£5.00	£15.00	£30.00
1272 Frosty the Snowman	*$4.30*	*$13.00*	*$26.00*	£2.80	£8.50	£17.00
1273 Hans Brinker; photo cover	*$10.50*	*$33.00*	*$65.00*	£7.25	£22.00	£44.00
1274 Santa Claus Funnies	*$4.30*	*$13.00*	*$26.00*	£2.80	£8.50	£17.00
1275 Rocky and his Friends	*$33.00*	*$97.50*	*$195.00*	£21.50	£65.00	£130.00
1276 Dondi	*$4.30*	*$13.00*	*$26.00*	£2.80	£8.50	£17.00
1278 King Leonardo	*$20.50*	*$62.50*	*$125.00*	£13.00	£40.00	£80.00
1279 Grandma Duck's Farm Friends	*$7.50*	*$23.00*	*$46.00*	£5.00	£15.00	£30.00
1280 Hennesey; photo cover	*$8.25*	*$25.00*	*$50.00*	£5.75	£17.50	£35.00
1281 Chilly Willy by Walter Lantz	*$3.80*	*$11.50*	*$23.00*	£2.50	£7.50	£15.00
1282 Babes in Toyland; photo cover	*$20.50*	*$62.50*	*$125.00*	£13.00	£40.00	£80.00
1283 Bonanza; photo cover	*$26.00*	*$77.50*	*$155.00*	£16.50	£50.00	£100.00
1284 Laramie; photo cover; Russ Heath art	*$8.25*	*$25.00*	*$50.00*	£5.75	£17.50	£35.00
1285 Leave It To Beaver; photo cover	*$24.00*	*$72.50*	*$145.00*	£15.50	£48.00	£95.00
1286 The Untouchables; photo cover	*$21.50*	*$65.00*	*$130.00*	£14.50	£44.00	£87.50
1287 The Man From Wells Fargo; photo cover	*$6.50*	*$19.50*	*$39.00*	£4.30	£13.00	£26.00
1288 The Twilight Zone; Crandall/Evans art	*$16.00*	*$49.00*	*$97.50*	£10.50	£33.00	£65.00
1289 Ellery Queen, Detective	*$10.50*	*$33.00*	*$65.00*	£7.25	£22.00	£44.00
1290 The Two Mouseketeers	*$3.15*	*$9.50*	*$19.00*	£2.15	£6.50	£13.00
1291 77 Sunset Strip; photo cover; Russ Manning art						

	$Good	$Fine	$N.Mint	£Good	£Fine	£N.Mint
	$12.50	*$39.00*	*$77.50*	£8.25	£25.00	£50.00
1293 Elmer Fudd	*$3.15*	*$9.50*	*$19.00*	£2.15	£6.50	£13.00
1294 Ripcord	*$8.25*	*$25.00*	*$50.00*	£5.75	£17.50	£35.00
1295 Mister Ed; photo cover	*$20.50*	*$62.50*	*$125.00*	£13.00	£40.00	£80.00
1296 Fury; photo cover	*$8.25*	*$25.00*	*$50.00*	£5.75	£17.50	£35.00
1297 The Little Rascals	*$4.30*	*$13.00*	*$26.00*	£2.80	£8.50	£17.00
1298 The Hathaways; photo cover	*$7.50*	*$23.00*	*$46.00*	£5.00	£15.00	£30.00
1299 Deputy Dawg	*$16.00*	*$49.00*	*$97.50*	£10.50	£33.00	£65.00
1300 The Comancheros; John Wayne photo cover	*$26.00*	*$77.50*	*$155.00*	£16.50	£50.00	£100.00
1301 Adventures in Paradise	*$6.50*	*$19.50*	*$39.00*	£4.30	£13.00	£26.00
1302 Johnny Jason, Teen Reporter	*$3.15*	*$9.50*	*$19.00*	£2.15	£6.50	£13.00
1303 Lad, A Dog; photo cover	*$5.50*	*$16.50*	*$33.00*	£3.65	£11.00	£22.00
1304 Nellie the Nurse	*$12.50*	*$39.00*	*$77.50*	£8.25	£25.00	£50.00
1305 Mister Magoo	*$10.50*	*$33.00*	*$65.00*	£7.25	£22.00	£44.00
1306 Target: The Corruptors; photo cover	*$7.50*	*$23.00*	*$46.00*	£5.00	£15.00	£30.00
1307 Margie	*$5.50*	*$16.50*	*$33.00*	£3.65	£11.00	£22.00
1308 Tales of the Wizard of Oz	*$16.00*	*$49.00*	*$97.50*	£10.50	£33.00	£65.00
1309 87th Precinct; photo cover	*$12.50*	*$39.00*	*$77.50*	£8.25	£25.00	£50.00
1310 Huckleberry Hound	*$8.25*	*$25.00*	*$50.00*	£5.75	£17.50	£35.00
1311 Rocky and his Friends	*$33.00*	*$97.50*	*$195.00*	£21.50	£65.00	£130.00
1312 National Velvet; photo cover	*$5.50*	*$16.50*	*$33.00*	£3.65	£11.00	£22.00
1313 Moon Pilot; photo cover	*$11.50*	*$35.00*	*$70.00*	£8.00	£24.00	£48.00
1328 The Underwater City; photo cover; George Evans art	*$10.50*	*$33.00*	*$65.00*	£7.25	£22.00	£44.00
1330 Brain Boy; Gil Kane art	*$15.50*	*$47.00*	*$110.00*	£10.00	£30.00	£70.00
1332 Bachelor Father	*$11.50*	*$35.00*	*$70.00*	£8.00	£24.00	£48.00
1333 Short Ribs	*$7.50*	*$23.00*	*$46.00*	£5.00	£15.00	£30.00
1335 Aggie Mack	*$5.50*	*$16.50*	*$33.00*	£3.65	£11.00	£22.00
1336 On Stage	*$6.50*	*$19.50*	*$39.00*	£4.30	£13.00	£26.00
1337 Dr. Kildare; photo cover	*$9.50*	*$29.00*	*$57.50*	£6.50	£19.50	£39.00
1341 The Andy Griffith Show; photo cover	*$38.00*	*$115.00*	*$230.00*	£25.00	£75.00	£150.00
1348 Yak Yak; Jack Davis art	*$10.50*	*$33.00*	*$65.00*	£7.25	£22.00	£44.00
1349 Yogi Bear Visits the U.N.	*$14.00*	*$43.00*	*$85.00*	£9.00	£28.00	£55.00
1350 Commanche; reprints #466 with title change	*$8.25*	*$25.00*	*$50.00*	£5.75	£17.50	£35.00
1354 scarce in the U.K. Calvin and the Colonel	*$11.50*	*$35.00*	*$70.00*	£8.00	£24.00	£48.00
Title Value:	*$22278.15*	*$67165.00*	*$155946.50*	£14956.35	£45108.50	£104818.00

FOUR KUNOICHI: BLOODLUST, THE

Lightning Comics; 1 Dec 1996-present

	$Good	$Fine	$N.Mint	£Good	£Fine	£N.Mint
1 ND John Cleary script and art; black and white	*$0.55*	*$1.65*	*$2.75*	£0.35	£1.05	£1.75
Title Value:	*$0.55*	*$1.65*	*$2.75*	£0.35	£1.05	£1.75

FOUR STAR BATTLE TALES

DC Comics; 1 Feb/Mar 1975-5 Nov/Dec 1975

	$Good	$Fine	$N.Mint	£Good	£Fine	£N.Mint
1-5 reprints	*$0.25*	*$0.75*	*$1.50*	£0.25	£0.75	£1.50
Title Value:	*$1.25*	*$3.75*	*$7.50*	£1.25	£3.75	£7.50

FOUR STAR SPECTACULAR

DC Comics; 1 Mar/Apr 1976-6 Jan/Feb 1977

	$Good	$Fine	$N.Mint	£Good	£Fine	£N.Mint
1 ND 68pgs	*$0.25*	*$0.75*	*$1.50*	£0.30	£1.00	£2.00
2-6 52pgs	*$0.25*	*$0.75*	*$1.50*	£0.25	£0.75	£1.50
Title Value:	*$1.50*	*$4.50*	*$9.00*	£1.55	£4.75	£9.50

FEATURES

Re-done GA Flash story in 1.

REPRINT FEATURES

Blackhawk in 6. Green Arrow, Vigilante in 5. Green Lantern, Supergirl/Superboy in 3. Hawkman in 1, 4. Kid Flash in 2. Superboy in 1, 2, 4-6. Wonder Woman in 1-6.

FOURTH WORLD GALLERY

DC Comics,OS; 1 Oct 1996

	$Good	$Fine	$N.Mint	£Good	£Fine	£N.Mint
1 ND pin-ups by John Byrne, Walt Simonson and others	*$0.70*	*$2.10*	*$3.50*	£0.50	£1.50	£2.50
Title Value:	*$0.70*	*$2.10*	*$3.50*	£0.50	£1.50	£2.50

FOX AND THE CROW

National Periodical Publications;62 Oct/Nov 1959-108 Feb/Mar 1968

(previous issues ND. Becomes Stanley and His Monster)

(See also TV Screen Cartoons)

	$Good	$Fine	$N.Mint	£Good	£Fine	£N.Mint
62-80 scarce in the U.K.	*$5.00*	*$15.00*	*$35.00*	£2.85	£8.50	£20.00

	$Good	$Fine	$N.Mint	£Good	£Fine	£N.Mint
81-94	$4.55	$13.50	$27.50	£2.50	£7.50	£15.00
95 origin and 1st appearance Stanley and His Monster						
	$5.00	$15.00	$30.00	£3.30	£10.00	£20.00
96-99	$2.50	$7.50	$15.00	£1.50	£4.50	£9.00
100	$2.90	$8.75	$17.50	£1.65	£5.00	£10.00
101-108	$2.50	$7.50	$15.00	£1.15	£3.50	£7.00
Title Value:	$196.60	$587.75	$1277.50	£109.30	£327.50	£712.00
FOXFIRE						
Night Wynd,MS; 1 Apr 1992-3 Jun 1992						
1-3 ND Barry Blair script and art						
	$0.50	$1.50	$2.50	£0.30	£0.90	£1.50
Title Value:	$1.50	$4.50	$7.50	£0.90	£2.70	£4.50
FOXFIRE						
Marvel Comics Group/Ultraverse; 1 Apr 1996-4 Jul 1996						
1 ND	$0.30	$0.90	$1.50	£0.20	£0.60	£1.00
1 Variant Cover Edition, ND painted cover by Glenn Fabry						
	$0.40	$1.20	$2.00	£0.30	£0.90	£1.50
2-3 ND painted cover by Glenn Fabry						
	$0.30	$0.90	$1.50	£0.20	£0.60	£1.00
4 ND origin of Foxfire						
	$0.30	$0.90	$1.50	£0.20	£0.60	£1.00
Title Value:	$1.60	$4.80	$8.00	£1.10	£3.30	£5.50
FRAGGLE ROCK						
Marvel Comics Group/Star; 1 Apr 1985-8 Sep 1986						
1-8	$0.15	$0.45	$0.75	£0.10	£0.30	£0.50
Title Value:	$1.20	$3.60	$6.00	£0.80	£2.40	£4.00
FRAGMENTS						
Screaming Cat Productions; 1 1986						
1 ND Gregg Hinlicky script/art; black and white						
	$0.30	$0.90	$1.50	£0.20	£0.60	£1.00
Title Value:	$0.30	$0.90	$1.50	£0.20	£0.60	£1.00
FRANCIS, BROTHER OF THE UNIVERSE						
Marvel Comics Group,OS; 1 1980						
1 ND scarce in the U.K. 52pgs, story of Francis Bernadone						
	$0.15	$0.45	$0.75	£0.10	£0.35	£0.60
Title Value:	$0.15	$0.45	$0.75	£0.10	£0.35	£0.60
FRANK						
Nemesis,MS; 1 Mar 1994-4 Jun 1994						
1-4 ND D.G. Chichester script, Denys Cowan and Mike Manley art						
	$0.35	$1.05	$1.75	£0.25	£0.75	£1.25
Title Value:	$1.40	$4.20	$7.00	£1.00	£3.00	£5.00
FRANK FRAZETTA'S THUN'DA						
(see Thun'da Tales)						
FRANKENSTEIN						
Dell; 12-283-305 Mar/May 1963; 1 Aug/Oct 1964;2 Sep 1966-4 Mar 1967						
12-283-305 scarce in the U.K. adapts film						
	$6.25	$19.00	$45.00	£3.10	£9.25	£22.00
1 1st regular issue rare in the U.K.						
	$5.50	$17.00	$40.00	£2.85	£8.50	£20.00
2 scarce in the U.K. becomes super-hero title (another crap idea - see Dracula)						
	$3.20	$9.50	$22.50	£1.40	£4.25	£10.00
3-4 scarce in the U.K.						
	$1.75	$5.25	$12.50	£0.50	£1.50	£3.50
Title Value:	$18.45	$56.00	$132.50	£8.35	£25.00	£59.00
Note: all distributed on the news-stands in the U.K.						
FRANKENSTEIN (2ND SERIES)						
Malibu,MS; 1-3 Dec 1994						
1 ND released to co-incide with Kenneth Branagh's film						
	$0.50	$1.50	$2.50	£0.30	£0.90	£1.50
1 Black Book Edition, ND (Dec 1994) - black cover on thicker stock paper; 2,500 copies						
	$1.00	$3.00	$5.00	£0.70	£2.10	£3.50
2-3 ND released to co-incide with Kenneth Branagh's film						
	$0.50	$1.50	$2.50	£0.30	£0.90	£1.50
Title Value:	$2.50	$7.50	$12.50	£1.60	£4.80	£8.00
FRANKENSTEIN BOOK AND RECORD SET						
Power Records;PR-14 1974						
PR-14, scarce in the U.K. 20pg booklet with 45 rpm record						
	$0.80	$2.50	$5.00	£0.80	£2.50	£5.00
Title Value:	$0.80	$2.50	$5.00	£0.80	£2.50	£5.00
Note: the item would be valued at about 50% less without record						
FRANKENSTEIN JNR.						
Gold Key; 1 Jan 1966						
1 scarce though distributed in the U.K. based on cartoon series						
	$5.50	$17.00	$40.00	£3.55	£10.50	£25.00
Title Value:	$5.50	$17.00	$40.00	£3.55	£10.50	£25.00
FRANKENSTEIN OR THE MODERN PROMETHEUS						
Caliber Press,OS; nn Oct 1994						
nn ND 48pgs, Charles Yates art, Vince Locke painted cover						
	$0.60	$1.80	$3.00	£0.40	£1.20	£2.00
Title Value:	$0.60	$1.80	$3.00	£0.40	£1.20	£2.00
FRANKENSTEIN PAGES, THE LOST						
Apple Comics,OS; 1 Jan 1992						
1 ND 48pgs, Bernie Wrightson reprint from Marvel Comics with unpublished pages						
	$1.40	$4.20	$7.00	£0.90	£2.70	£4.50
Title Value:	$1.40	$4.20	$7.00	£0.90	£2.70	£4.50
FRANKENSTEIN, MARY SHELLEY'S						
Topps,MS; 1 Oct 1994-4 Jan 1995						
1 ND adaptation of Kenneth Branagh film, Timothy Bradstreet cover						
	$0.40	$1.20	$2.00	£0.25	£0.75	£1.25
1 Direct Market Edition, ND (Oct 1994) - pre-bagged with trading card; John Bolton cover						
	$0.50	$1.50	$2.50	£0.30	£0.90	£1.50
2 ND adaptation of Kenneth Branagh film, Timothy Bradstreet cover						

	$Good	$Fine	$N.Mint	£Good	£Fine	£N.Mint
	$0.40	$1.20	$2.00	£0.25	£0.75	£1.25
2 Direct Market Edition, ND (Nov 1994) - pre-bagged with trading card; John Bolton cover						
	$0.50	$1.50	$2.50	£0.30	£0.90	£1.50
3 ND adaptation of Kenneth Branagh film, Timothy Bradstreet cover						
	$0.40	$1.20	$2.00	£0.25	£0.75	£1.25
3 Direct Market Edition, ND (Dec 1994) - pre-bagged with trading card; John Bolton cover						
	$0.50	$1.50	$2.50	£0.30	£0.90	£1.50
4 ND adaptation of Kenneth Branagh film, Timothy Bradstreet cover						
	$0.40	$1.20	$2.00	£0.25	£0.75	£1.25
4 Direct Market Edition, ND (Jan 1995) - pre-bagged with trading card; John Bolton cover						
	$0.50	$1.50	$2.50	£0.30	£0.90	£1.50
Title Value:	$3.60	$10.80	$18.00	£2.20	£6.60	£11.00
Mary Shelley's Frankenstein Deluxe (Mar 1995)						
Trade paperback reprints series with John Bolton covers and						
new wraparound cover by Tim Bradstreet				£1.30	£3.90	£6.50
FRANKENSTEIN, THE MONSTER OF						
Marvel Comics Group; 1 Jan 1973-18 Sep 1975						
(see Marvel Illustrated Books)						
1 ND Ploog art begins, ends #6						
	$3.00	$9.00	$18.00	£2.05	£6.25	£12.50
2 ND	$2.05	$6.25	$12.50	£1.25	£3.75	£7.50
3-4 ND	$1.65	$5.00	$10.00	£1.00	£3.00	£6.00
5 ND	$1.65	$5.00	$10.00	£0.80	£2.50	£5.00
6-7 ND	$1.25	$3.75	$7.50	£0.65	£2.00	£4.00
8-9 ND Dracula appears						
	$1.50	$4.50	$9.00	£0.75	£2.25	£4.50
10 ND	$1.25	$3.75	$7.50	£0.65	£2.00	£4.00
11 ND	$0.55	$1.75	$3.50	£0.40	£1.25	£2.50
12-18	$0.55	$1.75	$3.50	£0.35	£1.10	£2.25
Title Value:	$21.15	$64.50	$129.00	£12.40	£37.95	£76.25
FRANKENSTEIN/DRACULA WAR, THE						
Topps,MS; 1 Feb 1995-3 Apr 1995						
1-3 ND Roy Thomas script, Mike Mignola cover						
	$0.40	$1.20	$2.00	£0.25	£0.75	£1.25
Title Value:	$1.20	$3.60	$6.00	£0.75	£2.25	£3.75
FREAK FORCE						
Image; 1 Dec 1993-18 Jun 1995						
1 Erik Larsen script, Keith Giffen plot begins						
	$0.50	$1.50	$2.50	£0.30	£0.90	£1.50
2-3	$0.40	$1.20	$2.00	£0.25	£0.75	£1.25
4 features Vanguard						
	$0.40	$1.20	$2.00	£0.25	£0.75	£1.25
5	$0.40	$1.20	$2.00	£0.25	£0.75	£1.25
6 origin of Rapture	$0.40	$1.20	$2.00	£0.25	£0.75	£1.25
7	$0.40	$1.20	$2.00	£0.25	£0.75	£1.25
8 Vanguard appears						
	$0.40	$1.20	$2.00	£0.25	£0.75	£1.25
9 Cyberforce guest-stars						
	$0.40	$1.20	$2.00	£0.25	£0.75	£1.25
10 Savage Dragon guest-stars						
	$0.40	$1.20	$2.00	£0.25	£0.75	£1.25
11-18	$0.40	$1.20	$2.00	£0.25	£0.75	£1.25
Title Value:	$7.30	$21.90	$36.50	£4.55	£13.65	£22.75
Note: all Non-Distributed on the news-stands in the U.K.						
FREAKS						
Monster Comics,MS; 1 Jun 1992-3 1992						
1-3 ND Sam Kieth covers						
	$0.50	$1.50	$2.50	£0.30	£0.90	£1.50
Title Value:	$1.50	$4.50	$7.50	£0.90	£2.70	£4.50
FRED HEMBECK DESTROYS THE MARVEL UNIVERSE						
Marvel Comics Group,OS; 1 Jul 1989						
1 ND no advertisements						
	$0.30	$0.90	$1.50	£0.20	£0.60	£1.00
Title Value:	$0.30	$0.90	$1.50	£0.20	£0.60	£1.00
FRED HEMBECK SELLS THE MARVEL UNIVERSE						
Marvel Comics Group,OS; 1 Oct 1990						
1 ND reprints Marvel Age strips						
	$0.30	$0.90	$1.50	£0.20	£0.60	£1.00
Title Value:	$0.30	$0.90	$1.50	£0.20	£0.60	£1.00
FREDDY'S DEAD - THE FINAL NIGHTMARE						
Innovation,MS; 1 Nov 1991-3 Jan 1992						
1-2 ND based on film						
	$0.50	$1.50	$2.50	£0.30	£0.90	£1.50
3 ND based on film; part 3-D issue (as the 6th film in the series is part 3-D or "Freddyvision"); no glasses were issued with the comic as they were issued when seeing the film						
	$0.50	$1.50	$2.50	£0.30	£0.90	£1.50
Title Value:	$1.50	$4.50	$7.50	£0.90	£2.70	£4.50
Graphic Novel (Feb 1992),						
reprints mini-series with cover by John Dismukes				£0.90	£2.70	£4.50
FREEDOM AGENT						
Gold Key; 1 Apr 1963						
(see John Steele Secret Agent)						
1 scarce, distributed in the U.K. painted cover						
	$5.00	$15.00	$35.00	£2.85	£8.50	£20.00
Title Value:	$5.00	$15.00	$35.00	£2.85	£8.50	£20.00
FREEDOM FIGHTERS						
DC Comics; 1 Mar/Apr 1976-15 Jul/Aug 1978						
1 ND	$0.65	$2.00	$4.00	£0.50	£1.50	£3.00
2-3 scarce in the U.K.						
	$0.50	$1.50	$3.00	£0.30	£1.00	£2.00
4 scarce in the U.K. Wonder Woman appears						
	$0.30	$1.00	$2.00	£0.25	£0.75	£1.50

	$Good	$Fine	$N.Mint	£Good	£Fine	£N.Mint
5 Wonder Woman appears	$0.30	$1.00	$2.00	£0.20	£0.60	£1.25
6	$0.30	$1.00	$2.00	£0.20	£0.60	£1.25
7 Justice League of America appears	$0.30	$1.00	$2.00	£0.20	£0.60	£1.25
8-9 scarce in the U.K.	$0.30	$1.00	$2.00	£0.20	£0.60	£1.25
10 scarce in the U.K. origin Doll Man re-told	$0.30	$1.00	$2.00	£0.20	£0.60	£1.25
11 origin The Ray re-told	$0.25	$0.75	$1.50	£0.15	£0.50	£1.00
12-13	$0.25	$0.75	$1.50	£0.15	£0.50	£1.00
14 Batwoman and Batgirl guest-star	$0.25	$0.75	$1.50	£0.15	£0.50	£1.00
15	$0.25	$0.75	$1.50	£0.15	£0.50	£1.00
Title Value:	$5.00	$15.75	$31.50	£3.30	£10.35	£21.00

FEATURES
Freedom Fighters (Black Condor, Uncle Sam, The Ray, Doll Man, Phantom Lady, Human Bomb) in all.

FREEJACK
Now Comics,MS; 1 Apr 1992-3 Jun 1992

	$Good	$Fine	$N.Mint	£Good	£Fine	£N.Mint
1 ND based on film, bi-weekly	$0.40	$1.20	$2.00	£0.25	£0.75	£1.25
1 Direct Market Edition, ND - with free poster	$0.50	$1.50	$2.50	£0.30	£0.90	£1.50
2 ND bi-weekly	$0.40	$1.20	$2.00	£0.25	£0.75	£1.25
2 Direct Market Edition, ND - with free poster	$0.50	$1.50	$2.50	£0.30	£0.90	£1.50
3 ND bi-weekly	$0.40	$1.20	$2.00	£0.25	£0.75	£1.25
3 Direct Market Edition, ND - with free poster	$0.50	$1.50	$2.50	£0.30	£0.90	£1.50
Title Value:	$2.70	$8.10	$13.50	£1.65	£4.95	£8.25

FREEX
Malibu Ultraverse; 1 Jul 1993-18 Feb 1995

	$Good	$Fine	$N.Mint	£Good	£Fine	£N.Mint
1 pre-bagged with a trading card and large card coupon for Ultraverse #0	$0.50	$1.50	$2.50	£0.30	£0.90	£1.50
1 Limited Edition, : full hologram cover; 7,500 copies	$3.00	$9.00	$15.00	£1.50	£4.50	£7.50
1 without coupon/card	$0.45	$1.35	$2.25	£0.25	£0.75	£1.25
2-3	$0.50	$1.50	$2.50	£0.30	£0.90	£1.50
4 40pgs, Rune insert	$0.50	$1.50	$2.50	£0.30	£0.90	£1.50
5	$0.40	$1.20	$2.00	£0.25	£0.75	£1.25
6 Break-Thru X-over	$0.40	$1.20	$2.00	£0.25	£0.75	£1.25
7 Origins part 1: Pressure (ends #11)	$0.40	$1.20	$2.00	£0.25	£0.75	£1.25
8-11	$0.40	$1.20	$2.00	£0.25	£0.75	£1.25
12 Ultraforce tie-in	$0.40	$1.20	$2.00	£0.25	£0.75	£1.25
13-14	$0.40	$1.20	$2.00	£0.25	£0.75	£1.25
15 64pgs, flip-book format with Ultraverse Premiere #9	$0.70	$2.10	$3.50	£0.30	£0.90	£1.50
16 prelude to Godwheel story	$0.40	$1.20	$2.00	£0.25	£0.75	£1.25
17 Rune appears	$0.40	$1.20	$2.00	£0.25	£0.75	£1.25
18	$0.40	$1.20	$2.00	£0.25	£0.75	£1.25
Title Value:	$11.35	$34.05	$56.75	£6.50	£19.50	£32.50

Note: all Non-Distributed on the news-stands in the U.K.

FREEX, GIANT SIZE
Malibu Ultraverse; 1 Jul 1994

	$Good	$Fine	$N.Mint	£Good	£Fine	£N.Mint
1 ND 40pgs	$0.40	$1.20	$2.00	£0.25	£0.75	£1.25
Title Value:	$0.40	$1.20	$2.00	£0.25	£0.75	£1.25

FRENCH ICE
Renegade; 1 Jan 1987-13 Apr 1988

	$Good	$Fine	$N.Mint	£Good	£Fine	£N.Mint
1-13 ND Carmen Cru translated reprints; black and white	$0.40	$1.20	$2.00	£0.25	£0.75	£1.25
Title Value:	$5.20	$15.60	$26.00	£3.25	£9.75	£16.25

FRIENDS
Renegade; 1 May 1987-3 Sep 1987

	$Good	$Fine	$N.Mint	£Good	£Fine	£N.Mint
1-3 ND	$0.40	$1.20	$2.00	£0.25	£0.75	£1.25
Title Value:	$1.20	$3.60	$6.00	£0.75	£2.25	£3.75

FRIGHT
Atlas; 1 Jun 1975

	$Good	$Fine	$N.Mint	£Good	£Fine	£N.Mint
1 Son of Dracula by Frank Thorne; distributed in the U.K.	$0.30	$1.00	$2.00	£0.20	£0.60	£1.25
Title Value:	$0.30	$1.00	$2.00	£0.20	£0.60	£1.25

FRIGHT (2ND SERIES)
Eternity; 1 Jul 1988-13 Aug 1989

	$Good	$Fine	$N.Mint	£Good	£Fine	£N.Mint
1-13 ND black and white; mature readers label	$0.40	$1.20	$2.00	£0.25	£0.75	£1.25
Title Value:	$5.20	$15.60	$26.00	£3.25	£9.75	£16.25

FRIGHT NIGHT
Now Comics; 1 Oct 1988-22 Jul 1990

	$Good	$Fine	$N.Mint	£Good	£Fine	£N.Mint
1-6 ND adapts film	$0.40	$1.20	$2.00	£0.25	£0.75	£1.25
7-22 ND	$0.40	$1.20	$2.00	£0.25	£0.75	£1.25
Title Value:	$8.80	$26.40	$44.00	£5.50	£16.50	£27.50
Fright Night Annual (1993) includes centre-fold pin-up of all Fright Night covers				£0.30	£0.90	£1.50

FRIGHT NIGHT 3-D HALLOWEEN SPECIAL
Now Comics,OS; 1 Dec 1992

	$Good	$Fine	$N.Mint	£Good	£Fine	£N.Mint
1 ND pre-bagged with glasses (25% less without glasses)	$0.50	$1.50	$2.50	£0.30	£0.90	£1.50
Title Value:	$0.50	$1.50	$2.50	£0.30	£0.90	£1.50

FRIGHT NIGHT 3-D SPECIAL
Now Comics,OS; 1 Jun 1992

	$Good	$Fine	$N.Mint	£Good	£Fine	£N.Mint
1 ND with 3-D glasses (25% less without glasses)	$0.50	$1.50	$2.50	£0.30	£0.90	£1.50
Title Value:	$0.50	$1.50	$2.50	£0.30	£0.90	£1.50

FRIGHT NIGHT 3-D SUMMER SPECIAL
Now Comics,OS; 1 Aug 1993

	$Good	$Fine	$N.Mint	£Good	£Fine	£N.Mint
1 ND with 3-D glasses	$0.60	$1.80	$3.00	£0.40	£1.20	£2.00
Title Value:	$0.60	$1.80	$3.00	£0.40	£1.20	£2.00

FRIGHT NIGHT 3-D WINTER SPECIAL
Now Comics,OS; 1 May 1993

	$Good	$Fine	$N.Mint	£Good	£Fine	£N.Mint
1 ND pre-bagged with 3-D glasses (25% less without glasses)	$0.60	$1.80	$3.00	£0.40	£1.20	£2.00
Title Value:	$0.60	$1.80	$3.00	£0.40	£1.20	£2.00

FRIGHT NIGHT II
Now Comics,OS; 1 1989

	$Good	$Fine	$N.Mint	£Good	£Fine	£N.Mint
1 ND adapts film	$0.80	$2.40	$4.00	£0.50	£1.50	£2.50
Title Value:	$0.80	$2.40	$4.00	£0.50	£1.50	£2.50

FRINGE
Caliber Press; 1 Feb 1990-8 1992

	$Good	$Fine	$N.Mint	£Good	£Fine	£N.Mint
1-8 ND Paul Tobin script, Philip Hester art; black and white	$0.40	$1.20	$2.00	£0.25	£0.75	£1.25
Title Value:	$3.20	$9.60	$16.00	£2.00	£6.00	£10.00

FRISKY FROLICS
Renegade;(Revolver 13) 1 Nov 1986

	$Good	$Fine	$N.Mint	£Good	£Fine	£N.Mint
1 ND DS	$0.40	$1.20	$2.00	£0.25	£0.75	£1.25
Title Value:	$0.40	$1.20	$2.00	£0.25	£0.75	£1.25

Freex #1

Fright #1

From Beyond the Unknown #2

FROM BEYOND THE UNKNOWN

National Periodical Publications; 1 Oct/Nov 1969-25 Nov/Dec 1973

Issue	$Good	$Fine	$N.Mint	£Good	£Fine	£N.Mint
1 scarce in the U.K. reprints from Mystery in Space and Strange Adventures begin	$1.65	$5.00	$10.00	£0.90	£2.75	£5.50
2 scarce in the U.K. all reprint	$1.00	$3.00	$6.00	£0.55	£1.75	£3.50
3-5 scarce in the U.K. all reprint	$1.00	$3.00	$6.00	£0.50	£1.50	£3.00
6 scarce in the U.K. all reprint, Gil Kane art featured	$1.00	$3.00	$6.00	£0.40	£1.25	£2.50
7 64pgs, new 12pg story by O'Neil/Anderson plus reprints, Kubert cover	$1.00	$3.00	$6.00	£0.40	£1.25	£2.50
8 64pgs, new 12pg story by O'Neil/Anderson plus reprints	$1.00	$3.00	$6.00	£0.40	£1.25	£2.50
9-10 64pgs, all reprint	$1.00	$3.00	$6.00	£0.40	£1.25	£2.50
11 64pgs, all reprint	$0.75	$2.25	$4.50	£0.30	£1.00	£2.00
12-14 48pgs, all reprint, Kubert cover	$0.75	$2.25	$4.50	£0.30	£1.00	£2.00
15 scarce in the U.K. 48pgs, all reprint	$0.75	$2.25	$4.50	£0.40	£1.25	£2.50
16-17 48pgs, all reprint	$0.75	$2.25	$4.50	£0.30	£1.00	£2.00
18 all reprint	$0.75	$2.25	$4.50	£0.20	£0.60	£1.25
19 all reprint, Kaluta cover	$0.75	$2.25	$4.50	£0.25	£0.75	£1.50
20-21 all reprint	$0.75	$2.25	$4.50	£0.25	£0.75	£1.50
22 all reprint, photo cover	$0.65	$2.00	$4.00	£0.25	£0.75	£1.50
23-25 all reprint	$0.65	$2.00	$4.00	£0.25	£0.75	£1.50
Title Value:	$21.50	$64.75	$129.00	£9.10	£28.35	£56.75

FEATURES

All science-fiction reprints except one new story each in 7, 8

FROM BEYONDE

Studio Insidio; 1 Feb 1991

Issue	$Good	$Fine	$N.Mint	£Good	£Fine	£N.Mint
1 ND 48pgs, black and white horror anthology	$0.60	$1.80	$3.00	£0.40	£1.20	£2.00
Title Value:	$0.60	$1.80	$3.00	£0.40	£1.20	£2.00

FROM DUSK TILL DAWN

Tekno Comix/Big Entertainment,OS; nn Apr 1996

Issue	$Good	$Fine	$N.Mint	£Good	£Fine	£N.Mint
nn Deluxe Edition ND 48pgs, (Jul 1996), film adaptation plus behind the scenes material and interviews	$2.00	$6.00	$10.00	£1.30	£3.90	£6.50
nn Regular Edition ND 48pgs, adaptation of Quentin Tarantino film	$1.00	$3.00	$5.00	£0.65	£1.95	£3.25
Title Value:	$3.00	$9.00	$15.00	£1.95	£5.85	£9.75

FROM HELL

Tundra Publishing; 1 Apr 1991;2 Aug 1993;3 1993;Kitchen Sink;4 Mar 1994-present

Issue	$Good	$Fine	$N.Mint	£Good	£Fine	£N.Mint
1 ND collects first 2 episodes of Alan Moore and Eddie Campbell "Jack the Ripper" story from Taboo	$1.50	$4.50	$7.50	£0.80	£2.40	£4.00
1 2nd printing, ND (Jul 1992)	$0.90	$2.70	$4.50	£0.60	£1.80	£3.00
1 3rd printing ND	$0.90	$2.70	$4.50	£0.60	£1.80	£3.00
2 ND	$1.20	$3.60	$6.00	£0.70	£2.10	£3.50
2 2nd printing, ND (Aug 1994) - new cover logo, updated appendix	$1.00	$3.00	$5.00	£0.60	£1.80	£3.00
3-5 ND	$1.00	$3.00	$5.00	£0.60	£1.80	£3.00
6-10 ND	$1.00	$3.00	$5.00	£0.50	£1.50	£2.50
Title Value:	$13.50	$40.50	$67.50	£7.60	£22.80	£38.00

FROM THE DARK

Fantagor; 1 Apr 1991

Issue	$Good	$Fine	$N.Mint	£Good	£Fine	£N.Mint
1 ND Richard Corben, Bruce Jones, black and white	$0.40	$1.20	$2.00	£0.25	£0.75	£1.25
Title Value:	$0.40	$1.20	$2.00	£0.25	£0.75	£1.25

FROM THE DARKNESS

Eternity,MS; 1 Oct 1990-4 Jan 1991

Issue	$Good	$Fine	$N.Mint	£Good	£Fine	£N.Mint
1-4 ND black and white	$2.00	$6.00	$10.00	£0.30	£0.90	£1.50
Title Value:	$8.00	$24.00	$40.00	£1.20	£3.60	£6.00

FROM THE PIT

Fantagor; 1 Jul 1994

Issue	$Good	$Fine	$N.Mint	£Good	£Fine	£N.Mint
1 ND Richard Corben script and art	$1.00	$3.00	$5.00	£0.70	£2.10	£3.50
Title Value:	$1.00	$3.00	$5.00	£0.70	£2.10	£3.50

Note: issue #2 was advertised and solicited but never came out.

FROM THE VOID

Graphic Story Society; 1 1982

Issue	$Good	$Fine	$N.Mint	£Good	£Fine	£N.Mint
1 ND	$0.30	$0.90	$1.50	£0.20	£0.60	£1.00
Title Value:	$0.30	$0.90	$1.50	£0.20	£0.60	£1.00

FRONTIER

Slave Labor; 1 Jul 1994

Issue	$Good	$Fine	$N.Mint	£Good	£Fine	£N.Mint
1 ND Paul Duncan script, Steve Pugh art	$0.60	$1.80	$3.00	£0.40	£1.20	£2.00
Title Value:	$0.60	$1.80	$3.00	£0.40	£1.20	£2.00

FRONTIER FIGHTERS

National Periodical Publications; 1 Sep/Oct 1955-8 Nov/Dec 1956

Issue	$Good	$Fine	$N.Mint	£Good	£Fine	£N.Mint
1 very rare in the U.K. Buffalo Bill and Davy Crockett by Joe Kubert begin	$52.50	$155.00	$425.00	£36.00	£105.00	£285.00
2 rare in the U.K.	$44.00	$130.00	$310.00	£30.00	£90.00	£210.00
3-8 rare in the U.K.	$37.00	$110.00	$260.00	£25.00	£75.00	£175.00
Title Value:	$318.50	$945.00	$2295.00	£216.00	£645.00	£1545.00

Note: all Non-Distributed on the news-stands in the U.K.

FRONTIER ROMANCES

I.W. Super; 1,9 1964

Issue	$Good	$Fine	$N.Mint	£Good	£Fine	£N.Mint
1 scarce though distributed in the U.K. reprints Avon #1	$4.60	$13.50	$32.50	£2.10	£6.25	£15.00
9 scarce though distributed in the U.K. reprints Avon Periodicals title	$2.85	$8.50	$20.00	£1.25	£3.85	£9.00
Title Value:	$7.45	$22.00	$52.50	£3.35	£10.10	£24.00

FRONTIER SCOUT DANIEL BOONE

Charlton; 10 Jan 1956-13 Aug 1956; 14 Mar 1965

Issue	$Good	$Fine	$N.Mint	£Good	£Fine	£N.Mint
10 ND scarce in the U.K.	$8.50	$26.00	$60.00	£3.55	£10.50	£25.00
11-13 ND scarce in the U.K.	$5.00	$15.00	$35.00	£2.50	£7.50	£17.50
14 distributed in the U.K.	$3.20	$9.50	$22.50	£1.40	£4.25	£10.00
Title Value:	$26.70	$80.50	$187.50	£12.45	£37.25	£87.50

FRONTLINE COMBAT

E.C. Comics; 1 Jul/Aug 1951-15 Jan 1954

Issue	$Good	$Fine	$N.Mint	£Good	£Fine	£N.Mint
1 Harvey Kurtzman cover and art	$75.00	$225.00	$525.00	£50.00	£150.00	£350.00
2 Harvey Kurtzman cover and art	$43.00	$125.00	$300.00	£29.00	£85.00	£200.00
3 Harvey Kurtzman cover	$30.00	$90.00	$210.00	£20.00	£60.00	£140.00
4 Harvey Kurtzman cover	$29.00	$85.00	$200.00	£19.00	£57.50	£135.00
5 Harvey Kurtzman cover	$22.50	$67.50	$160.00	£15.50	£47.00	£110.00
6 Harvey Kurtzman cover	$18.50	$55.00	$130.00	£12.50	£38.00	£87.50
7 Iwo Jima issue, Harvey Kurtzman cover	$18.50	$55.00	$130.00	£12.50	£38.00	£87.50
8 Harvey Kurtzman cover	$18.50	$55.00	$130.00	£12.50	£38.00	£87.50
9 Civil War issue, Harvey Kurtzman cover	$18.50	$55.00	$130.00	£12.50	£38.00	£87.50
10 Harvey Kurtzman cover	$18.50	$55.00	$130.00	£12.50	£38.00	£87.50
11	$14.00	$43.00	$100.00	£9.50	£29.00	£67.50
12 Air Force issue	$14.00	$43.00	$100.00	£9.50	£29.00	£67.50
13	$14.00	$43.00	$100.00	£9.50	£29.00	£67.50
14-15 less common in the U.K.	$14.00	$43.00	$100.00	£10.00	£30.00	£70.00
Title Value:	$362.00	$1082.50	$2545.00	£244.50	£736.50	£1715.00

Note: all Non-Distributed on the news-stands in the U.K.

FRONTLINE COMBAT (2ND SERIES)

E.C. Comics/Russ Cochran; 1 Jun 1995-present

Issue	$Good	$Fine	$N.Mint	£Good	£Fine	£N.Mint
1 ND reprints begin from the original issue #1	$0.40	$1.20	$2.00	£0.25	£0.75	£1.25
2-4 ND	$0.40	$1.20	$2.00	£0.25	£0.75	£1.25
5 ND	$0.50	$1.50	$2.50	£0.30	£0.90	£1.50
Title Value:	$2.10	$6.30	$10.50	£1.30	£3.90	£6.50

FROST

Caliber Press,OS; 1 1990

Issue	$Good	$Fine	$N.Mint	£Good	£Fine	£N.Mint
1 ND	$0.30	$0.90	$1.50	£0.20	£0.60	£1.00
Title Value:	$0.30	$0.90	$1.50	£0.20	£0.60	£1.00
Frost Graphic Novel (1991), reprints issues #1,2 by Amazing Comics plus Caliber one-shot				£1.00	£3.00	£5.00

FROST: THE DYING BREED

Caliber Press,MS; 1 Jun 1991-4 Feb 1992

Issue	$Good	$Fine	$N.Mint	£Good	£Fine	£N.Mint
1-4 ND	$0.50	$1.50	$2.50	£0.30	£0.90	£1.50
Title Value:	$2.00	$6.00	$10.00	£1.20	£3.60	£6.00

FUGITIVE

Caliber Press,OS; 1 1989

Issue	$Good	$Fine	$N.Mint	£Good	£Fine	£N.Mint
1 ND 48pgs, black and white	$0.50	$1.50	$2.50	£0.30	£0.90	£1.50
Title Value:	$0.50	$1.50	$2.50	£0.30	£0.90	£1.50

FUGITOID

Mirage Studios,Magazine; 1 Jan 1986

Issue	$Good	$Fine	$N.Mint	£Good	£Fine	£N.Mint
1 ND ties in to Teenage Mutant Ninja Turtles #4-7, black and white	$1.20	$3.60	$6.00	£0.80	£2.40	£4.00
Title Value:	$1.20	$3.60	$6.00	£0.80	£2.40	£4.00

FULL THROTTLE

Aircel,MS; 1 Oct 1991-2 Nov 1991

Issue	$Good	$Fine	$N.Mint	£Good	£Fine	£N.Mint
1-2 ND black and white	$0.50	$1.50	$2.50	£0.30	£0.90	£1.50
Title Value:	$1.00	$3.00	$5.00	£0.60	£1.80	£3.00

FUN AND GAMES MAGAZINE

Marvel Comics Group; 1 Sep 1979-8? Apr 1980

Issue	$Good	$Fine	$N.Mint	£Good	£Fine	£N.Mint
1-8 ND	$0.25	$0.75	$1.50	£0.15	£0.50	£1.00
Title Value:	$2.00	$6.00	$12.00	£1.20	£4.00	£8.00

FUN COMICS

(see Bill Black's..)

FUN-IN

Gold Key, TV; 1 Feb 1970-10 Jan 1972; 11 Apr 1974-15 Dec 1974

Issue	$Good	$Fine	$N.Mint	£Good	£Fine	£N.Mint
1 ND Dastardly and Muttley, Penelope Pitstop	$4.15	$12.50	$25.00	£1.65	£5.00	£10.00
2-4 ND	$2.05	$6.25	$12.50	£0.80	£2.50	£5.00
5 ND Dastardly and Muttley	$2.50	$7.50	$15.00	£1.00	£3.00	£6.00

Issue	$Good	$Fine	$N.Mint	£Good	£Fine	£N.Mint
6 ND	$2.05	$6.25	$12.50	£0.80	£2.50	£5.00
7 ND Dastardly and Muttley	$2.50	$7.50	$15.00	£1.00	£3.00	£6.00
8 ND Harlem Globetrotters	$1.65	$5.00	$10.00	£0.65	£2.00	£4.00
9 ND Dastardly and Muttley	$2.50	$7.50	$15.00	£1.00	£3.00	£6.00
10 ND Harlem Globetrotters	$1.65	$5.00	$10.00	£0.65	£2.00	£4.00
11-15 ND	$1.50	$4.50	$9.00	£0.50	£1.50	£3.00
Title Value:	$30.65	$92.50	$185.00	£11.65	£35.50	£71.00

FUNKY PHANTOM, THE

Gold Key; 1 Mar 1972-13 Mar 1975

Issue	$Good	$Fine	$N.Mint	£Good	£Fine	£N.Mint
1 scarce distributed in the U.K. based on cartoon series	$3.65	$11.00	$22.00	£1.30	£4.00	£8.00
2-5	$2.00	$6.00	$12.00	£0.65	£2.00	£4.00
6-13	$1.25	$3.75	$7.50	£0.40	£1.25	£2.50
Title Value:	$21.65	$65.00	$130.00	£7.10	£22.00	£44.00

FUNNY STUFF STOCKING STUFFER

DC Comics,OS; 1 Mar 1985

Issue	$Good	$Fine	$N.Mint	£Good	£Fine	£N.Mint
1 48pgs, features most DC funny animals	$0.25	$0.75	$1.25	£0.15	£0.45	£0.75
Title Value:	$0.25	$0.75	$1.25	£0.15	£0.45	£0.75

FUNNYTIME FEATURES

Eenieweenie Comics; 1 1994-9 1996

Issue	$Good	$Fine	$N.Mint	£Good	£Fine	£N.Mint
1-6 ND	$0.50	$1.50	$2.50	£0.30	£0.90	£1.50
7 ND contains part 2 of X-over with Shi #7, art by Robb Bihun with black and white interior	$1.00	$3.00	$5.00	£0.70	£2.10	£3.50
7 Gold Edition, ND gold stamp on cover, limited to 3,000 copies (originally released as set containing both variant and standard Gold Editions)	$3.00	$9.00	$15.00	£2.00	£6.00	£10.00
7 Gold Edition Set, ND produced exclusively by Geoffrey's Comics; contains variant Gold Edition & standard Gold Edition; signed by Derek Drymon and Robb Bihun with certificate of authenticity; limited to 3,000 copies	$4.50	$13.50	$22.50	£3.00	£9.00	£15.00
7 Gold Variant Cover Edition, ND gold stamp on cover, limited to 3,000 copies (originally released as set containing both variant and standard Gold Editions)	$4.00	$12.00	$20.00	£2.50	£7.50	£12.50
7 Variant Cover Edition, ND black cover featuring Shi, cover art by Tucci	$3.00	$9.00	$15.00	£2.00	£6.00	£10.00
8-9 ND	$0.50	$1.50	$2.50	£0.30	£0.90	£1.50
Title Value:	$19.50	$58.50	$97.50	£12.60	£37.80	£63.00

FUNTASTIC WORLD OF HANNA-BARBERA, THE

Marvel Comics Group,Tabloid; 1 Dec 1977-3 Jun 1978

Issue	$Good	$Fine	$N.Mint	£Good	£Fine	£N.Mint
1 ND scarce in the U.K. Flintstones' Christmas Party	$1.00	$3.00	$6.00	£0.40	£1.25	£2.50
2 ND scarce in the U.K. Yogi Bear's Easter Parade	$1.00	$3.00	$6.00	£0.40	£1.25	£2.50
3 ND scarce in the U.K. Laff-a-Lympics	$1.00	$3.00	$6.00	£0.40	£1.25	£2.50
Title Value:	$3.00	$9.00	$18.00	£1.20	£3.75	£7.50

FURRLOUGH

Antarctic Press; 1 Jan 1992-present

Issue	$Good	$Fine	$N.Mint	£Good	£Fine	£N.Mint
1 ND 56pgs	$0.60	$1.80	$3.00	£0.40	£1.20	£2.00
2-20 ND 32pgs	$0.50	$1.50	$2.50	£0.30	£0.90	£1.50
21-22 ND 32pgs	$0.55	$1.65	$2.75	£0.35	£1.05	£1.75
23 ND 32pgs	$0.80	$2.40	$4.00	£0.50	£1.50	£2.50
24-34 ND 32pgs	$0.55	$1.65	$2.75	£0.35	£1.05	£1.75
35 ND 48pgs, 4th anniversary issue	$0.70	$2.10	$3.50	£0.50	£1.50	£2.50
36-43 ND	$0.60	$1.80	$3.00	£0.40	£1.20	£2.00
Title Value:	$23.55	$70.65	$117.75	£14.85	£44.55	£74.25
Best of Furrlough Volume 1 (Jan 1995) ND 64pgs, collection of selected best tales, special gate-fold cover				£0.50	£1.50	£2.50
Best of Furrlough Volume 2 (Jan 1996) ND 64pgs, collection of selected best tales				£0.50	£1.50	£2.50

FURY

Marvel Comics Group,OS; 1 May 1994

Issue	$Good	$Fine	$N.Mint	£Good	£Fine	£N.Mint
1 ND 64pgs, Nick Fury and his origin re-told; Wolverine and Iron Man guest-star	$0.60	$1.80	$3.00	£0.40	£1.20	£2.00
Title Value:	$0.60	$1.80	$3.00	£0.40	£1.20	£2.00

FURY OF FIRESTORM THE NUCLEAR MAN

(see Firestorm (2nd Series))

FURY OF S.H.I.E.L.D.

Marvel Comics Group; 1 Apr 1995-4 Jul 1995

Issue	$Good	$Fine	$N.Mint	£Good	£Fine	£N.Mint
1 foil-etched cover	$0.50	$1.50	$2.50	£0.30	£0.90	£1.50
2 Iron Man appears	$0.40	$1.20	$2.00	£0.25	£0.75	£1.25
3	$0.40	$1.20	$2.00	£0.25	£0.75	£1.25
4 bound-in decoder card	$0.50	$1.50	$2.50	£0.30	£0.90	£1.50
Title Value:	$1.80	$5.40	$9.00	£1.10	£3.30	£5.50

FUSION

Eclipse; 1 1987-17 1989

Issue	$Good	$Fine	$N.Mint	£Good	£Fine	£N.Mint
1-10 ND	$0.40	$1.20	$2.00	£0.20	£0.60	£1.00
11 ND 1st appearance Weasel Patrol	$0.40	$1.20	$2.00	£0.20	£0.60	£1.00
12-17 ND	$0.40	$1.20	$2.00	£0.20	£0.60	£1.00
Title Value:	$6.80	$20.40	$34.00	£3.40	£10.20	£17.00

FUTURIANS

Lodestone; 1 Oct 1985-3 1986

Issue	$Good	$Fine	$N.Mint	£Good	£Fine	£N.Mint
1-3 ND Dave Cockrum script and art	$0.40	$1.20	$2.00	£0.25	£0.75	£1.25
Title Value:	$1.20	$3.60	$6.00	£0.75	£2.25	£3.75

FUTURIANS (2ND SERIES)

Aardwolf Publications; 0 May 1995

Issue	$Good	$Fine	$N.Mint	£Good	£Fine	£N.Mint
0 ND reprints from original series; 50,000 print run	$0.60	$1.80	$3.00	£0.40	£1.20	£2.00
0 Signed Edition, ND (May 1995) - available to retailers for every 10 copies of issue #0 ordered	$0.70	$2.10	$3.50	£0.50	£1.50	£2.50
Title Value:	$1.30	$3.90	$6.50	£0.90	£2.70	£4.50

G

G-8 AND HIS BATTLE ACES

Gold Key; 1 Oct 1966

Issue	$Good	$Fine	$N.Mint	£Good	£Fine	£N.Mint
1 scarce, distributed in the U.K. painted cover	$4.25	$12.50	$30.00	£2.10	£6.25	£15.00
Title Value:	$4.25	$12.50	$30.00	£2.10	£6.25	£15.00

G-8 AND HIS BATTLE ACES (2ND SERIES)

Blazing Comics; 1 1991

Issue	$Good	$Fine	$N.Mint	£Good	£Fine	£N.Mint
1 ND Tim Truman cover and Sam Glanzman art, based on a 1940 story/characters; flip-book with The Spider's Web, all colour	$0.30	$0.90	$1.50	£0.20	£0.60	£1.00
Title Value:	$0.30	$0.90	$1.50	£0.20	£0.60	£1.00

G-8 AND HIS BATTLE ACES (3RD SERIES)

Millennium,MS; 1 Aug 1994-2 Sep 1994

Issue	$Good	$Fine	$N.Mint	£Good	£Fine	£N.Mint
1-2 ND new stories	$0.60	$1.80	$3.00	£0.40	£1.20	£2.00
Title Value:	$1.20	$3.60	$6.00	£0.80	£2.40	£4.00

G-MEN

Caliber Press; 1 Oct 1991

Issue	$Good	$Fine	$N.Mint	£Good	£Fine	£N.Mint
1 ND	$0.50	$1.50	$2.50	£0.30	£0.90	£1.50
Title Value:	$0.50	$1.50	$2.50	£0.30	£0.90	£1.50

G.I. COMBAT

National Periodical Publications;44 Jan 1957-288 Mar 1987

(previous issues #1-43 published by Quality Comics)

Issue	$Good	$Fine	$N.Mint	£Good	£Fine	£N.Mint
44 1st DC issue	$60.00	$180.00	$425.00	£42.00	£125.00	£295.00
45	$36.00	$105.00	$250.00	£26.00	£75.00	£180.00
46-50	$25.00	$75.00	$175.00	£17.00	£50.00	£120.00
51-60	$21.00	$62.50	$150.00	£12.00	£36.00	£85.00
61-66	$12.00	$36.00	$85.00	£5.50	£17.00	£40.00
67 1st appearance Tank Killer	$17.50	$52.50	$125.00	£7.75	£23.50	£55.00
1st official distribution in the U.K.						
68-80	$12.00	$36.00	$85.00	£4.25	£12.50	£30.00
81-82	$9.25	$28.00	$65.00	£3.55	£10.50	£25.00
83 scarce in the U.K. 1st appearances Big Al, Little Al, Charlie Cigar	$12.00	$36.00	$85.00	£3.90	£11.50	£27.50
84	$9.25	$28.00	$65.00	£3.55	£10.50	£25.00
85 painted (grey-tone) cover	$9.25	$28.00	$65.00	£3.55	£10.50	£25.00
86	$9.25	$28.00	$65.00	£3.55	£10.50	£25.00
87 scarce in the U.K. 1st appearance Haunted Tank (ends #246)	$38.00	$110.00	$300.00	£18.50	£55.00	£150.00
88-90 scarce in the U.K.	$9.25	$28.00	$65.00	£3.55	£10.50	£25.00
91-96 scarce in the U.K.	$7.75	$23.50	$55.00	£2.85	£8.50	£20.00
97-99	$7.75	$23.50	$55.00	£2.50	£7.50	£17.50
100	$7.75	$23.50	$55.00	£2.85	£8.50	£20.00
101-110	$7.00	$21.00	$50.00	£2.10	£6.25	£15.00
111-113	$5.50	$17.00	$40.00	£1.40	£4.25	£10.00
114 origin Haunted Tank	$10.50	$32.00	$75.00	£3.90	£11.50	£27.50
115-117	$5.50	$17.00	$40.00	£1.40	£4.25	£10.00
118-120 ND	$5.50	$17.00	$40.00	£1.75	£5.25	£12.50
121-135 ND	$4.25	$12.50	$30.00	£1.40	£4.25	£10.00
136 ND last 12¢ issue	$4.25	$12.50	$30.00	£1.40	£4.25	£10.00
137 ND	$4.25	$12.50	$30.00	£1.40	£4.25	£10.00
138 ND 1st appearance The Losers (Captain Storm, Gunner, Sarge and Johnny Cloud - see Losers Special)	$5.00	$15.00	$35.00	£1.75	£5.25	£12.50
139-140 ND	$5.00	$15.00	$30.00	£1.30	£4.00	£8.00
141-143 ND	$2.50	$7.50	$15.00	£1.00	£3.00	£6.00
144-146 ND 68pgs	$2.50	$7.50	$15.00	£1.25	£3.75	£7.50
147 scarce in the U.K. 68pgs	$2.50	$7.50	$15.00	£0.80	£2.50	£5.00
148-150 68pgs	$2.50	$7.50	$15.00	£0.55	£1.75	£3.50
151-152 52pgs	$1.65	$5.00	$10.00	£0.50	£1.50	£3.00
153 52pgs, Medal of Honour series by Maurer	$1.65	$5.00	$10.00	£0.50	£1.50	£3.00
154 52pgs	$1.65	$5.00	$10.00	£0.50	£1.50	£3.00
155-180	$1.65	$5.00	$10.00	£0.40	£1.25	£2.50
181-187	$1.00	$3.00	$6.00	£0.30	£1.00	£2.00
188 scarce in the U.K.	$1.00	$3.00	$6.00	£0.40	£1.25	£2.50
189-190	$1.00	$3.00	$6.00	£0.30	£1.00	£2.00
191 scarce in the U.K.	$1.00	$3.00	$6.00	£0.40	£1.25	£2.50
192	$1.00	$3.00	$6.00	£0.30	£1.00	£2.00
193-195 scarce in the U.K.	$1.00	$3.00	$6.00	£0.40	£1.25	£2.50
196-200	$1.00	$3.00	$6.00	£0.30	£1.00	£2.00

	$Good	$Fine	$N.Mint	£Good	£Fine	£N.Mint
201 ND 80pgs	*$1.00*	*$3.00*	*$5.00*	£0.60	£1.80	£3.00
202 scarce in the U.K. 80pgs						
	$1.00	*$3.00*	*$5.00*	£0.55	£1.65	£2.75
203-210 ND 80pgs	*$1.00*	*$3.00*	*$5.00*	£0.60	£1.80	£3.00
211-223 ND 68pgs	*$1.00*	*$3.00*	*$5.00*	£0.50	£1.50	£2.50
224-231 ND 52pgs	*$0.80*	*$2.40*	*$4.00*	£0.40	£1.20	£2.00
232 ND 52pgs, origin Kana the Ninja						
	$0.80	*$2.40*	*$4.00*	£0.40	£1.20	£2.00
233 ND 52pgs	*$0.80*	*$2.40*	*$4.00*	£0.40	£1.20	£2.00
234-242 52pgs	*$0.80*	*$2.40*	*$4.00*	£0.30	£0.90	£1.50
243 ND 52pgs	*$0.70*	*$2.10*	*$3.50*	£0.40	£1.20	£2.00
244 ND 52pgs, death of Slim Stryker, 1st appearance Mercenaries						
	$0.80	*$2.40*	*$4.00*	£0.50	£1.50	£2.50
245 ND 52pgs	*$0.70*	*$2.10*	*$3.50*	£0.40	£1.20	£2.00
246 ND 72pgs, 30th anniversary issue						
	$0.80	*$2.40*	*$4.00*	£0.50	£1.50	£2.50
247-256	*$0.60*	*$1.80*	*$3.00*	£0.20	£0.60	£1.00
257 1st appearance Stuart's Raiders						
	$0.70	*$2.10*	*$3.50*	£0.25	£0.75	£1.25
258-259	*$0.60*	*$1.80*	*$3.00*	£0.20	£0.60	£1.00
260-263 64pgs	*$0.70*	*$2.10*	*$3.50*	£0.30	£0.90	£1.50
264 64pgs, 1st appearance Sgt.Bullet & the Bravos of Vietnam; origin Kana retold						
	$0.80	*$2.40*	*$4.00*	£0.40	£1.20	£2.00
265-273 64pgs	*$0.70*	*$2.10*	*$3.50*	£0.30	£0.90	£1.50
274 64pgs, 1st full appearance of The Monitor (see New Teen Titans #21 and Crisis on Infinite Earths)						
	$0.70	*$2.10*	*$3.50*	£0.30	£0.90	£1.50
275-281 64pgs	*$0.70*	*$2.10*	*$3.50*	£0.30	£0.90	£1.50
282-288	*$0.60*	*$1.80*	*$3.00*	£0.20	£0.60	£1.00
Title Value:	*$1258.55*	*$3770.40*	*$8595.00*	£573.75	£1714.10	£3987.50

G.I. COMBAT (SPECIAL)

DC Comics; nn Sep 1980
(DC Special Series #22)

	$Good	$Fine	$N.Mint	£Good	£Fine	£N.Mint
nn ND 68pgs, features Haunted Tank						
	$0.60	*$1.80*	*$3.00*	£0.40	£1.20	£2.00
Title Value:	*$0.60*	*$1.80*	*$3.00*	£0.40	£1.20	£2.00

G.I. JOE

Marvel Comics Group; 1 Jun 1982-155 Dec 1994

	$Good	$Fine	$N.Mint	£Good	£Fine	£N.Mint
1 ND Baxter paper	*$1.00*	*$3.00*	*$5.00*	£0.70	£2.10	£3.50
2 ND scarce in the U.K.						
	$0.80	*$2.40*	*$4.00*	£0.80	£2.40	£4.00
2 2nd printing, ND 75 cents cover						
	$0.50	*$1.50*	*$2.50*	£0.30	£0.90	£1.50
3-4 ND	*$0.80*	*$2.40*	*$4.00*	£0.50	£1.50	£2.50
5-6 ND	*$0.60*	*$1.80*	*$3.00*	£0.40	£1.20	£2.00
6 2nd printing ND	*$0.40*	*$1.20*	*$2.00*	£0.25	£0.75	£1.25
7 ND	*$0.60*	*$1.80*	*$3.00*	£0.40	£1.20	£2.00
7 2nd printing ND	*$0.30*	*$0.90*	*$1.50*	£0.20	£0.60	£1.00
8 ND	*$0.60*	*$1.80*	*$3.00*	£0.40	£1.20	£2.00
8 2nd printing ND	*$0.30*	*$0.90*	*$1.50*	£0.20	£0.60	£1.00
9-10 ND	*$0.60*	*$1.80*	*$3.00*	£0.40	£1.20	£2.00
10 2nd printing ND	*$0.30*	*$0.90*	*$1.50*	£0.20	£0.60	£1.00
11 ND	*$0.50*	*$1.50*	*$2.50*	£0.30	£0.90	£1.50
11 2nd printing ND	*$0.30*	*$0.90*	*$1.50*	£0.20	£0.60	£1.00
12 ND	*$0.50*	*$1.50*	*$2.50*	£0.30	£0.90	£1.50
12 2nd printing ND	*$0.30*	*$0.90*	*$1.50*	£0.20	£0.60	£1.00
13-14 ND	*$0.50*	*$1.50*	*$2.50*	£0.30	£0.90	£1.50
14 2nd printing ND	*$0.30*	*$0.90*	*$1.50*	£0.20	£0.60	£1.00
15-17 ND	*$0.50*	*$1.50*	*$2.50*	£0.30	£0.90	£1.50
17 2nd printing ND	*$0.30*	*$0.90*	*$1.50*	£0.20	£0.60	£1.00
18 ND	*$0.50*	*$1.50*	*$2.50*	£0.30	£0.90	£1.50
18 2nd printing ND	*$0.30*	*$0.90*	*$1.50*	£0.20	£0.60	£1.00
19 ND	*$0.50*	*$1.50*	*$2.50*	£0.30	£0.90	£1.50
19 2nd printing ND	*$0.30*	*$0.90*	*$1.50*	£0.20	£0.60	£1.00
20 ND	*$0.50*	*$1.50*	*$2.50*	£0.30	£0.90	£1.50
21 ND	*$0.40*	*$1.20*	*$2.00*	£0.25	£0.75	£1.25
21 2nd printing ND	*$0.30*	*$0.90*	*$1.50*	£0.20	£0.60	£1.00
22-23 ND	*$0.40*	*$1.20*	*$2.00*	£0.25	£0.75	£1.25
23 2nd printing ND	*$0.30*	*$0.90*	*$1.50*	£0.20	£0.60	£1.00
24-25 ND	*$0.40*	*$1.20*	*$2.00*	£0.25	£0.75	£1.25
25 2nd printing ND	*$0.30*	*$0.90*	*$1.50*	£0.20	£0.60	£1.00
26 ND origin Snake Eyes						
	$0.40	*$1.20*	*$2.00*	£0.25	£0.75	£1.25
26 2nd printing ND	*$0.30*	*$0.90*	*$1.50*	£0.20	£0.60	£1.00
27 ND	*$0.40*	*$1.20*	*$2.00*	£0.25	£0.75	£1.25
27 2nd printing ND	*$0.30*	*$0.90*	*$1.50*	£0.20	£0.60	£1.00
28-30 ND	*$0.40*	*$1.20*	*$2.00*	£0.25	£0.75	£1.25
31-36 ND	*$0.40*	*$1.20*	*$2.00*	£0.20	£0.60	£1.00
36 2nd printing ND	*$0.30*	*$0.90*	*$1.50*	£0.15	£0.45	£0.75
37 ND	*$0.40*	*$1.20*	*$2.00*	£0.20	£0.60	£1.00
37 2nd printing ND	*$0.30*	*$0.90*	*$1.50*	£0.15	£0.45	£0.75
38-49 ND	*$0.40*	*$1.20*	*$2.00*	£0.20	£0.60	£1.00
50 ND DS, intro Special Missions						
	$0.50	*$1.50*	*$2.50*	£0.30	£0.90	£1.50
51 ND	*$0.35*	*$1.05*	*$1.75*	£0.20	£0.60	£1.00
51 2nd printing ND	*$0.30*	*$0.90*	*$1.50*	£0.15	£0.45	£0.75
52-59 ND	*$0.35*	*$1.05*	*$1.75*	£0.20	£0.60	£1.00
60 ND Todd McFarlane art						
	$0.40	*$1.20*	*$2.00*	£0.25	£0.75	£1.25
61-84 ND	*$0.30*	*$0.90*	*$1.50*	£0.15	£0.45	£0.75
85 ND Ninja story with no dialogue						
	$0.25	*$0.75*	*$1.25*	£0.15	£0.45	£0.75
86-99 ND	*$0.25*	*$0.75*	*$1.25*	£0.15	£0.45	£0.75
100 ND 48pgs	*$0.40*	*$1.20*	*$2.00*	£0.25	£0.75	£1.25
101-107 ND	*$0.25*	*$0.75*	*$1.25*	£0.15	£0.45	£0.75
108 ND G.I. Joe Dossier feature begins						
	$0.25	*$0.75*	*$1.25*	£0.15	£0.45	£0.75
109-115 ND	*$0.25*	*$0.75*	*$1.25*	£0.15	£0.45	£0.75
116-118 ND Destro: Search and Destroy, pre-bagged with trading card						
	$0.30	*$0.90*	*$1.50*	£0.20	£0.60	£1.00
119 ND	*$0.25*	*$0.75*	*$1.25*	£0.15	£0.45	£0.75
120 ND Sam Kieth art on G.I. Joe Dossier feature						
	$0.25	*$0.75*	*$1.25*	£0.15	£0.45	£0.75
121-123 ND	*$0.25*	*$0.75*	*$1.25*	£0.15	£0.45	£0.75
124 ND three stories						
	$0.25	*$0.75*	*$1.25*	£0.15	£0.45	£0.75
125-126 ND two stories						
	$0.25	*$0.75*	*$1.25*	£0.15	£0.45	£0.75
127-134 ND	*$0.25*	*$0.75*	*$1.25*	£0.15	£0.45	£0.75
135-138 ND pre-bagged with G.I. Joe photographic trading card						
	$0.30	*$0.90*	*$1.50*	£0.20	£0.60	£1.00
139 ND Transformers Generation 2 back-up begins						
	$0.25	*$0.75*	*$1.25*	£0.15	£0.45	£0.75
140-141 ND	*$0.25*	*$0.75*	*$1.25*	£0.15	£0.45	£0.75
142 ND leads into Transformers: Generation 2 #1						
	$0.25	*$0.75*	*$1.25*	£0.15	£0.45	£0.75
143-149 ND	*$0.25*	*$0.75*	*$1.25*	£0.15	£0.45	£0.75
150 ND 48pgs	*$0.30*	*$0.90*	*$1.50*	£0.20	£0.60	£1.00
151-154 ND	*$0.25*	*$0.75*	*$1.25*	£0.15	£0.45	£0.75
155 ND	*$0.30*	*$0.90*	*$1.50*	£0.20	£0.60	£1.00
Title Value:	*$59.20*	*$177.60*	*$292.50*	£35.15	£105.45	£175.75

G.I. JOE (2ND SERIES)

Dark Horse,MS; 1 Dec 1995-4 Mar 1996

	$Good	$Fine	$N.Mint	£Good	£Fine	£N.Mint
1 ND Frank Miller cover						
	$0.40	*$1.20*	*$2.00*	£0.25	£0.75	£1.25
2-4 ND Norm Breyfogle cover						
	$0.40	*$1.20*	*$2.00*	£0.25	£0.75	£1.25
Title Value:	*$1.60*	*$4.80*	*$8.00*	£1.00	£3.00	£5.00

G.I. JOE (3RD SERIES)

Dark Horse; 1 Jun 1996-4 Sep 1996

	$Good	$Fine	$N.Mint	£Good	£Fine	£N.Mint
1 ND Mike Barr script, Tatsuya Ishida and Scott Reed art						
	$0.50	*$1.50*	*$2.50*	£0.30	£0.90	£1.50
2-4 ND	*$0.50*	*$1.50*	*$2.50*	£0.30	£0.90	£1.50
Title Value:	*$2.00*	*$6.00*	*$10.00*	£1.20	£3.60	£6.00

G.I. JOE AND THE TRANSFORMERS

Marvel Comics Group,MS; 1 Jan 1987-4 Apr 1987

	$Good	$Fine	$N.Mint	£Good	£Fine	£N.Mint
1-4 ND	*$0.25*	*$0.75*	*$1.25*	£0.15	£0.45	£0.75
Title Value:	*$1.00*	*$3.00*	*$5.00*	£0.60	£1.80	£3.00
Bookshelf Edition (Apr 1993)						
ND 96pgs, Higgins, Trimpe and Coletta				£0.60	£1.80	£3.00

G.I. JOE COMICS MAGAZINE

Marvel Comics Group,Digest; 1 Dec 1986-13 1988

	$Good	$Fine	$N.Mint	£Good	£Fine	£N.Mint
1-13 ND	*$0.25*	*$0.75*	*$1.25*	£0.15	£0.45	£0.75
Title Value:	*$3.25*	*$9.75*	*$16.25*	£1.95	£5.85	£9.75

G.I. JOE EUROPEAN MISSIONS

Marvel Comics Group; 1 Oct 1988-15 Dec 1989

	$Good	$Fine	$N.Mint	£Good	£Fine	£N.Mint
1-15 ND	*$0.25*	*$0.75*	*$1.25*	£0.15	£0.45	£0.75
Title Value:	*$3.75*	*$11.25*	*$18.75*	£2.25	£6.75	£11.25

G.I. JOE IN 3-D

Blackthorne;(3-D Series #20,#26,#35,#39,#52); 1 Jul 1987-5 1988

	$Good	$Fine	$N.Mint	£Good	£Fine	£N.Mint
1-5 ND all with bound-in 3-D glasses (25% less if without glasses)						
	$0.50	*$1.50*	*$2.50*	£0.30	£0.90	£1.50
Title Value:	*$2.50*	*$7.50*	*$12.50*	£1.50	£4.50	£7.50

G.I. JOE ORDER OF BATTLE, THE

Marvel Comics Group,MS; 1 Dec 1986-4 Mar 1987

	$Good	$Fine	$N.Mint	£Good	£Fine	£N.Mint
1-4 ND	*$0.40*	*$1.20*	*$2.00*	£0.25	£0.75	£1.25
Title Value:	*$1.60*	*$4.80*	*$8.00*	£1.00	£3.00	£5.00

G.I. JOE SPECIAL MISSIONS

Marvel Comics Group; 1 Oct 1986-28 Dec 1989

	$Good	$Fine	$N.Mint	£Good	£Fine	£N.Mint
1-28 ND	*$0.25*	*$0.75*	*$1.25*	£0.15	£0.45	£0.75
Title Value:	*$7.00*	*$21.00*	*$35.00*	£4.20	£12.60	£21.00
Trade Paperback reprints issues #1-4				£0.75	£2.25	£3.75

G.I. JOE SPECIAL TREASURY EDITION

Marvel Comics Group; nn 1982

	$Good	$Fine	$N.Mint	£Good	£Fine	£N.Mint
nn ND extremely rare in the U.K. reprints issue #1						
	$0.80	*$2.40*	*$4.00*	£1.00	£3.00	£5.00
Title Value:	*$0.80*	*$2.40*	*$4.00*	£1.00	£3.00	£5.00

G.I. JOE THREE-PACK

Marvel Comics Group; nn Oct 1990

	$Good	$Fine	$N.Mint	£Good	£Fine	£N.Mint
nn ND scarce in the U.K. 2nd printings of Issues #2, #26 and #27; pre-bagged						
	$0.60	*$1.80*	*$3.00*	£0.40	£1.20	£2.00
Title Value:	*$0.60*	*$1.80*	*$3.00*	£0.40	£1.20	£2.00

G.I. JOE YEARBOOK

Marvel Comics Group; 1 Mar 1985-4 Feb 1988

	$Good	$Fine	$N.Mint	£Good	£Fine	£N.Mint
1 ND 48pgs, reprints issue #1 with selected history of subsequent events plus feature on G.I. Joe animated series, painted cover by Michael Golden						
	$0.40	*$1.20*	*$2.00*	£0.25	£0.75	£1.25
2 ND 48pgs, Mike Golden cover and art						
	$0.40	*$1.20*	*$2.00*	£0.25	£0.75	£1.25
3-4 ND 48pgs	*$0.40*	*$1.20*	*$2.00*	£0.25	£0.75	£1.25
Title Value:	*$1.60*	*$4.80*	*$8.00*	£1.00	£3.00	£5.00

Note: many copies of #1 were mis-cut

G.I. JOE, TALES OF

Marvel Comics Group; 1 Jan 1988-15 1989

1 ND DS, reprints from GI Joe begin

	$Good	$Fine	$N.Mint	£Good	£Fine	£N.Mint
	$0.25	*$0.75*	*$1.25*	£0.15	£0.45	£0.75
2-15 ND	*$0.25*	*$0.75*	*$1.25*	£0.15	£0.45	£0.75
Title Value:	*$3.75*	*$11.25*	*$18.75*	£2.25	£6.75	£11.25
G.I. WAR TALES						
DC Comics; 1 Mar/Apr 1973-4 Oct/Nov 1973						
1 reprints begin	*$0.65*	*$2.00*	*$4.00*	£0.30	£1.00	£2.00
2 Neal Adams reprint						
	$0.55	*$1.75*	*$3.50*	£0.30	£1.00	£2.00
3-4	*$0.50*	*$1.50*	*$3.00*	£0.25	£0.75	£1.50
Title Value:	*$2.20*	*$6.75*	*$13.50*	£1.10	£3.50	£7.00
G.I.JOE IN 3-D ANNUAL						
Blackthorne;(3-D Series #62) 1 1988						
1 ND	*$0.50*	*$1.50*	*$2.50*	£0.30	£0.90	£1.50
Title Value:	*$0.50*	*$1.50*	*$2.50*	£0.30	£0.90	£1.50
G.O.T.H.						
Verotik,MS; 1 Nov 1995-3 Mar 1996						
1-3 ND Glenn Danzig script, Liam Sharp art						
	$0.60	*$1.80*	*$3.00*	£0.40	£1.20	£2.00
Title Value:	*$1.80*	*$5.40*	*$9.00*	£1.20	£3.60	£6.00
G.R.I.P., THE						
Eclipse; 1 Apr 1994-2 1994						
1-2 ND Brad Gorby art						
	$0.50	*$1.50*	*$2.50*	£0.30	£0.90	£1.50
Title Value:	*$1.00*	*$3.00*	*$5.00*	£0.60	£1.80	£3.00
GABRIEL						
Caliber Press,OS; 1 Jul 1995						
1 ND 48pgs, black and white						
	$0.60	*$1.80*	*$3.00*	£0.40	£1.20	£2.00
1 Signed & Numbered Edition, ND limited to 1,000 copies						
	$0.80	*$2.40*	*$4.00*	£0.50	£1.50	£2.50
Title Value:	*$1.40*	*$4.20*	*$7.00*	£0.90	£2.70	£4.50
GAIJIN						
Caliber Press,OS; 1 Feb 1991						
1 ND 64pgs, black and white						
	$0.60	*$1.80*	*$3.00*	£0.40	£1.20	£2.00
Title Value:	*$0.60*	*$1.80*	*$3.00*	£0.40	£1.20	£2.00
GALACTIC GUARDIANS						
Marvel Comics Group,MS; 1 Jul 1994-4 Oct 1994						
1 Future History part 2, concluded in Guardians of the Galaxy Annual #4						
	$0.25	*$0.75*	*$1.25*	£0.15	£0.45	£0.75
2-4	*$0.25*	*$0.75*	*$1.25*	£0.15	£0.45	£0.75
Title Value:	*$1.00*	*$3.00*	*$5.00*	£0.60	£1.80	£3.00
GALACTIC PATROL						
Eternity,MS; 1 Jul 1990-5 Nov 1990						
(see Lensman)						
1-5 ND based on Lensman series						
	$0.40	*$1.20*	*$2.00*	£0.25	£0.75	£1.25
Title Value:	*$2.00*	*$6.00*	*$10.00*	£1.25	£3.75	£6.25
GALACTUS: THE ORIGIN						
(see Super Villain Classics)						
GALL FORCE: ETERNAL STORY						
CPM Comics; 1 Mar 1995-4 1995						
1-3 ND based on anime series						
	$0.60	*$1.80*	*$3.00*	£0.40	£1.20	£2.00
4 ND	*$0.60*	*$1.80*	*$3.00*	£0.40	£1.20	£2.00
Title Value:	*$2.40*	*$7.20*	*$12.00*	£1.60	£4.80	£8.00
GAMBIT						
Marvel Comics Group,MS; 1 Dec 1993-4 Mar 1994						
1 embossed gold foil stamped cover						
	$1.00	*$3.00*	*$5.00*	£0.70	£2.10	£3.50
1 Gold Edition ND	*$5.00*	*$15.00*	*$25.00*	£2.50	£7.50	£12.50

	$Good	$Fine	$N.Mint	£Good	£Fine	£N.Mint
2 Rogue appears	*$0.80*	*$2.40*	*$4.00*	£0.50	£1.50	£2.50
3-4	*$0.80*	*$2.40*	*$4.00*	£0.50	£1.50	£2.50
Title Value:	*$8.40*	*$25.20*	*$42.00*	£4.70	£14.10	£23.50
Gambit (Sep 1995) Trade Paperback						
collects four issue series, new Lee Weeks cover				£1.70	£5.10	£8.50
GAMBIT & THE X-TERNALS						
Marvel Comics Group; 1 Mar 1995-4 Jun 1995						
(title previously called X-Force)						
1 Fabian Nicieza script, Danial and Conrad art						
	$0.80	*$2.40*	*$4.00*	£0.50	£1.50	£2.50
2-3 Fabian Nicieza script, Danial and Conrad art						
	$0.50	*$1.50*	*$2.50*	£0.30	£0.90	£1.50
4 Fabian Nicieza script, Danial and Conrad art; continued in X-Men: Omega						
	$0.50	*$1.50*	*$2.50*	£0.30	£0.90	£1.50
Title Value:	*$2.30*	*$6.90*	*$11.50*	£1.40	£4.20	£7.00
The Ultimate Gambit & The X-Ternals (Jul 1995) 96pgs						
Bookshelf Edition collects issues #1-4 with etched gold cover				£1.20	£3.60	£6.00
GAMERA						
Dark Horse,MS; 1 Aug 1996-4 Nov 1996						
1-4 ND Dave Chipps script, Mozart Couto and Mike Sellers art						
	$0.60	*$1.80*	*$3.00*	£0.40	£1.20	£2.00
Title Value:	*$2.40*	*$7.20*	*$12.00*	£1.60	£4.80	£8.00
GAMMARAUDERS						
DC Comics, Game; 1 Jan 1989-10 Dec 1989						
1-10 ND	*$0.20*	*$0.60*	*$1.00*	£0.10	£0.35	£0.60
Title Value:	*$2.00*	*$6.00*	*$10.00*	£1.00	£3.50	£6.00
GARGOYLE						
Marvel Comics Group,MS; 1 Jun 1985-4 Sep 1985						
1-4 ND Badger art	*$0.30*	*$0.90*	*$1.50*	£0.20	£0.60	£1.00
Title Value:	*$1.20*	*$3.60*	*$6.00*	£0.80	£2.40	£4.00
GARGOYLES						
Marvel Comics Group,MS TV; 1 Feb 1995-17 Jun 1996						
1 ND based on US TV series; embossed UV-coated cover						
	$0.50	*$1.50*	*$2.50*	£0.30	£0.90	£1.50
2-7 ND	*$0.30*	*$0.90*	*$1.50*	£0.20	£0.60	£1.00
8-9 ND bi-weekly	*$0.30*	*$0.90*	*$1.50*	£0.20	£0.60	£1.00
10-17 ND	*$0.30*	*$0.90*	*$1.50*	£0.20	£0.60	£1.00
Title Value:	*$5.30*	*$15.90*	*$26.50*	£3.50	£10.50	£17.50
GASP!						
ACG; 1 Mar 1967-4 Aug 1967						
1 distributed in the U.K.						
	$3.55	*$10.50*	*$25.00*	£2.10	£6.25	£15.00
2-4 distributed in the U.K.						
	$2.10	*$6.25*	*$15.00*	£1.05	£3.20	£7.50
Title Value:	*$9.85*	*$29.25*	*$70.00*	£5.25	£15.85	£37.50
GATES OF THE NIGHT, THE						
Jademan,MS; 1 Oct 1990-6 Mar 1991						
1-6 ND 48pgs, squarebound						
	$0.70	*$2.10*	*$3.50*	£0.45	£1.35	£2.25
Title Value:	*$4.20*	*$12.60*	*$21.00*	£2.70	£8.10	£13.50
GEEK, BROTHER POWER, THE						
National Periodical Publications; 1 Sep/Oct 1968-2 Nov/Dec 1968						
1 scarce in the U.K.	*$3.55*	*$10.50*	*$25.00*	£2.10	£6.25	£15.00
2 scarce in the U.K.	*$2.50*	*$7.50*	*$17.50*	£1.40	£4.25	£10.00
Title Value:	*$6.05*	*$18.00*	*$42.50*	£3.50	£10.50	£25.00
Note: unusually cult comic owing to its focus on Sixties "flower power" culture, bizarre title and short-lived run						
GEEK, THE						
DC Comics/Vertigo,OS; 1 Jun 1993						
1 ND 64pgs	*$0.80*	*$2.40*	*$4.00*	£0.50	£1.50	£2.50
Title Value:	*$0.80*	*$2.40*	*$4.00*	£0.50	£1.50	£2.50

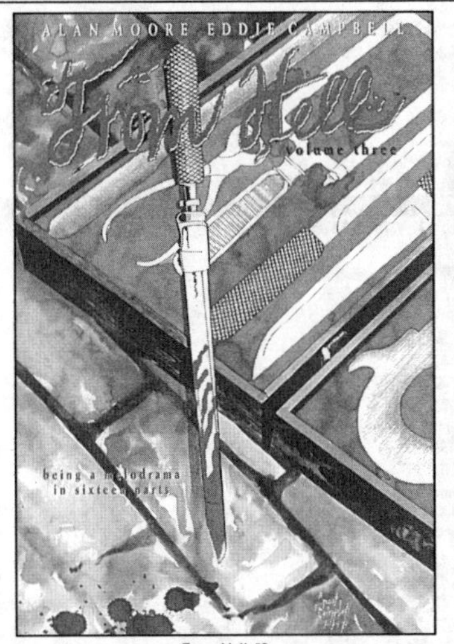

From Hell #3

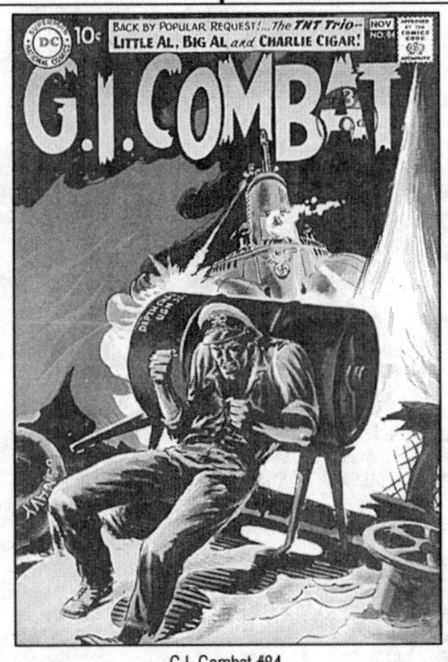

G.I. Combat #84

G.I. Joe #3

GEHENNA

White Wolf,MS; 1 Aug 1991

Issue	$Good	$Fine	$N.Mint	£Good	£Fine	£N.Mint
1 ND	$0.40	$1.20	$2.00	£0.25	£0.75	£1.25
Title Value:	$0.40	$1.20	$2.00	£0.25	£0.75	£1.25

Note: originally announced as a mini-series

GEMINI BLOOD

DC Comics/Helix; 1 Sep 1996-present

Issue	$Good	$Fine	$N.Mint	£Good	£Fine	£N.Mint
1-6 ND Walt Simonson covers						
	$0.45	$1.35	$2.25	£0.30	£0.90	£1.50
7 ND Bill Sienkiewicz guest inks; Walt Simonson covers						
	$0.50	$1.50	$2.50	£0.30	£0.90	£1.50
Title Value:	$3.20	$9.60	$16.50	£2.10	£6.30	£10.50

GEN 13

Image,MS; 0 Aug 1994; 1 Feb 1994-5 Jul 1994

Issue	$Good	$Fine	$N.Mint	£Good	£Fine	£N.Mint
½ ND produced in conjunction with Wizard Comics, issued in a protective Mylar with certificate of authenticity						
	$8.00	$24.00	$40.00	£5.00	£15.00	£25.00
0 ND (Aug 1994) short stories focusing on individual characters						
	$2.00	$6.00	$10.00	£1.20	£3.60	£6.00
1 ND Jim Lee and Brandon Choi script, J. Scott Campbell and Alex Garner art begins; fold-out poster at centre-fold						
	$8.00	$24.00	$40.00	£5.00	£15.00	£25.00
1 2nd printing, ND (Jul 1994)						
	$2.00	$6.00	$10.00	£1.20	£3.60	£6.00
2 ND	$8.00	$24.00	$40.00	£5.00	£15.00	£25.00
3 ND	$5.00	$15.00	$25.00	£3.00	£9.00	£15.00
4 ND	$3.50	$10.50	$17.50	£2.50	£7.50	£12.50
5 ND	$2.00	$6.00	$10.00	£1.60	£4.80	£8.00
5 Variant Cover Edition, ND Whilce Portacio cover art; cover forms larger picture when combined with variant covers of Deathblow #5, Kindred #3, Stormwatch #10, Team 7 #1, Union #0, Wetworks #2, WildC.A.T.S. #11						
	$4.00	$12.00	$20.00	£2.50	£7.50	£12.50
Title Value:	$42.50	$127.50	$212.50	£27.00	£81.00	£135.00
Gen 13 (Dec 1994) Trade paperback						
ND collects 5 issue mini-series				£1.70	£5.10	£8.50
ND 2nd/3rd printings				£1.30	£3.90	£6.50
Gen 13 Hardcover Collection (Jun 1995)						
ND reprints mini-series, case-bound limited edition signed and numbered; 1,000 copies				£5.20	£15.60	£26.00

GEN 13 (2ND SERIES)

Image; 1 Apr 1995-present

Issue	$Good	$Fine	$N.Mint	£Good	£Fine	£N.Mint
1 Cover A - "Charge", ND Brandon Choi script, J. Scott Campbell art; Fairchild, Grunge, Freefall, Burnout and Rainmaker begin						
	$1.20	$3.60	$6.00	£0.80	£2.40	£4.00
1 Cover B - "Thumbs Up" ND						
	$1.20	$3.60	$6.00	£0.80	£2.40	£4.00
1 Cover C - "Lil Gen", ND Arthur Adams cover art						
	$3.00	$9.00	$15.00	£2.00	£6.00	£10.00
1 Cover D - "Barbari-Gen", ND Simon Bisley cover art						
	$3.00	$9.00	$15.00	£2.00	£6.00	£10.00
1 Cover E -"Friendley Neighborhood Grunge", ND John Cleary cover art						
	$3.00	$9.00	$15.00	£2.00	£6.00	£10.00
1 Cover F - "Gen 13 Goes Madison Ave.", ND Michael Golden cover art						
	$3.00	$9.00	$15.00	£2.00	£6.00	£10.00
1 Cover G - "Lin-Gen-re", ND Michael Lopez cover art						
	$5.00	$15.00	$25.00	£3.00	£9.00	£15.00
1 Cover H - "Gen-et-Jackson", ND Jason Pearson cover art						
	$5.00	$15.00	$25.00	£3.00	£9.00	£15.00
1 Cover I - "That's the Way We Became Gen", ND J. Scott Campbell/Chuck Gibson cover art						
	$3.00	$9.00	$15.00	£2.00	£6.00	£10.00
1 Cover J - "All Dolled Up", ND J. Scott Campbell/Tom McWeeney cover art						
	$3.00	$9.00	$15.00	£2.00	£6.00	£10.00
1 Cover K - "Verti-Gen", ND Joe Dunn cover art						
	$3.00	$9.00	$15.00	£2.00	£6.00	£10.00
1 Cover L - "Picto-Fiction" ND						
	$3.00	$9.00	$15.00	£2.00	£6.00	£10.00
1 Cover M - "Do-It-Yourself-Cover" ND						
	$3.00	$9.00	$15.00	£2.00	£6.00	£10.00
2 ND Wildstorm Rising part 4, continued in Grifter #1; with two foil-bagged painted trading cards. Cover by Barry Windsor-Smith and extra cover by J. Scott Campbell						
	$1.00	$3.00	$5.00	£0.70	£2.10	£3.50
2 Newstand Edition, ND without trading cards						
	$0.60	$1.80	$3.00	£0.40	£1.20	£2.00
3-5 ND	$0.60	$1.80	$3.00	£0.40	£1.20	£2.00
6 ND	$0.50	$1.50	$2.50	£0.30	£0.90	£1.50
7 ND Jim Lee art	$0.50	$1.50	$2.50	£0.30	£0.90	£1.50
8 ND	$0.50	$1.50	$2.50	£0.30	£0.90	£1.50
9 ND The Dark Side, continued in Deathblow #25						
	$0.50	$1.50	$2.50	£0.30	£0.90	£1.50
10 ND Fire From Heaven part 3, continued in Wetworks #16						
	$0.50	$1.50	$2.50	£0.30	£0.90	£1.50
11 ND Fire From Heaven part 9, continued in Backlash #20						
	$0.50	$1.50	$2.50	£0.30	£0.90	£1.50
11 European Tour Edition, ND holo-chrome wraparound cover, limited to 5,000 copies; only released in Europe						
	$14.00	$42.00	$70.00	£5.00	£15.00	£25.00
12 ND	$0.50	$1.50	$2.50	£0.30	£0.90	£1.50
13 Version A, ND 16pgs						
	$0.25	$0.75	$1.30	£0.20	£0.60	£1.00
13 Version B, ND 16pgs, Bone appears						
	$0.25	$0.75	$1.30	£0.20	£0.60	£1.00
13 Version C, ND 16pgs						
	$0.25	$0.75	$1.30	£0.20	£0.60	£1.00
14 ND	$0.50	$1.50	$2.50	£0.30	£0.90	£1.50
Title Value:	$61.55	$184.65	$307.90	£35.90	£107.70	£179.50

Issue	$Good	$Fine	$N.Mint	£Good	£Fine	£N.Mint
Gen 13: Lost in Paradise (Jul 1996) Trade paperback						
ND 64pgs, collects issues #3-5 with pin-ups				£0.90	£2.70	£4.50

GEN 13 LIMITED EDITION COLLECTOR'S PACK

Image; nn 1995

Issue	$Good	$Fine	$N.Mint	£Good	£Fine	£N.Mint
nn Box Set - Alex Garner Chromium signed, ND Collector's Pack in slipcase featuring all 13 variant editions plus one chromium cover variant signed by Alex Garner						
	$40.00	$120.00	$200.00	£25.00	£75.00	£125.00
nn Box Set - Brandon Choi Chromium signed, ND Collector's Pack in slipcase featuring all 13 variant editions plus one chromium cover variant signed by Brandon Choi						
	$45.00	$135.00	$225.00	£30.00	£90.00	£150.00
nn Box Set - Jim Lee Chromium signed, ND Collector's Pack in slipcase featuring all 13 variant editions plus one chromium cover variant signed by Jim Lee						
	$50.00	$150.00	$250.00	£35.00	£105.00	£175.00
nn Box Set - Scott Campbell Chromium signed, ND Collector's Pack in slipcase featuring all 13 variant editions plus one chromium cover variant signed by J. Scott Campbell						
	$45.00	$135.00	$225.00	£30.00	£90.00	£150.00
nn Chromium Edition - Alex Garner ND Chromium Edition originally contained in Box Set, signed by Alex Garner						
	$10.00	$30.00	$50.00	£7.00	£21.00	£35.00
nn Chromium Edition - Brandon Choi ND Chromium Edition originally contained in Box Set, signed by Brandon Choi						
	$12.00	$36.00	$60.00	£8.00	£24.00	£40.00
nn Chromium Edition - J. Scott Campbell ND Chromium Edition originally contained in Box Set, signed by J. Scott Campbell						
	$12.00	$36.00	$60.00	£8.00	£24.00	£40.00
nn Chromium Edition - Jim Lee ND Chromium Edition originally contained in Box Set, signed by Jim Lee						
	$16.00	$48.00	$80.00	£10.00	£30.00	£50.00
Title Value:	$230.00	$690.00	$1150.00	£153.00	£459.00	£765.00

GEN 13 RAVE

Image,OS; nn Mar 1995

Issue	$Good	$Fine	$N.Mint	£Good	£Fine	£N.Mint
nn ND creator interviews and sketchbook showing the creation of Gen 13						
	$1.50	$4.50	$7.50	£1.20	£3.60	£6.00
Title Value:	$1.50	$4.50	$7.50	£1.20	£3.60	£6.00

GEN 13/MAXX

Image,OS; 1 Dec 1995

Issue	$Good	$Fine	$N.Mint	£Good	£Fine	£N.Mint
1 ND	$0.70	$2.10	$3.50	£0.50	£1.50	£2.50
Title Value:	$0.70	$2.10	$3.50	£0.50	£1.50	£2.50

GEN 13: BOOTLEG

Image; 1 Nov 1996-present

Issue	$Good	$Fine	$N.Mint	£Good	£Fine	£N.Mint
1-5 ND Mark Farmer and Alan Davis script and art begins						
	$0.50	$1.50	$2.50	£0.30	£0.90	£1.50
Title Value:	$2.50	$7.50	$12.50	£1.50	£4.50	£9.00

GEN 13: ORDINARY HEROES

Image,MS; 1 Feb 1996-2 Jul 1996

Issue	$Good	$Fine	$N.Mint	£Good	£Fine	£N.Mint
1-2 ND Adam Hughes cover and art						
	$0.50	$1.50	$2.50	£0.30	£0.90	£1.50
Title Value:	$1.00	$3.00	$5.00	£0.60	£1.80	£3.00

GEN 13: THE UNREAL WORLD

Image,OS; 1 Jul 1996

Issue	$Good	$Fine	$N.Mint	£Good	£Fine	£N.Mint
1 ND Mike Hesler script, Humberto Ramos and Alex Garner art						
	$0.60	$1.80	$3.00	£0.40	£1.20	£2.00
Title Value:	$0.60	$1.80	$3.00	£0.40	£1.20	£2.00

GENE DAY'S BLACK ZEPPELIN

(see Black Zeppelin)

GENE DOGS

Marvel UK,MS; 1 Oct 1993-3 Dec 1993

Issue	$Good	$Fine	$N.Mint	£Good	£Fine	£N.Mint
1 pre-bagged with trading cards and poster						
	$0.30	$0.90	$1.50	£0.20	£0.60	£1.00
2-3	$0.25	$0.75	$1.25	£0.15	£0.45	£0.75
Title Value:	$0.80	$2.40	$4.00	£0.50	£1.50	£2.50

GENERATION NEXT, THE

Marvel Comics Group; 1 Mar 1995-4 Jun 1995

(previously Generation X)

Issue	$Good	$Fine	$N.Mint	£Good	£Fine	£N.Mint
1 ND printing on glossy stock paper begins; Scott Lobdell script and Chris Bachalo art begin						
	$0.80	$2.40	$4.00	£0.50	£1.50	£2.50
2-3 ND	$0.50	$1.50	$2.50	£0.30	£0.90	£1.50
4 ND continued in X-Men: Omega						
	$0.50	$1.50	$2.50	£0.30	£0.90	£1.50
Title Value:	$2.30	$6.90	$11.50	£1.40	£4.20	£7.00
The Ultimate Generation Next (Jul 1995) 96pgs						
Bookshelf Edition collects issues #1-4 with etched gold cover				£1.20	£3.60	£6.00

GENERATION X

Marvel Comics Group; ½ 1996; 1 Nov 1994-4 Feb 1995; 5 Jul 1995-present

(becomes The Mutants: Generation Next)

Issue	$Good	$Fine	$N.Mint	£Good	£Fine	£N.Mint
½ ND 12pgs, - produced in conjunction with Overstreet's Fan magazine						
	$1.50	$4.50	$7.50	£1.00	£3.00	£5.00
1 ND 48pgs, chromium cover; Scott Lobdell, Chris Bachalo and Mark Buckingham creative team						
	$1.20	$3.60	$6.00	£0.80	£2.40	£4.00
2 ND	$0.50	$1.50	$2.50	£0.30	£0.90	£1.50
2 Deluxe Edition ND	$0.80	$2.40	$4.00	£0.50	£1.50	£2.50
3 ND	$0.50	$1.50	$2.50	£0.30	£0.90	£1.50
3 Deluxe Edition, ND - printed on glossy stock paper						
	$0.60	$1.80	$3.00	£0.40	£1.20	£2.00
4 ND	$0.50	$1.50	$2.50	£0.30	£0.90	£1.50
4 Deluxe Edition, ND : bound-in Fleer trading card; see Mutants: Generation Next #1						
	$0.60	$1.80	$3.00	£0.40	£1.20	£2.00
5 ND continued from X-Men: Prime; Scott Lobdell script, Chris Bachalo and Mark Buckingham art						
	$0.40	$1.20	$2.00	£0.25	£0.75	£1.25
6 ND Wolverine appears, continued in Wolverine #92						
	$0.40	$1.20	$2.00	£0.25	£0.75	£1.25
7-8 ND	$0.40	$1.20	$2.00	£0.25	£0.75	£1.25
9 ND Tom Grummett guest pencil art						

VERY GENERAL PERCENTAGE CONVERSION CHART WHICH MAY BE USED TO CALCULATE LOW AND INBETWEEN GRADES:

	$Good	$Fine	$N.Mint	£Good	£Fine	£N.Mint
	$0.40	$1.20	$2.00	£0.25	£0.75	£1.25
10 ND Banshee vs. Omega Red	$0.40	$1.20	$2.00	£0.25	£0.75	£1.25
11-13 ND	$0.40	$1.20	$2.00	£0.25	£0.75	£1.25
14 ND Bishop guest-stars	$0.40	$1.20	$2.00	£0.25	£0.75	£1.25
15-17 ND	$0.40	$1.20	$2.00	£0.25	£0.75	£1.25
18-19 ND 40pgs, Onslaught tie-in	$0.40	$1.20	$2.00	£0.25	£0.75	£1.25
20-24 ND	$0.40	$1.20	$2.00	£0.25	£0.75	£1.25
25 ND 48pgs	$0.60	$1.80	$3.00	£0.40	£1.20	£2.00
Title Value:	$14.80	$44.40	$74.00	£9.40	£28.20	£47.00
Origin of Generation X (Jul 1996) Trade paperback 336pgs, reprints Phalanx Covenant storyline and Generation X #1				£3.30	£9.90	£16.50

GENERATION X '95

Marvel Comics Group,OS; nn Nov 1995

	$Good	$Fine	$N.Mint	£Good	£Fine	£N.Mint
nn ND 64pgs, Scott Lobdell script, Ashley Wood art; Mondo joins team	$0.80	$2.40	$4.00	£0.50	£1.50	£2.50
Title Value:	$0.80	$2.40	$4.00	£0.50	£1.50	£2.50

Note: issued in place of Generation X Annual for 1995 (see X-Men '95)

GENERATION X '96

Marvel Comics Group; nn Nov 1996

	$Good	$Fine	$N.Mint	£Good	£Fine	£N.Mint
nn ND 64pgs, Michael Golden back-up story and cover art	$0.60	$1.80	$3.00	£0.40	£1.20	£2.00
Title Value:	$0.60	$1.80	$3.00	£0.40	£1.20	£2.00

GENERATION X ASHCAN

Marvel Comics Group,OS; nn Nov 1994

	$Good	$Fine	$N.Mint	£Good	£Fine	£N.Mint
nn ND 16pgs, previews Generation X	$0.30	$0.90	$1.50	£0.20	£0.60	£1.00
Title Value:	$0.30	$0.90	$1.50	£0.20	£0.60	£1.00

GENERATION X COLLECTOR'S PREVIEW

Marvel Comics Group,OS; 1 Oct 1994

	$Good	$Fine	$N.Mint	£Good	£Fine	£N.Mint
1 ND 48pgs, inside information on Generation X	$0.40	$1.20	$2.00	£0.50	£1.50	£2.50
Title Value:	$0.40	$1.20	$2.00	£0.50	£1.50	£2.50

GENERATION ZERO GRAPHIC NOVEL

DC Comics,OS; 1 Nov 1991

	$Good	$Fine	$N.Mint	£Good	£Fine	£N.Mint
1 ND 120pgs, reprints Pepe Moreno's Generation Zero, originally published in Marvel Comics' Epic Illustrated	$2.50	$7.50	$12.50	£1.50	£4.50	£7.50
Title Value:	$2.50	$7.50	$12.50	£1.50	£4.50	£7.50

GENERIC COMIC BOOK, THE

Marvel Comics Group,OS; 1 Apr 1984

	$Good	$Fine	$N.Mint	£Good	£Fine	£N.Mint
1 ND	$0.15	$0.45	$0.75	£0.10	£0.35	£0.60
Title Value:	$0.15	$0.45	$0.75	£0.10	£0.35	£0.60

GENESIS

Malibu,OS; 0 Oct 1993

	$Good	$Fine	$N.Mint	£Good	£Fine	£N.Mint
0 ND Widowmaker, Ex-Mutants, Dinosaurs for Hire and Protectors stories; all foil card-stock cover	$0.40	$1.20	$2.00	£0.25	£0.75	£1.25
Title Value:	$0.40	$1.20	$2.00	£0.25	£0.75	£1.25

GENETIX

Marvel UK,MS; 1 Oct 1993-6 Mar 1994

	$Good	$Fine	$N.Mint	£Good	£Fine	£N.Mint
1 pre-bagged with trading cards; Phil Gascoine art begins	$0.30	$0.90	$1.50	£0.20	£0.60	£1.00
2-3	$0.25	$0.75	$1.25	£0.15	£0.45	£0.75
4 Genetix vs. The Gene Dogs	$0.25	$0.75	$1.25	£0.15	£0.45	£0.75
5-6	$0.25	$0.75	$1.25	£0.15	£0.45	£0.75
Title Value:	$1.55	$4.65	$7.75	£0.95	£2.85	£4.75

GENOCYBER

Viz Communications,MS; 1 Jun 1993-6 Nov 1993

	$Good	$Fine	$N.Mint	£Good	£Fine	£N.Mint
1-6 ND	$0.55	$1.65	$2.75	£0.35	£1.05	£1.75
Title Value:	$3.30	$9.90	$16.50	£2.10	£6.30	£10.50

GENSAGA: ANCIENT WARRIOR

Entity Comics; 1 Aug 1995-3 1996 ?

	$Good	$Fine	$N.Mint	£Good	£Fine	£N.Mint
1 ND Raff Ienco script and art; Kabuki pin-up by David Mack	$0.50	$1.50	$2.50	£0.30	£0.90	£1.50
1 2nd printing, ND (Dec 1995	$0.40	$1.20	$2.00	£0.25	£0.75	£1.25
1 Videogame Edition, ND (Aug 1995) - pre-bagged with floppy disk game Sango Fighter	$1.40	$4.20	$7.00	£0.90	£2.70	£4.50
2-3 ND	$0.50	$1.50	$2.50	£0.30	£0.90	£1.50
Title Value:	$3.30	$9.90	$16.50	£2.05	£6.15	£10.25

GEOMANCER

Valiant; 1 Nov 1994-8 Jun 1995

	$Good	$Fine	$N.Mint	£Good	£Fine	£N.Mint
1 story continued from Eternal Warrior #27	$0.40	$1.20	$2.00	£0.25	£0.75	£1.25
2 Eternal Warrior vs. Geomancer	$0.40	$1.20	$2.00	£0.20	£0.60	£1.00
3-8	$0.40	$1.20	$2.00	£0.20	£0.60	£1.00
Title Value:	$3.20	$9.60	$16.00	£1.65	£4.95	£8.25

Note: all Non-Distributed on the news-stands in the U.K.

GET LOST

NCG; 1 Oct 1987-3 1988

	$Good	$Fine	$N.Mint	£Good	£Fine	£N.Mint
1 ND classic Ross Andru/Esposito humour reprints begin	$0.40	$1.20	$2.00	£0.25	£0.75	£1.25
2 ND	$0.40	$1.20	$2.00	£0.25	£0.75	£1.25
2 Gold Medal Edition, ND , signed and numbered (1200 copies)	$0.80	$2.40	$4.00	£0.50	£1.50	£2.50
3 ND	$0.40	$1.20	$2.00	£0.25	£0.75	£1.25
Title Value:	$2.00	$6.00	$10.00	£1.25	£3.75	£6.25

GET SMART

Dell,TV; 1 Jun 1966-8 Sep 1967

	$Good	$Fine	$N.Mint	£Good	£Fine	£N.Mint
1 scarce though distributed in the U.K.	$12.50	$39.00	$90.00	£7.00	£21.00	£50.00
2 scarce though distributed in the U.K. Steve Ditko art	$7.75	$23.50	$55.00	£4.60	£13.50	£32.50
3-8 scarce though distributed in the U.K. part Steve Ditko art	$7.00	$21.00	$50.00	£3.90	£11.50	£27.50
Title Value:	$62.25	$188.50	$445.00	£35.00	£103.50	£247.50

GETALONG GANG, THE

Marvel Comics Group/Star,TV; 1 May 1985-6 1986

	$Good	$Fine	$N.Mint	£Good	£Fine	£N.Mint
1-6 ND features Saturday morning TV characters	$0.15	$0.45	$0.75	£0.10	£0.30	£0.50
Title Value:	$0.90	$2.70	$4.50	£0.60	£1.80	£3.00

GHOST

Dark Horse; 1 Apr 1995-present

	$Good	$Fine	$N.Mint	£Good	£Fine	£N.Mint
1 ND Eric Luke script, Adam Hughes and Mark Farmer art begins; spin-off from Comics' Greatest World	$1.20	$3.60	$6.00	£0.70	£2.10	£3.50
2 ND	$0.80	$2.40	$4.00	£0.50	£1.50	£2.50
3-4 ND	$0.60	$1.80	$3.00	£0.30	£0.90	£1.50
5 ND Predator X-over (see Motorhead #1, X #18 and Agents of Law #6)	$0.50	$1.50	$2.50	£0.30	£0.90	£1.50
6-10 ND	$0.50	$1.50	$2.50	£0.30	£0.90	£1.50
11 ND David Bullock pencils begin	$0.50	$1.50	$2.50	£0.30	£0.90	£1.50
12-20 ND	$0.50	$1.50	$2.50	£0.30	£0.90	£1.50
Title Value:	$11.20	$33.60	$55.50	£6.60	£19.80	£33.00
Ghost Trade paperback 96pgs, reprints Ghost appearances from Comics' Greatest World, X #8 and Ghost Special plus sketches				£1.20	£3.60	£6.00
Ghost: Nocturnes (Apr 1996) Trade paperback reprints #1-4				£1.20	£3.60	£6.00

GHOST AND THE SHADOW SPECIAL

Dark Horse,OS; nn Dec 1995

	$Good	$Fine	$N.Mint	£Good	£Fine	£N.Mint
nn ND	$0.60	$1.80	$3.00	£0.40	£1.20	£2.00
Title Value:	$0.60	$1.80	$3.00	£0.40	£1.20	£2.00

GHOST IN THE SHELL, THE

Dark Horse,MS; 1 Feb 1995-8 Sep 1995

	$Good	$Fine	$N.Mint	£Good	£Fine	£N.Mint
1-8 ND Masamune Shirow script and art; colour and black and white	$0.80	$2.40	$4.00	£0.50	£1.50	£2.50
Title Value:	$6.40	$19.20	$32.00	£4.00	£12.00	£20.00

GHOST MANOR (1ST SERIES)

Charlton; 1 Jul 1968-19 Jul 1971

(becomes Ghostly Haunts #20 on)

	$Good	$Fine	$N.Mint	£Good	£Fine	£N.Mint
1 distributed in the U.K.	$1.40	$4.25	$10.00	£0.85	£2.55	£6.00
2 distributed in the U.K.	$0.85	$2.55	$6.00	£0.55	£1.70	£4.00
3 distributed in the U.K.	$0.70	$2.10	$5.00	£0.40	£1.25	£3.00
4-10 distributed in the U.K.	$0.55	$1.70	$4.00	£0.35	£1.05	£2.50
11-15 distributed in the U.K.	$0.65	$2.00	$4.00	£0.30	£1.00	£2.00
16 distributed in the U.K. Steve Ditko art	$0.75	$2.25	$4.50	£0.40	£1.25	£2.50
17 distributed in the U.K.	$0.65	$2.00	$4.00	£0.30	£1.00	£2.00
18-19 distributed in the U.K. Steve Ditko art	$0.75	$2.25	$4.50	£0.40	£1.25	£2.50
Title Value:	$12.95	$39.55	$86.50	£7.25	£22.60	£50.00

GHOST MANOR (2ND SERIES)

Charlton; 1 Oct 1971-32 Dec 1976; 33 Sep 1977-77 Nov 1984

	$Good	$Fine	$N.Mint	£Good	£Fine	£N.Mint
1 distributed in the U.K.	$1.65	$5.00	$10.00	£1.00	£3.00	£6.00
2 distributed in the U.K.	$1.00	$3.00	$6.00	£0.65	£2.00	£4.00
3-7 distributed in the U.K.	$0.80	$2.50	$5.00	£0.50	£1.50	£3.00
8 distributed in the U.K. Wally Wood art	$1.00	$3.00	$6.00	£0.55	£1.75	£3.50
9-10 distributed in the U.K.	$0.80	$2.50	$5.00	£0.50	£1.50	£3.00
11-17 distributed in the U.K.	$0.65	$2.00	$4.00	£0.30	£1.00	£2.00
18 distributed in the U.K. 1st professional work by Don Newton	$0.65	$2.00	$4.00	£0.40	£1.25	£2.50
19-20 distributed in the U.K.	$0.65	$2.00	$4.00	£0.30	£1.00	£2.00
21-56 distributed in the U.K.	$0.65	$2.00	$4.00	£0.25	£0.75	£1.50
57 distributed in the U.K. Steve Ditko art	$0.80	$2.40	$4.00	£0.50	£1.50	£2.50
58-60 distributed in the U.K.	$0.60	$1.80	$3.00	£0.30	£0.90	£1.50
61-77 distributed in the U.K.	$0.60	$1.80	$3.00	£0.20	£0.60	£1.00
Title Value:	$51.95	$158.90	$289.00	£22.60	£68.90	£133.00

GHOST RIDER

Marvel Comics Group; 1 Sep 1973-81 Jun 1983

(see Marvel Spotlight)

	$Good	$Fine	$N.Mint	£Good	£Fine	£N.Mint
1 Johnny Blaze as Ghost Rider begins; 1st appearance Daimon Hellstrom (cameo and face unseen)	$10.50	$32.00	$85.00	£5.50	£16.50	£45.00

2 2nd appearance Daimon Hellstrom (cameo - Son of Satan costume partially seen; face unseen); his appearance continues directly in Marvel Spotlight #12

	$Good	$Fine	$N.Mint	£Good	£Fine	£N.Mint
	$5.00	$15.00	$35.00	£2.85	£8.50	£20.00
3 new motorcycle, 2nd full appearance Son of Satan (see Marvel Spotlight #12/13)						
	$3.55	$10.50	$25.00	£1.75	£5.25	£12.50
4-5	$3.20	$9.50	$22.50	£1.40	£4.25	£10.00
6 ND	$2.50	$7.50	$17.50	£1.20	£3.60	£8.50
7	$2.10	$6.25	$15.00	£1.10	£3.40	£8.00
8 ND	$2.10	$6.25	$15.00	£1.20	£3.60	£8.50
9 Jesus Christ appears (called "friend")						
	$2.10	$6.25	$15.00	£1.05	£3.20	£7.50
10 Ploog art, reprints origin from Marvel Spotlight #5, Hulk appears						
	$2.10	$6.25	$15.00	£1.05	£3.20	£7.50
11 Ghost Rider vs. Hulk						
	$1.75	$5.25	$12.50	£0.70	£2.10	£5.00
12-16	$1.75	$5.25	$12.50	£0.70	£2.10	£5.00
17 team-up with Son of Satan						
	$1.75	$5.25	$12.50	£0.70	£2.10	£5.00
18 Spiderman, Thing, Hercules and Black Widow appear						
	$1.75	$5.25	$12.50	£0.70	£2.10	£5.00
19	$1.75	$5.25	$12.50	£0.70	£2.10	£5.00
20 ND John Byrne art, Death's Head appears, tie-in with Daredevil #138						
	$2.10	$6.25	$15.00	£0.85	£2.55	£6.00
21 ND Ghost Rider vs. The Gladiator, Gil Kane art						
	$1.05	$3.20	$7.50	£0.50	£1.50	£3.50
22 LD in the U.K.	$1.05	$3.20	$7.50	£0.40	£1.25	£3.00
23-25 ND	$1.05	$3.20	$7.50	£0.50	£1.50	£3.50
26 ND Ghost Rider vs. Dr. Druid						
	$1.25	$3.75	$7.50	£0.55	£1.75	£3.50
27 ND Hawkeye appears						
	$1.25	$3.75	$7.50	£0.55	£1.75	£3.50
28 ND	$1.25	$3.75	$7.50	£0.55	£1.75	£3.50
29-30 ND Ghost Rider vs. Dr. Strange						
	$1.25	$3.75	$7.50	£0.55	£1.75	£3.50
31 ND Dr. Strange appears						
	$1.00	$3.00	$6.00	£0.50	£1.50	£3.00
32-34 ND	$1.00	$3.00	$6.00	£0.50	£1.50	£3.00
35 ND Jim Starlin layouts						
	$1.00	$3.00	$6.00	£0.55	£1.75	£3.50
36-40	$1.00	$3.00	$6.00	£0.40	£1.25	£2.50
41-42	$0.80	$2.50	$5.00	£0.30	£1.00	£2.00
43 Infantino art, Ghost Rider vs. Johnny Blaze						
	$0.80	$2.50	$5.00	£0.30	£1.00	£2.00
44-49	$0.80	$2.50	$5.00	£0.30	£1.00	£2.00
50 ND 52pgs, Night Rider (original Ghost Rider) battles Ghost Rider						
	$1.25	$3.75	$7.50	£0.50	£1.50	£3.00
51 Infantino art	$0.80	$2.50	$5.00	£0.30	£1.00	£2.00
52-57	$0.80	$2.50	$5.00	£0.30	£1.00	£2.00
58 Sienkiewicz cover						
	$0.80	$2.50	$5.00	£0.30	£1.00	£2.00
59-67	$0.80	$2.50	$5.00	£0.30	£1.00	£2.00
68 origin retold	$1.00	$3.00	$6.00	£0.40	£1.25	£2.50
69-71	$0.80	$2.50	$5.00	£0.30	£1.00	£2.00
72-77 less common in the U.K.						
	$0.80	$2.50	$5.00	£0.40	£1.25	£2.50
78 LD in the U.K. Son of Satan, Dr. Strange and Dr. Druid cameos						
	$0.80	$2.50	$5.00	£0.50	£1.50	£3.00
79 ND	$0.80	$2.50	$5.00	£0.50	£1.50	£3.00
80 ND scarce in the U.K.						
	$0.80	$2.50	$5.00	£0.55	£1.75	£3.50
81 ND very scarce in the U.K.						
	$1.25	$3.75	$7.50	£0.65	£2.00	£4.00
Title Value:	$109.60	$332.75	$741.00	£49.55	£153.20	£343.00

Note: part origin stories of Ghost Rider in #6 and #68.

GHOST RIDER & BLAZE: SPIRITS OF VENGEANCE

Marvel Comics Group; 1 Aug 1992-23 Jun 1994

	$Good	$Fine	$N.Mint	£Good	£Fine	£N.Mint
1 ND 48pgs, pre-bagged, fold-out poster, ties in with Rise of the Midnight Sons						
	$0.50	$1.50	$2.50	£0.30	£0.90	£1.50
2-4 ND Rise of the Midnight Sons tie-in						
	$0.40	$1.20	$2.00	£0.25	£0.75	£1.25
5 ND Spirits of Venom part 2, continued in Web of Spiderman #96						
	$0.40	$1.20	$2.00	£0.25	£0.75	£1.25
6 ND Spirits of Venom part 4 (conclusion), Spiderman and Venom appear						
	$0.40	$1.20	$2.00	£0.25	£0.75	£1.25
7-8 ND	$0.40	$1.20	$2.00	£0.25	£0.75	£1.25
9 ND Adam Kubert cover, 1st appearance of Vengeance						
	$0.50	$1.50	$2.50	£0.30	£0.90	£1.50
10 ND Vengeance appears						
	$0.40	$1.20	$2.00	£0.25	£0.75	£1.25
11 ND	$0.30	$0.90	$1.50	£0.20	£0.60	£1.00
12 ND glow-in-the-dark cover by Andy and Adam Kubert, new logo						
	$0.30	$0.90	$1.50	£0.20	£0.60	£1.00
13 ND Midnight Massacre part 5 (conclusion), gold-printed black parchment outer cover						
	$0.30	$0.90	$1.50	£0.20	£0.60	£1.00
14 ND X-over with Ghost Rider #42						
	$0.30	$0.90	$1.50	£0.20	£0.60	£1.00
15 ND X-over with Ghost Rider #43						
	$0.30	$0.90	$1.50	£0.20	£0.60	£1.00
16 ND Road to Vengeance: The Missing Link conclusion, neon ink cover						
	$0.30	$0.90	$1.50	£0.20	£0.60	£1.00
17 ND Siege of Darkness part 8, black cover with enhanced inks						
	$0.30	$0.90	$1.50	£0.20	£0.60	£1.00
18 ND Siege of Darkness conclusion; Ghost Rider dies						
	$0.30	$0.90	$1.50	£0.20	£0.60	£1.00
19-21 ND	$0.30	$0.90	$1.50	£0.20	£0.60	£1.00
22 ND with free Spiderman and his Deadly Foes card sheet						
	$0.30	$0.90	$1.50	£0.20	£0.60	£1.00
23 ND	$0.30	$0.90	$1.50	£0.20	£0.60	£1.00
Title Value:	$8.10	$24.30	$40.50	£5.20	£15.60	£26.00

Ghost Rider & Spiderman: Spirits of Venom (Jan 1994)

				£Good	£Fine	£N.Mint
Trade paperback reprints Spirits of Vengeance #5 and Web of Spiderman #95, 96; new painted cover by Adam Kubert and Ken Steacy				£1.30	£3.90	£6.50

GHOST RIDER (2ND SERIES)

Marvel Comics Group; 1 May 1990-present

	$Good	$Fine	$N.Mint	£Good	£Fine	£N.Mint
1 ND 48pgs, Kingpin appears, Texeira art begins						
	$1.00	$3.00	$5.00	£0.80	£2.40	£4.00
1 2nd printing ND	$0.40	$1.20	$2.00	£0.30	£0.90	£1.50
2 ND Kingpin appears						
	$0.80	$2.40	$4.00	£0.60	£1.80	£3.00
3 ND scarce in the U.K. Kingpin appears						
	$0.80	$2.40	$4.00	£0.50	£1.50	£2.50
4 ND scarce in the U.K., scarce only in the U.S.						
	$0.80	$2.40	$4.00	£0.50	£1.50	£2.50
5 ND 1st Punisher/Ghost Rider team-up						
	$1.00	$3.00	$5.00	£0.60	£1.80	£3.00
5 2nd printing, ND Gold cover; this is the only gold edition available even though it's called 2nd print (ie. there's no 1st print Gold Edition)						
	$0.80	$2.40	$4.00	£0.50	£1.50	£2.50
6 ND Punisher co-stars						
	$0.80	$2.40	$4.00	£0.50	£1.50	£2.50
7-8 ND	$0.60	$1.80	$3.00	£0.40	£1.20	£2.00
9 ND X-Factor appear						
	$0.60	$1.80	$3.00	£0.40	£1.20	£2.00
10 ND	$0.60	$1.80	$3.00	£0.40	£1.20	£2.00
11 ND Dr. Strange appears						
	$0.50	$1.50	$2.50	£0.30	£0.90	£1.50
12 ND X-over with Dr. Strange #28						
	$0.50	$1.50	$2.50	£0.30	£0.90	£1.50
13-14 ND Ghost Rider vs. Johnny Blaze (original super-hero Ghost Rider)						
	$0.50	$1.50	$2.50	£0.30	£0.90	£1.50
15 ND Ghost Rider vs. Johnny Blaze (original super-hero Ghost Rider), glow-in-the-dark cover						
	$0.60	$1.80	$3.00	£0.40	£1.20	£2.00
15 2nd printing, ND different glow-in-the-dark cover						
	$0.50	$1.50	$2.50	£0.40	£1.20	£2.00
16 ND Johnny Blaze appears, Hobgoblin and Spiderman appear						
	$0.50	$1.50	$2.50	£0.30	£0.90	£1.50
17 ND Johnny Blaze appears, sequel to Spiderman #6,7 (Hobgoblin and Spiderman appear)						
	$0.50	$1.50	$2.50	£0.30	£0.90	£1.50
18-20 ND	$0.50	$1.50	$2.50	£0.30	£0.90	£1.50
21 ND Ron Wagner pencils, inks only by Texeira						
	$0.40	$1.20	$2.00	£0.25	£0.75	£1.25
22-23 ND	$0.40	$1.20	$2.00	£0.25	£0.75	£1.25
24 ND Johnny Blaze cameo						
	$0.40	$1.20	$2.00	£0.25	£0.75	£1.25
25 ND 48pgs, celebrates 20th anniversary, die-cut pop-up centre-spread						
	$0.50	$1.50	$2.50	£0.30	£0.90	£1.50
26 ND X-over with X-Men #9						
	$0.50	$1.50	$2.50	£0.30	£0.90	£1.50
27 ND X-Men guest-star, Jim Lee cover						
	$0.50	$1.50	$2.50	£0.30	£0.90	£1.50
28 ND Rise of the Midnight Sons part 1, pre-bagged with fold-out poster and gatefold centre-spread, Andy and Joe Kubert art						
	$0.50	$1.50	$2.50	£0.30	£0.90	£1.50
29 ND Wolverine and Beast appear, Rise of the Midnight Sons tie-in						
	$0.40	$1.20	$2.00	£0.25	£0.75	£1.25
30 ND more deatails of Ghost Rider's origin						
	$0.40	$1.20	$2.00	£0.25	£0.75	£1.25
31 ND pre-bagged, Rise of the Midnight Sons part 6 (conclusion), all characters in this storyline appear including Morbius and Dr. Strange						
	$0.50	$1.50	$2.50	£0.30	£0.90	£1.50
32 ND Dr. Strange guest-stars						
	$0.40	$1.20	$2.00	£0.25	£0.75	£1.25
33-36 ND	$0.40	$1.20	$2.00	£0.25	£0.75	£1.25
37 ND Archangel appears						
	$0.40	$1.20	$2.00	£0.25	£0.75	£1.25
38-39 ND	$0.40	$1.20	$2.00	£0.25	£0.75	£1.25
40 ND Midnight Massacre part 2, gold-ink black parchment outer cover						
	$0.40	$1.20	$2.00	£0.25	£0.75	£1.25
41 ND Road to Vengeance: The Missing Link begins, neon ink covers begin; continued in Ghost Rider & Blaze: Spirits of Vengeance #14						
	$0.40	$1.20	$2.00	£0.25	£0.75	£1.25
42 ND Road to Vengeance: The Missing Link story; continued in Ghost Rider & Blaze: Spirits of Vengeance #15						
	$0.40	$1.20	$2.00	£0.25	£0.75	£1.25
43 ND Road to Vengeance: The Missing Link story; continued in Ghost Rider & Blaze: Spirits of Vengeance #16						
	$0.40	$1.20	$2.00	£0.25	£0.75	£1.25
44 ND Siege of Darkness part 2, neon ink/spot varnish cover						
	$0.40	$1.20	$2.00	£0.25	£0.75	£1.25
45 ND Siege of Darkness part 10, neon ink/spot varnish cover						
	$0.40	$1.20	$2.00	£0.25	£0.75	£1.25
46 ND Vengeance becomes new Ghost Rider						
	$0.40	$1.20	$2.00	£0.25	£0.75	£1.25
47-48 ND	$0.40	$1.20	$2.00	£0.25	£0.75	£1.25
49 ND with free Spiderman and his Deadly Foes card sheet						
	$0.40	$1.20	$2.00	£0.25	£0.75	£1.25
50 ND 48pgs, John Blaze appears						
	$0.50	$1.50	$2.50	£0.30	£0.90	£1.50

	$Good	$Fine	$N.Mint	£Good	£Fine	£N.Mint
50 Collectors Edition, ND - John Blaze appears; die-cut foil stamped cover	$0.60	$1.80	$3.00	£0.40	£1.20	£2.00
51-54 ND	$0.40	$1.20	$2.00	£0.25	£0.75	£1.25
55 ND Werewolf By Night appears	$0.40	$1.20	$2.00	£0.25	£0.75	£1.25
56 ND	$0.40	$1.20	$2.00	£0.25	£0.75	£1.25
57 ND Wolverine appears, X-over with Wolverine #89	$0.40	$1.20	$2.00	£0.25	£0.75	£1.25
58 ND Nick Fury appears	$0.40	$1.20	$2.00	£0.25	£0.75	£1.25
59 ND Hulk appears	$0.40	$1.20	$2.00	£0.25	£0.75	£1.25
60 ND	$0.40	$1.20	$2.00	£0.25	£0.75	£1.25
61 ND 48pgs, Daredevil, Nick Fury and Punisher appear	$0.50	$1.50	$2.50	£0.30	£0.90	£1.50
62-63 ND Nick Fury appears	$0.40	$1.20	$2.00	£0.25	£0.75	£1.25
64 ND Avengers and Nick Fury appear	$0.40	$1.20	$2.00	£0.25	£0.75	£1.25
65 ND Over The Edge tie-in, Punisher appears	$0.40	$1.20	$2.00	£0.25	£0.75	£1.25
66 ND Ghost Rider vs. Blackout	$0.40	$1.20	$2.00	£0.25	£0.75	£1.25
67 ND Gambit guest-stars	$0.40	$1.20	$2.00	£0.25	£0.75	£1.25
68 ND Gambit and Wolverine appear	$0.40	$1.20	$2.00	£0.25	£0.75	£1.25
69-72 ND	$0.40	$1.20	$2.00	£0.25	£0.75	£1.25
73 ND the return of Johnny Blaze..	$0.40	$1.20	$2.00	£0.25	£0.75	£1.25
74-76 ND	$0.40	$1.20	$2.00	£0.25	£0.75	£1.25
77 ND Dr. Strange guest-stars	$0.30	$0.90	$1.50	£0.25	£0.75	£1.25
78 ND Ghost Rider's new costume and bike	$0.30	$0.90	$1.50	£0.25	£0.75	£1.25
79-80 ND Valkyrie guest-stars	$0.30	$0.90	$1.50	£0.20	£0.60	£1.00
81 ND Howard the Duck guest-stars	$0.30	$0.90	$1.50	£0.20	£0.60	£1.00
82 ND Devil Dinosaur appears (!)	$0.30	$0.90	$1.50	£0.20	£0.60	£1.00
83 ND	$0.40	$1.20	$2.00	£0.25	£0.75	£1.25
Title Value:	$40.30	$120.90	$200.50	£25.70	£77.10	£128.50
Ghost Rider: Ressurrected						
Trade paperback (Jan 1992) reprints issues #1-7				£1.60	£4.80	£8.00
(2nd printing - Dec 1992)				£1.50	£4.50	£7.50
Ghost Rider Poster Book (Jul 1992), magazine format with posters featuring the work of McFarlane, Lee, Texeira and Golden; sixteen of the posters are double-page spreads				£0.65	£1.95	£3.25
Ghost Rider: Midnight Sons (Aug 1993) Trade paperback reprints Ghost Rider #28,31, Morbius #1, Nightstalkers #1, Darkhold #1 and Spirits of Vengeance #1; wraparound cover with embossed gold logo				£2.75	£8.25	£13.75

GHOST RIDER (2ND SERIES) ANNUAL

Marvel Comics Group; 1 Sep 1993-present

	$Good	$Fine	$N.Mint	£Good	£Fine	£N.Mint
1 ND 64pgs, pre-bagged with trading card introducing Night Terror; Chris Bachalo and Mark Buckingham art	$0.50	$1.50	$2.50	£0.30	£0.90	£1.50
2 ND 64pgs, Warren Ellis script	$0.50	$1.50	$2.50	£0.30	£0.90	£1.50
Title Value:	$1.00	$3.00	$5.00	£0.60	£1.80	£3.00

GHOST RIDER 2099

Marvel Comics Group; 1 May 1994-25 May 1996

	$Good	$Fine	$N.Mint	£Good	£Fine	£N.Mint
1 ND Chris Bachalo and Mark Buckingham art begins	$0.30	$0.90	$1.50	£0.20	£0.60	£1.00
1 Collectors Edition, ND , prismatic foil enhanced cover; with free Spiderman's Amazing Powers card sheet	$0.50	$1.50	$2.50	£0.30	£0.90	£1.50
2-6 ND	$0.30	$0.90	$1.50	£0.20	£0.60	£1.00
7 ND Spiderman 2099 appears	$0.30	$0.90	$1.50	£0.20	£0.60	£1.00
8 ND	$0.30	$0.90	$1.50	£0.20	£0.60	£1.00
9 ND Mark Buckingham art	$0.30	$0.90	$1.50	£0.20	£0.60	£1.00
10 ND photographic cover	$0.30	$0.90	$1.50	£0.20	£0.60	£1.00
11 ND	$0.30	$0.90	$1.50	£0.20	£0.60	£1.00
12 ND computer-generated cover	$0.30	$0.90	$1.50	£0.20	£0.60	£1.00
13 ND $1.95 cover begin	$0.40	$1.20	$2.00	£0.25	£0.75	£1.25
14-15 ND	$0.40	$1.20	$2.00	£0.25	£0.75	£1.25
16 ND One Nation Under Doom	$0.40	$1.20	$2.00	£0.25	£0.75	£1.25
17-20 ND	$0.40	$1.20	$2.00	£0.25	£0.75	£1.25
21 ND ties-into 2099 Genesis	$0.40	$1.20	$2.00	£0.25	£0.75	£1.25
22 ND Ghost Rider 2099 vs. Vengeance 2099	$0.40	$1.20	$2.00	£0.25	£0.75	£1.25
23-24 ND	$0.40	$1.20	$2.00	£0.25	£0.75	£1.25
25 ND Hulk, Ravage and Punisher 2099 appear	$0.60	$1.80	$3.00	£0.40	£1.20	£2.00
Title Value:	$9.50	$28.50	$47.50	£6.10	£18.30	£30.50

GHOST RIDER AND THE MIDNIGHT SONS MAGAZINE

Marvel Comics Group,Magazine OS; 1 Dec 1993

	$Good	$Fine	$N.Mint	£Good	£Fine	£N.Mint
1 ND 48pgs, George Pratt cover	$0.80	$2.40	$4.00	£0.50	£1.50	£2.50
Title Value:	$0.80	$2.40	$4.00	£0.50	£1.50	£2.50

GHOST RIDER RIDES AGAIN, THE ORIGINAL

Marvel Comics Group,MS; 1 Jul 1991-7 Jan 1992

	$Good	$Fine	$N.Mint	£Good	£Fine	£N.Mint
1 ND reprints from Ghost Rider (super-hero) 1st series begin with issues #68,#69	$0.30	$0.90	$1.50	£0.20	£0.60	£1.00
2 ND reprints issues #70,#71	$0.30	$0.90	$1.50	£0.20	£0.60	£1.00
3 ND reprints issues #72,#73	$0.30	$0.90	$1.50	£0.20	£0.60	£1.00
4 ND reprints issues #74,#75	$0.30	$0.90	$1.50	£0.20	£0.60	£1.00
5 ND reprints issues #76,#77	$0.30	$0.90	$1.50	£0.20	£0.60	£1.00
6 ND reprints issues #78,#79	$0.30	$0.90	$1.50	£0.20	£0.60	£1.00
7 ND reprints issues #80,#81	$0.30	$0.90	$1.50	£0.20	£0.60	£1.00
Title Value:	$2.10	$6.30	$10.50	£1.40	£4.20	£7.00

GHOST RIDER, THE

Marvel Comics Group; 1 Feb 1967-7 Nov 1967

(see Nightrider, Western Gunfighters)

	$Good	$Fine	$N.Mint	£Good	£Fine	£N.Mint
1 origin and 1st appearance Ghost Rider (Western), Kid Colt begins	$6.25	$19.00	$45.00	£3.55	£10.50	£25.00
2	$2.85	$8.50	$20.00	£1.75	£5.25	£12.50
3-7	$2.50	$7.50	$17.50	£1.40	£4.25	£10.00
Title Value:	$21.60	$65.00	$152.50	£12.30	£37.00	£87.50

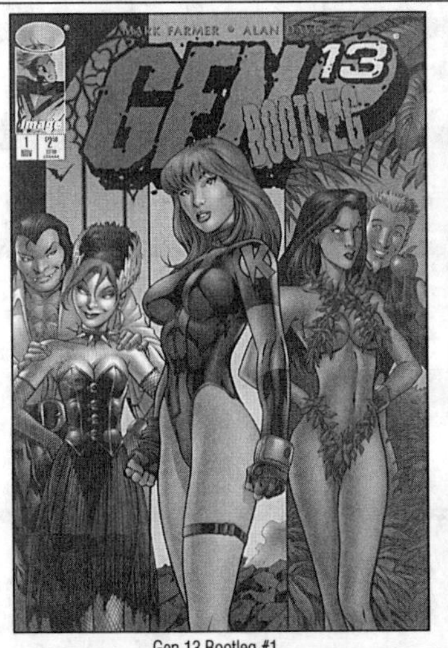

Gen 13 Bootleg #1

Generation Next #1

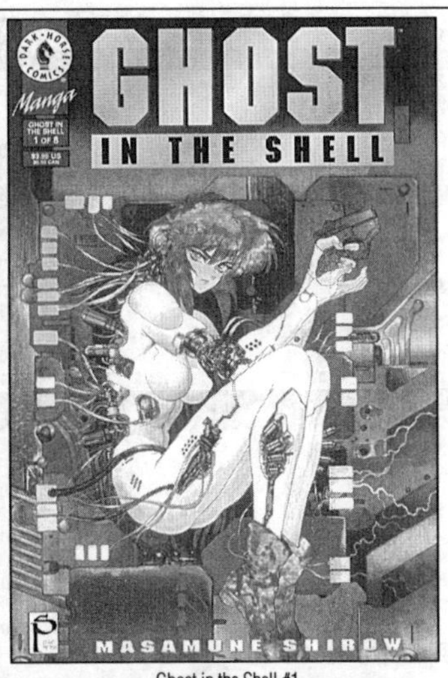

Ghost in the Shell #1

	$Good	$Fine	$N.Mint	£Good	£Fine	£N.Mint

Note: not to be confused with the later super-hero title. All the above were reprinted under the title "Night Rider".

GHOST RIDER, THE ORIGINAL

Marvel Comics Group; 1 Jul 1992-20 Feb 1994

Issue	$Good	$Fine	$N.Mint	£Good	£Fine	£N.Mint
1 ND reprints Marvel Spotlight (1st Series) #5 featuring the 1st appearance of Ghost Rider; reprints from this series begin in order	$0.30	$0.90	$1.50	£0.20	£0.60	£1.00
2-7 ND	$0.30	$0.90	$1.50	£0.20	£0.60	£1.00
8 ND reprints begin from Ghost Rider (1st series) #1	$0.30	$0.90	$1.50	£0.20	£0.60	£1.00
9 ND reprints Ghost Rider (1st Series) #2	$0.30	$0.90	$1.50	£0.20	£0.60	£1.00
10 ND reprints Marvel Spotlight (1st Series) #12 with the first full appearance of Son of Satan	$0.30	$0.90	$1.50	£0.20	£0.60	£1.00
11 ND reprints Ghost Rider #3, Hellstorm appears	$0.30	$0.90	$1.50	£0.20	£0.60	£1.00
12-17 ND	$0.30	$0.90	$1.50	£0.20	£0.60	£1.00
18 ND reprints Ghost Rider #11, Hulk appears	$0.30	$0.90	$1.50	£0.20	£0.60	£1.00
19 ND	$0.30	$0.90	$1.50	£0.20	£0.60	£1.00
20 ND Mike Ploog cover	$0.30	$0.90	$1.50	£0.20	£0.60	£1.00
Title Value:	$6.00	$18.00	$30.00	£4.00	£12.00	£20.00

GHOST RIDER/BALLISTIC

Marvel Comics Group/Top Cow Comics,OS; nn Feb 1997

Issue	$Good	$Fine	$N.Mint	£Good	£Fine	£N.Mint
nn ND Devil's Reign part 3, Warren Ellis script; continued in Ballistic/Wolverine	$0.60	$1.80	$3.00	£0.40	£1.20	£2.00
Title Value:	$0.60	$1.80	$3.00	£0.40	£1.20	£2.00

GHOST RIDER/CABLE SPECIAL

Marvel Comics Group,OS; 1 Sep 1992

Issue	$Good	$Fine	$N.Mint	£Good	£Fine	£N.Mint
1 ND reprints Marvel Comics Presents #90-98, new covers on heavier card-stock	$0.80	$2.40	$4.00	£0.50	£1.50	£2.50
Title Value:	$0.80	$2.40	$4.00	£0.50	£1.50	£2.50

GHOST RIDER/CYBLADE

Marvel Comics Group/Top Cow Comics,OS; nn Feb 1997

Issue	$Good	$Fine	$N.Mint	£Good	£Fine	£N.Mint
nn ND Devil's Reign part 2, continued in Ghost Rider/Ballistic; Ivan Velez Jnr. script, Anthony Chun art	$0.60	$1.80	$3.00	£0.40	£1.20	£2.00
Title Value:	$0.60	$1.80	$3.00	£0.40	£1.20	£2.00

GHOST RIDER/WOLVERINE/PUNISHER: THE DARK DESIGN

Marvel Comics Group,OS; 1 Feb 1995

Issue	$Good	$Fine	$N.Mint	£Good	£Fine	£N.Mint
1 ND 48pgs, sequel to Hearts of Darkness	$1.20	$3.60	$6.00	£0.80	£2.40	£4.00
Title Value:	$1.20	$3.60	$6.00	£0.80	£2.40	£4.00

GHOST RIDER: FEAR

Marvel Comics Group,OS; 1 Dec 1992

Issue	$Good	$Fine	$N.Mint	£Good	£Fine	£N.Mint
1 ND 48pgs, team-up with Captain America, gatefold cover	$1.00	$3.00	$5.00	£0.70	£2.10	£3.50
Title Value:	$1.00	$3.00	$5.00	£0.70	£2.10	£3.50

GHOST RIDERS: CROSS ROADS

Marvel Comics Group,OS; nn Dec 1995

Issue	$Good	$Fine	$N.Mint	£Good	£Fine	£N.Mint
nn ND 48pgs, features original Ghost Rider and Spirit of Vengeance, die-cut cover	$0.80	$2.40	$4.00	£0.50	£1.50	£2.50
Title Value:	$0.80	$2.40	$4.00	£0.50	£1.50	£2.50

GHOST SPECIAL

Dark Horse/Comics Greatest World,OS; 1 Jul 1994

Issue	$Good	$Fine	$N.Mint	£Good	£Fine	£N.Mint
1 ND 48pgs, Adam Hughes cover	$0.80	$2.40	$4.00	£0.50	£1.50	£2.50
Title Value:	$0.80	$2.40	$4.00	£0.50	£1.50	£2.50
Ghost Trade paperback (Feb 1995) reprints early appearances from Comics' Greatest World with Adam Hughes cover				£1.20	£3.60	£6.00

GHOST/HELLBOY SPECIAL

Dark Horse,MS; 1 May 1996-2 Jun 1996

Issue	$Good	$Fine	$N.Mint	£Good	£Fine	£N.Mint
1-2 ND Mike Mignola script and cover art	$0.50	$1.50	$2.50	£0.30	£0.90	£1.50
Title Value:	$1.00	$3.00	$5.00	£0.60	£1.80	£3.00

GHOSTBUSTERS

First,TV; 1 Feb 1986-6 Aug 1987

(see Real Ghostbusters)

Issue	$Good	$Fine	$N.Mint	£Good	£Fine	£N.Mint
1-6 ND based on animated TV show	$0.25	$0.75	$1.25	£0.15	£0.45	£0.75
Title Value:	$1.50	$4.50	$7.50	£0.90	£2.70	£4.50

GHOSTDANCING

DC Comics,MS; 1 Mar 1995-6 Sep 1995

Issue	$Good	$Fine	$N.Mint	£Good	£Fine	£N.Mint
1-2 Jamie Delano script, Richard Case art	$0.40	$1.20	$2.00	£0.25	£0.75	£1.25
3 Jamie Delano script, Richard Case art; upgraded paper format begins	$0.40	$1.20	$2.00	£0.25	£0.75	£1.25
4-6 Jamie Delano script, Richard Case art	$0.40	$1.20	$2.00	£0.25	£0.75	£1.25
Title Value:	$2.40	$7.20	$12.00	£1.50	£4.50	£7.50

GHOSTLY HAUNTS

Charlton;20 Sep 1971-53 Dec 1976; 54 Sep 1977-58 Apr 1978

(formerly Ghost Manor #1-19)

Issue	$Good	$Fine	$N.Mint	£Good	£Fine	£N.Mint
20-30 distributed in the U.K.	$0.65	$2.00	$4.00	£0.40	£1.25	£2.50
31-40 distributed in the U.K.	$0.55	$1.75	$3.50	£0.30	£1.00	£2.00
41-51 distributed in the U.K.	$0.50	$1.50	$3.00	£0.25	£0.75	£1.50
52 distributed in the U.K. Pat Boyette cover	$0.50	$1.50	$3.00	£0.25	£0.75	£1.50
53-58 distributed in the U.K.	$0.50	$1.50	$3.00	£0.25	£0.75	£1.50
Title Value:	$21.65	$66.50	$133.00	£11.90	£37.25	£74.50

Note: most issues have Steve Ditko art

GHOSTLY TALES

Charlton;55 Apr/May 1966-124 Dec 1976; 125 Sep 1977-169 Oct 1984

(previously Unusual Tales #1-49; Blue Beetle 2nd Series #50-54)

Issue	$Good	$Fine	$N.Mint	£Good	£Fine	£N.Mint
55 origin/1st appearance Dr. Graves	$1.25	$3.85	$9.00	£0.70	£2.10	£5.00
56-60 Dr. Graves appears	$0.70	$2.10	$5.00	£0.40	£1.25	£3.00
61-70 Dr. Graves appears	$0.60	$1.90	$4.50	£0.35	£1.05	£2.50
71-130	$0.65	$2.00	$4.00	£0.30	£1.00	£2.00
131-169	$0.60	$1.80	$3.00	£0.30	£0.90	£1.50
Title Value:	$73.15	$223.55	$421.00	£35.90	£113.95	£223.50

Note: most issues have Ditko art. All were distributed in the U.K.

GHOSTS

DC Comics; 1 Sep/Oct 1971-112 May 1982

(see DC Special Blue Ribbon Digest, Limited Collector's Edition)

Issue	$Good	$Fine	$N.Mint	£Good	£Fine	£N.Mint
1 48pgs	$2.50	$7.50	$15.00	£1.30	£4.00	£8.00
2 48pgs, Wood art	$1.15	$3.50	$7.00	£0.65	£2.00	£4.00
3-5 48pgs	$0.80	$2.50	$5.00	£0.40	£1.25	£2.50
6-10	$0.65	$2.00	$4.00	£0.30	£1.00	£2.00
11-20	$0.55	$1.75	$3.50	£0.25	£0.85	£1.75
21-30	$0.50	$1.50	$3.00	£0.25	£0.75	£1.50
31-39	$0.40	$1.25	$2.50	£0.20	£0.60	£1.25
40 scarce in the U.K. 64pgs, squarebound	$0.40	$1.25	$2.50	£0.25	£0.75	£1.50
41-42	$0.30	$1.00	$2.00	£0.15	£0.50	£1.00
43 ND	$0.30	$1.00	$2.00	£0.20	£0.60	£1.25
44-46	$0.30	$1.00	$2.00	£0.15	£0.50	£1.00
47-49 scarce in the U.K.	$0.30	$1.00	$2.00	£0.20	£0.60	£1.25
50-67	$0.30	$1.00	$2.00	£0.15	£0.50	£1.00
68-70 ND 44pgs	$0.30	$1.00	$2.00	£0.20	£0.60	£1.25
71-87	$0.30	$1.00	$2.00	£0.15	£0.50	£1.00
88 Golden art	$0.30	$1.00	$2.00	£0.15	£0.50	£1.00
89-96	$0.30	$1.00	$2.00	£0.15	£0.50	£1.00
97-99 Dr. Geist by Mike Nasser, Dr. 13 Ghostbreaker vs. The Spectre (back-up)	$0.60	$1.80	$3.00	£0.40	£1.20	£2.00
100	$0.40	$1.20	$2.00	£0.25	£0.75	£1.25
101-103	$0.30	$0.90	$1.50	£0.20	£0.60	£1.00
104 Giffen art	$0.30	$0.90	$1.50	£0.20	£0.60	£1.00
105-112	$0.30	$0.90	$1.50	£0.20	£0.60	£1.00
Title Value:	$46.40	$146.90	$288.00	£24.30	£77.15	£151.75

ARTISTS

Ditko in 77, 111. Nino in 35, 37, 57. Wood in 2.

FEATURES

All-new mystery stories except some reprints in 1-5, 40. Dr.13 in 95, 96, 101, 102. Dr.13/Spectre in 97-99.

GHOSTS SPECIAL

DC Comics; nn 1977

Issue	$Good	$Fine	$N.Mint	£Good	£Fine	£N.Mint
nn ND 52pgs, Alex Nino art	$0.50	$1.50	$3.00	£0.30	£1.00	£2.00
Title Value:	$0.50	$1.50	$3.00	£0.30	£1.00	£2.00

GHOUL GALLERY

AC Comics; 1 Apr 1994-2 1994

Issue	$Good	$Fine	$N.Mint	£Good	£Fine	£N.Mint
1-2 ND black and white	$0.60	$1.80	$3.00	£0.40	£1.20	£2.00
Title Value:	$1.20	$3.60	$6.00	£0.80	£2.40	£4.00

GIANT-SIZE MINI COMICS

Eclipse; 1 Aug 1986-4 Feb 1987

Issue	$Good	$Fine	$N.Mint	£Good	£Fine	£N.Mint
1-4 ND Mini-comics reprints in black and white featuring Ronald Reagan	$0.30	$0.90	$1.50	£0.20	£0.60	£1.00
Title Value:	$1.20	$3.60	$6.00	£0.80	£2.40	£4.00

GIFT, THE

First,OS; 1 Jan 1991

Issue	$Good	$Fine	$N.Mint	£Good	£Fine	£N.Mint
1 ND 48pgs, features Badger, Nexus, Grimjack, Meta-4, Squalor, Zero Tolerance	$1.20	$3.60	$6.00	£0.80	£2.40	£4.00
Title Value:	$1.20	$3.60	$6.00	£0.80	£2.40	£4.00

GIL KANE'S SAVAGE

Fantagraphics,Magazine; 1 1987

Issue	$Good	$Fine	$N.Mint	£Good	£Fine	£N.Mint
1 ND reprints "His Name Is Savage", new cover	$0.50	$1.50	$2.50	£0.30	£0.90	£1.50
Title Value:	$0.50	$1.50	$2.50	£0.30	£0.90	£1.50

GILGAMESH II

DC Comics,MS; 1 April 1989-4 July 1989

Issue	$Good	$Fine	$N.Mint	£Good	£Fine	£N.Mint
1-4 ND squarebound, Jim Starlin script/art	$0.60	$1.80	$3.00	£0.40	£1.20	£2.00
Title Value:	$2.40	$7.20	$12.00	£1.60	£4.80	£8.00

Note: Mature Readers

GINGER FOX

Comico,MS; 1 Sep 1988-4 Dec 1988

(see World of Ginger Fox)

Issue	$Good	$Fine	$N.Mint	£Good	£Fine	£N.Mint
1-4 ND Pander Bros. art	$0.40	$1.20	$2.00	£0.25	£0.75	£1.25
Title Value:	$1.60	$4.80	$8.00	£1.00	£3.00	£5.00

GIRL CRAZY

Dark Horse,MS; 1 May 1996-3 Jul 1996

Issue	$Good	$Fine	$N.Mint	£Good	£Fine	£N.Mint
1-2 ND Gilbert Hernandez script and art	$0.60	$1.80	$3.00	£0.40	£1.20	£2.00
3 ND	$0.60	$1.80	$3.00	£0.40	£1.20	£2.00
Title Value:	$1.80	$5.40	$9.00	£1.20	£3.60	£6.00

GIRL FROM U.N.C.L.E., THE

Gold Key,TV; 1 Oct 1966-5 Oct 1967
(see Man From Uncle)

Issue	$Good	$Fine	$N.Mint	£Good	£Fine	£N.Mint
1 scarce, distributed in the U.K.	$11.00	$34.00	$80.00	£7.00	£21.00	£50.00
2-5 scarce, distributed in the U.K.	$8.50	$26.00	$60.00	£5.00	£15.00	£35.00
Title Value:	$45.00	$138.00	$320.00	£27.00	£81.00	£190.00

GIRL'S LOVE STORIES

National Periodical Publications/DC Comics; 1 Aug/Sep 1949-180 Nov/Dec 1973

Issue	$Good	$Fine	$N.Mint	£Good	£Fine	£N.Mint
1 very scarce in the U.K. photo cover	$52.50	$155.00	$425.00	£36.00	£105.00	£285.00
2 very scarce in the U.K. photo cover	$32.00	$95.00	$225.00	£21.00	£62.50	£150.00
3-9 scarce in the U.K. photo cover	$21.00	$62.50	$150.00	£12.50	£39.00	£90.00
10 scarce in the U.K.	$21.00	$62.50	$150.00	£12.50	£39.00	£90.00
11-20 scarce in the U.K.	$15.50	$47.00	$110.00	£8.50	£26.00	£60.00
21-33 scarce in the U.K.	$8.50	$26.00	$60.00	£4.25	£12.50	£30.00
34-50 scarce in the U.K.	$6.25	$19.00	$45.00	£3.55	£10.50	£25.00
51-60 scarce in the U.K.	$5.00	$15.00	$35.00	£2.85	£8.50	£20.00
61-65 scarce in the U.K.	$4.60	$13.50	$32.50	£2.10	£6.25	£15.00
1st official distribution in the U.K.						
66-82 scarce in the U.K.	$4.60	$13.50	$32.50	£1.75	£5.25	£12.50
83 scarce in the U.K. last 10 cents issue	$4.25	$12.50	$30.00	£1.75	£5.25	£12.50
84-90 scarce in the U.K.	$4.25	$12.50	$30.00	£1.75	£5.25	£12.50
91-99	$4.25	$12.50	$30.00	£1.55	£4.70	£11.00
100	$5.00	$15.00	$35.00	£1.75	£5.25	£12.50
101-110	$2.50	$7.50	$15.00	£1.25	£3.75	£7.50
111-130	$2.50	$7.50	$15.00	£1.00	£3.00	£6.00
131-150	$2.00	$6.00	$12.00	£0.80	£2.50	£5.00
151-160	$1.00	$3.00	$6.00	£0.65	£2.00	£4.00
161-170 48pgs	$1.00	$3.00	$6.00	£0.75	£2.25	£4.50
171-180	$0.80	$2.50	$5.00	£0.55	£1.75	£3.50
Title Value:	$995.70	$2985.50	$6935.00	£524.05	£1583.05	£3684.00

GIRL'S ROMANCES

National Periodical Publications/DC Comics; 1 Feb/Mar 1950-160 Oct 1971

Issue	$Good	$Fine	$N.Mint	£Good	£Fine	£N.Mint
1 very scarce in the U.K. photo cover	$52.50	$160.00	$375.00	£36.00	£105.00	£250.00
2 very scarce in the U.K. photo cover	$30.00	$90.00	$210.00	£20.00	£60.00	£140.00
3-6 scarce in the U.K. photo cover	$21.00	$62.50	$150.00	£12.50	£39.00	£90.00
7-10 scarce in the U.K.	$21.00	$62.50	$150.00	£12.50	£39.00	£90.00
11-20 scarce in the U.K.	$15.00	$45.00	$105.00	£8.50	£26.00	£60.00
21-30 scarce in the U.K.	$7.75	$23.50	$55.00	£4.25	£12.50	£30.00
31-50 scarce in the U.K.	$6.75	$20.00	$47.50	£3.20	£9.50	£22.50
51-60 scarce in the U.K.	$5.00	$15.00	$35.00	£2.85	£8.50	£20.00
61-63 scarce in the U.K.	$4.60	$13.50	$32.50	£2.10	£6.25	£15.00
1st official distribution in the U.K.						
64-79 scarce in the U.K.	$4.60	$13.50	$32.50	£1.70	£5.00	£12.00
80 scarce in the U.K. last 10 cents issue	$4.60	$13.50	$32.50	£1.70	£5.00	£12.00
81-90	$4.60	$13.50	$32.50	£1.55	£4.70	£11.00
91-99	$4.25	$12.50	$30.00	£1.40	£4.25	£10.00
100	$5.25	$16.00	$37.50	£2.10	£6.25	£15.00
101-108	$3.75	$11.00	$22.50	£1.50	£4.50	£9.00
109 Beatles story and cover appearance	$12.50	$38.00	$75.00	£6.25	£18.50	£37.50
110-120	$3.75	$11.00	$22.50	£1.50	£4.50	£9.00
121-133	$2.05	$6.25	$12.50	£1.00	£3.00	£6.00
134 Neal Adams cover	$2.50	$7.50	$15.00	£1.25	£3.75	£7.50
135-140	$2.05	$6.25	$12.50	£1.00	£3.00	£6.00
141-158	$1.25	$3.75	$7.50	£0.65	£2.00	£4.00
159-160 scarce in the U.K. 48pgs	$1.25	$3.75	$7.50	£0.75	£2.25	£4.50
Title Value:	$994.70	$2966.75	$6872.50	£509.60	£1537.50	£3535.00

GIVE ME LIBERTY

Dark Horse,MS; 1 Aug 1990-4 Apr 1991

Issue	$Good	$Fine	$N.Mint	£Good	£Fine	£N.Mint
1-4 ND Frank Miller script, Dave Gibbons art	$1.00	$3.00	$5.00	£0.70	£2.10	£3.50
Title Value:	$4.00	$12.00	$20.00	£2.80	£8.40	£14.00
Trade paperback (Sep 1991 – published by Penguin Books) reprints #1-4				£1.80	£5.40	£9.00
Hardcover				£3.00	£9.00	£15.00
Hardcover distributed by Titan with signed plate by Miller and Gibbons				£3.50	£10.50	£17.50
Trade paperback (Feb 1992) - published by Dark Horse), reprints #1-4				£2.00	£6.00	£10.00
(2nd print - Sep 1994) $19.95 cover				£2.50	£7.50	£12.50
Signed and Numbered Limited Edition Hardcover (Dec 1994) with slipcase, new sketched included				£15.00	£45.00	£75.00
Give Me Liberty Trade Paperback - Dell Edition (Jul 1995) reprints mini-series. Note: only distributed in the U.S. not U.K.				£2.00	£6.00	£10.00

GIZMO

Chance,OS; 1 May 1985

Issue	$Good	$Fine	$N.Mint	£Good	£Fine	£N.Mint
1 ND Turtles X-over	$0.90	$2.70	$4.50	£0.60	£1.80	£3.00
Title Value:	$0.90	$2.70	$4.50	£0.60	£1.80	£3.00
Trade Paperback, reprints #1-6, plus new material				£1.70	£5.10	£8.50

GIZMO (2ND SERIES)

Mirage Studios; 1 Feb 1986-6 Jul 1987

Issue	$Good	$Fine	$N.Mint	£Good	£Fine	£N.Mint
1-6 ND black and white	$0.40	$1.20	$2.00	£0.25	£0.75	£1.25
Title Value:	$2.40	$7.20	$12.00	£1.50	£4.50	£7.50

GIZMO AND THE FUGITOID

Mirage Studios,MS; 1 Jun 1989-2 Jul 1989

Issue	$Good	$Fine	$N.Mint	£Good	£Fine	£N.Mint
1-2 ND	$0.40	$1.20	$2.00	£0.25	£0.75	£1.25
Title Value:	$0.80	$2.40	$4.00	£0.50	£1.50	£2.50

GLADIATOR/SUPREME

Marvel Comics Group/Image,OS; nn Mar 1997

Issue	$Good	$Fine	$N.Mint	£Good	£Fine	£N.Mint
nn ND 48pgs, Keith Giffen script, Andy Smith art	$1.00	$3.00	$5.00	£0.70	£2.10	£3.50
Title Value:	$1.00	$3.00	$5.00	£0.70	£2.10	£3.50

GLADSTONE COMIC ALBUM

Gladstone; 1 1987-28 1990

Issue	$Good	$Fine	$N.Mint	£Good	£Fine	£N.Mint
1 ND Uncle Scrooge: Mines of King Solomon, plus 2 shorts by Barks	$1.50	$4.50	$7.50	£1.00	£3.00	£5.00
2 ND Donald Duck: Terror of the River, plus 2 shorts by Barks	$1.40	$4.20	$7.00	£0.90	£2.70	£4.50
3 ND Mickey Mouse: Lair of Wolf Barker, Mickey's Nephew by Gottfredson	$1.40	$4.20	$7.00	£0.90	£2.70	£4.50
4 ND Uncle Scrooge: Back to the Klondike (includes restored artwork), plus 2 shorts by Barks	$1.40	$4.20	$7.00	£0.90	£2.70	£4.50
5 ND Donald Duck: Sheriff of Bullet Valley plus 2 shorts by Barks	$1.40	$4.20	$7.00	£0.90	£2.70	£4.50
6 ND Uncle Scrooge: Land Beneath the Ground & Pipeline to Danger by Barks	$1.20	$3.60	$6.00	£0.80	£2.40	£4.00
7 ND The Brittle Mastery of Donald Duck (5 shorts by Barks)	$1.20	$3.60	$6.00	£0.80	£2.40	£4.00
8 ND Mickey Mouse: Hoppy the Kangaroo, Mount Fishflake Expedition by Gottfredson	$1.20	$3.60	$6.00	£0.80	£2.40	£4.00
9 ND Bambi: movie adaptation	$1.20	$3.60	$6.00	£0.80	£2.40	£4.00
10 ND Donald Duck: In Ancient Persia, plus 2 shorts by Barks	$1.20	$3.60	$6.00	£0.80	£2.40	£4.00
11 ND Uncle Scrooge: Hawaiian Hideaway, plus 2 shorts by Barks	$1.20	$3.60	$6.00	£0.80	£2.40	£4.00
12 ND Donald and Daisy: 5 stories by Barks	$1.20	$3.60	$6.00	£0.80	£2.40	£4.00
13 ND Donald Duck: The Golden Helmet, plus 2 shorts by Barks	$1.20	$3.60	$6.00	£0.80	£2.40	£4.00
14 ND Uncle Scrooge	$1.20	$3.60	$6.00	£0.80	£2.40	£4.00
15-16 ND Donald Duck	$1.20	$3.60	$6.00	£0.80	£2.40	£4.00
17 ND Mickey Mouse	$1.20	$3.60	$6.00	£0.80	£2.40	£4.00
18 ND Junior Woodchucks	$1.20	$3.60	$6.00	£0.80	£2.40	£4.00
19-20 ND Uncle Scrooge	$1.20	$3.60	$6.00	£0.80	£2.40	£4.00
21 ND Duck Family	$1.20	$3.60	$6.00	£0.80	£2.40	£4.00
22 ND Mickey Mouse	$1.20	$3.60	$6.00	£0.80	£2.40	£4.00
23 ND Donald Duck/Halloween	$1.20	$3.60	$6.00	£0.80	£2.40	£4.00
24 ND Uncle Scrooge	$1.20	$3.60	$6.00	£0.80	£2.40	£4.00
25 ND Donald Duck, Christmas issue	$1.20	$3.60	$6.00	£0.80	£2.40	£4.00
26 ND Mickey and Donald	$1.20	$3.60	$6.00	£0.80	£2.40	£4.00
27 ND Donald Duck	$1.20	$3.60	$6.00	£0.80	£2.40	£4.00
28 ND Scrooge and Donald	$1.20	$3.60	$6.00	£0.80	£2.40	£4.00
Title Value:	$34.70	$104.10	$173.50	£23.00	£69.00	£115.00
Special 1 (1989) ND reprints Donald Duck Finds Pirate Gold from Four Color #9				£1.20	£3.60	£6.00
Special 2 (1989) ND Uncle Scrooge and Donald Duck, reprints Uncle Scrooge #5				£1.10	£3.30	£5.50
Special 3 (1990) ND Mickey Mouse reprint				£1.10	£3.30	£5.50
Special 4 (1990) ND Uncle Scrooge reprints 104pgs				£1.40	£4.20	£7.00

	$Good	$Fine	$N.Mint	£Good	£Fine	£N.Mint
Special 5 (1990)						
ND Donald Duck reprints 104pgs				£1.40	£4.20	£7.00
Special 6 (1990)						
ND Uncle Scrooge reprints 104pgs				£1.50	£4.50	£7.50
Special 7 (1990)						
ND Mickey Mouse reprints 104 pgs				£1.60	£4.80	£8.00

GLORY

Image; 0 Feb 1996; 1 Mar 1995-present

	$Good	$Fine	$N.Mint	£Good	£Fine	£N.Mint
0 ND (Feb 1996), origin of Glory	$0.50	$1.50	$2.50	£0.30	£0.90	£1.50
1 ND Mike Deodato Jnr. art begins	$0.80	$2.40	$4.00	£0.50	£1.50	£2.50
1 Variant Cover Edition ND	$1.40	$4.20	$7.00	£0.70	£2.10	£3.50
2 ND	$0.60	$1.80	$3.00	£0.40	£1.20	£2.00
3-4 ND	$0.50	$1.50	$2.50	£0.30	£0.90	£1.50
4 Variant Cover Edition, ND Joe Quesada/Jimmy Palmiotti cover art	$0.80	$2.40	$4.00	£0.50	£1.50	£2.50
5 ND Supreme Apocalypse part 3, continued in Brigade #22	$0.50	$1.50	$2.50	£0.30	£0.90	£1.50
6-7 ND	$0.50	$1.50	$2.50	£0.30	£0.90	£1.50
8 ND Extreme Babewatch	$0.50	$1.50	$2.50	£0.30	£0.90	£1.50
9 ND Extreme Destroyer part 5, continued in Knightstrike #1; Shaft guest-stars	$0.50	$1.50	$2.50	£0.30	£0.90	£1.50
10 ND Rage of Angels tie-in	$0.50	$1.50	$2.50	£0.30	£0.90	£1.50
11 ND	$0.50	$1.50	$2.50	£0.30	£0.90	£1.50
12 ND 48pgs	$0.70	$2.10	$3.50	£0.50	£1.50	£2.50
12 Variant Cover Edition ND	$0.70	$2.10	$3.50	£0.50	£1.50	£2.50
13-18 ND	$0.50	$1.50	$2.50	£0.30	£0.90	£1.50
Title Value:	$13.00	$39.00	$65.00	£7.90	£23.70	£39.50
Glory (Jul 1995) Trade paperback						
ND reprints issues #1-4 with new cover by Mike Deodato				£1.30	£3.90	£6.50
Glory Vol. II (Jul 1996) Trade paperback						
ND reprints Supreme: Glory days #1,2 and Brigade #17-21				£2.30	£6.90	£11.50

GLORY & FRIENDS BIKINI FEST

Image,OS; 1 Sep 1995

	$Good	$Fine	$N.Mint	£Good	£Fine	£N.Mint
1 ND pin-ups by Mike Deodato, Rob Liefeld, Stephen Platt, Dan Fraga and others	$0.50	$1.50	$2.50	£0.30	£0.90	£1.50
Title Value:	$0.50	$1.50	$2.50	£0.30	£0.90	£1.50

GLORY & FRIENDS CHRISTMAS SPECIAL

Image,OS; 1 Dec 1995

	$Good	$Fine	$N.Mint	£Good	£Fine	£N.Mint
1 ND	$0.50	$1.50	$2.50	£0.30	£0.90	£1.50
Title Value:	$0.50	$1.50	$2.50	£0.30	£0.90	£1.50

GLORY LINGERIE ISSUE

Image,OS; 1 Feb 1996

	$Good	$Fine	$N.Mint	£Good	£Fine	£N.Mint
1 ND features art by Rob Liefeld and Mike Deodato	$0.60	$1.80	$3.00	£0.40	£1.20	£2.00
Title Value:	$0.60	$1.80	$3.00	£0.40	£1.20	£2.00

GLORY/ANGELA: ANGELS IN HELL

Image,OS; 1 Apr 1996

	$Good	$Fine	$N.Mint	£Good	£Fine	£N.Mint
1 ND Rob Liefeld script, Jim Valentino lay-outs	$0.50	$1.50	$2.50	£0.30	£0.90	£1.50
Title Value:	$0.50	$1.50	$2.50	£0.30	£0.90	£1.50

GLORY/AVENGELYNE

Image,OS; 1 Oct 1995

	$Good	$Fine	$N.Mint	£Good	£Fine	£N.Mint
1 ND Rob Liefeld art, Robert Napton script; wraparound chromium cover	$0.80	$2.40	$4.00	£0.60	£1.80	£3.00
1 Variant Cover Edition, ND Rob Liefeld art, Glory in foreground on cover, Avengelyne in background	$0.90	$2.70	$4.50	£0.70	£2.10	£3.50
Title Value:	$1.70	$5.10	$8.50	£1.30	£3.90	£6.50
Glory/Avengelyne Signed Limited Edition Boxed Set (Dec 1995)						
ND both chromium covers and variants and a new special fifth ink cover edition; box signed by Rob Liefeld and John Stinsman				£6.50	£19.50	£32.50
Glory/Avengelyne, Avengelyne/Glory (May 1996)						
Trade paperback ND collects the cross-over between the two titles				£1.30	£3.90	£6.50

GLORY/CELESTINE: DARK ANGEL

Image,MS; 1 Sep 1996-3 Nov 1996

	$Good	$Fine	$N.Mint	£Good	£Fine	£N.Mint
1-3 ND Jo Duffy script, Pat Lee and Mike Miller art	$0.50	$1.50	$2.50	£0.30	£0.90	£1.50
Title Value:	$1.50	$4.50	$7.50	£0.90	£2.70	£4.50

GNAT RAT: THE DARK GNAT RETURNS

Prelude; 1 1986

(see also Happy Birthday Gnat Rat, Darerat)

	$Good	$Fine	$N.Mint	£Good	£Fine	£N.Mint
1 ND Dark Knight parody, Mark Martin art	$0.40	$1.20	$2.00	£0.25	£0.75	£1.25
Title Value:	$0.40	$1.20	$2.00	£0.25	£0.75	£1.25

GO-MAN!

Caliber Press; 1 Nov 1989-4 Jun 1990

	$Good	$Fine	$N.Mint	£Good	£Fine	£N.Mint
1-4 ND black and white	$0.40	$1.20	$2.00	£0.25	£0.75	£1.25
Title Value:	$1.60	$4.80	$8.00	£1.00	£3.00	£5.00

GOBBLEDYGOOK

Mirage Studios; 1,2 1984

	$Good	$Fine	$N.Mint	£Good	£Fine	£N.Mint
1 ND very scarce in the U.K. 1st appearance of Teenage Mutant Ninja Turtles	$40.00	$120.00	$200.00	£18.00	£52.50	£90.00
2 ND very scarce in the U.K.	$35.00	$105.00	$175.00	£15.00	£45.00	£75.00
Title Value:	$75.00	$225.00	$375.00	£33.00	£97.50	£165.00

Note: 1st Mirage comic title.

GOBBLEDYGOOK (2ND SERIES)

Mirage Studios,OS; 1 Dec 1986

	$Good	$Fine	$N.Mint	£Good	£Fine	£N.Mint
1 ND new 10pg Turtles story	$0.60	$1.80	$3.00	£0.40	£1.20	£2.00
Title Value:	$0.60	$1.80	$3.00	£0.40	£1.20	£2.00

GOBLIN, THE

Warren; 1 Jul 1982-4 Dec 1982

	$Good	$Fine	$N.Mint	£Good	£Fine	£N.Mint
1-4 ND	$0.60	$1.80	$3.00	£0.40	£1.20	£2.00
Title Value:	$2.40	$7.20	$12.00	£1.60	£4.80	£8.00

GOD'S HAMMER

Caliber Press; 1 Mar 1990-3 May 1990

	$Good	$Fine	$N.Mint	£Good	£Fine	£N.Mint
1-3 ND black and white	$0.30	$0.90	$1.50	£0.20	£0.60	£1.00
Title Value:	$0.90	$2.70	$4.50	£0.60	£1.80	£3.00

GODDESS

DC Comics,MS; 1 Jun 1995-8 Jan 1996

	$Good	$Fine	$N.Mint	£Good	£Fine	£N.Mint
1 Garth Ennis script, Phil Winslade art	$0.90	$2.70	$4.50	£0.60	£1.80	£3.00
2 Garth Ennis script, Phil Winslade art	$0.70	$2.10	$3.50	£0.50	£1.50	£2.50
3-8 Garth Ennis script, Phil Winslade art	$0.70	$2.10	$3.50	£0.40	£1.20	£2.00
Title Value:	$5.80	$17.40	$29.00	£3.50	£10.50	£17.50

GODWHEEL

Malibu Ultraverse,MS; 0-4 Mar 1995

	$Good	$Fine	$N.Mint	£Good	£Fine	£N.Mint
0-3 ND Lord Pumpkin, Rune, NecroMantra, Primevil appear, bi-weekly; Marvel's Thor appears; art by George Perez and Gary Frank amongst others	$0.50	$1.50	$2.50	£0.25	£0.75	£1.25
4 ND Lord Pumpkin, Rune, NecroMantra, Primevil appear; bi-weekly; Marvel's Thor appears; art by George Perez and Gary Frank amongst others	$0.50	$1.50	$2.50	£0.25	£0.75	£1.25
Title Value:	$2.50	$7.50	$12.50	£1.25	£3.75	£6.25
Godwheel: Wheel of Thunder (Apr 1995) Trade paperback						
reprints mini-series featuring Thor's debut as an Ultraverse character				£1.30	£3.90	£6.50

GODZILLA

Marvel Comics Group; 1 Aug 1977-24 Jul 1979

	$Good	$Fine	$N.Mint	£Good	£Fine	£N.Mint
1 ND	$1.65	$5.00	$10.00	£0.50	£1.50	£3.00
2 ND	$1.25	$3.75	$7.50	£0.30	£1.00	£2.00
3 ND Champions X-over	$0.80	$2.50	$5.00	£0.25	£0.75	£1.50
4-9 ND	$0.80	$2.50	$5.00	£0.25	£0.75	£1.50
10 ND Champions X-over	$0.80	$2.50	$5.00	£0.25	£0.75	£1.50
11-20 ND	$0.65	$2.00	$4.00	£0.20	£0.60	£1.25
21-22 ND Fantastic Four appear	$0.65	$2.00	$4.00	£0.20	£0.60	£1.25
23 ND Fantastic Four and Avengers appear	$0.65	$2.00	$4.00	£0.20	£0.60	£1.25
24 ND Fantastic Four, Spiderman and Avengers appear	$0.65	$2.00	$4.00	£0.20	£0.60	£1.25
Title Value:	$18.40	$56.75	$113.50	£5.60	£16.90	£34.50

GODZILLA (LIMITED SERIES 1)

Dark Horse,MS; 1 May 1988-6 Jan 1989

	$Good	$Fine	$N.Mint	£Good	£Fine	£N.Mint
1 ND Japanese art, American script, Mark Nelson covers begin	$1.20	$3.60	$6.00	£0.40	£1.20	£2.00
2-6 ND Japanese art, American script, Mark Nelson covers begin	$0.60	$1.80	$3.00	£0.30	£0.90	£1.50
Title Value:	$4.20	$12.60	$21.00	£1.90	£5.70	£9.50
Godzilla Collection (Aug 1990)						
Trade paperback reprints mini-series				£1.00	£3.00	£5.00
Godzilla (May 1995)						
Trade paperback 2nd Edition of the above with filmography and new painted cover by Bob Eggleton				£2.40	£7.20	£12.00

GODZILLA (LIMITED SERIES 2)

Dark Horse; 0 May 1995; 1 Jun 1995-present

	$Good	$Fine	$N.Mint	£Good	£Fine	£N.Mint
0 ND combination of new art and reprints from Dark Horse Comics #10 and 11	$0.50	$1.50	$2.50	£0.30	£0.90	£1.50
1 ND Kevin Maguire script, Brandon McKinney and Keith Aiken art; Art Adams covers begin	$0.50	$1.50	$2.50	£0.30	£0.90	£1.50
2-13 ND	$0.50	$1.50	$2.50	£0.30	£0.90	£1.50
14 ND	$0.60	$1.80	$3.00	£0.40	£1.20	£2.00
Title Value:	$7.60	$22.80	$38.00	£4.60	£13.80	£23.00

GODZILLA COLOUR SPECIAL

Dark Horse,OS; 1 Summer 1992

	$Good	$Fine	$N.Mint	£Good	£Fine	£N.Mint
1 ND 40pgs, Art Adams art	$0.90	$2.70	$4.50	£0.60	£1.80	£3.00
Title Value:	$0.90	$2.70	$4.50	£0.60	£1.80	£3.00

GODZILLA SPECIAL

Dark Horse,OS; 1 Aug 1987

	$Good	$Fine	$N.Mint	£Good	£Fine	£N.Mint
1 ND Bissette, Randall, Salmons art, Chadwick, Geary, Giffen, Vess, Alan Moore pin-ups	$0.50	$1.50	$2.50	£0.30	£0.90	£1.50
Title Value:	$0.50	$1.50	$2.50	£0.30	£0.90	£1.50

GODZILLA VS. BARKLEY

Dark Horse,OS; 1 Dec 1993

	$Good	$Fine	$N.Mint	£Good	£Fine	£N.Mint
1 ND Mike Baron script, Jeff Butler pencils	$0.60	$1.80	$3.00	£0.40	£1.20	£2.00
Title Value:	$0.60	$1.80	$3.00	£0.40	£1.20	£2.00

GODZILLA VS. HERO ZERO

Dark Horse,OS; 1 Jun 1995

	$Good	$Fine	$N.Mint	£Good	£Fine	£N.Mint
1 ND Art Adams cover	$0.50	$1.50	$2.50	£0.30	£0.90	£1.50
Title Value:	$0.50	$1.50	$2.50	£0.30	£0.90	£1.50

GOJIN

Antarctic Press,MS; 1 Apr 1995-8 Jun 1996

Issue	$Good	$Fine	$N.Mint	£Good	£Fine	£N.Mint
1-7 ND Kazuho Takizawa script, Yutaka Kondo art; black and white	*$0.60*	*$1.80*	*$3.00*	£0.40	£1.20	£2.00
8 ND Kazuho Takiwaza script, Yutaka Kondo art; black and white	*$0.60*	*$1.80*	*$3.00*	£0.40	£1.20	£2.00
Title Value:	*$4.80*	*$14.40*	*$24.00*	£3.20	£9.60	£16.00

GOKU

Antarctic Press; 1 Oct 1993-5 Feb 1994

Issue	$Good	$Fine	$N.Mint	£Good	£Fine	£N.Mint
1-5 ND Ippongi Bang script/art; black and white	*$0.60*	*$1.80*	*$3.00*	£0.40	£1.20	£2.00
Title Value:	*$3.00*	*$9.00*	*$15.00*	£2.00	£6.00	£10.00

GOLD DIGGER (1ST SERIES)

Antarctic Press,MS; 1 1992-4 1993 ?

Issue	$Good	$Fine	$N.Mint	£Good	£Fine	£N.Mint
1 ND	*$1.50*	*$4.50*	*$7.50*	£0.80	£2.40	£4.00
2 ND	*$1.20*	*$3.60*	*$6.00*	£0.60	£1.80	£3.00
3-4 ND	*$1.00*	*$3.00*	*$5.00*	£0.50	£1.50	£2.50
Title Value:	*$4.70*	*$14.10*	*$23.50*	£2.40	£7.20	£12.00

GOLD DIGGER (2ND SERIES)

Antarctic Press; 1 Jul 1993-present

Issue	$Good	$Fine	$N.Mint	£Good	£Fine	£N.Mint
1 ND Fred Perry script/art; black and white	*$1.50*	*$4.50*	*$7.50*	£0.60	£1.80	£3.00
2-3 ND Fred Perry script/art; black and white	*$1.00*	*$3.00*	*$5.00*	£0.50	£1.50	£2.50
4-10 ND Fred Perry script/art; black and white	*$0.80*	*$2.40*	*$4.00*	£0.40	£1.20	£2.00
11-28 ND Fred Perry script/art; black and white	*$0.60*	*$1.80*	*$3.00*	£0.35	£1.05	£1.75
29-32 ND Fred Perry script/art; black and white	*$0.60*	*$1.80*	*$3.00*	£0.40	£1.20	£2.00
Title Value:	*$22.30*	*$66.90*	*$105.25*	£12.30	£36.90	£61.50
Gold Digger Graphic Novel Volume 1 (Oct 1994)						
ND collects four issue limited series with new sketches and artwork				£1.30	£3.90	£6.50
(2nd/3rd printing)				£1.30	£3.90	£6.50
Signed Edition (May 1996)						
ND signed by artist Fred Perry				£2.10	£6.30	£10.50
Gold Digger Graphic Novel Volume 2 (Mar 1995)						
ND collects first four issues of on-going series with new cover				£1.30	£3.90	£6.50
(2nd printing)				£1.30	£3.90	£6.50
Gold Digger Graphic Novel Volume 3 (Oct 1995)						
ND collects issues #5-8				£1.30	£3.90	£6.50
Gold Digger Graphic Novel Volume 4 (Feb 1996)						
ND collects iddues #9-12				£1.30	£3.90	£6.50

GOLD DIGGER ANNUAL (2ND SERIES)

Antarctic Press; 1 Sep 1995-present

Issue	$Good	$Fine	$N.Mint	£Good	£Fine	£N.Mint
1 ND 48pgs, black and white	*$0.80*	*$2.40*	*$4.00*	£0.50	£1.50	£2.50
Title Value:	*$0.80*	*$2.40*	*$4.00*	£0.50	£1.50	£2.50

GOLD KEY CHAMPION

Gold Key; 1 Mar 1978-2 May 1978

Issue	$Good	$Fine	$N.Mint	£Good	£Fine	£N.Mint
1 scarce in the U.K. 48pgs, Space Family Robinson, painted cover	*$0.50*	*$1.50*	*$3.00*	£0.30	£1.00	£2.00
2 scarce in the U.K. 48pgs, Mighty Samson, painted cover	*$0.50*	*$1.50*	*$3.00*	£0.30	£1.00	£2.00
Title Value:	*$1.00*	*$3.00*	*$6.00*	£0.60	£2.00	£4.00

Note: thought not to be distributed in the U.K. but as yet unconfirmed. Part reprint

GOLD KEY SPOTLIGHT

Gold Key; 1 May 1976-11 Feb 1978

Issue	$Good	$Fine	$N.Mint	£Good	£Fine	£N.Mint
1 scarce in the U.K. Tom, Dick and Harriet	*$0.50*	*$1.50*	*$3.00*	£0.30	£1.00	£2.00
2 Wacky Adventures of Cracky	*$0.40*	*$1.25*	*$2.50*	£0.25	£0.75	£1.50
3 Wacky Witch	*$0.40*	*$1.25*	*$2.50*	£0.25	£0.75	£1.50
4 Tom, Dick and Harriet	*$0.30*	*$1.00*	*$2.00*	£0.20	£0.60	£1.25
5 Wacky Adventures of Cracky	*$0.30*	*$1.00*	*$2.00*	£0.20	£0.60	£1.25
6 Dagar the Invincible, painted cover	*$0.50*	*$1.50*	*$3.00*	£0.30	£1.00	£2.00
7 Wacky Witch and Greta Ghost	*$0.30*	*$1.00*	*$2.00*	£0.20	£0.60	£1.25
8 The Occult Files of Dr. Spektor, painted cover	*$0.50*	*$1.50*	*$3.00*	£0.30	£1.00	£2.00
9 Tragg and the Sky Gods, Dan Spiegle art, painted cover	*$0.50*	*$1.50*	*$3.00*	£0.30	£1.00	£2.00
10 O.G. Whiz	*$0.30*	*$1.00*	*$2.00*	£0.20	£0.60	£1.25
11 Tom, Dick and Harriet	*$0.30*	*$1.00*	*$2.00*	£0.20	£0.60	£1.25
Title Value:	*$4.30*	*$13.50*	*$27.00*	£2.70	£8.50	£17.25

Note: very irregular distribution in the U.K.

GOLDEN AGE GREATS

AC Comics; 1 Oct 1994-present

Issue	$Good	$Fine	$N.Mint	£Good	£Fine	£N.Mint
1 ND 76pgs, squarebound; reprints Catman and Kitten, Rocket-Man and Rocket-Girl, The Hood, Green Lama from over 45 years ago; black and white	*$2.00*	*$6.00*	*$10.00*	£1.30	£3.90	£6.50
2 ND 96pgs, Phantom Lady reprints with Matt Baker art; black and white	*$2.00*	*$6.00*	*$10.00*	£1.30	£3.90	£6.50
3 ND 80pgs, Lou Fine's The Flame, Will Eisner's Espionage: Black X; black and white	*$2.00*	*$6.00*	*$10.00*	£1.30	£3.90	£6.50
4 ND 96pgs, Bulletman, Mr. Scarlet, Ibis the Invincible, Minute Man	*$2.00*	*$6.00*	*$10.00*	£1.30	£3.90	£6.50
5 ND 80pgs, Iron Jaw vs. Crimebuster	*$2.50*	*$7.50*	*$12.50*	£1.50	£4.50	£7.50
6 ND 80pgs, Black Cat, Blonde Phantom, Lorna Queen of the Jungle	*$2.00*	*$6.00*	*$10.00*	£1.30	£3.90	£6.50
7 ND 80pgs, Best of the West featuring Ghost Rider, Black Mask, Durango Kid plus cover gallery	*$2.00*	*$6.00*	*$10.00*	£1.30	£3.90	£6.50
8 ND 80pgs, Phantom Lady, Miss Victory	*$2.00*	*$6.00*	*$10.00*	£1.30	£3.90	£6.50
9 ND 84pgs, Fiction House girls from Sheena to Sky Girl	*$2.00*	*$6.00*	*$10.00*	£1.30	£3.90	£6.50
Title Value:	*$18.50*	*$55.50*	*$92.50*	£11.90	£35.70	£59.50

GOLDEN AGE GREATS MYSTERY MEN

AC Comics; 1 Mar 1996-present ?

Issue	$Good	$Fine	$N.Mint	£Good	£Fine	£N.Mint
1 ND 44pgs, Golden Age reprints begin in black and white	*$1.40*	*$4.20*	*$7.00*	£0.90	£2.70	£4.50
Title Value:	*$1.40*	*$4.20*	*$7.00*	£0.90	£2.70	£4.50

GOLDEN AGE, THE

DC Comics/Elseworlds,MS; 1 Sep 1993-4 Dec 1993

Issue	$Good	$Fine	$N.Mint	£Good	£Fine	£N.Mint
1-4 ND 48pgs, squarebound, James Robinson script, Paul Smith art; embossed logo	*$1.00*	*$3.00*	*$5.00*	£0.70	£2.10	£3.50
Title Value:	*$4.00*	*$12.00*	*$20.00*	£2.80	£8.40	£14.00
The Golden Age (Sep 1995)						
Trade paperback reprints mini-series with Howard Chaykin intro				£2.70	£8.10	£13.50

GOLDYN IN 3-D

Blackthorne;(3-D Series #4) 1 Jun 1986

Issue	$Good	$Fine	$N.Mint	£Good	£Fine	£N.Mint
1 ND reprints	*$0.50*	*$1.50*	*$2.50*	£0.30	£0.90	£1.50
Title Value:	*$0.50*	*$1.50*	*$2.50*	£0.30	£0.90	£1.50

GOLGOTHIKA

Caliber Comics; 1 1996-present

Issue	$Good	$Fine	$N.Mint	£Good	£Fine	£N.Mint
1-2 ND John Bergin script and art; black and white	*$0.60*	*$1.80*	*$3.00*	£0.40	£1.20	£2.00

Girls' Love Stories #180

Godzilla #2

Gold Key Spotlight #8

	$Good	$Fine	$N.Mint	£Good	£Fine	£N.Mint
Title Value:	*$1.20*	*$3.60*	*$6.00*	£0.80	£2.40	£4.00

GOMER PYLE

Gold Key,TV; 1 Jul 1966-3 Jan 1967

	$Good	$Fine	$N.Mint	£Good	£Fine	£N.Mint
1 scarce though distributed in the U.K. photo cover	*$8.50*	*$26.00*	*$60.00*	£4.25	£12.50	£30.00
2-3 scarce though distributed in the U.K.	*$6.25*	*$19.00*	*$45.00*	£3.20	£9.50	£22.50
Title Value:	*$21.00*	*$64.00*	*$150.00*	£10.65	£31.50	£75.00

GON

DC Comics/Paradox Press,MS; 1 Aug 1996-4 Nov 1996

	$Good	$Fine	$N.Mint	£Good	£Fine	£N.Mint
1-4 ND Mashashi Tanaka script and art	*$1.20*	*$3.60*	*$6.00*	£0.80	£2.40	£4.00
Title Value:	*$4.80*	*$14.40*	*$24.00*	£3.20	£9.60	£16.00

GOOD GIRL ART QUARTERLY

AC Comics; 1 1990-18 1994

	$Good	$Fine	$N.Mint	£Good	£Fine	£N.Mint
1 ND new lead story plus classic "good girl art" reprints begin; black and white	*$0.70*	*$2.10*	*$3.50*	£0.45	£1.35	£2.25
2-8 ND	*$0.60*	*$1.80*	*$3.00*	£0.40	£1.20	£2.00
9 ND X-over with Femforce #52	*$0.60*	*$1.80*	*$3.00*	£0.40	£1.20	£2.00
10 ND $3.95 cover begins	*$0.80*	*$2.40*	*$4.00*	£0.50	£1.50	£2.50
11-16 ND	*$0.80*	*$2.40*	*$4.00*	£0.50	£1.50	£2.50
17 ND title becomes Good Girl Comics	*$0.80*	*$2.40*	*$4.00*	£0.50	£1.50	£2.50
18 ND	*$0.80*	*$2.40*	*$4.00*	£0.50	£1.50	£2.50
Title Value:	*$12.70*	*$38.10*	*$63.50*	£8.15	£24.45	£40.75

GOOD GIRLS

Fantagraphics; 1 Apr 1987-6 1987

	$Good	$Fine	$N.Mint	£Good	£Fine	£N.Mint
1 ND Carol Lay story and art	*$0.50*	*$1.50*	*$2.50*	£0.30	£0.90	£1.50
2-6 ND Carol Lay story and art	*$0.40*	*$1.20*	*$2.00*	£0.25	£0.75	£1.25
Title Value:	*$2.50*	*$7.50*	*$12.50*	£1.55	£4.65	£7.75

GOOD GUYS, THE

Defiant; 1 Nov 1993-9 Jul 1994

	$Good	$Fine	$N.Mint	£Good	£Fine	£N.Mint
1 ND part Jim Shooter script	*$0.60*	*$1.80*	*$3.00*	£0.30	£0.90	£1.50
1½ ND; reprints the story originally serialized in Previews magazine	*$0.50*	*$1.50*	*$2.50*	£0.25	£0.75	£1.25
2-9 ND part Jim Shooter script	*$0.60*	*$1.80*	*$3.00*	£0.30	£0.90	£1.50
Title Value:	*$5.90*	*$17.70*	*$29.50*	£2.95	£8.85	£14.75

Note: issues #10-12 were advertised and solicited but never appeared

GOOFY ADVENTURES

Disney; 1 Jun 1990-17 Sep 1991

	$Good	$Fine	$N.Mint	£Good	£Fine	£N.Mint
1-5 ND new stories	*$0.30*	*$0.90*	*$1.50*	£0.20	£0.60	£1.00
6 ND new stories, reprints Super Goof #1 (1965)	*$0.30*	*$0.90*	*$1.50*	£0.20	£0.60	£1.00
7 ND part reprints	*$0.30*	*$0.90*	*$1.50*	£0.20	£0.60	£1.00
8-17 ND	*$0.30*	*$0.90*	*$1.50*	£0.20	£0.60	£1.00
Title Value:	*$5.10*	*$15.30*	*$25.50*	£3.40	£10.20	£17.00

Note: banned from distribution in UK

GORE SHRIEK

Fantaco; 1 Sep 1986-6 1990

	$Good	$Fine	$N.Mint	£Good	£Fine	£N.Mint
1-3 ND	*$0.60*	*$1.80*	*$3.00*	£0.40	£1.20	£2.00
4 ND Mars Attacks special	*$0.80*	*$2.40*	*$4.00*	£0.50	£1.50	£2.50
5-6 ND	*$0.60*	*$1.80*	*$3.00*	£0.40	£1.20	£2.00
6 ½ ND very rare in the U.K 16pgs, , featuring unused art and stories, available only direct from the publisher	*$2.50*	*$7.50*	*$12.50*	£1.50	£4.50	£7.50
Title Value:	*$6.30*	*$18.90*	*$31.50*	£4.00	£12.00	£20.00

GORE SHRIEK ANNUAL

Fantaco,OS; 1 Dec 1990

	$Good	$Fine	$N.Mint	£Good	£Fine	£N.Mint
1 ND 100pgs, black and white humour/horror anthology featuring Gurchain Singh art	*$0.90*	*$2.70*	*$4.50*	£0.60	£1.80	£3.00
Title Value:	*$0.90*	*$2.70*	*$4.50*	£0.60	£1.80	£3.00

GORE SHRIEK VOLUME TWO

Eternity; 1 1990-4 1991

	$Good	$Fine	$N.Mint	£Good	£Fine	£N.Mint
1 ND	*$0.70*	*$2.10*	*$3.50*	£0.50	£1.50	£2.50
1 Limited Edition, ND : all pin-up edition of an amalgamated issue 1 and 2 by Gurchain Singh	*$0.80*	*$2.40*	*$4.00*	£0.50	£1.50	£2.50
2 ND	*$0.60*	*$1.80*	*$3.00*	£0.40	£1.20	£2.00
3 ND 3,000 copies printed	*$0.50*	*$1.50*	*$2.50*	£0.30	£0.90	£1.50
4 ND	*$0.50*	*$1.50*	*$2.50*	£0.30	£0.90	£1.50
Title Value:	*$3.10*	*$9.30*	*$15.50*	£2.00	£6.00	£10.00

GORE SHRIEK VOLUME TWO ANNUAL

Fantaco; 1 Jun 1995

	$Good	$Fine	$N.Mint	£Good	£Fine	£N.Mint
1 ND over 20 artists and writers feature; black and white	*$1.00*	*$3.00*	*$5.00*	£0.70	£2.10	£3.50
Title Value:	*$1.00*	*$3.00*	*$5.00*	£0.70	£2.10	£3.50

GORGO

Charlton; 1 May 1961-23 Sep 1965

(see Gorgo's Revenge,Return of...)

	$Good	$Fine	$N.Mint	£Good	£Fine	£N.Mint
1 very scarce in the U.K. Steve Ditko art	*$29.00*	*$85.00*	*$200.00*	£17.50	£52.50	£125.00
2-3 scarce in the U.K. Steve Ditko art	*$14.00*	*$43.00*	*$100.00*	£7.75	£23.50	£55.00
4 Steve Ditko cover	*$8.50*	*$26.00*	*$60.00*	£5.00	£15.00	£35.00
5	*$8.50*	*$26.00*	*$60.00*	£5.00	£15.00	£35.00
6-10	*$8.50*	*$26.00*	*$60.00*	£4.25	£12.50	£30.00
11 Steve Ditko art	*$6.25*	*$19.00*	*$45.00*	£3.90	£11.50	£27.50
12	*$3.20*	*$9.50*	*$22.50*	£1.75	£5.25	£12.50
13-16 Steve Ditko art	*$6.00*	*$18.00*	*$42.50*	£3.55	£10.50	£25.00
17-23	*$3.20*	*$9.50*	*$22.50*	£1.75	£5.25	£12.50
Title Value:	*$172.35*	*$520.00*	*$1215.00*	£96.35	£287.50	£682.50

Note: all distributed in the U.K.

GORGO'S REVENGE

Charlton; nn 1962

(becomes Return of Gorgo)

	$Good	$Fine	$N.Mint	£Good	£Fine	£N.Mint
nn distributed in the U.K.	*$5.00*	*$15.00*	*$35.00*	£2.85	£8.50	£20.00
Title Value:	*$5.00*	*$15.00*	*$35.00*	£2.85	£8.50	£20.00

GRACKLE, THE

Acclaim Comics,MS; 1 Jan 1997-4 Apr 1997

	$Good	$Fine	$N.Mint	£Good	£Fine	£N.Mint
1-4 ND Mike Baron script, Paul Gulacy art; black and white	*$0.60*	*$1.80*	*$3.00*	£0.40	£1.20	£2.00
Title Value:	*$2.40*	*$7.20*	*$12.00*	£1.60	£4.80	£8.00

GRAFIK MUZIK

Caliber Press; 1 Nov 1990-6 1991

	$Good	$Fine	$N.Mint	£Good	£Fine	£N.Mint
1 ND 48pgs, colour; Mike Allred script and art begins (see Madman Comics)	*$3.00*	*$9.00*	*$15.00*	£1.00	£3.00	£5.00
2-6 ND	*$2.50*	*$7.50*	*$12.50*	£0.80	£2.40	£4.00
Title Value:	*$15.50*	*$46.50*	*$77.50*	£5.00	£15.00	£25.00

Note: formerly published by Slave Labor

GRAPHIC

Fantaco; 1 Sep 1990

	$Good	$Fine	$N.Mint	£Good	£Fine	£N.Mint
1 ND horror anthology	*$0.70*	*$2.10*	*$3.50*	£0.50	£1.50	£2.50
Title Value:	*$0.70*	*$2.10*	*$3.50*	£0.50	£1.50	£2.50

GRAPHIC FANTASY

Ajax; 1 1982

(see Megaton)

	$Good	$Fine	$N.Mint	£Good	£Fine	£N.Mint
1 ND very rare in the U.K 1st draft appearance Savage Dragon (prior to Megaton #3 and #4). Self-published fanzine rather than a distributed comic	*$10.00*	*$30.00*	*$50.00*	£5.00	£15.00	£25.00
Title Value:	*$10.00*	*$30.00*	*$50.00*	£5.00	£15.00	£25.00

GRAPHIC STORY MONTHLY

Fantagraphics; 1 Feb 1990-12 1991

	$Good	$Fine	$N.Mint	£Good	£Fine	£N.Mint
1-4 ND Tardi, Ward Kimball, Paul Ollswang, Rick Geary work featured	*$0.70*	*$2.10*	*$3.50*	£0.50	£1.50	£2.50
5 ND Jacques Tardi's "Fog Over Tolbiac Bridge" concludes	*$0.60*	*$1.80*	*$3.00*	£0.40	£1.20	£2.00
6 ND Roger Langridge story	*$0.60*	*$1.80*	*$3.00*	£0.40	£1.20	£2.00
7 ND	*$0.60*	*$1.80*	*$3.00*	£0.40	£1.20	£2.00
8-9 ND 52pgs, Billie Holiday story by Carlos Sampayo and Jose Munoz	*$0.60*	*$1.80*	*$3.00*	£0.40	£1.20	£2.00
10 ND 48pgs, Billie Holiday plus Jacques Tardi's "Griffu"	*$0.60*	*$1.80*	*$3.00*	£0.40	£1.20	£2.00
11-12 ND	*$0.60*	*$1.80*	*$3.00*	£0.40	£1.20	£2.00
Title Value:	*$7.60*	*$22.80*	*$38.00*	£5.20	£15.60	£26.00

Note: black and white magazine format, 48pgs

GRAPHIQUE MUSIQUE

Slave Labor; 1 Dec 1989-3 May 1990

	$Good	$Fine	$N.Mint	£Good	£Fine	£N.Mint
1-3 ND 48pgs, black and white	*$4.00*	*$12.00*	*$20.00*	£0.60	£1.80	£3.00
Title Value:	*$12.00*	*$36.00*	*$50.00*	£1.80	£5.40	£9.00

GRATEFUL DEAD COMIX

Kitchen Sink,Magazine MS; 1 Jul 1991-6 1992

	$Good	$Fine	$N.Mint	£Good	£Fine	£N.Mint
1 ND Tim Truman art featured; 8" x 11"" format begins, painted cover by Dean Armstrong	*$1.50*	*$4.50*	*$7.50*	£1.00	£3.00	£5.00
2-3 ND Tim Truman art featured	*$1.00*	*$3.00*	*$5.00*	£0.70	£2.10	£3.50
4 ND Tim Truman and Mary Fleener art featured, Gilbert Shelton cover	*$1.00*	*$3.00*	*$5.00*	£0.70	£2.10	£3.50
5 ND Tim Truman art featured, painted cover by Dean Armstrong	*$1.00*	*$3.00*	*$5.00*	£0.70	£2.10	£3.50
6 ND	*$1.00*	*$3.00*	*$5.00*	£0.70	£2.10	£3.50
Title Value:	*$6.50*	*$19.50*	*$32.50*	£4.50	£13.50	£22.50
Grateful Dead Limited Edition (Dec 1992) signed, hardcover, 500 copies				£20.00	£60.00	£100.00

GRATEFUL DEAD COMIX (2ND SERIES)

Kitchen Sink; 1 Jun 1993-2 1993

	$Good	$Fine	$N.Mint	£Good	£Fine	£N.Mint
1-2 ND Tim Truman art featured	*$0.80*	*$2.40*	*$4.00*	£0.50	£1.50	£2.50
Title Value:	*$1.60*	*$4.80*	*$8.00*	£1.00	£3.00	£5.00

GRAVE TALES

Bruce Hamilton Publishing,Magazine; 1 Oct 1991-3 1992

	$Good	$Fine	$N.Mint	£Good	£Fine	£N.Mint
1-3 ND Joe Staton, Gray Morrow, Pat Boyette art featured; black and white	*$0.80*	*$2.40*	*$4.00*	£0.50	£1.50	£2.50
Title Value:	*$2.40*	*$7.20*	*$12.00*	£1.50	£4.50	£7.50

GRAVEDIGGERS

Acclaim Comics,MS; 1 Nov 1996-4 Feb 1997

	$Good	$Fine	$N.Mint	£Good	£Fine	£N.Mint
1-4 ND Mark Moretti script and art; black and white	*$0.60*	*$1.80*	*$3.00*	£0.40	£1.20	£2.00
Title Value:	*$2.40*	*$7.20*	*$12.00*	£1.60	£4.80	£8.00

GRAVESTONE

Malibu; 1 Jul 1993-7 Jan 1994

	$Good	$Fine	$N.Mint	£Good	£Fine	£N.Mint
1 Protectors spin-off	*$0.30*	*$0.90*	*$1.50*	£0.20	£0.60	£1.00

	$Good	$Fine	$N.Mint	£Good	£Fine	£N.Mint
2	*$0.30*	*$0.90*	*$1.50*	£0.20	£0.60	£1.00
3 Genesis Tie-In; pre-bagged with free Sky-Cap	*$0.30*	*$0.90*	*$1.50*	£0.20	£0.60	£1.00
4 Genesis Tie-In	*$0.30*	*$0.90*	*$1.50*	£0.20	£0.60	£1.00
5 Genesis Tie-In, Frank Miller cover	*$0.30*	*$0.90*	*$1.50*	£0.20	£0.60	£1.00
6-7 Genesis Tie-In	*$0.30*	*$0.90*	*$1.50*	£0.20	£0.60	£1.00
Title Value:	*$2.10*	*$6.30*	*$10.50*	£1.40	£4.20	£7.00

Note: all Non-Distributed on the news-stands in the U.K.

GREAT ACTION COMICS

IW Comics; 1,8,9 1958-1960

	$Good	$Fine	$N.Mint	£Good	£Fine	£N.Mint
1 scarce though distributed in the U.K. reprints	*$2.50*	*$7.50*	*$17.50*	£1.40	£4.25	£10.00
8 rare although distributed in the U.K. reprints Phantom Lady #15	*$12.50*	*$39.00*	*$90.00*	£5.50	£17.00	£40.00
9 rare although distributed in the U.K. reprints Phantom Lady #23	*$12.50*	*$39.00*	*$90.00*	£5.50	£17.00	£40.00
Title Value:	*$27.50*	*$85.50*	*$197.50*	£12.40	£38.25	£90.00

GREAT MOUSE DETECTIVE GRAPHIC NOVEL, THE

Disney,OS; 1 Apr 1991

	$Good	$Fine	$N.Mint	£Good	£Fine	£N.Mint
1 ND 48pgs, adaptation of film	*$0.90*	*$2.70*	*$4.50*	£0.60	£1.80	£3.00
Title Value:	*$0.90*	*$2.70*	*$4.50*	£0.60	£1.80	£3.00

GREAT WESTERN

I.W. Comics; 1,2,8,9 early 1960s

	$Good	$Fine	$N.Mint	£Good	£Fine	£N.Mint
1-2 distributed in the U.K. all reprints	*$2.50*	*$7.50*	*$17.50*	£1.05	£3.20	£7.50
8 distributed in the U.K. all reprint featuring origin Ghost Rider	*$3.20*	*$9.50*	*$22.50*	£1.40	£4.25	£10.00
9 distributed in the U.K.	*$2.50*	*$7.50*	*$17.50*	£1.05	£3.20	£7.50
Title Value:	*$10.70*	*$32.00*	*$75.00*	£4.55	£13.85	£32.50

GREATER MERCURY COMICS ACTION

Greater Mercury Comics; 1 1989-5 1990

	$Good	$Fine	$N.Mint	£Good	£Fine	£N.Mint
1-5 ND	*$0.40*	*$1.20*	*$2.00*	£0.25	£0.75	£1.25
Title Value:	*$2.00*	*$6.00*	*$10.00*	£1.25	£3.75	£6.25

GREATEST 1950s STORIES EVER TOLD, THE

DC Comics; nn Dec 1990

	$Good	$Fine	$N.Mint	£Good	£Fine	£N.Mint
nn Hardcover, ND 288pgs, Many stories never reprinted before	*$4.00*	*$12.00*	*$20.00*	£2.80	£8.25	£14.00
nn Softcover, ND 288pgs	*$3.00*	*$9.00*	*$15.00*	£2.00	£6.00	£10.00
Title Value:	*$7.00*	*$21.00*	*$35.00*	£4.80	£14.25	£24.00

GREATEST 1960s STORIES EVER TOLD

DC Comics; nn Mar 1992

	$Good	$Fine	$N.Mint	£Good	£Fine	£N.Mint
nn ND two volume slip-case set featuring the major DC characters with art by Neal Adams, Gil Kane, Carmine Infantino, Alex Toth etc.	*$9.00*	*$27.00*	*$45.00*	£6.00	£18.00	£30.00
Title Value:	*$9.00*	*$27.00*	*$45.00*	£6.00	£18.00	£30.00

GREATEST FLASH STORIES EVER TOLD, THE

DC Comics; nn Feb 1991

	$Good	$Fine	$N.Mint	£Good	£Fine	£N.Mint
nn ND 288pgs, Hardcover reprints of classic Flash stories inc. Showcase #4	*$4.00*	*$12.00*	*$20.00*	£2.80	£8.25	£14.00
Title Value:	*$4.00*	*$12.00*	*$20.00*	£2.80	£8.25	£14.00

GREATEST GOLDEN AGE STORIES EVER TOLD

DC Comics; nn Feb 1990

	$Good	$Fine	$N.Mint	£Good	£Fine	£N.Mint
nn ND 288pgs, Hardcover. Reprints of Golden Age stories, intro by Roy Thomas, new dust-jacket illustration by Jerry Ordway	*$4.00*	*$12.00*	*$20.00*	£2.80	£8.25	£14.00
Title Value:	*$4.00*	*$12.00*	*$20.00*	£2.80	£8.25	£14.00

GREATEST TEAM-UP STORIES EVER TOLD, THE

DC Comics; nn Jan 1990

	$Good	$Fine	$N.Mint	£Good	£Fine	£N.Mint
nn Hardcover ND 288pgs, 15 classic reprints including Flash #123	*$4.00*	*$12.00*	*$20.00*	£2.80	£8.25	£14.00
nn Softcover ND (Jul 1990)	*$3.00*	*$9.00*	*$15.00*	£2.00	£6.00	£10.00
Title Value:	*$7.00*	*$21.00*	*$35.00*	£4.80	£14.25	£24.00

GREEN ARROW

DC Comics; 0 Oct 1994; 1 Feb 1988-present

	$Good	$Fine	$N.Mint	£Good	£Fine	£N.Mint
0 (Oct 1994) Zero Hour X-over, origin retold	*$0.40*	*$1.20*	*$2.00*	£0.25	£0.75	£1.25
1 Mike Grell script begins	*$0.80*	*$2.40*	*$4.00*	£0.40	£1.20	£2.00
2-5 LD in the U.K.	*$0.60*	*$1.80*	*$3.00*	£0.30	£0.90	£1.50
6-15 LD in the U.K.	*$0.40*	*$1.20*	*$2.00*	£0.25	£0.75	£1.25
16-20	*$0.30*	*$0.90*	*$1.50*	£0.20	£0.60	£1.00
21-24 bi-weekly issues	*$0.30*	*$0.90*	*$1.50*	£0.20	£0.60	£1.00
25-26	*$0.30*	*$0.90*	*$1.50*	£0.20	£0.60	£1.00
27-28 The Warlord appears	*$0.30*	*$0.90*	*$1.50*	£0.20	£0.60	£1.00
29-34	*$0.30*	*$0.90*	*$1.50*	£0.20	£0.60	£1.00
35-38 Black Arrow saga, bi-weekly issues	*$0.30*	*$0.90*	*$1.50*	£0.20	£0.60	£1.00
39-43	*$0.30*	*$0.90*	*$1.50*	£0.20	£0.60	£1.00
44-45 Rock and Runes story	*$0.30*	*$0.90*	*$1.50*	£0.20	£0.60	£1.00
46-49	*$0.30*	*$0.90*	*$1.50*	£0.20	£0.60	£1.00
50 DS	*$0.50*	*$1.50*	*$2.50*	£0.30	£0.90	£1.50
51-54	*$0.30*	*$0.90*	*$1.50*	£0.20	£0.60	£1.00
55 ties in with Green Arrow: The Longbow Hunters	*$0.30*	*$0.90*	*$1.50*	£0.20	£0.60	£1.00
56-58	*$0.30*	*$0.90*	*$1.50*	£0.20	£0.60	£1.00
59 Predator part 1	*$0.30*	*$0.90*	*$1.50*	£0.20	£0.60	£1.00
60 Predator part 2, bi-weekly	*$0.30*	*$0.90*	*$1.50*	£0.20	£0.60	£1.00
61-62 bi-weekly	*$0.30*	*$0.90*	*$1.50*	£0.20	£0.60	£1.00
63 The Hunt for the Red Dragon story begins, "Mature Readers" label dropped from cover, bi-weekly	*$0.30*	*$0.90*	*$1.50*	£0.20	£0.60	£1.00
64-67	*$0.30*	*$0.90*	*$1.50*	£0.20	£0.60	£1.00
68 $1.75 cover begins	*$0.30*	*$0.90*	*$1.50*	£0.20	£0.60	£1.00
69-74	*$0.30*	*$0.90*	*$1.50*	£0.20	£0.60	£1.00
75 48pgs, Speedy appears; Green Arrow and Black Canary split up	*$0.50*	*$1.50*	*$2.50*	£0.30	£0.90	£1.50
76-84	*$0.30*	*$0.90*	*$1.50*	£0.20	£0.60	£1.00
85 Deathstroke the Terminator appears	*$0.30*	*$0.90*	*$1.50*	£0.20	£0.60	£1.00
86 Catwoman appears	*$0.30*	*$0.90*	*$1.50*	£0.20	£0.60	£1.00
87 $1.95 covers begin	*$0.40*	*$1.20*	*$2.00*	£0.25	£0.75	£1.25
88 Martian Manhunter and Blue Beetle appear	*$0.40*	*$1.20*	*$2.00*	£0.25	£0.75	£1.25
89	*$0.40*	*$1.20*	*$2.00*	£0.25	£0.75	£1.25
90 Zero Hour X-over	*$0.40*	*$1.20*	*$2.00*	£0.25	£0.75	£1.25
91-96	*$0.40*	*$1.20*	*$2.00*	£0.25	£0.75	£1.25
97 $2.25 covers begin	*$0.45*	*$1.35*	*$2.25*	£0.30	£0.90	£1.50
98-99	*$0.45*	*$1.35*	*$2.25*	£0.30	£0.90	£1.50
100 48pgs, holographic foil-stamped cover, Superman guest-stars	*$0.80*	*$2.40*	*$4.00*	£0.50	£1.50	£2.50
101 Superman and Black Canary guest-star and death (maybe) of Oliver Queen (original Green Arrow)	*$0.45*	*$1.35*	*$2.25*	£0.30	£0.90	£1.50
102-103 Underworld Unleashed tie-in	*$0.45*	*$1.35*	*$2.25*	£0.30	£0.90	£1.50
104 Green Lantern guest-stars	*$0.45*	*$1.35*	*$2.25*	£0.30	£0.90	£1.50
105 Robin guest-stars	*$0.45*	*$1.35*	*$2.25*	£0.30	£0.90	£1.50
106-107	*$0.45*	*$1.35*	*$2.25*	£0.30	£0.90	£1.50
108 Thorn appears	*$0.45*	*$1.35*	*$2.25*	£0.30	£0.90	£1.50
109 Superman appears	*$0.45*	*$1.35*	*$2.25*	£0.30	£0.90	£1.50
110 continued from Green Lantern #76, continued in Green Lantern #77	*$0.45*	*$1.35*	*$2.25*	£0.30	£0.90	£1.50
111 continued from Green Lantern #77	*$0.45*	*$1.35*	*$2.25*	£0.30	£0.90	£1.50
112-113	*$0.45*	*$1.35*	*$2.25*	£0.30	£0.90	£1.50
114 Final Night tie-in	*$0.45*	*$1.35*	*$2.25*	£0.30	£0.90	£1.50
115-117 ND	*$0.45*	*$1.35*	*$2.25*	£0.30	£0.90	£1.50
118-119 ND Dougie Braithwaite art	*$0.45*	*$1.35*	*$2.25*	£0.30	£0.90	£1.50
Title Value:	*$44.00*	*$132.00*	*$217.00*	£28.35	£85.05	£141.75

Note: all are New Format, Baxter paper. Mature Readers label.

GREEN ARROW (LIMITED SERIES)

DC Comics,MS; 1 May 1983-4 Aug 1983

(see Action, Adventure, Brave & the Bold, DC Super-Stars #17, Flash, Green Arrow: The Longbow Hunters, Green Lantern, World's Finest)

	$Good	$Fine	$N.Mint	£Good	£Fine	£N.Mint
1 Von Eeden art begins, origin retold, Speedy cameo	*$0.70*	*$2.10*	*$3.50*	£0.30	£0.90	£1.50
2-4	*$0.50*	*$1.50*	*$2.50*	£0.25	£0.75	£1.25
Title Value:	*$2.20*	*$6.60*	*$11.00*	£1.05	£3.15	£5.25

GREEN ARROW ANNUAL

DC Comics; 1 1988-present

	$Good	$Fine	$N.Mint	£Good	£Fine	£N.Mint
1 48pgs, ties in with Detective Annual #1, Question Annual #1	*$0.60*	*$1.80*	*$3.00*	£0.40	£1.20	£2.00
2 concluded from Question Annual #2	*$0.60*	*$1.80*	*$3.00*	£0.40	£1.20	£2.00
3-4 64pgs	*$0.60*	*$1.80*	*$3.00*	£0.40	£1.20	£2.00
5 64pgs, Eclipso: The Darkness Within, Batman appears	*$0.60*	*$1.80*	*$3.00*	£0.40	£1.20	£2.00
6 64pgs, Bloodlines (Wave Two) part 13, 1st appearance The Hook, continued in Detective Comics Annual #6	*$0.60*	*$1.80*	*$3.00*	£0.40	£1.20	£2.00
7 56pgs, Year One story	*$0.60*	*$1.80*	*$3.00*	£0.50	£1.50	£2.50
Title Value:	*$4.20*	*$12.60*	*$21.00*	£2.90	£8.70	£14.50

GREEN ARROW: THE LONGBOW HUNTERS

DC Comics,MS; 1 Aug 1987-3 Oct 1987

	$Good	$Fine	$N.Mint	£Good	£Fine	£N.Mint
1 ND Mike Grell cover/art begins	*$0.70*	*$2.10*	*$3.50*	£0.60	£1.80	£3.00
1 2nd printing ND	*$0.60*	*$1.80*	*$3.00*	£0.40	£1.20	£2.00
2 ND scarce in the U.K.	*$0.70*	*$2.10*	*$3.50*	£0.50	£1.50	£2.50
2 2nd printing ND	*$0.60*	*$1.80*	*$3.00*	£0.40	£1.20	£2.00
3 ND	*$0.70*	*$2.10*	*$3.50*	£0.50	£1.50	£2.50
Title Value:	*$3.30*	*$9.90*	*$16.50*	£2.40	£7.20	£12.00

Note: all are Prestige format, squarebound. Mature Readers label.

	$Good	$Fine	$N.Mint	£Good	£Fine	£N.Mint
Trade paperback (Jun 1989), 160 pgs. Reprints three issue MS with covers. New wraparound painted cover by Mike Grell				£1.00	£3.00	£5.00

GREEN ARROW: THE WONDER YEAR

DC Comics,MS; 1 Feb 1993-4 May 1993

	$Good	$Fine	$N.Mint	£Good	£Fine	£N.Mint
1 Mike Grell and Gray Morrow story presenting Green Arrow: Year One						
	$0.30	*$0.90*	*$1.50*	£0.20	£0.60	£1.00
2 Green Arrow meets Brianna Stone						
	$0.30	*$0.90*	*$1.50*	£0.20	£0.60	£1.00
3-4	*$0.30*	*$0.90*	*$1.50*	£0.20	£0.60	£1.00
Title Value:	*$1.20*	*$3.60*	*$6.00*	£0.80	£2.40	£4.00

GREEN CANDLES

DC Comics/Paradox Press,MS; 1 Nov 1995-3 Jan 1996

	$Good	$Fine	$N.Mint	£Good	£Fine	£N.Mint
1-3 ND 96pgs, Tom DeHaven script, Robin Smith art; Compact Format						
	$1.20	*$3.60*	*$6.00*	£0.80	£2.40	£4.00
Title Value:	*$3.60*	*$10.80*	*$18.00*	£2.40	£7.20	£12.00

GREEN GOBLIN

Marvel Comics Group; 1 Oct 1995-13 Oct 1996

	$Good	$Fine	$N.Mint	£Good	£Fine	£N.Mint
1 ND Tom DeFalco script, Scott McDaniel art; prismatic foil-stamped cover						
	$0.60	*$1.80*	*$3.00*	£0.40	£1.20	£2.00
2 ND Rhino appears						
	$0.40	*$1.20*	*$2.00*	£0.25	£0.75	£1.25
3 ND storyline tie-in from Amazing Scarlet Spider #2						
	$0.40	*$1.20*	*$2.00*	£0.25	£0.75	£1.25
4-5 ND Green Goblin vs. Hobgoblin						
	$0.40	*$1.20*	*$2.00*	£0.25	£0.75	£1.25
6 ND Green Goblin vs. Daredevil						
	$0.40	*$1.20*	*$2.00*	£0.25	£0.75	£1.25
7-11 ND	*$0.40*	*$1.20*	*$2.00*	£0.25	£0.75	£1.25
12 ND Onslaught tie-in						
	$0.40	*$1.20*	*$2.00*	£0.25	£0.75	£1.25
13 ND	*$0.40*	*$1.20*	*$2.00*	£0.25	£0.75	£1.25
Title Value:	*$5.40*	*$16.20*	*$27.00*	£3.40	£10.20	£17.00

GREEN HORNET

Gold Key,TV; 1 Feb 1967-3 Aug 1967

	$Good	$Fine	$N.Mint	£Good	£Fine	£N.Mint
1 scarce though distributed in the U.K. Bruce Lee cover						
	$32.00	*$95.00*	*$225.00*	£20.00	£60.00	£140.00
2 scarce though distributed in the U.K. Bruce Lee cover						
	$21.00	*$62.50*	*$150.00*	£12.50	£39.00	£90.00
3 scarce though distributed in the U.K. Bruce Lee cover						
	$21.00	*$62.50*	*$150.00*	£12.00	£36.00	£85.00
Title Value:	*$74.00*	*$220.00*	*$525.00*	£44.50	£135.00	£315.00

GREEN HORNET 3-D SPECIAL

Now Comics,OS; 1 Oct 1993

	$Good	$Fine	$N.Mint	£Good	£Fine	£N.Mint
1 ND with 3-D glasses						
	$0.60	*$1.80*	*$3.00*	£0.40	£1.20	£2.00
Title Value:	*$0.60*	*$1.80*	*$3.00*	£0.40	£1.20	£2.00

GREEN HORNET ANNIVERSARY SPECIAL, TALES OF THE

Now Comics; 1 Sep 1992

	$Good	$Fine	$N.Mint	£Good	£Fine	£N.Mint
1 ND pre-bagged with hologram trading card, direct market editions of 3rd Series Tales begins but cancelled after this one issue						
	$0.50	*$1.50*	*$2.50*	£0.30	£0.90	£1.50
Title Value:	*$0.50*	*$1.50*	*$2.50*	£0.30	£0.90	£1.50

GREEN HORNET ANNIVERSARY SPECIAL, THE

Now Comics; 1 Aug 1992-3 1992

	$Good	$Fine	$N.Mint	£Good	£Fine	£N.Mint
1 ND #12 (2nd Series), pre-bagged with badge, new cover						
	$0.50	*$1.50*	*$2.50*	£0.30	£0.90	£1.50
2 ND #13 (2nd Series), new cover						
	$0.50	*$1.50*	*$2.50*	£0.30	£0.90	£1.50
3 ND #14 (2nd Series), new cover						
	$0.50	*$1.50*	*$2.50*	£0.30	£0.90	£1.50
Title Value:	*$1.50*	*$4.50*	*$7.50*	£0.90	£2.70	£4.50

GREEN HORNET ANNUAL

Now Comics; 1 Dec 1992-3 1994

	$Good	$Fine	$N.Mint	£Good	£Fine	£N.Mint
1-2 ND	*$0.50*	*$1.50*	*$2.50*	£0.30	£0.90	£1.50
3 ND metallic green cover						
	$0.60	*$1.80*	*$3.00*	£0.40	£1.20	£2.00
Title Value:	*$1.60*	*$4.80*	*$8.00*	£1.00	£3.00	£5.00

GREEN HORNET LEGACY SPECIAL, THE

Now Comics,OS; 1 May 1993

	$Good	$Fine	$N.Mint	£Good	£Fine	£N.Mint
1 ND origin of Green Hornet II, pin-up of Van Williams, TV's Green Hornet						
	$0.50	*$1.50*	*$2.50*	£0.30	£0.90	£1.50
Title Value:	*$0.50*	*$1.50*	*$2.50*	£0.30	£0.90	£1.50

GREEN HORNET SPECIAL MINI SERIES

Now Comics,MS; 1 Jul 1990-2 Aug 1990

	$Good	$Fine	$N.Mint	£Good	£Fine	£N.Mint
1-2 ND script by Van Williams, TV's Green Hornet						
	$0.40	*$1.20*	*$2.00*	£0.25	£0.75	£1.25
Title Value:	*$0.80*	*$2.40*	*$4.00*	£0.50	£1.50	£2.50

GREEN HORNET, STING OF THE

Now Comics; 1 Jun 1992-4 Sep 1992

	$Good	$Fine	$N.Mint	£Good	£Fine	£N.Mint
1-4 ND	*$0.50*	*$1.50*	*$2.50*	£0.30	£0.90	£1.50
1-4 Collectors Editon, ND pre-bagged with poster						
	$0.55	*$1.65*	*$2.75*	£0.35	£1.05	£1.75
Title Value:	*$4.20*	*$12.60*	*$21.00*	£2.60	£7.80	£13.00

GREEN HORNET, TALES OF THE

Now Comics,MS; 1 Sep 1990-2 Oct 1990

	$Good	$Fine	$N.Mint	£Good	£Fine	£N.Mint
1-2 ND script by Van Williams (TV's Green Hornet); painted covers by Dell Barras						
	$0.40	*$1.20*	*$2.00*	£0.25	£0.75	£1.25
Title Value:	*$0.80*	*$2.40*	*$4.00*	£0.50	£1.50	£2.50

GREEN HORNET, TALES OF THE (2ND SERIES)

Now Comics; 1 Jan 1992-4 Apr 1992

	$Good	$Fine	$N.Mint	£Good	£Fine	£N.Mint
1 ND Neal Adams cover						
	$0.50	*$1.50*	*$2.50*	£0.30	£0.90	£1.50
2-4 ND	*$0.50*	*$1.50*	*$2.50*	£0.30	£0.90	£1.50
Title Value:	*$2.00*	*$6.00*	*$10.00*	£1.20	£3.60	£6.00

GREEN HORNET, TALES OF THE (3RD SERIES)

Now Comics; 1 Sep 1992-3 Nov 1992

	$Good	$Fine	$N.Mint	£Good	£Fine	£N.Mint
1-3 ND	*$0.50*	*$1.50*	*$2.50*	£0.30	£0.90	£1.50
Title Value:	*$1.50*	*$4.50*	*$7.50*	£0.90	£2.70	£4.50

GREEN HORNET, THE

Now Comics; 1 Nov 1989-18 Apr 1991

	$Good	$Fine	$N.Mint	£Good	£Fine	£N.Mint
1 DS painted cover by Jim Steranko						
	$1.50	*$4.50*	*$7.50*	£1.20	£3.60	£6.00
1 2nd printing, new cover						
	$0.70	*$2.10*	*$3.50*	£0.50	£1.50	£2.50
2	*$1.20*	*$3.60*	*$6.00*	£0.80	£2.40	£4.00
3-4	*$0.80*	*$2.40*	*$4.00*	£0.60	£1.80	£3.00
5 death original (1930s) Green Hornet						
	$0.80	*$2.40*	*$4.00*	£0.60	£1.80	£3.00
6	*$0.70*	*$2.10*	*$3.50*	£0.50	£1.50	£2.50
7 new Kato	*$0.70*	*$2.10*	*$3.50*	£0.50	£1.50	£2.50
8-10	*$0.60*	*$1.80*	*$3.00*	£0.40	£1.20	£2.00
11-18	*$0.50*	*$1.50*	*$2.50*	£0.30	£0.90	£1.50
Title Value:	*$13.00*	*$39.00*	*$65.00*	£8.90	£26.70	£44.50

Note: all Non-Distributed on the news-stands in the U.K.

Trade Paperback (1991), reprints issues #1-7 plus new cover £1.30 £3.90 £6.50

Note also: issue #1 depicts 1940s character, #2-4 depict 1960s television characters. Issues #15-18 were solicited and advertised but may not have appeared

GREEN HORNET, THE (2ND SERIES)

Now Comics; 1 Sep 1991-39 Dec 1994 ?

	$Good	$Fine	$N.Mint	£Good	£Fine	£N.Mint
1 ND	*$0.50*	*$1.50*	*$2.50*	£0.30	£0.90	£1.50
2-7 ND	*$0.40*	*$1.20*	*$2.00*	£0.25	£0.75	£1.25
8 ND intro new Black Beauty car						
	$0.40	*$1.20*	*$2.00*	£0.25	£0.75	£1.25
9-11 ND	*$0.40*	*$1.20*	*$2.00*	£0.25	£0.75	£1.25
12 ND 3rd anniversary edition, pre-bagged with Green Hornet badge						
	$0.50	*$1.50*	*$2.50*	£0.30	£0.90	£1.50
13-15 ND	*$0.40*	*$1.20*	*$2.00*	£0.25	£0.75	£1.25
16 ND ties-in to Green Hornet #8						
	$0.40	*$1.20*	*$2.00*	£0.25	£0.75	£1.25
17-18 ND	*$0.40*	*$1.20*	*$2.00*	£0.25	£0.75	£1.25
19 ND pre-bagged with Green Hornet hologram card (2 different covers available)						
	$0.80	*$2.40*	*$4.00*	£0.50	£1.50	£2.50
20-27 ND	*$0.40*	*$1.20*	*$2.00*	£0.25	£0.75	£1.25
27 Collectors Edition, ND pre-bagged with trading card - 1993 Anniversary Special						
	$0.60	*$1.80*	*$3.00*	£0.40	£1.20	£2.00
28-39 ND	*$0.40*	*$1.20*	*$2.00*	£0.25	£0.75	£1.25
Title Value:	*$16.80*	*$50.40*	*$84.00*	£10.50	£31.50	£52.50

Note: all Non-Distributed on the news-stands in the U.K.

Note also: issues #40-46 were solicited and advertised but never appeared owing to Now Comics liquidation

GREEN HORNET: DARK TOMORROW

Now Comics,MS; 1 Jun 1993-3 Aug 1993

	$Good	$Fine	$N.Mint	£Good	£Fine	£N.Mint
1-3 ND	*$0.50*	*$1.50*	*$2.50*	£0.30	£0.90	£1.50
Title Value:	*$1.50*	*$4.50*	*$7.50*	£0.90	£2.70	£4.50

GREEN HORNET: SOLITARY SENTINEL

Now Comics,MS; 1 Dec 1992-3 Feb 1993

	$Good	$Fine	$N.Mint	£Good	£Fine	£N.Mint
1-3 ND	*$0.50*	*$1.50*	*$2.50*	£0.30	£0.90	£1.50
Title Value:	*$1.50*	*$4.50*	*$7.50*	£0.90	£2.70	£4.50

GREEN LANTERN (1ST SERIES)

National Periodical Publications; 1 Sep 1941-38 May/Jun 1949

(see All American Comics, All Flash Quarterly, All Star Comics)

	$Good	$Fine	$N.Mint	£Good	£Fine	£N.Mint
1 scarce in the U.K. Green Lantern's origin retold; quarterly frequency begins (to #18)						
	$2900.00	*$8700.00*	*$29000.00*	£1925.00	£5800.00	£19350.00
			[Scarce in high grade - Very Fine+ or better]			
2	*$810.00*	*$2425.00*	*$6500.00*	£540.00	£1625.00	£4350.00
3	*$530.00*	*$1575.00*	*$4250.00*	£350.00	£1050.00	£2835.00
4 patriotic war cover						
	$360.00	*$1075.00*	*$2900.00*	£240.00	£720.00	£1935.00
5 scarce in the U.K. patriotic war cover						
	$240.00	*$730.00*	*$1950.00*	£160.00	£485.00	£1300.00
6-8	*$185.00*	*$560.00*	*$1500.00*	£125.00	£375.00	£1000.00
9	*$175.00*	*$520.00*	*$1400.00*	£115.00	£350.00	£935.00
10 origin Vandal Savage - "The Man Who Wanted The World"						
	$185.00	*$560.00*	*$1500.00*	£125.00	£375.00	£1000.00
11	*$150.00*	*$450.00*	*$1050.00*	£100.00	£300.00	£700.00
12 scarce in the U.K. 1st appearance The Gambler						
	$150.00	*$450.00*	*$1050.00*	£100.00	£300.00	£700.00
13-17	*$150.00*	*$450.00*	*$1050.00*	£100.00	£300.00	£700.00
18 classic Christmas cover						
	$160.00	*$490.00*	*$1150.00*	£110.00	£330.00	£775.00
19-20	*$150.00*	*$450.00*	*$1050.00*	£100.00	£300.00	£700.00
21-26	*$140.00*	*$425.00*	*$1000.00*	£95.00	£285.00	£670.00
27 Green Lantern vs. The Sky Pirate						
	$150.00	*$450.00*	*$1050.00*	£100.00	£300.00	£700.00
28 Green Lantern vs. The Sportsmaster						
	$140.00	*$425.00*	*$1000.00*	£95.00	£285.00	£670.00
29 Green Lantern vs. The Harlequin						
	$140.00	*$425.00*	*$1000.00*	£95.00	£285.00	£670.00
30 1st appearance Streak the Wonder Dog						
	$140.00	*$425.00*	*$1000.00*	£95.00	£285.00	£670.00
31-35	*$120.00*	*$360.00*	*$850.00*	£80.00	£240.00	£570.00
36-38 very scarce in the U.K., scarce in the U.S.						
	$130.00	*$395.00*	*$925.00*	£87.50	£265.00	£620.00
Title Value:	*$9665.00*	*$29065.00*	*$79675.00*	£6457.50	£19420.00	£53220.00

Note: all Non-Distributed on the news-stands in the U.K. but some issues may have come over with personnel movement during the Second World War or as cheap ballast on ships after the war. As in common with most Golden Age issues, these comics are generally scarce in the U.K.

GREEN LANTERN (2ND SERIES)

National Periodical Publications/DC Comics; 1 Jul/Aug 1960-89 Apr/May 1972; 90 Aug/Sep 1976-224 May 1988

(see Action, Adventure, Brave & the Bold, DC Comics Presents, DC Special, Emerald Dawn I & II, Five-Star Super-Hero Spectacular, Flash, Green Lantern: Mosaic, Showcase, Secret Origins, Super-Team Family, Tales of the Green Lantern Corps, World's Finest) (becomes Green Lantern Corps with issue #201)

Issue	$Good	$Fine	$N.Mint	£Good	£Fine	£N.Mint
1 origin retold, Gil Kane art begins	*$295.00*	*$880.00*	*$2950.00*	£195.00	£580.00	£1950.00
2 1st appearance Pieface	*$105.00*	*$315.00*	*$850.00*	£62.50	£185.00	£500.00
3	*$57.50*	*$175.00*	*$475.00*	£34.00	£100.00	£275.00
4 (Feb 1961)	*$47.00*	*$140.00*	*$375.00*	£21.50	£65.00	£175.00
5 1st appearance Hector Hammond	*$47.00*	*$140.00*	*$375.00*	£21.50	£65.00	£175.00
6 less common in the U.K. 1st appearance Tomar-re (alien Green Lantern)	*$41.00*	*$120.00*	*$325.00*	£18.50	£55.00	£150.00
7 origin and 1st appearance Sinestro	*$34.00*	*$100.00*	*$275.00*	£18.50	£55.00	£150.00
8 painted grey-tone cover	*$34.00*	*$100.00*	*$275.00*	£18.50	£55.00	£150.00
9 last 10 cents issue	*$31.00*	*$92.50*	*$250.00*	£15.50	£47.00	£125.00
10 (Jan 1962) the secret of Green Lantern's oath is told	*$31.00*	*$92.50*	*$250.00*	£15.50	£47.00	£125.00
11-12	*$25.00*	*$75.00*	*$175.00*	£13.50	£41.00	£95.00
13 Flash guest stars	*$29.00*	*$85.00*	*$200.00*	£15.50	£47.00	£110.00
14-15	*$21.00*	*$62.50*	*$150.00*	£11.00	£34.00	£80.00
16 origin and 1st appearance Star Sapphire	*$25.00*	*$75.00*	*$175.00*	£12.50	£39.00	£90.00
17	*$21.00*	*$62.50*	*$150.00*	£9.25	£28.00	£65.00
18 (Jan 1963)	*$21.00*	*$62.50*	*$150.00*	£9.25	£28.00	£65.00
19	*$21.00*	*$62.50*	*$150.00*	£9.25	£28.00	£65.00
20 Flash guest stars	*$21.00*	*$62.50*	*$150.00*	£9.25	£28.00	£65.00
21 origin Dr. Polaris	*$18.50*	*$55.00*	*$130.00*	£8.50	£26.00	£60.00
22	*$18.50*	*$55.00*	*$130.00*	£7.75	£23.50	£55.00
23 1st appearance Tattooed Man	*$18.50*	*$55.00*	*$130.00*	£8.50	£26.00	£60.00
24 origin Shark	*$18.50*	*$55.00*	*$130.00*	£8.50	£26.00	£60.00
25	*$18.50*	*$55.00*	*$130.00*	£7.75	£23.50	£55.00
26 (Jan 1964)	*$18.50*	*$55.00*	*$130.00*	£6.25	£19.00	£45.00
27-28	*$18.50*	*$55.00*	*$130.00*	£6.25	£19.00	£45.00
29 Justice League of America cameo	*$18.50*	*$55.00*	*$130.00*	£7.75	£23.50	£55.00
30	*$18.50*	*$55.00*	*$130.00*	£6.25	£19.00	£45.00
31-33	*$15.50*	*$47.00*	*$110.00*	£5.50	£17.00	£40.00
34 (Jan 1965)	*$15.50*	*$47.00*	*$110.00*	£5.50	£17.00	£40.00
35-37	*$15.50*	*$47.00*	*$110.00*	£5.50	£17.00	£40.00
38 Tomar-Re appears	*$15.50*	*$47.00*	*$110.00*	£5.50	£17.00	£40.00
39	*$15.50*	*$47.00*	*$110.00*	£5.50	£17.00	£40.00
40 1st appearance Crisis, origin of the Guardians, GA Green Lantern co-stars (1st full SA appearance in title. 2nd solo appearance in SA). (1st cameo in Flash 129, 1st full appearance in Flash #137)	*$50.00*	*$150.00*	*$500.00*	£17.50	£52.50	£175.00
[Prices may vary widely on this comic]						
41 Star Sapphire vs. Green Lantern; last Silver Age issue, indicia dated December 1965	*$10.50*	*$32.00*	*$75.00*	£4.25	£12.50	£30.00
42 (Jan 1966) 3rd appearance Zatanna	*$10.50*	*$32.00*	*$75.00*	£3.55	£10.50	£25.00
43-44	*$10.50*	*$32.00*	*$75.00*	£3.55	£10.50	£25.00
45 Golden Age Green Lantern appears (2nd full Silver Age appearance in title)	*$17.50*	*$52.50*	*$125.00*	£5.50	£17.00	£40.00
46-49	*$10.50*	*$32.00*	*$75.00*	£3.55	£10.50	£25.00
50 scarce in the U.K. (Jan 1967)	*$10.50*	*$32.00*	*$75.00*	£4.25	£12.50	£30.00
51	*$7.75*	*$23.50*	*$55.00*	£2.85	£8.50	£20.00
52 Golden Age Green Lantern X-over	*$11.00*	*$34.00*	*$80.00*	£3.55	£10.50	£25.00
53-55	*$7.75*	*$23.50*	*$55.00*	£2.85	£8.50	£20.00
56-57	*$7.75*	*$23.50*	*$55.00*	£2.10	£6.25	£15.00
58 (Jan 1968)	*$7.75*	*$23.50*	*$55.00*	£2.10	£6.25	£15.00
59 1st appearance Guy Gardner; in an imaginary story he becomes a Green Lantern (see #116)	*$28.00*	*$82.50*	*$220.00*	£10.50	£33.00	£87.50
60	*$5.50*	*$17.00*	*$40.00*	£1.75	£5.25	£12.50
61 Golden Age Green Lantern X-over	*$8.50*	*$26.00*	*$60.00*	£2.10	£6.25	£15.00
62	*$5.50*	*$17.00*	*$40.00*	£1.40	£4.25	£10.00
63 Neal Adams cover	*$5.50*	*$17.00*	*$40.00*	£1.40	£4.25	£10.00
64-65	*$5.50*	*$17.00*	*$40.00*	£1.40	£4.25	£10.00
66 (Jan 1969)	*$5.50*	*$17.00*	*$40.00*	£1.10	£3.40	£8.00
67-68	*$5.50*	*$17.00*	*$40.00*	£1.10	£3.40	£8.00
69 last 12 cents issue	*$5.50*	*$17.00*	*$40.00*	£1.10	£3.40	£8.00
70-72	*$3.55*	*$10.50*	*$25.00*	£0.90	£2.75	£6.50
73 Star Sapphire appears	*$3.55*	*$10.50*	*$25.00*	£0.90	£2.75	£6.50
74 (Jan 1970) Star Sapphire and Sinestro appear	*$3.55*	*$10.50*	*$25.00*	£0.90	£2.75	£6.50
75 less common in the U.K.	*$4.15*	*$12.50*	*$25.00*	£1.25	£3.75	£7.50
76 rare in the U.K. 1st Green Arrow/Green Lantern team-up, Neal Adams art and classic award-winning issue; comic generally credited as heralding the "Bronze Age" of comics' history	*$21.00*	*$62.50*	*$150.00*	£14.00	£43.00	£100.00
[Scarce in high grade - Very Fine+ or better]						
76 Silver Age Classic, ND (Mar 1992)	*$0.25*	*$0.75*	*$1.25*	£0.15	£0.45	£0.75
77 Neal Adams art	*$8.25*	*$25.00*	*$50.00*	£4.15	£12.50	£25.00
78-80 Neal Adams art	*$6.50*	*$20.00*	*$40.00*	£3.30	£10.00	£20.00
81 Neal Adams art	*$5.75*	*$17.50*	*$35.00*	£2.90	£8.75	£17.50
82 (Mar 1971) Neal Adams art	*$5.75*	*$17.50*	*$35.00*	£2.90	£8.75	£17.50
83 Neal Adams art	*$5.75*	*$17.50*	*$35.00*	£2.90	£8.75	£17.50
84 Neal Adams art; last 15 cents issue	*$5.75*	*$17.50*	*$35.00*	£2.90	£8.75	£17.50
85 scarce in the U.K. 48pgs, (says 52pgs on cover up to #89 as they count the covers in the U.S.), Neal Adams art, drugs issues	*$7.50*	*$22.50*	*$45.00*	£3.30	£10.00	£20.00
86 scarce in the U.K. 48pgs, Neal Adams art, drugs issues	*$7.50*	*$22.50*	*$45.00*	£3.30	£10.00	£20.00
87 48pgs, (Jan 1972) Neal Adams art, 2nd appearance Guy Gardner (cameo), 1st John Stewart Green Lantern	*$5.00*	*$15.00*	*$30.00*	£2.90	£8.75	£17.50
88 48pgs, Neal Adams art (1pg), reprint of Showcase #23 (2nd Silver Age Green Lantern), unpublished Golden Age Green Lantern story from unreleased #39	*$2.00*	*$6.00*	*$12.00*	£1.25	£3.75	£7.50
89 48pgs, story continues in Flash #217, Neal Adams art	*$2.50*	*$7.50*	*$15.00*	£1.50	£4.50	£9.00
90 scarce in the U.K.	*$0.80*	*$2.50*	*$5.00*	£0.55	£1.75	£3.50

Grafik Muzik #1

Green Lantern (2nd) #83

Green Lantern (3rd) #46

	$Good	$Fine	$N.Mint	£Good	£Fine	£N.Mint
91-92 scarce in the U.K.	*$0.80*	*$2.50*	*$5.00*	£0.40	£1.25	£2.50
93 scarce in the U.K. (Feb 1977)	*$0.80*	*$2.50*	*$5.00*	£0.40	£1.25	£2.50
94-96 scarce in the U.K.	*$0.80*	*$2.50*	*$5.00*	£0.40	£1.25	£2.50
97-98	*$0.80*	*$2.50*	*$5.00*	£0.30	£1.00	£2.00
99 ND	*$0.80*	*$2.50*	*$5.00*	£0.50	£1.50	£3.00
100 ND scarce in the U.K. 48pgs, (Jan 1978) 1st appearance Air Wave II	*$1.25*	*$3.75*	*$7.50*	£0.80	£2.50	£5.00
101-107	*$0.65*	*$2.00*	*$4.00*	£0.25	£0.75	£1.50
108-110 scarce in the U.K. 44pgs, Golden Age Green Lantern back-up	*$0.65*	*$2.00*	*$4.00*	£0.40	£1.25	£2.50
111 Green Lantern and Golden Age Green Lantern team-up	*$0.50*	*$1.50*	*$3.00*	£0.25	£0.75	£1.50
112 (Jan 1979) Golden Age Green Lantern origin retold	*$1.00*	*$3.00*	*$6.00*	£0.25	£0.75	£1.50
113-115	*$0.50*	*$1.50*	*$3.00*	£0.20	£0.60	£1.25
116 3rd appearance Guy Gardner, 1st as a Green Lantern	*$4.15*	*$12.50*	*$25.00*	£0.65	£2.00	£4.00
117-121	*$0.50*	*$1.50*	*$3.00*	£0.20	£0.60	£1.25
122 last Green Lantern/Green Arrow cover title, Guy Gardner appears, Superman and Flash appear	*$0.50*	*$1.50*	*$3.00*	£0.20	£0.60	£1.25
123 Green Lantern goes solo, Superman cameo, Gil Kane cover, Guy Gardner appears	*$0.80*	*$2.50*	*$5.00*	£0.25	£0.75	£1.50
124 (Jan 1980)	*$0.40*	*$1.20*	*$2.00*	£0.25	£0.75	£1.25
125-126	*$0.40*	*$1.20*	*$2.00*	£0.25	£0.75	£1.25
127 Bolland cover, his first published DC work	*$0.40*	*$1.20*	*$2.00*	£0.30	£0.90	£1.50
128 Cockrum art	*$0.40*	*$1.20*	*$2.00*	£0.25	£0.75	£1.25
129-130	*$0.40*	*$1.20*	*$2.00*	£0.25	£0.75	£1.25
131 Bolland cover (2nd DC work?)	*$0.40*	*$1.20*	*$2.00*	£0.25	£0.75	£1.25
132 Adam Strange back-up begins (ends #147)	*$0.40*	*$1.20*	*$2.00*	£0.25	£0.75	£1.25
133-135	*$0.40*	*$1.20*	*$2.00*	£0.25	£0.75	£1.25
136 (Jan 1981) Space Ranger and Eclipso appear; 1st appearance The Citadel	*$0.40*	*$1.20*	*$2.00*	£0.25	£0.75	£1.25
137 Space Ranger appears	*$0.40*	*$1.20*	*$2.00*	£0.25	£0.75	£1.25
138 Green Lantern vs. Eclipso	*$0.40*	*$1.20*	*$2.00*	£0.25	£0.75	£1.25
139-140	*$0.40*	*$1.20*	*$2.00*	£0.25	£0.75	£1.25
141 1st appearance Omega Men	*$0.60*	*$1.80*	*$3.00*	£0.30	£0.90	£1.50
142-144 Omega Men appear	*$0.40*	*$1.20*	*$2.00*	£0.25	£0.75	£1.25
145-147	*$0.40*	*$1.20*	*$2.00*	£0.25	£0.75	£1.25
148 (Jan 1982)	*$0.40*	*$1.20*	*$2.00*	£0.25	£0.75	£1.25
149	*$0.40*	*$1.20*	*$2.00*	£0.25	£0.75	£1.25
150 44pgs, anniversary issue	*$0.60*	*$1.80*	*$3.00*	£0.30	£0.90	£1.50
151-155	*$0.40*	*$1.20*	*$2.00*	£0.20	£0.60	£1.00
156 Gil Kane cover and art	*$0.40*	*$1.20*	*$2.00*	£0.20	£0.60	£1.00
157-159	*$0.40*	*$1.20*	*$2.00*	£0.20	£0.60	£1.00
160 (Jan 1983) Omega Men X-over	*$0.40*	*$1.20*	*$2.00*	£0.20	£0.60	£1.00
161 Dave Gibbons art, Omega Men X-over	*$0.40*	*$1.20*	*$2.00*	£0.20	£0.60	£1.00
162 Dave Gibbons art	*$0.40*	*$1.20*	*$2.00*	£0.20	£0.60	£1.00
163	*$0.40*	*$1.20*	*$2.00*	£0.20	£0.60	£1.00
164-167 Gibbons art	*$0.40*	*$1.20*	*$2.00*	£0.20	£0.60	£1.00
168-170	*$0.40*	*$1.20*	*$2.00*	£0.20	£0.60	£1.00
171 Gibbons art	*$0.40*	*$1.20*	*$2.00*	£0.20	£0.60	£1.00
172 (Jan 1984) Gibbons art	*$0.40*	*$1.20*	*$2.00*	£0.20	£0.60	£1.00
173-174 Gibbons art	*$0.40*	*$1.20*	*$2.00*	£0.20	£0.60	£1.00
175 Gibbons art; no number on cover	*$0.40*	*$1.20*	*$2.00*	£0.20	£0.60	£1.00
176 Gibbons art	*$0.40*	*$1.20*	*$2.00*	£0.20	£0.60	£1.00
177 Cockrum art	*$0.40*	*$1.20*	*$2.00*	£0.20	£0.60	£1.00
178-181 Gibbons art	*$0.40*	*$1.20*	*$2.00*	£0.20	£0.60	£1.00
182 John Stewart takes over as Green Lantern, Kevin O'Neill, Gibbons art	*$0.40*	*$1.20*	*$2.00*	£0.20	£0.60	£1.00
183 Gibbons art	*$0.40*	*$1.20*	*$2.00*	£0.20	£0.60	£1.00
184 (Jan 1985) John Stewart/Hal Jordan/Guy Gardner Green Lanterns appear	*$0.40*	*$1.20*	*$2.00*	£0.20	£0.60	£1.00
185 John Stewart origin as Green Lantern, Eclipso appears, Gibbons art	*$0.40*	*$1.20*	*$2.00*	£0.20	£0.60	£1.00
186 John Stewart vs. Eclipso	*$0.40*	*$1.20*	*$2.00*	£0.20	£0.60	£1.00
187 Marshall Rogers art	*$0.40*	*$1.20*	*$2.00*	£0.20	£0.60	£1.00
188 Moore script, Gibbons art	*$0.40*	*$1.20*	*$2.00*	£0.20	£0.60	£1.00
189-193	*$0.40*	*$1.20*	*$2.00*	£0.20	£0.60	£1.00
194 Crisis X-over	*$0.80*	*$2.40*	*$4.00*	£0.25	£0.75	£1.25
195 Crisis X-over, Guy Gardner becomes Green Lantern	*$1.50*	*$4.50*	*$7.50*	£0.50	£1.50	£2.50
196 (Jan 1986) unofficial Crisis X-over	*$0.40*	*$1.20*	*$2.00*	£0.20	£0.60	£1.00
197 Guy Gardner vs. John Stewart	*$0.40*	*$1.20*	*$2.00*	£0.20	£0.60	£1.00
198 DS, Crisis X-over, alien Green Lantern Tomar-Re dies	*$0.40*	*$1.20*	*$2.00*	£0.25	£0.75	£1.25
199 Hal Jordan returns as Green Lantern	*$0.40*	*$1.20*	*$2.00*	£0.20	£0.60	£1.00
200 DS, anniversary issue, various past Green Lantern friends and foes return in flashback	*$0.60*	*$1.80*	*$3.00*	£0.30	£0.90	£1.50
201 title becomes Green Lantern Corps (Jun 1986)	*$0.25*	*$0.75*	*$1.25*	£0.15	£0.45	£0.75
202-206	*$0.25*	*$0.75*	*$1.25*	£0.15	£0.45	£0.75
207 Legends X-over	*$0.25*	*$0.75*	*$1.25*	£0.15	£0.45	£0.75
208 (Jan 1987)	*$0.25*	*$0.75*	*$1.25*	£0.15	£0.45	£0.75
209-213	*$0.25*	*$0.75*	*$1.25*	£0.15	£0.45	£0.75
214-216 Ian Gibson art	*$0.25*	*$0.75*	*$1.25*	£0.15	£0.45	£0.75
217-219	*$0.25*	*$0.75*	*$1.25*	£0.15	£0.45	£0.75
220 (Jan 1988) Millennium X-over	*$0.25*	*$0.75*	*$1.25*	£0.15	£0.45	£0.75
221 Millennium X-over	*$0.25*	*$0.75*	*$1.25*	£0.15	£0.45	£0.75
222	*$0.25*	*$0.75*	*$1.25*	£0.15	£0.45	£0.75
223 LD in the U.K.	*$0.25*	*$0.75*	*$1.25*	£0.20	£0.60	£1.00
224 LD in the U.K. 48pgs	*$0.30*	*$0.90*	*$1.50*	£0.30	£0.90	£1.50
Title Value:	***$1774.30***	***$5318.85***	***$13835.50***	**£850.20**	**£2558.80**	**£6801.00**

Note: content changed to Green Lantern Corps with issue #201.

Green Lantern/Green Arrow Collection 1 (Jun 1992)

	£Good	£Fine	£N.Mint
Trade paperback, reprints issues #76-82, new intro by Denny O'Neill	£1.60	£4.80	£8.00

Green Lantern/Green Arrow Collection 2 (May 1993)

	£Good	£Fine	£N.Mint
Trade paperback, reprints issues #84-87, #89 and Flash #217-219, new Neal Adams cover, intro by Dick Giordano	£1.60	£4.80	£8.00

ARTISTS

Wrightson inks in 84.

FEATURES

Adam Strange in 132-147. Earth's First Green Lantern in 149. Green Lantern/Green Arrow in 76-86, 89-99, 101-122. Green Arrow solo in 87. Green Arrow/ Black Canary in 100. GA Green Lantern in 108-110. Tales of the Green Lantern Corps in 130-132, 148, 151-172, 188.

REPRINT FEATURES

Green Lantern in 85, 87, 88. GA Green Lantern in 86, 88, 89.

GREEN LANTERN (3RD SERIES)

DC Comics; 0 Oct 1994; 1 Jun 1990-present

	$Good	$Fine	$N.Mint	£Good	£Fine	£N.Mint
0 (Oct 1994) Zero Hour X-over, Kyle Rayner vs. Hal Jordan	*$0.40*	*$1.20*	*$2.00*	£0.25	£0.75	£1.25
1 Batman appears	*$0.60*	*$1.80*	*$3.00*	£0.40	£1.20	£2.00
2	*$0.40*	*$1.20*	*$2.00*	£0.30	£0.90	£1.50
3-8	*$0.40*	*$1.20*	*$2.00*	£0.25	£0.75	£1.25
9-10 origin G'Nort story	*$0.40*	*$1.20*	*$2.00*	£0.25	£0.75	£1.25
11-12 origin G'Nort story	*$0.30*	*$0.90*	*$1.50*	£0.20	£0.60	£1.00
13 48pgs, three story issue	*$0.40*	*$1.20*	*$2.00*	£0.25	£0.75	£1.25
14-17 John Stewart/Guardians story	*$0.30*	*$0.90*	*$1.50*	£0.20	£0.60	£1.00
18	*$0.30*	*$0.90*	*$1.50*	£0.20	£0.60	£1.00
19 48pgs, 50th anniversary issue, Golden Age Green Lantern appears, part art by Martin Nodell who originally drew G.L. in the 1940s	*$0.40*	*$1.20*	*$2.00*	£0.25	£0.75	£1.25
19 Signed & Numbered Edition, ND (Jul 1992), signed bt Marty Nodell. 2,000 copies only - one copy was issued per retailer's account by their distributor	*$3.00*	*$9.00*	*$15.00*	£2.00	£6.00	£10.00
20	*$0.30*	*$0.90*	*$1.50*	£0.20	£0.60	£1.00
21-24	*$0.25*	*$0.75*	*$1.25*	£0.15	£0.45	£0.75
25 48pgs, leads into Green Lantern: Mosaic #1	*$0.30*	*$0.90*	*$1.50*	£0.20	£0.60	£1.00
26-28 Evil Star Rising story	*$0.25*	*$0.75*	*$1.25*	£0.15	£0.45	£0.75
29	*$0.25*	*$0.75*	*$1.25*	£0.15	£0.45	£0.75
30 Gorilla Warfare part 1, Gorilla Grodd, Detective Chimp and Rex the Wonder Dog appear, continued in Flash [2nd Series] #69	*$0.25*	*$0.75*	*$1.25*	£0.15	£0.45	£0.75
31 Gorilla Warfare part 2, continued in Flash #70	*$0.25*	*$0.75*	*$1.25*	£0.15	£0.45	£0.75
32-33 bi-weekly	*$0.25*	*$0.75*	*$1.25*	£0.15	£0.45	£0.75
34 1st appearance Entropy	*$0.25*	*$0.75*	*$1.25*	£0.15	£0.45	£0.75
35-37	*$0.25*	*$0.75*	*$1.25*	£0.15	£0.45	£0.75
38 Adam Strange appears	*$0.25*	*$0.75*	*$1.25*	£0.15	£0.45	£0.75
39 Adam Strange appears, bi-weekly	*$0.25*	*$0.75*	*$1.25*	£0.15	£0.45	£0.75
40 Darkstar appears, bi-weekly	*$0.25*	*$0.75*	*$1.25*	£0.15	£0.45	£0.75
41 DC's Predator, Deathstroke and Eclipso appear, bi-weekly	*$0.25*	*$0.75*	*$1.25*	£0.15	£0.45	£0.75
42 DC's Predator, Deathstroke appear, bi-weekly						

VERY GENERAL PERCENTAGE CONVERSION CHART WHICH MAY BE USED TO CALCULATE LOW AND INBETWEEN GRADES:

	$Good	$Fine	$N.Mint	£Good	£Fine	£N.Mint
	$0.25	$0.75	$1.25	£0.15	£0.45	£0.75
43	$0.25	$0.75	$1.25	£0.15	£0.45	£0.75
44 Trinity part 2, continued in Legion '93 #57						
	$0.25	$0.75	$1.25	£0.15	£0.45	£0.75
45 Trinity part 5, continued in Legion '93 #58						
	$0.25	$0.75	$1.25	£0.15	£0.45	£0.75
46 Reign of the Supermen part 19, continued in Superman #82						
	$1.00	$3.00	$5.00	£0.50	£1.50	£2.50
46 2nd printing	$0.25	$0.75	$1.25	£0.15	£0.45	£0.75
47 Green Lantern and Green Arrow team returns						
	$0.25	$0.75	$1.25	£0.15	£0.45	£0.75
48 Emerald Twilight part 1						
	$0.60	$1.80	$3.00	£0.40	£1.20	£2.00
49 Emerald Twilight part 2						
	$0.50	$1.50	$2.50	£0.35	£1.05	£1.75
50 48pgs, Emerald Twilight part 3, Green Lantern vs. Sinestro, Green Lantern's new costume/powers; end of the Green lantern Corps and death of Killowog; green glow-in-the-dark cover						
	$0.80	$2.40	$4.00	£0.70	£2.10	£3.50
51 new Green Lantern takes over, cyborg Superman appears						
	$0.50	$1.50	$2.50	£0.30	£0.90	£1.50
52	$0.40	$1.20	$2.00	£0.25	£0.75	£1.25
53 Superman appears						
	$0.40	$1.20	$2.00	£0.25	£0.75	£1.25
54	$0.40	$1.20	$2.00	£0.25	£0.75	£1.25
55 Zero Hour X-over						
	$0.40	$1.20	$2.00	£0.25	£0.75	£1.25
56	$0.30	$0.90	$1.50	£0.20	£0.60	£1.00
57 continued in New Tians #116						
	$0.30	$0.90	$1.50	£0.20	£0.60	£1.00
58-59	$0.30	$0.90	$1.50	£0.20	£0.60	£1.00
60 Guy Gardner guest-stars						
	$0.30	$0.90	$1.50	£0.20	£0.60	£1.00
61-62	$0.30	$0.90	$1.50	£0.20	£0.60	£1.00
63 Parallax View: The ressurrection of Hal Jordan; Superman, Flash, Aquaman, Green Arrow, Black Canary, Martian Manhunter appear						
	$0.40	$1.20	$2.00	£0.25	£0.75	£1.25
64 Parallax View: The resurrection of Hal Jordan; Superman, Flash, Aquaman, Green Arrow, Black Canary, Martian Manhunter appear						
	$0.40	$1.20	$2.00	£0.25	£0.75	£1.25
65 The Siege of Zi Charam, continued in Darkstars #34. Ron Lim cover and art						
	$0.40	$1.20	$2.00	£0.25	£0.75	£1.25
66-67 Flash guest-stars						
	$0.40	$1.20	$2.00	£0.25	£0.75	£1.25
68-69 Underworld Unleashed tie-in						
	$0.40	$1.20	$2.00	£0.25	£0.75	£1.25
70 Supergirl guest-stars						
	$0.40	$1.20	$2.00	£0.25	£0.75	£1.25
71	$0.40	$1.20	$2.00	£0.25	£0.75	£1.25
72 Green Lantern teams with Captain Marvel						
	$0.40	$1.20	$2.00	£0.25	£0.75	£1.25
73 Wonder Woman and Donna Troy appear						
	$0.40	$1.20	$2.00	£0.25	£0.75	£1.25
74 Adam Strange guest-stars						
	$0.40	$1.20	$2.00	£0.25	£0.75	£1.25
75 Adam Strange guest-stars; bi-monthly						
	$0.40	$1.20	$2.00	£0.25	£0.75	£1.25
76 cover based on the classic Green Lantern [2nd Series] #76; bi-monthly						
	$0.40	$1.20	$2.00	£0.25	£0.75	£1.25
77 continued from Green Arrow #110, continued in Green Arrow #111						
	$0.40	$1.20	$2.00	£0.25	£0.75	£1.25
78-79	$0.35	$1.05	$1.75	£0.25	£0.75	£1.25
80 ND Final Night tie-in						
	$0.35	$1.05	$1.75	£0.25	£0.75	£1.25
81 ND the aftermath of The Final Night with a memorial for Hal Jordan						
	$0.35	$1.05	$1.75	£0.25	£0.75	£1.25
81 Collectors Edition, ND 48pgs, with 6 page reprint of Hal Jordan's 1st appearance plus 6 page new story						
	$0.80	$2.40	$4.00	£0.50	£1.50	£2.50
82-83 ND	$0.35	$1.05	$1.75	£0.25	£0.75	£1.25
84 ND John Stewart guest-stars						
	$0.35	$1.05	$1.75	£0.25	£0.75	£1.25
Title Value:	$33.95	$101.85	$169.75	£21.80	£65.40	£109.00

Note: early issues spotlight Hal Jordan/Guy Gardner/John Stewart incarnations of Green Lantern in rotation.

				£Good	£Fine	£N.Mint
Green Lantern: The Road Back (Jun 1992) Trade paperback						
ND reprints issues #1-8, new cover painting by Brian Stelfreeze				£1.10	£3.30	£5.50
Green Lantern/Green Arrow Collector's Set (Feb 1997)						
ND boxed set inc. Green lantern #77-79 and Green Arrow #110-111				£2.00	£6.00	£10.00

GREEN LANTERN ANNUAL

DC Comics; 1 Jul 1992-present

	$Good	$Fine	$N.Mint	£Good	£Fine	£N.Mint
1 64pgs, Eclipso: The Darkness Within tie-in						
	$0.50	$1.50	$2.50	£0.30	£0.90	£1.50
2 64pgs, Bloodlines part 7, 1st appearance Nightblade, continued in Batman Annual #17						
	$0.50	$1.50	$2.50	£0.30	£0.90	£1.50
3 64pgs, Elseworlds story, Adolf Hitler appears						
	$0.60	$1.80	$3.00	£0.35	£1.05	£1.75
4 64pgs, Year One	$0.80	$2.40	$4.00	£0.50	£1.50	£2.50
5 ND 48pgs, Legends of the Dead Earth tie-in						
	$0.60	$1.80	$3.00	£0.40	£1.20	£2.00
Title Value:	$3.00	$9.00	$15.00	£1.85	£5.55	£9.25

GREEN LANTERN ARCHIVES

DC Comics; 1 Jan 1993

	$Good	$Fine	$N.Mint	£Good	£Fine	£N.Mint
1 ND 224pgs, reprints Showcase #22-#24, Green Lantern #1-#5						
	$7.50	$22.50	$37.50	£5.00	£15.00	£25.00
Title Value:	$7.50	$22.50	$37.50	£5.00	£15.00	£25.00

GREEN LANTERN CORPS ANNUAL

DC Comics;2 Dec 1986-3 Aug 1987

(previously Tales of the ...)

	$Good	$Fine	$N.Mint	£Good	£Fine	£N.Mint
2 Moore script, Kev O'Neill art, non-code approved						
	$0.40	$1.20	$2.00	£0.25	£0.75	£1.25
3 Moore scripts, John Byrne, Kevin Nowlan art						
	$0.40	$1.20	$2.00	£0.25	£0.75	£1.25
Title Value:	$0.80	$2.40	$4.00	£0.50	£1.50	£2.50

Note: issue 3 titled "Green Lantern Annual".

GREEN LANTERN CORPS ANNUAL, TALES OF THE

DC Comics; 1 Jan 1985

(becomes Green Lantern Corps Annual)

	$Good	$Fine	$N.Mint	£Good	£Fine	£N.Mint
1 48pgs, Gil Kane cover/art						
	$0.50	$1.50	$2.50	£0.30	£0.90	£1.50
Title Value:	$0.50	$1.50	$2.50	£0.30	£0.90	£1.50

GREEN LANTERN CORPS QUARTERLY

DC Comics; 1 Jun 1992-8 Mar 1994

	$Good	$Fine	$N.Mint	£Good	£Fine	£N.Mint
1-6 64pgs, Golden Age Green Lantern appears						
	$0.50	$1.50	$2.50	£0.30	£0.90	£1.50
7 64pgs, Golden Age Green Lantern appears; special Halloween issue focusing on fear						
	$0.50	$1.50	$2.50	£0.30	£0.90	£1.50
8 64pgs, Golden Age Green Lantern appears						
	$0.50	$1.50	$2.50	£0.30	£0.90	£1.50
Title Value:	$4.00	$12.00	$20.00	£2.40	£7.20	£12.00

GREEN LANTERN CORPS, TALES OF THE

DC Comics,MS; 1 May 1981-3 Jul 1981

	$Good	$Fine	$N.Mint	£Good	£Fine	£N.Mint
1-3 origin Green Lantern & the Guardians retold						
	$0.30	$0.90	$1.50	£0.20	£0.60	£1.00
Title Value:	$0.90	$2.70	$4.50	£0.60	£1.80	£3.00

GREEN LANTERN GALLERY

DC Comics,OS; 1 Dec 1996

	$Good	$Fine	$N.Mint	£Good	£Fine	£N.Mint
1 ND pin-ups of Hal Jordan by George Perez, Walt Simonson, Bart Sears and others						
	$0.70	$2.10	$3.50	£0.50	£1.50	£2.50
Title Value:	$0.70	$2.10	$3.50	£0.50	£1.50	£2.50

GREEN LANTERN PLUS #1

DC Comics,OS; 1 Dec 1996

	$Good	$Fine	$N.Mint	£Good	£Fine	£N.Mint
1 ND 48pgs, The Ray appears; George Perez part cover art						
	$0.60	$1.80	$3.00	£0.40	£1.20	£2.00
Title Value:	$0.60	$1.80	$3.00	£0.40	£1.20	£2.00

GREEN LANTERN SPECIAL

DC Comics; 1 1988-2 1989

	$Good	$Fine	$N.Mint	£Good	£Fine	£N.Mint
1 48pgs	$0.30	$0.90	$1.50	£0.20	£0.60	£1.00
2 plotlines from Action Comics Weekly resolved						
	$0.30	$0.90	$1.50	£0.20	£0.60	£1.00
Title Value:	$0.60	$1.80	$3.00	£0.40	£1.20	£2.00

GREEN LANTERN/GREEN ARROW

DC Comics; 1 Oct 1983-7 Apr 1984

	$Good	$Fine	$N.Mint	£Good	£Fine	£N.Mint
1 52pgs, Neal Adams reprints begin from Green Lantern/Green Arrow #76						
	$0.60	$1.80	$3.00	£0.30	£0.90	£1.50
2-7 52pgs	$0.60	$1.80	$3.00	£0.30	£0.90	£1.50
Title Value:	$4.20	$12.60	$21.00	£2.10	£6.30	£10.50

GREEN LANTERN/SILVER SURFER

DC Comics/Marvel Comics Group,OS; 1 Jan 1996

	$Good	$Fine	$N.Mint	£Good	£Fine	£N.Mint
1 ND 48pgs, Ron Marz script, Darryl Banks and Terry Austin art						
	$1.00	$3.00	$5.00	£0.70	£2.10	£3.50
Title Value:	$1.00	$3.00	$5.00	£0.70	£2.10	£3.50

GREEN LANTERN: EMERALD DAWN

DC Comics,MS; 1 Dec 1989-6 May 1990

	$Good	$Fine	$N.Mint	£Good	£Fine	£N.Mint
1 origin retold	$0.60	$1.80	$3.00	£0.40	£1.20	£2.00
2-3	$0.50	$1.50	$2.50	£0.30	£0.90	£1.50
4-6	$0.40	$1.20	$2.00	£0.25	£0.75	£1.25
Title Value:	$2.80	$8.40	$14.00	£1.75	£5.25	£8.75
Trade Paperback (May 1991), reprints mini-series				£0.70	£2.10	£3.50

GREEN LANTERN: EMERALD DAWN II

DC Comics,MS; 1 Apr 1991-6 Sep 1991

	$Good	$Fine	$N.Mint	£Good	£Fine	£N.Mint
1-6	$0.40	$1.20	$2.00	£0.25	£0.75	£1.25
Title Value:	$2.40	$7.20	$12.00	£1.50	£4.50	£7.50

GREEN LANTERN: GANTHET'S TALE

DC Comics,OS; 1 Nov 1992

	$Good	$Fine	$N.Mint	£Good	£Fine	£N.Mint
1 64pgs, Larry Niven script, John Byrne art						
	$1.00	$3.00	$5.00	£0.70	£2.10	£3.50
Title Value:	$1.00	$3.00	$5.00	£0.70	£2.10	£3.50

GREEN LANTERN: MOSAIC

DC Comics; 1 Jun 1992-18 Nov 1993

	$Good	$Fine	$N.Mint	£Good	£Fine	£N.Mint
1 John Stewart (Green Lantern) begins						
	$0.25	$0.75	$1.25	£0.15	£0.45	£0.75
2	$0.25	$0.75	$1.25	£0.15	£0.45	£0.75
3 ties in with Eclipso: The Darkness Within and Guy Gardner: Reborn series						
	$0.25	$0.75	$1.25	£0.15	£0.45	£0.75
4-15	$0.25	$0.75	$1.25	£0.15	£0.45	£0.75
16 Flash, Power Girl and Martian Manhunter appear						
	$0.25	$0.75	$1.25	£0.15	£0.45	£0.75
17	$0.25	$0.75	$1.25	£0.15	£0.45	£0.75
18 Guy Gardner, Hal Jordan, Flash, Power Girl, Martian Manhunter appear with John Stewart						
	$0.25	$0.75	$1.25	£0.15	£0.45	£0.75
Title Value:	$4.50	$13.50	$22.50	£2.70	£8.10	£13.50

GREENHAVEN

Aircel; 1-3 1988

	$Good	$Fine	$N.Mint	£Good	£Fine	£N.Mint
1 ND Barry Blair script/art begins (colour)						
	$0.40	$1.20	$2.00	£0.25	£0.75	£1.25

	$Good	$Fine	$N.Mint	£Good	£Fine	£N.Mint
2 ND	*$0.40*	*$1.20*	*$2.00*	£0.25	£0.75	£1.25
3 ND conclusion in Elflord #21 (2nd Series)						
	$0.40	*$1.20*	*$2.00*	£0.25	£0.75	£1.25
Title Value:	*$1.20*	*$3.60*	*$6.00*	£0.75	£2.25	£3.75
GREENLOCK						
Aircel,OS; 1 Mar 1991						
1 ND Barry Blair script/art, black and white						
	$0.30	*$0.90*	*$1.50*	£0.20	£0.60	£1.00
Title Value:	*$0.30*	*$0.90*	*$1.50*	£0.20	£0.60	£1.00
GREGORY						
DC Comics/Piranha Press,OS; 1 1989						
1 ND Marc Hempel script/art						
	$1.50	*$4.50*	*$7.50*	£1.00	£3.00	£5.00
1 2nd printing, ND (1990)						
	$1.40	*$4.20*	*$7.00*	£0.90	£2.70	£4.50
Title Value:	*$2.90*	*$8.70*	*$14.50*	£1.90	£5.70	£9.50
GREGORY II						
DC Comics/Piranha Press,OS; 1993						
1 ND 64pgs, black and white						
	$0.90	*$2.70*	*$4.50*	£0.60	£1.80	£3.00
Title Value:	*$0.90*	*$2.70*	*$4.50*	£0.60	£1.80	£3.00
GREGORY III						
DC Comics/Piranha Press,OS; 1 Jul 1993						
1 ND 48pgs, Marc Hempel script/art						
	$1.00	*$3.00*	*$5.00*	£0.70	£2.10	£3.50
Title Value:	*$1.00*	*$3.00*	*$5.00*	£0.70	£2.10	£3.50
GREGORY IV: FAT BOY						
DC Comics/Piranha Press,OS; 1 Dec 1993						
1 ND Marc Hempel script/art						
	$1.00	*$3.00*	*$5.00*	£0.70	£2.10	£3.50
Title Value:	*$1.00*	*$3.00*	*$5.00*	£0.70	£2.10	£3.50
GRENDEL						
Comico; 1 Mar 1983-3 Feb 1984						
(see Primer #2)						
1 ND very scarce in the U.K.						
	$18.00	*$52.50*	*$90.00*	£10.00	£30.00	£50.00
2 ND scarce in the U.K.						
	$15.00	*$45.00*	*$75.00*	£8.00	£24.00	£40.00
3 ND scarce in the U.K.						
	$13.00	*$39.00*	*$65.00*	£7.00	£21.00	£35.00
Title Value:	*$46.00*	*$136.50*	*$230.00*	£25.00	£75.00	£125.00
GRENDEL (2ND SERIES)						
Comico; 1 Oct 1986-40 Feb 1990						
(see Mage)						
1 Christine Spar becomes Grendel, Wagner scripts, Pander Bros. art begins						
	$1.20	*$3.60*	*$6.00*	£0.80	£2.40	£4.00
1 2nd printing	*$0.80*	*$2.40*	*$4.00*	£0.50	£1.50	£2.50
2-3	*$0.80*	*$2.40*	*$4.00*	£0.60	£1.80	£3.00
4-10	*$0.70*	*$2.10*	*$3.50*	£0.50	£1.50	£2.50
11	*$0.60*	*$1.80*	*$3.00*	£0.40	£1.20	£2.00
12 last Pander Bros.						
	$0.60	*$1.80*	*$3.00*	£0.40	£1.20	£2.00
13-15 Bernie Mireault art						
	$0.60	*$1.80*	*$3.00*	£0.40	£1.20	£2.00
16 painted Mage back-up by Wagner begins						
	$1.20	*$3.60*	*$6.00*	£1.20	£3.60	£6.00
17-19 Mage back-up						
	$0.80	*$2.40*	*$4.00*	£0.60	£1.80	£3.00
20 Wagner art	*$0.60*	*$1.80*	*$3.00*	£0.30	£0.90	£1.50
21-22 Hannibal King art						
	$0.60	*$1.80*	*$3.00*	£0.30	£0.90	£1.50
23 Tim Sale art	*$0.60*	*$1.80*	*$3.00*	£0.30	£0.90	£1.50
24-25 Snyder/J.Geldhof art						
	$0.60	*$1.80*	*$3.00*	£0.30	£0.90	£1.50
26-32	*$0.60*	*$1.80*	*$3.00*	£0.30	£0.90	£1.50
33 44pgs	*$0.60*	*$1.80*	*$3.00*	£0.40	£1.20	£2.00
34-39	*$0.50*	*$1.50*	*$2.50*	£0.30	£0.90	£1.50
40 giant, scarce; flip-book featuring Grendel Tales Preview Special						
	$1.00	*$3.00*	*$5.00*	£0.70	£2.10	£3.50
Title Value:	*$27.50*	*$82.50*	*$136.50*	£17.80	£53.40	£89.00
Note: all Non-Distributed on the news-stands in the U.K.						
Grendel: Devil's Legacy Trade paperback						
(1988), reprints #1-12				£2.00	£6.00	£10.00
Hardcover, Limited Edition				£3.00	£9.00	£15.00
Grendel: Devil by the Deed, pink cover; re-tells story of original						
Grendel from Christine Spar's point of view				£1.50	£4.50	£7.50
2nd print, blue cover				£1.00	£3.00	£5.00
Dark Horse Edition (Aug 1993), new cover by Matt Wagner				£0.50	£1.50	£2.50
GRENDEL CLASSICS						
Dark Horse,MS; 1 Jul 1995-2 Aug 1995						
1 ND reprints issues 16 and 17 of original series with Matt Wagner art						
	$0.80	*$2.40*	*$4.00*	£0.50	£1.50	£2.50
2 ND reprints issues 18 and 19 from original series with Matt Wagner art						
	$0.80	*$2.40*	*$4.00*	£0.50	£1.50	£2.50
Title Value:	*$1.60*	*$4.80*	*$8.00*	£1.00	£3.00	£5.00
GRENDEL CYCLE						
Dark Horse,OS; nn Oct 1995						
nn ND 64pgs	*$1.20*	*$3.60*	*$6.00*	£0.80	£2.40	£4.00
Title Value:	*$1.20*	*$3.60*	*$6.00*	£0.80	£2.40	£4.00
GRENDEL TALES: DEVIL IN OUR MIDST						
Dark Horse,MS; 1 May 1994-5 Sep 1994						
1-5 ND Paul Grist art						

	$Good	$Fine	$N.Mint	£Good	£Fine	£N.Mint
	$0.60	*$1.80*	*$3.00*	£0.40	£1.20	£2.00
Title Value:	*$3.00*	*$9.00*	*$15.00*	£2.00	£6.00	£10.00
GRENDEL TALES: DEVIL MAY CARE						
Dark Horse,MS; 1 Dec 1995-6 May 1996						
1-6 ND Terry LaBan script, Peter Doherty art						
	$0.60	*$1.80*	*$3.00*	£0.40	£1.20	£2.00
Title Value:	*$3.60*	*$10.80*	*$18.00*	£2.40	£7.20	£12.00
GRENDEL TALES: DEVIL'S CHOICES						
Dark Horse,MS; 1 Mar 1995-4 Jun 1995						
1-4 ND Darko Macan script, Edvin Biukovic art with back-up feature by Matt Wagner						
	$0.60	*$1.80*	*$3.00*	£0.40	£1.20	£2.00
Title Value:	*$2.40*	*$7.20*	*$12.00*	£1.60	£4.80	£8.00
GRENDEL TALES: DEVILS & DEATHS						
Dark Horse,MS; 1 Oct 1994-2 Nov 1994						
1-2 ND Matt Wagner painted back-up story amd painted cover						
	$0.60	*$1.80*	*$3.00*	£0.40	£1.20	£2.00
Title Value:	*$1.20*	*$3.60*	*$6.00*	£0.80	£2.40	£4.00
GRENDEL TALES: FOUR DEVILS, ONE HELL						
Dark Horse,MS; 1 Aug 1993-6 Jan 1994						
1-6 ND Matt Wagner cover paintings and "creative direction"						
	$0.60	*$1.80*	*$3.00*	£0.40	£1.20	£2.00
Title Value:	*$3.60*	*$10.80*	*$18.00*	£2.40	£7.20	£12.00
Grendel Tales: Four Devils, One Hell (Nov 1994)						
Trade paperback reprints mini-series plus sketches				£2.40	£7.20	£12.00
GRENDEL TALES: HOMECOMING						
Dark Horse,MS; 1 Dec 1994-3 Feb 1995						
1-3 ND Pat McEwon script and art, painted cover by Matt Wagner						
	$0.60	*$1.80*	*$3.00*	£0.40	£1.20	£2.00
Title Value:	*$1.80*	*$5.40*	*$9.00*	£1.20	£3.60	£6.00
GRENDEL TALES: THE DEVIL'S HAMMER						
Dark Horse,MS; 1 Feb 1994-3 Apr 1994						
1-3 ND Bernie Mirault art						
	$0.60	*$1.80*	*$3.00*	£0.40	£1.20	£2.00
Title Value:	*$1.80*	*$5.40*	*$9.00*	£1.20	£3.60	£6.00
GRENDEL: DEVIL QUEST						
Dark Horse,OS; 1 Nov 1995						
1 ND 56pgs, Matt Wagner script and art						
	$1.00	*$3.00*	*$5.00*	£0.70	£2.10	£3.50
Title Value:	*$1.00*	*$3.00*	*$5.00*	£0.70	£2.10	£3.50
GRENDEL: DEVIL'S VAGARY						
Comico; nn 1987						
(see Comico Collection)						
nn rare in the U.K. 16pgs, Wagner script, Motter art, printed in black & red, published as part of the Comico Collection						
	$4.00	*$12.00*	*$20.00*	£5.00	£15.00	£25.00
Title Value:	*$4.00*	*$12.00*	*$20.00*	£5.00	£15.00	£25.00
GRENDEL: THE DEVIL INSIDE						
Comics,OS; 1 Jun 1989						
1 ND 80pgs, squarebound						
	$2.40	*$7.00*	*$12.00*	£1.60	£4.80	£8.00
Title Value:	*$2.40*	*$7.00*	*$12.00*	£1.60	£4.80	£8.00
GRENDEL: WAR CHILD						
Dark Horse,MS; 1 Aug 1992-10 Jun 1993						
1 ND Matt Wagner script and inks begin, Patrick McKeown pencils; picks up after events in Grendel #40, Simon Bisley painted covers begin						
	$0.90	*$2.70*	*$4.50*	£0.60	£1.80	£3.00
2 ND	*$0.80*	*$2.40*	*$4.00*	£0.50	£1.50	£2.50
3-9 ND	*$0.70*	*$2.10*	*$3.50*	£0.40	£1.20	£2.00
10 ND 48pgs, $3.50 cover						
	$0.90	*$2.70*	*$4.50*	£0.50	£1.50	£2.50
Title Value:	*$7.50*	*$22.50*	*$37.50*	£4.40	£13.20	£22.00
Grendel: War Child Limited Edition Hardcover (Oct 1994)						
1,000 signed and numbered copies, reprinting mini-series				£14.00	£42.00	£70.00
Grendel: War Child (1995)						
Trade paperback reprints mini-series plus covers				£2.40	£7.20	£12.00
(2nd print - Sep 1995)				£2.30	£6.90	£11.50
GREY						
Viz; 1 1988-9 1989						
1-9 ND 72pgs, black & white						
	$0.60	*$1.80*	*$3.00*	£0.40	£1.20	£2.00
Title Value:	*$5.40*	*$16.20*	*$27.00*	£3.60	£10.80	£18.00
GREYLORE						
Sirius; 1 Dec 1985-5 Sep 1986						
1-5 ND	*$0.40*	*$1.20*	*$2.00*	£0.25	£0.75	£1.25
Title Value:	*$2.00*	*$6.00*	*$10.00*	£1.25	£3.75	£6.25
GRID, THE						
Dark Horse; 1 Jul 1990-3 1990						
1 ND reprints Warlock 5 issues #1-5, new painted covers by Beauvais begin						
	$1.40	*$4.20*	*$7.00*	£0.90	£2.70	£4.50
2 ND reprints rest of Warlock 5 issues by Beauvais						
	$1.40	*$4.20*	*$7.00*	£0.90	£2.70	£4.50
3 ND new material	*$1.40*	*$4.20*	*$7.00*	£0.90	£2.70	£4.50
Title Value:	*$4.20*	*$12.60*	*$21.00*	£2.70	£8.10	£13.50
GRIFFIN						
Slave Labor; 1 Jul 1988-3 1988						
1-3 ND	*$0.40*	*$1.20*	*$2.00*	£0.25	£0.75	£1.25
Title Value:	*$1.20*	*$3.60*	*$6.00*	£0.75	£2.25	£3.75
GRIFFIN, THE						
DC Comics,MS; 1 Nov 1991-6 Apr 1992						
1-6 ND 48pgs, Matt Wagner cover						
	$0.80	*$2.40*	*$4.00*	£0.50	£1.50	£2.50
Title Value:	*$4.80*	*$14.40*	*$24.00*	£3.00	£9.00	£15.00

	$Good	$Fine	$N.Mint	£Good	£Fine	£N.Mint
Note: originally published by Slave Labor Graphics but never completed						

GRIFTER

Image; 1 May 1995-10 Mar 1996

	$Good	$Fine	$N.Mint	£Good	£Fine	£N.Mint
1 ND Wildstorm Rising part 5, continued in Deathblow #16; with two foil-bagged painted trading cards. Cover by Barry Windsor-Smith, Keith Giffen co-plot and pencils						
	$0.60	$1.80	$3.00	£0.40	£1.20	£2.00
1 Newstand Edition, ND without trading cards						
	$0.50	$1.50	$2.50	£0.30	£0.90	£1.50
2-10 ND	$0.50	$1.50	$2.50	£0.30	£0.90	£1.50
Title Value:	$5.60	$16.80	$28.00	£3.40	£10.20	£17.00

GRIFTER (2ND SERIES)

Image; 1 Jul 1996-present

	$Good	$Fine	$N.Mint	£Good	£Fine	£N.Mint
1-8 ND	$0.50	$1.50	$2.50	£0.30	£0.90	£1.50
Title Value:	$4.00	$12.00	$20.00	£2.40	£7.20	£12.00

GRIFTER AND THE MASK

Dark Horse,MS; 1 Sep 1996-2 Oct 1996

	$Good	$Fine	$N.Mint	£Good	£Fine	£N.Mint
1-2 ND Steven Seagle script, Luciano Lima and Joe Pimentel art						
	$0.50	$1.50	$2.50	£0.30	£0.90	£1.50
Title Value:	$1.00	$3.00	$5.00	£0.60	£1.80	£3.00

GRIFTER/BADROCK

Image,MS; 1 Oct 1995-3 Dec 1995

	$Good	$Fine	$N.Mint	£Good	£Fine	£N.Mint
1 ND Rob Liefeld script and art with Chap Yaep and Jonathan Sibal						
	$0.50	$1.50	$2.50	£0.30	£0.90	£1.50
2 ND	$0.50	$1.50	$2.50	£0.30	£0.90	£1.50
3 ND	$0.70	$2.10	$3.50	£0.50	£1.50	£2.50
Title Value:	$1.70	$5.10	$8.50	£1.10	£3.30	£5.50

GRIFTER/SHI

Image,MS; 1 Apr 1996-2 May 1996

	$Good	$Fine	$N.Mint	£Good	£Fine	£N.Mint
1 ND Brandon Choi and Peter Gutierrez script, Jim Lee, William Tucci and Travis Charest art						
	$0.60	$1.80	$3.00	£0.40	£1.20	£2.00
2 ND	$0.60	$1.80	$3.00	£0.40	£1.20	£2.00
Title Value:	$1.20	$3.60	$6.00	£0.80	£2.40	£4.00

GRIFTER/SHI HARDBOUND COLLECTOR'S EDITION

Image,OS; nn Dec 1995

	$Good	$Fine	$N.Mint	£Good	£Fine	£N.Mint
nn A, ND 64pgs, Jim Lee dust-jacket						
	$6.00	$18.00	$30.00	£4.00	£12.00	£20.00
nn B, ND 64pgs, William Tucci dust-jacket						
	$6.00	$18.00	$30.00	£4.00	£12.00	£20.00
nn Signed & Numbered A, ND 64pgs, - signed by Jim Lee, 500 copies						
	$15.00	$45.00	$75.00	£10.00	£30.00	£50.00
nn Signed & Numbered B, ND 64pgs, - signed by William Tucci						
	$15.00	$45.00	$75.00	£10.00	£30.00	£50.00
nn Signed & Numbered C, ND 64pgs, - signed by Travis Charest, 1000 copies						
	$9.00	$27.00	$45.00	£13.00	£39.00	£65.00
nn Signed & Numbered D, ND 64pgs, - signed by Troy Hubbs, 500 copies						
	$10.00	$30.00	$50.00	£7.00	£21.00	£35.00
Title Value:	$61.00	$183.00	$305.00	£48.00	£144.00	£240.00

GRIFTER: ONE-SHOT

Image,OS; 1 Jan 1995

	$Good	$Fine	$N.Mint	£Good	£Fine	£N.Mint
1 ND 48pgs, squarebound, Steve Seagle script, Dan Norton pencils						
	$1.00	$3.00	$5.00	£0.70	£2.10	£3.50
Title Value:	$1.00	$3.00	$5.00	£0.70	£2.10	£3.50

GRIM GHOST

Atlas; 1 Jan 1975-3 Jul 1975

	$Good	$Fine	$N.Mint	£Good	£Fine	£N.Mint
1-3 distributed in the U.K.						
	$0.25	$0.75	$1.50	£0.15	£0.50	£1.00
Title Value:	$0.75	$2.25	$4.50	£0.45	£1.50	£3.00

GRIMJACK

First; 1 Aug 1984-81 Jan 1991

(see Starslayer)

	$Good	$Fine	$N.Mint	£Good	£Fine	£N.Mint
1-21 ND	$0.40	$1.20	$2.00	£0.25	£0.75	£1.25
22 ND Brian Bolland backup (18pgs)						
	$0.40	$1.20	$2.00	£0.30	£0.90	£1.50
23-25 ND	$0.40	$1.20	$2.00	£0.25	£0.75	£1.25
26 ND 1st colour Teenage Mutant Ninja Turtles story						
	$0.50	$1.50	$2.50	£0.30	£0.90	£1.50
27-45 ND	$0.40	$1.20	$2.00	£0.25	£0.75	£1.25
46 ND Eddie Current in colour						
	$0.60	$1.80	$3.00	£0.40	£1.20	£2.00
47-50 ND	$0.40	$1.20	$2.00	£0.25	£0.75	£1.25
51-54 ND	$0.30	$0.90	$1.50	£0.20	£0.60	£1.00
55 ND 1st appearance new Grimjack						
	$0.30	$0.90	$1.50	£0.25	£0.75	£1.25
56-60 ND	$0.30	$0.90	$1.50	£0.20	£0.60	£1.00
61 ND no logo on cover						
	$0.30	$0.90	$1.50	£0.20	£0.60	£1.00
62-65 ND	$0.30	$0.90	$1.50	£0.20	£0.60	£1.00
66-67 ND Demon Wars						
	$0.30	$0.90	$1.50	£0.20	£0.60	£1.00
68-74 ND	$0.30	$0.90	$1.50	£0.20	£0.60	£1.00
75 ND 48pgs, squarebound, final confrontation with The Major, fold-out map of Cynosure						
	$0.80	$2.40	$4.00	£0.60	£1.80	£3.00
76-81 ND	$0.30	$0.90	$1.50	£0.20	£0.60	£1.00
Title Value:	$30.10	$90.30	$150.50	£19.40	£58.20	£97.00
Demon Knight Graphic Novel (1990)				£1.00	£3.00	£5.00

GRIMJACK CASEFILES

First; 1 Sep 1990-6 Feb 1991

	$Good	$Fine	$N.Mint	£Good	£Fine	£N.Mint
1 ND reprints from "Starslayer" begin						
	$0.40	$1.20	$2.00	£0.25	£0.75	£1.25
2 ND	$0.40	$1.20	$2.00	£0.25	£0.75	£1.25
3 ND reprints Grimjack #1						
	$0.40	$1.20	$2.00	£0.25	£0.75	£1.25
4 ND reprints Grimjack #2						
	$0.40	$1.20	$2.00	£0.25	£0.75	£1.25
5-6 ND	$0.40	$1.20	$2.00	£0.25	£0.75	£1.25
Title Value:	$2.40	$7.20	$12.00	£1.50	£4.50	£7.50

GRIMM TALES

Eclipse,OS; 1 Jul 1993

	$Good	$Fine	$N.Mint	£Good	£Fine	£N.Mint
1 ND	$1.20	$3.60	$6.00	£0.80	£2.40	£4.00
Title Value:	$1.20	$3.60	$6.00	£0.80	£2.40	£4.00

GRIMM'S GHOST STORIES

Gold Key; 1 Jan 1972-54 Nov 1979; Whitman; 55 Mar 1980-60 1982

	$Good	$Fine	$N.Mint	£Good	£Fine	£N.Mint
1 scarce in the U.K. painted covers begin (unless otherwise noted)						
	$1.25	$3.75	$7.50	£0.65	£2.00	£4.00
2	$0.65	$2.00	$4.00	£0.40	£1.25	£2.50
3-5	$0.55	$1.75	$3.50	£0.30	£1.00	£2.00
6-10	$0.50	$1.50	$3.00	£0.25	£0.75	£1.50
11-42	$0.40	$1.25	$2.50	£0.20	£0.60	£1.25
43 48pgs, photo cover						
	$0.40	$1.25	$2.50	£0.25	£0.75	£1.50
44 48pgs	$0.40	$1.25	$2.50	£0.25	£0.75	£1.50
45 photo cover	$0.30	$1.00	$2.00	£0.20	£0.60	£1.25
46-54	$0.30	$1.00	$2.00	£0.20	£0.60	£1.25
55 1st Whitman issue						
	$0.40	$1.20	$2.00	£0.25	£0.75	£1.25
56 last painted cover						
	$0.40	$1.20	$2.00	£0.25	£0.75	£1.25
57 line-drawn covers begin						
	$0.30	$0.90	$1.50	£0.20	£0.60	£1.00
58-60	$0.30	$0.90	$1.50	£0.20	£0.60	£1.00
Title Value:	$24.65	$77.00	$141.00	£13.40	£40.60	£82.00

Note: most issues distributed in the U.K. if irregularly

Green Lantern/Green Arrow #1

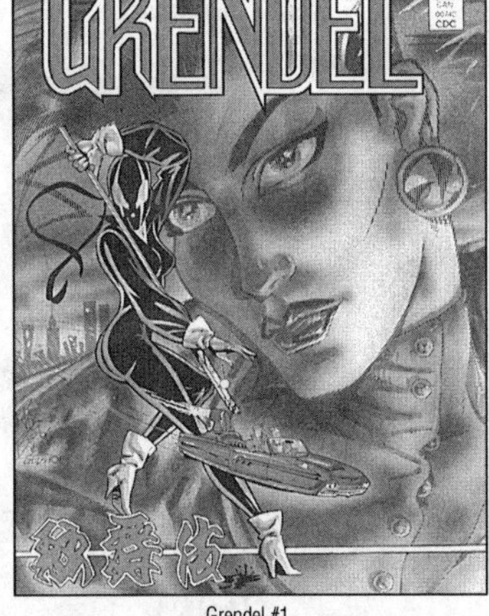

Grendel #1

Grifter One-Shot

GRIMMAX, THE GREAT

Defiant,OS; 0 Aug 1994

	$Good	$Fine	$N.Mint	£Good	£Fine	£N.Mint
0 ND 8pgs, free with Hero Illustrated; colour	$0.15	$0.45	$0.75	£0.10	£0.30	£0.50
Title Value:	$0.15	$0.45	$0.75	£0.10	£0.30	£0.50

GRIPS

Silverwolf/Greater Mercury Comics; 1 Sep 1986-4 1987

	$Good	$Fine	$N.Mint	£Good	£Fine	£N.Mint
1 ND Tim Vigil art	$2.00	$6.00	$10.00	£1.00	£3.00	£5.00
1 2nd printing, ND scarce in the U.K. (bootleg copy only)	$1.50	$4.50	$7.50	£0.70	£2.10	£3.50
2-4 ND Tim Vigil art	$1.50	$4.50	$7.50	£0.80	£2.40	£4.00
Title Value:	$8.00	$24.00	$40.00	£4.10	£12.30	£20.50

GRIPS (2ND SERIES)

Silverwolf/Greater Mercury Comics; 1 1989-12 1991

	$Good	$Fine	$N.Mint	£Good	£Fine	£N.Mint
1 ND black and white begins	$0.50	$1.50	$2.50	£0.30	£0.90	£1.50
1 Special Edition, ND (May 1992) - no cover copy or logos, 2,500 copies	$1.50	$4.50	$7.50	£0.80	£2.40	£4.00
2-6 ND	$0.40	$1.20	$2.00	£0.25	£0.75	£1.25
7-9 ND Web of the Spyder story	$0.40	$1.20	$2.00	£0.25	£0.75	£1.25
10-11 ND	$0.40	$1.20	$2.00	£0.25	£0.75	£1.25
12 ND Mistaken Identity story	$0.40	$1.20	$2.00	£0.25	£0.75	£1.25
Title Value:	$6.40	$19.20	$32.00	£3.85	£11.55	£19.25
Special Graphic Novel 1 (Nov 1990) 128pgs squarebound, black and white				£1.20	£3.60	£6.00
Gold Edition Special Graphic Novel 1 limited print run, gold-trimmed cover				£2.00	£6.00	£10.00
2nd printing (Aug 1991)				£1.10	£3.30	£5.50

GRIPS ADVENTURES

Greater Mercury Comics; 1 May 1989-10 1990

	$Good	$Fine	$N.Mint	£Good	£Fine	£N.Mint
1 ND DS featuring Legion X-II	$0.40	$1.20	$2.00	£0.25	£0.75	£1.25
2-6 ND	$0.40	$1.20	$2.00	£0.25	£0.75	£1.25
7-8 ND One Man's Army story	$0.40	$1.20	$2.00	£0.25	£0.75	£1.25
9-10 ND Chasing Time story	$0.40	$1.20	$2.00	£0.25	£0.75	£1.25
Title Value:	$4.00	$12.00	$20.00	£2.50	£7.50	£12.50

GRIPS SPECIAL

Greater Mercury Comics,OS; 1 Apr 1992

	$Good	$Fine	$N.Mint	£Good	£Fine	£N.Mint
1 ND anorexia nervosa story	$0.40	$1.20	$2.00	£0.25	£0.75	£1.25
Title Value:	$0.40	$1.20	$2.00	£0.25	£0.75	£1.25

GRIPS VOLUME TWO

Greater Mercury Comics; 1 Aug 1989-12 1991

	$Good	$Fine	$N.Mint	£Good	£Fine	£N.Mint
1 ND	$0.50	$1.50	$2.50	£0.30	£0.90	£1.50
1 Special Edition, ND 2,500 copies, alternate cover	$0.90	$2.70	$4.50	£0.60	£1.80	£3.00
2-7 ND	$0.40	$1.20	$2.00	£0.25	£0.75	£1.25
8-9 ND Web of the Spider story	$0.40	$1.20	$2.00	£0.25	£0.75	£1.25
10-11 ND River of Blood story	$0.40	$1.20	$2.00	£0.25	£0.75	£1.25
12 ND	$0.40	$1.20	$2.00	£0.25	£0.75	£1.25
Title Value:	$5.80	$17.40	$29.00	£3.65	£10.95	£18.25

GROO

Pacific; 1 Dec 1982-8 Mar 1984

(see Destroyer Duck #1, Groo [Marvel], Starslayer #5)

	$Good	$Fine	$N.Mint	£Good	£Fine	£N.Mint
1 ND	$7.00	$21.00	$35.00	£4.00	£12.00	£20.00
2 ND	$4.00	$12.00	$20.00	£2.50	£7.50	£12.50
3-6 ND	$3.00	$9.00	$15.00	£2.00	£6.00	£10.00
7 ND very scarce in the U.K.	$3.00	$9.00	$15.00	£2.50	£7.50	£12.50
8 ND scarce in the U.K.	$3.00	$9.00	$15.00	£2.00	£6.00	£10.00
Title Value:	$29.00	$87.00	$145.00	£19.00	£57.00	£95.00

GROO (2ND SERIES)

Image; 1 Dec 1994-12 Nov 1995

	$Good	$Fine	$N.Mint	£Good	£Fine	£N.Mint
1 ND Sergio Aragones with Mark Evanier begins	$0.40	$1.20	$2.00	£0.25	£0.75	£1.25
2-12 ND	$0.40	$1.20	$2.00	£0.25	£0.75	£1.25
Title Value:	$4.80	$14.40	$24.00	£3.00	£9.00	£15.00

GROO CHRONICLES

Marvel Comics Group/Epic,MS; 1 Jul 1989-6 Feb 1990

	$Good	$Fine	$N.Mint	£Good	£Fine	£N.Mint
1 ND squarebound, reprints of Pacific Groo/Eclipse Groo one-shot stories, re-coloured with new art by Aragones and new text by Evanier	$0.80	$2.40	$4.00	£0.50	£1.50	£2.50
2-6 ND	$0.60	$1.80	$3.00	£0.40	£1.20	£2.00
Title Value:	$3.80	$11.40	$19.00	£2.50	£7.50	£12.50
Hardback (by Graphitti), (1991), Signed.				£5.25	£15.75	£26.25

GROO SPECIAL

Eclipse,OS; 1 Oct 1984

	$Good	$Fine	$N.Mint	£Good	£Fine	£N.Mint
1 ND scarce in the U.K.	$6.00	$18.00	$30.00	£5.00	£15.00	£25.00
Title Value:	$6.00	$18.00	$30.00	£5.00	£15.00	£25.00

GROO THE WANDERER

Marvel Comics Group/Epic; 1 Mar 1985-120 Jan 1995

(see also Groo [Pacific], Groo Special [Eclipse], Destroyer Duck #1 [Eclipse], Starslayer #5 [First], Marvel Graphic Novel)

	$Good	$Fine	$N.Mint	£Good	£Fine	£N.Mint
1 ND Sergio Aragones art begins	$2.00	$6.00	$10.00	£2.00	£6.00	£10.00
2 ND	$1.20	$3.60	$6.00	£1.50	£4.50	£7.50
3 ND	$1.00	$3.00	$5.00	£1.20	£3.60	£6.00
4 ND	$1.00	$3.00	$5.00	£1.00	£3.00	£5.00
5-6 ND scarce in the U.K.	$1.00	$3.00	$5.00	£1.20	£3.60	£6.00
7 ND very scarce in the U.K.	$0.80	$2.40	$4.00	£1.30	£3.90	£6.50
8-10 ND	$0.80	$2.40	$4.00	£0.80	£2.40	£4.00
11-12 ND	$0.60	$1.80	$3.00	£0.60	£1.80	£3.00
13-30	$0.60	$1.80	$3.00	£0.40	£1.20	£2.00
31-38 ND	$0.40	$1.20	$2.00	£0.35	£1.05	£1.75
39-40	$0.40	$1.20	$2.00	£0.25	£0.75	£1.25
41-49	$0.30	$0.90	$1.50	£0.20	£0.60	£1.00
50 LD in the U.K. DS	$0.40	$1.20	$2.00	£0.25	£0.75	£1.25
51-54	$0.30	$0.90	$1.50	£0.20	£0.60	£1.00
55 LD in the U.K.	$0.30	$0.90	$1.50	£0.25	£0.75	£1.25
56-79	$0.30	$0.90	$1.50	£0.20	£0.60	£1.00
80 Thaiis the Warrior Woman introduced	$0.30	$0.90	$1.50	£0.20	£0.60	£1.00
81-86	$0.30	$0.90	$1.50	£0.20	£0.60	£1.00
87 ND $2.25 covers begin	$0.40	$1.20	$2.00	£0.25	£0.75	£1.25
88-99 ND	$0.40	$1.20	$2.00	£0.25	£0.75	£1.25
100 ND DS	$0.60	$1.80	$3.00	£0.40	£1.20	£2.00
101-120 ND	$0.40	$1.20	$2.00	£0.25	£0.75	£1.25
Title Value:	$54.10	$162.30	$264.50	£41.45	£124.35	£207.25
The Groo Adventurer Trade paperback (1991), reprints issues #1-4				£1.00	£3.00	£5.00
The Groo Adventurer Trade paperback (Mar 1992), reprints issues #5-8				£1.10	£3.00	£5.00
The Groo Carnival Trade paperback (Apr 1992), reprints issues #9-12, new foreword by Evanier				£1.00	£3.00	£5.00
The Groo Adventurer Trade paperback (1992), reprints issues #13-16				£1.00	£3.00	£5.00
Groo: Expose Trade paperback (Apr 1993), reprints issues #17-20				£1.00	£3.00	£5.00
Groo: Festival Trade paperback (Oct 1993), reprints issues #21-24				£1.50	£4.50	£7.50
Groo: Garden Trade paperback (Apr 1994), reprints issues #25-28				£1.50	£4.50	£7.50

Note: Evanier/Aragones scripts, Aragones art in all.

GROOTLORE

Fantagraphics,MS; 1 Mar 1989-2 Apr 1989

	$Good	$Fine	$N.Mint	£Good	£Fine	£N.Mint
1-2 ND Peter Gullerud script and art, black and white	$0.30	$0.90	$1.50	£0.20	£0.60	£1.00
Title Value:	$0.60	$1.80	$3.00	£0.40	£1.20	£2.00

GROOVY

Marvel Comics Group; 1 Mar 1968-3 Jul 1968

	$Good	$Fine	$N.Mint	£Good	£Fine	£N.Mint
1 rare in the U.K. features The Monkees	$5.00	$15.00	$35.00	£2.10	£6.25	£15.00
2-3 rare in the U.K.	$3.55	$10.50	$25.00	£1.40	£4.25	£10.00
Title Value:	$12.10	$36.00	$85.00	£4.90	£14.75	£35.00

Note: no CCA code on any of the comics

GROUND POUND COMIX

Blackthorne; nn Jan 1987

	$Good	$Fine	$N.Mint	£Good	£Fine	£N.Mint
nn ND 52pgs, all John Pound reprints	$0.50	$1.50	$2.50	£0.30	£0.90	£1.50
Title Value:	$0.50	$1.50	$2.50	£0.30	£0.90	£1.50

GROUND ZERO

Eternity,MS; 1 Nov 1991-4 Feb 1992

	$Good	$Fine	$N.Mint	£Good	£Fine	£N.Mint
1-4 ND	$0.50	$1.50	$2.50	£0.30	£0.90	£1.50
Title Value:	$2.00	$6.00	$10.00	£1.20	£3.60	£6.00

GROUP LARUE, THE

Innovation,MS; 1 Sep 1989-3 Nov 1989

	$Good	$Fine	$N.Mint	£Good	£Fine	£N.Mint
1-3 ND Mike Baron plot, colour	$0.30	$0.90	$1.50	£0.20	£0.60	£1.00
Title Value:	$0.90	$2.70	$4.50	£0.60	£1.80	£3.00

GRUNTS

Mirage Studios,OS; 1 Nov 1987

(see Teenage Mutant Ninja Turtles)

	$Good	$Fine	$N.Mint	£Good	£Fine	£N.Mint
1 ND Triceraton story	$0.90	$2.70	$4.50	£0.60	£1.80	£3.00
Title Value:	$0.90	$2.70	$4.50	£0.60	£1.80	£3.00

GUARDIANS OF METROPOLIS, THE

DC Comics,MS; 1 Nov 1994-4 Feb 1995

	$Good	$Fine	$N.Mint	£Good	£Fine	£N.Mint
1-4 The Guardian and The Newsboy Legion	$0.25	$0.75	$1.25	£0.15	£0.45	£0.75
Title Value:	$1.00	$3.00	$5.00	£0.60	£1.80	£3.00

GUARDIANS OF THE GALAXY

Marvel Comics Group; 1 Jul 1990-62 Jul 1995

(see Defenders, Marvel Team Up)

	$Good	$Fine	$N.Mint	£Good	£Fine	£N.Mint
1 ND Valentino art begins	$0.60	$1.80	$3.00	£0.50	£1.50	£2.50
2-3 ND	$0.50	$1.50	$2.50	£0.30	£0.90	£1.50
4-6 ND	$0.40	$1.20	$2.00	£0.25	£0.75	£1.25
7 ND George Perez inks (1st Marvel work for some years)	$0.40	$1.20	$2.00	£0.25	£0.75	£1.25
8 ND	$0.40	$1.20	$2.00	£0.25	£0.75	£1.25
9-10 ND World of Mutants						

Issue	$Good	$Fine	$N.Mint	£Good	£Fine	£N.Mint
	$0.40	*$1.20*	*$2.00*	£0.25	£0.75	£1.25
11-12 ND World of Mutants						
	$0.30	*$0.90*	*$1.50*	£0.20	£0.60	£1.00
13 Ghost Rider of the 31st Century appears						
	$0.30	*$0.90*	*$1.50*	£0.20	£0.60	£1.00
14 Ghost Rider of the 31st Century appears						
	$0.30	*$0.90*	*$1.50*	£0.25	£0.75	£1.25
15 LD in the U.K.	*$0.30*	*$0.90*	*$1.50*	£0.25	£0.75	£1.25
16 DS Martinex loses hand						
	$0.30	*$0.90*	*$1.50*	£0.25	£0.75	£1.25
17 new direction for title, 1st appearance Crazy Nate						
	$0.30	*$0.90*	*$1.50*	£0.20	£0.60	£1.00
18 Crazy Nate undergoes operation on eye - it is replaced with a bionic one; thought at one point to be the 1st origin of Cable but now disproved						
	$0.30	*$0.90*	*$1.50*	£0.20	£0.60	£1.00
19 1st appearance Talon, Crazy Nate shown with glowing eye (thought at one point to be proof that Nathan Summers is Cable and now not the case)						
	$0.30	*$0.90*	*$1.50*	£0.20	£0.60	£1.00
20	*$0.30*	*$0.90*	*$1.50*	£0.20	£0.60	£1.00
21 $1.25 cover begins						
	$0.25	*$0.75*	*$1.25*	£0.20	£0.60	£1.00
22 ND Starhawk returns						
	$0.25	*$0.75*	*$1.25*	£0.20	£0.60	£1.00
23 Starhawk appears, Mark Texeira art						
	$0.25	*$0.75*	*$1.25*	£0.20	£0.60	£1.00
24 LD in the U.K. Silver Surfer appears						
	$0.25	*$0.75*	*$1.25*	£0.25	£0.75	£1.25
25 LD in the U.K. 48pgs, Silver Surfer appears, foil-stamped cover ("prismatic")						
	$0.60	*$1.80*	*$3.00*	£0.40	£1.20	£2.00
25 2nd printing, non foil-cover						
	$0.50	*$1.50*	*$2.50*	£0.30	£0.90	£1.50
26 "secret" origin told						
	$0.25	*$0.75*	*$1.25*	£0.15	£0.45	£0.75
27-28 Infinity War X-over						
	$0.25	*$0.75*	*$1.25*	£0.15	£0.45	£0.75
29 Infinity War X-over, Dr. Octopus appears						
	$0.25	*$0.75*	*$1.25*	£0.15	£0.45	£0.75
30	*$0.25*	*$0.75*	*$1.25*	£0.15	£0.45	£0.75
31 Captain America appears						
	$0.25	*$0.75*	*$1.25*	£0.15	£0.45	£0.75
32-33 Dr. Strange appears						
	$0.25	*$0.75*	*$1.25*	£0.15	£0.45	£0.75
34-36	*$0.25*	*$0.75*	*$1.25*	£0.15	£0.45	£0.75
37 Dr. Doom appears						
	$0.25	*$0.75*	*$1.25*	£0.15	£0.45	£0.75
38 Inhumans appear						
	$0.25	*$0.75*	*$1.25*	£0.15	£0.45	£0.75
39 LD in the U.K. 48pgs, Rancor vs. Dr. Doom (wearing Wolverive's exo-skeleton)						
	$0.50	*$1.50*	*$2.50*	£0.30	£0.90	£1.50
40-43 Thor of 31st Century appears						
	$0.25	*$0.75*	*$1.25*	£0.15	£0.45	£0.75
44-47	*$0.25*	*$0.75*	*$1.25*	£0.15	£0.45	£0.75
48 with free Spiderman and his Deadly Foes card sheet						
	$0.25	*$0.75*	*$1.25*	£0.15	£0.45	£0.75
49	*$0.25*	*$0.75*	*$1.25*	£0.15	£0.45	£0.75
50	*$0.40*	*$1.20*	*$2.00*	£0.25	£0.75	£1.25
50 Direct Market Edition, ND 48pgs, - foil embossed cover; Future History part 1, continued in Galactic Guardians #1						
	$0.50	*$1.50*	*$2.50*	£0.30	£0.90	£1.50
51-53	*$0.25*	*$0.75*	*$1.25*	£0.15	£0.45	£0.75
54 Spiderman appears						
	$0.25	*$0.75*	*$1.25*	£0.15	£0.45	£0.75
55-59	*$0.25*	*$0.75*	*$1.25*	£0.15	£0.45	£0.75
60 30th Century Silver Surfer appears						
	$0.25	*$0.75*	*$1.25*	£0.15	£0.45	£0.75
61	*$0.25*	*$0.75*	*$1.25*	£0.15	£0.45	£0.75
62 48pgs	*$0.50*	*$1.50*	*$2.50*	£0.25	£0.75	£1.25
Title Value:	*$19.90*	*$59.70*	*$99.50*	£12.75	£38.25	£63.75
The Quest for the Shield (Apr 1992)						
Trade paperback, reprints issues #1-6, new cover by Jim Valentino				£1.40	£4.20	£7.00

GUARDIANS OF THE GALAXY ANNUAL

Marvel Comics Group; 1 Jul 1991-4 1994

Issue	$Good	$Fine	$N.Mint	£Good	£Fine	£N.Mint
1 ND The Korvac Quest, continued from Silver Surfer Annual #4						
	$0.50	*$1.50*	*$2.50*	£0.30	£0.90	£1.50
2 ND The System Bytes part 4 (of 4), Ghost Rider and Firelord appear, continued from Wonder Man Annual #1						
	$0.50	*$1.50*	*$2.50*	£0.30	£0.90	£1.50
3 ND 64pgs, pre-bagged with trading card introducing Cuchulain						
	$0.50	*$1.50*	*$2.50*	£0.30	£0.90	£1.50
4 ND 64pgs	*$0.50*	*$1.50*	*$2.50*	£0.30	£0.90	£1.50
Title Value:	*$2.00*	*$6.00*	*$10.00*	£1.20	£3.60	£6.00

GUMBY 3-D

Blackthorne;(3-D Series #10,#14,#17,#21,#28,#33,#38); 1 Oct 1986-7 Apr 1988

Issue	$Good	$Fine	$N.Mint	£Good	£Fine	£N.Mint
1-7 ND all come with 3-D bound-in glasses (25% less if without glasses)						
	$0.50	*$1.50*	*$2.50*	£0.30	£0.90	£1.50
Title Value:	*$3.50*	*$10.50*	*$17.50*	£2.10	£6.30	£10.50

GUMBY'S SUMMER FUN SPECIAL

Comico; 1 Jul 1987

Issue	$Good	$Fine	$N.Mint	£Good	£Fine	£N.Mint
1 ND Bob Burden script, Art Adams art and cover						
	$0.80	*$2.40*	*$4.00*	£0.50	£1.50	£2.50
Title Value:	*$0.80*	*$2.40*	*$4.00*	£0.50	£1.50	£2.50

GUMBY'S WINTER FUN SPECIAL

Comico; 1 Dec 1988

Issue	$Good	$Fine	$N.Mint	£Good	£Fine	£N.Mint
1 ND 40pgs, Steve Purcell script, Art Adams art						
	$0.80	*$2.40*	*$4.00*	£0.50	£1.50	£2.50
Title Value:	*$0.80*	*$2.40*	*$4.00*	£0.50	£1.50	£2.50

GUN FURY

Aircel; 1 Jan 1988-10 1988

Issue	$Good	$Fine	$N.Mint	£Good	£Fine	£N.Mint
1 ND	*$0.80*	*$2.40*	*$4.00*	£0.50	£1.50	£2.50
2-3 ND	*$0.60*	*$1.80*	*$3.00*	£0.40	£1.20	£2.00
4-10 ND	*$0.50*	*$1.50*	*$2.50*	£0.30	£0.90	£1.50
Title Value:	*$5.50*	*$16.50*	*$27.50*	£3.40	£10.20	£17.00

GUN FURY RETURNS

Aircel,MS; 1 Aug 1990-4 Nov 1990

Issue	$Good	$Fine	$N.Mint	£Good	£Fine	£N.Mint
1-4 ND	*$0.40*	*$1.20*	*$2.00*	£0.25	£0.75	£1.25
Title Value:	*$1.60*	*$4.80*	*$8.00*	£1.00	£3.00	£5.00

GUN RUNNER

Marvel UK,MS; 1 Oct 1993-3 Dec 1993

Issue	$Good	$Fine	$N.Mint	£Good	£Fine	£N.Mint
1 pre-bagged with trading cards, Dan Abnett/Andy Lanning script begins, Terry Clarke art; Ghost Rider appears						
	$0.50	*$1.50*	*$2.50*	£0.30	£0.90	£1.50
2 Ghost Rider appears; Anthony Williams art						
	$0.30	*$0.90*	*$1.50*	£0.20	£0.60	£1.00
3 Anthony Williams art						
	$0.30	*$0.90*	*$1.50*	£0.20	£0.60	£1.00
Title Value:	*$1.10*	*$3.30*	*$5.50*	£0.70	£2.10	£3.50

Note: originally solicited as a six issue mini-series

GUNFIGHTERS, THE

Charlton;51 Oct 1966-52 Oct 1967; 53 Jun 1979-85 Jul 1984

(formerly Kid Montana #1-50)

Issue	$Good	$Fine	$N.Mint	£Good	£Fine	£N.Mint
51-52 distributed in the U.K.						
	$0.85	*$2.55*	*$6.00*	£0.40	£1.25	£3.00
53-70 distributed in the U.K.						
	$0.65	*$2.00*	*$4.00*	£0.40	£1.25	£2.50
71-85 distributed in the U.K.						
	$0.60	*$1.80*	*$3.00*	£0.40	£1.20	£2.00
Title Value:	*$22.40*	*$68.10*	*$129.00*	£14.00	£43.00	£81.00

Note: Williamson reprints #53,54

GUNFIRE

DC Comics; 0 Oct 1994; 1 May 1994-13 Jun 1995

Issue	$Good	$Fine	$N.Mint	£Good	£Fine	£N.Mint
0 (Oct 1994) Zero Hour X-over, origin retold						
	$0.40	*$1.20*	*$2.00*	£0.25	£0.75	£1.25
1 Len Wein script, Steve Irwin and Brian Garvey art						
	$0.40	*$1.20*	*$2.00*	£0.25	£0.75	£1.25
2-5	*$0.30*	*$0.90*	*$1.50*	£0.20	£0.60	£1.00
6 new costume	*$0.30*	*$0.90*	*$1.50*	£0.20	£0.60	£1.00
7-13	*$0.30*	*$0.90*	*$1.50*	£0.20	£0.60	£1.00
Title Value:	*$4.40*	*$13.20*	*$22.00*	£2.90	£8.70	£14.50

GUNHAWKS, THE

Marvel Comics Group; 1 Oct 1972-7 Oct 1973

Issue	$Good	$Fine	$N.Mint	£Good	£Fine	£N.Mint
1 ND Reno Jones and Kid Cassidy begin; Gary Friedrich script and Sid Shores art begins						
	$0.80	*$2.50*	*$5.00*	£0.50	£1.50	£3.00
2-5 ND	*$0.55*	*$1.75*	*$3.50*	£0.30	£1.00	£2.00
6 ND Kid Cassidy dies; Dick Ayers and Vince Coletta art						
	$0.55	*$1.75*	*$3.50*	£0.30	£1.00	£2.00
7 titled Reno Jones, Gunhawk; Gardner Fox script						
	$0.55	*$1.75*	*$3.50*	£0.25	£0.85	£1.75
Title Value:	*$4.10*	*$13.00*	*$26.00*	£2.25	£7.35	£14.75

GUNHED

Viz,MS; 1 Jan 1991-3 May 1991

Issue	$Good	$Fine	$N.Mint	£Good	£Fine	£N.Mint
1-3 ND 48pgs, 1st full colour series from Viz, measures 7" x 9", squarebound; story and art by Kia Asamiya						
	$1.00	*$3.00*	*$5.00*	£0.70	£2.10	£3.50
Title Value:	*$3.00*	*$9.00*	*$15.00*	£2.10	£6.30	£10.50
Graphic Novel (Dec 1991), collects mini-series				£1.90	£5.70	£9.50

GUNMASTER

Charlton;84 Jul 1965-88 Mar/Apr 1966; 89 Oct 1967

(becomes Judomaster)

Issue	$Good	$Fine	$N.Mint	£Good	£Fine	£N.Mint
84-86 distributed in the U.K.						
	$1.40	*$4.25*	*$10.00*	£0.90	£2.75	£6.50
87-89 distributed in the U.K.						
	$1.05	*$3.20*	*$7.50*	£0.70	£2.10	£5.00
Title Value:	*$7.35*	*$22.35*	*$52.50*	£4.80	£14.55	£34.50

GUNS OF SHAR-PEI

Caliber Press,MS; 1 Dec 1991-3 Mar 1992

Issue	$Good	$Fine	$N.Mint	£Good	£Fine	£N.Mint
1-3 ND black and white						
	$0.50	*$1.50*	*$2.50*	£0.30	£0.90	£1.50
Title Value:	*$1.50*	*$4.50*	*$7.50*	£0.90	£2.70	£4.50

GUNSMITH CATS

Dark Horse,MS; 1 Apr 1995-10 Feb 1996

Issue	$Good	$Fine	$N.Mint	£Good	£Fine	£N.Mint
1 ND Kenichi Sonada script and art (translated by Dana Lewis and Toren Smith)						
	$0.70	*$2.10*	*$3.50*	£0.50	£1.50	£2.50
2-10 ND	*$0.60*	*$1.80*	*$3.00*	£0.40	£1.20	£2.00
Title Value:	*$6.10*	*$18.30*	*$30.50*	£4.10	£12.30	£20.50

GUNSMOKE WESTERN

Atlas/Marvel Comics Group;32 Dec 1955-77 Jul 1963 (Atlas #32-35)

Issue	$Good	$Fine	$N.Mint	£Good	£Fine	£N.Mint
32 scarce in the U.K. Wyatt Earp and Kid Colt begin						
	$13.50	*$41.00*	*$95.00*	£7.75	£23.50	£55.00
33 scarce in the U.K. Williamson art						
	$10.50	*$32.00*	*$75.00*	£5.50	£17.00	£40.00
34 scarce in the U.K. Matt Baker art						
	$7.75	*$23.50*	*$55.00*	£4.25	£12.50	£30.00
35-36 scarce in the U.K. Williamson art						
	$10.50	*$32.00*	*$75.00*	£5.50	£17.00	£40.00
37 scarce in the U.K.						
	$7.75	*$23.50*	*$55.00*	£4.25	£12.50	£30.00
38-39 scarce in the U.K.						

	$Good	$Fine	$N.Mint	£Good	£Fine	£N.Mint
	$6.00	*$18.00*	*$42.50*	£3.55	£10.50	£25.00
40 scarce in the U.K. Williamson art						
	$7.00	*$21.00*	*$50.00*	£3.90	£11.50	£27.50
41-49 scarce in the U.K.						
	$3.90	*$11.50*	*$27.50*	£2.10	£6.25	£15.00
50 scarce in the U.K. Reed Crandall art						
	$3.90	*$11.50*	*$27.50*	£2.10	£6.25	£15.00
51-55 scarce in the U.K.						
	$3.20	*$9.50*	*$22.50*	£1.70	£5.00	£12.00
56 scarce in the U.K. Matt Baker art						
	$3.55	*$10.50*	*$25.00*	£2.10	£6.25	£15.00
57 scarce in the U.K. 1st appearance Two Gun Kid by Stan Lee and Marie Severin						
	$3.55	*$10.50*	*$25.00*	£2.50	£7.50	£17.50
1st official distribution in the U.K.						
58 scarce in the U.K.						
	$3.20	*$9.50*	*$22.50*	£1.70	£5.00	£12.00
59-60 rare in the U.K.						
	$3.90	*$11.50*	*$27.50*	£2.50	£7.50	£17.50
61-64 rare in the U.K.						
	$3.20	*$9.50*	*$22.50*	£2.10	£6.25	£15.00
65-71	*$3.20*	*$9.50*	*$22.50*	£1.75	£5.25	£12.50
72 origin Kid Colt retold						
	$3.90	*$11.50*	*$27.50*	£2.10	£6.25	£15.00
73-77	*$2.85*	*$8.50*	*$20.00*	£1.25	£3.85	£9.00
Title Value:	*$205.95*	*$615.50*	*$1455.00*	£113.55	£340.50	£809.50

Note: issues after around 1958 distributed on the news-stands in the U.K. though irregularly before official distribution cover-date November 1959.

ARTISTS

Kirby art in 59, 32, 36, 65-67, 69-71, 73, 77. Ditko art in 66.

FEATURES

Kid Colt in all issues (origin in 72); Two-Gun Kid in 59-63, 66; Wyatt Earp in 58.

GUTTER RAT

Gauntlet Comics,MS; 1 Jul 1993

	$Good	$Fine	$N.Mint	£Good	£Fine	£N.Mint
1 ND	*$0.60*	*$1.80*	*$3.00*	£0.40	£1.20	£2.00
Title Value:	*$0.60*	*$1.80*	*$3.00*	£0.40	£1.20	£2.00

Note: cancelled after 1 issue

GUY GARDNER

DC Comics; 0 Oct 1994; 1 Oct 1992-44 Jun 1996

(see Green Lantern #59)

(becomes Guy Gardner: Warrior with #17)

	$Good	$Fine	$N.Mint	£Good	£Fine	£N.Mint
0 (Oct 1994) Zero Hour X-over, Guy Gardner's new powers revealed						
	$0.40	*$1.20*	*$2.00*	£0.25	£0.75	£1.25
1-4	*$0.30*	*$0.90*	*$1.50*	£0.20	£0.60	£1.00
5-7 Hal Jordan guest stars						
	$0.30	*$0.90*	*$1.50*	£0.20	£0.60	£1.00
8 Lobo vs. Guy Gardner						
	$0.30	*$0.90*	*$1.50*	£0.20	£0.60	£1.00
9-10	*$0.30*	*$0.90*	*$1.50*	£0.20	£0.60	£1.00
11-13 Guy Gardner: Year One						
	$0.30	*$0.90*	*$1.50*	£0.20	£0.60	£1.00
14 Guy Gardner: Year One, X-over Justice League America #72						
	$0.30	*$0.90*	*$1.50*	£0.20	£0.60	£1.00
15-16	*$0.30*	*$0.90*	*$1.50*	£0.20	£0.60	£1.00
17 Guy Gardner renames himself Warrior (1st appearance)						
	$0.30	*$0.90*	*$1.50*	£0.20	£0.60	£1.00
18	*$0.30*	*$0.90*	*$1.50*	£0.20	£0.60	£1.00
19 Golden Age Green Lantern appears						
	$0.30	*$0.90*	*$1.50*	£0.20	£0.60	£1.00
20 Green Lantern, Golden Age Green Lantern, Martian Manhunter, The Ray, Wonder Woman, Darkstar and Captain Atom appear						
	$0.30	*$0.90*	*$1.50*	£0.20	£0.60	£1.00
21 Green Lantern vs. Warrior						
	$0.30	*$0.90*	*$1.50*	£0.20	£0.60	£1.00
22-23	*$0.30*	*$0.90*	*$1.50*	£0.20	£0.60	£1.00
24 Zero Hour X-over						
	$0.30	*$0.90*	*$1.50*	£0.20	£0.60	£1.00
25 48pgs, Adam Hughes art featured						
	$0.30	*$0.90*	*$1.50*	£0.20	£0.60	£1.00
26-27	*$0.30*	*$0.90*	*$1.50*	£0.20	£0.60	£1.00
28 story concluded in Green Lantern #60						
	$0.30	*$0.90*	*$1.50*	£0.20	£0.60	£1.00
29	*$0.30*	*$0.90*	*$1.50*	£0.20	£0.60	£1.00
29 Collectors Edition, ND - barn-door style fold-out cover						
	$0.60	*$1.80*	*$3.00*	£0.40	£1.20	£2.00
30 story continued from Action Comics #709						
	$0.30	*$0.90*	*$1.50*	£0.20	£0.60	£1.00
31 Supergirl and Sentinel (the former Golden Age Green Lantern) guest-star						
	$0.35	*$1.05*	*$1.75*	£0.25	£0.75	£1.25
32 Way of the Warrior part 1, continued in Justice League America #101						
	$0.35	*$1.05*	*$1.75*	£0.25	£0.75	£1.25
33 Way of the Warrior part 4, continued in Justice League America #102						
	$0.35	*$1.05*	*$1.75*	£0.25	£0.75	£1.25
34 Way of the Warrior part 7 (conclusion)						
	$0.35	*$1.05*	*$1.75*	£0.25	£0.75	£1.25
35	*$0.35*	*$1.05*	*$1.75*	£0.25	£0.75	£1.25
36 Underworld Unleashed tie-in						
	$0.35	*$1.05*	*$1.75*	£0.25	£0.75	£1.25
37 Underworld Unleashed tie-in, continued in Darkstars #37						
	$0.35	*$1.05*	*$1.75*	£0.25	£0.75	£1.25
38-44	*$0.35*	*$1.05*	*$1.75*	£0.25	£0.75	£1.25
Title Value:	*$14.90*	*$44.70*	*$74.50*	£10.15	£30.45	£50.75

GUY GARDNER: REBORN

DC Comics,MS; 1 Jul 1992-3 Sep 1992

	$Good	$Fine	$N.Mint	£Good	£Fine	£N.Mint
1 ND 48pgs, aftermath of losing to the Hal Jordan Green Lantern in Green Lantern #25						
	$0.90	*$2.70*	*$4.50*	£0.60	£1.80	£3.00
2-3 ND 48pgs, Lobo appears						
	$0.90	*$2.70*	*$4.50*	£0.60	£1.80	£3.00
Title Value:	*$2.70*	*$8.10*	*$13.50*	£1.80	£5.40	£9.00

GUY GARDNER: WARRIOR ANNUAL

DC Comics; 1 Jul 1995-2 Jun 1996

	$Good	$Fine	$N.Mint	£Good	£Fine	£N.Mint
1 56pgs, Year One	*$0.80*	*$2.40*	*$4.00*	£0.50	£1.50	£2.50
2 48pgs, Legends of the Dead Earth tie-in						
	$0.60	*$1.80*	*$3.00*	£0.40	£1.20	£2.00
Title Value:	*$1.40*	*$4.20*	*$7.00*	£0.90	£2.70	£4.50

H

H.A.R.D. CORPS, THE

Valiant; 1 Nov 1992-30 May 1995

	$Good	$Fine	$N.Mint	£Good	£Fine	£N.Mint
1 ND gatefold cover by Jim Lee						
	$0.50	*$1.50*	*$2.50*	£0.30	£0.90	£1.50
1 Gold Edition ND	*$1.20*	*$3.60*	*$6.00*	£1.00	£3.00	£5.00
2-4 ND	*$0.50*	*$1.50*	*$2.50*	£0.25	£0.75	£1.25
5 ND Bloodshot appears						
	$0.50	*$1.50*	*$2.50*	£0.25	£0.75	£1.25
5 Comic Defense System Pro-Skins Giveaway, ND - red logo, no cover price						
	$0.80	*$2.40*	*$4.00*	£0.50	£1.50	£2.50
6 ND	*$0.50*	*$1.50*	*$2.50*	£0.25	£0.75	£1.25
7 ND Hotshot joins	*$0.50*	*$1.50*	*$2.50*	£0.25	£0.75	£1.25
8-9 ND	*$0.50*	*$1.50*	*$2.50*	£0.25	£0.75	£1.25
10 ND Turok, Dinosaur Hunter appears						
	$0.50	*$1.50*	*$2.50*	£0.25	£0.75	£1.25
11 ND Harbinger appear						
	$0.40	*$1.20*	*$2.00*	£0.25	£0.75	£1.25
12-16 ND	*$0.40*	*$1.20*	*$2.00*	£0.25	£0.75	£1.25
17 ND H.A.R.D. Corps vs. Armorines						
	$0.40	*$1.20*	*$2.00*	£0.25	£0.75	£1.25
18-19 ND	*$0.40*	*$1.20*	*$2.00*	£0.25	£0.75	£1.25
20 ND guest stars Harbinger; continued from Harbinger #31						
	$0.40	*$1.20*	*$2.00*	£0.25	£0.75	£1.25
21-22 ND	*$0.40*	*$1.20*	*$2.00*	£0.25	£0.75	£1.25
23 ND Chaos Effect tie-in						
	$0.40	*$1.20*	*$2.00*	£0.25	£0.75	£1.25
24-30 ND	*$0.40*	*$1.20*	*$2.00*	£0.25	£0.75	£1.25
Title Value:	*$15.00*	*$45.00*	*$75.00*	£9.05	£27.15	£45.25

H.P. LOVECRAFT'S CTHULHU

Millennium; 1 Feb 1992-3 Apr 1992

	$Good	$Fine	$N.Mint	£Good	£Fine	£N.Mint
1-3 ND bound-in trading card						
	$0.50	*$1.50*	*$2.50*	£0.30	£0.90	£1.50
Title Value:	*$1.50*	*$4.50*	*$7.50*	£0.90	£2.70	£4.50

H.P. LOVECRAFT'S CTHULHU: FESTIVAL OF DEATH

Millennium,MS; 1 Sep 1993-3 May 1994

	$Good	$Fine	$N.Mint	£Good	£Fine	£N.Mint
1-3 ND Roy Thomas script						
	$0.50	*$1.50*	*$2.50*	£0.30	£0.90	£1.50
Title Value:	*$1.50*	*$4.50*	*$7.50*	£0.90	£2.70	£4.50
H.P. Lovecraft's Cthulhu: The Festival Collection (Jan 1996)						
ND collects issues #1-3 with certificate; limited to 500 copies				£0.90	£2.70	£4.50

H.P. LOVECRAFT'S CTHULHU: THE FESTIVAL

Millennium,OS; nn Jun 1995

	$Good	$Fine	$N.Mint	£Good	£Fine	£N.Mint
nn ND 80pgs, David Mack script						
	$2.40	*$7.00*	*$12.00*	£1.60	£4.80	£8.00
Title Value:	*$2.40*	*$7.00*	*$12.00*	£1.60	£4.80	£8.00

H.P. LOVECRAFT'S CTHULHU: THE HOUNDS OF TINDALOS

Millennium,MS; 1 Jul 1992-2 Aug 1992

	$Good	$Fine	$N.Mint	£Good	£Fine	£N.Mint
1-2 ND	*$0.50*	*$1.50*	*$2.50*	£0.30	£0.90	£1.50
Title Value:	*$1.00*	*$3.00*	*$5.00*	£0.60	£1.80	£3.00

H.R. PUFNSTUF

Gold Key,TV; 1 Oct 1970-8 Jul 1972

	$Good	$Fine	$N.Mint	£Good	£Fine	£N.Mint
1 very scarce in the U.K.						
	$19.00	*$57.50*	*$135.00*	£10.50	£32.00	£75.00
2-8 very scarce in the U.K.						
	$8.50	*$26.00*	*$60.00*	£4.25	£12.50	£30.00
Title Value:	*$78.50*	*$239.50*	*$555.00*	£40.25	£119.50	£285.00

HACKER FILES, THE

DC Comics,MS; 1 Aug 1992-12 Jul 1993

	$Good	$Fine	$N.Mint	£Good	£Fine	£N.Mint
1 Mark Buckingham inks; computer-generated cover art begins						
	$0.25	*$0.75*	*$1.25*	£0.15	£0.45	£0.75
2-4 Mark Buckingham inks						
	$0.25	*$0.75*	*$1.25*	£0.15	£0.45	£0.75
5 1st appearance of Barbara Gordon appears as Oracle; Mark Buckingham inks						
	$0.30	*$0.90*	*$1.50*	£0.20	£0.60	£1.00
6 Barbara Gordon appears as Oracle, Green Lantern guest stars; Mark Buckingham inks						
	$0.25	*$0.75*	*$1.25*	£0.15	£0.45	£0.75
7-10 Mark Buckingham inks						
	$0.25	*$0.75*	*$1.25*	£0.15	£0.45	£0.75
11-12 Justice League appear; Mark Buckingham inks						
	$0.25	*$0.75*	*$1.25*	£0.15	£0.45	£0.75
Title Value:	*$3.05*	*$9.15*	*$15.25*	£1.85	£5.55	£9.25

HAGAR THE HORRIBLE

ACG,OS; 0 Jul 1995

	$Good	$Fine	$N.Mint	£Good	£Fine	£N.Mint
0 ND Frank Roberge script and art						
	$0.40	*$1.20*	*$2.00*	£0.25	£0.75	£1.25

	$Good	$Fine	$N.Mint	£Good	£Fine	£N.Mint
Title Value:	$0.40	$1.20	$2.00	£0.25	£0.75	£1.25
HAIRY CROWS						
Caliber Press; 1 Dec 1991						
1 ND horror anthology	$0.50	$1.50	$2.50	£0.30	£0.90	£1.50
Title Value:	$0.50	$1.50	$2.50	£0.30	£0.90	£1.50
HALLOWEEN HORROR						
Eclipse; 1 Oct 1987						
(Seduction of the Innocent #7)						
1 ND pre-Code horror reprints, colour	$0.30	$0.90	$1.50	£0.20	£0.60	£1.00
Title Value:	$0.30	$0.90	$1.50	£0.20	£0.60	£1.00
HALLOWEEN TERROR						
Eternity,OS; 1 Sep 1990						
1 ND horror anthology, black and white	$0.40	$1.20	$2.00	£0.25	£0.75	£1.25
Title Value:	$0.40	$1.20	$2.00	£0.25	£0.75	£1.25
HALO: AN ANGEL'S STORY						
Sirius Entertainment; 1 Jun 1996-4 Nov 1996						
1 ND 24pgs, Chris Knowles script and art begins	$0.60	$1.80	$3.00	£0.40	£1.20	£2.00
2-4 ND 24pgs	$0.60	$1.80	$3.00	£0.40	£1.20	£2.00
Title Value:	$2.40	$7.20	$12.00	£1.60	£4.80	£8.00
HAMMER HORROR						
Marvel Comics Group,Magazine; 1 Apr 1995-5 1995						
1 ND the history of Hammer films told in photo art	$1.00	$3.00	$5.00	£0.70	£2.10	£3.50
2-5 ND	$1.00	$3.00	$5.00	£0.70	£2.10	£3.50
Title Value:	$5.00	$15.00	$25.00	£3.50	£10.50	£17.50
HAMMER OF GOD						
First,MS; 1 Feb 1990-4 May 1990						
1-3 ND	$0.40	$1.20	$2.00	£0.25	£0.75	£1.25
Title Value:	$1.20	$3.60	$6.00	£0.75	£2.25	£3.75
HAMMER OF GOD: BUTCH						
Dark Horse,MS; 1 Apr 1994-3 Jun 1994						
1-3 ND Mike Baron script	$0.50	$1.50	$2.50	£0.30	£0.90	£1.50
Title Value:	$1.50	$4.50	$7.50	£0.90	£2.70	£4.50
HAMMER OF GOD: PENTATHLON						
Dark Horse,OS; 1 Dec 1993						
1 ND	$0.50	$1.50	$2.50	£0.30	£0.90	£1.50
Title Value:	$0.50	$1.50	$2.50	£0.30	£0.90	£1.50
HAMMER OF GOD: SWORD OF JUSTICE						
First,MS; 1 Feb 1991-2 Mar 1991						
1-2 ND 48pgs	$1.00	$3.00	$5.00	£0.70	£2.10	£3.50
Title Value:	$2.00	$6.00	$10.00	£1.40	£4.20	£7.00
HAMMERLOCKE						
DC Comics,MS; 1 Sep 1992-9 May 1993						
1 48pgs	$0.30	$0.90	$1.50	£0.20	£0.60	£1.00
2-9	$0.25	$0.75	$1.25	£0.15	£0.45	£0.75
Title Value:	$2.30	$6.90	$11.50	£1.40	£4.20	£7.00
HAMSTER VICE						
Blackthorne; 1 Jun 1986-9 1987						
1 ND Miami Vice parody begins; black and white	$0.40	$1.20	$2.00	£0.25	£0.75	£1.25
2-9 ND	$0.30	$0.90	$1.50	£0.20	£0.60	£1.00
Title Value:	$2.80	$8.40	$14.00	£1.85	£5.55	£9.25
HAMSTER VICE IN 3-D						
Blackthorne;(3-D Series #12,15); 1 Nov 1986-2 Dec 1986						
1-2 ND with bound-in 3-D glasses (25% less without glasses)	$0.50	$1.50	$2.50	£0.30	£0.90	£1.50

	$Good	$Fine	$N.Mint	£Good	£Fine	£N.Mint
Title Value:	$1.00	$3.00	$5.00	£0.60	£1.80	£3.00
HAND OF FATE						
Eclipse,MS; 1 Feb 1988-3 Apr 1988						
1-2 ND colour	$0.40	$1.20	$2.00	£0.25	£0.75	£1.25
3 ND black & white	$0.40	$1.20	$2.00	£0.25	£0.75	£1.25
Title Value:	$1.20	$3.60	$6.00	£0.75	£2.25	£3.75
HANDBOOK TO THE MALIBU ULTRAVERSE						
Marvel Comics Group,MS; 1 Mar 1996-2 Apr 1996						
1-2 ND 48pgs, information and character biographies	$0.60	$1.80	$3.00	£0.40	£1.20	£2.00
Title Value:	$1.20	$3.60	$6.00	£0.80	£2.40	£4.00
HANDS OF THE DRAGON						
Atlas; 1 Jun 1975						
1 scarce though distributed in the U.K.	$0.25	$0.75	$1.50	£0.15	£0.50	£1.00
Title Value:	$0.25	$0.75	$1.50	£0.15	£0.50	£1.00
HANDS OF THE MANDARIN						
Marvel Comics Group; 1994						
Cross-over storyline that ran throughout the following issues: **Force Works #6**, **War Machine #9**, **Iron Man 311**, **Force Works #7**, **War Machine #10**, **Iron Man #312**.						
HANNA-BARBERA SPOTLIGHT						
Marvel Comics Group; 1 Sep 1978-4 Mar 1979						
1 ND Huckleberry Hound	$0.20	$0.60	$1.25	£0.10	£0.35	£0.75
2 ND Quick Draw McGraw	$0.20	$0.60	$1.25	£0.10	£0.35	£0.75
3 ND The Jetsons	$0.20	$0.60	$1.25	£0.10	£0.35	£0.75
4 ND Magilla Gorilla	$0.20	$0.60	$1.25	£0.10	£0.35	£0.75
Title Value:	$0.80	$2.40	$5.00	£0.40	£1.40	£3.00
HANNA-BARBERA SUPER TV HEROES						
Gold Key; 1 Apr 1968-7 Oct 1969						
1 Birdman, Herculoids, Mighty Mightor, Young Sampson begin	$15.00	$45.00	$105.00	£9.25	£28.00	£65.00
2	$13.50	$41.00	$95.00	£7.75	£23.50	£55.00
3 Space Ghost appears	$12.00	$36.00	$85.00	£7.00	£21.00	£50.00
4	$12.00	$36.00	$85.00	£7.00	£21.00	£50.00
5-7 Space Ghost appears	$12.00	$36.00	$85.00	£7.00	£21.00	£50.00
Title Value:	$88.50	$266.00	$625.00	£52.00	£156.50	£370.00
Note: issues patchily distributed on the news-stands in the U.K.						
HAPPY BIRTHDAY GNATRAT						
Prelude; 1 1986						
(see Gnatrat, Darerat)						
1 ND Batman #400 parody, Mark Martin art	$0.60	$1.80	$3.00	£0.40	£1.20	£2.00
Title Value:	$0.60	$1.80	$3.00	£0.40	£1.20	£2.00
HAPPY BIRTHDAY MARTHA WASHINTON						
Dark Horse/Legend,OS; 1 Feb 1995						
1 ND Frank Miller script, Dave Gibbons art	$0.60	$1.80	$3.00	£0.40	£1.20	£2.00
Title Value:	$0.60	$1.80	$3.00	£0.40	£1.20	£2.00
HARBINGER						
Valiant; 0 1992; 1 Jan 1992-41 Jun 1995						
Note: all Non-Distributed on the news-stands in the U.K.						
0 rare in the U.K. (red cover); available from Valiant in return for coupons #1-6; print run estimated at approximately 5,000 copies	$1.50	$4.50	$7.50	£1.00	£3.00	£5.00
0 Blue Cover Edition, available from Valiant, a separate item poly-bagged together with Harbinger						

Grimm's Ghost Stories #60

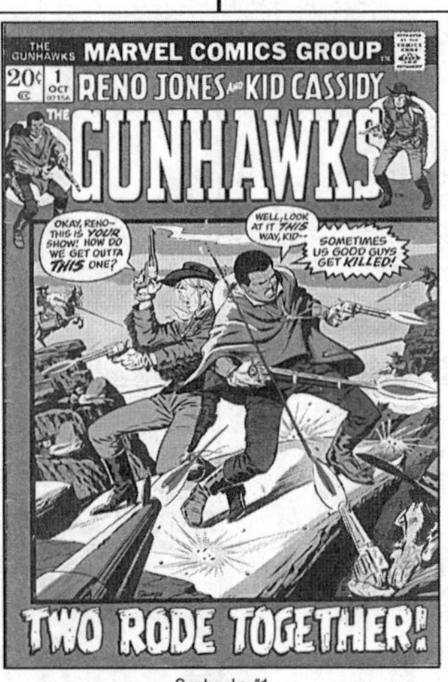

Gunhawks #1

Hanna-Barbera Spotlight #1

	$Good	$Fine	$N.Mint	£Good	£Fine	£N.Mint
Trade paperback	$1.00	$3.00	$5.00	£0.30	£0.90	£1.50
1 scarce in the U.K. (with coupon intact. Less approx. 30% without coupon for issues #1-6)	$1.00	$3.00	$5.00	£1.00	£3.00	£5.00
2 with coupon	$0.80	$2.40	$4.00	£0.60	£1.80	£3.00
3 with coupon	$0.80	$2.40	$4.00	£0.50	£1.50	£2.50
4 scarce in the U.K. with coupon	$1.00	$3.00	$5.00	£0.70	£2.10	£3.50
5 Sting vs. Solar, Man of the Atom; with coupon	$0.80	$2.40	$4.00	£0.50	£1.50	£2.50
6 scarce in the U.K. Torque dies; with coupon	$0.60	$1.80	$3.00	£0.40	£1.20	£2.00
7	$0.60	$1.80	$3.00	£0.40	£1.20	£2.00
8 Unity: Chapter 8	$0.60	$1.80	$3.00	£0.40	£1.20	£2.00
9 Unity: Chapter 9, Magnus Robot Fighter appears, Walt Simonson cover	$0.60	$1.80	$3.00	£0.40	£1.20	£2.00
10 1st appearance H.A.R.D. Corps	$0.60	$1.80	$3.00	£0.40	£1.20	£2.00
11 1st full appearance H.A.R.D. Corps	$0.50	$1.50	$2.50	£0.30	£0.90	£1.50
12-13	$0.50	$1.50	$2.50	£0.30	£0.90	£1.50
14 1st appearance Stronghold (cameo)	$0.50	$1.50	$2.50	£0.30	£0.90	£1.50
15 1st full appearance Stronghold and Livewire	$0.50	$1.50	$2.50	£0.30	£0.90	£1.50
16-21	$0.50	$1.50	$2.50	£0.25	£0.75	£1.25
22 Archer & Armstrong guest-star	$0.50	$1.50	$2.50	£0.25	£0.75	£1.25
23-24 Twilight of the Eighth Day story	$0.50	$1.50	$2.50	£0.25	£0.75	£1.25
25 Twilight of the Eighth Day story; Sting loses powers	$0.70	$2.10	$3.50	£0.30	£0.90	£1.50
26 titled "The New Harbingers", Sean Chen pencils begin	$0.50	$1.50	$2.50	£0.25	£0.75	£1.25
27-28	$0.50	$1.50	$2.50	£0.25	£0.75	£1.25
29 with free Valiant Upper Deck card bound-in at centre-fold	$0.50	$1.50	$2.50	£0.25	£0.75	£1.25
30	$0.50	$1.50	$2.50	£0.25	£0.75	£1.25
31 guest stars H.A.R.D Corps; continued in H.A.R.D. Corps #20	$0.50	$1.50	$2.50	£0.25	£0.75	£1.25
32 guest-stars Eternal Warrior	$0.50	$1.50	$2.50	£0.25	£0.75	£1.25
33 Dr. Eclipse appears	$0.50	$1.50	$2.50	£0.25	£0.75	£1.25
34 Chaos Effect tie-in	$0.50	$1.50	$2.50	£0.25	£0.75	£1.25
35-41	$0.50	$1.50	$2.50	£0.25	£0.75	£1.25
Title Value:	$25.60	$76.80	$128.00	£14.65	£43.95	£73.25

Note: a special issue "0" was made available by sending coupons from the first 6 issues of the title.

	£Good	£Fine	£N.Mint
Harbinger Trade paperback (Jan 1993) contains issue 0 and reprints issues #1-4	£2.00	£6.00	£10.00
(2nd print - Jul 1993), no Harbinger #0 included	£1.30	£3.90	£6.50
Harbinger Trade paperback (Feb 1993), as above but with blue logo specially produced by Diamond Distributors	£5.00	£15.00	£25.00
Harbinger #2 (Jun 1995) Trade paperback reprints issues #6,7,10,11	£1.30	£3.90	£6.50

HARBINGER FILES: HARADA

Valiant; 1 Jun 1994; 2 Feb 1995

	$Good	$Fine	$N.Mint	£Good	£Fine	£N.Mint
1 ND story continued directly after Solar Man of the Atom #3; features the origin of Harada	$0.40	$1.20	$2.00	£0.25	£0.75	£1.25
2 ND the debut of The Harbinger, Harada's secret weapon	$0.40	$1.20	$2.00	£0.25	£0.75	£1.25
Title Value:	$0.80	$2.40	$4.00	£0.50	£1.50	£2.50

HARD BOILED

Dark Horse,MS; 1 Sep 1990-3 May 1992

	$Good	$Fine	$N.Mint	£Good	£Fine	£N.Mint
1 ND Frank Miller script/Geoff Darrow art begins	$1.20	$3.60	$6.00	£0.70	£2.10	£3.50
2-3 ND larger format - $5.95 cover	$1.20	$3.60	$6.00	£0.70	£2.10	£3.50
Title Value:	$3.60	$10.80	$18.00	£2.10	£6.30	£10.50

Note: magazine format

	£Good	£Fine	£N.Mint
Hard Boiled Softcover Collection (Apr 1993) reprints mini-series with new cover	£2.00	£6.00	£10.00
Signed and Numbered Limited Edition Hardcover (Dec 1994) with slipcase and additional sketches	£13.50	£40.50	£67.50
Hard Boiled Trade Paperback - Dell Edition (Jul 1995) reprints mini-series with new cover by Geof Darrow. **Note:** only distributed in the U.S. not U.K.	£2.00	£6.00	£10.00

HARD LOOKS

Dark Horse; 1 Dec 1991-10 Sep 1993

	$Good	$Fine	$N.Mint	£Good	£Fine	£N.Mint
1 ND anthology series begins, Dave Gibbons art featured	$0.50	$1.50	$2.50	£0.30	£0.90	£1.50
2 ND David Lloyd art featured	$0.50	$1.50	$2.50	£0.30	£0.90	£1.50
3 ND George Pratt art featured	$0.50	$1.50	$2.50	£0.30	£0.90	£1.50
4-9 ND	$0.50	$1.50	$2.50	£0.30	£0.90	£1.50
10 ND 40pgs	$0.70	$2.10	$3.50	£0.50	£1.50	£2.50
Title Value:	$5.20	$15.60	$26.00	£3.20	£9.60	£16.00

	£Good	£Fine	£N.Mint
Andrew Vachss' Hard Looks Book One (Jun 1995) Trade paperback reprints plus four new stories	£2.00	£6.00	£10.00

HARDCASE

Malibu Ultraverse; 1 Jun 1993-26 Aug 1995

	$Good	$Fine	$N.Mint	£Good	£Fine	£N.Mint
1 Dave Gibbons cover, 1st appearance Hardcase; Ultraverse #0 card coupon	$0.70	$2.10	$3.50	£0.40	£1.20	£2.00
1 Limited Edition, (Jun 1993) - full hologram cover; 7,500 copies (re-offered by Marvel in Sep 1995)	$2.00	$6.00	$10.00	£1.00	£3.00	£5.00
2-3	$0.50	$1.50	$2.50	£0.25	£0.75	£1.25
4 gatefold cover, Hardcase & Strangers team up	$0.50	$1.50	$2.50	£0.25	£0.75	£1.25
5 40pgs, Rune insert	$0.50	$1.50	$2.50	£0.25	£0.75	£1.25
6	$0.40	$1.20	$2.00	£0.25	£0.75	£1.25
7 Break Thru X-over	$0.40	$1.20	$2.00	£0.25	£0.75	£1.25
8 Solution guest-stars; Solitaire origin by George Perez	$0.40	$1.20	$2.00	£0.25	£0.75	£1.25
9-10 The Origin of Choice	$0.40	$1.20	$2.00	£0.25	£0.75	£1.25
11-15	$0.40	$1.20	$2.00	£0.25	£0.75	£1.25
16 64pgs, flip-book format with Ultraverse Premiere #7	$0.50	$1.50	$2.50	£0.30	£0.90	£1.50
17-18	$0.40	$1.20	$2.00	£0.25	£0.75	£1.25
19 prelude to Godwheel story	$0.40	$1.20	$2.00	£0.25	£0.75	£1.25
20-22	$0.40	$1.20	$2.00	£0.25	£0.75	£1.25
23 Marvel's Loki appears, making his Ultraverse debut. The Loki Connection continues in Mantra #22	$0.40	$1.20	$2.00	£0.25	£0.75	£1.25
24	$0.40	$1.20	$2.00	£0.25	£0.75	£1.25
25 1st issue under Marvel Comics solicitation	$0.40	$1.20	$2.00	£0.25	£0.75	£1.25
26 $2.95 cover, no ads	$0.60	$1.80	$3.00	£0.30	£0.90	£1.50
Title Value:	$13.40	$40.20	$67.00	£7.75	£23.25	£38.75

Note: all Non-Distributed on the news-stands in the U.K.

HARDCORE

Cry For Dawn; 1 Aug 1995

	$Good	$Fine	$N.Mint	£Good	£Fine	£N.Mint
1 ND adult material; black and white	$0.60	$1.80	$3.00	£0.40	£1.20	£2.00
Title Value:	$0.60	$1.80	$3.00	£0.40	£1.20	£2.00

HARDKORR

Aircel,OS; 1 Jun 1991

	$Good	$Fine	$N.Mint	£Good	£Fine	£N.Mint
1 ND Barry Blair script/art, black and white	$0.50	$1.50	$2.50	£0.30	£0.90	£1.50
Title Value:	$0.50	$1.50	$2.50	£0.30	£0.90	£1.50

HARDWARE

DC Comics/Milestone; 1 Apr 1993-present

	$Good	$Fine	$N.Mint	£Good	£Fine	£N.Mint
1	$0.30	$0.90	$1.50	£0.20	£0.60	£1.00
1 Direct Market Edition, ND - pre-bagged with poster, profile, trading card and jig-saw puzzle pieces	$0.50	$1.50	$2.50	£0.30	£0.90	£1.50
1 Platinum Edition, ND - 6,000 copies available from Diamond Distributors	$1.00	$3.00	$5.00	£0.60	£1.80	£3.00
2-3 bi-weekly	$0.25	$0.75	$1.25	£0.15	£0.45	£0.75
4-10	$0.25	$0.75	$1.25	£0.15	£0.45	£0.75
11 Shadow War part 1, continued in Icon #9; spot-varnished cover by Walt Simonson	$0.30	$0.90	$1.50	£0.20	£0.60	£1.00
12-14	$0.30	$0.90	$1.50	£0.20	£0.60	£1.00
15 part Walt Simonson cover	$0.30	$0.90	$1.50	£0.20	£0.60	£1.00
16 John Byrne cover	$0.30	$0.90	$1.50	£0.20	£0.60	£1.00
16 Collectors Edition, ND 48pgs, "barn door" style gatefold cover by John Byrne	$0.80	$2.40	$4.00	£0.50	£1.50	£2.50
17 Worlds Collide X-over, continued in Superboy #6	$0.30	$0.90	$1.50	£0.20	£0.60	£1.00
18 Worlds Collide X-over, continued in Superman: The Man of Steel #36	$0.30	$0.90	$1.50	£0.20	£0.60	£1.00
19-24	$0.30	$0.90	$1.50	£0.20	£0.60	£1.00
25 48pgs, metallic ink cover	$0.50	$1.50	$2.50	£0.30	£0.90	£1.50
26-28	$0.30	$0.90	$1.50	£0.20	£0.60	£1.00
29 upgraded paper stock begins; cover priced at 99 cents	$0.20	$0.60	$1.00	£0.15	£0.45	£0.75
30-32	$0.50	$1.50	$2.50	£0.30	£0.90	£1.50
33 Howard Chaykin cover	$0.50	$1.50	$2.50	£0.30	£0.90	£1.50
34-43	$0.50	$1.50	$2.50	£0.30	£0.90	£1.50
44 The Heroes appear	$0.50	$1.50	$2.50	£0.30	£0.90	£1.50
45 ND Final Night tie-in	$0.50	$1.50	$2.50	£0.30	£0.90	£1.50
46-48 ND	$0.50	$1.50	$2.50	£0.30	£0.90	£1.50
49 ND Moebius cover	$0.50	$1.50	$2.50	£0.30	£0.90	£1.50
Title Value:	$20.65	$61.95	$103.25	£12.80	£38.40	£64.00

HARI KARI

Blackout Comics; 0 Sep 1995; 1 Nov 1995

	$Good	$Fine	$N.Mint	£Good	£Fine	£N.Mint
0 ND Gilbert King script, Guy Dorian art	$0.60	$1.80	$3.00	£0.40	£1.20	£2.00
0 Variant Cover Edition, ND (1996) red foil cover	$0.60	$1.80	$3.00	£0.40	£1.20	£2.00
1 ND Gilbert King script, Guy Dorian art	$0.60	$1.80	$3.00	£0.40	£1.20	£2.00

Issue	$Good	$Fine	$N.Mint	£Good	£Fine	£N.Mint
1 Commemorative Edition, ND (Dec 1995), platinum enhanced cover; 5,000 copies	$2.00	$6.00	$10.00	£1.30	£3.90	£6.50
Title Value:	$3.80	$11.40	$19.00	£2.50	£7.50	£12.50

HARI KARI PRIVATE GALLERY

Blackout Comics,OS; 1 Jan 1996

Issue	$Good	$Fine	$N.Mint	£Good	£Fine	£N.Mint
1 ND pin-ups by Gene Colan, Tim Vigil, Bill maus and others	$0.60	$1.80	$3.00	£0.40	£1.20	£2.00
1 Commemorative Edition, (Feb 1996), limited to 4,000 copies	$2.00	$6.00	$10.00	£1.30	£3.90	£6.50
Title Value:	$2.60	$7.80	$13.00	£1.70	£5.10	£8.50

HARI KARI: REBIRTH

Blackout Comics,OS; 1 1996

Issue	$Good	$Fine	$N.Mint	£Good	£Fine	£N.Mint
1 ND Tommy Castillo and David Mowry art	$0.60	$1.80	$3.00	£0.40	£1.20	£2.00
Title Value:	$0.60	$1.80	$3.00	£0.40	£1.20	£2.00

HARI KARI: THE SILENCE OF EVIL

Blackout Comics,MS; 0 Jun 1996

Issue	$Good	$Fine	$N.Mint	£Good	£Fine	£N.Mint
0 ND	$0.60	$1.80	$3.00	£0.40	£1.20	£2.00
Title Value:	$0.60	$1.80	$3.00	£0.40	£1.20	£2.00

HARLAN ELLISON'S DREAM CORRIDOR

Dark Horse; 1 Mar 1995-5 Jul 1995

Issue	$Good	$Fine	$N.Mint	£Good	£Fine	£N.Mint
1-3 ND sci-fi anthology featuring Harlan Ellison, John Byrne and Eric Shanower	$0.60	$1.80	$3.00	£0.40	£1.20	£2.00
4-5 ND Harlan Ellison, John Byrne and Eric Shanower, Peter David and Mike Deodato	$0.60	$1.80	$3.00	£0.40	£1.20	£2.00
Title Value:	$3.00	$9.00	$15.00	£2.00	£6.00	£10.00

Note: issue #6 was advertised and solicited but never appeared.

HARLAN ELLISON'S DREAM CORRIDOR (2ND SERIES)

Dark Horse; 1 Aug 1996-present

Issue	$Good	$Fine	$N.Mint	£Good	£Fine	£N.Mint
1 ND 64pgs, antholgy featuring art by Paul Chadwick, Matin Nodell and Neal Adams (13pgs - cool)	$1.20	$3.60	$6.00	£0.80	£2.40	£4.00
Title Value:	$1.20	$3.60	$6.00	£0.80	£2.40	£4.00

Note: quarterly frequency

HARLAN ELLISON'S DREAM CORRIDOR SPECIAL

Dark Horse,OS; 1 Jan 1995

Issue	$Good	$Fine	$N.Mint	£Good	£Fine	£N.Mint
1 ND 48pgs, sci-fi anthology	$1.00	$3.00	$5.00	£0.70	£2.10	£3.50
Title Value:	$1.00	$3.00	$5.00	£0.70	£2.10	£3.50

HAROLD HEDD

Kitchen Sink,MS; 1,2 1984

Issue	$Good	$Fine	$N.Mint	£Good	£Fine	£N.Mint
1-2 ND reprints underground colour strip from the 1970s	$0.80	$2.40	$4.00	£0.50	£1.50	£2.50
Title Value:	$1.60	$4.80	$8.00	£1.00	£3.00	£5.00

HARRIERS

Entity Comics,MS; 1 Jun 1995-3 Aug 1995

Issue	$Good	$Fine	$N.Mint	£Good	£Fine	£N.Mint
1 ND Aster/Harriers poster at centre-fold	$0.60	$1.80	$3.00	£0.40	£1.20	£2.00
2-3 ND	$0.60	$1.80	$3.00	£0.40	£1.20	£2.00
Title Value:	$1.80	$5.40	$9.00	£1.20	£3.60	£6.00

HARROWERS

Marvel Comics Group/Epic,MS; 1 Dec 1993-6 May 1994

Issue	$Good	$Fine	$N.Mint	£Good	£Fine	£N.Mint
1-6 ND Clive Barker's Pinhead featured	$0.40	$1.20	$2.00	£0.25	£0.75	£1.25
Title Value:	$2.40	$7.20	$12.00	£1.50	£4.50	£7.50

HARSH REALM

Harris Publications,MS; 1 Feb 1994-6 Jul 1994

Issue	$Good	$Fine	$N.Mint	£Good	£Fine	£N.Mint
1-6 ND John Ridgway inks	$0.60	$1.80	$3.00	£0.40	£1.20	£2.00
Title Value:	$3.60	$10.80	$18.00	£2.40	£7.20	£12.00

HARTE OF DARKNESS

Eternity,MS; 1 Oct 1991-4 Jan 1992

Issue	$Good	$Fine	$N.Mint	£Good	£Fine	£N.Mint
1-4 ND	$0.50	$1.50	$2.50	£0.30	£0.90	£1.50
Title Value:	$2.00	$6.00	$10.00	£1.20	£3.60	£6.00

HARVEY

Marvel Comics Group; 1 Oct 1970-6 Dec 1972

Issue	$Good	$Fine	$N.Mint	£Good	£Fine	£N.Mint
1 ND scarce in the U.K. Stan Lee scripts begin	$1.65	$5.00	$10.00	£0.80	£2.50	£5.00
2-6 ND scarce in the U.K.	$1.00	$3.00	$6.00	£0.65	£2.00	£4.00
Title Value:	$6.65	$20.00	$40.00	£4.05	£12.50	£25.00

HARVEY KURTZMAN'S STRANGE ADVENTURES HARDCOVER

Marvel Comics Group/Epic,OS; 1 Jan 1991

Issue	$Good	$Fine	$N.Mint	£Good	£Fine	£N.Mint
1 ND 80pgs, tribute to Kurtzman by a variety of leading artists including Gibbons/Aragones/ Moebius	$2.70	$8.00	$13.50	£1.80	£5.25	£9.00
Title Value:	$2.70	$8.00	$13.50	£1.80	£5.25	£9.00

HATARI

Dell/Movie Classics,OS Movie; 12-340-301 Jan 1963

Issue	$Good	$Fine	$N.Mint	£Good	£Fine	£N.Mint
12-340-301 distributed in the U.K. film adaptation; John Wayne photo cover	$10.50	$32.00	$75.00	£6.25	£19.00	£45.00
Title Value:	$10.50	$32.00	$75.00	£6.25	£19.00	£45.00

HATE

Fantagraphics; 1 Jun 1990-present

Issue	$Good	$Fine	$N.Mint	£Good	£Fine	£N.Mint
1 Peter Bagge script/art begins; black and white	$4.50	$13.50	$22.50	£1.20	£3.60	£6.00
1 2nd printing, (Jan 1992)	$0.50	$1.50	$2.50	£0.30	£0.90	£1.50
1 3rd /4th printing	$0.50	$1.50	$2.50	£0.30	£0.90	£1.50
2	$3.00	$9.00	$15.00	£0.80	£2.40	£4.00
2 2nd printing, (Feb 1992)	$0.50	$1.50	$2.50	£0.30	£0.90	£1.50
2 3rd /4th printing	$0.50	$1.50	$2.50	£0.30	£0.90	£1.50
3	$3.00	$9.00	$15.00	£0.70	£2.10	£3.50
3 2nd printing, (Mar 1992)	$0.50	$1.50	$2.50	£0.30	£0.90	£1.50
3 3rd printing	$0.50	$1.50	$2.50	£0.30	£0.90	£1.50
4	$1.60	$4.80	$8.00	£0.60	£1.80	£3.00
4 2nd printing, (Jun 1992)	$0.50	$1.50	$2.50	£0.30	£0.90	£1.50
4 3rd printing	$0.50	$1.50	$2.50	£0.30	£0.90	£1.50
5	$1.60	$4.80	$8.00	£0.60	£1.80	£3.00
5 2nd printing, (Aug 1992)	$0.50	$1.50	$2.50	£0.30	£0.90	£1.50
6	$1.60	$4.80	$8.00	£0.60	£1.80	£3.00
6 2nd printing, (1994)	$0.50	$1.50	$2.50	£0.30	£0.90	£1.50
6 3rd printing	$0.50	$1.50	$2.50	£0.30	£0.90	£1.50
7	$1.60	$4.80	$8.00	£0.60	£1.80	£3.00
7 2nd printing, (Nov 1994)	$0.50	$1.50	$2.50	£0.30	£0.90	£1.50
8	$1.60	$4.80	$8.00	£0.60	£1.80	£3.00
8 2nd printing, (Jul 1993)	$0.50	$1.50	$2.50	£0.30	£0.90	£1.50
8 3rd printing	$0.50	$1.50	$2.50	£0.30	£0.90	£1.50
9	$1.60	$4.80	$8.00	£0.60	£1.80	£3.00
9 2nd printing, (Jan 1994)	$0.50	$1.50	$2.50	£0.30	£0.90	£1.50
10	$1.60	$4.80	$8.00	£0.60	£1.80	£3.00
11 $2.50 cover begins	$0.80	$2.40	$4.00	£0.50	£1.50	£2.50
11 2nd printing, (Jan 1995)	$0.50	$1.50	$2.50	£0.30	£0.90	£1.50
12	$0.80	$2.40	$4.00	£0.50	£1.50	£2.50
12 2nd printing, (Oct 1995)	$0.50	$1.50	$2.50	£0.30	£0.90	£1.50
13-15	$0.80	$2.40	$4.00	£0.50	£1.50	£2.50
16	$0.60	$1.80	$3.00	£0.40	£1.20	£2.00
17 full colour begins	$0.60	$1.80	$3.00	£0.40	£1.20	£2.00
18-23	$0.60	$1.80	$3.00	£0.40	£1.20	£2.00
Title Value:	$39.00	$117.00	$195.00	£17.70	£53.10	£88.50

Note: all Non-Distributed on the news-stands in the U.K.

Note: Buddy Bradley character continues from Neat Stuff; bi-monthly

HAUNT OF FEAR

E.C. Comics; 1 May/Jun 1950-28 Nov/Dec 1954

(formerly Fat & Slat #1-4, becomes Gunfighter #5-14)

Issue	$Good	$Fine	$N.Mint	£Good	£Fine	£N.Mint
1 very scarce in the U.K., scarce in the U.S. has #15 on cover	$215.00	$650.00	$1750.00	£145.00	£440.00	£1175.00
2 scarce in the U.K. has #16 on cover	$100.00	$300.00	$700.00	£65.00	£200.00	£470.00
3 scarce in the U.K. has #17 on cover; origin Vault of Horror and Crypt of Terror	$105.00	$320.00	$750.00	£70.00	£210.00	£500.00
4	$75.00	$225.00	$525.00	£50.00	£150.00	£350.00
5 famous eye-injury panel	$55.00	$170.00	$400.00	£39.00	£115.00	£270.00
6-10	$39.00	$115.00	$275.00	£26.00	£77.50	£185.00
11-15	$29.00	$85.00	$200.00	£19.00	£57.50	£135.00
16 Ray Bradbury adaptation	$29.00	$85.00	$200.00	£19.00	£57.50	£135.00
17	$29.00	$85.00	$200.00	£19.00	£57.50	£135.00
18 Ray Bradbury adaptation	$29.00	$85.00	$200.00	£19.00	£57.50	£135.00
19 classic cover featuring bondage and beheading	$43.00	$125.00	$300.00	£29.00	£85.00	£200.00
20	$29.00	$85.00	$200.00	£19.00	£57.50	£135.00
21-27	$17.50	$52.50	$125.00	£12.00	£36.00	£85.00
28 scarce in both US and UK	$26.00	$75.00	$180.00	£17.00	£50.00	£120.00
Title Value:	$1197.50	$3572.50	$8655.00	£800.00	£2407.00	£5820.00

Note: all Non-Distributed on the news-stands in the U.K.

HAUNT OF FEAR (2ND SERIES)

Gladstone; 1 May 1991-2 1991

Issue	$Good	$Fine	$N.Mint	£Good	£Fine	£N.Mint
1 ND 64pgs, reprints Haunt of Fear #7 and Weird Science Fantasy #28	$0.40	$1.20	$2.00	£0.25	£0.75	£1.25
2 ND 64pgs, reprints Haunt of Fear #5 and Weird Science Fantasy #29	$0.40	$1.20	$2.00	£0.25	£0.75	£1.25
Title Value:	$0.80	$2.40	$4.00	£0.50	£1.50	£2.50

Note: sub-titled "Tales from the Crypt presents"..

Note also: issue #3 was advertised but never appeared.

HAUNT OF FEAR (3RD SERIES)

Russ Cochran/EC Comics; 1 Aug 1991-5 May 1992

Issue	$Good	$Fine	$N.Mint	£Good	£Fine	£N.Mint
1 ND reprints Haunt of Fear #14 and Weird Fantasy #13	$0.60	$1.80	$3.00	£0.40	£1.20	£2.00
2 ND reprints Haunt of Fear #18, Weird Fantasy #14	$0.40	$1.20	$2.00	£0.25	£0.75	£1.25
3 ND reprints Haunt of Fear #19, Weird Fantasy #18	$0.40	$1.20	$2.00	£0.25	£0.75	£1.25
4 ND reprints Haunt of Fear #16, Weird Fantasy #15	$0.40	$1.20	$2.00	£0.25	£0.75	£1.25
5 ND reprints Haunt of Fear #27, Weird Fantasy #22	$0.40	$1.20	$2.00	£0.25	£0.75	£1.25
Title Value:	$2.20	$6.60	$11.00	£1.40	£4.20	£7.00

Note: issues #6,7 were advertised but never appeared.

HAUNT OF FEAR (4TH SERIES)

Russ Cochran/EC Comics; 1 Nov 1992-present

Issue	$Good	$Fine	$N.Mint	£Good	£Fine	£N.Mint
1 ND reprints begin from original 1950s EC series with exact cover and interior reproduction	*$0.40*	*$1.20*	*$2.00*	£0.25	£0.75	£1.25
2-15 ND	*$0.40*	*$1.20*	*$2.00*	£0.25	£0.75	£1.25
16 ND	*$0.50*	*$1.50*	*$2.50*	£0.30	£0.90	£1.50
Title Value:	*$6.50*	*$19.50*	*$32.50*	£4.05	£12.15	£20.25
Haunt of Fear Annual 1 (Oct 1994) ND reprints issues #1-5 with covers				£1.20	£3.60	£6.00
Haunt of Fear Annual 2 (1995) ND reprints issues #6-10 with covers				£1.20	£3.60	£6.00
Haunt of Fear Annual 3 (Jun 1996) ND reprints issues #11-15 with covers				£1.20	£3.60	£6.00

HAUNT OF HORROR

Marvel Comics Group,Digest; 1 Jun 1973-2 Aug 1973

Issue	$Good	$Fine	$N.Mint	£Good	£Fine	£N.Mint
1-2 ND	*$0.65*	*$2.00*	*$4.00*	£0.40	£1.25	£2.50
Title Value:	*$1.30*	*$4.00*	*$8.00*	£0.80	£2.50	£5.00

HAUNT OF HORROR (2ND SERIES)

Marvel Comics Group,Magazine; 1 May 1974-5 Jan 1975

Issue	$Good	$Fine	$N.Mint	£Good	£Fine	£N.Mint
1 64pgs, Gabriel Devil-Hunter begins, Walt Simonson art featured	*$1.00*	*$3.00*	*$6.00*	£0.65	£2.00	£4.00
2 64pgs, Satana appears and in a text story, Gene Colan art featured; Earl Norem cover	*$0.80*	*$2.50*	*$5.00*	£0.40	£1.25	£2.50
3 64pgs	*$0.65*	*$2.00*	*$4.00*	£0.40	£1.25	£2.50
4 64pgs, Satana appears; Satana text story with illustrations by Pat Broderick and The Crusty Bunkers - a collection of inkers including Neal Adams	*$0.65*	*$2.00*	*$4.00*	£0.50	£1.50	£3.00
5 very scarce in the U.K. 64pgs, Satana appears, Dick Giordano cover	*$0.65*	*$2.00*	*$4.00*	£0.65	£2.00	£4.00
Title Value:	*$3.75*	*$11.50*	*$23.00*	£2.60	£8.00	£16.00

Note: a next issue was advertised but never appeared.

HAUNTED

Charlton; 1 Sep 1971-30 Nov 1976; 31 Sep 1977-75 Sep 1984
(becomes Baron Weirwulf's Haunted Library #20 on)

Issue	$Good	$Fine	$N.Mint	£Good	£Fine	£N.Mint
1 Steve Ditko art and cover	*$1.65*	*$5.00*	*$10.00*	£1.00	£3.00	£6.00
2 Steve Ditko art and cover	*$1.00*	*$3.00*	*$6.00*	£0.65	£2.00	£4.00
3-5 Steve Ditko art and cover	*$0.80*	*$2.50*	*$5.00*	£0.55	£1.75	£3.50
6-8 Steve Ditko art and cover	*$0.65*	*$2.00*	*$4.00*	£0.50	£1.50	£3.00
9-10	*$0.50*	*$1.50*	*$3.00*	£0.40	£1.25	£2.50
11 Steve Ditko art and cover	*$0.50*	*$1.50*	*$3.00*	£0.30	£1.00	£2.00
12-13 Steve Ditko art	*$0.50*	*$1.50*	*$3.00*	£0.30	£1.00	£2.00
14 Steve Ditko art and cover	*$0.50*	*$1.50*	*$3.00*	£0.30	£1.00	£2.00
15 Steve Ditko art	*$0.50*	*$1.50*	*$3.00*	£0.30	£1.00	£2.00
16 Steve Ditko art and cover	*$0.50*	*$1.50*	*$3.00*	£0.30	£1.00	£2.00
17	*$0.40*	*$1.25*	*$2.50*	£0.25	£0.75	£1.50
18 Steve Ditko art	*$0.50*	*$1.50*	*$3.00*	£0.30	£1.00	£2.00
19-20	*$0.40*	*$1.25*	*$2.50*	£0.25	£0.75	£1.50
21-22	*$0.30*	*$1.00*	*$2.00*	£0.20	£0.60	£1.25
23-24 Steve Ditko art	*$0.40*	*$1.25*	*$2.50*	£0.25	£0.75	£1.50
25-27	*$0.30*	*$1.00*	*$2.00*	£0.20	£0.60	£1.25
28 Steve Ditko art	*$0.40*	*$1.25*	*$2.50*	£0.20	£0.60	£1.25
29	*$0.30*	*$1.00*	*$2.00*	£0.20	£0.60	£1.25
30 Steve Ditko art and cover	*$0.40*	*$1.25*	*$2.50*	£0.20	£0.60	£1.25
31-40	*$0.25*	*$0.75*	*$1.50*	£0.15	£0.50	£1.00
41 Steve Ditko cover	*$0.25*	*$0.75*	*$1.50*	£0.15	£0.50	£1.00
42-46	*$0.25*	*$0.75*	*$1.50*	£0.15	£0.50	£1.00
47 Steve Ditko cover	*$0.25*	*$0.75*	*$1.50*	£0.15	£0.50	£1.00
48	*$0.25*	*$0.75*	*$1.50*	£0.15	£0.50	£1.00
49-50 Steve Ditko cover	*$0.25*	*$0.75*	*$1.50*	£0.15	£0.50	£1.00
51 Steve Ditko cover, reprints issue 1	*$0.30*	*$0.90*	*$1.50*	£0.20	£0.60	£1.00
52-56	*$0.30*	*$0.90*	*$1.50*	£0.20	£0.60	£1.00
57 Steve Ditko art	*$0.40*	*$1.20*	*$2.00*	£0.25	£0.75	£1.25
58-59	*$0.30*	*$0.90*	*$1.50*	£0.20	£0.60	£1.00
60 Steve Ditko art	*$0.40*	*$1.20*	*$2.00*	£0.25	£0.75	£1.25
61-75	*$0.30*	*$0.90*	*$1.50*	£0.20	£0.60	£1.00
Title Value:	*$28.80*	*$87.85*	*$168.00*	£18.65	£58.10	£111.50

Note: all Limited Distribution in the U.K.

HAUNTED LOVE

Charlton; 1 Apr 1973-11 Sep 1975

Issue	$Good	$Fine	$N.Mint	£Good	£Fine	£N.Mint
1	*$1.00*	*$3.00*	*$6.00*	£0.65	£2.00	£4.00
2-3	*$0.65*	*$2.00*	*$4.00*	£0.30	£1.00	£2.00
4-5 Steve Ditko art	*$0.75*	*$2.25*	*$4.50*	£0.40	£1.25	£2.50
6-11	*$0.50*	*$1.50*	*$3.00*	£0.25	£0.75	£1.50
Title Value:	*$6.80*	*$20.50*	*$41.00*	£3.55	£11.00	£22.00

Note: all Limited Distribution in the U.K.

HAVE GUN WILL TRAVEL

Dell;(Four Color #931) 1 Aug 1958-14 Sep 1962

Issue	$Good	$Fine	$N.Mint	£Good	£Fine	£N.Mint
1 (Four Color #931) photo cover	*$21.00*	*$62.50*	*$150.00*	£14.00	£43.00	£100.00
2 (Four Color #983) photo cover	*$15.50*	*$47.00*	*$110.00*	£10.50	£32.00	£75.00
3 (Four Color #1044) photo cover	*$15.50*	*$47.00*	*$110.00*	£10.50	£32.00	£75.00
4 all photo covers (ends #14)	*$12.00*	*$36.00*	*$85.00*	£8.00	£24.50	£57.50
5-14	*$12.00*	*$36.00*	*$85.00*	£8.00	£24.50	£57.50
Title Value:	*$184.00*	*$552.50*	*$1305.00*	£123.00	£376.50	£882.50

Note: all distributed on the news-stands in the U.K.

HAVOK AND WOLVERINE: MELTDOWN

Marvel Comics Group/Epic,MS; 1 Nov 1988-4 Jun 1989

Issue	$Good	$Fine	$N.Mint	£Good	£Fine	£N.Mint
1 ND 48pgs	*$1.00*	*$3.00*	*$5.00*	£0.60	£1.80	£3.00
2-3 ND 48pgs	*$0.80*	*$2.40*	*$4.00*	£0.50	£1.50	£2.50
4 ND scarce in the U.K. 48pgs	*$0.80*	*$2.40*	*$4.00*	£0.60	£1.80	£3.00
Title Value:	*$3.40*	*$10.20*	*$17.00*	£2.20	£6.60	£11.00

Note: Bookshelf Format. Walt/Louise Simonson script, Jon J. Muth/Kent Williams art

Issue	$Good	$Fine	$N.Mint	£Good	£Fine	£N.Mint
Trade Paperback (1991), reprints issues #1-4				£1.60	£4.80	£8.00

HAWK AND DOVE ANNUAL

DC Comics; 1 Sep 1990-2 1991

Issue	$Good	$Fine	$N.Mint	£Good	£Fine	£N.Mint
1 ND Rob Liefeld cover	*$0.50*	*$1.50*	*$2.50*	£0.30	£0.90	£1.50
2 ND Armageddon: 2001 tie-in	*$0.50*	*$1.50*	*$2.50*	£0.30	£0.90	£1.50
Title Value:	*$1.00*	*$3.00*	*$5.00*	£0.60	£1.80	£3.00

HAWK AND DOVE, THE

DC Comics,MS; 1 Oct 1988-5 Feb 1989

Issue	$Good	$Fine	$N.Mint	£Good	£Fine	£N.Mint
1 Rob Liefeld art	*$0.60*	*$1.80*	*$3.00*	£0.40	£1.20	£2.00
2-5 Rob Liefeld art	*$0.50*	*$1.50*	*$2.50*	£0.30	£0.90	£1.50
Title Value:	*$2.60*	*$7.80*	*$13.00*	£1.60	£4.80	£8.00
Hawk and Dove (Dec 1993) Trade paperback ND reprints 5 issue mini-series with unpublished costume designs				£1.30	£3.90	£6.50

Note: this volume was re-offered by DC Comics in November 1996.

HAWK AND DOVE, THE (2ND SERIES)

DC Comics; 1 Jun 1989-28 Oct 1991

Issue	$Good	$Fine	$N.Mint	£Good	£Fine	£N.Mint
1-10	*$0.25*	*$0.75*	*$1.25*	£0.15	£0.45	£0.75
11 New Titans guest-star	*$0.25*	*$0.75*	*$1.25*	£0.15	£0.45	£0.75
12-17	*$0.25*	*$0.75*	*$1.25*	£0.15	£0.45	£0.75
18-19 Creeper appears	*$0.25*	*$0.75*	*$1.25*	£0.15	£0.45	£0.75
20-24	*$0.25*	*$0.75*	*$1.25*	£0.15	£0.45	£0.75
25 48pgs	*$0.30*	*$0.90*	*$1.50*	£0.20	£0.60	£1.00
26-27	*$0.25*	*$0.75*	*$1.25*	£0.15	£0.45	£0.75
28 64pgs	*$0.30*	*$0.90*	*$1.50*	£0.20	£0.60	£1.00
Title Value:	*$7.10*	*$21.30*	*$35.50*	£4.30	£12.90	£21.50

HAWK AND THE DOVE, THE

National Periodical Publications; 1 Aug/Sep 1968-6 Jun/Jul 1969
(see Brave and the Bold, Showcase #75, Teen Titans)

Issue	$Good	$Fine	$N.Mint	£Good	£Fine	£N.Mint
1 Steve Ditko art	*$7.00*	*$21.00*	*$50.00*	£4.25	£12.50	£30.00
2 Steve Ditko art	*$6.25*	*$18.50*	*$37.50*	£3.30	£10.00	£20.00
3 Gil Kane art	*$6.25*	*$18.50*	*$37.50*	£3.30	£10.00	£20.00
4 Gil Kane art	*$6.25*	*$18.50*	*$37.50*	£2.90	£8.75	£17.50
5 Gil Kane art, Teen Titans cameo	*$6.25*	*$18.50*	*$37.50*	£2.90	£8.75	£17.50
6 Gil Kane art	*$6.25*	*$18.50*	*$37.50*	£2.90	£8.75	£17.50
Title Value:	*$38.25*	*$113.50*	*$237.50*	£19.55	£58.75	£122.50

Note: original Dove killed in Crisis on Infinite Earths.

HAWKEYE

Marvel Comics Group,MS; 1 Sep 1983-4 Dec 1983

Issue	$Good	$Fine	$N.Mint	£Good	£Fine	£N.Mint
1-2 ND scarce in the U.K.	*$0.40*	*$1.20*	*$2.00*	£0.40	£1.20	£2.00
3-4 ND	*$0.30*	*$0.90*	*$1.50*	£0.30	£0.90	£1.50
Title Value:	*$1.40*	*$4.20*	*$6.50*	£1.40	£4.20	£7.00
Trade Paperback, reprints #1-4				£1.00	£3.00	£5.00
(2nd print. 1991)				£1.00	£3.00	£5.00

HAWKEYE (2ND SERIES)

Marvel Comics Group,MS; 1 Jan 1994-4 Apr 1994

Issue	$Good	$Fine	$N.Mint	£Good	£Fine	£N.Mint
1-3	*$0.40*	*$1.20*	*$2.00*	£0.25	£0.75	£1.25
4 new costume	*$0.40*	*$1.20*	*$2.00*	£0.25	£0.75	£1.25
Title Value:	*$1.60*	*$4.80*	*$8.00*	£1.00	£3.00	£5.00

HAWKMAN

National Periodical Publications; 1 Apr/May 1964-27 Aug/Sep 1968
(see Atom and Hawkman, Brave and the Bold, DC Presents, Detective Mystery in Space, Shadow War of the..., Showcase, World's Finest)

Issue	$Good	$Fine	$N.Mint	£Good	£Fine	£N.Mint
1 Murphy Anderson art	*$57.50*	*$175.00*	*$525.00*	£39.00	£115.00	£350.00
2	*$25.00*	*$75.00*	*$200.00*	£13.00	£39.00	£105.00
3	*$15.50*	*$47.00*	*$125.00*	£8.00	£24.00	£65.00
4 1st appearance Zatanna	*$18.50*	*$55.00*	*$150.00*	£8.75	£26.00	£70.00
5	*$17.50*	*$52.50*	*$125.00*	£5.50	£17.00	£40.00
6-8	*$15.50*	*$47.00*	*$110.00*	£3.90	£11.50	£27.50
9 Atom X-over	*$12.00*	*$36.00*	*$85.00*	£3.90	£11.50	£27.50
10	*$12.00*	*$36.00*	*$85.00*	£3.90	£11.50	£27.50
11 last Silver Age issue, indicia dated Dec 1965/Jan 1966	*$8.50*	*$26.00*	*$60.00*	£3.20	£9.50	£22.50
12-15	*$10.00*	*$30.00*	*$60.00*	£3.30	£10.00	£20.00
16-17	*$8.25*	*$25.00*	*$50.00*	£2.90	£8.75	£17.50
18 Adam Strange appears	*$8.25*	*$25.00*	*$50.00*	£2.90	£8.75	£17.50
19-20	*$8.25*	*$25.00*	*$50.00*	£2.90	£8.75	£17.50
21-24	*$7.50*	*$22.50*	*$45.00*	£2.50	£7.50	£15.00

	$Good	$Fine	$N.Mint	£Good	£Fine	£N.Mint
25 Golden Age Hawkman reprint						
	$7.50	*$22.50*	*$45.00*	£2.50	£7.50	£15.00
26-27	*$7.50*	*$22.50*	*$45.00*	£2.50	£7.50	£15.00
Title Value:	*$346.75*	*$1046.00*	*$2455.00*	£142.15	£424.25	£1062.50
Trade Paperback (Sep 1989)						
Reprints classic Gardner Fox/Joe Kubert stories						
including Brave and the Bold #34				£2.80	£8.40	£14.00

HAWKMAN (2ND SERIES)

DC Comics; 1 Aug 1986-17 Dec 1987

	$Good	$Fine	$N.Mint	£Good	£Fine	£N.Mint
1	*$0.30*	*$0.90*	*$1.50*	£0.20	£0.60	£1.00
2-9	*$0.25*	*$0.75*	*$1.25*	£0.15	£0.45	£0.75
10 Superman cameo, John Byrne cover art						
	$0.25	*$0.75*	*$1.25*	£0.15	£0.45	£0.75
11-17	*$0.25*	*$0.75*	*$1.25*	£0.15	£0.45	£0.75
Title Value:	*$4.30*	*$12.90*	*$21.50*	£2.60	£7.80	£13.00

HAWKMAN (3RD SERIES)

DC Comics; 0 Oct 1994; 1 Sep 1993-33 Aug 1996

	$Good	$Fine	$N.Mint	£Good	£Fine	£N.Mint
0 (Oct 1994) Zero Hour X-over, Hawkman discovers new powers						
	$0.40	*$1.20*	*$2.00*	£0.25	£0.75	£1.25
1 new powers and new costume, gold foil embossed cover						
	$0.50	*$1.50*	*$2.50*	£0.30	£0.90	£1.50
2-3	*$0.40*	*$1.20*	*$2.00*	£0.25	£0.75	£1.25
4 Justice League of America appear						
	$0.40	*$1.20*	*$2.00*	£0.25	£0.75	£1.25
5	*$0.40*	*$1.20*	*$2.00*	£0.25	£0.75	£1.25
6 The Eradicator appears						
	$0.40	*$1.20*	*$2.00*	£0.25	£0.75	£1.25
7-8 King of the Netherworld story						
	$0.40	*$1.20*	*$2.00*	£0.25	£0.75	£1.25
9 prelude to Zero Hour mini-series begins						
	$0.40	*$1.20*	*$2.00*	£0.25	£0.75	£1.25
10-12	*$0.40*	*$1.20*	*$2.00*	£0.25	£0.75	£1.25
13 Zero Hour X-over						
	$0.40	*$1.20*	*$2.00*	£0.25	£0.75	£1.25
14 Hawkman with new powers discovered during Zero Hour						
	$0.40	*$1.20*	*$2.00*	£0.25	£0.75	£1.25
15 Hawkman vs. Aquaman						
	$0.40	*$1.20*	*$2.00*	£0.25	£0.75	£1.25
16 Diana Prince appears						
	$0.40	*$1.20*	*$2.00*	£0.25	£0.75	£1.25
17-18	*$0.40*	*$1.20*	*$2.00*	£0.25	£0.75	£1.25
19 Hawkwoman vs. Vigilante						
	$0.40	*$1.20*	*$2.00*	£0.25	£0.75	£1.25
20	*$0.40*	*$1.20*	*$2.00*	£0.25	£0.75	£1.25
21 Ron Lim cover and art						
	$0.45	*$1.35*	*$2.25*	£0.30	£0.90	£1.50
22 Way of the Warrior part 3, continued in Guy Gardner: Warrior #33. Cover by Ron Lim						
	$0.45	*$1.35*	*$2.25*	£0.30	£0.90	£1.50
23 Way of the Warrior part 3, continued in Guy Gardner: Warrior #34. Cover by Ron Lim						
	$0.45	*$1.35*	*$2.25*	£0.30	£0.90	£1.50
24 Ron Lim cover	*$0.45*	*$1.35*	*$2.25*	£0.30	£0.90	£1.50
25 Kent Williams painted cover						
	$0.45	*$1.35*	*$2.25*	£0.30	£0.90	£1.50
26 Underworld Unleashed tie-in, Scarecrow appears						
	$0.45	*$1.35*	*$2.25*	£0.30	£0.90	£1.50
27 Underworld Unleashed tie-in, Ron Lim cover						
	$0.45	*$1.35*	*$2.25*	£0.30	£0.90	£1.50
28 Hawkman vs. Doctor Polaris						
	$0.45	*$1.35*	*$2.25*	£0.30	£0.90	£1.50
29-30 Howard Chaykin cover						
	$0.45	*$1.35*	*$2.25*	£0.30	£0.90	£1.50
31-33	*$0.45*	*$1.35*	*$2.25*	£0.30	£0.90	£1.50
Title Value:	*$14.35*	*$43.05*	*$71.75*	£9.20	£27.60	£46.00

HAWKMAN ANNUAL

DC Comics; 1 Oct 1993-2 1994

	$Good	$Fine	$N.Mint	£Good	£Fine	£N.Mint
1 64pgs, Bloodlines (Wave Two) part 17, 1st appearance Mongrel, continued in Deathstroke the Terminator Annual #2						
	$0.70	*$2.10*	*$3.50*	£0.50	£1.50	£2.50
2 56pgs, Year One	*$0.80*	*$2.40*	*$4.00*	£0.50	£1.50	£2.50
Title Value:	*$1.50*	*$4.50*	*$7.50*	£1.00	£3.00	£5.00

HAWKMAN SPECIAL

DC Comics; 1 Mar 1986

	$Good	$Fine	$N.Mint	£Good	£Fine	£N.Mint
1 48pgs	*$0.30*	*$0.90*	*$1.50*	£0.20	£0.60	£1.00
Title Value:	*$0.30*	*$0.90*	*$1.50*	£0.20	£0.60	£1.00

HAWKMAN, SHADOW WAR OF

DC Comics,MS; 1 May 1985-4 Aug 1985

	$Good	$Fine	$N.Mint	£Good	£Fine	£N.Mint
1-4	*$0.25*	*$0.75*	*$1.25*	£0.15	£0.45	£0.75
Title Value:	*$1.00*	*$3.00*	*$5.00*	£0.60	£1.80	£3.00

HAWKMOON: THE JEWEL IN THE SKULL

First,MS; 1 May 1986-4 Nov 1986

	$Good	$Fine	$N.Mint	£Good	£Fine	£N.Mint
1-4 ND	*$0.50*	*$1.50*	*$2.50*	£0.30	£0.90	£1.50
Title Value:	*$2.00*	*$6.00*	*$10.00*	£1.20	£3.60	£6.00
Trade Paperback (1988), reprints #1-4				£1.00	£3.00	£5.00

HAWKMOON: THE MAD GOD'S AMULET

First,MS; 1 Jan 1987-4 Jul 1987

	$Good	$Fine	$N.Mint	£Good	£Fine	£N.Mint
1-4 ND	*$0.50*	*$1.50*	*$2.50*	£0.30	£0.90	£1.50
Title Value:	*$2.00*	*$6.00*	*$10.00*	£1.20	£3.60	£6.00

HAWKMOON: THE RUNESTAFF

First,MS; 1 Jun 1988-4 Dec 1988

	$Good	$Fine	$N.Mint	£Good	£Fine	£N.Mint
1-4 ND	*$0.50*	*$1.50*	*$2.50*	£0.30	£0.90	£1.50
Title Value:	*$2.00*	*$6.00*	*$10.00*	£1.20	£3.60	£6.00

HAWKMOON: THE SWORD OF THE DAWN

First,MS; 1 Sep 1987-4 Feb 1988

	$Good	$Fine	$N.Mint	£Good	£Fine	£N.Mint
1-4 ND	*$0.50*	*$1.50*	*$2.50*	£0.30	£0.90	£1.50
Title Value:	*$2.00*	*$6.00*	*$10.00*	£1.20	£3.60	£6.00

HAWKWORLD

DC Comics; 1 Jun 1990-32 Mar 1993

	$Good	$Fine	$N.Mint	£Good	£Fine	£N.Mint
1 Graham Nolan art begins						
	$0.40	*$1.20*	*$2.00*	£0.25	£0.75	£1.25
2-10	*$0.30*	*$0.90*	*$1.50*	£0.20	£0.60	£1.00
11-14	*$0.25*	*$0.75*	*$1.25*	£0.15	£0.45	£0.75
15-16 War of the Gods tie-in						
	$0.25	*$0.75*	*$1.25*	£0.15	£0.45	£0.75
17-20	*$0.25*	*$0.75*	*$1.25*	£0.15	£0.45	£0.75
21 Golden Age Hawkman guest-stars						
	$0.25	*$0.75*	*$1.25*	£0.15	£0.45	£0.75
22-24	*$0.25*	*$0.75*	*$1.25*	£0.15	£0.45	£0.75
25 new costumes	*$0.25*	*$0.75*	*$1.25*	£0.15	£0.45	£0.75
26	*$0.25*	*$0.75*	*$1.25*	£0.15	£0.45	£0.75
27-29 Flight's End story						
	$0.25	*$0.75*	*$1.25*	£0.15	£0.45	£0.75
30 Flight's End story, Tim Truman art begins						
	$0.25	*$0.75*	*$1.25*	£0.15	£0.45	£0.75
31-32 Flight's End story						
	$0.25	*$0.75*	*$1.25*	£0.15	£0.45	£0.75
Title Value:	*$8.60*	*$25.80*	*$43.00*	£5.35	£16.05	£26.75
Note: New Format						
Trade Paperback (Oct 1991),						
reprints four issue series, wraparound cover by Tim Truman				£2.10	£6.30	£10.50

HAWKWORLD (LIMITED SERIES)

DC Comics,MS; 1 Jun 1989-3 Aug 1989

	$Good	$Fine	$N.Mint	£Good	£Fine	£N.Mint
1-3 ND	*$1.00*	*$3.00*	*$5.00*	£0.60	£1.80	£3.00

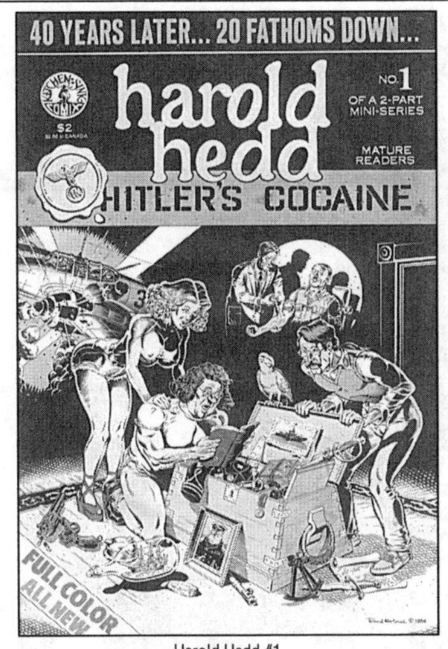

Harold Hedd #1

Harvey #1

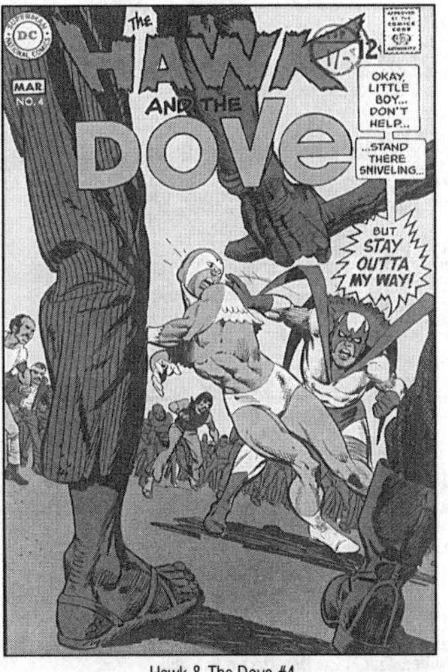

Hawk & The Dove #4

	$Good	$Fine	$N.Mint	£Good	£Fine	£N.Mint
Title Value:	*$3.00*	*$9.00*	*$15.00*	£1.80	£5.40	£9.00

Note: Bookshelf Format, 48pgs. Tim Truman story/art. Mature Readers label.

HAWKWORLD ANNUAL
DC Comics; 1 Nov 1990-3 1992

	$Good	$Fine	$N.Mint	£Good	£Fine	£N.Mint
1 48pgs, Flash guest-stars	*$0.50*	*$1.50*	*$2.50*	£0.30	£0.90	£1.50
2 64pgs, Armageddon: 2001 tie-in	*$0.50*	*$1.50*	*$2.50*	£0.30	£0.90	£1.50
2 2nd printing, silver ink cover	*$0.40*	*$1.20*	*$2.00*	£0.25	£0.75	£1.25
3 64pgs, Eclipso: The Darkness Within tie-in	*$0.50*	*$1.50*	*$2.50*	£0.30	£0.90	£1.50
Title Value:	*$1.90*	*$5.70*	*$9.50*	£1.15	£3.45	£5.75

HAYWIRE
DC Comics; 1 Oct 1988-13 Sep 1989

	$Good	$Fine	$N.Mint	£Good	£Fine	£N.Mint
1-13	*$0.15*	*$0.45*	*$0.75*	£0.10	£0.30	£0.50
Title Value:	*$1.95*	*$5.85*	*$9.75*	£1.30	£3.90	£6.50

Note: high quality paper

HAZARD
Image; 1 May 1996-present?

	$Good	$Fine	$N.Mint	£Good	£Fine	£N.Mint
1-5 ND	*$0.35*	*$1.05*	*$1.75*	£0.25	£0.75	£1.25
6-7 ND	*$0.45*	*$1.35*	*$2.25*	£0.30	£0.90	£1.50
Title Value:	*$2.65*	*$7.95*	*$13.25*	£1.85	£5.55	£9.25

HE-MAN, THE MOVIE
Marvel Comics Group/Star,Film; 1 Nov 1987

	$Good	$Fine	$N.Mint	£Good	£Fine	£N.Mint
1 scarce in the U.K. 48pgs, adapts film; George Tuska art	*$0.25*	*$0.75*	*$1.25*	£0.15	£0.45	£0.75
Title Value:	*$0.25*	*$0.75*	*$1.25*	£0.15	£0.45	£0.75

HEAP, THE
Skywald; 1 Sep 1971

	$Good	$Fine	$N.Mint	£Good	£Fine	£N.Mint
1 scarce though distributed in the U.K. giant, part reprint	*$0.80*	*$2.50*	*$5.00*	£0.80	£2.50	£5.00
Title Value:	*$0.80*	*$2.50*	*$5.00*	£0.80	£2.50	£5.00

HEART OF DARKNESS
Hardline Studios; 1 1994

	$Good	$Fine	$N.Mint	£Good	£Fine	£N.Mint
1 ND Mike Miller co-script and pencils, Matthew Osborne inks	*$0.60*	*$1.80*	*$3.00*	£0.40	£1.20	£2.00
Title Value:	*$0.60*	*$1.80*	*$3.00*	£0.40	£1.20	£2.00

HEART OF THE BEAST GRAPHIC NOVEL
DC Comics; nn Jul 1994

	$Good	$Fine	$N.Mint	£Good	£Fine	£N.Mint
nn ND 96pgs, Hardcover; Dean Motter script, Sean Phillips art and cover	*$4.00*	*$12.00*	*$20.00*	£2.50	£7.50	£12.50
Title Value:	*$4.00*	*$12.00*	*$20.00*	£2.50	£7.50	£12.50

HEART THROBS
National Periodical Publications;47 Apr/May 1959-146 Oct 1972

(previously published by Quality Comics; becomes Love Stories)

	$Good	$Fine	$N.Mint	£Good	£Fine	£N.Mint
47 scarce in the U.K. 1st DC issue	*$32.00*	*$95.00*	*$225.00*	£21.00	£62.50	£150.00
48-50 scarce in the U.K.	*$11.00*	*$34.00*	*$80.00*	£7.00	£21.00	£50.00
51-60 scarce in the U.K.	*$11.00*	*$34.00*	*$80.00*	£6.25	£19.00	£45.00
61 scarce in the U.K.	*$7.00*	*$21.00*	*$50.00*	£4.60	£13.50	£32.50
1st official distribution in the U.K.						
62-70 scarce in the U.K.	*$7.00*	*$21.00*	*$50.00*	£3.90	£11.50	£27.50
71-100 scarce in the U.K.	*$5.50*	*$17.00*	*$40.00*	£3.20	£9.50	£22.50
101 Beatles cover	*$11.00*	*$34.00*	*$80.00*	£5.50	£17.00	£40.00
102-119	*$3.30*	*$10.00*	*$20.00*	£1.65	£5.00	£10.00
120 Neal Adams cover	*$3.30*	*$10.00*	*$20.00*	£1.65	£5.00	£10.00
121-146	*$1.65*	*$5.00*	*$10.00*	£0.80	£2.50	£5.00
Title Value:	*$526.60*	*$1611.00*	*$3685.00*	£297.85	£894.50	£2065.00

HEARTBREAK COMICS
David Boswell; 1 Aug 1984

	$Good	$Fine	$N.Mint	£Good	£Fine	£N.Mint
1 ND	*$0.90*	*$2.70*	*$4.50*	£0.60	£1.80	£3.00
Title Value:	*$0.90*	*$2.70*	*$4.50*	£0.60	£1.80	£3.00

HEARTBREAK COMICS (2ND SERIES)
Eclipse; 1 May 1988

	$Good	$Fine	$N.Mint	£Good	£Fine	£N.Mint
1 ND magazine, Boswell art, Reid Flemming appears	*$0.50*	*$1.50*	*$2.50*	£0.30	£0.90	£1.50
Title Value:	*$0.50*	*$1.50*	*$2.50*	£0.30	£0.90	£1.50

HEARTBREAKERS
Dark Horse,MS; 1 Apr 1996-4 Jul 1996

	$Good	$Fine	$N.Mint	£Good	£Fine	£N.Mint
1-4 ND Anita Bennett script, Paul Guinan art	*$0.60*	*$1.80*	*$3.00*	£0.40	£1.20	£2.00
Title Value:	*$2.40*	*$7.20*	*$12.00*	£1.60	£4.80	£8.00

HEARTLAND
DC Comics/Vertigo,OS; 1 Mar 1997

	$Good	$Fine	$N.Mint	£Good	£Fine	£N.Mint
1 ND 64pgs, Garth Ennis script, Steve Dillon art	*$1.00*	*$3.00*	*$5.00*	£0.70	£2.10	£3.50
Title Value:	*$1.00*	*$3.00*	*$5.00*	£0.70	£2.10	£3.50

HEARTS OF DARKNESS
Marvel Comics Group,OS; 1 Feb 1992

	$Good	$Fine	$N.Mint	£Good	£Fine	£N.Mint
1 ND 48pgs, Ghost Rider, Punisher, Wolverine appear, John Romita Jnr and Klaus Janson art, double gatefold cover	*$0.90*	*$2.70*	*$4.50*	£0.60	£1.80	£3.00
Title Value:	*$0.90*	*$2.70*	*$4.50*	£0.60	£1.80	£3.00

HEARTSTOPPER
Millennium,MS; 1 Dec 1994-4 Oct 1995

	$Good	$Fine	$N.Mint	£Good	£Fine	£N.Mint
1-2 ND Steve Roman script, Uriel Caton part art	*$0.60*	*$1.80*	*$3.00*	£0.40	£1.20	£2.00
3-4 ND Fauve and Alan Larsen art	*$0.60*	*$1.80*	*$3.00*	£0.40	£1.20	£2.00
Title Value:	*$2.40*	*$7.20*	*$12.00*	£1.60	£4.80	£8.00

HEAT: DEADWORLD CHRONICLES
Caliber Press; 1 Jul 1994

	$Good	$Fine	$N.Mint	£Good	£Fine	£N.Mint
1 ND black and white	*$0.60*	*$1.80*	*$3.00*	£0.40	£1.20	£2.00
Title Value:	*$0.60*	*$1.80*	*$3.00*	£0.40	£1.20	£2.00

HEATHCLIFF
Marvel Comics Group/Star; 1 Apr 1985-57 1991

	$Good	$Fine	$N.Mint	£Good	£Fine	£N.Mint
1-49	*$0.15*	*$0.45*	*$0.75*	£0.10	£0.30	£0.50
50 48pgs	*$0.15*	*$0.50*	*$0.90*	£0.10	£0.35	£0.60
51-57	*$0.15*	*$0.45*	*$0.75*	£0.10	£0.30	£0.50
Title Value:	*$8.55*	*$25.70*	*$42.90*	£5.70	£17.15	£28.60

HEAVY HITTERS ANNUAL
Marvel Comics Group/Epic,OS; 1 Nov 1993

	$Good	$Fine	$N.Mint	£Good	£Fine	£N.Mint
1 ND 64pgs, features Spyke, Lawdog, Trouble With Girls, Alien Legion and Feud; bound-in trading card	*$0.80*	*$2.40*	*$4.00*	£0.50	£1.50	£2.50
Title Value:	*$0.80*	*$2.40*	*$4.00*	£0.50	£1.50	£2.50

HEAVY METAL
Heavy Metal; 1 Apr 1977-present

	£Good	£Fine	£N.Mint
Apr 1977	£4.00	£12.00	£20.00
May 1977	£3.00	£9.00	£15.00
Jun 1977	£1.50	£4.50	£7.50
Jul 1977-Dec 1979	£1.00	£3.00	£5.00
Jan 1980-Dec 1982	£0.70	£2.10	£3.50
Jan 1983-Dec 1985 (#105, last monthly)	£0.50	£1.50	£2.50
Winter 1986 1st Quarterly, squarebound	£0.80	£2.40	£4.00
Spring 1986-Winter 1989	£0.70	£2.10	£3.50
Mar 1989 1st bi-monthly	£0.70	£2.10	£3.50
May 1989 onwards	£0.60	£1.80	£3.00
Son of Heavy Metal (all new)	£0.70	£2.10	£3.50
Bride of Heavy Metal (all new)	£0.70	£2.10	£3.50
Best of Heavy Metal, all reprint	£0.70	£2.10	£3.50
Best of Heavy Metal II, all reprint	£0.70	£2.10	£3.50
Even Heavier Metal, all new	£0.70	£2.10	£3.50

HECKLER, THE
DC Comics; 1 Sep 1992-7 Mar 1993

	$Good	$Fine	$N.Mint	£Good	£Fine	£N.Mint
1 Keith Giffin script/art begins	*$0.25*	*$0.75*	*$1.25*	£0.15	£0.45	£0.75
2-7	*$0.25*	*$0.75*	*$1.25*	£0.15	£0.45	£0.75
Title Value:	*$1.75*	*$5.25*	*$8.75*	£1.05	£3.15	£5.25

HELL'S ANGEL
Marvel UK; 1 Jul 1992-17 Dec 1993

(see Overkill in British section) (title becomes Dark Angel with #8)

	$Good	$Fine	$N.Mint	£Good	£Fine	£N.Mint
1 origin Hell's Angel, X-Men guest-star; Jaye and Senior script/art	*$0.30*	*$0.90*	*$1.50*	£0.20	£0.60	£1.00
2-3	*$0.30*	*$0.90*	*$1.50*	£0.20	£0.60	£1.00
4-5 X-Men appear	*$0.30*	*$0.90*	*$1.50*	£0.20	£0.60	£1.00
6 becomes Dark Angel, X-Men appear	*$0.30*	*$0.90*	*$1.50*	£0.20	£0.60	£1.00
7 Psylocke guest-stars	*$0.30*	*$0.90*	*$1.50*	£0.20	£0.60	£1.00
8 Psylocke guest-stars; title change to "Dark Angel" owing to copyright problems actioned by Hell's Angels in America	*$0.30*	*$0.90*	*$1.50*	£0.20	£0.60	£1.00
9 Punisher appears	*$0.30*	*$0.90*	*$1.50*	£0.20	£0.60	£1.00
10 MyS-TECH Wars X-over, X-Men and the Avengers appear	*$0.30*	*$0.90*	*$1.50*	£0.20	£0.60	£1.00
11-12 X-Men appear	*$0.30*	*$0.90*	*$1.50*	£0.20	£0.60	£1.00
13 X-Men and Death's Head II appear	*$0.30*	*$0.90*	*$1.50*	£0.20	£0.60	£1.00
14-16 Death's Head II appears	*$0.30*	*$0.90*	*$1.50*	£0.20	£0.60	£1.00
17	*$0.30*	*$0.90*	*$1.50*	£0.20	£0.60	£1.00
Title Value:	*$5.10*	*$15.30*	*$25.50*	£3.40	£10.20	£17.00

HELLBLAZER
DC Comics; 1 Jan 1988-present

	$Good	$Fine	$N.Mint	£Good	£Fine	£N.Mint
1 John Constantine begins, John Ridgway art and Jamie Delano scripts begin	*$4.00*	*$12.00*	*$20.00*	£2.00	£6.00	£10.00
2	*$2.00*	*$6.00*	*$10.00*	£1.20	£3.60	£6.00
3 LD in the U.K. "Yuppies from Hell", Maggie Thatcher election issue	*$2.00*	*$6.00*	*$10.00*	£1.60	£4.80	£8.00
4-5	*$2.00*	*$6.00*	*$10.00*	£1.00	£3.00	£5.00
6-8	*$1.20*	*$3.60*	*$6.00*	£0.80	£2.40	£4.00
9 LD in the U.K. X-over Swamp Thing #76	*$1.20*	*$3.60*	*$6.00*	£0.90	£2.70	£4.50
10 story continued from Swamp Thing #76	*$1.20*	*$3.60*	*$6.00*	£0.80	£2.40	£4.00
11 Newcastle story, "origin"	*$1.00*	*$3.00*	*$5.00*	£0.70	£2.10	£3.50
12-15	*$1.00*	*$3.00*	*$5.00*	£0.70	£2.10	£3.50
16-20	*$0.90*	*$2.70*	*$4.50*	£0.60	£1.80	£3.00
21-24	*$0.80*	*$2.40*	*$4.00*	£0.50	£1.50	£2.50
25 Grant Morrison script	*$0.80*	*$2.40*	*$4.00*	£0.50	£1.50	£2.50
26 Grant Morrison script	*$0.70*	*$2.10*	*$3.50*	£0.40	£1.20	£2.00

	$Good	$Fine	$N.Mint	£Good	£Fine	£N.Mint
27 Gaiman script, McKean art						
	$1.60	$4.80	$8.00	£0.40	£1.20	£2.00
28-32	$0.70	$2.10	$3.50	£0.40	£1.20	£2.00
33 Dean Motter pencils						
	$0.70	$2.10	$3.50	£0.40	£1.20	£2.00
34-39	$0.70	$2.10	$3.50	£0.40	£1.20	£2.00
40 48pgs, previews Kid Eternity series						
	$0.80	$2.40	$4.00	£0.50	£1.50	£2.50
41 Garth Ennis script/Will Simpson art begins, John Constantine learns he has cancer						
	$1.00	$3.00	$5.00	£0.50	£1.50	£2.50
42-45	$0.60	$1.80	$3.00	£0.30	£0.90	£1.50
46 cancer story conclusion						
	$0.60	$1.80	$3.00	£0.30	£0.90	£1.50
47-49 painted photo cover						
	$0.60	$1.80	$3.00	£0.30	£0.90	£1.50
50 48pgs, painted photo cover, pin-ups by Will Simpson						
	$0.80	$2.40	$4.00	£0.40	£1.20	£2.00
51	$0.50	$1.50	$2.50	£0.30	£0.90	£1.50
52 Royal Blood part 1, Glenn Fabry painted covers begin						
	$0.50	$1.50	$2.50	£0.30	£0.90	£1.50
53-55 Royal Blood story						
	$0.50	$1.50	$2.50	£0.30	£0.90	£1.50
56 David Lloyd art	$0.50	$1.50	$2.50	£0.30	£0.90	£1.50
56 Free Edition, ND available in US only to advertisers and retailers; has "FREE" where price should be on cover						
	$1.00	$3.00	$5.00	£1.00	£3.00	£5.00
57-58 Steve Dillon art						
	$0.50	$1.50	$2.50	£0.30	£0.90	£1.50
59 Guys & Dolls story, Garth Ennis script						
	$0.50	$1.50	$2.50	£0.30	£0.90	£1.50
60 Guys & Dolls story, Garth Ennis script; Please Note new information has come to hand that reveals that this is not the 1st appearance of Genesis (see letters page of Preacher #18)						
	$1.00	$3.00	$5.00	£0.50	£1.50	£2.50
61 Guys & Dolls story, Garth Ennis script (see above)						
	$0.50	$1.50	$2.50	£0.30	£0.90	£1.50
62 Steve Dillon art, Garth Ennis script; Gaiman and McKean back-up AIDS story featuring Death						
	$0.40	$1.20	$2.00	£0.25	£0.75	£1.25
63 Steve Dillon art and Garth Ennis scripts begin under "Vertigo", metallic ink logo. 1st issue under "Vertigo" line of comics; Swamp Thing cameo						
	$0.40	$1.20	$2.00	£0.25	£0.75	£1.25
64-65 Fear & Loathing story						
	$0.40	$1.20	$2.00	£0.25	£0.75	£1.25
66 Fear & Loathing story, $1.95 cover begins						
	$0.40	$1.20	$2.00	£0.25	£0.75	£1.25
67-71	$0.40	$1.20	$2.00	£0.25	£0.75	£1.25
72-74 Damnation's Flame story						
	$0.40	$1.20	$2.00	£0.25	£0.75	£1.25
75 48pgs, Damnation's Flame conclusion						
	$0.60	$1.80	$3.00	£0.40	£1.20	£2.00
76-77	$0.40	$1.20	$2.00	£0.25	£0.75	£1.25
78 Rake At The Gates Of Hell story (ends #83)						
	$0.40	$1.20	$2.00	£0.25	£0.75	£1.25
79-83	$0.40	$1.20	$2.00	£0.25	£0.75	£1.25
84 1st Sean Philips art						
	$0.40	$1.20	$2.00	£0.25	£0.75	£1.25
85-88 Sean Philips cover and art						
	$0.40	$1.20	$2.00	£0.25	£0.75	£1.25
89-91 Sean Philips cover and art						
	$0.45	$1.35	$2.25	£0.30	£0.90	£1.50
92-96 Critical Mass story, Sean Philips cover and art						
	$0.45	$1.35	$2.25	£0.30	£0.90	£1.50
97-99	$0.45	$1.35	$2.25	£0.30	£0.90	£1.50
100 48pgs	$0.70	$2.10	$3.50	£0.50	£1.50	£2.50
101 Al Davison art	$0.45	$1.35	$2.25	£0.30	£0.90	£1.50
102-111	$0.45	$1.35	$2.25	£0.30	£0.90	£1.50
Title Value:	$78.20	$234.60	$391.00	£47.80	£143.40	£239.00

Note: all are New Format, Mature Readers label. Issue 36 previews World Without End series.

ARTISTS

John Ridgway art in #1-9. Richard Piers Rayner/Mark Buckingham art in 10, 11.

				£Good	£Fine	£N.Mint
Trade paperback (Titan) 1				£1.40	£4.20	£7.00
Trade paperback (Titan) 2				£1.30	£3.90	£6.50
Trade paperback (Titan) 3				£1.30	£3.90	£6.50
Trade paperback (Titan) 4				£1.30	£3.90	£6.50
Hellblazer: Original Sins Trade paperback						
ND reprints issues #1-9, new cover by Dave McKean				£2.70	£8.10	£13.50
Hellblazer: Dangerous Habits (Mar 1994) Trade paperback						
ND reprints issues #41-46, new cover by Glenn Fabry				£2.00	£6.00	£10.00
Hellblazer: Fear and Loathing (Mar 1997) Trade paperback						
ND reprints issues #62-67, new cover by Glenn Fabry				£2.00	£6.00	£10.00

HELLBLAZER ANNUAL

DC Comics; 1 Sep 1989

	$Good	$Fine	$N.Mint	£Good	£Fine	£N.Mint
1 ND Bryan Talbot art featured						
	$1.20	$3.60	$6.00	£0.70	£2.10	£3.50
Title Value:	$1.20	$3.60	$6.00	£0.70	£2.10	£3.50

HELLBLAZER SPECIAL

DC Comics; 1 Oct 1993

	$Good	$Fine	$N.Mint	£Good	£Fine	£N.Mint
1 64pgs, Garth Ennis and Steve Dillon						
	$1.20	$3.60	$6.00	£0.70	£2.10	£3.50
Title Value:	$1.20	$3.60	$6.00	£0.70	£2.10	£3.50

HELLBOY: SEED OF DESTRUCTION

Dark Horse/Legend,MS; 1 Mar 1994-4 Jun 1994

	$Good	$Fine	$N.Mint	£Good	£Fine	£N.Mint
1 ND scarce in the U.K. Mike Mignola script and cover, John Byrne art						
	$1.00	$3.00	$5.00	£0.50	£1.50	£2.50
2-4 ND Mike Mignola script and cover, John Byrne art						
	$0.90	$2.70	$4.50	£0.40	£1.20	£2.00
Title Value:	$3.70	$11.10	$18.50	£1.70	£5.10	£8.50
Hellboy: Seeds of Destruction (Oct 1995)						
Trade paperback reprints mini-series plus new artwork by Mignola				£2.40	£7.20	£12.00
Signed, Limited Hardcover Edition (Feb 1995)						
foil-embossed slipcase. 1,000 copies				£13.50	£40.50	£67.50

HELLBOY: THE CORPSE AND THE IRON SHOES

Dark Horse,OS; nn Jan 1996

	$Good	$Fine	$N.Mint	£Good	£Fine	£N.Mint
nn ND Mike Mignola script and painted cover, Matt Hollingsworth and James Sinclair art						
	$0.60	$1.80	$3.00	£0.40	£1.20	£2.00
Title Value:	$0.60	$1.80	$3.00	£0.40	£1.20	£2.00

HELLBOY: THE WOLVES OF ST. AUGUST

Dark Horse,OS; 1 Nov 1995

	$Good	$Fine	$N.Mint	£Good	£Fine	£N.Mint
1 ND 48pgs, Mike Mignola script and art						
	$1.00	$3.00	$5.00	£0.50	£1.50	£2.50
Title Value:	$1.00	$3.00	$5.00	£0.50	£1.50	£2.50

HELLBOY: WAKE THE DEVIL

Dark Horse,MS; 1 Jun 1996-5 Oct 1996

	$Good	$Fine	$N.Mint	£Good	£Fine	£N.Mint
1-5 ND Mike Mignola script and art						
	$0.60	$1.80	$3.00	£0.40	£1.20	£2.00
Title Value:	$3.00	$9.00	$15.00	£2.00	£6.00	£10.00

HELLHOUND

Marvel Comics Group/Epic,MS; 1 Dec 1993-4 Mar 1994

	$Good	$Fine	$N.Mint	£Good	£Fine	£N.Mint
1-4 ND John Miller and Floyd Hughes						
	$0.50	$1.50	$2.50	£0.30	£0.90	£1.50
Title Value:	$2.00	$6.00	$10.00	£1.20	£3.60	£6.00

HELLHOUNDS: PANZER COPS

Dark Horse; 1 Feb 1994-6 Jul 1994

	$Good	$Fine	$N.Mint	£Good	£Fine	£N.Mint
1-5 ND Mamoru Oshii and Kamui Fugiwara; black and white						
	$0.50	$1.50	$2.50	£0.30	£0.90	£1.50
6 ND 48pgs, Mamoru Oshii and Kamui Fugiwara; black and white						
	$0.60	$1.80	$3.00	£0.40	£1.20	£2.00
Title Value:	$3.10	$9.30	$15.50	£1.90	£5.70	£9.50

Note: title simply called Hellhounds for issues #1 and 2

HELLINA

Lightning Comics; 1 Sep 1994

	$Good	$Fine	$N.Mint	£Good	£Fine	£N.Mint
1 ND Steven Zyskowski script; black and white						
	$1.20	$3.60	$6.00	£0.60	£1.80	£3.00
1 2nd printing, ND (May 1995) - new cover and Hellina sketches						
	$0.55	$1.65	$2.75	£0.35	£1.05	£1.75
1 Commemorative Edition, ND Signed and Numbered, limited to 1500 copies						
	$3.00	$9.00	$15.00	£1.40	£4.20	£7.00
1 Gold Edition, ND (1996)						
	$1.20	$3.60	$6.00	£0.80	£2.40	£4.00
1 Nude Cover Editon ND						
	$2.00	$6.00	$10.00	£1.30	£3.90	£6.50
1 Signed & Numbered Edition, ND (May 1995) - pre-bagged in mylar, signed by Steven Zyskowski; 1,500 copies						
	$3.00	$9.00	$15.00	£1.40	£4.20	£7.00
Title Value:	$10.95	$32.85	$54.75	£5.85	£17.55	£29.25
Hellina (Feb 1995) Trade paperback						
ND reprints stories from Perg #4-7, Hellina #1 and Fury of Hellina #1				£1.20	£3.60	£6.00
Hellina Vol. II (Feb 1996) Trade paperback						
ND reprints four stories				£1.70	£5.10	£8.50

HELLINA, THE FURY OF

Lightning Comics; 1 Jan 1995

	$Good	$Fine	$N.Mint	£Good	£Fine	£N.Mint
1 ND Steven Zyskowski script; black and white						
	$0.60	$1.80	$3.00	£0.40	£1.20	£2.00
1 Commemorative Edition, ND (Jan 1995) - metallic silver ink cover, pre-bagged; limited to 1,000 copies						
	$2.00	$6.00	$10.00	£1.30	£3.90	£6.50
1 Signed & Numbered Edition, ND (Apr 1995) - signed and numbered by Steven Zyskowski, shipped in mylar bag						
	$2.00	$6.00	$10.00	£1.30	£3.90	£6.50
Title Value:	$4.60	$13.80	$23.00	£3.00	£9.00	£15.00

HELLINA/CATFIGHT

Lightning Comics,OS; 1 Oct 1995

	$Good	$Fine	$N.Mint	£Good	£Fine	£N.Mint
1 ND	$0.55	$1.65	$2.75	£0.35	£1.05	£1.75
1 Commemorative Edition, ND gold metallic ink cover pre-bagged with certificate of authenticity; limited to 2,500 copies						
	$2.50	$7.50	$12.50	£1.50	£4.50	£7.50
1 Nude Signed Edition, ND (Oct 1995) - Paul Abrams/Gary Barnes cover, signed						
	$2.00	$6.00	$10.00	£1.30	£3.90	£6.50
1 Signed & Numbered Edition, ND (Nov 1995) - 1,500 copies pre-bagged with certificate						
	$2.00	$6.00	$10.00	£1.30	£3.90	£6.50
1 Signed Edition, ND (Oct 1995) - gold metallic ink cover						
	$1.20	$3.60	$6.00	£0.80	£2.40	£4.00
Title Value:	$8.25	$24.75	$41.25	£5.25	£15.75	£26.25

HELLINA/DOUBLE IMPACT

Lightning Comics,OS; 1 Feb 1996

(see Double Impact/Hellina)

	$Good	$Fine	$N.Mint	£Good	£Fine	£N.Mint
1 Cover A, ND John Cleary cover art						
	$0.60	$1.80	$3.00	£0.40	£1.20	£2.00
1 Cover B, ND S. Clarke Hawbaker cover art						
	$0.60	$1.80	$3.00	£0.40	£1.20	£2.00
1 Gold Edition - Nude Cover, ND pre-bagged in Mylar sleeve with certificate; 5,000 copies						
	$2.60	$7.75	$13.00	£1.70	£5.00	£8.50
1 Gold Edition - Regular, ND gold dimensional metallic cover, pre-bagged with certificate; 10,000 copies						
	$1.20	$3.60	$6.00	£0.80	£2.40	£4.00
1 Nude Cover, ND wraparound nude cover by Paul Abrams						
	$2.00	$6.00	$10.00	£1.30	£3.90	£6.50
1 Platinum Nude Edition ND						

	$Good	$Fine	$N.Mint	£Good	£Fine	£N.Mint
	$4.00	$12.00	$20.00	£2.50	£7.50	£12.50
1 Signed & Numbered Edition, ND (Feb 1996) pre-bagged with certificate, limited to 1,500 copies						
	$2.00	$6.00	$10.00	£1.30	£3.90	£6.50
Title Value:	$13.00	$38.95	$65.00	£8.40	£25.10	£42.00

HELLINA/NIRA X: ANGELS OF DEATH

Lightning Comics,OS; 1 Aug 1996

	$Good	$Fine	$N.Mint	£Good	£Fine	£N.Mint
1 ND	$0.60	$1.80	$3.00	£0.40	£1.20	£2.00
1 Alternate Cover Edition, ND - cover by Paul Abrams						
	$0.60	$1.80	$3.00	£0.40	£1.20	£2.00
1 Signed & Numbered Edition ND						
	$2.00	$6.00	$10.00	£1.30	£3.90	£6.50
Title Value:	$3.20	$9.60	$16.00	£2.10	£6.30	£10.50

HELLINA: GENESIS

Lightning Comics,OS; 1 Apr 1996

	$Good	$Fine	$N.Mint	£Good	£Fine	£N.Mint
1 ND 48pgs, black and white reprints of early Hellina appearances						
	$0.70	$2.10	$3.50	£0.50	£1.50	£2.50
1 Nude Edition, ND with certificate						
	$2.00	$6.00	$10.00	£1.30	£3.90	£6.50
1 Platinum Edition, ND with certificate						
	$1.20	$3.60	$6.00	£0.80	£2.40	£4.00
1 Platinum Nude Edition ND						
	$4.00	$12.00	$20.00	£2.50	£7.50	£12.50
1 Signed & Limited Edition, ND pre-bagged in Mylar sleeve with certificate; limited to 1,000 copies						
	$2.00	$6.00	$10.00	£1.30	£3.90	£6.50
Title Value:	$9.90	$29.70	$49.50	£6.40	£19.20	£32.00

HELLINA: HEART OF THORNS

Lightning Comics,MS; 1 Jun 1996-2 Sep 1996

	$Good	$Fine	$N.Mint	£Good	£Fine	£N.Mint
1 ND	$0.60	$1.80	$3.00	£0.40	£1.20	£2.00
1 Nude Cover Edition ND						
	$2.00	$6.00	$10.00	£1.30	£3.90	£6.50
1 Signed & Numbered Edition, ND bagged with certificate						
	$2.00	$6.00	$10.00	£1.30	£3.90	£6.50
2 Nude Version A ND 24pgs						
	$2.00	$6.00	$10.00	£1.30	£3.90	£6.50
2 Nude version B ND 24pgs						
	$2.00	$6.00	$10.00	£1.30	£3.90	£6.50
2 Platinum Edition ND 24pgs						
	$1.20	$3.60	$6.00	£0.80	£2.40	£4.00
2 Version A, ND 24pgs, Paul Abrams cover						
	$0.55	$1.65	$2.75	£0.35	£1.05	£1.75
2 Version B, ND 24pgs, Ivan Reis cover						
	$0.55	$1.65	$2.75	£0.35	£1.05	£1.75
Title Value:	$10.90	$32.70	$54.50	£7.10	£21.30	£35.50

HELLINA: HELL'S ANGEL

Lightning Comics,MS; 1,2 Nov 1996

	$Good	$Fine	$N.Mint	£Good	£Fine	£N.Mint
1 ND Steven Vincent and Paul Abrams script, David Mowry and James M. Anderson art; black and white						
	$0.55	$1.65	$2.75	£0.35	£1.05	£1.75
1 Nude Edition ND	$2.00	$6.00	$10.00	£1.30	£3.90	£6.50
1 Platinum Edition, ND platinum cover; pre-bagged with certificate, limited to 1,000 copies						
	$2.00	$6.00	$10.00	£1.30	£3.90	£6.50
1 Platinum Nude Edition ND						
	$4.00	$12.00	$20.00	£2.50	£7.50	£12.50
2 ND	$0.55	$1.65	$2.75	£0.35	£1.05	£1.75
Title Value:	$9.10	$27.30	$45.50	£5.80	£17.40	£29.00

HELLINA: KISS OF DEATH

Lightning Comics; 1 Jul 1995

	$Good	$Fine	$N.Mint	£Good	£Fine	£N.Mint
1 ND Steven Zyskowski script, Paul Abrams and Gary Barnes art; black and white						
	$0.55	$1.65	$2.75	£0.35	£1.05	£1.75
1 Nude Version, ND pre-bagged with numbered certificate						
	$3.00	$9.00	$15.00	£1.50	£4.50	£7.50
1 Signed & Numbered Edition, ND (Aug 1995) - pre-bagged with certificate; 1,500 copies						
	$2.00	$6.00	$10.00	£1.30	£3.90	£6.50
1 Variant Cover Edition, ND limited to 20% of the print run						
	$1.50	$4.50	$7.50	£0.60	£1.80	£3.00
Title Value:	$7.05	$21.15	$35.25	£3.75	£11.25	£18.75

HELLINA: TAKING BACK THE NIGHT

Lightning Comics; 1 Apr 1995

	$Good	$Fine	$N.Mint	£Good	£Fine	£N.Mint
1 ND Lawrence and Anderson art, Clarke Hawbaker cover						
	$0.55	$1.65	$2.75	£0.35	£1.05	£1.75
1 Nude Edition, ND pre-bagged with certificate, Lawrence and Anderson art, Clarke Hawbaker cover						
	$2.00	$6.00	$10.00	£1.30	£3.90	£6.50
1 Signed & Numbered Edition, ND (Jun 1995) with certificate; limited to 1,500 copies						
	$2.00	$6.00	$10.00	£1.30	£3.90	£6.50
Title Value:	$4.55	$13.65	$22.75	£2.95	£8.85	£14.75

HELLINA: WICKED WAYS

Lightning Comics,OS; 1 Nov 1995

	$Good	$Fine	$N.Mint	£Good	£Fine	£N.Mint
1 ND black and white						
	$0.55	$1.65	$2.75	£0.35	£1.05	£1.75
1 Nude Cover Edition, ND signed by Joe Zyskowski						
	$2.00	$6.00	$10.00	£1.40	£4.20	£7.00
1 Variant Cover Edition, ND (Nov 1995) pre-bagged, pencilled and inked by Trent Kaniuga; black and white						
	$1.20	$3.60	$6.00	£0.80	£2.40	£4.00
Title Value:	$3.75	$11.25	$18.75	£2.55	£7.65	£12.75

HELLRAISER 1993 SPECIAL

Marvel Comics Group/Epic,OS; 1 Jan 1994

	$Good	$Fine	$N.Mint	£Good	£Fine	£N.Mint
1 ND 64pgs, anthology featuring work by Ann Nocenti and Scott Hampton; Scott Hampton painted cover						
	$1.50	$4.50	$7.50	£1.00	£3.00	£5.00
Title Value:	$1.50	$4.50	$7.50	£1.00	£3.00	£5.00

HELLRAISER HOLIDAY SPECIAL

Marvel Comics Group/Epic,OS; 1 Jan 1993

	$Good	$Fine	$N.Mint	£Good	£Fine	£N.Mint
1 ND 48pgs, anthology of Clive Barker stories						
	$0.90	$2.70	$4.50	£0.60	£1.80	£3.00
Title Value:	$0.90	$2.70	$4.50	£0.60	£1.80	£3.00

HELLRAISER III: HELL ON EARTH BOOKSHELF EDITION

Marvel Comics Group/Epic,OS; 1 Oct 1992

	$Good	$Fine	$N.Mint	£Good	£Fine	£N.Mint
1 ND 48pgs, adaptation of film						
	$0.90	$2.70	$4.50	£0.60	£1.80	£3.00
Title Value:	$0.90	$2.70	$4.50	£0.60	£1.80	£3.00

HELLRAISER III: HELL ON EARTH MAGAZINE EDITION

Marvel Comics Group/Epic,OS; 1 Oct 1992

	$Good	$Fine	$N.Mint	£Good	£Fine	£N.Mint
1 ND 48pgs, adaptation of film						
	$0.60	$1.80	$3.00	£0.40	£1.20	£2.00
Title Value:	$0.60	$1.80	$3.00	£0.40	£1.20	£2.00

HELLRAISER SPRING SLAUGHTER: RAZING HELL

Marvel Comics Group/Epic,OS; 1 May 1994

	$Good	$Fine	$N.Mint	£Good	£Fine	£N.Mint
1 ND 48pgs, three stories						
	$1.40	$4.20	$7.00	£0.90	£2.70	£4.50
Title Value:	$1.40	$4.20	$7.00	£0.90	£2.70	£4.50

HELLRAISER SUMMER SPECIAL

Marvel Comics Group/Epic,OS; 1 Sep 1992

	$Good	$Fine	$N.Mint	£Good	£Fine	£N.Mint
1 ND	$1.00	$3.00	$5.00	£0.70	£2.10	£3.50
Title Value:	$1.00	$3.00	$5.00	£0.70	£2.10	£3.50

HELLRAISER, CLIVE BARKER'S

Marvel Comics Group/Epic; 1 Feb 1990-20 1993

	$Good	$Fine	$N.Mint	£Good	£Fine	£N.Mint
1 ND Bolton art	$1.00	$3.00	$5.00	£0.70	£2.10	£3.50
2 ND Simon Bisley cover						
	$1.00	$3.00	$5.00	£0.70	£2.10	£3.50
3 ND features John Ridgway art						
	$1.00	$3.00	$5.00	£0.70	£2.10	£3.50
4 ND	$1.00	$3.00	$5.00	£0.70	£2.10	£3.50
5 ND Ted McKeever cover						
	$1.20	$3.60	$6.00	£0.80	£2.40	£4.00
6 ND Billy Mumy/Miguel Ferrer scripts featured						
	$1.20	$3.60	$6.00	£0.80	£2.40	£4.00
7 ND John Bolton/Kyle Baker art featured						
	$1.20	$3.60	$6.00	£0.80	£2.40	£4.00
8 ND Texeira art featured						
	$1.20	$3.60	$6.00	£0.80	£2.40	£4.00
9 ND Scott Hampton art featured						
	$1.20	$3.60	$6.00	£0.80	£2.40	£4.00
10 ND 48pgs, foil embossed cover						
	$1.00	$3.00	$5.00	£0.70	£2.10	£3.50
11-13 ND 48pgs	$1.00	$3.00	$5.00	£0.70	£2.10	£3.50
14 ND 48pgs, $4.95 cover begins						
	$1.00	$3.00	$5.00	£0.70	£2.10	£3.50
15-20 ND 48pgs	$1.00	$3.00	$5.00	£0.70	£2.10	£3.50
Title Value:	$21.00	$63.00	$105.00	£14.50	£43.50	£72.50
Trade Paperback (Apr 1991), selected stories reprinted from issues #1-4, new John Bolton cover				£1.60	£4.80	£8.00

Note: Mature Readers only. Based on the Hellraiser and Hellbound films. #1-9 64pgs. Issues #1-6 quarterly frequency. Bi-monthly from issue #7

HELLRAISER: BOOK OF THE DAMNED

Marvel Comics Group; 1 Oct 1991-4 1992

	$Good	$Fine	$N.Mint	£Good	£Fine	£N.Mint
1-4 ND 48pgs, journal format of photos, notes and press cuttings, foil embossed cover by Simon Bisley						
	$1.00	$3.00	$5.00	£0.70	£2.10	£3.50
Title Value:	$4.00	$12.00	$20.00	£2.80	£8.40	£14.00

HELLSHOCK

Image,MS; 1 Jul 1994-4 Oct 1994

	$Good	$Fine	$N.Mint	£Good	£Fine	£N.Mint
1-4 ND Jae Lee script and art						
	$0.50	$1.50	$2.50	£0.30	£0.90	£1.50
Title Value:	$2.00	$6.00	$10.00	£1.20	£3.60	£6.00

HELLSHOCK (2ND SERIES)

Image; 1 Jan 1997-present

	$Good	$Fine	$N.Mint	£Good	£Fine	£N.Mint
1-2 ND Jae Lee script and art						
	$0.50	$1.50	$2.50	£0.30	£0.90	£1.50
Title Value:	$1.00	$3.00	$5.00	£0.60	£1.80	£3.00

HELLSTORM

Marvel Comics Group; 1 Apr 1993-21 Dec 1994

	$Good	$Fine	$N.Mint	£Good	£Fine	£N.Mint
1 Daimon Hellstrom (Son of Satan) begins, parchment stock cover with thermographic (raised) red ink						
	$0.40	$1.20	$2.00	£0.25	£0.75	£1.25
2 Dr. Strange and Gargoyle appear						
	$0.40	$1.20	$2.00	£0.25	£0.75	£1.25
3	$0.40	$1.20	$2.00	£0.25	£0.75	£1.25
4 Ghost Rider appears						
	$0.40	$1.20	$2.00	£0.25	£0.75	£1.25
5	$0.40	$1.20	$2.00	£0.25	£0.75	£1.25
6 Mark Beachum guest pencils						
	$0.40	$1.20	$2.00	£0.25	£0.75	£1.25
7-13	$0.40	$1.20	$2.00	£0.25	£0.75	£1.25
14 with free Spiderman vs. Venom card sheet						
	$0.40	$1.20	$2.00	£0.25	£0.75	£1.25
15	$0.40	$1.20	$2.00	£0.25	£0.75	£1.25
16 Warren Ellis script begins, Brian Bolland cover						
	$0.40	$1.20	$2.00	£0.25	£0.75	£1.25
17 Satana returns	$0.40	$1.20	$2.00	£0.25	£0.75	£1.25
18-20	$0.40	$1.20	$2.00	£0.25	£0.75	£1.25
21 Duncan Fegredo cover						
	$0.40	$1.20	$2.00	£0.25	£0.75	£1.25
Title Value:	$8.40	$25.20	$42.00	£5.25	£15.75	£26.25

HEMBECK

Eclipse,Magazine; 1-2 1988?

	$Good	$Fine	$N.Mint	£Good	£Fine	£N.Mint
1-2 ND reprints	$0.30	$0.90	$1.50	£0.20	£0.60	£1.00
Title Value:	$0.60	$1.80	$3.00	£0.40	£1.20	£2.00

HENRY V

Caliber/Tome Press,MS; 1-3 1991

	$Good	$Fine	$N.Mint	£Good	£Fine	£N.Mint
1-3 ND black and white						
	$0.40	$1.20	$2.00	£0.25	£0.75	£1.25
Title Value:	$1.20	$3.60	$6.00	£0.75	£2.25	£3.75

HEPCATS

Double Diamond Press; 1 1989-12 1995

	$Good	$Fine	$N.Mint	£Good	£Fine	£N.Mint
1 Martin Wagner script and art begins; black and white						
	$2.00	$6.00	$10.00	£1.00	£3.00	£5.00
1 2nd printing	$0.50	$1.50	$2.50	£0.30	£0.90	£1.50
1 Special Edition, (Nov 1991) - reprints issue 1, 2,000 signed and numbered copies						
	$2.00	$6.00	$10.00	£0.80	£2.40	£4.00
1 Special Edition 2nd printing, (Aug 1994) - new cover, new back-up story						
	$0.50	$1.50	$2.50	£0.30	£0.90	£1.50
2	$1.50	$4.50	$7.50	£0.80	£2.40	£4.00
2 2nd printing	$0.50	$1.50	$2.50	£0.30	£0.90	£1.50
2 3rd printing	$0.50	$1.50	$2.50	£0.30	£0.90	£1.50
2 Special Edition, (Aug 1994) - contains L'il Hepcats story from Usagi Yojimbo #87						
	$1.50	$4.50	$7.50	£0.60	£1.80	£3.00
3 Martin Wagner script/art						
	$1.20	$3.60	$6.00	£0.60	£1.80	£3.00
4-6 Martin Wagner script/art						
	$1.00	$3.00	$5.00	£0.50	£1.50	£2.50
6 2nd printing, (Apr 1993)						
	$0.50	$1.50	$2.50	£0.30	£0.90	£1.50
7 Martin Wagner script/art						
	$1.00	$3.00	$5.00	£0.50	£1.50	£2.50
7 2nd printing, (Jun 1993)						
	$0.50	$1.50	$2.50	£0.30	£0.90	£1.50
8-9 Martin Wagner script/art						
	$1.00	$3.00	$5.00	£0.50	£1.50	£2.50
10-11 Martin Wagner script/art						
	$0.70	$2.10	$3.50	£0.40	£1.20	£2.00
12 40pgs, Martin Wagner script and art						
	$0.70	$2.10	$3.50	£0.40	£1.20	£2.00
Title Value:	$19.30	$57.90	$96.50	£9.80	£29.40	£49.00

Note: all Non-Distributed on the news-stands in the U.K.

Note also: issues #13-15 were adveritsed and solicited but never appeared.

				£Good	£Fine	£N.Mint
The First Hepcats Book (1991), reprints						
ND newspaper strips				£1.00	£3.00	£5.00
The Second Hepcats Book (1991), reprints						
ND newspaper strips				£1.00	£3.00	£5.00
The Collegiate Hepcats (1994)						
ND collects all early Hepcats strips from Martin Wagner's college days, signed				£1.30	£3.90	£6.50
Snowblind Part One (Mar 1995) Trade paperback						
ND reprints issues #3-10				£2.00	£6.00	£10.00

HEPCATS LITTERBOX, THE

Double Diamond Press,OS; nn Aug 1995

	$Good	$Fine	$N.Mint	£Good	£Fine	£N.Mint
nn ND sampler comic reprinting early excerpts and introducing characters						
	$0.50	$1.50	$2.50	£0.30	£0.90	£1.50
Title Value:	$0.50	$1.50	$2.50	£0.30	£0.90	£1.50

HERBIE

ACG; 1 Apr/May 1964-23 Feb 1967

	$Good	$Fine	$N.Mint	£Good	£Fine	£N.Mint
1	$19.00	$57.50	$135.00	£10.50	£32.00	£75.00
2-4	$10.50	$32.00	$75.00	£5.25	£16.00	£37.50
5 Beatles appear	$12.00	$36.00	$85.00	£6.25	£19.00	£45.00
6-7	$7.00	$21.00	$50.00	£4.25	£12.50	£30.00
8 origin	$9.25	$28.00	$65.00	£5.00	£15.00	£35.00
9-10	$7.00	$21.00	$50.00	£4.25	£12.50	£30.00
11-15	$5.00	$15.00	$35.00	£2.85	£8.50	£20.00
16-20	$5.00	$15.00	$35.00	£2.50	£7.50	£17.50
21-22	$5.00	$15.00	$35.00	£2.10	£6.25	£15.00
23 part reprint of 1st Herbie from Forbidden World's #73						
	$5.00	$15.00	$35.00	£2.10	£6.25	£15.00
Title Value:	$164.75	$496.50	$1165.00	£87.55	£262.75	£620.00

Note: all distributed in the U.K.

HERBIE (2ND SERIES)

A Plus Comics; 1 Oct 1990-6 1991

	$Good	$Fine	$N.Mint	£Good	£Fine	£N.Mint
1 ND 48pgs, reprints of original series begin, Trina Robbins cover that parodies Batman and Spiderman; black and white						
	$0.40	$1.20	$2.00	£0.25	£0.75	£1.25
2-5 ND 48pgs, Rog 2000 by John Byrne reprint; black and white						
	$0.40	$1.20	$2.00	£0.25	£0.75	£1.25
6 ND 48pgs, Star Trek parody cover; black and white						
	$0.40	$1.20	$2.00	£0.25	£0.75	£1.25
Title Value:	$2.40	$7.20	$12.00	£1.50	£4.50	£7.50

Note: copies of #1 were re-released in Apr 1996 at a cover price of $2.50.

HERBIE (3RD SERIES)

Dark Horse; 1 Sep 1992-2 Oct 1992

	$Good	$Fine	$N.Mint	£Good	£Fine	£N.Mint
1 ND Ogden Whitney art in colour begins; 8pgs John Byrne art, John Byrne cover						
	$0.50	$1.50	$2.50	£0.30	£0.90	£1.50
2 ND	$0.50	$1.50	$2.50	£0.30	£0.90	£1.50
Title Value:	$1.00	$3.00	$5.00	£0.60	£1.80	£3.00

Note: originally announced as a 12 issue series, only 7 issues were advertised and solicited but the series was cancelled after 2 issues due to poor sales.

HERCULES

Charlton; 1 Oct 1967-13 Sep 1969

	$Good	$Fine	$N.Mint	£Good	£Fine	£N.Mint
1 distributed in the U.K.						
	$1.40	$4.25	$10.00	£0.70	£2.10	£5.00
2-7 distributed in the U.K.						
	$1.05	$3.20	$7.50	£0.55	£1.70	£4.00
8 scarce in the U.S, very scarce in the U.K. magazine format; new Hercules story plus reprint of #1; black and white						
	$3.55	$10.50	$25.00	£2.10	£6.25	£15.00
9-13 distributed in the U.K.						
	$1.05	$3.20	$7.50	£0.40	£1.25	£3.00
Title Value:	$16.50	$49.95	$117.50	£8.10	£24.80	£59.00

HERCULES (2ND SERIES)

A Plus Comics; 1 Sep 1991-2 1991

	$Good	$Fine	$N.Mint	£Good	£Fine	£N.Mint
1-2 ND reprints Charlton series with new dialogue						
	$0.50	$1.50	$2.50	£0.30	£0.90	£1.50
Title Value:	$1.00	$3.00	$5.00	£0.60	£1.80	£3.00

HERCULES UNBOUND

DC Comics; 1 Oct/Nov 1975-12 Aug/Sep 1977

	$Good	$Fine	$N.Mint	£Good	£Fine	£N.Mint
1 Garcia Lopez art begins (ends #6), Wood inks begin						
	$0.65	$2.00	$4.00	£0.30	£1.00	£2.00
2-5	$0.50	$1.50	$3.00	£0.25	£0.75	£1.50
6 LD in the U.K.	$0.40	$1.25	$2.50	£0.20	£0.60	£1.25
7-9 Walt Simonson art						
	$0.40	$1.25	$2.50	£0.20	£0.60	£1.25
10 Walt Simonson art, Atomic Knights X-over						
	$0.40	$1.25	$2.50	£0.20	£0.60	£1.25
11-12 Walt Simonson art						
	$0.40	$1.25	$2.50	£0.20	£0.60	£1.25
Title Value:	$5.45	$16.75	$33.50	£2.70	£8.20	£16.75

HERCULES, PRINCE OF POWER

Marvel Comics Group,MS; 1 Sep 1982-4 Dec 1982

(see Marvel Graphic Novel)

	$Good	$Fine	$N.Mint	£Good	£Fine	£N.Mint
1-4 ND Bob Layton art						
	$0.25	$0.75	$1.25	£0.15	£0.45	£0.75
Title Value:	$1.00	$3.00	$5.00	£0.60	£1.80	£3.00

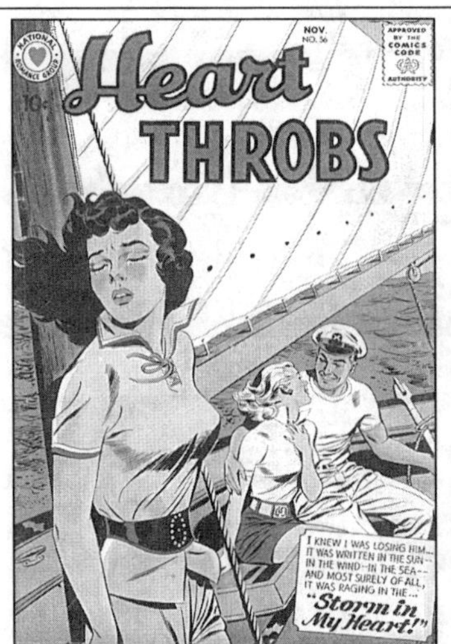

Heart Throbs #56

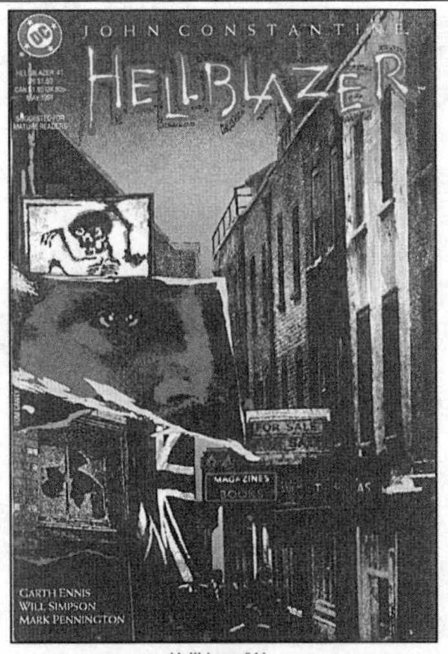

Hellblazer #41

Hercules Unbound #2

	$Good	$Fine	$N.Mint	£Good	£Fine	£N.Mint
Trade Paperback, reprints #1-4.				£0.70	£2.10	£3.50

HERCULES, PRINCE OF POWER (2ND SERIES)

Marvel Comics Group,MS; 1 Mar 1984-4 Jun 1984

	$Good	$Fine	$N.Mint	£Good	£Fine	£N.Mint
1-4 ND Bob Layton art	$0.25	$0.75	$1.25	£0.15	£0.45	£0.75
Title Value:	$1.00	$3.00	$5.00	£0.60	£1.80	£3.00

HERCULES: THE LEGENDARY JOURNEYS

Topps; 1 Jun 1996-4 Sep 1996

	$Good	$Fine	$N.Mint	£Good	£Fine	£N.Mint
1-2 ND based on US TV series; Michael Golden covers	$0.60	$1.80	$3.00	£0.40	£1.20	£2.00
3-4 ND based on US TV series	$0.60	$1.80	$3.00	£0.40	£1.20	£2.00
Title Value:	$2.40	$7.20	$12.00	£1.60	£4.80	£8.00

HERETIC, THE

Dark Horse/Blanc Noir,MS; 1 Nov 1996-3 Jan 1997

	$Good	$Fine	$N.Mint	£Good	£Fine	£N.Mint
1-3 ND Joseph Phillips script and art	$0.60	$1.80	$3.00	£0.40	£1.20	£2.00
Title Value:	$1.80	$5.40	$9.00	£1.20	£3.60	£6.00

HERMES VS. THE EYEBALL KID

Dark Horse,MS; 1 Dec 1994-3 Feb 1995

	$Good	$Fine	$N.Mint	£Good	£Fine	£N.Mint
1-3 ND Eddie Campbell script and art	$0.60	$1.80	$3.00	£0.40	£1.20	£2.00
Title Value:	$1.80	$5.40	$9.00	£1.20	£3.60	£6.00

HERO

Marvel Comics Group,MS; 1 May 1990-6 Oct 1990

	$Good	$Fine	$N.Mint	£Good	£Fine	£N.Mint
1-6 ND	$0.25	$0.75	$1.25	£0.15	£0.45	£0.75
Title Value:	$1.50	$4.50	$7.50	£0.90	£2.70	£4.50

Note: role-playing game tie-in

HERO ALLIANCE

Wonder,OS; 1 May 1987

	$Good	$Fine	$N.Mint	£Good	£Fine	£N.Mint
1 ND story continues from Pied Piper Graphic Novel	$0.50	$1.50	$2.50	£0.30	£0.90	£1.50
Title Value:	$0.50	$1.50	$2.50	£0.30	£0.90	£1.50
Graphic Novel, Hardcover				£1.70	£5.10	£8.50
Annual 1 (Jul 1990), wraparound cover by Paul Smith				£0.30	£0.90	£1.50

HERO ALLIANCE (2ND SERIES)

Innovation; 1 Sep 1989-18 1991

	$Good	$Fine	$N.Mint	£Good	£Fine	£N.Mint
1 ND Ron Lim art	$0.40	$1.20	$2.00	£0.25	£0.75	£1.25
2-9 ND	$0.40	$1.20	$2.00	£0.25	£0.75	£1.25
10 ND ties in with Annual #1	$0.40	$1.20	$2.00	£0.25	£0.75	£1.25
11-18 ND	$0.40	$1.20	$2.00	£0.25	£0.75	£1.25
Title Value:	$7.20	$21.60	$36.00	£4.50	£13.50	£22.50

HERO ALLIANCE QUARTERLY

Innovation; 1 Jun 1991-4 1992

	$Good	$Fine	$N.Mint	£Good	£Fine	£N.Mint
1 ND	$0.50	$1.50	$2.50	£0.30	£0.90	£1.50
2-3 ND Brian Stelfreeze cover	$0.50	$1.50	$2.50	£0.30	£0.90	£1.50
4 ND	$0.50	$1.50	$2.50	£0.30	£0.90	£1.50
Title Value:	$2.00	$6.00	$10.00	£1.20	£3.60	£6.00

HERO ALLIANCE SPECIAL

Innovation,OS; 1 Sep 1992

	$Good	$Fine	$N.Mint	£Good	£Fine	£N.Mint
1 ND prelude to re-vamped series	$0.50	$1.50	$2.50	£0.30	£0.90	£1.50
Title Value:	$0.50	$1.50	$2.50	£0.30	£0.90	£1.50

HERO ALLIANCE VS. JUSTICE MACHINE

Innovation,OS; 1 Nov 1990

	$Good	$Fine	$N.Mint	£Good	£Fine	£N.Mint
1 ND follows events after Annual #1	$0.80	$2.40	$4.00	£0.50	£1.50	£2.50
Title Value:	$0.80	$2.40	$4.00	£0.50	£1.50	£2.50

HERO ALLIANCE; END OF THE GOLDEN AGE

Innovation,MS; 1 Jul 1989-3 Aug 1989

	$Good	$Fine	$N.Mint	£Good	£Fine	£N.Mint
1-3 ND Bart Sears/Ron Lim art, part reprint	$0.50	$1.50	$2.50	£0.30	£0.90	£1.50
Title Value:	$1.50	$4.50	$7.50	£0.90	£2.70	£4.50

Note: bi-weekly

HERO FOR HIRE, LUKE CAGE

Marvel Comics Group; 1 Jun 1972-16 Dec 1973

(becomes Powerman with #17, Powerman and Iron Fist with #50)

	$Good	$Fine	$N.Mint	£Good	£Fine	£N.Mint
1 ND scarce in the U.K. origin and 1st appearance of Luke Cage	$5.75	$17.50	$35.00	£3.75	£11.00	£22.50
2 ND	$2.05	$6.25	$12.50	£1.30	£4.00	£8.00
3 ND 1st appearance Mace	$2.05	$6.25	$12.50	£1.25	£3.75	£7.50
4-5 ND	$2.05	$6.25	$12.50	£1.25	£3.75	£7.50
6-7 ND	$1.25	$3.75	$7.50	£0.80	£2.50	£5.00
8 ND Dr. Doom appears	$1.25	$3.75	$7.50	£0.80	£2.50	£5.00
9 ND Luke Cage vs. Dr. Doom	$1.25	$3.75	$7.50	£0.80	£2.50	£5.00
10 ND	$1.25	$3.75	$7.50	£0.80	£2.50	£5.00
11 ND	$1.15	$3.50	$7.00	£0.75	£2.25	£4.50
12 ND Spiderman cameo	$1.15	$3.50	$7.00	£0.75	£2.25	£4.50
13 ND	$1.15	$3.50	$7.00	£0.75	£2.25	£4.50
14 ND origin retold	$1.25	$3.75	$7.50	£0.80	£2.50	£5.00
15 ND includes Golden Age Sub-Mariner reprint by Everett	$1.25	$3.75	$7.50	£0.80	£2.50	£5.00
16 ND origin Stiletto	$1.15	$3.50	$7.00	£0.75	£2.25	£4.50
Title Value:	$27.30	$82.75	$165.50	£17.40	£52.75	£106.00

HERO HOTLINE

DC Comics,MS; 1 May 1989-6 Oct 1989

	$Good	$Fine	$N.Mint	£Good	£Fine	£N.Mint
1-6	$0.20	$0.60	$1.00	£0.10	£0.35	£0.60
Title Value:	$1.20	$3.60	$6.00	£0.60	£2.10	£3.60

HERO KILLERS

Marvel Comics Group; 1992

Cross-over storyline running throughout the following issues: **Amazing Spiderman Annual #26, Spectacular Spiderman Annual #12, Web of Spiderman Annual #8, New Warriors Annual #2**

HERO PREMIERE EDITION

Warrior Publications; 1 Jul 1993-11 1994?

	$Good	$Fine	$N.Mint	£Good	£Fine	£N.Mint
1 Premiere Edition #1 (issued with Hero Illustrated #1) - Star Trek: Deep Space Nine; all Ash Can 5.5" x 8.5" unless otherwise stated; blue cover, 8pgs	$0.60	$1.80	$3.00	£0.40	£1.20	£2.00
2 Premiere Edition #2 (issued with Hero Illustrated #1) - Batman/Grendel; red foil enhanced cover, 16pgs	$0.60	$1.80	$3.00	£0.40	£1.20	£2.00
3 Premiere Edition #3 (issued with Hero Illustrated #2) - Aliens: Deadliest of the Species; all red foil cover, 5.5" x 8.5" Ash Can size, 16pgs with 8 in coloyr and 8 in black and white	$0.60	$1.80	$3.00	£0.40	£1.20	£2.00
4 Premiere Edition #4 (issued with Hero Illustrated #2) - Madman Adventures; red foil enhanced cover, 16pgs	$0.60	$1.80	$3.00	£0.40	£1.20	£2.00
5 Premiere Edition #5 (issued with Hero Illustrated #3) - Q Unit; 16pgs	$0.60	$1.80	$3.00	£0.40	£1.20	£2.00
6 Premiere Edition #6 (issued with Hero Illustrated #3) - Horus, Lord of Light; 16pgs	$0.60	$1.80	$3.00	£0.40	£1.20	£2.00
7 Premiere Edition #7 - 2099 Unlimited #1; gold foil cover, 16pgs, numbered with seal of authenticity; 10,000	$0.80	$2.40	$4.00	£0.50	£1.50	£2.50
8 Premiere Edition #8 - Shadowhawk III #1	$0.60	$1.80	$3.00	£0.40	£1.20	£2.00
9 Premiere Edition #9 - Aliens vs. Predator: deadliest of the Species gold/blue foil cover	$0.60	$1.80	$3.00	£0.40	£1.20	£2.00
10 Premiere Edition #10 (issued with Hero Illustrated #6) - Pitt #3; red foil enhanced cover, 16pgs	$0.45	$1.35	$2.25	£0.30	£0.90	£1.50
11 Premiere Edition #11 (issued with Hero Illustrated #7) - Wetworks; 16pgs	$0.45	$1.35	$2.25	£0.30	£0.90	£1.50
11 Premiere Edition Holiday Special, (issued with Hero Illustrated #7) - Bone; 7" x 10" normal comic size	$0.60	$1.80	$3.00	£0.40	£1.20	£2.00
Title Value:	$7.10	$21.30	$35.50	£4.70	£14.10	£23.50

Note: only available with Hero Magazine; not distributed in the U.K.

HERO SANDWICH

Slave Labor; 1 1988-9 1990

	$Good	$Fine	$N.Mint	£Good	£Fine	£N.Mint
1-7 ND	$0.50	$1.50	$2.50	£0.30	£0.90	£1.50
7 Amalgamated Issue, ND - single issue amalgamation of issues #7 and #8 (Apr 1990)	$0.55	$1.65	$2.75	£0.35	£1.05	£1.75
8-9 ND	$0.50	$1.50	$2.50	£0.30	£0.90	£1.50
Title Value:	$5.05	$15.15	$25.25	£3.05	£9.15	£15.25
Hero Sandwich: Nobody Lives Forever (1989) Trade paperback ND collects issues #1-4				£1.00	£3.00	£5.00

HERO ZERO

Dark Horse,OS; 0 Sep 1994

	$Good	$Fine	$N.Mint	£Good	£Fine	£N.Mint
0 ND spin-off from Comics' Greatest World series	$0.50	$1.50	$2.50	£0.30	£0.90	£1.50
Title Value:	$0.50	$1.50	$2.50	£0.30	£0.90	£1.50

HEROES

DC Comics/Milestone,MS; 1 May 1996-6 Oct 1996

	$Good	$Fine	$N.Mint	£Good	£Fine	£N.Mint
1 ND Shadow Cabinet team members join up with Static	$0.50	$1.50	$2.50	£0.30	£0.90	£1.50
2-6 ND	$0.50	$1.50	$2.50	£0.30	£0.90	£1.50
Title Value:	$3.00	$9.00	$15.00	£1.80	£5.40	£9.00

HEROES AGAINST HUNGER

DC Comics,OS; nn 1986

(see Heroes For Hope)

	$Good	$Fine	$N.Mint	£Good	£Fine	£N.Mint
nn ND famine relief benefit book; Superman and Batman feature, Neal Adams cover and part art	$0.40	$1.20	$2.00	£0.25	£0.75	£1.25
Title Value:	$0.40	$1.20	$2.00	£0.25	£0.75	£1.25

HEROES FOR HOPE STARRING THE X-MEN

Marvel Comics Group,OS; nn Dec 1985

	$Good	$Fine	$N.Mint	£Good	£Fine	£N.Mint
nn ND 52pgs, proceeds donated to famine relief; Ellison, Morre and Stephen King scripts, Wrightson, Corben, Miller, Neal Adams and Bolton art	$1.00	$3.00	$5.00	£0.50	£1.50	£2.50
Title Value:	$1.00	$3.00	$5.00	£0.50	£1.50	£2.50

HERU, SON OF AUSAR

Afrocentric Comic Books; 1 Apr 1993-3 1993

	$Good	$Fine	$N.Mint	£Good	£Fine	£N.Mint
1 ND bound-in trading card by Erik Larsen	$0.40	$1.20	$2.00	£0.25	£0.75	£1.25
2-3 ND	$0.40	$1.20	$2.00	£0.25	£0.75	£1.25
Title Value:	$1.20	$3.60	$6.00	£0.75	£2.25	£3.75

HEX

DC Comics; 1 Sep 1985-18 Feb 1987

(see Jonah Hex, Jonah Hex Spectacular, Weird Western Tales)

	$Good	$Fine	$N.Mint	£Good	£Fine	£N.Mint
1 Mark Texeira art, new storyline, Hex in future continued from Jonah Hex #92	$0.40	$1.20	$2.00	£0.25	£0.75	£1.25
2-3 Mark Texira art	$0.40	$1.20	$2.00	£0.25	£0.75	£1.25
4 Mark Texeira cover	$0.40	$1.20	$2.00	£0.25	£0.75	£1.25
5 Mark Texeira cover and art	$0.40	$1.20	$2.00	£0.25	£0.75	£1.25
6 Mark Texeira cover and art, origin Stiletto	$0.40	$1.20	$2.00	£0.25	£0.75	£1.25
7 Mark Texeira cover and art	$0.40	$1.20	$2.00	£0.25	£0.75	£1.25
8	$0.40	$1.20	$2.00	£0.25	£0.75	£1.25
9 Mark Texeira cover and art						

	$Good	$Fine	$N.Mint	£Good	£Fine	£N.Mint
	$0.40	$1.20	$2.00	£0.25	£0.75	£1.25
10	$0.40	$1.20	$2.00	£0.25	£0.75	£1.25
11-12 Mark Texeira cover and art, Batman appears	$0.40	$1.20	$2.00	£0.25	£0.75	£1.25
13-14 Mark Texeira cover and art	$0.40	$1.20	$2.00	£0.25	£0.75	£1.25
15 Giffen cover and art	$0.40	$1.20	$2.00	£0.25	£0.75	£1.25
16-18 Giffen art	$0.40	$1.20	$2.00	£0.25	£0.75	£1.25
Title Value:	$7.20	$21.60	$36.00	£4.50	£13.50	£22.50

HEXBREAKER

(see Badger)

HI-ADVENTURE HEROES

Gold Key,TV; 1 May 1969-2 Aug 1969

	$Good	$Fine	$N.Mint	£Good	£Fine	£N.Mint
1 scarce though distributed in the U.K. Three Musketeers, Arabian Knights	$3.55	$10.50	$25.00	£2.10	£6.25	£15.00
2 scarce though distributed in the U.K. Three Musketeers, Arabian Knights	$2.85	$8.50	$20.00	£1.40	£4.25	£10.00
Title Value:	$6.40	$19.00	$45.00	£3.50	£10.50	£25.00

HIDING PLACE, THE

DC Comics/Piranha Press; nn Aug 1990

	$Good	$Fine	$N.Mint	£Good	£Fine	£N.Mint
nn ND 104pgs, Trade paperback format, Steve Parkhouse art	$2.30	$6.75	$11.50	£1.50	£4.50	£7.50
Title Value:	$2.30	$6.75	$11.50	£1.50	£4.50	£7.50

HIGH IMPACT STUDIOS LINGERIE SPECIAL

High Impact Studios,OS; nn May 1996

	$Good	$Fine	$N.Mint	£Good	£Fine	£N.Mint
nn ND pin-ups	$0.60	$1.80	$3.00	£0.40	£1.20	£2.00
nn Signed Edition ND signed by Ricky Carrelero, no certificate	$1.40	$4.20	$7.00	£1.00	£3.00	£5.00
Title Value:	$2.00	$6.00	$10.00	£1.40	£4.20	£7.00

HIGH SHINING BRASS

Apple Comics; 1 Aug 1990-4 Oct 1991

	$Good	$Fine	$N.Mint	£Good	£Fine	£N.Mint
1-4 ND story by Vietnam Veteran Don Lomax	$0.50	$1.50	$2.50	£0.30	£0.90	£1.50
Title Value:	$2.00	$6.00	$10.00	£1.20	£3.60	£6.00

HIGH VOLTAGE

Blackout Comics; 0 Mar 1996

	$Good	$Fine	$N.Mint	£Good	£Fine	£N.Mint
0 ND Mike Baron script	$0.60	$1.80	$3.00	£0.40	£1.20	£2.00
0 Commemorative Edition, ND (May 1996), pre-bagged with certificate; 3,000 copies	$2.00	$6.00	$10.00	£1.30	£3.90	£6.50
Title Value:	$2.60	$7.80	$13.00	£1.70	£5.10	£8.50

HIGHBROW ENTERTAINMENT ASHCAN

Image,OS; nn Aug 1994

	$Good	$Fine	$N.Mint	£Good	£Fine	£N.Mint
nn ND 16pgs, information on Erik Larsen's projects for 1995/96 inc. Savage Dragon; black and white	$0.30	$0.90	$1.50	£0.20	£0.60	£1.00
Title Value:	$0.30	$0.90	$1.50	£0.20	£0.60	£1.00

HIS NAME IS SAVAGE

Adventure House,Magazine; 1 Jun 1968

	$Good	$Fine	$N.Mint	£Good	£Fine	£N.Mint
1 ND Gil Kane art, black & white	$3.20	$9.50	$22.50	£2.10	£6.25	£15.00
Title Value:	$3.20	$9.50	$22.50	£2.10	£6.25	£15.00

HISTORY OF THE DC UNIVERSE

DC Comics,MS; 1 Sep 1986-2 Nov 1986

	$Good	$Fine	$N.Mint	£Good	£Fine	£N.Mint
1-2 ND 48pgs, George Perez art	$0.90	$2.70	$4.50	£0.60	£1.80	£3.00
Title Value:	$1.80	$5.40	$9.00	£1.20	£3.60	£6.00

Note: Dark Knight format, glossy paper (Silent Knight accidentally appears in 2 separate periods of history and Tommy Tomorrow is mis-coloured throughout as Rip Hunter).

	$Good	$Fine	$N.Mint	£Good	£Fine	£N.Mint
Deluxe Hardback Edition with dustjacket and limited edition enamel pin				£4.20	£12.60	£21.00
Deluxe Hardback Edition with dustjacket, signed and numbered with limited edition gold-plated pin				£12.00	£36.00	£60.00

HITCH-HIKER'S GUIDE TO THE GALAXY, THE

DC Comics,MS; 1 Nov 1993-3 Jan 1994

(see Restaurant at the End of the Universe)

	$Good	$Fine	$N.Mint	£Good	£Fine	£N.Mint
1-3 ND 48pgs, squarebound; John Carnell script, Steve Leialoha art	$1.00	$3.00	$5.00	£0.60	£1.80	£3.00
Title Value:	$3.00	$9.00	$15.00	£1.80	£5.40	£9.00

HITMAN

DC Comics; 1 Apr 1996-present

(see Demon 2nd series)

	$Good	$Fine	$N.Mint	£Good	£Fine	£N.Mint
1 ND Batman and The Joker appear; Garth Ennis script, John McCrea cover and art	$1.60	$4.80	$8.00	£1.00	£3.00	£5.00
2 ND	$1.20	$3.60	$6.00	£0.80	£2.40	£4.00
3 ND Batman appears	$1.00	$3.00	$5.00	£0.60	£1.80	£3.00
4 ND	$0.80	$2.40	$4.00	£0.50	£1.50	£2.50
5 ND	$0.80	$2.40	$4.00	£0.40	£1.20	£2.00
6 ND	$0.50	$1.50	$2.50	£0.30	£0.90	£1.50
7 ND bi-weekly	$0.50	$1.50	$2.50	£0.30	£0.90	£1.50
8 ND Final Night tie-in; bi-weekly	$0.50	$1.50	$2.50	£0.30	£0.90	£1.50
9 ND	$0.50	$1.50	$2.50	£0.30	£0.90	£1.50
10-12 ND Green Lantern appears	$0.50	$1.50	$2.50	£0.30	£0.90	£1.50
Title Value:	$8.90	$26.70	$44.00	£5.40	£16.20	£27.00
Hitman (Feb 1977) Trade paperback ND collects issues #1-3 with Demon Annual #2 and Batman Chronicles #4				£1.30	£3.90	£6.50

HITOMI II

Antarctic Press,MS; 1 Aug 1993-10 Sep 1995

	$Good	$Fine	$N.Mint	£Good	£Fine	£N.Mint
1 ND Dave Wilson script and art, black and white	$0.50	$1.50	$2.50	£0.30	£0.90	£1.50
2-6 ND black and white	$0.50	$1.50	$2.50	£0.30	£0.90	£1.50
7 ND title becomes "Hitomi: Geohammer"; black and white	$0.55	$1.65	$2.75	£0.35	£1.05	£1.75
8-9 ND black and white	$0.55	$1.65	$2.75	£0.35	£1.05	£1.75
10 ND 40pgs, black and white	$0.60	$1.80	$3.00	£0.40	£1.20	£2.00
Title Value:	$5.25	$15.75	$26.25	£3.25	£9.75	£16.25

HOBBIT, THE

Eclipse,MS; 1 Apr 1990-3 Jun 1990

	$Good	$Fine	$N.Mint	£Good	£Fine	£N.Mint
1 ND 48pgs, adaptation of Tolkien novel	$0.90	$2.70	$4.50	£0.60	£1.80	£3.00
1 2nd printing ND	$0.80	$2.40	$4.00	£0.50	£1.50	£2.50
2-3 ND 48pgs	$0.90	$2.70	$4.50	£0.60	£1.80	£3.00
Title Value:	$3.50	$10.50	$17.50	£2.30	£6.90	£11.50
Graphic Album (1991), softcover				£1.50	£4.50	£7.50
Graphic Album (1991), hardcover				£4.50	£1.50	£22.50

HOKUM & HEX

Marvel Comics Group/Razorline; 1 Sep 1993-9 May 1994

	$Good	$Fine	$N.Mint	£Good	£Fine	£N.Mint
1 ND prismatic foil cover	$0.45	$1.35	$2.25	£0.30	£0.90	£1.50
2-9 ND	$0.40	$1.20	$2.00	£0.25	£0.75	£1.25
Title Value:	$3.65	$10.95	$18.25	£2.30	£6.90	£11.50

HOLIDAY FOR SCREAMS

Malibu,OS; 1 Feb 1992

	$Good	$Fine	$N.Mint	£Good	£Fine	£N.Mint
1 ND 48pgs, squarebound, black and white horror anthology	$0.90	$2.70	$4.50	£0.60	£1.80	£3.00
Title Value:	$0.90	$2.70	$4.50	£0.60	£1.80	£3.00

HOLIDAY OUT

Renegade; 1 Mar 1987-4 Jun 1987

	$Good	$Fine	$N.Mint	£Good	£Fine	£N.Mint
1-4 ND	$0.40	$1.20	$2.00	£0.25	£0.75	£1.25
Title Value:	$1.60	$4.80	$8.00	£1.00	£3.00	£5.00

HOLLYWOOD DETECTIVES, THE

Eternity,OS; 1 Jul 1991

	$Good	$Fine	$N.Mint	£Good	£Fine	£N.Mint
1 ND Dan Turner, Queenie Smith feature	$0.80	$2.40	$4.00	£0.50	£1.50	£2.50
Title Value:	$0.80	$2.40	$4.00	£0.50	£1.50	£2.50

HOLLYWOOD SECRETS OF ROMANCE

I.W. Super;9 1964

	$Good	$Fine	$N.Mint	£Good	£Fine	£N.Mint
9 distributed in the U.K. reprints Quality Comics Title "Hollywood Secrets"; Reed Crandall art	$1.40	$4.25	$10.00	£0.70	£2.10	£5.00
Title Value:	$1.40	$4.25	$10.00	£0.70	£2.10	£5.00

HOLLYWOOD SUPERSTARS

Marvel Comics Group/Epic; 1 Dec 1990-5 Apr 1991

	$Good	$Fine	$N.Mint	£Good	£Fine	£N.Mint
1-5 ND 48pgs	$0.40	$1.20	$2.00	£0.25	£0.75	£1.25
Title Value:	$2.00	$6.00	$10.00	£1.25	£3.75	£6.25

HOLOCAUST

DC Comics/Milestone,MS; 1 Feb 1995-5 Jun 1995

	$Good	$Fine	$N.Mint	£Good	£Fine	£N.Mint
1-5	$0.30	$0.90	$1.50	£0.20	£0.60	£1.00
Title Value:	$1.50	$4.50	$7.50	£1.00	£3.00	£5.00

HOLY KNIGHT, THE

Pocket Change Comics; 1 1995-11 1996 ?

	$Good	$Fine	$N.Mint	£Good	£Fine	£N.Mint
1-8 ND 24pgs, Bob Dixon script, Xavier and Kaleb art; black and white	$0.50	$1.50	$2.50	£0.30	£0.90	£1.50
9 ND Bob Dixon script, Philip Xavier art; black and white	$0.50	$1.50	$2.50	£0.30	£0.90	£1.50
10-11 ND Bob Dixon script, Xavier and Austin art; black and white	$0.50	$1.50	$2.50	£0.30	£0.90	£1.50
Title Value:	$5.50	$16.50	$27.50	£3.30	£9.90	£16.50

HOMER THE HAPPY GHOST

Marvel Comics Group; 1 Nov 1969-5 Jul 1970

	$Good	$Fine	$N.Mint	£Good	£Fine	£N.Mint
1 scarce in the U.K.	$1.40	$4.25	$10.00	£0.55	£1.70	£4.00
2-5 scarce in the U.K.	$1.05	$3.20	$7.50	£0.40	£1.25	£3.00
Title Value:	$5.60	$17.05	$40.00	£2.15	£6.70	£16.00

HOMICIDE

Dark Horse,OS; 1 Apr 1990

	$Good	$Fine	$N.Mint	£Good	£Fine	£N.Mint
1 ND	$0.50	$1.50	$2.50	£0.30	£0.90	£1.50
Title Value:	$0.50	$1.50	$2.50	£0.30	£0.90	£1.50

HONEY WEST

Gold Key,TV; 1 Sep 1966

	$Good	$Fine	$N.Mint	£Good	£Fine	£N.Mint
1 scarce though distributed in the U.K. based on TV series starring Anne Francis (Alteira in Forbidden Planet)	$14.00	$43.00	$100.00	£7.00	£21.00	£50.00
Title Value:	$14.00	$43.00	$100.00	£7.00	£21.00	£50.00

HONEYMOONERS

Lodestone,TV; 1 Oct 1986

	$Good	$Fine	$N.Mint	£Good	£Fine	£N.Mint
1 ND	$0.50	$1.50	$2.50	£0.30	£0.90	£1.50
Title Value:	$0.50	$1.50	$2.50	£0.30	£0.90	£1.50

HONEYMOONERS (2ND SERIES)

Triad,TV; 1 Sep 1987-13 1988

	$Good	$Fine	$N.Mint	£Good	£Fine	£N.Mint
1 ND	$0.60	$1.80	$3.00	£0.40	£1.20	£2.00
2-3 ND	$0.50	$1.50	$2.50	£0.30	£0.90	£1.50
4 ND squarebound	$0.60	$1.80	$3.00	£0.40	£1.20	£2.00
5-13 ND	$0.50	$1.50	$2.50	£0.30	£0.90	£1.50
Title Value:	$6.70	$20.10	$33.50	£4.10	£12.30	£20.50

HONEYMOONERS CHRISTMAS SPECIAL

Triad,TV; 1 1988

	$Good	$Fine	$N.Mint	£Good	£Fine	£N.Mint
1 ND	$0.80	$2.40	$4.00	£0.50	£1.50	£2.50

	$Good	$Fine	$N.Mint	£Good	£Fine	£N.Mint
Title Value:	$0.80	$2.40	$4.00	£0.50	£1.50	£2.50

HONK!
Fantagraphics,Magazine; 1 1987-5 1988

	$Good	$Fine	$N.Mint	£Good	£Fine	£N.Mint
1-5 ND	$0.60	$1.80	$3.00	£0.40	£1.20	£2.00
Title Value:	$3.00	$9.00	$15.00	£2.00	£6.00	£10.00

HOODOO
The 3-D Zone,OS; 1 Nov 1988

	$Good	$Fine	$N.Mint	£Good	£Fine	£N.Mint
1 ND Mary Fleener art	$0.50	$1.50	$2.50	£0.30	£0.90	£1.50
Title Value:	$0.50	$1.50	$2.50	£0.30	£0.90	£1.50

HOOK
Marvel Comics Group,MS; 1 Jan 1992-4 Feb 1992

	$Good	$Fine	$N.Mint	£Good	£Fine	£N.Mint
1-4 adapted and inked by Charles Vess, bi-weekly	$0.15	$0.45	$0.75	£0.10	£0.35	£0.60
Title Value:	$0.60	$1.80	$3.00	£0.40	£1.40	£2.40

HOOK BOOKSHELF EDITION
Marvel Comics Group,OS; nn Jan 1992

	$Good	$Fine	$N.Mint	£Good	£Fine	£N.Mint
nn ND 64pgs, adaptation of Steven Spielberg film	$1.00	$3.00	$5.00	£0.70	£2.10	£3.50
Title Value:	$1.00	$3.00	$5.00	£0.70	£2.10	£3.50

HOOK SUPER SPECIAL
Marvel Comics Group,Magazine OS Film; 1 Jan 1992

	$Good	$Fine	$N.Mint	£Good	£Fine	£N.Mint
1 ND 80pgs, adaptation of Steven Spielberg film, John Ridgway and Charles Vess art	$0.60	$1.80	$3.00	£0.40	£1.20	£2.00
Title Value:	$0.60	$1.80	$3.00	£0.40	£1.20	£2.00

HOROBI
Viz; 1 Apr 1990-8 1991

	$Good	$Fine	$N.Mint	£Good	£Fine	£N.Mint
1-7 ND 64pgs, squarebound, Japanes manga adapted by Len Wein	$0.70	$2.10	$3.50	£0.45	£1.35	£2.25
8 ND 72pgs, squarebound, Japanes manga adapted by Len Wein	$0.80	$2.40	$4.00	£0.50	£1.50	£2.50
Title Value:	$5.70	$17.10	$28.50	£3.65	£10.95	£18.25

HOROBI BOOK TWO
Viz; 1 1991-7 1991

	$Good	$Fine	$N.Mint	£Good	£Fine	£N.Mint
1-7 ND	$0.80	$2.40	$4.00	£0.50	£1.50	£2.50
Title Value:	$5.60	$16.80	$28.00	£3.50	£10.50	£17.50

HORROR HOUSE
AC Comics; 1 Nov 1994

	$Good	$Fine	$N.Mint	£Good	£Fine	£N.Mint
1 ND horror anthology with classic Wally Wood cover; black and white	$0.60	$1.80	$3.00	£0.40	£1.20	£2.00
Title Value:	$0.60	$1.80	$3.00	£0.40	£1.20	£2.00

HORROR IN THE DARK
Fantagor,MS; 1 Aug 1991-5 Dec 1991

	$Good	$Fine	$N.Mint	£Good	£Fine	£N.Mint
1-5 ND Richard Corben art, black and white; painted covers	$0.40	$1.20	$2.00	£0.25	£0.75	£1.25
Title Value:	$2.00	$6.00	$10.00	£1.25	£3.75	£6.25

HORROR SHOW: TALES OF FEAR AND FANTASY
Caliber Press,OS; 1 Oct 1991

	$Good	$Fine	$N.Mint	£Good	£Fine	£N.Mint
1 ND 64pgs, Richard Sala cover, black and white	$0.60	$1.80	$3.00	£0.40	£1.20	£2.00
Title Value:	$0.60	$1.80	$3.00	£0.40	£1.20	£2.00

HORRORIST, THE
DC Comics/Vertigo,MS; 1 Dec 1995-2 Jan 1996

	$Good	$Fine	$N.Mint	£Good	£Fine	£N.Mint
1-2 ND 48pgs, John Constantine appears, Jamie Delano script, David Lloyd art	$1.20	$3.60	$6.00	£0.80	£2.40	£4.00
Title Value:	$2.40	$7.20	$12.00	£1.60	£4.80	£8.00

HORRORS OF THE HAUNTER
AC Comics; 1 Sep 1994

	$Good	$Fine	$N.Mint	£Good	£Fine	£N.Mint
1 ND Bill Black cover; black and white	$0.60	$1.80	$3.00	£0.40	£1.20	£2.00
Title Value:	$0.60	$1.80	$3.00	£0.40	£1.20	£2.00

HORSEMAN
Crusade Comics; 0 May 1996; 1 Mar 1996; Kevlar Studios; 1 Nov 1996-present

	$Good	$Fine	$N.Mint	£Good	£Fine	£N.Mint
0 ND 24pgs, (May 1996)	$0.60	$1.80	$3.00	£0.40	£1.20	£2.00
0 Ashcan Edition ND	$3.00	$9.00	$15.00	£2.00	£6.00	£10.00
1 ND Bill Tucci script, Mshindo art begins; Shi appears	$0.60	$1.80	$3.00	£0.40	£1.20	£2.00
1 Commemorative Edition ND	$5.00	$15.00	$25.00	£3.00	£9.00	£15.00
1 Kevlar Edition, ND Hank Kwon script, Mshindo Kuumba and Buzz art	$0.60	$1.80	$3.00	£0.40	£1.20	£2.00
1 Kevlar Variant Cover Edition, ND cover by Mshindo Kumba	$1.20	$3.60	$6.00	£0.70	£2.10	£3.50
Title Value:	$11.00	$33.00	$55.00	£6.90	£20.70	£34.50

Note: Crusade Comics originally planned Horseman as a mini-series but the character switched to Kevlar Studios after Crusade issue #1 and its variants.

HORUS, SON OF OSIRIS
Acme Comics,Magazine MS; 1 Apr 1991-3 Jun 1991

	$Good	$Fine	$N.Mint	£Good	£Fine	£N.Mint
1 ND 64pgs	$0.50	$1.50	$2.50	£0.30	£0.90	£1.50
1 Deluxe Edition, ND 64pgs, on high quality paper	$0.60	$1.80	$3.00	£0.40	£1.20	£2.00
2-3 ND 64pgs	$0.50	$1.50	$2.50	£0.30	£0.90	£1.50
Title Value:	$2.10	$6.30	$10.50	£1.30	£3.90	£6.50

HOSTILE TAKEOVER ASHCAN
Malibu Ultraverse,OS; nn Sep 1994

	$Good	$Fine	$N.Mint	£Good	£Fine	£N.Mint
nn ND 16pgs, black and white; previews storyline starting in Night Man #12	$0.15	$0.45	$0.75	£0.10	£0.30	£0.50
Title Value:	$0.15	$0.45	$0.75	£0.10	£0.30	£0.50

HOT AND COLD HEROES
A Plus Comics; 1 Oct 1990-2 1991

	$Good	$Fine	$N.Mint	£Good	£Fine	£N.Mint
1 ND 48pgs, John Byrne's "Rog 2000" reprinted plus other old and new heroes, Mike Zeck art featured; black and white	$0.40	$1.20	$2.00	£0.25	£0.75	£1.25
2 ND 48pgs, ACG reprints continue; black and white	$0.40	$1.20	$2.00	£0.25	£0.75	£1.25
Title Value:	$0.80	$2.40	$4.00	£0.50	£1.50	£2.50

HOT SHOTS: AVENGERS
Marvel Comics Group,OS; 1 Oct 1995

	$Good	$Fine	$N.Mint	£Good	£Fine	£N.Mint
1 ND fully painted pin-ups by Sienkiewicz, Steacy, Zeck, Golden, Jusko and others; fold-out format	$0.60	$1.80	$3.00	£0.40	£1.20	£2.00
Title Value:	$0.60	$1.80	$3.00	£0.40	£1.20	£2.00

HOT SHOTS: SPIDERMAN
Marvel Comics Group,OS; 1 Jan 1996

	$Good	$Fine	$N.Mint	£Good	£Fine	£N.Mint
1 ND pin-ups by Joe Jusko, Alex Ross, Charles Vess and others; fold-out format	$0.60	$1.80	$3.00	£0.40	£1.20	£2.00
Title Value:	$0.60	$1.80	$3.00	£0.40	£1.20	£2.00

HOT SHOTS: X-MEN
Marvel Comics Group; 1 Feb 1996

	$Good	$Fine	$N.Mint	£Good	£Fine	£N.Mint
1 ND pin-ups by Alan Davis, Bill Sienkiewicz, Alex Ross and others; fold-out format	$0.60	$1.80	$3.00	£0.40	£1.20	£2.00
Title Value:	$0.60	$1.80	$3.00	£0.40	£1.20	£2.00

HOT STUF'
Quartuccio,Magazine; 1 1975-8 1983?

	$Good	$Fine	$N.Mint	£Good	£Fine	£N.Mint
1-2 ND 64pgs	$0.90	$2.70	$4.50	£0.60	£1.80	£3.00
3 ND 64pgs, Tim Kirk and Richard Corben art	$1.00	$3.00	$5.00	£0.70	£2.10	£3.50
4 ND 64pgs, Alex Toth and Gray Morrow art	$0.90	$2.70	$4.50	£0.60	£1.80	£3.00
5-7 ND 64pgs	$0.90	$2.70	$4.50	£0.60	£1.80	£3.00
8 ND 64pgs, Erik Larsen art, Neal Adams painted cover	$0.90	$2.70	$4.50	£0.60	£1.80	£3.00
Title Value:	$7.30	$21.90	$36.50	£4.90	£14.70	£24.50

HOT WHEELS
DC Comics,TV Toy; 1 Mar/Apr 1970-6 Jan/Feb 1971

	$Good	$Fine	$N.Mint	£Good	£Fine	£N.Mint
1	$8.50	$26.00	$60.00	£3.55	£10.50	£25.00
2 rare in the U.K.	$3.55	$10.50	$25.00	£1.75	£5.25	£12.50
3 Neal Adams cover	$5.00	$15.00	$35.00	£1.75	£5.25	£12.50
4 rare in the U.K.	$3.55	$10.50	$25.00	£2.10	£6.25	£15.00
5	$3.55	$10.50	$25.00	£1.75	£5.25	£12.50
6 scarce in the U.K. Neal Adams art and cover	$5.50	$17.00	$40.00	£2.50	£7.50	£17.50
Title Value:	$29.65	$89.50	$210.00	£13.40	£40.00	£95.00

HOTEL HARBOUR VIEW
Viz; nn Dec 1990

	$Good	$Fine	$N.Mint	£Good	£Fine	£N.Mint
nn ND graphic album of Japanese manga material with a film noir look	$1.50	$4.50	$7.50	£1.00	£3.00	£5.00
Title Value:	$1.50	$4.50	$7.50	£1.00	£3.00	£5.00

HOTSPUR
Eclipse,MS; 1 Jun 1987-3 Oct 1987

	$Good	$Fine	$N.Mint	£Good	£Fine	£N.Mint
1-3 ND	$0.40	$1.20	$2.00	£0.20	£0.60	£1.00
Title Value:	$1.20	$3.60	$6.00	£0.60	£1.80	£3.00

HOUSE II - THE SECOND STORY
Marvel Comics Group,OS Film; 1 1987

	$Good	$Fine	$N.Mint	£Good	£Fine	£N.Mint
1 ND DS adaptation of film	$0.40	$1.20	$2.00	£0.25	£0.75	£1.25
Title Value:	$0.40	$1.20	$2.00	£0.25	£0.75	£1.25

HOUSE OF FRIGHTENSTEIN
AC Comics; 1 Dec 1994

	$Good	$Fine	$N.Mint	£Good	£Fine	£N.Mint
1 ND horror anthology; black and white	$0.60	$1.80	$3.00	£0.40	£1.20	£2.00
Title Value:	$0.60	$1.80	$3.00	£0.40	£1.20	£2.00

HOUSE OF MYSTERY
National Periodical Publications/DC Comics; 1 Dec/Jan 1951/52-321 Oct 1983

(see Brave and the Bold, Super DC Giant, Super-Star Holiday Special)

	$Good	$Fine	$N.Mint	£Good	£Fine	£N.Mint
1 scarce in the U.K.	$215.00	$650.00	$1750.00	£145.00	£435.00	£1170.00
2 scarce in the U.K.	$92.50	$280.00	$750.00	£62.50	£185.00	£500.00
3 scarce in the U.K.	$55.00	$170.00	$455.00	£38.00	£110.00	£305.00
4-5	$50.00	$150.00	$400.00	£34.00	£100.00	£270.00
6-10	$38.00	$110.00	$300.00	£25.00	£75.00	£200.00
11-15	$36.00	$105.00	$250.00	£24.00	£72.50	£170.00
16-25	$29.00	$85.00	$200.00	£19.00	£57.50	£135.00
26-35	$19.00	$57.50	$135.00	£12.50	£39.00	£90.00
36-49	$17.00	$50.00	$120.00	£11.00	£34.00	£80.00
50 features script of Orson Welles' War of the Worlds broadcast	$17.50	$52.50	$125.00	£12.00	£36.00	£85.00
51-60	$15.00	$45.00	$105.00	£10.00	£30.00	£70.00
61 Jack Kirby art	$15.50	$47.00	$110.00	£10.50	£32.00	£75.00
62	$12.00	$36.00	$85.00	£8.00	£24.50	£57.50
63 Jack Kirby art	$15.50	$47.00	$110.00	£10.50	£32.00	£75.00
64	$12.00	$36.00	$85.00	£8.00	£24.50	£57.50
65-66 Jack Kirby art	$15.50	$47.00	$110.00	£10.50	£32.00	£75.00
67-69	$12.00	$36.00	$85.00	£8.00	£24.50	£57.50
70 Jack Kirby art	$15.50	$47.00	$110.00	£10.50	£32.00	£75.00
71	$11.00	$34.00	$80.00	£7.75	£23.50	£55.00
72 Jack Kirby art	$15.50	$47.00	$110.00	£10.50	£32.00	£75.00
73-75	$11.00	$34.00	$80.00	£7.75	£23.50	£55.00
76 Jack Kirby art	$15.50	$47.00	$110.00	£10.50	£32.00	£75.00
77-83	$11.00	$34.00	$80.00	£7.75	£23.50	£55.00

Issue	$Good	$Fine	$N.Mint	£Good	£Fine	£N.Mint
84-85 Jack Kirby art	*$15.00*	*$45.00*	*$105.00*	£10.00	£30.00	£70.00
86-91	*$11.00*	*$34.00*	*$80.00*	£7.75	£23.50	£55.00
1st official distribution in the U.K.						
92-99	*$11.00*	*$34.00*	*$80.00*	£7.00	£21.00	£50.00
100	*$12.50*	*$39.00*	*$90.00*	£7.75	£23.50	£55.00
101-115	*$9.25*	*$28.00*	*$65.00*	£4.60	£13.50	£32.50
116 last 10 cents issue	*$9.25*	*$28.00*	*$65.00*	£4.60	£13.50	£32.50
117-119	*$8.50*	*$26.00*	*$60.00*	£3.90	£11.50	£27.50
120 Toth art	*$9.25*	*$28.00*	*$65.00*	£4.25	£12.50	£30.00
121-130	*$8.50*	*$26.00*	*$60.00*	£2.85	£8.50	£20.00
131-142	*$7.75*	*$23.50*	*$55.00*	£2.50	£7.50	£17.50
143 scarce in the U.K. Martian Manhunter series begins, ends #173; storyline continuation from Detective Comics #326	*$28.00*	*$82.50*	*$275.00*	£16.00	£48.00	£160.00
144	*$16.50*	*$50.00*	*$150.00*	£9.25	£28.00	£85.00
145-154	*$13.00*	*$39.00*	*$105.00*	£5.50	£16.50	£45.00
155 last Silver Age issue, indicia dated December 1965	*$13.00*	*$39.00*	*$105.00*	£5.50	£16.50	£45.00
156 1st Dial H For Hero, ends #173	*$15.00*	*$45.00*	*$120.00*	£6.75	£20.50	£55.00
157-159	*$12.50*	*$38.00*	*$100.00*	£3.75	£11.00	£30.00
160 Dial H for Hero as Plastic Man (see Plastic Man #1 for 1st Silver Age appearance)	*$16.50*	*$50.00*	*$150.00*	£6.50	£20.00	£60.00
161-172	*$8.75*	*$26.00*	*$70.00*	£3.40	£10.00	£27.50
173 last Martian Manhunter	*$8.00*	*$24.00*	*$65.00*	£3.40	£10.00	£27.50
174 change to mystery format, new-style cover	*$5.00*	*$15.00*	*$35.00*	£1.75	£5.25	£12.50
175-177	*$4.25*	*$12.50*	*$30.00*	£1.40	£4.25	£10.00
178 scarce in the U.K. Neal Adams art	*$4.25*	*$12.50*	*$30.00*	£2.10	£6.25	£15.00
179 scarce in the U.K. Neal Adams art, Wrightson art (1st pro work)	*$9.25*	*$28.00*	*$65.00*	£3.55	£10.50	£25.00
180 Wrightson art; last 12 cents issue	*$2.85*	*$8.50*	*$20.00*	£1.25	£3.85	£9.00
181 Wrightson art	*$2.85*	*$8.50*	*$20.00*	£1.25	£3.85	£9.00
182 Toth art	*$4.00*	*$12.00*	*$28.00*	£1.05	£3.20	£7.50
183 Wrightson art	*$2.85*	*$8.50*	*$20.00*	£1.25	£3.85	£9.00
184	*$2.90*	*$8.75*	*$17.50*	£1.00	£3.00	£6.00
185 Williamson/Kaluta art	*$2.90*	*$8.75*	*$17.50*	£1.25	£3.75	£7.50
186 Neal Adams, Wrightson art	*$2.90*	*$8.75*	*$17.50*	£1.30	£4.00	£8.00
187	*$1.65*	*$5.00*	*$10.00*	£0.65	£2.00	£4.00
188 Wrightson art	*$2.90*	*$8.75*	*$17.50*	£1.00	£3.00	£6.00
189 scarce in the U.K. Wood inks	*$1.50*	*$4.50*	*$9.00*	£0.80	£2.50	£5.00
190	*$1.65*	*$5.00*	*$10.00*	£0.65	£2.00	£4.00
191 Wrightson art	*$2.90*	*$8.75*	*$17.50*	£1.00	£3.00	£6.00
192-193	*$1.50*	*$4.50*	*$9.00*	£0.55	£1.75	£3.50
194 48pgs	*$1.50*	*$4.50*	*$9.00*	£0.65	£2.00	£4.00
195 48pgs, Wrightson art	*$2.90*	*$8.75*	*$17.50*	£1.00	£3.00	£6.00
196-198 48pgs	*$1.50*	*$4.50*	*$9.00*	£0.65	£2.00	£4.00
199 48pgs, (says 52pgs on the covers of #199-203 as in US they count the covers)	*$2.00*	*$6.00*	*$12.00*	£0.80	£2.50	£5.00
200 scarce in the U.K. 48pgs, Kaluta art	*$1.30*	*$4.00*	*$8.00*	£0.80	£2.50	£5.00
201 48pgs, features Wrightson art	*$1.30*	*$4.00*	*$8.00*	£0.75	£2.25	£4.50
202-203 48pgs	*$1.30*	*$4.00*	*$8.00*	£0.55	£1.75	£3.50
204 Wrightson art	*$1.30*	*$4.00*	*$8.00*	£0.55	£1.75	£3.50
205	*$1.00*	*$3.00*	*$6.00*	£0.40	£1.25	£2.50
206 Wrightson art	*$1.00*	*$3.00*	*$6.00*	£0.55	£1.75	£3.50
207 2pgs Jim Starlin art	*$1.00*	*$3.00*	*$6.00*	£0.55	£1.75	£3.50
208-210	*$1.00*	*$3.00*	*$6.00*	£0.40	£1.25	£2.50
211-220	*$1.00*	*$3.00*	*$6.00*	£0.30	£1.00	£2.00
221 Wrightson/Kaluta art	*$1.00*	*$3.00*	*$6.00*	£0.55	£1.75	£3.50
222-223	*$1.00*	*$3.00*	*$6.00*	£0.30	£1.00	£2.00
224-227 100pgs	*$1.65*	*$5.00*	*$10.00*	£0.80	£2.50	£5.00
228 100pgs, Neal Adams inks	*$1.30*	*$4.00*	*$8.00*	£0.80	£2.50	£5.00
229 100pgs	*$1.15*	*$3.50*	*$7.00*	£0.80	£2.50	£5.00
230-235	*$1.00*	*$3.00*	*$6.00*	£0.30	£1.00	£2.00
236 Neal Adams inks, part Ditko art; Wrightson cover	*$1.15*	*$3.50*	*$7.00*	£0.50	£1.50	£3.00
237-240	*$1.00*	*$3.00*	*$6.00*	£0.30	£1.00	£2.00
241-242 scarce in the U.K.	*$1.00*	*$3.00*	*$6.00*	£0.40	£1.25	£2.50
243 ND	*$1.00*	*$3.00*	*$6.00*	£0.50	£1.50	£3.00
244 scarce in the U.K.	*$1.00*	*$3.00*	*$6.00*	£0.40	£1.25	£2.50
245 ND	*$1.00*	*$3.00*	*$6.00*	£0.50	£1.50	£3.00
246-249 scarce in the U.K.	*$1.00*	*$3.00*	*$6.00*	£0.40	£1.25	£2.50
250-251	*$1.00*	*$3.00*	*$6.00*	£0.50	£1.50	£3.00
252 scarce in the U.K. 80pgs, Neal Adams cover; pin-up poster of The House	*$1.00*	*$3.00*	*$6.00*	£0.50	£1.50	£3.00
253 scarce in the U.K. 80pgs, Neal Adams cover	*$1.00*	*$3.00*	*$6.00*	£0.50	£1.50	£3.00
254 scarce in the U.K. 80pgs, Rogers art	*$1.00*	*$3.00*	*$6.00*	£0.50	£1.50	£3.00
255-256 ND 80pgs	*$1.00*	*$3.00*	*$6.00*	£0.50	£1.50	£3.00
257 ND 80pgs, Golden art	*$1.00*	*$3.00*	*$6.00*	£0.50	£1.50	£3.00
258 ND 80pgs	*$1.00*	*$3.00*	*$6.00*	£0.50	£1.50	£3.00
259 ND 80pgs, Golden art	*$1.00*	*$3.00*	*$6.00*	£0.50	£1.50	£3.00
260 scarce in the U.K. 44pgs	*$1.00*	*$3.00*	*$6.00*	£0.40	£1.25	£2.50
261-262 ND 44pgs	*$1.00*	*$3.00*	*$6.00*	£0.50	£1.50	£3.00
263-273	*$1.00*	*$3.00*	*$6.00*	£0.25	£0.75	£1.50
274 Rogers art	*$1.00*	*$3.00*	*$6.00*	£0.25	£0.75	£1.50
275	*$1.00*	*$3.00*	*$6.00*	£0.25	£0.75	£1.50
276 Nasser art	*$1.00*	*$3.00*	*$6.00*	£0.25	£0.75	£1.50
277-280	*$1.00*	*$3.00*	*$6.00*	£0.25	£0.75	£1.50
281	*$1.00*	*$3.00*	*$5.00*	£0.20	£0.60	£1.00
282 68pgs, Jim Starlin art on insert	*$1.00*	*$3.00*	*$5.00*	£0.30	£0.90	£1.50
283-300	*$1.00*	*$3.00*	*$5.00*	£0.20	£0.60	£1.00
301-321	*$0.80*	*$2.40*	*$4.00*	£0.15	£0.45	£0.75
Title Value:	*$3133.75*	*$9391.90*	*$22994.00*	£1840.85	£5555.75	£13647.75

ARTISTS

Adams inks reprint in 224. Ditko art in 236, 247, 254, 258, 276. Kaluta art (2pgs) in 195. Kirby reprints in 194, 199, 225. Nino art in 204, 212, 213, 220, 224, 225, 245, 250, 252-256, 283. Wood art in 180, 183-185, 189, 199, 251. Wrightson reprints in 224, 226, 228, 229.

Hex #18

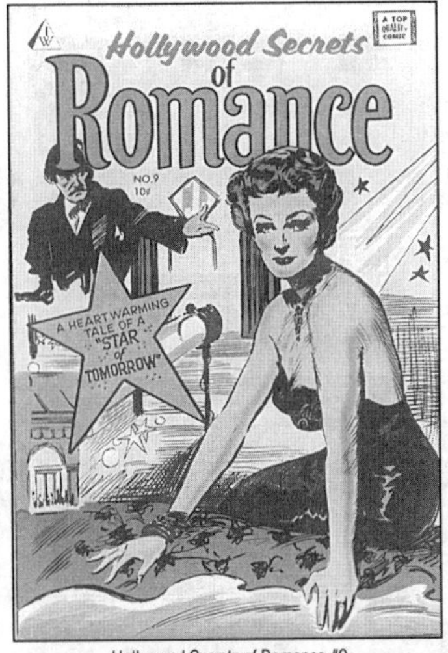

Hollywood Secrets of Romance #9

House Of Mystery #156

FEATURES
Dial H for Hero in 156-173. I...Vampire in 290, 291, 293, 295, 297, 299, 302-319. Martian Manhunter in 143-173. Remainder are mystery stories.
REPRINT FEATURES
Phantom Stranger in 225, 226. Spectre in 224, 225. Various Mystery stories in 174, 194-203, 224-229.

HOUSE OF SECRETS

National Periodical Publications/DC Comics; 1 Nov/Dec 1956-80 Sep/Oct 1966; 81 Aug/Sep 1969-140 Feb/Mar 1976; 141 Aug/Sep 1976-154 Oct/Nov 1978

	$Good	$Fine	$N.Mint	£Good	£Fine	£N.Mint
1 scarce in the U.K.	*$125.00*	*$375.00*	*$1250.00*	£82.50	£250.00	£835.00
2	*$50.00*	*$150.00*	*$450.00*	£33.00	£100.00	£300.00
3 Jack Kirby cover/art	*$44.00*	*$130.00*	*$400.00*	£30.00	£90.00	£270.00
4 Jack Kirby art	*$39.00*	*$115.00*	*$310.00*	£26.00	£77.50	£210.00
5-7	*$25.00*	*$75.00*	*$200.00*	£16.50	£50.00	£135.00
8 Jack Kirby art	*$39.00*	*$115.00*	*$310.00*	£26.00	£77.50	£210.00
9-11	*$21.50*	*$65.00*	*$175.00*	£15.00	£45.00	£120.00
12 Jack Kirby cover/art	*$26.00*	*$77.50*	*$185.00*	£17.50	£52.50	£125.00
13-15	*$17.00*	*$50.00*	*$120.00*	£11.00	£34.00	£80.00
16-20	*$15.00*	*$45.00*	*$105.00*	£10.00	£30.00	£70.00
21-22	*$13.50*	*$41.00*	*$95.00*	£9.25	£28.00	£65.00
23 origin and 1st appearance Mark Merlin	*$15.00*	*$45.00*	*$105.00*	£10.00	£30.00	£70.00
1st official distribution in the U.K.						
24-30	*$13.50*	*$41.00*	*$95.00*	£8.50	£26.00	£60.00
31-40	*$10.50*	*$32.00*	*$75.00*	£6.25	£19.00	£45.00
41-47	*$10.50*	*$32.00*	*$75.00*	£5.50	£17.00	£40.00
48 Toth art	*$10.50*	*$32.00*	*$75.00*	£5.50	£17.00	£40.00
49	*$10.50*	*$32.00*	*$75.00*	£5.50	£17.00	£40.00
50 last 10 cents issue	*$10.50*	*$32.00*	*$75.00*	£5.50	£17.00	£40.00
51-60	*$9.25*	*$28.00*	*$65.00*	£4.60	£13.50	£32.50
61 1st appearance Eclipso	*$25.00*	*$75.00*	*$175.00*	£12.00	£36.00	£85.00
62 2nd appearance Eclipso	*$15.00*	*$45.00*	*$105.00*	£7.00	£21.00	£50.00
63-65 Toth art	*$11.00*	*$34.00*	*$80.00*	£5.25	£16.00	£37.50
66 Toth art, 1st Eclipso cover	*$13.50*	*$41.00*	*$95.00*	£7.00	£21.00	£50.00
67 Toth art	*$11.00*	*$34.00*	*$80.00*	£5.25	£16.00	£37.50
68-70	*$7.75*	*$23.50*	*$55.00*	£3.55	£10.50	£25.00
71-74	*$7.75*	*$23.50*	*$55.00*	£3.20	£9.50	£22.50
75 last Silver Age issue, indicia dated Nov/Dec 1965	*$7.75*	*$23.50*	*$55.00*	£3.20	£9.50	£22.50
76-79	*$7.75*	*$23.50*	*$55.00*	£3.20	£9.50	£22.50
80 last Eclipso	*$7.75*	*$23.50*	*$55.00*	£3.20	£9.50	£22.50
81 1st mystery format, 1st appearance Abel	*$2.10*	*$6.25*	*$15.00*	£1.05	£3.20	£7.50
82 Neal Adams inks (cover)	*$2.05*	*$6.25*	*$12.50*	£0.80	£2.50	£5.00
83	*$2.05*	*$6.25*	*$12.50*	£0.65	£2.00	£4.00
84 Neal Adams cover	*$2.05*	*$6.25*	*$12.50*	£0.65	£2.00	£4.00
85 Neal Adams inks and cover	*$2.05*	*$6.25*	*$12.50*	£0.80	£2.50	£5.00
86 Neal Adams and cover	*$2.05*	*$6.25*	*$12.50*	£0.65	£2.00	£4.00
87 Wrightson/Kaluta art, Neal Adams cover	*$2.05*	*$6.25*	*$12.50*	£0.80	£2.50	£5.00
88 Neal Adams cover	*$2.05*	*$6.25*	*$12.50*	£0.65	£2.00	£4.00
89	*$2.05*	*$6.25*	*$12.50*	£0.65	£2.00	£4.00
90 Neal Adams inks, Buckler art (very early work)	*$2.05*	*$6.25*	*$12.50*	£1.00	£3.00	£6.00
91	*$2.05*	*$6.25*	*$12.50*	£0.65	£2.00	£4.00
92 scarce in the U.K. 1st appearance of Swamp Thing by Bernie Wrightson	*$50.00*	*$150.00*	*$460.00*	£33.00	£100.00	£300.00
[Scarce in high grade - Very Fine+ or better]						
92 Silver Age Classic, ND reprint (Mar 1992)	*$0.25*	*$0.75*	*$1.25*	£0.15	£0.45	£0.75
93 48pgs	*$1.25*	*$3.75*	*$7.50*	£0.45	£1.35	£2.75
94 48pgs, Wrightson inks	*$1.25*	*$3.75*	*$7.50*	£0.55	£1.75	£3.50
95 48pgs	*$1.25*	*$3.75*	*$7.50*	£0.45	£1.35	£2.75
96 48pgs, (says 52pgs on cover up to #98 as they count the covers in the U.S)	*$1.25*	*$3.75*	*$7.50*	£0.45	£1.35	£2.75
97 48pgs	*$1.25*	*$3.75*	*$7.50*	£0.45	£1.35	£2.75
98 48pgs, Kaluta art	*$1.25*	*$3.75*	*$7.50*	£0.45	£1.35	£2.75
99	*$1.25*	*$3.75*	*$7.50*	£0.30	£1.00	£2.00
100 scarce in the U.K. Bernie Wrightson cover	*$1.25*	*$3.75*	*$7.50*	£0.50	£1.50	£3.00
101 Kaluta cover	*$0.50*	*$1.50*	*$3.00*	£0.25	£0.85	£1.75
102	*$0.50*	*$1.50*	*$3.00*	£0.25	£0.85	£1.75
103 scarce in the U.K. Bernie Wrightson cover	*$0.50*	*$1.50*	*$3.00*	£0.40	£1.25	£2.50
104-105	*$0.50*	*$1.50*	*$3.00*	£0.25	£0.85	£1.75
106 Bernie Wrightson cover and 1pg art	*$0.50*	*$1.50*	*$3.00*	£0.25	£0.85	£1.75
107-110	*$0.50*	*$1.50*	*$3.00*	£0.25	£0.85	£1.75
111-120	*$0.50*	*$1.50*	*$3.00*	£0.25	£0.75	£1.50
121-134	*$0.50*	*$1.50*	*$3.00*	£0.20	£0.60	£1.25
135 Bernie Wrightson cover	*$0.40*	*$1.25*	*$2.50*	£0.20	£0.60	£1.25
136-139	*$0.40*	*$1.25*	*$2.50*	£0.20	£0.60	£1.25
140 origin Patchwork Man	*$0.40*	*$1.25*	*$2.50*	£0.25	£0.75	£1.50
141-147	*$0.40*	*$1.25*	*$2.50*	£0.15	£0.50	£1.00
148 Steve Ditko and Mike Golden art	*$0.40*	*$1.25*	*$2.50*	£0.15	£0.50	£1.00
149 Mike Golden art (1pg)	*$0.40*	*$1.25*	*$2.50*	£0.15	£0.50	£1.00
150	*$0.40*	*$1.25*	*$2.50*	£0.15	£0.50	£1.00
151 Mike Golden art	*$0.40*	*$1.25*	*$2.50*	£0.15	£0.50	£1.00
152-153	*$0.40*	*$1.25*	*$2.50*	£0.15	£0.50	£1.00
154 ND 44pgs	*$0.30*	*$1.00*	*$2.00*	£0.25	£0.75	£1.50
Title Value:	*$1333.50*	*$4019.25*	*$10245.75*	£790.15	£2388.95	£6183.50

ARTISTS
Ditko art in 139, 148. Nino art in 101, 103, 106, 109, 115, 117, 126, 128, 131, 147, 153. Wood art in 91, 96.
FEATURES
Eclipso in 61-80. Mark Merlin in 26-73 (origin in 58). Prince Ra-Man in 73-80. Swamp Thing in 92. Remainder are mystery stories.
REPRINT FEATURES
Various mystery stories in 93-98.

HOUSE OF SECRETS (2ND SERIES)

DC Comics; 1 Oct 1996-present

	$Good	$Fine	$N.Mint	£Good	£Fine	£N.Mint
1 ND Steven Seagle script and Teddy Kristiansen art begin	*$0.50*	*$1.50*	*$2.50*	£0.30	£0.90	£1.50
2-5 ND	*$0.50*	*$1.50*	*$2.50*	£0.30	£0.90	£1.50
6 ND Duncan Fegredo art	*$0.50*	*$1.50*	*$2.50*	£0.30	£0.90	£1.50
Title Value:	*$3.00*	*$9.00*	*$15.00*	£1.80	£5.40	£9.00

HOUSE OF YANG

Charlton; 1 Jul 1975-6 Jun 1976
(see Yang)

	$Good	$Fine	$N.Mint	£Good	£Fine	£N.Mint
1 distributed in the U.K. painted cover	*$0.40*	*$1.25*	*$2.50*	£0.20	£0.60	£1.25
1 reprint, ND scarce in the U.K. (1978) Modern Comics reprint, 35 cents cover	*$0.20*	*$0.60*	*$1.00*	£0.30	£0.90	£1.50
2-3 distributed in the U.K.	*$0.40*	*$1.25*	*$2.50*	£0.20	£0.60	£1.25
3 reprint, ND scarce in the U.K. (1978) Modern Comics reprint, 35 cents cover	*$0.20*	*$0.60*	*$1.00*	£0.30	£0.90	£1.50
4-6 distributed in the U.K.	*$0.40*	*$1.25*	*$2.50*	£0.20	£0.60	£1.25
Title Value:	*$2.80*	*$8.70*	*$17.00*	£1.80	£5.40	£10.50

HOW TO DRAW COMICS COMIC, THE

Solson Publications,OS; 1 1985

	$Good	$Fine	$N.Mint	£Good	£Fine	£N.Mint
1 ND John Byrne and John Romita guide to professional comic drawing; black and white sketches	*$0.40*	*$1.20*	*$2.00*	£0.25	£0.75	£1.25
Title Value:	*$0.40*	*$1.20*	*$2.00*	£0.25	£0.75	£1.25

HOWARD CHAYKIN'S AMERICAN FLAGG

(see American Flagg!)

HOWARD THE DUCK

Marvel Comics Group; 1 Jan 1976-31 May 1979; 32 Jan 1986-33 Sep 1986
(see Fear 19, Giant Size Man-Thing 4, 5,She-Hulk)

	$Good	$Fine	$N.Mint	£Good	£Fine	£N.Mint
1 scarce in the U.K. Brunner art, Spiderman appears	*$1.15*	*$3.50*	*$7.00*	£0.55	£1.75	£3.50
2 scarce in the U.K. Brunner art, Jim Starlin "script lay-out"	*$0.50*	*$1.50*	*$3.00*	£0.30	£1.00	£2.00
3 classic "Master of Quack Fu" story	*$0.30*	*$1.00*	*$2.00*	£0.20	£0.60	£1.25
4-7	*$0.30*	*$1.00*	*$2.00*	£0.20	£0.60	£1.25
8 Dr. Strange cameo	*$0.30*	*$1.00*	*$2.00*	£0.20	£0.60	£1.25
9-10	*$0.30*	*$1.00*	*$2.00*	£0.20	£0.60	£1.25
11	*$0.25*	*$0.75*	*$1.50*	£0.15	£0.50	£1.00
12 Kiss appear	*$1.65*	*$5.00*	*$10.00*	£0.40	£1.25	£2.50
13 Kiss and Son of Satan appear	*$2.05*	*$6.25*	*$12.50*	£0.40	£1.25	£2.50
14-15 Son of Satan appears	*$0.25*	*$0.75*	*$1.50*	£0.15	£0.50	£1.00
16-21	*$0.25*	*$0.75*	*$1.50*	£0.15	£0.50	£1.00
22 Man-Thing appears, Mayerik art	*$0.25*	*$0.75*	*$1.50*	£0.15	£0.50	£1.00
23 Star Wars parody, Mayerik art	*$0.25*	*$0.75*	*$1.50*	£0.15	£0.50	£1.00
24-31	*$0.25*	*$0.75*	*$1.50*	£0.15	£0.50	£1.00
32 ND Paul Smith art	*$0.25*	*$0.75*	*$1.50*	£0.15	£0.50	£1.00
33 ND	*$0.25*	*$0.75*	*$1.50*	£0.15	£0.50	£1.00
Title Value:	*$13.00*	*$40.00*	*$80.00*	£6.40	£20.55	£41.50

Note: Colan art 4-20, 24-27, 29, 30. Infantino art 21, 28. Also 32, 33 are high quality paper

HOWARD THE DUCK (2ND SERIES)

Marvel Comics Group,Magazine; 1 Oct 1979-9 Mar 1981

	$Good	$Fine	$N.Mint	£Good	£Fine	£N.Mint
1 ND Golden art	*$0.75*	*$2.25*	*$4.50*	£0.50	£1.50	£3.00
2-4 ND	*$0.50*	*$1.50*	*$3.00*	£0.30	£1.00	£2.00
5-6 ND Golden art	*$0.50*	*$1.50*	*$3.00*	£0.30	£1.00	£2.00
7 ND 1pg John Byrne art	*$0.65*	*$2.00*	*$4.00*	£0.40	£1.25	£2.50
8 ND Rogers art	*$0.50*	*$1.50*	*$3.00*	£0.30	£1.00	£2.00

	$Good	$Fine	$N.Mint	£Good	£Fine	£N.Mint
9 ND	$0.50	$1.50	$3.00	£0.30	£1.00	£2.00
Title Value:	$4.90	$14.75	$29.50	£3.00	£9.75	£19.50

HOWARD THE DUCK ANNUAL

Marvel Comics Group; 1 Sep 1977

	$Good	$Fine	$N.Mint	£Good	£Fine	£N.Mint
1 scarce in the U.K. 52pgs, Val Mayerik art	$0.30	$1.00	$2.00	£0.25	£0.75	£1.50
Title Value:	$0.30	$1.00	$2.00	£0.25	£0.75	£1.50

HOWARD THE DUCK HOLIDAY SPECIAL

Marvel Comics Group,OS; nn Feb 1997

	$Good	$Fine	$N.Mint	£Good	£Fine	£N.Mint
nn ND 48pgs, Larry Hama script, Pascual Ferry and Art Thibert art	$0.50	$1.50	$2.50	£0.30	£0.90	£1.50
Title Value:	$0.50	$1.50	$2.50	£0.30	£0.90	£1.50

HOWARD THE DUCK: THE MOVIE

Marvel Comics Group,MS Film; 1 Dec 1986-3 Feb 1987

	$Good	$Fine	$N.Mint	£Good	£Fine	£N.Mint
1-3 ND adapts film, Kyle Baker art	$0.25	$0.75	$1.25	£0.15	£0.45	£0.75
Title Value:	$0.75	$2.25	$3.75	£0.45	£1.35	£2.25

HOWL

Eternity; 1 Nov 1988-2 1989

	$Good	$Fine	$N.Mint	£Good	£Fine	£N.Mint
1-2 ND reprints	$0.40	$1.20	$2.00	£0.25	£0.75	£1.25
Title Value:	$0.80	$2.40	$4.00	£0.50	£1.50	£2.50

HUGGA BUNCH

Marvel Comics Group/Star; 1 Oct 1986-6 Aug 1987

	$Good	$Fine	$N.Mint	£Good	£Fine	£N.Mint
1-6 scarce in the U.K. based on cartoon series	$0.20	$0.60	$1.00	£0.15	£0.45	£0.75
Title Value:	$1.20	$3.60	$6.00	£0.90	£2.70	£4.50

HUGO

Fantagraphics; 1 Nov 1984-3 1985

	$Good	$Fine	$N.Mint	£Good	£Fine	£N.Mint
1-3 ND	$0.40	$1.20	$2.00	£0.25	£0.75	£1.25
Title Value:	$1.20	$3.60	$6.00	£0.75	£2.25	£3.75

HULK 2099

Marvel Comics Group; 1 Dec 1994-10 Sep 1995

	$Good	$Fine	$N.Mint	£Good	£Fine	£N.Mint
1 ND foil stamped cover	$0.40	$1.20	$2.00	£0.25	£0.75	£1.25
2-4 ND	$0.40	$1.20	$2.00	£0.20	£0.60	£1.00
5 ND The Hulk of 2099 mutates	$0.40	$1.20	$2.00	£0.20	£0.60	£1.00
6 ND	$0.40	$1.20	$2.00	£0.20	£0.60	£1.00
7 ND upgraded paper stock begins	$0.40	$1.20	$2.00	£0.20	£0.60	£1.00
8 ND	$0.40	$1.20	$2.00	£0.20	£0.60	£1.00
9-10 ND One Nation Under Doom	$0.40	$1.20	$2.00	£0.20	£0.60	£1.00
Title Value:	$4.00	$12.00	$20.00	£2.05	£6.15	£10.25

HUMAN FLY

IW Super; 1,10 1963, 1964

	$Good	$Fine	$N.Mint	£Good	£Fine	£N.Mint
1 rare although distributed in the U.K. reprint; reprints Blue Beetle from the 1940s	$1.75	$5.25	$12.50	£0.85	£2.55	£6.00
10 scarce though distributed in the U.K. reprint; reprints Blue Beetle and The Puppeteer (ie. no Human Fly at all!)	$1.40	$4.25	$10.00	£0.55	£1.70	£4.00
Title Value:	$3.15	$9.50	$22.50	£1.40	£4.25	£10.00

HUMAN FLY

Marvel Comics Group; 1 Sep 1977-19 Mar 1979

	$Good	$Fine	$N.Mint	£Good	£Fine	£N.Mint
1 Spiderman appears	$0.55	$1.75	$3.50	£0.15	£0.50	£1.00
2 Ghost Rider appears	$0.50	$1.50	$3.00	£0.10	£0.35	£0.75
3-7	$0.30	$1.00	$2.00	£0.10	£0.35	£0.75
8 White Tiger appears	$0.30	$1.00	$2.00	£0.10	£0.35	£0.75
9 Daredevil and White Tiger appear	$0.30	$1.00	$2.00	£0.10	£0.35	£0.75
10-19	$0.30	$1.00	$2.00	£0.10	£0.35	£0.75
Title Value:	$6.15	$20.25	$40.50	£1.95	£6.80	£14.50

HUMAN GARGOYLES

Eternity; 1-4 1988

	$Good	$Fine	$N.Mint	£Good	£Fine	£N.Mint
1-4 ND	$0.40	$1.20	$2.00	£0.25	£0.75	£1.25
Title Value:	$1.60	$4.80	$8.00	£1.00	£3.00	£5.00

HUMAN TARGET SPECIAL, THE

DC Comics,OS; 1 Nov 1991

	$Good	$Fine	$N.Mint	£Good	£Fine	£N.Mint
1 48pgs, tied in with U.S. TV series	$0.30	$0.90	$1.50	£0.20	£0.60	£1.00
Title Value:	$0.30	$0.90	$1.50	£0.20	£0.60	£1.00

HUMAN TORCH (1ST SERIES)

Timely/Atlas;2 Autumn 1940-15 Spring 1944; 16 Autumn 1944-35 Mar 1949; 36 Apr 1954-38 Aug 1954

(see Red Raven Comics for issue #1)

	$Good	$Fine	$N.Mint	£Good	£Fine	£N.Mint
2 scarce in the U.K. origin and 1st appearance Toro, Sub-Mariner back-up story begins (co-title on cover until #6); no number on cover (actually issue #1), Bill Everett cover and art	$2075.00	$6200.00	$23000.00	£1450.00	£4350.00	£16000.00
3 Bill Everett art; no number on cover (actually issue #2)	$520.00	$1575.00	$4750.00	£350.00	£1050.00	£3170.00
4 Alex Schomburg covers begin; no number on cover (actually issue #3)	$415.00	$1250.00	$3750.00	£275.00	£830.00	£2500.00
5 no number on cover (actually issue #4)	$510.00	$1525.00	$4100.00	£340.00	£1025.00	£2750.00
nn on cover, (the "real" issue #5), Human Torch vs. Sub-Mariner	$360.00	$1075.00	$2900.00	£240.00	£730.00	£1950.00
6 1st number on cover	$215.00	$650.00	$1750.00	£145.00	£440.00	£1175.00
7 1st Japanese war cover	$240.00	$730.00	$1950.00	£160.00	£485.00	£1300.00
8 Human Torch vs. Sub-Mariner	$350.00	$1050.00	$2800.00	£230.00	£700.00	£1875.00
9	$215.00	$650.00	$1750.00	£145.00	£440.00	£1175.00
10 Human Torch vs. Sub-Mariner	$290.00	$880.00	$2350.00	£195.00	£590.00	£1575.00
11-15	$170.00	$510.00	$1375.00	£115.00	£345.00	£920.00
16-19	$115.00	$355.00	$950.00	£77.50	£235.00	£635.00
20 1st war theme cover	$115.00	$355.00	$950.00	£77.50	£235.00	£635.00
21-30	$105.00	$315.00	$850.00	£70.00	£210.00	£570.00
31-32	$100.00	$300.00	$800.00	£65.00	£200.00	£535.00
33	$100.00	$305.00	$825.00	£67.50	£205.00	£550.00
34	$87.50	$260.00	$700.00	£57.50	£175.00	£470.00
35	$100.00	$305.00	$825.00	£67.50	£205.00	£550.00
36-38 scarce in the U.K.	$105.00	$315.00	$850.00	£70.00	£210.00	£570.00
Title Value:	$8467.50	$25475.00	$75725.00	£5725.00	£17255.00	£51295.00

Note: as with all Golden Age material, this title was not distributed on the news-stands in the U.K. but copies may have come over with personnel movements during the Second World War or as cheap ballast on ships. This title is generally scarce in the U.K.

HUMAN TORCH (2ND SERIES)

Marvel Comics Group; 1 Sep 1974-8 Nov 1975

(see Strange Tales)

	$Good	$Fine	$N.Mint	£Good	£Fine	£N.Mint
1 ND reprints from Strange Tales #101 onwards begin	$1.00	$3.00	$6.00	£0.40	£1.25	£2.50
2-6 ND	$0.65	$2.00	$4.00	£0.30	£1.00	£2.00
7 ND reprints, Strange Tales #107 (vs Sub-Mariner)	$0.55	$1.75	$3.50	£0.30	£1.00	£2.00
8 reprints Strange Tales #108 and Marvel Tales #16 (1948)	$0.55	$1.75	$3.50	£0.25	£0.85	£1.75
Title Value:	$5.35	$16.50	$31.00	£2.45	£8.10	£16.25

Note: Golden Age & 1960s reprints in all.

HUMAN TORCH, SAGA OF THE ORIGINAL

Marvel Comics Group,MS; 1 Apr 1990-4 Jul 1990

	$Good	$Fine	$N.Mint	£Good	£Fine	£N.Mint
1	$0.30	$0.90	$1.50	£0.20	£0.60	£1.00
2 Captain America/Sub-Mariner appear	$0.30	$0.90	$1.50	£0.20	£0.60	£1.00
3 Invaders/All Winners Squad/Liberty Legion appear	$0.30	$0.90	$1.50	£0.20	£0.60	£1.00
4	$0.30	$0.90	$1.50	£0.20	£0.60	£1.00
Title Value:	$1.20	$3.60	$6.00	£0.80	£2.40	£4.00

HUMANTS

Legacy Comics; 1 1992

	$Good	$Fine	$N.Mint	£Good	£Fine	£N.Mint
1 ND 48pgs, black and white	$0.50	$1.50	$2.50	£0.30	£0.90	£1.50
Title Value:	$0.50	$1.50	$2.50	£0.30	£0.90	£1.50

HUNTER'S HEART

DC Comics/Paradox Press,MS; 1 Aug 1995-3 Oct 1995

	$Good	$Fine	$N.Mint	£Good	£Fine	£N.Mint
1 ND 96pgs, Randy DuBurke script and art; black and white	$1.00	$3.00	$5.00	£0.60	£1.80	£3.00
2-3 ND 96pgs, Randy DuBurke script and art; black and white	$0.60	$1.80	$3.00	£0.40	£1.20	£2.00
Title Value:	$2.20	$6.60	$11.00	£1.40	£4.20	£7.00

HUNTRESS, THE

DC Comics; 1 Mar 1989-19 Sep 1990

	$Good	$Fine	$N.Mint	£Good	£Fine	£N.Mint
1	$0.30	$0.90	$1.50	£0.20	£0.60	£1.00
2-16	$0.25	$0.75	$1.25	£0.15	£0.45	£0.75
17-19 Batman appears	$0.25	$0.75	$1.25	£0.15	£0.45	£0.75
Title Value:	$4.80	$14.40	$24.00	£2.90	£8.70	£14.50

Note: Mature Readers label.

HUNTRESS, THE (2ND SERIES)

DC Comics,MS; 1 Jun 1994-4 Sep 1994

	$Good	$Fine	$N.Mint	£Good	£Fine	£N.Mint
1-4 Chuck Dixon script, Michael Netzer art	$0.25	$0.75	$1.25	£0.15	£0.45	£0.75
Title Value:	$1.00	$3.00	$5.00	£0.60	£1.80	£3.00

HURRICANE GIRLS

Antarctic Press,MS; 1 Jul 1995-7 Aug 1996

	$Good	$Fine	$N.Mint	£Good	£Fine	£N.Mint
1-7 ND Hiroshi Yakumo script and art; black and white	$0.70	$2.10	$3.50	£0.50	£1.50	£2.50
Title Value:	$4.90	$14.70	$24.50	£3.50	£10.50	£17.50

HYBRIDS

Continuity; 1 Sep 1992

	$Good	$Fine	$N.Mint	£Good	£Fine	£N.Mint
1 ND Neal Adams cover	$0.40	$1.20	$2.00	£0.25	£0.75	£1.25
Title Value:	$0.40	$1.20	$2.00	£0.25	£0.75	£1.25

HYBRIDS (2ND SERIES)

Continuity; 0 Apr 1993; 1 Apr 1993-5 Dec 1993

	$Good	$Fine	$N.Mint	£Good	£Fine	£N.Mint
0 Incentive Pack, Deathwatch 2000 part 2, silver foil embossed cover, part cover art by Neal Adams (pre-bagged with Megalith (3rd) #0)	$0.40	$1.20	$2.00	£0.40	£1.20	£2.00
0 Red Foil Embossed Cover, , part cover art by Neal Adams	$0.50	$1.50	$2.50	£0.50	£1.50	£2.50
1 Deathwatch 2000 part 4, pre-bagged with 2 trading cards, die-cut cover, Neal Adams plot	$0.40	$1.20	$2.00	£0.25	£0.75	£1.25
2 Deathwatch 2000 part 13, pre-bagged with trading card	$0.40	$1.20	$2.00	£0.25	£0.75	£1.25
3 Deathwatch 2000, pre-bagged with trading card, Tyvek "indestructible" cover	$0.40	$1.20	$2.00	£0.25	£0.75	£1.25
4-5 guest-stars Valeria the She-Bat and the Werebreds	$0.40	$1.20	$2.00	£0.25	£0.75	£1.25
Title Value:	$2.90	$8.70	$14.50	£2.15	£6.45	£10.75

Note; all Non-Distributed on the news-stands in the U.K.

HYBRIDS (3RD SERIES)

Continuity; 1 Jan 1994

	$Good	$Fine	$N.Mint	£Good	£Fine	£N.Mint
1 ND Rise of Magic X-over; parchment embossed cover; part Neal Adams cover and inks	*$0.40*	*$1.20*	*$2.00*	£0.25	£0.75	£1.25
Title Value:	*$0.40*	*$1.20*	*$2.00*	£0.25	£0.75	£1.25

HYDE-25

Harris Comics; 0 May 1995-1 1995

	$Good	$Fine	$N.Mint	£Good	£Fine	£N.Mint
0 ND spin-off from Vampirella series, Flint Henry cover	*$0.60*	*$1.80*	*$3.00*	£0.40	£1.20	£2.00
1 ND	*$0.60*	*$1.80*	*$3.00*	£0.40	£1.20	£2.00
Title Value:	*$1.20*	*$3.60*	*$6.00*	£0.80	£2.40	£4.00

HYPER VIOLENTS

CFD Productions; 1 Jul 1996

	$Good	$Fine	$N.Mint	£Good	£Fine	£N.Mint
1 ND anthology; black and white	*$0.60*	*$1.80*	*$3.00*	£0.40	£1.20	£2.00
Title Value:	*$0.60*	*$1.80*	*$3.00*	£0.40	£1.20	£2.00

HYPERKIND

Marvel Comics Group/Razorline; 1 Sep 1993-9 May 1994

	$Good	$Fine	$N.Mint	£Good	£Fine	£N.Mint
1 ND prismatic foil cover	*$0.40*	*$1.20*	*$2.00*	£0.25	£0.75	£1.25
2-9 ND	*$0.30*	*$0.90*	*$1.50*	£0.20	£0.60	£1.00
Title Value:	*$2.80*	*$8.40*	*$14.00*	£1.85	£5.55	£9.25

HYPERKIND UNLEASHED

Marvel Comics Group/Razorline; 1 Sep 1994

	$Good	$Fine	$N.Mint	£Good	£Fine	£N.Mint
1 ND	*$0.50*	*$1.50*	*$2.50*	£0.30	£0.90	£1.50
Title Value:	*$0.50*	*$1.50*	*$2.50*	£0.30	£0.90	£1.50

I

I AM COYOTE

(see Eclipse Graphic Album series #6)

I AM LEGEND

Eclipse,MS; 1 Apr 1991-4 Oct 1991

	$Good	$Fine	$N.Mint	£Good	£Fine	£N.Mint
1-4 ND 64pgs, squarebound, black and white	*$1.00*	*$3.00*	*$5.00*	£0.70	£2.10	£3.50
Title Value:	*$4.00*	*$12.00*	*$20.00*	£2.80	£8.40	£14.00

I BEFORE E

Fantagraphics,MS; 1 Aug 1991-2 Sep 1991

	$Good	$Fine	$N.Mint	£Good	£Fine	£N.Mint
1 ND 48pgs, Sam Kieth cover and art; black and white	*$0.90*	*$2.70*	*$4.50*	£0.60	£1.80	£3.00
1 2nd printing, ND 48pgs, (May 1994)	*$0.80*	*$2.40*	*$4.00*	£0.50	£1.50	£2.50
2 ND 48pgs, Sam Kieth cover and art; black and white	*$0.80*	*$2.40*	*$4.00*	£0.50	£1.50	£2.50
2 2nd printing, ND 48pgs, (Jun 1994)	*$0.80*	*$2.40*	*$4.00*	£0.50	£1.50	£2.50
Title Value:	*$3.30*	*$9.90*	*$16.50*	£2.10	£6.30	£10.50

I COME IN PEACE

Greater Mercury Comics,MS; 1 Oct 1991-2 Apr 1991

	$Good	$Fine	$N.Mint	£Good	£Fine	£N.Mint
1-2 ND colour, film adaptation	*$0.30*	*$0.90*	*$1.50*	£0.20	£0.60	£1.00
Title Value:	*$0.60*	*$1.80*	*$3.00*	£0.40	£1.20	£2.00

I LOVE LUCY

Eternity,MS; 1 May 1990-6 Oct 1990

	$Good	$Fine	$N.Mint	£Good	£Fine	£N.Mint
1-6 ND	*$0.50*	*$1.50*	*$2.50*	£0.30	£0.90	£1.50
Title Value:	*$3.00*	*$9.00*	*$15.00*	£1.80	£5.40	£9.00

I LOVE LUCY BOOK TWO

Eternity,MS; 1-3 1991

	$Good	$Fine	$N.Mint	£Good	£Fine	£N.Mint
1-3 ND	*$0.50*	*$1.50*	*$2.50*	£0.30	£0.90	£1.50
Title Value:	*$1.50*	*$4.50*	*$7.50*	£0.90	£2.70	£4.50

I LOVE YOU

Charlton;7 Sep 1955-121 Dec 1976; 122 Mar 1979-130 May 1980

(issues #1-6 called In Love)

	$Good	$Fine	$N.Mint	£Good	£Fine	£N.Mint
7 scarce in the U.K. Jack Kirby cover	*$10.00*	*$30.00*	*$70.00*	£6.50	£20.00	£47.00
8-10 scarce in the U.K.	*$3.55*	*$10.50*	*$25.00*	£2.50	£7.50	£17.50
11-16	*$1.75*	*$5.25*	*$12.50*	£1.25	£3.85	£9.00
17 giant	*$2.50*	*$7.50*	*$17.50*	£1.60	£4.90	£11.50
18-20	*$1.75*	*$5.25*	*$12.50*	£1.25	£3.85	£9.00
21-22	*$1.40*	*$4.25*	*$10.00*	£1.00	£3.00	£7.00
1st official distribution in the U.K.						
23-30	*$1.40*	*$4.25*	*$10.00*	£1.00	£3.00	£7.00
31-40	*$1.65*	*$5.00*	*$10.00*	£0.80	£2.50	£5.00
41-50	*$1.65*	*$5.00*	*$10.00*	£0.65	£2.00	£4.00
51-59	*$1.00*	*$3.00*	*$6.00*	£0.50	£1.50	£3.00
60 Elvis Presley cover and story	*$15.00*	*$45.00*	*$105.00*	£7.00	£21.00	£50.00
61-70	*$0.80*	*$2.50*	*$5.00*	£0.50	£1.50	£3.00
71-80	*$0.65*	*$2.00*	*$4.00*	£0.30	£1.00	£2.00
81-100	*$0.50*	*$1.50*	*$3.00*	£0.25	£0.75	£1.50
101-120	*$0.30*	*$1.00*	*$2.00*	£0.20	£0.60	£1.25
121-130	*$0.30*	*$0.90*	*$1.50*	£0.20	£0.60	£1.00
Title Value:	*$143.40*	*$434.75*	*$939.00*	£81.85	£249.55	£544.00

Note: most issues distributed in the U.K. after 1958

I WANT TO BE YOUR DOG

Eros Comix,MS; 1 Oct 1990-5 Mar 1991

	$Good	$Fine	$N.Mint	£Good	£Fine	£N.Mint
1-5 ND Ho Che Anderson script and art; black and white	*$0.40*	*$1.20*	*$2.00*	£0.25	£0.75	£1.25
Title Value:	*$2.00*	*$6.00*	*$10.00*	£1.25	£3.75	£6.25

Note: adult material

I, LUSHIPER

Mulehide Graphics,Magazine; 1 1991-7 1992

	$Good	$Fine	$N.Mint	£Good	£Fine	£N.Mint
1 ND Drew Hayes script and art begins	*$15.00*	*$45.00*	*$75.00*	£7.00	£21.00	£35.00
2 ND	*$10.00*	*$30.00*	*$50.00*	£5.00	£15.00	£25.00
3 ND scarce in the U.K, scarce in the U.S.	*$15.00*	*$45.00*	*$75.00*	£6.00	£18.00	£30.00
4-5 ND	*$9.00*	*$27.00*	*$45.00*	£5.00	£15.00	£25.00
6-7 ND	*$8.00*	*$24.00*	*$40.00*	£4.50	£13.50	£22.50
Title Value:	*$74.00*	*$222.00*	*$370.00*	£37.00	£111.00	£185.00

I-BOTS, ISAAC ASIMOV'S

Tekno Comix; 1 Dec 1995-7 May 1996

	$Good	$Fine	$N.Mint	£Good	£Fine	£N.Mint
1 ND Steven Grant script, George Perez cover and art begin	*$0.40*	*$1.20*	*$2.00*	£0.25	£0.75	£1.25
2 ND	*$0.40*	*$1.20*	*$2.00*	£0.25	£0.75	£1.25
3 ND	*$0.45*	*$1.35*	*$2.25*	£0.30	£0.90	£1.50
4 ND pre-bagged with Tekno back-issue comic	*$0.45*	*$1.35*	*$2.25*	£0.30	£0.90	£1.50
5-6 ND	*$0.45*	*$1.35*	*$2.25*	£0.30	£0.90	£1.50
Title Value:	*$2.60*	*$7.80*	*$13.00*	£1.70	£5.10	£8.50

I-BOTS, ISAAC ASIMOV'S (2ND SERIES)

Big Entertainment; 1 Jun 1996-present

	$Good	$Fine	$N.Mint	£Good	£Fine	£N.Mint
1 ND Lady Justice appears; Steven Grant script, Pat Broderick art begins	*$0.45*	*$1.35*	*$2.25*	£0.30	£0.90	£1.50
2 ND Gil Kane cover	*$0.45*	*$1.35*	*$2.25*	£0.30	£0.90	£1.50
3 ND	*$0.45*	*$1.35*	*$2.25*	£0.30	£0.90	£1.50
4 ND Pat Broderick cover in homage to Wally Wood	*$0.45*	*$1.35*	*$2.25*	£0.30	£0.90	£1.50
5-9 ND	*$0.50*	*$1.50*	*$2.50*	£0.30	£0.90	£1.50
Title Value:	*$4.30*	*$12.90*	*$21.25*	£2.70	£8.10	£13.50

I.F.S. ZONE

KBH; 1 Sep 1987

	$Good	$Fine	$N.Mint	£Good	£Fine	£N.Mint
1 ND b&w	*$0.25*	*$0.75*	*$1.25*	£0.15	£0.45	£0.75
Title Value:	*$0.25*	*$0.75*	*$1.25*	£0.15	£0.45	£0.75

ICARUS

Aircel; 1 1987-6 1988

	$Good	$Fine	$N.Mint	£Good	£Fine	£N.Mint
1-6 ND	*$0.40*	*$1.20*	*$2.00*	£0.25	£0.75	£1.25
Title Value:	*$2.40*	*$7.20*	*$12.00*	£1.50	£4.50	£7.50

ICE AGE - A MAGIC: THE GATHERING LIMITED SERIES

Acclaim Comics,MS; 1 Jul 1995-4 Oct 1995

	$Good	$Fine	$N.Mint	£Good	£Fine	£N.Mint
1-4 ND Jeff Gomez script, Rafael Kayanan art; painted cover by Charles Vess	*$0.50*	*$1.50*	*$2.50*	£0.30	£0.90	£1.50
Title Value:	*$2.00*	*$6.00*	*$10.00*	£1.20	£3.60	£6.00

Note: based on fantasy game Magic: The Gathering by Wizards of the Coast

	$Good	$Fine	$N.Mint	£Good	£Fine	£N.Mint
Ice Age on the World of Magic: The Gathering 1 (Sep 1995) Trade paperback collects issues #1,2				£0.65	£1.95	£3.25
Ice Age on the World of Magic: The Gathering 2 (Sep 1995) Trade paperback collects issues #3,4				£0.65	£1.95	£3.25

ICEMAN

Marvel Comics Group,MS; 1 Dec 1984-4 Jun 1985

	$Good	$Fine	$N.Mint	£Good	£Fine	£N.Mint
1-2 ND	*$0.50*	*$1.50*	*$2.50*	£0.30	£0.90	£1.50
3 ND original X-Men, Defenders and Champions appear	*$0.50*	*$1.50*	*$2.50*	£0.30	£0.90	£1.50
4 ND	*$0.50*	*$1.50*	*$2.50*	£0.30	£0.90	£1.50
Title Value:	*$2.00*	*$6.00*	*$10.00*	£1.20	£3.60	£6.00

ICICLE

Hero,MS; 1 Jul 1992-7 Jan 1993

	$Good	$Fine	$N.Mint	£Good	£Fine	£N.Mint
1 ND Flare and Lady Arcane appear	*$0.50*	*$1.50*	*$2.50*	£0.30	£0.90	£1.50
2-7 ND	*$0.50*	*$1.50*	*$2.50*	£0.30	£0.90	£1.50
Title Value:	*$3.50*	*$10.50*	*$17.50*	£2.10	£6.30	£10.50

ICON

DC Comics/Milestone; 1 May 1993-present

	$Good	$Fine	$N.Mint	£Good	£Fine	£N.Mint
1	*$0.30*	*$0.90*	*$1.50*	£0.20	£0.60	£1.00
1 Direct Market Edition, ND , pre-bagged with poster, trading card and jigsaw puzzle pieces	*$0.60*	*$1.80*	*$3.00*	£0.40	£1.20	£2.00
2-8	*$0.30*	*$0.90*	*$1.50*	£0.20	£0.60	£1.00
9 spot varnish ink cover by Walt Simonson, continued in Xombi #0	*$0.30*	*$0.90*	*$1.50*	£0.20	£0.60	£1.00
10-13	*$0.30*	*$0.90*	*$1.50*	£0.20	£0.60	£1.00
14 John Byrne cover	*$0.30*	*$0.90*	*$1.50*	£0.20	£0.60	£1.00
15 Worlds Collide X-over, continued in Steel #6	*$0.30*	*$0.90*	*$1.50*	£0.20	£0.60	£1.00
16 Worlds Collide X-over, continued in Steel #7	*$0.30*	*$0.90*	*$1.50*	£0.20	£0.60	£1.00
17-24	*$0.30*	*$0.90*	*$1.50*	£0.20	£0.60	£1.00
25 48pgs	*$0.60*	*$1.80*	*$3.00*	£0.40	£1.20	£2.00
26	*$0.40*	*$1.20*	*$2.00*	£0.25	£0.75	£1.25
27-30	*$0.45*	*$1.35*	*$2.25*	£0.30	£0.90	£1.50
31 Howard Chaykin cover; special price of 99 cents	*$0.20*	*$0.60*	*$1.00*	£0.15	£0.45	£0.75
32-42	*$0.45*	*$1.35*	*$2.25*	£0.30	£0.90	£1.50
43 ND Moebius cover in honour of Milestone's 250th issue	*$0.50*	*$1.50*	*$2.50*	£0.30	£0.90	£1.50
Title Value:	*$16.25*	*$48.75*	*$83.50*	£10.80	£32.40	£54.00

ICZER ONE, GOLDEN WARRIOR

Antarctic Press,MS; 1 Mar 1994-5 Aug 1994

	$Good	$Fine	$N.Mint	£Good	£Fine	£N.Mint
1-5 ND b&w	*$0.50*	*$1.50*	*$2.50*	£0.30	£0.90	£1.50
Title Value:	*$2.50*	*$7.50*	*$12.50*	£1.50	£4.50	£7.50

IDOL

Marvel Comics Group,MS; 1 May 1992-3 Jul 1992

	$Good	$Fine	$N.Mint	£Good	£Fine	£N.Mint
1-3 ND 48pgs	$0.50	$1.50	$2.50	£0.30	£0.90	£1.50
Title Value:	$1.50	$4.50	$7.50	£0.90	£2.70	£4.50

IGRAT

Verotik,MS; 1 Nov 1995-2 1996 ?

	$Good	$Fine	$N.Mint	£Good	£Fine	£N.Mint
1-2 ND Glenn Danzig script, Eric Canete art	$0.60	$1.80	$3.00	£0.40	£1.20	£2.00
Title Value:	$1.20	$3.60	$6.00	£0.80	£2.40	£4.00

IKE GARUDA, THE TRANSMUTATION OF

Marvel Comics Group/Epic,MS; 1 Sep 1991-2 Mar 1992

	$Good	$Fine	$N.Mint	£Good	£Fine	£N.Mint
1-2 ND	$0.80	$2.40	$4.00	£0.50	£1.50	£2.50
Title Value:	$1.60	$4.80	$8.00	£1.00	£3.00	£5.00

ILLEGAL ALIENS

Eclipse; 1 Sep 1992

	$Good	$Fine	$N.Mint	£Good	£Fine	£N.Mint
1 ND famous film monsters featured	$0.50	$1.50	$2.50	£0.30	£0.90	£1.50
Title Value:	$0.50	$1.50	$2.50	£0.30	£0.90	£1.50

ILLUMINATOR

Marvel Comics Group,MS; 1 Jan 1993-3 Apr 1994

	$Good	$Fine	$N.Mint	£Good	£Fine	£N.Mint
1-3 ND 48pgs, squarebound	$0.80	$2.40	$4.00	£0.50	£1.50	£2.50
Title Value:	$2.40	$7.20	$12.00	£1.50	£4.50	£7.50

Note: originally announced as "Crucible" but changed owing to a DC title of the same name appearing around the same time.

ILLUMINATUS!

Rip Off Press; 1,2 1990

	$Good	$Fine	$N.Mint	£Good	£Fine	£N.Mint
1 ND re-done art from original issue #1 dated July 1987, Robert Shea art	$0.50	$1.50	$2.50	£0.30	£0.90	£1.50
2 ND	$0.50	$1.50	$2.50	£0.30	£0.90	£1.50
Title Value:	$1.00	$3.00	$5.00	£0.60	£1.80	£3.00

IMAGE COMICS ANNUAL INFORMATION CATALOGUE

Image,OS; 1994

	$Good	$Fine	$N.Mint	£Good	£Fine	£N.Mint
1 ND details on titles, characters and artists up and coming for the year 1994	$0.50	$1.50	$2.50	£0.30	£0.90	£1.50
Title Value:	$0.50	$1.50	$2.50	£0.30	£0.90	£1.50

IMAGE COUPONS

Image; 1992/1993

The series of special Image Comics #0 coupons were bound-in with the following issues and all seven had to be sent away for the comic. The coupons are brightly coloured forms to be filled in and comics without the coupons are valued lower: **Coupon 1** - Shadowhawk #1, **Coupon 2** - Spawn #4, **Coupon 3** - Cyberforce #1, **Coupon 4** - Brigade #2, **Coupon 5** - WildC.A.T.S. #2, **Coupon 6** - Savage Dragon #3, **Coupon 7** - Youngblood #0

IMAGE PLUS

Image,OS; 1 May 1993

	$Good	$Fine	$N.Mint	£Good	£Fine	£N.Mint
1 ND information on Image artists and writers; embossed logo on cover	$0.40	$1.20	$2.00	£0.25	£0.75	£1.25
Title Value:	$0.40	$1.20	$2.00	£0.25	£0.75	£1.25

IMAGE SWIMSUIT SPECIAL

Image,OS; 1 Apr 1993

	$Good	$Fine	$N.Mint	£Good	£Fine	£N.Mint
1 ND pin-ups by Lee, Silvestri, Portacio and others; flip-cover by Lee and Silvestri	$0.40	$1.20	$2.00	£0.25	£0.75	£1.25
Title Value:	$0.40	$1.20	$2.00	£0.25	£0.75	£1.25

IMAGE ZERO

Image,OS; 0 Oct 1993

	$Good	$Fine	$N.Mint	£Good	£Fine	£N.Mint
0 ND features art by Silvestri, Larsen, Lee, Valentino & includes 1st appearance of Troll by Liefeld	$1.20	$3.60	$6.00	£1.00	£3.00	£5.00
Title Value:	$1.20	$3.60	$6.00	£1.00	£3.00	£5.00

IMMORTAL DR FATE, THE

(see Doctor Fate)

IMMORTALIS

Marvel UK/Frontier,MS; 1 Sep 1993-4 Dec 1993

	$Good	$Fine	$N.Mint	£Good	£Fine	£N.Mint
1-4 Mark Buckingham art	$0.40	$1.20	$2.00	£0.25	£0.75	£1.25
Title Value:	$1.60	$4.80	$8.00	£1.00	£3.00	£5.00

IMPACT COMICS WHO'S WHO

DC Comics/Impact,MS; 1 Sep 1991-2 Oct 1991; 3 May 1992

	$Good	$Fine	$N.Mint	£Good	£Fine	£N.Mint
1-2 ND 48pgs, loose-leaf format to fit in binder (issued separately)	$0.80	$2.40	$4.00	£0.50	£1.50	£2.50
3 ND 48pgs, loose-leaf format to fit in binder (issued separately), trading cards included	$0.80	$2.40	$4.00	£0.50	£1.50	£2.50
Title Value:	$2.40	$7.20	$12.00	£1.50	£4.50	£7.50

IMPACT COMICS WINTER SPECIAL

DC Comics/Impact,OS; 1 Jan 1992

	$Good	$Fine	$N.Mint	£Good	£Fine	£N.Mint
1 64pgs, features the Impact Line of heroes	$0.40	$1.20	$2.00	£0.25	£0.75	£1.25
Title Value:	$0.40	$1.20	$2.00	£0.25	£0.75	£1.25

IMPERIAL GUARD

Marvel Comics Group,MS; 1 Jan 1997-3 Mar 1997

	$Good	$Fine	$N.Mint	£Good	£Fine	£N.Mint
1-3 ND X-Men spin-off featuring the Shi'Ar Guard	$0.40	$1.20	$2.00	£0.25	£0.75	£1.25
Title Value:	$1.20	$3.60	$6.00	£0.75	£2.25	£3.75

IMPOSSIBLE MAN SUMMER VACATION SPECTACULAR

Marvel Comics Group; 1 Aug 1990; 2 Sep 1991

	$Good	$Fine	$N.Mint	£Good	£Fine	£N.Mint
1 ND 64pgs, Spiderman/Punisher appear, variety of artists/writers	$0.40	$1.20	$2.00	£0.25	£0.75	£1.25
2 ND Teenage Mutant Ninja Turtles parody cover by Golden	$0.40	$1.20	$2.00	£0.25	£0.75	£1.25
Title Value:	$0.80	$2.40	$4.00	£0.50	£1.50	£2.50

IMPULSE

DC Comics; 1 Apr 1995-present

(see Flash [2nd Series] #92/93)

	$Good	$Fine	$N.Mint	£Good	£Fine	£N.Mint
1 spin-off series from Flash (2nd Series) #100	$1.40	$4.20	$7.00	£0.60	£1.80	£3.00
2	$1.00	$3.00	$5.00	£0.40	£1.20	£2.00
3-5	$0.80	$2.40	$4.00	£0.30	£0.90	£1.50
6-7	$0.50	$1.50	$2.50	£0.25	£0.75	£1.25
8 Underworld Unleashed tie-in	$0.50	$1.50	$2.50	£0.25	£0.75	£1.25
9	$0.50	$1.50	$2.50	£0.25	£0.75	£1.25
10 Dead Heat part 3, continued in Flash #110	$0.50	$1.50	$2.50	£0.25	£0.75	£1.25
11 Dead Heat part 5, continued in Flash #111	$0.40	$1.20	$2.00	£0.25	£0.75	£1.25
12-13	$0.40	$1.20	$2.00	£0.25	£0.75	£1.25
14-15 The Trickster appears	$0.40	$1.20	$2.00	£0.25	£0.75	£1.25
16	$0.35	$1.05	$1.75	£0.25	£0.75	£1.25
17 Zatanna appears	$0.35	$1.05	$1.75	£0.25	£0.75	£1.25
18-20	$0.35	$1.05	$1.75	£0.25	£0.75	£1.25
21 ND Legion of Super-Heroes guest-star	$0.35	$1.05	$1.75	£0.25	£0.75	£1.25
22-23 ND	$0.35	$1.05	$1.75	£0.25	£0.75	£1.25
Title Value:	$12.10	$36.30	$58.50	£6.40	£19.20	£32.00

IMPULSE ANNUAL

DC Comics; 1 Jun 1996-present

	$Good	$Fine	$N.Mint	£Good	£Fine	£N.Mint
1 ND 48pgs, Legends of the Dead Earth tie-in; Steve Vance script, Mike Parobaek and John Nyberg art, cover by Humberto Ramos	$0.60	$1.80	$3.00	£0.40	£1.20	£2.00
Title Value:	$0.60	$1.80	$3.00	£0.40	£1.20	£2.00

House Of Secrets #82

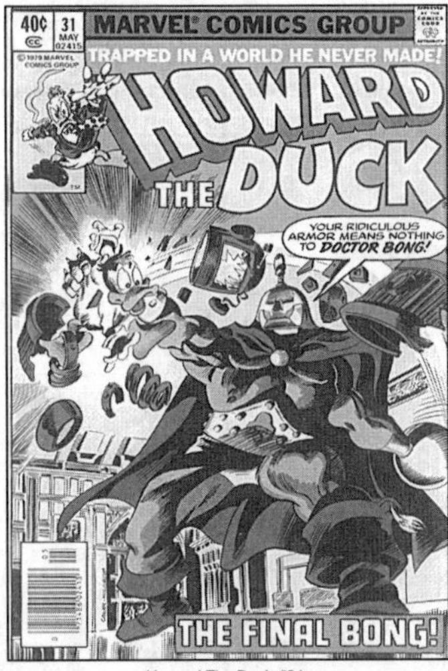

Howard The Duck #31

Impulse #1

IN HIS STEPS

Marvel Comics Group,OS; nn May 1994

Issue	$Good	$Fine	$N.Mint	£Good	£Fine	£N.Mint
nn ND 96pgs, Trade paperback; neighbourhood and community programme story published in conjunction with Thomas Nelson Publishing	*$2.00*	*$6.00*	*$10.00*	£1.30	£3.90	£6.50
Title Value:	*$2.00*	*$6.00*	*$10.00*	£1.30	£3.90	£6.50

IN SEARCH OF THE CASTAWAYS

Dell/Movie Comics,OS Movie; 10048-303 Mar 1963

Issue	$Good	$Fine	$N.Mint	£Good	£Fine	£N.Mint
10048-303 distributed in the U.K. film adaptation; Hayley Mills photo cover	*$9.25*	*$28.00*	*$65.00*	£5.50	£17.00	£40.00
Title Value:	*$9.25*	*$28.00*	*$65.00*	£5.50	£17.00	£40.00

IN THE DAYS OF THE MOB

DC Comics/Hampshire Distribution,Magazine; 1 Fall 1971

Issue	$Good	$Fine	$N.Mint	£Good	£Fine	£N.Mint
1 LD in the U.K. 48pgs, Jack Kirby art throughout, includes poster (John Dillinger); black and white	*$2.50*	*$7.50*	*$15.00*	£2.50	£7.50	£15.00
Title Value:	*$2.50*	*$7.50*	*$15.00*	£2.50	£7.50	£15.00

Note: a second issue was intended but never appeared. Some unpublished art by Kirby appears in The Amazing World of DC Comics #1

INCAL, THE

Marvel Comics Group/Epic;Graphic Novel; 1-3 1988

(see also Moebius)

Issue	$Good	$Fine	$N.Mint	£Good	£Fine	£N.Mint
1 ND 96pgs	*$1.50*	*$4.50*	*$7.50*	£1.00	£3.00	£5.00
2 ND 120pgs	*$1.80*	*$5.25*	*$9.00*	£1.20	£3.60	£6.00
3 ND 96pgs	*$1.50*	*$4.50*	*$7.50*	£1.00	£3.00	£5.00
Title Value:	*$4.80*	*$14.25*	*$24.00*	£3.20	£9.60	£16.00

Note: all have Moebius art. Titan (UK) editions also exist.

INCREDIBLE ASHCAN SET

Image,OS; nn Mar 1996

Issue	$Good	$Fine	$N.Mint	£Good	£Fine	£N.Mint
nn ND scarce in the U.K. Cyberforce #0, Cyberforce Mini-Series #1-4, Strykeforce #1, Ripclaw Mini-Series #1, Ballistic Studios Swimsuit Special	*$2.00*	*$6.00*	*$10.00*	£1.30	£3.90	£6.50
Title Value:	*$2.00*	*$6.00*	*$10.00*	£1.30	£3.90	£6.50

INCREDIBLE HULK & WOLVERINE

Marvel Comics Group,OS; 1 Oct 1986

Issue	$Good	$Fine	$N.Mint	£Good	£Fine	£N.Mint
1 ND reprints Hulk #180,#181 featuring the first appearance of Wolverine	*$2.00*	*$6.00*	*$10.00*	£1.20	£3.60	£6.00
1 2nd printing, (1991), squarebound, new cover art plus new pin-up inside back cover, titled "Wolverine Battles The Incredible Hulk"	*$1.00*	*$3.00*	*$5.00*	£0.70	£2.10	£3.50
Title Value:	*$3.00*	*$9.00*	*$15.00*	£1.90	£5.70	£9.50

INCREDIBLE HULK (1ST SERIES)

Marvel Comics Group; 1 May 1962-6 Mar 1963

(see Avengers, Marvel Fanfare, Marvel Team-Up, Marvel Treasury Edition, Rampaging Hulk)

Issue	$Good	$Fine	$N.Mint	£Good	£Fine	£N.Mint
1 origin and 1st appearance of The Hulk (grey); Jack Kirby cover and art	*$820.00*	*$2450.00*	*$11500.00*	£500.00	£1500.00	£7000.00
[Very rare in high grade - Very Fine+ or better]						
1 Marvel Milestone Edition, ND (May 1992), reprints original issue with ads	*$0.50*	*$1.50*	*$2.50*	£0.30	£0.90	£1.50
2 1st green Hulk; Jack Kirby and Steve Ditko cover and art	*$265.00*	*$800.00*	*$3200.00*	£130.00	£390.00	£1550.00
3 origin retold, 1st appearance Ringmaster; Jack Kirby cover and art	*$160.00*	*$480.00*	*$1600.00*	£87.50	£262.50	£875.00
4 origin re-told in brief; Jack Kirby cover and art	*$140.00*	*$420.00*	*$1400.00*	£75.00	£225.00	£750.00
5 scarce in the U.K. Jack Kirby cover and art	*$135.00*	*$410.00*	*$1375.00*	£80.00	£240.00	£800.00
6 less common in the U.K. 1st appearance Teen Brigade; all Steve Ditko cover and art	*$210.00*	*$630.00*	*$2100.00*	£100.00	£300.00	£1000.00
Title Value:	*$1730.50*	*$5191.50*	*$21177.50*	£972.80	£2918.40	£11976.50

Note: issue 1 has a dark blue cover which marks easily, particularly along the spine and edges and is therefore very rare in high grade. See also Fantastic Four #7.

ARTISTS

Kirby in 1-5, Ditko in 6.

INCREDIBLE HULK (2ND SERIES)

Marvel Comics Group; 102 Apr 1968-present

Issue	$Good	$Fine	$N.Mint	£Good	£Fine	£N.Mint
102 origin retold; Warriors Three and Odin appear; Thor and Silver Surfer cameos	*$27.00*	*$80.00*	*$190.00*	£17.00	£50.00	£120.00
103 scarce in the U.K.	*$10.50*	*$32.00*	*$75.00*	£6.25	£19.00	£45.00
104 Rhino appears	*$10.00*	*$30.00*	*$70.00*	£5.25	£16.00	£37.50
105 1st appearance Missing Link	*$7.75*	*$23.50*	*$55.00*	£4.25	£12.50	£30.00
106-108	*$7.75*	*$23.50*	*$55.00*	£4.25	£12.50	£30.00
109-110 Ka-Zar appears	*$5.50*	*$17.00*	*$40.00*	£2.85	£8.50	£20.00
111 (Jan 1969)	*$4.60*	*$13.50*	*$32.50*	£2.50	£7.50	£17.50
112-115	*$4.60*	*$13.50*	*$32.50*	£2.50	£7.50	£17.50
116	*$4.25*	*$12.50*	*$30.00*	£2.10	£6.25	£15.00
117 last 12¢ issue	*$4.25*	*$12.50*	*$30.00*	£2.10	£6.25	£15.00
118 Hulk battles Sub-Mariner	*$4.25*	*$12.50*	*$30.00*	£2.10	£6.25	£15.00
119	*$2.55*	*$7.50*	*$18.00*	£1.40	£4.25	£10.00
120 Inhumans appear, classic cover by Herb Trimpe	*$2.55*	*$7.50*	*$18.00*	£1.40	£4.25	£10.00
121	*$2.55*	*$7.50*	*$18.00*	£1.40	£4.25	£10.00
122 Hulk battles The Thing (see Fantastic Four #25), Fantastic Four appear	*$5.25*	*$16.00*	*$37.50*	£2.25	£6.75	£16.00
123 (Jan 1970), Fantastic Four appear	*$2.55*	*$7.50*	*$18.00*	£1.40	£4.25	£10.00
124-125	*$2.55*	*$7.50*	*$18.00*	£1.40	£4.25	£10.00
126 Dr. Strange appears	*$2.50*	*$7.50*	*$15.00*	£1.15	£3.50	£7.00
127	*$2.50*	*$7.50*	*$15.00*	£1.15	£3.50	£7.00
128 Hulk battles Avengers	*$2.50*	*$7.50*	*$15.00*	£1.25	£3.75	£7.50
129-130	*$2.50*	*$7.50*	*$15.00*	£1.15	£3.50	£7.00
131 Iron Man vs. The Hulk	*$2.05*	*$6.25*	*$12.50*	£1.00	£3.00	£6.00
132-133	*$2.05*	*$6.25*	*$12.50*	£1.00	£3.00	£6.00
134 1st appearance Golem I (see Strange Tales #174)	*$2.05*	*$6.25*	*$12.50*	£1.00	£3.00	£6.00
135 (Jan 1971)	*$2.05*	*$6.25*	*$12.50*	£1.00	£3.00	£6.00
136-139	*$2.05*	*$6.25*	*$12.50*	£1.00	£3.00	£6.00
140 Harlan Ellison script, 1st appearance Jarella; story continues from Avengers #88	*$2.05*	*$6.25*	*$12.50*	£1.00	£3.00	£6.00
141 less common in the U.K. 1st appearance Doc Samson	*$2.90*	*$8.75*	*$17.50*	£2.05	£6.25	£12.50
142-143	*$1.15*	*$3.50*	*$7.00*	£0.80	£2.50	£5.00
144 Iron Man and Dr. Doom appear, classic cover	*$1.15*	*$3.50*	*$7.00*	£0.80	£2.50	£5.00
145 52pgs, origin retold	*$1.65*	*$5.00*	*$10.00*	£1.05	£3.25	£6.50
146	*$1.15*	*$3.50*	*$7.00*	£0.80	£2.50	£5.00
147 (Jan 1972)	*$1.15*	*$3.50*	*$7.00*	£0.80	£2.50	£5.00
148 Nick Fury appears	*$1.15*	*$3.50*	*$7.00*	£0.80	£2.50	£5.00
149 1st appearance The Inheritor	*$1.15*	*$3.50*	*$7.00*	£0.80	£2.50	£5.00
150 Lorna Dane, Havok appear	*$1.15*	*$3.50*	*$7.00*	£0.80	£2.50	£5.00
151	*$1.00*	*$3.00*	*$6.00*	£0.65	£2.00	£4.00
152 scarce in the U.K. Captain America, Daredevil, Fantastic Four, Nick Fury appear: Hulk on trial	*$1.00*	*$3.00*	*$6.00*	£1.00	£3.00	£6.00
153 ND very scarce in the U.K. Hulk on trial continued with above guests plus Spiderman and the Avengers	*$1.00*	*$3.00*	*$6.00*	£1.25	£3.75	£7.50
154 ND	*$1.00*	*$3.00*	*$6.00*	£0.75	£2.25	£4.50
155 ND scarce in the U.K.	*$1.00*	*$3.00*	*$6.00*	£1.00	£3.00	£6.00
156-157 ND	*$1.00*	*$3.00*	*$6.00*	£0.75	£2.25	£4.50
158 ND Counter Earth story, various cameo appearances including Warlock	*$1.00*	*$3.00*	*$6.00*	£0.80	£2.50	£5.00
159 ND (Jan 1973)	*$1.00*	*$3.00*	*$6.00*	£0.75	£2.25	£4.50
160 ND	*$1.00*	*$3.00*	*$6.00*	£0.75	£2.25	£4.50
161 Beast appears, death of Mimic	*$1.00*	*$3.00*	*$6.00*	£0.65	£2.00	£4.00
162 1st appearance Wendigo	*$1.50*	*$4.50*	*$9.00*	£0.80	£2.50	£5.00
163-164	*$1.00*	*$3.00*	*$6.00*	£0.65	£2.00	£4.00
165 some issues have 4pg heavier paper insert with ads	*$1.00*	*$3.00*	*$6.00*	£0.65	£2.00	£4.00
166 1st appearance Zzzax, Hawkeye appears	*$1.00*	*$3.00*	*$6.00*	£0.65	£2.00	£4.00
167-170 ND	*$1.00*	*$3.00*	*$6.00*	£0.75	£2.25	£4.50
171 ND scarce in the U.K. (Jan 1974), Abomination/Rhino vs. Hulk	*$1.00*	*$3.00*	*$6.00*	£1.00	£3.00	£6.00
172 ND X-Men appear, ties in with Avengers #111	*$1.50*	*$4.50*	*$9.00*	£1.00	£3.00	£6.00
173-174 ND	*$1.00*	*$3.00*	*$6.00*	£0.55	£1.75	£3.50
175 ND Inhumans appear, Hulk vs. Black Bolt	*$1.00*	*$3.00*	*$6.00*	£0.55	£1.75	£3.50
176 ND Warlock X-over (cameo); same cover-date as Strange Tales #178	*$1.00*	*$3.00*	*$6.00*	£0.75	£2.25	£4.50
177 ND Warlock X-over; Warlock "dies" in last panel	*$1.15*	*$3.50*	*$7.00*	£0.80	£2.50	£5.00
178 ND Warlock X-over; rebirth of Warlock	*$1.65*	*$5.00*	*$10.00*	£1.00	£3.00	£6.00
179 ND	*$0.80*	*$2.50*	*$5.00*	£0.55	£1.75	£3.50
180 ND 1st appearance of Wolverine (one panel, last page)	*$11.00*	*$34.00*	*$80.00*	£7.00	£21.00	£50.00
181 ND 1st Wolverine story	*$50.00*	*$150.00*	*$400.00*	£31.00	£92.50	£250.00
182 ND Wolverine cameo only	*$9.25*	*$28.00*	*$65.00*	£5.00	£15.00	£35.00
183 ND (Jan 1975)	*$0.80*	*$2.50*	*$5.00*	£0.50	£1.50	£3.00
184-189 ND	*$0.80*	*$2.50*	*$5.00*	£0.50	£1.50	£3.00
190 ND 1st appearance Glorian	*$0.80*	*$2.50*	*$5.00*	£0.50	£1.50	£3.00
191-194 ND	*$0.65*	*$2.00*	*$4.00*	£0.40	£1.25	£2.50
195 ND (Jan 1976)	*$0.65*	*$2.00*	*$4.00*	£0.40	£1.25	£2.50
196-197 ND	*$0.65*	*$2.00*	*$4.00*	£0.40	£1.25	£2.50
198-199 ND Man-Thing appears	*$0.65*	*$2.00*	*$4.00*	£0.40	£1.25	£2.50
200 ND anniversary issue, Silver Surfer appears in dream sequence	*$3.55*	*$10.50*	*$25.00*	£1.05	£3.20	£7.50
201-203 ND	*$0.55*	*$1.75*	*$3.50*	£0.30	£1.00	£2.00
204 ND origin retold	*$0.55*	*$1.75*	*$3.50*	£0.30	£1.00	£2.00
205-206 ND	*$0.55*	*$1.75*	*$3.50*	£0.30	£1.00	£2.00
207 ND (Jan 1977), Hulk battles Defenders	*$0.55*	*$1.75*	*$3.50*	£0.30	£1.00	£2.00
208-211 ND	*$0.55*	*$1.75*	*$3.50*	£0.30	£1.00	£2.00
212 ND 1st appearance Constrictor	*$0.55*	*$1.75*	*$3.50*	£0.30	£1.00	£2.00

Issue	$Good	$Fine	$N.Mint	£Good	£Fine	£N.Mint
213 ND	*$0.55*	*$1.75*	*$3.50*	£0.30	£1.00	£2.00
214 ND Hulk battles Jack of Hearts	*$0.55*	*$1.75*	*$3.50*	£0.30	£1.00	£2.00
215-217 ND	*$0.55*	*$1.75*	*$3.50*	£0.30	£1.00	£2.00
218 ND 1st solo Doc Samson story	*$0.55*	*$1.75*	*$3.50*	£0.30	£1.00	£2.00
219 ND (Jan 1978)	*$0.55*	*$1.75*	*$3.50*	£0.30	£1.00	£2.00
220-221 ND	*$0.55*	*$1.75*	*$3.50*	£0.30	£1.00	£2.00
222 ND Jim Starlin layouts	*$0.65*	*$2.00*	*$4.00*	£0.40	£1.25	£2.50
223-226 ND	*$0.55*	*$1.75*	*$3.50*	£0.30	£1.00	£2.00
227 ND original Avengers appear	*$0.55*	*$1.75*	*$3.50*	£0.30	£1.00	£2.00
228 ND	*$0.55*	*$1.75*	*$3.50*	£0.30	£1.00	£2.00
229 ND Doc Samson appears	*$0.55*	*$1.75*	*$3.50*	£0.30	£1.00	£2.00
230 ND	*$0.55*	*$1.75*	*$3.50*	£0.30	£1.00	£2.00
231 ND (Jan 1979)	*$0.55*	*$1.75*	*$3.50*	£0.30	£1.00	£2.00
232 ND Captain America appears	*$0.55*	*$1.75*	*$3.50*	£0.30	£1.00	£2.00
233-234 ND	*$0.55*	*$1.75*	*$3.50*	£0.30	£1.00	£2.00
235-236 ND Machine Man appears	*$0.55*	*$1.75*	*$3.50*	£0.30	£1.00	£2.00
237-242 ND	*$0.55*	*$1.75*	*$3.50*	£0.30	£1.00	£2.00
243 ND (Jan 1980)	*$0.55*	*$1.75*	*$3.50*	£0.30	£1.00	£2.00
244 ND	*$0.55*	*$1.75*	*$3.50*	£0.30	£1.00	£2.00
245-246 ND Captain Marvel appears	*$0.55*	*$1.75*	*$3.50*	£0.30	£1.00	£2.00
247-248 ND	*$0.55*	*$1.75*	*$3.50*	£0.30	£1.00	£2.00
249 ND Steve Ditko art	*$0.55*	*$1.75*	*$3.50*	£0.30	£1.00	£2.00
250 ND 52pgs, Silver Surfer battles Hulk	*$1.65*	*$5.00*	*$10.00*	£0.80	£2.50	£5.00
251-252 ND	*$0.60*	*$1.80*	*$3.00*	£0.30	£0.90	£1.50
253 ND Doc Samson appears	*$0.60*	*$1.80*	*$3.00*	£0.30	£0.90	£1.50
254 ND	*$0.60*	*$1.80*	*$3.00*	£0.30	£0.90	£1.50
255 ND (Jan 1981), Hulk vs. Thor	*$0.60*	*$1.80*	*$3.00*	£0.30	£0.90	£1.50
256-257 ND	*$0.60*	*$1.80*	*$3.00*	£0.30	£0.90	£1.50
258 Frank Miller cover	*$0.60*	*$1.80*	*$3.00*	£0.25	£0.75	£1.25
259-260	*$0.60*	*$1.80*	*$3.00*	£0.25	£0.75	£1.25
261 Frank Miller cover	*$0.60*	*$1.80*	*$3.00*	£0.25	£0.75	£1.25
262-263	*$0.60*	*$1.80*	*$3.00*	£0.25	£0.75	£1.25
264 Frank Miller cover	*$0.60*	*$1.80*	*$3.00*	£0.25	£0.75	£1.25
265-266	*$0.60*	*$1.80*	*$3.00*	£0.25	£0.75	£1.25
267 (Jan 1982)	*$0.60*	*$1.80*	*$3.00*	£0.25	£0.75	£1.25
268 Frank Miller cover	*$0.60*	*$1.80*	*$3.00*	£0.25	£0.75	£1.25
269-270	*$0.60*	*$1.80*	*$3.00*	£0.25	£0.75	£1.25
271 20th anniversary issue, 1st appearance Rocket Raccoon	*$0.60*	*$1.80*	*$3.00*	£0.25	£0.75	£1.25
272 Alpha Flight and Wendigo appear	*$0.60*	*$1.80*	*$3.00*	£0.25	£0.75	£1.25
273 Sasquatch and Wendigo appear	*$0.60*	*$1.80*	*$3.00*	£0.25	£0.75	£1.25
274-276	*$0.60*	*$1.80*	*$3.00*	£0.25	£0.75	£1.25
277 many Marvel heroes make cameo appearances	*$0.60*	*$1.80*	*$3.00*	£0.25	£0.75	£1.25
278 X-Men and Avengers cameos plus many other Marvel heroes	*$0.60*	*$1.80*	*$3.00*	£0.25	£0.75	£1.25
279 (Jan 1983), Alpha Flight, X-Men cameos and many other Marvel heroes	*$0.60*	*$1.80*	*$3.00*	£0.25	£0.75	£1.25
280	*$0.60*	*$1.80*	*$3.00*	£0.25	£0.75	£1.25
281 Avengers cameo	*$0.50*	*$1.50*	*$2.50*	£0.25	£0.75	£1.25
282-284 Avengers appear	*$0.50*	*$1.50*	*$2.50*	£0.25	£0.75	£1.25
285-290	*$0.50*	*$1.50*	*$2.50*	£0.25	£0.75	£1.25
291 (Jan 1984)	*$0.50*	*$1.50*	*$2.50*	£0.25	£0.75	£1.25
292	*$0.50*	*$1.50*	*$2.50*	£0.25	£0.75	£1.25
293 Fantastic Four appear	*$0.50*	*$1.50*	*$2.50*	£0.25	£0.75	£1.25
294	*$0.50*	*$1.50*	*$2.50*	£0.25	£0.75	£1.25
295 Sienkiewicz cover	*$0.50*	*$1.50*	*$2.50*	£0.25	£0.75	£1.25
296 Rom appears	*$0.50*	*$1.50*	*$2.50*	£0.25	£0.75	£1.25
297-298 Dr. Strange appears	*$0.50*	*$1.50*	*$2.50*	£0.25	£0.75	£1.25
299 LD in the U.K. Dr. Strange appears	*$0.50*	*$1.50*	*$2.50*	£0.30	£0.90	£1.50
300 LD in the U.K. DS, Spiderman, Thor and Avengers battle a rampaging Hul; Dr. Strange, Daredevil, Luke Cage and Iron Fist appear	*$0.80*	*$2.40*	*$4.00*	£0.50	£1.50	£2.50
301 Dr. Strange appears, Sienkiewicz cover	*$0.60*	*$1.80*	*$3.00*	£0.25	£0.75	£1.25
302	*$0.60*	*$1.80*	*$3.00*	£0.25	£0.75	£1.25
303 (Jan 1985)	*$0.60*	*$1.80*	*$3.00*	£0.25	£0.75	£1.25
304	*$0.60*	*$1.80*	*$3.00*	£0.25	£0.75	£1.25
305 Dr. Strange and Avengers appear	*$0.60*	*$1.80*	*$3.00*	£0.25	£0.75	£1.25
306-311	*$0.60*	*$1.80*	*$3.00*	£0.25	£0.75	£1.25
312 LD in the U.K. Secret Wars X-over, origin retold	*$0.60*	*$1.80*	*$3.00*	£0.30	£0.90	£1.50
313 Alpha Flight	*$0.60*	*$1.80*	*$3.00*	£0.25	£0.75	£1.25
314 LD in the U.K. John Byrne art begins	*$1.00*	*$3.00*	*$5.00*	£0.40	£1.20	£2.00
315 (Jan 1986), John Byrne art	*$0.60*	*$1.80*	*$3.00*	£0.30	£0.90	£1.50
316 Hulk battles West and East Coast Avengers, John Byrne art	*$0.60*	*$1.80*	*$3.00*	£0.30	£0.90	£1.50
317-319 John Byrne art	*$0.60*	*$1.80*	*$3.00*	£0.30	£0.90	£1.50
320 LD in the U.K.	*$0.50*	*$1.50*	*$2.50*	£0.30	£0.90	£1.50
321-323 LD in the U.K. Avengers vs Hulk	*$0.50*	*$1.50*	*$2.50*	£0.30	£0.90	£1.50
324 1st modern grey Hulk (since 1962!)	*$2.00*	*$6.00*	*$10.00*	£0.70	£2.10	£3.50
325 grey Hulk, 1st Steve Geiger art	*$0.60*	*$1.80*	*$3.00*	£0.50	£1.50	£2.50
326 grey Hulk vs. green Hulk, Geiger art	*$1.00*	*$3.00*	*$5.00*	£0.50	£1.50	£2.50
327 (Jan 1987), Geiger art	*$0.60*	*$1.80*	*$3.00*	£0.30	£0.90	£1.50
328 1st Peter David scripting, Geiger cover	*$0.60*	*$1.80*	*$3.00*	£0.40	£1.20	£2.00
329	*$0.60*	*$1.80*	*$3.00*	£0.30	£0.90	£1.50
330 Todd McFarlane art begins (ends #346)	*$3.00*	*$9.00*	*$15.00*	£1.20	£3.60	£6.00
331 LD in the U.K. grey Hulk series begins, 2nd Peter David script (to present except #360 and #389), Todd McFarlane art	*$2.00*	*$6.00*	*$10.00*	£1.00	£3.00	£5.00
332-334 Todd McFarlane art	*$1.60*	*$4.80*	*$8.00*	£0.80	£2.40	£4.00
335 Ridgway art	*$0.50*	*$1.50*	*$2.50*	£0.30	£0.90	£1.50
336-337 LD in the U.K. X-Factor X-over, Todd McFarlane art	*$1.40*	*$4.20*	*$7.00*	£1.00	£3.00	£5.00
338 Todd McFarlane art	*$1.40*	*$4.20*	*$7.00*	£0.80	£2.40	£4.00
339 (Jan 1988), Todd McFarlane art	*$1.40*	*$4.20*	*$7.00*	£0.80	£2.40	£4.00
340 LD in the U.K. Hulk vs. Wolverine, Todd McFarlane art	*$7.00*	*$21.00*	*$35.00*	£2.00	£6.00	£10.00
341-343 Todd McFarlane art	*$1.20*	*$3.60*	*$6.00*	£0.70	£2.10	£3.50
344 LD in the U.K. Todd McFarlane art	*$1.20*	*$3.60*	*$6.00*	£0.80	£2.40	£4.00
345 very LD in the U.K. DS, Todd McFarlane art	*$1.20*	*$3.60*	*$6.00*	£0.90	£2.70	£4.50
346 part Todd McFarlane art	*$1.20*	*$3.60*	*$6.00*	£0.60	£1.80	£3.00
347-348 Jeff Purves art	*$0.60*	*$1.80*	*$3.00*	£0.30	£0.90	£1.50
349 Jeff Purves art, Spiderman appears; ties into Web of Spiderman #46	*$0.60*	*$1.80*	*$3.00*	£0.30	£0.90	£1.50
350 LD in the U.K. Thing vs Hulk	*$1.00*	*$3.00*	*$5.00*	£0.50	£1.50	£2.50
351 (Jan 1989)	*$0.60*	*$1.80*	*$3.00*	£0.30	£0.90	£1.50
352-358	*$0.60*	*$1.80*	*$3.00*	£0.30	£0.90	£1.50
359 Hulk vs. "illusion" Wolverine, John Byrne cover	*$1.00*	*$3.00*	*$5.00*	£0.30	£0.90	£1.50
360	*$0.60*	*$1.80*	*$3.00*	£0.30	£0.90	£1.50
361 Iron Man battles Hulk	*$0.60*	*$1.80*	*$3.00*	£0.30	£0.90	£1.50
362	*$0.60*	*$1.80*	*$3.00*	£0.30	£0.90	£1.50
363 Acts of Vengeance tie-in	*$0.60*	*$1.80*	*$3.00*	£0.30	£0.90	£1.50
364 Walt Simonson cover, part 1 "Countdown"	*$0.60*	*$1.80*	*$3.00*	£0.30	£0.90	£1.50
365 (Jan 1990), Hulk battles Thing; Ms. Marvel appears, Walt Simonson cover	*$0.60*	*$1.80*	*$3.00*	£0.30	£0.90	£1.50
366 Walt Simonson cover	*$0.60*	*$1.80*	*$3.00*	£0.30	£0.90	£1.50
367 LD in the U.K. 1st Dale Keown art, part 4 (conclusion) "Countdown", Walt Simonson cover	*$2.00*	*$6.00*	*$10.00*	£1.00	£3.00	£5.00
368 Sam Keith art	*$1.60*	*$4.80*	*$8.00*	£0.60	£1.80	£3.00
369 2nd Dale Keown art, Hulk battles Freedom Force	*$1.60*	*$4.80*	*$8.00*	£0.70	£2.10	£3.50
370 Dale Keown art, Dr. Strange, Sub-Mariner appear (the original Defenders)	*$1.60*	*$4.80*	*$8.00*	£0.70	£2.10	£3.50
371 Dale Keown art, Dr. Strange, Sub-Mariner appear	*$1.00*	*$3.00*	*$5.00*	£0.60	£1.80	£3.00
372 Dale Keown art, green hulk re-emerges	*$1.60*	*$4.80*	*$8.00*	£0.80	£2.40	£4.00
373-375 Dale Keown art	*$1.20*	*$3.60*	*$6.00*	£0.60	£1.80	£3.00
376 Dale Keown art, green hulk vs grey hulk	*$1.40*	*$4.20*	*$7.00*	£0.70	£2.10	£3.50
377 LD in the U.K. (Jan 1991), grey/green Hulks merge to form 1st all-new Hulk, Dale Keown art, "flourescent" cover	*$2.40*	*$7.00*	*$12.00*	£0.80	£2.40	£4.00

Issue	$Good	$Fine	$N.Mint	£Good	£Fine	£N.Mint
377 2nd printing, ND grey/green Hulks merge (gold cover)	*$1.20*	*$3.60*	*$6.00*	£0.60	£1.80	£3.00
377 3rd printing, ND reprints green cover (Nov 1994)	*$0.40*	*$1.20*	*$2.00*	£0.25	£0.75	£1.25
378 LD in the U.K. no Keown art	*$0.60*	*$1.80*	*$3.00*	£0.30	£0.90	£1.50
379 LD in the U.K. Dale Keown art	*$1.20*	*$3.60*	*$6.00*	£0.70	£2.10	£3.50
380 no Keown art, Doc Sampson appears	*$0.60*	*$1.80*	*$3.00*	£0.25	£0.75	£1.25
381-382 Dale Keown art	*$0.80*	*$2.40*	*$4.00*	£0.30	£0.90	£1.50
383-385 Infinity Gauntlet X-over, Dale Keown art	*$0.80*	*$2.40*	*$4.00*	£0.30	£0.90	£1.50
386-387 Dale Keown art	*$0.80*	*$2.40*	*$4.00*	£0.30	£0.90	£1.50
388 Dale Keown art, AIDS story	*$0.80*	*$2.40*	*$4.00*	£0.30	£0.90	£1.50
389 (Jan 1992), no Dale Keown art	*$0.60*	*$1.80*	*$3.00*	£0.25	£0.75	£1.25
390 X-Factor appear, $1.25 cover begins, Dale Keown art	*$0.80*	*$2.40*	*$4.00*	£0.30	£0.90	£1.50
391-392 X-Factor appear, Dale Keown art	*$0.60*	*$1.80*	*$3.00*	£0.25	£0.75	£1.25
393 64pgs, 30th anniversary issue, green foil back-ground, Dale Keown art plus Jim Starlin and Gil Kane	*$0.70*	*$2.10*	*$3.50*	£0.40	£1.20	£2.00
393 2nd printing, ND scarce in the U.K. grey cover	*$0.60*	*$1.80*	*$3.00*	£0.40	£1.20	£2.00
394 1st appearance Trauma, Andrew Wildman art	*$0.40*	*$1.20*	*$2.00*	£0.25	£0.75	£1.25
395 Punisher guest stars, Dale Keown art	*$0.40*	*$1.20*	*$2.00*	£0.25	£0.75	£1.25
396 Punisher and Dr. Octopus appear, Dale Keown art	*$0.40*	*$1.20*	*$2.00*	£0.25	£0.75	£1.25
397-398 Ghost of the Past story, Dale Keown art	*$0.40*	*$1.20*	*$2.00*	£0.25	£0.75	£1.25
399 Ghost of the Past story, Fantastic Four, Dr. Strange and Hank Pym appear; not Keown art	*$0.40*	*$1.20*	*$2.00*	£0.25	£0.75	£1.25
400 ND 64pgs, holo-grafix silver foil cover; reprints The Leader's 1st full appearance from Tales to Astonish #63; last Keown art	*$0.60*	*$1.80*	*$3.00*	£0.40	£1.20	£2.00
400 2nd printing, ND 64pgs, (May 1993), different back ground colour on cover	*$0.50*	*$1.50*	*$2.50*	£0.30	£0.90	£1.50
401 (Jan 1993)	*$0.40*	*$1.20*	*$2.00*	£0.25	£0.75	£1.25
402 Hulk vs. Juggernaut, Doc Samson returns	*$0.40*	*$1.20*	*$2.00*	£0.25	£0.75	£1.25
403 Red Skull and Avengers appear, Gary Frank pencils begin	*$0.40*	*$1.20*	*$2.00*	£0.25	£0.75	£1.25
404 Red Skull and Avengers appear	*$0.40*	*$1.20*	*$2.00*	£0.25	£0.75	£1.25
405-406	*$0.40*	*$1.20*	*$2.00*	£0.25	£0.75	£1.25
407 Ulysses origin in back-up story	*$0.40*	*$1.20*	*$2.00*	£0.25	£0.75	£1.25
408 Mad Man and Motormouth appear	*$0.40*	*$1.20*	*$2.00*	£0.25	£0.75	£1.25
409 Mad Man, Motormouth and Killpower appear	*$0.40*	*$1.20*	*$2.00*	£0.25	£0.75	£1.25
410 Nick Fury and SHIELD appear	*$0.40*	*$1.20*	*$2.00*	£0.25	£0.75	£1.25
411 Nick Fury and SHIELD appear	*$0.30*	*$0.90*	*$1.50*	£0.20	£0.60	£1.00
412	*$0.30*	*$0.90*	*$1.50*	£0.20	£0.60	£1.00
413 (Jan 1994), The Troyan War story	*$0.30*	*$0.90*	*$1.50*	£0.20	£0.60	£1.00
414 The Troyan War story	*$0.30*	*$0.90*	*$1.50*	£0.20	£0.60	£1.00
415 The Troyan War story, Silver Surfer appears	*$0.30*	*$0.90*	*$1.50*	£0.20	£0.60	£1.00
416 The Troyan War story; Future Imperfect storyline tie-in	*$0.30*	*$0.90*	*$1.50*	£0.20	£0.60	£1.00
417 with free Spiderman and his Deadly Foes card sheet	*$0.30*	*$0.90*	*$1.50*	£0.20	£0.60	£1.00
418 the wedding of Rick and Marlo	*$0.30*	*$0.90*	*$1.50*	£0.20	£0.60	£1.00
418 Collectors Edition, ND die-cut gate-fold wedding invitation cover; Rick and Marlo marry	*$0.60*	*$1.80*	*$3.00*	£0.30	£0.90	£1.50
419	*$0.30*	*$0.90*	*$1.50*	£0.20	£0.60	£1.00
420 AIDS story - death of Jim Wilson	*$0.30*	*$0.90*	*$1.50*	£0.20	£0.60	£1.00
421 Thor appears	*$0.30*	*$0.90*	*$1.50*	£0.20	£0.60	£1.00
422-424	*$0.30*	*$0.90*	*$1.50*	£0.20	£0.60	£1.00
425 48pgs, (Jan 1995), new art team of Liam Sharpe and Robin Riggs	*$0.50*	*$1.50*	*$2.50*	£0.30	£0.90	£1.50
425 Deluxe Edition, ND 48pgs, 2 channel holo-clear cover	*$0.80*	*$2.40*	*$4.00*	£0.50	£1.50	£2.50
426 the final fate of Betty Ross...	*$0.30*	*$0.90*	*$1.50*	£0.20	£0.60	£1.00
426 Deluxe Edition, ND superior paper stock and colouring	*$0.40*	*$1.20*	*$2.00*	£0.25	£0.75	£1.25
427 Man-Thing appears	*$0.30*	*$0.90*	*$1.50*	£0.20	£0.60	£1.00
427 Deluxe Edition, ND superior paper stock and colouring	*$0.40*	*$1.20*	*$2.00*	£0.25	£0.75	£1.25
428 Man-Thing appears	*$0.30*	*$0.90*	*$1.50*	£0.20	£0.60	£1.00
428 Deluxe Edition, ND superior paper stock and colouring	*$0.40*	*$1.20*	*$2.00*	£0.25	£0.75	£1.25
429-430	*$0.40*	*$1.20*	*$2.00*	£0.25	£0.75	£1.25
431 The Abomination returns	*$0.40*	*$1.20*	*$2.00*	£0.25	£0.75	£1.25
432 Hulk vs. The Abomination	*$0.40*	*$1.20*	*$2.00*	£0.25	£0.75	£1.25
433 Over The Edge tie-in, Punisher appears	*$0.40*	*$1.20*	*$2.00*	£0.25	£0.75	£1.25
434 Over The Edge Epilogue; Wolverine, Forge and Banshee appear; funeral of Nick Fury (see Double Edge: Omega for death of Nick Fury)	*$0.40*	*$1.20*	*$2.00*	£0.25	£0.75	£1.25
435 48pgs, Rhino appears; features excerpts from Peter David's Hulk novel, previews new storyline and the new The Savage Hulk title	*$0.50*	*$1.50*	*$2.50*	£0.30	£0.90	£1.50
436 Ghosts of the Future part 1, continued in Cutting Edge #1	*$0.40*	*$1.20*	*$2.00*	£0.25	£0.75	£1.25
437 (Jan 1996), Ghosts of the Future part 2, the return of The Leader?	*$0.40*	*$1.20*	*$2.00*	£0.25	£0.75	£1.25
438-439 Ghosts of the Future story	*$0.40*	*$1.20*	*$2.00*	£0.25	£0.75	£1.25
440 Ghosts of the Future story conclusion; Hulk vs. Thor	*$0.40*	*$1.20*	*$2.00*	£0.25	£0.75	£1.25
441 "Hulk Fiction" story, She-Hulk appears	*$0.40*	*$1.20*	*$2.00*	£0.25	£0.75	£1.25
442 She-Hulk appears	*$0.40*	*$1.20*	*$2.00*	£0.25	£0.75	£1.25
443	*$0.30*	*$0.90*	*$1.50*	£0.25	£0.75	£1.25
444 Onslaught tie-in, continued from Cable #34	*$0.30*	*$0.90*	*$1.50*	£0.25	£0.75	£1.25
445 Onslaught tie-in, continued in Onslaught: Marvel Universe	*$0.30*	*$0.90*	*$1.50*	£0.25	£0.75	£1.25
446 with bound-in Overpower cards	*$0.30*	*$0.90*	*$1.50*	£0.25	£0.75	£1.25
447 Mike Deodato Jnr. cover and art	*$0.30*	*$0.90*	*$1.50*	£0.20	£0.60	£1.00
447 Variant Cover Edition, ND Hulk with arms aloft; 25% of the print run	*$1.00*	*$3.00*	*$5.00*	£0.70	£2.10	£3.50
448 Hulk vs. Pantheon; Mike Deodato Jnr. art	*$0.30*	*$0.90*	*$1.50*	£0.20	£0.60	£1.00
449 intro The Thunderbolts	*$0.30*	*$0.90*	*$1.50*	£0.20	£0.60	£1.00
450 56pgs, Doctor Strange appears	*$0.60*	*$1.80*	*$3.00*	£0.40	£1.20	£2.00
451 ND	*$0.40*	*$1.20*	*$2.00*	£0.25	£0.75	£1.25
Title Value:	***$484.90***	***$1462.05***	***$3063.50***	**£269.35**	**£813.75**	**£1722.75**
Incredible Hulk: Ground Zero (Aug 1991) Trade paperback ND reprints issues #340-346, Todd McFarlane cover				£1.70	£5.10	£8.50
Incredible Hulk: Transformations (Jan 1997) Trade paperback ND 176pgs, features selected reprints with art by Dale Keown, John Byrne and Sal Buscema				£2.30	£6.90	£11.50
Incredible Hulk: Ghosts of the Past (Feb 1997) Trade paperback ND reprints issues #397-400				£1.70	£5.10	£8.50

INCREDIBLE HULK ANNUAL

Marvel Comics Group; 1 Oct 1968-2 Oct 1969; 3 Jan 1971-4 Jan 1972; 5 Oct 1976-present

Issue	$Good	$Fine	$N.Mint	£Good	£Fine	£N.Mint
1 68pgs, Steranko cover, Hulk vs. The Inhumans	*$10.50*	*$32.00*	*$75.00*	£5.50	£17.00	£40.00
2 68pgs, origin reprinted (3pgs), reprints Hulk (1st Series) #3	*$6.25*	*$19.00*	*$45.00*	£2.85	£8.50	£20.00
3 68pgs	*$2.05*	*$6.25*	*$12.50*	£1.25	£3.75	£7.50
4 ND scarce in the U.K. 52pgs, all reprint	*$1.50*	*$4.50*	*$9.00*	£0.80	£2.50	£5.00
5 ND 52pgs	*$1.00*	*$3.00*	*$6.00*	£0.50	£1.50	£3.00
6 ND 52pgs, Dr. Strange appears, Warlock cameo	*$1.00*	*$3.00*	*$5.00*	£0.60	£1.80	£3.00
7 ND 52pgs, John Byrne art, Iceman, Angel appear; Sentinels ("Master Mould") storyline	*$1.20*	*$3.60*	*$6.00*	£0.80	£2.40	£4.00
8 ND 52pgs, Sasquatch appears	*$0.60*	*$1.80*	*$3.00*	£0.50	£1.50	£2.50
9 ND 52pgs	*$0.60*	*$1.80*	*$3.00*	£0.40	£1.20	£2.00
10 ND 52pgs, Bruce Banner as Captain Universe	*$0.60*	*$1.80*	*$3.00*	£0.40	£1.20	£2.00
11 ND 52pgs, Frank Miller's first Marvel art (on a Doc Samson back-up story, drawn before John Carter of Mars #18) but not first published	*$0.80*	*$2.40*	*$4.00*	£0.50	£1.50	£2.50
12-13 ND	*$0.50*	*$1.50*	*$2.50*	£0.30	£0.90	£1.50
14 ND John Byrne story	*$0.50*	*$1.50*	*$2.50*	£0.30	£0.90	£1.50
15 ND Mike Zeck cover	*$0.50*	*$1.50*	*$2.50*	£0.30	£0.90	£1.50
16 ND Lifeform part 3, continues in Silver Surfer Annual #3, Peter David and Alan Grant	*$0.60*	*$1.80*	*$3.00*	£0.30	£0.90	£1.50
17 ND Subterranean Odyssey part 2, continues in Namor Annual #1	*$0.45*	*$1.35*	*$2.25*	£0.30	£0.90	£1.50
18 ND Return of the Defenders part 1, Dr. Strange, Silver Surfer and Sub-Mariner appear, continued in Namor Annual #2, cover and art by Kevin Maguire, 1st story art (Thing vs. Hulk) by Travis Charest	*$0.45*	*$1.35*	*$2.25*	£0.30	£0.90	£1.50
19 ND 64pgs, pre-bagged with trading card introducing Lazarus	*$0.60*	*$1.80*	*$3.00*	£0.40	£1.20	£2.00

TRADE PAPERBACKS, GRAPHIC NOVELS AND OTHER COLLECTIONS ARE PRICED IN POUNDS STERLING ONLY. CONVERT AT 1.5 FOR DOLLARS.

	$Good	$Fine	$N.Mint	£Good	£Fine	£N.Mint
20 ND 64pgs, Peter David script; Hulk's history retold through the eyes of The Abomination	$0.60	$1.80	$3.00	£0.40	£1.20	£2.00
Title Value:	$30.80	$93.25	$195.00	£17.00	£51.55	£106.00

INCREDIBLE HULK ASHCAN

Marvel Comics Group; nn Jun 1994

	$Good	$Fine	$N.Mint	£Good	£Fine	£N.Mint
nn ND 16pgs, background information on the wedding of Rick Jones and Marlo	$0.30	$0.90	$1.50	£0.20	£0.60	£1.00
Title Value:	$0.30	$0.90	$1.50	£0.20	£0.60	£1.00

INCREDIBLE HULK BOOK AND RECORD SET

Power Records;PR-11 1974

	$Good	$Fine	$N.Mint	£Good	£Fine	£N.Mint
PR-11 scarce in the U.K. 20pg booklet with 45 rpm record	$1.25	$3.75	$7.50	£0.80	£2.50	£5.00
Title Value:	$1.25	$3.75	$7.50	£0.80	£2.50	£5.00

Note: the item would be valued at approximately 50% less without record

INCREDIBLE HULK GIANT SIZE

Marvel Comics Group; 1 1975

	$Good	$Fine	$N.Mint	£Good	£Fine	£N.Mint
1 ND scarce in the U.K. 68pgs, all reprint	$2.05	$6.25	$12.50	£1.30	£4.00	£8.00
Title Value:	$2.05	$6.25	$12.50	£1.30	£4.00	£8.00

INCREDIBLE HULK MEGAZINE

Marvel Comics Group,OS; nn Dec 1996

	$Good	$Fine	$N.Mint	£Good	£Fine	£N.Mint
nn ND 96pgs, six selected reprints featuring art by McFarlane, Starlin, Buscema, Kane and Kirby	$0.80	$2.40	$4.00	£0.50	£1.50	£2.50
Title Value:	$0.80	$2.40	$4.00	£0.50	£1.50	£2.50

INCREDIBLE HULK VS. QUASIMODO

Marvel Comics Group,OS; 1 Mar 1983

	$Good	$Fine	$N.Mint	£Good	£Fine	£N.Mint
1 ND scarce in the U.K. based on cartoon	$0.40	$1.20	$2.00	£0.25	£0.75	£1.25
Title Value:	$0.40	$1.20	$2.00	£0.25	£0.75	£1.25

INCREDIBLE HULK VS. VENOM

Marvel Comics Group,OS; 1 Aug 1994

	$Good	$Fine	$N.Mint	£Good	£Fine	£N.Mint
1 ND produced in association with the National Council for the Prevention of Child Abuse; Peter David script	$0.80	$2.40	$4.00	£0.90	£2.70	£4.50
Title Value:	$0.80	$2.40	$4.00	£0.90	£2.70	£4.50

INCREDIBLE HULK/PITT

Marvel Comics Group,OS; nn Mar 1997

	$Good	$Fine	$N.Mint	£Good	£Fine	£N.Mint
nn ND 48pgs, Peter David script, Dale Keown art	$1.20	$3.60	$6.00	£0.80	£2.40	£4.00
Title Value:	$1.20	$3.60	$6.00	£0.80	£2.40	£4.00

INCREDIBLE HULK: FUTURE IMPERFECT

Marvel Comics Group,MS; 1 Feb 1993-2 Mar 1993

	$Good	$Fine	$N.Mint	£Good	£Fine	£N.Mint
1 ND 48pgs, squarebound, Peter David script, George Perez art; embossed cover	$1.00	$3.00	$5.00	£0.70	£2.10	£3.50
2 ND scarce in the U.K. (very?) 48pgs, squarebound, Peter David script, George Perez art; embossed cover	$1.00	$3.00	$5.00	£0.80	£2.40	£4.00
Title Value:	$2.00	$6.00	$10.00	£1.50	£4.50	£7.50
Incredible Hulk: Future Imperfect (Aug 1994) Trade paperback reprints 2 issue mini-series				£1.70	£5.10	£8.50
Marvel Limited: Incredible Hulk: Future Imperfect (Nov 1994) leather-bound hardcover, reprints 2 issue mini-series				£3.00	£5.00	£15.00

INCREDIBLE HULK: HERCULES UNLEASHED

Marvel Comics Group,OS; nn Oct 1996

	$Good	$Fine	$N.Mint	£Good	£Fine	£N.Mint
nn ND Hulk vs. Hercules in the aftermath of Onslaught; Peter David script, Mike Deodato Jnr. art	$0.50	$1.50	$2.50	£0.30	£0.90	£1.50
Title Value:	$0.50	$1.50	$2.50	£0.30	£0.90	£1.50

INCREDIBLE SCIENCE FICTION

E.C. Comics;30 Jul/Aug 1955-33 Jan/Feb 1956

(formerly Weird Science Fantasy)

	$Good	$Fine	$N.Mint	£Good	£Fine	£N.Mint
30 Jack Davis cover	$33.00	$97.50	$260.00	£21.50	£65.00	£175.00
31 Jack Davis cover, Wood and Williamson art	$34.00	$100.00	$275.00	£23.00	£67.50	£185.00
32 Jack Davis cover, Williamson art	$34.00	$100.00	$275.00	£23.00	£67.50	£185.00
33 Weird Fantasy #18 reprinted, Wally Wood cover and art	$33.00	$97.50	$260.00	£21.50	£65.00	£175.00
Title Value:	$134.00	$395.00	$1070.00	£89.00	£265.00	£720.00

Note: all Non-Distributed on the news-stands in the U.K.

INCREDIBLE SCIENCE FICTION (2ND SERIES)

Russ Cochran/EC Comics; 1 1993-11 1994

	$Good	$Fine	$N.Mint	£Good	£Fine	£N.Mint
1-11 ND	$0.30	$0.90	$1.50	£0.20	£0.60	£1.00
Title Value:	$3.30	$9.90	$16.50	£2.20	£6.60	£11.00

INDEPENDENCE DAY

Marvel Comics Group,MS; 0 Aug 1996-2 Sep 1996

	$Good	$Fine	$N.Mint	£Good	£Fine	£N.Mint
0 ND adaptation of film, Kevin Nowlan covers; bi-weekly	$0.40	$1.20	$2.00	£0.25	£0.75	£1.25
0 Black Cover Variant Edition, ND photo cover	$1.00	$3.00	$5.00	£1.00	£3.00	£5.00
1-2 ND adaptation of film, Kevin Nowlan covers; bi-weekly	$0.40	$1.20	$2.00	£0.25	£0.75	£1.25
Title Value:	$2.20	$6.60	$11.00	£1.75	£5.25	£8.75
Independence Day (Nov 1996) Trade paperback ND 96pgs, collects mini-series				£0.90	£2.70	£4.50

INDIANA JONES & THE IRON PHOENIX

Dark Horse,MS; 1 Dec 1994-4 Mar 1995

	$Good	$Fine	$N.Mint	£Good	£Fine	£N.Mint
1-4 ND Dave Dorman painted covers	$0.50	$1.50	$2.50	£0.30	£0.90	£1.50
Title Value:	$2.00	$6.00	$10.00	£1.20	£3.60	£6.00

INDIANA JONES & THE SHRINE OF THE SEA DEVIL

Dark Horse,OS; 1 Sep 1994

	$Good	$Fine	$N.Mint	£Good	£Fine	£N.Mint
1 ND reprints serial from Dark Horse Comics #3-6	$0.50	$1.50	$2.50	£0.30	£0.90	£1.50
Title Value:	$0.50	$1.50	$2.50	£0.30	£0.90	£1.50

INDIANA JONES AND THE ARMS OF GOLD

Dark Horse,MS; 1 Feb 1994-4 May 1994

	$Good	$Fine	$N.Mint	£Good	£Fine	£N.Mint
1-4 ND Lee Marrs script	$0.50	$1.50	$2.50	£0.30	£0.90	£1.50
Title Value:	$2.00	$6.00	$10.00	£1.20	£3.60	£6.00

INDIANA JONES AND THE FATE OF ATLANTIS

Dark Horse,MS; 1 May 1991-4 Nov 1991

	$Good	$Fine	$N.Mint	£Good	£Fine	£N.Mint
1 ND	$0.50	$1.50	$2.50	£0.30	£0.90	£1.50
1 2nd printing, ND (Dec 1991)	$0.40	$1.20	$2.00	£0.25	£0.75	£1.25
2-4 ND	$0.50	$1.50	$2.50	£0.30	£0.90	£1.50
Title Value:	$2.40	$7.20	$12.00	£1.45	£4.35	£7.25

INDIANA JONES AND THE GOLDEN FLEECE

Dark Horse,MS; 1 Jun 1994-2 Jul 1994

	$Good	$Fine	$N.Mint	£Good	£Fine	£N.Mint
1-2 ND	$0.50	$1.50	$2.50	£0.30	£0.90	£1.50
Title Value:	$1.00	$3.00	$5.00	£0.60	£1.80	£3.00

INDIANA JONES AND THE LAST CRUSADE

Marvel Comics Group,MS; 1 Oct 1989-3 Dec 1989

(see Further Adventures of...)

	$Good	$Fine	$N.Mint	£Good	£Fine	£N.Mint
1 ND	$0.40	$1.20	$2.00	£0.25	£0.75	£1.25
2 ND Todd McFarlane art	$0.40	$1.20	$2.00	£0.25	£0.75	£1.25
3 ND	$0.40	$1.20	$2.00	£0.25	£0.75	£1.25
Title Value:	$1.20	$3.60	$6.00	£0.75	£2.25	£3.75
Indiana Jones and the Last Crusade 80pg B&W magazine, David Michelinie and Bret Blevins				£0.40	£1.20	£2.00

INDIANA JONES AND THE SARGASSO PIRATES

Dark Horse,MS; 1 Dec 1995-4 Mar 1996

1-2 ND painted covers by Alex Ross

Incredible Hulk #428

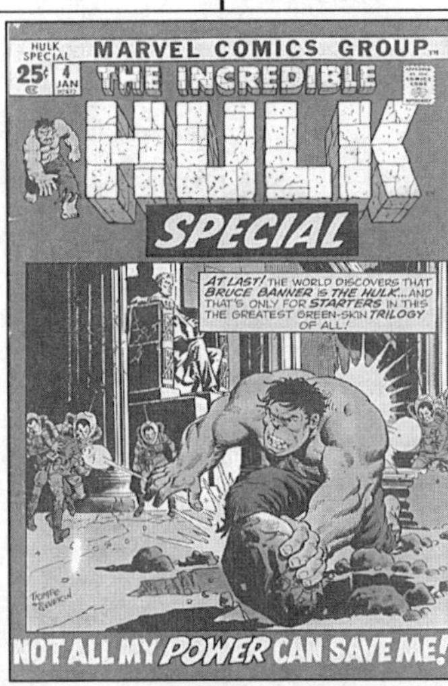

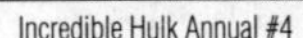
Incredible Hulk Annual #4

Incredible Hulk: Future Imperfect #2

	$Good	$Fine	$N.Mint	£Good	£Fine	£N.Mint
	$0.50	$1.50	$2.50	£0.30	£0.90	£1.50
3-4 ND pianted covers by Alex Ross	$0.50	$1.50	$2.50	£0.30	£0.90	£1.50
Title Value:	$2.00	$6.00	$10.00	£1.20	£3.60	£6.00

INDIANA JONES AND THE SPEAR OF DESTINY

Dark Horse,MS; 1 Apr 1995-4 Aug 1995

	$Good	$Fine	$N.Mint	£Good	£Fine	£N.Mint
1-4 ND Elaine Lee script, Will Simpson and Dan Spiegle art	$0.50	$1.50	$2.50	£0.30	£0.90	£1.50
Title Value:	$2.00	$6.00	$10.00	£1.20	£3.60	£6.00

INDIANA JONES AND THE TEMPLE OF DOOM

Marvel Comics Group,MS; 1 Sep 1984-3 Nov 1984

(see Further Adventures of ...)

	$Good	$Fine	$N.Mint	£Good	£Fine	£N.Mint
1-3 ND reprints Marvel Super Special #30, Guice art	$0.40	$1.20	$2.00	£0.25	£0.75	£1.25
Title Value:	$1.20	$3.60	$6.00	£0.75	£2.25	£3.75

INDIANA JONES, FURTHER ADVENTURES OF

Marvel Comics Group; 1 Jan 1983-34 Mar 1986

	$Good	$Fine	$N.Mint	£Good	£Fine	£N.Mint
1 ND John Byrne script and layouts	$0.30	$0.90	$1.50	£0.20	£0.60	£1.00
2 ND John Byrne layouts	$0.25	$0.75	$1.25	£0.15	£0.45	£0.75
3 ND Gene Day art	$0.25	$0.75	$1.25	£0.15	£0.45	£0.75
4-5	$0.25	$0.75	$1.25	£0.15	£0.45	£0.75
6 Chaykin art	$0.25	$0.75	$1.25	£0.15	£0.45	£0.75
7-8	$0.25	$0.75	$1.25	£0.15	£0.45	£0.75
9-10 Chaykin cover	$0.25	$0.75	$1.25	£0.15	£0.45	£0.75
11-20	$0.25	$0.75	$1.25	£0.15	£0.45	£0.75
21 Steve Ditko art	$0.25	$0.75	$1.25	£0.15	£0.45	£0.75
22-24	$0.25	$0.75	$1.25	£0.15	£0.45	£0.75
25 Steve Ditko art	$0.25	$0.75	$1.25	£0.15	£0.45	£0.75
26 Steve Ditko art, Sienkiewicz cover	$0.25	$0.75	$1.25	£0.15	£0.45	£0.75
27-28 ND Steve Ditko art	$0.25	$0.75	$1.25	£0.15	£0.45	£0.75
29-31 ND	$0.25	$0.75	$1.25	£0.15	£0.45	£0.75
32-34 ND Steve Ditko art	$0.25	$0.75	$1.25	£0.15	£0.45	£0.75
Title Value:	$8.55	$25.65	$42.75	£5.15	£15.45	£25.75

INDIANA JONES: THUNDER IN THE ORIENT

Dark Horse,MS; 1 Sep 1993-6 Feb 1994

	$Good	$Fine	$N.Mint	£Good	£Fine	£N.Mint
1-6 ND Dan Barry story and art; Dave Dorman cover	$0.50	$1.50	$2.50	£0.30	£0.90	£1.50
Title Value:	$3.00	$9.00	$15.00	£1.80	£5.40	£9.00

INDUSTRIAL GOTHIC

DC Comics/Vertigo,MS; 1 Dec 1995-5 Apr 1996

	$Good	$Fine	$N.Mint	£Good	£Fine	£N.Mint
1-5 ND 48pgs, Ted McKeever script and art	$0.50	$1.50	$2.50	£0.30	£0.90	£1.50
Title Value:	$2.50	$7.50	$12.50	£1.50	£4.50	£7.50

INFERIOR FIVE

National Periodical Publications; 1 Mar/Apr 1967-10 Sep/Oct 1968; 11 Aug/Sep 1972-12 Oct/Nov 1972

(see Showcase #62)

	$Good	$Fine	$N.Mint	£Good	£Fine	£N.Mint
1	$5.50	$17.00	$40.00	£3.20	£9.50	£22.50
2 Plastic Man X-over	$2.85	$8.50	$20.00	£1.75	£5.25	£12.50
3	$2.10	$6.25	$15.00	£1.40	£4.25	£10.00
4-6	$2.10	$6.25	$15.00	£1.10	£3.40	£8.00
7-9 ND	$2.10	$6.25	$15.00	£1.25	£3.85	£9.00
10 ND Superman appears; appearances by Spiderman and the Fantastic Four (unauthorised)	$2.10	$6.25	$15.00	£1.25	£3.85	£9.00
11 reprints Showcase #62 (1st appearance)	$2.10	$6.25	$15.00	£1.10	£3.40	£8.00
12 reprints Showcase #63 (2nd appearance)	$2.10	$6.25	$15.00	£1.10	£3.40	£8.00
Title Value:	$29.35	$88.00	$210.00	£16.85	£51.40	£121.00

INFERNO

Aircel,MS; 1 Oct 1990-4 Jan 1991

	$Good	$Fine	$N.Mint	£Good	£Fine	£N.Mint
1-4 ND horror anthology; pre-bagged	$0.40	$1.20	$2.00	£0.25	£0.75	£1.25
Title Value:	$1.60	$4.80	$8.00	£1.00	£3.00	£5.00

INFERNO

Marvel Comics Group; 1988

Cross-over storyline that ran throughout the following issues:

Uncanny X-Men #240, New Mutants #71, X-Factor #36, Uncanny X-Men #241, New Mutants #72, X-Factor #37, Uncanny X-Men #242, New Mutants #73, X-Factor #38.

INFERNO

Caliber Press; 1 1996-3 1996 ?

	$Good	$Fine	$N.Mint	£Good	£Fine	£N.Mint
1-3 ND Mike Carey script, Mike Taylor art; black and white	$0.60	$1.80	$3.00	£0.40	£1.20	£2.00
Title Value:	$1.80	$5.40	$9.00	£1.20	£3.60	£6.00

INFINITY CRUSADE, THE

Marvel Comics Group,MS; 1 Jun 1993-6 Nov 1993

	$Good	$Fine	$N.Mint	£Good	£Fine	£N.Mint
1 3rd part in the "Infinity trilogy", Jim Starlin script, Ron Lim art; Warlock, Silver Surfer and Thanos appear throughout	$0.50	$1.50	$2.50	£0.30	£0.90	£1.50
2-6	$0.50	$1.50	$2.50	£0.30	£0.90	£1.50
Title Value:	$3.00	$9.00	$15.00	£1.80	£5.40	£9.00

INFINITY CRUSADE, THE

Marvel Comics Group; 1993

Cross-over storyline that ran throughout the following issues:

Infinity Crusade #1, Warlock Chronicles #1, Warlock & The Infinity Watch #18, Avengers West Coast #96, Alpha Flight #122, Iron Man #294, Thor #464, Doctor Strange #55, Terror Inc. #13, Infinity Crusade #2, Warlock Chronicles #2, Warlock & The Infinity Watch #19, Avengers West Coast #97, Cage #17, Darkhawk #30, Alpha Flight #123, Infinity Crusade #3, Silver Surfer #83, Warlock Chronicles #3, Warlock & The Infinity Watch #20, Infinity Crusade #4, Warlock Chronicles #4, Warlock & The Infinity Watch #21, Web of Spiderman #105, Silver Sable #17, Alpha Flight #125, Deathlok #28, Infinity Crusade #5, Warlock Chronicles #5, Warlock & The Infinity Watch #22, Silver Surfer #85, Thor #467, Web of Spiderman #106, Alpha Flight #126, Deathlok #29, Infinity Crusade #6.

INFINITY GAUNTLET, THE

Marvel Comics Group,MS; 1 Jul 1991-6 Dec 1991

	$Good	$Fine	$N.Mint	£Good	£Fine	£N.Mint
1 ND 1st part in the "Infinity trilogy", Jim Starlin script and George Perez art; Thanos appears	$0.60	$1.80	$3.00	£0.50	£1.50	£2.50
1 Gold Edition, ND - 4,000 copies signed by George Perez in gold ink	$0.80	$2.40	$4.00	£0.50	£1.50	£2.50
1 Platinum Edition, ND - 3,500 copies signed by George Perez in platinum ink	$1.20	$3.60	$6.00	£1.00	£3.00	£5.00
2 ND Thanos, Warlock ,Doctor Strange, Galactus appear	$0.60	$1.80	$3.00	£0.40	£1.20	£2.00
3 ND Thanos; Galactus, Celestials and The Watcher appear	$0.60	$1.80	$3.00	£0.40	£1.20	£2.00
4 ND Thanos, Annihilus appear	$0.60	$1.80	$3.00	£0.40	£1.20	£2.00
5 ND Thanos, Warlock appear	$0.60	$1.80	$3.00	£0.40	£1.20	£2.00
6 ND Thanos, Warlock, Silver Surfer, Dr. Strange appear	$0.60	$1.80	$3.00	£0.40	£1.20	£2.00
Title Value:	$5.60	$16.80	$28.00	£4.00	£12.00	£20.00

Note: other tie-ins include: Dr. Strange #31-33, Hulk #383-385, Quasar #26, Silver Surfer #51-55.

Infinity Gauntlet

	$Good	$Fine	$N.Mint	£Good	£Fine	£N.Mint
Trade paperback reprints 6 issue mini-series				£3.00	£9.00	£15.00
(2nd print - Jun 1993)				£2.80	£8.40	£14.00

INFINITY INC.

DC Comics; 1 Mar 1984-53 Aug 1988

	$Good	$Fine	$N.Mint	£Good	£Fine	£N.Mint
1 ND Jerry Ordway cover and art begin (end #12), Fury, Jade, Brainwave Jnr, Huntress, Star Spangled Kid, Northwind, Nuklon, Power Girl, Obsidian, Silver Scarab begin	$0.40	$1.20	$2.00	£0.30	£0.90	£1.50
2 ND Dr. Mid-Nite Golden Age Flash, Wonderwoman, Dr. Fate, Hourman, Golden Age Green Lantern, Wildcat appear	$0.35	$1.05	$1.75	£0.25	£0.75	£1.25
3 ND	$0.35	$1.05	$1.75	£0.25	£0.75	£1.25
4-6 ND Justice Society of America appear	$0.35	$1.05	$1.75	£0.25	£0.75	£1.25
7 ND Golden Age Superman vs. Power Girl, Justice Society of America appear	$0.35	$1.05	$1.75	£0.25	£0.75	£1.25
8 ND	$0.35	$1.05	$1.75	£0.25	£0.75	£1.25
9 ND Justice Society of America cameo	$0.35	$1.05	$1.75	£0.25	£0.75	£1.25
10 ND Justice Society of America appear	$0.35	$1.05	$1.75	£0.25	£0.75	£1.25
11 ND origin Infinity Inc.	$0.35	$1.05	$1.75	£0.25	£0.75	£1.25
12 ND last Jerry Ordway cover and art	$0.35	$1.05	$1.75	£0.25	£0.75	£1.25
13 ND	$0.35	$1.05	$1.75	£0.25	£0.75	£1.25
14 ND Todd McFarlane art begins; his first professional mainstream art	$0.40	$1.20	$2.00	£0.30	£0.90	£1.50
15-17 ND Todd McFarlane art	$0.40	$1.20	$2.00	£0.30	£0.90	£1.50
18 ND Crisis X-over, Todd McFarlane art	$0.40	$1.20	$2.00	£0.30	£0.90	£1.50
19-20 ND scarce in the U.K. Crisis X-over; Justice Society of America and Infinity Inc. team-up, Todd McFarlane art	$0.40	$1.20	$2.00	£0.35	£1.05	£1.75
21 ND Crisis X-over, 1st appearance new Hourman and Dr. Midnight, Justice Society of America appear, Todd McFarlane art	$0.40	$1.20	$2.00	£0.30	£0.90	£1.50
22-24 ND Crisis X-over, Todd McFarlane art	$0.40	$1.20	$2.00	£0.30	£0.90	£1.50
25 ND unofficial Crisis X-over, Todd McFarlane art	$0.40	$1.20	$2.00	£0.30	£0.90	£1.50
26 ND 1st appearance new female Wildcat, Todd McFarlane art	$0.40	$1.20	$2.00	£0.30	£0.90	£1.50
27 ND Wonder Woman appears, Todd McFarlane art	$0.40	$1.20	$2.00	£0.30	£0.90	£1.50
28-29 ND Todd McFarlane art	$0.40	$1.20	$2.00	£0.30	£0.90	£1.50
30 ND Justice Society of America appear, Todd McFarlane art	$0.40	$1.20	$2.00	£0.30	£0.90	£1.50
31 ND Star Spangled Kid becomes Skyman, Todd McFarlane art	$0.40	$1.20	$2.00	£0.25	£0.75	£1.25
32 ND origin Northwind, Todd McFarlane art	$0.40	$1.20	$2.00	£0.25	£0.75	£1.25
33 ND origin Obsidian, Todd McFarlane art	$0.40	$1.20	$2.00	£0.25	£0.75	£1.25
34-36 ND Todd McFarlane art	$0.40	$1.20	$2.00	£0.25	£0.75	£1.25
37 ND last Todd McFarlane art	$0.40	$1.20	$2.00	£0.25	£0.75	£1.25
38-44 very LD in the U.K.	$0.35	$1.05	$1.75	£0.25	£0.75	£1.25
45 ND New Teen Titans guest-star	$0.35	$1.05	$1.75	£0.25	£0.75	£1.25
46 ND scarce in the U.K. Millennium X-over						

	$Good	$Fine	$N.Mint	£Good	£Fine	£N.Mint
	$0.35	$1.05	$1.75	£0.30	£0.90	£1.50
47 ND Millennium X-over	$0.35	$1.05	$1.75	£0.25	£0.75	£1.25
48 ND origin Nuklon	$0.35	$1.05	$1.75	£0.25	£0.75	£1.25
49 ND 1970s Sandman appears; Lyta appears (story ties into her appearances in Sandman 2nd series)	$0.35	$1.05	$1.75	£0.25	£0.75	£1.25
50 ND DS 1970s Sandman and Lyta appear	$0.50	$1.50	$2.50	£0.30	£0.90	£1.50
51-53 ND	$0.35	$1.05	$1.75	£0.20	£0.60	£1.00
Title Value:	$19.95	$59.85	$99.75	£14.20	£42.60	£71.00

Note: all 36 pgs, Baxter paper. Part McFarlane art in #20, 23, 24, 33.
Note also: issue #38 is particularly scarce owing to a possible lost shipment.

INFINITY INC. ANNUAL

DC Comics; 1 Dec 1985-2 1986

	$Good	$Fine	$N.Mint	£Good	£Fine	£N.Mint
1 ND 48pgs, Crisis X-over	$0.40	$1.20	$2.00	£0.25	£0.75	£1.25
2 ND 48pgs	$0.40	$1.20	$2.00	£0.25	£0.75	£1.25
Title Value:	$0.80	$2.40	$4.00	£0.50	£1.50	£2.50

INFINITY INC. SPECIAL

DC Comics; 1 1987

	$Good	$Fine	$N.Mint	£Good	£Fine	£N.Mint
1 ND	$0.40	$1.20	$2.00	£0.25	£0.75	£1.25
Title Value:	$0.40	$1.20	$2.00	£0.25	£0.75	£1.25

INFINITY WAR, THE

Marvel Comics Group,MS; 1 Jun 1992-6 Nov 1992

	$Good	$Fine	$N.Mint	£Good	£Fine	£N.Mint
1 ND 48pgs, 2nd part of the "Infinity trilogy", Jim Starlin script, Ron Lim art, Thanos, Silver Surfer, Spiderman, Wolverine, Warlock and many other Marvel characters appear, gatefold cover by Ron Lim	$0.50	$1.50	$2.50	£0.30	£0.90	£1.50
2 ND 48pgs, Jim Starlin script, Ron Lim art, Thanos, Silver Surfer, Galactus, Spiderman appear, gatefold cover by Ron Lim	$0.50	$1.50	$2.50	£0.30	£0.90	£1.50
3-6 ND 48pgs, Jim Starlin script, Ron Lim art, Thanos, Silver Surfer, Galactus, Spiderman appear	$0.50	$1.50	$2.50	£0.30	£0.90	£1.50
Title Value:	$3.00	$9.00	$15.00	£1.80	£5.40	£9.00

INFINITY WAR, THE

Marvel Comics Group; 1992

Cross-over storyline that ran throughout the following issues: **Infinity War #1**, **Doctor Strange #42**, **Infinity War #2**, **Alpha Flight #110**, **Doctor Strange #43**, **Fantastic Four #366**, **Silver Surfer #67**, **Silver Surfer #68**, **Spiderman #24**, **Infinity War #3**, **Alpha Flight #111**, **Doctor Strange #44**, **Fantastic Four #367**, **Guardians of the Galaxy #27**, **Marvel Comics Presents #108**, **Marvel Comics Presents #109**, **Moon Knight #41**, **Quasar #37**, **Silver Surfer #69**, **Infinity War #4**, **Alpha Flight #112**, **Doctor Strange #45**, **Fantastic Four #368**, **Guardians of the Galaxy #28**, **Marvel Comics Presents #110**, **Marvel Comics Presents #111**, **Moon Knight #42**, **New Warriors #27**, **Quasar #38**, **Silver Sable #4**, **Sleepwalker #18**, **Warlock #8**, **Wonder Man #13**, **Infinity War #5**, **Deathlok #16**, **Doctor Strange #46**, **Fantastic Four #369**, **Guardians of the Galaxy #29**, **Moon Knight #43**, **Quasar #39**, **Silver Sable #5**, **Warlock #9**, **Wonder Man #14**, **Infinity War #6**, **Doctor Strange #47**, **Fantastic Four #370**, **Nomad #7**, **Sleepwalker #18**, **Warlock #10**, **Wonder Man #15**.

INHUMANOIDS

Marvel Comics Group/Star,TV; 1 Jan 1987-4 Jul 1987

	$Good	$Fine	$N.Mint	£Good	£Fine	£N.Mint
1-4	$0.15	$0.45	$0.75	£0.10	£0.30	£0.50
Title Value:	$0.60	$1.80	$3.00	£0.40	£1.20	£2.00

Note: based on Hasbro toys

INHUMANS, THE

Marvel Comics Group; 1 Oct 1975-12 Aug 1977
(see Amazing Adventures, Marvel Graphic Novel)

	$Good	$Fine	$N.Mint	£Good	£Fine	£N.Mint
1 George Perez art	$1.15	$3.50	$7.00	£0.65	£2.00	£4.00
2 George Perez art	$0.80	$2.50	$5.00	£0.50	£1.50	£3.00
3 George Perez art, 1st Shatterstar (not to be confused with X-Force member of same name)	$0.65	$2.00	$4.00	£0.40	£1.25	£2.50
4 George Perez art	$0.55	$1.75	$3.50	£0.30	£1.00	£2.00
5-7 Gil Kane art	$0.55	$1.75	$3.50	£0.30	£1.00	£2.00
8 George Perez art	$0.50	$1.50	$3.00	£0.30	£1.00	£2.00
9 reprints Inhumans story from Amazing Adventures (2nd Series) 1,2	$0.50	$1.50	$3.00	£0.30	£1.00	£2.00
10-11 ND scarce in the U.K.	$0.50	$1.50	$3.00	£0.40	£1.25	£2.50
12 ND very scarce in the U.K. Inhumans vs. Hulk	$0.50	$1.50	$3.00	£0.50	£1.50	£3.00
Title Value:	$7.30	$22.50	$44.00	£4.65	£14.75	£29.50

INHUMANS, THE (2ND SERIES)

Marvel Comics Group,OS; 1 May 1995

	$Good	$Fine	$N.Mint	£Good	£Fine	£N.Mint
1 ND 64pgs, Atlantis Rising tie-in (see Fantastic Four #401)	$0.80	$2.40	$4.00	£0.50	£1.50	£2.50
Title Value:	$0.80	$2.40	$4.00	£0.50	£1.50	£2.50

INHUMANS: THE UNTOLD SAGA

Marvel Comics Group,OS; 1 Apr 1990

	$Good	$Fine	$N.Mint	£Good	£Fine	£N.Mint
1 ND DS	$0.30	$0.90	$1.50	£0.20	£0.60	£1.00
Title Value:	$0.30	$0.90	$1.50	£0.20	£0.60	£1.00

INNOCENTS

Radical Comics; 1 Oct 1995

	$Good	$Fine	$N.Mint	£Good	£Fine	£N.Mint
1 ND Simon Bisley cover	$0.50	$1.50	$2.50	£0.30	£0.90	£1.50
Title Value:	$0.50	$1.50	$2.50	£0.30	£0.90	£1.50

INNOVATION SOLICITATIONS

Innovation; 1 Mar 1989

	$Good	$Fine	$N.Mint	£Good	£Fine	£N.Mint
1 ND previews forthcoming releases like Hero Alliance	$0.20	$0.60	$1.00	£0.10	£0.30	£0.50
Title Value:	$0.20	$0.60	$1.00	£0.10	£0.30	£0.50

INNOVATION SPECTACULAR

Innovation,OS; 1 1991

	$Good	$Fine	$N.Mint	£Good	£Fine	£N.Mint
1 ND 100pgs, squarebound, Hero Alliance appear	$0.50	$1.50	$2.50	£0.30	£0.90	£1.50
Title Value:	$0.50	$1.50	$2.50	£0.30	£0.90	£1.50

INNOVATION'S SUMMER FUN SPECIAL

Innovation,OS; 1 Jul 1991

	$Good	$Fine	$N.Mint	£Good	£Fine	£N.Mint
1 ND	$0.60	$1.80	$3.00	£0.40	£1.20	£2.00
Title Value:	$0.60	$1.80	$3.00	£0.40	£1.20	£2.00

INSANE

Dark Horse; 1 Feb 1988-2 Sep 1988

	$Good	$Fine	$N.Mint	£Good	£Fine	£N.Mint
1 ND X-Men, Godzilla, Munden's Bar parodies	$0.60	$1.80	$3.00	£0.40	£1.20	£2.00
2 ND Concrete, Lone Wolf & Cub parodies	$0.50	$1.50	$2.50	£0.30	£0.90	£1.50
Title Value:	$1.10	$3.30	$5.50	£0.70	£2.10	£3.50

INSIDE IMAGE

Image; 1 Mar 1993-30 1994

	$Good	$Fine	$N.Mint	£Good	£Fine	£N.Mint
1 ND promotional; details up and coming comics, poster at centrefold	$0.15	$0.45	$0.75	£0.10	£0.30	£0.50
2-30 ND	$0.15	$0.45	$0.75	£0.10	£0.30	£0.50
Title Value:	$4.50	$13.50	$22.50	£3.00	£9.00	£15.00

INSTANT PIANO

Dark Horse; 1 Aug 1994-4 Nov 1994

	$Good	$Fine	$N.Mint	£Good	£Fine	£N.Mint
1-4 ND cartoon anthology featuring Kyle Baker and Evan Dorkin amongst others	$0.80	$2.40	$4.00	£0.50	£1.50	£2.50
Title Value:	$3.20	$9.60	$16.00	£2.00	£6.00	£10.00

INTERACTIVE COMICS

Adventure; 1 Feb 1991

	$Good	$Fine	$N.Mint	£Good	£Fine	£N.Mint
1 ND 56pgs, Dungeons and Dragons-game based	$0.90	$2.70	$4.50	£0.60	£1.80	£3.00
Title Value:	$0.90	$2.70	$4.50	£0.60	£1.80	£3.00

INTERFACE

Marvel Comics Group/Epic,MS; 1 Dec 1989-8 Feb 1991

	$Good	$Fine	$N.Mint	£Good	£Fine	£N.Mint
1-6 ND Paul Johnson art	$0.30	$0.90	$1.50	£0.20	£0.60	£1.00
7-8 ND	$0.30	$0.90	$1.50	£0.20	£0.60	£1.00
Title Value:	$2.40	$7.20	$12.00	£1.60	£4.80	£8.00

INTERPLANETARY LIZARDS OF THE TEXAS PLAIN

Leadbelly Publications; 0 Jun 1994; 1 1992-7 1993

	$Good	$Fine	$N.Mint	£Good	£Fine	£N.Mint
0 ND (Jun 1994)	$0.50	$1.50	$2.50	£0.30	£0.90	£1.50
1-7 ND	$0.50	$1.50	$2.50	£0.30	£0.90	£1.50
Title Value:	$4.00	$12.00	$20.00	£2.40	£7.20	£12.00

INTERVIEW WITH THE VAMPIRE

Innovation,MS; 1 Sep 1991-11 1994

	$Good	$Fine	$N.Mint	£Good	£Fine	£N.Mint
1 ND John Bolton cover	$1.00	$3.00	$5.00	£0.70	£2.10	£3.50
2 ND John Bolton cover	$0.60	$1.80	$3.00	£0.40	£1.20	£2.00
3 ND	$0.60	$1.80	$3.00	£0.40	£1.20	£2.00
4-11 ND	$0.50	$1.50	$2.50	£0.30	£0.90	£1.50
Title Value:	$6.20	$18.60	$31.00	£3.90	£11.70	£19.50

Note: issue #12 was produced but held in storage when Innovation went bankrupt. Some issue have been reported in circulation.

INTIMATE CONFESSIONS

I.W. Comics;9,10 1964

	$Good	$Fine	$N.Mint	£Good	£Fine	£N.Mint
9 scarce though distributed in the U.K. "Duncan's Love Story"	$1.10	$3.40	$8.00	£0.55	£1.70	£4.00
10 scarce though distributed in the U.K.	$1.10	$3.40	$8.00	£0.55	£1.70	£4.00
Title Value:	$2.20	$6.80	$16.00	£1.10	£3.40	£8.00

INTRON DEPOT DELUXE

Dark Horse,OS; nn 1995

	$Good	$Fine	$N.Mint	£Good	£Fine	£N.Mint
nn ND 148pgs, reprints the best of Masamune Shirow's work from 1981-1991	$8.00	$24.00	$40.00	£5.00	£15.00	£25.00
Title Value:	$8.00	$24.00	$40.00	£5.00	£15.00	£25.00

INTRUDER

TSR; 1-4 1990

	$Good	$Fine	$N.Mint	£Good	£Fine	£N.Mint
1-4 ND based on role-playing game	$0.40	$1.20	$2.00	£0.25	£0.75	£1.25
Title Value:	$1.60	$4.80	$8.00	£1.00	£3.00	£5.00

INVADERS

Gold Key,TV; 1 Oct 1967-4 Oct 1968

	$Good	$Fine	$N.Mint	£Good	£Fine	£N.Mint
1 distributed in the U.K.	$13.50	$41.00	$95.00	£8.50	£26.00	£60.00
2-4 distributed in the U.K.	$10.00	$30.00	$70.00	£5.50	£17.00	£40.00
Title Value:	$43.50	$131.00	$305.00	£25.00	£77.00	£180.00

INVADERS FROM HOME

DC Comics/Piranha Press,MS; 1 Aug 1990-6 Nov 1990

	$Good	$Fine	$N.Mint	£Good	£Fine	£N.Mint
1-6 ND John Blair Moore	$0.50	$1.50	$2.50	£0.30	£0.90	£1.50
Title Value:	$3.00	$9.00	$15.00	£1.80	£5.40	£9.00

INVADERS FROM MARS GRAPHIC NOVEL

Eternity; 1 Jun 1991

	$Good	$Fine	$N.Mint	£Good	£Fine	£N.Mint
1 ND adaptation of classic film	$1.50	$4.50	$7.50	£1.00	£3.00	£5.00
Title Value:	$1.50	$4.50	$7.50	£1.00	£3.00	£5.00

INVADERS FROM MARS II

Eternity,MS; 1 Aug 1991-3 Oct 1991

	$Good	$Fine	$N.Mint	£Good	£Fine	£N.Mint
1-3 ND	$0.40	$1.20	$2.00	£0.25	£0.75	£1.25
Title Value:	$1.20	$3.60	$6.00	£0.75	£2.25	£3.75

INVADERS, THE (1ST SERIES)

Marvel Comics Group; 1 Aug 1975-41 Sep 1979

	$Good	$Fine	$N.Mint	£Good	£Fine	£N.Mint
1 ND Captain America, Sub-Mariner, Human Torch begin in World War II setting	$2.85	$8.50	$20.00	£1.40	£4.25	£10.00

Issue	$Good	$Fine	$N.Mint	£Good	£Fine	£N.Mint
2 ND untold origin of Toro	$1.65	$5.00	$10.00	£1.00	£3.00	£6.00
3-4	$1.50	$4.50	$9.00	£0.65	£2.00	£4.00
5 ties into Marvel Premiere #29	$1.50	$4.50	$9.00	£0.65	£2.00	£4.00
6 Liberty Legion appears, 25 & 30 cent issues exist, ties into Marvel Premiere #30	$1.30	$4.00	$8.00	£0.50	£1.50	£3.00
7	$1.30	$4.00	$8.00	£0.50	£1.50	£3.00
8 1st appearance Union Jack	$1.30	$4.00	$8.00	£0.50	£1.50	£3.00
9	$1.30	$4.00	$8.00	£0.50	£1.50	£3.00
10 Golden Age Captain America reprint	$1.30	$4.00	$8.00	£0.50	£1.50	£3.00
11-13	$1.15	$3.50	$7.00	£0.40	£1.25	£2.50
14 1st appearance Crusaders	$1.15	$3.50	$7.00	£0.40	£1.25	£2.50
15	$1.15	$3.50	$7.00	£0.40	£1.25	£2.50
16 Destroyer appears	$1.15	$3.50	$7.00	£0.40	£1.25	£2.50
17 intro Warrior Woman	$1.15	$3.50	$7.00	£0.40	£1.25	£2.50
18	$1.15	$3.50	$7.00	£0.40	£1.25	£2.50
19 Adolf Hitler appears	$1.15	$3.50	$7.00	£0.40	£1.25	£2.50
20 1st appearance Union Jack II; also reprints the 1st ever appearance of Sub-Mariner from Motion Picture Funnies Weekly by Bill Everett (8pgs) with editiorial explanation	$1.30	$4.00	$8.00	£0.40	£1.25	£2.50
21 Golden Age Sub-Mariner reprint from Marvel Mystery #10	$1.00	$3.00	$6.00	£0.30	£1.00	£2.00
22 Golden Age Toro origin	$1.00	$3.00	$6.00	£0.30	£1.00	£2.00
23	$1.00	$3.00	$6.00	£0.30	£1.00	£2.00
24 reprints 1st Golden Age Human Torch and Sub-Mariner team-up from Marvel Mystery #17	$1.00	$3.00	$6.00	£0.30	£1.00	£2.00
25-30	$1.00	$3.00	$6.00	£0.30	£1.00	£2.00
31 Frankenstein appears	$0.80	$2.50	$5.00	£0.25	£0.75	£1.50
32-33 Thor, Adolf Hitler appear	$0.80	$2.50	$5.00	£0.25	£0.75	£1.50
34-37	$0.80	$2.50	$5.00	£0.25	£0.75	£1.50
38 1st appearance Lady Lotus	$0.80	$2.50	$5.00	£0.25	£0.75	£1.50
39-40	$0.80	$2.50	$5.00	£0.25	£0.75	£1.50
41 ND scarce in the U.K. 52pgs	$1.00	$3.00	$6.00	£0.40	£1.25	£2.50
Title Value:	$46.15	$140.50	$284.00	£16.75	£52.00	£105.50

INVADERS, THE (1ST SERIES) ANNUAL

Marvel Comics Group; 1 Sep 1977

Issue	$Good	$Fine	$N.Mint	£Good	£Fine	£N.Mint
1 ND 52pgs, Avengers appear	$1.00	$3.00	$6.00	£0.50	£1.50	£3.00
Title Value:	$1.00	$3.00	$6.00	£0.50	£1.50	£3.00

INVADERS, THE (1ST SERIES) GIANT SIZE

Marvel Comics Group; 1 Jun 1975

Issue	$Good	$Fine	$N.Mint	£Good	£Fine	£N.Mint
1 ND 68pgs, 1st appearance The Invaders (see Avengers #71), Golden Age Sub-Mariner reprint	$1.30	$4.00	$8.00	£1.00	£3.00	£6.00
Title Value:	$1.30	$4.00	$8.00	£1.00	£3.00	£6.00

Note: pre-dates first issue of regular series

INVADERS, THE(2ND SERIES)

Marvel Comics Group,MS; 1 May 1993-4 Aug 1993

Issue	$Good	$Fine	$N.Mint	£Good	£Fine	£N.Mint
1 Roy Thomas script begins	$0.40	$1.20	$2.00	£0.25	£0.75	£1.25
2 the original Vision returns	$0.40	$1.20	$2.00	£0.25	£0.75	£1.25
3-4	$0.40	$1.20	$2.00	£0.25	£0.75	£1.25
Title Value:	$1.60	$4.80	$8.00	£1.00	£3.00	£5.00

INVASION '55

Apple Comics,MS; 1 Oct 1990-3 Dec 1990

Issue	$Good	$Fine	$N.Mint	£Good	£Fine	£N.Mint
1-3 ND black and white	$0.40	$1.20	$2.00	£0.25	£0.75	£1.25
Title Value:	$1.20	$3.60	$6.00	£0.75	£2.25	£3.75

INVASION!

Cross-over series featuring most major DC heroes battling an invading alien force. The cross-over are listed below in alphabetical rather than chronological order:
Animal Man 6, Captain Atom 24,25, Checkmate 11,12, Detective Comics 595, Doom Patrol (2nd Series) 17,18, Firestorm 80,81, Flash 21,22, Justice League 22,23, Manhunter (2nd Series) 8,9, New Guardians 6, Spectre (2nd Series) 23, Starman 5,6, Superman 449, Superman (2nd Series) 26,27, Swamp Thing (2nd Series) 81, Wonder Woman (2nd Series) 25,26

INVASION! (LIMITED SERIES)

DC Comics,MS; 1 Oct 1988-3 Jan 1989

Issue	$Good	$Fine	$N.Mint	£Good	£Fine	£N.Mint
1 LD in the U.K. Todd McFarlane art	$0.80	$2.40	$4.00	£0.50	£1.50	£2.50
2 ND Iwo Jima cover, part Todd McFarlane art	$0.80	$2.40	$4.00	£0.50	£1.50	£2.50
3 Bart Sears art	$0.60	$1.80	$3.00	£0.40	£1.20	£2.00
Title Value:	$2.20	$6.60	$11.00	£1.40	£4.20	£7.00

Note: all 80pgs squarebound; fourth DC cross-over series (see Crisis, Legends, Millennium)

INVISIBLE PEOPLE

Kitchen Sink,MS; 1 Aug 1992-3 1992

Issue	$Good	$Fine	$N.Mint	£Good	£Fine	£N.Mint
1 ND part 1: Sanctum, script and art by Will Eisner	$0.50	$1.50	$2.50	£0.30	£0.90	£1.50
2 ND sub-titled "Power"	$0.50	$1.50	$2.50	£0.30	£0.90	£1.50
3 ND sub-titled "Mortal Combat"	$0.50	$1.50	$2.50	£0.30	£0.90	£1.50
Title Value:	$1.50	$4.50	$7.50	£0.90	£2.70	£4.50

INVISIBLES, THE

DC Comics/Vertigo; 1 Sep 1994-25 Oct 1996

Issue	$Good	$Fine	$N.Mint	£Good	£Fine	£N.Mint
1 48pgs, 1st appearance The Invisibles; Grant Morrison script and Steve Yeowell art begin	$0.70	$2.10	$3.50	£0.40	£1.20	£2.00
2-4	$0.50	$1.50	$2.50	£0.30	£0.90	£1.50
5 Jill Thompson and Dennis Cramer art begins; there are four variant covers, all printed on 'plain brown paper' cover with black ink graffiti slogans	$0.50	$1.50	$2.50	£0.30	£0.90	£1.50
6-15 painted cover by Sean Phillips	$0.50	$1.50	$2.50	£0.30	£0.90	£1.50
16-25	$0.50	$1.50	$2.50	£0.30	£0.90	£1.50
Title Value:	$12.70	$38.10	$63.50	£7.60	£22.80	£38.00

The Invisibles: Say You Want A Revolution (Jun 1996)

Issue	$Good	$Fine	$N.Mint	£Good	£Fine	£N.Mint
Trade paperback reprints issues #1-8				£2.30	£6.90	£11.50

INVISIBLES, THE (2ND SERIES)

DC Comics; 1 Feb 1997-present

Issue	$Good	$Fine	$N.Mint	£Good	£Fine	£N.Mint
1-2 ND Grant Morrison script, Phil Jiminez and John Stokes art; cover by Brian Bolland	$0.50	$1.50	$2.50	£0.30	£0.90	£1.50
Title Value:	$1.00	$3.00	$5.00	£0.60	£1.80	£3.00

IRON FIST

Marvel Comics Group; 1 Nov 1975-15 Sep 1977
(see Marvel Premiere, Powerman and Iron Fist)

Issue	$Good	$Fine	$N.Mint	£Good	£Fine	£N.Mint
1 ND Iron Man battles Iron Fist; John Byrne art	$5.00	$15.00	$35.00	£3.90	£11.50	£27.50
2 ND scarce in the U.K. John Byrne art	$3.30	$10.00	$20.00	£2.05	£6.25	£12.50
3 John Byrne art	$2.05	$6.25	$12.50	£1.65	£5.00	£10.00
4-7 John Byrne art	$1.65	$5.00	$10.00	£1.00	£3.00	£6.00
8-10 ND John Byrne art	$1.65	$5.00	$10.00	£1.05	£3.25	£6.50
11 ND John Byrne art	$1.50	$4.50	$9.00	£1.00	£3.00	£6.00
12 ND Captain America vs. Iron Fist; John Byrne art	$1.50	$4.50	$9.00	£1.00	£3.00	£6.00
13 ND John Byrne art	$1.50	$4.50	$9.00	£1.00	£3.00	£6.00
14 ND 1st appearance Sabretooth (see Powerman #66); John Byrne art	$22.50	$67.50	$160.00	£12.00	£36.00	£85.00
14 Marvel Milestone Edition, ND (Jan 1992) - silver border around cover	$0.25	$0.75	$1.25	£0.15	£0.50	£0.85
15 ND classic X-Men story, 30 cent cover; John Byrne art	$4.25	$12.50	$30.00	£2.50	£7.50	£17.50
15 35 cents cover, ND scarce in the U.K. , John Byrne art	$5.00	$15.00	$35.00	£2.85	£8.50	£20.00
Title Value:	$58.40	$175.50	$390.75	£35.25	£106.00	£234.85

IRON FIST (2ND SERIES)

Marvel Comics Group,MS; 1 Sep 1996-2 Oct 1996

Issue	$Good	$Fine	$N.Mint	£Good	£Fine	£N.Mint
1-2 ND James Felder script, Robert Brown and Ray Garcia art; spin-off from Spiderman Unlimited #13	$0.30	$0.90	$1.50	£0.20	£0.60	£1.00
Title Value:	$0.60	$1.80	$3.00	£0.40	£1.20	£2.00

IRON JAW

Atlas; 1 Jan 1975-4 Jul 1975
(see Barbarians)

Issue	$Good	$Fine	$N.Mint	£Good	£Fine	£N.Mint
1 distributed in the U.K. Mike Sekowsky art, part Neal Adams cover	$0.25	$0.75	$1.50	£0.15	£0.50	£1.00
2-4 distributed in the U.K. Pablo Marcos art	$0.25	$0.75	$1.50	£0.15	£0.50	£1.00
Title Value:	$1.00	$3.00	$6.00	£0.60	£2.00	£4.00

Note: Neal Adams cover on 2, origin in 4.

IRON MAN

Marvel Comics Group; 1 May 1968-332 Sep 1996
(see Avengers, Marvel Double Feature, Marvel Fanfare, Marvel Graphic Novel, Marvel Team Up, Marvel Two-In-One, Tales of Suspense)

Issue	$Good	$Fine	$N.Mint	£Good	£Fine	£N.Mint
1 origin retold; story continued from Iron Man and Sub-Mariner #1	$50.00	$150.00	$400.00	£31.00	£92.50	£250.00
2	$20.50	$62.50	$125.00	£12.50	£38.00	£75.00
3	$14.00	$43.00	$85.00	£9.00	£28.00	£55.00
4	$10.00	$30.00	$60.00	£6.25	£18.50	£37.50
5	$9.00	$28.00	$55.00	£5.75	£17.50	£35.00
6 The Crusher dies	$7.50	$22.50	$45.00	£4.55	£13.50	£27.50
7-8	$7.50	$22.50	$45.00	£4.55	£13.50	£27.50
9 Hulk appears (robot of the Mandarin)	$7.50	$22.50	$45.00	£4.55	£13.50	£27.50
10	$7.50	$22.50	$45.00	£4.55	£13.50	£27.50
11-15	$5.00	$15.00	$30.00	£2.90	£8.75	£17.50
16-17	$4.15	$12.50	$25.00	£2.50	£7.50	£15.00
18 Avengers appear	$4.15	$12.50	$25.00	£2.50	£7.50	£15.00
19-20	$4.15	$12.50	$25.00	£2.50	£7.50	£15.00
21	$3.30	$10.00	$20.00	£1.65	£5.00	£10.00
22 Janice Cord dies	$3.30	$10.00	$20.00	£1.65	£5.00	£10.00
23-24	$3.30	$10.00	$20.00	£1.65	£5.00	£10.00
25 Sub-Mariner battles Iron Man	$4.15	$12.50	$25.00	£2.50	£7.50	£15.00
26	$2.90	$8.75	$17.50	£1.65	£5.00	£10.00
27 1st appearance Fire Brand	$2.90	$8.75	$17.50	£1.65	£5.00	£10.00

	$Good	$Fine	$N.Mint	£Good	£Fine	£N.Mint
28-30	$2.90	$8.75	$17.50	£1.65	£5.00	£10.00
31-34	$2.50	$7.50	$15.00	£1.25	£3.75	£7.50
35 Daredevil and Nick Fury appear	$2.50	$7.50	$15.00	£1.25	£3.75	£7.50
36-39	$2.50	$7.50	$15.00	£1.25	£3.75	£7.50
40-42 scarce in the U.K.	$2.50	$7.50	$15.00	£1.40	£4.25	£8.50
43 ND scarce in the U.K. 52pgs	$2.90	$8.75	$17.50	£1.65	£5.00	£10.00
44 ND Ant-Man story	$2.50	$7.50	$15.00	£1.40	£4.25	£8.50
45 ND	$2.50	$7.50	$15.00	£1.40	£4.25	£8.50
46 ND	$2.05	$6.25	$12.50	£1.25	£3.75	£7.50
47 origin retold, Barry Smith art	$2.90	$8.75	$17.50	£1.40	£4.25	£8.50
48-50 scarce in the U.K.	$2.05	$6.25	$12.50	£1.25	£3.75	£7.50
51-52 scarce in the U.K.	$2.00	$6.00	$10.00	£1.30	£3.90	£6.50
53 scarce in the U.K. part Jim Starlin art	$2.00	$6.00	$10.00	£1.30	£3.90	£6.50
54 scarce in the U.K. Sub-Mariner battles Iron Man, part Bill Everett art; 1st appearance Moondragon	$3.00	$9.00	$15.00	£1.50	£4.50	£7.50
55 Jim Starlin art, origin and 1st appearance Thanos/Drax the Destroyer/Mentor/Starfox (cents copies seem to be scarce in the U.K.)	$10.00	$30.00	$50.00	£6.00	£18.00	£30.00
55 Marvel Milestone Edition, ND (Jan 1993) - silver border around cover	$0.50	$1.50	$2.50	£0.30	£0.90	£1.50
56 scarce in the U.K. Jim Starlin art	$4.00	$12.00	$20.00	£2.00	£6.00	£10.00
57-64	$2.00	$6.00	$10.00	£1.00	£3.00	£5.00
65 Thor appears (last panel)	$1.50	$4.50	$7.50	£1.00	£3.00	£5.00
66 Iron Man vs. Thor	$1.50	$4.50	$7.50	£0.80	£2.40	£4.00
67 ND	$1.50	$4.50	$7.50	£1.00	£3.00	£5.00
68 ND Jim Starlin cover, origin retold	$2.00	$6.00	$10.00	£1.20	£3.60	£6.00
69	$1.50	$4.50	$7.50	£0.80	£2.40	£4.00
70 ND scarce in the U.K.	$1.50	$4.50	$7.50	£1.20	£3.60	£6.00
71-75	$1.20	$3.60	$6.00	£0.60	£1.80	£3.00
76 reprints #9 (featuring Hulk)	$1.20	$3.60	$6.00	£0.60	£1.80	£3.00
77-79	$1.20	$3.60	$6.00	£0.60	£1.80	£3.00
80 Jack Kirby cover	$1.20	$3.60	$6.00	£0.60	£1.80	£3.00
81-82	$1.00	$3.00	$5.00	£0.50	£1.50	£2.50
83-84 Jack Kirby cover	$1.00	$3.00	$5.00	£0.50	£1.50	£2.50
85-87	$1.00	$3.00	$5.00	£0.50	£1.50	£2.50
88 Thanos appears in a flashback cameo	$1.00	$3.00	$5.00	£0.50	£1.50	£2.50
89 Daredevil appears	$1.00	$3.00	$5.00	£0.50	£1.50	£2.50
90 Avengers X-over, Jack Kirby cover	$1.00	$3.00	$5.00	£0.50	£1.50	£2.50
91-93	$1.00	$3.00	$5.00	£0.40	£1.20	£2.00
94-96 Jack Kirby cover	$1.00	$3.00	$5.00	£0.40	£1.20	£2.00
97	$1.00	$3.00	$5.00	£0.40	£1.20	£2.00
98 Iron Man vs. Sunfire	$1.00	$3.00	$5.00	£0.40	£1.20	£2.00
99	$1.00	$3.00	$5.00	£0.40	£1.20	£2.00
100 Jim Starlin cover	$1.60	$4.80	$8.00	£0.80	£2.40	£4.00
101 Frankenstein appears	$1.00	$3.00	$5.00	£0.40	£1.20	£2.00
102 1st appearance DreadKnight, George Perez cover	$1.00	$3.00	$5.00	£0.40	£1.20	£2.00
103-104 Jack of Hearts appears, George Perez cover	$1.00	$3.00	$5.00	£0.40	£1.20	£2.00
105-109 Jack of Hearts appears	$1.00	$3.00	$5.00	£0.40	£1.20	£2.00
110 LD in the U.K. Jack of Hearts appears (his origin retold)	$1.00	$3.00	$5.00	£0.50	£1.50	£2.50
111 Jack of Hearts appears	$1.00	$3.00	$5.00	£0.40	£1.20	£2.00
112 ND Jack of Hearts appears	$1.00	$3.00	$5.00	£0.50	£1.50	£2.50
113 ND	$1.00	$3.00	$5.00	£0.50	£1.50	£2.50
114 ND Giffen art, Avengers X-over	$1.00	$3.00	$5.00	£0.50	£1.50	£2.50
115 ND Avengers X-over, 1st John Romita Jnr. art	$1.00	$3.00	$5.00	£0.70	£2.10	£3.50
116 ND 2nd John Romita Jnr. art	$1.00	$3.00	$5.00	£0.60	£1.80	£3.00
117 ND 3rd John Romita Jnr. art	$1.00	$3.00	$5.00	£0.60	£1.80	£3.00
118 ND John Byrne art	$1.50	$4.50	$7.50	£0.70	£2.10	£3.50
119 ND John Byrne lay-outs	$1.00	$3.00	$5.00	£0.60	£1.80	£3.00
120 ND Iron Man vs. Sub-Mariner	$1.00	$3.00	$5.00	£0.60	£1.80	£3.00
121 ND Sub-Mariner appears	$0.60	$1.80	$3.00	£0.40	£1.20	£2.00
122 origin retold, Sub-Mariner appears	$0.60	$1.80	$3.00	£0.40	£1.20	£2.00
123-128 Tony Stark's alchohol struggle	$1.00	$3.00	$5.00	£0.45	£1.35	£2.25
129-130	$0.60	$1.80	$3.00	£0.40	£1.20	£2.00
131 Iron Man vs Hulk	$0.60	$1.80	$3.00	£0.30	£0.90	£1.50
132 LD in the U.K. Iron Man vs. Hulk	$0.60	$1.80	$3.00	£0.40	£1.20	£2.00
133 LD in the U.K. Hulk, Ant-Man appear	$0.60	$1.80	$3.00	£0.40	£1.20	£2.00
134-142	$0.60	$1.80	$3.00	£0.30	£0.90	£1.50
143 ND	$0.60	$1.80	$3.00	£0.40	£1.20	£2.00
144 ND Tony Stark's 1st meeting with Jim Rhodes re-told	$0.60	$1.80	$3.00	£0.40	£1.20	£2.00
145	$0.60	$1.80	$3.00	£0.30	£0.90	£1.50
146 ND	$0.60	$1.80	$3.00	£0.40	£1.20	£2.00
147-149	$0.60	$1.80	$3.00	£0.30	£0.90	£1.50
150 48pgs, Iron Man vs. Dr. Doom	$0.80	$2.40	$4.00	£0.40	£1.20	£2.00
151 Ant-Man appears	$0.50	$1.50	$2.50	£0.25	£0.75	£1.25
152 new armour, photo cover	$0.50	$1.50	$2.50	£0.25	£0.75	£1.25
153-158	$0.50	$1.50	$2.50	£0.25	£0.75	£1.25
159 Paul Smith art	$0.50	$1.50	$2.50	£0.25	£0.75	£1.25

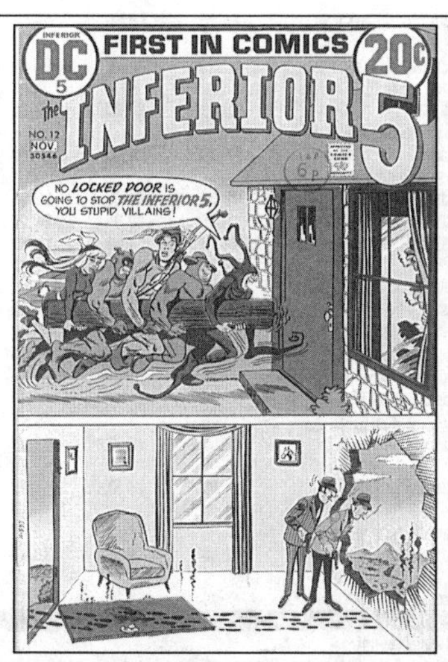

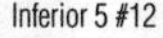
Inferior 5 #12

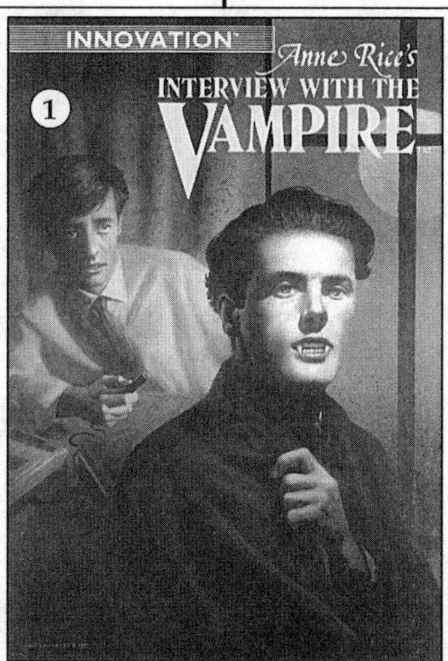

Interview With The Vampire #1

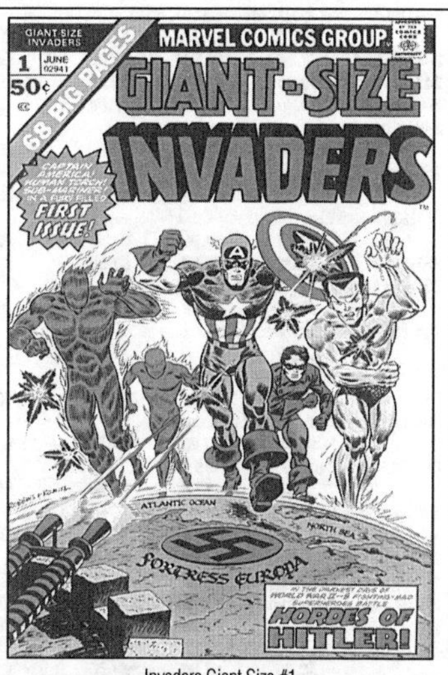

Invaders Giant Size #1

Issue	$Good	$Fine	$N.Mint	£Good	£Fine	£N.Mint
160 Steve Ditko and Marie Severin art	*$0.50*	*$1.50*	*$2.50*	£0.25	£0.75	£1.25
161 Moon Knight appears	*$0.50*	*$1.50*	*$2.50*	£0.25	£0.75	£1.25
162-164	*$0.50*	*$1.50*	*$2.50*	£0.25	£0.75	£1.25
165-167 LD in the U.K.	*$0.50*	*$1.50*	*$2.50*	£0.30	£0.90	£1.50
168 LD in the U.K. Machine Man appears	*$0.50*	*$1.50*	*$2.50*	£0.30	£0.90	£1.50
169 LD in the U.K. Jim Rhodes replaces Tony Stark as Iron Man, Daredevil cameo	*$0.80*	*$2.40*	*$4.00*	£0.50	£1.50	£2.50
170 LD in the U.K. 2nd appearance new Iron Man	*$0.60*	*$1.80*	*$3.00*	£0.40	£1.20	£2.00
171 LD in the U.K.	*$0.50*	*$1.50*	*$2.50*	£0.30	£0.90	£1.50
172 LD in the U.K. Captain America appears	*$0.50*	*$1.50*	*$2.50*	£0.30	£0.90	£1.50
173-174 LD in the U.K.	*$0.50*	*$1.50*	*$2.50*	£0.30	£0.90	£1.50
175-180	*$0.50*	*$1.50*	*$2.50*	£0.25	£0.75	£1.25
181-188	*$0.40*	*$1.20*	*$2.00*	£0.20	£0.60	£1.00
189 LD in the U.K.	*$0.40*	*$1.20*	*$2.00*	£0.25	£0.75	£1.25
190 LD in the U.K. Scarlet Witch appears	*$0.40*	*$1.20*	*$2.00*	£0.25	£0.75	£1.25
191 LD in the U.K. original Iron Man appears	*$0.40*	*$1.20*	*$2.00*	£0.25	£0.75	£1.25
192 LD in the U.K.	*$0.40*	*$1.20*	*$2.00*	£0.25	£0.75	£1.25
193-194 LD in the U.K. Hawkeye, Mockingbird X-over	*$0.40*	*$1.20*	*$2.00*	£0.25	£0.75	£1.25
195 LD in the U.K. Shaman appears	*$0.40*	*$1.20*	*$2.00*	£0.25	£0.75	£1.25
196 LD in the U.K.	*$0.40*	*$1.20*	*$2.00*	£0.25	£0.75	£1.25
197 Secret Wars X-over	*$0.40*	*$1.20*	*$2.00*	£0.20	£0.60	£1.00
198-199	*$0.40*	*$1.20*	*$2.00*	£0.20	£0.60	£1.00
200 LD in the U.K. DS Tony Stark returns as Iron Man in red/silver armour	*$0.80*	*$2.40*	*$4.00*	£0.40	£1.20	£2.00
201-207 LD in the U.K.	*$0.40*	*$1.20*	*$2.00*	£0.25	£0.75	£1.25
208-211	*$0.40*	*$1.20*	*$2.00*	£0.20	£0.60	£1.00
212 LD in the U.K. 1st appearance new Dominic Fortune (cameo)	*$0.40*	*$1.20*	*$2.00*	£0.25	£0.75	£1.25
213 1st full appearance new Dominic Fortune	*$0.40*	*$1.20*	*$2.00*	£0.20	£0.60	£1.00
214 Spiderwoman and Hawkeye appear	*$0.40*	*$1.20*	*$2.00*	£0.20	£0.60	£1.00
215 LD in the U.K.	*$0.40*	*$1.20*	*$2.00*	£0.25	£0.75	£1.25
216-222	*$0.40*	*$1.20*	*$2.00*	£0.20	£0.60	£1.00
223-224 build up to "Armour Wars"	*$0.40*	*$1.20*	*$2.00*	£0.25	£0.75	£1.25
225 LD in the U.K. DS, Armour Wars story begins, Ant-Man appears	*$0.80*	*$2.40*	*$4.00*	£0.40	£1.20	£2.00
226-231 Armour Wars	*$0.40*	*$1.20*	*$2.00*	£0.25	£0.75	£1.25
232 very LD Barry Smith art	*$0.40*	*$1.20*	*$2.00*	£0.30	£0.90	£1.50
233 LD in the U.K. Ant-Man appears	*$0.40*	*$1.20*	*$2.00*	£0.25	£0.75	£1.25
234 Spiderman appears	*$0.40*	*$1.20*	*$2.00*	£0.20	£0.60	£1.00
235-242	*$0.40*	*$1.20*	*$2.00*	£0.20	£0.60	£1.00
243 Tony Stark shot, Barry Smith inks	*$0.40*	*$1.20*	*$2.00*	£0.20	£0.60	£1.00
244 DS new armour and origin Iron Man part retold	*$0.70*	*$2.10*	*$3.50*	£0.30	£0.90	£1.50
245-246	*$0.40*	*$1.20*	*$2.00*	£0.20	£0.60	£1.00
247 Hulk appears	*$0.40*	*$1.20*	*$2.00*	£0.20	£0.60	£1.00
248	*$0.40*	*$1.20*	*$2.00*	£0.20	£0.60	£1.00
249 Dr. Doom appears	*$0.40*	*$1.20*	*$2.00*	£0.20	£0.60	£1.00
250 48pgs, Dr. Doom appears, Acts of Vengeance tie-in	*$0.40*	*$1.20*	*$2.00*	£0.25	£0.75	£1.25
251-252 Acts of Vengenance tie-in	*$0.30*	*$0.90*	*$1.50*	£0.15	£0.45	£0.75
253-257	*$0.30*	*$0.90*	*$1.50*	£0.15	£0.45	£0.75
258-263 Armour Wars II, John Byrne script	*$0.30*	*$0.90*	*$1.50*	£0.15	£0.45	£0.75
264-266 Armour Wars II extra, John Byrne script	*$0.30*	*$0.90*	*$1.50*	£0.15	£0.45	£0.75
267 John Byrne script	*$0.30*	*$0.90*	*$1.50*	£0.15	£0.45	£0.75
268 John Byrne script, more facts about origin	*$0.30*	*$0.90*	*$1.50*	£0.15	£0.45	£0.75
269 Black Widow appears, John Byrne script	*$0.30*	*$0.90*	*$1.50*	£0.15	£0.45	£0.75
270 John Byrne script	*$0.30*	*$0.90*	*$1.50*	£0.15	£0.45	£0.75
271 John Byrne script, Mandarin and Fin Fang Foom appear	*$0.30*	*$0.90*	*$1.50*	£0.15	£0.45	£0.75
272 John Byrne script, true origin Mandarin's rings	*$0.30*	*$0.90*	*$1.50*	£0.15	£0.45	£0.75
273 John Byrne script, Mandarin & Fin Fang Foom appear	*$0.30*	*$0.90*	*$1.50*	£0.15	£0.45	£0.75

Issue	$Good	$Fine	$N.Mint	£Good	£Fine	£N.Mint
274 John Byrne script	*$0.30*	*$0.90*	*$1.50*	£0.15	£0.45	£0.75
275 DS John Byrne script, Mandarin and Fin Fang Foom appear, back-up story and pin-up gallery	*$0.40*	*$1.20*	*$2.00*	£0.25	£0.75	£1.25
276 Black Widow appears	*$0.30*	*$0.90*	*$1.50*	£0.15	£0.45	£0.75
277 last John Byrne script, Black Widow appears, $1.25 cover begins	*$0.30*	*$0.90*	*$1.50*	£0.15	£0.45	£0.75
278 Galactic Storm part 6, Captain America appears	*$0.30*	*$0.90*	*$1.50*	£0.15	£0.45	£0.75
279 Galactic Storm part 13, guest stars Wonder Man, Hawkeye and the Avengers	*$0.30*	*$0.90*	*$1.50*	£0.15	£0.45	£0.75
280	*$0.30*	*$0.90*	*$1.50*	£0.15	£0.45	£0.75
281 1st appearance War Machine (cameo)	*$0.40*	*$1.20*	*$2.00*	£0.25	£0.75	£1.25
282 1st full appearance War Machine	*$0.80*	*$2.40*	*$4.00*	£0.30	£0.90	£1.50
283	*$0.30*	*$0.90*	*$1.50*	£0.15	£0.45	£0.75
284 Tony Stark cryogenically frozen	*$0.40*	*$1.20*	*$2.00*	£0.25	£0.75	£1.25
285-287	*$0.30*	*$0.90*	*$1.50*	£0.15	£0.45	£0.75
288 DS anniversary issue (Iron Man's 350th appearance)	*$0.60*	*$1.80*	*$3.00*	£0.30	£0.90	£1.50
289	*$0.30*	*$0.90*	*$1.50*	£0.15	£0.45	£0.75
290 DS Tony Stark returns as Iron Man, gold foil cover	*$0.60*	*$1.80*	*$3.00*	£0.40	£1.20	£2.00
291 Tony Stark vs. Jim Rhodes (War Machine)	*$0.30*	*$0.90*	*$1.50*	£0.20	£0.60	£1.00
292-293	*$0.30*	*$0.90*	*$1.50*	£0.20	£0.60	£1.00
294-295 Infinity Crusade X-over	*$0.30*	*$0.90*	*$1.50*	£0.20	£0.60	£1.00
296-299	*$0.30*	*$0.90*	*$1.50*	£0.20	£0.60	£1.00
300 64pgs, without foil cover	*$0.50*	*$1.50*	*$2.50*	£0.30	£0.90	£1.50
300 Collectors Edition, LD in the U.K. 64pgs, new armour debuts, War Machine guest-stars; double embossed red and gold foil cover	*$0.80*	*$2.40*	*$4.00*	£0.50	£1.50	£2.50
301-302	*$0.30*	*$0.90*	*$1.50*	£0.20	£0.60	£1.00
303 Venom appears	*$0.30*	*$0.90*	*$1.50*	£0.20	£0.60	£1.00
304 with free Spiderman and his Deadly Foes card sheet	*$0.30*	*$0.90*	*$1.50*	£0.20	£0.60	£1.00
305 Iron Man vs. Hulk	*$0.30*	*$0.90*	*$1.50*	£0.20	£0.60	£1.00
306-310	*$0.30*	*$0.90*	*$1.50*	£0.20	£0.60	£1.00
310 Collectors Edition, ND pre-bagged with acetate print from Marvel Action Hour TV series; neon ink cover; X-over War Machine #8	*$0.60*	*$1.80*	*$3.00*	£0.40	£1.20	£2.00
311 Hands of the Mandarin part 3, continued in Force Works #7	*$0.30*	*$0.90*	*$1.50*	£0.20	£0.60	£1.00
312 48pgs, Hands of the Mandarin part 6 (conclusion)	*$0.45*	*$1.35*	*$2.25*	£0.30	£0.90	£1.50
313-314	*$0.30*	*$0.90*	*$1.50*	£0.20	£0.60	£1.00
315-316 Black Widow guest-stars	*$0.30*	*$0.90*	*$1.50*	£0.20	£0.60	£1.00
317 48pgs, flip-book format, continued from War Machine #15	*$0.50*	*$1.50*	*$2.50*	£0.30	£0.90	£1.50
318	*$0.30*	*$0.90*	*$1.50*	£0.20	£0.60	£1.00
319 new Space Armour	*$0.30*	*$0.90*	*$1.50*	£0.20	£0.60	£1.00
320-321 Avengers: The Crossing tie-in; bi-weekly	*$0.30*	*$0.90*	*$1.50*	£0.20	£0.60	£1.00
322 Avengers: The Crossing tie-in	*$0.30*	*$0.90*	*$1.50*	£0.20	£0.60	£1.00
323-324 Iron Man vs. The Avengers	*$0.30*	*$0.90*	*$1.50*	£0.20	£0.60	£1.00
325 48pgs, Avengers: Timeslide tie-in; metallic fifth ink cover	*$0.60*	*$1.80*	*$3.00*	£0.40	£1.20	£2.00
326 The First Sign part 3, concludes in Avengers #396	*$0.30*	*$0.90*	*$1.50*	£0.20	£0.60	£1.00
327 "Iron Man: Day One" - new direction for character and title	*$0.30*	*$0.90*	*$1.50*	£0.20	£0.60	£1.00
328	*$0.30*	*$0.90*	*$1.50*	£0.20	£0.60	£1.00
329 new armour	*$0.30*	*$0.90*	*$1.50*	£0.20	£0.60	£1.00
330-331	*$0.30*	*$0.90*	*$1.50*	£0.20	£0.60	£1.00
332 Onslaught tie-in, continued in Onslaught: Marvel Universe	*$0.30*	*$0.90*	*$1.50*	£0.20	£0.60	£1.00
Title Value:	***$463.05***	***$1393.60***	***$2679.75***	**£262.60**	**£789.10**	**£1539.50**

Note: two versions of Iron Man #232 exist; a version printed on the incorrect paper exists but is very hard to find. The Guide cannot give a value to this anomaly at this stage.

	£Good	£Fine	£N.Mint
The Power of Iron Man Trade Paperback (1990), reprints Tony Stark's struggle with alcohol from issues #123-128	£1.10	£3.30	£5.50
(2nd printing - Apr 1991)	£1.00	£3.00	£5.00
Iron Man: Armor Wars (Jun 1990) Trade paperback 208pgs, reprints issues #225-232	£1.50	£4.50	£7.50
Iron Man: The Many Armours of Iron Man (Jan 1993) Trade paperback 208pgs, reprints stories showing the different types of armour over the years	£2.00	£6.00	£10.00
Iron Man vs. Dr. Doom (Feb 1995) Trade paperback 128pgs, reprints issues #149-150, #249-250	£1.70	£5.10	£8.50

IRON MAN (2ND SERIES)

Marvel Comics Group; 1 Nov 1996-present

1 ND 48pgs, The Hulk appears; Scott Lobdell and Jim Lee story, Whilce Portacio and Scott Williams art

	$Good	$Fine	$N.Mint	£Good	£Fine	£N.Mint
	$0.60	$1.80	$3.00	£0.40	£1.20	£2.00
1 Gold Stamped Signature Edition, ND (Jan 1997) pre-baaged with certificate featuring gold stamped signatures of Jim Lee, Scott Lobdell and Whilce Portacio; 5,000 copies						
	$5.00	$15.00	$25.00	£3.50	£10.50	£17.50
1 Signed & Numbered Edition, ND signed by Scott Lobdell, limited to 1,000 copies						
	$3.00	$9.00	$15.00	£2.00	£6.00	£10.00
1 Variant Cover Edition ND						
	$1.00	$3.00	$5.00	£0.80	£2.40	£4.00
2 ND	$0.40	$1.20	$2.00	£0.25	£0.75	£1.25
3 ND Iron Man vs. The Fantastic Four						
	$0.40	$1.20	$2.00	£0.25	£0.75	£1.25
4-5 ND	$0.40	$1.20	$2.00	£0.25	£0.75	£1.25
Title Value:	$11.20	$33.60	$56.00	£7.70	£23.10	£38.50

IRON MAN 2020

Marvel Comics Group,OS; nn Aug 1994

	$Good	$Fine	$N.Mint	£Good	£Fine	£N.Mint
nn ND 64pgs, Walt Simonson and Bob Wiacek						
	$1.20	$3.60	$6.00	£0.80	£2.40	£4.00
Title Value:	$1.20	$3.60	$6.00	£0.80	£2.40	£4.00

IRON MAN AND SUB-MARINER

Marvel Comics Group,OS; 1 Apr 1968

	$Good	$Fine	$N.Mint	£Good	£Fine	£N.Mint
1 stories continue from Tales to Astonish #101, Tales of Suspense #99, continue in Iron Man #1 and Sub-Mariner #1						
	$21.00	$62.50	$170.00	£13.50	£41.00	£110.00
Title Value:	$21.00	$62.50	$170.00	£13.50	£41.00	£110.00

IRON MAN ANNUAL

Marvel Comics Group; 1 Aug 1970-2 Nov 1971; 3 Jun 1976-4 Aug 1977; 5 Dec 1982-15 1994

	$Good	$Fine	$N.Mint	£Good	£Fine	£N.Mint
1 68pgs, all reprint inc. Iron Man vs. Sub-Mariner from Tales to Astonish #79,80,82						
	$4.15	$12.50	$25.00	£2.50	£7.50	£15.00
2 ND scarce in the U.K. 52pgs, reprints Tales of Suspense #81,92,91						
	$2.00	$6.00	$12.00	£1.25	£3.75	£7.50
3 ND 52pgs, Man-Thing appears						
	$1.20	$3.60	$6.00	£0.80	£2.40	£4.00
4 ND 52pgs, Champions (inc. Ghost Rider) appear						
	$1.00	$3.00	$5.00	£0.70	£2.10	£3.50
5 ND 52pgs, Black Panther appears						
	$0.60	$1.80	$3.00	£0.60	£1.80	£3.00
6 ND Eternals appear						
	$0.60	$1.80	$3.00	£0.50	£1.50	£2.50
7 ND West Coast Avengers X-over						
	$0.60	$1.80	$3.00	£0.50	£1.50	£2.50
8 ND X-Factor X-over						
	$0.60	$1.80	$3.00	£0.50	£1.50	£2.50
9 ND	$0.50	$1.50	$2.50	£0.30	£0.90	£1.50
10 ND Sub-Mariner appears, part 8 Atlantis Attacks						
	$0.50	$1.50	$2.50	£0.30	£0.90	£1.50
11 ND The Terminus Factor part 2, continues in Thor Annual #15, Machine Man appears						
	$0.50	$1.50	$2.50	£0.30	£0.90	£1.50
12 ND Subterranean Odyssey part 4, continues in Avengers West Coast Annual #6						
	$0.50	$1.50	$2.50	£0.30	£0.90	£1.50
13 ND Assault On Armor City part 3 (conclusion), Darkhawk appears						
	$0.50	$1.50	$2.50	£0.30	£0.90	£1.50
14 ND 64pgs, pre-bagged with trading card introducing Face Thief						
	$0.60	$1.80	$3.00	£0.40	£1.20	£2.00
15 ND 64pgs, The Controller appears						
	$0.60	$1.80	$3.00	£0.40	£1.20	£2.00
Title Value:	$14.45	$43.40	$78.50	£9.65	£28.95	£52.00

IRON MAN GIANT SIZE

Marvel Comics Group; 1 1975

	$Good	$Fine	$N.Mint	£Good	£Fine	£N.Mint
1 ND scarce in the U.K. 68pgs, all reprint from Tales of Suspense #49 (3rd X-Men), #57 (1st Hawkeye) and #58 (Iron Man vs. Captain America)						
	$1.65	$5.00	$10.00	£1.25	£3.75	£7.50
Title Value:	$1.65	$5.00	$10.00	£1.25	£3.75	£7.50

IRON MAN/FORCE WORKS COLLECTORS' PREVIEW

Marvel Comics Group,OS; 1 Nov 1994

	$Good	$Fine	$N.Mint	£Good	£Fine	£N.Mint
1 ND 48pgs, neon-ink wraparound cover						
	$0.40	$1.20	$2.00	£0.25	£0.75	£1.25
Title Value:	$0.40	$1.20	$2.00	£0.25	£0.75	£1.25

IRON MAN/X-O MANOWAR: HEAVY METAL

Marvel Comics Group/Acclaim Comics,OS; 1 Aug 1996

	$Good	$Fine	$N.Mint	£Good	£Fine	£N.Mint
1 ND Fabian Niceiza script, Tom Grindberg and Bill Anderson art						
	$0.50	$1.50	$2.50	£0.30	£0.90	£1.50
Title Value:	$0.50	$1.50	$2.50	£0.30	£0.90	£1.50

IRON MAN: AGE OF INNOCENCE

Marvel Comics Group,OS; 1 Feb 1996

	$Good	$Fine	$N.Mint	£Good	£Fine	£N.Mint
1 ND Avengers: Timeslide tie-in						
	$0.50	$1.50	$2.50	£0.30	£0.90	£1.50
Title Value:	$0.50	$1.50	$2.50	£0.30	£0.90	£1.50

IRON MAN: THE LEGEND

Marvel Comics Group,OS; 1 Sep 1996

	$Good	$Fine	$N.Mint	£Good	£Fine	£N.Mint
1 ND 48pgs, retells the life and times of Iron Man						
	$0.80	$2.40	$4.00	£0.50	£1.50	£2.50
Title Value:	$0.80	$2.40	$4.00	£0.50	£1.50	£2.50

IRON MANUAL

Marvel Comics Group,OS; 1 Mar 1993

	$Good	$Fine	$N.Mint	£Good	£Fine	£N.Mint
1 ND information on Iron Man technology, Bill Sienkiewicz painted cover						
	$0.30	$0.90	$1.50	£0.30	£0.90	£1.50
Title Value:	$0.30	$0.90	$1.50	£0.30	£0.90	£1.50

IRON MARSHAL

Jademan; 1 Jul 1990-33 Mar 1993

(see Jademan Special Issue)

	$Good	$Fine	$N.Mint	£Good	£Fine	£N.Mint
1-7 ND	$0.40	$1.20	$2.00	£0.25	£0.75	£1.25
8-20 ND	$0.30	$0.90	$1.50	£0.20	£0.60	£1.00
21-33 ND	$0.25	$0.75	$1.25	£0.15	£0.45	£0.75
Title Value:	$9.95	$29.85	$49.75	£6.30	£18.90	£31.50

IRON SAGA'S ANTHOLOGY

Iron Saga Productions; 1 Jan 1987-2 Mar 1987

	$Good	$Fine	$N.Mint	£Good	£Fine	£N.Mint
1-2 ND b&w	$0.30	$0.90	$1.50	£0.20	£0.60	£1.00
Title Value:	$0.60	$1.80	$3.00	£0.40	£1.20	£2.00

IRONHAND OF ALMURIC

Dark Horse,MS; 1 Sep 1991-4 Feb 1992

	$Good	$Fine	$N.Mint	£Good	£Fine	£N.Mint
1-4 ND Roy Thomas script						
	$0.40	$1.20	$2.00	£0.25	£0.75	£1.25
Title Value:	$1.60	$4.80	$8.00	£1.00	£3.00	£5.00

IRONWOLF

DC Comics; nn 1986

	$Good	$Fine	$N.Mint	£Good	£Fine	£N.Mint
nn 48pgs, reprints Chaykin's Ironwolf series from Weird Worlds #8-10						
	$0.60	$1.80	$3.00	£0.40	£1.20	£2.00
Title Value:	$0.60	$1.80	$3.00	£0.40	£1.20	£2.00

IRONWOLF: FIRES OF THE REVOLUTION

DC Comics; nn 1992

	$Good	$Fine	$N.Mint	£Good	£Fine	£N.Mint
nn Hardcover Edition ND 104pgs, Howard Chaykin script, Mike Mignola and P.Craig Russell art						
	$6.00	$18.00	$30.00	£4.00	£12.00	£20.00
nn Softcover Edition ND (May 1993), intro by Walt Simonson						
	$3.00	$9.00	$15.00	£2.00	£6.00	£10.00
Title Value:	$9.00	$27.00	$45.00	£6.00	£18.00	£30.00

ISIS, THE MIGHTY

DC Comics; 1 Oct/Nov 1976-8 Dec/Jan 1977/78

(see Shazam #25)

	$Good	$Fine	$N.Mint	£Good	£Fine	£N.Mint
1 scarce in the U.K. Wood inks						
	$0.80	$2.50	$5.00	£0.40	£1.25	£2.50
2 Nasser art	$0.55	$1.75	$3.50	£0.25	£0.75	£1.50
3-6	$0.55	$1.75	$3.50	£0.25	£0.75	£1.50
7 origin Isis	$0.55	$1.75	$3.50	£0.25	£0.75	£1.50
8	$0.55	$1.75	$3.50	£0.25	£0.75	£1.50
Title Value:	$4.65	$14.75	$29.50	£2.15	£6.50	£13.00

ISLAND OF DR. MOREAU

Marvel Comics Group,OS Film; 1 Oct 1977

	$Good	$Fine	$N.Mint	£Good	£Fine	£N.Mint
1 ND 52pgs, adapts film						
	$0.30	$0.90	$1.50	£0.20	£0.60	£1.00
Title Value:	$0.30	$0.90	$1.50	£0.20	£0.60	£1.00

IT! THE TERROR FROM BEYOND SPACE

Millennium,MS; 1 Nov 1992-4 Jul 1993

	$Good	$Fine	$N.Mint	£Good	£Fine	£N.Mint
1 ND adaptation of classic 1950s sci-fi film, said to have inspired "Alien", begins; die-cut cover						
	$0.50	$1.50	$2.50	£0.30	£0.90	£1.50
2-4 ND	$0.50	$1.50	$2.50	£0.30	£0.90	£1.50
Title Value:	$2.00	$6.00	$10.00	£1.20	£3.60	£6.00

IT'S SCIENCE WITH DR. RADIUM

Slave Labor; 1 Sep 1986-7 1987

	$Good	$Fine	$N.Mint	£Good	£Fine	£N.Mint
1-7 ND black and white; Samurai Penguin spin-off						
	$0.30	$0.90	$1.50	£0.20	£0.60	£1.00
Title Value:	$2.10	$6.30	$10.50	£1.40	£4.20	£7.00
Special 1 (1989)				£0.30	£0.90	£1.50
Dr. Radium's Big Book (1989)						
Trade paperback ND collects issues #1-7				£0.80	£2.40	£4.00
Dr. Radium and the Gizmo's of Boola Boola! (Jan 1992)						
one-shot				£0.30	£0.90	£1.50

ITCHY & SCRATCHY COMICS

Bongo Comics; 1 Jan 1994-3 1994

	$Good	$Fine	$N.Mint	£Good	£Fine	£N.Mint
1 ND Steve Vance script and Mike Milo art begin						
	$0.70	$2.10	$3.50	£0.50	£1.50	£2.50
2-3 ND	$0.50	$1.50	$2.50	£0.30	£0.90	£1.50
Title Value:	$1.70	$5.10	$8.50	£1.10	£3.30	£5.50

ITCHY & SCRATCHY'S HOLIDAY HIJINKS SPECIAL

Bongo Comics,OS; 1 Nov 1994

	$Good	$Fine	$N.Mint	£Good	£Fine	£N.Mint
1 ND	$0.50	$1.50	$2.50	£0.30	£0.90	£1.50
Title Value:	$0.50	$1.50	$2.50	£0.30	£0.90	£1.50

ITCHY PLANET

Fantagraphics; 1 Spring 1988-3 1989?

	$Good	$Fine	$N.Mint	£Good	£Fine	£N.Mint
1 ND Nuclear issue; all black and white						
	$0.50	$1.50	$2.50	£0.30	£0.90	£1.50
2 ND Politics	$0.50	$1.50	$2.50	£0.30	£0.90	£1.50
3 ND Elections	$0.50	$1.50	$2.50	£0.30	£0.90	£1.50
Title Value:	$1.50	$4.50	$7.50	£0.90	£2.70	£4.50

J

J.N. WILLIAMSON'S MASQUES

Innovation; 1 Jul 1992

	$Good	$Fine	$N.Mint	£Good	£Fine	£N.Mint
1 ND 48pgs, squarebound						
	$0.80	$2.40	$4.00	£0.50	£1.50	£2.50
Title Value:	$0.80	$2.40	$4.00	£0.50	£1.50	£2.50

JACK FROST

Amazing Comics; 1,2 1987

	$Good	$Fine	$N.Mint	£Good	£Fine	£N.Mint
1-2 ND	$0.40	$1.20	$2.00	£0.25	£0.75	£1.25
Title Value:	$0.80	$2.40	$4.00	£0.50	£1.50	£2.50

JACK KIRBY'S FOURTH WORLD

DC Comics; 1 Mar 1997-present

	$Good	$Fine	$N.Mint	£Good	£Fine	£N.Mint
1-2 ND John Byrne script and art; Walt Simonson covers						
	$0.40	$1.20	$2.00	£0.25	£0.75	£1.25
Title Value:	$0.80	$2.40	$4.00	£0.50	£1.50	£2.50

JACK KIRBY'S TEENAGENTS

Topps,MS; 1 Aug 1993-2 1993

1 pre-bagged with 3 trading cards (note: no Jack Kirby art)

	$Good	$Fine	$N.Mint	£Good	£Fine	£N.Mint
	$0.60	$1.80	$3.00	£0.40	£1.20	£2.00
2 pre-bagged with 2 trading cards (note: no Jack Kirby art)						
	$0.60	$1.80	$3.00	£0.40	£1.20	£2.00
Title Value:	$1.20	$3.60	$6.00	£0.80	£2.40	£4.00

JACK OF HEARTS

Marvel Comics Group,MS; 1 Jan 1984-4 Apr 1984

(see Deadly Hands of Kung Fu, Marvel Team Up)

	$Good	$Fine	$N.Mint	£Good	£Fine	£N.Mint
1 ND S.H.I.E.L.D. appear, George Freeman art begins						
	$0.30	$0.90	$1.50	£0.20	£0.60	£1.00
2-3 ND	$0.30	$0.90	$1.50	£0.20	£0.60	£1.00
4 ND scarce in the U.K.						
	$0.30	$0.90	$1.50	£0.25	£0.75	£1.25
Title Value:	$1.20	$3.60	$6.00	£0.85	£2.55	£4.25

JACK THE RIPPER

Eternity,MS; 1 Dec 1989-3 Apr 1990

	$Good	$Fine	$N.Mint	£Good	£Fine	£N.Mint
1-3 ND black and white						
	$0.50	$1.50	$2.50	£0.30	£0.90	£1.50
Title Value:	$1.50	$4.50	$7.50	£0.90	£2.70	£4.50
Graphic Album (Nov 1990), reprints #1-3				£1.00	£3.00	£5.00

JACKAROO

Eternity; 1 Mar 1990-3 May 1990

	$Good	$Fine	$N.Mint	£Good	£Fine	£N.Mint
1-3 ND Gary Chaloner script/art; black and white						
	$0.30	$0.90	$1.50	£0.20	£0.60	£1.00
Title Value:	$0.90	$2.70	$4.50	£0.60	£1.80	£3.00

JADEMAN COLLECTION

Jademan; 1 Dec 1989-4 Mar 1990

	$Good	$Fine	$N.Mint	£Good	£Fine	£N.Mint
1-4 ND 64pgs, anthology title edited by Len Wein, colour art, plastic-coated covers; bound-in poster						
	$0.50	$1.50	$2.50	£0.30	£0.90	£1.50
Title Value:	$2.00	$6.00	$10.00	£1.20	£3.60	£6.00

JADEMAN KUNG-FU SPECIAL

Jademan; 1 1988

	$Good	$Fine	$N.Mint	£Good	£Fine	£N.Mint
1 ND previews of Jademan titles						
	$0.30	$0.90	$1.50	£0.20	£0.60	£1.00
Title Value:	$0.30	$0.90	$1.50	£0.20	£0.60	£1.00

JADEMAN SPECIAL: GATES OF THE NIGHT

Jademan,MS; 1 Nov 1990-4 Feb 1991

	$Good	$Fine	$N.Mint	£Good	£Fine	£N.Mint
1-4 ND 68pgs, horror anthology						
	$0.80	$2.40	$4.00	£0.50	£1.50	£2.50
Title Value:	$3.20	$9.60	$16.00	£2.00	£6.00	£10.00

JAGUAR ANNUAL, THE

DC Comics/Impact; 1 Jun 1992

	$Good	$Fine	$N.Mint	£Good	£Fine	£N.Mint
1 64pgs, ties into Crusaders #1 (see other Impact annuals), trading cards included						
	$0.30	$0.90	$1.50	£0.20	£0.60	£1.00
Title Value:	$0.30	$0.90	$1.50	£0.20	£0.60	£1.00

JAGUAR GOD

Verotik; 1 1995-present

	$Good	$Fine	$N.Mint	£Good	£Fine	£N.Mint
0 ND (Aug 1995) Glenn Danzig script, Frank Teran art						
	$0.70	$2.10	$3.50	£0.50	£1.50	£2.50
1 ND Glenn Danzig script, Simon Bisley art; Frank Frazetta cover						
	$1.20	$3.60	$6.00	£0.70	£2.10	£3.50
2 ND Glenn Danzig script, Simon Bisley art						
	$0.80	$2.40	$4.00	£0.50	£1.50	£2.50
3 ND Glenn Danzig script, Simon Bisley art						
	$0.60	$1.80	$3.00	£0.40	£1.20	£2.00
4 ND new Frank Frazetta painted cover						
	$0.60	$1.80	$3.00	£0.40	£1.20	£2.00
5 ND Martin Edmond cover						
	$0.60	$1.80	$3.00	£0.40	£1.20	£2.00
Title Value:	$4.50	$13.50	$22.50	£2.90	£8.70	£14.50

JAGUAR STORIES

Comico; 1 Jul 1992-4 1992

	$Good	$Fine	$N.Mint	£Good	£Fine	£N.Mint
1-4 Steve Seagle script in all						
	$0.40	$1.20	$2.00	£0.25	£0.75	£1.25
Title Value:	$1.60	$4.80	$8.00	£1.00	£3.00	£5.00

JAGUAR, ADVENTURES OF THE

Archie; 1 Sep 1961-15 Nov 1963

	$Good	$Fine	$N.Mint	£Good	£Fine	£N.Mint
1	$21.00	$62.50	$150.00	£12.50	£39.00	£90.00
2-3 distributed in the U.K.						
	$10.50	$32.00	$75.00	£6.00	£18.00	£42.50
4-5 distributed in the U.K.						
	$8.50	$26.00	$60.00	£5.00	£15.00	£35.00
6-10 distributed in the U.K.						
	$6.25	$19.00	$45.00	£3.20	£9.50	£22.50
11-15 distributed in the U.K.						
	$5.00	$15.00	$35.00	£2.50	£7.50	£17.50
Title Value:	$115.25	$348.50	$820.00	£63.00	£190.00	£445.00

JAGUAR, THE

DC Comics/Impact; 1 Aug 1991-14 Oct 1992

	$Good	$Fine	$N.Mint	£Good	£Fine	£N.Mint
1-8	$0.15	$0.45	$0.75	£0.10	£0.35	£0.60
9 previews Crusaders #1 (see Web #9), trading cards included						
	$0.15	$0.45	$0.75	£0.10	£0.35	£0.60
10-14	$0.15	$0.45	$0.75	£0.10	£0.35	£0.60
Title Value:	$2.10	$6.30	$10.50	£1.40	£4.90	£8.40

Note: Archie character acquired (and revamped) by DC though events take place outside DC Universe continuity.

JAKE THRASH

Aircel,MS; 1 1988-3 1988

	$Good	$Fine	$N.Mint	£Good	£Fine	£N.Mint
1-3 ND Barry Blair script, Dave Cooper art, black and white						
	$0.40	$1.20	$2.00	£0.25	£0.75	£1.25
Title Value:	$1.20	$3.60	$6.00	£0.75	£2.25	£3.75
Book One (1989)						
80pgs squarebound, reprints issues #1-3 (published by Mailbu)				£0.50	£1.50	£2.50

JAM

Comico; 1 May 1988

	$Good	$Fine	$N.Mint	£Good	£Fine	£N.Mint
1 ND Bernie Mireault art in colour; sub-titled "Super Cool Colour-Injected Turbo Adventure from Hell!"						
	$0.50	$1.50	$2.50	£0.30	£0.90	£1.50
Title Value:	$0.50	$1.50	$2.50	£0.30	£0.90	£1.50

JAM SPECIAL

Matrix Graphics; 1 Oct 1987-2 1988

	$Good	$Fine	$N.Mint	£Good	£Fine	£N.Mint
1-2 ND 48pgs, Bernie Mireault script/art						
	$0.50	$1.50	$2.50	£0.30	£0.90	£1.50
Title Value:	$1.00	$3.00	$5.00	£0.60	£1.80	£3.00

JAM, THE

Slave Labor; 1 Nov 1989-4 May 1990; 5 May 1991; Dark Horse; 6-8 1994; Caliber Press; 9 Aug 1995-present

	$Good	$Fine	$N.Mint	£Good	£Fine	£N.Mint
1-5 ND Bernie Mireault script/art, black and white						
	$0.60	$1.80	$3.00	£0.40	£1.20	£2.00
6-9 ND Bernie Mireault script/art, black and white; sub-titled Urban Adventure						
	$0.60	$1.80	$3.00	£0.40	£1.20	£2.00
10-12 ND Bernie Mireault script/art; black and white						
	$0.60	$1.80	$3.00	£0.40	£1.20	£2.00
13 ND Jeff Lang and Bernie Mireault; black and white						
	$0.60	$1.80	$3.00	£0.40	£1.20	£2.00
Title Value:	$7.80	$23.40	$39.00	£5.20	£15.60	£26.00

JAMES BOND 007: QUASIMODO GAMBIT

Dark Horse,MS; 1 Jan 1995-3 Mar 1995

	$Good	$Fine	$N.Mint	£Good	£Fine	£N.Mint
1-3 ND Don McGregor script						
	$0.80	$2.40	$4.00	£0.50	£1.50	£2.50
Title Value:	$2.40	$7.20	$12.00	£1.50	£4.50	£7.50

JAMES BOND 007: SERPENT'S TOOTH

Dark Horse,MS; 1 Jul 1992-3 Dec 1992

	$Good	$Fine	$N.Mint	£Good	£Fine	£N.Mint
1-3 ND 48pgs, Doug Moench script, Paul Gulacy art						
	$0.90	$2.70	$4.50	£0.60	£1.80	£3.00
Title Value:	$2.70	$8.10	$13.50	£1.80	£5.40	£9.00
James Bond 007: Serpent's Tooth (Dec 1994)						
Trade paperback reprints mini-series, Paul Gulacy painted cover				£2.00	£6.00	£10.00

JAMES BOND 007: SHATTERED HELIX

Dark Horse,MS; 1 May 1994-2 Jun 1994

	$Good	$Fine	$N.Mint	£Good	£Fine	£N.Mint
1-2 ND David Lloyd cover and art						
	$0.50	$1.50	$2.50	£0.30	£0.90	£1.50
Title Value:	$1.00	$3.00	$5.00	£0.60	£1.80	£3.00

JAMES BOND JR.

Marvel Comics Group; 1 Feb 1992-12 Jan 1993

	$Good	$Fine	$N.Mint	£Good	£Fine	£N.Mint
1 based on animated U.S. series, Dan Abnett script begin, bi-weekly						
	$0.25	$0.75	$1.25	£0.15	£0.45	£0.75
2 bi-weekly	$0.25	$0.75	$1.25	£0.15	£0.45	£0.75
3-12	$0.25	$0.75	$1.25	£0.15	£0.45	£0.75
Title Value:	$3.00	$9.00	$15.00	£1.80	£5.40	£9.00

JAMES BOND: A SILENT ARMAGEDDON

Dark Horse,MS; 1 Mar 1993-2 Jun 1993

	$Good	$Fine	$N.Mint	£Good	£Fine	£N.Mint
1-2 ND Simon Jowett script and John Burns art						
	$0.60	$1.80	$3.00	£0.40	£1.20	£2.00
Title Value:	$1.20	$3.60	$6.00	£0.80	£2.40	£4.00

Note: it is not clear whether issues #3 and #4 ever appeared after Dark Horse put the series on hold waiting for the creators to finish the last issue.

JAMES BOND: GOLDENEYE

Topps,OS,Film; 1 Jan 1996

	$Good	$Fine	$N.Mint	£Good	£Fine	£N.Mint
1 ND adaptation of film; Don McGregor script, Claude St. Aubin and Rick Magyar art						
	$0.60	$1.80	$3.00	£0.40	£1.20	£2.00
Title Value:	$0.60	$1.80	$3.00	£0.40	£1.20	£2.00

Note: originally intended as a 3-part mini-series

JAMES BOND: PERMISSION TO DIE

Acme/Eclipse Books; 1,2 1989

	$Good	$Fine	$N.Mint	£Good	£Fine	£N.Mint
1-2 ND story/art by Mike Grell						
	$0.80	$2.40	$4.00	£0.50	£1.50	£2.50
Title Value:	$1.60	$4.80	$8.00	£1.00	£3.00	£5.00

JANUS DIRECTIVE, THE

(see in order)

Checkmate #15, Suicide Squad #27, Checkmate #16, Suicide Squad #28, Checkmate #17, Manhunter #14, Firestorm #86, Suicide Squad #29, Checkmate #18, Suicide Squad #30, Captain Atom #30

JASON AND THE ARGONAUTS

Dell/Movie Classics,OS Movie; 12-376-310 Aug/Oct 1963

	$Good	$Fine	$N.Mint	£Good	£Fine	£N.Mint
12-376-310 distributed in the U.K. film adaptation; photo cover						
	$12.00	$36.00	$85.00	£7.00	£21.00	£50.00
Title Value:	$12.00	$36.00	$85.00	£7.00	£21.00	£50.00

JASON AND THE ARGONAUTS (2ND SERIES)

Caliber/Tome Press; 1 Jul 1991-6 1991

	$Good	$Fine	$N.Mint	£Good	£Fine	£N.Mint
1-6 ND	$0.50	$1.50	$2.50	£0.30	£0.90	£1.50
Title Value:	$3.00	$9.00	$15.00	£1.80	£5.40	£9.00

JASON GOES TO HELL

Topps,MS; 1 Mar 1993-3 May 1993

	$Good	$Fine	$N.Mint	£Good	£Fine	£N.Mint
1 ND pre-bagged with 3 trading cards, glow-in-the-dark cover						
	$0.80	$2.40	$4.00	£0.50	£1.50	£2.50
2-3 ND pre-bagged with 3 trading cards						
	$0.60	$1.80	$3.00	£0.40	£1.20	£2.00
Title Value:	$2.00	$6.00	$10.00	£1.30	£3.90	£6.50

JASON VS. LEATHERFACE

Topps,MS; 1 Oct 1995-3 Dec 1995

	$Good	$Fine	$N.Mint	£Good	£Fine	£N.Mint
1 ND Nancy Collins script, Jeff Butler and Steve Montano script						
	$0.60	$1.80	$3.00	£0.40	£1.20	£2.00
2-3 ND Nancy Collins script, Jeff Butler and Steve Montano script; Simon Bisley cover						
	$0.60	$1.80	$3.00	£0.40	£1.20	£2.00
Title Value:	$1.80	$5.40	$9.00	£1.20	£3.60	£6.00

	$Good	$Fine	$N.Mint	£Good	£Fine	£N.Mint
JAVERTS						
Firstlight Comixx,MS; 1 Aug 1994-5 Dec 1994						
1 ND holo-foil enhanced cover by Bart Sears	$0.60	$1.80	$3.00	£0.40	£1.20	£2.00
1 Gold Edition, ND , available to retailers with every 15 copies of #1	$1.00	$3.00	$5.00	£0.60	£1.80	£3.00
2-5 ND	$0.60	$1.80	$3.00	£0.40	£1.20	£2.00
Title Value:	$4.00	$12.00	$20.00	£2.60	£7.80	£13.00
JAWBREAKER						
Marvel Comics Group,OS; 1 1996						
1 ND Hulk by Dave Gibbons reprint, Spiderman, Thor and Captain America reprints; available through mail-order in the U.K. by sending off 10 Jawbreaker sweet wrappers	$0.50	$1.50	$2.50	£0.30	£0.90	£1.50
Title Value:	$0.50	$1.50	$2.50	£0.30	£0.90	£1.50
JAZZ AGE CHRONICLES						
Caliber Press; 1 May 1990-6 1991						
1-6 ND	$0.40	$1.20	$2.00	£0.25	£0.75	£1.25
Title Value:	$2.40	$7.20	$12.00	£1.50	£4.50	£7.50
Note: issue #7 was advertised and solicited but the series was suddenly cancelled at #6.						
Graphic Novel (1991) ND reprints issues #1-3				£1.00	£3.00	£5.00
JAZZ: SOLO						
High Impact Studios,MS; 1 Mar 1996-3 Jun 1996						
1 ND Jude Millien art; black and white	$0.60	$1.80	$3.00	£0.40	£1.20	£2.00
1 Gold Edition ND	$2.00	$6.00	$10.00	£1.00	£3.00	£5.00
2 ND Jude Millien art; black and white	$0.60	$1.80	$3.00	£0.40	£1.20	£2.00
2 Variant Cover Edition, ND photo cover	$2.00	$6.00	$10.00	£1.30	£3.90	£6.50
3 ND Jude Millien art; black and white	$0.60	$1.80	$3.00	£0.40	£1.20	£2.00
3 Variant Cover Edition, ND signed with certificate	$2.00	$6.00	$10.00	£1.30	£3.90	£6.50
Title Value:	$7.80	$23.40	$39.00	£4.80	£14.40	£24.00
JEMM, SON OF SATURN						
DC Comics,MS; 1 Sep 1984-12 Aug 1985						
1-2	$0.15	$0.45	$0.75	£0.10	£0.35	£0.60
3 origin told	$0.15	$0.45	$0.75	£0.10	£0.35	£0.60
4 Superman appears	$0.15	$0.45	$0.75	£0.10	£0.35	£0.60
5-12	$0.15	$0.45	$0.75	£0.10	£0.35	£0.60
Title Value:	$1.80	$5.40	$9.00	£1.20	£4.20	£7.20
Note: Gene Colan art in all; series 1st intended to feature Martian Manhunter.						
JEREMIAH: A FISTFUL OF SAND						
Adventure,MS; 1,2 Aug 1991						
1-2 ND	$0.40	$1.20	$2.00	£0.25	£0.75	£1.25
Title Value:	$0.80	$2.40	$4.00	£0.50	£1.50	£2.50
JEREMIAH: BIRDS OF PREY						
Adventure,MS; 1,2 Jan 1991						
1-2 ND	$0.40	$1.20	$2.00	£0.25	£0.75	£1.25
Title Value:	$0.80	$2.40	$4.00	£0.50	£1.50	£2.50
JEREMIAH: EYES LIKE BURNING COALS						
Adventure,MS; 1,2 Oct 1991						
1-2 ND	$0.40	$1.20	$2.00	£0.25	£0.75	£1.25
Title Value:	$0.80	$2.40	$4.00	£0.50	£1.50	£2.50
JEREMIAH: THE HEIRS						
Adventure,MS; 1,2 Sep 1991						
1-2 ND	$0.40	$1.20	$2.00	£0.25	£0.75	£1.25
Title Value:	$0.80	$2.40	$4.00	£0.50	£1.50	£2.50
JEREMIAH: THE HUNTERS						
Adventure,MS; 1,2 Nov 1991						
1-2 ND	$0.40	$1.20	$2.00	£0.25	£0.75	£1.25
Title Value:	$0.80	$2.40	$4.00	£0.50	£1.50	£2.50
JERRY IGER'S FAMOUS FEATURES						
Pacific,OS; 1 Jul 1984						
1 ND Matt Baker Flamingo reprints; colour	$0.40	$1.20	$2.00	£0.25	£0.75	£1.25
Title Value:	$0.40	$1.20	$2.00	£0.25	£0.75	£1.25
JERRY IGER'S GOLDEN FEATURES						
Blackthorne; 1 Feb 1986-6 Dec 1986						
1 ND Flamingo by Matt Baker	$0.40	$1.20	$2.00	£0.25	£0.75	£1.25
2 ND Wonder Boy by Matt Baker	$0.40	$1.20	$2.00	£0.25	£0.75	£1.25
3 ND All-Girl issue	$0.40	$1.20	$2.00	£0.25	£0.75	£1.25
4 ND ZX-5 Spies in Action, Lou Fine, Jack Kirby art	$0.50	$1.50	$2.50	£0.30	£0.90	£1.50
5 ND All-Horror issue	$0.40	$1.20	$2.00	£0.25	£0.75	£1.25
6 ND All-Kids issue	$0.40	$1.20	$2.00	£0.25	£0.75	£1.25
Title Value:	$2.50	$7.50	$12.50	£1.55	£4.65	£7.75
JERRY LEWIS, THE ADVENTURES OF						
National Periodical Publications;41 Nov 1957-124 May/Jun 1971						
(see Super DC Giant)						
(previous issues #1-40 titled Adventures of Dean Martin and Jerry Lewis, all ND)						
41-60	$6.25	$19.00	$45.00	£3.55	£10.50	£25.00
61-63	$5.00	$15.00	$35.00	£2.85	£8.50	£20.00
1st official distribution in the U.K.						
64-73	$5.00	$15.00	$35.00	£2.50	£7.50	£17.50
74 ND	$5.00	$15.00	$35.00	£2.85	£8.50	£20.00
75-80	$5.00	$15.00	$35.00	£2.50	£7.50	£17.50
81-91 ND	$3.55	$10.50	$25.00	£1.75	£5.25	£12.50
92 ND Superman cameo	$4.25	$12.50	$30.00	£2.10	£6.25	£15.00
93-96 ND	$2.85	$8.50	$20.00	£1.40	£4.25	£10.00
97 scarce in the U.K. Batman and Robin X-over, Joker cover and story	$5.25	$16.00	$37.50	£2.85	£8.50	£20.00
98-100 ND	$2.85	$8.50	$20.00	£1.40	£4.25	£10.00
101 ND Neal Adams art	$5.25	$16.00	$37.50	£2.85	£8.50	£20.00
102 ND scarce in the U.K. Neal Adams art, Beatles appear	$5.50	$17.00	$40.00	£3.55	£10.50	£25.00
103-104 ND Neal Adams art	$5.25	$16.00	$37.50	£2.85	£8.50	£20.00
105 ND Superman appears	$4.25	$12.50	$30.00	£2.10	£6.25	£15.00
106-111 ND	$1.65	$5.00	$10.00	£1.00	£3.00	£6.00
112 ND Flash appears	$4.15	$12.50	$25.00	£1.65	£5.00	£10.00
113-116 ND	$1.65	$5.00	$10.00	£1.00	£3.00	£6.00
117 ND Wonder Woman appears	$2.90	$8.75	$17.50	£1.65	£5.00	£10.00
118-124 ND	$1.25	$3.75	$7.50	£1.00	£3.00	£6.00
Title Value:	$351.30	$1058.50	$2460.00	£190.90	£569.50	£1324.50
JESUS						
Spire,OS; nn 1979						
nn ND the story of Jesus written and illustrated by Al Hartley	$0.20	$0.60	$1.25	£0.10	£0.35	£0.75
Title Value:	$0.20	$0.60	$1.25	£0.10	£0.35	£0.75
JET POWER						
IW Super; 1,2 1963						
1-2 scarce, distributed in the U.K. all reprints	$3.20	$9.50	$22.50	£1.75	£5.25	£12.50

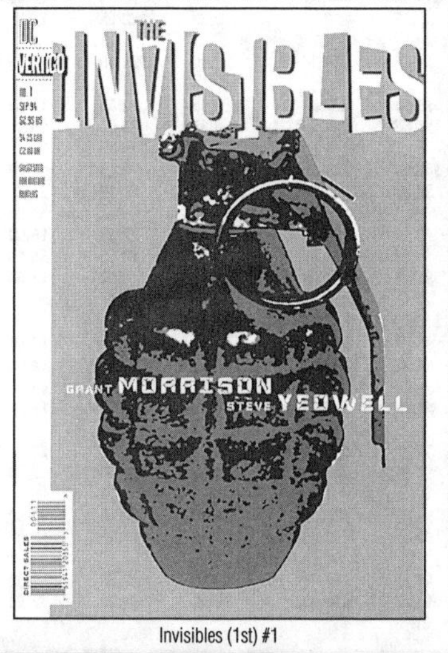

Invisibles (1st) #1

Iron Man Annual #2

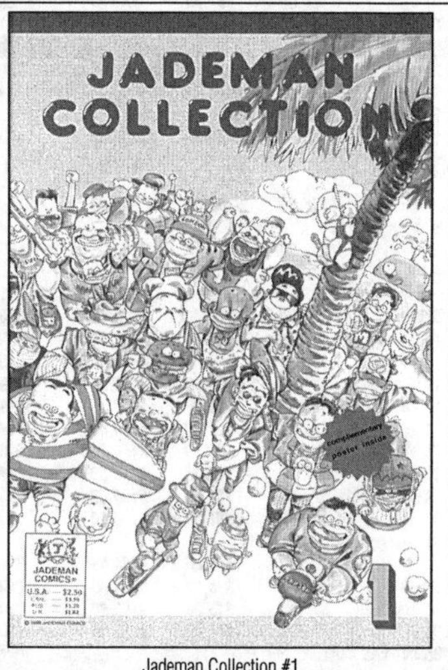

Jademan Collection #1

	$Good	$Fine	$N.Mint	£Good	£Fine	£N.Mint
Title Value:	$6.40	$19.00	$45.00	£3.50	£10.50	£25.00
JETSONS, THE						
Gold Key; 1 Jan 1963-36 Oct 1970						
1 scarce in the U.K	$32.00	$95.00	$225.00	£17.50	£52.50	£125.00
2 scarce in the U.K.	$17.50	$52.50	$125.00	£9.25	£28.00	£65.00
3 scarce in the U.K.	$13.50	$41.00	$95.00	£7.75	£23.50	£55.00
4-5	$13.50	$41.00	$95.00	£7.00	£21.00	£50.00
6-10	$13.50	$41.00	$95.00	£6.25	£19.00	£45.00
11-20	$9.25	$28.00	$65.00	£4.25	£12.50	£30.00
21-30	$7.75	$23.50	$55.00	£3.55	£10.50	£25.00
31-36	$7.00	$21.00	$50.00	£3.20	£9.50	£22.50
Title Value:	$369.50	$1116.50	$2610.00	£176.95	£528.00	£1255.00
Note: all distributed on the news-stands in the U.K.						
JETSONS, THE (2ND SERIES)						
Charlton; 1 Nov 1970-20 Jan 1974						
1 scarce in the U.K.	$10.00	$30.00	$60.00	£5.75	£17.50	£35.00
2-3 scarce in the U.K.	$5.00	$15.00	$30.00	£2.50	£7.50	£15.00
4-5	$4.15	$12.50	$25.00	£1.65	£5.00	£10.00
6-10	$3.75	$11.00	$22.50	£1.25	£3.75	£7.50
11-20	$2.50	$7.50	$15.00	£0.80	£2.50	£5.00
Title Value:	$72.05	$215.00	$427.50	£28.30	£86.25	£172.50
Note: most issues distributed on the news-stands in the U.K.						
JEZEBEL JADE						
Comico,MS; 1 Oct 1988-3 Dec 1988						
(see Jonny Quest)						
1-3 ND Messner-Loebs script, Adam Kubert cover and art	$0.60	$1.80	$3.00	£0.40	£1.20	£2.00
Title Value:	$1.80	$5.40	$9.00	£1.20	£3.60	£6.00
JIGSAW						
Harvey; 1 Sep 1966-2 Dec 1966						
1 distributed in the U.K. Reed Crandall art	$1.40	$4.25	$10.00	£0.70	£2.10	£5.00
2 distributed in the U.K.	$0.85	$2.55	$6.00	£0.40	£1.25	£3.00
Title Value:	$2.25	$6.80	$16.00	£1.10	£3.35	£8.00
JIHAD						
Marvel Comics Group,MS; 1 Dec 1991-2 Jan 1992						
1 ND features The Cenobites from Clive Barker's Nightbreed, Paul Johnson painted cover and art	$0.90	$2.70	$4.50	£0.60	£1.80	£3.00
2 ND	$0.90	$2.70	$4.50	£0.60	£1.80	£3.00
Title Value:	$1.80	$5.40	$9.00	£1.20	£3.60	£6.00
JIHAD						
White Wolf,MS; 1 Apr 1991						
1 ND (cancelled after 1 issue)	$0.50	$1.50	$2.50	£0.30	£0.90	£1.50
Title Value:	$0.50	$1.50	$2.50	£0.30	£0.90	£1.50
JIM						
Fantagraphics,Magazine; 1 1987-4 1990 ?						
1 ND Jim Woodring story/art begins	$2.50	$7.50	$12.50	£0.60	£1.80	£3.00
2 ND scarce in the U.K.	$2.00	$6.00	$10.00	£0.50	£1.50	£2.50
3-4 ND	$1.50	$4.50	$7.50	£0.40	£1.20	£2.00
Title Value:	$7.50	$22.50	$37.50	£1.90	£5.70	£9.50
JIMBO						
Bongo Comics; 1 Jun 1995-4 1995 ?						
1-4 ND Gary Panter art	$0.60	$1.80	$3.00	£0.40	£1.20	£2.00
Title Value:	$2.40	$7.20	$12.00	£1.60	£4.80	£8.00
JIMMY OLSEN, SUPERMAN'S PAL						
National Periodical Publications/DC Comics; 1 Sep/Oct 1954-163 Feb/Mar 1974						
(becomes Superman Family #164 on) (see also Superman, World's Finest)						
1 very scarce in the U.S. rare in the U.K.	$425.00	$1275.00	$4250.00	£300.00	£900.00	£3000.00
[Very scarce in high grade - Very Fine+ or better]						
2 very scarce in the U.K.	$155.00	$465.00	$1250.00	£110.00	£335.00	£900.00
3 very scarce in the U.K. (Jan/Feb 1955)	$82.50	$250.00	$675.00	£60.00	£180.00	£490.00
4-5 scarce in the U.K.	$57.50	$170.00	$460.00	£41.00	£120.00	£325.00
6-9	$41.00	$120.00	$325.00	£28.00	£82.50	£220.00
10 (Feb 1956)	$41.00	$120.00	$325.00	£28.00	£82.50	£220.00
11-17	$29.00	$85.00	$200.00	£19.00	£57.50	£135.00
18 (Feb 1957)	$29.00	$85.00	$200.00	£19.00	£57.50	£135.00
19-20	$29.00	$85.00	$200.00	£19.00	£57.50	£135.00
21-25	$21.00	$62.50	$150.00	£14.00	£43.00	£100.00
26 (Feb 1958)	$21.00	$62.50	$150.00	£14.00	£43.00	£100.00
27-28	$21.00	$62.50	$150.00	£14.00	£43.00	£100.00
29 Krypto appears	$21.00	$62.50	$150.00	£14.00	£43.00	£100.00
30	$21.00	$62.50	$150.00	£14.00	£43.00	£100.00
31 1st appearance Elastic Lad	$15.00	$45.00	$105.00	£10.00	£30.00	£70.00
32-33	$15.00	$45.00	$105.00	£10.00	£30.00	£70.00
34 (Feb 1959)	$15.00	$45.00	$105.00	£10.00	£30.00	£70.00
35	$15.00	$45.00	$105.00	£10.00	£30.00	£70.00
36 1st appearance Lucy Lane, sister of Lois Lane and long-time girl-friend of Jimmy	$15.00	$45.00	$105.00	£10.00	£30.00	£70.00
37-40	$15.00	$45.00	$105.00	£10.00	£30.00	£70.00
1st official distribution in the U.K.						
41	$11.00	$34.00	$80.00	£7.00	£21.00	£50.00
42 (Jan 1960)	$11.00	$34.00	$80.00	£7.00	£21.00	£50.00
43-45	$11.00	$34.00	$80.00	£7.00	£21.00	£50.00
46-47	$11.00	$34.00	$80.00	£6.25	£19.00	£45.00
48 1st Superman Emergency Squad	$11.00	$34.00	$80.00	£6.25	£19.00	£45.00
49 Congorilla appears	$11.00	$34.00	$80.00	£6.25	£19.00	£45.00
50 (Jan 1961), Bizarro and Supergirl appearances	$11.00	$34.00	$80.00	£6.25	£19.00	£45.00
51 Supergirl appears	$10.00	$30.00	$70.00	£5.00	£15.00	£35.00
52-55	$10.00	$30.00	$70.00	£5.00	£15.00	£35.00
56 last 10 cents issue	$10.00	$30.00	$70.00	£5.00	£15.00	£35.00
57 Supergirl appears	$6.25	$19.00	$45.00	£3.20	£9.50	£22.50
58 (Jan 1962)	$6.25	$19.00	$45.00	£3.20	£9.50	£22.50
59-60	$6.25	$19.00	$45.00	£3.20	£9.50	£22.50
61	$6.25	$19.00	$45.00	£2.50	£7.50	£17.50
62 Mon-El appearance	$6.25	$19.00	$45.00	£2.50	£7.50	£17.50
63 Legion of Super Villains appearance	$7.00	$21.00	$50.00	£2.85	£8.50	£20.00
64-65	$5.50	$17.00	$40.00	£1.75	£5.25	£12.50
66 (Jan 1963)	$5.50	$17.00	$40.00	£1.75	£5.25	£12.50
67-69	$5.50	$17.00	$40.00	£1.75	£5.25	£12.50
70 Element Lad X-over, 1st appearance Silver Kryponite (hoax)	$5.50	$17.00	$40.00	£1.75	£5.25	£12.50
71	$4.25	$12.50	$30.00	£1.40	£4.25	£10.00
72 Elastic Lad joins the Legion	$5.00	$15.00	$35.00	£1.75	£5.25	£12.50
73 Ultra Boy X-over	$5.00	$15.00	$35.00	£1.75	£5.25	£12.50
74 (Jan 1964)	$4.25	$12.50	$30.00	£1.40	£4.25	£10.00
75 Supergirl appears	$4.25	$12.50	$30.00	£1.40	£4.25	£10.00
76 Legion appears (Saturn Girl/Light Lass/Triplicate Girl)	$5.00	$15.00	$35.00	£1.75	£5.25	£12.50
77 Jimmy Olsen as Colossal Boy; Titano the Super-Ape appears	$5.00	$15.00	$35.00	£1.75	£5.25	£12.50
78 Aqualad appears	$4.25	$12.50	$30.00	£1.40	£4.25	£10.00
79 The Red Headed Beatle of 1,000 BC - cool!	$5.50	$17.00	$40.00	£1.75	£5.25	£12.50
80 Bizarro with Bizarro Lucy and Luthor appear	$4.25	$12.50	$30.00	£1.40	£4.25	£10.00
81	$3.55	$10.50	$25.00	£1.10	£3.40	£8.00
82 (Jan 1965)	$3.55	$10.50	$25.00	£1.10	£3.40	£8.00
83	$3.55	$10.50	$25.00	£1.10	£3.40	£8.00
84 Titano appears	$3.55	$10.50	$25.00	£1.10	£3.40	£8.00
85 Legion appear (3 panels)	$4.25	$12.50	$30.00	£1.40	£4.25	£10.00
86 Congorilla appears	$3.55	$10.50	$25.00	£1.10	£3.40	£8.00
87 Legion of Super Villains appear (inc. Brainiac and Luthor)	$4.25	$12.50	$30.00	£1.40	£4.25	£10.00
88 Star Boy appears (1 panel)	$4.25	$12.50	$30.00	£1.25	£3.85	£9.00
89 John F. Kennedy tribute; last Silver Age issue cover dated December 1965	$3.55	$10.50	$25.00	£1.05	£3.20	£7.50
90 (Jan 1966)	$3.55	$10.50	$25.00	£1.05	£3.20	£7.50
91	$2.85	$8.50	$20.00	£0.85	£2.55	£6.00
92 Batman, Robin and Supergirl appear	$2.85	$8.50	$20.00	£1.00	£3.00	£7.00
93 Jimmy as Super-Batman	$2.85	$8.50	$20.00	£0.85	£2.55	£6.00
94 Supergirl cameo	$2.85	$8.50	$20.00	£0.85	£2.55	£6.00
95 80pgs, Giant G-25	$4.25	$12.50	$30.00	£2.10	£6.25	£15.00
96-98	$2.85	$8.50	$20.00	£0.70	£2.10	£5.00
99 (Jan 1967), Jimmy Olsen as Star Boy, Lightning Lad, Sun Boy	$2.85	$8.50	$20.00	£0.85	£2.55	£6.00
100 Legion cameo	$2.85	$8.50	$20.00	£0.85	£2.55	£6.00
101-103	$1.40	$4.25	$10.00	£0.50	£1.50	£3.50
104 80pgs, Giant G-38	$4.25	$12.50	$30.00	£2.10	£6.25	£15.00
105	$1.40	$4.25	$10.00	£0.50	£1.50	£3.50
106 Legion appears	$1.40	$4.25	$10.00	£0.55	£1.70	£4.00
107	$1.40	$4.25	$10.00	£0.50	£1.50	£3.50
108 (Jan 1968)	$1.40	$4.25	$10.00	£0.50	£1.50	£3.50
109 Neal Adams cover	$1.40	$4.25	$10.00	£0.50	£1.50	£3.50
110	$1.40	$4.25	$10.00	£0.50	£1.50	£3.50
111 Batman and Robin appear	$1.40	$4.25	$10.00	£0.40	£1.25	£3.00
112	$1.40	$4.25	$10.00	£0.40	£1.25	£3.00
113 80pgs, Giant G-50	$2.10	$6.25	$15.00	£1.25	£3.85	£9.00
114	$1.40	$4.25	$10.00	£0.40	£1.25	£3.00
115 Aquaman appears, Neal Adams cover						

VERY GENERAL PERCENTAGE CONVERSION CHART WHICH MAY BE USED TO CALCULATE LOW AND INBETWEEN GRADES:

	$Good	$Fine	$N.Mint	£Good	£Fine	£N.Mint
	$1.40	$4.25	$10.00	£0.40	£1.25	£3.00
116 cover story reprints issue #10	$1.40	$4.25	$10.00	£0.40	£1.25	£3.00
117 (Jan 1969)	$1.40	$4.25	$10.00	£0.40	£1.25	£3.00
118-120	$1.40	$4.25	$10.00	£0.40	£1.25	£3.00
121	$1.40	$4.25	$10.00	£0.35	£1.05	£2.50
122 80pgs, Giant G-62	$2.85	$8.50	$20.00	£1.40	£4.25	£10.00
123-125	$1.40	$4.25	$10.00	£0.35	£1.05	£2.50
126 (Jan 1970)	$1.40	$4.25	$10.00	£0.35	£1.05	£2.50
127-130	$1.40	$4.25	$10.00	£0.35	£1.05	£2.50
131 80pgs, Giant G-74	$3.30	$10.00	$20.00	£1.65	£5.00	£10.00
132 scarce in the U.K.	$1.65	$5.00	$10.00	£0.55	£1.75	£3.50
133 1st of re-vamped series by Jack Kirby; Newsboy Legion appears	$3.30	$10.00	$20.00	£1.00	£3.00	£6.00
134 Jack Kirby art, 1st appearance Darkseid (cameo - 1 panel; see Forever People #1)	$5.00	$15.00	$30.00	£1.50	£4.50	£9.00
135 (Jan 1971), Jack Kirby art, 2nd appearance Darkseid (cameo)	$3.30	$10.00	$20.00	£1.15	£3.50	£7.00
136-139 Jack Kirby art	$1.00	$3.00	$6.00	£0.40	£1.25	£2.50
140 80pgs, Giant G-86	$3.30	$10.00	$20.00	£1.25	£3.75	£7.50
141 48pgs, (says 52pgs on cover to #150 as they count the covers in the U.S.), Jack Kirby art	$1.00	$3.00	$6.00	£0.40	£1.25	£2.50
142-144 48pgs, Jack Kirby art	$1.00	$3.00	$6.00	£0.40	£1.25	£2.50
145 48pgs, (Jan 1972), Jack Kirby art	$1.00	$3.00	$6.00	£0.40	£1.25	£2.50
146-148 48pgs, Jack Kirby art	$1.00	$3.00	$6.00	£0.40	£1.25	£2.50
149-150 48pgs, Golden Age Plastic Man reprints by Jack Cole	$0.80	$2.50	$5.00	£0.30	£1.00	£2.00
151-154	$0.80	$2.50	$5.00	£0.30	£1.00	£2.00
155 (Jan 1973)	$0.80	$2.50	$5.00	£0.30	£1.00	£2.00
156-161	$0.80	$2.50	$5.00	£0.30	£1.00	£2.00
162 (Jan 1974)	$0.80	$2.50	$5.00	£0.30	£1.00	£2.00
163	$0.80	$2.50	$5.00	£0.30	£1.00	£2.00
Title Value:	$2090.60	$6244.00	$16497.00	£1320.45	£3972.55	£10589.50

REPRINT FEATURES

Jimmy Olsen/Superman in 95, 104, 113, 122, 131, 140. Newsboy Legion by Simon & Kirby in 141-148.

JINX

Caliber Press; 1 Mar 1996-present

	$Good	$Fine	$N.Mint	£Good	£Fine	£N.Mint
1-5 ND Brian Michael Bendis script and art; black and white	$0.60	$1.80	$3.00	£0.40	£1.20	£2.00
Title Value:	$3.00	$9.00	$15.00	£2.00	£6.00	£10.00

JLA

DC Comics; 1 Jan 1997-present

	$Good	$Fine	$N.Mint	£Good	£Fine	£N.Mint
1 ND Superman, Batman, Wonder Woman, Flash, Green Lantern, Aquaman, Martian Manhunter begin; Grant Morrison script, Howard Porter and John Dell art	$1.00	$3.00	$5.00	£0.40	£1.20	£2.00
2-3 ND	$0.40	$1.20	$2.00	£0.25	£0.75	£1.25
Title Value:	$1.80	$5.40	$9.00	£0.90	£2.70	£4.50

JLX

DC Comics/Amalgam,OS; 1 May 1996

	$Good	$Fine	$N.Mint	£Good	£Fine	£N.Mint
1 ND a DC/Marvel amalgamation of the Justice League and the X-Men; Mark Waid and Gerard Jones script, Howard Porter and John Dell art	$0.50	$1.50	$2.50	£0.40	£1.20	£2.00
Title Value:	$0.50	$1.50	$2.50	£0.40	£1.20	£2.00

JOE R. LANSDALE'S BY BIZARRE HANDS

Dark Horse; 1 Mar 1994-3 1994

	$Good	$Fine	$N.Mint	£Good	£Fine	£N.Mint
1-3 ND black and white	$0.50	$1.50	$2.50	£0.30	£0.90	£1.50
Title Value:	$1.50	$4.50	$7.50	£0.90	£2.70	£4.50

JOE SINN

Caliber Press,MS; 1 Aug 1993-3 1993

	$Good	$Fine	$N.Mint	£Good	£Fine	£N.Mint
1-3 ND black and white	$0.50	$1.50	$2.50	£0.30	£0.90	£1.50
Title Value:	$1.50	$4.50	$7.50	£0.90	£2.70	£4.50

JOHN BOLTON HALLS OF HORROR

Eclipse,MS; 1,2 Jun 1985

	$Good	$Fine	$N.Mint	£Good	£Fine	£N.Mint
1-2 ND reprints	$0.40	$1.20	$2.00	£0.25	£0.75	£1.25
Title Value:	$0.80	$2.40	$4.00	£0.50	£1.50	£2.50

JOHN BYRNE'S 2112 GRAPHIC NOVEL

Dark Horse,OS; 1 Nov 1991

	$Good	$Fine	$N.Mint	£Good	£Fine	£N.Mint
1 ND 64pgs, John Byrne script and art, ties in with Next Men, squarebound	$2.00	$6.00	$10.00	£1.40	£4.20	£7.00
1 2nd printing, ND (Nov 1993)	$2.00	$6.00	$10.00	£1.30	£3.90	£6.50
1 3rd printing ND	$2.00	$6.00	$10.00	£1.30	£3.90	£6.50
Title Value:	$6.00	$18.00	$30.00	£4.00	£12.00	£20.00
Hardcover Limited Edition (Nov 1991), one copy issued free to retailers with every 100 copies of the regular graphic novel ordered. Diamond Distributors and Dark Horse silver stamps on cover.				£15.00	£45.00	£75.00

JOHN CARTER OF MARS

Gold Key; 1 Apr 1964-3 Oct 1964

	$Good	$Fine	$N.Mint	£Good	£Fine	£N.Mint
1 distributed in the U.K. reprints	$5.50	$17.00	$40.00	£2.85	£8.50	£20.00
2-3 distributed in the U.K. reprints	$4.25	$12.50	$30.00	£2.10	£6.25	£15.00
Title Value:	$14.00	$42.00	$100.00	£7.05	£21.00	£50.00

JOHN CARTER, WARLORD OF MARS

Marvel Comics Group; 1 Jun 1977-28 Oct 1979

	$Good	$Fine	$N.Mint	£Good	£Fine	£N.Mint
1 ND origin, Gil Kane art begins	$0.65	$2.00	$4.00	£0.25	£0.75	£1.50
2-10 ND Gil Kane art	$0.50	$1.50	$3.00	£0.20	£0.60	£1.25
11 ND origin Dejah Thoris	$0.30	$1.00	$2.00	£0.20	£0.60	£1.25
12-14 ND	$0.30	$1.00	$2.00	£0.20	£0.60	£1.25
15 ND Walt Simonson art	$0.30	$1.00	$2.00	£0.20	£0.60	£1.25
16-17 ND	$0.30	$1.00	$2.00	£0.20	£0.60	£1.25
18 ND Frank Miller's first published work for Marvel (see Hulk Annual #11)	$0.40	$1.25	$2.50	£0.30	£1.00	£2.00
19-28 ND	$0.30	$1.00	$2.00	£0.20	£0.60	£1.25
Title Value:	$10.65	$33.75	$61.00	£5.75	£17.35	£36.00

JOHN CARTER, WARLORD OF MARS ANNUAL

Marvel Comics Group; 1 Oct 1977-3 Oct 1979

	$Good	$Fine	$N.Mint	£Good	£Fine	£N.Mint
1-3 ND 52pgs	$0.40	$1.25	$2.50	£0.25	£0.75	£1.50
Title Value:	$1.20	$3.75	$6.50	£0.75	£2.25	£4.50

JOHN FORCE MAGIC AGENT

(see Magic Agent)

JOHN LAW, DETECTIVE

Eclipse; 1 Apr 1981

	$Good	$Fine	$N.Mint	£Good	£Fine	£N.Mint
1 ND previously unpublished Eisner work in colour	$0.40	$1.20	$2.00	£0.25	£0.75	£1.25
Title Value:	$0.40	$1.20	$2.00	£0.25	£0.75	£1.25

JOHN PAIN SPECIAL

Blackball Comics; 1 Aug 1994

	$Good	$Fine	$N.Mint	£Good	£Fine	£N.Mint
1 ND Kev O'Neill art, Mike Mignola pin-up	$0.60	$1.80	$3.00	£0.40	£1.20	£2.00
Title Value:	$0.60	$1.80	$3.00	£0.40	£1.20	£2.00

JOHN STEED AND EMMA PEEL

(see Avengers)

JOHN STEELE SECRET AGENT

Gold Key; 1 Dec 1964

(see Freedom Agent)

	$Good	$Fine	$N.Mint	£Good	£Fine	£N.Mint
1 scarce, distributed in the U.K.	$10.50	$32.00	$75.00	£6.25	£19.00	£45.00
Title Value:	$10.50	$32.00	$75.00	£6.25	£19.00	£45.00

JOHNNY ATOMIC

Eternity,MS; 1 Oct 1991

	$Good	$Fine	$N.Mint	£Good	£Fine	£N.Mint
1 ND (cancelled after 1 issue)	$1.00	$3.00	$5.00	£0.70	£2.10	£3.50
Title Value:	$1.00	$3.00	$5.00	£0.70	£2.10	£3.50

JOHNNY DEMON

Dark Horse,MS; 1 May 1994-3 Jul 1994

	$Good	$Fine	$N.Mint	£Good	£Fine	£N.Mint
1-3 ND Steve Leialoha cover	$0.50	$1.50	$2.50	£0.30	£0.90	£1.50
Title Value:	$1.50	$4.50	$7.50	£0.90	£2.70	£4.50

JOHNNY DYNAMITE

Dark Horse,MS; 1 Sep 1994-4 Dec 1994

	$Good	$Fine	$N.Mint	£Good	£Fine	£N.Mint
1-4 ND Max Allan Collins and Terry Beatty	$0.60	$1.80	$3.00	£0.40	£1.20	£2.00
Title Value:	$2.40	$7.20	$12.00	£1.60	£4.80	£8.00

JOHNNY NEMO MAGAZINE, THE

Eclipse; 1 Sep 1985-3 Feb 1986

(see Paradax, Strange Days)

	$Good	$Fine	$N.Mint	£Good	£Fine	£N.Mint
1-3 ND sub-titled "Strange Days present", Milligan/Brett Ewins art, colour	$1.00	$3.00	$5.00	£0.70	£2.10	£3.50
Title Value:	$3.00	$9.00	$15.00	£2.10	£6.30	£10.50

Note: originally announced as a 6 issue mini-series.

JOHNNY THUNDER

DC Comics; 1 Feb/Mar 1973-3 Jul/Aug 1973

(see All-Star Western, DC Comics Presents 28)

	$Good	$Fine	$N.Mint	£Good	£Fine	£N.Mint
1 scarce in the U.K. Alex Toth and Dan Barry art, Toth cover; reprints begin from All American Western	$0.40	$1.25	$2.50	£0.30	£1.00	£2.00
2-3	$0.40	$1.25	$2.50	£0.25	£0.75	£1.50
Title Value:	$1.20	$3.75	$7.50	£0.80	£2.50	£5.00

REPRINT FEATURES

Johnny Thunder, Nighthawk in 1-3. Trigger Twins in 2.

JOKER, THE

DC Comics; 1 May/Jun 1975-9 Sep/Oct 1976

(see Brave and the Bold, DC Comics Presents)

	$Good	$Fine	$N.Mint	£Good	£Fine	£N.Mint
1 Two Face appears	$2.50	$7.50	$15.00	£1.50	£4.50	£9.00
2	$1.50	$4.50	$9.00	£1.00	£3.00	£6.00
3 The Creeper appears	$1.25	$3.75	$7.50	£0.80	£2.50	£5.00
4 scarce in the U.K. Green Arrow appears	$1.15	$3.50	$7.00	£1.00	£3.00	£6.00
5 scarce in the U.K. Royal Flush Gang appears	$1.15	$3.50	$7.00	£1.00	£3.00	£6.00
6 scarce in the U.K. Sherlock Holmes appears	$1.15	$3.50	$7.00	£1.00	£3.00	£6.00
7 Lex Luthor appears	$1.00	$3.00	$6.00	£0.80	£2.50	£5.00
8 scarce in the U.K. Scarecrow appears	$1.00	$3.00	$6.00	£1.00	£3.00	£6.00
9 very scarce in the U.K. Catwoman appears	$1.00	$3.00	$6.00	£1.15	£3.50	£7.00

	$Good	$Fine	$N.Mint	£Good	£Fine	£N.Mint
Title Value:	*$11.70*	*$35.25*	*$70.50*	£9.25	£28.00	£56.00
Note: Garcia Lopez art in #2-4						
JOKER: DEVIL'S ADVOCATE, THE						
DC Comics,OS; nn Jan 1996; Nov 1996						
nn Hardcover ND 96pgs, Chuck Dixon script, Graham Nolan and Scott Hanna art	*$5.00*	*$15.00*	*$25.00*	£3.20	£9.50	£16.00
nn Softcover ND 96pgs, (Nov 1996)	*$2.60*	*$7.75*	*$13.00*	£1.70	£5.00	£8.50
Title Value:	*$7.60*	*$22.75*	*$38.00*	£4.90	£14.50	£24.50
JOKER: GREATEST STORIES EVER TOLD.						
DC Comics; nn 1989, 1990						
nn Hardover ND (1989) classic reprints	*$6.00*	*$18.00*	*$30.00*	£4.00	£12.00	£20.00
nn Hardover Expanded Edition ND (1990) expanded edition with extra stories, leather bound	*$9.00*	*$27.00*	*$45.00*	£6.00	£18.00	£30.00
nn Softcover ND	*$4.00*	*$12.00*	*$20.00*	£2.50	£7.50	£12.50
Title Value:	*$19.00*	*$57.00*	*$95.00*	£12.50	£37.50	£62.50
JON SABLE, FREELANCE						
First; 1 Jun 1983-56 Feb 1988						
(see Mike Grell's Sable)						
1 ND	*$0.40*	*$1.20*	*$2.00*	£0.25	£0.75	£1.25
2-24 ND	*$0.30*	*$0.90*	*$1.50*	£0.20	£0.60	£1.00
25 ND 1st Shatter backup, ends #30	*$0.30*	*$0.90*	*$1.50*	£0.20	£0.60	£1.00
26-33 ND	*$0.30*	*$0.90*	*$1.50*	£0.20	£0.60	£1.00
34-56 ND Deluxe Format	*$0.40*	*$1.20*	*$2.00*	£0.25	£0.75	£1.25
Title Value:	*$19.20*	*$57.60*	*$96.00*	£12.40	£37.20	£62.00
Note: Mike Grell art in #1-43.						
JONAH HEX						
DC Comics; 1 Mar/Apr 1977-92 Aug 1985						
(see All-Star Western, Weird Western Tales, Hex)						
1 scarce in the U.K.	*$5.50*	*$17.00*	*$40.00*	£4.25	£12.50	£30.00
2 scarce in the U.K.	*$2.50*	*$7.50*	*$15.00*	£1.65	£5.00	£10.00
3-5 scarce in the U.K.	*$2.00*	*$6.00*	*$12.00*	£1.25	£3.75	£7.50
6 scarce in the U.K.	*$2.00*	*$6.00*	*$12.00*	£0.80	£2.50	£5.00
7-8 scarce in the U.K. dis-figurement explained	*$2.00*	*$6.00*	*$12.00*	£0.80	£2.50	£5.00
9 scarce in the U.K. Wrightson cover	*$2.00*	*$6.00*	*$12.00*	£0.80	£2.50	£5.00
10	*$2.00*	*$6.00*	*$12.00*	£0.75	£2.25	£4.50
11	*$1.25*	*$3.75*	*$7.50*	£0.55	£1.75	£3.50
12 Jim Starlin cover	*$1.25*	*$3.75*	*$7.50*	£0.55	£1.75	£3.50
13-15	*$1.25*	*$3.75*	*$7.50*	£0.55	£1.75	£3.50
16-17 ND 44pgs	*$1.25*	*$3.75*	*$7.50*	£0.65	£2.00	£4.00
18-20 ND 44pgs	*$1.25*	*$3.75*	*$7.50*	£0.55	£1.75	£3.50
21-30 ND	*$1.00*	*$3.00*	*$5.00*	£0.60	£1.80	£3.00
31-32 ND origin retold	*$1.00*	*$3.00*	*$5.00*	£0.50	£1.50	£2.50
33-35 ND	*$1.00*	*$3.00*	*$5.00*	£0.50	£1.50	£2.50
36-44 ND	*$1.00*	*$3.00*	*$5.00*	£0.40	£1.20	£2.00
45 ND Jonah Hex weds	*$1.00*	*$3.00*	*$5.00*	£0.40	£1.20	£2.00
46-50 ND	*$1.00*	*$3.00*	*$5.00*	£0.40	£1.20	£2.00
51 ND Jonah Hex becomes a father	*$0.80*	*$2.40*	*$4.00*	£0.30	£0.90	£1.50
52-89 ND	*$0.80*	*$2.40*	*$4.00*	£0.30	£0.90	£1.50
90 Mark Texeira cover	*$0.70*	*$2.10*	*$3.50*	£0.30	£0.90	£1.50
91-92	*$0.70*	*$2.10*	*$3.50*	£0.30	£0.90	£1.50
Title Value:	*$99.80*	*$299.90*	*$538.00*	£46.40	£140.30	£258.50
FEATURES						
Bat Lash in 49, 51, 52. El Diablo in 48, 56-60. Scalphunter in 40, 41, 45-47. Tejano in 53-55.						
JONAH HEX AND OTHER WESTERN TALES						
DC Comics,Digest; 1 Sep/Oct 1979-3 Jan/Feb 1980						
1-3 scarce in the U.K. 100pgs	*$0.40*	*$1.25*	*$2.50*	£0.30	£1.00	£2.00
Title Value:	*$1.20*	*$3.75*	*$7.50*	£0.90	£3.00	£6.00
ARTISTS						
Adams reprints in 1, 2.						
REPRINT FEATURES						
Billy the Kid, El Diablo in 1, 2. Outlaw in 3. Jonah Hex, Scalphunter in 1-3.						
JONAH HEX SPECTACULAR						
DC Comics; nn Fall 1978						
(DC Special Series #16)						
nn ND scarce in the U.K. 68pgs, Jonah Hex dies, Scalphunter and Batlash appear	*$1.00*	*$3.00*	*$6.00*	£0.80	£2.50	£5.00
Title Value:	*$1.00*	*$3.00*	*$6.00*	£0.80	£2.50	£5.00
JONAH HEX: RIDERS OF THE WORM & SUCH						
DC Comics,MS; 1 Mar 1995-5 Jul 1995						
1-5 ND Joe R. Lansdale script, Tim Truman and Sam Glanzman art	*$0.60*	*$1.80*	*$3.00*	£0.40	£1.20	£2.00
Title Value:	*$3.00*	*$9.00*	*$15.00*	£2.00	£6.00	£10.00
JONAH HEX: TWO-GUN MOJO						
Vertigo,MS; 1 Aug 1993-5 Dec 1993						
1 ND Tim Truman art begins	*$1.20*	*$3.60*	*$6.00*	£0.60	£1.80	£3.00
1 Platinum Edition ND	*$3.00*	*$9.00*	*$15.00*	£1.50	£4.50	£7.50
2 ND	*$0.80*	*$2.40*	*$4.00*	£0.50	£1.50	£2.50
3-5 ND	*$0.70*	*$2.10*	*$3.50*	£0.40	£1.20	£2.00

	$Good	$Fine	$N.Mint	£Good	£Fine	£N.Mint
Title Value:	*$7.10*	*$21.30*	*$35.50*	£3.80	£11.40	£19.00
Jonah Hex: Two-Gun Mojo (Oct 1994) Trade paperback reprints mini-series, new painted cover by Tim Truman				£1.70	£5.10	£8.50
JONNI THUNDER						
DC Comics,MS; 1 Feb 1985-4 Aug 1985						
1-4	*$0.20*	*$0.60*	*$1.00*	£0.15	£0.45	£0.75
Title Value:	*$0.80*	*$2.40*	*$4.00*	£0.60	£1.80	£3.00
JONNY QUEST						
Gold Key,OS TV; 1 Dec 1964						
1 scarce though distributed in the U.K.	*$46.00*	*$135.00*	*$325.00*	£29.00	£85.00	£200.00
Title Value:	*$46.00*	*$135.00*	*$325.00*	£29.00	£85.00	£200.00
JONNY QUEST (2ND SERIES)						
Comico; 1 Jun 1986-31 Dec 1988						
1 ND Doug Wildey art	*$1.00*	*$3.00*	*$5.00*	£0.40	£1.20	£2.00
2 ND Wendi Pini art, Pini/Rude cover	*$0.60*	*$1.80*	*$3.00*	£0.30	£0.90	£1.50
3 ND Dave Stevens cover	*$0.60*	*$1.80*	*$3.00*	£0.30	£0.90	£1.50
4 ND	*$0.40*	*$1.20*	*$2.00*	£0.25	£0.75	£1.25
5 ND Dave Stevens cover	*$0.40*	*$1.20*	*$2.00*	£0.25	£0.75	£1.25
6 ND Adam Kubert cover and art	*$0.40*	*$1.20*	*$2.00*	£0.25	£0.75	£1.25
7 ND Dan Spiegle art, Doug Wildey cover	*$0.40*	*$1.20*	*$2.00*	£0.25	£0.75	£1.25
8 ND Ken Steacy painted cover	*$0.40*	*$1.20*	*$2.00*	£0.25	£0.75	£1.25
9 ND Murphy Anderson art, Truman cover	*$0.40*	*$1.20*	*$2.00*	£0.25	£0.75	£1.25
10 ND	*$0.40*	*$1.20*	*$2.00*	£0.25	£0.75	£1.25
11 ND Bandit solo story, Staton art, Sienkiewicz cover	*$0.30*	*$0.90*	*$1.50*	£0.20	£0.60	£1.00
12 ND Dan Spiegle art	*$0.30*	*$0.90*	*$1.50*	£0.20	£0.60	£1.00
13 ND Carmine Infantino art	*$0.30*	*$0.90*	*$1.50*	£0.20	£0.60	£1.00
14-31 ND	*$0.30*	*$0.90*	*$1.50*	£0.20	£0.60	£1.00
Title Value:	*$11.30*	*$33.90*	*$56.50*	£6.95	£20.85	£34.75
JONNY QUEST CLASSICS						
Comico; 1 May 1987-3 Jul 1987						
1-3 ND Doug Wildey cover and art	*$0.50*	*$1.50*	*$2.50*	£0.30	£0.90	£1.50
Title Value:	*$1.50*	*$4.50*	*$7.50*	£0.90	£2.70	£4.50
JONNY QUEST SPECIAL						
Comico; 1 Sep 1988-2 Oct 1988						
1-2 ND	*$0.40*	*$1.20*	*$2.00*	£0.25	£0.75	£1.25
Title Value:	*$0.80*	*$2.40*	*$4.00*	£0.50	£1.50	£2.50
JONTAR RETURNS						
Miller Publishing; 1-2 1990						
1-2 ND black and white	*$0.15*	*$0.45*	*$0.75*	£0.10	£0.30	£0.50
Title Value:	*$0.30*	*$0.90*	*$1.50*	£0.20	£0.60	£1.00
JOURNEY						
Aardvark/Fantagraphics; 1 Mar 1983-27 July 1986						
1 ND scarce in the U.K.	*$1.00*	*$3.00*	*$5.00*	£0.60	£1.80	£3.00
2 ND	*$0.60*	*$1.80*	*$3.00*	£0.40	£1.20	£2.00
3-6 ND	*$0.50*	*$1.50*	*$2.50*	£0.30	£0.90	£1.50
7-10 ND	*$0.30*	*$0.90*	*$1.50*	£0.25	£0.75	£1.25
11-13 ND	*$0.30*	*$0.90*	*$1.50*	£0.20	£0.60	£1.00
14 ND 44pgs	*$0.40*	*$1.20*	*$2.00*	£0.25	£0.75	£1.25
15-27 ND Fantagraphics issues	*$0.30*	*$0.90*	*$1.50*	£0.20	£0.60	£1.00
Title Value:	*$10.00*	*$30.00*	*$48.00*	£6.65	£19.95	£33.25
Journey Saga: Tall Tales, Trade paperback reprints #1-4 plus backups from Cerebus				£1.00	£3.00	£5.00
Book 2				£1.10	£3.30	£5.50
JOURNEY INTO MYSTERY						
Atlas/Marvel Comics Group; 1 Jun 1952-125 Feb 1966						
(becomes Thor)						
1 very scarce in the U.K.	*$250.00*	*$750.00*	*$2500.00*	£175.00	£520.00	£1750.00
2 very scarce in the U.K.	*$90.00*	*$270.00*	*$725.00*	£62.50	£185.00	£500.00
3-4 very scarce in the U.K.	*$67.50*	*$205.00*	*$550.00*	£46.00	£135.00	£370.00
5 very scarce in the U.K.	*$50.00*	*$150.00*	*$400.00*	£35.00	£105.00	£280.00
6-10 scarce in the U.K.	*$44.00*	*$130.00*	*$350.00*	£30.00	£90.00	£240.00
11-20	*$36.00*	*$105.00*	*$290.00*	£25.00	£75.00	£200.00
21 Kubert art	*$36.00*	*$105.00*	*$290.00*	£25.00	£75.00	£200.00
22 last pre-code issue	*$36.00*	*$105.00*	*$290.00*	£25.00	£75.00	£200.00
23-30	*$22.50*	*$67.50*	*$180.00*	£15.00	£45.00	£120.00
31-32	*$21.00*	*$62.50*	*$170.00*	£14.00	£43.00	£115.00
33 Ditko, Williamson art	*$24.00*	*$72.50*	*$195.00*	£16.00	£49.00	£130.00
34 Krigstein art	*$21.00*	*$62.50*	*$170.00*	£14.00	£43.00	£115.00
35-38	*$21.00*	*$62.50*	*$170.00*	£14.00	£43.00	£115.00

	$Good	$Fine	$N.Mint	£Good	£Fine	£N.Mint
39 Wood art	***$21.00***	***$62.50***	***$170.00***	£14.00	£43.00	£115.00
40	***$21.00***	***$62.50***	***$170.00***	£14.00	£43.00	£115.00
41 Reed Crandall art	***$21.00***	***$62.50***	***$170.00***	£14.00	£43.00	£115.00
42-50	***$20.00***	***$60.00***	***$160.00***	£13.50	£41.00	£110.00
51 Jack Kirby, Wally Wood art	***$25.00***	***$75.00***	***$200.00***	£16.50	£50.00	£135.00
52-57	***$18.00***	***$52.50***	***$145.00***	£11.50	£36.00	£95.00
1st official distribution in the U.K.						
58 cover similar to Fantastic Four #1 (was F.F. #1 based on this?)	***$18.00***	***$52.50***	***$145.00***	£11.00	£34.00	£90.00
59-61	***$18.00***	***$52.50***	***$145.00***	£11.00	£34.00	£90.00
62 1st appearance of Xemnu, called "The Hulk"	***$25.00***	***$75.00***	***$200.00***	£16.50	£50.00	£135.00
63-65	***$16.50***	***$50.00***	***$135.00***	£11.00	£34.00	£90.00
66 return of Xemnu, "The Hulk"	***$22.50***	***$67.50***	***$180.00***	£15.00	£45.00	£120.00
67-69	***$15.50***	***$47.00***	***$125.00***	£10.50	£32.00	£85.00
70 possible Sandman (Spiderman villain) prototype	***$17.50***	***$52.50***	***$140.00***	£10.50	£32.00	£85.00
71-72	***$15.50***	***$47.00***	***$125.00***	£10.50	£32.00	£85.00
73 possible Spiderman prototype - stronger similarities than most of these so-called prototypes	***$31.00***	***$92.50***	***$250.00***	£18.50	£55.00	£150.00
74	***$15.50***	***$47.00***	***$125.00***	£10.50	£32.00	£85.00
75 last 10 cents issue	***$15.50***	***$47.00***	***$125.00***	£10.50	£32.00	£85.00
76-77	***$14.00***	***$43.00***	***$115.00***	£9.25	£28.00	£75.00
78 features a young sorceror called Aaron who escapes from another dimension but loses his powers - Dr. Strange prototype? (see Strange Tales #79 and Tales of Suspense #32)	***$21.00***	***$62.50***	***$190.00***	£12.50	£38.00	£115.00
79 possible Mr. Hyde prototype	***$14.00***	***$43.00***	***$115.00***	£9.25	£28.00	£75.00
80-82	***$14.00***	***$43.00***	***$115.00***	£9.25	£28.00	£75.00
83 origin and 1st appearance of Thor by Stan Lee and Jack Kirby; Thor vs. The Stone Men from Saturn	***$380.00***	***$1150.00***	***$4600.00***	£245.00	£730.00	£2950.00
[Scarce in high grade - Very Fine+ or better]						
83 Reprint, ND very scarce in the U.K. (1966)	***$18.50***	***$55.00***	***$150.00***	£12.50	£38.00	£100.00
83 Reprint with Golden Record, ND very rare in the U.K to form complete sealed package	***$25.00***	***$75.00***	***$200.00***	£16.50	£50.00	£135.00
84 scarce in the U.K. 2nd appearance Thor	***$110.00***	***$330.00***	***$1100.00***	£70.00	£210.00	£700.00
[Scarce in high grade - Very Fine+ or better]						
85 1st appearance Loki, 1st appearance Heimdal, 1st appearance Odin (cameo)	***$77.50***	***$230.00***	***$625.00***	£50.00	£150.00	£400.00
86 1st full appearance Odin	***$48.00***	***$140.00***	***$380.00***	£28.00	£82.50	£225.00
87-88	***$33.00***	***$97.50***	***$260.00***	£20.00	£60.00	£160.00
89 reprints origin from #83	***$33.00***	***$97.50***	***$260.00***	£20.00	£60.00	£160.00
90 less common in the U.K. Steve Ditko art (note: no Jack Kirby art)	***$18.50***	***$55.00***	***$150.00***	£11.00	£34.00	£90.00
91 scarce in the U.K. Joe Sinnott art	***$16.00***	***$49.00***	***$130.00***	£10.50	£32.00	£85.00
92 Joe Sinnott art	***$16.00***	***$49.00***	***$130.00***	£10.00	£30.00	£80.00
93 Jack Kirby art	***$20.00***	***$60.00***	***$160.00***	£11.00	£34.00	£90.00
94-96 Joe Sinnott art	***$16.00***	***$49.00***	***$130.00***	£10.00	£30.00	£80.00
97 1st appearance Lava Man, Jack Kirby ar; "Tales of Asgard" begins, ends #125	***$21.00***	***$62.50***	***$170.00***	£11.00	£34.00	£90.00
98 1st appearance Cobra (first called Human Cobra later simply Cobra)	***$16.00***	***$49.00***	***$130.00***	£10.00	£30.00	£80.00
99 1st appearance Surtur, 1st appearance Mr.Hyde	***$16.00***	***$49.00***	***$130.00***	£10.00	£30.00	£80.00
100 less common in the U.K.	***$16.00***	***$49.00***	***$130.00***	£10.50	£32.00	£85.00
101 less common in the U.K. Avengers X-over	***$12.50***	***$39.00***	***$90.00***	£7.00	£21.00	£50.00
102 less common in the U.K. 1st appearance Lady Sif	***$12.50***	***$39.00***	***$90.00***	£7.00	£21.00	£50.00
103 1st appearance The Enchantress and The Executioner	***$12.50***	***$39.00***	***$90.00***	£7.00	£21.00	£50.00
104	***$12.50***	***$39.00***	***$90.00***	£7.00	£21.00	£50.00
105-106 Jack Kirby art	***$12.50***	***$39.00***	***$90.00***	£7.00	£21.00	£50.00
107 1st appearance Grey Gargoyle	***$12.50***	***$39.00***	***$90.00***	£7.00	£21.00	£50.00
108 Dr. Strange, Avengers appear; Jack Kirby art	***$12.50***	***$39.00***	***$90.00***	£7.00	£21.00	£50.00
109 very rare in the U.K. (historically so, though the situation is being monitored); Magneto/Scarlet Witch/Quicksilver appear; Magneto cover appearance and 1st X-over into title; Jack Kirby art	***$15.50***	***$47.00***	***$125.00***	£11.00	£34.00	£90.00
[Scarce in high grade - Very Fine+ or better]						
110 scarce in the U.K.	***$12.50***	***$39.00***	***$90.00***	£7.00	£21.00	£50.00
111 scarce in the U.K.	***$10.50***	***$32.00***	***$75.00***	£6.25	£19.00	£45.00
112 very scarce in the U.K. Thor vs. Hulk, origin Loki	***$21.00***	***$62.50***	***$170.00***	£12.50	£38.00	£100.00
113 origin Loki	***$10.50***	***$32.00***	***$75.00***	£6.00	£18.00	£42.50
114	***$10.50***	***$32.00***	***$75.00***	£6.00	£18.00	£42.50
115 origin Loki retold, reveals more facts about origin	***$13.50***	***$41.00***	***$95.00***	£6.25	£19.00	£45.00
116-117	***$10.50***	***$32.00***	***$75.00***	£5.50	£17.00	£40.00
118 1st appearance Destroyer	***$10.50***	***$32.00***	***$75.00***	£5.50	£17.00	£40.00
119 1st appearance Hogun, Fandrall, Volstagg (Warriors Three)	***$10.50***	***$32.00***	***$75.00***	£5.50	£17.00	£40.00
120	***$10.50***	***$32.00***	***$75.00***	£5.50	£17.00	£40.00
121-122	***$10.00***	***$30.00***	***$70.00***	£5.00	£15.00	£35.00
123 last Silver Age issue cover dated December 1965	***$10.00***	***$30.00***	***$70.00***	£5.00	£15.00	£35.00
124 Hercules appears	***$10.00***	***$30.00***	***$70.00***	£5.00	£15.00	£35.00
125 Hercules appears, lead into Thor #126	***$10.00***	***$30.00***	***$70.00***	£5.00	£15.00	£35.00
Title Value:	***$3577.00***	***$10704.00***	***$30815.00***	£2336.00	£7035.50	£20185.00

ARTISTS

Kirby (Thor) art in 83-89, 93, 97, 101-125.

JOURNEY INTO MYSTERY (2ND SERIES)

Marvel Comics Group; 1 Oct 1972-19 Oct 1975

	$Good	$Fine	$N.Mint	£Good	£Fine	£N.Mint
1 ND Gil Kane cover and art on Robert E. Howard adaptation, Jim Starlin art (6pgs)	***$1.15***	***$3.50***	***$7.00***	£0.65	£2.00	£4.00
2 ND Gil Kane art	***$0.55***	***$1.75***	***$3.50***	£0.40	£1.25	£2.50
3 ND Jim Starlin art	***$0.55***	***$1.75***	***$3.50***	£0.40	£1.25	£2.50
4 ND H.P.Lovecraft adaptation	***$0.50***	***$1.50***	***$3.00***	£0.30	£1.00	£2.00
5 ND last new material	***$0.40***	***$1.25***	***$2.50***	£0.25	£0.75	£1.50
6 ND horror/mystery reprints begin	***$0.40***	***$1.25***	***$2.50***	£0.25	£0.75	£1.50

Jimmy Olsen #5

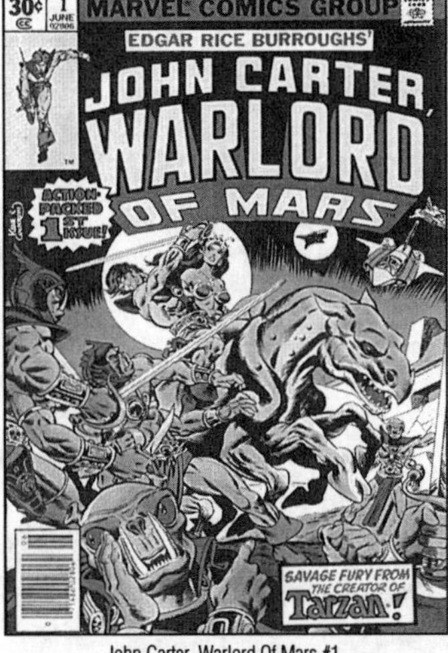

John Carter, Warlord Of Mars #1

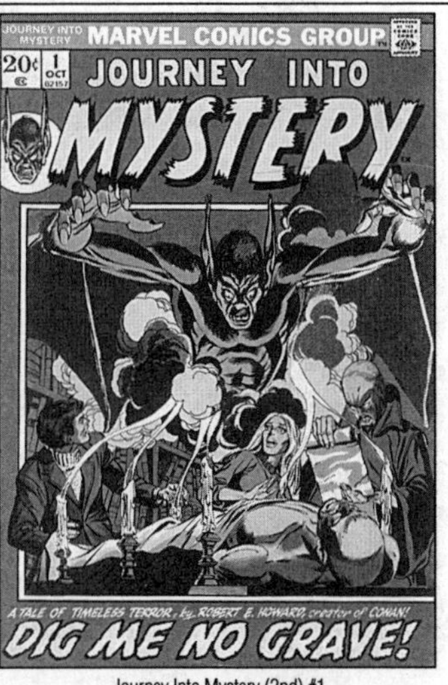

Journey Into Mystery (2nd) #1

	$Good	$Fine	$N.Mint	£Good	£Fine	£N.Mint
7-11 ND	$0.40	$1.25	$2.50	£0.25	£0.75	£1.50
12-18	$0.40	$1.25	$2.50	£0.20	£0.60	£1.25
19 ND scarce in the U.K.	$0.40	$1.25	$2.50	£0.25	£0.75	£1.50
Title Value:	$8.75	$27.25	$54.50	£5.15	£15.70	£31.75

JOURNEY INTO MYSTERY (3RD SERIES)

Marvel Comics Group;503 Nov 1996-present

	$Good	$Fine	$N.Mint	£Good	£Fine	£N.Mint
503 ND Tom DeFalco script, Mike Deodato Jnr. art begins	$0.30	$0.90	$1.50	£0.20	£0.60	£1.00
504 ND	$0.30	$0.90	$1.50	£0.20	£0.60	£1.00
505 ND Spiderman appears	$0.30	$0.90	$1.50	£0.20	£0.60	£1.00
506 ND	$0.30	$0.90	$1.50	£0.20	£0.60	£1.00
507 ND	$0.40	$1.20	$2.00	£0.25	£0.75	£1.25
Title Value:	$1.60	$4.80	$8.00	£1.05	£3.15	£5.25

JOURNEY INTO MYSTERY ANNUAL

Marvel Comics Group; 1 1965
(becomes Thor Annual)

	$Good	$Fine	$N.Mint	£Good	£Fine	£N.Mint
1 68pgs, 1st appearance Hercules, Thor vs. Hercules; Jack Kirby art	$20.00	$60.00	$160.00	£11.00	£34.00	£90.00
[Scarce in high grade - Very Fine+ or better]						
Title Value:	$20.00	$60.00	$160.00	£11.00	£34.00	£90.00

JOURNEY: WARDRUMS

Fantagraphics; 1 May 1987; 2 Oct 1990; 3 Sep 1991

	$Good	$Fine	$N.Mint	£Good	£Fine	£N.Mint
1-3 ND printed in sepia	$0.40	$1.20	$2.00	£0.25	£0.75	£1.25
Title Value:	$1.20	$3.60	$6.00	£0.75	£2.25	£3.75

JUDGE DREDD

DC Comics; 1 Aug 1994-18 Jan 1996

	$Good	$Fine	$N.Mint	£Good	£Fine	£N.Mint
1 ND Andrew Helfer and Mike Oeming creative team	$0.40	$1.20	$2.00	£0.30	£0.90	£1.50
2-10 ND	$0.40	$1.20	$2.00	£0.25	£0.75	£1.25
11-18 ND	$0.45	$1.35	$2.25	£0.30	£0.90	£1.50
Title Value:	$7.60	$22.80	$38.00	£4.95	£14.85	£24.75

JUDGE DREDD

(see British section for Eagle and Quality series)

JUDGE DREDD: LEGENDS OF THE LAW

DC Comics; 1 Dec 1994-13 Dec 1995

	$Good	$Fine	$N.Mint	£Good	£Fine	£N.Mint
1 ND Alan Grant and John Wagner script, Brent Anderson and Jimmy Palmiotti art. Painted cover by Dave Dorman	$0.40	$1.20	$2.00	£0.25	£0.75	£1.25
2-4 ND painted cover by Dave Dorman	$0.40	$1.20	$2.00	£0.25	£0.75	£1.25
5-6 ND painted cover by John Higgins	$0.40	$1.20	$2.00	£0.25	£0.75	£1.25
7 ND painted cover by John Higgins	$0.45	$1.35	$2.25	£0.30	£0.90	£1.50
8-10 ND John Byrne script	$0.45	$1.35	$2.25	£0.30	£0.90	£1.50
11-13 ND John Byrne cover	$0.45	$1.35	$2.25	£0.30	£0.90	£1.50
Title Value:	$5.55	$16.65	$27.75	£3.60	£10.80	£18.00

JUDGE DREDD: THE OFFICIAL MOVIE ADAPTATION

DC Comics,Film; nn Aug 1995

	$Good	$Fine	$N.Mint	£Good	£Fine	£N.Mint
nn ND 64pgs, Andrew Helfer script, Carlos Esquerra art	$1.20	$3.60	$6.00	£0.80	£2.40	£4.00
Title Value:	$1.20	$3.60	$6.00	£0.80	£2.40	£4.00

JUDGEMENT DAY

Lightning Comics; 1 Nov 1993-8 Apr 1994

	$Good	$Fine	$N.Mint	£Good	£Fine	£N.Mint
1 ND gold prism cover	$0.90	$2.70	$4.50	£0.60	£1.80	£3.00
2 ND pre-bagged with trading card	$0.60	$1.80	$3.00	£0.40	£1.20	£2.00
2 Signed & Numbered Edition ND	$1.80	$5.25	$9.00	£1.20	£3.60	£6.00
3-8 ND	$0.60	$1.80	$3.00	£0.40	£1.20	£2.00
Title Value:	$6.90	$20.55	$34.50	£4.60	£13.80	£23.00

JUDO MASTER

Charlton;89 May/Jun 1966-98 Dec 1967
(see Special War Series) (previously Gunmaster)

	$Good	$Fine	$N.Mint	£Good	£Fine	£N.Mint
89 distributed in the U.K. Judo Master vs. Mountain Storm; Frank McLaughlin art begins	$3.20	$9.50	$22.50	£1.40	£4.25	£10.00
90 distributed in the U.K.	$2.50	$7.50	$17.50	£1.05	£3.20	£7.50
91 distributed in the U.K. Judo Master vs. The Cat, distributed in the U.K.; Sarge Steel back-up begins (ends #98)	$2.10	$6.25	$15.00	£0.85	£2.55	£6.00
92 distributed in the U.K. The Smiling Skull appears	$2.10	$6.25	$15.00	£0.85	£2.55	£6.00
93 distributed in the U.K. intro The Tiger who becomes Judo Master's partner	$2.10	$6.25	$15.00	£0.85	£2.55	£6.00
94 distributed in the U.K. Mountain Storm appears	$2.10	$6.25	$15.00	£0.85	£2.55	£6.00
95-96 distributed in the U.K. The Acrobat appears	$2.10	$6.25	$15.00	£0.85	£2.55	£6.00
97-98 distributed in the U.K.	$2.10	$6.25	$15.00	£0.85	£2.55	£6.00
98 Modern Comics Reprint, LD in the U.K. (1977)	$0.20	$0.60	$1.25	£0.10	£0.35	£0.75
Title Value:	$22.70	$67.60	$161.25	£9.35	£28.20	£66.25

JUGULAR

Blackout Comics; 0 Dec 1995-1 1996

	$Good	$Fine	$N.Mint	£Good	£Fine	£N.Mint
0 ND Hari Kari appears; opening sequence by Mike Baron, cover by Christopher Moeller	$0.60	$1.80	$3.00	£0.40	£1.20	£2.00
0 Commemorative Edition, ND pre-bagged with certificate; 3,000 copies	$2.00	$6.00	$10.00	£1.30	£3.90	£6.50
1 ND Mike Baron script begins	$0.60	$1.80	$3.00	£0.40	£1.20	£2.00
Title Value:	$3.20	$9.60	$16.00	£2.10	£6.30	£10.50

JUNGLE ACTION

Marvel Comics Group; 1 Oct 1972-24 Nov 1976
(see Black Panther)

	$Good	$Fine	$N.Mint	£Good	£Fine	£N.Mint
1 ND scarce in the U.K. 1950s reprints of minor classic jungle characters begins	$1.15	$3.50	$7.00	£0.50	£1.50	£3.00
2 ND	$0.65	$2.00	$4.00	£0.30	£1.00	£2.00
3-4 ND	$0.50	$1.50	$3.00	£0.25	£0.75	£1.50
5 ND 1st of Black Panther series	$1.15	$3.50	$7.00	£0.50	£1.50	£3.00
6 ND	$0.65	$2.00	$4.00	£0.40	£1.25	£2.50
7 ND	$0.50	$1.50	$3.00	£0.30	£1.00	£2.00
8 ND origin retold	$0.50	$1.50	$3.00	£0.30	£1.00	£2.00
9-10 ND	$0.50	$1.50	$3.00	£0.30	£1.00	£2.00
11-13	$0.40	$1.25	$2.50	£0.25	£0.75	£1.50
14 Gil Kane dinosaur cover	$0.40	$1.25	$2.50	£0.25	£0.75	£1.50
15-22	$0.40	$1.25	$2.50	£0.25	£0.75	£1.50
23 Daredevil appears	$0.40	$1.25	$2.50	£0.25	£0.75	£1.50
24 ND	$0.40	$1.25	$2.50	£0.25	£0.75	£1.50
Title Value:	$12.20	$37.50	$75.00	£6.90	£21.25	£42.50

JUNGLE ADVENTURES

I.W. Super; 10,12,15,17,18 1963-1964

	$Good	$Fine	$N.Mint	£Good	£Fine	£N.Mint
10-15 distributed in the U.K. all reprints	$3.90	$11.50	$27.50	£1.75	£5.25	£12.50
17-18 distributed in the U.K. all reprints	$3.90	$11.50	$27.50	£1.55	£4.70	£11.00
Title Value:	$19.50	$57.50	$137.50	£8.35	£25.15	£59.50

JUNGLE BOOK GRAPHIC ALBUM, THE

Disney,OS; nn Sep 1990

	$Good	$Fine	$N.Mint	£Good	£Fine	£N.Mint
nn ND 64pgs, adaptation of film	$1.00	$3.00	$5.00	£0.70	£2.10	£3.50
Title Value:	$1.00	$3.00	$5.00	£0.70	£2.10	£3.50
Comic Book Edition				£0.35	£1.05	£1.75

JUNGLE COMICS

Blackthorne; 1 May 1988-6 1988

	$Good	$Fine	$N.Mint	£Good	£Fine	£N.Mint
1 ND Bruce Jones scripts begin, Dave Stevens cover	$0.40	$1.20	$2.00	£0.25	£0.75	£1.25
2-6 ND	$0.40	$1.20	$2.00	£0.25	£0.75	£1.25
Title Value:	$2.40	$7.20	$12.00	£1.50	£4.50	£7.50

JUNGLE GIRLS

AC Comics; 1 1991-16 1993

	$Good	$Fine	$N.Mint	£Good	£Fine	£N.Mint
1 ND new material begins plus "jungle girl art" reprints such as Nyoka the Jungle Girl and Cave Girl by Bob Powell	$0.40	$1.20	$2.00	£0.25	£0.75	£1.25
2-16 ND	$0.40	$1.20	$2.00	£0.25	£0.75	£1.25
Title Value:	$6.40	$19.20	$32.00	£4.00	£12.00	£20.00

JUNGLE TALES OF TARZAN

Charlton; 1 Dec 1964-4 Jul 1965; 5 Sep 1965 ?

	$Good	$Fine	$N.Mint	£Good	£Fine	£N.Mint
1 rare, distributed in the U.K.	$4.25	$12.50	$30.00	£2.50	£7.50	£17.50
2-4 scarce, distributed in the U.K.	$3.20	$9.50	$22.50	£1.75	£5.25	£12.50
5 extremely rare in the U.K. and U.S. (see note below)	$32.00	$95.00	$225.00	£21.00	£62.50	£150.00
Title Value:	$45.85	$136.00	$322.50	£28.75	£85.75	£205.00

Note: very few copies of issue No. 5 exist as virtually the entire print run was destroyed and it is therefore extremely rare in both the U.S. and U.K.

JUNGLE TWINS, THE (TONO AND KONO)

Gold Key; 1 Apr 1972-17 Nov 1975; Whitman; 18 May 1972

	$Good	$Fine	$N.Mint	£Good	£Fine	£N.Mint
1 scarce in the U.K. painted covers begin	$1.25	$3.75	$7.50	£0.80	£2.50	£5.00
2	$0.75	$2.25	$4.50	£0.50	£1.50	£3.00
3	$0.65	$2.00	$4.00	£0.40	£1.25	£2.50
4 16pg Fun Catalogue insert	$0.55	$1.75	$3.50	£0.35	£1.10	£2.25
5-11	$0.50	$1.50	$3.00	£0.30	£1.00	£2.00
12 dinosaur cover; 16pg Fun Catalogue insert	$0.55	$1.75	$3.50	£0.35	£1.10	£2.25
13 flying saucer cover	$0.50	$1.50	$3.00	£0.30	£1.00	£2.00
14-17	$0.50	$1.50	$3.00	£0.30	£1.00	£2.00
18 scarce in the U.K. reprint; line drawn cover	$0.50	$1.50	$3.00	£0.30	£1.00	£2.00
Title Value:	$10.25	$31.00	$62.00	£6.30	£20.45	£41.00

Note: irregularly distributed in the U.K.

JUNIOR CARROT PATROL

Dark Horse; 1 May 1989; 2 Nov 1990

	$Good	$Fine	$N.Mint	£Good	£Fine	£N.Mint
1-2 ND Rick Geary art	$0.50	$1.50	$2.50	£0.30	£0.90	£1.50
Title Value:	$1.00	$3.00	$5.00	£0.60	£1.80	£3.00

JUNIOR WOODCHUCKS

Disney,MS; 1 Jun 1991-4 Sep 1991

	$Good	$Fine	$N.Mint	£Good	£Fine	£N.Mint
1-4 ND Carl Bark reprints plus new material	$0.25	$0.75	$1.25	£0.15	£0.45	£0.75
Title Value:	$1.00	$3.00	$5.00	£0.60	£1.80	£3.00

JUNKWAFFEL

Last Gasp; 1-4 1988

	$Good	$Fine	$N.Mint	£Good	£Fine	£N.Mint
1-4 ND Vaughn Bode script and art; black and white	$0.25	$0.75	$1.25	£0.15	£0.45	£0.75
Title Value:	$1.00	$3.00	$5.00	£0.60	£1.80	£3.00

JURASSIC PARK

Topps,MS; 1 Jun 1993-4 Sep 1993

(becomes Jurassic Park Adventures)

	$Good	$Fine	$N.Mint	£Good	£Fine	£N.Mint
1 Gil Kane and George Perez art begins	$0.50	$1.50	$2.50	£0.30	£0.90	£1.50
1 Collectors Edition, - pre-bagged with 3 trading cards, Walt Simonson script with Gil Kane pencils and George Perez inks	$0.80	$2.40	$4.00	£0.50	£1.50	£2.50
1 Gold Edition, - gold prismatic cover	$1.60	$4.80	$8.00	£1.00	£3.00	£5.00
2	$0.50	$1.50	$2.50	£0.30	£0.90	£1.50
2 Collectors Edition, - pre-bagged with 3 trading cards, Walt Simonson script with Gil Kane pencils and George Perez inks	$0.60	$1.80	$3.00	£0.40	£1.20	£2.00
3	$0.50	$1.50	$2.50	£0.30	£0.90	£1.50
3 Collectors Edition, - pre-bagged with 3 trading cards, Walt Simonson script with Gil Kane pencils and George Perez inks	$0.60	$1.80	$3.00	£0.40	£1.20	£2.00
4	$0.50	$1.50	$2.50	£0.30	£0.90	£1.50
4 Collectors Edition, - pre-bagged with 3 trading cards, Walt Simonson script with Gil Kane pencils and George Perez inks	$1.50	$4.50	$3.00	£1.00	£3.00	£2.00
Title Value:	$7.10	$21.30	$31.00	£4.50	£13.50	£19.50

Note: all Non-Distributed on the news-stands in the U.K.

JURASSIC PARK ADVENTURES

Topps;5 Oct 1994-10 Feb 1995

	$Good	$Fine	$N.Mint	£Good	£Fine	£N.Mint
5-10 ND reprints Jurassic Park: Raptor titles	$0.40	$1.20	$2.00	£0.25	£0.75	£1.25
Title Value:	$2.40	$7.20	$12.00	£1.50	£4.50	£7.50

JURASSIC PARK ANNUAL

Topps; 1 May 1995

	$Good	$Fine	$N.Mint	£Good	£Fine	£N.Mint
1 ND two stories, Michael Golden cover	$0.80	$2.40	$4.00	£0.50	£1.50	£2.50
Title Value:	$0.80	$2.40	$4.00	£0.50	£1.50	£2.50

JURASSIC PARK, RETURN TO

Topps; 1 Apr 1995-9 1996 ?

	$Good	$Fine	$N.Mint	£Good	£Fine	£N.Mint
1 ND Steve Englehart script, Joe Staton and Rich Rankin art, Michael Golden cover	$0.50	$1.50	$2.50	£0.30	£0.90	£1.50
1 Direct Market Edition, ND - Steve Englehart script, Joe Staton and Rich Rankin art, Michael Golden cover	$0.50	$1.50	$2.50	£0.30	£0.90	£1.50
2 ND Steve Englehart script, Joe Staton and Rich Rankin art, Michael Golden cover	$0.50	$1.50	$2.50	£0.30	£0.90	£1.50
3-4 ND Steve Englehart script, Joe Staton and Rich Rankin art, Michael Golden cover; $2.95 cover	$0.60	$1.80	$3.00	£0.40	£1.20	£2.00
5 ND Tom and Mary Bierbaum script, Armando Gil and Fred Carillo art; Michael Golden cover	$0.60	$1.80	$3.00	£0.40	£1.20	£2.00
6-9 ND	$0.60	$1.80	$3.00	£0.40	£1.20	£2.00
Title Value:	$5.70	$17.10	$28.50	£3.70	£11.10	£18.50

JURASSIC PARK: RAPTOR

Topps,MS; 1 Nov 1993-2 Dec 1993

	$Good	$Fine	$N.Mint	£Good	£Fine	£N.Mint
1 ND pre-bagged with trading cards plus Zorro #0; Michael Golden cover	$0.50	$1.50	$2.50	£0.30	£0.90	£1.50
2 ND pre-bagged with trading cards; Michael Golden cover	$0.50	$1.50	$2.50	£0.30	£0.90	£1.50
Title Value:	$1.00	$3.00	$5.00	£0.60	£1.80	£3.00

JURASSIC PARK: RAPTOR'S ATTACK

Topps,MS; 1 Mar 1994-4 Jun 1994

	$Good	$Fine	$N.Mint	£Good	£Fine	£N.Mint
1-4 ND Steve Englehart script and Armando Gil art; covers by Michael Golden	$0.50	$1.50	$2.50	£0.30	£0.90	£1.50
Title Value:	$2.00	$6.00	$10.00	£1.20	£3.60	£6.00

JURASSIC PARK: RAPTOR'S HIJACK

Topps,MS; 1 Jul 1994-4 Oct 1994

	$Good	$Fine	$N.Mint	£Good	£Fine	£N.Mint
1-4 ND Steve Englehart script, Michael Golden cover	$0.50	$1.50	$2.50	£0.30	£0.90	£1.50
Title Value:	$2.00	$6.00	$10.00	£1.20	£3.60	£6.00

JUST IMAGINE COMICS AND STORIES

Just Imagine; 1 1987-12 1987

	$Good	$Fine	$N.Mint	£Good	£Fine	£N.Mint
1-12 ND	$0.25	$0.75	$1.25	£0.15	£0.45	£0.75
Title Value:	$3.00	$9.00	$15.00	£1.80	£5.40	£9.00

JUST IMAGINE COMICS AND STORIES SPECIAL

Just Imagine; 1 1987

	$Good	$Fine	$N.Mint	£Good	£Fine	£N.Mint
1 ND features The Mildly Micro-Waved Pre-Pubescent Kung-Fu Gophers	$0.30	$0.90	$1.50	£0.20	£0.60	£1.00
Title Value:	$0.30	$0.90	$1.50	£0.20	£0.60	£1.00

JUSTICE

Marvel Comics Group/New Universe; 1 Nov 1986-32 Jun 1989

	$Good	$Fine	$N.Mint	£Good	£Fine	£N.Mint
1-3 ND	$0.15	$0.45	$0.75	£0.10	£0.35	£0.60
4-5 ND Salmons art	$0.15	$0.45	$0.75	£0.10	£0.35	£0.60
6-8 ND	$0.15	$0.45	$0.75	£0.10	£0.35	£0.60
9-14 ND Giffen art	$0.15	$0.45	$0.75	£0.10	£0.35	£0.60
15 ND Peter David scripts begin (end 22), Nightmask X-over	$0.15	$0.45	$0.75	£0.10	£0.35	£0.60
16-17 ND	$0.15	$0.45	$0.75	£0.10	£0.35	£0.60
18 ND The Pitt X-over	$0.15	$0.45	$0.75	£0.10	£0.35	£0.60
19-28 ND	$0.15	$0.45	$0.75	£0.10	£0.35	£0.60
29 ND Psi-Force X-over	$0.15	$0.45	$0.75	£0.10	£0.35	£0.60
30-31 ND	$0.15	$0.45	$0.75	£0.10	£0.35	£0.60
32 ND unauthorised appearance of The Joker	$0.30	$0.90	$1.50	£0.20	£0.60	£1.00
Title Value:	$4.95	$14.85	$24.75	£3.30	£11.45	£19.60

Note: Peter David scripts #19-31

JUSTICE INC.

DC Comics; 1 May/Jun 1975-4 Nov/Dec 1975

	$Good	$Fine	$N.Mint	£Good	£Fine	£N.Mint
1 The Avenger begins	$0.50	$1.50	$3.00	£0.25	£0.75	£1.50
2-4 Jack Kirby art	$0.30	$1.00	$2.00	£0.25	£0.75	£1.50
Title Value:	$1.40	$4.50	$9.00	£1.00	£3.00	£6.00

JUSTICE INC. (2ND SERIES)

DC Comics,MS; 1 Aug 1989-2 Sep 1989

	$Good	$Fine	$N.Mint	£Good	£Fine	£N.Mint
1-2 ND 48pgs, squarebound	$0.70	$2.10	$3.50	£0.40	£1.20	£2.00
Title Value:	$1.40	$4.20	$7.00	£0.80	£2.40	£4.00

Note: Mature Readers label.

JUSTICE LEAGUE

DC Comics; 0 Oct 1994; 1 May 1987-113 Aug 1996

(see Legends #6)

(becomes Justice League International with issue #7) (reverts back to Justice League with issue #28)

	$Good	$Fine	$N.Mint	£Good	£Fine	£N.Mint
0 (Oct 1994) Zero Hour X-over, the formation of a new Justice League	$0.40	$1.20	$2.00	£0.25	£0.75	£1.25
1 LD in the U.K. new line-up: Batman, Blue Beetle, Captain Marvel, Black Canary, Green Lantern (Guy Gardner), Mister Miracle, Dr. Fate, Oberon, Martian Manhunter, Dr.Light; Giffen story, Maguire/Austin art begins	$1.00	$3.00	$5.00	£0.70	£2.10	£3.50
2 LD in the U.K.	$0.70	$2.10	$3.50	£0.50	£1.50	£2.50
3 regular cover	$0.60	$1.80	$3.00	£0.40	£1.20	£2.00
3 Test Cover Edition, ND very scarce in the U.K., scarce in the U.S. (see note below)	$12.00	$36.00	$60.00	£3.50	£10.50	£17.50
4 Booster Gold appears	$0.60	$1.80	$3.00	£0.40	£1.20	£2.00
5 The Creeper appears, Batman vs Guy Gardner	$0.60	$1.80	$3.00	£0.40	£1.20	£2.00
6 The Grey Man, Creeper appears	$0.50	$1.50	$2.50	£0.30	£0.90	£1.50
7 48pgs, Maguire art; new direction, Captain Marvel leaves, Captain Atom/Rocket Red/Booster Gold join, Superman/President Reagan cameo	$0.60	$1.80	$3.00	£0.40	£1.20	£2.00
8	$0.50	$1.50	$2.50	£0.30	£0.90	£1.50
9-10 Millennium X-over	$0.50	$1.50	$2.50	£0.30	£0.90	£1.50
11-12	$0.40	$1.20	$2.00	£0.25	£0.75	£1.25
13 X-over with Suicide Squad #13	$0.40	$1.20	$2.00	£0.25	£0.75	£1.25
14-15 no Maguire art	$0.40	$1.20	$2.00	£0.25	£0.75	£1.25
16-17	$0.40	$1.20	$2.00	£0.25	£0.75	£1.25
18 Lobo vs. Guy Gardner	$0.40	$1.20	$2.00	£0.25	£0.75	£1.25
19 Guy Gardner vs. Lobo	$0.40	$1.20	$2.00	£0.25	£0.75	£1.25
20 no Maguire art, Lobo appears	$0.40	$1.20	$2.00	£0.25	£0.75	£1.25
21 no Maguire art, Lobo appears	$0.30	$0.90	$1.50	£0.20	£0.60	£1.00
22-23 Invasion X-over	$0.30	$0.90	$1.50	£0.20	£0.60	£1.00
24 DS new team intro to become Justice League Europe spin off	$0.30	$0.90	$1.50	£0.20	£0.60	£1.00
25	$0.40	$1.20	$2.00	£0.25	£0.75	£1.25
26-30	$0.30	$0.90	$1.50	£0.20	£0.60	£1.00
31-32 Justice League Europe X-over	$0.30	$0.90	$1.50	£0.20	£0.60	£1.00
33-36	$0.30	$0.90	$1.50	£0.20	£0.60	£1.00
37 X-over with Justice League Europe #13	$0.30	$0.90	$1.50	£0.20	£0.60	£1.00
38-49	$0.30	$0.90	$1.50	£0.20	£0.60	£1.00
50 48pgs, conclusion General Glory story	$0.50	$1.50	$2.50	£0.30	£0.90	£1.50
51	$0.25	$0.75	$1.25	£0.15	£0.45	£0.75
52 Blue Beetle vs. Guy Gardner, Batman guest-stars	$0.25	$0.75	$1.25	£0.15	£0.45	£0.75
53	$0.25	$0.75	$1.25	£0.15	£0.45	£0.75
54 story continues in League Europe #30	$0.25	$0.75	$1.25	£0.15	£0.45	£0.75
55 War of the Gods tie-in	$0.25	$0.75	$1.25	£0.15	£0.45	£0.75
56 Breakdowns part 1, story continues in Justice League Europe #32	$0.25	$0.75	$1.25	£0.15	£0.45	£0.75
57 story continues in Justice League Europe #33	$0.25	$0.75	$1.25	£0.15	£0.45	£0.75
58 story continues in Justice League Europe #34	$0.25	$0.75	$1.25	£0.15	£0.45	£0.75
59 story continues in Justice League Europe #35	$0.25	$0.75	$1.25	£0.15	£0.45	£0.75
60 conclusion of Breakdowns story	$0.25	$0.75	$1.25	£0.15	£0.45	£0.75
61 new direction for title, cover based on the classic Justice League of America #1	$0.25	$0.75	$1.25	£0.15	£0.45	£0.75
62-68	$0.25	$0.75	$1.25	£0.15	£0.45	£0.75

Issue	$Good	$Fine	$N.Mint	£Good	£Fine	£N.Mint
69 LD in the U.K. Superman: Doomsday tie-in, story continued in Superman #74	$1.00	$3.00	$5.00	£0.50	£1.50	£2.50
69 2nd printing, II in box on cover	$0.25	$0.75	$1.25	£0.15	£0.45	£0.75
70 ties in with Superman #75; red card-stock part outer cover	$0.80	$2.40	$4.00	£0.40	£1.20	£2.00
70 2nd printing, II in box on cover	$0.25	$0.75	$1.25	£0.15	£0.45	£0.75
71	$0.25	$0.75	$1.25	£0.15	£0.45	£0.75
72 Justice League history re-told; Green Arrow, Black Canary and Atom return	$0.25	$0.75	$1.25	£0.15	£0.45	£0.75
73	$0.25	$0.75	$1.25	£0.15	£0.45	£0.75
74-75 original Justice League of America appear	$0.25	$0.75	$1.25	£0.15	£0.45	£0.75
76-78	$0.25	$0.75	$1.25	£0.15	£0.45	£0.75
79-80 bi-weekly	$0.25	$0.75	$1.25	£0.15	£0.45	£0.75
81	$0.25	$0.75	$1.25	£0.15	£0.45	£0.75
82 X-over Guy Gardner #14	$0.25	$0.75	$1.25	£0.15	£0.45	£0.75
83 X-over Guy Gardner #15	$0.25	$0.75	$1.25	£0.15	£0.45	£0.75
84-85	$0.25	$0.75	$1.25	£0.15	£0.45	£0.75
86-88 Cult of the Machine story	$0.25	$0.75	$1.25	£0.15	£0.45	£0.75
89 Judgement Day part 1, continued in Justice League Task Force #13	$0.25	$0.75	$1.25	£0.15	£0.45	£0.75
90 Judgement Day part 4, continued in Justice League Task Force #14	$0.25	$0.75	$1.25	£0.15	£0.45	£0.75
91 Aftershocks part 1, continued in Justice League Task Force #15	$0.30	$0.90	$1.50	£0.20	£0.60	£1.00
92 Zero Hour X-over	$0.30	$0.90	$1.50	£0.20	£0.60	£1.00
93-97	$0.30	$0.90	$1.50	£0.20	£0.60	£1.00
98 Blue Devil, Ice Maiden and the new Wonder Woman join the team	$0.30	$0.90	$1.50	£0.20	£0.60	£1.00
99	$0.30	$0.90	$1.50	£0.20	£0.60	£1.00
100 48pgs	$0.60	$1.80	$3.00	£0.40	£1.20	£2.00
100 Collectors Edition, 48pgs, holographic foil-enhanced cover (different art to Standard Edition)	$0.80	$2.40	$4.00	£0.50	£1.50	£2.50
101 Way of the Warrior part 2, continued in Hawkman #22	$0.35	$1.05	$1.75	£0.25	£0.75	£1.25
102 Way of the Warrior part 5, continued in Hawkman #23	$0.35	$1.05	$1.75	£0.25	£0.75	£1.25
103-104	$0.35	$1.05	$1.75	£0.25	£0.75	£1.25
105-106 Underworld Unleashed tie-in	$0.35	$1.05	$1.75	£0.25	£0.75	£1.25
107-113	$0.35	$1.05	$1.75	£0.25	£0.75	£1.25
Title Value:	$52.25	$156.75	$261.25	£29.25	£87.75	£146.25

JUSTICE LEAGUE AMERICA

(see Justice League)

JUSTICE LEAGUE ANNUAL

DC Comics; 1 Sep 1987-10 1996
(becomes Justice League International Annual with issue #2)
(becomes Justice League America Annual with issue #4)

Issue	$Good	$Fine	$N.Mint	£Good	£Fine	£N.Mint
1 48pgs, Giffen, P. Craig Russell and other art	$0.40	$1.20	$2.00	£0.25	£0.75	£1.25
2 48pgs, Joker appears	$0.40	$1.20	$2.00	£0.30	£0.90	£1.50
3 48pgs	$0.40	$1.20	$2.00	£0.25	£0.75	£1.25
4 64pgs, squarebound, intro Justice League Antarctica	$0.40	$1.20	$2.00	£0.25	£0.75	£1.25
5 64pgs, Armageddon 2001 tie-in	$0.40	$1.20	$2.00	£0.25	£0.75	£1.25
5 2nd printing, silver ink cover (Feb 1992)	$0.40	$1.20	$2.00	£0.25	£0.75	£1.25
6 64pgs, Eclipso: The Darkness Within tie-in, Wonder Woman guest stars	$0.50	$1.50	$2.50	£0.30	£0.90	£1.50
7 64pgs, Bloodlines (Wave Two) part 15, 1st appearance Terrorsmith, continued in Adventures of Superman Annual #5	$0.50	$1.50	$2.50	£0.30	£0.90	£1.50
8 64pgs, Elseworlds	$0.55	$1.65	$2.75	£0.35	£1.05	£1.75
9 64pgs, Year One	$0.80	$2.40	$4.00	£0.50	£1.50	£2.50
10 ND 48pgs, Legends of the Dead Earth story, Captain Atom stars	$0.60	$1.80	$3.00	£0.40	£1.20	£2.00
Title Value:	$5.35	$16.05	$26.75	£3.40	£10.20	£17.00

JUSTICE LEAGUE EUROPE

DC Comics; 1 Apr 1989-68 Sep 1994
(title becomes "Justice League International with #51)

Issue	$Good	$Fine	$N.Mint	£Good	£Fine	£N.Mint
1	$0.40	$1.20	$2.00	£0.25	£0.75	£1.25
2-6	$0.30	$0.90	$1.50	£0.20	£0.60	£1.00
7-8 Justice League America X-Over	$0.30	$0.90	$1.50	£0.20	£0.60	£1.00
9-10	$0.30	$0.90	$1.50	£0.20	£0.60	£1.00
11 Metamorpho appears	$0.25	$0.75	$1.25	£0.15	£0.45	£0.75
12 Metamorpho/Metal Men appear	$0.25	$0.75	$1.25	£0.15	£0.45	£0.75
13 X-over with Justice League America #37	$0.25	$0.75	$1.25	£0.15	£0.45	£0.75
14-20	$0.25	$0.75	$1.25	£0.15	£0.45	£0.75
21 line-up change	$0.25	$0.75	$1.25	£0.15	£0.45	£0.75
22-29	$0.25	$0.75	$1.25	£0.15	£0.45	£0.75
30 story continues in Justice League America #55	$0.25	$0.75	$1.25	£0.15	£0.45	£0.75
31 War of the Gods tie-in (unofficial)	$0.25	$0.75	$1.25	£0.15	£0.45	£0.75
32 new Doom Patrol cameo, story continued from Justice League America #56	$0.25	$0.75	$1.25	£0.15	£0.45	£0.75
33 story continued from Justice League America #57	$0.25	$0.75	$1.25	£0.15	£0.45	£0.75
34 story continued from Justice League America #58	$0.25	$0.75	$1.25	£0.15	£0.45	£0.75
35 story continued from Justice League America #59	$0.25	$0.75	$1.25	£0.15	£0.45	£0.75
36 Breakdowns epilogue, leads into Justice League Spectacular #1	$0.25	$0.75	$1.25	£0.15	£0.45	£0.75
37 Batman guest-stars, bi-weekly	$0.25	$0.75	$1.25	£0.15	£0.45	£0.75
38-40 bi-weekly	$0.25	$0.75	$1.25	£0.15	£0.45	£0.75
41 Wonder Woman and Metamorpho appear	$0.25	$0.75	$1.25	£0.15	£0.45	£0.75
42-44	$0.25	$0.75	$1.25	£0.15	£0.45	£0.75
45-49 Red Winter story	$0.25	$0.75	$1.25	£0.15	£0.45	£0.75
50 48pgs, Red Winter story conclusion	$0.30	$0.90	$1.50	£0.20	£0.60	£1.00
51 title becomes "Justice League International"	$0.25	$0.75	$1.25	£0.15	£0.45	£0.75
52-53	$0.25	$0.75	$1.25	£0.15	£0.45	£0.75
54-56 bi-weekly	$0.25	$0.75	$1.25	£0.15	£0.45	£0.75
57-60	$0.25	$0.75	$1.25	£0.15	£0.45	£0.75
61-64	$0.30	$0.90	$1.50	£0.20	£0.60	£1.00
65 continued from Justice League Task Force #13, continued in Justice League America #90	$0.30	$0.90	$1.50	£0.20	£0.60	£1.00
66 concluded from Justice League Task Force #14	$0.30	$0.90	$1.50	£0.20	£0.60	£1.00
67 Aftershocks part 3 (of 3)	$0.30	$0.90	$1.50	£0.20	£0.60	£1.00
68 Zero Hour X-over	$0.30	$0.90	$1.50	£0.20	£0.60	£1.00
Title Value:	$18.05	$54.15	$90.25	£11.20	£33.60	£56.00

JUSTICE LEAGUE EUROPE ANNUAL

DC Comics; 1 Jun 1990-5 1994
(becomes Justice League International Annual with issue #4)

Issue	$Good	$Fine	$N.Mint	£Good	£Fine	£N.Mint
1 48pgs, return of new Dr. Light	$0.40	$1.20	$2.00	£0.25	£0.75	£1.25
2 64pgs, Aramgeddon: 2001 tie-in, Bat-Lash, Jonah Hex, Demon and Legion of Super-Heroes appear	$0.40	$1.20	$2.00	£0.25	£0.75	£1.25
3 64pgs, Eclipso: The Darkness Within tie-in, Power Girl "eclipsed"	$0.50	$1.50	$2.50	£0.30	£0.90	£1.50
4 64pgs, Bloodlines part 9, 1st appearance Lionheart, continued in Robin Annual #2	$0.50	$1.50	$2.50	£0.30	£0.90	£1.50
5 64pgs, Elseworlds story, Gerard Jones script and Kiki Chansamone art	$0.60	$1.80	$3.00	£0.40	£1.20	£2.00
Title Value:	$2.40	$7.20	$12.00	£1.50	£4.50	£7.50

JUSTICE LEAGUE INTERNATIONAL

(see Justice League #7-28, and Justice League Europe #51 onwards)

JUSTICE LEAGUE INTERNATIONAL SPECIAL

DC Comics; 1 Feb 1990-2 1991

Issue	$Good	$Fine	$N.Mint	£Good	£Fine	£N.Mint
1 48pgs	$0.50	$1.50	$2.50	£0.30	£0.90	£1.50
2 48pgs, The Huntress appears	$0.50	$1.50	$2.50	£0.30	£0.90	£1.50
Title Value:	$1.00	$3.00	$5.00	£0.60	£1.80	£3.00

JUSTICE LEAGUE OF AMERICA

National Periodical Publications/DC Comics; 1 Oct/Nov 1960-261 Apr 1987

Issue	$Good	$Fine	$N.Mint	£Good	£Fine	£N.Mint
1 scarce in the U.K. origin and 1st appearance Despero	$325.00	$970.00	$3250.00	£225.00	£670.00	£2250.00
[Very scarce in high grade - Very Fine+ or better]						
2 (Dec/Jan 1961)	$87.50	$265.00	$800.00	£55.00	£165.00	£500.00
3 origin and 1st appearance Kanjar Ro; see Mystery in Space #75	$75.00	$225.00	$600.00	£50.00	£150.00	£400.00
[Scarce in high grade - Very Fine or better]						
4 Green Arrow joins	$52.50	$155.00	$425.00	£31.00	£92.50	£250.00
5 origin and 1st appearance Dr. Destiny	$44.00	$130.00	$350.00	£25.00	£75.00	£200.00
6 origin Professor Amos Fortune	$38.00	$110.00	$300.00	£20.00	£60.00	£160.00
7	$38.00	$110.00	$300.00	£18.50	£55.00	£150.00
8 (Jan 1962)	$38.00	$110.00	$300.00	£18.50	£55.00	£150.00
9 origin Justice League of America (origin untold in Brave and the Bold #28)	$47.00	$140.00	$425.00	£32.00	£95.00	£285.00
10 origin Felix Faust	$38.00	$110.00	$300.00	£18.50	£55.00	£150.00
11	$29.00	$85.00	$200.00	£13.50	£41.00	£95.00
12 origin and 1st appearance Dr. Light	$29.00	$85.00	$200.00	£13.50	£41.00	£95.00
13	$29.00	$85.00	$200.00	£13.50	£41.00	£95.00
14 Atom joins Justice League of America	$29.00	$85.00	$200.00	£13.50	£41.00	£95.00
15	$29.00	$85.00	$200.00	£13.50	£41.00	£95.00
16	$25.00	$75.00	$175.00	£10.50	£32.00	£75.00
17 (Feb 1963)	$25.00	$75.00	$175.00	£10.50	£32.00	£75.00

	$Good	$Fine	$N.Mint	£Good	£Fine	£N.Mint
18-20	$25.00	$75.00	$175.00	£10.50	£32.00	£75.00
21 1st re-appearance of Justice Society of America, 1st Silver Age Hourman and Dr. Fate, 1st appearance (as part of a team) Golden Age Green Lantern in Silver Age	$37.00	$110.00	$330.00	£19.00	£57.50	£175.00
22 Justice Society of America X-over, continues from #21, 2nd appearance (as part of a team) of Golden Age Green Lantern in Silver Age	$34.00	$100.00	$310.00	£16.50	£50.00	£150.00
23-24	$15.00	$45.00	$105.00	£5.00	£15.00	£35.00
25 (Feb 1964)	$15.00	$45.00	$105.00	£5.00	£15.00	£35.00
26-28	$15.00	$45.00	$105.00	£5.00	£15.00	£35.00
29 2nd Justice Society of America X-over, 1st Silver Age appearance of Golden Age Starman	$15.50	$47.00	$125.00	£5.50	£16.50	£45.00
30 Justice Society of America X-over continues from #29	$14.00	$43.00	$115.00	£5.00	£15.00	£40.00
31 Hawkman joins	$12.50	$39.00	$90.00	£3.90	£11.50	£27.50
32 1st appearance Brainstorm	$9.25	$28.00	$65.00	£3.20	£9.50	£22.50
33 (Feb 1965)	$8.50	$26.00	$60.00	£2.85	£8.50	£20.00
34 Joker cover and story	$9.25	$28.00	$65.00	£3.55	£10.50	£25.00
35-36	$8.50	$26.00	$60.00	£2.85	£8.50	£20.00
37 Justice Society of America X-over	$12.00	$36.00	$85.00	£4.00	£12.00	£28.00
38 Justice Society of America X-over, Mr. Terrific appears	$12.00	$36.00	$85.00	£4.00	£12.00	£28.00
39 80pgs, Giant G-16, reprints Brave and the Bold #28 (1st appearance Justice League of America) and #30 (3rd appearance)	$14.00	$43.00	$100.00	£5.00	£15.00	£35.00
40 3rd appearance Silver Age Penguin	$8.50	$26.00	$60.00	£2.85	£8.50	£20.00
41 last Silver Age issue, indicia dated December 1965	$8.50	$26.00	$60.00	£2.85	£8.50	£20.00
42 (Feb 1966)	$6.25	$19.00	$45.00	£1.75	£5.25	£12.50
43-45	$6.25	$19.00	$45.00	£1.75	£5.25	£12.50
46 Justice Society of America X-over, 1st appearance Silver Age Sandman, 3rd Silver Age appearance Golden Age Spectre	$10.50	$32.00	$85.00	£3.40	£10.00	£27.50
47 Justice Society of America X-over	$7.00	$21.00	$50.00	£2.10	£6.25	£15.00
48 80pgs, Giant G-29, reprints #2,#3, Brave and the Bold #29 (2nd appearance J.L.A.)	$6.00	$18.00	$42.00	£2.85	£8.50	£20.00
49-50	$5.50	$17.00	$40.00	£1.75	£5.25	£12.50
51 (Feb 1967)	$5.50	$17.00	$40.00	£1.40	£4.25	£10.00
52-54	$5.50	$17.00	$40.00	£1.40	£4.25	£10.00
55 1st Silver Age appearance of Golden Age Robin, Justice Society of America X-over	$6.75	$20.50	$55.00	£2.50	£7.50	£20.00
56 Justice Society of America X-over	$6.25	$19.00	$45.00	£1.40	£4.25	£10.00
57 United Nations story	$5.50	$17.00	$40.00	£1.40	£4.25	£10.00
58 80pgs, Giant G-41, reprints #1, #6, #8	$6.25	$19.00	$45.00	£1.75	£5.25	£12.50
59	$5.50	$17.00	$40.00	£1.40	£4.25	£10.00
60 (Feb 1968) Batgirl appears	$5.50	$17.00	$40.00	£1.40	£4.25	£10.00
61 all villain special	$4.25	$12.50	$30.00	£1.00	£3.00	£7.00
62	$4.25	$12.50	$30.00	£1.00	£3.00	£7.00
63 scarce in the U.K.	$4.25	$12.50	$30.00	£1.10	£3.40	£8.00
64 Justice Society of America X-over, origin and 1st appearance Red Tornado, Golden Age Black Canary, Dr. Fate, Flash, Starman and Hourman appear	$4.60	$13.50	$32.50	£1.10	£3.40	£8.00
65 Justice Society of America X-over	$4.25	$12.50	$30.00	£1.00	£3.00	£7.00
66 Neal Adams cover	$4.25	$12.50	$30.00	£1.00	£3.00	£7.00
67 80pgs, Giant G-53, reprints #4, #14, #31; Neal Adams cover	$5.00	$15.00	$35.00	£2.00	£6.00	£14.00
68	$4.25	$12.50	$30.00	£1.00	£3.00	£7.00
69 (Feb 1969)	$4.25	$12.50	$30.00	£1.00	£3.00	£7.00
70 Neal Adams cover, The Creeper (early appearance) vs. Justice League of America	$4.25	$12.50	$30.00	£1.00	£3.00	£7.00
71	$3.55	$10.50	$25.00	£0.85	£2.55	£6.00
72 last 12 cents issue; Joe Kubert cover	$3.55	$10.50	$25.00	£0.85	£2.55	£6.00
73 1st Silver Age appearance of the Golden Age Superman & Golden Age Black Canary; Justice Society of America X-over, Joe Kubert cover	$4.25	$12.50	$30.00	£1.40	£4.25	£10.00
74 Neal Adams cover, Justice Society of America X-over, Black Canary arrives on Earth 1 and is invited to stay	$1.40	$4.25	$10.00	£0.85	£2.55	£6.00
75 Black Canary replaces Wonder Woman	$1.40	$4.25	$10.00	£0.85	£2.55	£6.00
76 68pgs, Giant G-65, reprints #7, #12	$2.85	$8.50	$20.00	£1.40	£4.25	£10.00
77	$1.00	$3.00	$7.00	£0.60	£1.90	£4.50
78 (Feb 1970)	$1.40	$4.25	$10.00	£0.70	£2.10	£5.00
79 Neal Adams cover	$1.40	$4.25	$10.00	£0.70	£2.10	£5.00
80	$1.40	$4.25	$10.00	£0.70	£2.10	£5.00
81 Neal Adams cover inks	$1.10	$3.40	$8.00	£0.55	£1.70	£4.00
82 Neal Adams cover, Justice Society of America X-over	$1.10	$3.40	$8.00	£0.60	£1.90	£4.50
83 Justice Society of America X-over	$1.10	$3.40	$8.00	£0.60	£1.90	£4.50
84	$1.10	$3.40	$8.00	£0.55	£1.70	£4.00
85 68pgs, Giant G-77, reprints #10, #11	$2.85	$8.50	$20.00	£1.10	£3.40	£8.00
86 very scarce in the U.K. Neal Adams cover	$1.10	$3.40	$8.00	£0.70	£2.10	£5.00
87 scarce in the U.K. (Feb 1971) Neal Adams cover	$1.10	$3.40	$8.00	£0.60	£1.90	£4.50
88 very scarce in the U.K. Neal Adams cover	$1.10	$3.40	$8.00	£0.70	£2.10	£5.00
89 scarce in the U.K. Neal Adams cover	$1.10	$3.40	$8.00	£0.60	£1.90	£4.50
90 ecology theme issue	$1.10	$3.40	$8.00	£0.55	£1.70	£4.00
91-92 52pgs, Neal Adams cover	$1.00	$3.00	$7.00	£0.70	£2.10	£5.00
93 68pgs, Giant G-89, reprints #13, #18	$2.85	$8.50	$20.00	£1.10	£3.40	£8.00
94 52pgs, 4pgs Neal Adams art, reprints origin Sandman, Starman (Adventure #40, #61)	$5.25	$16.00	$37.50	£1.75	£5.25	£12.50
95 52pgs, Neal Adams cover, reprints origin Dr.Fate (More Fun #57), Dr.Midnight (All American #25)	$2.10	$6.25	$15.00	£0.85	£2.55	£6.00
96 52pgs, (Feb 1972) Neal Adams cover, reprints origin Hourman (Adventure #48)	$2.10	$6.25	$15.00	£0.85	£2.55	£6.00
97 52pgs, Neal Adams cover, reprints #9 (origin Justice League of America)	$1.75	$5.25	$12.50	£0.75	£2.35	£5.50

Jonah Hex #1

Jungle Action #4

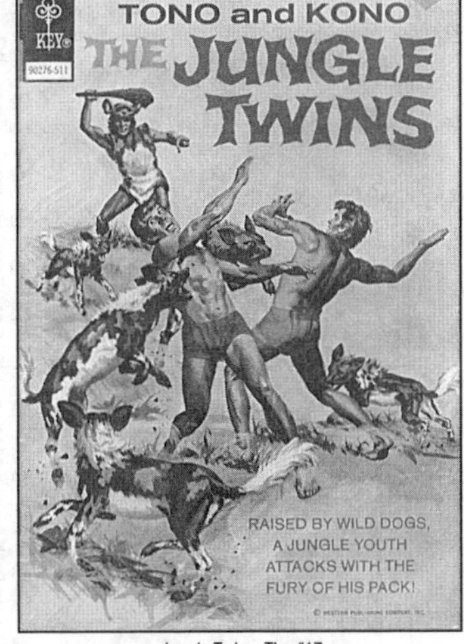

Jungle Twins, The #17

	$Good	$Fine	$N.Mint	£Good	£Fine	£N.Mint
98 52pgs, Neal Adams cover, Golden Age reprints	$1.75	$5.25	$12.50	£0.75	£2.35	£5.50
99 52pgs, Golden Age reprints	$1.75	$5.25	$12.50	£0.75	£2.35	£5.50
100 scarce in the U.K.	$1.40	$4.25	$10.00	£0.85	£2.55	£6.00
101 Justice Society of America X-over	$1.30	$4.00	$8.00	£0.65	£2.00	£4.00
102 Justice Society of America X-over, Red Tornado "dies"	$1.30	$4.00	$8.00	£0.65	£2.00	£4.00
103 Phantom Stranger joins	$0.80	$2.50	$5.00	£0.55	£1.75	£3.50
104 (Feb 1973)	$0.80	$2.50	$5.00	£0.55	£1.75	£3.50
105 Elongated Man joins	$0.80	$2.50	$5.00	£0.55	£1.75	£3.50
106 new Red Tornado joins	$0.80	$2.50	$5.00	£0.55	£1.75	£3.50
107 Justice Society of America X-over, Freedom Fighters return - 1st appearance since Golden Age (Human Bomb, Phantom Lady, Doll Man, Uncle Sam, The Ray, Black Condor), 1st mention Earth X	$0.80	$2.50	$5.00	£0.65	£2.00	£4.00
108 Justice Society of America X-over, Freedom Fighters on cover	$0.80	$2.50	$5.00	£0.65	£2.00	£4.00
109 (Feb 1974) Hawkman resigns	$0.80	$2.50	$5.00	£0.55	£1.75	£3.50
110-113 100pgs	$2.05	$6.25	$12.50	£1.25	£3.75	£7.50
114 100pgs, reprints #22 (2nd part 1st Silver Age Justice Society of America)	$2.05	$6.25	$12.50	£1.25	£3.75	£7.50
115 100pgs, (Feb 1975)	$2.05	$6.25	$12.50	£1.25	£3.75	£7.50
116 100pgs, 1st appearance Quizz, Joker appears	$2.05	$6.25	$12.50	£1.25	£3.75	£7.50
117 Hawkman rejoins	$0.65	$2.00	$4.00	£0.50	£1.50	£3.00
118-119	$0.65	$2.00	$4.00	£0.50	£1.50	£3.00
120 Adam Strange appears	$0.65	$2.00	$4.00	£0.50	£1.50	£3.00
121 Adam Strange marries Alanna	$0.55	$1.75	$3.50	£0.50	£1.50	£3.00
122 scarce in the U.K.	$0.55	$1.75	$3.50	£0.55	£1.75	£3.50
123-124 scarce in the U.K. Justice Society of America X-over	$0.55	$1.75	$3.50	£0.65	£2.00	£4.00
125 scarce in the U.K. Two Face appears	$0.55	$1.75	$3.50	£0.55	£1.75	£3.50
126 scarce in the U.K. (Jan 1976)	$0.55	$1.75	$3.50	£0.50	£1.50	£3.00
127	$0.55	$1.75	$3.50	£0.40	£1.25	£2.50
128 Wonder Woman rejoins	$0.55	$1.75	$3.50	£0.40	£1.25	£2.50
129-131	$0.55	$1.75	$3.50	£0.40	£1.25	£2.50
132-134 scarce in the U.K.	$0.55	$1.75	$3.50	£0.50	£1.50	£3.00
135 ND Justice Society of America X-over	$0.55	$1.75	$3.50	£0.55	£1.75	£3.50
136 scarce in the U.K. Justice Society of America X-over, Joker appears	$0.55	$1.75	$3.50	£0.50	£1.50	£3.00
137 scarce in the U.K. classic Superman vs. Shazam	$0.55	$1.75	$3.50	£0.50	£1.50	£3.00
138 scarce in the U.K. (Jan 1977) Neal Adams cover, Adam Strange appears	$0.55	$1.75	$3.50	£0.50	£1.50	£3.00
139 scarce in the U.K. 52pgs, Neal Adams cover	$0.65	$2.00	$4.00	£0.55	£1.75	£3.50
140 scarce in the U.K. 52pgs	$0.65	$2.00	$4.00	£0.55	£1.75	£3.50
141 ND 52pgs	$0.65	$2.00	$4.00	£0.65	£2.00	£4.00
142 scarce in the U.K. 52pgs	$0.65	$2.00	$4.00	£0.55	£1.75	£3.50
143 very scarce in the U.K. 52pgs, Superman vs. Wonder Woman	$0.65	$2.00	$4.00	£0.75	£2.25	£4.50
144 scarce in the U.K. 52pgs, cameo appearances of 30 past DC characters from the Challengers and Congorilla to Plastic Man and Rex the Wonder Dog	$0.65	$2.00	$4.00	£0.55	£1.75	£3.50
145 ND scarce in the U.K. 52pgs	$0.65	$2.00	$4.00	£0.75	£2.25	£4.50
146-147 ND 52pgs	$0.65	$2.00	$4.00	£0.65	£2.00	£4.00
148 scarce in the U.K. 52pgs, Justice Society of America X-over, Legion of Super-Heroes appear	$0.65	$2.00	$4.00	£0.65	£2.00	£4.00
149 scarce in the U.K. 52pgs	$0.65	$2.00	$4.00	£0.55	£1.75	£3.50
150 ND very scarce in the U.K. 52pgs, (Jan 1978)	$0.65	$2.00	$4.00	£0.80	£2.50	£5.00
151 scarce in the U.K. 52pgs	$0.55	$1.75	$3.50	£0.55	£1.75	£3.50
152-157 52pgs	$0.55	$1.75	$3.50	£0.40	£1.25	£2.50
158 scarce in the U.K. 44pgs	$0.55	$1.75	$3.50	£0.50	£1.50	£3.00
159 ND Jonah Hex, Enemy Ace, Viking Prince, Black Pirate, Miss Liberty, Justice Society of America appear	$0.50	$1.50	$3.00	£0.50	£1.50	£3.00
160 ND	$0.50	$1.50	$3.00	£0.40	£1.25	£2.50
161 Zatanna joins, new costume	$0.50	$1.50	$3.00	£0.25	£0.85	£1.75
162 (Jan 1979)	$0.50	$1.50	$3.00	£0.25	£0.85	£1.75
163-170	$0.50	$1.50	$3.00	£0.25	£0.85	£1.75
171 Justice Society of America X-over	$0.50	$1.50	$3.00	£0.25	£0.85	£1.75
172 Justice Society off America X-over, Mr. Terrific dies	$0.50	$1.50	$3.00	£0.25	£0.85	£1.75
173 Black Lightning refuses to join	$0.50	$1.50	$3.00	£0.25	£0.85	£1.75
174 (Jan 1980)	$0.50	$1.50	$3.00	£0.25	£0.85	£1.75
175-176	$0.50	$1.50	$3.00	£0.25	£0.85	£1.75
177 Martian Manhunter guest-stars, Despero appears	$0.50	$1.50	$3.00	£0.25	£0.85	£1.75
178 Martian Manhunter guest-stars, Despero appears; Jim Starlin cover	$0.50	$1.50	$3.00	£0.25	£0.85	£1.75
179 Firestorm joins; Jim Starlin cover	$0.50	$1.50	$3.00	£0.25	£0.85	£1.75
180 Jim Starlin cover	$0.50	$1.50	$3.00	£0.25	£0.85	£1.75
181	$0.50	$1.50	$2.50	£0.30	£0.90	£1.50
182 Green Arrow leaves, Elongated Man solo back-up	$0.50	$1.50	$2.50	£0.30	£0.90	£1.50
183 Justice Society of America X-over, Mr. Miracle, Darkseid and New Gods appear; Jim Starlin cover	$0.50	$1.50	$2.50	£0.30	£0.90	£1.50
184-185 Justice Society of America X-over, Darkseid appears; George Perez art, Jim Starlin cover	$0.50	$1.50	$2.50	£0.30	£0.90	£1.50
186 (Jan 1981) George Perez art	$0.50	$1.50	$2.50	£0.30	£0.90	£1.50
187-188	$0.50	$1.50	$2.50	£0.30	£0.90	£1.50
189-190 Brian Bolland covers featuring Starro the Conqueror	$0.50	$1.50	$2.50	£0.30	£0.90	£1.50
191	$0.50	$1.50	$2.50	£0.30	£0.90	£1.50
192 true origin of Red Tornado begins (ends #193); George Perez art	$0.50	$1.50	$2.50	£0.30	£0.90	£1.50
193 52pgs, 1st appearance All-Star Squadron (free insert); George Perez art	$0.50	$1.50	$2.50	£0.30	£0.90	£1.50
194 George Perez art	$0.50	$1.50	$2.50	£0.30	£0.90	£1.50
195-197 Justice Society of America X-over; George Perez art	$0.50	$1.50	$2.50	£0.30	£0.90	£1.50
198 (Jan 1982) Jonah Hex, Cinnamon, Bat Lash and Scalphunter appear	$0.50	$1.50	$2.50	£0.30	£0.90	£1.50
199 George Perez cover	$0.50	$1.50	$2.50	£0.30	£0.90	£1.50
200 76pgs, 1st Brian Bolland Batman (5pgs), Aparo/Infantino/Gil Kane/Kubert/George Perez art, Green Arrow rejoins (virtually all copies have crinkled spines owing to the binding process)	$0.80	$2.40	$4.00	£0.70	£2.10	£3.50
201-205 George Perez cover	$0.40	$1.20	$2.00	£0.25	£0.75	£1.25
206	$0.40	$1.20	$2.00	£0.25	£0.75	£1.25
207 20th annual Justice Society of America X-over, All Star Squadron appear; George Perez art	$0.40	$1.20	$2.00	£0.25	£0.75	£1.25
208 20th annual Justice Society of America X-over, All Star Squadron appear, Masters of the Universe insert; George Perez cover	$0.40	$1.20	$2.00	£0.25	£0.75	£1.25
209 20th annual Justice Society of America X-over, All Star Squadron appear; Goerge Perez cover	$0.40	$1.20	$2.00	£0.25	£0.75	£1.25
210 (Jan 1983)	$0.40	$1.20	$2.00	£0.25	£0.75	£1.25
211	$0.40	$1.20	$2.00	£0.25	£0.75	£1.25
212-215 George Perez cover	$0.40	$1.20	$2.00	£0.25	£0.75	£1.25
216	$0.40	$1.20	$2.00	£0.25	£0.75	£1.25
217 George Perez cover	$0.40	$1.20	$2.00	£0.25	£0.75	£1.25
217 SoMuchFun! Inc. Edition, ND rare in the U.K. (Aug 1983), same contents as above with same cover but the word "Classic" added to the logo	$0.80	$2.40	$4.00	£0.50	£1.50	£2.50
218	$0.40	$1.20	$2.00	£0.25	£0.75	£1.25
219-220 Justice Society of America X-over; George Perez cover	$0.40	$1.20	$2.00	£0.25	£0.75	£1.25
221	$0.30	$0.90	$1.50	£0.20	£0.60	£1.00
222 (Jan 1984)	$0.30	$0.90	$1.50	£0.20	£0.60	£1.00
223-230	$0.30	$0.90	$1.50	£0.20	£0.60	£1.00
231-232 Justice Society of America X-over	$0.30	$0.90	$1.50	£0.20	£0.60	£1.00
233 Rebirth begins (ends #236); Vibe, Vixen, Steel and Gypsy introduced	$0.30	$0.90	$1.50	£0.20	£0.60	£1.00
234 (Jan 1985)	$0.30	$0.90	$1.50	£0.20	£0.60	£1.00
235-242	$0.30	$0.90	$1.50	£0.20	£0.60	£1.00
243 Aquaman leaves	$0.30	$0.90	$1.50	£0.20	£0.60	£1.00
244-245 Crisis X-over, Justice Society of America and Infinity Inc. appear	$0.30	$0.90	$1.50	£0.20	£0.60	£1.00
246 (Jan 1986)	$0.30	$0.90	$1.50	£0.20	£0.60	£1.00
247-249	$0.30	$0.90	$1.50	£0.20	£0.60	£1.00
250 DS anniversary issue, Batman re-joins	$0.40	$1.20	$2.00	£0.25	£0.75	£1.25
251-252	$0.30	$0.90	$1.50	£0.20	£0.60	£1.00
253 origin Despero retold	$0.30	$0.90	$1.50	£0.20	£0.60	£1.00
254-257	$0.30	$0.90	$1.50	£0.20	£0.60	£1.00
258 (Jan 1987) Legends X-over, death of Vibe	$0.30	$0.90	$1.50	£0.20	£0.60	£1.00

	$Good	$Fine	$N.Mint	£Good	£Fine	£N.Mint
259 Legends X-over	*$0.30*	*$0.90*	*$1.50*	£0.20	£0.60	£1.00
260 Legends X-over, death of Steel	*$0.30*	*$0.90*	*$1.50*	£0.20	£0.60	£1.00
261 LD in the U.K. Legends X-over	*$0.50*	*$1.50*	*$2.50*	£0.30	£0.90	£1.50
Title Value:	*$1661.70*	*$4965.20*	*$13310.50*	£859.70	£2582.55	£7100.25

REPRINT FEATURES

Atom in 99. Black Canary in 116. Flash in 92. Hourman in 91, 96. Johnny Peril in 116. JLA in 39, 48, 58, 67, 76, 85, 93, 97, 110-113, 115, 116. JLA/JSA in 114. Justice Society of America in 110, 113, 115. Knights of the Galaxy in 91. Sandman in 94, 99. Sargon in 98. Seven Soldiers of Victory in 111, 112. Starman in 94, 98, 116. Dr.Fate, Dr.Mid-Nite in 95. Wildcat in 96.

JUSTICE LEAGUE OF AMERICA ANNUAL

DC Comics; 1 Jul 1983-3 Nov 1985

	$Good	$Fine	$N.Mint	£Good	£Fine	£N.Mint
1 Dr. Destiny appears	*$0.50*	*$1.50*	*$2.50*	£0.30	£0.90	£1.50
2 intro new Justice League of America	*$0.50*	*$1.50*	*$2.50*	£0.30	£0.90	£1.50
3 Crisis X-over	*$0.50*	*$1.50*	*$2.50*	£0.30	£0.90	£1.50
Title Value:	*$1.50*	*$4.50*	*$7.50*	£0.90	£2.70	£4.50

JUSTICE LEAGUE OF AMERICA ARCHIVES

DC Comics; 1 Apr 1992-present

	$Good	$Fine	$N.Mint	£Good	£Fine	£N.Mint
1 256pgs, hardcover reprint edition of Brave and the Bold #28-30, Justice League of America #1-6	*$7.50*	*$22.50*	*$37.50*	£5.00	£15.00	£25.00
2 256pgs, hardcover reprint edition of Justice League of America #7-14	*$7.50*	*$22.50*	*$37.50*	£5.00	£15.00	£25.00
3 256pgs, hardcover reprint edition of Justice League of America #15-22	*$7.50*	*$22.50*	*$37.50*	£5.00	£15.00	£25.00
Title Value:	*$22.50*	*$67.50*	*$112.50*	£15.00	£45.00	£75.00

JUSTICE LEAGUE QUARTERLY

DC Comics; 1 Winter 1990-17 Dec 1994

	$Good	$Fine	$N.Mint	£Good	£Fine	£N.Mint
1 80pgs, Booster Gold plus Maxi-Man, Praxis, Gypsy, Echo, Vapor and Reverb	*$0.60*	*$1.80*	*$3.00*	£0.40	£1.20	£2.00
2 80pgs, G'Nort appears	*$0.60*	*$1.80*	*$3.00*	£0.40	£1.20	£2.00
3 80pgs, original Justice League of America appears	*$0.60*	*$1.80*	*$3.00*	£0.40	£1.20	£2.00
4 80pgs, three complete stories	*$0.60*	*$1.80*	*$3.00*	£0.40	£1.20	£2.00
5 80pgs	*$0.60*	*$1.80*	*$3.00*	£0.40	£1.20	£2.00
6 80pgs, painted cover	*$0.60*	*$1.80*	*$3.00*	£0.40	£1.20	£2.00
7-12 80pgs	*$0.60*	*$1.80*	*$3.00*	£0.40	£1.20	£2.00
13 80pgs, Linsner cover art	*$2.00*	*$6.00*	*$10.00*	£0.60	£1.80	£3.00
14-16 80pgs	*$0.60*	*$1.80*	*$3.00*	£0.40	£1.20	£2.00
17 80pgs, special solo stories featuring Batman, Guy Gardner and others	*$0.60*	*$1.80*	*$3.00*	£0.40	£1.20	£2.00
Title Value:	*$11.60*	*$34.80*	*$58.00*	£7.00	£21.00	£35.00

JUSTICE LEAGUE SPECTACULAR

DC Comics,OS; 1 Apr 1992

	$Good	$Fine	$N.Mint	£Good	£Fine	£N.Mint
1 48pgs, ties in with Justice League America #61 and Justice League Europe #37, two different covers available depicting new Justice League of America and Justice League International teams	*$0.40*	*$1.20*	*$2.00*	£0.25	£0.75	£1.25
Title Value:	*$0.40*	*$1.20*	*$2.00*	£0.25	£0.75	£1.25

JUSTICE LEAGUE TASK FORCE

DC Comics; 0 Oct 1994; 1 Jun 1993-37 Aug 1996

	$Good	$Fine	$N.Mint	£Good	£Fine	£N.Mint
0 (Oct 1994) Zero Hour X-over, team re-formed	*$0.40*	*$1.20*	*$2.00*	£0.25	£0.75	£1.25
1-4	*$0.30*	*$0.90*	*$1.50*	£0.20	£0.60	£1.00
5 Knightquest: The Search part 1	*$0.40*	*$1.20*	*$2.00*	£0.25	£0.75	£1.25
6 Knightquest: The Search part 3	*$0.30*	*$0.90*	*$1.50*	£0.20	£0.60	£1.00
7-8 Peter David script	*$0.30*	*$0.90*	*$1.50*	£0.20	£0.60	£1.00
9	*$0.30*	*$0.90*	*$1.50*	£0.20	£0.60	£1.00
10-12 Purification story	*$0.30*	*$0.90*	*$1.50*	£0.20	£0.60	£1.00
13 Judgement Day part 2, continued in Justice League America #65	*$0.30*	*$0.90*	*$1.50*	£0.20	£0.60	£1.00
14 Judgement Day part 5, continued in Justice League America #66	*$0.30*	*$0.90*	*$1.50*	£0.20	£0.60	£1.00
15 Aftershocks part 2, continued in Justice League #67	*$0.30*	*$0.90*	*$1.50*	£0.20	£0.60	£1.00
16 Zero Hour X-over	*$0.30*	*$0.90*	*$1.50*	£0.20	£0.60	£1.00
17-20 Vandal Savage appears	*$0.30*	*$0.90*	*$1.50*	£0.20	£0.60	£1.00
21-23	*$0.30*	*$0.90*	*$1.50*	£0.20	£0.60	£1.00
24 $1.75 cover begin	*$0.35*	*$1.05*	*$1.75*	£0.25	£0.75	£1.25
25 Impulse and Damage guest-star	*$0.35*	*$1.05*	*$1.75*	£0.25	£0.75	£1.25
26	*$0.35*	*$1.05*	*$1.75*	£0.25	£0.75	£1.25
27-29 Despero appears	*$0.35*	*$1.05*	*$1.75*	£0.25	£0.75	£1.25
30 Underworld Unleashed tie-in	*$0.35*	*$1.05*	*$1.75*	£0.25	£0.75	£1.25
31-37	*$0.35*	*$1.05*	*$1.75*	£0.25	£0.75	£1.25
Title Value:	*$12.30*	*$36.90*	*$61.50*	£8.40	£25.20	£42.00

JUSTICE LEAGUE: A MIDSUMMER'S NIGHTMARE

DC Comics,MS; 1 Sep 1996-3 Nov 1996

	$Good	$Fine	$N.Mint	£Good	£Fine	£N.Mint
1-3 ND 48pgs, Mark Waid and Fabian Niceiza script, Jeff Johnson and Darick Robertson art	*$0.60*	*$1.80*	*$3.00*	£0.40	£1.20	£2.00
Title Value:	*$1.80*	*$5.40*	*$9.00*	£1.20	£3.60	£6.00
Justice League: A Midsummer's Nightmare (Feb 1997) Trade paperback ND collects mini-series with new Kevin Maguire cover				£1.10	£3.30	£5.50

JUSTICE MACHINE (1ST SERIES)

Noble/Texas; 1 Jun 1981-5 Nov 1983

	$Good	$Fine	$N.Mint	£Good	£Fine	£N.Mint
1 ND magazine size; John Byrne cover	*$1.20*	*$3.60*	*$6.00*	£0.80	£2.40	£4.00
2-3 ND magazine size	*$0.80*	*$2.40*	*$4.00*	£0.60	£1.80	£3.00
4-5 ND DS slightly larger than regular comic size	*$0.50*	*$1.50*	*$2.50*	£0.30	£0.90	£1.50
Title Value:	*$3.80*	*$11.40*	*$19.00*	£2.60	£7.80	£13.00

JUSTICE MACHINE (2ND SERIES)

Comico/Innovation; 1 Jan 1987-29 May 1989

	$Good	$Fine	$N.Mint	£Good	£Fine	£N.Mint
1-18 ND	*$0.40*	*$1.20*	*$2.00*	£0.25	£0.75	£1.25
19-25 ND The Earth/Georwell War	*$0.40*	*$1.20*	*$2.00*	£0.25	£0.75	£1.25
26-29 ND	*$0.40*	*$1.20*	*$2.00*	£0.25	£0.75	£1.25
Title Value:	*$11.60*	*$34.80*	*$58.00*	£7.25	£21.75	£36.25
Annual 1 (Jun 1989), last Comico issue				£0.40	£1.20	£2.00
Summer Spectacular (1990), 1st Innovation issue, part Byrne cover				£0.45	£1.35	£2.25

JUSTICE MACHINE (3RD SERIES)

Innovation; 1 Apr 1990-7 Apr 1991

	$Good	$Fine	$N.Mint	£Good	£Fine	£N.Mint
1-4 ND	*$0.40*	*$1.20*	*$2.00*	£0.25	£0.75	£1.25
5-7 ND The Demon Trilogy	*$0.40*	*$1.20*	*$2.00*	£0.25	£0.75	£1.25
Title Value:	*$2.80*	*$8.40*	*$14.00*	£1.75	£5.25	£8.75

JUSTICE MACHINE ANNUAL

Texas,OS; 1 1984

	$Good	$Fine	$N.Mint	£Good	£Fine	£N.Mint
1 ND 1st appearance Elementals, Willingham art, part Golden cover	*$1.00*	*$3.00*	*$5.00*	£0.80	£2.40	£4.00
Title Value:	*$1.00*	*$3.00*	*$5.00*	£0.80	£2.40	£4.00

JUSTICE MACHINE FEATURING THE ELEMENTALS

Comico,MS; 1 May 1986-4 Aug 1986

	$Good	$Fine	$N.Mint	£Good	£Fine	£N.Mint
1-4 ND	*$0.40*	*$1.20*	*$2.00*	£0.25	£0.75	£1.25
Title Value:	*$1.60*	*$4.80*	*$8.00*	£1.00	£3.00	£5.00

JUSTICE MACHINE MINI-SERIES, THE NEW

Innovation,MS; 1 Jan 1990-3 Mar 1990

	$Good	$Fine	$N.Mint	£Good	£Fine	£N.Mint
1-3 ND colour	*$0.40*	*$1.20*	*$2.00*	£0.25	£0.75	£1.25
Title Value:	*$1.20*	*$3.60*	*$6.00*	£0.75	£2.25	£3.75

JUSTICE MACHINE: THE CHIMERA CONSPIRACY

Millennium,MS; 1 Nov 1992-3 Jan 1993

	$Good	$Fine	$N.Mint	£Good	£Fine	£N.Mint
1-3 ND	*$0.50*	*$1.50*	*$2.50*	£0.30	£0.90	£1.50
Title Value:	*$1.50*	*$4.50*	*$7.50*	£0.90	£2.70	£4.50

JUSTICE RIDERS, THE

DC Comics/Elseworlds,OS; 1 Feb 1997

	$Good	$Fine	$N.Mint	£Good	£Fine	£N.Mint
1 ND 64pgs, Justice League in the Wild West	*$1.20*	*$3.60*	*$6.00*	£0.80	£2.40	£4.00
Title Value:	*$1.20*	*$3.60*	*$6.00*	£0.80	£2.40	£4.00

JUSTICE SOCIETY OF AMERICA (1ST SERIES)

DC Comics,MS; 1 Apr 1991-8 Nov 1991

(see Justice League of America #21)

	$Good	$Fine	$N.Mint	£Good	£Fine	£N.Mint
1 Golden Age Flash (Jay Garrick) appears	*$0.25*	*$0.75*	*$1.25*	£0.15	£0.45	£0.75
2 Golden Age Black Canary appears	*$0.25*	*$0.75*	*$1.25*	£0.15	£0.45	£0.75
3 Golden Age Green Lantern appears	*$0.25*	*$0.75*	*$1.25*	£0.15	£0.45	£0.75
4 Golden Age Hawkman appears	*$0.25*	*$0.75*	*$1.25*	£0.15	£0.45	£0.75
5 Golden Age Hawkman and Flash appear	*$0.25*	*$0.75*	*$1.25*	£0.15	£0.45	£0.75
6 Golden Age Black Canary and Green Lantern appear	*$0.25*	*$0.75*	*$1.25*	£0.15	£0.45	£0.75
7 Justice Society re-united	*$0.25*	*$0.75*	*$1.25*	£0.15	£0.45	£0.75
8 Justice Society vs. Vandal Savage	*$0.25*	*$0.75*	*$1.25*	£0.15	£0.45	£0.75
Title Value:	*$2.00*	*$6.00*	*$10.00*	£1.20	£3.60	£6.00

JUSTICE SOCIETY OF AMERICA (2ND SERIES)

DC Comics; 1 Aug 1992-10 May 1993

(see All Star Comics)

	$Good	$Fine	$N.Mint	£Good	£Fine	£N.Mint
1-10	*$0.25*	*$0.75*	*$1.25*	£0.15	£0.45	£0.75
Title Value:	*$2.50*	*$7.50*	*$12.50*	£1.50	£4.50	£7.50

JUSTICE: FOUR BALANCE

Marvel Comics Group,MS; 1 Sep 1994-4 Dec 1994

	$Good	$Fine	$N.Mint	£Good	£Fine	£N.Mint
1-4 Thing, Yancy Street Gang, Night Thrasher and Firestar	*$0.30*	*$0.90*	*$1.50*	£0.20	£0.60	£1.00
Title Value:	*$1.20*	*$3.60*	*$6.00*	£0.80	£2.40	£4.00

JUSTY

Viz,MS; 1 1988-9 1989

	$Good	$Fine	$N.Mint	£Good	£Fine	£N.Mint
1-9 ND Japanese manga material	*$0.40*	*$1.20*	*$2.00*	£0.25	£0.75	£1.25
Title Value:	*$3.60*	*$10.80*	*$18.00*	£2.25	£6.75	£11.25

K

KA-ZAR

Marvel Comics Group; 1 Aug 1970-3 Mar 1971
(see Savage Tales, X-Men #10)

Issue	$Good	$Fine	$N.Mint	£Good	£Fine	£N.Mint
1 68pgs, reprints X-Men #10 (1st Silver Age appearance), Daredevil #24; Hercules, Vision, Scarlet Witch, Quicksilver and Black Panther appear in new story	$2.90	$8.75	$17.50	£1.65	£5.00	£10.00
2 68pgs, reprints origin Ka-Zar; new Angel back-up story; Daredevil appears	$2.05	$6.25	$12.50	£1.15	£3.50	£7.00
3 68pgs, Daredevil appears (reprints issue #14); new Angel back-up continues in Marvel Tales #30	$2.05	$6.25	$12.50	£1.15	£3.50	£7.00
Title Value:	$7.00	$21.25	$42.50	£3.95	£12.00	£24.00

KA-ZAR (2ND SERIES)

Marvel Comics Group; 1 Jan 1974-20 Feb 1977

Issue	$Good	$Fine	$N.Mint	£Good	£Fine	£N.Mint
1 ND	$0.80	$2.50	$5.00	£0.40	£1.25	£2.50
2 ND	$0.55	$1.75	$3.50	£0.30	£1.00	£2.00
3 ND	$0.50	$1.50	$3.00	£0.25	£0.75	£1.50
4 ND Brunner cover	$0.50	$1.50	$3.00	£0.25	£0.75	£1.50
5-10	$0.50	$1.50	$3.00	£0.25	£0.75	£1.50
11	$0.40	$1.25	$2.50	£0.20	£0.60	£1.25
12 Russ Heath art	$0.40	$1.25	$2.50	£0.20	£0.60	£1.25
13-20	$0.40	$1.25	$2.50	£0.20	£0.60	£1.25
Title Value:	$9.35	$28.75	$57.50	£4.70	£14.25	£29.00

KA-ZAR OF THE SAVAGE LAND

Marvel Comics Group,OS; nn Feb 1997

Issue	$Good	$Fine	$N.Mint	£Good	£Fine	£N.Mint
nn ND 48pgs, Ka-Zar vs. Sauron	$0.50	$1.50	$2.50	£0.30	£0.90	£1.50
Title Value:	$0.50	$1.50	$2.50	£0.30	£0.90	£1.50

KA-ZAR THE SAVAGE

Marvel Comics Group; 1 Apr 1981-34 Oct 1984
(see Marvel Fanfare)

Issue	$Good	$Fine	$N.Mint	£Good	£Fine	£N.Mint
1 Brent Anderson art	$0.30	$0.90	$1.50	£0.20	£0.60	£1.00
2-9 Brent Anderson art	$0.25	$0.75	$1.25	£0.15	£0.45	£0.75
10 1st direct sale, Mando (heavier stock) paper begins, B. Anderson art	$0.25	$0.75	$1.25	£0.15	£0.45	£0.75
11-12 Brent Anderson art	$0.25	$0.75	$1.25	£0.15	£0.45	£0.75
13-20 ND	$0.25	$0.75	$1.25	£0.15	£0.45	£0.75
21-26 Spiderman appears	$0.25	$0.75	$1.25	£0.15	£0.45	£0.75
27-28 ND	$0.25	$0.75	$1.25	£0.15	£0.45	£0.75
29 DS, Ka-Zar and Shanna wed	$0.25	$0.75	$1.25	£0.15	£0.45	£0.75
30	$0.25	$0.75	$1.25	£0.15	£0.45	£0.75
31-33 Paul Neary art	$0.25	$0.75	$1.25	£0.15	£0.45	£0.75
34 Neary art; Steranko-parody cover, many cancelled characters appear (cameo)	$0.30	$0.90	$1.50	£0.20	£0.60	£1.00
Title Value:	$8.60	$25.80	$43.00	£5.20	£15.60	£26.00

Note: Tales of Zabu in 11, 12, 14-18.

FEATURES
Tales of Zabu in 11, 12, 14-18.

KABUKI COLOUR GALLERY

Caliber Press,OS; nn Aug 1995

Issue	$Good	$Fine	$N.Mint	£Good	£Fine	£N.Mint
nn ND painted pin-ups by David Mack, Tim Bradstreet, Colleen Doran and others	$0.60	$1.80	$3.00	£0.40	£1.20	£2.00
Title Value:	$0.60	$1.80	$3.00	£0.40	£1.20	£2.00

KABUKI COLOUR SPECIAL

Caliber Press,OS; nn Dec 1995

Issue	$Good	$Fine	$N.Mint	£Good	£Fine	£N.Mint
nn ND new story plus pin-ups by Billy Tucci and various	$0.60	$1.80	$3.00	£0.40	£1.20	£2.00
Title Value:	$0.60	$1.80	$3.00	£0.40	£1.20	£2.00

KABUKI: CIRCLE OF BLOOD

Caliber Press; 1 Jan 1995-6 Nov 1995

Issue	$Good	$Fine	$N.Mint	£Good	£Fine	£N.Mint
1 ND 48pgs, David Mack script and art; black and white	$1.20	$3.60	$6.00	£0.70	£2.10	£3.50
2-6 ND 48pgs, David Mack script and art; black and white	$0.60	$1.80	$3.00	£0.40	£1.20	£2.00
Title Value:	$4.20	$12.60	$21.00	£2.70	£8.10	£13.50
Kabuki: Circle of Blood (Feb 1996) Trade paperback ND collects mini-series				£2.30	£6.90	£13.50
Deluxe Edition (Feb 1996) ND signed and numbered with foil-enhanced cover				£3.30	£9.90	£16.50

KABUKI: DANCE OF DEATH

London Night Studios; 1 Jan 1995

Issue	$Good	$Fine	$N.Mint	£Good	£Fine	£N.Mint
1 ND David Mack script and art; black and white	$0.80	$2.40	$4.00	£0.50	£1.50	£2.50
1 Commemorative Edition ND	$1.20	$3.60	$6.00	£0.80	£2.40	£4.00
Title Value:	$2.00	$6.00	$10.00	£1.30	£3.90	£6.50

KABUKI: FEAR THE REAPER

Caliber Press,OS; 1 Nov 1994

Issue	$Good	$Fine	$N.Mint	£Good	£Fine	£N.Mint
1 ND 48pgs, 1st appearance of Kabuki; spin-off from Shi, David Mack script and art; black and white	$1.40	$4.20	$7.00	£0.70	£2.10	£3.50
Title Value:	$1.40	$4.20	$7.00	£0.70	£2.10	£3.50
Kabuki Compilation Graphic Novel (Jul 1995) 80pgs, reprints Fear The Reaper and Dance of Death; black and white				£1.00	£3.00	£5.00

KABUKI: MASKS OF NOH

Caliber Press,MS; 1 Apr 1996-present

Issue	$Good	$Fine	$N.Mint	£Good	£Fine	£N.Mint
1 Cover A, ND Joe Quesada cover; black and white	$0.60	$1.80	$3.00	£0.40	£1.20	£2.00
1 Cover B, ND David Mack cover; black and white	$0.60	$1.80	$3.00	£0.40	£1.20	£2.00
1 Cover C, ND Buzz cover; black and white	$0.60	$1.80	$3.00	£0.40	£1.20	£2.00
2-4 ND black and white	$0.60	$1.80	$3.00	£0.40	£1.20	£2.00
Title Value:	$3.60	$10.80	$18.00	£2.40	£7.20	£12.00

KABUKI: SKIN DEEP

Caliber Comics; 1 Oct 1996-present

Issue	$Good	$Fine	$N.Mint	£Good	£Fine	£N.Mint
1 ND David Mack script and art; colour	$0.60	$1.80	$3.00	£0.40	£1.20	£2.00
Title Value:	$0.60	$1.80	$3.00	£0.40	£1.20	£2.00

KAFKA

Renegade; 1 Apr 1987-6 Sep 1987

Issue	$Good	$Fine	$N.Mint	£Good	£Fine	£N.Mint
1-6 ND	$0.40	$1.20	$2.00	£0.25	£0.75	£1.25
Title Value:	$2.40	$7.20	$12.00	£1.50	£4.50	£7.50

KAMANDI THE LAST BOY ON EARTH

DC Comics; 1 Oct/Nov 1972-59 Sep/Oct 1978
(see Brave and the Bold 120, 157)

Issue	$Good	$Fine	$N.Mint	£Good	£Fine	£N.Mint
1 ND origin and 1st appearance Kamandi; Jack Kirby art	$7.50	$22.50	$45.00	£2.50	£7.50	£15.00
2 Jack Kirby art	$4.55	$13.50	$27.50	£1.30	£4.00	£8.00
3 Jack Kirby art	$2.90	$8.75	$17.50	£0.80	£2.50	£5.00
4 1st appearance Prince Tuftan of the Tigers; Jack Kirby art	$2.90	$8.75	$17.50	£0.80	£2.50	£5.00
5 Jack Kirby art	$2.90	$8.75	$17.50	£0.80	£2.50	£5.00
6-10 Jack Kirby art	$2.05	$6.25	$12.50	£0.65	£2.00	£4.00
11-20 Jack Kirby art	$1.25	$3.75	$7.50	£0.50	£1.50	£3.00
21-28 Jack Kirby art	$0.80	$2.50	$5.00	£0.40	£1.25	£2.50
29 Superman's costume appears, Jack Kirby art	$0.80	$2.50	$5.00	£0.40	£1.25	£2.50
30 Jack Kirby art	$0.80	$2.50	$5.00	£0.40	£1.25	£2.50
31 1st appearance Pyra, Jack Kirby art	$0.65	$2.00	$4.00	£0.30	£1.00	£2.00
32 scarce in the U.K. 68pgs, reprints issue #1; Jack Kirby art	$0.75	$2.25	$4.50	£0.50	£1.50	£3.00
33-39 Jack Kirby art	$0.65	$2.00	$4.00	£0.30	£1.00	£2.00
40 ND last Jack Kirby art	$0.65	$2.00	$4.00	£0.30	£1.00	£2.00
41-42	$0.50	$1.50	$3.00	£0.20	£0.60	£1.25
43 scarce in the U.K.	$0.50	$1.50	$3.00	£0.25	£0.75	£1.50
44 scarce in the U.K. Giffen art featured	$0.50	$1.50	$3.00	£0.25	£0.75	£1.50
45-46 scarce in the U.K. Giffen and Nasser art featured	$0.50	$1.50	$3.00	£0.25	£0.75	£1.50
47	$0.50	$1.50	$3.00	£0.20	£0.60	£1.25
48 scarce in the U.K.	$0.50	$1.50	$3.00	£0.25	£0.75	£1.50
49	$0.50	$1.50	$3.00	£0.20	£0.60	£1.25
50 Omac appears	$0.50	$1.50	$3.00	£0.25	£0.75	£1.50
51-57	$0.50	$1.50	$3.00	£0.20	£0.60	£1.25
58 Karate Kid appears	$0.50	$1.50	$3.00	£0.25	£0.75	£1.50
59 ND scarce in the U.K. 44pgs, Jim Starlin art on Omac; Kamandi story continued in Brave and the Bold #157	$0.70	$2.10	$3.50	£0.50	£1.50	£2.50
Title Value:	$67.80	$205.35	$410.50	£26.10	£80.35	£160.75

FEATURES
Omac in 59. Tales of the Great Disaster in 43-46.

KAMANDI: AT EARTH'S END

DC Comics,MS; 1 Jun 1993-6 Nov 1993

Issue	$Good	$Fine	$N.Mint	£Good	£Fine	£N.Mint
1 Tom Veitch script begins	$0.40	$1.20	$2.00	£0.25	£0.75	£1.25
2-3	$0.40	$1.20	$2.00	£0.25	£0.75	£1.25
4-5 Superman appears	$0.40	$1.20	$2.00	£0.25	£0.75	£1.25
6	$0.40	$1.20	$2.00	£0.25	£0.75	£1.25
Title Value:	$2.40	$7.20	$12.00	£1.50	£4.50	£7.50

KAMUI, LEGEND OF

Eclipse; 1 May 1987-38 Jul 1990

Issue	$Good	$Fine	$N.Mint	£Good	£Fine	£N.Mint
1 ND Saripei Shirato script/art begins (translated Japanese reprint); black and white	$0.80	$2.40	$4.00	£0.50	£1.50	£2.50
1 2nd printing ND	$0.45	$1.35	$2.25	£0.30	£0.90	£1.50
2 ND	$0.50	$1.50	$2.50	£0.30	£0.90	£1.50
2 2nd printing ND	$0.30	$0.90	$1.50	£0.20	£0.60	£1.00
3 ND	$0.40	$1.20	$2.00	£0.25	£0.75	£1.25
3 2nd printing ND	$0.30	$0.90	$1.50	£0.20	£0.60	£1.00
4-38 ND	$0.30	$0.90	$1.50	£0.20	£0.60	£1.00
Title Value:	$13.25	$39.75	$66.25	£8.75	£26.25	£43.75

KARATE KID

DC Comics; 1 Mar/Apr 1976-15 Jul/Aug 1978
(see Adventure, Legion of Super-Heroes, Superboy)

Issue	$Good	$Fine	$N.Mint	£Good	£Fine	£N.Mint
1 scarce in the U.K. Legion of Super-Heroes appear	$0.50	$1.50	$3.00	£0.50	£1.50	£3.00
2-3 scarce in the U.K.						

	$Good	$Fine	$N.Mint	£Good	£Fine	£N.Mint
	$0.40	$1.25	$2.50	£0.30	£1.00	£2.00
4-5	$0.40	$1.25	$2.50	£0.25	£0.75	£1.50
6 Legion of Super-Heroes appear	$0.40	$1.25	$2.50	£0.20	£0.60	£1.25
7	$0.40	$1.25	$2.50	£0.20	£0.60	£1.25
8 scarce in the U.K.	$0.40	$1.25	$2.50	£0.25	£0.75	£1.50
9 Princess Projectra appears	$0.40	$1.25	$2.50	£0.20	£0.60	£1.25
10 Princess Projectra and Legion appear	$0.40	$1.25	$2.50	£0.20	£0.60	£1.25
11	$0.30	$1.00	$2.00	£0.20	£0.60	£1.25
12-13 Legion of Super-Heroes appear	$0.30	$1.00	$2.00	£0.20	£0.60	£1.25
14 Robin appears	$0.30	$1.00	$2.00	£0.20	£0.60	£1.25
15 X-over Kamandi #58	$0.30	$1.00	$2.00	£0.20	£0.60	£1.25
Title Value:	$5.60	$17.75	$35.50	£3.65	£11.15	£22.75

Note: Legion of Super-Heroes appear in 1,2,4,6,10,12,13.

KATMANDU

Antarctic Press; 1 Oct 1995-6 1996 ?

	$Good	$Fine	$N.Mint	£Good	£Fine	£N.Mint
1-6 ND black and white	$0.55	$1.65	$2.75	£0.35	£1.05	£1.75
Title Value:	$3.30	$9.90	$16.50	£2.10	£6.30	£10.50

KATO OF THE GREEN HORNET

Now Comics,MS; 1 Nov 1991-4 Feb 1992

	$Good	$Fine	$N.Mint	£Good	£Fine	£N.Mint
1-4 ND	$0.40	$1.20	$2.00	£0.25	£0.75	£1.25
Title Value:	$1.60	$4.80	$8.00	£1.00	£3.00	£5.00

KATO OF THE GREEN HORNET II

Now Comics; 1 Nov 1992-4 Feb 1993

	$Good	$Fine	$N.Mint	£Good	£Fine	£N.Mint
1-4 ND	$0.50	$1.50	$2.50	£0.30	£0.90	£1.50
Title Value:	$2.00	$6.00	$10.00	£1.20	£3.60	£6.00

KATO OF THE GREEN HORNET III

Now Comics,MS; 1 Oct 1993-2 Nov 1993

	$Good	$Fine	$N.Mint	£Good	£Fine	£N.Mint
1-2 ND Mike Baron script	$0.50	$1.50	$2.50	£0.30	£0.90	£1.50
Title Value:	$1.00	$3.00	$5.00	£0.60	£1.80	£3.00

KATO: DRAGON'S IN EDEN GRAPHIC NOVEL

Now Comics,OS; nn Jul 1994

	$Good	$Fine	$N.Mint	£Good	£Fine	£N.Mint
nn ND 48pgs, Mike Baron script, Bob Bilau art	$1.00	$3.00	$5.00	£0.70	£2.10	£3.50
Title Value:	$1.00	$3.00	$5.00	£0.70	£2.10	£3.50

KATY KEENE SPECIAL

Red Circle/Archie Comics; 1 Sep 1983-33 1990

	$Good	$Fine	$N.Mint	£Good	£Fine	£N.Mint
1-33 ND	$0.20	$0.60	$1.00	£0.10	£0.30	£0.50
Title Value:	$6.60	$19.80	$33.00	£3.30	£9.90	£16.50

Note: becomes simply Katy Keen with #7.

KEGOR, MONSTER OF THE DEEP

A Plus Comics,MS; 1 Nov 1991

	$Good	$Fine	$N.Mint	£Good	£Fine	£N.Mint
1 ND 48pgs, Steve Ditko art and cover	$0.50	$1.50	$2.50	£0.30	£0.90	£1.50
Title Value:	$0.50	$1.50	$2.50	£0.30	£0.90	£1.50

Note: announced as a mini-series and cancelled

KEIF LLAMA - XENO TECH

Fantagraphics; 1 1988-6 1988

(see Particle Dreams)

	$Good	$Fine	$N.Mint	£Good	£Fine	£N.Mint
1-6 ND Matt Howarth script/art	$0.40	$1.20	$2.00	£0.25	£0.75	£1.25
Title Value:	$2.40	$7.20	$12.00	£1.50	£4.50	£7.50

KELVIN MACE

Vortex; 1 1986; 2 1987

	$Good	$Fine	$N.Mint	£Good	£Fine	£N.Mint
1 ND Schoenfeld art	$0.80	$2.40	$4.00	£0.50	£1.50	£2.50
1 2nd printing, ND (stamped on 1st page)	$0.40	$1.20	$2.00	£0.25	£0.75	£1.25
2 ND	$0.50	$1.50	$2.50	£0.30	£0.90	£1.50
Title Value:	$1.70	$5.10	$8.50	£1.05	£3.15	£5.25

KENDRA: LEGACY OF BLOOD

Perry Dog Press; 1 Feb/Mar 1987

	$Good	$Fine	$N.Mint	£Good	£Fine	£N.Mint
1 ND black and white	$0.25	$0.75	$1.25	£0.15	£0.45	£0.75
Title Value:	$0.25	$0.75	$1.25	£0.15	£0.45	£0.75

KI-GORR THE KILLER

AC Comics; 1 Feb 1995

	$Good	$Fine	$N.Mint	£Good	£Fine	£N.Mint
1 ND Bill Black script, Brad Gorby cover; black and white	$0.80	$2.40	$4.00	£0.50	£1.50	£2.50
Title Value:	$0.80	$2.40	$4.00	£0.50	£1.50	£2.50

KICKERS INC.

Marvel Comics Group/New Universe; 1 Nov 1986-12 Oct 1987

	$Good	$Fine	$N.Mint	£Good	£Fine	£N.Mint
1-12 ND	$0.15	$0.45	$0.75	£0.10	£0.35	£0.60
Title Value:	$1.80	$5.40	$9.00	£1.20	£4.20	£7.20

KID 'N PLAY

Marvel Comics Group,TV; 1 Feb 1992-9 Oct 1993

	$Good	$Fine	$N.Mint	£Good	£Fine	£N.Mint
1-9 ND	$0.15	$0.45	$0.75	£0.10	£0.30	£0.50
Title Value:	$1.35	$4.05	$6.75	£0.90	£2.70	£4.50

KID CANNIBAL

Eternity,MS; 1 Dec 1991-4 Mar 1992

	$Good	$Fine	$N.Mint	£Good	£Fine	£N.Mint
1-4 ND	$0.50	$1.50	$2.50	£0.30	£0.90	£1.50
Title Value:	$2.00	$6.00	$10.00	£1.20	£3.60	£6.00

KID CODY, WESTERN ACTION STARRING

Atlas; 1 Feb 1975

	$Good	$Fine	$N.Mint	£Good	£Fine	£N.Mint
1 distributed in the U.K. Doug Wildey art	$0.25	$0.75	$1.50	£0.15	£0.50	£1.00
Title Value:	$0.25	$0.75	$1.50	£0.15	£0.50	£1.00

KID COLT GIANT SIZE ANNUAL

Marvel Comics Group; 1 Jan 1975-3 Jul 1975

	$Good	$Fine	$N.Mint	£Good	£Fine	£N.Mint
1-3 ND 68pgs, part reprint	$0.80	$2.50	$5.00	£0.65	£2.00	£4.00
Title Value:	$2.40	$7.50	$15.00	£1.95	£6.00	£12.00

KID COLT OUTLAW

Atlas/Marvel Comics Group;91 Jul 1960-139 Mar 1968; 140 Nov 1969-229 Apr 1979

(previous issues ND)

	$Good	$Fine	$N.Mint	£Good	£Fine	£N.Mint
91	$3.20	$9.50	$22.50	£1.10	£3.40	£8.00
92-95 ND	$3.20	$9.50	$22.50	£1.40	£4.25	£10.00
96-99	$3.20	$9.50	$22.50	£1.10	£3.40	£8.00
100 scarce in the U.K.	$3.55	$10.50	$25.00	£1.75	£5.25	£12.50
101-104	$2.10	$6.25	$15.00	£0.85	£2.55	£6.00
105-108 very scarce in the U.K.	$2.10	$6.25	$15.00	£1.05	£3.20	£7.50
109	$2.10	$6.25	$15.00	£0.85	£2.55	£6.00
110 1st appearance Iron Mask	$2.10	$6.25	$15.00	£0.85	£2.55	£6.00
111-118	$2.10	$6.25	$15.00	£0.85	£2.55	£6.00
119-120 rare in the U.K.	$2.10	$6.25	$15.00	£1.40	£4.25	£10.00
121-129	$1.40	$4.25	$10.00	£0.50	£1.50	£3.50
130 64pgs, classic reprints including origin of Kid Colt	$1.40	$4.25	$10.00	£0.70	£2.10	£5.00
131-132 64pgs, classic reprints	$1.40	$4.25	$10.00	£0.70	£2.10	£5.00
133-139	$1.40	$4.25	$10.00	£0.40	£1.25	£3.00

Justice League of America #114

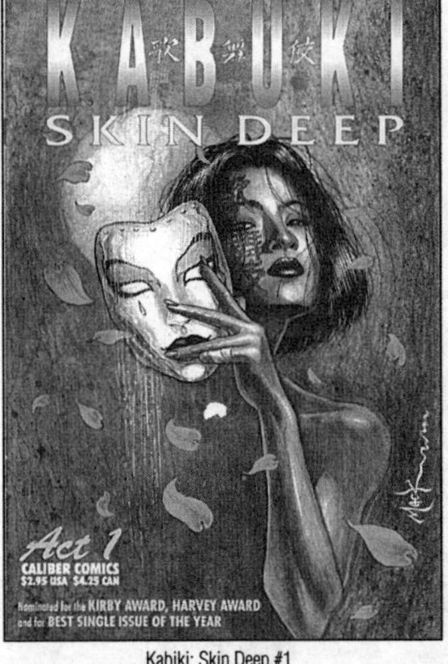

Kabiki: Skin Deep #1

Kamandi, The Last Boy On Earth #5

Issue	$Good	$Fine	$N.Mint	£Good	£Fine	£N.Mint
140-148 ND	*$1.65*	*$5.00*	*$10.00*	£0.55	£1.75	£3.50
149-154	*$1.00*	*$3.00*	*$6.00*	£0.40	£1.25	£2.50
155-156 ND scarce in the U.K.	*$0.80*	*$2.50*	*$5.00*	£0.50	£1.50	£3.00
157-169 ND	*$0.80*	*$2.50*	*$5.00*	£0.40	£1.25	£2.50
170 ND origin reprinted, Williamson art	*$0.65*	*$2.00*	*$4.00*	£0.45	£1.35	£2.75
171-199 ND	*$0.50*	*$1.50*	*$3.00*	£0.30	£1.00	£2.00
200 ND	*$0.30*	*$1.00*	*$2.00*	£0.40	£1.25	£2.50
201-229 ND	*$0.30*	*$1.00*	*$2.00*	£0.20	£0.60	£1.25
Title Value:	*$157.95*	*$477.75*	*$1024.50*	£70.05	£216.30	£478.50

Note: issues 140, 142-200, 202-229 are all reprint. New Two Gun Kid story in 141, new Kid Colt story in 201.

KID ETERNITY

DC Comics,MS; 1 Apr 1991-3 Nov 1991

(see Secret Origins [1st Series] #4)

Issue	$Good	$Fine	$N.Mint	£Good	£Fine	£N.Mint
1-3 ND 48pgs, Grant Morrison script/Duncan Fegredo art and design by Rian Hughes	*$1.00*	*$3.00*	*$5.00*	£0.70	£2.10	£3.50
Title Value:	*$3.00*	*$9.00*	*$15.00*	£2.10	£6.30	£10.50

Note: Prestige Format

KID ETERNITY (2ND SERIES)

DC Comics/Vertigo; 1 May 1993-16 Sep 1994

Issue	$Good	$Fine	$N.Mint	£Good	£Fine	£N.Mint
1 Sean Philips covers and art begins; under "Vertigo" banner	*$0.40*	*$1.20*	*$2.00*	£0.25	£0.75	£1.25
2-6	*$0.40*	*$1.20*	*$2.00*	£0.25	£0.75	£1.25
7 Sean Schoffield guest art	*$0.40*	*$1.20*	*$2.00*	£0.25	£0.75	£1.25
8-12	*$0.40*	*$1.20*	*$2.00*	£0.25	£0.75	£1.25
13-16 A Date In Hell story	*$0.40*	*$1.20*	*$2.00*	£0.25	£0.75	£1.25
Title Value:	*$6.40*	*$19.20*	*$32.00*	£4.00	£12.00	£20.00

KID MONTANA

Charlton;9 Nov 1957-50 Jan 1965

(called Davy Crockett, Frontier Fighter #1-8)

Issue	$Good	$Fine	$N.Mint	£Good	£Fine	£N.Mint
9 scarce in the U.K.	*$6.25*	*$19.00*	*$45.00*	£3.55	£10.50	£25.00
10 scarce in the U.K.	*$3.55*	*$10.50*	*$25.00*	£1.75	£5.25	£12.50
11-12	*$2.50*	*$7.50*	*$17.50*	£1.10	£3.40	£8.00
13 Williamson art	*$3.55*	*$10.50*	*$25.00*	£1.75	£5.25	£12.50
14-18	*$2.50*	*$7.50*	*$17.50*	£1.10	£3.40	£8.00
19-20 distributed in the U.K.	*$2.50*	*$7.50*	*$17.50*	£0.90	£2.75	£6.50
21-40 distributed in the U.K.	*$1.75*	*$5.25*	*$12.50*	£0.60	£1.90	£4.50
41-50 distributed in the U.K.	*$0.85*	*$2.55*	*$6.00*	£0.40	£1.25	£3.00
Title Value:	*$79.35*	*$238.00*	*$512.50*	£32.55	£100.80	£239.00

Note: reasonable distribution in the U.K. after 1959

KID SUPREME

Image; 1 Mar 1996-present

Issue	$Good	$Fine	$N.Mint	£Good	£Fine	£N.Mint
1 ND Dan Fraga and Eric Stephenson script, Dan Fraga and Marlo Alquiza art	*$0.50*	*$1.50*	*$2.50*	£0.30	£0.90	£1.50
2-8 ND	*$0.50*	*$1.50*	*$2.50*	£0.30	£0.90	£1.50
Title Value:	*$4.00*	*$12.00*	*$20.00*	£2.40	£7.20	£12.00

KIKU SAN

Aircel; 1 1988-6 1989

Issue	$Good	$Fine	$N.Mint	£Good	£Fine	£N.Mint
1-6 ND Barry Blair script and art	*$0.40*	*$1.20*	*$2.00*	£0.25	£0.75	£1.25
Title Value:	*$2.40*	*$7.20*	*$12.00*	£1.50	£4.50	£7.50

KILGORE

Renegade; 1 Nov 1987-5 1988

Issue	$Good	$Fine	$N.Mint	£Good	£Fine	£N.Mint
1-5 ND	*$0.40*	*$1.20*	*$2.00*	£0.25	£0.75	£1.25
Title Value:	*$2.00*	*$6.00*	*$10.00*	£1.25	£3.75	£6.25

KILL RAZOR SPECIAL

Image,OS; 1 Jun 1995

Issue	$Good	$Fine	$N.Mint	£Good	£Fine	£N.Mint
1 ND Codename: Strikeforce spin-off	*$0.50*	*$1.50*	*$2.50*	£0.30	£0.90	£1.50
Title Value:	*$0.50*	*$1.50*	*$2.50*	£0.30	£0.90	£1.50

KILL YOUR BOYFRIEND

DC Comics/Vertigo,OS; 1 Jun 1995

Issue	$Good	$Fine	$N.Mint	£Good	£Fine	£N.Mint
1 ND 64pgs, Grant Morrison script and Phillip Bond art	*$0.90*	*$2.70*	*$4.50*	£0.60	£1.80	£3.00
Title Value:	*$0.90*	*$2.70*	*$4.50*	£0.60	£1.80	£3.00

KILLER INSTINCT

Acclaim Comics,MS; 1 May 1996-3 Jul 1996

Issue	$Good	$Fine	$N.Mint	£Good	£Fine	£N.Mint
1-2 ND Doug Moench script, Paul Gulacy art	*$0.50*	*$1.50*	*$2.50*	£0.30	£0.90	£1.50
3 ND Art Holcomb script, Bart Sears art	*$0.50*	*$1.50*	*$2.50*	£0.30	£0.90	£1.50
Title Value:	*$1.50*	*$4.50*	*$7.50*	£0.90	£2.70	£4.50

KILLER INSTINCT - TIGER FURY SPECIAL

Acclaim Comics,OS; 1 Sep 1996

Issue	$Good	$Fine	$N.Mint	£Good	£Fine	£N.Mint
1 ND	*$0.50*	*$1.50*	*$2.50*	£0.30	£0.90	£1.50
Title Value:	*$0.50*	*$1.50*	*$2.50*	£0.30	£0.90	£1.50

KILLER INSTINCT SPECIAL

Acclaim Comics; 1 Sep 1996-present

Issue	$Good	$Fine	$N.Mint	£Good	£Fine	£N.Mint
1 ND issue #4 of Killer Instinct	*$0.50*	*$1.50*	*$2.50*	£0.30	£0.90	£1.50
2 ND issue #5 of Killer Instinct	*$0.50*	*$1.50*	*$2.50*	£0.30	£0.90	£1.50
3 ND issue #6 of Killer Instinct	*$0.50*	*$1.50*	*$2.50*	£0.30	£0.90	£1.50

Issue	$Good	$Fine	$N.Mint	£Good	£Fine	£N.Mint
Title Value:	*$1.50*	*$4.50*	*$7.50*	£0.90	£2.70	£4.50

KILLER SYNTHETIC TOADS

Artline Studios,OS; 1 Aug 1991

Issue	$Good	$Fine	$N.Mint	£Good	£Fine	£N.Mint
1 ND	*$0.40*	*$1.20*	*$2.00*	£0.25	£0.75	£1.25
Title Value:	*$0.40*	*$1.20*	*$2.00*	£0.25	£0.75	£1.25

KILLER...TALES BY TIM TRUMAN

Eclipse,OS; 1 Mar 1985

Issue	$Good	$Fine	$N.Mint	£Good	£Fine	£N.Mint
1 ND Tim Truman cover and art	*$0.40*	*$1.20*	*$2.00*	£0.25	£0.75	£1.25
Title Value:	*$0.40*	*$1.20*	*$2.00*	£0.25	£0.75	£1.25

KILLING STROKE, THE

Eternity,MS; 1 Jun 1991-4 Sep 1991

Issue	$Good	$Fine	$N.Mint	£Good	£Fine	£N.Mint
1 ND horror anthology featuring Mark Buckingham, D'Israeli, Shane Oakley, black and white; Intro by Jamie Delano	*$0.40*	*$1.20*	*$2.00*	£0.25	£0.75	£1.25
2-4 ND	*$0.40*	*$1.20*	*$2.00*	£0.25	£0.75	£1.25
Title Value:	*$1.60*	*$4.80*	*$8.00*	£1.00	£3.00	£5.00

KILLPOWER: THE EARLY YEARS

Marvel UK,MS; 1 Aug 1993-4 Dec 1993

Issue	$Good	$Fine	$N.Mint	£Good	£Fine	£N.Mint
1-4 Codename: Genetix appear	*$0.30*	*$0.90*	*$1.50*	£0.15	£0.45	£0.75
Title Value:	*$1.20*	*$3.60*	*$6.00*	£0.60	£1.80	£3.00

KILROY IS HERE

Caliber Press; 0 1995; 1 Apr 1995-10 1996 ?

Issue	$Good	$Fine	$N.Mint	£Good	£Fine	£N.Mint
0 ND black and white	*$0.60*	*$1.80*	*$3.00*	£0.40	£1.20	£2.00
1 ND Negative Burn spin-off; black and white	*$0.60*	*$1.80*	*$3.00*	£0.40	£1.20	£2.00
1 Signed Edition, ND (Sep 1995); black and white	*$0.60*	*$1.80*	*$3.00*	£0.40	£1.20	£2.00
2 ND Negative Burn spin-off; black and white	*$0.60*	*$1.80*	*$3.00*	£0.40	£1.20	£2.00
3-10 ND black and white	*$0.60*	*$1.80*	*$3.00*	£0.40	£1.20	£2.00
Title Value:	*$7.20*	*$21.60*	*$36.00*	£4.80	£14.40	£24.00

KILROY: REVELATIONS

Caliber Press,OS; 1 1994

Issue	$Good	$Fine	$N.Mint	£Good	£Fine	£N.Mint
1 ND black and white	*$0.60*	*$1.80*	*$3.00*	£0.40	£1.20	£2.00
Title Value:	*$0.60*	*$1.80*	*$3.00*	£0.40	£1.20	£2.00

KIMURA

Night Wynd,MS; 1 Dec 1991-4 Mar 1992

Issue	$Good	$Fine	$N.Mint	£Good	£Fine	£N.Mint
1-4 ND Barry Blair script and art	*$0.50*	*$1.50*	*$2.50*	£0.30	£0.90	£1.50
Title Value:	*$2.00*	*$6.00*	*$10.00*	£1.20	£3.60	£6.00

KINDRED, THE

Image; 1 Mar 1994-4 Jun 1994

Issue	$Good	$Fine	$N.Mint	£Good	£Fine	£N.Mint
1 ND Jim Lee and Brandon Choi script, Brett Booth art; bound-in scratch-off trading card	*$1.50*	*$4.50*	*$7.50*	£1.00	£3.00	£5.00
2 ND Jim Lee and Brandon Choi script, Brett Booth art	*$1.20*	*$3.60*	*$6.00*	£0.80	£2.40	£4.00
3 ND Jim Lee and Brandon Choi script, Brett Booth art; 1st appearance Team 7	*$0.80*	*$2.40*	*$4.00*	£0.60	£1.80	£3.00
3 Variant Cover Edition, ND - cover forms larger picture when combined with variant covers of Deathblow #5, Gen 13 #5, Stormwatch #10, Team 7 #1, Union #0, Wetworks #2. WildC.A.T.S. #11	*$1.60*	*$4.80*	*$8.00*	£1.00	£3.00	£5.00
4 ND Jim Lee and Brandon Choi script, Brett Booth art	*$0.60*	*$1.80*	*$3.00*	£0.50	£1.50	£2.50
Title Value:	*$5.70*	*$17.10*	*$28.50*	£3.90	£11.70	£19.50
Kindred (Feb 1995) Trade paperback reprints mini-series				£1.30	£3.90	£6.50

KING ARTHUR AND THE KNIGHTS OF JUSTICE

Marvel Comics Group,MS; 1 Dec 1993-3 Feb 1994

Issue	$Good	$Fine	$N.Mint	£Good	£Fine	£N.Mint
1 based on animated series; Michael Golden cover	*$0.25*	*$0.75*	*$1.25*	£0.15	£0.45	£0.75
2 Michael Golden cover	*$0.25*	*$0.75*	*$1.25*	£0.15	£0.45	£0.75
3	*$0.25*	*$0.75*	*$1.25*	£0.15	£0.45	£0.75
Title Value:	*$0.75*	*$2.25*	*$3.75*	£0.45	£1.35	£2.25

KING CONAN

Marvel Comics Group; 1 Mar 1980-55 Nov 1989

Issue	$Good	$Fine	$N.Mint	£Good	£Fine	£N.Mint
1 ND 52pgs	*$0.70*	*$2.10*	*$3.50*	£0.40	£1.20	£2.00
2-6 ND 52pgs	*$0.50*	*$1.50*	*$2.50*	£0.30	£0.90	£1.50
7 ND 52pgs, 1st Paul Smith art (2pgs)	*$0.60*	*$1.80*	*$3.00*	£0.40	£1.20	£2.00
8-19 ND 52pgs	*$0.45*	*$1.35*	*$2.25*	£0.30	£0.90	£1.50
20 ND 52pgs, title becomes Conan the King	*$0.50*	*$1.50*	*$2.50*	£0.25	£0.75	£1.25
21-30 ND 52pgs	*$0.40*	*$1.20*	*$2.00*	£0.25	£0.75	£1.25
31-55 ND 52pgs	*$0.30*	*$0.90*	*$1.50*	£0.20	£0.60	£1.00
Title Value:	*$21.20*	*$63.60*	*$108.75*	£13.65	£40.95	£68.25

KING KONG

Gold Key;30036-809 Sep 1968

Issue	$Good	$Fine	$N.Mint	£Good	£Fine	£N.Mint
30036-809 distributed in the U.K. painted cover	*$4.25*	*$12.50*	*$30.00*	£2.50	£7.50	£17.50
Title Value:	*$4.25*	*$12.50*	*$30.00*	£2.50	£7.50	£17.50

KING KONG (2ND SERIES)

Monster Comics,MS; 1 Dec 1990-6 Mar 1992

Issue	$Good	$Fine	$N.Mint	£Good	£Fine	£N.Mint
1-3 ND adaptation of film; includes stills from 1933 version; Dave Stevens cover	*$0.40*	*$1.20*	*$2.00*	£0.25	£0.75	£1.25
4-6 ND	*$0.40*	*$1.20*	*$2.00*	£0.25	£0.75	£1.25
Title Value:	*$2.40*	*$7.20*	*$12.00*	£1.50	£4.50	£7.50

VERY GENERAL PERCENTAGE CONVERSION CHART WHICH MAY BE USED TO CALCULATE LOW AND INBETWEEN GRADES:

KING OF THE DEAD
Fantaco; 1 1994-2 1994

	$Good	$Fine	$N.Mint	£Good	£Fine	£N.Mint
1-2 ND Steve Niles script, Brian Clark art; black and white	$0.40	$1.20	$2.00	£0.25	£0.75	£1.25
Title Value:	$0.80	$2.40	$4.00	£0.50	£1.50	£2.50

KING TIGER & MOTORHEAD
Dark Horse,MS; 1 Aug 1996-2 Sep 1996

	$Good	$Fine	$N.Mint	£Good	£Fine	£N.Mint
1-2 ND Comics' Greatest World spin-off	$0.60	$1.80	$3.00	£0.40	£1.20	£2.00
Title Value:	$1.20	$3.60	$6.00	£0.80	£2.40	£4.00

KINGDOM COME
DC Comics,MS; 1 Jun 1996-4 Oct 1996

	$Good	$Fine	$N.Mint	£Good	£Fine	£N.Mint
1 ND 48pgs, Mark Waid script, Alex Ross painted art; an Elseworlds type story on the eventual futures of the DC heroes	$1.20	$3.60	$6.00	£0.80	£2.40	£4.00
1 2nd printing ND	$1.00	$3.00	$5.00	£0.70	£2.10	£3.50
2-4 ND	$1.00	$3.00	$5.00	£0.70	£2.10	£3.50
Title Value:	$5.20	$15.60	$26.00	£3.60	£10.80	£18.00

Kingdom Come Collectors Set (Jan 1997)

	$Good	$Fine	$N.Mint	£Good	£Fine	£N.Mint
ND all four parts of the mini-series plus two trading cards				£2.60	£7.80	£13.00

KINGDOM OF THE DWARFS
Comico,OS; 1 May 1991

	$Good	$Fine	$N.Mint	£Good	£Fine	£N.Mint
1 ND 64pgs, squarebound; colour	$0.90	$2.70	$4.50	£0.60	£1.80	£3.00
Title Value:	$0.90	$2.70	$4.50	£0.60	£1.80	£3.00

KINGS IN DISGUISE
Kitchen Sink,MS; 1 Mar 1988-6 Aug 1988

	$Good	$Fine	$N.Mint	£Good	£Fine	£N.Mint
1-6 ND	$0.40	$1.20	$2.00	£0.25	£0.75	£1.25
Title Value:	$2.40	$7.20	$12.00	£1.50	£4.50	£7.50

KINGS OF PAIN
Marvel Comics Group; 1991

Cross-over storyline that ran throughout the following issues:
New Mutants Annual #7, **New Warriors Annual #1**, **X-Men Annual #15** and **X-Factor Annual #6**.

KINGS OF THE NIGHT
Dark Horse,MS; 1 Aug 1990-2 Sep 1990

	$Good	$Fine	$N.Mint	£Good	£Fine	£N.Mint
1-2 ND Roy and Dann Thomas script, painted covers by John Bolton	$0.40	$1.20	$2.00	£0.25	£0.75	£1.25
Title Value:	$0.80	$2.40	$4.00	£0.50	£1.50	£2.50

KISS CLASSIC
Marvel Comics Group; nn Apr 1995

	$Good	$Fine	$N.Mint	£Good	£Fine	£N.Mint
nn ND Trade paperback collecting Marvel Comics Super Special #1 and 5	$2.00	$6.00	$10.00	£1.30	£3.90	£6.50
Title Value:	$2.00	$6.00	$10.00	£1.30	£3.90	£6.50

KISS OF DEATH
(see British section)

KISSNATION
Marvel Comics Group,OS; 1 1996

	$Good	$Fine	$N.Mint	£Good	£Fine	£N.Mint
1 ND 96pgs, Kiss/X-Men team up with Gene Simmons and Paul Stanley plot, Stan Lee script	$2.00	$6.00	$10.00	£1.30	£3.90	£6.50
Title Value:	$2.00	$6.00	$10.00	£1.30	£3.90	£6.50

KISSYFUR
DC Comics,OS; 1 Sep 1989

	$Good	$Fine	$N.Mint	£Good	£Fine	£N.Mint
1 ND scarce in the U.K.	$0.25	$0.75	$1.25	£0.15	£0.45	£0.75
Title Value:	$0.25	$0.75	$1.25	£0.15	£0.45	£0.75

Note: based on TV cartoon

KITTY PRYDE AND WOLVERINE
Marvel Comics Group,MS; 1 Nov 1984-6 Apr 1985

(see X-Men)

	$Good	$Fine	$N.Mint	£Good	£Fine	£N.Mint
1 ND	$0.80	$2.40	$4.00	£0.60	£1.80	£3.00
2-4 ND	$0.60	$1.80	$3.00	£0.50	£1.50	£2.50
5 ND scarce in the U.K.	$0.60	$1.80	$3.00	£0.60	£1.80	£3.00
6 ND very scarce in the U.K.	$0.60	$1.80	$3.00	£0.70	£2.10	£3.50
Title Value:	$3.80	$11.40	$19.00	£3.40	£10.20	£17.00

KITZ 'N' KATZ KOMICS
Phantasy/Eclipse; 1 1985-5 1986

	$Good	$Fine	$N.Mint	£Good	£Fine	£N.Mint
1-5 ND	$0.30	$0.90	$1.50	£0.20	£0.60	£1.00
Title Value:	$1.50	$4.50	$7.50	£1.00	£3.00	£5.00

KLOWN SHOCK
Northstar,MS; 1 Aug 1990-4 1991

	$Good	$Fine	$N.Mint	£Good	£Fine	£N.Mint
1 ND 40pgs, horror material begins	$0.50	$1.50	$2.50	£0.30	£0.90	£1.50
2-4 ND 32pgs	$0.50	$1.50	$2.50	£0.30	£0.90	£1.50
Title Value:	$2.00	$6.00	$10.00	£1.20	£3.60	£6.00

KLOWNSHOCK (2ND SERIES)
Northstar,MS; 1 Sep 1991-2 1991?

	$Good	$Fine	$N.Mint	£Good	£Fine	£N.Mint
1-2 ND	$0.50	$1.50	$2.50	£0.30	£0.90	£1.50
Title Value:	$1.00	$3.00	$5.00	£0.60	£1.80	£3.00

KLOWNSHOCK MADHOUSE
Northstar,OS; 1 Apr 1995

	$Good	$Fine	$N.Mint	£Good	£Fine	£N.Mint
1 ND 48pgs, black and white	$1.00	$3.00	$5.00	£0.70	£2.10	£3.50
Title Value:	$1.00	$3.00	$5.00	£0.70	£2.10	£3.50

KLOWNSHOCK: FREAK SHOW
Northstar,OS; 1 Feb 1994

	$Good	$Fine	$N.Mint	£Good	£Fine	£N.Mint
1 ND 48pgs, foil-embossed cover logo; black and white	$1.00	$3.00	$5.00	£0.70	£2.10	£3.50
Title Value:	$1.00	$3.00	$5.00	£0.70	£2.10	£3.50

KNIGHT HAWKE INVESTIGATIONS
Entity Comics; 1 Dec 1995-2 1996

	$Good	$Fine	$N.Mint	£Good	£Fine	£N.Mint
1 ND black and white	$0.50	$1.50	$2.50	£0.30	£0.90	£1.50
1 Videogame Edition, ND pre-bagged with video game disk	$1.40	$4.20	$7.00	£0.90	£2.70	£4.50
2 ND	$0.50	$1.50	$2.50	£0.30	£0.90	£1.50
Title Value:	$2.40	$7.20	$12.00	£1.50	£4.50	£7.50

KNIGHT WATCHMAN: GRAVEYARD SHIFT
Caliber Press,OS; 1 Sep 1994

	$Good	$Fine	$N.Mint	£Good	£Fine	£N.Mint
1 ND black and white	$0.60	$1.80	$3.00	£0.40	£1.20	£2.00
Title Value:	$0.60	$1.80	$3.00	£0.40	£1.20	£2.00

KNIGHTHAWK
Acclaim Comics/Windjammer,MS; 1 May 1995-6 Jul 1995

	$Good	$Fine	$N.Mint	£Good	£Fine	£N.Mint
1-6 ND Neal Adams script and art with Peter Stone	$0.50	$1.50	$2.50	£0.30	£0.90	£1.50
Title Value:	$3.00	$9.00	$15.00	£1.80	£5.40	£9.00

Note: originally solicited in early 1994 by Continuity Comics

KNIGHTMARE
Antarctic Press; 1 Aug 1994-6 May 1995

	$Good	$Fine	$N.Mint	£Good	£Fine	£N.Mint
1-5 ND black and white	$0.55	$1.65	$2.75	£0.35	£1.05	£1.75
6 ND	$0.55	$1.65	$2.75	£0.35	£1.05	£1.75
Title Value:	$3.30	$9.90	$16.50	£2.10	£6.30	£10.50

KNIGHTMARE
Image; 0 Aug 1995; 1 Feb 1995-5 Dec 1995 ?

	$Good	$Fine	$N.Mint	£Good	£Fine	£N.Mint
0 ND (Aug 1995), origin; wraparound chromium cover	$0.70	$2.10	$3.50	£0.50	£1.50	£2.50
1-2 ND Marat Mychaels and Al Vey creative team	$0.50	$1.50	$2.50	£0.30	£0.90	£1.50
3 ND Marat Mychaels and Al Vey creative team; title becomes simply "Knightmare"	$0.50	$1.50	$2.50	£0.30	£0.90	£1.50
4 ND Marat Mychaels and Al Vey creative team	$0.50	$1.50	$2.50	£0.30	£0.90	£1.50
4 Variant Cover Edition, ND - Joe Quesada/Jimmy Palmiotti cover art	$0.60	$1.80	$3.00	£0.40	£1.20	£2.00
5 ND Rob Liefeld, Marat Mychaels and Al Vey	$0.50	$1.50	$2.50	£0.30	£0.90	£1.50
Title Value:	$3.80	$11.40	$19.00	£2.40	£7.20	£12.00

KNIGHTS OF PENDRAGON, THE
Marvel UK; 1 Jul 1990-18 Dec 1991

	$Good	$Fine	$N.Mint	£Good	£Fine	£N.Mint
1 Gary Erskine/Andy Lanning art begins; Captain Britain cameo	$0.30	$0.90	$1.50	£0.20	£0.60	£1.00
2-18	$0.30	$0.90	$1.50	£0.20	£0.60	£1.00
Title Value:	$5.40	$16.20	$27.00	£3.60	£10.80	£18.00

KNIGHTS OF PENDRAGON, THE (2ND SERIES)
Marvel UK; 1 Jul 1992-15 Sep 1993

(see Overkill in British section)

	$Good	$Fine	$N.Mint	£Good	£Fine	£N.Mint
1 Tomlinson and Abnett script, Gascoine and Buylla art; Iron Man co-stars	$0.30	$0.90	$1.50	£0.20	£0.60	£1.00
2 Black Knight appears	$0.30	$0.90	$1.50	£0.20	£0.60	£1.00
3-5	$0.30	$0.90	$1.50	£0.20	£0.60	£1.00
6-8 Spiderman guest-stars	$0.30	$0.90	$1.50	£0.20	£0.60	£1.00
9 Spiderman and the Warheads guest-star	$0.30	$0.90	$1.50	£0.20	£0.60	£1.00
10 origin Union Jack re-told, Baron Blood returns	$0.30	$0.90	$1.50	£0.20	£0.60	£1.00
11-12 MyS-Tech appear	$0.30	$0.90	$1.50	£0.20	£0.60	£1.00
13-15 Death's Head II appears	$0.30	$0.90	$1.50	£0.20	£0.60	£1.00
Title Value:	$4.50	$13.50	$22.50	£3.00	£9.00	£15.00

KNIGHTS ON BROADWAY
Broadway Comics; 1 Jul 1996-3 Sep 1996

	$Good	$Fine	$N.Mint	£Good	£Fine	£N.Mint
1-3 ND	$0.60	$1.80	$3.00	£0.40	£1.20	£2.00
Title Value:	$1.80	$5.40	$9.00	£1.20	£3.60	£6.00

KNIGHTSTRIKE
Image,OS; 1 Jan 1996

	$Good	$Fine	$N.Mint	£Good	£Fine	£N.Mint
1 ND Extreme Destroyer part 6, continued in Supreme #35; pre-bagged with trading card	$0.50	$1.50	$2.50	£0.30	£0.90	£1.50
Title Value:	$0.50	$1.50	$2.50	£0.30	£0.90	£1.50

KNUCKLES THE MALEVOLENT NUN
Fantagraphics; 1 Aug 1991-2 1991

	$Good	$Fine	$N.Mint	£Good	£Fine	£N.Mint
1-2 ND black and white	$0.40	$1.20	$2.00	£0.25	£0.75	£1.25
Title Value:	$0.80	$2.40	$4.00	£0.50	£1.50	£2.50

KOBALT
DC Comics/Milestone; 1 Jun 1994-16 Aug 1995

	$Good	$Fine	$N.Mint	£Good	£Fine	£N.Mint
1-15	$0.30	$0.90	$1.50	£0.20	£0.60	£1.00
16 48pgs	$0.50	$1.50	$2.50	£0.30	£0.90	£1.50
Title Value:	$5.00	$15.00	$25.00	£3.30	£9.90	£16.50

KOBRA
DC Comics; 1 Feb/Mar 1976-7 Mar/Apr 1977

(see Five-Star Super-Hero Spectacular)

	$Good	$Fine	$N.Mint	£Good	£Fine	£N.Mint
1 Jack Kirby art with faces redrawn by Pablo Marcos - part of Kirby's resignation from DC Comics	$0.65	$2.00	$4.00	£0.40	£1.25	£2.50
2 scarce in the U.K.	$0.50	$1.50	$3.00	£0.30	£1.00	£2.00
3 Giffen art	$0.40	$1.25	$2.50	£0.25	£0.75	£1.50
4-5	$0.40	$1.25	$2.50	£0.20	£0.60	£1.25
6 Nasser art	$0.40	$1.25	$2.50	£0.20	£0.60	£1.25
7 scarce in the U.K. Nasser art						

	$Good	$Fine	$N.Mint	£Good	£Fine	£N.Mint
	$0.40	$1.25	$2.50	£0.25	£0.75	£1.50
Title Value:	$3.15	$9.75	$19.50	£1.80	£5.55	£11.25

KOMAH
Anubis Press; 0 Oct 1994; 1 Dec 1994

	$Good	$Fine	$N.Mint	£Good	£Fine	£N.Mint
0 ND spin-off from Urban Decay; black and white, 5,000 copies	$0.55	$1.65	$2.75	£0.35	£1.05	£1.75
1 ND spin-off from Urban Decay; black and white	$0.55	$1.65	$2.75	£0.35	£1.05	£1.75
Title Value:	$1.10	$3.30	$5.50	£0.70	£2.10	£3.50

KONG THE UNTAMED
DC Comics; 1 Jun/Jul 1975-5 Feb/Mar 1976

	$Good	$Fine	$N.Mint	£Good	£Fine	£N.Mint
1 1st appearance Kong; Bernie Wrightson cover	$0.50	$1.50	$3.00	£0.30	£1.00	£2.00
2 Bernie Wrightson cover	$0.40	$1.25	$2.50	£0.25	£0.75	£1.50
3-5	$0.30	$1.00	$2.00	£0.20	£0.60	£1.25
Title Value:	$1.80	$5.75	$11.50	£1.15	£3.55	£7.25

KONGA
Charlton; 1 1960; 2 Aug 1961-23 Nov 1965
(becomes Fantastic Giants)

	$Good	$Fine	$N.Mint	£Good	£Fine	£N.Mint
1 rare in the U.K. Steve Ditko art	$32.00	$95.00	$225.00	£20.00	£60.00	£140.00
2 scarce in the U.K.	$17.50	$52.50	$125.00	£10.50	£32.00	£75.00
3-5 scarce in the U.K. Steve Ditko art	$12.50	$39.00	$90.00	£6.75	£20.00	£47.50
6-10 scarce in the U.K. Steve Ditko art	$8.50	$26.00	$60.00	£4.25	£12.50	£30.00
11-15 scarce in the U.K. Steve Ditko art	$7.00	$21.00	$50.00	£3.55	£10.50	£25.00
16-23	$5.50	$17.00	$40.00	£2.85	£8.50	£20.00
Title Value:	$208.50	$635.50	$1490.00	£112.55	£335.00	£792.50

Note: all distributed in the U.K.

KONGA'S REVENGE
Charlton;2 Summer 1963-3 Autumn 1963
(previously Return of Konga)

	$Good	$Fine	$N.Mint	£Good	£Fine	£N.Mint
1 reprints issue #3 (1968)	$3.20	$9.50	$22.50	£1.75	£5.25	£12.50
2-3 scarce in the U.K. Steve Ditko art	$6.25	$19.00	$45.00	£3.55	£10.50	£25.00
Title Value:	$15.70	$47.50	$112.50	£8.85	£26.25	£62.50

Note: all distributed in the U.K.

KONNY & CZU
Antarctic Press,MS; 1 Sep 1994-4 Mar 1995

	$Good	$Fine	$N.Mint	£Good	£Fine	£N.Mint
1-4 ND Matt Howarth script and art; black and white	$0.55	$1.65	$2.75	£0.35	£1.05	£1.75
Title Value:	$2.20	$6.60	$11.00	£1.40	£4.20	£7.00

KOOL-AID MAN, ADVENTURES OF
DC Comics,OS; 1 1983

	$Good	$Fine	$N.Mint	£Good	£Fine	£N.Mint
1 ND 36pgs, promotional giveaway in U.S.	$0.15	$0.45	$0.75	£0.10	£0.35	£0.60
Title Value:	$0.15	$0.45	$0.75	£0.10	£0.35	£0.60

KORAK, SON OF TARZAN (1ST SERIES)
Gold Key; 1 Jan 1964-45 Jan 1972
(published by DC issue #46 on)

	$Good	$Fine	$N.Mint	£Good	£Fine	£N.Mint
1 Russ Manning art	$7.75	$23.50	$55.00	£4.25	£12.50	£30.00
2-3 Russ Manning art	$5.00	$15.00	$35.00	£1.70	£5.00	£12.00
4-11 Russ Manning art	$4.60	$13.50	$32.50	£1.40	£4.25	£10.00
12-20	$3.20	$9.50	$22.50	£1.05	£3.20	£7.50
21-30	$2.50	$7.50	$17.50	£0.85	£2.55	£6.00
31-45	$2.05	$6.25	$12.50	£0.80	£2.50	£5.00
Title Value:	$139.10	$415.75	$950.00	£48.80	£148.30	£336.50

Note: all distributed in the U.K.

KORAK, SON OF TARZAN (2ND SERIES)
DC Comics;46 May/Jun 1972-56 Feb/Mar 1974; 57 May/Jun 1975-59 Sep/Oct 1975
(previously published by Gold Key; becomes Tarzan Family)

	$Good	$Fine	$N.Mint	£Good	£Fine	£N.Mint
46 52pgs, Kaluta art	$1.00	$3.00	$6.00	£0.40	£1.25	£2.50
47-59 ND Kaluta art	$0.55	$1.75	$3.50	£0.30	£1.00	£2.00
Title Value:	$8.15	$25.75	$51.50	£4.30	£14.25	£28.50

ARTISTS
Kaluta art in 46-56. Manning reprint in 57-59.
FEATURES
Carson of Venus in 46-56. Pellucidar in 46.

KORG: 70,000 BC
Charlton; 1 May 1975-9 Nov 1976

	$Good	$Fine	$N.Mint	£Good	£Fine	£N.Mint
1 scarce in the U.K. based on TV show	$0.80	$2.50	$5.00	£0.55	£1.75	£3.50
2 John Byrne text illustration; Pat Boyette painted cover	$0.55	$1.75	$3.50	£0.50	£1.50	£3.00
3	$0.50	$1.50	$3.00	£0.30	£1.00	£2.00
4 Pat Boyette painted cover	$0.50	$1.50	$3.00	£0.30	£1.00	£2.00
5-9	$0.50	$1.50	$3.00	£0.30	£1.00	£2.00
Title Value:	$4.85	$14.75	$29.50	£3.15	£10.25	£20.50

KORVAK QUEST, THE
Marvel Comics Group; 1991
Cross-over storyline running throughout the following titles: **Fantastic Four Annual #24, Thor Annual #16, Silver Surfer Annual #4, Guardians of the Galaxy Annual #1.**

KREE/SKRULL WAR STARRING THE AVENGERS
Marvel Comics Group,MS; 1 Sep 1983-2 Oct 1983

	$Good	$Fine	$N.Mint	£Good	£Fine	£N.Mint
1 ND 68pgs, reprints classic Neal Adams Avengers #93, #94	$0.60	$1.80	$3.00	£0.40	£1.20	£2.00
2 ND 68pgs, reprints classic Neal Adams Avengers #95-97	$0.60	$1.80	$3.00	£0.40	£1.20	£2.00
Title Value:	$1.20	$3.60	$6.00	£0.80	£2.40	£4.00

KREY
Gauntlet Comics,MS; 1 Sep 1992-5 Aug 1993

	$Good	$Fine	$N.Mint	£Good	£Fine	£N.Mint
1-5 ND	$0.50	$1.50	$2.50	£0.30	£0.90	£1.50
Title Value:	$2.50	$7.50	$12.50	£1.50	£4.50	£7.50

KREY SPECIAL
Caliber Press,OS; 1 Sep 1993

	$Good	$Fine	$N.Mint	£Good	£Fine	£N.Mint
1 ND ties up plot from series; flip-book format	$0.60	$1.80	$3.00	£0.40	£1.20	£2.00
Title Value:	$0.60	$1.80	$3.00	£0.40	£1.20	£2.00

KRULL
Marvel Comics Group,MS; 1 Nov 1983-2 Dec 1983

	$Good	$Fine	$N.Mint	£Good	£Fine	£N.Mint
1-2 ND adapts film	$0.30	$0.90	$1.50	£0.20	£0.60	£1.00
Title Value:	$0.60	$1.80	$3.00	£0.40	£1.20	£2.00

KRUSADA
Entity Comics; 1 Jun 1996

	$Good	$Fine	$N.Mint	£Good	£Fine	£N.Mint
1 ND Adam Arellano art; black and white	$0.55	$1.65	$2.75	£0.35	£1.05	£1.75
1 Commemorative Edition, ND pre-bagged with certificate; limited to 1,500 copies	$2.00	$6.00	$10.00	£1.30	£3.90	£6.50
Title Value:	$2.55	$7.65	$12.75	£1.65	£4.95	£8.25

KRUSTY COMICS
Bongo Comics,MS; 1 Jan 1995-3 Mar 1995

	$Good	$Fine	$N.Mint	£Good	£Fine	£N.Mint
1 ND Matt Groenig art	$0.50	$1.50	$2.50	£0.40	£1.20	£2.00
2-3 ND Matt Groenig art	$0.50	$1.50	$2.50	£0.30	£0.90	£1.50
Title Value:	$1.50	$4.50	$7.50	£1.00	£3.00	£5.00

KRYPTON CHRONICLES
DC Comics,MS; 1 Sep 1981-3 Nov 1981
(see World of Krypton)

	$Good	$Fine	$N.Mint	£Good	£Fine	£N.Mint
1-3	$0.25	$0.75	$1.25	£0.15	£0.45	£0.75
Title Value:	$0.75	$2.25	$3.75	£0.45	£1.35	£2.25

KULL AND THE BARBARIANS
Marvel Comics Group,Magazine; 1 May 1975-3 Sep 1975

	$Good	$Fine	$N.Mint	£Good	£Fine	£N.Mint
1 scarce in the U.K. 2pgs Neal Adams art, reprints Kull the Conqueror #1	$0.80	$2.50	$5.00	£0.80	£2.50	£5.00
2 scarce in the U.K. Neal Adams inks, Gil Kane art, Red Sonja by Chaykin	$0.50	$1.50	$3.00	£0.50	£1.50	£3.00
3 Neal Adams inks, Solomon Kane appears, origin Red Sonja by Chaykin	$0.30	$1.00	$2.00	£0.50	£1.50	£3.00
Title Value:	$1.60	$5.00	$10.00	£1.80	£5.50	£11.00

KULL IN 3-D
Blackthorne;(3-D Series #51,#67); 1 Autumn 1988-2 Spring 1989

	$Good	$Fine	$N.Mint	£Good	£Fine	£N.Mint
1-2 ND with bound-in 3-D glasses (25% less if without glasses)	$0.50	$1.50	$2.50	£0.30	£0.90	£1.50
Title Value:	$1.00	$3.00	$5.00	£0.60	£1.80	£3.00

KULL THE CONQUEROR
Marvel Comics Group; 1 Jun 1971-2 Sep 1971; 3 Jul 1972-15 Aug 1974; 16 Aug 1976-29 Oct 1978
(becomes Kull the Destroyer) (see Marvel Preview)

	$Good	$Fine	$N.Mint	£Good	£Fine	£N.Mint
1 origin and 2nd appearance Kull (see Creatures on the Loose #10), Wood inks	$1.65	$5.00	$10.00	£1.00	£3.00	£6.00
2 ND 3rd appearance Kull	$1.00	$3.00	$6.00	£0.55	£1.75	£3.50
3 ND	$0.80	$2.50	$5.00	£0.55	£1.75	£3.50
4-6 ND	$0.80	$2.50	$5.00	£0.30	£1.00	£2.00
7-10	$0.65	$2.00	$4.00	£0.25	£0.75	£1.50
11 Ploog art; title becomes "Kull the Destroyer"	$0.50	$1.50	$3.00	£0.30	£1.00	£2.00
12-15 ND Ploog art	$0.50	$1.50	$3.00	£0.25	£0.75	£1.50
16-17 ND	$0.50	$1.50	$3.00	£0.20	£0.60	£1.25
18	$0.50	$1.50	$3.00	£0.15	£0.50	£1.00
19-29 ND	$0.50	$1.50	$3.00	£0.20	£0.60	£1.25
Title Value:	$17.95	$54.50	$103.50	£8.05	£24.80	£50.25

Note: Severin art 2-10

KULL THE CONQUEROR (2ND SERIES)
Marvel Comics Group; 1 Dec 1982-2 Mar 1983

	$Good	$Fine	$N.Mint	£Good	£Fine	£N.Mint
1 ND Buscema art	$0.50	$1.50	$2.50	£0.30	£0.90	£1.50
2 ND Bolton art	$0.50	$1.50	$2.50	£0.30	£0.90	£1.50
Title Value:	$1.00	$3.00	$5.00	£0.60	£1.80	£3.00

Note: 52pgs, Baxter paper.

KULL THE CONQUEROR (3RD SERIES)
Marvel Comics Group; 1 May 1983-10 Jun 1985

	$Good	$Fine	$N.Mint	£Good	£Fine	£N.Mint
1 ND	$0.30	$0.90	$1.50	£0.20	£0.60	£1.00
2 ND Sienkiewicz art	$0.30	$0.90	$1.50	£0.20	£0.60	£1.00
3 ND	$0.30	$0.90	$1.50	£0.20	£0.60	£1.00
4 ND Sienkiewicz/Bolton art	$0.30	$0.90	$1.50	£0.20	£0.60	£1.00
5-10 ND	$0.30	$0.90	$1.50	£0.20	£0.60	£1.00
Title Value:	$3.00	$9.00	$15.00	£2.00	£6.00	£10.00

KUNG FU FIGHTER
(see Richard Dragon, Kung Fu Fighter)

	$Good	$Fine	$N.Mint	£Good	£Fine	£N.Mint
KUNG FU SPECIAL						
Marvel Comics Group,Magazine; 1 1974						
1 ND 84pgs, features Iron Fist (part Neal Adams inks), Shang-Chi, Sons of the Tiger						
	$0.65	$2.00	$4.00	£0.50	£1.50	£3.00
Title Value:	$0.65	$2.00	$4.00	£0.50	£1.50	£3.00
KYRA						
Elsewhere Productions; 1 Winter 1985-5 Spring 1987						
1 ND black and white begins; this issue slightly larger size than normal						
	$0.30	$0.90	$1.50	£0.20	£0.60	£1.00
2-5 ND	$0.30	$0.90	$1.50	£0.20	£0.60	£1.00
Title Value:	$1.50	$4.50	$7.50	£1.00	£3.00	£5.00

L

	$Good	$Fine	$N.Mint	£Good	£Fine	£N.Mint
L'IL GENIUS						
Charlton; 1 1954-52 Jan 1965; 53 Oct 1965; 54 Oct 1985-55 Jan 1986						
1 scarce in the U.K.	$8.50	$26.00	$60.00	£4.25	£12.50	£30.00
2 scarce in the U.K.	$4.25	$12.50	$30.00	£2.10	£6.25	£15.00
3 scarce in the U.K.	$2.85	$8.50	$20.00	£1.10	£3.40	£8.00
4-15	$2.85	$8.50	$20.00	£1.05	£3.20	£7.50
16-17 68pgs	$3.55	$10.50	$25.00	£1.75	£5.25	£12.50
18 scarce in the U.K. 100pgs						
	$5.50	$17.00	$40.00	£2.85	£8.50	£20.00
19-20	$2.85	$8.50	$20.00	£1.05	£3.20	£7.50
21-30	$2.10	$6.25	$15.00	£0.85	£2.55	£6.00
1st official distribution in the U.K.						
31-35	$2.10	$6.25	$15.00	£0.70	£2.10	£5.00
36-40	$1.40	$4.25	$10.00	£0.60	£1.90	£4.50
41-53	$1.10	$3.40	$8.00	£0.55	£1.70	£4.00
54-55 scarce in the U.K.						
	$0.30	$0.90	$1.50	£0.20	£0.60	£1.00
Title Value:	$121.50	$365.00	$862.00	£51.05	£154.75	£364.50

Note: distributed irregularly in the U.K. after 1958/59 prior to official distribution cover date November 1959

	$Good	$Fine	$N.Mint	£Good	£Fine	£N.Mint
L'IL GRUESOME						
United Way Comics/Eclipse; 1 1988						
1 ND colour volunteer community youth comic						
	$0.15	$0.45	$0.75	£0.10	£0.30	£0.50
Title Value:	$0.15	$0.45	$0.75	£0.10	£0.30	£0.50
L'IL KIDS						
Marvel Comics Group; 1 Aug 1970-2 Oct 1970; 3 Nov 1971-12 Jun 1973						
1 ND rare in the U.K.						
	$1.65	$5.00	$10.00	£1.00	£3.00	£6.00
2 ND rare in the U.K.						
	$1.00	$3.00	$6.00	£0.65	£2.00	£4.00
3-12 ND very scarce in the U.K.						
	$0.80	$2.50	$5.00	£0.50	£1.50	£3.00
Title Value:	$10.65	$33.00	$66.00	£6.65	£20.00	£40.00
L'IL PALS						
Marvel Comics Group; 1 Sep 1972-5 May 1973						
1 ND rare in the U.K.						
	$0.80	$2.50	$5.00	£0.50	£1.50	£3.00
2-5 ND rare in the U.K.						
	$0.65	$2.00	$4.00	£0.40	£1.25	£2.50
Title Value:	$3.40	$10.50	$21.00	£2.10	£6.50	£13.00
LA PACIFICA						
DC Comics/Paradox Press,MS; 1 Jan 1995-3 Mar 1995						
1-3 ND 96pgs, digest size; black and white						
	$0.90	$2.70	$4.50	£0.60	£1.80	£3.00
Title Value:	$2.70	$8.10	$13.50	£1.80	£5.40	£9.00

	$Good	$Fine	$N.Mint	£Good	£Fine	£N.Mint
LABMAN						
Image,OS; 1 Nov 1996						
1 ND 48pgs, Rudy Coby script, Mike Allred art						
	$0.70	$2.10	$3.50	£0.50	£1.50	£2.50
Title Value:	$0.70	$2.10	$3.50	£0.50	£1.50	£2.50
LABYRINTH						
Marvel Comics Group,Film; 1 Nov 1986-3 Jan 1987						
1-3 ND reprints Marvel Super Special #4						
	$0.25	$0.75	$1.25	£0.15	£0.45	£0.75
Title Value:	$0.75	$2.25	$3.75	£0.45	£1.35	£2.25
LADY ARCANE						
Hero,MS; 1 Jul 1992-6 1993						
1 ND Flare appears	$0.50	$1.50	$2.50	£0.30	£0.90	£1.50
2-5 ND	$0.50	$1.50	$2.50	£0.30	£0.90	£1.50
6 ND 44pgs	$0.55	$1.65	$2.75	£0.35	£1.05	£1.75
Title Value:	$3.05	$9.15	$15.25	£1.85	£5.55	£9.25
LADY CRIME						
AC Comics,OS; 1 Aug 1992						
1 ND	$0.50	$1.50	$2.50	£0.30	£0.90	£1.50
Title Value:	$0.50	$1.50	$2.50	£0.30	£0.90	£1.50
LADY DEATH						
Chaos Comics,MS; 1 Mar 1994-3 May 1994						
½ ND - produced in conjunction with Wizard Comics; issued in a Wizard protective Mylar with certificate of authenticity						
	$5.00	$15.00	$25.00	£2.50	£7.50	£12.50
½ Gold Edition, ND - Gold embossed logo, produced in conjunction with Wizard Comics; issued in a Wizard protective Mylar with certificate of authenticity						
	$9.00	$27.00	$45.00	£3.50	£10.50	£17.50
½ Red Velvet Edition, ND - Red velvet embossed logo, produced in conjunction with Wizard Comics; issued in a Wizard protective Mylar with certificate of authenticity						
	$10.00	$30.00	$50.00	£5.00	£15.00	£25.00
½ Signed & Numbered Edition, ND limted to 2,500 copies						
	$6.00	$18.00	$30.00	£4.00	£12.00	£20.00
1 ND Steven Hughes art; chromium enhanced cover; special guest appearance by Evil Ernie						
	$16.00	$48.00	$80.00	£8.00	£24.00	£40.00
1 Commemorative Edition, ND - Gold embossed logo, signed by creators on cover; limited to 5,000 copies						
	$16.00	$48.00	$80.00	£8.00	£24.00	£40.00
2 ND	$9.00	$27.00	$45.00	£5.00	£15.00	£25.00
3 ND	$5.00	$15.00	$25.00	£3.00	£9.00	£15.00
Title Value:	$76.00	$228.00	$380.00	£39.00	£117.00	£195.00
Lady Death: The Reckoning (Jul 1994) Trade paperback reprints mini-series with new cover by Steven Hughes				£0.90	£2.70	£4.50
Lady Death Limited Edition Hardcover (Jul 1994) reprints series, foil-stamped cover with dust-jacket plus interviews and unpublished artwork				£5.00	£15.00	£25.00
Lady Death: The Reckoning (Sep 1995) Trade paperback reprints mini-series plus Lady Death ½ and Swimsuit Special				£1.70	£5.10	£8.50
LADY DEATH & THE WOMEN OF CHAOS! GALLERY						
Chaos Comics,OS; 1 Nov 1996						
1 ND pin-ups	$0.50	$1.50	$2.50	£0.30	£0.90	£1.50
Title Value:	$0.50	$1.50	$2.50	£0.30	£0.90	£1.50
LADY DEATH ASHCAN						
Chaos Comics,OS; nn 1995; nn Feb 1996						
nn ND (Feb 1996), new Steven Hughes cover - limited to 2,000 copies						
	$2.50	$7.50	$12.50	£1.50	£4.50	£7.50
nn San Diego Edition ND - with blue foil logo cover; limited to 5,000 copies						
	$4.00	$12.00	$20.00	£3.00	£9.00	£15.00
Title Value:	$6.50	$19.50	$32.50	£4.50	£13.50	£22.50
LADY DEATH HALLOWEEN ASHCAN						
Chaos Comics,OS; nn 1996						

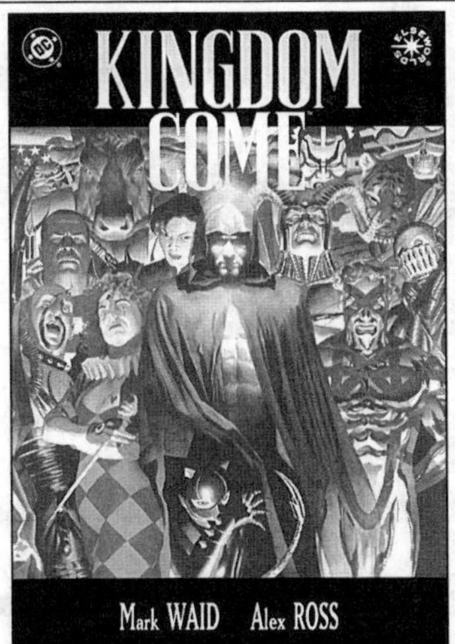

Kingdom Come #1

Korak, Son Of Tarzan (1st) #29

Korak, Son Of Tarzan (2nd) #46

	$Good	$Fine	$N.Mint	£Good	£Fine	£N.Mint
nn ND	$3.00	$9.00	$15.00	£2.00	£6.00	£10.00
Title Value:	$3.00	$9.00	$15.00	£2.00	£6.00	£10.00

LADY DEATH II: BETWEEN HEAVEN & HELL

Chaos Comics,MS; 1 Feb 1995-4 Jun 1995

	$Good	$Fine	$N.Mint	£Good	£Fine	£N.Mint
1 ND Brian Pulido script, Steven Hughes art; wraparound chromium cover	$1.60	$4.80	$8.00	£1.00	£3.00	£5.00
1 Black Velvet Edition, ND limited to 10,000 copies	$10.00	$30.00	$50.00	£4.00	£12.00	£20.00
1 Commemorative Edition, ND (Feb 1996) - produced in conjuction with Comic Cavalcade, gold foil logo - limited to 4,000 copies	$8.00	$24.00	$40.00	£4.00	£12.00	£20.00
1 Signed & Numbered Edition, ND (Mar 1995) - pre-bagged with certificate and mini-poster; limited to 5,000 copies	$8.00	$24.00	$40.00	£4.50	£13.50	£22.50
2-4 ND Brian Pulido script, Steven Hughes art	$1.00	$3.00	$5.00	£0.50	£1.50	£2.50
4 Variant Cover Edition, ND - Lady Demon variant cover	$6.00	$18.00	$30.00	£3.50	£10.50	£17.50
Title Value:	$36.60	$109.80	$180.00	£18.50	£55.50	£92.50
Lady Death: Between Heaven and Hell (Jun 1996) Trade paperback ND collects mini-series, new cover Jason Jensen				£1.70	£5.10	£8.50

LADY DEATH IN LINGERIE

Chaos Comics,OS; 1 Aug 1995

	$Good	$Fine	$N.Mint	£Good	£Fine	£N.Mint
1 ND Steven Hughes wraparound cover, pin-ups by Joe Quesada, Joe Linsner, David Mack, Tom Mandrake and others	$0.90	$2.70	$4.50	£0.50	£1.50	£2.50
1 Leather Edition, ND (Aug 1995) - available to retailers with every 50 copies ordered of the regular edition	$12.00	$36.00	$60.00	£7.00	£21.00	£35.00
1 Micro Premium, ND scarce in the U.K. Lady Demon cover, limited to 2,000 copies	$20.00	$60.00	$100.00	£12.00	£36.00	£60.00
1 Signed & Numbered Edition, ND pre-bagged with certificate	$10.00	$30.00	$50.00	£5.00	£15.00	£25.00
Title Value:	$42.90	$128.70	$214.50	£24.50	£73.50	£122.50

LADY DEATH SWIMSUIT SPECIAL

Chaos Comics,OS; 1 May 1994

	$Good	$Fine	$N.Mint	£Good	£Fine	£N.Mint
1 ND assorted eye-catching pin-ups...	$2.00	$6.00	$10.00	£1.00	£3.00	£5.00
1 Red Velvet Edition, ND - limited to 10,000 copies [May 1994]	$9.00	$27.00	$45.00	£5.00	£15.00	£25.00
1 Signed & Numbered Edition, ND (Sep 1994), pre-bagged with certificate	$5.00	$15.00	$25.00	£3.00	£9.00	£15.00
Title Value:	$16.00	$48.00	$80.00	£9.00	£27.00	£45.00

LADY DEATH: THE CRUCIBLE

Chaos Comics,MS; ½ Jul 1996-2 1996

	$Good	$Fine	$N.Mint	£Good	£Fine	£N.Mint
½ ND 24pgs, available from Wizard #60, issued in protective Mylar with certificate of authenticity	$2.00	$6.00	$10.00	£2.50	£7.50	£12.50
1 ND wraparound all silver cover - groovy	$0.70	$2.10	$3.50	£0.50	£1.50	£2.50
2 ND	$0.60	$1.80	$3.00	£0.40	£1.20	£2.00
Title Value:	$3.30	$9.90	$16.50	£3.40	£10.20	£17.00

LADY DEATH: THE ODYSSEY

Chaos Comics,MS; 1 Apr 1996-4 Jul 1996

	$Good	$Fine	$N.Mint	£Good	£Fine	£N.Mint
1 ND Brian Pulido script, Steven Hughes and Jason Jensen art begins; full embossed gold wraparound cover. Nice	$1.20	$3.60	$6.00	£0.80	£2.40	£4.00
1 Black Onyx Edition, ND limited to 200 copies	$20.00	$60.00	$100.00	£7.00	£21.00	£35.00
1 Limited Edition, ND pre-bagged, wraparound chromium cover; limited to 10,000 copies	$6.00	$18.00	$30.00	£4.00	£12.00	£20.00
1 Sneek Peek Preview, ND 16pgs, cover gallery and sketches	$0.30	$0.90	$1.50	£0.20	£0.60	£1.00
1 Sneek Peek Preview Micro Premium, ND 16pgs, cover gallery, sketches; limited to 2,500 copies	$8.00	$24.00	$40.00	£4.00	£12.00	£20.00
2-3 ND	$0.60	$1.80	$3.00	£0.40	£1.20	£2.00
4 ND new costume	$0.60	$1.80	$3.00	£0.40	£1.20	£2.00
Title Value:	$37.30	$111.90	$186.50	£17.20	£51.60	£86.00

LADY JUSTICE, NEIL GAIMAN'S

Tekno Comix; 1 May 1995-9 Jan 1995; Big Entertainment; 10 Feb 1996-11 Mar 1996

	$Good	$Fine	$N.Mint	£Good	£Fine	£N.Mint
1 ND Neil Gaiman script, Bill Sienkiewicz cover and art	$0.40	$1.20	$2.00	£0.25	£0.75	£1.25
2-4 ND	$0.40	$1.20	$2.00	£0.25	£0.75	£1.25
5 ND (non-Code approved issue)	$0.40	$1.20	$2.00	£0.25	£0.75	£1.25
6 ND (non-Code approved issue)	$0.45	$1.35	$2.25	£0.30	£0.90	£1.50
7 ND pre-bagged with Tekno back-issue comic	$0.45	$1.35	$2.25	£0.30	£0.90	£1.50
8-9 ND	$0.45	$1.35	$2.25	£0.30	£0.90	£1.50
10 ND painted cover by Daniel Brereton	$0.45	$1.35	$2.25	£0.30	£0.90	£1.50
11 ND	$0.45	$1.35	$2.25	£0.30	£0.90	£1.50
Title Value:	$4.70	$14.10	$23.50	£3.05	£9.15	£15.25

LADY JUSTICE, NEIL GAIMAN'S (2ND SERIES)

Big Entertainment; 1 Jun 1996-present

	$Good	$Fine	$N.Mint	£Good	£Fine	£N.Mint
1-9 ND Daniel Brereton covers	$0.45	$1.35	$2.25	£0.30	£0.90	£1.50
Title Value:	$4.05	$12.15	$20.25	£2.70	£8.10	£13.50

LADY PENDRAGON

Maximum Comic Press,MS; 1 Mar 1996-3 May 1996

	$Good	$Fine	$N.Mint	£Good	£Fine	£N.Mint
1-3 ND Matt Hawkins script, Hector Gomez and Mike Deodato art	$0.50	$1.50	$2.50	£0.30	£0.90	£1.50
Title Value:	$1.50	$4.50	$7.50	£0.90	£2.70	£4.50

LADY RAWHIDE

Topps,MS; 1 Jul 1995-5 Mar 1996

	$Good	$Fine	$N.Mint	£Good	£Fine	£N.Mint
½ ND available from Wizard #56, issued in protective Mylar with certificate of authenticity	$2.50	$7.50	$12.50	£1.50	£4.50	£7.50
1 ND Don McGregor script, Mayhew & Palmiotti art begins	$1.00	$3.00	$5.00	£0.60	£1.80	£3.00
1 Signed & Numbered Edition, ND (May 1996) - signed by Don McGregor; 1,500 copies	$2.00	$6.00	$10.00	£1.30	£3.90	£6.50
2 ND	$0.70	$2.10	$3.50	£0.50	£1.50	£2.50
3 ND	$0.60	$1.80	$3.00	£0.40	£1.20	£2.00
3 Signed & Numbered Edition, ND (May 1996) - signed by Adam Hughes; 750 copies	$3.50	$10.50	$17.50	£2.30	£6.75	£11.50
4 ND Michael Golden cover	$0.60	$1.80	$3.00	£0.40	£1.20	£2.00
5 ND painted cover by Julie Bell	$0.60	$1.80	$3.00	£0.40	£1.20	£2.00
Title Value:	$11.50	$34.50	$57.50	£7.40	£22.05	£37.00
Lady Rawhide (Apr 1996) Trade paperback ND collects mini-series plus covers				£1.30	£3.90	£6.50

LADY RAWHIDE (2ND SERIES)

Topps; 1 Oct 1996-present

	$Good	$Fine	$N.Mint	£Good	£Fine	£N.Mint
1 ND Don McGregor script, Esteban Maroto art	$0.60	$1.80	$3.00	£0.40	£1.20	£2.00
2 ND Lady Rawhide vs. Scarlet Fever	$0.60	$1.80	$3.00	£0.40	£1.20	£2.00
Title Value:	$1.20	$3.60	$6.00	£0.80	£2.40	£4.00

LADY RAWHIDE SPECIAL EDITION

Topps,OS; 1 Jun 1995

	$Good	$Fine	$N.Mint	£Good	£Fine	£N.Mint
1 ND 64pgs, reprints stories from Zorro #2, #3 with new Adam Hughes cover	$0.80	$2.40	$4.00	£0.50	£1.50	£2.50
Title Value:	$0.80	$2.40	$4.00	£0.50	£1.50	£2.50

LADY SUPREME

Image; 1 May 1996-2 Jun 1996

	$Good	$Fine	$N.Mint	£Good	£Fine	£N.Mint
1 ND Terry Moore script, Mike Deodato art, Glory guest-stars	$0.50	$1.50	$2.50	£0.30	£0.90	£1.50
1 Alternate Cover Edition ND	$0.50	$1.50	$2.50	£0.30	£0.90	£1.50
2 ND	$0.50	$1.50	$2.50	£0.30	£0.90	£1.50
Title Value:	$1.50	$4.50	$7.50	£0.90	£2.70	£4.50

LADY VAMPRE

Blackout Comics; 0 Mar 1995; 1 May 1995

	$Good	$Fine	$N.Mint	£Good	£Fine	£N.Mint
0 ND Bob Berry script and art; black and white	$0.60	$1.80	$3.00	£0.40	£1.20	£2.00
0 Commemorative Edition, ND (Jul 1995) - signed by Bob Berry with new cover plus certificate; limited to 5,000 copies	$2.00	$6.00	$10.00	£1.20	£3.60	£6.00
1 ND Bruce Schoengood script, Gutierrez and Moussa art; black and white	$0.60	$1.80	$3.00	£0.40	£1.20	£2.00
Title Value:	$3.20	$9.60	$16.00	£2.00	£6.00	£10.00
Lady Vampre Collector's Series (May 1996) ND pre-bagged collection with copies of issue #0, #1 and The Death of Lady Vampre plus mini-poster				£1.30	£3.90	£ 6.50
Lady Vampre Collector's Series Deluxe (May 1996) ND as above with Commemorative Edition of Death of Lady Vampre and signed mini-poster				£2.70	£8.10	£13.50

LADY VAMPRE, DEATH OF

Blackout Comics,OS; 1 Aug 1995

	$Good	$Fine	$N.Mint	£Good	£Fine	£N.Mint
1 ND Mike Migola and Gene Colan flip-cover	$0.60	$1.80	$3.00	£0.40	£1.20	£2.00
Title Value:	$0.60	$1.80	$3.00	£0.40	£1.20	£2.00

LADY VAMPRE: PLEASURES OF THE FLESH

Blackout Comics,OS; 1 Apr 1996

	$Good	$Fine	$N.Mint	£Good	£Fine	£N.Mint
1 ND Dave Guitierrez art; wraparound cover	$0.60	$1.80	$3.00	£0.40	£1.20	£2.00
Title Value:	$0.60	$1.80	$3.00	£0.40	£1.20	£2.00

LAFF-A-LYMPICS, HANNA-BARBERA'S

Marvel Comics Group,TV; 1 Mar 1978-13 Mar 1979

(see Funtastic World of Hanna-Barbera)

	$Good	$Fine	$N.Mint	£Good	£Fine	£N.Mint
1-13 ND	$0.10	$0.35	$0.75	£0.10	£0.30	£0.60
Title Value:	$1.30	$4.55	$9.75	£1.30	£3.90	£7.80

LAFFIN' GAS

Blackthorne; 1 May 1987-12 1988

	$Good	$Fine	$N.Mint	£Good	£Fine	£N.Mint
1 Adolescent Hamsters appear; parodies on every permutation of Mutant Turtles	$0.30	$0.90	$1.50	£0.20	£0.60	£1.00
2 Dark Knight parody	$0.30	$0.90	$1.50	£0.20	£0.60	£1.00
3 He-Man parody	$0.30	$0.90	$1.50	£0.20	£0.60	£1.00
5 Boris Bear revenge issue	$0.30	$0.90	$1.50	£0.20	£0.60	£1.00
6 (Blackthorne 3-D Series 16)	$0.50	$1.50	$2.50	£0.30	£0.90	£1.50
7-12	$0.30	$0.90	$1.50	£0.20	£0.60	£1.00
Title Value:	$3.50	$10.50	$17.50	£2.30	£6.90	£11.50

Note: all Non-Distributed on the news-stands in the U.K.

LANCE BARNES: POST-NUKE DICK

Marvel Comics Group,MS; 1 Apr 1993-4 Jul 1993

	$Good	$Fine	$N.Mint	£Good	£Fine	£N.Mint
1-4 ND	$0.40	$1.20	$2.00	£0.25	£0.75	£1.25
Title Value:	$1.60	$4.80	$8.00	£1.00	£3.00	£5.00

LANCE CARRIGAN OF THE GALACTIC LEGION

Quest Publications; 1 Jul 1983

	$Good	$Fine	$N.Mint	£Good	£Fine	£N.Mint
1 ND	$0.25	$0.75	$1.25	£0.15	£0.45	£0.75
Title Value:	$0.25	$0.75	$1.25	£0.15	£0.45	£0.75

LANCELOT AND GUINEVERE

Dell/Movie Classics,OS Movie; 12-416-310 Aug/Oct 1963

Issue	$Good	$Fine	$N.Mint	£Good	£Fine	£N.Mint
12-416-310 distributed in the U.K. film adaptation starring Cornel Wilde	$7.75	$23.50	$55.00	£5.00	£15.00	£35.00
Title Value:	$7.75	$23.50	$55.00	£5.00	£15.00	£35.00

LAND OF THE GIANTS

Gold Key,TV; 1 Nov 1968-5 Sep 1969

Issue	$Good	$Fine	$N.Mint	£Good	£Fine	£N.Mint
1 distributed in the U.K. photo cover	$7.00	$21.00	$50.00	£3.20	£9.50	£22.50
2 distributed in the U.K.	$4.25	$12.50	$30.00	£2.10	£6.25	£15.00
3-5 distributed in the U.K.	$3.55	$10.50	$25.00	£1.75	£5.25	£12.50
Title Value:	$21.90	$65.00	$155.00	£10.55	£31.50	£75.00

LARRY NIVEN'S A.R.M.

Adventure; 1 Sep 1990

Issue	$Good	$Fine	$N.Mint	£Good	£Fine	£N.Mint
1 ND	$0.50	$1.50	$2.50	£0.30	£0.90	£1.50
Title Value:	$0.50	$1.50	$2.50	£0.30	£0.90	£1.50

Note: based on novella "Death By Ecstasy"

LARS OF MARS 3-D

Eclipse;(3-D Special 19) 1 Apr 1987

Issue	$Good	$Fine	$N.Mint	£Good	£Fine	£N.Mint
1 ND with bound-in 3-D glasses (25% less if without glasses), painted cover; reprints featuring Murphy Anderson pencils	$0.50	$1.50	$2.50	£0.30	£0.90	£1.50
1 non 3-D issue, ND (100 copies, signed)	$0.90	$2.70	$4.50	£0.60	£1.80	£3.00
Title Value:	$1.40	$4.20	$7.00	£0.90	£2.70	£4.50

LASER ERASER & PRESSBUTTON

Eclipse; 1 Nov 1985-6 Jul 1986

(see Three-Dimensional...)

Issue	$Good	$Fine	$N.Mint	£Good	£Fine	£N.Mint
1 ND Steve Dillon art, Garry Leach cover	$0.40	$1.20	$2.00	£0.25	£0.75	£1.25
2 ND David Lloyd art, Garry Leach cover	$0.40	$1.20	$2.00	£0.25	£0.75	£1.25
3 ND Jerry Paris/Garry Leach art, Steve Dillon cover	$0.40	$1.20	$2.00	£0.25	£0.75	£1.25
4-5 ND Mike Collins and Mark Farmer art	$0.40	$1.20	$2.00	£0.25	£0.75	£1.25
6 ND Mike Collins and Mark Farmer art, Garry Leach cover	$0.40	$1.20	$2.00	£0.25	£0.75	£1.25
Title Value:	$2.40	$7.20	$12.00	£1.50	£4.50	£7.50

LASH LARUE WESTERN

Charlton;47 Mar/Apr 1954-84 Jun 1961

(#1-46 published by Fawcett Comics)

Issue	$Good	$Fine	$N.Mint	£Good	£Fine	£N.Mint
47 scarce in the U.K.	$17.50	$52.50	$125.00	£10.00	£30.00	£70.00
48	$12.50	$39.00	$90.00	£7.00	£21.00	£50.00
49-60	$8.50	$26.00	$60.00	£4.25	£12.50	£30.00
61-66	$7.00	$21.00	$50.00	£3.55	£10.50	£25.00
67-68 68pgs	$8.50	$26.00	$60.00	£4.25	£12.50	£30.00
69-70	$7.00	$21.00	$50.00	£3.55	£10.50	£25.00
71-73	$5.00	$15.00	$35.00	£2.10	£6.25	£15.00
1st official distribution in the U.K.						
74-83	$5.00	$15.00	$35.00	£2.10	£6.25	£15.00
84 scarce in the U.K.	$5.50	$17.00	$40.00	£2.50	£7.50	£17.50
Title Value:	$275.50	$835.50	$1950.00	£134.70	£398.75	£952.50

Note: some issues distributed in the U.K. after 1959/60 prior to official distribution with cover date November 1959

LASH LARUE WESTERN ANNUAL

AC Comics,OS; 1 Sep 1991

Issue	$Good	$Fine	$N.Mint	£Good	£Fine	£N.Mint
1 ND 40pgs, black and white cover and reprint art; $2.95 cover	$0.50	$1.50	$2.50	£0.40	£1.20	£2.00
Title Value:	$0.50	$1.50	$2.50	£0.40	£1.20	£2.00

LAST ACTION HERO, THE

Topps,MS; 1 Jun 1993-3 Aug 1993

Issue	$Good	$Fine	$N.Mint	£Good	£Fine	£N.Mint
1-3 ND pre-bagged with 3 trading cards, film adaptation	$0.60	$1.80	$3.00	£0.40	£1.20	£2.00
Title Value:	$1.80	$5.40	$9.00	£1.20	£3.60	£6.00

LAST AMERICAN, THE

Marvel Comics Group/Epic,MS; 1 Dec 1990-4 Mar 1991

Issue	$Good	$Fine	$N.Mint	£Good	£Fine	£N.Mint
1-4 ND script by John Wagner/Alan Grant, art by Steve McMahon	$0.40	$1.20	$2.00	£0.25	£0.75	£1.25
Title Value:	$1.60	$4.80	$8.00	£1.00	£3.00	£5.00

LAST AVENGERS STORY, THE

Marvel Comics Group,MS; 1 Nov 1995-2 Dec 1995

Issue	$Good	$Fine	$N.Mint	£Good	£Fine	£N.Mint
1-2 ND 48pgs, Peter David script, Ariel Olivetti painted art; acetate outer cover	$1.20	$3.60	$6.00	£0.80	£2.40	£4.00
Title Value:	$2.40	$7.20	$12.00	£1.60	£4.80	£8.00
The Last Avengers Story (Nov 1996) Trade paperback						
ND 96pgs, reprints above story in one volume				£1.70	£5.10	£8.50

LAST DAYS OF THE JUSTICE SOCIETY SPECIAL

DC Comics,OS; 1986

Issue	$Good	$Fine	$N.Mint	£Good	£Fine	£N.Mint
1 LD in the U.K. 68pgs	$0.50	$1.50	$2.50	£0.30	£0.90	£1.50
Title Value:	$0.50	$1.50	$2.50	£0.30	£0.90	£1.50

LAST GENERATION

Black Tie; 1 Summer 1987-3 1988

Issue	$Good	$Fine	$N.Mint	£Good	£Fine	£N.Mint
1-3 ND	$0.50	$1.50	$2.50	£0.30	£0.90	£1.50
Title Value:	$1.50	$4.50	$7.50	£0.90	£2.70	£4.50

LAST OF THE VIKING HEROES

Genesis West; 1 Mar 1987-12 1991?

Issue	$Good	$Fine	$N.Mint	£Good	£Fine	£N.Mint
1 ND Michael Thibodeaux art begins; part Jack Kirby cover	$0.50	$1.50	$2.50	£0.30	£0.90	£1.50
1 Signed Edition, ND (Dec 1992)	$0.60	$1.80	$3.00	£0.40	£1.20	£2.00
2-4 ND	$0.50	$1.50	$2.50	£0.30	£0.90	£1.50
5 ND (2 cover versions exist)	$0.50	$1.50	$2.50	£0.30	£0.90	£1.50
6-12 ND	$0.50	$1.50	$2.50	£0.30	£0.90	£1.50
Title Value:	$6.60	$19.80	$33.00	£4.00	£12.00	£20.00
Last of the Viking Heroes: Nidhogger Lives (Jun 1995)						
Hardcover, reprints issues #4-12; limited to 100 gold engraved copies				£6.50	£19.50	£32.50

LAST OF THE VIKING HEROES SUMMER SPECIAL

Genesis West; 1 Oct 1989-3 1991

Issue	$Good	$Fine	$N.Mint	£Good	£Fine	£N.Mint
1 ND Frank Frazetta cover	$0.60	$1.80	$3.00	£0.40	£1.20	£2.00
1 Signed Edition, ND (Jan 1993)	$0.60	$1.80	$3.00	£0.40	£1.20	£2.00
2-3 ND	$0.60	$1.80	$3.00	£0.40	£1.20	£2.00
Title Value:	$2.40	$7.20	$12.00	£1.60	£4.80	£8.00

LAST ONE, THE

DC Comics/Vertigo,MS; 1 Jul 1993-6 Dec 1993

Issue	$Good	$Fine	$N.Mint	£Good	£Fine	£N.Mint
1-6 ND J.M. DeMatteis script	$0.50	$1.50	$2.50	£0.30	£0.90	£1.50
Title Value:	$3.00	$9.00	$15.00	£1.80	£5.40	£9.00

LAST STARFIGHTER, THE

Marvel Comics Group,Film; 1 Oct 1984-3 Dec 1984

Issue	$Good	$Fine	$N.Mint	£Good	£Fine	£N.Mint
1-3 ND adapts film	$0.25	$0.75	$1.25	£0.15	£0.45	£0.75
Title Value:	$0.75	$2.25	$3.75	£0.45	£1.35	£2.25

LAUNCH

Elsewhere Productions; 1 1987

Issue	$Good	$Fine	$N.Mint	£Good	£Fine	£N.Mint
1 ND	$0.40	$1.20	$2.00	£0.25	£0.75	£1.25
Title Value:	$0.40	$1.20	$2.00	£0.25	£0.75	£1.25

LAUNDRYLAND

Fantagraphics; 1 Oct 1990-4 Oct 1992

Issue	$Good	$Fine	$N.Mint	£Good	£Fine	£N.Mint
1-4 ND black and white	$0.50	$1.50	$2.50	£0.30	£0.90	£1.50
Title Value:	$2.00	$6.00	$10.00	£1.20	£3.60	£6.00

LAUREL & HARDY IN 3-D

Blackthorne;(3-D Series #23,#34); 1 Autumn 1987-2 Dec 1987

Issue	$Good	$Fine	$N.Mint	£Good	£Fine	£N.Mint
1-2 ND with bound-in 3-D glasses (25% less if without glasses)	$0.50	$1.50	$2.50	£0.30	£0.90	£1.50
Title Value:	$1.00	$3.00	$5.00	£0.60	£1.80	£3.00

LAUREL AND HARDY

DC Comics,OS; 1 Jul/Aug 1972

Issue	$Good	$Fine	$N.Mint	£Good	£Fine	£N.Mint
1 ND very scarce in the U.K.	$0.65	$2.00	$4.00	£0.40	£1.25	£2.50
Title Value:	$0.65	$2.00	$4.00	£0.40	£1.25	£2.50

LAW & ORDER

Maximum Comic Press; 1 Sep 1995-4 1996 ?

Issue	$Good	$Fine	$N.Mint	£Good	£Fine	£N.Mint
1-4 ND	$0.50	$1.50	$2.50	£0.30	£0.90	£1.50
Title Value:	$2.00	$6.00	$10.00	£1.20	£3.60	£6.00

LAWDOG

Marvel Comics Group/Epic; 1 May 1993-10 Feb 1994

Issue	$Good	$Fine	$N.Mint	£Good	£Fine	£N.Mint
1 ND embossed metallic ink cover	$0.50	$1.50	$2.50	£0.30	£0.90	£1.50
2-8 ND	$0.40	$1.20	$2.00	£0.25	£0.75	£1.25
9-10 ND bound-in trading card	$0.40	$1.20	$2.00	£0.25	£0.75	£1.25
Title Value:	$4.10	$12.30	$20.50	£2.55	£7.65	£12.75

LAWDOG VS. GRIMROD

Marvel Comics Group/Epic,OS; 1 Nov 1993

Issue	$Good	$Fine	$N.Mint	£Good	£Fine	£N.Mint
1 ND 48pgs, bound-in trading card	$0.60	$1.80	$3.00	£0.40	£1.20	£2.00
Title Value:	$0.60	$1.80	$3.00	£0.40	£1.20	£2.00

LAWNMOWER MAN GRAPHIC NOVEL, THE

Innovation,OS; 1 Jun 1992

Issue	$Good	$Fine	$N.Mint	£Good	£Fine	£N.Mint
1 ND 80pgs, based on film including scenes cut from final version	$1.40	$4.20	$7.00	£0.90	£2.70	£4.50
Title Value:	$1.40	$4.20	$7.00	£0.90	£2.70	£4.50

LAZARUS CHURCHYARD

Tundra,MS; 1 Aug 1992-3 1992

Issue	$Good	$Fine	$N.Mint	£Good	£Fine	£N.Mint
1-3 ND reprints from British magazine "Blast!"	$0.80	$2.40	$4.00	£0.50	£1.50	£2.50
Title Value:	$2.40	$7.20	$12.00	£1.50	£4.50	£7.50

Note: all sorts of distribution and production problems as Tundra experienced its own problems in 1992 but issue #3 eventually came out.

LAZIEST SECRETARY IN THE WORLD, THE

DC Comics/Piranha Press,OS; 1 Oct 1990

Issue	$Good	$Fine	$N.Mint	£Good	£Fine	£N.Mint
1 ND 80pgs, Jennifer Waters and Gil Ashley	$2.00	$6.00	$10.00	£1.30	£3.90	£6.50
Title Value:	$2.00	$6.00	$10.00	£1.30	£3.90	£6.50

LEADING COMICS

National Periodical Publications; 1 Winter 1941-77 Aug/Sep 1955

Issue	$Good	$Fine	$N.Mint	£Good	£Fine	£N.Mint
1 origin and 1st appearance The Seven Soldiers of Victory (Star Spangled Kid & Stripsey, Crimson Avenger, Green Arrow & Speedy, Vigilante, Shining Knight)	$410.00	$1225.00	$3300.00	£275.00	£820.00	£2200.00
2	$175.00	$530.00	$1250.00	£115.00	£355.00	£835.00
3	$140.00	$425.00	$1000.00	£95.00	£285.00	£670.00
4-5	$105.00	$320.00	$750.00	£70.00	£210.00	£500.00
6-7	$85.00	$255.00	$600.00	£55.00	£170.00	£400.00
8 scarce in the U.K. classic hour-glass cover	$85.00	$255.00	$600.00	£55.00	£170.00	£400.00

	$Good	$Fine	$N.Mint	£Good	£Fine	£N.Mint
9-10	*$85.00*	*$255.00*	*$600.00*	£55.00	£170.00	£400.00
11-14	*$60.00*	*$180.00*	*$425.00*	£41.00	£120.00	£285.00
15 contents change to all funny animal material such as King Oscar's Court	*$29.00*	*$85.00*	*$200.00*	£19.00	£57.50	£135.00
16-18	*$12.50*	*$39.00*	*$90.00*	£8.50	£26.00	£60.00
19 scarce in the U.K.	*$12.50*	*$39.00*	*$90.00*	£9.50	£29.00	£67.50
20-22	*$12.50*	*$39.00*	*$90.00*	£8.50	£26.00	£60.00
23 1st appearance of Peter Porkchops who becomes the main feature	*$29.00*	*$85.00*	*$200.00*	£19.00	£57.50	£135.00
24-30	*$12.50*	*$39.00*	*$90.00*	£8.50	£26.00	£60.00
31-32	*$10.50*	*$32.00*	*$75.00*	£7.00	£21.00	£50.00
33 scarce in the U.S, very scarce in the U.K.	*$22.50*	*$67.50*	*$160.00*	£15.50	£47.00	£110.00
34 title changes to "Leading Screen Comics" though contents are still funny animal	*$10.00*	*$30.00*	*$70.00*	£6.75	£20.00	£47.50
35-41	*$10.00*	*$30.00*	*$70.00*	£6.75	£20.00	£47.50
42 title changed to Leading Screen Comics	*$10.00*	*$30.00*	*$70.00*	£6.75	£20.00	£47.50
43-77	*$7.75*	*$23.50*	*$55.00*	£5.25	£16.00	£37.50
Title Value:	*$2237.75*	*$6755.00*	*$16190.00*	£1496.00	£4521.00	£10912.50

Note: all Non-Distributed on the news-stands in the U.K. but it is possible that copies found their way over through G.I.'s, Red Cross Parcels etc. As with most Golden Age issues, they are generally scarce in the U.K.

LEAF

NAB; 1-4 1990

	$Good	$Fine	$N.Mint	£Good	£Fine	£N.Mint
1 ND black and white	*$0.30*	*$0.90*	*$1.50*	£0.20	£0.60	£1.00
1 Deluxe Edition, ND; black and white	*$0.80*	*$2.40*	*$4.00*	£0.50	£1.50	£2.50
2-4 ND black and white	*$0.30*	*$0.90*	*$1.50*	£0.20	£0.60	£1.00
Title Value:	*$2.00*	*$6.00*	*$10.00*	£1.30	£3.90	£6.50

LEAGUE OF CHAMPIONS, THE

Hero; 1 Oct 1990-15 1993

	$Good	$Fine	$N.Mint	£Good	£Fine	£N.Mint
1-3 ND	*$0.50*	*$1.50*	*$2.50*	£0.30	£0.90	£1.50
4 ND $3.50 cover begins	*$0.70*	*$2.10*	*$3.50*	£0.45	£1.35	£2.25
5-6 ND	*$0.70*	*$2.10*	*$3.50*	£0.45	£1.35	£2.25
7-10 ND pre-bagged with trading card	*$0.70*	*$2.10*	*$3.50*	£0.45	£1.35	£2.25
11-12 ND 44pgs, $3.95 cover; pre-bagged with trading card	*$0.80*	*$2.40*	*$4.00*	£0.50	£1.50	£2.50
13-15 ND 44pgs	*$0.60*	*$1.80*	*$3.00*	£0.40	£1.20	£2.00
Title Value:	*$9.80*	*$29.40*	*$49.00*	£6.25	£18.75	£31.25

LEAGUE OF JUSTICE

DC Comics/Elseworlds,MS; 1 Nov 1995-2 Dec 1995

	$Good	$Fine	$N.Mint	£Good	£Fine	£N.Mint
1-2 ND 48pgs, Elseworlds versions of the Justice League of America appear set in a medieval dimension	*$1.20*	*$3.60*	*$6.00*	£0.80	£2.40	£4.00
Title Value:	*$2.40*	*$7.20*	*$12.00*	£1.60	£4.80	£8.00

LEATHER AND LACE

Aircel; 1 Jul 1989-25 Nov 1991

	$Good	$Fine	$N.Mint	£Good	£Fine	£N.Mint
1 Barry Blair script and art begins, black and white	*$1.20*	*$3.60*	*$6.00*	£0.80	£2.40	£4.00
1 2nd printing	*$0.50*	*$1.50*	*$2.50*	£0.30	£0.90	£1.50
2	*$0.90*	*$2.70*	*$4.50*	£0.60	£1.80	£3.00
2 2nd printing	*$0.50*	*$1.50*	*$2.50*	£0.30	£0.90	£1.50
3	*$0.80*	*$2.40*	*$4.00*	£0.50	£1.50	£2.50
3 2nd printing	*$0.50*	*$1.50*	*$2.50*	£0.30	£0.90	£1.50
4	*$0.70*	*$2.10*	*$3.50*	£0.45	£1.35	£2.25
4 2nd printing	*$0.40*	*$1.20*	*$2.00*	£0.25	£0.75	£1.25
5	*$0.70*	*$2.10*	*$3.50*	£0.45	£1.35	£2.25
5 2nd printing	*$0.40*	*$1.20*	*$2.00*	£0.25	£0.75	£1.25
6	*$0.60*	*$1.80*	*$3.00*	£0.40	£1.20	£2.00
6 2nd printing	*$0.40*	*$1.20*	*$2.00*	£0.25	£0.75	£1.25
7	*$0.60*	*$1.80*	*$3.00*	£0.40	£1.20	£2.00
7 2nd printing	*$0.40*	*$1.20*	*$2.00*	£0.25	£0.75	£1.25
8	*$0.60*	*$1.80*	*$3.00*	£0.40	£1.20	£2.00
8 2nd printing	*$0.40*	*$1.20*	*$2.00*	£0.25	£0.75	£1.25
9	*$0.60*	*$1.80*	*$3.00*	£0.40	£1.20	£2.00
9 2nd printing	*$0.40*	*$1.20*	*$2.00*	£0.25	£0.75	£1.25
10	*$0.60*	*$1.80*	*$3.00*	£0.40	£1.20	£2.00
10 2nd printing	*$0.40*	*$1.20*	*$2.00*	£0.25	£0.75	£1.25
11 1st banned issue in U.K.	*$0.50*	*$1.50*	*$2.50*	£0.30	£0.90	£1.50
12-21	*$0.40*	*$1.20*	*$2.00*	£0.25	£0.75	£1.25
22 $2.95 cover begims	*$0.60*	*$1.80*	*$3.00*	£0.40	£1.20	£2.00
23-25	*$0.60*	*$1.80*	*$3.00*	£0.40	£1.20	£2.00
Title Value:	*$18.50*	*$55.50*	*$92.50*	£11.85	£35.55	£59.25

Note: all Non-Distributed on the news-stands in the U.K.

	£Good	£Fine	£N.Mint
Summer Special (Aug 1990)	£0.30	£0.90	£1.50
Search for Cindy Wilde Graphic Novel reprints issues #1-4, pre-bagged	£1.65	£4.95	£8.25
Holiday in Cambodia Graphic Album (Oct 1990) reprints #5-8 plus new 8pg story, pre-bagged	£1.65	£4.95	£8.25
Black Velvet Graphic Album (Jul 1991) reprints #9-12	£1.20	£3.60	£6.00

Note: adult content/nudity. Comics sealed in plastic bags. Opened bags would bring 50% of the above values. Artist on all, Barry Blair, also does a "tame" version of the same comics which sell for cover price. Back stocks at the time from Aircel generally very good for both.

LEATHER AND LACE II: BLOOD, SEX AND TEARS

Aircel,MS; 1 Dec 1991-4 Mar 1992

	$Good	$Fine	$N.Mint	£Good	£Fine	£N.Mint
1-4 ND	*$0.55*	*$1.65*	*$2.75*	£0.35	£1.05	£1.75
Title Value:	*$2.20*	*$6.60*	*$11.00*	£1.40	£4.20	£7.00

LEATHERFACE

Northstar; 1 Apr 1991-5 Jun 1992

	$Good	$Fine	$N.Mint	£Good	£Fine	£N.Mint
1 ND based on Texas Chainsaw Massacre film, Dave Dorman cover	*$0.50*	*$1.50*	*$2.50*	£0.30	£0.90	£1.50
2-5 ND	*$0.50*	*$1.50*	*$2.50*	£0.30	£0.90	£1.50
Title Value:	*$2.50*	*$7.50*	*$12.50*	£1.50	£4.50	£7.50

LEATHERFACE (2ND SERIES)

Comico; 1-3 1991; Northstar; 4 1992-8 1993

	$Good	$Fine	$N.Mint	£Good	£Fine	£N.Mint
1 ND	*$0.50*	*$1.50*	*$2.50*	£0.30	£0.90	£1.50
1 2nd printing, ND (Apr 1992)	*$0.45*	*$1.35*	*$2.25*	£0.30	£0.90	£1.50
2-8 ND	*$0.50*	*$1.50*	*$2.50*	£0.30	£0.90	£1.50
Title Value:	*$4.45*	*$13.35*	*$22.25*	£2.70	£8.10	£13.50

LEATHERFACE SPECIAL

Northstar,OS; 1 May 1992

	$Good	$Fine	$N.Mint	£Good	£Fine	£N.Mint
1 ND	*$0.50*	*$1.50*	*$2.50*	£0.30	£0.90	£1.50
Title Value:	*$0.50*	*$1.50*	*$2.50*	£0.30	£0.90	£1.50

LEAVE IT TO BINKY

(see Binky)

LEAVE IT TO CHANCE

Homage Comics; 1 Sep 1996-present

	$Good	$Fine	$N.Mint	£Good	£Fine	£N.Mint
1 ND James Robinson script, Paul Smith art	*$0.50*	*$1.50*	*$2.50*	£0.30	£0.90	£1.50
2-3 ND	*$0.50*	*$1.50*	*$2.50*	£0.30	£0.90	£1.50
Title Value:	*$1.50*	*$4.50*	*$7.50*	£0.90	£2.70	£4.50

LEGACY

Majestic Entertainment; 1 Oct 1993-6 1994

1 ND Tom Morgan and Stan Woch art begins; small glow in the dark image on cover

Lady Rawhide (2nd) #1

Leading Comics #3

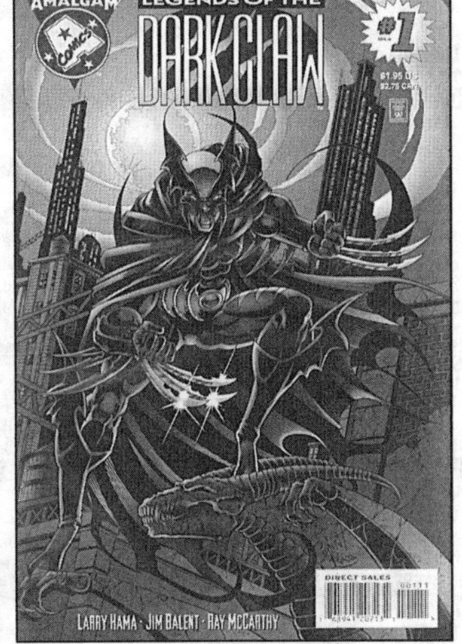

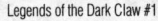

Legends of the Dark Claw #1

	$Good	$Fine	$N.Mint	£Good	£Fine	£N.Mint
	$0.50	$1.50	$2.50	£0.30	£0.90	£1.50
2-6 ND	$0.50	$1.50	$2.50	£0.30	£0.90	£1.50
Title Value:	$3.00	$9.00	$15.00	£1.80	£5.40	£9.00

LEGEND OF KAMUI

(see Kamui)

LEGEND OF MOTHER SARAH, THE

Dark Horse,MS; 1 Apr 1995-8 Nov 1995

	$Good	$Fine	$N.Mint	£Good	£Fine	£N.Mint
1-8 ND Katsuhiro Otomo script and art (translated by Dana Lewis and Toren Smith)	$0.50	$1.50	$2.50	£0.30	£0.90	£1.50
Title Value:	$4.00	$12.00	$20.00	£2.40	£7.20	£12.00

Legend of Mother Sarah: Tunnel Down (Feb 1996)

	£Good	£Fine	£N.Mint
Trade paperback ND 224pgs, collects mini-series	£2.50	£7.50	£12.50

LEGEND OF MOTHER SARAH: CITY OF THE CHILDREN

Dark Horse,MS; 1 Jan 1996-7 Jul 1996

	$Good	$Fine	$N.Mint	£Good	£Fine	£N.Mint
1-7 ND 48pgs, Katsuhiro Otomo script and art; black and white	$0.80	$2.40	$4.00	£0.50	£1.50	£2.50
Title Value:	$5.60	$16.80	$28.00	£3.50	£10.50	£17.50

LEGEND OF THE SHIELD

(see Shield...)

LEGEND OF WONDER WOMAN

(see Wonder Woman)

LEGENDLORE

Caliber Press; 1 1996-4 1996 ?

	$Good	$Fine	$N.Mint	£Good	£Fine	£N.Mint
1-4 ND Joe Martin script, Philip Xavier & Bill Nichols art	$0.60	$1.80	$3.00	£0.40	£1.20	£2.00

LEGENDS

Cross-over series that lead to the formation of the modern Suicide Squad and the new Justice League. The cross-overs are are listed outside the core mini-series of the same name in alphabetical rather than chronological order.

1) Batman 401
2) Blue Beetle 9
3) Blue Beetle 10
4) Cosmic Boy 1
5) Cosmic Boy 2
6) Cosmic Boy 3
7) Cosmic Boy 4
8) Detective Comics 568
9) Firestorm 55
10) Firestorm 56
11) Justice League of America 258
12) Justice League of America 259
13) Justice League of America 260
14) Secret Origins (3rd Series) 10
15) Shazam: The New Beginning 1
16) Shazam: The New Beginning 2
17) Shazam: The New Beginning 3
18) Shazam: The New Beginning 4
19) Superman, Adventures of 426
20) Warlord 114
21) Warlord 115

LEGENDS (LIMITED SERIES)

DC Comics,MS; 1 Nov 1986-6 Apr 1987

	$Good	$Fine	$N.Mint	£Good	£Fine	£N.Mint
1 1st appearance new Captain Marvel	$0.40	$1.20	$2.00	£0.20	£0.60	£1.00
2	$0.40	$1.20	$2.00	£0.20	£0.60	£1.00
3 1st appearance new Suicide Squad (see Brave and the Bold #25 for original team)	$0.40	$1.20	$2.00	£0.20	£0.60	£1.00
4	$0.40	$1.20	$2.00	£0.20	£0.60	£1.00
5 new Justice League appear in last panel though un-named	$0.40	$1.20	$2.00	£0.20	£0.60	£1.00
6 1st appearance new Justice League	$0.50	$1.50	$2.50	£0.40	£1.20	£2.00
Title Value:	$2.50	$7.50	$12.50	£1.40	£4.20	£7.00

Note: Byrne cover/art in all. Multi cross-over title similar to Crisis on Infinite, Earths and Millennium. Last panel #5 features 1st assembly of new Justice League

Legends (Jul 1993)

	£Good	£Fine	£N.Mint
Trade paperback reprints mini-series, new John Byrne cover	£1.85	£5.55	£9.25

LEGENDS OF LUXURA

Brainstorm Comics; 1 Feb 1996-3 1996 ?

	$Good	$Fine	$N.Mint	£Good	£Fine	£N.Mint
1 ND 40pgs, Kirk Lindo script and art; black and white	$0.60	$1.80	$3.00	£0.40	£1.20	£2.00
1 Gold Edition, ND (May 1996), gold foil cover; limited to 2,000 copies	$2.00	$6.00	$10.00	£1.30	£3.90	£6.50
1 Platinum Edition ND	$1.00	$3.00	$5.00	£0.70	£2.10	£3.50
2 ND	$0.60	$1.80	$3.00	£0.40	£1.20	£2.00
2 Gold Edition ND	$1.00	$3.00	$5.00	£0.70	£2.10	£3.50
3 ND	$0.60	$1.80	$3.00	£0.40	£1.20	£2.00
Title Value:	$5.80	$17.40	$29.00	£3.90	£11.70	£19.50

LEGENDS OF THE DARK CLAW

DC Comics/Amalgam,OS; 1 May 1996

	$Good	$Fine	$N.Mint	£Good	£Fine	£N.Mint
1 ND a DC/Marvel amalgamation of Batman and Wolverine; Larry Hama script, Jim Balent and Ray McCarthy art	$0.50	$1.50	$2.50	£0.40	£1.20	£2.00
Title Value:	$0.50	$1.50	$2.50	£0.40	£1.20	£2.00

LEGENDS OF THE STARGRAZERS

Innovation; 1 Jun 1989-5 1990

	$Good	$Fine	$N.Mint	£Good	£Fine	£N.Mint
1-5 ND colour; "good girl art in space" type story	$0.30	$0.90	$1.50	£0.20	£0.60	£1.00
Title Value:	$1.50	$4.50	$7.50	£1.00	£3.00	£5.00

LEGENDS OF THE WORLD'S FINEST

DC Comics,MS; 1 Feb 1994-3 Apr 1994

	$Good	$Fine	$N.Mint	£Good	£Fine	£N.Mint
1-3 ND 48pgs, squarebound; Walt Simonson script, Daniel Brereton painted art	$1.00	$3.00	$5.00	£0.60	£1.80	£3.00
Title Value:	$3.00	$9.00	$15.00	£1.80	£5.40	£9.00

Legends of the World's Finest (Apr 1995)

	£Good	£Fine	£N.Mint
Trade paperback 160pgs, reprints mini-series, new painted cover	£2.00	£6.00	£10.00

LEGION '89 (-'94)

DC Comics; 1 Feb 1989-70 Sep 1994

(Becomes Legion '90 with Jan 1990 issue, Legion '91 with Jan 1991 issue, Legion '92 with Jan 1992 issue, Legion '93 with Jan 1993 issue, Legion '94 with Jan 1994 issue)

	$Good	$Fine	$N.Mint	£Good	£Fine	£N.Mint
1 Barry Kitson art begins, Keith Giffen/Alan Grant script begins	$0.50	$1.50	$2.50	£0.30	£0.90	£1.50
2	$0.40	$1.20	$2.00	£0.25	£0.75	£1.25
3 Lobo joins; appears in most issues hereafter	$0.50	$1.50	$2.50	£0.30	£0.90	£1.50
4-10	$0.40	$1.20	$2.00	£0.25	£0.75	£1.25
11 1st Legion '90 issue	$0.30	$0.90	$1.50	£0.20	£0.60	£1.00
12-22	$0.30	$0.90	$1.50	£0.20	£0.60	£1.00
23 48pgs, 1st Legion '91 issue	$0.40	$1.20	$2.00	£0.25	£0.75	£1.25
24-30	$0.30	$0.90	$1.50	£0.20	£0.60	£1.00
31 Captain Marvel appears	$0.30	$0.90	$1.50	£0.20	£0.60	£1.00
32-33	$0.30	$0.90	$1.50	£0.20	£0.60	£1.00
34 1st Legion '92 issue	$0.30	$0.90	$1.50	£0.20	£0.60	£1.00
35 Lobo "dies"	$0.30	$0.90	$1.50	£0.20	£0.60	£1.00
36-37	$0.30	$0.90	$1.50	£0.20	£0.60	£1.00
38 Lobo vs. Ice Man	$0.30	$0.90	$1.50	£0.20	£0.60	£1.00
39	$0.30	$0.90	$1.50	£0.20	£0.60	£1.00
40 Barry Kitson scripts begin	$0.30	$0.90	$1.50	£0.20	£0.60	£1.00
41-44 bi-weekly	$0.30	$0.90	$1.50	£0.20	£0.60	£1.00
45-47 Green Lantern (Hal Jordan) guest stars	$0.30	$0.90	$1.50	£0.20	£0.60	£1.00
48 $1.75 cover begins	$0.40	$1.20	$2.00	£0.25	£0.75	£1.25
49	$0.40	$1.20	$2.00	£0.25	£0.75	£1.25
50 64pgs, Lobo and Dox vs. Ig'nea	$0.60	$1.80	$3.00	£0.40	£1.20	£2.00
51-52	$0.40	$1.20	$2.00	£0.25	£0.75	£1.25
53-56 bi-weekly	$0.40	$1.20	$2.00	£0.25	£0.75	£1.25
57 Trinity part 3, continued in Darkstars #11	$0.40	$1.20	$2.00	£0.25	£0.75	£1.25
59 Trinity part 6, continued in Darkstars #12	$0.40	$1.20	$2.00	£0.25	£0.75	£1.25
60	$0.40	$1.20	$2.00	£0.25	£0.75	£1.25
61-62 Barry Kitson cover	$0.40	$1.20	$2.00	£0.25	£0.75	£1.25
63 Superman appears, Barry Kitson cover	$0.40	$1.20	$2.00	£0.25	£0.75	£1.25
64-68 Barry Kitson cover	$0.40	$1.20	$2.00	£0.25	£0.75	£1.25
69	$0.40	$1.20	$2.00	£0.25	£0.75	£1.25
70 48pgs, Zero Hour X-over, previews new team Rebels '94	$0.45	$1.35	$2.25	£0.30	£0.90	£1.50
Title Value:	$24.45	$73.35	$122.25	£15.75	£47.25	£78.75

Note: spin-off from Invasion mini-series New Format

LEGION '90 (-'94) ANNUAL

DC Comics; 1 Aug 1990-5 1994

	$Good	$Fine	$N.Mint	£Good	£Fine	£N.Mint
1 48pgs, Superman guest-stars, Alan Grant script, continued from Adventures of Superman Annual 2	$0.50	$1.50	$2.50	£0.30	£0.90	£1.50
2 64pgs, Armageddon: 2001 tie-in	$0.50	$1.50	$2.50	£0.30	£0.90	£1.50
3 64pgs, Eclipso: The Darkness Within tie-in, Justice League appear	$0.50	$1.50	$2.50	£0.30	£0.90	£1.50
4 64pgs, Bloodlines (Wave Two) part 23, 1st appearance Pax, continued in Bloodbath Special #1	$0.50	$1.50	$2.50	£0.30	£0.90	£1.50
5 64pgs, Elseworlds story; Dick Sprang and Curt Swan art featured	$0.60	$1.80	$3.00	£0.40	£1.20	£2.00
Title Value:	$2.60	$7.80	$13.00	£1.60	£4.80	£8.00

LEGION ARCHIVES

DC Comics; 1 Dec 1991; 2 Dec 1992; 3 Oct 1993; 4 Oct 1994; 5 1995; 6 Dec 1996

	$Good	$Fine	$N.Mint	£Good	£Fine	£N.Mint
1 ND 256pgs, reprints Legion appearances in chronological order from Adventure Comics #247-#305	$7.50	$22.50	$37.50	£5.00	£15.00	£25.00
2 ND 256pgs, reprints Legion appearances in chronological order from Adventure Comics #306-#317	$7.50	$22.50	$37.50	£5.00	£15.00	£25.00
3 ND 256pgs, reprints Legion appearances in chronological order from Adventure Comics #318-330	$7.50	$22.50	$37.50	£5.00	£15.00	£25.00
4 ND 224pgs, reprints Legion appearances in chronological order from Adventure Comics #329-339	$7.50	$22.50	$37.50	£5.00	£15.00	£25.00
5 ND 224pgs, reprints Legion appearances in chronological order from Adventure Comics #340-349	$7.50	$22.50	$37.50	£5.00	£15.00	£25.00
6 ND reprints Adventure Comics #350-358 - classics one and all	$10.00	$30.00	$50.00	£6.00	£18.00	£30.00
Title Value:	$47.50	$142.50	$237.50	£31.00	£93.00	£155.00

LEGION OF MONSTERS

Marvel Comics Group,Magazine; 1 Sep 1975

	$Good	$Fine	$N.Mint	£Good	£Fine	£N.Mint
1 LD in the U.K. features Frankenstein, Dracula, Manphibian	$0.80	$2.50	$5.00	£0.65	£2.00	£4.00
Title Value:	$0.80	$2.50	$5.00	£0.65	£2.00	£4.00

LEGION OF NIGHT

Marvel Comics Group,MS; 1 Nov 1991-2 Dec 1991

	$Good	$Fine	$N.Mint	£Good	£Fine	£N.Mint
1-2 ND Steve Gerber script, Whilce Portacio art	*$1.00*	*$3.00*	*$5.00*	£0.60	£1.80	£3.00
Title Value:	*$2.00*	*$6.00*	*$10.00*	£1.20	£3.60	£6.00

LEGION OF STUPID HEROES

Blackthorne,OS; 1 Jan 1987

	$Good	$Fine	$N.Mint	£Good	£Fine	£N.Mint
1 ND Legion parody	*$0.30*	*$0.90*	*$1.50*	£0.20	£0.60	£1.00
Title Value:	*$0.30*	*$0.90*	*$1.50*	£0.20	£0.60	£1.00

LEGION OF SUBSTITUTE HEROES SPECIAL

DC Comics,OS; 1 Jul 1985

	$Good	$Fine	$N.Mint	£Good	£Fine	£N.Mint
1 Giffen cover, part art	*$0.40*	*$1.20*	*$2.00*	£0.25	£0.75	£1.25
Title Value:	*$0.40*	*$1.20*	*$2.00*	£0.25	£0.75	£1.25

LEGION OF SUPER-HEROES

(see Action Comics, Adventure Comics, All New Collector's Edition, Brave and the Bold, DC Comics Presents, DC Special, DC Special Blue Ribbon Digest, DC Super-Stars, Limited Collector's Edition, Secrets of the Legion of Super-Heroes, Secret Origins, Secret Origins of Super-Heroes, Superboy, Superboy and the Legion of Super-Heroes, Superman, Superman Annual, Super-Star Holiday Special)

Special Note: see Superboy #259-313 which was techically the third series of Legion adventures with the current one as the fourth. It was thought better to combine this third series as part of the Superboy run.

LEGION OF SUPER-HEROES

Special note: All appearances of the Legion prior to Adventure Comics #300 (Sep 1962, when they began their own regular series) are listed under the titles in which they occurred. For your information, here is a chronological list of all Legion appearances prior to Adventure #300:

1) Adventure Comics 247 (April 1958),
2) Adventure Comics 267 (December 1959),
3) Action Comics 267 (August 1960)
4) Superboy 86 (January 1961)
5) Adventure Comics 282 (March 1961)
6) Action Comics 276 (May 1961)
7) Superman 147 (August 1961)
8) Adventure Comics 289, statuettes in one panel only) (October 1961)
(Note: this is highly debateable as an actual appearance)
9) Adventure Comics 290 (November 1961)
10) Superman 149 (November 1961)
11) Superboy 93 (December 1961)
12) Superman Annual 4 (1961)
13) Action Comics 285 (February 1962)
14) Adventure Comics 293 (February 1962)
15) Action Comics 287 (April 1962)
16) Superman 152 (April 1962)
17) Action Comics 289 (June 1962)
18) Action Comics 290 (July 1962)
19) Superboy 98 (July 1962)
20) Superman 155 (August 1962)

Mon-El appearances prior to Adventure 300 are noted independently, as he was not a Legion member before that time. They are to be found in the following issues: Action Comics #284, 288; Jimmy Olsen #62; Lois Lane #33; Superboy #89 (1st appearance).

LEGION OF SUPER-HEROES (1ST SERIES)

DC Comics;259 Jan 1980-354 Dec 1987

	$Good	$Fine	$N.Mint	£Good	£Fine	£N.Mint
259 (Jan 1980,) Superboy leaves the Legion	*$0.40*	*$1.20*	*$2.00*	£0.25	£0.75	£1.25
260-264	*$0.40*	*$1.20*	*$2.00*	£0.25	£0.75	£1.25
265 68pgs, Jim Starlin art on free insert	*$0.50*	*$1.50*	*$2.50*	£0.30	£0.90	£1.50
266	*$0.30*	*$0.90*	*$1.50*	£0.20	£0.60	£1.00
267 LD in the U.K.	*$0.30*	*$0.90*	*$1.50*	£0.25	£0.75	£1.25
268-270	*$0.30*	*$0.90*	*$1.50*	£0.20	£0.60	£1.00
271 (Jan 1981)	*$0.30*	*$0.90*	*$1.50*	£0.20	£0.60	£1.00
272 48pgs, Dial H For Hero insert	*$0.40*	*$1.20*	*$2.00*	£0.25	£0.75	£1.25
273-279	*$0.30*	*$0.90*	*$1.50*	£0.20	£0.60	£1.00
280 Superboy rejoins the Legion	*$0.30*	*$0.90*	*$1.50*	£0.20	£0.60	£1.00
281-284	*$0.30*	*$0.90*	*$1.50*	£0.20	£0.60	£1.00
285-287 Giffen art	*$0.40*	*$1.20*	*$2.00*	£0.40	£1.20	£2.00
288-289	*$0.40*	*$1.20*	*$2.00*	£0.25	£0.75	£1.25
290 The Great Darkness Saga begins; Darkseid appears	*$0.40*	*$1.20*	*$2.00*	£0.25	£0.75	£1.25
291-293	*$0.40*	*$1.20*	*$2.00*	£0.25	£0.75	£1.25
294 LD in the U.K. 48pgs, Giffen art	*$0.50*	*$1.50*	*$2.50*	£0.50	£1.50	£2.50
295 (Jan 1983)	*$0.30*	*$0.90*	*$1.50*	£0.20	£0.60	£1.00
296-297	*$0.30*	*$0.90*	*$1.50*	£0.20	£0.60	£1.00
298 free 16 page insert, Amethyst Princess of Gemworld (1st appearance)	*$0.30*	*$0.90*	*$1.50*	£0.20	£0.60	£1.00
299	*$0.30*	*$0.90*	*$1.50*	£0.20	£0.60	£1.00
300 64pgs, anniversary issue, features work by many Legion artists	*$0.40*	*$1.20*	*$2.00*	£0.30	£0.90	£1.50
301-303	*$0.30*	*$0.90*	*$1.50*	£0.20	£0.60	£1.00
304 Karate Kid and Princess Projectra resign from Legion	*$0.30*	*$0.90*	*$1.50*	£0.20	£0.60	£1.00
305-306	*$0.30*	*$0.90*	*$1.50*	£0.20	£0.60	£1.00
307 (Jan 1984)	*$0.30*	*$0.90*	*$1.50*	£0.20	£0.60	£1.00
308-313	*$0.30*	*$0.90*	*$1.50*	£0.20	£0.60	£1.00
314 title becomes Tales of The Legion	*$0.25*	*$0.75*	*$1.25*	£0.15	£0.45	£0.75
315-318	*$0.25*	*$0.75*	*$1.25*	£0.15	£0.45	£0.75
319 (Jan 1985)	*$0.25*	*$0.75*	*$1.25*	£0.15	£0.45	£0.75
320-324	*$0.25*	*$0.75*	*$1.25*	£0.15	£0.45	£0.75
325 LD in the U.K.	*$0.25*	*$0.75*	*$1.25*	£0.20	£0.60	£1.00
326 reprints from Baxter (2nd) series begin (ends #354)	*$0.25*	*$0.75*	*$1.25*	£0.15	£0.45	£0.75
327-330	*$0.25*	*$0.75*	*$1.25*	£0.15	£0.45	£0.75
331 (Jan 1986)	*$0.25*	*$0.75*	*$1.25*	£0.15	£0.45	£0.75
332-336	*$0.25*	*$0.75*	*$1.25*	£0.15	£0.45	£0.75
337-338 LD in the U.K.	*$0.25*	*$0.75*	*$1.25*	£0.20	£0.60	£1.00
339	*$0.25*	*$0.75*	*$1.25*	£0.15	£0.45	£0.75
340 LD in the U.K.	*$0.25*	*$0.75*	*$1.25*	£0.20	£0.60	£1.00
341-342	*$0.25*	*$0.75*	*$1.25*	£0.15	£0.45	£0.75
343 LD in the U.K. (Jan 1987)	*$0.25*	*$0.75*	*$1.25*	£0.20	£0.60	£1.00
344-354	*$0.25*	*$0.75*	*$1.25*	£0.15	£0.45	£0.75
Title Value:	*$28.85*	*$86.55*	*$144.25*	£19.20	£57.60	£96.00

LEGION OF SUPER-HEROES (2ND SERIES)

DC Comics; 1 Aug 1984-63 Aug 1989

	$Good	$Fine	$N.Mint	£Good	£Fine	£N.Mint
1 ND	*$0.70*	*$2.10*	*$3.50*	£0.50	£1.50	£2.50
2-3 ND scarce in the U.K.	*$0.50*	*$1.50*	*$2.50*	£0.30	£0.90	£1.50
4 ND Karate Kid dies	*$0.40*	*$1.20*	*$2.00*	£0.25	£0.75	£1.25
5 ND Nemesis Kid dies	*$0.40*	*$1.20*	*$2.00*	£0.25	£0.75	£1.25
6-11 ND	*$0.40*	*$1.20*	*$2.00*	£0.25	£0.75	£1.25
12 ND Cosmic Boy, Lighting Lad, Saturn Girl resign	*$0.40*	*$1.20*	*$2.00*	£0.25	£0.75	£1.25
13 ND	*$0.40*	*$1.20*	*$2.00*	£0.25	£0.75	£1.25
14 ND 1st appearance Tellus, Sensor Girl, Quislet	*$0.40*	*$1.20*	*$2.00*	£0.25	£0.75	£1.25
15 ND	*$0.40*	*$1.20*	*$2.00*	£0.25	£0.75	£1.25
16 ND Supergirl's death foreseen/remembered, X-over with Crisis #7	*$0.40*	*$1.20*	*$2.00*	£0.25	£0.75	£1.25
17 ND	*$0.40*	*$1.20*	*$2.00*	£0.25	£0.75	£1.25
18 ND Crisis X-over	*$0.40*	*$1.20*	*$2.00*	£0.25	£0.75	£1.25
19-22 ND	*$0.40*	*$1.20*	*$2.00*	£0.25	£0.75	£1.25
23 ND last Superboy in Legion	*$0.40*	*$1.20*	*$2.00*	£0.25	£0.75	£1.25
24 ND	*$0.40*	*$1.20*	*$2.00*	£0.25	£0.75	£1.25
25 ND Sensor Girl revealed as Princess Projectra	*$0.40*	*$1.20*	*$2.00*	£0.25	£0.75	£1.25
26-31 ND	*$0.40*	*$1.20*	*$2.00*	£0.25	£0.75	£1.25
32-35 ND "The Universo Proj"	*$0.40*	*$1.20*	*$2.00*	£0.25	£0.75	£1.25
36 ND	*$0.40*	*$1.20*	*$2.00*	£0.25	£0.75	£1.25
37 ND scarce in the U.K. Superboy returns (post-Crisis)	*$1.60*	*$4.80*	*$8.00*	£1.20	£3.60	£6.00
38 ND very scarce in the U.K. Superboy dies	*$2.00*	*$6.00*	*$10.00*	£1.60	£4.80	£8.00
39-41 ND	*$0.40*	*$1.20*	*$2.00*	£0.25	£0.75	£1.25
42 ND Millennium X-over, Laurel Kent revealed as a Manhunter	*$0.40*	*$1.20*	*$2.00*	£0.25	£0.75	£1.25
43 ND Millennium X-over	*$0.40*	*$1.20*	*$2.00*	£0.25	£0.75	£1.25
44 ND	*$0.40*	*$1.20*	*$2.00*	£0.25	£0.75	£1.25
45 ND 64pgs, 30th anniversary issue	*$0.60*	*$1.80*	*$3.00*	£0.40	£1.20	£2.00
46-49 ND	*$0.40*	*$1.20*	*$2.00*	£0.25	£0.75	£1.25
50 ND 48pgs	*$0.50*	*$1.50*	*$2.50*	£0.30	£0.90	£1.50
51-59 ND	*$0.40*	*$1.20*	*$2.00*	£0.25	£0.75	£1.25
60-63 ND Magic Wars story	*$0.40*	*$1.20*	*$2.00*	£0.25	£0.75	£1.25
Title Value:	*$28.80*	*$86.40*	*$144.00*	£18.60	£55.80	£93.00

Note: unless otherwise stated, all 36pgs, ND, Deluxe Format Baxter paper

LEGION OF SUPER-HEROES (3RD SERIES)

DC Comics; 0 Oct 1994; 1 Oct 1989-present

	$Good	$Fine	$N.Mint	£Good	£Fine	£N.Mint
0 (Oct 1994) Zero Hour X-over, origin retold	*$0.40*	*$1.20*	*$2.00*	£0.25	£0.75	£1.25
1 events take place 5 years after Magic Wars storyline	*$0.50*	*$1.50*	*$2.50*	£0.30	£0.90	£1.50
2-5	*$0.40*	*$1.20*	*$2.00*	£0.25	£0.75	£1.25
6 new Legionnaires	*$0.40*	*$1.20*	*$2.00*	£0.25	£0.75	£1.25
7	*$0.40*	*$1.20*	*$2.00*	£0.25	£0.75	£1.25
8 origin re-worked	*$0.40*	*$1.20*	*$2.00*	£0.25	£0.75	£1.25
9-10	*$0.40*	*$1.20*	*$2.00*	£0.25	£0.75	£1.25
11 Matter-Eater Lad/Polar Boy appear	*$0.40*	*$1.20*	*$2.00*	£0.25	£0.75	£1.25
12 new costumes	*$0.40*	*$1.20*	*$2.00*	£0.25	£0.75	£1.25
13 Duo Damsel returns; gate-fold poster - compensate for comic being printed on Mando paper stock instead of its usual Standard stock	*$0.40*	*$1.20*	*$2.00*	£0.25	£0.75	£1.25
14 Matter-Eater Lad returns	*$0.40*	*$1.20*	*$2.00*	£0.25	£0.75	£1.25
15-18	*$0.40*	*$1.20*	*$2.00*	£0.25	£0.75	£1.25
19 continued from Adventures of Superman #478	*$0.40*	*$1.20*	*$2.00*	£0.25	£0.75	£1.25
20	*$0.40*	*$1.20*	*$2.00*	£0.25	£0.75	£1.25
21 The Quiet Darkness part 1, sequel to The Great Darkness Saga (Legion of Super-Heroes #290-294, Annual #2), Lobo and Darkseid appear	*$0.30*	*$0.90*	*$1.50*	£0.20	£0.60	£1.00
22 The Quiet Darkness part 2, Lobo and Darkseid appear	*$0.30*	*$0.90*	*$1.50*	£0.20	£0.60	£1.00
23 The Quiet Darkness part 3, Lobo vs. Timberwolf	*$0.30*	*$0.90*	*$1.50*	£0.20	£0.60	£1.00

	$Good	$Fine	$N.Mint	£Good	£Fine	£N.Mint
24 The Quiet Darkness part 4 (conclusion), Lobo vs. Timberwolf	$0.30	$0.90	$1.50	£0.20	£0.60	£1.00
25 original Legion from Adventure Comics appear	$0.30	$0.90	$1.50	£0.20	£0.60	£1.00
26-27	$0.30	$0.90	$1.50	£0.20	£0.60	£1.00
28 origin Sun Boy retold	$0.30	$0.90	$1.50	£0.20	£0.60	£1.00
29 intro Monica Sade	$0.30	$0.90	$1.50	£0.20	£0.60	£1.00
30	$0.30	$0.90	$1.50	£0.20	£0.60	£1.00
31 guest pencils by Colleen Doran	$0.30	$0.90	$1.50	£0.20	£0.60	£1.00
32-34	$0.30	$0.90	$1.50	£0.20	£0.60	£1.00
35-37 bi-weekly	$0.30	$0.90	$1.50	£0.20	£0.60	£1.00
38 bi-weekly, full page illustrations with text story; Earth destroyed in nuclear explosion	$0.30	$0.90	$1.50	£0.20	£0.60	£1.00
39	$0.30	$0.90	$1.50	£0.20	£0.60	£1.00
40 Legionnaires preview	$0.30	$0.90	$1.50	£0.20	£0.60	£1.00
41 1st solo adventure of teen Legionnaires	$0.30	$0.90	$1.50	£0.20	£0.60	£1.00
42	$0.30	$0.90	$1.50	£0.20	£0.60	£1.00
43 Mordru Arises story, Martian Manhunter appears	$0.30	$0.90	$1.50	£0.20	£0.60	£1.00
44-48 Mordru Arises story	$0.30	$0.90	$1.50	£0.20	£0.60	£1.00
49	$0.30	$0.90	$1.50	£0.20	£0.60	£1.00
50 64pgs, features a wedding, a death, a re-birth and the return of a lost Legionnaire	$0.50	$1.50	$2.50	£0.30	£0.90	£1.50
51-53	$0.30	$0.90	$1.50	£0.20	£0.60	£1.00
54 new direction for title; die-cut, foil-stamped cover	$0.50	$1.50	$2.50	£0.30	£0.90	£1.50
55-58	$0.30	$0.90	$1.50	£0.20	£0.60	£1.00
59 leads into End of an Era storyline and Zero Hour mini-series	$0.30	$0.90	$1.50	£0.20	£0.60	£1.00
60 End of an Era part 3, continued in Legionnaires #18	$0.40	$1.20	$2.00	£0.25	£0.75	£1.25
61 End of an Era part 6 (conclusion); Zero Hour X-over	$0.40	$1.20	$2.00	£0.25	£0.75	£1.25
62 new members introduced	$0.40	$1.20	$2.00	£0.25	£0.75	£1.25
63-68	$0.40	$1.20	$2.00	£0.25	£0.75	£1.25
69	$0.45	$1.35	$2.25	£0.30	£0.90	£1.50
70-71 Alan Davis and Mark Farmer cover	$0.45	$1.35	$2.25	£0.30	£0.90	£1.50
72 Alan Davis and Mark Farmer cover; storyline continued from Legionnaires Annual #2	$0.45	$1.35	$2.25	£0.30	£0.90	£1.50
73 Alan Davis and Mark Farmer cover; storyline continued from Legionnaires #30	$0.45	$1.35	$2.25	£0.30	£0.90	£1.50
74 Future Tense part 2, continued in Legionnaires #31	$0.45	$1.35	$2.25	£0.30	£0.90	£1.50
75 Two Timer part 1, continued in Legionnaires #32	$0.45	$1.35	$2.25	£0.30	£0.90	£1.50
76-84 Alan Davis and Mark Farmer cover	$0.45	$1.35	$2.25	£0.30	£0.90	£1.50
85 Superman guest-stars as the Legionnaires are thrown into the 20th Century - new direction for title; Alan Davis and Mark Farmer cover	$0.45	$1.35	$2.25	£0.30	£0.90	£1.50
86 ND Final Night tie-in, Alan Davis and Mark Farmer cover	$0.45	$1.35	$2.25	£0.30	£0.90	£1.50
87 ND Deadman appears	$0.45	$1.35	$2.25	£0.30	£0.90	£1.50
88 ND Impulse appears	$0.45	$1.35	$2.25	£0.30	£0.90	£1.50
89-90 ND	$0.45	$1.35	$2.25	£0.30	£0.90	£1.50
Title Value:	$34.10	$102.30	$170.50	£22.15	£66.45	£110.75

Note: Deluxe Format, high quality paper

LEGION OF SUPER-HEROES (LIMITED SERIES)

DC Comics; 1 Feb 1973-4 Jul/Aug 1973

	$Good	$Fine	$N.Mint	£Good	£Fine	£N.Mint
1 scarce in the U.K. Legion and Tommy Tomorrow reprints begin from Adventure and Action Comics respectively	$1.30	$4.00	$8.00	£0.80	£2.50	£5.00
2-4 scarce in the U.K.	$1.00	$3.00	$6.00	£0.65	£2.00	£4.00
Title Value:	$4.30	$13.00	$26.00	£2.75	£8.50	£17.00

LEGION OF SUPER-HEROES ANNUAL (1ST SERIES)

DC Comics; 1 1982-5 Oct 1987

(becomes Tales of the Legion of Super-Heroes Annual with #4)

	$Good	$Fine	$N.Mint	£Good	£Fine	£N.Mint
1 ND 52pgs, scarce, Giffen cover/art, 1st appearance new Invisible Kid	$0.40	$1.20	$2.00	£0.40	£1.20	£2.00
2 52pgs, scarce, Giffen cover Karate Kid, Princess Projectra wed	$0.40	$1.20	$2.00	£0.30	£0.90	£1.50
3 52pgs	$0.30	$0.90	$1.50	£0.25	£0.75	£1.25
4-5 48pgs	$0.30	$0.90	$1.50	£0.20	£0.60	£1.00
Title Value:	$1.70	$5.10	$8.50	£1.35	£4.05	£6.75

LEGION OF SUPER-HEROES ANNUAL (2ND SERIES)

DC Comics; 1 Oct 1985-4 1988

	$Good	$Fine	$N.Mint	£Good	£Fine	£N.Mint
1 ND	$0.50	$1.50	$2.50	£0.30	£0.90	£1.50
2 ND Dave Gibbons art	$0.50	$1.50	$2.50	£0.30	£0.90	£1.50
3 ND	$0.50	$1.50	$2.50	£0.30	£0.90	£1.50
4 ND Bolland cover, Gary Leach art (back-up)	$0.50	$1.50	$2.50	£0.30	£0.90	£1.50
Title Value:	$2.00	$6.00	$10.00	£1.20	£3.60	£6.00

Note: all 48pgs, Baxter paper

LEGION OF SUPER-HEROES ANNUAL (3RD SERIES)

DC Comics; 1 Aug 1990-present

	$Good	$Fine	$N.Mint	£Good	£Fine	£N.Mint
1-2 48pgs	$0.60	$1.80	$3.00	£0.40	£1.20	£2.00
3 64pgs, intro new-look Timber-Wolf	$0.70	$2.10	$3.50	£0.40	£1.20	£2.00
4 64pgs, Bloodlines (Wave Two) part 12, 1st appearance Jamm, continued in Green Arrow Annual #6	$0.70	$2.10	$3.50	£0.40	£1.20	£2.00
5 64pgs, Elseworlds story, features art by Colleen Doran and Ted McKeever	$0.70	$2.10	$3.50	£0.40	£1.20	£2.00
6 56pgs, Year One	$0.80	$2.40	$4.00	£0.50	£1.50	£2.50
7 ND 48pgs, Legends of the Dead Earth story; Mike Collins and Mark Farmer art; cover by Alan Davis and Mark Farmer	$0.70	$2.10	$3.50	£0.50	£1.50	£2.50
Title Value:	$4.80	$14.40	$24.50	£3.00	£9.00	£15.00

Note: Deluxe Format

LEGION OF SUPER-HEROES SPECIAL

DC Comics,OS; 1 Apr 1985

	$Good	$Fine	$N.Mint	£Good	£Fine	£N.Mint
1 48pgs, Giffen art	$0.40	$1.20	$2.00	£0.25	£0.75	£1.25
Title Value:	$0.40	$1.20	$2.00	£0.25	£0.75	£1.25

LEGION X-1

Greater Mercury Comics; 1 1989-2 1989

	$Good	$Fine	$N.Mint	£Good	£Fine	£N.Mint
1 ND b&w	$0.50	$1.50	$2.50	£0.30	£0.90	£1.50
2 ND rare in the U.K. black and white	$0.50	$1.50	$2.50	£0.40	£1.20	£2.00
Title Value:	$1.00	$3.00	$5.00	£0.70	£2.10	£3.50

LEGION X-1 (2ND SERIES)

Greater Mercury Comics; 1 Aug 1989-6 Dec 1990

	$Good	$Fine	$N.Mint	£Good	£Fine	£N.Mint
1-6 ND b&w	$0.40	$1.20	$2.00	£0.25	£0.75	£1.25
Title Value:	$2.40	$7.20	$12.00	£1.50	£4.50	£7.50

LEGION X-2

Greater Mercury Comics; 1 Aug 1989-10 1991

	$Good	$Fine	$N.Mint	£Good	£Fine	£N.Mint
1-8 ND b&w	$0.40	$1.20	$2.00	£0.25	£0.75	£1.25
9-10 ND Split Decision story, black and white	$0.40	$1.20	$2.00	£0.25	£0.75	£1.25
Title Value:	$4.00	$12.00	$20.00	£2.50	£7.50	£12.50

LEGIONNAIRES

DC Comics; 0 Oct 1994; 1 Apr 1993-present

	$Good	$Fine	$N.Mint	£Good	£Fine	£N.Mint
0 (Oct 1994) Zero Hour X-over origin retold	$0.40	$1.20	$2.00	£0.25	£0.75	£1.25
1 pre-bagged with trading card; spin-off from the destruction of Earth in Legion (3rd Series) #38; the covers of the first six issues make one giant montage	$0.30	$0.90	$1.50	£0.20	£0.60	£1.00
2-6	$0.30	$0.90	$1.50	£0.20	£0.60	£1.00
7 Adam Hughes pencils	$0.30	$0.90	$1.50	£0.20	£0.60	£1.00
8 Colleen Doran pencils	$0.30	$0.90	$1.50	£0.20	£0.60	£1.00
9	$0.30	$0.90	$1.50	£0.20	£0.60	£1.00
10 1st appearance new Kid Psycho	$0.30	$0.90	$1.50	£0.20	£0.60	£1.00
11 Kid Quantum joins	$0.30	$0.90	$1.50	£0.20	£0.60	£1.00
12-13	$0.30	$0.90	$1.50	£0.20	£0.60	£1.00
14-16 Adam Hughes cover	$0.30	$0.90	$1.50	£0.20	£0.60	£1.00
17 End of an Era part 1, continued in Valor #22; Adam Hughes cover	$0.30	$0.90	$1.50	£0.20	£0.60	£1.00
18 End of an Era part 4, continued in Valor #23; Adam Hughes cover	$0.30	$0.90	$1.50	£0.20	£0.60	£1.00
19-26	$0.30	$0.90	$1.50	£0.20	£0.60	£1.00
27 upgraded paper stock to Mando Format begins	$0.45	$1.35	$2.25	£0.30	£0.90	£1.50
28-29	$0.45	$1.35	$2.25	£0.30	£0.90	£1.50
30 continued from Legion of Super-Heroes #73	$0.45	$1.35	$2.25	£0.30	£0.90	£1.50
31 Future Tense part 3, continued from Legion of Super-Heroes #74	$0.45	$1.35	$2.25	£0.30	£0.90	£1.50
32 Underworld Unleashed tie-in, cover by Alan Davis and Mark Farmer	$0.45	$1.35	$2.25	£0.30	£0.90	£1.50
33-34 cover by Alan Davis and Mark Farmer	$0.45	$1.35	$2.25	£0.30	£0.90	£1.50
35-42	$0.45	$1.35	$2.25	£0.30	£0.90	£1.50
43 ND new Legionnaires inducted	$0.45	$1.35	$2.25	£0.30	£0.90	£1.50
44-46 ND	$0.45	$1.35	$2.25	£0.30	£0.90	£1.50
Title Value:	$17.20	$51.60	$86.00	£11.45	£34.35	£57.25

LEGIONNAIRES ANNUAL

DC Comics; 1 Jul 1994-present

	$Good	$Fine	$N.Mint	£Good	£Fine	£N.Mint
1 64pgs, Elseworlds story	$0.50	$1.50	$2.50	£0.30	£0.90	£1.50
2 56pgs, Year One	$0.80	$2.40	$4.00	£0.50	£1.50	£2.50
3 ND 48pgs, Legends of the Dead Earth story; cover by Alan Davis and Mark Farmer	$0.70	$2.10	$3.50	£0.50	£1.50	£2.50
Title Value:	$2.00	$6.00	$10.00	£1.30	£3.90	£6.50

LEGIONNAIRES THREE

DC Comics,MS; 1 Jan 1986-4 May 1986

	$Good	$Fine	$N.Mint	£Good	£Fine	£N.Mint
1-4	$0.25	$0.75	$1.25	£0.15	£0.45	£0.75
Title Value:	$1.00	$3.00	$5.00	£0.60	£1.80	£3.00

LENSMAN

Eternity; 1 Apr 1990-6 Oct 1990

	$Good	$Fine	$N.Mint	£Good	£Fine	£N.Mint
(see Galactic Patrol) (mini-series sub-titled The Secret of the Lens)						
1 ND adaptation of animated Japanese feature begins based on E.E. "Doc" Smith's sci-fi series; black and white	*$0.40*	*$1.20*	*$2.00*	£0.25	£0.75	£1.25
1 Collectors Edition, ND (Feb 1990) - 56pgs, gold foil embossed logo, heavier stock paper covers, additional information and art	*$0.80*	*$2.40*	*$4.00*	£0.50	£1.50	£2.50
2-6 ND	*$0.40*	*$1.20*	*$2.00*	£0.25	£0.75	£1.25
Title Value:	*$3.20*	*$9.60*	*$16.00*	£2.00	£6.00	£10.00
Birth of a Lensman Graphic Album (1991), reprints issues #1-3				£0.80	£2.40	£4.00
Secrets of the Lens Graphic Album, reprints issues #4-6				£0.80	£2.40	£4.00

LENSMAN: WAR OF THE GALAXIES
Eternity,MS; 1 Oct 1990-7 Apr 1991

	$Good	$Fine	$N.Mint	£Good	£Fine	£N.Mint
1-7 ND	*$0.40*	*$1.20*	*$2.00*	£0.25	£0.75	£1.25
Title Value:	*$2.80*	*$8.40*	*$14.00*	£1.75	£5.25	£8.75

LEONARDO
Mirage Studios,OS; 1 Dec 1986

	$Good	$Fine	$N.Mint	£Good	£Fine	£N.Mint
1 ND Teenage Mutant Ninja Turtles tie-in	*$1.00*	*$3.00*	*$5.00*	£0.60	£1.80	£3.00
Title Value:	*$1.00*	*$3.00*	*$5.00*	£0.60	£1.80	£3.00

LEOPARD
Millennium; 1 May 1995-2 1995

	$Good	$Fine	$N.Mint	£Good	£Fine	£N.Mint
1 ND Dan and David Day script and art	*$0.60*	*$1.80*	*$3.00*	£0.40	£1.20	£2.00
1 Variant Cover Edition Signed, ND (Jun 1995) - gold cover, signed by Dan and David Day	*$0.80*	*$2.40*	*$4.00*	£0.50	£1.50	£2.50
2 ND Dan and David Day script and art	*$0.60*	*$1.80*	*$3.00*	£0.40	£1.20	£2.00
Title Value:	*$2.00*	*$6.00*	*$10.00*	£1.30	£3.90	£6.50

LESTER GIRLS: THE LIZARD'S TRAIL
Eternity,MS; 1 Nov 1990-3 Jan 1991

	$Good	$Fine	$N.Mint	£Good	£Fine	£N.Mint
1 ND Gerard Jones and Tim Hamilton, black and white; ties up plots from Trouble With Girls	*$0.40*	*$1.20*	*$2.00*	£0.25	£0.75	£1.25
2-3 ND	*$0.40*	*$1.20*	*$2.00*	£0.25	£0.75	£1.25
Title Value:	*$1.20*	*$3.60*	*$6.00*	£0.75	£2.25	£3.75

LETHAL
Image,MS; 1 Feb 1996-2 Mar 1996

	$Good	$Fine	$N.Mint	£Good	£Fine	£N.Mint
1-2 ND Marat Mychaels script and art	*$0.50*	*$1.50*	*$2.50*	£0.30	£0.90	£1.50
Title Value:	*$1.00*	*$3.00*	*$5.00*	£0.60	£1.80	£3.00

LETHAL STRIKE
London Night Studios,MS; 0 Nov 1995; 1 Aug 1995-3 Nov 1995

	$Good	$Fine	$N.Mint	£Good	£Fine	£N.Mint
½ ND	*$1.00*	*$3.00*	*$5.00*	£0.80	£2.40	£4.00
½ Signed & Numbered Edition, ND (Dec 1995)	*$5.00*	*$15.00*	*$25.00*	£3.00	£9.00	£15.00
0 ND Collector's Edition (Nov 1995) - gold foil cover	*$1.20*	*$3.60*	*$6.00*	£0.80	£2.40	£4.00
1 ND	*$1.00*	*$3.00*	*$5.00*	£0.60	£1.80	£3.00
2-3 ND	*$0.60*	*$1.80*	*$3.00*	£0.40	£1.20	£2.00
Title Value:	*$9.40*	*$28.20*	*$47.00*	£6.00	£18.00	£30.00
Lethal Stryke (Jun 1996) Trade paperback ND 80pgs, collects mini-series				£1.70	£5.10	£8.50

LETHAL STRIKE ANNUAL
London Night Studios,OS; 1 Apr 1996

	$Good	$Fine	$N.Mint	£Good	£Fine	£N.Mint
1 ND Mike Shoemaker script, Leonard Kirk and Terry Pallot art	*$0.60*	*$1.80*	*$3.00*	£0.40	£1.20	£2.00
1 Platinum Edition ND	$2.00	$6.00	$10.00	£1.30	£3.90	£6.50
Title Value:	*$2.60*	*$7.80*	*$13.00*	£1.70	£5.10	£8.50

LETHAL STRYKE/DOUBLE IMPACT: LETHAL IMPACT
London Night Studios,OS; 1 Apr 1996

	$Good	$Fine	$N.Mint	£Good	£Fine	£N.Mint
1 ND	*$0.60*	*$1.80*	*$3.00*	£0.40	£1.20	£2.00
1 Natural Born Killer Edition, ND (Apr 1996), limited to 5,000 copies	*$2.00*	*$6.00*	*$10.00*	£1.30	£3.90	£6.50
Title Value:	*$2.60*	*$7.80*	*$13.00*	£1.70	£5.10	£8.50

LETHARGIC LAD
Crusade Comics,MS; 1 Jun 1996-3 Aug 1996

	$Good	$Fine	$N.Mint	£Good	£Fine	£N.Mint
1 ND Greg Hyland script and art; black and white; cover parody of Superman #1	*$0.60*	*$1.80*	*$3.00*	£0.40	£1.20	£2.00
2-3 ND	*$0.60*	*$1.80*	*$3.00*	£0.40	£1.20	£2.00
Title Value:	*$1.80*	*$5.40*	*$9.00*	£1.20	£3.60	£6.00

LEX LUTHOR, THE UNAUTHORISED BIOGRAPHY OF
DC Comics,OS; 1 Jun 1989

	$Good	$Fine	$N.Mint	£Good	£Fine	£N.Mint
1 ND 48pgs, squarebound	*$0.60*	*$1.80*	*$3.00*	£0.40	£1.20	£2.00
Title Value:	*$0.60*	*$1.80*	*$3.00*	£0.40	£1.20	£2.00

LIBBY ELLIS
Malibu,MS; 1 Jul 1987-4 Dec 1988

	$Good	$Fine	$N.Mint	£Good	£Fine	£N.Mint
1-4 ND	*$0.40*	*$1.20*	*$2.00*	£0.25	£0.75	£1.25
Title Value:	*$1.60*	*$4.80*	*$8.00*	£1.00	£3.00	£5.00

LIBBY ELLIS (2ND SERIES)
Eternity,MS; 1 Jun 1988-4 Dec 1988

	$Good	$Fine	$N.Mint	£Good	£Fine	£N.Mint
1-4 ND	*$0.40*	*$1.20*	*$2.00*	£0.25	£0.75	£1.25
Title Value:	*$1.60*	*$4.80*	*$8.00*	£1.00	£3.00	£5.00

LIBERATOR
Malibu/Eternity; 1 Dec 1987-6 Dec 1988

	$Good	$Fine	$N.Mint	£Good	£Fine	£N.Mint
1-6 ND Butch Burcham inks/covers	*$0.40*	*$1.20*	*$2.00*	£0.25	£0.75	£1.25
Title Value:	*$2.40*	*$7.20*	*$12.00*	£1.50	£4.50	£7.50

LIBERTY PROJECT
Eclipse; 1 Jun 1987-8 May 1988

	$Good	$Fine	$N.Mint	£Good	£Fine	£N.Mint
1-8 ND	*$0.40*	*$1.20*	*$2.00*	£0.25	£0.75	£1.25
Title Value:	*$3.20*	*$9.60*	*$16.00*	£2.00	£6.00	£10.00

LIBRA
Eternity; 1 1987

	$Good	$Fine	$N.Mint	£Good	£Fine	£N.Mint
1 ND	*$0.30*	*$0.90*	*$1.50*	£0.20	£0.60	£1.00
Title Value:	*$0.30*	*$0.90*	*$1.50*	£0.20	£0.60	£1.00

LIEUTENANT BLUEBERRY
Marvel Comics Group/Epic Graphic Novel; 1 1991

(see Blueberry, Moebius)

	$Good	$Fine	$N.Mint	£Good	£Fine	£N.Mint
1 ND Trail of the Sioux	*$1.60*	*$4.80*	*$8.00*	£1.00	£3.00	£5.00
Title Value:	*$1.60*	*$4.80*	*$8.00*	£1.00	£3.00	£5.00

LIFE OF CHRIST: THE CHRISTMAS STORY
Marvel Comics Group,MS; 1 Feb 1993-2 Mar 1993

	$Good	$Fine	$N.Mint	£Good	£Fine	£N.Mint
1-2 ND	*$0.50*	*$1.50*	*$2.50*	£0.30	£0.90	£1.50
Title Value:	*$1.00*	*$3.00*	*$5.00*	£0.60	£1.80	£3.00

LIFE OF POPE JOHN PAUL II, THE
Marvel Comics Group,OS; 1 Jan 1983

	$Good	$Fine	$N.Mint	£Good	£Fine	£N.Mint
1 ND 64pgs	*$0.15*	*$0.45*	*$0.75*	£0.10	£0.35	£0.60
Title Value:	*$0.15*	*$0.45*	*$0.75*	£0.10	£0.35	£0.60

LIFE, THE UNIVERSE AND EVERYTHING
DC Comics,MS; 1 May 1996-3 Jul 1996

	$Good	$Fine	$N.Mint	£Good	£Fine	£N.Mint
1-3 ND 48pgs, based on the third Hitchhiker's Guide to the Galaxy book; John Carnell script, Paris Cullins, Neil Vokes and John Nyberg art	*$1.40*	*$4.20*	*$7.00*	£0.90	£2.70	£4.50
Title Value:	*$4.20*	*$12.60*	*$21.00*	£2.70	£8.10	£13.50

LIFEFORM
Marvel Comics Group; 1990

Cross-over storyline running throughout the following issues:

Punisher Annual #3, Daredevil Annual #6, Incredible Hulk Annual #16, Silver Surfer Annual #3.

LIGHT AND DARKNESS WAR, THE
Marvel Comics Group/Epic,MS; 1 Oct 1988-6 Dec 1989

1 ND Cam Kennedy painted art begins

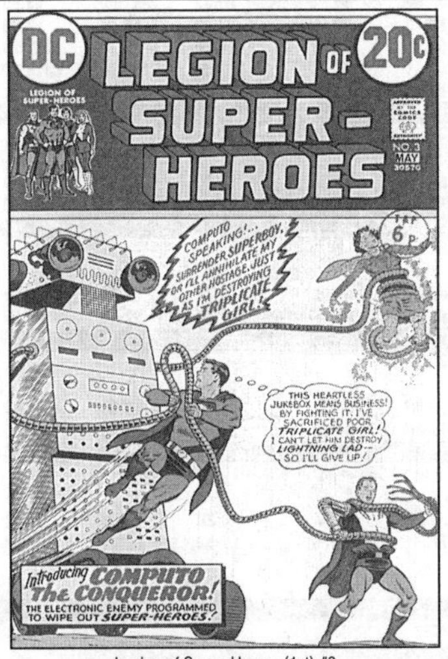

Legion of Super-Heroes (1st) #3

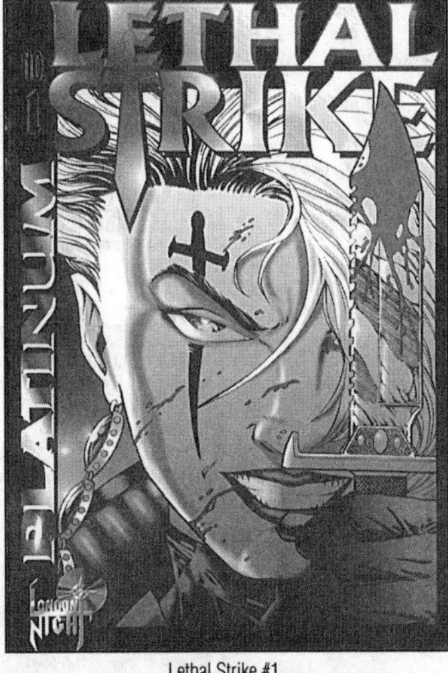

Lethal Strike #1

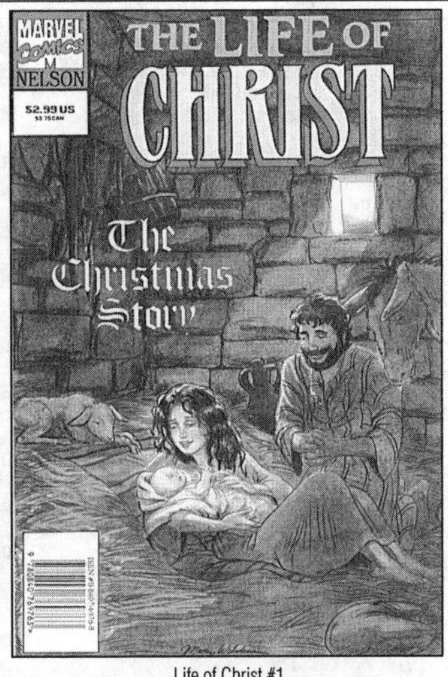

Life of Christ #1

	$Good	$Fine	$N.Mint	£Good	£Fine	£N.Mint
	$0.50	*$1.50*	*$2.50*	£0.30	£0.90	£1.50
2-6 ND	*$0.50*	*$1.50*	*$2.50*	£0.30	£0.90	£1.50
Title Value:	*$3.00*	*$9.00*	*$15.00*	£1.80	£5.40	£9.00

Note: Mature Readers

LIGHT FANTASTIC, THE

Innovation,MS; 1 Jun 1992-4 Sep 1992

1-4 ND adaptation of Terry Pratchett's 2nd Discworld novel; colour

	$Good	$Fine	$N.Mint	£Good	£Fine	£N.Mint
	$0.50	*$1.50*	*$2.50*	£0.30	£0.90	£1.50
Title Value:	*$2.00*	*$6.00*	*$10.00*	£1.20	£3.60	£6.00

LIGHTNING COMICS PRESENTS

Lightning Comics,OS; 1 May 1994

	$Good	$Fine	$N.Mint	£Good	£Fine	£N.Mint
1 Platinum Edition, ND - War Party and Dreadwolf appear						
	$0.80	*$2.40*	*$4.00*	£0.50	£1.50	£2.50
1 Red & Yellow Cover, ND - War Party and Dreadwolf appear; distributed by Heroes World						
	$0.80	*$2.40*	*$4.00*	£0.50	£1.50	£2.50
1 Red Foil Cover Edition, ND - War Party and Dreadwolf appear; distributed by Diamond Distributors						
	$0.80	*$2.40*	*$4.00*	£0.50	£1.50	£2.50
1 Yellow & Blue Cover, ND - War Party and Dreadwolf appear; black, distributed by Capital Distribution						
	$0.80	*$2.40*	*$4.00*	£0.50	£1.50	£2.50
Title Value:	*$3.20*	*$9.60*	*$16.00*	£2.00	£6.00	£10.00

LILITH

Antarctic Press,MS; 1 Sep 1996-3 Nov 1996

	$Good	$Fine	$N.Mint	£Good	£Fine	£N.Mint
1 ND	*$0.60*	*$1.80*	*$3.00*	£0.40	£1.20	£2.00
1 Alternate Cover Edition, ND cover by Henderson and Madison						
	$0.60	*$1.80*	*$3.00*	£0.40	£1.20	£2.00
2-3 ND	*$0.60*	*$1.80*	*$3.00*	£0.40	£1.20	£2.00
Title Value:	*$2.40*	*$7.20*	*$12.00*	£1.60	£4.80	£8.00

LIMITED COLLECTOR'S EDITION

DC Comics,Tabloid;C-21 Summer 1973-C-59 1978

(other numbers: see All New Collector's Editon and famous First Edition)

	$Good	$Fine	$N.Mint	£Good	£Fine	£N.Mint
C-21 distributed in the U.K. Shazam; reprints Captain Marvel Junior #11; cover by C.C. Beck						
	$1.20	*$3.60*	*$6.00*	£0.60	£1.80	£3.00
C-22 ND Tarzan; reprints origin from Tarzan #207-210 by Joe Kubert						
	$1.20	*$3.60*	*$6.00*	£0.80	£2.40	£4.00
C-23 distributed in the U.K. House of Mystery; selected reprints featuring art by Neal Adams, Bernie Wrightson, Wally Wood, Alex Toth and others						
	$1.00	*$3.00*	*$5.00*	£0.60	£1.80	£3.00
C-24 ND Rudolph the Red-Nosed Reindeer						
	$0.80	*$2.40*	*$4.00*	£0.40	£1.20	£2.00
C-25 ND Batman; selected reprints featuring work by Neal Adams, Carmine Infantino, Bob Kane, Jerry Robinson and Dick Sprang						
	$3.00	*$9.00*	*$15.00*	£3.00	£9.00	£15.00
C-27 ND Shazam; selected reprints featuring Captain Marvel and Mary Marvel						
	$1.00	*$3.00*	*$5.00*	£0.80	£2.40	£4.00
C-29 ND Tarzan; reprints from Tarzan #219-223 by Joe Kubert						
	$1.20	*$3.60*	*$6.00*	£0.80	£2.40	£4.00
C-31 ND Superman; 4pgs Neal Adams art; reprints orgin Superman 2001 from Superman #300; George Reeves photo feature						
	$1.50	*$4.50*	*$7.50*	£1.20	£3.60	£6.00
C-32 ND Ghosts; some new material						
	$1.20	*$3.60*	*$6.00*	£0.50	£1.50	£2.50
C-33 ND Rudolph the Red-Nosed Reindeer; some new material						
	$0.80	*$2.40*	*$4.00*	£0.40	£1.20	£2.00
C-34 ND Christmas with the Super-Heroes; reprints Frank Miller Batman from Five Star Super-Hero Spectacular and an unpublished Angel and the Ape story						
	$1.20	*$3.60*	*$6.00*	£0.70	£2.10	£3.50
C-35 ND Shazam; photo cover of TV's Captain Marvel						
	$1.00	*$3.00*	*$5.00*	£0.70	£2.10	£3.50
C-36 ND The Bible; adaptation by Joe Kubert and Nestor Redondo						
	$1.20	*$3.60*	*$6.00*	£0.60	£1.80	£3.00
C-37 ND scarce in the U.K. Batman; all villain issue with reprints featuring The Joker, Penguin, Two-Face, The Scarcecrow (origin) and Catwoman						
	$3.00	*$9.00*	*$15.00*	£3.00	£9.00	£15.00
C-38 ND scarce in the U.K. Superman; 2pgs Neal Adams art, part photo cover						
	$1.50	*$4.50*	*$7.50*	£0.80	£2.40	£4.00
C-39 ND Secret Origin of Super-Villains; reprints origin The Joker (Detective Comics #168) plus origins Luthor, Captain Cold, Dr. Sivana and Terra-Man						
	$1.50	*$4.50*	*$7.50*	£0.80	£2.40	£4.00
C-40 ND scarce in the U.K. Dick Tracy; newspaer strip reprints						
	$1.50	*$4.50*	*$7.50*	£1.00	£3.00	£5.00
C-41 distributed in the U.K. Super Friends; reprints from Justice League of America with Super Friends framing sequence						
	$0.80	*$2.40*	*$4.00*	£0.40	£1.20	£2.00
C-42 ND Rudolph the Red-Nosed Reindeer						
	$0.80	*$2.40*	*$4.00*	£0.40	£1.20	£2.00
C-43 ND Christmas with the Super-Heroes; Neal Adams Batman reprint plus Golden Age Superman, Wonder Woman, Sandman by Simon and Kirby and Bernie Wrightson on a House of Mystery short						
	$1.50	*$4.50*	*$7.50*	£0.60	£1.80	£3.00
C-44 ND scarce in the U.K. Batman; reprints by Infantino, Robinson, Sprang and Neal Adams						
	$3.00	*$9.00*	*$15.00*	£3.00	£9.00	£15.00
C-45 ND Secret Origins of Super-Villains; Catwoman, Mirror Master reprints Flash #105), Mr. Mxyzptlk and The Cheetah						
	$1.00	*$3.00*	*$5.00*	£0.80	£2.40	£4.00
C-46 ND Justice League of America						
	$1.50	*$4.50*	*$7.50*	£0.80	£2.40	£4.00
C-47 ND Superman Bicentennial; interior features Tomahawk reprints; 2pg new framing sequence with Superman						
	$0.80	*$2.40*	*$4.00*	£0.50	£1.50	£2.50
C-48 ND Superman vs. The Flash; reprints Superman #199 and Flash #175; 6 new pgs Neal Adams art						
	$2.00	*$6.00*	*$10.00*	£1.50	£4.50	£7.50
C-49 ND Superboy and the Legion of Super-Heroes						
	$1.00	*$3.00*	*$5.00*	£0.90	£2.70	£4.50
C-50 ND Rudolph the Red-Nosed Reindeer						
	$0.60	*$1.80*	*$3.00*	£0.30	£0.90	£1.50
C-51 ND Batman; full length story reprint from Batman #232 and #242-244 featuring the origin of R'as Al Ghul by Neal Adams						
	$2.00	*$6.00*	*$10.00*	£3.00	£9.00	£15.00
C-52 ND The Best of DC; classic reprints featuring Batman (Neal Adams), Flash (Carmine Infantino) and Firehair (Alex Toth)						
	$1.50	*$4.50*	*$7.50*	£0.50	£1.50	£2.50
C-57 ND scarce in the U.K. Welcome Back Kotter; based on US TV series						
	$0.60	*$1.80*	*$3.00*	£0.30	£0.90	£1.50
C-59 ND Batman's Strangest Cases; reprints include Swamp Thing #7 (Bernie Wrightson) and the Vow From the Grave story by Neal Adams						
	$2.00	*$6.00*	*$10.00*	£3.00	£9.00	£15.00
Title Value:	*$42.90*	*$128.70*	*$214.50*	£32.70	£98.10	£163.50

Note: all issues are reprint except some new stories in C-32-34. C-36 is all new material. Issues #21-34, 51-59 are all 80 pages, #35-41 are 64 pages and #42-50 are 56 pages, covers not being counted. Owing to their size and mail packaging and/or shop display, these items are rarely found in true Mint condition.

ARTISTS

Neal Adams reprints in C-23, 25, 39, 43, 44, 51, 59. Jack Kirby reprint in C-43. Bernie Wrightson reprints in C-23, 43, 59.

LION KING, THE

Marvel Comics Group,OS; 1 Jul 1994

1 ND 48pgs, adaptation of animated film

	$Good	$Fine	$N.Mint	£Good	£Fine	£N.Mint
	$0.50	*$1.50*	*$2.50*	£0.30	£0.90	£1.50
Title Value:	*$0.50*	*$1.50*	*$2.50*	£0.30	£0.90	£1.50

LION OF SPARTA

Dell/Movie Classics,OS Movie; 12-439-301 Jan 1963

12-439-301 distributed in the U.K. film adaptation with Richard Egan and Sir Ralph Richardson

	$Good	$Fine	$N.Mint	£Good	£Fine	£N.Mint
	$3.55	*$10.50*	*$25.00*	£1.75	£5.25	£12.50
Title Value:	*$3.55*	*$10.50*	*$25.00*	£1.75	£5.25	£12.50

LISA COMICS

Bongo Comics,OS; 1 Apr 1995

1 ND Lisa Simpson stars; Matt Groenig art

	$Good	$Fine	$N.Mint	£Good	£Fine	£N.Mint
	$0.50	*$1.50*	*$2.50*	£0.30	£0.90	£1.50
Title Value:	*$0.50*	*$1.50*	*$2.50*	£0.30	£0.90	£1.50

LITTLE DOT

Harvey; 1 Sep 1953-164 Apr 1976

1 1st appearance Little Dot and Richie Rich

	$Good	$Fine	$N.Mint	£Good	£Fine	£N.Mint
	$115.00	*$350.00*	*$825.00*	£77.50	£235.00	£550.00
2	*$46.00*	*$135.00*	*$325.00*	£31.00	£92.50	£220.00
3	*$29.00*	*$85.00*	*$200.00*	£19.00	£57.50	£135.00
4	*$21.00*	*$62.50*	*$150.00*	£14.00	£43.00	£100.00
5	*$30.00*	*$90.00*	*$210.00*	£20.00	£60.00	£140.00
6	*$25.00*	*$75.00*	*$175.00*	£17.00	£50.00	£120.00
7-10	*$17.50*	*$52.50*	*$125.00*	£12.00	£36.00	£85.00
11-20	*$12.50*	*$39.00*	*$90.00*	£8.50	£26.00	£60.00
21-40	*$7.00*	*$21.00*	*$50.00*	£5.00	£15.00	£35.00
41-60	*$3.55*	*$10.50*	*$25.00*	£2.50	£7.50	£17.50
61-80	*$2.10*	*$6.25*	*$15.00*	£1.40	£4.25	£10.00
81-100	*$1.05*	*$3.20*	*$7.50*	£0.70	£2.10	£5.00
101-141	*$0.80*	*$2.50*	*$5.00*	£0.50	£1.50	£3.00
142-145 giant	*$1.25*	*$3.75*	*$7.50*	£0.80	£2.50	£5.00
146-164	*$0.25*	*$0.75*	*$1.50*	£0.15	£0.50	£1.00
Title Value:	*$777.55*	*$2348.25*	*$5498.50*	£530.05	£1600.00	£3717.00

Note: most issues distributed in the U.K. after 1959

LITTLE DOT DOTLAND

Harvey; 1 Jul 1962-61 Dec 1973

	$Good	$Fine	$N.Mint	£Good	£Fine	£N.Mint
1	*$10.50*	*$32.00*	*$75.00*	£7.00	£21.00	£50.00
2-3	*$5.50*	*$17.00*	*$40.00*	£3.90	£11.50	£27.50
4-5	*$5.25*	*$16.00*	*$37.50*	£3.55	£10.50	£25.00
6-10	*$2.85*	*$8.50*	*$20.00*	£1.90	£5.75	£13.50
11-20	*$2.50*	*$7.50*	*$15.00*	£1.65	£5.00	£10.00
21-30	*$1.65*	*$5.00*	*$10.00*	£1.00	£3.00	£6.00
31-50	*$1.00*	*$3.00*	*$6.00*	£0.50	£1.50	£3.00
51-54 giant	*$1.65*	*$5.00*	*$10.00*	£0.80	£2.50	£5.00
55-61	*$0.50*	*$1.50*	*$3.00*	£0.25	£0.75	£1.50
Title Value:	*$117.85*	*$356.00*	*$761.00*	£72.85	£219.00	£473.00

Note: most issues distributed in the U.K.

LITTLE MERMAID COMIC EDITION, THE

Disney,OS; nn 1991

nn ND adaptation of film

	$Good	$Fine	$N.Mint	£Good	£Fine	£N.Mint
	$0.50	*$1.50*	*$2.50*	£0.30	£0.90	£1.50
Title Value:	*$0.50*	*$1.50*	*$2.50*	£0.30	£0.90	£1.50

LITTLE MERMAID GRAPHIC NOVEL, THE

Disney,OS; nn Nov 1990

nn ND 64pgs, adaptation of film

	$Good	$Fine	$N.Mint	£Good	£Fine	£N.Mint
	$1.00	*$3.00*	*$5.00*	£0.70	£2.10	£3.50
Title Value:	*$1.00*	*$3.00*	*$5.00*	£0.70	£2.10	£3.50

LITTLE MERMAID, THE

Disney; 1 Dec 1991-4 Apr 1992

1-4 ND Peter David script

	$Good	$Fine	$N.Mint	£Good	£Fine	£N.Mint
	$0.30	*$0.90*	*$1.50*	£0.20	£0.60	£1.00
Title Value:	*$1.20*	*$3.60*	*$6.00*	£0.80	£2.40	£4.00

LITTLE MERMAID, THE

Marvel Comics Group; 1 Sep 1994-13 Sep 1995

1-13 ND new adventures; Trina Robbins script

	$Good	$Fine	$N.Mint	£Good	£Fine	£N.Mint
	$0.30	*$0.90*	*$1.50*	£0.20	£0.60	£1.00
Title Value:	*$3.90*	*$11.70*	*$19.50*	£2.60	£7.80	£13.00

The Little Mermaid (Apr 1995)

	£Good	£Fine	£N.Mint
Trade paperback reprints issues #1-4	£1.30	£3.90	£6.50

LITTLE MONSTERS, THE

Gold Key; 1 Nov 1964-44 Feb 1978

1 scarce in the U.K. sub-titled 'Orrible Orvie and Awful Annie

VERY GENERAL PERCENTAGE CONVERSION CHART WHICH MAY BE USED TO CALCULATE LOW AND INBETWEEN GRADES:

	$Good	$Fine	$N.Mint	£Good	£Fine	£N.Mint
	$3.55	*$10.50*	*$25.00*	£1.75	£5.25	£12.50
2-5	*$1.65*	*$5.00*	*$10.00*	£0.80	£2.50	£5.00
6-10	*$1.25*	*$3.75*	*$7.50*	£0.55	£1.75	£3.50
11-20	*$0.55*	*$1.75*	*$3.50*	£0.25	£0.75	£1.50
21-44	*$0.25*	*$0.75*	*$1.50*	£0.15	£0.50	£1.00
Title Value:	*$27.90*	*$84.75*	*$173.50*	£13.80	£43.50	£89.00
LITTLE NEMO IN SLUMBERLAND						
Blackthorne;(3-D Series #11) nn Jan 1987						
nn ND reprints by Windsor McCay; with bound-in 3-D glasses (25% less if without glasses)	*$0.50*	*$1.50*	*$2.50*	£0.30	£0.90	£1.50
Title Value:	*$0.50*	*$1.50*	*$2.50*	£0.30	£0.90	£1.50
Note: see also Betty Boop in 3-D as this is also numbered Blackthorne 3-D Series in the indicia						
LITTLE NEMO IN SLUMBERLAND 3-D						
Blackthorne;(3-D Series #13) 1 Jan 1987						
1 ND indicia misprinted as #11	*$0.50*	*$1.50*	*$2.50*	£0.30	£0.90	£1.50
Title Value:	*$0.50*	*$1.50*	*$2.50*	£0.30	£0.90	£1.50
LITTLE NEMO IN THE PALACE OF ICE						
Dover; nn 1976						
nn ND	*$1.25*	*$3.75*	*$7.50*	£0.80	£2.50	£5.00
Title Value:	*$1.25*	*$3.75*	*$7.50*	£0.80	£2.50	£5.00
LITTLE NINJAS IN WONDERLAND						
Comax Productions; 1 1990						
1 ND Butch Burcham script and art; adult material, black and white	*$0.30*	*$0.90*	*$1.50*	£0.20	£0.60	£1.00
Title Value:	*$0.30*	*$0.90*	*$1.50*	£0.20	£0.60	£1.00
LITTLE SHOP OF HORRORS						
DC Comics,OS; 1 Feb 1987						
1 ND 68pgs, adapts film, Gene Colan art	*$0.30*	*$0.90*	*$1.50*	£0.20	£0.60	£1.00
Title Value:	*$0.30*	*$0.90*	*$1.50*	£0.20	£0.60	£1.00
LIVINGSTONE MOUNTAIN						
Adventure,MS; 1 Sep 1991-4 Dec 1991						
1-4 ND Steve Moncuse script/art	*$0.40*	*$1.20*	*$2.00*	£0.25	£0.75	£1.25
Title Value:	*$1.60*	*$4.80*	*$8.00*	£1.00	£3.00	£5.00
LIZARDS SUMMER FUN SPECIAL						
Alchemy Studios,OS; 1 Sep 1991						
1 ND 36pgs	*$0.50*	*$1.50*	*$2.50*	£0.30	£0.90	£1.50
Title Value:	*$0.50*	*$1.50*	*$2.50*	£0.30	£0.90	£1.50
LLOYD LLEWELLYN						
Fantagraphics,Magazine; 1 1986-6 1988						
1 ND Dan Clowes story/art begins	*$1.20*	*$3.60*	*$6.00*	£0.80	£2.40	£4.00
2 ND	*$0.90*	*$2.70*	*$4.50*	£0.70	£2.10	£3.50
3-6 ND	*$0.90*	*$2.70*	*$4.50*	£0.60	£1.80	£3.00
Title Value:	*$5.70*	*$17.10*	*$28.50*	£3.90	£11.70	£19.50
Collection (1990), reprints 13 stories				£1.10	£3.30	£5.50
The Many Worlds of Lloyd Llewellyn (May 1994) Hardcover collection of all stories published to date, 2,000 copies				£5.50	£16.50	£27.50
LLOYD LLEWELLYN SPECIAL						
Fantagraphics; 1 Dec 1988						
1 ND Dan Clowes story/art	*$0.60*	*$1.80*	*$3.00*	£0.40	£1.20	£2.00
1 2nd printing, ND (Dec 1992)	*$0.50*	*$1.50*	*$2.50*	£0.30	£0.90	£1.50
Title Value:	*$1.10*	*$3.30*	*$5.50*	£0.70	£2.10	£3.50
LOBO						
DC Comics,MS; 1 Nov 1990-4 Feb 1991						
(see Legion '89-'94,Omega Men,Superman #41)						
1 Keith Giffen/Alan Grant script, has cover splash with "only 99c", Simon Bisley art	*$1.00*	*$3.00*	*$5.00*	£0.60	£1.80	£3.00
1 2nd printing, has no cover splash?	*$0.50*	*$1.50*	*$2.50*	£0.30	£0.90	£1.50
2	*$0.80*	*$2.40*	*$4.00*	£0.50	£1.50	£2.50
3-4	*$0.60*	*$1.80*	*$3.00*	£0.40	£1.20	£2.00
Title Value:	*$3.50*	*$10.50*	*$17.50*	£2.20	£6.60	£11.00
Note: first issue sold at a special cut-price of 99 cents						
The Last Czarnian (Feb 1992) Trade paperback reprints issues #1-4 plus painted cover by Simon Bisley				£1.10	£3.30	£5.50
Lobo's Greatest Hits (Mar 1992) Trade paperback reprints early appearances from Omega Men, Justice League, Mister Miracle and Superman [2nd Series]				£1.60	£4.80	£8.00
Lobo Slipcase Package (Feb 1992), three trade paperbacks including The Wisdom of Lobo, pre-bagged in slipcase				£3.75	£11.25	£18.50
LOBO (2ND SERIES)						
DC Comics; 0 Oct 1994; 1 Dec 1993-present						
0 (Oct 1994) Zero Hour X-over	*$0.40*	*$1.20*	*$2.00*	£0.25	£0.75	£1.25
1 Alan Grant script begins; foil embossed cover	*$0.60*	*$1.80*	*$3.00*	£0.40	£1.20	£2.00
2-15	*$0.40*	*$1.20*	*$2.00*	£0.25	£0.75	£1.25
16-20	*$0.45*	*$1.35*	*$2.25*	£0.30	£0.90	£1.50
21 Kev O'Neill art	*$0.45*	*$1.35*	*$2.25*	£0.30	£0.90	£1.50
22 Underworld Unleahed tie-in	*$0.45*	*$1.35*	*$2.25*	£0.30	£0.90	£1.50
23-37	*$0.45*	*$1.35*	*$2.25*	£0.30	£0.90	£1.50
Title Value:	*$16.50*	*$49.50*	*$82.50*	£10.75	£32.25	£53.75
LOBO ANNUAL						
DC Comics; 1 Jul 1993-present						

	$Good	$Fine	$N.Mint	£Good	£Fine	£N.Mint
1 64pgs, Bloodlines part 1, continued in Superman: The Man of Steel Annual #2	*$0.80*	*$2.40*	*$4.00*	£0.50	£1.50	£2.50
2 64pgs, Elseworlds	*$0.80*	*$2.40*	*$4.00*	£0.50	£1.50	£2.50
3 56pgs, Year One	*$0.80*	*$2.40*	*$4.00*	£0.50	£1.50	£2.50
Title Value:	*$2.40*	*$7.20*	*$12.00*	£1.50	£4.50	£7.50
LOBO CONVENTION SPECIAL						
DC Comics,OS; 1 Sep 1993						
1 Keith Giffen and Alan Grant script, Kev O'Neill art	*$0.40*	*$1.20*	*$2.00*	£0.25	£0.75	£1.25
Title Value:	*$0.40*	*$1.20*	*$2.00*	£0.25	£0.75	£1.25
LOBO GOES TO HOLLYWOOD						
DC Comics; 1 Aug 1996						
1 ND Alan Grant script, Christian Alamy art	*$0.45*	*$1.35*	*$2.25*	£0.30	£0.90	£1.50
Title Value:	*$0.45*	*$1.35*	*$2.25*	£0.30	£0.90	£1.50
LOBO PARAMILITARY CHRISTMAS SPECIAL						
DC Comics,OS; 1 Jan 1992						
1 48pgs, Keith Giffen, Alan Grant and Simon Bisley	*$0.45*	*$1.35*	*$2.25*	£0.30	£0.90	£1.50
Title Value:	*$0.45*	*$1.35*	*$2.25*	£0.30	£0.90	£1.50
LOBO'S BACK						
DC Comics,MS; 1 May 1992-4 Sep 1992						
1 Simon Bisley cover and art, Lobo "dies"	*$0.50*	*$1.50*	*$2.50*	£0.30	£0.90	£1.50
2 Simon Bisley cover and art, Lobo reincarnated as a woman	*$0.40*	*$1.20*	*$2.00*	£0.25	£0.75	£1.25
3 Simon Bisley art with Sam Keith cover, Lobo reincarnated as a squirrel	*$0.40*	*$1.20*	*$2.00*	£0.25	£0.75	£1.25
4 Lobo reincarnated as Lobo again; (not Bisley art)	*$0.40*	*$1.20*	*$2.00*	£0.25	£0.75	£1.25
Title Value:	*$1.70*	*$5.10*	*$8.50*	£1.05	£3.15	£5.25
Lobo's Back Back (Sep 1993) Trade paperback 112pgs, reprints issues #1-4 with new die-cut cover				£1.30	£3.90	£6.50
LOBO'S BIG BABE SPRING BREAK SPECIAL						
DC Comics,OS; 1 May 1995						
1 Alan Grant script, Jim Balent art	*$0.45*	*$1.35*	*$2.25*	£0.30	£0.90	£1.50
Title Value:	*$0.45*	*$1.35*	*$2.25*	£0.30	£0.90	£1.50
LOBO/DEADMAN: THE BRAVE AND THE BALD						
DC Comics,OS; 1 Feb 1995						
1 Alan Grant script, Martin Edmond art	*$0.80*	*$2.40*	*$4.00*	£0.50	£1.50	£2.50
Title Value:	*$0.80*	*$2.40*	*$4.00*	£0.50	£1.50	£2.50
LOBO/DEMON: HELLOWE'EN						
DC Comics,OS; 1 Dec 1996						
1 ND Alan Grant script, Vince Giarrano art	*$0.45*	*$1.35*	*$2.25*	£0.30	£0.90	£1.50
Title Value:	*$0.45*	*$1.35*	*$2.25*	£0.30	£0.90	£1.50
LOBO/JUDGE DREDD: PSYCHO BIKERS VS. MUTANTS FROM HELL						
DC Comics,OS; 1 Jan 1996						
1 ND 48pgs, Alan Grant script, Val Semeiks and John Dell art	*$1.00*	*$3.00*	*$5.00*	£0.70	£2.10	£3.50
Title Value:	*$1.00*	*$3.00*	*$5.00*	£0.70	£2.10	£3.50
LOBO/MASK						
DC Comics/Dark Horse,MS; 1 Feb 1997-2 Mar 1997						
1-2 ND 48pgs, Alan Grant and John Arcudi script, Doug Mahnke and Keith Williams art	*$1.20*	*$3.60*	*$6.00*	£0.80	£2.40	£4.00
Title Value:	*$2.40*	*$7.20*	*$12.00*	£1.60	£4.80	£8.00
LOBO: A CONTRACT ON GAWD						
DC Comics,MS; 1 Apr 1994-4 Jul 1994						
1-4 Alan Grant script, Kieron Dwyer art	*$0.40*	*$1.20*	*$2.00*	£0.25	£0.75	£1.25
Title Value:	*$1.60*	*$4.80*	*$8.00*	£1.00	£3.00	£5.00
LOBO: BLAZING CHAIN OF LOVE						
DC Comics,OS; 1 Sep 1992						
1 Giffen, Grant and Cowan	*$0.40*	*$1.20*	*$2.00*	£0.25	£0.75	£1.25
Title Value:	*$0.40*	*$1.20*	*$2.00*	£0.25	£0.75	£1.25
LOBO: BOUNTY HUNTING FOR FUN & PROFIT						
DC Comics,OS; 1 Apr 1995						
1 ND 48pgs, Alan Grant script, Martin Edmond, Kev O'Neill among the artists	*$1.00*	*$3.00*	*$5.00*	£0.70	£2.10	£3.50
Title Value:	*$1.00*	*$3.00*	*$5.00*	£0.70	£2.10	£3.50
LOBO: DEATH & TAXES						
DC Comics,MS; 1 Oct 1994-4 Jan 1997						
1-4 ND Keith Giffen and Alan Grant script, Alex Horley art	*$0.45*	*$1.35*	*$2.25*	£0.30	£0.90	£1.50
Title Value:	*$1.80*	*$5.40*	*$9.00*	£1.20	£3.60	£6.00
LOBO: I QUIT						
DC Comics,OS; 1 Dec 1995						
1 ND Alan Grant script, Carlos Esquerra art	*$0.45*	*$1.35*	*$2.25*	£0.30	£0.90	£1.50
Title Value:	*$0.45*	*$1.35*	*$2.25*	£0.30	£0.90	£1.50
LOBO: IN THE CHAIR						
DC Comics,OS; 1 Aug 1994						
1 Alan Grant and Martin Edmond	*$0.40*	*$1.20*	*$2.00*	£0.25	£0.75	£1.25
Title Value:	*$0.40*	*$1.20*	*$2.00*	£0.25	£0.75	£1.25
LOBO: INFANTICIDE						
DC Comics,MS; 1 Oct 1992-4 Jan 1993						
1-4 Alan Grant script and Keith Giffen art						

	$Good	$Fine	$N.Mint	£Good	£Fine	£N.Mint
	$0.40	$1.20	$2.00	£0.25	£0.75	£1.25
Title Value:	$1.60	$4.80	$8.00	£1.00	£3.00	£5.00
LOBO: PORTRAITS OF A BASTICH						
DC Comics,OS; nn Sep 1995						
nn ND pin-ups by John Byrne, Carlos Esquerra, Kelley Jones, Barry Kitson, Mike Zeck and others; Simon Bisley cover						
	$0.80	$2.40	$4.00	£0.50	£1.50	£2.50
Title Value:	$0.80	$2.40	$4.00	£0.50	£1.50	£2.50
LOBO: PORTRAIT OF A VICTIM						
DC Comics,OS; 1 May 1993						
1 Alan Grant script	$0.40	$1.20	$2.00	£0.25	£0.75	£1.25
Title Value:	$0.40	$1.20	$2.00	£0.25	£0.75	£1.25
LOBO: UNAMERICAN GLADIATORS						
DC Comics,MS; 1 Jun 1993-4 Sep 1993						
1-4 Alan Grant and John Wagner script, Cam Kennedy art						
	$0.40	$1.20	$2.00	£0.25	£0.75	£1.25
Title Value:	$1.60	$4.80	$8.00	£1.00	£3.00	£5.00
LOBOCOP						
DC Comics,OS; 1 Feb 1994						
1 Alan Grant script, Martin Emond art						
	$0.40	$1.20	$2.00	£0.25	£0.75	£1.25
Title Value:	$0.40	$1.20	$2.00	£0.25	£0.75	£1.25
LOCO VERSUS PULVERINE						
Eclipse,OS; 1 Jul 1992						
1 ND parody of Lobo and Wolverine						
	$0.50	$1.50	$2.50	£0.30	£0.90	£1.50
Title Value:	$0.50	$1.50	$2.50	£0.30	£0.90	£1.50
LOGAN						
Marvel Comics Group,OS; 1 Feb 1996						
1 ND 48pgs, Logan before he was Weapon X and Wolverine						
	$1.20	$3.60	$6.00	£0.80	£2.40	£4.00
Title Value:	$1.20	$3.60	$6.00	£0.80	£2.40	£4.00
LOGAN'S RUN						
Adventure,MS; 1 Jun 1990-6 Apr 1991						
(see Marvel Comics title)						
1 ND Barry Blair art begins; black and white begins						
	$0.40	$1.20	$2.00	£0.25	£0.75	£1.25
1 2nd printing ND	$0.40	$1.20	$2.00	£0.25	£0.75	£1.25
2-3 ND	$0.40	$1.20	$2.00	£0.25	£0.75	£1.25
4-6 ND title becomes Logan's Run						
	$0.40	$1.20	$2.00	£0.25	£0.75	£1.25
Title Value:	$2.80	$8.40	$14.00	£1.75	£5.25	£8.75
LOGAN'S RUN						
Marvel Comics Group,Film; 1 Jan 1977-7 Jul 1977						
1 George Perez cover and art						
	$0.65	$2.00	$4.00	£0.30	£1.00	£2.00
2-5 George Perez cover and art						
	$0.40	$1.25	$2.50	£0.25	£0.75	£1.50
6 1st solo Thanos back-up story by Mike Zeck (very Starlinesque art)						
	$1.00	$3.00	$6.00	£0.40	£1.25	£2.50
7	$0.40	$1.25	$2.50	£0.25	£0.75	£1.50
Title Value:	$3.65	$11.25	$22.50	£1.95	£6.00	£12.00
Note: 1-5 adapts film. 6,7 new material.						
LOGAN'S WORLD						
Adventure; 1 Jul 1991-6 Dec 1991						
1-6 ND	$0.40	$1.20	$2.00	£0.25	£0.75	£1.25
Title Value:	$2.40	$7.20	$12.00	£1.50	£4.50	£7.50
LOGAN: SHADOW SOCIETY						
Marvel Comics Group,OS; nn Feb 1997						
nn ND 48pgs, pre-X-Men adventures of Wolverine						
	$1.20	$3.60	$6.00	£0.80	£2.40	£4.00
Title Value:	$1.20	$3.60	$6.00	£0.80	£2.40	£4.00
LOIS & CLARK: THE NEW ADVENTURES OF SUPERMAN						
DC Comics; nn Jul 1994						
nn Trade paperback, 192pgs; reprints highlighting Lois and Clark stories; intro by John Byrne						
	$2.00	$6.00	$10.00	£1.40	£4.20	£7.00
Title Value:	$2.00	$6.00	$10.00	£1.40	£4.20	£7.00
LOIS LANE						
DC Comics,MS; 1 Aug 1986-2 Sep 1986						
1-2 ND 52pgs, Gray Morrow art						
	$0.30	$0.90	$1.50	£0.20	£0.60	£1.00
Title Value:	$0.60	$1.80	$3.00	£0.40	£1.20	£2.00
LOIS LANE ANNUAL, SUPERMAN'S GIRLFRIEND						
National Periodical Publications; 1 Aug/Oct 1962-2 Aug/Oct 1963						
1 80pgs, reprints stories from Lois Lane #10, #11, Superman #131 and Adventure #261 among others						
	$22.00	$65.00	$200.00	£13.00	£40.00	£120.00
2 80pgs, reprints #14 and #16 among others						
	$12.00	$37.00	$110.00	£7.00	£21.50	£65.00
Title Value:	$34.00	$102.00	$310.00	£20.00	£61.50	£185.00
REPRINT FEATURES						
Lois Lane/Superman in 1, 2.						
LOIS LANE, SUPERMAN'S GIRLFRIEND						
National Periodical Publications/DC Comics; 1 Mar/Apr 1958-137 Sep/Oct 1974						
(see Brave and the Bold, 80-Page Giant, Lois Lane mini-series. Amalgamated with Superman Family after #137)						
1 very scarce in the U.K.						
	$250.00	$750.00	$2500.00	£175.00	£520.00	£1750.00
[Rare in high grade - Very Fine+ or better]						
2 very scarce in the U.K.						
	$100.00	$300.00	$800.00	£67.50	£205.00	£550.00
3 scarce in the U.K.						
	$65.00	$195.00	$525.00	£44.00	£130.00	£350.00

	$Good	$Fine	$N.Mint	£Good	£Fine	£N.Mint
4-5	$50.00	$150.00	$400.00	£34.00	£100.00	£270.00
6 (Jan 1959)	$45.00	$135.00	$360.00	£30.00	£90.00	£240.00
7-8	$45.00	$135.00	$360.00	£30.00	£90.00	£240.00
9-10	$36.00	$105.00	$285.00	£23.50	£70.00	£190.00
11-13	$26.00	$75.00	$180.00	£17.00	£50.00	£120.00
1st official distribution in the U.K.						
14 (Jan 1960), Supergirl appears, Lois as Batgirl						
	$26.00	$75.00	$180.00	£15.00	£45.00	£105.00
15 3-part story (black cover - scarce in high grade)						
	$26.00	$75.00	$180.00	£13.50	£41.00	£95.00
16-20	$26.00	$75.00	$180.00	£10.50	£32.00	£75.00
21	$20.00	$60.00	$140.00	£7.75	£23.50	£55.00
22 (Jan 1961), Supergirl appears						
	$20.00	$60.00	$140.00	£7.75	£23.50	£55.00
23-25	$20.00	$60.00	$140.00	£7.75	£23.50	£55.00
26	$20.00	$60.00	$140.00	£6.25	£19.00	£45.00
27 Bizarro appears						
	$20.00	$60.00	$140.00	£6.25	£19.00	£45.00
28	$20.00	$60.00	$140.00	£6.25	£19.00	£45.00
29 Aquaman, Batman, Green Arrow cameo; last 10 cents issue (Note: white cover shows wear and dirt easily - scarce in high grade)						
	$20.00	$60.00	$140.00	£7.00	£21.00	£50.00
30 (Jan 1962)	$11.00	$34.00	$80.00	£4.25	£12.50	£30.00
31-32	$11.00	$34.00	$80.00	£4.25	£12.50	£30.00
33 Mon El cameo	$12.50	$39.00	$90.00	£4.60	£13.50	£32.50
34-35	$11.00	$34.00	$80.00	£4.25	£12.50	£30.00
36-37	$10.50	$32.00	$75.00	£3.90	£11.50	£27.50
38 (Jan 1963)	$10.50	$32.00	$75.00	£3.90	£11.50	£27.50
39 Supergirl cameo						
	$10.50	$32.00	$75.00	£3.90	£11.50	£27.50
40	$10.50	$32.00	$75.00	£3.90	£11.50	£27.50
41-45	$10.50	$32.00	$75.00	£3.20	£9.50	£22.50
46 (Jan 1964)	$10.50	$32.00	$75.00	£3.20	£9.50	£22.50
47 scarce in the U.K. Legion cameo						
	$11.00	$34.00	$80.00	£3.55	£10.50	£25.00
48-49	$10.50	$32.00	$75.00	£3.20	£9.50	£22.50
50 Phantom Girl, Shrinking Violet, Triplicate Girl appear						
	$9.25	$28.00	$65.00	£3.90	£11.50	£27.50
51 Supergirl appears						
	$7.75	$23.50	$55.00	£2.50	£7.50	£17.50
52-53	$7.75	$23.50	$55.00	£2.50	£7.50	£17.50
54 (Jan 1965), classic "The Monster That Loved Lois Lane"						
	$7.75	$23.50	$55.00	£2.50	£7.50	£17.50
55	$7.75	$23.50	$55.00	£2.50	£7.50	£17.50
56 Saturn Girl appears						
	$7.75	$23.50	$55.00	£2.10	£6.25	£15.00
57-58	$7.75	$23.50	$55.00	£2.10	£6.25	£15.00
59 Batman appears						
	$7.75	$23.50	$55.00	£2.10	£6.25	£15.00
60	$7.75	$23.50	$55.00	£2.10	£6.25	£15.00
61 Supergirl appears; last Silver Age issue, cover-dated Nov/Dec 1965						
	$6.25	$19.00	$45.00	£2.10	£6.25	£15.00
62 (Jan 1966)	$6.25	$19.00	$45.00	£1.70	£5.00	£12.00
63-67	$6.25	$19.00	$45.00	£1.70	£5.00	£12.00
68 less common in the U.K. 80pgs, Giant G-26						
	$8.50	$26.00	$60.00	£3.20	£9.50	£22.50
69	$6.25	$19.00	$45.00	£1.70	£5.00	£12.00
70 1st Silver Age appearance of Catwoman (pre-dates Batman #197 by more than a year)						
	$39.00	$115.00	$275.00	£12.50	£39.00	£90.00
71 (Jan 1967), 2nd Silver Age Catwoman; Batman/Robin cameo						
	$25.00	$75.00	$175.00	£7.75	£23.50	£55.00
72-73	$4.25	$12.50	$30.00	£1.40	£4.25	£10.00
74 1st appearance Bizarro Flash, Justice League of America appear						
	$6.25	$19.00	$45.00	£1.40	£4.25	£10.00
75	$4.25	$12.50	$30.00	£1.25	£3.85	£9.00
76	$4.25	$12.50	$30.00	£1.10	£3.40	£8.00
77 80pgs, Giant G-39, reprints cover story of #1						
	$5.50	$17.00	$40.00	£2.50	£7.50	£17.50
78	$4.25	$12.50	$30.00	£1.05	£3.20	£7.50
79 Neal Adams covers begin						
	$2.85	$8.50	$20.00	£1.05	£3.20	£7.50
80 (Jan 1968), Neal Adams cover						
	$2.10	$6.25	$15.00	£0.85	£2.55	£6.00
81-85 Neal Adams covers						
	$2.10	$6.25	$15.00	£0.70	£2.10	£5.00
86 Neal Adams cover, 80pg Giant G-51						
	$3.55	$10.50	$25.00	£1.75	£5.25	£12.50
87-88 Neal Adams covers						
	$2.10	$6.25	$15.00	£0.70	£2.10	£5.00
89 (Jan 1969), Neal Adams cover, Batman appears						
	$2.10	$6.25	$15.00	£0.85	£2.55	£6.00
90-92 Neal Adams cover						
	$2.10	$6.25	$15.00	£0.70	£2.10	£5.00
93 Neal Adams cover, Wonder Woman appears						
	$2.10	$6.25	$15.00	£0.85	£2.55	£6.00
94 Neal Adams cover						
	$2.10	$6.25	$15.00	£0.70	£2.10	£5.00
95 Neal Adams cover, 80pg Giant G-63						
	$3.55	$10.50	$25.00	£1.75	£5.25	£12.50
96-97	$1.05	$3.20	$7.50	£0.55	£1.70	£4.00
98 (Jan 1970)	$1.05	$3.20	$7.50	£0.55	£1.70	£4.00
99-100 Batman appears						

	$Good	$Fine	$N.Mint	£Good	£Fine	£N.Mint
	$1.05	$3.20	$7.50	£0.55	£1.70	£4.00
101-103	$1.25	$3.75	$7.50	£0.50	£1.50	£3.00
104 scarce in the U.K. 80pgs, Giant G-75						
	$3.55	$10.50	$25.00	£1.75	£5.25	£12.50
105 1st appearance Rose and Thorn						
	$1.25	$3.75	$7.50	£0.40	£1.25	£2.50
106	$1.25	$3.75	$7.50	£0.40	£1.25	£2.50
107 (Jan 1971)	$1.25	$3.75	$7.50	£0.40	£1.25	£2.50
108 Neal Adams cover						
	$1.25	$3.75	$7.50	£0.40	£1.25	£2.50
109-110	$1.25	$3.75	$7.50	£0.40	£1.25	£2.50
111 Justice League of America appears						
	$1.25	$3.75	$7.50	£0.40	£1.25	£2.50
112 48pgs, (says 52pgs up to #123 as they count the covers in the U.S.)						
	$1.25	$3.75	$7.50	£0.50	£1.50	£3.00
113 80pgs, Giant G-87						
	$4.15	$12.50	$25.00	£1.65	£5.00	£10.00
114 48pgs	$1.25	$3.75	$7.50	£0.50	£1.50	£3.00
115 48pgs, Black Racer appears						
	$1.25	$3.75	$7.50	£0.50	£1.50	£3.00
116 48pgs, Darkseid cameo						
	$1.25	$3.75	$7.50	£0.50	£1.50	£3.00
117 48pgs	$1.25	$3.75	$7.50	£0.50	£1.50	£3.00
118 48pgs, (Jan 1972), Darkseid cameo, origin Morgan Edge						
	$1.25	$3.75	$7.50	£0.50	£1.50	£3.00
119 48pgs, Darkseid cameo						
	$1.25	$3.75	$7.50	£0.50	£1.50	£3.00
120-121 48pgs	$1.25	$3.75	$7.50	£0.50	£1.50	£3.00
122 48pgs, Thorn teams with Lois, solo Lois Lane story from Superman #30 reprinted						
	$1.25	$3.75	$7.50	£0.50	£1.50	£3.00
123 48pgs, reprints Golden Age Batman/Catwoman story from Batman #35						
	$1.25	$3.75	$7.50	£0.50	£1.50	£3.00
124 scarce in the U.K.						
	$0.80	$2.50	$5.00	£0.50	£1.50	£3.00
125-127 less common in the U.K.						
	$0.80	$2.50	$5.00	£0.40	£1.25	£2.50
128 less common in the U.K. Justice League of America appear (principally Batman and Aquaman)						
	$0.80	$2.50	$5.00	£0.50	£1.50	£3.00
129 (Feb 1973)	$0.80	$2.50	$5.00	£0.30	£1.00	£2.00
130-131	$0.80	$2.50	$5.00	£0.30	£1.00	£2.00
132 Zatanna appears						
	$0.80	$2.50	$5.00	£0.30	£1.00	£2.00
133-135	$0.80	$2.50	$5.00	£0.30	£1.00	£2.00
136 (Jan 1974), Wonder Woman appears						
	$0.80	$2.50	$5.00	£0.35	£1.10	£2.25
137	$0.80	$2.50	$5.00	£0.30	£1.00	£2.00
Title Value:	$1709.00	$5108.25	$13195.00	£872.65	£2609.50	£6977.75

FEATURES

Melba in 132. Rose & the Thorn in 105-112, 115-121, 123-130. Zatanna in 132.

LOMAX (POLICE ACTION FEATURING..)

Atlas; 1 Feb 1975

	$Good	$Fine	$N.Mint	£Good	£Fine	£N.Mint
1 distributed in the U.K. Mike Sekowsky art						
	$0.25	$0.75	$1.50	£0.15	£0.50	£1.00
Title Value:	$0.25	$0.75	$1.50	£0.15	£0.50	£1.00

LONDON NIGHT LINGERIE SPECIAL

London Night Studios,OS; 1 Apr 1996

	$Good	$Fine	$N.Mint	£Good	£Fine	£N.Mint
1 "Naughty Edition", ND J.J. North photo cover						
	$2.00	$6.00	$10.00	£1.30	£3.90	£6.50
1 "Nice Edition", ND J.J. North photo cover						
	$0.60	$1.80	$3.00	£0.40	£1.20	£2.00
Title Value:	$2.60	$7.80	$13.00	£1.70	£5.10	£8.50

LONE RANGER & TONTO: THE VELVET DRAGON

Topps,MS; 1 Apr 1996-5 Aug 1996

	$Good	$Fine	$N.Mint	£Good	£Fine	£N.Mint
1-5 ND Joe R. Lansdale script, Ted Naifeh art						
	$0.60	$1.80	$3.00	£0.40	£1.20	£2.00
Title Value:	$3.00	$9.00	$15.00	£2.00	£6.00	£10.00

LONE RANGER AND TONTO, THE

Topps,MS; 1 Aug 1994-4 Nov 1994

	$Good	$Fine	$N.Mint	£Good	£Fine	£N.Mint
1-4 ND Joe R. Lansdale script, Tim Truman cover and art						
	$0.50	$1.50	$2.50	£0.30	£0.90	£1.50
Title Value:	$2.00	$6.00	$10.00	£1.20	£3.60	£6.00
The Lone Ranger and Tonto (Jan 1995) Trade paperback r eprints mini-series with new wraparound cover by Tim Truman				£1.30	£3.90	£6.50

LONE WOLF & CUB

First; 1 May 1987-49 1991

	$Good	$Fine	$N.Mint	£Good	£Fine	£N.Mint
1 Frank Miller covers begin						
	$1.00	$3.00	$5.00	£0.80	£2.40	£4.00
1 2nd printing	$0.80	$2.40	$4.00	£0.50	£1.50	£2.50
1 3rd printing	$0.70	$2.10	$3.50	£0.40	£1.20	£2.00
2	$0.80	$2.40	$4.00	£0.60	£1.80	£3.00
2 2nd printing	$0.70	$2.10	$3.50	£0.40	£1.20	£2.00
3	$0.80	$2.40	$4.00	£0.50	£1.50	£2.50
3 2nd printing	$0.70	$2.10	$3.50	£0.40	£1.20	£2.00
4-5	$0.80	$2.40	$4.00	£0.50	£1.50	£2.50
6 origin issue	$0.80	$2.40	$4.00	£0.60	£1.80	£3.00
7-11	$0.80	$2.40	$4.00	£0.50	£1.50	£2.50
12 last Frank Miller cover						
	$0.80	$2.40	$4.00	£0.50	£1.50	£2.50
13-20 Bill Sienkiewicz covers						
	$0.80	$2.40	$4.00	£0.50	£1.50	£2.50
21-31	$0.80	$2.40	$4.00	£0.50	£1.50	£2.50
32 88pgs, Matt Wagner covers begin						
	$0.90	$2.70	$4.50	£0.60	£1.80	£3.00
33-36	$0.80	$2.40	$4.00	£0.50	£1.50	£2.50
37 Mike Ploog covers begin						
	$0.80	$2.40	$4.00	£0.50	£1.50	£2.50
38	$0.80	$2.40	$4.00	£0.50	£1.50	£2.50
39 120pgs	$1.20	$3.60	$6.00	£0.80	£2.40	£4.00
40	$0.80	$2.40	$4.00	£0.50	£1.50	£2.50
41 80pgs	$0.85	$2.55	$4.25	£0.55	£1.65	£2.75
42-48	$0.80	$2.40	$4.00	£0.50	£1.50	£2.50
49 Arthur Suydam cover						
	$0.80	$2.40	$4.00	£0.50	£1.50	£2.50
Title Value:	$42.85	$128.55	$214.25	£27.15	£81.45	£135.75

Note; all Non-Distributed on the news-stands in the U.K.

	$Good	$Fine	$N.Mint	£Good	£Fine	£N.Mint
Deluxe Edition, reprints #1-7, colour section; Miller/Sienkiewicz cover				£2.40	£7.20	£12.00

LONG HOT SUMMER, THE

DC Comics/Milestone,MS; 1 Jul 1995-3 Sep 1995

	$Good	$Fine	$N.Mint	£Good	£Fine	£N.Mint
1 ND holographic foil-stamped cover; mini-series involving all the Milestone titles						
	$0.60	$1.80	$3.00	£0.40	£1.20	£2.00
2-3 ND	$0.60	$1.80	$3.00	£0.40	£1.20	£2.00
Title Value:	$1.80	$5.40	$9.00	£1.20	£3.60	£6.00

LONGSHOT

Marvel Comics Group,MS; 1 Sep 1985-6 Feb 1986

	$Good	$Fine	$N.Mint	£Good	£Fine	£N.Mint
1 ND 1st appearance Longshot, Art Adams pencils and Whilce Portacio inks in all						
	$1.80	$5.25	$9.00	£1.20	£3.60	£6.00
2 ND scarce in the U.K.						
	$1.40	$4.20	$7.00	£1.00	£3.00	£5.00
3 ND	$1.20	$3.60	$6.00	£0.80	£2.40	£4.00
4 ND Spiderman, She-Hulk appear						
	$1.20	$3.60	$6.00	£0.80	£2.40	£4.00

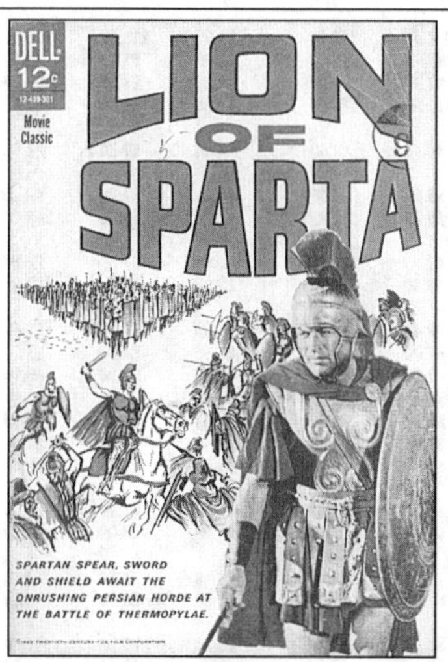

Lion of Sparta

Logan's Run (Adventure) #1

Lois Lane #10

	$Good	$Fine	$N.Mint	£Good	£Fine	£N.Mint
5 ND Dr. Strange appears	$1.20	$3.60	$6.00	£0.80	£2.40	£4.00
6 ND DS very scarce	$1.40	$4.20	$7.00	£1.20	£3.60	£6.00
Title Value:	$8.20	$24.45	$41.00	£5.80	£17.40	£29.00
Trade Paperback (1989) reprints issues #1-6				£2.50	£7.50	£12.50
2nd print (Dec 1992)				£2.25	£6.75	£11.25

LOONEY TUNES

DC Comics; 1 Apr 1994-present

	$Good	$Fine	$N.Mint	£Good	£Fine	£N.Mint
1 ND Bugs Bunny, Sylvester, Daffy Duck and others begin	$0.30	$0.90	$1.50	£0.20	£0.60	£1.00
2-19 ND	$0.30	$0.90	$1.50	£0.20	£0.60	£1.00
20 ND title goes bi-monthly	$0.30	$0.90	$1.50	£0.20	£0.60	£1.00
21-22 ND	$0.30	$0.90	$1.50	£0.20	£0.60	£1.00
23-28 ND	$0.35	$1.05	$1.75	£0.25	£0.75	£1.25
Title Value:	$8.70	$26.10	$43.50	£5.90	£17.70	£29.50

LOONEY TUNES MAGAZINE

DC Comics,Magazine; 1 Jan 1990-7 1990

	$Good	$Fine	$N.Mint	£Good	£Fine	£N.Mint
1-7 ND	$0.30	$0.90	$1.50	£0.20	£0.60	£1.00
Title Value:	$2.10	$6.30	$10.50	£1.40	£4.20	£7.00

Note: features Warner Bros cartoon characters like Bugs Bunny and Daffy Duck, other features and items, quarterly frequency.

LOOSE CANNON

DC Comics,MS; 1 Jun 1995-4 Sep 1995

	$Good	$Fine	$N.Mint	£Good	£Fine	£N.Mint
1 ND Jeph Loeb script and Adam Pollina art begins	$0.40	$1.20	$2.00	£0.25	£0.75	£1.25
2 ND The Eradicator appears	$0.40	$1.20	$2.00	£0.25	£0.75	£1.25
3-4 ND	$0.40	$1.20	$2.00	£0.25	£0.75	£1.25
Title Value:	$1.60	$4.80	$8.00	£1.00	£3.00	£5.00

LORD PUMPKIN

Malibu,OS; 0 Oct 1994

	$Good	$Fine	$N.Mint	£Good	£Fine	£N.Mint
0 ND 40pgs, spin-off from Sludge #9	$0.50	$1.50	$2.50	£0.30	£0.90	£1.50
0 Newstand Edition, ND (Feb 1995) - black etched cover	$0.50	$1.50	$2.50	£0.30	£0.90	£1.50
0 Signed & Numbered Edition, ND (Feb 1995) - signed with certificate; limited to 2,000 copies	$1.60	$4.80	$8.00	£0.80	£2.40	£4.00
Title Value:	$2.60	$7.80	$13.00	£1.40	£4.20	£7.00

LORDS OF THE ULTRA REALM

DC Comics,MS; 1 Jun 1986-6 Nov 1986

	$Good	$Fine	$N.Mint	£Good	£Fine	£N.Mint
1-6 ND scarce in the U.K.	$0.25	$0.75	$1.25	£0.15	£0.45	£0.75
Title Value:	$1.50	$4.50	$7.50	£0.90	£2.70	£4.50

LORDS OF THE ULTRA REALM SPECIAL

DC Comics; 1 Dec 1987

	$Good	$Fine	$N.Mint	£Good	£Fine	£N.Mint
1 ND	$0.40	$1.20	$2.00	£0.25	£0.75	£1.25
Title Value:	$0.40	$1.20	$2.00	£0.25	£0.75	£1.25

LOSERS SPECIAL

DC Comics,OS; 1 1985

(see Crisis On Infinite Earths, GI Combat #138, Our Fighting Forces #123)

	$Good	$Fine	$N.Mint	£Good	£Fine	£N.Mint
1 very LD 1st Crisis X-over comic, death of Captain Storm, Johnny Cloud and Gunner & Sarge	$0.30	$0.90	$1.50	£0.30	£0.90	£1.50
Title Value:	$0.30	$0.90	$1.50	£0.30	£0.90	£1.50

LOST CONTINENT, THE

Eclipse,MS; 1 Oct 1990-6 Mar 1991

	$Good	$Fine	$N.Mint	£Good	£Fine	£N.Mint
1-6 ND 64pgs, squarebound, Japanese material reprints of Akihiro Yamada work, black and white	$0.60	$1.80	$3.00	£0.40	£1.20	£2.00
Title Value:	$3.60	$10.80	$18.00	£2.40	£7.20	£12.00

LOST IN SPACE

Gold Key,TV;37 Oct 1973-54 Dec 1977; Whitman,TV; 55 Mar 1981-59 May 1982

(previously Space Family Robinson)

	$Good	$Fine	$N.Mint	£Good	£Fine	£N.Mint
37 full cover title now reads "Space Family Robinson Lost in Space on Space Staion One"	$0.80	$2.50	$5.00	£0.50	£1.50	£3.00
38 16pg Kenner cartoon insert	$0.80	$2.50	$5.00	£0.50	£1.50	£3.00
39-41	$0.80	$2.50	$5.00	£0.50	£1.50	£3.00
42 16pg Kenner cartoon insert	$0.80	$2.50	$5.00	£0.50	£1.50	£3.00
43-54	$0.80	$2.50	$5.00	£0.50	£1.50	£3.00
55 all reprints begin	$0.60	$1.80	$3.00	£0.40	£1.20	£2.00
56 new logo begins	$0.60	$1.80	$3.00	£0.40	£1.20	£2.00
57-58	$0.60	$1.80	$3.00	£0.40	£1.20	£2.00
59 scarce in the U.K. line drawn cover	$0.60	$1.80	$3.00	£0.50	£1.50	£2.50
Title Value:	$17.40	$54.00	$105.00	£11.10	£33.30	£64.50

Note: most issue distributed in the U.K.

LOST IN SPACE (2ND SERIES)

Innovation,MS; 1 Aug 1991-18 Nov 1993

	$Good	$Fine	$N.Mint	£Good	£Fine	£N.Mint
1 co-written by Billy Mumy ("Will" in TV series)	$0.60	$1.80	$3.00	£0.40	£1.20	£2.00
1 Special Edition Reprint, (Mar 1992) - extra pages, recoloured	$0.55	$1.65	$2.75	£0.35	£1.05	£1.75
2	$0.50	$1.50	$2.50	£0.30	£0.90	£1.50
2 Special Edition Reprint, (Oct 1992) - extra pages, recoloured	$0.55	$1.65	$2.75	£0.35	£1.05	£1.75
3-6	$0.50	$1.50	$2.50	£0.30	£0.90	£1.50
7 co-plotted by Mark Goddard	$0.50	$1.50	$2.50	£0.30	£0.90	£1.50
8	$0.50	$1.50	$2.50	£0.30	£0.90	£1.50
9 co-written by Billy Mumy	$0.50	$1.50	$2.50	£0.30	£0.90	£1.50
10-12	$0.50	$1.50	$2.50	£0.30	£0.90	£1.50
13 ND Voyage to the Bottom of the Soul story begins; gold foil cardstock cover with art by Mike Deodato	$0.50	$1.50	$2.50	£0.30	£0.90	£1.50
13 Gold Collectors Edition, ND (1993) pre-bagged with poster and gold embossed logo	$1.20	$3.60	$6.00	£0.60	£1.80	£3.00
14-18 ND Voyage to the Bottom of the Soul story; Mike Deodato cover	$0.50	$1.50	$2.50	£0.30	£0.90	£1.50
Title Value:	$11.40	$34.20	$57.00	£6.80	£20.40	£34.00

Note: all Non-Distributed on the news-stands in the U.K.

	$Good	$Fine	$N.Mint	£Good	£Fine	£N.Mint
Strangers Among Strangers Graphic Novel (Feb 1993) ND reprints issues #4-5 with new art, photo gallery and new cover painting				£0.75	£2.25	£3.75

Note also: the Voyage to the Bottom of the Soul story was originally intended to be a stand-alone 12 part mini-series.

LOST IN SPACE ANNUAL

Innovation; 1 1992-2 1993

	$Good	$Fine	$N.Mint	£Good	£Fine	£N.Mint
1 ND Miguel Ferrer appears	$0.50	$1.50	$2.50	£0.30	£0.90	£1.50
2 ND script by Peter David and Billy Mumy	$0.50	$1.50	$2.50	£0.30	£0.90	£1.50
Title Value:	$1.00	$3.00	$5.00	£0.60	£1.80	£3.00

LOST IN SPACE: PROJECT ROBINSON

Innovation,MS; 1 Nov 1993

	$Good	$Fine	$N.Mint	£Good	£Fine	£N.Mint
1 ND	$0.50	$1.50	$2.50	£0.30	£0.90	£1.50
Title Value:	$0.50	$1.50	$2.50	£0.30	£0.90	£1.50

Note: issue #2 was advertised and solicited but never came out.

LOST PLANET

Eclipse; 1 May 1987-5 Feb 1988; 6 Jan 1989

	$Good	$Fine	$N.Mint	£Good	£Fine	£N.Mint
1 ND Bo Hampton art, Scott Hampton art on back-up	$0.40	$1.20	$2.00	£0.25	£0.75	£1.25
2-3 ND Bo Hampton art	$0.40	$1.20	$2.00	£0.25	£0.75	£1.25
4 ND Bo Hampton art, Scott Hampton art on back-up	$0.40	$1.20	$2.00	£0.25	£0.75	£1.25
5-6 ND Bo Hampton art	$0.40	$1.20	$2.00	£0.25	£0.75	£1.25
Title Value:	$2.40	$7.20	$12.00	£1.50	£4.50	£7.50

LOST UNIVERSE, GENE RODDENBERRY'S

Tekno Comix; 0 Jul 1995; 1 Apr 1995-6 Nov 1995

	$Good	$Fine	$N.Mint	£Good	£Fine	£N.Mint
0 ND (Jul 1995), wraparound cover by Jae Lee	$0.45	$1.35	$2.25	£0.30	£0.90	£1.50
1 ND Lawrence Watts-Evans script, James Callahan and Aaron McClellan art; Bill Sienkiewicz painted cover	$0.40	$1.20	$2.00	£0.25	£0.75	£1.25
2-5 ND Bill Sienkiewicz painted cover	$0.40	$1.20	$2.00	£0.25	£0.75	£1.25
6 ND Bill Sienkiewicz painted cover	$0.45	$1.35	$2.25	£0.30	£0.90	£1.50
Title Value:	$2.90	$8.70	$14.50	£1.85	£5.55	£9.25

LOST WORLD

Millennium,MS; 1 Jan 1996-2 Feb 1996

	$Good	$Fine	$N.Mint	£Good	£Fine	£N.Mint
1-2 ND based on Arthur Conan Doyle story; black and white	$0.60	$1.80	$3.00	£0.40	£1.20	£2.00
Title Value:	$1.20	$3.60	$6.00	£0.80	£2.40	£4.00

LOVE AND ROCKETS

Hernandez Brothers/Fantagraphics; 1 Jul 1982-50 Mar 1996

(see Mechanics)

	$Good	$Fine	$N.Mint	£Good	£Fine	£N.Mint
1 black and white cover with no staples, $1.00 cover price, self-published, 800 copies	$11.00	$33.00	$55.00	£8.00	£24.00	£40.00
1 2nd printing, colour cover, 1st Fantagraphics issue	$8.00	$24.00	$40.00	£5.00	£15.00	£25.00
1 3rd printing	$0.90	$2.70	$4.50	£0.60	£1.80	£3.00
1 4th printing	$0.80	$2.40	$4.00	£0.50	£1.50	£2.50
2	$4.00	$12.00	$20.00	£3.00	£9.00	£15.00
2 2nd printing, (1990)	$0.80	$2.40	$4.00	£0.50	£1.50	£2.50
2 3rd printing, (May 1996)	$1.00	$3.00	$5.00	£0.65	£1.95	£3.25
3	$3.00	$9.00	$15.00	£2.00	£6.00	£10.00
3 2nd printing, (1991)	$0.80	$2.40	$4.00	£0.50	£1.50	£2.50
4	$3.00	$9.00	$15.00	£2.00	£6.00	£10.00
4 2nd printing, (1991)	$0.80	$2.40	$4.00	£0.50	£1.50	£2.50
5	$2.00	$6.00	$10.00	£1.50	£4.50	£7.50
6	$1.50	$4.50	$7.50	£1.00	£3.00	£5.00
6 2nd printing	$0.60	$1.80	$3.00	£0.40	£1.20	£2.00
7	$1.50	$4.50	$7.50	£1.00	£3.00	£5.00
7 2nd printing	$0.60	$1.80	$3.00	£0.40	£1.20	£2.00
8	$1.50	$4.50	$7.50	£1.00	£3.00	£5.00
8 2nd printing, (Oct 1991)	$0.60	$1.80	$3.00	£0.40	£1.20	£2.00
9	$1.50	$4.50	$7.50	£1.00	£3.00	£5.00
9 2nd printing, (Nov 1991)	$0.60	$1.80	$3.00	£0.40	£1.20	£2.00
10	$1.50	$4.50	$7.50	£1.00	£3.00	£5.00
10 2nd printing, (Jan 1992)	$0.50	$1.50	$2.50	£0.30	£0.90	£1.50
11	$1.20	$3.60	$6.00	£0.80	£2.40	£4.00

	$Good	$Fine	$N.Mint	£Good	£Fine	£N.Mint
11 2nd printing, (Feb 1992)	***$0.50***	***$1.50***	***$2.50***	**£0.30**	**£0.90**	**£1.50**
12	***$1.20***	***$3.60***	***$6.00***	**£0.80**	**£2.40**	**£4.00**
12 2nd printing, (Nov 1992)	***$0.50***	***$1.50***	***$2.50***	**£0.30**	**£0.90**	**£1.50**
13 Lloyd Llewellyn first ever story	***$1.20***	***$3.60***	***$6.00***	**£0.80**	**£2.40**	**£4.00**
13 2nd printing, (Dec 1992)	***$0.50***	***$1.50***	***$2.50***	**£0.30**	**£0.90**	**£1.50**
14	***$1.20***	***$3.60***	***$6.00***	**£0.80**	**£2.40**	**£4.00**
14 2nd printing, (Dec 1992)	***$0.50***	***$1.50***	***$2.50***	**£0.30**	**£0.90**	**£1.50**
15	***$1.20***	***$3.60***	***$6.00***	**£0.80**	**£2.40**	**£4.00**
15 2nd printing, (Nov 1993)	***$0.50***	***$1.50***	***$2.50***	**£0.30**	**£0.90**	**£1.50**
16	***$1.00***	***$3.00***	***$5.00***	**£0.70**	**£2.10**	**£3.50**
16 2nd printing, (Dec 1993)	***$0.50***	***$1.50***	***$2.50***	**£0.30**	**£0.90**	**£1.50**
17-20	***$1.00***	***$3.00***	***$5.00***	**£0.70**	**£2.10**	**£3.50**
21-25	***$0.90***	***$2.70***	***$4.50***	**£0.60**	**£1.80**	**£3.00**
26-28	***$0.60***	***$1.80***	***$3.00***	**£0.40**	**£1.20**	**£2.00**
28 2nd printing, (May 1995)	***$0.50***	***$1.50***	***$2.50***	**£0.30**	**£0.90**	**£1.50**
29	***$0.60***	***$1.80***	***$3.00***	**£0.40**	**£1.20**	**£2.00**
29 2nd printing, (May 1992)	***$0.50***	***$1.50***	***$2.50***	**£0.30**	**£0.90**	**£1.50**
30 bumper special	***$0.80***	***$2.40***	***$4.00***	**£0.50**	**£1.50**	**£2.50**
30 2nd printing, (Jun 1992)	***$0.60***	***$1.80***	***$3.00***	**£0.40**	**£1.20**	**£2.00**
31	***$0.60***	***$1.80***	***$3.00***	**£0.40**	**£1.20**	**£2.00**
31 2nd printing, (Jul 1992)	***$0.50***	***$1.50***	***$2.50***	**£0.30**	**£0.90**	**£1.50**
32-39	***$0.60***	***$1.80***	***$3.00***	**£0.40**	**£1.20**	**£2.00**
40 48pgs, Maggie returns	***$0.70***	***$2.10***	***$3.50***	**£0.50**	**£1.50**	**£2.50**
41-49	***$0.60***	***$1.80***	***$3.00***	**£0.40**	**£1.20**	**£2.00**
50 64pgs	***$1.20***	***$3.60***	***$6.00***	**£0.80**	**£2.40**	**£4.00**
Title Value:	***$83.00***	***$249.00***	***$415.00***	**£55.85**	**£167.55**	**£279.25**

Note: all Non-Distributed on the news-stands in the U.K.

	£Good	£Fine	£N.Mint
Book 1: Music For Mechanics, hardcover reprints #1,2	£4.00	£12.00	£20.00
(2nd,3rd printings)	£2.50	£7.50	£12.50
(4th printing - Mar 1993)	£1.90	£5.70	£9.50
Book 1 softcover	£1.80	£5.40	£9.00
Book 2: Chelo's Burden, hardback, reprints #3,4	£3.60	£10.80	£18.00
Book 2 softcover	£1.80	£5.40	£9.00
(2nd, 3rd printings)	£2.70	£8.10	£13.50
Book 3: Las Mujeres Perdidas, hardcover, reprints #5-8	£3.60	£10.80	£18.00
Book 3 softcover	£1.70	£5.10	£8.50
Book 4: Tears from Heaven, hardcover, reprints #9-12	£3.60	£10.80	£18.00
Book 4 softback	£1.70	£5.10	£8.50
Book 4 Deluxe	£5.00	£15.00	£25.00
[Book 4: softcover, hardcover, deluxe all reprinted Sep 1991]			
Book 4 3rd printing (Jun 1996)	£2.20	£6.60	£11.00
Book 5: House of Raging Women, reprints #13-16, hardcover	£4.50	£13.50	£22.50
Book 5 softcover	£1.70	£5.10	£8.50
Book 5 2nd print (Jul 1995)	£2.20	£6.60	£11.00
Book 5 Deluxe	£5.00	£15.00	£25.00
Book 6: Duck Feet	£4.20	£12.60	£21.00
Book 6 softcover	£1.70	£5.10	£8.50
Book 6 2nd print (Aug 1995)	£2.20	£6.60	£11.00
Book 6 Deluxe	£5.00	£15.00	£25.00
Book 7: The Death of Speedy, hardcover	£4.00	£12.00	£20.00
Book 7 limited hardcover	£5.00	£15.00	£25.00
Book 7 softcover	£1.65	£4.95	£8.25
Book 7 2nd print (Dec 1995)	£2.00	£6.00	£10.00
Book 8: Blood of Palomar, hardcover	£4.00	£12.00	£20.00
Book 8 limited hardcover	£5.00	£15.00	£25.00
Book 8 softcover	£1.65	£4.95	£8.25
Book 8 2nd print (Feb 1996)	£2.30	£6.90	£11.50
Book 9: Flies on the Ceiling, softcover	£1.50	£4.50	£7.50
Book 9: hardcover	£4.20	£12.60	£21.00
Book 10 softcover	£1.50	£4.50	£7.50
Book 11: Wig Wam Bam softcover	£1.70	£5.10	£8.50
Book 11 Hardcover	£4.50	£13.50	£22.50
Book 11 Limited Hardcover	£5.00	£15.00	£25.00
Book 12 soft cover	£2.20	£6.60	£11.00
Book 12: Poison River Signed & Numbered hardcover	£5.00	£15.00	£25.00
Book 13: Chester Square (Jun 1996)	£2.50	£7.50	£12.50
Book 13 Hardcover, signed	£5.30	£15.90	£26.50
Heartbreak Soup (Gilbert)	£1.50	£4.50	£7.50
The Reticent Heart (Gilbert)	£1.50	£4.50	£7.50
Short Stories (Jaimie)	£1.50	£4.50	£7.50
The Lost Women (Jaimie)	£1.50	£4.50	£7.50
TITAN BOOKS:			
Mechanics	£1.40	£4.20	£7.00
Love and Rockets	£1.30	£3.90	£6.50
Heartbreak Soup	£1.20	£3.60	£6.00
Duck Feet	£1.20	£3.60	£6.00
Human Diastrophism	£1.40	£4.20	£7.00
Ape Sex	£1.30	£3.90	£6.50

LOVE AND ROCKETS, TEN YEARS OF

Fantagraphics,OS; 1 Sep 1992

	$Good	$Fine	$N.Mint	£Good	£Fine	£N.Mint
1 ND character indexes and background information plus new and old strips	***$0.30***	***$0.90***	***$1.50***	**£0.20**	**£0.60**	**£1.00**
Title Value:	***$0.30***	***$0.90***	***$1.50***	**£0.20**	**£0.60**	**£1.00**

LOVE STORIES

DC Comics; 147 Nov 1972-152 Oct/Nov 1973

(previously Heart Throbs)

	$Good	$Fine	$N.Mint	£Good	£Fine	£N.Mint
147-152 ND	***$0.80***	***$2.50***	***$5.00***	**£0.50**	**£1.50**	**£3.00**
Title Value:	***$4.80***	***$15.00***	***$30.00***	**£3.00**	**£9.00**	**£18.00**

LOVECRAFT

Adventure,MS; 1 Dec 1991-4 May 1992

	$Good	$Fine	$N.Mint	£Good	£Fine	£N.Mint
1 ND The Lurking Fear	***$0.50***	***$1.50***	***$2.50***	**£0.30**	**£0.90**	**£1.50**
1 Limited Edition, ND - includes prose story, poster, embossed cover	***$0.80***	***$2.40***	***$4.00***	**£0.50**	**£1.50**	**£2.50**
2 ND Beyond The Wall of Sleep	***$0.50***	***$1.50***	***$2.50***	**£0.30**	**£0.90**	**£1.50**
3 ND The Tomb	***$0.50***	***$1.50***	***$2.50***	**£0.30**	**£0.90**	**£1.50**
4 ND The Alchemist	***$0.50***	***$1.50***	***$2.50***	**£0.30**	**£0.90**	**£1.50**
Title Value:	***$2.80***	***$8.40***	***$14.00***	**£1.70**	**£5.10**	**£8.50**

LOWLIFE

Caliber Press; 1 May 1991-3 1992; Aeon: 4 Oct 1994-6 1995

	$Good	$Fine	$N.Mint	£Good	£Fine	£N.Mint
1 ND Ed Brubaker script and art, black and white; Chester Brown art featured	***$0.50***	***$1.50***	***$2.50***	**£0.30**	**£0.90**	**£1.50**
2 ND Beat Generation story	***$0.50***	***$1.50***	***$2.50***	**£0.30**	**£0.90**	**£1.50**
3-6 ND	***$0.50***	***$1.50***	***$2.50***	**£0.30**	**£0.90**	**£1.50**
Title Value:	***$3.00***	***$9.00***	***$15.00***	**£1.80**	**£5.40**	**£9.00**
Portable Lowlife (Dec 1994) reprints issues #1 & 2 plus new 6pg story				£0.65	£1.95	£3.25

LUCIFER'S HAMMER

Innovation,MS; 1 Nov 1993-4 Feb 1994

	$Good	$Fine	$N.Mint	£Good	£Fine	£N.Mint
1 ND adaptation of Larry Niven and Jerry Pournelle novel begins	***$0.50***	***$1.50***	***$2.50***	**£0.30**	**£0.90**	**£1.50**
2-4 ND	***$0.50***	***$1.50***	***$2.50***	**£0.30**	**£0.90**	**£1.50**
Title Value:	***$2.00***	***$6.00***	***$10.00***	**£1.20**	**£3.60**	**£6.00**

LUGER

Eclipse,MS; 1 Oct 1986-3 Feb 1987

	$Good	$Fine	$N.Mint	£Good	£Fine	£N.Mint
1-3 ND Bo Hampton/Yeates art, colour	***$0.40***	***$1.20***	***$2.00***	**£0.25**	**£0.75**	**£1.25**
Title Value:	***$1.20***	***$3.60***	***$6.00***	**£0.75**	**£2.25**	**£3.75**

LUM

Viz; 1 1989-8 1990

	$Good	$Fine	$N.Mint	£Good	£Fine	£N.Mint
1-8 ND Urusei Yatsura art	***$0.60***	***$1.80***	***$3.00***	**£0.40**	**£1.20**	**£2.00**
Title Value:	***$4.80***	***$14.40***	***$24.00***	**£3.20**	**£9.60**	**£16.00**
Graphic Album 1, reprints				£1.65	£4.95	£8.25
Graphic Album 2, reprints				£1.65	£4.95	£8.25
Lum Urusei Yatsura Perfect Collection (Jul 1994) 400pgs, collects both the above in one volume; softcover, b&w				£2.60	£7.80	£13.00

LUNATIK

Marvel Comics Group; 1 Dec 1995-3 Feb 1996

	$Good	$Fine	$N.Mint	£Good	£Fine	£N.Mint
1 ND Thanos appears; Keith Giffen art begins	***$0.40***	***$1.20***	***$2.00***	**£0.25**	**£0.75**	**£1.25**
2 ND Lunatik vs. The Avengers	***$0.40***	***$1.20***	***$2.00***	**£0.25**	**£0.75**	**£1.25**
3 ND	***$0.40***	***$1.20***	***$2.00***	**£0.25**	**£0.75**	**£1.25**
Title Value:	***$1.20***	***$3.60***	***$6.00***	**£0.75**	**£2.25**	**£3.75**

LUST OF THE NAZI WEASEL WOMEN

Fantagraphics; 1 Oct 1990-5 1991

	$Good	$Fine	$N.Mint	£Good	£Fine	£N.Mint
1-5 ND Mitch Manzer script/art, black and white	***$0.40***	***$1.20***	***$2.00***	**£0.25**	**£0.75**	**£1.25**
Title Value:	***$2.00***	***$6.00***	***$10.00***	**£1.25**	**£3.75**	**£6.25**

LUTHER ARKWRIGHT

Dark Horse,MS; 1 Mar 1990-9 Jan 1991 (see British section)

	$Good	$Fine	$N.Mint	£Good	£Fine	£N.Mint
1-9 ND	***$0.40***	***$1.20***	***$2.00***	**£0.25**	**£0.75**	**£1.25**
Title Value:	***$3.60***	***$10.80***	***$18.00***	**£2.25**	**£6.75**	**£11.25**

Note: reprints original series with new covers by Bryan Talbot; issued every 6 weeks

LUX AND ALBY

Dark Horse,MS; 1 Apr 1993-9 Dec 1993

	$Good	$Fine	$N.Mint	£Good	£Fine	£N.Mint
1-9 ND Mark Millar script and Simon Fraser art	***$0.50***	***$1.50***	***$2.50***	**£0.30**	**£0.90**	**£1.50**
Title Value:	***$4.50***	***$13.50***	***$22.50***	**£2.70**	**£8.10**	**£13.50**

LUXURA LEATHER SPECIAL

Brainstorm Comics,OS; 1 Mar 1996

	$Good	$Fine	$N.Mint	£Good	£Fine	£N.Mint
1 ND pin-ups wearing leather; black and white	***$0.60***	***$1.80***	***$3.00***	**£0.40**	**£1.20**	**£2.00**
Title Value:	***$0.60***	***$1.80***	***$3.00***	**£0.40**	**£1.20**	**£2.00**

LYCANTHROPE LEO

Viz,MS; 1 May 1994-7 Nov 1994

	$Good	$Fine	$N.Mint	£Good	£Fine	£N.Mint
1-7 ND Kengo Kaji and Kenji Okamura; black and white	***$0.60***	***$1.80***	***$3.00***	**£0.40**	**£1.20**	**£2.00**
Title Value:	***$4.20***	***$12.60***	***$21.00***	**£2.80**	**£8.40**	**£14.00**

LYNCH MOB

Chaos Comics,MS; 1 Jun 1994-4 Sep 1994

	$Good	$Fine	$N.Mint	£Good	£Fine	£N.Mint
1 ND Brian Pulido script, Roman Morales art, cover by Greg Capullo	***$0.50***	***$1.50***	***$2.50***	**£0.30**	**£0.90**	**£1.50**
1 Special Edition, ND full foil cover	***$2.50***	***$7.50***	***$12.50***	**£1.00**	**£3.00**	**£5.00**
2-4 ND Brian Pulido script, Roman Morales art, cover by Greg Capullo	***$0.50***	***$1.50***	***$2.50***	**£0.30**	**£0.90**	**£1.50**
Title Value:	***$4.50***	***$13.50***	***$22.50***	**£2.20**	**£6.60**	**£11.00**

M

M

Eclipse,MS; 1 Oct 1990-4 Aug 1992

Issue	$Good	$Fine	$N.Mint	£Good	£Fine	£N.Mint
1 ND Jon J. Muth script/art; bound-in flexi-disc	*$0.80*	*$2.40*	*$4.00*	£0.50	£1.50	£2.50
2-4 ND Jon J. Muth script/art	*$0.80*	*$2.40*	*$4.00*	£0.50	£1.50	£2.50
Title Value:	*$3.20*	*$9.60*	*$16.00*	£2.00	£6.00	£10.00

M.A.R.S. PATROL TOTAL WAR

Gold Key; 3 Sep 1966-10 Aug 1969

(previously Total War)

Issue	$Good	$Fine	$N.Mint	£Good	£Fine	£N.Mint
3 distributed in the U.K. Wally Wood art, painted covers on all	*$6.25*	*$19.00*	*$45.00*	£3.90	£11.50	£27.50
4-10 distributed in the U.K.	*$3.55*	*$10.50*	*$25.00*	£2.10	£6.25	£15.00
Title Value:	*$31.10*	*$92.50*	*$220.00*	£18.60	£55.25	£132.50

Note: initials stand for Marine Attack Rescue Service - no, it's not a sci-fi book!

M.D. GEIST

CPM Comics,MS; 1 Jun 1995-3 Aug 1995

Issue	$Good	$Fine	$N.Mint	£Good	£Fine	£N.Mint
1-3 ND 24pgs, based on US animated video	*$0.60*	*$1.80*	*$3.00*	£0.40	£1.20	£2.00
Title Value:	*$1.80*	*$5.40*	*$9.00*	£1.20	£3.60	£6.00
M.D. Geist: Data Album 1 (Jun 1996) Trade paperback ND collects mini-series with new pin-ups				£1.30	£3.90	£6.50

M.D. GEIST: GROUND ZERO

CPM Comics,MS; 1 Dec 1995-3 May 1996

Issue	$Good	$Fine	$N.Mint	£Good	£Fine	£N.Mint
1-3 ND 24pgs	*$0.60*	*$1.80*	*$3.00*	£0.40	£1.20	£2.00
Title Value:	*$1.80*	*$5.40*	*$9.00*	£1.20	£3.60	£6.00

M.G.M'S MARVELOUS WIZARD OF OZ

Marvel Comics Group/DC Comics,OS Tabloid Film; 1 Nov 1975

(A Marvel/DC Co-Production)

Issue	$Good	$Fine	$N.Mint	£Good	£Fine	£N.Mint
1 ND 84pgs, adapts film; John Buscema art	*$0.80*	*$2.50*	*$5.00*	£0.50	£1.50	£3.00
Title Value:	*$0.80*	*$2.50*	*$5.00*	£0.50	£1.50	£3.00

M.I.C.R.A.

Comics Interview/Apple; 1 Nov 1986-8 1988

Issue	$Good	$Fine	$N.Mint	£Good	£Fine	£N.Mint
1-7 ND black and white	*$0.30*	*$0.90*	*$1.50*	£0.20	£0.60	£1.00
8 ND 1st Apple issue, black and white	*$0.30*	*$0.90*	*$1.50*	£0.20	£0.60	£1.00
Title Value:	*$2.40*	*$7.20*	*$12.00*	£1.60	£4.80	£8.00
Graphic Novel #1-3, reprints				£0.65	£1.95	£3.25

MACHINE MAN

Marvel Comics Group; 1 Apr 1978-9 Dec 1978; 10 Aug 1979-19 Feb 1981

(see 2001, A Space Odyssey)

Issue	$Good	$Fine	$N.Mint	£Good	£Fine	£N.Mint
1 ND Jack Kirby art	*$0.65*	*$2.00*	*$4.00*	£0.30	£1.00	£2.00
2-9 ND Jack Kirby art	*$0.30*	*$1.00*	*$2.00*	£0.25	£0.75	£1.50
10-13 Steve Ditko art	*$0.30*	*$1.00*	*$2.00*	£0.20	£0.60	£1.25
14 Steve Ditko art, John Byrne cover	*$0.25*	*$0.75*	*$1.50*	£0.20	£0.60	£1.25
15 Steve Ditko art, Fantastic Four appear	*$0.25*	*$0.75*	*$1.50*	£0.20	£0.60	£1.25
16-17 Steve Ditko art	*$0.25*	*$0.75*	*$1.50*	£0.20	£0.60	£1.25
18 Wendigo, Alpha Flight appear; ties in with X-Men #140, Steve Ditko art	*$0.80*	*$2.50*	*$5.00*	£0.25	£0.75	£1.50
19 ND 1st appearance Jack O'Lantern (Philip Macendale - later Hobgoblin II), Steve Ditko art and Frank Miller cover	*$2.50*	*$7.50*	*$15.00*	£0.80	£2.50	£5.00
Title Value:	*$8.55*	*$27.00*	*$52.50*	£4.95	£15.05	£30.50

ARTISTS

Ditko 10-19. Kirby 1-9.

MACHINE MAN (2ND SERIES)

Marvel Comics Group,MS; 1 Oct 1984-4 Jan 1985

Issue	$Good	$Fine	$N.Mint	£Good	£Fine	£N.Mint
1-2 ND Barry Windsor Smith inks	*$0.30*	*$0.90*	*$1.50*	£0.20	£0.60	£1.00
3-4 ND Barry Windsor Smith art	*$0.30*	*$0.90*	*$1.50*	£0.20	£0.60	£1.00
Title Value:	*$1.20*	*$3.60*	*$6.00*	£0.80	£2.40	£4.00
Trade Paperback, reprints #1-4, new cover by Barry Smith				£0.90	£2.70	£4.50

MACHINE MAN 2020

Marvel Comics Group,MS; 1 Aug 1994-2 Sep 1994

Issue	$Good	$Fine	$N.Mint	£Good	£Fine	£N.Mint
1 ND 48pgs, reprints mini-series issues #1,2	*$0.40*	*$1.20*	*$2.00*	£0.25	£0.75	£1.25
2 ND 48pgs, reprints mini-series issues #3,4	*$0.40*	*$1.20*	*$2.00*	£0.25	£0.75	£1.25
Title Value:	*$0.80*	*$2.40*	*$4.00*	£0.50	£1.50	£2.50

MACHINE, THE

Dark Horse; 1 Nov 1994-4 Feb 1995

Issue	$Good	$Fine	$N.Mint	£Good	£Fine	£N.Mint
1-4 ND spin-off from Comics'Greatest World series	*$0.50*	*$1.50*	*$2.50*	£0.30	£0.90	£1.50
Title Value:	*$2.00*	*$6.00*	*$10.00*	£1.20	£3.60	£6.00

MACKENZIE QUEEN

Matrix Graphics,MS; 1 Jun 1985-5 Apr 1986

Issue	$Good	$Fine	$N.Mint	£Good	£Fine	£N.Mint
1-5 ND Bernie Mireault art	*$0.40*	*$1.20*	*$2.00*	£0.25	£0.75	£1.25
Title Value:	*$2.00*	*$6.00*	*$10.00*	£1.25	£3.75	£6.25

MACKENZIE QUEEN TRADE PAPERBACK

Caliber Press; nn 1991

Issue	$Good	$Fine	$N.Mint	£Good	£Fine	£N.Mint
nn ND reprints issues #1-5 originally published by Matrix Graphics	*$2.50*	*$7.50*	*$12.50*	£1.50	£4.50	£7.50
Title Value:	*$2.50*	*$7.50*	*$12.50*	£1.50	£4.50	£7.50

MACROSS

Comico; 1 Dec 1984

(becomes Robotech: The Macross Saga)

Issue	$Good	$Fine	$N.Mint	£Good	£Fine	£N.Mint
1 ND colour, based on animated Japanese TV show	*$1.20*	*$3.60*	*$6.00*	£0.60	£1.80	£3.00
Title Value:	*$1.20*	*$3.60*	*$6.00*	£0.60	£1.80	£3.00

MACROSS II

Viz,MS; 1 Nov 1993-10 1994

Issue	$Good	$Fine	$N.Mint	£Good	£Fine	£N.Mint
1-10 ND	*$0.50*	*$1.50*	*$2.50*	£0.30	£0.90	£1.50
Title Value:	*$5.00*	*$15.00*	*$25.00*	£3.00	£9.00	£15.00
Macross II Graphic Novel (Jun 1994) 304pgs, collects mini-series; black and white				£2.20	£6.60	£11.00

MACROSS II: THE MICRON CONSPIRACY

Viz,MS; 1 Nov 1994-5 Mar 1995

Issue	$Good	$Fine	$N.Mint	£Good	£Fine	£N.Mint
1-5 ND James Hudnall and Schuloff Tam; black and white	*$0.50*	*$1.50*	*$2.50*	£0.30	£0.90	£1.50
Title Value:	*$2.50*	*$7.50*	*$12.50*	£1.50	£4.50	£7.50

MAD

Extra-Large Comics; 1 Aug 1991

Issue	$Good	$Fine	$N.Mint	£Good	£Fine	£N.Mint
1 ND reprints issues #1-6 of original series	*$3.50*	*$10.50*	*$17.50*	£2.50	£7.50	£12.50
Title Value:	*$3.50*	*$10.50*	*$17.50*	£2.50	£7.50	£12.50

Note: announced as an on-going series but cancelled after #1

MAD DOG

Marvel Comics Group,MS; 1 May 1993-6 Oct 1993

Issue	$Good	$Fine	$N.Mint	£Good	£Fine	£N.Mint
1-6 Evan Dorkin script and Ty Templeton art; based on US TV show	*$0.25*	*$0.75*	*$1.25*	£0.15	£0.45	£0.75
Title Value:	*$1.50*	*$4.50*	*$7.50*	£0.90	£2.70	£4.50

MAD DOG MAGAZINE

Blackthorne; 1 Nov 1986-3 1987

Issue	$Good	$Fine	$N.Mint	£Good	£Fine	£N.Mint
1-3 ND	*$0.25*	*$0.75*	*$1.25*	£0.15	£0.45	£0.75
Title Value:	*$0.75*	*$2.25*	*$3.75*	£0.45	£1.35	£2.25

MAD DOGS

Comico,MS; 1 Apr 1992-3 Jun 1992

Issue	$Good	$Fine	$N.Mint	£Good	£Fine	£N.Mint
1-3 ND	*$0.40*	*$1.20*	*$2.00*	£0.25	£0.75	£1.25
Title Value:	*$1.20*	*$3.60*	*$6.00*	£0.75	£2.25	£3.75

MAD MAGAZINE

E.C. Comics; 1 Oct/Nov 1952-present

Issue	$Good	$Fine	$N.Mint	£Good	£Fine	£N.Mint
1 very scarce in the U.K. comic format begins; classic cover by Harvey Kurtzman; sub-titled "Tales Calculated to Drive You.."	*$680.00*	*$2050.00*	*$5500.00*	£455.00	£1375.00	£3670.00
2 scarce in the U.K. Jack Davis cover	*$155.00*	*$470.00*	*$1100.00*	£105.00	£315.00	£735.00
3-4 Kurtzman cover	*$92.50*	*$275.00*	*$650.00*	£60.00	£185.00	£435.00
5 scarce in the U.K.	*$155.00*	*$470.00*	*$1100.00*	£105.00	£315.00	£735.00
6-10 Kurtzman cover	*$70.00*	*$210.00*	*$500.00*	£48.00	£140.00	£335.00
11 classic Basil Wolverton cover and art	*$70.00*	*$210.00*	*$500.00*	£48.00	£140.00	£335.00
12	*$55.00*	*$170.00*	*$400.00*	£39.00	£115.00	£270.00
13 Kurtzman cover	*$55.00*	*$170.00*	*$400.00*	£39.00	£115.00	£270.00
14 Kurtzman Mona Lisa cover	*$55.00*	*$170.00*	*$400.00*	£39.00	£115.00	£270.00
15	*$55.00*	*$170.00*	*$400.00*	£39.00	£115.00	£270.00
16 Kurtzman cover	*$43.00*	*$125.00*	*$300.00*	£29.00	£85.00	£200.00
17	*$43.00*	*$125.00*	*$300.00*	£29.00	£85.00	£200.00
18 Kurtzman cover	*$43.00*	*$125.00*	*$300.00*	£29.00	£85.00	£200.00
19-20	*$43.00*	*$125.00*	*$300.00*	£29.00	£85.00	£200.00
21 famous Alfred E. Neuman character appears on cover in "small ad" (1st)	*$43.00*	*$125.00*	*$300.00*	£29.00	£85.00	£200.00
22 special Art issue	*$43.00*	*$125.00*	*$300.00*	£29.00	£85.00	£200.00
23	*$43.00*	*$125.00*	*$300.00*	£29.00	£85.00	£200.00
24 scarce in the U.K. 1st magazine format (July 1955); sub-titled The New Mad	*$120.00*	*$360.00*	*$850.00*	£80.00	£240.00	£570.00
25	*$49.00*	*$145.00*	*$340.00*	£33.00	£97.50	£230.00
26-27	*$39.00*	*$115.00*	*$275.00*	£26.00	£77.50	£185.00
28-29	*$36.00*	*$105.00*	*$250.00*	£24.00	£72.50	£170.00
30 1st classic Alfred E. Neuman cover	*$60.00*	*$180.00*	*$425.00*	£41.00	£120.00	£285.00
31	*$29.00*	*$85.00*	*$200.00*	£19.00	£57.50	£135.00
32-33	*$25.00*	*$75.00*	*$175.00*	£17.00	£50.00	£120.00
34-35	*$20.00*	*$60.00*	*$140.00*	£13.50	£41.00	£95.00
36-40	*$12.50*	*$39.00*	*$90.00*	£8.50	£26.00	£60.00
41-50	*$10.50*	*$32.00*	*$75.00*	£7.00	£21.00	£50.00
51-60	*$8.50*	*$26.00*	*$60.00*	£5.50	£17.00	£40.00
61-70	*$7.50*	*$22.50*	*$45.00*	£5.00	£15.00	£30.00
71-80	*$6.50*	*$20.00*	*$40.00*	£4.15	£12.50	£25.00
81-90	*$5.75*	*$17.50*	*$35.00*	£3.75	£11.00	£22.50
91-100	*$5.00*	*$15.00*	*$30.00*	£2.90	£8.75	£17.50
101-104	*$3.75*	*$11.00*	*$22.50*	£2.05	£6.25	£12.50

105 Batman TV show parody

Issue	$Good	$Fine	$N.Mint	£Good	£Fine	£N.Mint
	$5.00	$15.00	$30.00	£2.90	£8.75	£17.50
106-120	$3.75	$11.00	$22.50	£2.05	£6.25	£12.50
121-150	$2.50	$7.50	$15.00	£1.65	£5.00	£10.00
151-170	$2.40	$7.00	$12.00	£1.60	£4.80	£8.00
171-200	$1.80	$5.25	$9.00	£1.20	£3.60	£6.00
201-220	$1.20	$3.60	$6.00	£0.80	£2.40	£4.00
221-250	$1.00	$3.00	$5.00	£0.60	£1.80	£3.00
251-300	$0.70	$2.10	$3.50	£0.50	£1.50	£2.50
301-320	$0.50	$1.50	$2.50	£0.30	£0.90	£1.50
321-350	$0.40	$1.20	$2.00	£0.25	£0.75	£1.25
Title Value:	$3521.25	$10564.50	$24767.50	£2352.35	£7033.50	£16467.50

Note: see Mad Magazine in the British section

MADAME XANADU

DC Comics,OS; 1 Jul 1981

(see Doorway to Nightmare, Unexpected)

Issue	$Good	$Fine	$N.Mint	£Good	£Fine	£N.Mint
1 32pgs, Bolland and Rogers art, Kaluta cover and art (2 pgs), includes poster, no ads	$0.40	$1.20	$2.00	£0.25	£0.75	£1.25
Title Value:	$0.40	$1.20	$2.00	£0.25	£0.75	£1.25

MADBALLS

Marvel Comics Group/Star; 1 Sep 1986-3 Nov 1986; 4 Jun 1987-10 Jun 1988

Issue	$Good	$Fine	$N.Mint	£Good	£Fine	£N.Mint
1-10	$0.15	$0.45	$0.75	£0.10	£0.30	£0.50
Title Value:	$1.50	$4.50	$7.50	£1.00	£3.00	£5.00

MADHOUSE

Red Circle (Archie); 95 Sep 1974-97 Jan 1975; 98 Aug 1975-130 Oct 1982

Issue	$Good	$Fine	$N.Mint	£Good	£Fine	£N.Mint
95-96 Gray Morrow cover and art	$0.65	$2.00	$4.00	£0.30	£1.00	£2.00
97 Williamson, Thorne, Morrow art	$0.30	$1.00	$2.00	£0.25	£0.75	£1.50
98-110	$0.30	$1.00	$2.00	£0.20	£0.60	£1.25
111-130	$0.40	$1.20	$2.00	£0.20	£0.60	£1.00
Title Value:	$13.50	$42.00	$76.00	£7.45	£22.55	£41.75

Note: all distributed in the U.K.

MADMAN

Tundra/Kitchen Sink; 1 May 1992-3 1992

Issue	$Good	$Fine	$N.Mint	£Good	£Fine	£N.Mint
1 ND 48pgs, squarebound	$2.00	$6.00	$10.00	£1.00	£3.00	£5.00
1 2nd printing, ND (1993)	$1.00	$3.00	$5.00	£0.50	£1.50	£2.50
1 3rd printing ND	$0.80	$2.40	$4.00	£0.50	£1.50	£2.50
2 ND 48pgs, squarebound	$1.60	$4.80	$8.00	£0.80	£2.40	£4.00
3 ND 48pgs, squarebound	$1.50	$4.50	$7.50	£0.70	£2.10	£3.50
Title Value:	$6.90	$20.70	$34.50	£3.50	£10.50	£17.50

MADMAN ADVENTURES

Tundra; 1 1992-3 1993

Issue	$Good	$Fine	$N.Mint	£Good	£Fine	£N.Mint
1 ND Mike Allred cover and art	$1.50	$4.50	$7.50	£0.70	£2.10	£3.50
2-3 ND Mike Allred cover and art	$1.20	$3.60	$6.00	£0.50	£1.50	£2.50
Title Value:	$3.90	$11.70	$18.50	£1.70	£5.10	£8.50
Madman Adventures Collection (Jan 1995) Trade paperback ND reprints mini-series with new cover by Mike Allred				£2.00	£6.00	£10.00

MADMAN COMICS

Dark Horse/Legend; 1 Apr 1994-present

Issue	$Good	$Fine	$N.Mint	£Good	£Fine	£N.Mint
1 ND Mike Allred script and art; back cover by Frank Miller	$1.40	$4.20	$7.00	£0.60	£1.80	£3.00
2 ND	$1.00	$3.00	$5.00	£0.50	£1.50	£2.50
3 ND Alex Toth back cover	$0.80	$2.40	$4.00	£0.40	£1.20	£2.00
4 ND Dave Stevens back cover	$0.60	$1.80	$3.00	£0.40	£1.20	£2.00
5 ND	$0.60	$1.80	$3.00	£0.40	£1.20	£2.00
6 ND Frank Miller script; Bruce Timm back cover	$0.60	$1.80	$3.00	£0.40	£1.20	£2.00
7 ND Frank Miller script	$0.60	$1.80	$3.00	£0.40	£1.20	£2.00
8 ND Peter Bagge back cover	$0.60	$1.80	$3.00	£0.40	£1.20	£2.00
9 ND Paul Chadwick back cover	$0.60	$1.80	$3.00	£0.40	£1.20	£2.00
10 ND Alex Ross cover	$0.60	$1.80	$3.00	£0.40	£1.20	£2.00
11 ND	$0.60	$1.80	$3.00	£0.40	£1.20	£2.00
Title Value:	$8.00	$24.00	$40.00	£4.70	£14.10	£23.50

MADRAVEN HALLOWEEN SPECIAL

Hamilton Comics,OS; 1 Oct 1995

Issue	$Good	$Fine	$N.Mint	£Good	£Fine	£N.Mint
1 ND features work by Nicola Cuti, Jan Duursema and Gray Morrow	$0.60	$1.80	$3.00	£0.40	£1.20	£2.00
Title Value:	$0.60	$1.80	$3.00	£0.40	£1.20	£2.00

MAELSTROM

Aircel; 1 1987-13 1988

Issue	$Good	$Fine	$N.Mint	£Good	£Fine	£N.Mint
1-13 ND	$0.30	$0.90	$1.50	£0.20	£0.60	£1.00
Title Value:	$3.90	$11.70	$19.50	£2.60	£7.80	£13.00

MAGE

Comico; 1 Feb 1984-15 Dec 1986

Issue	$Good	$Fine	$N.Mint	£Good	£Fine	£N.Mint
1 ND Comico's 1st colour comic, Matt Wagner script/art begins	$2.00	$6.00	$10.00	£2.00	£6.00	£10.00
2 ND	$1.50	$4.50	$7.50	£1.20	£3.60	£6.00
3-5 ND	$1.20	$3.60	$6.00	£1.00	£3.00	£5.00
6 ND 1st New Grendel (backup)	$4.00	$12.00	$20.00	£2.00	£6.00	£10.00
7 ND Grendel back up	$3.00	$9.00	$15.00	£1.50	£4.50	£7.50
8 ND Grendel back up	$1.50	$4.50	$7.50	£1.20	£3.60	£6.00
9-10 ND Grendel back up	$1.20	$3.60	$6.00	£0.80	£2.40	£4.00
11-14 ND Grendel back up	$1.00	$3.00	$5.00	£0.70	£2.10	£3.50
15 ND DS	$1.20	$3.60	$6.00	£1.00	£3.00	£5.00
Title Value:	$23.20	$69.60	$116.00	£16.30	£48.90	£81.50
Grendel: The Devil Inside (Jun 1989) Trade paperback, reprints issues #6-15				£1.10	£3.30	£5.50
Mage: The Hero Discovered, reprints				£2.00	£6.00	£10.00
Signed and Numbered Edition, slipcase				£20.00	£60.00	£100.00
Mage II, reprints				£2.00	£6.00	£10.00
Signed and Numbered Edition, slipcase				£20.00	£60.00	£100.00
Mage III, reprints				£2.00	£6.00	£10.00
Signed and Numbered Edition, slipcase				£20.00	£60.00	£100.00

MAGGIE THE CAT, MIKE GRELL'S

Image; 1 Feb 1996-2 1996 ?

Issue	$Good	$Fine	$N.Mint	£Good	£Fine	£N.Mint
1-2 ND Mike Grell script and art	$0.50	$1.50	$2.50	£0.30	£0.90	£1.50
Title Value:	$1.00	$3.00	$5.00	£0.60	£1.80	£3.00

MAGGOTS

Gladstone/Hamilton Comics; 1 Sep 1991-4 1992

Issue	$Good	$Fine	$N.Mint	£Good	£Fine	£N.Mint
1-4 ND 48pgs	$0.60	$1.80	$3.00	£0.40	£1.20	£2.00
Title Value:	$2.40	$7.20	$12.00	£1.60	£4.80	£8.00

MAGGOTS IN COLOUR

Hamilton Comics,OS; 1 Apr 1992

1 ND reprints in colour

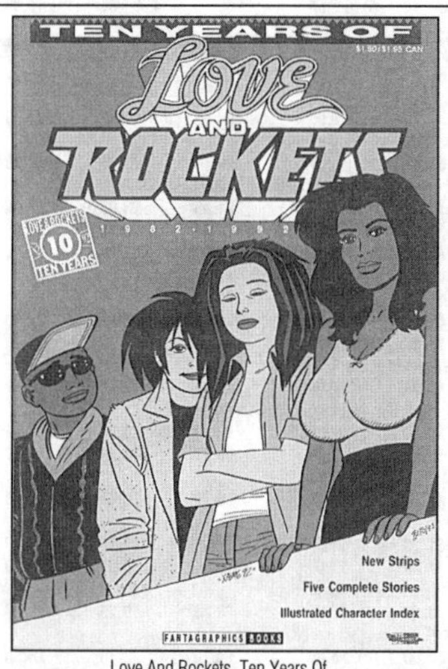

Love And Rockets, Ten Years Of

Low Life #1

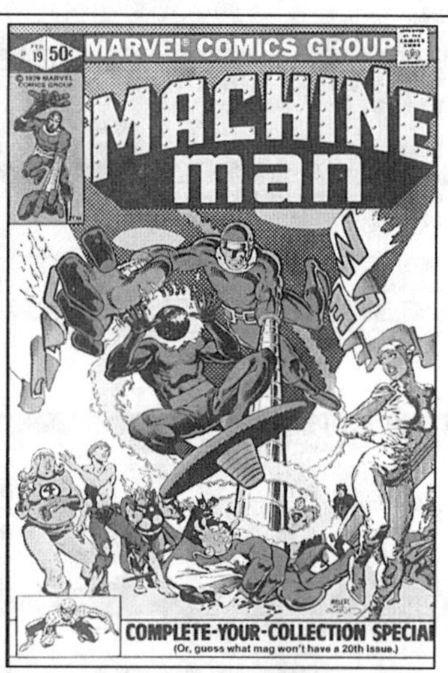

Machine Man #19

	$Good	$Fine	$N.Mint	£Good	£Fine	£N.Mint
	$0.25	$0.75	$1.25	£0.15	£0.45	£0.75
Title Value:	$0.25	$0.75	$1.25	£0.15	£0.45	£0.75

MAGIC AGENT, JOHN FORCE

ACG; 1 Jan/Feb 1961-3 May/Jun 1961

	$Good	$Fine	$N.Mint	£Good	£Fine	£N.Mint
1 distributed in the U.K.	$2.85	$8.50	$20.00	£2.00	£6.00	£14.00
2-3 distributed in the U.K.	$2.10	$6.25	$15.00	£1.40	£4.25	£10.00
Title Value:	$7.05	$21.00	$50.00	£4.80	£14.50	£34.00

MAGIC CARPET

Comix and Comix,Magazine; 1,2 1977

	$Good	$Fine	$N.Mint	£Good	£Fine	£N.Mint
1 ND Voltar appears	$0.30	$1.00	$2.00	£0.20	£0.60	£1.25
2 ND	$0.30	$1.00	$2.00	£0.20	£0.60	£1.25
Title Value:	$0.60	$2.00	$4.00	£0.40	£1.20	£2.50

MAGIC FLUTE, THE

Eclipse,MS; 1 Sep 1990-3 Nov 1990

	$Good	$Fine	$N.Mint	£Good	£Fine	£N.Mint
1-3 ND 64pgs, squarebound, P. Craig Russell art	$0.70	$2.10	$3.50	£0.50	£1.50	£2.50
Title Value:	$2.10	$6.30	$10.50	£1.50	£4.50	£7.50

MAGIC MAN

A Plus Comics; 1 1991

	$Good	$Fine	$N.Mint	£Good	£Fine	£N.Mint
1 ND 48pgs, Magic Man reprints from ACG comics; black and white	$0.40	$1.20	$2.00	£0.25	£0.75	£1.25
Title Value:	$0.40	$1.20	$2.00	£0.25	£0.75	£1.25

MAGIC: THE GATHERING - ARABIAN NIGHTS

Acclaim Comics/Armada,MS; 1 Dec 1995-2 Jan 1996

	$Good	$Fine	$N.Mint	£Good	£Fine	£N.Mint
1-2 ND	$0.50	$1.50	$2.50	£0.30	£0.90	£1.50
Title Value:	$1.00	$3.00	$5.00	£0.60	£1.80	£3.00

MAGIC: THE GATHERING - DAKKON BLACKBLADE

Acclaim Comics,OS; 1 Jun 1996

	$Good	$Fine	$N.Mint	£Good	£Fine	£N.Mint
1 ND 64pgs, includes Dakkon Blackblade trading card	$1.20	$3.60	$6.00	£0.90	£2.70	£4.50
Title Value:	$1.20	$3.60	$6.00	£0.90	£2.70	£4.50

MAGIC: THE GATHERING - HOMELANDS

Acclaim Comics/Armada,OS; 1 Feb 1996

	$Good	$Fine	$N.Mint	£Good	£Fine	£N.Mint
1 ND 64pgs, pre-bagged with one of three Magic: The Gathering cards	$1.20	$3.60	$6.00	£0.80	£2.40	£4.00
Title Value:	$1.20	$3.60	$6.00	£0.80	£2.40	£4.00

MAGIC: THE GATHERING - LEGEND OF JEDIT OJANEN

Acclaim Comics/Armada,MS; 1 Mar 1996-2 Apr 1996

	$Good	$Fine	$N.Mint	£Good	£Fine	£N.Mint
1-2 ND	$0.50	$1.50	$2.50	£0.30	£0.90	£1.50
Title Value:	$1.00	$3.00	$5.00	£0.60	£1.80	£3.00

MAGIC: THE GATHERING - LEGEND OF THE ELDER DRAGONS

Acclaim Comics,MS; 1 Apr 1996-2 May 1996

	$Good	$Fine	$N.Mint	£Good	£Fine	£N.Mint
1-2 ND	$0.50	$1.50	$2.50	£0.30	£0.90	£1.50
Title Value:	$1.00	$3.00	$5.00	£0.60	£1.80	£3.00

MAGIC: THE GATHERING - LEGEND OF THE FALLEN ANGEL

Acclaim Comics,OS; 1 May 1996

	$Good	$Fine	$N.Mint	£Good	£Fine	£N.Mint
1 ND 64pgs, Nancy Collins script, Richard Kane Ferguson art; Clyde Cauldwell painted cover	$1.20	$3.60	$6.00	£0.90	£2.70	£4.50
Title Value:	$1.20	$3.60	$6.00	£0.90	£2.70	£4.50

MAGIC: THE GATHERING - SHANDALAR

Acclaim Comics/Armada,MS; 1 Mar 1996-2 Apr 1996

	$Good	$Fine	$N.Mint	£Good	£Fine	£N.Mint
1-2 ND	$0.50	$1.50	$2.50	£0.30	£0.90	£1.50
Title Value:	$1.00	$3.00	$5.00	£0.60	£1.80	£3.00

MAGIC: THE GATHERING - THE SHADOW MAGE

Acclaim Comics/Armada,MS; 1 Jul 1995-4 Oct 1995

	$Good	$Fine	$N.Mint	£Good	£Fine	£N.Mint
1-4 ND Jeff Gomez script, Val Mayerik art and painted cover	$0.50	$1.50	$2.50	£0.30	£0.90	£1.50
Title Value:	$2.00	$6.00	$10.00	£1.20	£3.60	£6.00

Note: based on fantasy game Magic: The Gathering by Wizards of the Coast

Magic: The Gathering - Shadow Mage (Aug 1995)

	$Good	$Fine	$N.Mint	£Good	£Fine	£N.Mint
Trade paperback 48pgs, collects issues #1,2				£0.65	£1.95	£3.25

MAGIC: THE GATHERING - THE UZRA-MISHRA WAR

Acclaim Comics,MS; 1 Jul 1996-2 Aug 1996

	$Good	$Fine	$N.Mint	£Good	£Fine	£N.Mint
1-2 ND 64pgs, Bill Sienkiewicz cover and art	$1.20	$3.60	$6.00	£0.80	£2.40	£4.00
Title Value:	$2.40	$7.20	$12.00	£1.60	£4.80	£8.00

MAGIC: THE GATHERING - WAYFARER

Acclaim Comics/Armada,MS; 1 Nov 1995-5 Mar 1996

	$Good	$Fine	$N.Mint	£Good	£Fine	£N.Mint
1-2 ND Mike Kaluta painted covers	$0.50	$1.50	$2.50	£0.30	£0.90	£1.50
3-5 ND	$0.50	$1.50	$2.50	£0.30	£0.90	£1.50
Title Value:	$2.50	$7.50	$12.50	£1.50	£4.50	£7.50

MAGIC: THE GATHERING SPECIAL - NIGHTMARE

Acclaim Comics/Armada,OS; 1 Nov 1995

	$Good	$Fine	$N.Mint	£Good	£Fine	£N.Mint
1 ND Hilary Bader script	$0.50	$1.50	$2.50	£0.30	£0.90	£1.50
Title Value:	$0.50	$1.50	$2.50	£0.30	£0.90	£1.50

MAGICAL MATES

Antarctic Press,MS; 1 Feb 1996-3 Apr 1996

	$Good	$Fine	$N.Mint	£Good	£Fine	£N.Mint
1 ND Mio Odagi script and art; black and white	$0.70	$2.10	$3.50	£0.50	£1.50	£2.50
2 ND Mio Odagi script and art; black and white	$0.60	$1.80	$3.00	£0.40	£1.20	£2.00
3 ND	$0.60	$1.80	$3.00	£0.40	£1.20	£2.00
Title Value:	$1.90	$5.70	$9.50	£1.30	£3.90	£6.50

MAGIK: STORM AND ILLYANA

Marvel Comics Group,MS; 1 Dec 1983-4 Mar 1984

	$Good	$Fine	$N.Mint	£Good	£Fine	£N.Mint
1 ND Storm and Illyana (X-Men) begin	$0.80	$2.40	$4.00	£0.40	£1.20	£2.00
2 ND	$0.80	$2.40	$4.00	£0.40	£1.20	£2.00
3 ND scarce in the U.K.	$0.80	$2.40	$4.00	£0.50	£1.50	£2.50
4 ND rare in the U.K.	$0.80	$2.40	$4.00	£0.60	£1.80	£3.00
Title Value:	$3.20	$9.60	$16.00	£1.90	£5.70	£9.50

MAGILLA GORILLA

Gold Key,TV; 1 May 1964-10 Dec 1968

	$Good	$Fine	$N.Mint	£Good	£Fine	£N.Mint
1 scarce in the U.K. based on cartoon series	$8.50	$26.00	$60.00	£5.00	£15.00	£35.00
2-10 scarce in the U.K. based on cartoon series	$5.00	$15.00	$35.00	£2.50	£7.50	£17.50
Title Value:	$53.50	$161.00	$375.00	£27.50	£82.50	£192.50

MAGNA-MAN: THE LAST SUPER-HERO

Comics Interview,MS; 1 Summer 1988-3 Spring 1989

	$Good	$Fine	$N.Mint	£Good	£Fine	£N.Mint
1-3 ND	$0.40	$1.20	$2.00	£0.25	£0.75	£1.25
Title Value:	$1.20	$3.60	$6.00	£0.75	£2.25	£3.75

MAGNETO

Marvel Comics Group,OS; 0 Aug 1993

	$Good	$Fine	$N.Mint	£Good	£Fine	£N.Mint
0 ND promotional issue from Marvel; reprints from Classic X-Men #12,#19 featuring John Bolton art, 3 new pages of art by Duursema/Panosian; foil embossed cover by Sienkiewicz	$1.20	$3.60	$6.00	£0.80	£2.40	£4.00
Title Value:	$1.20	$3.60	$6.00	£0.80	£2.40	£4.00

MAGNETO & THE MAGNETIC MEN

Marvel Comics Group/Amalgam,OS; 1 Apr 1996

	$Good	$Fine	$N.Mint	£Good	£Fine	£N.Mint
1 ND a Marvel/DC amalgamation of The Brotherhood of Evil Mutants and Justice League of America; Mark Waid and Gerard Jones script, Jeff Matsuda and Art Thibert art	$0.50	$1.50	$2.50	£0.40	£1.20	£2.00
Title Value:	$0.50	$1.50	$2.50	£0.40	£1.20	£2.00

MAGNETO (2ND SERIES)

Marvel Comics Group,MS; 1 Nov 1996-4 Feb 1997

	$Good	$Fine	$N.Mint	£Good	£Fine	£N.Mint
1-4 ND Peter Milligan script, Kelley Jones and John Beatty art	$0.40	$1.20	$2.00	£0.25	£0.75	£1.25
Title Value:	$1.60	$4.80	$8.00	£1.00	£3.00	£5.00

MAGNUS ROBOT FIGHTER

Gold Key; 1 Feb 1963-46 Jan 1977

	$Good	$Fine	$N.Mint	£Good	£Fine	£N.Mint
1 Magnus by Russ Manning, Aliens back-up begin	$39.00	$115.00	$275.00	£25.00	£75.00	£175.00
2-3 distributed in the U.K.	$18.50	$55.00	$130.00	£12.00	£36.00	£85.00
4-5 distributed in the U.K.	$12.50	$39.00	$90.00	£8.50	£26.00	£60.00
6-10 distributed in the U.K.	$10.50	$32.00	$75.00	£7.00	£21.00	£50.00
11-15 distributed in the U.K.	$7.00	$21.00	$50.00	£5.00	£15.00	£35.00
16-20 distributed in the U.K.	$6.25	$19.00	$45.00	£4.25	£12.50	£30.00
21 distributed in the U.K. last new Russ Manning art on Magnus	$4.60	$13.50	$32.50	£2.85	£8.50	£20.00
22 distributed in the U.K. reprints #1; 12 and 15 cents versions exist; last Manning art on Aliens back-up	$4.25	$12.50	$30.00	£2.55	£7.50	£18.00
23 distributed in the U.K. 12 and 15 cents versions exist	$4.25	$12.50	$30.00	£2.55	£7.50	£18.00
24-27 distributed in the U.K.	$4.60	$13.50	$32.50	£2.85	£8.50	£20.00
28 distributed in the U.K. last Aliens feature	$4.60	$13.50	$32.50	£2.85	£8.50	£20.00
29-32 distributed in the U.K. all reprints	$2.50	$7.50	$15.00	£1.30	£4.00	£8.00
33-46 ND all reprints	$2.50	$7.50	$15.00	£1.40	£4.25	£8.50
Title Value:	$300.85	$904.00	$2072.00	£194.25	£583.00	£1347.00

Note: There was an 18-month gap in publication around issue #33-35.

MAGNUS ROBOT FIGHTER (2ND SERIES)

Valiant/Acclaim Comics; 0 1991; 1 May 1991-64 Jan 1996

	$Good	$Fine	$N.Mint	£Good	£Fine	£N.Mint
0 with trading card, - ordered mostly through mail	$2.50	$7.50	$12.50	£1.50	£4.50	£7.50
0 without trading card, - sold through shops	$1.20	$3.60	$6.00	£0.80	£2.40	£4.00
1 (with coupon intact. Less 30% without coupon for #1-8)	$1.50	$4.50	$7.50	£1.00	£3.00	£5.00
2	$1.00	$3.00	$5.00	£0.80	£2.40	£4.00
3-4	$0.80	$2.40	$4.00	£0.60	£1.80	£3.00
5 scarce in the U.K. Rai back-up feature begins (1st appearance - flip side cover says Rai #1)	$1.00	$3.00	$5.00	£0.90	£2.70	£4.50
6-8 Rai back-up	$0.60	$1.80	$3.00	£0.50	£1.50	£2.50
9-11	$0.50	$1.50	$2.50	£0.30	£0.90	£1.50
12 1st anniversary special, 1st modern appearance of Turok	$2.40	$7.00	$12.00	£1.30	£3.90	£6.50
13-14 The Asylum Saga part 1, ties in with Magnus Robot Fighter (1st Series) #18	$0.40	$1.20	$2.00	£0.30	£0.90	£1.50
15 Unity: Chapter 4	$0.40	$1.20	$2.00	£0.30	£0.90	£1.50
16 Unity: Chapter 12, true origin of Magnus, Walt Simonson cover	$0.40	$1.20	$2.00	£0.30	£0.90	£1.50
17-19 Steve Ditko art featured	$0.40	$1.20	$2.00	£0.30	£0.90	£1.50
20	$0.40	$1.20	$2.00	£0.30	£0.90	£1.50
21 new direction for title; ties-in with the 1st Series Magnus Robot Fighter #17 and the destruction of the Earth	$0.40	$1.20	$2.00	£0.25	£0.75	£1.25
21 Gold Edition, : 5,000 print run; gold logo and gold number/date box	$1.20	$3.60	$6.00	£0.70	£2.10	£3.50

	$Good	$Fine	$N.Mint	£Good	£Fine	£N.Mint
22-23	*$0.40*	*$1.20*	*$2.00*	£0.25	£0.75	£1.25
24 leads into Rai and the Future Force #9	*$0.40*	*$1.20*	*$2.00*	£0.25	£0.75	£1.25
25 silver foil cover	*$0.40*	*$1.20*	*$2.00*	£0.30	£0.90	£1.50
25 Valiant Validated Signature Series, (Feb 1994), signed by John Ostrander and Bob Layton; 5,500 copies with certificate in Mylar sleeve	*$1.50*	*$4.50*	*$7.50*	£1.00	£3.00	£5.00
26-28	*$0.40*	*$1.20*	*$2.00*	£0.25	£0.75	£1.25
29 Eternal Warrior appears	*$0.40*	*$1.20*	*$2.00*	£0.25	£0.75	£1.25
30-32	*$0.40*	*$1.20*	*$2.00*	£0.25	£0.75	£1.25
33 Ivar the Timewalker appears	*$0.40*	*$1.20*	*$2.00*	£0.25	£0.75	£1.25
34-36	*$0.40*	*$1.20*	*$2.00*	£0.25	£0.75	£1.25
37 continued in Rai #22	*$0.40*	*$1.20*	*$2.00*	£0.25	£0.75	£1.25
38-40	*$0.40*	*$1.20*	*$2.00*	£0.25	£0.75	£1.25
41 Chaos Effect tie-in	*$0.40*	*$1.20*	*$2.00*	£0.25	£0.75	£1.25
42 ties-in with Rai #27	*$0.40*	*$1.20*	*$2.00*	£0.25	£0.75	£1.25
43-48	*$0.40*	*$1.20*	*$2.00*	£0.25	£0.75	£1.25
49 1st Acclaim Comics issue; bi-weekly	*$0.50*	*$1.50*	*$2.50*	£0.30	£0.90	£1.50
50 bi-weekly	*$0.50*	*$1.50*	*$2.50*	£0.30	£0.90	£1.50
51-54 Return of the Robots story; bi-weekly	*$0.50*	*$1.50*	*$2.50*	£0.30	£0.90	£1.50
55-64 bi-weekly	*$0.50*	*$1.50*	*$2.50*	£0.30	£0.90	£1.50
Title Value:	*$39.60*	*$118.60*	*$198.00*	£25.85	£77.55	£129.25

Note: all Non-Distributed on the news-stands in the U.K.
Note: the first eight issues include 3 trading cards each.
Note also that a special "0" issue is available, ordered from the publishers through the mail and obtained by sending coupons collected from the first 8 issues. This is with the special trading card. Otherwise a copy of issue #0 was given free to retailers with every 100 copies of Magnus #1 ordered.
Note finally: There was also a #0 available on general sale in stores in America though how these differ, if at all, is unclear at this time.

	£Good	£Fine	£N.Mint
Steel Nation (Feb 1995) Trade paperback reprints issues #1-4	£1.30	£3.90	£6.50
Magnus Robot Fighter #2 Trade paperback reprints issues #5-8	£1.30	£3.90	£6.50

MAGNUS ROBOT FIGHTER YEARBOOK

Valiant; 1 Nov 1994

	$Good	$Fine	$N.Mint	£Good	£Fine	£N.Mint
1 ND Mike Baron script, Paul Smith art, Dave Dorman cover; story takes place between Magnus #1 and #2	*$0.80*	*$2.40*	*$4.00*	£0.40	£1.20	£2.00
Title Value:	*$0.80*	*$2.40*	*$4.00*	£0.40	£1.20	£2.00

MAGNUS ROBOT FIGHTER, THE ORIGINAL

Valiant/Western Publishing; 1 Apr 1995-3 Jun 1995

	$Good	$Fine	$N.Mint	£Good	£Fine	£N.Mint
1-3 ND reprints from the original Gold Key series begin featuring artwork by Russ Manning	*$0.40*	*$1.20*	*$2.00*	£0.25	£0.75	£1.25
Title Value:	*$1.20*	*$3.60*	*$6.00*	£0.75	£2.25	£3.75

MAGNUS ROBOT FIGHTER, THE VINTAGE

Valiant,MS; 1 May 1992-4 Aug 1992

	$Good	$Fine	$N.Mint	£Good	£Fine	£N.Mint
1 ND reprints from original Gold Key series begin; reprints issue #1	*$0.40*	*$1.20*	*$2.00*	£0.25	£0.75	£1.25
2 ND reprints issue #3	*$0.40*	*$1.20*	*$2.00*	£0.25	£0.75	£1.25
3 ND reprints issue #13	*$0.40*	*$1.20*	*$2.00*	£0.25	£0.75	£1.25
4 ND reprints issue #16	*$0.40*	*$1.20*	*$2.00*	£0.25	£0.75	£1.25
Title Value:	*$1.60*	*$4.80*	*$8.00*	£1.00	£3.00	£5.00

MAGNUS ROBOT FIGHTER/NEXUS

Valiant/Dark Horse,MS; 1 Dec 1993-2 Apr 1994

	$Good	$Fine	$N.Mint	£Good	£Fine	£N.Mint
1-2 ND Mike Baron script, Steve Rude art; card-stock cover; origin Magnus briefly re-told	*$0.50*	*$1.50*	*$2.50*	£0.30	£0.90	£1.50
Title Value:	*$1.00*	*$3.00*	*$5.00*	£0.60	£1.80	£3.00

MAI THE PSYCHIC GIRL

Eclipse; 1 May 1987-28 Jul 1988
(biweekly)

	$Good	$Fine	$N.Mint	£Good	£Fine	£N.Mint
1 all issues bi-weekly	*$0.50*	*$1.50*	*$2.50*	£0.30	£0.90	£1.50
1 2nd printing	*$0.40*	*$1.20*	*$2.00*	£0.25	£0.75	£1.25
2	*$0.40*	*$1.20*	*$2.00*	£0.25	£0.75	£1.25
2 2nd printing	*$0.40*	*$1.20*	*$2.00*	£0.25	£0.75	£1.25
3-5	*$0.40*	*$1.20*	*$2.00*	£0.25	£0.75	£1.25
6-28	*$0.30*	*$0.90*	*$1.50*	£0.20	£0.60	£1.00
Title Value:	*$9.80*	*$29.40*	*$49.00*	£6.40	£19.20	£32.00

Note: all Non-Distributed on the news-stands in the U.K.

	£Good	£Fine	£N.Mint
Mai the Psychic Girl Perfect Collection Vol 1 (Oct 1995) 368pgs, classic reprints in black and white	£2.70	£8.10	£13.50

MAISON IKKOKU

Viz Communications,MS; 1 Aug 1993-7 Feb 1994

	$Good	$Fine	$N.Mint	£Good	£Fine	£N.Mint
1-7 ND Rumiko Takahashi; black and white	*$0.60*	*$1.80*	*$3.00*	£0.40	£1.20	£2.00
Title Value:	*$4.20*	*$12.60*	*$21.00*	£2.80	£8.40	£14.00

	£Good	£Fine	£N.Mint
Maison Ikkoku Vol 1 (Dec 1994) 284pgs, reprints mini-series; black and white	£2.20	£6.60	£11.00

MAISON IKKOKU GRAPHIC NOVEL

Viz Communications,OS; nn Sep 1995

	$Good	$Fine	$N.Mint	£Good	£Fine	£N.Mint
nn ND 264pgs, Rumiko Takahashi script and art; black and white	*$3.40*	*$10.00*	*$17.00*	£2.40	£7.00	£12.00
Title Value:	*$3.40*	*$10.00*	*$17.00*	£2.40	£7.00	£12.00

MAISON IKKOKU PART 2

Viz Communications,MS; 1 Mar 1994-6 Aug 1994

	$Good	$Fine	$N.Mint	£Good	£Fine	£N.Mint
1-6 ND Rumiko Takahashi; black and white	*$0.60*	*$1.80*	*$3.00*	£0.40	£1.20	£2.00
Title Value:	*$3.60*	*$10.80*	*$18.00*	£2.40	£7.20	£12.00

MAISON IKKOKU PART 3

Viz Communications,MS; 1 Jul 1994-6 Dec 1994

	$Good	$Fine	$N.Mint	£Good	£Fine	£N.Mint
1-6 ND 48pgs, Rumiko Takahashi; black and white	*$0.60*	*$1.80*	*$3.00*	£0.40	£1.20	£2.00
Title Value:	*$3.60*	*$10.80*	*$18.00*	£2.40	£7.20	£12.00

MAISON IKKOKU PART 4

Viz Communications,MS; 1 Dec 1994-10 Sep 1995

	$Good	$Fine	$N.Mint	£Good	£Fine	£N.Mint
1-10 ND 40pgs, Rumiko Takahashi; black and white	*$0.60*	*$1.80*	*$3.00*	£0.40	£1.20	£2.00
Title Value:	*$6.00*	*$18.00*	*$30.00*	£4.00	£12.00	£20.00

MAISON IKKOKU PART 5

Viz Communications,MS; 1 Nov 1995-9 Jul 1996

	$Good	$Fine	$N.Mint	£Good	£Fine	£N.Mint
1-9 ND Rumiko Takahashi script and art; black and white	*$0.60*	*$1.80*	*$3.00*	£0.40	£1.20	£2.00
Title Value:	*$5.40*	*$16.20*	*$27.00*	£3.60	£10.80	£18.00

MAN CALLED A-X, THE

Malibu Bravura,MS; 0 Feb 1995; 1 Nov 1994-5 Mar 1995

	$Good	$Fine	$N.Mint	£Good	£Fine	£N.Mint
0 ND Marv Wolfman script, Shawn McManus art; facts about origin revealed	*$0.60*	*$1.80*	*$3.00*	£0.40	£1.20	£2.00
1 ND Marv Wolfman script, Shawn McManus art	*$0.60*	*$1.80*	*$3.00*	£0.40	£1.20	£2.00
1 Gold Edition, ND (Mar 1995) Gold foil cover	*$1.60*	*$4.80*	*$8.00*	£0.80	£2.40	£4.00
2-5 ND Marv Wolfman script, Shawn McManus art	*$0.50*	*$1.50*	*$2.50*	£0.30	£0.90	£1.50
Title Value:	*$4.80*	*$14.40*	*$24.00*	£2.80	£8.40	£14.00

	£Good	£Fine	£N.Mint
The Man Called A-X Ashcan Edition (Feb 1995) 1,000 copies, signed by Marv Wolfman and Shawn McManus. ND	£1.00	£3.00	£5.00

MAN CALLED LOCO, A

ACG,OS; nn Jul 1995

	$Good	$Fine	$N.Mint	£Good	£Fine	£N.Mint
nn ND Western reprints with scripts by Denny O'Neil and art by Pete Morisi	*$0.50*	*$1.50*	*$2.50*	£0.30	£0.90	£1.50
Title Value:	*$0.50*	*$1.50*	*$2.50*	£0.30	£0.90	£1.50

MAN FROG

Mad Dog Graphics; 1,2 1987

	$Good	$Fine	$N.Mint	£Good	£Fine	£N.Mint
1-2 ND	*$0.30*	*$0.90*	*$1.50*	£0.20	£0.60	£1.00
Title Value:	*$0.60*	*$1.80*	*$3.00*	£0.40	£1.20	£2.00

MAN FROM ATLANTIS

Marvel Comics Group,TV; 1 Feb 1978-7 Aug 1978

	$Good	$Fine	$N.Mint	£Good	£Fine	£N.Mint
1 ND 80pgs, origin	*$0.65*	*$2.00*	*$4.00*	£0.25	£0.75	£1.50
2-7 ND	*$0.40*	*$1.25*	*$2.50*	£0.20	£0.60	£1.25
Title Value:	*$3.05*	*$9.50*	*$19.00*	£1.45	£4.35	£9.00

Note: based on TV series starring Patrick Duffy

MAN FROM CIGURI, THE

Dark Horse,OS; nn May 1996

	$Good	$Fine	$N.Mint	£Good	£Fine	£N.Mint
nn ND 80pgs, reprints featuring work by Moebius	*$1.40*	*$4.20*	*$7.00*	£0.90	£2.70	£4.50
Title Value:	*$1.40*	*$4.20*	*$7.00*	£0.90	£2.70	£4.50

MAN FROM PLANET X REPRINT COMIC, THE

Robert Brosch; 1 1990

	$Good	$Fine	$N.Mint	£Good	£Fine	£N.Mint
1 ND reprints movie adaptation from 1951 with art by Kurt Schaffenberger, George Evans and Pete Costanza	*$0.50*	*$1.50*	*$2.50*	£0.30	£0.90	£1.50
Title Value:	*$0.50*	*$1.50*	*$2.50*	£0.30	£0.90	£1.50

MAN FROM U.N.C.L.E., THE

Gold Key,TV; 1 Feb 1965-22 Apr 1969

	$Good	$Fine	$N.Mint	£Good	£Fine	£N.Mint
1 scarce in the U.K. photo covers begin	*$19.00*	*$57.50*	*$135.00*	£11.00	£34.00	£80.00
2 scarce in the U.K.	*$11.00*	*$34.00*	*$80.00*	£6.25	£19.00	£45.00
3-5 scarce in the U.K.	*$8.50*	*$26.00*	*$60.00*	£4.25	£12.50	£30.00
6-10 scarce in the U.K.	*$7.00*	*$21.00*	*$50.00*	£3.90	£11.50	£27.50
11-15 scarce in the U.K.	*$6.25*	*$19.00*	*$45.00*	£3.20	£9.50	£22.50
16-20 scarce in the U.K.	*$6.00*	*$18.00*	*$42.50*	£2.85	£8.50	£20.00
21-22 scarce in the U.K. reprints	*$5.50*	*$17.00*	*$40.00*	£2.50	£7.50	£17.50
Title Value:	*$162.75*	*$493.50*	*$1162.50*	£84.75	£253.00	£600.00

Note: most issues distributed in the U.K.

MAN FROM U.N.C.L.E., THE (2ND SERIES)

Entertainment Publishing; 1 Feb 1987-11 1987

	$Good	$Fine	$N.Mint	£Good	£Fine	£N.Mint
1 ND black and white begins	*$0.40*	*$1.20*	*$2.00*	£0.25	£0.75	£1.25
2-4 ND	*$0.40*	*$1.20*	*$2.00*	£0.25	£0.75	£1.25
5 ND scarce in the U.K. never imported into U.K. comic shops	*$0.40*	*$1.20*	*$2.00*	£0.30	£0.90	£1.50
6-11 ND	*$0.30*	*$0.90*	*$1.50*	£0.20	£0.60	£1.00
Title Value:	*$3.80*	*$11.40*	*$19.00*	£2.50	£7.50	£12.50

MAN FROM U.N.C.L.E.: THE BIRDS OF PREY AFFAIR

Millennium,MS; 1 Mar 1993-2 Apr 1993

	$Good	$Fine	$N.Mint	£Good	£Fine	£N.Mint
1-2 ND	*$0.50*	*$1.50*	*$2.50*	£0.30	£0.90	£1.50
Title Value:	*$1.00*	*$3.00*	*$5.00*	£0.60	£1.80	£3.00

	£Good	£Fine	£N.Mint
The Man From U.N.C.L.E.: Birds of Prey Collection (Nov 1994) reprints mini-series with new wraparound cover	£1.00	£3.00	£5.00

MAN OF RUST
Blackthorne; 1A, 1B Nov 1986

Issue	$Good	$Fine	$N.Mint	£Good	£Fine	£N.Mint
1 ND (2 cover versions exist) parodies Man of Steel, Burchett art; cover 1A is chest emblem, cover 1B is rocket cover	$0.30	$0.90	$1.50	£0.20	£0.60	£1.00
Title Value:	$0.30	$0.90	$1.50	£0.20	£0.60	£1.00

MAN OF WAR
Eclipse; 1 Aug 1987-3 Feb 1988

Issue	$Good	$Fine	$N.Mint	£Good	£Fine	£N.Mint
1-3 ND Bruce Jones script, Rick Burchett art	$0.40	$1.20	$2.00	£0.25	£0.75	£1.25
Title Value:	$1.20	$3.60	$6.00	£0.75	£2.25	£3.75

MAN OF WAR (2ND SERIES)
Malibu; 1 Apr 1993-8 1993

Issue	$Good	$Fine	$N.Mint	£Good	£Fine	£N.Mint
1 ND	$0.30	$0.90	$1.50	£0.20	£0.60	£1.00
1 Direct Market Edition, ND - bound in poster and different cover	$0.40	$1.20	$2.00	£0.25	£0.75	£1.25
2 ND	$0.30	$0.90	$1.50	£0.20	£0.60	£1.00
2 Direct Market Edition, ND - bound in poster and different cover	$0.40	$1.20	$2.00	£0.25	£0.75	£1.25
3 ND	$0.30	$0.90	$1.50	£0.20	£0.60	£1.00
3 Direct Market Edition, ND - bound in poster and different cover	$0.40	$1.20	$2.00	£0.25	£0.75	£1.25
4 ND	$0.30	$0.90	$1.50	£0.20	£0.60	£1.00
4 Direct Market Edition, ND - bound in poster and different cover	$0.40	$1.20	$2.00	£0.25	£0.75	£1.25
5 ND	$0.30	$0.90	$1.50	£0.20	£0.60	£1.00
5 Direct Market Edition, ND - bound in poster and different cover	$0.40	$1.20	$2.00	£0.25	£0.75	£1.25
6 ND Genesis Tie-In; pre-bagged with free Sky Cap	$0.30	$0.90	$1.50	£0.20	£0.60	£1.00
7-8 ND	$0.30	$0.90	$1.50	£0.20	£0.60	£1.00
Title Value:	$4.40	$13.20	$22.00	£2.85	£8.55	£14.25

MAN-BAT
DC Comics; 1 Dec/Jan 1975/76-2 Feb/Mar 1976

(see Detective, Brave and the Bold, Batman Family)

Issue	$Good	$Fine	$N.Mint	£Good	£Fine	£N.Mint
1 Steve Ditko pencils, She Bat appears	$1.25	$3.75	$7.50	£1.00	£3.00	£6.00
2 scarce in the U.K.	$1.00	$3.00	$6.00	£0.80	£2.50	£5.00
Title Value:	$2.25	$6.75	$13.50	£1.80	£5.50	£11.00

MAN-BAT (2ND SERIES)
DC Comics,MS; 1 Feb 1996-3 Apr 1996

Issue	$Good	$Fine	$N.Mint	£Good	£Fine	£N.Mint
1-3 ND Chuck Dixon script, Flint Henry and Eduardo Barreto art	$0.45	$1.35	$2.25	£0.30	£0.90	£1.50
Title Value:	$1.35	$4.05	$6.75	£0.90	£2.70	£4.50

MAN-BAT (VERSUS BATMAN)
DC Comics,OS; 1 Dec 1984

(see Batman versus Man-bat)

Issue	$Good	$Fine	$N.Mint	£Good	£Fine	£N.Mint
1 ND 46pgs, reprints Neal Adams art from Detective Comics #400 and #402	$0.90	$2.70	$4.50	£0.60	£1.80	£3.00
Title Value:	$0.90	$2.70	$4.50	£0.60	£1.80	£3.00

MAN-EATING COW
New England Comics; 1 Jun 1992-10 1993

Issue	$Good	$Fine	$N.Mint	£Good	£Fine	£N.Mint
1-10 ND	$0.50	$1.50	$2.50	£0.30	£0.90	£1.50
Title Value:	$5.00	$15.00	$25.00	£3.00	£9.00	£15.00
Man-Eating Cow Bonanza (Apr 1996) Trade paperback ND 128pgs, collects issues #1-4				£0.65	£1.95	£3.25

MAN-THING
Marvel Comics Group; 1 Jan 1974-22 Oct 1975

(see Fear, Marvel Fanfare, Monsters Unleashed, Savage Tales)

Issue	$Good	$Fine	$N.Mint	£Good	£Fine	£N.Mint
1 ND 2nd Howard the Duck, continues from Fear #19	$3.30	$10.00	$20.00	£1.65	£5.00	£10.00
2 ND	$1.65	$5.00	$10.00	£0.80	£2.50	£5.00
3 ND 1st appearance original Foolkiller (see Omega The Unknown #8)	$1.00	$3.00	$6.00	£0.65	£2.00	£4.00
4 ND origin and 2nd appearance (final) original Foolkiller	$0.80	$2.50	$5.00	£0.55	£1.75	£3.50
5-7 ND Ploog art	$0.80	$2.50	$5.00	£0.55	£1.75	£3.50
8-11 Ploog art	$0.65	$2.00	$4.00	£0.50	£1.50	£3.00
12-19	$0.50	$1.50	$3.00	£0.30	£1.00	£2.00
20 Spiderman, Daredevil, Thing and Master of Kung Fu appear	$0.50	$1.50	$3.00	£0.30	£1.00	£2.00
21	$0.40	$1.25	$2.50	£0.25	£0.75	£1.50
22 Howard Duck cameo	$0.40	$1.25	$2.50	£0.25	£0.75	£1.50
Title Value:	$17.05	$52.00	$100.00	£10.50	£33.00	£66.00

MAN-THING (2ND SERIES)
Marvel Comics Group; 1 Nov 1979-11 Jul 1981

Issue	$Good	$Fine	$N.Mint	£Good	£Fine	£N.Mint
1	$0.25	$0.75	$1.50	£0.15	£0.50	£1.00
2-3 ND	$0.30	$0.90	$1.50	£0.15	£0.45	£0.75
4 ND ties into Dr. Strange (2nd Series) #41	$0.30	$0.90	$1.50	£0.15	£0.45	£0.75
5 ND	$0.30	$0.90	$1.50	£0.15	£0.45	£0.75
6 Michael Golden cover	$0.30	$0.90	$1.50	£0.15	£0.45	£0.75
7-10 ND	$0.30	$0.90	$1.50	£0.15	£0.45	£0.75
11 ND scarce in the U.K.	$0.30	$0.90	$1.50	£0.20	£0.60	£1.00
Title Value:	$3.25	$9.75	$16.50	£1.70	£5.15	£8.75

MAN-THING GIANT SIZE
Marvel Comics Group; 1 Aug 1974-5 Aug 1975

Issue	$Good	$Fine	$N.Mint	£Good	£Fine	£N.Mint
1 ND 64pgs, Ploog art; Steve Ditko and Jack Kirby pre-superhero reprints	$1.25	$3.75	$7.50	£0.80	£2.50	£5.00
2 ND 64pgs, Jack Kirby pre-superhero reprint	$1.00	$3.00	$6.00	£0.65	£2.00	£4.00
3 ND 64pgs, reprints Dr. Droom story from Amazing Adventures (1st Series) #6 and is re-named Dr. Druid (no relation to other Marvel character)	$0.80	$2.50	$5.00	£0.55	£1.75	£3.50
4 ND 64pgs, 2nd appearance Howard the Duck, Brunner art (see Fear #19)	$1.30	$4.00	$8.00	£1.00	£3.00	£6.00
5 ND 64pgs, 3rd appearance Howard the Duck, Brunner art	$1.15	$3.50	$7.00	£0.80	£2.50	£5.00
Title Value:	$5.50	$16.75	$33.50	£3.80	£11.75	£23.50

MANDRAKE
Marvel Comics Group,MS; 1 Apr 1995-3 Jun 1995

Issue	$Good	$Fine	$N.Mint	£Good	£Fine	£N.Mint
1-3 ND Rob Ortaleza art painted art on glossy stock paper	$0.50	$1.50	$2.50	£0.30	£0.90	£1.50
Title Value:	$1.50	$4.50	$7.50	£0.90	£2.70	£4.50

MANDRAKE
Pioneer Comics,MS; 1 Dec 1989-3 Feb 1990

Issue	$Good	$Fine	$N.Mint	£Good	£Fine	£N.Mint
1-3 ND never-before reprinted story	$1.20	$3.60	$6.00	£0.80	£2.40	£4.00
Title Value:	$3.60	$10.80	$18.00	£2.40	£7.20	£12.00

MANDRAKE THE MAGICIAN
King Comics; 1 Sep 1966-10 Nov 1967

Issue	$Good	$Fine	$N.Mint	£Good	£Fine	£N.Mint
1 scarce in the U.K.	$4.25	$12.50	$30.00	£2.85	£8.50	£20.00
2-7 scarce in the U.K.	$2.50	$7.50	$17.50	£1.75	£5.25	£12.50
8 4pgs Jeff Jones art	$3.20	$9.50	$22.50	£2.10	£6.25	£15.00
9	$2.50	$7.50	$17.50	£1.75	£5.25	£12.50
10 Rip Kirby appears; Alex Raymond art	$3.90	$11.50	$27.50	£2.50	£7.50	£17.50
Title Value:	$28.85	$86.00	$202.50	£19.70	£59.00	£140.00

Note: all distributed on the news-stands in the U.K.

MANGA MONTHLY
Fathom Press; 0 Aug 1991

Issue	$Good	$Fine	$N.Mint	£Good	£Fine	£N.Mint
0 ND 64pgs, Tim Tyler and Paris Cullins art	$0.50	$1.50	$2.50	£0.30	£0.90	£1.50
Title Value:	$0.50	$1.50	$2.50	£0.30	£0.90	£1.50

Note: series cancelled having been announced as ongoing

MANGA SHI: SHISEIJI
Crusade Comics; 1 Aug 1996

Issue	$Good	$Fine	$N.Mint	£Good	£Fine	£N.Mint
1 ND printed backwards, manga-style	$0.60	$1.80	$3.00	£0.40	£1.20	£2.00
Title Value:	$0.60	$1.80	$3.00	£0.40	£1.20	£2.00

MANGA VIZION VOL. 1
Viz Communications; 1 Mar 1995-present ?

Issue	$Good	$Fine	$N.Mint	£Good	£Fine	£N.Mint
1-10 ND 96pgs, anthology; black and white	$1.00	$3.00	$5.00	£0.60	£1.80	£3.00
Title Value:	$10.00	$30.00	$50.00	£6.00	£18.00	£30.00

MANGAZINE
Antarctic Press; 1 1985-5 Dec 1986

Issue	$Good	$Fine	$N.Mint	£Good	£Fine	£N.Mint
1 ND scarce in the U.K. paper cover	$0.50	$1.50	$2.50	£0.30	£0.90	£1.50
1 2nd printing, ND glossy cover	$0.40	$1.20	$2.00	£0.25	£0.75	£1.25
2-5 ND	$0.30	$0.90	$1.50	£0.20	£0.60	£1.00
Title Value:	$2.10	$6.30	$10.50	£1.35	£4.05	£6.75

MANGAZINE VOLUME TWO
Antarctic Press; 1 Sep 1989-present

Issue	$Good	$Fine	$N.Mint	£Good	£Fine	£N.Mint
1-9 ND	$0.40	$1.20	$2.00	£0.25	£0.75	£1.25
10-13 ND 40pgs	$0.45	$1.35	$2.25	£0.30	£0.90	£1.50
14-29 ND 40pgs	$0.55	$1.65	$2.75	£0.35	£1.05	£1.75
30-36 ND 32pgs	$0.60	$1.80	$3.00	£0.40	£1.20	£2.00
37 ND 48pgs, 10th anniversary issue; first time in full colour	$0.80	$2.40	$4.00	£0.50	£1.50	£2.50
38-39 ND 48pgs	$0.80	$2.40	$4.00	£0.50	£1.50	£2.50
40-43 ND 32pgs	$0.60	$1.80	$3.00	£0.40	£1.20	£2.00
44 ND 32pgs	$0.70	$2.10	$3.50	£0.50	£1.50	£2.50
Title Value:	$23.90	$71.70	$119.50	£15.45	£46.35	£77.25

MANGLE TANGLE TALES
Innovation,OS; 1 1990

Issue	$Good	$Fine	$N.Mint	£Good	£Fine	£N.Mint
1 ND funny animal material in colour, introduction by Harlan Ellison	$0.30	$0.90	$1.50	£0.20	£0.60	£1.00
Title Value:	$0.30	$0.90	$1.50	£0.20	£0.60	£1.00

MANHUNTER
DC Comics,OS; 1 May 1984

(see First Issue Special)

Issue	$Good	$Fine	$N.Mint	£Good	£Fine	£N.Mint
1 ND 76pgs, Walt Simonson reprints from Detective Comics #437-443, Batman appears	$0.90	$2.70	$4.50	£0.60	£1.80	£3.00
Title Value:	$0.90	$2.70	$4.50	£0.60	£1.80	£3.00

Note: high quality paper.

MANHUNTER (2ND SERIES)
DC Comics; 1 Jul 1988-24 Apr 1990

(see First Issue Special #5, Millennium)

Issue	$Good	$Fine	$N.Mint	£Good	£Fine	£N.Mint
1-3 part Sam Kieth art and cover	$0.25	$0.75	$1.25	£0.15	£0.45	£0.75
4-7	$0.25	$0.75	$1.25	£0.15	£0.45	£0.75
8-9 Invasion X-over, Flash appears	$0.25	$0.75	$1.25	£0.15	£0.45	£0.75
10-13	$0.25	$0.75	$1.25	£0.15	£0.45	£0.75
14 Kobra appears	$0.25	$0.75	$1.25	£0.15	£0.45	£0.75
15-16	$0.25	$0.75	$1.25	£0.15	£0.45	£0.75

	$Good	$Fine	$N.Mint	£Good	£Fine	£N.Mint
17 Batman appears	$0.25	$0.75	$1.25	£0.15	£0.45	£0.75
18-23 Saints and Sinners story	$0.25	$0.75	$1.25	£0.15	£0.45	£0.75
24	$0.25	$0.75	$1.25	£0.15	£0.45	£0.75
Title Value:	$6.00	$18.00	$30.00	£3.60	£10.80	£18.00
MANHUNTER (3RD SERIES)						
DC Comics; 0 Oct 1994; 1 Nov 1994-12 Nov 1995						
0 (Oct 1994) Zero Hour X-over, origin	$0.40	$1.20	$2.00	£0.25	£0.75	£1.25
1-6	$0.40	$1.20	$2.00	£0.25	£0.75	£1.25
7 Captain Atom appears	$0.40	$1.20	$2.00	£0.25	£0.75	£1.25
8-11	$0.40	$1.20	$2.00	£0.25	£0.75	£1.25
12 Underworld Unleashed tie-in	$0.40	$1.20	$2.00	£0.25	£0.75	£1.25
Title Value:	$5.20	$15.60	$26.00	£3.25	£9.75	£16.25
MANIMAL						
Renegade,OS; 1 Jan 1986						
1 ND reprints from Hot Stuf'; black and white, Ernie Colon art	$0.30	$0.90	$1.50	£0.20	£0.60	£1.00
Title Value:	$0.30	$0.90	$1.50	£0.20	£0.60	£1.00
MANOSAURS: THE ARMAGEDDON AGENDA						
Entity Comics,MS; 1 Sep 1994-3 Nov 1994						
1-3 ND foil-stamped cover; black and white	$0.60	$1.80	$3.00	£0.40	£1.20	£2.00
Title Value:	$1.80	$5.40	$9.00	£1.20	£3.60	£6.00
MANTECH: ROBOT WARRIORS						
Archie,MS; 1 Sep 1984-6 Jul 1985						
1-6 ND	$0.30	$0.90	$1.50	£0.20	£0.60	£1.00
Title Value:	$1.80	$5.40	$9.00	£1.20	£3.60	£6.00
MANTRA						
Malibu Ultraverse; 1 Jul 1993-24 Aug 1995						
1 pre-bagged with trading card plus large coupon for Ultraverse #0	$0.70	$2.10	$3.50	£0.40	£1.20	£2.00
1 Limited Edition, - full hologram cover; 7,500 copies	$2.00	$6.00	$10.00	£1.00	£3.00	£5.00
1 without coupon/card	$0.50	$1.50	$2.50	£0.30	£0.90	£1.50
2-3	$0.50	$1.50	$2.50	£0.30	£0.90	£1.50
4 40pgs, Rune insert; Mantra's wedding	$0.50	$1.50	$2.50	£0.30	£0.90	£1.50
5	$0.50	$1.50	$2.50	£0.30	£0.90	£1.50
6	$0.40	$1.20	$2.00	£0.25	£0.75	£1.25
7 origin Prototype by Dan Jurgens and Terry Austin; Prime rescues Mantra	$0.40	$1.20	$2.00	£0.25	£0.75	£1.25
8 Warstrike appears	$0.40	$1.20	$2.00	£0.25	£0.75	£1.25
9	$0.40	$1.20	$2.00	£0.25	£0.75	£1.25
10 64pgs, flip-book format with Ultraverse Premiere #2	$0.50	$1.50	$2.50	£0.30	£0.90	£1.50
11	$0.40	$1.20	$2.00	£0.25	£0.75	£1.25
12 Strangers and Mantra team up	$0.40	$1.20	$2.00	£0.25	£0.75	£1.25
13-14	$0.40	$1.20	$2.00	£0.25	£0.75	£1.25
15-16 Prime appears	$0.40	$1.20	$2.00	£0.25	£0.75	£1.25
17 prelude to Godwheel story	$0.40	$1.20	$2.00	£0.25	£0.75	£1.25
18 Mantra becomes pregnant	$0.40	$1.20	$2.00	£0.25	£0.75	£1.25
19-21	$0.40	$1.20	$2.00	£0.25	£0.75	£1.25
22 The Loki Connection, Primevil appears; continued in Night Man #22	$0.40	$1.20	$2.00	£0.25	£0.75	£1.25
23 1st issue under Marvel Comics solicitation	$0.40	$1.20	$2.00	£0.25	£0.75	£1.25
24 Ghoul and Topaz appear	$0.40	$1.20	$2.00	£0.25	£0.75	£1.25
Title Value:	$12.90	$38.70	$64.50	£7.70	£23.10	£38.50
Note: all Non-Distributed on the news-stands in the U.K.						
MANTRA (2ND SERIES)						
Marvel Comics Group; 1 Dec 1995-7 Apr 1996						
1 ND Mike Barr script, Dave Roberts and Jim Amash art	$0.30	$0.90	$1.50	£0.20	£0.60	£1.00
1 Variant Cover Edition, ND - computer painted cover by Chuck Maiden	$0.50	$1.50	$2.50	£0.30	£0.90	£1.50
2 ND flip-book format with Phoenix Ressurrection chapter	$0.30	$0.90	$1.50	£0.20	£0.60	£1.00
3-5 ND	$0.30	$0.90	$1.50	£0.20	£0.60	£1.00
6 ND Rush guest-stars; new costume for Mantra	$0.30	$0.90	$1.50	£0.20	£0.60	£1.00
7 ND Rush guest-stars	$0.30	$0.90	$1.50	£0.20	£0.60	£1.00
Title Value:	$2.60	$7.80	$13.00	£1.70	£5.10	£8.50
MANTRA, GIANT SIZE						
Malibu Ultraverse; 1 Jul 1994						
1 ND 40pgs	$0.50	$1.50	$2.50	£0.30	£0.90	£1.50
Title Value:	$0.50	$1.50	$2.50	£0.30	£0.90	£1.50
MANTRA: INFINITY						
Marvel Comics Group,OS; nn Nov 1995						
nn ND - Black September tie-in; introduces the new Mantra	$0.50	$1.50	$2.50	£0.30	£0.90	£1.50
nn Variant Cover Edition ND - 1 copy received for every 5 copies of the regular issue ordered	$0.60	$1.80	$3.00	£0.40	£1.20	£2.00
Title Value:	$1.10	$3.30	$5.50	£0.70	£2.10	£3.50
MANTRA: SPEAR OF DESTINY						
Malibu Ultraverse,MS; 1 Apr 1995-2 May 1995						
1-2 ND Joel Adams art	$0.50	$1.50	$2.50	£0.30	£0.90	£1.50
Title Value:	$1.00	$3.00	$5.00	£0.60	£1.80	£3.00
MANTUS FILES, THE						
Eternity,MS; 1 Aug 1991-4 Nov 1991						
1-4 ND black and white	$0.40	$1.20	$2.00	£0.25	£0.75	£1.25
Title Value:	$1.60	$4.80	$8.00	£1.00	£3.00	£5.00
MANY LOVES OF DOBIE GILLIS						
National Periodical Publications,TV; 1 May/Jun 1960-26 Oct 1964						
1 ND very scarce in the U.K.	$32.00	$95.00	$225.00	£21.00	£62.50	£150.00
2-5 ND scarce in the U.K.	$15.50	$47.00	$110.00	£10.50	£32.00	£75.00
6-10 ND	$12.00	$36.00	$85.00	£7.75	£23.50	£55.00
11-20 ND	$10.50	$32.00	$75.00	£6.25	£19.00	£45.00
21-26 ND	$10.00	$30.00	$70.00	£5.25	£16.00	£37.50
Title Value:	$319.00	$963.00	$2260.00	£195.75	£594.00	£1400.00
MARAUDER						
Caliber Press,OS; 1 Apr 1993						
1 ND	$0.40	$1.20	$2.00	£0.25	£0.75	£1.25
Title Value:	$0.40	$1.20	$2.00	£0.25	£0.75	£1.25
MARCH HARE						
Lodestone; 1 Aug 1986						
1 ND Keith Giffen art	$0.40	$1.20	$2.00	£0.25	£0.75	£1.25
Title Value:	$0.40	$1.20	$2.00	£0.25	£0.75	£1.25

Mage #1

Manga Vizion #1

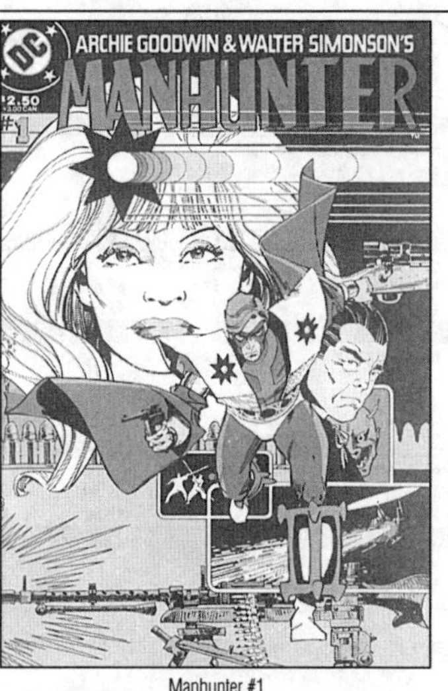

Manhunter #1

	$Good	$Fine	$N.Mint	£Good	£Fine	£N.Mint
MARINE WAR HEROES						
Charlton; 1 Jan 1964-18 Mar 1967						
1 distributed in the U.K.	*$2.10*	*$6.25*	*$15.00*	£1.40	£4.25	£10.00
2-10 distributed in the U.K.	*$1.05*	*$3.20*	*$7.50*	£0.70	£2.10	£5.00
11-18 distributed in the U.K.	*$1.05*	*$3.20*	*$7.50*	£0.60	£1.90	£4.50
Title Value:	*$19.95*	*$60.65*	*$142.50*	£12.50	£38.35	£91.00
MARK HAZZARD: MERC						
Marvel Comics Group/New Universe; 1 Nov 1986-12 Oct 1987						
1-2 ND Morrow art	*$0.15*	*$0.45*	*$0.75*	£0.10	£0.35	£0.60
3-4 ND Jack Fury art	*$0.15*	*$0.45*	*$0.75*	£0.10	£0.35	£0.60
5-6 ND Beechum art	*$0.15*	*$0.45*	*$0.75*	£0.10	£0.35	£0.60
7 ND Mayerick art	*$0.15*	*$0.45*	*$0.75*	£0.10	£0.35	£0.60
8-12 ND Morrow art	*$0.15*	*$0.45*	*$0.75*	£0.10	£0.35	£0.60
Title Value:	*$1.80*	*$5.40*	*$9.00*	£1.20	£4.20	£7.20
MARK HAZZARD: MERC ANNUAL						
Marvel Comics Group/New Universe; 1 Nov 1987						
1 ND Mark Hazzard dies	*$0.30*	*$0.90*	*$1.50*	£0.20	£0.60	£1.00
Title Value:	*$0.30*	*$0.90*	*$1.50*	£0.20	£0.60	£1.00
MARK, THE						
Dark Horse; 1 Sep 1987-6 Jan 1989						
1-6 ND	*$0.50*	*$1.50*	*$2.50*	£0.30	£0.90	£1.50
Title Value:	*$3.00*	*$9.00*	*$15.00*	£1.80	£5.40	£9.00
MARK, THE (2ND SERIES)						
Dark Horse,MS; 1 Dec 1993-4 Mar 1994						
1-4 ND	*$0.50*	*$1.50*	*$2.50*	£0.30	£0.90	£1.50
Title Value:	*$2.00*	*$6.00*	*$10.00*	£1.20	£3.60	£6.00
MARKSMAN						
Hero; 1 1987-5 Aug 1988						
1-5 ND spin-off from Champions	*$0.30*	*$0.90*	*$1.50*	£0.20	£0.60	£1.00
Title Value:	*$1.50*	*$4.50*	*$7.50*	£1.00	£3.00	£5.00
MARKSMAN ANNUAL						
Hero; 1 1988						
1 ND 52pgs	*$0.40*	*$1.20*	*$2.00*	£0.25	£0.75	£1.25
Title Value:	*$0.40*	*$1.20*	*$2.00*	£0.25	£0.75	£1.25
MARRIED WITH CHILDREN						
Now Comics; 1 Dec 1989-7 Jun 1990						
1 based on the US TV series	*$0.60*	*$1.80*	*$3.00*	£0.40	£1.20	£2.00
1 2nd printing	*$0.30*	*$0.90*	*$1.50*	£0.25	£0.75	£1.25
2 photo cover	*$0.40*	*$1.20*	*$2.00*	£0.30	£0.90	£1.50
2 2nd printing	*$0.30*	*$0.90*	*$1.50*	£0.20	£0.60	£1.00
3	*$0.30*	*$0.90*	*$1.50*	£0.30	£0.90	£1.50
3 2nd printing	*$0.30*	*$0.90*	*$1.50*	£0.20	£0.60	£1.00
4-7	*$0.30*	*$0.90*	*$1.50*	£0.30	£0.90	£1.50
Title Value:	*$3.40*	*$10.20*	*$17.00*	£2.85	£8.55	£14.25
Note: all Non-Distributed on the news-stands in the U.K.						
Married With Children Revisited Vol 1 (May 1991), 64pgs, reprints issues #1-3				£0.65	£1.95	£3.25
MARRIED WITH CHILDREN (2ND SERIES)						
Now Comics; 1 Sep 1991-13 Mar 1992						
1 ND based on US TV series, focusing more on character of Kelly Bundy (photo cover)	*$0.50*	*$1.50*	*$2.50*	£0.30	£0.90	£1.50
2-13 ND	*$0.40*	*$1.20*	*$2.00*	£0.25	£0.75	£1.25
Title Value:	*$5.30*	*$15.90*	*$26.50*	£3.30	£9.90	£16.50
MARRIED WITH CHILDREN 2099						
Now Comics,MS; 1 Jun 1993-3 Aug 1993						
1-3 ND	*$0.50*	*$1.50*	*$2.50*	£0.30	£0.90	£1.50
Title Value:	*$1.50*	*$4.50*	*$7.50*	£0.90	£2.70	£4.50
MARRIED WITH CHILDREN 3-D SPECIAL						
Now Comics,OS; 1 Jun 1993						
1 ND with 3-D glasses (25% less without glasses)	*$0.60*	*$1.80*	*$3.00*	£0.40	£1.20	£2.00
Title Value:	*$0.60*	*$1.80*	*$3.00*	£0.40	£1.20	£2.00
MARRIED WITH CHILDREN FLASHBACK SPECIAL						
Now Comics,MS; 1 Jan 1993-3 Mar 1993						
1-3 ND	*$0.50*	*$1.50*	*$2.50*	£0.30	£0.90	£1.50
Title Value:	*$1.50*	*$4.50*	*$7.50*	£0.90	£2.70	£4.50
MARRIED WITH CHILDREN: 2099 AND A HALF						
Now Comics,MS; 1 Apr 1995-2 May 1995						
1-2 ND sub-titled "Turgid Ordeals of Retchh and Slobb"	*$0.50*	*$1.50*	*$2.50*	£0.30	£0.90	£1.50
Title Value:	*$1.00*	*$3.00*	*$5.00*	£0.60	£1.80	£3.00
MARRIED WITH CHILDREN: BUCK'S TALE						
Now Comics; 1 Apr 1993-3 Jun 1994						
1-3 ND	*$0.50*	*$1.50*	*$2.50*	£0.30	£0.90	£1.50
Title Value:	*$1.50*	*$4.50*	*$7.50*	£0.90	£2.70	£4.50
MARRIED WITH CHILDREN: KELLY BUNDY SPECIAL						
Now Comics,MS; 1 Jul 1992-3 Sep 1993						
1-3 ND pre-bagged with poster	*$0.50*	*$1.50*	*$2.50*	£0.30	£0.90	£1.50
Title Value:	*$1.50*	*$4.50*	*$7.50*	£0.90	£2.70	£4.50
MARRIED WITH CHILDREN: KELLY GOES TO COLLEGE						
Now Comics,MS; 1 Jun 1994-3 Aug 1994						

	$Good	$Fine	$N.Mint	£Good	£Fine	£N.Mint
1-3 ND	*$0.60*	*$1.80*	*$3.00*	£0.40	£1.20	£2.00
Title Value:	*$1.80*	*$5.40*	*$9.00*	£1.20	£3.60	£6.00
MARRIED WITH CHILDREN: LOTTO FEVER!						
Now Comics,MS; 1 Oct 1994-3 Dec 1994						
1-3 ND	*$0.50*	*$1.50*	*$2.50*	£0.25	£0.75	£1.25
Title Value:	*$1.50*	*$4.50*	*$7.50*	£0.75	£2.25	£3.75
MARRIED WITH CHILDREN: QUANTUM QUARTET						
Now Comics,MS; 1 Oct 1993-2 Nov 1993; 3/4 Sep 1994						
1-2 ND	*$0.50*	*$1.50*	*$2.50*	£0.30	£0.90	£1.50
3 ND special flip-book format combining issues #3 and 4 that were originally solicited for Dec 1993/Jan 1994 cover date	*$0.60*	*$1.80*	*$3.00*	£0.40	£1.20	£2.00
Title Value:	*$1.60*	*$4.80*	*$8.00*	£1.00	£3.00	£5.00
MARRIED WITH CHILDREN: WE'RE DYSFUNCTIONAL						
Now Comics,MS; 1 Jan 1995-3 Mar 1995						
1-3 ND	*$0.50*	*$1.50*	*$2.50*	£0.30	£0.90	£1.50
Title Value:	*$1.50*	*$4.50*	*$7.50*	£0.90	£2.70	£4.50
MARRIED WITH: OFF BROADWAY						
Now Comics,OS; 1 Sep 1993						
1 ND	*$0.50*	*$1.50*	*$2.50*	£0.30	£0.90	£1.50
Title Value:	*$0.50*	*$1.50*	*$2.50*	£0.30	£0.90	£1.50
MARS						
First; 1 Jan 1984-12 Mar 1985						
1-12 ND	*$0.20*	*$0.60*	*$1.00*	£0.10	£0.30	£0.50
Title Value:	*$2.40*	*$7.20*	*$12.00*	£1.20	£3.60	£6.00
MARS ATTACKS						
Topps,MS; 1 May 1994-5 Sep 1994						
1 ND Keith Giffen script, Charlie Adlard art	*$1.40*	*$4.20*	*$7.00*	£1.20	£3.60	£6.00
2 ND Keith Giffen script, Charlie Adlard art	*$1.00*	*$3.00*	*$5.00*	£1.00	£3.00	£5.00
3-4 ND Keith Giffen script, Charlie Adlard art	*$0.80*	*$2.40*	*$4.00*	£0.60	£1.80	£3.00
5 ND Keith Giffen script, Charlie Adlard art; bound-in tattoos	*$0.80*	*$2.40*	*$4.00*	£0.60	£1.80	£3.00
Title Value:	*$4.80*	*$14.40*	*$24.00*	£4.00	£12.00	£20.00
Mars Attacks (Dec 1994) Trade paperback collects mini-series with Simon Bisley front cover, John Bolton back cover				£1.70	£5.10	£8.50
MARS ATTACKS (2ND SERIES)						
Topps; 1 Aug 1995-present						
1 ND Keith Giffen part script, Charlie Adlard art, Ken Steacy cover	*$0.80*	*$2.40*	*$4.00*	£0.60	£1.80	£3.00
1 Wizard Ace Edition, ND acetate outer cover; Wizard Ace Edition #11	*$5.00*	*$15.00*	*$25.00*	£3.00	£9.00	£15.00
2-7 ND	*$0.60*	*$1.80*	*$3.00*	£0.40	£1.20	£2.00
Title Value:	*$9.40*	*$28.20*	*$47.00*	£6.00	£18.00	£30.00
MARS ATTACKS BASEBALL SPECIAL						
Topps,OS; 1 Jun 1996						
1 ND Simon Bisley cover	*$0.60*	*$1.80*	*$3.00*	£0.40	£1.20	£2.00
Title Value:	*$0.60*	*$1.80*	*$3.00*	£0.40	£1.20	£2.00
MARS ATTACKS MINI-COMICS						
Pocket Comics; 1 Jul 1988-4 Oct 1988						
(mini-comics, cancelled 54-part series)						
1 ND scarce in the U.K.	*$2.00*	*$6.00*	*$10.00*	£2.00	£6.00	£10.00
2 ND scarce in the U.K.	*$1.50*	*$4.50*	*$7.50*	£1.50	£4.50	£7.50
3-4 ND scarce in the U.K.	*$1.20*	*$3.60*	*$6.00*	£1.20	£3.60	£6.00
Title Value:	*$5.90*	*$17.70*	*$29.50*	£5.90	£17.70	£29.50
MARS ON EARTH						
DC Comics/Piranha Press,OS; 1 1992						
1 ND	*$0.40*	*$1.20*	*$2.00*	£0.25	£0.75	£1.25
Title Value:	*$0.40*	*$1.20*	*$2.00*	£0.25	£0.75	£1.25
MARSHAL BLUEBERRY GRAPHIC NOVEL						
Marvel Comics Group,OS; 1 Dec 1991						
1 ND features the last two Blueberry tales by Charlier and Moebius	*$3.00*	*$9.00*	*$15.00*	£2.00	£6.00	£10.00
Title Value:	*$3.00*	*$9.00*	*$15.00*	£2.00	£6.00	£10.00
MARSHAL LAW						
Marvel Comics Group/Epic; 1 Dec 1987-6 May 1989						
(see British section)						
1 ND Pat Mills script, Kevin O'Neill painted art in all	*$0.50*	*$1.50*	*$2.50*	£0.50	£1.50	£2.50
2-3 ND	*$0.50*	*$1.50*	*$2.50*	£0.40	£1.20	£2.00
4-6 ND	*$0.50*	*$1.50*	*$2.50*	£0.30	£0.90	£1.50
Title Value:	*$3.00*	*$9.00*	*$15.00*	£2.20	£6.60	£11.00
Note: Mature Readers label						
Crime and Punishment: Marshal Law Takes Manhattan (Jan 1990) Pat Mills and Kev O'Neill; Mature Readers label				£0.60	£1.80	£3.00
Trade Paperback (Aug 1990), reprints issues #1-6, new cover by Kev O'Neill				£1.60	£4.80	£8.00
MARSHAL LAW: CAPE FEAR						
Dark Horse,MS; 1 Sep 1993-2 Oct 1993						
1-2 ND	*$0.50*	*$1.50*	*$2.50*	£0.30	£0.90	£1.50
Title Value:	*$1.00*	*$3.00*	*$5.00*	£0.60	£1.80	£3.00
MARSHAL LAW: SUPER BABYLON						
Dark Horse,OS; 1 May 1992						
1 ND	*$0.50*	*$1.50*	*$2.50*	£0.30	£0.90	£1.50
Title Value:	*$0.50*	*$1.50*	*$2.50*	£0.30	£0.90	£1.50

MARTHA SPLATTERHEAD'S MADDEST STORIES EVER TOLD

Monster Comics; 1 Feb 1994

Issue	$Good	$Fine	$N.Mint	£Good	£Fine	£N.Mint
1 ND with flexi-disc single; black and white	$0.70	$2.10	$3.50	£0.40	£1.20	£2.00
Title Value:	$0.70	$2.10	$3.50	£0.40	£1.20	£2.00

MARTHA WASHINGTON GOES TO WAR

Dark Horse/Legend,MS; 1 May 1994-5 Sep 1994

Issue	$Good	$Fine	$N.Mint	£Good	£Fine	£N.Mint
1 ND Frank Miller script and Dave Gibbons art begin	$0.60	$1.80	$3.00	£0.40	£1.20	£2.00
1 Blue Sky Edition, ND - produced in the UK by Chaos City Comics, signed by Dave Gibbons, limited to 500 copies	$1.50	$4.50	$7.50	£1.50	£4.50	£7.50
1 Sunset Red Edition, ND - produced in the UK by Chaos City Comics, signed by Dave Gibbons with 50% signed by Frank Miller, limited to 100 copies	$2.50	$7.50	$12.50	£2.50	£7.50	£12.50
2-5	$0.60	$1.80	$3.00	£0.40	£1.20	£2.00
Title Value:	$7.00	$21.00	$35.00	£6.00	£18.00	£30.00

Note: all Non-Distributed on the news-stands in the U.K.

Martha Washington Goes to Washington (Oct 1995)

Issue	$Good	$Fine	$N.Mint	£Good	£Fine	£N.Mint
Trade paperback collects issues #1-5				£2.40	£7.20	£12.00

MARTHA WASHINGTON STRANDED IN SPACE

Dark Horse,OS; 1 Nov 1995

Issue	$Good	$Fine	$N.Mint	£Good	£Fine	£N.Mint
1 ND Frank Miller script, Dave Gibbons art	$0.60	$1.80	$3.00	£0.40	£1.20	£2.00
Title Value:	$0.60	$1.80	$3.00	£0.40	£1.20	£2.00

MARTIAN MANHUNTER

DC Comics,MS; 1 May 1988-4 Aug 1988

(see Detective Comics, House of Mystery, Jemm Son of Saturn, Justice League, Justice League of America)

Issue	$Good	$Fine	$N.Mint	£Good	£Fine	£N.Mint
1 Mark Badger art begins, Batman appears	$0.25	$0.75	$1.25	£0.15	£0.45	£0.75
2 Batman appears	$0.25	$0.75	$1.25	£0.15	£0.45	£0.75
3-4	$0.25	$0.75	$1.25	£0.15	£0.45	£0.75
Title Value:	$1.00	$3.00	$5.00	£0.60	£1.80	£3.00

Note: all Deluxe Format.

MARTIAN MANHUNTER SPECIAL

DC Comics,OS; 1 Jun 1996

Issue	$Good	$Fine	$N.Mint	£Good	£Fine	£N.Mint
1 ND 64pgs, Paul Kupperberg script, Mike Collins and Hanibal Rodriguez art	$0.70	$2.10	$3.50	£0.50	£1.50	£2.50
Title Value:	$0.70	$2.10	$3.50	£0.50	£1.50	£2.50

MARTIAN MANHUNTER: AMERICAN SECRETS

DC Comics,MS; 1 Sep 1992-3 Nov 1992

Issue	$Good	$Fine	$N.Mint	£Good	£Fine	£N.Mint
1-3 ND 48pgs	$0.70	$2.10	$3.50	£0.50	£1.50	£2.50
Title Value:	$2.10	$6.30	$10.50	£1.50	£4.50	£7.50

MARVEL 1993 HOLIDAY SPECIAL

Marvel Comics Group,OS; 1 Jan 1994

Issue	$Good	$Fine	$N.Mint	£Good	£Fine	£N.Mint
1 ND 64pgs, features include Hulk by Peter David and Ron Lim, She-Hulk by John Byrne, Nick Fury by Howard Chaykin	$0.50	$1.50	$2.50	£0.30	£0.90	£1.50
Title Value:	$0.50	$1.50	$2.50	£0.30	£0.90	£1.50

MARVEL ACTION HOUR FEATURING FANTASTIC FOUR

Marvel Comics Group,TV; 1 Nov 1994-8 Jun 1995

Issue	$Good	$Fine	$N.Mint	£Good	£Fine	£N.Mint
1 ND based on US animated series	$0.30	$0.90	$1.50	£0.20	£0.60	£1.00
1 Collectors Edition, ND : pre-bagged with acetate print from TV series	$0.60	$1.80	$3.00	£0.40	£1.20	£2.00
2-3 ND Puppet Master appears	$0.30	$0.90	$1.50	£0.20	£0.60	£1.00
4-5 ND Sub-Mariner appears	$0.30	$0.90	$1.50	£0.20	£0.60	£1.00
6 ND The Skrulls appear	$0.30	$0.90	$1.50	£0.20	£0.60	£1.00
7 ND Dr. Doom appears	$0.30	$0.90	$1.50	£0.20	£0.60	£1.00
8 ND The Skrulls appear	$0.30	$0.90	$1.50	£0.20	£0.60	£1.00
Title Value:	$3.00	$9.00	$15.00	£2.00	£6.00	£10.00

MARVEL ACTION HOUR FEATURING IRON MAN

Marvel Comics Group,TV; 1 Nov 1994-8 Jun 1995

Issue	$Good	$Fine	$N.Mint	£Good	£Fine	£N.Mint
1 ND based on US animated series	$0.30	$0.90	$1.50	£0.20	£0.60	£1.00
1 Collectors Edition, ND : pre-bagged with acetate print from TV series	$0.60	$1.80	$3.00	£0.40	£1.20	£2.00
2 ND Iron Man vs. Mandarin	$0.30	$0.90	$1.50	£0.20	£0.60	£1.00
3 ND Hawkeye and Scarlet Witch appear	$0.30	$0.90	$1.50	£0.20	£0.60	£1.00
4 ND Force Works, Hawkeye and War Machine appear	$0.30	$0.90	$1.50	£0.20	£0.60	£1.00
5 ND origins of Iron man and Mandarin retold	$0.30	$0.90	$1.50	£0.20	£0.60	£1.00
6 ND Fin Fang Foom appears	$0.30	$0.90	$1.50	£0.20	£0.60	£1.00
7 ND origins of Iron Man and Mandarin retold	$0.30	$0.90	$1.50	£0.20	£0.60	£1.00
8 ND Mandarin and Modok appear	$0.30	$0.90	$1.50	£0.20	£0.60	£1.00
Title Value:	$3.00	$9.00	$15.00	£2.00	£6.00	£10.00

MARVEL ACTION UNIVERSE

Marvel Comics Group,OS TV; 1 Jan 1989

Issue	$Good	$Fine	$N.Mint	£Good	£Fine	£N.Mint
1 ND Spiderman, Iceman, Firestar appear	$0.25	$0.75	$1.25	£0.15	£0.45	£0.75
Title Value:	$0.25	$0.75	$1.25	£0.15	£0.45	£0.75

MARVEL ADVENTURE

Marvel Comics Group; 1 Dec 1975-6 Oct 1976

Issue	$Good	$Fine	$N.Mint	£Good	£Fine	£N.Mint
1 ND Daredevil reprints begin	$0.30	$1.00	$2.00	£0.25	£0.75	£1.50
2-5 ND	$0.30	$1.00	$2.00	£0.25	£0.75	£1.50
6 ND Spiderman appears (reprints Daredevil #27)	$0.30	$1.00	$2.00	£0.25	£0.75	£1.50
Title Value:	$1.80	$6.00	$12.00	£1.50	£4.50	£9.00

Note: reprints of Daredevil #22-27.

MARVEL AGE

Marvel Comics Group/Promotional; 1 Mar 1982-140 Aug 1994

Issue	$Good	$Fine	$N.Mint	£Good	£Fine	£N.Mint
1 ND	$0.30	$0.90	$1.50	£0.20	£0.60	£1.00
2-13 ND	$0.25	$0.75	$1.25	£0.15	£0.45	£0.75
14 ND John Byrne cover art	$0.25	$0.75	$1.25	£0.15	£0.45	£0.75
15-32 ND	$0.25	$0.75	$1.25	£0.15	£0.45	£0.75
33 ND Punisher (2pgs)	$0.25	$0.75	$1.25	£0.15	£0.45	£0.75
34-50 ND	$0.25	$0.75	$1.25	£0.15	£0.45	£0.75
51 ND Punisher	$0.25	$0.75	$1.25	£0.15	£0.45	£0.75
52 ND Silver Surfer issue	$0.25	$0.75	$1.25	£0.15	£0.45	£0.75
53-59 ND	$0.25	$0.75	$1.25	£0.15	£0.45	£0.75
60 ND Excalibur issue	$0.25	$0.75	$1.25	£0.15	£0.45	£0.75
61-66 ND	$0.25	$0.75	$1.25	£0.15	£0.45	£0.75
67 ND Punisher film preview	$0.25	$0.75	$1.25	£0.15	£0.45	£0.75
68 ND Havok and Wolverine	$0.25	$0.75	$1.25	£0.15	£0.45	£0.75
69-70 ND	$0.25	$0.75	$1.25	£0.15	£0.45	£0.75
71 ND Silver Surfer	$0.25	$0.75	$1.25	£0.15	£0.45	£0.75
72 ND Punisher film photo cover	$0.25	$0.75	$1.25	£0.15	£0.45	£0.75
73 ND	$0.25	$0.75	$1.25	£0.15	£0.45	£0.75
74 ND Moon Knight	$0.25	$0.75	$1.25	£0.15	£0.45	£0.75
75-87 ND	$0.25	$0.75	$1.25	£0.15	£0.45	£0.75
88 ND Guardians of the Galaxy	$0.25	$0.75	$1.25	£0.15	£0.45	£0.75
89-96 ND	$0.25	$0.75	$1.25	£0.15	£0.45	£0.75
97 ND Excalibur issue	$0.25	$0.75	$1.25	£0.15	£0.45	£0.75
98 ND	$0.25	$0.75	$1.25	£0.15	£0.45	£0.75
99 ND Infinity Gauntlet preview	$0.25	$0.75	$1.25	£0.15	£0.45	£0.75
100 ND Todd McFarlane/Jim Lee/Rob Liefeld interviews	$0.25	$0.75	$1.25	£0.15	£0.45	£0.75
101-103 ND	$0.25	$0.75	$1.25	£0.15	£0.45	£0.75
104 ND previews X-Men [2nd Series] #1 by Claremont/Lee	$0.25	$0.75	$1.25	£0.15	£0.45	£0.75
105-109 ND	$0.25	$0.75	$1.25	£0.15	£0.45	£0.75
110 ND Luke Cage preview	$0.25	$0.75	$1.25	£0.15	£0.45	£0.75
111 ND	$0.25	$0.75	$1.25	£0.15	£0.45	£0.75
112 ND Captain America special	$0.25	$0.75	$1.25	£0.15	£0.45	£0.75
113 ND Punisher and Captain America	$0.25	$0.75	$1.25	£0.15	£0.45	£0.75
114 ND Spiderman's 30th anniversary	$0.25	$0.75	$1.25	£0.15	£0.45	£0.75
115 ND Cable mini-series feature	$0.25	$0.75	$1.25	£0.15	£0.45	£0.75
116 ND X-Men feature	$0.25	$0.75	$1.25	£0.15	£0.45	£0.75
117 ND 2099 preview, new 2099 strip begins	$0.25	$0.75	$1.25	£0.15	£0.45	£0.75
118 ND pre-bagged with Hulk Marvel Masterpiece trading card, George Perez cover	$0.40	$1.20	$2.00	£0.25	£0.75	£1.25
119 ND	$0.25	$0.75	$1.25	£0.15	£0.45	£0.75
120 ND 10th anniversary issue	$0.25	$0.75	$1.25	£0.15	£0.45	£0.75
121 ND	$0.25	$0.75	$1.25	£0.15	£0.45	£0.75
122 ND $1.25 cover	$0.25	$0.75	$1.25	£0.15	£0.45	£0.75
123 ND Venom and Thunderstrike features	$0.25	$0.75	$1.25	£0.15	£0.45	£0.75
124 ND Infinity Crusade and Heavy Hitters features	$0.25	$0.75	$1.25	£0.15	£0.45	£0.75
125 ND flip-book covers	$0.25	$0.75	$1.25	£0.15	£0.45	£0.75
126 ND Marvel UK feature	$0.25	$0.75	$1.25	£0.15	£0.45	£0.75
127 ND Frank Miller cover	$0.25	$0.75	$1.25	£0.15	£0.45	£0.75
128 ND Wolverine cover	$0.25	$0.75	$1.25	£0.15	£0.45	£0.75
129 ND X-Men/Avengers poster part 1	$0.25	$0.75	$1.25	£0.15	£0.45	£0.75
130 ND X-Men/Avengers poster part 2	$0.25	$0.75	$1.25	£0.15	£0.45	£0.75

	$Good	$Fine	$N.Mint	£Good	£Fine	£N.Mint
131 ND Joe, Andy and Adam Kubert cover	*$0.25*	*$0.75*	*$1.25*	£0.15	£0.45	£0.75
132 ND Alan Davis cover	*$0.25*	*$0.75*	*$1.25*	£0.15	£0.45	£0.75
133 ND X-Men cover by Andy Kubert	*$0.25*	*$0.75*	*$1.25*	£0.15	£0.45	£0.75
134 ND 3 card insert sheet celebrating the wedding of Scott Summers and Jean Grey	*$0.30*	*$0.90*	*$1.50*	£0.20	£0.60	£1.00
135 ND	*$0.25*	*$0.75*	*$1.25*	£0.15	£0.45	£0.75
136 ND Neil Gaiman on Alice Cooper; with free Spiderman vs. Venom card sheet	*$0.25*	*$0.75*	*$1.25*	£0.15	£0.45	£0.75
137 ND 48pgs, article on Spiderman animated TV series	*$0.25*	*$0.75*	*$1.25*	£0.15	£0.45	£0.75
138-140 ND	*$0.25*	*$0.75*	*$1.25*	£0.15	£0.45	£0.75
Title Value:	*$35.25*	*$105.75*	*$176.25*	£21.20	£63.60	£106.00

MARVEL AGE ANNUAL

Marvel Comics Group/Promotional; 1 1986-4 1993

	$Good	$Fine	$N.Mint	£Good	£Fine	£N.Mint
1 ND Sabretooth appears (1 panel only, outside Marvel continuity)	*$0.25*	*$0.75*	*$1.25*	£0.15	£0.45	£0.75
2 ND celebrates 25th Anniversary	*$0.25*	*$0.75*	*$1.25*	£0.15	£0.45	£0.75
3 ND Fred Hembeck issue	*$0.25*	*$0.75*	*$1.25*	£0.15	£0.45	£0.75
4 ND squarebound	*$0.25*	*$0.75*	*$1.25*	£0.15	£0.45	£0.75
Title Value:	*$1.00*	*$3.00*	*$5.00*	£0.60	£1.80	£3.00

MARVEL AGE PREVIEW SPECIAL

Marvel Comics Group/Promotional; 1 May 1990; 2 Mar 1992

	$Good	$Fine	$N.Mint	£Good	£Fine	£N.Mint
1 ND 48pgs, no ads, previewing future Marvel comics	*$0.30*	*$0.90*	*$1.50*	£0.20	£0.60	£1.00
2 ND 64pgs, squarebound, no ads, previewing future Marvel comics	*$0.30*	*$0.90*	*$1.50*	£0.20	£0.60	£1.00
Title Value:	*$0.60*	*$1.80*	*$3.00*	£0.40	£1.20	£2.00

MARVEL AND DC PRESENT

Marvel Comics Group/DC Comics,OS; 1 Nov 1982

(Marvel/DC Co-Production)

	$Good	$Fine	$N.Mint	£Good	£Fine	£N.Mint
1 ND 64pgs, New Teen Titans and X-Men co-star, Darkseid and Dark Phoenix appear and Deathstroke (3rd ever appearance); Walt Simonson and Terry Austin art	*$2.40*	*$7.00*	*$12.00*	£1.20	£3.60	£6.00
Title Value:	*$2.40*	*$7.00*	*$12.00*	£1.20	£3.60	£6.00
(May 1996), ND 64pgs, reprints original edition with gold metallic border around cover				£0.50	£1.50	£2.50

MARVEL CHILLERS

Marvel Comics Group; 1 Oct 1975-7 Oct 1976

	$Good	$Fine	$N.Mint	£Good	£Fine	£N.Mint
1 1st appearance Modred the Mystic, Gil Kane cover	*$0.65*	*$2.00*	*$4.00*	£0.25	£0.85	£1.75
2 Modred the Mystic	*$0.55*	*$1.75*	*$3.50*	£0.25	£0.75	£1.50
3 Tigra the Were-Woman begins (origin); ends #7	*$0.40*	*$1.25*	*$2.50*	£0.20	£0.60	£1.25
4 Tigra vs. Kraven	*$0.40*	*$1.25*	*$2.50*	£0.20	£0.60	£1.25
5 Red Wolf appears	*$0.40*	*$1.25*	*$2.50*	£0.20	£0.60	£1.25
6 ND scarce in the U.K. Red Wolf appears, John Byrne art	*$0.40*	*$1.25*	*$2.50*	£0.25	£0.75	£1.50
7 Tigra vs. Super-Skrull, Jack Kirby cover	*$0.40*	*$1.25*	*$2.50*	£0.20	£0.60	£1.25
Title Value:	*$3.20*	*$10.00*	*$20.00*	£1.55	£4.75	£9.75

MARVEL CLASSICS COMICS

Marvel Comics Group; 1 1976-36 Dec 1978

(see Classics Illustrated in British section)

	$Good	$Fine	$N.Mint	£Good	£Fine	£N.Mint
1 Dr. Jekyll and Mr. Hyde; Nestor Redondo art, Gil Kane/Dan Adkins cover	*$0.65*	*$2.00*	*$4.00*	£0.30	£1.00	£2.00
2 The Time Machin; Alex Nino art, Gil Kane cover	*$0.40*	*$1.25*	*$2.50*	£0.25	£0.75	£1.50
3 The Hunchback of Notre Dame; Gil Kane/Klaus Janson cover	*$0.40*	*$1.25*	*$2.50*	£0.25	£0.75	£1.50
4 20,000 Leagues Under The Sea; Gil Kane/Dan Adkins cover	*$0.40*	*$1.25*	*$2.50*	£0.25	£0.75	£1.50
5 Black Beauty; Rudy Nebres art, Gil Kane cover	*$0.40*	*$1.25*	*$2.50*	£0.25	£0.75	£1.50
6 Gulliver's Travels; Gil Kane cover	*$0.40*	*$1.25*	*$2.50*	£0.25	£0.75	£1.50
7 Tom Sawyer; Gil Kane cover	*$0.40*	*$1.25*	*$2.50*	£0.25	£0.75	£1.50
8 Moby Dick; Alex Nino art	*$0.40*	*$1.25*	*$2.50*	£0.25	£0.75	£1.50
9 Dracula; Nestor Redondo art	*$0.40*	*$1.25*	*$2.50*	£0.25	£0.75	£1.50
10 Red Badge of Courage	*$0.40*	*$1.25*	*$2.50*	£0.25	£0.75	£1.50
11 Mysterious Island	*$0.40*	*$1.25*	*$2.50*	£0.25	£0.75	£1.50
12 The Three Musketeers; Alex Nino art	*$0.40*	*$1.25*	*$2.50*	£0.25	£0.75	£1.50
13 The Last of the Mohicans	*$0.40*	*$1.25*	*$2.50*	£0.25	£0.75	£1.50
14 The War of the Worlds, Alex Nino art	*$0.40*	*$1.25*	*$2.50*	£0.25	£0.75	£1.50
15 Treasure Island	*$0.40*	*$1.25*	*$2.50*	£0.25	£0.75	£1.50
16 Ivanhoe	*$0.40*	*$1.25*	*$2.50*	£0.25	£0.75	£1.50
17 The Count of Monte Cristo	*$0.40*	*$1.25*	*$2.50*	£0.25	£0.75	£1.50
18 The Odyssey	*$0.40*	*$1.25*	*$2.50*	£0.25	£0.75	£1.50
19 Robinson Crusoe	*$0.40*	*$1.25*	*$2.50*	£0.25	£0.75	£1.50
20 Frankenstein	*$0.40*	*$1.25*	*$2.50*	£0.25	£0.75	£1.50
21 Master of the World	*$0.40*	*$1.25*	*$2.50*	£0.25	£0.75	£1.50
22 Food of the Gods	*$0.40*	*$1.25*	*$2.50*	£0.25	£0.75	£1.50
23 The Moonstone	*$0.40*	*$1.25*	*$2.50*	£0.25	£0.75	£1.50
24 She	*$0.40*	*$1.25*	*$2.50*	£0.25	£0.75	£1.50
25 The Invisible Man, Alex Nino art	*$0.40*	*$1.25*	*$2.50*	£0.25	£0.75	£1.50
26 The Iliad	*$0.40*	*$1.25*	*$2.50*	£0.25	£0.75	£1.50
27 Kidnapped; John Romita Jnr. cover	*$0.40*	*$1.25*	*$2.50*	£0.25	£0.75	£1.50
28 The Pit and the Pendulum; part Michael Golden art	*$0.80*	*$2.50*	*$5.00*	£0.30	£1.00	£2.00
29 The Prisoner of Zenda	*$0.40*	*$1.25*	*$2.50*	£0.25	£0.75	£1.50
30 Arabian Nights	*$0.40*	*$1.25*	*$2.50*	£0.25	£0.75	£1.50
31 The First Men in the Moon	*$0.40*	*$1.25*	*$2.50*	£0.25	£0.75	£1.50
32 White Fang	*$0.40*	*$1.25*	*$2.50*	£0.25	£0.75	£1.50
33 The Prince and the Pauper	*$0.40*	*$1.25*	*$2.50*	£0.25	£0.75	£1.50
34 Robin Hood	*$0.40*	*$1.25*	*$2.50*	£0.25	£0.75	£1.50
35 Alice in Wonderland	*$0.40*	*$1.25*	*$2.50*	£0.25	£0.75	£1.50
36 A Christmas Carol	*$0.40*	*$1.25*	*$2.50*	£0.25	£0.75	£1.50
Title Value:	*$15.05*	*$47.00*	*$94.00*	£9.10	£27.50	£55.00

Note: all 52pgs, no ads.

MARVEL COLLECTOR'S ITEM CLASSICS

Marvel Comics Group; 1 Feb 1965-22 Aug 1969

(becomes Marvel's Greatest Comics)

	$Good	$Fine	$N.Mint	£Good	£Fine	£N.Mint
1 68pgs, reprints from Fantastic Four (#2), Thor, Spiderman (#3), Antman (Tales To Astonish #36)	*$8.75*	*$26.00*	*$70.00*	£5.00	£15.00	£40.00
2 68pgs, reprints F.F. #3, Spiderman #4, Tales To Astonish #37	*$5.50*	*$17.00*	*$40.00*	£3.20	£9.50	£22.50
3 68pgs, reprints F.F. #4, Hulk #6, Tales of Suspense #40, Strange Tales #110	*$5.00*	*$15.00*	*$35.00*	£2.85	£8.50	£20.00
4 68pgs, reprints F.F. #7, Hulk #4 (1 story), Tales of Suspense #41, Strange Tales #111	*$5.00*	*$15.00*	*$35.00*	£2.10	£6.25	£15.00
5 68pgs, reprints F.F. #8, Hulk #4 (1 story), Tales of Suspense #42, Strange Tales #114	*$4.25*	*$12.50*	*$30.00*	£1.40	£4.25	£10.00
6 68pgs, reprints F.F. #9, Hulk #5, Tales of Suspense #43, Strange Tales #116	*$3.55*	*$10.50*	*$25.00*	£1.40	£4.25	£10.00
7 68pgs, reprints F.F. #13, Hulk #5, Tales of Suspense #44, Strange Tales #117	*$3.55*	*$10.50*	*$25.00*	£1.40	£4.25	£10.00
8 68pgs, reprints F.F. #10, Hulk #2, Tales of Suspense #45, Strange Tales #118	*$3.55*	*$10.50*	*$25.00*	£1.40	£4.25	£10.00
9 68pgs, reprints F.F. #14, Hulk #2, Tales of Suspense #46, Strange Tales #118	*$3.55*	*$10.50*	*$25.00*	£1.40	£4.25	£10.00
10 68pgs, reprints F.F. #15, Hulk #2, Tales of Suspense #47, Strange Tales #119	*$3.55*	*$10.50*	*$25.00*	£1.40	£4.25	£10.00
11 68pgs, reprints F.F. #16, Hulk #6, Tales of Suspense #48, Strange Tales #120; cover repros of early Marvels on cover end	*$2.85*	*$8.50*	*$20.00*	£1.05	£3.20	£7.50
12-21 68pgs	*$2.85*	*$8.50*	*$20.00*	£1.05	£3.20	£7.50
22 68pgs, reprints 1st Ant-Man from Tales to Astonish #27	*$2.85*	*$8.50*	*$20.00*	£1.05	£3.20	£7.50
Title Value:	*$80.45*	*$240.00*	*$575.00*	£34.15	£103.15	£247.50

Note: all distributed in the U.K.

REPRINT FEATURES

Ant-Man in 1, 2, 22. Dr.Strange in 3-9, 11-22. Fantastic Four in 1-22. Hulk in 3-16. Iron Man in 3-22. Spiderman in 1, 2. Tales of Asgard in 1. Watcher in 3, 5, 10, 13, 21.

MARVEL COMICS

Timely/Atlas; 1 Oct/Nov 1939-92 Jun 1949

	$Good	$Fine	$N.Mint	£Good	£Fine	£N.Mint
1 origin and 1st distributed appearance Sub-Mariner, 1st appearance Human Torch, Ka-Zar and The Angel; most #1's have November cover with date blacked out, fewer have October. About 60 extant copies	*$10800.00*	*$32500.00*	*$97500.00*	£7200.00	£21600.00	£65000.00
[Prices may vary widely on this comic]						
2 origin re-told of Human Torch; traditionally rarer than #1 - about 50 extant copies	*$3000.00*	*$9000.00*	*$24000.00*	£2000.00	£6000.00	£16000.00
3	*$1250.00*	*$3750.00*	*$10000.00*	£830.00	£2500.00	£6675.00
4 1st appearance Electro	*$1000.00*	*$3000.00*	*$8000.00*	£660.00	£2000.00	£5350.00
5 very scarce in the U.K.	*$1875.00*	*$5600.00*	*$15000.00*	£1250.00	£3750.00	£10000.00
6-7	*$680.00*	*$2050.00*	*$5500.00*	£455.00	£1375.00	£3675.00
8 1st Human Torch and Sub-Mariner battle	*$1125.00*	*$3350.00*	*$9000.00*	£750.00	£2250.00	£6000.00
9 very scarce in the U.K. Human Torch vs. Sub-Mariner cover and story	*$2500.00*	*$7500.00*	*$20000.00*	£1650.00	£5000.00	£13350.00
10 Human Torch vs. Sub-Mariner	*$780.00*	*$2325.00*	*$6250.00*	£520.00	£1550.00	£4175.00
11	*$350.00*	*$1050.00*	*$2800.00*	£230.00	£700.00	£1875.00
12	*$435.00*	*$1300.00*	*$3500.00*	£290.00	£880.00	£2350.00
13 1st appearance Golden Age The Vision by Joe Simon and Jack Kirby	*$500.00*	*$1500.00*	*$4000.00*	£330.00	£1000.00	£2675.00
14-16	*$250.00*	*$750.00*	*$2000.00*	£165.00	£500.00	£1350.00
17 Human Torch and Sub-Mariner team up for 1st time cover and story	*$275.00*	*$820.00*	*$2200.00*	£180.00	£550.00	£1475.00

	$Good	$Fine	$N.Mint	£Good	£Fine	£N.Mint
18	*$210.00*	*$630.00*	*$1700.00*	£140.00	£430.00	£1150.00
19	*$250.00*	*$750.00*	*$2000.00*	£165.00	£500.00	£1350.00
20	*$240.00*	*$730.00*	*$1950.00*	£160.00	£485.00	£1300.00
21 1st appearance The Patriot	*$215.00*	*$650.00*	*$1750.00*	£145.00	£440.00	£1175.00
22-25	*$185.00*	*$560.00*	*$1500.00*	£125.00	£375.00	£1000.00
26-30	*$165.00*	*$495.00*	*$1325.00*	£110.00	£330.00	£885.00
31-33	*$135.00*	*$410.00*	*$1100.00*	£90.00	£275.00	£735.00
34	*$155.00*	*$465.00*	*$1250.00*	£100.00	£310.00	£835.00
35-40	*$135.00*	*$410.00*	*$1100.00*	£90.00	£275.00	£735.00
41-44	*$115.00*	*$355.00*	*$950.00*	£77.50	£235.00	£635.00
45-48	*$115.00*	*$345.00*	*$925.00*	£77.50	£230.00	£620.00
49 origin Miss America	*$155.00*	*$465.00*	*$1250.00*	£100.00	£310.00	£835.00
50	*$130.00*	*$390.00*	*$1050.00*	£87.50	£260.00	£700.00
51-60	*$115.00*	*$355.00*	*$950.00*	£77.50	£235.00	£635.00
61-62	*$105.00*	*$325.00*	*$875.00*	£72.50	£215.00	£585.00
63 Hitler on cover	*$110.00*	*$335.00*	*$900.00*	£75.00	£225.00	£600.00
64	*$105.00*	*$325.00*	*$875.00*	£72.50	£215.00	£585.00
65	*$110.00*	*$335.00*	*$900.00*	£75.00	£225.00	£600.00
66 last classic war cover	*$110.00*	*$335.00*	*$900.00*	£75.00	£225.00	£600.00
67-79	*$100.00*	*$300.00*	*$800.00*	£65.00	£200.00	£535.00
80 Captain America appears	*$150.00*	*$450.00*	*$1200.00*	£100.00	£300.00	£800.00
81 Captain America appears	*$100.00*	*$300.00*	*$800.00*	£65.00	£200.00	£535.00
82 origin and 1st appearance Namora	*$215.00*	*$650.00*	*$1750.00*	£145.00	£440.00	£1175.00
83	*$95.00*	*$290.00*	*$775.00*	£65.00	£195.00	£520.00
84 Captain America appears	*$130.00*	*$390.00*	*$1050.00*	£87.50	£260.00	£700.00
85	*$95.00*	*$290.00*	*$775.00*	£65.00	£195.00	£520.00
86 Captain America appears	*$115.00*	*$345.00*	*$925.00*	£77.50	£230.00	£620.00
87 Captain America/Golden Girl team	*$115.00*	*$355.00*	*$950.00*	£77.50	£235.00	£635.00
88 Captain America appears	*$110.00*	*$340.00*	*$915.00*	£75.00	£225.00	£610.00
89 Captain America solo story	*$115.00*	*$345.00*	*$925.00*	£77.50	£230.00	£620.00
90-91 Captain America appears	*$115.00*	*$355.00*	*$950.00*	£77.50	£235.00	£635.00
92 very scarce in the U.K. Captain America appears, Human Torch "origin"	*$280.00*	*$840.00*	*$2250.00*	£185.00	£560.00	£1500.00
Title Value:	***$35900.00***	***$108065.00***	***$299665.00***	**£23910.00**	**£72060.00**	**£200095.00**

Note: titled Marvel Mystery Comics from #2. Note also that these comics were not distributed on the news-stands in the U.K. like all Golden Age material but some copies have been noted with British pence stamps: these may have come over as ballast on ships during and after the war. As with most Golden Age comics, all these issues are at least generally scarce in the U.K.

MARVEL COMICS COLLECTION

Marvel Comics Group; 1-3 Jun 1992

	$Good	$Fine	$N.Mint	£Good	£Fine	£N.Mint
1-3 ND bound volumes of all the Marvel comics published for the month of June 1992 made available at the June Diamond Seminar; 600 sets made	*$6.00*	*$18.00*	*$30.00*	£4.00	£12.00	£20.00
Title Value:	***$18.00***	***$54.00***	***$90.00***	**£12.00**	**£36.00**	**£60.00**

MARVEL COMICS PRESENTS

Marvel Comics Group; 1 Sep 1988-175 Feb 1995

	$Good	$Fine	$N.Mint	£Good	£Fine	£N.Mint
1 ND Wolverine, Man-Thing, Master of Kung Fu, Silver Surfer	*$1.60*	*$4.80*	*$8.00*	£0.70	£2.10	£3.50
2-5 ND Wolverine	*$1.00*	*$3.00*	*$5.00*	£0.40	£1.20	£2.00
6-10 ND Wolverine	*$0.60*	*$1.80*	*$3.00*	£0.30	£0.90	£1.50
11-16 ND Colossus	*$0.40*	*$1.20*	*$2.00*	£0.25	£0.75	£1.25
17 ND Cyclops	*$0.40*	*$1.20*	*$2.00*	£0.25	£0.75	£1.25
18 ND She-Hulk, Cyclops, Byrne art	*$0.40*	*$1.20*	*$2.00*	£0.25	£0.75	£1.25
19-20 ND Cyclops	*$0.40*	*$1.20*	*$2.00*	£0.25	£0.75	£1.25
21-23 ND Cyclops	*$0.30*	*$0.90*	*$1.50*	£0.20	£0.60	£1.00
24 ND Cyclops,Havok	*$0.30*	*$0.90*	*$1.50*	£0.20	£0.60	£1.00
25 ND Havok; 1st appearance Nth Man, The Ultimate Ninja	*$0.30*	*$0.90*	*$1.50*	£0.20	£0.60	£1.00
26-28 ND Havok	*$0.30*	*$0.90*	*$1.50*	£0.20	£0.60	£1.00
29-30 ND Havok/Wolverine	*$0.30*	*$0.90*	*$1.50*	£0.20	£0.60	£1.00
31 ND Havok, Excalibur, Erik Larsen art	*$0.30*	*$0.90*	*$1.50*	£0.20	£0.60	£1.00
32 ND Excalibur, Erik Larsen art	*$0.30*	*$0.90*	*$1.50*	£0.20	£0.60	£1.00
33 ND Excalibur, Erik Larsen art; Jim Lee art on Namor	*$0.50*	*$1.50*	*$2.50*	£0.25	£0.75	£1.25
34-35 ND Excalibur	*$0.30*	*$0.90*	*$1.50*	£0.20	£0.60	£1.00
36-37 LD in the U.K. Excalibur, Erik Larsen art	*$0.30*	*$0.90*	*$1.50*	£0.20	£0.60	£1.00
38 LD in the U.K. Wolverine by Buscema, Excalibur by Larsen art	*$0.80*	*$2.40*	*$4.00*	£0.30	£0.90	£1.50
39 LD in the U.K. Wolverine, Spiderman	*$0.40*	*$1.20*	*$2.00*	£0.25	£0.75	£1.25
40-47 ND Wolverine	*$0.40*	*$1.20*	*$2.00*	£0.25	£0.75	£1.25
48-49 LD in the U.K. Wolverine, Spiderman, Larsen art	*$0.50*	*$1.50*	*$2.50*	£0.30	£0.90	£1.50
50 LD in the U.K. Wolverine, Spiderman, Silver Surfer appear, Larsen art	*$0.50*	*$1.50*	*$2.50*	£0.30	£0.90	£1.50
51-53 Wolverine, Wild Child, Rob Liefeld art	*$0.50*	*$1.50*	*$2.50*	£0.30	£0.90	£1.50
54-58 Wolverine, Hulk	*$0.50*	*$1.50*	*$2.50*	£0.25	£0.75	£1.25
59 Wolverine, Hulk; Punisher appears	*$0.50*	*$1.50*	*$2.50*	£0.25	£0.75	£1.25
60-61 Wolverine, Hulk	*$0.50*	*$1.50*	*$2.50*	£0.25	£0.75	£1.25
62 Wolverine, Deathlok story	*$0.50*	*$1.50*	*$2.50*	£0.25	£0.75	£1.25
63 Wolverine	*$0.40*	*$1.20*	*$2.00*	£0.25	£0.75	£1.25
64-67 Wolverine/Ghost Rider, Texeira art	*$0.40*	*$1.20*	*$2.00*	£0.30	£0.90	£1.50
68 ND Wolverine/Ghost Rider, Texeira art, bi-weekly	*$0.40*	*$1.20*	*$2.00*	£0.30	£0.90	£1.50
69-71 Wolverine/Ghost Rider, bi-weekly	*$0.40*	*$1.20*	*$2.00*	£0.30	£0.90	£1.50
72 LD in the U.K. Wolverine: Weapon X begins - Wolverine's origin, Barry Windsor-Smith art, bi-weekly issue	*$1.50*	*$4.50*	*$7.50*	£0.70	£2.10	£3.50
73 Weapon X story, bi-weekly issue	*$0.90*	*$2.70*	*$4.50*	£0.60	£1.80	£3.00
74 Weapon X story, bi-weekly issue	*$0.80*	*$2.40*	*$4.00*	£0.50	£1.50	£2.50
75 Weapon X story, bi-weekly issue						

Marvel Age #1

Marvel Classic Comics #20

Marvel Mystery Comics #12

	$Good	$Fine	$N.Mint	£Good	£Fine	£N.Mint
	$0.60	$1.80	$3.00	£0.40	£1.20	£2.00
76-83 Weapon X story, bi-weekly issue	$0.60	$1.80	$3.00	£0.30	£0.90	£1.50
84 Weapon X story, wraparound cover by Barry Windsor-Smith, bi-weekly issue	$0.50	$1.50	$2.50	£0.30	£0.90	£1.50
85 Wolverine by Peter David and Sam Keith begins (1st Sam Keith Wolverine), Liefeld art on X-Men back-up story, 1st Jae Lee art for Marvel, bi-weekly issue	$0.80	$2.40	$4.00	£0.40	£1.20	£2.00
86-89 Wolverine by Peter David, Sam Keith art, Jae Lee art, bi-weekly issue	$0.70	$2.10	$3.50	£0.30	£0.90	£1.50
90 Wolverine by Peter David, Sam Keith art, Jae Lee art, Ghost Rider and Cable begins, bi-weekly issue	$0.80	$2.40	$4.00	£0.30	£0.90	£1.50
91-92 Wolverine by Peter David, Sam Keith art, Jae Lee art, Ghost Rider and Cable, bi-weekly issue	$0.40	$1.20	$2.00	£0.25	£0.75	£1.25
93-96 Wolverine by Tim Truman, Nova, Ghost Rider and Cable, bi-weekly issue	$0.40	$1.20	$2.00	£0.25	£0.75	£1.25
97 Wolverine by Tim Truman, Ghost Rider and Cable, bi-weekly issue	$0.40	$1.20	$2.00	£0.25	£0.75	£1.25
98 Wolverine by Tim Truman, Ghost Rider, bi-weekly issue	$0.40	$1.20	$2.00	£0.25	£0.75	£1.25
99 Wolverine by Liefeld, Ghost Rider, Mary-Jane Parker, Captain America	$0.40	$1.20	$2.00	£0.25	£0.75	£1.25
100 Ghost Rider, Dr. Doom, Wolverine and Nightmare in one full length story	$0.50	$1.50	$2.50	£0.30	£0.90	£1.50
101-106 Ghost Rider and Dr. Strange, Wolverine and Nightcrawler, bi-weekly	$0.30	$0.90	$1.50	£0.20	£0.60	£1.00
107 Wolverine and Nightcrawler, Ghost Rider and Werewolf, bi-weekly	$0.30	$0.90	$1.50	£0.20	£0.60	£1.00
108 Infinity War X-over, Thanos appears, Wolverine and Nightcrawler, Ghost Rider and Werewolf, bi-weekly	$0.30	$0.90	$1.50	£0.20	£0.60	£1.00
109-111 Infinity War X-over, Thanos appears, Wolverine and Typhoid Mary, Ghost Rider and Werewolf, bi-weekly	$0.30	$0.90	$1.50	£0.20	£0.60	£1.00
112 Wolverine and Typhoid Mary, Ghost Rider and Werewolf, bi-weekly	$0.30	$0.90	$1.50	£0.20	£0.60	£1.00
113 Wolverine and Typhoid Mary, Giant Man vs. Goliath, Werewolf By Night vs. Wendigo, Ghost Rider and Man-Thing, bi-weekly	$0.30	$0.90	$1.50	£0.20	£0.60	£1.00
114-115 Wolverine and Typhoid Mary, Ghost Rider and Iron Fist, bi-weekly	$0.30	$0.90	$1.50	£0.20	£0.60	£1.00
116 Wolverine and Typhoid Mary, Ghost Rider and Iron Fist, Iron Fist solo story, bi-weekly	$0.30	$0.90	$1.50	£0.20	£0.60	£1.00
117 Wolverine and Venom by Sam Keith, Ghost Rider and Iron Fist, Sam Keith cover, bi-weekly; Ravage 2099 preview (1st appearance)	$0.50	$1.50	$2.50	£0.30	£0.90	£1.50
118 Wolverine and Venom by Sam Keith, Ghost Rider and Iron Fist, Sam Keith cover, bi-weekly	$0.30	$0.90	$1.50	£0.20	£0.60	£1.00
119 Wolverine and Venom by Sam Keith, Ghost Rider and Cloak and Dagger, Sam Keith cover, bi-weekly	$0.30	$0.90	$1.50	£0.20	£0.60	£1.00
120 Wolverine and Venom by Sam Keith, Ghost Rider and Cloak and Dagger, Spiderman solo story, Sam Keith cover, bi-weekly	$0.30	$0.90	$1.50	£0.20	£0.60	£1.00
121-122 Wolverine and Venom by Sam Keith, Ghost Rider and Cloak and Dagger, Sam Keith cover, bi-weekly	$0.30	$0.90	$1.50	£0.20	£0.60	£1.00
123-124 Wolverine and Lynx, Ghost Rider and Typhoid Mary, Sam Keith cover, bi-weekly	$0.30	$0.90	$1.50	£0.20	£0.60	£1.00
125-130 Wolverine and Lynx, Ghost Rider and Typhoid Mary, Iron Fist, Sam Keith cover, bi-weekly	$0.30	$0.90	$1.50	£0.20	£0.60	£1.00
131 Wolverine and Cyber, Ghost Rider and Cage, Iron Fist, Shadowcat, bi-weekly	$0.30	$0.90	$1.50	£0.20	£0.60	£1.00
132 Wolverine and Cyber, Ghost Rider and Cage, Iron Fist, Iron Man, bi-weekly	$0.30	$0.90	$1.50	£0.20	£0.60	£1.00
133 Wolverine and Cyber, Ghost Rider and Cage, Iron Fist, Cloak & Dagger, bi-weekly	$0.30	$0.90	$1.50	£0.20	£0.60	£1.00
134 Wolverine and Cyber, Ghost Rider and Cage, Iron Fist, Major Victory, bi-weekly	$0.30	$0.90	$1.50	£0.20	£0.60	£1.00
135 Wolverine and Cyber, Ghost Rider and Cage, Iron Fist, Daredevil, bi-weekly	$0.30	$0.90	$1.50	£0.20	£0.60	£1.00
136 Wolverine and Cyber, Ghost Rider and Cage, Iron Fist, Spiderman, bi-weekly	$0.30	$0.90	$1.50	£0.20	£0.60	£1.00
137 Wolverine and Cyber, Ghost Rider and The Masters of Silence, Iron Fist, Ant-Man, bi-weekly	$0.30	$0.90	$1.50	£0.20	£0.60	£1.00
138 Wolverine, Spellbound, Nightcrawler and Ghost Riddr/Masters of Silence	$0.30	$0.90	$1.50	£0.20	£0.60	£1.00
139 Wolverine, Spellbound, The Foreigner and Ghost Riddr/Masters of Silence	$0.30	$0.90	$1.50	£0.20	£0.60	£1.00
140 Wolverine, Spellbound, Captain Universe and Ghost Riddr/Masters of Silence	$0.30	$0.90	$1.50	£0.20	£0.60	£1.00
141 Wolverine, Spellbound, Iron Fist and Ghost Riddr/Masters of Silence	$0.30	$0.90	$1.50	£0.20	£0.60	£1.00
142 Wolverine, Spellbound, Mr. Fantastic and Ghost Riddr/Masters of Silence	$0.30	$0.90	$1.50	£0.20	£0.60	£1.00
143 Siege of Darkness part 3: Ghost Rider & Blaze, Werewolf, Scarlet Witch, Zarathos	$0.30	$0.90	$1.50	£0.20	£0.60	£1.00
144 Siege of Darkness part 6: Ghost Rider & Blaze, Werewolf, Scarlet Witch, Morbius	$0.30	$0.90	$1.50	£0.20	£0.60	£1.00
145 Siege of Darkness part 11: Ghost Rider & Blaze, Vengeance, Nightstalkers, Demonslayer, Morbius	$0.30	$0.90	$1.50	£0.20	£0.60	£1.00
146 Siege of Darkness part 14: Ghost Rider, Nightstalkers, Dr. Strange, Darkhold	$0.30	$0.90	$1.50	£0.20	£0.60	£1.00
147 Vengeance, American Eagle, Black Panther, Captain Universe	$0.30	$0.90	$1.50	£0.20	£0.60	£1.00
148 Vengeance, American Eagle, Saints & Sinners, The Masters of Silence	$0.30	$0.90	$1.50	£0.20	£0.60	£1.00
149 Wolverine vs. Typhoid Mary, Daredevil vs. Steel Shade	$0.30	$0.90	$1.50	£0.20	£0.60	£1.00
150 The Four Marys story featuring Wolverine and Daredevil	$0.30	$0.90	$1.50	£0.20	£0.60	£1.00
151-152 Vengeance, War Machine, Moon Knight, Wolverine	$0.30	$0.90	$1.50	£0.20	£0.60	£1.00
153 Vengeance, War Machine, Moon Knight, Wolverine; with free Spiderman vs. Venom card sheet	$0.30	$0.90	$1.50	£0.20	£0.60	£1.00
154 Vengeance, Namorita, War Machine, Wolverine	$0.30	$0.90	$1.50	£0.20	£0.60	£1.00
155 Ghost Rider, Hawk (previously Hawkeye), Namorita, Nick Fury; with free Spiderman vs. Venom card sheet	$0.30	$0.90	$1.50	£0.20	£0.60	£1.00
156 Vengeance, Hawkeye, New Warriors, Nick Fury	$0.30	$0.90	$1.50	£0.20	£0.60	£1.00
157 Vengeance, Hawkeye, New Warriors, The Destroyer	$0.30	$0.90	$1.50	£0.20	£0.60	£1.00
158 Vengeance, Master of Kung Fu, New Warriors, Clandestine by Alan Davis	$0.30	$0.90	$1.50	£0.20	£0.60	£1.00
159 Vengeance, Hawkeye, New Warriors, Thing	$0.30	$0.90	$1.50	£0.20	£0.60	£1.00
160-161 Vengeance, Hawkeye, New Warriors, Mace	$0.30	$0.90	$1.50	£0.20	£0.60	£1.00
162-163 Vengeance, New Warriors, Mace, Tigra	$0.30	$0.90	$1.50	£0.20	£0.60	£1.00
164 Vengeance, Speedball, Man-Thing, Tigra	$0.30	$0.90	$1.50	£0.20	£0.60	£1.00
165 Vengeance, Rage, Man-Thing, Tigra	$0.30	$0.90	$1.50	£0.20	£0.60	£1.00
166-167 Vengeance, Turbo, Man-Thing, Spiderwoman	$0.30	$0.90	$1.50	£0.20	£0.60	£1.00
168 Vengeance, Thing, Black Bolt, Spiderwoman	$0.30	$0.90	$1.50	£0.20	£0.60	£1.00
169 Vengeance, Mandarin, Century, It the Living Colossus	$0.30	$0.90	$1.50	£0.20	£0.60	£1.00
170 Vengeance, Mandarin, Force Works, Nick Fury	$0.30	$0.90	$1.50	£0.20	£0.60	£1.00
171 Vengeance, The Recorder, War Machine, Red Wolf	$0.30	$0.90	$1.50	£0.20	£0.60	£1.00
172 Vengeance, U.S Agent, Spiderwoman, Stingray	$0.30	$0.90	$1.50	£0.20	£0.60	£1.00
173 Vengeance, The Lunatics, Nick Fury, Sundragon	$0.30	$0.90	$1.50	£0.20	£0.60	£1.00
174 Vengeance, Lunatic/Silver Surfer, Nick Fury, Cage	$0.30	$0.90	$1.50	£0.20	£0.60	£1.00
175 Steel Raven, Lunatic/Silver Surfer, New Genix, Vengeance	$0.30	$0.90	$1.50	£0.20	£0.60	£1.00
Title Value:	$73.70	$221.10	$367.00	£43.45	£130.35	£217.25

Wolverine & Ghost Rider: Acts of Vengeance (Jan 1994)

				£Good	£Fine	£N.Mint
Trade paperback reprints Marvel Comics Presents #64-71				£0.90	£2.70	£4.50

Wolverine: Weapon X (Apr 1994)

				£Good	£Fine	£N.Mint
Trade paperback reprints Marvel Comics Presents #72-84				£1.70	£5.10	£8.50

FEATURES

American Eagle in 27. Ant-Man in 11,81. Aquarian in 46. Arabian Knight in 47. Beast in 85. Black Cat in 57. Black Knight in 72,73. Black Panther in 13-37. Black Widow and Silver Sable in 53. The Captain in 2. Captain America in 34, 47, 60, 80, 81. Clea in 20. Cloak in 9. Coldblood in 26-35. Collective Man in 55. Colossus in 10-17. Comet Man in 50-53. Cyclops in 17-24. Daughters of the Dragon in 42,80. Daredevil in 5,49,81. Death's Head in 76 Devilslayer in 37,46-49. Dr. Strange in 19, 20, 44, 61, 79, 80. El Aguila in 9. Excalibur in 31-38. Falcon in 23. Firestar in 82-85. Freedom Force in 41. Ghost Rider in 64-71. Gladiator in 49. Havok in 24-31. Hawkeye in 83. Hellcat in 36. Her in 35. Hercules in 12,39-41. Hulk in 6,26,38,45,52,54-61,75. Human Torch in 83. Iron Man in 8,43,51,58,78,82. Ka-Zar in 16. Leir in 30. Le Peregrine in 51. Longshot in 16. Machine Man in 10. Man-Thing in 1-12. Marvel Girl in 15. Master of Kung Fu in 1-8. Fantastic/Invisible Girl in 13. Namorita in 12. Nomad in 14. Nth Man in Overmind in 40. Paladin in 21. Poison in 60,61. Powerman in 82. Puma in 44. Punisher in 59. Quasar in 29. Red Wolf in 15. Rick Jones in 52. Scarlet Witch in 60, Shadowcat and Meggan in 78. Shamrock in 24. Shanna in 13,68-77. She-Hulk in 18. Shooting Star in 45. Sgt. Fury and Dracula in 77-79. Silver Surfer in 1,50. Sirya in 43. Slag in 11. Speedball in 14,56,85. Spiderman 39,48,50. Shroud in 54. Starfox in 22. Stingray in 53-56. Storm and Dr. Doom in 48. Sub-Mariner in 7,33,46,57-59,73,74. Sunfire in 32. Sunspot in 79. The Thing in 3,21. Thor in 4. Triton in 28. Union Jack in 42. Ursa Major in 25. Wasp in 48. Watcher in 17. Werewolf By Night in 54-59. Wheels of Wolfpack in 23. Willie Lumpkin in 18. Wolfsbane and Mirage in 22. Wolverine in 1-10,29,30,38-72. Wonderman in 38-45.

MARVEL DOUBLE FEATURE

Marvel Comics Group; 1 Dec 1973-21 Mar 1977

	$Good	$Fine	$N.Mint	£Good	£Fine	£N.Mint
1 ND Iron Man, Captain America reprints begin from Tales of Suspense #77 onwards	$0.80	$2.50	$5.00	£0.65	£2.00	£4.00
2 ND	$0.55	$1.75	$3.50	£0.40	£1.25	£2.50
3-9 ND	$0.55	$1.75	$3.50	£0.30	£1.00	£2.00
10	$0.50	$1.50	$3.00	£0.25	£0.85	£1.75
11-16 ND	$0.50	$1.50	$3.00	£0.30	£1.00	£2.00
17 ND reprints Iron Man and Sub-Mariner #1	$0.65	$2.00	$4.00	£0.30	£1.00	£2.00
18-19 ND reprints Iron Man #1	$0.80	$2.50	$5.00	£0.40	£1.25	£2.50
20-21 ND	$0.50	$1.50	$3.00	£0.30	£1.00	£2.00
Title Value:	$11.95	$37.00	$71.00	£6.90	£22.60	£45.25

MARVEL FAMILY, THE

Fawcett; 1 Dec 1945-89 Jan 1954

(see Captain Marvel Adventures, Mary Marvel Comics, Whiz Comics)

	$Good	$Fine	$N.Mint	£Good	£Fine	£N.Mint
1 scarce in the U.K. 1st appearance Black Adam; origins Captain Marvel, Mary Marvel, Captain Marvel Junior and Uncle Marvel retold	$130.00	$400.00	$1200.00	£87.50	£265.00	£800.00
2	$57.50	$175.00	$525.00	£39.00	£115.00	£350.00

	$Good	$Fine	$N.Mint	£Good	£Fine	£N.Mint
3	$47.00	$140.00	$375.00	£31.00	£92.50	£250.00
4-5	$38.00	$110.00	$300.00	£25.00	£75.00	£200.00
6-9	$28.00	$82.50	$225.00	£18.50	£55.00	£150.00
10 The Marvel Family vs. The Sivana Family	$28.00	$82.50	$225.00	£18.50	£55.00	£150.00
11-20	$26.00	$77.50	$185.00	£17.50	£52.50	£125.00
21-30	$20.00	$60.00	$140.00	£13.50	£41.00	£95.00
31-40	$17.00	$50.00	$120.00	£11.00	£34.00	£80.00
41-50	$14.00	$43.00	$100.00	£9.25	£28.00	£65.00
51-89	$12.50	$39.00	$90.00	£8.50	£26.00	£60.00
Title Value:	$1708.00	$5173.50	$12785.00	£1144.00	£3466.50	£8540.00

MARVEL FANFARE

Marvel Comics Group; 1 Mar 1982-60 Dec 1991

	$Good	$Fine	$N.Mint	£Good	£Fine	£N.Mint
1 ND Spiderman/Angel team-up, Paul Smith/Golden art	$1.20	$3.60	$6.00	£0.60	£1.80	£3.00
2 ND Spiderman, Ka-Zar, Angel team, origin FF retold, Golden art	$1.00	$3.00	$5.00	£0.70	£2.10	£3.50
3 ND X-Men, Ka-Zar	$0.80	$2.40	$4.00	£0.60	£1.80	£3.00
4 ND Paul Smith's 1st work on X-Men, Iron Man/Deathlok by Golden	$0.80	$2.40	$4.00	£0.60	£1.80	£3.00
5 ND Dr. Strange by Rogers, Captain America	$0.40	$1.20	$2.00	£0.25	£0.75	£1.25
6 ND Spiderman/Scarlet Witch	$0.40	$1.20	$2.00	£0.25	£0.75	£1.25
7 ND Hulk/Daredevil	$0.40	$1.20	$2.00	£0.25	£0.75	£1.25
8 ND Dr. Strange, Wolf Boy by Sienkiewicz	$0.40	$1.20	$2.00	£0.25	£0.75	£1.25
9 ND Man-Thing by Morrow	$0.40	$1.20	$2.00	£0.25	£0.75	£1.25
10-13 ND Black Widow by George Perez	$0.40	$1.20	$2.00	£0.25	£0.75	£1.25
14 ND Vision and Scarlet Witch, Fantastic Four appear; Inhumans back-up story	$0.40	$1.20	$2.00	£0.25	£0.75	£1.25
15 ND The Thing by Barry Windsor Smith	$0.50	$1.50	$2.50	£0.30	£0.90	£1.50
16 ND Skywolf; Sub-Mariner back-up story	$0.40	$1.20	$2.00	£0.25	£0.75	£1.25
17 ND Skywolf; Hulk back-up story	$0.40	$1.20	$2.00	£0.25	£0.75	£1.25
18 ND Captain America, Frank Miller art	$0.50	$1.50	$2.50	£0.30	£0.90	£1.50
19 ND scarce in the U.K. Cloak & Dagger	$0.50	$1.50	$2.50	£0.30	£0.90	£1.50
20 ND Thing/Hulk, Jim Starlin art	$0.50	$1.50	$2.50	£0.30	£0.90	£1.50
21 ND Thing vs. Hulk, Jim Starlin art	$0.50	$1.50	$2.50	£0.30	£0.90	£1.50
22-23 ND Iron Man Vs Dr Octopus, Steacy art	$0.40	$1.20	$2.00	£0.25	£0.75	£1.25
24 ND Weirdworld, Wolverine, Nick Fury, Binary	$0.50	$1.50	$2.50	£0.30	£0.90	£1.50
25-26 ND Weirdworld, Ploog/Russell art	$0.50	$1.50	$2.50	£0.30	£0.90	£1.50
27 ND Daredevil, Spiderman	$0.50	$1.50	$2.50	£0.30	£0.90	£1.50
28 ND Alpha Flight, Steacy painted cover	$0.50	$1.50	$2.50	£0.30	£0.90	£1.50
29 ND Hulk, John Byrne cover and art	$0.50	$1.50	$2.50	£0.30	£0.90	£1.50
30 ND Moon Knight, Anderson art and painted cover	$0.50	$1.50	$2.50	£0.30	£0.90	£1.50
31-32 ND Captain America	$0.50	$1.50	$2.50	£0.30	£0.90	£1.50
33 ND X-Men	$0.60	$1.80	$3.00	£0.35	£1.05	£1.75
34-37 ND Warriors Three, Vess art	$0.50	$1.50	$2.50	£0.30	£0.90	£1.50
38 ND Rogue/Dazzler, Moon Knight by Sienkewicz	$0.50	$1.50	$2.50	£0.30	£0.90	£1.50
39 ND Hawkeye	$0.50	$1.50	$2.50	£0.30	£0.90	£1.50
40 ND Angel/Storm	$0.50	$1.50	$2.50	£0.30	£0.90	£1.50
41 ND Dr.Strange, Dave Gibbons art and painted cover	$0.50	$1.50	$2.50	£0.30	£0.90	£1.50
42 ND Spiderman	$0.50	$1.50	$2.50	£0.30	£0.90	£1.50
43 ND Submariner, Human Torch, Mignola and Craig Russell art	$0.50	$1.50	$2.50	£0.30	£0.90	£1.50
44 ND Iron Man, Dr Doom; Steacy painted cover	$0.50	$1.50	$2.50	£0.30	£0.90	£1.50
45 ND All pin-up issue. Art by Nowlan, A.Adams, Simonson, Vess, Mignola, Kaluta, Zeck, Ordway and others	$0.50	$1.50	$2.50	£0.30	£0.90	£1.50
46 ND Fantastic Four	$0.50	$1.50	$2.50	£0.30	£0.90	£1.50
47 ND Hulk/Spiderman, Michael Golden art	$0.50	$1.50	$2.50	£0.30	£0.90	£1.50
48 ND She-Hulk, Byrne art	$0.50	$1.50	$2.50	£0.30	£0.90	£1.50
49 ND Dr. Strange, Nick Fury	$0.50	$1.50	$2.50	£0.30	£0.90	£1.50
50 ND X-Factor, pin-up painted pages by Mark Badger	$0.60	$1.80	$3.00	£0.35	£1.05	£1.75
51 ND 48pgs, Silver Surfer, originally meant as first issue of new Surfer series	$0.60	$1.80	$3.00	£0.35	£1.05	£1.75
52-54 ND Black Knight, Mature Readers label	$0.40	$1.20	$2.00	£0.25	£0.75	£1.25
55 ND Power Pack	$0.40	$1.20	$2.00	£0.25	£0.75	£1.25
56 ND Shanna the She-Devil by Steve Gerber, Bret Blevins art begins	$0.40	$1.20	$2.00	£0.25	£0.75	£1.25
57 ND Shanna the She-Devil, new Captain Marvel. Norm Breyfogle art gallery	$0.40	$1.20	$2.00	£0.25	£0.75	£1.25
58 ND Shanna the She-Devil, Vision and Scarlet Witch. Michael Golden art gallery	$0.40	$1.20	$2.00	£0.25	£0.75	£1.25
59 ND Shanna the She-Devil	$0.40	$1.20	$2.00	£0.25	£0.75	£1.25
60 ND	$0.40	$1.20	$2.00	£0.25	£0.75	£1.25
Title Value:	$29.80	$89.40	$149.00	£18.30	£54.90	£91.50

Note: all ND, direct sale, slick paper.

MARVEL FANFARE (2ND SERIES)

Marvel Comics Group; 1 Sep 1996-present

	$Good	$Fine	$N.Mint	£Good	£Fine	£N.Mint
1 ND Captain America and The Falcon	$0.20	$0.60	$1.00	£0.10	£0.35	£0.65
2 ND Wolverine, Ghost Rider, Hulk and Spiderman; the all-new Fantastic Four line-up from F.F. #347-349	$0.20	$0.60	$1.00	£0.10	£0.35	£0.65
3 ND Spiderman and Ghost Rider	$0.20	$0.60	$1.00	£0.15	£0.45	£0.75
4 ND Longshot appears	$0.20	$0.60	$1.00	£0.15	£0.45	£0.75
5 ND Longshot stars	$0.20	$0.60	$1.00	£0.15	£0.45	£0.75
6 ND Power Man and Iron Fist vs. Sabretooth	$0.20	$0.60	$1.00	£0.15	£0.45	£0.75
Title Value:	$1.20	$3.60	$6.00	£0.80	£2.50	£4.30

MARVEL FEATURE

Marvel Comics Group; 1 Dec 1971-12 Nov 1973

	$Good	$Fine	$N.Mint	£Good	£Fine	£N.Mint
1 ND 48pgs, squarebound, origin, 1st appearance of The Defenders, 1950s Sub-Mariner reprint, Neal Adams cover	$12.00	$36.00	$85.00	£7.00	£21.00	£50.00
2 ND 48pgs, squarebound, 1950s Sub-Mariner reprint	$6.50	$20.00	$40.00	£3.75	£11.00	£22.50
3 ND Defenders	$5.75	$17.50	$35.00	£3.30	£10.00	£20.00
4 ND Ant-Man begins (1st appearance since 1960s), brief origin, guest stars Peter Parker, Spiderman appears	$2.50	$7.50	$15.00	£1.30	£4.00	£8.00
5-7 ND Ant-Man	$1.00	$3.00	$6.00	£0.65	£2.00	£4.00
8 ND reprints Tales to Astonish #44 (origin Wasp), 3pgs Starlin/Russell art framing sequence	$1.00	$3.00	$6.00	£0.65	£2.00	£4.00
9-10 ND Ant-Man	$1.00	$3.00	$6.00	£0.65	£2.00	£4.00
11 ND Thing/Hulk, Starlin art. 1st Thing team up (pre Marvel Two in One title)	$1.65	$5.00	$10.00	£1.00	£3.00	£6.00
12 ND Thing/Iron Man battle Thanos, Jim Starlin art	$1.65	$5.00	$10.00	£1.05	£3.25	£6.50
Title Value:	$36.05	$109.00	$231.00	£21.30	£64.25	£137.00

MARVEL FEATURE (2ND SERIES)

Marvel Comics Group; 1 Nov 1975-7 Nov 1976

	$Good	$Fine	$N.Mint	£Good	£Fine	£N.Mint
1 ND Red Sonja begins (history retold), Neal Adams inks (reprint from Savage Sword of Conan)	$0.75	$2.25	$4.50	£0.50	£1.50	£3.00
2-6 Red Sonja	$0.40	$1.25	$2.50	£0.25	£0.75	£1.50
7 Conan appears	$0.40	$1.25	$2.50	£0.25	£0.75	£1.50
Title Value:	$3.15	$9.75	$19.50	£2.00	£6.00	£12.00

MARVEL FRONTIER COMICS UNLIMITED

Marvel UK,OS; 1 Jan 1994

	$Good	$Fine	$N.Mint	£Good	£Fine	£N.Mint
1 64pgs, Bloodseed, Children of the Voyager, Immortalis featured	$0.50	$1.50	$2.50	£0.30	£0.90	£1.50
Title Value:	$0.50	$1.50	$2.50	£0.30	£0.90	£1.50

MARVEL FUMETTI BOOK

Marvel Comics Group,OS; 1 Apr 1984

	$Good	$Fine	$N.Mint	£Good	£Fine	£N.Mint
1 ND photo-strips featuring the Marvel bullpen	$0.25	$0.75	$1.25	£0.15	£0.45	£0.75
Title Value:	$0.25	$0.75	$1.25	£0.15	£0.45	£0.75

MARVEL GRAPHIC NOVEL

Marvel Comics Group; 1 1982-nn Sep 1993

	$Good	$Fine	$N.Mint	£Good	£Fine	£N.Mint
1 DEATH OF CAPTAIN MARVEL ND Jim Starlin art	$4.00	$12.00	$20.00	£3.00	£9.00	£15.00
1 2nd printing, ND Thanos appears	$1.00	$3.00	$5.00	£1.50	£4.50	£7.50
1 3rd - 5th printings ND	$1.00	$3.00	$5.00	£0.80	£2.40	£4.00
2 ELRIC: THE DREAMING CITY ND scarce in the U.K. Roy Thomas script, P. Craig Russell art	$1.80	$5.25	$9.00	£1.00	£3.00	£5.00
3 DREADSTAR ND Jim Starlin cover and art	$1.60	$4.80	$8.00	£1.20	£3.60	£6.00
4 NEW MUTANTS ND origin and 1st appearance New Mutants; Chris Claremont script, Bob McLeod art	$3.00	$9.00	$15.00	£1.80	£5.25	£9.00
4 2nd printing ND	$1.20	$3.60	$6.00	£1.00	£3.00	£5.00
4 3rd printing, ND (Nov 1990)	$1.00	$3.00	$5.00	£0.80	£2.40	£4.00
5 X-MEN; GOD LOVES, MAN KILLS ND Chris Claremont script, Brent Anderson art	$2.80	$8.25	$14.00	£1.50	£4.50	£7.50
5 2nd/3rd printing ND	$1.00	$3.00	$5.00	£1.00	£3.00	£5.00
5 4th printing, ND (Nov 1990)	$1.00	$3.00	$5.00	£0.80	£2.40	£4.00
6 STAR SLAMMERS ND Walt Simonson script and art	$1.20	$3.60	$6.00	£0.70	£2.10	£3.50

Title	$Good	$Fine	$N.Mint	£Good	£Fine	£N.Mint
7 **KILLRAVEN: WARRIOR OF THE WORLDS** ND Don McGregor script, P.Craig Russell art	*$1.20*	*$3.60*	*$6.00*	£0.80	£2.40	£4.00
8 **SUPER BOXERS** ND John Byrne script, Ron Wilson and Armando Gil art	*$1.00*	*$3.00*	*$5.00*	£0.75	£2.25	£3.75
9 **THE FUTURIANS** ND Dave Cockrum art	*$1.20*	*$3.60*	*$6.00*	£1.00	£3.00	£5.00
10 **HEARTBURST** ND	*$1.00*	*$3.00*	*$5.00*	£0.70	£2.10	£3.50
11 **VOID INDIGO** ND scarce in the U.K. **Note**: at the time of printing, Marvel stipulated that this Graphic Novel would not be reprinted owing to its violent/sexual content	*$1.20*	*$3.60*	*$6.00*	£1.20	£3.60	£6.00
12 **DAZZLER: THE MOVIE** ND scarce in the U.K. Jim Shooter script, Frank Springer and Vince Coletta art	*$1.20*	*$3.60*	*$6.00*	£1.00	£3.00	£5.00
13 **STARSTRUCK** ND Mike Kaluta art	*$1.20*	*$3.60*	*$6.00*	£0.80	£2.40	£4.00
14 **SWORDS OF THE SWASHBUCKLERS** ND scarce in the U.K.	*$1.00*	*$3.00*	*$5.00*	£0.80	£2.40	£4.00
15 **THE RAVEN BANNER (Tales of Asgard)** ND Alan Zelenetz script, Charles Vess art	*$1.00*	*$3.00*	*$5.00*	£0.80	£2.40	£4.00
16 **THE ALADDIN EFFECT** ND Jim Shooter and Divid Michelinie script, Greg LaRocque and Vince Coletta art	*$1.00*	*$3.00*	*$5.00*	£0.70	£2.10	£3.50
17 **REVENGE OF THE LIVING MONOLITH** ND David Michelinie script, Marc Silvestri art	*$1.00*	*$3.00*	*$5.00*	£1.00	£3.00	£5.00
18 **SENSATIONAL SHE-HULK** (no number on cover), ND John Byrne script, DeMulder and Scotese art	*$1.20*	*$3.60*	*$6.00*	£1.20	£3.60	£6.00
18 2nd printing, ND (Sep 1991)	*$1.00*	*$3.00*	*$5.00*	£1.00	£3.00	£5.00
19 **CONAN: THE WITCH QUEEN OF ARCHERON** (no number on cover), ND Don Kraar script, Gary Kwapisz and Art Nichols art	*$1.20*	*$3.60*	*$6.00*	£0.80	£2.40	£4.00
20 **GREENBERG THE VAMPIRE** (no number on cover), ND J.M. DeMatteis acript, Mark Badger art	*$1.20*	*$3.60*	*$6.00*	£1.00	£3.00	£5.00
21 **MARADA THE SHE-WOLF** (no number on cover), ND Chris Claremont script, Jon Bolton art	*$1.60*	*$4.80*	*$8.00*	£1.20	£3.60	£6.00
22 **THE AMAZING SPIDERMAN: HOOKEY** (no number on cover), ND Sue Putney script, Bernie Wrightson art	*$1.50*	*$4.50*	*$7.50*	£1.20	£3.60	£6.00
23 **INTO SHAMBALLA (Dr. Strange)** (no number on cover), ND J.M. DeMatteis script, Dan Green art	*$1.20*	*$3.60*	*$6.00*	£0.70	£2.10	£3.50
24 **DAREDEVIL: LOVE AND WAR** (no number on cover), ND Frank Miller script, Bill Sienkiewicz art	*$1.50*	*$4.50*	*$7.50*	£1.00	£3.00	£5.00
25 **DRACULA: A SYMPHONY IN MOONLIGHT AND NIGHTMARES** (no number on cover), ND Jon J. Muth painted art	*$1.50*	*$4.50*	*$7.50*	£1.00	£3.00	£5.00
25 2nd printing ND	*$1.00*	*$3.00*	*$5.00*	£0.70	£2.10	£3.50
26 **ALIEN LEGION** (no number on cover), ND Carl Potts script, Cirocco and Austin art	*$1.20*	*$3.60*	*$6.00*	£0.80	£2.40	£4.00
27 **EMPEROR DOOM (The Avengers)** (no number on cover), ND David Michelinie script, Bob Hall art	*$1.20*	*$3.60*	*$6.00*	£0.70	£2.10	£3.50
28 **CONAN THE REAVER** (no number on cover), ND Don Kraar script, John and Marie Severin art	*$1.20*	*$3.60*	*$6.00*	£0.80	£2.40	£4.00
29 **THE THING AND THE HULK: THE BIG CHANGE** (no number on cover), ND Jim Starlin script, Bernie Wrightson art	*$1.20*	*$3.60*	*$6.00*	£1.00	£3.00	£5.00
30 **A SAILOR'S STORY** (no number on cover), ND Sam Glanzman script and art	*$1.00*	*$3.00*	*$5.00*	£0.65	£1.95	£3.25
31 **WOLFPACK** (no number on cover), ND origin and 1st appearance Wolfpack; Larry Hama script, Ron Wilson and Kyle Baker art	*$1.40*	*$4.20*	*$7.00*	£1.00	£3.00	£5.00
32 **THE DEATH OF GROO** (no number on cover), ND (see Life of Groo further down), Mark Evanier script, Sergio Aragones art	*$1.50*	*$4.50*	*$7.50*	£1.00	£3.00	£5.00
32 2nd printing ND	*$1.20*	*$3.60*	*$6.00*	£0.70	£2.10	£3.50
33 **THOR: I'M WHO THE GODS WOULD DESTROY** (no number on cover), ND Jim Shooter script, Owsley, Ryan and Coletta art	*$1.40*	*$4.20*	*$7.00*	£0.80	£2.40	£4.00
34 **CLOAK AND DAGGER: PREDATOR AND PREY** (no number on cover), ND Bill Mantlo script, Larry Stroman and Al Williamson art	*$1.40*	*$4.20*	*$7.00*	£0.80	£2.40	£4.00
35 **THE SHADOW: HITLER'S ASTROLOGER** (no number on cover), ND Denny O'Neill script, Mike Kaluta and Russ Heath art; hardcover with dust-jacket	*$3.00*	*$9.00*	*$15.00*	£2.00	£6.00	£10.00
35 2nd printing, ND (1990) Softcover reprint	*$2.20*	*$6.50*	*$11.00*	£1.50	£4.50	£7.50
36 **WILLOW** (no number on cover), ND adaptation of film; Bob Hall and Romeo Tanghal art	*$1.20*	*$3.60*	*$6.00*	£0.70	£2.10	£3.50
37 **HERCULES: FULL CIRCLE** (no number on cover), ND Bob Layton art	*$1.20*	*$3.60*	*$6.00*	£0.70	£2.10	£3.50
38 **SILVER SURFER: JUDGEMENT DAY** (no number on cover), ND Stan Lee script, John Buscema art; hardcover with dust-jacket	*$3.00*	*$9.00*	*$15.00*	£2.00	£6.00	£10.00
nn 2nd printing, ND softcover reprint	*$1.50*	*$4.50*	*$7.50*	£1.00	£3.00	£5.00
nn 2nd printing, ND (1991) reprint	*$1.20*	*$3.60*	*$6.00*	£1.80	£5.25	£9.00
nn **CRASH: IRON MAN** ND (1988) Mike Saenz art; some violence and nudity	*$2.60*	*$7.75*	*$13.00*	£1.50	£4.50	£7.50
nn **LAST OF THE DRAGONS** ND (1988) Carl Potts and Denny O'Neill script, Terry Austin and John Severin art	*$1.20*	*$3.60*	*$6.00*	£0.70	£2.10	£3.50
nn Limited Edition, ND - signed and numbered by Ann Nocenti and John Bolton	*$6.00*	*$18.00*	*$30.00*	£4.00	£12.00	£20.00

Title	$Good	$Fine	$N.Mint	£Good	£Fine	£N.Mint
nn **SOMEPLACE STRANGE** ND (1988) Anne Nocenti script, John Bolton art	*$1.50*	*$4.50*	*$7.50*	£1.00	£3.00	£5.00
nn **THE INHUMANS** ND (1988) Anne Nocenti script, Bret Blevins and Al Williamson art	*$1.50*	*$4.50*	*$7.50*	£0.70	£2.10	£3.50
nn **THE PUNISHER: ASSASSIN'S GUILD** ND Jo Duffy script, Jorge Zaffino and Julie Michel art	*$2.00*	*$6.00*	*$10.00*	£1.20	£3.60	£6.00
nn **THE PUNISHER HARDCOVER GRAPHIC NOVEL: RETURN TO BIG NOTHING** ND Steven Grant script, Mike Zeck art; all new material	*$3.40*	*$10.00*	*$17.00*	£2.20	£6.50	£11.00
nn 2nd printing, ND softcover reprint	*$1.80*	*$5.25*	*$9.00*	£1.20	£3.60	£6.00
nn **CONAN OF THE ISLES**ND adapts Carter/de Camp novel	*$1.20*	*$3.60*	*$6.00*	£0.80	£2.40	£4.00
nn **ARENA** ND Bruce Jones story and art	*$1.20*	*$3.60*	*$6.00*	£0.70	£2.10	£3.50
nn London Editions (U.K.), distributed in the U.K. and scarce in the U.S.; comic sized	*$0.30*	*$0.90*	*$1.50*	£0.20	£0.60	£1.00
nn **WHO FRAMED ROGER RABBIT?** Marvel Edition, ND (1989) Daan Jippes script, Ferguson and Spiegle art	*$1.40*	*$4.20*	*$7.00*	£0.70	£2.10	£3.50
nn **AX** ND Ernie Colon art	*$1.00*	*$3.00*	*$5.00*	£0.65	£1.95	£3.25
nn **DREAMWALKER** ND (announced as DREAMWAEVER); Billy Mumy and Miguel Ferrer script	*$1.00*	*$3.00*	*$5.00*	£0.65	£1.95	£3.25
nn **KING KULL**ND	*$1.00*	*$3.00*	*$5.00*	£0.65	£1.95	£3.25
nn **DR. DOOM/DR. STRANGE** ND Mike Mignola and Mark Badger art; hardcover	*$3.50*	*$10.50*	*$17.50*	£2.20	£6.50	£11.00
nn 2nd printing, ND softcover reprint	*$1.50*	*$4.50*	*$7.50*	£1.00	£3.00	£5.00
nn **NICK FURY/WOLVERINE: THE SCORPIO CONNECTION** 1st printing (Hardcover), ND Howard Chaykin art; hardcover	*$3.20*	*$9.50*	*$16.00*	£2.40	£7.00	£12.00
nn 1st printing (Softcover) ND	*$1.80*	*$5.25*	*$9.00*	£1.20	£3.60	£6.00
nn 2nd printing (Hardcover), ND (1991)	*$3.00*	*$9.00*	*$15.00*	£2.00	£6.00	£10.00
nn 2nd printing (Softcover), ND (Nov 1990)	*$1.60*	*$4.80*	*$8.00*	£1.00	£3.00	£5.00
nn **A SAILOR'S STORY 2** ND Sam Glanzman script and art	*$1.00*	*$3.00*	*$5.00*	£0.65	£1.95	£3.25
nn **VOYAGER** ND John Ridgway art, reprints from Dr. Who magazine #88 and #89	*$1.20*	*$3.60*	*$6.00*	£0.80	£2.40	£4.00
nn **CONAN: THE SKULL OF SET** ND	*$1.20*	*$3.60*	*$6.00*	£0.70	£2.10	£3.50
nn **THE SQUADRON SUPREME** ND	*$1.50*	*$4.50*	*$7.50*	£0.90	£2.70	£4.50
nn **ROGER RABBIT: THE RESURRECTION OF DOOM** ND (1989)	*$1.60*	*$4.80*	*$8.00*	£0.70	£2.10	£3.50
nn **SPIDERMAN: PARALLEL LIVES** ND Dr. Octopus appears; Alex Saviuk art	*$1.20*	*$3.60*	*$6.00*	£0.80	£2.40	£4.00
nn **PUNISHER: INTRUDER** ND Mike Baron script, Bill Reinhold art; hardcover	*$3.00*	*$9.00*	*$15.00*	£2.00	£6.00	£10.00
nn **CLOAK AND DAGGER/POWER PACK** ND Bill Mantlo script, Velluto and Farmer art	*$1.20*	*$3.60*	*$6.00*	£0.80	£2.40	£4.00
nn **NEUROMANCER** ND adaptation of William Gibson novel	*$1.20*	*$3.60*	*$6.00*	£0.80	£2.40	£4.00
nn **THE AGENT** ND 80pgs, John Ridgway art (Rick Mason as The Agent)	*$1.20*	*$3.60*	*$6.00*	£0.80	£2.40	£4.00
nn **RIO** ND Doug Wildey script and art	*$1.50*	*$4.50*	*$7.50*	£1.00	£3.00	£5.00
nn **SILVER SURFER: THE ENSLAVERS** ND hardcover	*$3.50*	*$10.50*	*$17.50*	£2.50	£7.50	£12.50
nn **JHEREG** ND adaptation of Steven Brust novel	*$1.50*	*$4.50*	*$7.50*	£1.00	£3.00	£5.00
nn **CONAN: THE HORN OF AZOTH** ND	*$1.50*	*$4.50*	*$7.50*	£1.00	£3.00	£5.00
nn **BLACK WIDOW: THE COLDEST WAR** ND Daredevil and The Avengers appear	*$1.50*	*$4.50*	*$7.50*	£1.00	£3.00	£5.00
nn **KA-ZAR: GUNS OF THE SAVAGE LAND** ND Chuck Dixon script, Tim Truman art	*$1.50*	*$4.50*	*$7.50*	£1.00	£3.00	£5.00
nn **ABSALOM DAAK: DALEK KILLER** ND	*$1.80*	*$5.25*	*$9.00*	£1.20	£3.60	£6.00
nn **SPIDERMAN: SPIRITS OF THE EARTH** ND painted art by Charles Vess; hardcover	*$3.00*	*$9.00*	*$15.00*	£2.00	£6.00	£10.00
nn **PUNISHER: KINGDOM COME** ND Chuck Dixon script, Jorge Zaffino art; hardcover	*$3.00*	*$9.00*	*$15.00*	£2.00	£6.00	£10.00
nn **DEATH'S HEAD: THE BODY IN QUESTION** ND reprints Death's Head serial from Strip #13-20, Walt Simonson cover	*$1.20*	*$3.60*	*$6.00*	£0.90	£2.70	£4.50
nn **X-MEN: PRYDE OF THE X-MEN** ND (see also X-Men Trade paperbacks) based on cartoon series	*$1.50*	*$4.50*	*$7.50*	£1.00	£3.00	£5.00
nn **EXCALIBUR: WEIRD WAR III** ND	*$1.40*	*$4.20*	*$7.00*	£0.90	£2.70	£4.50
nn **ELEKTRA LIVES AGAIN** ND Frank Miller script and art; hardcover	*$5.50*	*$16.50*	*$27.50*	£3.50	£10.50	£17.50
nn 2nd printing, ND (1991)	*$5.00*	*$15.00*	*$25.00*	£3.00	£9.00	£15.00
nn **HEARTS AND MINDS** ND Doug Murray script, Russ Heath art	*$1.50*	*$4.50*	*$7.50*	£1.00	£3.00	£5.00
nn **SPIDERMAN: FEAR ITSELF** ND Gerry Conway script, Ross Andru and Mike Esposito art	*$1.60*	*$4.80*	*$8.00*	£1.10	£3.30	£5.50

	$Good	$Fine	$N.Mint	£Good	£Fine	£N.Mint
nn **WOLVERINE: BLOODY CHOICES** ND Nick Fury co-stars; Tom DeFalco script, John Buscema art	*$2.80*	*$8.25*	*$14.00*	£1.60	£4.80	£8.00
nn 2nd printing, ND (Sep 1993)	*$2.50*	*$7.50*	*$12.50*	£1.50	£4.50	£7.50
nn **AVENGERS - DEATHTRAP: THE VAULT** ND Danny Fingeroth script, Ron Lim and Ron Emberlin art	*$1.80*	*$5.25*	*$9.00*	£1.20	£3.60	£6.00
nn **NIGHTRAVEN: HOUSE OF CARDS** ND Jamie Delano script, David Lloyd art	*$2.80*	*$8.25*	*$14.00*	£1.80	£5.25	£9.00
nn **CONAN THE ROGUE** ND Roy Thomas script, John Buscema art	*$1.60*	*$4.80*	*$8.00*	£1.10	£3.30	£5.50
nn **SILVER SURFER: HOMECOMING** ND Jim Starlin script, Bill Reinhold art	*$2.40*	*$7.00*	*$12.00*	£1.60	£4.80	£8.00
nn **WAR MAN** ND Chuck Dixon script, Zanotto art	*$1.60*	*$4.80*	*$8.00*	£1.10	£3.30	£5.50
nn **PUNISHER: BLOOD ON THE MOORS** ND Alan Grant and John Wagner script, Cam Kennedy art	*$3.00*	*$9.00*	*$15.00*	£2.00	£6.00	£10.00
nn **BOY'S RANCH HARDCOVER** ND Jack Kirby and Joe Simon	*$8.00*	*$24.00*	*$40.00*	£5.00	£15.00	£25.00
nn **CONAN AND THE RAVAGERS OF TIME** ND Roy Thomas script, Docherty and Alcala art	*$1.60*	*$4.80*	*$8.00*	£1.10	£3.30	£5.50
nn **PUNISHER/BLACK WIDOW: SPINNING DOOMSDAY'S WEB** ND Larry Stroman and Mark Farmer creative team	*$1.80*	*$5.25*	*$9.00*	£1.20	£3.60	£6.00
nn **LIFE OF GROO** ND Mark Evanier script, Sergio Aragones art (May 1993 - originally solicited in 1991)	*$2.40*	*$7.00*	*$12.00*	£1.60	£4.80	£8.00
nn **DAREDEVIL/BLACK WIDOW: ABATTOIR** ND (Sep 1993) Jim Starlin script, Joe Chiodo art	*$3.00*	*$9.00*	*$15.00*	£2.00	£6.00	£10.00
Title Value:	*$199.30*	*$595.70*	*$996.50*	£134.90	£403.85	£674.50

Note: owing to their size and card covers, true near mint copies are scarce. Having said that their collectibility lies a little outside comic book collecting and Graphic Novels, particularly the later ones, can be found in many a bargain bin at conventions and marts.

MARVEL GUIDE TO COLLECTING COMICS

Marvel Comics Group,OS; 1 1982

	$Good	$Fine	$N.Mint	£Good	£Fine	£N.Mint
1 ND features on comic book collecting, first appeared in Spiderman #234, paper cover	*$0.40*	*$1.20*	*$2.00*	£0.25	£0.75	£1.25
Title Value:	*$0.40*	*$1.20*	*$2.00*	£0.25	£0.75	£1.25

MARVEL HEROES & LEGENDS

Marvel Comics Group,OS; 1 Oct 1996

	$Good	$Fine	$N.Mint	£Good	£Fine	£N.Mint
1 ND 48pgs, an artists' jam featuring Fantastic Four, Spiderman, X-Men, Avengers and Daredevil	*$0.60*	*$1.80*	*$3.00*	£0.40	£1.20	£2.00
Title Value:	*$0.60*	*$1.80*	*$3.00*	£0.40	£1.20	£2.00

MARVEL HOLIDAY SPECIAL

Marvel Comics Group; 1 Jan 1992; 2 Jan 1994; 3 Jan 1995; 4 Jan 1996

	$Good	$Fine	$N.Mint	£Good	£Fine	£N.Mint
1 ND 64pgs, squarebound; X-Men, Captain America, Fantastic Four, Thor, Spiderman, Ghost Rider and others in Xmas season stories, cover by Art Adams (Note: many copies have crinkled spines)	*$0.50*	*$1.50*	*$2.50*	£0.30	£0.90	£1.50
2 ND 64pgs, Thanos and Wolverine appear in Christmas reprints	*$0.50*	*$1.50*	*$2.50*	£0.30	£0.90	£1.50
3 ND 64pgs, X-Men, Thing, Beast and Iceman appear in Christmas reprints	*$0.50*	*$1.50*	*$2.50*	£0.30	£0.90	£1.50
4 ND 48pgs, Spiderman, Rawhide Kid and Kitty Pryde feature	*$0.60*	*$1.80*	*$3.00*	£0.40	£1.20	£2.00
Title Value:	*$2.10*	*$6.30*	*$10.50*	£1.30	£3.90	£6.50

MARVEL ILLUSTRATED BOOKS

Marvel Comics Group; nn 1982

	$Good	$Fine	$N.Mint	£Good	£Fine	£N.Mint
nn ND Frankenstein; 40 illustrations by Bernie Wrightson	*$0.90*	*$2.70*	*$4.50*	£0.60	£1.80	£3.00
Title Value:	*$0.90*	*$2.70*	*$4.50*	£0.60	£1.80	£3.00

MARVEL ILLUSTRATED SWIMSUIT SPECIAL

Marvel Comics Group,Magazine OS; nn Mar 1991

	$Good	$Fine	$N.Mint	£Good	£Fine	£N.Mint
nn ND magazine format; Lee, Guice, Nowlan, Perez and Zeck art featured	*$0.80*	*$2.40*	*$4.00*	£0.50	£1.50	£2.50
nn 2nd printing ND (Sep 1991)	*$0.80*	*$2.40*	*$4.00*	£0.50	£1.50	£2.50
Title Value:	*$1.60*	*$4.80*	*$8.00*	£1.00	£3.00	£5.00

MARVEL MASTERPIECES COLLECTION 1, THE

Marvel Comics Group,MS; 1 May 1993-4 Aug 1993

	$Good	$Fine	$N.Mint	£Good	£Fine	£N.Mint
1-4 ND Joe Jusko's Marvel Masterpieces trading cards reprinted in comic book format; each issue also has half a dozen new paintings	*$0.60*	*$1.80*	*$3.00*	£0.40	£1.20	£2.00
Title Value:	*$2.40*	*$7.20*	*$12.00*	£1.60	£4.80	£8.00

MARVEL MASTERPIECES COLLECTION 2, THE

Marvel Comics Group,MS; 1 Jul 1994-3 Sep 1994

	$Good	$Fine	$N.Mint	£Good	£Fine	£N.Mint
1-3 ND reprints another collection of Marvel trading cards	*$0.50*	*$1.50*	*$2.50*	£0.30	£0.90	£1.50
Title Value:	*$1.50*	*$4.50*	*$7.50*	£0.90	£2.70	£4.50

MARVEL MASTERPIECES PREVIEW

Marvel Comics Group,OS; nn Dec 1995

	$Good	$Fine	$N.Mint	£Good	£Fine	£N.Mint
nn ND previews Fleer's painted trading card set	*$0.60*	*$1.80*	*$3.00*	£0.40	£1.20	£2.00
Title Value:	*$0.60*	*$1.80*	*$3.00*	£0.40	£1.20	£2.00

MARVEL MASTERWORKS

Marvel Comics Group; 1 Nov 1987-27 1994

	$Good	$Fine	$N.Mint	£Good	£Fine	£N.Mint
1 less common in the U.K. Spiderman #1-#10, Amazing Fantasy #15 (1st printing)	*$9.00*	*$27.00*	*$45.00*	£6.00	£18.00	£30.00
1 2nd printing	*$7.50*	*$22.50*	*$37.50*	£5.00	£15.00	£25.00
1 softcover, (May 1992), Spiderman #1-#10, Amazing Fantasy #15	*$2.50*	*$7.50*	*$12.50*	£1.50	£4.50	£7.50
1 softcover 2nd printing, (May 1993), Spiderman #1-#10, Amazing Fantasy #15	*$2.50*	*$7.50*	*$12.50*	£1.50	£4.50	£7.50
1 subsequent printings, (3rd-7th) (7th print in Oct 1994)	*$6.00*	*$18.00*	*$30.00*	£4.00	£12.00	£20.00
2 Fantastic Four #1-#10	*$7.50*	*$22.50*	*$37.50*	£5.00	£15.00	£25.00
3 X-Men #1-#10	*$6.00*	*$18.00*	*$30.00*	£4.00	£12.00	£20.00
3 2nd printing, (Jun 1994) X-Men #1-#10	*$6.00*	*$18.00*	*$30.00*	£4.00	£12.00	£20.00
3 softcover, (Apr 1993), X-Men #1-#5, new intro by Stan Lee	*$2.50*	*$7.50*	*$12.50*	£1.50	£4.50	£7.50
4 Avengers #1-#10	*$6.00*	*$18.00*	*$30.00*	£4.00	£12.00	£20.00
4 softcover, (Dec 1993), Avengers #1-5	*$2.50*	*$7.50*	*$12.50*	£1.50	£4.50	£7.50
5 Spiderman #11-#20	*$6.00*	*$18.00*	*$30.00*	£4.00	£12.00	£20.00
6 Fantastic Four #11-#20	*$6.00*	*$18.00*	*$30.00*	£4.00	£12.00	£20.00
7 X-Men #11-#21	*$6.00*	*$18.00*	*$30.00*	£4.00	£12.00	£20.00
8 Incredible Hulk #1-#6	*$6.00*	*$18.00*	*$30.00*	£4.00	£12.00	£20.00
9 Avengers #11-#20	*$6.00*	*$18.00*	*$30.00*	£4.00	£12.00	£20.00
10 Spiderman #21-#30, Annual #1	*$6.00*	*$18.00*	*$30.00*	£4.00	£12.00	£20.00
11 Giant Size X-Men #1, X-Men #94-#100	*$6.00*	*$18.00*	*$30.00*	£4.00	£12.00	£20.00
11 2nd printing, , Giant Size X-Men #1, X-Men #94-97 (Oct 1993); titled "X-Men: All New, All Different X-Men Masterworks Vol. 1"	*$2.50*	*$7.50*	*$12.50*	£1.50	£4.50	£7.50
12 X-Men #101-#110	*$6.00*	*$18.00*	*$30.00*	£4.00	£12.00	£20.00
13 Fantastic Four #21-#30, Annual #1	*$6.00*	*$18.00*	*$30.00*	£4.00	£12.00	£20.00

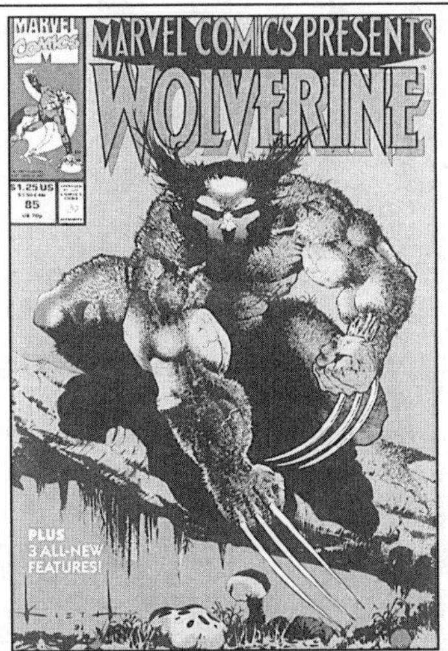

Marvel Comics Presents #85

Marvel Fanfare (1st) #60

Marvel Feature (1st) #4

Issue	$Good	$Fine	$N.Mint	£Good	£Fine	£N.Mint
14 Tales of Suspense #59-#81	$6.00	$18.00	$30.00	£4.00	£12.00	£20.00
15 Silver Surfer #1-#5	$6.00	$18.00	$30.00	£4.00	£12.00	£20.00
16 Spiderman #31-#40, Annual #2	$6.00	$18.00	$30.00	£4.00	£12.00	£20.00
17 Daredevil #1-#11	$6.00	$18.00	$30.00	£4.00	£12.00	£20.00
18 Journey Into Mystery #83-#100	$6.00	$18.00	$30.00	£4.00	£12.00	£20.00
19 Silver Surfer #6-#18	$8.50	$26.00	$42.50	£5.50	£16.50	£27.50
20 Tales of Suspense #39-#50	$6.00	$18.00	$30.00	£4.00	£12.00	£20.00
21 Fantastic Four #31-#40, Annual #2	$6.00	$18.00	$30.00	£4.00	£12.00	£20.00
22 Spiderman #41-#50, Annual #3	$6.00	$18.00	$30.00	£4.00	£12.00	£20.00
23 Strange Tales #110,#111,#114-141	$7.50	$22.50	$37.50	£5.00	£15.00	£25.00
24 Uncanny X-Men #111-120	$7.50	$22.50	$37.50	£5.00	£15.00	£25.00
25 Fantastic Four #41-50, Annual #3	$7.50	$22.50	$37.50	£5.00	£15.00	£25.00
26 Journey Into Mystery #101-110	$7.50	$22.50	$37.50	£5.00	£15.00	£25.00
27 Avengers #21-30	$7.50	$22.50	$37.50	£5.00	£15.00	£25.00
Title Value:	$208.50	$626.00	$1042.50	£138.00	£414.00	£690.00

Note: coffee-table high quality reprint books. Originally came shrink-wrapped in plastic and would perhaps command 10%more if unopened. The original stories have been re-coloured throughout. There are 2nd printings of 1-13 and 3rd printings of 1-4 available at much the same values. 4th printing Volume 1,2 in Dec 1992.

MARVEL MINI BOOKS

Marvel Comics Group; nn 1966

Issue	$Good	$Fine	$N.Mint	£Good	£Fine	£N.Mint
nn ND very scarce in the U.K. (six un-numbered issues): Captain America, Spiderman, Hulk, Millie the Model, Thor and Sgt. Fury	$5.00	$15.00	$35.00	£3.55	£10.50	£25.00
Title Value:	$5.00	$15.00	$35.00	£3.55	£10.50	£25.00

Note: all 22mm x 16mm: smallest comic books ever?

MARVEL MINI COMICS

Marvel Comics Group; nn Aug 1989

Issue	$Good	$Fine	$N.Mint	£Good	£Fine	£N.Mint
nn ND Spiderman, X-Men, Alf and Flintstone Kids comics available	$0.15	$0.45	$0.75	£0.10	£0.35	£0.60
Title Value:	$0.15	$0.45	$0.75	£0.10	£0.35	£0.60

Note: all intended for U.S. schools. Amazing Spiderman #1 is reprinted in the Spiderman comic as the 2nd story

MARVEL MOVIE PREMIERE

Marvel Comics Group,Magazine; 1 Sep 1975

Issue	$Good	$Fine	$N.Mint	£Good	£Fine	£N.Mint
1 ND scarce in the U.K. 68pgs, adapts Burroughs' Land That Time Forgot	$1.25	$3.75	$7.50	£1.00	£3.00	£6.00
Title Value:	$1.25	$3.75	$7.50	£1.00	£3.00	£6.00

MARVEL MOVIE SHOWCASE

Marvel Comics Group; 1 Nov 1982-2 Dec 1982

Issue	$Good	$Fine	$N.Mint	£Good	£Fine	£N.Mint
1 ND 68pgs, reprints Star Wars #1-3	$0.40	$1.20	$2.00	£0.25	£0.75	£1.25
2 ND 68pgs, reprints Star Wars #4-6	$0.40	$1.20	$2.00	£0.25	£0.75	£1.25
Title Value:	$0.80	$2.40	$4.00	£0.50	£1.50	£2.50

MARVEL MOVIE SPOTLIGHT

Marvel Comics Group; 1 Nov 1982

Issue	$Good	$Fine	$N.Mint	£Good	£Fine	£N.Mint
1 ND 68pgs, reprints Raiders of the Lost Ark	$0.40	$1.20	$2.00	£0.25	£0.75	£1.25
Title Value:	$0.40	$1.20	$2.00	£0.25	£0.75	£1.25

MARVEL MYSTERY #1 HARDCOVER

Marvel Comics Group; nn Dec 1990

Issue	$Good	$Fine	$N.Mint	£Good	£Fine	£N.Mint
nn Hardcover ND reprints in full the first Marvel comic in the Golden Age with the Human Torch and Sub-Mariner	$2.50	$7.50	$12.50	£1.50	£4.50	£7.50
Title Value:	$2.50	$7.50	$12.50	£1.50	£4.50	£7.50

MARVEL NO-PRIZE BOOK, THE

Marvel Comics Group,OS; 1 Jan 1983

Issue	$Good	$Fine	$N.Mint	£Good	£Fine	£N.Mint
1 ND Marvel's mistakes, Michael Golden Stan Lee/Dr.Doom cover	$0.30	$0.90	$1.50	£0.20	£0.60	£1.00
Title Value:	$0.30	$0.90	$1.50	£0.20	£0.60	£1.00

MARVEL PREMIERE

Marvel Comics Group; 1 Apr 1972-61 Aug 1981

Issue	$Good	$Fine	$N.Mint	£Good	£Fine	£N.Mint
1 ND origin Warlock by Gil Kane, first appearance as a super-hero; Thor, Hulk and Fantastic Four cameos (pre-dates Warlock #1)	$7.00	$21.00	$50.00	£5.00	£15.00	£35.00
2 ND Warlock, Gil Kane art, Jack Kirby reprint	$4.15	$12.50	$25.00	£2.50	£7.50	£15.00
3 ND Dr. Strange begins, Barry Smith art	$4.55	$13.50	$27.50	£2.90	£8.75	£17.50
4 ND Smith/Brunner art	$2.05	$6.25	$12.50	£1.25	£3.75	£7.50
5 ND	$1.50	$4.50	$9.00	£1.00	£3.00	£6.00
6 ND Brunner art	$1.25	$3.75	$7.50	£0.80	£2.50	£5.00
7 ND P. Craig Russell art	$1.25	$3.75	$7.50	£0.80	£2.50	£5.00
8 ND Jim Starlin/P. Craig Russell art	$1.25	$3.75	$7.50	£0.80	£2.50	£5.00
9 ND Brunner art	$1.25	$3.75	$7.50	£0.80	£2.50	£5.00
10 ND Brunner art, death of The Ancient One	$1.65	$5.00	$10.00	£1.00	£3.00	£6.00
11 ND reprints Dr. Strange origin by Steve Ditko	$0.80	$2.50	$5.00	£0.65	£2.00	£4.00
12-13 ND Brunner art	$0.80	$2.50	$5.00	£0.65	£2.00	£4.00
14 ND Frank Brunner, Neal Adams art	$0.80	$2.50	$5.00	£0.65	£2.00	£4.00
15 ND origin and 1st appearance of Iron Fist; Gil Kane art	$8.50	$26.00	$60.00	£5.00	£15.00	£35.00
16 ND 2nd appearance Iron Fist	$3.30	$10.00	$20.00	£2.05	£6.25	£12.50
17 ND	$2.50	$7.50	$15.00	£1.65	£5.00	£10.00
18-20 ND	$2.50	$7.50	$15.00	£1.00	£3.00	£6.00
21 ND scarce in the U.K.	$2.50	$7.50	$15.00	£1.05	£3.25	£6.50
22	$2.50	$7.50	$15.00	£0.80	£2.50	£5.00
23 ND scarce in the U.K.	$2.50	$7.50	$15.00	£1.00	£3.00	£6.00
24	$2.50	$7.50	$15.00	£0.80	£2.50	£5.00
25 ND John Byrne art on Iron Fist (1st)	$2.90	$8.75	$17.50	£1.65	£5.00	£10.00
26 Hercules	$0.80	$2.50	$5.00	£0.30	£1.00	£2.00
27 Satana, Daughter of Satan	$0.80	$2.50	$5.00	£0.30	£1.00	£2.00
28 Legion of Monsters - Ghost Rider, Werewolf, Man-Thing and Morbius (on cover also)	$1.65	$5.00	$10.00	£0.80	£2.50	£5.00
29 Liberty Legion, ties into Invaders #6	$0.30	$1.00	$2.00	£0.25	£0.75	£1.50
30 Liberty Legion	$0.30	$1.00	$2.00	£0.25	£0.75	£1.50
31 Woodgod, Giffen art	$0.30	$1.00	$2.00	£0.20	£0.60	£1.25
32 Monark Moonstalker, Chaykin art	$0.30	$1.00	$2.00	£0.20	£0.60	£1.25
33-34 Solomon Kane, Chaykin art	$0.30	$1.00	$2.00	£0.20	£0.60	£1.25
35 ND 1st appearance 3-D Man	$0.30	$1.00	$2.00	£0.20	£0.60	£1.25
36-37 ND 3-D Man	$0.30	$1.00	$2.00	£0.20	£0.60	£1.25
38 Weirdworld, Ploog art	$0.30	$1.00	$2.00	£0.20	£0.60	£1.25
39-40 The Torpedo	$0.30	$1.00	$2.00	£0.20	£0.60	£1.25
41 Seeker 3000	$0.30	$1.00	$2.00	£0.20	£0.60	£1.25
42 Tigra	$0.30	$1.00	$2.00	£0.20	£0.60	£1.25
43 Paladin	$0.30	$1.00	$2.00	£0.20	£0.60	£1.25
44 Jack of Hearts (1st solo story); some Giffen art	$0.30	$1.00	$2.00	£0.20	£0.60	£1.25
45-46 Man-Wolf, George Perez art	$0.30	$1.00	$2.00	£0.20	£0.60	£1.25
47 1st new Ant-Man, John Byrne art	$0.30	$1.00	$2.00	£0.20	£0.60	£1.25
48 Byrne art, Ant-Man	$0.30	$1.00	$2.00	£0.20	£0.60	£1.25
49 The Falcon; Captain America appears	$0.30	$1.00	$2.00	£0.20	£0.60	£1.25
50 Alice Cooper	$0.80	$2.50	$5.00	£0.55	£1.75	£3.50
51-53 Black Panther	$0.30	$1.00	$2.00	£0.20	£0.60	£1.25
54 Caleb Hammer, Chaykin art	$0.30	$1.00	$2.00	£0.20	£0.60	£1.25
55 Wonder Man	$0.30	$1.00	$2.00	£0.20	£0.60	£1.25
56 Dominic Fortune, Chaykin art	$0.30	$1.00	$2.00	£0.20	£0.60	£1.25
57 Dr. Who (1st U.S. appearance), Gibbons reprints begin, Simonson cover	$0.40	$1.25	$2.50	£0.25	£0.75	£1.50
58 ND Dr. Who	$0.30	$1.00	$2.00	£0.20	£0.60	£1.25
59 ND Dr. Who; Werewolf back-up story by Steven Grant	$0.30	$1.00	$2.00	£0.20	£0.60	£1.25
60 ND Dr. Who; Walt Simonson art on pin-ups	$0.30	$1.00	$2.00	£0.20	£0.60	£1.25
61 Starlord	$0.30	$1.00	$2.00	£0.20	£0.60	£1.25
Title Value:	$77.55	$237.25	$491.00	£44.95	£136.40	£284.25

FEATURES

Black Panther in 51-53. Caleb Hammer in 54. Dominic Fortune in 56. Falcon in 49. Jack of Hearts in 44. Paladin in 43. Seeker 3000 in 41. 3-D Man in 35-37. Tigra in 42. Torpedo in 39, 40. Wonder Man in 55.

MARVEL PRESENTS

Marvel Comics Group; 1 Oct 1975-12 Aug 1977

Issue	$Good	$Fine	$N.Mint	£Good	£Fine	£N.Mint
1 1st appearance Bloodstone	$0.75	$2.25	$4.50	£0.50	£1.50	£3.00
2 Bloodstone origin	$0.55	$1.75	$3.50	£0.30	£1.00	£2.00
3 Guardians of the Galaxy begin, Steve Gerber scripts begin	$2.50	$7.50	$15.00	£1.00	£3.00	£6.00
4 Guardians of the Galaxy	$1.65	$5.00	$10.00	£0.80	£2.50	£5.00
5 Guardians of the Galaxy	$1.65	$5.00	$10.00	£0.65	£2.00	£4.00
6-7 Guardians of the Galaxy	$1.65	$5.00	$10.00	£0.55	£1.75	£3.50

Issue	$Good	$Fine	$N.Mint	£Good	£Fine	£N.Mint
8 Guardians of the Galaxy, Silver Surfer part reprint (issue 2, 1st series)	$1.80	$5.50	$11.00	£0.55	£1.75	£3.50
9 Guardians of the Galaxy	$1.65	$5.00	$10.00	£0.55	£1.75	£3.50
10 ND Guardians of the Galaxy, part Jim Starlin art	$1.65	$5.00	$10.00	£0.65	£2.00	£4.00
11-12 ND Guardians of the Galaxy	$1.65	$5.00	$10.00	£0.65	£2.00	£4.00
Title Value:	$18.80	$57.00	$114.00	£7.40	£23.00	£46.00

MARVEL PREVIEW

Marvel Comics Group, Magazine; 1 1975-24 Feb 1981
(becomes Bizarre Adventures)

Issue	$Good	$Fine	$N.Mint	£Good	£Fine	£N.Mint
1 scarce in the U.K. 82pgs, squarebound, Man Gods from Beyond the Stars; Doug Moench script, Alex Nino art; Neal Adams art on cover; all black and white art from now on	$0.50	$1.50	$3.00	£0.40	£1.25	£2.50
2 LD in the U.K. 82pgs, squarebound; origin The Punisher, 1st appearance Dominic Fortune (Chaykin art)	$19.00	$57.50	$115.00	£6.50	£20.00	£40.00
3 82pgs, squarebound, Blade the Vampire Slayer	$0.40	$1.25	$2.50	£0.25	£0.75	£1.50
4 74pgs, squarebound, 1st appearance Starlord, Steve Englehart script	$0.40	$1.25	$2.50	£0.25	£0.75	£1.50
5 Sherlock Holmes; adaptation of Hound of the Baskervilles by Doug Moench and Val Mayerik	$0.40	$1.25	$2.50	£0.25	£0.75	£1.50
6 Sherlock Holmes	$0.40	$1.25	$2.50	£0.25	£0.75	£1.50
7 Satana by Nasser and Sword in the Star by Giffen	$0.40	$1.25	$2.50	£0.25	£0.75	£1.50
8 Legion of Monsters (featuring Morbius and Blade), Colan/Ploog art; Sword in the Star by Giffen	$1.30	$4.00	$8.00	£0.50	£1.50	£3.00
9 Man-God by Roy Thomas and Tony DeZuniga; Earl Norem painted cover	$0.40	$1.25	$2.50	£0.25	£0.75	£1.50
10 Thor, Jim Starlin art; Hercules back-up story	$0.40	$1.25	$2.50	£0.25	£0.75	£1.50
11 Starlord; Chris Claremont script, John Byrne art	$0.40	$1.25	$2.50	£0.25	£0.75	£1.50
12 Haunt of Horror featuring Dracula; Lilith story has 2pgs of George Perez art	$0.40	$1.25	$2.50	£0.25	£0.75	£1.50
13 UFO Connection; Jim Starlin cover	$0.40	$1.25	$2.50	£0.25	£0.75	£1.50
14 Starlord; Carmine Infantino art and Jim Starlin cover	$0.40	$1.25	$2.50	£0.25	£0.75	£1.50
15 Starlord; Carmine Infantino art and Joe Jusko cover	$0.40	$1.25	$2.50	£0.25	£0.75	£1.50
16 Masters of Terror featuring Hodiah Twist and Lilith	$0.40	$1.25	$2.50	£0.25	£0.75	£1.50
17 Black Mark by Gil Kane	$0.40	$1.25	$2.50	£0.25	£0.75	£1.50
18 ND Starlord	$0.40	$1.25	$2.50	£0.25	£0.75	£1.50
19 ND Kull by Buscema/DeZuniga	$0.40	$1.25	$2.50	£0.25	£0.75	£1.50
20 ND Bizarre Adventures featuring Dominic Fortune; Howard Chaykin cover and art	$0.40	$1.25	$2.50	£0.25	£0.75	£1.50
21 ND Moon Knight, Sienkiewicz art; The Shroud back-up story by Steve Ditko	$0.80	$2.50	$5.00	£0.55	£1.75	£3.50
22 ND Merlin by Doug Moench and John Buscema; Earl Norem painted cover	$0.40	$1.25	$2.50	£0.25	£0.75	£1.50
23 ND Bizarre Adventures; Frank Miller art	$0.80	$2.50	$5.00	£0.55	£1.75	£3.50
24 ND 1st appearance Paradox; Val Mayerik art, Paul Gulacy cover	$0.40	$1.25	$2.50	£0.25	£0.75	£1.50
Title Value:	$30.00	$91.75	$183.50	£13.25	£40.50	£81.00

ARTISTS
Adams art in 6 (1pg). Ditko in 21. Ploog in 8. Wrightson in 4 (1pg).

MARVEL PREVIEW 1993

Marvel Comics Group, Magazine OS; 1 Mar 1993

Issue	$Good	$Fine	$N.Mint	£Good	£Fine	£N.Mint
1 ND 48pgs, previews The Infinity Crusade and X-Men's 30th anniversary comics	$0.60	$1.80	$3.00	£0.40	£1.20	£2.00
Title Value:	$0.60	$1.80	$3.00	£0.40	£1.20	£2.00

MARVEL RIOT

Marvel Comics Group, OS; 1 Dec 1995

Issue	$Good	$Fine	$N.Mint	£Good	£Fine	£N.Mint
1 ND X-Men Age of Apocalypse spoof by Scott Lobdell, wraparound cover by Hilary Barta	$0.30	$0.90	$1.50	£0.20	£0.60	£1.00
Title Value:	$0.30	$0.90	$1.50	£0.20	£0.60	£1.00

MARVEL SAGA, THE

Marvel Comics Group; 1 Dec 1985-25 Dec 1987

Issue	$Good	$Fine	$N.Mint	£Good	£Fine	£N.Mint
1 ND new cameo origins of the major Marvel characters (5pgs); also part reprint Fantastic Four #1 and #2, Tales to Astonish #27 and reprint origin Guardian from Alpha Flight #12	$0.50	$1.50	$2.50	£0.30	£0.90	£1.50
2 ND part reprints of Spiderman's origin from Amazing Fantasy #15, Hulk's origin from Hulk #1 and Sub-Mariner from Fantastic Four #4	$0.40	$1.20	$2.00	£0.25	£0.75	£1.25
3 ND origin Dr. Doom re-told and history of Sub-Mariner from a variety of part reprints, conclusion origin Spiderman part reprinted from Amazing Fantasy #15	$0.40	$1.20	$2.00	£0.25	£0.75	£1.25
4 ND origin and history of X-Men re-told from a variety of reprint sources, origin Thor part reprint Journey into Mystery #83, origin Ant-Man in costume from Tales to Astonish #35	$0.40	$1.20	$2.00	£0.25	£0.75	£1.25
5 ND part reprints Fantastic Four #6,#7, Hulk #3, Strange Tales #101; origins Angel, Iceman and Loki from a variety of reprint sources	$0.40	$1.20	$2.00	£0.25	£0.75	£1.25
6 ND origins of Iron Man, Odin, Asgard and the Puppet Master from a variety of reprint sources; origins Iceman and Cyclops reprinted from X-Men 44-46	$0.40	$1.20	$2.00	£0.25	£0.75	£1.25
7 ND part reprint Spiderman #1, Iron Man's origin continued from Tales of Suspense #39; part reprints F.F. #9, Hulk #4, Strange Tales #103	$0.40	$1.20	$2.00	£0.25	£0.75	£1.25
8 ND continued part reprint Spiderman #1, part reprint F.F. 9-12, Hulk #6, Tales of Suspense #40; 3pgs new art by Bill Sienkiewicz Angel vs. Cyclops	$0.40	$1.20	$2.00	£0.25	£0.75	£1.25
9 ND origin Vulture, Wasp, Watcher and Dr. Octopus from part reprints; 4pgs new art by Steve Geiger Angel vs. Cyclops	$0.40	$1.20	$2.00	£0.25	£0.75	£1.25
10 ND origin Dr. Strange part reprint from Strange Tales #110, origins Jean Grey (Marvel Girl), Lizard, X-Men and Avengers from part reprints	$0.40	$1.20	$2.00	£0.25	£0.75	£1.25
11 ND 1st appearance Magneto part reprint from X-Men #1, origin Molecule Man from F.F. #20	$0.30	$0.90	$1.50	£0.20	£0.60	£1.00
12 ND history of Captain America reprinted from various including Avengers #4	$0.30	$0.90	$1.50	£0.20	£0.60	£1.00
13 ND history and origins Daredevil and Elektra from various part repints including Miller art	$0.30	$0.90	$1.50	£0.20	£0.60	£1.00
14 ND origin and 1st appearance Green Goblin part reprinted from Spiderman #14 and #40, F.F. meet the X-Men from F.F. #28	$0.30	$0.90	$1.50	£0.20	£0.60	£1.00
15 ND origins Hawkeye and Wonderman part reprinted	$0.30	$0.90	$1.50	£0.20	£0.60	£1.00
16 ND X-Men vs. Avengers part reprint from X-Men #9	$0.30	$0.90	$1.50	£0.20	£0.60	£1.00
17 ND origins Ka-Zar, The Leader and The Inhumans part reprint	$0.30	$0.90	$1.50	£0.20	£0.60	£1.00
18 ND origin Nick Fury Agent of Shield part reprint, 1st cameo Mary Jane Watson	$0.30	$0.90	$1.50	£0.20	£0.60	£1.00
19 ND 1st new Avengers line-up reprint	$0.30	$0.90	$1.50	£0.20	£0.60	£1.00
20 ND part reprint F.F. #39,#40 (powerless FF vs. Dr. Doom)	$0.30	$0.90	$1.50	£0.20	£0.60	£1.00
21 ND part reprint X-men vs. Juggernaut	$0.30	$0.90	$1.50	£0.20	£0.60	£1.00
22 ND scarce in the U.K. history in reprint of Mary Jane Watson leading up to her marriage to Peter Parker (Spiderman)	$0.30	$0.90	$1.50	£0.20	£0.60	£1.00
23 ND Reed Richards/Sue Storm wedding from F.F. Annual #3, Inhumans saga from F.F. #44-#47	$0.30	$0.90	$1.50	£0.20	£0.60	£1.00
24 ND origin Galactus re-told in reprint history	$0.30	$0.90	$1.50	£0.20	£0.60	£1.00
25 ND scarce in the U.K. origin Silver Surfer re-told in reprint history, Galactus appears	$0.40	$1.20	$2.00	£0.25	£0.75	£1.25
Title Value:	$8.70	$26.10	$43.50	£5.60	£16.80	£28.00

Note: reprints edited 1960s material in chronological order detailing origins and events in the Marvel Universe.

MARVEL SPECTACULAR

Marvel Comics Group; 1 Aug 1973-19 Nov 1975

Issue	$Good	$Fine	$N.Mint	£Good	£Fine	£N.Mint
1 ND scarce in the U.K. Jack Kirby Thor reprints begin (selected issues from Thor #128 on)	$0.50	$1.50	$3.00	£0.40	£1.25	£2.50
2-5	$0.40	$1.25	$2.50	£0.30	£1.00	£2.00
6-10	$0.30	$1.00	$2.00	£0.25	£0.75	£1.50
11-19	$0.30	$1.00	$2.00	£0.20	£0.60	£1.25
Title Value:	$6.30	$20.50	$41.00	£4.65	£14.40	£29.25

MARVEL SPOTLIGHT

Marvel Comics Group; 1 Nov 1971-33 Apr 1977

Issue	$Good	$Fine	$N.Mint	£Good	£Fine	£N.Mint
1 ND origin of Red Wolf (see Avengers #80), Wood inks, Neal Adams cover	$3.75	$11.00	$22.50	£2.50	£7.50	£15.00
2 ND 52pgs, 1st origin and appearance of Werewolf by Night, Ploog art; Venus reprint	$7.50	$22.50	$45.00	£4.55	£13.50	£27.50
3 ND 2nd appearance Werewolf, Ploog art	$2.50	$7.50	$15.00	£1.65	£5.00	£10.00
4 ND 3rd appearance Werewolf, Ploog art	$2.05	$6.25	$12.50	£1.25	£3.75	£7.50
5 ND scarce in the U.K. origin and 1st appearance Ghost Rider (super-hero)	$15.50	$47.00	$110.00	£7.00	£21.00	£50.00
6 ND 2nd appearance Ghost Rider, Ploog art	$7.50	$22.50	$45.00	£3.30	£10.00	£20.00
7 ND 3rd appearance Ghost Rider, Ploog art	$7.50	$22.50	$45.00	£1.65	£5.00	£10.00
8-11 Ghost Rider	$7.50	$22.50	$45.00	£1.15	£3.50	£7.00
12 origin and 1st full appearance Son of Satan (see Ghost Rider #2)	$1.65	$5.00	$10.00	£1.00	£3.00	£6.00
13 3rd full appearance Son of Satan (see Ghost Rider #3)	$0.80	$2.50	$5.00	£0.55	£1.75	£3.50
14 ND 4th appearance Son of Satan	$0.80	$2.50	$5.00	£0.55	£1.75	£3.50
15-19 ND	$0.80	$2.50	$5.00	£0.55	£1.75	£3.50
20 ND scarce in the U.K.	$0.80	$2.50	$5.00	£0.65	£2.00	£4.00
21 ND	$0.80	$2.50	$5.00	£0.50	£1.50	£3.00
22 ND Ghost Rider appears (cameo)	$1.25	$3.75	$7.50	£0.50	£1.50	£3.00
23 ND	$0.80	$2.50	$5.00	£0.50	£1.50	£3.00
24 ND last of Son of Satan series	$0.80	$2.50	$5.00	£0.50	£1.50	£3.00
25 ND Sinbad	$0.50	$1.50	$3.00	£0.30	£1.00	£2.00
26 Scarecrow	$0.50	$1.50	$3.00	£0.30	£1.00	£2.00
27 Sub-Mariner	$0.50	$1.50	$3.00	£0.30	£1.00	£2.00
28 Moon Knight (1st solo; see Werewolf by Night)	$1.65	$5.00	$10.00	£0.80	£2.50	£5.00

	$Good	$Fine	$N.Mint	£Good	£Fine	£N.Mint
29 Moon Knight (2nd solo; see Werewolf by Night), Kirby cover	$1.65	$5.00	$10.00	£0.65	£2.00	£4.00
30 Warriors Three	$0.40	$1.25	$2.50	£0.25	£0.75	£1.50
31 Nick Fury's longevity explained by Jim Starlin, Chaykin art	$0.40	$1.25	$2.50	£0.25	£0.75	£1.50
32 ND origin (true origin) and 1st appearance of Spiderwoman, Nick Fury appears	$1.30	$4.00	$8.00	£0.80	£2.50	£5.00
33 ND Deathlok, Devil-Slayer	$0.80	$2.50	$5.00	£0.50	£1.50	£3.00
Title Value:	$95.70	$289.00	$579.50	£38.15	£116.00	£240.50

MARVEL SPOTLIGHT (2ND SERIES)

Marvel Comics Group; 1 Jul 1979-11 Mar 1981

	$Good	$Fine	$N.Mint	£Good	£Fine	£N.Mint
1 Captain Marvel, Drax the Destroyer, Broderick art	$0.30	$1.00	$2.00	£0.20	£0.60	£1.25
2 Captain Marvel, Drax the Destroyer, Broderick art; Frank Miller cover	$0.25	$0.75	$1.50	£0.15	£0.50	£1.00
3 Captain Marvel, Broderick art	$0.25	$0.75	$1.50	£0.15	£0.50	£1.00
4 Captain Marvel	$0.25	$0.75	$1.50	£0.15	£0.50	£1.00
5 Dragonlord, Frank Miller cover	$0.25	$0.75	$1.50	£0.15	£0.50	£1.00
6 Starlord	$0.25	$0.75	$1.50	£0.15	£0.50	£1.00
7 Starlord, Miller cover	$0.25	$0.75	$1.50	£0.15	£0.50	£1.00
8 ND Captain Marvel, Frank Miller art	$0.25	$0.75	$1.50	£0.30	£1.00	£2.00
9 Captain Universe (see Spectacular Spiderman #158)	$0.25	$0.75	$1.50	£0.15	£0.50	£1.00
10-11 Captain Universe	$0.25	$0.75	$1.50	£0.15	£0.50	£1.00
Title Value:	$2.80	$8.50	$17.00	£1.85	£6.10	£12.25

Note: Spiderman's brief cosmic power derived from Captain Universe (see Spectacular Spiderman #158)

ARTISTS

Ditko in 4, 5, 9-11.

MARVEL SPOTLIGHT ON CAPTAIN AMERICA

Marvel Comics Group,MS; 1-4 Mar 1995

	$Good	$Fine	$N.Mint	£Good	£Fine	£N.Mint
1-4 ND 48pgs, classic reprints on glossy stock paper, weekly issues	$0.60	$1.80	$3.00	£0.40	£1.20	£2.00
Title Value:	$2.40	$7.20	$12.00	£1.60	£4.80	£8.00

MARVEL SPOTLIGHT ON DOCTOR STRANGE

Marvel Comics Group,MS; 1-4 Apr 1995

	$Good	$Fine	$N.Mint	£Good	£Fine	£N.Mint
1-4 ND 48pgs, classic reprints; weekly issues	$0.60	$1.80	$3.00	£0.40	£1.20	£2.00
Title Value:	$2.40	$7.20	$12.00	£1.60	£4.80	£8.00

MARVEL SPOTLIGHT ON SILVER SURFER

Marvel Comics Group,MS; 1-4 May 1995

	$Good	$Fine	$N.Mint	£Good	£Fine	£N.Mint
1-4 ND 48pgs, classic reprints; weekly issues	$0.60	$1.80	$3.00	£0.40	£1.20	£2.00
Title Value:	$2.40	$7.20	$12.00	£1.60	£4.80	£8.00

MARVEL SPRING SPECIAL

Marvel Comics Group,Magazine OS; 1 1989

(see Elvira)

	$Good	$Fine	$N.Mint	£Good	£Fine	£N.Mint
1 ND adaptation of Elvira The Movie	$0.50	$1.50	$2.50	£0.30	£0.90	£1.50
Title Value:	$0.50	$1.50	$2.50	£0.30	£0.90	£1.50

MARVEL SUPER ACTION

Marvel Comics Group,Magazine OS; 1 May 1976

	$Good	$Fine	$N.Mint	£Good	£Fine	£N.Mint
1 LD in the U.K. 72pgs, origin Dominic Fortune (Chaykin story/art) Punisher appears, 1st Weirdworld, Evans, Ploog art	$7.75	$23.50	$55.00	£3.55	£10.50	£25.00
Title Value:	$7.75	$23.50	$55.00	£3.55	£10.50	£25.00

MARVEL SUPER ACTION (2ND SERIES)

Marvel Comics Group; 1 May 1977-37 Nov 1981

	$Good	$Fine	$N.Mint	£Good	£Fine	£N.Mint
1 ND reprints Captain America #100	$0.65	$2.00	$4.00	£0.40	£1.25	£2.50
2-3 ND	$0.40	$1.25	$2.50	£0.30	£1.00	£2.00
4 ND Marvel Boy (now Quasar) #1 reprinted	$0.40	$1.25	$2.50	£0.30	£1.00	£2.00
5 ND	$0.40	$1.25	$2.50	£0.30	£1.00	£2.00
6-11 ND	$0.30	$1.00	$2.00	£0.25	£0.75	£1.50
12 reprints Captain America #110 (Steranko art)	$0.30	$1.00	$2.00	£0.20	£0.60	£1.25
13 reprints Captain America #111 (Steranko art)	$0.30	$1.00	$2.00	£0.20	£0.60	£1.25
14-20 ND Avengers reprints	$0.25	$0.75	$1.50	£0.25	£0.75	£1.50
21-30 ND Avengers reprints	$0.25	$0.75	$1.50	£0.20	£0.60	£1.25
31-37 Avengers reprints	$0.25	$0.75	$1.50	£0.15	£0.50	£1.00
Title Value:	$10.65	$33.00	$66.00	£8.30	£25.70	£52.00

Note: early Captain America and Avengers reprints.

REPRINT FEATURES

Avengers in 14-38. Captain America in 1-13.

MARVEL SUPER SPECIAL

Marvel Comics Group,Magazine,Film; 1 Sep 1977-41 Nov 1986

	$Good	$Fine	$N.Mint	£Good	£Fine	£N.Mint
1 ND scarce in the U.K. 66pgs, Kiss; story (38pgs) by Steve Gerber, pencils by Alan Weiss, inks by John & Sal Buscema and Rick Buckler, The Avengers, Defenders, Dr. Doom and Mephisto appear; plus photos, features	$10.50	$33.00	$65.00	£5.00	£15.00	£30.00
2 ND 66pgs, Savage Sword of Conan; John Buscema art, Earl Norem cover	$0.40	$1.25	$2.50	£0.25	£0.75	£1.50
3 LD in the U.K. 48pgs, Close Encounters film adaptation; Walt Simonson and Klaus Janson art	$0.40	$1.25	$2.50	£0.25	£0.85	£1.75
4 ND scarce in the U.K. 66pgs, the story of The Beatles; George Perez and Klaus Janson art; plus photos and features	$2.50	$7.50	$15.00	£1.65	£5.00	£10.00
5 ND 54pgs, Kiss; story art by John Romita Jnr plus photos and features; bound-in poster at centre-fold (often missing!)	$6.50	$20.00	$40.00	£3.30	£10.00	£20.00
6 ND 50pgs, Jaws II film adaptation; Gene Colan art	$0.40	$1.25	$2.50	£0.25	£0.75	£1.50
7 extremely rare in the U.K. and U.S. Sgt. Pepper's Lonely Heart's Club Band, only distributed in Japan (withdrawn from U.S. distribution)	$21.00	$62.50	$150.00	£10.50	£32.00	£75.00
8 ND 50pgs, Battlestar Galactica; Ernie Colon art; plus photos and features	$0.40	$1.25	$2.50	£0.25	£0.75	£1.50
9 LD in the U.K. 66pgs, Savage Sword of Conan; John Buscema art, Red Sonja back-up (15pgs) drawn by Howard Chaykin	$0.40	$1.25	$2.50	£0.25	£0.75	£1.50
10 ND 66pgs, Starlord; Gene Colon art	$0.40	$1.25	$2.50	£0.25	£0.75	£1.50
11 ND 56pgs, Warriors of the Shadow Realm Part I (Weirdworld); John Buscema and Rudy Nebres art	$0.40	$1.25	$2.50	£0.25	£0.75	£1.50
12 ND 56pgs, Warriors of the Shadow Realm Part II (Weirdworld); John Buscema and Rudy Nebres art	$0.40	$1.25	$2.50	£0.25	£0.75	£1.50
13 ND 56pgs, Warriors of the Shadow Realm Part III (Weirdworld); John Buscema and Rudy Nebres art; gatefold poster at centre-fold	$0.40	$1.25	$2.50	£0.25	£0.75	£1.50
14 ND 56pgs, Meteor film adaptation (series now settled as adaptations of films - ends #41)	$0.40	$1.25	$2.50	£0.30	£1.00	£2.00
15 ND 66pgs, Star Trek - The Motion Picture; Dave Cockrum and Klaus Janson art; plus photos and features	$0.40	$1.25	$2.50	£0.30	£1.00	£2.00
16 ND 96pgs, The Empire Strikes Back; Al Williamson and Carlos Garzon art	$0.40	$1.25	$2.50	£0.30	£1.00	£2.00
17 ND 66pgs, Xanadu; artists include Mike Nasser, Brent Anderson and Bill Sienkiewicz; plus photos and features	$0.40	$1.25	$2.50	£0.25	£0.75	£1.50
18 ND 64pgs, Raiders of the Lost Ark; Walt Simonson script, John Buscema and Klaus Janson art	$0.40	$1.25	$2.50	£0.25	£0.75	£1.50
19 LD in the U.K. 66pgs, For Your Eyes Only; Howard Chaykin and Vince Coletta art; plus photos and features	$0.40	$1.25	$2.50	£0.25	£0.75	£1.50
20 ND 66pgs, Dragonslayer; Marie Severin and John Tartaglione art	$0.40	$1.25	$2.50	£0.25	£0.75	£1.50
21 ND 66pgs, Conan the Movie	$0.40	$1.20	$2.00	£0.25	£0.75	£1.25
22 ND 64pgs, Bladerunner; Al Williamson and Carlos Garzon art (Note: regular comic size, not magazine size); plus photos and features	$0.40	$1.20	$2.00	£0.25	£0.75	£1.25
23 ND 64pgs, Annie; Win Mortimer and Vince Coletta art; plus photos and features	$0.40	$1.20	$2.00	£0.25	£0.75	£1.25
24 ND 64pgs, The Dark Crystal; Bret Blevins and Vince Coletta art; plus photos and features	$0.40	$1.20	$2.00	£0.25	£0.75	£1.25
25 ND 64pgs, Rock and Rule; specially adapted from the animated film plus photos and features	$0.40	$1.20	$2.00	£0.25	£0.75	£1.25
26 ND 64pgs, Octopussy; Paul Neary art; plus photos and features	$0.40	$1.20	$2.00	£0.25	£0.75	£1.25
27 ND 64pgs, Fire and Ice	$0.40	$1.20	$2.00	£0.25	£0.75	£1.25
28 ND 64pgs, Krull; Bret Blevins and Vince Coletta art	$0.40	$1.20	$2.00	£0.25	£0.75	£1.25
29 ND 64pgs, Greystoke - Tarzan of the Apes; Dan Spiegle art	$0.40	$1.20	$2.00	£0.25	£0.75	£1.25
30 ND 64pgs, Indiana Jones and the Temple of Doom; Jackson Guice art featured	$0.40	$1.20	$2.00	£0.25	£0.75	£1.25
31 ND 64pgs, The Last Starfighter; Bret Blevins and Tony Salmons art	$0.40	$1.20	$2.00	£0.25	£0.75	£1.25
32 ND 64pgs, The Muppets Take Manhattan	$0.40	$1.20	$2.00	£0.25	£0.75	£1.25
33 ND 64pgs, Buckeroo Banzai; Mark Texeira art	$0.40	$1.20	$2.00	£0.25	£0.75	£1.25
34 ND 64pgs, Sheena; Gray Morrow art	$0.40	$1.20	$2.00	£0.25	£0.75	£1.25
35 ND 64pgs, Conan the Destroyer; John Buscema art	$0.40	$1.20	$2.00	£0.25	£0.75	£1.25
36 ND 64pgs, Dune; Sienkiewicz art	$0.40	$1.20	$2.00	£0.25	£0.75	£1.25
37 ND 48pgs, 2010; Joe Barney, Larry Hama, Tom Palmer	$0.40	$1.20	$2.00	£0.25	£0.75	£1.25
38 ND 48pgs, Red Sonja; Louise Simonson and Mary Wilshire	$0.40	$1.20	$2.00	£0.25	£0.75	£1.25
39 ND 64pgs, Santa Claus: The Movie; Frank Springer art	$0.40	$1.20	$2.00	£0.25	£0.75	£1.25
40 ND 64pgs, Labyrinth; John Buscema art	$0.40	$1.20	$2.00	£0.25	£0.75	£1.25
41 ND 64pgs, Howard the Duck; Kyle Baker art	$0.40	$1.20	$2.00	£0.25	£0.75	£1.25
Title Value:	$55.30	$168.20	$352.00	£29.85	£90.60	£187.00

Note: #11-13 each had a 25 copy special press run with gold seal and signed by artists (therefore rare) valued at about **£30** or about **$60** in the U.S. Two different cover prices exist for #15 ($1.50 & $2.00). #22, 23 are normal comic size. #1-4 titled Marvel Comics Super Special.

MARVEL SUPER-HERO CONTEST OF CHAMPIONS

Marvel Comics Group,MS; 1 Jun 1982-3 Aug 1982

1 1st Marvel limited series; many Marvel heroes including X-Men appear

	$Good	$Fine	$N.Mint	£Good	£Fine	£N.Mint
	$1.00	$3.00	$5.00	£0.60	£1.80	£3.00
2	$1.00	$3.00	$5.00	£0.60	£1.80	£3.00
3 ND scarce in the U.K.	$1.00	$3.00	$5.00	£0.70	£2.10	£3.50
Title Value:	$3.00	$9.00	$15.00	£1.90	£5.70	£9.50

Note: most Marvel heroes appear.

MARVEL SUPER-HEROES

Marvel Comics Group; 12 Dec 1967-31 Nov 1971; 32 Sep 1972-106 Feb 1982
(previously Fantasy Masterpieces)

	$Good	$Fine	$N.Mint	£Good	£Fine	£N.Mint
12 68pgs, issues begin; origin and 1st appearance Captain Marvel of the Kree	$17.50	$52.50	$125.00	£10.50	£32.00	£75.00
13 2nd appearance Captain Marvel	$10.00	$30.00	$60.00	£5.75	£17.50	£35.00
14 Spiderman features in a new full length story	$17.50	$52.50	$125.00	£8.50	£26.00	£60.00
15 Medusa; Inhumans appear	$2.50	$7.50	$15.00	£1.65	£5.00	£10.00
16 origin and 1st appearance Phantom Eagle	$2.50	$7.50	$15.00	£1.65	£5.00	£10.00
17 origin Black Knight	$2.50	$7.50	$15.00	£1.65	£5.00	£10.00
18 origin and 1st appearance Guardians of the Galaxy	$11.50	$35.00	$70.00	£5.75	£17.50	£35.00
19 Ka-Zar, part Smith cover	$2.05	$6.25	$12.50	£1.25	£3.75	£7.50
20 Dr. Doom	$2.05	$6.25	$12.50	£1.25	£3.75	£7.50
21 X-Men #1 and #2 reprinted	$0.80	$2.50	$5.00	£0.55	£1.75	£3.50
22 X-Men #3, Daredevil #2 reprinted	$0.80	$2.50	$5.00	£0.55	£1.75	£3.50
23 new Watcher story, X-Men #4 reprinted (1st Brotherhood Evil Mutants/Scarlet Witch/Quicksilver), Daredevil #3	$0.80	$2.50	$5.00	£0.55	£1.75	£3.50
24 X-Men #5 reprinted, Daredevil #4	$0.80	$2.50	$5.00	£0.55	£1.75	£3.50
25 X-Men #6 reprinted, Daredevil #5	$0.80	$2.50	$5.00	£0.55	£1.75	£3.50
26 X-Men #7 reprinted, Daredevil #6	$0.80	$2.50	$5.00	£0.55	£1.75	£3.50
27 X-Men #8 reprinted, Daredevil #7	$0.80	$2.50	$5.00	£0.55	£1.75	£3.50
28 Iron Man and Daredevil reprints takeover cover credit	$0.80	$2.50	$5.00	£0.55	£1.75	£3.50
29-30	$0.80	$2.50	$5.00	£0.55	£1.75	£3.50
31 ND last 68pg issue	$0.80	$2.50	$5.00	£0.55	£1.75	£3.50
32 ND reprints featuring Sub-Mariner and Hulk from Tales to Astonish take over cover credit (ends #55)	$0.50	$1.50	$3.00	£0.30	£1.00	£2.00
33-40 ND	$0.50	$1.50	$3.00	£0.30	£1.00	£2.00
41-47 ND	$0.40	$1.25	$2.50	£0.25	£0.75	£1.50
48 ND reprints Tales to Astonish #93 (Hulk vs. Silver Surfer)	$0.40	$1.25	$2.50	£0.25	£0.75	£1.50
49-50 ND	$0.40	$1.25	$2.50	£0.25	£0.75	£1.50
51-55 ND	$0.30	$1.00	$2.00	£0.20	£0.60	£1.25
56 ND reprints Hulk #102, origin retold	$0.30	$1.00	$2.00	£0.20	£0.60	£1.25
57-70 ND	$0.30	$1.00	$2.00	£0.20	£0.60	£1.25
71-99 ND	$0.25	$0.75	$1.50	£0.15	£0.50	£1.00
100 ND 52pgs	$0.40	$1.20	$2.00	£0.25	£0.75	£1.25
101-106 ND	$0.30	$0.90	$1.50	£0.20	£0.60	£1.00
Title Value:	$100.85	$306.85	$651.50	£59.00	£182.10	£382.75

REPRINT FEATURES

All Winner's Squad in 17, 18. GA Black Knight in 12-16, 19. Black Marvel in 15. GA Captain America in 12 (by Romita), 13, 14, 15 (by Romita), 16, 20. Daredevil in 22-31. GA Destroyer in 12. Hulk in 21, 32-106. GA Human Torch in 12-14, 16, 17, 19, 20. Iron Man in 28-31. Marvel Boy in 19. Mercury in 14. Patriot in 16. GA Sub-Mariner in 12-20; Sub-Mariner in 21, 32-55. GA Vision in 13. X-Men in 21-27.

MARVEL SUPER-HEROES (2ND SERIES)

Marvel Comics Group; 1 May 1990-15 Dec 1993

	$Good	$Fine	$N.Mint	£Good	£Fine	£N.Mint
1 80pgs, Moon Knight, Hercules, Black Panther, Hell Cat, Magik, Brother Voodoo, Speedball, features Ron Lim and Steve Ditko art among others	$0.50	$1.50	$2.50	£0.30	£0.90	£1.50
2 80pgs, Iron Man, Tigra, Falcon, Red Wolf, Rogue, Speedball, Daredevil, Steve Ditko art on Iron Man and Speedball	$0.50	$1.50	$2.50	£0.30	£0.90	£1.50
3 80pgs, Captain America, Captain Marvel, Wasp, Hulk, Blue Shield, Ditko/Rogers art featured	$0.50	$1.50	$2.50	£0.30	£0.90	£1.50
4 80pgs, Spiderman and Nick Fury, Daredevil, Speedball, Wonder Man, Spitfire, Black Knight. John Byrne cover	$0.50	$1.50	$2.50	£0.30	£0.90	£1.50
5 80pgs, Thor, Thing, Speedball, Doctor Strange	$0.50	$1.50	$2.50	£0.30	£0.90	£1.50
6 80pgs, X-Men, Power Pack, Speedball, Sabra	$0.50	$1.50	$2.50	£0.30	£0.90	£1.50
7 80pgs, X-Men, Cloak and Dagger by Peter David	$0.50	$1.50	$2.50	£0.30	£0.90	£1.50
8 80pgs, X-Men, Iron Man (Ditko art), Namor; Erik Larsen cover	$0.50	$1.50	$2.50	£0.30	£0.90	£1.50
9 80pgs, Avengers West Coast, Thor, Iron Man; Sam Kieth cover	$0.50	$1.50	$2.50	£0.30	£0.90	£1.50
10 80pgs, Sub-Mariner, Fantastic Four, Thor appear; story and cover to Ms. Marvel #24 appear (never published before - it had what would have been Sabretooth's 2nd appearance!)	$0.50	$1.50	$2.50	£0.30	£0.90	£1.50
11 80pgs, Ghost Rider, Giant Man plus the never before published Ms. Marvel #25 with Rogue appearance, Mark Texeira cover	$0.50	$1.50	$2.50	£0.30	£0.90	£1.50
12 80pgs, Dr. Strange, Falcon, Iron Man	$0.50	$1.50	$2.50	£0.30	£0.90	£1.50
13 80pgs, all-Iron Man issue to celebrate 30th anniversary	$0.50	$1.50	$2.50	£0.30	£0.90	£1.50
14 80pgs, Iron Man, Speedball, Dr. Strange	$0.50	$1.50	$2.50	£0.30	£0.90	£1.50
15 80pgs, Volstagg by Walt Simonson, Thor, Iron Man	$0.50	$1.50	$2.50	£0.30	£0.90	£1.50
Title Value:	$7.50	$22.50	$37.50	£4.50	£13.50	£22.50

Note: all 80pgs, quarterly frequency

MARVEL SUPER-HEROES (ONE SHOT)

Marvel Comics Group,OS; 1 Oct 1966

	$Good	$Fine	$N.Mint	£Good	£Fine	£N.Mint
1 64pgs, reprints Daredevil #1 (origin), Avengers, Golden Age Sub-Mariner, Golden Age Human Torch reprint, 1st Marvel one-shot comic	$12.00	$36.00	$85.00	£7.00	£21.00	£50.00
Title Value:	$12.00	$36.00	$85.00	£7.00	£21.00	£50.00

MARVEL SUPER-HEROES 1992 HOLIDAY SPECIAL

Marvel Comics Group,OS; 1 Jan 1993

	$Good	$Fine	$N.Mint	£Good	£Fine	£N.Mint
1 ND 80pgs, stories featuring Hulk, Spiderman, Wolverine, Thanos, work by Sam Kieth, Jim Starlin and Golden	$0.50	$1.50	$2.50	£0.30	£0.90	£1.50
Title Value:	$0.50	$1.50	$2.50	£0.30	£0.90	£1.50

MARVEL SUPER-HEROES MAGAZINE

Marvel Comics Group; 1 Oct 1994-6 1995

	$Good	$Fine	$N.Mint	£Good	£Fine	£N.Mint
1 96pgs, reprints FF #232, Daredevil #159, Iron Man #115 and Hulk #314	$0.50	$1.50	$2.50	£0.30	£0.90	£1.50
2 96pgs, Human Torch, Daredevil and Hulk reprints; new Frank Miller cover	$0.50	$1.50	$2.50	£0.30	£0.90	£1.50
3 96pgs, Fantastic Four, Daredevil and Iron Man reprints; Michael Golden cover						

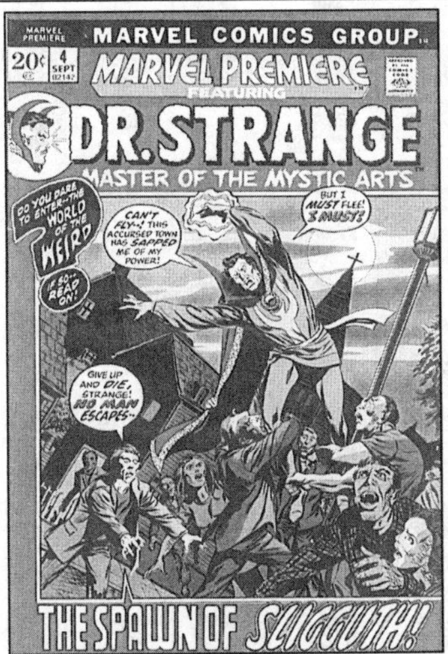

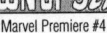

Marvel Premiere #4

Marvel Spotlight (1st) #28

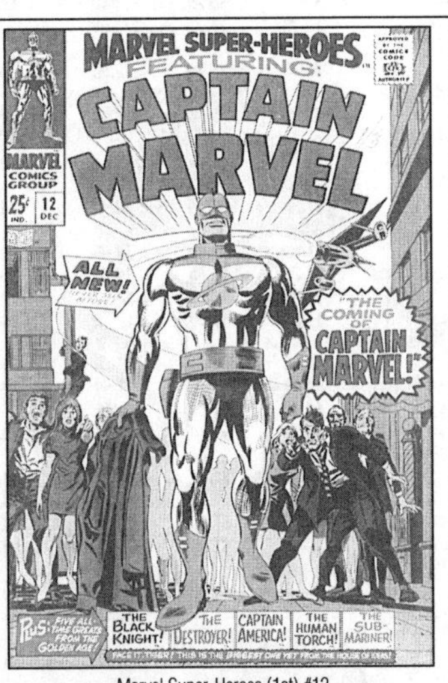

Marvel Super-Heroes (1st) #12

	$Good	$Fine	$N.Mint	£Good	£Fine	£N.Mint
	$0.50	$1.50	$2.50	£0.30	£0.90	£1.50
4 96pgs, Fantastic Four, Daredevil and Iron Man reprints						
	$0.50	$1.50	$2.50	£0.30	£0.90	£1.50
5 96pgs, all John Byrne issue with Fantastic Four, Thing and Hulk reprints; John Byrne cover						
	$0.50	$1.50	$2.50	£0.30	£0.90	£1.50
6 96pgs, Fantastic Four, Daredevil, Iron Man and Hulk reprints						
	$0.50	$1.50	$2.50	£0.30	£0.90	£1.50
Title Value:	$3.00	$9.00	$15.00	£1.80	£5.40	£9.00

MARVEL SUPER-HEROES SECRET WARS

Marvel Comics Group,MS; 1 May 1984-12 Apr 1985
(see Secret Wars II)

	$Good	$Fine	$N.Mint	£Good	£Fine	£N.Mint
1	$0.50	$1.50	$2.50	£0.50	£1.50	£2.50
1 2nd printing	$0.30	$0.90	$1.50	£0.30	£0.90	£1.50
1 3rd printing	$0.30	$0.90	$1.50	£0.30	£0.90	£1.50
2-3	$0.50	$1.50	$2.50	£0.40	£1.20	£2.00
4-5	$0.50	$1.50	$2.50	£0.30	£0.90	£1.50
6 Wasp dies	$0.50	$1.50	$2.50	£0.30	£0.90	£1.50
7 1st new Spiderwoman						
	$0.50	$1.50	$2.50	£0.30	£0.90	£1.50
8 origin Spiderman's black costume (see Spiderman #252, Spectacular Spiderman #90); costume later initiates origin of Venom						
	$4.00	$12.00	$20.00	£1.50	£4.50	£7.50
9-10	$0.50	$1.50	$2.50	£0.30	£0.90	£1.50
11 LD in the U.K.	$0.50	$1.50	$2.50	£0.35	£1.05	£1.75
12 LD in the U.K. DS						
	$0.50	$1.50	$2.50	£0.40	£1.20	£2.00
Title Value:	$10.10	$30.30	$50.50	£5.95	£17.85	£29.75
Secret Wars Trade paperback (Jun 1992), reprints issues #1-12, new cover by Mike Zeck				£2.50	£7.50	£12.50

MARVEL SWIMSUIT SPECIAL 1992

Marvel Comics Group,OS; 1 Aug 1992

	$Good	$Fine	$N.Mint	£Good	£Fine	£N.Mint
1 ND 48pgs	$0.60	$1.80	$3.00	£0.40	£1.20	£2.00
Title Value:	$0.60	$1.80	$3.00	£0.40	£1.20	£2.00

MARVEL SWIMSUIT SPECIAL 1993

Marvel Comics Group,Magazine OS; 1 Aug 1993

	$Good	$Fine	$N.Mint	£Good	£Fine	£N.Mint
1 ND 48pgs, Adam Hughes and Kevin Maguire art featured						
	$0.60	$1.80	$3.00	£0.40	£1.20	£2.00
Title Value:	$0.60	$1.80	$3.00	£0.40	£1.20	£2.00

MARVEL SWIMSUIT SPECIAL 1994

Marvel Comics Group,Magazine OS; 1 Aug 1994

	$Good	$Fine	$N.Mint	£Good	£Fine	£N.Mint
1 ND 48pgs, Adam Hughes cover						
	$0.60	$1.80	$3.00	£0.40	£1.20	£2.00
Title Value:	$0.60	$1.80	$3.00	£0.40	£1.20	£2.00

MARVEL SWIMSUIT SPECIAL 1995

Marvel Comics Group,Magazine OS; 1 Oct 1995

	$Good	$Fine	$N.Mint	£Good	£Fine	£N.Mint
1 ND 48pgs, Brian Stelfreeze, Gary Frank, Adam Hughes featured pin-ups, Gambit and Rogue cover by the Brothers Hildebrandt						
	$0.60	$1.80	$3.00	£0.40	£1.20	£2.00
Title Value:	$0.60	$1.80	$3.00	£0.40	£1.20	£2.00

MARVEL TAILS, PETER PORKER SPECTACULAR SPIDERHAM

Marvel Comics Group,OS; 1 Nov 1983

	$Good	$Fine	$N.Mint	£Good	£Fine	£N.Mint
1 ND	$0.25	$0.75	$1.25	£0.15	£0.45	£0.75
Title Value:	$0.25	$0.75	$1.25	£0.15	£0.45	£0.75

MARVEL TALES

Marvel Comics Group;3 Jul 1966-291 Nov 1994
(formerly Marvel Tales Annual)

	$Good	$Fine	$N.Mint	£Good	£Fine	£N.Mint
3 68pgs, reprints Spiderman #6 (1st Lizard), Journey into Mystery #84 (2nd Thor), Strange Tales #101 (1st Human Torch series)						
	$7.00	$21.00	$50.00	£3.55	£10.50	£25.00
4-5 68pgs	$3.55	$10.50	$25.00	£1.40	£4.25	£10.00
6 68pgs, reprints Spiderman #9 (1st Electro)						
	$1.75	$5.25	$12.50	£0.85	£2.55	£6.00
7 68pgs	$1.75	$5.25	$12.50	£0.85	£2.55	£6.00
8 68pgs, reprints Spiderman #13 (1st Mysterio)						
	$1.75	$5.25	$12.50	£0.85	£2.55	£6.00
9 68pgs, reprints Spiderman #14 (1st Green Goblin) plus cover						
	$1.75	$5.25	$12.50	£1.00	£3.00	£7.00
10 68pgs, reprints Spiderman #15 (1st Kraven)						
	$1.75	$5.25	$12.50	£0.85	£2.55	£6.00
11-12 scarce in the U.K. 68pgs						
	$1.25	$3.85	$9.00	£0.70	£2.10	£5.00
13 68pgs, Marvel Boy reprint						
	$1.25	$3.85	$9.00	£0.70	£2.10	£5.00
14-15 68pgs	$1.25	$3.85	$9.00	£0.70	£2.10	£5.00
16-20 68pgs	$1.05	$3.20	$7.50	£0.60	£1.90	£4.50
21-29 68pgs	$1.05	$3.20	$7.50	£0.55	£1.70	£4.00
30 68pgs, new Angel story, continued from Ka-Zar #3 (1st series)						
	$1.05	$3.20	$7.50	£0.55	£1.70	£4.00
31-32 68pgs	$1.05	$3.20	$7.50	£0.55	£1.70	£4.00
33 ND 48pgs	$0.60	$1.90	$4.50	£0.40	£1.25	£3.00
34-35 ND	$0.55	$1.70	$4.00	£0.35	£1.05	£2.50
36 ND reprints Spiderman #50 (1st Kingpin)						
	$0.55	$1.70	$4.00	£0.35	£1.05	£2.50
37-40 ND	$0.55	$1.70	$4.00	£0.35	£1.05	£2.50
41-60 ND	$0.40	$1.25	$3.00	£0.25	£0.85	£2.00
61-74 ND	$0.40	$1.25	$2.50	£0.25	£0.75	£1.50
75 ND reprints origin Spiderman						
	$0.50	$1.50	$3.00	£0.30	£1.00	£2.00
76 ND	$0.40	$1.25	$2.50	£0.25	£0.75	£1.50
77 ND reprints drug story (Spiderman #96)						
	$0.40	$1.25	$2.50	£0.25	£0.75	£1.50
78 ND reprints drug story (Spiderman #97)						
	$0.40	$1.25	$2.50	£0.25	£0.75	£1.50
79 ND reprints drug story (Spiderman #98)						
	$0.40	$1.25	$2.50	£0.25	£0.75	£1.50
80 ND	$0.40	$1.25	$2.50	£0.25	£0.75	£1.50
81 ND reprints newspaper strips as back-up						
	$0.25	$0.75	$1.50	£0.15	£0.50	£1.00
82-97	$0.25	$0.75	$1.50	£0.15	£0.50	£1.00
98 ND reprints death Gwen Stacy from Spiderman #121						
	$0.40	$1.25	$2.50	£0.25	£0.75	£1.50
99 ND reprints death Green Goblin from Spiderman #122						
	$0.40	$1.25	$2.50	£0.25	£0.75	£1.50
100 ND 52pgs, Nasser art on new Hawkeye/Two Gun Kid story						
	$0.40	$1.25	$2.50	£0.25	£0.75	£1.50
101-105	$0.25	$0.75	$1.50	£0.15	£0.50	£1.00
106 ND reprints 1st Punisher from Spiderman #129						
	$1.05	$3.25	$6.50	£0.40	£1.25	£2.50
107-110 ND	$0.30	$0.90	$1.50	£0.20	£0.60	£1.00
111 ND reprints Spiderman #134 (2nd appearance Punisher [cameo])						
	$0.30	$0.90	$1.50	£0.20	£0.60	£1.00
112 ND reprints Spiderman #135 (2nd full appearance Punisher)						
	$0.30	$0.90	$1.50	£0.20	£0.60	£1.00
113-122 ND	$0.30	$0.90	$1.50	£0.20	£0.60	£1.00
123 ND title becomes Marvel Tales Starring Spiderman						
	$0.30	$0.90	$1.50	£0.20	£0.60	£1.00
124-125 ND	$0.30	$0.90	$1.50	£0.20	£0.60	£1.00
126 reprints #149 Spiderman clone						
	$0.40	$1.20	$2.00	£0.30	£0.90	£1.50
127-136	$0.30	$0.90	$1.50	£0.20	£0.60	£1.00
137 reprints 1st Spiderman from Amazing Fantasy #15 with unused original cover, reprints ist Dr. Strange from Strange Tales #110						
	$1.00	$3.00	$5.00	£0.60	£1.80	£3.00
138 reprints Spiderman #1						
	$0.80	$2.40	$4.00	£0.50	£1.50	£2.50
139 reprints Spiderman #2						
	$0.40	$1.20	$2.00	£0.25	£0.75	£1.25
140 reprints Spiderman #3						
	$0.40	$1.20	$2.00	£0.25	£0.75	£1.25
141 reprints Spiderman #4						
	$0.40	$1.20	$2.00	£0.25	£0.75	£1.25
142 reprints Spiderman #5						
	$0.40	$1.20	$2.00	£0.25	£0.75	£1.25
143 reprints Spiderman #6						
	$0.40	$1.20	$2.00	£0.25	£0.75	£1.25
144 reprints Spiderman #7						
	$0.40	$1.20	$2.00	£0.25	£0.75	£1.25
145 reprints Spiderman #8						
	$0.40	$1.20	$2.00	£0.25	£0.75	£1.25
146 reprints Spiderman #9						
	$0.40	$1.20	$2.00	£0.25	£0.75	£1.25
147 reprints Spiderman #10						
	$0.40	$1.20	$2.00	£0.25	£0.75	£1.25
148-149	$0.30	$0.90	$1.50	£0.20	£0.60	£1.00
150 DS LD reprints Spiderman Annual #1 and #14						
	$0.50	$1.50	$2.50	£0.30	£0.90	£1.50
151	$0.30	$0.90	$1.50	£0.20	£0.60	£1.00
152 reprints Spiderman #14 (1st Green Goblin)						
	$0.30	$0.90	$1.50	£0.20	£0.60	£1.00
153-190	$0.30	$0.90	$1.50	£0.20	£0.60	£1.00
191 64pgs, reprints Spiderman #96-98						
	$0.30	$0.90	$1.50	£0.20	£0.60	£1.00
192 48pgs, reprints Spiderman #121, #122						
	$0.50	$1.50	$2.50	£0.30	£0.90	£1.50
193-197	$0.30	$0.90	$1.50	£0.20	£0.60	£1.00
198 new Spiderman/Thing story						
	$0.40	$1.20	$2.00	£0.25	£0.75	£1.25
199	$0.30	$0.90	$1.50	£0.20	£0.60	£1.00
200 DS Frank Miller reprint from Spiderman Annual #14						
	$0.40	$1.20	$2.00	£0.25	£0.75	£1.25
201-202 reprints Marvel Team Up #65, 66						
	$0.25	$0.75	$1.25	£0.15	£0.45	£0.75
203-208	$0.25	$0.75	$1.25	£0.15	£0.45	£0.75
209 reprints 1st Punisher from Spiderman #129						
	$0.30	$0.90	$1.50	£0.20	£0.60	£1.00
210 reprints Spiderman #134, Punisher appears (1 panel)						
	$0.25	$0.75	$1.25	£0.15	£0.45	£0.75
211-212 Punisher appears						
	$0.25	$0.75	$1.25	£0.15	£0.45	£0.75
213 Punisher, Jack Kirby's Silver Surfer appear						
	$0.25	$0.75	$1.25	£0.15	£0.45	£0.75
214-215 Punisher/Nightcrawler						
	$0.25	$0.75	$1.25	£0.15	£0.45	£0.75
216-222 Punisher appears						
	$0.25	$0.75	$1.25	£0.15	£0.45	£0.75
223 Death Captain Stacy, Todd McFarlane covers begin						
	$0.25	$0.75	$1.25	£0.15	£0.45	£0.75
224-232	$0.25	$0.75	$1.25	£0.15	£0.45	£0.75
233 reprints X-Men #35						
	$0.25	$0.75	$1.25	£0.15	£0.45	£0.75
234 reprints Marvel Team Up #4 (X-Men and Morbius)						
	$0.25	$0.75	$1.25	£0.15	£0.45	£0.75
235-236	$0.25	$0.75	$1.25	£0.15	£0.45	£0.75
237-238 reprints Marvel Team Up #150 with the X-Men						

VERY GENERAL PERCENTAGE CONVERSION CHART WHICH MAY BE USED TO CALCULATE LOW AND INBETWEEN GRADES:

	$Good	$Fine	$N.Mint	£Good	£Fine	£N.Mint
	$0.25	*$0.75*	*$1.25*	£0.15	£0.45	£0.75
239-240 Spiderman/Beast	*$0.25*	*$0.75*	*$1.25*	£0.15	£0.45	£0.75
241-242	*$0.25*	*$0.75*	*$1.25*	£0.15	£0.45	£0.75
243 reprints Marvel Team Up #117 with Wolverine	*$0.25*	*$0.75*	*$1.25*	£0.15	£0.45	£0.75
244 reprints Marvel Team Up #118 with Professor X	*$0.25*	*$0.75*	*$1.25*	£0.15	£0.45	£0.75
245-247	*$0.25*	*$0.75*	*$1.25*	£0.15	£0.45	£0.75
248 reprints Marvel Team Up Annual #6, new Rocket Racer back-up story	*$0.25*	*$0.75*	*$1.25*	£0.15	£0.45	£0.75
249	*$0.25*	*$0.75*	*$1.25*	£0.15	£0.45	£0.75
250 reprints Marvel Team Up #100	*$0.25*	*$0.75*	*$1.25*	£0.15	£0.45	£0.75
251 reprints Spiderman #100	*$0.25*	*$0.75*	*$1.25*	£0.15	£0.45	£0.75
252 reprints Spiderman #101	*$0.25*	*$0.75*	*$1.25*	£0.15	£0.45	£0.75
253 reprints Spiderman #102	*$0.25*	*$0.75*	*$1.25*	£0.15	£0.45	£0.75
254 reprints Marvel Team Up #15 (Ghost Rider)	*$0.25*	*$0.75*	*$1.25*	£0.15	£0.45	£0.75
255 reprints Marvel Team Up #58 (Ghost Rider)	*$0.25*	*$0.75*	*$1.25*	£0.15	£0.45	£0.75
256-257	*$0.25*	*$0.75*	*$1.25*	£0.15	£0.45	£0.75
258 reprints Spiderman #238 (1st Hobgoblin)	*$0.30*	*$0.90*	*$1.50*	£0.20	£0.60	£1.00
259-261 reprints Spiderman #239, George Perez cover	*$0.25*	*$0.75*	*$1.25*	£0.15	£0.45	£0.75
262-263	*$0.25*	*$0.75*	*$1.25*	£0.15	£0.45	£0.75
264-265 reprints lead story from Spiderman Annual #5 with Peter Parker's parents to tie in with 30th anniversary plot-lines	*$0.25*	*$0.75*	*$1.25*	£0.15	£0.45	£0.75
266 reprints Spiderman #252 (1st Black Costume)	*$0.25*	*$0.75*	*$1.25*	£0.15	£0.45	£0.75
267-276	*$0.25*	*$0.75*	*$1.25*	£0.15	£0.45	£0.75
277 reprints 1st Silver Sable fron Amazing Spiderman #265	*$0.25*	*$0.75*	*$1.25*	£0.15	£0.45	£0.75
278-284 Ron Lim cover	*$0.25*	*$0.75*	*$1.25*	£0.15	£0.45	£0.75
285 Ron Lim cover, Wendigo back-up by Charles Vess	*$0.25*	*$0.75*	*$1.25*	£0.15	£0.45	£0.75
286 Tom Lyle cover	*$0.25*	*$0.75*	*$1.25*	£0.15	£0.45	£0.75
286 Collectors Edtion, ND , pre-bagged with 16pg preview and animation cel from the Spiderman animated TV series; metallic ink cover	*$0.60*	*$1.80*	*$3.00*	£0.30	£0.90	£1.50
287-291	*$0.25*	*$0.75*	*$1.25*	£0.15	£0.45	£0.75
Title Value:	***$129.70***	***$392.80***	***$797.25***	**£75.60**	**£231.15**	**£463.50**

Note: issue 3 occasionally turns up with blank back and inside covers. These were originally subscription copies sent as leftovers (see also Spiderman Annual #1,2, Fantastic Four Annual #1-3, Sgt. Fury Annual #1 and Strange Tales Annual #2). With these white covers showing more easily signs of wear and soiling, near mint copies are extremely scarce in both the U.S. and U.K.

Note also: new Todd McFarlane covers begin from 223, new Spider-Ham back-up stories from 231.

REPRINT FEATURES

Ant-Man in 3-5. Dr.Strange in 28, 29, 31. Giant-Man in 13. Human Torch in 3-12, 14-27. Iron Man in 32. Marvel Boy in 13-16. Spiderman in 3-234. Thor in 3-27. Wasp in 6-12.

MARVEL TALES ANNUAL

Marvel Comics Group; 1 1964-2 1965

	$Good	$Fine	$N.Mint	£Good	£Fine	£N.Mint
1 scarce in the U.K. 68pgs, reprints first origins from first issues of Sgt. Fury, Spiderman, Hulk and Iron Man plus Giant Man origin (Astonish #49)	*$39.00*	*$115.00*	*$275.00*	£20.00	£60.00	£140.00
2 68pgs, reprints origins of Avengers (Avengers #1), Dr. Strange (Strange Tales #110), X-Men (X-Men #1), and a Hulk story	*$12.50*	*$39.00*	*$90.00*	£8.50	£26.00	£60.00
Title Value:	***$51.50***	***$154.00***	***$365.00***	**£28.50**	**£86.00**	**£200.00**

MARVEL TEAM-UP

Marvel Comics Group; 1 Mar 1972-150 Feb 1985

(see Marvel Treasury Edition 18, Official Marvel Index to...)

[Spiderman teamed with each of the following]

	$Good	$Fine	$N.Mint	£Good	£Fine	£N.Mint
1 ND Human Torch	*$11.00*	*$34.00*	*$80.00*	£7.00	£21.00	£50.00
2 ND Human Torch	*$5.25*	*$16.00*	*$32.50*	£3.30	£10.00	£20.00
3 ND Spiderman and Human Torch vs. Morbius the Living Vampire (Morbius on cover)	*$5.75*	*$17.50*	*$35.00*	£3.30	£10.00	£20.00
4 ND X-Men, Morbius the Living Vampire appears, Gil Kane part art	*$9.00*	*$28.00*	*$55.00*	£5.75	£17.50	£35.00
5 ND Vision	*$2.50*	*$7.50*	*$15.00*	£1.65	£5.00	£10.00
6 ND The Thing	*$2.50*	*$7.50*	*$15.00*	£1.25	£3.75	£7.50
7 ND Thor	*$2.50*	*$7.50*	*$15.00*	£1.25	£3.75	£7.50
8 ND scarce in the U.K. The Cat	*$2.50*	*$7.50*	*$15.00*	£1.40	£4.25	£8.50
9 ND Iron Man	*$2.50*	*$7.50*	*$15.00*	£1.25	£3.75	£7.50
10 ND Human Torch	*$2.50*	*$7.50*	*$15.00*	£1.25	£3.75	£7.50
11 ND Inhumans	*$1.65*	*$5.00*	*$10.00*	£1.00	£3.00	£6.00
12 ND Werewolf by Night	*$1.65*	*$5.00*	*$10.00*	£1.25	£3.75	£7.50
13 ND Captain America	*$1.65*	*$5.00*	*$10.00*	£1.00	£3.00	£6.00
14 ND Sub-Mariner	*$1.65*	*$5.00*	*$10.00*	£1.00	£3.00	£6.00
15 ND Ghost Rider	*$2.05*	*$6.25*	*$12.50*	£1.25	£3.75	£7.50
16 ND Captain Marvel	*$1.65*	*$5.00*	*$10.00*	£1.00	£3.00	£6.00
17 ND Mr. Fantastic	*$1.65*	*$5.00*	*$10.00*	£1.00	£3.00	£6.00
18 ND Human Torch and Hulk, no Spiderman	*$1.65*	*$5.00*	*$10.00*	£1.00	£3.00	£6.00
19 ND Ka-Zar	*$1.65*	*$5.00*	*$10.00*	£1.00	£3.00	£6.00
20 ND Black Panther	*$1.65*	*$5.00*	*$10.00*	£1.00	£3.00	£6.00
21 ND Dr. Strange	*$1.00*	*$3.00*	*$6.00*	£0.80	£2.50	£5.00
22 ND Hawkeye	*$1.00*	*$3.00*	*$6.00*	£0.80	£2.50	£5.00
23 ND Human Torch and Iceman, no Spiderman	*$1.00*	*$3.00*	*$6.00*	£0.80	£2.50	£5.00
24 Brother Voodoo	*$1.00*	*$3.00*	*$6.00*	£0.55	£1.75	£3.50
25 Daredevil	*$1.00*	*$3.00*	*$6.00*	£0.55	£1.75	£3.50
26 Human Torch and Thor, no Spiderman	*$1.00*	*$3.00*	*$6.00*	£0.55	£1.75	£3.50
27 Hulk	*$1.00*	*$3.00*	*$6.00*	£0.55	£1.75	£3.50
28 Hercules	*$1.00*	*$3.00*	*$6.00*	£0.55	£1.75	£3.50
29 Human Torch and Iron Man, no Spiderman	*$1.00*	*$3.00*	*$6.00*	£0.55	£1.75	£3.50
30 Falcon	*$1.00*	*$3.00*	*$6.00*	£0.55	£1.75	£3.50
31 Iron Fist	*$0.75*	*$2.25*	*$4.50*	£0.50	£1.50	£3.00
32 Human Torch and Son of Satan, no Spiderman	*$0.75*	*$2.25*	*$4.50*	£0.50	£1.50	£3.00
33 Nighthawk	*$0.75*	*$2.25*	*$4.50*	£0.50	£1.50	£3.00
34 Valkyrie; Nighthawk appears	*$0.75*	*$2.25*	*$4.50*	£0.50	£1.50	£3.00
35 Dr. Strange	*$0.75*	*$2.25*	*$4.50*	£0.50	£1.50	£3.00
36 Frankenstein; Man-Wolf appears	*$0.75*	*$2.25*	*$4.50*	£0.50	£1.50	£3.00
37 Man-Wolf; Frankenstein appears	*$0.75*	*$2.25*	*$4.50*	£0.50	£1.50	£3.00
38 ND The Beast	*$0.75*	*$2.25*	*$4.50*	£0.75	£2.25	£4.50
39 Human Torch	*$0.75*	*$2.25*	*$4.50*	£0.50	£1.50	£3.00
40 Sons of the Tiger; Human Torch appears	*$0.75*	*$2.25*	*$4.50*	£0.50	£1.50	£3.00
41 Scarlet Witch; Vision appears	*$0.65*	*$2.00*	*$4.00*	£0.40	£1.25	£2.50
42 Vision; Scarlet Witch appears	*$0.65*	*$2.00*	*$4.00*	£0.40	£1.25	£2.50
43 Dr. Doom; Vision and Scarlet Witch appear	*$0.65*	*$2.00*	*$4.00*	£0.40	£1.25	£2.50
44 Moondragon; Vision, Scarlet Witch and Iron Man appears	*$0.65*	*$2.00*	*$4.00*	£0.40	£1.25	£2.50
45 Killraven	*$0.65*	*$2.00*	*$4.00*	£0.40	£1.25	£2.50
46 Deathlok	*$0.65*	*$2.00*	*$4.00*	£0.40	£1.25	£2.50
47 The Thing	*$0.65*	*$2.00*	*$4.00*	£0.40	£1.25	£2.50
48-49 Iron Man	*$0.65*	*$2.00*	*$4.00*	£0.40	£1.25	£2.50
50 Dr. Strange	*$0.65*	*$2.00*	*$4.00*	£0.40	£1.25	£2.50
51 Iron Man; Dr. Strange appears	*$0.55*	*$1.75*	*$3.50*	£0.30	£1.00	£2.00
52 Captain America	*$0.55*	*$1.75*	*$3.50*	£0.30	£1.00	£2.00
53 Hulk, guest-stars New X-Men and Woodgod; John Byrne's 1st art on X-Men; story is linked Marvel Team-Up Annual #1	*$3.30*	*$10.00*	*$20.00*	£1.25	£3.75	£7.50
54 Hulk, John Byrne art	*$0.80*	*$2.50*	*$5.00*	£0.55	£1.75	£3.50
55 Warlock, John Byrne art	*$1.25*	*$3.75*	*$7.50*	£0.65	£2.00	£4.00
56 Daredevil	*$0.55*	*$1.75*	*$3.50*	£0.30	£1.00	£2.00
57 Black Widow, John Byrne cover	*$0.55*	*$1.75*	*$3.50*	£0.30	£1.00	£2.00
58 Ghost Rider	*$0.80*	*$2.50*	*$5.00*	£0.55	£1.75	£3.50
59 Yellowjacket; Wasp appears, John Byrne cover and art	*$0.80*	*$2.50*	*$5.00*	£0.55	£1.75	£3.50
60 Wasp; Yellowjacket appears, John Byrne art	*$0.80*	*$2.50*	*$5.00*	£0.55	£1.75	£3.50
61 Human Torch, John Byrne art	*$0.65*	*$2.00*	*$4.00*	£0.40	£1.25	£2.50
62 Ms. Marvel, John Byrne art	*$0.65*	*$2.00*	*$4.00*	£0.40	£1.25	£2.50
63 Iron Fist, John Byrne art	*$0.65*	*$2.00*	*$4.00*	£0.40	£1.25	£2.50
64 Daughters of the Dragon, Iron Fist appears, John Byrne art	*$0.65*	*$2.00*	*$4.00*	£0.40	£1.25	£2.50
65 1st Captain Britain U.S. appearance, John Byrne art	*$1.00*	*$3.00*	*$6.00*	£0.80	£2.50	£5.00
66 Captain Britain, John Byrne art	*$0.80*	*$2.50*	*$5.00*	£0.65	£2.00	£4.00
67 Tigra, John Byrne art	*$0.65*	*$2.00*	*$4.00*	£0.40	£1.25	£2.50
68 Man-Thing, John Byrne art	*$0.65*	*$2.00*	*$4.00*	£0.40	£1.25	£2.50
69 Havok, John Byrne art	*$0.65*	*$2.00*	*$4.00*	£0.40	£1.25	£2.50
70 Thor/Havok, John Byrne art	*$0.65*	*$2.00*	*$4.00*	£0.40	£1.25	£2.50
71 Falcon; Captain America appears						

	$Good	$Fine	$N.Mint	£Good	£Fine	£N.Mint
	$0.40	$1.25	$2.50	£0.25	£0.75	£1.50
72 Black Widow	$0.40	$1.25	$2.50	£0.25	£0.75	£1.50
73 Daredevil	$0.40	$1.25	$2.50	£0.25	£0.75	£1.50
74 The Not-Ready-For-Prime-Time Players	$0.40	$1.25	$2.50	£0.25	£0.75	£1.50
75 Powerman, John Byrne art	$0.40	$1.25	$2.50	£0.25	£0.75	£1.50
76-77 Dr. Strange, Ms. Marvel, part Chaykin art	$0.40	$1.25	$2.50	£0.25	£0.75	£1.50
78 Wonderman	$0.40	$1.25	$2.50	£0.25	£0.75	£1.50
79 Red Sonja, John Byrne cover and art	$0.40	$1.25	$2.50	£0.25	£0.75	£1.50
80 Dr. Strange	$0.40	$1.25	$2.50	£0.25	£0.75	£1.50
81 ND Satana	$0.40	$1.25	$2.50	£0.40	£1.25	£2.50
82 Black Widow	$0.30	$1.00	$2.00	£0.20	£0.60	£1.25
83 Nick Fury; Black Widow appears	$0.30	$1.00	$2.00	£0.20	£0.60	£1.25
84 Shang-Chi, Master of Kung Fu; Black Widow appears	$0.30	$1.00	$2.00	£0.20	£0.60	£1.25
85 Black Widow; Shang-Chi and Nick Fury appear	$0.30	$1.00	$2.00	£0.20	£0.60	£1.25
86 Guardians of the Galaxy	$0.50	$1.50	$3.00	£0.30	£1.00	£2.00
87 Black Panther	$0.30	$1.00	$2.00	£0.20	£0.60	£1.25
88 Invisible Girl	$0.30	$1.00	$2.00	£0.20	£0.60	£1.25
89 Nightcrawler, part Nasser art	$0.50	$1.50	$2.50	£0.30	£0.90	£1.50
90 The Beast	$0.40	$1.20	$2.00	£0.25	£0.75	£1.25
91 Ghost Rider	$0.50	$1.50	$2.50	£0.30	£0.90	£1.50
92 Hawkeye	$0.40	$1.20	$2.00	£0.25	£0.75	£1.25
93 Werewolf By Night	$0.40	$1.20	$2.00	£0.25	£0.75	£1.25
94 Shroud, Mike Zeck art	$0.40	$1.20	$2.00	£0.25	£0.75	£1.25
95 Mockingbird; Nick Fury appears, Frank Miller cover	$0.40	$1.20	$2.00	£0.25	£0.75	£1.25
96 Howard the Duck	$0.40	$1.20	$2.00	£0.25	£0.75	£1.25
97 Hulk and Spiderwoman, no Spiderman	$0.40	$1.20	$2.00	£0.25	£0.75	£1.25
98 Black Widow	$0.40	$1.20	$2.00	£0.25	£0.75	£1.25
99 Machine Man, Frank Miller cover	$0.40	$1.20	$2.00	£0.25	£0.75	£1.25
100 ND 52pgs, Fantastic Four, Miller art; Storm, Havok, Black Panther appear, John Byrne art, 1st appearance and origin Karma	$1.50	$4.50	$7.50	£0.70	£2.10	£3.50
101 Nighthawk, Steve Ditko art	$0.30	$0.90	$1.50	£0.20	£0.60	£1.00
102 ND Doc Samson	$0.30	$0.90	$1.50	£0.25	£0.75	£1.25
103 ND Ant-Man	$0.30	$0.90	$1.50	£0.25	£0.75	£1.25
104 ND Hulk and Ka-Zar, no Spiderman	$0.30	$0.90	$1.50	£0.25	£0.75	£1.25
105 ND Hulk and Powerman and Iron Fist, no Spiderman	$0.30	$0.90	$1.50	£0.25	£0.75	£1.25
106 ND Captain America	$0.30	$0.90	$1.50	£0.25	£0.75	£1.25
107 ND She-Hulk	$0.30	$0.90	$1.50	£0.25	£0.75	£1.25
108 ND Paladin	$0.30	$0.90	$1.50	£0.25	£0.75	£1.25
109 ND Dazzler	$0.30	$0.90	$1.50	£0.25	£0.75	£1.25
110 ND Iron Man	$0.30	$0.90	$1.50	£0.25	£0.75	£1.25
111 ND Devilslayer; Defenders and Dr. Strange appear	$0.30	$0.90	$1.50	£0.25	£0.75	£1.25
112 Kull; Dr. Strange appears	$0.30	$0.90	$1.50	£0.20	£0.60	£1.00
113 Quasar	$0.30	$0.90	$1.50	£0.20	£0.60	£1.00
114 Falcon, Mike Zeck cover	$0.30	$0.90	$1.50	£0.20	£0.60	£1.00
115 Thor	$0.30	$0.90	$1.50	£0.20	£0.60	£1.00
116 Valkyrie; Thor appears	$0.30	$0.90	$1.50	£0.20	£0.60	£1.00
117 Wolverine	$2.50	$7.50	$12.50	£1.20	£3.60	£6.00
118 Professor X; Wolverine appears	$0.80	$2.40	$4.00	£0.50	£1.50	£2.50
119 Gargoyle	$0.30	$0.90	$1.50	£0.20	£0.60	£1.00
120 Dominic Fortune	$0.30	$0.90	$1.50	£0.20	£0.60	£1.00
121 Human Torch	$0.30	$0.90	$1.50	£0.20	£0.60	£1.00
122 Man-Thing	$0.30	$0.90	$1.50	£0.20	£0.60	£1.00
123 Daredevil	$0.30	$0.90	$1.50	£0.20	£0.60	£1.00
124 The Beast	$0.30	$0.90	$1.50	£0.20	£0.60	£1.00
125 Tigra	$0.30	$0.90	$1.50	£0.20	£0.60	£1.00
126 Spiderman and Hulk; Powerman and Son of Satan	$0.30	$0.90	$1.50	£0.20	£0.60	£1.00
127 The Watcher; Captain America appears	$0.30	$0.90	$1.50	£0.20	£0.60	£1.00
128 Captain America	$0.30	$0.90	$1.50	£0.20	£0.60	£1.00
129 Vision, John Byrne cover	$0.30	$0.90	$1.50	£0.20	£0.60	£1.00
130 Scarlet Witch; The Vision appears	$0.30	$0.90	$1.50	£0.20	£0.60	£1.00
131 Frogman	$0.30	$0.90	$1.50	£0.20	£0.60	£1.00
132 Mr. Fantastic	$0.30	$0.90	$1.50	£0.20	£0.60	£1.00
133 Fantastic Four, John Byrne cover	$0.30	$0.90	$1.50	£0.20	£0.60	£1.00
134 Jack of Hearts; continued in Jack Of Hearts mini-series	$0.30	$0.90	$1.50	£0.20	£0.60	£1.00
135 Kitty Pryde, X-Men cameo	$0.40	$1.20	$2.00	£0.25	£0.75	£1.25
136 Wonderman	$0.30	$0.90	$1.50	£0.20	£0.60	£1.00
137 Aunt May, Franklin Richards; Thing cameo	$0.30	$0.90	$1.50	£0.20	£0.60	£1.00
138 Sandman	$0.30	$0.90	$1.50	£0.20	£0.60	£1.00
139 Nick Fury	$0.30	$0.90	$1.50	£0.20	£0.60	£1.00
140 Black Widow	$0.30	$0.90	$1.50	£0.20	£0.60	£1.00
141 Daredevil, new Black Widow appears; ties for 1st appearance of Spiderman black costume (see Amazing Spiderman #252)	$0.70	$2.10	$3.50	£0.40	£1.20	£2.00
142 Captain Marvel, Spiderman in black costume	$0.30	$0.90	$1.50	£0.20	£0.60	£1.00
143 Starfox, Spiderman in black costume	$0.30	$0.90	$1.50	£0.20	£0.60	£1.00
144 Moonknight, Spiderman in black costume	$0.30	$0.90	$1.50	£0.20	£0.60	£1.00
145 Iron Man, Spiderman in black costume	$0.30	$0.90	$1.50	£0.20	£0.60	£1.00
146 Nomad, Spiderman in black costume	$0.30	$0.90	$1.50	£0.20	£0.60	£1.00
147 Human Torch	$0.30	$0.90	$1.50	£0.20	£0.60	£1.00
148 LD in the U.K. Thor	$0.30	$0.90	$1.50	£0.25	£0.75	£1.25
149 Cannonball	$0.30	$0.90	$1.50	£0.25	£0.75	£1.25
150 LD in the U.K. DS, X-Men, Barry Smith cover	$1.00	$3.00	$5.00	£0.70	£2.10	£3.50
Title Value:	$135.55	$412.75	$812.00	£83.95	£255.45	£503.00

Note: Spiderman in black costume #141-146. Also issue #74 had no number on the cover.

MARVEL TEAM-UP ANNUAL

Marvel Comics Group; 1 1976-7 Oct 1984

	$Good	$Fine	$N.Mint	£Good	£Fine	£N.Mint
1 ND 52pgs, Spiderman, X-Men; story linked to Marvel Team-Up #53	$2.50	$7.50	$15.00	£1.65	£5.00	£10.00
2 ND 52pgs, Spiderman, Hulk	$0.50	$1.50	$3.00	£0.30	£1.00	£2.00
3 ND 52pgs, Hulk, Powerman, Iron Fist; Machine Man appears, Spiderman appears as cameo only; Frank Miller cover	$0.50	$1.50	$3.00	£0.30	£1.00	£2.00
4 ND 52pgs, Spiderman, Moonknight, Iron Fist, Daredevil, Powerman	$0.50	$1.50	$2.50	£0.30	£0.90	£1.50
5 ND 52pgs, Spiderman, Thing, Dr.Strange, Scarlet Witch, Quasar	$0.50	$1.50	$2.50	£0.30	£0.90	£1.50
6 ND 52pgs, Spiderman, New Mutants, Cloak and Dagger	$0.50	$1.50	$2.50	£0.30	£0.90	£1.50
7 ND 52pgs, Spiderman, Alpha Flight, John Byrne cover	$0.50	$1.50	$2.50	£0.30	£0.90	£1.50
Title Value:	$5.50	$16.50	$31.00	£3.45	£10.60	£20.00

MARVEL TEAM-UP, THE OFFICIAL MARVEL INDEX TO

Marvel Comics Group; 1 Jan 1986-6 Jul 1987

	$Good	$Fine	$N.Mint	£Good	£Fine	£N.Mint
1 ND scarce in the U.K. information and colour cover reproductions on Marvel Team-Up #1-#20	$0.50	$1.50	$2.50	£0.30	£0.90	£1.50
2 ND scarce in the U.K. information and colour cover reproductions on Marvel Team-Up #21-#42	$0.50	$1.50	$2.50	£0.30	£0.90	£1.50
3 ND scarce in the U.K. information and colour cover reproductions on Marvel Team-Up #43-#59, Annual #1; P. Craig Russell cover	$0.50	$1.50	$2.50	£0.30	£0.90	£1.50
4 ND scarce in the U.K. information and colour cover reproductions on Marvel Team-Up #60-#80	$0.50	$1.50	$2.50	£0.30	£0.90	£1.50
5 ND scarce in the U.K. information and colour cover reproductions on Marvel Team-Up #81-#98, Annual #2	$0.50	$1.50	$2.50	£0.30	£0.90	£1.50
6 ND scarce in the U.K. information and colour cover reproductions on Marvel Team-Up #99-#112, Annual #3,#4	$0.50	$1.50	$2.50	£0.30	£0.90	£1.50
Title Value:	$3.00	$9.00	$15.00	£1.80	£5.40	£9.00

MARVEL TREASURY EDITION

Marvel Comics Group,Tabloid; 1 1974-28 1981

	$Good	$Fine	$N.Mint	£Good	£Fine	£N.Mint
1 scarce in the U.K. Spiderman	$1.25	$3.75	$7.50	£0.80	£2.50	£5.00
2 Fantastic Four, issue #48 reprinted (origin Silver Surfer)	$0.80	$2.50	$5.00	£0.55	£1.75	£3.50
3 Thor	$0.80	$2.50	$5.00	£0.55	£1.75	£3.50
4 Conan, Smith reprints	$0.80	$2.50	$5.00	£0.55	£1.75	£3.50
5 Hulk, reprints origin	$0.80	$2.50	$5.00	£0.55	£1.75	£3.50
6 Dr. Strange	$0.65	$2.00	$4.00	£0.50	£1.50	£3.00
7 Avengers	$0.65	$2.00	$4.00	£0.50	£1.50	£3.00
8 Christmas Holiday Grab-Bag (Spiderman, Hulk, Nick Fury)	$0.65	$2.00	$4.00	£0.50	£1.50	£3.00
9 Super-Hero Team Up	$0.65	$2.00	$4.00	£0.50	£1.50	£3.00
10 Thor	$0.65	$2.00	$4.00	£0.50	£1.50	£3.00
11 Fantastic Four	$0.65	$2.00	$4.00	£0.50	£1.50	£3.00
12 Howard the Duck, one new story plus Brunner reprints from Giant Size Man-Thing	$0.65	$2.00	$4.00	£0.50	£1.50	£3.00
13 Christmas Holiday Grab-Bag						

	$Good	$Fine	$N.Mint	£Good	£Fine	£N.Mint
	$0.65	*$2.00*	*$4.00*	£0.50	£1.50	£3.00
14 less common in the U.K. Spiderman	*$0.65*	*$2.00*	*$4.00*	£0.50	£1.50	£3.00
15 Conan	*$0.65*	*$2.00*	*$4.00*	£0.50	£1.50	£3.00
16 Defenders, origin retold	*$0.65*	*$2.00*	*$4.00*	£0.50	£1.50	£3.00
17 Hulk	*$0.65*	*$2.00*	*$4.00*	£0.50	£1.50	£3.00
18 ND Spiderman, reprints 1st team-up with X-Men	*$0.65*	*$2.00*	*$4.00*	£0.50	£1.50	£3.00
19 ND Conan	*$0.65*	*$2.00*	*$4.00*	£0.50	£1.50	£3.00
20 ND Hulk	*$0.65*	*$2.00*	*$4.00*	£0.50	£1.50	£3.00
21 ND Fantastic Four	*$0.65*	*$2.00*	*$4.00*	£0.50	£1.50	£3.00
22 ND Spiderman	*$0.65*	*$2.00*	*$4.00*	£0.50	£1.50	£3.00
23 ND Conan	*$0.65*	*$2.00*	*$4.00*	£0.50	£1.50	£3.00
24 ND Hulk	*$0.65*	*$2.00*	*$4.00*	£0.50	£1.50	£3.00
25 ND Spiderman vs. Hulk	*$0.65*	*$2.00*	*$4.00*	£0.50	£1.50	£3.00
26 ND reprints Hulk #167-#170; new Wolverine and Hercules story (6pgs)	*$1.00*	*$3.00*	*$6.00*	£0.65	£2.00	£4.00
27 ND reprints Spiderman from Marvel Team Up #9-#11,#27, new Angel story (5pgs)	*$0.80*	*$2.50*	*$5.00*	£0.55	£1.75	£3.50
28 ND Superman and Spiderman, origins each retold	*$0.80*	*$2.50*	*$5.00*	£0.55	£1.75	£3.50
Title Value:	***$20.05***	***$61.75***	***$123.50***	**£14.75**	**£45.00**	**£90.00**

Note: owing to their large size and card covers, all are very scarce in true mint condition.

MARVEL TREASURY OF OZ

Marvel Comics Group,Tabloid; 1 1975

(see M.G.M.'s Marvelous...)

	$Good	$Fine	$N.Mint	£Good	£Fine	£N.Mint
1 ND The Marvelous Land of Oz, Buscema art	*$0.75*	*$2.25*	*$4.50*	£0.50	£1.50	£3.00
Title Value:	***$0.75***	***$2.25***	***$4.50***	**£0.50**	**£1.50**	**£3.00**

MARVEL TREASURY SPECIAL

Marvel Comics Group,Tabloid; 1974-1980

	$Good	$Fine	$N.Mint	£Good	£Fine	£N.Mint
1 2001: A Space Odyssey distributed in the U.K.	*$0.50*	*$1.50*	*$3.00*	£0.30	£1.00	£2.00
1 Amazing Spiderman, ND 80pgs, Steve Ditko reprints; titled Marvel Special Edition	*$0.75*	*$2.25*	*$4.50*	£0.50	£1.50	£3.00
Captain America's Bicentennnial Battles, distributed in the U.K. Jack Kirby art	*$0.65*	*$2.00*	*$4.00*	£0.40	£1.25	£2.50
1 Giant Super-Hero Holiday Grab-Bag distributed in the U.K.	*$0.65*	*$2.00*	*$4.00*	£0.40	£1.25	£2.50
1 Land of Oz ND	*$0.65*	*$2.00*	*$4.00*	£0.40	£1.25	£2.50
1 Savage Fist of Kung Fu ND	*$0.65*	*$2.00*	*$4.00*	£0.40	£1.25	£2.50
1 Star Wars, distributed in the U.K. 80pgs, reprints Star Wars #1-3	*$1.00*	*$3.00*	*$6.00*	£0.65	£2.00	£4.00
2 Star Wars, distributed in the U.K. 80pgs, reprints Star Wars #4-6	*$0.80*	*$2.50*	*$5.00*	£0.50	£1.50	£3.00
2 Star Wars: The Empire Strikes Back, ND reprints Star Wars #39-44	*$0.80*	*$2.50*	*$5.00*	£0.50	£1.50	£3.00
3 Close Encounters, distributed in the U.K. reprints Marvel Super Special #3	*$0.50*	*$1.50*	*$3.00*	£0.30	£1.00	£2.00
3 Star Wars, ND reprints Star Wars #1-6	*$1.00*	*$3.00*	*$6.00*	£0.80	£2.50	£5.00
Title Value:	***$7.95***	***$24.25***	***$48.50***	**£5.15**	**£16.00**	**£32.00**

MARVEL TRIPLE ACTION

Marvel Comics Group; 1 Feb 1972-24 Mar 1975; 25 Aug 1975-47 Apr 1979

	$Good	$Fine	$N.Mint	£Good	£Fine	£N.Mint
1 ND scarce in the U.K. 52pgs, Silver Surfer appears (reprints from Fantastic Four #57 onwards begin)	*$0.80*	*$2.50*	*$5.00*	£0.55	£1.75	£3.50
2-4 ND Silver Surfer appears	*$0.50*	*$1.50*	*$3.00*	£0.30	£1.00	£2.00
5 ND Avengers reprints begin (from #10 onwards omitting #11)	*$0.50*	*$1.50*	*$3.00*	£0.30	£1.00	£2.00
6-20 ND	*$0.40*	*$1.25*	*$2.50*	£0.25	£0.75	£1.50
21-40 ND	*$0.25*	*$0.75*	*$1.50*	£0.20	£0.60	£1.25
41-42 ND	*$0.20*	*$0.60*	*$1.25*	£0.15	£0.50	£1.00
43-44	*$0.20*	*$0.60*	*$1.25*	£0.10	£0.35	£0.75
45 includes X-Men reprint	*$0.20*	*$0.60*	*$1.25*	£0.10	£0.35	£0.75
46	*$0.20*	*$0.60*	*$1.25*	£0.10	£0.35	£0.75
47 ND	*$0.20*	*$0.60*	*$1.25*	£0.15	£0.50	£1.00
Title Value:	***$15.20***	***$46.45***	***$87.75***	**£10.35**	**£31.90**	**£65.00**

Note: Fantastic Four reprints #1-4, Avengers reprints #5-46.

REPRINT FEATURES

Avengers in 5-47. Fantastic Four in 1-4. Silver Surfer in 1-3. X-Men in 45.

MARVEL TRIPLE ACTION GIANT SIZE

Marvel Comics Group; 1 May 1975-2 Jul 1975

	$Good	$Fine	$N.Mint	£Good	£Fine	£N.Mint
1 ND very scarce in the U.K. 64pgs, reprints Avengers #31, Daredevil #20, Strange Tales #122	*$0.65*	*$2.00*	*$4.00*	£0.80	£2.50	£5.00
2 ND very scarce in the U.K. 64pgs, reprints Avengers #32, Daredevil #21, Strange Tales #123	*$0.55*	*$1.75*	*$3.50*	£0.65	£2.00	£4.00
Title Value:	***$1.20***	***$3.75***	***$7.50***	**£1.45**	**£4.50**	**£9.00**

Note: Avengers reprints in 1, 2.

MARVEL TRY-OUT BOOK

Marvel Comics Group,OS;Oversize; nn 1986

	$Good	$Fine	$N.Mint	£Good	£Fine	£N.Mint
nn ND illustrations and exercises to complete	*$3.50*	*$10.50*	*$17.50*	£2.50	£7.50	£12.50
Title Value:	***$3.50***	***$10.50***	***$17.50***	**£2.50**	**£7.50**	**£12.50**

Note: the value of the item depends on the extent of completion inside. Untouched copies are very scarce in both the U.K. and U.S.

MARVEL TRY-OUT BOOK, ALL NEW

Marvel Comics Group,OS; nn Jan 1997

	$Good	$Fine	$N.Mint	£Good	£Fine	£N.Mint
nn ND your chance to complete an X-Men adventure started by Andy Kubert and Art Thibert	*$5.00*	*$15.00*	*$25.00*	£3.00	£9.00	£15.00
Title Value:	***$5.00***	***$15.00***	***$25.00***	**£3.00**	**£9.00**	**£15.00**

MARVEL TWO-IN-ONE

Marvel Comics Group; 1 Jan 1974-100 Jun 1983

[The Thing appears in every issue teamed with each of the following]

	$Good	$Fine	$N.Mint	£Good	£Fine	£N.Mint
1 ND Man-Thing	*$5.00*	*$15.00*	*$30.00*	£3.30	£10.00	£20.00
2 ND Sub-Mariner	*$2.05*	*$6.25*	*$12.50*	£1.25	£3.75	£7.50
3 ND Daredevil	*$1.65*	*$5.00*	*$10.00*	£1.05	£3.25	£6.50
4 ND Captain America	*$1.65*	*$5.00*	*$10.00*	£1.05	£3.25	£6.50
5 ND Guardians of the Galaxy; Captain America appears	*$2.05*	*$6.25*	*$12.50*	£1.15	£3.50	£7.00
6 ND Dr. Strange, Jim Starlin cover	*$2.90*	*$8.75*	*$17.50*	£1.15	£3.50	£7.00
7 ND Valkyrie	*$1.30*	*$4.00*	*$8.00*	£0.80	£2.50	£5.00
8 ND Ghost Rider	*$2.05*	*$6.25*	*$12.50*	£1.05	£3.25	£6.50
9 ND Thor	*$1.30*	*$4.00*	*$8.00*	£0.80	£2.50	£5.00
10 ND Black Widow	*$1.30*	*$4.00*	*$8.00*	£0.80	£2.50	£5.00
11 Golem	*$0.65*	*$2.00*	*$4.00*	£0.40	£1.25	£2.50
12 Iron Man	*$0.65*	*$2.00*	*$4.00*	£0.40	£1.25	£2.50
13 Powerman	*$0.65*	*$2.00*	*$4.00*	£0.40	£1.25	£2.50
14 Son of Satan	*$0.65*	*$2.00*	*$4.00*	£0.40	£1.25	£2.50
15 Morbius	*$0.65*	*$2.00*	*$4.00*	£0.40	£1.25	£2.50
16 Ka-Zar	*$0.65*	*$2.00*	*$4.00*	£0.40	£1.25	£2.50
17 Spiderman; X-over Marvel Team Up #47	*$0.65*	*$2.00*	*$4.00*	£0.40	£1.25	£2.50
18 Scarecrow	*$0.65*	*$2.00*	*$4.00*	£0.40	£1.25	£2.50

Marvel Tales #6

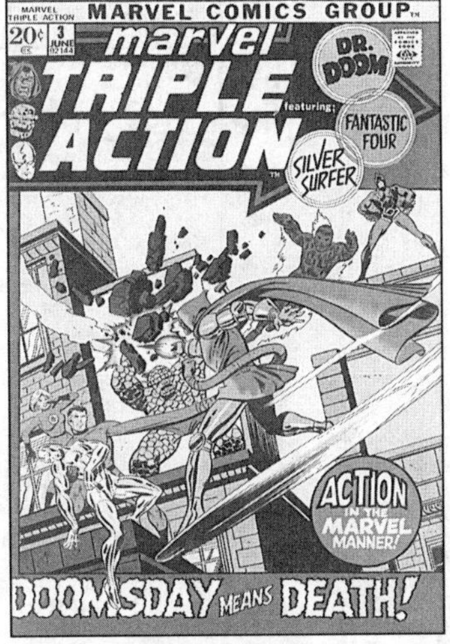

Marvel Triple Action #3

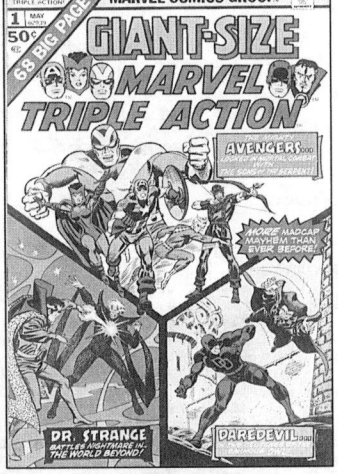

Marvel Triple Action Giant Size #1

	$Good	$Fine	$N.Mint	£Good	£Fine	£N.Mint
19 Tigra	*$0.65*	*$2.00*	*$4.00*	£0.40	£1.25	£2.50
20 Liberty Legion, continues from Fantastic Four Annual #11	*$0.65*	*$2.00*	*$4.00*	£0.40	£1.25	£2.50
21 Doc Savage	*$0.50*	*$1.50*	*$3.00*	£0.30	£1.00	£2.00
22 Thor; Human Torch appears	*$0.50*	*$1.50*	*$3.00*	£0.30	£1.00	£2.00
23 Thor	*$0.50*	*$1.50*	*$3.00*	£0.30	£1.00	£2.00
24 Black Goliath	*$0.50*	*$1.50*	*$3.00*	£0.30	£1.00	£2.00
25 Iron Fist	*$0.50*	*$1.50*	*$3.00*	£0.30	£1.00	£2.00
26 Nick Fury; Deathlok appears on last page	*$0.50*	*$1.50*	*$3.00*	£0.30	£1.00	£2.00
27 Deathlok; Fantastic Four and Impossible Man appear	*$0.65*	*$2.00*	*$4.00*	£0.40	£1.25	£2.50
28 Sub-Mariner; Deathlok cameo (2pgs)	*$0.50*	*$1.50*	*$3.00*	£0.30	£1.00	£2.00
29 Master of Kung Fu; Spiderman appears on last page	*$0.50*	*$1.50*	*$3.00*	£0.30	£1.00	£2.00
30 Spiderwoman (2nd appearance)	*$0.80*	*$2.50*	*$5.00*	£0.40	£1.25	£2.50
31 Spiderwoman (3rd appearance)	*$0.50*	*$1.50*	*$3.00*	£0.25	£0.75	£1.50
32 Invisible Girl; Spiderwoman appears	*$0.50*	*$1.50*	*$3.00*	£0.25	£0.75	£1.50
33 Modred the Mystic; Spiderwoman appears	*$0.50*	*$1.50*	*$3.00*	£0.25	£0.75	£1.50
34 Nighthawk; Deathlok cameo	*$0.50*	*$1.50*	*$3.00*	£0.25	£0.75	£1.50
35 Skull the Slayer	*$0.50*	*$1.50*	*$3.00*	£0.25	£0.75	£1.50
36 Mr. Fantastic; Skull the Slayer appears	*$0.50*	*$1.50*	*$3.00*	£0.25	£0.75	£1.50
37 Matt Murdock (Daredevil)	*$0.50*	*$1.50*	*$3.00*	£0.25	£0.75	£1.50
38 Daredevil	*$0.50*	*$1.50*	*$3.00*	£0.25	£0.75	£1.50
39 Vision; Daredevil and Yellowjacket appear	*$0.50*	*$1.50*	*$3.00*	£0.25	£0.75	£1.50
40 Black Panther	*$0.50*	*$1.50*	*$3.00*	£0.25	£0.75	£1.50
41 Brother Voodoo; Black Panther appears	*$0.40*	*$1.25*	*$2.50*	£0.25	£0.75	£1.50
42 Captain America; Wundarr appears	*$0.40*	*$1.25*	*$2.50*	£0.25	£0.75	£1.50
43 Man-Thing and Captain America, Cosmic Cube featured, John Byrne art	*$0.50*	*$1.50*	*$3.00*	£0.30	£1.00	£2.00
44 Hercules	*$0.40*	*$1.25*	*$2.50*	£0.25	£0.75	£1.50
45 Captain Marvel	*$0.40*	*$1.25*	*$2.50*	£0.25	£0.75	£1.50
46 Hulk	*$0.40*	*$1.25*	*$2.50*	£0.25	£0.75	£1.50
47 The Yancy Street Gang	*$0.40*	*$1.25*	*$2.50*	£0.25	£0.75	£1.50
48 Jack of Hearts	*$0.40*	*$1.25*	*$2.50*	£0.25	£0.75	£1.50
49 Dr. Strange	*$0.40*	*$1.25*	*$2.50*	£0.25	£0.75	£1.50
50 Thing vs. Thing, John Byrne art	*$0.50*	*$1.50*	*$3.00*	£0.30	£1.00	£2.00
51 Frank Miller art, Beast, Ms.Marvel, Nick Fury, Wonderman	*$0.65*	*$2.00*	*$4.00*	£0.40	£1.25	£2.50
52 Moon Knight	*$0.50*	*$1.50*	*$3.00*	£0.30	£1.00	£2.00
53 Quasar, Deathlok on last page, John Byrne art; The Pegasus Project begins (ends #58)	*$0.50*	*$1.50*	*$3.00*	£0.30	£1.00	£2.00
54 Deathlok dies, John Byrne art	*$1.25*	*$3.75*	*$7.50*	£0.55	£1.75	£3.50
55 Giant-Man, John Byrne art	*$0.50*	*$1.50*	*$3.00*	£0.30	£1.00	£2.00
56 Thundra; Giant-Man appears, George Perez and Gene Day art	*$0.40*	*$1.20*	*$2.00*	£0.25	£0.75	£1.25
57 Wundarr; Giant-Man appears, George Perez art	*$0.40*	*$1.20*	*$2.00*	£0.25	£0.75	£1.25
58 Aquarian; Giant-Man appears, George Perez art	*$0.40*	*$1.20*	*$2.00*	£0.25	£0.75	£1.25
59 Human Torch	*$0.40*	*$1.20*	*$2.00*	£0.25	£0.75	£1.25
60 Impossible Man, George Perez art	*$0.40*	*$1.20*	*$2.00*	£0.25	£0.75	£1.25
61 Starhawk, George Perez art	*$0.40*	*$1.20*	*$2.00*	£0.25	£0.75	£1.25
62 Moondragon; Starhawk appears, George Perez art	*$0.40*	*$1.20*	*$2.00*	£0.25	£0.75	£1.25
63 Warlock (dead), Starhawk appears, George Perez art	*$0.40*	*$1.20*	*$2.00*	£0.25	£0.75	£1.25
64 Stingray; Wundarr and Fantastic Four appear, George Perez art	*$0.40*	*$1.20*	*$2.00*	£0.25	£0.75	£1.25
65 Triton; Stingray and Thundra appear, George Perez art	*$0.40*	*$1.20*	*$2.00*	£0.25	£0.75	£1.25
66 Scarlet Witch	*$0.40*	*$1.20*	*$2.00*	£0.25	£0.75	£1.25
67 Hyperion; Quasar and Thundra appear	*$0.40*	*$1.20*	*$2.00*	£0.25	£0.75	£1.25
68 Angel	*$0.40*	*$1.20*	*$2.00*	£0.25	£0.75	£1.25
69 Guardians of the Galaxy; Fantastic Four appear	*$0.50*	*$1.50*	*$2.50*	£0.30	£0.90	£1.50
70 The Yancy Street Gang	*$0.40*	*$1.20*	*$2.00*	£0.25	£0.75	£1.25
71 Mr. Fantastic; Triton, Inhumans, Fantastic Four and Stingray appear; 1st appearance Maelstrom	*$0.30*	*$0.90*	*$1.50*	£0.20	£0.60	£1.00
72 ND Inhumans	*$0.30*	*$0.90*	*$1.50*	£0.20	£0.60	£1.00
73 ND Quasar	*$0.30*	*$0.90*	*$1.50*	£0.20	£0.60	£1.00
74 Puppet Master	*$0.30*	*$0.90*	*$1.50*	£0.20	£0.60	£1.00
75 52pgs, Avengers, Beast appears	*$0.30*	*$0.90*	*$1.50*	£0.20	£0.60	£1.00
76 Iceman; Black Goliath appears	*$0.30*	*$0.90*	*$1.50*	£0.20	£0.60	£1.00
77 Man-Thing; Sgt. Fury appears in flash-back	*$0.30*	*$0.90*	*$1.50*	£0.20	£0.60	£1.00
78 Wonderman	*$0.30*	*$0.90*	*$1.50*	£0.20	£0.60	£1.00
79 Blue Diamond	*$0.30*	*$0.90*	*$1.50*	£0.20	£0.60	£1.00
80 Ghost Rider; Fantastic Four appear	*$0.60*	*$1.80*	*$3.00*	£0.40	£1.20	£2.00
81 Sub-Mariner; Black Goliath and Quasar appear	*$0.30*	*$0.90*	*$1.50*	£0.20	£0.60	£1.00
82 Captain America; Black Goliath and Fantastic Four appear	*$0.30*	*$0.90*	*$1.50*	£0.20	£0.60	£1.00
83 Sasquatch; Black Goliath and Fantastic Four appear	*$0.40*	*$1.20*	*$2.00*	£0.25	£0.75	£1.25
84 Alpha Flight; Black Goliath and Fantastic Four appear	*$0.40*	*$1.20*	*$2.00*	£0.25	£0.75	£1.25
85 Spiderwoman	*$0.30*	*$0.90*	*$1.50*	£0.20	£0.60	£1.00
86 Sandman	*$0.30*	*$0.90*	*$1.50*	£0.20	£0.60	£1.00
87 Ant-Man	*$0.30*	*$0.90*	*$1.50*	£0.20	£0.60	£1.00
88 She-Hulk	*$0.30*	*$0.90*	*$1.50*	£0.20	£0.60	£1.00
89 Human Torch	*$0.30*	*$0.90*	*$1.50*	£0.20	£0.60	£1.00
90 Machine Man	*$0.30*	*$0.90*	*$1.50*	£0.20	£0.60	£1.00
91 Sphinx; Dr. Strange appears	*$0.30*	*$0.90*	*$1.50*	£0.20	£0.60	£1.00
92 Jocasta; Machine Man appears	*$0.30*	*$0.90*	*$1.50*	£0.20	£0.60	£1.00
93 Machine Man (Jocasta dies)	*$0.30*	*$0.90*	*$1.50*	£0.20	£0.60	£1.00
94 Powerman/Iron Fist	*$0.30*	*$0.90*	*$1.50*	£0.20	£0.60	£1.00
95 The Living Mummy	*$0.30*	*$0.90*	*$1.50*	£0.20	£0.60	£1.00
96 The Sandman (and virtually all Marvel characters)	*$0.30*	*$0.90*	*$1.50*	£0.20	£0.60	£1.00
97 Iron Man	*$0.30*	*$0.90*	*$1.50*	£0.20	£0.60	£1.00
98 Video Wars	*$0.30*	*$0.90*	*$1.50*	£0.20	£0.60	£1.00
99 Rom	*$0.30*	*$0.90*	*$1.50*	£0.20	£0.60	£1.00
100 LD in the U.K. DS, Ben Grimm, John Byrne script	*$0.40*	*$1.20*	*$2.00*	£0.25	£0.75	£1.25
Title Value:	*$61.50*	*$186.35*	*$357.00*	£36.70	£112.95	£215.75

ARTISTS

Gene Day inks on 58, 60-70. Byrne covers on 56-58, 98, 99. Kirby covers 12, 19, 25, 27. Perez covers on 42, 51-52, 54-55, 61-66. Perez art: 56-58, 60, 64, 65, 75.

MARVEL TWO-IN-ONE ANNUAL

Marvel Comics Group; 1 1976-7 Oct 1982

	$Good	$Fine	$N.Mint	£Good	£Fine	£N.Mint
1 ND Thing, Liberty Legion, continued from Fantastic Four Annual #11 and continues in Marvel Two-in-One #20; Jack Kirby cover	*$0.55*	*$1.75*	*$3.50*	£0.40	£1.25	£2.50
2 ND scarce in the U.K. Thing, Spiderman, Avengers, Warlock; Thanos dies, continues from Avengers Annual #7, Jim Starlin art	*$2.90*	*$8.75*	*$17.50*	£1.65	£5.00	£10.00
3 ND scarce in the U.K. Thing/Nova	*$0.40*	*$1.25*	*$2.50*	£0.30	£1.00	£2.00
4 ND Thing, Black Bolt	*$0.40*	*$1.20*	*$2.00*	£0.25	£0.75	£1.25
5 ND Thing, Hulk	*$0.40*	*$1.20*	*$2.00*	£0.25	£0.75	£1.25
6 ND Thing, American Eagle; Ka-Zar appears, Gene Day inks	*$0.40*	*$1.20*	*$2.00*	£0.25	£0.75	£1.25
7 ND Thing, X-Men appear; cameos of many other heroes	*$0.50*	*$1.50*	*$2.50*	£0.30	£0.90	£1.50
Title Value:	*$5.55*	*$16.85*	*$32.00*	£3.40	£10.40	£19.75

MARVEL UNIVERSE

Marvel Comics Group,OS; nn Feb 1997

	$Good	$Fine	$N.Mint	£Good	£Fine	£N.Mint
nn ND 48pgs, epilogue to the Onslaught Saga	*$0.60*	*$1.80*	*$3.00*	£0.40	£1.20	£2.00
Title Value:	*$0.60*	*$1.80*	*$3.00*	£0.40	£1.20	£2.00

MARVEL UNIVERSE - MASTER EDITION

Marvel Comics Group; 1 Dec 1990-36 Nov 1993

	$Good	$Fine	$N.Mint	£Good	£Fine	£N.Mint
1 ND 48pgs, loose-leaf spiral-bound format "who's who" of Marvel characters. Spiderman/Juggernaut featured	*$0.80*	*$2.40*	*$4.00*	£0.50	£1.50	£2.50
2 ND 48pgs, Captain America/Dr. Octopus featured	*$0.80*	*$2.40*	*$4.00*	£0.50	£1.50	£2.50
3 ND 48pgs, Ghost Rider/Elektra featured	*$0.80*	*$2.40*	*$4.00*	£0.50	£1.50	£2.50
4 ND 48pgs, Wolverine	*$0.80*	*$2.40*	*$4.00*	£0.50	£1.50	£2.50
5 ND 48pgs, Punisher/She-Hulk/Bullseye/ Nightcrawler featured	*$0.80*	*$2.40*	*$4.00*	£0.50	£1.50	£2.50
6 ND 48pgs, Hobgoblin	*$0.80*	*$2.40*	*$4.00*	£0.50	£1.50	£2.50
7 ND 48pgs, Daredevil/Callisto/Firestar/Nova/Black Knight featured	*$0.80*	*$2.40*	*$4.00*	£0.50	£1.50	£2.50
8 ND 48pgs, Hulk	*$0.80*	*$2.40*	*$4.00*	£0.50	£1.50	£2.50
9 ND 48pgs, Moon Knight/Scarlet Witch/Doc Samson featured	*$0.80*	*$2.40*	*$4.00*	£0.50	£1.50	£2.50
10 ND 48pgs, Captain Britain/Jigsaw/Wendigo/Odin featured	*$0.80*	*$2.40*	*$4.00*	£0.50	£1.50	£2.50
11 ND 48pgs, Storm, Madrox, Kid Nova featured	*$0.80*	*$2.40*	*$4.00*	£0.50	£1.50	£2.50

	$Good	$Fine	$N.Mint	£Good	£Fine	£N.Mint
12 ND 48pgs, Silver Surfer, Black Cat, Loki featured						
	$0.80	*$2.40*	*$4.00*	£0.50	£1.50	£2.50
13 ND 48pgs, High Evolutionary, Werewolf, Shroud, Mysterio featured						
	$0.80	*$2.40*	*$4.00*	£0.50	£1.50	£2.50
14 ND 48pgs, Captain America, Avengers, Thor, Fin Fang Foom featured						
	$0.80	*$2.40*	*$4.00*	£0.50	£1.50	£2.50
15-17 ND 48pgs	*$0.80*	*$2.40*	*$4.00*	£0.50	£1.50	£2.50
18 ND 48pgs, Thing, She-Hulk						
	$0.80	*$2.40*	*$4.00*	£0.50	£1.50	£2.50
19 ND 48pgs	*$0.80*	*$2.40*	*$4.00*	£0.50	£1.50	£2.50
20 ND 48pgs, Dr. Doom, Archangel						
	$0.80	*$2.40*	*$4.00*	£0.50	£1.50	£2.50
21 ND 48pgs, Gambit, Watcher						
	$0.80	*$2.40*	*$4.00*	£0.50	£1.50	£2.50
22 ND 48pgs, Speedball, Nick Fury, Rogue, Silver Sable, Invisible Woman plus Venom feature						
	$0.80	*$2.40*	*$4.00*	£0.50	£1.50	£2.50
23 ND 48pgs, Deathlok, Batroc, Psylocke, Sunfire						
	$0.80	*$2.40*	*$4.00*	£0.50	£1.50	£2.50
24 ND 48pgs, Johnny Blaze, Human Torch, Iron Fist, Red Skull						
	$0.80	*$2.40*	*$4.00*	£0.50	£1.50	£2.50
25 ND 48pgs, Deadpool, Night Thrasher, Black Widow						
	$0.80	*$2.40*	*$4.00*	£0.50	£1.50	£2.50
26 ND 48pgs, Morbius, Stryfe, Mystique, Ikaris						
	$0.80	*$2.40*	*$4.00*	£0.50	£1.50	£2.50
27 ND 48pgs, Beta Ray Bill, Pip the Troll, Wonderman, Green Goblin						
	$0.80	*$2.40*	*$4.00*	£0.50	£1.50	£2.50
28 ND 48pgs, Dr. Strange, Blade, Scarecrow, Hellfire Club, Man-Beast, Starhawk, X-Men						
	$0.80	*$2.40*	*$4.00*	£0.50	£1.50	£2.50
29 ND 48pgs, Carnage, Dazzler, Puma, Sabretooth						
	$0.80	*$2.40*	*$4.00*	£0.50	£1.50	£2.50
30 ND 48pgs, Bishop, Dracula, Longshot, Magik, Rage						
	$0.80	*$2.40*	*$4.00*	£0.50	£1.50	£2.50
31 ND 48pgs, War Machine, Cardiac, Feral, Sleepwalker, Molecule Man, Vision, Destroyer and Killraven						
	$0.80	*$2.40*	*$4.00*	£0.50	£1.50	£2.50
32 ND 48pgs, Maverick, Captain Universe, the Kree, Lord Chaos, Mephisto						
	$0.80	*$2.40*	*$4.00*	£0.50	£1.50	£2.50
33 ND 48pgs, Warpath, Gideon, Avalanche, Bloodaxe, Crippler and Living Tribunal						
	$0.80	*$2.40*	*$4.00*	£0.50	£1.50	£2.50
34 ND 48pgs, Thunderstrike, Deathwatch, Caliban, Henry Pym, Turbo, Living Laser						
	$0.80	*$2.40*	*$4.00*	£0.50	£1.50	£2.50
35 ND 48pgs, Hellstrom, Omega Red, Lilith, Beyonder, Spiderman 2099						
	$0.80	*$2.40*	*$4.00*	£0.50	£1.50	£2.50
36 ND 48pgs, Morbius, Ravage 2099, Sunspot, Zarathos						
	$0.80	*$2.40*	*$4.00*	£0.50	£1.50	£2.50
Title Value:	*$28.80*	*$86.40*	*$144.00*	£18.00	£54.00	£90.00

Note: binder issued separately

MARVEL VERSUS DC

Marvel Comics Group/DC Comics,MS;2 Feb 1996-3 Mar 1996

(see DC versus Marvel)

	$Good	$Fine	$N.Mint	£Good	£Fine	£N.Mint
2-3 ND	*$1.00*	*$3.00*	*$5.00*	£0.60	£1.80	£3.00
Title Value:	*$2.00*	*$6.00*	*$10.00*	£1.20	£3.60	£6.00

MARVEL X-MEN COLLECTION

Marvel Comics Group,MS; 1 Jan 1994-3 Mar 1994

	$Good	$Fine	$N.Mint	£Good	£Fine	£N.Mint
1-3 ND 32pgs, reprints Jim Lee's set of 96 trading cards; gatefold back cover						
	$0.60	*$1.80*	*$3.00*	£0.40	£1.20	£2.00
Title Value:	*$1.80*	*$5.40*	*$9.00*	£1.20	£3.60	£6.00

MARVEL'S GREATEST COMICS

Marvel Comics Group;23 Oct 1969-96 Jan 1981

(previously Marvel Collector's Item Classics)

	$Good	$Fine	$N.Mint	£Good	£Fine	£N.Mint
23-28 64pgs	*$0.55*	*$1.75*	*$3.50*	£0.40	£1.25	£2.50
29 64pgs, reprints Fantastic Four #12						
	$0.55	*$1.75*	*$3.50*	£0.40	£1.25	£2.50
30 64pgs	*$0.55*	*$1.75*	*$3.50*	£0.40	£1.25	£2.50
31 64pgs, reprints Fantastic Four #39, #40						
	$0.50	*$1.50*	*$3.00*	£0.30	£1.00	£2.00
32-33 ND scarce in the U.K. 64pgs						
	$0.50	*$1.50*	*$3.00*	£0.40	£1.25	£2.50
34 ND scarce in the U.K. 48pgs, last squarebound issue						
	$0.50	*$1.50*	*$3.00*	£0.40	£1.25	£2.50
35 ND reprints 1st Silver Surfer (FF #48)						
	$0.75	*$2.25*	*$4.50*	£0.50	£1.50	£3.00
36 ND reprints 2nd Silver Surfer (FF #49)						
	$0.55	*$1.75*	*$3.50*	£0.40	£1.25	£2.50
37 ND reprints 3rd Silver Surfer (FF #50)						
	$0.55	*$1.75*	*$3.50*	£0.40	£1.25	£2.50
38-40 ND	*$0.50*	*$1.50*	*$3.00*	£0.30	£1.00	£2.00
41 ND	*$0.40*	*$1.25*	*$2.50*	£0.25	£0.75	£1.50
42 ND reprints Fantastic Four #55						
	$0.40	*$1.25*	*$2.50*	£0.25	£0.75	£1.50
43-50 ND	*$0.40*	*$1.25*	*$2.50*	£0.25	£0.75	£1.50
51-96 ND	*$0.30*	*$1.00*	*$2.00*	£0.20	£0.60	£1.25
Title Value:	*$27.55*	*$88.75*	*$177.50*	£18.60	£56.85	£116.00

Note: Silver Surfer appears in #36, 37, 42

REPRINT FEATURES

Captain America 25-33. Dr.Strange 23-33. Fantastic Four in 23-96. Iron Man 23-33. Watcher in 23, 24.

MARVEL'S GREATEST SUPER-BATTLES

Marvel Comics Group; nn Aug 1994

	$Good	$Fine	$N.Mint	£Good	£Fine	£N.Mint
nn ND 176pgs, softcover trade paperback, reprints include X-Men #212/213, Spiderman #318/319 and Marvel Two in One Annual #7						
	$3.00	*$9.00*	*$15.00*	£2.00	£6.00	£10.00
Title Value:	*$3.00*	*$9.00*	*$15.00*	£2.00	£6.00	£10.00

MARVEL/ULTRAVERSE BATTLEZONES

Marvel Comics Group/Ultraverse,OS; 1 May 1996

	$Good	$Fine	$N.Mint	£Good	£Fine	£N.Mint
1 ND Prime vs. Wolverine, Lord Pumpkin vs. Ghost Rider, Necromantra vs. Storm, Hardcase vs. Captain America, Cayman vs. Thing; features art by George Perez, Gary Frank, Bryan Hitch and others						
	$0.80	*$2.40*	*$4.00*	£0.50	£1.50	£2.50
Title Value:	*$0.80*	*$2.40*	*$4.00*	£0.50	£1.50	£2.50

MARVEL: 1989-95 THE YEAR IN REVIEW

Marvel Comics Group,Magazine; nn Jan 1990; nn Feb 1991; nn Feb 1992; nn Feb 1993; nn Feb 1994; nn Feb 1995

	$Good	$Fine	$N.Mint	£Good	£Fine	£N.Mint
nn (1990) ND 48pgs, - based on Time Magazine format and style with articles and reviews; Todd McFarlane cover						
	$0.60	*$1.80*	*$3.00*	£0.40	£1.20	£2.00
nn (1991) ND 48pgs, - based on Time Magazine format and style with articles and reviews: Kevin Maguire cover						
	$0.60	*$1.80*	*$3.00*	£0.40	£1.20	£2.00
nn (1992) ND 48pgs, - based on Time Magazine format with articles and reviews						
	$0.60	*$1.80*	*$3.00*	£0.40	£1.20	£2.00
nn (1993) ND 48pgs, - comic sized format rather than magazine with articles and reviews						
	$0.60	*$1.80*	*$3.00*	£0.40	£1.20	£2.00
nn (1994) ND 48pgs, - more satirical than in previous years						
	$0.60	*$1.80*	*$3.00*	£0.40	£1.20	£2.00
nn (1995) ND 48pgs, - back to more factual review of the year with emphasis on art rather than text						
	$0.60	*$1.80*	*$3.00*	£0.40	£1.20	£2.00
Title Value:	*$3.60*	*$10.80*	*$18.00*	£2.40	£7.20	£12.00

MARVEL: PORTRAIT OF THE UNIVERSE

Marvel Comics Group,MS; 1 Mar 1995-4 Jun 1995

	$Good	$Fine	$N.Mint	£Good	£Fine	£N.Mint
1-4 Marvel history told in fully painted pin-ups; artists include Dave Gibbons, Brian Bolland, Simon Bisley and Mark Texeira						
	$0.60	*$1.80*	*$3.00*	£0.40	£1.20	£2.00
Title Value:	*$2.40*	*$7.20*	*$12.00*	£1.60	£4.80	£8.00

MARVELS

Marvel Comics Group,MS; 0 Aug 1994; 1 Jan 1994-4 Apr 1994

	$Good	$Fine	$N.Mint	£Good	£Fine	£N.Mint
0 ND (Aug 1994) 8pg Human Torch origin story from Marvel Age plus sketches and designs						
	$0.70	*$2.10*	*$3.50*	£0.50	£1.50	£2.50
1 ND 48pgs, acetate outer cover, Alex Ross painted art begins						
	$1.50	*$4.50*	*$7.50*	£1.00	£3.00	£5.00
1 2nd printing, ND 48pgs, (Jul 1996) no acetate outer cover; bi-weekly						
	$0.60	*$1.80*	*$3.00*	£0.40	£1.20	£2.00
2 ND 48pgs, acetate outer cover, Alex Ross painted art						
	$1.50	*$4.50*	*$7.50*	£1.00	£3.00	£5.00
2 2nd printing, ND 48pgs, (Jul 1996) no acetate outer cover; bi-weekly						
	$0.60	*$1.80*	*$3.00*	£0.40	£1.20	£2.00
3 ND 48pgs, acetate outer cover, Alex Ross painted art						
	$1.20	*$3.60*	*$6.00*	£0.80	£2.40	£4.00
3 2nd printing, ND 48pgs, (Aug 1996) no acetate outer cover; bi-weekly						
	$0.60	*$1.80*	*$3.00*	£0.40	£1.20	£2.00
4 ND 48pgs, acetate outer cover, Alex Ross painted art						
	$1.20	*$3.60*	*$6.00*	£0.70	£2.10	£3.50
4 2nd printing, ND 48pgs, (Aug 1996) no acetate outer cover; bi-weekly						
	$0.60	*$1.80*	*$3.00*	£0.40	£1.20	£2.00
Title Value:	*$8.50*	*$25.50*	*$42.50*	£5.60	£16.80	£28.00
Marvels Hardcover (Nov 1994) 216pgs, reprints mini-series with unpublished artwork and new Alex Ross painted cover				£4.50	£13.50	£22.50
Marvels (Jan 1995) Trade paperback 216pgs, reprints mini-series with new Alex Ross painted cover				£2.70	£8.10	£13.50

MARVELS: SHADOWS & LIGHT

Marvel Comics Group,OS; nn Feb 1997

	$Good	$Fine	$N.Mint	£Good	£Fine	£N.Mint
nn ND 48pgs, Wolverine, Dracula, Doctor Strange, Askani'Son in separate stories; black and white						
	$0.60	*$1.80*	*$3.00*	£0.40	£1.20	£2.00
Title Value:	*$0.60*	*$1.80*	*$3.00*	£0.40	£1.20	£2.00

MARY MARVEL COMICS

Fawcett; 1 Dec 1945-28 Sep 1948

	$Good	$Fine	$N.Mint	£Good	£Fine	£N.Mint
1 scarce in the U.K.						
	$165.00	*$500.00*	*$1350.00*	£110.00	£335.00	£900.00
2	*$75.00*	*$225.00*	*$600.00*	£50.00	£150.00	£400.00
3-4	*$47.00*	*$140.00*	*$375.00*	£31.00	£92.50	£250.00
5	*$41.00*	*$120.00*	*$325.00*	£28.00	£82.50	£220.00
6-10	*$32.00*	*$95.00*	*$225.00*	£21.00	£62.50	£150.00
11-20	*$21.00*	*$62.50*	*$150.00*	£14.00	£43.00	£100.00
21-26	*$17.50*	*$52.50*	*$125.00*	£12.00	£36.00	£85.00
27-28	*$16.00*	*$49.00*	*$115.00*	£10.50	£32.00	£75.00
Title Value:	*$882.00*	*$2638.00*	*$6630.00*	£588.00	£1775.00	£4430.00

MASK (1ST SERIES)

DC Comics, Toy; 1 Feb 1987-9 Oct 1987

	$Good	$Fine	$N.Mint	£Good	£Fine	£N.Mint
1-9	*$0.15*	*$0.45*	*$0.75*	£0.10	£0.30	£0.50
Title Value:	*$1.35*	*$4.05*	*$6.75*	£0.90	£2.70	£4.50

MASK (LIMITED SERIES)

DC Comics,MS TV Toy; 1 Dec 1985-4 Mar 1986

	$Good	$Fine	$N.Mint	£Good	£Fine	£N.Mint
1-4	*$0.15*	*$0.45*	*$0.75*	£0.10	£0.30	£0.50
Title Value:	*$0.60*	*$1.80*	*$3.00*	£0.40	£1.20	£2.00

MASK IN SCHOOL SPIRITS HARDCOVER STORYBOOK

Dark Horse,OS; nn Aug 1995

	$Good	$Fine	$N.Mint	£Good	£Fine	£N.Mint
nn ND Rick Geary script and art with Chris Chaloner						
	$2.20	*$6.50*	*$11.00*	£1.50	£4.50	£7.50
Title Value:	*$2.20*	*$6.50*	*$11.00*	£1.50	£4.50	£7.50

MASK RETURNS, THE

Dark Horse,MS; 1 Nov 1992-4 Feb 1993

	$Good	$Fine	$N.Mint	£Good	£Fine	£N.Mint
1 ND with cut-out mask						
	$0.70	*$2.10*	*$3.50*	£0.40	£1.20	£2.00
2 ND	*$0.60*	*$1.80*	*$3.00*	£0.30	£0.90	£1.50
3 ND origin	*$0.60*	*$1.80*	*$3.00*	£0.30	£0.90	£1.50
4 ND	*$0.60*	*$1.80*	*$3.00*	£0.30	£0.90	£1.50
Title Value:	*$2.50*	*$7.50*	*$12.50*	£1.30	£3.90	£6.50

The Mask Returns (Jul 1994)

Issue	$Good	$Fine	$N.Mint	£Good	£Fine	£N.Mint
Trade paperback reprints mini-series				£2.00	£6.00	£10.00

MASK STRIKES BACK, THE

Dark Horse,MS; 1 Feb 1995-5 Jun 1995

Issue	$Good	$Fine	$N.Mint	£Good	£Fine	£N.Mint
1-5 ND	*$0.50*	*$1.50*	*$2.50*	£0.30	£0.90	£1.50
Title Value:	*$2.50*	*$7.50*	*$12.50*	£1.50	£4.50	£7.50
The Mask Strikes Back (May 1996)						
Trade paperback collects mini-series				£2.00	£6.00	£10.00

MASK SUMMER VACATION HARDCOVER, THE

Dark Horse,OS; nn Jun 1995

Issue	$Good	$Fine	$N.Mint	£Good	£Fine	£N.Mint
nn ND 32pgs, hardcover, Rick Geary script and art	*$2.00*	*$6.00*	*$10.00*	£1.20	£3.60	£6.00
Title Value:	*$2.00*	*$6.00*	*$10.00*	£1.20	£3.60	£6.00

MASK, ADVENTURES OF THE

Dark Horse; 1 Jan 1996-present

Issue	$Good	$Fine	$N.Mint	£Good	£Fine	£N.Mint
1 ND based on Saturday morning animated show	*$0.50*	*$1.50*	*$2.50*	£0.30	£0.90	£1.50
2-7 ND	*$0.50*	*$1.50*	*$2.50*	£0.30	£0.90	£1.50
Title Value:	*$3.50*	*$10.50*	*$17.50*	£2.10	£6.30	£10.50

MASK, THE

Dark Horse,MS; 0 Dec 1991; 1 Aug 1991-4 Nov 1991

Issue	$Good	$Fine	$N.Mint	£Good	£Fine	£N.Mint
0 ND reprints from Dark Horse Presents	*$0.80*	*$2.40*	*$4.00*	£0.50	£1.50	£2.50
1 ND	*$1.20*	*$3.60*	*$6.00*	£0.70	£2.10	£3.50
2 ND	*$1.00*	*$3.00*	*$5.00*	£0.60	£1.80	£3.00
3-4 ND	*$0.80*	*$2.40*	*$4.00*	£0.50	£1.50	£2.50
Title Value:	*$4.60*	*$13.80*	*$23.00*	£2.80	£8.40	£14.00
The Mask Softcover Collection (May 1993)						
reprints mini-series plus new pages				£1.75	£5.25	£8.75
The Mask Limited Edition Collection (Jan 1995)						
2 volume hardcover edition in slipcase reprinting both The Mask and The Mask Returns mini-series, 1,500 sets signed and numbered by John Arcudi and Doug Mahnke				£13.50	£40.50	£67.50

MASK, THE (2ND SERIES)

Dark Horse,MS; 1 Feb 1995-9 Nov 1995

Issue	$Good	$Fine	$N.Mint	£Good	£Fine	£N.Mint
1 ND John Arcudi, Doug Mahnke and Keith Williams creative team	*$0.60*	*$1.80*	*$3.00*	£0.40	£1.20	£2.00
2-5 ND John Arcudi, Doug Mahnke and Keith Williams creative team	*$0.50*	*$1.50*	*$2.50*	£0.30	£0.90	£1.50
6 ND The Hunt for Green October story (cover says first issue of four)	*$0.50*	*$1.50*	*$2.50*	£0.30	£0.90	£1.50
7-9 ND The Hunt for Green October story	*$0.50*	*$1.50*	*$2.50*	£0.30	£0.90	£1.50
Title Value:	*$4.60*	*$13.80*	*$23.00*	£2.80	£8.40	£14.00

MASK: SOUTHERN DISCOMFORT

Dark Horse,MS; 1 Apr 1996-4 Jul 1996

Issue	$Good	$Fine	$N.Mint	£Good	£Fine	£N.Mint
1-4 ND	*$0.50*	*$1.50*	*$2.50*	£0.30	£0.90	£1.50
Title Value:	*$2.00*	*$6.00*	*$10.00*	£1.20	£3.60	£6.00

MASK: THE MOVIE, THE

Dark Horse,MS Film; 1 Jul 1994-2 Aug 1994

Issue	$Good	$Fine	$N.Mint	£Good	£Fine	£N.Mint
1-2 ND adaptation of film starring Jim Carrey	*$0.50*	*$1.50*	*$2.50*	£0.30	£0.90	£1.50
Title Value:	*$1.00*	*$3.00*	*$5.00*	£0.60	£1.80	£3.00

MASK: WORLD TOUR, THE

Dark Horse,MS; 1 Dec 1995-4 Mar 1996

Issue	$Good	$Fine	$N.Mint	£Good	£Fine	£N.Mint
1 ND The Mask meets Hero Zero	*$0.50*	*$1.50*	*$2.50*	£0.30	£0.90	£1.50
2 ND The Mask meets Barb Wire and The Machine	*$0.50*	*$1.50*	*$2.50*	£0.30	£0.90	£1.50
3-4 ND Mask meets X, King Tiger and Ghost	*$0.50*	*$1.50*	*$2.50*	£0.30	£0.90	£1.50
Title Value:	*$2.00*	*$6.00*	*$10.00*	£1.20	£3.60	£6.00

Note: the mini-series takes over from The Mask [2nd Series]. Issue #1 was solicited as Mask #10.

MASKED MAN

Eclipse; 1 Jan 1985-12 1987

Issue	$Good	$Fine	$N.Mint	£Good	£Fine	£N.Mint
1-12 ND	*$0.30*	*$0.90*	*$1.50*	£0.20	£0.60	£1.00
Title Value:	*$3.60*	*$10.80*	*$18.00*	£2.40	£7.20	£12.00

MASKED RIDER, THE

Marvel Comics Group; 1 Apr 1996

Issue	$Good	$Fine	$N.Mint	£Good	£Fine	£N.Mint
1 ND based on Saturday morning US cartoon show	*$0.30*	*$0.90*	*$1.50*	£0.20	£0.60	£1.00
Title Value:	*$0.30*	*$0.90*	*$1.50*	£0.20	£0.60	£1.00

MASKED WARRIOR X

Antarctic Press,MS; 1 Apr 1996-2 1996 ?

Issue	$Good	$Fine	$N.Mint	£Good	£Fine	£N.Mint
1 ND Masayuki Fujihara script and art; black and white	*$0.70*	*$2.10*	*$3.50*	£0.50	£1.50	£2.50
2 ND Masayuki Fujihara script and art; black and white	*$0.60*	*$1.80*	*$3.00*	£0.40	£1.20	£2.00
Title Value:	*$1.30*	*$3.90*	*$6.50*	£0.90	£2.70	£4.50

MASQUE OF THE RED DEATH

Dell/Movie Classics,OS,Movie; 12-490-410 Aug/Oct 1964

Note: published under Dell series "Movie Classics"

Issue	$Good	$Fine	$N.Mint	£Good	£Fine	£N.Mint
12-490-410 rare although distributed in the U.K., Vincent Price photo cover	*$6.50*	*$19.50*	*$45.00*	£3.40	£10.50	£24.00
Title Value:	*$6.50*	*$19.50*	*$45.00*	£3.40	£10.50	£24.00

MASTER COMICS

Fawcett; 1 Mar 1940-133 Apr 1953

Issue	$Good	$Fine	$N.Mint	£Good	£Fine	£N.Mint
1 very scarce in the U.K. and U.S. 52pgs, origin and 1st appearance of Master Man; no more than 120 extant copies in any condition	*$650.00*	*$1950.00*	*$6500.00*	£450.00	£1350.00	£4500.00
2 very scarce in the U.K. 52pgs	*$185.00*	*$560.00*	*$1500.00*	£125.00	£375.00	£1000.00
3 very scarce in the U.K. 52pgs	*$150.00*	*$450.00*	*$1200.00*	£100.00	£300.00	£800.00
4 very scarce in the U.K. cover price drops from 15 cents to 10 cents as page count drops to 36pgs	*$150.00*	*$450.00*	*$1200.00*	£100.00	£300.00	£800.00
5 very scarce in the U.K.	*$150.00*	*$450.00*	*$1200.00*	£100.00	£300.00	£800.00
6 last appearance of Master Man	*$150.00*	*$450.00*	*$1200.00*	£100.00	£300.00	£800.00
7 very scarce in the U.K. title combines with Slam Bang Comics; Bulletman from Nickel Comics begins	*$250.00*	*$750.00*	*$2000.00*	£165.00	£500.00	£1350.00
8	*$130.00*	*$390.00*	*$1050.00*	£87.50	£260.00	£700.00
9-10	*$100.00*	*$305.00*	*$825.00*	£67.50	£205.00	£550.00
11 very scarce in the U.K. origin and 1st appearance Minute-Man (no cover mention)	*$230.00*	*$690.00*	*$1850.00*	£155.00	£465.00	£1250.00
12	*$115.00*	*$355.00*	*$950.00*	£77.50	£235.00	£635.00
13 origin and 1st appearance Bulletgirl	*$175.00*	*$520.00*	*$1400.00*	£115.00	£350.00	£935.00
14-20	*$92.50*	*$280.00*	*$750.00*	£62.50	£185.00	£500.00
21 very scarce in the U.K. and U.S. Captain Marvel and Bulletman vs. Captain Nazi; Mac Raboy cover (1st); no more than 125 extant copies in any condition	*$465.00*	*$1400.00*	*$4200.00*	£310.00	£930.00	£2800.00
22 scarce in both US and UK X-over with Whiz Comics #25; Captain Marvel Jnr. appears	*$450.00*	*$1350.00*	*$3600.00*	£300.00	£900.00	£2400.00
23 Captain Marvel Jnr. cover stories begin	*$250.00*	*$750.00*	*$2000.00*	£165.00	£500.00	£1350.00
24-29	*$90.00*	*$270.00*	*$725.00*	£60.00	£180.00	£485.00
30 patriotic flag cover	*$92.50*	*$280.00*	*$750.00*	£62.50	£185.00	£500.00
31-35	*$55.00*	*$165.00*	*$450.00*	£38.00	£110.00	£300.00
36-39	*$50.00*	*$150.00*	*$400.00*	£34.00	£100.00	£270.00
40 patriotic flag cover	*$52.50*	*$155.00*	*$425.00*	£36.00	£105.00	£285.00
41 Captain Marvel Jnr, Bulletman, Bulletgirl and Minute-Man team-up	*$62.50*	*$185.00*	*$500.00*	£42.00	£125.00	£335.00
42-47	*$37.00*	*$110.00*	*$260.00*	£25.00	£75.00	£175.00
48 1st appearance Bulletboy	*$41.00*	*$120.00*	*$285.00*	£27.00	£80.00	£190.00
49	*$37.00*	*$110.00*	*$260.00*	£25.00	£75.00	£175.00
50 1st appearance Nyoka the Jungle Girl and Radar the International Policeman	*$32.00*	*$95.00*	*$225.00*	£21.00	£62.50	£150.00
51-60	*$21.00*	*$62.50*	*$150.00*	£14.00	£43.00	£100.00
61 Captain Marvel Jnr. meets Uncle Marvel	*$21.00*	*$62.50*	*$150.00*	£14.00	£43.00	£100.00
62-80	*$17.00*	*$50.00*	*$120.00*	£11.00	£34.00	£80.00
81-99	*$15.50*	*$47.00*	*$110.00*	£10.50	£32.00	£75.00
100	*$20.00*	*$60.00*	*$140.00*	£13.50	£41.00	£95.00
101-133	*$12.50*	*$39.00*	*$90.00*	£8.50	£26.00	£60.00
Title Value:	*$7183.00*	*$21612.50*	*$58085.00*	£4828.50	£14508.50	£39015.00

Note: most issues at least scarce in the U.K.

MASTER OF KUNG FU

Marvel Comics Group; 17 Apr 1974-125 Jun 1983

(previously Special Marvel Edition)

Issue	$Good	$Fine	$N.Mint	£Good	£Fine	£N.Mint
17 ND Jim Starlin art, 1st appearance Black Jack Tarr	*$3.30*	*$10.00*	*$20.00*	£2.05	£6.25	£12.50
18 ND 1st Gulacy art	*$2.50*	*$7.50*	*$15.00*	£1.25	£3.75	£7.50
19 ND Master of Kung Fu vs. Man-Thing, Gulacy art	*$2.05*	*$6.25*	*$12.50*	£1.05	£3.25	£6.50
20 ND Gulacy art	*$2.05*	*$6.25*	*$12.50*	£1.05	£3.25	£6.50
21-22 ND Gulacy art	*$1.25*	*$3.75*	*$7.50*	£0.65	£2.00	£4.00
23 ND	*$1.25*	*$3.75*	*$7.50*	£0.50	£1.50	£3.00
24 ND part Jim Starlin, part Walt Simonson art	*$1.00*	*$3.00*	*$6.00*	£0.55	£1.75	£3.50
25 ND Gulacy art	*$1.00*	*$3.00*	*$6.00*	£0.50	£1.50	£3.00
26-28 ND	*$1.00*	*$3.00*	*$6.00*	£0.50	£1.50	£3.00
29-30 ND Gulacy art	*$1.00*	*$3.00*	*$6.00*	£0.50	£1.50	£3.00
31 ND Gulacy art	*$0.80*	*$2.50*	*$5.00*	£0.40	£1.25	£2.50
32 ND	*$0.80*	*$2.50*	*$5.00*	£0.40	£1.25	£2.50
33-35 ND Gulacy art	*$0.80*	*$2.50*	*$5.00*	£0.40	£1.25	£2.50
36-37	*$0.80*	*$2.50*	*$5.00*	£0.30	£1.00	£2.00
38-40 Gulacy art	*$0.80*	*$2.50*	*$5.00*	£0.30	£1.00	£2.00
41	*$0.65*	*$2.00*	*$4.00*	£0.25	£0.75	£1.50
42-50 Gulacy art	*$0.65*	*$2.00*	*$4.00*	£0.25	£0.75	£1.50
51-59	*$0.50*	*$1.50*	*$3.00*	£0.20	£0.60	£1.25
60 Dr. Doom appears	*$0.50*	*$1.50*	*$3.00*	£0.20	£0.60	£1.25
61-70	*$0.50*	*$1.50*	*$3.00*	£0.20	£0.60	£1.25
71-89	*$0.60*	*$1.80*	*$3.00*	£0.20	£0.60	£1.00
90 Mike Zeck art	*$0.60*	*$1.80*	*$3.00*	£0.20	£0.60	£1.00
91-99	*$0.60*	*$1.80*	*$3.00*	£0.20	£0.60	£1.00
100 52pgs	*$0.60*	*$1.80*	*$3.00*	£0.30	£0.90	£1.50
101-117	*$0.50*	*$1.50*	*$2.50*	£0.20	£0.60	£1.00
118 DS	*$0.50*	*$1.50*	*$2.50*	£0.25	£0.75	£1.25
119-121	*$0.50*	*$1.50*	*$2.50*	£0.20	£0.60	£1.00
122-124 ND	*$0.50*	*$1.50*	*$2.50*	£0.25	£0.75	£1.25
125 ND scarce in the U.K. DS, Mike Mignola inks	*$0.50*	*$1.50*	*$2.50*	£0.30	£0.90	£1.50
Title Value:	*$75.65*	*$228.75*	*$427.00*	£32.15	£97.70	£185.00

ARTISTS

Gene Day in 76, 77, 79-118.

MASTER OF KUNG FU ANNUAL

Marvel Comics Group; 1 1976

	$Good	$Fine	$N.Mint	£Good	£Fine	£N.Mint
1 ND 52pgs, Iron Fist appears	$1.15	$3.50	$7.00	£0.50	£1.50	£3.00
Title Value:	$1.15	$3.50	$7.00	£0.50	£1.50	£3.00

MASTER OF KUNG FU GIANT SIZE

Marvel Comics Group; 1 Sep 1974-4 Jun 1975

	$Good	$Fine	$N.Mint	£Good	£Fine	£N.Mint
1 ND 68pgs, Gulacy art	$1.25	$3.75	$7.50	£0.80	£2.50	£5.00
2 ND 68pgs, Gulacy art	$0.80	$2.50	$5.00	£0.65	£2.00	£4.00
3 ND 68pgs, Gulacy art	$0.80	$2.50	$5.00	£0.55	£1.75	£3.50
4 ND 68pgs	$0.80	$2.50	$5.00	£0.50	£1.50	£3.00
Title Value:	$3.65	$11.25	$22.50	£2.50	£7.75	£15.50

MASTER OF KUNG FU: BLEEDING BLACK

Marvel Comics Group; nn Mar 1991

	$Good	$Fine	$N.Mint	£Good	£Fine	£N.Mint
nn ND 80pgs, Doug Moench script, David and Dan Day art	$0.50	$1.50	$2.50	£0.30	£0.90	£1.50
Title Value:	$0.50	$1.50	$2.50	£0.30	£0.90	£1.50

MASTER OF RAMPLING GATE, THE

Innovation,OS; 1 Jun 1991

	$Good	$Fine	$N.Mint	£Good	£Fine	£N.Mint
1 ND 76pgs, Colleen Doran art, adaptation of Anne Rice novel, painted cover by John Bolton	$1.20	$3.60	$6.00	£0.80	£2.40	£4.00
Title Value:	$1.20	$3.60	$6.00	£0.80	£2.40	£4.00
Anne Rice's Master of Rampling Gate Deluxe Edition (Aug1995) 64pgs, 150 copies sealed in archival bag with hand-embossed gold sticker				£8.00	£24.00	£60.00

MASTER, THE

New Comics Group; 1 1989-2 1989

	$Good	$Fine	$N.Mint	£Good	£Fine	£N.Mint
1-2 ND	$0.30	$0.90	$1.50	£0.20	£0.60	£1.00
Title Value:	$0.60	$1.80	$3.00	£0.40	£1.20	£2.00

MASTERS OF TERROR

Marvel Comics Group,Magazine; 1 Jul 1975-2 1975

	$Good	$Fine	$N.Mint	£Good	£Fine	£N.Mint
1 ND It!, all reprint, Neal Adams inks, Jim Starlin/Brunner/Smith art	$0.65	$2.00	$4.00	£0.40	£1.25	£2.50
2 ND Invisible Man, all reprint	$0.65	$2.00	$4.00	£0.40	£1.25	£2.50
Title Value:	$1.30	$4.00	$8.00	£0.80	£2.50	£5.00

MASTERS OF THE UNIVERSE

DC Comics,MS TV Toy; 1 Dec 1982-3 Feb 1983

(see Batman #353)

	$Good	$Fine	$N.Mint	£Good	£Fine	£N.Mint
1	$0.15	$0.45	$0.75	£0.10	£0.30	£0.50
2 origin He-Man	$0.15	$0.45	$0.75	£0.10	£0.30	£0.50
3	$0.15	$0.45	$0.75	£0.10	£0.30	£0.50
Title Value:	$0.45	$1.35	$2.25	£0.30	£0.90	£1.50

MASTERS OF THE UNIVERSE

Marvel Comics Group/Star,TV; 1 May 1986-13 May 1987

	$Good	$Fine	$N.Mint	£Good	£Fine	£N.Mint
1-12 ND	$0.15	$0.45	$0.75	£0.10	£0.30	£0.50
13 ND scarce in the U.K.	$0.15	$0.45	$0.75	£0.10	£0.35	£0.60
Title Value:	$1.95	$5.85	$9.75	£1.30	£3.95	£6.60

MASTERS OF THE UNIVERSE, THE MOTION PICTURE

Marvel Comics Group/Star,OS Film; 1 Nov 1987

	$Good	$Fine	$N.Mint	£Good	£Fine	£N.Mint
1 ND	$0.15	$0.45	$0.75	£0.10	£0.30	£0.50
Title Value:	$0.15	$0.45	$0.75	£0.10	£0.30	£0.50

MASTERWORKS SERIES OF GREAT COMIC BOOK ARTISTS

Seagate/DC Comics; 1 May 1983-3 Dec 1983

1-2 ND Shining Knight reprints by Frank Frazetta

	$Good	$Fine	$N.Mint	£Good	£Fine	£N.Mint
	$0.40	$1.20	$2.00	£0.25	£0.75	£1.25
3 ND Berni Wrightson reprints	$0.40	$1.20	$2.00	£0.25	£0.75	£1.25
Title Value:	$1.20	$3.60	$6.00	£0.75	£2.25	£3.75

Note: the planned Neal Adams issue (#4) featuring his mystery, suspense and horror stories was advertised but never appeared. Shame.

MATT CHAMPION

Metro Comics,MS; 1-4 1987

	$Good	$Fine	$N.Mint	£Good	£Fine	£N.Mint
1-4 ND	$0.25	$0.75	$1.25	£0.15	£0.45	£0.75
Title Value:	$1.00	$3.00	$5.00	£0.60	£1.80	£3.00

MAVERICK

Marvel Comics Group,OS; nn Jan 1997

	$Good	$Fine	$N.Mint	£Good	£Fine	£N.Mint
nn ND 48pgs, Larry Hama script, Wilfred Santiago art	$0.60	$1.80	$3.00	£0.40	£1.20	£2.00
Title Value:	$0.60	$1.80	$3.00	£0.40	£1.20	£2.00

MAVERICKS: THE NEW WAVE

Dagger Enterprises; 1 Jun 1994-4 Sep 1994

	$Good	$Fine	$N.Mint	£Good	£Fine	£N.Mint
1-4 ND Rich Buckler Snr. art	$0.40	$1.20	$2.00	£0.25	£0.75	£1.25
Title Value:	$1.60	$4.80	$8.00	£1.00	£3.00	£5.00

MAX THE MAGNIFICENT

Slave Labor,MS; 1 Jul 1987-3 Nov 1987

	$Good	$Fine	$N.Mint	£Good	£Fine	£N.Mint
1-3 ND Valentino art	$0.40	$1.20	$2.00	£0.25	£0.75	£1.25
Title Value:	$1.20	$3.60	$6.00	£0.75	£2.25	£3.75

MAXIMAGE

Image; 1 Dec 1995-present

	$Good	$Fine	$N.Mint	£Good	£Fine	£N.Mint
1 ND Rob Liefeld cover and story	$0.50	$1.50	$2.50	£0.30	£0.90	£1.50
2 ND Extreme Destroyer part 2, continued in New Man #1; pre-bagged with trading card	$0.50	$1.50	$2.50	£0.30	£0.90	£1.50
3 ND	$0.50	$1.50	$2.50	£0.30	£0.90	£1.50
4 ND Rage of Angels tie-in	$0.50	$1.50	$2.50	£0.30	£0.90	£1.50
5-8 ND	$0.50	$1.50	$2.50	£0.30	£0.90	£1.50
Title Value:	$4.00	$12.00	$20.00	£2.40	£7.20	£12.00

MAXIMORTAL, THE

Kind Hell Press/Tundra; 1 Aug 1992-7 1993

	$Good	$Fine	$N.Mint	£Good	£Fine	£N.Mint
1-2 ND card-stock embossed cover	$0.50	$1.50	$2.50	£0.30	£0.90	£1.50
3-7 ND	$0.50	$1.50	$2.50	£0.30	£0.90	£1.50
Title Value:	$3.50	$10.50	$17.50	£2.10	£6.30	£10.50

MAXIMUM OVERLOAD

Dark Horse,Magazine; 1 Feb 1994-5 Jun 1994

	$Good	$Fine	$N.Mint	£Good	£Fine	£N.Mint
1 ND 64pgs, with free Lemmings stickers and promo poster	$0.80	$2.40	$4.00	£0.50	£1.50	£2.50
2-5 ND 64pgs	$0.80	$2.40	$4.00	£0.50	£1.50	£2.50
Title Value:	$4.00	$12.00	$20.00	£2.50	£7.50	£12.50

MAXIMUM PRESS PREVIEW

Maximum Comic Press,OS; 1 Mar 1995

	$Good	$Fine	$N.Mint	£Good	£Fine	£N.Mint
1 ND review of Maximum Press titles	$0.30	$0.90	$1.50	£0.20	£0.60	£1.00
Title Value:	$0.30	$0.90	$1.50	£0.20	£0.60	£1.00

MAXWELL MOUSE FOLLIES

Renegade; 1 Feb 1986-5 Oct 1986

	$Good	$Fine	$N.Mint	£Good	£Fine	£N.Mint
1-5 ND	$0.40	$1.20	$2.00	£0.25	£0.75	£1.25
Title Value:	$2.00	$6.00	$10.00	£1.25	£3.75	£6.25

MAXX, FRIENDS OF

Image; 1 May 1996

	$Good	$Fine	$N.Mint	£Good	£Fine	£N.Mint
1 ND 48pgs, Dude Japan appears	$0.60	$1.80	$3.00	£0.40	£1.20	£2.00

Marvels #2

Mask, The (1st) #1

Master Comics #1

	$Good	$Fine	$N.Mint	£Good	£Fine	£N.Mint
Title Value:	$0.60	$1.80	$3.00	£0.40	£1.20	£2.00

MAXX, THE

Image; 1 Mar 1993-present

	$Good	$Fine	$N.Mint	£Good	£Fine	£N.Mint
1/2 ND available only with coupons sent from Wizard Price Guide magazine	$2.00	$6.00	$10.00	£1.20	£3.60	£6.00
1/2 with binder, ND as above in black folder with gold logo; 1,100 copies available at Diamond Distributors seminar in June 1993 in Atlanta	$4.00	$12.00	$20.00	£2.50	£7.50	£12.50
1 ND Sam Kieth story and art begins	$1.00	$3.00	$5.00	£0.60	£1.80	£3.00
1 Ashcan Edition, ND blue card cover, signed and numbered in gold pen on cover by Sam Keith, 8.5" x 5.5"	$3.00	$9.00	$15.00	£2.00	£6.00	£10.00
1 Blue Variant Edition ND	$3.00	$9.00	$15.00	£2.00	£6.00	£10.00
1 Glow in the Dark Edition ND	$4.00	$12.00	$20.00	£2.50	£7.50	£12.50
2 ND	$0.60	$1.80	$3.00	£0.40	£1.20	£2.00
2 Ashcan Edition, ND blue card cover, signed and numbered in gold pen on cover by Sam Keith, 8.5" x 5.5"	$2.50	$7.50	$12.50	£1.50	£4.50	£7.50
3-5 ND	$0.60	$1.80	$3.00	£0.40	£1.20	£2.00
6 ND	$0.50	$1.50	$2.50	£0.30	£0.90	£1.50
7 ND Maxx vs. Pitt	$0.50	$1.50	$2.50	£0.30	£0.90	£1.50
8-10 ND	$0.50	$1.50	$2.50	£0.30	£0.90	£1.50
11-20 ND	$0.40	$1.20	$2.00	£0.25	£0.75	£1.25
21 ND Alan Moore guest script	$0.40	$1.20	$2.00	£0.25	£0.75	£1.25
22-27 ND	$0.40	$1.20	$2.00	£0.25	£0.75	£1.25
Title Value:	$31.20	$93.60	$156.00	£19.65	£58.95	£98.25
Maxx (Mar 1995) Trade paperback ND reprints issues #1-6, new Sam Kieth cover				£1.70	£5.10	£8.50
(2nd printing - Aug 1996)				£1.70	£5.10	£8.50

MAYHEM

Dark Horse,MS; 1 May 1989-4 Sep 1989

	$Good	$Fine	$N.Mint	£Good	£Fine	£N.Mint
1 ND 48pgs, 1st time "The Mask" is used, previously "The Masque" (see Dark Horse Presents #10)	$3.00	$9.00	$15.00	£1.60	£4.80	£8.00
2 ND 48pgs, The Mask appears	$2.00	$6.00	$10.00	£1.00	£3.00	£5.00
3 ND 48pgs, The Mask appears	$2.00	$6.00	$10.00	£1.20	£3.60	£6.00
4 ND 48pgs, The Mask appears	$2.00	$6.00	$10.00	£1.00	£3.00	£5.00
Title Value:	$9.00	$27.00	$45.00	£4.80	£14.40	£24.00

MAZE AGENCY

Comico/Innovation; 1 Dec 1988-23 1992 (Innovation #8 On)

	$Good	$Fine	$N.Mint	£Good	£Fine	£N.Mint
1-15 ND	$0.40	$1.20	$2.00	£0.25	£0.75	£1.25
16 ND Russ Heath cover	$0.40	$1.20	$2.00	£0.25	£0.75	£1.25
17 ND Norm Breyfogle cover	$0.40	$1.20	$2.00	£0.25	£0.75	£1.25
18 ND Brian Bolland cover	$0.40	$1.20	$2.00	£0.25	£0.75	£1.25
19 ND Adam Hughes cover	$0.40	$1.20	$2.00	£0.25	£0.75	£1.25
20-23 ND	$0.40	$1.20	$2.00	£0.25	£0.75	£1.25
Title Value:	$9.20	$27.60	$46.00	£5.75	£17.25	£28.75
Trade Paperback, reprints #1-4				£1.20	£3.60	£6.00
Annual 1 (Nov 1990), colour, Ploog cover				£0.35	£1.05	£1.75
Special 1 (1990), colour, Joe Staton art; includes Maze Agency #0 with Alan Davis art				£0.50	£1.50	£2.50

MAZE AGENCY CHRISTMAS SPECIAL, THE

Innovation,OS; 1 Feb 1992

	$Good	$Fine	$N.Mint	£Good	£Fine	£N.Mint
1 ND Adam Hughes cover	$0.40	$1.20	$2.00	£0.25	£0.75	£1.25
Title Value:	$0.40	$1.20	$2.00	£0.25	£0.75	£1.25

MAZING MAN

DC Comics; 1 Jan 1986-12 Dec 1986

	$Good	$Fine	$N.Mint	£Good	£Fine	£N.Mint
1-6	$0.15	$0.45	$0.75	£0.10	£0.35	£0.60
7-8 Hembeck art	$0.15	$0.45	$0.75	£0.10	£0.35	£0.60
9-11	$0.15	$0.45	$0.75	£0.10	£0.35	£0.60
12 part Dark Knight cover by Frank Miller	$0.25	$0.75	$1.25	£0.10	£0.35	£0.60
Title Value:	$1.90	$5.70	$9.50	£1.20	£4.20	£7.20

MAZING MAN SPECIAL

DC Comics; 1 1987-2 Apr 1988; 3 Aug 1990

	$Good	$Fine	$N.Mint	£Good	£Fine	£N.Mint
1 LD in the U.K.	$0.15	$0.45	$0.75	£0.15	£0.45	£0.75
2	$0.15	$0.45	$0.75	£0.10	£0.35	£0.60
3 Kyle Baker/Todd McFarlane art featured	$0.25	$0.75	$1.25	£0.15	£0.45	£0.75
Title Value:	$0.55	$1.65	$2.75	£0.40	£1.25	£2.10

MAZINGER GRAPHIC NOVEL

First; nn 1990

	$Good	$Fine	$N.Mint	£Good	£Fine	£N.Mint
nn ND 64pgs, painted art by Go Nagi	$1.50	$4.50	$7.50	£1.00	£3.00	£5.00
Title Value:	$1.50	$4.50	$7.50	£1.00	£3.00	£5.00

MCA SATURDAY MORNING CARTOON'S GREATEST HITS: THE COMIC

Marvel Comics Group,OS; 1 Apr 1996

	$Good	$Fine	$N.Mint	£Good	£Fine	£N.Mint
1 ND based on the music accompanying Saturday morning US cartoon shows	$0.40	$1.20	$2.00	£0.25	£0.75	£1.25
Title Value:	$0.40	$1.20	$2.00	£0.25	£0.75	£1.25

MECHA

Dark Horse; 1 Jun 1987-6 Jan 1989

	$Good	$Fine	$N.Mint	£Good	£Fine	£N.Mint
1-6 ND Fong/Nichols art	$0.40	$1.20	$2.00	£0.25	£0.75	£1.25
Title Value:	$2.40	$7.20	$12.00	£1.50	£4.50	£7.50

MECHA ONE-SHOT SPECIAL

Dark Horse,OS; 1 May 1995

	$Good	$Fine	$N.Mint	£Good	£Fine	£N.Mint
1 ND Comics' Greatest World spin-off; Chris Warner cover	$0.50	$1.50	$2.50	£0.30	£0.90	£1.50
Title Value:	$0.50	$1.50	$2.50	£0.30	£0.90	£1.50

MECHANICS

Fantagraphics; 1 Oct 1985-3 Dec 1985

	$Good	$Fine	$N.Mint	£Good	£Fine	£N.Mint
1-3 ND reprints from Love & Rockets in colour plus new story	$0.60	$1.80	$3.00	£0.40	£1.20	£2.00
Title Value:	$1.80	$5.40	$9.00	£1.20	£3.60	£6.00

MECHANOID INVASION, THE

Caliber Press,MS; 1 Aug 1990-4 1990

	$Good	$Fine	$N.Mint	£Good	£Fine	£N.Mint
1-4 ND 48pgs	$0.40	$1.20	$2.00	£0.25	£0.75	£1.25
Title Value:	$1.60	$4.80	$8.00	£1.00	£3.00	£5.00

MECHANOIDS

Caliber Press,MS; 1 1990-5 1990

	$Good	$Fine	$N.Mint	£Good	£Fine	£N.Mint
1-5 ND 48pgs, based on role-playing game; black and white	$0.40	$1.20	$2.00	£0.25	£0.75	£1.25
Title Value:	$2.00	$6.00	$10.00	£1.25	£3.75	£6.25

MECHOVERSE

Airbrush Comics,MS; 1 Aug 1988-2 1988

	$Good	$Fine	$N.Mint	£Good	£Fine	£N.Mint
1-2 ND	$0.30	$0.90	$1.50	£0.20	£0.60	£1.00
Title Value:	$0.60	$1.80	$3.00	£0.40	£1.20	£2.00

MECHTHINGS

Renegade; 1 Jul 1987-4 Feb 1988

	$Good	$Fine	$N.Mint	£Good	£Fine	£N.Mint
1-4 ND	$0.40	$1.20	$2.00	£0.25	£0.75	£1.25
Title Value:	$1.60	$4.80	$8.00	£1.00	£3.00	£5.00

MEDAL OF HONOUR

Dark Horse,MS; 1 Oct 1994-5 Feb 1995

	$Good	$Fine	$N.Mint	£Good	£Fine	£N.Mint
1-5 ND text anthology of war heroism; Walt Simonson cover	$0.50	$1.50	$2.50	£0.30	£0.90	£1.50
Title Value:	$2.50	$7.50	$12.50	£1.50	£4.50	£7.50

MEDAL OF HONOUR SPECIAL

Dark Horse,OS; 1 Apr 1994

	$Good	$Fine	$N.Mint	£Good	£Fine	£N.Mint
1 ND Joe Kubert cover	$0.50	$1.50	$2.50	£0.30	£0.90	£1.50
Title Value:	$0.50	$1.50	$2.50	£0.30	£0.90	£1.50

MEDIA STARR

Innovation,MS; 1 Jul 1989-3 Oct 1989

	$Good	$Fine	$N.Mint	£Good	£Fine	£N.Mint
1-3 ND	$0.40	$1.20	$2.00	£0.25	£0.75	£1.25
Title Value:	$1.20	$3.60	$6.00	£0.75	£2.25	£3.75

MEDIEVAL SPAWN/WITCHBLADE

Image,MS; 1 May 1996-3 Jul 1996

	$Good	$Fine	$N.Mint	£Good	£Fine	£N.Mint
1 ND Garth Ennis script	$1.00	$3.00	$5.00	£0.60	£1.80	£3.00
1 Gold Edition, ND gold foil logo	$6.00	$18.00	$30.00	£3.00	£9.00	£15.00
1 Platinum Edition ND	$10.00	$30.00	$50.00	£6.00	£18.00	£30.00
2-3 ND Garth Ennis script	$0.60	$1.80	$3.00	£0.40	£1.20	£2.00
Title Value:	$18.20	$54.60	$91.00	£10.40	£31.20	£52.00

MEDUSA COMICS

Triangle Publications; 1 1986

	$Good	$Fine	$N.Mint	£Good	£Fine	£N.Mint
1 ND	$0.25	$0.75	$1.25	£0.15	£0.45	£0.75
Title Value:	$0.25	$0.75	$1.25	£0.15	£0.45	£0.75

MEET MERTON

I.W. Super;9 1964

	$Good	$Fine	$N.Mint	£Good	£Fine	£N.Mint
9 distributed in the U.K. reprints from Toby Press title	$1.00	$3.00	$6.00	£0.40	£1.25	£2.50
Title Value:	$1.00	$3.00	$6.00	£0.40	£1.25	£2.50

MEGALITH

Continuity; 1 Apr 1985-2 1985

(see Revengers featuring Megalith)

	$Good	$Fine	$N.Mint	£Good	£Fine	£N.Mint
1-2 ND Neal Adams art	$0.40	$1.20	$2.00	£0.25	£0.75	£1.25
Title Value:	$0.80	$2.40	$4.00	£0.50	£1.50	£2.50

MEGALITH (2ND SERIES)

Continuity; 1 1989-14 1992

	$Good	$Fine	$N.Mint	£Good	£Fine	£N.Mint
1-2 part Neal Adams art	$0.40	$1.20	$2.00	£0.25	£0.75	£1.25
3 painted issue	$0.40	$1.20	$2.00	£0.25	£0.75	£1.25
4-9	$0.40	$1.20	$2.00	£0.25	£0.75	£1.25
10 Neal Adams painted art, $2.50 cover begins	$0.40	$1.20	$2.00	£0.25	£0.75	£1.25
11 silver embossed cover by Neal Adams	$0.40	$1.20	$2.00	£0.25	£0.75	£1.25
12 painted art by Neal Adams	$0.40	$1.20	$2.00	£0.25	£0.75	£1.25
13-14	$0.40	$1.20	$2.00	£0.25	£0.75	£1.25
Title Value:	$5.60	$16.80	$28.00	£3.50	£10.50	£17.50

Note: all Non-Distributed on the news-stands in the U.K.

MEGALITH (3RD SERIES)

Continuity; 0 Apr 1993; 1 Apr 1993-7 1994

	$Good	$Fine	$N.Mint	£Good	£Fine	£N.Mint
0 Incentive Pack, Deathwatch 2000 part 1, silver foil embossed cover (pre-bagged with Hybrids (2nd) #0)	$0.40	$1.20	$2.00	£0.40	£1.20	£2.00
1 Deathwatch 2000 part 5, pre-bagged with 2 trading cards, Neal Adams plot; gatefold cover	$0.40	$1.20	$2.00	£0.25	£0.75	£1.25
2 Deathwatch 2000 part 10, pre-bagged with trading card, Neal Adams plot; gatefold cover opening out top and bottom	$0.40	$1.20	$2.00	£0.25	£0.75	£1.25

TRADE PAPERBACKS, GRAPHIC NOVELS AND OTHER COLLECTIONS ARE PRICED IN POUNDS STERLING ONLY. CONVERT AT 1.5 FOR DOLLARS.

	$Good	$Fine	$N.Mint	£Good	£Fine	£N.Mint
3 Deathwatch 200 part 16, pre-bagged with trading card; Tyvek indestructible cover	*$0.40*	*$1.20*	*$2.00*	£0.25	£0.75	£1.25
4 Rise of Magic X-over, embossed parchment cover by Neal Adams	*$0.40*	*$1.20*	*$2.00*	£0.25	£0.75	£1.25
5-6 Rise of Magic X-over, embossed parchment cover by Sienkiewicz	*$0.40*	*$1.20*	*$2.00*	£0.25	£0.75	£1.25
7 Rise of Magic X-over, embossed parchment cover by Neal Adams	*$0.40*	*$1.20*	*$2.00*	£0.25	£0.75	£1.25
Title Value:	*$3.20*	*$9.60*	*$16.00*	£2.15	£6.45	£10.75

Note: all Non-Distributed on the news-stands in the U.K.

MEGATON

Megaton Publications; 1 1983-8 1986

(see Graphic Fantasy)

	$Good	$Fine	$N.Mint	£Good	£Fine	£N.Mint
1 black and white, Erik Larsen's 1st pro work, 1st appearance Vanguard	*$1.00*	*$3.00*	*$5.00*	£1.00	£3.00	£5.00
2 black and white, 1st appearance Savage Dragon (cameo), Erik Larsen art	*$1.60*	*$4.80*	*$8.00*	£1.00	£3.00	£5.00
3 black and white, 1st full appearance Savage Dragon, Erik Larsen art	*$2.50*	*$7.50*	*$12.50*	£1.60	£4.80	£8.00
4 black and white, Savage Dragon appears, Erik Larsen art	*$1.60*	*$4.80*	*$8.00*	£1.20	£3.60	£6.00
5 black and white, 1st Rob Liefeld art inside front cover; Angel Medina art (June 1986)	*$1.00*	*$3.00*	*$5.00*	£0.50	£1.50	£2.50
6-7 black and white	*$0.60*	*$1.80*	*$3.00*	£0.40	£1.20	£2.00
8 black and white, Rob Liefeld Youngblood preview (1pg advert)	*$0.60*	*$1.80*	*$3.00*	£0.40	£1.20	£2.00
Title Value:	*$9.50*	*$28.50*	*$47.50*	£6.50	£19.50	£32.50

Note: all Non-Distributed on the news-stands in the U.K.

MEGATON (2ND SERIES)

Megaton Publications; 1 1986-3 1987

	$Good	$Fine	$N.Mint	£Good	£Fine	£N.Mint
1-3 ND colour	*$0.30*	*$0.90*	*$1.50*	£0.20	£0.60	£1.00
Title Value:	*$0.90*	*$2.70*	*$4.50*	£0.60	£1.80	£3.00

MEGATON EXPLOSION

Megaton Publications,OS; 1 Jun 1987

	$Good	$Fine	$N.Mint	£Good	£Fine	£N.Mint
1 very rare in the U.K., rare in the U.S. 16pgs, self published fanzine by Rob Liefeld and friends featuring the first concept of Youngblood, distributed free around colleges; approximately 200 copies printed	*$3.50*	*$10.50*	*$17.50*	£2.50	£7.50	£12.50
Title Value:	*$3.50*	*$10.50*	*$17.50*	£2.50	£7.50	£12.50

MEGATON MAN

Kitchen Sink; 1 Nov 1984-10 Jun 1986

(see Return of Megaton Man)

	$Good	$Fine	$N.Mint	£Good	£Fine	£N.Mint
1 ND scarce in the U.K.	*$0.60*	*$1.80*	*$3.00*	£0.50	£1.50	£2.50
1 2nd/3rd printing ND	*$0.50*	*$1.50*	*$2.50*	£0.30	£0.90	£1.50
2-3 ND	*$0.50*	*$1.50*	*$2.50*	£0.40	£1.20	£2.00
4-5 ND	*$0.50*	*$1.50*	*$2.50*	£0.30	£0.90	£1.50
6-10 ND Borderworlds back-up	*$0.50*	*$1.50*	*$2.50*	£0.30	£0.90	£1.50
Title Value:	*$5.60*	*$16.80*	*$28.00*	£3.70	£11.10	£18.50
Volume 1 (Sep 1990), reprints #1-4 softcover				£1.55	£4.65	£7.75
Signed Hardcover				£3.00	£9.00	£15.00
Megaton Man Meets The Uncategorizable X+Thems (Apr 1989)				£0.30	£0.60	£0.90

MELODY

Kitchen Sink; 1 May 1988-10 1992

	$Good	$Fine	$N.Mint	£Good	£Fine	£N.Mint
1 ND Sylvie Rancourt and Jacques Boivin; black and white begins	*$0.60*	*$1.80*	*$3.00*	£0.40	£1.20	£2.00
1 2nd printing ND	*$0.40*	*$1.20*	*$2.00*	£0.25	£0.75	£1.25
2 ND	*$0.50*	*$1.50*	*$2.50*	£0.30	£0.90	£1.50
2 2nd printing, ND (Jun 1993)	*$0.60*	*$1.80*	*$3.00*	£0.40	£1.20	£2.00
3 ND	*$0.50*	*$1.50*	*$2.50*	£0.30	£0.90	£1.50
3 2nd printing, ND (Jun 1993)	*$0.60*	*$1.80*	*$3.00*	£0.40	£1.20	£2.00
4-9 ND	*$0.40*	*$1.20*	*$2.00*	£0.25	£0.75	£1.25
10 ND	*$0.60*	*$1.80*	*$3.00*	£0.40	£1.20	£2.00
Title Value:	*$6.20*	*$18.60*	*$31.00*	£3.95	£11.85	£19.75
Melody Book 1 (Jun 1991), reprints #1-4						
Softcover				£1.80	£5.40	£9.00
Hardcover				£3.70	£11.10	£18.50

MELTING POT

Kitchen Sink,MS; 1 Jan 1994-4 Apr 1994

	$Good	$Fine	$N.Mint	£Good	£Fine	£N.Mint
1-3 ND Kevin Eastman, Eric Talbot and Simon Bisley	*$0.60*	*$1.80*	*$3.00*	£0.40	£1.20	£2.00
4 ND Kevin Eastman and Simon Bisley	*$0.60*	*$1.80*	*$3.00*	£0.40	£1.20	£2.00
Title Value:	*$2.40*	*$7.20*	*$12.00*	£1.60	£4.80	£8.00

MEMORIES

Marvel Comics Group/Epic,OS; 1 Oct 1992

	$Good	$Fine	$N.Mint	£Good	£Fine	£N.Mint
1 ND Katsuhiro Otomo companion piece to Akira	*$0.40*	*$1.20*	*$2.00*	£0.25	£0.75	£1.25
Title Value:	*$0.40*	*$1.20*	*$2.00*	£0.25	£0.75	£1.25

MEN IN BLACK, THE

Aircel,MS; 1-3 1991

	$Good	$Fine	$N.Mint	£Good	£Fine	£N.Mint
1-3 ND black and white	*$0.40*	*$1.20*	*$2.00*	£0.25	£0.75	£1.25
Title Value:	*$1.20*	*$3.60*	*$6.00*	£0.75	£2.25	£3.75
The Men in Black (Jun 1990) 80pgs squarebound, black and white, reprints issues #1-3				£1.00	£3.00	£5.00

MEN IN BLACK, THE (2ND SERIES)

Aircel,MS; 1 May 1991-3 Jul 1992

	$Good	$Fine	$N.Mint	£Good	£Fine	£N.Mint
1-3 ND black and white	*$0.40*	*$1.20*	*$2.00*	£0.25	£0.75	£1.25
Title Value:	*$1.20*	*$3.60*	*$6.00*	£0.75	£2.25	£3.75

MEN OF WAR

DC Comics; 1 Aug 1977-26 Mar 1980

	$Good	$Fine	$N.Mint	£Good	£Fine	£N.Mint
1 ND origin Gravedigger	*$0.40*	*$1.25*	*$2.50*	£0.25	£0.75	£1.50
2 origin continued	*$0.25*	*$0.75*	*$1.50*	£0.15	£0.50	£1.00
3-4	*$0.25*	*$0.75*	*$1.50*	£0.15	£0.50	£1.00
5-8 ND	*$0.25*	*$0.75*	*$1.50*	£0.20	£0.60	£1.25
9-10 ND 44pgs	*$0.25*	*$0.75*	*$1.50*	£0.25	£0.75	£1.50
11-26	*$0.20*	*$0.60*	*$1.25*	£0.10	£0.35	£0.75
Title Value:	*$5.85*	*$17.60*	*$36.00*	£3.60	£11.75	£24.50

FEATURES

Dateline: Frontline in 4-6, 9-11, 21-23. Enemy Ace in 1-3, 8-10, 12-14, 19, 20. Gravedigger in 1-26. Rosa, Master Spy in 17, 18, 24, 25.

MEPHISTO VS. FOUR HEROES

Marvel Comics Group,MS; 1 Apr 1987-4 Jul 1987

	$Good	$Fine	$N.Mint	£Good	£Fine	£N.Mint
1 ND Fantastic Four; John Buscema art begins	*$0.40*	*$1.20*	*$2.00*	£0.25	£0.75	£1.25
2 ND X-Factor	*$0.40*	*$1.20*	*$2.00*	£0.25	£0.75	£1.25
3 ND X-Men	*$0.40*	*$1.20*	*$2.00*	£0.25	£0.75	£1.25
4 ND Avengers	*$0.40*	*$1.20*	*$2.00*	£0.25	£0.75	£1.25
Title Value:	*$1.60*	*$4.80*	*$8.00*	£1.00	£3.00	£5.00

MERCEDES

Angus Publishing; 1 Jan 1996-present

	$Good	$Fine	$N.Mint	£Good	£Fine	£N.Mint
1-8 ND Mike Friedland script, Grant Fuhst art; black and white	*$0.60*	*$1.80*	*$3.00*	£0.40	£1.20	£2.00
9 ND	*$0.60*	*$1.80*	*$3.00*	£0.40	£1.20	£2.00
Title Value:	*$5.40*	*$16.20*	*$27.00*	£3.60	£10.80	£18.00

MERCY

DC Comics/Vertigo,OS; 1 Apr 1993

	$Good	$Fine	$N.Mint	£Good	£Fine	£N.Mint
1 ND 64pgs, Paul Johnson art	*$1.00*	*$3.00*	*$5.00*	£0.70	£2.10	£3.50
Title Value:	*$1.00*	*$3.00*	*$5.00*	£0.70	£2.10	£3.50

MERLIN

Adventure,MS; 1 Dec 1990-6 May 1991

	$Good	$Fine	$N.Mint	£Good	£Fine	£N.Mint
1-6 ND	*$0.40*	*$1.20*	*$2.00*	£0.25	£0.75	£1.25
Title Value:	*$2.40*	*$7.20*	*$12.00*	£1.50	£4.50	£7.50

MERLIN (2ND SERIES)

Adventure,MS; 1 Dec 1992-2 Jan 1993

	$Good	$Fine	$N.Mint	£Good	£Fine	£N.Mint
1-2 ND	*$0.40*	*$1.20*	*$2.00*	£0.25	£0.75	£1.25
Title Value:	*$0.80*	*$2.40*	*$4.00*	£0.50	£1.50	£2.50

MERLINREALM IN 3-D

Blackthorne;(3-D Series #2) 1 Oct 1985

	$Good	$Fine	$N.Mint	£Good	£Fine	£N.Mint
1 ND reprints, with 3-D glasses (25% less without glasses)	*$0.50*	*$1.50*	*$2.50*	£0.30	£0.90	£1.50
Title Value:	*$0.50*	*$1.50*	*$2.50*	£0.30	£0.90	£1.50

MERMAID FOREST

Viz Communications,MS; 1 Feb 1994-4 May 1994

	$Good	$Fine	$N.Mint	£Good	£Fine	£N.Mint
1-4 ND Rumiko Takahashi; black and white	*$0.50*	*$1.50*	*$2.50*	£0.30	£0.90	£1.50
Title Value:	*$2.00*	*$6.00*	*$10.00*	£1.20	£3.60	£6.00
Mermaid Forest graphic Novel (Nov 1994) Nine chapters collected from Animerica and final four from above series; 256pgs, black and white				£2.50	£7.50	£12.50

MERMAID'S DREAM

Viz Communications,MS; 1 Dec 1994-3 Feb 1995

	$Good	$Fine	$N.Mint	£Good	£Fine	£N.Mint
1-3 ND Rumiko Takahashi; black and white	*$0.50*	*$1.50*	*$2.50*	£0.30	£0.90	£1.50
Title Value:	*$1.50*	*$4.50*	*$7.50*	£0.90	£2.70	£4.50

MERMAID'S GAZE

Viz Communications,MS; 1 Mar 1995-4 Jun 1995

	$Good	$Fine	$N.Mint	£Good	£Fine	£N.Mint
1-4 ND Rumiko Takahashi script and art; black and white	*$0.50*	*$1.50*	*$2.50*	£0.30	£0.90	£1.50
Title Value:	*$2.00*	*$6.00*	*$10.00*	£1.20	£3.60	£6.00

MERMAID'S MASK

Viz Communications,MS; 1 Jul 1995-3 Sep 1995

	$Good	$Fine	$N.Mint	£Good	£Fine	£N.Mint
1-3 ND Rumiko Takahashi script and art; black and white	*$0.50*	*$1.50*	*$2.50*	£0.30	£0.90	£1.50
Title Value:	*$1.50*	*$4.50*	*$7.50*	£0.90	£2.70	£4.50

MERMAID'S PROMISE

Viz Communications,MS; 1 Aug 1994-4 Nov 1994

	$Good	$Fine	$N.Mint	£Good	£Fine	£N.Mint
1-4 ND Rumiko Takahashi; black and white	*$0.50*	*$1.50*	*$2.50*	£0.30	£0.90	£1.50
Title Value:	*$2.00*	*$6.00*	*$10.00*	£1.20	£3.60	£6.00

MERMAID'S SCAR

Viz Communications,MS; 1 Jun 1994-4 Sep 1994

	$Good	$Fine	$N.Mint	£Good	£Fine	£N.Mint
1-4 ND Rumiko Takahashi; black and white	*$0.50*	*$1.50*	*$2.50*	£0.30	£0.90	£1.50
Title Value:	*$2.00*	*$6.00*	*$10.00*	£1.20	£3.60	£6.00
Mermaid's Scar Graphic Novel (Oct 1995) 304pgs, reprints				£2.40	£7.20	£12.00

META-4

First,MS; 1 Feb 1991-3 Apr 1991

	$Good	$Fine	$N.Mint	£Good	£Fine	£N.Mint
1 ND 48pgs, Ian Gibson art begins, Gibson cover	*$0.50*	*$1.50*	*$2.50*	£0.30	£0.90	£1.50
2-3 ND Whilce Portacio cover	*$0.50*	*$1.50*	*$2.50*	£0.30	£0.90	£1.50
Title Value:	*$1.50*	*$4.50*	*$7.50*	£0.90	£2.70	£4.50

METACOPS
Monster Comics; 1 Feb 1991-3 1991

Issue	$Good	$Fine	$N.Mint	£Good	£Fine	£N.Mint
1-3 ND black and white	*$0.40*	*$1.20*	*$2.00*	£0.25	£0.75	£1.25
Title Value:	*$1.20*	*$3.60*	*$6.00*	£0.75	£2.25	£3.75

METAL BIKINI
Academy Comics; 0 Apr 1996-present

Issue	$Good	$Fine	$N.Mint	£Good	£Fine	£N.Mint
0 ND Jason Waltrip script and art begins; black and white	*$0.60*	*$1.80*	*$3.00*	£0.40	£1.20	£2.00
1-3 ND	*$0.60*	*$1.80*	*$3.00*	£0.40	£1.20	£2.00
Title Value:	*$2.40*	*$7.20*	*$12.00*	£1.60	£4.80	£8.00

METAL MEN
DC Comics; 1 Apr/May 1963-41 Dec/Jan 1969/70; 42 Mar 1973-44 Jul/Aug 1973; 45-Apr/May 1976-56 Feb/Mar 1978
(see Action, Brave and the Bold, DC Comics Presents, Showcase)

Issue	$Good	$Fine	$N.Mint	£Good	£Fine	£N.Mint
1	*$50.00*	*$150.00*	*$450.00*	£25.00	£75.00	£225.00
2	*$20.00*	*$60.00*	*$160.00*	£9.25	£28.00	£75.00
3-5	*$14.00*	*$43.00*	*$115.00*	£5.50	£16.50	£45.00
6-10	*$10.50*	*$32.00*	*$75.00*	£3.55	£10.50	£25.00
11-16	*$8.50*	*$26.00*	*$60.00*	£2.10	£6.25	£15.00
17 last Silver Age issue, indicia dated Dec 1965/Jan 1966	*$8.50*	*$26.00*	*$60.00*	£2.10	£6.25	£15.00
18-20	*$8.50*	*$26.00*	*$60.00*	£2.10	£6.25	£15.00
21-26	*$6.25*	*$19.00*	*$45.00*	£1.40	£4.25	£10.00
27 scarce in the U.K. origin Metal Men	*$10.00*	*$30.00*	*$70.00*	£1.75	£5.25	£12.50
28-30	*$6.25*	*$19.00*	*$45.00*	£1.40	£4.25	£10.00
31-36	*$5.00*	*$15.00*	*$35.00*	£1.05	£3.20	£7.50
37 1st "new" Metal Men; new direction for title	*$5.00*	*$15.00*	*$35.00*	£1.05	£3.20	£7.50
38-41	*$5.00*	*$15.00*	*$35.00*	£1.05	£3.20	£7.50
42-44 all reprint	*$2.50*	*$7.50*	*$15.00*	£0.55	£1.75	£3.50
45 Walt Simonson art	*$2.50*	*$7.50*	*$15.00*	£0.50	£1.50	£3.00
46 scarce in the U.K. Walt Simonson art	*$2.50*	*$7.50*	*$15.00*	£0.65	£2.00	£4.00
47 scarce in the U.K. Walt Simonson art; story titles "The X-Effect"	*$2.50*	*$7.50*	*$15.00*	£0.65	£2.00	£4.00
48 Walt Simonson art, Eclipso appears	*$2.50*	*$7.50*	*$15.00*	£0.50	£1.50	£3.00
49 Walt Simonson art	*$2.50*	*$7.50*	*$15.00*	£0.50	£1.50	£3.00
50 all reprint	*$2.50*	*$7.50*	*$15.00*	£0.50	£1.50	£3.00
51 Walt Simonson cover	*$2.50*	*$7.50*	*$15.00*	£0.40	£1.25	£2.50
52-53	*$2.50*	*$7.50*	*$15.00*	£0.40	£1.25	£2.50
54-55 Green Lantern X-over	*$2.50*	*$7.50*	*$15.00*	£0.40	£1.25	£2.50
56	*$2.50*	*$7.50*	*$15.00*	£0.40	£1.25	£2.50
Title Value:	*$408.25*	*$1237.50*	*$3015.00*	£122.75	£368.95	£940.50

METAL MEN (2ND SERIES)
DC Comics,MS; 1 Oct 1993-4 Jan 1994

Issue	$Good	$Fine	$N.Mint	£Good	£Fine	£N.Mint
1 Mike Carlin script, Dan Jurgens and Brett Breeding art begin; foil enhanced cover	*$0.30*	*$0.90*	*$1.50*	£0.20	£0.60	£1.00
2 true origin of the Metal Men explored	*$0.25*	*$0.75*	*$1.25*	£0.15	£0.45	£0.75
3	*$0.25*	*$0.75*	*$1.25*	£0.15	£0.45	£0.75
4 Dr. Will Magnus becomes a Metal Man	*$0.25*	*$0.75*	*$1.25*	£0.15	£0.45	£0.75
Title Value:	*$1.05*	*$3.15*	*$5.25*	£0.65	£1.95	£3.25

METAL MILITIA
Entity Comics,MS; 1 Aug 1995-4 Dec 1995

Issue	$Good	$Fine	$N.Mint	£Good	£Fine	£N.Mint
1 ND Hoang Nguyen plot and art, Lam Duy plot and script; Jae Lee cover	*$0.45*	*$1.35*	*$2.25*	£0.30	£0.90	£1.50
1 Encore Edition, ND (2nd printing), new cover by Hoang Nguyen	*$0.55*	*$1.65*	*$2.75*	£0.35	£1.05	£1.75
1 Videogame Edition, ND (Aug 1995) - pre-bagged with floppy disk game Sango Fighter	*$1.40*	*$4.20*	*$7.00*	£0.90	£2.70	£4.50
2-4 ND	*$0.50*	*$1.50*	*$2.50*	£0.30	£0.90	£1.50
Title Value:	*$3.90*	*$11.70*	*$19.50*	£2.45	£7.35	£12.25

METALLIC MEMORIES HARDCOVER GRAPHIC NOVEL
Marvel Comics Group,OS; 1 Jan 1993

Issue	$Good	$Fine	$N.Mint	£Good	£Fine	£N.Mint
1 ND 96pgs, companion volume to Chaos by Moebius	*$3.00*	*$9.00*	*$15.00*	£2.00	£6.00	£10.00
Title Value:	*$3.00*	*$9.00*	*$15.00*	£2.00	£6.00	£10.00

METAMORPHO
National Periodical Publications; 1 Jul/Aug 1965-17 Mar/Apr 1968
(see Action, Brave and the Bold, First Issue Special, World's Finest)

Issue	$Good	$Fine	$N.Mint	£Good	£Fine	£N.Mint
1	*$15.00*	*$45.00*	*$105.00*	£7.75	£23.50	£55.00
2	*$9.25*	*$28.00*	*$65.00*	£5.00	£15.00	£35.00
3 last Silver Age issue cover dated Nov/Dec 1965	*$8.50*	*$26.00*	*$60.00*	£3.55	£10.50	£25.00
4-6	*$6.25*	*$19.00*	*$45.00*	£2.10	£6.25	£15.00
7-9	*$5.50*	*$17.00*	*$40.00*	£1.75	£5.25	£12.50
10 origin and 1st appearance Element Girl	*$6.25*	*$19.00*	*$45.00*	£2.10	£6.25	£15.00
11-17	*$4.25*	*$12.50*	*$30.00*	£1.40	£4.25	£10.00
Title Value:	*$104.00*	*$313.50*	*$740.00*	£39.75	£119.50	£282.50

METAMORPHO (LIMITED SERIES)
DC Comics,MS; 1 Aug 1993-4 Nov 1993

Issue	$Good	$Fine	$N.Mint	£Good	£Fine	£N.Mint
1-4 Graham Nolan art	*$0.25*	*$0.75*	*$1.25*	£0.15	£0.45	£0.75
Title Value:	*$1.00*	*$3.00*	*$5.00*	£0.60	£1.80	£3.00

METAPHISIQUE
Eclipse,MS; 1 Jun 1992-2 Jul 1992

Issue	$Good	$Fine	$N.Mint	£Good	£Fine	£N.Mint
1-2 ND Norm Breyfogle script and art	*$0.40*	*$1.20*	*$2.00*	£0.25	£0.75	£1.25
Title Value:	*$0.80*	*$2.40*	*$4.00*	£0.50	£1.50	£2.50

METAPHYSIQUE
Malibu Bravura,MS; 1 Apr 1995-6 Dec 1995

Issue	$Good	$Fine	$N.Mint	£Good	£Fine	£N.Mint
1 ND Norm Breyfogle script and art begins	*$0.60*	*$1.80*	*$3.00*	£0.40	£1.20	£2.00
1 Ashcan Edition, ND (Apr 1995) - interviews and articles, black and white	*$0.30*	*$0.90*	*$1.50*	£0.20	£0.60	£1.00
1 Gold Foil Collectors Edition, ND (Apr 1995) - gold foil embossed cover	*$1.20*	*$3.60*	*$6.00*	£0.80	£2.40	£4.00
2-6 ND	*$0.60*	*$1.80*	*$3.00*	£0.40	£1.20	£2.00
Title Value:	*$5.10*	*$15.30*	*$25.50*	£3.40	£10.20	£17.00

METEOR MAN
Marvel Comics Group,MS Film; 1 Aug 1993-6 Jan 1994

Issue	$Good	$Fine	$N.Mint	£Good	£Fine	£N.Mint
1 based on film	*$0.25*	*$0.75*	*$1.25*	£0.15	£0.45	£0.75
1 pre-bagged, ND with copy of "Rap Sheet" magazine and square pin badge	*$0.40*	*$1.20*	*$2.00*	£0.25	£0.75	£1.25
2-3	*$0.25*	*$0.75*	*$1.25*	£0.15	£0.45	£0.75
4 Night Thrasher guest-stars	*$0.25*	*$0.75*	*$1.25*	£0.15	£0.45	£0.75
5-6	*$0.25*	*$0.75*	*$1.25*	£0.15	£0.45	£0.75
Title Value:	*$1.90*	*$5.70*	*$9.50*	£1.15	£3.45	£5.75

METEOR MAN MOVIE ADAPTATION
Marvel Comics Group,Film; 1 Apr 1993

Issue	$Good	$Fine	$N.Mint	£Good	£Fine	£N.Mint
1 64pgs	*$0.40*	*$1.20*	*$2.00*	£0.25	£0.75	£1.25
Title Value:	*$0.40*	*$1.20*	*$2.00*	£0.25	£0.75	£1.25

METROPOL
Marvel Comics Group/Epic; 1 Mar 1991-12 Feb 1992

Issue	$Good	$Fine	$N.Mint	£Good	£Fine	£N.Mint
1-8 ND Ted McKeever script/art	*$0.50*	*$1.50*	*$2.50*	£0.30	£0.90	£1.50
9-12 ND Eddy Current appears; Ted McKeever script/art	*$0.50*	*$1.50*	*$2.50*	£0.30	£0.90	£1.50
Title Value:	*$6.00*	*$18.00*	*$30.00*	£3.60	£10.80	£18.00

METROPOL A.D.
Marvel Comics Group/Epic,MS; 1 Oct 1992-3 Dec 1992

Issue	$Good	$Fine	$N.Mint	£Good	£Fine	£N.Mint
1-3 ND Ted McKeever sequel to Metropol	*$0.60*	*$1.80*	*$3.00*	£0.40	£1.20	£2.00
Title Value:	*$1.80*	*$5.40*	*$9.00*	£1.20	£3.60	£6.00

METROPOLIS S.C.U.
DC Comics,MS; 1 Nov 1994-4 Feb 1995

Issue	$Good	$Fine	$N.Mint	£Good	£Fine	£N.Mint
1-2 Lois Lane appears	*$0.30*	*$0.90*	*$1.50*	£0.20	£0.60	£1.00
3 Superman appears	*$0.30*	*$0.90*	*$1.50*	£0.20	£0.60	£1.00
4	*$0.30*	*$0.90*	*$1.50*	£0.20	£0.60	£1.00
Title Value:	*$1.20*	*$3.60*	*$6.00*	£0.80	£2.40	£4.00

MEZZ GALACTIC TOUR
Dark Horse,OS; 1 May 1994

Issue	$Good	$Fine	$N.Mint	£Good	£Fine	£N.Mint
1 ND spin-off from Nexus	*$0.50*	*$1.50*	*$2.50*	£0.30	£0.90	£1.50
Title Value:	*$0.50*	*$1.50*	*$2.50*	£0.30	£0.90	£1.50

MGM'S MARVELLOUS WIZARD OF OZ
Marvel Comics Group/DC Comics,Tabloid OS; 1 Nov 1975

Issue	$Good	$Fine	$N.Mint	£Good	£Fine	£N.Mint
1 ND scarce in the U.K. 80pgs, adapts film	*$0.80*	*$2.50*	*$5.00*	£0.55	£1.75	£3.50
Title Value:	*$0.80*	*$2.50*	*$5.00*	£0.55	£1.75	£3.50

MIAMI MICE
Rip Off Press; 1 1986-4 1987

Issue	$Good	$Fine	$N.Mint	£Good	£Fine	£N.Mint
1 ND Mark Bode art begins	*$0.40*	*$1.20*	*$2.00*	£0.25	£0.75	£1.25
1 2nd printing ND	*$0.30*	*$0.90*	*$1.50*	£0.20	£0.60	£1.00
1 3rd printing ND	*$0.30*	*$0.90*	*$1.50*	£0.20	£0.60	£1.00
2-3 ND	*$0.40*	*$1.20*	*$2.00*	£0.25	£0.75	£1.25
4 ND Teenage Mutant Ninja Turtles by Laird/ Eastman and Cerebus by Sim appear	*$0.50*	*$1.50*	*$2.50*	£0.30	£0.90	£1.50
Title Value:	*$2.30*	*$6.90*	*$11.50*	£1.45	£4.35	£7.25

MICHAEL MAUSER, THE NEW CRIME FILES OF
Apple Comics; 1 Aug 1991

Issue	$Good	$Fine	$N.Mint	£Good	£Fine	£N.Mint
1 ND Nicola Cuti, Joe Staton	*$0.40*	*$1.20*	*$2.00*	£0.25	£0.75	£1.25
Title Value:	*$0.40*	*$1.20*	*$2.00*	£0.25	£0.75	£1.25

MICHAELANGELO CHRISTMAS SPECIAL
Mirage Studios; nn Feb 1991

Issue	$Good	$Fine	$N.Mint	£Good	£Fine	£N.Mint
1 ND 48pgs, reprints Michaelangelo one-shot (1986) plus 14pgs of new story	*$0.40*	*$1.20*	*$2.00*	£0.25	£0.75	£1.25
Title Value:	*$0.40*	*$1.20*	*$2.00*	£0.25	£0.75	£1.25

MICHAELANGELO, TEENAGE MUTANT NINJA TURTLE
Mirage Studios,OS; 1 1986

Issue	$Good	$Fine	$N.Mint	£Good	£Fine	£N.Mint
1 ND	*$1.00*	*$3.00*	*$5.00*	£0.70	£2.10	£3.50
Title Value:	*$1.00*	*$3.00*	*$5.00*	£0.70	£2.10	£3.50

MICKEY & DONALD, WALT DISNEY'S
Gladstone; 1 Mar 1988-18 May 1990

Issue	$Good	$Fine	$N.Mint	£Good	£Fine	£N.Mint
1 ND Mickey, Goofy and Donald Duck begin; 1949 Firestone givaway plus Don Rosa art	*$0.80*	*$2.40*	*$4.00*	£0.20	£0.60	£1.00
2 ND	*$0.60*	*$1.80*	*$3.00*	£0.20	£0.60	£1.00
3 ND infinity cover	*$0.60*	*$1.80*	*$3.00*	£0.20	£0.60	£1.00
4-8 ND	*$0.40*	*$1.20*	*$2.00*	£0.20	£0.60	£1.00
9 ND Christmas issue						

	$Good	$Fine	$N.Mint	£Good	£Fine	£N.Mint
	$0.40	$1.20	$2.00	£0.20	£0.60	£1.00
10-13 ND	$0.40	$1.20	$2.00	£0.20	£0.60	£1.00
14 ND patriotic flag cover	$0.40	$1.20	$2.00	£0.20	£0.60	£1.00
15-16 ND	$0.40	$1.20	$2.00	£0.20	£0.60	£1.00
17 ND 68pgs, Christmas cover plus Rosa art	$0.50	$1.50	$2.50	£0.20	£0.60	£1.00
18 ND 68pgs	$0.50	$1.50	$2.50	£0.20	£0.60	£1.00
Title Value:	$8.20	$24.60	$41.00	£3.60	£10.80	£18.00

Note: Barks reprints in all.

MICKEY MOUSE

Gladstone;219 1986-256 Apr 1990
(previously published by Whitman)

	$Good	$Fine	$N.Mint	£Good	£Fine	£N.Mint
219 1st Gladstone issue, 75c cover; Gottfredson newspaper reprints begin	$0.80	$2.40	$4.00	£0.20	£0.60	£1.00
220-224 scarce in the U.K.	$0.60	$1.80	$3.00	£0.20	£0.60	£1.00
225 1st 95¢ issue	$0.60	$1.80	$3.00	£0.20	£0.60	£1.00
226-243	$0.40	$1.20	$2.00	£0.20	£0.60	£1.00
244 100pgs, 60th anniversary special	$0.50	$1.50	$2.50	£0.25	£0.75	£1.25
245-256	$0.40	$1.20	$2.00	£0.20	£0.60	£1.00
Title Value:	$16.90	$50.70	$85.50	£7.65	£22.95	£38.25

Note: all Non-Distributed on the news-stands in the U.K.

MICKEY MOUSE ADVENTURES

Disney; 1 Jun 1990-20 Jan 1992

	$Good	$Fine	$N.Mint	£Good	£Fine	£N.Mint
1 part reprint	$0.30	$0.90	$1.50	£0.20	£0.60	£1.00
2-7 new stories	$0.30	$0.90	$1.50	£0.20	£0.60	£1.00
8 new stories, John Byrne cover	$0.30	$0.90	$1.50	£0.20	£0.60	£1.00
9 adaptation of "The Sorcerer's Apprentice" from Fantasia film	$0.30	$0.90	$1.50	£0.20	£0.60	£1.00
10-20	$0.30	$0.90	$1.50	£0.20	£0.60	£1.00
Title Value:	$6.00	$18.00	$30.00	£4.00	£12.00	£20.00

Note: banned from distribution in UK

MICKEY MOUSE DIGEST

Gladstone; 1 1986-5 1987

	$Good	$Fine	$N.Mint	£Good	£Fine	£N.Mint
1-5 scarce in the U.K.	$0.30	$0.90	$1.50	£0.20	£0.60	£1.00
Title Value:	$1.50	$4.50	$7.50	£1.00	£3.00	£5.00

MICRONAUTS

Marvel Comics Group; 1 Jan 1979-59 Aug 1984

	$Good	$Fine	$N.Mint	£Good	£Fine	£N.Mint
1 ND Michael Golden's Wrightsonesque art begins	$0.40	$1.25	$2.50	£0.25	£0.75	£1.50
2-6 ND Golden art	$0.30	$1.00	$2.00	£0.20	£0.60	£1.25
7 ND Man-Thing appears, Golden art	$0.30	$1.00	$2.00	£0.20	£0.60	£1.25
8 ND Captain Universe appears, Golden art	$0.30	$1.00	$2.00	£0.20	£0.60	£1.25
9-10 ND Golden art	$0.30	$1.00	$2.00	£0.20	£0.60	£1.25
11-12 ND Golden art	$0.30	$0.90	$1.50	£0.20	£0.60	£1.00
13-14 ND	$0.30	$0.90	$1.50	£0.20	£0.60	£1.00
15-17 ND Fantastic Four appear	$0.30	$0.90	$1.50	£0.20	£0.60	£1.00
18-19 ND	$0.30	$0.90	$1.50	£0.20	£0.60	£1.00
20-21 ND Ant-Man appears	$0.30	$0.90	$1.50	£0.20	£0.60	£1.00
22-25 ND	$0.30	$0.90	$1.50	£0.20	£0.60	£1.00
26-29 ND Nick Fury appears	$0.30	$0.90	$1.50	£0.20	£0.60	£1.00
30	$0.30	$0.90	$1.50	£0.20	£0.60	£1.00
31-34 Dr. Strange appears	$0.25	$0.75	$1.25	£0.15	£0.45	£0.75
35 52pgs, Dr. Strange appears	$0.30	$0.90	$1.50	£0.20	£0.60	£1.00
36	$0.25	$0.75	$1.25	£0.15	£0.45	£0.75
37 X-Men appear	$0.40	$1.20	$2.00	£0.25	£0.75	£1.25
38	$0.25	$0.75	$1.25	£0.15	£0.45	£0.75
39 Steve Ditko art	$0.25	$0.75	$1.25	£0.15	£0.45	£0.75
40 Fantastic Four X-over	$0.25	$0.75	$1.25	£0.15	£0.45	£0.75
41 Dr. Doom appears; X-over Fantastic Four #236	$0.25	$0.75	$1.25	£0.15	£0.45	£0.75
42 Wasp appears	$0.25	$0.75	$1.25	£0.15	£0.45	£0.75
43 Avengers appear	$0.25	$0.75	$1.25	£0.15	£0.45	£0.75
44	$0.25	$0.75	$1.25	£0.15	£0.45	£0.75
45 Arcade appears	$0.25	$0.75	$1.25	£0.15	£0.45	£0.75
46-56	$0.25	$0.75	$1.25	£0.15	£0.45	£0.75
57 ND DS	$0.30	$0.90	$1.50	£0.20	£0.60	£1.00
58-59	$0.25	$0.75	$1.25	£0.15	£0.45	£0.75
Title Value:	$16.60	$50.75	$88.00	£10.60	£31.80	£55.50

Note: Chaykin in #13-18, Giffen in #36, 37, Gil Kane #40-45, Butch Guice #48-58. Mike Golden covers on #2-21, 23.

MICRONAUTS ANNUAL

Marvel Comics Group; 1 Dec 1979-2 Oct 1980

	$Good	$Fine	$N.Mint	£Good	£Fine	£N.Mint
1-2 ND Steve Ditko cover/art	$0.25	$0.75	$1.50	£0.15	£0.50	£1.00
Title Value:	$0.50	$1.50	$3.00	£0.30	£1.00	£2.00

MICRONAUTS SPECIAL EDITION

Marvel Comics Group; 1 Dec 1983-5 Apr 1984

	$Good	$Fine	$N.Mint	£Good	£Fine	£N.Mint
1 ND reprints from #1 begin	$0.40	$1.20	$2.00	£0.25	£0.75	£1.25
2-5 ND reprints	$0.40	$1.20	$2.00	£0.25	£0.75	£1.25
Title Value:	$2.00	$6.00	$10.00	£1.25	£3.75	£6.25

MICRONAUTS: THE NEW VOYAGES

Marvel Comics Group; 1 Oct 1984-20 May 1986

	$Good	$Fine	$N.Mint	£Good	£Fine	£N.Mint
1-15 LD in the U.K.	$0.25	$0.75	$1.25	£0.15	£0.45	£0.75
16 Secret Wars II X-over	$0.25	$0.75	$1.25	£0.15	£0.45	£0.75
17-20	$0.25	$0.75	$1.25	£0.15	£0.45	£0.75
Title Value:	$5.00	$15.00	$25.00	£3.00	£9.00	£15.00

MIDNIGHT EYE: GOKU P.I.

Viz Communications,MS; 1 Nov 1991-6 Apr 1992

	$Good	$Fine	$N.Mint	£Good	£Fine	£N.Mint
1-6 ND	$0.90	$2.70	$4.50	£0.60	£1.80	£3.00
Title Value:	$5.40	$16.20	$27.00	£3.60	£10.80	£18.00
Hardcover (1992), reprints #1-6				£4.00	£12.00	£20.00

MIDNIGHT MEN

Marvel Comics Group,MS; 1 Jun 1993-4 Sep 1993

	$Good	$Fine	$N.Mint	£Good	£Fine	£N.Mint
1 ND Howard Chaykin script and art begins, embossed cover with metallic ink	$0.40	$1.20	$2.00	£0.25	£0.75	£1.25
2-4 ND	$0.40	$1.20	$2.00	£0.25	£0.75	£1.25
Title Value:	$1.60	$4.80	$8.00	£1.00	£3.00	£5.00

MIDNIGHT MYSTERY

ACG; 1 Jan/Feb 1961-7 Oct 1961

	$Good	$Fine	$N.Mint	£Good	£Fine	£N.Mint
1 distributed in the U.K.	$11.00	$34.00	$80.00	£6.25	£19.00	£45.00
2-7 distributed in the U.K.	$5.50	$17.00	$40.00	£2.85	£8.50	£20.00

Men Of War #26

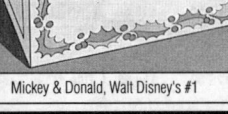

Mickey & Donald, Walt Disney's #1

Mighty Marvel Western #4

	$Good	$Fine	$N.Mint	£Good	£Fine	£N.Mint
Title Value:	$44.00	$136.00	$320.00	£23.35	£70.00	£165.00
MIDNIGHT SCREAMS						
Mystery Graphix Press,MS; 1 Sep 1991-2 Jan 1992						
1-2 ND black and white; includes uncut sheet of b/w trading cards						
	$0.40	$1.20	$2.00	£0.25	£0.75	£1.25
Title Value:	$0.80	$2.40	$4.00	£0.50	£1.50	£2.50
MIDNIGHT SONS ASHCAN EDITION						
Marvel Comics Group,OS; nn Jul 1994						
nn ND 16pgs, previews Blade the Vampire Hunter						
	$0.25	$0.75	$1.25	£0.15	£0.45	£0.75
Title Value:	$0.25	$0.75	$1.25	£0.15	£0.45	£0.75
MIDNIGHT SONS UNLIMITED						
Marvel Comics Group; 1 Apr 1993-9 May 1995						
1 64pgs, Ghost Rider, Morbius, Nightstalkers and Darkhold appear, Mark Texeira cover						
	$0.60	$1.80	$3.00	£0.40	£1.20	£2.00
2 64pgs, Ghost Rider, Morbius, Nightstalkers and Darkhold appear, Bill Sienkiewicz cover						
	$0.60	$1.80	$3.00	£0.40	£1.20	£2.00
3 64pgs, Ghost Rider, Morbius, Nightstalkers and Darkhold appear; Spiderman guest-stars; cover by John Romita Jnr						
	$0.60	$1.80	$3.00	£0.40	£1.20	£2.00
4 64pgs, Siege of Darkness part 17 (conclusion); spot varnished painted cover						
	$0.60	$1.80	$3.00	£0.40	£1.20	£2.00
5 64pgs, Dr. Strange and Midnight Sons						
	$0.60	$1.80	$3.00	£0.40	£1.20	£2.00
6 64pgs, Dr. Strange						
	$0.60	$1.80	$3.00	£0.40	£1.20	£2.00
7 64pgs, Man Thing						
	$0.60	$1.80	$3.00	£0.40	£1.20	£2.00
8 64pgs, Blade, Man-Thing and Scarlet Witch						
	$0.60	$1.80	$3.00	£0.40	£1.20	£2.00
9 64pgs, Ghost Rider, Legion of Night; Alex Ross painted cover						
	$0.60	$1.80	$3.00	£0.40	£1.20	£2.00
Title Value:	$5.40	$16.20	$27.00	£3.60	£10.80	£18.00
MIDNIGHT TALES						
Charlton; 1 Dec 1972-18 May 1976						
1 distributed in the U.K.						
	$0.75	$2.25	$4.50	£0.50	£1.50	£3.00
2-10 distributed in the U.K.						
	$0.50	$1.50	$3.00	£0.30	£1.00	£2.00
11 distributed in the U.K.						
	$0.40	$1.25	$2.50	£0.25	£0.75	£1.50
12 distributed in the U.K. reprint						
	$0.40	$1.25	$2.50	£0.20	£0.60	£1.25
13-16 distributed in the U.K.						
	$0.40	$1.25	$2.50	£0.25	£0.75	£1.50
17 distributed in the U.K. reprint						
	$0.40	$1.25	$2.50	£0.20	£0.60	£1.25
18 distributed in the U.K.						
	$0.40	$1.25	$2.50	£0.25	£0.75	£1.50
Title Value:	$8.45	$25.75	$51.50	£5.10	£16.20	£32.50
MIDNITE, THE REBEL SKUNK						
Blackthorne; 1 Nov 1986-3 Mar 1987						
1 ND Reform School Girl parody						
	$0.30	$0.90	$1.50	£0.20	£0.60	£1.00
2-3 ND	$0.30	$0.90	$1.50	£0.20	£0.60	£1.00
Title Value:	$0.90	$2.70	$4.50	£0.60	£1.80	£3.00
MIGHTY COMICS						
Archie;40 Nov 1966-50 Oct 1967						
(previously Flyman)						
40 distributed in the U.K.						
	$2.85	$8.50	$20.00	£1.70	£5.00	£12.00
41-49 distributed in the U.K.						
	$2.50	$7.50	$17.50	£1.40	£4.25	£10.00
50 rare although distributed in the U.K. Black Hood & Web appear						
	$2.10	$6.25	$15.00	£1.40	£4.25	£10.00
Title Value:	$27.45	$82.25	$182.50	£15.70	£47.50	£112.00
MIGHTY CRUSADERS						
Archie; 1 Nov 1965-7 Oct 1966						
1 distributed in the U.K.						
	$5.00	$15.00	$35.00	£2.85	£8.50	£20.00
2 distributed in the U.K.						
	$2.85	$8.50	$20.00	£1.75	£5.25	£12.50
3 distributed in the U.K.						
	$2.50	$7.50	$17.50	£1.40	£4.25	£10.00
4 distributed in the U.K.						
	$2.85	$8.50	$20.00	£1.75	£5.25	£12.50
5-7 distributed in the U.K.						
	$2.10	$6.25	$15.00	£1.40	£4.25	£10.00
Title Value:	$19.50	$58.25	$137.50	£11.95	£36.00	£85.00
MIGHTY CRUSADERS (2ND SERIES)						
Red Circle (Archie); 1 Mar 1983-13 Sep 1985						
1 distributed in the U.K.						
	$0.40	$1.20	$2.00	£0.25	£0.75	£1.25
2-10 distributed in the U.K.						
	$0.30	$0.90	$1.50	£0.20	£0.60	£1.00
11-13 distributed in the U.K.						
	$0.25	$0.75	$1.25	£0.15	£0.45	£0.75
Title Value:	$3.85	$11.55	$19.25	£2.50	£7.50	£12.50
MIGHTY HERCULES, THE						
Gold Key; 1 Jul 1963-2 Nov 1963						
1 scarce, limited distribution in the U.K.						
	$17.50	$52.50	$125.00	£8.50	£26.00	£60.00

	$Good	$Fine	$N.Mint	£Good	£Fine	£N.Mint
2 scarce, limited distribution in the U.K.						
	$15.00	$45.00	$105.00	£7.75	£23.50	£55.00
Title Value:	$32.50	$97.50	$230.00	£16.25	£49.50	£115.00
MIGHTY HEROES						
Dell; 1 Mar 1967-4 Jul 1967						
1 scarce in the U.K.						
	$19.00	$57.50	$135.00	£8.50	£26.00	£60.00
2-4	$15.00	$45.00	$105.00	£5.50	£17.00	£40.00
Title Value:	$64.00	$192.50	$450.00	£25.00	£77.00	£180.00
MIGHTY MAGNOR, THE						
Malibu; 1 Apr 1993-6 1994						
1 ND Sergio Aragones art begins						
	$0.50	$1.50	$2.50	£0.30	£0.90	£1.50
1 Direct Market Edition, ND pop-up cover feature						
	$0.80	$2.40	$4.00	£0.50	£1.50	£2.50
2-6 ND	$0.40	$1.20	$2.00	£0.25	£0.75	£1.25
Title Value:	$3.30	$9.90	$16.50	£2.05	£6.15	£10.25
MIGHTY MARVEL WESTERN, THE						
Marvel Comics Group; 1 Oct 1968-46 Sep 1976						
1 64pgs, Rawhide Kid, Kid Colt Outlaw and Two-Gun Kid reprints begin						
	$1.65	$5.00	$10.00	£1.00	£3.00	£6.00
2-5 64pgs	$0.80	$2.50	$5.00	£0.50	£1.50	£3.00
6-9 64pgs	$0.55	$1.75	$3.50	£0.30	£1.00	£2.00
10 scarce in the U.K. 64pgs						
	$0.55	$1.75	$3.50	£0.40	£1.25	£2.50
11-20 64pgs	$0.40	$1.25	$2.50	£0.25	£0.75	£1.50
21-46 ND	$0.30	$1.00	$2.00	£0.20	£0.60	£1.25
Title Value:	$19.40	$62.25	$124.50	£12.30	£37.35	£76.00
ARTISTS						
Williamson reprints in 32, 37.						
REPRINT FEATURES						
Kid Colt Outlaw in 1-24, 43-46. Rawhide Kid 1-46. Two-Gun Kid 1-46. Matt Slade 25-42.						
MIGHTY MITES, THE						
Eternity,OS; 1 1986						
1 ND X-Men parody (2 cover versions exist)						
	$0.40	$1.20	$2.00	£0.25	£0.75	£1.25
Title Value:	$0.40	$1.20	$2.00	£0.25	£0.75	£1.25
MIGHTY MITES, THE (2ND SERIES)						
Continuum Comics; 1 Aug 1993-4 1993						
1-4 ND	$0.40	$1.20	$2.00	£0.25	£0.75	£1.25
Title Value:	$1.60	$4.80	$8.00	£1.00	£3.00	£5.00
MIGHTY MORPHIN POWER RANGERS						
Hamilton Comics; 1 Nov 1994-6 Apr 1995						
1 ND Don Markstein script, Gray Morrow art; Brett Blevins and Terry Austin cover						
	$0.40	$1.20	$2.00	£0.25	£0.75	£1.25
2-6 ND	$0.40	$1.20	$2.00	£0.25	£0.75	£1.25
Title Value:	$2.40	$7.20	$12.00	£1.50	£4.50	£7.50
Mighty Morphin Power Rangers (May 1995)						
Trade paperback collects 6 issue series, photo cover				£1.30	£3.90	£6.50
MIGHTY MORPHIN POWER RANGERS (2ND SERIES)						
Hamilton Comics,MS; 1 May 1995-4 Aug 1995						
1-3 ND	$0.40	$1.20	$2.00	£0.25	£0.75	£1.25
4 ND Gray Morrow art						
	$0.40	$1.20	$2.00	£0.25	£0.75	£1.25
Title Value:	$1.60	$4.80	$8.00	£1.00	£3.00	£5.00
MIGHTY MORPHIN POWER RANGERS MAGAZINE, SABAN'S						
Marvel Comics Group,Magazine OS; 1 Nov 1995						
1 ND articles and features and pull-out poster						
	$0.40	$1.20	$2.00	£0.25	£0.75	£1.25
Title Value:	$0.40	$1.20	$2.00	£0.25	£0.75	£1.25
MIGHTY MORPHIN POWER RANGERS MOVIE ADAPTATION						
Marvel Comics Group,OS; nn Sep 1995						
nn ND 48pgs, adaptation of film, Ron Lim art; foil board cover						
	$0.80	$2.40	$4.00	£0.50	£1.50	£2.50
Title Value:	$0.80	$2.40	$4.00	£0.50	£1.50	£2.50
Mighty Morphin Power Rangers Two Pack (Sep 1995)						
film adaptation of above split into two comics, shrink-wrapped with bonus photos and pin-ups; ND				£0.30	£0.90	£1.50
MIGHTY MORPHIN POWER RANGERS SAGA						
Hamilton Comics,MS; 1 Jul 1995-6 1995						
1-6 ND Don Markstein script, John Heebink art						
	$0.40	$1.20	$2.00	£0.25	£0.75	£1.25
Title Value:	$2.40	$7.20	$12.00	£1.50	£4.50	£7.50
MIGHTY MORPHIN POWER RANGERS, SABAN'S						
Marvel Comics Group; 1 Nov 1995-7 May 1996						
1 ND Scott Lobdell and Fabian Nicieza script, Ron Lim and Mark McKenna art; 2 stories						
	$0.40	$1.20	$2.00	£0.25	£0.75	£1.25
2-7 ND	$0.40	$1.20	$2.00	£0.25	£0.75	£1.25
Title Value:	$2.80	$8.40	$14.00	£1.75	£5.25	£8.75
MIGHTY MORPHIN POWER RANGERS: NINJA TROOPERS/VR TROOPERS, SABAN'S						
Marvel Comics Group; 1 Dec 1995-5 Apr 1996						
1 ND flip-book format featuring Ron Lim art						
	$0.50	$1.50	$2.50	£0.30	£0.90	£1.50
2 ND flip-book format featuring Ron Lim art						
	$0.40	$1.20	$2.00	£0.25	£0.75	£1.25
3-5 ND	$0.40	$1.20	$2.00	£0.25	£0.75	£1.25
Title Value:	$2.10	$6.30	$10.50	£1.30	£3.90	£6.50
MIGHTY MORPHIN POWER RANGERS: THE MOVIE PHOTO ADAPTATION, SABAN'S						
Marvel Comics Group,OS; 1 Nov 1995						
1 ND 48pgs, movie adaptation with film stills						
	$0.60	$1.80	$3.00	£0.40	£1.20	£2.00
Title Value:	$0.60	$1.80	$3.00	£0.40	£1.20	£2.00

	$Good	$Fine	$N.Mint	£Good	£Fine	£N.Mint

MIGHTY MOUSE

Marvel Comics Group; 1 Oct 1990-10 Jul 1991

Issue	$Good	$Fine	$N.Mint	£Good	£Fine	£N.Mint
1-2 Dark Knight parody	$0.15	$0.45	$0.75	£0.10	£0.30	£0.50
3 John Byrne cover; Namor parody	$0.15	$0.45	$0.75	£0.10	£0.30	£0.50
4 George Perez cover; Crisis on Infinite Earths parody	$0.15	$0.45	$0.75	£0.10	£0.30	£0.50
5 Crisis parody continues	$0.15	$0.45	$0.75	£0.10	£0.30	£0.50
6 Todd McFarlane Spiderman parody	$0.15	$0.45	$0.75	£0.10	£0.30	£0.50
7 computer-generated issue	$0.15	$0.45	$0.75	£0.10	£0.30	£0.50
8-10	$0.15	$0.45	$0.75	£0.10	£0.30	£0.50
Title Value:	$1.50	$4.50	$7.50	£1.00	£3.00	£5.00

MIGHTY MOUSE

Spotlight; 1 1987

Issue	$Good	$Fine	$N.Mint	£Good	£Fine	£N.Mint
1 ND Paul Chadwick cover	$0.50	$1.50	$2.50	£0.30	£0.90	£1.50
Title Value:	$0.50	$1.50	$2.50	£0.30	£0.90	£1.50

Note: Buckler art in all.

MIGHTY MOUSE AND FRIENDS HOLIDAY SPECIAL

Spotlight; 1 1987

Issue	$Good	$Fine	$N.Mint	£Good	£Fine	£N.Mint
1 ND Deputy Dawg, Heckle & Jeckle appear	$0.40	$1.20	$2.00	£0.25	£0.75	£1.25
Title Value:	$0.40	$1.20	$2.00	£0.25	£0.75	£1.25

MIGHTY MUTANIMALS

Archie; 1 Mar 1991-3 May 1991

Issue	$Good	$Fine	$N.Mint	£Good	£Fine	£N.Mint
1 ND features Teenage Mutant Ninja Turtles	$0.25	$0.75	$1.25	£0.15	£0.45	£0.75
2-3 ND	$0.25	$0.75	$1.25	£0.15	£0.45	£0.75
Title Value:	$0.75	$2.25	$3.75	£0.45	£1.35	£2.25

MIGHTY MUTANIMALS (2ND SERIES)

Archie; 1 Mar 1992-9 1992

Issue	$Good	$Fine	$N.Mint	£Good	£Fine	£N.Mint
1-9 ND	$0.25	$0.75	$1.25	£0.15	£0.45	£0.75
Title Value:	$2.25	$6.75	$11.25	£1.35	£4.05	£6.75

MIGHTY MUTANIMALS INVASION FROM SPACE, THE

Archie,OS; 1 Jan 1992

Issue	$Good	$Fine	$N.Mint	£Good	£Fine	£N.Mint
1 ND 96pgs	$0.50	$1.50	$2.50	£0.30	£0.90	£1.50
Title Value:	$0.50	$1.50	$2.50	£0.30	£0.90	£1.50

MIGHTY SAMSON

Gold Key; 1 Jul 1964-20 Nov 1969; 21 Sep 1972-31 Mar 1976; 32 Aug 1982

(see Gold Key Champion)

Issue	$Good	$Fine	$N.Mint	£Good	£Fine	£N.Mint
1 origin; painted covers begin (to #32); Frank Thorne art begins	$5.50	$17.00	$40.00	£3.20	£9.50	£22.50
2-5	$2.85	$8.50	$20.00	£1.40	£4.25	£10.00
6-10	$2.10	$6.25	$15.00	£1.10	£3.40	£8.00
11-20	$1.75	$5.25	$12.50	£1.00	£3.00	£7.00
21-31	$1.25	$3.75	$7.50	£0.50	£1.50	£3.00
32	$1.50	$4.50	$7.50	£0.30	£0.90	£1.50
Title Value:	$60.15	$180.50	$410.00	£30.10	£90.90	£207.00

Note: most issues distributed on the news-stands in the U.K.

MIKE DANGER, MICKEY SPILLANE'S

Tekno Comix; 1 Sep 1995-9 Jan 1996; Big Entertainment; 10 Apr 1996-11 May 1996

Issue	$Good	$Fine	$N.Mint	£Good	£Fine	£N.Mint
1 ND Max Allan Collins script, Eduardo Barreto and Steve Leialoha art	$0.40	$1.20	$2.00	£0.25	£0.75	£1.25
2-5 ND	$0.40	$1.20	$2.00	£0.25	£0.75	£1.25
6 ND	$0.45	$1.35	$2.25	£0.30	£0.90	£1.50
7 ND pre-bagged with Tekno back-issue comic	$0.45	$1.35	$2.25	£0.30	£0.90	£1.50
8 ND Walt Simonson cover	$0.45	$1.35	$2.25	£0.30	£0.90	£1.50
9-11 ND	$0.45	$1.35	$2.25	£0.30	£0.90	£1.50
Title Value:	$4.70	$14.10	$23.50	£3.05	£9.15	£15.25

MIKE DANGER, MICKEY SPILLANE'S (2ND SERIES)

Big Entertainment; 1 Jun 1996-present

Issue	$Good	$Fine	$N.Mint	£Good	£Fine	£N.Mint
1-8 ND	$0.45	$1.35	$2.25	£0.30	£0.90	£1.50
Title Value:	$3.60	$10.80	$18.00	£2.40	£7.20	£12.00

MIKE GRELL'S SABLE

First; 1 Sep 1989-10 Dec 1990

Issue	$Good	$Fine	$N.Mint	£Good	£Fine	£N.Mint
1-10 ND Mike Grell art	$0.40	$1.20	$2.00	£0.25	£0.75	£1.25
Title Value:	$4.00	$12.00	$20.00	£2.50	£7.50	£12.50

MIKE MIST IN 3-D (MS. TREE'S..)

Eclipse,OS; 1 Aug 1985

Issue	$Good	$Fine	$N.Mint	£Good	£Fine	£N.Mint
1 ND with 3-D glasses (25% less without glasses)	$0.50	$1.50	$2.50	£0.30	£0.90	£1.50
Title Value:	$0.50	$1.50	$2.50	£0.30	£0.90	£1.50

MIKE MIST MINUTE MYSTERIES

Eclipse,OS; 1 1986

Issue	$Good	$Fine	$N.Mint	£Good	£Fine	£N.Mint
1 ND	$0.40	$1.20	$2.00	£0.25	£0.75	£1.25
Title Value:	$0.40	$1.20	$2.00	£0.25	£0.75	£1.25

MILK & CHEESE 666

Slave Labor,OS; 1 Apr 1995

Issue	$Good	$Fine	$N.Mint	£Good	£Fine	£N.Mint
1 ND Evan Dorkin script and art; black and white; number 6 of Milk and Cheese series	$2.00	$6.00	$10.00	£0.60	£1.80	£3.00
1 2nd printing, ND Sep 1996	$0.50	$1.50	$2.50	£0.30	£0.90	£1.50
Title Value:	$2.50	$7.50	$12.50	£0.90	£2.70	£4.50

MILK & CHEESE'S FIRST SECOND ISSUE

Slave Labor,OS; 1 Mar 1994

Issue	$Good	$Fine	$N.Mint	£Good	£Fine	£N.Mint
1 ND Evan Dorkin script and art; number #5 of the Milk and Cheese series	$2.00	$6.00	$10.00	£0.60	£1.80	£3.00
1 2nd printing, ND (Nov 1994)	$0.80	$2.40	$4.00	£0.50	£1.50	£2.50
1 3rd printing, ND (Feb 1996)	$0.60	$1.80	$3.00	£0.40	£1.20	£2.00
Title Value:	$3.40	$10.20	$17.00	£1.50	£4.50	£7.50

MILK AND CHEESE SPECIAL

Slave Labor,OS; 1 May 1991

Issue	$Good	$Fine	$N.Mint	£Good	£Fine	£N.Mint
1 ND Evan Dorkin script/art; black and white; number 1 of the Milk and Cheese series	$12.00	$36.00	$60.00	£2.00	£6.00	£10.00
1 2nd printing ND	$1.00	$3.00	$5.00	£0.60	£1.80	£3.00
1 3rd/4th printing ND	$0.80	$2.40	$4.00	£0.50	£1.50	£2.50
1 5th printing, ND (Oct 1994)	$0.60	$1.80	$3.00	£0.40	£1.20	£2.00
1 6th printing ND 24pgs	$0.50	$1.50	$2.50	£0.30	£0.90	£1.50
Title Value:	$14.90	$44.70	$74.50	£3.80	£11.40	£19.00

Note: originally solicited as a one shot, but due to overwhelming popularity in the States new series of one shots released (which combine to form #1-6)

The Milk and Cheese Experience (Mar 1994)
Trade paperback

Issue	$Good	$Fine	$N.Mint	£Good	£Fine	£N.Mint
ND reprints all strips in chronological order				£1.30	£3.90	£6.50

MILK AND CHEESE'S FOURTH NUMBER ONE

Slave Labor; 1 Jun 1993

Issue	$Good	$Fine	$N.Mint	£Good	£Fine	£N.Mint
1 ND Evan Dorkin script/art; number 4 of Milk and Cheese series	$2.00	$6.00	$10.00	£0.70	£2.10	£3.50
1 2nd printing, ND (Mar 1995)	$0.80	$2.40	$4.00	£0.50	£1.50	£2.50
1 3rd printing ND	$0.50	$1.50	$2.50	£0.30	£0.90	£1.50
Title Value:	$3.30	$9.90	$16.50	£1.50	£4.50	£7.50

Fun With Milk & Cheese (1994) Trade paperback

Issue	$Good	$Fine	$N.Mint	£Good	£Fine	£N.Mint
reprints all four "first" issues plus unpublished strips				£1.30	£3.90	£6.50
2nd print - Jan 1995				£1.30	£3.90	£6.50

MILK AND CHEESE'S OTHER

Slave Labor,OS; 1 Jan 1992

Issue	$Good	$Fine	$N.Mint	£Good	£Fine	£N.Mint
1 ND Evan Dorkin script/art; number 2 of Milk and Cheese series	$5.00	$15.00	$25.00	£1.00	£3.00	£5.00
1 2nd printing, ND (Jul 1993)	$0.80	$2.40	$4.00	£0.50	£1.50	£2.50
1 3rd printing ND	$0.60	$1.80	$3.00	£0.40	£1.20	£2.00
1 4th printing, ND (Jan 1996)	$0.55	$1.65	$2.75	£0.35	£1.05	£1.75
Title Value:	$6.95	$20.85	$34.75	£2.25	£6.75	£11.25

MILK AND CHEESE'S THIRD NUMBER ONE

Slave Labor,OS; 1 Oct 1992

Issue	$Good	$Fine	$N.Mint	£Good	£Fine	£N.Mint
1 ND Evan Dorkin script/art; number 3 of Milk and Cheese series	$3.50	$10.50	$17.50	£0.80	£2.40	£4.00
1 2nd printing, ND (Jun 1993)	$0.80	$2.40	$4.00	£0.50	£1.50	£2.50
1 3rd printing ND	$0.60	$1.80	$3.00	£0.40	£1.20	£2.00
1 4th printing, ND (Feb 1996)	$0.55	$1.65	$2.75	£0.35	£1.05	£1.75
Title Value:	$5.45	$16.35	$27.25	£2.05	£6.15	£10.25

MILLENNIUM

Cross-over series at the beginning of 1988 with a number of tie-ins around a core mini-series. The story revolves around the Manhunters, revealed as having been placed on Earth eons ago in order to assume positions of power and importance. The listings below are in alphabetical rather than chronological order.

1) Action Comics 596 - unofficial X-over
2) Adventures of Superman #436 - unofficial X-over
3) Adventures of Superman 437
4) Batman 415
5) Blue Beetle 20
6) Blue Beetle 21
7) Booster Gold 24
8) Booster Gold 25
9) Captain Atom 11
10) Detective Comics 582
11) Firestorm 67
12) Firestorm 68
13) Flash 8
14) Flash 9
15) Green Lantern #220
16) Green Lantern 221
17) Infinity Inc. 46
18) Infinity Inc. 47
19) Justice League International 9
20) Justice League International #10
21) Legion of Super-Heroes (2nd Series) 42 - unofficial X-over
22) Legion of Super-Heroes (2nd Series) 43
23) Outsiders 27
24) Outsiders 28
25) Secret Origins (2nd Series) 22
26) Secret Origins (2nd Series) 23
27) Spectre (2nd Series) 10
28) Spectre (2nd Series) 11
29) Suicide Squad 9
30) Superman 13
31) Superman 14
32) Teen Titans Spotlight 18

$Good | $Fine | $N.Mint | £Good | £Fine | £N.Mint

33) Teen Titans Spotlight 19
34) Wonder Woman 12
35) Wonder Woman 13
36) Young All Stars 8
37) Young All Stars 9
Note: unofficial cross-over means that the storyline may be referred to in the comic but not emblazoned on the cover with the "Millennium" logo.

MILLENNIUM (LIMITED SERIES)
DC Comics,MS; 1 Jan 1988-8 Feb 1988

Issue	$Good	$Fine	$N.Mint	£Good	£Fine	£N.Mint
1-8 Staton/Ian Gibson art	$0.25	$0.75	$1.25	£0.15	£0.45	£0.75
Title Value:	$2.00	$6.00	$10.00	£1.20	£3.60	£6.00

Note: multi-cross over series similar to Legends and Crisis on Infinite Earths

MILLENNIUM FEVER
DC Comics/Vertigo,MS; 1 Oct 1995-4 Jan 1996

Issue	$Good	$Fine	$N.Mint	£Good	£Fine	£N.Mint
1-4 ND Nick Abadzis script, Duncan Fegredo art	$0.45	$1.35	$2.25	£0.30	£0.90	£1.50
Title Value:	$1.80	$5.40	$9.00	£1.20	£3.60	£6.00

MILLENNIUM INDEX
ICG/Eclipse,MS; 1,2 Mar 1988

Issue	$Good	$Fine	$N.Mint	£Good	£Fine	£N.Mint
1 ND scarce in the U.K. information and colour cover reproductions Millennium maxi-series #1-#4 and X-overs weeks 1-4	$0.50	$1.50	$2.50	£0.30	£0.90	£1.50
2 ND scarce in the U.K. information and colour cover reproductions Millennium maxi-series #5-#8 and X-overs weeks 5-8	$0.50	$1.50	$2.50	£0.30	£0.90	£1.50
Title Value:	$1.00	$3.00	$5.00	£0.60	£1.80	£3.00

MILLENNIUM SHOWCASE
Millennium; 1 Jul 1991

Issue	$Good	$Fine	$N.Mint	£Good	£Fine	£N.Mint
1 ND Death Hawk	$0.40	$1.20	$2.00	£0.25	£0.75	£1.25
Title Value:	$0.40	$1.20	$2.00	£0.25	£0.75	£1.25

MILLIE ANNUAL, MAD ABOUT
Marvel Comics Group; 1 Nov 1971

Issue	$Good	$Fine	$N.Mint	£Good	£Fine	£N.Mint
1 very scarce in the U.K. 72pgs	$3.30	$10.00	$20.00	£1.25	£3.75	£7.50
Title Value:	$3.30	$10.00	$20.00	£1.25	£3.75	£7.50

MILLIE THE MODEL
Marvel Comics Group;79 Jul 1960-207 Dec 1973
(see Modelling with..., A Date with..., Life with..., Mad About..)

Issue	$Good	$Fine	$N.Mint	£Good	£Fine	£N.Mint
79-90 scarce in the U.K.	$3.90	$11.50	$27.50	£2.50	£7.50	£17.50
91-99 scarce in the U.K.	$3.55	$10.50	$25.00	£2.10	£6.25	£15.00
100 scarce in the U.K.	$5.00	$15.00	$35.00	£2.85	£8.50	£20.00
101-106	$2.85	$8.50	$20.00	£1.40	£4.25	£10.00
107 scarce in the U.K. Jack Kirby appears in story	$2.85	$8.50	$20.00	£1.40	£4.25	£10.00
108-150	$2.85	$8.50	$20.00	£1.40	£4.25	£10.00
151-153	$2.90	$8.75	$17.50	£1.50	£4.50	£9.00
154 scarce in the U.K. title re-vamped, new Millie	$3.75	$11.00	$22.50	£2.05	£6.25	£12.50
155-160 scarce in the U.K.	$3.30	$10.00	$20.00	£1.65	£5.00	£10.00
161-190 scarce in the U.K.	$2.90	$8.75	$17.50	£1.30	£4.00	£8.00
191 scarce in the U.K.	$1.65	$5.00	$10.00	£1.25	£3.75	£7.50
192 scarce in the U.K. 52pgs	$2.05	$6.25	$12.50	£1.30	£4.00	£8.00
193-207 scarce in the U.K.	$1.65	$5.00	$10.00	£1.25	£3.75	£7.50
Title Value:	$373.95	$1118.50	$2420.00	£198.50	£601.00	£1332.50

MILLIE THE MODEL ANNUAL
Marvel Comics Group; 1 1962-10 Nov 1971

Issue	$Good	$Fine	$N.Mint	£Good	£Fine	£N.Mint
1 very scarce in the U.K.	$21.00	$62.50	$150.00	£14.00	£43.00	£100.00
2 scarce in the U.K.	$16.00	$49.00	$115.00	£10.00	£30.00	£70.00
3-5 scarce in the U.K.	$11.00	$34.00	$80.00	£6.25	£19.00	£45.00
6-8 scarce in the U.K.	$5.50	$17.00	$40.00	£3.90	£11.50	£27.50
9-10 scarce in the U.K.	$6.25	$18.50	$37.50	£4.15	£12.50	£25.00
Title Value:	$99.00	$301.50	$670.00	£62.75	£189.50	£437.50

MILLIE THE MODEL QUEEN SIZE
Marvel Comics Group; 11 Sep 1974-12 1975
(formerly Millie the Model Annual)

Issue	$Good	$Fine	$N.Mint	£Good	£Fine	£N.Mint
11-12 scarce in the U.K.	$5.75	$17.50	$35.00	£3.30	£10.00	£20.00
Title Value:	$11.50	$35.00	$70.00	£6.60	£20.00	£40.00

MILLIE, A DATE WITH
Marvel Comics Group; 1 Oct 1959-7 Oct 1960
(previous series published by Atlas, 1956/1957)

Issue	$Good	$Fine	$N.Mint	£Good	£Fine	£N.Mint
1 ND scarce in the U.K.	$20.50	$60.00	$145.00	£12.00	£36.00	£85.00
2 ND scarce in the U.K.	$11.00	$34.00	$80.00	£6.25	£19.00	£45.00
3-7 ND scarce in the U.K.	$7.00	$21.00	$50.00	£4.25	£12.50	£30.00
Title Value:	$66.50	$199.00	$475.00	£39.50	£117.50	£280.00

MILLIE, LIFE WITH
Marvel Comics Group;8 Dec 1960-20 Dec 1962
(formerly Date with Millie; becomes Modelling with Millie)

Issue	$Good	$Fine	$N.Mint	£Good	£Fine	£N.Mint
8 ND scarce in the U.K.	$7.75	$23.50	$55.00	£4.25	£12.50	£30.00
9-10 ND scarce in the U.K.	$5.50	$17.00	$40.00	£3.20	£9.50	£22.50
11-20 ND scarce in the U.K.	$3.90	$11.50	$27.50	£2.50	£7.50	£17.50
Title Value:	$57.75	$172.50	$410.00	£35.65	£106.50	£250.00

MILLIE, MAD ABOUT
Marvel Comics Group; 1 Apr 1969-17 Dec 1970

Issue	$Good	$Fine	$N.Mint	£Good	£Fine	£N.Mint
1 rare in the U.K. 68pgs	$6.25	$18.50	$37.50	£4.15	£12.50	£25.00
2 rare in the U.K.	$3.75	$11.00	$22.50	£2.50	£7.50	£15.00
3-10 rare in the U.K.	$3.30	$10.00	$20.00	£2.05	£6.25	£12.50
11-15 rare in the U.K.	$2.90	$8.75	$17.50	£1.80	£5.50	£11.00
16-17 rare in the U.K. reprints	$2.50	$7.50	$15.00	£1.65	£5.00	£10.00
Title Value:	$55.90	$168.25	$337.50	£35.35	£107.50	£215.00

MILLIE, MODELLING WITH
Marvel Comics Group;21 Feb 1963-54 Jun 1967

Issue	$Good	$Fine	$N.Mint	£Good	£Fine	£N.Mint
21 very scarce in the U.K.	$9.25	$28.00	$65.00	£5.00	£15.00	£35.00
22-30 scarce in the U.K.	$5.25	$16.00	$37.50	£2.85	£8.50	£20.00
31-50 scarce in the U.K.	$3.90	$11.50	$27.50	£2.50	£7.50	£17.50
51-54 scarce in the U.K.	$3.20	$9.50	$22.50	£2.10	£6.25	£15.00
Title Value:	$147.30	$440.00	$1017.50	£89.05	£266.50	£625.00

MINDGAME GALLERY, THE
Mindgame Press; 1 Jul 1990-5 1991

Issue	$Good	$Fine	$N.Mint	£Good	£Fine	£N.Mint
1 ND Steve Bissette script, Rick Veitch art	$0.40	$1.20	$2.00	£0.25	£0.75	£1.25
2-4 ND	$0.40	$1.20	$2.00	£0.25	£0.75	£1.25
5 ND new Empire Lanes story	$0.40	$1.20	$2.00	£0.25	£0.75	£1.25
Title Value:	$2.00	$6.00	$10.00	£1.25	£3.75	£6.25

MIRACLE SQUAD
Upshot Graphics/Fantagraphics,MS; 1 Aug 1986-4 1987

Issue	$Good	$Fine	$N.Mint	£Good	£Fine	£N.Mint
1-4 ND Tidwell art	$0.40	$1.20	$2.00	£0.25	£0.75	£1.25
Title Value:	$1.60	$4.80	$8.00	£1.00	£3.00	£5.00

MIRACLE SQUAD: BLOOD AND DUST
Apple Comics,MS; 1 Jan 1989-4 Jul 1989

Issue	$Good	$Fine	$N.Mint	£Good	£Fine	£N.Mint
1-4 ND	$0.40	$1.20	$2.00	£0.25	£0.75	£1.25
Title Value:	$1.60	$4.80	$8.00	£1.00	£3.00	£5.00
Miracle Squad Bargain Pre-Pack (Jun 1991), reprints #1-4				£0.70	£2.10	£3.50

MIRACLEMAN
Eclipse; 1 Aug 1985-24 1992

Issue	$Good	$Fine	$N.Mint	£Good	£Fine	£N.Mint
1 ND Marvelman reprints from Warrior magazine begin; Alan Moore scripts, Leach and Davis art	$0.70	$2.10	$3.50	£0.50	£1.50	£2.50
1 U.K. Edition, distributed in the U.K. Quality advert on back	$0.60	$1.80	$3.00	£0.40	£1.20	£2.00
2 ND Leach, Davis art	$0.50	$1.50	$2.50	£0.40	£1.20	£2.00
3-5 ND Davis art	$0.50	$1.50	$2.50	£0.40	£1.20	£2.00
6 ND Davis, Beckum art	$0.40	$1.20	$2.00	£0.30	£0.90	£1.50
7 ND Beckum art	$0.40	$1.20	$2.00	£0.30	£0.90	£1.50
8 ND 50s reprints, New Wave preview	$0.40	$1.20	$2.00	£0.30	£0.90	£1.50
9 ND scarce in the U.K. contraversial birth issue	$0.40	$1.20	$2.00	£0.30	£0.90	£1.50
10 ND	$0.40	$1.20	$2.00	£0.30	£0.90	£1.50
11 ND John Totleben art	$0.40	$1.20	$2.00	£0.30	£0.90	£1.50
12 ND very scarce in the U.K. John Totleben art	$0.40	$1.20	$2.00	£0.60	£1.80	£3.00
13 ND John Totleben art, $1.75 cover price	$0.40	$1.20	$2.00	£0.30	£0.90	£1.50
14-15 ND John Totleben art	$0.40	$1.20	$2.00	£0.30	£0.90	£1.50
16 ND last Alan Moore script	$0.40	$1.20	$2.00	£0.30	£0.90	£1.50
17 ND 1st Neil Gaiman script, Mark Buckingham art	$0.40	$1.20	$2.00	£0.40	£1.20	£2.00
18-22 ND Neil Gaiman script, Mark Buckingham art	$0.40	$1.20	$2.00	£0.30	£0.90	£1.50
23-24 ND Neil Gaiman script, Mark Buckingham art, Barry Windsor-Smith painted cover	$0.50	$1.50	$2.50	£0.30	£0.90	£1.50
Title Value:	$11.10	$33.30	$57.50	£8.60	£25.80	£43.00

Note: a Gold and Silver logo edition of #1 is available and each would be priced at 25% more.
Note also: issue #25-28 were advertised and solicited but never came out.

	£Good	£Fine	£N.Mint
Graphic Album 1 "A Dream Of Flying" (1989) reprints issues #1-4, Garry Leach painted cover, hardcover	£4.00	£12.00	£20.00
(2nd print - Nov 1991)	£3.75	£11.25	£18.75
Softcover version	£1.20	£3.60	£6.00
Graphic Album 2 "The Red King Syndrome" (1990) reprints #5-8,9,10 with John Bolton painted cover, hardcover	£4.00	£12.00	£20.00

	$Good	$Fine	$N.Mint	£Good	£Fine	£N.Mint
(2nd print - Nov 1991)				£3.75	£11.25	£18.75
Softcover version				£1.60	£4.80	£8.00
Graphic Album 3 "Olympus" (1991), Softcover version				£1.60	£4.80	£8.00
Graphic Album 4 "The Golden Age" (Sep 1993) reprints #17-22						
Softcover				£1.60	£4.80	£8.00
Hardcover				£4.50	£13.50	£22.50

MIRACLEMAN 3-D SPECIAL

Eclipse; 1 Dec 1985

	$Good	$Fine	$N.Mint	£Good	£Fine	£N.Mint
1 ND reprints Marvelman Special (Quality), Alan Moore/Alan Davis framing sequence; glasses included (25% less if without glasses)	$0.40	$1.20	$2.00	£0.40	£1.20	£2.00
1 Non 3-D version ND scarce in the U.K.	$0.60	$1.80	$3.00	£0.70	£2.10	£3.50
Title Value:	$1.00	$3.00	$5.00	£1.10	£3.30	£5.50

MIRACLEMAN FAMILY

Eclipse,MS; 1 May 1988-2 Sep 1988

	$Good	$Fine	$N.Mint	£Good	£Fine	£N.Mint
1 ND reprints from Young Marvelman Adventures and Marvelman #361; story and art by the Mick Anglo Studios, colour; new Garry Leach cover	$0.40	$1.20	$2.00	£0.25	£0.75	£1.25
2 ND reprints from Young Marvelman #347, Marvelman Family #4; story and art by the Mick Anglo Studios, colour; new Paul Gulacy cover	$0.40	$1.20	$2.00	£0.25	£0.75	£1.25
Title Value:	$0.80	$2.40	$4.00	£0.50	£1.50	£2.50

Note: all references to "Marvelman" in original art re-lettered "Miracleman".

MIRACLEMAN TRIUMPHANT

Eclipse; 1 May 1994

	$Good	$Fine	$N.Mint	£Good	£Fine	£N.Mint
1 ND	$0.50	$1.50	$2.50	£0.30	£0.90	£1.50
Title Value:	$0.50	$1.50	$2.50	£0.30	£0.90	£1.50

MIRACLEMAN: THE APOCRYPHA

Eclipse,MS; 1 Nov 1991-3 Feb 1992

	$Good	$Fine	$N.Mint	£Good	£Fine	£N.Mint
1 ND features work by Matt Wagner, Norm Breyfogle, Neil Gaiman, Mark Buckingham	$0.50	$1.50	$2.50	£0.30	£0.90	£1.50
2 ND features work by Louise Simonson, Neil Gaiman, Mark Buckingham	$0.50	$1.50	$2.50	£0.30	£0.90	£1.50
3 ND features work by Steve Moore, Val Mayerik, Neil Gaiman, Mark Buckingham	$0.50	$1.50	$2.50	£0.30	£0.90	£1.50
Title Value:	$1.50	$4.50	$7.50	£0.90	£2.70	£4.50
Miracleman: The Apocrypha Trade paperback (Feb 1993) reprints mini-series, new Mark Buckingham cover				£2.00	£6.00	£10.00

MISEROTH: AMOK HELL

Northstar,MS; 1 Feb 1994-3 Apr 1994

	$Good	$Fine	$N.Mint	£Good	£Fine	£N.Mint
1-3 ND Frank Gomez script, Adam McDaniel art; black and white	$1.00	$3.00	$5.00	£0.60	£1.80	£3.00
Title Value:	$3.00	$9.00	$15.00	£1.80	£5.40	£9.00

MISS FURY

Adventure,MS; 1 Jun 1991-4 Feb 1992

	$Good	$Fine	$N.Mint	£Good	£Fine	£N.Mint
1-4 ND	$0.40	$1.20	$2.00	£0.25	£0.75	£1.25
Title Value:	$1.60	$4.80	$8.00	£1.00	£3.00	£5.00

MISS FURY QUARTERLY

A Plus Comics; 1 Jan 1992

	$Good	$Fine	$N.Mint	£Good	£Fine	£N.Mint
1 ND 48pgs	$0.40	$1.20	$2.00	£0.25	£0.75	£1.25
Title Value:	$0.40	$1.20	$2.00	£0.25	£0.75	£1.25

MISS VICTORY GOLDEN ANNIVERSARY SPECIAL

AC Comics,OS; 1 Nov 1991

	$Good	$Fine	$N.Mint	£Good	£Fine	£N.Mint
1 ND 68pgs, new colour Miss Victory story plus black and white Golden Age reprints	$0.70	$2.10	$3.50	£0.50	£1.50	£2.50
Title Value:	$0.70	$2.10	$3.50	£0.50	£1.50	£2.50

MISSION IMPOSSIBLE

Dell; 1 May 1967-5 Oct 1969

	$Good	$Fine	$N.Mint	£Good	£Fine	£N.Mint
1 scarce in the U.K. photo cover	$14.00	$43.00	$100.00	£5.50	£17.00	£40.00
2-5 photo covers	$9.25	$28.00	$65.00	£3.90	£11.50	£27.50
Title Value:	$51.00	$155.00	$360.00	£21.10	£63.00	£150.00

MISSION IMPOSSIBLE (2ND SERIES)

Marvel Comics Group,OS; 1 Jul 1996

	$Good	$Fine	$N.Mint	£Good	£Fine	£N.Mint
1 ND 48pgs, tie-in with film starring Tom Cruise; Rob Liefeld 6pg story and cover	$0.60	$1.80	$3.00	£0.40	£1.20	£2.00
Title Value:	$0.60	$1.80	$3.00	£0.40	£1.20	£2.00

MISTER E

DC Comics,MS; 1 May 1991-4 Sep 1991

	$Good	$Fine	$N.Mint	£Good	£Fine	£N.Mint
1 John K. Snyder III art begins	$0.40	$1.20	$2.00	£0.25	£0.75	£1.25
2-3	$0.40	$1.20	$2.00	£0.25	£0.75	£1.25
4 Dr. Fate/Phantom Stranger guest-star	$0.40	$1.20	$2.00	£0.25	£0.75	£1.25
Title Value:	$1.60	$4.80	$8.00	£1.00	£3.00	£5.00

Note: spin-off from Books of Magic. Delay between issues #3 and #4.

MISTER MIRACLE

DC Comics; 1 Mar/Apr 1971-18 Feb/Mar 1974; 19 Sep 1977-25 Aug/Sep 1978

(see Brave and the Bold, DC Comics Presents, Justice League)

	$Good	$Fine	$N.Mint	£Good	£Fine	£N.Mint
1 Jack Kirby art begins	$5.00	$15.00	$35.00	£2.85	£8.50	£20.00
2	$2.90	$8.75	$17.50	£1.65	£5.00	£10.00
3	$2.90	$8.75	$17.50	£1.25	£3.75	£7.50
4-8 52pgs, Joe Simon & Jack Kirby Boy Commandos reprints	$2.50	$7.50	$15.00	£1.00	£3.00	£6.00
9 scarce in the U.K. origin Mr. Miracle, Darkseid cameo	$2.05	$6.25	$12.50	£0.80	£2.50	£5.00
10	$2.05	$6.25	$12.50	£0.80	£2.50	£5.00
11-17	$2.05	$6.25	$12.50	£0.65	£2.00	£4.00
18 last Jack Kirby art, Darkseid cameo	$2.05	$6.25	$12.50	£0.65	£2.00	£4.00
19 scarce in the U.K. Rogers and Neal Adams art	$1.00	$3.00	$6.00	£0.50	£1.50	£3.00
20 scarce in the U.K. Rogers art	$0.80	$2.50	$5.00	£0.50	£1.50	£3.00
21-22 Rogers art	$0.80	$2.50	$5.00	£0.40	£1.25	£2.50
23-25 Golden art	$0.80	$2.50	$5.00	£0.40	£1.25	£2.50
Title Value:	$49.60	$150.50	$306.00	£20.55	£62.50	£128.00

MISTER MIRACLE (2ND SERIES)

DC Comics; 1 Jan 1989-28 Jun 1991

	$Good	$Fine	$N.Mint	£Good	£Fine	£N.Mint
1-2 Ian Gibson cover/art	$0.25	$0.75	$1.25	£0.15	£0.45	£0.75
3-4 Forever People appear	$0.25	$0.75	$1.25	£0.15	£0.45	£0.75
5	$0.25	$0.75	$1.25	£0.15	£0.45	£0.75
6 G'Nort appears	$0.25	$0.75	$1.25	£0.15	£0.45	£0.75
7-8 Blue Beetle, Booster Gold appear	$0.25	$0.75	$1.25	£0.15	£0.45	£0.75
9-12	$0.25	$0.75	$1.25	£0.15	£0.45	£0.75
13-14 Lobo appears	$0.25	$0.75	$1.25	£0.15	£0.45	£0.75
15-19	$0.25	$0.75	$1.25	£0.15	£0.45	£0.75
20 Ian Gibson art	$0.25	$0.75	$1.25	£0.15	£0.45	£0.75
21	$0.25	$0.75	$1.25	£0.15	£0.45	£0.75
22 new Mister Miracle, Shilo Norman, begins training by Scott Free the existing Mr. Miracle	$0.25	$0.75	$1.25	£0.15	£0.45	£0.75
23-28	$0.25	$0.75	$1.25	£0.15	£0.45	£0.75
Title Value:	$7.00	$21.00	$35.00	£4.20	£12.60	£21.00

MISTER MIRACLE (3RD SERIES)

DC Comics; 1 Apr 1996-7 Oct 1996

	$Good	$Fine	$N.Mint	£Good	£Fine	£N.Mint
1-4 ND	$0.40	$1.20	$2.00	£0.25	£0.75	£1.25

Millie The Model #136

Miracleman #9

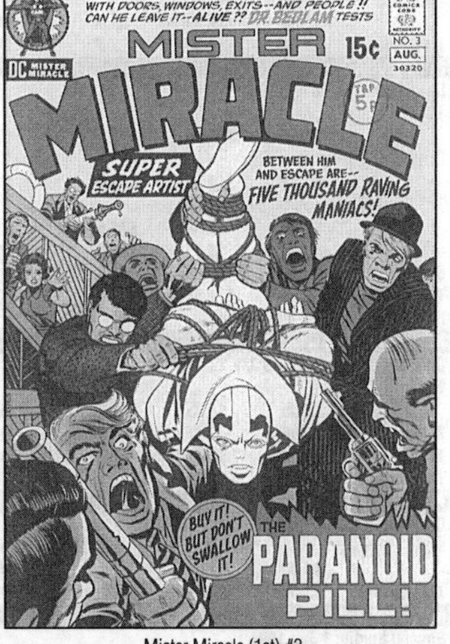

Mister Miracle (1st) #3

Issue	$Good	$Fine	$N.Mint	£Good	£Fine	£N.Mint
5 ND Marshall Rogers and Terry Austin cover	$0.40	$1.20	$2.00	£0.25	£0.75	£1.25
6 ND Walt Simonson cover	$0.40	$1.20	$2.00	£0.25	£0.75	£1.25
7 ND	$0.40	$1.20	$2.00	£0.25	£0.75	£1.25
Title Value:	$2.80	$8.40	$14.00	£1.75	£5.25	£8.75

MISTER MIRACLE SPECIAL

DC Comics; 1 1987

Issue	$Good	$Fine	$N.Mint	£Good	£Fine	£N.Mint
1 52pgs, Steve Rude art, Jack Kirby tribute	$0.30	$0.90	$1.50	£0.20	£0.60	£1.00
Title Value:	$0.30	$0.90	$1.50	£0.20	£0.60	£1.00

MISTER X

Vortex; 1 Jun 1984-14 Aug 1988

Issue	$Good	$Fine	$N.Mint	£Good	£Fine	£N.Mint
1 scarce in the U.K. J. Hernandez art	$0.80	$2.40	$4.00	£0.50	£1.50	£2.50
2 J. Hernandez art	$0.60	$1.80	$3.00	£0.40	£1.20	£2.00
3-4 J. Hernandez art	$0.50	$1.50	$2.50	£0.30	£0.90	£1.50
5 scarce in the U.K.	$0.50	$1.50	$2.50	£0.35	£1.05	£1.75
6-9	$0.50	$1.50	$2.50	£0.30	£0.90	£1.50
10 Dave McKean art	$0.50	$1.50	$2.50	£0.30	£0.90	£1.50
11-14	$0.50	$1.50	$2.50	£0.30	£0.90	£1.50
Title Value:	$7.40	$22.20	$37.00	£4.55	£13.65	£22.75
Note all Non-Distributed on the news-stands in the U.K.						
Special 1 (Nov 1990) ND Pete Milligan script, Brett Ewins art				£0.35	£1.05	£1.75
Trade paperback ND Vortex edition, collects #1-4				£1.70	£5.10	£8.50
Titan (UK) Edition distributed				£1.60	£4.80	£8.00
Warner Edition (Dec 1989) ND				£1.20	£3.60	£6.00
Hardback, Grafitti edition ND				£4.00	£12.00	£20.00

MISTER X VOLUME 2

Vortex; 1 Apr 1989-13 Jul 1991

Issue	$Good	$Fine	$N.Mint	£Good	£Fine	£N.Mint
1-13 ND	$0.50	$1.50	$2.50	£0.30	£0.90	£1.50
Title Value:	$6.50	$19.50	$32.50	£3.90	£11.70	£19.50

MISTER X VOLUME 3

Caliber Press; 1 Apr 1996-2 1996 ?

Issue	$Good	$Fine	$N.Mint	£Good	£Fine	£N.Mint
1 ND Deborah Marks script, Gene Gonzales art; black and white	$0.60	$1.80	$3.00	£0.40	£1.20	£2.00
2 ND	$0.60	$1.80	$3.00	£0.40	£1.20	£2.00
Title Value:	$1.20	$3.60	$6.00	£0.80	£2.40	£4.00

MISTS OF AVALON, THE

Eclipse,MS; 1 Mar 1994

Issue	$Good	$Fine	$N.Mint	£Good	£Fine	£N.Mint
1 ND 48pgs, Sarah Byam and Steve Parkhouse	$1.00	$3.00	$5.00	£0.70	£2.10	£3.50
Title Value:	$1.00	$3.00	$5.00	£0.70	£2.10	£3.50

Note: advertised and solicited but may not have come out

MISTY

Marvel Comics Group/Star; 1 Dec 1985-6 May 1986

Issue	$Good	$Fine	$N.Mint	£Good	£Fine	£N.Mint
1-6 ND Millie's niece	$0.15	$0.45	$0.75	£0.10	£0.30	£0.50
Title Value:	$0.90	$2.70	$4.50	£0.60	£1.80	£3.00

MOBFIRE

DC Comics/Vertigo,MS; 1 Dec 1994-6 May 1995

Issue	$Good	$Fine	$N.Mint	£Good	£Fine	£N.Mint
1-6 Gary Ushaw and Warren Pleece creative team	$0.40	$1.20	$2.00	£0.25	£0.75	£1.25
Title Value:	$2.40	$7.20	$12.00	£1.50	£4.50	£7.50

MOBILE SUIT GUNDAM 0083

Viz Communications,MS; 1 Jan 1994-13 Jan 1995

Issue	$Good	$Fine	$N.Mint	£Good	£Fine	£N.Mint
1-13 ND 48pgs, colour	$0.90	$2.70	$4.50	£0.60	£1.80	£3.00
Title Value:	$11.70	$35.10	$58.50	£7.80	£23.40	£39.00

MOD

Kitchen Sink; 1 1981

Issue	$Good	$Fine	$N.Mint	£Good	£Fine	£N.Mint
1 ND 5pgs Bob Burden art	$0.60	$1.80	$3.00	£0.40	£1.20	£2.00
Title Value:	$0.60	$1.80	$3.00	£0.40	£1.20	£2.00

MOD SQUAD

Dell; 1 Jan 1969-8 Apr 1971

Issue	$Good	$Fine	$N.Mint	£Good	£Fine	£N.Mint
1 based on TV series, photo cover	$6.00	$18.00	$42.50	£3.55	£10.50	£25.00
2 based on TV series, photo cover	$3.55	$10.50	$25.00	£1.75	£5.25	£12.50
3 based on TV series, photo cover	$2.85	$8.50	$20.00	£1.40	£4.25	£10.00
4-7	$2.85	$8.50	$20.00	£1.40	£4.25	£10.00
8 reprints #2	$2.50	$7.50	$17.50	£1.10	£3.40	£8.00
Title Value:	$26.30	$78.50	$185.00	£13.40	£40.40	£95.50

Note: very limited distribution in the U.K.

MOD WHEELS

Gold Key; 1 Mar 1971-19 Jan 1976

Issue	$Good	$Fine	$N.Mint	£Good	£Fine	£N.Mint
1 scarce in the U.K.	$2.05	$6.25	$12.50	£0.80	£2.50	£5.00
2-10	$1.00	$3.00	$6.00	£0.40	£1.25	£2.50
11-19	$0.80	$2.50	$5.00	£0.30	£1.00	£2.00
Title Value:	$18.25	$55.75	$111.50	£7.10	£22.75	£45.50

MODERN CLASSICS: FREAKS' AMOUR

Dark Horse,MS; 1 Jul 1992-3 Jan 1993

Issue	$Good	$Fine	$N.Mint	£Good	£Fine	£N.Mint
1-3 ND 48pgs, based on Tom DeHaven's cult novel, cover by Charles Burns	$0.80	$2.40	$4.00	£0.50	£1.50	£2.50
Title Value:	$2.40	$7.20	$12.00	£1.50	£4.50	£7.50

MODERN PULP

Special Studio; 1 Jan 1991

Issue	$Good	$Fine	$N.Mint	£Good	£Fine	£N.Mint
1 ND black and white	$0.40	$1.20	$2.00	£0.25	£0.75	£1.25
Title Value:	$0.40	$1.20	$2.00	£0.25	£0.75	£1.25

MODESTY BLAISE

DC Comics,MS; 1 Mar 1993-3 May 1993

Issue	$Good	$Fine	$N.Mint	£Good	£Fine	£N.Mint
1-3 ND 48pgs, Pete O'Donnell and Dick Giordano	$0.70	$2.10	$3.50	£0.50	£1.50	£2.50
Title Value:	$2.10	$6.30	$10.50	£1.50	£4.50	£7.50

MODESTY BLAZE GRAPHIC NOVEL

DC Comics,OS; nn Feb 1995

Issue	$Good	$Fine	$N.Mint	£Good	£Fine	£N.Mint
nn ND 144pgs, Peter O'Donnell script, Dick Giordano art	$3.50	$10.50	$17.50	£2.50	£7.50	£12.50
Title Value:	$3.50	$10.50	$17.50	£2.50	£7.50	£12.50

MOEBIUS

Marvel Comics Group/Epic Graphic Novel; 1 Oct 1987-8 1993

(see also The Incal)

Issue	$Good	$Fine	$N.Mint	£Good	£Fine	£N.Mint
1 ND 72pgs, Upon A Star				£1.10	£3.30	£5.50
(2nd print, Feb 1990)				£0.90	£2.70	£4.50
2 ND 72pgs, Arzach and Other Fantasy Stories				£1.00	£3.00	£5.00
(2nd print, Apr 1990)				£0.90	£2.70	£4.50
3 ND 120pgs, The Airtight Garage				£1.30	£3.90	£6.50
(2nd print, Apr 1990)				£1.20	£3.60	£6.00
4 ND 72pgs, The Long Tomorrow and other SF Stories				£1.00	£3.00	£5.00
5 ND 72pgs, The Gardens of Aedena				£1.00	£3.00	£5.00
6 ND72pgs, Pharagonesia and other Strange Stories				£1.00	£3.00	£5.00
7 ND 96pgs, The Goddess, links with Airtight Garage saga in "Elsewhere Prince"				£1.20	£3.60	£6.00
8 ND Mississippi River				£0.90	£2.70	£4.50
Note: there are also UK (Titan) editions of #5, #6.						
Art of Moebius Collection, text by Lofficier (Jan 1990)				£1.75	£3.50	£7.00

MOEBIUS 0: THE HORNY GOOF

Dark Horse; 0 1991

Issue	$Good	$Fine	$N.Mint	£Good	£Fine	£N.Mint
0 ND sci-fi story with Moebius art originally planned by Marvel Comics	$0.60	$1.80	$3.00	£0.40	£1.20	£2.00
Title Value:	$0.60	$1.80	$3.00	£0.40	£1.20	£2.00

MOEBIUS COMICS

Caliber Press; 1 Jun 1996-present

Issue	$Good	$Fine	$N.Mint	£Good	£Fine	£N.Mint
1-2 ND Moebius reprints in balck and white	$0.60	$1.80	$3.00	£0.40	£1.20	£2.00
3 ND Moebius reprints in black and white	$0.60	$1.80	$3.00	£0.40	£1.20	£2.00
Title Value:	$1.80	$5.40	$9.00	£1.20	£3.60	£6.00

MOEBIUS: CHAOS HARDCOVER

Marvel Comics Group,OS; 1 Dec 1991

Issue	$Good	$Fine	$N.Mint	£Good	£Fine	£N.Mint
1 ND rare in the U.K. 96pgs, Moebius material with new cover and introduction by Moebius	$3.50	$10.50	$17.50	£2.50	£7.50	£12.50
Title Value:	$3.50	$10.50	$17.50	£2.50	£7.50	£12.50

MOEBIUS: FUSION

Marvel Comics Group,OS; nn Nov 1995

Issue	$Good	$Fine	$N.Mint	£Good	£Fine	£N.Mint
nn ND 128pgs, collects sketches, paintings, poetry and Marvel posters by Moebius	$4.00	$12.00	$20.00	£2.80	£8.25	£14.00
Title Value:	$4.00	$12.00	$20.00	£2.80	£8.25	£14.00

MOEBIUS: STEL

Marvel Comics Group,OS; nn Jul 1994

Issue	$Good	$Fine	$N.Mint	£Good	£Fine	£N.Mint
nn ND 80pgs, softcover, sequel to Moebius #7: The Goddess	$3.00	$9.00	$15.00	£2.00	£6.00	£10.00
Title Value:	$3.00	$9.00	$15.00	£2.00	£6.00	£10.00

MONGREL

Northstar; 1 Oct 1994-2 1995

Issue	$Good	$Fine	$N.Mint	£Good	£Fine	£N.Mint
1 ND black and white	$0.40	$1.20	$2.00	£0.25	£0.75	£1.25
1 Deluxe Edition, ND with sketches; black and white	$0.50	$1.50	$2.50	£0.30	£0.90	£1.50
1 Gold Edition, ND (Oct 1994) - signed and numbered	$0.80	$2.40	$4.00	£0.50	£1.50	£2.50
2 ND	$0.40	$1.20	$2.00	£0.25	£0.75	£1.25
2 Prestige Format, ND - 8pg section on werewolf legends, foil logo on cover	$0.50	$1.50	$2.50	£0.30	£0.90	£1.50
Title Value:	$2.60	$7.80	$13.00	£1.60	£4.80	£8.00

MONKEES, THE

Dell,TV; 1 Mar 1967-17 Oct 1969

Issue	$Good	$Fine	$N.Mint	£Good	£Fine	£N.Mint
1 distributed in the U.K.	$14.00	$43.00	$100.00	£8.50	£26.00	£60.00
2-3 distributed in the U.K.	$8.50	$26.00	$60.00	£5.00	£15.00	£35.00
4-5 distributed in the U.K.	$6.75	$20.00	$47.50	£4.60	£13.50	£32.50
6-10 distributed in the U.K.	$6.25	$19.00	$45.00	£4.25	£12.50	£30.00
11-17 distributed in the U.K.	$6.00	$18.00	$42.50	£3.90	£11.50	£27.50
Title Value:	$117.75	$356.00	$827.50	£76.25	£226.00	£537.50

MONKEYMAN AND O'BRIEN

Dark Horse/Legend,MS; 1 Jul 1996-3 Sep 1996

Issue	$Good	$Fine	$N.Mint	£Good	£Fine	£N.Mint
1-3 ND Art Adams script and art	$0.60	$1.80	$3.00	£0.40	£1.20	£2.00
Title Value:	$1.80	$5.40	$9.00	£1.20	£3.60	£6.00

MONKEYMAN AND O'BRIEN SPECIAL

Dark Horse,OS; nn Feb 1996

Issue	$Good	$Fine	$N.Mint	£Good	£Fine	£N.Mint
nn ND Art Adams script and art	$0.50	$1.50	$2.50	£0.30	£0.90	£1.50
Title Value:	$0.50	$1.50	$2.50	£0.30	£0.90	£1.50

MONOLITH

Comico,MS; 1 Oct 1991-4 Jan 1992

Issue	$Good	$Fine	$N.Mint	£Good	£Fine	£N.Mint
1-4 ND colour, Kelley Jones covers	$0.40	$1.20	$2.00	£0.25	£0.75	£1.25
Title Value:	$1.60	$4.80	$8.00	£1.00	£3.00	£5.00

MONSTER FRAT HOUSE

Eternity,OS; 1 Oct 1989

Issue	$Good	$Fine	$N.Mint	£Good	£Fine	£N.Mint
1 ND Paul O'Conner script, John Grigni, Sandy Carruthers, Mike Roberts art; black and white	$0.30	$0.90	$1.50	£0.20	£0.60	£1.00
Title Value:	$0.30	$0.90	$1.50	£0.20	£0.60	£1.00

MONSTER HUNTERS

Charlton; 1 Aug 1975-18 Feb 1979

Issue	$Good	$Fine	$N.Mint	£Good	£Fine	£N.Mint
1	$1.05	$3.25	$6.50	£0.55	£1.75	£3.50
2 Steve Ditko art	$0.80	$2.50	$5.00	£0.55	£1.75	£3.50
3-5	$0.50	$1.50	$3.00	£0.30	£1.00	£2.00
6 Steve Ditko art	$0.50	$1.50	$3.00	£0.30	£1.00	£2.00
7	$0.50	$1.50	$3.00	£0.30	£1.00	£2.00
8 Steve Ditko art	$0.50	$1.50	$3.00	£0.30	£1.00	£2.00
9	$0.50	$1.50	$3.00	£0.30	£1.00	£2.00
10 Steve Ditko art	$0.50	$1.50	$3.00	£0.30	£1.00	£2.00
11-13	$0.50	$1.50	$3.00	£0.30	£1.00	£2.00
14 all Steve Ditko art	$0.65	$2.00	$4.00	£0.40	£1.25	£2.50
15-18	$0.50	$1.50	$3.00	£0.30	£1.00	£2.00
Title Value:	$10.00	$30.25	$60.50	£6.00	£19.75	£39.50

Note: reprints in #12-18. Distributed in the U.K.

MONSTER MASSACRE SPECIAL

Blackball Comics,OS; 1 Jan 1994

Issue	$Good	$Fine	$N.Mint	£Good	£Fine	£N.Mint
1 ND 48pgs, features art by Kev O'Neill, Keith Giffen and Simon Bisley; Bisley cover	$0.40	$1.20	$2.00	£0.25	£0.75	£1.25
Title Value:	$0.40	$1.20	$2.00	£0.25	£0.75	£1.25

MONSTER MASTERWORKS

Marvel Comics Group; nn Feb 1990

(see Marvel Masterworks)

Trade paperback

Issue	$Good	$Fine	$N.Mint	£Good	£Fine	£N.Mint
ND collection of Marvel pre-Superhero reprints with work by Lee, Kirby, Ditko and Everett. Cover by Walt Simonson				£1.40	£4.20	£7.00

MONSTER MENACE

Marvel Comics Group,MS; 1 Dec 1993-4 Mar 1994

Issue	$Good	$Fine	$N.Mint	£Good	£Fine	£N.Mint
1-4 pre-Marvel super-hero reprints begin featuring classics by Steve Ditko and Jack Kirby	$0.30	$0.90	$1.50	£0.20	£0.60	£1.00
Title Value:	$1.20	$3.60	$6.00	£0.80	£2.40	£4.00

MONSTER-HUNTER

Night Realm; 1 1990

Issue	$Good	$Fine	$N.Mint	£Good	£Fine	£N.Mint
1 ND black and white	$0.40	$1.20	$2.00	£0.25	£0.75	£1.25
Title Value:	$0.40	$1.20	$2.00	£0.25	£0.75	£1.25

MONSTERS FROM OUTER SPACE

Adventure,MS; 1 Feb 1993-3 Apr 1993

Issue	$Good	$Fine	$N.Mint	£Good	£Fine	£N.Mint
1-3 ND	$0.40	$1.20	$2.00	£0.25	£0.75	£1.25
Title Value:	$1.20	$3.60	$6.00	£0.75	£2.25	£3.75

MONSTERS ON THE PROWL

Marvel Comics Group,Magazine;9 Feb 1971-27 Nov 1973; 28 Jun 1974-30 Oct 1974

(formerly Chamber of Darkness)

Issue	$Good	$Fine	$N.Mint	£Good	£Fine	£N.Mint
9 Barry Smith inks	$0.65	$2.00	$4.00	£0.40	£1.25	£2.50
10-12	$0.30	$1.00	$2.00	£0.20	£0.60	£1.25
13-14 ND 52pgs	$0.40	$1.25	$2.50	£0.25	£0.75	£1.50
15	$0.30	$1.00	$2.00	£0.20	£0.60	£1.25
16 5th appearance Kull, 1st appearance Thulsa Doom, Severin art	$0.40	$1.25	$2.50	£0.25	£0.75	£1.50
17-30 ND	$0.30	$1.00	$2.00	£0.20	£0.60	£1.25
Title Value:	$7.25	$23.75	$47.50	£4.75	£14.30	£29.50

Note: all reprint except one new story in 9-13, 15, 16.

MONSTERS UNLEASHED

Marvel Comics Group,Magazine; 1 Jul 1973-11 Apr 1975

Issue	$Good	$Fine	$N.Mint	£Good	£Fine	£N.Mint
1 ND Frankenstein main feature begins	$1.00	$3.00	$6.00	£0.65	£2.00	£4.00
2 ND Frankenstein issue; Boris Karloff feature and Frankenstein painted cover by Boris	$0.80	$2.50	$5.00	£0.55	£1.75	£3.50
3 ND Frankenstein, Man-Thing stories, Son of Satan text story; Gil Kane art with part Neal Adams art (as "The Crusty Bunkers"), Neal Adams cover	$0.80	$2.50	$5.00	£0.55	£1.75	£3.50
4 scarce in the U.K. Frankenstein story, Gullivar Jones by Dave Cockrum, Ray Harryhausen feature; Werewolf cover	$0.65	$2.00	$4.00	£0.40	£1.25	£2.50
5 Frankenstein, Werewolf, Man-Thing	$0.65	$2.00	$4.00	£0.40	£1.25	£2.50
6 Werewolf by Night text story featuring illustrations by Mike Ploog, Frankenstein main feature and painted cover by Boris	$0.65	$2.00	$4.00	£0.40	£1.25	£2.50
7 Werewolf by Night text story featuring illustrations by Broderick and Janson; Frankenstein main feature	$0.65	$2.00	$4.00	£0.40	£1.25	£2.50
8 early George Perez work , Neal Adams reprint ("One Hungers"), Frankenstein main feature	$0.80	$2.50	$5.00	£0.50	£1.50	£3.00
9 Frankenstein, Man-Thing plus Wendigo back-up by Chris Claremont	$0.65	$2.00	$4.00	£0.40	£1.25	£2.50
10 Frankenstein plus Tigra back-up by Chris Claremont	$0.65	$2.00	$4.00	£0.40	£1.25	£2.50
11 Gabriel Devil-Hunter, Dave Cockrum Creature pin-up, Frank Brunner cover	$0.65	$2.00	$4.00	£0.40	£1.25	£2.50
Title Value:	$7.95	$24.50	$49.00	£5.05	£15.75	£31.50

ARTISTS

Adams reprint in 8. Ploog in 6,7. Williamson reprint in 9.

FEATURES

Frankenstein Monster in 2-5, 7-11. Wendigo in 9. Tigra (origin) in 10. Man-Thing in 3 (reprints origin), 4-11.

MONSTERS UNLEASHED ANNUAL

Marvel Comics Group,Magazine; 1 Summer 1975

Issue	$Good	$Fine	$N.Mint	£Good	£Fine	£N.Mint
1 ND 88pgs, squarebound, all reprint featuring Gene Colan and Gil Kane art; Neal Adams inks as part of "The Crusty Bunkers"	$0.65	$2.00	$4.00	£0.50	£1.50	£3.00
Title Value:	$0.65	$2.00	$4.00	£0.50	£1.50	£3.00

MONSTERS, NO SUCH THING AS

Choral Comics; 1,2 1986

Issue	$Good	$Fine	$N.Mint	£Good	£Fine	£N.Mint
1-2 ND	$0.25	$0.75	$1.25	£0.15	£0.45	£0.75
Title Value:	$0.50	$1.50	$2.50	£0.30	£0.90	£1.50

MOON KNIGHT

Marvel Comics Group; 1 Nov 1980-38 Jul 1984

(see Marvel Preview, Marvel Spotlight, Werewolf By Night #32)

Issue	$Good	$Fine	$N.Mint	£Good	£Fine	£N.Mint
1 Neal Adamsesque art by Bill Sienkiewicz begins, new origin	$0.50	$1.50	$2.50	£0.30	£0.90	£1.50
2-5 Sienkiewicz art	$0.40	$1.20	$2.00	£0.25	£0.75	£1.25
6 Sienkiewicz art, Earl Norem painted cover	$0.40	$1.20	$2.00	£0.25	£0.75	£1.25
7-8 Sienkiewicz art	$0.40	$1.20	$2.00	£0.25	£0.75	£1.25
9 Sienkiewicz art, Frank Miller cover	$0.40	$1.20	$2.00	£0.25	£0.75	£1.25
10 Sienkiewicz art	$0.40	$1.20	$2.00	£0.25	£0.75	£1.25
11-12 Sienkiewicz art	$0.30	$0.90	$1.50	£0.20	£0.60	£1.00
13 Sienkiewicz art, Daredevil appears	$0.30	$0.90	$1.50	£0.20	£0.60	£1.00
14 Sienkiewicz art	$0.30	$0.90	$1.50	£0.20	£0.60	£1.00
15 LD in the U.K. 1st Direct Sale issue, Sienkiewicz art, part Frank Miller cover	$0.30	$0.90	$1.50	£0.20	£0.60	£1.00
16 LD in the U.K. Thing appears	$0.30	$0.90	$1.50	£0.20	£0.60	£1.00
17-20 LD in the U.K. Sienkiewicz art	$0.30	$0.90	$1.50	£0.20	£0.60	£1.00
21 LD in the U.K. Brother Voodoo appears, Sienkiewicz cover only	$0.30	$0.90	$1.50	£0.20	£0.60	£1.00
22 LD in the U.K. Sienkiewicz cover only	$0.30	$0.90	$1.50	£0.20	£0.60	£1.00
23 LD in the U.K. Sienkiewicz art; art style begins to change from Neal Adamsesque to his own distinctive line-work	$0.30	$0.90	$1.50	£0.20	£0.60	£1.00
24 LD in the U.K. Sienkiewicz art	$0.30	$0.90	$1.50	£0.20	£0.60	£1.00
25 LD in the U.K. 52pgs, Sienkiewicz art	$0.50	$1.50	$2.50	£0.30	£0.90	£1.50
26 LD in the U.K. Sienkiewicz art	$0.30	$0.90	$1.50	£0.20	£0.60	£1.00
27 LD in the U.K. Frank Miller cover	$0.30	$0.90	$1.50	£0.20	£0.60	£1.00
28 LD in the U.K. Sienkiewicz art; 5pgs Kevin Nowlan art	$0.30	$0.90	$1.50	£0.20	£0.60	£1.00
29 LD in the U.K. Sienkiewicz art	$0.30	$0.90	$1.50	£0.20	£0.60	£1.00
30 LD in the U.K. Moon Knight battles Werewolf, Sienkiewicz art	$0.30	$0.90	$1.50	£0.25	£0.75	£1.25
31-32 LD in the U.K. Kevin Nowlan art	$0.30	$0.90	$1.50	£0.20	£0.60	£1.00
33 LD in the U.K. Kevin Nowlan art	$0.30	$0.90	$1.50	£0.25	£0.75	£1.25
34 LD in the U.K. Sienkiewicz art	$0.30	$0.90	$1.50	£0.25	£0.75	£1.25
35 LD in the U.K. DS X-Men and Fantastic Four appear, Kevin Nowlan art	$0.30	$0.90	$1.50	£0.30	£0.90	£1.50
36 LD in the U.K. Dr. Strange appears, Sienkiewicz art, Mike Kaluta cover	$0.30	$0.90	$1.50	£0.25	£0.75	£1.25
37-38 very LD/rare in the U.K. Scott Hampton art, Mike Kaluta cover	$0.30	$0.90	$1.50	£0.30	£0.90	£1.50
Title Value:	$12.70	$38.10	$63.50	£8.75	£26.25	£43.75

ARTISTS

Sienkiewicz in 1-15, 17-36. Hampton in 37, 38.

MOON KNIGHT SPECIAL

Marvel Comics Group,OS; 1 Oct 1992

Issue	$Good	$Fine	$N.Mint	£Good	£Fine	£N.Mint
1 ND 48pgs, Master of Kung Fu appears, pin-up gallery, Doug Moench script	$0.50	$1.50	$2.50	£0.30	£0.90	£1.50
Title Value:	$0.50	$1.50	$2.50	£0.30	£0.90	£1.50

MOON KNIGHT SPECIAL EDITION

Marvel Comics Group; 1 Nov 1983-3 Jan 1984

Issue	$Good	$Fine	$N.Mint	£Good	£Fine	£N.Mint
1 ND Hulk appears	$0.50	$1.50	$2.50	£0.30	£0.90	£1.50
2-3 ND	$0.50	$1.50	$2.50	£0.30	£0.90	£1.50
Title Value:	$1.50	$4.50	$7.50	£0.90	£2.70	£4.50

Note: all reprints of Sienkiewicz's magazine work, on Baxter paper

MOON KNIGHT, MARC SPECTOR

Marvel Comics Group; 1 Jun 1989-60 Mar 1994

Issue	$Good	$Fine	$N.Mint	£Good	£Fine	£N.Mint
1 ND	$0.50	$1.50	$2.50	£0.30	£0.90	£1.50
2 ND Spiderman appears (cameo)	$0.40	$1.20	$2.00	£0.25	£0.75	£1.25
3 ND	$0.40	$1.20	$2.00	£0.25	£0.75	£1.25
4-5 ND Black Cat appears	$0.40	$1.20	$2.00	£0.25	£0.75	£1.25

	$Good	$Fine	$N.Mint	£Good	£Fine	£N.Mint
6-7 ND	$0.40	$1.20	$2.00	£0.25	£0.75	£1.25
8-9 ND Acts of Vengeance tie-in, Punisher appears	$0.50	$1.50	$2.50	£0.25	£0.75	£1.25
10 ND Acts of Vengeance tie-in	$0.40	$1.20	$2.00	£0.25	£0.75	£1.25
11-14 ND	$0.40	$1.20	$2.00	£0.25	£0.75	£1.25
15-18 ND Trial of Marc Spector	$0.40	$1.20	$2.00	£0.25	£0.75	£1.25
19-21 ND Spiderman/Punisher appear	$0.60	$1.80	$3.00	£0.25	£0.75	£1.25
22-24 ND	$0.30	$0.90	$1.50	£0.20	£0.60	£1.00
25 ND DS Ghost Rider guest-stars	$0.50	$1.50	$2.50	£0.30	£0.90	£1.50
26-30 ND Scarlet Redemption story, Bill Sienkiewicz cover	$0.30	$0.90	$1.50	£0.20	£0.60	£1.00
31 ND Scarlet Redemption epilogue	$0.30	$0.90	$1.50	£0.20	£0.60	£1.00
32 ND Hobgoblin appears, Spiderman guset stars	$0.30	$0.90	$1.50	£0.20	£0.60	£1.00
33 ND Hobgoblin appears, Spiderman guest stars	$0.30	$0.90	$1.50	£0.20	£0.60	£1.00
34 ND	$0.30	$0.90	$1.50	£0.20	£0.60	£1.00
35 ND Punisher appears, $1.75 cover begins	$0.30	$0.90	$1.50	£0.20	£0.60	£1.00
36 ND	$0.30	$0.90	$1.50	£0.20	£0.60	£1.00
37 ND Punisher appears	$0.30	$0.90	$1.50	£0.20	£0.60	£1.00
38 ND Punisher appears, new logo	$0.30	$0.90	$1.50	£0.20	£0.60	£1.00
39 ND new direction for title, Dr. Doom appears	$0.30	$0.90	$1.50	£0.20	£0.60	£1.00
40 ND Dr. Doom appears	$0.30	$0.90	$1.50	£0.20	£0.60	£1.00
41-43 ND Infinity War X-over	$0.30	$0.90	$1.50	£0.20	£0.60	£1.00
44 ND Infinity War X-over, Dr. Strange and Mr. Fantastic appear	$0.30	$0.90	$1.50	£0.20	£0.60	£1.00
45-49 ND	$0.30	$0.90	$1.50	£0.20	£0.60	£1.00
50 ND DS die-cut cover	$0.50	$1.50	$2.50	£0.30	£0.90	£1.50
51 ND Gambit appears	$0.30	$0.90	$1.50	£0.20	£0.60	£1.00
52 ND Gambit and Werewolf appear	$0.30	$0.90	$1.50	£0.20	£0.60	£1.00
53-54 ND	$0.30	$0.90	$1.50	£0.20	£0.60	£1.00
55 ND 1st Stephen Platt art on Moon Knight	$1.60	$4.80	$8.00	£1.00	£3.00	£5.00
56 ND Stephen Platt art	$0.80	$2.40	$4.00	£0.50	£1.50	£2.50
57 ND Stephen Platt art, Infinity Crusade epilogue	$0.80	$2.40	$4.00	£0.50	£1.50	£2.50
58-59 ND Stephen Platt cover art	$0.50	$1.50	$2.50	£0.30	£0.90	£1.50
60 ND Stephen Platt cover and art	$0.50	$1.50	$2.50	£0.40	£1.20	£2.00
Title Value:	$24.30	$72.90	$121.50	£15.10	£45.30	£75.50

MOON KNIGHT, THE FIST OF KHONSHU

Marvel Comics Group; 1 Jun 1985-6 Dec 1985

	$Good	$Fine	$N.Mint	£Good	£Fine	£N.Mint
1 DS, new costume	$0.40	$1.20	$2.00	£0.25	£0.75	£1.25
2-4	$0.40	$1.20	$2.00	£0.20	£0.60	£1.00
5-6 LD in the U.K.	$0.40	$1.20	$2.00	£0.25	£0.75	£1.25
Title Value:	$2.40	$7.20	$12.00	£1.35	£4.05	£6.75

MOON KNIGHT: DIVIDED WE FALL

Marvel Comics Group,OS; 1 Jun 1992

	$Good	$Fine	$N.Mint	£Good	£Fine	£N.Mint
1 ND 48pgs	$0.80	$2.40	$4.00	£0.50	£1.50	£2.50
Title Value:	$0.80	$2.40	$4.00	£0.50	£1.50	£2.50

MOONSHADOW

Marvel Comics Group/Epic; 1 May 1985-12 Feb 1987

	$Good	$Fine	$N.Mint	£Good	£Fine	£N.Mint
1 ND "origin", Jon J. Muth art begins	$0.80	$2.40	$4.00	£0.50	£1.50	£2.50
2-5 ND	$0.60	$1.80	$3.00	£0.40	£1.20	£2.00
6-12 ND	$0.50	$1.50	$2.50	£0.30	£0.90	£1.50
Title Value:	$6.70	$20.10	$33.50	£4.20	£12.60	£21.00
Trade paperback (Jul 1989)						
Reprints 12 issue series with new ending				£2.00	£6.00	£10.00
2nd printing (Dec 1990)				£1.60	£4.80	£6.00
Hardback (by Graphitti) (1200 copies), Mar 1990.						
Signed and numbered				£5.00	£15.00	£25.00

MOONSHADOW (2ND SERIES)

DC Comics/Vertigo,MS; 1 Sep 1994-12 Aug 1995

	$Good	$Fine	$N.Mint	£Good	£Fine	£N.Mint
1 ND reprints of the original Marvel Epic series begin with new covers by Jon J. Muth	$0.50	$1.50	$2.50	£0.30	£0.90	£1.50
2-11 ND	$0.50	$1.50	$2.50	£0.30	£0.90	£1.50
12 ND	$0.60	$1.80	$3.00	£0.40	£1.20	£2.00
Title Value:	$6.10	$18.30	$30.50	£3.70	£11.10	£18.50

MOONTRAP

Caliber Press; 1 1988

	$Good	$Fine	$N.Mint	£Good	£Fine	£N.Mint
1 ND adapts film	$0.40	$1.20	$2.00	£0.25	£0.75	£1.25
Title Value:	$0.40	$1.20	$2.00	£0.25	£0.75	£1.25

MOONWALKER IN 3-D

Blackthorne;(3-D Series #75) 1 Summer 1989

	$Good	$Fine	$N.Mint	£Good	£Fine	£N.Mint
1 ND with bound-in 3-D glasses (25% less without glasses); based on Michael Jackson film						
	$0.50	$1.50	$2.50	£0.30	£0.90	£1.50
Title Value:	$0.50	$1.50	$2.50	£0.30	£0.90	£1.50

MORBID ANGEL

London Night Studios; ½ Jun 1996; 1 Mar 1996

	$Good	$Fine	$N.Mint	£Good	£Fine	£N.Mint
½ ND 24pgs	$0.60	$1.80	$3.00	£0.40	£1.20	£2.00
½ Limited Edition, ND 24pgs, (Jun 1996), limited to 5,000 copies	$2.00	$6.00	$10.00	£1.30	£3.90	£6.50
1 ND "Penance"	$0.80	$2.40	$4.00	£0.50	£1.50	£2.50
1 Red Foil Edition, ND 48pgs, spin-off from Razor: Torture series, limited to 2,000 copies	$2.00	$6.00	$10.00	£1.30	£3.90	£6.50
Title Value:	$5.40	$16.20	$27.00	£3.50	£10.50	£17.50

MORBID ANGEL: TO HELL AND BACK

London Night Studios,MS; 1 Oct 1996-3 Dec 1996

	$Good	$Fine	$N.Mint	£Good	£Fine	£N.Mint
1-3 ND Everette Hartsoe script, Shelley Robertson and Mike Taylor art; black and white	$0.60	$1.80	$3.00	£0.40	£1.20	£2.00
Title Value:	$1.80	$5.40	$9.00	£1.20	£3.60	£6.00

MORBIUS

Marvel Comics Group; 1 Sep 1992-32 Apr 1995

(see Adventure Into Fear, Amazing Spiderman #101/102)

	$Good	$Fine	$N.Mint	£Good	£Fine	£N.Mint
1 ND DS Rise of the Midnight Sons part 3, pre-bagged with colour poster	$0.40	$1.20	$2.00	£0.25	£0.75	£1.25
2 ND Rise of the Midnight Sons tie-in, Peter Parker appears	$0.40	$1.20	$2.00	£0.25	£0.75	£1.25
3 ND Spiderman vs. Morbius	$0.40	$1.20	$2.00	£0.25	£0.75	£1.25
4 ND Spiderman cameo	$0.40	$1.20	$2.00	£0.25	£0.75	£1.25
5 ND intro Basilisk II	$0.40	$1.20	$2.00	£0.25	£0.75	£1.25
6-9 ND	$0.30	$0.90	$1.50	£0.20	£0.60	£1.00
10 ND two stories, back-up art by Isaac Cordova	$0.30	$0.90	$1.50	£0.20	£0.60	£1.00
11 ND X-over with Nightstalkers #9	$0.30	$0.90	$1.50	£0.20	£0.60	£1.00
12 ND black parchment outer cover with gold ink, Werewolf By Night appears	$0.40	$1.20	$2.00	£0.20	£0.60	£1.00
13 ND	$0.30	$0.90	$1.50	£0.20	£0.60	£1.00
14 ND Werewolf By Night appears	$0.30	$0.90	$1.50	£0.20	£0.60	£1.00
15 ND Ghost Rider appears	$0.30	$0.90	$1.50	£0.20	£0.60	£1.00
16 ND Siege of Darkness part 5; neon ink/spot varnish cover	$0.30	$0.90	$1.50	£0.20	£0.60	£1.00
17 ND Siege of Darkness part 13; neon ink/spot varnish cover	$0.30	$0.90	$1.50	£0.20	£0.60	£1.00
18-19 ND Deathlok guest-stars	$0.30	$0.90	$1.50	£0.20	£0.60	£1.00
20 ND	$0.30	$0.90	$1.50	£0.20	£0.60	£1.00
21 ND Spiderman appears; with free Spiderman vs. Venom card sheet	$0.30	$0.90	$1.50	£0.20	£0.60	£1.00
22-23 ND Spiderman appears	$0.30	$0.90	$1.50	£0.20	£0.60	£1.00
24 ND	$0.30	$0.90	$1.50	£0.20	£0.60	£1.00
25 ND 48pgs, metallic fifth ink on cover	$0.40	$1.20	$2.00	£0.25	£0.75	£1.25
26-27 ND	$0.30	$0.90	$1.50	£0.20	£0.60	£1.00
28 ND Werewolf by Night appears	$0.30	$0.90	$1.50	£0.20	£0.60	£1.00
29 ND Werewolf by Night, Spiderman, Vengeamce, Dr. Strange and Ghost Rider appear	$0.30	$0.90	$1.50	£0.20	£0.60	£1.00
30-32 ND	$0.30	$0.90	$1.50	£0.20	£0.60	£1.00
Title Value:	$10.30	$30.90	$51.50	£6.70	£20.10	£33.50

MORBIUS REVISITED

Marvel Comics Group,MS; 1 Aug 1993-5 Dec 1993

	$Good	$Fine	$N.Mint	£Good	£Fine	£N.Mint
1 selected reprints from Adventure into Fear #20 onwards begin	$0.40	$1.20	$2.00	£0.25	£0.75	£1.25
2-5	$0.40	$1.20	$2.00	£0.25	£0.75	£1.25
Title Value:	$2.00	$6.00	$10.00	£1.25	£3.75	£6.25

MORE FUN COMICS

National Periodical Publications; 1 Feb 1935-127 Nov/Dec 1947

	$Good	$Fine	$N.Mint	£Good	£Fine	£N.Mint
1 very rare in both U.K. and U.S. 1st published DC comic, titled "New Fun Comics" (to issue #6), almost certainly less than 20 extant copies in any condition	$6000.00	$18000.00	($60000.00)	£4000.00	£12000.00	(£40000.00)
2 extremely rare in both U.K. and U.S; certainly less than 10 known copies, traditionally the rarest DC comic	$3100.00	$9300.00	($28000.00)	£2075.00	£6200.00	(£18675.00)
3 very rare in the U.K., rare in the U.S. about 30 extant copies, possibly the 1st ever sci-fi cover on a comic book (April 1935)	$1550.00	$4650.00	($14000.00)	£1025.00	£3100.00	(£9350.00)
4-5 very rare in the U.K., rare in the U.S. about 30 extant copies	$1550.00	$4650.00	($14000.00)	£1025.00	£3100.00	(£9350.00)
6 extremely rare in the U.K., very rare in the U.S. 1st appearance Dr. Occult by Jerry Siegel and Joe Shuster thought to be a prototype for Superman, less than 20 known copies	$3000.00	$9000.00	($30000.00)	£2000.00	£6000.00	(£20000.00)

(Note that values for Near Mint are theoretical only as no true near mint copies have yet been found. Issues #1-6 can only be considered to exist in up to a Very Fine grade)

	$Good	$Fine	$N.Mint	£Good	£Fine	£N.Mint
7 very rare in both U.K. and U.S. title changed to "More Fun Comics" as New Comics #1 was published in the same month (Dec. 1935). About 25 known copies; significantly none are known in Near Mint condition	$750.00	$2250.00	$6000.00	£500.00	£1500.00	£4000.00
8 very rare in both U.K. and U.S. probably less than 20 known copies	$680.00	$2050.00	$5500.00	£455.00	£1375.00	£3675.00
9 extremely rare in the U.K., very rare in the U.S. 1st comic-sized issue, probably less than 15 known copies	$780.00	$2325.00	$6250.00	£520.00	£1550.00	£4175.00

VERY GENERAL PERCENTAGE CONVERSION CHART WHICH MAY BE USED TO CALCULATE LOW AND INBETWEEN GRADES:

Issue	$Good	$Fine	$N.Mint	£Good	£Fine	£N.Mint
10 rare in the U.K., very scarce in the U.S.						
	$450.00	*$1350.00*	*$3600.00*	£300.00	£900.00	£2400.00
11 very rare in the U.K., rare in the U.S. last paper cover, about 30 extant copies						
	$450.00	*$1350.00*	*$3600.00*	£300.00	£900.00	£2400.00
12 rare in the U.K., very scarce in the U.S. 1st glossy cover						
	$340.00	*$1025.00*	*$2750.00*	£230.00	£690.00	£1850.00
13 rare in the U.K., very scarce in the U.S.						
	$300.00	*$900.00*	*$2400.00*	£200.00	£600.00	£1600.00
14 very rare in the U.K. 1st Dr. Occult in costume (skin-tight with cape - recognisable Superman prototype dated October 1936, 18 months before Action Comics #1); about 10 exant copies						
	$1325.00	*$4000.00*	*$12000.00*	£880.00	£2650.00	£8000.00
15 very rare in the U.K., rare in the U.S. about 30 extant copies						
	$620.00	*$1875.00*	*$5000.00*	£415.00	£1250.00	£3350.00
16 rare in the U.K., very scarce in the U.S. 1st numbering on cover (top left)						
	$620.00	*$1875.00*	*$5000.00*	£415.00	£1250.00	£3350.00
17 rare in the U.K., very scarce in the U.S.						
	$620.00	*$1875.00*	*$5000.00*	£415.00	£1250.00	£3350.00

[please note that the above are approximate values only as copies almost never come onto the UK market and as such prices are dictated by the American market. Also note that it would be more realistic to consider #1-20 ever being available on the market in no more that VFN condition]

Issue	$Good	$Fine	$N.Mint	£Good	£Fine	£N.Mint
18-20 very scarce in the U.K., scarce in the U.S.						
	$285.00	*$850.00*	*$2000.00*	£190.00	£570.00	£1350.00
21-24 very scarce in the U.K.						
	$260.00	*$790.00*	*$1850.00*	£175.00	£530.00	£1250.00
25-26 scarce in the U.K.						
	$255.00	*$770.00*	*$1800.00*	£170.00	£510.00	£1200.00
27 very scarce in the U.K. Christmas cover						
	$255.00	*$770.00*	*$1800.00*	£170.00	£510.00	£1200.00
28-29 scarce in the U.K.						
	$255.00	*$770.00*	*$1800.00*	£170.00	£510.00	£1200.00
30 scarce in the U.K. 1st adventure-type cover						
	$255.00	*$770.00*	*$1800.00*	£170.00	£510.00	£1200.00
31 advertisement showing cover of Action Comics #1						
	$255.00	*$770.00*	*$1800.00*	£170.00	£510.00	£1200.00
32-35	*$225.00*	*$680.00*	*$1600.00*	£150.00	£460.00	£1075.00
36-38	*$220.00*	*$660.00*	*$1550.00*	£150.00	£450.00	£1050.00
39 Christmas cover						
	$220.00	*$660.00*	*$1550.00*	£150.00	£450.00	£1050.00
40	*$220.00*	*$660.00*	*$1550.00*	£150.00	£450.00	£1050.00
41 last "funnies" cover						
	$175.00	*$530.00*	*$1250.00*	£115.00	£355.00	£835.00
42 adventure-type covers re-start (end #51)						
	$175.00	*$530.00*	*$1250.00*	£115.00	£355.00	£835.00
43-47	*$175.00*	*$530.00*	*$1250.00*	£115.00	£355.00	£835.00
48 dinosaur cover						
	$175.00	*$530.00*	*$1250.00*	£115.00	£355.00	£835.00
49-50	*$175.00*	*$530.00*	*$1250.00*	£115.00	£355.00	£835.00
51 scarce in the U.K. 1st appearance The Spectre (in costume in one panel announcing his arrival next issue)						
	$650.00	*$1950.00*	*$5250.00*	£435.00	£1300.00	£3500.00
52 rare in the U.K. origin and 1st full appearance The Spectre, in costume for 1 panel only, about 50 copies thought to exist						
	$5600.00	*$16800.00*	*$56000.00*	£3700.00	£11200.00	£37350.00
[Scarce in high grade - Very Fine+ or better]						
[Prices may vary widely on this comic]						
53 rare in the U.K. origin The Spectre continues, in costume at end of story						
	$4000.00	*$12000.00*	*$40000.00*	£2650.00	£8000.00	£26700.00
[Prices may vary widely on this comic]						
54	*$1375.00*	*$4150.00*	*$9750.00*	£920.00	£2750.00	£6500.00
55 scarce in the U.K. 1st appearance Dr. Fate, about 90 extant copies						
	$1700.00	*$5100.00*	*$13600.00*	£1125.00	£3400.00	£9100.00
56 2nd appearance Dr. Fate and 1st Dr. Fate cover (fab!); 1st appearance Congo Bill						
	$850.00	*$2550.00*	*$6000.00*	£570.00	£1700.00	£4000.00
57-60	*$460.00*	*$1375.00*	*$3250.00*	£310.00	£930.00	£2175.00
61-64	*$370.00*	*$1100.00*	*$2600.00*	£250.00	£750.00	£1750.00
65 classic Spectre-in-mirror cover						
	$370.00	*$1100.00*	*$2600.00*	£250.00	£750.00	£1750.00
66	*$370.00*	*$1100.00*	*$2600.00*	£250.00	£750.00	£1750.00
67 origin Dr. Fate						
	$250.00	*$750.00*	*$2000.00*	£165.00	£500.00	£1350.00
68-70	*$285.00*	*$850.00*	*$2000.00*	£190.00	£570.00	£1350.00
71 origin and 1st appearance Johnny Quick						
	$720.00	*$2175.00*	*$5800.00*	£480.00	£1450.00	£3875.00
72	*$250.00*	*$750.00*	*$1750.00*	£165.00	£500.00	£1175.00
73 scarce in the U.K. origin and 1st appearance Aquaman						
	$1550.00	*$4650.00*	*$14000.00*	£1025.00	£3100.00	£9350.00
74 2nd appearance Aquaman						
	$340.00	*$1025.00*	*$2400.00*	£225.00	£680.00	£1600.00
75-80	*$285.00*	*$850.00*	*$2000.00*	£190.00	£570.00	£1350.00
81	*$155.00*	*$470.00*	*$1100.00*	£105.00	£320.00	£750.00
82 1st small logo						
	$155.00	*$470.00*	*$1100.00*	£105.00	£320.00	£750.00
83-88	*$155.00*	*$470.00*	*$1100.00*	£105.00	£320.00	£750.00
89 origin Green Arrow and Speedy team						
	$165.00	*$500.00*	*$1175.00*	£110.00	£335.00	£785.00
90-99	*$110.00*	*$340.00*	*$800.00*	£75.00	£225.00	£535.00
100	*$155.00*	*$470.00*	*$1100.00*	£105.00	£315.00	£735.00
[Issues before #100 are generally at least scarce in the U.K.]						
101 origin and 1st appearance Superboy, last Spectre in title; Jerry Siegel and Joe Shuster not consulted about the creation of Superboy; it was the only part of a long law-suit against DC which they won						
	$600.00	*$1800.00*	*$7250.00*	£400.00	£1200.00	£4850.00
[Scarce in high grade - Very Fine+ or better]						
102 2nd appearance Superboy						
	$150.00	*$450.00*	*$1050.00*	£100.00	£300.00	£700.00
103 3rd appearance Superboy						
	$115.00	*$350.00*	*$825.00*	£77.50	£235.00	£550.00
104 1st Superboy cover						
	$100.00	*$300.00*	*$700.00*	£65.00	£200.00	£470.00
105	*$100.00*	*$300.00*	*$700.00*	£65.00	£200.00	£470.00
106 "funnies" covers begin again (end #127)						
	$100.00	*$300.00*	*$700.00*	£65.00	£200.00	£470.00
107 last Superboy story (Superboy #1 not set to appear for another 3 years until Mar/Apr 1949)						
	$100.00	*$300.00*	*$700.00*	£65.00	£200.00	£470.00
108-110	*$29.00*	*$85.00*	*$200.00*	£19.00	£57.50	£135.00
111-120	*$22.50*	*$67.50*	*$160.00*	£15.50	£47.00	£110.00
121-124	*$17.50*	*$52.50*	*$125.00*	£12.00	£36.00	£85.00
125 Superman on cover though he does not appear inside (it's almost as if he was stuck on as an accident or after-thought, perhaps to make a failing title sell better. A ludicrously over-priced comic)						
	$92.50	*$275.00*	*$650.00*	£60.00	£185.00	£435.00
126	*$17.50*	*$52.50*	*$125.00*	£12.00	£36.00	£85.00
127 very scarce in the U.K., scarce in the U.S.						
	$36.00	*$105.00*	*$250.00*	£24.00	£72.50	£170.00
Title Value:	*$59478.00*	*$178697.50*	*$507625.00*	£39648.50	£119460.00	£339460.00

Note: the first 8 issues were larger than normal comic size (8"x10"). Issues 1-6 were 10"x15" and issues 7 and 8 were 10"x12".

Note also: all Non-Distributed on the news-stands in the U.K. and while no British pence stamp copies have been recorded, it is probable that some copies came over as ballast on ships or through army personnel in the war. In common with all Golden Age issues, this title is generally scarce in the U.K.

MORLOCK 2001

Atlas; 1 Feb 1975-3 Jul 1975

Issue	$Good	$Fine	$N.Mint	£Good	£Fine	£N.Mint
1-2 distributed in the U.K.						
	$0.25	*$0.75*	*$1.50*	£0.15	£0.50	£1.00

Mod Squad #5

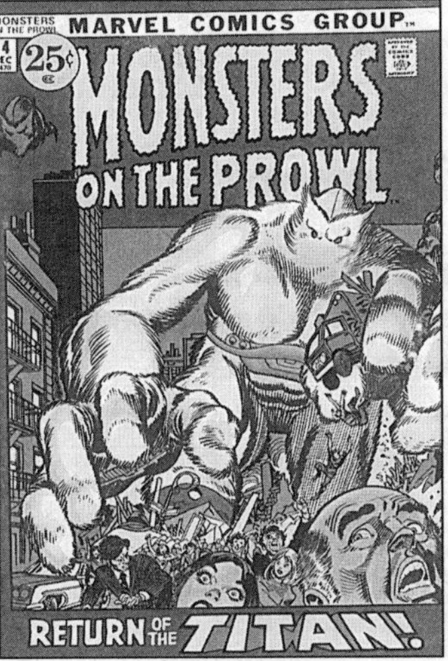

Monsters on the Prowl #14

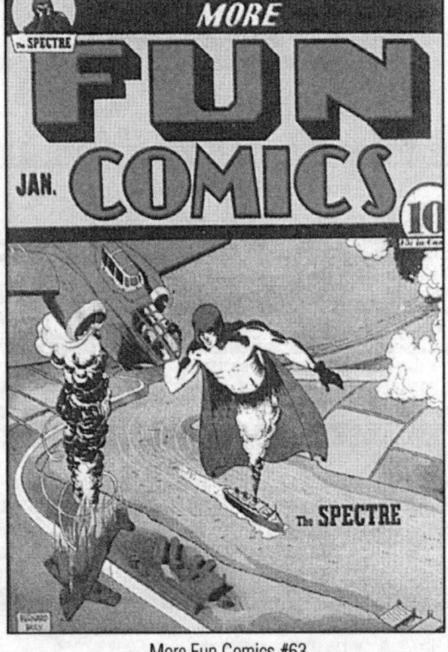

More Fun Comics #63

	$Good	$Fine	$N.Mint	£Good	£Fine	£N.Mint
3 distributed in the U.K. Steve Ditko and Bernie Wrightson art						
	$0.25	$0.75	$1.50	£0.15	£0.50	£1.00
Title Value:	$0.75	$2.25	$4.50	£0.45	£1.50	£3.00

Note: issue 3 titled "Moorlock 2001 and the Midnight Men"

MORNINGSTAR SPECIAL
DC Comics/Comico,OS; 1 Jun 1990

	$Good	$Fine	$N.Mint	£Good	£Fine	£N.Mint
1 ND	$0.40	$1.20	$2.00	£0.25	£0.75	£1.25
1 2nd printing, ND (Sep 1991)						
	$0.40	$1.20	$2.00	£0.25	£0.75	£1.25
Title Value:	$0.80	$2.40	$4.00	£0.50	£1.50	£2.50

MORPHOS THE SHAPECHANGER
Dark Horse,OS; 1 Jul 1996

	$Good	$Fine	$N.Mint	£Good	£Fine	£N.Mint
1 ND 48pgs, reprints Burne Hogarth strip						
	$1.00	$3.00	$5.00	£0.70	£2.10	£3.50
Title Value:	$1.00	$3.00	$5.00	£0.70	£2.10	£3.50

MORT THE DEAD TEENAGER
Marvel Comics Group,MS; 1 Dec 1993-4 Mar 1994

	$Good	$Fine	$N.Mint	£Good	£Fine	£N.Mint
1-4 ND Larry Hama script						
	$0.40	$1.20	$2.00	£0.25	£0.75	£1.25
Title Value:	$1.60	$4.80	$8.00	£1.00	£3.00	£5.00

MORTAL KOMBAT
Malibu; 0 Nov 1994; 1 Jul 1994-6 Dec 1994

	$Good	$Fine	$N.Mint	£Good	£Fine	£N.Mint
0 ND (Nov 1994)	$0.60	$1.80	$3.00	£0.40	£1.20	£2.00
1 ND	$0.60	$1.80	$3.00	£0.40	£1.20	£2.00
1 Gold Foil Edition, ND (Oct 1994)						
	$1.50	$4.50	$7.50	£1.00	£3.00	£5.00
1 Special Edition, ND (Nov 1994), expanded to 40pgs with interviews from the Mortal Kombat film personnel						
	$0.70	$2.10	$3.50	£0.50	£1.50	£2.50
2-6 ND	$0.60	$1.80	$3.00	£0.40	£1.20	£2.00
Title Value:	$6.40	$19.20	$32.00	£4.30	£12.90	£21.50

Note: based on video game

Mortal Kombat Kollection (Jul 1995)

	$Good	$Fine	$N.Mint	£Good	£Fine	£N.Mint
Trade Paperback collects 6 issue series				£1.70	£5.10	£8.50

MORTAL KOMBAT: BARAKA
Malibu,OS; 1 Jun 1995

	$Good	$Fine	$N.Mint	£Good	£Fine	£N.Mint
1 ND ti-in with Mortal Kombat: Battlewave						
	$0.60	$1.80	$3.00	£0.40	£1.20	£2.00
Title Value:	$0.60	$1.80	$3.00	£0.40	£1.20	£2.00

MORTAL KOMBAT: BATTLEWAVE
Malibu,MS; 1 Feb 1995-6 Jul 1995

	$Good	$Fine	$N.Mint	£Good	£Fine	£N.Mint
1-6 ND	$0.60	$1.80	$3.00	£0.40	£1.20	£2.00
Title Value:	$3.60	$10.80	$18.00	£2.40	£7.20	£12.00

MORTAL KOMBAT: GORO, PRINCE OF PAIN
Malibu Bravura,MS; 1 Sep 1994-3 Nov 1994

	$Good	$Fine	$N.Mint	£Good	£Fine	£N.Mint
1 ND based on video game movie						
	$0.60	$1.80	$3.00	£0.40	£1.20	£2.00
1 Platinum Edition, ND (Apr 1995) - platinum foil embossed cover						
	$1.50	$4.50	$7.50	£1.00	£3.00	£5.00
2-3 ND based on video game movie						
	$0.60	$1.80	$3.00	£0.40	£1.20	£2.00
Title Value:	$3.30	$9.90	$16.50	£2.20	£6.60	£11.00

MORTAL KOMBAT: KITANA & MILEENA
Malibu Bravura,OS; 1 Aug 1995

	$Good	$Fine	$N.Mint	£Good	£Fine	£N.Mint
1 ND ties into Mortal Kombat: Tournament Edition II #1 and Battlewave series						
	$0.60	$1.80	$3.00	£0.40	£1.20	£2.00
Title Value:	$0.60	$1.80	$3.00	£0.40	£1.20	£2.00

MORTAL KOMBAT: KUNG LAO
Marvel Comics Group/Malibu Comics,OS; 1 Jul 1995

	$Good	$Fine	$N.Mint	£Good	£Fine	£N.Mint
1 ND ties in with Battlewave series						
	$0.60	$1.80	$3.00	£0.40	£1.20	£2.00
Title Value:	$0.60	$1.80	$3.00	£0.40	£1.20	£2.00

MORTAL KOMBAT: RAYDEN/KANO
Malibu; 1 Mar 1995-3 May 1995

	$Good	$Fine	$N.Mint	£Good	£Fine	£N.Mint
1 ND based on video game						
	$0.60	$1.80	$3.00	£0.40	£1.20	£2.00
1 Foil Stamped Cover Edition, ND based on video game						
	$0.70	$2.10	$3.50	£0.50	£1.50	£2.50
2-3 ND based on video game						
	$0.60	$1.80	$3.00	£0.40	£1.20	£2.00
Title Value:	$2.50	$7.50	$12.50	£1.70	£5.10	£8.50

MORTAL KOMBAT: TOURNAMENT EDITION BATTLE FINALE
Malibu,OS; 1 Dec 1994

	$Good	$Fine	$N.Mint	£Good	£Fine	£N.Mint
1 ND DS	$0.60	$1.80	$3.00	£0.40	£1.20	£2.00
Title Value:	$0.60	$1.80	$3.00	£0.40	£1.20	£2.00

MORTAL KOMBAT: TOURNAMENT EDITION II
Malibu Bravura,OS; 1 Aug 1995

	$Good	$Fine	$N.Mint	£Good	£Fine	£N.Mint
1 ND 40pgs	$0.80	$2.40	$4.00	£0.50	£1.50	£2.50
Title Value:	$0.80	$2.40	$4.00	£0.50	£1.50	£2.50

MORTAL KOMBAT: U.S. SPECIAL FORCES
Malibu,MS; 1 Jan 1995-2 Feb 1995

	$Good	$Fine	$N.Mint	£Good	£Fine	£N.Mint
1-2 ND 40pgs	$0.60	$1.80	$3.00	£0.40	£1.20	£2.00
Title Value:	$1.20	$3.60	$6.00	£0.80	£2.40	£4.00

MOTORHEAD
Dark Horse; 1 Aug 1995-6 Jan 1996

	$Good	$Fine	$N.Mint	£Good	£Fine	£N.Mint
1 ND Predator X-over (see Ghost #5, Agents of Law #6 and X #18); Simon Bisley cover						
	$0.50	$1.50	$2.50	£0.30	£0.90	£1.50
2-6 ND Simon Bisley cover						
	$0.50	$1.50	$2.50	£0.30	£0.90	£1.50
Title Value:	$3.00	$9.00	$15.00	£1.80	£5.40	£9.00

MOTORHEAD SPECIAL
Dark Horse,OS; 1 Mar 1994

	$Good	$Fine	$N.Mint	£Good	£Fine	£N.Mint
1 ND 48pgs, Jae Lee cover; spin-off from Comics Greatest World						
	$0.80	$2.40	$4.00	£0.50	£1.50	£2.50
Title Value:	$0.80	$2.40	$4.00	£0.50	£1.50	£2.50

MOTORMOUTH
Marvel UK; 1 Jun 1992-13 Jun 1993
(see Overkill in British section)

	$Good	$Fine	$N.Mint	£Good	£Fine	£N.Mint
1 Marks, Frank and Lanning script/art						
	$0.30	$0.90	$1.50	£0.15	£0.45	£0.75
2 Nick Fury and Shield appear						
	$0.30	$0.90	$1.50	£0.15	£0.45	£0.75
3	$0.30	$0.90	$1.50	£0.15	£0.45	£0.75
4 Nick Fury and Shield appear						
	$0.30	$0.90	$1.50	£0.15	£0.45	£0.75
5 Excalibur and Archangel appear						
	$0.30	$0.90	$1.50	£0.15	£0.45	£0.75
6 Cable, Punisher, Badhand and Nick Fury appear						
	$0.30	$0.90	$1.50	£0.15	£0.45	£0.75
7 Nick Fury and Cable appear						
	$0.30	$0.90	$1.50	£0.15	£0.45	£0.75
8 Cable appears	$0.30	$0.90	$1.50	£0.15	£0.45	£0.75
9 Nick Fury and Cable appear						
	$0.30	$0.90	$1.50	£0.15	£0.45	£0.75
10 Red Sonja appears						
	$0.30	$0.90	$1.50	£0.15	£0.45	£0.75
11	$0.30	$0.90	$1.50	£0.15	£0.45	£0.75
12 Death's Head II appears						
	$0.30	$0.90	$1.50	£0.15	£0.45	£0.75
13 Death's Head II and Killpower appear						
	$0.30	$0.90	$1.50	£0.15	£0.45	£0.75
Title Value:	$3.90	$11.70	$19.50	£1.95	£5.85	£9.75

MOTORMOUTH & KILLPOWER
Marvel UK,MS; 1 Nov 1993-2 Dec 1993

	$Good	$Fine	$N.Mint	£Good	£Fine	£N.Mint
1 Andrew Cartmel script begins, Death's Head II appears; green foil stamped cover						
	$0.30	$0.90	$1.50	£0.15	£0.45	£0.75
2 Death's Head II appears						
	$0.30	$0.90	$1.50	£0.15	£0.45	£0.75
Title Value:	$0.60	$1.80	$3.00	£0.30	£0.90	£1.50

MOXI
Lightning Comics,OS; 1 Jul 1996

	$Good	$Fine	$N.Mint	£Good	£Fine	£N.Mint
1 Commemorative Edition, ND pre-bagged with certificate; dimensional platinum metallic ink cover						
	$2.00	$6.00	$10.00	£1.30	£3.90	£6.50
1 Cover A ND	$0.60	$1.80	$3.00	£0.40	£1.20	£2.00
1 Cover B, ND features Anguish on cover						
	$0.60	$1.80	$3.00	£0.40	£1.20	£2.00
Title Value:	$3.20	$9.60	$16.00	£2.10	£6.30	£10.50

MR. A
Comic Art,Magazine; 1 1973; 2 1975

	$Good	$Fine	$N.Mint	£Good	£Fine	£N.Mint
1 ND Steve Ditko script and art; something of a cult magazine for its satirical and political content; black and white begins						
	$1.25	$3.75	$7.50	£0.80	£2.50	£5.00
2 ND Steve Ditko script and art; black and white						
	$1.00	$3.00	$6.00	£0.65	£2.00	£4.00
Title Value:	$2.25	$6.75	$13.50	£1.45	£4.50	£9.00

MR. HERO - THE NEWMATIC MAN, NEIL GAIMAN'S
Tekno Comix; 1 Mar 1995-15 Jan 1996; Big Entertainment; 16 Apr 1996-17 May 1996

	$Good	$Fine	$N.Mint	£Good	£Fine	£N.Mint
1 ND James Vance script, Ted Slampyak and Bob McLeod art						
	$0.40	$1.20	$2.00	£0.25	£0.75	£1.25
2-11 ND	$0.40	$1.20	$2.00	£0.25	£0.75	£1.25
12 ND	$0.45	$1.35	$2.25	£0.30	£0.90	£1.50
13 ND pre-bagged with Tekno back-issue comic						
	$0.45	$1.35	$2.25	£0.30	£0.90	£1.50
14-17 ND	$0.45	$1.35	$2.25	£0.30	£0.90	£1.50
Title Value:	$7.10	$21.30	$35.50	£4.55	£13.65	£22.75

MR. HERO - THE NEWMATIC MAN, NEIL GAIMAN'S (2ND SERIES)
Big Entertainment; 1 Jun 1996-present

	$Good	$Fine	$N.Mint	£Good	£Fine	£N.Mint
1-3 ND	$0.45	$1.35	$2.25	£0.30	£0.90	£1.50
Title Value:	$1.35	$4.05	$6.75	£0.90	£2.70	£4.50

MR. LIZARD 1993 ANNUAL
Now Comics,OS; 1 Sep 1993

	$Good	$Fine	$N.Mint	£Good	£Fine	£N.Mint
1 ND pre-bagged with Instant Ralph Snart Action Figure Capsule						
	$0.50	$1.50	$2.50	£0.30	£0.90	£1.50
Title Value:	$0.50	$1.50	$2.50	£0.30	£0.90	£1.50

MR. LIZARD 3-D SPECIAL
Now Comics,OS; 1 May 1993

	$Good	$Fine	$N.Mint	£Good	£Fine	£N.Mint
1 ND pre-bagged with 3-D glasses (25% less without glasses)						
	$0.50	$1.50	$2.50	£0.30	£0.90	£1.50
Title Value:	$0.50	$1.50	$2.50	£0.30	£0.90	£1.50

MR. LIZARD SPECIAL
Now Comics,OS; 1 Aug 1992

	$Good	$Fine	$N.Mint	£Good	£Fine	£N.Mint
1 ND pre-bagged with badge (25% less without badge)						
	$0.50	$1.50	$2.50	£0.30	£0.90	£1.50
Title Value:	$0.50	$1.50	$2.50	£0.30	£0.90	£1.50

MR. MONSTER (1ST SERIES)
Eclipse; 1 Jan 1985-10 Jun 1987
(see Airboy/Mr.Monster Special, Vanguard Illustrated #7)

	$Good	$Fine	$N.Mint	£Good	£Fine	£N.Mint
1 ND scarce in the U.K. Michael T. Gilbert script/layouts begin						
	$1.00	$3.00	$5.00	£0.60	£1.80	£3.00
2 ND Dave Stevens cover						
	$0.60	$1.80	$3.00	£0.40	£1.20	£2.00
3 ND scarce in the U.K. Alan Moore script; Steve Bissette cover						
	$0.50	$1.50	$2.50	£0.70	£2.10	£3.50
4-9 ND	$0.50	$1.50	$2.50	£0.30	£0.90	£1.50
10 ND "6-D" issue	$0.50	$1.50	$2.50	£0.30	£0.90	£1.50

	$Good	$Fine	$N.Mint	£Good	£Fine	£N.Mint
Title Value:	$5.60	$16.80	$28.00	£3.80	£11.40	£19.00

MR. MONSTER (2ND SERIES)

Dark Horse; 1 Feb 1988-8 Sep 1991

	$Good	$Fine	$N.Mint	£Good	£Fine	£N.Mint
1 ND origin story; black and white begins	$0.40	$1.20	$2.00	£0.25	£0.75	£1.25
2 ND origin story continues	$0.40	$1.20	$2.00	£0.25	£0.75	£1.25
3-7 ND	$0.40	$1.20	$2.00	£0.25	£0.75	£1.25
8 ND DS squarebound	$0.80	$2.40	$4.00	£0.50	£1.50	£2.50
Title Value:	$3.60	$10.80	$18.00	£2.25	£6.75	£11.25

Note: big delay (nearly 3 years) between issues #7 and #8.

	£Good	£Fine	£N.Mint
Mr. Monster Origins (Dec 1995) Trade paperback collects mini-series, newly coloured in sepia tones. Produced by Graphitti	£2.70	£8.10	£13.50

MR. MONSTER SUPER-DUPER SPECIALS

Eclipse; 1 May 1986-8 Jul 1987

	$Good	$Fine	$N.Mint	£Good	£Fine	£N.Mint
1 Mr. Monster's 3-D High-Octane Horror #1 includes Wolverton, Evans	$0.60	$1.80	$3.00	£0.30	£0.90	£1.50
2 Mr. Monster's High-Octane Horror #2 includes Kubert, Powell	$0.50	$1.50	$2.50	£0.30	£0.90	£1.50
3-4 Mr. Monster's True Crime #1,2 all Jack Cole	$0.50	$1.50	$2.50	£0.30	£0.90	£1.50
5 Mr. Monster's High-Voltage Super-Science Atom Age Sci-Fi #1, Vic Torry by Powell	$0.50	$1.50	$2.50	£0.30	£0.90	£1.50
6 Mr. Monster's Hi-Shock Schlock #1	$0.50	$1.50	$2.50	£0.30	£0.90	£1.50
7 Mr. Monster's Hi-Shock Schlock #2	$0.50	$1.50	$2.50	£0.30	£0.90	£1.50
8 Mr. Monster's Weird Tales of the Future #1 Wolverton art	$0.50	$1.50	$2.50	£0.30	£0.90	£1.50
Title Value:	$4.10	$12.30	$20.50	£2.40	£7.20	£12.00

Note; all Non-Distributed on the news-stands in the U.K.

MR. MONSTER'S TRIPLE 3-D THREAT

3-D Zone,OS; 1 Sep 1993

	$Good	$Fine	$N.Mint	£Good	£Fine	£N.Mint
1 ND features work by Alan Moore, Paul Chadwick, Dave Stevens; with 3-D glasses (25% less without glasses)	$0.60	$1.80	$3.00	£0.40	£1.20	£2.00
Title Value:	$0.60	$1.80	$3.00	£0.40	£1.20	£2.00

MR. PUNCH HARDCOVER GRAPHIC NOVEL

DC Comics,OS; 1 Dec 1994

	$Good	$Fine	$N.Mint	£Good	£Fine	£N.Mint
1 ND 96pgs, Neil Gaiman script, Dave McKean art	$5.00	$15.00	$25.00	£3.00	£9.00	£15.00
Title Value:	$5.00	$15.00	$25.00	£3.00	£9.00	£15.00

	£Good	£Fine	£N.Mint
Mr. Punch Softcover Graphic Novel (Nov 1995) 96pgs, softcover reprint of the above hardcover with the stipulation of "available in North America only"	£2.00	£6.00	£10.00

MR. T AND THE T-FORCE

Now Comics; 1 Jun 1993-14 1994

	$Good	$Fine	$N.Mint	£Good	£Fine	£N.Mint
1 pre-bagged with Mr. T trading card, Neal Adams script and art begins	$0.40	$1.20	$2.00	£0.25	£0.75	£1.25
1 Advanced Edition, (Jun 1993), gold embossed logo, signed by Mr. T on cover	$0.80	$2.40	$4.00	£0.40	£1.20	£2.00
2-8 pre-bagged with trading card	$0.30	$0.90	$1.50	£0.20	£0.60	£1.00
2-8 pre-bagged, with gold foil stamped trading card	$0.40	$1.20	$2.00	£0.25	£0.75	£1.25
9-11	$0.30	$0.90	$1.50	£0.20	£0.60	£1.00
9-11 pre-bagged, with trading card						
12-14	$0.30	$0.90	$1.50	£0.20	£0.60	£1.00
Title Value:	$9.10	$27.30	$45.50	£5.75	£17.25	£28.75

Note: all Non-Distributed on the news-stands in the U.K.

MR. T AND THE T-FORCE ANNUAL

Now Comics; 1 Jul 1994

	$Good	$Fine	$N.Mint	£Good	£Fine	£N.Mint
1 ND metallic gold cover	$0.50	$1.50	$2.50	£0.30	£0.90	£1.50
Title Value:	$0.50	$1.50	$2.50	£0.30	£0.90	£1.50

MS. CYANIDE & ICE

Blackout Comics; 0 May 1995; 1 1995

	$Good	$Fine	$N.Mint	£Good	£Fine	£N.Mint
0 ND John R. Platt script, Bill Wylie and Scott Elmer art	$0.50	$1.50	$2.50	£0.30	£0.90	£1.50
1 ND	$0.50	$1.50	$2.50	£0.30	£0.90	£1.50
Title Value:	$1.00	$3.00	$5.00	£0.60	£1.80	£3.00

MS. MARVEL

Marvel Comics Group; 1 Jan 1977-23 Apr 1979

	$Good	$Fine	$N.Mint	£Good	£Fine	£N.Mint
1	$0.80	$2.50	$5.00	£0.40	£1.25	£2.50
2 origin	$0.50	$1.50	$3.00	£0.25	£0.75	£1.50
3-4	$0.30	$1.00	$2.00	£0.20	£0.60	£1.25
5 Ms. Marvel battles Vision	$0.30	$1.00	$2.00	£0.20	£0.60	£1.25
6-7	$0.30	$1.00	$2.00	£0.20	£0.60	£1.25
8 1st appearance Deathbird	$0.40	$1.25	$2.50	£0.25	£0.75	£1.50
9-10	$0.30	$1.00	$2.00	£0.20	£0.60	£1.25
11-14	$0.25	$0.75	$1.50	£0.15	£0.50	£1.00
15 Tiger Shark appears	$0.25	$0.75	$1.50	£0.15	£0.50	£1.00
16 Beast and Scarlet Witch appear, 1st appearance Mystique (cameo)	$1.65	$5.00	$10.00	£0.30	£1.00	£2.00
17 Mystique cameo	$1.65	$5.00	$10.00	£0.25	£0.75	£1.50
18 1st full appearance Mystique	$2.50	$7.50	$15.00	£0.40	£1.25	£2.50
19 Captain Marvel appears	$0.25	$0.75	$1.50	£0.15	£0.50	£1.00
20 new costume	$0.25	$0.75	$1.50	£0.15	£0.50	£1.00
21	$0.25	$0.75	$1.50	£0.15	£0.50	£1.00
22 Mike Zeck art	$0.25	$0.75	$1.50	£0.15	£0.50	£1.00
23 Vance Astro of Guardians of the Galaxy appears	$0.25	$0.75	$1.50	£0.15	£0.50	£1.00
Title Value:	$12.10	$37.25	$74.50	£4.75	£14.95	£30.25

Note: the intended issues #24 and #25 are published for the first time in Marvel Super-Heroes (2nd Series) 10 and 11.

MS. MYSTIC

Pacific; 1 Oct 1982-2 Feb 1984

(see Captain Victory #3)

	$Good	$Fine	$N.Mint	£Good	£Fine	£N.Mint
1-2 ND Neal Adams art	$0.30	$0.90	$1.50	£0.25	£0.75	£1.25
Title Value:	$0.60	$1.80	$3.00	£0.50	£1.50	£2.50

MS. MYSTIC (2ND SERIES)

Continuity; 1 Oct 1987-9 1992

	$Good	$Fine	$N.Mint	£Good	£Fine	£N.Mint
1 reprints Pacific issue #1	$0.40	$1.20	$2.00	£0.25	£0.75	£1.25
2 reprints Pacific issue #2	$0.40	$1.20	$2.00	£0.25	£0.75	£1.25
3 new material begins, part Neal Adams art	$0.40	$1.20	$2.00	£0.25	£0.75	£1.25
4 Neal Adams and Graham Nolan cover, Adams/Stone script	$0.40	$1.20	$2.00	£0.25	£0.75	£1.25
5 Dwayne Turner pencils and Neal Adams inks	$0.40	$1.20	$2.00	£0.25	£0.75	£1.25
6	$0.40	$1.20	$2.00	£0.25	£0.75	£1.25
7-8 Neal Adams cover	$0.40	$1.20	$2.00	£0.25	£0.75	£1.25
9 Dennis Beauvais art	$0.40	$1.20	$2.00	£0.25	£0.75	£1.25
Title Value:	$3.60	$10.80	$18.00	£2.25	£6.75	£11.25

MS. MYSTIC (3RD SERIES)

Continuity; 1 May 1993-3 Aug 1993

	$Good	$Fine	$N.Mint	£Good	£Fine	£N.Mint
1 ND Deathwatch 2000 part 8, pre-bagged with 2 trading cards, "dot-focus" cover; Neal Adams plot and cover	$0.40	$1.20	$2.00	£0.25	£0.75	£1.25
2 ND Deathwatch 2000 part 12, pre-bagged with trading card	$0.40	$1.20	$2.00	£0.25	£0.75	£1.25
3 ND Deathwatch 2000 part 17, pre-bagged with trading card; Tyvek indestructible cover	$0.40	$1.20	$2.00	£0.25	£0.75	£1.25
Title Value:	$1.20	$3.60	$6.00	£0.75	£2.25	£3.75

MS. MYSTIC (4TH SERIES)

Continuity; 1 Oct 1993-4 1994

	$Good	$Fine	$N.Mint	£Good	£Fine	£N.Mint
1 ND Vol.2 No 1 in indicia; Neal Adams co-inks	$0.40	$1.20	$2.00	£0.25	£0.75	£1.25
2 ND	$0.40	$1.20	$2.00	£0.25	£0.75	£1.25
3 ND Rise of Magic X-over; parchment embossed cover	$0.40	$1.20	$2.00	£0.25	£0.75	£1.25
4 ND Rise of Magic X-over; parchment embossed cover by Neal Adams	$0.40	$1.20	$2.00	£0.25	£0.75	£1.25
Title Value:	$1.60	$4.80	$8.00	£1.00	£3.00	£5.00

MS. TREE

Eclipse/Aardvark/Renegade; 1 Feb 1983-50 Jun 1989

(see The PI's)

	$Good	$Fine	$N.Mint	£Good	£Fine	£N.Mint
1 ND Eclipse issues begin; 2pg Frank Miller pin-up	$0.40	$1.20	$2.00	£0.20	£0.60	£1.00
2-9 ND	$0.40	$1.20	$2.00	£0.20	£0.60	£1.00
10 ND Aardvark issues begin	$0.40	$1.20	$2.00	£0.20	£0.60	£1.00
11-18 ND	$0.40	$1.20	$2.00	£0.20	£0.60	£1.00
19 ND Renegade issues begin	$0.40	$1.20	$2.00	£0.20	£0.60	£1.00
20-49 ND	$0.40	$1.20	$2.00	£0.20	£0.60	£1.00
50 ND scarce in the U.K. with flexidisc	$0.60	$1.80	$3.00	£0.40	£1.20	£2.00
Title Value:	$20.20	$60.60	$101.00	£10.20	£30.60	£51.00

Note: called Ms. Tree's Thrilling Detective Adventures on issues #1-3 Files of Ms. Tree:

	£Good	£Fine	£N.Mint
1 reprints #1-3	£1.00	£3.00	£5.00
2 The Cold Dish, reprints #4-8 plus new story	£1.00	£3.00	£5.00
3 Mike Mist's Casebook, collects all appearances	£1.00	£3.00	£5.00

MS. TREE 3-D

Renegade; 1 Aug 1985

	$Good	$Fine	$N.Mint	£Good	£Fine	£N.Mint
1 ND with bound-in 3-D glasses (25% less if without glasses)	$0.50	$1.50	$2.50	£0.30	£0.90	£1.50
Title Value:	$0.50	$1.50	$2.50	£0.30	£0.90	£1.50

MS. TREE QUARTERLY

DC Comics; 1 Jul 1990-8 Apr 1992; 9 Jul 1992-10 Oct 1992

	$Good	$Fine	$N.Mint	£Good	£Fine	£N.Mint
1 ND 80pgs, squarebound, Ms. Tree's origin by Max Allan Collins, Midnight begins with art by Graham Nolan, 11pg Batman illustrated prose story by Mike Grell	$0.60	$1.80	$3.00	£0.40	£1.20	£2.00
2 ND 80pgs, squarebound, John Butcher prose story by Mike Baron begins	$0.60	$1.80	$3.00	£0.40	£1.20	£2.00
3 ND 80pgs, squarebound, Frank Miller pin-up	$0.60	$1.80	$3.00	£0.40	£1.20	£2.00
4 ND 80pgs, cover by George Pratt	$0.60	$1.80	$3.00	£0.40	£1.20	£2.00
5-7 ND 80pgs	$0.60	$1.80	$3.00	£0.40	£1.20	£2.00
8-9 ND 64pgs	$0.55	$1.65	$2.75	£0.35	£1.05	£1.75
10 ND 80pgs, titled Ms. Tree Special	$0.60	$1.80	$3.00	£0.40	£1.20	£2.00
Title Value:	$5.90	$17.70	$29.50	£3.90	£11.70	£19.50

	$Good	$Fine	$N.Mint	£Good	£Fine	£N.Mint
Note: owing to the binding process, many copies of issues 1-3 have badly crinkled spines/covers.						
MS. TREE SUMMER SPECIAL						
Renegade; 1 Aug 1986						
1 ND	*$0.40*	*$1.20*	*$2.00*	£0.25	£0.75	£1.25
Title Value:	*$0.40*	*$1.20*	*$2.00*	£0.25	£0.75	£1.25
MS. TREE'S 1950s THREE-DIMENSIONAL CRIME						
Renegade; 1 Jul 1987						
1 ND reprints, new framing sequence; with bound-in 3-D glasses (25% less if without glasses)	*$0.50*	*$1.50*	*$2.50*	£0.30	£0.90	£1.50
Title Value:	*$0.50*	*$1.50*	*$2.50*	£0.30	£0.90	£1.50
MS. TREE'S CLASSIC CRIME						
Renegade; 1 1987						
1 ND reprints	*$0.40*	*$1.20*	*$2.00*	£0.25	£0.75	£1.25
Title Value:	*$0.40*	*$1.20*	*$2.00*	£0.25	£0.75	£1.25
MS. TREE'S ROCK & ROLL 3-D SPECIAL						
Renegade; 1 1986						
1 ND	*$0.50*	*$1.50*	*$2.50*	£0.30	£0.90	£1.50
Title Value:	*$0.50*	*$1.50*	*$2.50*	£0.30	£0.90	£1.50
MS. VICTORY SPECIAL						
AC Comics,OS; 1 1985						
1 ND	*$0.50*	*$1.50*	*$2.50*	£0.30	£0.90	£1.50
Title Value:	*$0.50*	*$1.50*	*$2.50*	£0.30	£0.90	£1.50
MUDWOG GRAPHIC NOVEL						
Continuity; 1 Nov 1991-2 1992						
1 ND reprints from Echo of Future Past featuring Arthur Suydam work	*$1.00*	*$3.00*	*$5.00*	£0.70	£2.10	£3.50
2 ND new material by Arthur Suydam	*$2.00*	*$6.00*	*$10.00*	£1.20	£3.60	£6.00
Title Value:	*$3.00*	*$9.00*	*$15.00*	£1.90	£5.70	£9.50
MULLKON EMPIRE, JOHN JAKE'S						
Tekno Comix; 1 Sep 1995-6 Feb 1996						
1 ND Kate Worley script, John Watkiss art and John Higgins colours	*$0.40*	*$1.20*	*$2.00*	£0.25	£0.75	£1.25
2-5 ND	*$0.40*	*$1.20*	*$2.00*	£0.25	£0.75	£1.25
6 ND	*$0.45*	*$1.35*	*$2.25*	£0.30	£0.90	£1.50
Title Value:	*$2.45*	*$7.35*	*$12.25*	£1.55	£4.65	£7.75
MUMMY ARCHIVES, THE						
Millennium,OS; 1 1992						
1 ND text and illustrations	*$0.40*	*$1.20*	*$2.00*	£0.25	£0.75	£1.25
Title Value:	*$0.40*	*$1.20*	*$2.00*	£0.25	£0.75	£1.25
MUMMY'S CURSE						
Aircel,MS; 1 Nov 1990-4 Feb 1991						
1-4 ND Barry Blair art, black and white	*$0.40*	*$1.20*	*$2.00*	£0.25	£0.75	£1.25
Title Value:	*$1.60*	*$4.80*	*$8.00*	£1.00	£3.00	£5.00
MUMMY, THE						
Dell/Movie Classics,OS Movie; 12-537-211 Sep/Nov 1962						
12-537-211 ND adaptation of movie; two different back covers are known to exist; limited distribution in the U.K.	*$5.00*	*$15.00*	*$35.00*	£3.20	£9.50	£22.50
Title Value:	*$5.00*	*$15.00*	*$35.00*	£3.20	£9.50	£22.50
MUMMY, THE (2ND SERIES)						
Millennium,MS; 1 Oct 1990-12 Dec 1991						
1-12 ND adaptation of Anne Rice novel	*$0.40*	*$1.20*	*$2.00*	£0.30	£0.90	£1.50
Title Value:	*$4.80*	*$14.40*	*$24.00*	£3.60	£10.80	£18.00
MUMMY, THE (LIMITED SERIES)						
Monster Comics,MS; 1 Mar 1991-4 Aug 1991						
1-4 ND Scott Beaderstadt adaptation of film	*$0.40*	*$1.20*	*$2.00*	£0.25	£0.75	£1.25
Title Value:	*$1.60*	*$4.80*	*$8.00*	£1.00	£3.00	£5.00
MUNDEN'S BAR ANNUAL						
First; 1 Apr 1988; 2 Mar 1991						
1 ND 48pgs, squarebound, Moncuse art (new Fish Police X-over), Rude, Staton, Ordway, Bolland (9pgs), Feazell reprints	*$0.80*	*$2.40*	*$4.00*	£0.50	£1.50	£2.50
2 ND 56pgs, squarebound, Reed Waller, Kate Worley, Evan Dorkin (6pgs of Milk & Cheese that pre-dates Milk & Cheese #1 as the 2nd appearance after Cerebus Bi-Weekly #20); Hilary Barta plus unseen TMNT story by Eastman/Laird	*$4.00*	*$12.00*	*$20.00*	£0.80	£2.40	£4.00
Title Value:	*$4.80*	*$14.40*	*$24.00*	£1.30	£3.90	£6.50
MUNSTERS, THE						
Gold Key; 1 Jan 1965-16 Jan 1968						
1 photo cover	*$29.00*	*$85.00*	*$200.00*	£15.50	£47.00	£110.00
2	*$15.00*	*$45.00*	*$105.00*	£7.75	£23.50	£55.00
3-5	*$10.50*	*$32.00*	*$75.00*	£5.50	£17.00	£40.00
6-16	*$8.50*	*$26.00*	*$60.00*	£5.00	£15.00	£35.00
Title Value:	*$169.00*	*$512.00*	*$1190.00*	£94.75	£286.50	£670.00
Note: very limited distribution on the news-stands in the U.K.						
MUPPET BABIES, THE						
Marvel Comics Group/Star,TV; 1 Aug 1985-26 Jul 1989						
1-26 ND	*$0.15*	*$0.45*	*$0.75*	£0.10	£0.30	£0.50
Title Value:	*$3.90*	*$11.70*	*$19.50*	£2.60	£7.80	£13.00
MUPPET TREASURE ISLAND						
Marvel Comics Group,OS; nn Apr 1996						
nn ND adaptation of film; Joey Cavalieri script, Marie Severin art	*$0.30*	*$0.90*	*$1.50*	£0.20	£0.60	£1.00
Title Value:	*$0.30*	*$0.90*	*$1.50*	£0.20	£0.60	£1.00
MUPPETS TAKE MANHATTAN, THE						
Marvel Comics Group,MS Film; 1 Nov 1984-3 Jan 1985						
1-3 ND	*$0.15*	*$0.45*	*$0.75*	£0.10	£0.30	£0.50

	$Good	$Fine	$N.Mint	£Good	£Fine	£N.Mint
Title Value:	*$0.45*	*$1.35*	*$2.25*	£0.30	£0.90	£1.50
MURDER						
Renegade; 1 Aug 1986-5 Dec 1986						
1-2 ND Dan Day, Steve Ditko, Toth art	*$0.40*	*$1.20*	*$2.00*	£0.25	£0.75	£1.25
3 ND Dan Day, Steve Ditko, Toth art/cover	*$0.40*	*$1.20*	*$2.00*	£0.25	£0.75	£1.25
4-5 ND Dan Day, Steve Ditko, Toth art	*$0.40*	*$1.20*	*$2.00*	£0.25	£0.75	£1.25
Title Value:	*$2.00*	*$6.00*	*$10.00*	£1.25	£3.75	£6.25
MURDER CITY						
Malibu; 1 1990						
1 ND 48pgs, squarebound, reprints newspaper strips	*$0.50*	*$1.50*	*$2.50*	£0.30	£0.90	£1.50
Title Value:	*$0.50*	*$1.50*	*$2.50*	£0.30	£0.90	£1.50
MUTANT CHRONICLES SOURCEBOOK						
Acclaim Comics,OS; 1 Sep 1996						
1 ND	*$0.60*	*$1.80*	*$3.00*	£0.40	£1.20	£2.00
Title Value:	*$0.60*	*$1.80*	*$3.00*	£0.40	£1.20	£2.00
MUTANT CHRONICLES: GOLGOTHA						
Academy Comics,MS; 1 May 1996-4 Aug 1996						
1-4 ND pre-bagged with trading card	*$0.60*	*$1.80*	*$3.00*	£0.40	£1.20	£2.00
Title Value:	*$2.40*	*$7.20*	*$12.00*	£1.60	£4.80	£8.00
MUTANT SUMMER FUN						
Marvel Comics Group,OS; 1 Aug 1990						
(see New Mutants)						
1 ND 80pgs, Anne Nocenti script, Brett Blevins art	*$0.40*	*$1.20*	*$2.00*	£0.25	£0.75	£1.25
Title Value:	*$0.40*	*$1.20*	*$2.00*	£0.25	£0.75	£1.25
MUTANTS VS. ULTRAS: FIRST ENCOUNTERS						
Marvel Comics Group/Ultraverse,OS; 1 Jan 1996						
1 ND 80pgs, X-Men vs. Exiles, Wolverine vs. Night Man, Prime vs. Hulk	*$1.40*	*$4.20*	*$7.00*	£0.90	£2.70	£4.50
Title Value:	*$1.40*	*$4.20*	*$7.00*	£0.90	£2.70	£4.50
MUTATIS						
Marvel Comics Group,MS; 1 Dec 1992-3 Feb 1993						
1-3 ND John Higgins cover and art	*$0.40*	*$1.20*	*$2.00*	£0.25	£0.75	£1.25
Title Value:	*$1.20*	*$3.60*	*$6.00*	£0.75	£2.25	£3.75
MY FAVOURITE MARTIAN						
Gold Key; 1 Jan 1964-9 Oct 1966						
1 photo covers begin	*$20.00*	*$60.00*	*$140.00*	£10.50	£32.00	£75.00
2	*$10.50*	*$32.00*	*$75.00*	£5.00	£15.00	£35.00
3-5	*$8.50*	*$26.00*	*$60.00*	£4.25	£12.50	£30.00
6-9	*$7.00*	*$21.00*	*$50.00*	£3.90	£11.50	£27.50
Title Value:	*$84.00*	*$254.00*	*$595.00*	£43.85	£130.50	£310.00
Note: limited distribution on the news-stands in the U.K.						
MY GREATEST ADVENTURE						
National Periodical Publications; 1 Jan/Feb 1955-85 Feb 1964						
(becomes Doom Patrol)						
1	*$125.00*	*$380.00*	*$1150.00*	£85.00	£255.00	£770.00
2	*$70.00*	*$210.00*	*$560.00*	£47.00	£140.00	£375.00
3-5	*$45.00*	*$135.00*	*$360.00*	£30.00	£90.00	£240.00
6-10	*$38.00*	*$110.00*	*$300.00*	£25.00	£75.00	£200.00
11-15	*$32.00*	*$95.00*	*$225.00*	£21.00	£62.50	£150.00
16-18 Jack Kirby art	*$38.00*	*$110.00*	*$265.00*	£26.00	£75.00	£180.00
19	*$30.00*	*$90.00*	*$210.00*	£20.00	£60.00	£140.00
20-21 Jack Kirby art	*$34.00*	*$100.00*	*$240.00*	£22.50	£67.50	£160.00
22-25	*$26.00*	*$75.00*	*$180.00*	£17.00	£50.00	£120.00
26-27	*$20.00*	*$60.00*	*$140.00*	£13.00	£40.00	£92.50
28 Jack Kirby art	*$29.00*	*$85.00*	*$200.00*	£19.00	£57.50	£135.00
29-30	*$20.00*	*$60.00*	*$140.00*	£13.00	£40.00	£92.50
31-36	*$16.00*	*$49.00*	*$115.00*	£10.50	£32.00	£75.00
1st official distribution in the U.K.						
37-40	*$16.00*	*$49.00*	*$115.00*	£10.50	£32.00	£75.00
41-50	*$12.50*	*$39.00*	*$90.00*	£7.00	£21.00	£50.00
51-57	*$12.50*	*$39.00*	*$90.00*	£6.25	£19.00	£45.00
58 Toth art	*$12.50*	*$39.00*	*$90.00*	£6.25	£19.00	£45.00
59	*$12.50*	*$39.00*	*$90.00*	£6.25	£19.00	£45.00
60 Toth art	*$12.50*	*$39.00*	*$90.00*	£6.25	£19.00	£45.00
61 Toth art; last 10 cents issue	*$12.50*	*$39.00*	*$90.00*	£6.25	£19.00	£45.00
62-70	*$7.75*	*$23.50*	*$55.00*	£3.90	£11.50	£27.50
71-76	*$7.75*	*$23.50*	*$55.00*	£3.20	£9.50	£22.50
77 Toth art	*$7.75*	*$23.50*	*$55.00*	£3.55	£10.50	£25.00
78-79	*$7.75*	*$23.50*	*$55.00*	£3.20	£9.50	£22.50
80 origin and 1st appearance Doom Patrol (Robotman, Negative Man, Elasti-Girl, The Chief)	*$50.00*	*$150.00*	*$400.00*	£31.00	£92.50	£250.00
[Scarce in high grade - Very Fine+ or better]						
81 2nd appearance Doom Patrol, Toth art	*$22.50*	*$67.50*	*$160.00*	£11.00	£34.00	£80.00
82 3rd appearance Doom Patrol	*$22.50*	*$67.50*	*$160.00*	£10.50	£32.00	£75.00
83-84	*$22.50*	*$67.50*	*$160.00*	£9.25	£28.00	£65.00
85 Toth art	*$22.50*	*$67.50*	*$160.00*	£10.00	£30.00	£70.00
Title Value:	*$1829.50*	*$5484.50*	*$13610.00*	£1123.00	£3363.50	£8402.50

FEATURES

Doom Patrol in 80-85. SF stories in 37-79, 81-85.

MY LITTLE MARGIE

Charlton; 1 Jul 1954-54 Nov 1964

	$Good	$Fine	$N.Mint	£Good	£Fine	£N.Mint
1 scarce in the U.K.	$26.00	$75.00	$180.00	£17.00	£50.00	£120.00
2 scarce in the U.K.	$12.50	$39.00	$90.00	£8.50	£26.00	£60.00
3-9 scarce in the U.K.	$6.25	$19.00	$45.00	£3.55	£10.50	£25.00
1st official distribution in the U.K.						
10	$6.25	$19.00	$45.00	£3.55	£10.50	£25.00
11-15	$5.50	$17.00	$40.00	£3.20	£9.50	£22.50
16-19	$4.25	$12.50	$30.00	£2.50	£7.50	£17.50
20 scarce in the U.K. 100pgs	$10.50	$32.00	$75.00	£6.25	£19.00	£45.00
21-38	$3.55	$10.50	$25.00	£2.10	£6.25	£15.00
39-53	$2.85	$8.50	$20.00	£1.40	£4.25	£10.00
54 scarce in the U.K. parody of Beatles and Beatles on front cover	$15.00	$45.00	$105.00	£8.50	£26.00	£60.00
Title Value:	$265.15	$794.50	$1870.00	£153.45	£458.75	£1087.50

Note: limited distribution on the news-stands in the U.K.

MY LOVE

Marvel Comics Group; 1 Sep 1969-39 Mar 1976

	$Good	$Fine	$N.Mint	£Good	£Fine	£N.Mint
1 ND scarce in the U.K.	$1.75	$5.25	$12.50	£1.05	£3.20	£7.50
2-5 ND	$1.25	$3.75	$7.50	£0.65	£2.00	£4.00
6-9 ND	$1.05	$3.25	$6.50	£0.55	£1.75	£3.50
10 ND Williamson reprint	$1.05	$3.25	$6.50	£0.55	£1.75	£3.50
11-13 ND	$0.65	$2.00	$4.00	£0.40	£1.25	£2.50
14 ND Morrow cover/art, part Jack Kirby reprint	$0.65	$2.00	$4.00	£0.40	£1.25	£2.50
15-20 ND	$0.65	$2.00	$4.00	£0.40	£1.25	£2.50
21-22 ND	$0.50	$1.50	$3.00	£0.30	£1.00	£2.00
23 ND scarce in the U.K. 7pg Steranko reprint of Our Love Story #5	$0.80	$2.50	$5.00	£0.40	£1.25	£2.50
24-37 ND	$0.50	$1.50	$3.00	£0.30	£1.00	£2.00
38-39 ND all reprint	$0.50	$1.50	$3.00	£0.30	£1.00	£2.00
Title Value:	$28.30	$86.00	$174.00	£16.20	£51.70	£104.50

MY LOVE SPECIAL

Marvel Comics Group; 1 Dec 1971

	$Good	$Fine	$N.Mint	£Good	£Fine	£N.Mint
1 ND scarce in the U.K. 52pgs	$1.00	$3.00	$6.00	£0.50	£1.50	£3.00
Title Value:	$1.00	$3.00	$6.00	£0.50	£1.50	£3.00

MY NAME IS CHAOS

DC Comics,MS; 1 Feb 1992-4 May 1992

	$Good	$Fine	$N.Mint	£Good	£Fine	£N.Mint
1 ND 48pgs, art by John Ridgway begins, script by Tom Veitch	$0.70	$2.10	$3.50	£0.50	£1.50	£2.50
2-4 ND 48pgs	$0.70	$2.10	$3.50	£0.50	£1.50	£2.50
Title Value:	$2.80	$8.40	$14.00	£2.00	£6.00	£10.00

MY NAME IS HOLOCAUST

DC Comics/Milestone,MS; 1 May 1995-5 Sep 1995

	$Good	$Fine	$N.Mint	£Good	£Fine	£N.Mint
1-5	$0.40	$1.20	$2.00	£0.25	£0.75	£1.25
Title Value:	$2.00	$6.00	$10.00	£1.25	£3.75	£6.25

MY OWN ROMANCE

Marvel Comics Group;76 Jul 1960

(previous issues ND)

	$Good	$Fine	$N.Mint	£Good	£Fine	£N.Mint
76 rare although distributed in the U.K.	$2.50	$7.50	$17.50	£1.40	£4.25	£10.00
Title Value:	$2.50	$7.50	$17.50	£1.40	£4.25	£10.00

MY SECRET MARRIAGE

IW Super;9 1964

	$Good	$Fine	$N.Mint	£Good	£Fine	£N.Mint
9 distributed in the U.K. reprints	$0.70	$2.10	$5.00	£0.35	£1.05	£2.50
Title Value:	$0.70	$2.10	$5.00	£0.35	£1.05	£2.50

MYRON MOOSE FUNNIES

Fantagraphics; 1-3 1987

	$Good	$Fine	$N.Mint	£Good	£Fine	£N.Mint
1-3 ND	$0.25	$0.75	$1.25	£0.15	£0.45	£0.75
Title Value:	$0.75	$2.25	$3.75	£0.45	£1.35	£2.25

MYS-TECH WARS

Marvel UK,MS; 1 Mar 1993-4 Jun 1993

	$Good	$Fine	$N.Mint	£Good	£Fine	£N.Mint
1 MysTech Wars cross-over story begins; Nick Fury, Fantastic Four, X-Men, X-Force appear; Bryan Hitch and Jeff Anderson art	$0.25	$0.75	$1.25	£0.15	£0.45	£0.75
2 Nick Fury appears	$0.25	$0.75	$1.25	£0.15	£0.45	£0.75
3-4 Death's Head II appears	$0.25	$0.75	$1.25	£0.15	£0.45	£0.75
Title Value:	$1.00	$3.00	$5.00	£0.60	£1.80	£3.00

Note: story runs through Motormouth #9, Dark Angel #10, Death's Head II #5, Warheads #11, Dark Angel #11, Knights of Pendragon #12.

MYSTERIES OF UNEXPLORED WORLDS

Charlton; 1 Aug 1956-48 Sep 1965

	$Good	$Fine	$N.Mint	£Good	£Fine	£N.Mint
1 scarce in the U.K.	$29.00	$85.00	$200.00	£19.00	£57.50	£135.00
2	$11.00	$34.00	$80.00	£7.75	£23.50	£55.00
3-4 Steve Ditko art	$20.50	$60.00	$145.00	£13.50	£42.00	£97.50
5-6 Steve Ditko cover and art	$22.50	$67.50	$160.00	£15.50	£47.00	£110.00
7 64pgs, Steve Ditko art featured	$22.50	$67.50	$160.00	£15.50	£47.00	£110.00
8-9 Steve Ditko art	$20.50	$60.00	$145.00	£13.50	£42.00	£97.50
10-11 Steve Ditko cover and art	$22.50	$67.50	$160.00	£15.50	£47.00	£110.00
12 Steve Ditko art	$15.00	$45.00	$105.00	£10.00	£30.00	£70.00
13-17	$4.60	$13.50	$32.50	£3.20	£9.50	£22.50
18 1st appearance of The Watcher prototype (May 1960); a discovery courtesy of Jonathan Ross, this prototype appears three years before The Watcher in Fantastic Four #13	$5.00	$15.00	$35.00	£3.55	£10.50	£25.00
19 Steve Ditko art	$15.00	$45.00	$105.00	£10.00	£30.00	£70.00
20	$4.60	$13.50	$32.50	£3.20	£9.50	£22.50
21-24 Steve Ditko art	$15.00	$45.00	$105.00	£10.00	£30.00	£70.00
25	$4.25	$12.50	$30.00	£2.85	£8.50	£20.00
26 Steve Ditko art	$14.00	$43.00	$100.00	£9.25	£28.00	£65.00
27-30	$4.25	$12.50	$30.00	£2.50	£7.50	£17.50
31-45	$2.10	$6.25	$15.00	£1.10	£3.40	£8.00
46 origin and 1st appearance Son of Vulcan	$3.55	$10.50	$25.00	£1.75	£5.25	£12.50
47-48 Son of Vulcan	$2.10	$6.25	$15.00	£1.05	£3.20	£7.50
Title Value:	$431.60	$1284.75	$3050.00	£283.45	£860.65	£2012.50

Note: most issues distributed in the U.K.after 1958

MYSTERIOUS SUSPENSE

Charlton; 1 Oct 1968

1 scarce, distributed in the U.K. The Question appears, Steve Ditko art

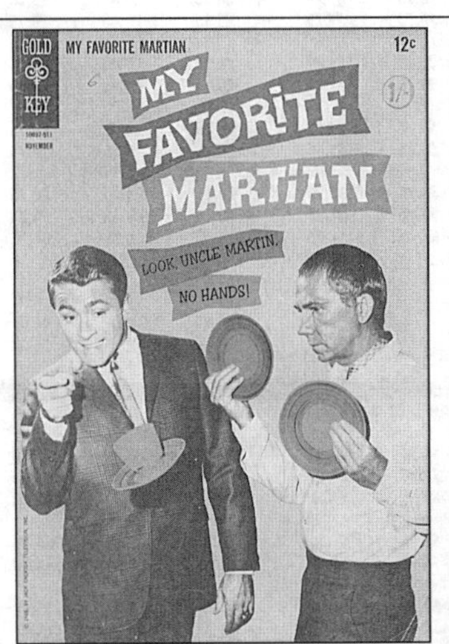

My Favourite Martian #6

My Greatest Adventure #69

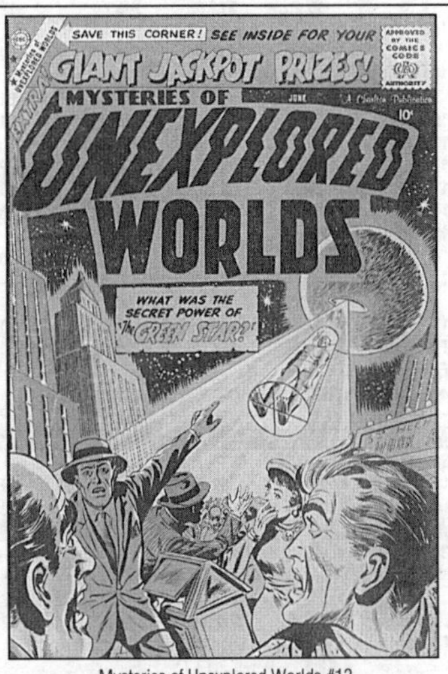

Mysteries of Unexplored Worlds #13

	$Good	$Fine	$N.Mint	£Good	£Fine	£N.Mint
	$5.00	*$15.00*	*$35.00*	£2.85	£8.50	£20.00
Title Value:	*$5.00*	*$15.00*	*$35.00*	£2.85	£8.50	£20.00

MYSTERY IN SPACE

National Periodical Publications/DC Comics; 1 Apr/May 1951-110 Sep 1966; 111 Sep 1980-117 Mar 1981
(see Adam Strange)

	$Good	$Fine	$N.Mint	£Good	£Fine	£N.Mint
1 Frazetta art (8pgs)	*$325.00*	*$970.00*	*$2600.00*	£215.00	£650.00	£1750.00
[Scarce in high grade - Very Fine+ or better]						
2	*$140.00*	*$425.00*	*$1000.00*	£95.00	£285.00	£670.00
3	*$110.00*	*$340.00*	*$800.00*	£75.00	£225.00	£535.00
4-5	*$95.00*	*$285.00*	*$675.00*	£62.50	£190.00	£450.00
6-10	*$77.50*	*$235.00*	*$550.00*	£52.50	£155.00	£370.00
11-15	*$55.00*	*$170.00*	*$400.00*	£39.00	£115.00	£270.00
16-25	*$52.50*	*$160.00*	*$375.00*	£36.00	£105.00	£250.00
26 1st appearance Space Cabbie (ends #47)	*$43.00*	*$125.00*	*$300.00*	£29.00	£85.00	£200.00
27-40	*$43.00*	*$125.00*	*$300.00*	£29.00	£85.00	£200.00
41-52	*$32.00*	*$95.00*	*$225.00*	£21.00	£62.50	£150.00
53 Adam Strange series begins (see Showcase #17 for 1st appearance)	*$130.00*	*$400.00*	*$1600.00*	£82.50	£250.00	£1000.00
1st official distribution in the U.K.						
54	*$50.00*	*$150.00*	*$400.00*	£33.00	£97.50	£260.00
55 Infantino Adam Strange begins; painted grey-tone cover	*$44.00*	*$130.00*	*$350.00*	£26.00	£77.50	£210.00
56-60	*$25.00*	*$75.00*	*$200.00*	£15.00	£45.00	£120.00
61 1st appearance Ulthoon	*$21.00*	*$62.50*	*$150.00*	£14.00	£43.00	£100.00
62 1st appearance Mortan	*$21.00*	*$62.50*	*$150.00*	£14.00	£43.00	£100.00
63 origin Vandor	*$21.00*	*$62.50*	*$150.00*	£14.00	£43.00	£100.00
64-65	*$21.00*	*$62.50*	*$150.00*	£10.50	£32.00	£75.00
66 Star Rovers begin	*$21.00*	*$62.50*	*$150.00*	£10.50	£32.00	£75.00
67-70	*$21.00*	*$62.50*	*$150.00*	£10.50	£32.00	£75.00
71 last 10 cents issue	*$21.00*	*$62.50*	*$150.00*	£10.50	£32.00	£75.00
72-74	*$15.00*	*$45.00*	*$105.00*	£7.75	£23.50	£55.00
75 scarce in the U.K. Justice League of America X-over (story continues from Justice League of America #3)	*$28.00*	*$82.50*	*$250.00*	£16.50	£50.00	£150.00
76-80	*$15.00*	*$45.00*	*$105.00*	£7.00	£21.00	£50.00
81-86	*$11.00*	*$34.00*	*$80.00*	£5.00	£15.00	£35.00
87 Hawkman appears (pre Hawkman #1)	*$26.00*	*$77.50*	*$210.00*	£15.00	£45.00	£120.00
88 Hawkman appears (pre Hawkman #1)	*$22.50*	*$67.50*	*$160.00*	£11.00	£34.00	£80.00
89 Hawkman appears (pre Hawkman #1)	*$21.00*	*$62.50*	*$150.00*	£10.00	£30.00	£70.00
90 Hawkman appears (pre Hawkman #1 by one month), 1st Hawkman and Adam Strange team-up	*$21.50*	*$65.00*	*$175.00*	£12.50	£38.00	£100.00
91 last Infantino art on Adam Strange	*$6.25*	*$19.00*	*$45.00*	£2.85	£8.50	£20.00
92 Space Ranger begins	*$6.25*	*$19.00*	*$45.00*	£2.85	£8.50	£20.00
93	*$6.25*	*$19.00*	*$45.00*	£2.10	£6.25	£15.00
94 Adam Strange/Space Ranger team up	*$6.25*	*$19.00*	*$45.00*	£2.85	£8.50	£20.00
95-97	*$6.25*	*$19.00*	*$45.00*	£2.10	£6.25	£15.00
98 Adam Strange/Space Ranger team up	*$6.25*	*$19.00*	*$45.00*	£2.10	£6.25	£15.00
99-101	*$6.25*	*$19.00*	*$45.00*	£2.10	£6.25	£15.00
102 Adam Strange ends	*$6.25*	*$19.00*	*$45.00*	£2.10	£6.25	£15.00
103 origin Ultra the Multi-Alien, Space Ranger ends	*$6.25*	*$19.00*	*$45.00*	£2.50	£7.50	£17.50
104 last Silver Age issue, indicia-dated December 1965	*$2.85*	*$8.50*	*$20.00*	£1.40	£4.25	£10.00
105-110	*$2.85*	*$8.50*	*$20.00*	£1.05	£3.20	£7.50
111 Rogers art	*$0.80*	*$2.40*	*$4.00*	£0.30	£0.90	£1.50
112	*$0.80*	*$2.40*	*$4.00*	£0.30	£0.90	£1.50
113 Golden art	*$0.80*	*$2.40*	*$4.00*	£0.30	£0.90	£1.50
114 Steve Ditko art	*$0.80*	*$2.40*	*$4.00*	£0.30	£0.90	£1.50
115 Bolland, Cowan, Steve Ditko art	*$0.80*	*$2.40*	*$4.00*	£0.30	£0.90	£1.50
116 Von Eeden, Craig, Steve Ditko art	*$0.80*	*$2.40*	*$4.00*	£0.30	£0.90	£1.50
117	*$0.80*	*$2.40*	*$4.00*	£0.30	£0.90	£1.50
Title Value:	*$3973.30*	*$11929.80*	*$29468.00*	£2550.00	£7581.50	£18748.00

FEATURES
Adam Strange in 55-100, 102. Adam Strange/Space Ranger in 94, 98. Hawkman in 87-90. Space Ranger in 92-103. Ultra, the Multi-Alien in 103-110. Most issues have science fiction back-up features.

MYSTERY MAN, THE

Slave Labor; 1 Jul 1988-5 1988

	$Good	$Fine	$N.Mint	£Good	£Fine	£N.Mint
1-5 ND	*$0.25*	*$0.75*	*$1.25*	£0.15	£0.45	£0.75
Title Value:	*$1.25*	*$3.75*	*$6.25*	£0.75	£2.25	£3.75

MYSTERY PLAY, THE

DC Comics/Vertigo,OS; nn Apr 1994

	$Good	$Fine	$N.Mint	£Good	£Fine	£N.Mint
nn ND 80pgs, Hardcover graphic novel; Grant Morrison script, Jon J. Muth art	*$4.00*	*$12.00*	*$20.00*	£2.50	£7.50	£12.50
Title Value:	*$4.00*	*$12.00*	*$20.00*	£2.50	£7.50	£12.50

The Mystery Play Softcover Graphic Novel (Aug 1995)

	£Good	£Fine	£N.Mint
softcover version of the above with Jon J. Muth painted cover	£1.30	£3.90	£6.50

MYTH ADVENTURES

Warp/Apple; 1 1984-12 1986

	$Good	$Fine	$N.Mint	£Good	£Fine	£N.Mint
1-4 ND magazine size	*$0.40*	*$1.20*	*$2.00*	£0.25	£0.75	£1.25
5-12 ND	*$0.40*	*$1.20*	*$2.00*	£0.25	£0.75	£1.25
Title Value:	*$4.80*	*$14.40*	*$24.00*	£3.00	£9.00	£15.00

MYTH CONCEPTIONS

Apple Comics; 1 Summer 1987-7 1988

	$Good	$Fine	$N.Mint	£Good	£Fine	£N.Mint
1-7 ND	*$0.40*	*$1.20*	*$2.00*	£0.25	£0.75	£1.25
Title Value:	*$2.80*	*$8.40*	*$14.00*	£1.75	£5.25	£8.75

MYTHOGRAPHY

Bardic Press; 1 Sep 1996-present

	$Good	$Fine	$N.Mint	£Good	£Fine	£N.Mint
1 ND 64pgs, anthology; black and white	*$0.80*	*$2.40*	*$4.00*	£0.50	£1.50	£2.50
Title Value:	*$0.80*	*$2.40*	*$4.00*	£0.50	£1.50	£2.50

MYTHOS: THE FINAL TOUR

DC Comics/Vertigo,MS; 1 Dec 1996-3 Feb 1997

	$Good	$Fine	$N.Mint	£Good	£Fine	£N.Mint
1-3 ND	*$1.20*	*$3.60*	*$6.00*	£0.80	£2.40	£4.00
Title Value:	*$3.60*	*$10.80*	*$18.00*	£2.40	£7.20	£12.00

McLINTOCK!

Gold Key/Movie Comics,OS Movie; 10110-403 Mar 1964

	$Good	$Fine	$N.Mint	£Good	£Fine	£N.Mint
10110-403 scarce in the U.K. John Wayne and Maureen O'Hara photo cover; film adaptation	*$15.50*	*$47.00*	*$110.00*	£8.50	£26.00	£60.00
Title Value:	*$15.50*	*$47.00*	*$110.00*	£8.50	£26.00	£60.00

N

NAIVE INTER-DIMENSIONAL COMMANDO KOALAS

Independent Comics Group,OS; 1 Oct 1986

	$Good	$Fine	$N.Mint	£Good	£Fine	£N.Mint
1 ND Black Belt Hamsters cameo; black and white	*$0.40*	*$1.20*	*$2.00*	£0.25	£0.75	£1.25
Title Value:	*$0.40*	*$1.20*	*$2.00*	£0.25	£0.75	£1.25

NAM MAGAZINE, THE

Marvel Comics Group,Magazine; 1 Aug 1988-10 May 1989

	$Good	$Fine	$N.Mint	£Good	£Fine	£N.Mint
1 ND reprints from regular series begin	*$0.40*	*$1.20*	*$2.00*	£0.20	£0.60	£1.00
2-10 ND	*$0.40*	*$1.20*	*$2.00*	£0.20	£0.60	£1.00
Title Value:	*$4.00*	*$12.00*	*$20.00*	£2.00	£6.00	£10.00

Note: black and white reprints

NAM, THE

Marvel Comics Group; 1 Dec 1986-84 Sep 1993

	$Good	$Fine	$N.Mint	£Good	£Fine	£N.Mint
1 ND	*$0.50*	*$1.50*	*$2.50*	£0.30	£0.90	£1.50
1 2nd printing ND	*$0.20*	*$0.60*	*$1.00*	£0.15	£0.45	£0.75
2 ND	*$0.40*	*$1.20*	*$2.00*	£0.25	£0.75	£1.25
3-5 ND	*$0.30*	*$0.90*	*$1.50*	£0.20	£0.60	£1.00
6-48 ND	*$0.25*	*$0.75*	*$1.25*	£0.15	£0.45	£0.75
49-51 ND 3 part story	*$0.25*	*$0.75*	*$1.25*	£0.15	£0.45	£0.75
52 ND Punisher appears	*$0.30*	*$0.90*	*$1.50*	£0.20	£0.60	£1.00
52 2nd printing, ND gold cover	*$0.25*	*$0.75*	*$1.25*	£0.15	£0.45	£0.75
53 ND Punisher appears	*$0.30*	*$0.90*	*$1.50*	£0.20	£0.60	£1.00
53 2nd printing, ND gold cover	*$0.25*	*$0.75*	*$1.25*	£0.15	£0.45	£0.75
54-58 ND The Death of Joe Hallen story	*$0.25*	*$0.75*	*$1.25*	£0.15	£0.45	£0.75
59-64 ND	*$0.25*	*$0.75*	*$1.25*	£0.15	£0.45	£0.75
65 ND $1.75 cover begins	*$0.25*	*$0.75*	*$1.25*	£0.15	£0.45	£0.75
66 ND	*$0.25*	*$0.75*	*$1.25*	£0.15	£0.45	£0.75
67-69 ND Punisher appears	*$0.25*	*$0.75*	*$1.25*	£0.15	£0.45	£0.75
70-74 ND	*$0.25*	*$0.75*	*$1.25*	£0.15	£0.45	£0.75
75 ND DS story of the My Lai Massacre	*$0.25*	*$0.75*	*$1.25*	£0.15	£0.45	£0.75
76-78 ND	*$0.25*	*$0.75*	*$1.25*	£0.15	£0.45	£0.75
79-81 ND Beginning of the End story; the 1968 TET Offensive, tryptych (ie 3-part) cover by Michael Golden	*$0.25*	*$0.75*	*$1.25*	£0.15	£0.45	£0.75
82-84 ND	*$0.25*	*$0.75*	*$1.25*	£0.15	£0.45	£0.75
Title Value:	*$22.35*	*$67.05*	*$111.75*	£13.55	£40.65	£67.75

Note: Limited series designed to last same length as Vietnam War, ie. about 10 years. It didn't.

Trade paperbacks:

	£Good	£Fine	£N.Mint
1 96pgs, reprints #1-4	£1.00	£3.00	£5.00
2nd print (Apr 1991)	£0.90	£2.70	£4.50
2 96pgs, reprints #5-8	£0.90	£2.70	£4.50
3 96pgs, reprints #9-12	£0.90	£2.70	£4.50

NAMOR

Marvel Comics Group; 1 Apr 1990-62 May 1995

	$Good	$Fine	$N.Mint	£Good	£Fine	£N.Mint
1 ND John Byrne script/art begins	*$0.50*	*$1.50*	*$2.50*	£0.30	£0.90	£1.50
2-3 ND	*$0.40*	*$1.20*	*$2.00*	£0.25	£0.75	£1.25
4 ND	*$0.30*	*$0.90*	*$1.50*	£0.20	£0.60	£1.00
5 ND Iron Man/Mr. Fantastic/Invisible Woman appear	*$0.30*	*$0.90*	*$1.50*	£0.20	£0.60	£1.00
6-7 ND	*$0.30*	*$0.90*	*$1.50*	£0.20	£0.60	£1.00
8 ND Iron Fist returns (cameo: not in costume)	*$0.30*	*$0.90*	*$1.50*	£0.20	£0.60	£1.00
9 ND	*$0.30*	*$0.90*	*$1.50*	£0.20	£0.60	£1.00
10 ND re-intro Iron Fist						

	$Good	$Fine	$N.Mint	£Good	£Fine	£N.Mint
	$0.30	$0.90	$1.50	£0.20	£0.60	£1.00
11 ND	$0.30	$0.90	$1.50	£0.20	£0.60	£1.00
12 ND DS re-intro Invaders	$0.40	$1.20	$2.00	£0.25	£0.75	£1.25
13 ND Fantastic Four appear	$0.30	$0.90	$1.50	£0.20	£0.60	£1.00
14 ND	$0.30	$0.90	$1.50	£0.20	£0.60	£1.00
15 ND Iron Fist (Skrull in disguise) on last page	$0.30	$0.90	$1.50	£0.20	£0.60	£1.00
16 ND Iron Fist (Skrull) vs. Sub-Mariner	$0.30	$0.90	$1.50	£0.20	£0.60	£1.00
17-18 ND	$0.30	$0.90	$1.50	£0.20	£0.60	£1.00
19 ND Punisher appears	$0.30	$0.90	$1.50	£0.20	£0.60	£1.00
20 ND	$0.30	$0.90	$1.50	£0.20	£0.60	£1.00
21-22 ND Wolverine appears	$0.30	$0.90	$1.50	£0.20	£0.60	£1.00
23 ND Wolverine appears, Iron Fist cameo, $1.25 cover begins	$0.30	$0.90	$1.50	£0.20	£0.60	£1.00
24 ND Namor vs. Wolverine, Iron Fist and Dr. Strange appear	$0.30	$0.90	$1.50	£0.20	£0.60	£1.00
25 ND Wolverine appears	$0.30	$0.90	$1.50	£0.20	£0.60	£1.00
26 ND Iron Fist appears, 1st Jae Lee art	$0.70	$2.10	$3.50	£0.40	£1.20	£2.00
27 ND Jae Lee art	$0.60	$1.80	$3.00	£0.30	£0.90	£1.50
28 ND Jae Lee art	$0.50	$1.50	$2.50	£0.25	£0.75	£1.25
29 ND Iron Fist and Human Torch appear, Jae Lee art	$0.40	$1.20	$2.00	£0.25	£0.75	£1.25
30 ND Jae Lee art	$0.40	$1.20	$2.00	£0.25	£0.75	£1.25
31-32 ND Namor vs. Dr. Doom, Jae Lee art	$0.30	$0.90	$1.50	£0.20	£0.60	£1.00
33 ND Jae Lee art	$0.30	$0.90	$1.50	£0.20	£0.60	£1.00
34 ND Jae Lee art; last John Byrne script	$0.30	$0.90	$1.50	£0.20	£0.60	£1.00
35-36 ND Jae Lee art	$0.30	$0.90	$1.50	£0.20	£0.60	£1.00
37 ND Jae Lee art, holo-grafix foil cover	$0.30	$0.90	$1.50	£0.20	£0.60	£1.00
38-39 ND Jae Lee art	$0.25	$0.75	$1.25	£0.15	£0.45	£0.75
40 ND last Jae Lee art	$0.25	$0.75	$1.25	£0.15	£0.45	£0.75
41 ND Shawn McManus art begins	$0.25	$0.75	$1.25	£0.15	£0.45	£0.75
42 ND	$0.25	$0.75	$1.25	£0.15	£0.45	£0.75
43 ND Namor vs. Stingray	$0.25	$0.75	$1.25	£0.15	£0.45	£0.75
44 ND Glenn Herdling, Geoff Isherwood and Jeff Albrecht as new creative team	$0.25	$0.75	$1.25	£0.15	£0.45	£0.75
45 ND	$0.25	$0.75	$1.25	£0.15	£0.45	£0.75
46-48 ND Starblast X-over	$0.25	$0.75	$1.25	£0.15	£0.45	£0.75
49 ND Valentine's Day issue; Namorita, Invisible Woman, Andromeda appear	$0.25	$0.75	$1.25	£0.15	£0.45	£0.75
50 ND 48pgs, love affair between Namor and Sue Richards (Invisible Woman)	$0.40	$1.20	$2.00	£0.25	£0.75	£1.25
50 Collectors Edition, ND 48pgs, love affair between Namor and Sue Richards (Invisible Woman); silver cover overprinted with transparent inks; with free Spiderman's Amazing Powers card sheet	$0.60	$1.80	$3.00	£0.40	£1.20	£2.00
51 X-over Fantastic Four #389 and Fantastic Four Unlimited #6	$0.25	$0.75	$1.25	£0.15	£0.45	£0.75
52-53	$0.25	$0.75	$1.25	£0.15	£0.45	£0.75
54 Llyra gives birth to Namor's son	$0.25	$0.75	$1.25	£0.15	£0.45	£0.75
55-56	$0.25	$0.75	$1.25	£0.15	£0.45	£0.75
57 Captain America guest-stars	$0.25	$0.75	$1.25	£0.15	£0.45	£0.75
58-59 Namor vs. The Abomination	$0.25	$0.75	$1.25	£0.15	£0.45	£0.75
60-61	$0.25	$0.75	$1.25	£0.15	£0.45	£0.75
62 Atlantis Rising prelude; Namor vs. Triton	$0.25	$0.75	$1.25	£0.15	£0.45	£0.75
Title Value:	$19.70	$59.10	$98.50	£12.35	£37.05	£61.75

NAMOR ANNUAL

Marvel Comics Group; 1 Sep 1991-4 1994

	$Good	$Fine	$N.Mint	£Good	£Fine	£N.Mint
1 ND Subterranean Odyssey part 3, continued in Iron Man Annual #12	$0.50	$1.50	$2.50	£0.30	£0.90	£1.50
2 ND Return of the Defenders part 2, continued in Silver Surfer Annual #5	$0.50	$1.50	$2.50	£0.30	£0.90	£1.50
3 ND 64pgs, pre-bagged with trading card introducing Assassin	$0.60	$1.80	$3.00	£0.35	£1.05	£1.75
4 ND 64pgs	$0.60	$1.80	$3.00	£0.35	£1.05	£1.75
Title Value:	$2.20	$6.60	$11.00	£1.30	£3.90	£6.50

NATHANIEL DUSK

DC Comics,MS; 1 Feb 1984-4 May 1984

	$Good	$Fine	$N.Mint	£Good	£Fine	£N.Mint
1-4 ND Gene Colan art	$0.25	$0.75	$1.25	£0.15	£0.45	£0.75
Title Value:	$1.00	$3.00	$5.00	£0.60	£1.80	£3.00

Note: all Direct Sale only, Baxter paper.

NATHANIEL DUSK II

DC Comics,MS; 1 Oct 1985-4 Jan 1986

	$Good	$Fine	$N.Mint	£Good	£Fine	£N.Mint
1-4 ND scarce in the U.K. Gene Colan art	$0.25	$0.75	$1.25	£0.15	£0.45	£0.75
Title Value:	$1.00	$3.00	$5.00	£0.60	£1.80	£3.00

Note: all Baxter paper

NATION OF SNITCHES

DC Comics/Piranha Press,OS; 1 Nov 1990

	$Good	$Fine	$N.Mint	£Good	£Fine	£N.Mint
1 ND Jon Hammer story/concept	$0.60	$1.80	$3.00	£0.40	£1.20	£2.00
Title Value:	$0.60	$1.80	$3.00	£0.40	£1.20	£2.00

NATURE OF THE BEAST

Caliber Press,MS; 1 May 1991-3 1991

	$Good	$Fine	$N.Mint	£Good	£Fine	£N.Mint
1-3 ND black and white	$0.40	$1.20	$2.00	£0.25	£0.75	£1.25
Title Value:	$1.20	$3.60	$6.00	£0.75	£2.25	£3.75

NAUSICAA OF THE VALLEY OF THE WIND

Viz Communications; 1 1988-7 1989

	$Good	$Fine	$N.Mint	£Good	£Fine	£N.Mint
1 ND 64pgs, squarebound begins, Hayau Miyazaki script/art; Moebius bound-in poster at front of book	$0.60	$1.80	$3.00	£0.40	£1.20	£2.00
2-7 ND	$0.60	$1.80	$3.00	£0.40	£1.20	£2.00
Title Value:	$4.20	$12.60	$21.00	£2.80	£8.40	£14.00
Graphic Album #1-4 (1990)				£1.55	£4.65	£7.75
Graphic Novel 5 (1993)				£2.00	£6.00	£10.00
Graphic Novel 6 (May 1995)				£2.00	£6.00	£10.00
Nausicaa of the Valley of Wind Perfect Collection 1 (May 1995) collects the first two volumes in one book				£2.40	£7.20	£12.00

NAUSICAA OF THE VALLEY OF THE WIND VOLUME 2

Viz Communications,MS; 1 1990-5 1991

	$Good	$Fine	$N.Mint	£Good	£Fine	£N.Mint
1-5 ND	$0.60	$1.80	$3.00	£0.40	£1.20	£2.00
Title Value:	$3.00	$9.00	$15.00	£2.00	£6.00	£10.00

NAUSICAA OF THE VALLEY OF THE WIND VOLUME 3

Viz Communications,MS; 1 Feb 1993-3 Apr 1993

	$Good	$Fine	$N.Mint	£Good	£Fine	£N.Mint
1-3 ND	$0.80	$2.40	$4.00	£0.50	£1.50	£2.50
Title Value:	$2.40	$7.20	$12.00	£1.50	£4.50	£7.50
Nausicaa of the Valley of Wind Perfect Collection 2 (Aug 1995) 284pgs, collects volumes 3 and 4				£2.40	£7.20	£12.00

NAUSICAA OF THE VALLEY OF WIND PART 4

Viz Communications,MS; 1 June 1994-5 Oct 1994

	$Good	$Fine	$N.Mint	£Good	£Fine	£N.Mint
1-5 ND Hayao Miyazaki; black and white	$0.60	$1.80	$3.00	£0.40	£1.20	£2.00
Title Value:	$3.00	$9.00	$15.00	£2.00	£6.00	£10.00

NAUSICAA VALLEY OF THE WIND PART 5

Viz Communications,MS; 1 Jul 1995-8 Feb 1996

	$Good	$Fine	$N.Mint	£Good	£Fine	£N.Mint
1 ND Hayao Miyazaki script and art; black and white	$0.50	$1.50	$2.50	£0.30	£0.90	£1.50
2-8 ND Hiyao Miyazaki script and art; black and white	$0.50	$1.50	$2.50	£0.30	£0.90	£1.50
Title Value:	$4.00	$12.00	$20.00	£2.40	£7.20	£12.00

NAVY WAR HEROES

Charlton; 1 Jan 1964-7 Mar/Apr 1965

	$Good	$Fine	$N.Mint	£Good	£Fine	£N.Mint
1 distributed in the U.K.	$1.25	$3.85	$9.00	£0.70	£2.10	£5.00
2-7 distributed in the U.K.	$0.55	$1.70	$4.00	£0.25	£0.85	£2.00
Title Value:	$4.55	$14.05	$33.00	£2.20	£7.20	£17.00

NAZA STONE AGE WARRIOR

Dell; 1 Jan/Mar 1965-9 Mar 1966

	$Good	$Fine	$N.Mint	£Good	£Fine	£N.Mint
1 painted cover	$2.85	$8.50	$20.00	£1.75	£5.25	£12.50
2-4 painted cover	$1.75	$5.25	$12.50	£1.00	£3.00	£7.00
5-8	$1.75	$5.25	$12.50	£1.00	£3.00	£7.00
9 dinosaur cover	$1.75	$5.25	$12.50	£1.00	£3.00	£7.00
Title Value:	$16.85	$50.50	$120.00	£9.75	£29.25	£68.50

Note: limited distribution on the news-stands in the U.K.

NAZRAT

Imperial/Eternity; 1 Dec 1987-6 1988

	$Good	$Fine	$N.Mint	£Good	£Fine	£N.Mint
1-4 ND	$0.30	$0.90	$1.50	£0.20	£0.60	£1.00
5-6 ND Eternity issues	$0.30	$0.90	$1.50	£0.20	£0.60	£1.00
Title Value:	$1.80	$5.40	$9.00	£1.20	£3.60	£6.00

NAZZ, THE

DC Comics,MS; 1 Oct 1990-4 Apr 1991

	$Good	$Fine	$N.Mint	£Good	£Fine	£N.Mint
1-4 ND 48pgs, Bryan Talbot art	$0.80	$2.40	$4.00	£0.50	£1.50	£2.50
Title Value:	$3.20	$9.60	$16.00	£2.00	£6.00	£10.00

Note: Mature Readers, Prestige Format. Delays occurred owing to production problems.

NEAR MYTHS

Rip Off Press,OS; 1 1990

	$Good	$Fine	$N.Mint	£Good	£Fine	£N.Mint
1 ND Trina Robbins script and art	$0.40	$1.20	$2.00	£0.25	£0.75	£1.25
Title Value:	$0.40	$1.20	$2.00	£0.25	£0.75	£1.25

NEAT STUFF

Fantagraphics,Magazine; 1 Jul 1985-15 1990

	$Good	$Fine	$N.Mint	£Good	£Fine	£N.Mint
1 ND scarce in the U.K. Bagge story/art begins; 8" x 11" black and white format begins	$1.50	$4.50	$7.50	£1.00	£3.00	£5.00
1 2nd printing ND	$0.60	$1.80	$3.00	£0.40	£1.20	£2.00
2 ND	$1.00	$3.00	$5.00	£0.70	£2.10	£3.50
2 2nd printing ND	$0.40	$1.20	$2.00	£0.25	£0.75	£1.25
3 ND	$0.60	$1.80	$3.00	£0.40	£1.20	£2.00
3 2nd printing, ND (Oct 1991)	$0.40	$1.20	$2.00	£0.25	£0.75	£1.25
4 ND	$0.60	$1.80	$3.00	£0.40	£1.20	£2.00
4 2nd printing, ND (Apr 1992)	$0.40	$1.20	$2.00	£0.25	£0.75	£1.25

	$Good	$Fine	$N.Mint	£Good	£Fine	£N.Mint
5 ND	$0.60	$1.80	$3.00	£0.40	£1.20	£2.00
5 2nd printing, ND (Jul 1992)	$0.40	$1.20	$2.00	£0.25	£0.75	£1.25
6 ND	$0.50	$1.50	$2.50	£0.30	£0.90	£1.50
6 2nd printing, ND (Dec 1992)	$0.40	$1.20	$2.00	£0.25	£0.75	£1.25
7-9 ND	$0.50	$1.50	$2.50	£0.30	£0.90	£1.50
9 2nd printing, ND (Apr 1994)	$0.40	$1.20	$2.00	£0.25	£0.75	£1.25
10-12 ND	$0.50	$1.50	$2.50	£0.30	£0.90	£1.50
12 2nd printing, ND (Jun 1994)	$0.40	$1.20	$2.00	£0.25	£0.75	£1.25
13-15 ND	$0.50	$1.50	$2.50	£0.30	£0.90	£1.50
15 2nd printing, ND (Nov 1994)	$0.40	$1.20	$2.00	£0.25	£0.75	£1.25
Title Value:	$13.10	$39.30	$65.50	£8.30	£24.90	£41.50

Note: all Non-Distributed on the news-stands in the U.K.

				£Good	£Fine	£N.Mint
Best of Neat Stuff collection from #1-5, 128pgs				£2.00	£6.00	£10.00

NECROMANCER: SEASON OF THE WITCH

Innovation,MS; 1 May 1991-3 Jul 1991

	$Good	$Fine	$N.Mint	£Good	£Fine	£N.Mint
1-3 ND bi-weekly	$0.40	$1.20	$2.00	£0.25	£0.75	£1.25
Title Value:	$1.20	$3.60	$6.00	£0.75	£2.25	£3.75

NECROMANTRA/LORD PUMPKIN

Malibu Ultraverse,MS; 1 Apr 1995-4 Jul 1995

	$Good	$Fine	$N.Mint	£Good	£Fine	£N.Mint
1-4 ND 40pgs, flip-book format with two stories, Gabriel Gecko and Kyle Hotz art; Godwheel tie-in	$0.50	$1.50	$2.50	£0.30	£0.90	£1.50
Title Value:	$2.00	$6.00	$10.00	£1.20	£3.60	£6.00

NECROPOLIS

Caliber Press,OS; 1 Dec 1995

	$Good	$Fine	$N.Mint	£Good	£Fine	£N.Mint
1 ND 64pgs, Deadworld spin-off; Joseph Micheal Linsner cover	$0.80	$2.40	$4.00	£0.50	£1.50	£2.50
Title Value:	$0.80	$2.40	$4.00	£0.50	£1.50	£2.50

NECROSCOPE

Malibu,MS; 1 Oct 1992-5 Aug 1993

	$Good	$Fine	$N.Mint	£Good	£Fine	£N.Mint
1 ND painted colour art by Daerick Gross begins	$0.60	$1.80	$3.00	£0.40	£1.20	£2.00
1 2nd printing, ND (Dec 1993) - skull hologram on cover	$0.50	$1.50	$2.50	£0.30	£0.90	£1.50
2-5 ND	$0.50	$1.50	$2.50	£0.30	£0.90	£1.50
Title Value:	$3.10	$9.30	$15.50	£1.90	£5.70	£9.50

Note: all Non-Distributed on the news-stands in the U.K.

				£Good	£Fine	£N.Mint
Necroscope Collection Softcover (Sep 1994) Trade paperback reprints mini-series				£2.60	£7.80	£13.00

NECROSCOPE BOOK II: WAMPHYRI

Malibu,MS; 1 Aug 1993-5 1993

	$Good	$Fine	$N.Mint	£Good	£Fine	£N.Mint
1-5 ND Dave Kendall art begins, 8" x 10" format	$0.50	$1.50	$2.50	£0.30	£0.90	£1.50
Title Value:	$2.50	$7.50	$12.50	£1.50	£4.50	£7.50

NEGATIVE BURN

Caliber Press; 1 1992-present

	$Good	$Fine	$N.Mint	£Good	£Fine	£N.Mint
1 ND black and white anthology begins	$0.80	$2.40	$4.00	£0.50	£1.50	£2.50
2 ND	$0.60	$1.80	$3.00	£0.40	£1.20	£2.00
3 ND Bone appears	$2.00	$6.00	$10.00	£1.20	£3.60	£6.00
4-8 ND	$0.50	$1.50	$2.50	£0.30	£0.90	£1.50
9-10 ND Alan Moore's "Songbook"	$0.50	$1.50	$2.50	£0.30	£0.90	£1.50
11 ND Bolland, Gaiman and Moore work featured; Moebius cover	$0.50	$1.50	$2.50	£0.30	£0.90	£1.50
12 ND Bolland, Gaiman and Moore work featured	$0.50	$1.50	$2.50	£0.30	£0.90	£1.50
13 ND 64pgs, Alan Moore's "Songbook" with Neil Gaiman art (!), Brian Bolland art; Strangers in Paradise story	$2.00	$6.00	$10.00	£1.20	£3.60	£6.00
14 ND 48pgs, Alan Moore's "Songbook", Michael T. Gilbert's Mr. Monster, Brian Bolland's Mr. Mamoulian all continue; Bob Burden Flaming Carrot cover	$0.50	$1.50	$2.50	£0.30	£0.90	£1.50
15-18 ND 48pgs, Alan Moore's "Songbook", Brian Bolland's Mr. Mamoulian both continue	$0.50	$1.50	$2.50	£0.30	£0.90	£1.50
19 ND 48pgs, Alan Moore's "Songbook", Brian Bolland's Mr. Mamoulian both continue and Flaming Carrot appears	$0.50	$1.50	$2.50	£0.30	£0.90	£1.50
20 ND 48pgs, Alan Moore's "Songbook", Brian Bolland's Mr. Mamoulian both continue	$0.50	$1.50	$2.50	£0.30	£0.90	£1.50
21 ND 48pgs, Brian Bolland's Mr. Mamoulian continues plus the return of Trollords	$0.50	$1.50	$2.50	£0.30	£0.90	£1.50
22 ND 48pgs, Brian Bolland's Mr. Mamoulian, Moebius painted cover	$0.50	$1.50	$2.50	£0.30	£0.90	£1.50
23 ND 40pgs, Brian Bolland's Mr. Mamoulian	$0.50	$1.50	$2.50	£0.30	£0.90	£1.50
24 ND 40pgs, Brian Bolland's Mr. Mamoulian, Mike Kaluta cover	$0.50	$1.50	$2.50	£0.30	£0.90	£1.50
25 ND 64pgs, Alan Moore and Dave Gibbons Songbook, Guy Davis' Baker Street and David Mack's Kabuki all feature	$0.60	$1.80	$3.00	£0.40	£1.20	£2.00
26 ND 48pgs, Alan Moore's Songbook and Brian Bolland's Mr. Mamoulian	$0.50	$1.50	$2.50	£0.30	£0.90	£1.50
27-29 ND 48pgs, Brian Bolland's Mr. Mamoulian	$0.50	$1.50	$2.50	£0.30	£0.90	£1.50
30 ND 64pgs, Adam Hughes sketchbook, Brian Bolland's Mr. Mamoulian continues	$0.80	$2.40	$4.00	£0.50	£1.50	£2.50
31 ND 64pgs, preview of Jinks by Michael Bendis	$0.80	$2.40	$4.00	£0.50	£1.50	£2.50
32-39 ND 64pgs	$0.80	$2.40	$4.00	£0.50	£1.50	£2.50
40 ND 64pgs, Steve Yeowell cover	$0.80	$2.40	$4.00	£0.50	£1.50	£2.50
Title Value:	$26.80	$80.40	$134.00	£16.40	£49.20	£82.00

				£Good	£Fine	£N.Mint
Negative Burn: Best of Year One (Feb 1995) Trade paperback ND 128pgs, collects best of the stories				£1.30	£3.90	£6.50
Negative Burn: Best of Year two (Feb 1996) Trade paperback ND 128pgs, collects best of the stories				£1.30	£3.90	£6.50

NEIL THE HORSE COMICS & STORIES

AV/Renegade; 1 Feb 1983-10 Dec 1984; 11 Apr 1985-15 1987 ?

(see Charlton Bullseye #2)

	$Good	$Fine	$N.Mint	£Good	£Fine	£N.Mint
1 ND Arn Saba script and art begins; black and white	$0.40	$1.20	$2.00	£0.25	£0.75	£1.25
1 2nd printing ND	$0.30	$0.90	$1.50	£0.20	£0.60	£1.00
2-10 ND	$0.30	$0.90	$1.50	£0.20	£0.60	£1.00
11 ND 1st Renegade issue	$0.30	$0.90	$1.50	£0.20	£0.60	£1.00
12-14 ND	$0.30	$0.90	$1.50	£0.20	£0.60	£1.00
15 ND double size	$0.30	$0.90	$1.50	£0.20	£0.60	£1.00
Title Value:	$4.90	$14.70	$24.50	£3.25	£9.75	£16.25

NEMESIS

A Plus Comics; 1 Sep 1991

	$Good	$Fine	$N.Mint	£Good	£Fine	£N.Mint
1 ND 48pgs, reprints ACG series, new Kurt Schaffenberger cover	$0.40	$1.20	$2.00	£0.25	£0.75	£1.25
Title Value:	$0.40	$1.20	$2.00	£0.25	£0.75	£1.25

NEOMEN

Slave Labor; 1 1987

	$Good	$Fine	$N.Mint	£Good	£Fine	£N.Mint
1 ND Cirocco layouts	$0.40	$1.20	$2.00	£0.25	£0.75	£1.25
Title Value:	$0.40	$1.20	$2.00	£0.25	£0.75	£1.25

NEON CITY

Innovation; 1 May 1991

	$Good	$Fine	$N.Mint	£Good	£Fine	£N.Mint
1 ND black and white	$0.40	$1.20	$2.00	£0.25	£0.75	£1.25
Title Value:	$0.40	$1.20	$2.00	£0.25	£0.75	£1.25

NEON CITY: AFTER THE FALL

Innovation; 1 Sep 1992

	$Good	$Fine	$N.Mint	£Good	£Fine	£N.Mint
1 ND	$0.40	$1.20	$2.00	£0.25	£0.75	£1.25
Title Value:	$0.40	$1.20	$2.00	£0.25	£0.75	£1.25

NEON KNIGHT

Now Comics; 1 Apr 1991

	$Good	$Fine	$N.Mint	£Good	£Fine	£N.Mint
1 ND	$0.40	$1.20	$2.00	£0.25	£0.75	£1.25
Title Value:	$0.40	$1.20	$2.00	£0.25	£0.75	£1.25
Direct Market Special (Apr 1991), reprints				£0.35	£1.05	£1.75

NERVOUS REX

Fantagraphics; 1 1985-10 1986?

	$Good	$Fine	$N.Mint	£Good	£Fine	£N.Mint
1 ND	$0.30	$0.90	$1.50	£0.20	£0.60	£1.00
1 2nd printing ND	$0.30	$0.90	$1.50	£0.20	£0.60	£1.00
2-10 ND	$0.30	$0.90	$1.50	£0.20	£0.60	£1.00
Title Value:	$3.30	$9.90	$16.50	£2.20	£6.60	£11.00
Graphic Novel (1986)				£0.50	£1.50	£2.50

NETHERWORLDS

Adventure; 1 Aug 1988-4 1988

	$Good	$Fine	$N.Mint	£Good	£Fine	£N.Mint
1-4 ND	$0.30	$0.90	$1.50	£0.20	£0.60	£1.00
Title Value:	$1.20	$3.60	$6.00	£0.80	£2.40	£4.00

NEURO JACK

Big Entertainment; 1 Aug 1996-present

	$Good	$Fine	$N.Mint	£Good	£Fine	£N.Mint
1 ND digital artwork by Erika Taguchi	$0.45	$1.35	$2.25	£0.30	£0.90	£1.50
Title Value:	$0.45	$1.35	$2.25	£0.30	£0.90	£1.50

NEUTRO

Dell; 1 Jan 1967

	$Good	$Fine	$N.Mint	£Good	£Fine	£N.Mint
1 rare although distributed in the U.K.	$3.55	$10.50	$25.00	£2.10	£6.25	£15.00
Title Value:	$3.55	$10.50	$25.00	£2.10	£6.25	£15.00

NEW ADVENTURE COMICS

(see Adventure Comics)

NEW ADVENTURES OF SUPERBOY, THE

(see Superboy)

NEW AMERICA

Eclipse,MS; 1 Nov 1987-4 Mar 1988

(see Scout)

	$Good	$Fine	$N.Mint	£Good	£Fine	£N.Mint
1-4 ND Scout spin-off	$0.40	$1.20	$2.00	£0.25	£0.75	£1.25
Title Value:	$1.60	$4.80	$8.00	£1.00	£3.00	£5.00

NEW BOOK OF COMICS

National Periodical Publications; 1 1937-2 Spring 1938

	$Good	$Fine	$N.Mint	£Good	£Fine	£N.Mint
1 rare in the U.S., very rare in the U.K. reprints New Comics #1-4 and More Fun Comics #9; this is the 2nd ever DC annual	$1500.00	$4500.00	$15000.00	£1000.00	£3000.00	£10000.00
2 very rare in the U.K., rare in the U.S. reprints More Fun Comics #15 and #16	$1000.00	$3000.00	$10000.00	£660.00	£2000.00	£6675.00
Title Value:	$2500.00	$7500.00	$25000.00	£1660.00	£5000.00	£16675.00

NEW COMICS

(see Adventure Comics)

NEW DNAGENTS

(see DNAgents)

NEW FORCE

Image,MS; 1 Jan 1996-4 Apr 1996

1 ND Extreme Destroyer part 8, continued in Extreme Destroyer Epilogue; pre-bagged with trading card; Rob Liefeld and Eric Stephenson script, Todd Nauck art

TRADE PAPERBACKS, GRAPHIC NOVELS AND OTHER COLLECTIONS ARE PRICED IN POUNDS STERLING ONLY. CONVERT AT 1.5 FOR DOLLARS.

	$Good	$Fine	$N.Mint	£Good	£Fine	£N.Mint
	$0.50	$1.50	$2.50	£0.30	£0.90	£1.50
2-4 ND	$0.50	$1.50	$2.50	£0.30	£0.90	£1.50
Title Value:	$2.00	$6.00	$10.00	£1.20	£3.60	£6.00

NEW FRONTIER, THE

Dark Horse,MS; 1 Dec 1992-3 Feb 1993

	$Good	$Fine	$N.Mint	£Good	£Fine	£N.Mint
1-3 ND spin-off from Heavy Metal magazine	$0.50	$1.50	$2.50	£0.30	£0.90	£1.50
Title Value:	$1.50	$4.50	$7.50	£0.90	£2.70	£4.50

NEW FRONTIERS

Evolution Comics; 1,2 1991

	$Good	$Fine	$N.Mint	£Good	£Fine	£N.Mint
1 ND	$0.40	$1.20	$2.00	£0.25	£0.75	£1.25
1 2nd printing, ND Curt Swan cover	$0.30	$0.90	$1.50	£0.20	£0.60	£1.00
2 ND	$0.40	$1.20	$2.00	£0.25	£0.75	£1.25
2 2nd printing ND	$0.30	$0.90	$1.50	£0.20	£0.60	£1.00
Title Value:	$1.40	$4.20	$7.00	£0.90	£2.70	£4.50

NEW FUN COMICS

(see More Fun Comics)

NEW GODS, THE

DC Comics; 1 Feb/Mar 1971-11 Oct/Nov 1972; 12 Jul 1977-19 Jul/Aug 1978

(see Adventure Comics, First Issue Special, Super-Team Family)

	$Good	$Fine	$N.Mint	£Good	£Fine	£N.Mint
1 Jack Kirby art begins, X-over Forever People #1, 1st full appearance Darkseid (see Forever People #1)	$7.00	$21.00	$50.00	£3.55	£10.50	£25.00
2 2nd full appearance Darkseid, Darkseid on cover	$5.00	$15.00	$30.00	£2.50	£7.50	£15.00
3	$3.75	$11.00	$22.50	£2.05	£6.25	£12.50
4-5 52pgs, Joe Simon & Jack Kirby Manhunter reprints	$2.50	$7.50	$15.00	£1.65	£5.00	£10.00
6 52pgs, Joe Simon & Jack Kirby Manhunter reprints	$2.50	$7.50	$15.00	£1.25	£3.75	£7.50
7 52pgs, Joe Simon & Jack Kirby Manhunter reprints, part origin Darkseid	$2.50	$7.50	$15.00	£1.25	£3.75	£7.50
8-9 52pgs, Joe Simon & Jack Kirby Manhunter reprints	$2.50	$7.50	$15.00	£1.25	£3.75	£7.50
10	$2.05	$6.25	$12.50	£1.00	£3.00	£6.00
11 last Jack Kirby art	$2.05	$6.25	$12.50	£1.00	£3.00	£6.00
12 scarce in the U.K.	$1.25	$3.75	$7.50	£0.50	£1.50	£3.00
13-19	$1.25	$3.75	$7.50	£0.40	£1.25	£2.50
Title Value:	$44.85	$134.50	$277.50	£21.70	£65.50	£135.00

Note: 12-19 titled "Return of the New Gods" on cover only.

FEATURES

New Gods in all issues. Young Gods in 5,7,8.

NEW GODS, THE (2ND SERIES)

DC Comics; 1 Feb 1989-28 Jul 1991

	$Good	$Fine	$N.Mint	£Good	£Fine	£N.Mint
1-6	$0.30	$0.90	$1.50	£0.20	£0.60	£1.00
7-10 Bloodline story	$0.30	$0.90	$1.50	£0.20	£0.60	£1.00
11-12 Bloodline story	$0.25	$0.75	$1.25	£0.15	£0.45	£0.75
13-24	$0.25	$0.75	$1.25	£0.15	£0.45	£0.75
25 Forever People guest-star	$0.25	$0.75	$1.25	£0.15	£0.45	£0.75
26-28	$0.25	$0.75	$1.25	£0.15	£0.45	£0.75
Title Value:	$7.50	$22.50	$37.50	£4.70	£14.10	£23.50

Note: New Format

NEW GODS, THE (3RD SERIES)

DC Comics; 1 Oct 1995-15 Feb 1997

	$Good	$Fine	$N.Mint	£Good	£Fine	£N.Mint
1 Darkseid appears; Tom Peyer and Rachel Pollack script, Luke Ross and Brian Garvey art begins	$0.40	$1.20	$2.00	£0.25	£0.75	£1.25
2-3 Darkseid appears	$0.40	$1.20	$2.00	£0.25	£0.75	£1.25
4-6	$0.40	$1.20	$2.00	£0.25	£0.75	£1.25
7-9 Darkseid appears	$0.40	$1.20	$2.00	£0.25	£0.75	£1.25
10 ND Darkseid appears, Superman guest-stars	$0.40	$1.20	$2.00	£0.25	£0.75	£1.25
11 ND	$0.40	$1.20	$2.00	£0.25	£0.75	£1.25
12 ND John Byrne script and art begins, Walt Simonson cover; special 99 cents cover price	$0.20	$0.60	$1.00	£0.10	£0.40	£0.70
13 ND Takion appears	$0.40	$1.20	$2.00	£0.25	£0.75	£1.25
14 ND Forever People appear	$0.40	$1.20	$2.00	£0.25	£0.75	£1.25
15 ND leads into Jack Kirby's Fourth World #1	$0.40	$1.20	$2.00	£0.25	£0.75	£1.25
Title Value:	$5.80	$17.40	$29.00	£3.60	£10.90	£18.20

NEW GODS, THE (LIMITED SERIES)

DC Comics,MS; 1 May 1984-6 Nov 1984

	$Good	$Fine	$N.Mint	£Good	£Fine	£N.Mint
1 48pgs, new Jack Kirby covers begin, reprints New Gods #1, #2; Darkseid cover	$0.50	$1.50	$2.50	£0.30	£0.90	£1.50
2 48pgs, reprints New Gods #3, #4	$0.50	$1.50	$2.50	£0.30	£0.90	£1.50
3 48pgs, reprints New Gods #5, #6	$0.50	$1.50	$2.50	£0.30	£0.90	£1.50
4 48pgs, reprints New Gods #7, #8	$0.50	$1.50	$2.50	£0.30	£0.90	£1.50
5 48pgs, reprints New Gods #9, #10	$0.50	$1.50	$2.50	£0.30	£0.90	£1.50
6 scarce in the U.K. 72pgs, new story and art by Jack Kirby (48pgs); reprints New Gods #11	$0.50	$1.50	$2.50	£0.40	£1.20	£2.00
Title Value:	$3.00	$9.00	$15.00	£1.90	£5.70	£9.50

Note: all Direct Sale, Baxter paper.

NEW GUARDIANS, THE

DC Comics; 1 Oct 1988-12 Sep 1989

(see Millennium)

	$Good	$Fine	$N.Mint	£Good	£Fine	£N.Mint
1 ND DS	$0.15	$0.45	$0.75	£0.10	£0.35	£0.60
2-5	$0.15	$0.45	$0.75	£0.10	£0.35	£0.60
6-7 Invasion X-over	$0.15	$0.45	$0.75	£0.10	£0.35	£0.60
8-12	$0.15	$0.45	$0.75	£0.10	£0.35	£0.60
Title Value:	$1.80	$5.40	$9.00	£1.20	£4.20	£7.20

Note: Deluxe Format, Mando paper

NEW HUMANS

Pied Piper; 1 Jul 1987-3 1987

	$Good	$Fine	$N.Mint	£Good	£Fine	£N.Mint
1-2 ND Ex-Mutants spin-off, Ron Lim cover and art	$0.40	$1.20	$2.00	£0.25	£0.75	£1.25
3 ND Ex-Mutants spin-off, Jack Snider and Jeff Dee art	$0.40	$1.20	$2.00	£0.25	£0.75	£1.25
Title Value:	$1.20	$3.60	$6.00	£0.75	£2.25	£3.75

NEW HUMANS (2ND SERIES)

Eternity; 1 Dec 1987-15 1989

	$Good	$Fine	$N.Mint	£Good	£Fine	£N.Mint
1-3 40pgs, reprints Pied Piper material, black and white	$0.40	$1.20	$2.00	£0.25	£0.75	£1.25
4 40pgs, all new material begins; sub-titled "The Shattered Earth Chronicles"	$0.40	$1.20	$2.00	£0.25	£0.75	£1.25
5-10 40pgs	$0.40	$1.20	$2.00	£0.25	£0.75	£1.25
11-15 40pgs	$0.30	$0.90	$1.50	£0.20	£0.60	£1.00
Title Value:	$5.50	$16.50	$27.50	£3.50	£10.50	£17.50

Note: all Non-Distributed on the news-stands in the U.K.

Mystery In Space #76

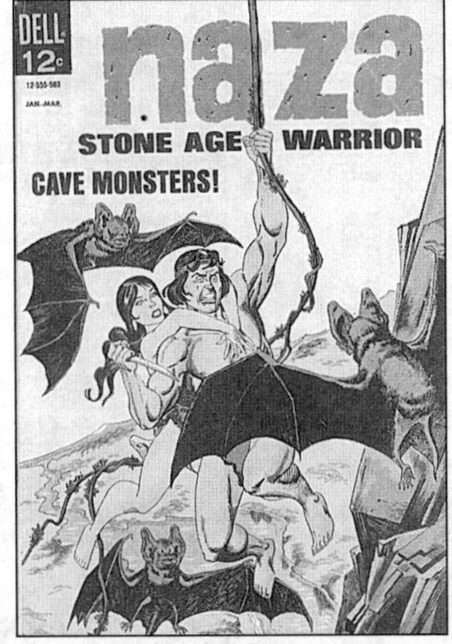

Naza, Stone Age Warrior #5

New Gods (1st) #4

NEW HUMANS ANNUAL

Eternity; 1 Jan 1989

	$Good	$Fine	$N.Mint	£Good	£Fine	£N.Mint
1 ND 60pgs, squarebound, black and white	$0.50	$1.50	$2.50	£0.30	£0.90	£1.50
Title Value:	$0.50	$1.50	$2.50	£0.30	£0.90	£1.50

NEW MAN

Image; 1 Jan 1996-4 1996

	$Good	$Fine	$N.Mint	£Good	£Fine	£N.Mint
1 ND Extreme Destroyer part 3, continued in Youngblood [2nd Series] #4; pre-bagged with trading card; Rob Liefeld script, Fabio Laguna art	$0.50	$1.50	$2.50	£0.30	£0.90	£1.50
2 ND guest-starring WildC.A.T.S.	$0.50	$1.50	$2.50	£0.30	£0.90	£1.50
3 ND	$0.50	$1.50	$2.50	£0.30	£0.90	£1.50
4 ND Shadowhunt part 5, guest-starring Youngblood	$0.50	$1.50	$2.50	£0.30	£0.90	£1.50
Title Value:	$2.00	$6.00	$10.00	£1.20	£3.60	£6.00

NEW MUTANTS

Marvel Comics Group; 1 Mar 1983-100 Apr 1991

(see Fallen Angels, Marvel Graphic Novel, Marvel Team Up #100 and Annual #6, Mutant Summer Fun, Rom Annual #2, Spellbound #4, Web of Spiderman Annual #2)

	$Good	$Fine	$N.Mint	£Good	£Fine	£N.Mint
1 ND	$1.40	$4.20	$7.00	£0.80	£2.40	£4.00
2-5 very LD	$0.80	$2.40	$4.00	£0.40	£1.20	£2.00
6	$0.60	$1.80	$3.00	£0.30	£0.90	£1.50
7 LD in the U.K.	$0.60	$1.80	$3.00	£0.40	£1.20	£2.00
8-13	$0.60	$1.80	$3.00	£0.30	£0.90	£1.50
14 LD in the U.K. X-over X-Men #180	$0.50	$1.50	$2.50	£0.40	£1.20	£2.00
15-16 LD in the U.K.	$0.50	$1.50	$2.50	£0.40	£1.20	£2.00
17 LD in the U.K. Sienkiewicz cover (with June Brigman)	$0.50	$1.50	$2.50	£0.40	£1.20	£2.00
18 1st Sienkiewicz art (ends #38), 1st New Mutants cybernetic Warlock (no relation to Adam Warlock), 1st full Sienkiewicz cover	$1.00	$3.00	$5.00	£0.50	£1.50	£2.50
19 2nd Sienkiewicz art	$0.50	$1.50	$2.50	£0.40	£1.20	£2.00
20 Sienkiewicz art	$0.60	$1.80	$3.00	£0.40	£1.20	£2.00
21 DS Sienkiewicz art	$1.00	$3.00	$5.00	£0.70	£2.10	£3.50
22 Nightcrawler and Cyclops appear; Sienkiewicz art	$0.50	$1.50	$2.50	£0.30	£0.90	£1.50
23 Cloak & Dagger, Nightcrawler and Cyclops appear, Sienkiewicz art	$0.50	$1.50	$2.50	£0.30	£0.90	£1.50
24 Cloak & Dagger appear, Sienkiewicz art	$0.50	$1.50	$2.50	£0.30	£0.90	£1.50
25 1st appearance Legion (cameo), Sienkiewicz art	$1.60	$4.80	$8.00	£0.80	£2.40	£4.00
26 1st full appearance Legion, Sienkiewicz art	$2.00	$6.00	$10.00	£1.00	£3.00	£5.00
27 1st appearance Legion in costume, Sienkiewicz art	$0.90	$2.70	$4.50	£0.60	£1.80	£3.00
28 origin of Legion, Sienkiewicz art	$0.90	$2.70	$4.50	£0.60	£1.80	£3.00
29 1st appearance Guido, Sienkiewicz art; ties into Secret Wars II #1	$0.50	$1.50	$2.50	£0.30	£0.90	£1.50
30 Secret Wars II X-over, Dazzler appears; Sienkiewicz art	$0.50	$1.50	$2.50	£0.30	£0.90	£1.50
31 LD in the U.K. Sienkiewicz cover	$0.40	$1.20	$2.00	£0.25	£0.75	£1.25
32-33 LD in the U.K. Storm appears	$0.40	$1.20	$2.00	£0.25	£0.75	£1.25
34 LD in the U.K. X-over New Mutants Special Edition, Storm appears	$0.40	$1.20	$2.00	£0.25	£0.75	£1.25
35 LD in the U.K. Sienkiewicz inks	$0.40	$1.20	$2.00	£0.25	£0.75	£1.25
36-37 LD in the U.K. Secret Wars X-over, Sienkiewicz inks	$0.40	$1.20	$2.00	£0.30	£0.90	£1.50
38 LD in the U.K. Sienkiewicz inks	$0.40	$1.20	$2.00	£0.25	£0.75	£1.25
39 LD in the U.K. Sienkiewicz cover	$0.40	$1.20	$2.00	£0.25	£0.75	£1.25
40 LD in the U.K. Magneto vs. Avengers	$0.40	$1.20	$2.00	£0.30	£0.90	£1.50
41-42	$0.30	$0.90	$1.50	£0.20	£0.60	£1.00
43 Whilce Portacio inks	$0.30	$0.90	$1.50	£0.20	£0.60	£1.00
44 Legion appears	$0.30	$0.90	$1.50	£0.20	£0.60	£1.00
45	$0.30	$0.90	$1.50	£0.20	£0.60	£1.00
46 X-Men appear, Mutant Massacre tie-in	$0.40	$1.20	$2.00	£0.25	£0.75	£1.25
47-49	$0.30	$0.90	$1.50	£0.20	£0.60	£1.00
50 DS	$0.50	$1.50	$2.50	£0.30	£0.90	£1.50
51 Kevin Nowlan art	$0.30	$0.90	$1.50	£0.20	£0.60	£1.00
52 Sienkiewicz cover	$0.30	$0.90	$1.50	£0.20	£0.60	£1.00
53-56	$0.30	$0.90	$1.50	£0.20	£0.60	£1.00
57 Kevin Nowlan art	$0.30	$0.90	$1.50	£0.20	£0.60	£1.00
58	$0.30	$0.90	$1.50	£0.20	£0.60	£1.00
59 ND Fall of the Mutants begins	$0.60	$1.80	$3.00	£0.40	£1.20	£2.00
60 DS, Fall of the Mutants	$0.50	$1.50	$2.50	£0.30	£0.90	£1.50
61 Fall of the Mutants	$0.40	$1.20	$2.00	£0.25	£0.75	£1.25
62 Jon J. Muth art, Miller cover	$0.30	$0.90	$1.50	£0.20	£0.60	£1.00
63 X-Men/Wolverine appear (clones)	$0.50	$1.50	$2.50	£0.30	£0.90	£1.50
64-70	$0.30	$0.90	$1.50	£0.20	£0.60	£1.00
71-72 LD in the U.K. Inferno x-over	$0.40	$1.20	$2.00	£0.25	£0.75	£1.25
73 LD in the U.K. DS Inferno x-over	$0.50	$1.50	$2.50	£0.30	£0.90	£1.50
74	$0.30	$0.90	$1.50	£0.20	£0.60	£1.00
75 Sabretooth appears, John Byrne art	$0.40	$1.20	$2.00	£0.25	£0.75	£1.25
76 X-Factor, X-Terminators appear	$0.40	$1.20	$2.00	£0.25	£0.75	£1.25
77	$0.30	$0.90	$1.50	£0.20	£0.60	£1.00
78 Dr. Strange appears	$0.30	$0.90	$1.50	£0.20	£0.60	£1.00
79-82	$0.30	$0.90	$1.50	£0.20	£0.60	£1.00
83-84 Acts of Vengeance tie-in	$0.30	$0.90	$1.50	£0.20	£0.60	£1.00
85 Acts of Vengeance tie-in; Rob Liefeld cover art	$0.30	$0.90	$1.50	£0.20	£0.60	£1.00
86 Acts of Vengeance tie-in, Rob Liefeld art begins, Cable appears in last panel though un-named	$2.00	$6.00	$10.00	£0.90	£2.70	£4.50
87 1st appearance Cable, Rob Liefeld art	$5.50	$16.50	$28.00	£1.20	£3.60	£6.00
87 2nd printing, ND Jan 1991, metallic ink cover	$0.50	$1.50	$2.50	£0.30	£0.90	£1.50
88 Rob Liefeld art, 2nd appearance Cable	$2.40	$7.00	$12.00	£0.80	£2.40	£4.00
89 Rob Liefeld art	$1.60	$4.80	$8.00	£0.70	£2.10	£3.50
90 Sabretooth appears, Rob Liefeld art	$1.60	$4.80	$8.00	£0.70	£2.10	£3.50
91 Sabretooth appears, Rob Liefeld art	$1.60	$4.80	$8.00	£0.60	£1.80	£3.00
92 Rob Liefeld cover only (not interior art)	$0.80	$2.40	$4.00	£0.50	£1.50	£2.50
93-94 Wolverine vs. Cable, Rob Liefeld art	$1.60	$4.80	$8.00	£0.60	£1.80	£3.00
95 The X-Tinction Agenda part 2 (see X-Men #270 for start of story), death of New Mutants' Warlock, Rob Liefeld art	$1.60	$4.80	$8.00	£0.70	£2.10	£3.50
95 2nd printing, ND The X-Tinction Agenda part 2 (gold cover)	$0.70	$2.10	$3.50	£0.40	£1.20	£2.00
96 The X-Tinction Agenda part 5, Rob Liefeld art	$1.60	$4.80	$8.00	£0.60	£1.80	£3.00
97 The X-Tinction Agenda part 8, Wolverine appears, Rob Liefeld cover	$1.60	$4.80	$8.00	£0.60	£1.80	£3.00
98 1st appearance Deadpool, Rob Liefeld art	$2.00	$6.00	$10.00	£0.70	£2.10	£3.50
99 LD in the U.K. 1st appearance Feral, Rob Liefeld art	$1.60	$4.80	$8.00	£0.60	£1.80	£3.00
100 48pgs, Cable assembles X-Force (see X-Force #1), Rob Liefeld art	$1.60	$4.80	$8.00	£0.50	£1.50	£2.50
100 2nd printing, ND 48pgs, (Aug 1990, gold cover)	$0.50	$1.50	$2.50	£0.30	£0.90	£1.50
100 3rd printing, ND 48pgs, (silver cover)	$0.40	$1.20	$2.00	£0.25	£0.75	£1.25
Title Value:	$72.40	$217.00	$359.00	£37.10	£111.30	£185.50

Demon Bear (1991),

	£Good	£Fine	£N.Mint
Trade paperback ND reprints, new Sienkiewicz cover	£1.00	£3.00	£5.00
ND 2nd print (Sep 1992), new cover by Bill Sienkiewicz	£1.20	£3.60	£6.00

X-Force Magazine (Nov 1996)

	£Good	£Fine	£N.Mint
ND 96pgs, reprints New Mutants #98-100	£0.50	£1.50	£2.50

NEW MUTANTS ANNUAL, THE

Marvel Comics Group; 1 1984-7 1991

	$Good	$Fine	$N.Mint	£Good	£Fine	£N.Mint
1 ND	$0.90	$2.70	$4.50	£0.50	£1.50	£2.50
2 ND Captain Britain and Psylocke (1st appearance) by Davis/Neary (pre Excalibur #1)	$2.00	$6.00	$10.00	£0.70	£2.10	£3.50
3 ND Davis/Neary art	$0.50	$1.50	$2.50	£0.30	£0.90	£1.50
4 ND 64pgs, Evolutionary War	$0.50	$1.50	$2.50	£0.30	£0.90	£1.50
5 ND squarebound, Atlantis Attacks part 9, 1st Rob Liefeld art on New Mutants	$1.00	$3.00	$5.00	£0.50	£1.50	£2.50
6 ND Days of Future Past/Present story, Cable appears, Rob Liefeld art; 1st appearance Shatterstar (cameo)	$0.50	$1.50	$2.50	£0.30	£0.90	£1.50
7 ND Kings of Pain part 1, continued in New Warriors Annual #1	$0.50	$1.50	$2.50	£0.30	£0.90	£1.50
Title Value:	$5.90	$17.70	$29.50	£2.90	£8.70	£14.50

NEW MUTANTS ONE-SHOT

Marvel Comics Group,OS; nn Oct 1994

	$Good	$Fine	$N.Mint	£Good	£Fine	£N.Mint
nn ND 48pgs, reprints Marvel Graphic Novel #4	$1.00	$3.00	$5.00	£0.70	£2.10	£3.50
Title Value:	$1.00	$3.00	$5.00	£0.70	£2.10	£3.50

NEW MUTANTS SPECIAL

Marvel Comics Group,OS; 1 1985

	$Good	$Fine	$N.Mint	£Good	£Fine	£N.Mint
1 ND 60pgs, Art Adams art, ties in with X-Men/Alpha Flight MS, X-Men Annual #9	*$1.00*	*$3.00*	*$5.00*	£0.70	£2.10	£3.50
Title Value:	*$1.00*	*$3.00*	*$5.00*	£0.70	£2.10	£3.50

NEW MUTANTS SUMMER SPECIAL

Marvel Comics Group,OS; 1 Summer 1990

	$Good	$Fine	$N.Mint	£Good	£Fine	£N.Mint
1 ND 80pgs	*$0.60*	*$1.80*	*$3.00*	£0.40	£1.20	£2.00
Title Value:	*$0.60*	*$1.80*	*$3.00*	£0.40	£1.20	£2.00

NEW ORDER HANDBOOK

Image,OS; nn Feb 1995

	$Good	$Fine	$N.Mint	£Good	£Fine	£N.Mint
nn ND guide to Image titles cover-dated February 1995; "New Order" is an attempt at tighter continuity and a jumping-off point for new readers at the time	*$0.30*	*$0.90*	*$1.50*	£0.20	£0.60	£1.00
Title Value:	*$0.30*	*$0.90*	*$1.50*	£0.20	£0.60	£1.00

NEW TALENT SHOWCASE

DC Comics; 1 Jan 1984-19 Oct 1985
(Talent Showcase #16 on)

	$Good	$Fine	$N.Mint	£Good	£Fine	£N.Mint
1 Scott Hampton art	*$0.15*	*$0.45*	*$0.75*	£0.10	£0.35	£0.60
2-3 Scott Hampton	*$0.15*	*$0.45*	*$0.75*	£0.10	£0.35	£0.60
4-17 features new strips and artists	*$0.15*	*$0.45*	*$0.75*	£0.10	£0.35	£0.60
18 Williamson cover	*$0.15*	*$0.45*	*$0.75*	£0.10	£0.35	£0.60
19 features new strips and artists	*$0.15*	*$0.45*	*$0.75*	£0.10	£0.35	£0.60
Title Value:	*$2.85*	*$8.55*	*$14.25*	£1.90	£6.65	£11.40

Note: Direct Sales only therefore not distributed on the news-stands in the U.K.

NEW TEEN TITANS (1ST SERIES)

DC Comics; 1 Nov 1980-91 Jul 1988
(see Best of DC #18, Teen Titans, The New Titans, Marvel and DC present)
(becomes Tales of the Teen Titans with issue #41)

	$Good	$Fine	$N.Mint	£Good	£Fine	£N.Mint
1 part origin	*$2.00*	*$6.00*	*$10.00*	£1.00	£3.00	£5.00
2 1st appearance Deathstroke the Terminator	*$2.00*	*$6.00*	*$10.00*	£1.00	£3.00	£5.00
3 scarce in the U.K. origin Starfire	*$1.00*	*$3.00*	*$5.00*	£0.70	£2.10	£3.50
4 scarce in the U.K. origin Starfire, Justice League of America X-over, Batman appears (see note below)	*$1.00*	*$3.00*	*$5.00*	£0.70	£2.10	£3.50
5	*$0.60*	*$1.80*	*$3.00*	£0.40	£1.20	£2.00
6 origin Raven	*$0.80*	*$2.40*	*$4.00*	£0.50	£1.50	£2.50
7 origin Cyborg	*$0.80*	*$2.40*	*$4.00*	£0.50	£1.50	£2.50
8 origin Kid Flash re-told	*$0.80*	*$2.40*	*$4.00*	£0.50	£1.50	£2.50
9 2nd appearance Deathstroke the Terminator	*$1.00*	*$3.00*	*$5.00*	£0.60	£1.80	£3.00
10 origin Changeling re-told, 3rd appearance of Deathstroke	*$1.50*	*$4.50*	*$7.50*	£0.50	£1.50	£2.50
11-12	*$0.50*	*$1.50*	*$2.50*	£0.40	£1.20	£2.00
13 very LD Captain Zahl, Madame Rouge appear, Robotman revived	*$0.50*	*$1.50*	*$2.50*	£0.50	£1.50	£2.50
14 LD in the U.K. origin Doom Patrol retold	*$0.50*	*$1.50*	*$2.50*	£0.30	£0.90	£1.50
15 very LD Captain Zahl, Madam Rouge die	*$0.50*	*$1.50*	*$2.50*	£0.30	£0.90	£1.50
16 52pgs, 1st appearance Captain Carrot in 16pg insert	*$0.50*	*$1.50*	*$2.50*	£0.30	£0.90	£1.50
17-18	*$0.50*	*$1.50*	*$2.50*	£0.30	£0.90	£1.50
19 Hawkman X-over	*$0.50*	*$1.50*	*$2.50*	£0.30	£0.90	£1.50
20	*$0.50*	*$1.50*	*$2.50*	£0.30	£0.90	£1.50
21 1st appearance Brother Blood, 1st appearance of The Monitor from Crisis on Infinite Earths (cameo - see G.I. Combat #274), 1st Night Force in 16pg insert	*$0.40*	*$1.20*	*$2.00*	£0.25	£0.75	£1.25
22	*$0.40*	*$1.20*	*$2.00*	£0.25	£0.75	£1,25
23 1st appearance Vigilante (no costume), Blackfire	*$0.40*	*$1.20*	*$2.00*	£0.25	£0.75	£1.25
24 Omega Men X-over	*$0.40*	*$1.20*	*$2.00*	£0.25	£0.75	£1.25
25 Omega Men cameo	*$0.40*	*$1.20*	*$2.00*	£0.25	£0.75	£1.25
26	*$0.40*	*$1.20*	*$2.00*	£0.25	£0.75	£1.25
27 1st appearance Atari Force in 16pg insert	*$0.40*	*$1.20*	*$2.00*	£0.25	£0.75	£1.25
28 1st appearance Terra	*$0.40*	*$1.20*	*$2.00*	£0.25	£0.75	£1.25
29 New Brotherhood of Evil, Speedy appears	*$0.40*	*$1.20*	*$2.00*	£0.25	£0.75	£1.25
30 Terra joins team	*$0.40*	*$1.20*	*$2.00*	£0.25	£0.75	£1.25
31-33	*$0.40*	*$1.20*	*$2.00*	£0.25	£0.75	£1.25
34 Deathstroke appears	*$0.50*	*$1.50*	*$2.50*	£0.25	£0.75	£1.25
35-36	*$0.40*	*$1.20*	*$2.00*	£0.25	£0.75	£1.25
37 X-over Batman and the Outsiders	*$0.40*	*$1.20*	*$2.00*	£0.25	£0.75	£1.25
38 origin Wonder Girl	*$0.40*	*$1.20*	*$2.00*	£0.25	£0.75	£1.25
39 last appearance Dick Grayson as Robin the Boy Wonder	*$0.40*	*$1.20*	*$2.00*	£0.25	£0.75	£1.25
40-41	*$0.40*	*$1.20*	*$2.00*	£0.25	£0.75	£1.25
42 "Judas Contract" story	*$0.40*	*$1.20*	*$2.00*	£0.25	£0.75	£1.25
43 "Judas Contract" story (note: some copies badly mis-cut in production process)	*$0.40*	*$1.20*	*$2.00*	£0.25	£0.75	£1.25
44 "Judas Contract" story continues in Annual #3; origin Terminator (see issue #2 for 1st appearance)	*$0.40*	*$1.20*	*$2.00*	£0.25	£0.75	£1.25
45	*$0.40*	*$1.20*	*$2.00*	£0.25	£0.75	£1.25
46 Aqualad, Aquagirl join	*$0.40*	*$1.20*	*$2.00*	£0.25	£0.75	£1.25
47	*$0.40*	*$1.20*	*$2.00*	£0.25	£0.75	£1.25
48 vs "The RECOMbatants" (unofficial DNAgents X-over)	*$0.40*	*$1.20*	*$2.00*	£0.25	£0.75	£1.25
49	*$0.40*	*$1.20*	*$2.00*	£0.25	£0.75	£1.25
50 DS, Wonder Girl (Donna Troy) weds	*$0.50*	*$1.50*	*$2.50*	£0.30	£0.90	£1.50
51-52	*$0.30*	*$0.90*	*$1.50*	£0.20	£0.60	£1.00
53 1st appearance Azreal (not to be confused with the Jean-Paul Valley character who becomes Azrael and dons the Batman costume)	*$0.30*	*$0.90*	*$1.50*	£0.20	£0.60	£1.00
54-55	*$0.30*	*$0.90*	*$1.50*	£0.20	£0.60	£1.00
56 1st appearance Jinx	*$0.30*	*$0.90*	*$1.50*	£0.20	£0.60	£1.00
57-58	*$0.30*	*$0.90*	*$1.50*	£0.20	£0.60	£1.00
59 reprints 1st appearance (from DC Presents #26)	*$0.30*	*$0.90*	*$1.50*	£0.20	£0.60	£1.00
60 reprints from Baxter (2nd) series begin	*$0.25*	*$0.75*	*$1.25*	£0.15	£0.45	£0.75
61-91 all reprints	*$0.25*	*$0.75*	*$1.25*	£0.15	£0.45	£0.75
Title Value:	*$39.40*	*$118.20*	*$197.00*	£23.95	£71.85	£119.75

Note: issue 4 often has ink-marks on the cover; see Batman 208, Superman 207. Perez art 1-4, 6-34, 37-47,49,50.

NEW TEEN TITANS (1ST SERIES) ANNUAL

DC Comics; 1 Nov 1982-4 1985
(becomes Tales of the Teen Titans Annual with issue #3)

	$Good	$Fine	$N.Mint	£Good	£Fine	£N.Mint
1 48pgs, George Perez art; Omega Men X-over	*$0.40*	*$1.20*	*$2.00*	£0.25	£0.75	£1.25
2 48pgs, George Perez art; 1st Vigilante in costume	*$0.40*	*$1.20*	*$2.00*	£0.25	£0.75	£1.25
3 LD in the U.K. 48pgs, "Judas Contract" story continues from issue #44 (1st Series)	*$0.40*	*$1.20*	*$2.00*	£0.30	£0.90	£1.50
4 48pgs, reprints New Teen Titans Annual #1	*$0.40*	*$1.20*	*$2.00*	£0.25	£0.75	£1.25
Title Value:	*$1.60*	*$4.80*	*$8.00*	£1.05	£3.15	£5.25

NEW TEEN TITANS (2ND SERIES)

DC Comics; 1 Aug 1984-49 Nov 1988
(becomes The New Titans)

	$Good	$Fine	$N.Mint	£Good	£Fine	£N.Mint
1 George Perez cover and art	*$0.80*	*$2.40*	*$4.00*	£0.50	£1.50	£2.50
2-5 George Perez cover and art	*$0.50*	*$1.50*	*$2.50*	£0.30	£0.90	£1.50
6	*$0.40*	*$1.20*	*$2.00*	£0.25	£0.75	£1.25
7 origin Lilith	*$0.40*	*$1.20*	*$2.00*	£0.25	£0.75	£1.25
8 1st appearance Kole (later killed in Crisis on Infinite Earths)	*$0.40*	*$1.20*	*$2.00*	£0.25	£0.75	£1.25
9-12	*$0.40*	*$1.20*	*$2.00*	£0.25	£0.75	£1.25
13-14 Crisis X-over	*$0.40*	*$1.20*	*$2.00*	£0.25	£0.75	£1.25
15	*$0.40*	*$1.20*	*$2.00*	£0.25	£0.75	£1.25
16 Omega Men X-over	*$0.40*	*$1.20*	*$2.00*	£0.25	£0.75	£1.25
17-18	*$0.40*	*$1.20*	*$2.00*	£0.25	£0.75	£1.25
19 George Perez cover	*$0.40*	*$1.20*	*$2.00*	£0.25	£0.75	£1.25
20 George Perez cover; old Titans appear	*$0.40*	*$1.20*	*$2.00*	£0.25	£0.75	£1.25
21-23 George Perez cover	*$0.40*	*$1.20*	*$2.00*	£0.25	£0.75	£1.25
24-36	*$0.40*	*$1.20*	*$2.00*	£0.25	£0.75	£1.25
37 1st $1.75 issue	*$0.40*	*$1.20*	*$2.00*	£0.25	£0.75	£1.25
38 Infinity Inc. appear	*$0.40*	*$1.20*	*$2.00*	£0.25	£0.75	£1.25
39 LD in the U.K.	*$0.40*	*$1.20*	*$2.00*	£0.30	£0.90	£1.50
40 Mike Collins art	*$0.40*	*$1.20*	*$2.00*	£0.25	£0.75	£1.25
41-43	*$0.40*	*$1.20*	*$2.00*	£0.25	£0.75	£1.25
44 old Doom Patrol cameo, Collins art	*$0.40*	*$1.20*	*$2.00*	£0.25	£0.75	£1.25
45-46	*$0.40*	*$1.20*	*$2.00*	£0.25	£0.75	£1.25
47 Titans' origins retold	*$0.40*	*$1.20*	*$2.00*	£0.25	£0.75	£1.25
48-49	*$0.40*	*$1.20*	*$2.00*	£0.25	£0.75	£1.25
Title Value:	*$20.40*	*$61.20*	*$102.00*	£12.75	£38.25	£63.75

Note: all Deluxe Format Baxter paper, all ND.
Perez art 1-5, 19-23; Dan Jurgens 6; Garcia Lopez 7-11

	$Good	$Fine	$N.Mint	£Good	£Fine	£N.Mint
Trade paperback, reprints The Judas Contract from issues #42-44, Annual #3. Also reprints issues #39-41.				£1.20	£3.60	£6.00

NEW TEEN TITANS (2ND SERIES) ANNUAL

DC Comics; 1 Sep 1985-4 1988
(becomes New Titans Annual)

	$Good	$Fine	$N.Mint	£Good	£Fine	£N.Mint
1 ND 48pgs, Superman, new Brainiac appear, 1st appearance Vanguard	*$0.50*	*$1.50*	*$2.50*	£0.30	£0.90	£1.50
2 ND 64pgs, John Byrne cover/art, Jim Baikie, Garcia Lopez art, origin Brother Blood, intro new Dr. Light	*$0.50*	*$1.50*	*$2.50*	£0.30	£0.90	£1.50
3 ND 48pgs, 1st appearance Godiva, Mike Collins art						

	$Good	$Fine	$N.Mint	£Good	£Fine	£N.Mint
	$0.50	$1.50	$2.50	£0.30	£0.90	£1.50
4 ND 48pgs, George Perez cover	$0.50	$1.50	$2.50	£0.30	£0.90	£1.50
Title Value:	$2.00	$6.00	$10.00	£1.20	£3.60	£6.00

NEW TEEN TITANS DRUG AWARENESS CAMPAIGN

Keebler/DC Comics; nn Nov 1983-3 1985

	$Good	$Fine	$N.Mint	£Good	£Fine	£N.Mint
nn George Perez art; white cover, Nancy Reagan foreword, intro The Protector (see note below)	$0.40	$1.20	$2.00	£0.25	£0.75	£1.25
2 ND scarce in the U.K. blue cover, Mando paper	$0.50	$1.50	$2.50	£0.30	£0.90	£1.50
3 ND very scarce in the U.K. orange cover, Mando paper	$0.50	$1.50	$2.50	£0.40	£1.20	£2.00
Title Value:	$1.40	$4.20	$7.00	£0.95	£2.85	£4.75

Note: These drug-propaganda comics were sponsored by Keebler, but after completion of the artwork it was discovered that Robin was licensed to Nabisco, a rival company. He was therefore re-drawn throughout (with no explanation) as "The Protector". Owing to the comics' intended distribution in schools, Starfire's costume was also re-designed to cover her cleavage.

NEW TEEN TITANS, TALES OF THE

DC Comics,MS; 1 Jun 1982-4 Sep 1982

	$Good	$Fine	$N.Mint	£Good	£Fine	£N.Mint
1 origin Cyborg	$0.30	$0.90	$1.50	£0.20	£0.60	£1.00
2 origin Raven	$0.30	$0.90	$1.50	£0.20	£0.60	£1.00
3 origin Changeling	$0.30	$0.90	$1.50	£0.20	£0.60	£1.00
4 origin Starfire	$0.30	$0.90	$1.50	£0.20	£0.60	£1.00
Title Value:	$1.20	$3.60	$6.00	£0.80	£2.40	£4.00

Note: Perez art in 1,2,4.

NEW TITANS

DC Comics; 0 Oct 1994; 50 Dec 1988-130 Feb 1996

(formerly The New Teen Titans [2nd Series])

	$Good	$Fine	$N.Mint	£Good	£Fine	£N.Mint
0 (Oct 1994) Zero Hour X-over, new team formation	$0.40	$1.20	$2.00	£0.25	£0.75	£1.25
50 LD in the U.K. George Perez art	$0.60	$1.80	$3.00	£0.50	£1.50	£2.50
51 LD in the U.K. George Perez art	$0.50	$1.50	$2.50	£0.40	£1.20	£2.00
52-59 George Perez art	$0.50	$1.50	$2.50	£0.30	£0.90	£1.50
60-61 LD in the U.K. X-over with Batman #440-442 (Tim Drake/new Robin story)	$1.00	$3.00	$5.00	£0.40	£1.20	£2.00
62-64 George Perez art	$0.40	$1.20	$2.00	£0.25	£0.75	£1.25
65 Tim Drake Robin and Batman appear	$0.40	$1.20	$2.00	£0.25	£0.75	£1.25
66-69	$0.40	$1.20	$2.00	£0.25	£0.75	£1.25
70 Terminator appears	$0.40	$1.20	$2.00	£0.25	£0.75	£1.25
71 48pgs, New Titans anniversary story begins	$0.50	$1.50	$2.50	£0.30	£0.90	£1.50
72 Aqualad appears; Golden Eagle dies	$0.40	$1.20	$2.00	£0.25	£0.75	£1.25
73-79	$0.40	$1.20	$2.00	£0.25	£0.75	£1.25
80 1st new line up from New Titans Annual 7	$0.40	$1.20	$2.00	£0.25	£0.75	£1.25
81 War of the Gods tie-in	$0.40	$1.20	$2.00	£0.25	£0.75	£1.25
82	$0.40	$1.20	$2.00	£0.25	£0.75	£1.25
83 Jericho vs. Deathstroke the Terminator; death of Jericho	$0.40	$1.20	$2.00	£0.25	£0.75	£1.25
84 death of Raven	$0.40	$1.20	$2.00	£0.25	£0.75	£1.25
85 Aquaman guest stars	$0.40	$1.20	$2.00	£0.25	£0.75	£1.25
86	$0.40	$1.20	$2.00	£0.25	£0.75	£1.25
87 Superman and Deathstroke appear	$0.40	$1.20	$2.00	£0.25	£0.75	£1.25
88-89	$0.40	$1.20	$2.00	£0.25	£0.75	£1.25
90 Total Chaos part 2, continued in Team Titans #1	$0.40	$1.20	$2.00	£0.25	£0.75	£1.25
91 Total Chaos part 5, continued in Team Titans #2	$0.40	$1.20	$2.00	£0.25	£0.75	£1.25
92 Total Chaos part 8, continued in Team Titans #3	$0.40	$1.20	$2.00	£0.25	£0.75	£1.25
93 Titans Sell-Out part 3, continued in Team Titans #4	$0.40	$1.20	$2.00	£0.25	£0.75	£1.25
94-96 Patriot Games story, triptych cover (one part of three that join together)	$0.40	$1.20	$2.00	£0.25	£0.75	£1.25
97 The Darkening part 1	$0.40	$1.20	$2.00	£0.25	£0.75	£1.25
98	$0.40	$1.20	$2.00	£0.25	£0.75	£1.25
99 Nightwing proposes to Starfire	$0.40	$1.20	$2.00	£0.25	£0.75	£1.25
100 48pgs, the wedding of Nightwing and Starfire, foil holografix cover, former Teen Titans guest-star	$0.70	$2.10	$3.50	£0.45	£1.35	£2.25
101 Nightwing and Starfire leave team	$0.40	$1.20	$2.00	£0.25	£0.75	£1.25
102-103	$0.40	$1.20	$2.00	£0.25	£0.75	£1.25
104-107 Terminus: The Fate of Cyborg story, bi-weekly	$0.40	$1.20	$2.00	£0.25	£0.75	£1.25
108 Supergirl, Flash, Lex Luthor and Sarge Steel appear	$0.40	$1.20	$2.00	£0.25	£0.75	£1.25
109	$0.40	$1.20	$2.00	£0.25	£0.75	£1.25
110 Flash and Sarge Steel guest-star	$0.40	$1.20	$2.00	£0.25	£0.75	£1.25
111-113	$0.40	$1.20	$2.00	£0.25	£0.75	£1.25
114 X-over with Damage #6	$0.40	$1.20	$2.00	£0.25	£0.75	£1.25
115 continued in Green Lantern #57	$0.40	$1.20	$2.00	£0.25	£0.75	£1.25
116 continued from Green Lantern #57	$0.40	$1.20	$2.00	£0.25	£0.75	£1.25
117-118	$0.40	$1.20	$2.00	£0.25	£0.75	£1.25
119 continued in Showcase '95 #2	$0.40	$1.20	$2.00	£0.25	£0.75	£1.25
120-121	$0.40	$1.20	$2.00	£0.25	£0.75	£1.25
122 $2.25 cover begin; The Crimelord/Syndicate War part 2, continued in Darkstars #32	$0.45	$1.35	$2.25	£0.40	£1.20	£2.00
123	$0.45	$1.35	$2.25	£0.40	£1.20	£2.00
124 The Siege of Zi Charam part 1, continued in Green Lantern #65	$0.45	$1.35	$2.25	£0.40	£1.20	£2.00
125 48pgs, The Siege of Zi Charam part 5 (conclusion); wraparound cover	$0.80	$2.40	$4.00	£0.50	£1.50	£2.50
126-128 Meltdown story	$0.45	$1.35	$2.25	£0.30	£0.90	£1.50
129	$0.45	$1.35	$2.25	£0.30	£0.90	£1.50
130 Meltdown conclusion, George Perez cover	$0.45	$1.35	$2.25	£0.30	£0.90	£1.50
Title Value:	$36.30	$108.90	$179.50	£22.80	£68.40	£114.00

Note: Deluxe Format

NEW TITANS ANNUAL

DC Comics;5 Aug 1989-11 1996

(formerly New Teen Titans Annual [2nd Series] #1-4)

	$Good	$Fine	$N.Mint	£Good	£Fine	£N.Mint
5 48pgs, George Perez cover	$0.60	$1.80	$3.00	£0.40	£1.20	£2.00
6 48pgs, Grindberg/Cullins/Swan art	$0.60	$1.80	$3.00	£0.40	£1.20	£2.00
7 64pgs, Armageddon: 2001 tie-in	$0.60	$1.80	$3.00	£0.40	£1.20	£2.00
8 64pgs, Eclipso: The Darkness Within tie-in	$0.60	$1.80	$3.00	£0.40	£1.20	£2.00
9 64pgs, Bloodlines part 5, 1st appearance Anima, continued in Superman Annual #5	$0.60	$1.80	$3.00	£0.40	£1.20	£2.00
10 64pgs, Elseworlds story; Marv Wolfman script	$0.60	$1.80	$3.00	£0.40	£1.20	£2.00
11 64pgs, Year One	$0.60	$1.80	$3.00	£0.40	£1.20	£2.00
Title Value:	$4.20	$12.60	$21.00	£2.80	£8.40	£14.00

Note: Deluxe Format

NEW TRIUMPH

Matrix Graphics; 1 Sep 1984-6 1988

	$Good	$Fine	$N.Mint	£Good	£Fine	£N.Mint
1 ND	$0.40	$1.20	$2.00	£0.25	£0.75	£1.25
1 2nd printing, ND ($1.75 cover)	$0.40	$1.20	$2.00	£0.25	£0.75	£1.25
2-6 ND	$0.40	$1.20	$2.00	£0.25	£0.75	£1.25
Title Value:	$2.80	$8.40	$14.00	£1.75	£5.25	£8.75
Annual 1				£0.40	£1.20	£2.00

NEW TRIUMPH FEATURING NORTHGUARD

Matrix Graphics; 1,2 1985

	$Good	$Fine	$N.Mint	£Good	£Fine	£N.Mint
1-2 ND black and white; Canadian independent comic	$0.30	$0.90	$1.50	£0.20	£0.60	£1.00
Title Value:	$0.60	$1.80	$3.00	£0.40	£1.20	£2.00

NEW WARRIORS

Marvel Comics Group; 1 Jul 1990-75 Sep 1996

	$Good	$Fine	$N.Mint	£Good	£Fine	£N.Mint
1 ND Night Thrasher, Namorita, Nova, Marvel Boy, Firestar, Speedball begin	$1.00	$3.00	$5.00	£1.00	£3.00	£5.00
1 2nd printing, ND (Jul 1991, gold ink cover)	$0.40	$1.20	$2.00	£0.30	£0.90	£1.50
2 ND	$0.70	$2.10	$3.50	£0.70	£2.10	£3.50
3 ND	$0.60	$1.80	$3.00	£0.60	£1.80	£3.00
4-5 ND	$0.50	$1.50	$2.50	£0.50	£1.50	£2.50
6 ND Inhumans appear	$0.50	$1.50	$2.50	£0.40	£1.20	£2.00
7-9 ND Punisher appears	$0.50	$1.50	$2.50	£0.40	£1.20	£2.00
10 ND	$0.50	$1.50	$2.50	£0.40	£1.20	£2.00
11-13 ND Forever Yesterday story	$0.50	$1.50	$2.50	£0.30	£0.90	£1.50
14 Namor and Darkhawk appear	$0.50	$1.50	$2.50	£0.30	£0.90	£1.50
15	$0.50	$1.50	$2.50	£0.30	£0.90	£1.50
16 Fantastic Four appear	$0.30	$0.90	$1.50	£0.20	£0.60	£1.00
17 Silver Surfer, Fantastic Four appear	$0.30	$0.90	$1.50	£0.20	£0.60	£1.00
18	$0.30	$0.90	$1.50	£0.20	£0.60	£1.00
19 New Warriors vs. Gideon, new facts about group's origin	$0.30	$0.90	$1.50	£0.20	£0.60	£1.00
20	$0.30	$0.90	$1.50	£0.20	£0.60	£1.00
21	$0.25	$0.75	$1.25	£0.15	£0.45	£0.75
22 Darkhawk and Rage appear	$0.25	$0.75	$1.25	£0.15	£0.45	£0.75
23-24	$0.25	$0.75	$1.25	£0.15	£0.45	£0.75
25 DS, Rage and Darkhawk appear, die-cut cover	$0.50	$1.50	$2.50	£0.30	£0.90	£1.50
26 Rage joins New Warriors	$0.25	$0.75	$1.25	£0.15	£0.45	£0.75
27 Infinity War X-over						

	$Good	$Fine	$N.Mint	£Good	£Fine	£N.Mint
	$0.25	*$0.75*	*$1.25*	£0.15	£0.45	£0.75
28 1st appearance Turbo	*$0.25*	*$0.75*	*$1.25*	£0.15	£0.45	£0.75
29-30	*$0.25*	*$0.75*	*$1.25*	£0.15	£0.45	£0.75
31 X-Force appear	*$0.25*	*$0.75*	*$1.25*	£0.15	£0.45	£0.75
32 Spiderman, Archangel and Dr. Strange appear	*$0.25*	*$0.75*	*$1.25*	£0.15	£0.45	£0.75
33 Cloak and Dagger, Darkhawk appear	*$0.25*	*$0.75*	*$1.25*	£0.15	£0.45	£0.75
34 Spiderman, Avengers, Thing, Torch and Darkhawk appear; concluded in New Warriors Annual #3	*$0.25*	*$0.75*	*$1.25*	£0.15	£0.45	£0.75
35-37	*$0.25*	*$0.75*	*$1.25*	£0.15	£0.45	£0.75
38 ties in to Night Thrasher #1 (on-going series)	*$0.25*	*$0.75*	*$1.25*	£0.15	£0.45	£0.75
39	*$0.25*	*$0.75*	*$1.25*	£0.15	£0.45	£0.75
40 Firelord, Air-Walker and Super-Nova appear	*$0.25*	*$0.75*	*$1.25*	£0.15	£0.45	£0.75
40 Direct Market Edition, ND gold foil enhanced cover	*$0.45*	*$1.35*	*$2.25*	£0.30	£0.90	£1.50
41-42	*$0.25*	*$0.75*	*$1.25*	£0.15	£0.45	£0.75
43 Marvel Boy returns	*$0.25*	*$0.75*	*$1.25*	£0.15	£0.45	£0.75
44	*$0.25*	*$0.75*	*$1.25*	£0.15	£0.45	£0.75
45 X-over with X-Force #32	*$0.25*	*$0.75*	*$1.25*	£0.15	£0.45	£0.75
46 X-Force appear	*$0.25*	*$0.75*	*$1.25*	£0.15	£0.45	£0.75
47 with free Spiderman vs. Venom card sheet	*$0.25*	*$0.75*	*$1.25*	£0.15	£0.45	£0.75
48-49	*$0.25*	*$0.75*	*$1.25*	£0.15	£0.45	£0.75
50 ND Direct Market Edition - 48pgs, glow-in-the-dark cover	*$0.60*	*$1.80*	*$3.00*	£0.40	£1.20	£2.00
50 Newstand Edition 48pgs	*$0.40*	*$1.20*	*$2.00*	£0.25	£0.75	£1.25
51-56	*$0.30*	*$0.90*	*$1.50*	£0.20	£0.60	£1.00
57 Sub-Mariner appears	*$0.30*	*$0.90*	*$1.50*	£0.20	£0.60	£1.00
58-59	*$0.30*	*$0.90*	*$1.50*	£0.20	£0.60	£1.00
60 48pgs, Nova Omega part 2 continued from Nova #18	*$0.45*	*$1.35*	*$2.25*	£0.30	£0.90	£1.50
61 Scarlet Spider joins the team; continued in Spectacular Spiderman #227	*$0.30*	*$0.90*	*$1.50*	£0.20	£0.60	£1.00
62 Maximum Clonage tie-in	*$0.30*	*$0.90*	*$1.50*	£0.20	£0.60	£1.00
63-64 bi-weekly	*$0.30*	*$0.90*	*$1.50*	£0.20	£0.60	£1.00
65 Scarlet Spider appears	*$0.30*	*$0.90*	*$1.50*	£0.20	£0.60	£1.00
66	*$0.30*	*$0.90*	*$1.50*	£0.20	£0.60	£1.00
67 continued from Web of Scarlet Spider #3 and concluded in Web of Scarlet Spider #4	*$0.30*	*$0.90*	*$1.50*	£0.20	£0.60	£1.00
68-69 Future Shock part 1, New Warriors vs. Guardians of the Galaxy	*$0.30*	*$0.90*	*$1.50*	£0.20	£0.60	£1.00
70 Future Shock part 3	*$0.30*	*$0.90*	*$1.50*	£0.20	£0.60	£1.00
71 Future Shock part 4 (conclusion)	*$0.30*	*$0.90*	*$1.50*	£0.20	£0.60	£1.00
72 Avengers appear	*$0.30*	*$0.90*	*$1.50*	£0.20	£0.60	£1.00
73 origin Torpedo	*$0.30*	*$0.90*	*$1.50*	£0.20	£0.60	£1.00
74 the return of Night Thrasher and Namorita	*$0.30*	*$0.90*	*$1.50*	£0.20	£0.60	£1.00
75 48pgs	*$0.50*	*$1.50*	*$2.50*	£0.30	£0.90	£1.50
Title Value:	*$27.00*	*$81.00*	*$135.00*	£18.75	£56.25	£93.75
New Warriors Trade paperback (Aug 1992) reprints Thor #411,412 and New Warriors #1-4, new cover by Mark Bagley				£1.40	£4.20	£7.00

NEW WARRIORS ANNUAL

Marvel Comics Group; 1 Jul 1991-4 1994

	$Good	$Fine	$N.Mint	£Good	£Fine	£N.Mint
1 ND Kings of Pain part 2, feature on origins of New Warriors, Cable and X-force appear	*$0.50*	*$1.50*	*$2.50*	£0.30	£0.90	£1.50
2 ND 64pgs, The Hero Killers part 4, continued from Web of Spiderman Annual #8, Spiderman appears	*$0.50*	*$1.50*	*$2.50*	£0.30	£0.90	£1.50
3 ND 64pgs, pre-bagged with trading card; Spiderman, Archangel, Cloak & Dagger and Darkhawk appear	*$0.60*	*$1.80*	*$3.00*	£0.40	£1.20	£2.00
4 ND 64pgs	*$0.60*	*$1.80*	*$3.00*	£0.40	£1.20	£2.00
Title Value:	*$2.20*	*$6.60*	*$11.00*	£1.40	£4.20	£7.00

NEW WARRIORS ASHCAN EDITION

Marvel Comics Group; nn Aug 1994

	$Good	$Fine	$N.Mint	£Good	£Fine	£N.Mint
nn ND 16pgs, black and white featuring a shorter history of the New Warriors	*$0.25*	*$0.75*	*$1.25*	£0.15	£0.45	£0.75
Title Value:	*$0.25*	*$0.75*	*$1.25*	£0.15	£0.45	£0.75

NEW WAVE

Eclipse; 1 Jun 1986-14 Apr 1987

	$Good	$Fine	$N.Mint	£Good	£Fine	£N.Mint
1 ND 16pgs, 50c cover, bi-weekly; Lee Weeks/Ty Templeton art begins, colour	*$0.25*	*$0.75*	*$1.25*	£0.15	£0.45	£0.75
1 as above with corrected pages, ND that were originally spoiled after printing	*$0.15*	*$0.45*	*$0.75*	£0.10	£0.30	£0.50
2-4 ND	*$0.25*	*$0.75*	*$1.25*	£0.15	£0.45	£0.75
5 ND origin New Wave Team concludes (begun in #1), Paul Gulacy cover	*$0.25*	*$0.75*	*$1.25*	£0.15	£0.45	£0.75
6-8 ND	*$0.25*	*$0.75*	*$1.25*	£0.15	£0.45	£0.75
9 ND 1st monthly issue, $1.50 cover	*$0.25*	*$0.75*	*$1.25*	£0.15	£0.45	£0.75
10-14 ND	*$0.25*	*$0.75*	*$1.25*	£0.15	£0.45	£0.75
Title Value:	*$3.65*	*$10.95*	*$18.25*	£2.20	£6.60	£11.00

NEW WAVE VS THE VOLUNTEERS 3-D

Eclipse; 1 Apr 1987-2 Jun 1987

	$Good	$Fine	$N.Mint	£Good	£Fine	£N.Mint
1-2 ND glasses included (25% less if without glasses)	*$0.40*	*$1.20*	*$2.00*	£0.25	£0.75	£1.25
Title Value:	*$0.80*	*$2.40*	*$4.00*	£0.50	£1.50	£2.50

NEW WORLDS

Caliber Press; 1 May 1996-present

	$Good	$Fine	$N.Mint	£Good	£Fine	£N.Mint
1-3 ND 64pgs, anthology; black and white	*$0.80*	*$2.40*	*$4.00*	£0.50	£1.50	£2.50
Title Value:	*$2.40*	*$7.20*	*$12.00*	£1.50	£4.50	£7.50

NEW YORK WORLD'S FAIR

National Periodical Publications; 1 1939-2 1940

	$Good	$Fine	$N.Mint	£Good	£Fine	£N.Mint
1 very scarce in the U.S. rare in the U.K. produced for the World's Fair; features Superman (only time with blond hair as depicted on cover) and 1st published appearance of the Golden Age Sandman prior to Adventure Comics #40; about 120 extant copies exist	*$2800.00*	*$8400.00*	*$28000.00*	£1875.00	£5600.00	£18750.00
[Very Rare in high grade - Very Fine+ or better]						
2 scarce in the U.K. Superman, Batman and Robin appear (1st time ever together on cover only and can be regarded as a forerunner of World's Best #1 that appeared about 15 months later), Hourman appears	*$1550.00*	*$4650.00*	*$15500.00*	£1025.00	£3050.00	£10250.00
Title Value:	*$4350.00*	*$13050.00*	*$43500.00*	£2900.00	£8650.00	£29000.00

Note: not distributed on the news-stands in the U.K. and no copies known with British pence stamps. As there was much U.K. company presence at the Fair, it is just possible that there are copies to discover in the U.K. – search those attics!

NEW YORK: YEAR ZERO

Eclipse,MS; 1 Aug 1988-3 Oct 1988

	$Good	$Fine	$N.Mint	£Good	£Fine	£N.Mint
1-3 ND	*$0.40*	*$1.20*	*$2.00*	£0.25	£0.75	£1.25

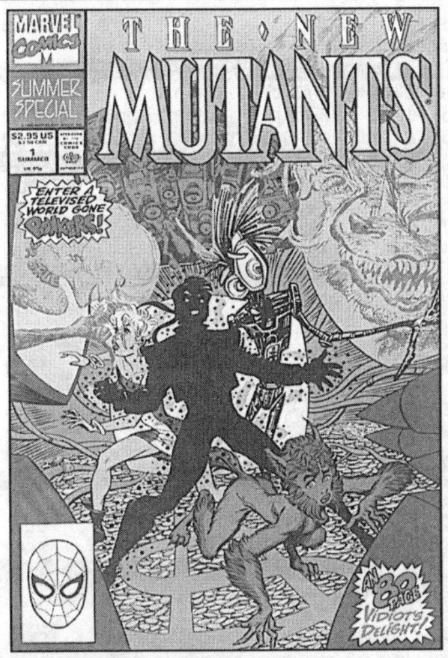

New Mutants Summer Special #1

New Triumph #1

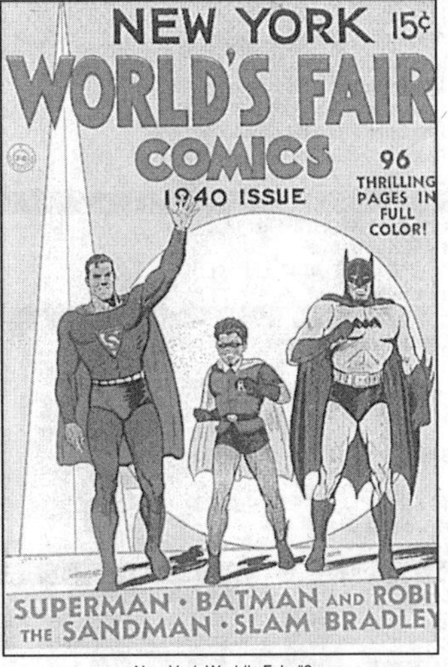

New York World's Fair #2

	$Good	$Fine	$N.Mint	£Good	£Fine	£N.Mint
Title Value:	*$1.20*	*$3.60*	*$6.00*	£0.75	£2.25	£3.75

NEWMAN

Legacy Comics,OS; 1 1991

	$Good	$Fine	$N.Mint	£Good	£Fine	£N.Mint
1 ND black and white	*$0.40*	*$1.20*	*$2.00*	£0.25	£0.75	£1.25
Title Value:	*$0.40*	*$1.20*	*$2.00*	£0.25	£0.75	£1.25

NEWMEN

Image; 1 Apr 1994-20 Nov 1995; 21 Aug 1996-present

	$Good	$Fine	$N.Mint	£Good	£Fine	£N.Mint
1 ND Rob Liefeld amd Eric Stephenson co-plot, Jeff Matsuda and Jonathan Sibal art; 1st appearance Newmen	*$0.50*	*$1.50*	*$2.50*	£0.30	£0.90	£1.50
2-3 ND	*$0.40*	*$1.20*	*$2.00*	£0.25	£0.75	£1.25
4 ND guest-stars Ripclaw	*$0.40*	*$1.20*	*$2.00*	£0.25	£0.75	£1.25
5 ND Newmen and Ripclaw vs. Ikonn	*$0.40*	*$1.20*	*$2.00*	£0.25	£0.75	£1.25
6-7 ND	*$0.40*	*$1.20*	*$2.00*	£0.25	£0.75	£1.25
8-9 ND New Blood story	*$0.40*	*$1.20*	*$2.00*	£0.25	£0.75	£1.25
10 ND Extreme Sacrifice part 4, continued in Team Youngblood #17; pre-bagged with trading card	*$0.40*	*$1.20*	*$2.00*	£0.25	£0.75	£1.25
11-16 ND	*$0.45*	*$1.35*	*$2.25*	£0.30	£0.90	£1.50
16 Variant Cover Edition ND	*$1.00*	*$3.00*	*$5.00*	£0.50	£1.50	£2.50
17-19 ND	*$0.45*	*$1.35*	*$2.25*	£0.30	£0.90	£1.50
20 ND Extreme Babewatch	*$0.50*	*$1.50*	*$2.50*	£0.30	£0.90	£1.50
21-22 ND	*$0.50*	*$1.50*	*$2.50*	£0.30	£0.90	£1.50
Title Value:	*$10.65*	*$31.95*	*$53.25*	£6.65	£19.95	£33.25
Newmen (Jan 1996)						
Trade paperback ND 124pgs, collects issues #1-5				£1.70	£8.50	£8.50

NEWSTIME - THE LIFE AND DEATH OF THE MAN OF STEEL

DC Comics,Magazine OS; 1 May 1993

	$Good	$Fine	$N.Mint	£Good	£Fine	£N.Mint
1 ND magazine based on Newsweek-type with features and interviews following Superman: Doomsday	*$0.60*	*$1.80*	*$3.00*	£0.40	£1.20	£2.00
Title Value:	*$0.60*	*$1.80*	*$3.00*	£0.40	£1.20	£2.00

NEWSTRALIA

Innovation; 1 Jul 1989

	$Good	$Fine	$N.Mint	£Good	£Fine	£N.Mint
1 ND 3pgs layouts by Tim Truman	*$0.30*	*$0.90*	*$1.50*	£0.20	£0.60	£1.00
Title Value:	*$0.30*	*$0.90*	*$1.50*	£0.20	£0.60	£1.00

NEXT MAN

Comico; 1 Mar 1985-5 Oct 1985

	$Good	$Fine	$N.Mint	£Good	£Fine	£N.Mint
1-5 ND	*$0.40*	*$1.20*	*$2.00*	£0.25	£0.75	£1.25
Title Value:	*$2.00*	*$6.00*	*$10.00*	£1.25	£3.75	£6.25

NEXT MEN

Dark Horse; 0 Apr 1992; 1 Jan 1992-30 Dec 1994

	$Good	$Fine	$N.Mint	£Good	£Fine	£N.Mint
0 (Apr 1992), reprints stories in Dark Horse Presents #54-57 in colour, new cover by John Byrne	*$1.00*	*$3.00*	*$5.00*	£0.70	£2.10	£3.50
1 John Byrne script and art begins, silver foil embossed (red) cover	*$1.00*	*$3.00*	*$5.00*	£0.70	£2.10	£3.50
1 2nd printing, (blue cover)	*$0.60*	*$1.80*	*$3.00*	£0.40	£1.20	£2.00
2	*$0.60*	*$1.80*	*$3.00*	£0.40	£1.20	£2.00
3-18	*$0.60*	*$1.80*	*$3.00*	£0.30	£0.90	£1.50
19-22 Faith story	*$0.50*	*$1.50*	*$2.50*	£0.30	£0.90	£1.50
23-26 Power story	*$0.50*	*$1.50*	*$2.50*	£0.30	£0.90	£1.50
27-30 Lies story	*$0.50*	*$1.50*	*$2.50*	£0.30	£0.90	£1.50
Title Value:	*$18.80*	*$56.40*	*$87.00*	£10.60	£31.80	£53.00

Note: all Non-Distributed on the news-stands in the U.K.

				£Good	£Fine	£N.Mint
John Byrne's Next Men Collection (Mar 1993)						
Softcover, reprints #0-6 with new painted cover				£2.00	£6.00	£10.00
Hardcover with dust-jacket				£3.50	£10.50	£17.50
John Byrne's Next Men Collection 2 (1993)						
Trade paperback reprints issues #7-12				£2.00	£6.00	£10.00
John Byrne's Next Men: Fame (Oct 1994)						
Trade paperback reprints issues #13-18, Gary Cody cover				£2.20	£6.60	£11.00
John Byrne's Next Men: Faith (Jan 1995)						
Trade paperback reprints issues #19-22, Gary Cody cover				£2.00	£6.00	£10.00
John Byrne's Next Men: Power (Mar 1995)						
Trade paperback reprints issues #1-4 of Next Men: Power, Gary Cody painted cover				£2.00	£6.00	£10.00

NEXT NEXUS

First,MS; 1 Jan 1989-4 Apr 1989

	$Good	$Fine	$N.Mint	£Good	£Fine	£N.Mint
1-4 ND Steve Rude art	*$0.40*	*$1.20*	*$2.00*	£0.25	£0.75	£1.25
Title Value:	*$1.60*	*$4.80*	*$8.00*	£1.00	£3.00	£5.00

NEXUS (1ST SERIES)

Capital,Magazine; 1 Mar 1981-3 Oct 1982

	$Good	$Fine	$N.Mint	£Good	£Fine	£N.Mint
1 ND scarce in the U.K.	*$3.50*	*$10.50*	*$17.50*	£2.00	£6.00	£10.00
2 ND scarce in the U.K.	*$2.00*	*$6.00*	*$10.00*	£1.50	£4.50	£7.50
3 ND includes the first flex-disc in comics	*$1.60*	*$4.80*	*$8.00*	£1.00	£3.00	£5.00
Title Value:	*$7.10*	*$21.30*	*$35.50*	£4.50	£13.50	£22.50
Nexus Book One						
Trade paperback, reprints #1-3				£1.50	£4.50	£7.50

NEXUS (2ND SERIES)

Capital/First; 1 May 1983-80 Feb 1991

	$Good	$Fine	$N.Mint	£Good	£Fine	£N.Mint
1	*$0.90*	*$2.70*	*$4.50*	£0.50	£1.50	£2.50
2	*$0.70*	*$2.10*	*$3.50*	£0.40	£1.20	£2.00
3 scarce in the U.K.	*$0.70*	*$2.10*	*$3.50*	£0.50	£1.50	£2.50
4-5	*$0.70*	*$2.10*	*$3.50*	£0.40	£1.20	£2.00
6 last Capital issue	*$0.70*	*$2.10*	*$3.50*	£0.40	£1.20	£2.00
7-10	*$0.50*	*$1.50*	*$2.50*	£0.40	£1.20	£2.00
11-20	*$0.40*	*$1.20*	*$2.00*	£0.30	£0.90	£1.50
21-49	*$0.40*	*$1.20*	*$2.00*	£0.25	£0.75	£1.25
50 bookshelf format, Crossroads X-over	*$0.80*	*$2.40*	*$4.00*	£0.50	£1.50	£2.50
51-80	*$0.40*	*$1.20*	*$2.00*	£0.25	£0.75	£1.25
Title Value:	*$34.80*	*$104.40*	*$174.00*	£22.45	£67.35	£112.25

Note: all Non-Distributed on the news-stands in the U.K.

				£Good	£Fine	£N.Mint
Nexus Book One Softcover Collection (Apr 1993)						
reprints issues #1-5 plus new matreial and new painted cover				£2.00	£6.00	£10.00
Nexus Book Two Trade Paperback (Sep 1993)						
reprints issues #6-10 plus new material				£2.00	£6.00	£10.00

NEXUS LEGENDS

First; 1 May 1988-23 Jan 1991

	$Good	$Fine	$N.Mint	£Good	£Fine	£N.Mint
1-23 ND reprints of original Nexus	*$0.30*	*$0.90*	*$1.50*	£0.20	£0.60	£1.00
Title Value:	*$6.90*	*$20.70*	*$34.50*	£4.60	£13.80	£23.00

NEXUS MEETS MADMAN

Dark Horse,OS; nn May 1996

	$Good	$Fine	$N.Mint	£Good	£Fine	£N.Mint
nn ND Mike Baron script, Mike Allred and Steve Rude art	*$0.60*	*$1.80*	*$3.00*	£0.40	£1.20	£2.00
Title Value:	*$0.60*	*$1.80*	*$3.00*	£0.40	£1.20	£2.00

NEXUS THE LIBERATOR

Dark Horse,MS; 1 Oct 1992-4 Jan 1993

	$Good	$Fine	$N.Mint	£Good	£Fine	£N.Mint
1 ND Whilce Portacio cover	*$0.50*	*$1.50*	*$2.50*	£0.30	£0.90	£1.50
2 ND Adam Hughes cover	*$0.50*	*$1.50*	*$2.50*	£0.30	£0.90	£1.50
3 ND Whilce Portacio cover	*$0.50*	*$1.50*	*$2.50*	£0.30	£0.90	£1.50
4 ND Adam Hughes cover	*$0.50*	*$1.50*	*$2.50*	£0.30	£0.90	£1.50
Title Value:	*$2.00*	*$6.00*	*$10.00*	£1.20	£3.60	£6.00

NEXUS: ALIEN JUSTICE

Dark Horse,MS; 1 Dec 1992-3 Feb 1993

	$Good	$Fine	$N.Mint	£Good	£Fine	£N.Mint
1-3 ND Mike Baron script, Steve Rude covers and art	*$0.70*	*$2.10*	*$3.50*	£0.40	£1.20	£2.00
Title Value:	*$2.10*	*$6.30*	*$10.50*	£1.20	£3.60	£6.00

NEXUS: EXECUTIONER'S SONG

Dark Horse,MS; 1 Jun 1996-4 Sep 1996

	$Good	$Fine	$N.Mint	£Good	£Fine	£N.Mint
1-4 ND Mike Baron script, Steve Rude art	*$0.60*	*$1.80*	*$3.00*	£0.40	£1.20	£2.00
Title Value:	*$2.40*	*$7.20*	*$12.00*	£1.60	£4.80	£8.00

NEXUS: OUT OF THE VORTEX

Dark Horse,MS; 1 Feb 1995-5 Jun 1995

	$Good	$Fine	$N.Mint	£Good	£Fine	£N.Mint
1-5 ND Joe Comstock and Brian Kane art	*$0.50*	*$1.50*	*$2.50*	£0.30	£0.90	£1.50
Title Value:	*$2.50*	*$7.50*	*$12.50*	£1.50	£4.50	£7.50

NEXUS: THE ORIGIN

Dark Horse,OS; 1 Jul 1992

	$Good	$Fine	$N.Mint	£Good	£Fine	£N.Mint
1 ND 48pgs, all new origin story by Mike Baron and Steve Rude	*$0.60*	*$1.80*	*$3.00*	£0.40	£1.20	£2.00
Title Value:	*$0.60*	*$1.80*	*$3.00*	£0.40	£1.20	£2.00

NEXUS: WAGES OF SIN

Dark Horse,MS; 1 Mar 1995-4 Jun 1995

	$Good	$Fine	$N.Mint	£Good	£Fine	£N.Mint
1-4 ND Mike Baron script, Steve Rude art	*$0.60*	*$1.80*	*$3.00*	£0.40	£1.20	£2.00
Title Value:	*$2.40*	*$7.20*	*$12.00*	£1.60	£4.80	£8.00

NFL PRO ACTION

Marvel Comics Group,Magazine OS; 1 Feb 1994

	$Good	$Fine	$N.Mint	£Good	£Fine	£N.Mint
1 ND 64pgs, bound-in sheet of trading cards	*$0.40*	*$1.20*	*$2.00*	£0.20	£0.60	£1.00
Title Value:	*$0.40*	*$1.20*	*$2.00*	£0.20	£0.60	£1.00

NFL PRO ACTION (2ND SERIES)

Marvel Comics Group,MS; 1 Aug 1994-4 Nov 1994

	$Good	$Fine	$N.Mint	£Good	£Fine	£N.Mint
1-4 ND 48pgs	*$0.50*	*$1.50*	*$2.50*	£0.20	£0.60	£1.00
Title Value:	*$2.00*	*$6.00*	*$10.00*	£0.80	£2.40	£4.00

NFL SUPERPRO

Marvel Comics Group,OS; 1 Mar 1991

	$Good	$Fine	$N.Mint	£Good	£Fine	£N.Mint
1 ND 48pgs, tied in with Superbowl promotion	*$0.50*	*$1.50*	*$2.50*	£0.20	£0.60	£1.00
Title Value:	*$0.50*	*$1.50*	*$2.50*	£0.20	£0.60	£1.00

NFL SUPERPRO (2ND SERIES)

Marvel Comics Group; 1 Oct 1991-12 1992

	$Good	$Fine	$N.Mint	£Good	£Fine	£N.Mint
1 Spiderman appears	*$0.15*	*$0.45*	*$0.75*	£0.10	£0.30	£0.50
2-4	*$0.15*	*$0.45*	*$0.75*	£0.10	£0.30	£0.50
5 $1.25 cover begins	*$0.15*	*$0.45*	*$0.75*	£0.10	£0.30	£0.50
6-12	*$0.15*	*$0.45*	*$0.75*	£0.10	£0.30	£0.50
Title Value:	*$1.80*	*$5.40*	*$9.00*	£1.20	£3.60	£6.00

NFL SUPERPRO SPECIAL

Marvel Comics Group,OS; 1 Aug 1991

	$Good	$Fine	$N.Mint	£Good	£Fine	£N.Mint
1 ND 48pgs	*$0.40*	*$1.20*	*$2.00*	£0.20	£0.60	£1.00
Title Value:	*$0.40*	*$1.20*	*$2.00*	£0.20	£0.60	£1.00

NICK FURY AND HIS AGENTS OF SHIELD

Marvel Comics Group; 1 Feb 1973-5 Oct 1973

	$Good	$Fine	$N.Mint	£Good	£Fine	£N.Mint
1 ND less common in the U.K. Steranko cover	*$0.80*	*$2.50*	*$5.00*	£0.55	£1.75	£3.50
2-5 ND less common in the U.K. Steranko cover						

	$Good	$Fine	$N.Mint	£Good	£Fine	£N.Mint
	$0.65	$2.00	$4.00	£0.50	£1.50	£3.00
Title Value:	$3.40	$10.50	$21.00	£2.55	£7.75	£15.50
Note: all reprints from Strange Tales #146-155						

NICK FURY ASHCAN

Marvel Comics Group,OS; nn Apr 1995

	$Good	$Fine	$N.Mint	£Good	£Fine	£N.Mint
nn ND 16pgs, black and white; history of Nick Fury and Shield						
	$0.15	$0.45	$0.75	£0.10	£0.30	£0.50
Title Value:	$0.15	$0.45	$0.75	£0.10	£0.30	£0.50

NICK FURY VS SHIELD

Marvel Comics Group,MS; 1 Jun 1988-6 Nov 1988

	$Good	$Fine	$N.Mint	£Good	£Fine	£N.Mint
1 ND Paul Neary art, Steranko cover						
	$1.00	$3.00	$5.00	£0.80	£2.40	£4.00
2 scarce in both US and UK Paul Neary art, Sienkiewicz cover						
	$1.00	$3.00	$5.00	£0.60	£1.80	£3.00
3 ND Paul Neary art, Joe Jusko cover						
	$0.80	$2.40	$4.00	£0.60	£1.80	£3.00
4-6 ND Paul Neary art						
	$0.80	$2.40	$4.00	£0.60	£1.80	£3.00
Title Value:	$5.20	$15.60	$26.00	£3.80	£11.40	£19.00
Note: all are 48pgs, bookshelf format. All painted covers						
Trade paperback (Aug 1989) 276pgs						
reprints 6 issue limited series				£1.60	£4.80	£8.00

NICK FURY, AGENT OF SHIELD

Marvel Comics Group; 1 Jun 1968-18 Mar 1971

(see Double Edge: Omega, Marvel Spotlight #31, Nick Fury Vs Shield, Strange Tales)

	$Good	$Fine	$N.Mint	£Good	£Fine	£N.Mint
1 Steranko art	$7.75	$23.50	$55.00	£5.00	£15.00	£35.00
2 Steranko art	$4.60	$13.50	$32.50	£2.50	£7.50	£17.50
3 Steranko art	$4.25	$12.50	$30.00	£2.10	£6.25	£15.00
4 origin Nick Fury and SHIELD retold						
	$4.25	$12.50	$30.00	£2.10	£6.25	£15.00
5 scarce in the U.K. Steranko art, classic psychedelia cover						
	$5.00	$15.00	$35.00	£2.50	£7.50	£17.50
6 Steranko cover	$2.85	$8.50	$20.00	£1.05	£3.20	£7.50
7 Steranko cover (Salvador Dali imitation)						
	$2.85	$8.50	$20.00	£1.05	£3.20	£7.50
8-9	$1.75	$5.25	$12.50	£0.85	£2.55	£6.00
10 2nd Barry Smith art in comics (3 pgs)						
	$1.75	$5.25	$12.50	£1.00	£3.00	£7.00
11	$1.40	$4.25	$10.00	£0.70	£2.10	£5.00
12 Barry Smith art	$1.75	$5.25	$12.50	£0.85	£2.55	£6.00
13 scarce in the U.K. classic patriotic cover						
	$1.40	$4.25	$10.00	£0.70	£2.10	£5.00
14 ND	$1.05	$3.20	$7.50	£0.70	£2.10	£5.00
15 scarce in the U.K. 1st appearance Bullseye (see Daredevil #131)						
	$3.55	$10.50	$25.00	£2.10	£6.25	£15.00
16 scarce in the U.K. 52pgs, all reprint						
	$0.40	$1.25	$3.00	£0.60	£1.90	£4.50
17-18 very scarce in the U.K. 52pgs, all reprint						
	$0.40	$1.25	$3.00	£0.70	£2.10	£5.00
Title Value:	$47.15	$140.95	$334.00	£26.05	£78.20	£184.50
Note: Steranko covers on #1-7						

NICK FURY, AGENT OF SHIELD (2ND SERIES)

Marvel Comics Group; 1 Sep 1989-47 May 1993

	$Good	$Fine	$N.Mint	£Good	£Fine	£N.Mint
1-5 ND	$0.40	$1.20	$2.00	£0.25	£0.75	£1.25
6 ND	$0.30	$0.90	$1.50	£0.20	£0.60	£1.00
7-9 ND The Chaos Serpent						
	$0.30	$0.90	$1.50	£0.20	£0.60	£1.00
10 ND The Chaos Serpent; Captain America appears						
	$0.30	$0.90	$1.50	£0.20	£0.60	£1.00
11 ND	$0.30	$0.90	$1.50	£0.20	£0.60	£1.00
12-14 ND The Hydra Affair						
	$0.30	$0.90	$1.50	£0.20	£0.60	£1.00
15 ND Fantastic Four appear, Apogee of Disaster begins						
	$0.30	$0.90	$1.50	£0.20	£0.60	£1.00
16-19 ND Apogee of Disaster story						
	$0.30	$0.90	$1.50	£0.20	£0.60	£1.00
20 ND Red Skull appears						
	$0.30	$0.90	$1.50	£0.20	£0.60	£1.00
21-25 ND	$0.30	$0.90	$1.50	£0.20	£0.60	£1.00
26 ND Wolverine cameo, Fantastic Four and Avengers appear						
	$0.30	$0.90	$1.50	£0.20	£0.60	£1.00
27-29 ND Wolverine appears						
	$0.40	$1.20	$2.00	£0.25	£0.75	£1.25
30 ND	$0.30	$0.90	$1.50	£0.20	£0.60	£1.00
31 ND Deathlok appears						
	$0.30	$0.90	$1.50	£0.20	£0.60	£1.00
32 ND $1.75 cover begins						
	$0.30	$0.90	$1.50	£0.20	£0.60	£1.00
33 ND intro New Super Agents of Shield						
	$0.30	$0.90	$1.50	£0.20	£0.60	£1.00
34 ND	$0.30	$0.90	$1.50	£0.20	£0.60	£1.00
35 ND Luke Cage appears						
	$0.30	$0.90	$1.50	£0.20	£0.60	£1.00
36-37 ND	$0.30	$0.90	$1.50	£0.20	£0.60	£1.00
38-41 ND Cold War of Nick Fury story						
	$0.30	$0.90	$1.50	£0.20	£0.60	£1.00
42-43 ND	$0.30	$0.90	$1.50	£0.20	£0.60	£1.00
44 ND Captain America appears						
	$0.30	$0.90	$1.50	£0.20	£0.60	£1.00
45 ND X-Force/Cable tie-in						
	$0.30	$0.90	$1.50	£0.20	£0.60	£1.00
46 ND X-Force tie-in						
	$0.30	$0.90	$1.50	£0.20	£0.60	£1.00
47 ND Nick Fury vs. Baron Strucker						
	$0.30	$0.90	$1.50	£0.20	£0.60	£1.00
Title Value:	$14.90	$44.70	$74.50	£9.80	£29.40	£49.00

NICK FURY, AGENT OF SHIELD SPECIAL EDITION

Marvel Comics Group; 1 Dec 1983-2 Jan 1984

	$Good	$Fine	$N.Mint	£Good	£Fine	£N.Mint
1-2 ND 48pgs, reprints classic Steranko art, new wraparound covers by Steranko, Baxter paper						
	$0.50	$1.50	$2.50	£0.30	£0.90	£1.50
Title Value:	$1.00	$3.00	$5.00	£0.60	£1.80	£3.00

NICK FURY/BLACK WIDOW: DEATH DUTY

Marvel Comics Group,OS; 1 Apr 1995

	$Good	$Fine	$N.Mint	£Good	£Fine	£N.Mint
1 ND 48pgs, Cefn Ridout script, Charlie Adlard art						
	$1.20	$3.60	$6.00	£0.80	£2.40	£4.00
Title Value:	$1.20	$3.60	$6.00	£0.80	£2.40	£4.00

NICK FURY/CAPTAIN AMERICA BOOKSHELF EDITION

Marvel Comics Group,OS; 1 Apr 1995

	$Good	$Fine	$N.Mint	£Good	£Fine	£N.Mint
1 ND 48pgs, Howard Chaykin script						
	$1.20	$3.60	$6.00	£0.80	£2.40	£4.00
Title Value:	$1.20	$3.60	$6.00	£0.80	£2.40	£4.00

NICK RYAN, THE SKULL

Antarctic Press,MS; 1 Dec 1994-3 1995

	$Good	$Fine	$N.Mint	£Good	£Fine	£N.Mint
1-3 ND black and white						
	$0.40	$1.20	$2.00	£0.25	£0.75	£1.25
Title Value:	$1.20	$3.60	$6.00	£0.75	£2.25	£3.75

NIGHT BEFORE CHRISTMASK, THE

Dark Horse,OS; 1 Oct 1995

	$Good	$Fine	$N.Mint	£Good	£Fine	£N.Mint
1 ND 32pgs, hardcover; Rick Geary story featuring a boy who discovers the mythical Mask						
	$2.00	$6.00	$10.00	£1.20	£3.60	£6.00
Title Value:	$2.00	$6.00	$10.00	£1.20	£3.60	£6.00

NIGHT FEARS

Millennium; 1 Jan 1994

	$Good	$Fine	$N.Mint	£Good	£Fine	£N.Mint
1 ND horror anthology; colour						
	$0.40	$1.20	$2.00	£0.25	£0.75	£1.25
Title Value:	$0.40	$1.20	$2.00	£0.25	£0.75	£1.25

NIGHT FORCE

DC Comics; 1 Aug 1982-14 Sep 1983

(see New Teen Titans #21)

	$Good	$Fine	$N.Mint	£Good	£Fine	£N.Mint
1 Gene Colan art begins						
	$0.15	$0.45	$0.75	£0.10	£0.35	£0.60
2-12	$0.15	$0.45	$0.75	£0.10	£0.35	£0.60
13 origin The Baron						
	$0.15	$0.45	$0.75	£0.10	£0.35	£0.60
14	$0.15	$0.45	$0.75	£0.10	£0.35	£0.60
Title Value:	$2.10	$6.30	$10.50	£1.40	£4.90	£8.40
Note: all Gene Colan art.						

NIGHT FORCE (2ND SERIES)

DC Comics; 1 Dec 1996-present

	$Good	$Fine	$N.Mint	£Good	£Fine	£N.Mint
1 ND Marv Wolfman script, Brent Anderson and Will Blyberg art begins						
	$0.45	$1.35	$2.25	£0.30	£0.90	£1.50
2-4 ND	$0.45	$1.35	$2.25	£0.30	£0.90	£1.50
Title Value:	$1.80	$5.40	$9.00	£1.20	£3.60	£6.00

NIGHT GLIDER

Topps,OS; 1 Apr 1993

	$Good	$Fine	$N.Mint	£Good	£Fine	£N.Mint
1 ND pre-bagged with coupon #4 for Secret City Saga #0 plus chrome trading card, Jack Kirby cover						
	$0.50	$1.50	$2.50	£0.30	£0.90	£1.50
1 without coupon/card ND						
	$0.40	$1.20	$2.00	£0.25	£0.75	£1.25
Title Value:	$0.90	$2.70	$4.50	£0.55	£1.65	£2.75

NIGHT LIFE

Strawberry Jam; 1 1986-7 1987; Caliber: 8 Jan 1992

	$Good	$Fine	$N.Mint	£Good	£Fine	£N.Mint
1-8 ND	$0.40	$1.20	$2.00	£0.25	£0.75	£1.25
Title Value:	$3.20	$9.60	$16.00	£2.00	£6.00	£10.00

NIGHT MAN

Malibu Ultraverse; 1 Oct 1993-23 Aug 1995

	$Good	$Fine	$N.Mint	£Good	£Fine	£N.Mint
1 ND 40pgs, Rune insert, Steve Englehart script and Darick Robertson art begins						
	$0.50	$1.50	$2.50	£0.30	£0.90	£1.50
1 Limited Edition, ND silver foil cover						
	$2.00	$6.00	$10.00	£1.00	£3.00	£5.00
2-3 ND	$0.40	$1.20	$2.00	£0.25	£0.75	£1.25
4 ND origin Firearm by Howard Chaykin						
	$0.40	$1.20	$2.00	£0.25	£0.75	£1.25
5-15 ND	$0.40	$1.20	$2.00	£0.25	£0.75	£1.25
16 ND flip-book format with Ultraverse Premiere #11						
	$0.50	$1.50	$2.50	£0.30	£0.90	£1.50
17 ND $2.50 cover begins						
	$0.40	$1.20	$2.00	£0.25	£0.75	£1.25
18-20 ND	$0.40	$1.20	$2.00	£0.25	£0.75	£1.25
21 ND cover by Mark Pacella and Art Thibert						
	$0.40	$1.20	$2.00	£0.25	£0.75	£1.25
22 ND Loki appears; 1st issue under Marvel Comics solicitation						
	$0.40	$1.20	$2.00	£0.25	£0.75	£1.25
23 ND	$0.40	$1.20	$2.00	£0.25	£0.75	£1.25
Title Value:	$11.40	$34.20	$57.00	£6.85	£20.55	£34.25

NIGHT MAN (2ND SERIES)

Marvel Comics Group; 1 Dec 1995-4 Mar 1996

	$Good	$Fine	$N.Mint	£Good	£Fine	£N.Mint
1 ND Steve Englehart script, M.C. Wyman art						
	$0.30	$0.90	$1.50	£0.20	£0.60	£1.00
1 Variant Cover Edition, ND computer painted cover by Chuck Maiden						
	$0.50	$1.50	$2.50	£0.30	£0.90	£1.50
2 ND flip-book format with Phoenix Ressurrection chapter						
	$0.30	$0.90	$1.50	£0.20	£0.60	£1.00
3 ND Lord Pumpkin returns						

	$Good	$Fine	$N.Mint	£Good	£Fine	£N.Mint
	$0.30	$0.90	$1.50	£0.20	£0.60	£1.00
4 ND Lord Pumpkin appears						
	$0.30	$0.90	$1.50	£0.20	£0.60	£1.00
Title Value:	$1.70	$5.10	$8.50	£1.10	£3.30	£5.50

NIGHT MAN ANNUAL, THE

Malibu Ultraverse; 1 Dec 1994

	$Good	$Fine	$N.Mint	£Good	£Fine	£N.Mint
1 ND 64pgs, continued in Strangers Annual #1						
	$0.50	$1.50	$2.50	£0.30	£0.90	£1.50
Title Value:	$0.50	$1.50	$2.50	£0.30	£0.90	£1.50

NIGHT MAN/GAMBIT, THE

Marvel Comics Group/Ultraverse; 1 Apr 1996-3 May 1996

	$Good	$Fine	$N.Mint	£Good	£Fine	£N.Mint
1 ND 3 page Foxfire flip-story						
	$0.40	$1.20	$2.00	£0.25	£0.75	£1.25
2-3 ND	$0.40	$1.20	$2.00	£0.25	£0.75	£1.25
Title Value:	$1.20	$3.60	$6.00	£0.75	£2.25	£3.75

NIGHT MAN: INFINITY, THE

Marvel Comics Group,OS; nn Nov 1995

	$Good	$Fine	$N.Mint	£Good	£Fine	£N.Mint
nn ND Black September tie-in; split by the Reality Gem, two versions of The Night Man are transported to the Marvel and Ultraverse universes						
	$0.50	$1.50	$2.50	£0.30	£0.90	£1.50
nn Variant Cover Edition ND 1 copy received for every 5 copies of the regular issue ordered						
	$0.60	$1.80	$3.00	£0.40	£1.20	£2.00
Title Value:	$1.10	$3.30	$5.50	£0.70	£2.10	£3.50

NIGHT MUSIC

Eclipse; 1 Dec 1984-3 Mar 1985

(see Pelleas & Melisande,Salome,Red Dog)

	$Good	$Fine	$N.Mint	£Good	£Fine	£N.Mint
1-3 ND P. Craig Russell						
	$0.40	$1.20	$2.00	£0.25	£0.75	£1.25
Title Value:	$1.20	$3.60	$6.00	£0.75	£2.25	£3.75

NIGHT NURSE

Marvel Comics Group; 1 Nov 1972-4 May 1973

	$Good	$Fine	$N.Mint	£Good	£Fine	£N.Mint
1 ND scarce in the U.K.						
	$0.50	$1.50	$3.00	£0.30	£1.00	£2.00
2-4 ND scarce in the U.K.						
	$0.50	$1.50	$3.00	£0.25	£0.75	£1.50
Title Value:	$2.00	$6.00	$12.00	£1.05	£3.25	£6.50

NIGHT OF THE LIVING DEAD

Fantaco,MS; 1 Nov 1990-4 1991

	$Good	$Fine	$N.Mint	£Good	£Fine	£N.Mint
1-4 ND 48pgs, Bissette art						
	$0.60	$1.80	$3.00	£0.40	£1.20	£2.00
Title Value:	$2.40	$7.20	$12.00	£1.60	£4.80	£8.00

Note: based on George Romero film

	£Good	£Fine	£N.Mint
Night of the Living Dead Limited Hardcover #1-#4 (1992) signed by Carlos Kastro and scripters Skulan and Stanway 200 copies of each only	£25.00	£45.00	£75.00

NIGHT OF THE LIVING DEAD (2ND SERIES)

Fantaco; 1 Mar 1994-3 1994

	$Good	$Fine	$N.Mint	£Good	£Fine	£N.Mint
1-3 ND black and white						
	$0.60	$1.80	$3.00	£0.40	£1.20	£2.00
Title Value:	$1.80	$5.40	$9.00	£1.20	£3.60	£6.00

NIGHT OF THE LIVING DEAD: AFTERMATH

Fantaco,OS; 1 Nov 1992

	$Good	$Fine	$N.Mint	£Good	£Fine	£N.Mint
1 ND black and white						
	$0.40	$1.20	$2.00	£0.25	£0.75	£1.25
Title Value:	$0.40	$1.20	$2.00	£0.25	£0.75	£1.25

NIGHT OF THE LIVING DEAD: LONDON - BLOODLINE

Fantaco,MS; 1 May 1993

	$Good	$Fine	$N.Mint	£Good	£Fine	£N.Mint
1 ND Clive Barker co-script; black and white						
	$0.60	$1.80	$3.00	£0.40	£1.20	£2.00
Title Value:	$0.60	$1.80	$3.00	£0.40	£1.20	£2.00

NIGHT RAVEN: HOUSE OF CARDS

Marvel Comics Group; 1991

	$Good	$Fine	$N.Mint	£Good	£Fine	£N.Mint
nn ND Jamie Delano script, David Lloyd art						
	$2.40	$7.00	$12.00	£1.50	£4.50	£7.50
nn new cover edition ND (Jan 1993), new format						
	$1.00	$3.00	$5.00	£0.75	£2.25	£3.75
Title Value:	$3.40	$10.00	$17.00	£2.25	£6.75	£11.25

Note: some remaindering in the U.K. and therefore tends to turn up in quantities at marts and shows

NIGHT THRASHER

Marvel Comics Group; 1 Jul 1993-21 Apr 1995

	$Good	$Fine	$N.Mint	£Good	£Fine	£N.Mint
1 48pgs, holo-grafix foil cover						
	$0.50	$1.50	$2.50	£0.25	£0.75	£1.25
2-9	$0.40	$1.20	$2.00	£0.25	£0.75	£1.25
10 with free Spiderman vs. Venom card sheet						
	$0.40	$1.20	$2.00	£0.25	£0.75	£1.25
11 X-over with Nova #6 and New Warriors #48						
	$0.40	$1.20	$2.00	£0.20	£0.60	£1.00
12 X-over with Nova #7 and New Warriors #49						
	$0.40	$1.20	$2.00	£0.20	£0.60	£1.00
13-14	$0.40	$1.20	$2.00	£0.20	£0.60	£1.00
15 Hulk guest-stars						
	$0.40	$1.20	$2.00	£0.20	£0.60	£1.00
16 The Prowler appears						
	$0.40	$1.20	$2.00	£0.20	£0.60	£1.00
17 War Machine appears						
	$0.40	$1.20	$2.00	£0.20	£0.60	£1.00
18 Nick Fury and Black Panther appear						
	$0.40	$1.20	$2.00	£0.20	£0.60	£1.00
19-21	$0.40	$1.20	$2.00	£0.20	£0.60	£1.00
Title Value:	$8.50	$25.50	$42.50	£4.70	£14.10	£23.50

NIGHT THRASHER: FOUR CONTROL

Marvel Comics Group,MS; 1 Oct 1992-Jan 1993

	$Good	$Fine	$N.Mint	£Good	£Fine	£N.Mint
1 follows on from events in New Warriors #25; issues 1-4 have "themes" respectively of strength/ money /power/ compassion						
	$0.40	$1.20	$2.00	£0.25	£0.75	£1.25
2-4	$0.40	$1.20	$2.00	£0.25	£0.75	£1.25
Title Value:	$1.60	$4.80	$8.00	£1.00	£3.00	£5.00

NIGHT'S CHILDREN

Fantaco,MS; 1 May 1991-4 Nov 1991

	$Good	$Fine	$N.Mint	£Good	£Fine	£N.Mint
1-4 ND	$0.60	$1.80	$3.00	£0.40	£1.20	£2.00
Title Value:	$2.40	$7.20	$12.00	£1.60	£4.80	£8.00

NIGHT'S CHILDREN: DOUBLE INDEMNITY

Fantaco,OS; 1 1992

	$Good	$Fine	$N.Mint	£Good	£Fine	£N.Mint
1 ND signed, limited edition						
	$2.00	$6.00	$10.00	£1.00	£3.00	£5.00
Title Value:	$2.00	$6.00	$10.00	£1.00	£3.00	£5.00

NIGHT'S CHILDREN: FOREPLAY

Fantaco,Magazine; 1 1991

	$Good	$Fine	$N.Mint	£Good	£Fine	£N.Mint
1 ND	$0.60	$1.80	$3.00	£0.40	£1.20	£2.00
Title Value:	$0.60	$1.80	$3.00	£0.40	£1.20	£2.00

NIGHT'S CHILDREN: LIASONS

Millennium,MS; 1 Sep 1994-2 Oct 1994

	$Good	$Fine	$N.Mint	£Good	£Fine	£N.Mint
1-2 ND reprints early material						
	$0.60	$1.80	$3.00	£0.40	£1.20	£2.00
Title Value:	$1.20	$3.60	$6.00	£0.80	£2.40	£4.00

NIGHT'S CHILDREN: ORIGINS

Millennium,OS; 1 1992?

	$Good	$Fine	$N.Mint	£Good	£Fine	£N.Mint
1 ND	$0.60	$1.80	$3.00	£0.40	£1.20	£2.00
Title Value:	$0.60	$1.80	$3.00	£0.40	£1.20	£2.00

NIGHT'S CHILDREN: THE RIPPER

Millennium,MS; 1 Oct 1995-2 Dec 1995

	$Good	$Fine	$N.Mint	£Good	£Fine	£N.Mint
1 ND 48pgs, Wendy Snow-Lang script and art; black and white						
	$0.80	$2.40	$4.00	£0.50	£1.50	£2.50
2 ND Wendy Snow-Lang script and art; black and white						
	$0.60	$1.80	$3.00	£0.40	£1.20	£2.00
Title Value:	$1.40	$4.20	$7.00	£0.90	£2.70	£4.50

NIGHT'S CHILDREN: THE VAMPIRE

Millennium; 1 Jul 1995-2 1995

	$Good	$Fine	$N.Mint	£Good	£Fine	£N.Mint
1-2 ND Wendy Snow-Lang script and art; black and white						
	$0.60	$1.80	$3.00	£0.40	£1.20	£2.00
Title Value:	$1.20	$3.60	$6.00	£0.80	£2.40	£4.00

NIGHT'S CHILDREN: VAMPYR

Fantaco,MS; 1 Jan 1993-4 Apr 1993

	$Good	$Fine	$N.Mint	£Good	£Fine	£N.Mint
1-4 ND	$0.60	$1.80	$3.00	£0.40	£1.20	£2.00
Title Value:	$2.40	$7.20	$12.00	£1.60	£4.80	£8.00

NIGHTBREED

Marvel Comics Group/Epic; 1 Apr 1990-25 1992

	$Good	$Fine	$N.Mint	£Good	£Fine	£N.Mint
1 ND story by John Wagner/Alan Grant, art by Jim Baikie						
	$0.60	$1.80	$3.00	£0.30	£0.90	£1.50
2-4 ND	$0.50	$1.50	$2.50	£0.30	£0.90	£1.50
5 ND new story lines based on film begins, Baikie art						
	$0.50	$1.50	$2.50	£0.30	£0.90	£1.50
6-10 ND Blevins art						
	$0.50	$1.50	$2.50	£0.30	£0.90	£1.50
11-12 ND Mark Nelson art						
	$0.40	$1.20	$2.00	£0.25	£0.75	£1.25
13 ND Texeira art	$0.40	$1.20	$2.00	£0.25	£0.75	£1.25
14 ND	$0.40	$1.20	$2.00	£0.25	£0.75	£1.25
15 ND 1st monthly issue						
	$0.40	$1.20	$2.00	£0.25	£0.75	£1.25
16-25 ND	$0.40	$1.20	$2.00	£0.25	£0.75	£1.25
Title Value:	$11.10	$33.30	$55.50	£6.75	£20.25	£33.75

Note: adaptation of horror film by Clive Barker

	£Good	£Fine	£N.Mint
Nightbreed Chronicles (Titan - 1990), based on film	£1.20	£3.60	£6.00
Trade Paperback (Nov 1991), reprints #1-4	£1.10	£3.30	£5.50

NIGHTCAT

Marvel Comics Group,OS; 1 Apr 1991

	$Good	$Fine	$N.Mint	£Good	£Fine	£N.Mint
1 ND based on American rock singer Jackie Tavar						
	$0.60	$1.80	$3.00	£0.40	£1.20	£2.00
Title Value:	$0.60	$1.80	$3.00	£0.40	£1.20	£2.00

NIGHTCRAWLER

Marvel Comics Group,MS; 1 Nov 1985-4 Feb 1986

(see X-Men)

	$Good	$Fine	$N.Mint	£Good	£Fine	£N.Mint
1-4 ND Cockrum art						
	$0.50	$1.50	$2.50	£0.30	£0.90	£1.50
Title Value:	$2.00	$6.00	$10.00	£1.20	£3.60	£6.00

NIGHTCRY

Visual Anarchy; 1 1994

	$Good	$Fine	$N.Mint	£Good	£Fine	£N.Mint
1 ND 64pgs, Razor story leads off a black and white anthology						
	$0.70	$2.10	$3.50	£0.50	£1.50	£2.50
Title Value:	$0.70	$2.10	$3.50	£0.50	£1.50	£2.50

NIGHTLINGER SPECIAL

Caliber Press,OS; 1 Aug 1994

	$Good	$Fine	$N.Mint	£Good	£Fine	£N.Mint
1 ND black and white						
	$0.50	$1.50	$2.50	£0.30	£0.90	£1.50
Title Value:	$0.50	$1.50	$2.50	£0.30	£0.90	£1.50

NIGHTMARE

Innovation; 1 Dec 1989

	$Good	$Fine	$N.Mint	£Good	£Fine	£N.Mint
1 ND Alex Nino art; colour						
	$0.30	$0.90	$1.50	£0.20	£0.60	£1.00
Title Value:	$0.30	$0.90	$1.50	£0.20	£0.60	£1.00

NIGHTMARE

Marvel Comics Group,MS; 1 Dec 1994-4 Mar 1995

1-4 spin-off from Dr. Strange series

	$Good	$Fine	$N.Mint	£Good	£Fine	£N.Mint
	$0.40	$1.20	$2.00	£0.25	£0.75	£1.25
Title Value:	$1.60	$4.80	$8.00	£1.00	£3.00	£5.00

NIGHTMARE CIRCUS

Marvel Comics Group; 1 Jan 1996-4 Apr 1996

	$Good	$Fine	$N.Mint	£Good	£Fine	£N.Mint
1-4 ND based on Sega video game	$0.50	$1.50	$2.50	£0.30	£0.90	£1.50
Title Value:	$2.00	$6.00	$10.00	£1.20	£3.60	£6.00

NIGHTMARE ON ELM STREET

Innovation,MS; 1 Jul 1991-6 Apr 1992

	$Good	$Fine	$N.Mint	£Good	£Fine	£N.Mint
1-2 ND	$0.50	$1.50	$2.50	£0.30	£0.90	£1.50
3 ND prequel to 6th film - Freddy's Dead	$0.50	$1.50	$2.50	£0.30	£0.90	£1.50
4-6 ND	$0.50	$1.50	$2.50	£0.30	£0.90	£1.50
Title Value:	$3.00	$9.00	$15.00	£1.80	£5.40	£9.00

NIGHTMARE ON ELM STREET

Marvel Comics Group,MS Film; 1 Oct 1989-2 Nov 1989

	$Good	$Fine	$N.Mint	£Good	£Fine	£N.Mint
1-2 ND 48pgs	$0.50	$1.50	$2.50	£0.30	£0.90	£1.50
Title Value:	$1.00	$3.00	$5.00	£0.60	£1.80	£3.00

Note: black and white, based on film of same name

NIGHTMARE ON ELM STREET: THE BEGINNING

Innovation,MS; 1 May 1992-3 Jun 1993

	$Good	$Fine	$N.Mint	£Good	£Fine	£N.Mint
1-3 ND	$0.50	$1.50	$2.50	£0.30	£0.90	£1.50
Title Value:	$1.50	$4.50	$7.50	£0.90	£2.70	£4.50

NIGHTMARES

Eclipse; 1,2 May 1985

	$Good	$Fine	$N.Mint	£Good	£Fine	£N.Mint
1-2 ND Moench script, Gulacy art	$0.40	$1.20	$2.00	£0.25	£0.75	£1.25
Title Value:	$0.80	$2.40	$4.00	£0.50	£1.50	£2.50

NIGHTMARK

Alpha Productions; 1 1991

	$Good	$Fine	$N.Mint	£Good	£Fine	£N.Mint
1 ND black and white	$0.30	$0.90	$1.50	£0.20	£0.60	£1.00
Title Value:	$0.30	$0.90	$1.50	£0.20	£0.60	£1.00

NIGHTMARK: BLOOD & HONOUR

Alpha Productions,MS; 1 Feb 1994-3 Jun 1994

	$Good	$Fine	$N.Mint	£Good	£Fine	£N.Mint
1-3 ND black and white	$0.50	$1.50	$2.50	£0.30	£0.90	£1.50
Title Value:	$1.50	$4.50	$7.50	£0.90	£2.70	£4.50
Nightmark: Blood & Honour Pre-Pack (1994) ND issues #1-3 in sealed white envelope				£1.00	£3.00	£5.00

NIGHTMASK

Marvel Comics Group/New Universe; 1 Nov 1986-12 Oct 1987

	$Good	$Fine	$N.Mint	£Good	£Fine	£N.Mint
1-12 ND	$0.15	$0.45	$0.75	£0.10	£0.30	£0.50
Title Value:	$1.80	$5.40	$9.00	£1.20	£3.60	£6.00

NIGHTRIDER

Marvel Comics Group; 1 Oct 1974-6 Aug 1975

	$Good	$Fine	$N.Mint	£Good	£Fine	£N.Mint
1 ND	$0.50	$1.50	$3.00	£0.25	£0.75	£1.50
2-6 ND	$0.30	$1.00	$2.00	£0.15	£0.50	£1.00
Title Value:	$2.00	$6.50	$13.00	£1.00	£3.25	£6.50

Note: re-lettered reprints of (western) Ghost Rider.

NIGHTSTALKERS

Marvel Comics Group; 1 Nov 1992-18 Apr 1994

	$Good	$Fine	$N.Mint	£Good	£Fine	£N.Mint
1 ND DS pre-bagged, Rise of the Midnight Sons part 5; Hannibal King, Frank Drake and Blade the Vampire Killer begin, includes fold-out poster	$0.50	$1.50	$2.50	£0.30	£0.90	£1.50
2-4	$0.40	$1.20	$2.00	£0.25	£0.75	£1.25
5 Punisher appears	$0.40	$1.20	$2.00	£0.25	£0.75	£1.25
6 Punisher appears	$0.30	$0.90	$1.50	£0.20	£0.60	£1.00
7 Ghost Rider appears	$0.30	$0.90	$1.50	£0.20	£0.60	£1.00
8 Morbius appears	$0.30	$0.90	$1.50	£0.20	£0.60	£1.00
9 Morbius appears, continued in Morbius #11	$0.30	$0.90	$1.50	£0.20	£0.60	£1.00
10 Midnight Massacre part 1, outer cover of black parchment and gold lettering	$0.30	$0.90	$1.50	£0.20	£0.60	£1.00
11	$0.30	$0.90	$1.50	£0.20	£0.60	£1.00
12 gold ink enhanced cover	$0.30	$0.90	$1.50	£0.20	£0.60	£1.00
13	$0.30	$0.90	$1.50	£0.20	£0.60	£1.00
14 Siege of Darkness part 1; Ghost Rider, Blaze, Morbius and the Darkhold Redeemers appear; spot varnish cover	$0.30	$0.90	$1.50	£0.20	£0.60	£1.00
15 Siege of Darkness part 9; spot varnish cover	$0.30	$0.90	$1.50	£0.20	£0.60	£1.00
16-17	$0.30	$0.90	$1.50	£0.20	£0.60	£1.00
18 Nightstalkers vs. Varnae	$0.30	$0.90	$1.50	£0.20	£0.60	£1.00
Title Value:	$6.00	$18.00	$30.00	£3.90	£11.70	£19.50

NIGHTSTREETS

Arrow; 1 1986-5 1987

	$Good	$Fine	$N.Mint	£Good	£Fine	£N.Mint
1-5 ND	$0.30	$0.90	$1.50	£0.20	£0.60	£1.00
Title Value:	$1.50	$4.50	$7.50	£1.00	£3.00	£5.00
Nightstreets Book I (1991), reprints issues #1-4 plus eight new pages				£1.00	£3.00	£5.00
Nightstreets Book II (1991), reprints issue 5 plus 60 new pages to conclude "Mob Rules" storyline				£1.00	£3.00	£5.00

NIGHTVEIL

AC Comics; 1 1984-7 1987

	$Good	$Fine	$N.Mint	£Good	£Fine	£N.Mint
1-7 ND scarce in the U.K.	$0.50	$1.50	$2.50	£0.30	£0.90	£1.50
Title Value:	$3.50	$10.50	$17.50	£2.10	£6.30	£10.50
Special 1				£0.30	£0.90	£1.50
Cauldron of Horror 1 (1989)				£0.25	£0.75	£1.25
Cauldron of Horror 2 (1990), b/w Joe Kubert reprint from Avon's Weird Horrors #9 (1953)				£0.30	£0.90	£1.50

NIGHTVISION

Rebel Studios,MS; 1 Feb 1993-3 1993

	$Good	$Fine	$N.Mint	£Good	£Fine	£N.Mint
1 ND 56pgs, David Quinn script begins, Tim Vigil cover	$0.50	$1.50	$2.50	£0.30	£0.90	£1.50
1 2nd printing, ND (Aug 1994)	$0.50	$1.50	$2.50	£0.30	£0.90	£1.50
2 ND 32pgs, Brian Stelfreeze cover	$0.50	$1.50	$2.50	£0.30	£0.90	£1.50
3 ND	$0.50	$1.50	$2.50	£0.30	£0.90	£1.50
Title Value:	$2.00	$6.00	$10.00	£1.20	£3.60	£6.00

NIGHTVISION

London Night Studios; 1 1996

	$Good	$Fine	$N.Mint	£Good	£Fine	£N.Mint
1 ND David Quinn script, Kyle Hotz art; black and white	$0.60	$1.80	$3.00	£0.40	£1.20	£2.00
Title Value:	$0.60	$1.80	$3.00	£0.40	£1.20	£2.00

NIGHTWATCH

Marvel Comics Group; 1 Apr 1994-12 Mar 1995

	$Good	$Fine	$N.Mint	£Good	£Fine	£N.Mint
1 Ron Lim covers and art begin	$0.30	$0.90	$1.50	£0.20	£0.60	£1.00
1 Collectors Edition, ND prismatic foil cover overlaid with black translucent ink	$0.45	$1.35	$2.25	£0.30	£0.90	£1.50
2 with free Spiderman and his Deadly Foes card sheet	$0.30	$0.90	$1.50	£0.20	£0.60	£1.00
3-5	$0.30	$0.90	$1.50	£0.20	£0.60	£1.00
6 Venom guest-stars	$0.30	$0.90	$1.50	£0.20	£0.60	£1.00
7-8 Cardiac appears						

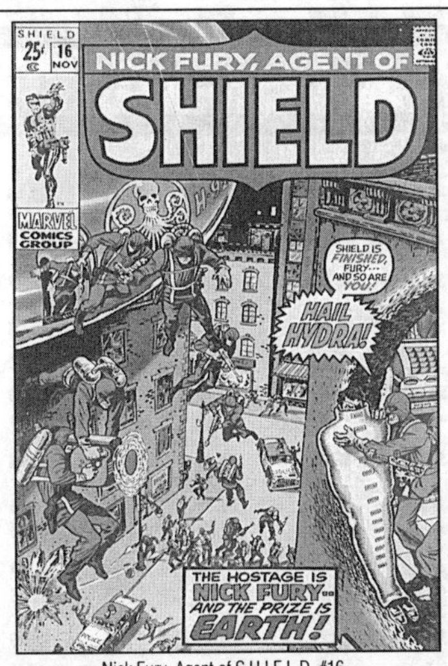

Nick Fury, Agent of S.H.I.E.L.D. #16

Night Glider #1

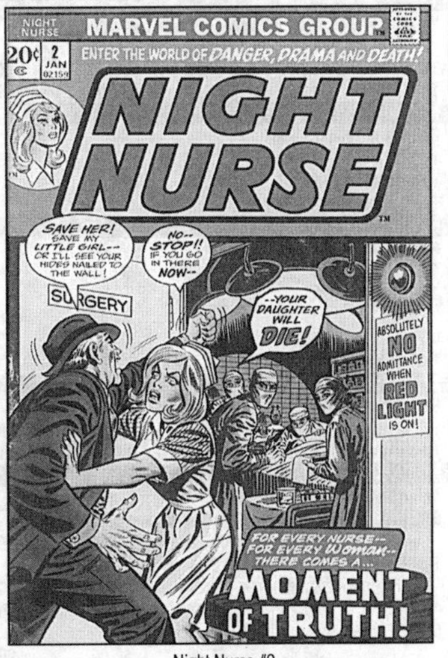

Night Nurse #2

	$Good	$Fine	$N.Mint	£Good	£Fine	£N.Mint
	$0.30	$0.90	$1.50	£0.20	£0.60	£1.00
9 origin told in more detail	$0.30	$0.90	$1.50	£0.20	£0.60	£1.00
10-12	$0.30	$0.90	$1.50	£0.20	£0.60	£1.00
Title Value:	$4.05	$12.15	$20.25	£2.70	£8.10	£13.50

NIGHTWING
DC Comics,MS; 1 Sep 1995-4 Dec 1995

	$Good	$Fine	$N.Mint	£Good	£Fine	£N.Mint
1 Denny O'Neil script, Greg Land and Mike Sellers art, Brian Stelfreeze covers all begin	$0.50	$1.50	$2.50	£0.30	£0.90	£1.50
2 new Nightwing costume	$0.50	$1.50	$2.50	£0.30	£0.90	£1.50
3-4	$0.50	$1.50	$2.50	£0.30	£0.90	£1.50
Title Value:	$2.00	$6.00	$10.00	£1.20	£3.60	£6.00

NIGHTWING (2ND SERIES)
DC Comics; 1 Oct 1996-present

	$Good	$Fine	$N.Mint	£Good	£Fine	£N.Mint
1 ND Chuck Dixon script and Scott McDaniel art begins	$0.40	$1.20	$2.00	£0.25	£0.75	£1.25
2 ND Final Night tie-in	$0.40	$1.20	$2.00	£0.25	£0.75	£1.25
3-5 ND	$0.40	$1.20	$2.00	£0.25	£0.75	£1.25
6 ND Robin guest-stars	$0.40	$1.20	$2.00	£0.25	£0.75	£1.25
Title Value:	$2.40	$7.20	$12.00	£1.50	£4.50	£7.50

NIGHTWING: ALFRED'S RETURN
DC Comics,OS; 1 Aug 1995

	$Good	$Fine	$N.Mint	£Good	£Fine	£N.Mint
1 ND 64pgs, Alan Grant script, Dick Giordano art	$0.80	$2.40	$4.00	£0.50	£1.50	£2.50
Title Value:	$0.80	$2.40	$4.00	£0.50	£1.50	£2.50

NINE PRINCES IN AMBER
DC Comics,MS; 1 Jun 1996-3 Aug 1996

	$Good	$Fine	$N.Mint	£Good	£Fine	£N.Mint
1-3 ND 48pgs, Terry Bission script, painted art by Lou Harrison; adaptation of Roger Zelazny story	$1.40	$4.20	$7.00	£0.90	£2.70	£4.50
Title Value:	$4.20	$12.60	$21.00	£2.70	£8.10	£13.50

1963
Image,MS; 1 Apr 1993-6 Oct 1993

	$Good	$Fine	$N.Mint	£Good	£Fine	£N.Mint
1 ND Mystery Incorporated; Alan Moore script with Rick Veitch and Dave Gibbons art	$0.40	$1.20	$2.00	£0.20	£0.60	£1.00
1 Bronze Edition, ND , as above but with bronze outer cover (20 copies); not signed however	$7.50	$22.50	$45.00	£5.75	£17.50	£35.00
1 Gold Edition, ND , produced in the U.K. by Chaos City Comics; gold outer cover, signed by Dave Gibbons (500 copies)	$1.25	$3.75	$7.50	£0.80	£2.50	£5.00
1 Platinum Edition, ND , as above but with Platinum outer cover (100 copies)	$3.30	$10.00	$20.00	£2.50	£7.50	£15.00
2 ND The Fury; Moore, Veitch, Bissette, Valentino and Gibbons	$0.40	$1.20	$2.00	£0.20	£0.60	£1.00
3 ND Tales of the Uncanny; Moore, Veitch, Bissette, Simpson and Brown	$0.40	$1.20	$2.00	£0.20	£0.60	£1.00
4 ND Tales From Beyond; Moore, Bissette, Totleben, Valentino and Workman	$0.40	$1.20	$2.00	£0.20	£0.60	£1.00
5 ND Horus, Lord of Light; Moore, Veitch, Totleben, Workman and Kilroy	$0.40	$1.20	$2.00	£0.20	£0.60	£1.00
6 ND Tomorrow Syndicate; Moore, Veitch, Gibbons and Kilroy	$0.40	$1.20	$2.00	£0.20	£0.60	£1.00
Title Value:	$14.45	$43.45	$84.50	£10.25	£31.10	£61.00

1984
Warren; 1 May 1978-10 Jan 1980
(becomes 1994)

	$Good	$Fine	$N.Mint	£Good	£Fine	£N.Mint
1 ND	$0.90	$2.70	$4.50	£0.60	£1.80	£3.00
2-10 ND	$0.60	$1.80	$3.00	£0.40	£1.20	£2.00
Title Value:	$6.30	$18.90	$31.50	£4.20	£12.60	£21.00

Note: Corben art in most issues

1994
Warren; 11 Feb 1980-29 1983
(previously 1984)

	$Good	$Fine	$N.Mint	£Good	£Fine	£N.Mint
11-29 ND	$0.60	$1.80	$3.00	£0.40	£1.20	£2.00
Title Value:	$11.40	$34.20	$57.00	£7.60	£22.80	£38.00

NINJA
Eternity; 1 1986-13 1987

	$Good	$Fine	$N.Mint	£Good	£Fine	£N.Mint
1-13 ND	$0.40	$1.20	$2.00	£0.25	£0.75	£1.25
Title Value:	$5.20	$15.60	$26.00	£3.25	£9.75	£16.25
Trade paperback, reprints				£0.85	£2.55	£4.25

NINJA ELITE
Adventure; 1 1987-7 Jul 1988

	$Good	$Fine	$N.Mint	£Good	£Fine	£N.Mint
1-3 ND	$0.30	$0.90	$1.50	£0.20	£0.60	£1.00
4 ND ties into Adventureres	$0.30	$0.90	$1.50	£0.20	£0.60	£1.00
5-7 ND	$0.30	$0.90	$1.50	£0.20	£0.60	£1.00
Title Value:	$2.10	$6.30	$10.50	£1.40	£4.20	£7.00

NINJA FUNNIES
Eternity; 1-5 1987

	$Good	$Fine	$N.Mint	£Good	£Fine	£N.Mint
1-5 ND 16pgs	$0.30	$0.90	$1.50	£0.20	£0.60	£1.00
Title Value:	$1.50	$4.50	$7.50	£1.00	£3.00	£5.00

NINJA HIGH SCHOOL
Antarctic/Eternity; 1 1986-present

	$Good	$Fine	$N.Mint	£Good	£Fine	£N.Mint
0 ND (Jan 1994), foil-enhanced UV card-stock cover	$0.40	$1.20	$2.00	£0.25	£0.75	£1.25
1-3 ND (#1-3 intended as mini-series)	$0.40	$1.20	$2.00	£0.25	£0.75	£1.25
4 ND	$0.40	$1.20	$2.00	£0.25	£0.75	£1.25
5-6 ND Eternity issues	$0.40	$1.20	$2.00	£0.25	£0.75	£1.25
6 2nd printing ND	$0.30	$0.90	$1.50	£0.20	£0.60	£1.00
7-43 ND	$0.40	$1.20	$2.00	£0.25	£0.75	£1.25
44-49 ND	$0.55	$1.65	$2.75	£0.35	£1.05	£1.75
50 ND 64pgs, coupons for silver foil Ninja High School Perfect Memory #1	$0.80	$2.40	$4.00	£0.50	£1.50	£2.50
51-52 ND	$0.60	$1.80	$3.00	£0.40	£1.20	£2.00
Title Value:	$23.20	$69.60	$115.74	£14.60	£43.80	£73.00
Annual 1 (Aug 1993) ND				£0.30	£0.90	£1.50
Trade paperback Vol 1 ND reprints #1-4				£0.90	£2.70	£4.50
Trade paperback, 2nd/3rd print				£0.85	£2.55	£4.25
Trade paperback Vol 1 (4th print - Feb 1992)				£1.00	£3.00	£5.00
Trade paperback Vol 2: A Boy and His Dog Supreme (Aug 1990) ND reprints #5-7				£1.00	£3.00	£5.00
2nd print (Mar 1996)				£0.90	£2.70	£4.50
Trade paperback Vol 3 (May 1991) ND reprints #8-11				£1.00	£3.00	£5.00
2nd print (Aug 1993)				£0.90	£2.70	£4.50
3rd print (May 1996)				£1.45	£4.35	£7.25
Trade paperback Vol 4: Of Rats and Men (Jul 1991) ND reprints #12-15				£1.00	£3.00	£5.00
Trade paperback Vol 5 (Dec 1994) ND reprints #16-18 plus new additional story				£1.00	£3.00	£5.00
Trade paperback Vol 6 (Jul 1995) ND reprints issues #19-21				£1.00	£3.00	£5.00
Trade paperback Vol 7 (Sep 1995) ND reprints issues #22-24				£1.00	£3.00	£5.00
Trade paperback Vol 8 (Jan 1996 ND reprints issues #25-27				£1.00	£3.00	£5.00

NINJA HIGH SCHOOL 1996, GIRLS OF
Antarctic Press,OS; nn May 1996

	$Good	$Fine	$N.Mint	£Good	£Fine	£N.Mint
nn ND 56pgs, black and white	$0.80	$2.40	$4.00	£0.50	£1.50	£2.50
Title Value:	$0.80	$2.40	$4.00	£0.50	£1.50	£2.50

NINJA HIGH SCHOOL IN COLOUR
Eternity,MS; 1 Aug 1992-14 1993

	$Good	$Fine	$N.Mint	£Good	£Fine	£N.Mint
1-14 ND reprints in colour, new covers by Ben Dunn	$0.40	$1.20	$2.00	£0.25	£0.75	£1.25
Title Value:	$5.60	$16.80	$28.00	£3.50	£10.50	£17.50

NINJA HIGH SCHOOL SWIMSUIT SPECIAL
Antarctic Press,OS; nn 1995

	$Good	$Fine	$N.Mint	£Good	£Fine	£N.Mint
nn ND Ben Dunn, Fred Perry and others	$0.60	$1.80	$3.00	£0.40	£1.20	£2.00
Title Value:	$0.60	$1.80	$3.00	£0.40	£1.20	£2.00

NINJA HIGH SCHOOL YEAR BOOK
Antarctic Press; 1 1989-7 1991

	$Good	$Fine	$N.Mint	£Good	£Fine	£N.Mint
1-6 ND black and white	$0.60	$1.80	$3.00	£0.40	£1.20	£2.00
7 ND 64pgs, titled Ninja High School Yearbook 1995; black and white	$0.60	$1.80	$3.00	£0.40	£1.20	£2.00
Title Value:	$4.20	$12.60	$21.00	£2.80	£8.40	£14.00

NINJA HIGH SCHOOL, BRENNER PRINTING PRESENTS
Antarctic Press; 1 1993

	$Good	$Fine	$N.Mint	£Good	£Fine	£N.Mint
1 ND rare in the U.K. promotional comic produced by Brenner and illustrating the process of printing up a comic book; available at 1993 San Diego Comicon	$0.80	$2.40	$4.00	£0.50	£1.50	£2.50
Title Value:	$0.80	$2.40	$4.00	£0.50	£1.50	£2.50

NINJA HIGH SCHOOL/SPEED RACER
Eternity,MS; 1 Jul 1993-2 Aug 1993

	$Good	$Fine	$N.Mint	£Good	£Fine	£N.Mint
1-2 ND	$0.60	$1.80	$3.00	£0.40	£1.20	£2.00
Title Value:	$1.20	$3.60	$6.00	£0.80	£2.40	£4.00

NINJA HIGH SCHOOL: THE PROM FORMULA
Eternity,MS; 1 Jun 1991-2 Jul 1991

	$Good	$Fine	$N.Mint	£Good	£Fine	£N.Mint
1-2 ND	$0.50	$1.50	$2.50	£0.30	£0.90	£1.50
Title Value:	$1.00	$3.00	$5.00	£0.60	£1.80	£3.00

NINJA SPECIAL
Eternity,OS; 1 1987

	$Good	$Fine	$N.Mint	£Good	£Fine	£N.Mint
1 ND	$0.40	$1.20	$2.00	£0.25	£0.75	£1.25
Title Value:	$0.40	$1.20	$2.00	£0.25	£0.75	£1.25

NINJAK
Valiant/Acclaim Comics; 0 and 00 Feb 1995; 1 Nov 1993-28 Nov 1995

	$Good	$Fine	$N.Mint	£Good	£Fine	£N.Mint
0 ND Mark Moretti script and art; origin of Ninjak	$0.45	$1.35	$2.25	£0.30	£0.90	£1.50
00 ND Mark Moretti script and art; origin of Ninjak	$0.45	$1.35	$2.25	£0.30	£0.90	£1.50
1 ND Joe Quesada art begins; all foil cover	$0.70	$2.10	$3.50	£0.40	£1.20	£2.00
1 Gold Premium Edition, gold logo, in Valiant logo stamped mylar pro-bag	$1.50	$4.50	$7.50	£1.00	£3.00	£5.00
1 Valiant Validated Signature Series, (May 1994), signed by Mark Moretti, Joe Quesada and Jimmy Palmiotti; 5,300 copies with certificate and Mylar sleeve	$1.50	$4.50	$7.50	£1.00	£3.00	£5.00
2-3 ND	$0.40	$1.20	$2.00	£0.25	£0.75	£1.25
4 ND bound-in Upper Deck trading card	$0.40	$1.20	$2.00	£0.25	£0.75	£1.25
5-6 ND guest stars X-O Manowar	$0.40	$1.20	$2.00	£0.25	£0.75	£1.25
7 ND	$0.40	$1.20	$2.00	£0.25	£0.75	£1.25
8 ND Chaos Effect tie-in	$0.40	$1.20	$2.00	£0.25	£0.75	£1.25
9-16 ND	$0.40	$1.20	$2.00	£0.25	£0.75	£1.25
17 ND 1st Acclaim Comics issue, Bart Sears cover; bi-weekly	$0.45	$1.35	$2.25	£0.30	£0.90	£1.50
18 ND Bart Sears cover; bi-weekly						

Issue	$Good	$Fine	$N.Mint	£Good	£Fine	£N.Mint
	$0.45	$1.35	$2.25	£0.30	£0.90	£1.50
19-21 ND Breaking the Web story; bi-weekly	$0.45	$1.35	$2.25	£0.30	£0.90	£1.50
22-28 ND bi-weekly	$0.45	$1.35	$2.25	£0.30	£0.90	£1.50
Title Value:	$16.00	$48.00	$80.00	£10.35	£31.05	£51.75

NINJAK (2ND SERIES)
Acclaim Comics; 1 Mar 1997-present

Issue	$Good	$Fine	$N.Mint	£Good	£Fine	£N.Mint
1 ND Kurt Busiek script, Neil Vokes and Mike Avon Oeming art begins	$0.50	$1.50	$2.50	£0.30	£0.90	£1.50
2,3 ND	$0.50	$1.50	$2.50	£0.30	£0.90	£1.50
Title Value:	$1.50	$4.50	$7.50	£0.90	£2.70	£4.50

NINJAK YEARBOOK
Valiant; 1 Dec 1994

Issue	$Good	$Fine	$N.Mint	£Good	£Fine	£N.Mint
1 ND Brian Hitch art	$0.60	$1.80	$3.00	£0.30	£0.90	£1.50
Title Value:	$0.60	$1.80	$3.00	£0.30	£0.90	£1.50

NINJUTSU, ART OF THE NINJA
Solson Publications; 1,2 1986

Issue	$Good	$Fine	$N.Mint	£Good	£Fine	£N.Mint
1-2 ND	$0.30	$0.90	$1.50	£0.20	£0.60	£1.00
Title Value:	$0.60	$1.80	$3.00	£0.40	£1.20	£2.00

NIRA X/CYNDER: ENDANGERED SPECIES
Entity Comics,OS; 1 Feb 1996

Issue	$Good	$Fine	$N.Mint	£Good	£Fine	£N.Mint
1 ND Bill Maus script, Cabin Boy art	$0.60	$1.80	$3.00	£0.40	£1.20	£2.00
1 Commemorative Edition, ND pre-bagged, gold-ink enhanced cover with certificate; 3,000 copies	$2.60	$7.75	$13.00	£1.70	£5.00	£8.50
Title Value:	$3.20	$9.55	$16.00	£2.10	£6.20	£10.50

NIRA X/HELLINA
Entity Comics,OS; 1 Aug 1996

Issue	$Good	$Fine	$N.Mint	£Good	£Fine	£N.Mint
1 Gold Foil cover, ND Bill Maus script and art	$0.60	$1.80	$3.00	£0.40	£1.20	£2.00
1 Platinum Edition ND	$2.50	$7.50	$12.50	£1.50	£4.50	£7.50
1 Red Foil cover, ND Bill Maus script and art	$0.60	$1.80	$3.00	£0.40	£1.20	£2.00
1 San Diego Edition, ND (Jul 1996), limited to 1,000 copies	$1.00	$3.00	$5.00	£1.00	£3.00	£5.00
Title Value:	$4.70	$14.10	$23.50	£3.30	£9.90	£16.50

NIRA X: CYBERANGEL
Entity Comics,MS; 1 Dec 1994-4 Jun 1995

Issue	$Good	$Fine	$N.Mint	£Good	£Fine	£N.Mint
1 ND Bill Maus script and art - foil stamped cover	$1.00	$3.00	$5.00	£0.60	£1.80	£3.00
1 2nd printing, ND (May 1995) - foil stamped cover	$0.60	$1.80	$3.00	£0.40	£1.20	£2.00
2-4 ND Bill Maus script and art, foil stamped cover	$0.60	$1.80	$3.00	£0.30	£0.90	£1.50
4 Collectors Edition, ND pre-bagged with video game	$1.40	$4.20	$7.00	£0.90	£2.70	£4.50
Title Value:	$4.80	$14.40	$23.00	£2.80	£8.40	£14.00
Nira X: Birth of the Cyberangel (sep 1995) Trade paperback collects four issue mini-series				£1.70	£5.10	£8.50

NIRA X: CYBERANGEL (2ND SERIES)
Entity Comics; 1 Jul 1995-4 1995

Issue	$Good	$Fine	$N.Mint	£Good	£Fine	£N.Mint
1 ND Bill Maus script and art; chromium cover	$0.80	$2.40	$4.00	£0.50	£1.50	£2.50
2-4 ND	$0.50	$1.50	$2.50	£0.30	£0.90	£1.50
Title Value:	$2.30	$6.90	$11.50	£1.40	£4.20	£7.00
Nira X: Heatwave (Dec 1995) Trade paperback ND collects mini-series				£1.70	£5.10	£8.50

NIRA X: CYBERANGEL (3RD SERIES)
Entity Comics; 0 Mar 1996-3 Jun 1996

Issue	$Good	$Fine	$N.Mint	£Good	£Fine	£N.Mint
0 ND Bill Maus script and art; black and white	$0.55	$1.65	$2.75	£0.35	£1.05	£1.75
0 Signed & Numbered Edition, ND (Mar 1996), pre-bagged with certificate; limited to 999 copies	$2.60	$7.75	$13.00	£1.50	£4.50	£7.50
1 ND	$0.50	$1.50	$2.50	£0.30	£0.90	£1.50
1 Collectors Edition, ND pre-bagged with video game	$1.40	$4.20	$7.00	£0.90	£2.70	£4.50
2 ND	$0.50	$1.50	$2.50	£0.30	£0.90	£1.50
3 ND	$0.60	$1.80	$3.00	£0.40	£1.20	£2.00
Title Value:	$6.15	$18.40	$30.75	£3.75	£11.25	£18.75

NIRA X: CYBERANGEL (4TH SERIES)
Entity Comics,MS; 1 Mar 1996-4 Aug 1996

Issue	$Good	$Fine	$N.Mint	£Good	£Fine	£N.Mint
1 ND	$0.55	$1.65	$2.75	£0.35	£1.05	£1.75
1 Collectors Edition, ND pre-bagged with video game	$1.50	$4.50	$7.50	£1.00	£3.00	£5.00
2-4 ND	$0.55	$1.65	$2.75	£0.35	£1.05	£1.75
4 Collectors Edition, ND pre-bagged with video game	$1.50	$4.50	$7.50	£1.00	£3.00	£5.00
Title Value:	$5.20	$15.60	$26.00	£3.40	£10.20	£17.00

NIRA X: CYBERANGEL (4TH SERIES) ANNUAL
Entity Comics; 1 1996

Issue	$Good	$Fine	$N.Mint	£Good	£Fine	£N.Mint
1 ND	$0.60	$1.80	$3.00	£0.40	£1.20	£2.00
1 Variant Cover Edition, ND "Snowman" cover	$1.50	$4.50	$7.50	£1.00	£3.00	£5.00
Title Value:	$2.10	$6.30	$10.50	£1.40	£4.20	£7.00

NO ESCAPE
Marvel Comics Group,MS; 1 Jun 1994-3 Aug 1994

Issue	$Good	$Fine	$N.Mint	£Good	£Fine	£N.Mint
1-3 film adaptation	$0.30	$0.90	$1.50	£0.20	£0.60	£1.00
Title Value:	$0.90	$2.70	$4.50	£0.60	£1.80	£3.00

NO GUTS OR GLORY
Fantaco,OS; 1 Aug 1991

Issue	$Good	$Fine	$N.Mint	£Good	£Fine	£N.Mint
1 ND Kevin Eastman script/art	$0.50	$1.50	$2.50	£0.30	£0.90	£1.50
Title Value:	$0.50	$1.50	$2.50	£0.30	£0.90	£1.50

NO TIME FOR SERGEANTS
Dell,TV; 1 Feb/Apr 1965-3 Aug/Oct 1965

Issue	$Good	$Fine	$N.Mint	£Good	£Fine	£N.Mint
1 scarce though distributed in the U.K. Sammy Jackson photo cover	$5.00	$15.00	$40.00	£3.10	£9.25	£25.00
2-3 scarce though distributed in the U.K.	$5.00	$15.00	$40.00	£3.10	£9.25	£25.00
Title Value:	$15.00	$45.00	$120.00	£9.30	£27.75	£75.00

NOCTURNAL EMISSIONS
Vortex; 1 Jun 1991-4 1992

Issue	$Good	$Fine	$N.Mint	£Good	£Fine	£N.Mint
1-4 ND Fiona Smyth script and art, black and white	$0.50	$1.50	$2.50	£0.30	£0.90	£1.50
Title Value:	$2.00	$6.00	$10.00	£1.20	£3.60	£6.00

NOCTURNALS, THE
Malibu Bravura,MS; 1 Jan 1995-6 Jun 1995

Issue	$Good	$Fine	$N.Mint	£Good	£Fine	£N.Mint
1 ND Daniel Brereton script and art	$0.60	$1.80	$3.00	£0.40	£1.20	£2.00
1 Glow in the Dark Edition, ND (Jan 1995) - limited to 2,500 copies	$1.50	$4.50	$7.50	£0.80	£2.40	£4.00
1 Newstand Edition, ND (Jan 1995) - with same interior but alternative cover	$0.60	$1.80	$3.00	£0.40	£1.20	£2.00
2-6 ND Daniel Brereton script and art	$0.60	$1.80	$3.00	£0.40	£1.20	£2.00
Title Value:	$5.70	$17.10	$28.50	£3.60	£10.80	£18.00

NOCTURNE
Aircel,MS; 1 Jun 1991-3 Aug 1991

Issue	$Good	$Fine	$N.Mint	£Good	£Fine	£N.Mint
1-3 ND Barry Blair art	$0.40	$1.20	$2.00	£0.25	£0.75	£1.25
Title Value:	$1.20	$3.60	$6.00	£0.75	£2.25	£3.75

NOCTURNE
Marvel Comics Group; 1 Jul 1995-4 Sep 1995

Issue	$Good	$Fine	$N.Mint	£Good	£Fine	£N.Mint
1 Dan Abnett script, Joe Fonteriz and John Stokes art all begin; Nocturne inherits the mantle of Night Raven	$0.30	$0.90	$1.50	£0.20	£0.60	£1.00
2	$0.30	$0.90	$1.50	£0.20	£0.60	£1.00
3-4 bi-weekly	$0.30	$0.90	$1.50	£0.20	£0.60	£1.00
Title Value:	$1.20	$3.60	$6.00	£0.80	£2.40	£4.00

NOMAD (1ST SERIES)
Marvel Comics Group,MS; 1 Nov 1990-4 Feb 1991

(see Captain America #180)

Issue	$Good	$Fine	$N.Mint	£Good	£Fine	£N.Mint
1 ND	$0.50	$1.50	$2.50	£0.30	£0.90	£1.50
2 ND	$0.40	$1.20	$2.00	£0.25	£0.75	£1.25
3-4 ND Captain America appears	$0.40	$1.20	$2.00	£0.25	£0.75	£1.25
Title Value:	$1.70	$5.10	$8.50	£1.05	£3.15	£5.25

Note: see Captain America for history of this character as sidekick

NOMAD (2ND SERIES)
Marvel Comics Group; 1 May 1992-25 May 1994

Issue	$Good	$Fine	$N.Mint	£Good	£Fine	£N.Mint
1 ND fold-out cover/map	$0.40	$1.20	$2.00	£0.25	£0.75	£1.25
2 ND	$0.30	$0.90	$1.50	£0.20	£0.60	£1.00
3 ND U.S.Agent appears	$0.30	$0.90	$1.50	£0.20	£0.60	£1.00
4 ND Dead Man's Hand part 2, Daredevil appears, continued in Punisher War Journal #45	$0.30	$0.90	$1.50	£0.20	£0.60	£1.00
5 ND Dead Man's Hand part 5, Punisher appears, continued in Punisher War Journal #46	$0.30	$0.90	$1.50	£0.20	£0.60	£1.00
6 ND Dead Man's Hand part 8, Punisher and Daredevil appear	$0.30	$0.90	$1.50	£0.20	£0.60	£1.00
7 ND Infinity War X-over	$0.30	$0.90	$1.50	£0.20	£0.60	£1.00
8-15 ND	$0.30	$0.90	$1.50	£0.20	£0.60	£1.00
16 ND Gambit appears	$0.30	$0.90	$1.50	£0.20	£0.60	£1.00
17 ND	$0.30	$0.90	$1.50	£0.20	£0.60	£1.00
18 ND continued from Captain America #420	$0.30	$0.90	$1.50	£0.20	£0.60	£1.00
19 ND Nomad vs. Captain America	$0.30	$0.90	$1.50	£0.20	£0.60	£1.00
20 ND	$0.30	$0.90	$1.50	£0.20	£0.60	£1.00
21 ND Man-Thing appears	$0.30	$0.90	$1.50	£0.20	£0.60	£1.00
22 ND Zaran the Weapons Master appears	$0.30	$0.90	$1.50	£0.20	£0.60	£1.00
23-24 ND	$0.30	$0.90	$1.50	£0.20	£0.60	£1.00
25 ND with free Spiderman vs. Venom card sheet	$0.30	$0.90	$1.50	£0.20	£0.60	£1.00
Title Value:	$7.60	$22.80	$38.00	£5.05	£15.15	£25.25

NOMAN
Tower; 1 Nov 1966-2 Mar 1967

(see Thunder Agents)

Issue	$Good	$Fine	$N.Mint	£Good	£Fine	£N.Mint
1 distributed in the U.K. Giant	$7.00	$21.00	$50.00	£4.25	£12.50	£30.00
2 distributed in the U.K. Giant	$5.00	$15.00	$35.00	£3.20	£9.50	£22.50
Title Value:	$12.00	$36.00	$85.00	£7.45	£22.00	£52.50

NORMALMAN
Aardvark/Renegade; 1 Jan 1984-12 1987

1 ND Valentino art begins

	$Good	$Fine	$N.Mint	£Good	£Fine	£N.Mint
	$0.50	$1.50	$2.50	£0.30	£0.90	£1.50
2-7 ND	$0.40	$1.20	$2.00	£0.25	£0.75	£1.25
8 ND last Aardvark issue						
	$0.40	$1.20	$2.00	£0.25	£0.75	£1.25
9 ND	$0.40	$1.20	$2.00	£0.25	£0.75	£1.25
10 ND Cerebus cameo						
	$0.50	$1.50	$2.50	£0.30	£0.90	£1.50
11-12 ND	$0.40	$1.20	$2.00	£0.25	£0.75	£1.25
Title Value:	$5.00	$15.00	$25.00	£3.10	£9.30	£15.50

NORMALMAN 3-D ANNUAL

Renegade; 1 1987

	$Good	$Fine	$N.Mint	£Good	£Fine	£N.Mint
1 ND with 3-D glasses (25% less if without glasses)						
	$0.50	$1.50	$2.50	£0.30	£0.90	£1.50
Title Value:	$0.50	$1.50	$2.50	£0.30	£0.90	£1.50

NORMALMAN/MEGATON SPECIAL

Image,OS; 1 Aug 1994

	$Good	$Fine	$N.Mint	£Good	£Fine	£N.Mint
1 ND Valentino, Simpson, Burden and Marder						
	$0.40	$1.20	$2.00	£0.25	£0.75	£1.25
Title Value:	$0.40	$1.20	$2.00	£0.25	£0.75	£1.25

NORMALMAN: THE NOVEL

Slave Labor; nn 1990

	$Good	$Fine	$N.Mint	£Good	£Fine	£N.Mint
nn ND reprints series of 12						
	$2.00	$6.00	$10.00	£1.50	£4.50	£7.50
Title Value:	$2.00	$6.00	$10.00	£1.50	£4.50	£7.50

NORTHGUARD: THE MANDES CONCLUSION

Caliber Press; 1-3 1989

	$Good	$Fine	$N.Mint	£Good	£Fine	£N.Mint
1-3 ND black and white						
	$0.30	$0.90	$1.50	£0.20	£0.60	£1.00
Title Value:	$0.90	$2.70	$4.50	£0.60	£1.80	£3.00

NORTHSTAR

Marvel Comics Group,MS; 1 Apr 1994-4 Jul 1994

	$Good	$Fine	$N.Mint	£Good	£Fine	£N.Mint
1 Simon Furman script begins; aftermath following Alpha Flight #130						
	$0.40	$1.20	$2.00	£0.25	£0.75	£1.25
2-4	$0.40	$1.20	$2.00	£0.25	£0.75	£1.25
Title Value:	$1.60	$4.80	$8.00	£1.00	£3.00	£5.00

Note: owing to poorer paper quality than usual, many copies appear crinkled

NORTHSTAR

Northstar; 1 1988

	$Good	$Fine	$N.Mint	£Good	£Fine	£N.Mint
1 ND rare in the U.K. signed by Tim Vigil, Mort Castle and Mark Bernard, black and white (spot red colour on cover) - limited to 1000 copies						
	$6.00	$18.00	$30.00	£5.00	£15.00	£25.00
Title Value:	$6.00	$18.00	$30.00	£5.00	£15.00	£25.00

NORTHSTAR 5TH ANNIVERSARY SPECIAL

Northstar,OS; 1 Jan 1995

	$Good	$Fine	$N.Mint	£Good	£Fine	£N.Mint
1 ND black and white collection of greatest hits						
	$0.40	$1.20	$2.00	£0.25	£0.75	£1.25
Title Value:	$0.40	$1.20	$2.00	£0.25	£0.75	£1.25

NORTHSTAR, BEST OF

Northstar; 1 Aug 1992-3 1993

	$Good	$Fine	$N.Mint	£Good	£Fine	£N.Mint
1 ND Tim Vigil, Mark Nelson art featured						
	$0.50	$1.50	$2.50	£0.30	£0.90	£1.50
2-3 ND	$0.50	$1.50	$2.50	£0.30	£0.90	£1.50
Title Value:	$1.50	$4.50	$7.50	£0.90	£2.70	£4.50

NOSFERATU

Dark Horse,OS; 1 May 1991

	$Good	$Fine	$N.Mint	£Good	£Fine	£N.Mint
1 ND 64pgs, Phillipe Druillet script/art						
	$0.80	$2.40	$4.00	£0.50	£1.50	£2.50
Title Value:	$0.80	$2.40	$4.00	£0.50	£1.50	£2.50

NOSFERATU (2ND SERIES)

Caliber Press,OS; 1 Mar 1995

	$Good	$Fine	$N.Mint	£Good	£Fine	£N.Mint
1 ND 48pgs, Rafael Nieves script and Ken Holewczynski art; film adaptation						
	$0.80	$2.40	$4.00	£0.50	£1.50	£2.50
Title Value:	$0.80	$2.40	$4.00	£0.50	£1.50	£2.50

NOSFERATU (LIMITED SERIES)

Caliber/Tome Press,MS; 1 Jul 1991-2 Aug 1991

	$Good	$Fine	$N.Mint	£Good	£Fine	£N.Mint
1-2 ND	$0.50	$1.50	$2.50	£0.30	£0.90	£1.50
Title Value:	$1.00	$3.00	$5.00	£0.60	£1.80	£3.00

NOSFERATU: PLAGUE OF TERROR

Millennium,MS; 1 May 1991-4 Aug 1991

	$Good	$Fine	$N.Mint	£Good	£Fine	£N.Mint
1-4 ND Mark Ellis and Rik Levins script/art						
	$0.40	$1.20	$2.00	£0.25	£0.75	£1.25
Title Value:	$1.60	$4.80	$8.00	£1.00	£3.00	£5.00
Nosferatu: Plague of Darkness (May 1995)						
collects four issue series with new blood red cover				£1.30	£3.90	£6.50

NOT BRAND ECHH

Marvel Comics Group; 1 Aug 1967-13 May 1969

	$Good	$Fine	$N.Mint	£Good	£Fine	£N.Mint
1	$5.50	$17.00	$40.00	£2.85	£8.50	£20.00
2 scarce in the U.K. "Gnatman & Rotten"						
	$2.85	$8.50	$20.00	£1.40	£4.25	£10.00
3	$2.85	$8.50	$20.00	£1.25	£3.85	£9.00
4 "The Ecchsmen"	$2.85	$8.50	$20.00	£1.25	£3.85	£9.00
5	$2.85	$8.50	$20.00	£1.25	£3.85	£9.00
6-7	$2.85	$8.50	$20.00	£1.05	£3.20	£7.50
8 "The Ecchsmen"	$2.85	$8.50	$20.00	£1.05	£3.20	£7.50
9-12 68pgs	$2.50	$7.50	$17.50	£1.05	£3.20	£7.50
13 scarce in the U.K. 68pgs						
	$2.50	$7.50	$17.50	£1.10	£3.40	£8.00
Title Value:	$37.95	$114.00	$267.50	£16.45	£50.10	£117.50

Note: Jack Kirby art in #1, 3, 5-7. Origin of Forbush Man in #5. #10 is all reprint.

NOVA

Marvel Comics Group; 1 Sep 1976-25 May 1979

(The Man Called Nova #22-25)

	$Good	$Fine	$N.Mint	£Good	£Fine	£N.Mint
1 origin	$0.80	$2.50	$5.00	£0.50	£1.50	£3.00
2-3	$0.40	$1.25	$2.50	£0.25	£0.75	£1.50
4 Nova vs. Thor, Jack Kirby cover						
	$0.40	$1.25	$2.50	£0.25	£0.75	£1.50
5-6	$0.40	$1.25	$2.50	£0.25	£0.75	£1.50
7 Jack Kirby cover	$0.40	$1.25	$2.50	£0.25	£0.75	£1.50
8-11	$0.40	$1.25	$2.50	£0.25	£0.75	£1.50
12 Nova vs. Spiderman, X-over Spiderman #171						
	$0.65	$2.00	$4.00	£0.30	£1.00	£2.00
13 1st appearance Crime-Buster						
	$0.40	$1.25	$2.50	£0.25	£0.75	£1.50
14	$0.40	$1.25	$2.50	£0.25	£0.75	£1.50
15 Spiderman, Iron Man, Hulk, Nick Fury and Captain America appear						
	$0.40	$1.25	$2.50	£0.25	£0.75	£1.50
16-18 Nick Fury appears						
	$0.40	$1.25	$2.50	£0.25	£0.75	£1.50
19-20 ND	$0.40	$1.25	$2.50	£0.25	£0.75	£1.50
21-23	$0.30	$1.00	$2.00	£0.20	£0.60	£1.25
24 1st full appearance new Champions						
	$0.30	$1.00	$2.00	£0.20	£0.60	£1.25
25 ND very scarce in the U.K. new Champions appear						
	$0.30	$1.00	$2.00	£0.80	£2.50	£5.00
Title Value:	$10.15	$32.00	$64.00	£6.90	£20.90	£42.00

Note: story continues in Fantastic Four #208-212.

NOVA (2ND SERIES)

Marvel Comics Group; 1 Jan 1994-18 Jun 1995

	$Good	$Fine	$N.Mint	£Good	£Fine	£N.Mint
1 48pgs, new costume and new powers						
	$0.50	$1.50	$2.50	£0.30	£0.90	£1.50
1 Collectors Edition, ND 48pgs, gold foil cover						
	$0.60	$1.80	$3.00	£0.40	£1.20	£2.00
2	$0.40	$1.20	$2.00	£0.25	£0.75	£1.25
3 Spiderman guest-stars						
	$0.40	$1.20	$2.00	£0.25	£0.75	£1.25
4	$0.40	$1.20	$2.00	£0.25	£0.75	£1.25
5 with free Spiderman and his Deadly Foes card sheet						
	$0.40	$1.20	$2.00	£0.25	£0.75	£1.25
6-10	$0.40	$1.20	$2.00	£0.25	£0.75	£1.25
11 Thing, Ant-Man and Dr. Doom appear						
	$0.40	$1.20	$2.00	£0.25	£0.75	£1.25
12 The Inhumans appear						
	$0.40	$1.20	$2.00	£0.25	£0.75	£1.25
13 Night Thrasher and Firestar appear						
	$0.40	$1.20	$2.00	£0.25	£0.75	£1.25
14 New Warriors appear						
	$0.40	$1.20	$2.00	£0.25	£0.75	£1.25
15-17	$0.40	$1.20	$2.00	£0.25	£0.75	£1.25
18 Nova Omega part 1, continued in New Warriors #60						
	$0.40	$1.20	$2.00	£0.25	£0.75	£1.25
Title Value:	$7.90	$23.70	$39.50	£4.95	£14.85	£24.75

NTH MAN, THE ULTIMATE NINJA

Marvel Comics Group; 1 Aug 1989-16 Sep 1990

(see Marvel Comics Presents #25)

	$Good	$Fine	$N.Mint	£Good	£Fine	£N.Mint
1-7 ND	$0.25	$0.75	$1.25	£0.15	£0.45	£0.75
8 early Dale Keown art						
	$0.30	$0.90	$1.50	£0.20	£0.60	£1.00
9-16	$0.25	$0.75	$1.25	£0.15	£0.45	£0.75
Title Value:	$4.05	$12.15	$20.25	£2.45	£7.35	£12.25

NUKLA

Dell; 1 Oct/Dec 1965-4 Sep 1966

	$Good	$Fine	$N.Mint	£Good	£Fine	£N.Mint
1 distributed in the U.K. origin of Nukla						
	$4.25	$12.50	$30.00	£2.10	£6.25	£15.00
2-3 distributed in the U.K.						
	$2.50	$7.50	$17.50	£1.05	£3.20	£7.50
4 distributed in the U.K. Steve Ditko art						
	$4.25	$12.50	$30.00	£2.10	£6.25	£15.00
Title Value:	$13.50	$40.00	$95.00	£6.30	£18.90	£45.00

NURSE BETSY CRANE

Charlton; 12 Sep 1961-27 Mar 1964

	$Good	$Fine	$N.Mint	£Good	£Fine	£N.Mint
12-13 distributed in the U.K.						
	$0.70	$2.10	$5.00	£0.40	£1.25	£3.00
14-20 distributed in the U.K.						
	$0.55	$1.70	$4.00	£0.35	£1.05	£2.50
21-27 distributed in the U.K.						
	$0.50	$1.50	$3.50	£0.25	£0.85	£2.00
Title Value:	$8.75	$26.60	$62.00	£5.00	£15.80	£37.50

NYOKA THE JUNGLE GIRL, THE FURTHER ADVENTURES OF

AC Comics; 1 1988-5 1989

	$Good	$Fine	$N.Mint	£Good	£Fine	£N.Mint
1-5 ND part 50s reprints						
	$0.40	$1.20	$2.00	£0.25	£0.75	£1.25
Title Value:	$2.00	$6.00	$10.00	£1.25	£3.75	£6.25

O

OBLIVION

Comico; 1 Jul 1995-4 1996

	$Good	$Fine	$N.Mint	£Good	£Fine	£N.Mint
1 ND Art Adams cover						
	$0.50	$1.50	$2.50	£0.30	£0.90	£1.50
2 ND pre-bagged with trading card						
	$0.50	$1.50	$2.50	£0.30	£0.90	£1.50
3 ND	$0.50	$1.50	$2.50	£0.30	£0.90	£1.50
4 ND Dave Gibbons cover						

	$Good	$Fine	$N.Mint	£Good	£Fine	£N.Mint
	$0.50	$1.50	$2.50	£0.30	£0.90	£1.50
Title Value:	$2.00	$6.00	$10.00	£1.20	£3.60	£6.00

OBLIVION CITY

Slave Labor; 1 Jun 1991-19 1993

	$Good	$Fine	$N.Mint	£Good	£Fine	£N.Mint
1 ND	$0.50	$1.50	$2.50	£0.30	£0.90	£1.50
1 2nd printing, ND (May 1992)	$0.40	$1.20	$2.00	£0.25	£0.75	£1.25
2-10 ND	$0.50	$1.50	$2.50	£0.30	£0.90	£1.50
11-19 ND	$0.40	$1.20	$2.00	£0.25	£0.75	£1.25
Title Value:	$9.00	$27.00	$45.00	£5.50	£16.50	£27.50
Oblivion City Starter Set, issues #1-4 offered at less than combined retail				£1.00	£3.00	£5.00
Big City: The Complete Oblivion City (Mar 1995) 250pgs, reprints all 19 issues				£2.70	£8.10	£13.50

OBNOXIO THE CLOWN

Marvel Comics Group,OS; 1 Apr 1983

	$Good	$Fine	$N.Mint	£Good	£Fine	£N.Mint
1 ND X-Men co-star	$0.50	$1.50	$2.50	£0.30	£0.90	£1.50
Title Value:	$0.50	$1.50	$2.50	£0.30	£0.90	£1.50

OCTOBER YEN

Antarctic Press,MS; 1 Jul 1996-3 Sep 1996

	$Good	$Fine	$N.Mint	£Good	£Fine	£N.Mint
1-3 ND Brandon Graham script and art	$0.70	$2.10	$3.50	£0.50	£1.50	£2.50
Title Value:	$2.10	$6.30	$10.50	£1.50	£4.50	£7.50

OFFCASTES

Marvel Comics Group/Epic,MS; 1 Jul 1993-3 Sep 1993

	$Good	$Fine	$N.Mint	£Good	£Fine	£N.Mint
1-3 ND Mike Vosburg script and art	$0.40	$1.20	$2.00	£0.25	£0.75	£1.25
Title Value:	$1.20	$3.60	$6.00	£0.75	£2.25	£3.75

OFFICIAL BUZ SAWYER

Pioneer; 1 Aug 1988-5 1989

	$Good	$Fine	$N.Mint	£Good	£Fine	£N.Mint
1-5 ND Roy Crane reprints from newspaper strip; black and white	$0.40	$1.20	$2.00	£0.25	£0.75	£1.25
Title Value:	$2.00	$6.00	$10.00	£1.25	£3.75	£6.25

OFFICIAL CRISIS ON INFINITE EARTHS CROSSOVER INDEX

I.C.G/Eclipse; 1 Jul 1986

(see Crisis on Infinite Earths)

	$Good	$Fine	$N.Mint	£Good	£Fine	£N.Mint
1 ND very scarce in the U.K. information and colour cover reproductions of Crisis X-overs plus continuity flow charts and character indexes	$0.50	$1.50	$2.50	£0.30	£0.90	£1.50
Title Value:	$0.50	$1.50	$2.50	£0.30	£0.90	£1.50

OFFICIAL CRISIS ON INFINITE EARTHS INDEX, THE

I.C.G/Eclipse; 1 Mar 1986

(see Crisis on Infinite Earths)

	$Good	$Fine	$N.Mint	£Good	£Fine	£N.Mint
1 ND scarce in the U.K. George Perez cover, information and colour cover reproductions Crisis on Infinite Earths maxi-series #1-12	$0.50	$1.50	$2.50	£0.30	£0.90	£1.50
Title Value:	$0.50	$1.50	$2.50	£0.30	£0.90	£1.50

OFFICIAL DOOM PATROL INDEX, THE

I.C.G/Eclipse; 1,2 Feb 1986

	$Good	$Fine	$N.Mint	£Good	£Fine	£N.Mint
1 ND information and colour cover reproductions My Greatest Adventure #80-#85, Doom Patrol #86-#98 plus synopses and character indexes	$0.50	$1.50	$2.50	£0.30	£0.90	£1.50
2 ND information and colour cover reproductions Doom Patrol #99-#124, Showcase #94-#96, Blue Ribbon Digest #19 plus synopses and character indexes; John Byrne cover	$0.50	$1.50	$2.50	£0.30	£0.90	£1.50
Title Value:	$1.00	$3.00	$5.00	£0.60	£1.80	£3.00

OFFICIAL HANDBOOK OF THE MARVEL UNIVERSE DELUXE EDITION, THE

Marvel Comics Group,MS; 1 Dec 1985-20 Jul 1986

(see Official Handbook of the Marvel Universe)

	$Good	$Fine	$N.Mint	£Good	£Fine	£N.Mint
1-5 ND	$0.80	$2.40	$4.00	£0.50	£1.50	£2.50
6-10 ND	$0.60	$1.80	$3.00	£0.40	£1.20	£2.00
11-20 ND	$0.50	$1.50	$2.50	£0.30	£0.90	£1.50
Title Value:	$12.00	$36.00	$60.00	£7.50	£22.50	£37.50
Trade paperback #1-10, 128pgs, reprints 2 of the above issues per book				£0.90	£2.70	£4.50

Note: covers of #1-15 and #16-20 were intended to fit together into continuous pictures. 2nd prints of #1-3 available (1991)

OFFICIAL HANDBOOK OF THE MARVEL UNIVERSE UPDATE '89

Marvel Comics Group,MS; 1 Jul 1989-6 Nov 1989; 7 Jan 1990-8 Feb 1990

	$Good	$Fine	$N.Mint	£Good	£Fine	£N.Mint
1-8 ND DS	$0.40	$1.20	$2.00	£0.25	£0.75	£1.25
Title Value:	$3.20	$9.60	$16.00	£2.00	£6.00	£10.00

Note: originally announced as a 6 issue run, extended by 2 further issues. Peter Sanderson text plus various artists.

OFFICIAL HANDBOOK OF THE MARVEL UNIVERSE, THE

Marvel Comics Group,MS; 1 Jan 1983-20 Jul 1986

	$Good	$Fine	$N.Mint	£Good	£Fine	£N.Mint
1 ND (A)	$0.80	$2.40	$4.00	£0.50	£1.50	£2.50
2 ND (B-C)	$0.60	$1.80	$3.00	£0.40	£1.20	£2.00
3-6 ND (B-L)	$0.60	$1.80	$3.00	£0.40	£1.20	£2.00
7-10 ND (M-Z)	$0.60	$1.80	$3.00	£0.40	£1.20	£2.00
11-12 ND (M-Z)	$0.50	$1.50	$2.50	£0.30	£0.90	£1.50
13-14 Book of the Dead	$0.50	$1.50	$2.50	£0.30	£0.90	£1.50
15 Weaponry Catalogue	$0.50	$1.50	$2.50	£0.30	£0.90	£1.50
Title Value:	$8.70	$26.10	$43.50	£5.60	£16.80	£28.00

Note: alphabetical listing of all Marvel characters. The covers of 1-12 fit together as a poster.

OFFICIAL HAWKMAN INDEX, THE

I.C.G/Eclipse; 1 Nov 1986-2 Dec 1986

	$Good	$Fine	$N.Mint	£Good	£Fine	£N.Mint
1 ND information and colour cover repros Brave and the Bold #34-#36, #42-#44, Mystery in Space #87-#90, Hawkman #1-#16 plus synopses and character indexes	$0.50	$1.50	$2.50	£0.30	£0.90	£1.50
2 ND information and colour cover repros Hawkman #17-#27, Atom #39-#45, Showcase #101-#103, plus synopses, character indexes and other appearances in Detective and World's Finest, Hawkman 2nd/Shadow War	$0.50	$1.50	$2.50	£0.30	£0.90	£1.50
Title Value:	$1.00	$3.00	$5.00	£0.60	£1.80	£3.00

OFFICIAL JOHNNY HAZARD

Pioneer; 1 Aug 1988-5 1989

	$Good	$Fine	$N.Mint	£Good	£Fine	£N.Mint
1-5 ND Frank Robbins reprints from newspaper strip; black and white	$0.40	$1.20	$2.00	£0.25	£0.75	£1.25
Title Value:	$2.00	$6.00	$10.00	£1.25	£3.75	£6.25

OFFICIAL JUNGLE JIM

Pioneer; 1 Jun 1988-16 1989

	$Good	$Fine	$N.Mint	£Good	£Fine	£N.Mint
1-16 ND black and white Alex Raymond reprints from newspaper strip, colour covers	$0.40	$1.20	$2.00	£0.25	£0.75	£1.25
Title Value:	$6.40	$19.20	$32.00	£4.00	£12.00	£20.00
Annual 1				£0.40	£1.20	£2.00

OFFICIAL JUNGLE JIM ANNUAL

Pioneer,OS; 1 Jan 1989

	$Good	$Fine	$N.Mint	£Good	£Fine	£N.Mint
1 ND 48pgs, black and white reprints, colour cover	$0.60	$1.80	$3.00	£0.40	£1.20	£2.00
Title Value:	$0.60	$1.80	$3.00	£0.40	£1.20	£2.00

OFFICIAL JUSTICE LEAGUE OF AMERICA INDEX, THE

I.C.G/Eclipse; 1 Apr 1986-8 Mar 1987

	$Good	$Fine	$N.Mint	£Good	£Fine	£N.Mint
1 scarce in the U.K. information and colour cover reproductions Brave and the Bold #28-#30, Justice League of America #1-#19 plus character synopses; George Perez cover	$0.50	$1.50	$2.50	£0.30	£0.90	£1.50
2 scarce in the U.K. information and colour cover reproductions Justice League of America #20-#56; George Perez cover	$0.50	$1.50	$2.50	£0.30	£0.90	£1.50
3 scarce in the U.K. information and colour cover reproductions Justice League of America #57-#95						

Nosferatu: Plague of Terror #1

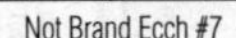

Not Brand Ecch #7

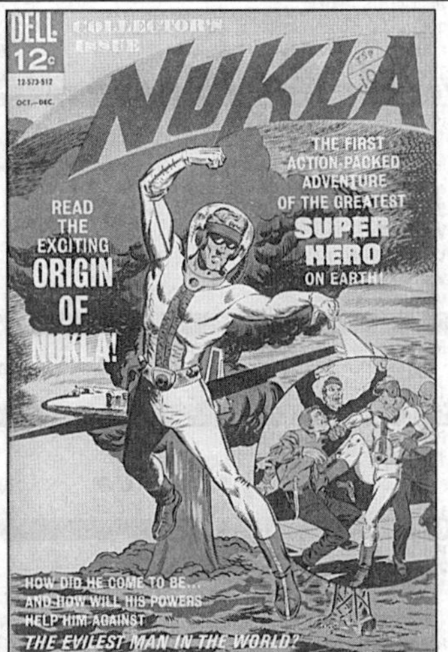

Nukla #1

	$Good	$Fine	$N.Mint	£Good	£Fine	£N.Mint
	$0.50	$1.50	$2.50	£0.30	£0.90	£1.50
4 scarce in the U.K. information and colour cover reproductions Justice League of America #96-#130						
	$0.50	$1.50	$2.50	£0.30	£0.90	£1.50
5 scarce in the U.K. information and colour cover reproductions Justice League of America #131-#167; Joe Staton cover						
	$0.50	$1.50	$2.50	£0.30	£0.90	£1.50
6 scarce in the U.K. information and colour cover reproductions Justice League of America #168-#203; Jerry Ordway cover featuring Darkseid						
	$0.50	$1.50	$2.50	£0.30	£0.90	£1.50
7 scarce in the U.K. information and colour cover reproductions Justice League of America #204-#237; Joe Staton cover						
	$0.50	$1.50	$2.50	£0.30	£0.90	£1.50
8 scarce in the U.K. information and colour cover reproductions Justice League of America #238-#261, 100pg Spectacular #6,#17, Justice League Digests and Tabloids, Red Tornado mini-series, Zatanna Special						
	$0.50	$1.50	$2.50	£0.30	£0.90	£1.50
Title Value:	$4.00	$12.00	$20.00	£2.40	£7.20	£12.00

Note: all Non-Distributed on the news-stands in the U.K.

OFFICIAL LEGION OF SUPER-HEROES INDEX

I.C.G/Eclipse; 1 Dec 1986-5 Apr 1987

	$Good	$Fine	$N.Mint	£Good	£Fine	£N.Mint
1 information and colour cover reproductions of Legion from Adventure #247 up to appearances prior to Adventure Comics #300 plus synopses and character breakdowns						
	$0.50	$1.50	$2.50	£0.30	£0.90	£1.50
2 information and colour cover reproductions of Legion appearances in Adventure Comics #301-#323 plus synopses and character breakdowns						
	$0.50	$1.50	$2.50	£0.30	£0.90	£1.50
3 information and colour cover reproductions of Legion appearances in Adventure Comics #324-#347 plus synopses and character breakdowns						
	$0.50	$1.50	$2.50	£0.30	£0.90	£1.50
4 information and colour cover reproductions of Legion appearances in Adventure Comics #348-#369 and Superboy #147 plus synopses and character breakdowns						
	$0.50	$1.50	$2.50	£0.30	£0.90	£1.50
5 information and colour cover reproductions of Legion appearances in Adventure Comics #370-#380 and Action #377-#390 plus synopses and character breakdowns						
	$0.50	$1.50	$2.50	£0.30	£0.90	£1.50
Title Value:	$2.50	$7.50	$12.50	£1.50	£4.50	£7.50

Note: all Non-Distributed on the news-stands in the U.K.

OFFICIAL MANDRAKE ANNUAL, THE

Pioneer,OS; 1 Feb 1987

	$Good	$Fine	$N.Mint	£Good	£Fine	£N.Mint
1 ND 48pgs, black and white cover and art, reprinting newspaper strips						
	$0.60	$1.80	$3.00	£0.40	£1.20	£2.00
Title Value:	$0.60	$1.80	$3.00	£0.40	£1.20	£2.00

OFFICIAL MANDRAKE KING SIZE, THE

Pioneer,OS; 1 1989

	$Good	$Fine	$N.Mint	£Good	£Fine	£N.Mint
1 ND 48pgs, black and white cover and art, reprinting newspaper strips						
	$0.60	$1.80	$3.00	£0.40	£1.20	£2.00
Title Value:	$0.60	$1.80	$3.00	£0.40	£1.20	£2.00

OFFICIAL MANDRAKE MONTHLY, THE

Pioneer; 1-3 1989

	$Good	$Fine	$N.Mint	£Good	£Fine	£N.Mint
1 ND 48pgs, squarebound, also features Buz Sawyer, Secret Agent and Jungle Jim; black and white covers and art						
	$0.80	$2.40	$4.00	£0.50	£1.50	£2.50
2-3 ND 48pgs, squarebound, also features Buz Sawyer, Secret Agent and Jungle Jim; black and white card-stock covers and art						
	$0.80	$2.40	$4.00	£0.50	£1.50	£2.50
Title Value:	$2.40	$7.20	$12.00	£1.50	£4.50	£7.50

OFFICIAL MANDRAKE, THE

Pioneer; 1 Jun 1988-15 1989

	$Good	$Fine	$N.Mint	£Good	£Fine	£N.Mint
1-15 ND Falk/Davis reprints from newspaper strip; black and white with colour covers						
	$0.40	$1.20	$2.00	£0.25	£0.75	£1.25
Title Value:	$6.00	$18.00	$30.00	£3.75	£11.25	£18.75

Note: #1-9 called The Official Mandrake the Magician

OFFICIAL MANDRAKE, THE (2ND SERIES)

Pioneer,OS; 1 1989

	$Good	$Fine	$N.Mint	£Good	£Fine	£N.Mint
1 ND black and white cover and art, reprinting newspaper strips						
	$0.80	$2.40	$4.00	£0.50	£1.50	£2.50
Title Value:	$0.80	$2.40	$4.00	£0.50	£1.50	£2.50

OFFICIAL MARVEL INDEX

Marvel Comics Group; 1 1985-5 1987

The series of five Official Marvel Indexes provide in-depth information on writers, artists, characters and features and was intended as an on-going concern. The titles and issue numbers covered are as follows and more details can be found under these respective titles:

Volume 1 - Amazing Spiderman #1-#9
Volume 2 - Fantastic Four #1-#12
Volume 3 - Marvel Team-Up #1-#6
Volume 4 - X-Men #1-#6
Volume 5 - Avengers #1-#7

OFFICIAL MARVEL TIMELINE

Marvel Comics Group,OS; nn Jan 1997

	$Good	$Fine	$N.Mint	£Good	£Fine	£N.Mint
nn ND	$1.20	$3.60	$6.00	£0.80	£2.40	£4.00
Title Value:	$1.20	$3.60	$6.00	£0.80	£2.40	£4.00

OFFICIAL MODESTY BLAISE

Pioneer; 1 Jul 1988-8 1989

	$Good	$Fine	$N.Mint	£Good	£Fine	£N.Mint
1-8 ND Peter O'Donnell strip reprints; black and white						
	$0.40	$1.20	$2.00	£0.25	£0.75	£1.25
Title Value:	$3.20	$9.60	$16.00	£2.00	£6.00	£10.00

OFFICIAL PRINCE VALIANT

Pioneer; 1 Jun 1988-18 1989

	$Good	$Fine	$N.Mint	£Good	£Fine	£N.Mint
1-18 ND Hal Foster reprints from newspaper strip; black and white						
	$0.40	$1.20	$2.00	£0.25	£0.75	£1.25
Title Value:	$7.20	$21.60	$36.00	£4.50	£13.50	£22.50
Annual 1, Hal Foster reprints				£0.45	£1.35	£2.25
King Size 1, Hal Foster reprints				£0.45	£1.35	£2.25

OFFICIAL PRINCE VALIANT MONTHLY

Pioneer; 1 1989

	$Good	$Fine	$N.Mint	£Good	£Fine	£N.Mint
1 ND newspaper strip reprints by Hal Foster						
	$0.60	$1.80	$3.00	£0.40	£1.20	£2.00
Title Value:	$0.60	$1.80	$3.00	£0.40	£1.20	£2.00

OFFICIAL RIP KIRBY

Pioneer; 1 Jun 1988-5 1989

	$Good	$Fine	$N.Mint	£Good	£Fine	£N.Mint
1-5 ND Alex Raymond reprints from newspaper strip						
	$0.40	$1.20	$2.00	£0.25	£0.75	£1.25
Title Value:	$2.00	$6.00	$10.00	£1.25	£3.75	£6.25

OFFICIAL SECRET AGENT

Pioneer; 1 Jun 1988-7 Dec 1988

	$Good	$Fine	$N.Mint	£Good	£Fine	£N.Mint
1-7 ND Archie Goodwin and Al Williamson reprints of newspaper strip; black and white						
	$0.40	$1.20	$2.00	£0.25	£0.75	£1.25
Title Value:	$2.80	$8.40	$14.00	£1.75	£5.25	£8.75

OFFICIAL TEEN TITANS INDEX

I.C.G/Eclipse; 1 Aug 1985-5 Dec 1985

	$Good	$Fine	$N.Mint	£Good	£Fine	£N.Mint
1 information and colour cover reproductions Brave and the Bold #54,#60, Showcase #59, Teen Titans (1st) #1-22 plus character synopses						
	$0.50	$1.50	$2.50	£0.30	£0.90	£1.50
2 information and colour cover reproductions Teen Titans (1st) #23-53, DC Super Stars #1, Showcase #75, Hawk and the Dove (1st) #1-6						
	$0.50	$1.50	$2.50	£0.30	£0.90	£1.50
3 information and colour cover reproductions DC Comics Presents #26, New Teen.Titans (1st) #1-25, Annual #1, Tales of the New Teen Titans #1-4, Marvel and DC Present #1						
	$0.50	$1.50	$2.50	£0.30	£0.90	£1.50
4 information and colour cover reproductions DC Comics Presents #26, New Teen Titans (1st) #26-50, Annual #2-3, Giveaway #1-3						
	$0.50	$1.50	$2.50	£0.30	£0.90	£1.50
5 information and colour cover reproductions DC Comics Presents #26, New Teen Titans (1st) #51-62, New Teen Titans (2nd) #1-16, Annual (2nd) #1						
	$0.50	$1.50	$2.50	£0.30	£0.90	£1.50
Title Value:	$2.50	$7.50	$12.50	£1.50	£4.50	£7.50

Note: all Non-Distributed on the news-stands in the U.K.

OGRE

Black Diamond Publishing,MS; 1 Jan 1994-4 Apr 1994

	$Good	$Fine	$N.Mint	£Good	£Fine	£N.Mint
1-4 ND Phil White script, Pete Ayala art						
	$0.50	$1.50	$2.50	£0.30	£0.90	£1.50
Title Value:	$2.00	$6.00	$10.00	£1.20	£3.60	£6.00

OH MY GODDESS!

Dark Horse,MS; 1 Aug 1994-6 Jan 1995

	$Good	$Fine	$N.Mint	£Good	£Fine	£N.Mint
1-6 ND Kosuke Fujishima script/art						
	$0.50	$1.50	$2.50	£0.30	£0.90	£1.50
Title Value:	$3.00	$9.00	$15.00	£1.80	£5.40	£9.00

OH MY GODDESS! PART 2

Dark Horse,MS; 1 Feb 1995-8 Sep 1995

	$Good	$Fine	$N.Mint	£Good	£Fine	£N.Mint
1-8 ND Kosuke Fujishima script and art; black and white						
	$0.50	$1.50	$2.50	£0.30	£0.90	£1.50
Title Value:	$4.00	$12.00	$20.00	£2.40	£7.20	£12.00

OH MY GODDESS! PART 3

Dark Horse,MS; 1 Nov 1995-5 Mar 1996

	$Good	$Fine	$N.Mint	£Good	£Fine	£N.Mint
1 ND Kosuke Fujishima script and art; black and white						
	$0.60	$1.80	$3.00	£0.40	£1.20	£2.00
2 ND sub-titled Love Potion Number Nine Special; Kosuke Fujishima script and art; black and white						
	$0.60	$1.80	$3.00	£0.40	£1.20	£2.00
3 ND sub-titled Sympathy For The Devil						
	$0.60	$1.80	$3.00	£0.40	£1.20	£2.00
4 ND sub-titled Mystical Engine						
	$0.60	$1.80	$3.00	£0.40	£1.20	£2.00
5 ND sub-titled Valentine Rhapsody						
	$0.60	$1.80	$3.00	£0.40	£1.20	£2.00
Title Value:	$3.00	$9.00	$15.00	£2.00	£6.00	£10.00

Note: originally solicited as a continuing mini-series, it became a series of one-off specials with #2.)

OH MY GODDESS!: TERRIBLE MASTER URD

Dark Horse,MS; 1 Apr 1996-6 Sep 1996

	$Good	$Fine	$N.Mint	£Good	£Fine	£N.Mint
1-6 ND Kosuke Fujishima script and art; black and white						
	$0.60	$1.80	$3.00	£0.40	£1.20	£2.00
Title Value:	$3.60	$10.80	$18.00	£2.40	£7.20	£12.00

OKTANE

Dark Horse,MS; 1 Aug 1995-4 Nov 1995

	$Good	$Fine	$N.Mint	£Good	£Fine	£N.Mint
1-4 ND Gerard Jones script, Gene Ha and Andrew Pepoy art						
	$0.50	$1.50	$2.50	£0.30	£0.90	£1.50
Title Value:	$2.00	$6.00	$10.00	£1.20	£3.60	£6.00

OKTOBERFEST COMICS

Now and Then,OS; 1 1986

	$Good	$Fine	$N.Mint	£Good	£Fine	£N.Mint
1 ND scarce in the U.K. Dave Sim, Gene Day art						
	$1.20	$3.60	$6.00	£0.80	£2.40	£4.00
Title Value:	$1.20	$3.60	$6.00	£0.80	£2.40	£4.00

OLYMPIANS

Marvel Comics Group/Epic,MS; 1 Jul 1991-2 Mar 1992

	$Good	$Fine	$N.Mint	£Good	£Fine	£N.Mint
1-2 ND super-hero spoof						
	$0.60	$1.80	$3.00	£0.40	£1.20	£2.00
Title Value:	$1.20	$3.60	$6.00	£0.80	£2.40	£4.00

OMAC

DC Comics; 1 Sep/Oct 1974-8 Nov/Dec 1975

(see Kamandi, Warlord)

	$Good	$Fine	$N.Mint	£Good	£Fine	£N.Mint
1 origin and 1st appearance Omac; Jack Kirby art						
	$2.50	$7.50	$15.00	£1.00	£3.00	£6.00
2 Jack Kirby art	$1.65	$5.00	$10.00	£0.65	£2.00	£4.00
3-8 Jack Kirby art	$1.65	$5.00	$10.00	£0.50	£1.50	£3.00
Title Value:	$14.05	$42.50	$77.50	£4.65	£14.00	£28.00

OMAC (2ND SERIES)

DC Comics,MS; 1 Nov 1991-4 Feb 1992

Issue	$Good	$Fine	$N.Mint	£Good	£Fine	£N.Mint
1 ND 48pgs, John Byrne script and two-tone black and white art	$0.80	$2.40	$4.00	£0.50	£1.50	£2.50
2-4 ND 48pgs, John Byrne script and two tone black and white art	$0.80	$2.40	$4.00	£0.50	£1.50	£2.50
Title Value:	$3.20	$9.60	$16.00	£2.00	£6.00	£10.00

Note: Prestige Format

OMAHA THE CAT DANCER

Steeldragon Press/Kitchen Sink; 0 Sep 1990; 1 Jun 1986-20 1994

Issue	$Good	$Fine	$N.Mint	£Good	£Fine	£N.Mint
0 ND originally published as Bizarre Sex #9 redesigned 44pg "origin" (Sep 1990)	$0.40	$1.20	$2.00	£0.25	£0.75	£1.25
0 2nd printing, ND of the original #0 (Mar 1995)	$0.40	$1.20	$2.00	£0.25	£0.75	£1.25
0 Expanded Edition, ND 48pgs, (Jan 1994), all new art featured in a squarebound format	$0.80	$2.40	$4.00	£0.50	£1.50	£2.50
1 ND	$1.20	$3.60	$6.00	£0.70	£2.10	£3.50
1 2nd printing ND	$0.40	$1.20	$2.00	£0.25	£0.75	£1.25
2 ND	$1.00	$3.00	$5.00	£0.40	£1.20	£2.00
3-4 ND	$0.60	$1.80	$3.00	£0.30	£0.90	£1.50
4 2nd printing, (May 1995)	$0.40	$1.20	$2.00	£0.25	£0.75	£1.25
5-11 ND	$0.60	$1.80	$3.00	£0.30	£0.90	£1.50
11 2nd printing, ND (Aug 1994) $2.95 cover	$0.60	$1.80	$3.00	£0.40	£1.20	£2.00
12 ND	$0.50	$1.50	$2.50	£0.30	£0.90	£1.50
12 2nd printing, ND (Oct 1994)	$0.40	$1.20	$2.00	£0.25	£0.75	£1.25
13-20 ND	$0.50	$1.50	$2.50	£0.30	£0.90	£1.50
Title Value:	$15.50	$46.50	$74.50	£8.65	£25.95	£43.25

Note: 2nd printings of #2-12 available at cover price.

	£Good	£Fine	£N.Mint
Collected Omaha Book 1, softcover, reprints 1,2 & stories from Snarf, Dope & Bizarre Sex	£2.00	£6.00	£10.00
Book 1 Limited Edition Hardcover	£3.60	£10.80	£18.00
Book 2 reprints #3-6	£1.70	£5.10	£8.50
Book 3 reprints #7-10	£1.70	£5.10	£8.50
2nd print - Feb 1995	£1.70	£5.10	£8.50
Book 4 reprints #11-14 plus new 8pg story	£1.70	£5.10	£8.50
Books #2-4, Hardcover	£3.20	£9.60	£16.00

OMAHA THE CAT DANCER (2ND SERIES)

Fantagraphics; 1 Jun 1994-6 1995?

Issue	$Good	$Fine	$N.Mint	£Good	£Fine	£N.Mint
1 ND black and white	$0.50	$1.50	$2.50	£0.30	£0.90	£1.50
1 2nd printing, ND (Sep 1994)	$0.40	$1.20	$2.00	£0.25	£0.75	£1.25
2-3 ND black and white	$0.50	$1.50	$2.50	£0.30	£0.90	£1.50
4-5 ND black and white	$0.55	$1.65	$2.75	£0.35	£1.05	£1.75
6 ND	$0.55	$1.65	$2.75	£0.35	£1.05	£1.75
Title Value:	$3.55	$10.65	$17.75	£2.20	£6.60	£11.00

Note: originally announced as being published by Kitchen Sink

	£Good	£Fine	£N.Mint
Collected Omaha Vol. 5 (1995) Trade paperback ND collects issues #15-18	£2.30	£6.90	£11.50
Collected Omaha Vol. 6 (Feb 1996) Trade paperback ND collects issues #19 and #20 plus issues #1-3 of Fantagraphics series	£2.30	£6.90	£11.50
(Signed Deluxe Hardcover Edition (Feb 1996)	£4.00	£12.00	£20.00

OMEGA

Rebel Studios; 1 Aug 1987-2 1987

Issue	$Good	$Fine	$N.Mint	£Good	£Fine	£N.Mint
1 ND rare in the U.K. Tim Vigil art; withdrawn after copyright problems with Marvel's Omega the Unknown and many were destroyed; covers of #1-3 of future Omen title appear as pin-ups	$7.00	$21.00	$35.00	£5.00	£15.00	£25.00
1 2nd printing, ND yellow cover	$3.00	$9.00	$15.00	£2.00	£6.00	£10.00
2 ND	$0.60	$1.80	$3.00	£0.40	£1.20	£2.00
Title Value:	$10.60	$31.80	$53.00	£7.40	£22.20	£37.00

OMEGA ELITE

Blackthorne; 1 1987

Issue	$Good	$Fine	$N.Mint	£Good	£Fine	£N.Mint
1 ND Jim Starlin cover	$0.30	$0.90	$1.50	£0.20	£0.60	£1.00
Title Value:	$0.30	$0.90	$1.50	£0.20	£0.60	£1.00

OMEGA FORCE

Entity Comics,OS; 1 Dec 1995

Issue	$Good	$Fine	$N.Mint	£Good	£Fine	£N.Mint
1 ND black and white	$0.50	$1.50	$2.50	£0.30	£0.90	£1.50
1 2nd printing, ND (Apr 1996)	$0.50	$1.50	$2.50	£0.30	£0.90	£1.50
1 Videogame Edition, ND pre-bagged with video game disk	$1.40	$4.20	$7.00	£0.90	£2.70	£4.50
Title Value:	$2.40	$7.20	$12.00	£1.50	£4.50	£7.50

OMEGA FORCE II

Entity Comics; 1 Jun 1996

Issue	$Good	$Fine	$N.Mint	£Good	£Fine	£N.Mint
1 ND Mike and Jonah Cagley creative team	$0.55	$1.65	$2.75	£0.35	£1.05	£1.75
1 Commemorative Edition, ND pre-bagged with certificate; limited to 1,500 copies	$2.00	$6.00	$10.00	£1.30	£3.90	£6.50
Title Value:	$2.55	$7.65	$12.75	£1.65	£4.95	£8.25

OMEGA MEN

DC Comics; 1 Dec 1982-38 May 1986
(see Green Lantern #141,Lobo)

Issue	$Good	$Fine	$N.Mint	£Good	£Fine	£N.Mint
1 ND	$0.40	$1.20	$2.00	£0.25	£0.75	£1.25
2 ND origin Broot, Lobo appears in ad for next issue (no name mentioned)	$0.40	$1.20	$2.00	£0.25	£0.75	£1.25
3 ND 1st appearance Lobo	$1.20	$3.60	$6.00	£0.70	£2.10	£3.50
4 ND	$0.40	$1.20	$2.00	£0.25	£0.75	£1.25
5 ND 2nd Lobo appearance (2pgs)	$0.60	$1.80	$3.00	£0.40	£1.20	£2.00
6-8 ND	$0.40	$1.20	$2.00	£0.25	£0.75	£1.25
9 ND 3rd Lobo appearance (2pgs)	$0.60	$1.80	$3.00	£0.40	£1.20	£2.00
10 ND 1st full Lobo story	$1.50	$4.50	$7.50	£0.80	£2.40	£4.00
11-18 ND	$0.30	$0.90	$1.50	£0.20	£0.60	£1.00
19 ND Lobo appearance	$0.50	$1.50	$2.50	£0.30	£0.90	£1.50
20 ND full Lobo story	$0.60	$1.80	$3.00	£0.40	£1.20	£2.00
21-23 ND	$0.30	$0.90	$1.50	£0.20	£0.60	£1.00
24 ND Kev O'Neill art	$0.30	$0.90	$1.50	£0.20	£0.60	£1.00
25 ND	$0.30	$0.90	$1.50	£0.20	£0.60	£1.00
26 ND McManus art, Alan Moore script	$0.40	$1.20	$2.00	£0.25	£0.75	£1.25
27 ND Alan Moore script	$0.40	$1.20	$2.00	£0.25	£0.75	£1.25
28-30 ND	$0.30	$0.90	$1.50	£0.20	£0.60	£1.00
31 ND Crisis X-over	$0.30	$0.90	$1.50	£0.20	£0.60	£1.00
32 ND	$0.30	$0.90	$1.50	£0.20	£0.60	£1.00
33 ND unofficial Crisis X-over, Dave Gibbons art	$0.30	$0.90	$1.50	£0.20	£0.60	£1.00
34-35 ND Titans X-over	$0.30	$0.90	$1.50	£0.20	£0.60	£1.00
36 ND	$0.30	$0.90	$1.50	£0.20	£0.60	£1.00
37 ND full Lobo story	$0.60	$1.80	$3.00	£0.40	£1.20	£2.00
38 ND	$0.30	$0.90	$1.50	£0.20	£0.60	£1.00
Title Value:	$15.70	$47.10	$78.50	£10.00	£30.00	£50.00

Note: all Deluxe Format Baxter paper

OMEGA MEN ANNUAL

DC Comics; 1 Nov 1984-2 Nov 1985

Issue	$Good	$Fine	$N.Mint	£Good	£Fine	£N.Mint
1 ND 52pgs	$0.40	$1.20	$2.00	£0.25	£0.75	£1.25
2 ND 52pgs, Kev O'Neill art (5pgs)	$0.40	$1.20	$2.00	£0.25	£0.75	£1.25
Title Value:	$0.80	$2.40	$4.00	£0.50	£1.50	£2.50

OMEGA THE UNKNOWN

Marvel Comics Group; 1 Mar 1976-10 Sep 1977

Issue	$Good	$Fine	$N.Mint	£Good	£Fine	£N.Mint
1	$0.50	$1.50	$3.00	£0.20	£0.60	£1.25
2 Omega battles Hulk	$0.30	$1.00	$2.00	£0.15	£0.50	£1.00
3-7	$0.30	$1.00	$2.00	£0.15	£0.50	£1.00
8 ND 1st appearance new Foolkiller (cameo)	$0.30	$1.00	$2.00	£0.20	£0.60	£1.25
9 ND FoolKiller (1st full appearance)	$0.40	$1.25	$2.50	£0.25	£0.75	£1.50
10 ND	$0.30	$1.00	$2.00	£0.15	£0.50	£1.00
Title Value:	$3.30	$10.75	$21.50	£1.70	£5.45	£11.00

Note: storyline completed in The Defenders.

OMEN

Northstar; 1 1987-4 1989

Issue	$Good	$Fine	$N.Mint	£Good	£Fine	£N.Mint
1 ND scarce in the U.K. Tim Vigil co-script and art begins, re-drawn from Omega Premiere Edition 1 (Rebel Studios), letter reprinted from Marvel stating copyright infringement problem	$1.00	$3.00	$5.00	£0.70	£2.10	£3.50
1 2nd printing, ND no letter	$0.60	$1.80	$3.00	£0.40	£1.20	£2.00
1 Signed & Numbered Edition, ND (? copies)	$10.00	$30.00	$50.00	£7.00	£21.00	£35.00
2-4 ND	$0.70	$2.10	$3.50	£0.50	£1.50	£2.50
Title Value:	$13.70	$41.10	$68.50	£9.60	£28.80	£48.00

ON A PALE HORSE

Innovation,MS; 1 Jun 1991-5 1991

Issue	$Good	$Fine	$N.Mint	£Good	£Fine	£N.Mint
1 ND 48pgs, squarebound, painted art adaptation of Piers Anthony novel begins	$0.80	$2.40	$4.00	£0.60	£1.80	£3.00
1 2nd printing, ND (Aug 1993), $4.95 cover	$0.60	$1.80	$3.00	£0.40	£1.20	£2.00
2 ND 48pgs, squarebound	$0.70	$2.10	$3.50	£0.50	£1.50	£2.50
2 2nd printing, ND (Sep 1993)	$0.60	$1.80	$3.00	£0.40	£1.20	£2.00
3-5 ND 48pgs, squarebound	$0.60	$1.80	$3.00	£0.40	£1.20	£2.00
Title Value:	$4.50	$13.50	$22.50	£3.10	£9.30	£15.50

Note: issue #6 was advertised and solicited but never appeared owing to the collapse of Innovation.

ONE HUNDRED AND ONE DALMATIANS GRAPHIC NOVEL

Disney,OS; 1 1991

Issue	$Good	$Fine	$N.Mint	£Good	£Fine	£N.Mint
1 ND 48pgs, adaptation of film	$1.00	$3.00	$5.00	£0.70	£2.10	£3.50
1 Newstand Edition, ND 48pgs, without trading cards	$0.55	$1.65	$2.75	£0.35	£1.05	£1.75
Title Value:	$1.55	$4.65	$7.75	£1.05	£3.15	£5.25

100% TRUE

DC Comics/Paradox Press; 1 Aug 1996; 2 Jan 1997

1-2 ND 64pgs, anthology of weird true stories

	$Good	$Fine	$N.Mint	£Good	£Fine	£N.Mint
	$0.70	$2.10	$3.50	£0.50	£1.50	£2.50
Title Value:	$1.40	$4.20	$7.00	£1.00	£3.00	£5.00

101 WAYS TO END THE CLONE SAGA

Marvel Comics Group,OS; nn Jan 1997

nn ND alternative endings to the Spiderman Clone Saga

	$Good	$Fine	$N.Mint	£Good	£Fine	£N.Mint
	$0.50	$1.50	$2.50	£0.30	£0.90	£1.50
Title Value:	$0.50	$1.50	$2.50	£0.30	£0.90	£1.50

ONE MILE UP

Eclipse,MS; 1 Feb 1992-2 1992

	$Good	$Fine	$N.Mint	£Good	£Fine	£N.Mint
1-2 ND	$0.40	$1.20	$2.00	£0.25	£0.75	£1.25
Title Value:	$0.80	$2.40	$4.00	£0.50	£1.50	£2.50

ONE SHOT WESTERN

Caliber Press,OS; 1 Feb 1992

	$Good	$Fine	$N.Mint	£Good	£Fine	£N.Mint
1 ND	$0.40	$1.20	$2.00	£0.25	£0.75	£1.25
Title Value:	$0.40	$1.20	$2.00	£0.25	£0.75	£1.25

1,001 NIGHTS OF BACCHUS, THE

Dark Horse,OS; 1 May 1993

1 ND 48pgs, Eddie Campbell script/art

	$Good	$Fine	$N.Mint	£Good	£Fine	£N.Mint
	$0.80	$2.40	$4.00	£0.50	£1.50	£2.50
Title Value:	$0.80	$2.40	$4.00	£0.50	£1.50	£2.50

ONE, THE

Marvel Comics Group/Epic,MS; 1 Jul 1985-6 Feb 1986

	$Good	$Fine	$N.Mint	£Good	£Fine	£N.Mint
1-6 ND	$0.40	$1.20	$2.00	£0.25	£0.75	£1.25
Title Value:	$2.40	$7.20	$12.00	£1.50	£4.50	£7.50

Trade paperback (Dec 1989)

	£Good	£Fine	£N.Mint
216pgs, black and white. Intro by Alan Moore	£1.60	£4.80	£8.00

Note: this trade paperback was re-offered by King Hell Press in Mar 1995

ONSLAUGHT, THE ROAD TO

Marvel Comics Group,OS; nn Oct 1996

nn ND behind the scenes look at the creative process regarding the Onslaught storyline

	$Good	$Fine	$N.Mint	£Good	£Fine	£N.Mint
	$0.50	$1.50	$2.50	£0.30	£0.90	£1.50
Title Value:	$0.50	$1.50	$2.50	£0.30	£0.90	£1.50

ONSLAUGHT: EPILOGUE

Marvel Comics Group,OS; nn Feb 1997

nn ND Larry Hama script, Randy Green and Jon Holredge art

	$Good	$Fine	$N.Mint	£Good	£Fine	£N.Mint
	$0.60	$1.80	$3.00	£0.40	£1.20	£2.00
Title Value:	$0.60	$1.80	$3.00	£0.40	£1.20	£2.00

ONSLAUGHT: MARVEL UNIVERSE

Marvel Comics Group,OS; nn Oct 1996

nn ND 48pgs, the conclusion of the Onslaught saga and lead into new first issues of Captain America, Iron Man, Fantastic Four and Avengers

	$Good	$Fine	$N.Mint	£Good	£Fine	£N.Mint
	$1.00	$3.00	$5.00	£0.70	£2.10	£3.50
Title Value:	$1.00	$3.00	$5.00	£0.70	£2.10	£3.50

ONSLAUGHT: X-MEN

Marvel Comics Group,OS; 1 Aug 1996

1 ND 48pgs, Mark Waid and Scott Lobdell script, Adam Kubert and Dan Green art

	$Good	$Fine	$N.Mint	£Good	£Fine	£N.Mint
	$1.00	$3.00	$5.00	£0.70	£2.10	£3.50

1 Gold Edition, ND scarce in the U.K. 48pgs, (Dec 1996) 22K gold embossed cover; pre-bagged with certificate, limited to 2,000 copies

	$Good	$Fine	$N.Mint	£Good	£Fine	£N.Mint
	$12.00	$36.00	$60.00	£8.00	£24.00	£40.00
Title Value:	$13.00	$39.00	$65.00	£8.70	£26.10	£43.50

	£Good	£Fine	£N.Mint
Onslaught: Book One (Feb 1997) Trade paperback ND 144pgs, collects X-Men #53,54, Uncanny X-Men #322,334 and Onslaught: X-Men	£1.70	£5.10	£8.50
Onslaught: Book Two (Feb 1997) Trade paperback ND 96pgs, collects X-Man #18,19, X-Force #57,58	£1.30	£3.90	£6.50
Onslaught: Book Three (Feb 1997) Trade paperback ND 96pgs, collects Uncanny X-Men #335, Avengers #401, Fantastic Four #415 and X-Men #55	£1.30	£3.90	£6.50
Onslaught: Book Four (Feb 1997) Trade paperback ND 96pgs, collects Incredible Hulk #444,445 and Cable #34,35	£1.30	£3.90	£6.50
Onslaught: Book Five (Feb 1997) Trade paperback ND 112pgs, collects X-Factor #125, Punisher #11, Green Goblin #12, Amazing Spiderman #415, Spiderman #72	£1.30	£3.90	£6.50
Onslaught: Book Six (Feb 1997) Trade paperback ND 144pgs, collects Uncanny X-Men #336, X-Men #56, Avengers #402, Fantastic Four #416 and Onslaught: Marvel Universe	£1.70	£5.10	£8.50
Onslaught Collection (Feb 1997) ND collects all six trade paperbacks in slipcase	£8.00	£24.00	£40.00

ONYX OVERLORD

Marvel Comics Group,MS; 1 Oct 1992-4 Jan 1993

1 ND Moebius and L'Officier sequel to "Airtight Garage"

	$Good	$Fine	$N.Mint	£Good	£Fine	£N.Mint
	$0.40	$1.20	$2.00	£0.25	£0.75	£1.25
2-4 ND	$0.40	$1.20	$2.00	£0.25	£0.75	£1.25
Title Value:	$1.60	$4.80	$8.00	£1.00	£3.00	£5.00

OPEN SEASON

Renegade/Strawberry Jam; 1 Dec 1986-6 Apr 1988; 7 1988

	$Good	$Fine	$N.Mint	£Good	£Fine	£N.Mint
1 ND story and art by Jim Bricker begins (all issues black and white)						
	$0.40	$1.20	$2.00	£0.25	£0.75	£1.25
2-5 ND	$0.40	$1.20	$2.00	£0.25	£0.75	£1.25
6 ND The Black Issue (for mourning the announcement it was being cancelled)						
	$0.40	$1.20	$2.00	£0.25	£0.75	£1.25
7 ND Strawberry Jam issue						
	$0.40	$1.20	$2.00	£0.25	£0.75	£1.25
Title Value:	$2.80	$8.40	$14.00	£1.75	£5.25	£8.75

OPEN SEASON: THE PLAY

Slave Labor,OS; 1 Nov 1990

1 ND based on stage play, intro by Neil Gaiman

	$Good	$Fine	$N.Mint	£Good	£Fine	£N.Mint
	$0.25	$0.75	$1.25	£0.15	£0.45	£0.75
Title Value:	$0.25	$0.75	$1.25	£0.15	£0.45	£0.75

Note: intended as a mini-series

OPEN SPACE

Marvel Comics Group/Marvel Graphics,MS; 1 Dec 1989-4 Aug 1990

1-4 ND squarebound

	$Good	$Fine	$N.Mint	£Good	£Fine	£N.Mint
	$0.60	$1.80	$3.00	£0.40	£1.20	£2.00
Title Value:	$2.40	$7.20	$12.00	£1.60	£4.80	£8.00

Note: collection of SF stories set in a shared universe by a variety of writers/artists inc. Steve Yeowell (#1). Paul Chadwick cover on #3. Bookshelf Format

OPERA

Eclipse,OS; 1 Sep 1991

1 ND 144pgs, collection of opera adaptations by P. Craig Russell

	$Good	$Fine	$N.Mint	£Good	£Fine	£N.Mint
	$2.50	$7.50	$12.50	£1.50	£4.50	£7.50
Title Value:	$2.50	$7.50	$12.50	£1.50	£4.50	£7.50

OPERATION KNIGHTSTRIKE

Image,MS; 1 May 1995-3 Jul 1995

1-3 ND Chapel, Al Simmons, Bravo, Dutch, Battlestone and Cabbot appear; Brian Witten script, Richard Horie and Jon Sibal art

	$Good	$Fine	$N.Mint	£Good	£Fine	£N.Mint
	$0.50	$1.50	$2.50	£0.30	£0.90	£1.50
Title Value:	$1.50	$4.50	$7.50	£0.90	£2.70	£4.50

OPERATION: GALACTIC STORM

Marvel Comics Group; 1991

Cross-over storyline running throughout the following issues:

Captain America #398,
Avengers West Coast #80,
Quasar #32,
Wonder Man #7,
Avengers #345,
Iron Man #278,
Thor #445,
Captain America #399,
Avengers West Coast #81,
Quasar #33,
Wonder Man #8,
Avengers #346,
Iron Man #279,
Thor #446,
Captain America #400,
Avengers West Coast #82,
Quasar #34,
Wonder Man #9,
Avengers #347,
Captain America #341 (Epilogue)
plus **What If [2nd Series] #55 and #56**.

OPERATION: URBAN STORM

Image,OS; 1 Jan 1993

1 ND benefit comic for the re-building of Los Angeles after the riots featuring work by Liefeld, Lee, Larsen, Portacio, Silvestri, McFarlane and others

	$Good	$Fine	$N.Mint	£Good	£Fine	£N.Mint
	$0.40	$1.20	$2.00	£0.25	£0.75	£1.25
Title Value:	$0.40	$1.20	$2.00	£0.25	£0.75	£1.25

OPTIC NERVE

Drawn and Quarterly; 1 Apr 1995-present

1 ND Adrian Tomine script and art begins

	$Good	$Fine	$N.Mint	£Good	£Fine	£N.Mint
	$1.50	$4.50	$7.50	£1.00	£3.00	£5.00
2 ND	$1.00	$3.00	$5.00	£0.60	£1.80	£3.00
3 ND	$0.60	$1.80	$3.00	£0.40	£1.20	£2.00
Title Value:	$3.10	$9.30	$15.50	£2.00	£6.00	£10.00

Note: bi-annual

ORBIT

Eclipse; 1 Aug 1990-3 1990

	$Good	$Fine	$N.Mint	£Good	£Fine	£N.Mint
1 ND 48pgs, Isaac Asimov story adapted by John Bolton, Dave Stevens cover						
	$0.70	$2.10	$3.50	£0.50	£1.50	£2.50
2 ND 48pgs, adaptations of Isaac Asimov and other SF writers continue						
	$0.70	$2.10	$3.50	£0.50	£1.50	£2.50
3 ND 48pgs, John Bolton art featured plus cover						
	$0.70	$2.10	$3.50	£0.50	£1.50	£2.50
Title Value:	$2.10	$6.30	$10.50	£1.50	£4.50	£7.50

Note: owing to scheduling problems, the original contents of issues #1 and #2 were swapped around

ORIENTAL HEROES

Jademan; 1 Aug 1988-56 Mar 1993

	$Good	$Fine	$N.Mint	£Good	£Fine	£N.Mint
1 ND	$0.40	$1.20	$2.00	£0.40	£1.20	£2.00
2 ND	$0.40	$1.20	$2.00	£0.30	£0.90	£1.50
3-56 ND	$0.40	$1.20	$2.00	£0.25	£0.75	£1.25
Title Value:	$22.40	$67.20	$112.00	£14.20	£42.60	£71.00

ORIGINAL ASTROBOY

Now Comics; 1 Jul 1987-20 1989

	$Good	$Fine	$N.Mint	£Good	£Fine	£N.Mint
1 ND Ken Steacy art begins						
	$0.40	$1.20	$2.00	£0.25	£0.75	£1.25
2-18 ND	$0.40	$1.20	$2.00	£0.25	£0.75	£1.25
19-20 ND Comic Code on cover						
	$0.40	$1.20	$2.00	£0.25	£0.75	£1.25
Title Value:	$8.00	$24.00	$40.00	£5.00	£15.00	£25.00

ORIGINAL SHIELD

Archie; 1 Apr 1984-2 Jun 1984

1-2 ND origin re-told, Dick Ayers art

	$Good	$Fine	$N.Mint	£Good	£Fine	£N.Mint
	$0.30	$0.90	$1.50	£0.20	£0.60	£1.00
Title Value:	$0.60	$1.80	$3.00	£0.40	£1.20	£2.00

ORIGINAL SWAMP THING SAGA

(see Swamp Thing)

ORION

Dark Horse,MS; 1 Aug 1992-6 Aug 1993

	$Good	$Fine	$N.Mint	£Good	£Fine	£N.Mint
1 ND 56pgs, Masamune Shirow script/art begins						
	$0.60	*$1.80*	*$3.00*	£0.40	£1.20	£2.00
2-6 ND 40pgs	*$0.60*	*$1.80*	*$3.00*	£0.40	£1.20	£2.00
Title Value:	*$3.60*	*$10.80*	*$18.00*	£2.40	£7.20	£12.00
Orion						
Trade paperback reprints mini-series, painted cover by Masamune Shirow				£2.00	£6.00	£10.00

ORLAK: FLESH AND STEEL

Caliber Press,OS; 1 Jan 1992

	$Good	$Fine	$N.Mint	£Good	£Fine	£N.Mint
1 ND	*$0.40*	*$1.20*	*$2.00*	£0.25	£0.75	£1.25
Title Value:	*$0.40*	*$1.20*	*$2.00*	£0.25	£0.75	£1.25

ORLAK: REDUX

Caliber Press,OS; 1 Sep 1991

	$Good	$Fine	$N.Mint	£Good	£Fine	£N.Mint
1 ND 64pgs, collects story from pages of Caliber Presents						
	$0.60	*$1.80*	*$3.00*	£0.40	£1.20	£2.00
Title Value:	*$0.60*	*$1.80*	*$3.00*	£0.40	£1.20	£2.00

OSBORN JOURNAL, THE

Marvel Comics Group,OS; nn Feb 1997

	$Good	$Fine	$N.Mint	£Good	£Fine	£N.Mint
nn ND written in journal form by Glenn Greenberg, art by Kyle Hotz						
	$0.60	*$1.80*	*$3.00*	£0.40	£1.20	£2.00
Title Value:	*$0.60*	*$1.80*	*$3.00*	£0.40	£1.20	£2.00

OTHERS, THE

Image; 0 Mar 1995; 1 Apr 1995-4 Jul 1995

	$Good	$Fine	$N.Mint	£Good	£Fine	£N.Mint
0 ND 16pgs, continuing from Shadowhawk #15 reprinting the stories from Shadowhawk #3 and #4 plus 5 new pages						
	$0.25	*$0.75*	*$1.25*	£0.15	£0.45	£0.75
1-3 ND Patrick Blaine and Jason Gorder art						
	$0.40	*$1.20*	*$2.00*	£0.25	£0.75	£1.25
4 ND	*$0.40*	*$1.20*	*$2.00*	£0.25	£0.75	£1.25
Title Value:	*$1.85*	*$5.55*	*$9.25*	£1.15	£3.45	£5.75

OUR ARMY AT WAR

National Periodical Publications/DC Comics; 1 Aug 1952-301 Feb 1977

(becomes Sgt.Rock)

	$Good	$Fine	$N.Mint	£Good	£Fine	£N.Mint
1	*$155.00*	*$465.00*	*$1250.00*	£100.00	£310.00	£835.00
2	*$87.50*	*$265.00*	*$625.00*	£60.00	£180.00	£420.00
3-4	*$62.50*	*$190.00*	*$450.00*	£43.00	£125.00	£300.00
5-10	*$50.00*	*$150.00*	*$350.00*	£34.00	£100.00	£235.00
11-20	*$39.00*	*$115.00*	*$275.00*	£26.00	£77.50	£185.00
21-31	*$29.00*	*$85.00*	*$200.00*	£19.00	£57.50	£135.00
32-40	*$21.00*	*$62.50*	*$150.00*	£14.00	£43.00	£100.00
41-60	*$18.50*	*$55.00*	*$130.00*	£12.00	£36.00	£85.00
61-70	*$15.00*	*$45.00*	*$105.00*	£10.00	£30.00	£70.00
71-80	*$12.00*	*$36.00*	*$85.00*	£7.75	£23.50	£55.00
81 very scarce in the U.K. 1st appearance Sgt. Rock						
	$200.00	*$600.00*	*$2000.00*	£135.00	£405.00	£1350.00
[Very scarce in high grade - Very Fine+ or better]						
82 scarce in the U.K. 2nd appearance Sgt. Rock (very brief)						
	$62.50	*$190.00*	*$515.00*	£43.00	£125.00	£345.00
83 scarce in the U.K. 1st Joe Kubert art on Sgt. Rock						
	$80.00	*$240.00*	*$800.00*	£52.50	£160.00	£535.00
84	*$23.50*	*$70.00*	*$190.00*	£15.50	£47.00	£125.00
85 origin Ice Cream soldier						
	$31.00	*$92.50*	*$250.00*	£20.50	£60.00	£165.00
86-87	*$23.50*	*$70.00*	*$190.00*	£15.50	£47.00	£125.00
1st official distribution in the U.K.						
88-90 scarce in the U.K.						
	$23.50	*$70.00*	*$190.00*	£15.50	£47.00	£125.00
91 scarce in the U.K. 1st all Sgt. Rock stories issue						
	$55.00	*$165.00*	*$450.00*	£31.00	£92.50	£250.00
92-99 scarce in the U.K.						
	$14.00	*$43.00*	*$115.00*	£8.00	£24.00	£65.00
100 scarce in the U.K.						
	$15.50	*$47.00*	*$125.00*	£9.25	£28.00	£75.00
101-110 scarce in the U.K.						
	$10.50	*$32.00*	*$75.00*	£5.00	£15.00	£35.00
111-120 scarce in the U.K.						
	$10.50	*$32.00*	*$75.00*	£4.25	£12.50	£30.00
121-127 scarce in the U.K.						
	$7.75	*$23.50*	*$55.00*	£3.55	£10.50	£25.00
128 combat training and partial origin Sgt. Rock shown in some panels only						
	$21.50	*$65.00*	*$175.00*	£10.50	£32.00	£85.00
129-130	*$7.75*	*$23.50*	*$55.00*	£3.55	£10.50	£25.00
131-150	*$7.75*	*$23.50*	*$55.00*	£2.85	£8.50	£20.00
151 Kubert art, 1st appearance Enemy Ace						
	$31.00	*$92.50*	*$250.00*	£15.50	£47.00	£125.00
152	*$6.75*	*$20.00*	*$47.50*	£2.10	£6.25	£15.00
153 2nd appearance Enemy Ace						
	$15.00	*$45.00*	*$105.00*	£7.00	£21.00	£50.00
154	*$6.75*	*$20.00*	*$47.50*	£2.10	£6.25	£15.00
155 3rd appearance Enemy Ace						
	$10.00	*$30.00*	*$70.00*	£4.25	£12.50	£30.00
156-157	*$6.75*	*$20.00*	*$47.50*	£2.10	£6.25	£15.00
158 1st appearance Iron Major						
	$7.75	*$23.50*	*$55.00*	£2.85	£8.50	£20.00
159-161	*$6.75*	*$20.00*	*$47.50*	£2.10	£6.25	£15.00
162 scarce in the U.K. Viking Prince guest-stars						
	$6.75	*$20.00*	*$47.50*	£2.50	£7.50	£17.50
163 Viking Prince guest-stars						
	$6.75	*$20.00*	*$47.50*	£2.10	£6.25	£15.00
164 scarce in the U.K. (very scarce?) 80pgs, Giant G-19						
	$10.50	*$32.00*	*$75.00*	£4.25	£12.50	£30.00
165-167 scarce in the U.K.						
	$6.75	*$20.00*	*$47.50*	£2.50	£7.50	£17.50
168-170 ND	*$6.75*	*$20.00*	*$47.50*	£2.85	£8.50	£20.00
171-176 ND	*$5.00*	*$15.00*	*$35.00*	£1.75	£5.25	£12.50
177 ND 80pgs, Giant G-32						
	$6.25	*$19.00*	*$45.00*	£2.85	£8.50	£20.00
178-181 ND	*$5.00*	*$15.00*	*$35.00*	£1.75	£5.25	£12.50
182-183 ND Neal Adams art						
	$5.25	*$16.00*	*$37.50*	£2.10	£6.25	£15.00
184-185 ND	*$6.00*	*$18.00*	*$30.00*	£2.00	£6.00	£10.00
186 ND Neal Adams art						
	$5.25	*$16.00*	*$37.50*	£2.10	£6.25	£15.00
187-189 ND	*$4.25*	*$12.50*	*$30.00*	£1.40	£4.25	£10.00
190 ND 80pgs, Giant G-44						
	$5.00	*$15.00*	*$35.00*	£2.10	£6.25	£15.00
191-199 ND	*$4.25*	*$12.50*	*$30.00*	£1.40	£4.25	£10.00
200 ND	*$3.55*	*$10.50*	*$25.00*	£1.05	£3.20	£7.50
201-202 ND	*$1.65*	*$5.00*	*$10.00*	£0.65	£2.00	£4.00
203 ND 80pgs, Giant G-56						
	$3.30	*$10.00*	*$20.00*	£1.25	£3.75	£7.50
204-205 ND all reprint						
	$1.30	*$4.00*	*$8.00*	£0.65	£2.00	£4.00
206-215 ND	*$1.30*	*$4.00*	*$8.00*	£0.65	£2.00	£4.00
216 ND 68pgs, (Giant G-68)						
	$3.30	*$10.00*	*$20.00*	£1.25	£3.75	£7.50
217-228 ND	*$1.00*	*$3.00*	*$6.00*	£0.50	£1.50	£3.00
229 ND 68pgs, (Giant G-80)						
	$3.30	*$10.00*	*$20.00*	£1.25	£3.75	£7.50
230-239 ND	*$1.00*	*$3.00*	*$6.00*	£0.40	£1.25	£2.50
240 52pgs, Neal Adams art						
	$1.30	*$4.00*	*$8.00*	£0.80	£2.50	£5.00

Official Secret Agent #1

Onslaught: X-Men

Our Army At War #30

	$Good	$Fine	$N.Mint	£Good	£Fine	£N.Mint
241 52pgs	$0.80	$2.50	$5.00	£0.40	£1.25	£2.50
242 less common in the U.K. 100pgs, DC-100pg Super Spectacular #9						
	$1.25	$3.75	$7.50	£0.80	£2.50	£5.00
243-248 52pgs	$0.80	$2.50	$5.00	£0.40	£1.25	£2.50
249 Wood art	$0.80	$2.50	$5.00	£0.40	£1.25	£2.50
250	$0.80	$2.50	$5.00	£0.40	£1.25	£2.50
251-268	$0.80	$2.50	$5.00	£0.30	£1.00	£2.00
269 100pgs	$0.80	$2.50	$5.00	£0.65	£2.00	£4.00
270	$0.80	$2.50	$5.00	£0.30	£1.00	£2.00
271-274	$0.80	$2.50	$5.00	£0.25	£0.75	£1.50
275 100pgs	$0.80	$2.50	$5.00	£0.65	£2.00	£4.00
276-279	$0.80	$2.50	$5.00	£0.25	£0.75	£1.50
280 68pgs, reprints 1st Sgt. Rock story & 1st Sgt. Rock by Kubert to celebrate 200th appearance of character						
	$0.80	$2.50	$5.00	£0.40	£1.25	£2.50
281-289	$0.80	$2.50	$5.00	£0.25	£0.75	£1.50
290-291 scarce in the U.K.						
	$0.80	$2.50	$5.00	£0.30	£1.00	£2.00
292	$0.80	$2.50	$5.00	£0.25	£0.75	£1.50
293 scarce in the U.K.						
	$0.80	$2.50	$5.00	£0.30	£1.00	£2.00
294-299	$0.80	$2.50	$5.00	£0.25	£0.75	£1.50
300 new celebratory Kanigher and Kubert story						
	$0.80	$2.50	$5.00	£0.25	£0.75	£1.50
301	$0.80	$2.50	$5.00	£0.25	£0.75	£1.50
Title Value:	$3779.15	$11315.75	$28023.50	£2265.35	£6797.45	£16923.00

FEATURES

Sgt.Rock in new stories in 88-163, 165-176, 178-189, 191-202, 206-215, 217-228, 230-239, 241, 234-301.

REPRINT FEATURES

Capt. Storm in 242. Frogman in 164, 177. Gunner & Sarge in 164, 177, 190, 203, 242. Haunted Tank in 164, 177, 190, 203, 216. Hunter's Hellcats in 269. Johnny Cloud in 164, 177, 190, 203, 242, 269. Mlle. Marie in 164, 177, 190, 203, 238. Sgt. Rock in 164, 177, 190, 203, 216, 229, 240, 269, 275, 280

OUR FIGHTING FORCES

National Periodical Publications/DC Comics; 1 Oct/Nov 1954-181 Sep/Oct 1978

	$Good	$Fine	$N.Mint	£Good	£Fine	£N.Mint
1 scarce in the U.K. Jerry Grandenetti art featured						
	$95.00	$290.00	$775.00	£65.00	£195.00	£520.00
2 scarce in the U.K.						
	$50.00	$150.00	$350.00	£34.00	£100.00	£235.00
3 scarce in the U.K. Joe Kubert cover						
	$43.00	$125.00	$300.00	£29.00	£85.00	£200.00
4-5 scarce in the U.K.						
	$32.00	$95.00	$225.00	£21.00	£62.50	£150.00
6-9 scarce in the U.K.						
	$26.00	$75.00	$180.00	£17.00	£50.00	£120.00
10 scarce in the U.K. Wally Wood art featured						
	$27.00	$80.00	$190.00	£17.50	£52.50	£125.00
11-20	$20.00	$60.00	$140.00	£13.50	£41.00	£95.00
21-30	$13.50	$41.00	$95.00	£9.25	£28.00	£65.00
31-40	$12.50	$39.00	$90.00	£8.50	£26.00	£60.00
41 possible Unknown Soldier prototype but highly debateable						
	$15.50	$47.00	$110.00	£7.00	£21.00	£50.00
42-44	$11.00	$34.00	$80.00	£7.00	£21.00	£50.00
45 1st appearance Gunner and Sarge						
	$41.00	$120.00	$285.00	£21.00	£62.50	£150.00
46	$17.00	$50.00	$120.00	£7.00	£21.00	£50.00
47	$12.00	$36.00	$85.00	£5.50	£17.00	£40.00
48	$9.25	$28.00	$65.00	£5.25	£16.00	£37.50
49 1st appearance The Pooch						
	$12.50	$39.00	$90.00	£7.75	£23.50	£55.00
50	$9.25	$28.00	$65.00	£5.25	£16.00	£37.50
1st official distribution in the U.K.						
51-64 scarce in the U.K.						
	$8.50	$26.00	$60.00	£3.55	£10.50	£25.00
65-70 scarce in the U.K.						
	$7.00	$21.00	$50.00	£2.85	£8.50	£20.00
71 scarce in the U.K. grey-tone cover						
	$3.55	$10.50	$25.00	£2.10	£6.25	£15.00
72-80	$3.55	$10.50	$25.00	£1.75	£5.25	£12.50
81-90	$2.85	$8.50	$20.00	£1.20	£3.60	£8.50
91-98	$2.10	$6.25	$15.00	£0.90	£2.75	£6.50
99-100 scarce in the U.K.						
	$2.10	$6.25	$15.00	£1.05	£3.20	£7.50
101-102 scarce in the U.K.						
	$2.00	$6.00	$12.00	£0.65	£2.00	£4.00
103-105 ND	$2.00	$6.00	$12.00	£0.75	£2.25	£4.50
106-120 ND	$2.00	$6.00	$12.00	£0.60	£1.85	£3.75
121-122 ND	$2.00	$6.00	$12.00	£0.55	£1.75	£3.50
123 ND 1st of Losers series						
	$2.00	$6.00	$12.00	£0.75	£2.25	£4.50
124-129 ND	$2.00	$6.00	$12.00	£0.55	£1.75	£3.50
130 scarce in the U.K.						
	$2.00	$6.00	$12.00	£0.50	£1.50	£3.00
131-132	$1.50	$4.50	$9.00	£0.40	£1.25	£2.50
133-137 52pgs	$1.50	$4.50	$9.00	£0.50	£1.50	£3.00
138-139	$1.50	$4.50	$9.00	£0.40	£1.25	£2.50
140 ND	$1.50	$4.50	$9.00	£0.50	£1.50	£3.00
141-150	$1.50	$4.50	$9.00	£0.30	£1.00	£2.00
151-158 Jack Kirby art						
	$1.25	$3.75	$7.50	£0.30	£1.00	£2.00
159 scarce in the U.K. Jack Kirby art						
	$1.25	$3.75	$7.50	£0.40	£1.25	£2.50
160-162 Jack Kirby art						
	$1.25	$3.75	$7.50	£0.30	£1.00	£2.00
163-164	$1.25	$3.75	$7.50	£0.25	£0.75	£1.50
165-166 ND	$1.25	$3.75	$7.50	£0.25	£0.85	£1.75
167-170	$1.25	$3.75	$7.50	£0.25	£0.75	£1.50
171	$1.25	$3.75	$7.50	£0.20	£0.60	£1.25
172-174 scarce in the U.K.						
	$1.25	$3.75	$7.50	£0.25	£0.75	£1.50
175-177	$1.25	$3.75	$7.50	£0.20	£0.60	£1.25
178-180 ND	$1.25	$3.75	$7.50	£0.25	£0.85	£1.75
181 ND 44pgs	$1.25	$3.75	$7.50	£0.30	£1.00	£2.00
Title Value:	$1367.25	$4113.75	$9607.50	£787.80	£2370.30	£5594.50

FEATURES

Captain Hunter in 99-106. Devil-Dog in 95-98. Gunner & Sarge in 51-94. Hunter's Hellcats in 106-122. Losers in 123-181. Super-Spy in 181.

OUR LOVE STORY

Marvel Comics Group; 1 Oct 1969-38 Feb 1976

	$Good	$Fine	$N.Mint	£Good	£Fine	£N.Mint
1 ND	$1.65	$5.00	$10.00	£1.00	£3.00	£6.00
2-4 ND	$0.80	$2.50	$5.00	£0.40	£1.25	£2.50
5 ND scarce in the U.K. 7pg Steranko story in famous psychedelia style						
	$2.50	$7.50	$15.00	£1.65	£5.00	£10.00
6-13 ND	$0.65	$2.00	$4.00	£0.30	£1.00	£2.00
14 ND	$1.00	$3.00	$6.00	£0.50	£1.50	£3.00
15-30 ND	$0.50	$1.50	$3.00	£0.25	£0.75	£1.50
31-38 ND	$0.50	$1.50	$3.00	£0.20	£0.60	£1.25
Title Value:	$24.75	$75.00	$150.00	£12.35	£38.05	£76.50

OUT OF THIS WORLD

Charlton; 1 Aug 1956-16 Dec 1959

	$Good	$Fine	$N.Mint	£Good	£Fine	£N.Mint
1 scarce in the U.K.						
	$21.00	$62.50	$150.00	£14.00	£43.00	£100.00
2 scarce in the U.K.						
	$12.00	$36.00	$85.00	£8.00	£24.50	£57.50
3-6 scarce in the U.K. Steve Ditko art						
	$25.00	$75.00	$175.00	£17.00	£50.00	£120.00
7 very scarce in the U.K. 68pgs, some Steve Ditko art						
	$25.00	$75.00	$175.00	£17.00	£50.00	£120.00
8 very scarce in the U.K. 68pgs, some Steve Ditko art						
	$21.00	$62.50	$150.00	£14.00	£43.00	£100.00
9-10 Steve Ditko art						
	$17.00	$50.00	$120.00	£11.00	£34.00	£80.00
11 Steve Ditko art						
	$20.00	$60.00	$140.00	£13.50	£41.00	£95.00
12 Steve Ditko art						
	$17.00	$50.00	$120.00	£11.00	£34.00	£80.00
13-15	$8.50	$26.00	$60.00	£5.50	£17.00	£40.00
16 Steve Ditko art						
	$17.00	$50.00	$120.00	£11.00	£34.00	£80.00
Title Value:	$292.50	$874.00	$2060.00	£195.00	£588.50	£1392.50

Note: issues #15 and #16 were the only ones officially distributed in the U.K.

OUTBREED 999

Blackout Comics; 1 May 1994-6 1995

	$Good	$Fine	$N.Mint	£Good	£Fine	£N.Mint
1-6 ND Bob Perry pencils and Dave Gutierrez ink						
	$0.50	$1.50	$2.50	£0.30	£0.90	£1.50
Title Value:	$3.00	$9.00	$15.00	£1.80	£5.40	£9.00
Commemorative Outbreed 999 Series Collection (Aug 1995)						
ND set of issues #1-5, plus limited signed poster				£2.00	£6.00	£10.00

OUTCAST SPECIAL, THE

Acclaim Comics,OS; 1 Aug 1995

	$Good	$Fine	$N.Mint	£Good	£Fine	£N.Mint
1 ND Norm Breyfogle art						
	$0.50	$1.50	$2.50	£0.30	£0.90	£1.50
Title Value:	$0.50	$1.50	$2.50	£0.30	£0.90	£1.50

OUTCASTS

DC Comics,MS; 1 Oct 1987-12 Sep 1988

	$Good	$Fine	$N.Mint	£Good	£Fine	£N.Mint
1-12 ND John Wagner and Alan Grant script, Cam Kennedy art						
	$0.25	$0.75	$1.25	£0.15	£0.45	£0.75
Title Value:	$3.00	$9.00	$15.00	£1.80	£5.40	£9.00

Note: Wagner/Grant scripts, Cam Kennedy/Steve Montano art in all; all Deluxe Format Baxter paper.

OUTER LIMITS, THE

Dell,TV; 1 Jan/Mar 1964-18 Oct 1969

	$Good	$Fine	$N.Mint	£Good	£Fine	£N.Mint
1 distributed in the U.K.						
	$10.50	$32.00	$75.00	£7.00	£21.00	£50.00
2 distributed in the U.K.						
	$6.25	$19.00	$45.00	£3.55	£10.50	£25.00
3-5 distributed in the U.K.						
	$5.00	$15.00	$35.00	£2.85	£8.50	£20.00
6-10 distributed in the U.K.						
	$4.60	$13.50	$32.50	£2.10	£6.25	£15.00
11-18 distributed in the U.K.						
	$3.90	$11.50	$27.50	£2.00	£6.00	£14.00
Title Value:	$85.95	$255.50	$607.50	£45.60	£136.25	£322.00

OUTER SPACE

Charlton; 17 May 1958-25 Dec 1959

	$Good	$Fine	$N.Mint	£Good	£Fine	£N.Mint
17	$11.00	$34.00	$80.00	£7.75	£23.50	£55.00
18-20 Steve Ditko art						
	$17.50	$52.50	$125.00	£12.00	£36.00	£85.00
21 Steve Ditko cover						
	$10.50	$32.00	$75.00	£7.00	£21.00	£50.00
22-24 pence-stamp copies known						
	$10.50	$32.00	$75.00	£7.00	£21.00	£50.00
1st official distribution in the U.K.						
25	$10.50	$32.00	$75.00	£7.00	£21.00	£50.00
Title Value:	$116.00	$351.50	$830.00	£78.75	£236.50	£560.00

Note: issues #24 and 25 were the only ones officially distributed in the U.K.

OUTER SPACE (2ND SERIES)

Charlton; 1 Nov 1968

Issue	$Good	$Fine	$N.Mint	£Good	£Fine	£N.Mint
1 scarce though distributed in the U.K. Steve Ditko art (10pgs), Pat Boyette cover	$5.00	$15.00	$35.00	£3.20	£9.50	£22.50
Title Value:	$5.00	$15.00	$35.00	£3.20	£9.50	£22.50

OUTLANDER

Malibu/Eternity; 1 Oct 1987-7 Jun 1988

Issue	$Good	$Fine	$N.Mint	£Good	£Fine	£N.Mint
1-7 ND black and white	$0.40	$1.20	$2.00	£0.25	£0.75	£1.25
Title Value:	$2.80	$8.40	$14.00	£1.75	£5.25	£8.75

OUTLANDERS

Dark Horse; 0 May 1992; 1 Jan 1989-33 Nov 1991

Issue	$Good	$Fine	$N.Mint	£Good	£Fine	£N.Mint
0 ND 40pgs, includes fold-out mini-poster	$0.55	$1.65	$2.75	£0.35	£1.05	£1.75
1-25 ND	$0.50	$1.50	$2.50	£0.30	£0.90	£1.50
26 ND 56pgs	$0.55	$1.65	$2.75	£0.35	£1.05	£1.75
27-33 ND	$0.50	$1.50	$2.50	£0.30	£0.90	£1.50
Title Value:	$17.10	$51.30	$85.50	£10.30	£30.90	£51.50

Note: issues #1-7 are black and white

Issue	$Good	$Fine	$N.Mint	£Good	£Fine	£N.Mint
Graphic Novel Collection 1, reprints #1-4				£1.40	£4.20	£7.00
Graphic Novel Collection 2 (Nov 1990), reprints issues #5-8 plus 20 new pages				£1.30	£3.90	£6.50
Graphic Novel Collection 3 (1992) reprints issues #9-12				£1.30	£3.90	£6.50
Outlanders Special 1 (Mar 1993), new material				£0.30	£0.90	£1.50
Outlander Volume 4 (Mar 1995) Trade paperback reprints issues #13-16, Ken Macklin painted cover				£1.70	£5.10	£8.50

OUTLANDERS EPILOGUE

Dark Horse,OS; 1 Mar 1994

Issue	$Good	$Fine	$N.Mint	£Good	£Fine	£N.Mint
1 ND black and white	$0.50	$1.50	$2.50	£0.30	£0.90	£1.50
Title Value:	$0.50	$1.50	$2.50	£0.30	£0.90	£1.50

OUTLAW KID, THE

Marvel Comics Group; 1 Aug 1970-30 Oct 1975

Issue	$Good	$Fine	$N.Mint	£Good	£Fine	£N.Mint
1-2	$1.00	$3.00	$6.00	£0.40	£1.25	£2.50
3 Williamson reprint	$0.40	$1.25	$2.50	£0.25	£0.75	£1.50
4-5	$0.40	$1.25	$2.50	£0.25	£0.75	£1.50
6	$0.40	$1.25	$2.50	£0.20	£0.60	£1.25
7-8 ND 52pgs	$0.40	$1.25	$2.50	£0.25	£0.75	£1.50
9 ND scarce in the U.K. Williamson reprint	$0.40	$1.25	$2.50	£0.25	£0.75	£1.50
10 ND scarce in the U.K. origin new Outlaw Kid	$0.40	$1.25	$2.50	£0.25	£0.75	£1.50
11-27 ND	$0.30	$1.00	$2.00	£0.20	£0.60	£1.25
28 ND Williamson reprint	$0.30	$1.00	$2.00	£0.20	£0.60	£1.25
29-30 ND	$0.30	$1.00	$2.00	£0.20	£0.60	£1.25
Title Value:	$11.20	$36.00	$71.00	£6.75	£20.35	£41.75

Note: all issues are reprint apart from one new story each in issue 10-16.

OUTLAWS

DC Comics,MS; 1 Sep 1991-8 Apr 1992

Issue	$Good	$Fine	$N.Mint	£Good	£Fine	£N.Mint
1-8	$0.25	$0.75	$1.25	£0.15	£0.45	£0.75
Title Value:	$2.00	$6.00	$10.00	£1.20	£3.60	£6.00

OUTLAWS OF THE WEST

Charlton; 11 Sep 1957-81 May 1970; 82 Jul 1979-88 Apr 1980

Issue	$Good	$Fine	$N.Mint	£Good	£Fine	£N.Mint
11 scarce in the U.K.	$7.00	$21.00	$50.00	£5.00	£15.00	£35.00
12-13	$3.55	$10.50	$25.00	£2.10	£6.25	£15.00
14 68pgs	$4.25	$12.50	$30.00	£2.85	£8.50	£20.00
15-17	$3.55	$10.50	$25.00	£2.10	£6.25	£15.00
18 Steve Ditko art	$9.25	$28.00	$65.00	£6.25	£19.00	£45.00
19-20	$3.55	$10.50	$25.00	£2.10	£6.25	£15.00
21-27	$2.55	$7.50	$18.00	£1.70	£5.00	£12.00
1st official distribution in the U.K.						
28-30	$2.55	$7.50	$18.00	£1.40	£4.25	£10.00
31-50	$2.05	$6.25	$12.50	£1.00	£3.00	£6.00
51-53	$1.00	$3.00	$6.00	£0.55	£1.75	£3.50
54 Kid Montana appears	$1.00	$3.00	$6.00	£0.55	£1.75	£3.50
55-63	$1.00	$3.00	$6.00	£0.55	£1.75	£3.50
64 1st appearance Captain Doom	$1.00	$3.00	$6.00	£0.55	£1.75	£3.50
65-70	$1.00	$3.00	$6.00	£0.55	£1.75	£3.50
71-72	$0.55	$1.75	$3.50	£0.30	£1.00	£2.00
73 1st appearance The Sharp Shooter	$0.55	$1.75	$3.50	£0.30	£1.00	£2.00
74-79	$0.55	$1.75	$3.50	£0.30	£1.00	£2.00
80-81 Steve Ditko art	$0.55	$1.75	$3.50	£0.40	£1.25	£2.50
82-88	$0.30	$1.00	$2.00	£0.20	£0.60	£1.25
Title Value:	$140.00	$421.25	$897.50	£80.80	£244.70	£540.75

Note: most issues after 1959 distributed on the new-stands in the U.K.

OUTSIDERS ANNUAL

DC Comics; 1 1986

Issue	$Good	$Fine	$N.Mint	£Good	£Fine	£N.Mint
1 ND Kevin Nowlan art featuring Batman	$0.50	$1.50	$2.50	£0.30	£0.90	£1.50
Title Value:	$0.50	$1.50	$2.50	£0.30	£0.90	£1.50

OUTSIDERS SPECIAL

DC Comics,OS; 1 Jul 1987

Issue	$Good	$Fine	$N.Mint	£Good	£Fine	£N.Mint
1 ND	$0.40	$1.20	$2.00	£0.25	£0.75	£1.25
Title Value:	$0.40	$1.20	$2.00	£0.25	£0.75	£1.25

OUTSIDERS, THE

DC Comics; 1 Nov 1985-28 Feb 1988

(see also Batman and the...)

Issue	$Good	$Fine	$N.Mint	£Good	£Fine	£N.Mint
1-10 ND	$0.40	$1.20	$2.00	£0.25	£0.75	£1.25
11 ND John Byrne art, Brian Bolland pin-up	$0.40	$1.20	$2.00	£0.25	£0.75	£1.25
12-17 ND	$0.30	$0.90	$1.50	£0.20	£0.60	£1.00
18-22 ND Batman appears	$0.30	$0.90	$1.50	£0.20	£0.60	£1.00
23-26 ND	$0.30	$0.90	$1.50	£0.20	£0.60	£1.00
27-28 ND Millennium X-over, Erik Larsen art	$0.30	$0.90	$1.50	£0.20	£0.60	£1.00
Title Value:	$9.50	$28.50	$47.50	£6.15	£18.45	£30.75

Note: all Deluxe Format Baxter paper.

OUTSIDERS, THE (2ND SERIES)

DC Comics; 0 Oct 1994; 1 Nov 1993-24 Nov 1995

Issue	$Good	$Fine	$N.Mint	£Good	£Fine	£N.Mint
0 (Oct 1994) Zero Hour X-over, The Eradicator forms a new team of Outsiders	$0.40	$1.20	$2.00	£0.25	£0.75	£1.25
1 Alpha; featuring Geo-Force, Technocrat and Faust; each issue has four common pages but can be read as stand-alone stories	$0.40	$1.20	$2.00	£0.25	£0.75	£1.25
1 Omega; featuring Halo, Katana and Looker; each issue has four common pages but can be read as stand-alone stories; both comics have Travis Charest covers	$0.40	$1.20	$2.00	£0.25	£0.75	£1.25
2	$0.40	$1.20	$2.00	£0.25	£0.75	£1.25
3-4 The Eradicator appears	$0.40	$1.20	$2.00	£0.25	£0.75	£1.25
5-6	$0.40	$1.20	$2.00	£0.25	£0.75	£1.25
7 Batman cameo	$0.40	$1.20	$2.00	£0.25	£0.75	£1.25
8 Batman appears	$0.40	$1.20	$2.00	£0.25	£0.75	£1.25
9-10	$0.40	$1.20	$2.00	£0.25	£0.75	£1.25
11 Zero Hour X-over	$0.40	$1.20	$2.00	£0.25	£0.75	£1.25
12-13	$0.40	$1.20	$2.00	£0.25	£0.75	£1.25
14 Lady Shiva appears	$0.40	$1.20	$2.00	£0.25	£0.75	£1.25
15	$0.40	$1.20	$2.00	£0.25	£0.75	£1.25
16 ties into Showcase '95 #3	$0.40	$1.20	$2.00	£0.25	£0.75	£1.25
17 Green Lantern, Darkstar and Arsenal appear	$0.40	$1.20	$2.00	£0.25	£0.75	£1.25
18-19	$0.40	$1.20	$2.00	£0.25	£0.75	£1.25
20 Outsiders vs. Metamorpho	$0.40	$1.20	$2.00	£0.25	£0.75	£1.25
21-23	$0.40	$1.20	$2.00	£0.25	£0.75	£1.25
24 Eradicator, Superboy, Supergirl and Steel appear	$0.40	$1.20	$2.00	£0.25	£0.75	£1.25
Title Value:	$10.40	$31.20	$52.00	£6.50	£19.50	£32.50

OVER THE EDGE

Marvel Comics Group; 1 Nov 1995-10 Aug 1996

Issue	$Good	$Fine	$N.Mint	£Good	£Fine	£N.Mint
1 ND Daredevil vs. Mr. Fear	$0.20	$0.60	$1.00	£0.10	£0.35	£0.65
2 ND Dr. Strange appears	$0.20	$0.60	$1.00	£0.10	£0.35	£0.65
3 ND Hulk appears	$0.20	$0.60	$1.00	£0.10	£0.35	£0.65
4 ND Ghost Rider appears	$0.20	$0.60	$1.00	£0.10	£0.35	£0.65
5 ND The Punisher appears	$0.20	$0.60	$1.00	£0.10	£0.35	£0.65
6 ND Daredevil and Black Panther appear; bi-monthly	$0.20	$0.60	$1.00	£0.10	£0.35	£0.65
7 ND Dr. Strange; bi-monthly	$0.20	$0.60	$1.00	£0.10	£0.35	£0.65
8 ND Elektra	$0.20	$0.60	$1.00	£0.10	£0.35	£0.65
9 ND Ghost Rider	$0.20	$0.60	$1.00	£0.10	£0.35	£0.65
10 ND Daredevil	$0.20	$0.60	$1.00	£0.10	£0.35	£0.65
Title Value:	$2.00	$6.00	$10.00	£1.00	£3.50	£6.50

OWL, THE

Gold Key; 1 Apr 1967-2 Apr 1968

Issue	$Good	$Fine	$N.Mint	£Good	£Fine	£N.Mint
1 distributed in the U.K.	$3.90	$11.50	$27.50	£2.25	£6.75	£16.00
2 distributed in the U.K.	$3.55	$10.50	$25.00	£2.10	£6.25	£15.00
Title Value:	$7.45	$22.00	$52.50	£4.35	£13.00	£31.00

OWLHOOTS

Kitchen Sink; 1,2 1991

Issue	$Good	$Fine	$N.Mint	£Good	£Fine	£N.Mint
1-2 ND James Vance script, John Garcia art; sepia colour	$0.30	$0.90	$1.50	£0.20	£0.60	£1.00
Title Value:	$0.60	$1.80	$3.00	£0.40	£1.20	£2.00

OZ-WONDERLAND WAR

DC Comics,MS; 1 Jan 1986-3 Mar 1986

(see also Captain Carrot)

Issue	$Good	$Fine	$N.Mint	£Good	£Fine	£N.Mint
1-2 ND DS	$0.25	$0.75	$1.25	£0.15	£0.45	£0.75
3 ND DS, Doom Patrol cameo	$0.25	$0.75	$1.25	£0.15	£0.45	£0.75
Title Value:	$0.75	$2.25	$3.75	£0.45	£1.35	£2.25

P

P.I'S: MICHAEL MAUSER & MR. TREE

First,MS; 1 Jan 1983-3 May 1985

	$Good	$Fine	$N.Mint	£Good	£Fine	£N.Mint
1-3 ND	$0.40	$1.20	$2.00	£0.25	£0.75	£1.25
Title Value:	$1.20	$3.60	$6.00	£0.75	£2.25	£3.75

P.J. WARLOCK

Eclipse; 1 Nov 1986-3 May 1987

	$Good	$Fine	$N.Mint	£Good	£Fine	£N.Mint
1-3 ND Bill Schorr art, black and white	$0.40	$1.20	$2.00	£0.25	£0.75	£1.25
Title Value:	$1.20	$3.60	$6.00	£0.75	£2.25	£3.75

PACIFIC PRESENTS

Pacific; 1 Oct 1982-4 Jun 1984

	$Good	$Fine	$N.Mint	£Good	£Fine	£N.Mint
1 ND Rocketeer by Dave Stevens, Missing Man by Steve Ditko	$1.00	$3.00	$5.00	£0.70	£2.10	£3.50
2 ND Rocketeer by Dave Stevens, Missing Man by Steve Ditko	$0.80	$2.40	$4.00	£0.60	£1.80	£3.00
3-4 ND Tim Conrad art	$0.40	$1.20	$2.00	£0.20	£0.60	£1.00
Title Value:	$2.60	$7.80	$13.00	£1.70	£5.10	£8.50

PACT, THE

Image,MS; 1 Feb 1994-3 Jun 1994

	$Good	$Fine	$N.Mint	£Good	£Fine	£N.Mint
1 ND Jim Valentino layout art, Walter McDanial pencils and Matt Banning inks	$0.40	$1.20	$2.00	£0.25	£0.75	£1.25
2 ND Youngblood appear	$0.40	$1.20	$2.00	£0.25	£0.75	£1.25
3 ND The Pact vs. The Renegades	$0.40	$1.20	$2.00	£0.25	£0.75	£1.25
Title Value:	$1.20	$3.60	$6.00	£0.75	£2.25	£3.75

PALADIN

Valiant; 1 Mar 1992

	$Good	$Fine	$N.Mint	£Good	£Fine	£N.Mint
1 ND 28pgs, three-panel gatefold cover, metallic silver ink logo	$0.40	$1.20	$2.00	£0.25	£0.75	£1.25
Title Value:	$0.40	$1.20	$2.00	£0.25	£0.75	£1.25

PALADIN ALPHA

Firstlight Comixx; 1 Dec 1994-2 Jan 1995

	$Good	$Fine	$N.Mint	£Good	£Fine	£N.Mint
1 ND Darryl Banks cover	$0.50	$1.50	$2.50	£0.30	£0.90	£1.50
2 ND	$0.50	$1.50	$2.50	£0.30	£0.90	£1.50
Title Value:	$1.00	$3.00	$5.00	£0.60	£1.80	£3.00

PANDORA

Avatar Press,MS; 1 Jan 1997-2 Feb 1997

	$Good	$Fine	$N.Mint	£Good	£Fine	£N.Mint
1-2 ND Richard Pollard and Jude Millien art; black and white	$0.60	$1.80	$3.00	£0.40	£1.20	£2.00
Title Value:	$1.20	$3.60	$6.00	£0.80	£2.40	£4.00

PARADAX

Vortex; 1 Apr 1987-2 Aug 1987

	$Good	$Fine	$N.Mint	£Good	£Fine	£N.Mint
1 ND Milligan/McCarthy art	$0.50	$1.50	$2.50	£0.30	£0.90	£1.50
2 ND reprints from Strange Days #1-3	$0.50	$1.50	$2.50	£0.30	£0.90	£1.50
Title Value:	$1.00	$3.00	$5.00	£0.60	£1.80	£3.00

PARADIGM

Gauntlet Comics; 1 1993-4 1994

	$Good	$Fine	$N.Mint	£Good	£Fine	£N.Mint
1-2 ND	$0.50	$1.50	$2.50	£0.30	£0.90	£1.50
2 Collectors Edition, ND (Oct 1993) - pre-bagged with limited edition print	$0.60	$1.80	$3.00	£0.40	£1.20	£2.00
3-4 ND	$0.50	$1.50	$2.50	£0.30	£0.90	£1.50
Title Value:	$2.60	$7.80	$13.00	£1.60	£4.80	£8.00

PARAGON: DARK APOCALYPSE

AC Comics,MS; 1 Apr 1993-4 Jun 1993

	$Good	$Fine	$N.Mint	£Good	£Fine	£N.Mint
1-4 ND	$0.50	$1.50	$2.50	£0.30	£0.90	£1.50
Title Value:	$2.00	$6.00	$10.00	£1.20	£3.60	£6.00

PARALLAX: EMERALD NIGHT

DC Comics,OS; 1 Nov 1996

	$Good	$Fine	$N.Mint	£Good	£Fine	£N.Mint
1 ND 48pgs, Final Night tie-in; Hal Jordan (original Green Lantern) dies	$0.60	$1.80	$3.00	£0.40	£1.20	£2.00
Title Value:	$0.60	$1.80	$3.00	£0.40	£1.20	£2.00

PARANOIA

Adventure,MS; 1 Nov 1991-6 Apr 1992

	$Good	$Fine	$N.Mint	£Good	£Fine	£N.Mint
1-6 ND colour	$0.50	$1.50	$2.50	£0.30	£0.90	£1.50
Title Value:	$3.00	$9.00	$15.00	£1.80	£5.40	£9.00

PARSIFAL

Star Reach; 1 May 1978

	$Good	$Fine	$N.Mint	£Good	£Fine	£N.Mint
1 ND P. Craig Russell, reprints Star Reach #8, #10	$0.40	$1.20	$2.00	£0.25	£0.75	£1.25
Title Value:	$0.40	$1.20	$2.00	£0.25	£0.75	£1.25

PARTICLE DREAMS

Fantagraphics; 1 Aug 1986-6 Jun 1987

	$Good	$Fine	$N.Mint	£Good	£Fine	£N.Mint
1-6 ND Kief Llama by Matt Howarth	$0.60	$1.80	$3.00	£0.40	£1.20	£2.00
Title Value:	$3.60	$10.80	$18.00	£2.40	£7.20	£12.00

PARTNERS IN PANDEMONIUM

Caliber Press,MS; 1 Nov 1991-3 1992

	$Good	$Fine	$N.Mint	£Good	£Fine	£N.Mint
1-3 ND	$0.40	$1.20	$2.00	£0.25	£0.75	£1.25
Title Value:	$1.20	$3.60	$6.00	£0.75	£2.25	£3.75

PARTS UNKNOWN

Eclipse/FX Comix,MS; 1 Jul 1992-4 Oct 1992

	$Good	$Fine	$N.Mint	£Good	£Fine	£N.Mint
1-4 ND based on film	$0.40	$1.20	$2.00	£0.25	£0.75	£1.25
Title Value:	$1.60	$4.80	$8.00	£1.00	£3.00	£5.00

Parts Unknown Volume One Limited Hardcover (Feb 1996)

	$Good	$Fine	$N.Mint	£Good	£Fine	£N.Mint
ND collects series, hardcover				£3.30	£9.90	£16.50

Note: published by Knight Press

PARTS UNKNOWN II: THE NEXT INVASION

Eclipse; 1 Dec 1993-3 Feb 1994

	$Good	$Fine	$N.Mint	£Good	£Fine	£N.Mint
1-3 ND Brad Gorby art; black and white	$0.50	$1.50	$2.50	£0.30	£0.90	£1.50
Title Value:	$1.50	$4.50	$7.50	£0.90	£2.70	£4.50

PARTS UNKNOWN: DARK INTENTIONS

Knight Press; 0 Aug 1995; 1 1995-present

	$Good	$Fine	$N.Mint	£Good	£Fine	£N.Mint
0 ND Beau Smith script, Brad Gorby and Mark Heike art; black and white	$0.50	$1.50	$2.50	£0.30	£0.90	£1.50
1-3 ND Beau Smith script, Brad Gorby art; black and white	$0.50	$1.50	$2.50	£0.30	£0.90	£1.50
4 ND Beau Smith script, Brad Gorby art; balck and white	$0.60	$1.80	$3.00	£0.40	£1.20	£2.00
Title Value:	$2.60	$7.80	$13.00	£1.60	£4.80	£8.00

PASSOVER

Maximum Comic Press,MS; 1 Dec 1996-2 Jan 1997

	$Good	$Fine	$N.Mint	£Good	£Fine	£N.Mint
1-2 ND Jeff Rebner script and pencils	$0.60	$1.80	$3.00	£0.40	£1.20	£2.00
Title Value:	$1.20	$3.60	$6.00	£0.80	£2.40	£4.00

PAT BOONE

National Periodical Publications,TV; 1 Sep/Oct 1959-5 May/Jun 1960

(see also Lois Lane #9)

	$Good	$Fine	$N.Mint	£Good	£Fine	£N.Mint
1 photo cover	$46.00	$135.00	$325.00	£31.00	£92.50	£220.00
	1st official distribution in the U.K.					
2-5	$36.00	$105.00	$250.00	£23.50	£70.00	£165.00
Title Value:	$190.00	$555.00	$1325.00	£125.00	£372.50	£880.00

PAT SAVAGE: WOMAN OF BRONZE SPECIAL

Millennium,OS; 1 Sep 1992

	$Good	$Fine	$N.Mint	£Good	£Fine	£N.Mint
1 ND the cousin of Doc Savage, cover/art by Brian Stelfreeze with Adam Hughes	$0.40	$1.20	$2.00	£0.25	£0.75	£1.25
Title Value:	$0.40	$1.20	$2.00	£0.25	£0.75	£1.25

PATHWAYS TO FANTASY

Pacific; 1 Jul 1984

	$Good	$Fine	$N.Mint	£Good	£Fine	£N.Mint
1 ND John Bolton, Scott Hampton, Jeff Jones, Barry Smith, Leila Dowling art	$0.60	$1.80	$3.00	£0.40	£1.20	£2.00
Title Value:	$0.60	$1.80	$3.00	£0.40	£1.20	£2.00

PATSY AND HEDY ANNUAL

Marvel Comics Group; 1 1963

	$Good	$Fine	$N.Mint	£Good	£Fine	£N.Mint
1 scarce in the U.K. 68pgs	$6.25	$19.00	$45.00	£4.25	£12.50	£30.00
Title Value:	$6.25	$19.00	$45.00	£4.25	£12.50	£30.00

PATSY AND HEDY CAREER GIRLS

Marvel Comics Group;70 Jun/Jul 1960-110 Feb 1967

(previous issues ND)

	$Good	$Fine	$N.Mint	£Good	£Fine	£N.Mint
70-110	$1.70	$5.00	$12.00	£0.85	£2.55	£6.00
Title Value:	$69.70	$205.00	$472.00	£34.85	£104.55	£246.00

PATSY WALKER

Marvel Comics Group;51 Nov 1959-124 Dec 1965

(previous issues ND)

	$Good	$Fine	$N.Mint	£Good	£Fine	£N.Mint
51-57	$4.25	$12.50	$30.00	£2.85	£8.50	£20.00
58-60	$3.20	$9.50	$22.50	£2.10	£6.25	£15.00
61-80	$3.20	$9.50	$22.50	£1.75	£5.25	£12.50
81-91	$2.10	$6.25	$15.00	£1.25	£3.85	£9.00
92 Millie X-over	$2.10	$6.25	$15.00	£1.25	£3.85	£9.00
93-97	$2.10	$6.25	$15.00	£1.25	£3.85	£9.00
98 Millie X-over	$2.10	$6.25	$15.00	£1.25	£3.85	£9.00
99	$2.10	$6.25	$15.00	£1.25	£3.85	£9.00
100	$2.50	$7.50	$17.50	£1.40	£4.25	£10.00
101-124	$1.40	$4.25	$10.00	£0.85	£2.55	£6.00
Title Value:	$179.35	$534.25	$1245.00	£106.80	£321.85	£760.00

PATSY WALKER FASHION PARADE

Marvel Comics Group; 1 1966

	$Good	$Fine	$N.Mint	£Good	£Fine	£N.Mint
1 rare in the U.K. 68pgs	$6.25	$19.00	$45.00	£4.25	£12.50	£30.00
Title Value:	$6.25	$19.00	$45.00	£4.25	£12.50	£30.00

PAUL THE SAMURAI

New England Comics,MS; 1 Oct 1990-3 Sep 1991

	$Good	$Fine	$N.Mint	£Good	£Fine	£N.Mint
1-3 ND	$0.70	$2.10	$3.50	£0.50	£1.50	£2.50
Title Value:	$2.10	$6.30	$10.50	£1.50	£4.50	£7.50

PAUL THE SAMURAI (2ND SERIES)

New England Comics; 1 Jun 1992-10 1994

	$Good	$Fine	$N.Mint	£Good	£Fine	£N.Mint
1 ND oversized "Tick" format, more serious treatment of character	$0.70	$2.10	$3.50	£0.50	£1.50	£2.50
2-3 ND	$0.60	$1.80	$3.00	£0.40	£1.20	£2.00
4-10 ND	$0.55	$1.65	$2.75	£0.35	£1.05	£1.75
Title Value:	$5.75	$17.25	$28.75	£3.75	£11.25	£18.75

PEACEMAKER

Charlton; 1 Mar 1967-5 Nov 1967

	$Good	$Fine	$N.Mint	£Good	£Fine	£N.Mint
1 distributed in the U.K.	$3.55	$10.50	$25.00	£2.10	£6.25	£15.00
2-3 distributed in the U.K.	$2.10	$6.25	$15.00	£1.10	£3.40	£8.00
4 distributed in the U.K. origin told	$3.55	$10.50	$25.00	£2.10	£6.25	£15.00
5 distributed in the U.K.	$2.10	$6.25	$15.00	£1.10	£3.40	£8.00
Title Value:	$13.40	$39.75	$95.00	£7.50	£22.70	£54.00

PEACEMAKER

DC Comics,MS; 1 Jan 1988-4 Apr 1988

SOME INDEPENDENT COMICS MAY NOT HAVE APPEARED ALTHOUGH THEY WERE ADVERTISED AND SOLICITED.

Issue	$Good	$Fine	$N.Mint	£Good	£Fine	£N.Mint
1-4	$0.15	$0.45	$0.75	£0.10	£0.30	£0.50
Title Value:	$0.60	$1.80	$3.00	£0.40	£1.20	£2.00

Note: Deluxe Format

PELLEAS & MELISANDE

Eclipse;(Night Music 4,5); 1,2 1986

Issue	$Good	$Fine	$N.Mint	£Good	£Fine	£N.Mint
1-2 ND P. Craig Russell art	$0.40	$1.20	$2.00	£0.25	£0.75	£1.25
Title Value:	$0.80	$2.40	$4.00	£0.50	£1.50	£2.50

PENDULUM

Adventure,MS; 1 Nov 1992-4 Feb 1993

Issue	$Good	$Fine	$N.Mint	£Good	£Fine	£N.Mint
1-4 ND	$0.40	$1.20	$2.00	£0.25	£0.75	£1.25
Title Value:	$1.60	$4.80	$8.00	£1.00	£3.00	£5.00

PENDULUM PRESS CLASSICS

Pendulum Press; 1 Jan 1991-6 1991

Issue	$Good	$Fine	$N.Mint	£Good	£Fine	£N.Mint
1 ND Moby Dick, 64pgs	$0.70	$2.10	$3.50	£0.50	£1.50	£2.50
2 ND Treasure Island, 64pgs	$0.70	$2.10	$3.50	£0.50	£1.50	£2.50
3 ND Dr. Jekyll and Mr. Hyde	$0.70	$2.10	$3.50	£0.50	£1.50	£2.50
4 ND 20,000 Leagues Under The Sea	$0.70	$2.10	$3.50	£0.50	£1.50	£2.50
5 ND A Christmas Carol	$0.70	$2.10	$3.50	£0.50	£1.50	£2.50
6 ND A Midsummer Night's Dream	$0.70	$2.10	$3.50	£0.50	£1.50	£2.50
Title Value:	$4.20	$12.60	$21.00	£3.00	£9.00	£15.00
Pendulum Press Collectors Kit: each of the above comes with a 30 minute audio cassette and illustrated pamphlet				£0.85	£2.55	£4.25

PENTACLE: SIGN OF THE FIVE

Eternity,MS; 1 Jan 1991-4 Apr 1991

Issue	$Good	$Fine	$N.Mint	£Good	£Fine	£N.Mint
1-4 ND continues story of Warlock 5 (Aircel), black and white	$0.40	$1.20	$2.00	£0.25	£0.75	£1.25
Title Value:	$1.60	$4.80	$8.00	£1.00	£3.00	£5.00

PENTHOUSE COMIX

General Media International,Magazine; 1 1994-present

Issue	$Good	$Fine	$N.Mint	£Good	£Fine	£N.Mint
1 ND adult material	$5.00	$15.00	$25.00	£3.00	£9.00	£15.00
2-3 ND adult material	$3.00	$9.00	$15.00	£2.00	£6.00	£10.00
4-20 ND adult material	$1.00	$3.00	$5.00	£0.60	£1.80	£3.00
Title Value:	$28.00	$84.00	$140.00	£17.20	£51.60	£86.00

PENTHOUSE MAX

General Media International,Magazine; 1 Jul 1996-present
(formerly Penthouse Men's Adventure Comix)

Issue	$Good	$Fine	$N.Mint	£Good	£Fine	£N.Mint
1 ND Bart Sears, Keith Giffen and Kevin Maguire art; adult material	$1.00	$3.00	$5.00	£0.60	£1.80	£3.00
2 ND adult material	$1.00	$3.00	$5.00	£0.60	£1.80	£3.00
Title Value:	$2.00	$6.00	$10.00	£1.20	£3.60	£6.00

PENTHOUSE MEN'S ADVENTURE COMIX

General Media International; 1 1995-7 1996
(becomes Penthouse Max)

Issue	$Good	$Fine	$N.Mint	£Good	£Fine	£N.Mint
1 Comic Edition, ND adult material	$1.00	$3.00	$5.00	£0.60	£1.80	£3.00
1 Magazine Edition, ND adult material	$1.00	$3.00	$5.00	£0.60	£1.80	£3.00
2 Comic Edition, ND adult material	$1.00	$3.00	$5.00	£0.60	£1.80	£3.00
2 Magazine Edition, ND adult material	$1.00	$3.00	$5.00	£0.60	£1.80	£3.00
3 Comic Edition, ND adult material	$1.00	$3.00	$5.00	£0.60	£1.80	£3.00
3 Magazine Edition, ND adult material	$1.00	$3.00	$5.00	£0.60	£1.80	£3.00
4 Comic Edition, ND adult material	$1.00	$3.00	$5.00	£0.60	£1.80	£3.00
4 Magazine Edition, ND adult material	$1.00	$3.00	$5.00	£0.60	£1.80	£3.00
5 Comic Edition, ND adult material	$1.00	$3.00	$5.00	£0.60	£1.80	£3.00
5-7 Magazine Edition, ND adult material	$1.00	$3.00	$5.00	£0.60	£1.80	£3.00
Title Value:	$12.00	$36.00	$60.00	£7.20	£21.60	£36.00

PERG

Lightning Comics; 1 Dec 1993-8 May 1994

Issue	$Good	$Fine	$N.Mint	£Good	£Fine	£N.Mint
1 ND glow in the dark flip-cover	$0.70	$2.10	$3.50	£0.40	£1.20	£2.00
1 Platinum Edition, ND (Sep 1994), signed and limited to 2,000 copies	$1.20	$3.60	$6.00	£0.80	£2.40	£4.00
2 ND	$0.60	$1.80	$3.00	£0.30	£0.90	£1.50
2 Platinum Edition ND	$1.00	$3.00	$5.00	£0.70	£2.10	£3.50
3 ND	$0.60	$1.80	$3.00	£0.30	£0.90	£1.50
3 Platinum Edition ND	$1.00	$3.00	$5.00	£0.70	£2.10	£3.50
4 ND 1st appearance Hellina	$1.00	$3.00	$5.00	£0.50	£1.50	£2.50
4 Platinum Edition, ND (Jan 1995) - metallic ink cover, signed by Joseph Zyskowski; 1,500 copies	$2.00	$6.00	$10.00	£1.20	£3.60	£6.00
4 Signed & Numbered Edition, ND (Jul 1995) - pre-bagged in mylar sleeve, 500 copies	$1.50	$4.50	$7.50	£1.00	£3.00	£5.00
5-6 ND	$0.50	$1.50	$2.50	£0.30	£0.90	£1.50
6 Nude Edition, ND (Sep 1996)	$2.00	$6.00	$10.00	£1.30	£3.90	£6.50
7-8 ND	$0.50	$1.50	$2.50	£0.30	£0.90	£1.50
Title Value:	$13.60	$40.80	$68.00	£8.40	£25.20	£42.00

PETER CANNON: THUNDERBOLT

DC Comics; 1 Sep 1992-12 Aug 1993

Issue	$Good	$Fine	$N.Mint	£Good	£Fine	£N.Mint
1 Michael Collins script/art begins	$0.25	$0.75	$1.25	£0.10	£0.35	£0.60
2-8	$0.25	$0.75	$1.25	£0.10	£0.35	£0.60
9 Justice League Europe appear, $1.50 cover begins	$0.25	$0.75	$1.25	£0.10	£0.35	£0.60
10 Justice League Europe appear	$0.25	$0.75	$1.25	£0.10	£0.35	£0.60
11-12	$0.25	$0.75	$1.25	£0.10	£0.35	£0.60
Title Value:	$3.00	$9.00	$15.00	£1.20	£4.20	£7.20

PETER PAN GRAPHIC NOVEL

Disney,OS; nn Nov 1990

Issue	$Good	$Fine	$N.Mint	£Good	£Fine	£N.Mint
nn ND 64pgs, adaptation of film	$1.00	$3.00	$5.00	£0.70	£2.10	£3.50
Title Value:	$1.00	$3.00	$5.00	£0.70	£2.10	£3.50

PETER PAN GRAPHIC NOVEL, COMPLETE

Adventure,OS; 1 Feb 1992

Issue	$Good	$Fine	$N.Mint	£Good	£Fine	£N.Mint
1 ND 40pgs, collects 2-part mini-series	$1.00	$3.00	$5.00	£0.70	£2.10	£3.50
Title Value:	$1.00	$3.00	$5.00	£0.70	£2.10	£3.50

PETER PAN: RETURN TO NEVER NEVER LAND

Adventure,MS; 1,2 Sep 1991

Our Fighting Forces #17

Our Love Story #7

Patsy And Hedy, Career Girls #108

Issue	$Good	$Fine	$N.Mint	£Good	£Fine	£N.Mint
1-2 ND adaptation of classic story	*$0.40*	*$1.20*	*$2.00*	£0.25	£0.75	£1.25
Title Value:	*$0.80*	*$2.40*	*$4.00*	£0.50	£1.50	£2.50

PETER PORKCHOPS

National Periodical Publications;61 Sep/Nov 1959; 62 Oct/Dec 1960

(Previous issues ND)

Issue	$Good	$Fine	$N.Mint	£Good	£Fine	£N.Mint
61-62 very scarce in the U.K.	*$7.75*	*$23.50*	*$55.00*	£5.00	£15.00	£35.00
Title Value:	*$15.50*	*$47.00*	*$110.00*	£10.00	£30.00	£70.00

Note: character becomes Pig-Iron in Captain Carrot

PETER RABBIT 3-D

Eternity,OS; 1 Apr 1990

Issue	$Good	$Fine	$N.Mint	£Good	£Fine	£N.Mint
1 ND reprints by Harrison Cady; with bound-in 3-D glasses (25% less if without glasses)	*$0.50*	*$1.50*	*$2.50*	£0.30	£0.90	£1.50
Title Value:	*$0.50*	*$1.50*	*$2.50*	£0.30	£0.90	£1.50

PETER THE LITTLE PEST

Marvel Comics Group; 1 Nov 1969-4 May 1970

Issue	$Good	$Fine	$N.Mint	£Good	£Fine	£N.Mint
1 ND	*$1.40*	*$4.25*	*$10.00*	£0.85	£2.55	£6.00
2-4 ND reprints	*$1.00*	*$3.00*	*$6.00*	£0.55	£1.75	£3.50
Title Value:	*$4.40*	*$13.25*	*$28.00*	£2.50	£7.80	£16.50

PHAGE: SHADOW DEATH, NEIL GAIMAN'S

Big Entertainment,MS; 1 Jun 1996-6 Nov 1996

Issue	$Good	$Fine	$N.Mint	£Good	£Fine	£N.Mint
1-6 ND Bryan Talbot script and covers, David Pugh and Tim Perkins art	*$0.45*	*$1.35*	*$2.25*	£0.30	£0.90	£1.50
Title Value:	*$2.70*	*$8.10*	*$13.50*	£1.80	£5.40	£9.00

PHANTOM

Marvel Comics Group,MS; 1 Feb 1995-3 Apr 1995

Issue	$Good	$Fine	$N.Mint	£Good	£Fine	£N.Mint
1-3 ties in with US animated TV series; Glen Lumsden art	*$0.60*	*$1.80*	*$3.00*	£0.40	£1.20	£2.00
Title Value:	*$1.80*	*$5.40*	*$9.00*	£1.20	£3.60	£6.00

PHANTOM

Pioneer,MS; 1 May 1990-4 Aug 1990

Issue	$Good	$Fine	$N.Mint	£Good	£Fine	£N.Mint
1-4 ND material never-before reprinted	*$0.90*	*$2.70*	*$4.50*	£0.60	£1.80	£3.00
Title Value:	*$3.60*	*$10.80*	*$18.00*	£2.40	£7.20	£12.00

PHANTOM 2040

Marvel Comics Group,MS; 1 May 1995-4 Aug 1995

Issue	$Good	$Fine	$N.Mint	£Good	£Fine	£N.Mint
1 ND based on US TV cartoon; Steve Ditko art; centrespread poster by Steve Ditko and John Romita (1st time ever collaboration)	*$0.30*	*$0.90*	*$1.50*	£0.20	£0.60	£1.00
2-4 ND based on US TV cartoon; Steve Ditko art	*$0.30*	*$0.90*	*$1.50*	£0.20	£0.60	£1.00
Title Value:	*$1.20*	*$3.60*	*$6.00*	£0.80	£2.40	£4.00

PHANTOM FORCE

Image,MS; 1 Dec 1993-2 May 1994; Genesis West; 0 Mar 1994; 3 May 1994-10 1995

Issue	$Good	$Fine	$N.Mint	£Good	£Fine	£N.Mint
0 (Mar 1994) Jack Kirby pencils (8pgs), cover by Jack Kirby and Jim Lee	*$0.40*	*$1.20*	*$2.00*	£0.25	£0.75	£1.25
1 pre-bagged with trading card (5 different); Jack Kirby plot and pencils, inks by Liefeld, Larsen, McFarlane, Williams and Lee	*$0.40*	*$1.20*	*$2.00*	£0.25	£0.75	£1.25
2 64pgs, Jack Kirby pencils (8pgs), inked by Liefeld, Larsen, Gordon, Ordway, Giffen; cover by Kirby and Larsen	*$0.50*	*$1.50*	*$2.50*	£0.30	£0.90	£1.50
3 Jack Kirby pencils (8pgs), inked by Liefeld, Larsen, Thibideaux, Giffen, Ordway and Gordon; cover by Kirby and McFarlane	*$0.40*	*$1.20*	*$2.00*	£0.25	£0.75	£1.25
4 Jack Kirby and Michael Thibodeaux cover, Kirby splash page	*$0.40*	*$1.20*	*$2.00*	£0.25	£0.75	£1.25
5-8 Michael Thibodeaux script	*$0.40*	*$1.20*	*$2.00*	£0.25	£0.75	£1.25
9 Michael Thibodeaux script and art, Jack Kirby cover (one of his last?)	*$0.40*	*$1.20*	*$2.00*	£0.25	£0.75	£1.25
10 Michael Thibodeaux art; origin of Kublak	*$0.40*	*$1.20*	*$2.00*	£0.25	£0.75	£1.25
Title Value:	*$4.50*	*$13.50*	*$22.50*	£2.80	£8.40	£14.00

Note: all Non-Distributed on the news-stands in the U.K.

PHANTOM OF FEAR CITY

Claypool Comics; 1 May 1993-12 May 1995

Issue	$Good	$Fine	$N.Mint	£Good	£Fine	£N.Mint
1-12 ND Steve Englehart scripts	*$0.40*	*$1.20*	*$2.00*	£0.25	£0.75	£1.25
Title Value:	*$4.80*	*$14.40*	*$24.00*	£3.00	£9.00	£15.00

PHANTOM SPECIAL EDITION

Pioneer,MS; 1 May 1990-4 Jul 1990

Issue	$Good	$Fine	$N.Mint	£Good	£Fine	£N.Mint
1-4 ND reprints of Sunday paper strips	*$2.00*	*$6.00*	*$10.00*	£1.40	£4.20	£7.00
Title Value:	*$8.00*	*$24.00*	*$40.00*	£5.60	£16.80	£28.00

PHANTOM STRANGER

National Periodical Publications; 1 May/Jun 1969-41 Feb/Mar 1976

(see Brave and the Bold, DC Comics Presents, DC Super-Stars, Saga of Swamp Thing, Showcase #80)

Issue	$Good	$Fine	$N.Mint	£Good	£Fine	£N.Mint
1	*$9.25*	*$28.00*	*$65.00*	£5.00	£15.00	£35.00
2	*$5.00*	*$15.00*	*$30.00*	£2.50	£7.50	£15.00
3 Neal Adams cover	*$5.00*	*$15.00*	*$30.00*	£2.50	£7.50	£15.00
4 Neal Adams art	*$5.00*	*$15.00*	*$30.00*	£2.50	£7.50	£15.00
5-10 Neal Adams cover	*$2.90*	*$8.75*	*$17.50*	£1.65	£5.00	£10.00
11-13 Neal Adams cover	*$2.05*	*$6.25*	*$12.50*	£1.30	£4.00	£8.00
14 last 15 cent cover; Neal Adams cover	*$2.05*	*$6.25*	*$12.50*	£1.30	£4.00	£8.00
15-19 52pgs, Neal Adams cover	*$1.25*	*$3.75*	*$7.50*	£0.80	£2.50	£5.00
20-22	*$0.80*	*$2.50*	*$5.00*	£0.55	£1.75	£3.50
23 Kaluta art, Spawn of Frankenstein begins (ends #30)	*$0.80*	*$2.50*	*$5.00*	£0.55	£1.75	£3.50
24-25 Kaluta art	*$0.80*	*$2.50*	*$5.00*	£0.55	£1.75	£3.50
26-30	*$0.80*	*$2.50*	*$5.00*	£0.55	£1.75	£3.50
31 Black Orchid begins	*$0.80*	*$2.50*	*$5.00*	£0.50	£1.50	£3.00
32	*$0.80*	*$2.50*	*$5.00*	£0.50	£1.50	£3.00
33 Deadman appears	*$0.80*	*$2.50*	*$5.00*	£0.50	£1.50	£3.00
34-38	*$0.80*	*$2.50*	*$5.00*	£0.50	£1.50	£3.00
39-41 Deadman appears	*$0.80*	*$2.50*	*$5.00*	£0.50	£1.50	£3.00
Title Value:	*$73.70*	*$224.25*	*$450.00*	£43.15	£131.75	£268.50

FEATURES

Black Orchid in 31, 32, 35, 36, 38-41. Dr.13 in 12-16, 18, 19, 21, 22, 34. Phantom Stranger in 11-25, 27-41. P.Stranger/Dr.13 in 1-10. P.Stranger/Dr.13/ Spawn of Frankenstein in 26. Spawn of Frankenstein in 23-25, 27-30.

REPRINT FEATURES

Dr.13 in 1-3, 17. Mark Merlin in 16, 18, 19. Phantom Stranger (1950s) in 1-3.

PHANTOM STRANGER (2ND SERIES)

DC Comics,OS; 1 Oct 1993

Issue	$Good	$Fine	$N.Mint	£Good	£Fine	£N.Mint
1 64pgs, Guy Davis art	*$0.60*	*$1.80*	*$3.00*	£0.40	£1.20	£2.00
Title Value:	*$0.60*	*$1.80*	*$3.00*	£0.40	£1.20	£2.00

PHANTOM STRANGER (LIMITED SERIES)

DC Comics,MS; 1 Oct 1987-4 Jan 1988

Issue	$Good	$Fine	$N.Mint	£Good	£Fine	£N.Mint
1-4 Mike Mignola art, P. Craig Russell inks, Eclipso appears	*$0.25*	*$0.75*	*$1.25*	£0.15	£0.45	£0.75
Title Value:	*$1.00*	*$3.00*	*$5.00*	£0.60	£1.80	£3.00

PHANTOM ZONE

DC Comics,MS; 1 Jan 1982-4 Apr 1982

Issue	$Good	$Fine	$N.Mint	£Good	£Fine	£N.Mint
1 Superman appears	*$0.25*	*$0.75*	*$1.25*	£0.15	£0.45	£0.75
2-4 Batman, Green Lantern, Wonder Woman, Zatanna and Supergirl appear	*$0.25*	*$0.75*	*$1.25*	£0.15	£0.45	£0.75
Title Value:	*$1.00*	*$3.00*	*$5.00*	£0.60	£1.80	£3.00

Note: Superman in all, Gene Colan art.

PHANTOM, THE

Gold Key/King; 1 Nov 1962-28 Dec 1967; Charlton; 30 Feb 1969-74 Dec 1976

Issue	$Good	$Fine	$N.Mint	£Good	£Fine	£N.Mint
1 rare in the U.K. Russ Manning art; painted covers begin (ends #17)	*$15.00*	*$45.00*	*$105.00*	£9.25	£28.00	£65.00
2 rare in the U.K.	*$7.75*	*$23.50*	*$55.00*	£5.00	£15.00	£35.00
3-10 rare in the U.K	*$5.50*	*$17.00*	*$40.00*	£3.55	£10.50	£25.00
11-17 rare in the U.K.	*$5.00*	*$15.00*	*$35.00*	£2.85	£8.50	£20.00
18 rare in the U.K. Flash Gordon by Wally Wood	*$5.25*	*$16.00*	*$37.50*	£3.20	£9.50	£22.50
19-20 rare in the U.K. Flash Gordon	*$3.20*	*$9.50*	*$22.50*	£1.75	£5.25	£12.50
21 scarce in the U.K.	*$3.20*	*$9.50*	*$22.50*	£2.10	£6.25	£15.00
22	*$3.20*	*$9.50*	*$22.50*	£1.75	£5.25	£12.50
23 scarce in the U.K.	*$3.20*	*$9.50*	*$22.50*	£2.10	£6.25	£15.00
24	*$3.20*	*$9.50*	*$22.50*	£1.75	£5.25	£12.50
25 Jeff Jones art	*$3.20*	*$9.50*	*$22.50*	£1.75	£5.25	£12.50
26-28	*$3.20*	*$9.50*	*$22.50*	£1.75	£5.25	£12.50
30-35 scarce in the U.K.	*$2.90*	*$8.75*	*$17.50*	£1.65	£5.00	£10.00
36 scarce in the U.K. Steve Ditko art	*$2.90*	*$8.75*	*$17.50*	£1.50	£4.50	£9.00
37-38 scarce in the U.K.	*$2.90*	*$8.75*	*$17.50*	£1.30	£4.00	£8.00
39 scarce in the U.K. Steve Ditko art	*$2.90*	*$8.75*	*$17.50*	£1.50	£4.50	£9.00
40 scarce in the U.K.	*$2.90*	*$8.75*	*$17.50*	£1.30	£4.00	£8.00
41-45 scarce in the U.K.	*$2.05*	*$6.25*	*$12.50*	£1.00	£3.00	£6.00
46 scarce in the U.K. 1st appearance Pirana (see Thrill-o-Rama)	*$2.05*	*$6.25*	*$12.50*	£1.00	£3.00	£6.00
47-54 scarce in the U.K.	*$2.05*	*$6.25*	*$12.50*	£1.00	£3.00	£6.00
55-66	*$1.65*	*$5.00*	*$10.00*	£0.80	£2.50	£5.00
67-69 scarce in the U.K. Newton art	*$1.65*	*$5.00*	*$10.00*	£0.80	£2.50	£5.00
70 scarce in the U.K. Maltese Falcon/Casablanca tribute; Bogart, Bacall, Greenstreet, Lorre appear, Newton art	*$1.65*	*$5.00*	*$10.00*	£0.80	£2.50	£5.00
71 scarce in the U.K. Newton art	*$1.25*	*$3.75*	*$7.50*	£0.80	£2.50	£5.00
72	*$1.25*	*$3.75*	*$7.50*	£0.50	£1.50	£3.00
73 Newton art	*$1.25*	*$3.75*	*$7.50*	£0.50	£1.50	£3.00
74 scarce in the U.K. Newton art	*$1.25*	*$3.75*	*$7.50*	£0.65	£2.00	£4.00
Title Value:	*$231.00*	*$699.25*	*$1535.00*	£130.05	£391.00	£873.50

Note: all distributed in the U.K.

PHANTOM, THE (1ST SERIES)

DC Comics,MS; 1 May 1988-4 Aug 1988

Issue	$Good	$Fine	$N.Mint	£Good	£Fine	£N.Mint
1-4	*$0.25*	*$0.75*	*$1.25*	£0.15	£0.45	£0.75
Title Value:	*$1.00*	*$3.00*	*$5.00*	£0.60	£1.80	£3.00

Note: Deluxe Format

PHANTOM, THE (2ND SERIES)

DC Comics; 1 Mar 1989-13 Mar 1990

Issue	$Good	$Fine	$N.Mint	£Good	£Fine	£N.Mint
1-13	$0.25	$0.75	$1.25	£0.15	£0.45	£0.75
Title Value:	$3.25	$9.75	$16.25	£1.95	£5.85	£9.75

PHAZE

Eclipse; 1 Apr 1988-2 Oct 1988

Issue	$Good	$Fine	$N.Mint	£Good	£Fine	£N.Mint
1 ND Sienkiewicz cover, painted colour art	$0.40	$1.20	$2.00	£0.25	£0.75	£1.25
2 ND Gulacy cover, painted colour art	$0.40	$1.20	$2.00	£0.25	£0.75	£1.25
Title Value:	$0.80	$2.40	$4.00	£0.50	£1.50	£2.50

PHOENIX

Atlas; 1 Jan 1975-4 Oct 1975

Issue	$Good	$Fine	$N.Mint	£Good	£Fine	£N.Mint
1-2 distributed in the U.K. origin	$0.25	$0.75	$1.50	£0.15	£0.50	£1.00
3 distributed in the U.K.	$0.25	$0.75	$1.50	£0.15	£0.50	£1.00
4 distributed in the U.K. new costume, Estrada art	$0.25	$0.75	$1.50	£0.15	£0.50	£1.00
Title Value:	$1.00	$3.00	$6.00	£0.60	£2.00	£4.00

PHOENIX - THE UNTOLD STORY

Marvel Comics Group,OS; 1 Apr 1984

Issue	$Good	$Fine	$N.Mint	£Good	£Fine	£N.Mint
1 ND scarce in the U.K. reprints X-Men #137 in unpublished original version, John Byrne art	$2.50	$7.50	$12.50	£1.50	£4.50	£7.50
Title Value:	$2.50	$7.50	$12.50	£1.50	£4.50	£7.50

PHOENIX RESURRECTION

Marvel Comics Group/Ultraverse,OS; 0 Dec 1995

Issue	$Good	$Fine	$N.Mint	£Good	£Fine	£N.Mint
0 ND collects back-up stories from the November 1995 Ultraverse titles plus a new Phoenix story; Bryan Hitch cover	$0.40	$1.20	$2.00	£0.25	£0.75	£1.25
Title Value:	$0.40	$1.20	$2.00	£0.25	£0.75	£1.25

PHOENIX RESURRECTION - AFTERMATH, THE

Marvel Comics Group,OS; 1 Mar 1996

Issue	$Good	$Fine	$N.Mint	£Good	£Fine	£N.Mint
1 ND 48pgs, intro Foxfire	$0.80	$2.40	$4.00	£0.50	£1.50	£2.50
Title Value:	$0.80	$2.40	$4.00	£0.50	£1.50	£2.50

PHOENIX RESURRECTION - GENESIS, THE

Marvel Comics Group,OS; 1 Feb 1996

Issue	$Good	$Fine	$N.Mint	£Good	£Fine	£N.Mint
1 ND 48pgs, X-Men appear; art by Bryan Hitch, Mark Pacella, Randy Green and others	$0.80	$2.40	$4.00	£0.50	£1.50	£2.50
Title Value:	$0.80	$2.40	$4.00	£0.50	£1.50	£2.50
The Phoenix Resurrection (Jun 1996) Trade paperback collects both Genesis and Revelations series				£0.90	£2.70	£4.50

PHOENIX RESURRECTION - REVELATIONS, THE

Marvel Comics Group/Ultraverse,OS; 1 Feb 1996

Issue	$Good	$Fine	$N.Mint	£Good	£Fine	£N.Mint
1 ND 48pgs, X-Men appear; art by John Royle, Jeff Matsuda and others	$0.80	$2.40	$4.00	£0.50	£1.50	£2.50
Title Value:	$0.80	$2.40	$4.00	£0.50	£1.50	£2.50

PHONY PAGES

Renegade,MS; 1 May 1986-2 Jun 1986

Issue	$Good	$Fine	$N.Mint	£Good	£Fine	£N.Mint
1-2 ND Terry Beaty parody reprints	$0.40	$1.20	$2.00	£0.25	£0.75	£1.25
Title Value:	$0.80	$2.40	$4.00	£0.50	£1.50	£2.50

PILGRIM'S PROGRESS, THE

Marvel Comics Group,OS; 1 May 1993

Issue	$Good	$Fine	$N.Mint	£Good	£Fine	£N.Mint
1 ND 96pgs, softcover	$1.50	$4.50	$7.50	£1.00	£3.00	£5.00
Title Value:	$1.50	$4.50	$7.50	£1.00	£3.00	£5.00

PINEAPPLE ARMY

Viz Communications; 1 Dec 1988-10 1989

Issue	$Good	$Fine	$N.Mint	£Good	£Fine	£N.Mint
1-10 ND Naohi Urasawa script/art, black and white; bi-weekly with painted covers	$0.80	$2.40	$4.00	£0.50	£1.50	£2.50
Title Value:	$8.00	$24.00	$40.00	£5.00	£15.00	£25.00
Graphic Novel (Oct 1990), reprints #1-10, softcover				£1.90	£5.70	£9.50

PINHEAD

Marvel Comics Group/Epic; 1 Dec 1993-7 1994

Issue	$Good	$Fine	$N.Mint	£Good	£Fine	£N.Mint
1 ND based on Clive Barker charcter from Hellraiser films; red foil embossed cover	$0.50	$1.50	$2.50	£0.30	£0.90	£1.50
2-7 ND	$0.50	$1.50	$2.50	£0.30	£0.90	£1.50
Title Value:	$3.50	$10.50	$17.50	£2.10	£6.30	£10.50

PINHEAD/MARSHALL LAW: LAW IN HELL

Marvel Comics Group/Epic,MS; 1 Nov 1993-2 Dec 1993

Issue	$Good	$Fine	$N.Mint	£Good	£Fine	£N.Mint
1 ND Pat Mills and Kev O'Neill	$0.60	$1.80	$3.00	£0.40	£1.20	£2.00
2 ND Pat Mills and Kev O'Neill; silver foil embossed cover	$0.60	$1.80	$3.00	£0.40	£1.20	£2.00
Title Value:	$1.20	$3.60	$6.00	£0.80	£2.40	£4.00

PINK FLOYD EXPERIENCE, THE

Revolutionary Comics,MS; 1 Jan 1991-5 1991

Issue	$Good	$Fine	$N.Mint	£Good	£Fine	£N.Mint
1-5 ND	$0.40	$1.20	$2.00	£0.25	£0.75	£1.25
Title Value:	$2.00	$6.00	$10.00	£1.25	£3.75	£6.25

PINK PANTHER, THE

Gold Key; 1 Apr 1971-87 1984

Issue	$Good	$Fine	$N.Mint	£Good	£Fine	£N.Mint
1 scarce in the U.K.	$4.15	$12.50	$25.00	£2.05	£6.25	£12.50
2-3	$2.05	$6.25	$12.50	£1.00	£3.00	£6.00
4-10	$2.05	$6.25	$12.50	£0.80	£2.50	£5.00
11-20	$1.65	$5.00	$10.00	£0.55	£1.75	£3.50
21-30	$1.25	$3.75	$7.50	£0.40	£1.25	£2.50
31-60	$1.00	$3.00	$5.00	£0.30	£0.90	£1.50
61-87	$0.70	$2.10	$3.50	£0.20	£0.60	£1.00
Title Value:	$100.50	$302.95	$557.00	£33.55	£102.95	£191.50

Note: most issues distributed in the U.K.

PINKY AND THE BRAIN

DC Comics; 1 Jun 1996-present

Issue	$Good	$Fine	$N.Mint	£Good	£Fine	£N.Mint
1-8 ND Walter Carzon and Mike DeCarlo art; based on US cartoon	$0.35	$1.05	$1.75	£0.25	£0.75	£1.25
9-10 ND	$0.35	$1.05	$1.75	£0.25	£0.75	£1.25
Title Value:	$3.50	$10.50	$17.50	£2.50	£7.50	£12.50

PINKY AND THE BRAIN CHRISTMAS SPECIAL

DC Comics,OS; 1 Jan 1996

Issue	$Good	$Fine	$N.Mint	£Good	£Fine	£N.Mint
1 ND based on US animated TV show	$0.30	$0.90	$1.50	£0.20	£0.60	£1.00
Title Value:	$0.30	$0.90	$1.50	£0.20	£0.60	£1.00

PINOCCHIO AND THE EMPEROR OF THE NIGHT

Marvel Comics Group,OS; 1 Mar 1986

Issue	$Good	$Fine	$N.Mint	£Good	£Fine	£N.Mint
1 scarce in the U.K.	$0.20	$0.60	$1.00	£0.15	£0.45	£0.75
Title Value:	$0.20	$0.60	$1.00	£0.15	£0.45	£0.75

Note: high quality paper.

PIRANHA IS LOOSE

Special Studio,OS; 1 Jan 1991

Issue	$Good	$Fine	$N.Mint	£Good	£Fine	£N.Mint
1 ND black and white	$0.30	$0.90	$1.50	£0.20	£0.60	£1.00
Title Value:	$0.30	$0.90	$1.50	£0.20	£0.60	£1.00

PIRATE CORPS!

Eternity; 1 Jul 1987-4 1988

Issue	$Good	$Fine	$N.Mint	£Good	£Fine	£N.Mint
1-4 ND	$0.30	$0.90	$1.50	£0.20	£0.60	£1.00
Title Value:	$1.20	$3.60	$6.00	£0.80	£2.40	£4.00

PIRATE CORPS! (2ND SERIES)

Slave Labor; 1 1989-5 1990

Issue	$Good	$Fine	$N.Mint	£Good	£Fine	£N.Mint
1 ND Evan Dorkin script/art begins; black and white	$0.40	$1.20	$2.00	£0.25	£0.75	£1.25
1 2nd printing ND	$0.40	$1.20	$2.00	£0.25	£0.75	£1.25
1 3rd printing, ND (Jul 1995)	$0.30	$0.90	$1.50	£0.20	£0.60	£1.00
2 ND	$0.40	$1.20	$2.00	£0.25	£0.75	£1.25
2 2nd printing, ND (Feb 1993)	$0.40	$1.20	$2.00	£0.25	£0.75	£1.25
2 3rd printing, ND (Jul 1995)	$0.30	$0.90	$1.50	£0.20	£0.60	£1.00
3 ND	$0.40	$1.20	$2.00	£0.25	£0.75	£1.25
3 2nd printing, ND (Feb 1993)	$0.40	$1.20	$2.00	£0.25	£0.75	£1.25
3 3rd printing, ND (Jul 1995)	$0.30	$0.90	$1.50	£0.20	£0.60	£1.00
4 ND	$0.40	$1.20	$2.00	£0.25	£0.75	£1.25
4 2nd printing, ND (Oct 1993)	$0.40	$1.20	$2.00	£0.25	£0.75	£1.25
4 3rd printing, ND (Jul 1995)	$0.30	$0.90	$1.50	£0.20	£0.60	£1.00
5 ND	$0.40	$1.20	$2.00	£0.25	£0.75	£1.25
5 2nd printing, ND (Apr 1994)	$0.40	$1.20	$2.00	£0.25	£0.75	£1.25
Title Value:	$5.20	$15.60	$26.00	£3.30	£9.90	£16.50
Special 1				£0.30	£0.90	£1.50

PIRATE CORPS: THE BLUNDER YEARS

Slave Labor; 1 Jul 1993-2 1993

Issue	$Good	$Fine	$N.Mint	£Good	£Fine	£N.Mint
1 ND 56pgs, reprints Pirate Corps #1 & 2	$0.90	$2.70	$4.50	£0.60	£1.80	£3.00
2 ND 56pgs, reprints Pirate Corps #3 & 4	$0.90	$2.70	$4.50	£0.60	£1.80	£3.00
Title Value:	$1.80	$5.40	$9.00	£1.20	£3.60	£6.00

PIRATES OF DARK WATER, THE

Marvel Comics Group,MS; 1 Nov 1991-9 Jul 1992

Issue	$Good	$Fine	$N.Mint	£Good	£Fine	£N.Mint
1 series adapts first five episodes of U.S. animated show	$0.15	$0.45	$0.75	£0.10	£0.35	£0.60
2-3	$0.15	$0.45	$0.75	£0.10	£0.35	£0.60
4 $1.25 cover begins	$0.15	$0.45	$0.75	£0.10	£0.35	£0.60
5-8	$0.15	$0.45	$0.75	£0.10	£0.35	£0.60
9 Charles Vess cover	$0.15	$0.45	$0.75	£0.10	£0.35	£0.60
Title Value:	$1.35	$4.05	$6.75	£0.90	£3.15	£5.40

PISTOLERO

Eternity,OS; nn Jul 1990

Issue	$Good	$Fine	$N.Mint	£Good	£Fine	£N.Mint
nn ND 56pgs	$1.00	$3.00	$5.00	£0.70	£2.10	£3.50
Title Value:	$1.00	$3.00	$5.00	£0.70	£2.10	£3.50

PITT

Image; 1 Jan 1993-9 1996; Full Bleed Studios; 10 1996-present

Issue	$Good	$Fine	$N.Mint	£Good	£Fine	£N.Mint
½ ND 24pgs, (Dec 1995) Brian Hotton script, Dale Keown art	$0.30	$0.90	$1.50	£0.20	£0.60	£1.00
1 ND Brian Hotton script and Dale Keown art begins	$1.00	$3.00	$5.00	£0.60	£1.80	£3.00
1 Ashcan Edition, ND 8.5" x 5.5" red card cover, black and white interior, limited to 5,500 copies (numbered in silver bottom right of cover), each signed in silver ink on cover by Keown and Hotton	$2.50	$7.50	$12.50	£1.50	£4.50	£7.50
2 ND ties-in to Youngblood #4	$0.60	$1.80	$3.00	£0.40	£1.20	£2.00
2 Black Ashcan Edition, ND 8.5" x 5.5" black card cover, black and white interior	$2.50	$7.50	$12.50	£1.50	£4.50	£7.50
2 Olive Ashcan Edition, ND 8.5" x 5.5" olive card cover, black and white interior	$2.50	$7.50	$12.50	£1.50	£4.50	£7.50
2 Platinum Ashcan Edition, ND 8.5" x 5.5" platinum card cover, black and white interior						

	$Good	$Fine	$N.Mint	£Good	£Fine	£N.Mint
	$2.50	*$7.50*	*$12.50*	£1.50	£4.50	£7.50
3 ND scarce in the U.K, scarce in the U.S.						
	$1.20	*$3.60*	*$6.00*	£1.20	£3.60	£6.00
3 Ashcan Edition, ND 24pgs, silver foil cover, signed by Dale Keown and Brian Hotton; black and white						
	$3.00	*$9.00*	*$15.00*	£2.00	£6.00	£10.00
4 ND less common	*$0.50*	*$1.50*	*$2.50*	£0.60	£1.80	£3.00
5-10 ND	*$0.50*	*$1.50*	*$2.50*	£0.30	£0.90	£1.50
11-12 ND	*$0.40*	*$1.20*	*$2.00*	£0.25	£0.75	£1.25
Title Value:	*$20.40*	*$61.20*	*$102.00*	£13.30	£39.90	£66.50

Pitt (Feb 1996)

	$Good	$Fine	$N.Mint	£Good	£Fine	£N.Mint
Trade paperback ND collects issues ½ plus #1-4				£1.30	£3.90	£6.50

PITT, THE

New Universe,OS; nn 1988

(see The Draft)

	$Good	$Fine	$N.Mint	£Good	£Fine	£N.Mint
nn ND John Byrne story; ties into Starbrand and DP7						
	$0.70	*$2.10*	*$3.50*	£0.50	£1.50	£2.50
Title Value:	*$0.70*	*$2.10*	*$3.50*	£0.50	£1.50	£2.50

Note: 48pgs, Bookshelf Format

PITT: IN THE BLOOD

Full Bleed Comics,OS; 1 Aug 1996

	$Good	$Fine	$N.Mint	£Good	£Fine	£N.Mint
1 ND Richard Pace script and art						
	$0.50	*$1.50*	*$2.50*	£0.30	£0.90	£1.50
Title Value:	*$0.50*	*$1.50*	*$2.50*	£0.30	£0.90	£1.50

PIXY JUNKET

Viz Communications,MS; 1 Sep 1993-6 Feb 1994

	$Good	$Fine	$N.Mint	£Good	£Fine	£N.Mint
1-6 ND	*$0.50*	*$1.50*	*$2.50*	£0.30	£0.90	£1.50
Title Value:	*$3.00*	*$9.00*	*$15.00*	£1.80	£5.40	£9.00

PLAN 9 FRON OUTER SPACE MOVIE ADAPTATION

Eternity,OS; nn May 1990

	$Good	$Fine	$N.Mint	£Good	£Fine	£N.Mint
nn ND 64pgs, squarebound, adapts cult film						
	$0.90	*$2.70*	*$4.50*	£0.60	£1.80	£3.00
Title Value:	*$0.90*	*$2.70*	*$4.50*	£0.60	£1.80	£3.00
2nd print (1991)				£0.65	£1.95	£3.25

PLANET 29

Caliber Press,MS; 1 Oct 1991-3 1992

	$Good	$Fine	$N.Mint	£Good	£Fine	£N.Mint
1-3 ND	*$0.40*	*$1.20*	*$2.00*	£0.25	£0.75	£1.25
Title Value:	*$1.20*	*$3.60*	*$6.00*	£0.75	£2.25	£3.75

PLANET COMICS

I.W. Comics; 1,8,9 1959-1961

	$Good	$Fine	$N.Mint	£Good	£Fine	£N.Mint
1 rare although distributed in the U.K. reprints						
	$8.50	*$26.00*	*$60.00*	£5.00	£15.00	£35.00
8-9 rare although distributed in the U.K. reprints						
	$6.25	*$19.00*	*$45.00*	£4.25	£12.50	£30.00
Title Value:	*$21.00*	*$64.00*	*$150.00*	£13.50	£40.00	£95.00

PLANET COMICS

Fiction House Magazines, Sci-Fi; 1 Jan 1940-73 Winter 1953/54

	$Good	$Fine	$N.Mint	£Good	£Fine	£N.Mint
1 scarce in the U.K. origins and 1st appearances of Flint Baker, The Red Comet - Planet Ranger and Auro - Lord of Jupiter; a line of classic covers featuring beautiful women and space monsters begins						
	$1050.00	*$3150.00*	*$9500.00*	£720.00	£2150.00	£6500.00
2 very scarce in the U.K., scarce in the U.S. cover by Lou Fine						
	$385.00	*$1150.00*	*$3500.00*	£265.00	£800.00	£2400.00
3 cover by Will Eisner						
	$280.00	*$840.00*	*$2250.00*	£190.00	£580.00	£1550.00
4 Gale Allen of the Girls' Space Patrol begins						
	$225.00	*$670.00*	*$1800.00*	£150.00	£455.00	£1225.00
5 very scarce in the U.K., scarce in the U.S. cover by Lou Fine and Will Eisner						
	$215.00	*$650.00*	*$1750.00*	£145.00	£440.00	£1175.00
6 very scarce in the U.K., scarce in the U.S.				*$210.00*	*$630.00*	*$1700.00*
	£140.00	£430.00	£1150.00			
7-12	*$175.00*	*$520.00*	*$1400.00*	£115.00	£350.00	£940.00
13-14	*$125.00*	*$380.00*	*$1025.00*	£85.00	£255.00	£690.00
15 very scarce in the U.K., scarce in the U.S. Mars God of War begins						
	$275.00	*$820.00*	*$2200.00*	£185.00	£560.00	£1500.00
16 Mars God of War cover						
	$150.00	*$450.00*	*$1200.00*	£100.00	£300.00	£800.00
17-20	*$125.00*	*$375.00*	*$1000.00*	£82.50	£250.00	£670.00
21-30	*$105.00*	*$315.00*	*$850.00*	£70.00	£210.00	£570.00
31-35	*$77.50*	*$230.00*	*$625.00*	£52.50	£155.00	£420.00
36-50	*$65.00*	*$195.00*	*$525.00*	£44.00	£130.00	£350.00
51-60	*$57.50*	*$175.00*	*$475.00*	£40.00	£120.00	£320.00
61 last 52pg issue						
	$57.50	*$175.00*	*$475.00*	£40.00	£120.00	£320.00
62-70	*$44.00*	*$130.00*	*$350.00*	£29.00	£87.50	£235.00
71-73	*$32.00*	*$95.00*	*$225.00*	£21.00	£62.50	£150.00
Title Value:	*$8127.00*	*$24345.00*	*$66900.00*	£5471.50	£16445.00	£45135.00

PLANET COMICS (2ND SERIES)

Pacific; 1 Jul 1984

	$Good	$Fine	$N.Mint	£Good	£Fine	£N.Mint
1 ND 76pgs, squarebound						
	$1.50	*$4.50*	*$7.50*	£1.00	£3.00	£5.00
Title Value:	*$1.50*	*$4.50*	*$7.50*	£1.00	£3.00	£5.00

PLANET COMICS (3RD SERIES)

Blackthorne; 1-5 1988

	$Good	$Fine	$N.Mint	£Good	£Fine	£N.Mint
1 ND Dave Stevens cover						
	$0.40	*$1.20*	*$2.00*	£0.25	£0.75	£1.25
2-3 ND Bill Stout cover						
	$0.40	*$1.20*	*$2.00*	£0.25	£0.75	£1.25
4-5 ND	*$0.40*	*$1.20*	*$2.00*	£0.25	£0.75	£1.25
Title Value:	*$2.00*	*$6.00*	*$10.00*	£1.25	£3.75	£6.25

PLANET OF THE APES

Adventure; 1 Apr 1990-24 Jul 1992

	$Good	$Fine	$N.Mint	£Good	£Fine	£N.Mint
1 ND Charles Marshall script, Kent Burles and Barb Kaalberg art; available with green, pink or yellow wraparound extra half cover						
	$0.80	*$2.40*	*$4.00*	£0.40	£1.20	£2.00
1 2nd printing ND	*$0.60*	*$1.80*	*$3.00*	£0.40	£1.20	£2.00
1 3rd printing ND	*$0.40*	*$1.20*	*$2.00*	£0.25	£0.75	£1.25
1 Limited Edition, ND (Apr 1990), gold embossed logo, sponsored by American Entertainment						
	$1.20	*$3.60*	*$6.00*	£0.80	£2.40	£4.00
2-5 ND	*$0.50*	*$1.50*	*$2.50*	£0.30	£0.90	£1.50
6-13 ND	*$0.40*	*$1.20*	*$2.00*	£0.25	£0.75	£1.25
14-17 ND Countdown Zero story						
	$0.40	*$1.20*	*$2.00*	£0.25	£0.75	£1.25
18 ND	*$0.40*	*$1.20*	*$2.00*	£0.25	£0.75	£1.25
19 ND ties in to Conquest of the Planet of the Apes						
	$0.40	*$1.20*	*$2.00*	£0.25	£0.75	£1.25
20 ND	*$0.40*	*$1.20*	*$2.00*	£0.25	£0.75	£1.25
21-24 ND tie-in with Conquest of the Planet of the Apes						
	$0.40	*$1.20*	*$2.00*	£0.25	£0.75	£1.25
Title Value:	*$12.60*	*$37.80*	*$63.00*	£7.80	£23.40	£39.00

Annual 1 (Nov 1991)

	$Good	$Fine	$N.Mint	£Good	£Fine	£N.Mint
ND 48pgs, six stories, cover by Mark Pennington				£0.45	£1.35	£2.25

Graphic Novel (Dec 1990)

	$Good	$Fine	$N.Mint	£Good	£Fine	£N.Mint
ND 144pgs reprints, adaptation of film				£1.10	£3.30	£5.50

PLANET OF THE APES

Marvel Comics Group,Magazine Film; 1 Aug 1974-29 Feb 1977

(see Adventures on the Planet of the Apes)

	$Good	$Fine	$N.Mint	£Good	£Fine	£N.Mint
1	*$1.65*	*$5.00*	*$10.00*	£0.80	£2.50	£5.00
2-5 ND	*$0.80*	*$2.50*	*$5.00*	£0.40	£1.25	£2.50
6-10 ND	*$0.65*	*$2.00*	*$4.00*	£0.30	£1.00	£2.00
11-15 ND	*$0.50*	*$1.50*	*$3.00*	£0.25	£0.75	£1.50
16-29 ND	*$0.50*	*$1.50*	*$3.00*	£0.20	£0.60	£1.25
Title Value:	*$17.60*	*$53.50*	*$95.00*	£7.95	£24.65	£50.00

Note: issues 1-10 are 84pgs, 11-13 are 76pgs, 14-29 are 52pgs.

ARTISTS

Ploog art in 1-4, 6, 8, 11, 13, 14, 19.

PLANET OF THE APES, TERROR ON

Adventure,MS; 1 Aug 1991-4 Nov 1991

	$Good	$Fine	$N.Mint	£Good	£Fine	£N.Mint
1 ND Doug Moench script, Mike Ploog art begins (from 1970s Marvel magazines)						
	$0.40	*$1.20*	*$2.00*	£0.25	£0.75	£1.25
2-4 ND	*$0.40*	*$1.20*	*$2.00*	£0.25	£0.75	£1.25
Title Value:	*$1.60*	*$4.80*	*$8.00*	£1.00	£3.00	£5.00

PLANET OF THE APES: FORBIDDEN ZONE

Adventure,MS; 1 Feb 1993-4 May 1993

	$Good	$Fine	$N.Mint	£Good	£Fine	£N.Mint
1-4 ND	*$0.40*	*$1.20*	*$2.00*	£0.25	£0.75	£1.25
Title Value:	*$1.60*	*$4.80*	*$8.00*	£1.00	£3.00	£5.00

PLANET OF THE APES: SINS OF THE FATHERS

Adventure,OS; 1 May 1992

	$Good	$Fine	$N.Mint	£Good	£Fine	£N.Mint
1 ND prequel to Planet of the Apes series						
	$0.40	*$1.20*	*$2.00*	£0.25	£0.75	£1.25
Title Value:	*$0.40*	*$1.20*	*$2.00*	£0.25	£0.75	£1.25

PLANET OF THE APES: URCHAK'S FOLLY

Adventure,MS; 1 Mar 1991-4 Jun 1991

	$Good	$Fine	$N.Mint	£Good	£Fine	£N.Mint
1-4 ND	*$0.40*	*$1.20*	*$2.00*	£0.25	£0.75	£1.25
Title Value:	*$1.60*	*$4.80*	*$8.00*	£1.00	£3.00	£5.00

PLANET OF VAMPIRES

Atlas; 1 Feb 1975-3 Jun 1975

	$Good	$Fine	$N.Mint	£Good	£Fine	£N.Mint
1-2 distributed in the U.K. part Neal Adams covers						
	$0.25	*$0.75*	*$1.50*	£0.15	£0.50	£1.00
3 distributed in the U.K. Russ Heath art						
	$0.25	*$0.75*	*$1.50*	£0.15	£0.50	£1.00
Title Value:	*$0.75*	*$2.25*	*$4.50*	£0.45	£1.50	£3.00

PLANET TERRY

Marvel Comics Group/Star; 1 Apr 1985-9 Jan 1986

	$Good	$Fine	$N.Mint	£Good	£Fine	£N.Mint
1-9	*$0.15*	*$0.45*	*$0.75*	£0.10	£0.30	£0.50
Title Value:	*$1.35*	*$4.05*	*$6.75*	£0.90	£2.70	£4.50

PLANET-X

Eternity,OS; 1 Sep 1991

	$Good	$Fine	$N.Mint	£Good	£Fine	£N.Mint
1 ND horror anthology						
	$0.40	*$1.20*	*$2.00*	£0.25	£0.75	£1.25
Title Value:	*$0.40*	*$1.20*	*$2.00*	£0.25	£0.75	£1.25

PLASMA BABY

Caliber Press; 1 Jan 1992-3 1992

	$Good	$Fine	$N.Mint	£Good	£Fine	£N.Mint
1-3 ND	*$0.50*	*$1.50*	*$2.50*	£0.30	£0.90	£1.50
Title Value:	*$1.50*	*$4.50*	*$7.50*	£0.90	£2.70	£4.50

PLASMA BABY: VENGEANCE OF THE AZTECS

Caliber Press; 1 1993-4 1993

	$Good	$Fine	$N.Mint	£Good	£Fine	£N.Mint
1-3 ND	*$0.50*	*$1.50*	*$2.50*	£0.30	£0.90	£1.50
4 ND double issue book #4 & 5						
	$0.60	*$1.80*	*$3.00*	£0.40	£1.20	£2.00
Title Value:	*$2.10*	*$6.30*	*$10.50*	£1.30	£3.90	£6.50

PLASMER

Marvel UK,MS; 1 Nov 1993-2 Dec 1993

	$Good	$Fine	$N.Mint	£Good	£Fine	£N.Mint
1 pre-bagged with 4 trading cards, Captain America guest-stars						
	$0.40	*$1.20*	*$2.00*	£0.20	£0.60	£1.00
2 Captain Britain and Black Knight appear						
	$0.40	*$1.20*	*$2.00*	£0.20	£0.60	£1.00
Title Value:	*$0.80*	*$2.40*	*$4.00*	£0.40	£1.20	£2.00

PLASTIC FORKS

Marvel Comics Group/Epic,MS; 1 Apr 1990-5 Aug 1990

	$Good	$Fine	$N.Mint	£Good	£Fine	£N.Mint
1-5 ND 64pgs, Ted McKeever art						
	$0.90	*$2.70*	*$4.50*	£0.60	£1.80	£3.00
Title Value:	*$4.50*	*$13.50*	*$22.50*	£3.00	£9.00	£15.00

Note: Creator owned title.

	$Good	$Fine	$N.Mint	£Good	£Fine	£N.Mint
Hardback (by Graphitti), 1991. Signed.				£5.00	£15.00	£25.00

PLASTIC MAN

National Periodical Publications; 1 Nov/Dec 1966-10 May/Jun 1968; 11 Feb/Mar 1976-20 Oct/Nov 1977

(see Action, Adventure, Brave and the Bold, DC Presents, DC Special, Superfriends, World's Finest)

Issue	$Good	$Fine	$N.Mint	£Good	£Fine	£N.Mint
1 Gil Kane cover/art, 1st Silver Age Plastic Man (see House of Mystery #160)	$9.25	$28.00	$65.00	£5.50	£17.00	£40.00
2 scarce in the U.K.	$4.60	$13.50	$32.50	£2.85	£8.50	£20.00
3-5 scarce in the U.K.	$3.90	$11.50	$27.50	£2.10	£6.25	£15.00
6-7 scarce in the U.K.	$2.50	$7.50	$17.50	£1.40	£4.25	£10.00
8-10 scarce in the U.K.	$2.50	$7.50	$17.50	£1.05	£3.20	£7.50
11-12	$1.25	$3.75	$7.50	£0.50	£1.50	£3.00
13 scarce in the U.K.	$1.25	$3.75	$7.50	£0.55	£1.75	£3.50
14	$1.25	$3.75	$7.50	£0.50	£1.50	£3.00
15 scarce in the U.K.	$1.25	$3.75	$7.50	£0.55	£1.75	£3.50
16-20	$1.25	$3.75	$7.50	£0.50	£1.50	£3.00
Title Value:	$50.55	$151.00	$342.50	£25.70	£77.85	£178.50

PLASTIC MAN

Super Comics; 11,16,18 1963-1964

Issue	$Good	$Fine	$N.Mint	£Good	£Fine	£N.Mint
11 rare in the U.K. reprints	$6.25	$19.00	$45.00	£3.20	£9.50	£22.50
16 reprints #18 and #21 from original series	$7.50	$22.50	$45.00	£3.30	£10.00	£20.00
18 Spirit appearance, reprint	$7.50	$22.50	$45.00	£3.30	£10.00	£20.00
Title Value:	$21.25	$64.00	$135.00	£9.80	£29.50	£62.50

Note: all distributed on the news-stands in the U.K.

PLASTIC MAN (2ND SERIES)

DC Comics,MS; 1 Nov 1988-4 Feb 1989

Issue	$Good	$Fine	$N.Mint	£Good	£Fine	£N.Mint
1-4 part Nowlan art	$0.25	$0.75	$1.25	£0.15	£0.45	£0.75
Title Value:	$1.00	$3.00	$5.00	£0.60	£1.80	£3.00

PLASTRON CAFE

Mirage Studios; 1 Feb 1993-5 1993

Issue	$Good	$Fine	$N.Mint	£Good	£Fine	£N.Mint
1 ND anthology featuring Eastman, Laird and Rick Veitch	$0.40	$1.20	$2.00	£0.25	£0.75	£1.25
2-5 ND	$0.40	$1.20	$2.00	£0.25	£0.75	£1.25
Title Value:	$2.00	$6.00	$10.00	£1.25	£3.75	£6.25

PLAYGROUND

Caliber Press,OS; 1 Oct 1990

Issue	$Good	$Fine	$N.Mint	£Good	£Fine	£N.Mint
1 ND black and white	$0.40	$1.20	$2.00	£0.25	£0.75	£1.25
Title Value:	$0.40	$1.20	$2.00	£0.25	£0.75	£1.25

PLOP!

DC Comics; 1 Sep/Oct 1973-24 Nov/Dec 1976

Issue	$Good	$Fine	$N.Mint	£Good	£Fine	£N.Mint
1 Bernie Wrightson art	$1.00	$3.00	$6.00	£0.55	£1.75	£3.50
2-4	$0.80	$2.50	$5.00	£0.40	£1.25	£2.50
5 Bernie Wrightson art	$0.80	$2.50	$5.00	£0.40	£1.25	£2.50
6-10	$0.80	$2.50	$5.00	£0.40	£1.25	£2.50
11-13	$0.80	$2.50	$5.00	£0.30	£1.00	£2.00
14 Wood art	$0.80	$2.50	$5.00	£0.30	£1.00	£2.00
15	$0.80	$2.50	$5.00	£0.30	£1.00	£2.00
16 ND Steve Ditko/Wally Wood art	$0.80	$2.50	$5.00	£0.40	£1.25	£2.50
17-20	$0.80	$2.50	$5.00	£0.30	£1.00	£2.00
21-22 ND 52pgs	$0.75	$2.25	$4.50	£0.40	£1.25	£2.50
23 ND 52pgs, no Segio Aragones art	$0.50	$1.50	$3.00	£0.40	£1.25	£2.50
24 52pgs	$0.65	$2.00	$4.00	£0.40	£1.25	£2.50
Title Value:	$18.85	$58.50	$117.00	£8.85	£28.25	£56.50

POISON ELVES

Sirius Entertainment; 1 1995-present

Issue	$Good	$Fine	$N.Mint	£Good	£Fine	£N.Mint
1 ND Drew Hayes script and art begins; 24pgs, black and white	$2.00	$6.00	$10.00	£1.20	£3.60	£6.00
1 2nd printing, ND (Jan 1996)	$0.60	$1.80	$3.00	£0.40	£1.20	£2.00
1 Commemorative Edition, ND features a foil enhanced cover, limited to 1,000 copies	$4.00	$12.00	$20.00	£2.00	£6.00	£10.00
2 ND	$1.50	$4.50	$7.50	£0.70	£2.10	£3.50
3-4 ND	$1.20	$3.60	$6.00	£0.50	£1.50	£2.50
5 ND	$1.20	$3.60	$6.00	£0.40	£1.20	£2.00
6-17 ND	$0.50	$1.50	$2.50	£0.30	£0.90	£1.50
Title Value:	$17.70	$53.10	$88.50	£9.30	£27.90	£46.50
Poison Elves Requiem for an Elf (Mar 1996)						
Trade paperback ND reprints issues #1-6				£2.00	£6.00	£10.00
Poison Elves Traumatic Dogs (Nov 1996)						
Trade paperback ND reprints issues #7-12				£2.00	£6.00	£10.00

POIZON: LOST CHILD

London Night Studios; ½ Sep 1995; 1 Mar 1996-present

Issue	$Good	$Fine	$N.Mint	£Good	£Fine	£N.Mint
½ ND Razor appears	$1.00	$3.00	$5.00	£0.60	£1.80	£3.00
0 ND	$0.60	$1.80	$3.00	£0.40	£1.20	£2.00
0 Signed & Numbered "Gothchik" Edition ND	$2.50	$7.50	$12.50	£1.40	£4.20	£7.00
0 Variant Cover Edition, ND cover by Everette Hartsoe	$1.60	$4.80	$8.00	£1.00	£3.00	£5.00
1 ND Razor and Stryke appear; wraparound cover	$0.60	$1.80	$3.00	£0.40	£1.20	£2.00
1 "Green Death" Edition, ND (Jun 1996), signed by George Jeanty with certificate, available in day-glow green envelope;limited to 3,000 copies	$3.00	$9.00	$15.00	£2.00	£6.00	£10.00
1 "Necro-Nude" Edition, ND (Mar 1996), protective outer cover; adult material	$2.00	$6.00	$10.00	£1.20	£3.60	£6.00
2 ND Razor and Stryke appear	$0.60	$1.80	$3.00	£0.40	£1.20	£2.00
3 ND Razor appears	$0.60	$1.80	$3.00	£0.40	£1.20	£2.00
Title Value:	$12.50	$37.50	$62.50	£7.80	£23.40	£39.00

POLICE ACADEMY

Marvel Comics Group; 1 Nov 1989-9 Jul 1990

Issue	$Good	$Fine	$N.Mint	£Good	£Fine	£N.Mint
1-9	$0.15	$0.45	$0.75	£0.10	£0.30	£0.50
Title Value:	$1.35	$4.05	$6.75	£0.90	£2.70	£4.50

POLICE ACTION

Atlas; 1 Feb 1975-3 Jun 1975

Issue	$Good	$Fine	$N.Mint	£Good	£Fine	£N.Mint
1-3 distributed in the U.K. Mike Sekowsky and Mike Ploog art	$0.25	$0.75	$1.50	£0.15	£0.50	£1.00
Title Value:	$0.75	$2.25	$4.50	£0.45	£1.50	£3.00

POLICE COMICS

Quality Comics; 1 Aug 1941-127 Oct 1953

Issue	$Good	$Fine	$N.Mint	£Good	£Fine	£N.Mint
1 origin and 1st appearance of Plastic Man by Jack Cole; also features The Human Bomb, Phantom Lady and The Mouthpiece; 1st appearance The Firebrand	$660.00	$2000.00	$6000.00	£440.00	£1325.00	£4000.00
2	$275.00	$820.00	$2200.00	£180.00	£550.00	£1475.00
3-4	$175.00	$520.00	$1400.00	£115.00	£355.00	£950.00

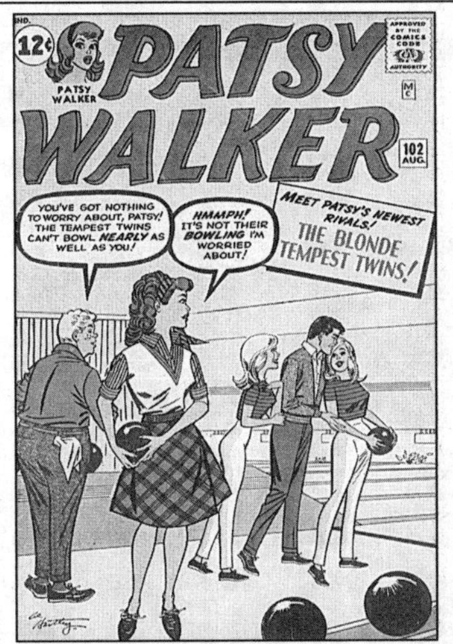

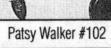

Patsy Walker #102

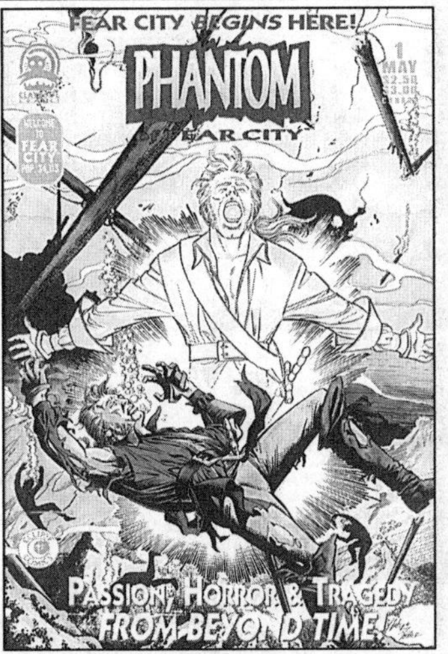

Phantom of Fear City #1

Planet Comics #1

Issue	$Good	$Fine	$N.Mint	£Good	£Fine	£N.Mint
5 1st Plastic Man cover						
	$155.00	$465.00	$1250.00	£105.00	£315.00	£850.00
6-7	$140.00	$420.00	$1125.00	£92.50	£280.00	£750.00
8 origin and 1st appearance Manhunter (no cover mention)						
	$185.00	$560.00	$1500.00	£125.00	£375.00	£1000.00
9-10	$130.00	$390.00	$1050.00	£87.50	£260.00	£700.00
11 The Spirit by Will Eisner begins from newspaper strip reprints						
	$215.00	$650.00	$1750.00	£150.00	£450.00	£1200.00
12 Ebony appears (1st time in comics)						
	$130.00	$390.00	$1050.00	£87.50	£260.00	£700.00
13 Woozy Winks appears (1st time in comics)						
	$130.00	$390.00	$1050.00	£87.50	£260.00	£700.00
14	$87.50	$260.00	$700.00	£57.50	£175.00	£470.00
15 cover style changes with Plastic Man and The Spirit interacting						
	$87.50	$260.00	$700.00	£57.50	£175.00	£470.00
16-19	$87.50	$260.00	$700.00	£57.50	£175.00	£470.00
20	$80.00	$240.00	$650.00	£52.50	£160.00	£435.00
21-30	$65.00	$195.00	$525.00	£44.00	£130.00	£350.00
31-40	$44.00	$130.00	$350.00	£29.00	£87.50	£235.00
41 last Spirit reprint by Will Eisner						
	$44.00	$130.00	$350.00	£29.00	£87.50	£235.00
42-50	$36.00	$105.00	$250.00	£24.00	£72.50	£170.00
51-60	$29.00	$85.00	$200.00	£19.00	£57.50	£135.00
61-89	$21.00	$62.50	$150.00	£14.00	£43.00	£100.00
90 The Spirit by Lou Fine						
	$25.00	$75.00	$175.00	£17.50	£52.50	£125.00
91	$21.00	$62.50	$150.00	£14.00	£43.00	£100.00
92 The Spirit by Lou Fine						
	$25.00	$75.00	$175.00	£17.50	£52.50	£125.00
93	$21.00	$62.50	$150.00	£14.00	£43.00	£100.00
94-99 The Spirit by Will Eisner						
	$32.00	$95.00	$225.00	£21.00	£62.50	£150.00
100	$43.00	$125.00	$300.00	£29.00	£85.00	£200.00
101-102 The Spirit by Will Eisner						
	$32.00	$95.00	$225.00	£21.00	£62.50	£150.00
103 becomes crime title; intro Ken Shannon, Private Eye and T-Man Trask						
	$21.00	$62.50	$150.00	£14.00	£43.00	£100.00
104-110	$15.50	$47.00	$110.00	£10.50	£32.00	£75.00
111-127	$14.00	$43.00	$100.00	£9.25	£28.00	£65.00
Title Value:	$6360.50	$19005.00	$49870.00	£4238.25	£12791.00	£33425.00

Note: most issues at least scarce in the U.K.

POPEYE

Charlton;94 Jul 1969-138 Dec 1976

Issue	$Good	$Fine	$N.Mint	£Good	£Fine	£N.Mint
94-100 distributed in the U.K.						
	$2.50	$7.50	$17.50	£1.40	£4.25	£10.00
101-120 distributed in the U.K.						
	$2.05	$6.25	$12.50	£1.15	£3.50	£7.00
121-138 distributed in the U.K.						
	$2.05	$6.25	$12.50	£0.80	£2.50	£5.00
Title Value:	$95.40	$290.00	$557.50	£47.20	£144.75	£300.00

POPEYE SPECIAL

Ocean; 1 Summer 1987-2 Sep 1988

Issue	$Good	$Fine	$N.Mint	£Good	£Fine	£N.Mint
1 ND origin	$0.40	$1.20	$2.00	£0.25	£0.75	£1.25
2 ND 60th anniversary special						
	$0.40	$1.20	$2.00	£0.25	£0.75	£1.25
Title Value:	$0.80	$2.40	$4.00	£0.50	£1.50	£2.50

PORTIA PRINZ OF THE GLAMAZONS

Eclipse; 1 Dec 1986-6 Oct 1987

Issue	$Good	$Fine	$N.Mint	£Good	£Fine	£N.Mint
1-6 ND Howell art	$0.40	$1.20	$2.00	£0.25	£0.75	£1.25
Title Value:	$2.40	$7.20	$12.00	£1.50	£4.50	£7.50

POST BROS. THOSE ANNOYING

Vortex/Rip Off Press; 1 Jan 1985-38 1993; Aeon; 39 Aug 1994-present

Issue	$Good	$Fine	$N.Mint	£Good	£Fine	£N.Mint
1 ND	$0.50	$1.50	$2.50	£0.30	£0.90	£1.50
1 2nd printing, ND (Jan 1994)						
	$0.40	$1.20	$2.00	£0.25	£0.75	£1.25
2-38 ND	$0.40	$1.20	$2.00	£0.25	£0.75	£1.25
39 ND 1st Aeon issue						
	$0.50	$1.50	$2.50	£0.30	£0.90	£1.50
40-46 ND	$0.50	$1.50	$2.50	£0.30	£0.90	£1.50
47-49 ND	$0.60	$1.80	$3.00	£0.40	£1.20	£2.00
50 ND 48pgs	$1.00	$3.00	$5.00	£0.65	£1.95	£3.25
Title Value:	$22.50	$67.50	$112.50	£14.05	£42.15	£70.25
Those Annoying Post Bros. In: Das Loot (Aug 1994)						
Trade paperback reprints issues #1-5 plus 8pg unpublished story				£2.00	£6.00	£10.00
Those Annoying Post Bros.: Disturb the Neighbours (Sep 1995)						
reprints issues #6-8				£1.30	£3.90	£6.50

POST BROTHERS ANNUAL, THOSE ANNOYING

Aeon; 1 Aug 1995

Issue	$Good	$Fine	$N.Mint	£Good	£Fine	£N.Mint
1 ND 56pgs, Matt Howarth with Nancy Collins; black and white						
	$0.90	$2.70	$4.50	£0.60	£1.80	£3.00
Title Value:	$0.90	$2.70	$4.50	£0.60	£1.80	£3.00

POST-MORTEM

Brave New Words,OS; 1 1991

Issue	$Good	$Fine	$N.Mint	£Good	£Fine	£N.Mint
1 ND 64pgs, squarebound, Matt Howarth script and art, black and white; features Savage Henry and Those Annoying Post Brothers						
	$0.90	$2.70	$4.50	£0.60	£1.80	£3.00
Title Value:	$0.90	$2.70	$4.50	£0.60	£1.80	£3.00

POWER & GLORY

Malibu Bravura; 1 Feb 1994-4 May 1994

Issue	$Good	$Fine	$N.Mint	£Good	£Fine	£N.Mint
1 Blue Foil Edition, ND (Oct 1994) - limited to 10,000 copies						
	$1.50	$4.50	$7.50	£1.00	£3.00	£5.00
1 Cover A, ND Howard Chaykin script, art and cover						
	$0.50	$1.50	$2.50	£0.30	£0.90	£1.50
1 Cover B, ND (photo collage) Howard Chaykin script, art and cover						
	$0.50	$1.50	$2.50	£0.30	£0.90	£1.50
1 Serigraph Edition, ND (Apr 1994) - limited to 3,000 copies						
	$1.50	$4.50	$7.50	£1.00	£3.00	£5.00
2-4 ND	$0.50	$1.50	$2.50	£0.30	£0.90	£1.50
Title Value:	$5.50	$16.50	$27.50	£3.50	£10.50	£17.50
Power & Glory Softcover Collection (Oct 1994)						
Trade paperback reprints mini-series with new text/features				£1.70	£5.10	£8.50
Power & Glory Softcover Collection Signed (Oct 1994)						
as above, signed by Howard Chaykin. 500 copies				£4.00	£12.00	£20.00

POWER & GLORY WINTER SPECIAL

Malibu,OS; 1 Dec 1994

Issue	$Good	$Fine	$N.Mint	£Good	£Fine	£N.Mint
1 ND Howard Chaykin script and art						
	$0.50	$1.50	$2.50	£0.30	£0.90	£1.50
Title Value:	$0.50	$1.50	$2.50	£0.30	£0.90	£1.50

Note: Non-Distributed on the news-stands in the U.K.

POWER COMICS

Power Comics; 1 1977-5 1979

Issue	$Good	$Fine	$N.Mint	£Good	£Fine	£N.Mint
1 ND First Dave Sim Aardvark story						
	$1.65	$5.00	$10.00	£1.25	£3.75	£7.50
1 reprint, ND of above (Mar 1977)						
	$0.80	$2.40	$4.00	£0.50	£1.50	£2.50
2 ND Cobalt Blue appears						
	$0.30	$1.00	$2.00	£0.20	£0.60	£1.25
3-5 ND	$0.30	$1.00	$2.00	£0.20	£0.60	£1.25
Title Value:	$3.65	$11.40	$22.00	£2.55	£7.65	£15.00

POWER COMICS (2ND SERIES)

Eclipse,MS; 1 Mar 1988-4 Sep 1988

Issue	$Good	$Fine	$N.Mint	£Good	£Fine	£N.Mint
1-4 ND Brian Bolland and Dave Gibbons reprints						
	$0.40	$1.20	$2.00	£0.25	£0.75	£1.25
Title Value:	$1.60	$4.80	$8.00	£1.00	£3.00	£5.00

Note: series features black super-hero Powerman (renamed Powerbolt by Eclipse) and reprints early Bolland and Gibbons work that was specially commissioned and published in Nigeria in 1975.

POWER FACTOR

Wonder Color Comics/Pied Piper Comics; 1 May 1987-2 1988

Issue	$Good	$Fine	$N.Mint	£Good	£Fine	£N.Mint
1 ND colour	$0.25	$0.75	$1.25	£0.15	£0.45	£0.75
2 ND colour, published by Pied Piper						
	$0.25	$0.75	$1.25	£0.15	£0.45	£0.75
Title Value:	$0.50	$1.50	$2.50	£0.30	£0.90	£1.50

POWER FACTOR (2ND SERIES)

Innovation; 1 Nov 1990-3 1991

Issue	$Good	$Fine	$N.Mint	£Good	£Fine	£N.Mint
1-3 ND colour	$0.40	$1.20	$2.00	£0.25	£0.75	£1.25
Title Value:	$1.20	$3.60	$6.00	£0.75	£2.25	£3.75

POWER GIRL

DC Comics,MS; 1 Jun 1988-4 Sep 1988

(see All Star Comics, Justice League Europe, 1986 Secret Origins #11, Showcase #97-100)

Issue	$Good	$Fine	$N.Mint	£Good	£Fine	£N.Mint
1-2	$0.25	$0.75	$1.25	£0.15	£0.45	£0.75
3-4 Phantom Stranger appears						
	$0.25	$0.75	$1.25	£0.15	£0.45	£0.75
Title Value:	$1.00	$3.00	$5.00	£0.60	£1.80	£3.00

POWER LORDS

DC Comics,MS Toy; 1 Dec 1983-3 Feb 1984

Issue	$Good	$Fine	$N.Mint	£Good	£Fine	£N.Mint
1-3 Mark Texeira art						
	$0.15	$0.45	$0.75	£0.10	£0.30	£0.50
Title Value:	$0.45	$1.35	$2.25	£0.30	£0.90	£1.50

POWER OF THE ATOM

(see Atom, Power of The)

POWER PACHYDERMS

Marvel Comics Group,OS; 1 Sep 1989

Issue	$Good	$Fine	$N.Mint	£Good	£Fine	£N.Mint
1 ND X-Men parody						
	$0.30	$0.90	$1.50	£0.20	£0.60	£1.00
Title Value:	$0.30	$0.90	$1.50	£0.20	£0.60	£1.00

Note: parody of X-Men characters as elephants

POWER PACK

Marvel Comics Group; 1 Aug 1984-62 Feb 1991

Issue	$Good	$Fine	$N.Mint	£Good	£Fine	£N.Mint
1 DS	$0.40	$1.20	$2.00	£0.25	£0.75	£1.25
2-5	$0.30	$0.90	$1.50	£0.20	£0.60	£1.00
6 Spiderman appears						
	$0.30	$0.90	$1.50	£0.20	£0.60	£1.00
7-8 Cloak & Dagger appear						
	$0.30	$0.90	$1.50	£0.20	£0.60	£1.00
9 Spiderman appears						
	$0.30	$0.90	$1.50	£0.20	£0.60	£1.00
10	$0.30	$0.90	$1.50	£0.20	£0.60	£1.00
11	$0.25	$0.75	$1.25	£0.15	£0.45	£0.75
12 Kitty Pryde/Nightcrawler/Leech appear						
	$0.25	$0.75	$1.25	£0.15	£0.45	£0.75
13-14	$0.25	$0.75	$1.25	£0.15	£0.45	£0.75
15 Thor (Beta Ray Bill) appears						
	$0.25	$0.75	$1.25	£0.15	£0.45	£0.75
16 painted cover	$0.25	$0.75	$1.25	£0.15	£0.45	£0.75
17	$0.25	$0.75	$1.25	£0.15	£0.45	£0.75
18 LD in the U.K. Secret Wars X-over, ties into Thor #363						
	$0.25	$0.75	$1.25	£0.15	£0.45	£0.75
19 DS, Cloak and Dagger, Thor (Beta Ray Bill), Wolverine, Kitty Pryde appear; Guice cover						
	$0.60	$1.80	$3.00	£0.30	£0.90	£1.50
20 New Mutants appear						
	$0.25	$0.75	$1.25	£0.15	£0.45	£0.75
21 Spiderman cameo						
	$0.25	$0.75	$1.25	£0.15	£0.45	£0.75
22	$0.25	$0.75	$1.25	£0.15	£0.45	£0.75

	$Good	$Fine	$N.Mint	£Good	£Fine	£N.Mint
23 Fantastic Four cameo	$0.25	$0.75	$1.25	£0.15	£0.45	£0.75
24 Cloak cameo	$0.25	$0.75	$1.25	£0.15	£0.45	£0.75
25 LD in the U.K. DS, Fantastic Four cameo	$0.30	$0.90	$1.50	£0.20	£0.60	£1.00
26 ND	$0.25	$0.75	$1.25	£0.15	£0.45	£0.75
27 ND scarce in the U.K. Mutant Massacre, Wolverine and Sabretooth appear	$1.00	$3.00	$5.00	£0.40	£1.20	£2.00
28 ND scarce in the U.K. Avengers and Fantastic Four appear	$0.25	$0.75	$1.25	£0.15	£0.45	£0.75
29 ND Spiderman vs. Hobgoblin	$0.25	$0.75	$1.25	£0.15	£0.45	£0.75
30-32 ND	$0.25	$0.75	$1.25	£0.15	£0.45	£0.75
33 ND New Mutants appear (some)	$0.25	$0.75	$1.25	£0.15	£0.45	£0.75
34 ND	$0.25	$0.75	$1.25	£0.15	£0.45	£0.75
35 ND Fall of Mutants, X-Factor appear	$0.25	$0.75	$1.25	£0.15	£0.45	£0.75
36 ND Sentinels story	$0.25	$0.75	$1.25	£0.15	£0.45	£0.75
37-38 ND	$0.25	$0.75	$1.25	£0.15	£0.45	£0.75
39 ND 1st format change/slick cover	$0.25	$0.75	$1.25	£0.15	£0.45	£0.75
40 ND New Mutants appear	$0.25	$0.75	$1.25	£0.15	£0.45	£0.75
41 ND	$0.25	$0.75	$1.25	£0.15	£0.45	£0.75
42-44 ND Inferno tie-in	$0.25	$0.75	$1.25	£0.15	£0.45	£0.75
45 ND	$0.25	$0.75	$1.25	£0.15	£0.45	£0.75
46 ND Punisher appears, Whilce Portacio art	$0.25	$0.75	$1.25	£0.15	£0.45	£0.75
47-49 ND	$0.25	$0.75	$1.25	£0.15	£0.45	£0.75
50 ND DS	$0.30	$0.90	$1.50	£0.20	£0.60	£1.00
51-52 ND	$0.25	$0.75	$1.25	£0.15	£0.45	£0.75
53 ND Acts of Vengeance tie-in	$0.25	$0.75	$1.25	£0.15	£0.45	£0.75
54-62 ND	$0.25	$0.75	$1.25	£0.15	£0.45	£0.75
Title Value:	$17.30	$51.90	$86.50	£10.35	£31.05	£51.75

Note: Direct Sales (ND) from 26 on. Format change/slick cover from #39 on

POWER PACK HOLIDAY SPECIAL

Marvel Comics Group,OS; nn Feb 1992

	$Good	$Fine	$N.Mint	£Good	£Fine	£N.Mint
nn 64pgs	$0.40	$1.20	$2.00	£0.25	£0.75	£1.25
Title Value:	$0.40	$1.20	$2.00	£0.25	£0.75	£1.25

POWER PLAY

Millennium,MS; 1 Feb 1995-4 Aug 1995

	$Good	$Fine	$N.Mint	£Good	£Fine	£N.Mint
1-4 ND black and white	$0.60	$1.80	$3.00	£0.40	£1.20	£2.00
Title Value:	$2.40	$7.20	$12.00	£1.60	£4.80	£8.00

POWER PLAYS

AC Comics; 1 1987-2 1987

	$Good	$Fine	$N.Mint	£Good	£Fine	£N.Mint
1-2 ND 52pgs	$0.40	$1.20	$2.00	£0.25	£0.75	£1.25
Title Value:	$0.80	$2.40	$4.00	£0.50	£1.50	£2.50

POWER, THE

Aircel,MS; 1 Mar 1991-4 Jun 1991

	$Good	$Fine	$N.Mint	£Good	£Fine	£N.Mint
1-4 ND Barry Blair script, Dave Cooper art, black and white	$0.30	$0.90	$1.50	£0.20	£0.60	£1.00
Title Value:	$1.20	$3.60	$6.00	£0.80	£2.40	£4.00

POWERLINE

Marvel Comics Group/Epic; 1 May 1988-8 Jul 1989

(see Dr.Zero, St.George)

	$Good	$Fine	$N.Mint	£Good	£Fine	£N.Mint
1-8 ND	$0.40	$1.20	$2.00	£0.20	£0.60	£1.00
Title Value:	$3.20	$9.60	$16.00	£1.60	£4.80	£8.00

Note: art by D. Ross/Williamson/Gray Morrow

POWERMAN

Marvel Comics Group; 17 Feb 1974-125 Sep 1986

(formerly Hero for Hire; becomes Powerman and Iron Fist with issue #50)

	$Good	$Fine	$N.Mint	£Good	£Fine	£N.Mint
17 ND Iron Man appears	$2.00	$6.00	$12.00	£1.00	£3.00	£6.00
18-20 ND	$1.00	$3.00	$6.00	£0.65	£2.00	£4.00
21 Luke Cage vs. original Powerman	$0.65	$2.00	$4.00	£0.30	£1.00	£2.00
22-23	$0.65	$2.00	$4.00	£0.30	£1.00	£2.00
24 1st appearance Black Goliath	$0.65	$2.00	$4.00	£0.40	£1.25	£2.50
25 Black Goliath appears	$0.65	$2.00	$4.00	£0.30	£1.00	£2.00
26	$0.65	$2.00	$4.00	£0.30	£1.00	£2.00
27 George Perez art	$0.65	$2.00	$4.00	£0.30	£1.00	£2.00
28-30	$0.65	$2.00	$4.00	£0.30	£1.00	£2.00
31 Neal Adams inks (credited as "The Crusty Bunkers" which was his art studio team at the time)	$0.65	$2.00	$4.00	£0.30	£1.00	£2.00
32-44	$0.50	$1.50	$3.00	£0.25	£0.75	£1.50
45 Jim Starlin cover	$0.50	$1.50	$3.00	£0.25	£0.75	£1.50
46-47	$0.50	$1.50	$3.00	£0.25	£0.75	£1.50
48 1st appearance of Iron Fist in title, John Byrne art	$0.50	$1.50	$3.00	£0.30	£1.00	£2.00
49 John Byrne art	$0.50	$1.50	$3.00	£0.30	£1.00	£2.00
50 John Byrne art, logo changes to "Powerman and Iron Fist" from here on	$0.50	$1.50	$3.00	£0.50	£1.50	£3.00
51-52 Mike Zeck art	$0.30	$1.00	$2.00	£0.20	£0.60	£1.25
53-56	$0.30	$1.00	$2.00	£0.20	£0.60	£1.25
57 X-Men appear	$0.80	$2.50	$5.00	£0.50	£1.50	£3.00
58-65 ND	$0.30	$1.00	$2.00	£0.25	£0.75	£1.50
66 2nd appearance Sabretooth (see Iron Fist #14)	$7.50	$22.50	$45.00	£1.65	£5.00	£10.00
67-72 ND	$0.40	$1.20	$2.00	£0.25	£0.75	£1.25
73 Rom X-over, Frank Miller cover	$0.40	$1.20	$2.00	£0.25	£0.75	£1.25
74 Frank Miller cover	$0.40	$1.20	$2.00	£0.25	£0.75	£1.25
75 52pgs	$0.45	$1.35	$2.25	£0.30	£0.90	£1.50
76 2pgs Frank Miller art	$0.40	$1.20	$2.00	£0.25	£0.75	£1.25
77 Daredevil guest-stars (X-over Daredevil #178)	$0.40	$1.20	$2.00	£0.25	£0.75	£1.25
78 3rd appearance Sabretooth. Referred to as "The Slasher" and heavily disguised with sacking over his head. Claws exposed in a few panels...	$3.30	$10.00	$20.00	£0.65	£2.00	£4.00
79 Dr. Who parody	$0.40	$1.20	$2.00	£0.25	£0.75	£1.25
80-83	$0.40	$1.20	$2.00	£0.25	£0.75	£1.25
84 4th appearance Sabretooth	$3.30	$10.00	$20.00	£0.65	£2.00	£4.00
85-86	$0.40	$1.20	$2.00	£0.25	£0.75	£1.25
87 Moon Knight appears	$0.40	$1.20	$2.00	£0.25	£0.75	£1.25
88-99	$0.40	$1.20	$2.00	£0.25	£0.75	£1.25
100 52pgs	$0.55	$1.65	$2.75	£0.35	£1.05	£1.75
101-117	$0.30	$0.90	$1.50	£0.20	£0.60	£1.00
118-120 ND	$0.30	$0.90	$1.50	£0.30	£0.90	£1.50
121 ND Secret Wars X-over	$0.30	$0.90	$1.50	£0.30	£0.90	£1.50
122-124 ND scarce in the U.K.	$0.30	$0.90	$1.50	£0.40	£1.20	£2.00
125 ND scarce in the U.K. DS	$0.50	$1.50	$2.50	£0.60	£1.80	£3.00
Title Value:	$61.45	$186.60	$352.50	£32.65	£99.50	£184.75

ARTISTS

Byrne covers on 104, 106, 107, 113-116.

POWERMAN ANNUAL

Marvel Comics Group; 1 Nov 1976

	$Good	$Fine	$N.Mint	£Good	£Fine	£N.Mint
1 ND 52pgs, Punisher appears in a flashback sequence	$0.65	$2.00	$4.00	£0.50	£1.50	£3.00
Title Value:	$0.65	$2.00	$4.00	£0.50	£1.50	£3.00

POWERMAN GIANT SIZE

Marvel Comics Group; 1 1975

	$Good	$Fine	$N.Mint	£Good	£Fine	£N.Mint
1 ND 68pgs, all reprint	$1.25	$3.75	$7.50	£0.80	£2.50	£5.00
Title Value:	$1.25	$3.75	$7.50	£0.80	£2.50	£5.00

POWERS THAT BE

Broadway Comics; 1 Nov 1995-present

	$Good	$Fine	$N.Mint	£Good	£Fine	£N.Mint
1 ND 1st appearance Star Seed and Fatale, Jim Shooter script	$0.80	$2.40	$4.00	£0.50	£1.50	£2.50
2-4 ND	$0.50	$1.50	$2.50	£0.30	£0.90	£1.50
5-6 ND	$0.60	$1.80	$3.00	£0.40	£1.20	£2.00
7 ND title becomes Star Seed	$0.60	$1.80	$3.00	£0.40	£1.20	£2.00
8-9 ND	$0.60	$1.80	$3.00	£0.40	£1.20	£2.00
Title Value:	$5.30	$15.90	$26.50	£3.40	£10.20	£17.00

PRARIE MOON AND OTHER STORIES

Dark Horse,OS; 1 Aug 1992

	$Good	$Fine	$N.Mint	£Good	£Fine	£N.Mint
1 ND Rick Geary story and art; black and white	$0.30	$0.90	$1.50	£0.20	£0.60	£1.00
Title Value:	$0.30	$0.90	$1.50	£0.20	£0.60	£1.00

PRE-TEEN DIRTY GENE KUNG-FU KANGAROOS

Blackthorne; 1 Aug 1986

	$Good	$Fine	$N.Mint	£Good	£Fine	£N.Mint
1 ND Teenage Mutant Ninja Turtles appear, Lee Marrs script/art, black and white	$0.40	$1.20	$2.00	£0.25	£0.75	£1.25
Title Value:	$0.40	$1.20	$2.00	£0.25	£0.75	£1.25

PREACHER

DC Comics/Vertigo; 1 Apr 1995-present

	$Good	$Fine	$N.Mint	£Good	£Fine	£N.Mint
1 ND Garth Ennis script and Steve Dillon art begins; Glenn Fabry painted covers	$6.50	$19.50	$32.50	£3.50	£10.50	£17.50
2 ND	$5.00	$15.00	$25.00	£2.50	£7.50	£12.50
3 ND	$4.00	$12.00	$20.00	£2.00	£6.00	£10.00
4 ND	$3.00	$9.00	$15.00	£1.50	£4.50	£7.50
5 ND	$2.50	$7.50	$12.50	£1.00	£3.00	£5.00
6-7 ND	$2.00	$6.00	$10.00	£0.80	£2.40	£4.00
8 ND "All in the Family" begins	$1.50	$4.50	$7.50	£0.60	£1.80	£3.00
9-10 ND	$1.50	$4.50	$7.50	£0.60	£1.80	£3.00
11 ND	$1.00	$3.00	$5.00	£0.50	£1.50	£2.50
12 ND polybagged, conclusion of "All in the Family" story	$1.00	$3.00	$5.00	£0.50	£1.50	£2.50
13-15 ND	$0.70	$2.10	$3.50	£0.40	£1.20	£2.00
16-23 ND	$0.50	$1.50	$2.50	£0.30	£0.90	£1.50
Title Value:	$37.60	$112.80	$188.00	£18.50	£55.50	£92.50

Preacher: Gone To Texas (Apr 1996)

	$Good	$Fine	$N.Mint	£Good	£Fine	£N.Mint
Trade paperback ND reprints issues #1-7				£2.00	£6.00	£10.00
Preacher: Until the End of the World (Feb 1997) Trade paperback ND reprints issues #8-17				£2.00	£6.00	£10.00

PREACHER SPECIAL: SAINT OF KILLERS

DC Comics,MS; 1 Aug 1996-4 Nov 1996

	$Good	$Fine	$N.Mint	£Good	£Fine	£N.Mint
1 ND Garth Ennis script, Steve Pugh art	$0.70	$2.10	$3.50	£0.40	£1.20	£2.00
2-4 ND Garth Ennis script, Steve Pugh art	$0.50	$1.50	$2.50	£0.30	£0.90	£1.50
Title Value:	$2.20	$6.60	$11.00	£1.30	£3.90	£6.50

PREACHER SPECIAL: THE STORY OF YOU-KNOW-WHO

DC Comics,OS; 1 Dec 1996

	$Good	$Fine	$N.Mint	£Good	£Fine	£N.Mint
1 ND 64pgs, Garth Ennis script, Richard Case art; the origin of Arseface	$1.00	$3.00	$5.00	£0.65	£1.95	£3.25
Title Value:	$1.00	$3.00	$5.00	£0.65	£1.95	£3.25

PREDATOR

Dark Horse,MS; 1 May 1989-4 1990

	$Good	$Fine	$N.Mint	£Good	£Fine	£N.Mint
1 ND	$3.00	$9.00	$15.00	£1.50	£4.50	£7.50
1 2nd printing ND	$0.80	$2.40	$4.00	£0.50	£1.50	£2.50
2 ND	$1.50	$4.50	$7.50	£0.80	£2.40	£4.00
2 2nd printing ND	$0.50	$1.50	$2.50	£0.30	£0.90	£1.50
3 ND	$1.00	$3.00	$5.00	£0.60	£1.80	£3.00
3 2nd printing ND	$0.50	$1.50	$2.50	£0.30	£0.90	£1.50
4 ND	$1.00	$3.00	$5.00	£0.60	£1.80	£3.00
Title Value:	$8.30	$24.90	$41.50	£4.60	£13.80	£23.00
Predator Collection (Sep 1990), reprints issues #1-4, new cover				£1.50	£4.50	£7.50
Limited Edition Hardcover (Apr 1991), signed and numbered, 2500 copies				£10.00	£30.00	£50.00
Predator Volume One: Concrete Jungle						
2nd printing (1992)				£1.75	£5.25	£8.75
3rd printing (Apr 1996)				£2.00	£6.00	£10.00

PREDATOR 2

Dark Horse,MS; 1 Feb 1991-2 Mar 1991

	$Good	$Fine	$N.Mint	£Good	£Fine	£N.Mint
1-2 ND adaptation of film, Dan Barry pencils; with 2 trading cards	$0.50	$1.50	$2.50	£0.30	£0.90	£1.50
Title Value:	$1.00	$3.00	$5.00	£0.60	£1.80	£3.00

PREDATOR VS. MAGNUS ROBOT FIGHTER

Dark Horse,MS; 1 Dec 1992-2 Jan 1993

	$Good	$Fine	$N.Mint	£Good	£Fine	£N.Mint
1 ND Jim Shooter script, Barry Windsor-Smith cover; contains bound-in trading cards	$0.50	$1.50	$2.50	£0.30	£0.90	£1.50
1 Platinum Edition, ND (Dec 1992) - "Platinum Edtion" banner on bottom of platinum-coloured cover	$1.50	$4.50	$7.50	£1.00	£3.00	£5.00
2 ND Jim Shooter script, Barry Windsor-Smith cover; contains bound-in trading cards	$0.50	$1.50	$2.50	£0.30	£0.90	£1.50
Title Value:	$2.50	$7.50	$12.50	£1.60	£4.80	£8.00
Predator vs. Magnus Robot Fighter (Sep 1994) Trade paperback 64pgs, reprints mini-series				£1.00	£3.00	£5.00

PREDATOR: BAD BLOOD

Dark Horse,MS; 1 Dec 1993-4 Mar 1994

	$Good	$Fine	$N.Mint	£Good	£Fine	£N.Mint
1-4 ND Derek Thompson cover and art	$0.50	$1.50	$2.50	£0.30	£0.90	£1.50
Title Value:	$2.00	$6.00	$10.00	£1.20	£3.60	£6.00

PREDATOR: BIG GAME

Dark Horse,MS; 1 Mar 1991-4 Jun 1991

	$Good	$Fine	$N.Mint	£Good	£Fine	£N.Mint
1-4 ND Evan Dorkin art	$0.50	$1.50	$2.50	£0.30	£0.90	£1.50
Title Value:	$2.00	$6.00	$10.00	£1.20	£3.60	£6.00
Predator: Big Game Trade paperback (Aug 1992) reprints issues #1-#4				£1.70	£5.10	£8.50
2nd printing (Apr 1996)				£1.90	£5.40	£9.00

PREDATOR: BLOODY SANDS OF TIME

Dark Horse,MS; 1 Feb 1992-2 Mar 1992

	$Good	$Fine	$N.Mint	£Good	£Fine	£N.Mint
1-2 ND script/pencils by Dan Barry, inks and covers by Chris Warner	$0.50	$1.50	$2.50	£0.30	£0.90	£1.50
Title Value:	$1.00	$3.00	$5.00	£0.60	£1.80	£3.00

PREDATOR: COLD WAR

Dark Horse,MS; 1 Nov 1991-4 Feb 1992

	$Good	$Fine	$N.Mint	£Good	£Fine	£N.Mint
1-4 ND Brian Stelfreeze covers	$0.50	$1.50	$2.50	£0.30	£0.90	£1.50
Title Value:	$2.00	$6.00	$10.00	£1.20	£3.60	£6.00
Predator: Cold War Softcover Collection (May 1993) reprints mini-series with new cover by Ray Lago				£1.65	£4.95	£8.25

PREDATOR: DARK RIVER

Dark Horse,MS; 1 Jul 1996-4 Oct 1996

	$Good	$Fine	$N.Mint	£Good	£Fine	£N.Mint
1-4 ND Mark Verheiden script, Ron Randall and Rick Magyar art; covers by Miran Kim	$0.60	$1.80	$3.00	£0.40	£1.20	£2.00
Title Value:	$2.40	$7.20	$12.00	£1.60	£4.80	£8.00

PREDATOR: INVADERS FROM THE FOURTH DIMENSION

Dark Horse,OS; 1 Jul 1994

	$Good	$Fine	$N.Mint	£Good	£Fine	£N.Mint
1 ND 48pgs	$0.80	$2.40	$4.00	£0.50	£1.50	£2.50
Title Value:	$0.80	$2.40	$4.00	£0.50	£1.50	£2.50

PREDATOR: JUNGLE TALES

Dark Horse,OS; 1 Mar 1995

	$Good	$Fine	$N.Mint	£Good	£Fine	£N.Mint
1 ND reprints stories from Dark Horse Comics #1,2 and #10-12; Val Mayerik cover	$0.60	$1.80	$3.00	£0.40	£1.20	£2.00
Title Value:	$0.60	$1.80	$3.00	£0.40	£1.20	£2.00

PREDATOR: KINDRED

Dark Horse,MS; 1 Dec 1996-4 Mar 1997

	$Good	$Fine	$N.Mint	£Good	£Fine	£N.Mint
1-4 ND Brian O'Connell and Bruce Patterson art	$0.50	$1.50	$2.50	£0.30	£0.90	£1.50
Title Value:	$2.00	$6.00	$10.00	£1.20	£3.60	£6.00

PREDATOR: RACE WAR

Dark Horse,MS; 0 Apr 1993; 1 Feb 1993-4 Aug 1993

	$Good	$Fine	$N.Mint	£Good	£Fine	£N.Mint
0 ND (Apr 1993), reprints prologue from Dark Horse Presents #67-69	$0.50	$1.50	$2.50	£0.30	£0.90	£1.50
1-4 ND Dave Dorman covers	$0.50	$1.50	$2.50	£0.30	£0.90	£1.50
Title Value:	$2.50	$7.50	$12.50	£1.50	£4.50	£7.50
Predator: Race War (Jul 1995) Trade paperback reprints mini-series with new cover by Ray Lago				£2.40	£7.20	£12.00

PREDATOR: STRANGE ROUX

Dark Horse,OS; 1 Nov 1996

	$Good	$Fine	$N.Mint	£Good	£Fine	£N.Mint
1 ND Brian McDonald script, Mitch Byrd and Jasen Rodriguez art	$0.60	$1.80	$3.00	£0.40	£1.20	£2.00
Title Value:	$0.60	$1.80	$3.00	£0.40	£1.20	£2.00

PRELUDE TO WAR - TWILIGHT ON THE WORLD OF MAGIC: THE GATHERING

Acclaim Comics,OS; nn Nov 1996

	$Good	$Fine	$N.Mint	£Good	£Fine	£N.Mint
nn, ND, 64pgs	$1.20	$3.60	$6.00	£0.80	£2.40	£4.00
Title Value:	$1.20	$3.60	$6.00	£0.80	£2.40	£4.00

PRESSBUTTON

Eclipse; 1 1984-6 1985

	$Good	$Fine	$N.Mint	£Good	£Fine	£N.Mint
1-2 ND	$0.40	$1.20	$2.00	£0.30	£0.90	£1.50
3-5 ND	$0.40	$1.20	$2.00	£0.25	£0.75	£1.25
6 ND scarce in the U.K.	$0.40	$1.20	$2.00	£0.30	£0.90	£1.50
Title Value:	$2.40	$7.20	$12.00	£1.65	£4.95	£8.25

PREZ

DC Comics; 1 Aug/Sep 1973-4 Feb/Mar 1974

(see Supergirl #10)

	$Good	$Fine	$N.Mint	£Good	£Fine	£N.Mint
1 Joe Simon scripts begin, origin and 1st appearance Prez	$0.65	$2.00	$4.00	£0.30	£1.00	£2.00
2-4	$0.40	$1.25	$2.50	£0.25	£0.75	£1.50
Title Value:	$1.85	$5.75	$11.50	£1.05	£3.25	£6.50

PREZ (2ND SERIES)

DC Comics/Vertigo,OS; 1 Sep 1994

	$Good	$Fine	$N.Mint	£Good	£Fine	£N.Mint
1 ND 64pgs, Ed Brubaker script, Eric Shanower art; photo cover	$0.80	$2.40	$4.00	£0.50	£1.50	£2.50
Title Value:	$0.80	$2.40	$4.00	£0.50	£1.50	£2.50

PRICE, THE

(see Eclipse Graphic Album Series #5)

PRIEST

Maximum Comic Press; 1 Aug 1996-present

	$Good	$Fine	$N.Mint	£Good	£Fine	£N.Mint
1 ND Robert Napton script, Mark Pajarillo and Sean Parsons art begins	$0.60	$1.80	$3.00	£0.40	£1.20	£2.00
2 ND	$0.60	$1.80	$3.00	£0.40	£1.20	£2.00
Title Value:	$1.20	$3.60	$6.00	£0.80	£2.40	£4.00

PRIMAL

Dark Horse,MS; 1 Oct 1992-2 Nov 1992

	$Good	$Fine	$N.Mint	£Good	£Fine	£N.Mint
1-2 ND continuation from Graphic Novel by Barker and Chichester, photo cover	$0.50	$1.50	$2.50	£0.30	£0.90	£1.50
Title Value:	$1.00	$3.00	$5.00	£0.60	£1.80	£3.00

PRIMAL FORCE

DC Comics; 0 Oct 1994; 1 Nov 1994-14 Dec 1995

	$Good	$Fine	$N.Mint	£Good	£Fine	£N.Mint
0 (Oct 1994) Zero Hour X-over; Tornado, Jack O'Lantern, Meridian, Golem and Claw begin; spin-off from Zero Hour	$0.40	$1.20	$2.00	£0.25	£0.75	£1.25
1-6	$0.40	$1.20	$2.00	£0.25	£0.75	£1.25
7 Superman, Green lantern, Wonder Woman and Batman (Azrael) guest-star	$0.40	$1.20	$2.00	£0.25	£0.75	£1.25
8-12	$0.40	$1.20	$2.00	£0.25	£0.75	£1.25
13-14 Underworld Unleashed tie-in	$0.40	$1.20	$2.00	£0.25	£0.75	£1.25
Title Value:	$6.00	$18.00	$30.00	£3.75	£11.25	£18.75

PRIMAL RAGE

Sirius Entertainment; 1 1996

	$Good	$Fine	$N.Mint	£Good	£Fine	£N.Mint
1 ND based on game	$0.60	$1.80	$3.00	£0.40	£1.20	£2.00
Title Value:	$0.60	$1.80	$3.00	£0.40	£1.20	£2.00

PRIMAL: FROM THE CRADLE TO THE GRAVE

Dark Horse,OS; 1 Oct 1992

	$Good	$Fine	$N.Mint	£Good	£Fine	£N.Mint
1 ND 64pgs, Clive Barker and Dan Chichester	$1.50	$4.50	$7.50	£1.00	£3.00	£5.00
Title Value:	$1.50	$4.50	$7.50	£1.00	£3.00	£5.00

PRIME

Malibu Ultraverse; 1 Jun 1993-26 Aug 1995

	$Good	$Fine	$N.Mint	£Good	£Fine	£N.Mint
½ 24pgs, (May 1994), produced in association with Wizard Press, Norm Breyfogle art, small Wizard logo hologram on cover; pre-bagged in mylar with certificate	$3.00	$9.00	$15.00	£1.20	£3.60	£6.00
1 Norm Breyfogle covers and art begin; 1st appearance Prime and Prototype, Ultraverse #0 coupon card	$1.00	$3.00	$5.00	£0.50	£1.50	£2.50
1 Gold Hologram Edition ND	$2.00	$6.00	$10.00	£1.00	£3.00	£5.00
1 Limited Edition, full hologram cover, 7,500 copies produced	$2.00	$6.00	$10.00	£1.00	£3.00	£5.00
1 Ultra-Limited Foil Edition ND	$2.50	$7.50	$12.50	£1.20	£3.60	£6.00
2 pre-bagged with trading card	$0.70	$2.10	$3.50	£0.40	£1.20	£2.00
2 unbagged, without trading card	$0.50	$1.50	$2.50	£0.30	£0.90	£1.50
3 origin Prime	$0.50	$1.50	$2.50	£0.30	£0.90	£1.50
4 two covers available; the postions of Prime and Prototype are inter-changed on each cover; Prime vs. Prototype	$0.50	$1.50	$2.50	£0.30	£0.90	£1.50

	$Good	$Fine	$N.Mint	£Good	£Fine	£N.Mint
5 40pgs, Rune insert	$0.50	$1.50	$2.50	£0.30	£0.90	£1.50
6 continued in Break-Thru #1; President Bill Clinton appears	$0.40	$1.20	$2.00	£0.25	£0.75	£1.25
7 Break-Thru X-over	$0.40	$1.20	$2.00	£0.25	£0.75	£1.25
8 Freex origin by Walt Simonson; Mantra appears	$0.40	$1.20	$2.00	£0.25	£0.75	£1.25
9 continued in Firearm #6	$0.40	$1.20	$2.00	£0.25	£0.75	£1.25
10 continued from Firearm #6, new look and costume for Prime	$0.40	$1.20	$2.00	£0.25	£0.75	£1.25
11	$0.40	$1.20	$2.00	£0.25	£0.75	£1.25
12 64pgs, anniversary issue with silver logos	$0.55	$1.65	$2.75	£0.35	£1.05	£1.75
13 48pgs	$0.50	$1.50	$2.50	£0.30	£0.90	£1.50
14-19	$0.40	$1.20	$2.00	£0.25	£0.75	£1.25
20 reveals identity to Kelly	$0.40	$1.20	$2.00	£0.25	£0.75	£1.25
21	$0.40	$1.20	$2.00	£0.25	£0.75	£1.25
22 Godwheel tie-in; Mark Pacella and Art Thibert cover	$0.40	$1.20	$2.00	£0.25	£0.75	£1.25
23 Pat Broderick guest art, leads into Power of Prime mini-series; bi-weekly	$0.40	$1.20	$2.00	£0.25	£0.75	£1.25
24 leads into Power of Prime mini-series; bi-weekly	$0.40	$1.20	$2.00	£0.25	£0.75	£1.25
25 1st issue under Marvel Comics solicitation; Chelsea Clinton appears	$0.40	$1.20	$2.00	£0.25	£0.75	£1.25
26	$0.40	$1.20	$2.00	£0.25	£0.75	£1.25
Title Value:	$21.85	$65.55	$109.25	£11.90	£35.70	£59.50

Note: all Non-Distributed on the news-stands in the U.K.

	£Good	£Fine	£N.Mint
Prime Collection Sofcover (Aug 1994) reprints issues #1-4, Alex Ross painted cover	£1.30	£3.90	£6.50
Prime Collection Hardcover (Aug 1994), limited to 2,000 copies with signed plate	£3.50	£10.50	£17.50

PRIME (2ND SERIES)

Marvel Comics Group; 1 Dec 1995-present

	$Good	$Fine	$N.Mint	£Good	£Fine	£N.Mint
1 ND Gerard Jones and Len Strazewski script, Kevin West and John Statema art; Spiderman and Spider-Prime vs. The new lizard	$0.30	$0.90	$1.50	£0.20	£0.60	£1.00
1 Signed Edition, ND (Mar 1996) - limited to 2,000 copies with certificate	$1.50	$4.50	$7.50	£1.00	£3.00	£5.00
1 Variant Cover Edition, ND computer painted cover by Chuck Maiden	$0.50	$1.50	$2.50	£0.30	£0.90	£1.50
1 Variant Cover Signed Edition, ND (Jun 1996), limited to 2,000 copies, signed by Kevin West and Philip Moy with certificate of authenticity	$2.20	$6.50	$11.00	£1.50	£4.50	£7.50
2 ND flip-book format with Phoenix Ressurrection chapter	$0.30	$0.90	$1.50	£0.20	£0.60	£1.00
3-4 ND	$0.30	$0.90	$1.50	£0.20	£0.60	£1.00
5 ND Freex return	$0.30	$0.90	$1.50	£0.20	£0.60	£1.00
6 ND Solitaire guest-stars	$0.30	$0.90	$1.50	£0.20	£0.60	£1.00
7 ND Prime vs. Solitaire	$0.30	$0.90	$1.50	£0.20	£0.60	£1.00
8 ND Primal Rage part 3 (conclusion)	$0.30	$0.90	$1.50	£0.20	£0.60	£1.00
9-10 ND Norm Breyfogle art	$0.30	$0.90	$1.50	£0.20	£0.60	£1.00
11 ND Keith Giffen art, Humberto Ramos cover	$0.30	$0.90	$1.50	£0.20	£0.60	£1.00
12-14 ND Humberto Ramos cover	$0.30	$0.90	$1.50	£0.20	£0.60	£1.00
15 ND Lord Pumpkin returns; Humberto Ramos cover	$0.30	$0.90	$1.50	£0.20	£0.60	£1.00
Title Value:	$8.70	$26.00	$43.50	£5.80	£17.40	£29.00

PRIME ANNUAL

Malibu Ultraverse; 1 Oct 1994

	$Good	$Fine	$N.Mint	£Good	£Fine	£N.Mint
1 ND 64pgs, Boris Vallejo painted cover	$0.50	$1.50	$2.50	£0.30	£0.90	£1.50
Title Value:	$0.50	$1.50	$2.50	£0.30	£0.90	£1.50

PRIME CUTS

Fantagraphics,Magazine; 1 Jun 1987-10 1988

	$Good	$Fine	$N.Mint	£Good	£Fine	£N.Mint
1-10 ND	$0.80	$2.40	$4.00	£0.50	£1.50	£2.50
Title Value:	$8.00	$24.00	$40.00	£5.00	£15.00	£25.00

PRIME MONTH ASHCAN

Malibu,OS; nn Oct 1994

	$Good	$Fine	$N.Mint	£Good	£Fine	£N.Mint
nn ND 16pgs, black and white; information and sketches of the character Prime	$0.15	$0.45	$0.75	£0.10	£0.30	£0.50
Title Value:	$0.15	$0.45	$0.75	£0.10	£0.30	£0.50

PRIME SLIME TALES

Mirage/Now Comics; 1 Apr 1986-4 Jan 1987

	$Good	$Fine	$N.Mint	£Good	£Fine	£N.Mint
1-4 ND	$0.40	$1.20	$2.00	£0.25	£0.75	£1.25
Title Value:	$1.60	$4.80	$8.00	£1.00	£3.00	£5.00

PRIME, POWER OF

Marvel Comics Group/Malibu Ultraverse,MS; 1 Jul 1995-4 Oct 1995

	$Good	$Fine	$N.Mint	£Good	£Fine	£N.Mint
1-4 ND Godwheel tie-in	$0.40	$1.20	$2.00	£0.25	£0.75	£1.25
Title Value:	$1.60	$4.80	$8.00	£1.00	£3.00	£5.00

PRIME/CAPTAIN AMERICA

Marvel Comics Group/Ultraverse,OS; 1 May 1996

	$Good	$Fine	$N.Mint	£Good	£Fine	£N.Mint
1 ND Gerard Jones script, Norm Breyfogle art	$0.80	$2.40	$4.00	£0.50	£1.50	£2.50
Title Value:	$0.80	$2.40	$4.00	£0.50	£1.50	£2.50

PRIME: INFINITY

Marvel Comics Group,OS; nn Nov 1995

	$Good	$Fine	$N.Mint	£Good	£Fine	£N.Mint
nn ND Black September tie-in; Spiderman and Spider-Prime vs. The new Lizard	$0.40	$1.20	$2.00	£0.20	£0.60	£1.00
nn Signed & Numbered Edition ND (Dec 1995); limited to 2,000 copies with certificate	$2.00	$6.00	$10.00	£1.00	£3.00	£5.00
nn Variant Cover Edition ND 1 copy received for every 5 copies of the regular issue ordered	$0.60	$1.80	$3.00	£0.40	£1.20	£2.00
Title Value:	$3.00	$9.00	$15.00	£1.60	£4.80	£8.00

PRIMER

Comico; 1 Oct 1982-6 Feb 1984

	$Good	$Fine	$N.Mint	£Good	£Fine	£N.Mint
1 1st appearances Victor, Slaughterman, Az, Skrog, Mr. Justice; black and white "showcase" comic for "talented amateurs"	$0.90	$2.70	$4.50	£0.60	£1.80	£3.00
2 scarce in the U.K. 1st appearance Grendel by Matt Wagner	$15.50	$48.00	$95.00	£8.25	£25.00	£50.00
3	$1.00	$3.00	$5.00	£0.60	£1.80	£3.00
4 1st Sam Kieth art in comics? (1 preview page announcing feature for next issue)	$1.00	$3.00	$5.00	£0.60	£1.80	£3.00
5 1st appearance The Maxx by Sam Kieth	$5.00	$15.00	$30.00	£2.05	£6.25	£12.50
6 scarce in the U.K. 1st appearance Evangeline	$1.00	$3.00	$5.00	£1.00	£3.00	£5.00
Title Value:	$24.40	$74.70	$144.50	£13.10	£39.65	£76.50

Note: all Non-Distributed on the news-stands in the U.K.

PRIMER (2ND SERIES)

Comico; 1 Nov 1995-present

1 ND 1st appearance Lady Bathory

Power Man and Iron Fist #100

Powers That Be #1

Preacher #1

	$Good	$Fine	$N.Mint	£Good	£Fine	£N.Mint
	$0.60	$1.80	$3.00	£0.40	£1.20	£2.00
2-3 ND Lady Bathory appears						
	$0.60	$1.80	$3.00	£0.40	£1.20	£2.00
Title Value:	$1.80	$5.40	$9.00	£1.20	£3.60	£6.00

PRIMORTALS ORIGINS, LEONARD NIMOY'S

Tekno Comix,MS; 1 Nov 1995-2 Dec 1995

	$Good	$Fine	$N.Mint	£Good	£Fine	£N.Mint
1 ND pre-bagged with copy of Neil Gaiman's Mr. Hero						
	$0.60	$1.80	$3.00	£0.30	£0.90	£1.50
2 ND origin of the Primortals concluded; Art Adams cover						
	$0.45	$1.35	$2.25	£0.30	£0.90	£1.50
Title Value:	$1.05	$3.15	$5.25	£0.60	£1.80	£3.00

Note: this mini-series replaced issues the on-going title for two months between issues #12 and #13

PRIMORTALS, LEONARD NIMOY'S

Tekno Comix; 1 Mar 1995-13 Jan 1996; Big Entertainment; 14 Apr 1996-15 May 1996

	$Good	$Fine	$N.Mint	£Good	£Fine	£N.Mint
1 ND Kate Worley script, Scot Eaton and Mike Barreiro art begins						
	$0.40	$1.20	$2.00	£0.25	£0.75	£1.25
2-11 ND	$0.40	$1.20	$2.00	£0.25	£0.75	£1.25
12 ND	$0.45	$1.35	$2.25	£0.30	£0.90	£1.50
13-14 ND Arthur Adams cover						
	$0.45	$1.35	$2.25	£0.30	£0.90	£1.50
15 ND	$0.45	$1.35	$2.25	£0.30	£0.90	£1.50
Title Value:	$6.20	$18.60	$31.00	£3.95	£11.85	£19.75

PRIMORTALS, LEONARD NIMOY'S (2ND SERIES)

Big Entertainment; 1 Jun 1996-present

	$Good	$Fine	$N.Mint	£Good	£Fine	£N.Mint
1 ND Walt Simonson cover						
	$0.45	$1.35	$2.25	£0.30	£0.90	£1.50
2-8 ND	$0.45	$1.35	$2.25	£0.30	£0.90	£1.50
Title Value:	$3.60	$10.80	$18.00	£2.40	£7.20	£12.00

PRIMUS

Charlton,TV; 1 Feb 1972-7 Oct 1972

	$Good	$Fine	$N.Mint	£Good	£Fine	£N.Mint
1 distributed in the U.K. Joe Staton art						
	$1.50	$4.50	$9.00	£1.00	£3.00	£6.00
2-7 distributed in the U.K. Joe Staton art						
	$1.00	$3.00	$6.00	£0.55	£1.75	£3.50
Title Value:	$7.50	$22.50	$45.00	£4.30	£13.50	£27.00

PRINCE AND THE PAUPER GRAPHIC NOVEL, THE

Disney; nn Dec 1990

	$Good	$Fine	$N.Mint	£Good	£Fine	£N.Mint
nn ND 64pgs, adaptation of film						
	$1.00	$3.00	$5.00	£0.60	£1.80	£3.00
Title Value:	$1.00	$3.00	$5.00	£0.60	£1.80	£3.00

PRINCE VALIANT

Marvel Comics Group,MS; 1 Dec 1994-4 Mar 1995

	$Good	$Fine	$N.Mint	£Good	£Fine	£N.Mint
1-4 Charles Vess script, John Ridway art and cover by Mike Kaluta						
	$0.60	$1.80	$3.00	£0.40	£1.20	£2.00
Title Value:	$2.40	$7.20	$12.00	£1.60	£4.80	£8.00

PRINCE VALIANT

Pioneer; 1 Apr 1990

(see Official Prince Valiant)

	$Good	$Fine	$N.Mint	£Good	£Fine	£N.Mint
1 ND material never-before reprinted						
	$1.00	$3.00	$5.00	£0.70	£2.10	£3.50
Title Value:	$1.00	$3.00	$5.00	£0.70	£2.10	£3.50

PRINCE VANDAL

Triumphant Comics; 0 Jul 1994; 1 Nov 1993-12 Oct 1994

	$Good	$Fine	$N.Mint	£Good	£Fine	£N.Mint
0 (Jul 1994) origin/life story of Prince Vandal						
	$0.40	$1.20	$2.00	£0.25	£0.75	£1.25
0 Signed Edition, (Oct 1994) - pre-bagged with mini-poster photo-print and backing board						
	$1.00	$3.00	$5.00	£0.50	£1.50	£2.50
1 serially numbered each time at top of cover; Bobby Rae pencils begin; Unleashed X-over						
	$0.40	$1.20	$2.00	£0.25	£0.75	£1.25
2-6 serially numbered at top						
	$0.40	$1.20	$2.00	£0.25	£0.75	£1.25
7	$0.40	$1.20	$2.00	£0.25	£0.75	£1.25
8 dual issue with Chromium Man #11 (Note: there is only the one comic between the two titles)						
	$0.40	$1.20	$2.00	£0.25	£0.75	£1.25
9 dual issue with Chromium Man #12 (Note: there is only the one comic between the two titles)						
	$0.40	$1.20	$2.00	£0.25	£0.75	£1.25
10-12	$0.40	$1.20	$2.00	£0.25	£0.75	£1.25
Title Value:	$6.20	$18.60	$31.00	£3.75	£11.25	£18.75

Note: all Non-Distributed on the news-stands in the U.K.

PRINCE: ALTER EGO

DC Comics/Piranha Press,OS; 1 1991

	$Good	$Fine	$N.Mint	£Good	£Fine	£N.Mint
1 ND Brian Bolland cover, Denys Cowan/Kent Williams art, promotional tie-in with album "Diamonds and Pearls"	$0.80	$2.40	$4.00	£0.50	£1.50	£2.50
1 2nd printing ND	$0.50	$1.50	$2.50	£0.30	£0.90	£1.50
1 3rd printing, ND (Aug 1992)						
	$0.40	$1.20	$2.00	£0.25	£0.75	£1.25
Title Value:	$1.70	$5.10	$8.50	£1.05	£3.15	£5.25

PRINCE: THREE CHAINS OF GOLD

DC Comics/Piranha Press,OS; 1 Jun 1994

	$Good	$Fine	$N.Mint	£Good	£Fine	£N.Mint
1 ND 48pgs, Dwayne McDuffie script, David Williams, Steve Carr and Joe Rubenstein art						
	$0.60	$1.80	$3.00	£0.40	£1.20	£2.00
Title Value:	$0.60	$1.80	$3.00	£0.40	£1.20	£2.00

PRISONER, THE

DC Comics,MS; 1 Dec 1988-4 Mar 1989

	$Good	$Fine	$N.Mint	£Good	£Fine	£N.Mint
1-4 ND 48pgs, Dean Motter script/art						
	$0.70	$2.10	$3.50	£0.40	£1.20	£2.00
Title Value:	$2.80	$8.40	$14.00	£1.60	£4.80	£8.00

Note: all Prestige Format,squarebound. Uses concepts from the television series.

	$Good	$Fine	$N.Mint	£Good	£Fine	£N.Mint
Trade paperback (Jul 1990), 208 pgs, new wraparound painted cover by Dean Motter				£1.90	£5.70	£9.50

PRIVATE BEACH

Antarctic Press,MS; 1 Jan 1995-3 May 1995

	$Good	$Fine	$N.Mint	£Good	£Fine	£N.Mint
1-3 ND David Hahn script and art; black and white						
	$0.55	$1.65	$2.75	£0.35	£1.05	£1.75
Title Value:	$1.65	$4.95	$8.25	£1.05	£3.15	£5.25

PRIVATEERS

Vanguard; 1 Aug 1987

	$Good	$Fine	$N.Mint	£Good	£Fine	£N.Mint
1 ND	$0.30	$0.90	$1.50	£0.20	£0.60	£1.00
Title Value:	$0.30	$0.90	$1.50	£0.20	£0.60	£1.00

PROFESSIONAL: GOGOL 13, THE

Viz,MS; 1-4 1991

	$Good	$Fine	$N.Mint	£Good	£Fine	£N.Mint
1-4 ND 48pgs, squarebound, Takao Saito material adapted by James Hudnall						
	$0.90	$2.70	$4.50	£0.60	£1.80	£3.00
Title Value:	$3.60	$10.80	$18.00	£2.40	£7.20	£12.00

PROFESSOR XAVIER AND THE X-MEN

Marvel Comics Group; 1 Nov 1995-present

	$Good	$Fine	$N.Mint	£Good	£Fine	£N.Mint
1 ND Fred Schiller script, Jan Duursema and Rick Magyar art; the X-Men's early adventures seen through the eyes of the characters who were there; 99 cents cover price begins						
	$0.25	$0.75	$1.25	£0.15	£0.45	£0.75
2-3 ND	$0.20	$0.60	$1.00	£0.15	£0.45	£0.75
4-6 ND Magneto and the Brotherhood of Evil Mutants appear						
	$0.20	$0.60	$1.00	£0.15	£0.45	£0.75
7 ND Sub-Mariner with Magneto and the Brotherhood of Evil Mutants appear						
	$0.20	$0.60	$1.00	£0.15	£0.45	£0.75
8 ND Blob and Magneto appear						
	$0.20	$0.60	$1.00	£0.15	£0.45	£0.75
9 ND Beast vs. Unus the Untouchable						
	$0.20	$0.60	$1.00	£0.15	£0.45	£0.75
10 ND The Avengers appear						
	$0.20	$0.60	$1.00	£0.15	£0.45	£0.75
11 ND	$0.20	$0.60	$1.00	£0.15	£0.45	£0.75
12 ND Ka-Zar appears						
	$0.20	$0.60	$1.00	£0.15	£0.45	£0.75
13-14 ND Juggernaut appears						
	$0.20	$0.60	$1.00	£0.15	£0.45	£0.75
15 ND Quicksilver and Scarlet Witch appear						
	$0.20	$0.60	$1.00	£0.15	£0.45	£0.75
16-17 ND	$0.20	$0.60	$1.00	£0.15	£0.45	£0.75
Title Value:	$3.45	$10.35	$17.25	£2.55	£7.65	£12.75

note: originally announced as X-Men Dollar Book

PROJECT A-KO

Malibu,MS; 1,2 Mar 1994; 3,4 Apr 1994

	$Good	$Fine	$N.Mint	£Good	£Fine	£N.Mint
1-4 ND based on Japanese anime series						
	$0.60	$1.80	$3.00	£0.40	£1.20	£2.00
Title Value:	$2.40	$7.20	$12.00	£1.60	£4.80	£8.00
Project A-KO Graphic Novel (Mar 1995) collects four issue mini-series plus new 8pg battle sequence (Note: published by CPM Comics)				£1.30	£3.90	£6.50

PROJECT A-KO 2

CPM Comics,MS; 1 Apr 1995-3 Aug 1995

	$Good	$Fine	$N.Mint	£Good	£Fine	£N.Mint
1-3 ND 24pgs, Tim Eldred art						
	$0.60	$1.80	$3.00	£0.40	£1.20	£2.00
Title Value:	$1.80	$5.40	$9.00	£1.20	£3.60	£6.00

PROJECT A-KO: VERSUS THE UNIVERSE

CPM Comics,MS; 1 Oct 1995-5 Jun 1996

	$Good	$Fine	$N.Mint	£Good	£Fine	£N.Mint
1-3 ND 24pgs, John Ott script and Studio Go! art						
	$0.60	$1.80	$3.00	£0.40	£1.20	£2.00
4-5 ND Tim Eldred script and Studio Go! art						
	$0.60	$1.80	$3.00	£0.40	£1.20	£2.00
Title Value:	$3.00	$9.00	$15.00	£2.00	£6.00	£10.00

PROJECT X

Kitchen Sink; 1 1993

	$Good	$Fine	$N.Mint	£Good	£Fine	£N.Mint
1 ND issue #1 of Thump 'N Guts, poster, trading card and 100 dollar bill flyer in envelope all pre-bagged in gold; Kevin Eastman and Simon Bisley						
	$1.00	$3.00	$5.00	£0.60	£1.80	£3.00
Title Value:	$1.00	$3.00	$5.00	£0.60	£1.80	£3.00

PROJECT, THE

DC Comics/Paradox Press,MS; 1 May 1996-2 Jun 1996

	$Good	$Fine	$N.Mint	£Good	£Fine	£N.Mint
1-2 ND 96pgs, John Figueroa script, Kirk Albert art; Compact Format (digest size)						
	$1.20	$3.60	$6.00	£0.80	£2.40	£4.00
Title Value:	$2.40	$7.20	$12.00	£1.60	£4.80	£8.00

PROJECT: NEWMAN

Legacy Comics,OS; 1 1991

	$Good	$Fine	$N.Mint	£Good	£Fine	£N.Mint
1 ND black and white						
	$0.15	$0.45	$0.75	£0.10	£0.30	£0.50
Title Value:	$0.15	$0.45	$0.75	£0.10	£0.30	£0.50

PROMISE

Viz,OS; 1 Apr 1994

	$Good	$Fine	$N.Mint	£Good	£Fine	£N.Mint
1 ND 80pgs, Keiko Nishi script and art; black and white						
	$1.20	$3.60	$6.00	£0.80	£2.40	£4.00
Title Value:	$1.20	$3.60	$6.00	£0.80	£2.40	£4.00

PROPELLERMAN

Dark Horse,MS; 1 Jan 1993-8 Mar 1994

	$Good	$Fine	$N.Mint	£Good	£Fine	£N.Mint
1-8 ND Matthias Schultheiss script and art						
	$0.60	$1.80	$3.00	£0.40	£1.20	£2.00
Title Value:	$4.80	$14.40	$24.00	£3.20	£9.60	£16.00

PROPHET

Image; 0 Jul 1994; 1 Oct 1993-10 Jan 1995

	$Good	$Fine	$N.Mint	£Good	£Fine	£N.Mint
0 San Diego Edition, ND released at the San Diego comic convention						
	$2.00	$6.00	$10.00	£1.50	£4.50	£7.50
1 ND Rob Liefeld script/layouts, Dan Panosian pencils/inks						
	$0.50	$1.50	$2.50	£0.30	£0.90	£1.50
1 Gold Edition, ND foil embossed cover						
	$1.50	$4.50	$7.50	£1.00	£3.00	£5.00

Issue	$Good	$Fine	$N.Mint	£Good	£Fine	£N.Mint
2-4 ND	$0.40	$1.20	$2.00	£0.25	£0.75	£1.25
4 Variant Cover Edition, ND less common Platt cover art	$2.00	$6.00	$10.00	£1.20	£3.60	£6.00
5-7 ND	$0.40	$1.20	$2.00	£0.25	£0.75	£1.25
8 ND War Games part 2, X-over with Bloodstrike #15/16	$0.40	$1.20	$2.00	£0.25	£0.75	£1.25
9 ND Extreme Sacrifices prologue	$0.40	$1.20	$2.00	£0.25	£0.75	£1.25
10 ND Extreme Sacrifice part 6, pre-bagged with trading card	$0.40	$1.20	$2.00	£0.25	£0.75	£1.25
Title Value:	$9.60	$28.80	$48.00	£6.25	£18.75	£31.25
Prophet (Jan 1996) Trade paperback ND collects issues #1-7, new cover by Stephen Platt				£2.20	£6.60	£11.00

PROPHET (2ND SERIES)

Image; 1 Aug 1995-present

Issue	$Good	$Fine	$N.Mint	£Good	£Fine	£N.Mint
1 ND Chuck Dixon script and Stephen Platt art begins; wraparound chromium cover by Platt	$0.50	$1.50	$2.50	£0.30	£0.90	£1.50
2 ND Chuck Dixon and Stephen Platt	$0.50	$1.50	$2.50	£0.30	£0.90	£1.50
3 ND	$0.50	$1.50	$2.50	£0.30	£0.90	£1.50
4 ND guest-starring The NewMen	$0.50	$1.50	$2.50	£0.30	£0.90	£1.50
5 ND guest-starring Youngblood	$0.50	$1.50	$2.50	£0.30	£0.90	£1.50
6 ND	$0.50	$1.50	$2.50	£0.30	£0.90	£1.50
7 ND guest-stars Youngblood and Bloodpool	$0.50	$1.50	$2.50	£0.30	£0.90	£1.50
8 ND	$0.50	$1.50	$2.50	£0.30	£0.90	£1.50
Title Value:	$4.00	$12.00	$20.00	£2.40	£7.20	£12.00
Prophet: War Games (Jul 1996) Trade paperback ND collects issues #1-3				£0.90	£2.70	£4.50

PROPHET ANNUAL

Image; 1 Sep 1995

Issue	$Good	$Fine	$N.Mint	£Good	£Fine	£N.Mint
1 ND Supreme Apocalypse part 2, continued in Glory 5; Chuck Dixon script, Stephen Platt art	$0.50	$1.50	$2.50	£0.30	£0.90	£1.50
Title Value:	$0.50	$1.50	$2.50	£0.30	£0.90	£1.50

PROPHET BABEWATCH SPECIAL

Image,OS; 1 Dec 1995

Issue	$Good	$Fine	$N.Mint	£Good	£Fine	£N.Mint
1 ND	$0.50	$1.50	$2.50	£0.30	£0.90	£1.50
Title Value:	$0.50	$1.50	$2.50	£0.30	£0.90	£1.50

PROPHET SOURCEBOOK

Image; 1 Oct 1994

Issue	$Good	$Fine	$N.Mint	£Good	£Fine	£N.Mint
1 ND information on the character featuring Stephen Platt art	$0.60	$1.80	$3.00	£0.40	£1.20	£2.00
Title Value:	$0.60	$1.80	$3.00	£0.40	£1.20	£2.00

PROPHET/AVENGELYNE

Image,OS; 1 May 1996

Issue	$Good	$Fine	$N.Mint	£Good	£Fine	£N.Mint
1 ND Rob Liefeld and Robert Napton script, Rob Liefeld and Mike Deodato Jnr. art	$0.60	$1.80	$3.00	£0.40	£1.20	£2.00
Title Value:	$0.60	$1.80	$3.00	£0.40	£1.20	£2.00

PROPHET/CABLE

Image,OS; 1 Jan 1997

Issue	$Good	$Fine	$N.Mint	£Good	£Fine	£N.Mint
1 ND Robert Napton script, Mark Pajarillo and Rob Liefeld art	$1.00	$3.00	$5.00	£0.70	£2.10	£3.50
Title Value:	$1.00	$3.00	$5.00	£0.70	£2.10	£3.50

PROPHET/CHAPEL: SUPER SOLDIERS

Image,MS; 1 May 1996-2 Jun 1996

Issue	$Good	$Fine	$N.Mint	£Good	£Fine	£N.Mint
1 ND	$0.50	$1.50	$2.50	£0.30	£0.90	£1.50
1 Variant Cover Edition, ND Liefeld & Platt cover	$0.50	$1.50	$2.50	£0.30	£0.90	£1.50
2 ND	$0.50	$1.50	$2.50	£0.30	£0.90	£1.50
Title Value:	$1.50	$4.50	$7.50	£0.90	£2.70	£4.50

PROTECTORS

New York Comics; 1 1986

Issue	$Good	$Fine	$N.Mint	£Good	£Fine	£N.Mint
1 ND black and white	$0.15	$0.45	$0.75	£0.10	£0.35	£0.60
Title Value:	$0.15	$0.45	$0.75	£0.10	£0.35	£0.60

PROTECTORS HANDBOOK, THE

Malibu,OS; 1 Dec 1992

Issue	$Good	$Fine	$N.Mint	£Good	£Fine	£N.Mint
1 ND information on the Protectors plus interview with the creators	$0.40	$1.20	$2.00	£0.25	£0.75	£1.25
Title Value:	$0.40	$1.20	$2.00	£0.25	£0.75	£1.25

PROTECTORS, THE

Malibu; 1 Sep 1992-20 Apr 1994

Issue	$Good	$Fine	$N.Mint	£Good	£Fine	£N.Mint
1-12	$0.30	$0.90	$1.50	£0.20	£0.60	£1.00
1-12 Direct Market Edition, with bound-in poster and wraparound protective cover	$0.40	$1.20	$2.00	£0.25	£0.75	£1.25
13 Genesis tie-in; pre-bagged with free Sky-Cap	$0.30	$0.90	$1.50	£0.20	£0.60	£1.00
14-15 Genesis tie-in	$0.30	$0.90	$1.50	£0.20	£0.60	£1.00
16-17	$0.30	$0.90	$1.50	£0.20	£0.60	£1.00
18 Genesis tie-in	$0.30	$0.90	$1.50	£0.20	£0.60	£1.00
19-20	$0.30	$0.90	$1.50	£0.20	£0.60	£1.00
Title Value:	$10.80	$32.40	$54.00	£7.00	£21.00	£35.00

Note: all Non-Distributed on the news-stands in the U.K.

PROTHEUS, MIKE DEODATO'S

Caliber Press,MS; 1 Apr 1996-present

Issue	$Good	$Fine	$N.Mint	£Good	£Fine	£N.Mint
1 ND Mike Deodato art	$0.60	$1.80	$3.00	£0.40	£1.20	£2.00
2 ND	$0.60	$1.80	$3.00	£0.40	£1.20	£2.00
Title Value:	$1.20	$3.60	$6.00	£0.80	£2.40	£4.00

PROTOTYPE

Malibu Ultraverse; 0 Aug 1994; 1 Aug 1993-18 Feb 1995

Issue	$Good	$Fine	$N.Mint	£Good	£Fine	£N.Mint
0 40pgs, Joe Quesada and Jimmy Palmiotti cover	$0.40	$1.20	$2.00	£0.25	£0.75	£1.25
1 pre-bagged with trading card	$0.60	$1.80	$3.00	£0.40	£1.20	£2.00
1 Gold Hologram Edition	$2.00	$6.00	$10.00	£1.00	£3.00	£5.00
1 Limited Edition, hologram cover	$2.00	$6.00	$10.00	£1.00	£3.00	£5.00
1 Ultra-Limited Foil Edition	$2.50	$7.50	$12.50	£1.20	£3.60	£6.00
2	$0.50	$1.50	$2.50	£0.30	£0.90	£1.50
3 40pgs, Rune insert	$0.40	$1.20	$2.00	£0.25	£0.75	£1.25
4-5	$0.40	$1.20	$2.00	£0.25	£0.75	£1.25
6 origins month X-over	$0.40	$1.20	$2.00	£0.25	£0.75	£1.25
7-12	$0.40	$1.20	$2.00	£0.25	£0.75	£1.25
13 48pgs, flip-book format with Ultraverse Premiere #6	$0.55	$1.65	$2.75	£0.35	£1.05	£1.75
14-18	$0.40	$1.20	$2.00	£0.25	£0.75	£1.25
Title Value:	$14.55	$43.65	$72.75	£8.25	£24.75	£41.25

Note: all Non-Distributed on the news-stands in the U.K.

PROTOTYPE, GIANT SIZE

Malibu Ultraverse; 1 Sep 1994

Issue	$Good	$Fine	$N.Mint	£Good	£Fine	£N.Mint
1 ND 40pgs, Hostile Takeover part 4 (of 4)	$0.50	$1.50	$2.50	£0.30	£0.90	£1.50
Title Value:	$0.50	$1.50	$2.50	£0.30	£0.90	£1.50

PROTOTYPE: TURF WAR

Malibu Ultraverse,MS; 1 Apr 1995-4 Jul 1995

Issue	$Good	$Fine	$N.Mint	£Good	£Fine	£N.Mint
1-4 ND Gabriel Gecko and Stephen Baskerville art	$0.40	$1.20	$2.00	£0.25	£0.75	£1.25
Title Value:	$1.60	$4.80	$8.00	£1.00	£3.00	£5.00

PROWLER

Eclipse; 1 Jul 1987-4 Oct 1987

(see Revenge of the Prowler)

Issue	$Good	$Fine	$N.Mint	£Good	£Fine	£N.Mint
1 ND Tim Truman script, John K. Snyder III art begins, colour	$0.40	$1.20	$2.00	£0.25	£0.75	£1.25
2-4 ND Graham Nolan back-up detailing origin Prowler	$0.40	$1.20	$2.00	£0.25	£0.75	£1.25
Title Value:	$1.60	$4.80	$8.00	£1.00	£3.00	£5.00

Note: although the next issue was advertised, the series was suddenly cancelled.

PROWLER

Marvel Comics Group,MS; 1 Nov 1994-4 Feb 1995

Issue	$Good	$Fine	$N.Mint	£Good	£Fine	£N.Mint
1-3	$0.30	$0.90	$1.50	£0.20	£0.60	£1.00
4 The Prowler vs. The Vulture	$0.30	$0.90	$1.50	£0.20	£0.60	£1.00
Title Value:	$1.20	$3.60	$6.00	£0.80	£2.40	£4.00

PROWLER IN WHITE ZOMBIE, THE

Eclipse,OS; 1 Oct 1988

Issue	$Good	$Fine	$N.Mint	£Good	£Fine	£N.Mint
1 ND features Graham Nolan art, black and white	$0.40	$1.20	$2.00	£0.25	£0.75	£1.25
Title Value:	$0.40	$1.20	$2.00	£0.25	£0.75	£1.25

PRUDENCE & CAUTION

Defiant; 1 May 1994-6 Oct 1994

Issue	$Good	$Fine	$N.Mint	£Good	£Fine	£N.Mint
1 ND 48pgs, Chris Claremont script begins	$0.40	$1.20	$2.00	£0.25	£0.75	£1.25
2-3 ND	$0.40	$1.20	$2.00	£0.25	£0.75	£1.25
4 ND Schism X-over	$0.40	$1.20	$2.00	£0.25	£0.75	£1.25
5-6 ND	$0.40	$1.20	$2.00	£0.25	£0.75	£1.25
Title Value:	$2.40	$7.20	$12.00	£1.50	£4.50	£7.50

PSI FORCE

Marvel Comics Group/New Universe; 1 Nov 1986-32 Jun 1989

Issue	$Good	$Fine	$N.Mint	£Good	£Fine	£N.Mint
1-5 ND Mark Texeira art	$0.15	$0.45	$0.75	£0.10	£0.35	£0.60
6-7 ND	$0.15	$0.45	$0.75	£0.10	£0.35	£0.60
8 Mark Texeira art	$0.15	$0.45	$0.75	£0.10	£0.35	£0.60
9-12	$0.15	$0.45	$0.75	£0.10	£0.35	£0.60
13 Williamson inks	$0.15	$0.45	$0.75	£0.10	£0.35	£0.60
14-15	$0.15	$0.45	$0.75	£0.10	£0.35	£0.60
16-22 Ron Lim art	$0.15	$0.45	$0.75	£0.10	£0.35	£0.60
23-32 ND	$0.15	$0.45	$0.75	£0.10	£0.35	£0.60
Title Value:	$4.80	$14.40	$24.00	£3.20	£11.20	£19.20

PSI FORCE ANNUAL

Marvel Comics Group/New Universe; 1 1987

Issue	$Good	$Fine	$N.Mint	£Good	£Fine	£N.Mint
1 ND	$0.25	$0.75	$1.25	£0.15	£0.45	£0.75
Title Value:	$0.25	$0.75	$1.25	£0.15	£0.45	£0.75

PSI-LORDS

Valiant; 1 Sep 1994-10 Jun 1995

Issue	$Good	$Fine	$N.Mint	£Good	£Fine	£N.Mint
1 Mike Leeke pencils, Dick Giordano inks, wraparound chrome cover	$0.50	$1.50	$2.50	£0.30	£0.90	£1.50
2 Valiant Vision issue (3-D effect)	$0.40	$1.20	$2.00	£0.25	£0.75	£1.25
3-10	$0.40	$1.20	$2.00	£0.25	£0.75	£1.25
Title Value:	$4.10	$12.30	$20.50	£2.55	£7.65	£12.75

PSYBA-RATS, THE

DC Comics,MS; 1 Apr 1995-3 Jun 1995

	$Good	$Fine	$N.Mint	£Good	£Fine	£N.Mint
1-3 48pgs	$0.40	$1.20	$2.00	£0.25	£0.75	£1.25
Title Value:	$1.20	$3.60	$6.00	£0.75	£2.25	£3.75
PSYCHO						
DC Comics,MS; 1 Sep 1991-3 Nov 1991						
1-3 ND 48pgs, painted art by Dan Brereton	$0.80	$2.40	$4.00	£0.50	£1.50	£2.50
Title Value:	$2.40	$7.20	$12.00	£1.50	£4.50	£7.50
Note: Prestige Format						
PSYCHO-PATH						
Greater Mercury Comics; 1 Dec 1990						
1 ND black and white	$0.30	$0.90	$1.50	£0.20	£0.60	£1.00
Title Value:	$0.30	$0.90	$1.50	£0.20	£0.60	£1.00
PSYCHOBLAST						
First; 1 Nov 1987-9 Jul 1988						
1-9 ND Steven Grant script	$0.40	$1.20	$2.00	£0.25	£0.75	£1.25
Title Value:	$3.60	$10.80	$18.00	£2.25	£6.75	£11.25
PSYCHONAUTS						
Marvel Comics Group/Epic,MS; 1 Oct 1993-4 Jan 1994						
1-4 ND 48pgs, Alan Grant co-script, art by Yasuo Yazaki	$0.80	$2.40	$4.00	£0.50	£1.50	£2.50
Title Value:	$3.20	$9.60	$16.00	£2.00	£6.00	£10.00
PTERANO-MAN						
Kitchen Sink; 1 Aug 1990						
1 ND Don Simpson script and art	$0.40	$1.20	$2.00	£0.25	£0.75	£1.25
Title Value:	$0.40	$1.20	$2.00	£0.25	£0.75	£1.25
PUBLIC ENEMIES						
Malibu,OS; 1 Nov 1989						
1 ND 48pgs, squarebound; black and white reprints of 40s and 50s crime comics	$0.50	$1.50	$2.50	£0.30	£0.90	£1.50
Title Value:	$0.50	$1.50	$2.50	£0.30	£0.90	£1.50
PULP DREAMS						
Eros Comix; 1 May 1991						
1 ND adult pin-ups, black and white	$0.30	$0.90	$1.50	£0.20	£0.60	£1.00
Title Value:	$0.30	$0.90	$1.50	£0.20	£0.60	£1.00
PUMA BLUES						
Aardvark/Mirage; 1 Jun 1986-26 1988						
1 ND	$0.50	$1.50	$2.50	£0.30	£0.90	£1.50
1 2nd printing ND	$0.40	$1.20	$2.00	£0.25	£0.75	£1.25
2-19 ND	$0.40	$1.20	$2.00	£0.25	£0.75	£1.25
20 ND features work by Alan Moore, Frank Miller, Mike Grell	$0.80	$2.40	$4.00	£0.50	£1.50	£2.50
21 ND 1st Mirage issue	$0.40	$1.20	$2.00	£0.25	£0.75	£1.25
22-26 ND	$0.40	$1.20	$2.00	£0.25	£0.75	£1.25
Title Value:	$11.30	$33.90	$56.50	£7.05	£21.15	£35.25
Trade Paperback (1988), reprints				£1.80	£5.40	£9.00
PUMPKINHEAD: THE RITES OF EXORCISM						
Dark Horse,MS; 1 Sep 1993-3 Nov 1993						
1-3 ND	$0.50	$1.50	$2.50	£0.30	£0.90	£1.50
Title Value:	$1.50	$4.50	$7.50	£0.90	£2.70	£4.50
PUNISHER (1ST SERIES)						
Marvel Comics Group; 1 Jul 1987-104 Jul 1995						
1 ND	$2.00	$6.00	$10.00	£1.50	£4.50	£7.50
2 ND	$1.40	$4.20	$7.00	£0.80	£2.40	£4.00
3-5 ND	$1.00	$3.00	$5.00	£0.70	£2.10	£3.50
6 ND Kevin Nowlan inks	$0.80	$2.40	$4.00	£0.50	£1.50	£2.50
7 ND	$0.80	$2.40	$4.00	£0.50	£1.50	£2.50
8-9 ND Whilce Portacio art	$0.80	$2.40	$4.00	£0.50	£1.50	£2.50
10 ND scarce in the U.K. X-over with Daredevil #257, Whilce Portacio art	$1.20	$3.60	$6.00	£1.20	£3.60	£6.00
11 ND Whilce Portacio art	$0.70	$2.10	$3.50	£0.40	£1.20	£2.00
12 ND Whlice Portacio art	$0.70	$2.10	$3.50	£0.40	£1.20	£2.00
13 LD in the U.K. Whilce Portacio art	$0.70	$2.10	$3.50	£0.40	£1.20	£2.00
14 drugs overdose cover, Whilce Portacio art	$0.70	$2.10	$3.50	£0.40	£1.20	£2.00
15-18 Kingpin appears, Whilce Portacio art	$0.70	$2.10	$3.50	£0.40	£1.20	£2.00
19 Larry Stroman art	$0.70	$2.10	$3.50	£0.40	£1.20	£2.00
20	$0.70	$2.10	$3.50	£0.40	£1.20	£2.00
21 Erik Larsen art	$0.50	$1.50	$2.50	£0.30	£0.90	£1.50
22-23	$0.50	$1.50	$2.50	£0.30	£0.90	£1.50
24 LD in the U.K. 1st appearance Shadowmasters	$0.60	$1.80	$3.00	£0.40	£1.20	£2.00
25 LD in the U.K. DS	$0.60	$1.80	$3.00	£0.40	£1.20	£2.00
26	$0.40	$1.20	$2.00	£0.25	£0.75	£1.25
27 Acts of Vengeance tie-in	$0.40	$1.20	$2.00	£0.25	£0.75	£1.25
28-29 Acts of Vengeance tie-in, Dr. Doom appears	$0.40	$1.20	$2.00	£0.25	£0.75	£1.25
30	$0.40	$1.20	$2.00	£0.25	£0.75	£1.25
31-34	$0.30	$0.90	$1.50	£0.20	£0.60	£1.00
35 Jigsaw Puzzle story, bi-weekly	$0.30	$0.90	$1.50	£0.20	£0.60	£1.00
36-37 Jigsaw Puzzle story, Mark Texeira, bi-weekly	$0.30	$0.90	$1.50	£0.20	£0.60	£1.00
38-40 Jigsaw Puzzle story, bi-weekly	$0.30	$0.90	$1.50	£0.20	£0.60	£1.00
41	$0.30	$0.90	$1.50	£0.20	£0.60	£1.00
42 Mark Texeira art	$0.30	$0.90	$1.50	£0.20	£0.60	£1.00
43-48	$0.30	$0.90	$1.50	£0.20	£0.60	£1.00
49 Ron Wagner art begins	$0.30	$0.90	$1.50	£0.20	£0.60	£1.00
50 48pgs	$0.40	$1.20	$2.00	£0.25	£0.75	£1.25
51-52	$0.30	$0.90	$1.50	£0.20	£0.60	£1.00
53-56 bi-weekly issue	$0.30	$0.90	$1.50	£0.20	£0.60	£1.00
57 bi-weekly issue, brown card "wanted poster" outer cover	$0.40	$1.20	$2.00	£0.25	£0.75	£1.25
57 without outer cover	$0.30	$0.90	$1.50	£0.20	£0.60	£1.00
58 painted cover, bi-weekly issue	$0.30	$0.90	$1.50	£0.20	£0.60	£1.00
59 bi-weekly issue, Punisher has skin grafted on and becomes black	$0.30	$0.90	$1.50	£0.20	£0.60	£1.00
60 Luke Cage returns, $1.25 cover begins	$0.30	$0.90	$1.50	£0.20	£0.60	£1.00
61-62 Luke Cage appears	$0.25	$0.75	$1.25	£0.15	£0.45	£0.75
63	$0.25	$0.75	$1.25	£0.15	£0.45	£0.75
64 Eurohit part 1 (ends #70), Dougie Braithwaite pencils begin, Dan Abnett scripts begin, bi-weekly	$0.25	$0.75	$1.25	£0.15	£0.45	£0.75
65-70 bi-weekly	$0.25	$0.75	$1.25	£0.15	£0.45	£0.75
71 new creative team Abnett with Lanning, Braithwaite with Williamson take over	$0.25	$0.75	$1.25	£0.15	£0.45	£0.75
72 LD in the U.K.	$0.25	$0.75	$1.25	£0.20	£0.60	£1.00
73-74	$0.25	$0.75	$1.25	£0.15	£0.45	£0.75
75 DS	$0.40	$1.20	$2.00	£0.25	£0.75	£1.25
76-85	$0.25	$0.75	$1.25	£0.15	£0.45	£0.75
86 48pgs, Suicide Run part 3, foil embossed cover by Michael Golden	$0.40	$1.20	$2.00	£0.25	£0.75	£1.25
87 Suicide Run part 6, continued in Punisher War Journal #63; Michael Golden cover	$0.25	$0.75	$1.25	£0.15	£0.45	£0.75
88 Suicide Run part 9, continued in Punisher War Journal #64; Michael Golden cover	$0.25	$0.75	$1.25	£0.15	£0.45	£0.75
89 Russ Heath art	$0.25	$0.75	$1.25	£0.15	£0.45	£0.75
90 Russ Heath art; with free Spiderman and his Deadly Foes card sheet	$0.25	$0.75	$1.25	£0.15	£0.45	£0.75
91-92 Russ Heath art	$0.25	$0.75	$1.25	£0.15	£0.45	£0.75
93 Bill Sienkiewicz cover	$0.25	$0.75	$1.25	£0.15	£0.45	£0.75
94-99	$0.25	$0.75	$1.25	£0.15	£0.45	£0.75
100 64pgs	$0.40	$1.20	$2.00	£0.25	£0.75	£1.25
100 Enhanced Cover Edition, 64pgs, prismatic-foil enhanced cover	$0.50	$1.50	$2.50	£0.30	£0.90	£1.50
101-102 Bullseye appears	$0.25	$0.75	$1.25	£0.15	£0.45	£0.75
103 Countdown: 4, continued in Punisher War Journal #79	$0.25	$0.75	$1.25	£0.15	£0.45	£0.75
104 Countdown:14, continued in Punisher War Journal #80; Kingpin and Bullseye appear; Jae Lee cover	$0.25	$0.75	$1.25	£0.15	£0.45	£0.75
Title Value:	$43.95	$131.85	$219.75	£28.10	£84.30	£140.50
PUNISHER (2ND SERIES)						
Marvel Comics Group; 1 Nov 1995-present						
1 ND John Ostrander script, Tom Lyle and Chris Ivy art; Doc Samson, Avengers and Bullseye appear, metallic foil-stamped cover	$0.60	$1.80	$3.00	£0.40	£1.20	£2.00
2-3 ND	$0.40	$1.20	$2.00	£0.25	£0.75	£1.25
4 ND Daredevil appears	$0.40	$1.20	$2.00	£0.25	£0.75	£1.25
5-12 ND	$0.40	$1.20	$2.00	£0.25	£0.75	£1.25
13-16 ND	$0.30	$0.90	$1.50	£0.20	£0.60	£1.00
17 ND Daredevil, Doc Samson and Spiderman appear	$0.40	$1.20	$2.00	£0.25	£0.75	£1.25
Title Value:	$6.60	$19.80	$31.00	£4.20	£12.60	£21.00
PUNISHER (LIMITED SERIES)						
Marvel Comics Group,MS; 1 Jan 1986-5 May 1986						
(see Spiderman, Captain America, Daredevil, Marvel Graphic Novel, Marvel Preview, Marvel Super-Action, Punisher War Journal, Spectacular Spiderman)						
1 ND scarce in the U.K. Mike Zeck art	$4.00	$12.00	$20.00	£3.00	£9.00	£15.00
2 ND scarce in the U.K. Mike Zeck art	$2.00	$6.00	$10.00	£1.50	£4.50	£7.50
3 ND Mike Zeck art (75 and 95 cents versions available)	$1.00	$3.00	$5.00	£1.00	£3.00	£5.00
4-5 ND Mike Zeck art	$1.00	$3.00	$5.00	£0.80	£2.40	£4.00
Title Value:	$9.00	$27.00	$45.00	£7.10	£21.30	£35.50
Note: 75 cents and 95 cents cover versions of issue #3 available. No differentiation in value at this time.						
Hardback, oversize, ND scarce in the U.K.; reprints #1,2 of mini-series				£0.80	£2.40	£4.00
Circle of Blood						

Issue	$Good	$Fine	$N.Mint	£Good	£Fine	£N.Mint
Trade paperback, 144pgs, ND, reprints #1-5				£1.00	£3.00	£5.00
(2nd print. Sep 1989)				£1.20	£3.60	£6.00
(3rd print. Dec 1990)				£1.10	£3.30	£5.50

Note: #1-4 labelled as 4-issue series, #5 labelled as 5-issue series. Mike Zeck art in #1-4.

PUNISHER 2099

Marvel Comics Group; 1 Feb 1993-34 Nov 1995

Issue	$Good	$Fine	$N.Mint	£Good	£Fine	£N.Mint
1 ND Pat Mills script begins, foil-stamped cover	$0.40	$1.20	$2.00	£0.25	£0.75	£1.25
2-12 ND	$0.30	$0.90	$1.50	£0.20	£0.60	£1.00
13 ND Spiderman 2099 appears	$0.30	$0.90	$1.50	£0.20	£0.60	£1.00
14-15 ND	$0.30	$0.90	$1.50	£0.20	£0.60	£1.00
16 ND with free Spiderman and his Deadly Foes card sheet	$0.30	$0.90	$1.50	£0.20	£0.60	£1.00
17-25 ND	$0.30	$0.90	$1.50	£0.20	£0.60	£1.00
25 Enhanced Edition, ND multi-level foil-enhanced cover	$0.40	$1.20	$2.00	£0.25	£0.75	£1.25
26-29 ND	$0.30	$0.90	$1.50	£0.20	£0.60	£1.00
30-31 ND One Nation Under Doom	$0.30	$0.90	$1.50	£0.20	£0.60	£1.00
32-33 ND One Nation Under Doom; bi-weekly	$0.30	$0.90	$1.50	£0.20	£0.60	£1.00
34 ND One Nation Under Doom	$0.30	$0.90	$1.50	£0.20	£0.60	£1.00
Title Value:	$10.70	$32.10	$53.50	£7.10	£21.30	£35.50

PUNISHER AND CAPTAIN AMERICA: BLOOD AND GLORY

Marvel Comics Group,MS; 1 Oct 1992-3 Dec 1992

Issue	$Good	$Fine	$N.Mint	£Good	£Fine	£N.Mint
1 ND 48pgs, embossed cover	$0.90	$2.70	$4.50	£0.60	£1.80	£3.00
2-3 ND 48pgs	$0.90	$2.70	$4.50	£0.60	£1.80	£3.00
Title Value:	$2.70	$8.10	$13.50	£1.80	£5.40	£9.00

PUNISHER ANNIVERSARY MAGAZINE

Marvel Comics Group,OS; 1 Feb 1994

Issue	$Good	$Fine	$N.Mint	£Good	£Fine	£N.Mint
1 ND 48pgs, celebrates 20 years with articles and profiles; Michael Golden cover	$0.80	$2.40	$4.00	£0.50	£1.50	£2.50
Title Value:	$0.80	$2.40	$4.00	£0.50	£1.50	£2.50

PUNISHER ANNUAL

Marvel Comics Group; 1 1988-7 1994

Issue	$Good	$Fine	$N.Mint	£Good	£Fine	£N.Mint
1 ND scarce in the U.K. 64pgs, Evolutionary War, Mark Texeira art	$0.60	$1.80	$3.00	£0.40	£1.20	£2.00
2 ND squarebound, Moon Knight appears, Atlantis Attacks part 5, Jim Lee art	$0.50	$1.50	$2.50	£0.30	£0.90	£1.50
3 ND Lifeform story begins, continues in Daredevil Annual #6, Mark Texeira art	$0.50	$1.50	$2.50	£0.30	£0.90	£1.50
4 ND Baron Strucker story, continued in Captain America Annual #10	$0.40	$1.20	$2.00	£0.25	£0.75	£1.25
5 ND The System Bytes by Peter David	$0.40	$1.20	$2.00	£0.25	£0.75	£1.25
6 ND 64pgs, pre-bagged with trading card, 1st appearance Phalanx	$0.50	$1.50	$2.50	£0.30	£0.90	£1.50
7 ND 64pgs, sequel to "Eurohit" storyline from Punisher #64-70	$0.50	$1.50	$2.50	£0.30	£0.90	£1.50
Title Value:	$3.40	$10.20	$17.00	£2.10	£6.30	£10.50

PUNISHER ARMORY

Marvel Comics Group; 1 Jul 1990-10 1994

Issue	$Good	$Fine	$N.Mint	£Good	£Fine	£N.Mint
1 ND part reprints from Punisher War Journal	$0.50	$1.50	$2.50	£0.30	£0.90	£1.50
2 ND Jim Lee cover	$0.40	$1.20	$2.00	£0.25	£0.75	£1.25
3 ND Joe Jusko painted cover	$0.40	$1.20	$2.00	£0.25	£0.75	£1.25
4 ND Dougie Braithwaite cover	$0.40	$1.20	$2.00	£0.25	£0.75	£1.25
5-6 ND Eliot R. Brown cover	$0.40	$1.20	$2.00	£0.25	£0.75	£1.25
7-8 ND Dougie Braithwaite cover	$0.40	$1.20	$2.00	£0.25	£0.75	£1.25
9-10 ND Michael Golden cover	$0.40	$1.20	$2.00	£0.25	£0.75	£1.25
Title Value:	$4.10	$12.30	$20.50	£2.55	£7.65	£12.75

PUNISHER ASHCAN

Marvel Comics Group,OS; nn Dec 1994

Issue	$Good	$Fine	$N.Mint	£Good	£Fine	£N.Mint
nn ND history of The Punisher	$0.15	$0.45	$0.75	£0.10	£0.30	£0.50
Title Value:	$0.15	$0.45	$0.75	£0.10	£0.30	£0.50

PUNISHER BACK-TO-SCHOOL SPECIAL

Marvel Comics Group; 1 Nov 1992; 2 Oct 1993; 3 Oct 1994

Issue	$Good	$Fine	$N.Mint	£Good	£Fine	£N.Mint
1 ND 64pgs, features John Ridgway art	$0.50	$1.50	$2.50	£0.30	£0.90	£1.50
2 ND 64pgs, Bill Sienkiewicz cover	$0.50	$1.50	$2.50	£0.30	£0.90	£1.50
3 ND 64pgs	$0.50	$1.50	$2.50	£0.30	£0.90	£1.50
Title Value:	$1.50	$4.50	$7.50	£0.90	£2.70	£4.50

PUNISHER CLASSICS

Marvel Comics Group,OS; 1 Dec 1989

Issue	$Good	$Fine	$N.Mint	£Good	£Fine	£N.Mint
1 ND 68pgs, squarebound, reprints black and white Marvel Preview #2 (5th appearance) and Marvel Super Action #1, Larry Stroman cover	$0.90	$2.70	$4.50	£0.60	£1.80	£3.00
Title Value:	$0.90	$2.70	$4.50	£0.60	£1.80	£3.00

Note: originally announced as "Punisher Classics" and appeared with "Classic Punisher" on the cover.

PUNISHER HOLIDAY SPECIAL

Marvel Comics Group; 1 Jan 1993; 2 Jan 1994; 3 Jan 1995

Issue	$Good	$Fine	$N.Mint	£Good	£Fine	£N.Mint
1 ND foil stamped cover	$0.60	$1.80	$3.00	£0.40	£1.20	£2.00
2 ND 64pgs, Bill Sienkiewicz cover	$0.60	$1.80	$3.00	£0.40	£1.20	£2.00
3 ND 64pgs, Dale Eaglesham art	$0.60	$1.80	$3.00	£0.40	£1.20	£2.00
Title Value:	$1.80	$5.40	$9.00	£1.20	£3.60	£6.00

PUNISHER IN NAM: FINAL INVASION

Marvel Comics Group,OS; nn Apr 1994

Issue	$Good	$Fine	$N.Mint	£Good	£Fine	£N.Mint
nn ND 80pgs, Frank Castle (Punisher) and his last mission in Vietnam; Don Lomax script	$1.20	$3.60	$6.00	£0.80	£2.40	£4.00
Title Value:	$1.20	$3.60	$6.00	£0.80	£2.40	£4.00

PUNISHER KILLS THE MARVEL UNIVERSE

Marvel Comics Group,OS; 1 Feb 1996

Issue	$Good	$Fine	$N.Mint	£Good	£Fine	£N.Mint
1 ND 48pgs, Garth Ennis script, Dougie Braithwaite art	$1.20	$3.60	$6.00	£0.80	£2.40	£4.00
Title Value:	$1.20	$3.60	$6.00	£0.80	£2.40	£4.00

PUNISHER MAGAZINE

Marvel Comics Group; 1 Oct 1989-16 1990

Issue	$Good	$Fine	$N.Mint	£Good	£Fine	£N.Mint
1 ND 64pgs, reprints Mini-Series #½; black and white begins	$0.70	$2.10	$3.50	£0.40	£1.20	£2.00
2 ND reprints Mini-Series #3/4	$0.50	$1.50	$2.50	£0.30	£0.90	£1.50
3 ND reprints Mini-Series #5, Punisher regular series #1	$0.40	$1.20	$2.00	£0.25	£0.75	£1.25
4 ND reprints issues #2, #3 of Punisher regular series	$0.40	$1.20	$2.00	£0.25	£0.75	£1.25
5 ND reprints issues #4, #5 of Punisher regular series	$0.40	$1.20	$2.00	£0.25	£0.75	£1.25
6 ND reprints issues #6, #7 of Punisher regular series						

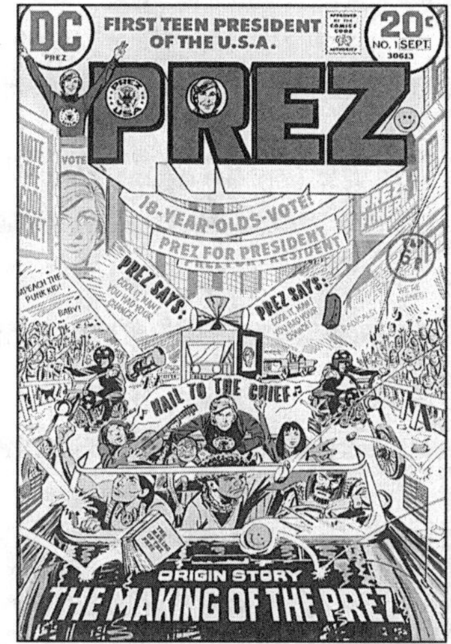

Prez (1st) #1

Pumpkinhead #1

Punisher (Limted Series) #5

	$Good	$Fine	$N.Mint	£Good	£Fine	£N.Mint
	$0.40	$1.20	$2.00	£0.25	£0.75	£1.25
7 ND reprints issues #8, #9 of Punisher regular series	$0.40	$1.20	$2.00	£0.25	£0.75	£1.25
8-13 ND reprints from regular series	$0.40	$1.20	$2.00	£0.25	£0.75	£1.25
14 ND Punisher War Journal reprints begin	$0.40	$1.20	$2.00	£0.25	£0.75	£1.25
15 ND reprints Punisher War Journal #2, Punisher Annual #2	$0.40	$1.20	$2.00	£0.25	£0.75	£1.25
16 ND reprints Punisher War Journal #3,8	$0.40	$1.20	$2.00	£0.25	£0.75	£1.25
Title Value:	$6.80	$20.40	$34.00	£4.20	£12.60	£21.00

PUNISHER MEETS ARCHIE: WHEN WORLDS COLLIDE

Marvel Comics Group/Archie Comics,OS; 1 Aug 1994

	$Good	$Fine	$N.Mint	£Good	£Fine	£N.Mint
1 Archie Edition, ND 48pgs, "Archie Meets the Punisher"	$0.50	$1.50	$2.50	£0.30	£0.90	£1.50
1 Direct Market Edition, ND 48pgs, die-cut cover	$0.70	$2.10	$3.50	£0.40	£1.20	£2.00
1 Marvel Edition, ND 48pgs, "Punisher Meets Archie"	$0.40	$1.20	$2.00	£0.25	£0.75	£1.25
Title Value:	$1.60	$4.80	$8.00	£0.95	£2.85	£4.75

PUNISHER MOVIE ADAPTATION

Marvel Comics Group,OS; 1 Aug 1990

	$Good	$Fine	$N.Mint	£Good	£Fine	£N.Mint
1 ND 48pgs, adaptation of the movie by Potts/Anderson	$0.90	$2.70	$4.50	£0.60	£1.80	£3.00
Title Value:	$0.90	$2.70	$4.50	£0.60	£1.80	£3.00

Note: Bookshelf Format

PUNISHER SUMMER SPECIAL

Marvel Comics Group; 1 Aug 1991; 2 Aug 1992; 3 Aug 1993; 4 Jul 1994

	$Good	$Fine	$N.Mint	£Good	£Fine	£N.Mint
1 ND 48pgs, four new stories featuring scripts by Pat Mills and Peter David, Mark Texeira art	$0.50	$1.50	$2.50	£0.30	£0.90	£1.50
2 ND 48pgs, Pat Mills script, Simon Bisley painted cover	$0.50	$1.50	$2.50	£0.30	£0.90	£1.50
3 ND 48pgs, Brian Stelfreeze cover	$0.50	$1.50	$2.50	£0.30	£0.90	£1.50
4 ND 48pgs, John Romita Jnr. cover	$0.50	$1.50	$2.50	£0.30	£0.90	£1.50
Title Value:	$2.00	$6.00	$10.00	£1.20	£3.60	£6.00

PUNISHER VS WOLVERINE: THE AFRICAN SAGA

Marvel Comics Group,OS; nn 1990

	$Good	$Fine	$N.Mint	£Good	£Fine	£N.Mint
nn ND 48pgs, reprints Punisher War Journal #6,7, Jim Lee art	$1.20	$3.60	$6.00	£0.80	£2.40	£4.00
Title Value:	$1.20	$3.60	$6.00	£0.80	£2.40	£4.00

PUNISHER WAR JOURNAL

Marvel Comics Group; 1 Nov 1988-80 Jul 1995

	$Good	$Fine	$N.Mint	£Good	£Fine	£N.Mint
1 ND origin retold, Jim Lee art	$1.50	$4.50	$7.50	£1.00	£3.00	£5.00
2 ND scarce in the U.K. Daredevil, Jim Lee art	$1.00	$3.00	$5.00	£0.70	£2.10	£3.50
3 ND scarce in the U.K. Daredevil, Jim Lee art	$0.80	$2.40	$4.00	£0.60	£1.80	£3.00
4-5 ND Jim Lee art	$0.80	$2.40	$4.00	£0.60	£1.80	£3.00
6 ND 1st Punisher/Wolverine story, Jim Lee art	$1.20	$3.60	$6.00	£0.80	£2.40	£4.00
7 ND 2nd Punisher/Wolverine story, Jim Lee art	$1.00	$3.00	$5.00	£0.70	£2.10	£3.50
8 ND Shadowmasters appear, Jim Lee art	$0.60	$1.80	$3.00	£0.40	£1.20	£2.00
9-10 ND Jim Lee art	$0.60	$1.80	$3.00	£0.40	£1.20	£2.00
11 ND Jim Lee art	$0.50	$1.50	$2.50	£0.30	£0.90	£1.50
12 ND Acts of Vengeance tie-in, Jim Lee art	$0.50	$1.50	$2.50	£0.30	£0.90	£1.50
13 ND Acts of Vengeance tie-in, Jim Lee cover	$0.50	$1.50	$2.50	£0.30	£0.90	£1.50
14-15 ND Spiderman appears, Jim Lee cover	$0.50	$1.50	$2.50	£0.30	£0.90	£1.50
16 ND Mark Texeira inks	$0.50	$1.50	$2.50	£0.30	£0.90	£1.50
17-19 ND Jim Lee art	$0.50	$1.50	$2.50	£0.30	£0.90	£1.50
20-24 ND	$0.40	$1.20	$2.00	£0.25	£0.75	£1.25
25-28 ND Texeira inks	$0.40	$1.20	$2.00	£0.25	£0.75	£1.25
29-30 ND Ghost Rider appears, Texeira inks	$0.40	$1.20	$2.00	£0.25	£0.75	£1.25
31-33 ND The Kamchatkan Konspiracy, Andy Kubert and Joe Kubert art	$0.40	$1.20	$2.00	£0.25	£0.75	£1.25
34 ND	$0.40	$1.20	$2.00	£0.25	£0.75	£1.25
35 ND scarce in the U.K.	$0.40	$1.20	$2.00	£0.30	£0.90	£1.50
36 ND photo cover	$0.40	$1.20	$2.00	£0.25	£0.75	£1.25
37-39 ND	$0.40	$1.20	$2.00	£0.25	£0.75	£1.25
40 ND painted cover by Michael Golden	$0.40	$1.20	$2.00	£0.25	£0.75	£1.25
41-44 ND	$0.40	$1.20	$2.00	£0.25	£0.75	£1.25
45 ND Dead Man's Hand part 3, continued in Daredevil 408	$0.40	$1.20	$2.00	£0.25	£0.75	£1.25
46 ND Dead Man's Hand part 6, continued in Daredevil 409	$0.40	$1.20	$2.00	£0.25	£0.75	£1.25
47 ND Dead Man's Hand part 9 (conclusion), Daredevil and Nomad appear	$0.40	$1.20	$2.00	£0.25	£0.75	£1.25
48-49 ND	$0.40	$1.20	$2.00	£0.25	£0.75	£1.25
50 ND DS embossed cover by Mark Texeira, preview of Punisher 2099	$0.50	$1.50	$2.50	£0.30	£0.90	£1.50
51-56 ND	$0.40	$1.20	$2.00	£0.25	£0.75	£1.25
57-58 ND Ghost Rider and Daredevil appear	$0.40	$1.20	$2.00	£0.25	£0.75	£1.25
59-60 ND	$0.40	$1.20	$2.00	£0.25	£0.75	£1.25
61 ND 48pgs, Suicide Run part 1, embossed foil cover by Michael Golden	$0.80	$2.40	$4.00	£0.50	£1.50	£2.50
62 ND Suicide Run part 4	$0.40	$1.20	$2.00	£0.25	£0.75	£1.25
63 ND Suicide Run part 7	$0.40	$1.20	$2.00	£0.25	£0.75	£1.25
64 ND 48pgs, Suicide Run part 10 (conclusion)	$0.40	$1.20	$2.00	£0.25	£0.75	£1.25
64 Collectors Edition, ND 48pgs, Suicide Run part 10, die-cut cover by Michael Golden	$0.50	$1.50	$2.50	£0.30	£0.90	£1.50
65 ND Pariah story	$0.40	$1.20	$2.00	£0.25	£0.75	£1.25
66 ND Pariah story, with free Spiderman vs. Venom card sheet	$0.40	$1.20	$2.00	£0.25	£0.75	£1.25
67-74 ND	$0.40	$1.20	$2.00	£0.25	£0.75	£1.25
75 ND 48pgs, new logo and cover design painted by Mark Texeira	$0.50	$1.50	$2.50	£0.30	£0.90	£1.50
76-78 ND	$0.40	$1.20	$2.00	£0.25	£0.75	£1.25
79 ND Countdown: 3, continued in Punisher War Zone #41; Jae Lee cover	$0.40	$1.20	$2.00	£0.25	£0.75	£1.25
80 ND Countdown: 0; Punisher vs. Bullseye, Nick Fury appears	$0.40	$1.20	$2.00	£0.25	£0.75	£1.25
Title Value:	$38.90	$116.70	$194.50	£24.85	£74.55	£124.25
An Eye For An Eye (Feb 1992) Trade paperback reprints issues #1-3, new Jim Lee cover				£1.10	£3.30	£5.50

PUNISHER WAR ZONE

Marvel Comics Group; 1 Mar 1992-41 Jul 1995

	$Good	$Fine	$N.Mint	£Good	£Fine	£N.Mint
1 ND die-cut cover giving bullet-ridden effect, John Romita Jnr. art begins	$0.60	$1.80	$3.00	£0.40	£1.20	£2.00
2-10 ND	$0.40	$1.20	$2.00	£0.25	£0.75	£1.25
11 ND last John Romita Jnr. art	$0.30	$0.90	$1.50	£0.20	£0.60	£1.00
12 ND Abnett and Lanning script begin, Mike McKone pencils begin	$0.30	$0.90	$1.50	£0.20	£0.60	£1.00
13-18 ND	$0.30	$0.90	$1.50	£0.20	£0.60	£1.00
19 ND Wolverine guest-stars	$0.30	$0.90	$1.50	£0.20	£0.60	£1.00
20-22 ND	$0.30	$0.90	$1.50	£0.20	£0.60	£1.00
23 ND 48pgs, Suicide Run part 2, foil embossed cover by Michael Golden	$0.50	$1.50	$2.50	£0.30	£0.90	£1.50
24 ND Suicide Run part 5, continued in Punisher #87	$0.30	$0.90	$1.50	£0.20	£0.60	£1.00
25 ND 48pgs, Suicide Run part 8, continued in Punisher #88	$0.30	$0.90	$1.50	£0.20	£0.60	£1.00
26 ND John Buscema art	$0.30	$0.90	$1.50	£0.20	£0.60	£1.00
27 ND John Buscema art, with free Spiderman vs. Venom card sheet	$0.30	$0.90	$1.50	£0.20	£0.60	£1.00
28-30 ND John Buscema art	$0.30	$0.90	$1.50	£0.20	£0.60	£1.00
31-36 ND Joe Kubert art	$0.30	$0.90	$1.50	£0.20	£0.60	£1.00
37 ND Mark Texeira art	$0.30	$0.90	$1.50	£0.20	£0.60	£1.00
38-40 ND	$0.30	$0.90	$1.50	£0.20	£0.60	£1.00
41 ND Countdown: 2, continued in Punisher #104; Jae Lee cover	$0.30	$0.90	$1.50	£0.20	£0.60	£1.00
Title Value:	$13.70	$41.10	$68.50	£8.95	£26.85	£44.75

PUNISHER WAR ZONE ANNUAL

Marvel Comics Group; 1 Aug 1993-2 1994

	$Good	$Fine	$N.Mint	£Good	£Fine	£N.Mint
1 ND 64pgs, pre-bagged with trading card introducing Phalanx	$0.50	$1.50	$2.50	£0.30	£0.90	£1.50
2 ND 64pgs	$0.50	$1.50	$2.50	£0.30	£0.90	£1.50
Title Value:	$1.00	$3.00	$5.00	£0.60	£1.80	£3.00

PUNISHER/BATMAN: DEADLY KNIGHTS

Marvel Comics Group/DC Comics,OS; 1 Oct 1994

	$Good	$Fine	$N.Mint	£Good	£Fine	£N.Mint
1 ND 48pgs, squarebound, Chuck Dixon, John Romita Jnr and Klaus Janson	$0.90	$2.70	$4.50	£0.60	£1.80	£3.00
Title Value:	$0.90	$2.70	$4.50	£0.60	£1.80	£3.00

PUNISHER: A MAN NAMED FRANK

Marvel Comics Group,OS; 1 Aug 1994

	$Good	$Fine	$N.Mint	£Good	£Fine	£N.Mint
1 ND 48pgs, Chuck Dixon and John Buscema	$1.20	$3.60	$6.00	£0.80	£2.40	£4.00
Title Value:	$1.20	$3.60	$6.00	£0.80	£2.40	£4.00

PUNISHER: BLOODLINES

Marvel Comics Group,OS; 1 Feb 1992

	$Good	$Fine	$N.Mint	£Good	£Fine	£N.Mint
1 ND 48pgs	$0.90	$2.70	$4.50	£0.60	£1.80	£3.00
Title Value:	$0.90	$2.70	$4.50	£0.60	£1.80	£3.00

PUNISHER: CRUISE HARD

Marvel Comics Group,OS; 1 Feb 1995

	$Good	$Fine	$N.Mint	£Good	£Fine	£N.Mint
1 ND Dan Abnett and Andy Lanning script	$0.60	$1.80	$3.00	£0.40	£1.20	£2.00
Title Value:	$0.60	$1.80	$3.00	£0.40	£1.20	£2.00

PUNISHER: DIE HARD IN THE BIG EASY
Marvel Comics Group,OS; 1 Jan 1993

Issue	$Good	$Fine	$N.Mint	£Good	£Fine	£N.Mint
1 ND 48pgs, John Wagner script	$0.90	$2.70	$4.50	£0.60	£1.80	£3.00
Title Value:	$0.90	$2.70	$4.50	£0.60	£1.80	£3.00

PUNISHER: EMPTY QUARTER
Marvel Comics Group,OS; 1 Jan 1995

Issue	$Good	$Fine	$N.Mint	£Good	£Fine	£N.Mint
1 ND 64pgs, Mike Baron script, Bill Reinhold art	$1.20	$3.60	$6.00	£0.80	£2.40	£4.00
Title Value:	$1.20	$3.60	$6.00	£0.80	£2.40	£4.00

PUNISHER: FAMILY AFFAIR SPECIAL
Marvel Comics Group,OS; 1 Oct 1991

Issue	$Good	$Fine	$N.Mint	£Good	£Fine	£N.Mint
1 ND 64pgs	$0.50	$1.50	$2.50	£0.30	£0.90	£1.50
Title Value:	$0.50	$1.50	$2.50	£0.30	£0.90	£1.50

PUNISHER: G-FORCE BOOKSHELF EDITION
Marvel Comics Group,OS; 1 Apr 1992

Issue	$Good	$Fine	$N.Mint	£Good	£Fine	£N.Mint
1 ND 48pgs, Mike Baron script	$0.90	$2.70	$4.50	£0.60	£1.80	£3.00
Title Value:	$0.90	$2.70	$4.50	£0.60	£1.80	£3.00

PUNISHER: NO ESCAPE
Marvel Comics Group,OS; 1 Aug 1990

Issue	$Good	$Fine	$N.Mint	£Good	£Fine	£N.Mint
1 ND 48pgs, Todd Smith art, The Captain/Paladin appear	$0.90	$2.70	$4.50	£0.60	£1.80	£3.00
Title Value:	$0.90	$2.70	$4.50	£0.60	£1.80	£3.00

Note: Bookshelf Format

PUNISHER: ORIGIN OF MICRO-CHIP
Marvel Comics Group,MS; 1 Jul 1993-2 Aug 1993

Issue	$Good	$Fine	$N.Mint	£Good	£Fine	£N.Mint
1 Dougie Braithwaite cover	$0.40	$1.20	$2.00	£0.25	£0.75	£1.25
2	$0.40	$1.20	$2.00	£0.25	£0.75	£1.25
Title Value:	$0.80	$2.40	$4.00	£0.50	£1.50	£2.50

PUNISHER: P.O.V.
Marvel Comics Group,MS; 1 Jul 1991-4 Oct 1991

Issue	$Good	$Fine	$N.Mint	£Good	£Fine	£N.Mint
1 ND Jim Starlin script/Bernie Wrightson art; Nick Fury co-stars	$0.70	$2.10	$3.50	£0.50	£1.50	£2.50
2 ND Kingpin appears	$0.70	$2.10	$3.50	£0.50	£1.50	£2.50
3 ND	$0.70	$2.10	$3.50	£0.50	£1.50	£2.50
4 ND Nick Fury appears	$0.70	$2.10	$3.50	£0.50	£1.50	£2.50
Title Value:	$2.80	$8.40	$14.00	£2.00	£6.00	£10.00

Note: Bookshelf Format

PUNISHER: THE GHOSTS OF INNOCENTS
Marvel Comics Group,MS; 1 Jan 1993-2 Feb 1993

Issue	$Good	$Fine	$N.Mint	£Good	£Fine	£N.Mint
1-2 ND 48pgs, Jim Starlin script	$0.90	$2.70	$4.50	£0.60	£1.80	£3.00
Title Value:	$1.80	$5.40	$9.00	£1.20	£3.60	£6.00

PUNISHER: THE PRIZE
Marvel Comics Group,OS; 1 Dec 1990

Issue	$Good	$Fine	$N.Mint	£Good	£Fine	£N.Mint
1 ND 64pgs, Iron Man's armour featured	$0.70	$2.10	$3.50	£0.50	£1.50	£2.50
Title Value:	$0.70	$2.10	$3.50	£0.50	£1.50	£2.50

PUNISHER: YEAR ONE
Marvel Comics Group,MS; 1 Dec 1994-4 Mar 1995

Issue	$Good	$Fine	$N.Mint	£Good	£Fine	£N.Mint
1-4 Dan Abnett and Andy Lanning tell Punisher's origin	$0.40	$1.20	$2.00	£0.25	£0.75	£1.25
Title Value:	$1.60	$4.80	$8.00	£1.00	£3.00	£5.00

PUNX
Acclaim Comics,MS; 1 Jul 1995-4 Oct 1995

Issue	$Good	$Fine	$N.Mint	£Good	£Fine	£N.Mint
1-4 ND Keith Giffen script and pencil art, Claude St. Aubain inks	$0.50	$1.50	$2.50	£0.30	£0.90	£1.50
Title Value:	$2.00	$6.00	$10.00	£1.20	£3.60	£6.00

PUNX REDUX
Acclaim Comics,MS; 1 Jul 1996-4 Oct 1996

Issue	$Good	$Fine	$N.Mint	£Good	£Fine	£N.Mint
1-4 ND Keith Giffen script and art	$0.50	$1.50	$2.50	£0.30	£0.90	£1.50
Title Value:	$2.00	$6.00	$10.00	£1.20	£3.60	£6.00

PUNX SPECIAL
Valiant/Acclaim Comics,OS; 1 Nov 1995

Issue	$Good	$Fine	$N.Mint	£Good	£Fine	£N.Mint
1 ND Keith Giffen script and art with Claude St. Aubain	$0.50	$1.50	$2.50	£0.30	£0.90	£1.50
Title Value:	$0.50	$1.50	$2.50	£0.30	£0.90	£1.50

PUPPET MASTER
Eternity,MS; 1 Dec 1990-4 Mar 1991

Issue	$Good	$Fine	$N.Mint	£Good	£Fine	£N.Mint
1-4 ND	$0.40	$1.20	$2.00	£0.25	£0.75	£1.25
Title Value:	$1.60	$4.80	$8.00	£1.00	£3.00	£5.00
Puppet Master Comic Companion, 48pgs, articles and photos (1991)				£0.70	£2.10	£3.50

PUPPET MASTER 2
Eternity,MS Film; 1,2 Oct 1991

Issue	$Good	$Fine	$N.Mint	£Good	£Fine	£N.Mint
1-2 ND film adaptation	$0.40	$1.20	$2.00	£0.25	£0.75	£1.25
Title Value:	$0.80	$2.40	$4.00	£0.50	£1.50	£2.50

PURE IMAGES
Pure Imagination; 1 Nov 1990-6 1991

Issue	$Good	$Fine	$N.Mint	£Good	£Fine	£N.Mint
1 ND article/unseen artwork on Spiderman detailing how the character originated	$0.40	$1.20	$2.00	£0.25	£0.75	£1.25
2 ND article/unseen artwork on The Hulk and The Fantastic Four	$0.40	$1.20	$2.00	£0.25	£0.75	£1.25
3-4 ND Monsterama	$0.40	$1.20	$2.00	£0.25	£0.75	£1.25
5 ND Jack Kirby issue, Dave Gibbons pin-up	$0.40	$1.20	$2.00	£0.25	£0.75	£1.25
6 ND Mechanical Dinosaurs	$0.40	$1.20	$2.00	£0.25	£0.75	£1.25
Title Value:	$2.40	$7.20	$12.00	£1.50	£4.50	£7.50

PUREHEART THE POWERFUL, ARCHIE AS
Archie; 1 Sep 1966-6 Nov 1967

Issue	$Good	$Fine	$N.Mint	£Good	£Fine	£N.Mint
1 versus The Octopus	$9.25	$28.00	$65.00	£5.50	£17.00	£40.00
2	$6.25	$19.00	$45.00	£3.55	£10.50	£25.00
3-6	$4.60	$13.50	$32.50	£2.85	£8.50	£20.00
Title Value:	$33.90	$101.00	$240.00	£20.45	£61.50	£145.00

Note: all distributed on the news-stands in the U.K.

PURGATORI
Chaos Comics,MS;-1 May 1996-3 Dec 1996

Issue	$Good	$Fine	$N.Mint	£Good	£Fine	£N.Mint
-1 ND 16pgs, spin-off from Lady Death	$0.30	$0.90	$1.50	£0.20	£0.60	£1.00
1 ND wraparound cover	$0.60	$1.80	$3.00	£0.40	£1.20	£2.00
1 Limited Edition, ND; limited to 10,000 copies	$4.00	$12.00	$20.00	£2.00	£6.00	£10.00
2-3 ND	$0.60	$1.80	$3.00	£0.40	£1.20	£2.00
3 Variant Cover Edition ND	$1.40	$4.20	$7.00	£1.00	£3.00	£5.00
Title Value:	$7.50	$22.50	$37.50	£4.40	£13.20	£22.00

PURPLE CLAW
I.W. Comics;8 (early 1960s)

Issue	$Good	$Fine	$N.Mint	£Good	£Fine	£N.Mint
8 scarce distributed in the U.K. 50s reprints	$2.55	$7.50	$18.00	£1.70	£5.00	£12.00
Title Value:	$2.55	$7.50	$18.00	£1.70	£5.00	£12.00

PURPLE CLAW MYSTERIES
AC Comics; 1 Oct 1994

Issue	$Good	$Fine	$N.Mint	£Good	£Fine	£N.Mint
1 ND Bill Black script, Dick Ayers art; black and white	$0.60	$1.80	$3.00	£0.40	£1.20	£2.00
Title Value:	$0.60	$1.80	$3.00	£0.40	£1.20	£2.00

PURPLE SNIT, THE TWISTED TANTRUMS OF THE
Blackthorne; 1 Oct 1986-2 1986

Issue	$Good	$Fine	$N.Mint	£Good	£Fine	£N.Mint
1-2 ND black and white	$0.25	$0.75	$1.25	£0.15	£0.45	£0.75
Title Value:	$0.50	$1.50	$2.50	£0.30	£0.90	£1.50

PURSUIT
Marvel Comics Group; 1994

Cross-over storyline running throughout the following titles:
Spiderman #45,
Spectacular Spiderman #211,
Web of Spiderman #122,
Amazing Spiderman #389.

PUSSYCAT
Marvel Comics Group,Magazine OS; 1 1968

Issue	$Good	$Fine	$N.Mint	£Good	£Fine	£N.Mint
1 ND scarce in the U.K. Men's magazine reprint, Wood and Everett art	$18.50	$55.00	$130.00	£12.00	£36.00	£85.00
Title Value:	$18.50	$55.00	$130.00	£12.00	£36.00	£85.00

Q

QUACK
Star Reach; 1 Jul 1976-6 Dec 1977

Issue	$Good	$Fine	$N.Mint	£Good	£Fine	£N.Mint
1 ND Frank Brunner and Howard Chaykin art	$0.75	$2.25	$4.50	£0.50	£1.50	£3.00
2-6 ND	$0.40	$1.25	$2.50	£0.25	£0.75	£1.50
Title Value:	$2.75	$8.50	$17.00	£1.75	£5.25	£10.50

QUADRANT
Quadrant; 1 1983-8 1986

Issue	$Good	$Fine	$N.Mint	£Good	£Fine	£N.Mint
1 ND scarce in the U.K. magazine	$1.20	$3.60	$6.00	£0.80	£2.40	£4.00
1 1st comic format ND scarce in the U.K.	$1.20	$3.60	$6.00	£0.80	£2.40	£4.00
2 ND scarce in the U.K.	$0.50	$1.50	$2.50	£0.40	£1.20	£2.00
3-8 ND scarce in the U.K.	$0.50	$1.50	$2.50	£0.30	£0.90	£1.50
Title Value:	$5.90	$17.70	$29.50	£3.80	£11.40	£19.00
Trade Paperback reprints issues #1-8, the "Hellrazor Saga" plus "Hellrazor" saga, new 8pg story, new cover pre-bagged				£1.75	£5.50	£9.00
2nd printing				£1.50	£5.00	£8.00

QUANTUM LEAP
Innovation; 1 Sep 1991-12 Jun 1993

Issue	$Good	$Fine	$N.Mint	£Good	£Fine	£N.Mint
1 based on TV series	$1.50	$4.50	$7.50	£2.50	£7.50	£12.50
1 Special Edition Reprint, (Sep 1992) - features 8pgs of articles and photos from Quantum Leap Convention	$0.50	$1.50	$2.50	£0.60	£1.80	£3.00
2	$1.00	$3.00	$5.00	£1.50	£4.50	£7.50
2 2nd printing, (Oct 1992)	$0.50	$1.50	$2.50	£0.40	£1.20	£2.00
3	$0.70	$2.10	$3.50	£1.00	£3.00	£5.00
4-5	$0.50	$1.50	$2.50	£0.80	£2.40	£4.00
6-10	$0.50	$1.50	$2.50	£0.70	£2.10	£3.50
11-12	$0.50	$1.50	$2.50	£0.50	£1.50	£2.50
Title Value:	$8.70	$26.10	$43.50	£12.10	£36.30	£60.50

Note: all Non-Distributed on the news-stands in the U.K.

Issue	$Good	$Fine	$N.Mint	£Good	£Fine	£N.Mint
Annual 1 (Jun 1993), pin-up gallery included				£0.40	£1.20	£2.00

QUANTUM LEAP TIME AND SPACE SPECIAL

Innovation; 1 Aug 1993

	$Good	$Fine	$N.Mint	£Good	£Fine	£N.Mint
1 ND silver foil logo and card-stock cover; number 13 on cover						
	$0.50	*$1.50*	*$2.50*	£0.80	£2.40	£4.00
Title Value:	*$0.50*	*$1.50*	*$2.50*	£0.80	£2.40	£4.00

QUANTUM LEAP: SECOND CHILDHOOD

Innovation,MS; 1 Mar 1994-3 May 1994

	$Good	$Fine	$N.Mint	£Good	£Fine	£N.Mint
1-3 ND	*$0.40*	*$1.20*	*$2.00*	£0.50	£1.50	£2.50
Title Value:	*$1.20*	*$3.60*	*$6.00*	£1.50	£4.50	£7.50

QUASAR

Marvel Comics Group; 1 Oct 1989-60 Jul 1994

(see Avengers #302)

	$Good	$Fine	$N.Mint	£Good	£Fine	£N.Mint
1 ND origin	*$0.30*	*$0.90*	*$1.50*	£0.20	£0.60	£1.00
2 ND	*$0.25*	*$0.75*	*$1.25*	£0.15	£0.45	£0.75
3 ND Quasar vs. Human Torch						
	$0.25	*$0.75*	*$1.25*	£0.15	£0.45	£0.75
4 ND	*$0.25*	*$0.75*	*$1.25*	£0.15	£0.45	£0.75
5 LD in the U.K. Acts of Vengeance tie-in						
	$0.25	*$0.75*	*$1.25*	£0.15	£0.45	£0.75
6 LD in the U.K. Acts of Vengeance tie-in, Venom cameo (2pgs)						
	$0.25	*$0.75*	*$1.25*	£0.15	£0.45	£0.75
7 Quasar vs. cosmic-powered Spiderman						
	$0.25	*$0.75*	*$1.25*	£0.15	£0.45	£0.75
8 New Mutants appear						
	$0.25	*$0.75*	*$1.25*	£0.15	£0.45	£0.75
9-10	*$0.25*	*$0.75*	*$1.25*	£0.15	£0.45	£0.75
11 Excalibur guest-stars						
	$0.25	*$0.75*	*$1.25*	£0.15	£0.45	£0.75
12	*$0.25*	*$0.75*	*$1.25*	£0.15	£0.45	£0.75
13 Journey Into Mystery story, Squadron Supreme appear						
	$0.25	*$0.75*	*$1.25*	£0.15	£0.45	£0.75
14-15 Journey Into Mystery story						
	$0.25	*$0.75*	*$1.25*	£0.15	£0.45	£0.75
16 DS Journey Into Mystery story concludes, many guest-stars						
	$0.30	*$0.90*	*$1.50*	£0.20	£0.60	£1.00
17 Neal Adams cover, "Speedster" guest-stars (Flash parody)						
	$0.25	*$0.75*	*$1.25*	£0.15	£0.45	£0.75
18	*$0.25*	*$0.75*	*$1.25*	£0.15	£0.45	£0.75
19 Cosmos in Collision part 1 (of 7); Quasar vs. Jack of Hearts						
	$0.25	*$0.75*	*$1.25*	£0.15	£0.45	£0.75
20 Fantastic Four guest-star						
	$0.25	*$0.75*	*$1.25*	£0.15	£0.45	£0.75
21-22 ND	*$0.25*	*$0.75*	*$1.25*	£0.15	£0.45	£0.75
23 ND Ghost Rider appears						
	$0.25	*$0.75*	*$1.25*	£0.15	£0.45	£0.75
24 ND Galactus, Thanos and the Celestials appear						
	$0.25	*$0.75*	*$1.25*	£0.15	£0.45	£0.75
25 ND DS Cosmos In Collision conclusion						
	$0.30	*$0.90*	*$1.50*	£0.20	£0.60	£1.00
26 ND Infinity Gauntlet X-over, Thanos appears						
	$0.25	*$0.75*	*$1.25*	£0.15	£0.45	£0.75
27 ND Infinity Gauntlet X-over						
	$0.25	*$0.75*	*$1.25*	£0.15	£0.45	£0.75
28 ND Thor, Wonderman, Captain America, Hulk, Doc Samson, Hercules and others appear						
	$0.25	*$0.75*	*$1.25*	£0.15	£0.45	£0.75
29 ND	*$0.25*	*$0.75*	*$1.25*	£0.15	£0.45	£0.75
30 ND What If? story featuring The Watcher						
	$0.25	*$0.75*	*$1.25*	£0.15	£0.45	£0.75
31 ND Quasar in the New Universe, DP 7 appear						
	$0.25	*$0.75*	*$1.25*	£0.15	£0.45	£0.75
32 ND scarce in the U.K. Galactic Storm part 3						
	$0.25	*$0.75*	*$1.25*	£0.20	£0.60	£1.00
33 ND Galactic Storm part 10						
	$0.25	*$0.75*	*$1.25*	£0.15	£0.45	£0.75
34 ND Galactic Storm part 17						
	$0.25	*$0.75*	*$1.25*	£0.15	£0.45	£0.75
35-36 ND Galactic Storm: Aftermath						
	$0.25	*$0.75*	*$1.25*	£0.15	£0.45	£0.75
37 ND Infinity War X-over						
	$0.25	*$0.75*	*$1.25*	£0.15	£0.45	£0.75
38 ND Infinity War X-over, Wolverine, Nova and Hulk appear						
	$0.25	*$0.75*	*$1.25*	£0.15	£0.45	£0.75
39-40 ND Infinity War X-over						
	$0.25	*$0.75*	*$1.25*	£0.15	£0.45	£0.75
41 ND	*$0.25*	*$0.75*	*$1.25*	£0.15	£0.45	£0.75
42-43 ND Quasar vs. Blue Marvel (Marvel Boy)						
	$0.25	*$0.75*	*$1.25*	£0.15	£0.45	£0.75
44-49 ND	*$0.25*	*$0.75*	*$1.25*	£0.15	£0.45	£0.75
50 ND DS gold-holo-grafix foil cover, Silver Surfer appears						
	$0.40	*$1.20*	*$2.00*	£0.25	£0.75	£1.25
51-52 ND Squadron Supreme guest-stars						
	$0.25	*$0.75*	*$1.25*	£0.15	£0.45	£0.75
53 ND Warlock appears						
	$0.25	*$0.75*	*$1.25*	£0.15	£0.45	£0.75
54 ND Starblast part 2						
	$0.25	*$0.75*	*$1.25*	£0.15	£0.45	£0.75
55 ND Starblast part 6						
	$0.25	*$0.75*	*$1.25*	£0.15	£0.45	£0.75
56 ND Starblast part 10						
	$0.25	*$0.75*	*$1.25*	£0.15	£0.45	£0.75
57 ND Starblast epilogue						
	$0.25	*$0.75*	*$1.25*	£0.15	£0.45	£0.75
58 ND with free Spiderman and his Deadly Foes card sheet						
	$0.25	*$0.75*	*$1.25*	£0.15	£0.45	£0.75
59 ND	*$0.25*	*$0.75*	*$1.25*	£0.15	£0.45	£0.75
60 ND Nova guest-stars						
	$0.25	*$0.75*	*$1.25*	£0.15	£0.45	£0.75
Title Value:	*$15.30*	*$45.90*	*$76.50*	£9.30	£27.90	£46.50

QUASAR SPECIAL EDITION

Marvel Comics Group; 1 Mar 1992-3 May 1992

	$Good	$Fine	$N.Mint	£Good	£Fine	£N.Mint
1 Galactic Storm part 3, same as issue #32 but news-stand as opposed to Direct Market						
	$0.25	*$0.75*	*$1.25*	£0.15	£0.45	£0.75
2 Galactic Storm part 10 reprinted for news-stand						
	$0.25	*$0.75*	*$1.25*	£0.15	£0.45	£0.75
3 Galactic Storm part 17 reprinted for news-stand						
	$0.25	*$0.75*	*$1.25*	£0.15	£0.45	£0.75
Title Value:	*$0.75*	*$2.25*	*$3.75*	£0.45	£1.35	£2.25

QUEEN OF THE DAMNED, ANNE RICE'S

Innovation,MS; 1 Oct 1991-11 1993

	$Good	$Fine	$N.Mint	£Good	£Fine	£N.Mint
1 ND Vampire Lestat spin-off begins						
	$0.50	*$1.50*	*$2.50*	£0.50	£1.50	£2.50
2-11 ND	*$0.50*	*$1.50*	*$2.50*	£0.40	£1.20	£2.00
Title Value:	*$5.50*	*$16.50*	*$27.50*	£4.50	£13.50	£22.50

Note: issue #12 was advertised and solicited but never cme out. It is rumoured that the issue was just about to ship as Innovation went under and that the copies remained locked in a warehouse...

QUESTION

DC Comics; 1 Feb 1987-36 Mar 1990

	$Good	$Fine	$N.Mint	£Good	£Fine	£N.Mint
1 ND painted cover						
	$0.50	*$1.50*	*$2.50*	£0.30	£0.90	£1.50
2 ND scarce in the U.K. Batman appears						
	$0.50	*$1.50*	*$2.50*	£0.30	£0.90	£1.50
3-5 ND	*$0.50*	*$1.50*	*$2.50*	£0.30	£0.90	£1.50
6-20 ND	*$0.40*	*$1.20*	*$2.00*	£0.25	£0.75	£1.25
21-25 ND	*$0.30*	*$0.90*	*$1.50*	£0.20	£0.60	£1.00
26 ND Riddler appears						
	$0.30	*$0.90*	*$1.50*	£0.20	£0.60	£1.00
27-35 ND	*$0.30*	*$0.90*	*$1.50*	£0.20	£0.60	£1.00
36 ND ties in with Green Arrow Annual #3						
	$0.30	*$0.90*	*$1.50*	£0.20	£0.60	£1.00
Title Value:	*$13.30*	*$39.90*	*$66.50*	£8.45	£25.35	£42.25

Note: Deluxe Format Baxter paper. For Mature Readers

Question: Thunder Over The Abyss

	$Good	$Fine	$N.Mint	£Good	£Fine	£N.Mint
Trade paperback (Mar 1992), reprints issues #1-5				£1.60	£4.80	£8.00

QUESTION ANNUAL, THE

DC Comics; 1 1988-2 1989

	$Good	$Fine	$N.Mint	£Good	£Fine	£N.Mint
1 ND 48pgs, ties in with Green Arrow Annual #1 and Detective Comics Annual #1 (Batman appears)						
	$0.50	*$1.50*	*$2.50*	£0.30	£0.90	£1.50
2 ND 48pgs, ties in with Green Arrow Annual #2						
	$0.50	*$1.50*	*$2.50*	£0.30	£0.90	£1.50
Title Value:	*$1.00*	*$3.00*	*$5.00*	£0.60	£1.80	£3.00

QUESTION QUARTERLY, THE

DC Comics; 1 Nov 1990-5 Spring 1992

	$Good	$Fine	$N.Mint	£Good	£Fine	£N.Mint
1-5 ND 48pgs	*$0.50*	*$1.50*	*$2.50*	£0.30	£0.90	£1.50
Title Value:	*$2.50*	*$7.50*	*$12.50*	£1.50	£4.50	£7.50

Note: issue 2 delayed owing to production problems. Quarterly frequency.

QUESTION RETURNS, THE

DC Comics,OS; 1 Feb 1997

	$Good	$Fine	$N.Mint	£Good	£Fine	£N.Mint
1 ND 48pgs, Denny O'Neil script, Ed Barreto art, Dan Brereton cover						
	$0.70	*$2.10*	*$3.50*	£0.50	£1.50	£2.50
Title Value:	*$0.70*	*$2.10*	*$3.50*	£0.50	£1.50	£2.50

QUESTPROBE

Marvel Comics Group,OS; 1 Aug 1984

	$Good	$Fine	$N.Mint	£Good	£Fine	£N.Mint
1 ND	*$0.30*	*$0.90*	*$1.50*	£0.20	£0.60	£1.00
Title Value:	*$0.30*	*$0.90*	*$1.50*	£0.20	£0.60	£1.00

QUESTPROBE (2ND SERIES)

Marvel Comics Group,MS; 1 Sep 1985-3 Nov 1985

	$Good	$Fine	$N.Mint	£Good	£Fine	£N.Mint
1 ND Hulk appears	*$0.30*	*$0.90*	*$1.50*	£0.20	£0.60	£1.00
2 ND Spiderman appears						
	$0.30	*$0.90*	*$1.50*	£0.20	£0.60	£1.00
3 ND Human Torch and Thing appear						
	$0.30	*$0.90*	*$1.50*	£0.20	£0.60	£1.00
Title Value:	*$0.90*	*$2.70*	*$4.50*	£0.60	£1.80	£3.00

Note: issue #4 was announced but it eventually appeared in Marvel Fanfare #33

R

R.A.Z.E.

Firstlight Comixx; 1 Dec 1994-2 1994

	$Good	$Fine	$N.Mint	£Good	£Fine	£N.Mint
1-2 ND	*$0.60*	*$1.80*	*$3.00*	£0.40	£1.20	£2.00
Title Value:	*$1.20*	*$3.60*	*$6.00*	£0.80	£2.40	£4.00

R.E.B.E.L.S. '94-'96

DC Comics; 0 Oct 1994; 1 Nov 1994-17 Mar 1996

	$Good	$Fine	$N.Mint	£Good	£Fine	£N.Mint
0 (Oct 1994) Zero Hour X-over, origin						
	$0.40	*$1.20*	*$2.00*	£0.25	£0.75	£1.25
1-2	*$0.40*	*$1.20*	*$2.00*	£0.25	£0.75	£1.25
3 title becomes R.E.B.E.L.S. '95						
	$0.40	*$1.20*	*$2.00*	£0.25	£0.75	£1.25
4-10	*$0.40*	*$1.20*	*$2.00*	£0.25	£0.75	£1.25
11 Captain Comet appears						
	$0.40	*$1.20*	*$2.00*	£0.25	£0.75	£1.25
12	*$0.40*	*$1.20*	*$2.00*	£0.25	£0.75	£1.25
13 Underworld Unleashed tie-in						
	$0.40	*$1.20*	*$2.00*	£0.25	£0.75	£1.25

	$Good	$Fine	$N.Mint	£Good	£Fine	£N.Mint
14-17	$0.40	$1.20	$2.00	£0.25	£0.75	£1.25
Title Value:	$7.20	$21.60	$36.00	£4.50	£13.50	£22.50

R.I.P. BRASHER, AVENGER OF THE DEAD
TSR; 1 1990-4 1991

	$Good	$Fine	$N.Mint	£Good	£Fine	£N.Mint
1-4 ND role-playing game; Doug Moench script, cover design by George Perez	$0.50	$1.50	$2.50	£0.30	£0.90	£1.50
Title Value:	$2.00	$6.00	$10.00	£1.20	£3.60	£6.00

R.O.B.O.T. BATTALION 2050
Eclipse,OS; 1 Mar 1988

	$Good	$Fine	$N.Mint	£Good	£Fine	£N.Mint
1 ND Bill Sienkiewicz cover; black and white	$0.30	$0.90	$1.50	£0.20	£0.60	£1.00
Title Value:	$0.30	$0.90	$1.50	£0.20	£0.60	£1.00

RACE OF SCORPIONS
Dark Horse; 1 Sep 1991-4 Dec 1991

	$Good	$Fine	$N.Mint	£Good	£Fine	£N.Mint
Book 1 (1991), 48pgs squarebound, reprints from Dark Horse Presents				£0.50	£1.50	£2.50
Book 2 (1991), 48pgs, reprints as above				£0.50	£1.50	£2.50

RACER-X
Now Comics; 0 May 1988; 1 Jul 1988-11 Aug 1989

	$Good	$Fine	$N.Mint	£Good	£Fine	£N.Mint
0 ND $3.50 cover	$0.50	$1.50	$2.50	£0.30	£0.90	£1.50
1 ND	$0.50	$1.50	$2.50	£0.30	£0.90	£1.50
2-11 ND	$0.40	$1.20	$2.00	£0.25	£0.75	£1.25
Title Value:	$5.00	$15.00	$25.00	£3.10	£9.30	£15.50

RACER-X VOLUME TWO
Now Comics; 1 Sep 1989-9 1990

	$Good	$Fine	$N.Mint	£Good	£Fine	£N.Mint
1-9 ND	$0.30	$0.90	$1.50	£0.20	£0.60	£1.00
Title Value:	$2.70	$8.10	$13.50	£1.80	£5.40	£9.00

RACK & PAIN
Dark Horse,MS; 1 Feb 1994-4 May 1994

	$Good	$Fine	$N.Mint	£Good	£Fine	£N.Mint
1-4 ND Greg Capullo covers	$0.50	$1.50	$2.50	£0.30	£0.90	£1.50
Title Value:	$2.00	$6.00	$10.00	£1.20	£3.60	£6.00

RACK & PAIN: KILLERS
Chaos Comics,MS; 1 Sep 1996-4 Jan 1997

	$Good	$Fine	$N.Mint	£Good	£Fine	£N.Mint
1-4 ND Brian Pulido script, Leonard Jimenez art	$0.60	$1.80	$3.00	£0.40	£1.20	£2.00
Title Value:	$2.40	$7.20	$12.00	£1.60	£4.80	£8.00

RADICAL DREAMER
Blackball Comics;-1 Dec 1994; 0 May 1994; 1 Jun 1994-4 1995

	$Good	$Fine	$N.Mint	£Good	£Fine	£N.Mint
-1 ND immediately precedes issue #0; Poster Format	$0.50	$1.50	$2.50	£0.30	£0.90	£1.50
0-2 ND Mark Wheatley script and art	$0.40	$1.20	$2.00	£0.25	£0.75	£1.25
3-4 ND Mark Wheatley script and art; Poster Format as 16pgs fold out into 2 eight page posters	$0.40	$1.20	$2.00	£0.25	£0.75	£1.25
Title Value:	$2.50	$7.50	$12.50	£1.55	£4.65	£7.75

Note: issue #5 was advertised and solicited but never came out with the collapse of Blackball.

	$Good	$Fine	$N.Mint	£Good	£Fine	£N.Mint
Radical Dreamer: The Dream Collection (Aug 1994) ND pre-bagged set of issues #0 and #1; 10,000 sets				£0.50	£1.50	£2.50

RADICAL DREAMER (2ND SERIES)
Mark's Giant Economy Size Comics; 1 Jun 1995-3 1995

	$Good	$Fine	$N.Mint	£Good	£Fine	£N.Mint
1 ND Mark Wheatley script and art begins; utilizes unpublished material from Blackball series plus new art; black and white	$0.60	$1.80	$3.00	£0.40	£1.20	£2.00
2-3 ND	$0.60	$1.80	$3.00	£0.40	£1.20	£2.00
Title Value:	$1.80	$5.40	$9.00	£1.20	£3.60	£6.00

RADIO BOY
Eclipse,OS; 1 Mar 1987

	$Good	$Fine	$N.Mint	£Good	£Fine	£N.Mint
1 ND Japanimation parody	$0.40	$1.20	$2.00	£0.25	£0.75	£1.25
Title Value:	$0.40	$1.20	$2.00	£0.25	£0.75	£1.25

RADIOACTIVE MAN
Bongo Comics,MS; 1 Dec 1993-6 Oct 1994

	$Good	$Fine	$N.Mint	£Good	£Fine	£N.Mint
1 ND fluorescent red skeleton cover, pull-out poster	$0.70	$2.10	$3.50	£0.50	£1.50	£2.50
2 ND '60s Marvel parody	$0.60	$1.80	$3.00	£0.40	£1.20	£2.00
3 ND 1970s theme issue	$0.50	$1.50	$2.50	£0.30	£0.90	£1.50
4 ND 1980s "dark phoenix" parody	$0.50	$1.50	$2.50	£0.30	£0.90	£1.50
5 ND Watchmen parody	$0.50	$1.50	$2.50	£0.30	£0.90	£1.50
6 ND last issues spoof	$0.50	$1.50	$2.50	£0.30	£0.90	£1.50
Title Value:	$3.30	$9.90	$16.50	£2.10	£6.30	£10.50

RADIOACTIVE MAN 80 PAGE COLOSSAL
Bongo Comics,OS; nn Jul 1995

	$Good	$Fine	$N.Mint	£Good	£Fine	£N.Mint
nn ND 80pgs, contains four stories plus pin-ups	$1.00	$3.00	$5.00	£0.60	£1.80	£3.00
Title Value:	$1.00	$3.00	$5.00	£0.60	£1.80	£3.00

RADIUM AND HIS INTERGALACTIC ODD SQUAD
Fantasy General Comics; 1 1985

	$Good	$Fine	$N.Mint	£Good	£Fine	£N.Mint
1 ND black and white	$0.30	$0.90	$1.50	£0.20	£0.60	£1.00
Title Value:	$0.30	$0.90	$1.50	£0.20	£0.60	£1.00

RAFFERTY ASHCAN
Malibu,OS; nn Nov 1994

	$Good	$Fine	$N.Mint	£Good	£Fine	£N.Mint
nn ND previews Rafferty cross-over storyline; Howard Chaykin cover; black and white	$0.15	$0.45	$0.75	£0.10	£0.30	£0.50
Title Value:	$0.15	$0.45	$0.75	£0.10	£0.30	£0.50

RAGAMUFFINS
Eclipse,OS; 1 Jan 1985

	$Good	$Fine	$N.Mint	£Good	£Fine	£N.Mint
1 ND Gene Colan reprints	$0.40	$1.20	$2.00	£0.25	£0.75	£1.25
Title Value:	$0.40	$1.20	$2.00	£0.25	£0.75	£1.25

RAGMAN
DC Comics; 1 Aug/Sep 1976-5 Jun/Jul 1977

(see Batman Family #20)

	$Good	$Fine	$N.Mint	£Good	£Fine	£N.Mint
1 scarce in the U.K. origin and 1st appearance Ragman	$0.55	$1.75	$3.50	£0.40	£1.25	£2.50
2 scarce in the U.K. origin	$0.40	$1.25	$2.50	£0.30	£1.00	£2.00
3 ND	$0.40	$1.25	$2.50	£0.30	£1.00	£2.00
4-5 very scarce in the U.K. Kubert art	$0.40	$1.25	$2.50	£0.30	£1.00	£2.00
Title Value:	$2.15	$6.75	$13.50	£1.60	£5.25	£10.50

RAGMAN (2ND SERIES)
DC Comics,MS; 1 Oct 1991-8 May 1992

	$Good	$Fine	$N.Mint	£Good	£Fine	£N.Mint
1-2	$0.25	$0.75	$1.25	£0.15	£0.45	£0.75
3 origin	$0.25	$0.75	$1.25	£0.15	£0.45	£0.75
4-5	$0.25	$0.75	$1.25	£0.15	£0.45	£0.75
6-8 Batman appears	$0.25	$0.75	$1.25	£0.15	£0.45	£0.75
Title Value:	$2.00	$6.00	$10.00	£1.20	£3.60	£6.00

RAGMAN: CRY OF THE DEAD
DC Comics,MS; 1 Aug 1993-6 Jan 1994

	$Good	$Fine	$N.Mint	£Good	£Fine	£N.Mint
1-6 Joe Kubert covers	$0.30	$0.90	$1.50	£0.20	£0.60	£1.00
Title Value:	$1.80	$5.40	$9.00	£1.20	£3.60	£6.00

RAI
Valiant; 0 Oct 1992; 1 Mar 1992-8 Sep 1992; 9 Apr 1993-33 Apr 1995

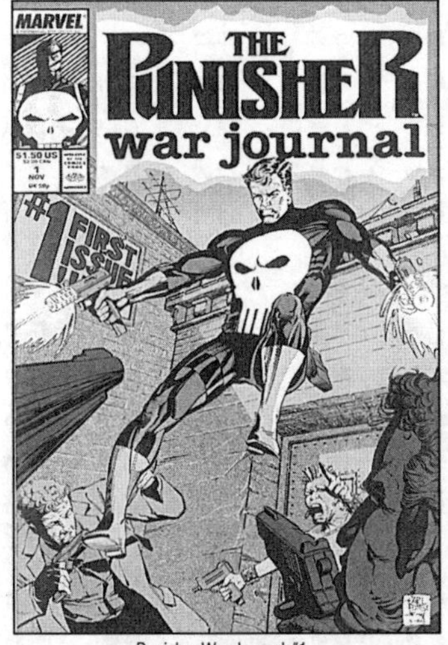

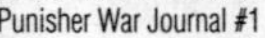
Punisher War Journal #1

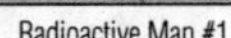
Radioactive Man #1

Ragman (1st) #3

Issue	$Good	$Fine	$N.Mint	£Good	£Fine	£N.Mint
0 (Oct 1992), origin of Rising Spirit, guest-stars all Valiant heroes; joint 1st appearance (cameo) Bloodshot (see Eternal Warrior #4). Note: shipped before Eternal Warrior #4 though same cover date	$1.50	$4.50	$7.50	£1.00	£3.00	£5.00
0 glossy cover, as above	$2.00	$6.00	$10.00	£1.20	£3.60	£6.00
1	$1.50	$4.50	$7.50	£1.00	£3.00	£5.00
2	$1.50	$4.50	$7.50	£0.80	£2.40	£4.00
3 scarce in both US and UK	$1.50	$4.50	$7.50	£1.00	£3.00	£5.00
4 very scarce in the U.K., scarce in the U.S. (the scarcest Valiant comic)	$2.00	$6.00	$10.00	£1.20	£3.60	£6.00
5	$0.80	$2.40	$4.00	£0.40	£1.20	£2.00
6 Unity: Chapter 7	$0.80	$2.40	$4.00	£0.40	£1.20	£2.00
7 Unity: Chapter 15, Sting appears, Walt Simonson cover; death of Rai	$0.80	$2.40	$4.00	£0.40	£1.20	£2.00
8 Unity aftermath, exploring the consequences of the death of Rai during Unity	$0.80	$2.40	$4.00	£0.40	£1.20	£2.00
9 title returns as "Rai & the Future Force"; story continued from Magnus #24; Magnus now appears throughout	$0.50	$1.50	$2.50	£0.30	£0.90	£1.50
9 Gold Edition, ND 5,000 print run	$1.50	$4.50	$7.50	£1.00	£3.00	£5.00
10	$0.50	$1.50	$2.50	£0.30	£0.90	£1.50
11-20	$0.40	$1.20	$2.00	£0.25	£0.75	£1.25
21 with free Upper Deck trading card	$0.40	$1.20	$2.00	£0.25	£0.75	£1.25
22 continued from Magnus #37	$0.40	$1.20	$2.00	£0.25	£0.75	£1.25
23-24	$0.40	$1.20	$2.00	£0.25	£0.75	£1.25
25 sub-titled "The New.."	$0.40	$1.20	$2.00	£0.25	£0.75	£1.25
26 Chaos Effect tie-in	$0.40	$1.20	$2.00	£0.25	£0.75	£1.25
27 ties-in with Magnus Robot Fighter #42	$0.40	$1.20	$2.00	£0.25	£0.75	£1.25
28-33	$0.40	$1.20	$2.00	£0.25	£0.75	£1.25
Title Value:	$24.90	$74.70	$124.50	£15.15	£45.45	£75.75

Note: all ND in the U.K.

Issue	$Good	$Fine	$N.Mint	£Good	£Fine	£N.Mint
Rai (1994) Trade paperback reprints issues #0-4				£1.60	£4.80	£8.00

RAIDERS OF THE LOST ARK

Marvel Comics Group,MS Film; 1 Sep 1981-3 Nov 1981

Issue	$Good	$Fine	$N.Mint	£Good	£Fine	£N.Mint
1-2 ND adapts film, Walt Simonson script	$0.25	$0.75	$1.25	£0.15	£0.45	£0.75
3 ND adapts film, Walt Simonson script and cover art	$0.25	$0.75	$1.25	£0.15	£0.45	£0.75
Title Value:	$0.75	$2.25	$3.75	£0.45	£1.35	£2.25

RAIN

Tundra Publishing,MS; 1 May 1991-5 1991

Issue	$Good	$Fine	$N.Mint	£Good	£Fine	£N.Mint
1-5 ND	$0.40	$1.20	$2.00	£0.25	£0.75	£1.25
Title Value:	$2.00	$6.00	$10.00	£1.25	£3.75	£6.25

RAINBOW BRITE AND THE STAR STEALER

DC Comics,OS TV Toy; nn 1985

Issue	$Good	$Fine	$N.Mint	£Good	£Fine	£N.Mint
nn ND very scarce in the U.K. adapts animated film	$0.15	$0.45	$0.75	£0.10	£0.35	£0.60
Title Value:	$0.15	$0.45	$0.75	£0.10	£0.35	£0.60

RALPH SNART - THE LOST ISSUES

Now Comics,MS; 1 Apr 1993-3 Jun 1993

Issue	$Good	$Fine	$N.Mint	£Good	£Fine	£N.Mint
1 ND pre-bagged with trading card; features the issues originally meant to be #27-29 of the 1990 series (note: two different trading cards available)	$0.30	$0.90	$1.50	£0.20	£0.60	£1.00
2-3 ND	$0.30	$0.90	$1.50	£0.20	£0.60	£1.00
Title Value:	$0.90	$2.70	$4.50	£0.60	£1.80	£3.00

RALPH SNART ADVENTURES

Now Comics,MS; 1 Jun 1986-3 Oct 1986

Issue	$Good	$Fine	$N.Mint	£Good	£Fine	£N.Mint
1-3 ND	$0.30	$0.90	$1.50	£0.20	£0.60	£1.00
Title Value:	$0.90	$2.70	$4.50	£0.60	£1.80	£3.00

RALPH SNART ADVENTURES (2ND SERIES)

Now Comics; 1 Nov 1986-9 Jul 1987

Issue	$Good	$Fine	$N.Mint	£Good	£Fine	£N.Mint
1-7 ND	$0.30	$0.90	$1.50	£0.20	£0.60	£1.00
8-9 ND 1st colour issues	$0.30	$0.90	$1.50	£0.20	£0.60	£1.00
Title Value:	$2.70	$8.10	$13.50	£1.80	£5.40	£9.00
Ralph Snart Adventures (Oct 1992) Trade paperback reprints issues #1-3, new cover by Marc Hansen				£1.00	£3.00	£5.00
Ralph Snart Adventures II Trade paperback reprints issues #5-7, new cover by Marc Hansen				£1.00	£3.00	£5.00

RALPH SNART ADVENTURES (3RD SERIES)

Now Comics; 1 Sep 1988-31 1992

Issue	$Good	$Fine	$N.Mint	£Good	£Fine	£N.Mint
1 ND reprints vol 2 in colour	$0.40	$1.20	$2.00	£0.25	£0.75	£1.25
2-7 ND reprints vol 2 in colour	$0.30	$0.90	$1.50	£0.20	£0.60	£1.00
8-23 ND Comics Code on cover	$0.30	$0.90	$1.50	£0.20	£0.60	£1.00
24 ND Comics Code on cover, 3-D issue with glasses (25% less without glasses)	$0.30	$0.90	$1.50	£0.20	£0.60	£1.00
25-31 ND Comics Code on cover	$0.30	$0.90	$1.50	£0.20	£0.60	£1.00
Title Value:	$9.40	$28.20	$47.00	£6.25	£18.75	£31.25
Trade Paperback (1989) reprints #1-7, full colour; comic book size				£1.70	£5.10	£8.50
black and white paperback size				£0.60	£1.80	£3.00

RALPH SNART ADVENTURES (4TH SERIES)

Now Comics,MS; 1 May 1992-3 Jul 1992

Issue	$Good	$Fine	$N.Mint	£Good	£Fine	£N.Mint
1-3 ND pre-bagged, 4 different trading cards available, one in each variant	$0.30	$0.90	$1.50	£0.20	£0.60	£1.00
Title Value:	$0.90	$2.70	$4.50	£0.60	£1.80	£3.00

RALPH SNART ADVENTURES (5TH SERIES)

Now Comics; 1 Jul 1993-12 May 1994

Issue	$Good	$Fine	$N.Mint	£Good	£Fine	£N.Mint
1-12 Direct Market Edition - pre-bagged with trading card	$0.30	$0.90	$1.50	£0.20	£0.60	£1.00
1-12 Newstand Edition, un-bagged/without card	$0.25	$0.75	$1.25	£0.15	£0.45	£0.75
Title Value:	$6.35	$19.05	$31.75	£4.05	£12.15	£20.25

Note: all Non-Distributed on the news-stands in the U.K.

RALPH SNART ADVENTURES (6TH SERIES)

Now Comics; 1 Aug 1994

Issue	$Good	$Fine	$N.Mint	£Good	£Fine	£N.Mint
1 ND Marc Hansen script and art; colour	$0.30	$0.90	$1.50	£0.20	£0.60	£1.00
Title Value:	$0.30	$0.90	$1.50	£0.20	£0.60	£1.00

RALPH SNART ADVENTURES 3-D SPECIAL

Now Comics,OS; 1 Oct 1992

Issue	$Good	$Fine	$N.Mint	£Good	£Fine	£N.Mint
1 ND pre-bagged with glasses (25% less without glasses)	$0.40	$1.20	$2.00	£0.25	£0.75	£1.25
1 Special Edition, ND as above plus 12 trading cards	$0.50	$1.50	$2.50	£0.30	£0.90	£1.50
Title Value:	$0.90	$2.70	$4.50	£0.55	£1.65	£2.75

RAMAR OF THE JUNGLE

Charlton; 1 1954; 2 Sep 1955-5 Sep 1956

Issue	$Good	$Fine	$N.Mint	£Good	£Fine	£N.Mint
1 ND scarce in the U.K. based on 1950s TV series starring Jon Hall as a great white hunter	$13.50	$41.00	$110.00	£9.25	£28.00	£75.00
2-5 ND	$9.25	$28.00	$75.00	£6.25	£18.50	£50.00
Title Value:	$50.50	$153.00	$410.00	£34.25	£102.00	£275.00

Note: all Non-Distributed on the news-stands in the U.K.

RAMBO IN 3-D

Blackthorne;(3-D Series #49) 1 Autumn 1988

Issue	$Good	$Fine	$N.Mint	£Good	£Fine	£N.Mint
1 ND based on Stallone film; with bound-in 3-D glasses (25% less if without glasses)	$0.50	$1.50	$2.50	£0.30	£0.90	£1.50
Title Value:	$0.50	$1.50	$2.50	£0.30	£0.90	£1.50

RAMM

Megaton Comics; 1 May 1987-2 Sep 1987

Issue	$Good	$Fine	$N.Mint	£Good	£Fine	£N.Mint
1 ND scarce in the U.K. 1st appearance of Youngblood by Rob Liefeld and Hank Kanalz in a 1pg advert; black and white	$0.60	$1.80	$3.00	£0.80	£2.40	£4.00
2 ND scarce in the U.K. 1pg advert for Youngblood	$0.40	$1.20	$2.00	£0.40	£1.20	£2.00
Title Value:	$1.00	$3.00	$5.00	£1.20	£3.60	£6.00

RAMPAGE (VALIANT)

Valiant; 1995

Cross-over storyline running throughout the following issues:
Bloodshot #27,
Secret Weapons #20,
Bloodshot #28,
Secret Weapons #28,
Bloodshot #29.

RAMPAGING HULK

Marvel Comics Group,Magazine; 1 Jan 1977-27 Jun 1981

(titled Rampaging Hulk #1-9; becomes The Hulk with #10)

Issue	$Good	$Fine	$N.Mint	£Good	£Fine	£N.Mint
1 LD in the U.K. Walt Simonson art	$1.00	$3.00	$6.00	£0.65	£2.00	£4.00
2 original X-Men appear, X-Men article, Walt Simonson art	$1.65	$5.00	$10.00	£0.65	£2.00	£4.00
3 Iron Man appears in Bloodstone back-up story, Walt Simonson art; Earl Norem painted cover	$0.50	$1.50	$3.00	£0.30	£1.00	£2.00
4 Jim Starlin and Nino art; Giffen art on super-villain histories and Marshall Rogers art on 2pg intro to Bloodstone story	$0.50	$1.50	$3.00	£0.30	£1.00	£2.00
5-6 Sub-Mariner vs. Hulk	$0.50	$1.50	$3.00	£0.30	£1.00	£2.00
7 Gerber script and Jim Starlin art on Man-Thing back-up story	$0.50	$1.50	$3.00	£0.30	£1.00	£2.00
8 LD in the U.K. original Avengers appear, George Perez art (1pg)	$0.50	$1.50	$3.00	£0.30	£1.00	£2.00
9 original Avengers appear; Shanna She-Devil ckecklist and portfolio	$0.50	$1.50	$3.00	£0.30	£1.00	£2.00
10 ND	$0.50	$1.50	$3.00	£0.30	£1.00	£2.00
11-12 ND Moon Knight story	$0.50	$1.50	$3.00	£0.30	£1.00	£2.00
13 ND Moon Knight; Sienkiewicz art	$0.50	$1.50	$3.00	£0.30	£1.00	£2.00
14 ND Moon Knight story; Sienkiewicz art	$0.50	$1.50	$3.00	£0.30	£1.00	£2.00
15 ND Moon Knight story; Sienkiewicz art	$0.50	$1.50	$2.50	£0.30	£0.90	£1.50
16 ND Mike Zeck art, Bissette art (1pg)	$0.50	$1.50	$2.50	£0.30	£0.90	£1.50
17-18 ND Moon Knight story; Sienkiewicz art	$0.50	$1.50	$2.50	£0.30	£0.90	£1.50
19 ND	$0.50	$1.50	$2.50	£0.30	£0.90	£1.50
20 ND Moon Knight story; Sienkiewicz art	$0.50	$1.50	$2.50	£0.30	£0.90	£1.50
21-24 ND	$0.50	$1.50	$2.50	£0.30	£0.90	£1.50
25 ND Chaykin art	$0.50	$1.50	$2.50	£0.30	£0.90	£1.50

Issue	$Good	$Fine	$N.Mint	£Good	£Fine	£N.Mint
26 ND	$0.50	$1.50	$2.50	£0.30	£0.90	£1.50
27 ND Walt Simonson art (1pg)	$0.50	$1.50	$2.50	£0.30	£0.90	£1.50
Title Value:	$15.15	$45.50	$84.50	£8.80	£27.70	£51.50

FEATURES

Bloodstone in 1-6,8. Dominic Fortune by Chaykin in 21-25. Hulk in 1-27. Man-Thing in 7. Moon Knight in 11-15,17,18,20. Shanna in 9.

RAMTHAR, MIKE DEODATO'S

Caliber Press,OS; 1 Mar 1996

Issue	$Good	$Fine	$N.Mint	£Good	£Fine	£N.Mint
1 ND Mike Deodato cover and art; black and white	$0.60	$1.80	$3.00	£0.40	£1.20	£2.00
Title Value:	$0.60	$1.80	$3.00	£0.40	£1.20	£2.00

RANMA ½

Viz Communications,MS; 1 Jul 1992-7 Jan 1993

Issue	$Good	$Fine	$N.Mint	£Good	£Fine	£N.Mint
1 ND Rumiko Takahashi; black and white	$2.00	$6.00	$10.00	£0.80	£2.40	£4.00
2 ND Rumiko Takahashi; black and white	$1.20	$3.60	$6.00	£0.70	£2.10	£3.50
3-7 ND Rumiko Takahashi; black and white	$0.90	$2.70	$4.50	£0.60	£1.80	£3.00
Title Value:	$7.70	$23.10	$38.50	£4.50	£13.50	£22.50
Ranma ½ Graphic Novel (Jul 1993) reprints series; 300pgs				£2.30	£6.90	£11.50

RANMA ½ PART 2

Viz Communications,MS; 1 Mar 1993-11 Jan 1994

Issue	$Good	$Fine	$N.Mint	£Good	£Fine	£N.Mint
1 ND Rumiko Takahashi; black and white	$0.80	$2.40	$4.00	£0.40	£1.20	£2.00
2-11 ND Rumiko Takahashi; black and white	$0.50	$1.50	$2.50	£0.30	£0.90	£1.50
Title Value:	$5.80	$17.40	$29.00	£3.40	£10.20	£17.00
Ranma ½ Graphic Novel 2 (June 1994) reprints first half of series, black and white				£2.00	£6.00	£10.00
Ranma ½ Graphic Novel 3 Aug 1994) reprints second half of series, black and white				£2.00	£6.00	£10.00

RANMA ½ PART 3

Viz Communications,MS; 1 Feb 1994-13 Feb 1995

Issue	$Good	$Fine	$N.Mint	£Good	£Fine	£N.Mint
1-13 ND Rumiko Takahashi; black and white	$0.50	$1.50	$2.50	£0.30	£0.90	£1.50
Title Value:	$6.50	$19.50	$32.50	£3.90	£11.70	£19.50
Ranma ½ Volume 4 (Jul 1995) collects the first half of part three				£2.10	£6.30	£10.50
Ranma ½ Volume 5 (Sep 1995) collects second half of part three				£2.10	£6.30	£10.50

RANMA ½ PART 4

Viz Communications,MS; 1 Jan 1995-11 Nov 1995

Issue	$Good	$Fine	$N.Mint	£Good	£Fine	£N.Mint
1-11 ND Rumiko Takahashi; black and white	$0.50	$1.50	$2.50	£0.30	£0.90	£1.50
Title Value:	$5.50	$16.50	$27.50	£3.30	£9.90	£16.50

RANMA ½ PART 5

Viz Communications,MS; 1 Dec 1995-12 Nov 1996

Issue	$Good	$Fine	$N.Mint	£Good	£Fine	£N.Mint
1-12 ND Rumiko Takahashi script and art; black and white	$0.60	$1.80	$3.00	£0.40	£1.20	£2.00
Title Value:	$7.20	$21.60	$36.00	£4.80	£14.40	£24.00

RAPHAEL

Mirage Studios,Oversized; 1 1985

(see Teenage Mutant Ninja Turtles)

Issue	$Good	$Fine	$N.Mint	£Good	£Fine	£N.Mint
1 ND orange/black/white cover, 1st appearance Casey Jones	$1.00	$3.00	$5.00	£0.70	£2.10	£3.50
1 2nd printing, ND new 10 page story, new painted cover (blue)	$0.60	$1.80	$3.00	£0.40	£1.20	£2.00
Title Value:	$1.60	$4.80	$8.00	£1.10	£3.30	£5.50

RAPLH SNART ADVENTURES SUMMER SPECIAL

Now Comics,OS; 1 Jul 1994

Issue	$Good	$Fine	$N.Mint	£Good	£Fine	£N.Mint
1 ND Marc Hansen script and art	$0.40	$1.20	$2.00	£0.25	£0.75	£1.25
Title Value:	$0.40	$1.20	$2.00	£0.25	£0.75	£1.25

RAPTUS

Knight Angel Studios; 1 Dec 1995

Issue	$Good	$Fine	$N.Mint	£Good	£Fine	£N.Mint
1 ND Juan Alcantara art; black and white	$1.00	$3.00	$5.00	£0.60	£1.80	£3.00
1 Variant Cover Edition, ND (Jan 1996), Ricky Carrelero cover, limited to 1,000 copies	$1.40	$4.20	$7.00	£0.90	£2.70	£4.50
Title Value:	$2.40	$7.20	$12.00	£1.50	£4.50	£7.50

RARE BIT FIENDS

King Hell; 1 Jul 1994-present

Issue	$Good	$Fine	$N.Mint	£Good	£Fine	£N.Mint
1-20 ND Rick Veitch script and art; black and white	$0.60	$1.80	$3.00	£0.40	£1.20	£2.00
Title Value:	$12.00	$36.00	$60.00	£8.00	£24.00	£40.00

RASCALS IN PARADISE

Dark Horse,MS; 1 Jul 1994-3 Nov 1994

Issue	$Good	$Fine	$N.Mint	£Good	£Fine	£N.Mint
1-3 ND Jim Silke script and art; oversize format	$0.80	$2.40	$4.00	£0.50	£1.50	£2.50
Title Value:	$2.40	$7.20	$12.00	£1.50	£4.50	£7.50
Rascals in Paradise (Oct 1995) Trade paperback collects issues #1-3 with Dave Stevens/Geof Darrow introduction				£2.30	£6.90	£11.50
Rascals in Paradise Limited Edition Hardcover (May 1996) ND 104pgs, with new plate and dust-jacket				£11.00	£33.00	£66.00

RATMAN: DARK CIRCLE

Comico,MS; 1 Jul 1993-4 Oct 1993

Issue	$Good	$Fine	$N.Mint	£Good	£Fine	£N.Mint
1 ND Elementals spin-off	$0.40	$1.20	$2.00	£0.25	£0.75	£1.25
1 Limited Edition, ND - with poster	$0.50	$1.50	$2.50	£0.30	£0.90	£1.50
2-4 ND	$0.40	$1.20	$2.00	£0.25	£0.75	£1.25
Title Value:	$2.10	$6.30	$10.50	£1.30	£3.90	£6.50

RAVAGE

Fathom Press; 1 Jun 1992

Issue	$Good	$Fine	$N.Mint	£Good	£Fine	£N.Mint
1 ND black and white	$0.30	$0.90	$1.50	£0.20	£0.60	£1.00
Title Value:	$0.30	$0.90	$1.50	£0.20	£0.60	£1.00

RAVAGE 2099

Marvel Comics Group; 1 Dec 1992-33 Aug 1995

Issue	$Good	$Fine	$N.Mint	£Good	£Fine	£N.Mint
1 ND Stan Lee script begins, gold foil-stamped cover	$0.30	$0.90	$1.50	£0.20	£0.60	£1.00
2-9 ND	$0.25	$0.75	$1.25	£0.15	£0.45	£0.75
10 ND new direction for title with Pat Mills scripting	$0.25	$0.75	$1.25	£0.15	£0.45	£0.75
11-13 ND	$0.25	$0.75	$1.25	£0.15	£0.45	£0.75
14 ND Punisher 2099 appears	$0.25	$0.75	$1.25	£0.15	£0.45	£0.75
15 ND continued in X-Men 2099 #5	$0.25	$0.75	$1.25	£0.15	£0.45	£0.75
16-17 ND	$0.25	$0.75	$1.25	£0.15	£0.45	£0.75
18 ND with free Spiderman vs. Venom card sheet	$0.25	$0.75	$1.25	£0.15	£0.45	£0.75
19-24 ND	$0.25	$0.75	$1.25	£0.15	£0.45	£0.75
25 ND 48pgs	$0.30	$0.90	$1.50	£0.20	£0.60	£1.00
26-30 ND	$0.25	$0.75	$1.25	£0.15	£0.45	£0.75
31 ND upgraded paper stock begins	$0.25	$0.75	$1.25	£0.15	£0.45	£0.75
32 ND	$0.25	$0.75	$1.25	£0.15	£0.45	£0.75
33 ND Doom vs. Ravage	$0.25	$0.75	$1.25	£0.15	£0.45	£0.75
Title Value:	$8.35	$25.05	$41.75	£5.05	£15.15	£25.25

RAVEN, THE

Dell/Movie Classics,OS Movie; 12-680-309 Sep 1963

Issue	$Good	$Fine	$N.Mint	£Good	£Fine	£N.Mint
12-680-309 distributed in the U.K. film adaptation with Vincent Price; photo cover	$7.00	$21.00	$50.00	£3.55	£10.50	£25.00
Title Value:	$7.00	$21.00	$50.00	£3.55	£10.50	£25.00

RAVENS & RAINBOWS

Pacific,OS; 1 1983

Issue	$Good	$Fine	$N.Mint	£Good	£Fine	£N.Mint
1 ND Jeff Jones reprints	$0.30	$0.90	$1.50	£0.20	£0.60	£1.00
Title Value:	$0.30	$0.90	$1.50	£0.20	£0.60	£1.00

RAVER

Malibu,MS; 1 Apr 1993-3 Jun 1993

Issue	$Good	$Fine	$N.Mint	£Good	£Fine	£N.Mint
1 Walter Koenig ("Chekov" in Star Trek) script begins, foil-enhanced "oil-slick" cover; Direct Sales Edition	$0.50	$1.50	$2.50	£0.30	£0.90	£1.50
1 Newstand Edition	$0.40	$1.20	$2.00	£0.25	£0.75	£1.25
2-3	$0.40	$1.20	$2.00	£0.25	£0.75	£1.25
Title Value:	$1.70	$5.10	$8.50	£1.05	£3.15	£5.25

Note: all Non-Distributed on the news-stands in the U.K.

RAVER, WALTER KOENIG'S

Millennium; 0 Dec 1995; 1 Nov 1994

Issue	$Good	$Fine	$N.Mint	£Good	£Fine	£N.Mint
0 ND (Dec 1995) story continues from issue #1	$0.40	$1.20	$2.00	£0.25	£0.75	£1.25
0 Collectors Edition, ND (Dec 1995)	$1.00	$3.00	$5.00	£0.70	£2.10	£3.50
1 ND	$0.40	$1.20	$2.00	£0.25	£0.75	£1.25
1 Deluxe Edition, ND - with foil cover designed by Walter Koenig	$0.50	$1.50	$2.50	£0.30	£0.90	£1.50
Title Value:	$2.30	$6.90	$11.50	£1.50	£4.50	£7.50

RAWHIDE KID

Atlas/Marvel Comics Group; 1 Mar 1955-151 May 1979

Issue	$Good	$Fine	$N.Mint	£Good	£Fine	£N.Mint
1 scarce in the U.K. Wyatt Earp appears	$72.50	$220.00	$515.00	£50.00	£150.00	£350.00
2 scarce in the U.K.	$30.00	$90.00	$210.00	£21.00	£62.50	£150.00
3-5	$19.00	$57.50	$135.00	£12.50	£39.00	£90.00
6-10	$15.50	$47.00	$110.00	£10.50	£32.00	£75.00
11-16	$12.50	$39.00	$90.00	£8.50	£26.00	£60.00
1st official distribution in the U.K.						
17 origin, Jack Kirby art	$21.00	$62.50	$150.00	£11.00	£34.00	£80.00
18-20 rare in the U.K.	$10.50	$32.00	$75.00	£5.50	£17.00	£40.00
21-22 scarce in the U.K.	$9.25	$28.00	$65.00	£5.25	£16.00	£37.50
23 scarce in the U.K. origin retold by Jack Kirby	$19.00	$57.50	$135.00	£10.00	£30.00	£70.00
24-30 scarce in the U.K.	$9.25	$28.00	$65.00	£5.25	£16.00	£37.50
31-39	$7.75	$23.50	$55.00	£4.25	£12.50	£30.00
40 Two-Gun Kid X-over	$7.75	$23.50	$55.00	£4.25	£12.50	£30.00
41-44	$7.00	$21.00	$50.00	£3.55	£10.50	£25.00
45 origin retold	$8.50	$26.00	$60.00	£4.25	£12.50	£30.00
46 Toth art	$5.00	$15.00	$35.00	£2.50	£7.50	£17.50
47-50	$5.00	$15.00	$35.00	£2.50	£7.50	£17.50
51-60	$4.55	$13.50	$27.50	£2.30	£7.00	£14.00
61-68	$3.75	$11.00	$22.50	£2.05	£6.25	£12.50
69-70 ND	$3.75	$11.00	$22.50	£2.25	£6.75	£13.50

	$Good	$Fine	$N.Mint	£Good	£Fine	£N.Mint
71-74 ND	$2.50	$7.50	$15.00	£1.40	£4.25	£8.50
75-78	$2.50	$7.50	$15.00	£1.15	£3.50	£7.00
79 Williamson reprints	$2.50	$7.50	$15.00	£1.15	£3.50	£7.00
80-85	$2.50	$7.50	$15.00	£1.15	£3.50	£7.00
86 Williamson reprints	$1.65	$5.00	$10.00	£1.00	£3.00	£6.00
87-88	$1.65	$5.00	$10.00	£1.00	£3.00	£6.00
89-92 ND	$1.65	$5.00	$10.00	£1.05	£3.25	£6.50
93 ND 52pgs	$2.05	$6.25	$12.50	£1.15	£3.50	£7.00
94	$1.65	$5.00	$10.00	£1.00	£3.00	£6.00
95 ND Williamson reprint	$1.65	$5.00	$10.00	£1.05	£3.25	£6.50
96-99	$1.65	$5.00	$10.00	£0.80	£2.50	£5.00
100	$2.50	$7.50	$15.00	£1.25	£3.75	£7.50
101-110	$1.00	$3.00	$6.00	£0.65	£2.00	£4.00
111 ND Williamson reprint	$1.00	$3.00	$6.00	£0.65	£2.00	£4.00
112-125	$1.00	$3.00	$6.00	£0.50	£1.50	£3.00
126-151	$1.00	$3.00	$6.00	£0.40	£1.25	£2.50
Title Value:	$803.25	$2428.75	$5476.00	£471.75	£1431.50	£3250.00

Note: Kirby art in 17-32, 34, 42, 43. Most later issues are entirely reprint.

RAWHIDE KID (2ND SERIES)

Marvel Comics Group,MS; 1 Aug 1985-4 Nov 1985

	$Good	$Fine	$N.Mint	£Good	£Fine	£N.Mint
1-4 ND	$0.25	$0.75	$1.25	£0.15	£0.45	£0.75
Title Value:	$1.00	$3.00	$5.00	£0.60	£1.80	£3.00

RAWHIDE KID ANNUAL

Marvel Comics Group; 1 Sep 1971

	$Good	$Fine	$N.Mint	£Good	£Fine	£N.Mint
1 ND scarce in the U.K. 72pgs, all reprint	$1.25	$3.75	$7.50	£0.80	£2.50	£5.00
Title Value:	$1.25	$3.75	$7.50	£0.80	£2.50	£5.00

RAY BRADBURY COMICS

Topps,MS; 1 Apr 1993-5 Aug 1993

	$Good	$Fine	$N.Mint	£Good	£Fine	£N.Mint
1 pre-bagged with 3 trading cards, all-dinosaur issue with work by Richard Corben and Al Williamson	$0.60	$1.80	$3.00	£0.40	£1.20	£2.00
2 pre-bagged with 3 trading cards, all-horror issue with work by Sean Phillips	$0.60	$1.80	$3.00	£0.40	£1.20	£2.00
3 pre-bagged with 3 trading cards, all-dinosaur issue; Jurassic Park preview	$0.60	$1.80	$3.00	£0.40	£1.20	£2.00
4 pre-bagged with 3 trading cards, all-Mars Attacks issue; Jurassic Park preview	$0.60	$1.80	$3.00	£0.40	£1.20	£2.00
5 pre-bagged with 3 trading cards	$0.60	$1.80	$3.00	£0.40	£1.20	£2.00
Title Value:	$3.00	$9.00	$15.00	£2.00	£6.00	£10.00

Note: all Non-Distributed on the news-stands in the U.K.

RAY BRADBURY COMICS SPECIAL: TALES OF HORROR

Topps,OS; 1 May 1994

	$Good	$Fine	$N.Mint	£Good	£Fine	£N.Mint
1 ND adaptations of Bradbury horror stories, Kelley Jones cover	$0.40	$1.20	$2.00	£0.25	£0.75	£1.25
Title Value:	$0.40	$1.20	$2.00	£0.25	£0.75	£1.25

RAY BRADBURY COMICS SPECIAL: THE ILLUSTRATED MAN

Topps,OS; 1 Apr 1994

	$Good	$Fine	$N.Mint	£Good	£Fine	£N.Mint
1 ND Ray Bradbury stories adapted by Guy Davis, P. Craig Russell and Michael Lark; foil etched cover	$0.60	$1.80	$3.00	£0.40	£1.20	£2.00
Title Value:	$0.60	$1.80	$3.00	£0.40	£1.20	£2.00

RAY BRADBURY'S MARTIAN CHRONICLES SPECIAL EDITION

Topps,OS; 1 Jun 1994

	$Good	$Fine	$N.Mint	£Good	£Fine	£N.Mint
1 ND adaptations of Bradbury's Martian Chronicles; foreword by Mike Kaluta, cover by Jim Steranko	$0.40	$1.20	$2.00	£0.25	£0.75	£1.25
Title Value:	$0.40	$1.20	$2.00	£0.25	£0.75	£1.25

RAY, THE

DC Comics,MS; 1 Feb 1992-6 Jul 1992

	$Good	$Fine	$N.Mint	£Good	£Fine	£N.Mint
1 Joe Quesada art begins	$0.80	$2.40	$4.00	£0.50	£1.50	£2.50
2-3	$0.50	$1.50	$2.50	£0.30	£0.90	£1.50
4-6	$0.40	$1.20	$2.00	£0.25	£0.75	£1.25
Title Value:	$3.00	$9.00	$15.00	£1.85	£5.55	£9.25
The Ray: In A Blaze of Power (May 1994) Trade paperback reprints mini-series with new cover by Joe Quesada and Brian Stelfreeze				£1.30	£3.90	£6.50

RAY, THE (2ND SERIES)

DC Comics; 0 Oct 1994; 1 May 1994-28 Oct 1996

	$Good	$Fine	$N.Mint	£Good	£Fine	£N.Mint
0 (Oct 1994) Zero Hour X-over, origin retold	$0.40	$1.20	$2.00	£0.25	£0.75	£1.25
1 Howard Porter and Robert Jones art, Christopher Priest script, Joe Quesada cover	$0.40	$1.20	$2.00	£0.25	£0.75	£1.25
1 Collectors Edition, ND gold foil embossed cover by Joe Quesada	$0.60	$1.80	$3.00	£0.40	£1.20	£2.00
2-5	$0.40	$1.20	$2.00	£0.25	£0.75	£1.25
6-7 Black Canary appears	$0.40	$1.20	$2.00	£0.25	£0.75	£1.25
8 Lobo appears	$0.40	$1.20	$2.00	£0.25	£0.75	£1.25
9-15	$0.40	$1.20	$2.00	£0.25	£0.75	£1.25
16-17	$0.45	$1.35	$2.25	£0.30	£0.90	£1.50
18-19 Underworld Unleashed tie-in	$0.45	$1.35	$2.25	£0.30	£0.90	£1.50
20-21 Black Condor guest-stars	$0.45	$1.35	$2.25	£0.30	£0.90	£1.50
22-24	$0.45	$1.35	$2.25	£0.30	£0.90	£1.50
25 48pgs	$0.70	$2.10	$3.50	£0.50	£1.50	£2.50
26-28	$0.45	$1.35	$2.25	£0.30	£0.90	£1.50
Title Value:	$13.10	$39.30	$65.50	£8.50	£25.50	£42.50

RAY, THE (2ND SERIES) ANNUAL

DC Comics; 1 Jun 1995

	$Good	$Fine	$N.Mint	£Good	£Fine	£N.Mint
1 64pgs, Year One	$0.80	$2.40	$4.00	£0.50	£1.50	£2.50
Title Value:	$0.80	$2.40	$4.00	£0.50	£1.50	£2.50

RAZOR

London Night Studios; ½ Apr 1995; 0 May 1992; 1 Sep 1992-present

	$Good	$Fine	$N.Mint	£Good	£Fine	£N.Mint
½ ND (Apr 1995), Joseph Michael Linsner cover art, produced in conjunction with Fan magazine, 1st appearance Poizon; colour, 16 pages	$4.00	$12.00	$20.00	£2.50	£7.50	£12.50
0 ND 1st appearance Razor	$10.00	$30.00	$50.00	£6.00	£18.00	£30.00
0 2nd printing, ND (Aug 1992)	$0.80	$2.40	$4.00	£0.50	£1.50	£2.50
0 London Night Special Edition, ND (May 1995) - features the first Razor story, re-drawn by Richard Pollard; black and white	$0.80	$2.40	$4.00	£0.50	£1.50	£2.50
1 ND Everett Hartsoe script begins; 1st appearance Stryke, black and white	$9.00	$27.00	$45.00	£6.00	£18.00	£30.00
1 2nd printing, ND photo cover	$1.50	$4.50	$7.50	£1.00	£3.00	£5.00
2 ND	$6.00	$18.00	$30.00	£3.50	£10.50	£17.50
2 2nd printing, ND (1996) card-stock cover	$0.60	$1.80	$3.00	£0.40	£1.20	£2.00
2 Limited Edition, ND red and blue cover variants	$10.00	$30.00	$50.00	£5.00	£15.00	£25.00
2 Platinum Edition, ND no price box on cover	$9.00	$27.00	$45.00	£4.50	£13.50	£22.50
3 ND Jim Balent cover	$5.00	$15.00	$25.00	£3.00	£9.00	£15.00
3 Limited Edition, ND with poster	$10.00	$30.00	$50.00	£4.00	£12.00	£20.00
4 ND Tim Vigil cover	$2.00	$6.00	$10.00	£1.20	£3.60	£6.00
4 Limited Edition, ND with poster	$3.00	$9.00	$15.00	£1.50	£4.50	£7.50
5 ND Joseph Michael Linsner cover art; Achilles Storm 4 page preview	$5.00	$15.00	$25.00	£2.00	£6.00	£10.00
5 Platinum Edition ND	$8.00	$24.00	$40.00	£3.00	£9.00	£15.00
6 ND origin Razor	$2.00	$6.00	$10.00	£1.00	£3.00	£5.00
7-8 ND	$2.00	$6.00	$10.00	£0.80	£2.40	£4.00
8 Variant Cover Edition, ND photo-cover	$2.50	$7.50	$12.50	£1.50	£4.50	£7.50
9 ND	$1.20	$3.60	$6.00	£0.80	£2.40	£4.00
10 ND origin of Stryke; ties into Razor: The Suffering	$1.20	$3.60	$6.00	£0.80	£2.40	£4.00
11-12 ND more of Razor's origin revealed	$0.60	$1.80	$3.00	£0.40	£1.20	£2.00
12 Collectors Edition, ND (Nov 1995) - red foil embossed cover	$0.80	$2.40	$4.00	£0.50	£1.50	£2.50
13 ND title becomes "Razor Uncut"	$0.60	$1.80	$3.00	£0.40	£1.20	£2.00
14 ND Kevin Sharpe cover	$0.60	$1.80	$3.00	£0.40	£1.20	£2.00
15 ND title becomes Razor Uncut	$0.60	$1.80	$3.00	£0.40	£1.20	£2.00
16 ND Interview with Death story	$0.60	$1.80	$3.00	£0.40	£1.20	£2.00
17-18 ND	$0.60	$1.80	$3.00	£0.40	£1.20	£2.00
19 ND Kiss of a Rose story	$0.60	$1.80	$3.00	£0.40	£1.20	£2.00
20 ND Kiss of a Rise story	$0.60	$1.80	$3.00	£0.40	£1.20	£2.00
21 ND Kiss of a Rose story	$0.60	$1.80	$3.00	£0.40	£1.20	£2.00
22-24 ND	$0.60	$1.80	$3.00	£0.40	£1.20	£2.00
25 ND photo cover	$0.60	$1.80	$3.00	£0.40	£1.20	£2.00
26-30 ND	$0.60	$1.80	$3.00	£0.40	£1.20	£2.00
Title Value:	$108.40	$325.20	$542.00	£58.80	£176.40	£294.00

RAZOR AND SHI SPECIAL

London Night Studios,OS; 1 Aug 1994

	$Good	$Fine	$N.Mint	£Good	£Fine	£N.Mint
1 ND reprints Razor Annual #1 with new artwork and pin-ups	$2.00	$6.00	$10.00	£1.20	£3.60	£6.00
1 Platinum Edition, ND available to retailers for every 10 copies ordered of the above	$3.00	$9.00	$15.00	£1.50	£4.50	£7.50
Title Value:	$5.00	$15.00	$25.00	£2.70	£8.10	£13.50

RAZOR ANNUAL

London Night Studios; 1 1993-present

	$Good	$Fine	$N.Mint	£Good	£Fine	£N.Mint
1 ND 1st appearance of Shi; black and white	$9.00	$27.00	$45.00	£5.50	£16.50	£27.50
1 Gold Edition, ND 1,200 copies printed	$12.00	$36.00	$60.00	£6.50	£19.50	£32.50
2 ND more facts about origin; black and white	$1.20	$3.60	$6.00	£0.70	£2.10	£3.50
Title Value:	$22.20	$66.60	$111.00	£12.70	£38.10	£63.50

RAZOR SWIMSUIT SPECIAL

London Night Studios,OS; 1 Apr 1995

	$Good	$Fine	$N.Mint	£Good	£Fine	£N.Mint
1 ND pin-ups by Bill Tucci, Everette Hartsoe, Kevin Taylor and others	$0.70	$2.10	$3.50	£0.50	£1.50	£2.50
1 Platinum Edition ND	$3.00	$9.00	$15.00	£2.00	£6.00	£10.00
Title Value:	$3.70	$11.10	$18.50	£2.50	£7.50	£12.50

RAZOR VS. DARK ANGEL

London Night Studios/Boneyard Press,OS; 1 Oct 1994

	$Good	$Fine	$N.Mint	£Good	£Fine	£N.Mint
1 ND reprints The Final Nail #1 plus new art and new ending; pre-bagged with death certificate (randomly inserted)	*$1.00*	*$3.00*	*$5.00*	£0.70	£2.10	£3.50
Title Value:	*$1.00*	*$3.00*	*$5.00*	£0.70	£2.10	£3.50

RAZOR VS. DARK ANGEL TO THE DEATH

Boneyard Press,OS; nn Jun 1995

	$Good	$Fine	$N.Mint	£Good	£Fine	£N.Mint
nn ND reprints Razor vs. Dark Angel with new pages, computer colours and new Kyle Hotz cover; pre-bagged	*$0.60*	*$1.80*	*$3.00*	£0.40	£1.20	£2.00
Title Value:	*$0.60*	*$1.80*	*$3.00*	£0.40	£1.20	£2.00

RAZOR/AREALA WARRIOR NUN: FAITH

London Night Studios,OS; 1 May 1996

(see Warrior Nun Areala vs. Razor)

	$Good	$Fine	$N.Mint	£Good	£Fine	£N.Mint
1 ND Everette Hartsoe script, Jude Millien art	*$0.80*	*$2.40*	*$4.00*	£0.50	£1.50	£2.50
1 Holy Virgin Cover Edition, ND (May 1996)	*$2.00*	*$6.00*	*$10.00*	£1.30	£3.90	£6.50
Title Value:	*$2.80*	*$8.40*	*$14.00*	£1.80	£5.40	£9.00

RAZOR/DARK ANGEL: THE FINAL NAIL

London Night Studios/Boneyard Press; 1 1994-2 1994

	$Good	$Fine	$N.Mint	£Good	£Fine	£N.Mint
1-2 ND inter company X-over	*$0.70*	*$2.10*	*$3.50*	£0.50	£1.50	£2.50
Title Value:	*$1.40*	*$4.20*	*$7.00*	£1.00	£3.00	£5.00

RAZOR/MORBID ANGEL: SOUL SEARCH

London Night Studios,MS; 1 Sep 1996-3 Jan 1997

	$Good	$Fine	$N.Mint	£Good	£Fine	£N.Mint
1 ND Everette Hartsoe script, George Jeanty art	*$0.60*	*$1.80*	*$3.00*	£0.40	£1.20	£2.00
1 Platinum Edition ND	*$2.00*	*$6.00*	*$10.00*	£1.30	£3.90	£6.50
2-3 ND	*$0.60*	*$1.80*	*$3.00*	£0.40	£1.20	£2.00
Title Value:	*$3.80*	*$11.40*	*$19.00*	£2.50	£7.50	£12.50

RAZOR: BURN

London Night Studios; 1 Dec 1994-5 Jul 1995

	$Good	$Fine	$N.Mint	£Good	£Fine	£N.Mint
1 ND Everette Hartsoe script, Mike Taylor art; black and white	*$1.50*	*$4.50*	*$7.50*	£0.80	£2.40	£4.00
1 Commemorative Edition, ND signed and limited to 3,000 copies, issued with certificate of authenticity	*$3.00*	*$9.00*	*$15.00*	£1.50	£4.50	£7.50
2 ND Everette Hartsoe script, Mike Taylor art; black and white	*$1.00*	*$3.00*	*$5.00*	£0.60	£1.80	£3.00
2 Platinum Edition ND	*$4.00*	*$12.00*	*$20.00*	£2.00	£6.00	£10.00
3-4 ND Everette Hartsoe script, Slick art; black and white	*$0.80*	*$2.40*	*$4.00*	£0.50	£1.50	£2.50
5 ND Everette Hartsoe script, Mike Wolfer art; black and white	*$0.70*	*$2.10*	*$3.50*	£0.50	£1.50	£2.50
Title Value:	*$11.80*	*$35.40*	*$58.50*	£6.40	£19.20	£32.00

Razor: Burn (May 1996)

	£Good	£Fine	£N.Mint
Trade paperback ND collects issues #1-5 and Razor #½	£2.00	£6.00	£10.00

RAZOR: CRY NO MORE

London Night Studios,OS; 1 Feb 1996

	$Good	$Fine	$N.Mint	£Good	£Fine	£N.Mint
1 ND 48pgs, origin of Razor	*$0.80*	*$2.40*	*$4.00*	£0.50	£1.50	£2.50
Title Value:	*$0.80*	*$2.40*	*$4.00*	£0.50	£1.50	£2.50

RAZOR: FLESH & BLOOD CONVENTION BOOK

London Night Studios,OS; nn Oct 1994

	$Good	$Fine	$N.Mint	£Good	£Fine	£N.Mint
nn ND pin-up book with photo cover; 5,000 copies signed and numbered	*$4.00*	*$12.00*	*$20.00*	£2.00	£6.00	£10.00
Title Value:	*$4.00*	*$12.00*	*$20.00*	£2.00	£6.00	£10.00

RAZOR: THE SUFFERING

London Night Studios,MS; 1 Jun 1994-3 Sep 1994

	$Good	$Fine	$N.Mint	£Good	£Fine	£N.Mint
1 ND Everette Hartsoe script and art; black and white	*$0.70*	*$2.10*	*$3.50*	£0.50	£1.50	£2.50
1 Director's Cut, ND reprints issue #1 with some new art and new cover by Everette Hartsoe to celebrate publisher's third year	*$1.00*	*$3.00*	*$5.00*	£0.70	£2.10	£3.50
2-3 ND Everette Hartsoe script and art; black and white	*$0.70*	*$2.10*	*$3.50*	£0.50	£1.50	£2.50
Title Value:	*$3.10*	*$9.30*	*$15.50*	£2.20	£6.60	£11.00

RAZOR: TORTURE

London Night Studios,MS; 0 Dec 1995-6 1996

	$Good	$Fine	$N.Mint	£Good	£Fine	£N.Mint
0 ND features every London Night Studios character; pre-bagged with 3 chromium cards	*$0.80*	*$2.40*	*$4.00*	£0.50	£1.50	£2.50
0 Signed Promo Edition, ND (Mar 1996), pre-bagged with up to 5 trading cards; limited to 2,000 copies	*$4.00*	*$12.00*	*$20.00*	£2.70	£8.00	£13.50
1-6 ND 24pgs	*$0.60*	*$1.80*	*$3.00*	£0.40	£1.20	£2.00
Title Value:	*$8.40*	*$25.20*	*$42.00*	£5.60	£16.70	£28.00

RAZOR: TORTURE PREQUEL

London Night Studios,OS; nn 1996

	$Good	$Fine	$N.Mint	£Good	£Fine	£N.Mint
nn ND 12pgs, - limited to 10,000 copies	*$3.00*	*$9.00*	*$15.00*	£2.00	£6.00	£10.00
Title Value:	*$3.00*	*$9.00*	*$15.00*	£2.00	£6.00	£10.00

RAZORLINE: THE FIRST CUT

Marvel Comics Group,OS; 1 Sep 1993

	$Good	$Fine	$N.Mint	£Good	£Fine	£N.Mint
1 previews of Hyperkind, Ectokid, Hokum & Hex and Saint Sinner; Clive Barker interview	*$0.30*	*$0.90*	*$1.50*	£0.20	£0.60	£1.00
Title Value:	*$0.30*	*$0.90*	*$1.50*	£0.20	£0.60	£1.00

RE-ANIMATOR

Adventure,MS; 1 Oct 1991-3 Dec 1991

	$Good	$Fine	$N.Mint	£Good	£Fine	£N.Mint
1 ND based on film, colour, Dave Dorman painted covers	*$0.40*	*$1.20*	*$2.00*	£0.25	£0.75	£1.25
2-3 ND	*$0.40*	*$1.20*	*$2.00*	£0.25	£0.75	£1.25
Title Value:	*$1.20*	*$3.60*	*$6.00*	£0.75	£2.25	£3.75

RE-ANIMATOR, DAWN OF THE

Adventure,MS; 1 Mar 1992-4 Jun 1992

	$Good	$Fine	$N.Mint	£Good	£Fine	£N.Mint
1-4 ND prequel based on film	*$0.40*	*$1.20*	*$2.00*	£0.25	£0.75	£1.25
Title Value:	*$1.60*	*$4.80*	*$8.00*	£1.00	£3.00	£5.00

RE-ANIMATOR: TALES OF HERBERT WEST

Adventure,OS; 1 Dec 1991

	$Good	$Fine	$N.Mint	£Good	£Fine	£N.Mint
1 ND 48pgs, squarebound, six stories of H.P. Lovecraft	*$0.70*	*$2.10*	*$3.50*	£0.50	£1.50	£2.50
Title Value:	*$0.70*	*$2.10*	*$3.50*	£0.50	£1.50	£2.50

REACTOMAN

B-Movie; 1 Feb 1987-3 Jun 1987

	$Good	$Fine	$N.Mint	£Good	£Fine	£N.Mint
1-3 ND	*$0.30*	*$0.90*	*$1.50*	£0.20	£0.60	£1.00
Title Value:	*$0.90*	*$2.70*	*$4.50*	£0.60	£1.80	£3.00

REAGAN'S RAIDERS

Solson Productions; 1-3 1986

	$Good	$Fine	$N.Mint	£Good	£Fine	£N.Mint
1-3 ND Rich Buckler art	*$0.25*	*$0.75*	*$1.25*	£0.10	£0.30	£0.50
Title Value:	*$0.75*	*$2.25*	*$3.75*	£0.30	£0.90	£1.50

REAL FACT COMICS

National Periodical Publications; 1 Mar/Apr 1946-21 Jul/Aug 1949

	$Good	$Fine	$N.Mint	£Good	£Fine	£N.Mint
1 very scarce in the U.K. Harry Houdini life-story; Simon and Kirby cover and art	*$57.50*	*$175.00*	*$475.00*	£41.00	£120.00	£325.00
2 very scarce in the U.K. P.T. Barnum and Rin-Tin-Tin features; Simon and Kirby art	*$41.00*	*$120.00*	*$325.00*	£28.00	£82.50	£225.00
3 H.G. Wells feature - "Mr. Future"; claimed to be the first DC letter/fan column	*$34.00*	*$100.00*	*$275.00*	£24.00	£72.50	£195.00
4 James Stewart feature; "Just Imagine" back-up stories begin	*$41.00*	*$120.00*	*$325.00*	£28.00	£82.50	£225.00
5 very scarce in the U.K. Batman and Robin origin feature with Bob Kane; cover based on Batman #9	*$185.00*	*$560.00*	*$1500.00*	£135.00	£410.00	£1100.00

Ramm #1

Rawhide Kid #58

Real Fact Comics #3

Issue	$Good	$Fine	$N.Mint	£Good	£Fine	£N.Mint
6 origin and 1st appearance of Tommy Tomorrow by Virgil Finley; Harlan Ellison fan column appears	$110.00	$335.00	$900.00	£75.00	£225.00	£600.00
7 Douglas Fairbanks - Stuntman Star feature	$18.50	$55.00	$150.00	£12.50	£38.00	£100.00
8 2nd appearance Tommy Tomorrow	$62.50	$185.00	$500.00	£42.00	£125.00	£335.00
9 Glenn Miller feature	$28.00	$82.50	$225.00	£18.50	£55.00	£150.00
10 Vigilante by Mort Meskin	$25.00	$75.00	$200.00	£16.50	£50.00	£135.00
11 The G-Men, The F.B.I., Annie Oakley	$15.50	$47.00	$125.00	£10.50	£32.00	£85.00
12 The G-Men	$15.50	$47.00	$125.00	£10.50	£32.00	£85.00
13 3rd appearance Tommy Tomorrow; Dale Evans	$55.00	$165.00	$450.00	£38.00	£110.00	£300.00
14 Will Rogers life-story	$12.50	$38.00	$100.00	£8.00	£24.00	£65.00
15 Last War on Earth - nuclear war feature	$18.50	$55.00	$150.00	£10.50	£32.00	£85.00
16 Tommy Tomorrow and The Planteers	$47.00	$140.00	$375.00	£31.00	£92.50	£250.00
17 The Hatfields vs. The McCoys	$12.50	$38.00	$100.00	£8.00	£24.00	£65.00
18 Wyatt Earp and Doc Holliday	$12.50	$38.00	$100.00	£8.00	£24.00	£65.00
19 Sir Arthur Conan Doyle feature	$15.50	$47.00	$125.00	£10.50	£32.00	£85.00
20 The Real Daniel Boone story; some Joe Kubert art	$16.50	$50.00	$135.00	£11.00	£34.00	£90.00
21 Kit Carson - Indian Scout story; some Joe Kubert art	$12.50	$38.00	$100.00	£8.00	£24.00	£65.00
Title Value:	$836.00	$2510.50	$6760.00	£574.50	£1721.00	£4630.00

Note: all at least scarce in the U.K.

REAL GHOSTBUSTERS 3-D HALLOWEEN SPECIAL
Now Comics,OS; 1 Dec 1992

Issue	$Good	$Fine	$N.Mint	£Good	£Fine	£N.Mint
1 ND pre-bagged with 3-D glasses (25% less without glasses)	$0.40	$1.20	$2.00	£0.25	£0.75	£1.25
Title Value:	$0.40	$1.20	$2.00	£0.25	£0.75	£1.25

REAL GHOSTBUSTERS 3D SLIMER SPECIAL
Now Comics,OS; 1 Jul 1993

Issue	$Good	$Fine	$N.Mint	£Good	£Fine	£N.Mint
1 ND includes 3-D glasses (25% less without glasses)	$0.40	$1.20	$2.00	£0.25	£0.75	£1.25
Title Value:	$0.40	$1.20	$2.00	£0.25	£0.75	£1.25

REAL GHOSTBUSTERS SUPER 3-D SPECIAL
Now Comics,OS; 1 Oct 1991

Issue	$Good	$Fine	$N.Mint	£Good	£Fine	£N.Mint
1 ND pre-bagged with 3-D glasses (25% less without glasses)	$0.40	$1.20	$2.00	£0.25	£0.75	£1.25
Title Value:	$0.40	$1.20	$2.00	£0.25	£0.75	£1.25

REAL GHOSTBUSTERS, THE
Now Comics; 1 Jun 1988-28 1990

Issue	$Good	$Fine	$N.Mint	£Good	£Fine	£N.Mint
1-8 ND scarce in the U.K.	$0.40	$1.20	$2.00	£0.25	£0.75	£1.25
9-10 ND Comics Code on cover	$0.40	$1.20	$2.00	£0.25	£0.75	£1.25
11-28 ND Comics Code on cover	$0.30	$0.90	$1.50	£0.20	£0.60	£1.00
Title Value:	$9.40	$28.20	$47.00	£6.10	£18.30	£30.50

REAL GHOSTBUSTERS, THE (2ND SERIES)
Now Comics; 1 Nov 1991-8 1992

Issue	$Good	$Fine	$N.Mint	£Good	£Fine	£N.Mint
1-8 ND	$0.30	$0.90	$1.50	£0.20	£0.60	£1.00
Title Value:	$2.40	$7.20	$12.00	£1.60	£4.80	£8.00

REAL WAR STORIES
Eclipse; 1 Jul 1987; 2 Dec 1990

Issue	$Good	$Fine	$N.Mint	£Good	£Fine	£N.Mint
1 ND 48pgs, Alan Moore script, Bolland, Bissette, Totleben art; some copies have cutting defects on centre-fold, colour	$0.60	$1.80	$3.00	£0.40	£1.20	£2.00
1 2nd printing ND	$0.55	$1.65	$2.75	£0.35	£1.05	£1.75
2 ND 48pgs, features work by Sienkiewicz, Badger, Motter, cover by Gulacy, colour	$0.60	$1.80	$3.00	£0.40	£1.20	£2.00
Title Value:	$1.75	$5.25	$8.75	£1.15	£3.45	£5.75

REALM HANDBOOK, THE
Caliber Press,OS; 1 Sep 1993

Issue	$Good	$Fine	$N.Mint	£Good	£Fine	£N.Mint
1 ND complete reference work on the world of Realm	$0.50	$1.50	$2.50	£0.30	£0.90	£1.50
Title Value:	$0.50	$1.50	$2.50	£0.30	£0.90	£1.50

REALM OF THE DEAD
Caliber Press,MS; 1 Aug 1993-3 Oct 1993

Issue	$Good	$Fine	$N.Mint	£Good	£Fine	£N.Mint
1 Cover A, ND Chris Morea art, black and white; features Realm characters	$0.50	$1.50	$2.50	£0.30	£0.90	£1.50
1 Cover B, ND Chris Morea art, black and white; features Deadworld characters	$0.50	$1.50	$2.50	£0.30	£0.90	£1.50
2 ND	$0.50	$1.50	$2.50	£0.30	£0.90	£1.50
2 Limited Edition, ND - 2,500 copies, signed and embossed stamped	$0.60	$1.80	$3.00	£0.40	£1.20	£2.00
3 ND	$0.50	$1.50	$2.50	£0.30	£0.90	£1.50
3 Limited Edition, ND - 2,500 copies, signed and embossed stamped	$0.60	$1.80	$3.00	£0.40	£1.20	£2.00
Title Value:	$3.20	$9.60	$16.00	£2.00	£6.00	£10.00
Realm of the Dead Graphic Novel (Dec 1994) reprints mini-series plus free copy of Deadworld Collection that reprints Deadworld #1-7				£2.00	£6.00	£10.00

REALM, SAGA OF THE
Caliber Press; 1 Dec 1992-5 1993

Issue	$Good	$Fine	$N.Mint	£Good	£Fine	£N.Mint
1 ND reprints of Realm begin	$0.40	$1.20	$2.00	£0.25	£0.75	£1.25
2-5 ND	$0.40	$1.20	$2.00	£0.25	£0.75	£1.25
Title Value:	$2.00	$6.00	$10.00	£1.25	£3.75	£6.25

REALM, THE
Arrow/Innovation/Caliber; 1 1986-24 1992

Issue	$Good	$Fine	$N.Mint	£Good	£Fine	£N.Mint
1 ND black and white begins	$0.60	$1.80	$3.00	£0.40	£1.20	£2.00
2-3 ND	$0.50	$1.50	$2.50	£0.30	£0.90	£1.50
4 ND 1st Deadworld story (see Caliber Presents #8)	$1.00	$3.00	$5.00	£0.60	£1.80	£3.00
5-9 ND	$0.40	$1.20	$2.00	£0.25	£0.75	£1.25
10-13 ND	$0.30	$0.90	$1.50	£0.20	£0.60	£1.00
14 ND 1st Caliber issue ($1.75)	$0.30	$0.90	$1.50	£0.20	£0.60	£1.00
15-19 ND	$0.30	$0.90	$1.50	£0.20	£0.60	£1.00
20-24 ND Daemonstorm story	$0.30	$0.90	$1.50	£0.20	£0.60	£1.00
Title Value:	$9.10	$27.30	$45.50	£5.85	£17.55	£29.25
Book 1, reprints #1-4				£0.65	£1.95	£3.25
Book 2, reprints #5-8				£0.90	£2.70	£4.50
Book 3, reprints #9-12				£1.10	£3.30	£5.50
Book 4, reprints #13-15 plus others from Caliber Presents				£1.60	£4.80	£8.00

REALM, THE (2ND SERIES)
Caliber Press; 1 Jun 1993-13 1995 ?

Issue	$Good	$Fine	$N.Mint	£Good	£Fine	£N.Mint
1 ND glossy covers begin; black and white	$0.40	$1.20	$2.00	£0.25	£0.75	£1.25
2-7 ND	$0.30	$0.90	$1.50	£0.20	£0.60	£1.00
7 Limited Edition, ND - signed by one creator with trading card	$0.50	$1.50	$2.50	£0.30	£0.90	£1.50
8-11 ND	$0.30	$0.90	$1.50	£0.20	£0.60	£1.00
12-13 ND David Mack cover	$0.30	$0.90	$1.50	£0.20	£0.60	£1.00
Title Value:	$4.50	$13.50	$22.50	£2.95	£8.85	£14.75

REALM, THE: THE SHINDE IMAS
Caliber Press; 1 Sep 1993

Issue	$Good	$Fine	$N.Mint	£Good	£Fine	£N.Mint
1 ND pre-bagged with print, Guy Davis script and art	$1.50	$4.50	$7.50	£0.90	£2.70	£4.50
Title Value:	$1.50	$4.50	$7.50	£0.90	£2.70	£4.50

REBEL SWORD PART ONE, THE
Dark Horse,MS; 1 Oct 1994-6 Mar 1995

Issue	$Good	$Fine	$N.Mint	£Good	£Fine	£N.Mint
1-6 ND 40pgs, Yoshikazu Yasuhiko script/art; black and white	$0.60	$1.80	$3.00	£0.40	£1.20	£2.00
Title Value:	$3.60	$10.80	$18.00	£2.40	£7.20	£12.00

RED CIRCLE SORCERY
Red Circle (Archie);6 Apr 1974-11 Feb 1975

(previously Chilling Adventures in Sorcery)

Issue	$Good	$Fine	$N.Mint	£Good	£Fine	£N.Mint
6 Morrow, Chaykin art	$0.30	$1.00	$2.00	£0.20	£0.60	£1.25
7 Morrow, Bruce Jones art; Morrow cover	$0.25	$0.75	$1.50	£0.15	£0.50	£1.00
8 Thorne, Morrow, Toth art; Morrow cover	$0.25	$0.75	$1.50	£0.15	£0.50	£1.00
9 Toth art; Morrow cover	$0.25	$0.75	$1.50	£0.15	£0.50	£1.00
10 Thorne, Morrow, Chaykin, Al Williamson art	$0.25	$0.75	$1.50	£0.15	£0.50	£1.00
11 rare in the U.K. Gray Morrow art	$0.30	$1.00	$2.00	£0.20	£0.60	£1.25
Title Value:	$1.60	$5.00	$10.00	£1.00	£3.20	£6.50

Note: all distributed on the news-stands in the U.K.

RED DOG
Eclipse; 1 Feb 1988

(Night Music #7)

Issue	$Good	$Fine	$N.Mint	£Good	£Fine	£N.Mint
1 ND Kipling adaptation, P. Craig Russell art	$0.40	$1.20	$2.00	£0.25	£0.75	£1.25
Title Value:	$0.40	$1.20	$2.00	£0.25	£0.75	£1.25

RED DRAGON
Comico; 1 Oct 1995-4 1996 ?

Issue	$Good	$Fine	$N.Mint	£Good	£Fine	£N.Mint
1 ND Brian Azzarello script, Tony Akins art	$0.50	$1.50	$2.50	£0.30	£0.90	£1.50
2-4 ND	$0.50	$1.50	$2.50	£0.30	£0.90	£1.50
Title Value:	$2.00	$6.00	$10.00	£1.20	£3.60	£6.00

RED FOX
(see British section)

RED HEAT IN 3-D
Blackthorne;(3-D Series #45) 1 Jul 1988

Issue	$Good	$Fine	$N.Mint	£Good	£Fine	£N.Mint
1 ND based on Arnold Schwarzenegger film by Carolco; with bound-in 3-D glasses (25% less without glasses)	$0.50	$1.50	$2.50	£0.30	£0.90	£1.50
Title Value:	$0.50	$1.50	$2.50	£0.30	£0.90	£1.50

RED MASK OF THE RIO GRANDE
AC Comics,MS; 1-3 1992

Issue	$Good	$Fine	$N.Mint	£Good	£Fine	£N.Mint
1-3 ND Red Mask reprints, art by Frank Bolle; 2,000 copies	$0.50	$1.50	$2.50	£0.30	£0.90	£1.50
Title Value:	$1.50	$4.50	$7.50	£0.90	£2.70	£4.50

RED MOON
Millennium,MS; 1 Feb 1995-2 Apr 1995

Issue	$Good	$Fine	$N.Mint	£Good	£Fine	£N.Mint
1-2 ND black and white; wraparound cover by John Bolton	$0.60	$1.80	$3.00	£0.40	£1.20	£2.00
Title Value:	$1.20	$3.60	$6.00	£0.80	£2.40	£4.00

RED RAVEN COMICS
Timely Comics; 1 Aug 1940
(see Human Torch #2)

	$Good	$Fine	$N.Mint	£Good	£Fine	£N.Mint
1 scarce in the U.K. origin and 1st appearance of Red Raven; Jack Kirby cover art (1st cover he ever signed)	*$1375.00*	*$4150.00*	*$12500.00*	£880.00	£2650.00	£8000.00
Title Value:	*$1375.00*	*$4150.00*	*$12500.00*	£880.00	£2650.00	£8000.00

RED SONJA
Marvel Comics Group; 1 Jan 1977-15 May 1979
(see Conan, Marvel Feature, Savage Sword of Conan)

	$Good	$Fine	$N.Mint	£Good	£Fine	£N.Mint
1	*$0.65*	*$2.00*	*$4.00*	£0.30	£1.00	£2.00
2-10 ND	*$0.40*	*$1.25*	*$2.50*	£0.25	£0.75	£1.50
11	*$0.30*	*$1.00*	*$2.00*	£0.20	£0.60	£1.25
12-15 Brunner cover	*$0.30*	*$1.00*	*$2.00*	£0.20	£0.60	£1.25
Title Value:	*$5.75*	*$18.25*	*$36.50*	£3.55	£10.75	£21.75

RED SONJA (2ND SERIES)
Marvel Comics Group; 1 Feb 1983-2 Mar 1983

	$Good	$Fine	$N.Mint	£Good	£Fine	£N.Mint
1-2 ND	*$0.30*	*$0.90*	*$1.50*	£0.20	£0.60	£1.00
Title Value:	*$0.60*	*$1.80*	*$3.00*	£0.40	£1.20	£2.00

RED SONJA (3RD SERIES)
Marvel Comics Group; 1 Aug 1983-13 1986

	$Good	$Fine	$N.Mint	£Good	£Fine	£N.Mint
1 ND	*$0.30*	*$0.90*	*$1.50*	£0.20	£0.60	£1.00
2-13 ND	*$0.25*	*$0.75*	*$1.25*	£0.15	£0.45	£0.75
Title Value:	*$3.30*	*$9.90*	*$16.50*	£2.00	£6.00	£10.00

RED SONJA (4TH SERIES)
Marvel Comics Group,OS; 1 Dec 1995

	$Good	$Fine	$N.Mint	£Good	£Fine	£N.Mint
1 ND Glenn Herdling script, Ken Lashley and Harry Candelario art; painted cover by Brothers Hildebrandt	*$0.50*	*$1.50*	*$2.50*	£0.30	£0.90	£1.50
Title Value:	*$0.50*	*$1.50*	*$2.50*	£0.30	£0.90	£1.50

RED SONJA IN 3-D
Blackthorne;(3-D Series #53) 1 Autumn 1988-2 1988

	$Good	$Fine	$N.Mint	£Good	£Fine	£N.Mint
1-2 ND with bound-in 3-D glasses (25% less without glasses)	*$0.50*	*$1.50*	*$2.50*	£0.30	£0.90	£1.50
Title Value:	*$1.00*	*$3.00*	*$5.00*	£0.60	£1.80	£3.00

RED SONJA: SCAVENGER HUNT
Marvel Comics Group,OS; 1 Dec 1995

	$Good	$Fine	$N.Mint	£Good	£Fine	£N.Mint
1 ND 48pgs	*$0.50*	*$1.50*	*$2.50*	£0.30	£0.90	£1.50
Title Value:	*$0.50*	*$1.50*	*$2.50*	£0.30	£0.90	£1.50

RED SONJA: THE MOVIE
Marvel Comics Group,MS Film; 1 Nov 1985-2 Dec 1985

	$Good	$Fine	$N.Mint	£Good	£Fine	£N.Mint
1-2 ND adapts film, Conan appears	*$0.40*	*$1.20*	*$2.00*	£0.25	£0.75	£1.25
Title Value:	*$0.80*	*$2.40*	*$4.00*	£0.50	£1.50	£2.50

RED TORNADO
DC Comics,MS; 1 Jul 1985-4 Oct 1985

	$Good	$Fine	$N.Mint	£Good	£Fine	£N.Mint
1 Infantino art, Justice League of America (inc. Superman and Batman) appear	*$0.25*	*$0.75*	*$1.25*	£0.15	£0.45	£0.75
2 Infantino art, Superman appears	*$0.25*	*$0.75*	*$1.25*	£0.15	£0.45	£0.75
3-4 Infantino art	*$0.25*	*$0.75*	*$1.25*	£0.15	£0.45	£0.75
Title Value:	*$1.00*	*$3.00*	*$5.00*	£0.60	£1.80	£3.00

RED TRAILS WEST
Millennium,MS; 1 Dec 1994-2 Feb 1995

	$Good	$Fine	$N.Mint	£Good	£Fine	£N.Mint
1-2 ND Wendy Snow-Lang script, black and white	*$0.50*	*$1.50*	*$2.50*	£0.30	£0.90	£1.50
Title Value:	*$1.00*	*$3.00*	*$5.00*	£0.60	£1.80	£3.00

RED WOLF
Marvel Comics Group; 1 May 1972-9 Sep 1973
(see Avengers #80, Marvel Spotlight #1)

	$Good	$Fine	$N.Mint	£Good	£Fine	£N.Mint
1 ND scarce in the U.K.	*$0.80*	*$2.50*	*$5.00*	£0.40	£1.25	£2.50
2 ND scarce in the U.K. Gil Kane cover	*$0.40*	*$1.25*	*$2.50*	£0.25	£0.75	£1.50
3-4 ND scarce in the U.K.	*$0.40*	*$1.25*	*$2.50*	£0.25	£0.75	£1.50
5 ND scarce in the U.K. Gil Kane cover	*$0.40*	*$1.25*	*$2.50*	£0.25	£0.75	£1.50
6 ND scarce in the U.K.	*$0.30*	*$1.00*	*$2.00*	£0.20	£0.60	£1.25
7 ND scarce in the U.K. story moves to present day	*$0.30*	*$1.00*	*$2.00*	£0.20	£0.60	£1.25
8-9 ND scarce in the U.K.	*$0.30*	*$1.00*	*$2.00*	£0.20	£0.60	£1.25
Title Value:	*$3.60*	*$11.50*	*$23.00*	£2.20	£6.65	£13.50

REDBLADE
Dark Horse,MS; 1 Apr 1993-3 Jun 1993

	$Good	$Fine	$N.Mint	£Good	£Fine	£N.Mint
1-3 ND Vince Garriano script and art	*$0.50*	*$1.50*	*$2.50*	£0.30	£0.90	£1.50
Title Value:	*$1.50*	*$4.50*	*$7.50*	£0.90	£2.70	£4.50

REESE'S PIECES
Eclipse,MS; 1,2 Oct 1985

	$Good	$Fine	$N.Mint	£Good	£Fine	£N.Mint
1-2 ND Ralph Reese reprints	*$0.40*	*$1.20*	*$2.00*	£0.25	£0.75	£1.25
Title Value:	*$0.80*	*$2.40*	*$4.00*	£0.50	£1.50	£2.50

REGULATORS
Image; 1 Jun 1995-3 Aug 1995

	$Good	$Fine	$N.Mint	£Good	£Fine	£N.Mint
1 ND Kurt Busiek script, Ron Randall and Dan Davis art	*$0.50*	*$1.50*	*$2.50*	£0.30	£0.90	£1.50
2-3 ND	*$0.50*	*$1.50*	*$2.50*	£0.30	£0.90	£1.50
Title Value:	*$1.50*	*$4.50*	*$7.50*	£0.90	£2.70	£4.50

REID FLEMING, WORLD'S TOUGHEST MILKMAN
David Boswell; 1 Oct 1980
(see Heartbreak Comics)
(continued from David Boswell publications)

	$Good	$Fine	$N.Mint	£Good	£Fine	£N.Mint
1 ND (Oct '80)	*$0.90*	*$2.70*	*$4.50*	£0.60	£1.80	£3.00
1 2nd printing, ND (Jul '85)	*$0.70*	*$2.10*	*$3.50*	£0.40	£1.20	£2.00
Title Value:	*$1.60*	*$4.80*	*$8.00*	£1.00	£3.00	£5.00

REID FLEMING, WORLD'S TOUGHEST MILKMAN VOLUME TWO
Eclipse; 1 Aug 1986-5 1987

	$Good	$Fine	$N.Mint	£Good	£Fine	£N.Mint
1 ND comic size (4th print of original David Boswell comic)	*$0.50*	*$1.50*	*$2.50*	£0.30	£0.90	£1.50
1 2nd/3rd printing ND	*$0.40*	*$1.20*	*$2.00*	£0.25	£0.75	£1.25
2 ND	*$0.40*	*$1.20*	*$2.00*	£0.25	£0.75	£1.25
2 2nd/3rd printing ND	*$0.40*	*$1.20*	*$2.00*	£0.25	£0.75	£1.25
3-5 ND	*$0.40*	*$1.20*	*$2.00*	£0.25	£0.75	£1.25
Title Value:	*$2.90*	*$8.70*	*$14.50*	£1.80	£5.40	£9.00

REIGN OF THE DRAGON LORD
Eternity; 1,2 1986

	$Good	$Fine	$N.Mint	£Good	£Fine	£N.Mint
1-2 ND	*$0.30*	*$0.90*	*$1.50*	£0.20	£0.60	£1.00
Title Value:	*$0.60*	*$1.80*	*$3.00*	£0.40	£1.20	£2.00

REIKI WARRIORS
Heroic Publishing; 1 Aug 1993

	$Good	$Fine	$N.Mint	£Good	£Fine	£N.Mint
1 ND	*$0.60*	*$1.80*	*$3.00*	£0.40	£1.20	£2.00
Title Value:	*$0.60*	*$1.80*	*$3.00*	£0.40	£1.20	£2.00

REN & STIMPY
Marvel Comics Group,TV; 1 Dec 1992-44 Jul 1996

	$Good	$Fine	$N.Mint	£Good	£Fine	£N.Mint
1 ND pre-bagged, includes free-gift scratch and sniff "air-fouler" card; based on animated US TV series	*$1.00*	*$3.00*	*$5.00*	£1.20	£3.60	£6.00
1 2nd printing ND	*$0.60*	*$1.80*	*$3.00*	£0.40	£1.20	£2.00
2 ND	*$0.60*	*$1.80*	*$3.00*	£0.60	£1.80	£3.00
3-5 ND	*$0.40*	*$1.20*	*$2.00*	£0.40	£1.20	£2.00
6-10 ND	*$0.40*	*$1.20*	*$2.00*	£0.30	£0.90	£1.50
11-12 ND	*$0.40*	*$1.20*	*$2.00*	£0.25	£0.75	£1.25
13 ND Halloween issue	*$0.40*	*$1.20*	*$2.00*	£0.25	£0.75	£1.25
14-24 ND	*$0.40*	*$1.20*	*$2.00*	£0.25	£0.75	£1.25
25 ND die-cut cover	*$0.60*	*$1.80*	*$3.00*	£0.40	£1.20	£2.00
26-44 ND	*$0.40*	*$1.20*	*$2.00*	£0.25	£0.75	£1.25
Title Value:	*$19.20*	*$57.60*	*$96.00*	£13.55	£40.65	£67.75
Ren & Stimpy: Pick of the Litter (Jul 1993) Trade paperback reprints issues #1-4 plus new material				£1.60	£4.80	£8.00
Ren & Stimpy: Running Joke (Nov 1993) Trade paperback reprints issues #5-8 plus new material				£1.60	£4.80	£8.00
Ren & Stimpy: Don't Try This At Home Trade paperback reprints issues #9-12 plus new material				£1.70	£5.10	£8.50
Ren & Stimpy: Your Pals (Oct 1994) Trade paperback reprints issues #13-16				£1.70	£5.10	£8.50
Ren & Stimpy: Seeck Little Monkey (Mar 1995) Trade paperback reprints issues #17-20				£1.70	£5.10	£8.50

REN & STIMPY HOLIDAY SPECIAL
Marvel Comics Group,OS; 1 Feb 1995

	$Good	$Fine	$N.Mint	£Good	£Fine	£N.Mint
1 ND reprints issues #3 and #15 plus new material	*$0.60*	*$1.80*	*$3.00*	£0.40	£1.20	£2.00
Title Value:	*$0.60*	*$1.80*	*$3.00*	£0.40	£1.20	£2.00

REN & STIMPY SPECIAL: AROUND THE WORLD IN A DAZE
Marvel Comics Group,OS; 1 Jan 1996

	$Good	$Fine	$N.Mint	£Good	£Fine	£N.Mint
1 ND 48pgs	*$0.60*	*$1.80*	*$3.00*	£0.40	£1.20	£2.00
Title Value:	*$0.60*	*$1.80*	*$3.00*	£0.40	£1.20	£2.00

REN & STIMPY SPECIAL: FANTASTIC FOURS
Marvel Comics Group,OS; 1 Jan 1995

	$Good	$Fine	$N.Mint	£Good	£Fine	£N.Mint
1 ND 48pgs, Powdered Toast man appears	*$0.60*	*$1.80*	*$3.00*	£0.40	£1.20	£2.00
Title Value:	*$0.60*	*$1.80*	*$3.00*	£0.40	£1.20	£2.00

REN & STIMPY SPECIAL: HISTORY OF MUSIC
Marvel Comics Group,OS; 1 Oct 1995

	$Good	$Fine	$N.Mint	£Good	£Fine	£N.Mint
1 ND 48pgs	*$0.60*	*$1.80*	*$3.00*	£0.40	£1.20	£2.00
Title Value:	*$0.60*	*$1.80*	*$3.00*	£0.40	£1.20	£2.00

REN & STIMPY SPECIAL: VIRTUAL STUPIDITY
Marvel Comics Group,OS; 1 Jul 1995

	$Good	$Fine	$N.Mint	£Good	£Fine	£N.Mint
1 ND 48pgs	*$0.60*	*$1.80*	*$3.00*	£0.40	£1.20	£2.00
Title Value:	*$0.60*	*$1.80*	*$3.00*	£0.40	£1.20	£2.00

REN & STIMPY SUMMER JOBS SPECIAL
Marvel Comics Group,OS; 1 Jul 1994

	$Good	$Fine	$N.Mint	£Good	£Fine	£N.Mint
1 ND 48pgs	*$0.60*	*$1.80*	*$3.00*	£0.40	£1.20	£2.00
Title Value:	*$0.60*	*$1.80*	*$3.00*	£0.40	£1.20	£2.00

REN & STIMPY TIME AND SPACE SPECIAL
Marvel Comics Group,OS; 1 Oct 1994

	$Good	$Fine	$N.Mint	£Good	£Fine	£N.Mint
1 ND 48pgs	*$0.60*	*$1.80*	*$3.00*	£0.40	£1.20	£2.00
Title Value:	*$0.60*	*$1.80*	*$3.00*	£0.40	£1.20	£2.00

REN & STIMPY: POWDERED TOAST MAN
Marvel Comics Group,OS; 1 Apr 1994

	$Good	$Fine	$N.Mint	£Good	£Fine	£N.Mint
1 ND 48pgs	*$0.60*	*$1.80*	*$3.00*	£0.40	£1.20	£2.00
Title Value:	*$0.60*	*$1.80*	*$3.00*	£0.40	£1.20	£2.00

REN & STIMPY: POWDERED TOASTMAN'S CEREAL SERIAL SPECIAL
Marvel Comics Group,OS; 1 Apr 1995

	$Good	$Fine	$N.Mint	£Good	£Fine	£N.Mint
1 ND 48pgs	*$0.60*	*$1.80*	*$3.00*	£0.40	£1.20	£2.00
Title Value:	*$0.60*	*$1.80*	*$3.00*	£0.40	£1.20	£2.00

REN & STIMPY: RADIO DAZED & CONFUSED
Marvel Comics Group,OS; 1 Nov 1995

1 ND tie-in with Ren & Stimpy CD and cassette

	$Good	$Fine	$N.Mint	£Good	£Fine	£N.Mint
	$0.40	$1.20	$2.00	£0.25	£0.75	£1.25
Title Value:	$0.40	$1.20	$2.00	£0.25	£0.75	£1.25
RENEGADE RABBIT						
Printed Matter Comics; 1 Dec 1986-2 1987						
1-2 ND 9.5" x 7" format (slightly smaller than normal comic size)						
	$0.30	$0.90	$1.50	£0.20	£0.60	£1.00
Title Value:	$0.60	$1.80	$3.00	£0.40	£1.20	£2.00
RENEGADE ROMANCE						
Renegade; 1 Jun 1987-2 1988						
1 ND 64pgs, Mary Wilshire, DeStefano, Williamson art, G. Hernandez cover						
	$0.50	$1.50	$2.50	£0.30	£0.90	£1.50
2 ND 64pgs, Mary Wilshire, Steve Leialoha art, J. Hernandez cover						
	$0.50	$1.50	$2.50	£0.30	£0.90	£1.50
Title Value:	$1.00	$3.00	$5.00	£0.60	£1.80	£3.00
RENFIELD						
Caliber Press,MS; 1 Aug 1994-3 1995						
1-3 ND black and white						
	$0.50	$1.50	$2.50	£0.30	£0.90	£1.50
Title Value:	$1.50	$4.50	$7.50	£0.90	£2.70	£4.50
Renfield Graphic Novel (Sep 1995) collects six issue series				£1.20	£3.60	£6.00
Note: series cancelled in comic book format after 3 issues. Caliber Press decided to issue the last three instalments as a graphic novel and they then decided to include the first three issues as one publication						
REPLACEMENT GOD, THE						
Slave Labor/Amaze Ink; 1 Jun 1995-present						
1-6 ND Zander Cannon script and art; black and white						
	$0.60	$1.80	$3.00	£0.40	£1.20	£2.00
Title Value:	$3.60	$10.80	$18.00	£2.40	£7.20	£12.00
REPTILICUS						
Charlton; 1 Aug 1961-2 Oct 1961						
(becomes Reptisaurus)						
1 rare, distributed in the U.K. based on a "B" movie "The Beast from 20,000 Fathoms"						
	$12.50	$39.00	$90.00	£8.50	£26.00	£60.00
2 scarce, distributed in the U.K						
	$10.00	$30.00	$60.00	£6.50	£20.00	£40.00
Title Value:	$22.50	$69.00	$150.00	£15.00	£46.00	£100.00
REPTISAURUS						
Charlton;3 Jan 1962-8 Dec 1962						
3-8 distributed in the U.K.						
	$5.25	$16.00	$37.50	£3.55	£10.50	£25.00
Title Value:	$31.50	$96.00	$225.00	£21.30	£63.00	£150.00
Special 1 (Summer 1963)				£1.40	£5.20	£7.00
RESCUERS DOWN UNDER GRAPHIC NOVEL, THE						
Disney; nn Nov 1990						
nn ND 64pgs, adaptation of film						
	$0.90	$2.70	$4.50	£0.60	£1.80	£3.00
Title Value:	$0.90	$2.70	$4.50	£0.60	£1.80	£3.00
RESCUERS DOWN UNDER, THE						
Disney,OS; 1 Aug 1991						
1 ND 64pgs, adaptation of film						
	$0.90	$2.70	$4.50	£0.60	£1.80	£3.00
Title Value:	$0.90	$2.70	$4.50	£0.60	£1.80	£3.00
RESIDENTS: FREAK SHOW						
Dark Horse,OS; 1 Jun 1992						
1 ND 80pgs, anthology featuring John Bolton, Dave McKean, Matt Howarth and Kyle Baker, cover by Charles Burns	$1.50	$4.50	$7.50	£1.00	£3.00	£5.00
Title Value:	$1.50	$4.50	$7.50	£1.00	£3.00	£5.00
RESTAURANT AT THE END OF THE UNIVERSE, THE						
DC Comics,MS; 1 Mar 1995-3 May 1995						
(see Hitchiker's Guide to the Galaxy)						
1-3 ND John Carnell script, Steve Leialoha art. The second book of The Hitch-Hiker's Guide						
	$1.20	$3.60	$6.00	£0.80	£2.40	£4.00
Title Value:	$3.60	$10.80	$18.00	£2.40	£7.20	£12.00
RETALIATOR, THE						
Eclipse/FX Comix,MS; 1 Sep 1992-4 Dec 1992						
1-4 ND based on film						
	$0.40	$1.20	$2.00	£0.25	£0.75	£1.25
Title Value:	$1.60	$4.80	$8.00	£1.00	£3.00	£5.00
RETIEF						
Adventure,MS; 1 Apr 1991-6 Sep 1991						
1-6 ND	$0.40	$1.20	$2.00	£0.25	£0.75	£1.25
Title Value:	$2.40	$7.20	$12.00	£1.50	£4.50	£7.50
Retief Graphic Novel reprints issues #1-6, Bob Fugitake art				£1.65	£4.95	£8.25
RETIEF (KEITH LAUMER'S...)						
Mad Dog Graphics; 1 Apr 1987-6 Mar 1988						
1-6 ND Bob Fujitake art, black and white						
	$0.40	$1.20	$2.00	£0.25	£0.75	£1.25
Title Value:	$2.40	$7.20	$12.00	£1.50	£4.50	£7.50
Retief Graphic Novel (1990)						
reprints issues #1-6 with new Bob Fugitake cover				£1.65	£4.95	£8.25
Note: the above published by Apple Comics						
RETIEF (KEITH LAUMER'S...) (2ND SERIES)						
Adventure; 1 Dec 1989-6 May 1990						
1-6 ND newsprint paper, black and white						
	$0.40	$1.20	$2.00	£0.25	£0.75	£1.25
Title Value:	$2.40	$7.20	$12.00	£1.50	£4.50	£7.50
RETIEF AND THE WARLORDS						
Eternity,MS; 1 Jan 1991-3 Mar 1991						
1-3 ND black and white						
	$0.40	$1.20	$2.00	£0.25	£0.75	£1.25
Title Value:	$1.20	$3.60	$6.00	£0.75	£2.25	£3.75
RETIEF OF THE C.D.T.						
Mad Dog Graphics,OS; 1 1988						

	$Good	$Fine	$N.Mint	£Good	£Fine	£N.Mint
1 ND	$0.40	$1.20	$2.00	£0.25	£0.75	£1.25
Title Value:	$0.40	$1.20	$2.00	£0.25	£0.75	£1.25
RETIEF: GIANT KILLER						
Adventure; 1 Dec 1991						
1 ND	$0.40	$1.20	$2.00	£0.25	£0.75	£1.25
Title Value:	$0.40	$1.20	$2.00	£0.25	£0.75	£1.25
RETIEF: GRIME AND PUNISHMENT						
Adventure,OS; 1 Nov 1991						
1 ND	$0.40	$1.20	$2.00	£0.25	£0.75	£1.25
Title Value:	$0.40	$1.20	$2.00	£0.25	£0.75	£1.25
RETIEF: THE GARBAGE INVASION						
Adventure,OS; 1 Oct 1991						
1 ND	$0.40	$1.20	$2.00	£0.25	£0.75	£1.25
Title Value:	$0.40	$1.20	$2.00	£0.25	£0.75	£1.25
RETURN OF DR. FATE						
(see Dr.Fate)						
RETURN OF GORGO, THE						
Charlton;2 Summer 1963-3 Autumn 1964						
(previously Gorgo's Revenge)						
2-3 scarce, distributed in the U.K. Steve Ditko art						
	$7.75	$23.50	$55.00	£5.00	£15.00	£35.00
Title Value:	$15.50	$47.00	$110.00	£10.00	£30.00	£70.00
RETURN OF KONGA, THE						
Charlton; nn 1962						
(becomes Konga's Revenge)						
nn distributed in the U.K.						
	$7.75	$23.50	$55.00	£5.00	£15.00	£35.00
Title Value:	$7.75	$23.50	$55.00	£5.00	£15.00	£35.00
RETURN OF LUM: URUSEI YATSURA, THE						
Viz Communications,MS; 1 Dec 1994-8 Jul 1995						
(see Lum)						
1-8 ND 40pgs, Rumiko Takahashi; black and white						
	$0.60	$1.80	$3.00	£0.40	£1.20	£2.00
Title Value:	$4.80	$14.40	$24.00	£3.20	£9.60	£16.00
Return of Lum Vol. 1 Graphic Novel (Mar 1995)						
collection of self-contained stories				£2.00	£6.00	£10.00
RETURN OF LUM: URUSEI YATSURA, THE PART TWO						
Viz Communications,MS; 1 Aug 1995-9 Apr 1996						
1-9 ND Rumiko Takahashi script and art; black and white						
	$0.55	$1.65	$2.75	£0.35	£1.05	£1.75
Title Value:	$4.95	$14.85	$24.75	£3.15	£9.45	£15.75
RETURN OF MEGATON MAN						
Kitchen Sink; 1 Jul 1988-3 Sep 1988						
(see Megaton Man)						
1-3 ND	$0.40	$1.20	$2.00	£0.25	£0.75	£1.25
Title Value:	$1.20	$3.60	$6.00	£0.75	£2.25	£3.75
RETURN OF THE DEFENDERS						
Marvel Comics Group; 1992						
Cross-over storyline running throughout the following issues:						
Incredible Hulk Annual #18,						
Namor Annual #2,						
Silver Surfer Annual #5,						
Doctor Strange Annual #2.						
RETURN OF THE JEDI						
Marvel Comics Group,MS Film; 1 Oct 1983-4 Jan 1984						
1-4 ND adapts film, Williamson art						
	$1.00	$3.00	$5.00	£0.50	£1.50	£2.50
Title Value:	$4.00	$12.00	$20.00	£2.00	£6.00	£10.00
RETURN OF THE NEW GODS						
(see New Gods)						
REVENGE OF THE PROWLER						
Eclipse; 1 Feb 1988-4 Jun 1988						
1 ND Tim Truman script, John K. Snyder III art begins						
	$0.40	$1.20	$2.00	£0.25	£0.75	£1.25
2 ND Flexi-disc double-sided single attached (25% less if disc missing)						
	$0.50	$1.50	$2.50	£0.30	£0.90	£1.50
3 ND	$0.40	$1.20	$2.00	£0.25	£0.75	£1.25
4 ND continues in Total Eclipse #1						
	$0.40	$1.20	$2.00	£0.25	£0.75	£1.25
Title Value:	$1.70	$5.10	$8.50	£1.05	£3.15	£5.25
REVENGERS						
Continuity; 1 Apr 1985-6 1989						
1 Neal Adams cover, script, pencil layouts and inks; origin and 1st appearance The Ultimate Man Megalith						
	$0.40	$1.20	$2.00	£0.25	£0.75	£1.25
2 1st appearance Armor and The Silver Streak, Neal Adams cover, script, pencil layouts and inks; Megalith appears	$0.40	$1.20	$2.00	£0.25	£0.75	£1.25
3 Neal Adams script, cover and pencils; features Megalith, Armor and The Silver Streak						
	$0.40	$1.20	$2.00	£0.25	£0.75	£1.25
4 Neal Adams part script and pencils; features Megalith, Armor and The Silver Streak; 1st appearance The New Clear Warlock						
	$0.40	$1.20	$2.00	£0.25	£0.75	£1.25
5 Neal Adams part script and pencils; features Megalith and New Clear Warlock						
	$0.40	$1.20	$2.00	£0.25	£0.75	£1.25
6 Neal Adams part script, Larry Stroman pencils and cover						
	$0.40	$1.20	$2.00	£0.25	£0.75	£1.25
Title Value:	$2.40	$7.20	$12.00	£1.50	£4.50	£7.50
Note: all Non-Distributed on the news-stands in the U.K.						
REVENGERS SPECIAL						
Continuity,MS; 1 Jul 1992-2 Aug 1992						
1 ND 48pgs, Neal Adams story, features pre-X-Factor Larry Stroman art, previews Hybrids series						
	$0.60	$1.80	$3.00	£0.40	£1.20	£2.00
1 2nd printing, ND (Nov 1993)						

	$Good	$Fine	$N.Mint	£Good	£Fine	£N.Mint
	$0.50	$1.50	$2.50	£0.30	£0.90	£1.50
2 ND 48pgs, Larry Stroman art, Neal Adams cover						
	$0.50	$1.50	$2.50	£0.30	£0.90	£1.50
Title Value:	$1.60	$4.80	$8.00	£1.00	£3.00	£5.00

REVEREND ABLACK

CFD Productions,MS; 1,2 May 1996

	$Good	$Fine	$N.Mint	£Good	£Fine	£N.Mint
1-2 ND bi-weekly; black and white						
	$0.50	$1.50	$2.50	£0.30	£0.90	£1.50
Title Value:	$1.00	$3.00	$5.00	£0.60	£1.80	£3.00

REVOLVER

Renegade; 1 Nov 1985-12 Oct 1986

	$Good	$Fine	$N.Mint	£Good	£Fine	£N.Mint
1 Star Guider, Steve Ditko cover and part art, black and white (all issues)						
	$0.30	$0.90	$1.50	£0.20	£0.60	£1.00
2 Star Guider, Steve Ditko part art						
	$0.30	$0.90	$1.50	£0.20	£0.60	£1.00
3 Star Guider, Boyette cover						
	$0.30	$0.90	$1.50	£0.20	£0.60	£1.00
4 Fantastic Fables, Steve Ditko cover and part art						
	$0.30	$0.90	$1.50	£0.20	£0.60	£1.00
5 Fantastic Fables	$0.30	$0.90	$1.50	£0.20	£0.60	£1.00
6 Fantastic Fables, Bissette cover						
	$0.30	$0.90	$1.50	£0.20	£0.60	£1.00
7-9 Steve Ditko cover						
	$0.30	$0.90	$1.50	£0.20	£0.60	£1.00
10	$0.30	$0.90	$1.50	£0.20	£0.60	£1.00
11 Carmine Infantino cover						
	$0.30	$0.90	$1.50	£0.20	£0.60	£1.00
12 Alex Toth cover	$0.30	$0.90	$1.50	£0.20	£0.60	£1.00
Title Value:	$3.60	$10.80	$18.00	£2.40	£7.20	£12.00

Note: all Non-Distributed on the news-stands in the U.K.

REVOLVER ANNUAL

Renegade; 1 Nov 1986

	$Good	$Fine	$N.Mint	£Good	£Fine	£N.Mint
1 ND (issue #13 of Revolver) Alex Toth cover, Steve Ditko art featured plus checklist of all Revolver issue credits						
	$0.30	$0.90	$1.50	£0.20	£0.60	£1.00
Title Value:	$0.30	$0.90	$1.50	£0.20	£0.60	£1.00

REVOLVING DOORS

Blackthorne; 1 Oct 1986-3 Feb 1987

	$Good	$Fine	$N.Mint	£Good	£Fine	£N.Mint
1-3 ND	$0.30	$0.90	$1.50	£0.20	£0.60	£1.00
Title Value:	$0.90	$2.70	$4.50	£0.60	£1.80	£3.00
Graphic Novel (1987)				£0.50	£1.50	£2.50

REX THE WONDER DOG

National Periodical Publications; 1 Jan/Feb 1952-46 Sep/Oct 1959 (cover-date Nov)

(see DC Comics Presents #35)

	$Good	$Fine	$N.Mint	£Good	£Fine	£N.Mint
1 rare in the U.K. Alex Toth art						
	$100.00	$300.00	$800.00	£70.00	£215.00	£575.00
2 rare in the U.K. Alex Toth art						
	$55.00	$170.00	$400.00	£37.00	£110.00	£260.00
3 rare in the U.K. Alex Toth art						
	$43.00	$125.00	$300.00	£29.00	£85.00	£200.00
4-5 very scarce in the U.K.						
	$32.00	$95.00	$225.00	£21.00	£62.50	£150.00
6-10 very scarce in the U.K.						
	$24.00	$72.50	$170.00	£15.50	£47.00	£110.00
11 very scarce in the U.K.						
	$26.00	$75.00	$180.00	£17.00	£50.00	£120.00
12-20 very scarce in the U.K.						
	$12.50	$39.00	$90.00	£8.50	£26.00	£60.00
21-30 very scarce in the U.K.						
	$10.00	$30.00	$70.00	£6.25	£19.00	£45.00
31-45 very scarce in the U.K.						
	$9.25	$28.00	$65.00	£6.00	£18.00	£42.50
1st official distribution in the U.K.						
46 rare in the U.K.	$9.25	$28.00	$65.00	£6.00	£18.00	£42.50
Title Value:	$768.50	$2321.50	$5530.00	£507.50	£1532.00	£3675.00

RIBIT!

Comico,MS; 1 Jan 1989-4 Apr 1989

	$Good	$Fine	$N.Mint	£Good	£Fine	£N.Mint
1-4 ND Frank Thorne Red Sonja-esque character/art in colour						
	$0.40	$1.20	$2.00	£0.25	£0.75	£1.25
Title Value:	$1.60	$4.80	$8.00	£1.00	£3.00	£5.00

RICH BUCKLER'S SECRETS OF DRAWING COMICS

Showcase Publications; 1-4 1986

	$Good	$Fine	$N.Mint	£Good	£Fine	£N.Mint
1-4 ND black and white; all hints and tips for would-be comic artists						
	$0.15	$0.45	$0.75	£0.10	£0.35	£0.60
Title Value:	$0.60	$1.80	$3.00	£0.40	£1.40	£2.40

RICHARD DRAGON KUNG FU FIGHTER

DC Comics; 1 Apr/May 1975-18 Nov/Dec 1977

(see Brave and the Bold, DC Comics Presents #39)

	$Good	$Fine	$N.Mint	£Good	£Fine	£N.Mint
1	$0.50	$1.50	$3.00	£0.25	£0.75	£1.50
2 Jim Starlin art	$0.30	$1.00	$2.00	£0.20	£0.60	£1.25
3 Jack Kirby art	$0.25	$0.75	$1.50	£0.15	£0.50	£1.00
4-7 Wood inks	$0.25	$0.75	$1.50	£0.15	£0.50	£1.00
8 scarce in the U.K. Wood inks						
	$0.25	$0.75	$1.50	£0.20	£0.60	£1.25
9	$0.25	$0.75	$1.50	£0.15	£0.50	£1.00
10 scarce in the U.K.						
	$0.25	$0.75	$1.50	£0.20	£0.60	£1.25
11-18	$0.25	$0.75	$1.50	£0.15	£0.50	£1.00
Title Value:	$4.80	$14.50	$28.75	£2.95	£9.55	£19.25

RICHIE RICH

Harvey; 1 Nov 1960-254 Jan 1991

	$Good	$Fine	$N.Mint	£Good	£Fine	£N.Mint
1 scarce in the U.K.						
	$135.00	$405.00	$1350.00	£95.00	£285.00	£950.00
2 scarce in the U.K.						
	$62.50	$185.00	$500.00	£47.00	£140.00	£375.00
3-5 scarce in the U.K.						
	$39.00	$115.00	$275.00	£26.00	£77.50	£185.00
6-10	$26.00	$75.00	$180.00	£17.00	£50.00	£120.00
11-20	$12.50	$39.00	$90.00	£8.50	£26.00	£60.00
21-30	$11.00	$34.00	$80.00	£7.75	£23.50	£55.00
31-40	$9.25	$28.00	$65.00	£5.50	£17.00	£40.00
41-50	$6.25	$19.00	$45.00	£4.25	£12.50	£30.00
51-60	$5.00	$15.00	$30.00	£3.30	£10.00	£20.00
61-80	$3.30	$10.00	$20.00	£2.00	£6.00	£12.00
81-99	$2.50	$7.50	$15.00	£1.30	£4.00	£8.00
100	$2.90	$8.75	$17.50	£1.65	£5.00	£10.00
101-111	$1.65	$5.00	$10.00	£1.00	£3.00	£6.00
112-116 giant	$1.80	$5.50	$11.00	£1.15	£3.50	£7.00
117-120	$1.65	$5.00	$10.00	£1.00	£3.00	£6.00
121-140	$1.15	$3.50	$7.00	£0.65	£2.00	£4.00
141-160	$0.65	$2.00	$4.00	£0.40	£1.25	£2.50
161-180	$0.50	$1.50	$2.50	£0.40	£1.20	£2.00
181-200	$0.40	$1.20	$2.00	£0.30	£0.90	£1.50
201-225	$0.30	$0.90	$1.50	£0.20	£0.60	£1.00
226-254	$0.25	$0.75	$1.25	£0.15	£0.45	£0.75
Title Value:	$1103.40	$3322.00	$7966.25	£729.45	£2196.05	£5303.75

Note: all distributed on the news-stands in the U.K. though later issues more erratically

RICHIE RICH AND CASPER IN 3-D

Blackthorne;(3-D Series #32) 1 Dec 1987

	$Good	$Fine	$N.Mint	£Good	£Fine	£N.Mint
1 ND colour, with bound-in 3-D glasses (25% less without glasses)						
	$0.50	$1.50	$2.50	£0.30	£0.90	£1.50
Title Value:	$0.50	$1.50	$2.50	£0.30	£0.90	£1.50

Red Circle Sorcery #7

Red Wolf #9

Rima, The Jungle Girl #7

RICHIE RICH MOVIE ADAPTATION

Marvel Comics Group,Film; 1 Mar 1995

	$Good	$Fine	$N.Mint	£Good	£Fine	£N.Mint
1 ND 48pgs, Film adaptation starring Macauley Culkin	$0.60	$1.80	$3.00	£0.40	£1.20	£2.00
Title Value:	$0.60	$1.80	$3.00	£0.40	£1.20	£2.00

RIFLEMAN, THE

Dell;(Four Color #1009) 1 Sep 1959-20 Oct 1964

	$Good	$Fine	$N.Mint	£Good	£Fine	£N.Mint
1 (Four Color #1009) photo cover Chuck Connors	$32.00	$95.00	$225.00	£21.00	£62.50	£150.00
2	$15.50	$47.00	$110.00	£10.50	£32.00	£75.00
3 Alex Toth art featured	$17.50	$52.50	$125.00	£12.00	£36.00	£85.00
4-5	$14.00	$43.00	$100.00	£9.25	£28.00	£65.00
6 Alex Toth art	$15.00	$45.00	$105.00	£10.00	£30.00	£70.00
7-10	$14.00	$43.00	$100.00	£9.25	£28.00	£65.00
11-20	$10.50	$32.00	$75.00	£6.25	£19.00	£45.00
Title Value:	$269.00	$817.50	$1915.00	£171.50	£518.50	£1220.00

Note: all distributed on the news-stands in the U.K.

RIMA THE JUNGLE GIRL

DC Comics; 1 Apr/May 1974-7 Apr/May 1975

	$Good	$Fine	$N.Mint	£Good	£Fine	£N.Mint
1 ND origin, Alex Nino art begins, Space Voyagers begin	$0.50	$1.50	$3.00	£0.30	£1.00	£2.00
2-4 scarce in the U.K. origin	$0.40	$1.25	$2.50	£0.25	£0.75	£1.50
5 last Nino art, last Space Voyagers	$0.40	$1.25	$2.50	£0.25	£0.75	£1.50
6	$0.40	$1.25	$2.50	£0.25	£0.75	£1.50
7 Space Marshall appears	$0.40	$1.25	$2.50	£0.25	£0.75	£1.50
Title Value:	$2.90	$9.00	$18.00	£1.80	£5.50	£11.00

RING OF ROSES

Dark Horse,MS; 1 Jan 1993-4 Apr 1993

	$Good	$Fine	$N.Mint	£Good	£Fine	£N.Mint
1-4 ND black and white	$0.50	$1.50	$2.50	£0.30	£0.90	£1.50
Title Value:	$2.00	$6.00	$10.00	£1.20	£3.60	£6.00

RING, THE

DC Comics,MS; 1 Jan 1990-4 Apr 1990

	$Good	$Fine	$N.Mint	£Good	£Fine	£N.Mint
1-4 ND squarebound	$0.80	$2.40	$4.00	£0.50	£1.50	£2.50
Title Value:	$3.20	$9.60	$16.00	£2.00	£6.00	£10.00
Trade paperback (Jun 1991), 200pgs				£2.80	£5.60	£11.20

Note: adaptation of Richard Wagner's The Ring by Roy Thomas and Gil Kane. Mature Readers label. Full title: The Ring of Nibelung.

RINGO KID, THE

Marvel Comics Group; 1 Jan 1970-23 Nov 1973; 24 Nov 1975-30 Nov 1976

	$Good	$Fine	$N.Mint	£Good	£Fine	£N.Mint
1 Williamson reprint	$0.80	$2.50	$5.00	£0.50	£1.50	£3.00
2-3 scarce in the U.K.	$0.50	$1.50	$3.00	£0.30	£1.00	£2.00
4-30	$0.40	$1.25	$2.50	£0.25	£0.75	£1.50
Title Value:	$12.60	$39.25	$78.00	£7.85	£23.75	£47.50

Note: all issues are reprint. Williamson reprint in #20.

RIO

Comico;Graphic Novel; nn Jun 1987

	$Good	$Fine	$N.Mint	£Good	£Fine	£N.Mint
nn ND Doug Wildey art	$1.50	$4.50	$7.50	£1.00	£3.00	£5.00
Title Value:	$1.50	$4.50	$7.50	£1.00	£3.00	£5.00

RIO AT BAY

Dark Horse; 1 Jul 1992-2 Oct 1992

	$Good	$Fine	$N.Mint	£Good	£Fine	£N.Mint
1-2 ND Doug Wildey script and art	$0.50	$1.50	$2.50	£0.30	£0.90	£1.50
Title Value:	$1.00	$3.00	$5.00	£0.60	£1.80	£3.00
Rio At Bay Softcover Collection (Jun 1993) reprints mini-series, silver foil embossed logo on cover, 10pg section previously unpublished material				£1.00	£3.00	£5.00

RIO KID

Eternity,MS; 1 Nov 1991-2 1991

	$Good	$Fine	$N.Mint	£Good	£Fine	£N.Mint
1-2 ND	$0.40	$1.20	$2.00	£0.25	£0.75	£1.25
Title Value:	$0.80	$2.40	$4.00	£0.50	£1.50	£2.50

RIOT

Viz Communications,MS; 1 Oct 1995-6 Mar 1996

	$Good	$Fine	$N.Mint	£Good	£Fine	£N.Mint
1-6 ND Satoshi Shiki script and art; black and white	$0.55	$1.65	$2.75	£0.35	£1.05	£1.75
Title Value:	$3.30	$9.90	$16.50	£2.10	£6.30	£10.50

RIOT GEAR

Triumphant Comics; 1 Aug 1993-14 Sep 1994

	$Good	$Fine	$N.Mint	£Good	£Fine	£N.Mint
1 coupon for Riot Gear #0; 25,000 copies with serial number on front cover	$0.40	$1.20	$2.00	£0.25	£0.75	£1.25
1 Limited Edition, (Feb 1994) - signed by creators with mini-poster photo-print; pre-bagged with backing board	$0.50	$1.50	$2.50	£0.30	£0.90	£1.50
2	$0.40	$1.20	$2.00	£0.25	£0.75	£1.25
3 Unleashed X-over	$0.40	$1.20	$2.00	£0.25	£0.75	£1.25
4-12	$0.40	$1.20	$2.00	£0.25	£0.75	£1.25
13 Kelley Jones cover	$0.40	$1.20	$2.00	£0.25	£0.75	£1.25
14	$0.40	$1.20	$2.00	£0.25	£0.75	£1.25
Title Value:	$6.10	$18.30	$30.50	£3.80	£11.40	£19.00

Note: all Non-Distributed on the news-stands in the U.K.

RIOT GEAR: VIOLENT PAST

Triumphant Comics,MS; 1,2 Feb 1994

	$Good	$Fine	$N.Mint	£Good	£Fine	£N.Mint
1-2 ND	$0.40	$1.20	$2.00	£0.25	£0.75	£1.25
Title Value:	$0.80	$2.40	$4.00	£0.50	£1.50	£2.50

RIP HUNTER TIME MASTER

National Periodical Publications; 1 Mar/Apr 1961-29 Nov/Dec 1965

(see DC Comics Presents #37, Showcase, Time Masters)

	$Good	$Fine	$N.Mint	£Good	£Fine	£N.Mint
1 dinosaur cover	$62.50	$185.00	$500.00	£44.00	£130.00	£350.00
2	$34.00	$100.00	$240.00	£21.00	£62.50	£150.00
3-5	$20.50	$60.00	$145.00	£12.00	£36.00	£85.00
6-8 Toth art	$15.00	$45.00	$105.00	£9.25	£28.00	£65.00
9-10	$12.50	$39.00	$90.00	£7.00	£21.00	£50.00
11-15	$10.00	$30.00	$70.00	£6.25	£19.00	£45.00
16-19	$9.25	$28.00	$65.00	£5.50	£17.00	£40.00
20 Hitler on cover	$9.25	$28.00	$65.00	£5.50	£17.00	£40.00
21-28	$7.75	$23.50	$55.00	£5.00	£15.00	£35.00
29 Gil Kane cover	$7.75	$23.50	$55.00	£5.00	£15.00	£35.00
Title Value:	$394.00	$1179.50	$2840.00	£246.50	£741.50	£1790.00

RIP IN TIME

Fantagor,MS; 1 Aug 1986-5 1987

	$Good	$Fine	$N.Mint	£Good	£Fine	£N.Mint
1-5 ND Richard Corben art	$0.40	$1.20	$2.00	£0.25	£0.75	£1.25
Title Value:	$2.00	$6.00	$10.00	£1.25	£3.75	£6.25
Trade Paperback (Oct 1990), reprints #1-5				£1.00	£3.00	£5.00

RIPCLAW

Image,MS; 1 Apr 1995-4 Jul 1995

	$Good	$Fine	$N.Mint	£Good	£Fine	£N.Mint
½ ND produced in conjunction with Wizard Comics	$2.00	$6.00	$10.00	£1.00	£3.00	£5.00
½ Chicago Edition, ND released at the Chicago comic convention	$2.40	$7.00	$12.00	£1.60	£4.80	£8.00
½ Gold Edition ND	$2.40	$7.00	$12.00	£1.60	£4.80	£8.00
½ San Diego Edition, ND realeased at the 1995 San Diego comic convention; features the San Diego comic convention insignia (a parrot) in gold at bottom right of cover	$2.40	$7.00	$12.00	£1.60	£4.80	£8.00
1 ND Marc Silvestri script, Brian Peterson and Al Vey art	$0.60	$1.80	$3.00	£0.40	£1.20	£2.00
2 ND Marc Silvestri script, Brian Peterson and Al Vey art	$0.50	$1.50	$2.50	£0.30	£0.90	£1.50
3-4 ND Cyberforce appear; Marc Silvestri script, Brian Peterson and Al Vey art	$0.50	$1.50	$2.50	£0.30	£0.90	£1.50
Title Value:	$11.30	$33.30	$56.50	£7.10	£21.30	£35.50

RIPCLAW (2ND SERIES)

Image; 1 Dec 1995-present

	$Good	$Fine	$N.Mint	£Good	£Fine	£N.Mint
1-2 ND	$0.50	$1.50	$2.50	£0.30	£0.90	£1.50
3 ND Cyblade appears	$0.50	$1.50	$2.50	£0.30	£0.90	£1.50
4-6 ND	$0.50	$1.50	$2.50	£0.30	£0.90	£1.50
Title Value:	$3.00	$9.00	$15.00	£1.80	£5.40	£9.00

RIPCLAW SPECIAL

Image,OS; 1 Aug 1995

	$Good	$Fine	$N.Mint	£Good	£Fine	£N.Mint
1 ND Marc Silvestri script	$0.60	$1.80	$3.01	£0.40	£1.20	£2.00
Title Value:	$0.60	$1.80	$3.01	£0.40	£1.20	£2.00

RIPFIRE

Malibu; 0 Jan 1995

	$Good	$Fine	$N.Mint	£Good	£Fine	£N.Mint
0 ND 40pgs	$0.40	$1.20	$2.00	£0.25	£0.75	£1.25
Title Value:	$0.40	$1.20	$2.00	£0.25	£0.75	£1.25

RIPLASH

Pocket Change Comics; 1 Jan 1996-2 1996?

	$Good	$Fine	$N.Mint	£Good	£Fine	£N.Mint
1 ND Bob Dixon script, Scott Shriver art begins; black and white	$0.50	$1.50	$2.50	£0.30	£0.90	£1.50
2 ND	$0.50	$1.50	$2.50	£0.30	£0.90	£1.50
Title Value:	$1.00	$3.00	$5.00	£0.60	£1.80	£3.00

RIPLEY'S BELIEVE IT OR NOT

Gold Key;4 Apr 1967-94 Feb 1980

(True War Stories #1-3)

	$Good	$Fine	$N.Mint	£Good	£Fine	£N.Mint
4	$3.55	$10.50	$25.00	£2.10	£6.25	£15.00
5-10	$2.50	$7.50	$17.50	£1.40	£4.25	£10.00
11-20	$1.75	$5.25	$12.50	£1.05	£3.20	£7.50
21-30	$1.65	$5.00	$10.00	£0.80	£2.50	£5.00
31-50	$1.00	$3.00	$6.00	£0.55	£1.75	£3.50
51-70	$0.75	$2.25	$4.50	£0.50	£1.50	£3.00
71-94	$0.55	$1.75	$3.50	£0.40	£1.25	£2.50
Title Value:	$100.75	$305.00	$639.00	£59.60	£183.75	£390.00

Note: most issues distributed on the news-stands in the U.K.

RIPLEY'S BELIEVE IT OR NOT: ANIMAL ODDITIES

Schanes Products; 1 Sep 1993

	$Good	$Fine	$N.Mint	£Good	£Fine	£N.Mint
1 ND black and white	$0.50	$1.50	$2.50	£0.30	£0.90	£1.50
Title Value:	$0.50	$1.50	$2.50	£0.30	£0.90	£1.50

RIPLEY'S BELIEVE IT OR NOT: BEAUTY & GROOMING

Schanes Products; 1 Aug 1993

	$Good	$Fine	$N.Mint	£Good	£Fine	£N.Mint
1 ND black and white	$0.50	$1.50	$2.50	£0.30	£0.90	£1.50
Title Value:	$0.50	$1.50	$2.50	£0.30	£0.90	£1.50

RIPLEY'S BELIEVE IT OR NOT: CHILD PRODIGIES

Schanes Products; 1 May 1993-2 Jun 1993

	$Good	$Fine	$N.Mint	£Good	£Fine	£N.Mint
1-2 ND Scott Hampton cover; black and white	$0.50	$1.50	$2.50	£0.30	£0.90	£1.50
Title Value:	$1.00	$3.00	$5.00	£0.60	£1.80	£3.00

RIPLEY'S BELIEVE IT OR NOT: COINCIDENCES

Schanes Products; 1 Oct 1993

	$Good	$Fine	$N.Mint	£Good	£Fine	£N.Mint
1 ND black and white	$0.50	$1.50	$2.50	£0.30	£0.90	£1.50
Title Value:	$0.50	$1.50	$2.50	£0.30	£0.90	£1.50

RIPLEY'S BELIEVE IT OR NOT: CRIME & MURDER

Schanes Products; 1 May 1993-2 Jun 1993

	$Good	$Fine	$N.Mint	£Good	£Fine	£N.Mint
1-2 ND Scott Hampton cover; black and white	$0.50	$1.50	$2.50	£0.30	£0.90	£1.50
Title Value:	$1.00	$3.00	$5.00	£0.60	£1.80	£3.00

RIPLEY'S BELIEVE IT OR NOT: CRUELTY

Schanes Products; 1 May 1993-2 Jun 1993

	$Good	$Fine	$N.Mint	£Good	£Fine	£N.Mint
1 ND Scott Hampton cover (says Unusual Deaths in indicia); black and white	$0.50	$1.50	$2.50	£0.30	£0.90	£1.50
2 ND Scott Hampton cover; black and white	$0.50	$1.50	$2.50	£0.30	£0.90	£1.50
Title Value:	$1.00	$3.00	$5.00	£0.60	£1.80	£3.00

RIPLEY'S BELIEVE IT OR NOT: DEATH

Schanes Products; 1 Aug 1993

	$Good	$Fine	$N.Mint	£Good	£Fine	£N.Mint
1 ND black and white	$0.50	$1.50	$2.50	£0.30	£0.90	£1.50
Title Value:	$0.50	$1.50	$2.50	£0.30	£0.90	£1.50

RIPLEY'S BELIEVE IT OR NOT: FAIRY TALES & LITERATURE

Schanes Products; 1 Jun 1993-2 Jul 1993

	$Good	$Fine	$N.Mint	£Good	£Fine	£N.Mint
1-2 ND Scott Hampton design photo cover; black and white	$0.50	$1.50	$2.50	£0.30	£0.90	£1.50
Title Value:	$1.00	$3.00	$5.00	£0.60	£1.80	£3.00

RIPLEY'S BELIEVE IT OR NOT: FEATS OF WONDER

Schanes Products; 1 Jun 1993-2 Jul 1993

	$Good	$Fine	$N.Mint	£Good	£Fine	£N.Mint
1-2 ND Scott Hampton cover; black and white	$0.50	$1.50	$2.50	£0.30	£0.90	£1.50
Title Value:	$1.00	$3.00	$5.00	£0.60	£1.80	£3.00

RIPLEY'S BELIEVE IT OR NOT: MODERN WONDERS

Schanes Products; 1 Sep 1993

	$Good	$Fine	$N.Mint	£Good	£Fine	£N.Mint
1 ND black and white; large cover stamp attached announcing US TV programme on Ripley	$0.50	$1.50	$2.50	£0.30	£0.90	£1.50
Title Value:	$0.50	$1.50	$2.50	£0.30	£0.90	£1.50

RIPLEY'S BELIEVE IT OR NOT: PERSONAL HYGIENE

Schanes Products; 1 Aug 1993

	$Good	$Fine	$N.Mint	£Good	£Fine	£N.Mint
1 ND black and white	$0.50	$1.50	$2.50	£0.30	£0.90	£1.50
Title Value:	$0.50	$1.50	$2.50	£0.30	£0.90	£1.50

RIPLEY'S BELIEVE IT OR NOT: RECORDS

Schanes Products; 1 Jun 1993-2 Jul 1993

	$Good	$Fine	$N.Mint	£Good	£Fine	£N.Mint
1-2 ND black and white	$0.50	$1.50	$2.50	£0.30	£0.90	£1.50
Title Value:	$1.00	$3.00	$5.00	£0.60	£1.80	£3.00

RIPLEY'S BELIEVE IT OR NOT: SPORTS FEATS

Schanes Products; 1 Jun 1993-2 Jul 1993

	$Good	$Fine	$N.Mint	£Good	£Fine	£N.Mint
1-2 ND Scott Hampton cover, black and white	$0.50	$1.50	$2.50	£0.30	£0.90	£1.50
Title Value:	$1.00	$3.00	$5.00	£0.60	£1.80	£3.00

RIPLEY'S BELIEVE IT OR NOT: STRANGE DEATHS

Schanes Products; 1 Jun 1993

	$Good	$Fine	$N.Mint	£Good	£Fine	£N.Mint
1 ND reprints famous newspaper cartoons, black and white; Scott Hampton cover (says Unusual Deaths in indicia)	$0.50	$1.50	$2.50	£0.30	£0.90	£1.50
Title Value:	$0.50	$1.50	$2.50	£0.30	£0.90	£1.50

RIPLEY'S BELIEVE IT OR NOT: STRANGE PEOPLE

Schanes Products; 1 Sep 1993

	$Good	$Fine	$N.Mint	£Good	£Fine	£N.Mint
1 ND black and white	$0.50	$1.50	$2.50	£0.30	£0.90	£1.50
Title Value:	$0.50	$1.50	$2.50	£0.30	£0.90	£1.50

RIPLEY'S BELIEVE IT OR NOT: STRANGE RELIGIONS

Schanes Products; 1 Sep 1993-2 Oct 1993

	$Good	$Fine	$N.Mint	£Good	£Fine	£N.Mint
1-2 ND black and white	$0.50	$1.50	$2.50	£0.30	£0.90	£1.50
Title Value:	$1.00	$3.00	$5.00	£0.60	£1.80	£3.00

RIPLEY'S BELIEVE IT OR NOT: THE MACABRE

Schanes Products; 1 Oct 1993

	$Good	$Fine	$N.Mint	£Good	£Fine	£N.Mint
1 ND black and white	$0.50	$1.50	$2.50	£0.30	£0.90	£1.50
Title Value:	$0.50	$1.50	$2.50	£0.30	£0.90	£1.50

RIPLEY'S BELIEVE IT OR NOT: THE ORIENT

Schanes Products; 1 Sep 1993

	$Good	$Fine	$N.Mint	£Good	£Fine	£N.Mint
1 ND black and white	$0.50	$1.50	$2.50	£0.30	£0.90	£1.50
Title Value:	$0.50	$1.50	$2.50	£0.30	£0.90	£1.50

RIPLEY'S BELIEVE IT OR NOT: WILD ANIMALS

Schanes Products; 1 Aug 1993

	$Good	$Fine	$N.Mint	£Good	£Fine	£N.Mint
1 ND black and white	$0.50	$1.50	$2.50	£0.30	£0.90	£1.50
Title Value:	$0.50	$1.50	$2.50	£0.30	£0.90	£1.50

RIPPER

Aircel,MS; 1 Nov 1989-6 Apr 1990

	$Good	$Fine	$N.Mint	£Good	£Fine	£N.Mint
1 ND Barry Blair script/art begins, black and white	$0.40	$1.20	$2.00	£0.25	£0.75	£1.25
1 2nd printing ND	$0.30	$0.90	$1.50	£0.20	£0.60	£1.00
2 ND	$0.40	$1.20	$2.00	£0.25	£0.75	£1.25
2 2nd printing ND	$0.30	$0.90	$1.50	£0.20	£0.60	£1.00
3-6 ND	$0.40	$1.20	$2.00	£0.25	£0.75	£1.25
Title Value:	$3.00	$9.00	$15.00	£1.90	£5.70	£9.50

Note: owing to the content of extreme violence, issue shipped pre-bagged. Approximately 75% value for un-bagged issues

RIPTIDE

Image,MS; 1 Sep 1995-2 Oct 1995

	$Good	$Fine	$N.Mint	£Good	£Fine	£N.Mint
1-2 ND Rob Liefeld script; origin told	$0.50	$1.50	$2.50	£0.30	£0.90	£1.50
Title Value:	$1.00	$3.00	$5.00	£0.60	£1.80	£3.00

RISE OF THE MIDNIGHT SONS

Marvel Comics Group; 1992

Cross-over storyline running throughout the following titles:
Ghost Rider [2nd Series] #28,
Ghost Rider & Blaze: Spirits of Vengeance #1,
Morbius #1,
Darkhold #1,
Nightstalkers #1,
Ghost Rider [2nd Series] #31.

RISK

Maximum Comic Press; 1 Oct 1995

	$Good	$Fine	$N.Mint	£Good	£Fine	£N.Mint
1 ND Robert Napton script, Fabian Ribiero art	$0.50	$1.50	$2.50	£0.30	£0.90	£1.50
Title Value:	$0.50	$1.50	$2.50	£0.30	£0.90	£1.50

ROACHMILL

Blackthorne; 1 Dec 1986-6 Aug 1987

	$Good	$Fine	$N.Mint	£Good	£Fine	£N.Mint
1 ND	$0.40	$1.20	$2.00	£0.40	£1.20	£2.00
2-6 ND	$0.30	$0.90	$1.50	£0.30	£0.90	£1.50
Title Value:	$1.90	$5.70	$9.50	£1.90	£5.70	£9.50
Trade Paperback (Dark Horse), reprints #1-4				£0.80	£2.40	£4.00

ROACHMILL (2ND SERIES)

Dark Horse; 1 May 1988-10 Dec 1990

(see Dark Horse Presents #17)

	$Good	$Fine	$N.Mint	£Good	£Fine	£N.Mint
1 ND	$0.60	$1.80	$3.00	£0.40	£1.20	£2.00
2-10 ND	$0.50	$1.50	$2.50	£0.30	£0.90	£1.50
Title Value:	$5.10	$15.30	$25.50	£3.10	£9.30	£15.50
Collection 1 (1991) ND				£0.80	£2.40	£4.00

ROADKILL: DEADWORLD CHRONICLES

Caliber Press; 1 Jan 1994

	$Good	$Fine	$N.Mint	£Good	£Fine	£N.Mint
1 Direct Market Edition, ND - pre-bagged with trading card	$0.70	$2.10	$3.50	£0.50	£1.50	£2.50
1 Newstand Edition ND	$0.60	$1.80	$3.00	£0.40	£1.20	£2.00
Title Value:	$1.30	$3.90	$6.50	£0.90	£2.70	£4.50

ROBIN

DC Comics,MS; 1 Jan 1991-5 May 1991

(see Batman, Detective)

	$Good	$Fine	$N.Mint	£Good	£Fine	£N.Mint
1 Batman, Lady Shiva appearances begin, poster by Neal Adams; covers by Brian Bolland begin	$0.80	$2.40	$4.00	£0.50	£1.50	£2.50
1 2nd printing, Roman numerals in date box	$0.30	$0.90	$1.50	£0.20	£0.60	£1.00
1 3rd printing	$0.25	$0.75	$1.25	£0.15	£0.45	£0.75
2	$0.40	$1.20	$2.00	£0.25	£0.75	£1.25
3-5	$0.30	$0.90	$1.50	£0.20	£0.60	£1.00
Title Value:	$2.65	$7.95	$13.25	£1.70	£5.10	£8.50
Robin: A Hero Reborn (Jul 1991) Trade paperback reprints Batman #455-#457 and Robin mini-series #1-5 new cover by Brian Bolland				£0.70	£2.10	£3.50
Robin: Tragedy and Triumph (Nov 1993) Trade paperback reprints Detective Comics #618-621 & Robin II: Joker's Wild #1-4				£1.30	£3.90	£6.50

ROBIN (2ND SERIES)

DC Comics; 0 Oct 1994; 1 Nov 1993-present

	$Good	$Fine	$N.Mint	£Good	£Fine	£N.Mint
0 (Oct 1994) Zero Hour X-over, origins of all three Robins	$0.40	$1.20	$2.00	£0.25	£0.75	£1.25
1	$0.30	$0.90	$1.50	£0.20	£0.60	£1.00
1 Collectors Edition, ND - embossed foil enhanced cover	$0.60	$1.80	$3.00	£0.40	£1.20	£2.00
2-5	$0.30	$0.90	$1.50	£0.20	£0.60	£1.00
6 X-over with Showcase'94 #6/7	$0.30	$0.90	$1.50	£0.20	£0.60	£1.00
7 Knightquest storyline concludes, continued in Batman #509	$0.30	$0.90	$1.50	£0.20	£0.60	£1.00
8 Knightsend part 5, continued in Catwoman #12	$0.30	$0.90	$1.50	£0.20	£0.60	£1.00
9 Knightsend: Aftermath, continued in Catwoman #13	$0.30	$0.90	$1.50	£0.20	£0.60	£1.00
10 Zero Hour X-over	$0.30	$0.90	$1.50	£0.20	£0.60	£1.00
11 Two Face appears	$0.30	$0.90	$1.50	£0.20	£0.60	£1.00
12-13	$0.30	$0.90	$1.50	£0.20	£0.60	£1.00
14 The Troika part 4 (conclusion)	$0.30	$0.90	$1.50	£0.20	£0.60	£1.00
14 Collectors Edition, ND embossed black cover	$0.50	$1.50	$2.50	£0.30	£0.90	£1.50
15-16	$0.30	$0.90	$1.50	£0.20	£0.60	£1.00
17 upgraded coated paper stock (Miraweb Format) begins	$0.40	$1.20	$2.00	£0.25	£0.75	£1.25
18-22	$0.40	$1.20	$2.00	£0.25	£0.75	£1.25
23 Underworld Unleashed tie-in, Killer Moth appears	$0.40	$1.20	$2.00	£0.25	£0.75	£1.25
24	$0.40	$1.20	$2.00	£0.25	£0.75	£1.25
25 Green Arrow guest-stars	$0.40	$1.20	$2.00	£0.25	£0.75	£1.25
26 bi-monthly	$0.40	$1.20	$2.00	£0.25	£0.75	£1.25
27 Contagion part 3, continued in Catwoman #31						

	$Good	$Fine	$N.Mint	£Good	£Fine	£N.Mint
	$0.40	$1.20	$2.00	£0.25	£0.75	£1.25
28 Contagion conclusion, continued from Azrael #16						
	$0.40	$1.20	$2.00	£0.25	£0.75	£1.25
29-30	$0.40	$1.20	$2.00	£0.25	£0.75	£1.25
31 Golden Age Wildcat appears						
	$0.40	$1.20	$2.00	£0.25	£0.75	£1.25
32 Legacy part 3, continued in Batman: Shadow of the Bat #54						
	$0.40	$1.20	$2.00	£0.25	£0.75	£1.25
33 Legacy conclusion, continued from Detective Comics #701						
	$0.40	$1.20	$2.00	£0.25	£0.75	£1.25
34	$0.40	$1.20	$2.00	£0.25	£0.75	£1.25
35 ND Final Night tie-in						
	$0.40	$1.20	$2.00	£0.25	£0.75	£1.25
36-37 ND The Toyman appears						
	$0.40	$1.20	$2.00	£0.25	£0.75	£1.25
38-39 ND	$0.40	$1.20	$2.00	£0.25	£0.75	£1.25
Title Value:	$15.50	$46.50	$77.50	£9.90	£29.70	£49.50
ROBIN 3000						
DC Comics,MS; 1,2 Jan 1993						
1-2 ND 48pgs, squarebound, P. Craig Russell cover and art						
	$0.90	$2.70	$4.50	£0.60	£1.80	£3.00
Title Value:	$1.80	$5.40	$9.00	£1.20	£3.60	£6.00
ROBIN ANNUAL						
DC Comics; 1 Sep 1992-present						
1 64pgs, Sam Kieth cover, Eclipso: The Darkness Within tie-in						
	$0.50	$1.50	$2.50	£0.30	£0.90	£1.50
2 64pgs, Bloodlines part 10, 1st appearance Razorsharp, continued in Action Comics Annual #5						
	$0.50	$1.50	$2.50	£0.30	£0.90	£1.50
3 64pgs, Elseworlds						
	$0.60	$1.80	$3.00	£0.40	£1.20	£2.00
4 64pgs, Year One	$0.60	$1.80	$3.00	£0.40	£1.20	£2.00
5 ND 48pgs, Legends of the Dead Earth story						
	$0.60	$1.80	$3.00	£0.40	£1.20	£2.00
Title Value:	$2.80	$8.40	$14.00	£1.80	£5.40	£9.00
ROBIN HOOD						
Eclipse,MS; 1 Sep 1991-3 Nov 1991						
1-3 ND	$0.40	$1.20	$2.00	£0.25	£0.75	£1.25
Title Value:	$1.20	$3.60	$6.00	£0.75	£2.25	£3.75
ROBIN HOOD TALES						
National Periodical Publications;7 Jan/Feb 1957-14 Mar/Apr 1958						
(issues #1-6 published by Quality)						
7 rare in the U.K.	$30.00	$90.00	$240.00	£22.50	£67.50	£180.00
8-14 rare in the U.K.						
	$26.00	$75.00	$205.00	£17.50	£52.50	£140.00
Title Value:	$212.00	$615.00	$1675.00	£145.00	£435.00	£1160.00
ROBIN III - CRY OF THE HUNTRESS						
DC Comics,MS; 1 Dec 1992-6 Mar 1993						
1 Mike Zeck cover	$0.40	$1.20	$2.00	£0.25	£0.75	£1.25
1 Collectors Edition:, ND pre-bagged with mini-poster and "movement-enhanced" cover						
	$0.45	$1.35	$2.25	£0.30	£0.90	£1.50
2 Mike Zeck cover	$0.40	$1.20	$2.00	£0.25	£0.75	£1.25
2 Collectors Edition:, ND pre-bagged with mini-poster and "movement-enhanced" cover						
	$0.45	$1.35	$2.25	£0.30	£0.90	£1.50
3 Mike Zeck cover	$0.40	$1.20	$2.00	£0.25	£0.75	£1.25
3 Collectors Edition:, ND pre-bagged with mini-poster and "movement-enhanced" cover						
	$0.45	$1.35	$2.25	£0.30	£0.90	£1.50
4 Mike Zeck cover	$0.40	$1.20	$2.00	£0.25	£0.75	£1.25
4 Collectors Edition:, ND pre-bagged with mini-poster and "movement-enhanced" cover						
	$0.45	$1.35	$2.25	£0.30	£0.90	£1.50
5 Mike Zeck cover	$0.40	$1.20	$2.00	£0.25	£0.75	£1.25
5 Collectors Edition:, ND pre-bagged with mini-poster and "movement-enhanced" cover						
	$0.45	$1.35	$2.25	£0.30	£0.90	£1.50
6	$0.40	$1.20	$2.00	£0.25	£0.75	£1.25
6 Collectors Edition:, ND pre-bagged with mini-poster and "movement-enhanced" cover						
	$0.45	$1.35	$2.25	£0.30	£0.90	£1.50
Title Value:	$5.10	$15.30	$25.50	£3.30	£9.90	£16.50
Note: bi-weekly frequency						
ROBIN MINI-SERIES MULTI-PACK						
DC Comics,OS; 1 Oct 1991						
1 ND scarce in the U.K. shrink-wrapped set of 5 issue mini-series; issue #1 (3rd print), issue #2 (2nd print), illustrated card titled DC Classic Comics						
	$1.00	$3.00	$5.00	£0.70	£2.10	£3.50
Title Value:	$1.00	$3.00	$5.00	£0.70	£2.10	£3.50
ROBIN PLUS #1						
DC Comics,OS; 1 Dec 1996						
1 ND 48pgs, Robin and Impulse appear						
	$0.60	$1.80	$3.00	£0.40	£1.20	£2.00
Title Value:	$0.60	$1.80	$3.00	£0.40	£1.20	£2.00
ROBIN: THE JOKER'S WILD						
DC Comics,MS; 1 Dec 1991-4 Mar 1992						
1 sequel to Robin mini-series, Joker appears						
	$0.25	$0.75	$1.25	£0.15	£0.45	£0.75
1 Direct Market Edition, ND of the above, four cover variations with same hologram but each on a different part of the cover						
	$0.30	$0.90	$1.50	£0.20	£0.60	£1.00
2	$0.25	$0.75	$1.25	£0.15	£0.45	£0.75
2 Direct Market Edition, ND of the above, three cover variations with the same hologram but each on a different part of the cover						
	$0.30	$0.90	$1.50	£0.20	£0.60	£1.00
3	$0.25	$0.75	$1.25	£0.15	£0.45	£0.75
3 Direct Market Edition, ND of the above, two cover variations with same hologram but each on a different part of the cover						
	$0.30	$0.90	$1.50	£0.20	£0.60	£1.00
4	$0.25	$0.75	$1.25	£0.15	£0.45	£0.75
4 Direct Market Edition, ND of the above, hologram cover						
	$0.30	$0.90	$1.50	£0.20	£0.60	£1.00
Title Value:	$2.20	$6.60	$11.00	£1.40	£4.20	£7.00
Robin: The Joker's Wild #1 Collector's Set (Dec 1991), ND pre-bagged, contains the news-stand edition plus all four direct-sale hologram editions with hologram trading card				£1.25	£3.75	£6.25
Robin: The Joker's Wild #2 Collector's Set (Jan 1992), ND pre-bagged, contains the news-stand edition plus all three direct-sale hologram editions with hologram trading card				£1.00	£3.00	£5.00
Robin: The Joker's Wild #3 Collector's Set (Jan 1992), ND pre-bagged, contains the news-stand edition plus the direct-sale hologram editions with hologram trading card				£0.75	£2.25	£3.75
Robin: The Joker's Wild #4 Collector's Set (Feb 1992), ND contains the news-stand and Direct sale editions plus hologram trading card				£0.50	£1.50	£2.50
Robin: The Joker's Wild Deluxe Complete Set (Dec 1991), ND pre-bagged, all 14 variant covers from the 4 issue mini-series; gift certificate (issued in advance) and limited to 25,000 editions, 13.7cm x 15.2cm "R" hologram on slipcase				£5.00	£15.00	£25.00
Robin: The Joker's Wild Multi-Pack (Sep 1992), ND contains issues #1-4 direct-sales editions (with holograms), 1st printings				£0.50	£1.50	£2.50
ROBOCOP						
Marvel Comics Group; 1 Mar 1990-23 Jan 1992						
1 ND Alan Grant script begins						
	$0.30	$0.90	$1.50	£0.20	£0.60	£1.00
2-10 ND						
	$0.30	$0.90	$1.50	£0.20	£0.60	£1.00
11 ND last Alan Grant						
	$0.25	$0.75	$1.25	£0.15	£0.45	£0.75
12-15 ND Robocop Army story						
	$0.25	$0.75	$1.25	£0.15	£0.45	£0.75
16-20 ND	$0.25	$0.75	$1.25	£0.15	£0.45	£0.75
21-23 ND Beyond The Law story						
	$0.25	$0.75	$1.25	£0.15	£0.45	£0.75
Title Value:	$6.25	$18.75	$31.25	£3.95	£11.85	£19.75
Bookshelf Special (Jul 1990), 48pgs				£0.65	£1.95	£3.25
Note: based on Movie character, High quality paper						
ROBOCOP 2						
Marvel Comics Group,OS Film; 1 Aug 1990						
1 ND 48pgs, based on Frank Miller screenplay, Alan Grant script						
	$0.80	$2.40	$4.00	£0.50	£1.50	£2.50
Title Value:	$0.80	$2.40	$4.00	£0.50	£1.50	£2.50
Note: Bookshelf Format						
ROBOCOP 2 (LIMITED SERIES)						
Marvel Comics Group,MS Film; 1 Aug 1990-3 Oct 1990						
1-3 ND Alan Grant script based on Frank Miller screenplay						
	$0.30	$0.90	$1.50	£0.20	£0.60	£1.00
Title Value:	$0.90	$2.70	$4.50	£0.60	£1.80	£3.00
ROBOCOP 2 BOOKSHELF FORMAT						
Marvel Comics Group,OS Film; 1 Aug 1991						
1 ND 48pgs, adaptation of film						
	$1.00	$3.00	$5.00	£0.70	£2.10	£3.50
Title Value:	$1.00	$3.00	$5.00	£0.70	£2.10	£3.50
ROBOCOP 2 MAGAZINE						
Marvel Comics Group,OS Film; 1 Aug 1991						
1 ND 48pgs, black and white reprint of the above						
	$0.40	$1.20	$2.00	£0.25	£0.75	£1.25
Title Value:	$0.40	$1.20	$2.00	£0.25	£0.75	£1.25
ROBOCOP 3						
Dark Horse,MS; 1 Aug 1992-3 Oct 1993						
1-3 ND adaptation of film, bi-weekly						
	$0.50	$1.50	$2.50	£0.30	£0.90	£1.50
Title Value:	$1.50	$4.50	$7.50	£0.90	£2.70	£4.50
ROBOCOP VERSUS TERMINATOR						
Dark Horse,MS; 1 May 1992-4 Aug 1992						
1 ND Frank Miller and Walt Simonson script/art begins; contains bound-in trading cards						
	$0.50	$1.50	$2.50	£0.30	£0.90	£1.50
1 Platinum Edition ND	$2.00	$6.00	$10.00	£1.20	£3.60	£6.00
1 Sealed envelope, ND (Dark Horse imprinted) containing Platinum Edition, 2 numbered prints and an un-cut sheet of trading cards						
	$3.00	$9.00	$15.00	£2.00	£6.00	£10.00
2-4 ND	$0.50	$1.50	$2.50	£0.30	£0.90	£1.50
Title Value:	$7.00	$21.00	$35.00	£4.40	£13.20	£22.00
Robocop vs. Terminator Compilation (1994)						
Trade paperback reprints mini-series, new Walt Simonson cover				£1.70	£5.10	£8.50
ROBOCOP: MORTAL COILS						
Dark Horse,MS; 1 Sep 1993-4 Dec 1993						
1-4 ND	$0.50	$1.50	$2.50	£0.30	£0.90	£1.50
Title Value:	$2.00	$6.00	$10.00	£1.20	£3.60	£6.00
ROBOCOP: PRIME SUSPECT						
Dark Horse,MS; 1 Oct 1992-4 Jan 1993						
1-4 ND	$0.50	$1.50	$2.50	£0.30	£0.90	£1.50
Title Value:	$2.00	$6.00	$10.00	£1.20	£3.60	£6.00
ROBOCOP: ROULETTE						
Dark Horse,MS; 1 Jan 1994-4 Apr 1994						
1-4 ND Nelson painted covers						
	$0.50	$1.50	$2.50	£0.30	£0.90	£1.50
Title Value:	$2.00	$6.00	$10.00	£1.20	£3.60	£6.00

	$Good	$Fine	$N.Mint	£Good	£Fine	£N.Mint
ROBOT COMICS						
Renegade; 0 Jun 1987						
0 ND Bob Burden script and art						
	$0.50	*$1.50*	*$2.50*	£0.30	£0.90	£1.50
Title Value:	*$0.50*	*$1.50*	*$2.50*	£0.30	£0.90	£1.50
ROBOTECH						
Academy Comics,OS; 0 Sep 1994						
0 ND Bill Spangler script, William Jang art; outlines history of characters plus interviews with creators						
	$0.40	*$1.20*	*$2.00*	£0.25	£0.75	£1.25
Title Value:	*$0.40*	*$1.20*	*$2.00*	£0.25	£0.75	£1.25
ROBOTECH DEFENDERS						
DC Comics,MS; 1 Mar 1985-2 Apr 1985						
(see Robotech Masters, Macross [Comico])						
1-2	*$0.15*	*$0.45*	*$0.75*	£0.10	£0.35	£0.60
Title Value:	*$0.30*	*$0.90*	*$1.50*	£0.20	£0.70	£1.20
ROBOTECH II: SENTINELS CRYSTAL WORLD - PRISONERS OF SPHERIS						
Academy Comics; 1 Jun 1996						
1 ND John and Jason Waltrip; black and white						
	$0.60	*$1.80*	*$3.00*	£0.40	£1.20	£2.00
Title Value:	*$0.60*	*$1.80*	*$3.00*	£0.40	£1.20	£2.00
ROBOTECH II: THE SENTINELS						
Eternity; 1 Nov 1988-16 1990						
1-3 ND	*$0.40*	*$1.20*	*$2.00*	£0.25	£0.75	£1.25
3 2nd printing ND	*$0.30*	*$0.90*	*$1.50*	£0.20	£0.60	£1.00
4-10 ND	*$0.40*	*$1.20*	*$2.00*	£0.25	£0.75	£1.25
11-16 ND	*$0.30*	*$0.90*	*$1.50*	£0.20	£0.60	£1.00
Title Value:	*$6.10*	*$18.30*	*$30.50*	£3.90	£11.70	£19.50
The Sentinels Graphic Album (1990) reprints issues #1-4				£2.20	£6.60	£11.00
Limited Edition, reprints issues #1-4 (850 copies)				£5.50	£16.50	£27.50
The Sentinels Hardcover 2 (Aug 1990)						
reprints issues #5,6 plus Wedding Special #1,2				£2.20	£6.60	£11.00
Softcover, reprints issues #1-4				£1.05	£3.75	£5.25
Hardcover				£5.50	£16.50	£27.50
Signed and Numbered Edition				£7.00	£21.00	£35.00
Robotech II - The Sentinels: Operation Tirol						
reprints issues #7-10				£1.05	£3.75	£5.25
Robotech II - The Sentinels: Mission Impossible!						
reprints issues #11-14				£1.30	£3.90	£6.50
ROBOTECH II: THE SENTINELS - BOOK 2						
Eternity; 1 Jun 1990-21 Jul 1993						
1-10 ND	*$0.40*	*$1.20*	*$2.00*	£0.25	£0.75	£1.25
11-21 ND	*$0.30*	*$0.90*	*$1.50*	£0.20	£0.60	£1.00
Title Value:	*$7.30*	*$21.90*	*$36.50*	£4.70	£14.10	£23.50
ROBOTECH II: THE SENTINELS - BOOK 3						
Eternity,MS; 1 Aug 1993-8 Mar 1994; Academy Comics; 9 Sep 1994-22 Oct 1995						
1 ND	*$0.50*	*$1.50*	*$2.50*	£0.30	£0.90	£1.50
1 The Untold Story Edition, ND (Dec 1993) - special one-shot edition featuring 8 uncensored pages						
	$0.45	*$1.35*	*$2.25*	£0.30	£0.90	£1.50
2-15 ND	*$0.50*	*$1.50*	*$2.50*	£0.30	£0.90	£1.50
16-17 ND	*$0.60*	*$1.80*	*$3.00*	£0.40	£1.20	£2.00
18 ND $2.95 cover begins						
	$0.60	*$1.80*	*$3.00*	£0.40	£1.20	£2.00
19-22 ND	*$0.60*	*$1.80*	*$3.00*	£0.40	£1.20	£2.00
Title Value:	*$12.15*	*$36.45*	*$60.75*	£7.60	£22.80	£38.00
ROBOTECH II: THE SENTINELS - BOOK 4						
Academy Comics,MS; 1 Dec 1995-7 1996						
1-7 ND black and white						
	$0.60	*$1.80*	*$3.00*	£0.40	£1.20	£2.00
Title Value:	*$4.20*	*$12.60*	*$21.00*	£2.80	£8.40	£14.00
ROBOTECH II: THE SENTINELS - CYBERPIRATES						
Eternity,MS; 1 Apr 1991-4 Jul 1991						
1-4 ND black and white						
	$0.40	*$1.20*	*$2.00*	£0.25	£0.75	£1.25
Title Value:	*$1.60*	*$4.80*	*$8.00*	£1.00	£3.00	£5.00
ROBOTECH II: THE SENTINELS - SWIMSUIT SPECTACULAR						
Eternity,OS; 1 Jul 1992						
1 ND	*$0.50*	*$1.50*	*$2.50*	£0.30	£0.90	£1.50
Title Value:	*$0.50*	*$1.50*	*$2.50*	£0.30	£0.90	£1.50
ROBOTECH II: THE SENTINELS - THE ILLUSTRATED HANDBOOK						
Eternity,MS; 1 Jul 1991-3 Sep 1991						
1-3 ND black and white						
	$0.40	*$1.20*	*$2.00*	£0.25	£0.75	£1.25
Title Value:	*$1.20*	*$3.60*	*$6.00*	£0.75	£2.25	£3.75
ROBOTECH II: THE SENTINELS - THE MALCONTENT UPRISINGS						
Eternity,MS; 1 Apr 1989-12 Dec 1990						
1-12 ND black and white						
	$0.40	*$1.20*	*$2.00*	£0.25	£0.75	£1.25
Title Value:	*$4.80*	*$14.40*	*$24.00*	£3.00	£9.00	£15.00
ROBOTECH II: THE SENTINELS SCRIPT BOOK						
Eternity; 1 Aug 1991-2 1991						
1 ND script of unfilmed TV series, episodes #1-4						
	$1.50	*$4.50*	*$7.50*	£1.00	£3.00	£5.00
1 2nd printing, ND (Aug 1992)						
	$1.20	*$3.60*	*$6.00*	£0.80	£2.40	£4.00
2 ND script of unfilmed TV series, episodes #5-8						
	$1.50	*$4.50*	*$7.50*	£1.00	£3.00	£5.00
Title Value:	*$4.20*	*$12.60*	*$21.00*	£2.80	£8.40	£14.00
ROBOTECH IN 3-D						
Comico,OS; 1 Aug 1987						
1 ND Ken Steacy wraparound cover; with bound-in 3-D glasses (25% less without glasses)						
	$0.50	*$1.50*	*$2.50*	£0.30	£0.90	£1.50
Title Value:	*$0.50*	*$1.50*	*$2.50*	£0.30	£0.90	£1.50
ROBOTECH MASTERS						
Comico; 1 Jul 1985-23 Apr 1988						
1-23 ND colour	*$0.30*	*$0.90*	*$1.50*	£0.20	£0.60	£1.00
Title Value:	*$6.90*	*$20.70*	*$34.50*	£4.60	£13.80	£23.00
ROBOTECH METAL SWARM						
Academy Comics,OS; 1 Dec 1995						
1 ND black and white						
	$0.60	*$1.80*	*$3.00*	£0.40	£1.20	£2.00
Title Value:	*$0.60*	*$1.80*	*$3.00*	£0.40	£1.20	£2.00
ROBOTECH SPECIAL						
Comico,OS; 1 May 1988						
1 ND 40pgs, sub-titled "Dana's Story"; photo-collage cover						
	$0.50	*$1.50*	*$2.50*	£0.30	£0.90	£1.50
Title Value:	*$0.50*	*$1.50*	*$2.50*	£0.30	£0.90	£1.50
ROBOTECH SPECIAL: MACROSS MISSIONS - DESTROID						
Academy Comics,OS; 1 Jul 1995						
1 ND William Jang script and art; black and white						
	$0.60	*$1.80*	*$3.00*	£0.40	£1.20	£2.00
Title Value:	*$0.60*	*$1.80*	*$3.00*	£0.40	£1.20	£2.00
ROBOTECH, THE OFFICIAL HOW TO DRAW						
Blackthorne,MS; 1 Jan 1987-2 Mar 1987						
1-2 ND black and white						
	$0.25	*$0.75*	*$1.25*	£0.15	£0.45	£0.75
Title Value:	*$0.50*	*$1.50*	*$2.50*	£0.30	£0.90	£1.50
ROBOTECH, WORLDS OF						
Academy Comics,OS; 1 Sep 1995						
0 reprints four classic stories; black and white						
	$2.50	*$7.50*	*$12.50*	£1.50	£4.50	£7.50
Title Value:	*$2.50*	*$7.50*	*$12.50*	£1.50	£4.50	£7.50

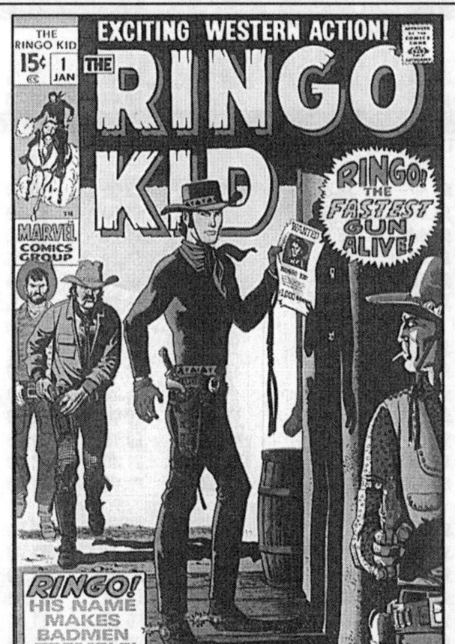

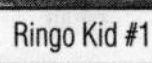

Ringo Kid #1

Rip Hunter, Time Master #1

Robotech II: The Sentinels #1

ROBOTECH: ACADEMY BLUES

Academy Comics,OS; 0 May 1995; 1 Jun 1995-5 1996 ?

Issue	$Good	$Fine	$N.Mint	£Good	£Fine	£N.Mint
0 ND Robert Gibson script, Sean Bishop art begins; bi-monthly and black and white	$0.60	$1.80	$3.00	£0.40	£1.20	£2.00
1-5 ND bi-monthly; black and white	$0.60	$1.80	$3.00	£0.40	£1.20	£2.00
Title Value:	$3.60	$10.80	$18.00	£2.40	£7.20	£12.00

ROBOTECH: AMAZON WORLD - ESCAPE FROM PRAXIS

Academy Comics; 1 Nov 1994

Issue	$Good	$Fine	$N.Mint	£Good	£Fine	£N.Mint
1 ND black and white	$0.60	$1.80	$3.00	£0.40	£1.20	£2.00
Title Value:	$0.60	$1.80	$3.00	£0.40	£1.20	£2.00

ROBOTECH: CLONE

Academy Comics; 0 Dec 1994; 1 Jan 1995-present

Issue	$Good	$Fine	$N.Mint	£Good	£Fine	£N.Mint
0 ND story continues from Robotech: Invid War: Aftermath #7-9; black and white	$0.60	$1.80	$3.00	£0.40	£1.20	£2.00
1 ND black and white	$0.60	$1.80	$3.00	£0.40	£1.20	£2.00
1 Special Edition, ND (Jun 1995), John Schearman art	$0.80	$2.40	$4.00	£0.50	£1.50	£2.50
2-5 ND black and white	$0.60	$1.80	$3.00	£0.40	£1.20	£2.00
Title Value:	$4.40	$13.20	$22.00	£2.90	£8.70	£14.50
Robotech: The Threadbare Heart Graphic Novel (Apr 1995) reprints three issue story arc of Robotech that lead directly into Robotech: Clone				£1.30	£3.90	£6.50

ROBOTECH: CYBERWORLD - SECRETS OF HAYDON IV

Academy Comics; 1 Jul 1995

Issue	$Good	$Fine	$N.Mint	£Good	£Fine	£N.Mint
1 ND black and white	$0.60	$1.80	$3.00	£0.40	£1.20	£2.00
Title Value:	$0.60	$1.80	$3.00	£0.40	£1.20	£2.00

ROBOTECH: FIREWALKERS

Eternity,OS; 1 Mar 1993

Issue	$Good	$Fine	$N.Mint	£Good	£Fine	£N.Mint
1 ND spin-off from Invid War	$0.40	$1.20	$2.00	£0.25	£0.75	£1.25
Title Value:	$0.40	$1.20	$2.00	£0.25	£0.75	£1.25

ROBOTECH: GENESIS

Eternity,MS; 1 Mar 1992-6 Jan 1993

Issue	$Good	$Fine	$N.Mint	£Good	£Fine	£N.Mint
1 ND	$0.50	$1.50	$2.50	£0.30	£0.90	£1.50
1 Limited Edition, ND (Mar 1992) - includes two trading cards, 8 extra pages, foil embossed cover. 10,000 copies, sequentially numbered on front cover	$0.70	$2.10	$3.50	£0.50	£1.50	£2.50
2-6 ND	$0.50	$1.50	$2.50	£0.30	£0.90	£1.50
Title Value:	$3.70	$11.10	$18.50	£2.30	£6.90	£11.50

ROBOTECH: HOSHQ'S STORY

Academy Comics,OS; 1 Nov 1994

Issue	$Good	$Fine	$N.Mint	£Good	£Fine	£N.Mint
1 ND Bruce Lewis script and art; black and white	$0.60	$1.80	$3.00	£0.40	£1.20	£2.00
Title Value:	$0.60	$1.80	$3.00	£0.40	£1.20	£2.00

ROBOTECH: INVID WAR

Eternity,MS; 1 Jul 1992-18 Dec 1993

Issue	$Good	$Fine	$N.Mint	£Good	£Fine	£N.Mint
1-5 ND	$0.50	$1.50	$2.50	£0.30	£0.90	£1.50
6-11 ND	$0.40	$1.20	$2.00	£0.25	£0.75	£1.25
12 ND announced as an extended series	$0.40	$1.20	$2.00	£0.25	£0.75	£1.25
13-18 ND	$0.40	$1.20	$2.00	£0.25	£0.75	£1.25
Title Value:	$7.70	$23.10	$38.50	£4.75	£14.25	£23.75

ROBOTECH: INVID WAR AFTERMATH

Eternity; 1 Jan 1994-6 Jun 1994; Academy Comics; 7 Sep 1994-13 1995 ?

Issue	$Good	$Fine	$N.Mint	£Good	£Fine	£N.Mint
1-5 ND black and white	$0.50	$1.50	$2.50	£0.30	£0.90	£1.50
6 ND black and white	$0.40	$1.20	$2.00	£0.25	£0.75	£1.25
7-13 ND black and white, $2.95 cover	$0.40	$1.20	$2.00	£0.25	£0.75	£1.25
Title Value:	$5.70	$17.10	$28.50	£3.50	£10.50	£17.50

ROBOTECH: MACROSS TEMPEST

Academy Comics,OS; 1 Sep 1995

Issue	$Good	$Fine	$N.Mint	£Good	£Fine	£N.Mint
1 ND Gary Terry script and art; black and white	$0.60	$1.80	$3.00	£0.40	£1.20	£2.00
Title Value:	$0.60	$1.80	$3.00	£0.40	£1.20	£2.00

ROBOTECH: MECHANGEL

Academy Comics,MS; 0 Sep 1995; 1 Jan 1996-3 Mar 1996

Issue	$Good	$Fine	$N.Mint	£Good	£Fine	£N.Mint
0 ND Bill Spangler script, Jim Reddington art; black and white	$0.60	$1.80	$3.00	£0.40	£1.20	£2.00
1-3 ND black and white	$0.60	$1.80	$3.00	£0.40	£1.20	£2.00
Title Value:	$2.40	$7.20	$12.00	£1.60	£4.80	£8.00

ROBOTECH: MORDECAI

Academy Comics; 1 Feb 1996-2 Apr 1996 ?

Issue	$Good	$Fine	$N.Mint	£Good	£Fine	£N.Mint
1 ND black and white	$0.60	$1.80	$3.00	£0.40	£1.20	£2.00
2 ND	$0.60	$1.80	$3.00	£0.40	£1.20	£2.00
Title Value:	$1.20	$3.60	$6.00	£0.80	£2.40	£4.00

ROBOTECH: OPTERA, INVID WAR

Academy Comics,OS; 1 Oct 1994

Issue	$Good	$Fine	$N.Mint	£Good	£Fine	£N.Mint
1 ND information, diagrams and text on Robotech	$0.60	$1.80	$3.00	£0.40	£1.20	£2.00
Title Value:	$0.60	$1.80	$3.00	£0.40	£1.20	£2.00

ROBOTECH: RETURN TO MACROSS

Eternity; 1 May 1993-12 Apr 1994; Academy Comics; 13 Sep 1994-present

Issue	$Good	$Fine	$N.Mint	£Good	£Fine	£N.Mint
1-5 ND black and white	$0.50	$1.50	$2.50	£0.30	£0.90	£1.50
6-14 ND black and white	$0.40	$1.20	$2.00	£0.25	£0.75	£1.25
15 ND black and white; flip-book format with Robotech Warrior #0	$0.40	$1.20	$2.00	£0.25	£0.75	£1.25
16-20 ND black and white	$0.40	$1.20	$2.00	£0.25	£0.75	£1.25
21 ND black and white	$0.50	$1.50	$2.50	£0.30	£0.90	£1.50
22 ND $2.95 cover begins, War of the Believers story; black and white	$0.50	$1.50	$2.50	£0.30	£0.90	£1.50
23-24 ND War of the Believers story; black and white	$0.50	$1.50	$2.50	£0.30	£0.90	£1.50
25 ND 40pgs, $3.75 cover, War of the Believers story; silver foil enhanced cover; black and white	$0.60	$1.80	$3.00	£0.40	£1.20	£2.00
25 Special Edition, ND pre-bagged with un-cut sheet of cards	$0.90	$2.70	$4.50	£0.50	£1.50	£2.50
26-33 ND black and white	$0.60	$1.80	$3.00	£0.40	£1.20	£2.00
Title Value:	$16.80	$50.40	$84.00	£10.55	£31.65	£52.75

ROBOTECH: SMITH WORLD - SABOTAGE ON KARBARRA

Academy Comics; 1 Mar 1995

Issue	$Good	$Fine	$N.Mint	£Good	£Fine	£N.Mint
1 ND black and white	$0.60	$1.80	$3.00	£0.40	£1.20	£2.00
Title Value:	$0.60	$1.80	$3.00	£0.40	£1.20	£2.00

ROBOTECH: THE GRAPHIC NOVEL

Comico; 1 Aug 1986

Issue	$Good	$Fine	$N.Mint	£Good	£Fine	£N.Mint
1 ND	$1.00	$3.00	$5.00	£0.70	£2.10	£3.50
Title Value:	$1.00	$3.00	$5.00	£0.70	£2.10	£3.50

ROBOTECH: THE MACROSS SAGA

Comico;2 Feb 1985-36 Feb 1989

(previously Macross)

Issue	$Good	$Fine	$N.Mint	£Good	£Fine	£N.Mint
2-5 ND	$0.50	$1.50	$2.50	£0.30	£0.90	£1.50
6-36 ND	$0.40	$1.20	$2.00	£0.25	£0.75	£1.25
Title Value:	$14.40	$43.20	$72.00	£8.95	£26.85	£44.75

ROBOTECH: THE MACROSS SAGA - BOOBY TRAP

Academy Comics; 1 Mar 1996

Issue	$Good	$Fine	$N.Mint	£Good	£Fine	£N.Mint
1 ND Sean Bishop script and art; black and white	$0.60	$1.80	$3.00	£0.40	£1.20	£2.00
Title Value:	$0.60	$1.80	$3.00	£0.40	£1.20	£2.00

ROBOTECH: THE NEW GENERATION

Comico; 1 Jul 1985-25 Jul 1988

Issue	$Good	$Fine	$N.Mint	£Good	£Fine	£N.Mint
1-5 ND based on Harmony-Gold TV series, colour	$0.50	$1.50	$2.50	£0.30	£0.90	£1.50
6-25 ND based on Harmony-Gold TV series, colour	$0.40	$1.20	$2.00	£0.25	£0.75	£1.25
Title Value:	$10.50	$31.50	$52.50	£6.50	£19.50	£32.50

ROBOTECH: THE SENTINELS PRESENTS FERAL WORLD: NIGHTMARE ON G

Academy Comics,OS; 1 Jan 1996

Issue	$Good	$Fine	$N.Mint	£Good	£Fine	£N.Mint
1 ND black and white	$0.60	$1.80	$3.00	£0.40	£1.20	£2.00
Title Value:	$0.60	$1.80	$3.00	£0.40	£1.20	£2.00

ROBOTECH: WAR OF THE BELIEVERS GRAPHIC NOVEL

Academy Comics,OS; nn Apr 1996

Issue	$Good	$Fine	$N.Mint	£Good	£Fine	£N.Mint
nn ND 100pgs, Bill Spangler script, Wes Abbott art; black and white	$2.60	$7.75	$13.00	£1.70	£5.00	£8.50
Title Value:	$2.60	$7.75	$13.00	£1.70	£5.00	£8.50

ROBOTECH: WARRIORS

Academy Comics; 1 Feb 1995-3 1995

Issue	$Good	$Fine	$N.Mint	£Good	£Fine	£N.Mint
1-3 ND black and white	$0.60	$1.80	$3.00	£0.40	£1.20	£2.00
Title Value:	$1.80	$5.40	$9.00	£1.20	£3.60	£6.00

ROBOTIX

Marvel Comics Group,OS Toy; 1 Feb 1986

Issue	$Good	$Fine	$N.Mint	£Good	£Fine	£N.Mint
1 ND scarce in the U.K.	$0.25	$0.75	$1.25	£0.15	£0.45	£0.75
Title Value:	$0.25	$0.75	$1.25	£0.15	£0.45	£0.75

ROCK N' ROLL COMICS

Revolutionary Comics; 1 Jun 1989-71 1994

Issue	$Good	$Fine	$N.Mint	£Good	£Fine	£N.Mint
1 features Guns and Roses	$1.60	$4.80	$8.00	£1.00	£3.00	£5.00
1 2nd printing	$0.80	$2.40	$4.00	£0.50	£1.50	£2.50
1 3rd printing	$0.60	$1.80	$3.00	£0.40	£1.20	£2.00
1 4th printing	$0.60	$1.80	$3.00	£0.40	£1.20	£2.00
1 5th printing	$0.50	$1.50	$2.50	£0.30	£0.90	£1.50
1 6th printing	$0.40	$1.20	$2.00	£0.25	£0.75	£1.25
1 7th printing, new group biography/pin-ups	$0.40	$1.20	$2.00	£0.25	£0.75	£1.25
2 features Metallica	$1.00	$3.00	$5.00	£0.70	£2.10	£3.50
2 2nd printing	$0.60	$1.80	$3.00	£0.40	£1.20	£2.00
2 3rd printing	$0.50	$1.50	$2.50	£0.30	£0.90	£1.50
2 4th-6th printings	$0.40	$1.20	$2.00	£0.25	£0.75	£1.25
3 features Bon Jovi	$0.90	$2.70	$4.50	£0.60	£1.80	£3.00
3 2nd printing	$0.50	$1.50	$2.50	£0.30	£0.90	£1.50
4 features Motley Crue	$0.60	$1.80	$3.00	£0.40	£1.20	£2.00
4 2nd printing	$0.50	$1.50	$2.50	£0.30	£0.90	£1.50
5 Def Leppard	$0.50	$1.50	$2.50	£0.30	£0.90	£1.50
5 2nd printing	$0.50	$1.50	$2.50	£0.30	£0.90	£1.50
6 Rolling Stones	$0.50	$1.50	$2.50	£0.30	£0.90	£1.50
6 2nd-4th printings	$0.40	$1.20	$2.00	£0.25	£0.75	£1.25
7 The Who	$0.50	$1.50	$2.50	£0.30	£0.90	£1.50

	$Good	$Fine	$N.Mint	£Good	£Fine	£N.Mint
7 2nd/3rd printing	$0.40	$1.20	$2.00	£0.25	£0.75	£1.25
Never published, reason unknown at time of going to press						
9 Kiss	$0.50	$1.50	$2.50	£0.30	£0.90	£1.50
9 2nd-4th printings	$0.40	$1.20	$2.00	£0.25	£0.75	£1.25
10 Warrant/Whitesnake	$0.50	$1.50	$2.50	£0.30	£0.90	£1.50
10 2nd printing	$0.40	$1.20	$2.00	£0.25	£0.75	£1.25
11 Aerosmith	$0.30	$0.90	$1.50	£0.30	£0.90	£1.50
11 2nd printing	$0.40	$1.20	$2.00	£0.25	£0.75	£1.25
12 New Kids on the Block	$0.30	$0.90	$1.50	£0.30	£0.90	£1.50
12 2nd/3rd printing	$0.40	$1.20	$2.00	£0.25	£0.75	£1.25
13 Led Zepplin	$0.40	$1.20	$2.00	£0.25	£0.75	£1.25
14 The Sex Pistols	$0.40	$1.20	$2.00	£0.25	£0.75	£1.25
15 Poison	$0.40	$1.20	$2.00	£0.25	£0.75	£1.25
16 Van Halen	$0.40	$1.20	$2.00	£0.25	£0.75	£1.25
17 Madonna/Blondie/Paula Abdul, 1st colour issue	$0.40	$1.20	$2.00	£0.25	£0.75	£1.25
18 Alice Cooper	$0.40	$1.20	$2.00	£0.25	£0.75	£1.25
19 Live Crew/Public Enemy	$0.40	$1.20	$2.00	£0.25	£0.75	£1.25
20 Queensryche	$0.40	$1.20	$2.00	£0.25	£0.75	£1.25
21 Prince	$0.40	$1.20	$2.00	£0.25	£0.75	£1.25
22 AC/DC	$0.40	$1.20	$2.00	£0.25	£0.75	£1.25
23 Living Color	$0.40	$1.20	$2.00	£0.25	£0.75	£1.25
24 Anthrax	$0.40	$1.20	$2.00	£0.25	£0.75	£1.25
25 ZZ Top	$0.40	$1.20	$2.00	£0.25	£0.75	£1.25
26 The Doors	$0.40	$1.20	$2.00	£0.25	£0.75	£1.25
27-28 Black Sabbath/Ozzy Osbourne	$0.40	$1.20	$2.00	£0.25	£0.75	£1.25
29-30 The Cure	$0.40	$1.20	$2.00	£0.25	£0.75	£1.25
31 Vanilla Ice	$0.40	$1.20	$2.00	£0.25	£0.75	£1.25
32 Frank Zappa	$0.40	$1.20	$2.00	£0.25	£0.75	£1.25
33 Guns 'n Roses	$0.40	$1.20	$2.00	£0.25	£0.75	£1.25
34 The Black Crowes	$0.40	$1.20	$2.00	£0.25	£0.75	£1.25
35 R.E.M.	$0.40	$1.20	$2.00	£0.25	£0.75	£1.25
36 Michael Jackson	$0.40	$1.20	$2.00	£0.25	£0.75	£1.25
37 Ice Cube, Ice T	$0.40	$1.20	$2.00	£0.25	£0.75	£1.25
38 Rod Stewart	$0.40	$1.20	$2.00	£0.25	£0.75	£1.25
39 R 'n R	$0.40	$1.20	$2.00	£0.25	£0.75	£1.25
40 N.W.A., Ice Cube	$0.40	$1.20	$2.00	£0.25	£0.75	£1.25
41 Paula Abdul	$0.40	$1.20	$2.00	£0.25	£0.75	£1.25
42 Metallica	$0.40	$1.20	$2.00	£0.25	£0.75	£1.25
43 Guns 'n Roses: Tales from the Tour	$1.20	$2.00		£0.25	£0.75	£1.25
44 The Skorpions	$0.40	$1.20	$2.00	£0.25	£0.75	£1.25
45 The Grateful Dead	$0.40	$1.20	$2.00	£0.25	£0.75	£1.25
46 The Grateful Dead	$0.50	$1.50	$2.50	£0.30	£0.90	£1.50
46 2nd printing, (Jan 1994)	$0.40	$1.20	$2.00	£0.25	£0.75	£1.25
47 The Grateful Dead	$0.40	$1.20	$2.00	£0.25	£0.75	£1.25
48 Queen	$0.40	$1.20	$2.00	£0.25	£0.75	£1.25
49 Rush	$0.40	$1.20	$2.00	£0.25	£0.75	£1.25
50-52 Bob Dylan	$0.40	$1.20	$2.00	£0.25	£0.75	£1.25
53 Bruce Springsteen	$0.40	$1.20	$2.00	£0.25	£0.75	£1.25
54 U2	$0.50	$1.50	$2.50	£0.30	£0.90	£1.50
54 2nd printing, U2 (May 1994)	$0.40	$1.20	$2.00	£0.25	£0.75	£1.25
55 U2	$0.40	$1.20	$2.00	£0.25	£0.75	£1.25
56 David Bowie	$0.40	$1.20	$2.00	£0.25	£0.75	£1.25
57 Aerosmith (continues on from #11)	$0.40	$1.20	$2.00	£0.25	£0.75	£1.25
58 Kate Bush	$0.40	$1.20	$2.00	£0.25	£0.75	£1.25
59 Eric Clapton	$0.40	$1.20	$2.00	£0.25	£0.75	£1.25
60 Genesis - The '70s	$0.40	$1.20	$2.00	£0.25	£0.75	£1.25
61 Yes - The '70s	$0.40	$1.20	$2.00	£0.25	£0.75	£1.25
62 Elton John	$0.40	$1.20	$2.00	£0.25	£0.75	£1.25
63 Janis Joplin	$0.40	$1.20	$2.00	£0.25	£0.75	£1.25
64 San Francisco issue (Grateful Dead, Joplin, Miller, Jefferson Airplane etc)	$0.40	$1.20	$2.00	£0.25	£0.75	£1.25
65 Sci-Fi Space Rockers (Marillion, Genesis, Yes etc)	$0.40	$1.20	$2.00	£0.25	£0.75	£1.25
66 Allman Bros. and Lynard Skynard	$0.40	$1.20	$2.00	£0.25	£0.75	£1.25
67 John Mellencamp	$0.40	$1.20	$2.00	£0.25	£0.75	£1.25
68 Tom Petty	$0.40	$1.20	$2.00	£0.25	£0.75	£1.25
69 Neil Young	$0.40	$1.20	$2.00	£0.25	£0.75	£1.25
70 Police/Sting and Iggy Pop	$0.40	$1.20	$2.00	£0.25	£0.75	£1.25
71 Meatloaf, Lenny Kravitz, Mozart	$0.40	$1.20	$2.00	£0.25	£0.75	£1.25
Title Value:	$40.50	$121.50	$202.50	£25.60	£76.80	£128.00

Note: all Non-Distributed on the news-stands in the U.K.

	$Good	$Fine	$N.Mint	£Good	£Fine	£N.Mint
Annual 1: Encyclopedia Metallica (Dec 1990) reprints, squarebound magazine				£0.75	£2.25	£3.75
Trade Paperback (May 1991)				£1.35	£4.05	£6.75

ROCK N' ROLL COMICS MAGAZINE

Revolutionary Comics; 1 Sep 1990-9 1991

	$Good	$Fine	$N.Mint	£Good	£Fine	£N.Mint
1 ND reprints featuring Kiss plus new material	$0.40	$1.20	$2.00	£0.25	£0.75	£1.25
2 ND reprints from New Kids on the Block	$0.40	$1.20	$2.00	£0.25	£0.75	£1.25
3 ND reprints issue #1 (7th print)	$0.40	$1.20	$2.00	£0.25	£0.75	£1.25
4 ND reprints issue #2 (Metallica)	$0.40	$1.20	$2.00	£0.25	£0.75	£1.25
5 ND reprints issue #11 (Aerosmith)	$0.40	$1.20	$2.00	£0.25	£0.75	£1.25
6 ND reprints issue #15 (Poison)	$0.40	$1.20	$2.00	£0.25	£0.75	£1.25
7 ND reprints issue #17 (Madonna)	$0.40	$1.20	$2.00	£0.25	£0.75	£1.25
8 ND reprints issue #12 (New Kids on the Block)?	$0.40	$1.20	$2.00	£0.25	£0.75	£1.25
9 ND 68pgs, reprints issues #4,15	$0.50	$1.50	$2.50	£0.30	£0.90	£1.50
Title Value:	$3.70	$11.10	$18.50	£2.30	£6.90	£11.50

Note: issues #1-3 released in same month

ROCKET RACCOON

Marvel Comics Group,MS; 1 May 1985-4 Aug 1985

	$Good	$Fine	$N.Mint	£Good	£Fine	£N.Mint
1-4 ND Mike Mignola art	$0.25	$0.75	$1.25	£0.15	£0.45	£0.75
Title Value:	$1.00	$3.00	$5.00	£0.60	£1.80	£3.00

ROCKET RANGER

Adventure,MS; 1 Sep 1991-6 Sep 1992

	$Good	$Fine	$N.Mint	£Good	£Fine	£N.Mint
1-6 ND based on computer game	$0.50	$1.50	$2.50	£0.30	£0.90	£1.50
Title Value:	$3.00	$9.00	$15.00	£1.80	£5.40	£9.00

ROCKETEER

Eclipse;(Graphic Novel 7); nn 1987

	$Good	$Fine	$N.Mint	£Good	£Fine	£N.Mint
nn 1st printing ND reprints from Pacific Presents #1 & 2, Starslayer #2,3 and Rocketeer Special; Dave Stevens art	$2.40	$7.00	$12.00	£1.60	£4.80	£8.00
nn 2nd printing ND	$1.80	$5.25	$9.00	£1.20	£3.60	£6.00
nn 3rd printing ND (Apr 1991)	$1.70	$5.00	$8.50	£1.10	£3.30	£5.50
nn 3rd printing Hardcover ND (Apr 1991)	$6.00	$18.00	$30.00	£4.00	£12.00	£20.00
Title Value:	$11.90	$35.25	$59.50	£7.90	£23.70	£39.50
Rocketeer Graphic Novel (Aug 1991), reprints Adventure Magazine 1,2				£1.10	£3.30	£5.50
Rocketeer Graphic Novel Hardcover (Aug 1991)				£3.00	£9.00	£15.00
Rocketeer Graphic Novel Signed, Numbered Hardcover (Oct 1991), 1,000 copies				£7.00	£21.00	£35.00

ROCKETEER ADVENTURE MAGAZINE

Comico; 1,2 1988; Dark Horse; 3 Jan 1995

	$Good	$Fine	$N.Mint	£Good	£Fine	£N.Mint
1 ND Rocketeer by Stevens, Galactic Girl Guides by Kaluta (see Starstruck); Dave Stevens cover	$1.00	$3.00	$5.00	£0.70	£2.10	£3.50
2 ND Stevens/Kaluta art; Dave Stevens cover	$0.60	$1.80	$3.00	£0.40	£1.20	£2.00
3 ND Dave Stevens, Mike Kaluta, Art Adams art	$0.50	$1.50	$2.50	£0.30	£0.90	£1.50
Title Value:	$2.10	$6.30	$10.50	£1.40	£4.20	£7.00

Note: issue #3 was originally solicited by Dark Horse cover dated September 1991

ROCKETEER GRAPHIC NOVEL

Eclipse; nn 1991

	$Good	$Fine	$N.Mint	£Good	£Fine	£N.Mint
nn ND reprints Rocketeer Adventure Magazine #1 & 2	$1.70	$5.00	$8.50	£1.10	£3.30	£5.50
nn Hardcover ND (Aug 1991)	$5.00	$15.00	$25.00	£3.00	£9.00	£15.00
nn Signed & Numbered Hardcover ND (Oct 1991) 1,000 copies	$12.00	$36.00	$60.00	£7.00	£21.00	£35.00
Title Value:	$18.70	$56.00	$93.50	£11.10	£33.30	£55.50

ROCKETEER GRAPHIC NOVEL, THE

Disney,OS; 1 Jul 1991

	$Good	$Fine	$N.Mint	£Good	£Fine	£N.Mint
1 ND 64pgs, adaptation of Disney film, Peter David script, Russ Heath art, Dave Stevens cover	$1.00	$3.00	$5.00	£0.70	£2.10	£3.50
1 Newstand Edition ND	$0.40	$1.20	$2.00	£0.25	£0.75	£1.25
Title Value:	$1.40	$4.20	$7.00	£0.95	£2.85	£4.75

ROCKETEER SPECIAL EDITION

Eclipse,OS; 1 Nov 1984

	$Good	$Fine	$N.Mint	£Good	£Fine	£N.Mint
1 ND scarce in the U.K. Chapter 5; intended for Pacific Presents #5; pin-ups by Wildey, Morrow, Anderson, Heath, Stout, Williamson, Jones	$2.00	$6.00	$10.00	£1.20	£3.60	£6.00
Title Value:	$2.00	$6.00	$10.00	£1.20	£3.60	£6.00

ROCKETMAN ASHCAN EDITION

AC Comics,OS; nn Aug 1995

	$Good	$Fine	$N.Mint	£Good	£Fine	£N.Mint
nn ND 36pgs, reprints classic Rocketman and Jetgirl stories from the 1940s; black and white	$1.20	$3.60	$6.00	£0.80	£2.40	£4.00
Title Value:	$1.20	$3.60	$6.00	£0.80	£2.40	£4.00

ROCKETMAN: KING OF THE ROCKET MEN

Innovation,MS; 1 Aug 1991-4 Oct 1991

	$Good	$Fine	$N.Mint	£Good	£Fine	£N.Mint
1-4 ND based on 1940s movie serial; Chris Moeller script and painted art	$0.40	$1.20	$2.00	£0.25	£0.75	£1.25

	$Good	$Fine	$N.Mint	£Good	£Fine	£N.Mint
Title Value:	$1.60	$4.80	$8.00	£1.00	£3.00	£5.00
Graphic Novel (Feb 1992), collects mini-series				£1.10	£3.30	£5.50
Signed Edition by Chris Moeller (May 1993)				£1.20	£3.60	£6.00

ROCKO'S MODERN LIFE

Marvel Comics Group,TV; 1 Jun 1994-7 Dec 1994

	$Good	$Fine	$N.Mint	£Good	£Fine	£N.Mint
1-7 based on TV cartoon	$0.40	$1.20	$2.00	£0.25	£0.75	£1.25
Title Value:	$2.80	$8.40	$14.00	£1.75	£5.25	£8.75

ROCKOLA

Mirage Studios; 1 May 1987

	$Good	$Fine	$N.Mint	£Good	£Fine	£N.Mint
1 ND	$0.30	$0.90	$1.50	£0.20	£0.60	£1.00
Title Value:	$0.30	$0.90	$1.50	£0.20	£0.60	£1.00

ROCKY AND HIS FIENDISH FRIENDS

Gold Key; 1 Oct 1962-5 Sep 1963

	$Good	$Fine	$N.Mint	£Good	£Fine	£N.Mint
1 very scarce in the U.K. 80pgs, based on cartoon	$34.00	$100.00	$240.00	£22.50	£67.50	£160.00
2-3 scarce in the U.K. 80pgs, based on cartoon	$23.50	$70.00	$165.00	£15.50	£47.00	£110.00
4-5 scarce in the U.K.	$15.50	$47.00	$110.00	£9.25	£28.00	£65.00
Title Value:	$112.00	$334.00	$790.00	£72.00	£217.50	£510.00

ROCKY HORROR PICTURE SHOW

Caliber Press,MS; 1 Jul 1990-3 Nov 1990

	$Good	$Fine	$N.Mint	£Good	£Fine	£N.Mint
1 ND 64pgs	$0.60	$1.80	$3.00	£0.40	£1.20	£2.00
1 2nd printing ND	$0.50	$1.50	$2.50	£0.30	£0.90	£1.50
2-3 ND 64pgs	$0.60	$1.80	$3.00	£0.40	£1.20	£2.00
Title Value:	$2.30	$6.90	$11.50	£1.50	£4.50	£7.50

Note: adaptation of film

	$Good	$Fine	$N.Mint	£Good	£Fine	£N.Mint
Rocky Horror Picture Show Trade Paperback (Feb 1992), collects mini-series, new photo cover				£0.65	£1.95	£3.25

ROCKY LANE WESTERN

Charlton;56 Feb 1954-87 Nov 1959

	$Good	$Fine	$N.Mint	£Good	£Fine	£N.Mint
56 1st Charlton issue (previously published by Fawcett)	$15.50	$47.00	$110.00	£10.50	£32.00	£75.00
57 photo cover	$9.25	$28.00	$65.00	£6.25	£19.00	£45.00
58-59	$6.25	$19.00	$45.00	£4.25	£12.50	£30.00
60 photo cover	$9.25	$28.00	$65.00	£6.25	£19.00	£45.00
61-64	$6.25	$19.00	$45.00	£4.25	£12.50	£30.00
65 reprints Fawcett issue #29	$7.00	$21.00	$50.00	£4.25	£12.50	£30.00
66 reprints Fawcett issue #30	$6.25	$19.00	$45.00	£4.25	£12.50	£30.00
67 reprints Fawcett issue #31	$6.25	$19.00	$45.00	£4.25	£12.50	£30.00
68 reprints Fawcett issue #32	$6.25	$19.00	$45.00	£4.25	£12.50	£30.00
69-78	$6.25	$19.00	$45.00	£4.25	£12.50	£30.00
79 scarce in the U.K. 64pgs, squarebound	$8.50	$26.00	$60.00	£5.25	£16.00	£37.50
80-86	$6.25	$19.00	$45.00	£3.90	£11.50	£27.50
87 scarce in the U.K.	$7.00	$21.00	$50.00	£4.25	£12.50	£30.00
Title Value:	$219.00	$665.00	$1570.00	£144.80	£429.00	£1025.00

Note: all Non-Distributed in the U.K. though a few of the last issues may have been just prior to official distribution in November 1959

ROG 2000, THE COMPLETE

Pacific,Magazine; nn Jul 1982

	$Good	$Fine	$N.Mint	£Good	£Fine	£N.Mint
nn ND 40pgs, all reprint; all John Byrne art	$0.90	$2.70	$4.50	£0.60	£1.80	£3.00
Title Value:	$0.90	$2.70	$4.50	£0.60	£1.80	£3.00

ROGAN GOSH GRAPHIC NOVEL

DC Comics; nn May 1994

	$Good	$Fine	$N.Mint	£Good	£Fine	£N.Mint
nn ND 56pgs, reprints Peter Milligan and Brendan McCarthy story from Revolver magazine	$1.40	$4.20	$7.00	£0.90	£2.70	£4.50
Title Value:	$1.40	$4.20	$7.00	£0.90	£2.70	£4.50

ROGER RABBIT

Disney; 1 Jul 1990-19 Nov 1991

	$Good	$Fine	$N.Mint	£Good	£Fine	£N.Mint
1-10 ND	$0.40	$1.20	$2.00	£0.25	£0.75	£1.25
11-19 ND	$0.30	$0.90	$1.50	£0.20	£0.60	£1.00
Title Value:	$6.70	$20.10	$33.50	£4.30	£12.90	£21.50

Note: banned from distibution in UK

ROGER RABBIT'S TOON TOWN

Disney; 1 Jul 1991-6 Jan 1992

	$Good	$Fine	$N.Mint	£Good	£Fine	£N.Mint
1-6 ND	$0.30	$0.90	$1.50	£0.20	£0.60	£1.00
Title Value:	$1.80	$5.40	$9.00	£1.20	£3.60	£6.00

ROGER WILCO

Adventure,MS; 1 Apr 1992-3 Aug 1992

	$Good	$Fine	$N.Mint	£Good	£Fine	£N.Mint
1-3 ND based on computer game	$0.50	$1.50	$2.50	£0.30	£0.90	£1.50
Title Value:	$1.50	$4.50	$7.50	£0.90	£2.70	£4.50

ROGUE

Marvel Comics Group,MS; 1 Jan 1995-4 Apr 1995

	$Good	$Fine	$N.Mint	£Good	£Fine	£N.Mint
1 foil stamped cover	$0.70	$2.10	$3.50	£0.50	£1.50	£2.50
2-4 foil stamped cover	$0.60	$1.80	$3.00	£0.40	£1.20	£2.00
Title Value:	$2.50	$7.50	$12.50	£1.70	£5.10	£8.50
Rogue (Jan 1996) Trade paperback reprints mini-series				£1.60	£4.80	£8.00

ROGUE'S GALLERY

DC Comics,OS; 1 Jun 1996

	$Good	$Fine	$N.Mint	£Good	£Fine	£N.Mint
1 ND features pin-ups of DC villains	$0.70	$2.10	$3.50	£0.50	£1.50	£2.50
Title Value:	$0.70	$2.10	$3.50	£0.50	£1.50	£2.50

ROJA FUSION

Antarctic Press; 1 Apr 1995

	$Good	$Fine	$N.Mint	£Good	£Fine	£N.Mint
1 ND 40pgs, black and white	$0.60	$1.80	$3.00	£0.40	£1.20	£2.00
Title Value:	$0.60	$1.80	$3.00	£0.40	£1.20	£2.00

ROLLING STONES: VOODOO LOUNGE

Marvel Comics Group,OS; nn Nov 1995

	$Good	$Fine	$N.Mint	£Good	£Fine	£N.Mint
nn ND 48pgs, Dave McKean painted art, pull out poster and interactive computer disc	$2.00	$6.00	$10.00	£1.30	£3.90	£6.50
Title Value:	$2.00	$6.00	$10.00	£1.30	£3.90	£6.50

ROM

Marvel Comics Group; 1 Dec 1979-75 Feb 1986

	$Good	$Fine	$N.Mint	£Good	£Fine	£N.Mint
1 1st appearance Rom - based on toy	$0.60	$1.80	$3.00	£0.25	£0.75	£1.25
2-7	$0.30	$0.90	$1.50	£0.20	£0.60	£1.00
8-12 ND Golden cover	$0.30	$0.90	$1.50	£0.20	£0.60	£1.00
13-16 ND	$0.30	$0.90	$1.50	£0.20	£0.60	£1.00
17-18 X-Men appear	$0.50	$1.50	$2.50	£0.30	£0.90	£1.50
19-22	$0.25	$0.75	$1.25	£0.15	£0.45	£0.75
23 ND Luke Cage and Iron Fist appear	$0.30	$0.90	$1.50	£0.20	£0.60	£1.00
24 Nova appears with the new Champions	$0.30	$0.90	$1.50	£0.20	£0.60	£1.00
25 DS	$0.30	$0.90	$1.50	£0.20	£0.60	£1.00
26-27 Galactus appears	$0.25	$0.75	$1.25	£0.15	£0.45	£0.75
28-30	$0.25	$0.75	$1.25	£0.15	£0.45	£0.75
31-32 Rogue appears	$0.30	$0.90	$1.50	£0.20	£0.60	£1.00
33	$0.25	$0.75	$1.25	£0.15	£0.45	£0.75
34-35 Sub-Mariner appears	$0.25	$0.75	$1.25	£0.15	£0.45	£0.75
36-37	$0.25	$0.75	$1.25	£0.15	£0.45	£0.75
38-39 Master of Kung Fu appears	$0.25	$0.75	$1.25	£0.15	£0.45	£0.75
40	$0.25	$0.75	$1.25	£0.15	£0.45	£0.75
41-42 LD in the U.K. Dr. Strange appears	$0.25	$0.75	$1.25	£0.15	£0.45	£0.75
43-49	$0.25	$0.75	$1.25	£0.15	£0.45	£0.75
50 DS Torpedo dies	$0.30	$0.90	$1.50	£0.20	£0.60	£1.00
51	$0.25	$0.75	$1.25	£0.15	£0.45	£0.75
52 Sienkiewicz cover	$0.25	$0.75	$1.25	£0.15	£0.45	£0.75
53 Nick Fury appears, Sienkiewicz cover	$0.25	$0.75	$1.25	£0.15	£0.45	£0.75
54 Nick Fury and Dr. Strange cameos, Sienkiewicz cover	$0.25	$0.75	$1.25	£0.15	£0.45	£0.75
55 Sienkiewicz cover	$0.25	$0.75	$1.25	£0.15	£0.45	£0.75
56 Alpha Flight appears	$0.25	$0.75	$1.25	£0.15	£0.45	£0.75
57 Alpha Flight appears, John Byrne cover	$0.25	$0.75	$1.25	£0.15	£0.45	£0.75
58 Ant-Man and Alpha Flight appear, Guice cover	$0.25	$0.75	$1.25	£0.15	£0.45	£0.75
59 Ant-Man appears; Steve Ditko pencils	$0.25	$0.75	$1.25	£0.15	£0.45	£0.75
60 Ditko pencils, Guice cover	$0.25	$0.75	$1.25	£0.15	£0.45	£0.75
61 Forge appears, Steve Ditko and Jackson Guice art	$0.25	$0.75	$1.25	£0.15	£0.45	£0.75
62 Forge appears, Steve Ditko pencils	$0.25	$0.75	$1.25	£0.15	£0.45	£0.75
63 Forge appears, Steve Ditko pencils, Neary cover	$0.25	$0.75	$1.25	£0.15	£0.45	£0.75
64 Steve Ditko and P.Craig Russell art, Russell cover	$0.25	$0.75	$1.25	£0.15	£0.45	£0.75
65 X-Men, Avengers, West Coast Avengers and Defenders appear; Steve Ditko and Russell art, part Russell cover	$0.25	$0.75	$1.25	£0.15	£0.45	£0.75
66 All Earth's Heroes story; Steve Ditko pencils, Russell cover	$0.30	$0.90	$1.50	£0.20	£0.60	£1.00
67 Steve Ditko and Russell art	$0.25	$0.75	$1.25	£0.15	£0.45	£0.75
68 Steve Ditko pencils, Sienkiewicz cover	$0.25	$0.75	$1.25	£0.15	£0.45	£0.75
69 Steve Ditko and Russell art	$0.25	$0.75	$1.25	£0.15	£0.45	£0.75
70 Steve Ditko pencils, Guice and Ordway cover	$0.25	$0.75	$1.25	£0.15	£0.45	£0.75
71 Steve Ditko and Russell art, Russell and Sienkiewicz cover	$0.25	$0.75	$1.25	£0.15	£0.45	£0.75
72 Secret Wars X-over; Steve Ditko pencils	$0.25	$0.75	$1.25	£0.15	£0.45	£0.75
73 Steve Ditko pencils	$0.25	$0.75	$1.25	£0.15	£0.45	£0.75
74 Steve Ditko pencils, John Byrne inks						

VERY GENERAL PERCENTAGE CONVERSION CHART WHICH MAY BE USED TO CALCULATE LOW AND INBETWEEN GRADES:

	$Good	$Fine	$N.Mint	£Good	£Fine	£N.Mint
	$0.25	$0.75	$1.25	£0.15	£0.45	£0.75
75 Steve Ditko and Russell art, Russell cover						
	$0.25	$0.75	$1.25	£0.15	£0.45	£0.75
Title Value:	$20.70	$62.10	$103.50	£12.75	£38.25	£63.75

FEATURES

Galactus in 26, 27. Jack of Hearts in 12. Nova in 24. Powerman and Iron Fist in 23. Rogue in 31, 32. Tales of the Space Knights in 13, 14, 16, 19-21. Torpedo in 21, 22.

ROM ANNUAL

Marvel Comics Group; 1 Nov 1982-4 1985

	$Good	$Fine	$N.Mint	£Good	£Fine	£N.Mint
1-2	$0.30	$0.90	$1.50	£0.20	£0.60	£1.00
3 ND New Mutants appear						
	$0.40	$1.20	$2.00	£0.25	£0.75	£1.25
4 ND Gladiator appears						
	$0.30	$0.90	$1.50	£0.20	£0.60	£1.00
Title Value:	$1.30	$3.90	$6.50	£0.85	£2.55	£4.25

ROMAN HOLIDAYS, THE

Gold Key; 1 Feb 1973-4 Nov 1973

	$Good	$Fine	$N.Mint	£Good	£Fine	£N.Mint
1 very scarce in the U.K.						
	$2.90	$8.75	$17.50	£1.25	£3.75	£7.50
2 scarce in the U.K.						
	$2.50	$7.50	$15.00	£0.80	£2.50	£5.00
3-4	$2.00	$6.00	$12.00	£0.55	£1.75	£3.50
Title Value:	$9.40	$28.25	$56.50	£3.15	£9.75	£19.50

ROMANTIC SECRETS

Charlton;5 Oct 1955-52 Nov 1964

(issues #1-4 formerly Negro Romances)

	$Good	$Fine	$N.Mint	£Good	£Fine	£N.Mint
5 scarce in the U.K.						
	$6.00	$18.00	$42.00	£3.55	£10.50	£25.00
6-10	$3.20	$9.50	$22.50	£1.75	£5.25	£12.50
11-20	$1.70	$5.00	$12.00	£1.05	£3.20	£7.50
21-22	$1.05	$3.20	$7.50	£0.70	£2.10	£5.00
1st official distribution in the U.K.						
23-30	$1.05	$3.20	$7.50	£0.70	£2.10	£5.00
31-40	$0.70	$2.10	$5.00	£0.50	£1.50	£3.50
41-52	$0.50	$1.50	$3.50	£0.35	£1.05	£2.50
Title Value:	$62.50	$186.50	$441.50	£39.00	£117.35	£277.50

ROMANTIC STORY

Fawcett; 1 Nov 1949-22 Sum 1953; Charlton; 23 May 1954-27 Dec 1954; 28 Aug 1955-130 Nov 1973

	$Good	$Fine	$N.Mint	£Good	£Fine	£N.Mint
1 scarce in the U.K.						
	$12.50	$39.00	$90.00	£7.75	£23.50	£55.00
2 scarce in the U.K.						
	$6.25	$19.00	$45.00	£4.25	£12.50	£30.00
3-5 scarce in the U.K.						
	$5.50	$17.00	$40.00	£3.55	£10.50	£25.00
6-14	$4.25	$12.50	$30.00	£2.50	£7.50	£17.50
15 George Evans art						
	$5.25	$16.00	$37.50	£3.20	£9.50	£22.50
16-34	$2.85	$8.50	$20.00	£1.70	£5.00	£12.00
1st official distribution in the U.K.						
35-39	$2.85	$8.50	$20.00	£1.70	£5.00	£12.00
40 scarce in the U.K. 100pgs						
	$5.25	$16.00	$37.50	£3.20	£9.50	£22.50
41-50	$2.25	$6.75	$16.00	£1.40	£4.25	£10.00
51-60	$1.10	$3.40	$8.00	£0.70	£2.10	£5.00
61-70	$1.10	$3.40	$8.00	£0.55	£1.70	£4.00
71-90	$0.70	$2.10	$5.00	£0.50	£1.50	£3.50
91-100	$0.50	$1.50	$3.50	£0.25	£0.85	£2.00
101-110	$0.40	$1.25	$2.50	£0.25	£0.75	£1.50
111-130	$0.30	$1.00	$2.00	£0.20	£0.60	£1.25
Title Value:	$225.90	$682.50	$1600.00	£137.85	£412.50	£970.50

RONIN

DC Comics,MS; 1 Jul 1983-6 Apr 1984

	$Good	$Fine	$N.Mint	£Good	£Fine	£N.Mint
1 ND Frank Miller art; DC's 1st full-process separation comic						
	$1.00	$3.00	$5.00	£0.60	£1.80	£3.00
2-3 ND Frank Miller art						
	$0.80	$2.40	$4.00	£0.50	£1.50	£2.50
4-5 ND scarce in the U.K. Frank Miller art						
	$0.80	$2.40	$4.00	£0.60	£1.80	£3.00
6 ND very scarce in the U.K., scarce in the U.S. Frank Miller art, fold out page of panoramic art ("gatefold")						
	$1.20	$3.60	$6.00	£1.00	£3.00	£5.00
Title Value:	$5.40	$16.20	$27.00	£3.80	£11.40	£19.00
Trade Paperback						
reprints #1-6				£1.40	£4.20	£7.00

ROOK

Warren; 1 Nov 1979-14 Apr 1982

(see Eerie)

	$Good	$Fine	$N.Mint	£Good	£Fine	£N.Mint
1	$0.50	$1.50	$2.50	£0.30	£0.90	£1.50
2-14	$0.40	$1.20	$2.00	£0.25	£0.75	£1.25
Title Value:	$5.70	$17.10	$28.50	£3.55	£10.65	£17.75

Note: distributed in the U.K.

ROOK, THE

Harris Comics; 0 Jun 1995; 1 Aug 1995-4 1995

	$Good	$Fine	$N.Mint	£Good	£Fine	£N.Mint
0 ND (Jun 1995), includes designs and character sketches						
	$0.60	$1.80	$3.00	£0.40	£1.20	£2.00
1 ND Tom Sniegoski script, Kirk van Wormer and Joe Weems art						
	$0.60	$1.80	$3.00	£0.40	£1.20	£2.00
2-4 ND	$0.60	$1.80	$3.00	£0.40	£1.20	£2.00
Title Value:	$3.00	$9.00	$15.00	£2.00	£6.00	£10.00

ROOKIE COP

Charlton; 27 Nov 1955-33 Jul 1957

(Crime & Justice #1-26)

	$Good	$Fine	$N.Mint	£Good	£Fine	£N.Mint
27 ND	$7.00	$21.00	$50.00	£5.00	£15.00	£35.00
28-33 ND	$5.00	$15.00	$35.00	£3.20	£9.50	£22.50
Title Value:	$37.00	$111.00	$260.00	£24.20	£72.00	£170.00

ROOM 222

Dell; 1 Jan 1970-4 Jan 1971

	$Good	$Fine	$N.Mint	£Good	£Fine	£N.Mint
1 scarce in the U.K. based on US TV series						
	$8.25	$25.00	$50.00	£3.30	£10.00	£20.00
2-4 scarce in the U.K.						
	$5.00	$15.00	$30.00	£1.65	£5.00	£10.00
Title Value:	$23.25	$70.00	$140.00	£8.25	£25.00	£50.00

ROOTS OF THE SWAMP THING

DC Comics,MS; 1 Jul 1986-5 Nov 1986

	$Good	$Fine	$N.Mint	£Good	£Fine	£N.Mint
1 ND DS	$0.90	$2.70	$4.50	£0.60	£1.80	£3.00
2-5 ND DS	$0.80	$2.40	$4.00	£0.50	£1.50	£2.50
Title Value:	$4.10	$12.30	$20.50	£2.60	£7.80	£13.00

Note: reprints original Swamp Thing series #1-10, Berni Wrightson art. Deluxe Format Baxter paper.

ROSCOE! THE DAWG DETECTIVE

Renegade; 1 Jul 1987-4 Jan 1988

	$Good	$Fine	$N.Mint	£Good	£Fine	£N.Mint
1-4 ND black and white						
	$0.20	$0.60	$1.00	£0.10	£0.35	£0.60
Title Value:	$0.80	$2.40	$4.00	£0.40	£1.40	£2.40

ROSE & GUNN

Bishop Press; 1 Jan 1995-7 1996

	$Good	$Fine	$N.Mint	£Good	£Fine	£N.Mint
1 ND features art by Everett Hartsoe and London Night Studios; black and white						
	$0.60	$1.80	$3.00	£0.40	£1.20	£2.00
2-7 ND black and white						
	$0.60	$1.80	$3.00	£0.40	£1.20	£2.00
Title Value:	$4.20	$12.60	$21.00	£2.80	£8.40	£14.00

ROSE & GUNN (2ND SERIES)

London Night Studios; 1 Jun 1996-present

ROM #1

Ronin #1

Rudolph, The Red-Nosed Reindeer (1950)

	$Good	$Fine	$N.Mint	£Good	£Fine	£N.Mint
1 ND 24pgs, black and white	$0.60	$1.80	$3.00	£0.40	£1.20	£2.00
Title Value:	$0.60	$1.80	$3.00	£0.40	£1.20	£2.00

ROSE, THE

Hero,OS; 1 Dec 1992

	$Good	$Fine	$N.Mint	£Good	£Fine	£N.Mint
1 ND spin-off from The Champions, Mark Beachum art; black and white	$0.30	$0.90	$1.50	£0.20	£0.60	£1.00
Title Value:	$0.30	$0.90	$1.50	£0.20	£0.60	£1.00

ROSWELL: LITTLE GREEN MAN

Bongo Comics; 1 1996-present

	$Good	$Fine	$N.Mint	£Good	£Fine	£N.Mint
1-2 ND	$0.60	$1.80	$3.00	£0.40	£1.20	£2.00
Title Value:	$1.20	$3.60	$6.00	£0.80	£2.40	£4.00

ROUGH RAIDERS ANNUAL

Blue Comet Press; 1 1990

	$Good	$Fine	$N.Mint	£Good	£Fine	£N.Mint
1 ND black and white	$0.40	$1.20	$2.00	£0.25	£0.75	£1.25
Title Value:	$0.40	$1.20	$2.00	£0.25	£0.75	£1.25

ROVERS

Malibu; 1 Sep 1987-6 Feb 1988

	$Good	$Fine	$N.Mint	£Good	£Fine	£N.Mint
1-6 ND	$0.30	$0.90	$1.50	£0.20	£0.60	£1.00
Title Value:	$1.80	$5.40	$9.00	£1.20	£3.60	£6.00

ROVERS, THE

Mindgame Corporation; 1 Dec 1990

	$Good	$Fine	$N.Mint	£Good	£Fine	£N.Mint
1 ND 40pgs	$0.40	$1.20	$2.00	£0.25	£0.75	£1.25
Title Value:	$0.40	$1.20	$2.00	£0.25	£0.75	£1.25

ROYAL ROY

Marvel Comics Group/Star; 1 Jun 1985-5 Feb 1986

	$Good	$Fine	$N.Mint	£Good	£Fine	£N.Mint
1-5	$0.15	$0.45	$0.75	£0.10	£0.30	£0.50
Title Value:	$0.75	$2.25	$3.75	£0.50	£1.50	£2.50

RUDOLPH, THE RED-NOSED REINDEER

National Periodical Publications; 1950-1962

	$Good	$Fine	$N.Mint	£Good	£Fine	£N.Mint
1950 (#1)	$18.00	$54.00	$125.00	£12.00	£36.00	£85.00
1951-1954	$10.00	$30.00	$75.00	£7.00	£21.00	£50.00
1955-1962	$7.00	$21.00	$50.00	£5.00	£15.00	£35.00
Title Value:	$114.00	$342.00	$798.00	£80.00	£240.00	£560.00

RUINS

Marvel Comics Group,MS; 1 Aug 1995-2 Sep 1995

	$Good	$Fine	$N.Mint	£Good	£Fine	£N.Mint
1-2 ND photo-journalist Phil Seldon (from Marvels mini-series) appears; Warren Ellis script, Cliff and Terese Neilsen art; acetate outer cover	$1.00	$3.00	$5.00	£0.70	£2.10	£3.50
Title Value:	$2.00	$6.00	$10.00	£1.40	£4.20	£7.00

RUNE

Malibu Ultraverse; 1 Jan 1994-9 Apr 1995

	$Good	$Fine	$N.Mint	£Good	£Fine	£N.Mint
0 ND obtained with Solution #0 by sending off coupons contained within 11 Ultraverse issues	$1.50	$4.50	$7.50	£1.00	£3.00	£5.00
1 Barry Windsor Smith script and art begins; origin Rune	$0.50	$1.50	$2.50	£0.30	£0.90	£1.50
1 Ashcan Edition, 16pgs, (Jan 1994) flip sided with Wrath	$0.30	$0.90	$1.50	£0.20	£0.60	£1.00
1 Limited Edition, ND full hologram cover, 5,000 copies produced	$1.50	$4.50	$7.50	£1.00	£3.00	£5.00
2	$0.40	$1.20	$2.00	£0.25	£0.75	£1.25
3 64pgs, flip side is Ultraverse Premiere #1 featuring Warstrike and Ripfire	$0.50	$1.50	$2.50	£0.30	£0.90	£1.50
4-8	$0.40	$1.20	$2.00	£0.25	£0.75	£1.25
9 prelude to Godwheel story	$0.40	$1.20	$2.00	£0.25	£0.75	£1.25
Title Value:	$7.10	$21.30	$35.50	£4.55	£13.65	£22.75

Note: all Non-Distributed on the news-stands in the U.K.

	£Good	£Fine	£N.Mint
Rune: The Awakening (Apr 1995) Trade paperback collects issues #1-5, Barry Windsor-Smith cover	£1.70	£5.10	£8.50
Rune: The Awakening Limited Edition (Apr 1995) as above but with foil-stamped cover, shrink-wrapped with sticker that announces 1,000 copies plus Rune #1 Ultra Limitedcomic	£4.00	£12.00	£20.00

RUNE (2ND SERIES)

Marvel Comics Group; 1 Dec 1995-7 Jun 1996

	$Good	$Fine	$N.Mint	£Good	£Fine	£N.Mint
1 ND Len Kaminski script, Kyle Hotz art, cover by Kyle Hotz and Tim Vigil; Rune vs. Annihilus, Adam Warlock appears	$0.30	$0.90	$1.50	£0.20	£0.60	£1.00
1 Signed Limited Edition, ND (Jan 1996), with certificate; 2,000 copies	$1.50	$4.50	$7.50	£1.00	£3.00	£5.00
1 Variant Cover Edition, ND computer painted cover by Chuck Maiden	$0.50	$1.50	$2.50	£0.30	£0.90	£1.50
2 ND Adam Warlock guest-stars, flip-book format with Phoenix Ressurrection chapter	$0.30	$0.90	$1.50	£0.20	£0.60	£1.00
3 ND Adam Warlock guest-stars	$0.30	$0.90	$1.50	£0.20	£0.60	£1.00
4-5 ND	$0.30	$0.90	$1.50	£0.20	£0.60	£1.00
6-7 ND Warlock appears	$0.30	$0.90	$1.50	£0.20	£0.60	£1.00
Title Value:	$4.10	$12.30	$20.50	£2.70	£8.10	£13.50

RUNE ASHCAN EDITION

Malibu Ultraverse,OS; nn Apr 1994

	$Good	$Fine	$N.Mint	£Good	£Fine	£N.Mint
nn ND 16pgs, black and white	$0.15	$0.45	$0.75	£0.10	£0.30	£0.50
Title Value:	$0.15	$0.45	$0.75	£0.10	£0.30	£0.50

RUNE INDEX

Malibu; 1993

Barry Windsor-Smith's Rune story was available as inserts in particular issues of Malibu comics across certain months.

The list in alphabetical order is as follows:

Exiles #3
Firearm #2
Freex #4
Hardcase #5
Mantra #4
Night Man #1
Prime #5
Prototype #3
Sludge #1 (part 1)
Strangers #5
along with Rune #0 and The Solution #0

which were available direct from Malibu in return for coupons from all the above comics sent back.

RUNE VS. VENOM

Marvel Comics Group,OS; 1 Feb 1996

	$Good	$Fine	$N.Mint	£Good	£Fine	£N.Mint
1 ND 48pgs, Chris Ulm script	$0.90	$2.70	$4.50	£0.60	£1.80	£3.00
1 Signed & Numbered Edition, ND (Feb 1996) - with certificate; limited to 2,000 copies	$2.00	$6.00	$10.00	£1.20	£3.60	£6.00
Title Value:	$2.90	$8.70	$14.50	£1.80	£5.40	£9.00

RUNE, CURSE OF

Malibu Ultraverse,MS; 1 May 1995-4 Jul 1995

	$Good	$Fine	$N.Mint	£Good	£Fine	£N.Mint
1 Cover A, ND the left-hand side of a complete poster; Chris Ulm script, Kyle Hotz art; ties into Rune/ Silver Surfer #1 and Warlock and the Infinity Watch #42	$0.40	$1.20	$2.00	£0.25	£0.75	£1.25
1 Cover B, ND the right-hand side of a complete poster; Chris Ulm script, Kyle Hotz art; ties into Rune/ Silver Surfer #1 and Warlock and the Infinity Watch #42	$0.40	$1.20	$2.00	£0.25	£0.75	£1.25
2 ND Rune has Adam Warlock's soul-gem imbedded in his skull	$0.40	$1.20	$2.00	£0.25	£0.75	£1.25
3 ND Loki appears, Gemini vs. Rune	$0.40	$1.20	$2.00	£0.25	£0.75	£1.25
4 ND Rune enters the Negative Zone, Adam Warlock crosses to the Ultraverse	$0.40	$1.20	$2.00	£0.25	£0.75	£1.25
Title Value:	$2.00	$6.00	$10.00	£1.25	£3.75	£6.25

RUNE, GIANT SIZE

Malibu Ultraverse; 1 Sep 1994

	$Good	$Fine	$N.Mint	£Good	£Fine	£N.Mint
1 ND 40pgs, Rune discovers he must exclusively feed on ultrahumans	$0.50	$1.50	$2.50	£0.30	£0.90	£1.50
Title Value:	$0.50	$1.50	$2.50	£0.30	£0.90	£1.50

RUNE/SILVER SURFER

Marvel Comics Group/Malibu Ultraverse,OS; 1 Apr 1995

	$Good	$Fine	$N.Mint	£Good	£Fine	£N.Mint
1 Collectors Edition, ND (Apr 1995) - foil-stamped cover, limited to 5,000 copies	$1.60	$4.80	$8.00	£1.00	£3.00	£5.00
1 Direct Market Edition, ND 48pgs, Chris Ulm script, Flint Henry art; Barry Windsor-Smith cover (flip-book format)	$0.90	$2.70	$4.50	£0.60	£1.80	£3.00
1 Newstand Edition, ND without cover enhancement	$0.60	$1.80	$3.00	£0.40	£1.20	£2.00
Title Value:	$3.10	$9.30	$15.50	£2.00	£6.00	£10.00

RUNE: HEARTS OF DARKNESS

Marvel Comics Group,MS; 1 Nov 1996-3 Jan 1997

	$Good	$Fine	$N.Mint	£Good	£Fine	£N.Mint
1-3 ND	$0.30	$0.90	$1.50	£0.20	£0.60	£1.00
Title Value:	$0.90	$2.70	$4.50	£0.60	£1.80	£3.00

RUNE: INFINITY

Marvel Comics Group,OS; nn Nov 1995

	$Good	$Fine	$N.Mint	£Good	£Fine	£N.Mint
nn ND Black September tie-in; Rune vs. Annihilus, Adam Warlock establishes his home in the Ultraverse	$0.50	$1.50	$2.50	£0.30	£0.90	£1.50
nn Variant Cover Edition ND 1 copy received for every 5 copies of the regular issue ordered	$0.60	$1.80	$3.00	£0.40	£1.20	£2.00
Title Value:	$1.10	$3.30	$5.50	£0.70	£2.10	£3.50

RUNE: THE DARK GOD

Malibu,OS; nn Jan 1995

	$Good	$Fine	$N.Mint	£Good	£Fine	£N.Mint
nn ND originally issued with Spin Magazine; Barry Windsor Smith art	$0.90	$2.70	$4.50	£0.60	£1.80	£3.00
Title Value:	$0.90	$2.70	$4.50	£0.60	£1.80	£3.00

RUST

Now Comics; 1 Jul 1987-13 Sep 1988

	$Good	$Fine	$N.Mint	£Good	£Fine	£N.Mint
1-11 ND	$0.40	$1.20	$2.00	£0.25	£0.75	£1.25
12 ND Terminator preview (5pgs)	$0.80	$2.40	$4.00	£0.50	£1.50	£2.50
13 ND	$0.40	$1.20	$2.00	£0.25	£0.75	£1.25
Title Value:	$5.60	$16.80	$28.00	£3.50	£10.50	£17.50

RUST (2ND SERIES)

Now Comics; 1 Feb 1989-7 Jun 1989

	$Good	$Fine	$N.Mint	£Good	£Fine	£N.Mint
1-7 ND painted artwork	$0.40	$1.20	$2.00	£0.25	£0.75	£1.25
Title Value:	$2.80	$8.40	$14.00	£1.75	£5.25	£8.75

RUST (3RD SERIES)

Adventure; 1 Apr 1992-4 Sep 1992

	$Good	$Fine	$N.Mint	£Good	£Fine	£N.Mint
1 ND painted cover by Dave Dorman	$0.50	$1.50	$2.50	£0.30	£0.90	£1.50
1 Limited Edition, ND (Apr 1992) - gold foil-embossed cover and serial numbered on back cover	$0.70	$2.10	$3.50	£0.50	£1.50	£2.50
2 ND	$0.50	$1.50	$2.50	£0.30	£0.90	£1.50
2 2nd printing, ND (Sep 1992)	$0.40	$1.20	$2.00	£0.25	£0.75	£1.25
3-4 ND	$0.50	$1.50	$2.50	£0.30	£0.90	£1.50
Title Value:	$3.10	$9.30	$15.50	£1.95	£5.85	£9.75
	$0.50	$1.50	$2.50	£0.30	£0.90	£1.50

S

S.T.A.R. CORPS

DC Comics,MS; 1 Nov 1993-6 Apr 1994

Issue	$Good	$Fine	$N.Mint	£Good	£Fine	£N.Mint
1 Superman appears	$0.30	$0.90	$1.50	£0.20	£0.60	£1.00
2-6	$0.30	$0.90	$1.50	£0.20	£0.60	£1.00
Title Value:	$1.80	$5.40	$9.00	£1.20	£3.60	£6.00

SABER TIGER

Viz,OS; 1 Jul 1991

Issue	$Good	$Fine	$N.Mint	£Good	£Fine	£N.Mint
1 ND 80pgs	$1.20	$3.60	$6.00	£0.80	£2.40	£4.00
Title Value:	$1.20	$3.60	$6.00	£0.80	£2.40	£4.00

SABLE

First; 1 Mar 1988-27 May 1990

(formerly Jon Sable, Freelance; see also Mike Grell's Sable)

Issue	$Good	$Fine	$N.Mint	£Good	£Fine	£N.Mint
1 ND	$0.30	$0.90	$1.50	£0.20	£0.60	£1.00
2 ND scarce in the U.K.	$0.30	$0.90	$1.50	£0.25	£0.75	£1.25
3-27 ND	$0.30	$0.90	$1.50	£0.20	£0.60	£1.00
Title Value:	$8.10	$24.30	$40.50	£5.45	£16.35	£27.25

SABRE

Eclipse; 1 Sep 1982-14 1985

Issue	$Good	$Fine	$N.Mint	£Good	£Fine	£N.Mint
1 ND Don McGregor script begins, Kent Williams covers	$0.40	$1.20	$2.00	£0.25	£0.75	£1.25
2-14 ND	$0.40	$1.20	$2.00	£0.25	£0.75	£1.25
Title Value:	$5.60	$16.80	$28.00	£3.50	£10.50	£17.50

SABRE (2ND SERIES)

Eclipse; (Graphic Novel) nn Oct 1978

Issue	$Good	$Fine	$N.Mint	£Good	£Fine	£N.Mint
nn ND Don McGregor script, Paul Gulacy art	$1.50	$4.50	$7.50	£1.00	£3.00	£5.00
Title Value:	$1.50	$4.50	$7.50	£1.00	£3.00	£5.00
2nd print (Jan 1979)				£0.90	£2.70	£4.50
3rd print				£0.85	£2.55	£4.25

SABRETOOTH

Marvel Comics Group,MS; 1 Aug 1993-4 Nov 1993

Issue	$Good	$Fine	$N.Mint	£Good	£Fine	£N.Mint
1 die-cut logo giving "shredded" effect	$1.00	$3.00	$5.00	£0.70	£2.10	£3.50
1 Dynamic Forces Edition, ND - signed by Mark Texeira limited to 10,000 copies	$3.00	$9.00	$15.00	£2.00	£6.00	£10.00
2 Wolverine appears, card stock cover	$0.80	$2.40	$4.00	£0.60	£1.80	£3.00
3-4	$0.80	$2.40	$4.00	£0.60	£1.80	£3.00
Title Value:	$6.40	$19.20	$32.00	£4.50	£13.50	£22.50
Sabretooth: Death Hunt (Feb 1995) Trade paperback reprints four issue mini-series				£1.70	£5.10	£8.50

SABRETOOTH & MYSTIQUE

Marvel Comics Group,MS; 1 Dec 1996-4 Mar 1997

Issue	$Good	$Fine	$N.Mint	£Good	£Fine	£N.Mint
1-4 ND Jorge Gonzalez script, Ariel Olivetti art	$0.40	$1.20	$2.00	£0.25	£0.75	£1.25
Title Value:	$1.60	$4.80	$8.00	£1.00	£3.00	£5.00

SABRETOOTH CLASSICS

Marvel Comics Group; 1 May 1994-15 Jul 1995

Issue	$Good	$Fine	$N.Mint	£Good	£Fine	£N.Mint
1 reprints Sabretooth's 2nd appearance from Powerman and Iron Fist #66	$0.30	$0.90	$1.50	£0.20	£0.60	£1.00
2 reprints Sabretooth's 3rd appearance from Powerman and Iron Fist #78	$0.30	$0.90	$1.50	£0.20	£0.60	£1.00
3 reprints Sabretooth's 4th appearance from Powerman and Iron Fist #84	$0.30	$0.90	$1.50	£0.20	£0.60	£1.00
4 reprints Sabretooth's 5th appearance from Spectacular Spiderman #116	$0.30	$0.90	$1.50	£0.20	£0.60	£1.00
5 reprints from Spectacular Spiderman #119	$0.30	$0.90	$1.50	£0.20	£0.60	£1.00
6 reprints from X-Factor #10	$0.30	$0.90	$1.50	£0.20	£0.60	£1.00
7 reprints from Thor #374	$0.30	$0.90	$1.50	£0.20	£0.60	£1.00
8 reprints X-Men #212	$0.30	$0.90	$1.50	£0.20	£0.60	£1.00
9 reprints X-Men #213	$0.30	$0.90	$1.50	£0.20	£0.60	£1.00
10 reprints X-Men #214	$0.30	$0.90	$1.50	£0.20	£0.60	£1.00
11 reprints Daredevil #238	$0.30	$0.90	$1.50	£0.20	£0.60	£1.00
12	$0.30	$0.90	$1.50	£0.20	£0.60	£1.00
13 reprints X-Men #219	$0.30	$0.90	$1.50	£0.20	£0.60	£1.00
14 reprints X-Men #220	$0.30	$0.90	$1.50	£0.20	£0.60	£1.00
15 reprints X-Men #221	$0.30	$0.90	$1.50	£0.20	£0.60	£1.00
Title Value:	$4.50	$13.50	$22.50	£3.00	£9.00	£15.00

SABRETOOTH SPECIAL

Marvel Comics Group,OS; 1 Jan 1996

Issue	$Good	$Fine	$N.Mint	£Good	£Fine	£N.Mint
1 ND 48pgs, X-Men appear, Gary Frank art; wraparound chromium cover; continued from Uncanny X-Men #328 and X-Men #48	$1.00	$3.00	$5.00	£0.70	£2.10	£3.50
Title Value:	$1.00	$3.00	$5.00	£0.70	£2.10	£3.50

SACHS & VIOLENS

Marvel Comics Group/Epic,MS; 1 Nov 1993-4 Jul 1994

1 ND Peter David script and George Perez art begins; embossed cover and bound-in trading card

Issue	$Good	$Fine	$N.Mint	£Good	£Fine	£N.Mint
	$0.50	$1.50	$2.50	£0.30	£0.90	£1.50
1 Silver Premium Edition ND	$1.50	$4.50	$7.50	£1.00	£3.00	£5.00
2-4 ND	$0.50	$1.50	$2.50	£0.30	£0.90	£1.50
Title Value:	$3.50	$10.50	$17.50	£2.20	£6.60	£11.00

SAD SACK AND THE SARGE

Harvey; 1 Sep 1957-155 Jun 1982

Issue	$Good	$Fine	$N.Mint	£Good	£Fine	£N.Mint
1 scarce in the U.K.	$13.00	$40.00	$120.00	£8.75	£27.00	£80.00
2 scarce in the U.K.	$6.50	$20.00	$60.00	£4.40	£13.00	£40.00
3-10 scarce in the U.K.	$5.00	$15.00	$40.00	£3.35	£10.00	£27.00
11-20	$4.35	$13.00	$35.00	£2.90	£8.75	£23.50
21-30	$2.85	$8.50	$20.00	£1.90	£5.75	£13.50
31-40	$2.50	$7.50	$15.00	£1.65	£5.00	£10.00
41-50	$2.05	$6.25	$12.50	£1.40	£4.25	£8.50
51-70	$1.50	$4.50	$9.00	£1.00	£3.00	£6.00
71-90	$1.25	$3.75	$7.50	£0.80	£2.50	£5.00
91-96 48pgs	$1.50	$4.50	$9.00	£1.00	£3.00	£6.00
97-100	$1.25	$3.75	$7.50	£0.80	£2.50	£5.00
101-125	$0.80	$2.50	$5.00	£0.55	£1.65	£3.35
126-155	$0.70	$2.10	$3.50	£0.40	£1.20	£2.00
Title Value:	$287.00	$865.00	$1969.00	£189.40	£572.75	£1310.75

Note: although the title is dated well before official distribution in the U.K. cover-dated November 1959, it is possible that all issues from #1 came over

SAD SACK IN 3-D

Blackthorne;(3-D Series #49) 1 Autumn 1988

Issue	$Good	$Fine	$N.Mint	£Good	£Fine	£N.Mint
1 ND with bound-in 3-D glasses (25% less without glasses)	$0.50	$1.50	$2.50	£0.30	£0.90	£1.50
Title Value:	$0.50	$1.50	$2.50	£0.30	£0.90	£1.50

SAD SACK LAUGH SPECIAL

Harvey; 1 Nov 1958-93 Feb 1977

Issue	$Good	$Fine	$N.Mint	£Good	£Fine	£N.Mint
1 scarce in the U.K. 64pgs	$15.00	$45.00	$105.00	£10.00	£30.00	£70.00
2 scarce in the U.K. 64pgs	$9.00	$28.00	$55.00	£6.25	£18.50	£37.50
3-10 64pgs	$5.75	$17.50	$35.00	£3.90	£11.50	£23.50
11-30 64pgs	$3.30	$10.00	$20.00	£2.25	£6.75	£13.50
31-60 64pgs	$2.05	$6.25	$12.50	£1.35	£4.10	£8.25
61-76 48pgs	$1.50	$4.50	$7.50	£1.00	£3.00	£5.00
77 regular 32pg issues begin	$1.00	$3.00	$5.00	£0.60	£1.80	£3.00
78-93	$1.00	$3.00	$5.00	£0.60	£1.80	£3.00
Title Value:	$238.50	$723.50	$1420.00	£159.15	£477.10	£944.00

Note: all distributed in the U.K. though more experimentally for the first few issues

SAD SACK WITH SARGE AND SADIE

Harvey; 1 Sep 1972-8 Nov 1973

Issue	$Good	$Fine	$N.Mint	£Good	£Fine	£N.Mint
1 distributed in the U.K. 48pgs	$1.15	$3.50	$7.00	£0.75	£2.25	£4.50
2 distributed in the U.K.	$0.80	$2.50	$5.00	£0.50	£1.50	£3.00
3-8 distributed in the U.K.	$0.65	$2.00	$4.00	£0.40	£1.25	£2.50
Title Value:	$5.85	$18.00	$36.00	£3.65	£11.25	£22.50

SAD SACK'S ARMY LIFE (PARADE/TODAY)

Harvey; 1 Oct 1963-60 Nov 1975; 61 May 1976

(...Parade to #57; ...Today from #58 on)

Issue	$Good	$Fine	$N.Mint	£Good	£Fine	£N.Mint
1 scarce in the U.K.	$7.75	$23.50	$55.00	£5.25	£16.00	£37.50
2 scarce in the U.K. 64pgs	$5.00	$15.00	$30.00	£3.30	£10.00	£20.00
3-10 scarce in the U.K. 64pgs	$4.15	$12.50	$25.00	£2.75	£8.25	£16.50
11-20 64pgs	$2.50	$7.50	$15.00	£1.65	£5.00	£10.00
21-34 64pgs	$2.00	$6.00	$10.00	£1.30	£3.90	£6.50
35-40 48pgs	$1.50	$4.50	$7.50	£1.00	£3.00	£5.00
41-51 48pgs	$1.00	$3.00	$5.00	£0.65	£2.00	£3.35
52 regular 32pgs begins	$0.60	$1.80	$3.00	£0.40	£1.20	£2.00
53-60	$0.60	$1.80	$3.00	£0.40	£1.20	£2.00
61 scarce in the U.K.	$0.60	$1.80	$3.00	£0.30	£0.90	£1.50
Title Value:	$124.95	$375.50	$705.00	£82.30	£248.30	£466.85

Note: all distributed on the news-stands in the U.K.

SADE

Bishop Press; 0 Jul 1995-2 1996

Issue	$Good	$Fine	$N.Mint	£Good	£Fine	£N.Mint
0 ND	$0.60	$1.80	$3.00	£0.40	£1.20	£2.00
1-2 ND black and white	$0.60	$1.80	$3.00	£0.40	£1.20	£2.00
Title Value:	$1.80	$5.40	$9.00	£1.20	£3.60	£6.00

SADE (2ND SERIES)

London Night Studios; 1 Jun 1996-present

Issue	$Good	$Fine	$N.Mint	£Good	£Fine	£N.Mint
1 ND black and white	$0.60	$1.80	$3.00	£0.40	£1.20	£2.00
1 "Balance of Pain" Edition, ND black and white	$1.00	$3.00	$5.00	£0.60	£1.80	£3.00
2-4 ND black and white	$0.60	$1.80	$3.00	£0.40	£1.20	£2.00
Title Value:	$3.40	$10.20	$17.00	£2.20	£6.60	£11.00

SADE SPECIAL

London Night Studios; 1 1996

Issue	$Good	$Fine	$N.Mint	£Good	£Fine	£N.Mint
1 ND 40pgs, Razor appears	$1.00	$3.00	$5.00	£0.70	£2.10	£3.50
1 Encore Edition, ND 40pgs, (Apr 1996) new cover and Razor pin-ups	$0.60	$1.80	$3.00	£0.40	£1.20	£2.00
Title Value:	$1.60	$4.80	$8.00	£1.10	£3.30	£5.50

SADE/ROSE AND GUNN: CONFEDERATE MIST
Bishop Press,MS; 1 Mar 1996

Issue	$Good	$Fine	$N.Mint	£Good	£Fine	£N.Mint
1 ND black and white	$0.60	$1.80	$3.00	£0.40	£1.20	£2.00
Title Value:	$0.60	$1.80	$3.00	£0.40	£1.20	£2.00

SAFEST PLACE, THE
Dark Horse,OS; nn Jun 1993

Issue	$Good	$Fine	$N.Mint	£Good	£Fine	£N.Mint
nn ND Steve Ditko script and art	$0.50	$1.50	$2.50	£0.30	£0.90	£1.50
Title Value:	$0.50	$1.50	$2.50	£0.30	£0.90	£1.50

SAFETY-BELT MAN: ALL HELL
Sirius Entertainment; 1 Apr 1996-6 Sep 1996

Issue	$Good	$Fine	$N.Mint	£Good	£Fine	£N.Mint
1-3 ND	$0.80	$2.40	$4.00	£0.40	£1.20	£2.00
4 ND Linsner back up story	$1.00	$3.00	$5.00	£0.50	£1.50	£2.50
5-6 ND	$0.60	$1.80	$3.00	£0.40	£1.20	£2.00
Title Value:	$4.60	$13.80	$21.00	£2.50	£7.50	£12.50

SAGA OF RA'S AL GHUL
DC Comics,MS; 1 Jan 1988-4 Apr 1988

(see Batman)

Issue	$Good	$Fine	$N.Mint	£Good	£Fine	£N.Mint
1 ND scarce in the U.K. Neal Adams art, reprints 1st appearance in Batman #232	$0.70	$2.10	$3.50	£0.40	£1.20	£2.00
2 ND scarce in the U.K.	$0.70	$2.10	$3.50	£0.40	£1.20	£2.00
3 ND scarce in the U.K. Neal Adams art, reprints Batman #243	$0.70	$2.10	$3.50	£0.40	£1.20	£2.00
4 ND scarce in the U.K. Neal Adams art, reprints Batman #244	$0.70	$2.10	$3.50	£0.40	£1.20	£2.00
Title Value:	$2.80	$8.40	$14.00	£1.60	£4.80	£8.00

SAGA OF SWAMP THING
(see Swamp Thing)

SAGE
Fantaco; 1 Oct 1995

Issue	$Good	$Fine	$N.Mint	£Good	£Fine	£N.Mint
1 ND Tom Simonton script and art; black and white	$1.00	$3.00	$5.00	£0.60	£1.80	£3.00
Title Value:	$1.00	$3.00	$5.00	£0.60	£1.80	£3.00

SAIGON CHRONICLES, THE
A Plus Comics; 1 Sep 1991-2 1991

Issue	$Good	$Fine	$N.Mint	£Good	£Fine	£N.Mint
1-2 ND 48pgs, new and reprint war stories	$0.40	$1.20	$2.00	£0.25	£0.75	£1.25
Title Value:	$0.80	$2.40	$4.00	£0.50	£1.50	£2.50

SAINT SINNER
Marvel Comics Group/Razorline; 1 Oct 1993-7 Apr 1994

Issue	$Good	$Fine	$N.Mint	£Good	£Fine	£N.Mint
1-7 ND based on Clive Barker characters	$0.30	$0.90	$1.50	£0.20	£0.60	£1.00
Title Value:	$2.10	$6.30	$10.50	£1.40	£4.20	£7.00

SALIMBA 3-D
Blackthorne,MS;(3-D Series #6,#9); 1 Aug 1986-2 Sep 1986

Issue	$Good	$Fine	$N.Mint	£Good	£Fine	£N.Mint
1-2 ND all Paul Chadwick wraparound cover/art; with 3-D glasses (25% less if without glasses)	$0.60	$1.80	$3.00	£0.40	£1.20	£2.00
Title Value:	$1.20	$3.60	$6.00	£0.80	£2.40	£4.00

SALOME
Eclipse;(Night Music 5) 1 1987

Issue	$Good	$Fine	$N.Mint	£Good	£Fine	£N.Mint
1 ND P. Craig Russell art	$0.40	$1.20	$2.00	£0.25	£0.75	£1.25
Title Value:	$0.40	$1.20	$2.00	£0.25	£0.75	£1.25

SAM & MAX COLOUR COLLECTION
Marvel Comics Group,OS; 1 Sep 1992

Issue	$Good	$Fine	$N.Mint	£Good	£Fine	£N.Mint
1 ND 64pgs	$0.80	$2.40	$4.00	£0.50	£1.50	£2.50
Title Value:	$0.80	$2.40	$4.00	£0.50	£1.50	£2.50

SAM & MAX FREELANCE POLICE SPECIAL
Comico; 1 Jan 1989

Issue	$Good	$Fine	$N.Mint	£Good	£Fine	£N.Mint
1 ND 40pgs, colour	$0.40	$1.20	$2.00	£0.25	£0.75	£1.25
Title Value:	$0.40	$1.20	$2.00	£0.25	£0.75	£1.25

SAM & MAX FREELANCE POLICE SPECIAL EDITION
Fishwrap Productions; 1 1987

Issue	$Good	$Fine	$N.Mint	£Good	£Fine	£N.Mint
1 ND Steve Purcell script and art, black & white	$0.40	$1.20	$2.00	£0.25	£0.75	£1.25
Title Value:	$0.40	$1.20	$2.00	£0.25	£0.75	£1.25

SAM & MAX GO TO THE MOON DIRT BAG SPECIAL
Marvel Comics Group,OS; 1 Jun 1992

Issue	$Good	$Fine	$N.Mint	£Good	£Fine	£N.Mint
1 ND pre-bagged, Sam & Max comic, "Dirt" magazine, pop music cassette	$0.70	$2.10	$3.50	£0.40	£1.20	£2.00
Title Value:	$0.70	$2.10	$3.50	£0.40	£1.20	£2.00

SAM & MAX SHOW, THE
Marvel Comics Group,MS; 1 May 1993-3 Jul 1993

Issue	$Good	$Fine	$N.Mint	£Good	£Fine	£N.Mint
1-3 ND Mike Mignola and Art Adams art featured	$0.50	$1.50	$2.50	£0.30	£0.90	£1.50
Title Value:	$1.50	$4.50	$7.50	£0.90	£2.70	£4.50

SAMURAI
Aircel; 1 1985-23 1987

Issue	$Good	$Fine	$N.Mint	£Good	£Fine	£N.Mint
1 scarce in the U.K.	$0.50	$1.50	$2.50	£0.30	£0.90	£1.50
1 2nd printing, (1986)	$0.40	$1.20	$2.00	£0.25	£0.75	£1.25
1 3rd printing	$0.40	$1.20	$2.00	£0.25	£0.75	£1.25
2	$0.40	$1.20	$2.00	£0.25	£0.75	£1.25
2 2nd printing	$0.40	$1.20	$2.00	£0.25	£0.75	£1.25
3-12	$0.40	$1.20	$2.00	£0.25	£0.75	£1.25
13 Dale Keown cover and art (1st pro work?)	$0.80	$2.40	$4.00	£0.40	£1.20	£2.00
14-16 Dale Keown cover and art	$0.60	$1.80	$3.00	£0.30	£0.90	£1.50
17-18 Dale Keown inks only	$0.50	$1.50	$2.50	£0.30	£0.90	£1.50
19-23	$0.40	$1.20	$2.00	£0.25	£0.75	£1.25
Title Value:	$11.70	$35.10	$58.50	£6.95	£20.85	£34.75

Note: all Non-Distributed on the news-stands in the U.K.

SAMURAI (2ND SERIES)
Aircel; 1 Aug 1988-2 1988 ?

Issue	$Good	$Fine	$N.Mint	£Good	£Fine	£N.Mint
1 ND 1st colour issue	$0.40	$1.20	$2.00	£0.25	£0.75	£1.25
2 ND	$0.40	$1.20	$2.00	£0.25	£0.75	£1.25
Title Value:	$0.80	$2.40	$4.00	£0.50	£1.50	£2.50

SAMURAI (3RD SERIES)
Aircel; 1 1989-7 1990 ?

Issue	$Good	$Fine	$N.Mint	£Good	£Fine	£N.Mint
1-7 ND	$0.40	$1.20	$2.00	£0.25	£0.75	£1.25
Title Value:	$2.80	$8.40	$14.00	£1.75	£5.25	£8.75

SAMURAI CAT
Marvel Comics Group/Epic,MS; 1 Jun 1991-3 Aug 1991

Issue	$Good	$Fine	$N.Mint	£Good	£Fine	£N.Mint
1-3 ND Frank Cirocco art	$0.40	$1.20	$2.00	£0.25	£0.75	£1.25
Title Value:	$1.20	$3.60	$6.00	£0.75	£2.25	£3.75

SAMURAI FUNNIES
Solson Publications;2-3 1987

Issue	$Good	$Fine	$N.Mint	£Good	£Fine	£N.Mint
2 ND Friday 13th film parody ("Samurai the 13th")	$0.30	$0.90	$1.50	£0.15	£0.45	£0.75
3 ND scarce in the U.K.	$0.30	$0.90	$1.50	£0.20	£0.60	£1.00
Title Value:	$0.60	$1.80	$3.00	£0.35	£1.05	£1.75

SAMURAI PENGUIN
Slave Labor; 1 1986-8 1988

Issue	$Good	$Fine	$N.Mint	£Good	£Fine	£N.Mint
1 ND	$0.30	$0.90	$1.50	£0.20	£0.60	£1.00
2 ND intro Dr. Radium	$0.30	$0.90	$1.50	£0.20	£0.60	£1.00
3 ND	$0.30	$0.90	$1.50	£0.20	£0.60	£1.00
4 ND Boris the Bear parody	$0.30	$0.90	$1.50	£0.20	£0.60	£1.00
5 ND	$0.30	$0.90	$1.50	£0.20	£0.60	£1.00
6 ND colour issue; says number 7 in indicia	$0.30	$0.90	$1.50	£0.20	£0.60	£1.00
7-8 ND	$0.30	$0.90	$1.50	£0.20	£0.60	£1.00
Title Value:	$2.40	$7.20	$12.00	£1.60	£4.80	£8.00
Food Chain Follies (Jun 1991)						
Trade paperback ND 64pgs, reprints #1-3				£0.50	£1.50	£2.50

SAMURAI SANTA
Solson Publications,OS; 1 1987

(becomes Samurai Funnies)

Issue	$Good	$Fine	$N.Mint	£Good	£Fine	£N.Mint
1 ND Jim Lee art, his 1st in comics (black and white)	$0.80	$2.40	$4.00	£0.50	£1.50	£2.50
Title Value:	$0.80	$2.40	$4.00	£0.50	£1.50	£2.50

SAMURAI SEVEN
Caliber Press; 1 Jul 1992-4 Jan 1993

Issue	$Good	$Fine	$N.Mint	£Good	£Fine	£N.Mint
1-4 ND	$0.40	$1.20	$2.00	£0.25	£0.75	£1.25
Title Value:	$1.60	$4.80	$8.00	£1.00	£3.00	£5.00

SAMURAI SQUIRREL
Spotlight; 1 1986-2 1987

Issue	$Good	$Fine	$N.Mint	£Good	£Fine	£N.Mint
1-2 ND	$0.40	$1.20	$2.00	£0.25	£0.75	£1.25
Title Value:	$0.80	$2.40	$4.00	£0.50	£1.50	£2.50

SAMURAI, SON OF DEATH
Eclipse;(Graphic Novel 14); 1 1987

Issue	$Good	$Fine	$N.Mint	£Good	£Fine	£N.Mint
1 ND	$0.80	$2.40	$4.00	£0.50	£1.50	£2.50
1 2nd printing ND	$0.70	$2.10	$3.50	£0.40	£1.20	£2.00
Title Value:	$1.50	$4.50	$7.50	£0.90	£2.70	£4.50

SAMURAI: DEATH OF A LEGEND
Night Wynd,MS; 1 Apr 1993-4 Jul 1993

Issue	$Good	$Fine	$N.Mint	£Good	£Fine	£N.Mint
1-4 ND Barry Blair and Dale Keown	$0.40	$1.20	$2.00	£0.25	£0.75	£1.25
Title Value:	$1.60	$4.80	$8.00	£1.00	£3.00	£5.00

SAMURAI: DEMON SWORD
Night Wynd,MS; 1 Aug 1993-4 Nov 1993

Issue	$Good	$Fine	$N.Mint	£Good	£Fine	£N.Mint
1-4 ND Barry Blair script and art begins; black and white	$0.40	$1.20	$2.00	£0.25	£0.75	£1.25
Title Value:	$1.60	$4.80	$8.00	£1.00	£3.00	£5.00

SAMURAI: MYSTIC CULT
Night Wynd,MS; 1 Nov 1992-4 Mar 1993

Issue	$Good	$Fine	$N.Mint	£Good	£Fine	£N.Mint
1-4 ND Barry Blair script and art	$0.40	$1.20	$2.00	£0.25	£0.75	£1.25
Title Value:	$1.60	$4.80	$8.00	£1.00	£3.00	£5.00

SAMURAI: VAMPIRE'S HUNT
Night Wynd,MS; 1 Jul 1992-4 Oct 1992

Issue	$Good	$Fine	$N.Mint	£Good	£Fine	£N.Mint
1-4 ND Barry Blair script and art	$0.40	$1.20	$2.00	£0.25	£0.75	£1.25
Title Value:	$1.60	$4.80	$8.00	£1.00	£3.00	£5.00

SAMURAI: YAKUZA'S REVENGE
Night Wynd,MS; 1 Apr 1993-4 Jul 1993

Issue	$Good	$Fine	$N.Mint	£Good	£Fine	£N.Mint
1-4 ND Barry Blair and Patrick McEown	$0.40	$1.20	$2.00	£0.25	£0.75	£1.25

	$Good	$Fine	$N.Mint	£Good	£Fine	£N.Mint
Title Value:	*$1.60*	*$4.80*	*$8.00*	£1.00	£3.00	£5.00

SAMUREE

Continuity; 1 May 1987-13 1992

	$Good	$Fine	$N.Mint	£Good	£Fine	£N.Mint
1 Neal Adams script, Mark Beachum art	*$0.40*	*$1.20*	*$2.00*	£0.25	£0.75	£1.25
2-3 Neal Adams cover	*$0.40*	*$1.20*	*$2.00*	£0.25	£0.75	£1.25
4 Neal Adams part pencils	*$0.40*	*$1.20*	*$2.00*	£0.25	£0.75	£1.25
5 Neal Adams plot	*$0.40*	*$1.20*	*$2.00*	£0.25	£0.75	£1.25
6-13	*$0.40*	*$1.20*	*$2.00*	£0.25	£0.75	£1.25
Title Value:	*$5.20*	*$15.60*	*$26.00*	£3.25	£9.75	£16.25

Note: all Non-Distributed on the news-stands in the U.K.

SAMUREE (2ND SERIES)

Continuity; 1 Aug 1993-4 1994

	$Good	$Fine	$N.Mint	£Good	£Fine	£N.Mint
1 ND Rise of Magic X-over, Neal Adams co-plot begins	*$0.40*	*$1.20*	*$2.00*	£0.25	£0.75	£1.25
2-4 ND Rise of Magic X-over, embossed parchment cover	*$0.40*	*$1.20*	*$2.00*	£0.25	£0.75	£1.25
Title Value:	*$1.60*	*$4.80*	*$8.00*	£1.00	£3.00	£5.00

SAMUREE (3RD SERIES)

Acclaim Comics/Windjammer,MS; 1 Jun 1995-3 Aug 1995

	$Good	$Fine	$N.Mint	£Good	£Fine	£N.Mint
1-3 ND Neal Adams pencils	*$0.40*	*$1.20*	*$2.00*	£0.25	£0.75	£1.25
Title Value:	*$1.20*	*$3.60*	*$6.00*	£0.75	£2.25	£3.75

SAN DIEGO COMICON COMICS

Dark Horse,OS; 1 Aug 1992-3 1994

	$Good	$Fine	$N.Mint	£Good	£Fine	£N.Mint
1 ND special comic-convention jam featuring art by Joe Quesada, John Byrne, Moebius, Paul Chadwick, Steve Rude and many others; Paul Chadwick cover; available only at the convention	*$1.00*	*$3.00*	*$5.00*	£0.60	£1.80	£3.00
2 ND (1993) 1st appearance of Danger Unlimited, Monkeyman & O'Brien, Big Guy	*$1.20*	*$3.60*	*$6.00*	£0.70	£2.10	£3.50
3 ND (1994) Barb Wire, Grendel, Mask appear	*$1.00*	*$3.00*	*$5.00*	£0.60	£1.80	£3.00
Title Value:	*$3.20*	*$9.60*	*$16.00*	£1.90	£5.70	£9.50

SANCTUARY

Viz Communications,MS; 1 May 1992-9 Jan 1993

	$Good	$Fine	$N.Mint	£Good	£Fine	£N.Mint
1-9 ND 80pgs, black and white	*$0.90*	*$2.70*	*$4.50*	£0.60	£1.80	£3.00
Title Value:	*$8.10*	*$24.30*	*$40.50*	£5.40	£16.20	£27.00
Sanctuary Graphic Novel Vol 1 (1993) reprints from series begin; black and white				£2.40	£7.20	£12.00
Sanctuary Graphic Novel Vol 2 (1994) reprints from series continue; black and white				£2.40	£7.20	£12.00
Sanctuary Graphic Novel Vol 3 (Jan 1995) reprints from series continue; black and white				£2.40	£7.20	£12.00
Sanctuary Graphic Novel Vol 4 (Mar 1995) reprints from series continue; black and white				£2.40	£7.20	£12.00

SANCTUARY PART 2

Viz Communications,MS; 1 Jul 1993-9 Mar 1994

	$Good	$Fine	$N.Mint	£Good	£Fine	£N.Mint
1-9 ND black and white	*$0.90*	*$2.70*	*$4.50*	£0.60	£1.80	£3.00
Title Value:	*$8.10*	*$24.30*	*$40.50*	£5.40	£16.20	£27.00

SANCTUARY PART 3

Viz Communications,MS; 1 Dec 1994-8 Jul 1995

	$Good	$Fine	$N.Mint	£Good	£Fine	£N.Mint
1-8 ND 48pgs, Sho Fumimura; black and white	*$0.60*	*$1.80*	*$3.00*	£0.40	£1.20	£2.00
Title Value:	*$4.80*	*$14.40*	*$24.00*	£3.20	£9.60	£16.00

SANCTUARY PART 4

Viz Communications,MS; 1 Aug 1995-7 Feb 1996

	$Good	$Fine	$N.Mint	£Good	£Fine	£N.Mint
1-7 ND Sho Fumimura and Ryoichi Ikegami script and art; black and white	*$0.60*	*$1.80*	*$3.00*	£0.40	£1.20	£2.00
Title Value:	*$4.20*	*$12.60*	*$21.00*	£2.80	£8.40	£14.00

SANDMAN

DC Comics; 1 Winter 1974; 2 Apr/May 1975-6 Dec/Jan 1975/76

	$Good	$Fine	$N.Mint	£Good	£Fine	£N.Mint
1 ND very scarce in the U.K. Jack Kirby art	*$2.00*	*$6.00*	*$12.00*	£1.15	£3.50	£7.00
2 Ernie Chua art	*$1.15*	*$3.50*	*$7.00*	£0.65	£2.00	£4.00
3 Ernie Chua art	*$1.00*	*$3.00*	*$6.00*	£0.55	£1.75	£3.50
4-5 Jack Kirby art	*$1.00*	*$3.00*	*$6.00*	£0.55	£1.75	£3.50
6 Jack Kirby/Wally Wood art	*$1.00*	*$3.00*	*$6.00*	£0.55	£1.75	£3.50
Title Value:	*$7.15*	*$21.50*	*$43.00*	£4.00	£12.50	£25.00

SANDMAN (2ND SERIES)

DC Comics/Vertigo; 1 Jan 1989-75 Mar 1996

(see Best of DC #22)

	$Good	$Fine	$N.Mint	£Good	£Fine	£N.Mint
1 LD in the U.K. DS Neil Gaiman scripts, Sam Keith/Mike Dringenberg art, Dave McKean paint & collage covers begin	*$15.00*	*$45.00*	*$75.00*	£4.00	£12.00	£20.00
2 very LD Sam Keith art	*$8.00*	*$24.00*	*$40.00*	£2.00	£6.00	£10.00
3 LD in the U.K. Sam Kieth art	*$7.00*	*$21.00*	*$35.00*	£1.40	£4.20	£7.00
4-5 LD in the U.K. Sam Keith art	*$6.00*	*$18.00*	*$30.00*	£1.20	£3.60	£6.00
6-7 LD in the U.K.	*$5.00*	*$15.00*	*$25.00*	£1.00	£3.00	£5.00
8 LD in the U.K. (see note below), 1st appearance Death (Sandman's sister)	*$10.00*	*$30.00*	*$50.00*	£1.80	£5.25	£9.00
8 Variant Edition, ND (see notes below Trade paperbacks)	*$35.00*	*$105.00*	*$175.00*	£20.00	£60.00	£100.00
9-10 LD in the U.K.	*$3.00*	*$9.00*	*$15.00*	£0.80	£2.40	£4.00
11-13 LD in the U.K.	*$3.00*	*$9.00*	*$15.00*	£0.70	£2.10	£3.50
14 LD in the U.K. DS	*$3.00*	*$9.00*	*$15.00*	£0.80	£2.40	£4.00
15-18 ND	*$2.00*	*$6.00*	*$10.00*	£0.60	£1.80	£3.00
18 Misprint Edition, ND - first 3 panels on page 1 are coloured in blue ink	*$13.00*	*$39.00*	*$65.00*	£5.00	£15.00	£25.00
19 ND	*$2.00*	*$6.00*	*$10.00*	£0.60	£1.80	£3.00
20 ND Element Girl appears and "dies"	*$2.00*	*$6.00*	*$10.00*	£0.60	£1.80	£3.00
21 ND Season of Mists story begins (part 0)	*$2.00*	*$6.00*	*$10.00*	£1.20	£3.60	£6.00
22 ND previews World Without End series, Season of Mists part 1 (ends #28); 1st appearance of Daniel later becomes the new Sandman	*$5.00*	*$15.00*	*$25.00*	£1.20	£3.60	£6.00
23 ND	*$2.00*	*$6.00*	*$10.00*	£0.70	£2.10	£3.50
24 ND Phantom Stranger appears	*$2.00*	*$6.00*	*$10.00*	£0.70	£2.10	£3.50
25 ND	*$2.00*	*$6.00*	*$10.00*	£0.70	£2.10	£3.50
26-29 ND	*$1.50*	*$4.50*	*$7.50*	£0.60	£1.80	£3.00
30 ND Bryan Talbot art, Dave McKean cover	*$1.50*	*$4.50*	*$7.50*	£0.60	£1.80	£3.00
31 ND	*$1.20*	*$3.60*	*$6.00*	£0.50	£1.50	£2.50
32 ND The Game of You part 1	*$1.20*	*$3.60*	*$6.00*	£0.50	£1.50	£2.50
33-36 ND	*$1.20*	*$3.60*	*$6.00*	£0.50	£1.50	£2.50
37 ND The Game of You part 6 (conclusion)	*$0.80*	*$2.40*	*$4.00*	£0.40	£1.20	£2.00
38 ND Duncan Eagleson/Vince Locke art	*$0.80*	*$2.40*	*$4.00*	£0.40	£1.20	£2.00

Ruins #2

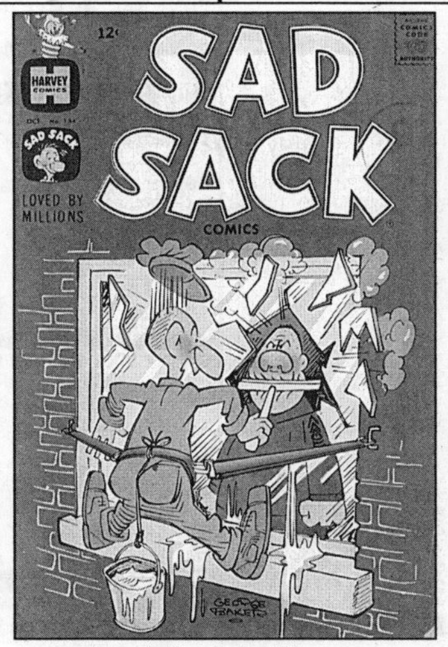

Sad Sack Comics #134

Samuree #1

	$Good	$Fine	$N.Mint	£Good	£Fine	£N.Mint
39 ND	*$0.80*	*$2.40*	*$4.00*	£0.40	£1.20	£2.00
40 ND Jill Thompson art begins						
	$0.80	*$2.40*	*$4.00*	£0.40	£1.20	£2.00
41 ND	*$0.60*	*$1.80*	*$3.00*	£0.30	£0.90	£1.50
42 ND Dave McKean painted covers begin						
	$0.60	*$1.80*	*$3.00*	£0.30	£0.90	£1.50
43-44 ND	*$0.60*	*$1.80*	*$3.00*	£0.30	£0.90	£1.50
45 ND $1.75 cover begins						
	$0.60	*$1.80*	*$3.00*	£0.30	£0.90	£1.50
46 ND Gaiman and McKean AIDS awareness back-up story						
	$0.60	*$1.80*	*$3.00*	£0.30	£0.90	£1.50
47 ND 1st issue under the "Vertigo" banner						
	$0.60	*$1.80*	*$3.00*	£0.30	£0.90	£1.50
48-49 ND	*$0.60*	*$1.80*	*$3.00*	£0.30	£0.90	£1.50
50 ND 48pgs, anniversary issue with pin-ups by McFarlane, McKean, Kaluta and many others; wraparound black cover with gold metallic inks						
	$0.80	*$2.40*	*$4.00*	£0.40	£1.20	£2.00
50 Limited Edition, ND - all black cover with gold titles						
	$10.00	*$30.00*	*$50.00*	£6.00	£18.00	£30.00
51-56 ND Bryan Talbot art featured						
	$0.50	*$1.50*	*$2.50*	£0.30	£0.90	£1.50
57 ND Marc Hempel art; American Freak preview; The Kindly Ones story						
	$0.50	*$1.50*	*$2.50*	£0.30	£0.90	£1.50
58-63 ND Marc Hempel art; The Kindly Ones story						
	$0.50	*$1.50*	*$2.50*	£0.30	£0.90	£1.50
64-68 ND	*$0.50*	*$1.50*	*$2.50*	£0.30	£0.90	£1.50
69 ND The Kindly Ones storyline concludes, death of Sandman (Morpheus), Daniel takes over as the new Sandman						
	$1.00	*$3.00*	*$5.00*	£0.50	£1.50	£2.50
70-72 ND The Wake, Michael Zulli art						
	$0.50	*$1.50*	*$2.50*	£0.30	£0.90	£1.50
73 ND The Wake epilogue, Michael Zulli art						
	$0.50	*$1.50*	*$2.50*	£0.30	£0.90	£1.50
74 ND	*$0.50*	*$1.50*	*$2.50*	£0.30	£0.90	£1.50
75 ND 48pgs, Charles Vess art plus 2pg "farewell" by Neil Gaiman						
	$0.80	*$2.40*	*$4.00*	£0.50	£1.50	£2.50
Title Value:	***$200.40***	***$601.20***	***$1001.00***	**£75.80**	**£227.25**	**£379.00**

Note: New Format, Mature Readers label

	£Good	£Fine	£N.Mint
Preludes and Nocturnes (1991)			
Trade paperback ND reprints issues #1-8, 240pgs	£1.85	£5.55	£9.25
Preludes and Nocturnes Hardcover (Oct 1995)			
ND reprints issues #1-8 with new cover design by Dave McKean	£4.00	£12.00	£20.00
The Doll's House (1990)			
Trade paperback ND reprints issues #8-16, 256pgs	£1.60	£4.80	£8.00
The Doll's House Hardcover (Dec 1995)			
ND reprints issues #8-16 with new cover design by Dave McKean	£4.00	£12.00	£20.00
Dream Country (1991)			
Trade paperback ND reprints issuesd #17-27, 160pgs	£1.85	£5.55	£9.25
Dream Country Hardcover (Feb 1996)			
ND new cover and slipcase designed by Dave McKean	£4.00	£12.00	£20.00
Sandman Slipcase Package (Nov 1991)			
ND designed for the above three trade paperbacks though this package only included Preludes and Dream Country - room available for Doll's House	£3.75	£11.25	£18.75
Seasons of Mists Hardcover (Sep 1992)			
ND 224pgs, reprints issues #22-28 painted cover by Dave McKean	£3.75	£11.25	£18.75
Seasons of Mists Softcover (Sep 1992)			
ND 224pgs, reprints issues #22-28 new cover painting by Dave McKean	£2.50	£7.50	£12.50
A Game of You Hardcover (Jun 1993)			
ND 192pgs, reprints issues #32-37 contributions from Dave McKean, Dick Giordano, George Pratt, Bryan Talbot	£3.75	£11.25	£18.75
A Game of You Softcover (Sep 1993)			
ND 192pgs, reprints issues #32-37	£2.50	£7.50	£12.50
Fables and Reflections Hardcover (Oct 1993)			
ND reprints #29-31, #38-40, #50, Sandman Special #1 and Vertigo Preview	£3.75	£11.25	£18.75
Fables and Reflections Softcover (Feb 1994)			
ND reprints #29-31, #38-40, #50, Sandman Special #1 and Vertigo Preview; new Dave McKean cover	£2.50	£7.50	£12.50
Brief Lives Hardcover (Aug 1994)			
ND 256pgs, reprints issues #41-49	£4.00	£12.00	£20.00
Brief Lives Softcover (Jan 1995)			
ND reprints issues #41-49	£2.70	£8.10	£13.50
World's End Softcover (Jun 1995)			
Trade paperback ND reprints issues #51-56 with new Dave McKean cover	£2.70	£8.10	£13.50
World's End Hardcover (Dec 1995)			
ND reprints issues #51-56 with new Dave McKean cover	£3.75	£11.25	£18.75
The Kindly Ones Hardcover (Mar 1996)			
ND reprints issues #57-69 and The Castle story from Vertigo Jam, new cover and dust-jacket by Dave McKean	£4.70	£14.10	£23.50
The Kindly Ones Softcover (Sep 1996)			
ND reprints issues #57-69 and The Castle	£2.70	£8.10	£13.50
The Sandman: The Wake Hardcover (Jan 1997)			
ND reprints issues #70-75 with dust-jacket design by Dave McKean	£4.00	£12.00	£20.00

Note also: #8 accidentally had two separate printings: a 1st printing with regular DC inside front and back covers and a 2nd print which used an editorial by Karen Berger on the inside front cover and a pin up/ad for the next issue drawn by Mike Dringenberg. About 600 copies of the 2nd print were run off when DC asked for such copies for copyright purposes.

SANDMAN MIDNIGHT THEATRE

DC Comics,OS; nn Sep 1995

	$Good	$Fine	$N.Mint	£Good	£Fine	£N.Mint
nn ND Neil Gaiman and Matt wagner script, Teddy Kristiansen art; the Golden Age Sandman meets the current Sandman/Dream/Morpheus						
	$1.40	*$4.20*	*$7.00*	£0.90	£2.70	£4.50
Title Value:	***$1.40***	***$4.20***	***$7.00***	**£0.90**	**£2.70**	**£4.50**

SANDMAN MYSTERY THEATRE

DC Comics/Vertigo; 1 Apr 1993-present

	$Good	$Fine	$N.Mint	£Good	£Fine	£N.Mint
1 Matt Wagner script/art, Golden Age Sandman (Wesley Dodds) begins; part of the "Vertigo" banner, painted photo collage covers begin						
	$0.40	*$1.20*	*$2.00*	£0.25	£0.75	£1.25
2-24	*$0.40*	*$1.20*	*$2.00*	£0.25	£0.75	£1.25
25 The Butcher story	*$0.40*	*$1.20*	*$2.00*	£0.25	£0.75	£1.25
26-28 The Butcher story	*$0.45*	*$1.35*	*$2.25*	£0.30	£0.90	£1.50
29-32 Golden Age Hourman features						
	$0.45	*$1.35*	*$2.25*	£0.30	£0.90	£1.50
33-36	*$0.45*	*$1.35*	*$2.25*	£0.30	£0.90	£1.50
37 The Mist part 1 (of 4), origin of The Mist retold in more detail						
	$0.45	*$1.35*	*$2.25*	£0.30	£0.90	£1.50
38-44	*$0.45*	*$1.35*	*$2.25*	£0.30	£0.90	£1.50
45 ND The Blackhawk story; details about the origin of Blackhawk revealed						
	$0.50	*$1.50*	*$2.50*	£0.30	£0.90	£1.50
46-48 ND The Blackhawk story						
	$0.50	*$1.50*	*$2.50*	£0.30	£0.90	£1.50
Title Value:	***$20.55***	***$61.65***	***$103.25***	**£13.15**	**£39.45**	**£65.75**
Sandman Mystery Theatre: The Tarantula (May 1995)						
Trade paperback reprints issues #1-4 with new painted cover				£2.00	£6.00	£10.00

SANDMAN MYSTERY THEATRE ANNUAL

DC Comics/Vertigo; 1 Oct 1994-present

	$Good	$Fine	$N.Mint	£Good	£Fine	£N.Mint
1 64pgs, features work by Alex Ross, John Bolton, George Pratt, David Lloyd						
	$0.60	*$1.80*	*$3.00*	£0.40	£1.20	£2.00
Title Value:	***$0.60***	***$1.80***	***$3.00***	**£0.40**	**£1.20**	**£2.00**

SANDMAN SPECIAL

DC Comics,OS; 1 Nov 1991

	$Good	$Fine	$N.Mint	£Good	£Fine	£N.Mint
1 ND script by Neil Gaiman, art by Talbot and Buckingham, pin-ups by other artists including P. Craig Russell, white spot varnish face cover						
	$0.90	*$2.70*	*$4.50*	£0.60	£1.80	£3.00
Title Value:	***$0.90***	***$2.70***	***$4.50***	**£0.60**	**£1.80**	**£3.00**

SANTA CLAWS

Eternity,OS; 1 Dec 1991

	$Good	$Fine	$N.Mint	£Good	£Fine	£N.Mint
1 ND black and white						
	$0.50	*$1.50*	*$2.50*	£0.30	£0.90	£1.50
Title Value:	***$0.50***	***$1.50***	***$2.50***	**£0.30**	**£0.90**	**£1.50**

SANTA THE BARBARIAN

Maximum Comic Press,OS; 1 Dec 1996

	$Good	$Fine	$N.Mint	£Good	£Fine	£N.Mint
1 ND Dan Fraga script and art						
	$0.60	*$1.80*	*$3.00*	£0.40	£1.20	£2.00
Title Value:	***$0.60***	***$1.80***	***$3.00***	**£0.40**	**£1.20**	**£2.00**

SAPPHIRE

Aircel; 1 Feb 1990-10 1991

	$Good	$Fine	$N.Mint	£Good	£Fine	£N.Mint
1 ND Barry Blair script/art begins, black and white						
	$0.60	*$1.80*	*$3.00*	£0.40	£1.20	£2.00
1 2nd printing ND	*$0.40*	*$1.20*	*$2.00*	£0.25	£0.75	£1.25
2 ND	*$0.50*	*$1.50*	*$2.50*	£0.30	£0.90	£1.50
2 2nd printing ND	*$0.40*	*$1.20*	*$2.00*	£0.25	£0.75	£1.25
3 ND	*$0.50*	*$1.50*	*$2.50*	£0.30	£0.90	£1.50
3 2nd printing ND	*$0.40*	*$1.20*	*$2.00*	£0.25	£0.75	£1.25
4 ND	*$0.50*	*$1.50*	*$2.50*	£0.30	£0.90	£1.50
4 2nd printing ND	*$0.40*	*$1.20*	*$2.00*	£0.25	£0.75	£1.25
5-10 ND	*$0.40*	*$1.20*	*$2.00*	£0.25	£0.75	£1.25
Title Value:	***$6.10***	***$18.30***	***$30.50***	**£3.80**	**£11.40**	**£19.00**

Note: shipped pre-bagged owing to sexual content

	£Good	£Fine	£N.Mint
Graphic Novel: War of the Elves (Nov 1990)			
pre-bagged, reprints #1-4	£1.10	£3.30	£5.50
Graphic Novel: A Wizard's Quest (Aug 1991)			
reprints #5-8	£1.10	£3.30	£5.50

SARGE SNORKEL, BEETLE BAILEY FEATURING

Charlton; 1 Oct 1973-17 Dec 1976

	$Good	$Fine	$N.Mint	£Good	£Fine	£N.Mint
1 distributed in the U.K.						
	$1.00	*$3.00*	*$6.00*	£0.55	£1.75	£3.50
2 distributed in the U.K.						
	$0.55	*$1.75*	*$3.50*	£0.30	£1.00	£2.00
3-10 distributed in the U.K.						
	$0.50	*$1.50*	*$3.00*	£0.25	£0.75	£1.50
11-17 distributed in the U.K.						
	$0.40	*$1.25*	*$2.50*	£0.20	£0.60	£1.25
Title Value:	***$8.35***	***$25.50***	***$51.00***	**£4.25**	**£12.95**	**£26.25**

SARGE STEEL

Charlton; 1 Dec 1964-8 Mar/Apr 1966

(becomes Secret Agent)
(all distributed in the U.K.)

	$Good	$Fine	$N.Mint	£Good	£Fine	£N.Mint
1 Giordano art	*$2.50*	*$7.50*	*$17.50*	£1.40	£4.25	£10.00
2 Giordano art	*$1.70*	*$5.00*	*$12.00*	£1.00	£3.00	£7.00
3-5 Giordano art	*$1.10*	*$3.40*	*$8.00*	£0.70	£2.10	£5.00
6 rare in the U.K. Giordano art, Judomaster appears						
	$2.10	*$6.25*	*$15.00*	£1.40	£4.25	£10.00
7-8 Giordano art	*$1.10*	*$3.40*	*$8.00*	£0.70	£2.10	£5.00
Title Value:	***$11.80***	***$35.75***	***$84.50***	**£7.30**	**£22.00**	**£52.00**

SATAN'S SIX

Topps,MS; 1 Apr 1993-4 July 1993

1 pre-bagged with coupon #1 for Secret City Saga #0 plus chrome trading card; Jack Kirby and Todd McFarlane cover

VERY GENERAL PERCENTAGE CONVERSION CHART WHICH MAY BE USED TO CALCULATE LOW AND INBETWEEN GRADES:

	$Good	$Fine	$N.Mint	£Good	£Fine	£N.Mint
	$0.40	*$1.20*	*$2.00*	£0.25	£0.75	£1.25
1 without coupon/card						
	$0.30	*$0.90*	*$1.50*	£0.20	£0.60	£1.00
2-4 pre-bagged with 3 trading cards						
	$0.40	*$1.20*	*$2.00*	£0.25	£0.75	£1.25
Title Value:	*$1.90*	*$5.70*	*$9.50*	£1.20	£3.60	£6.00

Note: all Non-Distributed on the news-stands in the U.K.

SATAN'S SIX: HELLSPAWN

Topps,MS; 1 Jun 1994-4 Sep 1994

	$Good	$Fine	$N.Mint	£Good	£Fine	£N.Mint
1-4 ND adult material						
	$0.40	*$1.20*	*$2.00*	£0.25	£0.75	£1.25
Title Value:	*$1.60*	*$4.80*	*$8.00*	£1.00	£3.00	£5.00

SATANIKA

Verotik; 0 Jun 1995-present

	$Good	$Fine	$N.Mint	£Good	£Fine	£N.Mint
0 ND Glenn Danzig script, Simon Bisley art						
	$1.20	*$3.60*	*$6.00*	£1.00	£3.00	£5.00
1 ND Glenn Danzig script, Duke Mighten art						
	$3.00	*$9.00*	*$15.00*	£1.40	£4.20	£7.00
2 ND Glenn Danzig script, Duke Mighten art						
	$1.40	*$4.20*	*$7.00*	£1.00	£3.00	£5.00
3-6 ND Glenn Danzig script, Duke Mighten art						
	$0.80	*$2.40*	*$4.00*	£0.80	£2.40	£4.00
Title Value:	*$8.80*	*$26.40*	*$44.00*	£6.60	£19.80	£33.00
Satanika (Oct 1995)						
Trade paperback collects mini-series, new Simon Bisley cover				£1.30	£3.90	£6.50

SATANIKA VS. SHILENE

Verotik,OS; nn Apr 1996

	$Good	$Fine	$N.Mint	£Good	£Fine	£N.Mint
nn ND 48pgs, Glenn Danzig script, Eric Canete art; oversize format with 2 and 3 page pull-outs						
	$2.00	*$6.00*	*$10.00*	£1.30	£3.90	£6.50
Title Value:	*$2.00*	*$6.00*	*$10.00*	£1.30	£3.90	£6.50

SAVAGE COMBAT TALES

Atlas; 1 Feb 1975-3 Jul 1975

	$Good	$Fine	$N.Mint	£Good	£Fine	£N.Mint
1-3 distributed in the U.K.						
	$0.30	*$1.00*	*$2.00*	£0.20	£0.60	£1.00
Title Value:	*$0.90*	*$3.00*	*$6.00*	£0.60	£1.80	£3.00

SAVAGE DRAGON

Image,MS; 1 Jul 1992-3 Dec 1992

(see Dragon, The)

	$Good	$Fine	$N.Mint	£Good	£Fine	£N.Mint
1 Erik Larsen script/art begins, bound-in poster (4 variants)						
	$0.80	*$2.40*	*$4.00*	£0.60	£1.80	£3.00
2	*$0.70*	*$2.10*	*$3.50*	£0.50	£1.50	£2.50
3 Savage Dragon vs. Bedrock; contains Image #0 coupon 6 and bound-in poster (25% less without coupon)						
	$0.70	*$2.10*	*$3.50*	£0.50	£1.50	£2.50
Title Value:	*$2.20*	*$6.60*	*$11.00*	£1.60	£4.80	£8.00

Note: all Non-Distributed on the news-stands in the U.K.

	$Good	$Fine	$N.Mint	£Good	£Fine	£N.Mint
Savage Dragon Trade paperback (Jul 1993)						
reprints mini-series plus material from Image #0				£1.30	£3.90	£6.50

SAVAGE DRAGON (2ND SERIES)

Image; 1 Jun 1993-present

	$Good	$Fine	$N.Mint	£Good	£Fine	£N.Mint
1 ND Erik Larsen script and art begins						
	$0.50	*$1.50*	*$2.50*	£0.30	£0.90	£1.50
2 ND 48pgs, Savage Dragon vs. Teenage Mutant Ninja Turtles; flip-book with Vanguard #0						
	$0.50	*$1.50*	*$2.50*	£0.30	£0.90	£1.50
3-11 ND	*$0.50*	*$1.50*	*$2.50*	£0.30	£0.90	£1.50
12 ND pull out poster by Joe Quesada and Jimmy Palmiotti						
	$0.50	*$1.50*	*$2.50*	£0.30	£0.90	£1.50
13 ND Image X Month tie-in						
	$0.50	*$1.50*	*$2.50*	£0.30	£0.90	£1.50
13 2nd printing, ND 2nd version by Erik Larsen (May 1995) - Star, Mighty Man, Overpower, Rapture and the 1st appearance of Widow						
	$0.40	*$1.20*	*$2.00*	£0.25	£0.75	£1.25
14-16 ND Possessed story						
	$0.50	*$1.50*	*$2.50*	£0.30	£0.90	£1.50
17-21 ND	*$0.50*	*$1.50*	*$2.50*	£0.30	£0.90	£1.50
22 ND Teenage Mutant Ninja Turtles appear						
	$0.50	*$1.50*	*$2.50*	£0.30	£0.90	£1.50
23 ND	*$0.50*	*$1.50*	*$2.50*	£0.30	£0.90	£1.50
24 ND Gang War story						
	$0.50	*$1.50*	*$2.50*	£0.30	£0.90	£1.50
25 ND 48pgs, Freak Force and Super Patriot appear; 2 stories						
	$0.80	*$2.40*	*$4.00*	£0.50	£1.50	£2.50
26 ND Freak Force and Star appear; 2 stories						
	$0.50	*$1.50*	*$2.50*	£0.30	£0.90	£1.50
27 ND	*$0.50*	*$1.50*	*$2.50*	£0.30	£0.90	£1.50
28 ND Maxx guest-stars						
	$0.50	*$1.50*	*$2.50*	£0.30	£0.90	£1.50
29 ND Wildstar guest-stars						
	$0.50	*$1.50*	*$2.50*	£0.30	£0.90	£1.50
30 ND continued from Spawn #52						
	$0.50	*$1.50*	*$2.50*	£0.30	£0.90	£1.50
31-32 ND	*$0.50*	*$1.50*	*$2.50*	£0.30	£0.90	£1.50
33 ND Savage Dragon has a baby; pin-up at centrefold by Andy Smith and Tim Townsend						
	$0.50	*$1.50*	*$2.50*	£0.30	£0.90	£1.50
Title Value:	*$17.20*	*$51.60*	*$86.00*	£10.35	£31.05	£51.75
The Savage Dragon: A Force To Be Reckoned With (Jan 1996)						
Trade paperback ND 144pgs, collects issues #1-6 plus 10 new story pages				£2.00	£6.00	£10.00
Signed, Limited Edition (Jan 1996)						
ND Hardcover, signed and numbered by Erik Larsen				£5.40	£16.20	£27.00

SAVAGE DRAGON VS. THE SAVAGE MEGATON MAN

Image,OS; 1 Apr 1993

	$Good	$Fine	$N.Mint	£Good	£Fine	£N.Mint
1 ND Erik Larsen and Don Simpson script/art						
	$0.40	*$1.20*	*$2.00*	£0.25	£0.75	£1.25
1 Gold Edition, ND - foil embossed cover						
	$3.00	*$9.00*	*$15.00*	£1.50	£4.50	£7.50
Title Value:	*$3.40*	*$10.20*	*$17.00*	£1.75	£5.25	£8.75

SAVAGE DRAGON/DESTROYER DUCK

Image,OS; 1 Nov 1996

	$Good	$Fine	$N.Mint	£Good	£Fine	£N.Mint
1 ND Steve Gerber script, Chris Marrinan and Erik Larsen art						
	$0.80	*$2.40*	*$4.00*	£0.50	£1.50	£2.50
Title Value:	*$0.80*	*$2.40*	*$4.00*	£0.50	£1.50	£2.50

SAVAGE DRAGON/TEENAGE MUTANT NINJA TURTLES CROSSOVER

Image,OS; 1 Sep 1993

	$Good	$Fine	$N.Mint	£Good	£Fine	£N.Mint
1 ND Michael Dooney script and art						
	$0.50	*$1.50*	*$2.50*	£0.30	£0.90	£1.50
Title Value:	*$0.50*	*$1.50*	*$2.50*	£0.30	£0.90	£1.50

SAVAGE HENRY

Vortex/Rip Off Press; 1 Jan 1987-31 1993

	$Good	$Fine	$N.Mint	£Good	£Fine	£N.Mint
1 ND Matt Howarth script and art begins; black and white						
	$0.40	*$1.20*	*$2.00*	£0.25	£0.75	£1.25
1 2nd printing, ND (Feb 1994), new painted cover						
	$0.30	*$0.90*	*$1.50*	£0.20	£0.60	£1.00
2-14 ND	*$0.40*	*$1.20*	*$2.00*	£0.25	£0.75	£1.25
14 2nd printing, ND (Apr 1994)						
	$0.30	*$0.90*	*$1.50*	£0.20	£0.60	£1.00
15-31 ND	*$0.40*	*$1.20*	*$2.00*	£0.25	£0.75	£1.25
Title Value:	*$13.00*	*$39.00*	*$65.00*	£8.15	£24.45	£40.75

SAVAGE HENRY (2ND SERIES)

Caliber Press; 1 Jul 1994-3 Oct 1994

	$Good	$Fine	$N.Mint	£Good	£Fine	£N.Mint
1-3 ND Matt Howarth script and art; black and white						
	$0.60	*$1.80*	*$3.00*	£0.40	£1.20	£2.00
Title Value:	*$1.80*	*$5.40*	*$9.00*	£1.20	£3.60	£6.00

SAVAGE HENRY: HEAD STRONG

Caliber Press; 1 Feb 1995-3 1995

	$Good	$Fine	$N.Mint	£Good	£Fine	£N.Mint
1-3 ND Matt Howarth script and art; black and white						
	$0.60	*$1.80*	*$3.00*	£0.40	£1.20	£2.00
Title Value:	*$1.80*	*$5.40*	*$9.00*	£1.20	£3.60	£6.00

SAVAGE HULK

Marvel Comics Group,OS; 1 Jan 1996

	$Good	$Fine	$N.Mint	£Good	£Fine	£N.Mint
1 ND 64pgs, features work by Peter David, Dave Gibbons, Mike Golden, Sam Kieth, Scott Lobdell, Matt Wagner and others; painted cover by Adam Kubert and Simon Bisley						
	$1.40	*$4.20*	*$7.00*	£0.90	£2.70	£4.50
Title Value:	*$1.40*	*$4.20*	*$7.00*	£0.90	£2.70	£4.50

SAVAGE TALES

Marvel Comics Group,Magazine; 1 May 1971; 2 Oct 1973; 3 Feb 1974-11 Jul 1975; 12 Summer 1975

	$Good	$Fine	$N.Mint	£Good	£Fine	£N.Mint
1 ND Conan by Barry Smith, 1st appearance of Man-Thing						
	$20.00	*$60.00*	*$140.00*	£9.25	£28.00	£65.00
2 ND Smith, Morrow, Brunner, Williamson art						
	$8.25	*$25.00*	*$50.00*	£4.15	£12.50	£25.00
3 scarce in the U.K. Williamson, Steranko, Brunner, Smith art						
	$5.75	*$17.50*	*$35.00*	£3.30	£10.00	£20.00
4 becomes Savage Tales Featuring Conan; part Neal Adams art, Barry Smith, Williamson reprints						
	$3.75	*$11.00*	*$22.50*	£2.05	£6.25	£12.50
5 Jim Starlin art	*$3.75*	*$11.00*	*$22.50*	£2.05	£6.25	£12.50
6 becomes Savage Tales Featuring Ka-Zar; Williamson reprint; Neal Adams cover						
	$1.25	*$3.75*	*$7.50*	£0.80	£2.50	£5.00
7 Neal Adams inks, Boris painted cover						
	$1.00	*$3.00*	*$6.00*	£0.65	£2.00	£4.00
8 scarce in the U.K. Shanna She-Devil back-up						
	$1.00	*$3.00*	*$6.00*	£0.65	£2.00	£4.00
9 Shanna She-Devil back-up						
	$0.75	*$2.25*	*$4.50*	£0.50	£1.50	£3.00
10 Russ Heath art, Neal Adams inks; Boris painted cover and Shanna She-Devil back-up						
	$0.75	*$2.25*	*$4.50*	£0.50	£1.50	£3.00
11 Heath art on back-up story ("Intruder!")						
	$0.75	*$2.25*	*$4.50*	£0.50	£1.50	£3.00
12 ND 88pgs, squarebound, all reprint, titled Savage Tales Annual #1 on cover, Gil Kane/BarrySmith/Gray Morrow art						
	$1.00	*$3.00*	*$6.00*	£0.65	£2.00	£4.00
Title Value:	*$48.00*	*$144.00*	*$309.00*	£25.05	£76.00	£161.00

FEATURES

Brak the Barbarian in 5-8. Conan in 1-5. Ka-Zar in 6-12. Shanna in 9,10.

REPRINT FEATURES

Jann of the Jungle in 6-8. Ka-Zar in 1, 5. Kull by Wrightson in 2. Femizons in 1-3.

SAVAGE TALES (2ND SERIES)

Marvel Comics Group,Magazine; 1 Nov 1985-9 Mar 1987

	$Good	$Fine	$N.Mint	£Good	£Fine	£N.Mint
1 ND Larry Hama script, Michael Golden art begins on 'Nam try-out						
	$0.50	*$1.50*	*$2.50*	£0.30	£0.90	£1.50
2-9 ND	*$0.30*	*$0.90*	*$1.50*	£0.20	£0.60	£1.00
Title Value:	*$2.90*	*$8.70*	*$14.50*	£1.90	£5.70	£9.50

SAVIOUR

(see British section)

SCARAB

DC Comics/Vertigo,MS; 1 Nov 1993-8 Jun 1994

	$Good	$Fine	$N.Mint	£Good	£Fine	£N.Mint
1 ND Scot Eaton pencils begin, painted covers by Glenn Fabry begin						
	$0.40	*$1.20*	*$2.00*	£0.25	£0.75	£1.25
2-8 ND	*$0.40*	*$1.20*	*$2.00*	£0.25	£0.75	£1.25
Title Value:	*$3.20*	*$9.60*	*$16.00*	£2.00	£6.00	£10.00

SCARAMOUCH

Innovation; 1 Dec 1990-2 Jan 1991

	$Good	$Fine	$N.Mint	£Good	£Fine	£N.Mint
1-2 ND black and white						
	$0.40	*$1.20*	*$2.00*	£0.25	£0.75	£1.25
Title Value:	*$0.80*	*$2.40*	*$4.00*	£0.50	£1.50	£2.50

SCARE TATICS
DC Comics; 1 Dec 1996-present

	$Good	$Fine	$N.Mint	£Good	£Fine	£N.Mint
1 ND Len Kaminski script, Anthony Williams and Andy Lanning art begins	$0.45	$1.35	$2.25	£0.30	£0.90	£1.50
2-4 ND	$0.45	$1.35	$2.25	£0.30	£0.90	£1.50
Title Value:	$1.80	$5.40	$9.00	£1.20	£3.60	£6.00

SCARLET IN GASLIGHT
Eternity; 1 Nov 1987-4 Jun 1988

	$Good	$Fine	$N.Mint	£Good	£Fine	£N.Mint
1-4 ND Sherlock Holmes vs. Dracula; black and white	$0.40	$1.20	$2.00	£0.25	£0.75	£1.25
Title Value:	$1.60	$4.80	$8.00	£1.00	£3.00	£5.00
Graphic Novel Collection (1988)				£0.90	£2.70	£4.50

SCARLET SCORPION/DARKSHADE
AC Comics; 1 Apr 1995-2 1995

	$Good	$Fine	$N.Mint	£Good	£Fine	£N.Mint
1 ND black and white; flip-book format begins	$0.80	$2.40	$4.00	£0.50	£1.50	£2.50
1 pre-bagged, ND with trading card by Jerry Ordway	$1.00	$3.00	$5.00	£0.70	£2.10	£3.50
2 ND black and white	$0.80	$2.40	$4.00	£0.50	£1.50	£2.50
Title Value:	$2.60	$7.80	$13.00	£1.70	£5.10	£8.50

SCARLET SPIDER
Marvel Comics Group; 1 Nov 1995-2 Dec 1995

	$Good	$Fine	$N.Mint	£Good	£Fine	£N.Mint
1 ND Howard Mackie script, Gil Kane and Tom Palmer art, continued in Spectacular Scarlet Spider #1; metallic ink cover	$0.40	$1.20	$2.00	£0.25	£0.75	£1.25
2 ND continued in Spectacular Scarlet Spider #2	$0.40	$1.20	$2.00	£0.25	£0.75	£1.25
Title Value:	$0.80	$2.40	$4.00	£0.50	£1.50	£2.50

SCARLET SPIDER UNLIMITED
Marvel Comics Group; 1 Nov 1995

	$Good	$Fine	$N.Mint	£Good	£Fine	£N.Mint
1 ND 64pgs, Glenn Herdling script, Tod Smith and John Nyberg art; metallic ink cover	$0.80	$2.40	$4.00	£0.50	£1.50	£2.50
Title Value:	$0.80	$2.40	$4.00	£0.50	£1.50	£2.50

SCARLET WITCH
Marvel Comics Group,MS; 1 Jan 1994-4 Apr 1994

	$Good	$Fine	$N.Mint	£Good	£Fine	£N.Mint
1 John Higgins art begins	$0.40	$1.20	$2.00	£0.25	£0.75	£1.25
2-3 West Coast Avengers appear	$0.40	$1.20	$2.00	£0.25	£0.75	£1.25
4 Spiderwoman and Iron Man appear	$0.40	$1.20	$2.00	£0.25	£0.75	£1.25
Title Value:	$1.60	$4.80	$8.00	£1.00	£3.00	£5.00

SCARLETT
DC Comics; 1 Jan 1993-14 Feb 1994

	$Good	$Fine	$N.Mint	£Good	£Fine	£N.Mint
1 spin-off from Batman: Legends of the Dark Knight	$0.25	$0.75	$1.25	£0.15	£0.45	£0.75
2-4	$0.25	$0.75	$1.25	£0.15	£0.45	£0.75
5 Gray Morrow art	$0.25	$0.75	$1.25	£0.15	£0.45	£0.75
6-14	$0.25	$0.75	$1.25	£0.15	£0.45	£0.75
Title Value:	$3.50	$10.50	$17.50	£2.10	£6.30	£10.50

SCARY BOOK, THE
Caliber Press; 1 Jul 1992-4 1992

	$Good	$Fine	$N.Mint	£Good	£Fine	£N.Mint
1-4 ND	$0.40	$1.20	$2.00	£0.25	£0.75	£1.25
Title Value:	$1.60	$4.80	$8.00	£1.00	£3.00	£5.00

SCARY TALES
Charlton; 1 Aug 1975-9 Jan 1977; 10 Oct 1977-20 Jun 1979; 21 Aug 1980-46 Oct 1984

	$Good	$Fine	$N.Mint	£Good	£Fine	£N.Mint
1 distributed in the U.K. Joe Staton painted cover	$0.65	$2.00	$4.00	£0.40	£1.25	£2.50
2-3 distributed in the U.K.	$0.40	$1.25	$2.50	£0.25	£0.75	£1.50
4-20 distributed in the U.K.	$0.30	$1.00	$2.00	£0.20	£0.60	£1.25
21-46 distributed in the U.K.	$0.30	$0.90	$1.50	£0.20	£0.60	£1.00
Title Value:	$14.35	$44.90	$82.00	£9.50	£28.55	£52.75

Note: many later issues all reprint

SCAVENGERS
Triumphant Comics; 0 Mar 1994; 1 Sep 1993-16 Dec 1994

	$Good	$Fine	$N.Mint	£Good	£Fine	£N.Mint
0 (Mar 1994) serial numbered at top of cover	$0.40	$1.20	$2.00	£0.25	£0.75	£1.25
1 20,000 copies, serial numbered at top of cover begins	$0.40	$1.20	$2.00	£0.25	£0.75	£1.25
2 20,000 copies	$0.40	$1.20	$2.00	£0.25	£0.75	£1.25
2 Limited Edition, signed by creators with mini-poster photo-print; pre-bagged with backing board	$1.00	$3.00	$5.00	£0.50	£1.50	£2.50
3-4	$0.40	$1.20	$2.00	£0.25	£0.75	£1.25
5 Unleashed X-over	$0.40	$1.20	$2.00	£0.25	£0.75	£1.25
6-16	$0.40	$1.20	$2.00	£0.25	£0.75	£1.25
Title Value:	$7.80	$23.40	$39.00	£4.75	£14.25	£23.75

Note: all Non-Distributed on the news-stands in the U.K.

SCHISM
Defiant Comics; 1,2 Jul 1994; 3,4 Aug 1994

	$Good	$Fine	$N.Mint	£Good	£Fine	£N.Mint
1-4 ND 48pgs, Jim Shooter script, David Lapham art	$0.40	$1.20	$2.00	£0.25	£0.75	£1.25
Title Value:	$1.60	$4.80	$8.00	£1.00	£3.00	£5.00

SCIMIDAR
Eternity,MS; 1 Dec 1988-4 Mar 1989

	$Good	$Fine	$N.Mint	£Good	£Fine	£N.Mint
1 ND (2 cover versions exist)	$0.50	$1.50	$2.50	£0.30	£0.90	£1.50
2-3 ND	$0.50	$1.50	$2.50	£0.30	£0.90	£1.50
4 "hot" cover ND	$0.50	$1.50	$2.50	£0.30	£0.90	£1.50
4 "mild" cover ND	$0.50	$1.50	$2.50	£0.30	£0.90	£1.50
Title Value:	$2.50	$7.50	$12.50	£1.50	£4.50	£7.50
Book I: Pleasure and Pain				£1.20	£3.60	£6.00
2nd print (1990), new cover				£1.10	£3.30	£5.50

Note: pre-bagged owing to sexual content. Unsealed copies would bring 25% less.

SCIMIDAR
CFD Productions; 1 Oct 1995-4 1996 ?

	$Good	$Fine	$N.Mint	£Good	£Fine	£N.Mint
1 ND 24pgs, Tom Derenick art begins; black and white	$0.50	$1.50	$2.50	£0.30	£0.90	£1.50
2-4 ND	$0.50	$1.50	$2.50	£0.30	£0.90	£1.50
Title Value:	$2.00	$6.00	$10.00	£1.20	£3.60	£6.00

SCIMIDAR II
Eternity,MS; 1 May 1989-4 Aug 1989

	$Good	$Fine	$N.Mint	£Good	£Fine	£N.Mint
1 ND	$0.40	$1.20	$2.00	£0.25	£0.75	£1.25
1 2nd printing ND	$0.30	$0.90	$1.50	£0.20	£0.60	£1.00
2-4 ND	$0.40	$1.20	$2.00	£0.25	£0.75	£1.25
Title Value:	$1.90	$5.70	$9.50	£1.20	£3.60	£6.00
Trade paperback: Feast and Famine, reprints #1-4				£1.15	£3.45	£5.75
(2nd print - 1991)				£1.10	£3.30	£5.50

Note: sealed in plastic bags. Unsealed copies would bring 25% less.

SCIMIDAR III
Eternity,MS; 1 Jan 1990-4 Apr 1990

	$Good	$Fine	$N.Mint	£Good	£Fine	£N.Mint
1 ND	$0.40	$1.20	$2.00	£0.25	£0.75	£1.25
1 2nd printing ND	$0.30	$0.90	$1.50	£0.20	£0.60	£1.00
2-4 ND	$0.40	$1.20	$2.00	£0.25	£0.75	£1.25
Title Value:	$1.90	$5.70	$9.50	£1.20	£3.60	£6.00

Note: pre-bagged owing to sexual content

	$Good	$Fine	$N.Mint	£Good	£Fine	£N.Mint
Trade Paperback# (Jun 1991), reprints #1-4				£1.00	£3.00	£5.00

SCIMIDAR IV: WILD THING
Eternity,MS; 1 Aug 1990-4 Nov 1990

	$Good	$Fine	$N.Mint	£Good	£Fine	£N.Mint
1 ND nude cover; has black and white wraparound outer cover advising content	$0.40	$1.20	$2.00	£0.25	£0.75	£1.25
1 clothed cover ND	$0.40	$1.20	$2.00	£0.25	£0.75	£1.25
2-4 ND	$0.40	$1.20	$2.00	£0.25	£0.75	£1.25
Title Value:	$2.00	$6.00	$10.00	£1.25	£3.75	£6.25

Note: pre-bagged owing to sexual content

SCIMIDAR PIN-UP BOOK
Eternity,OS; 1 Oct 1990

	$Good	$Fine	$N.Mint	£Good	£Fine	£N.Mint
1 ND seven loose pin-ups (no staples)	$0.50	$1.50	$2.50	£0.30	£0.90	£1.50
Title Value:	$0.50	$1.50	$2.50	£0.30	£0.90	£1.50

SCIMIDAR V: LIVING COLOUR
Eternity,MS; 1 Apr 1991-4 Jul 1991

	$Good	$Fine	$N.Mint	£Good	£Fine	£N.Mint
1 ND regular cover	$0.40	$1.20	$2.00	£0.25	£0.75	£1.25
1 nude cover, ND - has black and white wraparound outer cover advising content	$0.40	$1.20	$2.00	£0.25	£0.75	£1.25
2-4 ND	$0.40	$1.20	$2.00	£0.25	£0.75	£1.25
Title Value:	$2.00	$6.00	$10.00	£1.25	£3.75	£6.25

Note: all Non-Distributed on the news-stands in the U.K.

SCIMIDAR VI: SLASHDANCE
Aircel,MS; 1 Oct 1992-4 Jan 1993

	$Good	$Fine	$N.Mint	£Good	£Fine	£N.Mint
1 ND	$0.40	$1.20	$2.00	£0.25	£0.75	£1.25
1 Deluxe Edition, ND - extra story, sketches and pin-ups	$0.50	$1.50	$2.50	£0.30	£0.90	£1.50
2-4 ND	$0.40	$1.20	$2.00	£0.25	£0.75	£1.25
Title Value:	$2.10	$6.30	$10.50	£1.30	£3.90	£6.50

SCOOBY-DOO
Gold Key; 1 Mar 1970-30 Feb 1975

	$Good	$Fine	$N.Mint	£Good	£Fine	£N.Mint
1 scarce in the U.K.	$7.50	$22.50	$45.00	£3.75	£11.00	£22.50
2-5	$4.15	$12.50	$25.00	£2.05	£6.25	£12.50
6-10	$3.30	$10.00	$20.00	£1.65	£5.00	£10.00
11-15	$2.50	$7.50	$15.00	£1.25	£3.75	£7.50
16-20	$2.05	$6.25	$12.50	£0.80	£2.50	£5.00
21-30	$1.65	$5.00	$10.00	£0.65	£2.00	£4.00
Title Value:	$79.85	$241.25	$482.50	£36.95	£112.25	£225.00

SCOOBY-DOO (2ND SERIES)
Charlton; 1 Apr 1975-11 Dec 1976

	$Good	$Fine	$N.Mint	£Good	£Fine	£N.Mint
1 scarce in the U.K.	$2.90	$8.75	$17.50	£1.50	£4.50	£9.00
2-5	$1.65	$5.00	$10.00	£0.65	£2.00	£4.00
6-11	$1.25	$3.75	$7.50	£0.40	£1.25	£2.50
Title Value:	$17.00	$51.25	$102.50	£6.50	£20.00	£40.00

SCOOBY-DOO, HANNA-BARBERA'S
Marvel Comics Group,TV; 1 Oct 1977-9 Feb 1979

	$Good	$Fine	$N.Mint	£Good	£Fine	£N.Mint
1 ND	$0.65	$2.00	$4.00	£0.30	£1.00	£2.00
2-9 ND	$0.30	$1.00	$2.00	£0.15	£0.50	£1.00
Title Value:	$3.05	$10.00	$20.00	£1.50	£5.00	£10.00

SCORCHED EARTH
Tundra Publishing,MS; 1 May 1991-4 1991

	$Good	$Fine	$N.Mint	£Good	£Fine	£N.Mint
1-4 ND ecology/S.F. theme	$0.50	$1.50	$2.50	£0.30	£0.90	£1.50
Title Value:	$2.00	$6.00	$10.00	£1.20	£3.60	£6.00

SCORE, THE
DC Comics/Piranha Press,MS; 1-4 1990

	$Good	$Fine	$N.Mint	£Good	£Fine	£N.Mint
1-4 ND 48pgs, squarebound, Gerard Jones/Mark Badger	$0.80	$2.40	$4.00	£0.50	£1.50	£2.50
Title Value:	$3.20	$9.60	$16.00	£2.00	£6.00	£10.00

SCORPIO ROSE
Eclipse; 1 Jan 1983-2 Oct 1983

	$Good	$Fine	$N.Mint	£Good	£Fine	£N.Mint
1-2 ND Steve Englehart scripts, Marshall Rogers art; Dr. Orient backup by Rogers & Adam Kubert	$0.40	$1.20	$2.00	£0.25	£0.75	£1.25
Title Value:	$0.80	$2.40	$4.00	£0.50	£1.50	£2.50

SCORPION

Atlas; 1 Feb 1975-3 Jul 1975

	$Good	$Fine	$N.Mint	£Good	£Fine	£N.Mint
1 distributed in the U.K. Chaykin story/art (Dominic Fortune prototype)						
	$0.50	*$1.50*	*$2.50*	£0.30	£0.90	£1.50
2 distributed in the U.K. Chaykin story/art,Kaluta/Wrightson part inks						
	$0.50	*$1.50*	*$2.50*	£0.30	£0.90	£1.50
3 distributed in the U.K. new costume, no Chaykin						
	$0.50	*$1.50*	*$2.50*	£0.30	£0.90	£1.50
Title Value:	*$1.50*	*$4.50*	*$7.50*	£0.90	£2.70	£4.50

SCORPION CORPS

Dagger Comics; 1 Dec 1993-11 1994

	$Good	$Fine	$N.Mint	£Good	£Fine	£N.Mint
1-11 ND	*$0.40*	*$1.20*	*$2.00*	£0.25	£0.75	£1.25
Title Value:	*$4.40*	*$13.20*	*$22.00*	£2.75	£8.25	£13.75

SCOUT

Eclipse; 1 Sep 1985-24 Oct 1987

(see New America, Scout: War Shaman, Swords of Texas)

	$Good	$Fine	$N.Mint	£Good	£Fine	£N.Mint
1 ND scarce in the U.K. Tim Truman art begins						
	$0.50	*$1.50*	*$2.50*	£0.30	£0.90	£1.50
2 ND scarce in the U.K.						
	$0.40	*$1.20*	*$2.00*	£0.30	£0.90	£1.50
3-8 ND	*$0.40*	*$1.20*	*$2.00*	£0.25	£0.75	£1.25
9 ND ($1.25) Airboy preview						
	$0.40	*$1.20*	*$2.00*	£0.25	£0.75	£1.25
10-15 ND	*$0.40*	*$1.20*	*$2.00*	£0.25	£0.75	£1.25
16 ND 3-D issue (Eclipse 3-D Special #16), with bound-in 3-D glasses (25% less without glasses)						
	$0.50	*$1.50*	*$2.50*	£0.30	£0.90	£1.50
17 ND Beanworld X-over, Larry Marder part art						
	$0.40	*$1.20*	*$2.00*	£0.25	£0.75	£1.25
18 ND	*$0.40*	*$1.20*	*$2.00*	£0.25	£0.75	£1.25
19 ND with flexi-disc						
	$0.40	*$1.20*	*$2.00*	£0.25	£0.75	£1.25
20-24 ND	*$0.40*	*$1.20*	*$2.00*	£0.25	£0.75	£1.25
Title Value:	*$9.80*	*$29.40*	*$49.00*	£6.15	£18.45	£30.75
Trade Paperback, reprints #1-7				£2.00	£6.00	£10.00

SCOUT HANDBOOK

Eclipse; 1 Aug 1987

	$Good	$Fine	$N.Mint	£Good	£Fine	£N.Mint
1 ND maps, weapons, personal data etc; Tim Truman cover						
	$0.40	*$1.20*	*$2.00*	£0.25	£0.75	£1.25
Title Value:	*$0.40*	*$1.20*	*$2.00*	£0.25	£0.75	£1.25

SCOUT WAR SHAMAN

Eclipse; 1 Mar 1988-16 Oct 1989

	$Good	$Fine	$N.Mint	£Good	£Fine	£N.Mint
1-16 ND	*$0.40*	*$1.20*	*$2.00*	£0.25	£0.75	£1.25
Title Value:	*$6.40*	*$19.20*	*$32.00*	£4.00	£12.00	£20.00

SCREEN PLAY

Slave Labor; 1 Jun 1989-3 1989

	$Good	$Fine	$N.Mint	£Good	£Fine	£N.Mint
1-3 ND	*$0.30*	*$0.90*	*$1.50*	£0.20	£0.60	£1.00
Title Value:	*$0.90*	*$2.70*	*$4.50*	£0.60	£1.80	£3.00

SCREWTAPE LETTERS, THE

Marvel Comics Group,OS; 1 Oct 1993

	$Good	$Fine	$N.Mint	£Good	£Fine	£N.Mint
1 ND 96pgs, adaptation of C.S. Lewis work by Charles E. Hall and Pat Redding						
	$1.50	*$4.50*	*$7.50*	£1.00	£3.00	£5.00
Title Value:	*$1.50*	*$4.50*	*$7.50*	£1.00	£3.00	£5.00

SCYTHE

Caliber Press,OS; 1 Feb 1996

	$Good	$Fine	$N.Mint	£Good	£Fine	£N.Mint
1 ND Gregg Kendrick script, Ed Herrera art; black and white						
	$0.60	*$1.80*	*$3.00*	£0.40	£1.20	£2.00
Title Value:	*$0.60*	*$1.80*	*$3.00*	£0.40	£1.20	£2.00

SEA DEVILS

National Periodical Publications; 1 Sep/Oct 1961-35 May/Jun 1967

(see Showcase #27-29)

	$Good	$Fine	$N.Mint	£Good	£Fine	£N.Mint
1 Russ Heath art; painted cover						
	$60.00	*$180.00*	*$485.00*	£38.00	£110.00	£300.00
2 Russ Heath art; painted cover						
	$34.00	*$100.00*	*$235.00*	£18.50	£55.00	£130.00
3 Russ Heath art; painted cover						
	$21.00	*$62.50*	*$150.00*	£12.50	£39.00	£90.00
4-5 Russ Heath art; painted cover						
	$19.00	*$57.50*	*$135.00*	£12.00	£36.00	£85.00
6-10 Russ Heath art						
	$11.00	*$34.00*	*$80.00*	£6.25	£19.00	£45.00
11-12	*$8.50*	*$26.00*	*$60.00*	£5.00	£15.00	£35.00
13 Joe Kubert and Gene Colan art						
	$8.50	*$26.00*	*$60.00*	£5.00	£15.00	£35.00
14-20	*$8.50*	*$26.00*	*$60.00*	£5.00	£15.00	£35.00
21-30	*$6.25*	*$19.00*	*$45.00*	£3.90	£11.50	£27.50
31-35	*$5.25*	*$16.00*	*$37.50*	£3.55	£10.50	£25.00
Title Value:	*$381.75*	*$1157.50*	*$2752.50*	£231.00	£688.50	£1665.00

SEADRAGON

Elite Comics; 1 May 1986-8 Dec 1986

	$Good	$Fine	$N.Mint	£Good	£Fine	£N.Mint
1 ND Butch Burcham inks begin						
	$0.30	*$0.90*	*$1.50*	£0.20	£0.60	£1.00
1 2nd printing ND	*$0.30*	*$0.90*	*$1.50*	£0.20	£0.60	£1.00
2-8 ND	*$0.30*	*$0.90*	*$1.50*	£0.20	£0.60	£1.00
Title Value:	*$2.70*	*$8.10*	*$13.50*	£1.80	£5.40	£9.00

SEAQUEST DSV

Nemesis; 1 Mar 1994-4 1994

	$Good	$Fine	$N.Mint	£Good	£Fine	£N.Mint
1-4 ND Keith Pollard and Alfredo Alcala art; based on TV series with Roy Scheider						
	$0.40	*$1.20*	*$2.00*	£0.25	£0.75	£1.25
Title Value:	*$1.60*	*$4.80*	*$8.00*	£1.00	£3.00	£5.00

SEBASTIAN O

DC Comics/Vertigo,MS; 1 May 1993-3 Jul 1993

	$Good	$Fine	$N.Mint	£Good	£Fine	£N.Mint
1-3 ND Grant Morrison script, Steve Yeowell art						
	$0.40	*$1.20*	*$2.00*	£0.25	£0.75	£1.25
Title Value:	*$1.20*	*$3.60*	*$6.00*	£0.75	£2.25	£3.75

SECRET AGENT

Charlton;9 Oct 1966-10 Oct 1967

(previously Sarge Steel)

	$Good	$Fine	$N.Mint	£Good	£Fine	£N.Mint
9 distributed in the U.K.						
	$1.70	*$5.00*	*$12.00*	£0.85	£2.55	£6.00
10 distributed in the U.K.						
	$0.85	*$2.55*	*$6.00*	£0.50	£1.50	£3.50
Title Value:	*$2.55*	*$7.55*	*$18.00*	£1.35	£4.05	£9.50

Note: from the Danger Man TV series.

SECRET AGENT (2ND SERIES)

Gold Key; 1 Nov 1966-2 Jan 1968

	$Good	$Fine	$N.Mint	£Good	£Fine	£N.Mint
1 rare, distributed in the U.K.						
	$17.00	*$50.00*	*$120.00*	£10.00	£30.00	£70.00
2 rare, distributed in the U.K.						
	$10.00	*$30.00*	*$70.00*	£5.00	£15.00	£35.00
Title Value:	*$27.00*	*$80.00*	*$190.00*	£15.00	£45.00	£105.00

SECRET CITY SAGA, JACK KIRBY'S

Topps,MS; 0 Apr 1993; 1 May 1993-4 Aug 1993

	$Good	$Fine	$N.Mint	£Good	£Fine	£N.Mint
0 Walt Simonson cover - originally available free from Topps with the 8 coupons from this series and the four other Jack Kirby titles						
	$0.40	*$1.20*	*$2.00*	£0.25	£0.75	£1.25
0 Gold Edition	*$1.50*	*$4.50*	*$7.50*	£0.80	£2.40	£4.00
1 pre-bagged with coupon #5 for Secret City Saga #0 plus 3 trading cards, Steve Ditko art and cover						
	$0.40	*$1.20*	*$2.00*	£0.25	£0.75	£1.25
1 without coupon/cards						
	$0.30	*$0.90*	*$1.50*	£0.20	£0.60	£1.00
2 pre-bagged with 3 trading cards inked by John Byrne, Sienkiewicz and Gibbons; cover by Steve Ditko and John Byrne						

Sandman (2nd) #30

Scooby Doo #1

Secret Agent #9

Issue	$Good	$Fine	$N.Mint	£Good	£Fine	£N.Mint
	$0.40	$1.20	$2.00	£0.25	£0.75	£1.25
2 without coupon/cards	$0.30	$0.90	$1.50	£0.20	£0.60	£1.00
3 pre-bagged with 3 trading cards inked by John Byrne, Sienkiewicz and Gibbons; cover by Steve Ditko and John Byrne	$0.40	$1.20	$2.00	£0.25	£0.75	£1.25
3 without coupon/cards	$0.30	$0.90	$1.50	£0.20	£0.60	£1.00
4 pre-bagged with 3 trading cards inked by Hughes, Steve Ditko/Art Adams and Jim Valentino; cover by Steve Ditko and George Perez	$0.40	$1.20	$2.00	£0.25	£0.75	£1.25
4 without coupon/cards	$0.30	$0.90	$1.50	£0.20	£0.60	£1.00
Title Value:	$4.70	$14.10	$23.50	£2.85	£8.55	£14.25

Note: all Non-Distributed on the news-stands in the U.K.

SECRET DEFENDERS

Marvel Comics Group; 1 Mar 1993-25 Mar 1995

Issue	$Good	$Fine	$N.Mint	£Good	£Fine	£N.Mint
1 Dr. Strange assembles rotating teams: Nomad, Darkhawk, Wolverine, Spiderwoman begin; red foil cover, Roy Thomas script begins	$0.40	$1.20	$2.00	£0.25	£0.75	£1.25
2-3	$0.30	$0.90	$1.50	£0.20	£0.60	£1.00
4 new team of Ghost Rider, Namorita and Sleepwalker	$0.30	$0.90	$1.50	£0.20	£0.60	£1.00
5	$0.30	$0.90	$1.50	£0.20	£0.60	£1.00
6 new team of Scarlet Witch, Spiderman and Captain America	$0.30	$0.90	$1.50	£0.20	£0.60	£1.00
7-8	$0.30	$0.90	$1.50	£0.20	£0.60	£1.00
9 new team of War Machine, Thunderstrike and Silver Surfer	$0.30	$0.90	$1.50	£0.20	£0.60	£1.00
10	$0.30	$0.90	$1.50	£0.20	£0.60	£1.00
11 Starblast part 3	$0.30	$0.90	$1.50	£0.20	£0.60	£1.00
12 Thanos appears, prismatic foil cover	$0.30	$0.90	$1.50	£0.20	£0.60	£1.00
13-14 Thanos appears	$0.30	$0.90	$1.50	£0.20	£0.60	£1.00
15 Thanos and Silver Surfer appear; with free Spiderman vs. Venom card sheet	$0.30	$0.90	$1.50	£0.20	£0.60	£1.00
16-17	$0.30	$0.90	$1.50	£0.20	£0.60	£1.00
18-19 Archangel and Iceman appear	$0.30	$0.90	$1.50	£0.20	£0.60	£1.00
20 Venom appears	$0.30	$0.90	$1.50	£0.20	£0.60	£1.00
21-23	$0.30	$0.90	$1.50	£0.20	£0.60	£1.00
24 the original Defenders vs. The Secret Defenders	$0.30	$0.90	$1.50	£0.20	£0.60	£1.00
25 48pgs, Secret Defenders Sepulchre, Cadaver, Deathlok, Dagger and Drax team with Hulk, Namor and Silver Surfer against Dr. Druid	$0.40	$1.20	$2.00	£0.25	£0.75	£1.25
Title Value:	$7.70	$23.10	$38.50	£5.10	£15.30	£25.50

SECRET HEARTS

National Periodical Publications/DC Comics;40 Jun/Jul 1957-153 Jul 1971

(previous issues ND)

Issue	$Good	$Fine	$N.Mint	£Good	£Fine	£N.Mint
40-50 scarce in the U.K.	$5.00	$15.00	$35.00	£2.85	£8.50	£20.00
51-58 scarce in the U.K.	$4.25	$12.50	$30.00	£2.50	£7.50	£17.50
1st official distribution in the U.K.						
59-60 scarce in the U.K.	$4.25	$12.50	$30.00	£2.50	£7.50	£17.50
61-70 scarce in the U.K.	$3.55	$10.50	$25.00	£2.10	£6.25	£15.00
71-74	$2.85	$8.50	$20.00	£1.75	£5.25	£12.50
75 last 10 cents issue	$2.85	$8.50	$20.00	£1.75	£5.25	£12.50
76-80	$2.85	$8.50	$20.00	£1.75	£5.25	£12.50
81-100	$2.50	$7.50	$17.50	£1.40	£4.25	£10.00
101-110	$2.10	$6.25	$15.00	£1.05	£3.20	£7.50
111-119	$1.75	$5.25	$12.50	£0.85	£2.55	£6.00
120 Neal Adams cover	$1.75	$5.25	$12.50	£0.85	£2.55	£6.00
121-133	$1.40	$4.25	$10.00	£0.70	£2.10	£5.00
134 Neal Adams cover	$1.40	$4.25	$10.00	£0.70	£2.10	£5.00
135-140	$1.40	$4.25	$10.00	£0.70	£2.10	£5.00
141-142 Toth art	$1.25	$3.85	$9.00	£0.60	£1.90	£4.50
143	$1.25	$3.85	$9.00	£0.60	£1.90	£4.50
144 Morrow art	$1.25	$3.85	$9.00	£0.60	£1.90	£4.50
145-148	$1.25	$3.85	$9.00	£0.60	£1.90	£4.50
149 Toth art	$1.25	$3.85	$9.00	£0.70	£2.10	£5.00
150-153	$1.25	$3.85	$9.00	£0.60	£1.90	£4.50
Title Value:	$294.25	$880.05	$2077.00	£163.75	£492.90	£1164.00

Note: issues pre #40 not included as yet as the author doesn't have them as yet!

SECRET OF THE DWARFS

Comico,OS; 1 Dec 1992

Issue	$Good	$Fine	$N.Mint	£Good	£Fine	£N.Mint
1 ND 48pgs	$0.80	$2.40	$4.00	£0.50	£1.50	£2.50
Title Value:	$0.80	$2.40	$4.00	£0.50	£1.50	£2.50

SECRET OF THE SALAMANDER, THE

Dark Horse,OS; 1 Mar 1992

Issue	$Good	$Fine	$N.Mint	£Good	£Fine	£N.Mint
1 ND 48pgs, Jacques Tardi script, art and cover	$0.50	$1.50	$2.50	£0.30	£0.90	£1.50
Title Value:	$0.50	$1.50	$2.50	£0.30	£0.90	£1.50

SECRET ORIGINS (1ST SERIES)

National Periodical Publications; 1 1961

(see Eighty Page Giant Magazine)

Issue	$Good	$Fine	$N.Mint	£Good	£Fine	£N.Mint
1 scarce in the U.K. 80pgs, reprints Green Lantern #1, Detective #225 (Jonn Jonzz), Showcase #4, Showcase #6 (part), Showcase #17, Wonder Woman #105, World's Finest #94	$45.00	$135.00	$495.00	£27.00	£80.00	£300.00
Title Value:	$45.00	$135.00	$495.00	£27.00	£80.00	£300.00

REPRINT FEATURES

Origins of the Superman/Batman team, Adam Strange, Green Lantern, Challengers of the Unknown, Wonder Woman, The Flash, Manhunter from Mars

SECRET ORIGINS (2ND SERIES)

DC Comics; 1 Feb/Mar 1973-6 Jan/Feb 1974; 7 Oct/Nov 1974

Issue	$Good	$Fine	$N.Mint	£Good	£Fine	£N.Mint
1 origin of Superman (from Action No #1), Batman (from Detective Comics #33), The Ghost, Silver Age Flash from Showcase #4	$2.30	$7.00	$14.00	£1.15	£3.50	£7.00
2 origin Silver Age Atom from Showcase #34, Green Lantern from Showcase #22, Supergirl from Action #252	$1.15	$3.50	$7.00	£0.65	£2.00	£4.00
3 origin Wonder Woman from Wonder Woman #1, Wildcat from Sensation Comics #1	$1.15	$3.50	$7.00	£0.65	£2.00	£4.00
4 origin Vigilante from Action Comics #42, Kid Eternity from Hit Comics #25	$1.15	$3.50	$7.00	£0.65	£2.00	£4.00
5 origin The Spectre from More Fun #52-53	$1.15	$3.50	$7.00	£0.65	£2.00	£4.00
6 origin Blackhawk from Military Comics #1, Legion of Super-Heroes from Adventure Comics #247	$1.15	$3.50	$7.00	£0.65	£2.00	£4.00
7 origin Robin from Detective Comics #38, Aquaman from More Fun Comics #73	$1.15	$3.50	$7.00	£0.65	£2.00	£4.00
Title Value:	$9.20	$28.00	$56.00	£5.05	£15.50	£31.00

SECRET ORIGINS (3RD SERIES)

DC Comics; 1 Apr 1986-50 Aug 1990

Issue	$Good	$Fine	$N.Mint	£Good	£Fine	£N.Mint
1 LD in the U.K. Superman; Jerry Ordway art	$0.80	$2.40	$4.00	£0.30	£0.90	£1.50
2 Blue Beetle; Gil Kane art	$0.50	$1.50	$2.50	£0.25	£0.75	£1.25
3 Captain Marvel	$0.50	$1.50	$2.50	£0.25	£0.75	£1.25
4 Firestorm	$0.50	$1.50	$2.50	£0.25	£0.75	£1.25
5 Crimson Avenger	$0.50	$1.50	$2.50	£0.25	£0.75	£1.25
6 Batman; Marshall Rogers and Alan Davis art	$0.50	$1.50	$2.50	£0.25	£0.75	£1.25
7 Green Lantern, Golden Age Sandman; Brian Bolland cover	$0.50	$1.50	$2.50	£0.25	£0.75	£1.25
8 Dollman	$0.50	$1.50	$2.50	£0.25	£0.75	£1.25
9 Flash, Skyman	$0.50	$1.50	$2.50	£0.25	£0.75	£1.25
10 Phantom Stranger; Legends X-over; part Alan Moore script, part Garcia Lopez art	$0.50	$1.50	$2.50	£0.25	£0.75	£1.25
11 Hawkman, Power Girl	$0.40	$1.20	$2.00	£0.20	£0.60	£1.00
12 Challengers of the Unknown, Golden Age Fury	$0.40	$1.20	$2.00	£0.20	£0.60	£1.00
13 Nightwing, Johnny Thunder	$0.40	$1.20	$2.00	£0.20	£0.60	£1.00
14 Suicide Squad	$0.40	$1.20	$2.00	£0.20	£0.60	£1.00
15 Spectre, Deadman; Kevin Maguire art	$0.40	$1.20	$2.00	£0.20	£0.60	£1.00
16 Golden Age Hourman, Warlord, 'Mazing Man	$0.40	$1.20	$2.00	£0.20	£0.60	£1.00
17 Adam Strange, Dr. Occult; Kevin Nowlan cover	$0.40	$1.20	$2.00	£0.20	£0.60	£1.00
18 The Creeper by Giffen, Golden Age Green Lantern	$0.40	$1.20	$2.00	£0.20	£0.60	£1.00
19 Uncle Sam, The Guardian	$0.40	$1.20	$2.00	£0.20	£0.60	£1.00
20 Batgirl, Golden Age Dr.Mid-Nite	$0.40	$1.20	$2.00	£0.20	£0.60	£1.00
21 Jonah Hex, Black Condor; Gray Morrow art	$0.40	$1.20	$2.00	£0.20	£0.60	£1.00
22 Manhunters, Millennium X-over	$0.40	$1.20	$2.00	£0.20	£0.60	£1.00
23 Floronic Man, Guardians of the Universe; Millennium X-over; Brett Ewins art	$0.40	$1.20	$2.00	£0.20	£0.60	£1.00
24 Blue Devil, Dr. Fate; Ty Templeton art	$0.40	$1.20	$2.00	£0.20	£0.60	£1.00
25 Legion of Super-Heroes, Golden Age Atom	$0.40	$1.20	$2.00	£0.20	£0.60	£1.00
26 Black Lightning, Miss America, Hourman appears, X-over with Young All Stars #12	$0.40	$1.20	$2.00	£0.20	£0.60	£1.00
27 Zatara, Zatanna	$0.40	$1.20	$2.00	£0.20	£0.60	£1.00
28 Midnight, Nightshade; Rob Liefeld art	$0.40	$1.20	$2.00	£0.20	£0.60	£1.00
29 Power of the Atom, Mr. America, Golden Age Red Tornado	$0.40	$1.20	$2.00	£0.20	£0.60	£1.00
30 Plastic Man, Elongated Man; Ty Templeton art	$0.40	$1.20	$2.00	£0.20	£0.60	£1.00
31 Justice Society of America	$0.40	$1.20	$2.00	£0.20	£0.60	£1.00
32 Justice League of America	$0.40	$1.20	$2.00	£0.20	£0.60	£1.00
33 Justice League of America; Art Adams part inks	$0.40	$1.20	$2.00	£0.20	£0.60	£1.00
34 Justice League International; covers fit together as poster; Keith Giffen art featured	$0.40	$1.20	$2.00	£0.20	£0.60	£1.00

Issue	$Good	$Fine	$N.Mint	£Good	£Fine	£N.Mint
35 Justice League International; covers fit together as poster	$0.40	$1.20	$2.00	£0.20	£0.60	£1.00
36 Poison Ivy by Neil Gaiman, Green Lantern	$0.40	$1.20	$2.00	£0.20	£0.60	£1.00
37 Legion of Substitute Heroes, Dr. Light; Ty Templeton art	$0.40	$1.20	$2.00	£0.20	£0.60	£1.00
38 Green Arrow, Speedy	$0.40	$1.20	$2.00	£0.20	£0.60	£1.00
39 Animal Man by Grant Morrison, Man-Bat	$0.40	$1.20	$2.00	£0.20	£0.60	£1.00
40 Gorilla City, Detective Chimp, Congorilla; Carmine Infantino art	$0.40	$1.20	$2.00	£0.20	£0.60	£1.00
41 Flash's Rogues Gallery (Captain Cold/Heat Wave/Pied Piper/Trickster/Weather Wizard), cover based on Flash #174	$0.40	$1.20	$2.00	£0.20	£0.60	£1.00
42 Phantom Girl, Grim Ghost	$0.40	$1.20	$2.00	£0.20	£0.60	£1.00
43 Hawk and the Dove, Cave Carson	$0.40	$1.20	$2.00	£0.20	£0.60	£1.00
44 The Four Clay Faces	$0.40	$1.20	$2.00	£0.20	£0.60	£1.00
45 Blackhawk, El Diablo	$0.40	$1.20	$2.00	£0.20	£0.60	£1.00
46 Justice League/Teen Titans/Legion of Super Heroes Headquarters	$0.40	$1.20	$2.00	£0.20	£0.60	£1.00
47 Ferro Lad, Chemical King, Karate Kid; Curt Swan and Mark Badger art	$0.40	$1.20	$2.00	£0.20	£0.60	£1.00
48 Ambush Bug (Giffen art)/Rex the WonderDog/Stanley and his Monster	$0.40	$1.20	$2.00	£0.20	£0.60	£1.00
49 Cadmus Project/Silent Knight/Legion of Super-Heroes (2 pgs)	$0.40	$1.20	$2.00	£0.20	£0.60	£1.00
50 96pgs, Batman by O'Neil/George Perez, Flash story by Grant Morrison, Black Canary/Dolphin/Johnny Thunder, Space Museum drawn by Infantino/George Perez	$0.60	$1.80	$3.00	£0.40	£1.20	£2.00
Title Value:	$21.50	$64.50	$107.50	£10.75	£32.25	£53.75

Note: all 48pgs from #6-49

Trade paperback (Mar 1990) new origin of Batman by O'Neill and Giordano, reprints new origins of Flash, Green Lantern, JLA, Martian Manhunter and Superman; Brian Bolland cover — £0.60 £1.80 £3.00

SECRET ORIGINS ANNUAL

DC Comics; 1 Aug 1987-3 1989

Issue	$Good	$Fine	$N.Mint	£Good	£Fine	£N.Mint
1 Doom Patrol; John Byrne cover and art	$0.40	$1.20	$2.00	£0.25	£0.75	£1.25
2 48pgs, Flash II, Flash III; Infantino and Anderson art	$0.40	$1.20	$2.00	£0.25	£0.75	£1.25
3 64pgs, Teen Titans; George Perez art	$0.50	$1.50	$2.50	£0.30	£0.90	£1.50
Title Value:	$1.30	$3.90	$6.50	£0.80	£2.40	£4.00

SECRET ORIGINS OF SUPER-HEROES

DC Comics; nn Autumn 1979

(DC Special Series #19)

Issue	$Good	$Fine	$N.Mint	£Good	£Fine	£N.Mint
nn ND 100pgs	$0.50	$1.50	$3.00	£0.30	£1.00	£2.00
Title Value:	$0.50	$1.50	$3.00	£0.30	£1.00	£2.00

FEATURES

Wonder Woman

REPRINT FEATURES

Superman/Batman, Elongated Man, Hawkman, Robin, Supergirl, Aquaman, Lightning Lad/Lass.

SECRET ORIGINS OF SUPER-HEROES SPECIAL

DC Comics; nn 1978

(DC Special Series #10)

Issue	$Good	$Fine	$N.Mint	£Good	£Fine	£N.Mint
nn ND 52pgs, Dr. Fate, Lightray and Black Canary; Joe Staton and Mike Nasser art	$0.50	$1.50	$3.00	£0.30	£1.00	£2.00
Title Value:	$0.50	$1.50	$3.00	£0.30	£1.00	£2.00

SECRET ORIGINS SPECIAL

DC Comics; 1 Aug 1989

Issue	$Good	$Fine	$N.Mint	£Good	£Fine	£N.Mint
1 LD in the U.K. 64pgs, squarebound, Sam Kieth art featured, Brian Bolland cover, Neil Gaiman/Alan Grant story, origins of Two Face, Penguin and The Riddler	$0.80	$2.40	$4.00	£0.50	£1.50	£2.50
Title Value:	$0.80	$2.40	$4.00	£0.50	£1.50	£2.50

SECRET SIX

National Periodical Publications; 1 Apr/May 1968-7 Apr/May 1969

Issue	$Good	$Fine	$N.Mint	£Good	£Fine	£N.Mint
1 origin and 1st appearance of Secret Six	$6.25	$19.00	$45.00	£3.55	£10.50	£25.00
2-7	$3.90	$11.50	$27.50	£2.10	£6.25	£15.00
Title Value:	$29.65	$88.00	$210.00	£16.15	£48.00	£115.00

SECRET SOCIETY OF SUPER-VILLAINS

DC Comics; 1 May/Jun 1976-15 Jun/Jul 1978

Issue	$Good	$Fine	$N.Mint	£Good	£Fine	£N.Mint
1	$0.80	$2.50	$5.00	£0.40	£1.25	£2.50
2-3 ND	$0.50	$1.50	$3.00	£0.30	£1.00	£2.00
4	$0.40	$1.25	$2.50	£0.25	£0.75	£1.50
5 Green Lantern appears	$0.40	$1.25	$2.50	£0.25	£0.75	£1.50
6-8	$0.30	$1.00	$2.00	£0.20	£0.60	£1.25
9 scarce in the U.K.	$0.30	$1.00	$2.00	£0.25	£0.75	£1.50
10 Creeper appears	$0.30	$1.00	$2.00	£0.20	£0.60	£1.25
11 Captain Comet appears	$0.30	$1.00	$2.00	£0.20	£0.60	£1.25
12-14	$0.30	$1.00	$2.00	£0.20	£0.60	£1.25
15 Justice Society of America appear	$0.30	$1.00	$2.00	£0.20	£0.60	£1.25
Title Value:	$5.60	$18.00	$35.50	£3.55	£10.90	£22.25

Note: features Gorilla Grodd, Mirror Master, Sinestro, Star Sapphire, Captain Cold, Captain Boomerang, Copperhead and Manhunter

SECRET SOCIETY OF SUPER-VILLAINS SPECIAL

DC Comics; nn 1977

(DC Special Series #6)

Issue	$Good	$Fine	$N.Mint	£Good	£Fine	£N.Mint
nn ND 52pgs	$0.50	$1.50	$3.00	£0.30	£1.00	£2.00
Title Value:	$0.50	$1.50	$3.00	£0.30	£1.00	£2.00

SECRET SQUIRREL

Gold Key; 1 Oct 1966

Issue	$Good	$Fine	$N.Mint	£Good	£Fine	£N.Mint
1 scarce in the U.K. based on cartoon	$14.00	$43.00	$100.00	£8.50	£26.00	£60.00
Title Value:	$14.00	$43.00	$100.00	£8.50	£26.00	£60.00

SECRET WARS II

Marvel Comics Group,MS; 1 Jul 1985-9 Mar 1986

Issue	$Good	$Fine	$N.Mint	£Good	£Fine	£N.Mint
1 ND 1st appearance The Beyonder	$0.30	$0.90	$1.50	£0.25	£0.75	£1.25
2-7 LD in the U.K.	$0.30	$0.90	$1.50	£0.20	£0.60	£1.00
8 LD in the U.K. Spiderman in black costume	$0.30	$0.90	$1.50	£0.20	£0.60	£1.00
9 LD in the U.K. DS	$0.35	$1.05	$1.75	£0.25	£0.75	£1.25
Title Value:	$2.75	$8.25	$13.75	£1.90	£5.70	£9.50

SECRET WARS II

Marvel Comics Group; 1985

Cross-over storyline with The Beyonder that ran throughout the following titles:

Secret Wars II #1, New Mutants #39, Captain America #308, Uncanny X-Men #196, Iron Man #197, Secret Wars II #2, Web of Spiderman #6, Amazing Spiderman #268, Fantastic Four #282, Secret Wars II #3, Daredevil #223, Hulk #312, Avengers #260, Secret Wars II #4, Dazzler #40, Alpha Flight #28, Rom #72, Avengers #261, Secret Wars II #5, The Thing #30, Doctor Strange #74, Fantastic Four #285, Secret Wars II #6, Cloak & Dagger #4, Power Pack #18, Micronauts #16, Thor #363, Power Man & Iron Fist #121, Secret Wars II #7, New Mutants #36, Amazing Spiderman #273, Uncanny X-Men #202, Defenders #152, Spectacular Spiderman #111, Secret Wars II #8, New Mutants #37, Amazing Spiderman #274, Avengers #256, Uncanny X-Men #203, Fantastic Four #288, Secret Wars II #9, Avengers #266.

SECRET WEAPONS

Valiant; 1 Sep 1993-23 Aug 1995

Issue	$Good	$Fine	$N.Mint	£Good	£Fine	£N.Mint
1 The Coming of the Darque Age part 1; X-O, Bloodshot, Eternal Warrior, Livewire and Stronghold vs. Dr. Eclipse	$0.30	$0.90	$1.50	£0.20	£0.60	£1.00
2 The Coming of the Darque Age story concludes	$0.30	$0.90	$1.50	£0.20	£0.60	£1.00
3 Empirircal Dynasty part 1, continued in Bloodshot #11	$0.30	$0.90	$1.50	£0.20	£0.60	£1.00
4	$0.30	$0.90	$1.50	£0.20	£0.60	£1.00
5 Ninjak featured	$0.30	$0.90	$1.50	£0.20	£0.60	£1.00
6-8	$0.30	$0.90	$1.50	£0.20	£0.60	£1.00
9 with free Upper Deck trading card	$0.30	$0.90	$1.50	£0.20	£0.60	£1.00
10	$0.30	$0.90	$1.50	£0.20	£0.60	£1.00
11 pre-bagged in brown wrapper marked Top Secret Eyes Only; new direction for title	$0.30	$0.90	$1.50	£0.20	£0.60	£1.00
12 Bloodshot appears	$0.30	$0.90	$1.50	£0.20	£0.60	£1.00
13 Chaos Effect tie-in	$0.30	$0.90	$1.50	£0.20	£0.60	£1.00
14-23	$0.30	$0.90	$1.50	£0.20	£0.60	£1.00
Title Value:	$6.90	$20.70	$34.50	£4.60	£13.80	£23.00

Note: all Non-Distributed on the news-stands in the U.K.

SECRET WEAPONS: PLAYING WITH FIRE

Valiant/Acclaim Comics,MS; 1,2 Nov 1995

Issue	$Good	$Fine	$N.Mint	£Good	£Fine	£N.Mint
1-2 ND	$0.40	$1.20	$2.00	£0.25	£0.75	£1.25
Title Value:	$0.80	$2.40	$4.00	£0.50	£1.50	£2.50

SECRETS OF HAUNTED HOUSE

DC Comics; 1 Apr/May 1975-5 Dec/Jan 1975/76; 6 Jun/Jul 1977-14 Oct/Nov 1978; 15 Aug 1979-46 Mar 1982

Issue	$Good	$Fine	$N.Mint	£Good	£Fine	£N.Mint
1 Cain and Abel appear	$1.00	$3.00	$6.00	£0.55	£1.75	£3.50
2	$0.65	$2.00	$4.00	£0.30	£1.00	£2.00
3-9	$0.40	$1.25	$2.50	£0.25	£0.75	£1.50
10 Golden art	$0.40	$1.25	$2.50	£0.25	£0.75	£1.50
11-13	$0.40	$1.25	$2.50	£0.25	£0.75	£1.50
14 scarce in the U.K. 44pgs	$0.50	$1.50	$3.00	£0.25	£0.85	£1.75
15-23 ND	$0.40	$1.20	$2.00	£0.25	£0.75	£1.25
24 Nasser art	$0.40	$1.20	$2.00	£0.25	£0.75	£1.25
25-30	$0.40	$1.20	$2.00	£0.25	£0.75	£1.25
31-41 Mister E stars	$0.40	$1.20	$2.00	£0.25	£0.75	£1.25
42-46	$0.40	$1.20	$2.00	£0.25	£0.75	£1.25
Title Value:	$19.35	$58.65	$104.50	£11.85	£35.85	£63.75

ARTISTS

Ditko in 9, 12, 41, 45. Nino in 1, 13, 19.

SECRETS OF HAUNTED HOUSE SPECIAL

DC Comics; nn Spring 1978

(DC Special Series #12)

Issue	$Good	$Fine	$N.Mint	£Good	£Fine	£N.Mint
nn, ND scarce in the U.K., 52pgs	$0.80	$2.50	$5.00	£0.55	£1.75	£3.50
Title Value:	$0.80	$2.50	$5.00	£0.55	£1.75	£3.50

SECRETS OF SINISTER HOUSE

DC Comics;5 Jun/Jul 1972-18 Jun/Jul 1974

(previously Sinister House of Secret Love)

	$Good	$Fine	$N.Mint	£Good	£Fine	£N.Mint
5 ND 52pgs	***$0.65***	***$2.00***	***$4.00***	**£0.30**	**£1.00**	**£2.00**
6-9 ND	***$0.50***	***$1.50***	***$3.00***	**£0.25**	**£0.75**	**£1.50**
10 ND Neal Adams inks	***$1.00***	***$3.00***	***$6.00***	**£0.55**	**£1.75**	**£3.50**
11-18 ND	***$0.40***	***$1.25***	***$2.50***	**£0.25**	**£0.75**	**£1.50**
Title Value:	***$6.85***	***$21.00***	***$42.00***	**£3.85**	**£11.75**	**£23.50**

ARTISTS

Nino art in 8, 11-13

SECRETS OF THE LEGION OF SUPER-HEROES

DC Comics,MS; 1 Jan 1981-3 Mar 1981

(see Legion of Super-Heroes)

	$Good	$Fine	$N.Mint	£Good	£Fine	£N.Mint
1 Legion origin retold	***$0.30***	***$0.90***	***$1.50***	**£0.20**	**£0.60**	**£1.00**
2 Brainiac 5, Bouncing Boy, Dream Girl, Sun Boy, Karate Kid, Matter-Eater Lad, Shrinking Violet, Mon-El origins retold	***$0.30***	***$0.90***	***$1.50***	**£0.20**	**£0.60**	**£1.00**
3	***$0.30***	***$0.90***	***$1.50***	**£0.20**	**£0.60**	**£1.00**
Title Value:	***$0.90***	***$2.70***	***$4.50***	**£0.60**	**£1.80**	**£3.00**

SECRETS OF THE VALIANT UNIVERSE

Valiant; 1 Sep 1994-3 Nov 1994

	$Good	$Fine	$N.Mint	£Good	£Fine	£N.Mint
1 ND available with Wizard's "Valiant Universe Special"	***$0.30***	***$0.90***	***$1.50***	**£0.20**	**£0.60**	**£1.00**
2 ND Chaos Effect tie-in	***$0.30***	***$0.90***	***$1.50***	**£0.20**	**£0.60**	**£1.00**
3 ND features Sho Sugino the 2nd Rai	***$0.30***	***$0.90***	***$1.50***	**£0.20**	**£0.60**	**£1.00**
Title Value:	***$0.90***	***$2.70***	***$4.50***	**£0.60**	**£1.80**	**£3.00**

SECTAURS

Marvel Comics Group, Toy; 1 Jun 1985-8 1986

	$Good	$Fine	$N.Mint	£Good	£Fine	£N.Mint
1 ND Mark Texeira art	***$0.15***	***$0.45***	***$0.75***	**£0.10**	**£0.30**	**£0.50**
1 1985 Coleco Toys Giveaway, ND rare in the U.K. (banner across bottom left corner)	***$0.30***	***$0.90***	***$1.50***	**£0.20**	**£0.60**	**£1.00**
2 ND Mark Texeira art	***$0.15***	***$0.45***	***$0.75***	**£0.10**	**£0.30**	**£0.50**
3-8 ND	***$0.15***	***$0.45***	***$0.75***	**£0.10**	**£0.30**	**£0.50**
Title Value:	***$1.50***	***$4.50***	***$7.50***	**£1.00**	**£3.00**	**£5.00**

SEDUCTION OF THE INNOCENT

Eclipse,MS; 1 Nov 1985-6 Apr 1986

(see Three-Dimensional Seduction of the Innocent)

(#1-3 marked as 3-issue mini-series)

	$Good	$Fine	$N.Mint	£Good	£Fine	£N.Mint
1 all pre-code horror reprints	***$0.40***	***$1.20***	***$2.00***	**£0.25**	**£0.75**	**£1.25**
1 3-D issue, (Oct 1985), Dave Stevens cover; with bound-in 3-D glasses (25% less without glasses)	***$0.50***	***$1.50***	***$2.50***	**£0.30**	**£0.90**	**£1.50**
2 all pre-code horror reprints	***$0.40***	***$1.20***	***$2.00***	**£0.25**	**£0.75**	**£1.25**
2 3-D issue, (Apr 1986), Berni Wrightson cover, Alex Toth reprint; with bound-in 3-D glasses (25% less without glasses)	***$0.50***	***$1.50***	***$2.50***	**£0.30**	**£0.90**	**£1.50**
3-6 all pre-code horror reprints	***$0.40***	***$1.20***	***$2.00***	**£0.25**	**£0.75**	**£1.25**
Title Value:	***$3.40***	***$10.20***	***$17.00***	**£2.10**	**£6.30**	**£10.50**

Note: all Non-Distributed on the news-stands in the U.K.

SEEKER, JOE MARTIN'S

Sky Comics; 1 Nov 1993-2 Apr 1994

	$Good	$Fine	$N.Mint	£Good	£Fine	£N.Mint
1 ND sub-titled Seeker: Vengeance	***$0.40***	***$1.20***	***$2.00***	**£0.25**	**£0.75**	**£1.25**
2 ND plastic acetate cover	***$0.40***	***$1.20***	***$2.00***	**£0.25**	**£0.75**	**£1.25**
Title Value:	***$0.80***	***$2.40***	***$4.00***	**£0.50**	**£1.50**	**£2.50**

SEEKERS: INTO THE MYSTERY

DC Comics/Vertigo; 1 Jan 1996-15 Mar 1997

	$Good	$Fine	$N.Mint	£Good	£Fine	£N.Mint
1-8 ND J.M. DeMatteis script, Glen Barr art	***$0.50***	***$1.50***	***$2.50***	**£0.30**	**£0.90**	**£1.50**
9 ND J.M. DeMatteis script, Michael Zulli painted art	***$0.50***	***$1.50***	***$2.50***	**£0.30**	**£0.90**	**£1.50**
10 ND J.M. DeMatteis script, Jon J. Muth painted cover and art	***$0.50***	***$1.50***	***$2.50***	**£0.30**	**£0.90**	**£1.50**
11-13 ND	***$0.50***	***$1.50***	***$2.50***	**£0.30**	**£0.90**	**£1.50**
14 ND J.M. DeMatteis script, Jill Thompson art; cover by John Bolton	***$0.50***	***$1.50***	***$2.50***	**£0.30**	**£0.90**	**£1.50**
15 ND	***$0.60***	***$1.80***	***$3.00***	**£0.40**	**£1.20**	**£2.00**
Title Value:	***$7.60***	***$22.80***	***$38.00***	**£4.60**	**£13.80**	**£23.00**

SEMPER FI

Marvel Comics Group; 1 Dec 1988-9 Aug 1989

	$Good	$Fine	$N.Mint	£Good	£Fine	£N.Mint
1-9 ND	***$0.20***	***$0.60***	***$1.00***	**£0.10**	**£0.35**	**£0.60**
Title Value:	***$1.80***	***$5.40***	***$9.00***	**£0.90**	**£3.15**	**£5.40**

SENSATION COMICS

National Periodical Publications; 1 Jan 1942-116 Jul/Aug 1953

	$Good	$Fine	$N.Mint	£Good	£Fine	£N.Mint
1 Wonder Woman's adventures continue from All Star Comics #8, origin/1st appearance Mr. Terrific, 1st appearance Wildcat	***$2750.00***	***$8200.00***	***$27500.00***	**£1825.00**	**£5500.00**	**£18350.00**
2	***$430.00***	***$1300.00***	***$3900.00***	**£285.00**	**£860.00**	**£2600.00**
3	***$250.00***	***$750.00***	***$2000.00***	**£165.00**	**£500.00**	**£1350.00**
4	***$170.00***	***$510.00***	***$1375.00***	**£115.00**	**£345.00**	**£920.00**
5	***$140.00***	***$430.00***	***$1150.00***	**£95.00**	**£285.00**	**£770.00**
6 origin and 1st appearance the magic lasso (used on cover)	***$150.00***	***$450.00***	***$1200.00***	**£100.00**	**£300.00**	**£800.00**
7-10	***$95.00***	***$285.00***	***$760.00***	**£62.50**	**£190.00**	**£510.00**
11-12	***$95.00***	***$285.00***	***$675.00***	**£62.50**	**£190.00**	**£450.00**
13 Hitler, Mussolini and Emperor Tojo parody cover	***$125.00***	***$385.00***	***$900.00***	**£85.00**	**£255.00**	**£600.00**
14-20	***$95.00***	***$285.00***	***$675.00***	**£62.50**	**£190.00**	**£450.00**
21-30	***$75.00***	***$230.00***	***$540.00***	**£50.00**	**£150.00**	**£360.00**
31-33	***$60.00***	***$180.00***	***$420.00***	**£40.00**	**£120.00**	**£280.00**
34 Sargon the Sorceror back-up	***$62.50***	***$190.00***	***$450.00***	**£43.00**	**£125.00**	**£300.00**
35-36 Sargon the Sorceror back-up	***$52.50***	***$160.00***	***$375.00***	**£36.00**	**£105.00**	**£250.00**
37	***$52.50***	***$160.00***	***$375.00***	**£36.00**	**£105.00**	**£250.00**
38 Christmas cover	***$52.50***	***$160.00***	***$375.00***	**£36.00**	**£105.00**	**£250.00**
39-40	***$52.50***	***$160.00***	***$375.00***	**£36.00**	**£105.00**	**£250.00**
41 Red Cross cover	***$43.00***	***$125.00***	***$300.00***	**£29.00**	**£85.00**	**£200.00**
42-50	***$43.00***	***$125.00***	***$300.00***	**£29.00**	**£85.00**	**£200.00**
51-60	***$37.00***	***$110.00***	***$260.00***	**£25.00**	**£75.00**	**£175.00**
61-67	***$35.00***	***$105.00***	***$245.00***	**£23.50**	**£70.00**	**£165.00**
68 origin and 1st appearance of the Huntress	***$39.00***	***$115.00***	***$275.00***	**£26.00**	**£77.50**	**£185.00**
69-80	***$35.00***	***$105.00***	***$245.00***	**£23.50**	**£70.00**	**£165.00**
81 B. Krigstein art	***$32.00***	***$95.00***	***$225.00***	**£21.00**	**£62.50**	**£150.00**
82	***$29.00***	***$85.00***	***$200.00***	**£19.00**	**£57.50**	**£135.00**
83 scarce in the U.S, very scarce in the U.K. B. Krigstein art	***$28.00***	***$82.50***	***$225.00***	**£18.50**	**£55.00**	**£150.00**
84-90	***$29.00***	***$85.00***	***$200.00***	**£19.00**	**£57.50**	**£135.00**
91-93	***$27.00***	***$80.00***	***$190.00***	**£18.50**	**£55.00**	**£130.00**
94 cover logo change, new features announced including Dr. Pat and other romance-orientated stories	***$45.00***	***$135.00***	***$315.00***	**£30.00**	**£90.00**	**£210.00**
95-99	***$41.00***	***$120.00***	***$285.00***	**£27.00**	**£80.00**	**£190.00**
100 scarce in the U.K.	***$55.00***	***$170.00***	***$400.00***	**£39.00**	**£115.00**	**£270.00**
101-105 scarce in the U.K.	***$41.00***	***$120.00***	***$285.00***	**£27.00**	**£80.00**	**£190.00**
106 scarce in the U.K. last Wonder Woman in title and on cover	***$41.00***	***$120.00***	***$285.00***	**£27.00**	**£80.00**	**£190.00**
107 scarce in the U.S, very scarce in the U.K. title becomes mystery anthology	***$55.00***	***$165.00***	***$450.00***	**£38.00**	**£110.00**	**£300.00**
108 scarce in the U.S, very scarce in the U.K.	***$50.00***	***$150.00***	***$400.00***	**£34.00**	**£100.00**	**£270.00**
109 scarce in the U.S, very scarce in the U.K.	***$55.00***	***$165.00***	***$450.00***	**£38.00**	**£110.00**	**£300.00**
110 very scarce in the U.K. title becomes "Sensation Mystery" on cover	***$39.00***	***$115.00***	***$275.00***	**£26.00**	**£77.50**	**£185.00**
111-116 very scarce in the U.K.	***$36.00***	***$105.00***	***$250.00***	**£24.00**	**£72.50**	**£170.00**
Title Value:	***$9400.50***	***$28127.50***	***$76575.00***	**£6267.00**	**£18797.50**	**£51205.00**

Note: in common with all Golden Age material, this title was not officially distributed on the news-stands in the U.K. but copies may have found their way over through personnel movements during the war or as cheap ballast on ships after the war. No reports of copies with British pence stamps on as yet.

SENSATIONAL SPIDERMAN

Marvel Comics Group; 0 Jan 1996; 1 Feb 1996-present

	$Good	$Fine	$N.Mint	£Good	£Fine	£N.Mint
0 ND 48pgs, The Return of Spiderman part 1, continued in Amazing Spiderman #407; 1st new costume; "moving image" lenticular cover	***$1.00***	***$3.00***	***$5.00***	**£0.70**	**£2.10**	**£3.50**
1 ND Media Blizzard part 1, continued in Amazing Spiderman #408; new Spiderman vs. new Mysterio	***$0.40***	***$1.20***	***$2.00***	**£0.30**	**£0.90**	**£1.50**
2 ND The Return of Kaine part 2, continued in Amazing Spiderman #409	***$0.40***	***$1.20***	***$2.00***	**£0.30**	**£0.90**	**£1.50**
3 ND Web of Carnage part 1, continued in Amazing Spiderman #410; Carnage appears	***$0.40***	***$1.20***	***$2.00***	**£0.30**	**£0.90**	**£1.50**
4 ND Blood Brothers part 1, continued in Amazing Spiderman #411	***$0.40***	***$1.20***	***$2.00***	**£0.30**	**£0.90**	**£1.50**
5-6 ND Blood Brothers part 5, continued in Amazing Spiderman #412	***$0.40***	***$1.20***	***$2.00***	**£0.30**	**£0.90**	**£1.50**
7-8 ND 40pgs	***$0.40***	***$1.20***	***$2.00***	**£0.30**	**£0.90**	**£1.50**
9 ND Peter Parker and Mary Jane's baby - boy, girl or spider! with bound-in Overpower cards	***$0.40***	***$1.20***	***$2.00***	**£0.30**	**£0.90**	**£1.50**
10 ND	***$0.40***	***$1.20***	***$2.00***	**£0.30**	**£0.90**	**£1.50**
11 ND Revelations part 2, continued in Amazing Spiderman #418	***$0.40***	***$1.20***	***$2.00***	**£0.25**	**£0.75**	**£1.25**
11 Polybag Promotion Edition, ND pre-bagged with trading card and redemption card for one copy of Spiderman #75, Amazing Spiderman #418 or Spectacular Spiderman #241	***$1.40***	***$4.20***	***$7.00***	**£0.90**	**£2.70**	**£4.50**
12 ND The Trapster returns	***$0.40***	***$1.20***	***$2.00***	**£0.25**	**£0.75**	**£1.25**
13-14 ND Ka-Zar appears	***$0.40***	***$1.20***	***$2.00***	**£0.25**	**£0.75**	**£1.25**
Title Value:	***$8.00***	***$24.00***	***$40.00***	**£5.60**	**£16.80**	**£28.00**

SENSATIONAL SPIDERMAN '96

Marvel Comics Group; nn Nov 1996

	$Good	$Fine	$N.Mint	£Good	£Fine	£N.Mint
nn ND 64pgs, retells the first meeting of Spiderman and Kraven the Hunter	***$0.60***	***$1.80***	***$3.00***	**£0.40**	**£1.20**	**£2.00**
Title Value:	***$0.60***	***$1.80***	***$3.00***	**£0.40**	**£1.20**	**£2.00**

SENSEI

First,MS; 1 Sep 1989-4 Dec 1989

(see Squalor, Twilight Man)

	$Good	$Fine	$N.Mint	£Good	£Fine	£N.Mint
1 ND Val Mayerik cover and art begins, sub-titled "First Fiction Volume 2"; glossy heavier stock paper covers begin	***$0.40***	***$1.20***	***$2.00***	**£0.25**	**£0.75**	**£1.25**
2-4 ND	***$0.40***	***$1.20***	***$2.00***	**£0.25**	**£0.75**	**£1.25**
Title Value:	***$1.60***	***$4.80***	***$8.00***	**£1.00**	**£3.00**	**£5.00**

SENTAI
Antarctic Press; 1 Mar 1994-5 1995

Issue	$Good	$Fine	$N.Mint	£Good	£Fine	£N.Mint
1-5 ND information and features on Asian sci-fi and fantasy	*$0.50*	*$1.50*	*$2.50*	£0.30	£0.90	£1.50
Title Value:	*$2.50*	*$7.50*	*$12.50*	£1.50	£4.50	£7.50

SENTINELS OF JUSTICE
AC Comics; 1 1985-5 1986

Issue	$Good	$Fine	$N.Mint	£Good	£Fine	£N.Mint
1-5 ND	*$0.40*	*$1.20*	*$2.00*	£0.25	£0.75	£1.25
Title Value:	*$2.00*	*$6.00*	*$10.00*	£1.25	£3.75	£6.25

SENTRY SPECIAL
Innovation,OS; 1 Jun 1991

Issue	$Good	$Fine	$N.Mint	£Good	£Fine	£N.Mint
1 ND spin-off from Hero Alliance, black and white	*$0.40*	*$1.20*	*$2.00*	£0.25	£0.75	£1.25
Title Value:	*$0.40*	*$1.20*	*$2.00*	£0.25	£0.75	£1.25

SERAPHIM
Innovation,MS; 1 May 1990-2 Jun 1990

Issue	$Good	$Fine	$N.Mint	£Good	£Fine	£N.Mint
1-2 ND painted art by Doug Talalla	*$0.40*	*$1.20*	*$2.00*	£0.25	£0.75	£1.25
Title Value:	*$0.80*	*$2.40*	*$4.00*	£0.50	£1.50	£2.50

SERGEANT BILKO
National Periodical Publications,TV; 1 May/Jun 1957-18 Mar/Apr 1960

Issue	$Good	$Fine	$N.Mint	£Good	£Fine	£N.Mint
1 scarce in the U.K.	*$62.50*	*$185.00*	*$500.00*	£44.00	£130.00	£350.00
2 scarce in the U.K.	*$38.00*	*$110.00*	*$265.00*	£26.00	£75.00	£180.00
3-5 scarce in the U.K.	*$30.00*	*$90.00*	*$210.00*	£20.00	£60.00	£140.00
6-15	*$25.00*	*$75.00*	*$175.00*	£16.00	£49.00	£115.00
1st official distribution in the U.K.						
16-18	*$25.00*	*$75.00*	*$175.00*	£16.00	£49.00	£115.00
Title Value:	*$515.50*	*$1540.00*	*$3670.00*	£338.00	£1022.00	£2445.00

SERGIO ARAGONES DESTROYS DC
DC Comics,OS; 1 Jun 1996

Issue	$Good	$Fine	$N.Mint	£Good	£Fine	£N.Mint
1 ND 48pgs	*$0.70*	*$2.10*	*$3.50*	£0.50	£1.50	£2.50
Title Value:	*$0.70*	*$2.10*	*$3.50*	£0.50	£1.50	£2.50

SERGIO MASSACRES MARVEL
Marvel Comics Group,OS; 1 Jun 1996

Issue	$Good	$Fine	$N.Mint	£Good	£Fine	£N.Mint
1 ND	*$0.70*	*$2.10*	*$3.50*	£0.50	£1.50	£2.50
Title Value:	*$0.70*	*$2.10*	*$3.50*	£0.50	£1.50	£2.50

Note: originally solicited two months previously and called Sergio Aragones Massacres Marvel

SERINA
Antarctic Press,MS; 1 Apr 1996-3 Jun 1996

Issue	$Good	$Fine	$N.Mint	£Good	£Fine	£N.Mint
1-3 ND David Hahn script and art	*$0.60*	*$1.80*	*$3.00*	£0.40	£1.20	£2.00
Title Value:	*$1.80*	*$5.40*	*$9.00*	£1.20	£3.60	£6.00

SERPENT RISING
Caliber Press,OS; 1 Jul 1992

Issue	$Good	$Fine	$N.Mint	£Good	£Fine	£N.Mint
1 ND ecological theme; black and white	*$0.40*	*$1.20*	*$2.00*	£0.25	£0.75	£1.25
Title Value:	*$0.40*	*$1.20*	*$2.00*	£0.25	£0.75	£1.25

SERPENTYNE
Night Wynd,MS; 1 Apr 1992-3 Jun 1992

Issue	$Good	$Fine	$N.Mint	£Good	£Fine	£N.Mint
1-3 ND Barry Blair; black and white	*$0.40*	*$1.20*	*$2.00*	£0.25	£0.75	£1.25
Title Value:	*$1.20*	*$3.60*	*$6.00*	£0.75	£2.25	£3.75

SERRA ANGEL ON THE WORLD OF MAGIC: THE GATHERING
Acclaim Comics,OS; 1 Aug 1996

Issue	$Good	$Fine	$N.Mint	£Good	£Fine	£N.Mint
1 64pgs, pre-bagged with trading card	*$1.20*	*$3.60*	*$6.00*	£0.80	£2.40	£4.00
Title Value:	*$1.20*	*$3.60*	*$6.00*	£0.80	£2.40	£4.00

SEVEN BLOCK BOOKSHELF EDITION
Marvel Comics Group/Epic,OS; 1 Oct 1990

Issue	$Good	$Fine	$N.Mint	£Good	£Fine	£N.Mint
1 ND 48pgs, Dixon script, Zaffino art	*$0.50*	*$1.50*	*$2.50*	£0.30	£0.90	£1.50
Title Value:	*$0.50*	*$1.50*	*$2.50*	£0.30	£0.90	£1.50

77 SUNSET STRIP
Gold Key;1 Nov 1962-2 Feb 1963

(see Four Colour #1066, #1106, #1211, #1263, #1291)

Issue	$Good	$Fine	$N.Mint	£Good	£Fine	£N.Mint
1 distributed in the U.K. Russ Manning art	*$14.00*	*$43.00*	*$100.00*	£7.00	£21.00	£50.00
2 distributed in the U.K. Russ Manning art	*$12.50*	*$39.00*	*$90.00*	£6.25	£19.00	£45.00
Title Value:	*$26.50*	*$82.00*	*$190.00*	£13.25	£40.00	£95.00

SEX WARRIOR
Dark Horse,MS; 1 Apr 1993-2 May 1993

Issue	$Good	$Fine	$N.Mint	£Good	£Fine	£N.Mint
1-2 ND Mills and Skinner, McKone and Erasmus	*$0.50*	*$1.50*	*$2.50*	£0.30	£0.90	£1.50
Title Value:	*$1.00*	*$3.00*	*$5.00*	£0.60	£1.80	£3.00

SF SHORT STORIES
Webb Graphics; 1 1991

Issue	$Good	$Fine	$N.Mint	£Good	£Fine	£N.Mint
1 ND black and white	*$0.25*	*$0.75*	*$1.25*	£0.15	£0.45	£0.75
Title Value:	*$0.25*	*$0.75*	*$1.25*	£0.15	£0.45	£0.75

SGT. BILKO'S PVT. DOBERMAN
National Periodical Publications,TV; 1 Jun/Jul 1958-11 Feb/Mar 1960

Issue	$Good	$Fine	$N.Mint	£Good	£Fine	£N.Mint
1 scarce in the U.K.	*$36.00*	*$105.00*	*$285.00*	£25.00	£75.00	£200.00
2 scarce in the U.K.	*$23.00*	*$67.50*	*$185.00*	£13.50	£41.00	£110.00
3-5 scarce in the U.K.	*$15.50*	*$47.00*	*$125.00*	£10.50	£32.00	£85.00
6-8	*$11.50*	*$36.00*	*$95.00*	£8.75	£26.00	£70.00
1st official distribution in the U.K.						
9-11	*$11.50*	*$36.00*	*$95.00*	£8.75	£26.00	£70.00
Title Value:	*$174.50*	*$529.50*	*$1415.00*	£122.50	£368.00	£985.00

SGT. FURY AND HIS HOWLING COMMANDOS
Marvel Comics Group; 1 May 1963-167 Dec 1981

Issue	$Good	$Fine	$N.Mint	£Good	£Fine	£N.Mint
1 scarce in the U.K. 1st appearance Sgt. Fury, Jack Kirby art begins, Dick Ayers inks	*$95.00*	*$285.00*	*$950.00*	£55.00	£170.00	£570.00
2 scarce in the U.K. Jack Kirby art	*$38.00*	*$110.00*	*$300.00*	£22.50	£67.50	£180.00
3 scarce in the U.K. Jack Kirby art, Reed Richards appears	*$23.50*	*$70.00*	*$165.00*	£11.00	£34.00	£80.00
4 Jack Kirby art	*$23.50*	*$70.00*	*$165.00*	£11.00	£34.00	£80.00
5 1st appearance Baron Strucker, Jack Kirby art	*$23.50*	*$70.00*	*$165.00*	£11.00	£34.00	£80.00
6-7 Jack Kirby art	*$16.00*	*$49.00*	*$115.00*	£7.00	£21.00	£50.00
8-9	*$16.00*	*$49.00*	*$115.00*	£7.00	£21.00	£50.00
10 1st appearance Captain Savage	*$16.00*	*$49.00*	*$115.00*	£7.00	£21.00	£50.00
11 rare in the U.K.	*$10.00*	*$30.00*	*$70.00*	£5.00	£15.00	£35.00
12 scarce in the U.K.	*$10.00*	*$30.00*	*$70.00*	£4.60	£13.50	£32.50
13 Captain America guest-stars, classic cover, Jack Kirby art	*$33.00*	*$100.00*	*$300.00*	£11.00	£33.00	£100.00
14	*$10.00*	*$30.00*	*$70.00*	£4.25	£12.50	£30.00
15 Steve Ditko art	*$10.00*	*$30.00*	*$70.00*	£4.25	£12.50	£30.00
16-20	*$10.00*	*$30.00*	*$70.00*	£4.25	£12.50	£30.00

Secret Hearts #62

Sectaurs #1

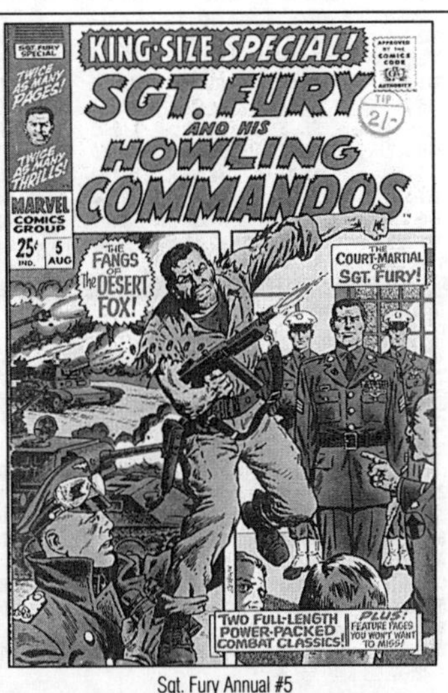

Sgt. Fury Annual #5

	$Good	$Fine	$N.Mint	£Good	£Fine	£N.Mint
21-24	$6.75	$20.00	$47.50	£2.85	£8.50	£20.00
25 Red Skull appears						
	$6.75	$20.00	$47.50	£2.85	£8.50	£20.00
26	$6.75	$20.00	$47.50	£2.85	£8.50	£20.00
27 origin Fury's eye-patch						
	$6.75	$20.00	$47.50	£2.85	£8.50	£20.00
28-30	$6.75	$20.00	$47.50	£2.85	£8.50	£20.00
31-33	$4.25	$12.50	$30.00	£2.10	£6.25	£15.00
34 origin Howling Commandoes						
	$4.25	$12.50	$30.00	£2.10	£6.25	£15.00
35-40	$4.25	$12.50	$30.00	£2.10	£6.25	£15.00
41-42	$3.55	$10.50	$25.00	£1.75	£5.25	£12.50
43 Bob Hope, Glen Miller cameos						
	$3.55	$10.50	$25.00	£1.75	£5.25	£12.50
44-50	$3.55	$10.50	$25.00	£1.75	£5.25	£12.50
51 Churchill, Roosevelt, Stalin cameos						
	$3.30	$10.00	$20.00	£1.65	£5.00	£10.00
52-60	$3.30	$10.00	$20.00	£1.65	£5.00	£10.00
61-63	$2.90	$8.75	$17.50	£1.25	£3.75	£7.50
64 Captain Savage X-over						
	$2.90	$8.75	$17.50	£1.25	£3.75	£7.50
65-68	$2.90	$8.75	$17.50	£1.25	£3.75	£7.50
69 scarce in the U.K.						
	$2.90	$8.75	$17.50	£1.40	£4.25	£8.50
70	$2.90	$8.75	$17.50	£1.25	£3.75	£7.50
71-80 scarce in the U.K.						
	$2.50	$7.50	$15.00	£1.00	£3.00	£6.00
81-91	$2.05	$6.25	$12.50	£0.80	£2.50	£5.00
92 ND 48pgs, squarebound						
	$2.05	$6.25	$12.50	£1.00	£3.00	£6.00
93-99 ND	$2.05	$6.25	$12.50	£0.80	£2.50	£5.00
100 ND Captain America, Fantastic Four, Stan Lee cameos plus scripter and artist Gary Friedrich and Dick Ayers cameos						
	$2.05	$6.25	$12.50	£1.00	£3.00	£6.00
101 ND origin retold						
	$1.65	$5.00	$10.00	£0.65	£2.00	£4.00
102-106 ND	$1.65	$5.00	$10.00	£0.65	£2.00	£4.00
107-117	$1.65	$5.00	$10.00	£0.55	£1.75	£3.50
118-120 ND	$1.65	$5.00	$10.00	£0.65	£2.00	£4.00
121-130 ND	$1.25	$3.75	$7.50	£0.50	£1.50	£3.00
131-140 ND	$1.00	$3.00	$6.00	£0.40	£1.25	£2.50
141-162 ND	$0.80	$2.50	$5.00	£0.30	£1.00	£2.00
163-166	$0.80	$2.50	$5.00	£0.25	£0.85	£1.75
167 scarce in the U.K. reprints issue #1						
	$0.80	$2.50	$5.00	£0.40	£1.25	£2.50
Title Value:	$757.10	$2272.50	$5520.00	£347.30	£1053.90	£2613.50

Note: Ditko inks in #15. Most issues from #80-120 are reprint. All issues from 121 on are reprint.

SGT. FURY ANNUAL

Marvel Comics Group; 1 1965-7 1971

	$Good	$Fine	$N.Mint	£Good	£Fine	£N.Mint
1 scarce in the U.K. 72pgs, one new story plus reprints of #4, #5						
	$17.50	$52.50	$125.00	£10.50	£32.00	£75.00
2 72pgs	$7.75	$23.50	$55.00	£5.00	£15.00	£35.00
3 72pgs	$5.00	$15.00	$35.00	£2.85	£8.50	£20.00
4 72pgs	$3.75	$11.00	$22.50	£2.05	£6.25	£12.50
5-6 64pgs, all reprint						
	$2.05	$6.25	$12.50	£1.25	£3.75	£7.50
7 ND scarce in the U.K. 48pgs, all reprint (Note: almost all copies ink-stained)						
	$2.05	$6.25	$12.50	£1.25	£3.75	£7.50
Title Value:	$40.15	$120.75	$275.00	£24.15	£73.00	£165.00

SGT. ROCK

DC Comics;302 Mar 1977-422 Jul 1988

(see Brave and the Bold, Brave and Bold Special, DC Comics Presents, DC Super Stars, One-Hundred Page Super Spectacular, Sgt. Rock Special, Showcase) (previously Our Army At War)

	$Good	$Fine	$N.Mint	£Good	£Fine	£N.Mint
302	$2.90	$8.75	$17.50	£1.05	£3.25	£6.50
303-310	$2.05	$6.25	$12.50	£0.65	£2.00	£4.00
311-312	$1.65	$5.00	$10.00	£0.40	£1.25	£2.50
313-317 ND	$1.65	$5.00	$10.00	£0.50	£1.50	£3.00
318 ND all reprint	$1.65	$5.00	$10.00	£0.50	£1.50	£3.00
319-322 ND	$1.65	$5.00	$10.00	£0.50	£1.50	£3.00
323-350	$1.50	$4.50	$7.50	£0.50	£1.50	£2.50
351-370	$1.00	$3.00	$5.00	£0.40	£1.20	£2.00
371-400	$1.00	$3.00	$5.00	£0.35	£1.05	£1.75
401-422	$0.90	$2.70	$4.50	£0.30	£0.90	£1.50
Title Value:	$150.90	$454.15	$776.50	£51.15	£154.05	£269.00

SGT. ROCK ANNUAL

DC Comics;2 1982-4 1984

(previously Sgt. Rock's Prize Battle Tales)

	$Good	$Fine	$N.Mint	£Good	£Fine	£N.Mint
2-4 ND 52pgs	$1.00	$3.00	$5.00	£0.40	£1.20	£2.00
Title Value:	$3.00	$9.00	$15.00	£1.20	£3.60	£6.00

SGT. ROCK SPECIAL

DC Comics; nn 1977; 2 1988; 3 1989-21 Jan 1992

	$Good	$Fine	$N.Mint	£Good	£Fine	£N.Mint
nn ND 52pgs, reprints begin						
	$0.55	$1.75	$3.50	£0.30	£1.00	£2.00
2 ND 48pgs, Chaykin cover, Chaykin reprint from Weird War Tales						
	$0.50	$1.50	$2.50	£0.30	£0.90	£1.50
3 48pgs	$0.50	$1.50	$2.50	£0.30	£0.90	£1.50
4 48pgs, Walt Simonson cover						
	$0.50	$1.50	$2.50	£0.30	£0.90	£1.50
5 48pgs	$0.50	$1.50	$2.50	£0.30	£0.90	£1.50
6 48pgs, Frank Miller reprint						
	$0.50	$1.50	$2.50	£0.30	£0.90	£1.50
7 48pgs, Jack Kirby reprint						
	$0.50	$1.50	$2.50	£0.25	£0.75	£1.25
8 48pgs, Neal Adams/Toth reprints						
	$0.50	$1.50	$2.50	£0.25	£0.75	£1.25
9-10 48pgs	$0.50	$1.50	$2.50	£0.25	£0.75	£1.25
11 48pgs, new Kubert cover						
	$0.50	$1.50	$2.50	£0.25	£0.75	£1.25
12-15 48pgs	$0.50	$1.50	$2.50	£0.25	£0.75	£1.25
16 48pgs, 1st monthly						
	$0.50	$1.50	$2.50	£0.25	£0.75	£1.25
17 48pgs, Kubert, Russ Heath art						
	$0.50	$1.50	$2.50	£0.25	£0.75	£1.25
18 48pgs, new Joe Kubert cover						
	$0.50	$1.50	$2.50	£0.25	£0.75	£1.25
19 48pgs, classic Batman and Sgt. Rock team-up reprinted, new Batman/Sgt. Rock cover by Kubert						
	$0.50	$1.50	$2.50	£0.25	£0.75	£1.25
20 48pgs, 50th anniversary of attack on Pearl Harbour commemorated						
	$0.50	$1.50	$2.50	£0.25	£0.75	£1.25
21 48pgs, Kubert, Heath art						
	$0.50	$1.50	$2.50	£0.25	£0.75	£1.25
Title Value:	$10.55	$31.75	$53.50	£5.55	£16.75	£28.25

Note: issued monthly as of issue #12.

SGT. ROCK SPECIAL (2ND SERIES)

DC Comics; 1 Nov 1992; 2 Dec 1994

	$Good	$Fine	$N.Mint	£Good	£Fine	£N.Mint
1 previously unseen Kanigher/Kubert story plus new stories by P. Craig Russell, Matt Wagner, George Pratt, Mike Golden, Tim Truman; Walt Simonson cover						
	$0.70	$2.10	$3.50	£0.40	£1.20	£2.00
2 features art by Russ Heath, Howard Chaykin, Brian Bolland, Eduardo Barreto, Graham Nolan						
	$0.70	$2.10	$3.50	£0.40	£1.20	£2.00
Title Value:	$1.40	$4.20	$7.00	£0.80	£2.40	£4.00

SGT. ROCK SPECTACULAR

DC Comics; nn Spring 1978

(DC Special Series #13)

	$Good	$Fine	$N.Mint	£Good	£Fine	£N.Mint
nn ND 80pgs	$0.65	$2.00	$4.00	£0.30	£1.00	£2.00
Title Value:	$0.65	$2.00	$4.00	£0.30	£1.00	£2.00

SGT. ROCK'S PRIZE BATTLE TALES

National Periodical Publications; 1 Winter 1964

(becomes Sgt. Rock Annual)

	$Good	$Fine	$N.Mint	£Good	£Fine	£N.Mint
1 rare in the U.K. 80pgs, new Kubert cover, Sgt. Rock, Unknown Soldier, Enemy Ace reprints						
	$28.00	$82.50	$225.00	£18.50	£55.00	£150.00
Title Value:	$28.00	$82.50	$225.00	£18.50	£55.00	£150.00

SGT. ROCK'S PRIZE BATTLE TALES (2ND SERIES)

DC Comics,Digest; nn Fall 1979

(DC Special Series #18)

	$Good	$Fine	$N.Mint	£Good	£Fine	£N.Mint
nn ND 100pgs, digest size						
	$0.80	$2.50	$5.00	£0.30	£1.00	£2.00
Title Value:	$0.80	$2.50	$5.00	£0.30	£1.00	£2.00

SHADE SPECIAL

AC Comics,OS; nn 1985

	$Good	$Fine	$N.Mint	£Good	£Fine	£N.Mint
nn ND 52pgs, black and white						
	$0.40	$1.20	$2.00	£0.25	£0.75	£1.25
Title Value:	$0.40	$1.20	$2.00	£0.25	£0.75	£1.25

SHADE, THE CHANGING MAN

DC Comics; 1 Jun/Jul 1977-8 Aug/Sep 1978

	$Good	$Fine	$N.Mint	£Good	£Fine	£N.Mint
1 ND Steve Ditko art						
	$0.80	$2.50	$5.00	£0.50	£1.50	£3.00
2-8 Steve Ditko art						
	$0.50	$1.50	$3.00	£0.30	£1.00	£2.00
Title Value:	$4.30	$13.00	$26.00	£2.60	£8.50	£17.00

SHADE, THE CHANGING MAN (2ND SERIES)

DC Comics; 1 Jul 1990-70 Apr 1996

	$Good	$Fine	$N.Mint	£Good	£Fine	£N.Mint
1 LD in the U.K. 48pgs, scripts by Pete Milligan, painted covers by Brendan McCarthy begin						
	$0.70	$2.10	$3.50	£0.50	£1.50	£2.50
2-3 LD in the U.K.	$0.50	$1.50	$2.50	£0.30	£0.90	£1.50
4-5	$0.40	$1.20	$2.00	£0.25	£0.75	£1.25
6 previews World Without End series						
	$0.40	$1.20	$2.00	£0.25	£0.75	£1.25
7-14	$0.40	$1.20	$2.00	£0.25	£0.75	£1.25
15 Jamie Hewlett cover						
	$0.40	$1.20	$2.00	£0.25	£0.75	£1.25
16-17	$0.40	$1.20	$2.00	£0.25	£0.75	£1.25
18 American Scream concludes						
	$0.40	$1.20	$2.00	£0.25	£0.75	£1.25
19	$0.40	$1.20	$2.00	£0.25	£0.75	£1.25
20 Off The Road story begins, painted cover by Jamie Hewlett						
	$0.40	$1.20	$2.00	£0.25	£0.75	£1.25
21-25 painted cover by Jamie Hewlett						
	$0.40	$1.20	$2.00	£0.25	£0.75	£1.25
26	$0.40	$1.20	$2.00	£0.25	£0.75	£1.25
27-29 Shade the Changing Woman story						
	$0.40	$1.20	$2.00	£0.25	£0.75	£1.25
30 Duncan Eagleson guest art						
	$0.40	$1.20	$2.00	£0.25	£0.75	£1.25
31-32 Ernest & Jim story						
	$0.40	$1.20	$2.00	£0.25	£0.75	£1.25
33 Birth Pains part 1, Shade reborn; 1st issue under "Vertigo" line of comics						
	$0.40	$1.20	$2.00	£0.25	£0.75	£1.25
34-41	$0.40	$1.20	$2.00	£0.25	£0.75	£1.25
42-44 John Constantine appears						
	$0.40	$1.20	$2.00	£0.25	£0.75	£1.25
45-49	$0.40	$1.20	$2.00	£0.25	£0.75	£1.25
50 48pgs, with pin-up gallery featuring Brian Bolland						
	$0.60	$1.80	$3.00	£0.40	£1.20	£2.00

	$Good	$Fine	$N.Mint	£Good	£Fine	£N.Mint
51-53 Sean Philips art	$0.40	$1.20	$2.00	£0.25	£0.75	£1.25
54-60	$0.40	$1.20	$2.00	£0.25	£0.75	£1.25
61-64	$0.45	$1.35	$2.25	£0.30	£0.90	£1.50
65 Richard Case art begins	$0.45	$1.35	$2.25	£0.30	£0.90	£1.50
66-70	$0.45	$1.35	$2.25	£0.30	£0.90	£1.50
Title Value:	$29.20	$87.60	$146.00	£18.50	£55.50	£92.50

Note: New Format

SHADES OF GREY COMICS AND STORIES

Caliber Press/Tapestry; 1 1996-present

	$Good	$Fine	$N.Mint	£Good	£Fine	£N.Mint
1 ND Jimmy Gownley script and art begins; black and white	$0.60	$1.80	$3.00	£0.40	£1.20	£2.00
Title Value:	$0.60	$1.80	$3.00	£0.40	£1.20	£2.00

SHADO: SONG OF THE DRAGON

DC Comics,MS; 1 Mar 1991-4 Jun 1992

	$Good	$Fine	$N.Mint	£Good	£Fine	£N.Mint
1-4 ND 48pgs	$0.80	$2.40	$4.00	£0.50	£1.50	£2.50
Title Value:	$3.20	$9.60	$16.00	£2.00	£6.00	£10.00

Note: Prestige Format

SHADOW & THE MYSTERIOUS THREE, THE

Dark Horse,OS; 1 Sep 1994

	$Good	$Fine	$N.Mint	£Good	£Fine	£N.Mint
1 ND three stories; features Mike Kaluta art	$0.60	$1.80	$3.00	£0.40	£1.20	£2.00
Title Value:	$0.60	$1.80	$3.00	£0.40	£1.20	£2.00

SHADOW AND DOC SAVAGE, THE

Dark Horse,MS; 1 Jul 1995-2 Aug 1995

	$Good	$Fine	$N.Mint	£Good	£Fine	£N.Mint
1-2 ND Steve Vance script, Stan Manoukian and Vince Roucher art	$0.60	$1.80	$3.00	£0.40	£1.20	£2.00
Title Value:	$1.20	$3.60	$6.00	£0.80	£2.40	£4.00

SHADOW CABINET

DC Comics/Milestone; 0 Jan 1994; 1 Jun 1994-17 Oct 1995

	$Good	$Fine	$N.Mint	£Good	£Fine	£N.Mint
0 48pgs, (Jan 1994) spot-varnished cover by Walt Simonson, conclusion of Milestone cross-over story Shadow War (see Static #8)	$0.45	$1.35	$2.25	£0.30	£0.90	£1.50
1 John Byrne cover	$0.40	$1.20	$2.00	£0.25	£0.75	£1.25
2-17	$0.30	$0.90	$1.50	£0.20	£0.60	£1.00
Title Value:	$5.65	$16.95	$28.25	£3.75	£11.25	£18.75

SHADOW EMPIRES: FAITH CONQUERS

Dark Horse,MS; 1 Jul 1994-4 Oct 1994

	$Good	$Fine	$N.Mint	£Good	£Fine	£N.Mint
1-4 ND Chris Moeller script and painted art	$0.60	$1.80	$3.00	£0.40	£1.20	£2.00
Title Value:	$2.40	$7.20	$12.00	£1.60	£4.80	£8.00

SHADOW MOVIE ADAPTATION, THE

Dark Horse,MS Film; 1 Jun 1994-2 Jul 1994

	$Good	$Fine	$N.Mint	£Good	£Fine	£N.Mint
1-2 ND Mike Kaluta's adaptation of the film starring Alec Baldwin	$0.50	$1.50	$2.50	£0.30	£0.90	£1.50
Title Value:	$1.00	$3.00	$5.00	£0.60	£1.80	£3.00

SHADOW OF THE BATMAN

(see Batman: Shadow of the Bat)

SHADOW OF THE TORTURER, THE

Innovation,MS; 1 Jul 1991-6 Dec 1991

	$Good	$Fine	$N.Mint	£Good	£Fine	£N.Mint
1-6 ND colour	$0.40	$1.20	$2.00	£0.25	£0.75	£1.25
Title Value:	$2.40	$7.20	$12.00	£1.50	£4.50	£7.50

SHADOW RIDERS

Marvel UK,MS; 1 Jun 1993-4 Sep 1993

	$Good	$Fine	$N.Mint	£Good	£Fine	£N.Mint
1 Cable and Ghost Rider appear, Ross Dearsley art begins	$0.30	$0.90	$1.50	£0.15	£0.45	£0.75
2 Ghost Rider appears	$0.30	$0.90	$1.50	£0.15	£0.45	£0.75
3-4 Cable appears	$0.30	$0.90	$1.50	£0.15	£0.45	£0.75
Title Value:	$1.20	$3.60	$6.00	£0.60	£1.80	£3.00

SHADOW SLASHER

Pocket Change Comics; 1 1995-9 Apr 1996

	$Good	$Fine	$N.Mint	£Good	£Fine	£N.Mint
1-9 ND 24pgs, Bob Dixon script, Scott Shriver art; black and white	$0.50	$1.50	$2.50	£0.30	£0.90	£1.50
Title Value:	$4.50	$13.50	$22.50	£2.70	£8.10	£13.50

SHADOW STATE

Broadway Comics; 1 Dec 1995-5 Apr 1996

	$Good	$Fine	$N.Mint	£Good	£Fine	£N.Mint
1 ND Jim Shooter script, BloodS.C.R.E.A.M. and Fatale feature	$0.50	$1.50	$2.50	£0.30	£0.90	£1.50
2-5 ND	$0.50	$1.50	$2.50	£0.30	£0.90	£1.50
Title Value:	$2.50	$7.5	$12.50	£1.50	£5.50	£7.50

SHADOW STRIKES! ANNUAL, THE

DC Comics; 1 Dec 1989

	$Good	$Fine	$N.Mint	£Good	£Fine	£N.Mint
1 ND	$0.50	$1.50	$2.50	£0.30	£0.90	£1.50
Title Value:	$0.50	$1.50	$2.50	£0.30	£0.90	£1.50

SHADOW STRIKES!, THE

DC Comics; 1 Sep 1989-31 May 1992

	$Good	$Fine	$N.Mint	£Good	£Fine	£N.Mint
1-4 ND	$0.40	$1.20	$2.00	£0.25	£0.75	£1.25
5-6 ND X-over with Doc Savage #17, #18	$0.40	$1.20	$2.00	£0.25	£0.75	£1.25
7-10 ND	$0.40	$1.20	$2.00	£0.25	£0.75	£1.25
11-17 ND	$0.30	$0.90	$1.50	£0.20	£0.60	£1.00
18-19 ND Mark Badger art	$0.30	$0.90	$1.50	£0.20	£0.60	£1.00
20-29 ND	$0.30	$0.90	$1.50	£0.20	£0.60	£1.00
30 ND The Shadow: Year One part 1, bi-weekly	$0.30	$0.90	$1.50	£0.20	£0.60	£1.00
31 ND The Shadow: Year One part 2, bi-weekly	$0.30	$0.90	$1.50	£0.20	£0.60	£1.00
Title Value:	$10.30	$30.90	$51.50	£6.70	£20.10	£33.50

SHADOW WAR OF HAWKMAN

(see Hawkman, Shadow War of the)

SHADOW, THE

Archie; 1 Aug 1964-8 Sep 1965

	$Good	$Fine	$N.Mint	£Good	£Fine	£N.Mint
1 scarce, distributed in the U.K.	$5.25	$16.00	$37.50	£3.55	£10.50	£25.00
2-7 distributed in the U.K.	$3.55	$10.50	$25.00	£2.10	£6.25	£15.00
8 scarce, distributed in the U.K.	$3.55	$10.50	$25.00	£2.25	£6.75	£16.00
Title Value:	$30.10	$89.50	$212.50	£18.40	£54.75	£131.00

SHADOW, THE

DC Comics; 1 Oct/Nov 1973-12 Apr/May 1975

	$Good	$Fine	$N.Mint	£Good	£Fine	£N.Mint
1 scarce in the U.K. Kaluta art	$5.00	$15.00	$30.00	£2.05	£6.25	£12.50
2 Kaluta art	$2.90	$8.75	$17.50	£1.25	£3.75	£7.50
3 Kaluta/Wrightson art	$2.90	$8.75	$17.50	£1.25	£3.75	£7.50
4 Kaluta art	$2.05	$6.25	$12.50	£0.80	£2.50	£5.00
5	$1.30	$4.00	$8.00	£0.65	£2.00	£4.00
6 Kaluta art	$2.05	$6.25	$12.50	£0.80	£2.50	£5.00
7-10	$1.25	$3.75	$7.50	£0.50	£1.50	£3.00
11 The Shadow vs. The Avenger	$1.25	$3.75	$7.50	£0.50	£1.50	£3.00
12	$1.25	$3.75	$7.50	£0.50	£1.50	£3.00
Title Value:	$23.70	$71.50	$143.00	£9.80	£29.75	£59.50

SHADOW, THE (2ND SERIES)

DC Comics; 1 Aug 1987-19 Jan 1989

(becomes revamped into The Shadow Strikes!)

	$Good	$Fine	$N.Mint	£Good	£Fine	£N.Mint
1-6 ND Sienkiewicz art	$0.30	$0.90	$1.50	£0.20	£0.60	£1.00
7 ND Marshall Rogers art	$0.30	$0.90	$1.50	£0.20	£0.60	£1.00
8-12 ND Kyle Baker art	$0.30	$0.90	$1.50	£0.20	£0.60	£1.00
13 ND Kyle Baker art, Shadow dies	$0.30	$0.90	$1.50	£0.20	£0.60	£1.00
14-19 ND Kyle Baker art	$0.30	$0.90	$1.50	£0.20	£0.60	£1.00
Title Value:	$5.70	$17.10	$28.50	£3.80	£11.40	£19.00

Note: Deluxe Format. Sienkiewicz painted covers on #1-6.

SHADOW, THE (2ND SERIES) ANNUAL

DC Comics; 1 Dec 1987-2 Dec 1988

	$Good	$Fine	$N.Mint	£Good	£Fine	£N.Mint
1-2 ND	$0.50	$1.50	$2.50	£0.30	£0.90	£1.50
Title Value:	$1.00	$3.00	$5.00	£0.60	£1.80	£3.00

SHADOW, THE (LIMITED SERIES)

DC Comics,MS; 1 May 1986-4 Aug 1986

	$Good	$Fine	$N.Mint	£Good	£Fine	£N.Mint
1 ND scarce in the U.K. Chaykin art	$0.50	$1.50	$2.50	£0.30	£0.90	£1.50
2-4 ND Chaykin art	$0.50	$1.50	$2.50	£0.25	£0.75	£1.25
Title Value:	$2.00	$6.00	$10.00	£1.05	£3.15	£5.25

Note: Deluxe Format, Baxter paper. Mature Readers label

	$Good	$Fine	$N.Mint	£Good	£Fine	£N.Mint
Trade paperback reprints #1-4 plus eight new pages				£1.40	£4.20	£7.00

SHADOW, THE PRIVATE FILES OF THE

DC Comics; nn Apr 1989

	$Good	$Fine	$N.Mint	£Good	£Fine	£N.Mint
nn ND Hardcover reprint of issues #1-4 and 6 of 1970s Kaluta series; new story in b/w by Kaluta, new essay by Denny O'Neil	$4.50	$13.50	$22.50	£3.00	£9.00	£15.00
Title Value:	$4.50	$13.50	$22.50	£3.00	£9.00	£15.00

SHADOW: HELL'S HEAT WAVE, THE

Dark Horse,MS; 1 Apr 1995-3 Jun 1995

	$Good	$Fine	$N.Mint	£Good	£Fine	£N.Mint
1-3 ND Mike Kaluta script, Joel Goss and Gary Gianni art	$0.60	$1.80	$3.00	£0.40	£1.20	£2.00
Title Value:	$1.80	$5.40	$9.00	£1.20	£3.60	£6.00

SHADOW: IN THE COILS OF THE LEVIATHAN, THE

Dark Horse,MS; 1 Oct 1993-4 Apr 1994

	$Good	$Fine	$N.Mint	£Good	£Fine	£N.Mint
1-4 ND Mike Kaluta script and Gary Gianni art	$0.60	$1.80	$3.00	£0.40	£1.20	£2.00
Title Value:	$2.40	$7.20	$12.00	£1.60	£4.80	£8.00

The Shadow: In The Coils of the Leviathan (Sep 1993)

	$Good	$Fine	$N.Mint	£Good	£Fine	£N.Mint
Trade paperback reprints mini-series with painted cover by Mike Kaluta				£1.75	£5.25	£8.75

SHADOWALKER

Aircel; 1 Aug 1988-3 1991

	$Good	$Fine	$N.Mint	£Good	£Fine	£N.Mint
1-3 ND	$0.30	$0.90	$1.50	£0.20	£0.60	£1.00
Title Value:	$0.90	$2.70	$4.50	£0.60	£1.80	£3.00

SHADOWALKER CHRONICLES, THE

Ground Zero Graphics,MS; 1 Sep 1991-5 May 1992

	$Good	$Fine	$N.Mint	£Good	£Fine	£N.Mint
1-5 ND	$0.40	$1.20	$2.00	£0.25	£0.75	£1.25
Title Value:	$2.00	$6.00	$10.00	£1.25	£3.75	£6.25

SHADOWBLADE

Hot Comics; 1-4 1987

	$Good	$Fine	$N.Mint	£Good	£Fine	£N.Mint
1-4 ND	$0.25	$0.75	$1.25	£0.15	£0.45	£0.75
Title Value:	$1.00	$3.00	$5.00	£0.60	£1.80	£3.00

SHADOWDRAGON ANNUAL

DC Comics,OS; 1 Oct 1995

	$Good	$Fine	$N.Mint	£Good	£Fine	£N.Mint
1 ND Year One story	$0.80	$2.40	$4.00	£0.50	£1.50	£2.50
Title Value:	$0.80	$2.40	$4.00	£0.50	£1.50	£2.50

SHADOWHAWK

Image,MS; 1 Oct 1992-4 Mar 1993

1 Jim Valentino script/art begins, black cover with silver embossed logo and character figure; 1st of the series

	$Good	$Fine	$N.Mint	£Good	£Fine	£N.Mint
of coupons to send away for Image Comics #0	$1.00	$3.00	$5.00	£0.60	£1.80	£3.00
1 without coupon	$0.60	$1.80	$3.00	£0.40	£1.20	£2.00
2 wraparound cover with silver ink highlights plus poster inked by McFarlane	$0.60	$1.80	$3.00	£0.40	£1.20	£2.00
3 glow-in-dark cover	$0.50	$1.50	$2.50	£0.30	£0.90	£1.50
4 Savage Dragon guest-stars	$0.50	$1.50	$2.50	£0.30	£0.90	£1.50
Title Value:	$3.20	$9.60	$16.00	£2.00	£6.00	£10.00

Note: all Non-Distributed on the news-stands in the U.K.

Shadowhawk: Out of the Shadows (1994)

	$Good	$Fine	$N.Mint	£Good	£Fine	£N.Mint
Trade paperback reprints mini-series plus stories in Youngblood #2 and Image #0				£2.60	£7.80	£13.00

SHADOWHAWK GALLERY

Image,OS; 1 Apr 1994

	$Good	$Fine	$N.Mint	£Good	£Fine	£N.Mint
1 ND pin-ups by various Image artists	$0.40	$1.20	$2.00	£0.25	£0.75	£1.25
Title Value:	$0.40	$1.20	$2.00	£0.25	£0.75	£1.25

SHADOWHAWK II

Image,MS; 1 May 1993-3 Aug 1993

	$Good	$Fine	$N.Mint	£Good	£Fine	£N.Mint
1 all black embossed outer cover which is die-cut to reveal silver foil beneath; Jim Valentino script and art begins	$0.60	$1.80	$3.00	£0.40	£1.20	£2.00
2	$0.50	$1.50	$2.50	£0.30	£0.90	£1.50
2 Gold Edition	$2.00	$6.00	$10.00	£1.00	£3.00	£5.00
3 fold-out poster cover	$0.50	$1.50	$2.50	£0.30	£0.90	£1.50
Title Value:	$3.60	$10.80	$18.00	£2.00	£6.00	£10.00

Note: all Non-Distributed on the news-stands in the U.K.

Shadowhawk: Secret Revealed/Fact File (1994)

	$Good	$Fine	$N.Mint	£Good	£Fine	£N.Mint
Trade paperback flip-book format reprinting mini-series with fact file revealing untold facts				£1.70	£5.10	£8.50

SHADOWHAWK III

Image; 0 Sep 1994; 1 Nov 1993-4 Mar 1994; 12 Aug 1994-18 Mar 1995

	$Good	$Fine	$N.Mint	£Good	£Fine	£N.Mint
0 Image X tie-in	$0.40	$1.20	$2.00	£0.25	£0.75	£1.25
1 Jim Valentino script and art begins; red foil enhanced logo	$0.40	$1.20	$2.00	£0.25	£0.75	£1.25
2-4	$0.40	$1.20	$2.00	£0.25	£0.75	£1.25
12 the 5th issue of the series, numbered as 12. The Monster Within story begins, Chapel guest-stars	$0.40	$1.20	$2.00	£0.25	£0.75	£1.25
13 WildC.A.T.S. guest-star	$0.40	$1.20	$2.00	£0.25	£0.75	£1.25
14 1963 characters guest-star	$0.40	$1.20	$2.00	£0.25	£0.75	£1.25
15	$0.40	$1.20	$2.00	£0.25	£0.75	£1.25
16 Shadowhawk vs. Supreme	$0.40	$1.20	$2.00	£0.25	£0.75	£1.25
17 Spawn guest-stars	$0.40	$1.20	$2.00	£0.25	£0.75	£1.25
18	$0.40	$1.20	$2.00	£0.25	£0.75	£1.25
Title Value:	$4.80	$14.40	$24.00	£3.00	£9.00	£15.00

Note: all Non-Distributed on the news-stands in the U.K.

SHADOWHAWK SPECIAL

Image,OS; 1 Dec 1994

	$Good	$Fine	$N.Mint	£Good	£Fine	£N.Mint
1 ND 48pgs, flip-book format showing the Shadowhawks of both past and future	$0.50	$1.50	$2.50	£0.30	£0.90	£1.50
Title Value:	$0.50	$1.50	$2.50	£0.30	£0.90	£1.50

SHADOWHAWK, IMAGES OF

Image,MS; 1 Sep 1993-3 1994

	$Good	$Fine	$N.Mint	£Good	£Fine	£N.Mint
1 ND Alan Grant and Keith Giffen script, Keith Giffen art begins	$0.40	$1.20	$2.00	£0.25	£0.75	£1.25
2-3 ND	$0.40	$1.20	$2.00	£0.25	£0.75	£1.25
Title Value:	$1.20	$3.60	$6.00	£0.75	£2.25	£3.75

SHADOWHAWK, THE NEW

Image; 1 Jun 1995-7 May 1996 ?

	$Good	$Fine	$N.Mint	£Good	£Fine	£N.Mint
1 ND Kurt Busiek script, James Fry and Andrew Pepoy art	$0.50	$1.50	$2.50	£0.30	£0.90	£1.50
2-7 ND	$0.50	$1.50	$2.50	£0.30	£0.90	£1.50
Title Value:	$3.50	$10.50	$17.50	£2.10	£6.30	£10.50

SHADOWHAWK/VAMPIRELLA

Image/Harris Comics,MS; 1,2 Feb 1995

	$Good	$Fine	$N.Mint	£Good	£Fine	£N.Mint
1 ND 48pgs, Jim Valentino script and art; fully painted cover by Joe Jusko	$1.00	$3.00	$5.00	£0.60	£1.80	£3.00
2 ND 48pgs, Jim Valentino script and art; fully painted cover by Mark Texeira	$1.00	$3.00	$5.00	£0.60	£1.80	£3.00
Title Value:	$2.00	$6.00	$10.00	£1.20	£3.60	£6.00

SHADOWHAWKS OF LEGEND

Image,OS; 1 Nov 1995

	$Good	$Fine	$N.Mint	£Good	£Fine	£N.Mint
1 ND 48pgs, four stories featuring work by Alan Moore, Kurt Busiek, Stan Sakai and Jim Valentino among others	$1.00	$3.00	$5.00	£0.60	£1.80	£3.00
Title Value:	$1.00	$3.00	$5.00	£0.60	£1.80	£3.00

SHADOWHUNT SPECIAL

Image,OS; 1 May 1996

	$Good	$Fine	$N.Mint	£Good	£Fine	£N.Mint
1 ND Jim Valentino script, Jay Morrigan art; continued in Chapel #7	$0.50	$1.50	$2.50	£0.30	£0.90	£1.50
Title Value:	$0.50	$1.50	$2.50	£0.30	£0.90	£1.50

SHADOWLAND

Fantagraphics; 1 Oct 1989-2 1990 ?

	$Good	$Fine	$N.Mint	£Good	£Fine	£N.Mint
1-2 ND adult material	$0.40	$1.20	$2.00	£0.25	£0.75	£1.25

	$Good	$Fine	$N.Mint	£Good	£Fine	£N.Mint
Title Value:	$0.80	$2.40	$4.00	£0.50	£1.50	£2.50

SHADOWMAN

Valiant/Acclaim Comics; 0 Apr 1994; 1 May 1992-43 Oct 1995

	$Good	$Fine	$N.Mint	£Good	£Fine	£N.Mint
0	$0.30	$0.90	$1.50	£0.20	£0.60	£1.00
0 Deluxe Edition, (Apr 1994), origin of Shadowman, Master D'Arque appears; all foil cover	$0.50	$1.50	$2.50	£0.30	£0.90	£1.50
0 Valiant Validated Signature Series, (Jun 1994), signed by at least one creator; 5,300 copies with certificate and Mylar sleeve	$1.50	$4.50	$7.50	£1.00	£3.00	£5.00
1 scarce in the U.K. Steve Engelhart script begins	$1.60	$4.80	$8.00	£1.00	£3.00	£5.00
2	$1.00	$3.00	$5.00	£0.60	£1.80	£3.00
3	$0.80	$2.40	$4.00	£0.40	£1.20	£2.00
4 Unity: Chapter 6, team-up with Solar Man of the Atom	$0.60	$1.80	$3.00	£0.30	£0.90	£1.50
5 Unity: Chapter 14, Eternal Warrior and Magnus Robot Fighter appear, Walt Simonson cover	$0.60	$1.80	$3.00	£0.30	£0.90	£1.50
6-7	$0.60	$1.80	$3.00	£0.30	£0.90	£1.50
8 1st appearance Master D'Arque	$0.80	$2.40	$4.00	£0.50	£1.50	£2.50
9-10	$0.40	$1.20	$2.00	£0.25	£0.75	£1.25
11 new costume	$0.40	$1.20	$2.00	£0.25	£0.75	£1.25
12-15	$0.40	$1.20	$2.00	£0.25	£0.75	£1.25
16 1st appearance of Dr. Mirage	$0.50	$1.50	$2.50	£0.30	£0.90	£1.50
17-18 Archer & Armstrong appear	$0.40	$1.20	$2.00	£0.25	£0.75	£1.25
19 Aerosmith rock group appear	$0.40	$1.20	$2.00	£0.25	£0.75	£1.25
20-22 Master D'Arque appears	$0.40	$1.20	$2.00	£0.25	£0.75	£1.25
23 Doctor Mirage guest-stars; Shadowman vs. Master D'Arque	$0.40	$1.20	$2.00	£0.25	£0.75	£1.25
24	$0.40	$1.20	$2.00	£0.25	£0.75	£1.25
25 with free Valiant Upper Deck card bound-in at centre-fold	$0.40	$1.20	$2.00	£0.25	£0.75	£1.25
26-27	$0.40	$1.20	$2.00	£0.25	£0.75	£1.25
28 Shadowman vs. Master D'Arque	$0.40	$1.20	$2.00	£0.25	£0.75	£1.25
29 Chaos Effect X-over	$0.40	$1.20	$2.00	£0.25	£0.75	£1.25
30-36	$0.40	$1.20	$2.00	£0.25	£0.75	£1.25
37 X-O Manowar appears	$0.40	$1.20	$2.00	£0.25	£0.75	£1.25
38 1st Acclaim Comics issue	$0.40	$1.20	$2.00	£0.25	£0.75	£1.25
39-43	$0.40	$1.20	$2.00	£0.25	£0.75	£1.25
Title Value:	$23.00	$69.00	$115.00	£14.00	£42.00	£70.00

Note: all Non-Distributed on the news-stands in the U.K.

Shadowman (1994)

	$Good	$Fine	$N.Mint	£Good	£Fine	£N.Mint
Trade paperback reprints issues #1-3 & 6				£1.30	£3.90	£6.50

SHADOWMAN (2ND SERIES)

Acclaim Comics; 1 Mar 1997-present

	$Good	$Fine	$N.Mint	£Good	£Fine	£N.Mint
1-4 ND Garth Ennis script, Ashley Wood art begins	$0.50	$1.50	$2.50	£0.30	£0.90	£1.50
Title Value:	$2.00	$6.00	$10.00	£1.20	£3.60	£6.00

SHADOWMAN YEARBOOK

Valiant; 1 Jan 1995

	$Good	$Fine	$N.Mint	£Good	£Fine	£N.Mint
1 ND story set in Edwardian London starring the turn-of-the-century Shadowman	$0.50	$1.50	$2.50	£0.30	£0.90	£1.50
Title Value:	$0.50	$1.50	$2.50	£0.30	£0.90	£1.50

SHADOWMASTERS

Marvel Comics Group,MS; 1 Oct 1989-4 Jan 1990

	$Good	$Fine	$N.Mint	£Good	£Fine	£N.Mint
1 ND 48pgs, squarebound, Russ Heath inks, part Jim Lee covers begin	$0.60	$1.80	$3.00	£0.40	£1.20	£2.00
2-4 ND squarebound	$0.60	$1.80	$3.00	£0.40	£1.20	£2.00
Title Value:	$2.40	$7.20	$12.00	£1.60	£4.80	£8.00

Note: ties in with Punisher and Punisher War Journal

SHADOWS FALL

DC Comics,MS; 1 Nov 1994-6 Apr 1995

	$Good	$Fine	$N.Mint	£Good	£Fine	£N.Mint
1-6	$0.60	$1.80	$3.00	£0.40	£1.20	£2.00
Title Value:	$3.60	$10.80	$18.00	£2.40	£7.20	£12.00

SHADOWS FROM THE GRAVE

Renegade,MS; 1 May 1987-2 Mar 1988

	$Good	$Fine	$N.Mint	£Good	£Fine	£N.Mint
1-2 ND	$0.30	$0.90	$1.50	£0.20	£0.60	£1.00
Title Value:	$0.60	$1.80	$3.00	£0.40	£1.20	£2.00

SHAIANA

Entity Comics,MS; 1 Jul 1995-4 Feb 1996

	$Good	$Fine	$N.Mint	£Good	£Fine	£N.Mint
1 ND chromium cover	$0.80	$2.40	$4.00	£0.50	£1.50	£2.50
2-4 ND	$0.60	$1.80	$3.00	£0.40	£1.20	£2.00
Title Value:	$2.60	$7.80	$13.00	£1.70	£5.10	£8.50

SHAMAN

Continuity; 0 Jan 1994

	$Good	$Fine	$N.Mint	£Good	£Fine	£N.Mint
0 ND Neal Adams script and art; previews Shaman graphic novel	$0.30	$0.90	$1.50	£0.25	£0.75	£1.25
Title Value:	$0.30	$0.90	$1.50	£0.25	£0.75	£1.25

SHAMAN GRAPHIC NOVEL

Continuity,OS; 1 Aug 1994

	$Good	$Fine	$N.Mint	£Good	£Fine	£N.Mint
1 ND 48pgs	$0.60	$1.80	$3.00	£0.40	£1.20	£2.00
Title Value:	$0.60	$1.80	$3.00	£0.40	£1.20	£2.00

SOME INDEPENDENT COMICS MAY NOT HAVE APPEARED ALTHOUGH THEY WERE ADVERTISED AND SOLICITED.

SHAMAN'S TEARS

Image; 0 Nov 1995; 1 May 1993-2 Aug 1993; 3 Jun 1994-12 Mar 1996

	$Good	$Fine	$N.Mint	£Good	£Fine	£N.Mint
0 origin of Shaman	*$0.50*	*$1.50*	*$2.50*	£0.30	£0.90	£1.50
1 Mike Grell script and art begins, red foil embossed cover	*$0.50*	*$1.50*	*$2.50*	£0.30	£0.90	£1.50
2 double gate-fold poster cover	*$0.50*	*$1.50*	*$2.50*	£0.30	£0.90	£1.50
3	*$0.40*	*$1.20*	*$2.00*	£0.25	£0.75	£1.25
4 Jon Sable returns	*$0.40*	*$1.20*	*$2.00*	£0.25	£0.75	£1.25
5-8 Jon Sable appears	*$0.40*	*$1.20*	*$2.00*	£0.25	£0.75	£1.25
9 The Becoming of Broadarrow story	*$0.40*	*$1.20*	*$2.00*	£0.25	£0.75	£1.25
10-11 The Becoming of Broadarrow story	*$0.45*	*$1.35*	*$2.25*	£0.30	£0.90	£1.50
12 ND	*$0.45*	*$1.35*	*$2.25*	£0.30	£0.90	£1.50
Title Value:	*$5.65*	*$16.95*	*$28.25*	£3.55	£10.65	£17.75

Note: all Non-Distributed on the news-stands in the U.K.

Note also: issues #3 and #4 were solicited by Axis but never appeared

SHANDA

Antarctic Press; 1 Jul 1994-present

	$Good	$Fine	$N.Mint	£Good	£Fine	£N.Mint
1-11 ND black and white	*$0.50*	*$1.50*	*$2.50*	£0.30	£0.90	£1.50
12-13 ND black and white	*$0.60*	*$1.80*	*$3.00*	£0.40	£1.20	£2.00
14 ND	*$0.50*	*$1.50*	*$2.50*	£0.30	£0.90	£1.50
Title Value:	*$7.20*	*$21.60*	*$36.00*	£4.40	£13.20	£22.00

SHANNA THE SHE-DEVIL

Marvel Comics Group; 1 Dec 1972-5 Aug 1973

(see Ka-Zar, Marvel Fanfare, Savage Tales)

	$Good	$Fine	$N.Mint	£Good	£Fine	£N.Mint
1 ND Steranko cover	*$1.40*	*$4.25*	*$8.50*	£0.80	£2.50	£5.00
2 ND Steranko cover	*$0.65*	*$2.00*	*$4.00*	£0.40	£1.25	£2.50
3-5 ND	*$0.50*	*$1.50*	*$3.00*	£0.30	£1.00	£2.00
Title Value:	*$3.55*	*$10.75*	*$21.50*	£2.10	£6.75	£13.50

SHATTER

First; 1 Jun 1985-14 Apr 1988

	$Good	$Fine	$N.Mint	£Good	£Fine	£N.Mint
1-14 ND scarce in the U.K. computer generated art	*$0.40*	*$1.20*	*$2.00*	£0.25	£0.75	£1.25
Title Value:	*$5.60*	*$16.80*	*$28.00*	£3.50	£10.50	£17.50

SHATTER POINT

Eternity,MS; 1 Dec 1990-4 Mar 1991

	$Good	$Fine	$N.Mint	£Good	£Fine	£N.Mint
1-4 ND black and white	*$0.40*	*$1.20*	*$2.00*	£0.25	£0.75	£1.25
Title Value:	*$1.60*	*$4.80*	*$8.00*	£1.00	£3.00	£5.00

SHATTER SPECIAL

First; 1 Jun 1985

(see Jon Sable #25-31)

	$Good	$Fine	$N.Mint	£Good	£Fine	£N.Mint
1 ND 1st computer generated comic	*$0.50*	*$1.50*	*$2.50*	£0.30	£0.90	£1.50
1 2nd printing ND	*$0.40*	*$1.20*	*$2.00*	£0.25	£0.75	£1.25
Title Value:	*$0.90*	*$2.70*	*$4.50*	£0.55	£1.65	£2.75

SHATTERED IMAGE

Image,MS; 1 Aug 1996-4 Dec 1996

	$Good	$Fine	$N.Mint	£Good	£Fine	£N.Mint
1 ND Kurt Busiek script, Tony Daniel and Kevin Conrad art begins	*$0.50*	*$1.50*	*$2.50*	£0.30	£0.90	£1.50
2-4 ND	*$0.50*	*$1.50*	*$2.50*	£0.30	£0.90	£1.50
Title Value:	*$2.00*	*$6.00*	*$10.00*	£1.20	£3.60	£6.00

SHATTERSHOT

Marvel Comics Group; 1992

Cross-over storyline that ran throughout the following issues:

X-Men Annual #1, **Uncanny X-Men Annual 16**, **X-Factor Annual #7**, **X-Force Annual #4**.

SHAZAM!

DC Comics; 1 Feb 1973-35 May/Jun 1978

(see All-New Collector's Edition, Limited Collector's Edition, Shazam: The New Beginning, World's Finest)

	$Good	$Fine	$N.Mint	£Good	£Fine	£N.Mint
1 origin Captain Marvel retold	*$1.65*	*$5.00*	*$10.00*	£0.65	£2.00	£4.00
2 photo cover	*$0.80*	*$2.50*	*$5.00*	£0.40	£1.25	£2.50
3	*$0.80*	*$2.50*	*$5.00*	£0.40	£1.25	£2.50
4-5	*$0.65*	*$2.00*	*$4.00*	£0.30	£1.00	£2.00
6 photo cover	*$0.55*	*$1.75*	*$3.50*	£0.25	£0.75	£1.50
7	*$0.55*	*$1.75*	*$3.50*	£0.25	£0.75	£1.50
8 100pgs	*$0.65*	*$2.00*	*$4.00*	£0.40	£1.25	£2.50
9-11	*$0.55*	*$1.75*	*$3.50*	£0.25	£0.75	£1.50
12-14 100pgs	*$0.65*	*$2.00*	*$4.00*	£0.40	£1.25	£2.50
15 100pgs, Lex Luthor appears, Superman cameo	*$0.65*	*$2.00*	*$4.00*	£0.40	£1.25	£2.50
16-17 100pgs	*$0.65*	*$2.00*	*$4.00*	£0.40	£1.25	£2.50
18-19	*$0.55*	*$1.75*	*$3.50*	£0.25	£0.75	£1.50
20 ND	*$0.55*	*$1.75*	*$3.50*	£0.30	£1.00	£2.00
21	*$0.55*	*$1.75*	*$3.50*	£0.25	£0.75	£1.50
22 scarce in the U.K.	*$0.55*	*$1.75*	*$3.50*	£0.30	£1.00	£2.00
23	*$0.55*	*$1.75*	*$3.50*	£0.25	£0.75	£1.50
24 ND	*$0.55*	*$1.75*	*$3.50*	£0.30	£1.00	£2.00
25 1st appearance Isis	*$0.55*	*$1.75*	*$3.50*	£0.25	£0.75	£1.50
26	*$0.55*	*$1.75*	*$3.50*	£0.25	£0.75	£1.50
27-28 scarce in the U.K.	*$0.55*	*$1.75*	*$3.50*	£0.30	£1.00	£2.00
29	*$0.55*	*$1.75*	*$3.50*	£0.25	£0.75	£1.50
30-31 scarce in the U.K.	*$0.55*	*$1.75*	*$3.50*	£0.30	£1.00	£2.00
32-34	*$0.55*	*$1.75*	*$3.50*	£0.25	£0.75	£1.50
35 story continued in World's Finest Comics #253; Don Newton art	*$0.55*	*$1.75*	*$3.50*	£0.25	£0.75	£1.50
Title Value:	*$21.75*	*$68.25*	*$136.50*	£10.95	£34.25	£68.50

Note: issues 8, 21-24 are all reprint.

ARTISTS

New C.C.Beck art in 1-7, 9, 10.

FEATURES

Captain Marvel in 1-7, 9-13, 15, 16, 18, 19, 26-33. Cap. Marvel/Captain Marvel Jr. in 34. Cap.Marvel Jr. in 9, 12, 15, 18. Isis in 25. Mary Marvel in 10, 13, 16, 19. Marvel Family in 11, 14, 17, 20, 35.

REPRINT FEATURES

Captain Marvel in 1, 2, 4, 8, 12-17, 21, 22, 24, 25. Capt. Marvel Jr. in 5, 8, 13, 14, 16, 17, 21, 24. Marvel Family in 3, 6-8, 12, 13, 15, 16, 23. Mary Marvel in 8, 12, 14, 17, 22.

SHAZAM! ARCHIVES, THE

DC Comics; nn Nov 1992

	$Good	$Fine	$N.Mint	£Good	£Fine	£N.Mint
nn ND 208pgs, Hardcover; reprints the very rare Flash Comics ash-can issue plus Whiz Comics #2-15 with covers and ads	*$8.00*	*$24.00*	*$40.00*	£5.50	£16.50	£27.50
Title Value:	*$8.00*	*$24.00*	*$40.00*	£5.50	£16.50	£27.50

SHAZAM, THE POWER OF

DC Comics; nn Mar 1994

	$Good	$Fine	$N.Mint	£Good	£Fine	£N.Mint
nn ND 96pgs, Hardcover; Jerry Ordway script, art and painted cover	*$4.50*	*$13.50*	*$22.50*	£3.00	£9.00	£15.00
Title Value:	*$4.50*	*$13.50*	*$22.50*	£3.00	£9.00	£15.00

The Power of Shazam Softcover Graphic Novel (Feb 1995)

	$Good	$Fine	$N.Mint	£Good	£Fine	£N.Mint
96pgs, Jerry Ordway cover and art				£1.30	£3.90	£6.50

Shadow, The (Archie) #5

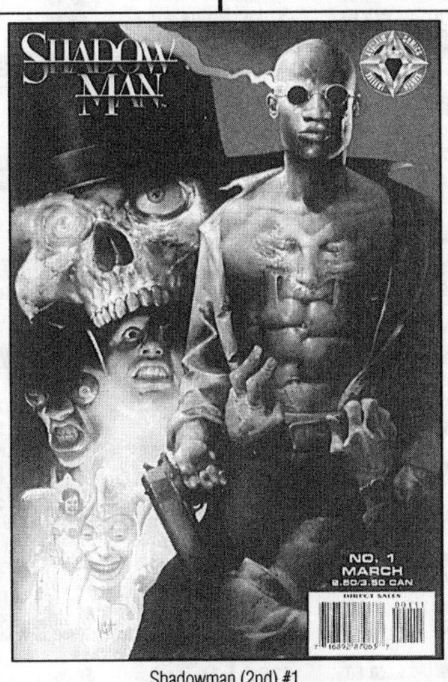

Shadowman (2nd) #1

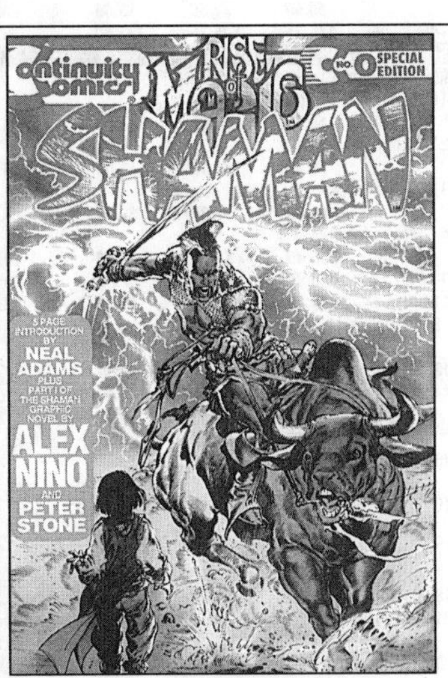

Shaman #0

SHAZAM, THE POWER OF (2ND SERIES)

DC Comics; 1 Mar 1995-present

Issue	$Good	$Fine	$N.Mint	£Good	£Fine	£N.Mint
1 Jerry Ordway script begins, Jerry Ordway painted covers begin	*$0.40*	*$1.20*	*$2.00*	£0.30	£0.90	£1.50
2-13	*$0.35*	*$1.05*	*$1.75*	£0.25	£0.75	£1.25
14 Gil Kane art	*$0.35*	*$1.05*	*$1.75*	£0.25	£0.75	£1.25
15-18	*$0.35*	*$1.05*	*$1.75*	£0.25	£0.75	£1.25
19 Gil Kane and Mike Manley art	*$0.35*	*$1.05*	*$1.75*	£0.25	£0.75	£1.25
20 Final Night tie-in, Superman guest-stars	*$0.35*	*$1.05*	*$1.75*	£0.25	£0.75	£1.25
21 ND Plastic Man appears	*$0.35*	*$1.05*	*$1.75*	£0.25	£0.75	£1.25
22 ND Batman guest-stars	*$0.35*	*$1.05*	*$1.75*	£0.25	£0.75	£1.25
23-24 ND	*$0.35*	*$1.05*	*$1.75*	£0.25	£0.75	£1.25
Title Value:	*$8.45*	*$25.35*	*$42.25*	£6.05	£18.15	£30.25

SHAZAM, THE POWER OF (2ND SERIES) ANNUAL

DC Comics; 1 Oct 1996-present

Issue	$Good	$Fine	$N.Mint	£Good	£Fine	£N.Mint
1 ND 48pgs, Legends of the Dead Earth story; Jerry Ordway script and cover art, Mike Manley art	*$0.60*	*$1.80*	*$3.00*	£0.40	£1.20	£2.00
Title Value:	*$0.60*	*$1.80*	*$3.00*	£0.40	£1.20	£2.00

SHAZAM: THE NEW BEGINNING

DC Comics,MS; 1 Apr 1987-4 Jul 1987

Issue	$Good	$Fine	$N.Mint	£Good	£Fine	£N.Mint
1-4 Legends tie-in	*$0.25*	*$0.75*	*$1.25*	£0.15	£0.45	£0.75
Title Value:	*$1.00*	*$3.00*	*$5.00*	£0.60	£1.80	£3.00

SHE-CAT

AC Comics; 1 Mar 1990-4 1990; 5 Sep 1994

Issue	$Good	$Fine	$N.Mint	£Good	£Fine	£N.Mint
1 ND black and white begins	*$0.40*	*$1.20*	*$2.00*	£0.25	£0.75	£1.25
2 ND	*$0.40*	*$1.20*	*$2.00*	£0.25	£0.75	£1.25
3 ND Colt of Femforce appears	*$0.40*	*$1.20*	*$2.00*	£0.25	£0.75	£1.25
4 ND	*$0.40*	*$1.20*	*$2.00*	£0.25	£0.75	£1.25
5 ND very scarce in the U.K. as most copies were mis-cut at the printing stage and destroyed by the publisher	*$0.40*	*$1.20*	*$2.00*	£0.30	£0.90	£1.50
5 reprinted issue, ND 48pgs, (Mar 1995) with new cover by Brad Gorby and an 8pg origin recap; 1,500 copies only	*$0.50*	*$1.50*	*$2.50*	£0.30	£0.90	£1.50
Title Value:	*$2.50*	*$7.50*	*$12.50*	£1.60	£4.80	£8.00
She-Cat Chronicles (Jul 1995) Trade paperback reprints issues #1-4, signed by Bill Marimon; 400 copies				£1.60	£4.80	£8.00

SHE-HULK, THE SAVAGE

Marvel Comics Group; 1 Feb 1980-25 Feb 1982

Issue	$Good	$Fine	$N.Mint	£Good	£Fine	£N.Mint
1 ND origin and 1st appearance, written by Stan Lee	*$1.25*	*$3.75*	*$7.50*	£0.40	£1.25	£2.50
2 ND	*$1.00*	*$3.00*	*$5.00*	£0.40	£1.20	£2.00
3-5 ND	*$0.80*	*$2.40*	*$4.00*	£0.30	£0.90	£1.50
6 ND Iron Man appears	*$0.60*	*$1.80*	*$3.00*	£0.30	£0.90	£1.50
7 ND	*$0.60*	*$1.80*	*$3.00*	£0.30	£0.90	£1.50
8 ND Man-Thing appears, Golden cover	*$0.60*	*$1.80*	*$3.00*	£0.30	£0.90	£1.50
9 Morbius appears	*$0.60*	*$1.80*	*$3.00*	£0.25	£0.75	£1.25
10	*$0.60*	*$1.80*	*$3.00*	£0.25	£0.75	£1.25
11-12 ND Morbius appears	*$0.50*	*$1.50*	*$2.50*	£0.20	£0.60	£1.00
13-14 ND Man-Wolf and Hell Cat appear	*$0.50*	*$1.50*	*$2.50*	£0.20	£0.60	£1.00
15-24 ND	*$0.50*	*$1.50*	*$2.50*	£0.20	£0.60	£1.00
25 ND scarce in the U.K. 52pgs	*$0.60*	*$1.80*	*$3.00*	£0.30	£0.90	£1.50
Title Value:	*$15.25*	*$45.75*	*$77.50*	£6.20	£18.65	£31.50

SHE-HULK, THE SENSATIONAL

Marvel Comics Group; 1 May 1989-60 Feb 1994

Issue	$Good	$Fine	$N.Mint	£Good	£Fine	£N.Mint
1 ND John Byrne story/art	*$0.50*	*$1.50*	*$2.50*	£0.30	£0.90	£1.50
2 ND John Byrne story/art	*$0.40*	*$1.20*	*$2.00*	£0.25	£0.75	£1.25
3 ND Spiderman appears, John Byrne story/art	*$0.40*	*$1.20*	*$2.00*	£0.25	£0.75	£1.25
4-8 ND John Byrne story/art	*$0.40*	*$1.20*	*$2.00*	£0.25	£0.75	£1.25
9-10 ND	*$0.40*	*$1.20*	*$2.00*	£0.25	£0.75	£1.25
11 ND	*$0.30*	*$0.90*	*$1.50*	£0.20	£0.60	£1.00
12 ND Peter David script, Leialoha/Trina Robbins art	*$0.30*	*$0.90*	*$1.50*	£0.20	£0.60	£1.00
13 ND	*$0.30*	*$0.90*	*$1.50*	£0.20	£0.60	£1.00
14 ND The Cosmic Squish Principle part 1, Bolland cover announced but did not appear: issued separately (with re-ordered issues of comic) explaining the delay; Howard the Duck appears	*$0.30*	*$0.90*	*$1.50*	£0.20	£0.60	£1.00
15 ND part 2, Bolland cover, Howard the Duck	*$0.30*	*$0.90*	*$1.50*	£0.20	£0.60	£1.00
16 ND part 3, Howard the Duck appears	*$0.30*	*$0.90*	*$1.50*	£0.20	£0.60	£1.00
17 ND part 4, Howard the Duck appears	*$0.30*	*$0.90*	*$1.50*	£0.20	£0.60	£1.00
18-20 ND	*$0.30*	*$0.90*	*$1.50*	£0.20	£0.60	£1.00
21-22 ND Return of the Blonde Phantom, featuring 1940s Timely super-heroes	*$0.30*	*$0.90*	*$1.50*	£0.20	£0.60	£1.00
23 ND Return of the Blonde Phantom, featuring 1940s Timely super-heroes	*$0.30*	*$0.90*	*$1.50*	£0.20	£0.60	£1.00
24 ND Death's Head appears	*$0.30*	*$0.90*	*$1.50*	£0.20	£0.60	£1.00
25 ND Hercules appears	*$0.30*	*$0.90*	*$1.50*	£0.20	£0.60	£1.00
26-28 ND	*$0.30*	*$0.90*	*$1.50*	£0.20	£0.60	£1.00
29 ND Wolverine, Hulk, Spiderman appear	*$0.30*	*$0.90*	*$1.50*	£0.20	£0.60	£1.00
30 ND a host of Marvel character cameos	*$0.30*	*$0.90*	*$1.50*	£0.20	£0.60	£1.00
31 ND John Byrne script/pencils begin (again), John Byrne on cover	*$0.30*	*$0.90*	*$1.50*	£0.20	£0.60	£1.00
32-35 ND	*$0.30*	*$0.90*	*$1.50*	£0.20	£0.60	£1.00
36 ND $1.75 cover begins	*$0.30*	*$0.90*	*$1.50*	£0.20	£0.60	£1.00
37-49 ND	*$0.30*	*$0.90*	*$1.50*	£0.20	£0.60	£1.00
50 ND 48pgs, anniversary issue, green foil-stamped cover, last John Byrne script/art; features work by Gibbons, Simonson, Chaykin, Austin, Hughes	*$0.50*	*$1.50*	*$2.50*	£0.30	£0.90	£1.50
51 ND Scott Benshaw and Tom Morgan guest creative team	*$0.30*	*$0.90*	*$1.50*	£0.20	£0.60	£1.00
52 ND Mr. Fantastic and The Thing appear, cover by Adam Hughes	*$0.30*	*$0.90*	*$1.50*	£0.20	£0.60	£1.00
53 ND cover by Adam Hughes	*$0.30*	*$0.90*	*$1.50*	£0.20	£0.60	£1.00
54 ND cover by Michael Golden	*$0.30*	*$0.90*	*$1.50*	£0.20	£0.60	£1.00
55-60 ND	*$0.30*	*$0.90*	*$1.50*	£0.20	£0.60	£1.00
Title Value:	*$19.30*	*$57.90*	*$96.50*	£12.65	£37.95	£63.25
She-Hulk Trade paperback (May 1992) reprints issues #1-8, new cover by John Byrne				£1.40	£4.20	£7.00

SHE-HULK: CEREMONY

Marvel Comics Group,MS; 1 Apr 1990-2 May 1990

Issue	$Good	$Fine	$N.Mint	£Good	£Fine	£N.Mint
1-2 ND 48pgs, She-Hulk proposes to Wyatt Wingfoot	*$0.80*	*$2.40*	*$4.00*	£0.50	£1.50	£2.50
Title Value:	*$1.60*	*$4.80*	*$8.00*	£1.00	£3.00	£5.00

Note: bi-weekly frequency

SHEENA

IW Comics;9 1963

Issue	$Good	$Fine	$N.Mint	£Good	£Fine	£N.Mint
9 scarce distributed in the U.K. 1950s reprints	*$5.25*	*$16.00*	*$37.50*	£3.90	£11.50	£27.50
Title Value:	*$5.25*	*$16.00*	*$37.50*	£3.90	£11.50	£27.50

SHEENA 3-D SPECIAL

Blackthorne;(3-D Series #1) 1 May 1985

Issue	$Good	$Fine	$N.Mint	£Good	£Fine	£N.Mint
1 ND all reprint, Dave Stevens cover; with 3-D glasses (25% less without glasses)	*$0.50*	*$1.50*	*$2.50*	£0.30	£0.90	£1.50
1 non 3-D issue ND scarce in the U.K.	*$0.60*	*$1.80*	*$3.00*	£0.40	£1.20	£2.00
Title Value:	*$1.10*	*$3.30*	*$5.50*	£0.70	£2.10	£3.50

SHEENA, QUEEN OF THE JUNGLE

Marvel Comics Group,MS Film; 1 Dec 1984-2 Feb 1985

Issue	$Good	$Fine	$N.Mint	£Good	£Fine	£N.Mint
1-2 ND adapts film	*$0.25*	*$0.75*	*$1.25*	£0.15	£0.45	£0.75
Title Value:	*$0.50*	*$1.50*	*$2.50*	£0.30	£0.90	£1.50

SHERLOCK HOLMES

DC Comics; 1 Sep/Oct 1975

Issue	$Good	$Fine	$N.Mint	£Good	£Fine	£N.Mint
1 ND Walt Simonson cover	*$0.40*	*$1.25*	*$2.50*	£0.25	£0.75	£1.50
Title Value:	*$0.40*	*$1.25*	*$2.50*	£0.25	£0.75	£1.50

SHERLOCK HOLMES

Eternity; 1 Jun 1988-22 1990

(see Cases of...)

Issue	$Good	$Fine	$N.Mint	£Good	£Fine	£N.Mint
1-22 ND newspaper strip reprints	*$0.40*	*$1.20*	*$2.00*	£0.25	£0.75	£1.25
Title Value:	*$8.80*	*$26.40*	*$44.00*	£5.50	£16.50	£27.50
Book I, reprints				£0.40	£1.20	£2.00

SHERLOCK HOLMES IN THE CASE OF THE MISSING MARTIAN

Eternity,MS; 1 Sep 1990-4 Dec 1990

Issue	$Good	$Fine	$N.Mint	£Good	£Fine	£N.Mint
1-4 ND	*$0.40*	*$1.20*	*$2.00*	£0.25	£0.75	£1.25
Title Value:	*$1.60*	*$4.80*	*$8.00*	£1.00	£3.00	£5.00

Note: bi-weekly

SHERLOCK HOLMES IN THE CURIOUS CASE OF THE VANISHING VILLAIN

Tundra,OS; 1 Aug 1992

Issue	$Good	$Fine	$N.Mint	£Good	£Fine	£N.Mint
1 ND	*$0.60*	*$1.80*	*$3.00*	£0.40	£1.20	£2.00
Title Value:	*$0.60*	*$1.80*	*$3.00*	£0.40	£1.20	£2.00

SHERLOCK HOLMES OF THE '30S

Eternity,MS; 1 Mar 1990-7 Sep 1990

Issue	$Good	$Fine	$N.Mint	£Good	£Fine	£N.Mint
1-7 ND	*$0.40*	*$1.20*	*$2.00*	£0.25	£0.75	£1.25
Title Value:	*$2.80*	*$8.40*	*$14.00*	£1.75	£5.25	£8.75

SHERLOCK HOLMES, NEW ADVENTURES OF

Dell; 1169, 1245-1961-1962

Issue	$Good	$Fine	$N.Mint	£Good	£Fine	£N.Mint
1169 scarce though distributed in the U.K. (Four Colour #1169)	*$20.50*	*$60.00*	*$145.00*	£13.50	£41.00	£95.00
1245 scarce though distributed in the U.K. (Four Colour #1245)	*$20.50*	*$60.00*	*$145.00*	£13.50	£41.00	£95.00
Title Value:	*$41.00*	*$120.00*	*$290.00*	£27.00	£82.00	£190.00

SHERLOCK HOLMES: A CASE OF BLIND FEAR

Eternity,MS; 1 Feb 1989-4 Aug 1989

Issue	$Good	$Fine	$N.Mint	£Good	£Fine	£N.Mint
1-4 ND b&w	*$0.40*	*$1.20*	*$2.00*	£0.25	£0.75	£1.25
Title Value:	*$1.60*	*$4.80*	*$8.00*	£1.00	£3.00	£5.00
Trade Paperback (Jul 1990), reprints				£1.10	£3.30	£5.50

SHERLOCK HOLMES: A STUDY IN SCARLET

Innovation; nn 1990

Issue	$Good	$Fine	$N.Mint	£Good	£Fine	£N.Mint
1 ND reprints	*$1.20*	*$3.60*	*$6.00*	£0.80	£2.40	£4.00

	$Good	$Fine	$N.Mint	£Good	£Fine	£N.Mint
Title Value:	$1.20	$3.60	$6.00	£0.80	£2.40	£4.00

SHERLOCK HOLMES: ADVENTURES OF THE OPERA GHOST

Caliber Press,MS; 1,2 Oct 1994	$Good	$Fine	$N.Mint	£Good	£Fine	£N.Mint
1-2 ND Steven Jones script, Aldin Baroza art; black and white	$0.50	$1.50	$2.50	£0.30	£0.90	£1.50
Title Value:	$1.00	$3.00	$5.00	£0.60	£1.80	£3.00

SHERLOCK HOLMES: CHRONICLES OF CRIME & MYSTERY

Northstar; 1 Mar 1992-3 1992	$Good	$Fine	$N.Mint	£Good	£Fine	£N.Mint
1 ND The Speckled Band	$0.40	$1.20	$2.00	£0.25	£0.75	£1.25
1 2nd printing, ND (May 1993)	$0.40	$1.20	$2.00	£0.25	£0.75	£1.25
2-3 ND	$0.40	$1.20	$2.00	£0.25	£0.75	£1.25
Title Value:	$1.60	$4.80	$8.00	£1.00	£3.00	£5.00

SHERLOCK HOLMES: HOUND OF THE BASKERVILLES GRAPHIC NOVEL

Innovation,OS; nn Apr 1993	$Good	$Fine	$N.Mint	£Good	£Fine	£N.Mint
nn ND 68pgs, squarebound, painted cover by Jim Steranko	$1.20	$3.60	$6.00	£0.80	£2.40	£4.00
Title Value:	$1.20	$3.60	$6.00	£0.80	£2.40	£4.00

SHERLOCK HOLMES: RETURN OF THE DEVIL

Adventure,MS; 1 Nov 1992-2 Dec 1992	$Good	$Fine	$N.Mint	£Good	£Fine	£N.Mint
1-2 ND	$0.40	$1.20	$2.00	£0.25	£0.75	£1.25
Title Value:	$0.80	$2.40	$4.00	£0.50	£1.50	£2.50

SHERLOCK HOLMES: TALES OF MYSTERY & SUSPENSE

Northstar; 1 Aug 1992-4 1993; 5 Oct 1994	$Good	$Fine	$N.Mint	£Good	£Fine	£N.Mint
1-3 ND black and white	$0.40	$1.20	$2.00	£0.25	£0.75	£1.25
3 with poster, ND black and white	$0.50	$1.50	$2.50	£0.30	£0.90	£1.50
4 ND black and white	$0.40	$1.20	$2.00	£0.25	£0.75	£1.25
5 ND black and white; cover by Jon J. Muth	$0.40	$1.20	$2.00	£0.25	£0.75	£1.25
Title Value:	$2.50	$7.50	$12.50	£1.55	£4.65	£7.75

SHERLOCK HOLMES: THE MUSGRAVE RITUAL

Caliber/Tome Press; 1 1992	$Good	$Fine	$N.Mint	£Good	£Fine	£N.Mint
1 ND black and white	$0.40	$1.20	$2.00	£0.25	£0.75	£1.25
Title Value:	$0.40	$1.20	$2.00	£0.25	£0.75	£1.25

SHERLOCK HOLMES: THE RED-HEADED LEAGUE AND OTHER STORIES

Eternity; nn Aug 1990	$Good	$Fine	$N.Mint	£Good	£Fine	£N.Mint
nn ND 6 stories reprinted from 1950s U.S. newspaper strips	$2.50	$7.50	$12.50	£1.50	£4.50	£7.50
Title Value:	$2.50	$7.50	$12.50	£1.50	£4.50	£7.50

SHERLOCK JNR.

Eternity,MS; 1 Oct 1990-3 Nov 1990	$Good	$Fine	$N.Mint	£Good	£Fine	£N.Mint
1-3 ND reprints	$0.40	$1.20	$2.00	£0.25	£0.75	£1.25
Title Value:	$1.20	$3.60	$6.00	£0.75	£2.25	£3.75

Note: first two issues bi-weekly

SHI VS. TOMOE

Crusade Comics,OS; 1 Aug 1996	$Good	$Fine	$N.Mint	£Good	£Fine	£N.Mint
1 ND 48pgs, Bill Tucci script, Peter Guttierrez art; wraparound chromium cover; links between Shi #8 and #9	$0.80	$2.40	$4.00	£0.50	£1.50	£2.50
Title Value:	$0.80	$2.40	$4.00	£0.50	£1.50	£2.50

SHI/CYBLADE SPECIAL - THE BATTLE FOR INDEPENDENTS

Crusade Comics,OS; nn Aug 1995	$Good	$Fine	$N.Mint	£Good	£Fine	£N.Mint
nn ND co-written and co-pencilled by Marc Silvestri and William Tucci; cover by William Tucci	$1.00	$3.00	$5.00	£0.40	£1.20	£2.00
nn Variant Cover Edition ND Marc Silvestri cover art, Shi on left of cover back to back with Cyblade	$1.50	$4.50	$7.50	£0.80	£2.40	£4.00
Title Value:	$2.50	$7.50	$12.50	£1.20	£3.60	£6.00

SHI: KAIDAN

Crusade Comics,OS; 1 Oct 1996	$Good	$Fine	$N.Mint	£Good	£Fine	£N.Mint
1 ND Peter Gutierrez script; black and white	$0.60	$1.80	$3.00	£0.40	£1.20	£2.00
Title Value:	$0.60	$1.80	$3.00	£0.40	£1.20	£2.00

SHI: SENRYAKU

Crusade Comics,MS; 1 Aug 1995-3 Nov 1995	$Good	$Fine	$N.Mint	£Good	£Fine	£N.Mint
1 ND William Tucci cover art, backgrounds and philosophies on Shi	$0.80	$2.40	$4.00	£0.50	£1.50	£2.50
1 Variant Cover Edition, ND cover as regular but with no Crusade logo	$1.60	$4.80	$8.00	£0.90	£2.70	£4.50
2 ND William Tucci cover art, backgrounds and philosophies on Shi	$0.60	$1.80	$3.00	£0.40	£1.20	£2.00
3 ND Joe Jusko cover art, backgrounds and philosophies on Shi	$0.60	$1.80	$3.00	£0.40	£1.20	£2.00
Title Value:	$3.60	$10.80	$18.00	£2.20	£6.60	£11.00

Shi: Senryaku Hardcover (Dec 1995)

				£Good	£Fine	£N.Mint
ND collects mini-series, limited to 5,000 copies				£3.30	£9.90	£16.50

Shi: Senryaku (Mar 1996)

				£Good	£Fine	£N.Mint
Trade paperback ND softcover version of the above				£1.80	£5.40	£9.00

SHI: THE WAY OF THE WARRIOR

Crusade Comics; 1 Mar 1994-present	$Good	$Fine	$N.Mint	£Good	£Fine	£N.Mint
1 ND William Tucci script and art; colour	$8.50	$26.00	$42.50	£5.00	£15.00	£25.00
1 Ashcan Editon, ND 24pgs, signed bt Bill Tucci, 500 copies only; black and white	$8.00	$24.00	$40.00	£6.00	£18.00	£30.00
1 Commemorative Edition, ND - avaialble at the 1994 San Diego Comic convention	$10.00	$30.00	$50.00	£6.00	£18.00	£30.00
1 Fan Appreciation Edition, ND (Apr 1995) - reprints issue #1 with new cover by William Tucci and poster at centrefold	$1.20	$3.60	$6.00	£0.50	£1.50	£2.50
1 Fan Appreciation Edition - Gold Variant, ND as regular issue but with gold Crusade Comics logo on cover	$5.00	$15.00	$25.00	£3.00	£9.00	£15.00
1 Fan Appreciation Edition - Variant Cover, ND as regular issue but with no Crusade Comics logo on cover	$2.00	$6.00	$10.00	£1.00	£3.00	£5.00
2 ND	$5.00	$15.00	$25.00	£3.00	£9.00	£15.00
2 Ashcan Edition, ND contains never seen before Shi prototype	$3.00	$9.00	$15.00	£2.00	£6.00	£10.00
2 Commemorative Edition, ND available at the San Diego comic convention, limited to 3,000 copies signed by William Tucci; black and white	$8.00	$24.00	$40.00	£4.00	£12.00	£20.00
2 Fan Appreciation Edition, ND reprints issue #2 with new cover by William Tucci	$1.00	$3.00	$5.00	£0.40	£1.20	£2.00
3 ND	$3.00	$9.00	$15.00	£1.20	£3.60	£6.00
4 ND 1st appearance Tomoe	$1.20	$3.60	$6.00	£0.80	£2.40	£4.00
4 Ashcan Edition, ND white cover composed of rice paper, signed by William Tucci	$8.00	$24.00	$40.00	£5.00	£15.00	£25.00
4 Wizard Ace Edition, ND acetate outer cover	$3.00	$9.00	$15.00	£1.50	£4.50	£7.50
5 ND 1st appearance Tomoe in costume	$1.00	$3.00	$5.00	£0.60	£1.80	£3.00
5 Black Gold Version ND	$9.00	$27.00	$45.00	£4.50	£13.50	£22.50
5 Variant Cover Edition, ND Marc Silvestri cover art, black cover	$3.20	$9.50	$16.00	£2.00	£6.00	£10.00
6 ND Tomoe #1 cover	$1.40	$4.20	$7.00	£1.00	£3.00	£5.00
7 ND part 1 of two part story, X-over in Funnytime Features #7	$0.80	$2.40	$4.00	£0.40	£1.20	£2.00
7 Chromium Edition, ND limited to 5,000 copies	$4.00	$12.00	$20.00	£3.00	£9.00	£15.00
8 ND new costume	$0.60	$1.80	$3.00	£0.40	£1.20	£2.00
9-11 ND	$0.60	$1.80	$3.00	£0.40	£1.20	£2.00
Title Value:	$88.70	$266.50	$443.50	£52.50	£157.50	£262.50

Shi - The Way of the Warrior (Dec 1994)

				£Good	£Fine	£N.Mint
Trade paperback ND reprints issues #1-4 plus unpublished artwork				£1.70	£5.10	£8.50

Shi - The Way of the Warrior (Jan 1996)

				£Good	£Fine	£N.Mint
Trade paperback Revised Edition ND reprints mini-series with unpublished artwork and new Julie Bell cover				£2.00	£6.00	£10.00

SHIELD

Red Circle (Archie); 1 Jun 1983-7 Jul 1984

(see Original Shield)

	$Good	$Fine	$N.Mint	£Good	£Fine	£N.Mint
1 ND titled Lancelot Strong, the...	$0.30	$0.90	$1.50	£0.20	£0.60	£1.00
2 ND Rudy Nebres art	$0.30	$0.90	$1.50	£0.20	£0.60	£1.00
3 ND titled Shield - Steel Sterling, Alex Nino art	$0.30	$0.90	$1.50	£0.20	£0.60	£1.00
4 ND title becomes Steel Sterling (Jan 1984), Kanigher script and Barreto art	$0.30	$0.90	$1.50	£0.20	£0.60	£1.00
5 ND	$0.30	$0.90	$1.50	£0.20	£0.60	£1.00
6 ND Infantino/Barreto art	$0.30	$0.90	$1.50	£0.20	£0.60	£1.00
7 ND	$0.30	$0.90	$1.50	£0.20	£0.60	£1.00
Title Value:	$2.10	$6.30	$10.50	£1.40	£4.20	£7.00

SHIELD ANNUAL, LEGEND OF THE

DC Comics/Impact; 1 May 1992	$Good	$Fine	$N.Mint	£Good	£Fine	£N.Mint
1 Neal Adams cover, leads into Crusaders #1 (see other Impact annuals), includes trading cards	$0.25	$0.75	$1.25	£0.15	£0.45	£0.75
Title Value:	$0.25	$0.75	$1.25	£0.15	£0.45	£0.75

SHIELD, LEGEND OF THE

DC Comics/Impact; 1 Jul 1991-16 Oct 1992

(see The Comet/Fly/Jaguar/Web)

	$Good	$Fine	$N.Mint	£Good	£Fine	£N.Mint
1-10	$0.15	$0.45	$0.75	£0.10	£0.35	£0.60
11 previews Crusaders #1 (see Jaguar #9), includes trading cards	$0.15	$0.45	$0.75	£0.10	£0.35	£0.60
12-16	$0.15	$0.45	$0.75	£0.10	£0.35	£0.60
Title Value:	$2.40	$7.20	$12.00	£1.60	£5.60	£9.60

Note: Archie character acquired by DC though events takes place outside DC Universe continuity

SHIP OF FOOLS

Caliber Press; 1 1996-present	$Good	$Fine	$N.Mint	£Good	£Fine	£N.Mint
1-4 ND black and white	$0.60	$1.80	$3.00	£0.40	£1.20	£2.00
Title Value:	$2.40	$7.20	$12.00	£1.60	£5.60	£8.00

SHOCK SUSPENSTORIES (1ST SERIES)

E.C. Comics; 1 Feb/Mar 1952-18 Dec/Jan 1954/1955	$Good	$Fine	$N.Mint	£Good	£Fine	£N.Mint
1 scarce in the U.K.	$72.50	$215.00	$585.00	£47.00	£140.00	£375.00
2	$44.00	$130.00	$350.00	£28.00	£82.50	£225.00
3-4	$31.00	$92.50	$250.00	£21.50	£65.00	£175.00
5	$28.00	$82.50	$225.00	£18.50	£55.00	£150.00
6 classic bondage cover	$34.00	$100.00	$275.00	£23.00	£67.50	£185.00
7 classic "melting face" cover, Ray Bradbury adaptation	$33.00	$97.50	$265.00	£21.50	£65.00	£175.00
8 classic "knife-to-girl's-throat" cover	$28.00	$82.50	$225.00	£18.50	£55.00	£150.00
9 Ray Bradbury adaptation	$22.50	$67.50	$180.00	£15.50	£47.00	£125.00
10-11	$22.50	$67.50	$180.00	£15.50	£47.00	£125.00
12 drug story/cover	$22.50	$67.50	$180.00	£15.50	£47.00	£125.00

	$Good	$Fine	$N.Mint	£Good	£Fine	£N.Mint
13 Frazetta story	*$33.00*	*$97.50*	*$260.00*	£23.00	£67.50	£185.00
14-15	*$18.50*	*$55.00*	*$150.00*	£12.50	£38.00	£100.00
16-18	*$17.50*	*$52.50*	*$140.00*	£11.50	£36.00	£95.00
Title Value:	*$514.00*	*$1527.50*	*$4125.00*	£344.00	£1034.50	£2780.00

Note: all Non-Distributed on the news-stands in the U.K.

SHOCK SUSPENSTORIES (2ND SERIES)

Russ Cochran/EC Comics; 1 Sep 1991-2 1991

	$Good	$Fine	$N.Mint	£Good	£Fine	£N.Mint
1 ND reprints Shock Suspense Stories #1,2						
	$0.60	*$1.80*	*$3.00*	£0.40	£1.20	£2.00
2 ND	*$0.30*	*$0.90*	*$1.50*	£0.20	£0.60	£1.00
Title Value:	*$0.90*	*$2.70*	*$4.50*	£0.60	£1.80	£3.00

SHOCK SUSPENSTORIES (3RD SERIES)

Russ Cochran/EC Comics; 1 Sep 1992-present

	$Good	$Fine	$N.Mint	£Good	£Fine	£N.Mint
1 ND reprints begin from original 1950s EC series with exact cover and interior reproduction						
	$0.40	*$1.20*	*$2.00*	£0.25	£0.75	£1.25
2-15 ND	*$0.40*	*$1.20*	*$2.00*	£0.25	£0.75	£1.25
Title Value:	*$6.00*	*$18.00*	*$30.00*	£3.75	£11.25	£18.75
Shock Suspenstories Annual #1 (Aug 1994)						
ND reprints five stories with covers, softcover				£1.20	£3.60	£6.00
Shock Suspenstories Annual #2 (Dec 1994)						
ND reprints five stories with covers, softcover				£1.20	£3.60	£6.00
Shock Suspenstories Annual #3 (Dec 1995)						
reprints five stories with covers, softcover				£1.20	£3.60	£6.00

SHOCKING TALES DIGEST

Harvey; 1 Oct 1981

	$Good	$Fine	$N.Mint	£Good	£Fine	£N.Mint
1 ND all reprint	*$0.40*	*$1.20*	*$2.00*	£0.25	£0.75	£1.25
Title Value:	*$0.40*	*$1.20*	*$2.00*	£0.25	£0.75	£1.25

SHOGUN WARRIORS

Marvel Comics Group; 1 Feb 1979-20 Sep 1980

	$Good	$Fine	$N.Mint	£Good	£Fine	£N.Mint
1 ND	*$0.40*	*$1.25*	*$2.50*	£0.20	£0.60	£1.25
2-10 ND	*$0.30*	*$0.90*	*$1.50*	£0.20	£0.60	£1.00
11-18	*$0.30*	*$0.90*	*$1.50*	£0.15	£0.45	£0.75
19-20 Fantastic Four appear						
	$0.30	*$0.90*	*$1.50*	£0.15	£0.45	£0.75
Title Value:	*$6.10*	*$18.35*	*$31.00*	£3.50	£10.50	£17.75

SHOGUNAUT

Firstlight Comixx; 1 Dec 1994-2 1995

	$Good	$Fine	$N.Mint	£Good	£Fine	£N.Mint
1-2 ND	*$0.50*	*$1.50*	*$2.50*	£0.30	£0.90	£1.50
Title Value:	*$1.00*	*$3.00*	*$5.00*	£0.60	£1.80	£3.00

SHOTGUN MARY

Antarctic Press,MS; 1 Sep 1995-3 Jan 1996

	$Good	$Fine	$N.Mint	£Good	£Fine	£N.Mint
1 ND Warrior Nun Areala tie-in; Herb Mallette and Joseph Wight						
	$0.60	*$1.80*	*$3.00*	£0.40	£1.20	£2.00
1 CD Soundtrack Signed Edition, ND pre-bagged with CD						
	$3.20	*$9.50*	*$16.00*	£2.20	£6.50	£11.00
1 Signed Edition, ND pre-bagged with certificate						
	$2.00	*$6.00*	*$10.00*	£1.30	£3.90	£6.50
1 Variant Cover Edition, ND (Sep 1995) - pre-baaged with CD soundtrack by Pink Filth						
	$1.80	*$5.25*	*$9.00*	£1.20	£3.60	£6.00
2-3 ND	*$0.60*	*$1.80*	*$3.00*	£0.40	£1.20	£2.00
Title Value:	*$8.80*	*$26.15*	*$44.00*	£5.90	£17.60	£29.50

SHOTGUN MARY: DEVILTOWN

Antarctic Press,OS; 1 Jul 1996

	$Good	$Fine	$N.Mint	£Good	£Fine	£N.Mint
1 ND	*$0.60*	*$1.80*	*$3.00*	£0.60	£1.80	£3.00
Title Value:	*$0.60*	*$1.80*	*$3.00*	£0.60	£1.80	£3.00

SHOTGUN MARY: SHOOTING GALLERY

Antarctic Press,OS; nn Jun 1996

	$Good	$Fine	$N.Mint	£Good	£Fine	£N.Mint
nn ND pin-ups and information	*$0.60*	*$1.80*	*$3.00*	£0.40	£1.20	£2.00
Title Value:	*$0.60*	*$1.80*	*$3.00*	£0.40	£1.20	£2.00

SHOWCASE

National Periodical Publications/DC Comics; 1 Mar/Apr 1956-93 Sep 1970; 94 Aug/Sep 1977-104 Sep 1978

	$Good	$Fine	$N.Mint	£Good	£Fine	£N.Mint
1 Fire Fighters starring Fireman Farrell						
	$315.00	*$940.00*	*$3150.00*	£210.00	£630.00	£2100.00
2 King of the Wild; Jack Kirby art						
	$100.00	*$305.00*	*$825.00*	£67.50	£205.00	£550.00
3 The Frogmen; Robert Kanigher script, Russ Heath art featuring a painted (grey-tone) cover						
	$100.00	*$300.00*	*$810.00*	£67.50	£200.00	£540.00
4 origin and 1st appearance of Silver Age Flash: generally regarded as the comic that started the Silver Age (Sep/Oct 1956)						
	$1400.00	*$4200.00*	*$28000.00*	£930.00	£2800.00	£18700.00
[Prices may vary widely on this comic]						
[Rare in high grade - Very Fine+ or better]						
4 Silver Age Classic, ND (Mar 1992)						
	$0.25	*$0.75*	*$1.25*	£0.15	£0.45	£0.80
5 Manhunters	*$110.00*	*$335.00*	*$900.00*	£75.00	£225.00	£600.00
6 origin and 1st appearance Challengers of the Unknown by Jack Kirby (1st DC Silver Age super-hero team)						
	$290.00	*$870.00*	*$3500.00*	£190.00	£580.00	£2335.00
7 2nd appearance Challengers of the Unknown; Jack Kirby art						
	$160.00	*$480.00*	*$1600.00*	£105.00	£320.00	£1075.00
8 scarce in the U.K. 2nd Silver Age Flash, origin and 1st appearance Captain Cold						
	$930.00	*$2800.00*	*$15000.00*	£620.00	£1875.00	£10000.00
[Prices vary widely on this comic. Scarcer than Showcase #4]						
9 rare in the U.K. 1st Lois Lane solo comic (pre-dates Lois Lane #1)						
	$550.00	*$1650.00*	*$5500.00*	£365.00	£1100.00	£3675.00
[Very rare in high grade - Very Fine+ or better]						
10 scarce in the U.K. 2nd Lois Lane solo comic (pre-dates Lois Lane #1); Jor-El appears						
	$255.00	*$760.00*	*$2550.00*	£170.00	£510.00	£1700.00
11 3rd appearance Challengers of the Unknown, Jack Kirby art						
	$140.00	*$425.00*	*$1425.00*	£95.00	£285.00	£950.00
12 4th appearance Challengers of the Unknown, Jack Kirby art						
	$140.00	*$420.00*	*$1400.00*	£92.50	£280.00	£935.00
13 3rd Silver Age Flash, 1st appearance Mr. Element						
	$375.00	*$1125.00*	*$3750.00*	£250.00	£750.00	£2500.00
14 4th Silver Age Flash, Mr. Element becomes Dr. Alchemy (1st appearance)						
[Note: this issue is scarcer than #13]						
	$440.00	*$1300.00*	*$4400.00*	£295.00	£880.00	£2950.00
[Scarce in high grade - Very Fine+ or better]						
15 1st appearance Space Ranger						
	$170.00	*$510.00*	*$1700.00*	£115.00	£345.00	£1150.00
[Scarce in high grade - Very Fine+ or better]						
16 2nd appearance Space Ranger						
	$100.00	*$300.00*	*$900.00*	£65.00	£200.00	£600.00
17 origin and 1st appearance of Adam Strange (see Mystery in Space #53); sub-titled Adventures on Other Worlds						
	$225.00	*$670.00*	*$2250.00*	£150.00	£450.00	£1500.00
[Scarce in high grade - Very Fine+ or better]						
18 2nd appearance Adam Strange; sub-titled Adventures on Other Worlds						
	$135.00	*$410.00*	*$1100.00*	£90.00	£275.00	£735.00
19 3rd appearance Adam Strange						
	$135.00	*$410.00*	*$1100.00*	£90.00	£275.00	£735.00
20 scarce in the U.K. 1st appearance Rip Hunter Time Master						
	$100.00	*$305.00*	*$925.00*	£67.50	£205.00	£620.00
21 2nd appearance Rip Hunter Time Master						
	$62.50	*$185.00*	*$500.00*	£42.00	£125.00	£335.00
22 origin and 1st appearance of Silver Age Green Lantern						
	$415.00	*$1250.00*	*$5000.00*	£275.00	£830.00	£3350.00
1st official distribution in the U.K.						
22 SIlver Age Classic, ND (Mar 1992)						
	$0.25	*$0.75*	*$1.25*	£0.15	£0.45	£0.80
23 2nd appearance Green Lantern, nuclear explosion cover						
	$165.00	*$495.00*	*$1650.00*	£110.00	£330.00	£1100.00
24 3rd appearance Green Lantern						
	$160.00	*$480.00*	*$1600.00*	£105.00	£320.00	£1075.00
25 3rd appearance Rip Hunter; painted (grey-tone) cover						
	$44.00	*$130.00*	*$350.00*	£28.00	£82.50	£225.00
26 4th appearance Rip Hunter						
	$41.00	*$120.00*	*$325.00*	£25.00	£75.00	£200.00
27 1st appearance Sea Devils; painted (grey-tone) cover; Russ Heath art						
	$105.00	*$315.00*	*$850.00*	£67.50	£205.00	£550.00
28 2nd appearance Sea Devils; painted (grey-tone) cover; Russ heath art						
	$52.50	*$155.00*	*$425.00*	£33.00	£97.50	£265.00
29 3rd appearance Sea Devils; painted (grey-tone) cover; Russ Heath art						
	$50.00	*$150.00*	*$400.00*	£31.00	£92.50	£250.00
30 Aquaman appears, origin retold (see Adventure Comics #260 for 1st Silver Age appearance)						
	$82.50	*$245.00*	*$825.00*	£50.00	£150.00	£500.00
31-32 Aquaman	*$45.00*	*$135.00*	*$450.00*	£25.00	£75.00	£250.00
33 Aquaman	*$43.00*	*$125.00*	*$425.00*	£22.50	£67.50	£225.00
34 origin & 1st appearance Silver Age Atom; Gil Kane and Murphy Anderson art						
	$140.00	*$420.00*	*$1400.00*	£82.50	£245.00	£825.00
35 2nd appearance Silver Age Atom; last 10 cents issue						
	$97.50	*$290.00*	*$780.00*	£55.00	£170.00	£455.00
36 3rd appearance Silver Age Atom (pre Atom #1)						
	$75.00	*$225.00*	*$600.00*	£44.00	£130.00	£350.00
37 1st appearance the Metal Men						
	$75.00	*$225.00*	*$600.00*	£43.00	£125.00	£340.00
38 2nd appearance the Metal Men						
	$57.50	*$175.00*	*$475.00*	£31.00	£90.00	£245.00
39 3rd appearance the Metal Men						
	$45.00	*$135.00*	*$360.00*	£22.50	£67.50	£180.00
40 4th appearance the Metal Men						
	$41.00	*$120.00*	*$325.00*	£20.50	£60.00	£165.00
41-42 Tommy Tomorrow						
	$21.00	*$62.50*	*$170.00*	£9.25	£28.00	£75.00
43 Dr. No (film adaptation), no ads, originally published as British Classics Illustrated 158A, 1st major Silver Age film adaptation						
	$49.00	*$145.00*	*$390.00*	£26.00	£77.50	£210.00
44 Tommy Tomorrow						
	$15.50	*$47.00*	*$125.00*	£7.50	£22.50	£60.00
45 rare in the U.K. Sgt. Rock; origin retold; Russ Heath cover						
	$28.00	*$82.50*	*$225.00*	£16.50	£50.00	£135.00
46-47 Tommy Tomorrow						
	$13.00	*$39.00*	*$105.00*	£6.75	£20.50	£55.00
48-49 Cave Carson						
	$10.50	*$32.00*	*$85.00*	£4.35	£13.00	£35.00
50 I-Spy	*$9.25*	*$28.00*	*$75.00*	£5.00	£15.00	£40.00
51 I-Spy	*$9.25*	*$28.00*	*$75.00*	£4.35	£13.00	£35.00
52 Cave Carson	*$8.75*	*$26.00*	*$70.00*	£3.75	£11.00	£30.00
53-54 scarce in the U.K. G.I.Joe; Russ Heath art						
	$9.25	*$28.00*	*$75.00*	£4.35	£13.00	£35.00
55 Dr. Fate/Hourman, 1st solo (ie. not part of a team) Golden Age Green Lantern in Silver Age (see Green Lantern [1st Series] #40), 1st Silver Age Solomon Grundy						
	$28.00	*$82.50*	*$250.00*	£15.00	£45.00	£135.00
56 Dr. Fate/Hourman						
	$12.50	*$38.00*	*$100.00*	£5.50	£16.50	£45.00
57 scarce in the U.K. Enemy Ace by Joe Kubert (see Our Army at War #155)						
	$20.50	*$60.00*	*$165.00*	£11.00	£34.00	£90.00
58 scarce in the U.K. Enemy Ace by Kubert						
	$17.50	*$52.50*	*$140.00*	£8.00	£24.00	£65.00
59 3rd Teen Titans (see Brave and the Bold #54, #60)						
	$11.50	*$35.00*	*$105.00*	£7.00	£21.50	£65.00
60 1st Silver Age appearance The Spectre (last seen 20 years before in More Fun Comics #101 dated February 1945)						

Issue	$Good	$Fine	$N.Mint	£Good	£Fine	£N.Mint
	$29.00	*$85.00*	*$260.00*	£13.00	£40.00	£120.00
61 2nd Silver Age appearance The Spectre, Murphy Anderson art	*$17.50*	*$52.50*	*$160.00*	£8.25	£25.00	£75.00
62 1st appearance Inferior Five	*$12.50*	*$38.00*	*$100.00*	£6.25	£18.50	£50.00
63 2nd appearance Inferior Five; Incredible Hulk parody	*$7.50*	*$22.50*	*$60.00*	£3.75	£11.00	£30.00
64 The Spectre by Murphy Anderson	*$17.50*	*$52.50*	*$140.00*	£8.00	£24.00	£65.00
65 Inferior Five, X-Men parody	*$7.50*	*$22.50*	*$60.00*	£3.75	£11.00	£30.00
66 1st appearance B'wana Beast	*$5.00*	*$15.00*	*$40.00*	£2.15	£6.50	£17.50
67 B'wana Beast	*$5.00*	*$15.00*	*$40.00*	£1.85	£5.50	£15.00
68 Maniaks (1st appearance)	*$4.35*	*$13.00*	*$35.00*	£1.85	£5.50	£15.00
69 Maniaks	*$4.35*	*$13.00*	*$35.00*	£1.85	£5.50	£15.00
70 rare in the U.K. Binky	*$5.00*	*$15.00*	*$40.00*	£3.10	£9.25	£25.00
71 scarce in the U.K. Maniaks (Woody Allen appears)	*$4.35*	*$13.00*	*$35.00*	£1.85	£5.50	£15.00
72 Top Gun; Alex Toth art	*$4.35*	*$13.00*	*$35.00*	£1.55	£4.65	£12.50
73 origin & 1st appearance of the Creeper; Steve Ditko art	*$13.50*	*$42.00*	*$125.00*	£6.50	£20.00	£60.00
74 1st appearance Anthro	*$9.25*	*$28.00*	*$75.00*	£4.35	£13.00	£35.00
75 1st appearance Hawk and the Dove; Steve Ditko art	*$13.50*	*$41.00*	*$110.00*	£6.25	£18.50	£50.00
76 1st appearance Bat Lash	*$7.50*	*$22.50*	*$60.00*	£3.75	£11.00	£30.00
77 1st appearance Angel and the Ape	*$7.50*	*$22.50*	*$60.00*	£3.75	£11.00	£30.00
78 1st appearance Johnny Double	*$4.35*	*$13.00*	*$35.00*	£1.85	£5.50	£15.00
79 1st appearance Dolphin; Aqualad origin reprint	*$8.00*	*$24.00*	*$65.00*	£3.10	£9.25	£25.00
80 Phantom Stranger (part reprint); Neal Adams cover	*$5.25*	*$16.00*	*$37.50*	£2.50	£7.50	£17.50
81 rare in the U.K. Windy & Willy	*$4.35*	*$13.00*	*$35.00*	£2.80	£8.25	£22.50
82 1st appearance Nightmaster by Jerry Grandenetti	*$8.00*	*$24.00*	*$65.00*	£3.75	£11.00	£30.00
83 Nightmaster; Wrightson, Jones and Kaluta art	*$6.75*	*$20.50*	*$55.00*	£2.80	£8.25	£22.50
84 Nightmaster; Wrightson, Jones & Kaluta art	*$6.75*	*$20.50*	*$55.00*	£2.80	£8.25	£22.50
85-87 Firehair byJoe Kubert	*$3.75*	*$11.00*	*$30.00*	£1.10	£3.35	£9.00
88-90 Jason's Quest	*$2.85*	*$8.50*	*$20.00*	£0.50	£1.50	£3.50
91-93 Manhunter (science-fiction character, not to be confused with super-hero)	*$1.40*	*$4.25*	*$10.00*	£0.50	£1.50	£3.50
94 1st appearance New Doom Patrol	*$1.25*	*$3.75*	*$7.50*	£0.80	£2.50	£5.00
95 2nd appearance New Doom Patrol	*$0.85*	*$2.60*	*$5.25*	£0.55	£1.75	£3.50
96 Doom Patrol	*$0.75*	*$2.25*	*$4.50*	£0.50	£1.50	£3.00
97 origin Power Girl, "headlights" cover	*$0.65*	*$2.00*	*$4.00*	£0.40	£1.25	£2.50
98 origin Power Girl	*$0.65*	*$2.00*	*$4.00*	£0.30	£1.00	£2.00
99 scarce in the U.K. Power Girl	*$0.65*	*$2.00*	*$4.00*	£0.40	£1.25	£2.50
100 scarce in the U.K. 52pgs, features almost every character ever to appear in title	*$1.00*	*$3.00*	*$6.00*	£0.65	£2.00	£4.00
101-103 Hawkman	*$0.65*	*$2.00*	*$4.00*	£0.30	£1.00	£2.00
104 ND 44pgs, OSS Spies at War	*$0.65*	*$2.00*	*$4.00*	£0.50	£1.50	£3.00
Title Value:	***$8580.25***	***$25727.85***	***$103216.25***	**£5519.50**	**£16620.60**	**£67321.10**

REPRINT FEATURES

(50, 51, 70, 72, 81 are entirely reprint, 79, 80 are partly reprint), Aquaman in 79. Binky in 70. Johnny Thunder, Trigger Twins in 72. King Faraday in 50, 51. Part 1950s Phantom Stranger in 80. 1950s/1960s humour title with some art changes in 81.

The Essential Showcase Volume 1 (Jan 1993)

ND Softcover, 192pgs, reprints selected issues from #1-#19 £2.50 £7.50 £12.50

SHOWCASE '93

DC Comics,MS; 1 Jan 1993-12 Dec 1993

Issue	$Good	$Fine	$N.Mint	£Good	£Fine	£N.Mint
1 ND Arthur Adams and Terry Austin cover; features Catwoman, Blue Devil, Cyborg stories	*$0.40*	*$1.20*	*$2.00*	£0.25	£0.75	£1.25
2 ND Kevin Maguire and Terry Austin cover; features Catwoman (Robin cameo), Blue Devil, Cyborg stories	*$0.40*	*$1.20*	*$2.00*	£0.25	£0.75	£1.25
3 ND Brian Bolland cover; features Catwoman, Blue Devil plus Flash by Travis Charest	*$0.40*	*$1.20*	*$2.00*	£0.25	£0.75	£1.25
4 ND Michael Golden cover; features Catwoman, Blue Devil plus Geo-Force	*$0.40*	*$1.20*	*$2.00*	£0.25	£0.75	£1.25
5 ND features Robin, Blue Devil and Geo-Force	*$0.40*	*$1.20*	*$2.00*	£0.25	£0.75	£1.25
6 ND Mike Zeck cover; features Robin, Blue Devil and Deathstroke the Terminator	*$0.40*	*$1.20*	*$2.00*	£0.25	£0.75	£1.25
7 ND Knightfall part 13 - Batman vs. Two-Face; also features Kobra, Deathstroke, Peacemaker, Jade and Obsidian, bi-weekly	*$0.50*	*$1.50*	*$2.50*	£0.30	£0.90	£1.50
8 ND Knightfall part 14 - Batman vs. Two-Face; also features Kobra, Deathstroke, Peacemaker, Fire and Ice, bi-weekly; continued in Batman #498	*$0.50*	*$1.50*	*$2.50*	£0.30	£0.90	£1.50
9 ND Howard Chaykin cover; features Huntress, Kobra, Shining Knight	*$0.40*	*$1.20*	*$2.00*	£0.25	£0.75	£1.25
10 ND Paul Gulacy cover; features Huntress, Kobra, Martian Manhunter	*$0.40*	*$1.20*	*$2.00*	£0.25	£0.75	£1.25
11 ND George Perez cover; features Robin and Nightwing, Kobra, Wonder Woman	*$0.40*	*$1.20*	*$2.00*	£0.25	£0.75	£1.25
12 ND Alan Davis and Mark Farmer cover; features Robin And Nightwing, Green Lantern, The Creeper	*$0.40*	*$1.20*	*$2.00*	£0.25	£0.75	£1.25
Title Value:	***$5.00***	***$15.00***	***$25.00***	**£3.10**	**£9.30**	**£15.50**

SHOWCASE '94

DC Comics,MS; 1 Jan 1994-12 Dec 1994

Issue	$Good	$Fine	$N.Mint	£Good	£Fine	£N.Mint
1 ND 48pgs, Graham Nolan cover; features Joker, Gunfire, Orion & Metron	*$0.40*	*$1.20*	*$2.00*	£0.25	£0.75	£1.25
2 ND 48pgs, Kevin O'Neill cover; features Joker, Gunfire, Blue Beetle	*$0.40*	*$1.20*	*$2.00*	£0.25	£0.75	£1.25
3 ND 48pgs, Mike Mignola cover; features Two-Face, Riddler, Scarecrow and Mad Hatter, Razorsharpe, Blue Beetle	*$0.40*	*$1.20*	*$2.00*	£0.25	£0.75	£1.25
4 ND 48pgs, Kyle Baker cover; features Two-Face, Riddler, Scarecrow and Mad Hatter, Razorsharpe, Blue Beetle	*$0.40*	*$1.20*	*$2.00*	£0.25	£0.75	£1.25
5 ND 48pgs, Robin and The Huntress; Bloodwynd, Loose Cannon; continued in Robin #7; bi-weekly	*$0.40*	*$1.20*	*$2.00*	£0.25	£0.75	£1.25
6 ND 48pgs, Robin and The Huntress; Bloodwynd, Loose Cannon; continued from Robin #7; bi-weekly	*$0.40*	*$1.20*	*$2.00*	£0.25	£0.75	£1.25
7 ND 48pgs, Penguin by Peter David with art by P. Craig Russell and Michael T. Gilbert; Terrorsmith, Arsenal						

Shazam #12

Shock SuspenStories (3rd) #3

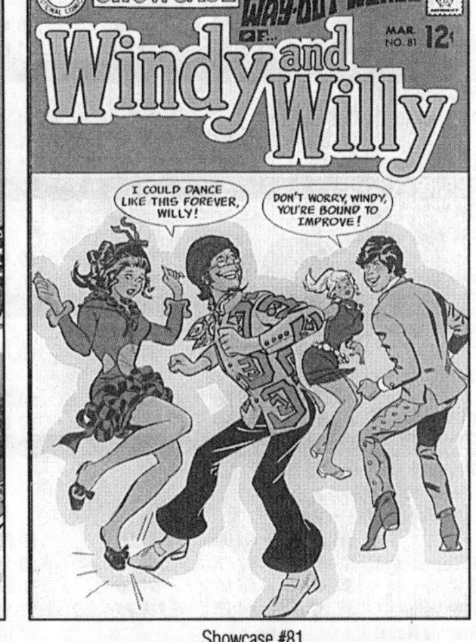

Showcase #81

	$Good	$Fine	$N.Mint	£Good	£Fine	£N.Mint
	$0.40	$1.20	$2.00	£0.25	£0.75	£1.25
8 ND 48pgs, Origin of Scarface by Alan Grant & John Wagner, Ted McKeever art; Wildcat, Zero Hour prelude	$0.40	$1.20	$2.00	£0.25	£0.75	£1.25
9 ND 48pgs, Origin of Scarface by Alan Grant & John Wagner; Zero Hour prelude featuring Waverider and Monarch	$0.40	$1.20	$2.00	£0.25	£0.75	£1.25
10 ND 48pgs, Azrael, Black Condor; Zero Hour X-over; Joe Quesada cover	$0.40	$1.20	$2.00	£0.25	£0.75	£1.25
11 ND 48pgs, Man-Bat, Condor, Starfire; Geof Darrow cover	$0.40	$1.20	$2.00	£0.25	£0.75	£1.25
12 ND 48pgs, Barbara Gordon/Oracle, Ballistic, Triumph	$0.40	$1.20	$2.00	£0.25	£0.75	£1.25
Title Value:	$4.80	$14.40	$24.00	£3.00	£9.00	£15.00

SHOWCASE '95

DC Comics,MS; 1 Jan 1995-12 Dec 1995

	$Good	$Fine	$N.Mint	£Good	£Fine	£N.Mint
1 ND Supergirl, Argus and the Golden Age Green Lantern	$0.50	$1.50	$2.50	£0.30	£0.90	£1.50
2 ND Supergirl, Argus and the Metal Men	$0.50	$1.50	$2.50	£0.30	£0.90	£1.50
3 ND The Eradicator, Claw of Primal Force and The Question	$0.50	$1.50	$2.50	£0.30	£0.90	£1.50
4 ND Thorn, Catwoman and Green Arrow	$0.50	$1.50	$2.50	£0.30	£0.90	£1.50
5 ND 48pgs, Thorn, The Spoiler, Firehawk	$0.60	$1.80	$3.00	£0.30	£0.90	£1.50
6 ND 48pgs, Lobo, Leviathan, Andromeda	$0.60	$1.80	$3.00	£0.30	£0.90	£1.50
7 ND 48pgs, Mongul, Arion, New Gods	$0.60	$1.80	$3.00	£0.30	£0.90	£1.50
8 ND 48pgs, Mongul, Spectre, Arsenal	$0.60	$1.80	$3.00	£0.30	£0.90	£1.50
9 ND 48pgs, Lois Lane, Lobo, Martian Manhunter	$0.60	$1.80	$3.00	£0.30	£0.90	£1.50
10 ND 48pgs, Gangbuster, Darkstars, Hi-Tech; bi-weekly	$0.60	$1.80	$3.00	£0.30	£0.90	£1.50
11 ND 48pgs, Agent Liberty, Arkham Asylum, Hi-Tech	$0.60	$1.80	$3.00	£0.30	£0.90	£1.50
12 ND 48pgs, Supergirl, Maitresse, The Shade (an Underworld Unleashed story)	$0.60	$1.80	$3.00	£0.30	£0.90	£1.50
Title Value:	$6.80	$20.40	$34.00	£3.60	£10.80	£18.00

SHOWCASE '96

DC Comics,MS; 1 Jan 1996-12 Jan 1997

	$Good	$Fine	$N.Mint	£Good	£Fine	£N.Mint
1 ND 48pgs, Steel and Warrior team-up, Aqualad and Metropolis S.C.U. feature in separate stories	$0.60	$1.80	$3.00	£0.40	£1.20	£2.00
2 ND Steel and Warrior team-up, Circe vs. Ares	$0.60	$1.80	$3.00	£0.40	£1.20	£2.00
3 ND Black Canary, Oracle and Lois Lane team, Lightray and Deadman	$0.60	$1.80	$3.00	£0.40	£1.20	£2.00
4 ND Firebrand vs. Guardian, Golden Age Shade vs. Doctor Fate, Demon	$0.60	$1.80	$3.00	£0.40	£1.20	£2.00
5 ND Green Arrow and Thorn, New Gods, Golden Age Shade	$0.60	$1.80	$3.00	£0.40	£1.20	£2.00
6 ND Superboy, Firestorm, The Atom	$0.60	$1.80	$3.00	£0.40	£1.20	£2.00
7 ND Mary Marvel and Gangbuster, Fire, Firestorm	$0.60	$1.80	$3.00	£0.40	£1.20	£2.00
8 ND Superman and Superboy, Legionnaires, Supergirl	$0.60	$1.80	$3.00	£0.40	£1.20	£2.00
9 ND Lady Shiva and Shadowdragon, Martian Manhunter, Dr. Light	$0.60	$1.80	$3.00	£0.40	£1.20	£2.00
10 ND Bibbo, Ultra Boy, Captain Comet	$0.60	$1.80	$3.00	£0.40	£1.20	£2.00
11 ND Brainiac 5 and the Legion of Super Heroes, Scare Tactics, Golden Age Wildcat	$0.60	$1.80	$3.00	£0.40	£1.20	£2.00
12 ND Brainiac 5, Jesse Quick, King Faraday and Sarge Steel	$0.60	$1.80	$3.00	£0.40	£1.20	£2.00
Title Value:	$7.20	$21.60	$36.00	£4.80	£14.40	£24.00

SHRIEK

Fantaco; 1 1989

	$Good	$Fine	$N.Mint	£Good	£Fine	£N.Mint
1 ND magazine size; features work by Gurchain Singh, Kevin Eastman and Steve Bissette; black and white	$1.50	$4.50	$7.50	£1.00	£3.00	£5.00
Title Value:	$1.50	$4.50	$7.50	£1.00	£3.00	£5.00

SHRIKE

Cat Wild; 1 Jan 1991

	$Good	$Fine	$N.Mint	£Good	£Fine	£N.Mint
1 ND black and white	$0.25	$0.75	$1.25	£0.15	£0.45	£0.75
Title Value:	$0.25	$0.75	$1.25	£0.15	£0.45	£0.75

SHROUD, THE

Marvel Comics Group,MS; 1 Mar 1994-4 Jun 1994

	$Good	$Fine	$N.Mint	£Good	£Fine	£N.Mint
1-3	$0.30	$0.90	$1.50	£0.20	£0.60	£1.00
4 Spiderman guest-stars	$0.30	$0.90	$1.50	£0.20	£0.60	£1.00
Title Value:	$1.20	$3.60	$6.00	£0.80	£2.40	£4.00

SHURIKEN

Victory; 1 1985-10 May 1987

(see Blade of Shuriken)

	$Good	$Fine	$N.Mint	£Good	£Fine	£N.Mint
1 ND black and white begins	$0.30	$0.90	$1.50	£0.20	£0.60	£1.00
1 2nd printing ND	$0.25	$0.75	$1.25	£0.15	£0.45	£0.75
2-10 ND	$0.30	$0.90	$1.50	£0.20	£0.60	£1.00
Title Value:	$3.25	$9.75	$16.25	£2.15	£6.45	£10.75
Graphic Novel (Blackthorne), reprints				£1.10	£3.30	£5.50

SHURIKEN (2ND SERIES)

Eternity,MS; 1 Aug 1991-6 Jan 1992

	$Good	$Fine	$N.Mint	£Good	£Fine	£N.Mint
1-6 ND	$0.40	$1.20	$2.00	£0.25	£0.75	£1.25
Title Value:	$2.40	$7.20	$12.00	£1.50	£4.50	£7.50

SHURIKEN: COLD STEEL

Eternity; 1-4 1987

	$Good	$Fine	$N.Mint	£Good	£Fine	£N.Mint
1-4 ND 16pgs	$0.40	$1.20	$2.00	£0.25	£0.75	£1.25
Title Value:	$1.60	$4.80	$8.00	£1.00	£3.00	£5.00

SIDNEY MELLON'S THUNDERSKULL!

Slave Labor; 1 1989

	$Good	$Fine	$N.Mint	£Good	£Fine	£N.Mint
1 ND black and white	$0.40	$1.20	$2.00	£0.25	£0.75	£1.25
Title Value:	$0.40	$1.20	$2.00	£0.25	£0.75	£1.25

SIEGE OF DARKNESS

Marvel Comics Group; 1993

Cross-over storyline running throughout the following titles:
Nightstalkers #14, Ghost Rider [2nd Series] #44, Marvel Comics Presents #143, Darkhold #15, Morbius #16, Marvel Comics Presents #144, Doctor Strange [3rd Series] #60, Ghost Rider & Blaze: Spirits of Vengeance #17, Nightstalkers #15, Ghost Rider [2nd Series] #45, Marvel Comics Presents #145, Darkhold #16, Morbius #17, Marvel Comics Presents #146, Doctor Strange [3rd Series] #61, Ghost Rider & Blaze: Spirits of Vengeance #18, Midnight Sons Unlimited #4.

SIEGEL & SHUSTER: DATELINE 1930S

Eclipse; 1 Nov 1984-2 1985

	$Good	$Fine	$N.Mint	£Good	£Fine	£N.Mint
1 ND pre-Superman reprints, includes interview	$0.40	$1.20	$2.00	£0.25	£0.75	£1.25
2 ND reprints	$0.40	$1.20	$2.00	£0.25	£0.75	£1.25
Title Value:	$0.80	$2.40	$4.00	£0.50	£1.50	£2.50

SIGMA

Image; 1 Mar 1996-3 Jun 1996

	$Good	$Fine	$N.Mint	£Good	£Fine	£N.Mint
1 ND Brandon Choi script, Tomm Coker art; leads into Deathblow #26; Fire From Heaven X-over	$0.50	$1.50	$2.50	£0.30	£0.90	£1.50
2 ND Fire From Heaven part 6, continued in WildC.A.T.S. #27	$0.50	$1.50	$2.50	£0.30	£0.90	£1.50
3 ND Fire From Heaven part 14, continued in Deathblow #28	$0.50	$1.50	$2.50	£0.30	£0.90	£1.50
Title Value:	$1.50	$4.50	$7.50	£0.90	£2.70	£4.50

SIGNAL TO NOISE GRAPHIC NOVEL

Dark Horse,OS; nn Dec 1992

	$Good	$Fine	$N.Mint	£Good	£Fine	£N.Mint
nn ND 80pgs, Neil Gaiman script, Dave McKean art; originally published in the U.K.	$3.00	$9.00	$15.00	£2.00	£6.00	£10.00
nn 2nd printing, ND 80pgs, (Mar 1996)	$3.00	$9.00	$15.00	£2.00	£6.00	£10.00
Title Value:	$6.00	$18.00	$30.00	£4.00	£12.00	£20.00

SILBUSTER

Antarctic Press; 1 Jan 1994-present

	$Good	$Fine	$N.Mint	£Good	£Fine	£N.Mint
1-4 ND 40pgs, Kazumitsu Sahara; black and white	$0.60	$1.80	$3.00	£0.40	£1.20	£2.00
5-14 ND 40pgs, Ikkou Sahara; black and white	$0.60	$1.80	$3.00	£0.40	£1.20	£2.00
15-16 ND	$0.60	$1.80	$3.00	£0.40	£1.20	£2.00
Title Value:	$9.60	$28.80	$48.00	£6.40	£19.20	£32.00
Collected Silbuster (Aug 1995) 136pgs, collects issues #1-4, black and white				£1.50	£4.50	£7.50

SILENCERS, THE

Caliber Press,MS; 1 Sep 1991-4 Dec 1991

	$Good	$Fine	$N.Mint	£Good	£Fine	£N.Mint
1-4 ND	$0.40	$1.20	$2.00	£0.25	£0.75	£1.25
Title Value:	$1.60	$4.80	$8.00	£1.00	£3.00	£5.00

SILENT INVASION

Renegade; 1 Jul 1986-12 1988

	$Good	$Fine	$N.Mint	£Good	£Fine	£N.Mint
1-12 ND	$0.40	$1.20	$2.00	£0.25	£0.75	£1.25
Title Value:	$4.80	$14.40	$24.00	£3.00	£9.00	£15.00
Book 1, reprints #1-4				£1.20	£3.60	£6.00
Book 2, reprints #5-8				£1.20	£3.60	£6.00

SILENT INVASION (2ND SERIES)

Caliber Press; 1 May 1996-present

	$Good	$Fine	$N.Mint	£Good	£Fine	£N.Mint
1 ND reprints from the Renegade series begin; black and white	$0.60	$1.80	$3.00	£0.40	£1.20	£2.00
2-5 ND	$0.60	$1.80	$3.00	£0.40	£1.20	£2.00
Title Value:	$3.00	$9.00	$15.00	£2.00	£6.00	£10.00

SILENT MOBIUS

Viz Communications,MS; 1 Aug 1991-6 Jan 1992

	$Good	$Fine	$N.Mint	£Good	£Fine	£N.Mint
1 ND 40pgs, Japanese material begins; Kia Asamiya script and art, black and white	$1.00	$3.00	$5.00	£0.60	£1.80	£3.00
2-6 ND	$1.00	$3.00	$5.00	£0.60	£1.80	£3.00
Title Value:	$6.00	$18.00	$30.00	£3.60	£10.80	£18.00
Silent Mobius Graphic Novel Vol 1 (Oct 1992) 120pgs, reprints mini-series				£2.00	£6.00	£10.00

SILENT MOBIUS PART 2

Viz Communications,MS; 1 Feb 1992-5 Jun 1992

	$Good	$Fine	$N.Mint	£Good	£Fine	£N.Mint
1 ND Kia Asamiya script and art begins, black and white	$0.90	$2.70	$4.50	£0.60	£1.80	£3.00
2-5 ND	$0.90	$2.70	$4.50	£0.60	£1.80	£3.00
Title Value:	$4.50	$13.50	$22.50	£3.00	£9.00	£15.00
Silent Mobius Graphic Novel Vol 2 (Nov 1992) 120pgs, reprints mini-series				£2.00	£6.00	£10.00

SILENT MOBIUS PART 3

Viz Communications,MS; 1 Oct 1992-5 Feb 1993

	$Good	$Fine	$N.Mint	£Good	£Fine	£N.Mint
1 ND Kia Asamiya script and art begins, black and white	$0.60	$1.80	$3.00	£0.40	£1.20	£2.00
2-5 ND	$0.60	$1.80	$3.00	£0.40	£1.20	£2.00
Title Value:	$3.00	$9.00	$15.00	£2.00	£6.00	£10.00

SILENT MOBIUS PART 4

Viz Communications,MS; 1 Sep 1993-5 Jan 1994

Issue	$Good	$Fine	$N.Mint	£Good	£Fine	£N.Mint
1 ND Kia Asamiya script and art, black and white						
	$0.60	$1.80	$3.00	£0.40	£1.20	£2.00
2-5 ND	$0.60	$1.80	$3.00	£0.40	£1.20	£2.00
Title Value:	$3.00	$9.00	$15.00	£2.00	£6.00	£10.00

SILENT MOBIUS PART 5

Viz Communications,MS; 1 Feb 1994-5 Jun 1994

Issue	$Good	$Fine	$N.Mint	£Good	£Fine	£N.Mint
1-5 ND	$0.60	$1.80	$3.00	£0.40	£1.20	£2.00
Title Value:	$3.00	$9.00	$15.00	£2.00	£6.00	£10.00

SILENT RAPTURE

Avatar Press,MS; 1 Jan 1997-3 Mar 1997

Issue	$Good	$Fine	$N.Mint	£Good	£Fine	£N.Mint
1-3 ND Jude Millien script and art; black and white						
	$0.60	$1.80	$3.00	£0.40	£1.20	£2.00
Title Value:	$1.80	$5.40	$9.00	£1.20	£3.60	£6.00

SILVER SABLE

Marvel Comics Group; 1 Jun 1992-35 Apr 1995

Issue	$Good	$Fine	$N.Mint	£Good	£Fine	£N.Mint
1 ND silver foil-stamped embossed cover, Peter Parker appears						
	$0.30	$0.90	$1.50	£0.20	£0.60	£1.00
2-3 ND	$0.25	$0.75	$1.25	£0.15	£0.45	£0.75
4-5 ND Infinity War X-over, Dr. Doom appears						
	$0.25	$0.75	$1.25	£0.15	£0.45	£0.75
6-7 ND Deathlok appears						
	$0.25	$0.75	$1.25	£0.15	£0.45	£0.75
8 ND	$0.25	$0.75	$1.25	£0.15	£0.45	£0.75
9 ND origin Silver Sable						
	$0.25	$0.75	$1.25	£0.15	£0.45	£0.75
10 ND Punisher appears						
	$0.25	$0.75	$1.25	£0.15	£0.45	£0.75
11 ND back-up feature begins						
	$0.25	$0.75	$1.25	£0.15	£0.45	£0.75
12 ND	$0.25	$0.75	$1.25	£0.15	£0.45	£0.75
13 ND Cage appears, continued in Terror Inc. #12						
	$0.25	$0.75	$1.25	£0.15	£0.45	£0.75
14 ND Cage and Terror appear						
	$0.25	$0.75	$1.25	£0.15	£0.45	£0.75
15 ND Captain America appears						
	$0.25	$0.75	$1.25	£0.15	£0.45	£0.75
16-17 ND Infinity Crusade X-over						
	$0.25	$0.75	$1.25	£0.15	£0.45	£0.75
18 ND Venom appears						
	$0.25	$0.75	$1.25	£0.15	£0.45	£0.75
19 ND Siege of Darkness tie-in						
	$0.25	$0.75	$1.25	£0.15	£0.45	£0.75
20-23 ND	$0.25	$0.75	$1.25	£0.15	£0.45	£0.75
24 ND with free Spiderman vs. Venom card sheet						
	$0.25	$0.75	$1.25	£0.15	£0.45	£0.75
25 ND 48pgs	$0.30	$0.90	$1.50	£0.20	£0.60	£1.00
26 ND Sandman and Trapster appear						
	$0.25	$0.75	$1.25	£0.15	£0.45	£0.75
27 ND Sandman appears						
	$0.25	$0.75	$1.25	£0.15	£0.45	£0.75
28-35 ND	$0.25	$0.75	$1.25	£0.15	£0.45	£0.75
Title Value:	$8.85	$26.55	$44.25	£5.35	£16.05	£26.75

SILVER SCREAM, THE

Lorne-Harvey Publications/Recollections; 1 Jun 1991-3 Nov 1991

Issue	$Good	$Fine	$N.Mint	£Good	£Fine	£N.Mint
1-3 ND horror reprints; black and white						
	$0.30	$0.90	$1.50	£0.20	£0.60	£1.00
Title Value:	$0.90	$2.70	$4.50	£0.60	£1.80	£3.00

SILVER STAR

Pacific; 1 Feb 1983-6 Jul 1983

Issue	$Good	$Fine	$N.Mint	£Good	£Fine	£N.Mint
1 ND Last of the Viking Heroes backup; Jack Kirby art						
	$0.30	$0.90	$1.50	£0.20	£0.60	£1.00
2 ND Jack Kirby art and Steve Ditko art on back-up						
	$0.30	$0.90	$1.50	£0.20	£0.60	£1.00
3 ND Jack Kirby art and Flynn backup						
	$0.30	$0.90	$1.50	£0.20	£0.60	£1.00
4-6 ND Jack Kirby art						
	$0.30	$0.90	$1.50	£0.20	£0.60	£1.00
Title Value:	$1.80	$5.40	$9.00	£1.20	£3.60	£6.00

SILVER STAR (2ND SERIES)

Topps,MS; 1 Oct 1993; 2 Jul 1994-4 Sep 1994

Issue	$Good	$Fine	$N.Mint	£Good	£Fine	£N.Mint
1 ND pre-bagged with 3 trading cards; James Fry and Terry Austin art						
	$0.40	$1.20	$2.00	£0.25	£0.75	£1.25
2-4 ND James Fry and Terry Austin art						
	$0.40	$1.20	$2.00	£0.25	£0.75	£1.25
Title Value:	$1.60	$4.80	$8.00	£1.00	£3.00	£5.00

SILVER SURFER (1ST SERIES)

Marvel Comics Group; 1 Aug 1968-18 Sep 1970

(see Fantastic Four, Fantasy Masterpieces, Marvel Graphic Novel, Marvel Presents #8, Marvel's Greatest Comics, Tales to Astonish)

Issue	$Good	$Fine	$N.Mint	£Good	£Fine	£N.Mint
1 72pgs, squarebound, origin Silver Surfer, Watcher begins (origin)						
	$55.00	$165.00	$450.00	£38.00	£110.00	£300.00
2 72pgs, squarebound						
	$21.50	$65.00	$175.00	£14.00	£43.00	£115.00
3 72pgs, squarebound, 1st appearance Mephisto						
	$18.50	$55.00	$150.00	£12.50	£38.00	£100.00
4 scarce in the U.K. 72pgs, squarebound, Thor appears						
	$52.50	$155.00	$425.00	£37.00	£110.00	£295.00
5 scarce in the U.K. 72pgs, squarebound, The Stranger appears, Fantastic Four cameo						
	$11.00	$34.00	$90.00	£7.50	£22.50	£60.00
6 72pgs, squarebound, Brunner inks						
	$10.50	$32.00	$85.00	£6.75	£20.50	£55.00
7 72pgs, squarebound, Brunner cover						
	$10.50	$32.00	$85.00	£6.75	£20.50	£55.00
8-10	$8.50	$26.00	$60.00	£5.50	£17.00	£40.00
11-13	$7.00	$21.00	$50.00	£4.60	£13.50	£32.50
14 Spiderman X-over						
	$10.00	$30.00	$70.00	£5.50	£17.00	£40.00
15 scarce in the U.K. Human Torch X-over						
	$7.00	$21.00	$50.00	£5.00	£15.00	£35.00
16-17	$6.25	$19.00	$45.00	£4.25	£12.50	£30.00
18 very scarce in the U.K. Inhumans appear, Jack Kirby cover/art						
	$6.25	$19.00	$45.00	£5.00	£15.00	£35.00
Title Value:	$261.75	$787.00	$2045.00	£176.80	£528.00	£1367.50

Note: #1-17 John Buscema pencils

SILVER SURFER (2ND SERIES)

Marvel Comics Group,OS; 1 Jun 1982

Issue	$Good	$Fine	$N.Mint	£Good	£Fine	£N.Mint
1 ND scarce in the U.K. 52pgs, John Byrne art, Stan Lee script						
	$1.50	$4.50	$9.00	£1.15	£3.50	£7.00
Title Value:	$1.50	$4.50	$9.00	£1.15	£3.50	£7.00

SILVER SURFER (3RD SERIES)

Marvel Comics Group; 1 Jul 1987-present

Issue	$Good	$Fine	$N.Mint	£Good	£Fine	£N.Mint
1 ND DS, Marshall Rogers art begins, ends #12, Englehart scripts						
	$1.00	$3.00	$5.00	£0.80	£2.40	£4.00
2 ND	$0.70	$2.10	$3.50	£0.40	£1.20	£2.00
3-5	$0.50	$1.50	$2.50	£0.30	£0.90	£1.50
6	$0.40	$1.20	$2.00	£0.25	£0.75	£1.25
7 LD in the U.K.	$0.40	$1.20	$2.00	£0.30	£0.90	£1.50
8	$0.40	$1.20	$2.00	£0.25	£0.75	£1.25
9-10 Galactus appears						
	$0.40	$1.20	$2.00	£0.25	£0.75	£1.25
11 Galactus appears						
	$0.30	$0.90	$1.50	£0.20	£0.60	£1.00
12	$0.30	$0.90	$1.50	£0.20	£0.60	£1.00
13 Staton art	$0.30	$0.90	$1.50	£0.20	£0.60	£1.00
14 Staton art, Surfer battles Surfer; ties into Silver Surfer Annual #1						
	$0.30	$0.90	$1.50	£0.20	£0.60	£1.00
15 1st Ron Lim art on series, Fantastic Four appear						
	$0.50	$1.50	$2.50	£0.30	£0.90	£1.50
16 2nd Ron Lim art on series						
	$0.40	$1.20	$2.00	£0.25	£0.75	£1.25
17 Ron Lim art	$0.40	$1.20	$2.00	£0.25	£0.75	£1.25
18 Ron Lim art, Galactus vs. The In-Betweener						
	$0.40	$1.20	$2.00	£0.25	£0.75	£1.25
19 LD in the U.K. Surfer battles Firelord, Ron Lim art						
	$0.40	$1.20	$2.00	£0.25	£0.75	£1.25
20 Ron Lim art	$0.40	$1.20	$2.00	£0.25	£0.75	£1.25
21 Rogers art	$0.40	$1.20	$2.00	£0.25	£0.75	£1.25
22-24 Ron Lim art	$0.40	$1.20	$2.00	£0.25	£0.75	£1.25
25 LD in the U.K. DS Ron Lim art						
	$0.50	$1.50	$2.50	£0.30	£0.90	£1.50
26-30 Ron Lim art						
	$0.40	$1.20	$2.00	£0.25	£0.75	£1.25
31 LD in the U.K. DS Ron Lim art						
	$0.50	$1.50	$2.50	£0.30	£0.90	£1.50
32 Ron Frenz art	$0.40	$1.20	$2.00	£0.25	£0.75	£1.25
33 Impossible Man appears, Ron Lim art						
	$0.40	$1.20	$2.00	£0.25	£0.75	£1.25
34 Thanos returns (cover and cameo), (1st) Starlin script/Ron Lim art begins						
	$0.80	$2.40	$4.00	£0.50	£1.50	£2.50
35 Ron Lim art, 1st full re-appearance Thanos, Drax the Destroyer re-introduced on last page						
	$1.00	$3.00	$5.00	£0.60	£1.80	£3.00
36 Ron Lim art, history of Thanos						
	$0.80	$2.40	$4.00	£0.50	£1.50	£2.50
37 Ron Lim art	$0.60	$1.80	$3.00	£0.40	£1.20	£2.00
38 Ron Lim art, Silver Surfer vs. Thanos						
	$0.80	$2.40	$4.00	£0.50	£1.50	£2.50
39 Alan Grant script (no Jim Starlin/Ron Lim)						
	$0.40	$1.20	$2.00	£0.25	£0.75	£1.25
40-43 Jim Starlin script, Ron Lim art						
	$0.40	$1.20	$2.00	£0.25	£0.75	£1.25
44-45 Jim Starlin script, Ron Lim art, Thanos appears						
	$0.40	$1.20	$2.00	£0.25	£0.75	£1.25
46 Warlock returns, Jim Starlin script, Ron Lim art						
	$0.70	$2.10	$3.50	£0.40	£1.20	£2.00
47 Warlock appears, Jim Starlin script, Ron Lim art						
	$0.60	$1.80	$3.00	£0.30	£0.90	£1.50
48 Jim Starlin script, Ron Lim art						
	$0.40	$1.20	$2.00	£0.25	£0.75	£1.25
49 Jim Starlin script, Ron Lim art, Thanos appears						
	$0.40	$1.20	$2.00	£0.25	£0.75	£1.25
50 Silver Surfer vs. Thanos, special silver-embossed cover, Ron Lim art						
	$0.80	$2.40	$4.00	£0.50	£1.50	£2.50
50 2nd printing, scarce in the U.K. Silver Surfer vs. Thanos, Ron Lim art						
	$0.50	$1.50	$2.50	£0.30	£0.90	£1.50
50 3rd printing, very scarce in the U.K. not embossed						
	$0.50	$1.50	$2.50	£0.30	£0.90	£1.50
50 misprint, rare in the U.K. - silver over-lay production problem resulting in a pure all white Silver Surfer and logo (other misprints have only part of silver foil missing)						
	$1.20	$3.60	$6.00	£0.80	£2.40	£4.00
51 Infinity Gauntlet X-over, Ron Lim art						
	$0.50	$1.50	$2.50	£0.30	£0.90	£1.50
52-53 Infinity Gauntlet X-over, Ron Lim art, bi-weekly						

Issue	$Good	$Fine	$N.Mint	£Good	£Fine	£N.Mint
	$0.50	*$1.50*	*$2.50*	£0.30	£0.90	£1.50
54 Infinity Gauntlet X-over, Ron Lim art, bi-weekly; Silver Surfer vs. Rhino	*$0.50*	*$1.50*	*$2.50*	£0.30	£0.90	£1.50
55 Infinity Gauntlet X-over, Ron Lim art, bi-weekly; Thanos appears	*$0.50*	*$1.50*	*$2.50*	£0.30	£0.90	£1.50
56-57 Infinity Gauntlet X-over, Ron Lim art, bi-weekly; Thanos appears	*$0.40*	*$1.20*	*$2.00*	£0.25	£0.75	£1.25
58 Infinity Gauntlet X-over, Dr. Strange and Hulk appear (return of the old Defenders), Ron Lim art, bi-weekly issue	*$0.50*	*$1.50*	*$2.50*	£0.30	£0.90	£1.50
59 Infinity Gauntlet X-over, Dr. Strange, Warlock appear, Ron Lim art, bi-weekly issue	*$0.50*	*$1.50*	*$2.50*	£0.30	£0.90	£1.50
60 Infinity Gauntlet epilogue, Ron Lim art, bi-weekly issue	*$0.40*	*$1.20*	*$2.00*	£0.25	£0.75	£1.25
61 Ron Lim art	*$0.30*	*$0.90*	*$1.50*	£0.20	£0.60	£1.00
62 $1.25 cover begins, Ron Lim art	*$0.30*	*$0.90*	*$1.50*	£0.20	£0.60	£1.00
63 Captain Marvel "returns", Ron Lim art	*$0.30*	*$0.90*	*$1.50*	£0.20	£0.60	£1.00
64 Silver Surfer vs. Dark Silver Surfer, Ron Lim art	*$0.30*	*$0.90*	*$1.50*	£0.20	£0.60	£1.00
65-66 Ron Lim art	*$0.30*	*$0.90*	*$1.50*	£0.20	£0.60	£1.00
67-69 Infinity War X-over, Galactus appears, Ron Lim cover, bi-weekly	*$0.30*	*$0.90*	*$1.50*	£0.20	£0.60	£1.00
70 The Herald War begins, bi-weekly	*$0.30*	*$0.90*	*$1.50*	£0.20	£0.60	£1.00
71 Firelord appears, bi-weekly; 1st appearance Morg	*$0.25*	*$0.75*	*$1.25*	£0.15	£0.45	£0.75
72-73 Firelord appears, bi-weekly	*$0.25*	*$0.75*	*$1.25*	£0.15	£0.45	£0.75
74 Firelord and Nova appear	*$0.25*	*$0.75*	*$1.25*	£0.15	£0.45	£0.75
75 conclusion to The Herald Ordeal, foil embossed cover	*$0.40*	*$1.20*	*$2.00*	£0.25	£0.75	£1.25
76-78 Jack of Hearts appears	*$0.25*	*$0.75*	*$1.25*	£0.15	£0.45	£0.75
79	*$0.25*	*$0.75*	*$1.25*	£0.15	£0.45	£0.75
80 1st appearance Ganymede	*$0.25*	*$0.75*	*$1.25*	£0.15	£0.45	£0.75
81	*$0.25*	*$0.75*	*$1.25*	£0.15	£0.45	£0.75
82 Jack of Hearts and Beta Ray Bill appear	*$0.25*	*$0.75*	*$1.25*	£0.15	£0.45	£0.75
83-85 Infinity Crusade X-over	*$0.25*	*$0.75*	*$1.25*	£0.15	£0.45	£0.75
85 pre-bagged, ND - with Dirt Magazine and sticker	*$0.60*	*$1.80*	*$3.00*	£0.40	£1.20	£2.00
86	*$0.25*	*$0.75*	*$1.25*	£0.15	£0.45	£0.75
87 Blood and Thunder part 6; Dr. Strange, Warlock and the Infinity Watch appear	*$0.25*	*$0.75*	*$1.25*	£0.15	£0.45	£0.75
88 Blood and Thunder part 10; Silver Surfer and Thanos team-up	*$0.25*	*$0.75*	*$1.25*	£0.15	£0.45	£0.75
89-90	*$0.25*	*$0.75*	*$1.25*	£0.15	£0.45	£0.75
91 Ron Lim cover and art	*$0.25*	*$0.75*	*$1.25*	£0.15	£0.45	£0.75
92 Ron Lim cover and art; with free Spiderman and his Deadly Foes card sheet	*$0.25*	*$0.75*	*$1.25*	£0.15	£0.45	£0.75
93 Down to Earth story begins as Silver Surfer returns to Earth...	*$0.25*	*$0.75*	*$1.25*	£0.15	£0.45	£0.75
94 Adam Warlock and Fantastic Four appear	*$0.25*	*$0.75*	*$1.25*	£0.15	£0.45	£0.75
95	*$0.25*	*$0.75*	*$1.25*	£0.15	£0.45	£0.75
96 Fantastic Four appear	*$0.25*	*$0.75*	*$1.25*	£0.15	£0.45	£0.75
97-99	*$0.25*	*$0.75*	*$1.25*	£0.15	£0.45	£0.75
100 48pgs, Silver Surfer vs. Mephisto	*$0.50*	*$1.50*	*$2.50*	£0.30	£0.90	£1.50
100 Hologram cover 48pgs	*$0.80*	*$2.40*	*$4.00*	£0.50	£1.50	£2.50
101-104	*$0.30*	*$0.90*	*$1.50*	£0.20	£0.60	£1.00
105 Silver Surfer vs. Skrull	*$0.30*	*$0.90*	*$1.50*	£0.20	£0.60	£1.00
106 Legacy and Morg guest-star	*$0.30*	*$0.90*	*$1.50*	£0.20	£0.60	£1.00
107 Galactus, Morg and Tyrant appear	*$0.30*	*$0.90*	*$1.50*	£0.20	£0.60	£1.00
108-109 Galactus vs. Tyrant; bi-weekly	*$0.30*	*$0.90*	*$1.50*	£0.20	£0.60	£1.00
110 Nebula appears, John Buscema art	*$0.30*	*$0.90*	*$1.50*	£0.20	£0.60	£1.00
111 George Perez scripts begin; $1.95 cover begins	*$0.40*	*$1.20*	*$2.00*	£0.25	£0.75	£1.25
112-117	*$0.40*	*$1.20*	*$2.00*	£0.25	£0.75	£1.25
118-122	*$0.30*	*$0.90*	*$1.50*	£0.20	£0.60	£1.00
123 George Perez script and Ron Garney art begins	*$0.30*	*$0.90*	*$1.50*	£0.20	£0.60	£1.00
124	*$0.30*	*$0.90*	*$1.50*	£0.20	£0.60	£1.00
125 48pgs, Silver Surfer vs. The Incredible Hulk	*$0.60*	*$1.80*	*$3.00*	£0.40	£1.20	£2.00
126 ND Dr. Strange appears	*$0.40*	*$1.20*	*$2.00*	£0.25	£0.75	£1.25
Title Value:	*$52.10*	*$156.30*	*$260.50*	£32.75	£98.25	£163.75

Issue	$Good	$Fine	$N.Mint	£Good	£Fine	£N.Mint
Silver Surfer: Rebirth of Thanos (Jun 1993) Trade paperback reprints issues #34-38				£1.60	£4.80	£8.00

SILVER SURFER (3RD SERIES) ANNUAL

Marvel Comics Group; 1 1988-present

Issue	$Good	$Fine	$N.Mint	£Good	£Fine	£N.Mint
1 ND scarce in the U.K. squarebound, Evolutionary War; 1st Ron Lim art on the Silver Surfer	*$0.80*	*$2.40*	*$4.00*	£0.50	£1.50	£2.50
2 ND squarebound Atlantis Attacks part 1	*$0.50*	*$1.50*	*$2.50*	£0.30	£0.90	£1.50
3 ND Lifeform story conclusion	*$0.50*	*$1.50*	*$2.50*	£0.30	£0.90	£1.50
4 ND story continues in Guardians of the Galaxy Annual #1 (many copies have crinkled spine owing to production process)	*$0.50*	*$1.50*	*$2.50*	£0.30	£0.90	£1.50
5 ND Return of the Defenders part 3, guest stars Dr. Strange, Hulk, Sub-Mariner, continued in Dr. Strange Annual #2	*$0.50*	*$1.50*	*$2.50*	£0.30	£0.90	£1.50
6 ND 64pgs, pre-bagged with trading card, 1st appearance Legacy	*$0.60*	*$1.80*	*$3.00*	£0.40	£1.20	£2.00
7 ND 64pgs, Firelord, Air-Walker and Galactus appear	*$0.60*	*$1.80*	*$3.00*	£0.40	£1.20	£2.00
Title Value:	*$4.00*	*$12.00*	*$20.00*	£2.50	£7.50	£12.50

SILVER SURFER (LIMITED SERIES)

Marvel Comics Group,MS; 1 Dec 1988-2 Jan 1989

Issue	$Good	$Fine	$N.Mint	£Good	£Fine	£N.Mint
1 ND scarce in the U.K. Stan Lee script, Moebius art	*$0.60*	*$1.80*	*$3.00*	£0.50	£1.50	£2.50
2 ND scarce in the U.K. Stan Lee script, Moebius art	*$0.60*	*$1.80*	*$3.00*	£0.40	£1.20	£2.00
Title Value:	*$1.20*	*$3.60*	*$6.00*	£0.90	£2.70	£4.50
Silver Surfer: Parable Hardback (Apr 1989) Reprints 2 issue mini-series				£2.40	£7.20	£12.00
Silver Surfer: Parable Softback (Jul 1991) reprints mini-series plus new material				£1.20	£3.60	£6.00

SILVER SURFER ASHCAN EDITION

Marvel Comics Group,OS; nn May 1995

Issue	$Good	$Fine	$N.Mint	£Good	£Fine	£N.Mint
nn ND 16pgs, black and white	*$0.15*	*$0.45*	*$0.75*	£0.10	£0.30	£0.50
Title Value:	*$0.15*	*$0.45*	*$0.75*	£0.10	£0.30	£0.50

SILVER SURFER VS. DRACULA

Marvel Comics Group,OS; 1 Feb 1994

Issue	$Good	$Fine	$N.Mint	£Good	£Fine	£N.Mint
1 ND reprints Tomb of Dracula #50, new Ron Lim cover	*$0.30*	*$0.90*	*$1.50*	£0.20	£0.60	£1.00
Title Value:	*$0.30*	*$0.90*	*$1.50*	£0.20	£0.60	£1.00

SILVER SURFER/SUPERMAN

Marvel Comics Group/DC Comics,OS; nn Jan 1997

Issue	$Good	$Fine	$N.Mint	£Good	£Fine	£N.Mint
nn ND 48pgs, squarebound; Goerge Perez script, Ron Lim and Terry Austin art	*$1.20*	*$3.60*	*$6.00*	£0.80	£2.40	£4.00
Title Value:	*$1.20*	*$3.60*	*$6.00*	£0.80	£2.40	£4.00

SILVER SURFER/WARLOCK: RESURRECTION

Marvel Comics Group,MS; 1 Mar 1993-4 Jun 1993

Issue	$Good	$Fine	$N.Mint	£Good	£Fine	£N.Mint
1-4 Jim Starlin script and art with Terry Austin	*$0.40*	*$1.20*	*$2.00*	£0.25	£0.75	£1.25
Title Value:	*$1.60*	*$4.80*	*$8.00*	£1.00	£3.00	£5.00

SILVER SURFER/WEAPON ZERO

Marvel Comics Group/Top Cow Comics,OS; nn Mar 1997

Issue	$Good	$Fine	$N.Mint	£Good	£Fine	£N.Mint
nn ND Devil's Reign part 8 (conclusion); Brian Holguin script, Joe Benitez and Aaron Sowd art	*$0.60*	*$1.80*	*$3.00*	£0.40	£1.20	£2.00
Title Value:	*$0.60*	*$1.80*	*$3.00*	£0.40	£1.20	£2.00

SILVER SURFER: DANGEROUS ARTIFACTS

Marvel Comics Group,OS; nn Jun 1996

Issue	$Good	$Fine	$N.Mint	£Good	£Fine	£N.Mint
nn ND 48pgs, Thanos and Galactus appear; Ron Marz script, Claudio Castellini art	*$0.80*	*$2.40*	*$4.00*	£0.50	£1.50	£2.50
Title Value:	*$0.80*	*$2.40*	*$4.00*	£0.50	£1.50	£2.50

SILVER SURFER: THE FIRST COMING OF GALACTUS

Marvel Comics Group,OS; 1 Feb 1993

Issue	$Good	$Fine	$N.Mint	£Good	£Fine	£N.Mint
1 ND 64pgs, reprints Fantastic Four #48-#50, Ron Lim cover	*$1.00*	*$3.00*	*$5.00*	£0.70	£2.10	£3.50
Title Value:	*$1.00*	*$3.00*	*$5.00*	£0.70	£2.10	£3.50

SILVER SURFER: THE ULTIMATE COSMIC EXPERIENCE

Marvel Comics Group; nn 1978

Issue	$Good	$Fine	$N.Mint	£Good	£Fine	£N.Mint
nn ND rare in the U.K., scarce in the U.S. 114pgs, Stan Lee script Jack Kirby art (all new material), Earl Norem cover	*$24.00*	*$72.50*	*$170.00*	£12.00	£36.00	£85.00
Title Value:	*$24.00*	*$72.50*	*$170.00*	£12.00	£36.00	£85.00

SILVERBACK

Comico,MS; 1 Oct 1989-3 Dec 1989

Issue	$Good	$Fine	$N.Mint	£Good	£Fine	£N.Mint
1-3 ND Matt Wagner plot, John Beck art	*$0.40*	*$1.20*	*$2.00*	£0.25	£0.75	£1.25
Title Value:	*$1.20*	*$3.60*	*$6.00*	£0.75	£2.25	£3.75

SILVERBLADE

DC Comics,MS; 1 Sep 1987-12 Aug 1988

Issue	$Good	$Fine	$N.Mint	£Good	£Fine	£N.Mint
1 Gene Colan art begins; includes bound-in poster	*$0.15*	*$0.45*	*$0.75*	£0.10	£0.35	£0.60
2-12	*$0.15*	*$0.45*	*$0.75*	£0.10	£0.35	£0.60
Title Value:	*$1.80*	*$5.40*	*$9.00*	£1.20	£4.20	£7.20

SILVERHAWKS

Marvel Comics Group/Star; 1 Aug 1987-6 Jun 1988

Issue	$Good	$Fine	$N.Mint	£Good	£Fine	£N.Mint
1-6 ND	*$0.15*	*$0.45*	*$0.75*	£0.10	£0.35	£0.60
Title Value:	*$0.90*	*$2.70*	*$4.50*	£0.60	£2.10	£3.60

SILVERHEELS

Pacific; 1 Dec 1983-3 May 1984

Issue	$Good	$Fine	$N.Mint	£Good	£Fine	£N.Mint
1 ND Bruce Jones script, Scott Hampton, Ken Steacy art	*$0.40*	*$1.20*	*$2.00*	£0.25	£0.75	£1.25

	$Good	$Fine	$N.Mint	£Good	£Fine	£N.Mint
2 ND Scott Hampton, Ken Steacy art	$0.40	$1.20	$2.00	£0.25	£0.75	£1.25
3 ND Scott Hampton art, Ken Steacy, J. Hernandez back-ups	$0.40	$1.20	$2.00	£0.25	£0.75	£1.25
Title Value:	$1.20	$3.60	$6.00	£0.75	£2.25	£3.75

SILVERHEELS (2ND SERIES)

Eclipse;(Graphic Novel 12); 1 1987

	$Good	$Fine	$N.Mint	£Good	£Fine	£N.Mint
1 ND Jones/Campbell/Scott Hampton; completes story	$2.00	$6.00	$10.00	£1.40	£4.20	£7.00
Title Value:	$2.00	$6.00	$10.00	£1.40	£4.20	£7.00

SILVERSTORM

Aircel; 1 Jul 1990-4 1990

	$Good	$Fine	$N.Mint	£Good	£Fine	£N.Mint
1-4 ND Steven Butler art	$0.40	$1.20	$2.00	£0.25	£0.75	£1.25
Title Value:	$1.60	$4.80	$8.00	£1.00	£3.00	£5.00
Silverstorm Collection (1991) reprints issues #1-4, new cover by Dave Dorman				£1.05	£3.15	£5.25

SIMONSON, THE ART OF WALTER

DC Comics; nn Aug 1989

	$Good	$Fine	$N.Mint	£Good	£Fine	£N.Mint
nn ND 208pgs, Trade paperback; reprints include Detective Comics #450, new intro by Howard Chaykin	$4.00	$12.00	$20.00	£2.50	£7.50	£12.50
Title Value:	$4.00	$12.00	$20.00	£2.50	£7.50	£12.50

SIMPSONS COMICS

Bongo Comics; 1 Dec 1993-present

	$Good	$Fine	$N.Mint	£Good	£Fine	£N.Mint
1 ND pull-out poster; cover parody of Fantastic Four #1	$0.80	$2.40	$4.00	£0.50	£1.50	£2.50
2-10 ND	$0.50	$1.50	$2.50	£0.30	£0.90	£1.50
11 ND 1st monthly issue	$0.45	$1.35	$2.25	£0.30	£0.90	£1.50
12-27 ND	$0.45	$1.35	$2.25	£0.30	£0.90	£1.50
Title Value:	$12.95	$38.85	$65.00	£8.30	£24.90	£41.50
Simpsons Comics Extravaganza (1995) ND 128pgs, selected reprints				£1.30	£3.90	£6.50
Simpsons Comics Spectacular (Jun 1995) ND 128pgs, selected reprints				£1.30	£3.90	£6.50

SIMPSONS COMICS AND STORIES

Welsh Publishing,OS; 1 Apr 1993

	$Good	$Fine	$N.Mint	£Good	£Fine	£N.Mint
1 ND pre-bagged with poster	$0.90	$2.70	$4.50	£0.60	£1.80	£3.00
Title Value:	$0.90	$2.70	$4.50	£0.60	£1.80	£3.00

SIMPSONS ILLUSTRATED 1992 ANNUAL

Marvel Comics Group,Magazine OS; 1 Apr 1992

	$Good	$Fine	$N.Mint	£Good	£Fine	£N.Mint
1 ND pre-bagged with 3-D glasses	$0.60	$1.80	$3.00	£0.40	£1.20	£2.00
Title Value:	$0.60	$1.80	$3.00	£0.40	£1.20	£2.00

SIN CITY: A DAME TO KILL FOR

Dark Horse,MS; 1 Nov 1993-6 Apr 1994

	$Good	$Fine	$N.Mint	£Good	£Fine	£N.Mint
1 ND Frank Miller script and art	$1.20	$3.60	$6.00	£0.70	£2.10	£3.50
1 2nd printing, ND (Jul 1994)	$0.60	$1.80	$3.00	£0.40	£1.20	£2.00
2 ND Frank Miller script and art	$0.90	$2.70	$4.50	£0.60	£1.80	£3.00
2 2nd printing, ND (Jul 1994)	$0.60	$1.80	$3.00	£0.40	£1.20	£2.00
3 ND Frank Miller script and art	$0.80	$2.40	$4.00	£0.50	£1.50	£2.50
3 2nd printing, ND (Jul 1994)	$0.60	$1.80	$3.00	£0.40	£1.20	£2.00
4-6 ND Frank Miller script and art	$0.60	$1.80	$3.00	£0.40	£1.20	£2.00
Title Value:	$6.50	$19.50	$32.50	£4.20	£12.60	£21.00
Sin City: A Dame To Kill For Collection (Oct 1994) Trade paperback reprints mini-series with extra new pages by Frank Miller						
Softcover				£2.00	£6.00	£10.00
Hardcover				£3.50	£10.50	£17.50
Signed, Limited Edition (Nov 1994)				£12.00	£36.00	£60.00

SIN CITY: LOST, LONELY & LETHAL

Dark Horse,OS; 1 Dec 1996

	$Good	$Fine	$N.Mint	£Good	£Fine	£N.Mint
1 ND Frank Miller script and art; black and white	$0.60	$1.80	$3.00	£0.40	£1.20	£2.00
Title Value:	$0.60	$1.80	$3.00	£0.40	£1.20	£2.00

SIN CITY: SILENT NIGHT

Dark Horse,OS; 1 Nov 1995

	$Good	$Fine	$N.Mint	£Good	£Fine	£N.Mint
1 ND Frank Miller's wordless tale; black and white; card-stock cover	$0.60	$1.80	$3.00	£0.40	£1.20	£2.00
Title Value:	$0.60	$1.80	$3.00	£0.40	£1.20	£2.00

SIN CITY: THAT YELLOW BASTARD

Dark Horse,MS; 1 Feb 1996-6 Jul 1996

	$Good	$Fine	$N.Mint	£Good	£Fine	£N.Mint
1-5 ND Frank Miller script and art; black and white	$0.60	$1.80	$3.00	£0.40	£1.20	£2.00
6 ND 48pgs, Frank Miller script and art; black and white	$0.70	$2.10	$3.50	£0.50	£1.50	£2.50
Title Value:	$3.70	$11.10	$18.50	£2.50	£7.50	£12.50

SIN CITY: THE BABE WORE RED & OTHER STORIES

Dark Horse,OS; 1 Nov 1994

	$Good	$Fine	$N.Mint	£Good	£Fine	£N.Mint
1 ND Frank Miller script and art; black and white	$0.60	$1.80	$3.00	£0.40	£1.20	£2.00
Title Value:	$0.60	$1.80	$3.00	£0.40	£1.20	£2.00

SIN CITY: THE BIG FAT KILL

Dark Horse,MS; 1 Nov 1994-5 Mar 1995

	$Good	$Fine	$N.Mint	£Good	£Fine	£N.Mint
1 ND Frank Miller script and art, black and white	$0.80	$2.40	$4.00	£0.50	£1.50	£2.50
2-5 ND Frank Miller script and art, black and white	$0.60	$1.80	$3.00	£0.40	£1.20	£2.00
Title Value:	$3.20	$9.60	$16.00	£2.10	£6.30	£10.50
Sin City: Big Fat Kill Hardcover Collection (Dec 1995) ND collects mini-series with additional new pages				£3.30	£9.90	£16.50
Sin City: Big Fat Kill (May 1996) Trade paperback ND 184pgs, collects mini-series				£2.00	£6.00	£10.00
Sin City Limited Edition Hardcover (Jul 1996) ND 184pgs, limited to 1,000 copies				£12.00	£36.00	£60.00

SINBAD

Adventure,MS; 1 Feb 1990-4 May 1990

	$Good	$Fine	$N.Mint	£Good	£Fine	£N.Mint
1-4 ND	$0.40	$1.20	$2.00	£0.25	£0.75	£1.25
Title Value:	$1.60	$4.80	$8.00	£1.00	£3.00	£5.00

SINBAD, THE FANTASTIC VOYAGES OF

Gold Key; 1 Oct 1965; 2 Jun 1967

	$Good	$Fine	$N.Mint	£Good	£Fine	£N.Mint
1 rare although distributed in the U.K. painted cover	$5.50	$17.00	$40.00	£3.55	£10.50	£25.00
2 scarce distributed in the U.K. painted cover	$5.00	$15.00	$35.00	£2.85	£8.50	£20.00
Title Value:	$10.50	$32.00	$75.00	£6.40	£19.00	£45.00

SINBAD: HOUSE OF GOD

Adventure,MS; 1 Mar 1991-4 Jun 1991

	$Good	$Fine	$N.Mint	£Good	£Fine	£N.Mint
1-4 ND	$0.40	$1.20	$2.00	£0.25	£0.75	£1.25
Title Value:	$1.60	$4.80	$8.00	£1.00	£3.00	£5.00

SINERGY

Caliber Press; 1 Apr 1993-5 Oct 1993

	$Good	$Fine	$N.Mint	£Good	£Fine	£N.Mint
1 ND	$0.50	$1.50	$2.50	£0.30	£0.90	£1.50
1 Signed & Numbered Edition, ND - limited to 2,000 copies	$0.80	$2.40	$4.00	£0.50	£1.50	£2.50

Silver Star #1

Silver Surfer (Limited) #2

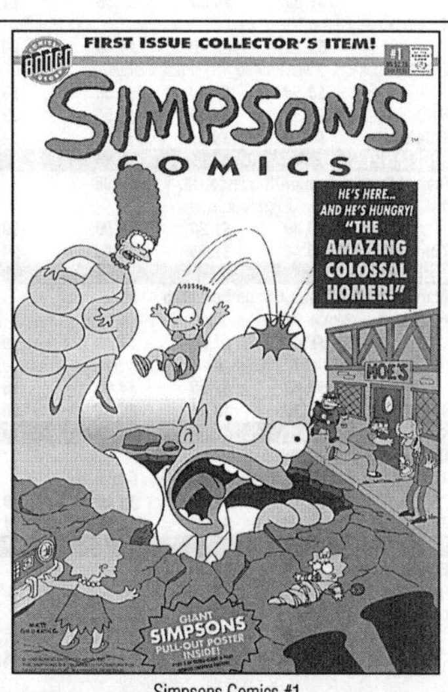

Simpsons Comics #1

	$Good	$Fine	$N.Mint	£Good	£Fine	£N.Mint
2 ND	$0.50	$1.50	$2.50	£0.30	£0.90	£1.50
2 Limited Edition, ND - signed by different creators; 2,000 copies	$0.60	$1.80	$3.00	£0.40	£1.20	£2.00
3 ND	$0.50	$1.50	$2.50	£0.30	£0.90	£1.50
3 Limited Edition, ND - signed by different creators; 2,000 copies	$0.60	$1.80	$3.00	£0.40	£1.20	£2.00
4 ND	$0.50	$1.50	$2.50	£0.30	£0.90	£1.50
4 Limited Edition, ND - signed by different creators; 2,000 copies	$0.60	$1.80	$3.00	£0.40	£1.20	£2.00
5 ND	$0.50	$1.50	$2.50	£0.30	£0.90	£1.50
5 Limited Edition, ND - signed by different creators; 2,000 copies	$0.60	$1.80	$3.00	£0.40	£1.20	£2.00
Title Value:	$5.70	$17.10	$28.50	£3.60	£10.80	£18.00
Sinergy Graphic Novel (Jul 1994) 176pgs collects mini-series				£2.00	£6.00	£10.00
Deluxe Edition, signed with print				£2.70	£8.10	£13.50

SINISTER HOUSE OF SECRET LOVE

DC Comics; 1 Oct/Nov 1971-4 Apr/May 1972
(becomes Secrets of Sinister House)

	$Good	$Fine	$N.Mint	£Good	£Fine	£N.Mint
1 ND 52pgs, gothic romance/mysteries begin	$2.05	$6.25	$12.50	£1.05	£3.25	£6.50
2-4 ND 52pgs	$1.25	$3.75	$7.50	£0.55	£1.75	£3.50
Title Value:	$5.80	$17.50	$35.00	£2.70	£8.50	£17.00

SINJA: DEADLY SINS

Lightning Comics,OS; 1 May 1996

	$Good	$Fine	$N.Mint	£Good	£Fine	£N.Mint
1 Commemorative Edition, ND pre-bagged with certificate; dimensional platinum metallic ink cover (!)	$1.20	$3.60	$6.00	£0.70	£2.10	£3.50
1 Cover A, ND Sinja alone	$0.60	$1.80	$3.00	£0.40	£1.20	£2.00
1 Cover B, ND group of female assassins	$0.60	$1.80	$3.00	£0.40	£1.20	£2.00
1 Nude Cover, ND pre-bagged with certificate	$2.00	$6.00	$10.00	£1.30	£3.90	£6.50
1 Signed Edition, ND (Jun 1996), pre-bagged with certificate; limited to 2,000 copies	$2.00	$6.00	$10.00	£1.30	£3.90	£6.50
Title Value:	$6.40	$19.20	$32.00	£4.10	£12.30	£20.50

SINJA: RESURRECTION

Lightning Comics,OS; 1 Aug 1996

	$Good	$Fine	$N.Mint	£Good	£Fine	£N.Mint
1 ND John Cleary art	$0.60	$1.80	$3.00	£0.40	£1.20	£2.00
1 Platinum Edition, ND pre-bagged with certificate, platinum/silver cover	$2.00	$6.00	$10.00	£1.30	£3.90	£6.50
Title Value:	$2.60	$7.80	$13.00	£1.70	£5.10	£8.50

SINKING GRAPHIC NOVEL

Marvel Comics Group,OS; nn Dec 1992

	$Good	$Fine	$N.Mint	£Good	£Fine	£N.Mint
nn ND 80pgs, James Hudnall script, Rob Ortelezah art	$3.00	$9.00	$15.00	£2.00	£6.00	£10.00
Title Value:	$3.00	$9.00	$15.00	£2.00	£6.00	£10.00

SINNAMON

Catfish Comics; 1 1995-7 1996 ?

	$Good	$Fine	$N.Mint	£Good	£Fine	£N.Mint
1-7 ND Angelo Furan script, Gerald Delaney art; black and white	$0.55	$1.65	$2.75	£0.35	£1.05	£1.75
Title Value:	$3.85	$11.55	$19.25	£2.45	£7.35	£12.25

SINNER

Fantagraphics,Magazine; 1 Spring 1987-7 1990

	$Good	$Fine	$N.Mint	£Good	£Fine	£N.Mint
1-7 ND Munoz art	$0.60	$1.80	$3.00	£0.40	£1.20	£2.00
Title Value:	$4.20	$12.60	$21.00	£2.80	£8.40	£14.00

SIREN

Marvel Comics Group; 1 Dec 1995-3 Feb 1996

	$Good	$Fine	$N.Mint	£Good	£Fine	£N.Mint
1 ND Hank Kanaiz script, Kevin West and Bob Almond art; Siren and Diamondback vs. War Machine	$0.30	$0.90	$1.50	£0.20	£0.60	£1.00
1 Signed Limited Edition, ND (Jan 1996), with certificate; 2,000 copies	$1.50	$4.50	$7.50	£1.00	£3.00	£5.00
1 Variant Cover Edition, ND - computer painted cover by Chuck Maiden	$0.80	$2.40	$4.00	£0.50	£1.50	£2.50
2 ND flip-book format with Phoenix Ressurrection chapter	$0.30	$0.90	$1.50	£0.20	£0.60	£1.00
3 ND	$0.30	$0.90	$1.50	£0.20	£0.60	£1.00
Title Value:	$3.20	$9.60	$16.00	£2.10	£6.30	£10.50

SIREN SPECIAL

Marvel Comics Group/Ultraverse,OS; 1 Apr 1996

	$Good	$Fine	$N.Mint	£Good	£Fine	£N.Mint
1 ND Siren vs. Shuriken, Juggernaut appears	$0.40	$1.20	$2.00	£0.25	£0.75	£1.25
Title Value:	$0.40	$1.20	$2.00	£0.25	£0.75	£1.25

SIREN: INFINITY

Marvel Comics Group,OS; nn Nov 1995

	$Good	$Fine	$N.Mint	£Good	£Fine	£N.Mint
nn ND Black September tie-in; spin-off from Ultraforce/Avengers X-over, War Machine appears	$0.50	$1.50	$2.50	£0.30	£0.90	£1.50
nn Variant Cover Edition ND 1 copy received for every 5 copies of the regular issue ordered	$0.80	$2.40	$4.00	£0.50	£1.50	£2.50
Title Value:	$1.30	$3.90	$6.50	£0.80	£2.40	£4.00

SIRENS

Caliber Press; 1,2 1993

	$Good	$Fine	$N.Mint	£Good	£Fine	£N.Mint
1-2 ND Sid Williams script, John Drury and Chuck Bordell art	$0.80	$2.40	$4.00	£0.50	£1.50	£2.50
Title Value:	$1.60	$4.80	$8.00	£1.00	£3.00	£5.00

SISTERHOOD OF STEEL

Eclipse;(Graphic Novel 13); 1 1987
(see Marvel series)

	$Good	$Fine	$N.Mint	£Good	£Fine	£N.Mint
nn ND Christy Marx, Pete Ledger	$1.50	$4.50	$7.50	£1.00	£3.00	£5.00
Title Value:	$1.50	$4.50	$7.50	£1.00	£3.00	£5.00

SISTERHOOD OF STEEL, THE

Marvel Comics Group/Epic; 1 Dec 1984-8 Apr 1986
(see Marvel Graphic Novel)

	$Good	$Fine	$N.Mint	£Good	£Fine	£N.Mint
1-8 ND Baxter paper	$0.30	$0.90	$1.50	£0.20	£0.60	£1.00
Title Value:	$2.40	$7.20	$12.00	£1.60	£4.80	£8.00

SISTERS OF MERCY

No Mercy Comics; 1 Mar 1996-5 Oct 1996

	$Good	$Fine	$N.Mint	£Good	£Fine	£N.Mint
1-5 ND Mark Williams and Rikki Rockett script and art	$0.50	$1.50	$2.50	£0.30	£0.90	£1.50
Title Value:	$2.50	$7.50	$12.50	£1.50	£4.50	£7.50

SIX DEGREES

(see British Section)

SIX FROM SIRIUS

Marvel Comics Group/Epic,MS; 1 Jul 1984-4 Oct 1984

	$Good	$Fine	$N.Mint	£Good	£Fine	£N.Mint
1-4 ND Gulacy art	$0.40	$1.20	$2.00	£0.25	£0.75	£1.25
Title Value:	$1.60	$4.80	$8.00	£1.00	£3.00	£5.00
Trade paperback, reprints #1-4				£1.00	£3.00	£5.00

SIX FROM SIRIUS II

Marvel Comics Group/Epic,MS; 1 Feb 1986-4 May 1986

	$Good	$Fine	$N.Mint	£Good	£Fine	£N.Mint
1-4 ND Gulacy art	$0.40	$1.20	$2.00	£0.25	£0.75	£1.25
Title Value:	$1.60	$4.80	$8.00	£1.00	£3.00	£5.00

SIX MILLION DOLLAR MAN

Charlton; 1 Jun 1976-9 Jul 1978

	$Good	$Fine	$N.Mint	£Good	£Fine	£N.Mint
1 scarce in the U.K. Joe Staton art begins, Staton painted cover	$0.50	$1.50	$3.00	£0.30	£1.00	£2.00
2 scarce in the U.K. Neal Adams cover	$0.40	$1.25	$2.50	£0.25	£0.75	£1.50
3 scarce in the U.K.	$0.30	$1.00	$2.00	£0.20	£0.60	£1.25
4-6	$0.25	$0.75	$1.50	£0.15	£0.50	£1.00
7-9 scarce in the U.K.	$0.25	$0.75	$1.50	£0.20	£0.60	£1.25
Title Value:	$2.70	$8.25	$16.50	£1.80	£5.65	£11.50

Note: all distributed in the U.K. though irregularly published

SIX MILLION DOLLAR MAN (MAGAZINE)

Charlton,Magazine; 1 Jun 1976-8 Mar 1978

	$Good	$Fine	$N.Mint	£Good	£Fine	£N.Mint
1 ND Neal Adams art	$0.50	$1.50	$3.00	£0.30	£1.00	£2.00
2-8 ND	$0.30	$1.00	$2.00	£0.25	£0.75	£1.50
Title Value:	$2.60	$8.50	$17.00	£2.05	£6.25	£12.50

SIX-GUN HEROES

Charlton;24 Jan 1954-83 Apr 1965

	$Good	$Fine	$N.Mint	£Good	£Fine	£N.Mint
24 scarce in the U.K.	$17.50	$52.50	$125.00	£11.50	£35.00	£82.50
25 scarce in the U.K.	$8.50	$26.00	$60.00	£5.50	£17.00	£40.00
26-30	$7.00	$21.00	$50.00	£4.25	£12.50	£30.00
31-40	$6.00	$18.00	$42.50	£3.55	£10.50	£25.00
41-50	$5.50	$17.00	$40.00	£3.20	£9.50	£22.50
51-56	$4.25	$12.50	$30.00	£2.50	£7.50	£17.50
57 1st appearance Gunmaster	$5.00	$15.00	$35.00	£3.20	£9.50	£22.50
58-60	$4.25	$12.50	$30.00	£2.50	£7.50	£17.50
61-70	$2.85	$8.50	$20.00	£1.75	£5.25	£12.50
71-83	$2.10	$6.25	$15.00	£1.40	£4.25	£10.00
Title Value:	$275.05	$827.25	$1960.00	£167.15	£499.25	£1182.50

Note: reasonable distribution of issues in the U.K. after 1959/60

SIX-GUN HEROES (2ND SERIES)

A Plus Comics; 1 Jul 1991

	$Good	$Fine	$N.Mint	£Good	£Fine	£N.Mint
1 ND 48pgs, western reprints including Steve Ditko art	$0.40	$1.20	$2.00	£0.25	£0.75	£1.25
Title Value:	$0.40	$1.20	$2.00	£0.25	£0.75	£1.25

SIXTY SEVEN SECONDS GRAPHIC NOVEL

Marvel Comics Group,OS; nn Dec 1992

	$Good	$Fine	$N.Mint	£Good	£Fine	£N.Mint
nn ND 80pgs, Robinson script, Steve Yeowell art	$3.00	$9.00	$15.00	£2.00	£6.00	£10.00
Title Value:	$3.00	$9.00	$15.00	£2.00	£6.00	£10.00

SKATEMAN

Pacific; 1 Nov 1983

	$Good	$Fine	$N.Mint	£Good	£Fine	£N.Mint
1 ND Neal Adams story and art	$0.30	$0.90	$1.50	£0.20	£0.60	£1.00
Title Value:	$0.30	$0.90	$1.50	£0.20	£0.60	£1.00

SKELETON WARRIORS

Marvel Comics Group,MS; 1 Apr 1995-4 Jul 1995

	$Good	$Fine	$N.Mint	£Good	£Fine	£N.Mint
1-4 ND based on US animated series	$0.25	$0.75	$1.25	£0.15	£0.45	£0.75
Title Value:	$1.00	$3.00	$5.00	£0.60	£1.80	£3.00

SKIDMARKS

Tundra,MS; 1 Aug 1992

	$Good	$Fine	$N.Mint	£Good	£Fine	£N.Mint
1 ND reprints British independent comic from the '80s	$0.50	$1.50	$2.50	£0.30	£0.90	£1.50
Title Value:	$0.50	$1.50	$2.50	£0.30	£0.90	£1.50

SKIN GRAFT

DC Comics/Vertigo,MS; 1 Jul 1993-4 Oct 1993

	$Good	$Fine	$N.Mint	£Good	£Fine	£N.Mint
1 ND Warren Pleece art begins, photo covers begin; sub-titled "The Adventures of a Tattooed Man" (note: Green Lantern villain)	$0.50	$1.50	$2.50	£0.35	£1.05	£1.75
2-4 ND	$0.50	$1.50	$2.50	£0.30	£0.90	£1.50
Title Value:	$2.00	$6.00	$10.00	£1.25	£3.75	£6.25

SKREEMER

DC Comics,MS; 1 May 1989-6 Oct 1989

	$Good	$Fine	$N.Mint	£Good	£Fine	£N.Mint
1-6 ND	$0.25	$0.75	$1.25	£0.15	£0.45	£0.75

	$Good	$Fine	$N.Mint	£Good	£Fine	£N.Mint
Title Value:	$1.50	$4.50	$7.50	£0.90	£2.70	£4.50

Note: Mature Readers label. 1st DC creator-owned project (see Tempus Fugitives); Peter Milligan script/Brett Ewins art

SKROG
Comico; 1 1984

	$Good	$Fine	$N.Mint	£Good	£Fine	£N.Mint
1 ND black and white	$0.40	$1.20	$2.00	£0.25	£0.75	£1.25
Title Value:	$0.40	$1.20	$2.00	£0.25	£0.75	£1.25

SKROG (YIP YIP YAY) SPECIAL
Crystal; 1 Dec 1987

	$Good	$Fine	$N.Mint	£Good	£Fine	£N.Mint
1 ND 64pgs, black and white	$0.40	$1.20	$2.00	£0.25	£0.75	£1.25
Title Value:	$0.40	$1.20	$2.00	£0.25	£0.75	£1.25

SKRULL KILL KREW
Marvel Comics Group,MS; 1 Sep 1995-5 Jan 1996

	$Good	$Fine	$N.Mint	£Good	£Fine	£N.Mint
1-5 ND Grant Morrison and Mark Millar script, Steve Yeowell and Chris Ivy art	$0.60	$1.80	$3.00	£0.40	£1.20	£2.00
Title Value:	$3.00	$9.00	$15.00	£2.00	£6.00	£10.00

SKULL AND BONES
DC Comics,MS; 1 Feb 1992-3 Apr 1992

	$Good	$Fine	$N.Mint	£Good	£Fine	£N.Mint
1-3 ND 48pgs	$0.80	$2.40	$4.00	£0.50	£1.50	£2.50
Title Value:	$2.40	$7.20	$12.00	£1.50	£4.50	£7.50

SKULL THE SLAYER
Marvel Comics Group; 1 Aug 1975-8 Nov 1976

	$Good	$Fine	$N.Mint	£Good	£Fine	£N.Mint
1 ND 1st appearance Skull the Slayer; Marv Wolfman script begins	$0.65	$2.00	$4.00	£0.30	£1.00	£2.00
2-3	$0.50	$1.50	$3.00	£0.25	£0.75	£1.50
4-5 Black Knight appears	$0.30	$1.00	$2.00	£0.20	£0.60	£1.25
6-8	$0.30	$1.00	$2.00	£0.20	£0.60	£1.25
Title Value:	$3.15	$10.00	$20.00	£1.80	£5.50	£11.25

SKY GAL
AC Comics; 1 Sep 1993-3 1994

	$Good	$Fine	$N.Mint	£Good	£Fine	£N.Mint
1 ND pre-bagged with trading card	$0.60	$1.80	$3.00	£0.40	£1.20	£2.00
2-3 ND	$0.60	$1.80	$3.00	£0.40	£1.20	£2.00
Title Value:	$1.80	$5.40	$9.00	£1.20	£3.60	£6.00

SKY WOLF
Eclipse,MS; 1 Mar 1988-3 Oct 1988

(see Airboy)

	$Good	$Fine	$N.Mint	£Good	£Fine	£N.Mint
1-3 ND Tom Lyle cover and art; colour	$0.40	$1.20	$2.00	£0.25	£0.75	£1.25
Title Value:	$1.20	$3.60	$6.00	£0.75	£2.25	£3.75

SKY-HOPPER
Illuminated Comics; 1 Feb 1991

	$Good	$Fine	$N.Mint	£Good	£Fine	£N.Mint
1 ND black and white	$0.15	$0.45	$0.75	£0.10	£0.30	£0.50
Title Value:	$0.15	$0.45	$0.75	£0.10	£0.30	£0.50

SLAPSTICK
Marvel Comics Group,MS; 1 Nov 1992-4 Feb 1993

	$Good	$Fine	$N.Mint	£Good	£Fine	£N.Mint
1-3	$0.25	$0.75	$1.25	£0.15	£0.45	£0.75
4 Ghost Rider, Daredevil, Captain America, Fantastic Four and Speedball appear	$0.25	$0.75	$1.25	£0.15	£0.45	£0.75
Title Value:	$1.00	$3.00	$5.00	£0.60	£1.80	£3.00

SLASH
Northstar; 1 Aug 1992-4 1993

	$Good	$Fine	$N.Mint	£Good	£Fine	£N.Mint
1 ND horror anthology	$0.50	$1.50	$2.50	£0.30	£0.90	£1.50
1 Red Embossed Cover Edition ND	$0.80	$2.40	$4.00	£0.50	£1.50	£2.50
2-4 ND	$0.50	$1.50	$2.50	£0.30	£0.90	£1.50
Title Value:	$2.80	$8.40	$14.00	£1.70	£5.10	£8.50

SLASH ANNUAL
Northstar; 1 Jan 1994

	$Good	$Fine	$N.Mint	£Good	£Fine	£N.Mint
1 ND 48pgs, black and white	$0.90	$2.70	$4.50	£0.60	£1.80	£3.00
Title Value:	$0.90	$2.70	$4.50	£0.60	£1.80	£3.00

SLASH MARAUD
DC Comics,MS; 1 Nov 1987-6 Apr 1988

	$Good	$Fine	$N.Mint	£Good	£Fine	£N.Mint
1-6 ND Gulacy art	$0.25	$0.75	$1.25	£0.15	£0.45	£0.75
Title Value:	$1.50	$4.50	$7.50	£0.90	£2.70	£4.50

Note: Mature Readers, Deluxe Format.

SLAUGHTERHOUSE USA
Innovation,OS; 1 Jun 1991

	$Good	$Fine	$N.Mint	£Good	£Fine	£N.Mint
1 ND	$0.40	$1.20	$2.00	£0.25	£0.75	£1.25
Title Value:	$0.40	$1.20	$2.00	£0.25	£0.75	£1.25

SLAUGHTERMAN
Comico; 1 Feb 1983-2 Apr 1983

	$Good	$Fine	$N.Mint	£Good	£Fine	£N.Mint
1-2 ND	$0.40	$1.20	$2.00	£0.25	£0.75	£1.25
Title Value:	$0.80	$2.40	$4.00	£0.50	£1.50	£2.50

SLEDGE HAMMER
Marvel Comics Group,MS TV; 1 Feb 1988-2 Mar 1988

	$Good	$Fine	$N.Mint	£Good	£Fine	£N.Mint
1 Satana appears	$0.25	$0.75	$1.25	£0.15	£0.45	£0.75
2 "Spiderman" appears	$0.25	$0.75	$1.25	£0.15	£0.45	£0.75
Title Value:	$0.50	$1.50	$2.50	£0.30	£0.90	£1.50

SLEEPWALKER
Marvel Comics Group; 1 Jun 1991-33 Mar 1994

	$Good	$Fine	$N.Mint	£Good	£Fine	£N.Mint
1 ND Blevins art begins	$0.30	$0.90	$1.50	£0.20	£0.60	£1.00
2 ND Blevins art	$0.25	$0.75	$1.25	£0.15	£0.45	£0.75
3 ND X-Factor/X-Men/Fantastic Four/Avengers appear in dream sequence, Blevins art	$0.25	$0.75	$1.25	£0.15	£0.45	£0.75
4 ND Leonardi art	$0.25	$0.75	$1.25	£0.15	£0.45	£0.75
5 ND Blevins art, Spiderman, Kingpin appear	$0.25	$0.75	$1.25	£0.15	£0.45	£0.75
6 ND Blevins art, Infinity Gauntlet X-over, Spiderman appears	$0.25	$0.75	$1.25	£0.15	£0.45	£0.75
7 ND Infinity Gauntlet X-over	$0.25	$0.75	$1.25	£0.15	£0.45	£0.75
8 ND Deathlok appears	$0.25	$0.75	$1.25	£0.15	£0.45	£0.75
9 $1.25 cover begins	$0.25	$0.75	$1.25	£0.15	£0.45	£0.75
10	$0.25	$0.75	$1.25	£0.15	£0.45	£0.75
11 Sleepwalker vs. Ghost Rider	$0.25	$0.75	$1.25	£0.15	£0.45	£0.75
12 Nightmare appears, upside down logo	$0.25	$0.75	$1.25	£0.15	£0.45	£0.75
13	$0.25	$0.75	$1.25	£0.15	£0.45	£0.75
14 intro Spectra	$0.25	$0.75	$1.25	£0.15	£0.45	£0.75
15 Fantastic Four guest star	$0.25	$0.75	$1.25	£0.15	£0.45	£0.75
16 Mr. Fantastic and The Thing appear	$0.25	$0.75	$1.25	£0.15	£0.45	£0.75
17 X-over Darkhawk #20, Darkhawk and Spiderman appear	$0.25	$0.75	$1.25	£0.15	£0.45	£0.75
18 Infinity War X-over, Professor Xavier appears, Joe Quesada cover	$0.25	$0.75	$1.25	£0.15	£0.45	£0.75
19 Halloween issue with pop-out mask on cover	$0.30	$0.90	$1.50	£0.20	£0.60	£1.00
20 Sam Kieth cover	$0.25	$0.75	$1.25	£0.15	£0.45	£0.75
21 Hobgoblin appears, Sam Kieth cover	$0.25	$0.75	$1.25	£0.15	£0.45	£0.75
22 Hobgoblin appears	$0.25	$0.75	$1.25	£0.15	£0.45	£0.75
23-24	$0.25	$0.75	$1.25	£0.15	£0.45	£0.75
25 48pgs, "oil-slick" holo-grafix cover; new direction for title	$0.30	$0.90	$1.50	£0.20	£0.60	£1.00
26	$0.25	$0.75	$1.25	£0.15	£0.45	£0.75
27 Avengers guest-star	$0.25	$0.75	$1.25	£0.15	£0.45	£0.75
28-33	$0.25	$0.75	$1.25	£0.15	£0.45	£0.75
Title Value:	$8.40	$25.20	$42.00	£5.10	£15.30	£25.50

SLEEPWALKER HOLIDAY SPECIAL
Marvel Comics Group,OS; 1 Jan 1993

	$Good	$Fine	$N.Mint	£Good	£Fine	£N.Mint
1 ND 48pgs	$0.30	$0.90	$1.50	£0.20	£0.60	£1.00
Title Value:	$0.30	$0.90	$1.50	£0.20	£0.60	£1.00

SLEEZE BROTHERS
Marvel Comics Group/Epic,MS; 1 Aug 1989-6 Jan 1990

	$Good	$Fine	$N.Mint	£Good	£Fine	£N.Mint
1 ND Andy Lanning pencils begin	$0.25	$0.75	$1.25	£0.15	£0.45	£0.75
2-6 ND	$0.25	$0.75	$1.25	£0.15	£0.45	£0.75
Title Value:	$1.50	$4.50	$7.50	£0.90	£2.70	£4.50
Trade paperback						
reprints issues #1-6 plus 8pgs new material				£1.90	£5.70	£9.50

SLEEZE BROTHERS SPECIAL
Marvel Comics Group,OS; 1 Nov 1991

	$Good	$Fine	$N.Mint	£Good	£Fine	£N.Mint
1 ND 48pgs	$0.60	$1.80	$3.00	£0.40	£1.20	£2.00
Title Value:	$0.60	$1.80	$3.00	£0.40	£1.20	£2.00

SLIDERS
Acclaim Comics,MS; 1 Jun 1996-2 Jul 1996

	$Good	$Fine	$N.Mint	£Good	£Fine	£N.Mint
1-2 ND D.G. Chichester script, Dick Giordano and Mike DeCarlo art; based on TV series	$0.50	$1.50	$2.50	£0.30	£0.90	£1.50
Title Value:	$1.00	$3.00	$5.00	£0.60	£1.80	£3.00

SLIDERS SPECIAL
Acclaim Comics,OS; 1 Nov 1996

	$Good	$Fine	$N.Mint	£Good	£Fine	£N.Mint
1 ND 48pgs, features Jackson Guice art	$0.80	$2.40	$4.00	£0.50	£1.50	£2.50
Title Value:	$0.80	$2.40	$4.00	£0.50	£1.50	£2.50

SLIDERS SPECIAL: DEADLY SECRETS
Acclaim Comics,OS; 1 Mar 1997

	$Good	$Fine	$N.Mint	£Good	£Fine	£N.Mint
1 ND 48pgs	$0.80	$2.40	$4.00	£0.50	£1.50	£2.50
Title Value:	$0.80	$2.40	$4.00	£0.50	£1.50	£2.50

SLIDERS: DARKEST HOUR
Acclaim Comics,MS; 1 Oct 1996-3 Dec 1996

	$Good	$Fine	$N.Mint	£Good	£Fine	£N.Mint
1-3 ND D.G. Chichester script, Dick Giordano art	$0.50	$1.50	$2.50	£0.30	£0.90	£1.50
Title Value:	$1.50	$4.50	$7.50	£0.90	£2.70	£4.50

SLIDERS: ULTIMATUM
Acclaim Comics,MS; 1 Aug 1996-2 Sep 1996

	$Good	$Fine	$N.Mint	£Good	£Fine	£N.Mint
1-2 ND based on TV show	$0.50	$1.50	$2.50	£0.30	£0.90	£1.50
Title Value:	$1.00	$3.00	$5.00	£0.60	£1.80	£3.00

SLOW DANCE WITH DEATH
Comico,OS; 1 May 1992

	$Good	$Fine	$N.Mint	£Good	£Fine	£N.Mint
1 ND 48pgs, duo-tone art	$0.80	$2.40	$4.00	£0.50	£1.50	£2.50
Title Value:	$0.80	$2.40	$4.00	£0.50	£1.50	£2.50

SLUDGE
Malibu Ultraverse; 1 Oct 1993-13 Nov 1994

	$Good	$Fine	$N.Mint	£Good	£Fine	£N.Mint
1 40pgs, Rune part 1, Steve Gerber script begins	$0.50	$1.50	$2.50	£0.30	£0.90	£1.50

Issue	$Good	$Fine	$N.Mint	£Good	£Fine	£N.Mint
2	$0.40	$1.20	$2.00	£0.25	£0.75	£1.25
3 Break Thru tie-in	$0.40	$1.20	$2.00	£0.25	£0.75	£1.25
4 origin of Mantra	$0.40	$1.20	$2.00	£0.25	£0.75	£1.25
5-8	$0.40	$1.20	$2.00	£0.25	£0.75	£1.25
9-10 origin of Sludge	$0.40	$1.20	$2.00	£0.25	£0.75	£1.25
11	$0.40	$1.20	$2.00	£0.25	£0.75	£1.25
12 64pgs, flip-book format with Ultraverse Premiere #8	$0.50	$1.50	$2.50	£0.30	£0.90	£1.50
13	$0.40	$1.20	$2.00	£0.25	£0.75	£1.25
Title Value:	$5.40	$16.20	$27.00	£3.35	£10.05	£16.75

Note: all Non-Distributed on the news-stands in the U.K.

SLUDGE: RED XMAS

Malibu Ultraverse, OS; 1 Dec 1994

Issue	$Good	$Fine	$N.Mint	£Good	£Fine	£N.Mint
1 ND Steve Gerber script, Mike Ploog art	$0.50	$1.50	$2.50	£0.30	£0.90	£1.50
Title Value:	$0.50	$1.50	$2.50	£0.30	£0.90	£1.50

SMURFS

Marvel Comics Group, TV; 1 Dec 1982-3 Feb 1983

Issue	$Good	$Fine	$N.Mint	£Good	£Fine	£N.Mint
1-3 ND	$0.15	$0.45	$0.75	£0.10	£0.35	£0.60
Title Value:	$0.45	$1.35	$2.25	£0.30	£1.05	£1.80

SNAKE EYES

Fantagraphics, OS; nn Feb 1991

Issue	$Good	$Fine	$N.Mint	£Good	£Fine	£N.Mint
nn ND 80pgs, anthology featuring Charles Burns and David Mazzuchelli	$1.20	$3.60	$6.00	£0.80	£2.40	£4.00
nn 2nd printing ND (Oct 1992)	$1.00	$3.00	$5.00	£0.70	£2.10	£3.50
Title Value:	$2.20	$6.60	$11.00	£1.50	£4.50	£7.50

SNAKE PLISSKEN, THE ADVENTURES OF

Marvel Comics Group, OS; nn Mar 1997

Issue	$Good	$Fine	$N.Mint	£Good	£Fine	£N.Mint
nn ND featuring the Kurt Russell character from Escape From New York	$0.50	$1.50	$2.50	£0.30	£0.90	£1.50
Title Value:	$0.50	$1.50	$2.50	£0.30	£0.90	£1.50

SNAKE, THE

Anubis Press; 0 Jan 1994; 1 Mar 1994

Issue	$Good	$Fine	$N.Mint	£Good	£Fine	£N.Mint
0 ND black and white	$0.40	$1.20	$2.00	£0.25	£0.75	£1.25
0 Ashcan Edition, ND (Feb 1994), 10,000 copies; black and white	$0.50	$1.50	$2.50	£0.30	£0.90	£1.50
1 ND Edward Morges script and art	$0.40	$1.20	$2.00	£0.25	£0.75	£1.25
1 Ashcan Edition, ND (Sep 1994) - 5,000 copies, black and white	$0.50	$1.50	$2.50	£0.30	£0.90	£1.50
Title Value:	$1.80	$5.40	$9.00	£1.10	£3.30	£5.50

SNARF

Kitchen Sink; 1 1988-25 1990

Issue	$Good	$Fine	$N.Mint	£Good	£Fine	£N.Mint
1-25 ND black and white	$0.25	$0.75	$1.25	£0.15	£0.45	£0.75
Title Value:	$6.25	$18.75	$31.25	£3.75	£11.25	£18.75

SNOW WHITE AND THE SEVEN DWARFS

Gladstone, Magazine OS; 1 1987

Issue	$Good	$Fine	$N.Mint	£Good	£Fine	£N.Mint
1 ND 50th anniversary; adapts film	$0.80	$2.40	$4.00	£0.50	£1.50	£2.50
Title Value:	$0.80	$2.40	$4.00	£0.50	£1.50	£2.50

SNOW WHITE SPECIAL EDITION

Marvel Comics Group, Film; nn Jan 1995

Issue	$Good	$Fine	$N.Mint	£Good	£Fine	£N.Mint
nn ND 48pgs, uses original artwork from 1937	$0.40	$1.20	$2.00	£0.25	£0.75	£1.25
Title Value:	$0.40	$1.20	$2.00	£0.25	£0.75	£1.25

SNOWMAN

Hall of Heroes; 1 Jul 1996-Sep 1996

Issue	$Good	$Fine	$N.Mint	£Good	£Fine	£N.Mint
1 ND Matt Martin script and art; black and white begins	$3.00	$9.00	$15.00	£1.20	£3.60	£6.00
1 San Diego '96 Edition, ND reprints Hall of Heroes #1 with new cover	$3.00	$9.00	$15.00	£2.00	£6.00	£10.00
1 Variant Cover Edition, ND cover by Ethan van Sciver	$5.00	$15.00	$25.00	£3.00	£9.00	£15.00
2 ND	$1.00	$3.00	$5.00	£0.60	£1.80	£3.00
2 Variant Cover Edition, ND cover by Trent Kanuiga	$2.00	$6.00	$10.00	£1.30	£3.90	£6.50
3 ND	$0.50	$1.50	$2.50	£0.30	£0.90	£1.50
3 Variant Cover Edition, ND cover by Jamie Hood	$1.00	$3.00	$5.00	£0.60	£1.80	£3.00
Title Value:	$15.50	$46.50	$77.50	£9.00	£27.00	£45.00

SNOWMAN: 1944

Entity Comics; 1 Oct 1996-present

Issue	$Good	$Fine	$N.Mint	£Good	£Fine	£N.Mint
1-2 ND Matt Martin script and art; black and white	$0.55	$1.65	$2.75	£0.35	£1.05	£1.75
Title Value:	$1.10	$3.30	$5.50	£0.70	£2.10	£3.50

SOAP OPERA ROMANCES

Charlton; 1 Jul 1982-5 Mar 1983

Issue	$Good	$Fine	$N.Mint	£Good	£Fine	£N.Mint
1 Nurse Betsy Crane reprints from the early 60s begin; distributed in the U.K.	$0.25	$0.75	$1.25	£0.15	£0.45	£0.75
2-5 distributed in the U.K.	$0.25	$0.75	$1.25	£0.15	£0.45	£0.75
Title Value:	$1.25	$3.75	$6.25	£0.75	£2.25	£3.75

SOJOURN

White Cliffs Publishing Co., Tabloid; 1 1977-2 Sep 1977

Issue	$Good	$Fine	$N.Mint	£Good	£Fine	£N.Mint
1-2 ND John Severin, Sergio Aragones, Doug Wildey, Steve Bissette, Joe Kubert art; black and white	$0.30	$1.00	$2.00	£0.20	£0.60	£1.25
Title Value:	$0.60	$2.00	$4.00	£0.40	£1.20	£2.50

Note: magazine size which folds out to what can best be described as tabloid size. Joe Kubert covers

SOLAR, MAN OF THE ATOM

Valiant/Acclaim Comics; 1 Sep 1991-60 Apr 1996

(see Doctor Solar)

Issue	$Good	$Fine	$N.Mint	£Good	£Fine	£N.Mint
1 return of the first Gold Key hero, script by Jim Shooter telling origin Solar	$1.50	$4.50	$7.50	£1.00	£3.00	£5.00
2	$1.20	$3.60	$6.00	£0.80	£2.40	£4.00
3 scarce in the U.K. 1st appearance Harada	$1.40	$4.20	$7.00	£1.00	£3.00	£5.00
4	$1.00	$3.00	$5.00	£0.60	£1.80	£3.00
5	$0.80	$2.40	$4.00	£0.50	£1.50	£2.50
6	$0.60	$1.80	$3.00	£0.40	£1.20	£2.00
7 X-O Manowar armour appears	$0.60	$1.80	$3.00	£0.40	£1.20	£2.00
8	$0.60	$1.80	$3.00	£0.40	£1.20	£2.00
9 Solar vs. God-Child	$0.60	$1.80	$3.00	£0.40	£1.20	£2.00
10 48pgs, black cover, title-embossed on heavier stock paper, Alpha & Omega by Barry Windsor-Smith concludes, 1st appearance Eternal Warrior, leads into Unity; only 2nd print Valiant comic	$2.00	$6.00	$10.00	£1.30	£3.90	£6.50
10 2nd printing, Oct 1992	$0.50	$1.50	$2.50	£0.30	£0.90	£1.50
11 Unity prelude, Eternal Warrior (1st full appearance) vs. Harbinger	$0.60	$1.80	$3.00	£0.40	£1.20	£2.00
12 Unity: Chapter 9, Frank Miller cover	$0.50	$1.50	$2.50	£0.30	£0.90	£1.50
13 Unity: Chapter 17, the conclusion guest-starring all Valiant characters, Walt Simonson cover	$0.50	$1.50	$2.50	£0.30	£0.90	£1.50
14 1st appearence of Fred Bender a.k.a. Dr. Eclipse	$0.60	$1.80	$3.00	£0.40	£1.20	£2.00
15	$0.50	$1.50	$2.50	£0.30	£0.90	£1.50
16 Bob Layton scripts begin	$0.50	$1.50	$2.50	£0.30	£0.90	£1.50
17 continued from X-O Manowar #12	$0.50	$1.50	$2.50	£0.30	£0.90	£1.50
18 X-O Manowar appears	$0.50	$1.50	$2.50	£0.30	£0.90	£1.50
19-20	$0.50	$1.50	$2.50	£0.30	£0.90	£1.50
21-22 Master Darque appears	$0.40	$1.20	$2.00	£0.25	£0.75	£1.25
23 1st appearance of Solar the Destroyer as Solar splits into two beings	$0.40	$1.20	$2.00	£0.25	£0.75	£1.25
24	$0.40	$1.20	$2.00	£0.25	£0.75	£1.25
25 The Coming of the Darque Age story; Solar vs. Dr. Eclipse, continued in Secret Weapons #2	$0.40	$1.20	$2.00	£0.25	£0.75	£1.25
26-28	$0.40	$1.20	$2.00	£0.25	£0.75	£1.25
29 produced in Valiant Vision (3-D effect without altering basic art of comic)	$0.40	$1.20	$2.00	£0.25	£0.75	£1.25
30-32	$0.40	$1.20	$2.00	£0.25	£0.75	£1.25
33 with free Upper Deck trading card; in Valiant Vision (no glasses included)	$0.40	$1.20	$2.00	£0.25	£0.75	£1.25
34-35 in Valiant Vision (no glasses included)	$0.40	$1.20	$2.00	£0.25	£0.75	£1.25
36 Dr. Eclipse appears	$0.40	$1.20	$2.00	£0.25	£0.75	£1.25
37	$0.40	$1.20	$2.00	£0.25	£0.75	£1.25
38 Chaos Effect tie-in	$0.40	$1.20	$2.00	£0.25	£0.75	£1.25
39-40	$0.40	$1.20	$2.00	£0.25	£0.75	£1.25
41 Solar vs. Harada	$0.40	$1.20	$2.00	£0.25	£0.75	£1.25
42-45	$0.40	$1.20	$2.00	£0.25	£0.75	£1.25
46 1st Acclaim Comics issue, Dan Jurgens script and art begin; Brave New Worlds story	$0.50	$1.50	$2.50	£0.30	£0.90	£1.50
47 Brave New Worlds story	$0.50	$1.50	$2.50	£0.30	£0.90	£1.50
48-49 Brave New Worlds story; bi-weekly	$0.50	$1.50	$2.50	£0.30	£0.90	£1.50
50 DS, Brave New Worlds story conclusion	$0.60	$1.80	$3.00	£0.40	£1.20	£2.00
51-59 bi-weekly	$0.50	$1.50	$2.50	£0.30	£0.90	£1.50
60	$0.50	$1.50	$2.50	£0.30	£0.90	£1.50
Title Value:	$34.10	$102.30	$170.50	£21.45	£64.35	£107.25

Note: all Non-Distributed on the news-stands in the U.K.

	£Good	£Fine	£N.Mint
Solar, Man of the Atom #0 (1994) Trade paperback reprints 8pgs inserts from issues #1-10	£1.30	£3.90	£6.50
Solar, Man of the Atom #1 (Jan 1995) Trade paperback reprints issues #1-4	£1.30	£3.90	£6.50

SOLARMAN

Marvel Comics Group; 1 Jan 1989; 2 May 1990

Issue	$Good	$Fine	$N.Mint	£Good	£Fine	£N.Mint
1 Stan Lee script, Jim Mooney art	$0.25	$0.75	$1.25	£0.15	£0.45	£0.75
2 Stan Lee script, Mike Zeck art	$0.25	$0.75	$1.25	£0.15	£0.45	£0.75
Title Value:	$0.50	$1.50	$2.50	£0.30	£0.90	£1.50

SOLD OUT

Fantaco; 1,2 1986

Issue	$Good	$Fine	$N.Mint	£Good	£Fine	£N.Mint
1-2 ND	$0.30	$0.90	$1.50	£0.20	£0.60	£1.00
Title Value:	$0.60	$1.80	$3.00	£0.40	£1.20	£2.00

SOLITAIRE

Malibu Ultraverse; 1 Nov 1993-12 Nov 1994

Issue	$Good	$Fine	$N.Mint	£Good	£Fine	£N.Mint
1 Gerard Jones script and Jeff Johnson art begin	$0.40	$1.20	$2.00	£0.25	£0.75	£1.25

	$Good	$Fine	$N.Mint	£Good	£Fine	£N.Mint
1 Collectors Edition, pre-bagged in black with a special edition playing card (Ace of Spades one being the rarest)	*$0.50*	*$1.50*	*$2.50*	£0.30	£0.90	£1.50
2	*$0.40*	*$1.20*	*$2.00*	£0.25	£0.75	£1.25
3 Night Man origin by Kevin Maguire	*$0.40*	*$1.20*	*$2.00*	£0.25	£0.75	£1.25
4-12	*$0.40*	*$1.20*	*$2.00*	£0.25	£0.75	£1.25
Title Value:	*$5.30*	*$15.90*	*$26.50*	£3.30	£9.90	£16.50

Note: all Non-Distributed on the news-stands in the U.K.

SOLO

Marvel Comics Group,MS; 1 Sep 1994-4 Dec 1994

	$Good	$Fine	$N.Mint	£Good	£Fine	£N.Mint
1-4 Spiderman guest-stars	*$0.30*	*$0.90*	*$1.50*	£0.20	£0.60	£1.00
Title Value:	*$1.20*	*$3.60*	*$6.00*	£0.80	£2.40	£4.00

SOLO

Dark Horse,MS; 1 Jul 1996-2 Aug 1996

	$Good	$Fine	$N.Mint	£Good	£Fine	£N.Mint
1-2 ND Rick Geary script adaptation of Mario van Peebles film	*$0.50*	*$1.50*	*$2.50*	£0.30	£0.90	£1.50
Title Value:	*$1.00*	*$3.00*	*$5.00*	£0.60	£1.80	£3.00

SOLO AVENGERS (AVENGERS SPOTLIGHT)

Marvel Comics Group; 1 Dec 1987-40 Jan 1991

(becomes Avengers Spotlight 21 on)

	$Good	$Fine	$N.Mint	£Good	£Fine	£N.Mint
1 ND 2nd Jim Lee art for Marvel (see Alpha Flight #51)	*$0.50*	*$1.50*	*$2.50*	£0.25	£0.75	£1.25
2-3 ND	*$0.30*	*$0.90*	*$1.50*	£0.20	£0.60	£1.00
4 ND Ron Lim art	*$0.30*	*$0.90*	*$1.50*	£0.20	£0.60	£1.00
5-7 LD in the U.K.	*$0.30*	*$0.90*	*$1.50*	£0.20	£0.60	£1.00
8-11	*$0.25*	*$0.75*	*$1.25*	£0.15	£0.45	£0.75
12-13 Ron Lim art	*$0.25*	*$0.75*	*$1.25*	£0.15	£0.45	£0.75
14 Alan Davis She Hulk	*$0.25*	*$0.75*	*$1.25*	£0.15	£0.45	£0.75
15-20	*$0.25*	*$0.75*	*$1.25*	£0.15	£0.45	£0.75
21 title becomes Avengers Spotlight	*$0.25*	*$0.75*	*$1.25*	£0.15	£0.45	£0.75
22-24	*$0.25*	*$0.75*	*$1.25*	£0.15	£0.45	£0.75
25 Acts of Vengeance part 1	*$0.25*	*$0.75*	*$1.25*	£0.15	£0.45	£0.75
26-28 ND Acts of Vengeance tie-in	*$0.25*	*$0.75*	*$1.25*	£0.15	£0.45	£0.75
29 ND Acts of Vengeance epilogue	*$0.25*	*$0.75*	*$1.25*	£0.15	£0.45	£0.75
30 LD in the U.K. new costume/direction for Hawkeye	*$0.25*	*$0.75*	*$1.25*	£0.15	£0.45	£0.75
31-34 LD in the U.K. back-up story U.S.Agent	*$0.25*	*$0.75*	*$1.25*	£0.15	£0.45	£0.75
35 LD in the U.K. Tigra back-up begins (ends #37)	*$0.25*	*$0.75*	*$1.25*	£0.15	£0.45	£0.75
36-39 LD in the U.K. Avengers Re-Born story; Gilgamesh/Dr. Druid/Tigra/Black Knight featured	*$0.25*	*$0.75*	*$1.25*	£0.15	£0.45	£0.75
40 LD in the U.K. Avengers Re-Born epilogue	*$0.25*	*$0.75*	*$1.25*	£0.15	£0.45	£0.75
Title Value:	*$10.55*	*$31.65*	*$52.25*	£6.40	£19.20	£32.00

ARTISTS

Grindberg in 6. Guice in 7, 13. Ron Lim in 4, 13. John Ridgway in 5.

FEATURES

Black Knight in 4. Black Widow in 7, 14. Captain Marvel in 2. Dr.Druid in 10. Falcon in 6. Hawkeye in all. Hellcat in 9. Hercules in 11. Mockingbird in 1. Moondragon in 16. Moonknight in 3. Scarlet Witch in 5. Sub-Mariner in 17. Wasp in 15. Wonderman in 13. Yellowjacket in 12.

SOLO EX-MUTANTS

Eternity; 1 Jan 1988-6 1989

(see Ex-Mutants)

	$Good	$Fine	$N.Mint	£Good	£Fine	£N.Mint
1 ND reprints Ex-Mutants #1 (Pied Piper issue) with new Ron Lim cover	*$0.40*	*$1.20*	*$2.00*	£0.25	£0.75	£1.25
2-6 ND	*$0.40*	*$1.20*	*$2.00*	£0.25	£0.75	£1.25
Title Value:	*$2.40*	*$7.20*	*$12.00*	£1.50	£4.50	£7.50

Note: black and white

SOLOMON KANE IN 3-D

Blackthorne; (3-D Series #60) 1 Winter 1988

	$Good	$Fine	$N.Mint	£Good	£Fine	£N.Mint
1 ND with bound-in 3-D glasses (25% less without glasses)	*$0.50*	*$1.50*	*$2.50*	£0.30	£0.90	£1.50
Title Value:	*$0.50*	*$1.50*	*$2.50*	£0.30	£0.90	£1.50

SOLOMON KANE, THE SWORD OF

Marvel Comics Group,MS; 1 Sep 1985-6 Mar 1986

	$Good	$Fine	$N.Mint	£Good	£Fine	£N.Mint
1 ND DS	*$0.30*	*$0.90*	*$1.50*	£0.20	£0.60	£1.00
2-6 ND	*$0.25*	*$0.75*	*$1.25*	£0.15	£0.45	£0.75
Title Value:	*$1.55*	*$4.65*	*$7.75*	£0.95	£2.85	£4.75

ARTISTS

Mignola in 3. Nowlan cover on 4. Ridgway in 6. Williamson in 3, 4.

SOLUTION, THE

Malibu Ultraverse; 1 Sep 1993-17 Feb 1995

	$Good	$Fine	$N.Mint	£Good	£Fine	£N.Mint
0 obtained with Rune #0 by sending off coupons contained within 11 Ultraverse issues	*$1.50*	*$4.50*	*$7.50*	£1.00	£3.00	£5.00
1 Darick Robertson/John Lowe art begins	*$0.50*	*$1.50*	*$2.50*	£0.30	£0.90	£1.50
1 Limited Edition - full hologram cover, 5,000 copies produced	*$2.00*	*$6.00*	*$10.00*	£1.00	£3.00	£5.00
2 40pgs, Rune insert	*$0.50*	*$1.50*	*$2.50*	£0.30	£0.90	£1.50
3	*$0.40*	*$1.20*	*$2.00*	£0.25	£0.75	£1.25
4 Break-Thru X-over; gatefold cover	*$0.40*	*$1.20*	*$2.00*	£0.25	£0.75	£1.25
5 origin The Strangers by Adam Hughes	*$0.40*	*$1.20*	*$2.00*	£0.25	£0.75	£1.25
6 origin of Tech	*$0.40*	*$1.20*	*$2.00*	£0.25	£0.75	£1.25
7-8 origin of The Solution	*$0.40*	*$1.20*	*$2.00*	£0.25	£0.75	£1.25
9-12	*$0.40*	*$1.20*	*$2.00*	£0.25	£0.75	£1.25
13 Hostile Takeover part 3	*$0.40*	*$1.20*	*$2.00*	£0.25	£0.75	£1.25
14-15	*$0.40*	*$1.20*	*$2.00*	£0.25	£0.75	£1.25
16 64pgs, flip-book format with Ultraverse Premiere #10	*$0.50*	*$1.50*	*$2.50*	£0.30	£0.90	£1.50
17	*$0.40*	*$1.20*	*$2.00*	£0.25	£0.75	£1.25
Title Value:	*$10.60*	*$31.80*	*$53.00*	£6.40	£19.20	£32.00

Note: all Non-Distributed on the news-stands in the U.K.

SOMERSET HOLMES

Pacific; 1 Sep 1983-4 Apr 1984; Eclipse; 5 Nov 1984-6 Dec 1985

	$Good	$Fine	$N.Mint	£Good	£Fine	£N.Mint
1-5 ND Jones/Campbell/Brent Anderson begin, Cliff Hanger by Williamson	*$0.40*	*$1.20*	*$2.00*	£0.25	£0.75	£1.25
6 ND scarce in the U.K. Jones/Campbell/Brent Anderson begin, Cliff Hanger by Williamson	*$0.40*	*$1.20*	*$2.00*	£0.30	£0.90	£1.50
Title Value:	*$2.40*	*$7.20*	*$12.00*	£1.55	£4.65	£7.75

SOMERSET HOLMES (2ND SERIES)

Eclipse;Graphic Novel 10; 1986

	$Good	$Fine	$N.Mint	£Good	£Fine	£N.Mint
1 ND reprints issues #1-6, new cover	*$2.50*	*$7.50*	*$12.50*	£1.50	£4.50	£7.50
Title Value:	*$2.50*	*$7.50*	*$12.50*	£1.50	£4.50	£7.50

SON OF AMBUSH BUG

(see Ambush Bug, Son of)

SON OF CELLULOID

Eclipse,OS; nn 1991

nn ND 64pgs, Hardcover, adaptation of Clive Barker material by Steve Niles, painted art by Les Edwards

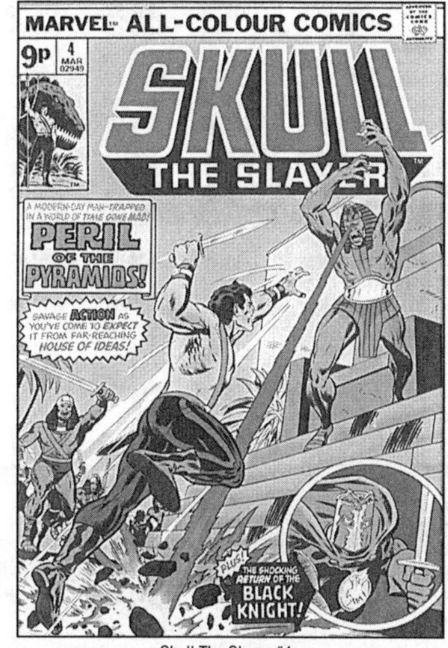

Skull The Slayer #4

Somerset Holmes #1

Soul Searchers and Company #1

	$Good	$Fine	$N.Mint	£Good	£Fine	£N.Mint
	$4.50	$13.50	$22.50	£3.00	£9.00	£15.00
Title Value:	$4.50	$13.50	$22.50	£3.00	£9.00	£15.00

SON OF MUTANT WORLD

Fantagor,MS; 1 Summer 1990-5 Feb 1991

	$Good	$Fine	$N.Mint	£Good	£Fine	£N.Mint
1-5 ND Richard Corben/Bruce Jones art, Richard Corben cover	$0.40	$1.20	$2.00	£0.25	£0.75	£1.25
Title Value:	$2.00	$6.00	$10.00	£1.25	£3.75	£6.25

Note: bi-monthly frequency

SON OF SATAN

Marvel Comics Group; 1 Dec 1975-8 Feb 1977
(see Marvel Spotlight)

	$Good	$Fine	$N.Mint	£Good	£Fine	£N.Mint
1 splash page by Jim Starlin	$2.05	$6.25	$12.50	£1.00	£3.00	£6.00
2	$1.25	$3.75	$7.50	£0.50	£1.50	£3.00
3-7	$1.00	$3.00	$6.00	£0.40	£1.25	£2.50
8 ND Russ Heath art	$1.00	$3.00	$6.00	£0.40	£1.25	£2.50
Title Value:	$9.30	$28.00	$56.00	£3.90	£12.00	£24.00

ARTISTS
Part P.Craig Russell art in 4, 5. Russ Heath in 8.

SON OF VULCAN

Charlton;49 Nov 1965-50 Jan 1966
(becomes Thunderbolt)

	$Good	$Fine	$N.Mint	£Good	£Fine	£N.Mint
49-50 distributed in the U.K.	$2.25	$6.75	$16.00	£1.55	£4.70	£11.00
Title Value:	$4.50	$13.50	$32.00	£3.10	£9.40	£22.00

SONG OF THE CID

Caliber/Tome Press,MS; 1 Jul 1991-2 Aug 1991

	$Good	$Fine	$N.Mint	£Good	£Fine	£N.Mint
1-2 ND	$0.40	$1.20	$2.00	£0.25	£0.75	£1.25
Title Value:	$0.80	$2.40	$4.00	£0.50	£1.50	£2.50

SONIC DISRUPTERS

DC Comics,MS; 1 Dec 1987-7 Jul 1988

	$Good	$Fine	$N.Mint	£Good	£Fine	£N.Mint
1-7 ND	$0.15	$0.45	$0.75	£0.10	£0.35	£0.60
Title Value:	$1.05	$3.15	$5.25	£0.70	£2.45	£4.20

Note: Mike Baron story, Mature Readers, Deluxe format (planned 12-issue series, cancelled with #7).

SONS OF KATIE ELDER, THE

Dell/Movie Classics,OS Movie; 12-748-511 Sep/Nov 1965

	$Good	$Fine	$N.Mint	£Good	£Fine	£N.Mint
12-748-511 12-748-511, distributed in the U.K. film adaptation; John Wayne photo cover	$17.00	$50.00	$120.00	£10.50	£32.00	£75.00
Title Value:	$17.00	$50.00	$120.00	£10.50	£32.00	£75.00

SOULQUEST

Innovation; 1 Apr 1989

	$Good	$Fine	$N.Mint	£Good	£Fine	£N.Mint
1 ND 48pgs, squarebound, based on role playing game	$0.40	$1.20	$2.00	£0.25	£0.75	£1.25
Title Value:	$0.40	$1.20	$2.00	£0.25	£0.75	£1.25

SOULSEARCHERS AND COMPANY

Claypool Comics; 1 Jun 1993-present

	$Good	$Fine	$N.Mint	£Good	£Fine	£N.Mint
1-18 ND Peter David script	$0.50	$1.50	$2.50	£0.30	£0.90	£1.50
Title Value:	$9.00	$27.00	$45.00	£5.40	£16.20	£27.00

SOUTHERN KNIGHTS

Guild/Comics Interview;2 Jan 1983-35 1987 ?
(previously Crusaders)

	$Good	$Fine	$N.Mint	£Good	£Fine	£N.Mint
2 ND scarce in the U.K. magazine size, black and white begins	$0.40	$1.20	$2.00	£0.40	£1.20	£2.00
3-7 ND scarce in the U.K.	$0.30	$0.90	$1.50	£0.30	£0.90	£1.50
8 ND 1st Comics Interview issue	$0.30	$0.90	$1.50	£0.25	£0.75	£1.25
9-33 ND	$0.30	$0.90	$1.50	£0.25	£0.75	£1.25
34 ND Christmas issue	$0.30	$0.90	$1.50	£0.25	£0.75	£1.25
35 ND 100pgs, squarebound, actually bound-together copies of Champions #1 and Eternity Smith; George Perez cover art	$0.40	$1.20	$2.00	£0.30	£0.90	£1.50
Title Value:	$10.40	$31.20	$52.00	£8.95	£26.85	£44.75
Dread Halloween Special 1				£0.40	£1.20	£2.00
Special 1 (1989), reprints				£0.25	£0.75	£1.25
Graphic Novel #1-4 (more?)				£0.65	£1.95	£3.25

SOUTHERN SQUADRON

Aircel,MS; 1 Jul 1990-4 Oct 1990

	$Good	$Fine	$N.Mint	£Good	£Fine	£N.Mint
1 ND Mike Grell cover and introduction; David de Vries script, Gary Chaloner and Glenn Lumsden art; black and white	$0.40	$1.20	$2.00	£0.25	£0.75	£1.25
2 ND	$0.40	$1.20	$2.00	£0.25	£0.75	£1.25
3 ND Jerry Ordway introduction and cover	$0.40	$1.20	$2.00	£0.25	£0.75	£1.25
4 ND	$0.40	$1.20	$2.00	£0.25	£0.75	£1.25
Title Value:	$1.60	$4.80	$8.00	£1.00	£3.00	£5.00

SOUTHERN SQUADRON: FREEDOM OF INFORMATION ACT

Eternity,MS; 1 Jan 1992-4 Apr 1992

	$Good	$Fine	$N.Mint	£Good	£Fine	£N.Mint
1-4 ND	$0.40	$1.20	$2.00	£0.25	£0.75	£1.25
Title Value:	$1.60	$4.80	$8.00	£1.00	£3.00	£5.00

SOVEREIGN SEVEN

DC Comics; 1 Jul 1995-present

	$Good	$Fine	$N.Mint	£Good	£Fine	£N.Mint
1 Cascade, Network, Reflex, Rampart, Finale, Indigo and Cruiser begin and Darkseid appears; script by Chris Claremont, art by Dwayne Turner	$0.40	$1.20	$2.00	£0.30	£0.90	£1.50
1 Gold Edition ND	$1.50	$4.50	$7.50	£1.00	£3.00	£5.00
2 Cascade dies	$0.40	$1.20	$2.00	£0.25	£0.75	£1.25
3-9	$0.40	$1.20	$2.00	£0.25	£0.75	£1.25
10 Impulse appears	$0.40	$1.20	$2.00	£0.25	£0.75	£1.25
11-13	$0.40	$1.20	$2.00	£0.25	£0.75	£1.25
14 Ron Lim and Art Thibert art	$0.40	$1.20	$2.00	£0.25	£0.75	£1.25
15	$0.40	$1.20	$2.00	£0.25	£0.75	£1.25
16 Final Night tie-in	$0.40	$1.20	$2.00	£0.25	£0.75	£1.25
17 ND Lady Blackhawk appears	$0.40	$1.20	$2.00	£0.25	£0.75	£1.25
18-19 ND	$0.40	$1.20	$2.00	£0.25	£0.75	£1.25
20 ND Superman appears in back-up story	$0.40	$1.20	$2.00	£0.25	£0.75	£1.25
21 ND	$0.40	$1.20	$2.00	£0.25	£0.75	£1.25
Title Value:	$9.90	$29.70	$49.50	£6.30	£18.90	£31.50
Sovereign Seven (Dec 1996) Trade paperback ND collects issues #1-5, Annual #1 and story from Showcase '95 #12				£1.70	£5.10	£8.50

SOVEREIGN SEVEN ANNUAL

DC Comics; 1 Dec 1995-present

	$Good	$Fine	$N.Mint	£Good	£Fine	£N.Mint
1 ND 56pgs, Year One story, Lobo appears	$0.80	$2.40	$4.00	£0.50	£1.50	£2.50
2 ND 48pgs, Legends of the Dead Earth story	$0.60	$1.80	$3.00	£0.40	£1.20	£2.00
Title Value:	$1.40	$4.20	$7.00	£0.90	£2.70	£4.50

SOVEREIGN SEVEN PLUS #1

DC Comics,OS; 1 Feb 1997

	$Good	$Fine	$N.Mint	£Good	£Fine	£N.Mint
1 ND 48pgs, Sovereign Seven and The Legion of Super-Heroes team up	$0.60	$1.80	$3.00	£0.40	£1.20	£2.00
Title Value:	$0.60	$1.80	$3.00	£0.40	£1.20	£2.00

SOVIET SUPER SOLDIERS

Marvel Comics Group,OS; 1 Nov 1992

	$Good	$Fine	$N.Mint	£Good	£Fine	£N.Mint
1	$0.40	$1.20	$2.00	£0.25	£0.75	£1.25
Title Value:	$0.40	$1.20	$2.00	£0.25	£0.75	£1.25

SPACE 1999

Charlton; 1 Nov 1975-7 Nov 1976

	$Good	$Fine	$N.Mint	£Good	£Fine	£N.Mint
1	$0.65	$2.00	$4.00	£0.40	£1.25	£2.50
2	$0.50	$1.50	$3.00	£0.30	£1.00	£2.00
3-7 John Byrne art	$0.75	$2.25	$4.50	£0.50	£1.50	£3.00
Title Value:	$4.90	$14.75	$29.50	£3.20	£9.75	£19.50

Note: all distributed in the U.K.

SPACE 1999 (MAGAZINE)

Charlton,Magazine; 1 Nov 1975-8 Nov 1976

	$Good	$Fine	$N.Mint	£Good	£Fine	£N.Mint
1 ND	$0.80	$2.40	$4.00	£0.60	£1.80	£3.00
2-8 ND	$0.60	$1.80	$3.00	£0.50	£1.50	£2.50
Title Value:	$5.00	$15.00	$25.00	£4.10	£12.30	£20.50

SPACE ADVENTURES

Charlton; 1 Jul 1952-59 Nov 1964; 60 Oct 1967

	$Good	$Fine	$N.Mint	£Good	£Fine	£N.Mint
1 scarce in the U.K.	$42.00	$125.00	$335.00	£28.00	£82.50	£225.00
2	$22.50	$67.50	$160.00	£15.00	£45.00	£105.00
3-5	$17.50	$52.50	$125.00	£11.50	£35.00	£82.50
6-9	$15.50	$47.00	$110.00	£10.00	£31.00	£72.50
10-11 Steve Ditko cover and art	$40.00	$120.00	$280.00	£26.00	£77.50	£185.00
12 rare in the U.K. Steve Ditko cover	$50.00	$150.00	$350.00	£34.00	£100.00	£235.00
13-14 Blue Beetle reprint from Fox title	$17.00	$50.00	$120.00	£11.00	£34.00	£80.00
15	$17.00	$50.00	$120.00	£11.00	£34.00	£80.00
16 Krigstein art	$18.50	$55.00	$130.00	£12.50	£38.00	£87.50
17-18	$17.00	$50.00	$120.00	£11.00	£34.00	£80.00
19	$11.00	$34.00	$80.00	£7.50	£22.50	£52.50
20 reprints Destination Moon from Fawcett title	$26.00	$77.50	$185.00	£17.50	£52.50	£125.00
21	$11.00	$34.00	$80.00	£7.50	£22.50	£52.50
22 titled "War At Sea"	$4.25	$12.50	$30.00	£2.85	£8.50	£20.00
23 reprints Destination Moon from Fawcett title	$20.00	$60.00	$140.00	£13.50	£41.00	£95.00
24-27 Steve Ditko art	$18.50	$55.00	$130.00	£12.50	£38.00	£87.50
28-30	$6.25	$19.00	$45.00	£4.25	£12.50	£30.00
1st official distribution in the U.K.						
31-32 Steve Ditko art	$17.50	$52.50	$125.00	£11.00	£34.00	£80.00
33 1st appearance of Captain Atom by Steve Ditko	$46.00	$135.00	$325.00	£26.00	£75.00	£180.00
34-40 Captain Atom by Steve Ditko	$18.50	$55.00	$130.00	£10.00	£30.00	£70.00
41 1st appearance Mercury Man	$3.55	$10.50	$25.00	£1.75	£5.25	£12.50
42 Captain Atom by Steve Ditko	$13.50	$41.00	$95.00	£9.25	£28.00	£65.00
43	$2.55	$7.50	$18.00	£1.70	£5.00	£12.00
44-45 Mercury Man	$3.55	$10.50	$25.00	£1.75	£5.25	£12.50
46-59	$3.55	$10.50	$25.00	£1.75	£5.25	£12.50
60 1st Paul Mann and the Saucers from the Future	$5.00	$15.00	$30.00	£2.90	£8.75	£17.50
Title Value:	$869.40	$2595.00	$6173.00	£544.20	£1640.00	£3882.00

Note: most issues distributed in the U.K. after 1959

SPACE ARK

AC/Apple; 1 1985-5 1988

Issue	$Good	$Fine	$N.Mint	£Good	£Fine	£N.Mint
1-2 ND	$0.40	$1.20	$2.00	£0.25	£0.75	£1.25
3 ND 1st Apple issue	$0.40	$1.20	$2.00	£0.25	£0.75	£1.25
4-5 ND	$0.40	$1.20	$2.00	£0.25	£0.75	£1.25
Title Value:	$2.00	$6.00	$10.00	£1.25	£3.75	£6.25

SPACE BEAVER

Ten Buck Comics; 1 Oct 1986-11 1988

Issue	$Good	$Fine	$N.Mint	£Good	£Fine	£N.Mint
1-11 ND	$0.30	$0.90	$1.50	£0.20	£0.60	£1.00
Title Value:	$3.30	$9.90	$16.50	£2.20	£6.60	£11.00

SPACE FAMILY ROBINSON

Gold Key; 1 Dec 1962-36 Oct 1969

(becomes Lost in Space #37 onwards)

Issue	$Good	$Fine	$N.Mint	£Good	£Fine	£N.Mint
1 rare in the U.K. painted covers begin	$34.00	$100.00	$240.00	£23.50	£70.00	£165.00
2 scarce in the U.K.	$17.00	$50.00	$120.00	£11.00	£34.00	£80.00
3-5 scarce in the U.K.	$8.50	$26.00	$60.00	£5.50	£17.00	£40.00
6-10 scarce in the U.K.	$7.75	$23.50	$55.00	£5.25	£16.00	£37.50
11-20 scarce in the U.K.	$5.50	$17.00	$40.00	£3.55	£10.50	£25.00
21-30 scarce in the U.K.	$3.55	$10.50	$25.00	£2.10	£6.25	£15.00
31-36 scarce in the U.K.	$3.55	$10.50	$25.00	£1.75	£5.25	£12.50
Title Value:	$227.05	$683.50	$1615.00	£144.25	£434.00	£1027.50

Note: all distributed in the U.K.

SPACE GHOST

Gold Key,OS; 1 Mar 1967

Issue	$Good	$Fine	$N.Mint	£Good	£Fine	£N.Mint
1 rare although distributed in the U.K.	$48.00	$140.00	$335.00	£31.00	£90.00	£215.00
Title Value:	$48.00	$140.00	$335.00	£31.00	£90.00	£215.00

SPACE GHOST

Comico,OS; 1 Sep 1987

Issue	$Good	$Fine	$N.Mint	£Good	£Fine	£N.Mint
1 ND bookshelf format, Steve Rude art	$0.80	$2.40	$4.00	£0.50	£1.50	£2.50
Title Value:	$0.80	$2.40	$4.00	£0.50	£1.50	£2.50

SPACE JAM

DC Comics,OS; nn Dec 1996

Issue	$Good	$Fine	$N.Mint	£Good	£Fine	£N.Mint
nn ND 48pgs,Film adaptation starring Michael Jordan	$1.20	$3.60	$6.00	£0.80	£2.40	£4.00
Title Value:	$1.20	$3.60	$6.00	£0.80	£2.40	£4.00

SPACE MAN

Dell; 1253 Jan/Mar 1962; Gold Key; 2 Apr/Jun 1962-8 Mar/May 1964; 9 Jul 1972-10 Oct 1972

Issue	$Good	$Fine	$N.Mint	£Good	£Fine	£N.Mint
1 very scarce with limited distribution in the U.K. (Four Color #1253)	$10.50	$32.00	$75.00	£7.00	£21.00	£50.00
2 scarce though distributed in the U.K. painted cover	$5.50	$17.00	$40.00	£4.25	£12.50	£30.00
3 scarce though distributed in the U.K. painted cover	$5.00	$15.00	$35.00	£3.55	£10.50	£25.00
4-8 scarce though distributed in the U.K. painted cover	$4.25	$12.50	$30.00	£2.85	£8.50	£20.00
9-10 LD in the U.K. reprints issue #1	$1.25	$3.75	$7.50	£0.80	£2.50	£5.00
Title Value:	$44.75	$134.00	$315.00	£30.65	£91.50	£215.00

SPACE PATROL

Adventure,MS; 1 Jan 1993-3 Mar 1993

Issue	$Good	$Fine	$N.Mint	£Good	£Fine	£N.Mint
1-3 ND	$0.40	$1.20	$2.00	£0.25	£0.75	£1.25
Title Value:	$1.20	$3.60	$6.00	£0.75	£2.25	£3.75

SPACE USAGI

Mirage Studios,MS; 1 Aug 1992-3 Oct 1992

Issue	$Good	$Fine	$N.Mint	£Good	£Fine	£N.Mint
1-3 ND features Usagi Yojimbo by Stan Sakai	$0.40	$1.20	$2.00	£0.25	£0.75	£1.25
Title Value:	$1.20	$3.60	$6.00	£0.75	£2.25	£3.75

SPACE USAGI

Dark Horse,MS; 1 Jan 1996-3 Mar 1996

Issue	$Good	$Fine	$N.Mint	£Good	£Fine	£N.Mint
1-3 ND Stan Sakai script and art	$0.60	$1.80	$3.00	£0.40	£1.20	£2.00
Title Value:	$1.80	$5.40	$9.00	£1.20	£3.60	£6.00

SPACE USAGI II

Mirage Studios,MS; 1 Jan 1994-3 Mar 1994

Issue	$Good	$Fine	$N.Mint	£Good	£Fine	£N.Mint
1-3 ND Stan Sakai with Mary Woodring	$0.50	$1.50	$2.50	£0.30	£0.90	£1.50
Title Value:	$1.50	$4.50	$7.50	£0.90	£2.70	£4.50

SPACE WAR

Charlton; 1 Oct 1959-27 Mar 1964; 28 Mar 1978-34 Mar 1979

Issue	$Good	$Fine	$N.Mint	£Good	£Fine	£N.Mint
1 ND	$17.00	$50.00	$120.00	£11.00	£34.00	£80.00
2-3 distributed in the U.K.	$8.50	$26.00	$60.00	£5.50	£17.00	£40.00
4-6 distributed in the U.K. Steve Ditko art	$17.00	$50.00	$120.00	£11.00	£34.00	£80.00
7 distributed in the U.K.	$4.25	$12.50	$30.00	£2.85	£8.50	£20.00
8 distributed in the U.K. Steve Ditko art	$15.50	$47.00	$110.00	£10.00	£31.00	£72.50
9 distributed in the U.K.	$4.25	$12.50	$30.00	£2.85	£8.50	£20.00
10 distributed in the U.K. Steve Ditko art	$15.50	$47.00	$110.00	£10.00	£31.00	£72.50
11-15 distributed in the U.K.	$3.90	$11.50	$27.50	£2.50	£7.50	£17.50
16-27 distributed in the U.K.	$3.55	$10.50	$25.00	£2.10	£6.25	£15.00
28-29 distributed in the U.K. Steve Ditko reprint	$7.50	$22.50	$45.00	£4.55	£13.50	£27.50
30 distributed in the U.K. Steve Ditko reprint and Wally Wood art	$8.25	$25.00	$50.00	£5.00	£15.00	£30.00
31 distributed in the U.K. Steve Ditko reprint, atomic bomb cover	$8.25	$25.00	$50.00	£5.00	£15.00	£30.00
32 distributed in the U.K.	$0.80	$2.50	$5.00	£0.50	£1.50	£3.00
33-34 distributed in the U.K. Steve Ditko reprint	$7.00	$21.00	$42.50	£3.75	£11.00	£22.50
Title Value:	$232.90	$694.00	$1580.00	£145.50	£442.00	£1015.50

SPACE: ABOVE & BEYOND

Topps,MS; 1 Jan 1996-3 Mar 1996

Issue	$Good	$Fine	$N.Mint	£Good	£Fine	£N.Mint
1-3 ND Roy Thomas script, Paquette and Gil art, Ken Steacy cover; based on US TV series	$0.60	$1.80	$3.00	£0.40	£1.20	£2.00
Title Value:	$1.80	$5.40	$9.00	£1.20	£3.60	£6.00

SPACE: ABOVE & BEYOND: THE GAUNTLET

Topps; 1 May 1996-2 Jun 1996

Issue	$Good	$Fine	$N.Mint	£Good	£Fine	£N.Mint
1-2 ND Roy Thomas script, Yanick Paquette and Michel Lacombe art, Mark Harrison cover	$0.60	$1.80	$3.00	£0.40	£1.20	£2.00
Title Value:	$1.20	$3.60	$6.00	£0.80	£2.40	£4.00

SPACED

Unbridled Ambition/Eclipse; 1 1985-13 1988

Issue	$Good	$Fine	$N.Mint	£Good	£Fine	£N.Mint
1 ND scarce in the U.K.	$2.50	$7.50	$12.50	£1.50	£4.50	£7.50
2 ND scarce in the U.K.	$1.60	$4.80	$8.00	£1.00	£3.00	£5.00
3 ND scarce in the U.K.	$1.20	$3.60	$6.00	£0.70	£2.10	£3.50
4 ND scarce in the U.K.	$1.00	$3.00	$5.00	£0.60	£1.80	£3.00
5 ND	$0.60	$1.80	$3.00	£0.40	£1.20	£2.00
6-7 ND	$0.50	$1.50	$2.50	£0.30	£0.90	£1.50
8-13 ND	$0.40	$1.20	$2.00	£0.25	£0.75	£1.25
Title Value:	$10.30	$30.90	$51.50	£6.30	£18.90	£31.50

SPANNER'S GALAXY

DC Comics,MS; 1 Dec 1984-6 May 1985

Issue	$Good	$Fine	$N.Mint	£Good	£Fine	£N.Mint
1-6	$0.15	$0.45	$0.75	£0.10	£0.35	£0.60
Title Value:	$0.90	$2.70	$4.50	£0.60	£2.10	£3.60

Note: flexographically-printed DC comic.

SPARKPLUG

Hero,MS; 1 Mar 1993-3 1993

Issue	$Good	$Fine	$N.Mint	£Good	£Fine	£N.Mint
1-3 ND	$0.50	$1.50	$2.50	£0.30	£0.90	£1.50
Title Value:	$1.50	$4.50	$7.50	£0.90	£2.70	£4.50

SPARROW

DC Comics/Piranha Press,OS; 1 Mar 1990

Issue	$Good	$Fine	$N.Mint	£Good	£Fine	£N.Mint
1 ND 104pgs, Alison Marek script/art; black and white	$1.50	$4.50	$7.50	£1.00	£3.00	£5.00
Title Value:	$1.50	$4.50	$7.50	£1.00	£3.00	£5.00

SPARTAN: WARRIOR SPIRIT

Image,MS; 1 Aug 1995-4 Nov 1995

Issue	$Good	$Fine	$N.Mint	£Good	£Fine	£N.Mint
1-4 ND Kurt Busiek script	$0.50	$1.50	$2.50	£0.30	£0.90	£1.50
Title Value:	$2.00	$6.00	$10.00	£1.20	£3.60	£6.00

SPAWN

Image; 1 May 1992-present

Issue	$Good	$Fine	$N.Mint	£Good	£Fine	£N.Mint
1 ND Todd McFarlane script/art begins; 1st appearance Spawn and 1st appearance Pitt (as a pin-up)	$3.50	$10.50	$17.50	£1.60	£4.80	£8.00
2 ND 1st appearance Violator	$2.50	$7.50	$12.50	£1.50	£4.50	£7.50
3 ND some details of origin told	$2.50	$7.50	$12.50	£1.20	£3.60	£6.00
4 ND contains Image #0 coupon 2; new powers detailed	$3.00	$9.00	$15.00	£1.50	£4.50	£7.50
4 without coupon ND	$1.60	$4.80	$8.00	£0.70	£2.10	£3.50
5 ND	$1.80	$5.25	$9.00	£1.00	£3.00	£5.00
6 ND 1st appearance Overkill	$1.40	$4.20	$7.00	£0.80	£2.40	£4.00
7 ND	$1.20	$3.60	$6.00	£0.70	£2.10	£3.50
8 ND features Alan Moore's 1st super-hero script for some years plus poster by Frank Miller; cover in classic Spiderman #1 pose	$1.20	$3.60	$6.00	£0.70	£2.10	£3.50
9 ND Neil Gaiman script, 1st appearance Angela	$2.00	$6.00	$10.00	£1.20	£3.60	£6.00
10 ND Dave Sim script, Cerebus the Aardvark appears	$1.00	$3.00	$5.00	£0.50	£1.50	£2.50
11 ND Frank Miller script, Geoff Darrow poster	$1.00	$3.00	$5.00	£0.50	£1.50	£2.50
12 ND the conclusion to Spawn's origin and Spawn's killer revealed to be Chapel	$1.00	$3.00	$5.00	£0.50	£1.50	£2.50
13 ND Spawn vs. Chapel	$1.00	$3.00	$5.00	£0.50	£1.50	£2.50
14 ND Violator appears	$1.00	$3.00	$5.00	£0.50	£1.50	£2.50
15 ND 1st appearance Medieval Spawn, Violator appears	$1.00	$3.00	$5.00	£1.00	£3.00	£5.00
16 ND 1st Greg Capullo Spawn						

	$Good	$Fine	$N.Mint	£Good	£Fine	£N.Mint
	$1.00	*$3.00*	*$5.00*	£1.00	£3.00	£5.00
17 ND 1st appearance Redeemer	*$1.00*	*$3.00*	*$5.00*	£0.80	£2.40	£4.00
18 ND less common	*$1.20*	*$3.60*	*$6.00*	£0.80	£2.40	£4.00
19-20 ND issued Oct 1994 after issue #24	*$1.20*	*$3.60*	*$6.00*	£0.80	£2.40	£4.00
21 ND less common	*$1.40*	*$4.20*	*$7.00*	£0.80	£2.40	£4.00
22-23 ND	*$0.60*	*$1.80*	*$3.00*	£0.40	£1.20	£2.00
24 ND leads into Angela mini-series	*$0.60*	*$1.80*	*$3.00*	£0.40	£1.20	£2.00
25 ND Image X Month tie-in	*$0.90*	*$2.70*	*$4.50*	£0.50	£1.50	£2.50
26-30 ND	*$0.60*	*$1.80*	*$3.00*	£0.40	£1.20	£2.00
31 ND	*$0.50*	*$1.50*	*$2.50*	£0.30	£0.90	£1.50
32 ND new costume and 6pg preview of Spawn mini-series	*$0.50*	*$1.50*	*$2.50*	£0.30	£0.90	£1.50
33-34 ND Spawn vs. Violator	*$0.50*	*$1.50*	*$2.50*	£0.30	£0.90	£1.50
35 ND Violator appears	*$0.50*	*$1.50*	*$2.50*	£0.30	£0.90	£1.50
36 ND	*$0.40*	*$1.20*	*$2.00*	£0.25	£0.75	£1.25
37 ND intro The Freak; Alan Moore script	*$0.40*	*$1.20*	*$2.00*	£0.25	£0.75	£1.25
38 ND bi-weekly	*$0.40*	*$1.20*	*$2.00*	£0.25	£0.75	£1.25
39 ND Christmas story special; bi-weekly	*$0.40*	*$1.20*	*$2.00*	£0.25	£0.75	£1.25
40-46 ND bi-weekly	*$0.40*	*$1.20*	*$2.00*	£0.25	£0.75	£1.25
47 ND bi-weekly	*$0.50*	*$1.50*	*$2.50*	£0.30	£0.90	£1.50
48-49 ND bi-weekly	*$0.40*	*$1.20*	*$2.00*	£0.25	£0.75	£1.25
50 ND 48pgs	*$0.80*	*$2.40*	*$4.00*	£0.50	£1.50	£2.50
51 ND	*$0.40*	*$1.20*	*$2.00*	£0.25	£0.75	£1.25
52 ND continued in Savage Dragon #30	*$0.40*	*$1.20*	*$2.00*	£0.25	£0.75	£1.25
53-54 ND	*$0.40*	*$1.20*	*$2.00*	£0.25	£0.75	£1.25
55 ND	*$0.60*	*$1.80*	*$3.00*	£0.40	£1.20	£2.00
56 ND	*$0.40*	*$1.20*	*$2.00*	£0.25	£0.75	£1.25
Title Value:	***$51.00***	***$152.85***	***$255.00***	**£30.30**	**£90.90**	**£151.50**
Spawn (May 1995) Trade paperback ND reprints issues #1-5, new cover by Todd McFarlane				£1.30	£3.90	£6.50
Spawn II (May 1996) Trade paperback ND reprints issues #6-9 and 11, new cover by McFarlane				£1.30	£3.90	£6.50

SPAWN BIBLE

Image,OS; 1 Aug 1996

	$Good	$Fine	$N.Mint	£Good	£Fine	£N.Mint
1 ND character profiles and histories	*$0.40*	*$1.20*	*$2.00*	£0.25	£0.75	£1.25
Title Value:	***$0.40***	***$1.20***	***$2.00***	**£0.25**	**£0.75**	**£1.25**

SPAWN FAN EDITION

Image,OS; 1 Aug 1996

	$Good	$Fine	$N.Mint	£Good	£Fine	£N.Mint
1 ND 12pgs, available with Overstreet's Fan #16	*$0.40*	*$1.20*	*$2.00*	£0.20	£0.60	£1.00
2 ND 12 pgs, available with Overstreet's Fan #17	*$0.40*	*$1.20*	*$2.00*	£0.20	£0.60	£1.00
3 ND 12 pgs, available with Overstreet's Fan #18	*$0.40*	*$1.20*	*$2.00*	£0.20	£0.60	£1.00
Title Value:	***$1.20***	***$3.60***	***$6.00***	**£0.60**	**£1.80**	**£3.00**

SPAWN THE IMPALER

Image,MS; 1 Oct 1996-3 Dec 1996

	$Good	$Fine	$N.Mint	£Good	£Fine	£N.Mint
1-3 ND Mike Grell script and art with Rob Prior	*$0.60*	*$1.80*	*$3.00*	£0.40	£1.20	£2.00
Title Value:	***$1.80***	***$5.40***	***$9.00***	**£1.20**	**£3.60**	**£6.00**

SPAWN, CURSE OF THE

Image; 1 Sep 1996-present

	$Good	$Fine	$N.Mint	£Good	£Fine	£N.Mint
1 ND Alan McElroy script, Dwayne Turner and Danny Miki art	*$0.60*	*$1.80*	*$3.00*	£0.40	£1.20	£2.00
2 ND	*$0.50*	*$1.50*	*$2.50*	£0.30	£0.90	£1.50
3-6 ND	*$0.40*	*$1.20*	*$2.00*	£0.25	£0.75	£1.25
Title Value:	***$2.70***	***$8.10***	***$13.50***	**£1.70**	**£5.10**	**£8.50**

SPAWN/BATMAN

Image,OS; 1 May 1994

	$Good	$Fine	$N.Mint	£Good	£Fine	£N.Mint
1 ND 48pgs, Frank Miller script, Todd McFarlane art	*$1.00*	*$3.00*	*$5.00*	£0.70	£2.10	£3.50
Title Value:	***$1.00***	***$3.00***	***$5.00***	**£0.70**	**£2.10**	**£3.50**

SPAWN/WILDC.A.T.S.

Image,MS; 1 Jan 1996-4 Apr 1996

	$Good	$Fine	$N.Mint	£Good	£Fine	£N.Mint
1-4 ND Alan Moore script	*$0.50*	*$1.50*	*$2.50*	£0.30	£0.90	£1.50
Title Value:	***$2.00***	***$6.00***	***$10.00***	**£1.20**	**£3.60**	**£6.00**

SPAWN: BLOOD FEUD

Image,MS; 1 Jun 1995-4 Sep 1995

	$Good	$Fine	$N.Mint	£Good	£Fine	£N.Mint
1 ND Alan Moore script, Tony Daniel and Kevin Conrad art	*$0.60*	*$1.80*	*$3.00*	£0.40	£1.20	£2.00
2-4 ND Alan Moore script, Tony Daniel and Kevin Conrad art	*$0.50*	*$1.50*	*$2.50*	£0.30	£0.90	£1.50
Title Value:	***$2.10***	***$6.30***	***$10.50***	**£1.30**	**£3.90**	**£6.50**

SPECIAL MARVEL EDITION

Marvel Comics Group; 1 Jan 1971-16 Feb 1974

	$Good	$Fine	$N.Mint	£Good	£Fine	£N.Mint
(becomes Master of Kung Fu)						
1 68pgs, Jack Kirby Thor reprints begin (continued from Marvel Tales #27) from Journey Into Mystery #117 onwards (3 per issue)	*$1.25*	*$3.75*	*$7.50*	£0.80	£2.50	£5.00
2-4 ND 68pgs, Thor reprints	*$0.80*	*$2.50*	*$5.00*	£0.55	£1.75	£3.50
5 ND Jack Kirby Sgt. Fury reprints begin from Sgt. Fury #3 onwards	*$0.80*	*$2.50*	*$5.00*	£0.50	£1.50	£3.00
6-10 ND Sgt. Fury reprints	*$0.65*	*$2.00*	*$4.00*	£0.40	£1.25	£2.50
11 ND reprints Sgt. Fury #13 (Captain America)	*$0.65*	*$2.00*	*$4.00*	£0.40	£1.25	£2.50
12-14 ND Sgt.Fury reprints	*$0.65*	*$2.00*	*$4.00*	£0.40	£1.25	£2.50
15 ND scarce in the U.K. 1st appearance Master of Kung Fu, Jim Starlin art	*$6.25*	*$19.00*	*$45.00*	£4.25	£12.50	£30.00
16 ND 2nd appearance Master of Kung Fu, Jim Starlin art	*$4.15*	*$12.50*	*$25.00*	£2.90	£8.75	£17.50
Title Value:	***$20.70***	***$63.25***	***$133.50***	**£13.70**	**£41.75**	**£88.50**

SPECIAL WAR SERIES

Charlton; 1 Aug 1965-4 Nov 1965

	$Good	$Fine	$N.Mint	£Good	£Fine	£N.Mint
1 distributed in the U.K.	*$2.10*	*$6.25*	*$15.00*	£1.40	£4.25	£10.00
2-3 distributed in the U.K.	*$1.40*	*$4.25*	*$10.00*	£0.90	£2.75	£6.50
4 distributed in the U.K. 1st appearance of Judo Master	*$5.00*	*$15.00*	*$35.00*	£2.85	£8.50	£20.00
Title Value:	***$9.90***	***$29.75***	***$70.00***	**£6.05**	**£18.25**	**£43.00**

SPECIES

Dark Horse,MS; 1 Jun 1995-4 Sep 1995

	$Good	$Fine	$N.Mint	£Good	£Fine	£N.Mint
1-4 ND adapation of film by Dennis Feldman, John Bolton painted covers	*$0.50*	*$1.50*	*$2.50*	£0.30	£0.90	£1.50
Title Value:	***$2.00***	***$6.00***	***$10.00***	**£1.20**	**£3.60**	**£6.00**

SPECIES: HUMAN RACE

Dark Horse,MS; 1 Nov 1996-4 Feb 1997

	$Good	$Fine	$N.Mint	£Good	£Fine	£N.Mint
1-4 ND 48pgs, Phil Hester and Ande Parks art	*$0.80*	*$2.40*	*$4.00*	£0.50	£1.50	£2.50
Title Value:	***$3.20***	***$9.60***	***$16.00***	**£2.00**	**£6.00**	**£10.00**

SPECTACULAR SCARLET SPIDERMAN

Marvel Comics Group; 1 Nov 1995-2 Dec 1995

	$Good	$Fine	$N.Mint	£Good	£Fine	£N.Mint
1 ND Todd Dezago script, Sal Buscema and Bill Sienkiewicz art; metallic ink cover	*$0.40*	*$1.20*	*$2.00*	£0.25	£0.75	£1.25
2 ND Ben Reilly ends his career as The Scarlet Spider	*$0.40*	*$1.20*	*$2.00*	£0.25	£0.75	£1.25
Title Value:	***$0.80***	***$2.40***	***$4.00***	**£0.50**	**£1.50**	**£2.50**

SPECTACULAR SPIDERMAN

Marvel Comics Group; 1 Dec 1976-229 Oct 1995; 230 Jan 1996-present

	$Good	$Fine	$N.Mint	£Good	£Fine	£N.Mint
1 distributed in the U.K. Tarantula appears and Spiderman origin retold	*$8.50*	*$26.00*	*$60.00*	£3.90	£11.50	£27.50
2 ND Kraven the Hunter appears	*$5.00*	*$15.00*	*$30.00*	£2.15	£6.50	£13.00
3 ND 1st appearance Lightmaster	*$3.30*	*$10.00*	*$20.00*	£1.30	£4.00	£8.00
4-5 ND	*$2.90*	*$8.75*	*$17.50*	£1.15	£3.50	£7.00
6 ND part reprint Marvel Team Up #4 with X-Men and Morbius	*$2.90*	*$8.75*	*$17.50*	£1.15	£3.50	£7.00
7 ND Morbius appears	*$2.90*	*$8.75*	*$17.50*	£1.15	£3.50	£7.00
8 ND Morbius appears, Gulacy cover	*$2.90*	*$8.75*	*$17.50*	£1.15	£3.50	£7.00
9 ND 1st appearance White Tiger	*$1.65*	*$5.00*	*$10.00*	£0.80	£2.50	£5.00
10 ND George Perez cover	*$1.65*	*$5.00*	*$10.00*	£0.80	£2.50	£5.00
11 ND Inhumans appear	*$1.30*	*$4.00*	*$8.00*	£0.65	£2.00	£4.00
12 ND scarce in the U.K.	*$1.30*	*$4.00*	*$8.00*	£0.80	£2.50	£5.00
13-16 ND	*$1.30*	*$4.00*	*$8.00*	£0.65	£2.00	£4.00
17 ND scarce in the U.K. Angel and X-Men appear, The Champions appear	*$1.30*	*$4.00*	*$8.00*	£1.25	£3.75	£7.50
18 ND Angel, Iceman and X-Men appear, Champions disband	*$1.30*	*$4.00*	*$8.00*	£1.05	£3.25	£6.50
19-21 ND	*$1.30*	*$4.00*	*$8.00*	£0.65	£2.00	£4.00
22 ND Moon Knight appears, Zeck art	*$1.30*	*$4.00*	*$8.00*	£0.80	£2.50	£5.00
23 ND Moon Knight appears	*$1.30*	*$4.00*	*$8.00*	£0.75	£2.25	£4.50
24-25 ND	*$1.15*	*$3.50*	*$7.00*	£0.65	£2.00	£4.00
26 ND Daredevil appears	*$1.15*	*$3.50*	*$7.00*	£0.75	£2.25	£4.50
27 ND 1st Frank Miller art on Daredevil	*$2.50*	*$7.50*	*$15.00*	£1.30	£4.00	£8.00
28 ND Frank Miller Daredevil	*$2.05*	*$6.25*	*$12.50*	£1.15	£3.50	£7.00
29-30 ND	*$1.00*	*$3.00*	*$6.00*	£0.65	£2.00	£4.00
31-35 ND	*$1.00*	*$3.00*	*$5.00*	£0.70	£2.10	£3.50
36 ND 1st appearance Swarm	*$1.00*	*$3.00*	*$5.00*	£0.70	£2.10	£3.50
37 ND	*$1.00*	*$3.00*	*$5.00*	£0.70	£2.10	£3.50
38 ND Morbius appears	*$1.00*	*$3.00*	*$5.00*	£0.70	£2.10	£3.50

	$Good	$Fine	$N.Mint	£Good	£Fine	£N.Mint
39 ND Morbius appears (flashback), Bingham cover	$1.00	$3.00	$5.00	£0.70	£2.10	£3.50
40-52 ND	$1.00	$3.00	$5.00	£0.70	£2.10	£3.50
53	$0.80	$2.40	$4.00	£0.50	£1.50	£2.50
54 Frank Miller cover	$0.80	$2.40	$4.00	£0.50	£1.50	£2.50
55	$0.80	$2.40	$4.00	£0.50	£1.50	£2.50
56 2nd appearance Jack O'Lantern, 1st battle between Spiderman and Jack O'Lantern, Miller cover	$1.50	$4.50	$7.50	£0.70	£2.10	£3.50
57 Frank Miller cover	$0.80	$2.40	$4.00	£0.50	£1.50	£2.50
58 John Byrne art	$1.00	$3.00	$5.00	£0.60	£1.80	£3.00
59	$0.80	$2.40	$4.00	£0.50	£1.50	£2.50
60 DS, origin retold with new facts, Miller cover	$1.00	$3.00	$5.00	£0.70	£2.10	£3.50
61-63	$0.60	$1.80	$3.00	£0.40	£1.20	£2.00
64 1st appearance Cloak and Dagger	$1.40	$4.20	$7.00	£0.70	£2.10	£3.50
65-68	$0.60	$1.80	$3.00	£0.40	£1.20	£2.00
69 2nd appearance Cloak and Dagger	$1.00	$3.00	$5.00	£0.60	£1.80	£3.00
70 3rd appearance Cloak and Dagger	$0.80	$2.40	$4.00	£0.50	£1.50	£2.50
71-74	$0.60	$1.80	$3.00	£0.40	£1.20	£2.00
75 DS	$0.80	$2.40	$4.00	£0.50	£1.50	£2.50
76 LD in the U.K.	$0.60	$1.80	$3.00	£0.50	£1.50	£2.50
77 very LD/rare in the U.K.	$0.60	$1.80	$3.00	£0.60	£1.80	£3.00
78-80 LD in the U.K.	$0.60	$1.80	$3.00	£0.50	£1.50	£2.50
81-82 Punisher, Cloak & Dagger appear	$1.00	$3.00	$5.00	£0.70	£2.10	£3.50
83 origin Punisher retold	$1.50	$4.50	$7.50	£1.00	£3.00	£5.00
84	$0.60	$1.80	$3.00	£0.40	£1.20	£2.00
85 1st Hobgoblin (Ned Leeds) origin	$4.00	$12.00	$20.00	£1.20	£3.60	£6.00
86-88	$0.60	$1.80	$3.00	£0.40	£1.20	£2.00
89 Fantastic Four and Captain America cameos	$0.60	$1.80	$3.00	£0.40	£1.20	£2.00
90 LD in the U.K. Avengers cameo	$0.60	$1.80	$3.00	£0.40	£1.20	£2.00
91-93 LD in the U.K.	$0.60	$1.80	$3.00	£0.40	£1.20	£2.00
94-96 Cloak & Dagger	$0.60	$1.80	$3.00	£0.35	£1.05	£1.75
97-99	$0.60	$1.80	$3.00	£0.35	£1.05	£1.75
100 DS	$0.80	$2.40	$4.00	£0.40	£1.20	£2.00
101-102 John Byrne cover	$0.50	$1.50	$2.50	£0.30	£0.90	£1.50
103 Human Torch appears; Peter David's 1st commissioned script for Marvel Comics (see Spiderman #266)	$0.50	$1.50	$2.50	£0.30	£0.90	£1.50
104-106	$0.50	$1.50	$2.50	£0.30	£0.90	£1.50
107-110 LD in the U.K. Death of Jean DeWolff story, Daredevil appears	$0.50	$1.50	$2.50	£0.35	£1.05	£1.75
111 LD in the U.K. Secret Wars X-over	$0.50	$1.50	$2.50	£0.35	£1.05	£1.75
112 LD in the U.K. Beechum art	$0.50	$1.50	$2.50	£0.35	£1.05	£1.75
113-114 LD in the U.K.	$0.50	$1.50	$2.50	£0.35	£1.05	£1.75

	$Good	$Fine	$N.Mint	£Good	£Fine	£N.Mint
115 LD in the U.K. Dr. Strange appears, Beechum art	$0.50	$1.50	$2.50	£0.35	£1.05	£1.75
116 5th appearance Sabretooth	$1.20	$3.60	$6.00	£0.80	£2.40	£4.00
117 LD in the U.K. Dr. Strange appears	$0.50	$1.50	$2.50	£0.35	£1.05	£1.75
118 LD in the U.K. Mike Zeck layouts	$0.50	$1.50	$2.50	£0.35	£1.05	£1.75
119 Sabretooth appears	$1.00	$3.00	$5.00	£0.60	£1.80	£3.00
120-129	$0.50	$1.50	$2.50	£0.30	£0.90	£1.50
130 Hobgoblin story and cover	$0.60	$1.80	$3.00	£0.30	£0.90	£1.50
131 Kraven Saga, Zeck art	$1.00	$3.00	$5.00	£0.60	£1.80	£3.00
132 Kraven Saga, Zeck art	$1.00	$3.00	$5.00	£0.50	£1.50	£2.50
133 very LD/rare in the U.K. Sienkiewicz cover	$0.50	$1.50	$2.50	£0.35	£1.05	£1.75
134 LD scarce in the U.K.	$0.50	$1.50	$2.50	£0.35	£1.05	£1.75
135-138 LD in the U.K.	$0.50	$1.50	$2.50	£0.30	£0.90	£1.50
139 LD in the U.K. origin Tombstone	$0.50	$1.50	$2.50	£0.30	£0.90	£1.50
140 1pg Punisher appearance	$0.50	$1.50	$2.50	£0.30	£0.90	£1.50
141 Punisher appears	$0.60	$1.80	$3.00	£0.35	£1.05	£1.75
142 1pg Punisher	$0.50	$1.50	$2.50	£0.30	£0.90	£1.50
143 Punisher appears	$0.60	$1.80	$3.00	£0.35	£1.05	£1.75
144 LD in the U.K.	$0.50	$1.50	$2.50	£0.30	£0.90	£1.50
145	$0.50	$1.50	$2.50	£0.25	£0.75	£1.25
146 Inferno X-over, Hobgoblin appears (cameo)	$0.50	$1.50	$2.50	£0.30	£0.90	£1.50
147 Inferno X-over, Hobgoblin appears, 1st appearance demonic Hobgoblin	$3.50	$10.50	$17.50	£0.70	£2.10	£3.50
148 Inferno X-over	$0.50	$1.50	$2.50	£0.25	£0.75	£1.25
149 story continues from Annual #7	$0.50	$1.50	$2.50	£0.25	£0.75	£1.25
150-157	$0.50	$1.50	$2.50	£0.25	£0.75	£1.25
158 LD in the U.K. Spiderman acquires the powers of Captain Universe to become the strongest hero in the Marvel Universe; Acts of Vengeance tie-in	$0.80	$2.40	$4.00	£0.40	£1.20	£2.00
159 Acts of Vengeance tie-in, Cosmic Spiderman	$0.80	$2.40	$4.00	£0.30	£0.90	£1.50
160 Acts of Vengeance tie-in, Cosmic Spiderman	$0.40	$1.20	$2.00	£0.25	£0.75	£1.25
161-164 Hobgoblin appears	$0.40	$1.20	$2.00	£0.25	£0.75	£1.25
165-167	$0.40	$1.20	$2.00	£0.25	£0.75	£1.25
168 LD in the U.K. Thor, Captain America appear	$0.40	$1.20	$2.00	£0.25	£0.75	£1.25
169 LD in the U.K. Thor, Iron Man and Captain America appear	$0.40	$1.20	$2.00	£0.25	£0.75	£1.25
170 ND Thor, Captain America, She-Hulk, Quasar and Sersi appear; conclusion of Spiderman's refusal to join Avengers (3 part)	$0.40	$1.20	$2.00	£0.25	£0.75	£1.25
171-173 ND	$0.30	$0.90	$1.50	£0.20	£0.60	£1.00

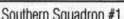

Southern Squadron #1

Space Adventures #28

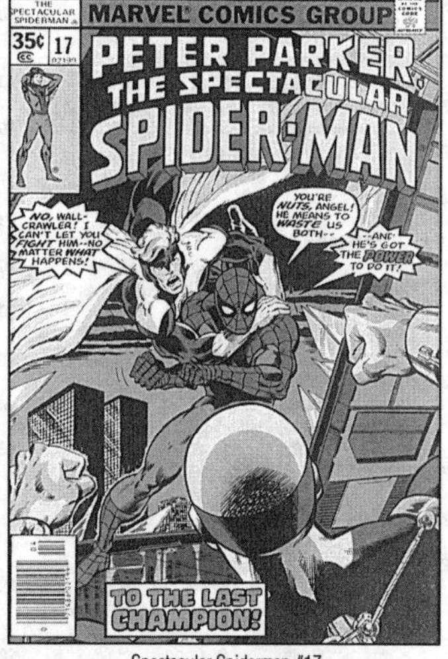

Spectacular Spiderman #17

	$Good	$Fine	$N.Mint	£Good	£Fine	£N.Mint
174	$0.30	$0.90	$1.50	£0.15	£0.45	£0.75
175-177 LD in the U.K.	$0.30	$0.90	$1.50	£0.20	£0.60	£1.00
178 LD in the U.K. The Child Within story; The Green Goblin returns	$0.30	$0.90	$1.50	£0.20	£0.60	£1.00
179 LD in the U.K. The Child Within story; The Green Goblin appears	$0.30	$0.90	$1.50	£0.20	£0.60	£1.00
180 The Child Within story, Vermin, Green Goblin appear	$0.30	$0.90	$1.50	£0.20	£0.60	£1.00
181-183 The Child Within story, Vermin, Green Goblin appear	$0.25	$0.75	$1.25	£0.15	£0.45	£0.75
184 The Child Within epilogue, Green Goblin, Vermin, Molten Man appear	$0.25	$0.75	$1.25	£0.15	£0.45	£0.75
185 Frog Man appears, $1.25 cover begins	$0.25	$0.75	$1.25	£0.15	£0.45	£0.75
186-188 Funeral Arrangements story, Vulture appears	$0.25	$0.75	$1.25	£0.15	£0.45	£0.75
189 48pgs, 30th anniversary issue, origin retold thru' Aunt May's eyes, Green Goblin appears, card cover with Spiderman hologram (scarcest of the 4 hologram anniversary covers)	$0.80	$2.40	$4.00	£0.50	£1.50	£2.50
189 2nd printing, (Nov 1992) - gold foil hologram cover	$0.60	$1.80	$3.00	£0.40	£1.20	£2.00
190-193	$0.25	$0.75	$1.25	£0.15	£0.45	£0.75
194-195 Death of Vermin story	$0.25	$0.75	$1.25	£0.15	£0.45	£0.75
195 pre-bagged, ND - with copy of Dirt magazine and audio cassette	$0.55	$1.65	$2.75	£0.35	£1.05	£1.75
196 Death of Vermin story	$0.25	$0.75	$1.25	£0.15	£0.45	£0.75
197-198 Cyclops, Iceman, Beast and Archangel (original X-Men) appear	$0.25	$0.75	$1.25	£0.15	£0.45	£0.75
199 X-Men and Green Goblin appear	$0.25	$0.75	$1.25	£0.15	£0.45	£0.75
200 card-stock holo-grafix cover, death of Harry Osborn (Green Goblin II)	$0.60	$1.80	$3.00	£0.40	£1.20	£2.00
201 Maximum Carnage part 5, continued in Amazing Spiderman #379	$0.25	$0.75	$1.25	£0.15	£0.45	£0.75
202 Maximum Carnage part 9, continued in Web of Spiderman #102	$0.25	$0.75	$1.25	£0.15	£0.45	£0.75
203 Maximum Carnage part 13, continued in Spiderman Unlimited #2	$0.25	$0.75	$1.25	£0.15	£0.45	£0.75
204-206	$0.25	$0.75	$1.25	£0.15	£0.45	£0.75
207 Siege of Darkness tie-in, Ghost Rider appears	$0.25	$0.75	$1.25	£0.15	£0.45	£0.75
208 Siege of Darkness tie-in, Black Cat back-up story	$0.25	$0.75	$1.25	£0.15	£0.45	£0.75
209	$0.25	$0.75	$1.25	£0.15	£0.45	£0.75
210 Black Cat appears	$0.25	$0.75	$1.25	£0.15	£0.45	£0.75
211 Pursuit part 2	$0.25	$0.75	$1.25	£0.15	£0.45	£0.75
212 with free Spiderman vs. Venom card sheet	$0.30	$0.90	$1.50	£0.20	£0.60	£1.00
213	$0.30	$0.90	$1.50	£0.20	£0.60	£1.00
213 Collectors Edition, ND - pre-bagged with 16pg preview and animation cel from Spiderman animated TV series; metallic ink cover	$0.60	$1.80	$3.00	£0.40	£1.20	£2.00
214 Typhoid Mary appears	$0.30	$0.90	$1.50	£0.20	£0.60	£1.00
215-216	$0.30	$0.90	$1.50	£0.20	£0.60	£1.00
217 Power and Responsibility part 4	$0.30	$0.90	$1.50	£0.20	£0.60	£1.00
217 Collectors Edition, - Power and Responsibility part 4, foil stamped cover, incorporates 16pg flip-book and second foil stamped cover	$0.60	$1.80	$3.00	£0.40	£1.20	£2.00
218 Puma appears	$0.30	$0.90	$1.50	£0.20	£0.60	£1.00
219 Spiderman and Daredevil vs. The Vulture and The Owl (see Spiderman #396)	$0.30	$0.90	$1.50	£0.20	£0.60	£1.00
220 48pgs, Web of Death part 2, continued in Spiderman #398	$0.60	$1.80	$3.00	£0.40	£1.20	£2.00
221 Web of Death part 4; Dr. Octopus dies	$0.30	$0.90	$1.50	£0.20	£0.60	£1.00
222 The Jackal appears; leads into Spiderman #400	$0.30	$0.90	$1.50	£0.20	£0.60	£1.00
223 48pgs, Aftershocks part 2 (see Spiderman 2nd Series #57)	$0.50	$1.50	$2.50	£0.30	£0.90	£1.50
223 Enhanced Edition, ND 48pgs, - multi-level debossed cover	$0.60	$1.80	$3.00	£0.40	£1.20	£2.00
224 The Mark of Kaine part 4, continued in Spiderman Unlimited #9	$0.30	$0.90	$1.50	£0.20	£0.60	£1.00
225 48pgs, 1st appearance all new Green Goblin	$0.60	$1.80	$3.00	£0.40	£1.20	£2.00
225 3-D holodisc cover, ND 48pgs, - 1st appearance new green Goblin	$0.80	$2.40	$4.00	£0.50	£1.50	£2.50
226 The Trial of Peter Parker part 4 (conclusion), Peter Parker/Spiderman revealed to be a clone	$0.30	$0.90	$1.50	£0.20	£0.60	£1.00
227 Maximum Clonage part 5, continued in Spiderman: Maximum Clonage Omega	$0.30	$0.90	$1.50	£0.20	£0.60	£1.00
228 Timebomb part 1, continued in Web of Spiderman #129; Bill Sienkiewicz inks and cover art; bi-weekly	$0.30	$0.90	$1.50	£0.20	£0.60	£1.00
229 ND continued from Spiderman #63; Peter Parker gives up being Spiderman; wraparound acetate cover; bi-weekly	$0.80	$2.40	$4.00	£0.50	£1.50	£2.50
229 Newstand Edition, ND - no cover enhancements	$0.45	$1.35	$2.25	£0.30	£0.90	£1.50
230 ND The Return of Spiderman part 4 (conclusion)	$0.30	$0.90	$1.50	£0.20	£0.60	£1.00
231 ND The Return of Kaine part 1, continued in Sensational Spiderman #2	$0.30	$0.90	$1.50	£0.20	£0.60	£1.00
232 ND	$0.30	$0.90	$1.50	£0.20	£0.60	£1.00
233 ND Web of Carnage part 4 (conclusion from Spiderman #67); Carnage appears; bi-monthly	$0.30	$0.90	$1.50	£0.20	£0.60	£1.00
234 ND Blood Brothers part 4 (conclusion)	$0.30	$0.90	$1.50	£0.20	£0.60	£1.00
235-236 ND	$0.30	$0.90	$1.50	£0.20	£0.60	£1.00
237 ND The Lizard appears	$0.30	$0.90	$1.50	£0.20	£0.60	£1.00
238 ND Onslaught tie-in, The Lizard appears	$0.30	$0.90	$1.50	£0.20	£0.60	£1.00
239 ND with bound-in Overpower cards; Luke Ross art begins	$0.30	$0.90	$1.50	£0.20	£0.60	£1.00
240 ND Revelations part 1, continued in Spiderman #75 - the return of Peter Parker	$0.30	$0.90	$1.50	£0.20	£0.60	£1.00
240 Variant Cover Edition ND	$0.80	$2.40	$4.00	£0.50	£1.50	£2.50
241 ND	$0.30	$0.90	$1.50	£0.20	£0.60	£1.00
242-243 ND The Chameleon appears	$0.30	$0.90	$1.50	£0.20	£0.60	£1.00
244 ND The Chameleon appears	$0.40	$1.20	$2.00	£0.25	£0.75	£1.25
Title Value:	$189.85	$572.05	$1017.25	£109.60	£330.25	£585.75

Spiderman and Daredevil Special Edition

	$Good	$Fine	$N.Mint	£Good	£Fine	£N.Mint
ND, reprints #26-28 (1st Miller Daredevil)				£0.35	£1.05	£1.75

Note: Black Cat appears in 75, 76, 82, 83, 85-90, 93, 95, 112, 113, 115, 116, 117, 119.

SPECTACULAR SPIDERMAN ANNUAL

Marvel Comics Group; 1 1980-present

	$Good	$Fine	$N.Mint	£Good	£Fine	£N.Mint
1 ND 52pgs, Dr. Octopus appears	$1.40	$4.20	$7.00	£1.00	£3.00	£5.00
2 ND 52pgs	$1.00	$3.00	$5.00	£0.70	£2.10	£3.50
3 ND 52pgs, Man-Wolf gemstone destroyed	$1.00	$3.00	$5.00	£0.70	£2.10	£3.50
4 ND 52pgs, more background details of Aunt May	$0.80	$2.40	$4.00	£0.60	£1.80	£3.00
5 ND Beechum art	$0.80	$2.40	$4.00	£0.60	£1.80	£3.00
6 ND Beechum art	$0.70	$2.10	$3.50	£0.50	£1.50	£2.50
7 ND	$0.60	$1.80	$3.00	£0.40	£1.20	£2.00
8 ND 64pgs, squarebound, Evolutionary War, 1st appearance Speedball	$0.60	$1.80	$3.00	£0.40	£1.20	£2.00
9 ND squarebound, Atlantis Attacks part 6, Cloak and Dagger appear	$0.60	$1.80	$3.00	£0.40	£1.20	£2.00
10 ND Spiderman's Totally Tiny Adventure part 2, continued from Spiderman Annual #24, solo Prowler story by Todd McFarlane	$0.60	$1.80	$3.00	£0.40	£1.20	£2.00
11 ND The Vibranium Vendetta part 2, continued in Web of Spiderman Annual #7	$0.50	$1.50	$2.50	£0.30	£0.90	£1.50
12 ND The Hero Killers part 2, New Warriors appear, Venom appears, continued in Web of Spiderman Annual #8	$0.50	$1.50	$2.50	£0.30	£0.90	£1.50
13 ND 64pgs, pre-bagged with trading card introducing Nocturne	$0.60	$1.80	$3.00	£0.40	£1.20	£2.00
14 ND	$0.60	$1.80	$3.00	£0.40	£1.20	£2.00
Title Value:	$10.30	$30.90	$51.50	£7.10	£21.30	£35.50

SPECTACULAR SPIDERMAN SUPER-SIZE SPECIAL

Marvel Comics Group,OS; 1 Sep 1995

	$Good	$Fine	$N.Mint	£Good	£Fine	£N.Mint
1 ND 64pgs, Planet of Symbiotes part 4, continued in Web of Spiderman Super-Size Special #1; metallic ink cover	$0.80	$2.40	$4.00	£0.50	£1.50	£2.50
Title Value:	$0.80	$2.40	$4.00	£0.50	£1.50	£2.50

SPECTACULAR SPIDERMAN, THE

Marvel Comics Group,Magazine; 1 Jul 1968-2 Nov 1968

	$Good	$Fine	$N.Mint	£Good	£Fine	£N.Mint
1 scarce in the U.K. John Romita art, origin re-told and up-dated, black and white	$10.50	$32.00	$75.00	£7.75	£23.50	£55.00
2 scarce in the U.K. Green Goblin appears in full length story, colour throughout	$13.50	$41.00	$95.00	£9.25	£28.00	£65.00
Title Value:	$24.00	$73.00	$170.00	£17.00	£51.50	£120.00

Note: Very Limited distribution on the news-stands in the U.K.

SPECTRE, THE

National Periodical Publications; 1 Nov/Dec 1967-10 May/Jun 1969

(see Adventure, Brave and the Bold, DC Comics Presents, Showcase, Wrath of the Spectre)

	$Good	$Fine	$N.Mint	£Good	£Fine	£N.Mint
1	$13.50	$41.00	$95.00	£7.75	£23.50	£55.00
2 Neal Adams cover and art	$10.50	$32.00	$75.00	£4.60	£13.50	£32.50
3-5 Neal Adams cover and art	$10.00	$30.00	$70.00	£4.25	£12.50	£30.00
6	$6.25	$19.00	$45.00	£2.85	£8.50	£20.00
7 Hourman appears	$6.25	$19.00	$45.00	£2.85	£8.50	£20.00
8	$6.25	$19.00	$45.00	£2.85	£8.50	£20.00
9 Bernie Wrightson art	$6.25	$19.00	$45.00	£3.20	£9.50	£22.50
10	$6.25	$19.00	$45.00	£2.85	£8.50	£20.00
Title Value:	$85.25	$258.00	$605.00	£39.70	£118.00	£280.00

SPECTRE, THE (2ND SERIES)

DC Comics; 1 Apr 1987-31 Oct 1989

1-3 Gene Colan art, Mike Kaluta cover

Issue	$Good	$Fine	$N.Mint	£Good	£Fine	£N.Mint
	$0.25	$0.75	$1.25	£0.15	£0.45	£0.75
4-6 Colan art	$0.25	$0.75	$1.25	£0.15	£0.45	£0.75
7-8 Cam Kennedy art, Mignola cover	$0.25	$0.75	$1.25	£0.15	£0.45	£0.75
9 Gray Morrow art, Mike Mignola cover; 1st DC comic featuring nudity without Mature Readers label (production error)	$0.25	$0.75	$1.25	£0.15	£0.45	£0.75
10-11 Millennium X-over	$0.25	$0.75	$1.25	£0.15	£0.45	£0.75
12	$0.25	$0.75	$1.25	£0.15	£0.45	£0.75
13 Charles Vess cover	$0.25	$0.75	$1.25	£0.15	£0.45	£0.75
14-22	$0.25	$0.75	$1.25	£0.15	£0.45	£0.75
23 Invasion X-over	$0.25	$0.75	$1.25	£0.15	£0.45	£0.75
24-29 Ghost in the Machine story	$0.25	$0.75	$1.25	£0.15	£0.45	£0.75
30	$0.25	$0.75	$1.25	£0.15	£0.45	£0.75
31 LD in the U.K.	$0.25	$0.75	$1.25	£0.20	£0.60	£1.00
Title Value:	$7.75	$23.25	$38.75	£4.70	£14.10	£23.50

Note: Kaluta covers #1-3, Garcia Lopez covers #5, #6, Mignola covers #7-9

SPECTRE, THE (2ND SERIES) ANNUAL

DC Comics; 1 1988

Issue	$Good	$Fine	$N.Mint	£Good	£Fine	£N.Mint
1 ND 48pgs, Baikie art, Art Adams cover includes Marvel/Indie character cameos	$0.40	$1.20	$2.00	£0.25	£0.75	£1.25
Title Value:	$0.40	$1.20	$2.00	£0.25	£0.75	£1.25

SPECTRE, THE (3RD SERIES)

DC Comics; 0 Oct 1994; 1 Dec 1992-present

Issue	$Good	$Fine	$N.Mint	£Good	£Fine	£N.Mint
0 (Oct 1994) Zero Hour X-over, origin retold	$0.40	$1.20	$2.00	£0.25	£0.75	£1.25
1 Tom Mandrake art begins; glow-in-the-dark cover	$1.20	$3.60	$6.00	£0.60	£1.80	£3.00
2	$0.80	$2.40	$4.00	£0.30	£0.90	£1.50
3 Madame Xanadu appears	$0.80	$2.40	$4.00	£0.30	£0.90	£1.50
4	$0.40	$1.20	$2.00	£0.25	£0.75	£1.25
5 Charles Vess cover	$0.40	$1.20	$2.00	£0.25	£0.75	£1.25
6 Garry Leach cover	$0.40	$1.20	$2.00	£0.25	£0.75	£1.25
7 Madame Xanadu becomes The Spectre (temporarily)	$0.40	$1.20	$2.00	£0.25	£0.75	£1.25
8 glow-in-the-dark cover	$0.80	$2.40	$4.00	£0.40	£1.20	£2.00
9 Matt Wagner cover	$0.40	$1.20	$2.00	£0.25	£0.75	£1.25
10 Kaluta cover	$0.40	$1.20	$2.00	£0.25	£0.75	£1.25
11-12	$0.40	$1.20	$2.00	£0.25	£0.75	£1.25
13 glow-in-the-dark cover	$0.80	$2.40	$4.00	£0.40	£1.20	£2.00
14 Phantom Stranger appears	$0.40	$1.20	$2.00	£0.25	£0.75	£1.25
15 Phantom Stranger, Demon, Dr. Fate and John Constantine appear	$0.40	$1.20	$2.00	£0.25	£0.75	£1.25
16-21	$0.40	$1.20	$2.00	£0.25	£0.75	£1.25
22 Superman guest-stars; painted cover by Alex Ross	$0.40	$1.20	$2.00	£0.25	£0.75	£1.25
23-26	$0.40	$1.20	$2.00	£0.25	£0.75	£1.25
27 Simon Bisley painted cover	$0.40	$1.20	$2.00	£0.25	£0.75	£1.25
28-29	$0.40	$1.20	$2.00	£0.25	£0.75	£1.25
30-34	$0.45	$1.35	$2.25	£0.30	£0.90	£1.50
35-36 Underworld Unleashed tie-in	$0.45	$1.35	$2.25	£0.30	£0.90	£1.50
37-38	$0.45	$1.35	$2.25	£0.30	£0.90	£1.50
39 painted cover by Kev O'Neill	$0.45	$1.35	$2.25	£0.30	£0.90	£1.50
40-41	$0.45	$1.35	$2.25	£0.30	£0.90	£1.50
42-43 painted cover by Brian Bolland	$0.45	$1.35	$2.25	£0.30	£0.90	£1.50
44-46	$0.45	$1.35	$2.25	£0.30	£0.90	£1.50
47 ND Final Night tie-in	$0.45	$1.35	$2.25	£0.30	£0.90	£1.50
48-49 ND	$0.60	$1.80	$3.00	£0.40	£1.20	£2.00
50 ND John Bolton cover	$0.50	$1.50	$2.50	£0.30	£0.90	£1.50
51 ND Batman guest-stars	$0.50	$1.50	$2.50	£0.30	£0.90	£1.50
Title Value:	$24.70	$74.10	$123.50	£15.05	£45.15	£75.25

The Spectre: Crimes & Punishments (Dec 1993)

	£Good	£Fine	£N.Mint
Trade paperback reprints issues #1-4 with new glow-in-the-dark cover	£1.30	£3.90	£6.50

SPECTRE, THE (3RD SERIES) ANNUAL

DC Comics; 1 Nov 1995-present

Issue	$Good	$Fine	$N.Mint	£Good	£Fine	£N.Mint
1 ND 56pgs, Year One, Dr. Fate appears	$0.80	$2.40	$4.00	£0.50	£1.50	£2.50
Title Value:	$0.80	$2.40	$4.00	£0.50	£1.50	£2.50

SPECTRE, WRATH OF THE

DC Comics,MS; 1 May 1988-4 Aug 1988

Issue	$Good	$Fine	$N.Mint	£Good	£Fine	£N.Mint
1-3 ND 48pgs, reprints Adventure #431-440	$0.50	$1.50	$2.50	£0.30	£0.90	£1.50
4 ND 48pgs, 3 new stories originally intended for Adventure Comics #441-443	$0.50	$1.50	$2.50	£0.30	£0.90	£1.50

Issue	$Good	$Fine	$N.Mint	£Good	£Fine	£N.Mint
Title Value:	$2.00	$6.00	$10.00	£1.20	£3.60	£6.00

SPEED DEMON

Marvel Comics Group/Amalgam,OS; 1 Apr 1996

Issue	$Good	$Fine	$N.Mint	£Good	£Fine	£N.Mint
1 ND a Marvel/DC amalgamation of Ghost Rider and Flash; Howard Mackie and James Felder script, Sal Larocca and Al Milgrom art	$0.50	$1.50	$2.50	£0.40	£1.20	£2.00
Title Value:	$0.50	$1.50	$2.50	£0.40	£1.20	£2.00

SPEED RACER

Now Comics; 1 Aug 1987-42 1992 ?

Issue	$Good	$Fine	$N.Mint	£Good	£Fine	£N.Mint
1 ND	$0.40	$1.20	$2.00	£0.25	£0.75	£1.25
1 2nd printing ND	$0.30	$0.90	$1.50	£0.20	£0.60	£1.00
2-19 ND	$0.40	$1.20	$2.00	£0.25	£0.75	£1.25
20-42 ND Comics Code on cover	$0.40	$1.20	$2.00	£0.25	£0.75	£1.25
Title Value:	$17.10	$51.30	$85.50	£10.70	£32.10	£53.50

SPEED RACER (2ND SERIES)

Now Comics,MS; 1 Jul 1992-3 Sep 1992

Issue	$Good	$Fine	$N.Mint	£Good	£Fine	£N.Mint
1 ND includes cut-out model	$0.40	$1.20	$2.00	£0.25	£0.75	£1.25
1 Newstand Edition, ND, pre-bagged with badge, signed and numbered by creators	$0.50	$1.50	$2.50	£0.30	£0.90	£1.50
1 Prestige Edition, ND, pre-bagged with badge, 16 extra pages, 500 copies signed and numbered by creators, numbered neon label on front cover	$0.50	$1.50	$2.50	£0.30	£0.90	£1.50
2-3 ND	$0.40	$1.20	$2.00	£0.25	£0.75	£1.25
Title Value:	$2.20	$6.60	$11.00	£1.35	£4.05	£6.75

SPEED RACER 3-D SPECIAL

Now Comics; 1 Jan 1993-2 1993

Issue	$Good	$Fine	$N.Mint	£Good	£Fine	£N.Mint
1-2 ND pre-bagged with glasses (25% less without glasses)	$0.50	$1.50	$2.50	£0.30	£0.90	£1.50
Title Value:	$1.00	$3.00	$5.00	£0.60	£1.80	£3.00

SPEED RACER FEATURING NINJA HIGH SCHOOL

Now Comics,MS; 1 Aug 1993-2 1994

Issue	$Good	$Fine	$N.Mint	£Good	£Fine	£N.Mint
1 ND	$0.50	$1.50	$2.50	£0.30	£0.90	£1.50
2 ND pre-bagged with trading card; part 3 - part 4 published by Eternity the same month	$0.50	$1.50	$2.50	£0.30	£0.90	£1.50
Title Value:	$1.00	$3.00	$5.00	£0.60	£1.80	£3.00

SPEED RACER SPECIAL

Now Comics; 1 1987-2 1988

Issue	$Good	$Fine	$N.Mint	£Good	£Fine	£N.Mint
1 ND	$0.40	$1.20	$2.00	£0.25	£0.75	£1.25
2 ND	$0.60	$1.80	$3.00	£0.40	£1.20	£2.00
Title Value:	$1.00	$3.00	$5.00	£0.65	£1.95	£3.25

SPEED RACER, THE NEW ADVENTURES OF

Now Comics; 0 Nov 1993; 1 Dec 1993-11 1994 ?

Issue	$Good	$Fine	$N.Mint	£Good	£Fine	£N.Mint
0 ND pre-bagged with trading card	$0.50	$1.50	$2.50	£0.30	£0.90	£1.50
1-11 ND	$0.40	$1.20	$2.00	£0.25	£0.75	£1.25
Title Value:	$4.90	$14.70	$24.50	£3.05	£9.15	£15.25

SPEEDBALL THE MASKED MARVEL

Marvel Comics Group; 1 Sep 1988-11 Jul 1989

(see New Warriors)

Issue	$Good	$Fine	$N.Mint	£Good	£Fine	£N.Mint
1 ND Steve Ditko story/art begins	$0.30	$0.90	$1.50	£0.20	£0.60	£1.00
2-11	$0.25	$0.75	$1.25	£0.15	£0.45	£0.75
Title Value:	$2.80	$8.40	$14.00	£1.70	£5.10	£8.50

SPELLBOUND

Marvel Comics Group,MS; 1 Jan 1988-6 Mar 1988

Issue	$Good	$Fine	$N.Mint	£Good	£Fine	£N.Mint
1-3 ND	$0.25	$0.75	$1.25	£0.15	£0.45	£0.75
4 ND New Mutants appear	$0.25	$0.75	$1.25	£0.15	£0.45	£0.75
5-6 ND	$0.25	$0.75	$1.25	£0.15	£0.45	£0.75
Title Value:	$1.50	$4.50	$7.50	£0.90	£2.70	£4.50

Note: all high quality paper, bi-weekly frequency

SPELLJAMMER COMICS

DC Comics; 1 Sep 1990-18 Feb 1992

Issue	$Good	$Fine	$N.Mint	£Good	£Fine	£N.Mint
1-7 ND	$0.40	$1.20	$2.00	£0.25	£0.75	£1.25
8 ND Joe Quesada art (1st professional work?)	$0.55	$1.65	$2.75	£0.35	£1.05	£1.75
9 ND Joe Quesada art	$0.50	$1.50	$2.50	£0.30	£0.90	£1.50
10 ND part prose, Joe Quesada art	$0.40	$1.20	$2.00	£0.25	£0.75	£1.25
11-13 ND Joe Quesada art	$0.40	$1.20	$2.00	£0.25	£0.75	£1.25
14-18 ND	$0.40	$1.20	$2.00	£0.25	£0.75	£1.25
Title Value:	$7.45	$22.35	$37.25	£4.65	£13.95	£23.25

Note: New Format

SPENCER SPOOK, THE ADVENTURES OF

Ace; 1 Oct 1986-4 1987

Issue	$Good	$Fine	$N.Mint	£Good	£Fine	£N.Mint
1-4 ND Pat Boyette art	$0.30	$0.90	$1.50	£0.20	£0.60	£1.00
Title Value:	$1.20	$3.60	$6.00	£0.80	£2.40	£4.00

SPICY DETECTIVE STORIES

Eternity; nn 1987

Issue	$Good	$Fine	$N.Mint	£Good	£Fine	£N.Mint
nn ND 1930s detective pulp reprints	$1.20	$3.60	$6.00	£0.80	£2.40	£4.00
Title Value:	$1.20	$3.60	$6.00	£0.80	£2.40	£4.00
2nd print (1990)				£0.85	£2.55	£4.25

SPICY HORROR STORIES

Eternity; nn Oct 1990

Issue	$Good	$Fine	$N.Mint	£Good	£Fine	£N.Mint
nn ND 1930s/1940s horror pulp reprints	$1.50	$4.50	$7.50	£1.00	£3.00	£5.00

	$Good	$Fine	$N.Mint	£Good	£Fine	£N.Mint
Title Value:	**$1.50**	**$4.50**	**$7.50**	**£1.00**	**£3.00**	**£5.00**

SPICY MYSTERY STORIES TRADE PAPERBACK

Eternity; nn Jun 1990

	$Good	$Fine	$N.Mint	£Good	£Fine	£N.Mint
nn ND 10 classic pulp tales from the 1930s	$1.50	$4.50	$7.50	£1.00	£3.00	£5.00
Title Value:	$1.50	$4.50	$7.50	£1.00	£3.00	£5.00

SPICY TALES

Eternity; 1 Feb 1989-17 1991

	$Good	$Fine	$N.Mint	£Good	£Fine	£N.Mint
1 ND reprint detective anthology begins	$0.40	$1.20	$2.00	£0.25	£0.75	£1.25
2-17 ND	$0.40	$1.20	$2.00	£0.25	£0.75	£1.25
Title Value:	$6.80	$20.40	$34.00	£4.25	£12.75	£21.25
Special 1,2				£0.30	£0.90	£1.50
Collection (1990), reprints				£1.10	£3.30	£5.50
Graphic Album, new reprints (1990)				£1.10	£3.30	£5.50

SPICY WESTERN STORIES TRADE PAPERBACK

Eternity; nn Jul 1990

	$Good	$Fine	$N.Mint	£Good	£Fine	£N.Mint
nn ND reprints 1930s western pulps	$1.50	$4.50	$7.50	£1.00	£3.00	£5.00
Title Value:	$1.50	$4.50	$7.50	£1.00	£3.00	£5.00

SPIDER, THE

Eclipse,MS; 1 Jun 1991-3 Oct 1991

	$Good	$Fine	$N.Mint	£Good	£Fine	£N.Mint
1-3 ND 48pgs, Tim Truman and Alcatena (see DC's Hawkworld)	$0.80	$2.40	$4.00	£0.50	£1.50	£2.50
Title Value:	$2.40	$7.20	$12.00	£1.50	£4.50	£7.50

SPIDER-BOY

Marvel Comics Group/Amalgam,OS; 1 Apr 1996

	$Good	$Fine	$N.Mint	£Good	£Fine	£N.Mint
1 ND a Marvel/DC amalgamation of Spiderman and Superboy; Karl Kesel script, Mike Wieringo art	$0.50	$1.50	$2.50	£0.40	£1.20	£2.00
Title Value:	$0.50	$1.50	$2.50	£0.40	£1.20	£2.00

SPIDER: REIGN OF THE VAMPIRE KING, THE

Eclipse,MS; 1 Aug 1992-3 Oct 1992

	$Good	$Fine	$N.Mint	£Good	£Fine	£N.Mint
1-3 ND 48pgs, Truman and Alcatena	$0.80	$2.40	$4.00	£0.50	£1.50	£2.50
Title Value:	$2.40	$7.20	$12.00	£1.50	£4.50	£7.50

SPIDERMAN

Marvel Comics Group; 1 Aug 1990-63 Oct 1995; 64 Jan 1996-present

	$Good	$Fine	$N.Mint	£Good	£Fine	£N.Mint
1 2nd printing, ND, Direct Sales only, gold cover (Note: Marvel have stated no bagged 2nd prints were produced)	$0.90	$2.70	$4.50	£0.60	£1.80	£3.00
1 Green Cover Edition, ND - Todd McFarlane art begins, Lizard appears	$0.90	$2.70	$4.50	£0.60	£1.80	£3.00
1 Green Cover Edition, pre-bagged, ND with bar-code lines in bottom left hand corner	$1.20	$3.60	$6.00	£0.80	£2.40	£4.00
1 Green Cover Edition, pre-bagged with, ND Spidey face in bottom left hand corner	$1.80	$5.25	$9.00	£1.20	£3.60	£6.00
1 Green Cover Signed Edition, ND - signed by McFarlane with letter of authenticity (20,000 copies)	$4.50	$13.50	$22.50	£3.00	£9.00	£15.00
1 Platinum Edition, ND - limited to 10,000 copies sent by Marvel to distributors in U.S. and U.K. as "thankyou". (Most copies damaged through the mail, however...)	$32.00	$95.00	$160.00	£20.00	£60.00	£100.00
1 Silver Cover Edition, ND - Direct Sales only to comic shops	$1.20	$3.60	$6.00	£0.80	£2.40	£4.00
1 Silver Cover Edition, pre-bagged ND	$2.00	$6.00	$10.00	£1.40	£4.20	£7.00
1 Silver Cover Signed Edition, ND - signed by McFarlane with letter of authenticity, limited to 20,000 copies	$4.50	$13.50	$22.50	£3.00	£9.00	£15.00
2 ND Lizard appears	$0.90	$2.70	$4.50	£0.60	£1.80	£3.00
3 ND Lizard appears, origin Spiderman retold	$0.90	$2.70	$4.50	£0.60	£1.80	£3.00
4-5 ND Lizard appears	$0.80	$2.40	$4.00	£0.50	£1.50	£2.50
6 ND Ghost Rider appears	$0.90	$2.70	$4.50	£0.60	£1.80	£3.00
6 2nd printing, ND Ghost Rider appears	$0.40	$1.20	$2.00	£0.25	£0.75	£1.25
7 ND Ghost Rider appears	$0.80	$2.40	$4.00	£0.50	£1.50	£2.50
8 ND Perceptions story; Wolverine appears last page	$0.60	$1.80	$3.00	£0.40	£1.20	£2.00
9-12 ND Perceptions story, Wolverine/Wendigo appear	$0.60	$1.80	$3.00	£0.40	£1.20	£2.00
13-14 ND Morbius the Living Vampire appears	$0.50	$1.50	$2.50	£0.30	£0.90	£1.50
15 ND Impossible Man appears	$0.50	$1.50	$2.50	£0.30	£0.90	£1.50
16 ND X-over with X-Force #4; entire issue printed sideways, last McFarlane art	$0.50	$1.50	$2.50	£0.30	£0.90	£1.50
17 ND Thanos appears, Nocenti script, Leonardi and Austin art	$0.50	$1.50	$2.50	£0.30	£0.90	£1.50
18 ND Erik Larsen script and art begins, Sinister Six appear	$0.50	$1.50	$2.50	£0.30	£0.90	£1.50
19 ND Erik Larsen script and art, Deathlok, Hulk, Sinister Six appear	$0.50	$1.50	$2.50	£0.30	£0.90	£1.50
20 ND Erik Larsen script and art, Sinister Six appear	$0.50	$1.50	$2.50	£0.30	£0.90	£1.50
21 ND Erik Larsen script and art, Sinister Six appear, Deathlok and Hulk appear	$0.40	$1.20	$2.00	£0.25	£0.75	£1.25
22 ND Erik Larsen script and art, Sinister Six appear, Deathlok, Ghost Rider and Sleepwalker appear	$0.40	$1.20	$2.00	£0.25	£0.75	£1.25
23 ND Erik Larsen script and art, Sinister Six appear plus Ghost Rider, Solo, Deathlok, Hulk, Nova, Fantastic Four, gatefold cover	$0.40	$1.20	$2.00	£0.25	£0.75	£1.25
24 ND Infinity War X-over	$0.40	$1.20	$2.00	£0.25	£0.75	£1.25
25 ND Excalibur appear	$0.40	$1.20	$2.00	£0.25	£0.75	£1.25
26 ND 30th anniversary issue, hologram cover, gatefold centre-spread, Spiderman's origin as seen through the eyes of Peter Parker, Larsen art	$0.80	$2.40	$4.00	£0.50	£1.50	£2.50
27-31 ND	$0.40	$1.20	$2.00	£0.25	£0.75	£1.25
32-34 ND Punisher guest-stars	$0.40	$1.20	$2.00	£0.25	£0.75	£1.25
35 ND Maximum Carnage part 4, continued in Spectacular Spiderman #201	$0.40	$1.20	$2.00	£0.25	£0.75	£1.25
36 ND Maximum Carnage part 8, continued in Spectacular Spiderman #202	$0.40	$1.20	$2.00	£0.25	£0.75	£1.25
37 ND Maximum Carnage part 12, continued in Spectacular Spiderman #203	$0.40	$1.20	$2.00	£0.25	£0.75	£1.25
38-40 ND Electro appears	$0.40	$1.20	$2.00	£0.25	£0.75	£1.25
41-43 ND Iron Fist appears; Jae Lee art	$0.30	$0.90	$1.50	£0.20	£0.60	£1.00
44 ND Howard Mackie, Tom Lyle and Scott Hanna creative team begins	$0.30	$0.90	$1.50	£0.20	£0.60	£1.00
45 ND Pursuit part 1, continued in Spectacular Spiderman #211	$0.30	$0.90	$1.50	£0.20	£0.60	£1.00
46 ND Hobgoblin and Demogoblin appear	$0.30	$0.90	$1.50	£0.20	£0.60	£1.00
46 Collectors Edition, ND pre-bagged with 16pg preview and animation cel from the Spiderman animated TV series, metallic ink cover	$0.60	$1.80	$3.00	£0.40	£1.20	£2.00
47 ND Hobgoblin and Demogoblin appear	$0.30	$0.90	$1.50	£0.20	£0.60	£1.00
48-49	$0.30	$0.90	$1.50	£0.20	£0.60	£1.00
50 48pgs, holo-grafix foil cover	$0.80	$2.40	$4.00	£0.50	£1.50	£2.50
51 Power and responsibility part 3	$0.30	$0.90	$1.50	£0.20	£0.60	£1.00
51 Collectors Edition, ND - Power and responsibility part 3, incorporates 16pg flip-book with second foil stamped cover; contimued in Spectacular Spiderman #217	$0.60	$1.80	$3.00	£0.40	£1.20	£2.00
52-53 Venom appears	$0.30	$0.90	$1.50	£0.20	£0.60	£1.00
54 48pgs, Web of Life part 2, continued in Web of Spiderman #121	$0.55	$1.65	$2.75	£0.35	£1.05	£1.75
55 Web of Life part 4 (conclusion)	$0.40	$1.20	$2.00	£0.25	£0.75	£1.25
56 The Jackal appears	$0.40	$1.20	$2.00	£0.25	£0.75	£1.25
57 48pgs, Aftershocks part 1, continued in Spectacular Spiderman #223	$0.50	$1.50	$2.50	£0.30	£0.90	£1.50
57 Collectors Edition, ND 48pgs, - multi-level embossed cover	$0.60	$1.80	$3.00	£0.40	£1.20	£2.00
58 The Mark of Kaine part 3, continued in Spectacular Spiderman #224; Spiderman and The Scarlet Spider vs. Kaine	$0.40	$1.20	$2.00	£0.25	£0.75	£1.25
59 continued from Amazing Spiderman #402	$0.40	$1.20	$2.00	£0.25	£0.75	£1.25
60 The Trial of Peter Parker part 3, continued in Spectacular Spiderman #226	$0.40	$1.20	$2.00	£0.25	£0.75	£1.25
61 Maximum Clonage part 4, continued in Spectacular Spiderman #227	$0.40	$1.20	$2.00	£0.25	£0.75	£1.25
62 Exiled part 3, continued in Spiderman Unlimited #10	$0.40	$1.20	$2.00	£0.25	£0.75	£1.25
63 The Great Responsibility part 2, continued in Spectacular Spiderman #229	$0.40	$1.20	$2.00	£0.25	£0.75	£1.25
64 The Return of Spiderman part 3, continued in Spectacular Spiderman #230	$0.40	$1.20	$2.00	£0.25	£0.75	£1.25
65 Media Blizzard part 3 (conclusion), continued from Amazing Spiderman #408	$0.40	$1.20	$2.00	£0.25	£0.75	£1.25
66 The Return of Kaine part 4 (conclusion from Amazing Spiderman #409)	$0.40	$1.20	$2.00	£0.25	£0.75	£1.25
67 Web of Carnage part 3, continued in Spectacular Spiderman #233; Carnage appears	$0.40	$1.20	$2.00	£0.25	£0.75	£1.25
68 Blood Brothers part 3, continued in Spectacular Spiderman #234	$0.40	$1.20	$2.00	£0.25	£0.75	£1.25
69-71	$0.40	$1.20	$2.00	£0.25	£0.75	£1.25
72 Onslaught tie-in	$0.40	$1.20	$2.00	£0.25	£0.75	£1.25
73	$0.40	$1.20	$2.00	£0.25	£0.75	£1.25
74 Spiderman and Daredevil team-up	$0.40	$1.20	$2.00	£0.25	£0.75	£1.25
75 48pgs, Revelations part 4, the one true Spiderman revealed...	$0.60	$1.80	$3.00	£0.40	£1.20	£2.00
76	$0.40	$1.20	$2.00	£0.25	£0.75	£1.25
77 Morbius appears	$0.40	$1.20	$2.00	£0.25	£0.75	£1.25
78 ND title becomes "Peter Parker, Spiderman"	$0.40	$1.20	$2.00	£0.25	£0.75	£1.25
Title Value:	$86.55	$258.50	$432.75	£55.25	£165.75	£276.25

Note: a print run of over 2.5 million copies makes this one of the best selling comics of modern times.

Blue Lizard Edition: Note also that a printing defect on the silver ink/black cover unbagged (and

VERY GENERAL PERCENTAGE CONVERSION CHART WHICH MAY BE USED TO CALCULATE LOW AND INBETWEEN GRADES:

possibly bagged) editions that came to this country (apparently only to the North of England) shows a blue-coloured Lizard in a couple of panels. The number of copies is alledged to be anything from 200–1,500 but more are suspected. This anomaly is duly noted but no firmly established value can be given for it even though isolated copies have been sold at a wide range of premium prices. An average now seems to be **£5.00–£10.00**.

Note also that pre-bagged copies of the gold edition have been sighted but these have been constructed outside Marvel Comics as they never officially designed this package.

Note also that up to 40,000 copies of the regular green and silver editions were officially signed by Todd McFarlane in gold ink on the cover. They would have an added value though counterfeits have been known. Genuine copies should be accompanied by a signed letter of authentication and a red spider-web seal on the back.

The Platinum Edition: this is a special edition of Spiderman #1 with no ads + 10 pages of sketches and pin-ups. They were made available by Marvel in the Spring of 1991 to (mostly US) retailers only. 10,000 were officially printed. It has very glossy cardstock (stiffer) covers.

AS MANY OF THESE WERE MAILED THROUGH THE POST, MOST SUFFER FROM SCRATCHES OR CRUMPLED CORNERS. ABSOLUTELY NEAR MINT COPIES ARE VERY RARE IN BOTH THE U.K. AND U.S.

	$Good	$Fine	$N.Mint	£Good	£Fine	£N.Mint
Spiderman Mini-Masterpiece (Dec 1995) ND boxed set collecting Spiderman #45 & #50, Spectacular Spiderman #211, Web of Spiderman #112, Amazing Spiderman #389				£1.30	£3.90	£6.50

SPIDERMAN '97, PETER PARKER

Marvel Comics Group; 1 Mar 1997

	$Good	$Fine	$N.Mint	£Good	£Fine	£N.Mint
1 ND Glenn Herdling script, Shawn McManus art, Calypso appears; title replaces Spiderman [2nd Series] Annual	$0.60	$1.80	$3.00	£0.40	£1.20	£2.00
Title Value:	$0.60	$1.80	$3.00	£0.40	£1.20	£2.00

SPIDERMAN 2099

Marvel Comics Group; 1 Nov 1992-46 Aug 1996

(see Doom 2099, Ghost Rider 2099, Hulk 2099, Punisher 2099, Ravage 2099, X-Men 2099)

	$Good	$Fine	$N.Mint	£Good	£Fine	£N.Mint
1 ND Peter David script, Leonardi/Williamson art begins, red-foil border cover on heavier stock paper; origin begins	$0.40	$1.20	$2.00	£0.25	£0.75	£1.25
2 ND origin continues	$0.30	$0.90	$1.50	£0.20	£0.60	£1.00
3 ND origin concludes	$0.30	$0.90	$1.50	£0.20	£0.60	£1.00
4 ND Doom 2099 appears	$0.25	$0.75	$1.25	£0.15	£0.45	£0.75
5-7 ND	$0.25	$0.75	$1.25	£0.15	£0.45	£0.75
8 ND 1st appearance Vulture 2099	$0.25	$0.75	$1.25	£0.15	£0.45	£0.75
9-15 ND	$0.25	$0.75	$1.25	£0.15	£0.45	£0.75
16 ND Peter David script, continued in Ravage 2099 #15	$0.25	$0.75	$1.25	£0.15	£0.45	£0.75
17-18 ND	$0.25	$0.75	$1.25	£0.15	£0.45	£0.75
19 ND with free Spiderman's Amazing Powers card sheet	$0.25	$0.75	$1.25	£0.15	£0.45	£0.75
20-25 ND	$0.25	$0.75	$1.25	£0.15	£0.45	£0.75
25 Collectors Edition, ND multi-level embossed foil stamped cover; 8pg Hulk 2099 preview	$0.60	$1.80	$3.00	£0.40	£1.20	£2.00
26-31 ND	$0.30	$0.90	$1.50	£0.20	£0.60	£1.00
32 ND $1.95 begin	$0.40	$1.20	$2.00	£0.25	£0.75	£1.25
33 ND	$0.40	$1.20	$2.00	£0.25	£0.75	£1.25
34-35 ND One Nation Under Doom	$0.40	$1.20	$2.00	£0.25	£0.75	£1.25
36 Cover A, ND One Nation Under Doom; cover high-lighting Spiderman 2099 that joins to Cover B	$0.40	$1.20	$2.00	£0.25	£0.75	£1.25
36 Cover B, ND One Nation Under Doom; cover high-lighting Venom 2099 that joins to Cover A	$0.40	$1.20	$2.00	£0.25	£0.75	£1.25
37 Cover A, ND One Nation Under Doom; cover high-lighting Spiderman 2099 being attacked by Venom 2099	$0.40	$1.20	$2.00	£0.25	£0.75	£1.25
37 Cover B, ND One Nation Under Doom; cover high-lighting Venom 2099 in the classic "Amazing Fantasy #15 pose"	$0.40	$1.20	$2.00	£0.25	£0.75	£1.25
38 Cover A, ND Venom 2099 saga concludes; cover shows Spiderman 2099	$0.40	$1.20	$2.00	£0.25	£0.75	£1.25
38 Cover B, ND Venom 2099 saga concludes; cover shows Venom 2099	$0.40	$1.20	$2.00	£0.25	£0.75	£1.25
39 ND intro Goblin 2099, ties into 2099 Genesis	$0.40	$1.20	$2.00	£0.25	£0.75	£1.25
40 ND	$0.40	$1.20	$2.00	£0.25	£0.75	£1.25
41 ND Goblin 2099 vs. Vulture 2099	$0.40	$1.20	$2.00	£0.25	£0.75	£1.25
42 ND	$0.40	$1.20	$2.00	£0.25	£0.75	£1.25
43-44 ND Sub-Mariner 2099 appears; Ron Lim art	$0.40	$1.20	$2.00	£0.25	£0.75	£1.25
45-46 ND	$0.40	$1.20	$2.00	£0.25	£0.75	£1.25
Title Value:	$16.10	$48.30	$80.50	£10.05	£30.15	£50.25

SPIDERMAN 2099 ANNUAL

Marvel Comics Group; 1 Sep 1994

	$Good	$Fine	$N.Mint	£Good	£Fine	£N.Mint
1 ND Peter David Script	$0.60	$1.80	$3.00	£0.40	£1.20	£2.00
Title Value:	$0.60	$1.80	$3.00	£0.40	£1.20	£2.00

SPIDERMAN 2099 SPECIAL

Marvel Comics Group; 1 Nov 1995

	$Good	$Fine	$N.Mint	£Good	£Fine	£N.Mint
1 ND 64pgs, One Nation Under Doom, painted cover by the Brothers Hildebrandt	$0.80	$2.40	$4.00	£0.50	£1.50	£2.50
Title Value:	$0.80	$2.40	$4.00	£0.50	£1.50	£2.50

SPIDERMAN ADVENTURES

Marvel Comics Group; 1 Dec 1994-15 Mar 1996

	$Good	$Fine	$N.Mint	£Good	£Fine	£N.Mint
1 ND based on newest animated series, foil stamped and embossed cover	$0.60	$1.80	$3.00	£0.40	£1.20	£2.00
2 ND The Scorpion appears	$0.30	$0.90	$1.50	£0.20	£0.60	£1.00
3-4 ND Spider-Slayer appears	$0.30	$0.90	$1.50	£0.20	£0.60	£1.00
5 ND Mysterio appears	$0.30	$0.90	$1.50	£0.20	£0.60	£1.00
6 ND Kraven the Hunter appears	$0.30	$0.90	$1.50	£0.20	£0.60	£1.00
7 ND Dr. Octopus origin retold	$0.30	$0.90	$1.50	£0.20	£0.60	£1.00
8-9 ND origin of Venom retold	$0.30	$0.90	$1.50	£0.20	£0.60	£1.00
10 ND Spiderman vs. Venom; bi-weekly	$0.30	$0.90	$1.50	£0.20	£0.60	£1.00
11 ND Spiderman vs. Hobgoblin; bi-weekly	$0.30	$0.90	$1.50	£0.20	£0.60	£1.00
12 ND Hobgoblin and Kingpin appear	$0.30	$0.90	$1.50	£0.20	£0.60	£1.00
13 ND Chameleon appears	$0.30	$0.90	$1.50	£0.20	£0.60	£1.00
14 ND origin of Spiderman retold as brand new adventures not seen on the animated show begin	$0.30	$0.90	$1.50	£0.20	£0.60	£1.00
15 ND The Lizard appears	$0.30	$0.90	$1.50	£0.20	£0.60	£1.00
Title Value:	$4.80	$14.40	$24.00	£3.20	£9.60	£16.00
Spiderman Adventures (Nov 1995) Trade paperback 112pgs, collects issues #1-5, computer animated cel cover				£1.20	£3.60	£6.00

SPIDERMAN AND HIS AMAZING FRIENDS

Marvel Comics Group,OS TV; 1 Dec 1981

Spectre (1st) #5

Spiderman and Power Pack Giveaway

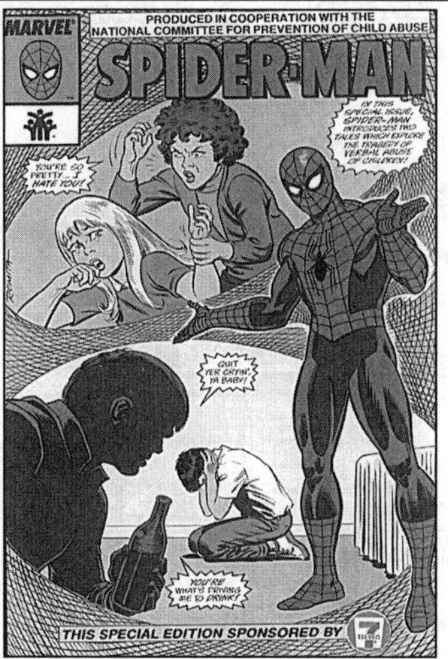

Spiderman Child Abuse Giveaway

	$Good	$Fine	$N.Mint	£Good	£Fine	£N.Mint
1 ND adapts TV cartoon, 1st appearance of Firestar but outside Marvel continuity	*$0.60*	*$1.80*	*$3.00*	£0.40	£1.20	£2.00
Title Value:	*$0.60*	*$1.80*	*$3.00*	£0.40	£1.20	£2.00

SPIDERMAN ASHCAN, AMAZING

Marvel Comics Group; nn Jun 1994

	$Good	$Fine	$N.Mint	£Good	£Fine	£N.Mint
nn ND 16pgs, origin retold and profiles on Spiderman villains	*$0.25*	*$0.75*	*$1.25*	£0.15	£0.45	£0.75
Title Value:	*$0.25*	*$0.75*	*$1.25*	£0.15	£0.45	£0.75

SPIDERMAN BOOK AND RECORD SET

Power Records;PR-24 1974

	$Good	$Fine	$N.Mint	£Good	£Fine	£N.Mint
PR-24 ND scarce in the U.K. 20pg booklet with 45 rpm record	*$1.65*	*$5.00*	*$10.00*	£1.00	£3.00	£6.00
PR-24 without record	*$0.80*	*$2.50*	*$5.00*	£0.40	£1.25	£2.50
Title Value:	*$2.45*	*$7.50*	*$15.00*	£1.40	£4.25	£8.50

SPIDERMAN CLASSICS

Marvel Comics Group; 1 Apr 1993-16 Jul 1994

	$Good	$Fine	$N.Mint	£Good	£Fine	£N.Mint
1 ND reprints Amazing Fantasy #15 and Strange Tales #115	*$0.25*	*$0.75*	*$1.25*	£0.15	£0.45	£0.75
2 ND reprints Amazing Spiderman #1	*$0.25*	*$0.75*	*$1.25*	£0.15	£0.45	£0.75
3 ND reprints Amazing Spiderman #2	*$0.25*	*$0.75*	*$1.25*	£0.15	£0.45	£0.75
4 ND reprints Amazing Spiderman #3, Ron Lim cover	*$0.25*	*$0.75*	*$1.25*	£0.15	£0.45	£0.75
5 ND reprints Amazing Spiderman #4	*$0.25*	*$0.75*	*$1.25*	£0.15	£0.45	£0.75
6 ND reprints Amazing Spiderman #5	*$0.25*	*$0.75*	*$1.25*	£0.15	£0.45	£0.75
7 ND reprints Amazing Spiderman #6	*$0.25*	*$0.75*	*$1.25*	£0.15	£0.45	£0.75
8 ND reprints Amazing Spiderman #7	*$0.25*	*$0.75*	*$1.25*	£0.15	£0.45	£0.75
9 ND reprints Amazing Spiderman #8	*$0.25*	*$0.75*	*$1.25*	£0.15	£0.45	£0.75
10 ND reprints Amazing Spiderman #9	*$0.25*	*$0.75*	*$1.25*	£0.15	£0.45	£0.75
11 ND reprints Amazing Spiderman #10	*$0.25*	*$0.75*	*$1.25*	£0.15	£0.45	£0.75
12 ND reprints Amazing Spiderman #11	*$0.25*	*$0.75*	*$1.25*	£0.15	£0.45	£0.75
13 ND reprints Amazing Spiderman #12	*$0.25*	*$0.75*	*$1.25*	£0.15	£0.45	£0.75
14 ND reprints Amazing Spiderman #13	*$0.25*	*$0.75*	*$1.25*	£0.15	£0.45	£0.75
15 ND reprints Amazing Spiderman #14	*$0.25*	*$0.75*	*$1.25*	£0.15	£0.45	£0.75
15 Collectors Edition, ND; pre-bagged with animation cel from Spiderman TV series; reprints Amazing Spiderman #14; metallic ink cover	*$0.60*	*$1.80*	*$3.00*	£0.40	£1.20	£2.00
16 ND reprints Amazing Spiderman #15	*$0.25*	*$0.75*	*$1.25*	£0.15	£0.45	£0.75
Title Value:	*$4.60*	*$13.80*	*$23.00*	£2.80	£8.40	£14.00

SPIDERMAN COLLECTORS' PREVIEW

Marvel Comics Group,OS; 1 Dec 1994

	$Good	$Fine	$N.Mint	£Good	£Fine	£N.Mint
1 ND previews the storylines leading up to Spiderman #400 plus news and features	*$0.30*	*$0.90*	*$1.50*	£0.20	£0.60	£1.00
Title Value:	*$0.30*	*$0.90*	*$1.50*	£0.20	£0.60	£1.00

SPIDERMAN COMICS DIGEST

Marvel Comics Group,Digest; 1 Jan 1987-10 Oct 1987

	$Good	$Fine	$N.Mint	£Good	£Fine	£N.Mint
1-10 ND scarce in the U.K. reprints	*$0.30*	*$0.90*	*$1.50*	£0.20	£0.60	£1.00
Title Value:	*$3.00*	*$9.00*	*$15.00*	£2.00	£6.00	£10.00

SPIDERMAN GIANT SIZE

Marvel Comics Group; 1 Jul 1974-6 Sep 1975

	$Good	$Fine	$N.Mint	£Good	£Fine	£N.Mint
1 ND 68pgs, Spiderman vs. Dracula; reprints Spiderman/Human Torch from Strange Tales Annual #2	*$4.15*	*$12.50*	*$25.00*	£2.50	£7.50	£15.00
2-3 ND 68pgs	*$2.05*	*$6.25*	*$12.50*	£1.25	£3.75	£7.50
4 ND 68pgs, 3rd full appearance of The Punisher	*$7.50*	*$22.50*	*$45.00*	£5.00	£15.00	£30.00
5-6 ND 68pgs	*$1.65*	*$5.00*	*$10.00*	£1.05	£3.25	£6.50
Title Value:	*$19.05*	*$57.50*	*$115.00*	£12.10	£36.50	£73.00

SPIDERMAN GIVEAWAY

Marvel Comics Group; 1980-1984

(all ND)

	£Good	£Fine	£N.Mint
1979 32pgs, All Detergent Promotion; reprints Amazing Spiderman #23 and origin re-told	£0.50	£1.50	£3.00
1979 16pgs, Columbus Despatch Spiderman and Hulk Giveaway	£0.30	£0.90	£1.50
1980 32pgs, Aim Toothpaste Promotion, Green Goblin appears	£0.30	£0.90	£1.50
1980 16pgs, Chicago Tribune Spiderman and Hulk Giveaway; origin re-told	£0.30	£0.90	£1.50
nn Dallas Times Herald Spiderman and Hulk Giveaway; Kingpin and Sandman appear	£0.30	£0.90	£1.50
1982 16pgs, Aim Toothpaste Promotion, Dr. Octopus appears	£0.30	£0.90	£1.50
1982 16pgs, American Cancer Society; Storm and Powerman appear	£0.30	£0.90	£1.50
1983 32pgs, Dallas Times Herald Giveaway, Kingpin appears	£0.30	£0.90	£1.50
1983 32pgs, Dallas Times Herald Giveaway, Dallas Cowboys /Ringmaster/Crime Circus appear	£0.30	£0.90	£1.50
1983 32pgs, Dallas Times Herald Giveaway; Firestar and Iceman appear	£0.30	£0.90	£1.50
1984 16pgs, National Education Association; Power Pack appear, highlights problem of Child Abuse	£0.25	£0.75	£1.25
1987 32pgs, National Committee for Prevention of Child Abuse; Hobgoblin appears	£0.30	£0.90	£1.50

SPIDERMAN HOLIDAY SPECIAL '95

Marvel Comics Group,OS; 1 Feb 1996

	$Good	$Fine	$N.Mint	£Good	£Fine	£N.Mint
1 ND four stories featuring Venom and Human Torch among others; cover by Adam Kubert	*$0.60*	*$1.80*	*$3.00*	£0.40	£1.20	£2.00
Title Value:	*$0.60*	*$1.80*	*$3.00*	£0.40	£1.20	£2.00

SPIDERMAN MAGAZINE

Marvel Comics Group,Magazine; 1 Mar 1994-15 May 1995

	$Good	$Fine	$N.Mint	£Good	£Fine	£N.Mint
1 puzzles and games magazine for a younger audience; bound-in sheet of 8 trading cards; cover by John Romita Jnr. Characters and stories are not considered part of the Marvel Universe continuity	*$0.40*	*$1.20*	*$2.00*	£0.25	£0.75	£1.25
2-7 ND	*$0.40*	*$1.20*	*$2.00*	£0.25	£0.75	£1.25
8 ND bound-in trading cards	*$0.40*	*$1.20*	*$2.00*	£0.25	£0.75	£1.25
9-13 ND	*$0.40*	*$1.20*	*$2.00*	£0.25	£0.75	£1.25
14-15 ND with bound-in trading cards	*$0.40*	*$1.20*	*$2.00*	£0.25	£0.75	£1.25
Title Value:	*$6.00*	*$18.00*	*$30.00*	£3.75	£11.25	£18.75

SPIDERMAN MAGAZINE (2ND SERIES)

Marvel Comics Group,Magazine; 1 Nov 1995

	$Good	$Fine	$N.Mint	£Good	£Fine	£N.Mint
1 ND She-Hulk appears; Pulp Fiction film poster parody cover	*$0.45*	*$1.35*	*$2.25*	£0.30	£0.90	£1.50
Title Value:	*$0.45*	*$1.35*	*$2.25*	£0.30	£0.90	£1.50

SPIDERMAN MEGAZINE

Marvel Comics Group; 1 Oct 1994-6 Mar 1995

	$Good	$Fine	$N.Mint	£Good	£Fine	£N.Mint
1 ND 96pgs, reprints Amazing Spiderman #15, 220-223 and Marvel Team Up #1	*$0.60*	*$1.80*	*$3.00*	£0.40	£1.20	£2.00
2 ND 96pgs, reprints featuring Black Cat, Green Goblin and Human Torch	*$0.60*	*$1.80*	*$3.00*	£0.40	£1.20	£2.00
3 ND 96pgs, reprints featuring Juggernaut, Human Torch, Morbius and Sandman	*$0.60*	*$1.80*	*$3.00*	£0.40	£1.20	£2.00
4 ND 96pgs, reprints featuring X-Men, Morbius, Human Torch and Sandman	*$0.60*	*$1.80*	*$3.00*	£0.40	£1.20	£2.00
5 ND 96pgs, reprints featuring Vision, Tarantula and Puppet Master	*$0.60*	*$1.80*	*$3.00*	£0.40	£1.20	£2.00
6 ND 96pgs, reprints featuring Thing, Human Torch and Tarantula	*$0.60*	*$1.80*	*$3.00*	£0.40	£1.20	£2.00
Title Value:	*$3.60*	*$10.80*	*$18.00*	£2.40	£7.20	£12.00

SPIDERMAN SAGA

Marvel Comics Group,MS; 1 Nov 1991-4 Feb 1992

	$Good	$Fine	$N.Mint	£Good	£Fine	£N.Mint
1 ND scarce in the U.K. history of Spiderman using panels from Amazing Fantasy #15 onwards, McFarlane cover	*$0.50*	*$1.50*	*$2.50*	£0.30	£0.90	£1.50
2 ND scarce in the U.K. covers Spiderman issues #101-175	*$0.50*	*$1.50*	*$2.50*	£0.30	£0.90	£1.50
3 ND scarce in the U.K. covers Spiderman issues #176-238	*$0.50*	*$1.50*	*$2.50*	£0.30	£0.90	£1.50
4 ND scarce in the U.K. covers Spiderman issues #239-300	*$0.50*	*$1.50*	*$2.50*	£0.30	£0.90	£1.50
Title Value:	*$2.00*	*$6.00*	*$10.00*	£1.20	£3.60	£6.00

Note: series delayed from original solicitation

SPIDERMAN SPECIAL EDITION - TRIAL OF VENOM

Marvel Comics Group/Unicef,OS; 1 Nov 1992

	$Good	$Fine	$N.Mint	£Good	£Fine	£N.Mint
1 ND scarce in the U.K. Peter David script, card stock glossy cover, bound-in poster; comes with certificate and black commemorative card plaque	*$1.50*	*$4.50*	*$7.50*	£1.00	£3.00	£5.00
Title Value:	*$1.50*	*$4.50*	*$7.50*	£1.00	£3.00	£5.00

Note: special promotional giveaway obtained by sending $5 to Unicef (the International Children's Fund). Estimated 10,000 print run and therefore scarce in the U.K., particularly as Unicef would only send copies to American postal addresses and not UK or European ones.

SPIDERMAN SUPER SIZE SPECIAL

Marvel Comics Group,OS; 1 Jul 1995

	$Good	$Fine	$N.Mint	£Good	£Fine	£N.Mint
1 ND Planet of the Symbiotes part 2, continued in Venom Super Size Special; Phil Gosier art	*$0.80*	*$2.40*	*$4.00*	£0.50	£1.50	£2.50
Title Value:	*$0.80*	*$2.40*	*$4.00*	£0.50	£1.50	£2.50

SPIDERMAN TEAM-UP

Marvel Comics Group; 1 Dec 1995-present

	$Good	$Fine	$N.Mint	£Good	£Fine	£N.Mint
1 ND 48pgs, Mark Waid script, Ken Lashley art; Cyclops, Phoenix, Beast, Psylocke and Archangel appear	*$0.60*	*$1.80*	*$3.00*	£0.40	£1.20	£2.00
2 ND Spiderman and Silver Surfer	*$0.60*	*$1.80*	*$3.00*	£0.40	£1.20	£2.00
3 ND 48pgs, Spiderman and Fantastic Four	*$0.60*	*$1.80*	*$3.00*	£0.40	£1.20	£2.00
4 ND Spiderman and The Avengers; George Perez cover and script	*$0.60*	*$1.80*	*$3.00*	£0.40	£1.20	£2.00
5 ND Spiderman and X-Man and Spiderman and Howard the Duck	*$0.60*	*$1.80*	*$3.00*	£0.40	£1.20	£2.00
6 ND 64pgs, Incredible Hulk and Dr. Strange appear; Bob Larkin painted cover	*$0.60*	*$1.80*	*$3.00*	£0.40	£1.20	£2.00
Title Value:	*$3.60*	*$10.80*	*$18.00*	£2.40	£7.20	£12.00

SPIDERMAN UNLIMITED

Marvel Comics Group; 1 May 1993-present

	$Good	$Fine	$N.Mint	£Good	£Fine	£N.Mint
1 ND 64pgs, Maximum Carnage part 1, continued in Web of Spiderman #101; Ron Lim cover and art begins	*$0.80*	*$2.40*	*$4.00*	£0.50	£1.50	£2.50
2 ND 64pgs, Maximum Carnage part 14 (conclusion), Ron Lim cover and art	*$0.80*	*$2.40*	*$4.00*	£0.50	£1.50	£2.50
3 ND 64pgs, Dr. Octopus origin explored in more detail, Ron Lim cover and art	*$0.80*	*$2.40*	*$4.00*	£0.50	£1.50	£2.50
4 ND 64pgs, Mysterio and Rhino appear	*$0.80*	*$2.40*	*$4.00*	£0.50	£1.50	£2.50

TRADE PAPERBACKS, GRAPHIC NOVELS AND OTHER COLLECTIONS ARE PRICED IN POUNDS STERLING ONLY. CONVERT AT 1.5 FOR DOLLARS.

	$Good	$Fine	$N.Mint	£Good	£Fine	£N.Mint
5 ND 64pgs, Human Torch appears						
	$0.80	*$2.40*	*$4.00*	£0.50	£1.50	£2.50
6 ND 64pgs, Thunderstrike appears						
	$0.80	*$2.40*	*$4.00*	£0.50	£1.50	£2.50
7-8 ND 64pgs	*$0.80*	*$2.40*	*$4.00*	£0.50	£1.50	£2.50
9 ND 64pgs, The Mark of Kaine part 5 (conclusion)						
	$0.80	*$2.40*	*$4.00*	£0.50	£1.50	£2.50
10 ND 64pgs, Exiled part 4 (conclusion)						
	$0.80	*$2.40*	*$4.00*	£0.50	£1.50	£2.50
11 ND 64pgs, The Black Cat appears (and meets Ben Reilly the new Spiderman for 1st time)						
	$0.80	*$2.40*	*$4.00*	£0.50	£1.50	£2.50
12 ND 64pgs, Scorpion, Beetle, Puma, Rhino, Silver Sable and Black Cat appear						
	$0.80	*$2.40*	*$4.00*	£0.50	£1.50	£2.50
13 ND 64pgs, Luke Cage and Iron Fist appear						
	$0.80	*$2.40*	*$4.00*	£0.50	£1.50	£2.50
14 ND 64pgs	*$0.80*	*$2.40*	*$4.00*	£0.50	£1.50	£2.50
15 ND 64pgs, Puma appears						
	$0.60	*$1.80*	*$3.00*	£0.40	£1.20	£2.00
Title Value:	*$11.80*	*$35.40*	*$59.00*	£7.40	£22.20	£37.00

SPIDERMAN UNMASKED

Marvel Comics Group,OS; nn Feb 1997

	$Good	$Fine	$N.Mint	£Good	£Fine	£N.Mint
nn ND 64pgs, information and statistics all about Spiderman						
	$1.20	*$3.60*	*$6.00*	£0.80	£2.40	£4.00
Title Value:	*$1.20*	*$3.60*	*$6.00*	£0.80	£2.40	£4.00

SPIDERMAN VS. DRACULA

Marvel Comics Group,OS; 1 Jan 1994

	$Good	$Fine	$N.Mint	£Good	£Fine	£N.Mint
1 ND 48pgs, reprints Spiderman Giant Size #1						
	$0.30	*$0.90*	*$1.50*	£0.20	£0.60	£1.00
Title Value:	*$0.30*	*$0.90*	*$1.50*	£0.20	£0.60	£1.00

SPIDERMAN VS. WOLVERINE

Marvel Comics Group,OS; 1 Feb 1987

	$Good	$Fine	$N.Mint	£Good	£Fine	£N.Mint
1 ND 64pgs, Japanese Connection story in which Spiderman kills, Bright/Williamson art						
	$3.00	*$9.00*	*$15.00*	£2.00	£6.00	£10.00
Title Value:	*$3.00*	*$9.00*	*$15.00*	£2.00	£6.00	£10.00
Bookshelf Special (Aug 1990)						
reprints the above with new Mark Bright cover				£0.75	£2.25	£3.75
(2nd printing - May 1991)				£0.70	£2.10	£3.50

SPIDERMAN, ADVENTURES IN READING

Marvel Comics Group,OS; 1 Dec 1990

	$Good	$Fine	$N.Mint	£Good	£Fine	£N.Mint
1 ND promotional comic exploring illiteracy in America						
	$0.30	*$0.90*	*$1.50*	£0.20	£0.60	£1.00
Title Value:	*$0.30*	*$0.90*	*$1.50*	£0.20	£0.60	£1.00

SPIDERMAN, DEADLY FOES OF

Marvel Comics Group,MS; 1 May 1991-4 Aug 1991

	$Good	$Fine	$N.Mint	£Good	£Fine	£N.Mint
1 ND scarce in the U.K. Beetle, Rhino, Hydroman, Boomerang, Speed Demon featured						
	$0.40	*$1.20*	*$2.00*	£0.25	£0.75	£1.25
2-3 ND scarce in the U.K.						
	$0.40	*$1.20*	*$2.00*	£0.25	£0.75	£1.25
4 ND scarce in the U.K. Kingpin appears						
	$0.40	*$1.20*	*$2.00*	£0.25	£0.75	£1.25
Title Value:	*$1.60*	*$4.80*	*$8.00*	£1.00	£3.00	£5.00
Deadly Foes of Spiderman (Apr 1994)						
Trade paperback reprints issues #1-4 with new cover				£1.70	£5.10	£8.50

SPIDERMAN, LETHAL FOES OF

Marvel Comics Group,MS; 1 Sep 1993-4 Dec 1993

	$Good	$Fine	$N.Mint	£Good	£Fine	£N.Mint
1 ND origin of Dr. Octopus explored						
	$0.40	*$1.20*	*$2.00*	£0.25	£0.75	£1.25
2-4 ND Dr. Octopus appears						
	$0.40	*$1.20*	*$2.00*	£0.25	£0.75	£1.25
Title Value:	*$1.60*	*$4.80*	*$8.00*	£1.00	£3.00	£5.00

SPIDERMAN, THE ADVENTURES OF

Marvel Comics Group; 1 Apr 1996-present

	$Good	$Fine	$N.Mint	£Good	£Fine	£N.Mint
1 ND based on animated television show; Nel Yomtov script, Alex Saviuk art						
	$0.20	*$0.60*	*$1.00*	£0.15	£0.45	£0.75
2 ND	*$0.20*	*$0.60*	*$1.00*	£0.15	£0.45	£0.75
3 ND continued from The Adventures of X-Men #3						
	$0.20	*$0.60*	*$1.00*	£0.15	£0.45	£0.75
4 ND	*$0.20*	*$0.60*	*$1.00*	£0.15	£0.45	£0.75
5 ND The Vulture appears						
	$0.20	*$0.60*	*$1.00*	£0.15	£0.45	£0.75
6 ND	*$0.20*	*$0.60*	*$1.00*	£0.15	£0.45	£0.75
7-8 ND Kingpin appears						
	$0.20	*$0.60*	*$1.00*	£0.15	£0.45	£0.75
9 ND Dr. Strange appears						
	$0.20	*$0.60*	*$1.00*	£0.15	£0.45	£0.75
10 ND The Beetle appears						
	$0.20	*$0.60*	*$1.00*	£0.15	£0.45	£0.75
11-12 ND Dr. Octopus and Venom appear						
	$0.20	*$0.60*	*$1.00*	£0.15	£0.45	£0.75
Title Value:	*$2.40*	*$7.20*	*$12.00*	£1.80	£5.40	£9.00

SPIDERMAN, THE BEST OF

Marvel Comics Group/Ballantine,OS; nn 1986

	$Good	$Fine	$N.Mint	£Good	£Fine	£N.Mint
nn ND Trade paperback, oversize; reprints newspaper strip						
	$1.80	*$5.25*	*$9.00*	£1.20	£3.60	£6.00
Title Value:	*$1.80*	*$5.25*	*$9.00*	£1.20	£3.60	£6.00

SPIDERMAN, THE OFFICIAL MARVEL INDEX TO

Marvel Comics Group,MS; 1 Apr 1985-9 Dec 1985

	$Good	$Fine	$N.Mint	£Good	£Fine	£N.Mint
1 ND information and colour cover repros Amazing Fantasy #15, Amazing Spiderman #1-#29, King Size Annual #1,#2; Byrne cover						
	$0.50	*$1.50*	*$2.50*	£0.30	£0.90	£1.50
2 ND information and colour cover repros Amazing Spiderman #30-#58, King Size Annual #3,#4; Romita Snr. cover						
	$0.50	*$1.50*	*$2.50*	£0.30	£0.90	£1.50
3 ND information and colour cover repros Amazing Spiderman #59-#84, King Size Annual #5, Spectacular Spiderman (magazine) #1,#2; Paul Neary cover						
	$0.50	*$1.50*	*$2.50*	£0.30	£0.90	£1.50
4 ND information and colour cover repros Amazing Spiderman #85-#112, King Size Annual #7,#8						
	$0.50	*$1.50*	*$2.50*	£0.30	£0.90	£1.50
5 ND information and colour cover repros Amazing Spiderman #114-#137, King Size Annual #9, Giant Size Super-Heroes #1						
	$0.50	*$1.50*	*$2.50*	£0.30	£0.90	£1.50
6 ND information and colour cover repros Amazing Spiderman #138-#155, Giant Size Annual #1-#6						
	$0.50	*$1.50*	*$2.50*	£0.30	£0.90	£1.50
7 ND information and colour cover repros Amazing Spiderman #156-#174, Annuals #10,#11						
	$0.50	*$1.50*	*$2.50*	£0.30	£0.90	£1.50
8 ND information and colour cover repros Amazing Spiderman #175-#195, Annuals #12						
	$0.50	*$1.50*	*$2.50*	£0.30	£0.90	£1.50
9 ND information and colour cover repros Amazing Spiderman #196-#215, Annuals #13,#14						
	$0.50	*$1.50*	*$2.50*	£0.30	£0.90	£1.50
Title Value:	*$4.50*	*$13.50*	*$22.50*	£2.70	£8.10	£13.50

Note: Volume 1 in Official Marvel Index Series of 5.

SPIDERMAN, UNTOLD TALES OF

Marvel Comics Group; 1 Sep 1995-present

	$Good	$Fine	$N.Mint	£Good	£Fine	£N.Mint
1 ND Kurt Busiek script, Pat Oliffe and Al Vey art begins; Spiderman's adventures in the early days; cover priced at 99 cents						
	$0.20	*$0.60*	*$1.00*	£0.15	£0.45	£0.75
2 ND	*$0.20*	*$0.60*	*$1.00*	£0.15	£0.45	£0.75
3 ND Sandman appears						
	$0.20	*$0.60*	*$1.00*	£0.15	£0.45	£0.75
4 ND	*$0.20*	*$0.60*	*$1.00*	£0.15	£0.45	£0.75
5 ND The Vulture appears						
	$0.20	*$0.60*	*$1.00*	£0.15	£0.45	£0.75
6 ND Human Torch appears						
	$0.20	*$0.60*	*$1.00*	£0.15	£0.45	£0.75
7 ND	*$0.20*	*$0.60*	*$1.00*	£0.15	£0.45	£0.75
8 ND The Enforcers appear						
	$0.20	*$0.60*	*$1.00*	£0.15	£0.45	£0.75
9 ND The Lizard appears						
	$0.20	*$0.60*	*$1.00*	£0.15	£0.45	£0.75
10 ND	*$0.20*	*$0.60*	*$1.00*	£0.15	£0.45	£0.75
11 ND Electro and The Eel appear						
	$0.20	*$0.60*	*$1.00*	£0.15	£0.45	£0.75
12-17 ND	*$0.20*	*$0.60*	*$1.00*	£0.15	£0.45	£0.75
18 ND Green Goblin appears						
	$0.20	*$0.60*	*$1.00*	£0.15	£0.45	£0.75
19 ND Dr. Octopus appears						
	$0.20	*$0.60*	*$1.00*	£0.15	£0.45	£0.75
Title Value:	*$3.80*	*$11.40*	*$19.00*	£2.85	£8.55	£14.25
Untold Tales of Spiderman (Mar 1997)						
Trade paperback ND 176pgs, collects issues #1-8				£2.20	£6.60	£11.00

SPIDERMAN, UNTOLD TALES OF '96

Marvel Comics Group,OS; nn Dec 1996

	$Good	$Fine	$N.Mint	£Good	£Fine	£N.Mint
nn ND 48pgs, Kurt Busiek script, Mike Allred and Joe Sinnott art						
	$0.40	*$1.20*	*$2.00*	£0.25	£0.75	£1.25
Title Value:	*$0.40*	*$1.20*	*$2.00*	£0.25	£0.75	£1.25

SPIDERMAN/BATMAN

Marvel Comics Group/DC Comics,OS; 1 Nov 1995

	$Good	$Fine	$N.Mint	£Good	£Fine	£N.Mint
1 ND 48pgs, J.M. DeMatteis script, Mark Bagley and Mark Farmer art; Carnage and The Joker appear; card-stock embossed cover						
	$1.20	*$3.60*	*$6.00*	£0.80	£2.40	£4.00
Title Value:	*$1.20*	*$3.60*	*$6.00*	£0.80	£2.40	£4.00

SPIDERMAN/DR. STRANGE: THE WAY TO DUSTY DEATH

Marvel Comics Group,OS; 1 Feb 1993

	$Good	$Fine	$N.Mint	£Good	£Fine	£N.Mint
1 ND 64pgs	*$1.00*	*$3.00*	*$5.00*	£0.70	£2.10	£3.50
Title Value:	*$1.00*	*$3.00*	*$5.00*	£0.70	£2.10	£3.50

SPIDERMAN/GEN 13

Marvel Comics Group,OS; nn Jan 1997

	$Good	$Fine	$N.Mint	£Good	£Fine	£N.Mint
nn ND 48pgs, Peter David script, Stuart Immomen and Cam Smith art						
	$1.00	*$3.00*	*$5.00*	£0.70	£2.10	£3.50
Title Value:	*$1.00*	*$3.00*	*$5.00*	£0.70	£2.10	£3.50

SPIDERMAN/PUNISHER

Marvel Comics Group,MS; 1,2 Feb 1996

	$Good	$Fine	$N.Mint	£Good	£Fine	£N.Mint
1-2 ND Tom Lyle script, Shawn McManus art; bi-weekly						
	$0.60	*$1.80*	*$3.00*	£0.40	£1.20	£2.00
Title Value:	*$1.20*	*$3.60*	*$6.00*	£0.80	£2.40	£4.00

SPIDERMAN/PUNISHER/SABRETOOTH: DESIGNER GENES

Marvel Comics Group,OS; 1 Jun 1993

	$Good	$Fine	$N.Mint	£Good	£Fine	£N.Mint
1 ND 64pgs, bookshelf format, McDaniel and Williams art						
	$1.50	*$4.50*	*$7.50*	£1.00	£3.00	£5.00
Title Value:	*$1.50*	*$4.50*	*$7.50*	£1.00	£3.00	£5.00

SPIDERMAN/SPIDERMAN 2099

Marvel Comics Group,OS; nn Jan 1996

	$Good	$Fine	$N.Mint	£Good	£Fine	£N.Mint
nn ND 48pgs, Peter David script, Rick Leonardi and Al Williamson art						
	$1.20	*$3.60*	*$6.00*	£0.80	£2.40	£4.00
Title Value:	*$1.20*	*$3.60*	*$6.00*	£0.80	£2.40	£4.00

SPIDERMAN/ULTRAFORCE

Marvel Comics Group,OS; 1 Mar 1996

	$Good	$Fine	$N.Mint	£Good	£Fine	£N.Mint
1 Version A, ND 48pgs, features half of Ultraforce with Green Goblin						
	$0.80	*$2.40*	*$4.00*	£0.50	£1.50	£2.50
1 Version B, ND 48pgs, features other half of Ultraforce with Spiderman						
	$0.80	*$2.40*	*$4.00*	£0.50	£1.50	£2.50
Title Value:	*$1.60*	*$4.80*	*$8.00*	£1.00	£3.00	£5.00

SPIDERMAN/X-FACTOR: SHADOWGAMES

Marvel Comics Group,MS; 1 May 1994-3 Jul 1994

	$Good	$Fine	$N.Mint	£Good	£Fine	£N.Mint
1-3 ND Pat Broderick art	$0.40	$1.20	$2.00	£0.25	£0.75	£1.25
Title Value:	$1.20	$3.60	$6.00	£0.75	£2.25	£3.75

SPIDERMAN: CHAOS IN CALGARY

Marvel Comics Group,OS; 4 1990; 4 Feb 1993

	$Good	$Fine	$N.Mint	£Good	£Fine	£N.Mint
4 ND distributed in Canada only safety-conscious story for motorcyclists	$2.50	$7.50	$12.50	£1.50	£4.50	£7.50
4 reprint of Canadian giveaway ND	$0.40	$1.20	$2.00	£0.25	£0.75	£1.25
Title Value:	$2.90	$8.70	$14.50	£1.75	£5.25	£8.75

SPIDERMAN: DOUBLE TROUBLE

Marvel Comics Group,OS; 2 1990; 2 Feb 1993

	$Good	$Fine	$N.Mint	£Good	£Fine	£N.Mint
2 ND only distributed in Canada (not U.S. or U.K.), anti-drugs	$2.50	$7.50	$12.50	£1.50	£4.50	£7.50
2 reprint of Canadian giveaway ND	$0.40	$1.20	$2.00	£0.25	£0.75	£1.25
Title Value:	$2.90	$8.70	$14.50	£1.75	£5.25	£8.75

SPIDERMAN: FRIENDS & ENEMIES

Marvel Comics Group,MS; 1 Jan 1995-4 Apr 1995

	$Good	$Fine	$N.Mint	£Good	£Fine	£N.Mint
1-4 ND Spiderman, Darkhawk, Nova and Speedball appear; Ron Lim art	$0.40	$1.20	$2.00	£0.25	£0.75	£1.25
Title Value:	$1.60	$4.80	$8.00	£1.00	£3.00	£5.00

SPIDERMAN: FUNERAL FOR AN OCTOPUS

Marvel Comics Group,MS; 1 Mar 1995-3 May 1995

	$Good	$Fine	$N.Mint	£Good	£Fine	£N.Mint
1 ND spin-off from Spectacular Spiderman #221; Scarlet Spider and Sinister Six appear	$0.40	$1.20	$2.00	£0.25	£0.75	£1.25
2 ND	$0.40	$1.20	$2.00	£0.25	£0.75	£1.25
3 ND Mark of Kaine tie-in (see Web of Spiderman Unlimited #9)	$0.40	$1.20	$2.00	£0.25	£0.75	£1.25
Title Value:	$1.20	$3.60	$6.00	£0.75	£2.25	£3.75

SPIDERMAN: HIT AND RUN

Marvel Comics Group,OS; 3 1990; 3 Feb 1993

	$Good	$Fine	$N.Mint	£Good	£Fine	£N.Mint
3 ND only distributed in Canada (not in U.S. or U.K.), anti-hit and run drivers, Ghost Rider appears	$2.50	$7.50	$12.50	£1.50	£4.50	£7.50
3 reprint of Canadian giveaway, ND, Ghost Rider appears	$0.40	$1.20	$2.00	£0.25	£0.75	£1.25
Title Value:	$2.90	$8.70	$14.50	£1.75	£5.25	£8.75

SPIDERMAN: HOBGOBLIN LIVES!

Marvel Comics Group,MS; 1 Jan 1997-3 Mar 1997

	$Good	$Fine	$N.Mint	£Good	£Fine	£N.Mint
1-3 ND Roger Stern script, Ron Frenz and George Perez art	$0.50	$1.50	$2.50	£0.30	£0.90	£1.50
Title Value:	$1.50	$4.50	$7.50	£0.90	£2.70	£4.50

SPIDERMAN: LEGACY OF EVIL

Marvel Comics Group,OS; 1 Jun 1996

	$Good	$Fine	$N.Mint	£Good	£Fine	£N.Mint
1 ND 48pgs, Green Goblin and Molten Man appear; Kurt Busiek script, Mark Texeira painted art and cover	$0.80	$2.40	$4.00	£0.50	£1.50	£2.50
Title Value:	$0.80	$2.40	$4.00	£0.50	£1.50	£2.50

SPIDERMAN: MAXIMUM CLONAGE ALPHA

Marvel Comics Group,OS; 1 Aug 1995

	$Good	$Fine	$N.Mint	£Good	£Fine	£N.Mint
1 ND 48pgs, Maximum Clonage part 1, continued in Web of Spiderman #127; clear chromium cover	$1.20	$3.60	$6.00	£0.80	£2.40	£4.00
Title Value:	$1.20	$3.60	$6.00	£0.80	£2.40	£4.00

SPIDERMAN: MAXIMUM CLONAGE OMEGA

Marvel Comics Group,OS; 1 Sep 1995

	$Good	$Fine	$N.Mint	£Good	£Fine	£N.Mint
1 ND 48pgs, Maximum Clonage part 6 (conclusion) with Scarlet Spider and Spiderman vs. The Jackal and his Clone Assassin; chromium cover	$1.20	$3.60	$6.00	£0.80	£2.40	£4.00
Title Value:	$1.20	$3.60	$6.00	£0.80	£2.40	£4.00

SPIDERMAN: MUTANT AGENDA

Marvel Comics Group,MS; 0 Feb 1994-3 May 1994

	$Good	$Fine	$N.Mint	£Good	£Fine	£N.Mint
0-3 ND 48pgs, sections allocated to paste in Spiderman newspaper strip (**Note:** item would be valued more if the strips are pasted in)	$0.30	$0.90	$1.50	£0.20	£0.60	£1.00
Title Value:	$1.20	$3.60	$6.00	£0.80	£2.40	£4.00

SPIDERMAN: REDEMPTION

Marvel Comics Group,MS; 1 Sep 1996-4 Dec 1996

	$Good	$Fine	$N.Mint	£Good	£Fine	£N.Mint
1-4 ND Mike Zeck art	$0.30	$0.90	$1.50	£0.20	£0.60	£1.00
Title Value:	$1.20	$3.60	$6.00	£0.80	£2.40	£4.00

SPIDERMAN: SKATING ON THIN ICE

Marvel Comics Group,OS; 1 1990; 1 Feb 1993

	$Good	$Fine	$N.Mint	£Good	£Fine	£N.Mint
1 ND only distributed in Canada, (not in U.S. or in U.K.), Todd McFarlane cover, anti-drug issue	$2.50	$7.50	$12.50	£1.50	£4.50	£7.50
1 reprint of Canadian giveaway ND	$0.40	$1.20	$2.00	£0.25	£0.75	£1.25
Title Value:	$2.90	$8.70	$14.50	£1.75	£5.25	£8.75

SPIDERMAN: SOUL OF THE HUNTER

Marvel Comics Group,OS; 1 Oct 1992

	$Good	$Fine	$N.Mint	£Good	£Fine	£N.Mint
1 ND 48pgs, Spiderman vs. the ghost of Kraven, Mike Zeck art	$1.00	$3.00	$5.00	£0.70	£2.10	£3.50
Title Value:	$1.00	$3.00	$5.00	£0.70	£2.10	£3.50

SPIDERMAN: THE ARACHNIS PROJECT

Marvel Comics Group,MS; 1 Aug 1994-6 Jan 1995

	$Good	$Fine	$N.Mint	£Good	£Fine	£N.Mint
1 ND series tied in with Smithsonian Institute exhibition on Spiderman	$0.30	$0.90	$1.50	£0.20	£0.60	£1.00
2-5 ND	$0.30	$0.90	$1.50	£0.20	£0.60	£1.00
6 ND Venom appears	$0.30	$0.90	$1.50	£0.20	£0.60	£1.00
Title Value:	$1.80	$5.40	$9.00	£1.20	£3.60	£6.00

SPIDERMAN: THE CLONE JOURNALS

Marvel Comics Group,OS; 1 Mar 1995

	$Good	$Fine	$N.Mint	£Good	£Fine	£N.Mint
1 ND edited reprints deatailing the story of the Spiderman clones plus new material	$0.40	$1.20	$2.00	£0.25	£0.75	£1.25
Title Value:	$0.40	$1.20	$2.00	£0.25	£0.75	£1.25

SPIDERMAN: THE FINAL ADVENTURE

Marvel Comics Group,MS; 1 Dec 1995-4 Mar 1996

	$Good	$Fine	$N.Mint	£Good	£Fine	£N.Mint
1-3 ND Fabian Nicieza script, Darick Robertson and Chris Ivy art; foil stamped cover	$0.60	$1.80	$3.00	£0.40	£1.20	£2.00
4 ND Fabian Nicieza script, Darick Robertson and Jeff Albrecht art; foil stamped cover	$0.60	$1.80	$3.00	£0.40	£1.20	£2.00
Title Value:	$2.40	$7.20	$12.00	£1.60	£4.80	£8.00

SPIDERMAN: THE JACKAL FILES

Marvel Comics Group,OS; 1 Aug 1995

	$Good	$Fine	$N.Mint	£Good	£Fine	£N.Mint
1 ND The Jackal appears, Maximum Clonage tie-in	$0.40	$1.20	$2.00	£0.25	£0.75	£1.25
Title Value:	$0.40	$1.20	$2.00	£0.25	£0.75	£1.25

SPIDERMAN: THE LOST YEARS

Marvel Comics Group,MS; 0 Jan 1996; 1 Aug 1995-3 Oct 1995

	$Good	$Fine	$N.Mint	£Good	£Fine	£N.Mint
0 ND 64pgs, reprints the 4-part "Birth of Spiderman" and 3-part "Parker Legacy"	$0.80	$2.40	$4.00	£0.50	£1.50	£2.50
1-2 ND J.M. DeMatteis script, John Romita Jnr. art	$0.60	$1.80	$3.00	£0.40	£1.20	£2.00
3 ND Ben (Scarlet Spider) Reilly vs. Kaine; J.M. DeMatteis script, John Romita Jnr. art	$0.60	$1.80	$3.00	£0.40	£1.20	£2.00
Title Value:	$2.60	$7.80	$13.00	£1.70	£5.10	£8.50

SPIDERMAN: THE PARKER YEARS

Marvel Comics Group,OS; 1 Nov 1995

	$Good	$Fine	$N.Mint	£Good	£Fine	£N.Mint
1 ND Evan Skolnick script, Joe St. Pierre art, wraparound cover by John Romita Jnr. with no ads; Venom and Carnage appear	$0.50	$1.50	$2.50	£0.30	£0.90	£1.50
Title Value:	$0.50	$1.50	$2.50	£0.30	£0.90	£1.50

SPIDERMAN: THE POWER OF TERROR

Marvel Comics Group,MS; 1 Jan 1995-4 Apr 1995

	$Good	$Fine	$N.Mint	£Good	£Fine	£N.Mint
1-3 ND Silvermane and Deathlok appear	$0.40	$1.20	$2.00	£0.25	£0.75	£1.25
4 ND Silvermane, Deathlok, Daredevil and Punisher appear	$0.40	$1.20	$2.00	£0.25	£0.75	£1.25
Title Value:	$1.60	$4.80	$8.00	£1.00	£3.00	£5.00

SPIDERMAN: WEB OF DOOM

Marvel Comics Group,MS; 1 Aug 1994-3 Oct 1994

	$Good	$Fine	$N.Mint	£Good	£Fine	£N.Mint
1-3 ND	$0.30	$0.90	$1.50	£0.20	£0.60	£1.00
Title Value:	$0.90	$2.70	$4.50	£0.60	£1.80	£3.00

SPIDERWOMAN

Marvel Comics Group; 1 Apr 1978-50 Jun 1983

(see Marvel Spotlight #32)

	$Good	$Fine	$N.Mint	£Good	£Fine	£N.Mint
1 ND new origin	$1.20	$3.60	$6.00	£0.50	£1.50	£2.50
2 ND	$0.50	$1.50	$2.50	£0.30	£0.90	£1.50
3-4 ND	$0.40	$1.20	$2.00	£0.25	£0.75	£1.25
5	$0.40	$1.20	$2.00	£0.20	£0.60	£1.00
6 Werewolf By Night appears	$0.40	$1.20	$2.00	£0.20	£0.60	£1.00
7-18	$0.40	$1.20	$2.00	£0.20	£0.60	£1.00
19 Werewolf By Night appears	$0.40	$1.20	$2.00	£0.20	£0.60	£1.00
20 Spiderman appears	$0.40	$1.20	$2.00	£0.20	£0.60	£1.00
21-25	$0.40	$1.20	$2.00	£0.20	£0.60	£1.00
26 Spiderman cameo	$0.40	$1.20	$2.00	£0.20	£0.60	£1.00
27	$0.40	$1.20	$2.00	£0.20	£0.60	£1.00
28-29 Spiderman appears	$0.40	$1.20	$2.00	£0.20	£0.60	£1.00
30-31	$0.40	$1.20	$2.00	£0.20	£0.60	£1.00
32 Werewolf By Night appears, photo montage cover	$0.40	$1.20	$2.00	£0.20	£0.60	£1.00
33-34	$0.40	$1.20	$2.00	£0.20	£0.60	£1.00
35-36 ND	$0.40	$1.20	$2.00	£0.25	£0.75	£1.25
37 1st appearance Syrin, X-Men cameo appearance, origin retold	$0.80	$2.40	$4.00	£0.40	£1.20	£2.00
38 scarce in the U.K. X-Men appear	$0.80	$2.40	$4.00	£0.50	£1.50	£2.50
39 ND Storm, Angel, Colossus appear; leads into X-Men #148	$0.60	$1.80	$3.00	£0.30	£0.90	£1.50
40	$0.40	$1.20	$2.00	£0.20	£0.60	£1.00
41-44 scarce in the U.K.	$0.40	$1.20	$2.00	£0.25	£0.75	£1.25
45 scarce in the U.K. Impossible Man appears	$0.40	$1.20	$2.00	£0.25	£0.75	£1.25
46-48 scarce in the U.K.	$0.40	$1.20	$2.00	£0.25	£0.75	£1.25
49 scarce in the U.K. Tigra and Werewolf By Night appear	$0.40	$1.20	$2.00	£0.25	£0.75	£1.25
50 scarce in the U.K. DS	$0.70	$2.10	$3.50	£0.40	£1.20	£2.00
Title Value:	$22.20	$66.60	$111.00	£11.85	£35.55	£59.25

ARTISTS

Miller cover on 32. Sienkiewicz covers on 16, 27. Von Eeden art in 23, 24.

SPIDERWOMAN (2ND SERIES)

Marvel Comics Group,MS; 1 Nov 1993-4 Feb 1994

	$Good	$Fine	$N.Mint	£Good	£Fine	£N.Mint
1	$0.40	$1.20	$2.00	£0.25	£0.75	£1.25
2 origin re-explored in more detail	$0.40	$1.20	$2.00	£0.25	£0.75	£1.25
3	$0.40	$1.20	$2.00	£0.25	£0.75	£1.25
4 U.S.Agent guest-stars						

	$Good	$Fine	$N.Mint	£Good	£Fine	£N.Mint
	$0.40	$1.20	$2.00	£0.25	£0.75	£1.25
Title Value:	$1.60	$4.80	$8.00	£1.00	£3.00	£5.00

SPIDEY SUPER STORIES

Marvel Comics Group,TV; 1 Oct 1974-57 Mar 1982

	$Good	$Fine	$N.Mint	£Good	£Fine	£N.Mint
1 ND origin retold	$0.80	$2.50	$5.00	£0.40	£1.25	£2.50
2 ND	$0.50	$1.50	$3.00	£0.30	£1.00	£2.00
3-4 ND	$0.40	$1.25	$2.50	£0.25	£0.75	£1.50
5 ND Iceman appears	$0.40	$1.25	$2.50	£0.25	£0.75	£1.50
6-10 ND	$0.40	$1.25	$2.50	£0.25	£0.75	£1.50
11-14 ND	$0.30	$1.00	$2.00	£0.20	£0.60	£1.25
15 ND Storm appears	$0.30	$1.00	$2.00	£0.20	£0.60	£1.25
16-22 ND	$0.30	$1.00	$2.00	£0.20	£0.60	£1.25
23 ND Green Goblin appears	$0.30	$1.00	$2.00	£0.20	£0.60	£1.25
24 ND Thundra appears	$0.30	$1.00	$2.00	£0.20	£0.60	£1.25
25 ND Dr. Doom appears	$0.30	$1.00	$2.00	£0.20	£0.60	£1.25
26 ND	$0.30	$1.00	$2.00	£0.20	£0.60	£1.25
27 ND Thor and Loki appear	$0.30	$1.00	$2.00	£0.20	£0.60	£1.25
28 ND	$0.30	$1.00	$2.00	£0.20	£0.60	£1.25
29 ND Kingpin appears	$0.30	$1.00	$2.00	£0.20	£0.60	£1.25
30 ND Kang appears	$0.30	$1.00	$2.00	£0.20	£0.60	£1.25
31-33 ND	$0.30	$1.00	$2.00	£0.20	£0.60	£1.25
34 ND Sub-Mariner appears	$0.30	$1.00	$2.00	£0.20	£0.60	£1.25
35-38 ND	$0.30	$1.00	$2.00	£0.20	£0.60	£1.25
39 ND Thanos appears in back-up story (outside Marvel continuity)	$0.30	$1.00	$2.00	£0.20	£0.60	£1.25
40-50 ND	$0.30	$1.00	$2.00	£0.20	£0.60	£1.25
51-57 ND	$0.40	$1.20	$2.00	£0.20	£0.60	£1.00
Title Value:	$19.30	$62.40	$122.00	£12.10	£36.45	£73.50

Note: contains simplified Spiderman stories for younger children; published in association with Children's Television Workshop

SPIDEY'S TOTALLY TINY ADVENTURE

Marvel Comics Group; 1990

Cross-over storyline that ran throughout the following titles:
Amazing Spiderman Annual #24, **Spectacular Spiderman Annual #10**, **Web of Spiderman Annual #6**.

SPINE-TINGLING TALES, DR. SPEKTOR PRESENTS

Gold Key; 1 May 1975-4 Jan 1976

	$Good	$Fine	$N.Mint	£Good	£Fine	£N.Mint
1 distributed in the U.K. though scarce painted covers begin	$0.40	$1.25	$2.50	£0.25	£0.75	£1.50
2-3 distributed in the U.K.	$0.30	$1.00	$2.00	£0.20	£0.60	£1.25
4 distributed in the U.K. features Baron Tibor - Vampire	$0.30	$1.00	$2.00	£0.20	£0.60	£1.25
Title Value:	$1.30	$4.25	$8.50	£0.85	£2.55	£5.25

SPIRAL PATH

Eclipse,MS; 1,2 Jul 1986

	$Good	$Fine	$N.Mint	£Good	£Fine	£N.Mint
1-2 ND reprints from Warrior in colour; Steve Parkhouse script/John Ridgway art	$0.40	$1.20	$2.00	£0.25	£0.75	£1.25
Title Value:	$0.80	$2.40	$4.00	£0.50	£1.50	£2.50

SPIRAL ZONE

DC Comics,Magazine MS,Toy; 1 Oct 1987-4 Jan 1988

	$Good	$Fine	$N.Mint	£Good	£Fine	£N.Mint
1-4	$0.15	$0.45	$0.75	£0.10	£0.30	£0.50

	$Good	$Fine	$N.Mint	£Good	£Fine	£N.Mint
Title Value:	$0.60	$1.80	$3.00	£0.40	£1.20	£2.00

SPIRIT

Kitchen Sink; 1 Oct 1983-87 Mar 1992

(see Will Eisner's 3-D Classics)

	$Good	$Fine	$N.Mint	£Good	£Fine	£N.Mint
1 ND	$0.60	$1.80	$3.00	£0.40	£1.20	£2.00
2-9 ND	$0.50	$1.50	$2.50	£0.30	£0.90	£1.50
10 ND last colour issue	$0.50	$1.50	$2.50	£0.30	£0.90	£1.50
11-40 ND	$0.40	$1.20	$2.00	£0.25	£0.75	£1.25
41 ND Frederick Wertham parody	$0.40	$1.20	$2.00	£0.25	£0.75	£1.25
42-76 ND	$0.40	$1.20	$2.00	£0.25	£0.75	£1.25
77-87 ND new Eisner covers	$0.40	$1.20	$2.00	£0.25	£0.75	£1.25
Title Value:	$35.90	$107.70	$179.50	£22.35	£67.05	£111.75

SPIRIT DAILYS

Ken Pierce; 1-4 1980

	$Good	$Fine	$N.Mint	£Good	£Fine	£N.Mint
1-4 ND	$1.00	$3.00	$5.00	£0.70	£2.10	£3.50
Title Value:	$4.00	$12.00	$20.00	£2.80	£8.40	£14.00

Note: reprints all 738 Daily strips.

SPIRIT MAGAZINE, THE

Warren; 1 Apr 1974-16 Oct 1976; Kitchen Sink; 17 Winter 1977-41 1983

	$Good	$Fine	$N.Mint	£Good	£Fine	£N.Mint
1	$1.50	$4.50	$9.00	£1.00	£3.00	£6.00
2	$1.00	$3.00	$6.00	£0.65	£2.00	£4.00
3-5	$0.80	$2.50	$5.00	£0.55	£1.75	£3.50
6-9	$0.65	$2.00	$4.00	£0.50	£1.50	£3.00
10 origin	$0.65	$2.00	$4.00	£0.50	£1.50	£3.00
11-16	$0.55	$1.75	$3.50	£0.40	£1.25	£2.50
17	$0.50	$1.50	$3.00	£0.30	£1.00	£2.00
18 scarce in the U.K.	$0.40	$1.25	$2.50	£0.40	£1.25	£2.50
19-20	$0.40	$1.25	$2.50	£0.30	£1.00	£2.00
21-29	$0.40	$1.20	$2.00	£0.30	£0.90	£1.50
30 Eisner, Canniff, Kurtzman, Corben, John Byrne, Frank Miller, Austin, Rogers art	$0.80	$2.40	$4.00	£0.50	£1.50	£2.50
31-35	$0.40	$1.20	$2.00	£0.30	£0.90	£1.50
36 $2.95 cover begin	$0.60	$1.80	$3.00	£0.40	£1.20	£2.00
37-41	$0.60	$1.80	$3.00	£0.40	£1.20	£2.00
Title Value:	$23.15	$70.75	$131.50	£16.60	£50.80	£94.50

Note: all Non-Distributed on the news-stands in the U.K.

Spirit Color Special, scarce in the U.K., reprints colour sections £1.40 £4.20 £7.00

SPIRIT OF WONDER

Dark Horse,MS; 1 Apr 1996-5 Aug 1996

	$Good	$Fine	$N.Mint	£Good	£Fine	£N.Mint
1-5 ND Kenji Tsuruta script and art; black and white	$0.60	$1.80	$3.00	£0.40	£1.20	£2.00
Title Value:	$3.00	$9.00	$15.00	£2.00	£6.00	£10.00

SPIRIT SPECIAL, THE

Warren; nn 1975

	$Good	$Fine	$N.Mint	£Good	£Fine	£N.Mint
nn ND scarce in the U.K. Will Eisner art	$0.80	$2.50	$5.00	£0.65	£2.00	£4.00
Title Value:	$0.80	$2.50	$5.00	£0.65	£2.00	£4.00

SPIRIT WORLD

Hampshire/DC,Magazine; 1 Fall 1971

(see In the Days of the Mob)

	$Good	$Fine	$N.Mint	£Good	£Fine	£N.Mint
1 distributed in the U.K. though scarce 48pgs, Jack Kirby art throughout; came with psychedelic Souls poster	$1.25	$3.75	$7.50	£1.25	£3.75	£7.50
Title Value:	$1.25	$3.75	$7.50	£1.25	£3.75	£7.50

SPIRIT, THE

I.W. Super; 11 1963-12 1964

11 rare, distributed in the U.K. 40s/50s Will Eisner reprints

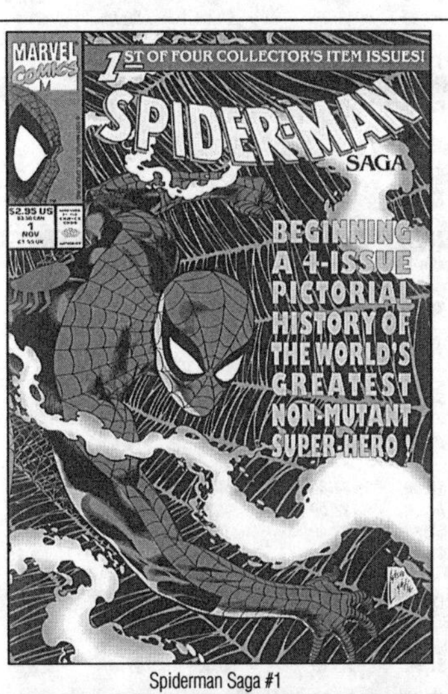

Spiderman Saga #1

Spidey Super Stories #3

Spirit (2nd) #2

	$Good	$Fine	$N.Mint	£Good	£Fine	£N.Mint
	$3.55	*$10.50*	*$25.00*	£2.10	£6.25	£15.00
12 rare, distributed in the U.K. 40s/50s Will Eisner reprints						
	$3.20	*$9.50*	*$22.50*	£1.75	£5.25	£12.50
Title Value:	*$6.75*	*$20.00*	*$47.50*	£3.85	£11.50	£27.50

Note: all reprint except one new story in each issue.

SPIRIT, THE (2ND SERIES)

Harvey; 1 Oct 1966-2 Mar 1967

	$Good	$Fine	$N.Mint	£Good	£Fine	£N.Mint
1 scarce though distributed in the U.K. giant, Will Eisner art						
	$7.75	*$23.50*	*$55.00*	£5.00	£15.00	£35.00
2 distributed in the U.K. giant, Will Eisner art						
	$7.00	*$21.00*	*$50.00*	£4.25	£12.50	£30.00
Title Value:	*$14.75*	*$44.50*	*$105.00*	£9.25	£27.50	£65.00

SPIRIT, THE (3RD SERIES)

Kitchen Sink; 1 Jan 1973-2 Sep 1973

	$Good	$Fine	$N.Mint	£Good	£Fine	£N.Mint
1-2 ND Will Eisner art						
	$2.00	*$6.00*	*$12.00*	£1.30	£4.00	£8.00
Title Value:	*$4.00*	*$12.00*	*$24.00*	£2.60	£8.00	£16.00

SPIRIT: THE ORIGIN YEARS

Kitchen Sink; 1 Jul 1992-10 1993

	$Good	$Fine	$N.Mint	£Good	£Fine	£N.Mint
1 ND new cover designs by Will Eisner begin						
	$0.50	*$1.50*	*$2.50*	£0.30	£0.90	£1.50
2-10 ND	*$0.50*	*$1.50*	*$2.50*	£0.30	£0.90	£1.50
Title Value:	*$5.00*	*$15.00*	*$25.00*	£3.00	£9.00	£15.00

SPITFIRE AND THE TROUBLESHOOTERS

Marvel Comics Group/New Universe; 1 Oct 1986-13 Oct 1987

	$Good	$Fine	$N.Mint	£Good	£Fine	£N.Mint
1-3 ND	*$0.15*	*$0.45*	*$0.75*	£0.10	£0.35	£0.60
4 ND Todd McFarlane art						
	$0.15	*$0.45*	*$0.75*	£0.10	£0.35	£0.60
5-9 ND	*$0.15*	*$0.45*	*$0.75*	£0.10	£0.35	£0.60
10 title becomes Codename: Spitfire						
	$0.15	*$0.45*	*$0.75*	£0.10	£0.35	£0.60
11-13	*$0.15*	*$0.45*	*$0.75*	£0.10	£0.35	£0.60
Title Value:	*$1.95*	*$5.85*	*$9.75*	£1.30	£4.55	£7.80

SPLAT!

Mad Dog Graphics; 1 Feb 1987-3 Aug 1987

	$Good	$Fine	$N.Mint	£Good	£Fine	£N.Mint
1 ND features Peter Bagge and Hunt Emerson art						
	$0.40	*$1.20*	*$2.00*	£0.25	£0.75	£1.25
2 ND	*$0.40*	*$1.20*	*$2.00*	£0.25	£0.75	£1.25
3 ND 1st appearance Eddy Current by Ted McKeever, Lone Wolf parody by Fujitake						
	$0.80	*$2.40*	*$4.00*	£0.50	£1.50	£2.50
Title Value:	*$1.60*	*$4.80*	*$8.00*	£1.00	£3.00	£5.00

SPLATTER

Arpad Publishing/Northstar; 1 May 1991-9 1993 ?

	$Good	$Fine	$N.Mint	£Good	£Fine	£N.Mint
1 horror anthology, Tim Vigil art featured; black and white						
	$0.60	*$1.80*	*$3.00*	£0.40	£1.20	£2.00
1 2nd printing	*$0.50*	*$1.50*	*$2.50*	£0.30	£0.90	£1.50
1 3rd printing	*$0.50*	*$1.50*	*$2.50*	£0.30	£0.90	£1.50
1 Gold Edition, - (Feb 1993); 3,000 copies						
	$1.00	*$3.00*	*$5.00*	£0.60	£1.80	£3.00
2-4 Tim Vigil art; black and white						
	$0.50	*$1.50*	*$2.50*	£0.30	£0.90	£1.50
5 black and white	*$0.50*	*$1.50*	*$2.50*	£0.30	£0.90	£1.50
6-9	*$0.50*	*$1.50*	*$2.50*	£0.30	£0.90	£1.50
Title Value:	*$6.60*	*$19.80*	*$33.00*	£4.00	£12.00	£20.00

Note: all Non-Distributed on the news-stands in the U.K.

				£Good	£Fine	£N.Mint
The Splatter Collection (Apr 1993), reprints #2-5				£1.50	£4.50	£7.50

SPLATTER ANNUAL

Northstar; 1 1993-2 1994

	$Good	$Fine	$N.Mint	£Good	£Fine	£N.Mint
1-2 ND 48pgs, black and white						
	$0.80	*$2.40*	*$4.00*	£0.50	£1.50	£2.50
Title Value:	*$1.60*	*$4.80*	*$8.00*	£1.00	£3.00	£5.00

SPLATTER: HOLIDAY IN HELL

Northstar,OS; 1 Nov 1994

	$Good	$Fine	$N.Mint	£Good	£Fine	£N.Mint
1 ND 48pgs, black and white						
	$0.80	*$2.40*	*$4.00*	£0.50	£1.50	£2.50
Title Value:	*$0.80*	*$2.40*	*$4.00*	£0.50	£1.50	£2.50

SPLITTING IMAGE

Image; 1 Jan 1993-2 Apr 1993

	$Good	$Fine	$N.Mint	£Good	£Fine	£N.Mint
1-2 ND parodies of Image characters by Valentino and Liefeld plus covers by other Image artists						
	$0.40	*$1.20*	*$2.00*	£0.25	£0.75	£1.25
Title Value:	*$0.80*	*$2.40*	*$4.00*	£0.50	£1.50	£2.50

SPOOF

Marvel Comics Group; 1 Oct 1970; 2 Nov 1972-5 May 1973

	$Good	$Fine	$N.Mint	£Good	£Fine	£N.Mint
1 ND scarce in the U.K. Marie Severin art						
	$1.00	*$3.00*	*$6.00*	£0.65	£2.00	£4.00
2-5 ND scarce in the U.K.						
	$0.65	*$2.00*	*$4.00*	£0.40	£1.25	£2.50
Title Value:	*$3.60*	*$11.00*	*$22.00*	£2.25	£7.00	£14.00

Note: TV and film parodies.

SPOOKY

Harvey; 1 Nov 1955-161 Sep 1980

	$Good	$Fine	$N.Mint	£Good	£Fine	£N.Mint
1	*$34.00*	*$100.00*	*$275.00*	£23.00	£67.50	£185.00
2	*$21.00*	*$62.50*	*$150.00*	£14.00	£43.00	£100.00
3-5	*$11.00*	*$34.00*	*$80.00*	£7.50	£22.50	£52.50
6-10	*$10.00*	*$30.00*	*$70.00*	£6.25	£19.00	£45.00
11-20	*$5.50*	*$17.00*	*$40.00*	£3.20	£9.50	£22.50
21-40	*$3.55*	*$10.50*	*$25.00*	£1.75	£5.25	£12.50
41-60	*$2.10*	*$6.25*	*$15.00*	£1.05	£3.20	£7.50
61-80	*$1.65*	*$5.00*	*$10.00*	£0.80	£2.50	£5.00
81-100	*$1.50*	*$4.50*	*$7.50*	£0.70	£2.10	£3.50
101-120	*$1.20*	*$3.60*	*$6.00*	£0.60	£1.80	£3.00
121-126	*$0.70*	*$2.10*	*$3.50*	£0.40	£1.20	£2.00
127-132 48pgs	*$1.20*	*$3.60*	*$6.00*	£0.50	£1.50	£2.50
133-140	*$0.70*	*$2.10*	*$3.50*	£0.40	£1.20	£2.00
141-150	*$0.40*	*$1.20*	*$2.00*	£0.25	£0.75	£1.25
151-161	*$0.40*	*$1.20*	*$2.00*	£0.20	£0.60	£1.00
Title Value:	*$418.40*	*$1257.70*	*$2812.00*	£234.05	£704.90	£1589.00

Note: some issues distributed in the U.K. after 1959/60

SPOTLIGHT

Heroic Publishing; 0 Aug 1993

	$Good	$Fine	$N.Mint	£Good	£Fine	£N.Mint
0 ND pre-bagged with trading card and signed by creators						
	$0.50	*$1.50*	*$2.50*	£0.30	£0.90	£1.50
Title Value:	*$0.50*	*$1.50*	*$2.50*	£0.30	£0.90	£1.50

SPRING-HEEL JACK

Dark Horse,MS; 1,2 1991

	$Good	$Fine	$N.Mint	£Good	£Fine	£N.Mint
1-2 ND David Barbour and Wayne Tanaka script/art						
	$0.40	*$1.20*	*$2.00*	£0.25	£0.75	£1.25
Title Value:	*$0.80*	*$2.40*	*$4.00*	£0.50	£1.50	£2.50

SPRING-HEEL JACK: REVENGE OF THE RIPPER

Rebel Studios,MS; 1 May 1993-3 Feb 1994

	$Good	$Fine	$N.Mint	£Good	£Fine	£N.Mint
1-3 ND Wayne Tanaka art						
	$0.40	*$1.20*	*$2.00*	£0.25	£0.75	£1.25
Title Value:	*$1.20*	*$3.60*	*$6.00*	£0.75	£2.25	£3.75

SPUMCO COMIC BOOK

Marvel Comics Group; 1 Oct 1995-4 Jan 1996

	$Good	$Fine	$N.Mint	£Good	£Fine	£N.Mint
1-4 ND 64pgs, cartoon adventures from the Ren & Stimpy studio; 9" x 12" format						
	$1.40	*$4.20*	*$7.00*	£0.90	£2.70	£4.50
Title Value:	*$5.60*	*$16.80*	*$28.00*	£3.60	£10.80	£18.00
Spumco (Feb 1996)						
Trade paperback 256pgs, reprints mini-series				£3.30	£9.90	£16.50

SPUMCO COMIC BOOK (2ND SERIES)

Dark Horse; 1 Jan 1997-present

	$Good	$Fine	$N.Mint	£Good	£Fine	£N.Mint
1-2 ND 64pgs, oversize format						
	$1.20	*$3.60*	*$6.00*	£0.80	£2.40	£4.00
Title Value:	*$2.40*	*$7.20*	*$12.00*	£1.60	£4.80	£8.00

SPYKE

Marvel Comics Group/Epic,MS; 1 Jul 1993-4 Oct 1993

	$Good	$Fine	$N.Mint	£Good	£Fine	£N.Mint
1 ND Mike Baron script begins, embossed cover with metallic ink						
	$0.40	*$1.20*	*$2.00*	£0.25	£0.75	£1.25
2-4 ND	*$0.40*	*$1.20*	*$2.00*	£0.25	£0.75	£1.25
Title Value:	*$1.60*	*$4.80*	*$8.00*	£1.00	£3.00	£5.00

SPYMAN, TOP SECRET PRESENTS

Harvey; 1 Sep 1966-3 Feb 1967

	$Good	$Fine	$N.Mint	£Good	£Fine	£N.Mint
1 distributed in the U.K. Jim Steranko art, his first professional work in comics (**Note:** has Top Secret Adventures on cover)						
	$5.25	*$16.00*	*$37.50*	£3.55	£10.50	£25.00
2 distributed in the U.K. Jim Steranko art						
	$3.90	*$11.50*	*$27.50*	£2.50	£7.50	£17.50
3 distributed in the U.K. Joe Simon cover						
	$3.90	*$11.50*	*$27.50*	£2.50	£7.50	£17.50
Title Value:	*$13.05*	*$39.00*	*$92.50*	£8.55	£25.50	£60.00

SQUAD: A HARDCASE MINI-SERIES, THE

Malibu Ultraverse; 0 Nov 1994-2 Jan 1995

	$Good	$Fine	$N.Mint	£Good	£Fine	£N.Mint
0 ND numbered #0-A						
	$0.40	*$1.20*	*$2.00*	£0.25	£0.75	£1.25
1 ND numbered #0-B						
	$0.40	*$1.20*	*$2.00*	£0.25	£0.75	£1.25
2 ND numbered #0-C						
	$0.40	*$1.20*	*$2.00*	£0.25	£0.75	£1.25
Title Value:	*$1.20*	*$3.60*	*$6.00*	£0.75	£2.25	£3.75

SQUADRON SUPREME

Marvel Comics Group,MS; 1 Sep 1985-12 Aug 1986

(see Avengers #69, Quasar)

	$Good	$Fine	$N.Mint	£Good	£Fine	£N.Mint
1 ND	*$0.40*	*$1.20*	*$2.00*	£0.25	£0.75	£1.25
2-11 ND	*$0.30*	*$0.90*	*$1.50*	£0.20	£0.60	£1.00
12 ND DS	*$0.40*	*$1.20*	*$2.00*	£0.25	£0.75	£1.25
Title Value:	*$3.80*	*$11.40*	*$19.00*	£2.50	£7.50	£12.50

SQUALOR

First,MS; 1 Dec 1989-4 Aug 1990

(see Sensei, Twilight Man)

	$Good	$Fine	$N.Mint	£Good	£Fine	£N.Mint
1 ND sub-titled "First Fiction Volume Three"; glossy heavier stock paper covers						
	$0.40	*$1.20*	*$2.00*	£0.25	£0.75	£1.25
2-4 ND	*$0.40*	*$1.20*	*$2.00*	£0.25	£0.75	£1.25
Title Value:	*$1.60*	*$4.80*	*$8.00*	£1.00	£3.00	£5.00

ST. GEORGE

Marvel Comics Group/Epic; 1 Jun 1988-8 Aug 1989

	$Good	$Fine	$N.Mint	£Good	£Fine	£N.Mint
1 ND Klaus Janson art begins, Sienkiewicz cover						
	$0.30	*$0.90*	*$1.50*	£0.20	£0.60	£1.00
2 ND Jon Muth cover						
	$0.30	*$0.90*	*$1.50*	£0.20	£0.60	£1.00
3 ND Nowlan cover						
	$0.30	*$0.90*	*$1.50*	£0.20	£0.60	£1.00
4 ND Chiarello cover						
	$0.30	*$0.90*	*$1.50*	£0.20	£0.60	£1.00
5 ND Kev O'Neill cover						
	$0.30	*$0.90*	*$1.50*	£0.20	£0.60	£1.00
6-7 ND	*$0.30*	*$0.90*	*$1.50*	£0.20	£0.60	£1.00
8 ND Jim Lee art	*$0.40*	*$1.20*	*$2.00*	£0.25	£0.75	£1.25
Title Value:	*$2.50*	*$7.50*	*$12.50*	£1.65	£4.95	£8.25

Note: all painted covers

STAINLESS STEEL ARMADILLO

Antarctic Press,MS; 1 Feb 1995-6 Dec 1995

	$Good	$Fine	$N.Mint	£Good	£Fine	£N.Mint
1-6 ND Ryukihei script and art; black and white						
	$0.60	*$1.80*	*$3.00*	£0.40	£1.20	£2.00

VERY GENERAL PERCENTAGE CONVERSION CHART WHICH MAY BE USED TO CALCULATE LOW AND INBETWEEN GRADES:

Issue	$Good	$Fine	$N.Mint	£Good	£Fine	£N.Mint
Title Value:	$3.60	$10.80	$18.00	£2.40	£7.20	£12.00
STALKER						
DC Comics; 1 Jun/Jul 1975-4 Dec/Jan 1975						
1 origin and 1st appearance; Steve Ditko and Wally Wood art	$0.60	$1.80	$3.00	£0.40	£1.20	£2.00
2-4 Steve Ditko and Wally Wood art	$0.50	$1.50	$2.50	£0.30	£0.90	£1.50
Title Value:	$2.10	$6.30	$10.50	£1.30	£3.90	£6.50
STALKERS						
Marvel Comics Group/Epic,MS; 1 Apr 1990-12 Mar 1991						
1 ND Chadwick cover, Mark Texeira art begins (ends #7)	$0.30	$0.90	$1.50	£0.20	£0.60	£1.00
2 ND	$0.30	$0.90	$1.50	£0.20	£0.60	£1.00
3-6 ND two stories per issue	$0.30	$0.90	$1.50	£0.20	£0.60	£1.00
7 ND two stories, last Texeira art	$0.30	$0.90	$1.50	£0.20	£0.60	£1.00
8-12 ND two stories per issue	$0.30	$0.90	$1.50	£0.20	£0.60	£1.00
Title Value:	$3.60	$10.80	$18.00	£2.40	£7.20	£12.00
STAN SHAW'S BEAUTY & THE BEAST						
Dark Horse,OS; 1 Nov 1993						
1 ND 48pgs	$0.90	$2.70	$4.50	£0.60	£1.80	£3.00
Title Value:	$0.90	$2.70	$4.50	£0.60	£1.80	£3.00
STANLEY AND HIS MONSTER						
National Periodical Publications; 109 Apr/May 1968-112 Oct/Nov 1968 (formerly The Fox and the Crow; see Secret Origins #48)						
109-112 scarce in the U.K.	$2.50	$7.50	$17.50	£1.75	£5.25	£12.50
Title Value:	$10.00	$30.00	$70.00	£7.00	£21.00	£50.00
STANLEY AND HIS MONSTER (2ND SERIES)						
DC Comics,MS; 1 Feb 1993-4 May 1993						
1-4	$0.25	$0.75	$1.25	£0.15	£0.45	£0.75
Title Value:	$1.00	$3.00	$5.00	£0.60	£1.80	£3.00
STAR						
Image,MS; 1 Jun 1995-4 Sep 1995						
1-4 ND Tom and Mary Bierbaum script, Ben Herrera art	$0.50	$1.50	$2.50	£0.30	£0.90	£1.50
Title Value:	$2.00	$6.00	$10.00	£1.20	£3.60	£6.00
STAR BLAZERS						
Argo Press; 1 Aug 1995-2 1995						
1 ND sub-titled "The Magazine of the Battleship Yamato"	$0.60	$1.80	$3.00	£0.40	£1.20	£2.00
2 ND	$0.60	$1.80	$3.00	£0.40	£1.20	£2.00
Title Value:	$1.20	$3.60	$6.00	£0.80	£2.40	£4.00
STAR BRAND, THE						
Marvel Comics Group/New Universe; 1 Oct 1986-19 May 1989						
1-6 Romita Jr./Williamson art	$0.25	$0.75	$1.25	£0.15	£0.45	£0.75
7-9	$0.25	$0.75	$1.25	£0.15	£0.45	£0.75
10-11 ND John Byrne art	$0.25	$0.75	$1.25	£0.15	£0.45	£0.75
12 ND John Byrne art, The Pitt begins, Byrne self-cameo	$0.25	$0.75	$1.25	£0.15	£0.45	£0.75
13 ND John Byrne art, Pitt X-over	$0.25	$0.75	$1.25	£0.15	£0.45	£0.75
14-19 ND John Byrne art	$0.25	$0.75	$1.25	£0.15	£0.45	£0.75
Title Value:	$4.75	$14.25	$23.75	£2.85	£8.55	£14.25
STAR BRAND, THE ANNUAL						
Marvel Comics Group/New Universe; 1 Oct 1987						
1 ND	$0.30	$0.90	$1.50	£0.20	£0.60	£1.00
Title Value:	$0.30	$0.90	$1.50	£0.20	£0.60	£1.00
STAR FEMS						
AC Comics,OS; nn 1987						
nn ND Black Blaze appears; Paul Gulacy cover	$0.40	$1.20	$2.00	£0.25	£0.75	£1.25
Title Value:	$0.40	$1.20	$2.00	£0.25	£0.75	£1.25
STAR HUNTERS						
DC Comics; 1 Oct/Nov 1977-7 Oct/Nov 1978 (see DC Super-Stars #16)						
1 scarce in the U.K.	$0.50	$1.50	$3.00	£0.25	£0.75	£1.50
2-6	$0.25	$0.75	$1.50	£0.15	£0.50	£1.00
7 ND 44pgs	$0.30	$1.00	$2.00	£0.20	£0.60	£1.25
Title Value:	$2.05	$6.25	$12.50	£1.20	£3.85	£7.75
STAR MASTERS						
AC Comics; 1 Mar 1984						
1 ND Tom Lyle script and art	$0.30	$0.90	$1.50	£0.20	£0.60	£1.00
Title Value:	$0.30	$0.90	$1.50	£0.20	£0.60	£1.00
STAR MASTERS						
Marvel Comics Group; 1 Dec 1995-3 Feb 1996						
1 ND Silver Surfer, Beta Ray Thor and Quasar begin	$0.40	$1.20	$2.00	£0.25	£0.75	£1.25
2 ND ties into Thor #494	$0.40	$1.20	$2.00	£0.25	£0.75	£1.25
3 ND concludes in Cosmic Powers Unlimited #4	$0.40	$1.20	$2.00	£0.25	£0.75	£1.25
Title Value:	$1.20	$3.60	$6.00	£0.75	£2.25	£3.75
STAR POLICE						
Sky Comics; 1 Jul 1994						

Issue	$Good	$Fine	$N.Mint	£Good	£Fine	£N.Mint
1 ND Michael Brown script	$0.40	$1.20	$2.00	£0.25	£0.75	£1.25
Title Value:	$0.40	$1.20	$2.00	£0.25	£0.75	£1.25
STAR RANGERS						
Adventure; 1 Oct 1987-4 Feb 1988						
1 ND Jim Mooney art	$0.40	$1.20	$2.00	£0.25	£0.75	£1.25
2-3 ND Adam Hughes art	$0.40	$1.20	$2.00	£0.25	£0.75	£1.25
4 ND Dave Dorman cover	$0.40	$1.20	$2.00	£0.25	£0.75	£1.25
Title Value:	$1.60	$4.80	$8.00	£1.00	£3.00	£5.00
STAR REACH						
Star Reach; 1 Apr 1974-18 Oct 1979						
1 ND Cody Starbuck by Chaykin, Jim Starlin art	$0.80	$2.50	$5.00	£0.55	£1.75	£3.50
1 2nd printing, ND (Nov 1975)	$0.50	$1.50	$3.00	£0.30	£1.00	£2.00
1 3rd/4th printing ND	$0.30	$1.00	$2.00	£0.20	£0.60	£1.25
2 ND Jim Starlin, Workman art, Stephanie Star by Friedrich/Giordano; Neal Adams cover	$0.65	$2.00	$4.00	£0.40	£1.25	£2.50
2 2nd printing ND	$0.40	$1.25	$2.50	£0.25	£0.75	£1.50
2 3rd printing ND	$0.30	$1.00	$2.00	£0.20	£0.60	£1.25
3 ND Brunner art	$0.50	$1.50	$3.00	£0.30	£1.00	£2.00
3 2nd printing ND	$0.40	$1.25	$2.50	£0.25	£0.75	£1.50
3 3rd printing ND	$0.30	$1.00	$2.00	£0.20	£0.60	£1.25
4 ND Chaykin art	$0.50	$1.50	$3.00	£0.30	£1.00	£2.00
4 2nd printing ND	$0.40	$1.25	$2.50	£0.25	£0.75	£1.50
4 3rd printing ND	$0.30	$1.00	$2.00	£0.20	£0.60	£1.25
5 ND Chaykin art	$0.50	$1.50	$3.00	£0.30	£1.00	£2.00
5 2nd printing ND	$0.40	$1.25	$2.50	£0.25	£0.75	£1.50
5 3rd printing ND	$0.30	$1.00	$2.00	£0.20	£0.60	£1.25
6 ND Jeff Jones art	$0.45	$1.35	$2.75	£0.25	£0.85	£1.75
6 2nd printing ND	$0.40	$1.25	$2.50	£0.25	£0.75	£1.50
6 3rd printing ND	$0.30	$1.00	$2.00	£0.20	£0.60	£1.25
7 ND Dave Sim script, Bonivert, Staton art, Barry Smith cover	$0.40	$1.25	$2.50	£0.25	£0.75	£1.50
7 2nd printing ND	$0.30	$1.00	$2.00	£0.20	£0.60	£1.25
8 ND P. Craig Russell, Gene Day art	$0.40	$1.25	$2.50	£0.25	£0.75	£1.50
8 2nd printing ND	$0.30	$1.00	$2.00	£0.20	£0.60	£1.25
9 ND	$0.40	$1.25	$2.50	£0.25	£0.75	£1.50
9 2nd printing ND	$0.30	$1.00	$2.00	£0.20	£0.60	£1.25
10 ND Brunner art	$0.40	$1.25	$2.50	£0.25	£0.75	£1.50
10 2nd printing ND	$0.30	$1.00	$2.00	£0.20	£0.60	£1.25
11-15 ND	$0.30	$1.00	$2.00	£0.20	£0.60	£1.25
16-18 ND magazine size	$0.40	$1.25	$2.50	£0.25	£0.75	£1.50
Title Value:	$13.20	$41.85	$83.75	£8.40	£25.85	£52.50
Greatest Hits Graphic Novel (1979) 124pgs				£1.20	£3.60	£6.00
STAR REACH CLASSICS						
Eclipse; 1 Mar 1984-6 Aug 1984						
1 ND Jim Starlin and Dave Sim reprints; Starlin cover	$0.40	$1.20	$2.00	£0.25	£0.75	£1.25
2 ND Sergio Aragones reprints	$0.40	$1.20	$2.00	£0.25	£0.75	£1.25
3 ND P. Craig Russell reprint/cover	$0.40	$1.20	$2.00	£0.25	£0.75	£1.25
4 ND Frank Brunner reprint/cover	$0.40	$1.20	$2.00	£0.25	£0.75	£1.25
5 ND Ditko reprint, Chaykin cover	$0.40	$1.20	$2.00	£0.25	£0.75	£1.25
6 ND P. Craig Russell reprint/cover	$0.40	$1.20	$2.00	£0.25	£0.75	£1.25
Title Value:	$2.40	$7.20	$12.00	£1.50	£4.50	£7.50
STAR SEED						
(see Powers That Be)						
STAR SLAMMERS						
Malibu Bravura,MS; 1 May 1994-5 Nov 1994						
1-5 ND Walter Simonson script and art	$0.40	$1.20	$2.00	£0.25	£0.75	£1.25
Title Value:	$2.00	$6.00	$10.00	£1.25	£3.75	£6.25
STAR SLAMMERS SPECIAL						
Dark Horse,OS; 1 Jun 1996						
1 ND Walt Simonson script and art	$0.60	$1.80	$3.00	£0.40	£1.20	£2.00
Title Value:	$0.60	$1.80	$3.00	£0.40	£1.20	£2.00
STAR TREK						
Gold Key; 1 Jul 1967-61 Mar 1979						
1 photo cover	$62.50	$185.00	$500.00	£41.00	£120.00	£325.00
2 photo cover	$43.00	$125.00	$300.00	£29.00	£85.00	£200.00
3-5 photo cover	$29.00	$85.00	$200.00	£19.00	£57.50	£135.00
6-9 photo cover	$25.00	$75.00	$175.00	£16.00	£49.00	£115.00
10 painted covers begin (ends #59)	$12.50	$39.00	$90.00	£8.50	£26.00	£60.00
11-14	$12.50	$39.00	$90.00	£8.50	£26.00	£60.00
15-20 distributed in the U.K.	$11.00	$34.00	$80.00	£7.75	£23.50	£55.00
21 scarce though distributed in the U.K.	$8.50	$26.00	$60.00	£6.00	£18.00	£42.50
22-23 distributed in the U.K.						

	$Good	$Fine	$N.Mint	£Good	£Fine	£N.Mint
	$8.50	$26.00	$60.00	£5.50	£17.00	£40.00
24 scarce though distributed in the U.K.						
	$8.50	$26.00	$60.00	£6.00	£18.00	£42.50
25-26 distributed in the U.K.						
	$8.50	$26.00	$60.00	£5.50	£17.00	£40.00
27 scarce though distributed in the U.K.						
	$8.50	$26.00	$60.00	£6.00	£18.00	£42.50
28-29 distributed in the U.K.						
	$8.50	$26.00	$60.00	£5.50	£17.00	£40.00
30 scarce though distributed in the U.K.						
	$8.50	$26.00	$60.00	£6.00	£18.00	£42.50
31-40 distributed in the U.K.						
	$7.50	$22.50	$45.00	£5.00	£15.00	£30.00
41-44	$5.00	$15.00	$30.00	£3.30	£10.00	£20.00
45 same photo cover as #7						
	$5.00	$15.00	$30.00	£3.30	£10.00	£20.00
46-50	$5.00	$15.00	$30.00	£3.30	£10.00	£20.00
51-59	$4.55	$13.50	$27.50	£2.90	£8.75	£17.50
60-61 scarce in the U.K. line-drawn cover						
	$4.55	$13.50	$27.50	£3.30	£10.00	£20.00
Title Value:	$681.05	$2047.50	$4680.00	£452.70	£1367.25	£3127.50

Note: irregular distribution in the U.K.

STAR TREK

Marvel Comics Group; 1 Apr 1980-18 Feb 1982

	$Good	$Fine	$N.Mint	£Good	£Fine	£N.Mint
1 ND reprints movie adaptation from Super Special #15						
	$1.20	$3.60	$6.00	£0.80	£2.40	£4.00
2-3 ND reprints movie adaptation from Super Special #15						
	$0.80	$2.40	$4.00	£0.50	£1.50	£2.50
4-12 ND	$0.80	$2.40	$4.00	£0.50	£1.50	£2.50
13-14	$0.80	$2.40	$4.00	£0.40	£1.20	£2.00
15 ND	$0.80	$2.40	$4.00	£0.50	£1.50	£2.50
16-17	$0.80	$2.40	$4.00	£0.40	£1.20	£2.00
18 ND	$0.80	$2.40	$4.00	£0.50	£1.50	£2.50
Title Value:	$14.80	$44.40	$74.00	£8.90	£26.70	£44.50

STAR TREK (1ST SERIES)

DC Comics; 1 Feb 1984-56 Nov 1988

	$Good	$Fine	$N.Mint	£Good	£Fine	£N.Mint
1 George Perez cover art, Mando paper begins						
	$2.50	$7.50	$12.50	£1.40	£4.20	£7.00
2	$1.50	$4.50	$7.50	£0.80	£2.40	£4.00
3-5	$1.20	$3.60	$6.00	£0.60	£1.80	£3.00
6-10	$1.00	$3.00	$5.00	£0.50	£1.50	£2.50
11-20	$0.80	$2.40	$4.00	£0.40	£1.20	£2.00
21-30	$0.60	$1.80	$3.00	£0.35	£1.05	£1.75
31-32	$0.50	$1.50	$2.50	£0.30	£0.90	£1.50
33 DS anniversary issue						
	$0.80	$2.40	$4.00	£0.50	£1.50	£2.50
34-48	$0.50	$1.50	$2.50	£0.30	£0.90	£1.50
49 Who Killed Captain Kirk story begins by Peter David (ends #55)						
	$0.50	$1.50	$2.50	£0.30	£0.90	£1.50
50 DS painted cover						
	$0.60	$1.80	$3.00	£0.40	£1.20	£2.00
51-55	$0.40	$1.20	$2.00	£0.25	£0.75	£1.25
56 Gray Morrow art						
	$0.40	$1.20	$2.00	£0.25	£0.75	£1.25
Title Value:	$39.40	$118.20	$197.00	£21.80	£65.40	£109.00
Star Trek: The Mirror Universe Trade paperback (Jun 1991)						
reprints issues #9-16, new painted cover				£2.40	£7.20	£12.00
The Best of Star Trek Trade paperback (Dec 1991), 240pgs				£2.50	£7.50	£12.50
Star Trek: Who Killed Captain Kirk (Aug 1993)						
Trade paperback reprints issues #49-55 by Peter David,						
new painted cover by Jason Palmer				£2.10	£6.30	£10.50

STAR TREK (1ST SERIES) ANNUAL

DC Comics; 1 Oct 1985-3 1988

	$Good	$Fine	$N.Mint	£Good	£Fine	£N.Mint
1	$0.80	$2.40	$4.00	£0.50	£1.50	£2.50
2-3	$0.70	$2.10	$3.50	£0.40	£1.20	£2.00
Title Value:	$2.20	$6.60	$11.00	£1.30	£3.90	£6.50

STAR TREK (2ND SERIES)

DC Comics; 1 Oct 1989-80 Jan 1996

	$Good	$Fine	$N.Mint	£Good	£Fine	£N.Mint
1	$1.70	$5.00	$8.50	£1.00	£3.00	£5.00
2	$1.00	$3.00	$5.00	£0.60	£1.80	£3.00
3	$0.80	$2.40	$4.00	£0.50	£1.50	£2.50
4-10	$0.70	$2.10	$3.50	£0.40	£1.20	£2.00
11-12	$0.60	$1.80	$3.00	£0.35	£1.05	£1.75
13 Return of the Worthy story, part written by Billy Mumy						
	$0.60	$1.80	$3.00	£0.35	£1.05	£1.75
14 Return of the Worthy story, part written by Billy Mumy						
	$0.60	$1.80	$3.00	£0.35	£1.05	£1.75
15 Return of the Worthy story, part written by Billy Mumy						
	$0.60	$1.80	$3.00	£0.35	£1.05	£1.75
16-20	$0.60	$1.80	$3.00	£0.35	£1.05	£1.75
21-23	$0.60	$1.80	$3.00	£0.30	£0.90	£1.50
24 DS 25th anniversary salute						
	$0.70	$2.10	$3.50	£0.40	£1.20	£2.00
25-29	$0.60	$1.80	$3.00	£0.30	£0.90	£1.50
30-33 Veritas story						
	$0.60	$1.80	$3.00	£0.30	£0.90	£1.50
34	$0.50	$1.50	$2.50	£0.30	£0.90	£1.50
35-40 The Tabukan Syndrome, bi-weekly						
	$0.50	$1.50	$2.50	£0.30	£0.90	£1.50
41-45	$0.50	$1.50	$2.50	£0.30	£0.90	£1.50
46-49 bi-weekly	$0.50	$1.50	$2.50	£0.30	£0.90	£1.50
50 64pgs	$0.90	$2.70	$4.50	£0.50	£1.50	£2.50
51-60	$0.50	$1.50	$2.50	£0.30	£0.90	£1.50
61-70	$0.40	$1.20	$2.00	£0.25	£0.75	£1.25
71 $2.50 cover begin						
	$0.50	$1.50	$2.50	£0.30	£0.90	£1.50
72-74	$0.50	$1.50	$2.50	£0.30	£0.90	£1.50
75 56pgs	$0.80	$2.40	$4.00	£0.50	£1.50	£2.50
76-80	$0.50	$1.50	$2.50	£0.30	£0.90	£1.50
Title Value:	$45.50	$136.40	$226.00	£26.40	£79.20	£132.00
Note: New Format						
Star Trek: Tests of Courage (Oct 1994)						
Trade paperback reprints issues #35-40				£2.40	£7.20	£12.00

STAR TREK (2ND SERIES) ANNUAL

DC Comics; 1 Jun 1990-6 1995

	$Good	$Fine	$N.Mint	£Good	£Fine	£N.Mint
1 48pgs, Gray Morrow art, script by Peter David/George Takei						
	$0.80	$2.40	$4.00	£0.50	£1.50	£2.50
2 LD in the U.K. 64pgs						
	$0.70	$2.10	$3.50	£0.50	£1.50	£2.50
3-5 64pgs	$0.60	$1.80	$3.00	£0.40	£1.20	£2.00
6 64pgs, Convergence part 1, continued in Star Trek: The Next Generation Annual #6						
	$0.80	$2.40	$4.00	£0.50	£1.50	£2.50
Title Value:	$4.10	$12.30	$20.50	£2.70	£8.10	£13.50

STAR TREK DYNABRITE COMICS

Whitman; 11357, 11358 1978

	$Good	$Fine	$N.Mint	£Good	£Fine	£N.Mint
11357 scarce in the U.K. 48pgs, reprints Gold Key Star Trek issues #33, #41						
	$1.25	$3.75	$7.50	£1.25	£3.75	£7.50
11358 scarce in the U.K. 48pgs, reprints Gold Key Star Trek issues #34, #36						
	$1.25	$3.75	$7.50	£1.25	£3.75	£7.50
Title Value:	$2.50	$7.50	$15.00	£2.50	£7.50	£15.00

STAR TREK MOVIE SPECIAL

DC Comics; 1 1984; 2 1987

	$Good	$Fine	$N.Mint	£Good	£Fine	£N.Mint
1 68pgs, adapts Star Trek III						
	$0.50	$1.50	$2.50	£0.30	£0.90	£1.50
2 68pgs, adapts Star Trek IV						
	$0.50	$1.50	$2.50	£0.30	£0.90	£1.50
Title Value:	$1.00	$3.00	$5.00	£0.60	£1.80	£3.00

STAR TREK SPECIAL

DC Comics; 1 May 1994-3 1995

	$Good	$Fine	$N.Mint	£Good	£Fine	£N.Mint
1 64pgs, Peter David script; also features script and art by Mike Collins; painted cover by Bill Sienkiewicz						
	$0.80	$2.40	$4.00	£0.50	£1.50	£2.50
2 64pgs, painted cover by Dan Curry						
	$0.80	$2.40	$4.00	£0.50	£1.50	£2.50
3 64pgs	$0.80	$2.40	$4.00	£0.50	£1.50	£2.50
Title Value:	$2.40	$7.20	$12.00	£1.50	£4.50	£7.50

STAR TREK V MOVIE ADAPTATION

DC Comics; nn Aug 1989

	$Good	$Fine	$N.Mint	£Good	£Fine	£N.Mint
nn adapts Star Trek V film						
	$0.50	$1.50	$2.50	£0.30	£0.90	£1.50
Title Value:	$0.50	$1.50	$2.50	£0.30	£0.90	£1.50

STAR TREK VI MOVIE ADAPTATION

DC Comics; 1 Feb 1992

	$Good	$Fine	$N.Mint	£Good	£Fine	£N.Mint
1 64pgs, Peter David script						
	$0.60	$1.80	$3.00	£0.40	£1.20	£2.00
1 Direct Sales Edition, ND 64pgs, - Peter David script, photo gallery of stills from the film						
	$1.00	$3.00	$5.00	£0.70	£2.10	£3.50
Title Value:	$1.60	$4.80	$8.00	£1.10	£3.30	£5.50

STAR TREK/X-MEN

Top Cow/Marvel Comics Group,OS; 1 Dec 1996

	$Good	$Fine	$N.Mint	£Good	£Fine	£N.Mint
1 ND 64pgs, Scott Lobdell script, Marc Silvestri part art						
	$1.00	$3.00	$5.00	£0.60	£1.80	£3.00
Title Value:	$1.00	$3.00	$5.00	£0.60	£1.80	£3.00

STAR TREK: ASHES OF EDEN

DC Comics,OS; nn Jul 1995

	$Good	$Fine	$N.Mint	£Good	£Fine	£N.Mint
nn ND adaptation of William Shatner novel						
	$3.00	$9.00	$15.00	£2.00	£6.00	£10.00
Title Value:	$3.00	$9.00	$15.00	£2.00	£6.00	£10.00

STAR TREK: DEBT OF HONOUR

DC Comics,OS; 1 Aug 1992

	$Good	$Fine	$N.Mint	£Good	£Fine	£N.Mint
1 ND 96pgs, Adam Hughes art, Chris Claremont script; 25th anniversary celebration, painted cover by Dave Dorman						
	$4.50	$13.50	$22.50	£3.00	£9.00	£15.00
Title Value:	$4.50	$13.50	$22.50	£3.00	£9.00	£15.00
Softcover Graphic Novel (Dec 1992)						
96pgs, new painted cover by Jason Palmer				£2.00	£6.00	£10.00

STAR TREK: DEEP SPACE NINE

Malibu/Marvel Comics Group; 0 Jan 1995; 1 Sep 1993-32 Jan 1996

	$Good	$Fine	$N.Mint	£Good	£Fine	£N.Mint
0 ND sub-titled Terok Nor; fully painted art by Trevor Goring						
	$0.60	$1.80	$3.00	£0.40	£1.20	£2.00
1 ND	$0.50	$1.50	$2.50	£0.50	£1.50	£2.50
1 Dual Foil Edition, ND (May 1994) - gold and silver foil logo on black matte finish						
	$3.00	$9.00	$15.00	£2.00	£6.00	£10.00
1 Gold Edition, ND (May 1994) - gold foil cover, limited to 2,400 copies						
	$3.00	$9.00	$15.00	£2.00	£6.00	£10.00
1 Limited Edition, ND - all black cover						
	$2.50	$7.50	$12.50	£1.50	£4.50	£7.50
1 Newstand Edition, ND photo cover						
	$0.50	$1.50	$2.50	£0.50	£1.50	£2.50
2 ND pre-bagged with trading card						
	$0.50	$1.50	$2.50	£0.30	£0.90	£1.50
3-21 ND	$0.50	$1.50	$2.50	£0.30	£0.90	£1.50
22-23 ND bi-weekly						
	$0.50	$1.50	$2.50	£0.30	£0.90	£1.50
24 ND	$0.50	$1.50	$2.50	£0.30	£0.90	£1.50

Issue	$Good	$Fine	$N.Mint	£Good	£Fine	£N.Mint
25 ND 48pgs, bi-weekly						
	$0.80	*$2.40*	*$4.00*	£0.50	£1.50	£2.50
26-27 ND	*$0.50*	*$1.50*	*$2.50*	£0.30	£0.90	£1.50
28 ND 1st issue solicited under Marvel Comics banner						
	$0.50	*$1.50*	*$2.50*	£0.30	£0.90	£1.50
29-30 ND	*$0.50*	*$1.50*	*$2.50*	£0.30	£0.90	£1.50
31 ND 48pgs	*$0.80*	*$2.40*	*$4.00*	£0.50	£1.50	£2.50
32 ND	*$0.50*	*$1.50*	*$2.50*	£0.30	£0.90	£1.50
Title Value:	*$26.20*	*$78.60*	*$131.00*	£16.60	£49.80	£83.00

Note: all Non-Distributed on the news-stands in the U.K.

STAR TREK: DEEP SPACE NINE (2ND SERIES)

Marvel Comics Group; 1 Nov 1996-present

Issue	$Good	$Fine	$N.Mint	£Good	£Fine	£N.Mint
1 ND Howard Weinstein script, Tom Grindberg and Al Milgrom art begins						
	$0.40	*$1.20*	*$2.00*	£0.25	£0.75	£1.25
2-5 ND	*$0.40*	*$1.20*	*$2.00*	£0.25	£0.75	£1.25
Title Value:	*$2.00*	*$6.00*	*$10.00*	£1.25	£3.75	£6.25

STAR TREK: DEEP SPACE NINE - BLOOD AND HONOUR

Malibu,OS; 1 May 1995

Issue	$Good	$Fine	$N.Mint	£Good	£Fine	£N.Mint
1 ND Mark Lenard (Sarek in Star Trek) script, Ken Penders art						
	$0.60	*$1.80*	*$3.00*	£0.40	£1.20	£2.00
1 Signed & Numbered Edition, ND (Jun 1995) - limited to 500 copies, signed by Mark Lenard with certificate						
	$2.50	*$7.50*	*$12.50*	£1.50	£4.50	£7.50
Title Value:	*$3.10*	*$9.30*	*$15.50*	£1.90	£5.70	£9.50

STAR TREK: DEEP SPACE NINE - THE RULES OF DIPLOMACY

Malibu,OS; 1 Aug 1995

Issue	$Good	$Fine	$N.Mint	£Good	£Fine	£N.Mint
1 ND script by Aron Eisenberg (Nog in DS9)						
	$0.60	*$1.80*	*$3.00*	£0.40	£1.20	£2.00
1 Signed & Numbered Edition, ND; limited to 1,000 copies with certificate						
	$2.50	*$7.50*	*$12.50*	£1.50	£4.50	£7.50
Title Value:	*$3.10*	*$9.30*	*$15.50*	£1.90	£5.70	£9.50

STAR TREK: DEEP SPACE NINE - WORF

Marvel Comics Group,OS; 0 Feb 1996

Issue	$Good	$Fine	$N.Mint	£Good	£Fine	£N.Mint
0 ND 48pgs, biography and pin-up section to tie in with Worf joining the series on television						
	$0.80	*$2.40*	*$4.00*	£0.50	£1.50	£2.50
Title Value:	*$0.80*	*$2.40*	*$4.00*	£0.50	£1.50	£2.50

STAR TREK: DEEP SPACE NINE ANNUAL

Malibu; 1 Dec 1994

Issue	$Good	$Fine	$N.Mint	£Good	£Fine	£N.Mint
1 ND	*$0.60*	*$1.80*	*$3.00*	£0.40	£1.20	£2.00
1 Gold Edition, ND (Mar 1996)						
	$2.50	*$7.50*	*$12.50*	£1.50	£4.50	£7.50
Title Value:	*$3.10*	*$9.30*	*$15.50*	£1.90	£5.70	£9.50

STAR TREK: DEEP SPACE NINE HEARTS AND MINDS

Malibu,MS; 1 June 1994-4 Sep 1994

Issue	$Good	$Fine	$N.Mint	£Good	£Fine	£N.Mint
1 ND	*$0.50*	*$1.50*	*$2.50*	£0.30	£0.90	£1.50
1 Deluxe Edition, ND, holographic cover (Nov 1994)						
	$1.20	*$3.60*	*$6.00*	£0.80	£2.40	£4.00
2-4 ND	*$0.50*	*$1.50*	*$2.50*	£0.30	£0.90	£1.50
Title Value:	*$3.20*	*$9.60*	*$16.00*	£2.00	£6.00	£10.00

Note: the Holographic Edition of #1 was re-solicited by Marvel Comics Group cover date Feb 1996 at $14.95 with specific information that the issue would not be available outside the U.S and Canada

STAR TREK: DEEP SPACE NINE SPECIAL

Malibu,OS; 1 Jun 1995

Issue	$Good	$Fine	$N.Mint	£Good	£Fine	£N.Mint
1 ND 48pgs, five complete stories						
	$0.80	*$2.40*	*$4.00*	£0.50	£1.50	£2.50
Title Value:	*$0.80*	*$2.40*	*$4.00*	£0.50	£1.50	£2.50

STAR TREK: DEEP SPACE NINE THE MAQUIS

Malibu,MS; 1 Feb 1995-3 Apr 1995

Issue	$Good	$Fine	$N.Mint	£Good	£Fine	£N.Mint
1 ND	*$0.50*	*$1.50*	*$2.50*	£0.30	£0.90	£1.50
1 Photo Cover Edition, ND (Feb 1995)						
	$0.50	*$1.50*	*$2.50*	£0.30	£0.90	£1.50
2-3 ND	*$0.50*	*$1.50*	*$2.50*	£0.30	£0.90	£1.50
Title Value:	*$2.00*	*$6.00*	*$10.00*	£1.20	£3.60	£6.00

STAR TREK: DEEP SPACE NINE/STAR TREK: NEXT GENERATION

Malibu/DC Comics,MS; 1 Oct 1994-2 Nov 1994

Issue	$Good	$Fine	$N.Mint	£Good	£Fine	£N.Mint
1 ND	*$0.50*	*$1.50*	*$2.50*	£0.30	£0.90	£1.50
1 Gold Foil Edition ND						
	$2.50	*$7.50*	*$12.50*	£1.50	£4.50	£7.50
2 ND	*$0.50*	*$1.50*	*$2.50*	£0.30	£0.90	£1.50
Title Value:	*$3.50*	*$10.50*	*$17.50*	£2.10	£6.30	£10.50

Note: a cross collaboration between DC and Malibu. Both companies published issues #1 and 2 though the story is structured over 4 parts

STAR TREK: DEEP SPACE NINE: LIGHTSTORM

Malibu,OS; 1 Nov 1994

Issue	$Good	$Fine	$N.Mint	£Good	£Fine	£N.Mint
1 ND sequel to Star Trek: Deep Space Nine Hearts and Minds						
	$0.80	*$2.40*	*$4.00*	£0.50	£1.50	£2.50
1 Silver Foil Logo Edition, ND (Nov 1994) - limited to 2,500 copies						
	$2.50	*$7.50*	*$12.50*	£1.50	£4.50	£7.50
Title Value:	*$3.30*	*$9.90*	*$16.50*	£2.00	£6.00	£10.00

STAR TREK: DEEP SPACE NINE: LIGHTSTORM

Marvel Comics Group/Ultraverse,OS; 1 Apr 1996

Issue	$Good	$Fine	$N.Mint	£Good	£Fine	£N.Mint
1 ND 48pgs, ties into Star Trek: Generations						
	$0.70	*$2.10*	*$3.50*	£0.50	£1.50	£2.50
Title Value:	*$0.70*	*$2.10*	*$3.50*	£0.50	£1.50	£2.50

STAR TREK: EARLY VOYAGES

Marvel Comics Group; 1 Feb 1997-present

Issue	$Good	$Fine	$N.Mint	£Good	£Fine	£N.Mint
1 ND 48pgs, Dan Abnett and Ian Edington script; the Enterprise under the command of Captain Pike						
	$0.60	*$1.80*	*$3.00*	£0.40	£1.20	£2.00
2 ND	*$0.40*	*$1.20*	*$2.00*	£0.25	£0.75	£1.25
Title Value:	*$1.00*	*$3.00*	*$5.00*	£0.65	£1.95	£3.25

STAR TREK: FIRST CONTACT MOVIE ADAPTATION

Marvel Comics Group,OS; nn Jan 1997

Issue	$Good	$Fine	$N.Mint	£Good	£Fine	£N.Mint
nn ND 48pgs, John Vornholt script, Terry Pallott art						
	$1.20	*$3.60*	*$6.00*	£0.80	£2.40	£4.00
Title Value:	*$1.20*	*$3.60*	*$6.00*	£0.80	£2.40	£4.00

STAR TREK: GENERATIONS

DC Comics,OS; 1 Jan 1995

Issue	$Good	$Fine	$N.Mint	£Good	£Fine	£N.Mint
1 ND 64pgs, adaptation of the seventh Star Trek film						
	$0.80	*$2.40*	*$4.00*	£0.50	£1.50	£2.50
1 Prestige Format ND 64pgs						
	$1.20	*$3.60*	*$6.00*	£0.80	£2.40	£4.00
Title Value:	*$2.00*	*$6.00*	*$10.00*	£1.30	£3.90	£6.50

STAR TREK: MIRROR, MIRROR

Marvel Comics Group,OS; nn Feb 1997

Issue	$Good	$Fine	$N.Mint	£Good	£Fine	£N.Mint
nn ND 48pgs, Tom DeFalco script, Mark Bagley art						
	$0.80	*$2.40*	*$4.00*	£0.50	£1.50	£2.50
Title Value:	*$0.80*	*$2.40*	*$4.00*	£0.50	£1.50	£2.50

STAR TREK: STARFLEET ACADEMY

Marvel Comics Group; 1 Dec 1996-present

Issue	$Good	$Fine	$N.Mint	£Good	£Fine	£N.Mint
1 ND Chris Cooper script, Chris Renaud and Andy Lanning art begins						
	$0.40	*$1.20*	*$2.00*	£0.25	£0.75	£1.25
2-4 ND	*$0.40*	*$1.20*	*$2.00*	£0.25	£0.75	£1.25
Title Value:	*$1.60*	*$4.80*	*$8.00*	£1.00	£3.00	£5.00

STAR TREK: THE MODALA IMPERATIVE

DC Comics,MS; 1 Jul 1991-4 Aug 1991

Issue	$Good	$Fine	$N.Mint	£Good	£Fine	£N.Mint
1-4 LD in the U.K. bi-weekly 25th anniversary series						
	$0.50	*$1.50*	*$2.50*	£0.30	£0.90	£1.50
Title Value:	*$2.00*	*$6.00*	*$10.00*	£1.20	£3.60	£6.00

STAR TREK: THE NEXT GENERATION

DC Comics,MS; 1 Feb 1988-6 Jul 1988

Issue	$Good	$Fine	$N.Mint	£Good	£Fine	£N.Mint
1 DS	*$2.00*	*$6.00*	*$10.00*	£1.30	£3.90	£6.50
2-6	*$1.50*	*$4.50*	*$7.50*	£0.70	£2.10	£3.50
Title Value:	*$9.50*	*$28.50*	*$47.50*	£4.80	£14.40	£24.00

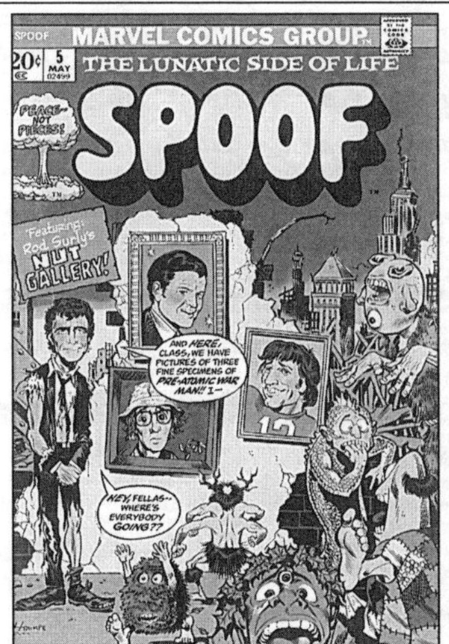

Spoof #5

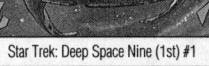

Star Trek: Deep Space Nine (1st) #1

Star Trek: The Next Generation (1st) #2

	$Good	$Fine	$N.Mint	£Good	£Fine	£N.Mint
Note: New Format						
Star Trek: The Next Generation - Beginnings (Jul 1995)						
Trade paperback reprints mini-series with new Bill Sienkiewicz cover				£2.70	£8.10	£13.50

STAR TREK: THE NEXT GENERATION (2ND SERIES)

DC Comics; 1 Oct 1989-80 Jan 1996

	$Good	$Fine	$N.Mint	£Good	£Fine	£N.Mint
1	$2.40	$7.00	$12.00	£1.30	£3.90	£6.50
2	$1.50	$4.50	$7.50	£0.80	£2.40	£4.00
3-5	$1.20	$3.60	$6.00	£0.60	£1.80	£3.00
6-10	$0.80	$2.40	$4.00	£0.50	£1.50	£2.50
11-12	$0.60	$1.80	$3.00	£0.40	£1.20	£2.00
13 written by Peter David/Billy Mumy	$0.60	$1.80	$3.00	£0.40	£1.20	£2.00
14-20	$0.60	$1.80	$3.00	£0.40	£1.20	£2.00
21-23	$0.50	$1.50	$2.50	£0.30	£0.90	£1.50
24 DS	$0.60	$1.80	$3.00	£0.40	£1.20	£2.00
25-29	$0.50	$1.50	$2.50	£0.30	£0.90	£1.50
30 The Rift part 1	$0.50	$1.50	$2.50	£0.30	£0.90	£1.50
31 The Rift part 2	$0.50	$1.50	$2.50	£0.30	£0.90	£1.50
32	$0.50	$1.50	$2.50	£0.30	£0.90	£1.50
33-38 bi-weekly	$0.50	$1.50	$2.50	£0.30	£0.90	£1.50
39 Divergence story	$0.50	$1.50	$2.50	£0.30	£0.90	£1.50
40-49	$0.50	$1.50	$2.50	£0.30	£0.90	£1.50
50 64pgs	$0.80	$2.40	$4.00	£0.50	£1.50	£2.50
51-58	$0.50	$1.50	$2.50	£0.30	£0.90	£1.50
59-60 Children of Chaos story	$0.50	$1.50	$2.50	£0.30	£0.90	£1.50
61 Children of Chaos story	$0.40	$1.20	$2.00	£0.25	£0.75	£1.25
62-70	$0.40	$1.20	$2.00	£0.25	£0.75	£1.25
71 $2.50 begin	$0.50	$1.50	$2.50	£0.30	£0.90	£1.50
72-74	$0.50	$1.50	$2.50	£0.30	£0.90	£1.50
75 56pgs	$0.80	$2.40	$4.00	£0.50	£1.50	£2.50
76-80	$0.50	$1.50	$2.50	£0.30	£0.90	£1.50
Title Value:	$47.20	$141.40	$234.00	£28.40	£85.20	£142.00
The Star Lost (Apr 1993)						
Trade paperback reprints issues #20-24, introduction by Ron Moore, producer of Star Trek: The Next Generation				£1.90	£5.70	£9.50
The Best of Star Trek: The Next Generation (Mar 1994)						
Trade paperback reprints issues #5,6,19 and Annual #2				£2.70	£8.10	£13.50
Star Trek: Revisitations (Dec 1995)						
Trade paperback reprints issues #22-24 and #49-50, painted cover				£2.70	£8.10	£13.50

STAR TREK: THE NEXT GENERATION (2ND SERIES) ANNUAL

DC Comics; 1 Aug 1990-6 1995

	$Good	$Fine	$N.Mint	£Good	£Fine	£N.Mint
1 ND 48pgs, script by John de Lancie ("Q") from TV series	$0.80	$2.40	$4.00	£0.50	£1.50	£2.50
2-5 ND 64pgs	$0.80	$2.40	$4.00	£0.50	£1.50	£2.50
6 ND 56pgs, Convergence part 2 continued from Star Trek Annual #6	$0.80	$2.40	$4.00	£0.50	£1.50	£2.50
Title Value:	$4.80	$14.40	$24.00	£3.00	£9.00	£15.00

Note: New Format

STAR TREK: THE NEXT GENERATION - ILL WIND

DC Comics,MS; 1 Nov 1995-4 Feb 1996

	$Good	$Fine	$N.Mint	£Good	£Fine	£N.Mint
1-4 ND painted covers by Hugh Fleming	$0.50	$1.50	$2.50	£0.30	£0.90	£1.50
Title Value:	$2.00	$6.00	$10.00	£1.20	£3.60	£6.00

STAR TREK: THE NEXT GENERATION - OPERATION: ASSIMILATION

Marvel Comics Group,OS; nn Feb 1997

	$Good	$Fine	$N.Mint	£Good	£Fine	£N.Mint
nn ND Paul Jenkins script, painted cover by Sorayama, interview with Jonathan Frakes (director of Star Trek: First Contact)	$0.60	$1.80	$3.00	£0.40	£1.20	£2.00
Title Value:	$0.60	$1.80	$3.00	£0.40	£1.20	£2.00

STAR TREK: THE NEXT GENERATION - SEASON FINALE

DC Comics,OS; 1 Aug 1994

	$Good	$Fine	$N.Mint	£Good	£Fine	£N.Mint
1 ND 64pgs, adaptation of the last ever episode	$0.80	$2.40	$4.00	£0.50	£1.50	£2.50
Title Value:	$0.80	$2.40	$4.00	£0.50	£1.50	£2.50

STAR TREK: THE NEXT GENERATION - SHADOWHEART

DC Comics,MS; 1 Dec 1994-4 Mar 1995

	$Good	$Fine	$N.Mint	£Good	£Fine	£N.Mint
1-4 ND	$0.50	$1.50	$2.50	£0.30	£0.90	£1.50
Title Value:	$2.00	$6.00	$10.00	£1.20	£3.60	£6.00

STAR TREK: THE NEXT GENERATION SPECIAL

DC Comics; 1 Nov 1993; 2 Sep 1994; 3 Oct 1995

	$Good	$Fine	$N.Mint	£Good	£Fine	£N.Mint
1 ND 64pgs, three stories	$0.80	$2.40	$4.00	£0.50	£1.50	£2.50
2 ND 64pgs, three stories featuring a Chris Claremont script	$0.80	$2.40	$4.00	£0.50	£1.50	£2.50
3 ND 64pgs, one story based on unused plot from TV series	$0.80	$2.40	$4.00	£0.50	£1.50	£2.50
Title Value:	$2.40	$7.20	$12.00	£1.50	£4.50	£7.50

STAR TREK: THE NEXT GENERATION/STAR TREK: DEEP SPACE NINE

DC Comics,MS; 1 Dec 1994-2 Jan 1995

	$Good	$Fine	$N.Mint	£Good	£Fine	£N.Mint
1-2 ND inter-company X-over with Malibu Comics	$0.50	$1.50	$2.50	£0.30	£0.90	£1.50
Title Value:	$1.00	$3.00	$5.00	£0.60	£1.80	£3.00

STAR TREK: THE NEXT GENERATION: THE MODALA IMPERATIVE

DC Comics,MS; 1 Sep 1991-4 Oct 1991

	$Good	$Fine	$N.Mint	£Good	£Fine	£N.Mint
1-4 bi-weekly	$0.50	$1.50	$2.50	£0.30	£0.90	£1.50
Title Value:	$2.00	$6.00	$10.00	£1.20	£3.60	£6.00

Note: story continued from The Modala Imperative mini-series

STAR TREK: UNLIMITED

Marvel Comics Group; 1 Nov 1996-present

	$Good	$Fine	$N.Mint	£Good	£Fine	£N.Mint
1 ND 56pgs, Dan Abnett and Ian Edgington scripts, Mark Buckingham and Jerome Moore, Kev Sutherland and Al Williamson art; bi-monthly	$0.60	$1.80	$3.00	£0.40	£1.20	£2.00
2-3 ND	$0.60	$1.80	$3.00	£0.40	£1.20	£2.00
Title Value:	$1.80	$5.40	$9.00	£1.20	£3.60	£6.00

STAR TREK: VOYAGER

Marvel Comics Group; 1 Nov 1996-present

	$Good	$Fine	$N.Mint	£Good	£Fine	£N.Mint
1 ND Laurie Sutton script, Jesus Redondo art	$0.40	$1.20	$2.00	£0.25	£0.75	£1.25
2-5 ND	$0.40	$1.20	$2.00	£0.25	£0.75	£1.25
Title Value:	$2.00	$6.00	$10.00	£1.25	£3.75	£6.25

STAR TREK: VOYAGER PREMIERE EPISODE ADAPTATION

Malibu,MS; 1,2 Jan 1995

	$Good	$Fine	$N.Mint	£Good	£Fine	£N.Mint
1 Cover A, ND - Mike Barr script, Rob Davis and Terry Pallot art begin	$0.50	$1.50	$2.50	£0.30	£0.90	£1.50
1 Cover A Newstand Edition, ND, same interior but with photo cover	$0.50	$1.50	$2.50	£0.30	£0.90	£1.50
2 Cover B ND	$0.50	$1.50	$2.50	£0.30	£0.90	£1.50
2 Cover B Newstand Edition, ND, same interior but with photo cover	$0.50	$1.50	$2.50	£0.30	£0.90	£1.50
Title Value:	$2.00	$6.00	$10.00	£1.20	£3.60	£6.00

STAR WARS

Marvel Comics Group; 1 Jul 1977-107 Sep 1986

(see Droids, Ewoks, Marvel Movie Showcase, Marvel Special Edition)

	$Good	$Fine	$N.Mint	£Good	£Fine	£N.Mint
1 ND 30c cover price (three variants with/without UPC code?)	$10.00	$30.00	$70.00	£5.00	£15.00	£35.00
1 35 cents cover, very rare in the U.K. with UPC code on cover (Note: documented sales on this item are very few and far between)	$62.50	$190.00	$450.00	£43.00	£125.00	£300.00
2	$6.50	$20.00	$40.00	£2.50	£7.50	£15.00
3	$5.00	$15.00	$30.00	£2.05	£6.25	£12.50
4-5	$5.00	$15.00	$30.00	£1.65	£5.00	£10.00
6 ND	$4.15	$12.50	$25.00	£1.30	£4.00	£8.00
7 ND new stories begin	$4.15	$12.50	$25.00	£1.30	£4.00	£8.00
8-10 ND	$4.15	$12.50	$25.00	£1.30	£4.00	£8.00
11-12 ND	$3.75	$11.00	$22.50	£1.25	£3.75	£7.50
13 ND John Byrne cover	$3.75	$11.00	$22.50	£1.25	£3.75	£7.50
14-15 ND	$3.75	$11.00	$22.50	£1.25	£3.75	£7.50
16 ND Walt Simonson art	$3.75	$11.00	$22.50	£1.25	£3.75	£7.50
17-20 ND	$3.75	$11.00	$22.50	£1.25	£3.75	£7.50
21-37 ND	$3.30	$10.00	$20.00	£1.00	£3.00	£6.00
38 ND Golden art	$3.30	$10.00	$20.00	£1.00	£3.00	£6.00
39-44 ND reprints Empire Strikes Back from Super Special 16, Williamson art	$3.75	$11.00	$22.50	£1.05	£3.25	£6.50
45-48 ND	$3.30	$10.00	$20.00	£1.00	£3.00	£6.00
49 ND Walt Simonson art	$3.30	$10.00	$20.00	£1.00	£3.00	£6.00
50 ND 52pgs, Williamson art	$4.15	$12.50	$25.00	£1.15	£3.50	£7.00
51-60 ND Walt Simonson art	$2.90	$8.75	$17.50	£0.80	£2.50	£5.00
61-63 ND Walt Simonson art	$2.90	$8.75	$17.50	£0.65	£2.00	£4.00
64 ND no Simonson	$2.90	$8.75	$17.50	£0.65	£2.00	£4.00
65-66 ND Walt Simonson art	$2.90	$8.75	$17.50	£0.65	£2.00	£4.00
67-80 ND	$2.90	$8.75	$17.50	£0.65	£2.00	£4.00
81-91 ND	$2.50	$7.50	$15.00	£0.55	£1.75	£3.50
92 ND Sienkiewicz cover (with Cynthia Martin)	$2.50	$7.50	$15.00	£0.55	£1.75	£3.50
93-99 ND	$2.50	$7.50	$15.00	£0.55	£1.75	£3.50
100 ND scarce in the U.K. DS	$4.15	$12.50	$25.00	£1.00	£3.00	£6.00
101-106 ND very scarce in the U.K., scarce in the U.S.	$4.15	$12.50	$25.00	£2.05	£6.25	£12.50
107 ND rare in the U.K., scarce in the U.S. Whilce Portacio inks	$9.00	$28.00	$55.00	£6.50	£20.00	£40.00
Title Value:	$427.35	$1286.50	$2660.00	£156.55	£472.00	£999.00

Note: #1-6 adapt Star Wars movie. 2nd prints of #1-6 have "Reprint" printed on the covers.

ARTISTS

Chaykin in 1-10. Infantino/Gene Day in 18, 21, 25. Simonson art in 16, 49, 51, 52, 55-66.

STAR WARS ANNUAL

Marvel Comics Group; 1 1979; 2 1982-3 Dec 1983

	$Good	$Fine	$N.Mint	£Good	£Fine	£N.Mint
1 ND 52pgs	$2.50	$7.50	$15.00	£1.30	£4.00	£8.00
2-3 ND 52pgs	$2.05	$6.25	$12.50	£1.05	£3.25	£6.50
Title Value:	$6.60	$20.00	$40.00	£3.40	£10.50	£21.00

STAR WARS GALAXY MAGAZINE

Topps,Magazine; 1 Oct 1994-present

	$Good	$Fine	$N.Mint	£Good	£Fine	£N.Mint
1 ND news, features and articles on Star Wars	$0.90	$2.70	$4.50	£0.60	£1.80	£3.00
1 Direct Market Edition, ND (Oct 1994) - pre-bagged with trading card, poster and ashcan edition of Star Wars: Dark Lords of Sith #1	$1.00	$3.00	$5.00	£0.70	£2.10	£3.50
2 ND news, features and articles on Star Wars	$0.90	$2.70	$4.50	£0.60	£1.80	£3.00
2 Direct Market Edition, ND (Jan 1995) - pre-bagged with X-Files #1 ashcan edition, Star Wars poster and Mastervision card, Star Wars trading card	$6.00	$18.00	$30.00	£4.00	£12.00	£20.00

	$Good	$Fine	$N.Mint	£Good	£Fine	£N.Mint
3 ND pre-bagged with Star Wars trading card and Skycap	*$0.90*	*$2.70*	*$4.50*	£0.60	£1.80	£3.00
3 Direct Market Edition, ND pre-bagged with trading cards	*$1.00*	*$3.00*	*$5.00*	£0.70	£2.10	£3.50
4 ND pre-bagged with three trading cards	*$0.90*	*$2.70*	*$4.50*	£0.60	£1.80	£3.00
4 Direct Market Edition, ND pre-bagged with trading cards	*$1.00*	*$3.00*	*$5.00*	£0.70	£2.10	£3.50
5 ND pre-bagged with three trading cards	*$0.90*	*$2.70*	*$4.50*	£0.60	£1.80	£3.00
5 Direct Market Edition, ND pre-bagged with trading cards	*$1.00*	*$3.00*	*$5.00*	£0.70	£2.10	£3.50
6 ND pre-bagged with promo-card and collectible	*$0.90*	*$2.70*	*$4.50*	£0.60	£1.80	£3.00
6 Direct Market Edition, ND pre-bagged with trading cards	*$1.00*	*$3.00*	*$5.00*	£0.70	£2.10	£3.50
7 ND pre-bagged with promo-cards	*$0.90*	*$2.70*	*$4.50*	£0.60	£1.80	£3.00
7 Direct Market Edition, ND pre-bagged with trading cards	*$1.00*	*$3.00*	*$5.00*	£0.70	£2.10	£3.50
8-10 ND pre-bagged with promo-card and collectible	*$0.90*	*$2.70*	*$4.50*	£0.60	£1.80	£3.00
Title Value:	*$21.00*	*$63.00*	*$105.00*	£14.20	£42.60	£71.00

STAR WARS IN 3-D

Blackthorne;(3-D Series #30,#47,#48); 1 Winter 1987-4 1988

	$Good	$Fine	$N.Mint	£Good	£Fine	£N.Mint
1 ND all with bound-in 3-D glasses (25% less without glasses)	*$1.00*	*$3.00*	*$5.00*	£0.60	£1.80	£3.00
2-4 ND	*$0.80*	*$2.40*	*$4.00*	£0.50	£1.50	£2.50
Title Value:	*$3.40*	*$10.20*	*$17.00*	£2.10	£6.30	£10.50

STAR WARS: BATTLE OF THE BOUNTY HUNTERS POP-UP COMIC BOOK

Dark Horse,OS; nn Jun 1996

	$Good	$Fine	$N.Mint	£Good	£Fine	£N.Mint
nn ND features Boba Fett; Christopher Moeller painted art; 7" x 10" format	*$3.60*	*$10.50*	*$18.00*	£2.40	£7.00	£12.00
Title Value:	*$3.60*	*$10.50*	*$18.00*	£2.40	£7.00	£12.00

STAR WARS: BOBA FETT

Dark Horse; 1 Dec 1995; 2 Sep 1996

	$Good	$Fine	$N.Mint	£Good	£Fine	£N.Mint
1 ND 48pgs, sub-titled "Bounty on Bar-Kooda"; John Wagner script, Cam Kennedy art	*$1.00*	*$3.00*	*$5.00*	£0.70	£2.10	£3.50
2 ND sub-titled "When the Fat Lady Swings"; John Wagner script, Cam Kennedy art	*$0.80*	*$2.40*	*$4.00*	£0.50	£1.50	£2.50
Title Value:	*$1.80*	*$5.40*	*$9.00*	£1.20	£3.60	£6.00

STAR WARS: BOBA FETT: TWIN ENGINES OF DESTRUCTION

Dark Horse,OS; 1 Jan 1997

	$Good	$Fine	$N.Mint	£Good	£Fine	£N.Mint
1 ND Andy Mangels script, John Nadeau and Jordi Ensign art	*$0.60*	*$1.80*	*$3.00*	£0.40	£1.20	£2.00
Title Value:	*$0.60*	*$1.80*	*$3.00*	£0.40	£1.20	£2.00

STAR WARS: DARK EMPIRE

Dark Horse,MS; 1 Feb 1992-6 Dec 1992

	$Good	$Fine	$N.Mint	£Good	£Fine	£N.Mint
1 Tom Veitch script, Cam Kennedy art begins, cover paintings by Dave Dorman begin	*$2.50*	*$7.50*	*$12.50*	£1.60	£4.80	£8.00
1 2nd printing, Aug 1992	*$0.80*	*$2.40*	*$4.00*	£0.50	£1.50	£2.50
2 scarce in the U.K.	*$3.00*	*$9.00*	*$15.00*	£1.60	£4.80	£8.00
2 2nd printing, Aug 1992	*$0.80*	*$2.40*	*$4.00*	£0.50	£1.50	£2.50
3	*$1.50*	*$4.50*	*$7.50*	£1.00	£3.00	£5.00
3 2nd printing, Oct 1992	*$0.60*	*$1.80*	*$3.00*	£0.40	£1.20	£2.00
4	*$1.00*	*$3.00*	*$5.00*	£0.70	£2.10	£3.50
5-6	*$0.80*	*$2.40*	*$4.00*	£0.60	£1.80	£3.00
Title Value:	*$11.80*	*$35.40*	*$59.00*	£7.50	£22.50	£37.50

Note: all Non-Distributed on the news-stands in the U.K.

				£Good	£Fine	£N.Mint
Star Wars: Dark Empire Softcover Collection (Apr 1993) reprints mini-series with text and sketch pages				£2.40	£7.20	£12.00
(2nd print - Jul 1994)				£2.20	£6.60	£11.00
Signed, Limited Hardcover Edition (May 1993), gold foil embossed cover, 1000 copies				£15.00	£45.00	£75.00

STAR WARS: DARK EMPIRE II

Dark Horse,MS; 1 Dec 1994-6 May 1995

	$Good	$Fine	$N.Mint	£Good	£Fine	£N.Mint
1 ND Tom Veitch script, Cam Kennedy art; painted covers by Dave Dorman	*$0.80*	*$2.40*	*$4.00*	£0.50	£1.50	£2.50
2-6 ND Tom Veitch script, Cam Kennedy art; painted covers by Dave Dorman	*$0.60*	*$1.80*	*$3.00*	£0.40	£1.20	£2.00
Title Value:	*$3.80*	*$11.40*	*$19.00*	£2.50	£7.50	£12.50
Star Wars: Dark Empire II (Aug 1995) Trade paperback reprints issues #1-6 plus cover paintings				£2.40	£7.20	£12.00
Star Wars: Dark Empire II Hardcover Limited Edition (Feb 1996) foil-stamped leather cover and signature plate				£11.00	£33.00	£66.00

STAR WARS: DARK EMPIRE TRADE PAPERBACK PREVIEW

Dark Horse,OS; nn Mar 1996

	$Good	$Fine	$N.Mint	£Good	£Fine	£N.Mint
nn ND preview of Star Wars: Dark Empire collection in comic book form reprinting the first chapter of the story	*$0.20*	*$0.60*	*$1.00*	£0.10	£0.35	£0.65
Title Value:	*$0.20*	*$0.60*	*$1.00*	£0.10	£0.35	£0.65

STAR WARS: DROIDS

Dark Horse,MS; 1 Apr 1994-6 Sep 1994

	$Good	$Fine	$N.Mint	£Good	£Fine	£N.Mint
1 ND	*$0.60*	*$1.80*	*$3.00*	£0.60	£1.80	£3.00
2-6 ND	*$0.50*	*$1.50*	*$2.50*	£0.30	£0.90	£1.50
Title Value:	*$3.10*	*$9.30*	*$15.50*	£2.10	£6.30	£10.50
Special (Jan 1995)				£0.30	£0.90	£1.50
Star Wars: Droids (Apr 1995) Trade paperback collects story from Dark Horse Comics #17-19, Star Wars: Droids #1-6 and 8pg story from Star Wars Galaxy Magazine				£2.40	£7.20	£12.00
Star Wars: Droids - The Kalarba Adventures Limited Edition Hardcover (Jun 1996) collects mini-series, with dust-jacket and signature plate				£11.00	£33.00	£66.00

STAR WARS: DROIDS (2ND SERIES)

Dark Horse,MS; 1 Apr 1995-8 Nov 1995

	$Good	$Fine	$N.Mint	£Good	£Fine	£N.Mint
1-7 ND Ian Gibson art	*$0.50*	*$1.50*	*$2.50*	£0.30	£0.90	£1.50
8 ND	*$0.50*	*$1.50*	*$2.50*	£0.30	£0.90	£1.50
Title Value:	*$4.00*	*$12.00*	*$20.00*	£2.40	£7.20	£12.00

STAR WARS: EMPIRE'S END

Dark Horse,MS; 1 Oct 1995-2 Nov 1995

	$Good	$Fine	$N.Mint	£Good	£Fine	£N.Mint
1-2 ND Tom Veitch script, Jim Baikie art; painted covers by Dave Dorman	*$0.60*	*$1.80*	*$3.00*	£0.40	£1.20	£2.00
Title Value:	*$1.20*	*$3.60*	*$6.00*	£0.80	£2.40	£4.00

STAR WARS: HEIR TO THE EMPIRE

Dark Horse,MS; 1 Oct 1995-6 Mar 1996

	$Good	$Fine	$N.Mint	£Good	£Fine	£N.Mint
1 ND Mike Baron script, Olivier Vatine and Fred Blanchard art begins	*$0.60*	*$1.80*	*$3.00*	£0.40	£1.20	£2.00
2-6 ND	*$0.60*	*$1.80*	*$3.00*	£0.40	£1.20	£2.00
Title Value:	*$3.60*	*$10.80*	*$18.00*	£2.40	£7.20	£12.00

STAR WARS: JABBA THE HUTT

Dark Horse,OS; 1 Mar 1995

	$Good	$Fine	$N.Mint	£Good	£Fine	£N.Mint
1 ND Jim Woodring script, Art Wetherell art; cover by Steve Bissette and Cam Kennedy	*$0.50*	*$1.50*	*$2.50*	£0.30	£0.90	£1.50
Title Value:	*$0.50*	*$1.50*	*$2.50*	£0.30	£0.90	£1.50

STAR WARS: JABBA THE HUTT - BETRAYAL

Dark Horse,OS; nn Feb 1996

	$Good	$Fine	$N.Mint	£Good	£Fine	£N.Mint
nn ND painted cover by Mark Harrison	*$0.50*	*$1.50*	*$2.50*	£0.30	£0.90	£1.50
Title Value:	*$0.50*	*$1.50*	*$2.50*	£0.30	£0.90	£1.50

STAR WARS: JABBA THE HUTT - THE DYNASTY TRAP

Dark Horse,OS; 1 Aug 1995

	$Good	$Fine	$N.Mint	£Good	£Fine	£N.Mint
1 ND	*$0.50*	*$1.50*	*$2.50*	£0.30	£0.90	£1.50
Title Value:	*$0.50*	*$1.50*	*$2.50*	£0.30	£0.90	£1.50

STAR WARS: JABBA THE HUTT: THE HUNGER OF PRINCESS NAMPI

Dark Horse,OS; 1 Jun 1995

	$Good	$Fine	$N.Mint	£Good	£Fine	£N.Mint
1 ND Jim Woodring script, Art Wetherell art	*$0.50*	*$1.50*	*$2.50*	£0.30	£0.90	£1.50
Title Value:	*$0.50*	*$1.50*	*$2.50*	£0.30	£0.90	£1.50

STAR WARS: RIVER OF CHAOS

Dark Horse,MS; 1 May 1995-4 Aug 1995

	$Good	$Fine	$N.Mint	£Good	£Fine	£N.Mint
1-4 ND June Brigman and Roy Richardson art	*$0.50*	*$1.50*	*$2.50*	£0.30	£0.90	£1.50
Title Value:	*$2.00*	*$6.00*	*$10.00*	£1.20	£3.60	£6.00

STAR WARS: SHADOWS OF THE EMPIRE

Dark Horse,MS; 1 May 1996-6 Oct 1996

	$Good	$Fine	$N.Mint	£Good	£Fine	£N.Mint
1-6 ND John Wagner script, Killian Plunkett and P. Craig Russell art	*$0.60*	*$1.80*	*$3.00*	£0.40	£1.20	£2.00
Title Value:	*$3.60*	*$10.80*	*$18.00*	£2.40	£7.20	£12.00

STAR WARS: SPLINTER OF THE MIND'S EYE

Dark Horse,MS; 1 Dec 1995-4 Mar 1996

	$Good	$Fine	$N.Mint	£Good	£Fine	£N.Mint
1-4 ND Terry Austin script, Chris Sprouse art	*$0.50*	*$1.50*	*$2.50*	£0.30	£0.90	£1.50
Title Value:	*$2.00*	*$6.00*	*$10.00*	£1.20	£3.60	£6.00

STAR WARS: TALES FROM MOS EISLEY

Dark Horse,OS; nn Mar 1996

	$Good	$Fine	$N.Mint	£Good	£Fine	£N.Mint
nn ND collects stories originally published in Topps Comics Star Wars Galaxy Magazine	*$0.60*	*$1.80*	*$3.00*	£0.40	£1.20	£2.00
Title Value:	*$0.60*	*$1.80*	*$3.00*	£0.40	£1.20	£2.00

STAR WARS: TALES OF THE JEDI

Dark Horse,MS; 1 Oct 1993-5 Feb 1994

	$Good	$Fine	$N.Mint	£Good	£Fine	£N.Mint
1 ND	*$0.80*	*$2.40*	*$4.00*	£0.50	£1.50	£2.50
2-5 ND	*$0.60*	*$1.80*	*$3.00*	£0.40	£1.20	£2.00
Title Value:	*$3.20*	*$9.60*	*$16.00*	£2.10	£6.30	£10.50
Star Wars: Tales of the Jedi (Jul 1994) Trade paperback reprints mini-series, painted cover by Dave Dorman				£2.00	£6.00	£10.00

STAR WARS: TALES OF THE JEDI - DARK LORDS OF SITH BOOK 1

Dark Horse,MS; 1 Oct 1994-6 Mar 1995

	$Good	$Fine	$N.Mint	£Good	£Fine	£N.Mint
1-6 ND Tom Veitch script, Kevin Anderson art; pre-bagged with trading card	*$0.50*	*$1.50*	*$2.50*	£0.30	£0.90	£1.50
Title Value:	*$3.00*	*$9.00*	*$15.00*	£1.80	£5.40	£9.00
Star Wars: Dark Lords of the Sith (Dec 1995) Trade paperback reprints mini-series with new pianted cover by Hugh Fleming				£2.40	£7.20	£12.00

STAR WARS: TALES OF THE JEDI - THE FREEDON NADD UPRISING

Dark Horse,MS; 1 Jul 1994-2 Aug 1994

	$Good	$Fine	$N.Mint	£Good	£Fine	£N.Mint
1-2 ND Dave Dorman painted cover	*$0.50*	*$1.50*	*$2.50*	£0.30	£0.90	£1.50
Title Value:	*$1.00*	*$3.00*	*$5.00*	£0.60	£1.80	£3.00

STAR WARS: TALES OF THE JEDI - THE GOLDEN AGE OF SITH

Dark Horse,MS; 0 Jul 1996; 1 Oct 1996-5 Feb 1997

	$Good	$Fine	$N.Mint	£Good	£Fine	£N.Mint
0 ND 16pgs	*$0.20*	*$0.60*	*$1.00*	£0.10	£0.35	£0.65
1-5 ND Kevin J. Anderson script, Dario Carrasco art	*$0.60*	*$1.80*	*$3.00*	£0.40	£1.20	£2.00
Title Value:	*$3.20*	*$9.60*	*$16.00*	£2.10	£6.35	£10.65

STAR WARS: TALES OF THE JEDI - THE SITH WAR

Dark Horse,MS; 1 Aug 1995-6 Jan 1996

	$Good	$Fine	$N.Mint	£Good	£Fine	£N.Mint
1-6 ND Kevin Anderson script, Dario Carrasco and Jordi Ensign art	*$0.50*	*$1.50*	*$2.50*	£0.30	£0.90	£1.50
Title Value:	*$3.00*	*$9.00*	*$15.00*	£1.80	£5.40	£9.00

Star Wars: Tales of the Jedi - The Sith War (Jun 1996)

	$Good	$Fine	$N.Mint	£Good	£Fine	£N.Mint
collects mini-series with new cover by Mathieu Lauffrey				£2.40	£7.20	£12.00

STAR WARS: X-WING - ROGUE SQUADRON: THE PHANTOM AFFAIR

Dark Horse,MS; 1 Feb 1995-4 May 1996

	$Good	$Fine	$N.Mint	£Good	£Fine	£N.Mint
1-4 ND	$0.60	$1.80	$3.00	£0.40	£1.20	£2.00
Title Value:	$2.40	$7.20	$12.00	£1.60	£4.80	£8.00

STAR WARS: X-WING ROGUE SQUADRON

Dark Horse,MS; 1 Jul 1995-4 Oct 1995

	$Good	$Fine	$N.Mint	£Good	£Fine	£N.Mint
1 ND Mike Baron script, Allen Nunis and Andy Mushynsky art begins; Dave Dorman painted covers	$0.60	$1.80	$3.00	£0.40	£1.20	£2.00
2-4 ND	$0.60	$1.80	$3.00	£0.40	£1.20	£2.00
Title Value:	$2.40	$7.20	$12.00	£1.60	£4.80	£8.00

STAR WARS: X-WING ROGUE SQUADRON: THE WARRIOR PRINCESS

Dark Horse,MS; 1 Oct 1996-4 Jan 1997

	$Good	$Fine	$N.Mint	£Good	£Fine	£N.Mint
1-4 ND	$0.60	$1.80	$3.00	£0.40	£1.20	£2.00
Title Value:	$2.40	$7.20	$12.00	£1.60	£4.80	£8.00

STAR WARS: X-WING SQUADRON - BATTLEGROUND: TATTOINE

Dark Horse; 1 Jun 1996-4 Sep 1996

	$Good	$Fine	$N.Mint	£Good	£Fine	£N.Mint
1-4 ND Mark Harrison covers	$0.60	$1.80	$3.00	£0.40	£1.20	£2.00
Title Value:	$2.40	$7.20	$12.00	£1.60	£4.80	£8.00

STAR-SPANGLED WAR STORIES

National Periodical Publications/DC Comics; 1 (#131) Aug 1952-204 Feb/Mar 1977

(issues #1 & #2 called Star Spangled Comics, numbered #131 & #132)
(becomes Unknown Soldier)

	$Good	$Fine	$N.Mint	£Good	£Fine	£N.Mint
1 scarce in the U.K. number 131 on cover, continuing the numbering of Star Spangled Comics	$85.00	$260.00	$780.00	£57.50	£170.00	£520.00
2 scarce in the U.K. number 132 on cover	$67.50	$205.00	$550.00	£46.00	£135.00	£370.00
3 scarce in the U.K. number 133 on cover	$31.00	$92.50	$250.00	£21.00	£62.50	£170.00
3 no number on cover scarce in the U.K.	$28.00	$82.50	$225.00	£18.50	£55.00	£150.00
4 no number on cover	$31.00	$92.50	$250.00	£21.00	£62.50	£170.00
5 numbers on cover begin	$31.00	$92.50	$250.00	£21.00	£62.50	£170.00
6	$31.00	$92.50	$250.00	£21.00	£62.50	£170.00
7-10	$25.00	$75.00	$200.00	£16.50	£50.00	£135.00
11-20	$21.50	$65.00	$175.00	£15.00	£45.00	£120.00
21-30	$20.00	$60.00	$160.00	£13.50	£41.00	£110.00
31 1st Code approved issue	$13.50	$41.00	$110.00	£9.25	£28.00	£75.00
32-40	$13.50	$41.00	$110.00	£9.25	£28.00	£75.00
41-44	$13.50	$41.00	$95.00	£9.25	£28.00	£65.00
45 1st painted (grey-tone) cover by DC, starting a long collectible line that lasted into the 1960s	$17.50	$52.50	$125.00	£12.00	£36.00	£85.00
46-50	$13.50	$41.00	$95.00	£9.25	£28.00	£65.00
51-60	$11.00	$34.00	$80.00	£7.50	£22.50	£52.50
61-70	$10.50	$32.00	$75.00	£7.00	£21.00	£50.00
71-83	$10.00	$30.00	$70.00	£6.25	£19.00	£45.00
84 origin and 1st appearance Mlle. Marie	$22.00	$65.00	$155.00	£15.00	£45.00	£105.00
85-86 Mille. Marie	$12.50	$39.00	$90.00	£7.75	£23.50	£55.00
1st official distribution in the U.K.						
87-88 scarce in the U.K. Mille. Marie	$12.50	$39.00	$90.00	£7.75	£23.50	£55.00
89 scarce in the U.K. fab Mille. Marie cover	$12.50	$39.00	$90.00	£7.75	£23.50	£55.00
90 scarce in the U.K. 1st War That Time Forgot (ends #137), classic dinosaur covers begin	$48.00	$140.00	$380.00	£28.00	£82.50	£225.00
91 scarce in the U.K.	$9.25	$28.00	$65.00	£5.50	£17.00	£40.00
92 scarce in the U.K. 2nd dinosaur cover	$19.00	$57.50	$135.00	£11.00	£34.00	£80.00
93 scarce in the U.K.	$9.25	$28.00	$65.00	£5.50	£17.00	£40.00
94-99 scarce in the U.K. dinosaur covers	$19.00	$57.50	$135.00	£11.00	£34.00	£80.00
100 very scarce in the U.K. dinosaur cover	$22.50	$67.50	$160.00	£12.50	£39.00	£90.00
101-106 scarce in the U.K. dinosaur covers	$13.50	$41.00	$95.00	£8.00	£24.50	£57.50
107-110	$13.50	$41.00	$95.00	£8.00	£24.50	£57.50
111-125	$13.50	$41.00	$95.00	£6.75	£20.00	£47.50
126	$8.50	$26.00	$60.00	£5.00	£15.00	£35.00
127-133 ND	$12.00	$36.00	$85.00	£6.75	£20.00	£47.50
134 ND Neal Adams art	$12.50	$39.00	$90.00	£7.00	£21.00	£50.00
135-136 ND	$12.00	$36.00	$85.00	£6.25	£19.00	£45.00
137 ND last dinosaur cover	$12.00	$36.00	$85.00	£6.25	£19.00	£45.00
138 ND 1st appearance Enemy Ace (series ends #150), Kubert art	$15.50	$47.00	$110.00	£8.50	£26.00	£60.00
139 ND 2nd appearance Enemy Ace	$12.00	$36.00	$85.00	£6.25	£19.00	£45.00
140-143 ND Enemy Ace	$9.25	$28.00	$65.00	£4.60	£13.50	£32.50
144 ND Enemy Ace, Neal Adams and Kubert art	$10.00	$30.00	$70.00	£5.00	£15.00	£35.00
145 ND Enemy Ace	$9.25	$28.00	$65.00	£4.60	£13.50	£32.50
146-150 ND Enemy Ace	$7.00	$21.00	$50.00	£3.90	£11.50	£27.50
151 ND 1st appearance Unknown Soldier; Enemy Ace reprints begin (to #161)	$8.50	$26.00	$60.00	£5.25	£16.00	£37.50
152-153 ND	$2.85	$8.50	$20.00	£1.75	£5.25	£12.50
154 ND origin Unknown Soldier	$6.25	$19.00	$45.00	£3.20	£9.50	£22.50
155 ND	$2.85	$8.50	$20.00	£1.75	£5.25	£12.50
156 scarce in the U.K.	$2.10	$6.25	$15.00	£0.85	£2.55	£6.00
157 Sgt. Rock appears in Unknown Soldier story	$1.40	$4.25	$10.00	£0.55	£1.70	£4.00
158-164 48pgs	$1.40	$4.25	$10.00	£0.70	£2.10	£5.00
165-167	$1.65	$5.00	$10.00	£0.65	£2.00	£4.00
168 scarce in the U.K.	$1.65	$5.00	$10.00	£0.80	£2.50	£5.00
169-170	$1.65	$5.00	$10.00	£0.65	£2.00	£4.00
171-180	$1.00	$3.00	$6.00	£0.40	£1.25	£2.50
181-183 Enemy Ace vs. The Balloon Buster	$0.80	$2.50	$5.00	£0.40	£1.25	£2.50
184-191	$0.80	$2.50	$5.00	£0.40	£1.25	£2.50
192-195	$0.80	$2.50	$5.00	£0.30	£1.00	£2.00
196 scarce in the U.K.	$0.80	$2.50	$5.00	£0.40	£1.25	£2.50
197 scarce in the U.K. Kaluta inks	$0.80	$2.50	$5.00	£0.40	£1.25	£2.50
198-199	$0.80	$2.50	$5.00	£0.30	£1.00	£2.00
200 scarce in the U.K.	$0.80	$2.50	$5.00	£0.40	£1.25	£2.50
201-203	$0.80	$2.50	$5.00	£0.30	£1.00	£2.00
204 scarce in the U.K.	$0.80	$2.50	$5.00	£0.40	£1.25	£2.50
Title Value:	$2417.95	$7313.75	$18080.00	£1511.50	£4551.95	£11453.00

FEATURES

Enemy Ace in 138-150 (2pgs only in 146, remainder reprint), 181-183, 200. Mlle.Marie in 84-91. Suicide Squadron in 110, 116-121, 125, 127, 128. Unknown Soldier in 151-204. War That Time Forgot in 90, 92, 94-137.

REPRINT FEATURES

Ballon Buster in 160, 163. Enemy Ace in 151-159, 161. Viking Prince in 149, 150.

STARBLAST

Marvel Comics Group,MS; 1 Jan 1994-4 Apr 1994

	$Good	$Fine	$N.Mint	£Good	£Fine	£N.Mint
1 48pgs, Starblast part 1, Nova, Quasar, Hyperion, Black Bolt appear	$0.40	$1.20	$2.00	£0.25	£0.75	£1.25
2 Starblast part 4	$0.35	$1.05	$1.75	£0.20	£0.60	£1.00
3 Starblast part 8	$0.35	$1.05	$1.75	£0.20	£0.60	£1.00
4 Starblast part 12	$0.35	$1.05	$1.75	£0.20	£0.60	£1.00
Title Value:	$1.45	$4.35	$7.25	£0.85	£2.55	£4.25

STARBLAST CROSSOVER INDEX

Marvel Comics Group; 1994

Cross-over storyline running throughout the following titles: **Starblast #1**, **Quasar #54**, **Fantastic Four #385**, **Namor #46**, **Starblast #2**, **Quasar #55**, **Fantastic Four #386**, **Namor #47**, **Starblast #3**, **Quasar #56**, **Namor #48**, **Quasar #57**, **Starblast #4**.

STARBLAZERS (1ST SERIES)

Comico,MS; 1 Apr 1987-4 Jul 1987

	$Good	$Fine	$N.Mint	£Good	£Fine	£N.Mint
1-4 ND	$0.40	$1.20	$2.00	£0.25	£0.75	£1.25
Title Value:	$1.60	$4.80	$8.00	£1.00	£3.00	£5.00
Trade paperback (Sep 1991) reprints series with new Ken Steacy cover				£2.20	£6.60	£11.00

STARBLAZERS (2ND SERIES)

Comico,MS; 1 1989-5 1989

	$Good	$Fine	$N.Mint	£Good	£Fine	£N.Mint
1-5 ND Steacy wraparound covers; colour	$0.40	$1.20	$2.00	£0.25	£0.75	£1.25
Title Value:	$2.00	$6.00	$10.00	£1.25	£3.75	£6.25

STARDUSTERS

Night Wynd,MS; 1 Dec 1991-4 Mar 1992

	$Good	$Fine	$N.Mint	£Good	£Fine	£N.Mint
1-4 ND	$0.40	$1.20	$2.00	£0.25	£0.75	£1.25
Title Value:	$1.60	$4.80	$8.00	£1.00	£3.00	£5.00

STARFIRE

DC Comics; 1 Aug/Sep 1976-8 Oct/Nov 1977

	$Good	$Fine	$N.Mint	£Good	£Fine	£N.Mint
1 scarce in the U.K. origin and 1st appearance Starfire (not to be confused with Teen Titans Starfire)	$0.30	$1.00	$2.00	£0.20	£0.60	£1.25
2-8	$0.25	$0.75	$1.50	£0.15	£0.50	£1.00
Title Value:	$2.05	$6.25	$12.50	£1.25	£4.10	£8.25

STARFORCE SIX SPECIAL

AC Comics,OS; nn 1985

	$Good	$Fine	$N.Mint	£Good	£Fine	£N.Mint
nn ND	$0.40	$1.20	$2.00	£0.25	£0.75	£1.25
Title Value:	$0.40	$1.20	$2.00	£0.25	£0.75	£1.25

STARGATE

Entity Comics,MS; 1 Jul 1996-4 Oct 1996

	$Good	$Fine	$N.Mint	£Good	£Fine	£N.Mint
1 ND adaptation of film	$0.60	$1.80	$3.00	£0.40	£1.20	£2.00
1 Special Edition, ND foil enhanced photo covers plus behind the scenes photos	$0.70	$2.10	$3.50	£0.50	£1.50	£2.50
2 ND adaptation of film	$0.60	$1.80	$3.00	£0.40	£1.20	£2.00
2 Special Edition, ND foil enhanced photo covers plus behind the scenes photos	$0.70	$2.10	$3.50	£0.50	£1.50	£2.50
3 ND adaptation of film	$0.60	$1.80	$3.00	£0.40	£1.20	£2.00
3 Special Edition, ND foil enhanced photo covers plus behind the scenes photos	$0.70	$2.10	$3.50	£0.50	£1.50	£2.50
4 ND adaptation of film						

	$Good	$Fine	$N.Mint	£Good	£Fine	£N.Mint
	$0.60	$1.80	$3.00	£0.40	£1.20	£2.00
4 Special Edition, ND foil enhanced photo covers plus behind the scenes photos						
	$0.70	$2.10	$3.50	£0.50	£1.50	£2.50
Title Value:	$5.20	$15.60	$26.00	£3.60	£10.80	£18.00

STARGATE DOOMSDAY WORLD

Entity Comics; 1 Nov 1996-present

	$Good	$Fine	$N.Mint	£Good	£Fine	£N.Mint
1 ND Raff Ienco script and art with John Migliore begins						
	$0.60	$1.80	$3.00	£0.40	£1.20	£2.00
1 Collectors Edtion, ND prism foil card-stock cover						
	$0.70	$2.10	$3.50	£0.50	£1.50	£2.50
2 ND	$0.60	$1.80	$3.00	£0.40	£1.20	£2.00
Title Value:	$1.90	$5.70	$9.50	£1.30	£3.90	£6.50

STARJAMMERS

Marvel Comics Group,MS; 1 Oct 1995-4 Jan 1996

	$Good	$Fine	$N.Mint	£Good	£Fine	£N.Mint
1-4 ND Warren Ellis script, Carlos Pacheco and Cam Smith art; foil stamped cover						
	$0.60	$1.80	$3.00	£0.40	£1.20	£2.00
Title Value:	$2.40	$7.20	$12.00	£1.60	£4.80	£8.00

STARK: FUTURE

Aircel; 1 1986-17 1987

	$Good	$Fine	$N.Mint	£Good	£Fine	£N.Mint
1-17 ND	$0.40	$1.20	$2.00	£0.25	£0.75	£1.25
Title Value:	$6.80	$20.40	$34.00	£4.25	£12.75	£21.25

STARLIGHT AGENCY

Antarctic Press,MS; 1 Sep 1991-3 Nov 1991

	$Good	$Fine	$N.Mint	£Good	£Fine	£N.Mint
1-3 ND	$0.40	$1.20	$2.00	£0.25	£0.75	£1.25
Title Value:	$1.20	$3.60	$6.00	£0.75	£2.25	£3.75

STARLORD

Marvel Comics Group,MS; 1 Dec 1996-3 Feb 1997

	$Good	$Fine	$N.Mint	£Good	£Fine	£N.Mint
1-3 ND Timothy Zahn script, Dan Lawlis art						
	$0.50	$1.50	$2.50	£0.30	£0.90	£1.50
Title Value:	$1.50	$4.50	$7.50	£0.90	£2.70	£4.50

STARLORD MEGAZINE

Marvel Comics Group,OS; nn Nov 1996

	$Good	$Fine	$N.Mint	£Good	£Fine	£N.Mint
nn ND 64pgs, reprints Starlord by Claremont, Byrne and Austin with new John Byrne cover						
	$0.60	$1.80	$3.00	£0.40	£1.20	£2.00
Title Value:	$0.60	$1.80	$3.00	£0.40	£1.20	£2.00

STARLORD, THE SPECIAL EDITION

Marvel Comics Group,OS; 1 Feb 1982

(see Marvel Comics Super Special #10, Marvel Premiere, Marvel Preview, Marvel Spotlight #6, #7)

	$Good	$Fine	$N.Mint	£Good	£Fine	£N.Mint
1 ND John Byrne art reprinted from Marvel Preview, additional pages by Golden; Gibbons Dr.Who back-up reprint						
	$1.00	$3.00	$5.00	£0.70	£2.10	£3.50
Title Value:	$1.00	$3.00	$5.00	£0.70	£2.10	£3.50

Note: Direct Sales; 1st Marvel Baxter paper comic.

STARMAN

DC Comics; 1 Oct 1988-46 May 1992

(see First Issue Special #12)

	$Good	$Fine	$N.Mint	£Good	£Fine	£N.Mint
1-4	$0.25	$0.75	$1.25	£0.15	£0.45	£0.75
5-6 Invasion X-over						
	$0.25	$0.75	$1.25	£0.15	£0.45	£0.75
7-8	$0.25	$0.75	$1.25	£0.15	£0.45	£0.75
9 Batman appears	$0.25	$0.75	$1.25	£0.15	£0.45	£0.75
10 Blockbuster appears						
	$0.25	$0.75	$1.25	£0.15	£0.45	£0.75
11-13	$0.25	$0.75	$1.25	£0.15	£0.45	£0.75
14 Superman appears						
	$0.25	$0.75	$1.25	£0.15	£0.45	£0.75
15-16	$0.25	$0.75	$1.25	£0.15	£0.45	£0.75
17-18 Power Girl appears						
	$0.25	$0.75	$1.25	£0.15	£0.45	£0.75
19-27	$0.25	$0.75	$1.25	£0.15	£0.45	£0.75
28 LD in the U.K. "Superman" appears, ties in with Superman #50						
	$0.25	$0.75	$1.25	£0.20	£0.60	£1.00
29	$0.25	$0.75	$1.25	£0.15	£0.45	£0.75
30-33 The Seduction of Starman story						
	$0.25	$0.75	$1.25	£0.15	£0.45	£0.75
34-37	$0.25	$0.75	$1.25	£0.15	£0.45	£0.75
38 War of the Gods tie-in						
	$0.25	$0.75	$1.25	£0.15	£0.45	£0.75
39-41	$0.25	$0.75	$1.25	£0.15	£0.45	£0.75
42 origin Starman begins, Eclipso appears						
	$0.25	$0.75	$1.25	£0.15	£0.45	£0.75
43 origin Starman continued, Eclipso, Lobo appear						
	$0.25	$0.75	$1.25	£0.15	£0.45	£0.75
44 Starman and Eclipso vs. Lobo						
	$0.25	$0.75	$1.25	£0.15	£0.45	£0.75
45 Power Girl appears						
	$0.25	$0.75	$1.25	£0.15	£0.45	£0.75
46	$0.25	$0.75	$1.25	£0.15	£0.45	£0.75
Title Value:	$11.50	$34.50	$57.50	£6.95	£20.85	£34.75

Note: 18 has free 16pg insert (see Batman #443, Superman #39)

STARMAN (2ND SERIES)

DC Comics; 0 Oct 1994; 1 Nov 1994-present

	$Good	$Fine	$N.Mint	£Good	£Fine	£N.Mint
0 (Oct 1994) Zero Hour X-over, origin						
	$1.60	$4.80	$8.00	£0.70	£2.10	£3.50
1	$1.60	$4.80	$8.00	£0.80	£2.40	£4.00
2	$1.20	$3.60	$6.00	£0.60	£1.80	£3.00
3	$0.50	$1.50	$2.50	£0.30	£0.90	£1.50
4	$0.80	$2.40	$4.00	£0.40	£1.20	£2.00
5 Starman vs. Starman						
	$0.80	$2.40	$4.00	£0.40	£1.20	£2.00
6 guest artist Teddy Kristiansen on a one-off story						
	$0.50	$1.50	$2.50	£0.30	£0.90	£1.50
7	$0.50	$1.50	$2.50	£0.30	£0.90	£1.50
8 becomes a Vertigo title						
	$0.50	$1.50	$2.50	£0.30	£0.90	£1.50
9-12	$0.50	$1.50	$2.50	£0.30	£0.90	£1.50
13 Underworld Unleashed						
	$0.45	$1.35	$2.25	£0.30	£0.90	£1.50
14-17	$0.45	$1.35	$2.25	£0.30	£0.90	£1.50
18 Starman vs. The Mist						
	$0.45	$1.35	$2.25	£0.30	£0.90	£1.50
19-23	$0.45	$1.35	$2.25	£0.30	£0.90	£1.50
24 covers fit together to form a painted tryptych (go look it up)						
	$0.45	$1.35	$2.25	£0.30	£0.90	£1.50
25-26 ND	$0.45	$1.35	$2.25	£0.30	£0.90	£1.50
27 ND Steve Yeowell guest art						
	$0.45	$1.35	$2.25	£0.30	£0.90	£1.50
28 ND	$0.45	$1.35	$2.25	£0.30	£0.90	£1.50
Title Value:	$17.20	$51.60	$85.25	£10.10	£30.30	£50.50
Starman: Sins of the Father (Jan 1996) Trade paperback collects issues #0-5, new painted cover by Tony Harris				£1.70	£5.10	£8.50

STARMAN ANNUAL

DC Comics; 1 Nov 1996-present

	$Good	$Fine	$N.Mint	£Good	£Fine	£N.Mint
1 ND 48pgs, Legends of the Dead Earth story						
	$0.70	$2.10	$3.50	£0.50	£1.50	£2.50
Title Value:	$0.70	$2.10	$3.50	£0.50	£1.50	£2.50

STARRIORS

Marvel Comics Group,MS Toy; 1 Aug 1984-4 Feb 1985

	$Good	$Fine	$N.Mint	£Good	£Fine	£N.Mint
1-4 ND	$0.15	$0.45	$0.75	£0.10	£0.30	£0.50
Title Value:	$0.60	$1.80	$3.00	£0.40	£1.20	£2.00

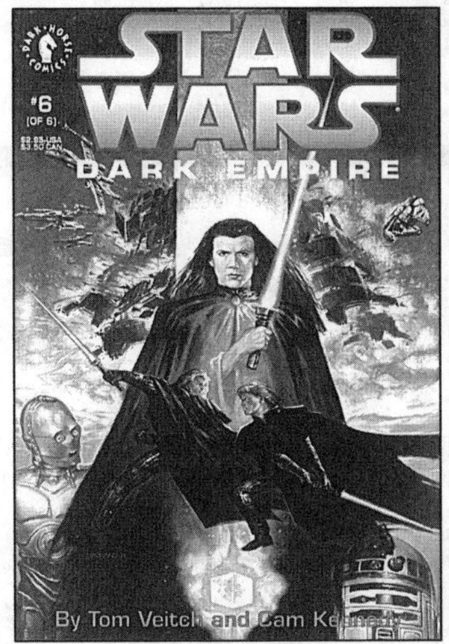

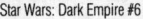

Star Wars: Dark Empire #6

Star-Spangled War Stories #89

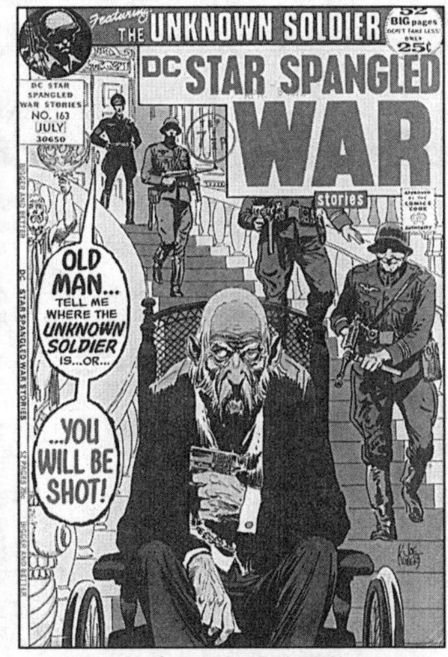

Star-Spangled War Stories #163

STARSLAYER

Pacific/First; 1 Feb 1982-34 Nov 1985

	$Good	$Fine	$N.Mint	£Good	£Fine	£N.Mint
1 Grell art begins	*$0.60*	*$1.80*	*$3.00*	£0.40	£1.20	£2.00
2 scarce in the U.K. origin and 1st appearance Rocketeer by Dave Stevens	*$1.50*	*$4.50*	*$7.50*	£1.00	£3.00	£5.00
3 2nd appearance Rocketeer by Stevens	*$1.20*	*$3.60*	*$6.00*	£0.80	£2.40	£4.00
4	*$0.60*	*$1.80*	*$3.00*	£0.40	£1.20	£2.00
5 2nd appearance Groo	*$1.50*	*$4.50*	*$7.50*	£1.00	£3.00	£5.00
6 last Pacific issue	*$0.50*	*$1.50*	*$2.50*	£0.30	£0.90	£1.50
7 1st First issue, last Grell art	*$0.50*	*$1.50*	*$2.50*	£0.30	£0.90	£1.50
8-9	*$0.30*	*$0.90*	*$1.50*	£0.20	£0.60	£1.00
10 1st appearance Grimjack	*$0.40*	*$1.20*	*$2.00*	£0.25	£0.75	£1.25
11-17	*$0.30*	*$0.90*	*$1.50*	£0.20	£0.60	£1.00
18 Starslayer meets Grimjack	*$0.30*	*$0.90*	*$1.50*	£0.20	£0.60	£1.00
19-20	*$0.30*	*$0.90*	*$1.50*	£0.20	£0.60	£1.00
21-34	*$0.25*	*$0.75*	*$1.25*	£0.15	£0.45	£0.75
Title Value:	*$13.90*	*$41.70*	*$69.50*	£8.95	£26.85	£44.75

Note: all Non-Distributed on the news-stands in the U.K.

STARSLAYER: THE DIRECTOR'S CUT

Valiant/Windjammer,MS; 1 Jun 1995-8 Oct 1995

	$Good	$Fine	$N.Mint	£Good	£Fine	£N.Mint
1-8 ND new story, pencil art and cover by Mike Grell; bi-weekly	*$0.50*	*$1.50*	*$2.50*	£0.30	£0.90	£1.50
Title Value:	*$4.00*	*$12.00*	*$20.00*	£2.40	£7.20	£12.00

STARSTREAM

Whitman; 1-4 1976

	$Good	$Fine	$N.Mint	£Good	£Fine	£N.Mint
1 ND scarce in the U.K. adaptations of sci-fi classics begins: "Who Goes There?" adapted by John W. Campbell Jnr. plus other stories featuring Frank Bolle and Garcia Lopez art; heavy stock paper covers begin	*$0.40*	*$1.25*	*$2.50*	£0.25	£0.75	£1.50
2-4 ND scarce in the U.K. Bolle and McWilliams art	*$0.40*	*$1.25*	*$2.50*	£0.25	£0.75	£1.50
Title Value:	*$1.60*	*$5.00*	*$10.00*	£1.00	£3.00	£6.00

STARSTRUCK

Dark Horse,MS; 1 Aug 1990-4 Mar 1991

(sub-titled "The Expanding Universe")

	$Good	$Fine	$N.Mint	£Good	£Fine	£N.Mint
1-3 ND 48pgs, reprints Marvel mini-series, Mike Kaluta art, black and white	*$0.60*	*$1.80*	*$3.00*	£0.40	£1.20	£2.00
4 ND 64pgs, reprints Marvel mini-series, Mike Kaluta art, black and white; includes two bound-in trading cards at centre-fold	*$0.90*	*$2.70*	*$4.50*	£0.60	£1.80	£3.00
Title Value:	*$2.70*	*$8.10*	*$13.50*	£1.80	£5.40	£9.00

STARSTRUCK

Marvel Comics Group/Epic,MS; 1 Mar 1985-6 Feb 1986

(see Marvel Graphic Novel; Rocketeer Adventure Magazine [Comico])

	$Good	$Fine	$N.Mint	£Good	£Fine	£N.Mint
1-6 ND Kaluta art and cover	*$0.50*	*$1.50*	*$2.50*	£0.30	£0.90	£1.50
Title Value:	*$3.00*	*$9.00*	*$15.00*	£1.80	£5.40	£9.00

STARTLING CRIME ILLUSTRATED

Arts Industria; 1 Jan 1991

	$Good	$Fine	$N.Mint	£Good	£Fine	£N.Mint
1 ND black and white, photo cover	*$0.25*	*$0.75*	*$1.25*	£0.15	£0.45	£0.75
Title Value:	*$0.25*	*$0.75*	*$1.25*	£0.15	£0.45	£0.75

STARWATCHERS

Valiant; 1 Sep 1994-3 Nov 1994

	$Good	$Fine	$N.Mint	£Good	£Fine	£N.Mint
1-2 ND Mike Leeke and Dick Giordano art	*$0.40*	*$1.20*	*$2.00*	£0.25	£0.75	£1.25
3 ND Chaos Effect tie-in; Mike Leeke and Dick Giordano art	*$0.40*	*$1.20*	*$2.00*	£0.25	£0.75	£1.25
Title Value:	*$1.20*	*$3.60*	*$6.00*	£0.75	£2.25	£3.75

STATE

Majestic Entertainment; 1 Dec 1993

	$Good	$Fine	$N.Mint	£Good	£Fine	£N.Mint
1 ND Phil Hester and Mike Sellers art begins	*$0.40*	*$1.20*	*$2.00*	£0.25	£0.75	£1.25
Title Value:	*$0.40*	*$1.20*	*$2.00*	£0.25	£0.75	£1.25

STATIC

DC Comics/Milestone; 1 Jun 1993-present

	$Good	$Fine	$N.Mint	£Good	£Fine	£N.Mint
1	*$0.30*	*$0.90*	*$1.50*	£0.20	£0.60	£1.00
1 Direct Market Edition, ND - pre-bagged with poster and the 4th set of jigsaw puzzle pieces	*$0.50*	*$1.50*	*$2.50*	£0.30	£0.90	£1.50
1 Platinum Edition, ND - platinum logo	*$1.20*	*$3.60*	*$6.00*	£0.80	£2.40	£4.00
2-7	*$0.30*	*$0.90*	*$1.50*	£0.20	£0.60	£1.00
8 spot varnished cover by Walt Simonson, continued in Shadow Cabinet #0	*$0.30*	*$0.90*	*$1.50*	£0.20	£0.60	£1.00
9-12	*$0.30*	*$0.90*	*$1.50*	£0.20	£0.60	£1.00
13 John Byrne cover	*$0.30*	*$0.90*	*$1.50*	£0.20	£0.60	£1.00
14 48pgs, Worlds Collide part 14 (conclusion)	*$0.45*	*$1.35*	*$2.25*	£0.30	£0.90	£1.50
15-20	*$0.30*	*$0.90*	*$1.50*	£0.20	£0.60	£1.00
21 The Blood Syndicate appear	*$0.30*	*$0.90*	*$1.50*	£0.20	£0.60	£1.00
22-24	*$0.30*	*$0.90*	*$1.50*	£0.20	£0.60	£1.00
25 48pgs, Hardware guest-stars	*$0.55*	*$1.65*	*$2.75*	£0.35	£1.05	£1.75
26	*$0.50*	*$1.50*	*$2.50*	£0.30	£0.90	£1.50
27 special 99 cents issue	*$0.20*	*$0.60*	*$1.00*	£0.15	£0.45	£0.75
28	*$0.50*	*$1.50*	*$2.50*	£0.30	£0.90	£1.50
29 Howard Chaykin cover	*$0.50*	*$1.50*	*$2.50*	£0.30	£0.90	£1.50
30	*$0.50*	*$1.50*	*$2.50*	£0.30	£0.90	£1.50
31 special 99 cents issue	*$0.20*	*$0.60*	*$1.00*	£0.15	£0.45	£0.75
32-44	*$0.50*	*$1.50*	*$2.50*	£0.30	£0.90	£1.50
45 ND Moebius cover	*$0.50*	*$1.50*	*$2.50*	£0.30	£0.90	£1.50
Title Value:	*$19.00*	*$57.00*	*$95.00*	£12.05	£36.15	£60.25

STATIC, CHARLTON ACTION FEATURING

Charlton; 11 Oct 1985-12 Dec 1985

	$Good	$Fine	$N.Mint	£Good	£Fine	£N.Mint
11-12 Steve Ditko cover and art	*$0.40*	*$1.20*	*$2.00*	£0.25	£0.75	£1.25
Title Value:	*$0.80*	*$2.40*	*$4.00*	£0.50	£1.50	£2.50

Note: very Limited Distribution in the U.K.

STEALTH FORCE

Malibu/Eternity; 1 Jul 1987-8 Apr 1988

	$Good	$Fine	$N.Mint	£Good	£Fine	£N.Mint
1-7 ND	*$0.40*	*$1.20*	*$2.00*	£0.25	£0.75	£1.25
8 ND 1st Eternity issue	*$0.40*	*$1.20*	*$2.00*	£0.25	£0.75	£1.25
Title Value:	*$3.20*	*$9.60*	*$16.00*	£2.00	£6.00	£10.00

STEED AND MRS. PEEL

Eclipse,MS; 1 Dec 1990-3 Jun 1991

(see The Avengers [Gold Key])

	$Good	$Fine	$N.Mint	£Good	£Fine	£N.Mint
1-3 ND 48pgs, Grant Morrison script, Ian Gibson art	*$1.00*	*$3.00*	*$5.00*	£0.70	£2.10	£3.50
Title Value:	*$3.00*	*$9.00*	*$15.00*	£2.10	£6.30	£10.50

STEEL

DC Comics; 0 Oct 1994; 1 Feb 1994-present

	$Good	$Fine	$N.Mint	£Good	£Fine	£N.Mint
0 (Oct 1994), Zero Hour X-over, Steel's armour takes on new capabilities	*$0.40*	*$1.20*	*$2.00*	£0.25	£0.75	£1.25
1 spin-off from The Reign of the Supermen; Louise Simonson script and Jon Bogdanove art begin	*$0.30*	*$0.90*	*$1.50*	£0.20	£0.60	£1.00
2-5	*$0.30*	*$0.90*	*$1.50*	£0.20	£0.60	£1.00
6 Worlds Collide X-over, continued in Blood Syndicate #16	*$0.30*	*$0.90*	*$1.50*	£0.20	£0.60	£1.00
7 Worlds Collide X-over, continued in Blood Syndicate #17	*$0.30*	*$0.90*	*$1.50*	£0.20	£0.60	£1.00
8 Zero Hour X-over	*$0.30*	*$0.90*	*$1.50*	£0.20	£0.60	£1.00
9-13	*$0.30*	*$0.90*	*$1.50*	£0.20	£0.60	£1.00
14 story continued from Superman #99 and continued in Adventures of Superman #522	*$0.30*	*$0.90*	*$1.50*	£0.20	£0.60	£1.00
15	*$0.30*	*$0.90*	*$1.50*	£0.20	£0.60	£1.00
16 upgraded coated paper stock (Miraweb Format) begins	*$0.40*	*$1.20*	*$2.00*	£0.25	£0.75	£1.25
17-20	*$0.40*	*$1.20*	*$2.00*	£0.25	£0.75	£1.25
21 Underworld Unleashed tie-in, Steel vs. Metallo	*$0.40*	*$1.20*	*$2.00*	£0.25	£0.75	£1.25
22-31	*$0.40*	*$1.20*	*$2.00*	£0.25	£0.75	£1.25
32 Steel vs. Blockbuster	*$0.40*	*$1.20*	*$2.00*	£0.25	£0.75	£1.25
33 ND	*$0.40*	*$1.20*	*$2.00*	£0.25	£0.75	£1.25
34 ND Christopher Priest scripts begin	*$0.40*	*$1.20*	*$2.00*	£0.25	£0.75	£1.25
35-36 ND	*$0.40*	*$1.20*	*$2.00*	£0.25	£0.75	£1.25
Title Value:	*$13.30*	*$39.90*	*$66.50*	£8.50	£25.50	£42.50

STEEL ANGEL

Caliber Press,MS; 1 Sep 1992-3 Jan 1993

	$Good	$Fine	$N.Mint	£Good	£Fine	£N.Mint
1-3 ND	*$0.40*	*$1.20*	*$2.00*	£0.25	£0.75	£1.25
Title Value:	*$1.20*	*$3.60*	*$6.00*	£0.75	£2.25	£3.75

STEEL ANNUAL

DC Comics; 1 Jul 1994-present

	$Good	$Fine	$N.Mint	£Good	£Fine	£N.Mint
1 64pgs, Elseworlds	*$0.60*	*$1.80*	*$3.00*	£0.40	£1.20	£2.00
2 64pgs, Year One	*$0.80*	*$2.40*	*$4.00*	£0.50	£1.50	£2.50
Title Value:	*$1.40*	*$4.20*	*$7.00*	£0.90	£2.70	£4.50

STEEL PULSE

True Fiction Publications; 1 Spring 1986

	$Good	$Fine	$N.Mint	£Good	£Fine	£N.Mint
1 ND	*$0.30*	*$0.90*	*$1.50*	£0.20	£0.60	£1.00
Title Value:	*$0.30*	*$0.90*	*$1.50*	£0.20	£0.60	£1.00

STEEL STERLING

(see Shield)

STEEL, THE INDESTRUCTIBLE MAN

DC Comics; 1 Mar 1978-5 Oct/Nov 1978

(see Justice League of America)

	$Good	$Fine	$N.Mint	£Good	£Fine	£N.Mint
1	*$0.50*	*$1.50*	*$3.00*	£0.25	£0.75	£1.50
2-4	*$0.30*	*$1.00*	*$2.00*	£0.15	£0.50	£1.00
5 ND 44pgs	*$0.50*	*$1.50*	*$3.00*	£0.25	£0.75	£1.50
Title Value:	*$1.90*	*$6.00*	*$12.00*	£0.95	£3.00	£6.00

STEELGRIP STARKEY

Marvel Comics Group/Epic,MS; 1 Jul 1986-6 Jun 1987

	$Good	$Fine	$N.Mint	£Good	£Fine	£N.Mint
1-6 ND Baxter paper	*$0.30*	*$0.90*	*$1.50*	£0.20	£0.60	£1.00
Title Value:	*$1.80*	*$5.40*	*$9.00*	£1.20	£3.60	£6.00

STEELTOWN ROCKERS

Marvel Comics Group,MS; 1 Apr 1990-6 Sep 1990

	$Good	$Fine	$N.Mint	£Good	£Fine	£N.Mint
1-6	*$0.15*	*$0.45*	*$0.75*	£0.10	£0.30	£0.50
Title Value:	*$0.90*	*$2.70*	*$4.50*	£0.60	£1.80	£3.00

STEVE CANYON 3-D

Kitchen Sink; 1 Jun 1986

Issue	$Good	$Fine	$N.Mint	£Good	£Fine	£N.Mint
1 ND Milton Caniff reprints; with bound-in 3-D glasses (25% less without glasses)	*$0.50*	*$1.50*	*$2.50*	£0.30	£0.90	£1.50
Title Value:	*$0.50*	*$1.50*	*$2.50*	£0.30	£0.90	£1.50

STEVE CANYON MAGAZINE

Kitchen Sink; 1 1986-24 1987 ?

Issue	$Good	$Fine	$N.Mint	£Good	£Fine	£N.Mint
1-18 ND	*$1.00*	*$3.00*	*$5.00*	£0.70	£2.10	£3.50
19 ND DS,40th Anniversary Special	*$1.50*	*$4.50*	*$7.50*	£1.00	£3.00	£5.00
20-21 ND	*$1.50*	*$4.50*	*$7.50*	£1.00	£3.00	£5.00
22-24 ND book form	*$2.50*	*$7.50*	*$12.50*	£1.50	£4.50	£7.50
Title Value:	*$30.00*	*$90.00*	*$150.00*	£20.10	£60.30	£100.50

STEVE ZODIAC AND THE FIREBALL XL-5

Gold Key; 1 Jan 1964

Issue	$Good	$Fine	$N.Mint	£Good	£Fine	£N.Mint
1 rare though distributed in the U.K.	*$10.00*	*$30.00*	*$70.00*	£7.00	£21.00	£50.00
Title Value:	*$10.00*	*$30.00*	*$70.00*	£7.00	£21.00	£50.00

STICKBOY

Revolutionary Comics/Fantagraphics; 1 1990-6 May 1993

Issue	$Good	$Fine	$N.Mint	£Good	£Fine	£N.Mint
1 ND	*$0.40*	*$1.20*	*$2.00*	£0.25	£0.75	£1.25
1 2nd printing ND	*$0.30*	*$0.90*	*$1.50*	£0.20	£0.60	£1.00
2-5 ND	*$0.40*	*$1.20*	*$2.00*	£0.25	£0.75	£1.25
6 ND 1st Fantagraphics issue (May 1993)	*$0.40*	*$1.20*	*$2.00*	£0.25	£0.75	£1.25
Title Value:	*$2.70*	*$8.10*	*$13.50*	£1.70	£5.10	£8.50

STIG'S INFERNO

Vortex/Eclipse; 1 May 1984-7 Mar 1987

Issue	$Good	$Fine	$N.Mint	£Good	£Fine	£N.Mint
1 ND scarce in the U.K. Ty Templeton art begins; black and white	*$0.40*	*$1.20*	*$2.00*	£0.30	£0.90	£1.50
2 ND scarce in the U.K.	*$0.40*	*$1.20*	*$2.00*	£0.30	£0.90	£1.50
3 ND	*$0.40*	*$1.20*	*$2.00*	£0.25	£0.75	£1.25
4 ND says number 5 in indicia	*$0.40*	*$1.20*	*$2.00*	£0.25	£0.75	£1.25
5 ND last Vortex issue	*$0.40*	*$1.20*	*$2.00*	£0.25	£0.75	£1.25
6-7 ND	*$0.40*	*$1.20*	*$2.00*	£0.25	£0.75	£1.25
Title Value:	*$2.80*	*$8.40*	*$14.00*	£1.85	£5.55	£9.25
Trade paperback (1988), reprints #1-5				£0.85	£2.55	£4.25

STORM

Marvel Comics Group,MS; 1 Feb 1996-4 May 1996

Issue	$Good	$Fine	$N.Mint	£Good	£Fine	£N.Mint
1-4 ND Warren Ellis script, Terry Dodson and Karl Story art; foil stamped cover	*$0.60*	*$1.80*	*$3.00*	£0.40	£1.20	£2.00
Title Value:	*$2.40*	*$7.20*	*$12.00*	£1.60	£4.80	£8.00

STORMQUEST

Caliber Press; 1 Nov 1994-6 Jun 1995

Issue	$Good	$Fine	$N.Mint	£Good	£Fine	£N.Mint
1-6 ND Barricade, Soulfire, Time-Stepper, Shalimar, Tremblor, Shrike and Brightblade	*$0.40*	*$1.20*	*$2.00*	£0.25	£0.75	£1.25
Title Value:	*$2.40*	*$7.20*	*$12.00*	£1.50	£4.50	£7.50

STORMWATCH

Image; 0 Jun 1993; 1 Mar 1993-present

Issue	$Good	$Fine	$N.Mint	£Good	£Fine	£N.Mint
0 ND pre-bagged with trading card	*$0.50*	*$1.50*	*$2.50*	£0.30	£0.90	£1.50
1 ND Jim Lee and Brandon Choi script begins, Jim Lee covers begin; includes coupon (send all three) for limited edition Stormwatch trading card	*$0.50*	*$1.50*	*$2.50*	£0.30	£0.90	£1.50
2 ND 1st appearance Cannon and Farenheit	*$0.40*	*$1.20*	*$2.00*	£0.25	£0.75	£1.25
3 ND 1st appearance Backlash	*$0.60*	*$1.80*	*$3.00*	£0.40	£1.20	£2.00
4-7 ND	*$0.40*	*$1.20*	*$2.00*	£0.25	£0.75	£1.25
8 ND 1st appearance Sarah Rainmaker (later joins Gen 13), Ripclaw appears	*$0.60*	*$1.80*	*$3.00*	£0.40	£1.20	£2.00
9 ND 1st appearance Defile	*$0.50*	*$1.50*	*$2.50*	£0.30	£0.90	£1.50
10 ND	*$0.40*	*$1.20*	*$2.00*	£0.25	£0.75	£1.25
10 Variant Cover Edition, ND cover forms larger picture when combined with variant covers of Deathblow #5, Gen 13 #5, Kindred #3, Team 7 #1, Union #0, Wetworks #2, WildC.A.T.S. #11	*$1.50*	*$4.50*	*$7.50*	£1.00	£3.00	£5.00
11 ND	*$0.50*	*$1.50*	*$2.50*	£0.30	£0.90	£1.50
12 ND Stormwatch vs. Hellstrike	*$0.50*	*$1.50*	*$2.50*	£0.30	£0.90	£1.50
13-16 ND	*$0.50*	*$1.50*	*$2.50*	£0.30	£0.90	£1.50
17 ND team mourn the death of their leader Battalion	*$0.50*	*$1.50*	*$2.50*	£0.30	£0.90	£1.50
18-20 ND	*$0.50*	*$1.50*	*$2.50*	£0.30	£0.90	£1.50
21 ND Stormwatch vs. Wildc.a.t.s.	*$0.50*	*$1.50*	*$2.50*	£0.30	£0.90	£1.50
22 ND Wildstorm Rising part 9, continued in Wildstorm Rising #10; with two foil-bagged painted trading cards. Cover by Barry Windsor-Smith	*$0.50*	*$1.50*	*$2.50*	£0.30	£0.90	£1.50
22 Newstand Edition, ND (without trading cards)	*$0.40*	*$1.20*	*$2.00*	£0.25	£0.75	£1.25
23-24 ND bi-weekly	*$0.50*	*$1.50*	*$2.50*	£0.30	£0.90	£1.50
25 ND cover-dated May 1994, issued between #9 and 10 as part of "Images of Tomorrow" previewing the 25th issue and how it reads/looks	*$0.50*	*$1.50*	*$2.50*	£0.30	£0.90	£1.50
25 2nd printing, ND (Aug 1995)	*$0.50*	*$1.50*	*$2.50*	£0.30	£0.90	£1.50
26 ND bi-weekly	*$0.50*	*$1.50*	*$2.50*	£0.30	£0.90	£1.50
27-34 ND	*$0.50*	*$1.50*	*$2.50*	£0.30	£0.90	£1.50
35 ND Fire From Heaven part 5, continued in Sigma #2	*$0.50*	*$1.50*	*$2.50*	£0.30	£0.90	£1.50
36 ND Fire From Heaven part 12, continued in WildC.A.T.S. #30	*$0.50*	*$1.50*	*$2.50*	£0.30	£0.90	£1.50
37 ND 40pgs, Warren Ellis script begins	*$0.70*	*$2.10*	*$3.50*	£0.50	£1.50	£2.50
38-43 ND	*$0.50*	*$1.50*	*$2.50*	£0.30	£0.90	£1.50
Title Value:	*$24.20*	*$72.60*	*$121.00*	£14.85	£44.55	£74.25

STORMWATCH SPECIAL

Image; 1 Jan 1994-present

Issue	$Good	$Fine	$N.Mint	£Good	£Fine	£N.Mint
1 ND Dwayne Turner, Richard Johnson and Kevin Nowlan art	*$0.80*	*$2.40*	*$4.00*	£0.50	£1.50	£2.50
2 ND Ron Marz script, Cully Hammer art	*$0.80*	*$2.40*	*$4.00*	£0.50	£1.50	£2.50
Title Value:	*$1.60*	*$4.80*	*$8.00*	£1.00	£3.00	£5.00

STORMWATCHER

(see British section)

STRANGE ADVENTURES

National Periodical Publications/DC Comics; 1 Aug/Sep 1950-244 Nov 1973

Issue	$Good	$Fine	$N.Mint	£Good	£Fine	£N.Mint
1 52pgs, cover and adaptation of film "Destination Moon", part painted cover	*$275.00*	*$830.00*	*$2500.00*	£185.00	£550.00	£1675.00
[Scarce in high grade - Very Fine+ or better]						
2 52pgs	*$135.00*	*$410.00*	*$1100.00*	£90.00	£275.00	£735.00
3 52pgs	*$100.00*	*$300.00*	*$800.00*	£65.00	£200.00	£535.00
4 52pgs	*$87.50*	*$260.00*	*$700.00*	£57.50	£175.00	£470.00
5-8 52pgs	*$77.50*	*$235.00*	*$635.00*	£52.50	£155.00	£425.00
9 52pgs, origin and 1st appearance Captain Comet	*$160.00*	*$480.00*	*$1450.00*	£105.00	£325.00	£975.00
10 52pgs, Captain Comet cover	*$77.50*	*$235.00*	*$635.00*	£52.50	£155.00	£425.00
11-12 52pgs, Captain Comet cover	*$57.50*	*$170.00*	*$460.00*	£39.00	£115.00	£310.00
13-14 Captain Comet covers	*$52.50*	*$160.00*	*$435.00*	£36.00	£105.00	£290.00
15-17	*$52.50*	*$160.00*	*$435.00*	£36.00	£105.00	£290.00
18-19 Captain Comet covers	*$52.50*	*$160.00*	*$435.00*	£36.00	£105.00	£290.00
20	*$52.50*	*$160.00*	*$435.00*	£36.00	£105.00	£290.00
21-25	*$45.00*	*$135.00*	*$360.00*	£30.00	£90.00	£240.00
26-27 Captain Comet covers	*$45.00*	*$135.00*	*$360.00*	£30.00	£90.00	£240.00
28-30	*$45.00*	*$135.00*	*$360.00*	£30.00	£90.00	£240.00
31-34	*$39.00*	*$115.00*	*$315.00*	£26.00	£77.50	£210.00
35 Captain Comet cover	*$39.00*	*$115.00*	*$315.00*	£26.00	£77.50	£210.00
36-40	*$39.00*	*$115.00*	*$315.00*	£26.00	£77.50	£210.00
41-50	*$35.00*	*$105.00*	*$280.00*	£23.50	£70.00	£190.00
51-52	*$28.00*	*$82.50*	*$225.00*	£18.50	£55.00	£150.00
53 last pre Comic Code issue	*$28.00*	*$82.50*	*$225.00*	£18.50	£55.00	£150.00
54-60	*$28.00*	*$82.50*	*$225.00*	£18.50	£55.00	£150.00
61-70	*$22.50*	*$67.50*	*$180.00*	£15.00	£45.00	£120.00
71-80	*$17.50*	*$52.50*	*$140.00*	£11.50	£36.00	£95.00
81-90	*$15.50*	*$47.00*	*$125.00*	£10.50	£32.00	£85.00
91-99	*$14.00*	*$43.00*	*$115.00*	£9.25	£28.00	£75.00
100	*$16.00*	*$49.00*	*$130.00*	£10.50	£32.00	£85.00
101-109	*$12.50*	*$39.00*	*$90.00*	£7.00	£21.00	£50.00
1st official distribution in the U.K.						
110	*$12.50*	*$39.00*	*$90.00*	£7.00	£21.00	£50.00
111-113	*$12.00*	*$36.00*	*$85.00*	£5.50	£17.00	£40.00
114 Star Hawkins begins (ends #185), Heath art	*$12.00*	*$36.00*	*$85.00*	£5.50	£17.00	£40.00
115-116	*$12.00*	*$36.00*	*$85.00*	£5.50	£17.00	£40.00
117 origin and 1st appearance Atomic Knights (ends #160)	*$70.00*	*$215.00*	*$575.00*	£41.00	£120.00	£325.00
118-119	*$12.00*	*$36.00*	*$85.00*	£5.50	£17.00	£40.00
120 2nd appearance Atomic Knights	*$27.00*	*$80.00*	*$240.00*	£13.50	£42.00	£125.00
121-122	*$10.50*	*$32.00*	*$75.00*	£3.55	£10.50	£25.00
123 3rd appearance Atomic Knights	*$16.50*	*$50.00*	*$150.00*	£7.75	£23.00	£70.00
124 1st appearance Faceless Creature	*$10.50*	*$32.00*	*$75.00*	£3.55	£10.50	£25.00
125	*$10.50*	*$32.00*	*$75.00*	£3.55	£10.50	£25.00
126 Atomic Knights appear	*$15.50*	*$47.00*	*$140.00*	£6.50	£20.00	£60.00
127-128	*$10.50*	*$32.00*	*$75.00*	£3.55	£10.50	£25.00
129 Atomic Knights appear	*$12.50*	*$39.00*	*$90.00*	£4.25	£12.50	£30.00
130-131	*$10.50*	*$32.00*	*$75.00*	£3.55	£10.50	£25.00
132 Atomic Knights appear	*$12.50*	*$39.00*	*$90.00*	£2.85	£8.50	£20.00
133-134	*$10.50*	*$32.00*	*$75.00*	£3.20	£9.50	£22.50
135 Atomic Knights appear	*$12.50*	*$39.00*	*$90.00*	£3.55	£10.50	£25.00
136-137	*$7.75*	*$23.50*	*$55.00*	£2.85	£8.50	£20.00
138 Atomic Knights appear	*$12.50*	*$39.00*	*$90.00*	£3.55	£10.50	£25.00
139-140	*$7.75*	*$23.50*	*$55.00*	£2.85	£8.50	£20.00
141 Atomic Knights appear						

	$Good	$Fine	$N.Mint	£Good	£Fine	£N.Mint
	$12.50	$39.00	$90.00	£3.20	£9.50	£22.50
142 return of the Faceless Creature						
	$7.75	$23.50	$55.00	£2.50	£7.50	£17.50
143	$7.75	$23.50	$55.00	£2.50	£7.50	£17.50
144 Atomic Knights appear						
	$12.50	$39.00	$90.00	£3.20	£9.50	£22.50
145-146	$7.75	$23.50	$55.00	£2.50	£7.50	£17.50
147 Atomic Knights appear						
	$12.50	$39.00	$90.00	£3.20	£9.50	£22.50
148-149	$7.75	$23.50	$55.00	£2.50	£7.50	£17.50
150 Atomic Knights appear, painted cover						
	$9.25	$28.00	$65.00	£3.20	£9.50	£22.50
151-152	$7.75	$23.50	$55.00	£2.50	£7.50	£17.50
153 Atomic Knights appear						
	$9.25	$28.00	$65.00	£3.20	£9.50	£22.50
154-155	$7.75	$23.50	$55.00	£2.50	£7.50	£17.50
156 Atomic Knights appear						
	$9.25	$28.00	$65.00	£3.20	£9.50	£22.50
157-158	$7.75	$23.50	$55.00	£2.50	£7.50	£17.50
159 Star Rovers	$7.75	$23.50	$55.00	£2.50	£7.50	£17.50
160 last Atomic Knights						
	$9.25	$28.00	$65.00	£3.20	£9.50	£22.50
161 last Space Museum						
	$6.25	$19.00	$45.00	£2.10	£6.25	£15.00
162	$6.25	$19.00	$45.00	£2.10	£6.25	£15.00
163 Star Rovers	$6.25	$19.00	$45.00	£2.10	£6.25	£15.00
164-170	$6.25	$19.00	$45.00	£2.10	£6.25	£15.00
171-179	$5.50	$17.00	$40.00	£1.75	£5.25	£12.50
180 origin and 1st appearance Animal Man, Carmine Infantino art						
	$26.00	$77.50	$210.00	£15.00	£45.00	£120.00
181-182	$3.20	$9.50	$22.50	£1.25	£3.85	£9.00
183 last Silver Age issue, indicia-dated December 1965						
	$3.20	$9.50	$22.50	£1.25	£3.85	£9.00
184 2nd appearance Animal Man, Gil Kane art						
	$17.50	$52.50	$140.00	£7.50	£22.50	£60.00
185-188	$2.85	$8.50	$20.00	£1.05	£3.20	£7.50
189 Steve Ditko art featured						
	$2.85	$8.50	$20.00	£1.05	£3.20	£7.50
190 1st Animal Man in costume, 3rd appearance						
	$20.00	$60.00	$160.00	£10.00	£30.00	£80.00
191-194	$2.10	$6.25	$15.00	£0.70	£2.10	£5.00
195 1st full Animal Man story						
	$12.50	$38.00	$100.00	£5.00	£15.00	£40.00
196-200	$2.10	$6.25	$15.00	£0.70	£2.10	£5.00
201 last Animal Man in title (full length story)						
	$7.00	$21.00	$50.00	£2.85	£8.50	£20.00
202-204	$1.75	$5.25	$12.50	£0.55	£1.70	£4.00
205 origin and 1st appearance Deadman, Carmine Infantino art						
	$12.00	$36.00	$85.00	£5.50	£17.00	£40.00
206 Deadman, Neal Adams art						
	$7.75	$23.50	$55.00	£2.85	£8.50	£20.00
207-210 Deadman, Neal Adams art						
	$6.25	$19.00	$45.00	£2.10	£6.25	£15.00
211-215 Deadman, Neal Adams art						
	$5.50	$17.00	$40.00	£1.75	£5.25	£12.50
216 scarce in the U.K. Deadman, Neal Adams art; story concludes in Brave and the Bold #86						
	$5.50	$17.00	$40.00	£2.10	£6.25	£15.00
217 Adam Strange and Atomic Knights reprints begin						
	$1.50	$4.50	$9.00	£0.50	£1.50	£3.00
218-221	$1.50	$4.50	$9.00	£0.50	£1.50	£3.00
222 new Adam Strange story by Gil Kane and Murphy Anderson						
	$2.50	$7.50	$15.00	£0.80	£2.50	£5.00
223-225	$1.50	$4.50	$9.00	£0.40	£1.25	£2.50
226 scarce in the U.K. 64pgs, squarebound, new 8pg illustrated Adam Strange text story; rest reprints including Adam Strange and Atomic Knights						
	$1.50	$4.50	$9.00	£0.50	£1.50	£3.00
227 64pgs, new 6pg sci-fi illustrated text story by O'Neil and Anderson; rest reprint including Adam Strange and Atomic Knights						
	$1.50	$4.50	$9.00	£0.40	£1.25	£2.50
228-231 64pgs, seven reprint stories including Adam Strange and Atomic Knights						
	$1.50	$4.50	$9.00	£0.40	£1.25	£2.50
232-233 48pgs, four reprint stories including Adam Strange						
	$1.00	$3.00	$6.00	£0.40	£1.25	£2.50
234 48pgs, four reprint stories including Adam Strange, Kubert cover						
	$1.00	$3.00	$6.00	£0.40	£1.25	£2.50
235 48pgs, reprints Mystery in Space #75 (co-starring Justice League of America) plus two reprint stories						
	$1.00	$3.00	$6.00	£0.50	£1.50	£3.00
236 48pgs, four reprint stories including Adam Strange						
	$1.00	$3.00	$6.00	£0.40	£1.25	£2.50
237-244 scarce in the U.K.						
	$1.00	$3.00	$6.00	£0.40	£1.25	£2.50
Title Value:	$4915.50	$14812.50	$39389.00	£3006.75	£9006.30	£24302.50

FEATURES

Adam Strange in 222, 226 (text story with illustrations). Animal Man in 180, 184, 190, 195, 201. Atomic Knights in 117, 120, 123, 126, 129, 132, 135, 138, 141, 144, 147, 150, 153, 156, 160. Darwin Jones in 149, 160. Deadman in 205-216. Enchantress in 187, 191, 200. Immortal Man in 177, 185, 190, 198. Space Museum in 112, 115, 118, 121, 124, 127, 130, 133, 136, 139, 142, 145, 148, 151, 154, 157, 161. Star Hawkins in 114, 116, 119, 122, 125, 128, 131, 134, 137, 140, 143, 146, 149, 152, 155, 158, 162, 173, 176, 179, 182, 185. Star Rovers in 159, 163.

REPRINT FEATURES

Adam Strange in 217-221, 223-244. Atomic Knights in 217-231.

STRANGE ATTRACTORS

RetroGraphix; 1 1993-present

	$Good	$Fine	$N.Mint	£Good	£Fine	£N.Mint
1 ND Mark Sherman and Michael Cohen; black and white						
	$0.60	$1.80	$3.00	£0.40	£1.20	£2.00
2-15 ND black and white						
	$0.60	$1.80	$3.00	£0.40	£1.20	£2.00
Title Value:	$9.00	$27.00	$45.00	£6.00	£18.00	£30.00
Chaos Jitterbug: The Collected Strange Attractors (1995)						
Trade paperback ND collects issues #1-7				£1.70	£5.10	£8.50

STRANGE BREW

Aardvark-Vanaheim; 1 Dec 1982

	$Good	$Fine	$N.Mint	£Good	£Fine	£N.Mint
1 ND (Jan 1983 in indicia)						
	$0.60	$1.80	$3.00	£0.40	£1.20	£2.00
Title Value:	$0.60	$1.80	$3.00	£0.40	£1.20	£2.00

STRANGE COMBAT TALES

Marvel Comics Group/Epic,MS; 1 Oct 1993-4 Jan 1994

	$Good	$Fine	$N.Mint	£Good	£Fine	£N.Mint
1-4 ND	$0.40	$1.20	$2.00	£0.25	£0.75	£1.25
Title Value:	$1.60	$4.80	$8.00	£1.00	£3.00	£5.00

STRANGE DAYS

Eclipse; 1 Oct 1984-3 Apr 1985

	$Good	$Fine	$N.Mint	£Good	£Fine	£N.Mint
1 ND Johnny Nemo, Freakwave by Milligan, Ewins, McCarthy begin						
	$1.20	$3.60	$6.00	£0.80	£2.40	£4.00
2 ND scarce in the U.K.						
	$1.20	$3.60	$6.00	£0.90	£2.70	£4.50
3 ND	$1.20	$3.60	$6.00	£0.80	£2.40	£4.00
Title Value:	$3.60	$10.80	$18.00	£2.50	£7.50	£12.50

STRANGE DAYS MOVIE ADAPTATION

Marvel Comics Group,OS; 1 Jan 1996

	$Good	$Fine	$N.Mint	£Good	£Fine	£N.Mint
1 ND film adaptation of Jim Cameron film by Dan Chichester and Bill Reinhold						
	$1.20	$3.60	$6.00	£0.80	£2.40	£4.00
Title Value:	$1.20	$3.60	$6.00	£0.80	£2.40	£4.00

STRANGE MYSTERIES

I.W. Super;9 1963-18 1964

	$Good	$Fine	$N.Mint	£Good	£Fine	£N.Mint
9-18 scarce though distributed in the U.K. reprint						
	$2.50	$7.50	$17.50	£1.70	£5.00	£12.00
Title Value:	$20.00	$60.00	$140.00	£13.60	£40.00	£96.00

STRANGE PLANETS

I.W. Super; 1,8-12,15-18 1958-1964

	$Good	$Fine	$N.Mint	£Good	£Fine	£N.Mint
1 scarce in the U.K. reprints Incredible Science Fiction #8 (EC)						
	$7.50	$22.50	$60.00	£5.00	£15.00	£40.00
9 scarce in the U.K. Wood art						
	$11.00	$34.00	$80.00	£7.75	£23.50	£55.00
10 scarce in the U.K. Wood art						
	$10.50	$32.00	$75.00	£7.00	£21.00	£50.00
11 scarce in the U.K. reprints An Earthman on Venus, Wood art						
	$12.50	$39.00	$90.00	£8.50	£26.00	£60.00
12 scarce in the U.K. reprints Rocket to the Moon						
	$10.00	$30.00	$70.00	£6.25	£19.00	£45.00
15 scarce in the U.K.						
	$3.90	$11.50	$27.50	£2.50	£7.50	£17.50
16 scarce in the U.K. reprints Strange Worlds #6						
	$5.00	$15.00	$35.00	£3.20	£9.50	£22.50
18 scarce in the U.K. reprints Daring Adventures #6						
	$3.55	$10.50	$25.00	£2.25	£6.75	£16.00
Title Value:	$63.95	$194.50	$462.50	£42.45	£128.25	£306.00

Note: all distributed in the U.K.

STRANGE SPORTS STORIES

Adventure; 1 May 1992-3 Jul 1992

	$Good	$Fine	$N.Mint	£Good	£Fine	£N.Mint
1-3 ND includes two trading cards bound on outside						
	$0.40	$1.20	$2.00	£0.25	£0.75	£1.25
Title Value:	$1.20	$3.60	$6.00	£0.75	£2.25	£3.75

STRANGE SPORTS STORIES

DC Comics; 1 Sep/Oct 1973-6 Jul/Aug 1974

(see Brave and the Bold, DC Special, DC Special Blue Ribbon Digest, DC Super Stars)

	$Good	$Fine	$N.Mint	£Good	£Fine	£N.Mint
1	$1.50	$4.50	$9.00	£0.50	£1.50	£3.00
2-6	$1.00	$3.00	$6.00	£0.30	£1.00	£2.00
Title Value:	$6.50	$19.50	$39.00	£2.00	£6.50	£13.00

STRANGE SUSPENSE STORIES

Fawcett/Charlton; 1 Jun 1952-77 Oct 1965

(becomes Captain Atom)

	$Good	$Fine	$N.Mint	£Good	£Fine	£N.Mint
1 scarce in the U.K.						
	$57.50	$175.00	$475.00	£40.00	£120.00	£320.00
2 scarce in the U.K.						
	$41.00	$120.00	$290.00	£28.00	£82.50	£195.00
3-5 scarce in the U.K.						
	$36.00	$105.00	$250.00	£24.00	£72.50	£170.00
10 titled Lawbreaker's Suspense Stories						
	$23.50	$70.00	$165.00	£15.50	£47.00	£110.00
11 scarce in the U.K. titled Lawbreaker's Suspense Stories; famous severed tongue panel						
	$57.50	$170.00	$405.00	£39.00	£115.00	£270.00
12-14 titled Lawbreaker's Suspense Stories						
	$10.00	$30.00	$70.00	£6.25	£19.00	£45.00
15 scarce in the U.K. titled Lawbreaker's Suspense Stories; famous acid thrown in face story						
	$36.00	$105.00	$250.00	£24.00	£72.50	£170.00
16	$21.00	$62.50	$150.00	£14.00	£43.00	£100.00
17	$17.50	$52.50	$125.00	£12.00	£36.00	£85.00
18 Steve Ditko art						
	$31.00	$92.50	$220.00	£20.50	£60.00	£145.00
19 Steve Ditko art; famous electric chair cover						
	$41.00	$120.00	$285.00	£27.00	£80.00	£190.00
20 Steve Ditko art						
	$30.00	$90.00	$210.00	£20.00	£60.00	£140.00

	$Good	$Fine	$N.Mint	£Good	£Fine	£N.Mint
21	$17.50	$52.50	$125.00	£12.00	£36.00	£85.00
22 titled This Is Suspense, Steve Ditko cover	$26.00	$77.50	$185.00	£17.50	£52.50	£125.00
23 titled This Is Suspense, Wood art	$22.50	$67.50	$160.00	£15.50	£47.00	£110.00
24 titled This Is Suspense, Evans art	$12.50	$39.00	$90.00	£8.50	£26.00	£60.00
25-26 titled This Is Suspense	$9.25	$28.00	$65.00	£6.25	£19.00	£45.00
27	$13.50	$41.00	$95.00	£9.25	£28.00	£65.00
28-30	$8.50	$26.00	$60.00	£5.50	£17.00	£40.00
31-33 Steve Ditko art	$17.50	$52.50	$125.00	£12.00	£36.00	£85.00
34 story featuring William Gaines satire; Steve Ditko art	$41.00	$120.00	$285.00	£27.00	£80.00	£190.00
35 Steve Ditko art	$17.50	$52.50	$125.00	£12.00	£36.00	£85.00
36 64pgs, Steve Ditko art	$19.00	$57.50	$135.00	£12.50	£39.00	£90.00
37 Steve Ditko art	$17.50	$52.50	$125.00	£12.00	£36.00	£85.00
38	$8.50	$26.00	$60.00	£5.50	£17.00	£40.00
39 Steve Ditko art	$14.00	$43.00	$100.00	£9.50	£29.00	£67.50
40 Steve Ditko art	$17.50	$52.50	$125.00	£12.00	£36.00	£85.00
41 Steve Ditko art	$14.00	$43.00	$100.00	£9.50	£29.00	£67.50
42-44	$6.25	$19.00	$45.00	£4.25	£12.50	£30.00
45 Steve Ditko art	$11.00	$34.00	$80.00	£7.75	£23.50	£55.00
46	$6.25	$19.00	$45.00	£4.25	£12.50	£30.00
47-48 Steve Ditko art	$11.00	$34.00	$80.00	£7.75	£23.50	£55.00
49	$6.25	$19.00	$45.00	£4.25	£12.50	£30.00
1st official distribution in the U.K.						
50-51 Steve Ditko art	$11.00	$34.00	$80.00	£7.75	£23.50	£55.00
52-53 Steve Ditko art	$14.00	$43.00	$100.00	£9.50	£29.00	£67.50
54-60	$5.00	$15.00	$35.00	£3.55	£10.50	£25.00
61-74	$2.50	$7.50	$17.50	£1.40	£4.25	£10.00
75 reprints Space Aventures #33 (1st Captain Atom)	$15.50	$47.00	$110.00	£9.25	£28.00	£65.00
76-77 Captain Atom reprints	$7.00	$21.00	$50.00	£3.20	£9.50	£22.50
Title Value:	$1045.25	$3128.50	$7455.00	£697.60	£2097.00	£4975.00

Note: most issues distributed in the U.K.after 1958/59

STRANGE TALES

Atlas/Marvel Comics Group; 1 Jun 1951-168 May 1968; 169 Sep 1973-188 Nov 1976
(previous issues ND, becomes Dr.Strange)

	$Good	$Fine	$N.Mint	£Good	£Fine	£N.Mint
1 scarce in the U.K.	$235.00	$700.00	$2350.00	£155.00	£470.00	£1575.00
2	$100.00	$300.00	$800.00	£65.00	£200.00	£535.00
3-5	$75.00	$225.00	$600.00	£50.00	£150.00	£400.00
6-9	$52.50	$160.00	$430.00	£36.00	£105.00	£285.00
10 Krigstein art	$52.50	$160.00	$430.00	£36.00	£105.00	£285.00
11-14	$38.00	$110.00	$300.00	£25.00	£75.00	£200.00
15 Krigstein art	$38.00	$110.00	$300.00	£25.00	£75.00	£200.00
16-20	$38.00	$110.00	$300.00	£25.00	£75.00	£200.00
21-25	$28.00	$82.50	$225.00	£18.50	£55.00	£150.00
26-34	$25.00	$75.00	$200.00	£16.50	£50.00	£135.00
35-40	$21.50	$65.00	$175.00	£14.00	£43.00	£115.00
41-45	$20.00	$60.00	$160.00	£13.00	£39.00	£105.00
46-60	$18.50	$55.00	$150.00	£12.50	£38.00	£100.00
61-66	$18.50	$55.00	$150.00	£11.50	£35.00	£92.50
67 possible Quicksilver prototype; Ditko and Kirby art	$21.50	$65.00	$175.00	£14.00	£43.00	£115.00
68 Ditko and Kirby art	$18.50	$55.00	$150.00	£11.50	£35.00	£92.50
69 possible Professor X prototype; Ditko and Kirby art	$21.50	$65.00	$175.00	£14.00	£43.00	£115.00
70 possible Giant Man prototype; Ditko and Kirby art	$21.50	$65.00	$175.00	£14.00	£43.00	£115.00
71-72 Ditko and Kirby art	$18.50	$55.00	$150.00	£11.50	£35.00	£92.50
73 possible Ant-Man prototype; Ditko and Kirby art	$21.50	$65.00	$175.00	£14.00	£43.00	£115.00
74 Ditko and Kirby art	$18.50	$55.00	$150.00	£11.50	£35.00	£92.50
1st official distribution in the U.K.						
75 possible Iron Man prototype; Ditko and Kirby art	$21.50	$65.00	$175.00	£13.00	£39.00	£105.00
76 possible Human Torch prototype; Ditko and Kirby art	$21.50	$65.00	$175.00	£13.00	£39.00	£105.00
77 scarce in the U.K. Ditko and Kirby art	$18.50	$55.00	$150.00	£11.50	£35.00	£92.50
78 rare in the U.K. possible Ant-Man prototype; Ditko and Kirby art	$22.50	$67.50	$180.00	£15.00	£45.00	£120.00
79 features an early Marvel - Dr. Strange prototype? (see Journey Into Mystery #78), Ditko and Kirby art	$22.50	$67.50	$180.00	£13.50	£41.00	£110.00
80 Ditko and Kirby art	$18.50	$55.00	$150.00	£11.00	£34.00	£90.00
81-83 Ditko and Kirby art	$16.00	$49.00	$130.00	£9.25	£28.00	£75.00
84 Magneto prototype (as American guides claim)? Nonsense! It's a monster not a mutant man..; Steve Ditko and Jack Kirby art	$20.00	$60.00	$160.00	£11.00	£34.00	£90.00
85-88 Ditko and Kirby art	$16.00	$49.00	$130.00	£9.25	£28.00	£75.00
89 1st appearance Fin Fang Foom, classic Jack Kirby monster art and cover, Ditko art also	$42.00	$125.00	$375.00	£25.00	£75.00	£225.00
90-91 Ditko and Kirby art	$16.00	$49.00	$130.00	£8.75	£26.00	£70.00
92 (Jan 1962), last 10 cents issue	$16.00	$49.00	$130.00	£8.75	£26.00	£70.00
93-96 Jack Kirby art	$16.00	$49.00	$130.00	£8.75	£26.00	£70.00
97 early Aunt May/Uncle Ben (Spiderman's foster parents) prototypes, three months prior to the publication of Amazing Fantasy #15	$41.00	$120.00	$325.00	£22.50	£67.50	£180.00
98-99 Jack Kirby art	$16.00	$49.00	$130.00	£8.75	£26.00	£70.00
100 Jack Kirby art	$18.50	$55.00	$150.00	£10.00	£30.00	£80.00
101 scarce in the U.K. 1st of Human Torch series by Jack Kirby; origin of Fantastic Four briefly re-told	$120.00	$365.00	$975.00	£65.00	£200.00	£535.00
102 1st appearance The Wizard (later leader of The Frightful Four)	$43.00	$125.00	$300.00	£23.50	£70.00	£165.00
103	$39.00	$115.00	$275.00	£19.00	£57.50	£135.00
104 (Jan 1963), 1st appearance Paste-Pot Pete (later The Trapster)	$39.00	$115.00	$275.00	£19.00	£57.50	£135.00

Steel, The Indestructible Man #2

Strange Adventures #117

Strange Tales #156

	$Good	$Fine	$N.Mint	£Good	£Fine	£N.Mint
105	$39.00	$115.00	$275.00	£19.00	£57.50	£135.00
106 less common in the U.K. Fantastic Four appear	$25.00	$75.00	$175.00	£13.50	£41.00	£95.00
107 Human Torch/Sub-Mariner battle; 4th Silver Age Sub-Mariner appearance	$30.00	$90.00	$210.00	£17.50	£52.50	£125.00
108-109 less common in the U.K.	$25.00	$75.00	$175.00	£13.50	£41.00	£95.00
110 1st appearance Dr. Strange by Steve Ditko; as a back-up story only (with no mention on cover!)	$110.00	$330.00	$1100.00	£55.00	£165.00	£550.00
110 Marvel Milestone Edition, ND (Apr 1995) - metallic ink cover	$0.60	$1.80	$3.00	£0.40	£1.20	£2.00
111 scarce in the U.K. 2nd appearance Dr. Strange	$50.00	$150.00	$350.00	£29.00	£85.00	£200.00
112-113	$17.50	$52.50	$125.00	£10.50	£32.00	£75.00
114 The Acrobat appears, disguised as Captain America; the first appearance of Captain America since the 1950s, 3rd appearance Dr. Strange as his regular back-up stories begin	$48.00	$140.00	$385.00	£28.00	£82.50	£220.00
115 origin Dr. Strange, Spiderman appears, 2nd appearance and origin Sandman	$52.50	$160.00	$490.00	£31.00	£90.00	£275.00
116 less common in the U.K. (Jan 1964), Human Torch battles The Thing; painted (grey-tone) cover	$17.00	$50.00	$120.00	£10.00	£30.00	£70.00
117 less common in the U.K.	$11.00	$34.00	$80.00	£6.25	£19.00	£45.00
118 less common in the U.K. Fantastic Four guest-star	$11.00	$34.00	$80.00	£6.25	£19.00	£45.00
119 less common in the U.K. Spiderman appears	$21.00	$62.50	$150.00	£10.50	£32.00	£75.00
120 less common in the U.K. Iceman appears, Angel, Marvel Girl, Professor X cameos	$11.00	$34.00	$80.00	£6.25	£19.00	£45.00
121 less common in the U.K. Human Torch and Dr. Strange team up	$10.00	$30.00	$70.00	£5.00	£15.00	£35.00
122 less common in the U.K.	$10.00	$30.00	$70.00	£5.00	£15.00	£35.00
123 less common in the U.K. 1st appearance The Beetle; Thor appears (1st outside own magazine); Loki and Odin also appear	$10.50	$32.00	$75.00	£5.25	£16.00	£37.50
124 less common in the U.K. 1st Human Torch and Thing team-up (ends #134)	$10.00	$30.00	$70.00	£5.00	£15.00	£35.00
125 less common in the U.K. Sub-Mariner vs. Thing and The Human Torch	$9.25	$28.00	$65.00	£5.00	£15.00	£35.00
126 scarce in the U.K. 1st appearance Clea	$9.25	$28.00	$65.00	£5.00	£15.00	£35.00
127 rare in the U.K.	$9.25	$28.00	$65.00	£5.25	£16.00	£37.50
128 scarce in the U.K. (Jan 1965), Scarlet Witch and Quicksilver appear	$9.25	$28.00	$65.00	£4.25	£12.50	£30.00
129	$9.25	$28.00	$65.00	£3.55	£10.50	£25.00
130 very scarce in the U.K. Beatles cameo	$9.25	$28.00	$65.00	£5.00	£15.00	£35.00
131-133	$9.25	$28.00	$65.00	£3.55	£10.50	£25.00
134 The Watcher appears	$9.25	$28.00	$65.00	£3.55	£10.50	£25.00
135 origin and 1st appearance Nick Fury, Agent of Shield	$14.00	$43.00	$115.00	£7.00	£21.50	£57.50
136 2nd appearance Nick Fury, Agent of Shield	$7.00	$21.00	$50.00	£3.20	£9.50	£22.50
137 less common in the U.K.	$7.00	$21.00	$50.00	£3.20	£9.50	£22.50
138	$7.00	$21.00	$50.00	£2.85	£8.50	£20.00
139 last Silver Age issue indicia-dated December 1965	$7.00	$21.00	$50.00	£2.85	£8.50	£20.00
140 (Jan 1966)	$7.00	$21.00	$50.00	£2.85	£8.50	£20.00
141-145	$6.25	$19.00	$45.00	£2.50	£7.50	£17.50
146 Steve Ditko cover	$6.25	$19.00	$45.00	£2.50	£7.50	£17.50
147	$6.25	$19.00	$45.00	£2.50	£7.50	£17.50
148 origin The Ancient One	$10.50	$32.00	$75.00	£3.55	£10.50	£25.00
149	$6.25	$19.00	$45.00	£2.50	£7.50	£17.50
150 John Buscema's 1st work for Marvel	$6.25	$19.00	$45.00	£2.50	£7.50	£17.50
151 scarce in the U.K. Jim Steranko art on Shield, his first Marvel work	$9.25	$28.00	$65.00	£3.90	£11.50	£27.50
152 (Jan 1967), Steranko art	$5.50	$17.00	$40.00	£2.85	£8.50	£20.00
153-156 Steranko art	$5.50	$17.00	$40.00	£2.50	£7.50	£17.50
157 Steranko art, Living Tribunal appears (cameo)	$5.50	$17.00	$40.00	£2.50	£7.50	£17.50
158 Steranko art, 1st full appearance Living Tribunal	$5.50	$17.00	$40.00	£2.50	£7.50	£17.50
159 origin Nick Fury retold, Nick Fury vs. Captain America, Steranko art	$6.25	$19.00	$45.00	£2.85	£8.50	£20.00
160 classic Steranko art	$4.60	$13.50	$32.50	£2.10	£6.25	£15.00
161-163 classic Steranko art	$4.60	$13.50	$32.50	£1.75	£5.25	£12.50
164 (Jan 1968), classic Steranko art	$4.60	$13.50	$32.50	£1.75	£5.25	£12.50
165-166 classic Steranko art	$4.60	$13.50	$32.50	£1.75	£5.25	£12.50
167 classic Steranko art, classic patriotic cover	$7.00	$21.00	$50.00	£2.50	£7.50	£17.50
168 classic Steranko art	$4.60	$13.50	$32.50	£1.75	£5.25	£12.50
169 ND origin and 1st appearance Brother Voodoo	$0.80	$2.50	$5.00	£0.50	£1.50	£3.00
170 ND origin Brother Voodoo continued	$0.65	$2.00	$4.00	£0.30	£1.00	£2.00
171 ND	$0.65	$2.00	$4.00	£0.30	£1.00	£2.00
172 ND (Feb 1974)	$0.65	$2.00	$4.00	£0.30	£1.00	£2.00
173 ND	$0.65	$2.00	$4.00	£0.30	£1.00	£2.00
174 ND 1st appearance Golem II (origin); see Hulk #134	$0.65	$2.00	$4.00	£0.40	£1.25	£2.50
175 scarce in the U.K. monster reprints from Amazing Aventures (1st Series) #1	$0.65	$2.00	$4.00	£0.25	£0.75	£1.50
176-177 Golem	$0.65	$2.00	$4.00	£0.25	£0.75	£1.50
178 (Feb 1975), Warlock by Jim Starlin begins, 1st appearance Magus	$3.30	$10.00	$20.00	£1.25	£3.75	£7.50
179-181 Warlock, Jim Starlin art	$1.65	$5.00	$10.00	£0.55	£1.75	£3.50
182 reprints Dr. Strange	$0.55	$1.75	$3.50	£0.25	£0.75	£1.50
183 (Jan 1976), reprints Dr. Strange	$0.55	$1.75	$3.50	£0.25	£0.75	£1.50
184-187 reprints Dr. Strange	$0.55	$1.75	$3.50	£0.25	£0.75	£1.50
188 ND reprint Dr. Strange	$0.55	$1.75	$3.50	£0.40	£1.25	£2.50
Title Value:	$3964.25	$11861.55	$31939.50	£2404.25	£7237.95	£19469.50

ARTISTS

Kirby in 75-105, 108, 109, 114, 120, 135-150, 151-153 with Steranko. Ditko in 75-146.

FEATURES

Brother Voodoo in 169-173. Dr. Strange in 114-134. Golem in 174, 176, 177. Human Torch in 101-123. Human Torch/Thing in 124-134. Nick Fury, Agent of Shield in 135-168. Warlock in 178-181 (series continues in Warlock 9). Monster/Fantasy stories in 75-109, 111, 112 (back-ups only in 101-109, 111, 112).

REPRINT FEATURES

Monster/fantasy in 175. Dr. Strange in 182-188.

STRANGE TALES (2ND SERIES)

Marvel Comics Group; 1 Apr 1987-19 Oct 1988

	$Good	$Fine	$N.Mint	£Good	£Fine	£N.Mint
1 ND Cloak & Dagger/Dr Strange in separate stories begin	$0.25	$0.75	$1.25	£0.15	£0.45	£0.75
2-8 ND	$0.25	$0.75	$1.25	£0.15	£0.45	£0.75
9 Dazzler appears	$0.25	$0.75	$1.25	£0.15	£0.45	£0.75
10 Black Cat appears	$0.25	$0.75	$1.25	£0.15	£0.45	£0.75
11-12	$0.25	$0.75	$1.25	£0.15	£0.45	£0.75
13-14 Punisher appears	$0.25	$0.75	$1.25	£0.15	£0.45	£0.75
15-17	$0.25	$0.75	$1.25	£0.15	£0.45	£0.75
18 X-Factor appears, Kevin Nowlan inks	$0.25	$0.75	$1.25	£0.15	£0.45	£0.75
19	$0.25	$0.75	$1.25	£0.15	£0.45	£0.75
Title Value:	$4.75	$14.25	$23.75	£2.85	£8.55	£14.25

STRANGE TALES (3RD SERIES)

Marvel Comics Group,OS; 1 Feb 1995

	$Good	$Fine	$N.Mint	£Good	£Fine	£N.Mint
1 ND 64pgs, The Thing, Dr. Strange, Nick Fury, Human Torch feature, painted art by Ricardo Villagran; card-stock cover with protective acetate over-lay	$1.40	$4.20	$7.00	£0.90	£2.70	£4.50
Title Value:	$1.40	$4.20	$7.00	£0.90	£2.70	£4.50

STRANGE TALES ANNUAL

Marvel Comics Group; 1 1962-2 1963

	$Good	$Fine	$N.Mint	£Good	£Fine	£N.Mint
1 very rare in the U.K. 72pgs, '50s/'60s monster/fantasy reprints including Strange Tales #73 ("Grottu"), #92 ("Serpent Creature"), Tales To Astonish #7 ("Shadow Thing"), #9 ("Diablo"); Kirby, Ditko art	$52.50	$155.00	$425.00	£38.00	£110.00	£300.00
[Very rare in high grade - Very Fine+ or better]						
2 rare in the U.K. 72pgs, Spiderman vs. Human Torch, (joint 4th appearance of Spiderman with Spiderman #3 dated July 1963) by Jack Kirby/Steve Ditko, monster/fantasy reprints	$62.50	$185.00	$500.00	£41.00	£120.00	£325.00
[Very scarce in high grade - Very Fine+ or better]						
Title Value:	$115.00	$340.00	$925.00	£79.00	£230.00	£625.00

Note: Annual #2 occasionally turns up with a blank back and inside front covers (see Fantastic Four Annual #1-3, Sgt. Fury Annual #1, Spiderman Annual #1,2). These were subscription copies sent over to this country as left-overs and are very scarce in both the U.K. and U.S. With their white back covers which show soiling and wear that much more easily, they are **very rare** in near mint condition.

STRANGE WORLDS

Atlas; 1 Dec 1958-5 Aug 1959

	$Good	$Fine	$N.Mint	£Good	£Fine	£N.Mint
1 ND scarce in the U.K. classic flying saucer cover, Jack Kirby, Steve Ditko art	$75.00	$225.00	$600.00	£50.00	£150.00	£400.00
2 ND scarce in the U.K. Steve Ditko cover and art	$41.00	$120.00	$325.00	£28.00	£82.50	£220.00
3 ND scarce in the U.K. part Jack Kirby art	$31.00	$92.50	$250.00	£21.00	£62.50	£170.00
4 ND scarce in the U.K. Williamson art	$28.00	$82.50	$225.00	£18.50	£55.00	£150.00
5 ND scarce in the U.K. Steve Ditko art	$23.00	$67.50	$185.00	£15.50	£47.00	£125.00
Title Value:	$198.00	$587.50	$1585.00	£133.00	£397.00	£1065.00

STRANGE WORLDS

Eternity; 1 Apr 1990

	$Good	$Fine	$N.Mint	£Good	£Fine	£N.Mint
1 ND 60pgs, squarebound anthology of 1950s sci-fi reprints	$0.60	$1.80	$3.00	£0.40	£1.20	£2.00
Title Value:	$0.60	$1.80	$3.00	£0.40	£1.20	£2.00

STRANGEHAVEN

(see British section)

VERY GENERAL PERCENTAGE CONVERSION CHART WHICH MAY BE USED TO CALCULATE LOW AND INBETWEEN GRADES:

STRANGELOVE

Entity Comics; 1 Aug 1995-5 1995

Issue	$Good	$Fine	$N.Mint	£Good	£Fine	£N.Mint
1 ND Stacy Freeman script, Tatsuya Ishida art; black and white	*$0.50*	*$1.50*	*$2.50*	£0.30	£0.90	£1.50
1 Encore Edition, ND (2nd printing), new sketches	*$0.55*	*$1.65*	*$2.75*	£0.35	£1.05	£1.75
1 Fan Appreciation Edition, ND includes new sketches and commentary	*$0.50*	*$1.50*	*$2.50*	£0.30	£0.90	£1.50
2 ND	*$0.50*	*$1.50*	*$2.50*	£0.30	£0.90	£1.50
2 Encore Edition, ND (2nd printing), new sketches	*$0.55*	*$1.65*	*$2.75*	£0.35	£1.05	£1.75
3-5 ND	*$0.50*	*$1.50*	*$2.50*	£0.30	£0.90	£1.50
Title Value:	*$4.10*	*$12.30*	*$20.50*	£2.50	£7.50	£12.50

STRANGERS IN PARADISE

Antarctic Press; 1 Nov 1993-3 Feb 1994

Issue	$Good	$Fine	$N.Mint	£Good	£Fine	£N.Mint
1 ND Terry Moore art	*$11.00*	*$33.00*	*$55.00*	£6.00	£18.00	£30.00
1 2nd printing ND	*$2.00*	*$6.00*	*$10.00*	£1.30	£3.90	£6.50
1 3rd printing, ND (Apr 1994)	*$1.50*	*$4.50*	*$7.50*	£0.80	£2.40	£4.00
2 ND	*$8.00*	*$24.00*	*$40.00*	£4.00	£12.00	£20.00
3 ND	*$6.00*	*$18.00*	*$30.00*	£3.50	£10.50	£17.50
Title Value:	*$28.50*	*$85.50*	*$142.50*	£15.60	£46.80	£78.00

STRANGERS IN PARADISE (2ND SERIES)

Abstract Studios; 1 Sep 1994-14 Jul 1996

Issue	$Good	$Fine	$N.Mint	£Good	£Fine	£N.Mint
1 ND 24pgs, black and white begins	*$3.50*	*$10.50*	*$17.50*	£1.50	£4.50	£7.50
1 2nd printing ND	*$0.60*	*$1.80*	*$3.00*	£0.40	£1.20	£2.00
2 ND	*$2.50*	*$7.50*	*$12.50*	£1.20	£3.60	£6.00
2 2nd printing ND	*$0.60*	*$1.80*	*$3.00*	£0.40	£1.20	£2.00
3 ND	*$1.60*	*$4.80*	*$8.00*	£0.80	£2.40	£4.00
3 2nd printing ND	*$0.55*	*$1.65*	*$2.75*	£0.35	£1.05	£1.75
4 ND	*$1.00*	*$3.00*	*$5.00*	£0.60	£1.80	£3.00
4 2nd printing ND	*$0.55*	*$1.65*	*$2.75*	£0.35	£1.05	£1.75
5 ND	*$1.00*	*$3.00*	*$5.00*	£0.60	£1.80	£3.00
5 2nd printing ND	*$0.55*	*$1.65*	*$2.75*	£0.35	£1.05	£1.75
6 ND	*$0.60*	*$1.80*	*$3.00*	£0.40	£1.20	£2.00
6 2nd printing ND	*$0.55*	*$1.65*	*$2.75*	£0.35	£1.05	£1.75
7-10 ND	*$0.60*	*$1.80*	*$3.00*	£0.40	£1.20	£2.00
11-14 ND	*$0.55*	*$1.65*	*$2.75*	£0.35	£1.05	£1.75
Title Value:	*$18.20*	*$54.60*	*$91.00*	£10.30	£30.90	£51.50
Strangers in Paradise (Feb 1996) Trade paperback ND collects issues #1-8				£2.30	£6.90	£16.50

STRANGERS IN PARADISE (3RD SERIES)

Homage Comics; 1 Nov 1996-present

Issue	$Good	$Fine	$N.Mint	£Good	£Fine	£N.Mint
1-2 ND Terry Moore script and art	*$0.55*	*$1.65*	*$2.75*	£0.40	£1.20	£2.00
Title Value:	*$1.10*	*$3.30*	*$5.50*	£0.80	£2.40	£4.00

STRANGERS, THE

Malibu Ultraverse; 1 Jun 1993-26 May 1995

Issue	$Good	$Fine	$N.Mint	£Good	£Fine	£N.Mint
1 1st appearance Atom Bob, Electrocute, Grenade, Lady Killer, Spectral, Zip Zap and Yrial	*$0.70*	*$2.10*	*$3.50*	£0.40	£1.20	£2.00
1 Limited Edition, (Jun 1993) - full hologram cover; 7,500 copies (offered again by Marvel Comics in Sep 1995)	*$2.00*	*$6.00*	*$10.00*	£1.00	£3.00	£5.00
2 pre-bagged with trading card	*$0.50*	*$1.50*	*$2.50*	£0.30	£0.90	£1.50
2 un-bagged, (without card)	*$0.40*	*$1.20*	*$2.00*	£0.25	£0.75	£1.25
3	*$0.50*	*$1.50*	*$2.50*	£0.30	£0.90	£1.50
4 Hardcase appears	*$0.40*	*$1.20*	*$2.00*	£0.25	£0.75	£1.25
5 40pgs, Rune insert	*$0.50*	*$1.50*	*$2.50*	£0.30	£0.90	£1.50
6	*$0.40*	*$1.20*	*$2.00*	£0.25	£0.75	£1.25
7 Prototype appears	*$0.40*	*$1.20*	*$2.00*	£0.25	£0.75	£1.25
8 origin Solution by Art Nichols	*$0.40*	*$1.20*	*$2.00*	£0.25	£0.75	£1.25
9-11	*$0.40*	*$1.20*	*$2.00*	£0.25	£0.75	£1.25
12 anniversary issue with silver logos	*$0.40*	*$1.20*	*$2.00*	£0.25	£0.75	£1.25
13 64pgs, flip-book format with Ultraverse Premiere #4; Strangers team up with Mantra	*$0.50*	*$1.50*	*$2.50*	£0.30	£0.90	£1.50
14-24	*$0.40*	*$1.20*	*$2.00*	£0.25	£0.75	£1.25
25 Godwheel tie-in	*$0.40*	*$1.20*	*$2.00*	£0.25	£0.75	£1.25
26 1st issue under Marvel Comics solicitation; Godwheel tie-in	*$0.40*	*$1.20*	*$2.00*	£0.25	£0.75	£1.25
Title Value:	*$13.50*	*$40.50*	*$67.50*	£8.10	£24.30	£40.50

Note: all Non-Distributed on the news-stands in the U.K.

Issue	$Good	$Fine	$N.Mint	£Good	£Fine	£N.Mint
The Strangers Collection: Jumpstart Softcover (Oct 1994) Trade paperback reprints issues #1-4				£1.30	£3.90	£6.50
The Strangers Collection: Jumpstart Signed Edition (Oct 1994) as above, signed by Steve Englehart and Rick Hoberg, 500 copies				£4.00	£12.00	£20.00

STRANGERS ANNUAL, THE

Malibu Ultraverse; 1 Dec 1994

Issue	$Good	$Fine	$N.Mint	£Good	£Fine	£N.Mint
1 ND 64pgs, continued from Night Man Annual #1	*$0.60*	*$1.80*	*$3.00*	£0.40	£1.20	£2.00
Title Value:	*$0.60*	*$1.80*	*$3.00*	£0.40	£1.20	£2.00

STRATA

Renegade; 1 Jan 1986-6 Apr 1987

Issue	$Good	$Fine	$N.Mint	£Good	£Fine	£N.Mint
1-6 ND	*$0.40*	*$1.20*	*$2.00*	£0.25	£0.75	£1.25
Title Value:	*$2.40*	*$7.20*	*$12.00*	£1.50	£4.50	£7.50

STRATONAUT

Night Wynd,MS; 1 Jan 1992-4 Apr 1992

Issue	$Good	$Fine	$N.Mint	£Good	£Fine	£N.Mint
1-4 ND Barry Blair script/art; black and white	*$0.40*	*$1.20*	*$2.00*	£0.25	£0.75	£1.25
Title Value:	*$1.60*	*$4.80*	*$8.00*	£1.00	£3.00	£5.00

STRAW MEN

All American Comics; 1 1989-8 1990

Issue	$Good	$Fine	$N.Mint	£Good	£Fine	£N.Mint
1-8 ND	*$0.30*	*$0.90*	*$1.50*	£0.20	£0.60	£1.00
Title Value:	*$2.40*	*$7.20*	*$12.00*	£1.60	£4.80	£8.00

STRAWBERRY SHORTCAKE

Marvel Comics Group/Star; 1 Jun 1985-7 Apr 1986

Issue	$Good	$Fine	$N.Mint	£Good	£Fine	£N.Mint
1-7 ND	*$0.15*	*$0.45*	*$0.75*	£0.10	£0.30	£0.50
Title Value:	*$1.05*	*$3.15*	*$5.25*	£0.70	£2.10	£3.50

STRAY BULLETS

El Capitan Books; 1 1995-present

Issue	$Good	$Fine	$N.Mint	£Good	£Fine	£N.Mint
1 ND David Lapham art and covers begins	*$5.00*	*$15.00*	*$25.00*	£3.50	£10.50	£17.50
1 2nd/3rd/4th printings ND	*$0.60*	*$1.80*	*$3.00*	£0.40	£1.20	£2.00
2 ND	*$3.00*	*$9.00*	*$15.00*	£2.00	£6.00	£10.00
3 ND	*$2.40*	*$7.00*	*$12.00*	£1.20	£3.60	£6.00
4-5 ND	*$0.80*	*$2.40*	*$4.00*	£0.60	£1.80	£3.00
6-7 ND	*$0.70*	*$2.10*	*$3.50*	£0.50	£1.50	£2.50
8-11 ND	*$0.60*	*$1.80*	*$3.00*	£0.40	£1.20	£2.00
Title Value:	*$16.40*	*$49.00*	*$82.00*	£10.90	£32.70	£54.50

STRAY TOASTERS

Marvel Comics Group/Epic,MS; 1 1988-4 Apr 1989

Issue	$Good	$Fine	$N.Mint	£Good	£Fine	£N.Mint
1 ND Bill Sienkiewicz story and painted art	*$0.80*	*$2.40*	*$4.00*	£0.50	£1.50	£2.50
2 ND scarce in the U.K. Bill Sienkiewicz story and painted art	*$0.80*	*$2.40*	*$4.00*	£0.60	£1.80	£3.00
3-4 ND Bill Sienkiewicz story and painted art	*$0.80*	*$2.40*	*$4.00*	£0.50	£1.50	£2.50
Title Value:	*$3.20*	*$9.60*	*$16.00*	£2.10	£6.30	£10.50
Trade paperback (May 1991), reprints mini-series				£2.00	£6.00	£10.00

Note: all 48pg squarebound Bookshelf Format

STREET FIGHTER

Malibu; 1 Aug 1993-3 1994

Issue	$Good	$Fine	$N.Mint	£Good	£Fine	£N.Mint
1 ND	*$0.50*	*$1.50*	*$2.50*	£0.30	£0.90	£1.50
1 Gold Edition, ND (Oct 1994)	*$1.00*	*$3.00*	*$5.00*	£0.70	£2.10	£3.50
2 ND bound-in poster at centrefold	*$0.50*	*$1.50*	*$2.50*	£0.30	£0.90	£1.50
2 Gold Edition, ND (Oct 1994)	*$1.00*	*$3.00*	*$5.00*	£0.70	£2.10	£3.50
3 ND	*$0.50*	*$1.50*	*$2.50*	£0.30	£0.90	£1.50
3 Gold Edition, ND (Oct 1994)	*$1.00*	*$3.00*	*$5.00*	£0.70	£2.10	£3.50
Title Value:	*$4.50*	*$13.50*	*$22.50*	£3.00	£9.00	£15.00

Note: based on video game

STREET FIGHTER II

Viz Communications,MS; 1 Jun 1994-8 Jan 1995

Issue	$Good	$Fine	$N.Mint	£Good	£Fine	£N.Mint
1-8 ND Masaomi Kanzaki	*$0.60*	*$1.80*	*$3.00*	£0.40	£1.20	£2.00
Title Value:	*$4.80*	*$14.40*	*$24.00*	£3.20	£9.60	£16.00

STREET MUSIC

Fantagraphics,Magazine; 1 1988-6 1989 ?

Issue	$Good	$Fine	$N.Mint	£Good	£Fine	£N.Mint
1-6 ND	*$0.50*	*$1.50*	*$2.50*	£0.30	£0.90	£1.50
Title Value:	*$3.00*	*$9.00*	*$15.00*	£1.80	£5.40	£9.00

STREET POET-RAY

Marvel Comics Group/Epic; 1 Apr 1990-5 Dec 1990

Issue	$Good	$Fine	$N.Mint	£Good	£Fine	£N.Mint
1 ND Michael Redmond rap-poetry/Junko Hoshizawa art begins	*$0.40*	*$1.20*	*$2.00*	£0.25	£0.75	£1.25
2 ND 20th International Earth Day special	*$0.40*	*$1.20*	*$2.00*	£0.25	£0.75	£1.25
3 ND Amnesty International special	*$0.40*	*$1.20*	*$2.00*	£0.25	£0.75	£1.25
4 ND Rock and Roll Hall of Fame	*$0.40*	*$1.20*	*$2.00*	£0.25	£0.75	£1.25
5 ND Amnesty International	*$0.40*	*$1.20*	*$2.00*	£0.25	£0.75	£1.25
Title Value:	*$2.00*	*$6.00*	*$10.00*	£1.25	£3.75	£6.25

Note: bi-monthly frequency Bookshelf Format

STREET SHADOWS

Caliber Press,MS; 1 Apr 1992-2 1992

Issue	$Good	$Fine	$N.Mint	£Good	£Fine	£N.Mint
1 ND spin-off from Caliber Presents	*$0.50*	*$1.50*	*$2.50*	£0.30	£0.90	£1.50
2 ND	*$0.50*	*$1.50*	*$2.50*	£0.30	£0.90	£1.50
Title Value:	*$1.00*	*$3.00*	*$5.00*	£0.60	£1.80	£3.00

STREET WOLF

Blackthorne; 1 Jul 1986-3 Dec 1986

Issue	$Good	$Fine	$N.Mint	£Good	£Fine	£N.Mint
1-3 ND	*$0.40*	*$1.20*	*$2.00*	£0.25	£0.75	£1.25
Title Value:	*$1.20*	*$3.60*	*$6.00*	£0.75	£2.25	£3.75

STREETFIGHTER: THE BATTLE FOR SHADALOO

DC Comics,Film; 1 Feb 1995

Issue	$Good	$Fine	$N.Mint	£Good	£Fine	£N.Mint
1 ND 64pgs, adaptation of film based on Nintendo game starring Jean Claude Van Damme	*$0.80*	*$2.40*	*$4.00*	£0.50	£1.50	£2.50
Title Value:	*$0.80*	*$2.40*	*$4.00*	£0.50	£1.50	£2.50

STREETS

DC Comics,MS; 1 Oct 1993-3 Dec 1993

Issue	$Good	$Fine	$N.Mint	£Good	£Fine	£N.Mint
1-3 ND 48pgs, painted art						
	$0.80	*$2.40*	*$4.00*	£0.50	£1.50	£2.50
Title Value:	*$2.40*	*$7.20*	*$12.00*	£1.50	£4.50	£7.50

STRIKE

Eclipse; 1 Aug 1987-6 Feb 1988

Issue	$Good	$Fine	$N.Mint	£Good	£Fine	£N.Mint
1-6 ND	*$0.40*	*$1.20*	*$2.00*	£0.25	£0.75	£1.25
Title Value:	*$2.40*	*$7.20*	*$12.00*	£1.50	£4.50	£7.50

STRIKE FORCE AMERICA

Comico; 1 May 1992-5 1992

Issue	$Good	$Fine	$N.Mint	£Good	£Fine	£N.Mint
1 ND Sam Kieth cover						
	$0.40	*$1.20*	*$2.00*	£0.25	£0.75	£1.25
2 ND pin-up gallery included						
	$0.40	*$1.20*	*$2.00*	£0.25	£0.75	£1.25
3-5 ND	*$0.40*	*$1.20*	*$2.00*	£0.25	£0.75	£1.25
Title Value:	*$2.00*	*$6.00*	*$10.00*	£1.25	£3.75	£6.25
The Strike Force Files (Feb 1993)						
shrink-wrapped pack of issues #1 & #2 and Elementals #16				£1.60	£4.80	£8.00

STRIKE FORCE AMERICA (2ND SERIES)

Comico; 1 Sep 1995-3 1996 ?

Issue	$Good	$Fine	$N.Mint	£Good	£Fine	£N.Mint
1-2 ND	*$0.50*	*$1.50*	*$2.50*	£0.30	£0.90	£1.50
3 ND	*$0.60*	*$1.80*	*$3.00*	£0.40	£1.20	£2.00
Title Value:	*$1.60*	*$4.80*	*$8.00*	£1.00	£3.00	£5.00

STRIKE FORCE LEGACY

Comico; 1 Oct 1993

Issue	$Good	$Fine	$N.Mint	£Good	£Fine	£N.Mint
1 ND 48pgs, gold embossed logo; Mike Leeke and Mike Chen art						
	$0.60	*$1.80*	*$3.00*	£0.40	£1.20	£2.00
Title Value:	*$0.60*	*$1.80*	*$3.00*	£0.40	£1.20	£2.00

STRIKE VS. SGT. STRIKE SPECIAL

Eclipse,OS; 1 May 1988

Issue	$Good	$Fine	$N.Mint	£Good	£Fine	£N.Mint
1 ND Tom Lyle art, colour						
	$0.40	*$1.20*	*$2.00*	£0.25	£0.75	£1.25
Title Value:	*$0.40*	*$1.20*	*$2.00*	£0.25	£0.75	£1.25

STRIKEBACK!

Malibu Bravura,MS; 1 Oct 1994-4 Jan 1995

Issue	$Good	$Fine	$N.Mint	£Good	£Fine	£N.Mint
1 ND Kevin Maguire art						
	$0.60	*$1.80*	*$3.00*	£0.40	£1.20	£2.00
1 Gold Foil Edition, ND (Feb 1995)						
	$1.50	*$4.50*	*$7.50*	£1.00	£3.00	£5.00
2-4 ND Kevin Maguire art						
	$0.60	*$1.80*	*$3.00*	£0.40	£1.20	£2.00
Title Value:	*$3.90*	*$11.70*	*$19.50*	£2.60	£7.80	£13.00

STRIKEBACK! (2ND SERIES)

Image,MS; 1 Jan 1996-5 May 1996

Issue	$Good	$Fine	$N.Mint	£Good	£Fine	£N.Mint
1 ND Jonathan Peterson script, Kevin Maguire and Joe Rubenstein art						
	$0.50	*$1.50*	*$2.50*	£0.30	£0.90	£1.50
2-3 ND re-presenting Jonathan Peterson script, Kevin Maguire and Joe Rubenstein art with added pages						
	$0.50	*$1.50*	*$2.50*	£0.30	£0.90	£1.50
4-5 ND	*$0.50*	*$1.50*	*$2.50*	£0.30	£0.90	£1.50
Title Value:	*$2.50*	*$7.50*	*$12.50*	£1.50	£4.50	£7.50

STRIKEBACK! SPECIAL

Malibu Bravura,OS; 1 Apr 1995

Issue	$Good	$Fine	$N.Mint	£Good	£Fine	£N.Mint
1 ND 48pgs, climax to the mini-series						
	$0.80	*$2.40*	*$4.00*	£0.50	£1.50	£2.50
Title Value:	*$0.80*	*$2.40*	*$4.00*	£0.50	£1.50	£2.50

STRIKEFORCE: MORITURI

Marvel Comics Group; 1 Dec 1986-31 Jul 1989

Issue	$Good	$Fine	$N.Mint	£Good	£Fine	£N.Mint
1 ND Brent Anderson art begins, 3pgs Whilce Portacio art						
	$0.25	*$0.75*	*$1.25*	£0.15	£0.45	£0.75
2-9 ND	*$0.25*	*$0.75*	*$1.25*	£0.15	£0.45	£0.75
10 ND Whilce Portacio inks						
	$0.25	*$0.75*	*$1.25*	£0.15	£0.45	£0.75
11-12 ND	*$0.25*	*$0.75*	*$1.25*	£0.15	£0.45	£0.75
13 ND DS	*$0.25*	*$0.75*	*$1.25*	£0.15	£0.45	£0.75
14-15 ND	*$0.25*	*$0.75*	*$1.25*	£0.15	£0.45	£0.75
16 ND Whilce Portacio inks						
	$0.25	*$0.75*	*$1.25*	£0.15	£0.45	£0.75
17-20 ND	*$0.25*	*$0.75*	*$1.25*	£0.15	£0.45	£0.75
21 ND format change to higher quality paper						
	$0.25	*$0.75*	*$1.25*	£0.15	£0.45	£0.75
22-31 ND	*$0.25*	*$0.75*	*$1.25*	£0.15	£0.45	£0.75
Title Value:	*$7.75*	*$23.25*	*$38.75*	£4.65	£13.95	£23.25

STRIKER: SECRET OF THE BERSERKER

Viz Communications,MS; 1 Apr 1995-4 Jul 1995

Issue	$Good	$Fine	$N.Mint	£Good	£Fine	£N.Mint
1-4 ND Takashige & Mingawa script and art; black and white						
	$0.50	*$1.50*	*$2.50*	£0.30	£0.90	£1.50
Title Value:	*$2.00*	*$6.00*	*$10.00*	£1.20	£3.60	£6.00

STRIKER: THE ARMOURED WARRIOR

Viz Communications,MS; 1 Jun 1992-4 Sep 1992

Issue	$Good	$Fine	$N.Mint	£Good	£Fine	£N.Mint
1-4 ND	*$0.50*	*$1.50*	*$2.50*	£0.30	£0.90	£1.50
Title Value:	*$2.00*	*$6.00*	*$10.00*	£1.20	£3.60	£6.00

STRIKER: THE ARMOURED WARRIOR (2ND SERIES)

Viz Communications,MS; 1 Dec 1992

Issue	$Good	$Fine	$N.Mint	£Good	£Fine	£N.Mint
1 ND	*$0.50*	*$1.50*	*$2.50*	£0.30	£0.90	£1.50
Title Value:	*$0.50*	*$1.50*	*$2.50*	£0.30	£0.90	£1.50

STRONG MAN, THE POWER OF

AC Comics; 1 1989

Issue	$Good	$Fine	$N.Mint	£Good	£Fine	£N.Mint
1 ND 40pgs, (16 in colour), Cave Girl and Thun'da appear						
	$0.50	*$1.50*	*$2.50*	£0.30	£0.90	£1.50
Title Value:	*$0.50*	*$1.50*	*$2.50*	£0.30	£0.90	£1.50

STRYFE'S STRIKE FILE

Marvel Comics Group,OS; 1 Jan 1993

Issue	$Good	$Fine	$N.Mint	£Good	£Fine	£N.Mint
1 ND information on the mutant heroes and villains, metallic ink cover; Larry Stroman, Andy Kubert and Greg Capullo art featured						
	$0.50	*$1.50*	*$2.50*	£0.30	£0.90	£1.50
1 2nd printing, ND Jul 1993; gold and silver metallic cover						
	$0.40	*$1.20*	*$2.00*	£0.25	£0.75	£1.25
Title Value:	*$0.90*	*$2.70*	*$4.50*	£0.55	£1.65	£2.75

STRYKE

London Night Studios; 0 Mar 1995; ½ 1995

Issue	$Good	$Fine	$N.Mint	£Good	£Fine	£N.Mint
½ ND Everette hartsoe script, Jude Millien art; pre-bagged with tarot card						
	$0.60	*$1.80*	*$3.00*	£0.40	£1.20	£2.00
0 ND Everette Hartsoe script, Keith Pollard art						
	$0.90	*$2.70*	*$4.50*	£0.60	£1.80	£3.00
0 Commemorative Edition, ND with certificate of authenticity						
	$3.00	*$9.00*	*$15.00*	£2.00	£6.00	£10.00
0 Variant Cover Edition ND						
	$1.00	*$3.00*	*$5.00*	£0.70	£2.10	£3.50
Title Value:	*$5.50*	*$16.50*	*$27.50*	£3.70	£11.10	£18.50

STRYKE: NATURAL BORN KILLER

London Night Studios,MS; 1 Jun 1995

Issue	$Good	$Fine	$N.Mint	£Good	£Fine	£N.Mint
1 ND Everette Hartsoe script, Jude Millien art						
	$0.60	*$1.80*	*$3.00*	£0.40	£1.20	£2.00
Title Value:	*$0.60*	*$1.80*	*$3.00*	£0.40	£1.20	£2.00

STUCK RUBBER BABY GRAPHIC NOVEL

DC Comics/Paradox Press,OS; nn Oct 1995

Issue	$Good	$Fine	$N.Mint	£Good	£Fine	£N.Mint
nn Hardcover ND 224pgs, Howard Cruse script and art						
	$4.50	*$13.50*	*$22.50*	£3.00	£9.00	£15.00
nn Softcover ND 224pgs, (Oct 1996)						
	$3.00	*$9.00*	*$15.00*	£2.00	£6.00	£10.00
Title Value:	*$7.50*	*$22.50*	*$37.50*	£5.00	£15.00	£25.00

STUPID

Image; 1 Jul 1993

Issue	$Good	$Fine	$N.Mint	£Good	£Fine	£N.Mint
1 ND Hilary Barta and Doug Rice; Spawn parody						
	$0.40	*$1.20*	*$2.00*	£0.25	£0.75	£1.25
1 Ashcan Edition, ND (Oct 1993)						
	$0.80	*$2.40*	*$4.00*	£0.50	£1.50	£2.50
Title Value:	*$1.20*	*$3.60*	*$6.00*	£0.75	£2.25	£3.75

STUPID HEROES

Mirage/Next Comics; 1 Aug 1994-3 1994

Issue	$Good	$Fine	$N.Mint	£Good	£Fine	£N.Mint
1 ND Peter Laird script and art						
	$0.40	*$1.20*	*$2.00*	£0.25	£0.75	£1.25
2 ND	*$0.40*	*$1.20*	*$2.00*	£0.25	£0.75	£1.25
3 ND with two bound-in trading cards						
	$0.40	*$1.20*	*$2.00*	£0.25	£0.75	£1.25
Title Value:	*$1.20*	*$3.60*	*$6.00*	£0.75	£2.25	£3.75

STYGMATA

Entity Comics; 0 Apr 1994; 1 Jul 1994-3 Sep 1994

Issue	$Good	$Fine	$N.Mint	£Good	£Fine	£N.Mint
0 ND foil-stamped cover						
	$0.60	*$1.80*	*$3.00*	£0.40	£1.20	£2.00
1 ND foil enhanced logo						
	$0.60	*$1.80*	*$3.00*	£0.40	£1.20	£2.00
1 Gold Signed & Numbered Edition, ND (Jul 1994)						
	$1.50	*$4.50*	*$7.50*	£1.00	£3.00	£5.00
2 ND	*$0.60*	*$1.80*	*$3.00*	£0.40	£1.20	£2.00
3 ND foil-stamped cover						
	$0.60	*$1.80*	*$3.00*	£0.40	£1.20	£2.00
Title Value:	*$3.90*	*$11.70*	*$19.50*	£2.60	£7.80	£13.00
Stygmata: Dragon Prophet (Mar 1995)						
Trade paperback reprints mini-series, gold foil enhanced cover				£0.90	£2.70	£4.50

STYGMATA YEARBOOK

Entity Comics; 1 Dec 1994

Issue	$Good	$Fine	$N.Mint	£Good	£Fine	£N.Mint
1 ND foil-stamped enhanced cover						
	$0.60	*$1.80*	*$3.00*	£0.40	£1.20	£2.00
Title Value:	*$0.60*	*$1.80*	*$3.00*	£0.40	£1.20	£2.00

SUB-MARINER (1ST) COMICS

Timely/Atlas; 1 Spring 1941-25 Spring 1948; 26 Jun 1948-32 Jun 1949; 33 Apr 1954-42 Oct 1955

Issue	$Good	$Fine	$N.Mint	£Good	£Fine	£N.Mint
1 Sub-Mariner begins, 20pg Angel back-up story begins (ends #21)						
	$2400.00	*$7200.00*	*$24000.00*	£1600.00	£4800.00	£16000.00
2	*$620.00*	*$1875.00*	*$5000.00*	£415.00	£1250.00	£3350.00
3	*$400.00*	*$1200.00*	*$3200.00*	£265.00	£800.00	£2150.00
4	*$350.00*	*$1050.00*	*$2800.00*	£230.00	£700.00	£1875.00
5	*$235.00*	*$710.00*	*$1900.00*	£155.00	£475.00	£1275.00
6-10	*$225.00*	*$680.00*	*$1600.00*	£150.00	£460.00	£1075.00
11-15	*$170.00*	*$510.00*	*$1200.00*	£110.00	£340.00	£800.00
16	*$150.00*	*$450.00*	*$1050.00*	£100.00	£300.00	£700.00
17 1st war theme cover						
	$150.00	*$450.00*	*$1050.00*	£100.00	£300.00	£700.00
18-20	*$150.00*	*$450.00*	*$1050.00*	£100.00	£300.00	£700.00
21	*$105.00*	*$320.00*	*$750.00*	£70.00	£210.00	£500.00
22-23	*$120.00*	*$360.00*	*$850.00*	£80.00	£240.00	£570.00
24 Namora appears (cover)						
	$120.00	*$360.00*	*$850.00*	£80.00	£240.00	£570.00
25 Namora appears (cover), The Blonde Phantom begins						
	$150.00	*$450.00*	*$1050.00*	£100.00	£300.00	£700.00
26-28 Namora appears (cover)						
	$120.00	*$360.00*	*$850.00*	£80.00	£240.00	£570.00
29 Namora appears (cover) and shares co-title (only time)						
	$120.00	*$360.00*	*$850.00*	£80.00	£240.00	£570.00
30-31	*$120.00*	*$360.00*	*$850.00*	£80.00	£240.00	£570.00
32 scarce in the U.S, very scarce in the U.K. origin Sub-Mariner re-told						
	$200.00	*$600.00*	*$1400.00*	£130.00	£400.00	£935.00
33 scarce in the U.K. 1st Atlas issue, origin re-told						
	$110.00	*$340.00*	*$800.00*	£75.00	£225.00	£535.00

TRADE PAPERBACKS, GRAPHIC NOVELS AND OTHER COLLECTIONS ARE PRICED IN POUNDS STERLING ONLY. CONVERT AT 1.5 FOR DOLLARS.

	$Good	$Fine	$N.Mint	£Good	£Fine	£N.Mint
34-37	***$85.00***	***$260.00***	***$610.00***	**£57.50**	**£175.00**	**£410.00**
38	***$100.00***	***$300.00***	***$700.00***	**£65.00**	**£200.00**	**£470.00**
39-41	***$85.00***	***$255.00***	***$600.00***	**£55.00**	**£170.00**	**£400.00**
42 scarce in the U.K.						
	$100.00	***$310.00***	***$725.00***	**£67.50**	**£205.00**	**£485.00**
Title Value:	***$9170.00***	***$27600.00***	***$73465.00***	**£6087.50**	**£18435.00**	**£49120.00**

Note: all Non-Distributed on the news-stands in the U.K. though it is possible that copies came over via American G.I's or U.S. relatives of U.K. citizens. As with all Golden Age comics, these issues are generally scarce in the U.K.

SUB-MARINER (2ND SERIES)

Marvel Comics Group; 1 May 1968-72 Sep 1974

(see Namor, The Sub-Mariner, Tales to Astonish and Sub-Mariner Comics in the Independent section)

	$Good	$Fine	$N.Mint	£Good	£Fine	£N.Mint
1 origin retold, Fantastic Four appear						
	$21.00	***$62.50***	***$150.00***	**£13.50**	**£41.00**	**£95.00**
2 scarce in the U.K. Inhumans appear						
	$7.75	***$23.50***	***$55.00***	**£4.25**	**£12.50**	**£30.00**
3 Triton appears	***$5.00***	***$15.00***	***$35.00***	**£2.50**	**£7.50**	**£17.50**
4	***$5.00***	***$15.00***	***$35.00***	**£2.10**	**£6.25**	**£15.00**
5 1st appearance Tiger Shark						
	$5.00	***$15.00***	***$35.00***	**£2.50**	**£7.50**	**£17.50**
6	***$4.60***	***$13.50***	***$32.50***	**£1.75**	**£5.25**	**£12.50**
7 photo cover (Sub-Mariner in flight across cityscape)						
	$4.60	***$13.50***	***$32.50***	**£1.75**	**£5.25**	**£12.50**
8 scarce in the U.K. Thing vs Sub-Mariner						
	$5.00	***$15.00***	***$35.00***	**£2.85**	**£8.50**	**£20.00**
9 1st Serpent Crown						
	$4.60	***$13.50***	***$32.50***	**£1.75**	**£5.25**	**£12.50**
10	***$4.60***	***$13.50***	***$32.50***	**£1.75**	**£5.25**	**£12.50**
11-13	***$3.75***	***$11.00***	***$22.50***	**£1.65**	**£5.00**	**£10.00**
14 Sub-Mariner vs. Golden Age Human Torch, Toro dies						
	$5.75	***$17.50***	***$35.00***	**£2.50**	**£7.50**	**£15.00**
15	***$3.75***	***$11.00***	***$22.50***	**£1.65**	**£5.00**	**£10.00**
16-17	***$2.05***	***$6.25***	***$12.50***	**£1.15**	**£3.50**	**£7.00**
18 Triton appears	***$2.05***	***$6.25***	***$12.50***	**£1.15**	**£3.50**	**£7.00**
19 1st appearance Sting Ray						
	$2.05	***$6.25***	***$12.50***	**£1.15**	**£3.50**	**£7.00**
20 Sub-Mariner vs. Dr. Doom						
	$2.05	***$6.25***	***$12.50***	**£1.15**	**£3.50**	**£7.00**
21	***$1.30***	***$4.00***	***$8.00***	**£0.80**	**£2.50**	**£5.00**
22 Dr. Strange (as masked super-hero) appears						
	$1.30	***$4.00***	***$8.00***	**£0.80**	**£2.50**	**£5.00**
23 1st appearance Orka						
	$1.30	***$4.00***	***$8.00***	**£0.80**	**£2.50**	**£5.00**
24-25	***$1.30***	***$4.00***	***$8.00***	**£0.80**	**£2.50**	**£5.00**
26 Sub-Mariner vs. Red Raven						
	$1.25	***$3.75***	***$7.50***	**£0.65**	**£2.00**	**£4.00**
27 1st appearance Commander Kraken						
	$1.25	***$3.75***	***$7.50***	**£0.65**	**£2.00**	**£4.00**
28	***$1.25***	***$3.75***	***$7.50***	**£0.65**	**£2.00**	**£4.00**
29 Sub-Mariner vs. Hercules						
	$1.25	***$3.75***	***$7.50***	**£0.65**	**£2.00**	**£4.00**
30 Sub-Mariner vs. Captain Marvel						
	$1.25	***$3.75***	***$7.50***	**£0.65**	**£2.00**	**£4.00**
31-33	***$1.25***	***$3.75***	***$7.50***	**£0.65**	**£2.00**	**£4.00**
34 Hulk, Silver Surfer, Sub-Mariner team-up: 1st Defenders, though not yet named						
	$3.30	***$10.00***	***$20.00***	**£1.65**	**£5.00**	**£10.00**
35 Hulk, Silver Surfer, Sub-Mariner team-up: 2nd Defenders, though not yet named						
	$2.90	***$8.75***	***$17.50***	**£1.30**	**£4.00**	**£8.00**
36 Berni Wrightson inks						
	$1.25	***$3.75***	***$7.50***	**£0.65**	**£2.00**	**£4.00**
37 death of Lady Dorma						
	$1.25	***$3.75***	***$7.50***	**£0.65**	**£2.00**	**£4.00**
38 origin retold	***$1.25***	***$3.75***	***$7.50***	**£0.65**	**£2.00**	**£4.00**
39	***$1.25***	***$3.75***	***$7.50***	**£0.65**	**£2.00**	**£4.00**
40 Spiderman appears						
	$1.25	***$3.75***	***$7.50***	**£0.65**	**£2.00**	**£4.00**
41	***$1.00***	***$3.00***	***$6.00***	**£0.55**	**£1.75**	**£3.50**
42 last 15 cents issue						
	$1.00	***$3.00***	***$6.00***	**£0.55**	**£1.75**	**£3.50**
43 scarce in the U.K. 52pgs, (almost all copies ink-stained)						
	$1.00	***$3.00***	***$6.00***	**£0.80**	**£2.50**	**£5.00**
44 Sub-Mariner vs. Human Torch						
	$1.00	***$3.00***	***$6.00***	**£0.55**	**£1.75**	**£3.50**
45 Human Torch appears						
	$1.00	***$3.00***	***$6.00***	**£0.55**	**£1.75**	**£3.50**
46 Namor's father appears						
	$1.00	***$3.00***	***$6.00***	**£0.55**	**£1.75**	**£3.50**
47-48 Dr. Doom appears						
	$1.00	***$3.00***	***$6.00***	**£0.55**	**£1.75**	**£3.50**
49 Dr. Doom appears with the Cosmic Cube						
	$1.00	***$3.00***	***$6.00***	**£0.55**	**£1.75**	**£3.50**
50 1st appearance Namorita (later Nita in New Warriors), Bill Everett art						
	$1.25	***$3.75***	***$7.50***	**£0.80**	**£2.50**	**£5.00**
51 scarce in the U.K. Bill Everett art						
	$0.80	***$2.50***	***$5.00***	**£0.55**	**£1.75**	**£3.50**
52 scarce in the U.K.						
	$0.80	***$2.50***	***$5.00***	**£0.55**	**£1.75**	**£3.50**
53 scarce in the U.K. Bill Everett Sub-Mariner reprint from 1950s						
	$0.80	***$2.50***	***$5.00***	**£0.55**	**£1.75**	**£3.50**
54-56	***$0.80***	***$2.50***	***$5.00***	**£0.50**	**£1.50**	**£3.00**
57 Bill Everett art; classic cover with bondage thrown in for good measure						
	$0.80	***$2.50***	***$5.00***	**£0.55**	**£1.75**	**£3.50**
58 Bill Everett art (with Sam Kweskin); part Gil Kane cover						
	$0.80	***$2.50***	***$5.00***	**£0.50**	**£1.50**	**£3.00**
59 Sub-Mariner vs. Thor (no Everett art)						
	$0.80	***$2.50***	***$5.00***	**£0.50**	**£1.50**	**£3.00**
60 Bill Everett art	***$0.80***	***$2.50***	***$5.00***	**£0.50**	**£1.50**	**£3.00**
61 part Everett art (last ever original work?)						
	$0.80	***$2.50***	***$5.00***	**£0.50**	**£1.50**	**£3.00**
62-63 Everett script, Chaykin art on back-up						
	$0.80	***$2.50***	***$5.00***	**£0.50**	**£1.50**	**£3.00**
64 Chaykin art on back-up						
	$0.80	***$2.50***	***$5.00***	**£0.50**	**£1.50**	**£3.00**
65-66	***$0.80***	***$2.50***	***$5.00***	**£0.50**	**£1.50**	**£3.00**
67 Fantastic Four and Triton appear; 1st new costume						
	$0.80	***$2.50***	***$5.00***	**£0.50**	**£1.50**	**£3.00**
68	***$0.80***	***$2.50***	***$5.00***	**£0.50**	**£1.50**	**£3.00**
69 Sub-Mariner vs. Spiderman, Dr. Strange appears						
	$0.80	***$2.50***	***$5.00***	**£0.50**	**£1.50**	**£3.00**
70-72 ND	***$0.80***	***$2.50***	***$5.00***	**£0.50**	**£1.50**	**£3.00**
Title Value:	***$154.95***	***$466.00***	***$1009.00***	**£82.15**	**£249.75**	**£536.00**

Note: Everett art in #49-55, 57, 60. Tales of Atlantis in #62-66.

SUB-MARINER (2ND SERIES) ANNUAL

Marvel Comics Group; 1 1971-2 1972

	$Good	$Fine	$N.Mint	£Good	£Fine	£N.Mint
1 scarce in the U.K. 68pgs, reprints Tales to Astonish #70-73						
	$1.25	***$3.75***	***$7.50***	**£1.00**	**£3.00**	**£6.00**
2 ND scarce in the U.K. 68pgs, reprints Tales to Astonish #74-75						
	$1.15	***$3.50***	***$7.00***	**£0.80**	**£2.50**	**£5.00**
Title Value:	***$2.40***	***$7.25***	***$14.50***	**£1.80**	**£5.50**	**£11.00**

SUB-MARINER (LIMITED SERIES)

Marvel Comics Group,MS; 1 Sep 1984-4 Dec 1984

	$Good	$Fine	$N.Mint	£Good	£Fine	£N.Mint
1-4 ND	***$0.30***	***$0.90***	***$1.50***	**£0.20**	**£0.60**	**£1.00**

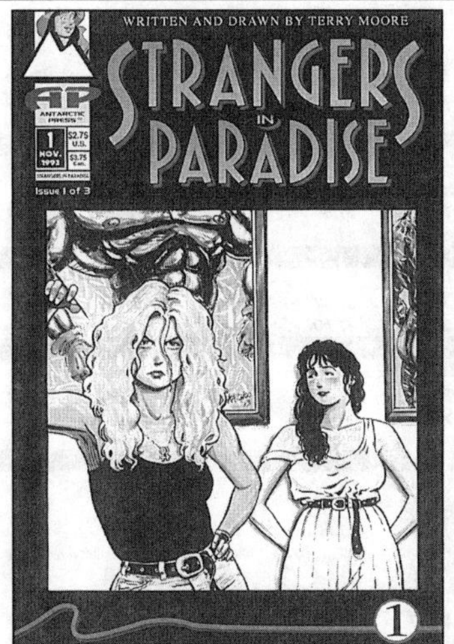

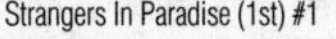
Strangers In Paradise (1st) #1

Sub-Mariner Annual #1

Sugar and Spike #98

	$Good	$Fine	$N.Mint	£Good	£Fine	£N.Mint
Title Value:	$1.20	$3.60	$6.00	£0.80	£2.40	£4.00

SUB-MARINER, SAGA OF THE

Marvel Comics Group,MS; 1 Nov 1988-12 Oct 1989

	$Good	$Fine	$N.Mint	£Good	£Fine	£N.Mint
1-4 ND	$0.30	$0.90	$1.50	£0.20	£0.60	£1.00
5 ND Invaders appear	$0.30	$0.90	$1.50	£0.20	£0.60	£1.00
6 ND	$0.30	$0.90	$1.50	£0.20	£0.60	£1.00
7 ND Fantastic Four appear	$0.30	$0.90	$1.50	£0.20	£0.60	£1.00
8 ND Avengers appear	$0.30	$0.90	$1.50	£0.20	£0.60	£1.00
9 ND original X-Men appear	$0.30	$0.90	$1.50	£0.20	£0.60	£1.00
10-12 ND	$0.30	$0.90	$1.50	£0.20	£0.60	£1.00
Title Value:	$3.60	$10.80	$18.00	£2.40	£7.20	£12.00

SUBMARINE ATTACK

Charlton; 11 May 1958-54 Feb/Mar 1966

(previously Speed Demons)

	$Good	$Fine	$N.Mint	£Good	£Fine	£N.Mint
11	$3.55	$10.50	$25.00	£2.25	£6.75	£16.00
12-20	$2.50	$7.50	$17.50	£1.75	£5.25	£12.50
21-30	$2.10	$6.25	$15.00	£1.40	£4.25	£10.00
31-54	$1.75	$5.25	$12.50	£1.05	£3.20	£7.50
Title Value:	$89.05	$266.50	$632.50	£57.20	£173.30	£408.50

Note: all distributed on the news-stands in the U.K. including the first few issues that technically fall outside official distribution

SUBSPECIES

Eternity,MS; 1 May 1991-4 Aug 1991

	$Good	$Fine	$N.Mint	£Good	£Fine	£N.Mint
1-4 ND based on film, colour	$0.40	$1.20	$2.00	£0.25	£0.75	£1.25
Title Value:	$1.60	$4.80	$8.00	£1.00	£3.00	£5.00

SUBTERRANEAN WARS

Marvel Comics Group; 1991

Cross-over storyline running throughout the following issues: **Avengers Annual #20**, **Incredible Hulk Annual #17**, **Namor Annual #1**, **Iron Man Annual #12**, **West Coast Avengers Annual #6**.

SUBURBAN HIGH LIFE

Slave Labor; 1 Jun 1987-3 1988

	$Good	$Fine	$N.Mint	£Good	£Fine	£N.Mint
1 ND Frank Cirocco, Mark Martin, Rick Geary, Trina Robbins art	$0.40	$1.20	$2.00	£0.25	£0.75	£1.25
1 2nd printing, ND (Jun 1987)	$0.30	$0.90	$1.50	£0.20	£0.60	£1.00
2-3 ND	$0.40	$1.20	$2.00	£0.25	£0.75	£1.25
Title Value:	$1.50	$4.50	$7.50	£0.95	£2.85	£4.75
Trade paperback, reprints				£0.65	£1.95	£3.25

SUBURBAN HIGHLIFE (2ND SERIES)

Slave Labor; 1 1996

	$Good	$Fine	$N.Mint	£Good	£Fine	£N.Mint
1 ND magazine format begins	$0.60	$1.80	$3.00	£0.40	£1.20	£2.00
Title Value:	$0.60	$1.80	$3.00	£0.40	£1.20	£2.00

SUBURBAN NIGHTMARES

Renegade,MS; 1 May 1988-4 Aug 1988

	$Good	$Fine	$N.Mint	£Good	£Fine	£N.Mint
1-4 ND	$0.40	$1.20	$2.00	£0.25	£0.75	£1.25
Title Value:	$1.60	$4.80	$8.00	£1.00	£3.00	£5.00

SUBURBAN NINJA SHE-DEVILS, THE

Marvel Comics Group,OS; 1 Jan 1992

	$Good	$Fine	$N.Mint	£Good	£Fine	£N.Mint
1 ND Turtles parody by Steve Gerber	$0.30	$0.90	$1.50	£0.20	£0.60	£1.00
Title Value:	$0.30	$0.90	$1.50	£0.20	£0.60	£1.00

SUE AND SALLY SMITH, FLYING NURSES

Charlton;48 Nov 1962-54 Nov 1963

	$Good	$Fine	$N.Mint	£Good	£Fine	£N.Mint
48-54 distributed in the U.K.	$1.05	$3.20	$7.50	£0.70	£2.10	£5.00
Title Value:	$7.35	$22.40	$52.50	£4.90	£14.70	£35.00

SUGAR AND SPIKE

National Periodical Publications/DC Comics; 1 Apr/May 1956-98 Oct/Nov 1971; 99 Mar 1992

(see also The Best of DC)

	$Good	$Fine	$N.Mint	£Good	£Fine	£N.Mint
1 very scarce in the U.K., scarce in the U.S.	$135.00	$410.00	$1100.00	£92.50	£280.00	£750.00
2 scarce in the U.K.	$57.50	$170.00	$460.00	£41.00	£120.00	£325.00
3-5 scarce in the U.K.	$50.00	$150.00	$400.00	£34.00	£100.00	£275.00
6-10	$36.00	$105.00	$250.00	£24.00	£72.50	£170.00
11-14	$32.00	$95.00	$225.00	£21.00	£62.50	£150.00
1st official distribution in the U.K.						
15-20 scarce in the U.K.	$32.00	$95.00	$225.00	£21.00	£62.50	£150.00
21-29 rare in the U.K.	$19.00	$57.50	$135.00	£11.00	£34.00	£80.00
30 rare in the U.K. Scribbly guest stars	$21.00	$62.50	$150.00	£11.00	£34.00	£80.00
31-40 rare in the U.K.	$18.50	$55.00	$130.00	£10.50	£32.00	£75.00
41-50 rare in the U.K.	$12.00	$36.00	$85.00	£6.25	£19.00	£45.00
51-60 rare in the U.K.	$10.50	$32.00	$75.00	£5.50	£17.00	£40.00
61-70 rare in the U.K.	$7.75	$23.50	$55.00	£4.25	£12.50	£30.00
71 rare in the U.K.	$7.75	$23.50	$55.00	£3.90	£11.50	£27.50
72 rare in the U.K. 1st Bernie the Brain	$7.75	$23.50	$55.00	£3.90	£11.50	£27.50
73-80 rare in the U.K.	$7.75	$23.50	$55.00	£3.90	£11.50	£27.50
81-84 rare in the U.K.	$5.00	$15.00	$35.00	£2.50	£7.50	£17.50
85 very scarce in the U.K. 68pgs	$5.00	$15.00	$35.00	£2.10	£6.25	£15.00
86-95 rare in the U.K.	$5.00	$15.00	$35.00	£2.50	£7.50	£17.50
96 very scarce in the U.K. 68pgs	$5.00	$15.00	$35.00	£2.10	£6.25	£15.00
97-98 scarce in the U.K. 52pgs	$5.00	$15.00	$35.00	£1.75	£5.25	£12.50
99 ND Silver Age Classic (Mar 1992) featuring material originally intended for this issue before the series was cancelled	$0.25	$0.75	$1.25	£0.15	£0.45	£0.75
Title Value:	$1689.75	$5055.75	$12256.25	£1022.35	£3075.95	£7525.75

Note: all issues by Sheldon Mayer.

SUICIDE SQUAD

DC Comics; 1 May 1987-66 Jun 1992

(see Deadshot)

	$Good	$Fine	$N.Mint	£Good	£Fine	£N.Mint
1 Howard Chaykin cover	$0.25	$0.75	$1.25	£0.15	£0.45	£0.75
2-8	$0.25	$0.75	$1.25	£0.15	£0.45	£0.75
9 Millennium X-over	$0.25	$0.75	$1.25	£0.15	£0.45	£0.75
10	$0.25	$0.75	$1.25	£0.15	£0.45	£0.75
11 Speedy and The Vixen appear	$0.25	$0.75	$1.25	£0.15	£0.45	£0.75
12	$0.25	$0.75	$1.25	£0.15	£0.45	£0.75
13 X-over with Justice League International #13	$0.25	$0.75	$1.25	£0.15	£0.45	£0.75
14-15	$0.25	$0.75	$1.25	£0.15	£0.45	£0.75
16 Shade the Changing Man returns	$0.25	$0.75	$1.25	£0.15	£0.45	£0.75
17-20	$0.25	$0.75	$1.25	£0.15	£0.45	£0.75
21 Bonus Book 16pg insert featuring The Bronze Tiger	$0.25	$0.75	$1.25	£0.15	£0.45	£0.75
22-25	$0.25	$0.75	$1.25	£0.15	£0.45	£0.75
26-28 The Janus Directive X-over with Checkmate #15, #16	$0.25	$0.75	$1.25	£0.15	£0.45	£0.75
29-30 Janus Directive	$0.25	$0.75	$1.25	£0.15	£0.45	£0.75
31-39	$0.25	$0.75	$1.25	£0.15	£0.45	£0.75
40 part 1 The Phoenix Gambit, Batman guest-stars, features free poster, one year gap in storyline after #39	$0.25	$0.75	$1.25	£0.15	£0.45	£0.75
41-43 parts 2-4 The Phoenix Gambit, Batman guest-stars	$0.25	$0.75	$1.25	£0.15	£0.45	£0.75
44-47	$0.25	$0.75	$1.25	£0.15	£0.45	£0.75
48-49 ties into The Killing Joke; Joker appears	$0.25	$0.75	$1.25	£0.15	£0.45	£0.75
50 48pgs, 50 year history of Suicide Squad	$0.30	$0.90	$1.50	£0.20	£0.60	£1.00
51-52	$0.25	$0.75	$1.25	£0.15	£0.45	£0.75
53 The Dragon's Horde part 1, Katana/Manhunter guest-star	$0.25	$0.75	$1.25	£0.15	£0.45	£0.75
54-57 The Dragon's Horde story	$0.25	$0.75	$1.25	£0.15	£0.45	£0.75
58 War of the Gods tie-in	$0.25	$0.75	$1.25	£0.15	£0.45	£0.75
59 Mystery of the Atom begins, Superman, Batman, Aquaman appear	$0.25	$0.75	$1.25	£0.15	£0.45	£0.75
60 Superman, Batman, Aquaman appear	$0.25	$0.75	$1.25	£0.15	£0.45	£0.75
61 Superman, Batman, Aquaman appear, intro Adam Cray the new Atom	$0.25	$0.75	$1.25	£0.15	£0.45	£0.75
62 Superman, Batman, Aquaman appear, Adam Cray dies, Ray Palmer (the Atom) returns	$0.25	$0.75	$1.25	£0.15	£0.45	£0.75
63-66	$0.25	$0.75	$1.25	£0.15	£0.45	£0.75
Title Value:	$16.55	$49.65	$82.75	£9.95	£29.85	£49.75

SUICIDE SQUAD ANNUAL

DC Comics; 1 1988

	$Good	$Fine	$N.Mint	£Good	£Fine	£N.Mint
1 ND Keith Giffen backup, new Manhunter appears	$0.30	$0.90	$1.50	£0.20	£0.60	£1.00
Title Value:	$0.30	$0.90	$1.50	£0.20	£0.60	£1.00

SULTRY TEENAGE SUPER FOXES

Solson Publications; 1 1987

	$Good	$Fine	$N.Mint	£Good	£Fine	£N.Mint
1 ND	$0.30	$0.90	$1.50	£0.20	£0.60	£1.00
Title Value:	$0.30	$0.90	$1.50	£0.20	£0.60	£1.00

SUN DEVILS

DC Comics,MS; 1 Jul 1984-12 Jun 1985

	$Good	$Fine	$N.Mint	£Good	£Fine	£N.Mint
1-12 ND	$0.20	$0.60	$1.00	£0.15	£0.45	£0.75
Title Value:	$2.40	$7.20	$12.00	£1.80	£5.40	£9.00

Note: high quality paper

SUN RUNNERS

Pacific/Eclipse; 1 Feb 1984-7 Dec 1985

	$Good	$Fine	$N.Mint	£Good	£Fine	£N.Mint
1 ND Pat Broderick cover and art, colour	$0.30	$0.90	$1.50	£0.20	£0.60	£1.00
2-4 ND Pat Broderick cover and art, colour; Mike Mahoney back-up strip by Roger McKenzie and Paul Smith	$0.30	$0.90	$1.50	£0.20	£0.60	£1.00
5 ND Pat Broderick cover and art, colour	$0.30	$0.90	$1.50	£0.20	£0.60	£1.00
6-7 ND	$0.30	$0.90	$1.50	£0.20	£0.60	£1.00
Title Value:	$2.10	$6.30	$10.50	£1.40	£4.20	£7.00

Note: although the next issue was advertised, the series was suddenly cancelled.

SUN RUNNERS CHRISTMAS SPECIAL

Amazing Comics; 1 1987

Issue	$Good	$Fine	$N.Mint	£Good	£Fine	£N.Mint
1 ND	$0.40	$1.20	$2.00	£0.25	£0.75	£1.25
Title Value:	$0.40	$1.20	$2.00	£0.25	£0.75	£1.25

SUNGLASSES AFTER DARK

Verotik; 1 Nov 1995-present

Issue	$Good	$Fine	$N.Mint	£Good	£Fine	£N.Mint
1 ND Nancy Collins script, Stan Shaw art begins	$0.60	$1.80	$3.00	£0.40	£1.20	£2.00
2-6 ND	$0.60	$1.80	$3.00	£0.40	£1.20	£2.00
Title Value:	$3.60	$10.80	$18.00	£2.40	£7.20	£12.00

SUPER COPS

Red Circle (Archie),Film; 1 Jul 1974

Issue	$Good	$Fine	$N.Mint	£Good	£Fine	£N.Mint
1 distributed in the U.K. Gray Morrow and Frank Thorne art	$0.40	$1.25	$2.50	£0.25	£0.75	£1.50
Title Value:	$0.40	$1.25	$2.50	£0.25	£0.75	£1.50

SUPER DC GIANT

DC Comics; 13 Sep/Oct 1970-26 Jul/Aug 1971; 27 Summer 1976

(No issues numbered #1-12 were published)

Issue	$Good	$Fine	$N.Mint	£Good	£Fine	£N.Mint
13 ND Binky	$0.65	$2.00	$4.00	£0.50	£1.50	£3.00
14 Top Guns of the West, Joe Kubert cover	$0.65	$2.00	$4.00	£0.30	£1.00	£2.00
15 Western Comics; new Warrior Breed story, Joe Kubert cover	$0.80	$2.50	$5.00	£0.30	£1.00	£2.00
16 Best of The Brave and the Bold; 2 new framing pages featuring Batman and Flash; reprints Brave and the Bold #58, #67	$0.80	$2.50	$5.00	£0.65	£2.00	£4.00
17 ND scarce in the U.K, scarce in the U.S. Love 1970	$0.65	$2.00	$4.00	£0.40	£1.25	£2.50
18 ND Three Mouseketeers	$0.65	$2.00	$4.00	£0.30	£1.00	£2.00
19 ND scarce in the U.K. Neal Adams reprint, Jerry Lewis	$0.65	$2.00	$4.00	£0.65	£2.00	£4.00
20 House of Mystery	$0.80	$2.50	$5.00	£0.30	£1.00	£2.00
21 ND scarce in the U.K, scarce in the U.S. Love 1971	$0.65	$2.00	$4.00	£0.40	£1.25	£2.50
22 Top Guns of the West, features Batlash/Johnny Thunder/Night Hawk/Matt Savage; Joe Kubert cover	$0.65	$2.00	$4.00	£0.30	£1.00	£2.00
23 Unexpected	$0.65	$2.00	$4.00	£0.30	£1.00	£2.00
24 Supergirl; reprints back-up stories from Action Comics #295-298	$0.65	$2.00	$4.00	£0.40	£1.25	£2.50
25 scarce in the U.K. Challengers of the Unknown	$0.65	$2.00	$4.00	£0.65	£2.00	£4.00
26 Aquaman	$0.65	$2.00	$4.00	£0.50	£1.50	£3.00
27 ND 48pgs, and scarce in the U.K., Strange Flying Saucer Stories	$0.65	$2.00	$4.00	£0.50	£1.50	£3.00
Title Value:	$10.20	$31.50	$63.00	£6.45	£20.25	£40.50

Note: Issues 13-26 are 68pgs. S-13, 14, 16-27 are all reprint.

ARTISTS

Kirby reprints in 20, 25.

REPRINT FEATURES

Bat Lash in 22. Batman/Flash in 16. Buffalo Bill in 15. Johnny Thunder in 14, 22. Matt Savage in 14, 22. Metamorpho in 16. Nighthawk in 14, 22. Pow-Wow Smith in 15. Trigger Twins in 14. Vigilante in 15. Wyoming Kid in 14.

SUPER FRIENDS

DC Comics,TV; 1 Nov 1975-47 Aug 1981

(see Best of DC Limited Collector's Edition)

Issue	$Good	$Fine	$N.Mint	£Good	£Fine	£N.Mint
1 scarce in the U.K. Superman, Batman, Robin, Wonder Woman, Aquaman plus Zan and Jayna the Wonder Twins begin; based on Saturday morning cartoon show	$0.80	$2.50	$5.00	£0.50	£1.50	£3.00
2 scarce in the U.K.	$0.50	$1.50	$3.00	£0.30	£1.00	£2.00
3 scarce in the U.K.	$0.40	$1.25	$2.50	£0.25	£0.75	£1.50
4 scarce in the U.K. Riddler appears	$0.40	$1.25	$2.50	£0.25	£0.75	£1.50
5-7	$0.40	$1.25	$2.50	£0.25	£0.75	£1.50
8 Red Tornado appears; dinosaur cover	$0.40	$1.25	$2.50	£0.25	£0.75	£1.50
9 1st appearance Ice (though outside DC continuity)	$0.40	$1.25	$2.50	£0.25	£0.75	£1.50
10	$0.40	$1.25	$2.50	£0.25	£0.75	£1.50
11-13	$0.40	$1.25	$2.50	£0.20	£0.60	£1.25
14 scarce in the U.K. 44pgs	$0.40	$1.25	$2.50	£0.25	£0.75	£1.50
15-21	$0.40	$1.25	$2.50	£0.20	£0.60	£1.25
22 Chronos appears	$0.40	$1.25	$2.50	£0.20	£0.60	£1.25
23 Mirror Master appears	$0.40	$1.25	$2.50	£0.20	£0.60	£1.25
24	$0.40	$1.25	$2.50	£0.20	£0.60	£1.25
25 1st appearance Fire (though outside DC continuity)	$0.40	$1.25	$2.50	£0.20	£0.60	£1.25
26-27	$0.40	$1.25	$2.50	£0.20	£0.60	£1.25
28 Bizarro, Demon, Man-Bat, Solomon Grundy and Swamp Thing appear	$0.40	$1.25	$2.50	£0.20	£0.60	£1.25
29	$0.40	$1.25	$2.50	£0.20	£0.60	£1.25
30 Gorilla Grodd appears	$0.40	$1.25	$2.50	£0.20	£0.60	£1.25
31 Black Orchid guest-stars	$0.40	$1.25	$2.50	£0.20	£0.60	£1.25
32 The Scarecrow appears	$0.40	$1.25	$2.50	£0.20	£0.60	£1.25
33 Hawkman appears	$0.40	$1.25	$2.50	£0.20	£0.60	£1.25
34-36	$0.40	$1.25	$2.50	£0.20	£0.60	£1.25
37 Supergirl appears	$0.40	$1.25	$2.50	£0.20	£0.60	£1.25
38-40	$0.40	$1.25	$2.50	£0.20	£0.60	£1.25
41 The Toyman appears	$0.40	$1.25	$2.50	£0.20	£0.60	£1.25
42	$0.40	$1.25	$2.50	£0.20	£0.60	£1.25
43 Plastic Man back-up	$0.40	$1.25	$2.50	£0.20	£0.60	£1.25
44	$0.40	$1.25	$2.50	£0.20	£0.60	£1.25
45 Sinestro appears; Plastic Man back-up	$0.40	$1.25	$2.50	£0.20	£0.60	£1.25
46-47	$0.40	$1.25	$2.50	£0.20	£0.60	£1.25
Title Value:	$19.30	$60.25	$120.50	£10.25	£30.85	£63.50

FEATURES

Super Friends (Superman, Batman, Robin, Wonder Woman, Aquaman) in all issues. Jack O'Lantern in 37, 40, 44. Plastic Man in 43, 45. The Seraph in 38, 41, 46. Wonder Twins in 14, 29, 34, 36, 39, 42.

SUPER FRIENDS SPECIAL, THE

DC Comics,OS; 1 1981

Issue	$Good	$Fine	$N.Mint	£Good	£Fine	£N.Mint
1 ND scarce in the U.K. giveaway	$0.40	$1.20	$2.00	£0.30	£0.90	£1.50
Title Value:	$0.40	$1.20	$2.00	£0.30	£0.90	£1.50

SUPER GOOF

Gold Key/Whitman; 1 Oct 1965-74 1982

Issue	$Good	$Fine	$N.Mint	£Good	£Fine	£N.Mint
1 scarce in the U.K.	$3.55	$10.50	$25.00	£2.10	£6.25	£15.00
2-5	$1.75	$5.25	$12.50	£0.85	£2.55	£6.00
6-10	$1.05	$3.20	$7.50	£0.50	£1.50	£3.50
11-30	$0.80	$2.50	$5.00	£0.30	£1.00	£2.00
31-57	$0.55	$1.75	$3.50	£0.25	£0.75	£1.50
58 1st Whitman issue	$0.40	$1.20	$2.00	£0.20	£0.60	£1.00
59-74	$0.40	$1.20	$2.00	£0.20	£0.60	£1.00
Title Value:	$53.45	$165.15	$341.00	£24.15	£74.40	£154.00

SUPER GREEN BERET (TED HOLTON..)

Milson Publishing; 1 Apr 1967-2 Jun 1967

Issue	$Good	$Fine	$N.Mint	£Good	£Fine	£N.Mint
1-2 ND	$3.20	$9.50	$22.50	£2.10	£6.25	£15.00
Title Value:	$6.40	$19.00	$45.00	£4.20	£12.50	£30.00

SUPER HEROES

Dell; 1 Jan 1967-4 Jun 1967

Issue	$Good	$Fine	$N.Mint	£Good	£Fine	£N.Mint
1 distributed in the U.K. 1st appearance The Fab Four (Marvel rip-off!)	$4.25	$12.50	$30.00	£2.85	£8.50	£20.00
2-4 distributed in the U.K.	$2.50	$7.50	$17.50	£1.75	£5.25	£12.50
Title Value:	$11.75	$35.00	$82.50	£8.10	£24.25	£57.50

SUPER POWERS

DC Comics,MS; 1 Jul 1984-5 Nov 1984

Issue	$Good	$Fine	$N.Mint	£Good	£Fine	£N.Mint
1 Jack Kirby plot and covers begin; Joker, Luthor, Penguin cover; Batman appears	$0.40	$1.20	$2.00	£0.25	£0.75	£1.25
2 Batman, Joker, Pengiun, Luthor appear	$0.40	$1.20	$2.00	£0.25	£0.75	£1.25
3-4 Batman, Joker, Pengiun, Luthor appear; Darkseid appears	$0.40	$1.20	$2.00	£0.25	£0.75	£1.25
5 Jack Kirby art and script (not just plot); Batman, Joker, Pengiun, Luthor, Darkseid all appear	$0.40	$1.20	$2.00	£0.25	£0.75	£1.25
Title Value:	$2.00	$6.00	$10.00	£1.25	£3.75	£6.25

SUPER POWERS (2ND SERIES)

DC Comics,MS; 1 Sep 1985-6 Feb 1986

Issue	$Good	$Fine	$N.Mint	£Good	£Fine	£N.Mint
1 Jack Kirby cover and art; Darkseid appears (and on cover), Justice League of Ameerica inc. Batman appear	$0.40	$1.20	$2.00	£0.25	£0.75	£1.25
2-3 Jack Kirby cover and art	$0.40	$1.20	$2.00	£0.25	£0.75	£1.25
4-6 Jack Kirby cover and art, Batman appears	$0.40	$1.20	$2.00	£0.25	£0.75	£1.25
Title Value:	$2.40	$7.20	$12.00	£1.50	£4.50	£7.50

SUPER POWERS (3RD SERIES)

DC Comics,MS; 1 Sep 1986-4 Dec 1986

Issue	$Good	$Fine	$N.Mint	£Good	£Fine	£N.Mint
1 Batman appears; Infantino art	$0.30	$0.90	$1.50	£0.20	£0.60	£1.00
2-3 Batman and Darkseid appear; Infantino art	$0.30	$0.90	$1.50	£0.20	£0.60	£1.00
4 Batman appears; Infantino art	$0.30	$0.90	$1.50	£0.20	£0.60	£1.00
Title Value:	$1.20	$3.60	$6.00	£0.80	£2.40	£4.00

SUPER SOLDIER

DC Comics/Amalgam,OS; 1 May 1996

Issue	$Good	$Fine	$N.Mint	£Good	£Fine	£N.Mint
1 ND a DC/Marvel amalgamation of Superman and Captain America; Mark Waid script, Dave Gibbons art	$0.50	$1.50	$2.50	£0.40	£1.20	£2.00
Title Value:	$0.50	$1.50	$2.50	£0.40	£1.20	£2.00

SUPER SOLDIERS

Marvel UK; 1 Apr 1993-10 Jan 1994

Issue	$Good	$Fine	$N.Mint	£Good	£Fine	£N.Mint
1 Bennet/Stevens and Currie/Ramos, USAgent appears; silver-embossed logo	$0.40	$1.20	$2.00	£0.20	£0.60	£1.00
2-3	$0.30	$0.90	$1.50	£0.15	£0.45	£0.75
4 Avengers, USAgent and Captain America appear	$0.30	$0.90	$1.50	£0.15	£0.45	£0.75
5 Captain America and West Coast Anengers appear	$0.30	$0.90	$1.50	£0.15	£0.45	£0.75

Issue	$Good	$Fine	$N.Mint	£Good	£Fine	£N.Mint
6 origin Hauer, Nick Fury appears; day-glow cover	*$0.30*	*$0.90*	*$1.50*	£0.15	£0.45	£0.75
7 Nick Fury and X-Men appear	*$0.30*	*$0.90*	*$1.50*	£0.15	£0.45	£0.75
8-9 Punisher appears	*$0.30*	*$0.90*	*$1.50*	£0.15	£0.45	£0.75
10	*$0.30*	*$0.90*	*$1.50*	£0.15	£0.45	£0.75
Title Value:	*$3.10*	*$9.30*	*$15.50*	£1.55	£4.65	£7.75

SUPER VILLAIN CLASSICS

Marvel Comics Group,OS; 1 May 1983

Issue	$Good	$Fine	$N.Mint	£Good	£Fine	£N.Mint
1 ND Galactus the Origin by Jack Kirby, extra art by John Byrne	*$0.60*	*$1.80*	*$3.00*	£0.40	£1.20	£2.00
1 2nd printing, ND (Feb 1996), with new colour separations and extra pin-ups	*$0.50*	*$1.50*	*$2.50*	£0.30	£0.90	£1.50
Title Value:	*$1.10*	*$3.30*	*$5.50*	£0.70	£2.10	£3.50

SUPER-HEROES BATTLE SUPER-GORILLAS

DC Comics,OS; 1 Winter 1976

(see DC Special #16)

Issue	$Good	$Fine	$N.Mint	£Good	£Fine	£N.Mint
1 ND 52pgs, Superman, Batman, Flash reprints	*$0.50*	*$1.50*	*$3.00*	£0.30	£1.00	£2.00
Title Value:	*$0.50*	*$1.50*	*$3.00*	£0.30	£1.00	£2.00

SUPER-HEROES GIANT SIZE

Marvel Comics Group; 1 Jun 1974

Issue	$Good	$Fine	$N.Mint	£Good	£Fine	£N.Mint
1 ND 52pgs, Spiderman vs. Man-Wolf, Morbius appears, Gil Kane art	*$6.25*	*$18.50*	*$37.50*	£3.30	£10.00	£20.00
Title Value:	*$6.25*	*$18.50*	*$37.50*	£3.30	£10.00	£20.00

SUPER-HEROES PUZZLES AND GAMES

Marvel Comics Group; nn 1979

Issue	$Good	$Fine	$N.Mint	£Good	£Fine	£N.Mint
nn ND 32pgs, cereal giveaway; features origins of Spiderman, Spiderwoman, Hulk and Captain America	*$1.00*	*$3.00*	*$6.00*	£0.50	£1.50	£3.00
Title Value:	*$1.00*	*$3.00*	*$6.00*	£0.50	£1.50	£3.00

SUPER-STAR HOLIDAY SPECIAL

DC Comics; nn Spring 1980

(DC Special Series #21)

Issue	$Good	$Fine	$N.Mint	£Good	£Fine	£N.Mint
nn ND 64pgs, new Batman story by Frank Miller (1st Frank Miller Batman), House of Mystery, Sgt. Rock, Superboy and the Legion of Super-Heroes	*$2.00*	*$6.00*	*$10.00*	£1.50	£4.50	£7.50
Title Value:	*$2.00*	*$6.00*	*$10.00*	£1.50	£4.50	£7.50

SUPER-STARS GIANT SIZE

Marvel Comics Group; 1 May 1974

(becomes Fantastic Four Giant Size)

Issue	$Good	$Fine	$N.Mint	£Good	£Fine	£N.Mint
1 ND 52pgs, features Fantastic Four; Thing vs. Hulk	*$2.50*	*$7.50*	*$15.00*	£1.65	£5.00	£10.00
Title Value:	*$2.50*	*$7.50*	*$15.00*	£1.65	£5.00	£10.00

SUPER-TEAM FAMILY

DC Comics; 1 Oct Nov 1975-15 Mar Apr 1978

Issue	$Good	$Fine	$N.Mint	£Good	£Fine	£N.Mint
1 68pgs, new Teen Titans story o/w reprints inc. a Neal Adams reprint	*$0.50*	*$1.50*	*$3.00*	£0.50	£1.50	£3.00
2 68pgs, new Creeper/Wildcat story o/w reprints inc. Neal Adams reprints	*$0.30*	*$1.00*	*$2.00*	£0.40	£1.25	£2.50
3 68pgs, new Flash/Hawkman story o/w reprints inc. Neal Adams reprints	*$0.30*	*$1.00*	*$2.00*	£0.30	£1.00	£2.00
4 68pgs, all reprint begins	*$0.30*	*$1.00*	*$2.00*	£0.25	£0.75	£1.50
5 52pgs, Batman/Eclipso reprint from Brave and the Bold #64, new 1pg origin Eclipso	*$0.30*	*$1.00*	*$2.00*	£0.30	£1.00	£2.00
6 scarce in the U.K. 52pgs	*$0.25*	*$0.75*	*$1.50*	£0.25	£0.75	£1.50
7 52pgs	*$0.25*	*$0.75*	*$1.50*	£0.20	£0.60	£1.25
8 52pgs, new Challengers of the Unknown story, Doom patrol origin sequence reprinted from Doom Patrol #86, Doom Patrol #87 reprinted	*$0.40*	*$1.25*	*$2.50*	£0.20	£0.60	£1.25
9 ND 52pgs, new Challengers of the Unknown story	*$0.40*	*$1.25*	*$2.50*	£0.25	£0.85	£1.75
10 52pgs, new Challengers of the Unknown story	*$0.40*	*$1.25*	*$2.50*	£0.20	£0.60	£1.25
11 52pgs	*$0.25*	*$0.75*	*$1.50*	£0.20	£0.60	£1.25
12-15 ND 52pgs	*$0.25*	*$0.75*	*$1.50*	£0.25	£0.75	£1.50
Title Value:	*$4.65*	*$14.50*	*$29.00*	£4.05	£12.50	£25.25

FEATURES

Aquaman/Captain Comet/Atom in 13. Creeper/Wildcat in 2. Challengers of the Unknown in 8-10. Flash/Hawkman in 3. Flash/New Gods in 15. Flash/Supergirl Atom in 11. Green Lantern/Hawkman/Atom in 12. Wonder Woman/Atom in 14.

REPRINT FEATURES

Aquaman/Green Arrow, Batman/Deadman, Green Arrow in 2. Batman/Eclipso, Superboy in 5. Doom Patrol in 7-10. Flash in 1. Justice Society of America in 4. Marvel Family in 6. Superman/Batman in 1, 3, 4, 6. Teen Titans in 1, 7.

SUPER-VILLAIN TEAM-UP

Marvel Comics Group; 1 Aug 1975-14 Oct 1977; 15 Nov 1978; 16 Sep 1979; 17 Jun 1980

Issue	$Good	$Fine	$N.Mint	£Good	£Fine	£N.Mint
1 ND	*$0.80*	*$2.50*	*$5.00*	£0.55	£1.75	£3.50
2 ND	*$0.50*	*$1.50*	*$3.00*	£0.30	£1.00	£2.00
3-4	*$0.50*	*$1.50*	*$3.00*	£0.20	£0.60	£1.25
5-7 Fantastic Four appear	*$0.50*	*$1.50*	*$3.00*	£0.20	£0.60	£1.25
8 Giffen art	*$0.50*	*$1.50*	*$3.00*	£0.20	£0.60	£1.25
9 Avengers tie-in to #155	*$0.50*	*$1.50*	*$3.00*	£0.30	£1.00	£2.00
10 ND Avengers appear	*$0.50*	*$1.50*	*$3.00*	£0.30	£1.00	£2.00
11-12 ND Captain America appears	*$0.40*	*$1.25*	*$2.50*	£0.30	£1.00	£2.00
13 ND	*$0.40*	*$1.25*	*$2.50*	£0.25	£0.85	£1.75
14 ND X-Men cameo, Magneto appears; The Champions guest-star (tie-in to Champions #16), John Byrne cover	*$0.40*	*$1.25*	*$2.50*	£0.30	£1.00	£2.00
15 ND rare in the U.K. reprint	*$0.40*	*$1.25*	*$2.50*	£0.40	£1.25	£2.50
16-17 ND	*$0.40*	*$1.25*	*$2.50*	£0.25	£0.75	£1.50
Title Value:	*$8.10*	*$24.75*	*$49.50*	£4.70	£14.95	£30.25

FEATURES

Dr.Doom/Sub-Mariner in 1-15. Red Skull/Hate Monger in 16, 17. Avengers tie-in issue 9.

SUPER-VILLAIN TEAM-UP GIANT SIZE

Marvel Comics Group; 1 Oct 1974-2 Jul 1975

Issue	$Good	$Fine	$N.Mint	£Good	£Fine	£N.Mint
1 ND 68pgs, pre-dates Super-Villain Team Up #1	*$1.25*	*$3.75*	*$7.50*	£0.80	£2.50	£5.00
2 ND 68pgs	*$1.00*	*$3.00*	*$6.00*	£0.65	£2.00	£4.00
Title Value:	*$2.25*	*$6.75*	*$13.50*	£1.45	£4.50	£9.00

Note: Dr. Doom and Sub-Mariner in both.

SUPERBOY

National Periodical Publications/DC Comics; 1 Mar/Apr 1949-258 Dec 1979

(see Action, Adventure, DC Superstars, Legion of Super-Heroes)
(becomes Superboy and the Legion of Super-Heroes with #231)
(see Legion of Super-Heroes (1st series) for issues #259 onwards)

Issue	$Good	$Fine	$N.Mint	£Good	£Fine	£N.Mint
1 scarce in the U.K. Superman appears on cover; cover "illusion" of page being turned back	*$670.00*	*$2025.00*	*$6750.00*	£450.00	£1350.00	£4500.00
[Prices may vary widely on this comic]						
2	*$185.00*	*$560.00*	*$1500.00*	£125.00	£375.00	£1000.00
3	*$140.00*	*$420.00*	*$1125.00*	£92.50	£280.00	£750.00
4	*$92.50*	*$280.00*	*$750.00*	£62.50	£185.00	£500.00
5	*$90.00*	*$270.00*	*$725.00*	£60.00	£180.00	£485.00
6 (Jan/Feb 1950)	*$82.50*	*$250.00*	*$675.00*	£55.00	£165.00	£450.00
7	*$82.50*	*$250.00*	*$675.00*	£55.00	£165.00	£450.00
8 1st appearance Superbaby	*$82.50*	*$250.00*	*$675.00*	£55.00	£165.00	£450.00
9	*$82.50*	*$250.00*	*$675.00*	£55.00	£165.00	£450.00
10 1st appearance Lana Lang	*$82.50*	*$250.00*	*$675.00*	£55.00	£165.00	£450.00
11	*$62.50*	*$185.00*	*$500.00*	£42.00	£125.00	£335.00
12 (Jan/Feb 1951)	*$62.50*	*$185.00*	*$500.00*	£42.00	£125.00	£335.00
13-15	*$62.50*	*$185.00*	*$500.00*	£42.00	£125.00	£335.00
16-17	*$41.00*	*$120.00*	*$325.00*	£28.00	£82.50	£220.00
18 (Feb/Mar 1952)	*$41.00*	*$120.00*	*$325.00*	£28.00	£82.50	£220.00
19-20	*$41.00*	*$120.00*	*$325.00*	£28.00	£82.50	£220.00
21-23	*$31.00*	*$92.50*	*$250.00*	£21.00	£62.50	£170.00
24 (Feb/Mar 1953)	*$31.00*	*$92.50*	*$250.00*	£21.00	£62.50	£170.00
25-26	*$31.00*	*$92.50*	*$250.00*	£21.00	£62.50	£170.00
27 scarce in the U.S, very scarce in the U.K.	*$38.00*	*$110.00*	*$300.00*	£25.00	£75.00	£200.00
28-29	*$31.00*	*$92.50*	*$250.00*	£21.00	£62.50	£170.00
30 (Jan 1954)	*$31.00*	*$92.50*	*$250.00*	£21.00	£62.50	£170.00
31-37	*$23.00*	*$67.50*	*$185.00*	£15.50	£47.00	£125.00
38 (Jan 1955)	*$23.00*	*$67.50*	*$185.00*	£15.50	£47.00	£125.00
39-40	*$23.00*	*$67.50*	*$185.00*	£15.50	£47.00	£125.00
41-45	*$21.00*	*$62.50*	*$170.00*	£14.00	£43.00	£115.00
46 (Jan 1956)	*$21.00*	*$62.50*	*$170.00*	£14.00	£43.00	£115.00
47-48	*$21.00*	*$62.50*	*$170.00*	£14.00	£43.00	£115.00
49 1st appearance Metallo (robot guardian of Kal-El on Krypton)	*$23.50*	*$70.00*	*$190.00*	£16.00	£49.00	£130.00
50	*$21.00*	*$62.50*	*$170.00*	£14.00	£43.00	£115.00
51-53	*$16.50*	*$50.00*	*$135.00*	£11.00	£34.00	£90.00
54 (Jan 1957)	*$16.50*	*$50.00*	*$135.00*	£11.00	£34.00	£90.00
55-60	*$16.50*	*$50.00*	*$135.00*	£11.00	£34.00	£90.00
61	*$15.00*	*$45.00*	*$120.00*	£10.00	£30.00	£80.00
62 (Jan 1958)	*$15.00*	*$45.00*	*$120.00*	£10.00	£30.00	£80.00
63-67	*$15.00*	*$45.00*	*$120.00*	£10.00	£30.00	£80.00
68 origin and 1st appearance original Bizarro	*$52.50*	*$160.00*	*$490.00*	£36.00	£105.00	£325.00
69	*$12.50*	*$38.00*	*$100.00*	£8.00	£24.00	£65.00
70 (Jan 1959)	*$12.50*	*$38.00*	*$100.00*	£8.00	£24.00	£65.00
71-75	*$12.50*	*$38.00*	*$100.00*	£8.00	£24.00	£65.00
76 1st appearance Beppo the Super-Monkey; copies known with distribution stamps	*$12.50*	*$38.00*	*$100.00*	£8.00	£24.00	£65.00
1st official distribution in the U.K.						
77	*$12.50*	*$38.00*	*$100.00*	£8.00	£24.00	£65.00
78 (Jan 1960), origin Mr. Mxyzptlk re-told (see Superman #30 for 1st appearance)	*$20.00*	*$60.00*	*$160.00*	£11.50	£36.00	£95.00
79	*$12.50*	*$38.00*	*$100.00*	£7.50	£22.50	£60.00
80 Superboy and Supergirl 1st meet	*$17.50*	*$52.50*	*$140.00*	£10.50	£32.00	£85.00
81	*$12.00*	*$36.00*	*$85.00*	£6.75	£20.00	£47.50
82 1st appearance Bizarro Krypto	*$12.50*	*$39.00*	*$90.00*	£6.75	£20.00	£47.50
83 1st appearance Kryptonite Kid	*$12.00*	*$36.00*	*$85.00*	£6.75	£20.00	£47.50
84-85	*$12.00*	*$36.00*	*$85.00*	£6.75	£20.00	£47.50
86 (Jan 1961), 4th appearance of Legion, 1st appearance Pete Ross	*$16.00*	*$49.00*	*$130.00*	£9.50	£29.00	£77.50
87-88	*$12.00*	*$36.00*	*$85.00*	£6.75	£20.00	£47.50
89 1st appearance Mon-El	*$34.00*	*$100.00*	*$275.00*	£17.50	£52.50	£140.00
90 Pete Ross discovers Superboy's secret identity						

Issue	$Good	$Fine	$N.Mint	£Good	£Fine	£N.Mint
	$12.00	$36.00	$85.00	£6.75	£20.00	£47.50
91	$12.00	$36.00	$85.00	£6.75	£20.00	£47.50
92 last 10 cents issue	$12.00	$36.00	$85.00	£6.75	£20.00	£47.50
93 11th Legion appearance	$10.50	$32.00	$75.00	£6.75	£20.00	£47.50
94 (Jan 1962)	$8.50	$26.00	$60.00	£4.25	£12.50	£30.00
95-97	$8.50	$26.00	$60.00	£4.25	£12.50	£30.00
98 19th Legion; origin and 1st appearance Ultra Boy	$10.00	$30.00	$70.00	£5.00	£15.00	£35.00
99	$8.50	$26.00	$60.00	£4.25	£12.50	£30.00
100 origin of Superboy retold, Ultra Boy appears, Pete Ross in Legion	$23.50	$70.00	$190.00	£12.50	£38.00	£100.00
101	$7.00	$21.00	$50.00	£3.20	£9.50	£22.50
102 (Jan 1963)	$7.00	$21.00	$50.00	£3.20	£9.50	£22.50
103-109	$7.00	$21.00	$50.00	£3.20	£9.50	£22.50
110 (Jan 1964)	$7.00	$21.00	$50.00	£3.20	£9.50	£22.50
111-116	$6.25	$19.00	$45.00	£2.50	£7.50	£17.50
117 Legion of Super-Heroes appears	$6.25	$19.00	$45.00	£2.50	£7.50	£17.50
118 (Jan 1965)	$6.25	$19.00	$45.00	£2.50	£7.50	£17.50
119-120	$6.25	$19.00	$45.00	£2.50	£7.50	£17.50
121-124	$5.50	$17.00	$40.00	£2.10	£6.25	£15.00
125 last Silver Age issue, indicia dated December 1965	$5.50	$17.00	$40.00	£2.10	£6.25	£15.00
126 (Jan 1966), origin Krypto	$5.50	$17.00	$40.00	£2.10	£6.25	£15.00
127-128	$5.50	$17.00	$40.00	£2.10	£6.25	£15.00
129 80pgs, Giant G-22, reprints Superboy #89 (1st Mon-El)	$6.25	$18.50	$50.00	£2.80	£8.25	£22.50
130-134	$4.25	$12.50	$30.00	£1.40	£4.25	£10.00
135 (Jan 1967)	$4.25	$12.50	$30.00	£1.40	£4.25	£10.00
136-137	$4.25	$12.50	$30.00	£1.40	£4.25	£10.00
138 80pgs, Giant G-35	$6.25	$18.50	$50.00	£2.80	£8.25	£22.50
139-140	$4.25	$12.50	$30.00	£1.40	£4.25	£10.00
141-142	$2.50	$7.50	$17.50	£1.10	£3.40	£8.00
143 Neal Adams cover	$2.50	$7.50	$17.50	£1.10	£3.40	£8.00
144 (Jan 1968)	$2.50	$7.50	$17.50	£1.10	£3.40	£8.00
145	$2.50	$7.50	$17.50	£1.10	£3.40	£8.00
146 2pg Superboy Legend at centrefold (often missing!)	$2.50	$7.50	$17.50	£1.10	£3.40	£8.00
147 80pgs, Giant G-47, Legion origin retold in new story, reprints Superman #147, Adventure Comics #290 (origin Sun Boy and 9th Legion appearance)	$3.10	$9.25	$25.00	£1.85	£5.50	£15.00
148-149 Neal Adams cover	$2.50	$7.50	$17.50	£1.00	£3.00	£7.00
150	$2.50	$7.50	$17.50	£1.00	£3.00	£7.00
151-152 Neal Adams cover	$2.50	$7.50	$17.50	£1.00	£3.00	£7.00
153 (Jan 1969), Neal Adams cover	$2.50	$7.50	$17.50	£1.00	£3.00	£7.00
154	$2.50	$7.50	$17.50	£1.00	£3.00	£7.00
155 Neal Adams cover	$2.50	$7.50	$17.50	£1.00	£3.00	£7.00
156 80pgs, Giant G-59	$2.85	$8.50	$20.00	£1.75	£5.25	£12.50
157	$2.50	$7.50	$17.50	£1.00	£3.00	£7.00
158 Wood inks	$2.50	$7.50	$17.50	£1.00	£3.00	£7.00
159-161	$2.50	$7.50	$17.50	£1.00	£3.00	£7.00
162 (Jan 1970)	$2.50	$7.50	$17.50	£1.00	£3.00	£7.00
163-164 Neal Adams cover	$2.50	$7.50	$17.50	£1.00	£3.00	£7.00
165 80pgs, Giant G-71, reprints Adventure Comics #210 (1st Krypto)	$3.10	$9.25	$25.00	£1.55	£4.65	£12.50
166-168 Neal Adams cover	$2.50	$7.50	$15.00	£1.00	£3.00	£6.00
169-170	$2.50	$7.50	$15.00	£1.00	£3.00	£6.00
171 (Jan 1971), 1st appearance Aquaboy	$2.50	$7.50	$15.00	£0.80	£2.50	£5.00
172 new Legion stories	$2.50	$7.50	$15.00	£0.80	£2.50	£5.00
173 Neal Adams cover, new Legion stories	$2.50	$7.50	$15.00	£0.80	£2.50	£5.00
174 80pgs, Giant G-83	$3.30	$10.00	$20.00	£1.65	£5.00	£10.00
175 Neal Adams cover	$1.65	$5.00	$10.00	£0.75	£2.25	£4.50
176 Neal Adams cover, new Legion stories	$1.65	$5.00	$10.00	£0.75	£2.25	£4.50
177 48pgs, (the Americans count the covers and make it 52)	$1.65	$5.00	$10.00	£0.75	£2.25	£4.50
178 48pgs, Neal Adams cover	$1.65	$5.00	$10.00	£0.75	£2.25	£4.50
179-180 48pgs	$1.65	$5.00	$10.00	£0.75	£2.25	£4.50
181 48pgs, (Jan 1972)	$1.65	$5.00	$10.00	£0.75	£2.25	£4.50
182 48pgs, Superboy meets young Bruce Wayne (Batman)	$1.65	$5.00	$10.00	£0.90	£2.75	£5.50
183-184 48pgs, new Legion stories	$1.65	$5.00	$10.00	£0.75	£2.25	£4.50
185 100pgs, DC-100pg Super Spectacular #12; Legion reprints, reprints Brave and Bold #60 (2nd Teen Titans)	$2.10	$6.25	$15.00	£1.10	£3.40	£8.00
186-187 48pgs	$1.65	$5.00	$10.00	£0.65	£2.00	£4.00
188 new Legion stories	$0.55	$1.75	$3.50	£0.50	£1.50	£3.00
189	$0.55	$1.75	$3.50	£0.40	£1.25	£2.50
190 new Legion stories	$0.55	$1.75	$3.50	£0.50	£1.50	£3.00
191 origin Sun Boy retold	$0.55	$1.75	$3.50	£0.50	£1.50	£3.00
192	$0.55	$1.75	$3.50	£0.40	£1.25	£2.50
193 (Jan 1973), new Legion stories	$0.55	$1.75	$3.50	£0.50	£1.50	£3.00
194	$0.50	$1.50	$3.00	£0.40	£1.25	£2.50
195 new Legion stories	$0.50	$1.50	$3.00	£0.50	£1.50	£3.00
196	$0.50	$1.50	$3.00	£0.40	£1.25	£2.50
197 scarce in the U.K. 1st of new Legion series	$1.50	$4.50	$9.00	£1.15	£3.50	£7.00
198-199 scarce in the U.K.	$0.80	$2.50	$5.00	£1.00	£3.00	£6.00
200 scarce in the U.K. (Jan 1974), Bouncing Boy, Duo Damsel wed	$1.25	$3.75	$7.50	£1.00	£3.00	£6.00
201	$0.50	$1.50	$3.00	£0.50	£1.50	£3.00
202 100pgs, squarebound	$0.70	$2.10	$5.00	£0.85	£2.55	£6.00
203 original Invisible Kid dies	$0.50	$1.50	$3.00	£0.50	£1.50	£3.00
204	$0.50	$1.50	$3.00	£0.50	£1.50	£3.00
205 100pgs, squarebound						

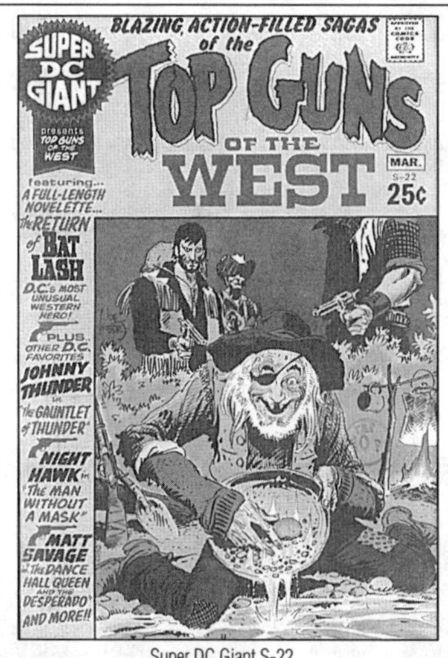

Super DC Giant S-22

Superboy #62

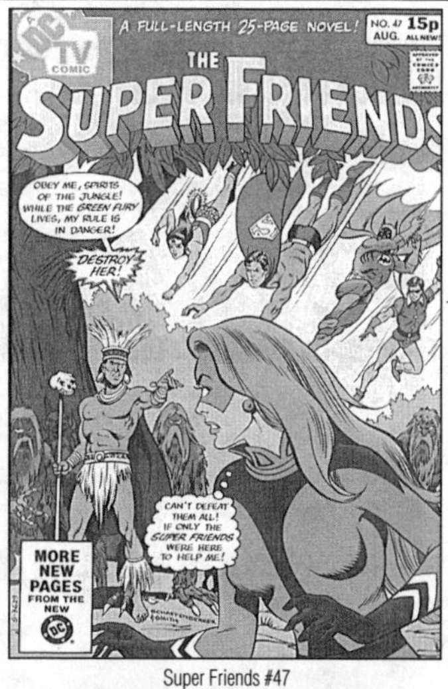

Super Friends #47

	$Good	$Fine	$N.Mint	£Good	£Fine	£N.Mint
	$0.70	*$2.10*	*$5.00*	£0.85	£2.55	£6.00
206 (Jan 1975)	*$0.50*	*$1.50*	*$3.00*	£0.50	£1.50	£3.00
207	*$0.50*	*$1.50*	*$3.00*	£0.50	£1.50	£3.00
208 scarce in the U.K. 68pgs, squarebound	*$0.70*	*$2.10*	*$5.00*	£0.75	£2.35	£5.50
209	*$0.50*	*$1.50*	*$3.00*	£0.50	£1.50	£3.00
210 origin Karate Kid	*$0.50*	*$1.50*	*$3.00*	£0.50	£1.50	£3.00
211 ND	*$0.40*	*$1.25*	*$2.50*	£0.80	£2.50	£5.00
212-213 scarce in the U.K.	*$0.40*	*$1.25*	*$2.50*	£0.55	£1.75	£3.50
214 (Jan 1976)	*$0.40*	*$1.25*	*$2.50*	£0.40	£1.25	£2.50
215-216	*$0.40*	*$1.25*	*$2.50*	£0.40	£1.25	£2.50
217	*$0.40*	*$1.25*	*$2.50*	£0.30	£1.00	£2.00
218 ND	*$0.40*	*$1.25*	*$2.50*	£0.55	£1.75	£3.50
219-222 scarce in the U.K.	*$0.40*	*$1.25*	*$2.50*	£0.50	£1.50	£3.00
223 scarce in the U.K. (Jan 1977)	*$0.30*	*$1.00*	*$2.00*	£0.50	£1.50	£3.00
224-226 scarce in the U.K.	*$0.30*	*$1.00*	*$2.00*	£0.50	£1.50	£3.00
227 ND	*$0.30*	*$1.00*	*$2.00*	£0.55	£1.75	£3.50
228-229	*$0.30*	*$1.00*	*$2.00*	£0.30	£1.00	£2.00
230 scarce in the U.K.	*$0.30*	*$1.00*	*$2.00*	£0.50	£1.50	£3.00
231 52pgs	*$0.30*	*$1.00*	*$2.00*	£0.30	£1.00	£2.00
232 ND 52pgs	*$0.30*	*$1.00*	*$2.00*	£0.40	£1.25	£2.50
233-234 52pgs	*$0.30*	*$1.00*	*$2.00*	£0.30	£1.00	£2.00
235 scarce in the U.K. 52pgs, (Jan 1978)	*$0.30*	*$1.00*	*$2.00*	£0.40	£1.25	£2.50
236-238 52pgs	*$0.30*	*$1.00*	*$2.00*	£0.25	£0.75	£1.50
239 52pgs, Jim Starlin script/layouts	*$0.30*	*$1.00*	*$2.00*	£0.25	£0.85	£1.75
240 scarce in the U.K. 52pgs, Chaykin art	*$0.30*	*$1.00*	*$2.00*	£0.25	£0.85	£1.75
241-242 52pgs	*$0.30*	*$1.00*	*$2.00*	£0.25	£0.75	£1.50
243-245 ND 44pgs	*$0.30*	*$1.00*	*$2.00*	£0.30	£1.00	£2.00
246	*$0.30*	*$1.00*	*$2.00*	£0.20	£0.60	£1.25
246 Whitman Cover Variant, ND Whitman symbol in place of the DC symbol and the price blanked out - issued free with other Whitman comics	*$0.30*	*$0.90*	*$1.50*	£0.30	£0.90	£1.50
247 (Jan 1979)	*$0.30*	*$1.00*	*$2.00*	£0.20	£0.60	£1.25
248-249	*$0.30*	*$1.00*	*$2.00*	£0.20	£0.60	£1.25
250-251 Jim Starlin layouts	*$0.30*	*$1.00*	*$2.00*	£0.25	£0.75	£1.50
252	*$0.30*	*$1.00*	*$2.00*	£0.20	£0.60	£1.25
253 1st appearance Blok	*$0.30*	*$1.00*	*$2.00*	£0.20	£0.60	£1.25
254 LD in the U.K.	*$0.30*	*$1.00*	*$2.00*	£0.25	£0.75	£1.50
255-258	*$0.30*	*$1.00*	*$2.00*	£0.20	£0.60	£1.25
Title Value:	*$3980.40*	*$11944.70*	*$32940.00*	£2554.95	£7671.00	£21216.50
The Great Darkness Saga (Nov 1989) Trade paperback reprints #290-294, Annual #2, Darkseid appears; also with fold-out poster which is a reprint of the original Keith Giffen one				£2.40	£7.20	£12.00

ARTISTS

Ditko art in 257, 267, 268, 272, 274, 276, 281. Nasser art in 222, 225, 226, 230, 233, 236. Wood inks in 153-155, 157-161.

FEATURES

Legion of Super-Heroes 147, 172, 173, 176, 183, 184, 188, 190, 191, 193, 195, 197-354. Superboy in 1-128, 130-137, 139-146, 148-155, 157-164, 166- 173, 175-184, 186-197.

REPRINT FEATURES

Dial H for Hero in 184, 186, 187. Legion in 177, 178, 181, 185. Star Spangled Kid, Teen Titans, Kid Eternity, Little Boy Blue in 185. Superboy in 129, 138, 156, 165, 174, 179, 182, 183, 185. Superboy/Legion in 147, 202, 205, 208. Superman in 147.

SUPERBOY & THE RAVERS

DC Comics; 1 Sep 1996-present

	$Good	$Fine	$N.Mint	£Good	£Fine	£N.Mint
1 ND Karl Kesel script, Paul Petellier and Dan Davis art	*$0.40*	*$1.20*	*$2.00*	£0.25	£0.75	£1.25
2-3 ND	*$0.40*	*$1.20*	*$2.00*	£0.25	£0.75	£1.25
4 ND Adam Strange guest-stars	*$0.40*	*$1.20*	*$2.00*	£0.25	£0.75	£1.25
5 ND the origin of Hero and finding the legendary "H" dial	*$0.40*	*$1.20*	*$2.00*	£0.25	£0.75	£1.25
6 ND	*$0.40*	*$1.20*	*$2.00*	£0.25	£0.75	£1.25
7 ND Impulse guest-stars	*$0.40*	*$1.20*	*$2.00*	£0.25	£0.75	£1.25
Title Value:	*$2.80*	*$8.40*	*$14.00*	£1.75	£5.25	£8.75

SUPERBOY (2ND SERIES)

DC Comics,TV; 1 Feb 1990-22 Feb 1992

	$Good	$Fine	$N.Mint	£Good	£Fine	£N.Mint
1 photocover of Gerard Christopher, 1st TV series Superboy	*$0.25*	*$0.75*	*$1.25*	£0.15	£0.45	£0.75
2-12	*$0.25*	*$0.75*	*$1.25*	£0.15	£0.45	£0.75
13 Mr. Mxyzptlk appears	*$0.25*	*$0.75*	*$1.25*	£0.15	£0.45	£0.75
14-21	*$0.25*	*$0.75*	*$1.25*	£0.15	£0.45	£0.75
22 Metallo appears	*$0.25*	*$0.75*	*$1.25*	£0.15	£0.45	£0.75
Title Value:	*$5.50*	*$16.50*	*$27.50*	£3.30	£9.90	£16.50

Note: continuity takes place outside DC Comics universe.

SUPERBOY (3RD SERIES)

DC Comics; 0 Oct 1994; 1 Feb 1994-present

	$Good	$Fine	$N.Mint	£Good	£Fine	£N.Mint
0 (Oct 1994) Zero Hour X-over, origin retold	*$0.30*	*$0.90*	*$1.50*	£0.20	£0.60	£1.00
1 new series set in Hawaii by Karl Kesel, Tom Grummett and Doug Hazelwood	*$0.30*	*$0.90*	*$1.50*	£0.20	£0.60	£1.00
2-5	*$0.30*	*$0.90*	*$1.50*	£0.20	£0.60	£1.00
6 Worlds Collide X-over, continued in Icon #15	*$0.30*	*$0.90*	*$1.50*	£0.20	£0.60	£1.00
7 Worlds Collide X-over, continued in Hardware #18	*$0.30*	*$0.90*	*$1.50*	£0.20	£0.60	£1.00
8 Zero Hour X-over	*$0.30*	*$0.90*	*$1.50*	£0.20	£0.60	£1.00
9-15	*$0.30*	*$0.90*	*$1.50*	£0.20	£0.60	£1.00
16 Loose Cannon guest-stars; upgraded coated paper (Miraweb Format) begins	*$0.40*	*$1.20*	*$2.00*	£0.25	£0.75	£1.25
17-20	*$0.40*	*$1.20*	*$2.00*	£0.25	£0.75	£1.25
21 Future Tense part 1; the new Superboy meets the original Superboy and The Legion of Super-Heroes for the 1st time	*$0.40*	*$1.20*	*$2.00*	£0.25	£0.75	£1.25
22 Underworld Unleashed tie-in	*$0.40*	*$1.20*	*$2.00*	£0.25	£0.75	£1.25
23-24	*$0.40*	*$1.20*	*$2.00*	£0.25	£0.75	£1.25
25 48pgs, Losin' It story; origin Knockout	*$0.60*	*$1.80*	*$3.00*	£0.40	£1.20	£2.00
26-30 Losin' It story	*$0.40*	*$1.20*	*$2.00*	£0.25	£0.75	£1.25
31-32	*$0.40*	*$1.20*	*$2.00*	£0.25	£0.75	£1.25
33 ND Final Night tie-in	*$0.40*	*$1.20*	*$2.00*	£0.25	£0.75	£1.25
34-37 ND	*$0.40*	*$1.20*	*$2.00*	£0.25	£0.75	£1.25
Title Value:	*$13.80*	*$41.40*	*$69.00*	£8.85	£26.55	£44.25

SUPERBOY (3RD SERIES) ANNUAL

DC Comics; 1 1994-present

	$Good	$Fine	$N.Mint	£Good	£Fine	£N.Mint
1 64pgs, squarebound, Elseworlds story continued from Adventures of Superman Annual #6	*$0.60*	*$1.80*	*$3.00*	£0.40	£1.20	£2.00
2 56pgs, Year One, Superboy learns who he was cloned from	*$0.80*	*$2.40*	*$4.00*	£0.50	£1.50	£2.50
3 ND Legends of the Dead Earth story	*$0.60*	*$1.80*	*$3.00*	£0.40	£1.20	£2.00
Title Value:	*$2.00*	*$6.00*	*$10.00*	£1.30	£3.90	£6.50

SUPERBOY ANNUAL

National Periodical Publications; 1 Summer 1964

	$Good	$Fine	$N.Mint	£Good	£Fine	£N.Mint
1 80pgs, reprints including part origin Krypto from Adventure Comics #259	*$15.00*	*$45.00*	*$135.00*	£10.00	£30.00	£90.00
Title Value:	*$15.00*	*$45.00*	*$135.00*	£10.00	£30.00	£90.00

SUPERBOY PLUS #1

DC Comics,OS; 1 Jan 1997

	$Good	$Fine	$N.Mint	£Good	£Fine	£N.Mint
1 ND Superboy and Captain Marvel Jnr. team up; Gary Frank and Cam Smith cover	*$0.60*	*$1.80*	*$3.00*	£0.40	£1.20	£2.00
Title Value:	*$0.60*	*$1.80*	*$3.00*	£0.40	£1.20	£2.00

SUPERBOY SPECIAL

DC Comics,OS; 1 Jun 1992

	$Good	$Fine	$N.Mint	£Good	£Fine	£N.Mint
1 ties up plot lines from Superboy (2nd Series)	*$0.25*	*$0.75*	*$1.25*	£0.15	£0.45	£0.75
Title Value:	*$0.25*	*$0.75*	*$1.25*	£0.15	£0.45	£0.75

SUPERBOY SPECTACULAR

DC Comics; 1 1980

	$Good	$Fine	$N.Mint	£Good	£Fine	£N.Mint
1 ND 68pgs, new 8pg story with 6 Silver Age reprints	*$0.40*	*$1.20*	*$2.00*	£0.40	£1.20	£2.00
Title Value:	*$0.40*	*$1.20*	*$2.00*	£0.40	£1.20	£2.00

Note: All reprint apart from one new story. This comic was only distributed via specialist comic shops and related outlets - it was not put on general news-stand sale. This was the first direct-sales only comic by either DC or Marvel.

SUPERBOY, THE NEW ADVENTURES OF

DC Comics; 1 Jan 1980-54 Jun 1984

	$Good	$Fine	$N.Mint	£Good	£Fine	£N.Mint
1-6	*$0.15*	*$0.45*	*$0.75*	£0.10	£0.35	£0.60
7 68pgs, Jim Starlin art on insert	*$0.15*	*$0.45*	*$0.75*	£0.10	£0.35	£0.60
8-14	*$0.15*	*$0.45*	*$0.75*	£0.10	£0.35	£0.60
15 intro Superboy's new parents	*$0.15*	*$0.45*	*$0.75*	£0.10	£0.35	£0.60
16-27	*$0.15*	*$0.45*	*$0.75*	£0.10	£0.35	£0.60
28 Dial H for Hero begins (ends 49)	*$0.15*	*$0.45*	*$0.75*	£0.10	£0.35	£0.60
29-44	*$0.15*	*$0.45*	*$0.75*	£0.10	£0.35	£0.60
45 1st appearance Sunburst	*$0.15*	*$0.45*	*$0.75*	£0.10	£0.35	£0.60
46-49	*$0.15*	*$0.45*	*$0.75*	£0.10	£0.35	£0.60
50 52pgs, Giffen art, Legion co-stars	*$0.20*	*$0.60*	*$1.00*	£0.15	£0.45	£0.75
51-54	*$0.15*	*$0.45*	*$0.75*	£0.10	£0.35	£0.60
Title Value:	*$8.15*	*$24.45*	*$40.75*	£5.45	£19.00	£32.55

FEATURES

Dial H for Hero in 28-49. Krypto in 10, 17, 22. Misadventures of Superbaby in 11, 14, 19, 24. Superboy's Secret Diary 9, 12, 18, 23.

SUPERCAR

Gold Key; 1 Nov 1962-4 Aug 1963

	$Good	$Fine	$N.Mint	£Good	£Fine	£N.Mint
1 rare although distributed in the U.K.	*$36.00*	*$105.00*	*$250.00*	£25.00	£75.00	£175.00
2-3 rare although distributed in the U.K.	*$17.50*	*$52.50*	*$125.00*	£11.00	£34.00	£80.00
4 very rare though distributed in the U.K.	*$24.00*	*$72.50*	*$170.00*	£15.50	£47.00	£110.00
Title Value:	*$95.00*	*$282.50*	*$670.00*	£62.50	£190.00	£445.00

TRADE PAPERBACKS, GRAPHIC NOVELS AND OTHER COLLECTIONS ARE PRICED IN POUNDS STERLING ONLY. CONVERT AT 1.5 FOR DOLLARS.

SUPERCOPS

Now Comics; 1 Sep 1990-4 Dec 1990

Issue	$Good	$Fine	$N.Mint	£Good	£Fine	£N.Mint
1 ND 48pgs, Chuck Dixon script, Peter Grau art; Dave Dorman painted cover	$0.40	$1.20	$2.00	£0.25	£0.75	£1.25
1 2nd printing ND	$0.30	$0.90	$1.50	£0.20	£0.60	£1.00
2-4 ND	$0.40	$1.20	$2.00	£0.25	£0.75	£1.25
Title Value:	$1.90	$5.70	$9.50	£1.20	£3.60	£6.00

SUPERGIRL

DC Comics; 1 Nov 1972-9 Dec/Jan 1973/74; 10 Sep 1974

(see Action, Adventure, Best of DC, Brave and the Bold, Crisis, DC Comics Presents, Super DC Giant, Superman Family, Secret Origins of Super-Heroes, Super-Team Family)

Issue	$Good	$Fine	$N.Mint	£Good	£Fine	£N.Mint
1 Zatanna back-up begins	$2.50	$7.50	$15.00	£0.80	£2.50	£5.00
2	$1.30	$4.00	$8.00	£0.55	£1.75	£3.50
3	$1.25	$3.75	$7.50	£0.50	£1.50	£3.00
4 last Zatanna back-up	$1.25	$3.75	$7.50	£0.50	£1.50	£3.00
5	$1.25	$3.75	$7.50	£0.50	£1.50	£3.00
6	$1.25	$3.75	$7.50	£0.40	£1.25	£2.50
7 Zatanna guest-stars	$1.25	$3.75	$7.50	£0.40	£1.25	£2.50
8 Batman, Hawkman and Green Lantern appear	$1.25	$3.75	$7.50	£0.40	£1.25	£2.50
9	$1.25	$3.75	$7.50	£0.40	£1.25	£2.50
10 Prez appears	$1.25	$3.75	$7.50	£0.40	£1.25	£2.50
Title Value:	$13.80	$41.50	$83.00	£4.85	£15.00	£30.00

Note: Hawkman Zatanna reprint in 5. Melba in 6.

SUPERGIRL (2ND SERIES)

DC Comics; 1 Nov 1982-23 Sep 1984

(titled Daring New Adventures of Supergirl #1-13)

Issue	$Good	$Fine	$N.Mint	£Good	£Fine	£N.Mint
1 origin retold	$0.50	$1.50	$2.50	£0.30	£0.90	£1.50
2-12	$0.40	$1.20	$2.00	£0.20	£0.60	£1.00
13 new costume	$0.40	$1.20	$2.00	£0.20	£0.60	£1.00
14-15	$0.40	$1.20	$2.00	£0.20	£0.60	£1.00
16 Ambush Bug X-over	$0.40	$1.20	$2.00	£0.20	£0.60	£1.00
17-19	$0.40	$1.20	$2.00	£0.20	£0.60	£1.00
20 New Titans appear	$0.40	$1.20	$2.00	£0.20	£0.60	£1.00
21-23	$0.40	$1.20	$2.00	£0.20	£0.60	£1.00
Title Value:	$9.30	$27.90	$46.50	£4.70	£14.10	£23.50

SUPERGIRL (3RD SERIES)

DC Comics,MS; 1 Feb 1994-4 May 1994

Issue	$Good	$Fine	$N.Mint	£Good	£Fine	£N.Mint
1 June Brigman pencils, Jackson Guice inks begin; The Matrix Supergirl orgin retold	$0.40	$1.20	$2.00	£0.25	£0.75	£1.25
2-3	$0.40	$1.20	$2.00	£0.25	£0.75	£1.25
4 Superman appears	$0.40	$1.20	$2.00	£0.25	£0.75	£1.25
Title Value:	$1.60	$4.80	$8.00	£1.00	£3.00	£5.00

SUPERGIRL (4TH SERIES)

DC Comics; 1 Sep 1996-present

Issue	$Good	$Fine	$N.Mint	£Good	£Fine	£N.Mint
1 ND Peter David script, Gary Frank and Cam Smith art	$1.00	$3.00	$5.00	£0.70	£2.10	£3.50
2 ND	$0.60	$1.80	$3.00	£0.50	£1.50	£2.50
3 ND Final Night tie-in; Supergirl vs. Gorilla Grodd	$0.50	$1.50	$2.50	£0.40	£1.20	£2.00
4 ND Gorilla Grodd appears	$0.50	$1.50	$2.50	£0.30	£0.90	£1.50
5 ND	$0.40	$1.20	$2.00	£0.25	£0.75	£1.25
6 ND Supergirl vs. Rampage	$0.40	$1.20	$2.00	£0.25	£0.75	£1.25
7 ND	$0.40	$1.20	$2.00	£0.25	£0.75	£1.25
Title Value:	$3.80	$11.40	$19.00	£2.65	£7.95	£13.25

SUPERGIRL (4TH SERIES) ANNUAL

DC Comics; 1 Jun 1996-present

Issue	$Good	$Fine	$N.Mint	£Good	£Fine	£N.Mint
1 ND 48pgs, Legends of the Dead Earth story	$0.60	$1.80	$3.00	£0.40	£1.20	£2.00
Title Value:	$0.60	$1.80	$3.00	£0.40	£1.20	£2.00

SUPERGIRL MOVIE SPECIAL

DC Comics,OS; 1 1985

Issue	$Good	$Fine	$N.Mint	£Good	£Fine	£N.Mint
1 Gray Morrow art, adaptation of film starring Helen Slater	$0.30	$0.90	$1.50	£0.20	£0.60	£1.00
Title Value:	$0.30	$0.90	$1.50	£0.20	£0.60	£1.00

SUPERGIRL PLUS #1

DC Comics,OS; 1 Feb 1997

Issue	$Good	$Fine	$N.Mint	£Good	£Fine	£N.Mint
1 ND 48pgs, Supergirl and Mary Marvel team up	$0.60	$1.80	$3.00	£0.40	£1.20	£2.00
Title Value:	$0.60	$1.80	$3.00	£0.40	£1.20	£2.00

SUPERGIRL/TEAM LUTHOR SPECIAL

DC Comics,OS; 1 Apr 1993

Issue	$Good	$Fine	$N.Mint	£Good	£Fine	£N.Mint
1 64pgs	$0.50	$1.50	$2.50	£0.30	£0.90	£1.50
Title Value:	$0.50	$1.50	$2.50	£0.30	£0.90	£1.50

SUPERHEROES VS SUPERVILLAINS

Archie; 1 1966

Issue	$Good	$Fine	$N.Mint	£Good	£Fine	£N.Mint
1 distributed in the U.K. giant, all reprint	$7.00	$21.00	$50.00	£5.00	£15.00	£35.00
Title Value:	$7.00	$21.00	$50.00	£5.00	£15.00	£35.00

SUPERHUMAN SAMURAI CYBER SQUAD

Hamilton Comics; 0 Oct 1995

Issue	$Good	$Fine	$N.Mint	£Good	£Fine	£N.Mint
0 ND Jack C. Harris script, Joe Staton art	$0.60	$1.80	$3.00	£0.40	£1.20	£2.00
Title Value:	$0.60	$1.80	$3.00	£0.40	£1.20	£2.00

SUPERMAN (1ST SERIES) (ADVENTURES OF SUPERMAN)

National Periodical Publications/DC Comics; 0 Oct 1994; 1 Summer 1939-423 Sep 1986; 424 Jan 1987-499 Feb 1993; 500 Jun 1993-present

(see Action Comics, All-New Collector's Edition, Best of DC, DC Comics Presents, Eighty Page Giant Magazine, Famous First Edition, Limited Collector's Edition, One Hundred Page Super Spectacular,Super-Heroes Battle Super-Gorillas, Super Powers, Superman Family, Super Team Family, World's Finest Comics) (becomes Adventures of Superman with #424)

Issue	$Good	$Fine	$N.Mint	£Good	£Fine	£N.Mint
0 (Oct 1994) Zero Hour X-over, origin retold; concluded in Action Comics #0	$0.40	$1.20	$2.00	£0.25	£0.75	£1.25
1 stories from Action Comics #1-4 reprinted with 4 new preceding pages, new 2 page origin of Superman; around 200 extant copies in any condition	$12000.00	$36000.00	$120000.00	£8000.00	£24000.00	£80000.00
[Prices may vary widely on this comic]						
2	$1200.00	$3650.00	$11000.00	£810.00	£2450.00	£7350.00
3	$810.00	$2450.00	$7350.00	£540.00	£1625.00	£4900.00
4 (Spring 1940), 2nd appearance Lex Luthor (suddenly bald! see Action Comics #23 for 1st appearance), 1st Luthor on cover (see Action Comics #47)	$700.00	$2100.00	$5600.00	£465.00	£1400.00	£3750.00
5	$480.00	$1425.00	$3850.00	£320.00	£960.00	£2575.00
6	$310.00	$930.00	$2500.00	£205.00	£620.00	£1675.00
7 1st war cover	$310.00	$930.00	$2500.00	£205.00	£620.00	£1675.00
8 (Jan/Feb 1941)	$265.00	$800.00	$2150.00	£180.00	£540.00	£1450.00
9	$265.00	$800.00	$2150.00	£180.00	£540.00	£1450.00
10 Lex Luthor appears	$265.00	$800.00	$2150.00	£180.00	£540.00	£1450.00
11-12	$195.00	$590.00	$1575.00	£130.00	£390.00	£1050.00
13 early appearance Jimmy Olsen (as office boy - see Action Comics #6)	$195.00	$590.00	$1575.00	£130.00	£390.00	£1050.00
14 (Jan/Feb 1942), classic patriotic cover: Superman and American Eagle; cover concept re-used on issue #424	$360.00	$1075.00	$3250.00	£240.00	£720.00	£2175.00
[Scarce in high grade - Very Fine+ or better]						
15	$190.00	$580.00	$1550.00	£130.00	£390.00	£1040.00
16	$165.00	$500.00	$1350.00	£110.00	£335.00	£900.00
17 Emperor Hirohito and Adolf Hitler on cover; Superman loses powers for the 1st time as he battles Luthor and the Powerstone (see Action Comics #47)	$165.00	$500.00	$1350.00	£110.00	£335.00	£900.00
18 patriotic cover: "Do The Job On The Japanazis!"	$165.00	$500.00	$1350.00	£110.00	£335.00	£900.00
19	$165.00	$500.00	$1350.00	£110.00	£335.00	£900.00
20 (Jan/Feb 1943)	$165.00	$500.00	$1350.00	£110.00	£335.00	£900.00
21-23	$125.00	$375.00	$1000.00	£82.50	£250.00	£670.00
24 classic patriotic flag cover	$170.00	$510.00	$1375.00	£115.00	£345.00	£920.00
25	$120.00	$365.00	$975.00	£80.00	£240.00	£650.00
26 (Jan/Feb 1944)	$110.00	$335.00	$900.00	£75.00	£225.00	£600.00
27-28	$110.00	$335.00	$900.00	£75.00	£225.00	£600.00
28 Armed Forces Edition scarce in the U.K.	$120.00	$365.00	$975.00	£80.00	£240.00	£650.00
29	$110.00	$335.00	$900.00	£75.00	£225.00	£600.00
30 1st appearance Mr. Mxyztplk (the "t" and the "p" became reversed in spelling in the Silver Age)	$165.00	$500.00	$1500.00	£110.00	£330.00	£1000.00
31	$100.00	$300.00	$800.00	£65.00	£200.00	£535.00
32 (Jan/Feb 1945)	$100.00	$300.00	$800.00	£65.00	£200.00	£535.00
33 3rd appearance Mr. Mxyztplk	$100.00	$300.00	$800.00	£65.00	£200.00	£535.00
34-36	$100.00	$300.00	$800.00	£65.00	£200.00	£535.00
37 Prankster cover and story	$100.00	$300.00	$800.00	£65.00	£200.00	£535.00
38 (Jan/Feb 1946), contraversial Atom Bomb story	$100.00	$300.00	$800.00	£65.00	£200.00	£535.00
39	$100.00	$300.00	$800.00	£65.00	£200.00	£535.00
40 Mr. Mxyztplk cover and story	$100.00	$300.00	$800.00	£65.00	£200.00	£535.00
41-43	$75.00	$225.00	$600.00	£50.00	£150.00	£400.00
44 (Jan/Feb 1947), Toyman cover and story	$75.00	$225.00	$600.00	£50.00	£150.00	£400.00
45 Lois Lane as Superwoman (see Action Comics #60 for 1st appearance of this plus Action #156 and Superman #123)	$75.00	$225.00	$600.00	£50.00	£150.00	£400.00
46-49	$75.00	$225.00	$600.00	£50.00	£150.00	£400.00
50 (Jan/Feb 1948)	$75.00	$225.00	$600.00	£50.00	£150.00	£400.00
51-52	$62.50	$185.00	$500.00	£42.00	£125.00	£335.00
53 10th anniversay issue, origin Superman retold in new detail	$220.00	$660.00	$2000.00	£150.00	£450.00	£1350.00
54-55	$62.50	$185.00	$500.00	£42.00	£125.00	£335.00
56 (Jan/Feb 1949)	$62.50	$185.00	$500.00	£42.00	£125.00	£335.00
57 Lois Lane as Superwoman (see Action Comics #60, Superman #45)	$62.50	$185.00	$500.00	£42.00	£125.00	£335.00
58-60	$62.50	$185.00	$500.00	£42.00	£125.00	£335.00
61 1st appearance Green Kryptonite, Superman 1st learns he's from Krypton	$125.00	$375.00	$1000.00	£82.50	£250.00	£670.00
[Scarce in high grade - Very Fine+ or better]						
62 (Jan/Feb 1950), Orsen Welles on cover, his famous Martian Invasion broadcast featured	$62.50	$185.00	$500.00	£42.00	£125.00	£335.00
63-64	$62.50	$185.00	$500.00	£42.00	£125.00	£335.00

Issue	$Good	$Fine	$N.Mint	£Good	£Fine	£N.Mint
65 1st foes to come from Krypton (see Action Comics #194)	*$67.50*	*$205.00*	*$550.00*	£46.00	£135.00	£370.00
66	*$62.50*	*$185.00*	*$500.00*	£42.00	£125.00	£335.00
67 singer Perry Como appears	*$62.50*	*$185.00*	*$500.00*	£42.00	£125.00	£335.00
68 (Jan/Feb 1951), Lex Luthor cover and story	*$62.50*	*$185.00*	*$500.00*	£42.00	£125.00	£335.00
69 Prankster cover and story	*$62.50*	*$185.00*	*$500.00*	£42.00	£125.00	£335.00
70	*$62.50*	*$185.00*	*$500.00*	£42.00	£125.00	£335.00
71-72	*$57.50*	*$175.00*	*$475.00*	£40.00	£120.00	£320.00
72 giveaway issue, rare in both U.S. and U.K. with cover banner and price blacked out	*$110.00*	*$335.00*	*$900.00*	£75.00	£225.00	£600.00
73	*$57.50*	*$175.00*	*$475.00*	£40.00	£120.00	£320.00
74 (Jan/Feb 1952), Lex Luthor cover and story	*$57.50*	*$175.00*	*$475.00*	£40.00	£120.00	£320.00
75 unknown percentage have number 74 on cover	*$57.50*	*$175.00*	*$475.00*	£40.00	£120.00	£320.00
76 1st Superman Batman team-up story, Batman on cover	*$170.00*	*$510.00*	*$1375.00*	£115.00	£345.00	£920.00
77-78	*$57.50*	*$170.00*	*$460.00*	£39.00	£115.00	£310.00
79 Lex Luthor cover and story	*$57.50*	*$170.00*	*$460.00*	£39.00	£115.00	£310.00
80 (Jan/Feb 1953)	*$57.50*	*$170.00*	*$460.00*	£39.00	£115.00	£310.00
81	*$52.50*	*$155.00*	*$425.00*	£36.00	£105.00	£285.00
82 Mr. Mxyztplk appears	*$52.50*	*$155.00*	*$425.00*	£36.00	£105.00	£285.00
83-84	*$52.50*	*$155.00*	*$425.00*	£36.00	£105.00	£285.00
85 Lex Luthor story	*$52.50*	*$155.00*	*$425.00*	£36.00	£105.00	£285.00
86 (Jan 1954)	*$52.50*	*$155.00*	*$425.00*	£36.00	£105.00	£285.00
87	*$52.50*	*$155.00*	*$425.00*	£36.00	£105.00	£285.00
88 Lex Luthor, Prankster, Toyman cover and story	*$52.50*	*$160.00*	*$435.00*	£36.00	£105.00	£290.00
89-90	*$52.50*	*$155.00*	*$425.00*	£36.00	£105.00	£285.00
91-93	*$44.00*	*$130.00*	*$350.00*	£29.00	£87.50	£235.00
94 (Jan 1955)	*$44.00*	*$130.00*	*$350.00*	£29.00	£87.50	£235.00
95	*$44.00*	*$130.00*	*$350.00*	£29.00	£87.50	£235.00
96 Mr. Mxyztplk cover and story	*$44.00*	*$130.00*	*$350.00*	£29.00	£87.50	£235.00
97-99	*$44.00*	*$130.00*	*$350.00*	£29.00	£87.50	£235.00
100 scarce in the U.K. cover has reproductions of issues #1, #25, #50, #75 (see Batman #100)	*$175.00*	*$520.00*	*$1750.00*	£115.00	£350.00	£1175.00
101 scarce in the U.K.	*$38.00*	*$110.00*	*$300.00*	£25.00	£75.00	£200.00
102 scarce in the U.K. (Jan 1956)	*$38.00*	*$110.00*	*$300.00*	£25.00	£75.00	£200.00
103-105 scarce in the U.K.	*$38.00*	*$110.00*	*$300.00*	£25.00	£75.00	£200.00
106 scarce in the U.K. Lex Luthor cover and story	*$38.00*	*$110.00*	*$300.00*	£25.00	£75.00	£200.00
107-109	*$38.00*	*$110.00*	*$300.00*	£25.00	£75.00	£200.00
110 (Jan 1957)	*$38.00*	*$110.00*	*$300.00*	£25.00	£75.00	£200.00
111-112	*$29.00*	*$85.00*	*$230.00*	£19.00	£57.50	£155.00
113 1st full length 3-part story	*$29.00*	*$85.00*	*$230.00*	£19.00	£57.50	£155.00
114-117	*$29.00*	*$85.00*	*$230.00*	£19.00	£57.50	£155.00
118 (Jan 1958)	*$29.00*	*$85.00*	*$230.00*	£19.00	£57.50	£155.00
119-120	*$29.00*	*$85.00*	*$230.00*	£19.00	£57.50	£155.00
121-122	*$25.00*	*$75.00*	*$200.00*	£16.50	£50.00	£135.00
123 Supergirl try-out (blonde on cover, brunette inside - see Action Comics #156), 3 part story	*$31.00*	*$92.50*	*$250.00*	£21.00	£62.50	£170.00
124-125	*$25.00*	*$75.00*	*$200.00*	£16.50	£50.00	£135.00
126 (Jan 1959)	*$25.00*	*$75.00*	*$200.00*	£16.50	£50.00	£135.00
127 1st appearance Lori Lemaris, 1st appearance Titano the Super-Ape	*$28.00*	*$82.50*	*$225.00*	£18.50	£55.00	£150.00
128	*$25.00*	*$75.00*	*$200.00*	£16.50	£50.00	£135.00
129	*$28.00*	*$82.50*	*$225.00*	£18.50	£55.00	£150.00
130	*$25.00*	*$75.00*	*$200.00*	£16.50	£50.00	£135.00
131	*$20.00*	*$60.00*	*$160.00*	£13.50	£41.00	£110.00
1st official distribution in the U.K.						
132 Batman and Robin cameo	*$20.00*	*$60.00*	*$160.00*	£13.50	£41.00	£110.00
133	*$20.00*	*$60.00*	*$160.00*	£13.50	£41.00	£110.00
134 (Jan 1960)	*$20.00*	*$60.00*	*$160.00*	£13.50	£41.00	£110.00
135-137	*$20.00*	*$60.00*	*$160.00*	£13.50	£41.00	£110.00
138 Aquaman appears	*$20.00*	*$60.00*	*$160.00*	£13.50	£41.00	£110.00
139	*$20.00*	*$60.00*	*$160.00*	£13.50	£41.00	£110.00
140 1st appearance Blue Kryptonite, 1st appearance Bizarro Supergirl, 1st appearance Bizarro Junior	*$21.50*	*$65.00*	*$175.00*	£15.00	£45.00	£120.00
141 classic story: Superman's Return to Krypton	*$17.50*	*$52.50*	*$140.00*	£10.50	£32.00	£85.00
142 (Jan 1961), Batman appears (1st time since issue #76)	*$17.50*	*$52.50*	*$140.00*	£10.50	£32.00	£85.00
143-145	*$17.50*	*$52.50*	*$140.00*	£10.50	£32.00	£85.00
146 scarce in the U.K. Superman's life story	*$20.00*	*$60.00*	*$160.00*	£12.50	£38.00	£100.00
147 7th appearance of Legion of Super-Heroes, 1st Legion of Super Villains, Adult Legion appear; Krypto vs. Titano	*$18.50*	*$55.00*	*$150.00*	£11.50	£36.00	£95.00

Issue	$Good	$Fine	$N.Mint	£Good	£Fine	£N.Mint
148	*$17.50*	*$52.50*	*$140.00*	£10.50	£32.00	£85.00
149 10th Legion, classic Death of Superman story, last 10 cents issue; answers to Great Superman Boo Boo Contest!	*$17.50*	*$52.50*	*$140.00*	£10.50	£32.00	£85.00
150 (Jan 1962), Superman, Supergirl and Krypto origins briefly retold, Bizarros and Brainiac cameo appearances; creation of artificial Krypton	*$11.00*	*$34.00*	*$80.00*	£7.00	£21.00	£50.00
151	*$11.00*	*$34.00*	*$80.00*	£7.00	£21.00	£50.00
152 16th Legion appearance	*$11.00*	*$34.00*	*$80.00*	£7.00	£21.00	£50.00
153-154	*$11.00*	*$34.00*	*$80.00*	£7.00	£21.00	£50.00
155 20th Legion appearance	*$11.00*	*$34.00*	*$80.00*	£7.00	£21.00	£50.00
156 Legion appears	*$11.00*	*$34.00*	*$80.00*	£6.25	£19.00	£45.00
157 Mon-El, Lightning Lad cameo	*$11.00*	*$34.00*	*$80.00*	£6.25	£19.00	£45.00
158 (Jan 1963), 1st appearance Flamebird and Nightwing (Jimmy Olsen and Superman as crime-fighters in Kandor)	*$11.00*	*$34.00*	*$80.00*	£6.25	£19.00	£45.00
159-160	*$11.00*	*$34.00*	*$80.00*	£6.25	£19.00	£45.00
161 Ma & Pa Kent death 1st told	*$10.50*	*$32.00*	*$75.00*	£5.00	£15.00	£35.00
162 Legion appears	*$10.50*	*$32.00*	*$75.00*	£5.00	£15.00	£35.00
163-165	*$10.50*	*$32.00*	*$75.00*	£5.00	£15.00	£35.00
166 (Jan 1964)	*$10.50*	*$32.00*	*$75.00*	£5.00	£15.00	£35.00
167 Luthor and Brainiac team-up; 1st appearance Tixaria later to marry Lex Luthor	*$13.50*	*$41.00*	*$95.00*	£7.00	£21.00	£50.00
168	*$10.50*	*$32.00*	*$75.00*	£5.00	£15.00	£35.00
169 Batman appears; The Great DC Contest (answers in #174)	*$10.50*	*$32.00*	*$75.00*	£5.00	£15.00	£35.00
170 President Kennedy story originally prepared for #168	*$10.50*	*$32.00*	*$75.00*	£5.00	£15.00	£35.00
171	*$8.50*	*$26.00*	*$60.00*	£4.25	£12.50	£30.00
172 Luthor and Brainiac team-up, Legion cameo	*$8.50*	*$26.00*	*$60.00*	£4.25	£12.50	£30.00
173 Luthor and Brainiac team-up, Legion cameo and Batman cameo (with wierd chest emblem and eyes seen through mask!); Tales of Green Kryptonite begin (also #176,#177,#179)	*$8.50*	*$26.00*	*$60.00*	£4.25	£12.50	£30.00
174 (Jan 1965), Bizarro appears and Batman cameo (with another weird chest emblem!)	*$8.50*	*$26.00*	*$60.00*	£4.25	£12.50	£30.00
175	*$8.50*	*$26.00*	*$60.00*	£4.25	£12.50	£30.00
176 Green Kryptonite deadly to humans (1st and only appearance)	*$8.50*	*$26.00*	*$60.00*	£4.25	£12.50	£30.00
177-180	*$8.50*	*$26.00*	*$60.00*	£4.25	£12.50	£30.00
181 1st appearance Superman 2965; last Silver Age issue, indicia-dated November 1965	*$7.00*	*$21.00*	*$50.00*	£3.55	£10.50	£25.00
182 (Jan 1966)	*$7.00*	*$21.00*	*$50.00*	£3.55	£10.50	£25.00
183 80pgs, Giant G-18, rare Golden Age reprints inc. Superman #30 (1st Golden Age Mr. Mxyztplk)	*$6.75*	*$20.50*	*$55.00*	£4.35	£13.00	£35.00
184 Fortress of Solitude feature at centre-spread (often missing!)	*$7.00*	*$21.00*	*$50.00*	£3.55	£10.50	£25.00
185	*$7.00*	*$21.00*	*$50.00*	£3.55	£10.50	£25.00
186 Batman cameo	*$7.00*	*$21.00*	*$50.00*	£3.55	£10.50	£25.00
187 80pgs, Giant G-23	*$6.75*	*$20.50*	*$55.00*	£3.75	£11.00	£30.00
188	*$7.00*	*$21.00*	*$50.00*	£3.55	£10.50	£25.00
189 Batman cameo, Supergirl origin briefly retold	*$7.00*	*$21.00*	*$50.00*	£3.55	£10.50	£25.00
190	*$7.00*	*$21.00*	*$50.00*	£3.55	£10.50	£25.00
191	*$7.00*	*$21.00*	*$50.00*	£3.20	£9.50	£22.50
192 (Jan 1967), Justice League of America appear	*$7.00*	*$21.00*	*$50.00*	£3.20	£9.50	£22.50
193 80pgs, Giant G-31, reprints #149	*$6.75*	*$20.50*	*$55.00*	£3.75	£11.00	£30.00
194-195	*$7.00*	*$21.00*	*$50.00*	£3.20	£9.50	£22.50
196 classic The Thing From 40,000AD (reprint of #87), Superman vs. Superman cover	*$7.00*	*$21.00*	*$50.00*	£3.20	£9.50	£22.50
197 80pgs, Giant G-36	*$6.75*	*$20.50*	*$55.00*	£3.75	£11.00	£30.00
198	*$7.00*	*$21.00*	*$50.00*	£3.20	£9.50	£22.50
199 1st Superman/Flash race (see Flash #175, World's Finest #198/199; see also Adv. of Superman #463 for updated version of the race)	*$26.00*	*$77.50*	*$210.00*	£12.50	£38.00	£100.00
[Scarce in high grade - Very Fine+ or better]						
200 Krypton history	*$7.00*	*$21.00*	*$50.00*	£3.55	£10.50	£25.00
201	*$6.25*	*$19.00*	*$45.00*	£2.50	£7.50	£17.50
202 scarce in the U.K. 80pgs, Giant G-42, all Bizarro reprints	*$5.00*	*$15.00*	*$40.00*	£3.10	£9.25	£25.00
203 (Jan 1968)	*$6.25*	*$19.00*	*$45.00*	£2.50	£7.50	£17.50
204 Neal Adams cover art, 1st appearance Q-Energy, lethal to Superman	*$6.25*	*$19.00*	*$45.00*	£2.50	£7.50	£17.50
205 Neal Adams cover art, more facts about the destruction of Krypton	*$6.25*	*$19.00*	*$45.00*	£2.50	£7.50	£17.50
206 Neal Adams cover	*$6.25*	*$19.00*	*$45.00*	£2.50	£7.50	£17.50
207 80pgs, Giant G-48, 30th anniversary with classic reprints	*$5.00*	*$15.00*	*$40.00*	£3.10	£9.25	£25.00

Issue	$Good	$Fine	$N.Mint	£Good	£Fine	£N.Mint
208 Neal Adams cover	$6.25	$19.00	$45.00	£2.50	£7.50	£17.50
209-211	$6.25	$19.00	$45.00	£2.50	£7.50	£17.50
212 80pgs, Giant G-54	$5.00	$15.00	$40.00	£2.50	£7.50	£20.00
213 (Jan 1969)	$5.50	$17.00	$40.00	£2.10	£6.25	£15.00
214-215 Neal Adams cover	$5.50	$17.00	$40.00	£2.10	£6.25	£15.00
216	$3.55	$10.50	$25.00	£1.75	£5.25	£12.50
217 80pgs, Giant G-60, reprints #123	$5.00	$15.00	$40.00	£2.50	£7.50	£20.00
218-220	$3.55	$10.50	$25.00	£1.75	£5.25	£12.50
221	$3.55	$10.50	$25.00	£1.40	£4.25	£10.00
222 80pgs, Giant G-66	$5.00	$15.00	$40.00	£2.15	£6.50	£17.50
223 (Jan 1970)	$3.55	$10.50	$25.00	£1.40	£4.25	£10.00
224	$3.55	$10.50	$25.00	£1.40	£4.25	£10.00
225 2pgs text: The Superman Legend	$3.55	$10.50	$25.00	£1.40	£4.25	£10.00
226	$4.15	$12.50	$25.00	£1.65	£5.00	£10.00
227 80pgs, Giant G-72, all kryptonite issue	$5.00	$15.00	$40.00	£2.15	£6.50	£17.50
228-230	$4.15	$12.50	$25.00	£1.65	£5.00	£10.00
231	$4.15	$12.50	$25.00	£1.50	£4.50	£9.00
232 scarce in the U.K. 80pgs, Giant G-78, reprints #141	$4.35	$13.00	$35.00	£1.85	£5.50	£15.00
233 (Jan 1971), 1st new look: Clark Kent becomes TV reporter, "Kryptonite No More" - all kryptonite turned to lead; 1st appearance Sand Creature Superman; Neal Adams cover	$3.30	$10.00	$20.00	£1.65	£5.00	£10.00
234 Neal Adams cover	$2.50	$7.50	$15.00	£1.25	£3.75	£7.50
235-236	$2.50	$7.50	$15.00	£1.25	£3.75	£7.50
237 Neal Adams cover	$2.50	$7.50	$15.00	£1.25	£3.75	£7.50
238 Gray Morrow art	$2.50	$7.50	$15.00	£1.25	£3.75	£7.50
239 scarce in the U.K. 80pgs, Giant G-84, reprints #127 (1st Titano)	$5.00	$15.00	$35.00	£2.10	£6.25	£15.00
240 Mike Kaluta art	$1.65	$5.00	$10.00	£1.00	£3.00	£6.00
241 52pgs	$1.25	$3.75	$7.50	£0.80	£2.50	£5.00
242 52pgs, Neal Adams cover	$1.25	$3.75	$7.50	£0.80	£2.50	£5.00
243-244 52pgs	$1.25	$3.75	$7.50	£0.80	£2.50	£5.00
245 scarce in the U.K. 100pgs, DC 100pg Super Spectacular #7; reprints Atom #3	$2.50	$7.50	$15.00	£1.25	£3.75	£7.50
246 52pgs	$1.25	$3.75	$7.50	£0.80	£2.50	£5.00
247 52pgs, (Jan 1972)	$1.25	$3.75	$7.50	£0.80	£2.50	£5.00
248 52pgs, Cockrum art	$1.25	$3.75	$7.50	£0.80	£2.50	£5.00
249 52pgs, Neal Adams inks, origin and 1st appearance Terra-Man	$1.50	$4.50	$9.00	£1.00	£3.00	£6.00
250 52pgs	$1.25	$3.75	$7.50	£0.80	£2.50	£5.00
251 52pgs	$1.00	$3.00	$6.00	£0.65	£2.00	£4.00
252 very scarce in the U.K. 100pgs, DC-100pg Super Spectacular #13; reprints Superman #17 and Action Comics #47; Neal Adams cover	$2.10	$6.25	$15.00	£1.75	£5.25	£12.50
253 52pgs	$1.00	$3.00	$6.00	£0.65	£2.00	£4.00
254 scarce in the U.K. Neal Adams art	$1.65	$5.00	$10.00	£1.00	£3.00	£6.00
255-259	$0.65	$2.00	$4.00	£0.40	£1.25	£2.50
260 (Jan 1973)	$0.65	$2.00	$4.00	£0.40	£1.25	£2.50
261-262	$0.65	$2.00	$4.00	£0.40	£1.25	£2.50
263 photo cover	$0.65	$2.00	$4.00	£0.40	£1.25	£2.50
264 1st appearance Steve Lombard, Cockrum art	$0.65	$2.00	$4.00	£0.40	£1.25	£2.50
265-267	$0.65	$2.00	$4.00	£0.40	£1.25	£2.50
268 Batgirl co-stars	$0.65	$2.00	$4.00	£0.40	£1.25	£2.50
269-270	$0.65	$2.00	$4.00	£0.40	£1.25	£2.50
271 (Jan 1974)	$0.65	$2.00	$4.00	£0.40	£1.25	£2.50
272 100pgs	$1.65	$5.00	$10.00	£0.90	£2.75	£5.50
273-277	$0.50	$1.50	$3.00	£0.30	£1.00	£2.00
278 100pgs	$1.65	$5.00	$10.00	£0.90	£2.75	£5.50
279-282	$0.50	$1.50	$3.00	£0.30	£1.00	£2.00
283 (Jan 1975)	$0.50	$1.50	$3.00	£0.30	£1.00	£2.00
284 100pgs	$1.65	$5.00	$10.00	£0.90	£2.75	£5.50
285-289	$0.50	$1.50	$3.00	£0.30	£1.00	£2.00
290-293 very scarce in the U.K.	$0.50	$1.50	$3.00	£0.50	£1.50	£3.00
294 scarce in the U.K.	$0.50	$1.50	$3.00	£0.40	£1.25	£2.50
295 scarce in the U.K. (Jan 1976)	$0.50	$1.50	$3.00	£0.40	£1.25	£2.50
296-299 scarce in the U.K.	$0.50	$1.50	$3.00	£0.40	£1.25	£2.50
300 scarce in the U.K. origin Superman 2001	$1.65	$5.00	$10.00	£0.55	£1.75	£3.50
301-304 scarce in the U.K.	$0.50	$1.50	$3.00	£0.30	£1.00	£2.00
305 scarce in the U.K. Bizarro appears	$0.50	$1.50	$3.00	£0.30	£1.00	£2.00
306 scarce in the U.K.	$0.50	$1.50	$3.00	£0.30	£1.00	£2.00
307 scarce in the U.K. (Jan 1977)	$0.50	$1.50	$3.00	£0.30	£1.00	£2.00
308-310 scarce in the U.K.	$0.50	$1.50	$3.00	£0.30	£1.00	£2.00
311-312 scarce in the U.K.	$0.50	$1.50	$3.00	£0.25	£0.85	£1.75
313-314 scarce in the U.K. Neal Adams covers	$0.50	$1.50	$3.00	£0.25	£0.85	£1.75
315-316 scarce in the U.K.	$0.50	$1.50	$3.00	£0.25	£0.85	£1.75
317 scarce in the U.K. Neal Adams cover	$0.50	$1.50	$3.00	£0.25	£0.85	£1.75
318 scarce in the U.K.	$0.50	$1.50	$3.00	£0.25	£0.85	£1.75
319 scarce in the U.K. (Jan 1978)	$0.50	$1.50	$3.00	£0.25	£0.85	£1.75
320 scarce in the U.K.	$0.50	$1.50	$3.00	£0.25	£0.85	£1.75
321-326	$0.40	$1.25	$2.50	£0.25	£0.75	£1.50
327-329 ND 44pgs	$0.40	$1.25	$2.50	£0.25	£0.85	£1.75
330	$0.40	$1.25	$2.50	£0.25	£0.75	£1.50
331 (Jan 1979)	$0.40	$1.25	$2.50	£0.25	£0.75	£1.50
332	$0.40	$1.25	$2.50	£0.25	£0.75	£1.50
333 Bizarro appears	$0.40	$1.25	$2.50	£0.25	£0.75	£1.50
334-337	$0.40	$1.25	$2.50	£0.25	£0.75	£1.50
338 40th anniversary issue						

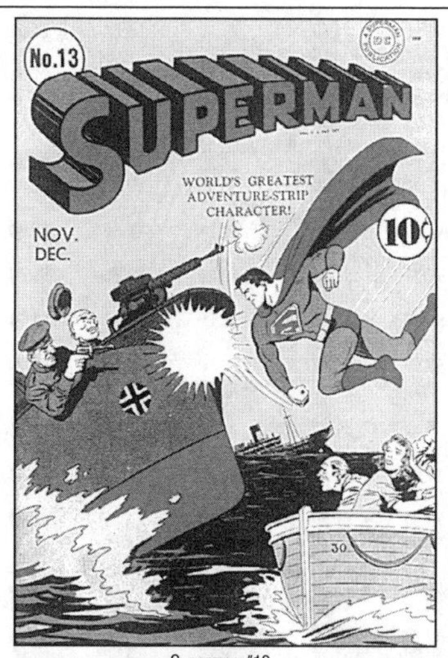

Superman #13

Superman #95

Superman #108

	$Good	$Fine	$N.Mint	£Good	£Fine	£N.Mint
	$0.40	$1.25	$2.50	£0.25	£0.75	£1.50
339-342	$0.40	$1.25	$2.50	£0.25	£0.75	£1.50
343 (Jan 1980)	$0.40	$1.25	$2.50	£0.25	£0.75	£1.50
344-350	$0.40	$1.25	$2.50	£0.25	£0.75	£1.50
351-353	$0.50	$1.50	$2.50	£0.25	£0.75	£1.25
354 1st appearance Superman 2020						
	$0.50	$1.50	$2.50	£0.25	£0.75	£1.25
355 (Jan 1981)	$0.50	$1.50	$2.50	£0.25	£0.75	£1.25
356-363	$0.50	$1.50	$2.50	£0.25	£0.75	£1.25
364 George Perez cover						
	$0.50	$1.50	$2.50	£0.25	£0.75	£1.25
365-366	$0.50	$1.50	$2.50	£0.25	£0.75	£1.25
367 (Jan 1982)	$0.50	$1.50	$2.50	£0.25	£0.75	£1.25
368-375	$0.50	$1.50	$2.50	£0.25	£0.75	£1.25
376 X-over Supergirl (2nd Series) #1						
	$0.50	$1.50	$2.50	£0.25	£0.75	£1.25
377 Masters of the Universe insert						
	$0.50	$1.50	$2.50	£0.25	£0.75	£1.25
378	$0.50	$1.50	$2.50	£0.25	£0.75	£1.25
379 (Jan 1983), Bizarro appears						
	$0.50	$1.50	$2.50	£0.25	£0.75	£1.25
380 X-over Superboy (2nd Series) #38						
	$0.50	$1.50	$2.50	£0.30	£0.90	£1.50
381-386	$0.50	$1.50	$2.50	£0.25	£0.75	£1.25
387 X-over Action Comics #547						
	$0.50	$1.50	$2.50	£0.25	£0.75	£1.25
388-390	$0.50	$1.50	$2.50	£0.25	£0.75	£1.25
391 (Jan 1984)	$0.50	$1.50	$2.50	£0.25	£0.75	£1.25
392-399	$0.50	$1.50	$2.50	£0.25	£0.75	£1.25
400 scarce in the U.K. 68pgs, top artists' tributes inc. 10pgs of new Steranko art, 1pg John Byrne art						
	$1.50	$4.50	$7.50	£1.00	£3.00	£5.00
401-402	$0.50	$1.50	$2.50	£0.25	£0.75	£1.25
403 (Jan 1985)	$0.50	$1.50	$2.50	£0.25	£0.75	£1.25
404-410	$0.50	$1.50	$2.50	£0.25	£0.75	£1.25
411 LD in the U.K. tribute to Julius Schwartz issue						
	$0.50	$1.50	$2.50	£0.30	£0.90	£1.50
412	$0.50	$1.50	$2.50	£0.25	£0.75	£1.25
413 unofficial Crisis X-over						
	$0.50	$1.50	$2.50	£0.25	£0.75	£1.25
414 Crisis X-over	$0.50	$1.50	$2.50	£0.30	£0.90	£1.50
415 (Jan 1986), Crisis X-over						
	$0.50	$1.50	$2.50	£0.30	£0.90	£1.50
416-422	$0.50	$1.50	$2.50	£0.25	£0.75	£1.25
423 George Perez and Curt Swan art, Alan Moore story, ties in with Action #583 last pre-John Byrne Superman						
	$2.00	$6.00	$10.00	£0.70	£2.10	£3.50
424 LD in the U.K. (Jan 1987), title becomes The Adventures of Superman, patriotic cover based on issue #14						
	$0.60	$1.80	$3.00	£0.30	£0.90	£1.50
425	$0.40	$1.20	$2.00	£0.20	£0.60	£1.00
426 Legends X-over						
	$0.40	$1.20	$2.00	£0.20	£0.60	£1.00
427-435	$0.40	$1.20	$2.00	£0.20	£0.60	£1.00
436 (Jan 1988), Millennium X-over						
	$0.40	$1.20	$2.00	£0.20	£0.60	£1.00
437-440 John Byrne scripts						
	$0.40	$1.20	$2.00	£0.20	£0.60	£1.00
441 John Byrne script and art						
	$0.40	$1.20	$2.00	£0.20	£0.60	£1.00
442 John Byrne script and cover art						
	$0.40	$1.20	$2.00	£0.20	£0.60	£1.00
443-448	$0.40	$1.20	$2.00	£0.20	£0.60	£1.00
449 (Jan 1989), Invasion X-over, Captain Atom, Guardians, Newsboy Legion appear						
	$0.40	$1.20	$2.00	£0.20	£0.60	£1.00
450-461	$0.40	$1.20	$2.00	£0.20	£0.60	£1.00
462 (Jan 1990), George Perez art						
	$0.40	$1.20	$2.00	£0.20	£0.60	£1.00
463 4th Superman/Flash race (see Superman #199, Flash #175, World's Finest Comics #198/199)						
	$1.00	$3.00	$5.00	£0.30	£0.90	£1.50
464 X-over with Superman #41, Lobo appears						
	$0.50	$1.50	$2.50	£0.20	£0.60	£1.00
465 Art Thibert inks; X-over with Superman #42, Action Comics #652						
	$0.25	$0.75	$1.25	£0.15	£0.45	£0.75
466 "Fantastic Four" type story; 1st appearance Hank Henshaw later The Cyborg Superman						
	$0.50	$1.50	$2.50	£0.30	£0.90	£1.50
467 Dark Knight Over Metropolis, Batman appears, continued in Action Comics #654, bi-weekly						
	$0.25	$0.75	$1.25	£0.15	£0.45	£0.75
468 Art Thilbert co-artist, 8pg insert re-telling origin						
	$0.25	$0.75	$1.25	£0.15	£0.45	£0.75
469 Art Thibert co-artist						
	$0.25	$0.75	$1.25	£0.15	£0.45	£0.75
470 Art Thibert co-artist, continued from Superman #47						
	$0.25	$0.75	$1.25	£0.15	£0.45	£0.75
471 The Sinbad Contract part 2, continued in Action Comics #658						
	$0.25	$0.75	$1.25	£0.15	£0.45	£0.75
472 Krisis of the Krimson Kryptonite part 2, continued in Action Comics #659						
	$0.25	$0.75	$1.25	£0.15	£0.45	£0.75
473 Art Thilbert inks, Green Lantern(s) guest-star						
	$0.25	$0.75	$1.25	£0.15	£0.45	£0.75
474 (Jan 1991), Art Thibert inks						
	$0.25	$0.75	$1.25	£0.15	£0.45	£0.75
475	$0.25	$0.75	$1.25	£0.15	£0.45	£0.75
476 Time and Time Again part 1, Booster Gold appears, continued in Action Comics #663						
	$0.25	$0.75	$1.25	£0.15	£0.45	£0.75
477 Time and Time Again part 4, guest-stars "middle period" Legion of Super-Heroes						
	$0.25	$0.75	$1.25	£0.15	£0.45	£0.75
478 Time and Time Again part 7 (conclusion)						
	$0.25	$0.75	$1.25	£0.15	£0.45	£0.75
479 The Red Glass trilogy part 2						
	$0.25	$0.75	$1.25	£0.15	£0.45	£0.75
480 DS	$0.40	$1.20	$2.00	£0.25	£0.75	£1.25
481	$0.25	$0.75	$1.25	£0.15	£0.45	£0.75
482 The Parasite appears, cover based on Action Comics #360						
	$0.25	$0.75	$1.25	£0.15	£0.45	£0.75
483 The Parasite appears						
	$0.25	$0.75	$1.25	£0.15	£0.45	£0.75
484 Blackout part 1, continues in Action Comics #671						
	$0.25	$0.75	$1.25	£0.15	£0.45	£0.75
485 Blackout part 5 (conclusion)						
	$0.25	$0.75	$1.25	£0.15	£0.45	£0.75
486 (Jan 1992)	$0.25	$0.75	$1.25	£0.15	£0.45	£0.75
487	$0.25	$0.75	$1.25	£0.15	£0.45	£0.75
488 Panic in the Sky part 3, continued in Action Comics #675						
	$0.25	$0.75	$1.25	£0.15	£0.45	£0.75
489 Panic in the Sky epilogue, continued in Action Comics #676						
	$0.25	$0.75	$1.25	£0.15	£0.45	£0.75
490	$0.25	$0.75	$1.25	£0.15	£0.45	£0.75
491 Metallo returns						
	$0.25	$0.75	$1.25	£0.15	£0.45	£0.75
492 continued from Superman #69, Agent Liberty appears						
	$0.25	$0.75	$1.25	£0.15	£0.45	£0.75
493 The Blaze/Satanus War part 1, continued in Action Comics #680						
	$0.25	$0.75	$1.25	£0.15	£0.45	£0.75
494 The Blaze/Satanus War epilogue						
	$0.25	$0.75	$1.25	£0.15	£0.45	£0.75
495 Forever People appear						
	$0.25	$0.75	$1.25	£0.15	£0.45	£0.75
496 Doomsday cameo						
	$1.00	$3.00	$5.00	£0.30	£0.90	£1.50
496 2nd printing	$0.25	$0.75	$1.25	£0.15	£0.45	£0.75
497 Superman: Doomsday part 3						
	$1.00	$3.00	$5.00	£0.40	£1.20	£2.00
497 2nd printing	$0.25	$0.75	$1.25	£0.15	£0.45	£0.75
498 (Jan 1993), Funeral for a Friend part 1, continued in Action Comics #685						
	$0.60	$1.80	$3.00	£0.30	£0.90	£1.50
498 2nd printing, (II in date/number box)						
	$0.25	$0.75	$1.25	£0.15	£0.45	£0.75
498 3rd printing	$0.25	$0.75	$1.25	£0.15	£0.45	£0.75
499 Funeral for a Friend part 5, continued in Action Comics #686						
	$0.60	$1.80	$3.00	£0.15	£0.45	£0.75
500 64pgs, squarebound, the return of Superman (though in four variations), 1st appearance of the new Superboy; bi-weekly						
	$0.30	$0.90	$1.50	£0.20	£0.60	£1.00
500 Collectors Edition, ND 64pgs, squarebound, translucent cover panel, extra 8pg section; pre-bagged in white plastic; bi-weekly						
	$0.60	$1.80	$3.00	£0.40	£1.20	£2.00
500 Platinum Edition, ND pre-bagged in black with "S" emblem in platinum on front						
	$7.00	$21.00	$35.00	£5.00	£15.00	£25.00
501 Reign of the Supermen part 2, bi-weekly						
	$0.50	$1.50	$2.50	£0.30	£0.90	£1.50
501 Collectors Edition, ND Reign of the Supermen part 2, die-cut outer cover, bound-in mini-poster; bi-weekly						
	$0.70	$2.10	$3.50	£0.40	£1.20	£2.00
501 Dynamic Forces Edition, ND signed by Kesel and Grummett; 10,000 copies						
	$3.00	$9.00	$15.00	£2.00	£6.00	£10.00
502 Reign of the Supermen part 8, Supergirl appears						
	$0.30	$0.90	$1.50	£0.20	£0.60	£1.00
503 Reign of the Supermen part 12, continued in Action Comics #690						
	$0.30	$0.90	$1.50	£0.20	£0.60	£1.00
504 Reign of the Supermen part 16, continued in Action Comics #691						
	$0.30	$0.90	$1.50	£0.20	£0.60	£1.00
505 Superman returns! (ties in with Green Lantern #46 and Superman #82)						
	$0.30	$0.90	$1.50	£0.20	£0.60	£1.00
505 Collectors Edition, ND foil enhanced cover, continued in Action Comics #691						
	$0.45	$1.35	$2.25	£0.30	£0.90	£1.50
506	$0.30	$0.90	$1.50	£0.20	£0.60	£1.00
507 Barry Kitson pencils begin; story continued in Action Comics #494						
	$0.30	$0.90	$1.50	£0.20	£0.60	£1.00
508 (Jan 1994), Challengers of the Unknown appear						
	$0.30	$0.90	$1.50	£0.20	£0.60	£1.00
509 death of Auron						
	$0.30	$0.90	$1.50	£0.20	£0.60	£1.00
510 Bizarro appears, continued in Action Comics #697						
	$0.30	$0.90	$1.50	£0.20	£0.60	£1.00
511	$0.30	$0.90	$1.50	£0.20	£0.60	£1.00
512 Parasite appears						
	$0.30	$0.90	$1.50	£0.20	£0.60	£1.00
513 The Battle for Metropolis part 4 (conclusion)						
	$0.30	$0.90	$1.50	£0.20	£0.60	£1.00
514 concluded in Action Comics #701						
	$0.30	$0.90	$1.50	£0.20	£0.60	£1.00
515	$0.30	$0.90	$1.50	£0.20	£0.60	£1.00
516 Zero Hour X-over						
	$0.30	$0.90	$1.50	£0.20	£0.60	£1.00
517-518	$0.30	$0.90	$1.50	£0.20	£0.60	£1.00
519 (Jan 1995)	$0.30	$0.90	$1.50	£0.20	£0.60	£1.00
520-521	$0.30	$0.90	$1.50	£0.20	£0.60	£1.00

VERY GENERAL PERCENTAGE CONVERSION CHART WHICH MAY BE USED TO CALCULATE LOW AND INBETWEEN GRADES:

$Good ***$Fine*** ***$N.Mint*** **£Good** **£Fine** **£N.Mint**

522 story continued from Steel #14
$0.30 ***$0.90*** ***$1.50*** **£0.20** **£0.60** **£1.00**
523 The Death of Clark Kent part 2, continued in Action Comics #710
$0.30 ***$0.90*** ***$1.50*** **£0.20** **£0.60** **£1.00**
524 The Death of Clark Kent part 6, continued in Action Comics #711; upgraded coated paper stock (Miraweb Format) begins
$0.40 ***$1.20*** ***$2.00*** **£0.25** **£0.75** **£1.25**
525-526 ***$0.40*** ***$1.20*** ***$2.00*** **£0.25** **£0.75** **£1.25**
527 The Joker appears on the last page
$0.40 ***$1.20*** ***$2.00*** **£0.25** **£0.75** **£1.25**
528 ***$0.40*** ***$1.20*** ***$2.00*** **£0.25** **£0.75** **£1.25**
529 The Trial of Superman, continued in Action Comics #716
$0.40 ***$1.20*** ***$2.00*** **£0.25** **£0.75** **£1.25**
530 The Trial of Superman, continued in Superman: The Man of Tomorrow #3; Underworld Unleashed tie-in
$0.40 ***$1.20*** ***$2.00*** **£0.25** **£0.75** **£1.25**
531 (Jan 1996), The Trial of Superman concluded from Superman #108
$0.40 ***$1.20*** ***$2.00*** **£0.25** **£0.75** **£1.25**
532 Lori Lemaris returns
$0.40 ***$1.20*** ***$2.00*** **£0.25** **£0.75** **£1.25**
533 Impulse guest-stars
$0.40 ***$1.20*** ***$2.00*** **£0.25** **£0.75** **£1.25**
534-535 ***$0.40*** ***$1.20*** ***$2.00*** **£0.25** **£0.75** **£1.25**
536 Brainiac appears
$0.40 ***$1.20*** ***$2.00*** **£0.25** **£0.75** **£1.25**
537-539 ***$0.40*** ***$1.20*** ***$2.00*** **£0.25** **£0.75** **£1.25**
540 Final Night tie-in; Ferro Lad of the Legion of Super-Heroes appears
$0.40 ***$1.20*** ***$2.00*** **£0.25** **£0.75** **£1.25**
541 ND Misa of The Outsiders appears
$0.40 ***$1.20*** ***$2.00*** **£0.25** **£0.75** **£1.25**
542-544 ND ***$0.40*** ***$1.20*** ***$2.00*** **£0.25** **£0.75** **£1.25**
Title Value: *$27187.20* *$81599.55* *$244612.00* £18022.20 £54162.90 £162448.75
Note: #207 is often found with printing ink smears on cover (see Batman #208, New Teen Titans #4).

FEATURES

Bruce (Superman) Wayne in 353, 358, 363. Mr & Mrs Superman in 327, 329. Private Life of Clark Kent in 247, 254, 356, 258, 260, 262, 267, 270, 273, 277, 280, 285, 287, 289, 292, 294, 328, 371, 373. Superman: The In-Between Years in 359, 362, 365, 366, 370, 374. Superman 2020/1 in 354, 355, 357, 361, 364, 368, 372. Terra-Man in 249. World of Krypton in 233, 234, 236, 238, 240, 243, 246, 248, 251, 255, 257, 263, 264, 266, 268, 271, 275, 279, 282, 352, 356, 360, 367.

REPRINT FEATURES

Bizarro World in 193, 202. Captain Comet in 244. Dr. Fate, Hawkman, Black Condor, Spectre in 252. Jimmy Olsen, Green Lantern in 272. Kid Eternity, Atom, Super-Chief, Air Wave, Hawkman in 245. Lois Lane in 207, 212. Starman The Ray in 252. Superboy 212, 222, 227, 232. Supergirl in 212. Superman in 183, 187, 193, 197, 207, 212, 222, 227, 229-232, 239, 241-253, 272, 278, 284.

SUPERMAN (1ST SERIES) ANNUAL

National Periodical Publications/DC Comics; 1 1960-8 Winter 1963/64; 9 Sep 1983-12 Aug 1986
(becomes Adventures of Superman Annual re-starting at #1)
1 rare in the U.K. 80pgs, (not to be confused with 80pg Giant #1!); reprints Lois lane #1 (cover story) and Action Comics #252 (Supergirl's origin); 1st Silver Age DC annual
$92.50 ***$275.00*** ***$925.00*** **£52.50** **£155.00** **£525.00**
[Scarce in high grade - Very Fine+ or better]
2 80pgs, Villains issue, reprints Action #242 (1st Brainiac), origin Metallo (Action #252), origin Bizarro (Superboy #68), Titano (Superman #127)
$47.00 ***$140.00*** ***$425.00*** **£27.00** **£80.00** **£240.00**
3 80pgs ***$33.00*** ***$100.00*** ***$300.00*** **£19.00** **£57.50** **£175.00**
4 scarce in the U.K. 80pgs, 12th Legion of Super-Heroes (2pgs of portraits and powers - debateable as to being a full Legion story appearance)
$29.00 ***$85.00*** ***$260.00*** **£18.50** **£55.00** **£170.00**
5 80pgs, Krypton issue
$23.00 ***$70.00*** ***$210.00*** **£13.00** **£40.00** **£120.00**
6 80pgs, Monsters, reprints Adventure #247 (1st Legion), reprints Superman #123
$20.50 ***$60.00*** ***$185.00*** **£11.50** **£35.00** **£105.00**
7 80pgs, Silver anniversary issue, Batman appears
$15.50 ***$47.00*** ***$140.00*** **£9.25** **£28.00** **£85.00**
8 scarce in the U.K. 80pgs
$13.00 ***$40.00*** ***$120.00*** **£8.25** **£25.00** **£75.00**
9 Toth and Austin art, Batman appears; Curt Swan self-appearance back-up story
$1.20 ***$3.60*** ***$6.00*** **£0.60** **£1.80** **£3.00**
10 ***$1.00*** ***$3.00*** ***$5.00*** **£0.40** **£1.20** **£2.00**
11 Alan Moore script, Dave Gibbons art
$1.00 ***$3.00*** ***$5.00*** **£0.70** **£2.10** **£3.50**
12 Brian Bolland cover
$1.00 ***$3.00*** ***$5.00*** **£0.40** **£1.20** **£2.00**
Title Value: *$277.70* *$829.60* *$2586.00* £161.10 £481.80 £1505.50

SUPERMAN (2ND SERIES)

DC Comics; 1 Jan 1987-77 Mar 1993; 78 Jun 1993-present
0 (Oct 1994) Zero Hour X-over, origin retold; continued in Adventures of Superman #0
$0.40 ***$1.20*** ***$2.00*** **£0.25** **£0.75** **£1.25**
1 John Byrne art ***$0.40*** ***$1.20*** ***$2.00*** **£0.25** **£0.75** **£1.25**
2-3 John Byrne art
$0.30 ***$0.90*** ***$1.50*** **£0.20** **£0.60** **£1.00**
4 John Byrne art, 1st appearance Bloodsport
$0.30 ***$0.90*** ***$1.50*** **£0.20** **£0.60** **£1.00**
5-7 John Byrne art
$0.30 ***$0.90*** ***$1.50*** **£0.20** **£0.60** **£1.00**
8 John Byrne art, Legion of Super-Heroes appear
$0.30 ***$0.90*** ***$1.50*** **£0.20** **£0.60** **£1.00**
9 John Byrne art, Joker appears
$0.50 ***$1.50*** ***$2.50*** **£0.30** **£0.90** **£1.50**
10 John Byrne art ***$0.30*** ***$0.90*** ***$1.50*** **£0.20** **£0.60** **£1.00**
11 John Byrne art, "Beyonder" appears (Ben DeRoy)
$0.30 ***$0.90*** ***$1.50*** **£0.20** **£0.60** **£1.00**

$Good ***$Fine*** ***$N.Mint*** **£Good** **£Fine** **£N.Mint**

12 John Byrne art ***$0.30*** ***$0.90*** ***$1.50*** **£0.20** **£0.60** **£1.00**
13-14 John Byrne art, Millennium X-over
$0.30 ***$0.90*** ***$1.50*** **£0.20** **£0.60** **£1.00**
15-17 John Byrne art
$0.30 ***$0.90*** ***$1.50*** **£0.20** **£0.60** **£1.00**
18 Mike Mignola art, Hawkman appears
$0.30 ***$0.90*** ***$1.50*** **£0.20** **£0.60** **£1.00**
19-21 John Byrne art
$0.30 ***$0.90*** ***$1.50*** **£0.20** **£0.60** **£1.00**
22 John Byrne art, Superman kills! Condemns to death General Zod, Quex-Ul and Zaora
$0.30 ***$0.90*** ***$1.50*** **£0.20** **£0.60** **£1.00**
23 Mike Mignola art, Batman X-over
$0.30 ***$0.90*** ***$1.50*** **£0.20** **£0.60** **£1.00**
24-25 ***$0.30*** ***$0.90*** ***$1.50*** **£0.20** **£0.60** **£1.00**
26-27 Invasion X-over
$0.30 ***$0.90*** ***$1.50*** **£0.20** **£0.60** **£1.00**
28-36 ***$0.30*** ***$0.90*** ***$1.50*** **£0.20** **£0.60** **£1.00**
37 Guardian and Newsboy Legion appear, cover based on Jack Kirby's Jimmy Olsen #133
$0.30 ***$0.90*** ***$1.50*** **£0.20** **£0.60** **£1.00**
38 ***$0.30*** ***$0.90*** ***$1.50*** **£0.20** **£0.60** **£1.00**
39 free 16pg insert (see Batman #443, Starman #18)
$0.30 ***$0.90*** ***$1.50*** **£0.20** **£0.60** **£1.00**
40 ***$0.30*** ***$0.90*** ***$1.50*** **£0.20** **£0.60** **£1.00**
41 LD in the U.K. X-over with Adventures of Superman #464, Lobo appears
$0.40 ***$1.20*** ***$2.00*** **£0.25** **£0.75** **£1.25**
42 X-over Adventures of Superman #465/Action Comics #652
$0.30 ***$0.90*** ***$1.50*** **£0.20** **£0.60** **£1.00**
43 ***$0.30*** ***$0.90*** ***$1.50*** **£0.20** **£0.60** **£1.00**
44 part 1 Dark Knight Over Metropolis, X-over Adventures of Superman #467/Action #654
$0.30 ***$0.90*** ***$1.50*** **£0.20** **£0.60** **£1.00**
45 free 8pg insert ***$0.30*** ***$0.90*** ***$1.50*** **£0.20** **£0.60** **£1.00**
46 Jade/Obsidian guest-star
$0.30 ***$0.90*** ***$1.50*** **£0.20** **£0.60** **£1.00**
47 continues in Adventures of Superman #470
$0.30 ***$0.90*** ***$1.50*** **£0.20** **£0.60** **£1.00**
48 continues in Adventures of Superman #471
$0.30 ***$0.90*** ***$1.50*** **£0.20** **£0.60** **£1.00**
49 Krisis of the Krimson Kryptonite part 1, continues in Adventures of Superman #472
$0.30 ***$0.90*** ***$1.50*** **£0.20** **£0.60** **£1.00**
50 48pgs, Krisis of the Krimson Kryptonite part 4; Clark Kent proposes to Lois Lane; Byrne co-artist and inks
$0.60 ***$1.80*** ***$3.00*** **£0.40** **£1.20** **£2.00**
50 2nd printing, (many copies were mis-cut), has "Historic Engagement Issue" on front cover
$0.30 ***$0.90*** ***$1.50*** **£0.20** **£0.60** **£1.00**
51-52 ***$0.30*** ***$0.90*** ***$1.50*** **£0.20** **£0.60** **£1.00**
53 Superman reveals identity to Lois Lane
$0.50 ***$1.50*** ***$2.50*** **£0.30** **£0.90** **£1.50**
53 2nd printing ***$0.25*** ***$0.75*** ***$1.25*** **£0.15** **£0.45** **£0.75**
54 Time and Time Again part 3, Newsboy Legion back-up stories begin
$0.30 ***$0.90*** ***$1.50*** **£0.20** **£0.60** **£1.00**
55 Time and Time Again part 6
$0.30 ***$0.90*** ***$1.50*** **£0.20** **£0.60** **£1.00**
56 The Red Glass Trilogy part 1
$0.30 ***$0.90*** ***$1.50*** **£0.20** **£0.60** **£1.00**
57 48pgs, Revenge of the Krypton Man part 2, continues in Adventures of Superman #480
$0.30 ***$0.90*** ***$1.50*** **£0.20** **£0.60** **£1.00**
58-59 ***$0.30*** ***$0.90*** ***$1.50*** **£0.20** **£0.60** **£1.00**
60 continued from Man of Steel #4, intro Agent Liberty
$0.30 ***$0.90*** ***$1.50*** **£0.20** **£0.60** **£1.00**
61 Armageddon: 2001 epilogue, Metal Men appear
$0.30 ***$0.90*** ***$1.50*** **£0.20** **£0.60** **£1.00**
62 Blackout part 4, continues in Adventures of Superman #485
$0.30 ***$0.90*** ***$1.50*** **£0.20** **£0.60** **£1.00**
63 Aquaman appears
$0.30 ***$0.90*** ***$1.50*** **£0.20** **£0.60** **£1.00**
64 Christmas issue
$0.30 ***$0.90*** ***$1.50*** **£0.20** **£0.60** **£1.00**
65 Panic in the Sky part 2, continues in Adventures of Superman #488
$0.30 ***$0.90*** ***$1.50*** **£0.20** **£0.60** **£1.00**
66 Panic in the Sky part 6, continues in Adventures of Superman #489; Doomsday device launched
$0.30 ***$0.90*** ***$1.50*** **£0.20** **£0.60** **£1.00**
67 ***$0.30*** ***$0.90*** ***$1.50*** **£0.20** **£0.60** **£1.00**
68 X-over with Deathstroke the Terminator #12/13
$0.30 ***$0.90*** ***$1.50*** **£0.20** **£0.60** **£1.00**
69 Agent Liberty appears
$0.30 ***$0.90*** ***$1.50*** **£0.20** **£0.60** **£1.00**
70 Robin appears, continues from Superman The Man of Steel #14
$0.30 ***$0.90*** ***$1.50*** **£0.20** **£0.60** **£1.00**
71 The Blaze/Satanus War part 4 (conclusion), continued from Superman: The Man of Steel #15
$0.30 ***$0.90*** ***$1.50*** **£0.20** **£0.60** **£1.00**
72 Crisis at Hand part 2, continued from Superman: The Man of Steel #16
$0.30 ***$0.90*** ***$1.50*** **£0.20** **£0.60** **£1.00**
73 Doomsday cameo
$0.60 ***$1.80*** ***$3.00*** **£0.30** **£0.90** **£1.50**
74 Superman: Doomsday part 2, continued in Adventures of Superman #497
$0.80 ***$2.40*** ***$4.00*** **£0.50** **£1.50** **£2.50**
74 2nd printing ***$0.25*** ***$0.75*** ***$1.25*** **£0.15** **£0.45** **£0.75**
75 Superman: Doomsday part 6 (conclusion), the death of Superman drawn in full splash pages with special fold-out last page, continued in Adventures of Superman #498
$0.80 ***$2.40*** ***$4.00*** **£0.50** **£1.50** **£2.50**
75 2nd-4th printings
$0.25 ***$0.75*** ***$1.25*** **£0.15** **£0.45** **£0.75**
75 Collectors Edition, ND pre-bagged in black with satin Superman arm-band, Daily Planet obituary page and

	$Good	$Fine	$N.Mint	£Good	£Fine	£N.Mint
commemorative Superman stamp						
	$2.50	*$7.50*	*$12.50*	£1.50	£4.50	£7.50
75 Collectors Edition un-sealed, as above, contents complete						
	$0.90	*$2.70*	*$4.50*	£0.60	£1.80	£3.00
75 Platinum Edition, ND (Apr 1993) - 10,000 copies, pre-bagged in black with trading card						
	$10.00	*$30.00*	*$50.00*	£7.00	£21.00	£35.00
76 Funeral for a Friend part 4, continued in Adventures of Superman #499						
	$0.30	*$0.90*	*$1.50*	£0.20	£0.60	£1.00
77 Funeral for a Friend part 8 (conclusion)						
	$0.30	*$0.90*	*$1.50*	£0.20	£0.60	£1.00
78 Reign of the Supermen part 3						
	$0.30	*$0.90*	*$1.50*	£0.20	£0.60	£1.00
78 Collectors Edition, ND Reign of the Supermen part 3, die-cut outer cover, bound-in mini-poster						
	$0.40	*$1.20*	*$2.00*	£0.25	£0.75	£1.25
78 Dynamic Forces Edition, ND signed by Jurgens and Breeding; 10,000 copies						
	$2.50	*$7.50*	*$12.50*	£1.50	£4.50	£7.50
79 Reign of the Supermen part 7						
	$0.30	*$0.90*	*$1.50*	£0.20	£0.60	£1.00
80 Reign of the Supermen part 11, continued in Adventures of Superman #503						
	$0.30	*$0.90*	*$1.50*	£0.20	£0.60	£1.00
81 Reign of the Supermen part 15, continued in Adventures of Superman #504						
	$0.30	*$0.90*	*$1.50*	£0.20	£0.60	£1.00
82 Reign of the Supermen part 20 - the one, true Superman revealed!						
	$0.30	*$0.90*	*$1.50*	£0.20	£0.60	£1.00
82 Collectors Edition, ND chromium cover and no ads						
	$0.60	*$1.80*	*$3.00*	£0.40	£1.20	£2.00
83 Justice League America appear						
	$0.30	*$0.90*	*$1.50*	£0.20	£0.60	£1.00
84-85 The (new) Toyman appears						
	$0.30	*$0.90*	*$1.50*	£0.20	£0.60	£1.00
86 Superman's powers increase including the ability to travel through space (again! In the good old days of the Silver Age, unlimited space and time travel was dead easy)						
	$0.30	*$0.90*	*$1.50*	£0.20	£0.60	£1.00
87 Bizarro World part 1; Bizarro appears, continued in Superman (1st Series) #510						
	$0.30	*$0.90*	*$1.50*	£0.20	£0.60	£1.00
88 Bizaro World part 5 (conclusion), Bizarro appears; continued from Superman: The Man of Steel #31						
	$0.30	*$0.90*	*$1.50*	£0.20	£0.60	£1.00
89	*$0.30*	*$0.90*	*$1.50*	£0.20	£0.60	£1.00
90 The Battle for Metropolis part 3, continued in Superman (1st Series) #513						
	$0.30	*$0.90*	*$1.50*	£0.20	£0.60	£1.00
91 continued in Superman (1st series) #514						
	$0.30	*$0.90*	*$1.50*	£0.20	£0.60	£1.00
92 continued in Superman (1st series) #515						
	$0.30	*$0.90*	*$1.50*	£0.20	£0.60	£1.00
93 Zero Hour X-over						
	$0.30	*$0.90*	*$1.50*	£0.20	£0.60	£1.00
94-97	*$0.30*	*$0.90*	*$1.50*	£0.20	£0.60	£1.00
98 The Toyman appears						
	$0.30	*$0.90*	*$1.50*	£0.20	£0.60	£1.00
99 tie-in with Steel #15, Gil Kane guest art						
	$0.30	*$0.90*	*$1.50*	£0.20	£0.60	£1.00
100 64pgs, The Death of Clark Kent part 1, continued in Superman [2nd Series] #523; Standard Edition						
	$0.60	*$1.80*	*$3.00*	£0.40	£1.20	£2.00
100 Collectors Edition, 64pgs, The Death of Clark Kent part 1, continued in Superman [2nd Series] #523; with holographic foil-enhanced cover						
	$0.80	*$2.40*	*$4.00*	£0.50	£1.50	£2.50
101 The Death of Clark Kent part 5, continued in Superman [2nd Series] #524. Upgraded coated paper stock (Miraweb Format) begins						
	$0.40	*$1.20*	*$2.00*	£0.25	£0.75	£1.25
102 Captain Marvel guest-stars						
	$0.40	*$1.20*	*$2.00*	£0.25	£0.75	£1.25
103-104	*$0.40*	*$1.20*	*$2.00*	£0.25	£0.75	£1.25
105 Green Lantern guest-stars; Superman's origin retold in part						
	$0.40	*$1.20*	*$2.00*	£0.25	£0.75	£1.25
106 The Trial of Superman, continued in Superman [1st Series] #529; Ron Frenz art begins						
	$0.40	*$1.20*	*$2.00*	£0.25	£0.75	£1.25
107	*$0.40*	*$1.20*	*$2.00*	£0.25	£0.75	£1.25
108 The Trial of Superman, concluded in Superman [1st series] #531						
	$0.40	*$1.20*	*$2.00*	£0.25	£0.75	£1.25
109	*$0.40*	*$1.20*	*$2.00*	£0.25	£0.75	£1.25
110 Plastic Man guest-stars						
	$0.40	*$1.20*	*$2.00*	£0.25	£0.75	£1.25
111-113	*$0.40*	*$1.20*	*$2.00*	£0.25	£0.75	£1.25
114 Brainiac appears						
	$0.40	*$1.20*	*$2.00*	£0.25	£0.75	£1.25
115 Lois Lane leaves Superman and Metropolis (temporarily)						
	$0.40	*$1.20*	*$2.00*	£0.25	£0.75	£1.25
116 8pg preview of the (new) Teen Titans by George Perez						
	$0.40	*$1.20*	*$2.00*	£0.25	£0.75	£1.25
117 Final Night tie-in						
	$0.40	*$1.20*	*$2.00*	£0.25	£0.75	£1.25
118 ND Legion of Super Heroes appear						
	$0.40	*$1.20*	*$2.00*	£0.25	£0.75	£1.25
119 ND Legion of Super-Heroes appear						
	$0.40	*$1.20*	*$2.00*	£0.25	£0.75	£1.25
120-121 ND	*$0.40*	*$1.20*	*$2.00*	£0.25	£0.75	£1.25
Title Value:	*$59.95*	*$179.85*	*$299.75*	£39.30	£117.90	£196.50
Multi-Pack (1990)						
Three issues from #19-#21 or #20-#22. ND pre-bagged with illustrated header card				£0.30	£0.90	£1.50
Superman: The Death of Superman (1993)						
Trade paperback ND reprints Superman: The Man of Steel #17-19, Superman #73-75, Adventures of Superman #496-497, Action Comics #683-684				£0.65	£1.95	£3.25
Signed, Numbered Edition (1993)						
Trade paperback ND as above though signed by Dan Jurgens, Brett Breeding and Jon Bogdanove; limited to 5,000 copies				£5.00	£15.00	£25.00
Platinum Edition (Jun 1993)						
ND scarce in the U.K. - available to Retailers only who responded to a questionnaire from DC. Same content as Trade paperback but with platinum strip on cover				£5.00	£15.00	£25.00
Superman: Panic in the Sky (May 1993)						
Trade paperback ND 192pgs, reprints Action Comics #674/675, Superman: The Man of Steel #9/10, Superman #65/66, Adventures of Superman #488/489				£1.30	£3.90	£6.50
World Without a Superman						
Trade paperback (Jul 1993) ND reprints Funeral For A Friend storyline from Adventures of Superman #498-500, Action Comics #685,686, Superman: The Man of Steel #20,21, Superman #76,77				£1.00	£3.00	£5.00
Superman: The Return of Superman (Mar 1994)						
Trade paperback ND 480pgs, reprints The Reign of the Supermen storyline from the four Superman titles				£2.00	£6.00	£10.00
Superman: Time & Time Again (Sep 1994)						
Trade paperback ND reprints Action #663-665, Adventures of Superman #476-478 and Superman #54,55,61 and #63				£1.00	£3.00	£5.00
Superman: Eradication! The Origin of the Eradicator (Jan 1996)						
Trade paperback ND reprints Adventures of Superman #460, 464,465, Superman #41,42 and Action Comics #651				£1.70	£5.10	£8.50
Superman: Bizarro's World (Apr 1996)						
Trade paperback ND reprints issues #87,88, Adventures of Superman #510, Action Comics #697, Superman: The Man of Steel #32				£1.30	£3.90	£6.50
Superman's Greatest Foes Collector's Set (Apr 1996)						
ND collectors' pack with Adventures of Superman #520, Superman #104, Superman: Man of Steel #30, Action Comics #713, Superman: Man of Tomorrow #1 and Superman/Toyman #1				£2.00	£6.00	£10.00
Superman: Krisis of the Krimson Kryptonite (Oct 1996)						
Trade paperback ND reprints Superman #49,50, Adventures of Superman #472,473, Action Comics #659,660 and Starman #28				£1.70	£5.10	£8.50

SUPERMAN (2ND SERIES) ANNUAL

DC Comics; 1 Aug 1987-2 1988; 3 Jun 1991-present

	$Good	$Fine	$N.Mint	£Good	£Fine	£N.Mint
1 48pgs, (no John Byrne art)						
	$0.40	*$1.20*	*$2.00*	£0.25	£0.75	£1.25
2 48pgs, John Byrne back-up						
	$0.40	*$1.20*	*$2.00*	£0.25	£0.75	£1.25
3 64pgs, Armageddon: 2001 tie-in, Batman appears						
	$0.40	*$1.20*	*$2.00*	£0.25	£0.75	£1.25
3 2nd/3rd printings	*$0.40*	*$1.20*	*$2.00*	£0.25	£0.75	£1.25
4 64pgs, Eclipso: The Darkness Within tie-in, Joe Quesada cover						
	$0.50	*$1.50*	*$2.50*	£0.30	£0.90	£1.50
5 64pgs, Bloodlines part 6, 1st appearance Myriad, continued in Green Lantern Annual #2						
	$0.50	*$1.50*	*$2.50*	£0.30	£0.90	£1.50
6 64pgs, Elseworlds story, Mike Mignola cover						
	$0.60	*$1.80*	*$3.00*	£0.40	£1.20	£2.00
7 64pgs, Year One, Superman's first encounter with magic						
	$0.80	*$2.40*	*$4.00*	£0.50	£1.50	£2.50
8 Legends of the Dead Earth story						
	$0.60	*$1.80*	*$3.00*	£0.40	£1.20	£2.00
Title Value:	*$4.60*	*$13.80*	*$23.00*	£2.90	£8.70	£14.50

SUPERMAN ADVENTURES

DC Comics; 1 Nov 1996-present

	$Good	$Fine	$N.Mint	£Good	£Fine	£N.Mint
1 ND Rick Burchett and Terry Austin art and Bruce Timm covers begin; based on animated show						
	$0.35	*$1.05*	*$1.75*	£0.25	£0.75	£1.25
2-5 ND	*$0.35*	*$1.05*	*$1.75*	£0.25	£0.75	£1.25
Title Value:	*$1.75*	*$5.25*	*$8.75*	£1.25	£3.75	£6.25

SUPERMAN AND HIS INCREDIBLE FORTRESS OF SOLITUDE

DC Comics,Tabloid;(DC Special Series 26); nn Summer 1981

	$Good	$Fine	$N.Mint	£Good	£Fine	£N.Mint
nn ND 64pgs, all new stories featuring Supergirl and Green Lantern cameo appearances						
	$1.00	*$3.00*	*$5.00*	£0.70	£2.10	£3.50
Title Value:	*$1.00*	*$3.00*	*$5.00*	£0.70	£2.10	£3.50

SUPERMAN AND SPIDERMAN

Marvel Comics Group/DC Comics,Tabloid; nn (Marvel Treasury Edition #28) 1981

	$Good	$Fine	$N.Mint	£Good	£Fine	£N.Mint
nn ND 68pgs, Parasite and Dr. Doom appear (not to be confused with Superman vs. The Amazing Spiderman)						
	$2.50	*$7.50*	*$15.00*	£1.65	£5.00	£10.00
Title Value:	*$2.50*	*$7.50*	*$15.00*	£1.65	£5.00	£10.00
Note: A British has also been published, which is worth around 50%. (May 1996), ND 64pgs, reprints tabloid in comic form with gold metallic border around cover				£0.50	£1.50	£2.50

SUPERMAN ANNUAL, THE ADVENTURES OF

DC Comics; 1 Sep 1987; 2 Aug 1990-present

	$Good	$Fine	$N.Mint	£Good	£Fine	£N.Mint
1 48pgs, Jim Starlin script						
	$0.40	*$1.20*	*$2.00*	£0.25	£0.75	£1.25
2 48pgs, Legion '90 appear						
	$0.40	*$1.20*	*$2.00*	£0.25	£0.75	£1.25
3 64pgs, Armageddon: 2001 tie-in						
	$0.40	*$1.20*	*$2.00*	£0.25	£0.75	£1.25
4 64pgs, Eclipso: The Darkness Within tie-in, Lobo and Guy Gardner appear						
	$0.50	*$1.50*	*$2.50*	£0.30	£0.90	£1.50
5 64pgs, Bloodlines (Wave Two) part 16, 1st appearance Sparx; continued in Hawkman Annual #1						
	$0.50	*$1.50*	*$2.50*	£0.30	£0.90	£1.50
6 64pgs, Elseworlds, continued in Superboy Annual #1						
	$0.60	*$1.80*	*$3.00*	£0.40	£1.20	£2.00
7 64pgs, Year One, Superman and Maggie Sawyer first meet						
	$0.80	*$2.40*	*$4.00*	£0.50	£1.50	£2.50

	$Good	$Fine	$N.Mint	£Good	£Fine	£N.Mint
8 ND Legends of the Dead Earth story						
	$0.60	*$1.80*	*$3.00*	£0.40	£1.20	£2.00
Title Value:	*$4.20*	*$12.60*	*$21.00*	£2.65	£7.95	£13.25

SUPERMAN ARCHIVES

DC Comics; 1 Dec 1989; 2 Nov 1990; 3 Nov 1991; 4 Jun 1994

	$Good	$Fine	$N.Mint	£Good	£Fine	£N.Mint
1 ND reprints Superman #1-#4 by Siegel and Shuster plus covers and ads. Intro by Jim Steranko. Hardcover.						
	$7.50	*$22.50*	*$37.50*	£5.00	£15.00	£25.00
1 2nd printing, ND (Dec 1991)						
	$7.50	*$22.50*	*$37.50*	£5.00	£15.00	£25.00
2 ND reprints Superman #5-#8 by Siegel and Shuster plus covers and ads. Intro by Ron Goulart. Hardcover						
	$7.50	*$22.50*	*$37.50*	£5.00	£15.00	£25.00
2 2nd printing, ND (Dec 1990)						
	$7.50	*$22.50*	*$37.50*	£5.00	£15.00	£25.00
3 ND reprints Superman #9-#12 by Siegel and Shuster plus covers and ads. Intro by Golden Age artist Jack Burnley						
	$7.50	*$22.50*	*$37.50*	£5.00	£15.00	£25.00
4 ND reprints Superman #13-#16 by Siegel and Shuster plus covers and ads. Intro by Golden Age artist Jack Burnley						
	$7.50	*$22.50*	*$37.50*	£5.00	£15.00	£25.00
Title Value:	*$45.00*	*$135.00*	*$225.00*	£30.00	£90.00	£150.00

SUPERMAN BOOK AND RECORD SET

Power Records;PR-28, PR-33 1974

	$Good	$Fine	$N.Mint	£Good	£Fine	£N.Mint
PR-28 scarce in the U.K. 20pg booklet with 45 rpm record						
	$1.65	*$5.00*	*$10.00*	£1.25	£3.75	£7.50
PR-33 scarce in the U.K. 20pg booklet with 45 rpm record						
	$1.65	*$5.00*	*$10.00*	£1.25	£3.75	£7.50
Title Value:	*$3.30*	*$10.00*	*$20.00*	£2.50	£7.50	£15.00

Note: item would be valued at 50% less without record.

SUPERMAN FAMILY

DC Comics; 164 Apr May 1974-222 Sep 1982

(previously Jimmy Olsen)

	$Good	$Fine	$N.Mint	£Good	£Fine	£N.Mint
164 100pgs	*$0.65*	*$2.00*	*$4.00*	£0.50	£1.50	£3.00
165-170 100pgs	*$0.55*	*$1.75*	*$3.50*	£0.40	£1.25	£2.50
171 68pgs, Batgirl and Justice League of America appear						
	$0.50	*$1.50*	*$3.00*	£0.30	£1.00	£2.00
172-180 scarce in the U.K. 68pgs						
	$0.50	*$1.50*	*$3.00*	£0.40	£1.25	£2.50
181 52pgs	*$0.40*	*$1.25*	*$2.50*	£0.30	£1.00	£2.00
182 ND 80pgs, Rogers art						
	$0.50	*$1.50*	*$3.00*	£0.55	£1.75	£3.50
183 80pgs	*$0.40*	*$1.25*	*$2.50*	£0.30	£1.00	£2.00
184 ND scarce in the U.K. 80pgs						
	$0.40	*$1.25*	*$2.50*	£0.40	£1.25	£2.50
185-187 ND 80pgs						
	$0.40	*$1.25*	*$2.50*	£0.35	£1.10	£2.25
188 ND 80pgs, Nightwing and Flamebird appear						
	$0.40	*$1.25*	*$2.50*	£0.35	£1.10	£2.25
189-190 ND 80pgs						
	$0.40	*$1.25*	*$2.50*	£0.35	£1.10	£2.25
191-193 scarce in the U.K. 68pgs						
	$0.40	*$1.25*	*$2.50*	£0.30	£1.00	£2.00
194 ND 68pgs, Rogers art						
	$0.50	*$1.50*	*$3.00*	£0.50	£1.50	£3.00
195-200 ND 68pgs						
	$0.40	*$1.25*	*$2.50*	£0.30	£1.00	£2.00
201-210 ND 68pgs						
	$0.50	*$1.50*	*$2.50*	£0.35	£1.05	£1.75
211 52pgs, Earth 2 Batman and Catwoman marry (see Adventure Comics #462)						
	$0.60	*$1.80*	*$3.00*	£0.50	£1.50	£2.50
212-222 52pgs	*$0.40*	*$1.20*	*$2.00*	£0.30	£0.90	£1.50
Title Value:	*$27.15*	*$83.00*	*$155.50*	£20.95	£65.25	£123.50

FEATURES

Clark Kent in 195-197, 199-222. Jimmy Olsen in 164, 167, 170, 173, 176, 179 182-222. Krypto in 182-192. Lois Lane in 166, 169, 172, 175, 178, 181-222. Mr. and Mrs. Superman in 195, 196, 198-222. Nightwing & Flamebird in 183-194. Perry White in 183. Superbaby in 182, 216. Superboy in 191-198. Super- girl in 165, 168, 171, 177, 180, 182-199, 200 (Superwoman), 210-222. Superman in 184-193. World of Krypton in 182.

REPRINT FEATURES

Bizarro World in 166, 169. Jimmy Olsen in 164-169, 171, 172, 174, 175, 177, 178, 180, 181. Lois Lane in 164, 165, 167, 168, 170, 171, 173, 174, 176, 177, 179, 180. Superbaby in 165-167. Superboy in 164-170, 173, 176. Supergirl in 164, 166, 167, 169, 170, 172, 173, 175, 176, 178, 179. Superman in 165, 168, 174, 175.

SUPERMAN GALLERY, THE

DC Comics,OS; 1 Apr 1993

	$Good	$Fine	$N.Mint	£Good	£Fine	£N.Mint
1 ND pin-ups by Frank Miller, Todd McFarlane, Steve Rude, George Perez, Jerry Ordway, John Byrne, Mike Zeck and others						
	$0.50	*$1.50*	*$2.50*	£0.30	£0.90	£1.50
Title Value:	*$0.50*	*$1.50*	*$2.50*	£0.30	£0.90	£1.50

SUPERMAN II THE ADVENTURE CONTINUES

DC Comics,Tabloid; Summer 1981

(DC Special Series #25)

	$Good	$Fine	$N.Mint	£Good	£Fine	£N.Mint
nn ND 64pgs, mainly film stills and interviews with the stars						
	$1.00	*$3.00*	*$5.00*	£0.70	£2.10	£3.50
Title Value:	*$1.00*	*$3.00*	*$5.00*	£0.70	£2.10	£3.50

SUPERMAN III MOVIE SPECIAL

DC Comics,OS; 1 Sep 1983

	$Good	$Fine	$N.Mint	£Good	£Fine	£N.Mint
1 48pgs, adapts film						
	$0.40	*$1.20*	*$2.00*	£0.25	£0.75	£1.25
Title Value:	*$0.40*	*$1.20*	*$2.00*	£0.25	£0.75	£1.25

SUPERMAN IV MOVIE SPECIAL

DC Comics,OS; nn Oct 1987

	$Good	$Fine	$N.Mint	£Good	£Fine	£N.Mint
nn 64pgs	*$0.40*	*$1.20*	*$2.00*	£0.25	£0.75	£1.25
Title Value:	*$0.40*	*$1.20*	*$2.00*	£0.25	£0.75	£1.25

SUPERMAN MEETS THE QUIK BUNNY

DC Comics,OS; nn 1987

	$Good	$Fine	$N.Mint	£Good	£Fine	£N.Mint
nn ND scarce in the U.K. Infantino and Giordano art, Mike Carlin script; promotional giveaway from Nestle						
	$0.30	*$0.90*	*$1.50*	£0.20	£0.60	£1.00
Title Value:	*$0.30*	*$0.90*	*$1.50*	£0.20	£0.60	£1.00

SUPERMAN METROPOLIS EDITION, THE AMAZING WORLD OF

DC Comics,Tabloid; nn 1973

	$Good	$Fine	$N.Mint	£Good	£Fine	£N.Mint
nn ND 64pgs, includes photo-features and poster (map of Krypton), reprints origin from #300 and classic story "Superman in Superman Land" from Action Comics #210						
	$1.25	*$3.75*	*$7.50*	£0.80	£2.50	£5.00
Title Value:	*$1.25*	*$3.75*	*$7.50*	£0.80	£2.50	£5.00

SUPERMAN PIZZA HUT GIVEAWAYS

DC Comics/Pizza Hut; 97,113 1977

(see Batman, Wonder Woman)

	$Good	$Fine	$N.Mint	£Good	£Fine	£N.Mint
97 ND original issue #97 reprinted in its entirety but with different ads and Pizza Hut banner on the cover						
	$1.25	*$3.75*	*$7.50*	£0.80	£2.50	£5.00
113 ND original issue #113 reprinted in its entirety but with different ads and Pizza Hut banner on the cover						
	$1.25	*$3.75*	*$7.50*	£0.80	£2.50	£5.00
Title Value:	*$2.50*	*$7.50*	*$15.00*	£1.60	£5.00	£10.00

SUPERMAN PLUS #1

DC Comics,OS; 1 Feb 1997

	$Good	$Fine	$N.Mint	£Good	£Fine	£N.Mint
1 ND Superman and The Legion of Super-Heroes team up						
	$0.60	*$1.80*	*$3.00*	£0.40	£1.20	£2.00
Title Value:	*$0.60*	*$1.80*	*$3.00*	£0.40	£1.20	£2.00

SUPERMAN RADIO SHACK

DC Comics/Radio Shack; nn Jul 1980-Jul 1982

	$Good	$Fine	$N.Mint	£Good	£Fine	£N.Mint
nn "Computer Masters of Metropolis" ND 32pgs, Wonder Woman and Lex Luthor appear						
	$0.30	*$0.90*	*$1.50*	£0.20	£0.60	£1.00
nn "The Computers That Saved Metropolis" ND 32pgs, appeared as an insert in Action Comics #509, Superboy						

Superman Annual (1st) #6

Superman Radio Shack: The Computer Masters of Metropolis

Superman Radio Shack: Victory by Computer

	$Good	$Fine	$N.Mint	£Good	£Fine	£N.Mint

(New Adventures) #7, Superboy #265, House of Mystery #282
$0.30 $0.90 $1.50 £0.20 £0.60 £1.00
nn "Victory By Computer" ND 32pgs, guest-stars Supergirl
$0.30 $0.90 $1.50 £0.20 £0.60 £1.00
Title Value: $0.90 $2.70 $4.50 £0.60 £1.80 £3.00

SUPERMAN RECORD COMIC
DC Comics; nn 1966
nn ND scarce in the U.K. set contains iron-on patch, decoder, membership card and badge plus 45 rpm record reading origin
$21.00 $62.50 $150.00 £14.00 £43.00 £100.00
Title Value: $21.00 $62.50 $150.00 £14.00 £43.00 £100.00
Note: set would be de-valued by any of the above missing; at least 50% if the record was missing.

SUPERMAN SPECIAL
DC Comics; 1 1983-3 1985
1 48pgs, Gil Kane story and art
$0.50 $1.50 $2.50 £0.30 £0.90 £1.50
2-3 48pgs $0.50 $1.50 $2.50 £0.30 £0.90 £1.50
Title Value: $1.50 $4.50 $7.50 £0.90 £2.70 £4.50

SUPERMAN SPECIAL (2ND SERIES)
DC Comics; 1 Oct 1992
1 64pgs, Walt Simonson script and art, a re-working of "Kryptonite No More" from Superman #233
$0.70 $2.10 $3.50 £0.40 £1.20 £2.00
Title Value: $0.70 $2.10 $3.50 £0.40 £1.20 £2.00
Note: originally meant for the 1991 Superman Annual (No. 3)

SUPERMAN SPECTACULAR
DC Comics; nn 1977
(DC Special Series #5)
nn ND 80pgs $0.50 $1.50 $3.00 £0.30 £1.00 £2.00
Title Value: $0.50 $1.50 $3.00 £0.30 £1.00 £2.00

SUPERMAN VS. ALIENS
Dark Horse/DC Comics,MS; 1 May 1995-3 Jul 1995
1-3 ND 48pgs, squarebound, Dan Jurgens script and Kevin Nowlan art
$1.00 $3.00 $5.00 £0.70 £2.10 £3.50
Title Value: $3.00 $9.00 $15.00 £2.10 £6.30 £10.50
Superman Vs. Aliens (May 1996)
Trade paperback ND 152pgs, collects mini-series £2.00 £6.00 £10.00

SUPERMAN VS. THE AMAZING SPIDERMAN
Marvel Comics Group/DC Comics,Tabloid; nn 1976
(see Superman and Spiderman)
nn distributed in the U.K. 96pgs, Doctor Octopus, Lex Luthor and Wonder Woman appear; Ross Andru art
$2.50 $7.50 $15.00 £2.05 £6.25 £12.50
Title Value: $2.50 $7.50 $15.00 £2.05 £6.25 £12.50

SUPERMAN'S GIRL FRIEND, LOIS LANE
(see Lois Lane, Superman's Girlfriend)

SUPERMAN'S METROPOLIS
DC Comics,OS; nn Jan 1997
nn ND 64pgs, painted art and cover by Ted McKeever
$1.20 $3.60 $6.00 £0.80 £2.40 £4.00
Title Value: $1.20 $3.60 $6.00 £0.80 £2.40 £4.00

SUPERMAN'S PAL, JIMMY OLSEN
(see Jimmy Olsen, Superman's Pal)

SUPERMAN, THE ADVENTURES OF
(see Superman (1st Series) (Adventures of Superman) #424 onwards)

SUPERMAN, THE LEGACY OF
DC Comics,OS; 1 Mar 1993
1 64pgs, antholgy by such as Jerry Ordway, Roger Stern, Curt Swan, Walt Simonson, Karl Kesel, William Messner-Loebs and Art Adams, Art Adams cover
$0.50 $1.50 $2.50 £0.30 £0.90 £1.50
Title Value: $0.50 $1.50 $2.50 £0.30 £0.90 £1.50

SUPERMAN/BATMAN: ALTERNATE HISTORIES
DC Comics/Elseworlds,OS; nn May 1996
nn ND 224pgs, Trade paperback; reprints Elseworlds stories from Action Comics Annual #6, Steel Annual #1, Batman: Legends of the Dark Knight Annual #7, Detective Comics Annual #7
$3.00 $9.00 $15.00 £2.00 £6.00 £10.00
Title Value: $3.00 $9.00 $15.00 £2.00 £6.00 £10.00

SUPERMAN/DOOMSDAY: HUNTER/PREY
DC Comics,MS; 1 Mar 1994-3 Jul 1994
1 48pgs, Dan Jurgens and Brett Breeding; bi-weekly, set 1 year after Doomsday "killed" by Superman
$1.00 $3.00 $5.00 £0.70 £2.10 £3.50
2 48pgs, Dan Jurgens and Brett Breeding; bi-weekly, origin of Doomsday explored
$1.00 $3.00 $5.00 £0.70 £2.10 £3.50
3 48pgs, Dan Jurgens and Brett Breeding; bi-weekly
$1.00 $3.00 $5.00 £0.70 £2.10 £3.50
Title Value: $3.00 $9.00 $15.00 £2.10 £6.30 £10.50
Superman/Doomsday: Hunter/Prey (Oct 1995)
Trade paperback reprints mini-series, new cover £2.00 £6.00 £10.00

SUPERMAN/TOYMAN
DC Comics,OS; 1 Jan 1996
1 ND tie-in with the release of Superman figures by Kenner
$0.40 $1.20 $2.00 £0.25 £0.75 £1.25
Title Value: $0.40 $1.20 $2.00 £0.25 £0.75 £1.25

SUPERMAN/WONDER WOMAN: WHOM GODS DESTROY
DC Comics/Elseworlds,MS; 1 Dec 1996-4 Mar 1997
1-4 ND 48pgs, Elseworlds story; Chris Claremont script, Dusty Abell covers and art
$1.00 $3.00 $5.00 £0.70 £2.10 £3.50
Title Value: $4.00 $12.00 $20.00 £2.80 £8.40 £14.00

SUPERMAN: AT EARTH'S END
DC Comics/Elseworlds,OS; 1 Nov 1995
1 ND Tom Veitch script, Frank Gomez art
$1.00 $3.00 $5.00 £0.70 £2.10 £3.50
Title Value: $1.00 $3.00 $5.00 £0.70 £2.10 £3.50

SUPERMAN: DOOMSDAY
The multi-part story that lead up to the death of Superman and record sales of Superman titles and Superman #75 becoming one of the biggest selling comics of all time at 4 million copies. The parts of the story are as follows:
Part 1 - Superman, The Man of Steel #18
X-over 1 - Justice League of America #69
Part 2 - Superman #74
Part 3 - Adventures of Superman #497
Part 4 - Action Comics #684
Part 5 - Superman, The Man of Steel #19
Part 6 - Superman #75
The aftermath continues as Funeral For A Friend in the following:
X-over 1 - Justice League of America #70
Part 1 - Adventures of Superman #498
Part 2 - Action Comics #685
Part 3 - Superman, The Man of Steel #20
Part 4 - Superman #76
Part 5 - Adventures of Superman #499
Part 6 - Action Comics #686
Part 7 - Superman, The Man of Steel #21
Part 8 - Superman #77

SUPERMAN: FOR EARTH
DC Comics,OS; 1 May 1991
1 48pgs, ecology theme
$0.90 $2.70 $4.50 £0.60 £1.80 £3.00
Title Value: $0.90 $2.70 $4.50 £0.60 £1.80 £3.00
Note: Prestige Format. Originally announced as Superman: Earth Day 1991. Printed on re-cycled paper.

SUPERMAN: GREATEST STORIES EVER TOLD
DC Comics; nn 1987; nn Mar 1993
nn Hardcover Edition, ND classic reprints including Superman (1st series) #30, #53, #123 and #149
$6.00 $18.00 $30.00 £4.00 £12.00 £20.00
nn Softcover Edition ND
$3.00 $9.00 $15.00 £2.00 £6.00 £10.00
Title Value: $9.00 $27.00 $45.00 £6.00 £18.00 £30.00

SUPERMAN: KAL
DC Comics,OS; 1 Mar 1995
1 ND 48pgs, squarebound, Dave Gibbons script, Jose Garcia Lopez art
$1.20 $3.60 $6.00 £0.80 £2.40 £4.00
Title Value: $1.20 $3.60 $6.00 £0.80 £2.40 £4.00

SUPERMAN: SPEEDING BULLETS
DC Comics/Elseworlds,OS; 1 Nov 1993
1 ND 48pgs, Superman adopted by Thomas and Martha Wayne to become Batman
$1.00 $3.00 $5.00 £0.70 £2.10 £3.50
Title Value: $1.00 $3.00 $5.00 £0.70 £2.10 £3.50

SUPERMAN: THE EARTH STEALERS
DC Comics,OS; 1 Feb 1988
1 ND 48pgs, squarebound, John Byrne script, Curt Swan and Jerry Ordway art
$0.80 $2.40 $4.00 £0.50 £1.50 £2.50
1 2nd printing, ND (Jun 1989)
$0.60 $1.80 $3.00 £0.40 £1.20 £2.00
Title Value: $1.40 $4.20 $7.00 £0.90 £2.70 £4.50

SUPERMAN: THE MAN OF STEEL (1ST SERIES)
DC Comics,MS; 1 Jun 1986-6 Aug 1986
1 re-vamped origin, "rocket" cover
$0.25 $0.75 $1.25 £0.15 £0.45 £0.75
1 Direct Sales Edition, ND "S" emblem cover
$0.40 $1.20 $2.00 £0.25 £0.75 £1.25
1 Silver Edition, ND (1993), silver border around cover
$0.30 $0.90 $1.50 £0.20 £0.60 £1.00
2 intro new Lois Lane
$0.25 $0.75 $1.25 £0.15 £0.45 £0.75
2 Silver Edition, ND (1993), silver border around cover
$0.30 $0.90 $1.50 £0.20 £0.60 £1.00
3 Batman appears $0.25 $0.75 $1.25 £0.15 £0.45 £0.75
4 intro new Lex Luthor
$0.25 $0.75 $1.25 £0.15 £0.45 £0.75
5 intro new Bizarro
$0.25 $0.75 $1.25 £0.15 £0.45 £0.75
6 intro new Lana Lang
$0.25 $0.75 $1.25 £0.15 £0.45 £0.75
Title Value: $2.50 $7.50 $12.50 £1.55 £4.65 £7.75
Note: a very small quantity of the Non-Distributed "S" emblem-cover first issues did appear in UK newsagents.
MPI Audio Edition (1986)
same issues with stiffer card covers featuring Superman and Action Silver Age covers. Each comic came with a 30 minute audio cassette of that particular part of the story. Smaller than standard comic size. ND very scarce in the U.K. £1.00 £3.00 £5.00
Superman: The Man of Steel
Trade paperback ND reprints #1-6 with new story and art £1.60 £4.80 £8.00
Limited Edition, as above, very scarce in the U.K. £5.00 £15.00 £25.00
Superman: The Man of Steel (Aug 1993)
Trade paperback ND reprints issues #1-6 with new format and new cover, intro by Ray Bradbury £1.00 £3.00 £5.00
Note: all John Byrne story/art, updates entire Superman legend.

SUPERMAN: THE MAN OF STEEL (2ND SERIES)
DC Comics; 0 Oct 1994; 1 Jul 1991-21 Mar 1993; 22 Jun 1993-present
0 (Oct 1994) Zero Hour X-over, origin retold; continued in Superman #0
$0.40 $1.20 $2.00 £0.25 £0.75 £1.25
1 48pgs, Revenge of the Krypton Man part 1, continued in Superman #57
$0.40 $1.20 $2.00 £0.25 £0.75 £1.25
2 $0.30 $0.90 $1.50 £0.20 £0.60 £1.00

	$Good	$Fine	$N.Mint	£Good	£Fine	£N.Mint
3 War of the Gods tie-in						
	$0.30	*$0.90*	*$1.50*	£0.20	£0.60	£1.00
4	*$0.25*	*$0.75*	*$1.25*	£0.15	£0.45	£0.75
5 continued from Action Comics #670, issue reads sideways						
	$0.25	*$0.75*	*$1.25*	£0.15	£0.45	£0.75
6 Blackout part 3, continues in Superman #62						
	$0.25	*$0.75*	*$1.25*	£0.15	£0.45	£0.75
7-8	*$0.25*	*$0.75*	*$1.25*	£0.15	£0.45	£0.75
9 Panic in the Sky part 1, continues in Superman #65						
	$0.25	*$0.75*	*$1.25*	£0.15	£0.45	£0.75
10 Panic in the Sky part 5, continues in Superman #66						
	$0.25	*$0.75*	*$1.25*	£0.15	£0.45	£0.75
11-13	*$0.25*	*$0.75*	*$1.25*	£0.15	£0.45	£0.75
14 Robin guest-stars, continues in Superman #70						
	$0.25	*$0.75*	*$1.25*	£0.15	£0.45	£0.75
15 The Blaze/Satanus War part 3, continued in Superman #71						
	$0.25	*$0.75*	*$1.25*	£0.15	£0.45	£0.75
16 Crisis at Hand part 1, continued in Superman #72						
	$0.25	*$0.75*	*$1.25*	£0.15	£0.45	£0.75
17 cameo appearance Doomsday, continued in Superman #73						
	$0.60	*$1.80*	*$3.00*	£0.40	£1.20	£2.00
18 1st full appearance Doomsday, Superman: Doomsday part 1, continued in Justice League America #69						
	$0.80	*$2.40*	*$4.00*	£0.50	£1.50	£2.50
18 2nd/3rd printing	*$0.25*	*$0.75*	*$1.25*	£0.15	£0.45	£0.75
19 Superman: Doomsday part 5, continued in Superman #75						
	$0.50	*$1.50*	*$2.50*	£0.30	£0.90	£1.50
20 Funeral for a Friend part 3, continued in Superman #76						
	$0.30	*$0.90*	*$1.50*	£0.20	£0.60	£1.00
21 Funeral for a Friend part 7, continued in Superman #77						
	$0.30	*$0.90*	*$1.50*	£0.20	£0.60	£1.00
22 Reign of the Supermen part 4						
	$0.30	*$0.90*	*$1.50*	£0.20	£0.60	£1.00
22 Collectors Edition, ND Reign of the Supermen part 4, die-cut outer cover, bound-in mini-poster						
	$0.40	*$1.20*	*$2.00*	£0.25	£0.75	£1.25
22 Dynamic Forces Edition, ND signed by Simonson and Bogdanove; 10,000 copies						
	$3.00	*$9.00*	*$15.00*	£1.50	£4.50	£7.50
23 Reign of the Supermen part 6						
	$0.30	*$0.90*	*$1.50*	£0.20	£0.60	£1.00
24 Reign of the Supermen part 10, continued in Superman #80						
	$0.30	*$0.90*	*$1.50*	£0.20	£0.60	£1.00
25 Reign of the Supermen part 14, continued in Superman #81						
	$0.30	*$0.90*	*$1.50*	£0.20	£0.60	£1.00
26 Reign of the Supermen epilogue (part 18), continued finally in Superman #82 (and X-over with Green Lantern #46)						
	$0.30	*$0.90*	*$1.50*	£0.20	£0.60	£1.00
27-28	*$0.30*	*$0.90*	*$1.50*	£0.20	£0.60	£1.00
29 continued from Action Comics #694						
	$0.30	*$0.90*	*$1.50*	£0.20	£0.60	£1.00
30 Superman vs. Lobo						
	$0.30	*$0.90*	*$1.50*	£0.20	£0.60	£1.00
30 Collectors Edition, ND pre-bagged with sheet of "vinyl clings" of Superman and Lobo to make your own cover - great fun!						
	$0.50	*$1.50*	*$2.50*	£0.30	£0.90	£1.50
31	*$0.30*	*$0.90*	*$1.50*	£0.20	£0.60	£1.00
32 Bizarro appears, concluded in Superman (2nd Series) #88						
	$0.30	*$0.90*	*$1.50*	£0.20	£0.60	£1.00
33 Parasite appears						
	$0.30	*$0.90*	*$1.50*	£0.20	£0.60	£1.00
34 The Battle for Metropolis, continued in Superman (2nd Series) #90						
	$0.30	*$0.90*	*$1.50*	£0.20	£0.60	£1.00
35 Worlds Collide X-over, continued in Hardware #17						
	$0.30	*$0.90*	*$1.50*	£0.20	£0.60	£1.00
36 Worlds Collide X-over, continued in Ilcon #16						
	$0.30	*$0.90*	*$1.50*	£0.20	£0.60	£1.00
37 Zero Hour X-over, Batman appears						
	$0.30	*$0.90*	*$1.50*	£0.20	£0.60	£1.00
38-42	*$0.30*	*$0.90*	*$1.50*	£0.20	£0.60	£1.00
43 Mister Miracle appears						
	$0.30	*$0.90*	*$1.50*	£0.20	£0.60	£1.00
44 prologue to The Death of Clark Kent (see Superman [2nd Series] #100)						
	$0.30	*$0.90*	*$1.50*	£0.20	£0.60	£1.00
45 The Death of Clark Kent part 4, continued in Superman #101; upgraded coated paper stock (Miraweb Format) begins						
	$0.40	*$1.20*	*$2.00*	£0.25	£0.75	£1.25
46-47	*$0.40*	*$1.20*	*$2.00*	£0.25	£0.75	£1.25
48 Aquaman guest-stars						
	$0.40	*$1.20*	*$2.00*	£0.25	£0.75	£1.25
49	*$0.40*	*$1.20*	*$2.00*	£0.25	£0.75	£1.25
50 The Trial of Superman begins, continued in Superman #106						
	$0.60	*$1.80*	*$3.00*	£0.40	£1.20	£2.00
51 The Trial of Superman, continued in Superman #107						
	$0.40	*$1.20*	*$2.00*	£0.25	£0.75	£1.25
52 The Trial of Superman, continued in Superman #108						
	$0.40	*$1.20*	*$2.00*	£0.25	£0.75	£1.25
53	*$0.40*	*$1.20*	*$2.00*	£0.25	£0.75	£1.25
54 Spectre guest-stars						
	$0.40	*$1.20*	*$2.00*	£0.25	£0.75	£1.25
55	*$0.40*	*$1.20*	*$2.00*	£0.25	£0.75	£1.25
56 Mr. Mxyzptlk appears						
	$0.40	*$1.20*	*$2.00*	£0.25	£0.75	£1.25
57	*$0.40*	*$1.20*	*$2.00*	£0.25	£0.75	£1.25
58 Brainiac appears						
	$0.40	*$1.20*	*$2.00*	£0.25	£0.75	£1.25
59-61	*$0.40*	*$1.20*	*$2.00*	£0.25	£0.75	£1.25
62 ND Final Night tie-in						
	$0.40	*$1.20*	*$2.00*	£0.25	£0.75	£1.25
63-64 ND Metron, Barda and Mister Miracle appear						
	$0.40	*$1.20*	*$2.00*	£0.25	£0.75	£1.25
65 ND	*$0.40*	*$1.20*	*$2.00*	£0.25	£0.75	£1.25
Title Value:	*$26.80*	*$80.40*	*$134.00*	£16.65	£49.95	£83.25

SUPERMAN: THE MAN OF STEEL ANNUAL

DC Comics; 1 Jul 1992-present

	$Good	$Fine	$N.Mint	£Good	£Fine	£N.Mint
1 64pgs, Eclipso: The Darkness Within tie-in, Starman appears						
	$0.50	*$1.50*	*$2.50*	£0.30	£0.90	£1.50
2 64pgs, Bloodlines part 2, 1st appearance Edge, continued in Batman: Shadow of the Bat Anual #1						
	$0.50	*$1.50*	*$2.50*	£0.30	£0.90	£1.50
3 64pgs, Elseworlds story						
	$0.50	*$1.50*	*$2.50*	£0.30	£0.90	£1.50
4 64pgs, Year One story, how Superman met members of the Justice League of America; Walt Simonson cover						
	$0.60	*$1.80*	*$3.00*	£0.40	£1.20	£2.00
5 ND 48pgs, Legends of the Dead Earth story; Kurt Busiek script, Jerry Ordway cover						
	$0.60	*$1.80*	*$3.00*	£0.40	£1.20	£2.00
Title Value:	*$2.70*	*$8.10*	*$13.50*	£1.70	£5.10	£8.50

SUPERMAN: THE MAN OF STEEL GALLERY

DC Comics,OS; 1 Dec 1995

	$Good	$Fine	$N.Mint	£Good	£Fine	£N.Mint
1 ND pin-ups by various artists including Alan Davis, Dave Gibbons, Michael Golden, Curt Swan						
	$0.80	*$2.40*	*$4.00*	£0.50	£1.50	£2.50
Title Value:	*$0.80*	*$2.40*	*$4.00*	£0.50	£1.50	£2.50

SUPERMAN: THE MAN OF TOMORROW

DC Comics; 1 Summer 1995-present

	$Good	$Fine	$N.Mint	£Good	£Fine	£N.Mint
1 ND Lex Luthor returns; Roger Stern script, Tom Grummett and Brett Breeding art						
	$0.40	*$1.20*	*$2.00*	£0.25	£0.75	£1.25
2 ND	*$0.40*	*$1.20*	*$2.00*	£0.25	£0.75	£1.25
3 ND Underworld Unleashed tie-in, continued in Action Comics #717						
	$0.40	*$1.20*	*$2.00*	£0.25	£0.75	£1.25
4 ND Captain Marvel guest-stars						
	$0.40	*$1.20*	*$2.00*	£0.25	£0.75	£1.25
5 ND Lex Luthor and the Contessa wed						
	$0.40	*$1.20*	*$2.00*	£0.25	£0.75	£1.25
6 ND Superman vs. The Jackal						
	$0.40	*$1.20*	*$2.00*	£0.25	£0.75	£1.25
7-8 ND	*$0.40*	*$1.20*	*$2.00*	£0.25	£0.75	£1.25
Title Value:	*$3.20*	*$9.60*	*$16.00*	£2.00	£6.00	£10.00

SUPERMAN: THE REIGN OF THE SUPERMEN

Multi-part storyline that re-introduces Superman, back from the dead, in four incarnations. The parts of the story are as follows:

Part 1 - Action Comics #687
Part 2 - Superman (1st) #501
Part 3 - Superman (2nd) #78
Part 4 - Superman: The Man of Steel #22
Part 5 - Action Comics #688
Part 6 - Superman: The Man of Steel #23
Part 7 - Superman (2nd) #79
Part 8 - Superman (1st) #502
Part 9 - Action Comics #689
Part 10 - Superman: The Man of Steel #24
Part 11 - Superman (2nd) #80
Part 12 - Superman (1st) #503
Part 13 - Action Comics #690
Part 14 - Superman: The Man of Steel #25
Part 15 - Superman (2nd) #81
Part 16 - Superman (1st) #504
Part 17 - Action Comics #691
Part 18 - Superman: The Man of Steel #26
Part 19 - Green Lantern (2nd) #46
Part 20 - Superman #82

SUPERMAN: THE SECRET YEARS

DC Comics,MS; 1 Feb 1985-4 May 1985

	$Good	$Fine	$N.Mint	£Good	£Fine	£N.Mint
1-4 Frank Miller cover art						
	$0.30	*$0.90*	*$1.50*	£0.20	£0.60	£1.00
Title Value:	*$1.20*	*$3.60*	*$6.00*	£0.80	£2.40	£4.00

SUPERMAN: THE WEDDING ALBUM

DC Comics,OS; 1 Dec 1996

	$Good	$Fine	$N.Mint	£Good	£Fine	£N.Mint
1 ND 88pgs, Superman and Lois Lane finally marry...; Superman artists past and present contribute; gate-fold back cover						
	$1.00	*$3.00*	*$5.00*	£0.65	£1.95	£3.25
1 Collectors Edition, ND as above with white embossed cover						
	$1.00	*$3.00*	*$5.00*	£0.70	£2.10	£3.50
Title Value:	*$2.00*	*$6.00*	*$10.00*	£1.35	£4.05	£6.75

SUPERMAN: UNDER A YELLOW SUN

DC Comics,OS; nn Mar 1994

	$Good	$Fine	$N.Mint	£Good	£Fine	£N.Mint
nn ND 64pgs, squarebound, J.F. Moore script, Barreto and Gammill art						
	$1.00	*$3.00*	*$5.00*	£0.70	£2.10	£3.50
Title Value:	*$1.00*	*$3.00*	*$5.00*	£0.70	£2.10	£3.50

SUPERMAN: WHATEVER HAPPENED TO THE MAN OF TOMORROW?

DC Comics,OS; nn Feb 1997

	$Good	$Fine	$N.Mint	£Good	£Fine	£N.Mint
nn ND 64pgs, collects the classic two-parter in Superman #423 and Action Comics #583 with art by Curt Swan, Kurt Schaffenberger and George Perez						
	$1.20	*$3.60*	*$6.00*	£0.80	£2.40	£4.00
Title Value:	*$1.20*	*$3.60*	*$6.00*	£0.80	£2.40	£4.00

SUPERNATURAL THRILLERS

Marvel Comics Group; 1 Dec 1972-6 Nov 1973; 7 Jul 1974-15 Oct 1975

	$Good	$Fine	$N.Mint	£Good	£Fine	£N.Mint
1 ND Theodore Sturgeon adaptation						
	$0.50	*$1.50*	*$3.00*	£0.30	£1.00	£2.00

Issue	$Good	$Fine	$N.Mint	£Good	£Fine	£N.Mint
2 ND The Invisible Man adapted by Ron Goulart	***$0.40***	***$1.25***	***$2.50***	**£0.25**	**£0.75**	**£1.50**
3 ND Valley of the Worm by Robert E. Howard, Gil Kane art and cover	***$0.40***	***$1.25***	***$2.50***	**£0.25**	**£0.75**	**£1.50**
4 ND Dr. Jekyll and Mr. Hyde adaptation	***$0.40***	***$1.25***	***$2.50***	**£0.25**	**£0.75**	**£1.50**
5 ND The Living Mummy begins (ends #15)	***$0.40***	***$1.25***	***$2.50***	**£0.25**	**£0.75**	**£1.50**
6 ND The Headless Horseman	***$0.40***	***$1.25***	***$2.50***	**£0.25**	**£0.75**	**£1.50**
7-12 ND	***$0.40***	***$1.25***	***$2.50***	**£0.25**	**£0.75**	**£1.50**
13	***$0.40***	***$1.25***	***$2.50***	**£0.20**	**£0.60**	**£1.25**
14 ND	***$0.40***	***$1.25***	***$2.50***	**£0.25**	**£0.75**	**£1.50**
15	***$0.40***	***$1.25***	***$2.50***	**£0.20**	**£0.60**	**£1.25**
Title Value:	***$6.10***	***$19.00***	***$38.00***	**£3.70**	**£11.20**	**£22.50**

Note: Steranko covers on 1, 2

FEATURES

Dr. Jekyll and Mr. Hyde in 4. Headless Horseman in 6. Invisible Man in 2. It! in 1. Living Mummy in 7-15.

SUPERPATRIOT

Image,MS; 1 Jul 1993-4 Oct 1995

Issue	$Good	$Fine	$N.Mint	£Good	£Fine	£N.Mint
1 ND Erik Larsen script, Keith Giffen plot begins	***$0.40***	***$1.20***	***$2.00***	**£0.25**	**£0.75**	**£1.25**
2-4 ND	***$0.40***	***$1.20***	***$2.00***	**£0.25**	**£0.75**	**£1.25**
Title Value:	***$1.60***	***$4.80***	***$8.00***	**£1.00**	**£3.00**	**£5.00**

SUPERPATRIOT: LIBERTY & JUSTICE

Image,MS; 1 Jun 1995-4 Sep 1995

Issue	$Good	$Fine	$N.Mint	£Good	£Fine	£N.Mint
1-4 ND Dave Johnson art	***$0.50***	***$1.50***	***$2.50***	**£0.30**	**£0.90**	**£1.50**
Title Value:	***$2.00***	***$6.00***	***$10.00***	**£1.20**	**£3.60**	**£6.00**

SUPREME

Image; 0 Aug 1995; 1 Nov 1992-present

Issue	$Good	$Fine	$N.Mint	£Good	£Fine	£N.Mint
0 ND (Aug 1995), origin of Supreme	***$0.50***	***$1.50***	***$2.50***	**£0.30**	**£0.90**	**£1.50**
1 ND Rob Liefeld and Brian Murray script/art begins, silver embossed cover	***$0.50***	***$1.50***	***$2.50***	**£0.30**	**£0.90**	**£1.50**
1 Gold Edition ND	***$1.60***	***$4.80***	***$8.00***	**£1.00**	**£3.00**	**£5.00**
2-4 ND	***$0.40***	***$1.20***	***$2.00***	**£0.25**	**£0.75**	**£1.25**
5 ND Supreme vs. Krome	***$0.40***	***$1.20***	***$2.00***	**£0.25**	**£0.75**	**£1.25**
6-10 ND	***$0.40***	***$1.20***	***$2.00***	**£0.25**	**£0.75**	**£1.25**
11 ND Extreme Prejudice part 4	***$0.40***	***$1.20***	***$2.00***	**£0.25**	**£0.75**	**£1.25**
12 ND Aftermath of Extreme Prejudice	***$0.40***	***$1.20***	***$2.00***	**£0.25**	**£0.75**	**£1.25**
13 ND Supreme Madness story begins; guest-stars Pitt, Spawn, Stormwatch and Union	***$0.50***	***$1.50***	***$2.50***	**£0.30**	**£0.90**	**£1.50**
14 ND Supreme Madness story, Supreme vs. Union	***$0.50***	***$1.50***	***$2.50***	**£0.30**	**£0.90**	**£1.50**
15 ND Supreme Madness story, Spawn appears	***$0.50***	***$1.50***	***$2.50***	**£0.30**	**£0.90**	**£1.50**
16 ND Supreme Madness story, Supreme vs. Stormwatch	***$0.50***	***$1.50***	***$2.50***	**£0.30**	**£0.90**	**£1.50**
17 ND Supreme Madness story, Supreme vs. Pitt	***$0.50***	***$1.50***	***$2.50***	**£0.30**	**£0.90**	**£1.50**
18 ND Supreme Madness story, Pitt appears	***$0.50***	***$1.50***	***$2.50***	**£0.30**	**£0.90**	**£1.50**
19-22 ND	***$0.50***	***$1.50***	***$2.50***	**£0.30**	**£0.90**	**£1.50**
23 ND Extreme Sacrifice part 1, continued in Bloodstrike #18; pre-bagged with trading card	***$0.50***	***$1.50***	***$2.50***	**£0.30**	**£0.90**	**£1.50**
24 ND	***$0.50***	***$1.50***	***$2.50***	**£0.30**	**£0.90**	**£1.50**
25 ND cover-dated May 1994, issued between #12 and #13 as part of "Images of Tomorrow" previewing the 25th issue and how it reads/looks	***$0.50***	***$1.50***	***$2.50***	**£0.30**	**£0.90**	**£1.50**
26-27 ND	***$0.50***	***$1.50***	***$2.50***	**£0.30**	**£0.90**	**£1.50**
28 ND A Supreme Apocalypse - Prelude	***$0.50***	***$1.50***	***$2.50***	**£0.30**	**£0.90**	**£1.50**
28 Variant Cover Edition, ND Joe Quesada/Jimmy Palmiotti cover art	***$0.60***	***$1.80***	***$3.00***	**£0.50**	**£1.50**	**£2.50**
29 ND Supreme Apocalypse part 1, continued in Brigade #22	***$0.50***	***$1.50***	***$2.50***	**£0.30**	**£0.90**	**£1.50**
30 ND scarce in the U.K. Supreme Apocalypse part 5	***$0.50***	***$1.50***	***$2.50***	**£0.80**	**£2.40**	**£4.00**
31-32 ND	***$0.50***	***$1.50***	***$2.50***	**£0.30**	**£0.90**	**£1.50**
33 ND Extreme Babewatch tie-in	***$0.50***	***$1.50***	***$2.50***	**£0.30**	**£0.90**	**£1.50**
34 ND She-Supreme appears	***$0.50***	***$1.50***	***$2.50***	**£0.30**	**£0.90**	**£1.50**
35 ND Extreme Destroyer part 7, continued in New Force #1	***$0.50***	***$1.50***	***$2.50***	**£0.30**	**£0.90**	**£1.50**
36 ND	***$0.50***	***$1.50***	***$2.50***	**£0.30**	**£0.90**	**£1.50**
37 ND ties into Kid Supreme #1	***$0.50***	***$1.50***	***$2.50***	**£0.30**	**£0.90**	**£1.50**
38 ND	***$0.50***	***$1.50***	***$2.50***	**£0.30**	**£0.90**	**£1.50**
39 ND guest-stars Lady Supreme	***$0.50***	***$1.50***	***$2.50***	**£0.30**	**£0.90**	**£1.50**
40 ND	***$0.50***	***$1.50***	***$2.50***	**£0.30**	**£0.90**	**£1.50**
Title Value:	***$21.60***	***$64.80***	***$108.00***	**£13.75**	**£41.25**	**£68.75**
Supreme Madness (Apr 1996) Trade paperback ND collects 6 part storyline guest-starring Pitt, Stormwatch, Union and Spawn				£2.00	£6.00	£10.00

SUPREME ANNUAL

Image; 1 May 1995-present

Issue	$Good	$Fine	$N.Mint	£Good	£Fine	£N.Mint
1 ND Keith Giffen co-plot and pencil art, Charlie Adlard inks	***$0.60***	***$1.80***	***$3.00***	**£0.40**	**£1.20**	**£2.00**
Title Value:	***$0.60***	***$1.80***	***$3.00***	**£0.40**	**£1.20**	**£2.00**

SUPREME, LEGEND OF

Image,MS; 1 Dec 1994-3 Feb 1995

Issue	$Good	$Fine	$N.Mint	£Good	£Fine	£N.Mint
1-3 ND	***$0.50***	***$1.50***	***$2.50***	**£0.30**	**£0.90**	**£1.50**
Title Value:	***$1.50***	***$4.50***	***$7.50***	**£0.90**	**£2.70**	**£4.50**

SUPREME: GLORY DAYS

Image,MS; 1 Oct 1994-2 Nov 1994

Issue	$Good	$Fine	$N.Mint	£Good	£Fine	£N.Mint
1-2 ND Supreme in World War II, Rob Liefeld script	***$0.60***	***$1.80***	***$3.00***	**£0.40**	**£1.20**	**£2.00**
Title Value:	***$1.20***	***$3.60***	***$6.00***	**£0.80**	**£2.40**	**£4.00**

SURGE

Eclipse,MS; 1 Jul 1984-4 Jan 1985

Issue	$Good	$Fine	$N.Mint	£Good	£Fine	£N.Mint
1-4 ND DNAgents spin-off series, Mark Evanier script, Rick Hoberg art, colour	***$0.30***	***$0.90***	***$1.50***	**£0.20**	**£0.60**	**£1.00**
Title Value:	***$1.20***	***$3.60***	***$6.00***	**£0.80**	**£2.40**	**£4.00**

SURVIVE!

Apple Comics; 1 Oct 1991

Issue	$Good	$Fine	$N.Mint	£Good	£Fine	£N.Mint
1 ND Don Lomax script and art	***$0.40***	***$1.20***	***$2.00***	**£0.25**	**£0.75**	**£1.25**
Title Value:	***$0.40***	***$1.20***	***$2.00***	**£0.25**	**£0.75**	**£1.25**

SURVIVORS, THE

Spectrum Comics; 1 Jun 1983-4 Mar 1984

Issue	$Good	$Fine	$N.Mint	£Good	£Fine	£N.Mint
1 ND Steve Woron script and art; black and white	***$0.20***	***$0.60***	***$1.00***	**£0.10**	**£0.35**	**£0.60**
2 ND colour begins	***$0.20***	***$0.60***	***$1.00***	**£0.10**	**£0.35**	**£0.60**
3-4 ND	***$0.20***	***$0.60***	***$1.00***	**£0.10**	**£0.35**	**£0.60**
Title Value:	***$0.80***	***$2.40***	***$4.00***	**£0.40**	**£1.40**	**£2.40**

SURVIVORS, THE (2ND SERIES)

Burnside Comics,OS; 1 Dec 1987

Issue	$Good	$Fine	$N.Mint	£Good	£Fine	£N.Mint
1 ND Steve Woron script, Darren Goodhart and Bob Lewis art; black and white	***$0.30***	***$0.90***	***$1.50***	**£0.20**	**£0.60**	**£1.00**
Title Value:	***$0.30***	***$0.90***	***$1.50***	**£0.20**	**£0.60**	**£1.00**

SUSHI

Shunga Comix; 1 Feb 1990-2 1990

Issue	$Good	$Fine	$N.Mint	£Good	£Fine	£N.Mint
1-2 ND adult material, black and white	***$0.40***	***$1.20***	***$2.00***	**£0.25**	**£0.75**	**£1.25**
Title Value:	***$0.80***	***$2.40***	***$4.00***	**£0.50**	**£1.50**	**£2.50**

SUSSEX VAMPIRE, THE

Caliber Press,OS; nn 1996

Issue	$Good	$Fine	$N.Mint	£Good	£Fine	£N.Mint
nn ND Warren Ellis script, Criag Gilmore art; black and white	***$0.60***	***$1.80***	***$3.00***	**£0.40**	**£1.20**	**£2.00**
Title Value:	***$0.60***	***$1.80***	***$3.00***	**£0.40**	**£1.20**	**£2.00**

SWAMP THING

DC Comics; 1 Oct/Nov 1972-24 Aug/Sep 1976

(see Brave and the Bold, DC Comics Presents, House of Secrets #92, Original Swamp Thing Saga, Saga of the Swamp Thing)

Issue	$Good	$Fine	$N.Mint	£Good	£Fine	£N.Mint
1 scarce in the U.K. 2nd appearance Swamp Thing (see House of Secrets #92), Berni Wrightson art begins	***$9.25***	***$28.00***	***$65.00***	**£4.25**	**£12.50**	**£30.00**
2 3rd appearance Swamp Thing, Wrightson art	***$6.50***	***$20.00***	***$40.00***	**£2.90**	**£8.75**	**£17.50**
3 Wrightson art	***$4.15***	***$12.50***	***$25.00***	**£2.05**	**£6.25**	**£12.50**
4 Wrightson art	***$3.30***	***$10.00***	***$20.00***	**£1.65**	**£5.00**	**£10.00**
5-6 Wrightson art	***$3.30***	***$10.00***	***$20.00***	**£1.25**	**£3.75**	**£7.50**
7 Wrightson art, Batman X-over	***$3.75***	***$11.00***	***$22.50***	**£1.65**	**£5.00**	**£10.00**
8 Wrightson art	***$2.90***	***$8.75***	***$17.50***	**£1.25**	**£3.75**	**£7.50**
9-10 ND Wrightson art	***$2.90***	***$8.75***	***$17.50***	**£1.30**	**£4.00**	**£8.00**
11-12 scarce in the U.K.	***$0.80***	***$2.50***	***$5.00***	**£0.40**	**£1.25**	**£2.50**
13-19	***$0.80***	***$2.50***	***$5.00***	**£0.30**	**£1.00**	**£2.00**
20-21 scarce in the U.K.	***$0.80***	***$2.50***	***$5.00***	**£0.40**	**£1.25**	**£2.50**
22 ND scarce in the U.K.	***$0.80***	***$2.50***	***$5.00***	**£0.55**	**£1.75**	**£3.50**
23 very scarce in the U.K.	***$0.80***	***$2.50***	***$5.00***	**£0.50**	**£1.50**	**£3.00**
24 ND scarce in the U.K.	***$0.80***	***$2.50***	***$5.00***	**£0.55**	**£1.75**	**£3.50**
Title Value:	***$53.45***	***$162.75***	***$335.00***	**£24.15**	**£73.75**	**£152.50**

Note: Kaluta inks in 9.

SWAMP THING (2ND SERIES)

DC Comics/Vertigo; 1 May 1982-171 Oct 1996

(sub-titled "Saga of the...")

(see Challengers of the Unknown, DC Comics Presents, House of Secrets #92, Original Swamp Thing Saga, Roots of the Swamp Thing, Swamp Thing)

Issue	$Good	$Fine	$N.Mint	£Good	£Fine	£N.Mint
1 origin retold, Phantom Stranger series begins (ends #13)	***$0.60***	***$1.80***	***$3.00***	**£0.40**	**£1.20**	**£2.00**
2 photo cover from movie	***$0.50***	***$1.50***	***$2.50***	**£0.30**	**£0.90**	**£1.50**
3-10	***$0.50***	***$1.50***	***$2.50***	**£0.30**	**£0.90**	**£1.50**
11-14 LD in the U.K.	***$0.40***	***$1.20***	***$2.00***	**£0.40**	**£1.20**	**£2.00**
15 LD in the U.K. Bissette art	***$0.40***	***$1.20***	***$2.00***	**£0.50**	**£1.50**	**£2.50**
16-19 LD in the U.K. Bissette art	***$0.40***	***$1.20***	***$2.00***	**£0.40**	**£1.20**	**£2.00**
20 1st Alan Moore script	***$2.90***	***$8.75***	***$17.50***	**£1.65**	**£5.00**	**£10.00**

	$Good	$Fine	$N.Mint	£Good	£Fine	£N.Mint
21 new origin	*$2.50*	*$7.50*	*$15.00*	£1.30	£4.00	£8.00
22	*$1.65*	*$5.00*	*$10.00*	£1.00	£3.00	£6.00
23-24 scarce in the U.K.	*$1.50*	*$4.50*	*$7.50*	£1.00	£3.00	£5.00
25 scarce in the U.K. Demon trilogy begins	*$1.50*	*$4.50*	*$7.50*	£1.00	£3.00	£5.00
26-27 Demon trilogy	*$1.00*	*$3.00*	*$5.00*	£1.00	£3.00	£5.00
28-30 last code-approved issues	*$1.00*	*$3.00*	*$5.00*	£0.80	£2.40	£4.00
31 title changes to Swamp Thing, no code	*$0.80*	*$2.40*	*$4.00*	£0.70	£2.10	£3.50
32	*$0.80*	*$2.40*	*$4.00*	£0.70	£2.10	£3.50
33 mostly reprints House of Secrets #92	*$0.80*	*$2.40*	*$4.00*	£0.70	£2.10	£3.50
34	*$1.50*	*$4.50*	*$7.50*	£1.00	£3.00	£5.00
35-36	*$0.80*	*$2.40*	*$4.00*	£0.60	£1.80	£3.00
37 1st appearance John Constantine	*$3.50*	*$10.50*	*$17.50*	£1.50	£4.50	£7.50
38 2nd appearance John Constantine	*$2.00*	*$6.00*	*$10.00*	£0.80	£2.40	£4.00
39-40 John Constantine appears	*$1.60*	*$4.80*	*$8.00*	£0.60	£1.80	£3.00
41-43	*$0.60*	*$1.80*	*$3.00*	£0.40	£1.20	£2.00
44 American Gothic story begins (ends 50), unofficial Crisis X-over; John Constantine appears (thru' to #51)	*$0.60*	*$1.80*	*$3.00*	£0.40	£1.20	£2.00
45	*$0.60*	*$1.80*	*$3.00*	£0.40	£1.20	£2.00
46 Crisis X-over featuring Batman, Hawkman and Phantom Stranger	*$0.60*	*$1.80*	*$3.00*	£0.40	£1.20	£2.00
47-49	*$0.50*	*$1.50*	*$2.50*	£0.30	£0.90	£1.50
50 DS	*$0.60*	*$1.80*	*$3.00*	£0.50	£1.50	£2.50
51	*$0.50*	*$1.50*	*$2.50*	£0.30	£0.90	£1.50
52 Batman last page, 1 panel Joker	*$0.50*	*$1.50*	*$2.50*	£0.30	£0.90	£1.50
53 DS Batman appears, Arkham Asylum	*$0.80*	*$2.40*	*$4.00*	£0.50	£1.50	£2.50
54 Batman 1 panel	*$0.50*	*$1.50*	*$2.50*	£0.30	£0.90	£1.50
55-59	*$0.50*	*$1.50*	*$2.50*	£0.30	£0.90	£1.50
60 1st New Format	*$0.50*	*$1.50*	*$2.50*	£0.30	£0.90	£1.50
61-63	*$0.40*	*$1.20*	*$2.00*	£0.25	£0.75	£1.25
64 last Alan Moore script	*$0.40*	*$1.20*	*$2.00*	£0.25	£0.75	£1.25
65 Batman 2 panels, Arkham Asylum	*$0.40*	*$1.20*	*$2.00*	£0.25	£0.75	£1.25
66 Batman, Arkham Asylum	*$0.40*	*$1.20*	*$2.00*	£0.25	£0.75	£1.25
67 Hellblazer preview, Arkham Asylum	*$0.60*	*$1.80*	*$3.00*	£0.40	£1.20	£2.00
68-69	*$0.40*	*$1.20*	*$2.00*	£0.25	£0.75	£1.25
70 Rick Veitch/Brett Ewins art, Hellblazer	*$0.40*	*$1.20*	*$2.00*	£0.25	£0.75	£1.25
71-75 LD in the U.K.	*$0.40*	*$1.20*	*$2.00*	£0.30	£0.90	£1.50
76 LD in the U.K. X-over with Hellblazer #10	*$0.40*	*$1.20*	*$2.00*	£0.30	£0.90	£1.50
77-78 LD in the U.K.	*$0.40*	*$1.20*	*$2.00*	£0.30	£0.90	£1.50
79 Superman appears	*$0.40*	*$1.20*	*$2.00*	£0.25	£0.75	£1.25

	$Good	$Fine	$N.Mint	£Good	£Fine	£N.Mint
80	*$0.40*	*$1.20*	*$2.00*	£0.25	£0.75	£1.25
81 Invasion X-over	*$0.40*	*$1.20*	*$2.00*	£0.25	£0.75	£1.25
82 Sgt. Rock X-over	*$0.40*	*$1.20*	*$2.00*	£0.25	£0.75	£1.25
83 Enemy Ace appears	*$0.40*	*$1.20*	*$2.00*	£0.25	£0.75	£1.25
84 modern Sandman appears (3rd ever?)	*$1.50*	*$4.50*	*$7.50*	£0.50	£1.50	£2.50
85 DC Western Heroes appear	*$0.30*	*$0.90*	*$1.50*	£0.20	£0.60	£1.00
86 Tomahawk appears	*$0.30*	*$0.90*	*$1.50*	£0.20	£0.60	£1.00
87 Demon appears	*$0.30*	*$0.90*	*$1.50*	£0.20	£0.60	£1.00
88-99	*$0.30*	*$0.90*	*$1.50*	£0.20	£0.60	£1.00
100 48pgs	*$0.50*	*$1.50*	*$2.50*	£0.30	£0.90	£1.50
101	*$0.30*	*$0.90*	*$1.50*	£0.20	£0.60	£1.00
102 previews World Without End series	*$0.30*	*$0.90*	*$1.50*	£0.20	£0.60	£1.00
103	*$0.30*	*$0.90*	*$1.50*	£0.20	£0.60	£1.00
104-109 Quest for the Elementals story	*$0.30*	*$0.90*	*$1.50*	£0.20	£0.60	£1.00
110-113	*$0.30*	*$0.90*	*$1.50*	£0.20	£0.60	£1.00
114-115 John Constantine appears	*$0.30*	*$0.90*	*$1.50*	£0.20	£0.60	£1.00
116 Dick Foreman guest writer, photo cover	*$0.30*	*$0.90*	*$1.50*	£0.20	£0.60	£1.00
117-118 John Higgins cover	*$0.30*	*$0.90*	*$1.50*	£0.20	£0.60	£1.00
119-120	*$0.30*	*$0.90*	*$1.50*	£0.20	£0.60	£1.00
121-124 John Higgins cover	*$0.30*	*$0.90*	*$1.50*	£0.20	£0.60	£1.00
125 DS Arcane returns, John Higgins painted cover	*$0.60*	*$1.80*	*$3.00*	£0.40	£1.20	£2.00
126 Dick Foreman script, John Higgins painted cover	*$0.30*	*$0.90*	*$1.50*	£0.20	£0.60	£1.00
127-128 Project Proteus	*$0.30*	*$0.90*	*$1.50*	£0.20	£0.60	£1.00
129 Swamp Fever part 1, 1st issue under the "Vertigo" banner, painted covers by Charles Vess begin	*$0.40*	*$1.20*	*$2.00*	£0.25	£0.75	£1.25
130 Swamp Fever part 2 (conclusion)	*$0.40*	*$1.20*	*$2.00*	£0.25	£0.75	£1.25
131 Swamp Thing changes in appearance	*$0.40*	*$1.20*	*$2.00*	£0.25	£0.75	£1.25
132	*$0.40*	*$1.20*	*$2.00*	£0.25	£0.75	£1.25
133 pin-up by Paul Chadwick	*$0.40*	*$1.20*	*$2.00*	£0.25	£0.75	£1.25
134-135	*$0.40*	*$1.20*	*$2.00*	£0.25	£0.75	£1.25
136-138 painted covers by Charles Vess	*$0.40*	*$1.20*	*$2.00*	£0.25	£0.75	£1.25
139 Black Orchid appears, continued from Black Orchid #5; painted cover by Charles Vess	*$0.40*	*$1.20*	*$2.00*	£0.25	£0.75	£1.25
140 Grant Morrison and Mark Millar scripts begin; Alec Holland awakes thinking being the Swamp Thing was all a dream like that bit in Dallas..	*$0.40*	*$1.20*	*$2.00*	£0.25	£0.75	£1.25
141-147	*$0.40*	*$1.20*	*$2.00*	£0.25	£0.75	£1.25
148-149 Sargon the Sorceror appears	*$0.40*	*$1.20*	*$2.00*	£0.25	£0.75	£1.25
150 48pgs, Swamp Thing vs. Sargon the Sorceror	*$0.60*	*$1.80*	*$3.00*	£0.40	£1.20	£2.00

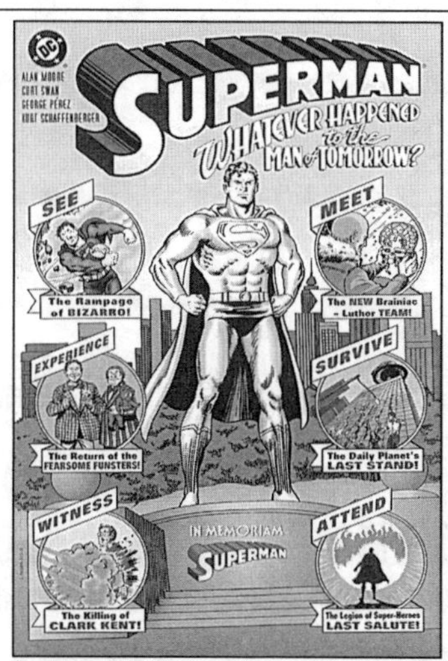

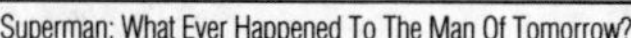
Superman: What Ever Happened To The Man Of Tomorrow?

Supernatural Thrillers #4

Swamp Thing (1st) #21

	$Good	$Fine	$N.Mint	£Good	£Fine	£N.Mint
151-153 Brian Bolland painted cover	$0.40	$1.20	$2.00	£0.25	£0.75	£1.25
154	$0.40	$1.20	$2.00	£0.25	£0.75	£1.25
155 $2.25 cover begin	$0.45	$1.35	$2.25	£0.30	£0.90	£1.50
156-164	$0.45	$1.35	$2.25	£0.30	£0.90	£1.50
165 Curt Swan cover and art	$0.45	$1.35	$2.25	£0.30	£0.90	£1.50
166-171 Trial By Fire storyline	$0.45	$1.35	$2.25	£0.30	£0.90	£1.50
Title Value:	$93.00	$279.10	$469.75	£60.40	£181.35	£306.25

Note: most distributed copies of issues #60, #61 have large white Co-Mag distribution labels. Issues #30 on are Mature Readers in content though only labelled as such from #57.

				£Good	£Fine	£N.Mint
Trade paperback DC Edition ND, colour, Ramsey Campbell foreword, reprints #21-27 plus 15 pages of new material				£2.00	£6.00	£10.00
Trade paperback Warner Books Edition, as above, ND scarce				£2.25	£6.75	£11.25
Swamp Thing: Love and Death (Nov 1990) Trade paperback reprints #28-34 and Annual #2, all recoloured				£1.80	£5.40	£9.00
Trade paperback Titan (UK) Edition Books #1-11, all black and white, as follows:						
1 James Herbert foreword (reprints #21-24)				£1.40	£4.20	£7.00
2 Clive Barker foreword (reprints #25-28)				£2.50	£7.50	£12.50
3 (reprints #29-31, Annual #2)				£1.40	£4.20	£7.00
4 (reprints #32-36)				£1.30	£3.90	£6.50
5 (reprints #37-40)				£1.10	£3.30	£5.50
6 (reprints #41-44)				£1.10	£3.30	£5.50
7 (reprints #45-47)				£1.00	£3.00	£5.00
8 (reprints #48-51)				£1.10	£3.30	£5.50
9 (reprints #52-55)				£1.10	£3.30	£5.50
10 (reprints #56-59)				£1.10	£3.30	£5.50
11 (reprints #60-64)				£1.30	£3.90	£6.50
Swamp Thing: Dark Genesis, Trade paperback (Mar 1992) reprints Swamp Thing (1st Series) #1-10, House of Secrets #92, cover painting by Berni Wrightson				£2.50	£7.50	£12.50

SWAMP THING (2ND SERIES) ANNUAL

DC Comics; 1 Nov 1982-7 1993

(sub-titled "Saga of the...")

	$Good	$Fine	$N.Mint	£Good	£Fine	£N.Mint
1 52pgs, adapts film	$0.40	$1.20	$2.00	£0.30	£0.90	£1.50
2 LD in the U.K. continues from Saga of Swamp Thing #31, Moore script, title changes to Swamp Thing Annual	$0.60	$1.80	$3.00	£0.50	£1.50	£2.50
3	$0.40	$1.20	$2.00	£0.30	£0.90	£1.50
4 LD in the U.K. Batman appears cover and story	$0.60	$1.80	$3.00	£0.40	£1.20	£2.00
5 Neil Gaiman story, Floronic Man and Brother Power The Geek appear, Batman cameo	$0.60	$1.80	$3.00	£0.40	£1.20	£2.00
6 ND 64pgs, Nancy Collins script, John Higgins cover	$0.60	$1.80	$3.00	£0.40	£1.20	£2.00
7 ND 64pgs, The Children's Crusade part 4, painted cover by Charles Vess	$0.80	$2.40	$4.00	£0.50	£1.50	£2.50
Title Value:	$4.00	$12.00	$20.00	£2.80	£8.40	£14.00

Note: some copies of Annual 2 have a pin-sized burn-mark in the cover. All Mature Readers label.

SWAMP THING SAGA, ORIGINAL

DC Comics;2 1977; 14 Summer 1978; 17 Sep 1979; 20 Feb 1980

(DC Special Series #2, #14, #17, #20)

	$Good	$Fine	$N.Mint	£Good	£Fine	£N.Mint
2-20 ND 52pgs	$0.80	$2.50	$5.00	£0.50	£1.50	£3.00
Title Value:	$3.20	$10.00	$20.00	£2.00	£6.00	£12.00

REPRINT FEATURES

All are Wrightson reprints. 2 reprints Swamp Thing 1, 2. 14 reprints Swamp Thing 3, 4. 17 reprints ST 5, 6, 7. 20 reprints ST 8, 9, 10.

SWEET XVI

Marvel Comics Group,MS; 1 Apr 1991-6 Sep 1991

	$Good	$Fine	$N.Mint	£Good	£Fine	£N.Mint
1 ND Barbara Slate script/art begins	$0.15	$0.45	$0.75	£0.10	£0.35	£0.60
2-6 ND	$0.15	$0.45	$0.75	£0.10	£0.35	£0.60
Title Value:	$0.90	$2.70	$4.50	£0.60	£2.10	£3.60

SWEET XVI BACK-TO-SCHOOL SPECIAL

Marvel Comics Group,OS; 1 Nov 1992

	$Good	$Fine	$N.Mint	£Good	£Fine	£N.Mint
1 ND 64pgs, Barbarar Slate script/art	$0.40	$1.20	$2.00	£0.25	£0.75	£1.25
Title Value:	$0.40	$1.20	$2.00	£0.25	£0.75	£1.25

SWING WITH SCOOTER

National Periodical Publications/DC Comics; 1 Jun/Jul 1966-35 Aug/Sep 1971; 36 Oct/Nov 1972

	$Good	$Fine	$N.Mint	£Good	£Fine	£N.Mint
1	$2.85	$8.50	$20.00	£1.75	£5.25	£12.50
2-3	$1.75	$5.25	$12.50	£1.05	£3.20	£7.50
4-10	$1.55	$4.70	$11.00	£0.85	£2.55	£6.00
11-20	$1.50	$4.50	$9.00	£0.80	£2.50	£5.00
21-36	$1.25	$3.75	$7.50	£0.65	£2.00	£4.00
Title Value:	$52.20	$156.90	$323.00	£28.20	£86.50	£183.50

SWORD OF DAMOCLES

Image; 1,2 Mar 1996

	$Good	$Fine	$N.Mint	£Good	£Fine	£N.Mint
1 ND Warren Ellis script, Randy Green art; leads into Sigma #1; Fire From Heaven X-over	$0.50	$1.50	$2.50	£0.30	£0.90	£1.50
2 ND Fire From Heaven part 16, concluded in Fire From Heaven #2	$0.50	$1.50	$2.50	£0.30	£0.90	£1.50
Title Value:	$1.00	$3.00	$5.00	£0.60	£1.80	£3.00

SWORD OF SORCERY

DC Comics; 1 Feb/Mar 1973-5 Nov/Dec 1973

(see Wonder Woman #202)

	$Good	$Fine	$N.Mint	£Good	£Fine	£N.Mint
1 scarce in the U.K. Howard Chaykin art, some Neal Adams inks, (credited as The Crusty Bunkers); Fafhrd and Grey Mouser begin	$1.00	$3.00	$6.00	£0.40	£1.25	£2.50
2 part Neal Adams inks	$0.55	$1.75	$3.50	£0.30	£1.00	£2.00
3 Bernie Wrightson art (5 pages)	$0.40	$1.25	$2.50	£0.25	£0.75	£1.50
4 Howard Chaykin art	$0.50	$1.50	$3.00	£0.30	£1.00	£2.00
5 Jim Starlin and Walt Simonson art	$0.50	$1.50	$3.00	£0.30	£1.00	£2.00
Title Value:	$2.95	$9.00	$18.00	£1.55	£5.00	£10.00

SWORD OF THE ATOM

(see Atom, Sword of The)

SWORD OF THE SAMURAI

Avalon Communications,MS; 1 Feb 1996-4 May 1996

	$Good	$Fine	$N.Mint	£Good	£Fine	£N.Mint
1-4 ND	$0.50	$1.50	$2.50	£0.30	£0.90	£1.50
Title Value:	$2.00	$6.00	$10.00	£1.20	£3.60	£6.00

SWORDS OF CEREBUS

(see Cerebus)

SWORDS OF SHA-PEI

Caliber Press,MS; 1 Jul 1991-3 Sep 1991

	$Good	$Fine	$N.Mint	£Good	£Fine	£N.Mint
1-3 ND	$0.40	$1.20	$2.00	£0.25	£0.75	£1.25
Title Value:	$1.20	$3.60	$6.00	£0.75	£2.25	£3.75
Swords of Shar-Pei Compilation (Feb 1992) collects 3 issue mini-series 3 issue mini-series plus intro story from Caliber Presents				£0.65	£1.95	£3.25

SWORDS OF TEXAS

Eclipse,MS; 1 Oct 1987-4 Jan 1988

	$Good	$Fine	$N.Mint	£Good	£Fine	£N.Mint
1 ND Scout spin-off	$0.40	$1.20	$2.00	£0.25	£0.75	£1.25
2-4 ND	$0.40	$1.20	$2.00	£0.25	£0.75	£1.25
Title Value:	$1.60	$4.80	$8.00	£1.00	£3.00	£5.00

SWORDS OF THE SWASHBUCKLERS

Marvel Comics Group/Epic,MS; 1 Apr 1985-12 Jun 1987

(see Marvel Graphic Novel)

	$Good	$Fine	$N.Mint	£Good	£Fine	£N.Mint
1-12 ND Jackson Guice art	$0.40	$1.20	$2.00	£0.25	£0.75	£1.25
Title Value:	$4.80	$14.40	$24.00	£3.00	£9.00	£15.00

SWORDS OF VALOR

A Plus Comics,OS; 1 Sep 1991

	$Good	$Fine	$N.Mint	£Good	£Fine	£N.Mint
1 ND 48pgs, Robin Hood reprints from Charlton comics, black and white	$0.40	$1.20	$2.00	£0.25	£0.75	£1.25
Title Value:	$0.40	$1.20	$2.00	£0.25	£0.75	£1.25

SYMBOLS OF JUSTICE

High Impact Studios; 1 May 1995-3 1996 ?

	$Good	$Fine	$N.Mint	£Good	£Fine	£N.Mint
1 ND Rick Lyon script and Ricky Carralero art	$0.60	$1.80	$3.00	£0.40	£1.20	£2.00
2 ND black and white	$0.60	$1.80	$3.00	£0.40	£1.20	£2.00
3 ND	$0.60	$1.80	$3.00	£0.40	£1.20	£2.00
Title Value:	$1.80	$5.40	$9.00	£1.20	£3.60	£6.00

SYPHONS

Now Comics; 1 Jul 1986-7 1987

	$Good	$Fine	$N.Mint	£Good	£Fine	£N.Mint
1 ND Caputo cover	$0.30	$0.90	$1.50	£0.20	£0.60	£1.00
2-7 ND	$0.30	$0.90	$1.50	£0.20	£0.60	£1.00
Title Value:	$2.10	$6.30	$10.50	£1.40	£4.20	£7.00

SYPHONS (2ND SERIES)

Now Comics,MS; 1 Mar 1994-3 May 1994

	$Good	$Fine	$N.Mint	£Good	£Fine	£N.Mint
1-3 ND Allen Curtis script, Mark Beachum art	$0.40	$1.20	$2.00	£0.25	£0.75	£1.25
Title Value:	$1.20	$3.60	$6.00	£0.75	£2.25	£3.75
Syphons (Aug 1994) Trade paperback reprints issues #1-3, new cover				£0.80	£2.40	£4.00

SYPHONS ANNUAL

Now Comics; 1 1995

	$Good	$Fine	$N.Mint	£Good	£Fine	£N.Mint
1 ND Rich Buckler art	$0.50	$1.50	$2.50	£0.30	£0.90	£1.50
Title Value:	$0.50	$1.50	$2.50	£0.30	£0.90	£1.50

SYPHONS: COUNTDOWN TO ARMAGEDDON

Now Comics,MS; 1 Feb 1995-3 Apr 1995

	$Good	$Fine	$N.Mint	£Good	£Fine	£N.Mint
1-3 ND Rick Buckler art	$0.50	$1.50	$2.50	£0.30	£0.90	£1.50
Title Value:	$1.50	$4.50	$7.50	£0.90	£2.70	£4.50

SYPHONS: THE SYGATE STRATAGEM

Now Comics; 1 Oct 1994-3 Dec 1994

	$Good	$Fine	$N.Mint	£Good	£Fine	£N.Mint
1-3 ND	$0.50	$1.50	$2.50	£0.30	£0.90	£1.50
Title Value:	$1.50	$4.50	$7.50	£0.90	£2.70	£4.50

SYSTEM BYTES, THE

Marvel Comics Group; 1992

Cross-over storyline that ran throughout the following issues:

Punisher Annual #5, Daredevil Annual #8, Wonderman Annual #1, Guardians of the Galaxy Annual #2.

T

T MINUS 1

Renegade; 1,2 Sep 1988

	$Good	$Fine	$N.Mint	£Good	£Fine	£N.Mint
1-2 ND bi-weekly	$0.40	$1.20	$2.00	£0.25	£0.75	£1.25
Title Value:	$0.80	$2.40	$4.00	£0.50	£1.50	£2.50

	$Good	$Fine	$N.Mint	£Good	£Fine	£N.Mint
T.H.U.N.D.E.R.						
Solson Publications; 1 1987						
1 ND black and white	$0.30	$0.90	$1.50	£0.20	£0.60	£1.00
Title Value:	$0.30	$0.90	$1.50	£0.20	£0.60	£1.00
TABOO						
Spiderbaby Grafix; 1 Autumn 1988-5 1992; Tundra Publishing; 6 1993; King Hell Press; 7,8 1994; Kitchen Sink Press; 9 1995						
1 ND Stephen Bissette, S. Clay Wilson, Paul Chadwick plus others; adult horror stories begin, 144pgs	$1.50	$4.50	$7.50	£1.00	£3.00	£5.00
1 2nd printing ND	$1.20	$3.60	$6.00	£0.80	£2.40	£4.00
2 ND	$1.50	$4.50	$7.50	£1.00	£3.00	£5.00
2 2nd printing ND	$1.20	$3.60	$6.00	£0.80	£2.40	£4.00
3 ND	$1.50	$4.50	$7.50	£1.00	£3.00	£5.00
3 2nd printing ND	$1.20	$3.60	$6.00	£0.80	£2.40	£4.00
4 ND 160pgs, Moebius art featured, part 3 From Hell by Alan Moore/Eddie Campbell, also Charles Vess, Neil Gaiman	$2.00	$6.00	$10.00	£1.50	£4.50	£7.50
5 ND 130pgs, part 4 From Hell featured	$2.00	$6.00	$10.00	£1.50	£4.50	£7.50
6 ND 122pgs, 1st Tundra issue, part 5 From Hell featured plus Neil Gaiman's Sweeny Todd Penny Dreadful (16pgs)	$2.00	$6.00	$10.00	£1.50	£4.50	£7.50
7 ND 128pgs, part 6 From Hell	$2.50	$7.50	$12.50	£1.80	£5.25	£9.00
8 ND 128pgs, work by David Lloyd, P. Craig Russell, Greg Capullo	$2.50	$7.50	$12.50	£1.80	£5.25	£9.00
9 ND stories by Tim Truman and Matt Howarth; introduction by Steve Bissette	$3.00	$9.00	$15.00	£2.00	£6.00	£10.00
Title Value:	$22.10	$66.30	$110.50	£15.50	£46.20	£77.50
Note: all Non-Distributed on the news-stands in the U.K.						
TAILGUNNER JO						
DC Comics,MS; 1 Sep 1988-6 Feb 1989						
1-6	$0.15	$0.45	$0.75	£0.10	£0.30	£0.50
Title Value:	$0.90	$2.70	$4.50	£0.60	£1.80	£3.00
Note: New Format						
TAINTED						
DC Comics/Vertigo,OS; 1 Feb 1995						
1 ND Jamie Delano script, Al Davison art	$0.90	$2.70	$4.50	£0.60	£1.80	£3.00
Title Value:	$0.90	$2.70	$4.50	£0.60	£1.80	£3.00
TAKEN UNDER						
Caliber Press; 1 Apr 1992						
1 ND spin-off from Caliber Presents	$0.50	$1.50	$2.50	£0.30	£0.90	£1.50
Title Value:	$0.50	$1.50	$2.50	£0.30	£0.90	£1.50
TAKING A.I.M.						
Marvel Comics Group; 1995						
Cross-over storyline throughout the following issues: **Avengers #386 Prelude**, **Captain America #440**, **Avengers #387**, **Captain America #441**, **Avengers #388**.						
TAKION						
DC Comics; 1 Jun 1996-7 Dec 1996						
1 ND Paul Kupperberg script, Aaron Lopresti art	$0.35	$1.05	$1.75	£0.25	£0.75	£1.25
2 ND Green Lantern, Flash and Captain Atom appear	$0.35	$1.05	$1.75	£0.25	£0.75	£1.25
3-5 ND	$0.35	$1.05	$1.75	£0.25	£0.75	£1.25
6 ND Final Night tie-in	$0.35	$1.05	$1.75	£0.25	£0.75	£1.25
7 ND	$0.35	$1.05	$1.75	£0.25	£0.75	£1.25
Title Value:	$2.45	$7.35	$12.25	£1.75	£5.25	£8.75
TALE OF ONE BAD RAT						
Dark Horse,MS; 1 Oct 1994-4 Jan 1995						
1-4 ND Bryan Talbot script and art	$0.60	$1.80	$3.00	£0.40	£1.20	£2.00
Title Value:	$2.40	$7.20	$12.00	£1.60	£4.80	£8.00
The Tale of One Bad Rat (Sep 1995)						
Trade paperback reprints issues #1-4 with new painted cover				£2.00	£6.00	£10.00
TALES FROM THE ANIVERSE (1ST SERIES)						
Arrow; 1 Apr 1985-6 Feb 1986						
1-6 ND black and white	$0.30	$0.90	$1.50	£0.20	£0.60	£1.00
Title Value:	$1.80	$5.40	$9.00	£1.20	£3.60	£6.00
TALES FROM THE ANIVERSE (2ND SERIES)						
Massive Comics Group; 1 Sep 1991-5 1992						
1 ND	$0.40	$1.20	$2.00	£0.25	£0.75	£1.25
2 ND 48pgs	$0.50	$1.50	$2.50	£0.30	£0.90	£1.50
3-5 ND	$0.40	$1.20	$2.00	£0.25	£0.75	£1.25
Title Value:	$2.10	$6.30	$10.50	£1.30	£3.90	£6.50
TALES FROM THE CRYPT						
E.C. Comics; 20 Oct/Nov 1950-46 Feb/Mar 1955						
(formerly International Comics #1-5, becomes International Crime Patrol #6, becomes Crime Patrol #7-16, becomes Crypt of Terror #17-19)						
20	$120.00	$365.00	$975.00	£80.00	£240.00	£650.00
21	$100.00	$305.00	$825.00	£67.50	£205.00	£550.00
22	$77.50	$235.00	$635.00	£52.50	£155.00	£425.00
23-25	$60.00	$180.00	$480.00	£40.00	£120.00	£320.00
26-30	$44.00	$130.00	$350.00	£29.00	£87.50	£235.00
31 1st ever Williamson art at E.C.	$47.00	$140.00	$375.00	£31.00	£92.50	£250.00
32	$36.00	$105.00	$290.00	£24.00	£72.50	£195.00
33 origin Crypt Keeper	$67.50	$205.00	$550.00	£46.00	£135.00	£365.00
34 Ray Bradbury adaptaion	$36.00	$105.00	$290.00	£24.00	£72.50	£195.00
35-45	$36.00	$105.00	$290.00	£24.00	£72.50	£195.00
46 scarce in both US and UK	$41.00	$120.00	$325.00	£27.00	£80.00	£215.00
Title Value:	$1321.00	$3925.00	$10645.00	£881.00	£2647.50	£7125.00
Note: all Non-Distributed on the news-stands in the U.K.						
TALES FROM THE CRYPT (2ND SERIES)						
Gladstone; 1 Jul 1990-6 Jan 1992						
1-6 ND DS	$0.50	$1.50	$2.50	£0.30	£0.90	£1.50
Title Value:	$3.00	$9.00	$15.00	£1.80	£5.40	£9.00
Note: reprints from classic 1950s EC material featuring such artists as Wally Wood, Jack Davis and Harvey Kurtzman. **Note also**: issue #7 was advertised but never appeared.						
TALES FROM THE CRYPT (3RD SERIES)						
Russ Cochran/EC Comics; 1 Sep 1991-6 1992						
1 ND 64pgs, reprints Tales from the Crypt #31 and Crime Suspense Stories 12; published in extra-large format rather than normal comic size	$0.50	$1.50	$2.50	£0.30	£0.90	£1.50
2 ND 64pgs, reprints Tales from the Crypt #34, Crime Suspense Stories #15	$0.50	$1.50	$2.50	£0.30	£0.90	£1.50
3 ND 64pgs, reprints Tales from the Crypt #24, Crime Suspense Stories #21	$0.50	$1.50	$2.50	£0.30	£0.90	£1.50
4 ND 64pgs, reprints Tales from the Crypt #43, Crime Suspense Stories #18	$0.50	$1.50	$2.50	£0.30	£0.90	£1.50
5 ND 64pgs, reprints Tales from the Crypt #22, Crime Suspense Stories #23	$0.50	$1.50	$2.50	£0.30	£0.90	£1.50
6 ND 64pgs, reprints Tales from the Crypt #36, Crime Suspense Stories #6	$0.50	$1.50	$2.50	£0.30	£0.90	£1.50
Title Value:	$3.00	$9.00	$15.00	£1.80	£5.40	£9.00
Note: issues #7-9 were advertised but never appeared.						
TALES FROM THE CRYPT (4TH SERIES)						
Russ Cochran/EC Comics; 1 Sep 1992-present						
1 ND reprints from the original 1950s EC series begin with exact cover and interior reproduction	$0.40	$1.20	$2.00	£0.25	£0.75	£1.25
2-14 ND	$0.40	$1.20	$2.00	£0.25	£0.75	£1.25
Title Value:	$5.60	$16.80	$28.00	£3.50	£10.50	£17.50
Tales from the Crypt Annual 1 (Aug 1994)						
reprints issues #1-5 with covers, softcover				£1.20	£3.60	£6.00
Tales from the Crypt Annual 2 (Dec 1994)						
reprints issues #6-10 with covers, softcover				£1.20	£3.60	£6.00
TALES FROM THE HEART						
Slave Labor; 1 1987-6 1989; 7 Nov 1990-9 1991						
1-6 ND	$0.40	$1.20	$2.00	£0.25	£0.75	£1.25
7 ND Matt Wagner cover	$0.40	$1.20	$2.00	£0.25	£0.75	£1.25
8 ND	$0.40	$1.20	$2.00	£0.25	£0.75	£1.25
9 ND $2.95 cover begins	$0.60	$1.80	$3.00	£0.40	£1.20	£2.00
Title Value:	$3.80	$11.40	$19.00	£2.40	£7.20	£12.00
Note: #1,2 published by Entropy						
Hearts of Africa (1995)						
Trade paperback ND collects issues #1-3				£1.30	£3.90	£6.50
TALES FROM THE HEART OF AFRICA - TEMPORARY NATIVES						
Marvel Comics Group/Epic,OS; 1 Aug 1990						
1 ND 48pgs	$0.60	$1.80	$3.00	£0.40	£1.20	£2.00
Title Value:	$0.60	$1.80	$3.00	£0.40	£1.20	£2.00
TALES FROM THE MUMMY'S TOMB						
Millennium,OS; 1 Jul 1991						
1 ND 48pgs, Frank Frazetta cover	$0.60	$1.80	$3.00	£0.40	£1.20	£2.00
Title Value:	$0.60	$1.80	$3.00	£0.40	£1.20	£2.00
TALES OF ASGARD						
Marvel Comics Group,OS; 1 Oct 1968						
1 scarce in the U.K. 72pgs, classic Jack Kirby reprints from Journey into Mystery back-ups in issues #97-106	$4.60	$13.50	$32.50	£3.20	£9.50	£22.50
Title Value:	$4.60	$13.50	$32.50	£3.20	£9.50	£22.50
TALES OF ASGARD (2ND SERIES)						
Marvel Comics Group,OS; 1 Feb 1984						
1 ND 48pgs, Thor reprints, Simonson cover	$0.50	$1.50	$2.50	£0.30	£0.90	£1.50
Title Value:	$0.50	$1.50	$2.50	£0.30	£0.90	£1.50
TALES OF EVIL						
Atlas; 1 Feb 1975-3 Jul 1975						
1-2 distributed in the U.K.	$0.25	$0.75	$1.50	£0.15	£0.50	£1.00
3 distributed in the U.K. origin Man Monster, Buckler/Vosburg art	$0.25	$0.75	$1.50	£0.15	£0.50	£1.00
Title Value:	$0.75	$2.25	$4.50	£0.45	£1.50	£3.00
TALES OF GHOST CASTLE						
DC Comics; 1 May/Jun 1975-3 Sep/Oct 1975						
1	$0.50	$1.50	$3.00	£0.30	£1.00	£2.00
2-3	$0.40	$1.25	$2.50	£0.25	£0.75	£1.50
Title Value:	$1.30	$4.00	$8.00	£0.80	£2.50	£5.00
TALES OF LETHARGY						
Alpha Productions,MS; 1 Oct 1993-3 Dec 1993						
1-3 ND	$0.40	$1.20	$2.00	£0.25	£0.75	£1.25
Title Value:	$1.20	$3.60	$6.00	£0.75	£2.25	£3.75
TALES OF ORDINARY MADNESS						
Dark Horse,MS; 1 Jan 1992-4 Apr 1992						
1-4 ND Malcolm Bourne script, painted covers by John Bolton						

$Good $Fine $N.Mint £Good £Fine £N.Mint

$0.50 $1.50 $2.50 £0.30 £0.90 £1.50
Title Value: $2.00 $6.00 $10.00 £1.20 £3.60 £6.00

TALES OF SUSPENSE (1ST SERIES)

Atlas/Marvel Comics Group; 1 Jan 1959-99 Mar 1968
(becomes Captain America)
1 scarce in the U.K. part Williamson art
$150.00 $450.00 $1350.00 £100.00 £300.00 £900.00
2 Steve Ditko cover
$65.00 $195.00 $525.00 £44.00 £130.00 £350.00
3 flying saucer cover
$62.50 $185.00 $500.00 £42.00 £125.00 £335.00
4 Williamson/Jack Kirby/Bill Everett art
$57.50 $175.00 $475.00 £39.00 £115.00 £315.00
5 the 1st in a long line of Jack Kirby monster covers
$41.00 $120.00 $325.00 £27.00 £80.00 £215.00
6 $41.00 $120.00 $325.00 £27.00 £80.00 £215.00
7 possible Lava Man prototype in the story "I Fought the Molten Man-Thing", pre-figuring Journey into Mystery #97. Note that the two cover layouts are remarkably similar
$41.00 $120.00 $325.00 £27.00 £80.00 £215.00
8 $41.00 $120.00 $325.00 £27.00 £80.00 £215.00
9 possible Iron Man prototype
$41.00 $120.00 $325.00 £27.00 £80.00 £215.00

1st official distribution in the U.K.

10 $41.00 $120.00 $325.00 £27.00 £80.00 £215.00
11-15 ND scarce in the U.K.
$31.00 $92.50 $250.00 £20.50 £60.00 £165.00
16 1st appearance Metallo (see DC's Action #252), Iron Man prototype? Metallo here is actually a gigantic robot used by a criminal who becomes trapped inside forever
$38.00 $110.00 $300.00 £25.00 £75.00 £200.00
17-20 $31.00 $92.50 $250.00 £20.50 £60.00 £165.00
21-24 $23.50 $70.00 $190.00 £15.50 £47.00 £125.00
25 (Jan 1962), last 10 cents issue
$23.50 $70.00 $190.00 £15.50 £47.00 £125.00
26-27 $21.50 $65.00 $175.00 £13.00 £39.00 £105.00
28 possible Stone Men from Saturn prototype
$23.00 $67.50 $185.00 £14.00 £43.00 £115.00
29-30 $21.50 $65.00 $175.00 £13.00 £39.00 £105.00
31 Dr. Doom prototype? "The Monster in the Iron Mask" is exactly that, not a disfigured man/ruler turned evil
$21.50 $65.00 $175.00 £13.00 £39.00 £105.00
32 1st Sazzik the Sorcerer, prototype of Dr. Strange? Debatable as Sazzik is 15th century, evil and grotesque-looking! (see also Strange Tales #79 and Journey Into Mystery #78). Ant-Man prototype more in keeping with the cover story "The Man in the Bee-Hive"
$21.50 $65.00 $175.00 £13.00 £39.00 £105.00
33-34 $21.50 $65.00 $175.00 £13.00 £39.00 £105.00
35 Watcher prototype? More possible than other "prototypes"! Zarkorr is a humanoid alien who wears a Watcher-like disguise to preach world peace to humanity
$20.00 $60.00 $160.00 £11.50 £36.00 £95.00
36 $20.00 $60.00 $160.00 £11.50 £36.00 £95.00
37 (Jan 1963) $20.00 $60.00 $160.00 £11.50 £36.00 £95.00
38 $20.00 $60.00 $160.00 £11.50 £36.00 £95.00
39 origin & 1st appearance Iron Man, part Kirby art
$400.00 $1200.00 $4000.00 £260.00 £780.00 £2600.00
[Prices may vary widely on this comic]
39 Marvel Milestone Edition, ND (Oct 1994) - silver border around cover
$0.60 $1.80 $3.00 £0.40 £1.20 £2.00
40 scarce in the U.K. 2nd Iron Man and new Iron Man armour (gold rather than grey)
$160.00 $480.00 $1450.00 £92.50 £280.00 £850.00
41 features villain called Dr. Strange, two months before Strange Tales #110 (Jul 1963) with 1st appearance of the hero Dr. Strange
$95.00 $285.00 $675.00 £60.00 £180.00 £425.00
42 $44.00 $130.00 $310.00 £26.00 £77.50 £185.00
43 less common in the U.K.
$44.00 $130.00 $310.00 £28.00 £82.50 £195.00
44 scarce in the U.K. "Pharaoh" mis-spelt on cover
$44.00 $130.00 $310.00 £29.00 £85.00 £200.00
45 less common in the U.K.
$44.00 $130.00 $310.00 £26.00 £77.50 £185.00
46 less common in the U.K. 1st appearance Crimson Dynamo
$29.00 $85.00 $200.00 £17.50 £52.50 £125.00
47 $27.00 $80.00 $190.00 £15.50 £47.00 £110.00
48 Iron Man's new armour (red and gold)
$32.00 $95.00 $225.00 £19.00 £57.50 £135.00
49 (Jan 1964), joint 3rd appearance X-Men; came out same month (Jan. 1964) as X-Men #3 and Avengers #3; The Watcher back-up story (2nd appearance)
$28.00 $82.50 $195.00 £17.00 £50.00 £120.00
50 1st appearance Mandarin
$17.50 $52.50 $125.00 £11.00 £34.00 £80.00
51 1st appearance Scarecrow (note: not DC's long-time villain)
$15.00 $45.00 $105.00 £10.00 £30.00 £70.00
52 1st appearance Black Widow
$19.00 $57.50 $135.00 £11.00 £34.00 £80.00
53 2nd appearance Black Widow, origin and 3rd appearance The Watcher
$17.00 $50.00 $120.00 £10.00 £30.00 £70.00
54 The Mandarin returns
$11.00 $34.00 $80.00 £7.00 £21.00 £50.00
55 extra 5 page section on inside information about Iron Man
$11.00 $34.00 $80.00 £7.00 £21.00 £50.00
56 1st appearance Unicorn
$11.00 $34.00 $80.00 £7.00 £21.00 £50.00
57 scarce in the U.K. origin and 1st appearance of Hawkeye, Black Widow appears
$22.50 $67.50 $160.00 £14.00 £43.00 £100.00
58 scarce in the U.K. Captain America vs. Iron Man
$40.00 $120.00 $280.00 £21.00 £62.50 £150.00
59 scarce in the U.K. 1st solo Silver Age Captain America series begins
$40.00 $120.00 $280.00 £21.00 £62.50 £150.00
60 very scarce in the U.K. 2nd appearance Hawkeye
$18.50 $55.00 $130.00 £10.50 £32.00 £75.00
61 less common in the U.K. (Jan 1965)
$11.00 $34.00 $80.00 £6.25 £19.00 £45.00
62 less common in the U.K. origin Mandarin
$11.00 $34.00 $80.00 £6.25 £19.00 £45.00
63 1st Silver Age origin Captain America
$30.00 $90.00 $210.00 £15.50 £47.00 £110.00
64 1st new Black Widow (1st costume)
$11.00 $34.00 $80.00 £6.25 £19.00 £45.00
65 1st appearance Silver Age Red Skull (since Captain America Comics #74 in 1949)
$16.50 $50.00 $135.00 £6.75 £20.50 £55.00
66 2nd Silver Age Red Skull, origin retold
$16.00 $49.00 $130.00 £6.25 £18.50 £50.00
67-68 $8.00 $24.50 $57.50 £4.25 £12.50 £30.00
69 1st appearance Titanium Man
$8.00 $24.50 $57.50 £4.25 £12.50 £30.00
70 $8.00 $24.50 $57.50 £4.25 £12.50 £30.00
71 $7.75 $23.50 $55.00 £3.55 £10.50 £25.00
72 Quicksilver and Scarlet Witch appear; last Silver Age issue cover dated December 1965
$7.75 $23.50 $55.00 £3.55 £10.50 £25.00
73 (Jan 1966) $7.75 $23.50 $55.00 £3.55 £10.50 £25.00
74-75 $7.75 $23.50 $55.00 £3.55 £10.50 £25.00
76-77 $7.75 $23.50 $55.00 £2.85 £8.50 £20.00
78 Nick Fury appears
$7.75 $23.50 $55.00 £2.85 £8.50 £20.00
79 Iron Man battles Sub-Mariner; 1st appearance of the Cosmic Cube
$7.75 $23.50 $55.00 £2.85 £8.50 £20.00
80 Iron Man battles Sub-Mariner, X-over with Tales to Astonish #82
$9.25 $28.00 $65.00 £3.20 £9.50 £22.50
81-83 $7.75 $23.50 $55.00 £2.50 £7.50 £17.50
84 scarce in the U.K.
$7.75 $23.50 $55.00 £2.85 £8.50 £20.00
85 scarce in the U.K. (Jan 1967)
$7.75 $23.50 $55.00 £2.85 £8.50 £20.00
86-94 $7.75 $23.50 $55.00 £2.50 £7.50 £17.50
95 Iron Man vs. Grey Gargoyle
$7.75 $23.50 $55.00 £2.50 £7.50 £17.50
96 $7.75 $23.50 $55.00 £2.50 £7.50 £17.50
97 (Jan 1968), Black Panther appears, 1st appearance Whiplash
$7.75 $23.50 $55.00 £2.50 £7.50 £17.50
98 Captain America battles Black Panther
$7.75 $23.50 $55.00 £2.50 £7.50 £17.50
99 less common in the U.K. leads into Captain America #100 and Iron Man #1
$10.00 $30.00 $70.00 £3.55 £10.50 £25.00
Title Value: $2816.60 $8425.30 $22843.00 £1704.25 £5097.20 £13934.50

ARTISTS
Ditko in 10-15, 17-44, 46, 48, 49. Kirby in 10-35, 40, 41, 43, 59-68, 78-86, 92-99.

FEATURES
Captain America in 59-99. Iron Man in 39-99. Tales of the Watcher in 48-58. Monster/fantasy stories in 10-47 (as back-ups in 39-47).

TALES OF SUSPENSE (2ND SERIES)

Marvel Comics Group,OS; 1 Jan 1995
1 ND 64pgs, Iron Man and Captain America appear, Colin MacNeil painted art; card-stock cover with protective acetate overlay
$1.40 $4.20 $7.00 £0.90 £2.70 £4.50
Title Value: $1.40 $4.20 $7.00 £0.90 £2.70 £4.50

TALES OF TERROR

Eclipse; 1 Aug 1985-13 Jul 1987
1-4 ND $0.40 $1.20 $2.00 £0.25 £0.75 £1.25
5 ND Dowling, Weeks art, Conrad cover
$0.40 $1.20 $2.00 £0.25 £0.75 £1.25
6 ND $0.40 $1.20 $2.00 £0.25 £0.75 £1.25
7 ND David Lloyd, Bolton art
$0.40 $1.20 $2.00 £0.25 £0.75 £1.25
8 ND $0.40 $1.20 $2.00 £0.25 £0.75 £1.25
9 ND Bolton, Geary, Ridgway art
$0.40 $1.20 $2.00 £0.25 £0.75 £1.25
10-13 ND $0.40 $1.20 $2.00 £0.25 £0.75 £1.25
Title Value: $5.20 $15.60 $26.00 £3.25 £9.75 £16.25

TALES OF TERROR

Dell/Movie Classics,OS Movie; 12-793-302 Feb 1963
12-793-302 distributed in the U.K. film adaptation with Vincent Price; photo cover
$3.55 $10.50 $25.00 £1.75 £5.25 £12.50
Title Value: $3.55 $10.50 $25.00 £1.75 £5.25 £12.50

TALES OF THE AGE OF APOCALYPSE

Marvel Comics Group,OS; nn Feb 1997
nn ND 48pgs, Scott Lobdell script, Joe Bennett art
$1.20 $3.60 $6.00 £0.80 £2.40 £4.00
Title Value: $1.20 $3.60 $6.00 £0.80 £2.40 £4.00

TALES OF THE BEANWORLD

Beanworld/Eclipse; 1 Feb 1985-21 1993
(see Scout #17)
1 ND scarce in the U.K. Larry Marder story/art begins; black and white
$0.80 $2.40 $4.00 £0.50 £1.50 £2.50
2-3 ND scarce in the U.K.
$0.60 $1.80 $3.00 £0.40 £1.20 £2.00
4 ND scarce in the U.K.
$0.50 $1.50 $2.50 £0.35 £1.05 £1.75

	$Good	$Fine	$N.Mint	£Good	£Fine	£N.Mint
5 ND	***$0.50***	***$1.50***	***$2.50***	**£0.30**	**£0.90**	**£1.50**
6-19 ND	***$0.40***	***$1.20***	***$2.00***	**£0.25**	**£0.75**	**£1.25**
20 ND $2.50 cover	***$0.50***	***$1.50***	***$2.50***	**£0.30**	**£0.90**	**£1.50**
21 ND $2.95 cover	***$0.60***	***$1.80***	***$3.00***	**£0.40**	**£1.20**	**£2.00**
Title Value:	***$9.70***	***$29.10***	***$48.50***	**£6.15**	**£18.45**	**£30.75**
Book 1 - Trade paperback (reprints #1-4)				£1.20	£3.60	£6.00
2nd printing (1990)				£1.10	£3.30	£5.50
Book 2 - Trade paperback (Dec 1992), reprints #5-7						
Softcover				£1.10	£3.30	£5.50
Hardcover				£4.00	£12.00	£20.00
Larry Marder's Beanworld: Book One (Mar 1995) reprints issues #1-4; introduction by Scott McCloud				£1.30	£3.90	£6.50

TALES OF THE FEHNNIK

Antarctic Press; 1 Aug 1995

1 ND Elin Winkler script, Pat Kelley art; black and white

	$Good	$Fine	$N.Mint	£Good	£Fine	£N.Mint
1	***$0.55***	***$1.65***	***$2.75***	**£0.35**	**£1.05**	**£1.75**
Title Value:	***$0.55***	***$1.65***	***$2.75***	**£0.35**	**£1.05**	**£1.75**

TALES OF THE GREEN LANTERN CORPS

(see Green Lantern Corps, Tales of The)

TALES OF THE JACKALOPE

Blackthorne; 1 Feb 1986-8 Dec 1986

1-8 ND Bob Crabb art; black and white

	$Good	$Fine	$N.Mint	£Good	£Fine	£N.Mint
1-8	***$0.40***	***$1.20***	***$2.00***	**£0.25**	**£0.75**	**£1.25**
Title Value:	***$3.20***	***$9.60***	***$16.00***	**£2.00**	**£6.00**	**£10.00**

TALES OF THE LEGION

(see Legion of Super-Heroes (1st Series) #314 onwards)

TALES OF THE MARVELS: BLOCKBUSTER

Marvel Comics Group,OS; nn Jun 1995

nn ND 48pgs, Mike Baron script, Shawn Martinbrough art; story stems from F.F. #260 with battle between Silver Surfer and Terrax; acetate outer cover

	$Good	$Fine	$N.Mint	£Good	£Fine	£N.Mint
nn	***$1.20***	***$3.60***	***$6.00***	**£0.80**	**£2.40**	**£4.00**
Title Value:	***$1.20***	***$3.60***	***$6.00***	**£0.80**	**£2.40**	**£4.00**

TALES OF THE MARVELS: INNER DEMONS

Marvel Comics Group,OS; 1 Feb 1996

1 ND 48pgs, Human Torch, Sub-Mariner (origin re-examined) and The Enforcers appear; painted art by Bob Wakelin

	$Good	$Fine	$N.Mint	£Good	£Fine	£N.Mint
1	***$1.20***	***$3.60***	***$6.00***	**£0.80**	**£2.40**	**£4.00**
Title Value:	***$1.20***	***$3.60***	***$6.00***	**£0.80**	**£2.40**	**£4.00**

TALES OF THE MARVELS: WONDER YEARS

Marvel Comics Group,MS; 1 Oct 1995-2 Nov 1995

1-2 ND Dan Abnett and Andy Lanning script, painted art by Igor Kordey, Wonder Man stars; acetate outer cover

	$Good	$Fine	$N.Mint	£Good	£Fine	£N.Mint
1-2	***$1.00***	***$3.00***	***$5.00***	**£0.70**	**£2.10**	**£3.50**
Title Value:	***$2.00***	***$6.00***	***$10.00***	**£1.40**	**£4.20**	**£7.00**

TALES OF THE MYSTERIOUS TRAVELLER

Charlton; 1 Aug 1956-13 Jun 1959; 14 Oct 1985-15 Dec 1985

	$Good	$Fine	$N.Mint	£Good	£Fine	£N.Mint
1 ND scarce in the U.K.	***$46.00***	***$135.00***	***$320.00***	**£31.00**	**£90.00**	**£215.00**
2 ND scarce in the U.K. part Steve Ditko art	***$36.00***	***$105.00***	***$250.00***	**£23.50**	**£70.00**	**£165.00**
3 ND scarce in the U.K. Steve Ditko cover and part art	***$32.00***	***$95.00***	***$225.00***	**£21.00**	**£62.50**	**£150.00**
4-6 ND scarce in the U.K. Steve Ditko cover and art	***$39.00***	***$115.00***	***$275.00***	**£26.00**	**£77.50**	**£185.00**
7-9 ND Steve Ditko cover and art	***$32.00***	***$95.00***	***$225.00***	**£21.00**	**£62.50**	**£150.00**
10 ND Steve Ditko cover and art	***$36.00***	***$105.00***	***$250.00***	**£23.50**	**£70.00**	**£165.00**
11 distributed in the U.K. (note cover date of February 1959, before official distribution of cover-date November 1959) Steve Ditko cover and art	***$36.00***	***$105.00***	***$250.00***	**£23.50**	**£70.00**	**£165.00**
12 distributed in the U.K. (note cover date of April 1959, before official distribution in November 1959)	***$17.50***	***$52.50***	***$125.00***	**£10.50**	**£32.00**	**£75.00**
13 distributed in the U.K. (note cover date of June 1959, before official distribution in November 1959)	***$17.50***	***$52.50***	***$125.00***	**£10.50**	**£32.00**	**£75.00**
14-15 LD in the U.K. Steve Ditko cover and art (reprints)	***$0.40***	***$1.20***	***$2.00***	**£0.25**	**£0.75**	**£1.25**
Title Value:	***$434.80***	***$1282.40***	***$3049.00***	**£285.00**	**£848.00**	**£2017.50**

TALES OF THE SUN RUNNERS

Sirius/Amazing; 1 Jul 1986-3 Jan 1987

1-3 ND black and white

	$Good	$Fine	$N.Mint	£Good	£Fine	£N.Mint
1-3	***$0.40***	***$1.20***	***$2.00***	**£0.25**	**£0.75**	**£1.25**
Title Value:	***$1.20***	***$3.60***	***$6.00***	**£0.75**	**£2.25**	**£3.75**

TALES OF THE TEEN TITANS

(see New Teen Titans (1st Series) #41 onwards)

TALES OF THE TEEN TITANS ANNUAL

(see New Teen Titans (1st series) Annual #3 onwards)

TALES OF THE TEENAGE MUTANT NINJA TURTLES

Mirage Studios; 1 May 1987-7 Apr 1989

(merges with Teenage Mutant Ninja Turtles)

	$Good	$Fine	$N.Mint	£Good	£Fine	£N.Mint
1 ND	***$0.50***	***$1.50***	***$2.50***	**£0.35**	**£1.05**	**£1.75**
1 2nd printing ND	***$0.50***	***$1.50***	***$2.50***	**£0.30**	**£0.90**	**£1.50**
2-7 ND	***$0.50***	***$1.50***	***$2.50***	**£0.30**	**£0.90**	**£1.50**
Title Value:	***$4.00***	***$12.00***	***$20.00***	**£2.45**	**£7.35**	**£12.25**
Collected Edition (1990), reprints #1-7				£1.60	£4.80	£8.00

TALES OF THE UNEXPECTED

National Periodical Publications; 1 Feb/Mar 1956-104 Dec/Jan 1967/68

(becomes The Unexpected)

	$Good	$Fine	$N.Mint	£Good	£Fine	£N.Mint
1 scarce in the U.K.	***$105.00***	***$325.00***	***$975.00***	**£70.00**	**£215.00**	**£650.00**
2 scarce in the U.K.	***$60.00***	***$180.00***	***$490.00***	**£41.00**	**£120.00**	**£325.00**
3-5 scarce in the U.K.	***$41.00***	***$120.00***	***$330.00***	**£28.00**	**£82.50**	**£220.00**
6-10	***$34.00***	***$100.00***	***$275.00***	**£23.00**	**£67.50**	**£185.00**
11	***$21.50***	***$65.00***	***$175.00***	**£14.00**	**£43.00**	**£115.00**
12-13 Jack Kirby art	***$24.00***	***$72.50***	***$195.00***	**£16.00**	**£49.00**	**£130.00**
14	***$21.50***	***$65.00***	***$175.00***	**£14.00**	**£43.00**	**£115.00**
15-18 Jack Kirby art	***$24.00***	***$72.50***	***$195.00***	**£16.00**	**£49.00**	**£130.00**
19-20	***$21.50***	***$65.00***	***$175.00***	**£14.00**	**£43.00**	**£115.00**
21-24 Jack Kirby art	***$23.00***	***$67.50***	***$185.00***	**£15.50**	**£47.00**	**£125.00**
25-30	***$18.50***	***$55.00***	***$150.00***	**£12.50**	**£38.00**	**£100.00**
31-39	***$16.00***	***$49.00***	***$130.00***	**£10.50**	**£33.00**	**£87.50**
40 1st of Space Ranger series (see Showcase #15/16); no mention on cover	***$95.00***	***$290.00***	***$875.00***	**£62.50**	**£190.00**	**£580.00**
41 Space Ranger	***$44.00***	***$130.00***	***$350.00***	**£25.00**	**£75.00**	**£200.00**
42 Space Ranger	***$35.00***	***$105.00***	***$280.00***	**£23.00**	**£67.50**	**£185.00**
1st official distribution in the U.K.						
43 1st Space Ranger series cover; painted (grey-tone) cover	***$75.00***	***$225.00***	***$675.00***	**£47.00**	**£140.00**	**£425.00**
44-46	***$29.00***	***$85.00***	***$200.00***	**£16.00**	**£49.00**	**£115.00**
47-50	***$20.50***	***$60.00***	***$145.00***	**£12.50**	**£39.00**	**£90.00**
51-60	***$17.50***	***$52.50***	***$125.00***	**£11.00**	**£34.00**	**£80.00**
61-66	***$15.00***	***$45.00***	***$105.00***	**£9.25**	**£28.00**	**£65.00**
67 last 10 cents issue	***$15.00***	***$45.00***	***$105.00***	**£9.25**	**£28.00**	**£65.00**
68-70	***$10.00***	***$30.00***	***$70.00***	**£5.50**	**£17.00**	**£40.00**
71-81	***$8.50***	***$26.00***	***$60.00***	**£4.60**	**£13.50**	**£32.50**
82 last Space Ranger	***$8.50***	***$26.00***	***$60.00***	**£4.60**	**£13.50**	**£32.50**

Syphons (2nd) #3

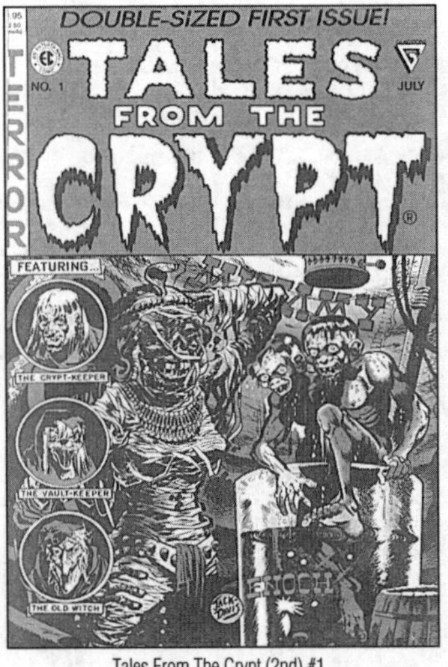

Tales From The Crypt (2nd) #1

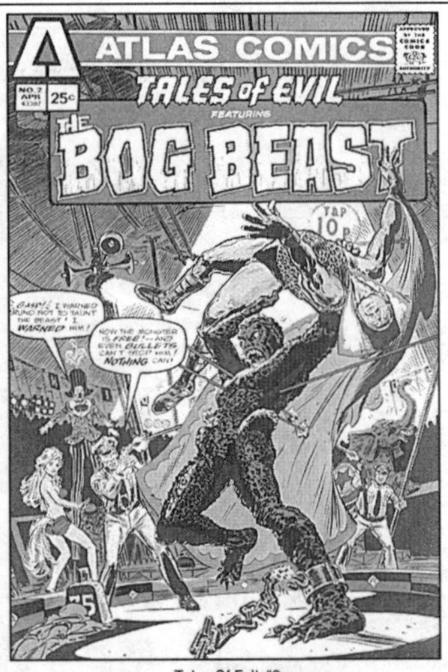

Tales Of Evil #2

Issue	$Good	$Fine	$N.Mint	£Good	£Fine	£N.Mint
83-90	$7.00	$21.00	$50.00	£3.55	£10.50	£25.00
91	$7.00	$21.00	$50.00	£2.85	£8.50	£20.00
92 last Silver Age issue indicia dated Dec 1965/Jan 1966	$7.00	$21.00	$50.00	£2.85	£8.50	£20.00
93-100	$7.00	$21.00	$50.00	£2.85	£8.50	£20.00
101-104	$5.25	$16.00	$37.50	£2.10	£6.25	£15.00
Title Value:	$2012.00	$6030.00	$15835.00	£1260.75	£3817.50	£10007.50

TALES OF THE VOYAGER

White Wolf; 1 Aug 1991

Issue	$Good	$Fine	$N.Mint	£Good	£Fine	£N.Mint
1 ND	$0.40	$1.20	$2.00	£0.25	£0.75	£1.25
Title Value:	$0.40	$1.20	$2.00	£0.25	£0.75	£1.25

TALES OF THE ZOMBIE

Marvel Comics Group,Magazine; 1 Aug 1973-10 Mar 1975

Issue	$Good	$Fine	$N.Mint	£Good	£Fine	£N.Mint
1 ND scarce in the U.K. 72pgs, The Zombie by Steve Gerber and Pablo Marcos begins; back-up stories begin with Voodoo themes, all black and white	$3.30	$10.00	$20.00	£2.05	£6.25	£12.50
2-3 ND 72pgs, Boris painted cover	$2.05	$6.25	$12.50	£1.05	£3.25	£6.50
4 64pgs, James Bond feature (v2 #1 in indicia)	$2.00	$6.00	$12.00	£0.90	£2.75	£5.50
5 64pgs	$2.00	$6.00	$12.00	£0.90	£2.75	£5.50
6 64pgs, Brother Voodoo back-up with Gene Colan art	$1.65	$5.00	$10.00	£0.80	£2.50	£5.00
7-8 64pgs	$1.65	$5.00	$10.00	£0.80	£2.50	£5.00
9 scarce in the U.K. 64pgs, double-length Zombie story	$1.65	$5.00	$10.00	£0.90	£2.75	£5.50
10 64pgs, Brother Voodoo main feature	$1.65	$5.00	$10.00	£0.80	£2.50	£5.00
Title Value:	$19.65	$59.50	$119.00	£10.05	£31.00	£62.00

ARTISTS

Kaluta art in 8.

FEATURES

Brother Voodoo in 5 (text only), 6, 10. Zombie in 1-9. Photos and text of Bond movie Live and Let Die in 4.

Note: a next issue was advertised but never appeared.

TALES OF THE ZOMBIE ANNUAL

Marvel Comics Group,Magazine; 1 Summer 1975

Issue	$Good	$Fine	$N.Mint	£Good	£Fine	£N.Mint
1 ND 88pgs, squarebound, all reprint	$1.25	$3.75	$7.50	£0.80	£2.50	£5.00
Title Value:	$1.25	$3.75	$7.50	£0.80	£2.50	£5.00

TALES OF UNSUPERVISED EXISTENCE

Fantagraphics; 1 1990-7 1992 ?

Issue	$Good	$Fine	$N.Mint	£Good	£Fine	£N.Mint
1-7 ND	$0.50	$1.50	$2.50	£0.30	£0.90	£1.50
Title Value:	$3.50	$10.50	$17.50	£2.10	£6.30	£10.50

TALES TO ASTONISH (1ST SERIES)

Atlas/Marvel Comics Group; 1 Jan 1959-101 Mar 1968

(becomes The Incredible Hulk)

Issue	$Good	$Fine	$N.Mint	£Good	£Fine	£N.Mint
1 scarce in the U.K. Jack Davis art	$170.00	$510.00	$1550.00	£110.00	£340.00	£1025.00
2 Steve Ditko flying saucer cover	$75.00	$230.00	$615.00	£50.00	£150.00	£410.00
3-4	$50.00	$150.00	$400.00	£33.00	£97.50	£265.00
5 possible Stone Men from Saturn prototypes in the story "The Things on Easter Island", part Williamson art	$52.50	$155.00	$425.00	£36.00	£105.00	£285.00
6 lead story called "I Saw the Invasion of the Stone Men" but their appearance does not suggest prototypes for The Stone Men from Saturn	$44.00	$130.00	$350.00	£29.00	£87.50	£235.00
7 possible Toad Men prototypes in the story "We Met In The Swamp", pre-figuring Hulk #2	$44.00	$130.00	$350.00	£29.00	£87.50	£235.00
8-9	$39.00	$115.00	$310.00	£26.00	£75.00	£205.00
1st official distribution in the U.K.						
10	$39.00	$115.00	$310.00	£26.00	£75.00	£205.00
11-14 ND scarce in the U.K.	$31.00	$92.50	$250.00	£21.50	£65.00	£175.00
15 Electro prototype?? More like a prototype for the Hulk villain/monster Zzzax (see Tales of Suspense #13 for a monster called "Elektro")	$31.00	$92.50	$250.00	£20.50	£60.00	£165.00
16 lead story "Thorr the Unbelievable" has characters that pre-figure The Stone Men from Saturn who appeared in Thor's first adventure in Journey into Mystery #83. Also Mole Men prototypes pre-figuring their appearance in Fantastic Four #1	$34.00	$100.00	$275.00	£23.00	£67.50	£185.00
17-20	$31.00	$92.50	$250.00	£20.50	£60.00	£165.00
21-26	$21.50	$65.00	$175.00	£14.00	£43.00	£115.00
27 very scarce in the U.K. (Jan 1962), origin and 1st appearance of Ant-Man (in fantasy/horror story; no costume); last 10 cents issue. It is traditionally the hardest key Marvel to find in high grade	$350.00	$1050.00	$3500.00	£250.00	£750.00	£2500.00
[Prices may vary widely on this comic] **[Very rare in high grade - Very Fine+ or better]**						
28 possible Stone Men from Saturn prototypes appear in the story "Back From The Dead" and refer to themselves as "stone men"	$20.50	$60.00	$165.00	£13.00	£39.00	£105.00
29-30	$20.50	$60.00	$165.00	£13.00	£39.00	£105.00
31-34	$18.50	$55.00	$150.00	£12.50	£38.00	£100.00
35 1st costumed Ant-Man, series begins	$160.00	$480.00	$1600.00	£100.00	£300.00	£1000.00
36 2nd costumed Ant-Man	$75.00	$225.00	$600.00	£47.00	£140.00	£375.00
37	$50.00	$150.00	$350.00	£26.00	£77.50	£185.00
38 less common in the U.K. 1st appearance Egghead	$50.00	$150.00	$360.00	£29.00	£85.00	£200.00
39 less common in the U.K. (Jan 1963)	$50.00	$150.00	$350.00	£27.00	£80.00	£190.00
40	$50.00	$150.00	$350.00	£26.00	£77.50	£185.00
41-43	$30.00	$90.00	$210.00	£17.50	£52.50	£125.00
44 originand 1st appearance of The Wasp	$34.00	$100.00	$240.00	£20.50	£60.00	£145.00
45-48	$19.00	$57.50	$135.00	£11.00	£34.00	£80.00
49 Ant-Man becomes Giant-Man	$23.50	$70.00	$165.00	£14.00	£43.00	£100.00
50 1st origin and appearance Human Top	$14.00	$43.00	$100.00	£7.75	£23.50	£55.00
51 (Jan 1964), Giant Man vs. Human Top	$14.00	$43.00	$100.00	£7.00	£21.00	£50.00
52 origin and 1st appearance Black Knight	$14.00	$43.00	$100.00	£7.75	£23.50	£55.00
53-54	$14.00	$43.00	$100.00	£7.00	£21.00	£50.00
55 less common in the U.K.	$14.00	$43.00	$100.00	£7.50	£22.50	£52.50
56	$14.00	$43.00	$100.00	£6.25	£19.00	£45.00
57 scarce in the U.K. Spiderman appears (early X-over)	$17.50	$52.50	$140.00	£10.00	£30.00	£80.00
58	$14.00	$43.00	$100.00	£6.25	£19.00	£45.00
59 Giant Man vs. Hulk, Avengers cameo; 1st appearance of Hulk in this title	$21.00	$62.50	$150.00	£12.00	£36.00	£85.00
60 Hulk series begins, Giant-Man series continues	$25.00	$75.00	$175.00	£14.00	£43.00	£100.00
61 scarce in the U.K. Steve Ditko cover and art	$9.25	$28.00	$65.00	£6.25	£19.00	£45.00
62 rare in the U.K. 1st appearance The Leader (cameo)	$10.00	$30.00	$70.00	£7.00	£21.00	£50.00
63 (Jan 1965), 1st full appearance The Leader (see Incredible Hulk #400)	$9.25	$28.00	$65.00	£6.00	£18.00	£42.50
64	$9.25	$28.00	$65.00	£5.50	£17.00	£40.00
65 1st new Giant Man (new costume)	$9.25	$28.00	$65.00	£6.00	£18.00	£42.50
66	$9.25	$28.00	$65.00	£5.00	£15.00	£35.00
67 one of those great Marvel story titles: "Where Strides The Behemoth"	$9.25	$28.00	$65.00	£5.00	£15.00	£35.00
68	$9.25	$28.00	$65.00	£5.00	£15.00	£35.00
69 last of Giant-Man series	$9.25	$28.00	$65.00	£5.00	£15.00	£35.00
70 Sub-Mariner series begins	$12.50	$39.00	$90.00	£6.25	£19.00	£45.00
71-73	$7.75	$23.50	$55.00	£3.55	£10.50	£25.00
74 last Silver Age issue cover dated December 1965	$7.75	$23.50	$55.00	£3.55	£10.50	£25.00
75 (Jan 1966)	$7.75	$23.50	$55.00	£3.20	£9.50	£22.50
76-78	$7.75	$23.50	$55.00	£3.20	£9.50	£22.50
79 Hulk vs Hercules (1st Hulk/Hercules battle)	$7.75	$23.50	$55.00	£3.55	£10.50	£25.00
80	$7.75	$23.50	$55.00	£3.20	£9.50	£22.50
81	$7.00	$21.00	$50.00	£2.85	£8.50	£20.00
82 Sub-Mariner battles Iron Man, X-over with Tales of Suspense #79/80	$9.25	$28.00	$65.00	£3.55	£10.50	£25.00
83-84	$7.00	$21.00	$50.00	£2.85	£8.50	£20.00
85-86 scarce in the U.K.	$7.00	$21.00	$50.00	£3.20	£9.50	£22.50
87 (Jan 1967)	$7.00	$21.00	$50.00	£2.85	£8.50	£20.00
88-89	$7.00	$21.00	$50.00	£2.85	£8.50	£20.00
90 1st appearance The Abomination	$8.50	$26.00	$60.00	£3.55	£10.50	£25.00
91	$7.00	$21.00	$50.00	£2.50	£7.50	£17.50
92 4th appearance Silver Surfer, cameo only (pre-dates Silver Surfer #1)	$9.25	$28.00	$65.00	£3.55	£10.50	£25.00
93 5th appearance Silver Surfer (pre-dates Silver Surfer #1), battles Hulk	$10.00	$30.00	$70.00	£4.25	£12.50	£30.00
94-96 High Evolutionary appears	$7.00	$21.00	$50.00	£2.50	£7.50	£17.50
97-98 scarce in the U.K.	$7.00	$21.00	$50.00	£2.85	£8.50	£20.00
99 scarce in the U.K. (Jan 1968)	$7.00	$21.00	$50.00	£2.85	£8.50	£20.00
100 scarce in the U.K. Hulk vs. Sub-Mariner	$9.25	$28.00	$65.00	£3.55	£10.50	£25.00
101 scarce in the U.K. lead into Hulk #102 and Iron Man/Sub-Mariner #1	$11.00	$33.00	$77.50	£4.60	£13.50	£32.50
Title Value:	$2700.25	$8097.50	$22022.50	£1666.85	£4996.00	£13792.50

Note: Kirby art in 10-40, 44, 49-51, 68-70, 82, 83. Everett art in 78-84, 87-91, 94-96.

ARTISTS

Ditko art in 10-48, 60-67; inks in 50. Kirby art in 10-40, 44, 49-51, 68-70, 82, 83.

FEATURES

Ant-Man in 27, 35-48. Giant-Man in 49-69. Hulk in 60-101. Sub-Mariner in 70-101. Hulk vs Sub-Mariner in 100. Monster/fantasy stories in 10-59 (as back-ups in 35-59).

TALES TO ASTONISH (2ND SERIES)

Marvel Comics Group; 1 Dec 1979-14 Jan 1981

Issue	$Good	$Fine	$N.Mint	£Good	£Fine	£N.Mint
1 ND reprints Sub-Mariner #1 etc.	$0.40	$1.25	$2.50	£0.25	£0.75	£1.50
2-3 ND	$0.40	$1.20	$2.00	£0.25	£0.75	£1.25
4-14	$0.30	$0.90	$1.50	£0.20	£0.60	£1.00
Title Value:	$4.50	$13.55	$23.00	£2.95	£8.85	£15.00

TALES TO ASTONISH (3RD SERIES)

Marvel Comics Group,OS; 1 Dec 1994

Issue	$Good	$Fine	$N.Mint	£Good	£Fine	£N.Mint
1 ND 64pgs, squarebound. Peter David script, John Estes art. The Hulk, Hank Pym and The Wasp appear; painted cover with protective acetate outer cover	$1.40	$4.20	$7.00	£0.90	£2.70	£4.50

	$Good	$Fine	$N.Mint	£Good	£Fine	£N.Mint
Title Value:	*$1.40*	*$4.20*	*$7.00*	£0.90	£2.70	£4.50

TALES TOO TERRIBLE TO TELL

New England Comics; 1 Winter 1989-11 1993; 13 May 1996-present ?

	$Good	$Fine	$N.Mint	£Good	£Fine	£N.Mint
1 pre-Code horror reprints	*$0.80*	*$2.40*	*$4.00*	£0.50	£1.50	£2.50
1 2nd printing, Jun 1993	*$0.60*	*$1.80*	*$3.00*	£0.40	£1.20	£2.00
2 pre-Code horror reprints	*$0.60*	*$1.80*	*$3.00*	£0.40	£1.20	£2.00
3 pre-Code horror reprints, Bissette cover	*$0.60*	*$1.80*	*$3.00*	£0.40	£1.20	£2.00
4-8 pre Code horror reprints	*$0.60*	*$1.80*	*$3.00*	£0.40	£1.20	£2.00
9 pre Code horror reprints, $3.95 cover	*$0.80*	*$2.40*	*$4.00*	£0.50	£1.50	£2.50
10-11 pre Code horror reprints	*$0.60*	*$1.80*	*$3.00*	£0.40	£1.20	£2.00
13 ND 104pgs	*$0.90*	*$2.70*	*$4.50*	£0.60	£1.80	£3.00
Title Value:	*$8.50*	*$25.50*	*$42.50*	£5.60	£16.80	£28.00

Note: reprints of 1950s horror stories plus articles, cover gallery and new material. Quarterly frequency. Non-Distributed in the U.K.

Note also: issues #12 and #13 were advertised and issue #12 was solicited but neither of these issues came out. Issue #12 was then missed out when New England re-launched the title with issue #13.

TALESPIN

Disney,MS; 1 Dec 1990-4 Mar 1991

	$Good	$Fine	$N.Mint	£Good	£Fine	£N.Mint
1-4 ND	*$0.30*	*$0.90*	*$1.50*	£0.20	£0.60	£1.00
Title Value:	*$1.20*	*$3.60*	*$6.00*	£0.80	£2.40	£4.00

TALESPIN (2ND SERIES)

Disney; 1 May 1991-9 Jan 1992

	$Good	$Fine	$N.Mint	£Good	£Fine	£N.Mint
1-9 ND	*$0.30*	*$0.90*	*$1.50*	£0.20	£0.60	£1.00
Title Value:	*$2.70*	*$8.10*	*$13.50*	£1.80	£5.40	£9.00

TALOS OF THE WILDERNESS SEA

DC Comics,OS; 1 Jun 1987

	$Good	$Fine	$N.Mint	£Good	£Fine	£N.Mint
1 48pgs, Gil Kane art, no adverts	*$0.30*	*$0.90*	*$1.50*	£0.20	£0.60	£1.00
Title Value:	*$0.30*	*$0.90*	*$1.50*	£0.20	£0.60	£1.00

TANK GIRL

Dark Horse,MS; 1 Jul 1991-4 Oct 1991

	$Good	$Fine	$N.Mint	£Good	£Fine	£N.Mint
1 ND reprints from U.K.'s Deadline magazine, Jamie Hewlett art	*$0.60*	*$1.80*	*$3.00*	£0.40	£1.20	£2.00
2-4 ND reprints from U.K.'s Deadline magazine, Jamie Hewlett art	*$0.50*	*$1.50*	*$2.50*	£0.30	£0.90	£1.50
Title Value:	*$2.10*	*$6.30*	*$10.50*	£1.30	£3.90	£6.50
Tank Girl Volume One (1994) Trade paperback reprints mini-series, painted cover by Jamie Hewlett				£2.00	£6.00	£10.00

TANK GIRL II

Dark Horse,MS; 1 Jun 1993-4 Sep 1993

	$Good	$Fine	$N.Mint	£Good	£Fine	£N.Mint
1-4 ND Alan Martin and Jamie Hewlett	*$0.50*	*$1.50*	*$2.50*	£0.30	£0.90	£1.50
Title Value:	*$2.00*	*$6.00*	*$10.00*	£1.20	£3.60	£6.00
Tank Girl II (Jan 1995) Trade paperback reprints mini-series, Jamie Hewlett painted cover				£2.40	£7.20	£12.00

TANK GIRL MOVIE ADAPTATION

DC Comics,OS; 1 May 1995

	$Good	$Fine	$N.Mint	£Good	£Fine	£N.Mint
1 ND 64pgs, Peter Milligan and Andy Pritchett adaptation of film, John Bolton cover	*$1.00*	*$3.00*	*$5.00*	£0.70	£2.10	£3.50
Title Value:	*$1.00*	*$3.00*	*$5.00*	£0.70	£2.10	£3.50

TANK GIRL: APOCALYPSE

DC Comics,MS; 1 Nov 1995-4 Feb 1996

	$Good	$Fine	$N.Mint	£Good	£Fine	£N.Mint
1-4 ND Alan Grant script, Brian Bolland covers	*$0.50*	*$1.50*	*$2.50*	£0.30	£0.90	£1.50
Title Value:	*$2.00*	*$6.00*	*$10.00*	£1.20	£3.60	£6.00

TANK GIRL: THE ODYSSEY

DC Comics/Vertigo,MS; 1 Jun 1995-4 Sep 1995

	$Good	$Fine	$N.Mint	£Good	£Fine	£N.Mint
1-4 ND Peter Milligan script, Jamie Hewlett art; painted cover by Brian Bolland	*$0.50*	*$1.50*	*$2.50*	£0.30	£0.90	£1.50
Title Value:	*$2.00*	*$6.00*	*$10.00*	£1.20	£3.60	£6.00

TAPPING THE VEIN

(see Clive Barker's Tapping The Vein)

TARGET: AIRBOY

Eclipse; 1 Mar 1988

	$Good	$Fine	$N.Mint	£Good	£Fine	£N.Mint
1 ND Sam Kieth cover and art, Clint of the Radioactive Hamsters appears, card covers; continuity ties in these events before Airboy #37	*$0.80*	*$2.40*	*$4.00*	£0.50	£1.50	£2.50
Title Value:	*$0.80*	*$2.40*	*$4.00*	£0.50	£1.50	£2.50

TARGITT

Atlas; 1 Mar 1975-2 Jul 1975

	$Good	$Fine	$N.Mint	£Good	£Fine	£N.Mint
1-3 distributed in the U.K. "John Targitt, Man-Stalker" on cover	*$0.30*	*$0.90*	*$1.50*	£0.20	£0.60	£1.00
Title Value:	*$0.90*	*$2.70*	*$4.50*	£0.60	£1.80	£3.00

TARZAN

DC Comics; 207 Apr 1972-258 Feb 1977

(see Limited Collector's Edition, One Hundred Page Super Spectacular) (previously published by Gold Key)

	$Good	$Fine	$N.Mint	£Good	£Fine	£N.Mint
207 52pgs, origin begins	*$2.50*	*$7.50*	*$15.00*	£1.25	£3.75	£7.50
208-209 52pgs, origin	*$1.65*	*$5.00*	*$10.00*	£0.80	£2.50	£5.00
210 ND origin ends	*$1.65*	*$5.00*	*$10.00*	£0.75	£2.25	£4.50
211-215 ND	*$1.65*	*$5.00*	*$10.00*	£0.75	£2.25	£4.50
216 ND Chaykin back-up	*$1.65*	*$5.00*	*$10.00*	£0.75	£2.25	£4.50
217-220 ND	*$1.65*	*$5.00*	*$10.00*	£0.75	£2.25	£4.50
221-229 ND	*$1.50*	*$4.50*	*$9.00*	£0.65	£2.00	£4.00
230 ND 100pgs, Kaluta art	*$1.65*	*$5.00*	*$10.00*	£0.75	£2.25	£4.50
231-234 ND 100pgs, Nino art	*$1.50*	*$4.50*	*$9.00*	£0.65	£2.00	£4.00
235-237 very LD 100pgs	*$1.50*	*$4.50*	*$9.00*	£0.65	£2.00	£4.00
238 ND 68pgs	*$1.65*	*$5.00*	*$10.00*	£0.75	£2.25	£4.50
239-240 ND	*$1.50*	*$4.50*	*$9.00*	£0.65	£2.00	£4.00
241-258 ND	*$1.30*	*$4.00*	*$8.00*	£0.55	£1.75	£3.50
Title Value:	*$77.65*	*$235.50*	*$471.00*	£34.20	£105.50	£211.00

FEATURES

Beyond the Furthest Star in 213-218. Carson of Venus in 230. John Carter in 207-209. Korak in 230-234. Tarzan in 207-225, 227-236, 239-256.

REPRINT FEATURES

Congo Bill in 230-235. Detective Chimp in 230-235. Rex the Wonder Dog in 232, 233. Tarzan by Hal Foster in 207-209, 211, 215, 221. Tarzan by Hogarth in 211. Tarzan by Manning in 226, 230-235, 237, 238. Tarzan in 252, 253, 257, 258. Simba (Bomba re-titled) in 230, 231.

TARZAN

Dell/Gold Key; 1 Feb 1948-131 Aug 1962; Gold Key; 132 Nov 1962-206 Feb 1972

(transfers to DC Comics #207 on)

	$Good	$Fine	$N.Mint	£Good	£Fine	£N.Mint
1 Jesse Marsh art begins	*$115.00*	*$345.00*	*$925.00*	£77.50	£230.00	£620.00
2-5	*$52.50*	*$160.00*	*$375.00*	£36.00	£105.00	£250.00
6-10	*$43.00*	*$125.00*	*$300.00*	£29.00	£85.00	£200.00
11-12	*$37.00*	*$110.00*	*$260.00*	£25.00	£75.00	£175.00
13 1st photo cover (Lex Barker)	*$37.00*	*$110.00*	*$260.00*	£25.00	£75.00	£175.00
14-15	*$37.00*	*$110.00*	*$260.00*	£25.00	£75.00	£175.00
16-20	*$28.00*	*$82.50*	*$195.00*	£18.50	£55.00	£130.00
21-24	*$21.00*	*$62.50*	*$150.00*	£14.00	£43.00	£100.00
25 1st appearance Brothers of the Spear (see their own title)	*$25.00*	*$75.00*	*$175.00*	£16.00	£49.00	£115.00
26-30	*$21.00*	*$62.50*	*$150.00*	£14.00	£43.00	£100.00
31-38	*$15.00*	*$45.00*	*$105.00*	£10.00	£30.00	£70.00
39 1st Russ Manning art on Brothers of the Spear	*$15.00*	*$45.00*	*$105.00*	£10.00	£30.00	£70.00
40	*$15.00*	*$45.00*	*$105.00*	£10.00	£30.00	£70.00
41-50	*$10.50*	*$32.00*	*$75.00*	£7.00	£21.00	£50.00
51-53	*$7.75*	*$23.50*	*$55.00*	£5.25	£15.50	£37.00
54 last Lex Barker photo cover	*$7.75*	*$23.50*	*$55.00*	£5.25	£15.50	£37.00
55 painted covers restart	*$7.75*	*$23.50*	*$55.00*	£5.25	£15.50	£37.00
56-60	*$7.75*	*$23.50*	*$55.00*	£5.25	£15.50	£37.00
61-70	*$5.50*	*$17.00*	*$40.00*	£3.85	£11.50	£27.00
71-78	*$3.90*	*$11.50*	*$27.50*	£2.50	£7.50	£17.50
79 last painted cover	*$3.90*	*$11.50*	*$27.50*	£2.50	£7.50	£17.50
80 Gordon Scott photo covers begin	*$4.25*	*$12.50*	*$30.00*	£2.85	£8.50	£20.00
81-90	*$4.25*	*$12.50*	*$30.00*	£2.85	£8.50	£20.00
91-99	*$3.90*	*$11.50*	*$27.50*	£2.50	£7.50	£17.50
100	*$5.00*	*$15.00*	*$35.00*	£3.20	£9.50	£22.50
101-109	*$3.20*	*$9.50*	*$22.50*	£2.10	£6.25	£15.00
110 scarce in both US and UK last photo cover	*$4.25*	*$12.50*	*$30.00*	£2.85	£8.50	£20.00
111 painted covers restart	*$2.85*	*$8.50*	*$20.00*	£2.00	£6.00	£14.00
112-114	*$2.85*	*$8.50*	*$20.00*	£2.00	£6.00	£14.00
1st official distribution in the U.K.						
115-120	*$2.85*	*$8.50*	*$20.00*	£2.00	£6.00	£14.00
121-130	*$2.10*	*$6.25*	*$15.00*	£1.40	£4.25	£10.00
131 last Dell issue	*$2.10*	*$6.25*	*$15.00*	£1.40	£4.25	£10.00
132 1st Gold Key issue	*$3.20*	*$9.50*	*$22.50*	£2.10	£6.25	£15.00
133-137	*$2.50*	*$7.50*	*$17.50*	£1.75	£5.25	£12.50
138 title becomes "Tarzan of the Apes"	*$2.50*	*$7.50*	*$17.50*	£1.75	£5.25	£12.50
139 1st appearance Korak	*$3.55*	*$10.50*	*$25.00*	£2.10	£6.25	£15.00
140	*$2.50*	*$7.50*	*$17.50*	£1.75	£5.25	£12.50
141-150	*$2.10*	*$6.25*	*$15.00*	£1.40	£4.25	£10.00
151-154	*$2.50*	*$7.50*	*$15.00*	£1.30	£4.00	£8.00
155 origin	*$4.15*	*$12.50*	*$25.00*	£2.50	£7.50	£15.00
156-160	*$2.50*	*$7.50*	*$15.00*	£1.30	£4.00	£8.00
161-177	*$2.05*	*$6.25*	*$12.50*	£1.15	£3.50	£7.00
178 origin, reprints #155	*$2.40*	*$7.00*	*$12.00*	£1.60	£4.80	£8.00
179-180	*$2.00*	*$6.00*	*$10.00*	£1.40	£4.20	£7.00
181-199	*$1.65*	*$5.00*	*$10.00*	£0.80	£2.50	£5.00
200 scarce in both US and UK	*$2.50*	*$7.50*	*$15.00*	£1.30	£4.00	£8.00
201-205	*$1.65*	*$5.00*	*$10.00*	£0.80	£2.50	£5.00
206 numbering continued in DC title	*$1.65*	*$5.00*	*$10.00*	£0.80	£2.50	£5.00
Title Value:	*$1830.00*	*$5469.00*	*$12904.50*	£1213.60	£3624.95	£8541.00

Note: issues from about 1958 distributed on the news-stands in the U.K. and then officially distributed from cover-date November 1959

TARZAN

Marvel Comics Group; 1 Jun 1977-29 Oct 1979

	$Good	$Fine	$N.Mint	£Good	£Fine	£N.Mint
1 ND John Buscema art begins (ends #18)	$0.65	$2.00	$4.00	£0.40	£1.25	£2.50
2-5 ND	$0.55	$1.75	$3.50	£0.30	£1.00	£2.00
6-18 ND	$0.50	$1.50	$3.00	£0.25	£0.75	£1.50
19 ND Sal Buscema art begins (to #29)	$0.50	$1.50	$3.00	£0.25	£0.75	£1.50
20 ND	$0.50	$1.50	$3.00	£0.25	£0.75	£1.50
21-29 ND	$0.40	$1.25	$2.50	£0.20	£0.60	£1.25
Title Value:	$13.95	$42.75	$85.50	£7.15	£21.90	£44.25

TARZAN ANNUAL

Marvel Comics Group; 1 1977-3 1979

	$Good	$Fine	$N.Mint	£Good	£Fine	£N.Mint
1 ND 52pgs	$0.50	$1.50	$3.00	£0.30	£1.00	£2.00
2-3 ND 52pgs	$0.40	$1.25	$2.50	£0.25	£0.75	£1.50
Title Value:	$1.30	$4.00	$8.00	£0.80	£2.50	£5.00

TARZAN DIGEST

DC Comics,Digest; 1 Autumn 1972

	$Good	$Fine	$N.Mint	£Good	£Fine	£N.Mint
1 ND 160pgs, reprints	$1.25	$3.75	$7.50	£0.80	£2.50	£5.00
Title Value:	$1.25	$3.75	$7.50	£0.80	£2.50	£5.00

TARZAN FAMILY

DC Comics; 60 Nov/Dec 1975-66 Nov/Dec 1976

(previously Korak, Son of Tarzan)

	$Good	$Fine	$N.Mint	£Good	£Fine	£N.Mint
60-62 ND 68pgs	$0.55	$1.75	$3.50	£0.30	£1.00	£2.00
63-66 ND 52pgs	$0.50	$1.50	$3.00	£0.25	£0.75	£1.50
Title Value:	$3.65	$11.25	$22.50	£1.90	£6.00	£12.00

ARTISTS

Kaluta reprints in 60-65.

FEATURES

Korak in 60-66. John Carter in 62-64. Pellucidar in 66.

REPRINT FEATURES

Carson of Venus in 60-65. John Carter in 65, 66. Tarzan in 60-64.

TARZAN OF THE APES

Marvel Comics Group,MS; 1 Jul 1984-2 Aug 1984

	$Good	$Fine	$N.Mint	£Good	£Fine	£N.Mint
1-2 ND reprints Marvel Super Special #29	$0.30	$0.90	$1.50	£0.20	£0.60	£1.00
Title Value:	$0.60	$1.80	$3.00	£0.40	£1.20	£2.00

TARZAN THE WARRIOR

Malibu,MS; 1 Apr 1992-5 Aug 1992

	$Good	$Fine	$N.Mint	£Good	£Fine	£N.Mint
1 ND Simon Bisley cover	$0.50	$1.50	$2.50	£0.30	£0.90	£1.50
1 2nd printing, ND (Nov 1992)	$0.40	$1.20	$2.00	£0.25	£0.75	£1.25
2-5 ND	$0.50	$1.50	$2.50	£0.30	£0.90	£1.50
Title Value:	$2.90	$8.70	$14.50	£1.75	£5.25	£8.75

TARZAN VS. PREDATOR: AT EARTH'S CORE

Dark Horse,MS; 1 Jan 1996-4 Apr 1995

	$Good	$Fine	$N.Mint	£Good	£Fine	£N.Mint
1-4 ND Walt Simonson script, Lee Weeks art	$0.50	$1.50	$2.50	£0.30	£0.90	£1.50
Title Value:	$2.00	$6.00	$10.00	£1.20	£3.60	£6.00

TARZAN, EDGAR RICE BURROUGH'S

Dark Horse; 1 Jun 1996-6 Nov 1996

	$Good	$Fine	$N.Mint	£Good	£Fine	£N.Mint
1-6 ND Bruce Jones script, Chris Schenck and Tom Yeates art	$0.60	$1.80	$3.00	£0.40	£1.20	£2.00
Title Value:	$3.60	$10.80	$18.00	£2.40	£7.20	£12.00

TARZAN, LORD OF THE JUNGLE

Gold Key; 1 Sep 1965

	$Good	$Fine	$N.Mint	£Good	£Fine	£N.Mint
1 rare in the U.K. giant size reprint	$10.50	$32.00	$75.00	£6.25	£19.00	£45.00
Title Value:	$10.50	$32.00	$75.00	£6.25	£19.00	£45.00

TARZAN/JOHN CARTER: WARLORDS OF MARS

Dark Horse,MS; 1 Dec 1995-4 Mar 1996

	$Good	$Fine	$N.Mint	£Good	£Fine	£N.Mint
1-4 ND Bruce Jones script, Bret Blevins art	$0.50	$1.50	$2.50	£0.30	£0.90	£1.50
Title Value:	$2.00	$6.00	$10.00	£1.20	£3.60	£6.00

TARZAN: LOVE, LIES AND THE LOST CITY

Malibu,MS; 1 Aug 1992-3 Dec 1992

	$Good	$Fine	$N.Mint	£Good	£Fine	£N.Mint
1-3 ND	$0.50	$1.50	$2.50	£0.30	£0.90	£1.50
Title Value:	$1.50	$4.50	$7.50	£0.90	£2.70	£4.50

TARZAN: MUGAMBI, EDGAR RICE BURROUGHS'

Dark Horse,OS; 1 May 1995

	$Good	$Fine	$N.Mint	£Good	£Fine	£N.Mint
1 ND Darko Macan script, Igor Kordej art	$0.60	$1.80	$3.00	£0.40	£1.20	£2.00
Title Value:	$0.60	$1.80	$3.00	£0.40	£1.20	£2.00

TARZAN: THE BECKONING

Malibu,MS; 1 Nov 1992-7 May 1993

	$Good	$Fine	$N.Mint	£Good	£Fine	£N.Mint
1-7 ND Tom Yeates art	$0.50	$1.50	$2.50	£0.30	£0.90	£1.50
Title Value:	$3.50	$10.50	$17.50	£2.10	£6.30	£10.50

TARZAN: THE LAND THAT TIME FORGOT

Dark Horse,OS; nn May 1996

	$Good	$Fine	$N.Mint	£Good	£Fine	£N.Mint
nn ND Trade paperback collection featuring a story by Russ Manning and re-coloured	$2.60	$7.75	$13.00	£1.70	£5.00	£8.50
Title Value:	$2.60	$7.75	$13.00	£1.70	£5.00	£8.50

TARZAN: THE LOST ADVENTURE, EDGAR RICE BURROUGHS'

Dark Horse,MS; 1 Jan 1995-4 Apr 1995

	$Good	$Fine	$N.Mint	£Good	£Fine	£N.Mint
1 ND 64pgs, Joe R. Lansdale script. Tom Yeates art	$0.60	$1.80	$3.00	£0.40	£1.20	£2.00
2 ND 64pgs, Joe R. Lansdale script. Charles Vess art	$0.60	$1.80	$3.00	£0.40	£1.20	£2.00
3 ND 64pgs, Joe R. Lansdale script. Gary Gianni art	$0.60	$1.80	$3.00	£0.40	£1.20	£2.00
4 ND 64pgs, Joe R. Lansdale script. Mike Kaluta art	$0.60	$1.80	$3.00	£0.40	£1.20	£2.00
Title Value:	$2.40	$7.20	$12.00	£1.60	£4.80	£8.00

Note: unusual 6.5" x 9.5" pulp magazine size format. Painted covers by Arthur Suydam

Tarzan: The Lost Adventure Hardcover (Mar 1996)

	$Good	$Fine	$N.Mint	£Good	£Fine	£N.Mint
ND 208pgs, with bookplate and dust-jacket				£2.70	£8.10	£13.50

TASK FORCE ALPHA: FORGED IN FIRE

Alpha Productions,MS; 1 Jan 1995-2 Feb 1995

	$Good	$Fine	$N.Mint	£Good	£Fine	£N.Mint
1-2 ND 48pgs, Paul Pelletier flip-covers	$0.40	$1.20	$2.00	£0.25	£0.75	£1.25
Title Value:	$0.80	$2.40	$4.00	£0.50	£1.50	£2.50

TATTOO

Caliber Press; 1 Dec 1995-3 1996 ?

	$Good	$Fine	$N.Mint	£Good	£Fine	£N.Mint
1-3 ND black and white	$0.60	$1.80	$3.00	£0.40	£1.20	£2.00
Title Value:	$1.80	$5.40	$9.00	£1.20	£3.60	£6.00

TEAM 1: STORMWATCH 1

Image,MS; 1 Jul 1995-2 Aug 1995

	$Good	$Fine	$N.Mint	£Good	£Fine	£N.Mint
1-2 ND Steven Seagle script, Tom Raney art	$0.50	$1.50	$2.50	£0.30	£0.90	£1.50
Title Value:	$1.00	$3.00	$5.00	£0.60	£1.80	£3.00

TEAM 1: WILDC.A.T.S. 1

Image,MS; 1 Jul 1995-2 Aug 1995

	$Good	$Fine	$N.Mint	£Good	£Fine	£N.Mint
1-2 ND James Robinson script, Rich Johnson art	$0.50	$1.50	$2.50	£0.30	£0.90	£1.50
Title Value:	$1.00	$3.00	$5.00	£0.60	£1.80	£3.00

TEAM 7

Image,MS; 1 Oct 1994-4 Jan 1995

	$Good	$Fine	$N.Mint	£Good	£Fine	£N.Mint
1 ND Grifter, Backlash, Deathblow, Lynch and Dane	$1.00	$3.00	$5.00	£0.70	£2.10	£3.50
1 Variant Cover Edition, ND cover forms larger picture when combined with variant covers of Deathblow #5, Gen 13 #5, Kindred #3, Stormwatch #10, Wetworks #2, WildC.A.T.S. #11	$1.50	$4.50	$7.50	£1.00	£3.00	£5.00
2-4 ND Grifter, Backlash, Deathblow, Lynch and Dane	$0.60	$1.80	$3.00	£0.40	£1.20	£2.00
Title Value:	$4.30	$12.90	$21.50	£2.90	£8.70	£14.50

Team 7 (Jun 1995)

	$Good	$Fine	$N.Mint	£Good	£Fine	£N.Mint
Trade paperback collects mini-series				£1.30	£3.90	£6.50

TEAM 7 - OBJECTIVE HELL

Image,MS; 1 May 1995-3 Jul 1995

	$Good	$Fine	$N.Mint	£Good	£Fine	£N.Mint
1 ND Wildstorm Rising Prologue, continued in Wildstorm Rising #1; with two foil-bagged painted trading cards. Cover by Barry Windsor-Smith	$0.50	$1.50	$2.50	£0.30	£0.90	£1.50
1 Newstand Edition, ND without trading cards	$0.40	$1.20	$2.00	£0.25	£0.75	£1.25
2-3 ND	$0.50	$1.50	$2.50	£0.30	£0.90	£1.50
Title Value:	$1.90	$5.70	$9.50	£1.15	£3.45	£5.75

TEAM 7: DEAD RECKONING

Image,MS; 1 Jan 1996-4 Apr 1996

	$Good	$Fine	$N.Mint	£Good	£Fine	£N.Mint
1-4 ND Chuck Dixon script	$0.50	$1.50	$2.50	£0.30	£0.90	£1.50
Title Value:	$2.00	$6.00	$10.00	£1.20	£3.60	£6.00

TEAM AMERICA

Marvel Comics Group, Toy; 1 Jun 1982-12 May 1983

(see Captain America #269)

	$Good	$Fine	$N.Mint	£Good	£Fine	£N.Mint
1 ND origin	$0.15	$0.45	$0.75	£0.10	£0.30	£0.50
2-8 ND	$0.15	$0.45	$0.75	£0.10	£0.30	£0.50
9 ND Iron Man appears	$0.15	$0.45	$0.75	£0.10	£0.30	£0.50
10 ND	$0.15	$0.45	$0.75	£0.10	£0.30	£0.50
11 ND Team America vs. Ghost Rider	$0.30	$0.90	$1.50	£0.10	£0.30	£0.50
12 ND	$0.15	$0.45	$0.75	£0.10	£0.30	£0.50
Title Value:	$1.95	$5.85	$9.75	£1.20	£3.60	£6.00

TEAM ANARCHY

Dagger Enterprises; 1 Oct 1993-12 Sep 1994

	$Good	$Fine	$N.Mint	£Good	£Fine	£N.Mint
1-12 ND Rick Buckler Jnr. art	$0.40	$1.20	$2.00	£0.25	£0.75	£1.25
Title Value:	$4.80	$14.40	$24.00	£3.00	£9.00	£15.00

TEAM HELIX

Marvel UK,MS; 1 Jan 1993-4 Apr 1993

	$Good	$Fine	$N.Mint	£Good	£Fine	£N.Mint
1-2 Wolverine appears	$0.30	$0.90	$1.50	£0.15	£0.45	£0.75
3-4 Wolverine and Ka-Zar appear; re-titled "Codename: Genetix"	$0.30	$0.90	$1.50	£0.15	£0.45	£0.75
Title Value:	$1.20	$3.60	$6.00	£0.60	£1.80	£3.00

TEAM TITANS

DC Comics; 1 Sep 1992-24 Sep 1994

	$Good	$Fine	$N.Mint	£Good	£Fine	£N.Mint
1 Killowat Cover:, 48pgs, Total Chaos part 3, Killowat origin plus bonus 21pg story	$0.40	$1.20	$2.00	£0.25	£0.75	£1.25
1 Mirage Cover:, 48pgs, Total Chaos part 3, Mirage origin plus bonus 21pg story	$0.40	$1.20	$2.00	£0.25	£0.75	£1.25
1 Nightrider Cover:, 48pgs, Total Chaos part 3, Nightrider origin plus bonus 21pg story	$0.40	$1.20	$2.00	£0.25	£0.75	£1.25
1 Redwing Cover:, 48pgs, Total Chaos part 3, Redwing origin plus bonus 21pg story	$0.40	$1.20	$2.00	£0.25	£0.75	£1.25
1 Terra Cover:, 48pgs, Total Chaos part 3, Terra origin plus bonus 21pg story	$0.40	$1.20	$2.00	£0.25	£0.75	£1.25
2 Total Chaos part 6, continued in Deathstroke the Terminator #16	$0.40	$1.20	$2.00	£0.25	£0.75	£1.25
3 Total Chaos part 9 (conclusion)	$0.40	$1.20	$2.00	£0.25	£0.75	£1.25
4 Titans Sell-Out part 4 (conclusion)						

	$Good	$Fine	$N.Mint	£Good	£Fine	£N.Mint
	$0.40	$1.20	$2.00	£0.25	£0.75	£1.25
5	$0.40	$1.20	$2.00	£0.25	£0.75	£1.25
6 Christmas issue	$0.30	$0.90	$1.50	£0.20	£0.60	£1.00
7-9	$0.30	$0.90	$1.50	£0.20	£0.60	£1.00
10 The Darkening part 4 (conclusion), continued from New Titans #100	$0.30	$0.90	$1.50	£0.20	£0.60	£1.00
11-19	$0.30	$0.90	$1.50	£0.20	£0.60	£1.00
20-23 prelude to Zero Hour	$0.30	$0.90	$1.50	£0.20	£0.60	£1.00
24 Zero Hour X-over	$0.30	$0.90	$1.50	£0.20	£0.60	£1.00
Title Value:	$9.30	$27.90	$46.50	£6.05	£18.15	£30.25

TEAM TITANS ANNUAL

DC Comics; 1 Nov 1993-2 1994

	$Good	$Fine	$N.Mint	£Good	£Fine	£N.Mint
1 64pgs, Bloodlines (Wave Two) part 22, 1st appearance Chimera, continued in Legion '93 Annual #4	$0.60	$1.80	$3.00	£0.40	£1.20	£2.00
2 64pgs, Luke Ross and Kevin Conrad art; Elseworlds story	$0.60	$1.80	$3.00	£0.40	£1.20	£2.00
Title Value:	$1.20	$3.60	$6.00	£0.80	£2.40	£4.00

TEAM X/TEAM 7

Marvel Comics Group,OS; nn Jan 1997

	$Good	$Fine	$N.Mint	£Good	£Fine	£N.Mint
nn ND 48pgs, squarebound; Larry Hama script, Steve Epting and Klaus Janson art	$1.00	$3.00	$5.00	£0.70	£2.10	£3.50
Title Value:	$1.00	$3.00	$5.00	£0.70	£2.10	£3.50

TEAM YANKEE

First,MS; 1 Jan 1989-6 Feb 1989

	$Good	$Fine	$N.Mint	£Good	£Fine	£N.Mint
1-6 ND	$0.40	$1.20	$2.00	£0.25	£0.75	£1.25
Title Value:	$2.40	$7.20	$12.00	£1.50	£4.50	£7.50
Trade Paperback				£1.70	£5.10	£8.50

TEAM YOUNGBLOOD

Image; 1 Sep 1993-22 Sep 1995

	$Good	$Fine	$N.Mint	£Good	£Fine	£N.Mint
1 ND Rob Liefeld script, Chap Yaep pencils and Norm Rapmund inks begin	$0.40	$1.20	$2.00	£0.25	£0.75	£1.25
2-8 ND	$0.40	$1.20	$2.00	£0.25	£0.75	£1.25
9 ND Rob Liefeld returns to Extreme Studios work with this issue; Liefeld script and wraparound cover	$0.50	$1.50	$2.50	£0.30	£0.90	£1.50
10 ND $2.50 cover begin	$0.45	$1.35	$2.25	£0.30	£0.90	£1.50
11 ND story continued from Team Youngblood #10 and Youngblood #7	$0.50	$1.50	$2.50	£0.30	£0.90	£1.50
12 ND story continued from Youngblood #7 and Team Youngblood #11	$0.50	$1.50	$2.50	£0.30	£0.90	£1.50
13 ND Riptide poses nude in a men's magazine	$0.50	$1.50	$2.50	£0.30	£0.90	£1.50
14 ND	$0.50	$1.50	$2.50	£0.30	£0.90	£1.50
15 ND New Blood story, continued from Newmen #8	$0.50	$1.50	$2.50	£0.30	£0.90	£1.50
16 ND guest-stars Bloodpool	$0.50	$1.50	$2.50	£0.30	£0.90	£1.50
17 ND Extreme Sacrifice part 5, continued in Prophet #10; pre-bagged with trading card	$0.50	$1.50	$2.50	£0.30	£0.90	£1.50
18 ND team line-up changes begin decided by reader poll	$0.50	$1.50	$2.50	£0.30	£0.90	£1.50
19 ND	$0.50	$1.50	$2.50	£0.30	£0.90	£1.50
20 ND Contact part 1, Extreme 3000 prologue	$0.50	$1.50	$2.50	£0.30	£0.90	£1.50
21 ND Rage of Angels tie-in; guest-starring Glory and Angela	$0.50	$1.50	$2.50	£0.30	£0.90	£1.50
22 ND Shadowhunt part 4, New Man guest stars; continued in New Man #4	$0.50	$1.50	$2.50	£0.30	£0.90	£1.50
Title Value:	$10.15	$30.45	$50.75	£6.20	£18.60	£31.00

TEEN BEAM

National Periodical Publications; 2 Jan/Feb 1968

(previously Teen Beat)

	$Good	$Fine	$N.Mint	£Good	£Fine	£N.Mint
2 rare in the U.K, scarce in the U.S. Monkees photo cover	$3.20	$9.50	$22.50	£2.10	£6.25	£15.00
Title Value:	$3.20	$9.50	$22.50	£2.10	£6.25	£15.00

Note: Pop star photos, features, cartoons. Note also that just recently a copy has surfaced in the U.K. with a distribution stamp suggesting very limited distribution in newsagents to co-incide with the showing of the TV series on UK television.

TEEN BEAT

National Periodical Publications; 1 Nov/Dec 1967

(becomes Teen Beam)

	$Good	$Fine	$N.Mint	£Good	£Fine	£N.Mint
1 rare in the U.K, scarce in the U.S. Monkees photo cover	$4.25	$12.50	$30.00	£2.85	£8.50	£20.00
Title Value:	$4.25	$12.50	$30.00	£2.85	£8.50	£20.00

Note: Pop star photos, features, cartoons.

TEEN TITANS

National Periodical Publications/DC Comics; 1 Jan/Feb 1966-43 Jan/Feb 1973; 44 Nov 1976-53 Feb 1978

(see Brave and the Bold, DC Super-Stars, New Teen Titans, Showcase, Tales of the New Teen Titans, World's Finest)

	$Good	$Fine	$N.Mint	£Good	£Fine	£N.Mint
1 Batman, Flash, Aquaman, Wonder Woman cameos	$25.00	$75.00	$200.00	£15.50	£47.00	£125.00
2	$14.00	$43.00	$100.00	£7.75	£23.50	£55.00
3	$8.50	$26.00	$60.00	£4.25	£12.50	£30.00
4 Speedy appears	$8.50	$26.00	$60.00	£4.25	£12.50	£30.00
5	$8.50	$26.00	$60.00	£4.25	£12.50	£30.00
6-10	$7.00	$21.00	$50.00	£3.20	£9.50	£22.50
11 Speedy appears	$4.60	$13.50	$32.50	£2.25	£6.75	£16.00
12-18	$4.60	$13.50	$32.50	£2.25	£6.75	£16.00
19 Speedy joins; Wood inks	$4.60	$13.50	$32.50	£2.25	£6.75	£16.00
20 Neal Adams art	$5.00	$15.00	$35.00	£2.50	£7.50	£17.50
21 Neal Adams art, Hawk & Dove X-over	$5.00	$15.00	$35.00	£2.50	£7.50	£17.50
22 Neal Adams art, origin Wonder Girl	$5.00	$15.00	$35.00	£2.50	£7.50	£17.50
23 Wonder Girl dons new costume	$2.50	$7.50	$17.50	£1.25	£3.85	£9.00
24	$2.50	$7.50	$17.50	£1.25	£3.85	£9.00
25 Hawk & Dove, Flash, Green Arrow, Green Lantern, Aquaman, Batman, Superman X-over	$2.50	$7.50	$17.50	£1.25	£3.85	£9.00
26-28	$2.50	$7.50	$17.50	£1.25	£3.85	£9.00
29 Hawk & Dove X-over	$2.50	$7.50	$17.50	£1.25	£3.85	£9.00
30 Aquagirl appears	$2.50	$7.50	$17.50	£1.25	£3.85	£9.00
31 Hawk & Dove X-over	$2.05	$6.25	$12.50	£1.05	£3.25	£6.50
32-39	$2.05	$6.25	$12.50	£1.05	£3.25	£6.50
40	$2.05	$6.25	$12.50	£1.00	£3.00	£6.00
41-43	$2.05	$6.25	$12.50	£0.80	£2.50	£5.00
44 1st appearance Guardian	$1.00	$3.00	$6.00	£0.50	£1.50	£3.00
45 scarce in the U.K.	$1.00	$3.00	$6.00	£0.55	£1.75	£3.50
46 ND 1st appearance Joker's daughter	$2.05	$6.25	$12.50	£0.80	£2.50	£5.00
47 Joker's daughter appears	$1.65	$5.00	$10.00	£0.65	£2.00	£4.00

Tales Of The Unexpected #26

Tarzan #207

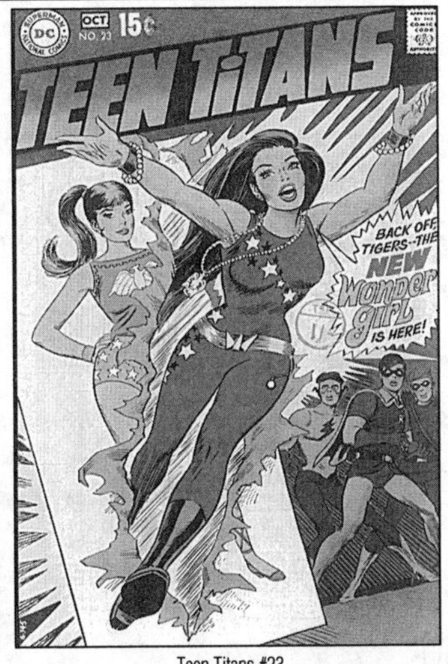

Teen Titans #23

	$Good	$Fine	$N.Mint	£Good	£Fine	£N.Mint
48 1st Bumblebee, Joker's daughter becomes Harlequin	*$1.65*	*$5.00*	*$10.00*	£0.65	£2.00	£4.00
49 scarce in the U.K.	*$1.00*	*$3.00*	*$6.00*	£0.55	£1.75	£3.50
50 1st Teen Titans West, 1st return original Bat-Girl (see Batman #139)	*$2.05*	*$6.25*	*$12.50*	£0.75	£2.25	£4.50
51-52	*$1.00*	*$3.00*	*$6.00*	£0.40	£1.25	£2.50
53 origin retold	*$1.00*	*$3.00*	*$6.00*	£0.50	£1.50	£3.00
Title Value:	*$215.95*	*$649.25*	*$1511.00*	£108.35	£327.05	£766.00

FEATURES

Aqualad in 30, 36. Hawk and the Dove in 31. Lilith in 36, 38.

REPRINT FEATURES

Aquaman/Aqualad in 35, 38. Green Arrow/Speedy in 35, 38. Hawk and the Dove in 39. Superboy in 36, 37.

TEEN TITANS SPOTLIGHT

DC Comics; 1 Aug 1986-21 Apr 1988

	$Good	$Fine	$N.Mint	£Good	£Fine	£N.Mint
1-2 Starfire, Apartheid story	*$0.25*	*$0.75*	*$1.25*	£0.15	£0.45	£0.75
3-6	*$0.25*	*$0.75*	*$1.25*	£0.15	£0.45	£0.75
7 1st Jackson Guice's art for DC, Hawk appears	*$0.25*	*$0.75*	*$1.25*	£0.15	£0.45	£0.75
8 Hawk appears	*$0.25*	*$0.75*	*$1.25*	£0.15	£0.45	£0.75
9	*$0.25*	*$0.75*	*$1.25*	£0.15	£0.45	£0.75
10 Erik Larsen art	*$0.25*	*$0.75*	*$1.25*	£0.15	£0.45	£0.75
11 "Asterix" issue	*$0.25*	*$0.75*	*$1.25*	£0.15	£0.45	£0.75
12-13	*$0.25*	*$0.75*	*$1.25*	£0.15	£0.45	£0.75
14 Batman appears	*$0.25*	*$0.75*	*$1.25*	£0.15	£0.45	£0.75
15 Erik Larsen art	*$0.25*	*$0.75*	*$1.25*	£0.15	£0.45	£0.75
16-17	*$0.25*	*$0.75*	*$1.25*	£0.15	£0.45	£0.75
18 Art Thibert cover and art (1st in comics?); Millennium X-over	*$0.25*	*$0.75*	*$1.25*	£0.15	£0.45	£0.75
19 Millennium X-over	*$0.25*	*$0.75*	*$1.25*	£0.15	£0.45	£0.75
20-21	*$0.25*	*$0.75*	*$1.25*	£0.15	£0.45	£0.75
Title Value:	*$5.25*	*$15.75*	*$26.25*	£3.15	£9.45	£15.75

Note: Aqualad in 10,18. Brotherhood of Evil in 11. Changeling in 9. Cyborg in 13,20. Hawk in 7,8. Jericho in 3-6. Magenta in 17. Nightwing in 14. Omega Men in 15. Starfire in 1,2 19. Teen Titans (old) in 21. Thunder and Lightning in 16. Wonder Girl in 12.

TEEN TITANS, THE

DC Comics; 1 Oct 1996-present

	$Good	$Fine	$N.Mint	£Good	£Fine	£N.Mint
1 ND Dan Jurgens script and pencil art, George Perez inks begin	*$0.40*	*$1.20*	*$2.00*	£0.25	£0.75	£1.25
2-3 ND	*$0.40*	*$1.20*	*$2.00*	£0.25	£0.75	£1.25
4 ND Nightwing, Supergirl and Captain Marvel Jnr. appear	*$0.40*	*$1.20*	*$2.00*	£0.25	£0.75	£1.25
5-6 ND	*$0.40*	*$1.20*	*$2.00*	£0.25	£0.75	£1.25
Title Value:	*$2.40*	*$7.20*	*$12.00*	£1.50	£4.50	£7.50

TEEN-AGE ROMANCE

Atlas/Marvel Comics Group; 77 Sep 1960-86 Mar 1962

(formerly My Own Romance)

	$Good	$Fine	$N.Mint	£Good	£Fine	£N.Mint
77-86 scarce in the U.K.	*$2.85*	*$8.50*	*$20.00*	£1.75	£5.25	£12.50
Title Value:	*$28.50*	*$85.00*	*$200.00*	£17.50	£52.50	£125.00

TEENAGE MUTANT NINJA TURTLES

Mirage Studios; 1 1984-62 Sep 1993

(see Donatello, Fugitoid, Grimjack #26, Grunts,Gobbledeygook, How to Draw TMNT Leonardo, Michaelangelo, Raphael, Turtle Soup, TMNT Martial Arts Training Manual)

	$Good	$Fine	$N.Mint	£Good	£Fine	£N.Mint
1 scarce in the U.K. magazine size, red and white cover (see Warning below regarding counterfeit issue)	*$30.00*	*$90.00*	*$180.00*	£16.50	£50.00	£100.00
1 2nd printing, scarce (6,000 copies)	*$3.30*	*$10.00*	*$20.00*	£1.65	£5.00	£10.00
1 3rd printing	*$1.00*	*$3.00*	*$6.00*	£0.65	£2.00	£4.00
1 4th printing	*$0.80*	*$2.40*	*$4.00*	£0.50	£1.50	£2.50
1 5th printing, new back-up with two pages out of sequence	*$0.40*	*$1.20*	*$2.00*	£0.25	£0.75	£1.25
2 scarce in the U.K. blue/black and white cover, magazine size	*$7.50*	*$22.50*	*$45.00*	£5.00	£15.00	£30.00
2 2nd printing scarce in the U.K.	*$1.50*	*$4.50*	*$7.50*	£1.00	£3.00	£5.00
2 3rd printing	*$0.80*	*$2.40*	*$4.00*	£0.50	£1.50	£2.50
3 scarce in the U.K. 1st Party Wagon, magazine size	*$3.75*	*$11.00*	*$22.50*	£2.05	£6.25	£12.50
3 2nd printing, new back-up, new cover	*$0.90*	*$2.70*	*$4.50*	£0.60	£1.80	£3.00
4 1st Triceratons, magazine size	*$1.65*	*$5.00*	*$10.00*	£1.05	£3.25	£6.50
4 2nd printing, new back-up, new cover	*$0.40*	*$1.20*	*$2.00*	£0.25	£0.75	£1.25
5	*$1.25*	*$3.75*	*$7.50*	£0.80	£2.50	£5.00
5 2nd printing, new back-up, new cover	*$0.40*	*$1.20*	*$2.00*	£0.25	£0.75	£1.25
6	*$1.20*	*$3.60*	*$6.00*	£0.80	£2.40	£4.00
6 2nd printing, new back-up	*$0.40*	*$1.20*	*$2.00*	£0.25	£0.75	£1.25
7 4 page colour insert by Corben, 1st Bade Biker by Lawson	*$1.20*	*$3.60*	*$6.00*	£0.80	£2.40	£4.00
7 2nd printing	*$0.40*	*$1.20*	*$2.00*	£0.25	£0.75	£1.25
8 Cerebus by Sim X-over	*$1.20*	*$3.60*	*$6.00*	£0.80	£2.40	£4.00
9 Rip in Time preview by Corben	*$0.90*	*$2.70*	*$4.50*	£0.60	£1.80	£3.00
10	*$0.90*	*$2.70*	*$4.50*	£0.60	£1.80	£3.00
11-14	*$0.70*	*$2.10*	*$3.50*	£0.50	£1.50	£2.50
15 Golden Age Parody cover, printed to appear damaged and worn	*$0.70*	*$2.10*	*$3.50*	£0.50	£1.50	£2.50
16 (published before issue #15)	*$0.60*	*$1.80*	*$3.00*	£0.40	£1.20	£2.00
17-20	*$0.60*	*$1.80*	*$3.00*	£0.40	£1.20	£2.00
21	*$0.50*	*$1.50*	*$2.50*	£0.30	£0.90	£1.50
22-23 Mark Martin art	*$0.50*	*$1.50*	*$2.50*	£0.30	£0.90	£1.50
24-25 Rick Veitch art	*$0.50*	*$1.50*	*$2.50*	£0.30	£0.90	£1.50
26 Rick Veitch art	*$0.40*	*$1.20*	*$2.00*	£0.25	£0.75	£1.25
27-32	*$0.40*	*$1.20*	*$2.00*	£0.25	£0.75	£1.25
32 2nd printing, (Jul 1992) - in colour with wraparound cover	*$0.50*	*$1.50*	*$2.50*	£0.30	£0.90	£1.50
33	*$0.40*	*$1.20*	*$2.00*	£0.25	£0.75	£1.25
34-36 The Soul's Triad	*$0.40*	*$1.20*	*$2.00*	£0.25	£0.75	£1.25
37 The Twilight of the Rings	*$0.40*	*$1.20*	*$2.00*	£0.25	£0.75	£1.25
38 George Bush appears	*$0.40*	*$1.20*	*$2.00*	£0.25	£0.75	£1.25
39-40	*$0.40*	*$1.20*	*$2.00*	£0.25	£0.75	£1.25
41 Matt Howarth script/art	*$0.40*	*$1.20*	*$2.00*	£0.25	£0.75	£1.25
42-47	*$0.40*	*$1.20*	*$2.00*	£0.25	£0.75	£1.25
48 Shades of Gray part 1, plotted by Eastman and Laird	*$0.40*	*$1.20*	*$2.00*	£0.25	£0.75	£1.25
49 Shades of Gray part 2, plotted by Eastman and Laird	*$0.40*	*$1.20*	*$2.00*	£0.25	£0.75	£1.25
50 48pgs, City at War part 1, pin-ups by Larsen, Todd McFarlane and Walt Simonson	*$0.40*	*$1.20*	*$2.00*	£0.25	£0.75	£1.25
50 2nd printing, (Aug 1993)	*$0.40*	*$1.20*	*$2.00*	£0.25	£0.75	£1.25
51	*$0.40*	*$1.20*	*$2.00*	£0.25	£0.75	£1.25
51 2nd printing, (Sep 1993)	*$0.40*	*$1.20*	*$2.00*	£0.25	£0.75	£1.25
52 $2.25 cover begins	*$0.45*	*$1.35*	*$2.25*	£0.30	£0.90	£1.50
53-62	*$0.45*	*$1.35*	*$2.25*	£0.30	£0.90	£1.50
Title Value:	*$85.50*	*$256.40*	*$476.25*	£51.75	£156.15	£288.25

Note: all Non-Distributed on the news-stands in the U.K.

WARNING: there are counterfeit copies of issues #1 and 2 available. The cover is blue/black instead of solid black and the pages are unusually white. Issue #2 has a glossy cover instead of the original matt coating. In this instance the Guide does not give a value for either of these and thereby promote forgery.

Books published by First/Penguin:

	£Good	£Fine	£N.Mint
Book 1, reprints #1-3 plus 2 new stories, colour	£1.50	£4.50	£7.50
Book 2, reprints #4-6 plus 3 new pages, colour	£1.40	£4.20	£7.00
Book 3, reprints #7-9 plus 12 new pages, colour	£1.40	£4.20	£7.00
Book 4, reprints #10,11 plus Leonardo OS, gatefold, colour	£1.40	£4.20	£7.00

Trade paperbacks published by Mirage:

	£Good	£Fine	£N.Mint
Limited Edition hardback (1,000 copies) reprints #1-11 plus all 4 micro series	£7.00	£21.00	£35.00
Limited Edition softback (5,000 copies), as above	£2.50	£7.50	£12.50
Movie Adaptation (Jun 1990) 64pgs plus 10pg commentary by Eastman/Laird	£0.50	£1.50	£2.50
The Collected TMNT 1 (May 1990), reprints issues #9-11	£0.80	£2.40	£4.00
The Collected TMNT 2 (Jun 1990), reprints issues #12-14	£0.80	£2.40	£4.00
The Collected TMNT 3 (Jul 1990), reprints issues #15,#17,#18	£0.80	£2.40	£4.00
The Collected TMNT 4 (Aug 1990), reprints issues #19-21	£0.80	£2.40	£4.00
The Collected TMNT 5 (Sep 1990), reprints issues #16,#22,#23	£0.80	£2.40	£4.00
The Collected TMNT 6: The River (Sep 1991) reprints issues #24-26	£0.80	£2.40	£4.00
The Collected TMNT 7 (1991), reprints issues #27-29	£0.80	£2.40	£4.00
Challenges Graphic Novel (Nov 1991) six all-new stories, origin retold	£0.80	£2.40	£4.00
Deluxe TMNT Book 1 (Oct 1992) Facsimile Edition of #1, in duo-shade, introduction by Harlan Ellison	£0.75	£2.25	£3.75

TEENAGE MUTANT NINJA TURTLES (2ND SERIES)

Mirage Studios; 1 Oct 1993-13 1995 ?

	$Good	$Fine	$N.Mint	£Good	£Fine	£N.Mint
1 ND Jim Lawson story and pencils begin	*$0.50*	*$1.50*	*$2.50*	£0.30	£0.90	£1.50
2-13 ND	*$0.50*	*$1.50*	*$2.50*	£0.30	£0.90	£1.50
Title Value:	*$6.50*	*$19.50*	*$32.50*	£3.90	£11.70	£19.50

TEENAGE MUTANT NINJA TURTLES (3RD SERIES)

Image; 1 Jun 1996-present

	$Good	$Fine	$N.Mint	£Good	£Fine	£N.Mint
1 ND Gary Carlson script, Frank Fosco and Erik Larsen art; Larsen cover	*$0.40*	*$1.20*	*$2.00*	£0.25	£0.75	£1.25
2-4 ND	*$0.40*	*$1.20*	*$2.00*	£0.25	£0.75	£1.25
Title Value:	*$1.60*	*$4.80*	*$8.00*	£1.00	£3.00	£5.00

TEENAGE MUTANT NINJA TURTLES ADVENTURES

Archie; 1 Dec 1988-74 Nov 1995

	$Good	$Fine	$N.Mint	£Good	£Fine	£N.Mint
1 ND	*$0.40*	*$1.20*	*$2.00*	£0.25	£0.75	£1.25
2-10 ND	*$0.30*	*$0.90*	*$1.50*	£0.20	£0.60	£1.00
11-31 ND	*$0.25*	*$0.75*	*$1.25*	£0.15	£0.45	£0.75
32 ND Peter Laird cover	*$0.25*	*$0.75*	*$1.25*	£0.15	£0.45	£0.75
33-47 ND	*$0.25*	*$0.75*	*$1.25*	£0.15	£0.45	£0.75
48-50 ND The Black Hole Trilogy	*$0.25*	*$0.75*	*$1.25*	£0.15	£0.45	£0.75
51-61 ND	*$0.25*	*$0.75*	*$1.25*	£0.15	£0.45	£0.75
62-66 ND Dreamland story	*$0.25*	*$0.75*	*$1.25*	£0.15	£0.45	£0.75

Issue	$Good	$Fine	$N.Mint	£Good	£Fine	£N.Mint
67-74 ND	$0.25	$0.75	$1.25	£0.15	£0.45	£0.75
Title Value:	$19.10	$57.30	$95.50	£11.65	£34.95	£58.25
Spring Special, 64pgs				£0.35	£1.05	£1.75

TEENAGE MUTANT NINJA TURTLES ADVENTURES (LIMITED SERIES)

Archie,MS; 1 Sep 1988-3 Nov 1988

Issue	$Good	$Fine	$N.Mint	£Good	£Fine	£N.Mint
1-3 ND	$0.50	$1.50	$2.50	£0.30	£0.90	£1.50
Title Value:	$1.50	$4.50	$7.50	£0.90	£2.70	£4.50

Note: all colour Nestle Nespray drink version, no cover price, same indicia dates and valued the same as printings #2-5.

TEENAGE MUTANT NINJA TURTLES ADVENTURES SPECIAL

Archie; 1 Jun 1992-11 1993 ?

Issue	$Good	$Fine	$N.Mint	£Good	£Fine	£N.Mint
1 ND 64pgs	$0.40	$1.20	$2.00	£0.25	£0.75	£1.25
2 ND 64pgs, Peter Laird cover	$0.40	$1.20	$2.00	£0.25	£0.75	£1.25
3-11 ND 64pgs	$0.40	$1.20	$2.00	£0.25	£0.75	£1.25
Title Value:	$4.40	$13.20	$22.00	£2.75	£8.25	£13.75

TEENAGE MUTANT NINJA TURTLES II MOVIE ADAPTATION

Tundra Publishing,OS; 1 Jul 1991

Issue	$Good	$Fine	$N.Mint	£Good	£Fine	£N.Mint
1 ND includes four pages of material not available in Archie version	$1.00	$3.00	$5.00	£0.60	£1.80	£3.00
Title Value:	$1.00	$3.00	$5.00	£0.60	£1.80	£3.00

TEENAGE MUTANT NINJA TURTLES III MOVIE ADAPTATION

Archie,OS; 1 May 1993

Issue	$Good	$Fine	$N.Mint	£Good	£Fine	£N.Mint
1 Direct Market Edition ND 48pgs	$0.60	$1.80	$3.00	£0.40	£1.20	£2.00
1 Newstand Edition ND 48pgs	$0.50	$1.50	$2.50	£0.30	£0.90	£1.50
Title Value:	$1.10	$3.30	$5.50	£0.70	£2.10	£3.50

TEENAGE MUTANT NINJA TURTLES MARTIAL ARTS TRAINING MANUAL

Solson Publications; 1-4 1986

Issue	$Good	$Fine	$N.Mint	£Good	£Fine	£N.Mint
1-4 ND	$0.80	$2.40	$4.00	£0.50	£1.50	£2.50
Title Value:	$3.20	$9.60	$16.00	£2.00	£6.00	£10.00

TEENAGE MUTANT NINJA TURTLES MOVIE ADAPTATION

Archie; nn Jun 1990

Issue	$Good	$Fine	$N.Mint	£Good	£Fine	£N.Mint
nn Direct Market Edition, ND, 48pgs	$0.70	$2.10	$3.50	£0.50	£1.50	£2.50
nn Newstand Edition, ND, 64pgs	$0.50	$1.50	$2.50	£0.30	£0.90	£1.50
Title Value:	$1.20	$3.60	$6.00	£0.80	£2.40	£4.00

TEENAGE MUTANT NINJA TURTLES MOVIE PARODY

Mirage Studios; nn Jul 1990

Issue	$Good	$Fine	$N.Mint	£Good	£Fine	£N.Mint
nn ND Mark Martin script and art	$0.50	$1.50	$2.50	£0.30	£0.90	£1.50
Title Value:	$0.50	$1.50	$2.50	£0.30	£0.90	£1.50

TEENAGE MUTANT NINJA TURTLES MOVIE SPECIAL 2

Archie; 1 May 1991

Issue	$Good	$Fine	$N.Mint	£Good	£Fine	£N.Mint
1 ND adaptation of The Secret of the Ooze	$0.40	$1.20	$2.00	£0.25	£0.75	£1.25
Title Value:	$0.40	$1.20	$2.00	£0.25	£0.75	£1.25

TEENAGE MUTANT NINJA TURTLES VOLUMES

Tundra Publishing; 1 Feb 1991

Issue	$Good	$Fine	$N.Mint	£Good	£Fine	£N.Mint
1 ND 150pgs, reprints Teenage Mutant Ninja Turtles Adventures #1-4 recoloured plus adaptation of first Teenage Mutant Ninja Turtles animated episode	$1.50	$4.50	$7.50	£1.00	£3.00	£5.00
Title Value:	$1.50	$4.50	$7.50	£1.00	£3.00	£5.00

TEENAGE MUTANT NINJA TURTLES VOLUMES (2ND SERIES)

Tundra Publishing; 1-4 Jul 1991

Issue	$Good	$Fine	$N.Mint	£Good	£Fine	£N.Mint
1-4 ND reprints Archie issues #5-16; each volume has a different Turtle on cover	$1.00	$3.00	$5.00	£0.70	£2.10	£3.50
Title Value:	$4.00	$12.00	$20.00	£2.80	£8.40	£14.00

TEENAGE MUTANT NINJA TURTLES WINTER SPECIAL

Archie; 1 Jan 1991

Issue	$Good	$Fine	$N.Mint	£Good	£Fine	£N.Mint
1 ND	$0.40	$1.20	$2.00	£0.25	£0.75	£1.25
Title Value:	$0.40	$1.20	$2.00	£0.25	£0.75	£1.25

TEENAGE MUTANT NINJA TURTLES/SAVAGE DRAGON CROSSOVER

Mirage Studios,OS; 1 Aug 1995

Issue	$Good	$Fine	$N.Mint	£Good	£Fine	£N.Mint
1 ND Mike Dooney script, Erik Lasen art; continued in Savage Dragon #22	$0.50	$1.50	$2.50	£0.30	£0.90	£1.50
Title Value:	$0.50	$1.50	$2.50	£0.30	£0.90	£1.50

TEENAGE MUTANT NINJA TURTLES: HAUNTED PIZZA

Mirage Studios,OS; 1 Dec 1992

Issue	$Good	$Fine	$N.Mint	£Good	£Fine	£N.Mint
1 ND Matt Howarth script/art	$0.40	$1.20	$2.00	£0.25	£0.75	£1.25
Title Value:	$0.40	$1.20	$2.00	£0.25	£0.75	£1.25

TEENAGE MUTANT NINJA TURTLES: THE COMIC STRIP

Express Press; 1 Aug 1991

Issue	$Good	$Fine	$N.Mint	£Good	£Fine	£N.Mint
1 ND 24pgs, reprints from U.K. Daily Express newspaper	$0.40	$1.20	$2.00	£0.25	£0.75	£1.25
Title Value:	$0.40	$1.20	$2.00	£0.25	£0.75	£1.25
Special Edition 1, printed in green inks				£0.30	£0.90	£1.50

TEENAGE MUTANT NINJA TURTLES: THE MALTESE TURTLE

Mirage Studios,OS; 1 Mar 1993

Issue	$Good	$Fine	$N.Mint	£Good	£Fine	£N.Mint
1 ND 48pgs	$0.40	$1.20	$2.00	£0.25	£0.75	£1.25
Title Value:	$0.40	$1.20	$2.00	£0.25	£0.75	£1.25

TEENAGE MUTANT NINJA TURTLES: YEAR OF THE TURTLE

Archie Comics,MS; 1 Oct 1995-3 Dec 1995

Issue	$Good	$Fine	$N.Mint	£Good	£Fine	£N.Mint
1-3 ND Dan Slott script, Hugh Haynes art	$0.30	$0.90	$1.50	£0.20	£0.60	£1.00
Title Value:	$0.90	$2.70	$4.50	£0.60	£1.80	£3.00

TEKNO COMIX HANDBOOK

Tekno Comix/Big Entertainment,OS; 1 Mar 1996

Issue	$Good	$Fine	$N.Mint	£Good	£Fine	£N.Mint
1 ND 48pgs, blueprints, diagrams and information	$0.80	$2.40	$4.00	£0.50	£1.50	£2.50
Title Value:	$0.80	$2.40	$4.00	£0.50	£1.50	£2.50

TEKNOPHAGE VERSUS ZEERUS

Big Entertainment,OS; 1 Jul 1996

Issue	$Good	$Fine	$N.Mint	£Good	£Fine	£N.Mint
1 ND 48pgs	$0.65	$1.95	$3.25	£0.45	£1.35	£2.25
Title Value:	$0.65	$1.95	$3.25	£0.45	£1.35	£2.25

TEKNOPHAGE, NEIL GAIMAN'S

Tekno Comix; 1 Aug 1995-present

Issue	$Good	$Fine	$N.Mint	£Good	£Fine	£N.Mint
1 ND Rick Veitch script, Bryan Talbot and Angus McKie art	$0.40	$1.20	$2.00	£0.25	£0.75	£1.25
1 Steel Edition, ND (Dec 1995) - silver embossed card-stock cover; 25,000 copies	$1.50	$4.50	$7.50	£1.00	£3.00	£5.00
2-5 ND	$0.40	$1.20	$2.00	£0.25	£0.75	£1.25
6 ND (non-Code approved issue)	$0.40	$1.20	$2.00	£0.25	£0.75	£1.25
7 ND (non-Code approved issue)	$0.45	$1.35	$2.25	£0.30	£0.90	£1.50
8 ND pre-bagged with Tekno back- issue comic	$0.45	$1.35	$2.25	£0.30	£0.90	£1.50
9-10 ND	$0.45	$1.35	$2.25	£0.30	£0.90	£1.50
Title Value:	$5.70	$17.10	$28.50	£3.70	£11.10	£18.50

TEKQ

Caliber Press,MS; 1 Jul 1992-3 1992

Issue	$Good	$Fine	$N.Mint	£Good	£Fine	£N.Mint
1-3 ND	$0.50	$1.50	$2.50	£0.30	£0.90	£1.50
Title Value:	$1.50	$4.50	$7.50	£0.90	£2.70	£4.50

TEKWORLD, WILLIAM SHATNER'S

Marvel Comics Group/Epic; 1 Sep 1992-24 Aug 1994

Issue	$Good	$Fine	$N.Mint	£Good	£Fine	£N.Mint
1-24 ND based on Tekworld novels	$0.30	$0.90	$1.50	£0.20	£0.60	£1.00
Title Value:	$7.20	$21.60	$36.00	£4.80	£14.40	£24.00
William Shatner's Tekworld (Feb 1994) Trade paperback, 120pgs, collects 5 issue adaptation of Tekworld plus Shatner interview and preview of TV films				£1.70	£5.10	£8.50

TELL ME DARK HARDCOVER GRAPHIC NOVEL

DC Comics,OS; nn Dec 1992

Issue	$Good	$Fine	$N.Mint	£Good	£Fine	£N.Mint
nn Hardcover ND script by Karl Edward Wagner, painted cover and art by Kent Williams	$5.50	$16.50	$28.00	£3.70	£11.00	£18.50
nn Softcover ND (Jul 1993), as above	$2.80	$8.25	$14.00	£1.80	£5.25	£9.00
Title Value:	$8.30	$24.75	$42.00	£5.50	£16.25	£27.50

TEMPEST

DC Comics,MS; 1 Nov 1996-4 Feb 1997

Issue	$Good	$Fine	$N.Mint	£Good	£Fine	£N.Mint
1-4 ND the former Aqualad stars; covers and art by Phil Jimenez and John Stokes	$0.35	$1.05	$1.75	£0.25	£0.75	£1.25
Title Value:	$1.40	$4.20	$7.00	£1.00	£3.00	£5.00

TEMPUS FUGITIVE

DC Comics,MS; 1 Apr 1990-4 Sep 1991

Issue	$Good	$Fine	$N.Mint	£Good	£Fine	£N.Mint
1-4 ND 48pgs	$0.90	$2.70	$4.50	£0.60	£1.80	£3.00
Title Value:	$3.60	$10.80	$18.00	£2.40	£7.20	£12.00

Note: Prestige Format, painted art by Ken Steacy. Creator-owned project (see Skreemer). Publication delays as series went on.

TERMINAL CITY

DC Comics,MS; 1 Jun 1996-9 Mar 1997

Issue	$Good	$Fine	$N.Mint	£Good	£Fine	£N.Mint
1-5 ND Dean Motter script, Michael Lark art, Mark Chiarello painted covers	$0.50	$1.50	$2.50	£0.30	£0.90	£1.50
6-9 ND Dean Motter script, Michael Lark art	$0.50	$1.50	$2.50	£0.30	£0.90	£1.50
Title Value:	$4.50	$13.50	$22.50	£2.70	£8.10	£13.50

TERMINAL POINT

Dark Horse,MS; 1 Feb 1993-3 Apr 1993

Issue	$Good	$Fine	$N.Mint	£Good	£Fine	£N.Mint
1-3 ND Bruce Zick script and art	$0.50	$1.50	$2.50	£0.30	£0.90	£1.50
Title Value:	$1.50	$4.50	$7.50	£0.90	£2.70	£4.50

TERMINATOR

Now Comics; 1 Sep 1988-17 Feb 1990

Issue	$Good	$Fine	$N.Mint	£Good	£Fine	£N.Mint
1 movie tie-in begins, sub-titled "Tempest"	$1.60	$4.80	$8.00	£1.20	£3.60	£6.00
2 scarce in the U.K.	$1.20	$3.60	$6.00	£0.80	£2.40	£4.00
3 scarce in the U.K.	$0.90	$2.70	$4.50	£0.60	£1.80	£3.00
4-5	$0.60	$1.80	$3.00	£0.50	£1.50	£2.50
6-9	$0.60	$1.80	$3.00	£0.40	£1.20	£2.00
10 scarce in the U.K.	$0.60	$1.80	$3.00	£0.50	£1.50	£2.50
11	$0.60	$1.80	$3.00	£0.40	£1.20	£2.00
12 52pgs	$0.70	$2.10	$3.50	£0.50	£1.50	£2.50
13-15	$0.60	$1.80	$3.00	£0.40	£1.20	£2.00
16 52pgs	$0.60	$1.80	$3.00	£0.45	£1.35	£2.25
17	$0.60	$1.80	$3.00	£0.40	£1.20	£2.00
Title Value:	$12.20	$36.60	$61.00	£8.65	£25.95	£43.25

Note: Comics Code on cover from issue #8. All Non-Distributed on the news-stands in the U.K.

Issue	$Good	$Fine	$N.Mint	£Good	£Fine	£N.Mint
The Terminator: Tempest Collection (1994) Trade paperback reprints issues #1-4, John Bolton cover				£1.70	£5.10	£8.50

TERMINATOR (LIMITED SERIES)

Dark Horse,MS; 1 Aug 1990-4 Nov 1990

Issue	$Good	$Fine	$N.Mint	£Good	£Fine	£N.Mint
1 ND Chris Warner pencils	$0.80	$2.40	$4.00	£0.50	£1.50	£2.50
2-4 ND Chris Warner pencils	$0.60	$1.80	$3.00	£0.40	£1.20	£2.00
Title Value:	$2.60	$7.80	$13.00	£1.70	£5.10	£8.50

The Terminator Collection (Aug 1991)

	$Good	$Fine	$N.Mint	£Good	£Fine	£N.Mint
reprints #1-4, new John Bolton cover				£0.75	£2.25	£3.75
Limited Hardcover (Nov 1991) signed and numbered (2,000 copies)				£9.00	£27.00	£45.00

TERMINATOR 2
Marvel Comics Group,MS; 1 Sep 1991-3 Oct 1991

	$Good	$Fine	$N.Mint	£Good	£Fine	£N.Mint
1 based on Arnold Schwarzenegger film, bi-weekly	$0.15	$0.45	$0.75	£0.10	£0.35	£0.60
2-3 bi-weekly	$0.15	$0.45	$0.75	£0.10	£0.35	£0.60
Title Value:	$0.45	$1.35	$2.25	£0.30	£1.05	£1.80

TERMINATOR 2 MOVIE ADAPTATION BOOKSHELF FORMAT
Marvel Comics Group,OS; 1 Sep 1991

	$Good	$Fine	$N.Mint	£Good	£Fine	£N.Mint
1 ND based on Arnold Schwarzenegger film screenplay, photo cover	$0.80	$2.40	$4.00	£0.50	£1.50	£2.50
Title Value:	$0.80	$2.40	$4.00	£0.50	£1.50	£2.50

TERMINATOR 2 MOVIE ADAPTATION MAGAZINE
Marvel Comics Group,OS; 1 Sep 1991

	$Good	$Fine	$N.Mint	£Good	£Fine	£N.Mint
1 ND based on Arnold Schwarzenegger film screenplay	$0.40	$1.20	$2.00	£0.25	£0.75	£1.25
Title Value:	$0.40	$1.20	$2.00	£0.25	£0.75	£1.25

TERMINATOR 2: FUTURE WAR - NUCLEAR TWILIGHT
Marvel Comics Group,MS; 1 Jan 1996-4 Apr 1996

	$Good	$Fine	$N.Mint	£Good	£Fine	£N.Mint
1-4 ND Mark Paniccia script, Gary Erskine art	$0.50	$1.50	$2.50	£0.30	£0.90	£1.50
Title Value:	$2.00	$6.00	$10.00	£1.20	£3.60	£6.00

TERMINATOR 2: PRESENT WAR - CYBERNETIC DAWN
Marvel Comics Group,MS; 1 Jan 1996-4 Apr 1996

	$Good	$Fine	$N.Mint	£Good	£Fine	£N.Mint
1-4 ND Dan Abnett script, Keith Conroy and Jack Snider art	$0.50	$1.50	$2.50	£0.30	£0.90	£1.50
Title Value:	$2.00	$6.00	$10.00	£1.20	£3.60	£6.00

TERMINATOR ONE SHOT, THE
Dark Horse,OS; 1 Jul 1991

	$Good	$Fine	$N.Mint	£Good	£Fine	£N.Mint
1 ND 48pgs, Matt Wagner art, pop-up section	$1.20	$3.60	$6.00	£0.80	£2.40	£4.00
Title Value:	$1.20	$3.60	$6.00	£0.80	£2.40	£4.00

TERMINATOR: END GAME
Dark Horse,MS; 1 Sep 1992-3 Dec 1992

	$Good	$Fine	$N.Mint	£Good	£Fine	£N.Mint
1-3 ND Jackson Guice art, John Higgins cover	$0.50	$1.50	$2.50	£0.30	£0.90	£1.50
Title Value:	$1.50	$4.50	$7.50	£0.90	£2.70	£4.50
Terminator: Endgame (1994) Trade paperback reprints mini-series				£1.30	£3.90	£6.50

TERMINATOR: ENEMY WITHIN, THE
Dark Horse,MS; 1 Jan 1992-4 Apr 1992

	$Good	$Fine	$N.Mint	£Good	£Fine	£N.Mint
1-4 ND Simon Bisley covers	$0.50	$1.50	$2.50	£0.30	£0.90	£1.50
Title Value:	$2.00	$6.00	$10.00	£1.20	£3.60	£6.00
The Terminator: The Enemy Within (1994) Trade paperback reprints mini-series, Simon Bisley cover				£2.00	£6.00	£10.00

TERMINATOR: HUNTERS & KILLERS, THE
Dark Horse,MS; 1 Mar 1992-3 May 1992

	$Good	$Fine	$N.Mint	£Good	£Fine	£N.Mint
1-3 ND	$0.50	$1.50	$2.50	£0.30	£0.90	£1.50
Title Value:	$1.50	$4.50	$7.50	£0.90	£2.70	£4.50
Terminator: Hunters and Killers (1994) Trade paperback reprints mini-series				£1.30	£3.90	£6.50

TERMINATOR: SECONDARY OBJECTIVES
Dark Horse,MS; 1 Sep 1991-4 Dec 1991

	$Good	$Fine	$N.Mint	£Good	£Fine	£N.Mint
1-4 ND	$0.50	$1.50	$2.50	£0.30	£0.90	£1.50
Title Value:	$2.00	$6.00	$10.00	£1.20	£3.60	£6.00
The Terminator: Secondary Objectives Collection (Oct 1992) reprints issues #1-4 with new cover painting by Paul Gulacy				£1.70	£5.10	£8.50

TERMINATOR: SPECIAL MINI-SERIES
Now Comics; 1 Jun 1990-2 Jul 1990

	$Good	$Fine	$N.Mint	£Good	£Fine	£N.Mint
1-2 ND sub-titled All My Futures Past	$0.50	$1.50	$2.50	£0.30	£0.90	£1.50
Title Value:	$1.00	$3.00	$5.00	£0.60	£1.80	£3.00

TERMINATOR: THE BURNING EARTH
Now Comics,MS; 1 Mar 1990-5 Jul 1990

	$Good	$Fine	$N.Mint	£Good	£Fine	£N.Mint
1 ND	$0.50	$1.50	$2.50	£0.70	£2.10	£3.50
2 ND	$0.40	$1.20	$2.00	£0.60	£1.80	£3.00
3-5 ND	$0.40	$1.20	$2.00	£0.50	£1.50	£2.50
Title Value:	$2.10	$6.30	$10.50	£2.80	£8.40	£14.00

TERMINUS FACTOR, THE
Marvel Comics Group; 1990

Cross-over storyline that ran throughout the following issues:
Captain America Annual #9, **Iron Man Annual #11**, **Thor Annual #15**, **Avengers West Coast Annual #5**, **Avengers Annual #19**.

TERRAFORMERS
Wonder Color Comics; 1 Apr 1987-2 May 1987

	$Good	$Fine	$N.Mint	£Good	£Fine	£N.Mint
1-2 ND Kelley Jones art	$0.40	$1.20	$2.00	£0.25	£0.75	£1.25
Title Value:	$0.80	$2.40	$4.00	£0.50	£1.50	£2.50

TERRARISTS
Marvel Comics Group,MS; 1 Nov 1993-4 Feb 1994

	$Good	$Fine	$N.Mint	£Good	£Fine	£N.Mint
1 ND Pat Mills and Tony Skinner script; bound-in trading card	$0.40	$1.20	$2.00	£0.25	£0.75	£1.25
2-4 ND bound-in trading card	$0.40	$1.20	$2.00	£0.25	£0.75	£1.25
Title Value:	$1.60	$4.80	$8.00	£1.00	£3.00	£5.00

TERROR INC.
Marvel Comics Group; 1 Jul 1992-13 Jul 1993

	$Good	$Fine	$N.Mint	£Good	£Fine	£N.Mint
1-3 ND	$0.25	$0.75	$1.25	£0.15	£0.45	£0.75
4-5 ND Dr. Strange guest-stars	$0.25	$0.75	$1.25	£0.15	£0.45	£0.75
6-7 ND Terror vs. Punisher	$0.25	$0.75	$1.25	£0.15	£0.45	£0.75
8-11 ND	$0.25	$0.75	$1.25	£0.15	£0.45	£0.75
12 ND Cage and Silver Sable appear; X-over Cage #16 and Silver Sable #14	$0.25	$0.75	$1.25	£0.15	£0.45	£0.75
13 ND Infinity Crusade X-over	$0.25	$0.75	$1.25	£0.15	£0.45	£0.75
Title Value:	$3.25	$9.75	$16.25	£1.95	£5.85	£9.75

TERROR TALES
Eternity; 1 Jun 1991

	$Good	$Fine	$N.Mint	£Good	£Fine	£N.Mint
1 ND	$0.40	$1.20	$2.00	£0.25	£0.75	£1.25
Title Value:	$0.40	$1.20	$2.00	£0.25	£0.75	£1.25

TERRORESS
Anger Helps; 1 Dec 1990

	$Good	$Fine	$N.Mint	£Good	£Fine	£N.Mint
1 ND black and white	$0.15	$0.45	$0.75	£0.10	£0.35	£0.60
Title Value:	$0.15	$0.45	$0.75	£0.10	£0.35	£0.60

TEX AVERY'S COMICS AND STORIES
Dark Horse,MS; 1 Apr 1996-4 Jul 1996

	$Good	$Fine	$N.Mint	£Good	£Fine	£N.Mint
1-4 ND	$0.60	$1.80	$3.00	£0.40	£1.20	£2.00
Title Value:	$2.40	$7.20	$12.00	£1.60	£4.80	£8.00

TEX AVERY'S SCREWBALL SQUIRREL
Dark Horse,MS; 1 Jul 1995-3 Sep 1995

	$Good	$Fine	$N.Mint	£Good	£Fine	£N.Mint
1-3 ND	$0.50	$1.50	$2.50	£0.30	£0.90	£1.50
Title Value:	$1.50	$4.50	$7.50	£0.90	£2.70	£4.50

TEX BENSON
Metro Comics,MS; 1 Nov 1986-4 Feb 1987

	$Good	$Fine	$N.Mint	£Good	£Fine	£N.Mint
1-4 ND	$0.40	$1.20	$2.00	£0.25	£0.75	£1.25
Title Value:	$1.60	$4.80	$8.00	£1.00	£3.00	£5.00

TEX DAWSON, GUNSLINGER
Marvel Comics Group; 1 Jan 1973-3 Jun 1973

(#2, #3 titled Gunslinger)

	$Good	$Fine	$N.Mint	£Good	£Fine	£N.Mint
1 ND Williamson reprint, Steranko cover	$0.50	$1.50	$3.00	£0.30	£1.00	£2.00
2-3 ND reprints	$0.40	$1.25	$2.50	£0.25	£0.75	£1.50
Title Value:	$1.30	$4.00	$8.00	£0.80	£2.50	£5.00

TEXAS CHAINSAW MASSACRE
Northstar,MS; 1 Apr 1992-3 1992

	$Good	$Fine	$N.Mint	£Good	£Fine	£N.Mint
1-3 ND based on film	$0.50	$1.50	$2.50	£0.30	£0.90	£1.50
Title Value:	$1.50	$4.50	$7.50	£0.90	£2.70	£4.50

THANATOS SYNDROME: THE JACKAL, THE
Boneyard Press; 1 Mar 1992

	$Good	$Fine	$N.Mint	£Good	£Fine	£N.Mint
1 ND black and white; smaller than regular comic size	$0.25	$0.75	$1.25	£0.15	£0.45	£0.75
Title Value:	$0.25	$0.75	$1.25	£0.15	£0.45	£0.75

THANOS QUEST
Marvel Comics Group,MS; 1 Sep 1990-2 Oct 1990

(see Captain Marvel, Silver Surfer)

	$Good	$Fine	$N.Mint	£Good	£Fine	£N.Mint
1 ND 48pgs, Jim Starlin script, Ron Lim art	$1.30	$3.90	$6.50	£0.80	£2.40	£4.00
1 2nd printing ND 48pgs	$0.90	$2.70	$4.50	£0.60	£1.80	£3.00
2 ND 48pgs, Jim Starlin script, Ron Lim art; 1st appearance Infinity Gauntlet	$1.20	$3.60	$6.00	£0.80	£2.40	£4.00
Title Value:	$3.40	$10.20	$17.00	£2.20	£6.60	£11.00

THAT DARN CAT
Gold Key/Movie Comics,OS Movie; 10171-602 Feb 1966

	$Good	$Fine	$N.Mint	£Good	£Fine	£N.Mint
10171-602 distributed in the U.K. film adaptation; Hayley Mills photo cover	$7.75	$23.50	$55.00	£4.25	£12.50	£30.00
Title Value:	$7.75	$23.50	$55.00	£4.25	£12.50	£30.00

THE MIGHTY I
Image; 1 May 1995

	$Good	$Fine	$N.Mint	£Good	£Fine	£N.Mint
1 ND 48pgs, interviews and articles on Image product	$0.30	$0.90	$1.50	£0.20	£0.60	£1.00
Title Value:	$0.30	$0.90	$1.50	£0.20	£0.60	£1.00

THE PRICE
Eclipse; Graphic Novel 5, Oct 1981

	$Good	$Fine	$N.Mint	£Good	£Fine	£N.Mint
nn ND Jim Starlin art, Dreadstar featured	$1.20	$3.60	$6.00	£0.80	£2.40	£4.00
Title Value:	$1.20	$3.60	$6.00	£0.80	£2.40	£4.00

THE STARS MY DESTINATION
Epic Graphic Novel; nn Jul 1992

	$Good	$Fine	$N.Mint	£Good	£Fine	£N.Mint
nn ND 160pgs, Howard Chaykin art	$3.00	$9.00	$15.00	£2.00	£6.00	£10.00
Title Value:	$3.00	$9.00	$15.00	£2.00	£6.00	£10.00

THEY CAME FROM THE '50S
Eternity; nn Sep 1990

	$Good	$Fine	$N.Mint	£Good	£Fine	£N.Mint
nn ND collection of pre-Code horror stories	$1.50	$4.50	$7.50	£1.00	£3.00	£5.00
Title Value:	$1.50	$4.50	$7.50	£1.00	£3.00	£5.00

THEY WERE ELEVEN
Viz Communications,MS; 1 Feb 1995-4 May 1995

	$Good	$Fine	$N.Mint	£Good	£Fine	£N.Mint
1-4 ND Moto Hagio script and art; black and white	$0.50	$1.50	$2.50	£0.30	£0.90	£1.50
Title Value:	$2.00	$6.00	$10.00	£1.20	£3.60	£6.00

THIEF OF SHERWOOD, THE
A Plus Comics,MS; 1 Aug 1991-3 Oct 1991

	$Good	$Fine	$N.Mint	£Good	£Fine	£N.Mint
1-3 ND Sam Glanzman art	$0.40	$1.20	$2.00	£0.25	£0.75	£1.25
Title Value:	$1.20	$3.60	$6.00	£0.75	£2.25	£3.75

VERY GENERAL PERCENTAGE CONVERSION CHART WHICH MAY BE USED TO CALCULATE LOW AND INBETWEEN GRADES:

THIEVES & KINGS

I Box Publishing; 1 Jul 1994-present

Issue	$Good	$Fine	$N.Mint	£Good	£Fine	£N.Mint
1 ND Mark Oakley script and art; black and white						
	$0.70	*$2.10*	*$3.50*	£0.50	£1.50	£2.50
1 2nd printing ND	*$0.60*	*$1.80*	*$3.00*	£0.40	£1.20	£2.00
2-10 ND	*$0.60*	*$1.80*	*$3.00*	£0.40	£1.20	£2.00
11-15 ND	*$0.45*	*$1.35*	*$2.25*	£0.30	£0.90	£1.50
Title Value:	*$8.95*	*$26.85*	*$44.75*	£6.00	£18.00	£30.00
Thieves & Kings (Oct 1996)						
Trade paperback ND collects issues #1-6				£1.50	£4.50	£7.50

THING FROM ANOTHER WORLD

Dark Horse,MS; 1 Feb 1992-2 May 1992

Issue	$Good	$Fine	$N.Mint	£Good	£Fine	£N.Mint
1-2 ND John Higgins painted art, based on John Carpenter film						
	$0.60	*$1.80*	*$3.00*	£0.40	£1.20	£2.00
Title Value:	*$1.20*	*$3.60*	*$6.00*	£0.80	£2.40	£4.00

THING FROM ANOTHER WORLD: CLIMATE OF FEAR

Dark Horse; 1 Sep 1992-4 Dec 1992

Issue	$Good	$Fine	$N.Mint	£Good	£Fine	£N.Mint
1-4 ND based on John Carpenter's "The Thing", painted cover by John Higgins						
	$0.50	*$1.50*	*$2.50*	£0.30	£0.90	£1.50
Title Value:	*$2.00*	*$6.00*	*$10.00*	£1.20	£3.60	£6.00

THING FROM ANOTHER WORLD: ETERNAL VOWS

Dark Horse,MS; 1 Dec 1993-4 Mar 1994

Issue	$Good	$Fine	$N.Mint	£Good	£Fine	£N.Mint
1-4 ND Paul Gulacy cover and art						
	$0.50	*$1.50*	*$2.50*	£0.30	£0.90	£1.50
Title Value:	*$2.00*	*$6.00*	*$10.00*	£1.20	£3.60	£6.00

THING, THE

Marvel Comics Group; 1 Jul 1983-36 Jun 1986

(see Fantastic Four, Marvel Fanfare, Marvel Graphic Novel, Marvel Two-In-One)

Issue	$Good	$Fine	$N.Mint	£Good	£Fine	£N.Mint
1 ND John Byrne story						
	$0.40	*$1.20*	*$2.00*	£0.20	£0.60	£1.00
2 John Byrne inks/story						
	$0.30	*$0.90*	*$1.50*	£0.15	£0.45	£0.75
3-4 Inhumans appear, John Byrne story						
	$0.25	*$0.75*	*$1.25*	£0.15	£0.45	£0.75
5 Spiderman, Wonderman, She-Hulk appear, John Byrne story						
	$0.25	*$0.75*	*$1.25*	£0.15	£0.45	£0.75
6 John Byrne story	*$0.25*	*$0.75*	*$1.25*	£0.15	£0.45	£0.75
7 John Byrne art on back-up story, Byrne script on Thing story						
	$0.25	*$0.75*	*$1.25*	£0.15	£0.45	£0.75
8-9 She-Hulk appears, John Byrne scripts						
	$0.25	*$0.75*	*$1.25*	£0.15	£0.45	£0.75
10 Fantastic Four appear, John Byrne script						
	$0.25	*$0.75*	*$1.25*	£0.15	£0.45	£0.75
11 John Byrne script						
	$0.25	*$0.75*	*$1.25*	£0.15	£0.45	£0.75
12 Dr. Doom appears, John Byrne script						
	$0.25	*$0.75*	*$1.25*	£0.15	£0.45	£0.75
13 John Byrne script						
	$0.25	*$0.75*	*$1.25*	£0.15	£0.45	£0.75
14-18	*$0.25*	*$0.75*	*$1.25*	£0.15	£0.45	£0.75
19-22 John Byrne scripts						
	$0.25	*$0.75*	*$1.25*	£0.15	£0.45	£0.75
23 Fantastic Four appear, Mike Carlin scripts begin						
	$0.25	*$0.75*	*$1.25*	£0.15	£0.45	£0.75
24 Thing vs. Rhino	*$0.25*	*$0.75*	*$1.25*	£0.15	£0.45	£0.75
25	*$0.25*	*$0.75*	*$1.25*	£0.15	£0.45	£0.75
26 Vance Astro (as a young boy) appears						
	$0.25	*$0.75*	*$1.25*	£0.15	£0.45	£0.75
27-29	*$0.25*	*$0.75*	*$1.25*	£0.15	£0.45	£0.75
30 Secret Wars X-over						
	$0.25	*$0.75*	*$1.25*	£0.15	£0.45	£0.75
31	*$0.25*	*$0.75*	*$1.25*	£0.15	£0.45	£0.75
32 Vance Astro of Guardians of the Galaxy appears						
	$0.25	*$0.75*	*$1.25*	£0.15	£0.45	£0.75
33	*$0.25*	*$0.75*	*$1.25*	£0.15	£0.45	£0.75
34 last Carlin script, Neary art						
	$0.25	*$0.75*	*$1.25*	£0.15	£0.45	£0.75
35 1st new Ms. Marvel, Byrne script, Neary art						
	$0.25	*$0.75*	*$1.25*	£0.15	£0.45	£0.75
36 She-Hulk vs. new Ms. Marvel, John Byrne script, Neary art; story completed in West Coast Avengers #10						
	$0.25	*$0.75*	*$1.25*	£0.15	£0.45	£0.75
Title Value:	*$9.20*	*$27.60*	*$46.00*	£5.45	£16.35	£27.25

THING, THE (2ND SERIES)

Marvel Comics Group,MS; 1 Apr 1992-4 Jul 1992

Issue	$Good	$Fine	$N.Mint	£Good	£Fine	£N.Mint
1 reprints Marvel Two-In-One #8 featuring Ghost Rider						
	$0.25	*$0.75*	*$1.25*	£0.15	£0.45	£0.75
2 reprints Marvel Two-In-One #80 featuring Ghost Rider						
	$0.25	*$0.75*	*$1.25*	£0.15	£0.45	£0.75
3 reprints Marvel Two-In-One #51 featuring Beast, Nick Fury, Wonderman and Ms. Marvel, Frank Miller art						
	$0.25	*$0.75*	*$1.25*	£0.15	£0.45	£0.75
4 reprints Marvel Two In One #77 featuring Man-Thing and Nick Fury						
	$0.25	*$0.75*	*$1.25*	£0.15	£0.45	£0.75
Title Value:	*$1.00*	*$3.00*	*$5.00*	£0.60	£1.80	£3.00

THOR

Marvel Comics Group; 126 Mar 1966-502 Oct 1996

(formerly Journey Into Mystery)(becomes Journey Into Mystery again with #503) (see Marvel Graphic Novel, Marvel Preview, Marvel Special, Marvel Treasury Edition, Special Marvel Edition, Tales of Asgard)

Issue	$Good	$Fine	$N.Mint	£Good	£Fine	£N.Mint
126 Thor vs. Hercules; story continued from Journey Into Mystery #125						
	$19.00	*$57.50*	*$135.00*	£10.50	£32.00	£75.00
127-130	*$7.00*	*$21.00*	*$50.00*	£3.55	£10.50	£25.00
131-132	*$6.75*	*$20.00*	*$47.50*	£3.20	£9.50	£22.50
133 scarce in the U.K.						
	$6.75	*$20.00*	*$47.50*	£3.55	£10.50	£25.00
134 scarce in the U.K. 1st appearance High Evolutionary; Quicksilver and Scarlet Witch appear						
	$8.50	*$26.00*	*$60.00*	£4.25	£12.50	£30.00
135 scarce in the U.K.						
	$6.75	*$20.00*	*$47.50*	£3.55	£10.50	£25.00
136-140	*$6.75*	*$20.00*	*$47.50*	£3.20	£9.50	£22.50
141	*$5.00*	*$15.00*	*$35.00*	£2.50	£7.50	£17.50
142 Thor battles Super-Skrull						
	$5.00	*$15.00*	*$35.00*	£2.50	£7.50	£17.50
143	*$5.00*	*$15.00*	*$35.00*	£2.50	£7.50	£17.50
144 scarce in the U.K.						
	$5.00	*$15.00*	*$35.00*	£2.85	£8.50	£20.00
145	*$5.00*	*$15.00*	*$35.00*	£2.50	£7.50	£17.50
146-147 The Inhumans origin told						
	$5.00	*$15.00*	*$35.00*	£2.50	£7.50	£17.50
148 start origin Black Bolt, 1st appearance The Wrecker						
	$5.00	*$15.00*	*$35.00*	£2.50	£7.50	£17.50
149 origins Black Bolt, Medusa, Crystal, Maximus, Gorgon, Karnak						
	$5.00	*$15.00*	*$35.00*	£2.50	£7.50	£17.50
150	*$5.00*	*$15.00*	*$35.00*	£2.50	£7.50	£17.50
151-157	*$5.25*	*$16.00*	*$32.50*	£2.50	£7.50	£15.00
158 origin reprinted in part from Journey into Mystery #83						
	$10.50	*$33.00*	*$65.00*	£5.00	£15.00	£30.00
159 more details of Thor's origin and secret identity of Don Blake						
	$5.25	*$16.00*	*$32.50*	£2.50	£7.50	£15.00
160 Galactus appears						
	$5.25	*$16.00*	*$32.50*	£2.50	£7.50	£15.00
161-162 Galactus appears						
	$4.15	*$12.50*	*$25.00*	£2.05	£6.25	£12.50
163	*$4.15*	*$12.50*	*$25.00*	£2.05	£6.25	£12.50

Tenn Titans Spotlight #21

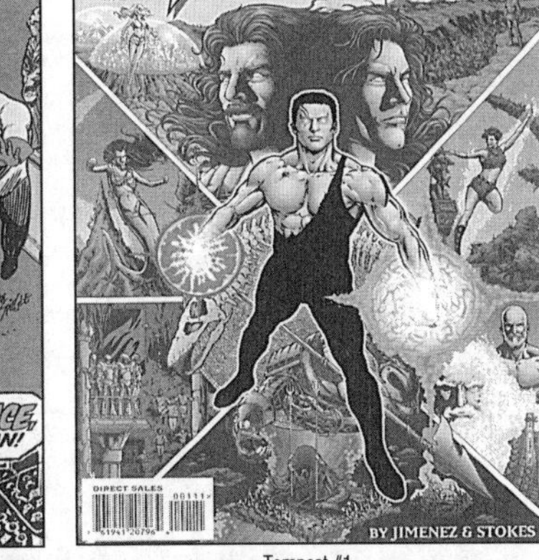

Tempest #1

Thing Fromn Another World: Eternal Vows #1

Issue	$Good	$Fine	$N.Mint	£Good	£Fine	£N.Mint
164 coccoon seen in last panel						
	$4.15	*$12.50*	*$25.00*	£2.05	£6.25	£12.50
165 1st full appearance "Him" - later Warlock (see Fantastic Four #66/67)						
	$7.50	*$22.50*	*$45.00*	£5.00	£15.00	£30.00
166 2nd full appearance "Him" - later Warlock; Thor vs. "Him"						
	$6.50	*$20.00*	*$40.00*	£4.55	£13.50	£27.50
167-169 Galactus appears						
	$4.15	*$12.50*	*$25.00*	£2.05	£6.25	£12.50
170	*$4.15*	*$12.50*	*$25.00*	£2.05	£6.25	£12.50
171-179	*$3.75*	*$11.00*	*$22.50*	£1.65	£5.00	£10.00
180-181 Neal Adams art						
	$2.50	*$7.50*	*$15.00*	£1.65	£5.00	£10.00
182 Dr. Doom appears						
	$1.65	*$5.00*	*$10.00*	£1.00	£3.00	£6.00
183 Thor vs. Dr. Doom						
	$1.65	*$5.00*	*$10.00*	£1.00	£3.00	£6.00
184-186	*$1.65*	*$5.00*	*$10.00*	£1.00	£3.00	£6.00
187-191 scarce in the U.K.						
	$1.65	*$5.00*	*$10.00*	£1.05	£3.25	£6.50
192 scarce in the U.K. Silver Surfer appears at end of story (cameo)						
	$1.25	*$3.75*	*$7.50*	£1.05	£3.25	£6.50
193 very scarce in the U.K. 52pgs, Silver Surfer appears; 25 cents cover price						
	$6.50	*$20.00*	*$40.00*	£4.55	£13.50	£27.50
194-199 scarce in the U.K.						
	$1.25	*$3.75*	*$7.50*	£1.05	£3.25	£6.50
200 very scarce in the U.K. Thor vs. Loki						
	$1.25	*$3.75*	*$7.50*	£1.25	£3.75	£7.50
201-204 scarce in the U.K.						
	$1.00	*$3.00*	*$6.00*	£0.75	£2.25	£4.50
205 scarce in the U.K. Mephisto appears						
	$1.00	*$3.00*	*$6.00*	£0.75	£2.25	£4.50
206 scarce in the U.K. Thor vs. Absorbing Man						
	$1.00	*$3.00*	*$6.00*	£0.75	£2.25	£4.50
207-209 scarce in the U.K.						
	$1.00	*$3.00*	*$6.00*	£0.75	£2.25	£4.50
210-216	*$1.00*	*$3.00*	*$6.00*	£0.55	£1.75	£3.50
217 Thor vs. Odin	*$1.00*	*$3.00*	*$6.00*	£0.55	£1.75	£3.50
218-220	*$1.00*	*$3.00*	*$6.00*	£0.55	£1.75	£3.50
221 Thor vs. Hercules						
	$0.80	*$2.50*	*$5.00*	£0.55	£1.75	£3.50
222-224 ND	*$0.80*	*$2.50*	*$5.00*	£0.75	£2.25	£4.50
225 ND 1st appearance Firelord (Galactus' 2nd herald)						
	$1.25	*$3.75*	*$7.50*	£0.80	£2.50	£5.00
226 Galactus appears						
	$0.80	*$2.50*	*$5.00*	£0.40	£1.25	£2.50
227-228 Galactus appears, Rich Buckler's Kirbyesque art						
	$0.80	*$2.50*	*$5.00*	£0.40	£1.25	£2.50
229 Buckler's Kirbyesque art						
	$0.80	*$2.50*	*$5.00*	£0.40	£1.25	£2.50
230 Iron Man cameo, Buckler's Kirbyesque art						
	$0.80	*$2.50*	*$5.00*	£0.40	£1.25	£2.50
231	*$0.80*	*$2.50*	*$5.00*	£0.30	£1.00	£2.00
232 Thor vs. Firelord, Iron Man appears						
	$0.80	*$2.50*	*$5.00*	£0.30	£1.00	£2.00
233	*$0.80*	*$2.50*	*$5.00*	£0.30	£1.00	£2.00
234 Firelord appears						
	$0.80	*$2.50*	*$5.00*	£0.30	£1.00	£2.00
235-245	*$0.80*	*$2.50*	*$5.00*	£0.30	£1.00	£2.00
246 Thor vs. Firelord						
	$0.65	*$2.00*	*$4.00*	£0.30	£1.00	£2.00
247 Firelord appears						
	$0.65	*$2.00*	*$4.00*	£0.30	£1.00	£2.00
248-250	*$0.65*	*$2.00*	*$4.00*	£0.30	£1.00	£2.00
251-253	*$0.65*	*$2.00*	*$4.00*	£0.25	£0.75	£1.50
254 reprints issue #159						
	$0.65	*$2.00*	*$4.00*	£0.25	£0.75	£1.50
255-258	*$0.65*	*$2.00*	*$4.00*	£0.25	£0.75	£1.50
259 Walt Simonson layouts/pencils begin (ends #271)						
	$0.65	*$2.00*	*$4.00*	£0.25	£0.75	£1.50
260-270	*$0.65*	*$2.00*	*$4.00*	£0.25	£0.75	£1.50
271 Iron Man, Beast, Vision, Scarlet Witch and Nick Fury appear; last Walt Simonson layouts/pencils						
	$0.50	*$1.50*	*$3.00*	£0.25	£0.75	£1.50
272-282	*$0.50*	*$1.50*	*$3.00*	£0.25	£0.75	£1.50
283-284 ND Eternals appear						
	$0.50	*$1.50*	*$3.00*	£0.25	£0.85	£1.75
285-289 Eternals appear						
	$0.50	*$1.50*	*$3.00*	£0.25	£0.75	£1.50
290	*$0.50*	*$1.50*	*$3.00*	£0.25	£0.75	£1.50
291-292 Eternals appear						
	$0.50	*$1.50*	*$3.00*	£0.25	£0.75	£1.50
293	*$0.50*	*$1.50*	*$3.00*	£0.25	£0.75	£1.50
294 origin Odin/Asgard retold						
	$0.50	*$1.50*	*$3.00*	£0.25	£0.75	£1.50
295-299	*$0.50*	*$1.50*	*$3.00*	£0.25	£0.75	£1.50
300 ND 52pgs, end of Asgard (origin Odin retold)						
	$1.05	*$3.25*	*$6.50*	£0.80	£2.50	£5.00
301-303	*$0.40*	*$1.20*	*$2.00*	£0.25	£0.75	£1.25
304 ND	*$0.40*	*$1.20*	*$2.00*	£0.30	£0.90	£1.50
305 ND Gabriel the Air-Walker appears						
	$0.40	*$1.20*	*$2.00*	£0.30	£0.90	£1.50
306 Firelord appears						
	$0.40	*$1.20*	*$2.00*	£0.25	£0.75	£1.25

Issue	$Good	$Fine	$N.Mint	£Good	£Fine	£N.Mint
307-315	*$0.40*	*$1.20*	*$2.00*	£0.25	£0.75	£1.25
316 Iron Man appears						
	$0.40	*$1.20*	*$2.00*	£0.25	£0.75	£1.25
317-332	*$0.40*	*$1.20*	*$2.00*	£0.25	£0.75	£1.25
333 Dracula and Dr. Strange appear						
	$0.40	*$1.20*	*$2.00*	£0.25	£0.75	£1.25
334-336	*$0.40*	*$1.20*	*$2.00*	£0.25	£0.75	£1.25
337 1st issue of classic Walt Simonson run, Beta Ray Bill becomes new Thor						
	$1.00	*$3.00*	*$5.00*	£0.50	£1.50	£2.50
338 2nd Walt Simonson art						
	$0.60	*$1.80*	*$3.00*	£0.40	£1.20	£2.00
339 3rd Walt Simonson art						
	$0.50	*$1.50*	*$2.50*	£0.30	£0.90	£1.50
340-350 Walt Simonson art						
	$0.40	*$1.20*	*$2.00*	£0.25	£0.75	£1.25
351 Walt Simonson art						
	$0.30	*$0.90*	*$1.50*	£0.20	£0.60	£1.00
352 Walt Simonson art, Fantastic Four appear						
	$0.30	*$0.90*	*$1.50*	£0.20	£0.60	£1.00
353-354 Walt Simonson art						
	$0.30	*$0.90*	*$1.50*	£0.20	£0.60	£1.00
355 Walt Simonson story						
	$0.30	*$0.90*	*$1.50*	£0.20	£0.60	£1.00
356 Guice cover and art						
	$0.30	*$0.90*	*$1.50*	£0.20	£0.60	£1.00
357-362 Walt Simonson art						
	$0.30	*$0.90*	*$1.50*	£0.20	£0.60	£1.00
363 Secret Wars II X-over, Walt Simonson art						
	$0.30	*$0.90*	*$1.50*	£0.20	£0.60	£1.00
364 Walt Simonson art						
	$0.30	*$0.90*	*$1.50*	£0.20	£0.60	£1.00
365 Walt Simonson art, new secret identity						
	$0.30	*$0.90*	*$1.50*	£0.20	£0.60	£1.00
366-367 Walt Simonson art						
	$0.30	*$0.90*	*$1.50*	£0.20	£0.60	£1.00
368-369 Walt Simonson story						
	$0.30	*$0.90*	*$1.50*	£0.20	£0.60	£1.00
370 P. Craig Russell inks						
	$0.30	*$0.90*	*$1.50*	£0.20	£0.60	£1.00
371-372 Judge Dredd parody, Simonson story						
	$0.30	*$0.90*	*$1.50*	£0.20	£0.60	£1.00
373 LD in the U.K. Mutant Massacre, Simonson story						
	$0.70	*$2.10*	*$3.50*	£0.40	£1.20	£2.00
374 LD in the U.K. Mutant Massacre, X-Factor X-over, Simonson story						
	$1.10	*$3.30*	*$5.50*	£0.70	£2.10	£3.50
375-376 Simonson story						
	$0.30	*$0.90*	*$1.50*	£0.20	£0.60	£1.00
377 X-Factor cameo, Simonson story						
	$0.30	*$0.90*	*$1.50*	£0.20	£0.60	£1.00
378-380 Simonson story						
	$0.30	*$0.90*	*$1.50*	£0.20	£0.60	£1.00
381 Avengers appear, Simonson story						
	$0.25	*$0.75*	*$1.25*	£0.15	£0.45	£0.75
382 LD in the U.K. 52pgs, last Simonson, 300th Thor anniversary						
	$0.50	*$1.50*	*$2.50*	£0.30	£0.90	£1.50
383 Secret Wars X-over						
	$0.25	*$0.75*	*$1.25*	£0.15	£0.45	£0.75
384 1st appearance Dargo, new (future) Thor						
	$0.25	*$0.75*	*$1.25*	£0.15	£0.45	£0.75
385 Thor vs. Hulk, Erik Larsen art						
	$0.25	*$0.75*	*$1.25*	£0.15	£0.45	£0.75
386-390	*$0.25*	*$0.75*	*$1.25*	£0.15	£0.45	£0.75
391 Spiderman appears						
	$0.25	*$0.75*	*$1.25*	£0.15	£0.45	£0.75
392-393 Daredevil appears						
	$0.25	*$0.75*	*$1.25*	£0.15	£0.45	£0.75
394-395	*$0.25*	*$0.75*	*$1.25*	£0.15	£0.45	£0.75
396 Black Knight appears						
	$0.25	*$0.75*	*$1.25*	£0.15	£0.45	£0.75
397-399	*$0.25*	*$0.75*	*$1.25*	£0.15	£0.45	£0.75
400 LD in the U.K. 64pgs, Charles Vess art						
	$0.50	*$1.50*	*$2.50*	£0.30	£0.90	£1.50
401-406	*$0.25*	*$0.75*	*$1.25*	£0.15	£0.45	£0.75
407-410 Tales of Asgard back-up						
	$0.25	*$0.75*	*$1.25*	£0.15	£0.45	£0.75
411 Acts of Vengeance tie-in, 1st appearance The New Warriors (cameo), Thor vs. Juggernaut, Ron Lim art						
	$0.60	*$1.80*	*$3.00*	£0.40	£1.20	£2.00
412 LD in the U.K. Acts of Vengeance tie-in, 1st full appearance The New Warriors, Ron Lim art in back-up story						
	$1.50	*$4.50*	*$7.50*	£0.90	£2.70	£4.50
413 Ron Lim art	*$0.25*	*$0.75*	*$1.25*	£0.15	£0.45	£0.75
414	*$0.25*	*$0.75*	*$1.25*	£0.15	£0.45	£0.75
415 true origin Thor's identity as Don Blake						
	$0.25	*$0.75*	*$1.25*	£0.15	£0.45	£0.75
416 Texiera art	*$0.25*	*$0.75*	*$1.25*	£0.15	£0.45	£0.75
417-418	*$0.25*	*$0.75*	*$1.25*	£0.15	£0.45	£0.75
419-424 The Black Galaxy Saga, bi-weekly issue						
	$0.25	*$0.75*	*$1.25*	£0.15	£0.45	£0.75
425 The Black Galaxy Saga epilogue						
	$0.25	*$0.75*	*$1.25*	£0.15	£0.45	£0.75
426 Lost Asgard storyline resolved						
	$0.25	*$0.75*	*$1.25*	£0.15	£0.45	£0.75
427-428 Captain Britain and Excalibur guest-star						

	$Good	$Fine	$N.Mint	£Good	£Fine	£N.Mint
	$0.25	$0.75	$1.25	£0.15	£0.45	£0.75
429 Ghost Rider guest stars (and some of Excalibur)	$0.30	$0.90	$1.50	£0.15	£0.45	£0.75
430 Ghost Rider guest stars	$0.30	$0.90	$1.50	£0.15	£0.45	£0.75
431 Enchantress appears	$0.25	$0.75	$1.25	£0.15	£0.45	£0.75
432 LD in the U.K. DS, 350th appearance of Thor, Loki killed and Thor banished; Eric Masterson becomes new Thor; Journey into Mystery #83 reprinted	$0.50	$1.50	$2.50	£0.30	£0.90	£1.50
433 new Thor begins	$0.80	$2.40	$4.00	£0.40	£1.20	£2.00
434 Captain America, Balder, Sif, Warriors Three appear	$0.25	$0.75	$1.25	£0.15	£0.45	£0.75
435 Warriors Three appear	$0.25	$0.75	$1.25	£0.15	£0.45	£0.75
436 Titania/Absorbing Man appear	$0.25	$0.75	$1.25	£0.15	£0.45	£0.75
437 Thor vs. Quasar	$0.25	$0.75	$1.25	£0.15	£0.45	£0.75
438 Dargo the Thor of the Future appears, bi-weekly issue, 1st Thor Corps	$0.25	$0.75	$1.25	£0.15	£0.45	£0.75
439 Dargo the Future Thor vs. new Thor, bi-weekly issue	$0.25	$0.75	$1.25	£0.15	£0.45	£0.75
440 bi-weekly issue	$0.25	$0.75	$1.25	£0.15	£0.45	£0.75
441 Thor vs. Ego, Celestials appear, bi-weekly issue	$0.25	$0.75	$1.25	£0.15	£0.45	£0.75
442 bi-weekly issue	$0.25	$0.75	$1.25	£0.15	£0.45	£0.75
443 Silver Surfer, Dr. Strange appear, bi-weekly	$0.25	$0.75	$1.25	£0.15	£0.45	£0.75
444 $1.25 cover begins	$0.25	$0.75	$1.25	£0.15	£0.45	£0.75
445 Galactic Storm part 7	$0.25	$0.75	$1.25	£0.15	£0.45	£0.75
446 Galactic Storm part 14	$0.25	$0.75	$1.25	£0.15	£0.45	£0.75
447	$0.25	$0.75	$1.25	£0.15	£0.45	£0.75
448 Spiderman guest stars	$0.25	$0.75	$1.25	£0.15	£0.45	£0.75
449	$0.25	$0.75	$1.25	£0.15	£0.45	£0.75
450 64pgs, double gatefold cover	$0.50	$1.50	$2.50	£0.30	£0.90	£1.50
451-452	$0.30	$0.90	$1.50	£0.20	£0.60	£1.00
453-454 bi-weekly	$0.30	$0.90	$1.50	£0.20	£0.60	£1.00
455 Dr. Strange guest-stars, bi-weekly	$0.30	$0.90	$1.50	£0.20	£0.60	£1.00
456 bi-weekly	$0.30	$0.90	$1.50	£0.20	£0.60	£1.00
457 original Thor returns, bi-weekly	$0.30	$0.90	$1.50	£0.20	£0.60	£1.00
458 original Thor vs. Eric Masterson Thor, bi-weekly	$0.30	$0.90	$1.50	£0.20	£0.60	£1.00
459 last Tom DeFalco/Ron Frenz creative team; intro Thunderstrike	$0.30	$0.90	$1.50	£0.20	£0.60	£1.00
460 Jim Starlin script begins, intro new Valkyrie	$0.30	$0.90	$1.50	£0.20	£0.60	£1.00
461 Thor vs. Beta Ray Bill	$0.30	$0.90	$1.50	£0.20	£0.60	£1.00
462	$0.30	$0.90	$1.50	£0.20	£0.60	£1.00
463 Infinity Crusade X-over	$0.30	$0.90	$1.50	£0.20	£0.60	£1.00
464 Infinity Crusade X-over; Loki returns	$0.30	$0.90	$1.50	£0.20	£0.60	£1.00
465-467 Infinity Crusade X-over	$0.30	$0.90	$1.50	£0.20	£0.60	£1.00
468 Blood and Thunder part 1, Silver Surfer and Warlock appear	$0.30	$0.90	$1.50	£0.20	£0.60	£1.00
468 pre-bagged, ND with audio cassette and copy of "Dirt" Magazine	$0.60	$1.80	$3.00	£0.40	£1.20	£2.00
469 Blood and Thunder part 5, Warlock and Silver Surfer appear	$0.30	$0.90	$1.50	£0.20	£0.60	£1.00
470 Blood and Thunder part 9, Dr. Strange, Warlock and Silver Surfer appear	$0.30	$0.90	$1.50	£0.20	£0.60	£1.00
471 Blood and Thunder part 13 (conclusion), Warlock and Silver Surfer appear	$0.30	$0.90	$1.50	£0.20	£0.60	£1.00
472	$0.30	$0.90	$1.50	£0.20	£0.60	£1.00
473 Loki returns	$0.30	$0.90	$1.50	£0.20	£0.60	£1.00
474 Loki appears; with free Spiderman and his Deadly Foes card sheet	$0.30	$0.90	$1.50	£0.20	£0.60	£1.00
475 48pgs, new costume	$0.40	$1.20	$2.00	£0.25	£0.75	£1.25
475 Collectors Edition, ND new costume, foil stamped embossed cover	$0.45	$1.35	$2.25	£0.30	£0.90	£1.50
476	$0.30	$0.90	$1.50	£0.20	£0.60	£1.00
477 Thunderstrike appears	$0.30	$0.90	$1.50	£0.20	£0.60	£1.00
478-479	$0.30	$0.90	$1.50	£0.20	£0.60	£1.00
480 High Evolutionary appears	$0.30	$0.90	$1.50	£0.20	£0.60	£1.00
481	$0.30	$0.90	$1.50	£0.20	£0.60	£1.00
482-483 Loki appears	$0.30	$0.90	$1.50	£0.20	£0.60	£1.00
484	$0.30	$0.90	$1.50	£0.20	£0.60	£1.00
485 Thor vs. The Thing	$0.30	$0.90	$1.50	£0.20	£0.60	£1.00
486-487	$0.30	$0.90	$1.50	£0.20	£0.60	£1.00
488 Thor and Lady Sif separate	$0.30	$0.90	$1.50	£0.20	£0.60	£1.00
489 Hulk appears; bi-weekly	$0.30	$0.90	$1.50	£0.20	£0.60	£1.00
490 bi-weekly	$0.30	$0.90	$1.50	£0.20	£0.60	£1.00
491 Warren Ellis scripts and Mike Deodato art (ends #494); new costume	$1.00	$3.00	$5.00	£0.70	£2.10	£3.50
492	$0.80	$2.40	$4.00	£0.60	£1.80	£3.00
493	$0.60	$1.80	$3.00	£0.50	£1.50	£2.50
494	$0.40	$1.20	$2.00	£0.40	£1.20	£2.00
495 Avengers: Timeslide tie-in	$0.30	$0.90	$1.50	£0.20	£0.60	£1.00
496 The First Sign part 2, continued in Iron Man #326	$0.30	$0.90	$1.50	£0.20	£0.60	£1.00
497	$0.30	$0.90	$1.50	£0.20	£0.60	£1.00
498-499 Mike Deodato Jnr. art	$0.30	$0.90	$1.50	£0.20	£0.60	£1.00
500 48pgs, Mike Deodato Jnr. art	$0.50	$1.50	$2.50	£0.30	£0.90	£1.50
501 ND	$0.50	$1.50	$2.50	£0.30	£0.90	£1.50
502 ND Onslaught tie-in, continued in Onslaught: Marvel Universe	$0.50	$1.50	$2.50	£0.30	£0.90	£1.50
Title Value:	$486.00	$1463.90	$3025.00	£261.20	£788.30	£1622.75

Note: #194 has back-up reprint. #254 is a reprint. **Note also**: Hercules appears in 128, 221, 229-231, 235-239, 289, 356, 400. Inhumans appear in 146-152.

	£Good	£Fine	£N.Mint
Trade paperback (Apr 1990) ND reprints #337-#340, new cover by Simonson	£1.00	£3.00	£5.00
Thor: Worldengine (Oct 1996) Trade paperback ND collects issues #491-494	£1.30	£3.90	£6.50

ARTISTS

Note: *Buckler art in 227-230. Gene Day art in 300, 310-315 (mainly inks).*

THOR ANNUAL

Marvel Comics Group; 2 1966-3 1967; 4 Dec 1971; 5 1976-8 1979; 9 1981-19 1994

(formerly Journey into Mystery Annual)

	$Good	$Fine	$N.Mint	£Good	£Fine	£N.Mint
2 scarce in the U.K. 68pgs, back up reprint	$7.75	$23.50	$55.00	£5.00	£15.00	£35.00
3-4 scarce in the U.K. 68pgs, all reprint	$1.75	$5.25	$12.50	£1.10	£3.40	£8.00
5 ND 52pgs, Hercules appears	$1.65	$5.00	$10.00	£0.80	£2.50	£5.00
6 ND 52pgs, Guardians of the Galaxy appear	$1.65	$5.00	$10.00	£0.80	£2.50	£5.00
7 ND 52pgs, Walt Simonson art	$1.25	$3.75	$7.50	£0.55	£1.75	£3.50
8 ND 52pgs, Thor vs. Zeus	$1.25	$3.75	$7.50	£0.55	£1.75	£3.50
9 ND 52pgs	$1.00	$3.00	$5.00	£0.50	£1.50	£2.50
10 ND 52pgs, map of Asgard	$0.70	$2.10	$3.50	£0.40	£1.20	£2.00
11-12 ND	$0.60	$1.80	$3.00	£0.40	£1.20	£2.00
13 ND	$0.50	$1.50	$2.50	£0.30	£0.90	£1.50
14 ND Atlantis Attacks part 13, continues in Fantastic Four Annual #22	$0.50	$1.50	$2.50	£0.30	£0.90	£1.50
15 ND The Terminus Factor part 3, continued in West Coast Avengers Annual #5, Dr. Strange, Quasar and Thing appear	$0.50	$1.50	$2.50	£0.30	£0.90	£1.50
16 ND Korvac Quest, Guardians of the Galaxy appear	$0.50	$1.50	$2.50	£0.30	£0.90	£1.50
17 ND 64pgs, Citizen Kang part 2, Avengers appear, continued in Fantastic Four Annual #25	$0.50	$1.50	$2.50	£0.30	£0.90	£1.50
18 ND 64pgs, pre-bagged with trading card introducing The Flame	$0.60	$1.80	$3.00	£0.40	£1.20	£2.00
19 ND 64pgs, Thor vs. Pluto	$0.60	$1.80	$3.00	£0.40	£1.20	£2.00
Title Value:	$23.65	$71.30	$148.00	£13.90	£42.30	£88.00

THOR CORPS, THE

Marvel Comics Group,MS; 1 Sep 1993-4 Dec 1993

	$Good	$Fine	$N.Mint	£Good	£Fine	£N.Mint
1	$0.40	$1.20	$2.00	£0.25	£0.75	£1.25
2 Franklin Richards appears	$0.40	$1.20	$2.00	£0.25	£0.75	£1.25
3 Spiderman 2099, Guardians of the Galaxy, Rawhide Kid, Two-Gun Kid and Kid Colt Outlaw appear	$0.40	$1.20	$2.00	£0.25	£0.75	£1.25
4	$0.40	$1.20	$2.00	£0.25	£0.75	£1.25
Title Value:	$1.60	$4.80	$8.00	£1.00	£3.00	£5.00

THOR GIANT SIZE

Marvel Comics Group; 1 1975

	$Good	$Fine	$N.Mint	£Good	£Fine	£N.Mint
1 ND very scarce in the U.K. 68pgs, all reprint (Jack Kirby)	$1.25	$3.75	$7.50	£1.25	£3.75	£7.50
Title Value:	$1.25	$3.75	$7.50	£1.25	£3.75	£7.50

THOR: ALONE AGAINST THE CELESTIALS

Marvel Comics Group,OS; 1 Aug 1992

	$Good	$Fine	$N.Mint	£Good	£Fine	£N.Mint
1 64pgs, reprints Thor #387-389	$1.00	$3.00	$5.00	£0.70	£2.10	£3.50
Title Value:	$1.00	$3.00	$5.00	£0.70	£2.10	£3.50

THOR: THE LEGEND

Marvel Comics Group,OS; 1 Sep 1996

Issue	$Good	$Fine	$N.Mint	£Good	£Fine	£N.Mint
1 ND 48pgs, retells the life and times of Thor	*$0.80*	*$2.40*	*$4.00*	£0.50	£1.50	£2.50
Title Value:	*$0.80*	*$2.40*	*$4.00*	£0.50	£1.50	£2.50

THORR-SVERD, THE SWORD OF THOR
Vincent Creations; 1-3 1987

Issue	$Good	$Fine	$N.Mint	£Good	£Fine	£N.Mint
1 ND	*$0.30*	*$0.90*	*$1.50*	£0.20	£0.60	£1.00
1 2nd printing ND	*$0.25*	*$0.75*	*$1.25*	£0.15	£0.45	£0.75
2-3 ND	*$0.30*	*$0.90*	*$1.50*	£0.20	£0.60	£1.00
Title Value:	*$1.15*	*$3.45*	*$5.75*	£0.75	£2.25	£3.75

THOSE ANNOYING POST BROTHERS
(see Post Bros, Those Annoying)

THRAX
Event Comics; nn Jul 1996; 1 Nov 1996-present

Issue	$Good	$Fine	$N.Mint	£Good	£Fine	£N.Mint
nn Ashcan Edition, ND 16pgs, Mike Baron script, Dave Ross art; black and white; signed & numbered, limited to 500 copies	*$2.00*	*$6.00*	*$10.00*	£1.30	£3.90	£6.50
1 ND Mike Baron script, Dave Ross and Tom Wergryzn art	*$0.60*	*$1.80*	*$3.00*	£0.40	£1.20	£2.00
Title Value:	*$2.60*	*$7.80*	*$13.00*	£1.70	£5.10	£8.50

THREAT
Fantagraphics,Magazine; 1 1985-10 1987

Issue	$Good	$Fine	$N.Mint	£Good	£Fine	£N.Mint
1-10 ND	*$0.50*	*$1.50*	*$2.50*	£0.30	£0.90	£1.50
Title Value:	*$5.00*	*$15.00*	*$25.00*	£3.00	£9.00	£15.00

THREE MOUSEKETEERS, THE
National Periodical Publications; 25 Aug/Sep 1960-26 Oct/Nov 1960

(previous issues ND)

Issue	$Good	$Fine	$N.Mint	£Good	£Fine	£N.Mint
25-26 very scarce in the U.K.	*$8.50*	*$26.00*	*$60.00*	£5.50	£17.00	£40.00
Title Value:	*$17.00*	*$52.00*	*$120.00*	£11.00	£34.00	£80.00

THREE MOUSEKETEERS, THE (2ND SERIES)
DC Comics; 1 May/Jun 1970-7 May/Jun 1971

Issue	$Good	$Fine	$N.Mint	£Good	£Fine	£N.Mint
1 very scarce in the U.K.	*$2.90*	*$8.75*	*$17.50*	£1.65	£5.00	£10.00
2 very scarce in the U.K.	*$2.00*	*$6.00*	*$10.00*	£1.50	£4.50	£7.50
3-7 very scarce in the U.K.	*$2.00*	*$6.00*	*$10.00*	£1.20	£3.60	£6.00
Title Value:	*$14.90*	*$44.75*	*$77.50*	£9.15	£27.50	£47.50

THREE MUSKETEERS
Eternity; 1 Dec 1988-3 1989

Issue	$Good	$Fine	$N.Mint	£Good	£Fine	£N.Mint
1-3 ND	*$0.40*	*$1.20*	*$2.00*	£0.25	£0.75	£1.25
Title Value:	*$1.20*	*$3.60*	*$6.00*	£0.75	£2.25	£3.75
Graphic Album, reprints				£1.10	£3.30	£5.50

THREE MUSKETEERS GRAPHIC ALBUM, THE
Malibu,OS; 1 1990

Issue	$Good	$Fine	$N.Mint	£Good	£Fine	£N.Mint
1 ND 100pgs, squarebound, black and white	*$1.50*	*$4.50*	*$7.50*	£1.00	£3.00	£5.00
Title Value:	*$1.50*	*$4.50*	*$7.50*	£1.00	£3.00	£5.00

THREE MUSKETEERS, THE
Marvel Comics Group,MS; 1,2 Feb 1994

Issue	$Good	$Fine	$N.Mint	£Good	£Fine	£N.Mint
1-2 ND adaptation of Disney film	*$0.30*	*$0.90*	*$1.50*	£0.20	£0.60	£1.00
Title Value:	*$0.60*	*$1.80*	*$3.00*	£0.40	£1.20	£2.00

THREE STOOGES, THE
Gold Key; 10 Oct 1962-55 Jun 1972

Issue	$Good	$Fine	$N.Mint	£Good	£Fine	£N.Mint
10 scarce in the U.K.	*$12.00*	*$36.00*	*$85.00*	£7.75	£23.50	£55.00
11-20	*$10.50*	*$32.00*	*$75.00*	£7.00	£21.00	£50.00
21-30	*$8.50*	*$26.00*	*$60.00*	£5.50	£17.00	£40.00
31-40	*$7.00*	*$21.00*	*$50.00*	£5.00	£15.00	£35.00
41-55	*$6.75*	*$20.00*	*$47.50*	£4.60	£13.50	£32.50
Title Value:	*$373.25*	*$1126.00*	*$2647.50*	£251.75	£756.00	£1792.50

Note: all distributed in the U.K.

3-D ADVENTURE COMICS
Stats Etc; 1 Aug 1986

Issue	$Good	$Fine	$N.Mint	£Good	£Fine	£N.Mint
1 ND promotional material, with bound-in 3-D glasses (25% less without glasses); smaller size (5"x7")	*$0.50*	*$1.50*	*$2.50*	£0.30	£0.90	£1.50
Title Value:	*$0.50*	*$1.50*	*$2.50*	£0.30	£0.90	£1.50

3-D ALIEN TERROR
Eclipse; 1 Jun 1986

Issue	$Good	$Fine	$N.Mint	£Good	£Fine	£N.Mint
1 ND Pound, Castrillo, Morrow art; Tom Yeates cover. Issued with bound-in 3-D glasses (25% less without glasses)	*$0.50*	*$1.50*	*$2.50*	£0.30	£0.90	£1.50
1 non 3-D issue ND scarce in the U.K.	*$0.60*	*$1.80*	*$3.00*	£0.40	£1.20	£2.00
Title Value:	*$1.10*	*$3.30*	*$5.50*	£0.70	£2.10	£3.50

3-D EXOTIC BEAUTIES
3-D Zone,OS; 1 1990

Issue	$Good	$Fine	$N.Mint	£Good	£Fine	£N.Mint
1 ND illustrations and story featuring belly-dancers and other such sordid stuff!	*$0.30*	*$0.90*	*$1.50*	£0.20	£0.60	£1.00
Title Value:	*$0.30*	*$0.90*	*$1.50*	£0.20	£0.60	£1.00

3-D HEAVY METAL MONSTERS
3-D Zone,OS; 1 Sep 1993

Issue	$Good	$Fine	$N.Mint	£Good	£Fine	£N.Mint
1 ND with 3-D glasses (25% less without glasses)	*$0.80*	*$2.40*	*$4.00*	£0.50	£1.50	£2.50
Title Value:	*$0.80*	*$2.40*	*$4.00*	£0.50	£1.50	£2.50

3-D HEROES
Blackthorne; (3-D Series #3) 1 Feb 1986

Issue	$Good	$Fine	$N.Mint	£Good	£Fine	£N.Mint
1 ND Steve Huston painted cover and art	*$0.50*	*$1.50*	*$2.50*	£0.30	£0.90	£1.50
Title Value:	*$0.50*	*$1.50*	*$2.50*	£0.30	£0.90	£1.50

3-D LASER ERASER AND PRESSBUTTON
Eclipse; 1 Aug 1986

Issue	$Good	$Fine	$N.Mint	£Good	£Fine	£N.Mint
1 ND Mike Collins and Mark Farmer art, Jerry Paris/Garry Leach cover; with 3-D glasses (25% less without glasses)	*$0.60*	*$1.80*	*$3.00*	£0.40	£1.20	£2.00
1 non 3-D issue ND scarce in the U.K.	*$0.90*	*$2.70*	*$4.50*	£0.60	£1.80	£3.00
Title Value:	*$1.50*	*$4.50*	*$7.50*	£1.00	£3.00	£5.00

3-D SUBSTANCE
The 3-D Zone; nn 1990; 2 Dec 1991

Issue	$Good	$Fine	$N.Mint	£Good	£Fine	£N.Mint
nn ND Steve Ditko art, with 3-D glasses (25% less without glasses)	*$0.60*	*$1.80*	*$3.00*	£0.40	£1.20	£2.00
2 ND Steve Ditko art featured, with 3-D glasses (25% less without glasses)	*$0.80*	*$2.40*	*$4.00*	£0.50	£1.50	£2.50
Title Value:	*$1.40*	*$4.20*	*$7.00*	£0.90	£2.70	£4.50

3-D THREE STOOGES
Eclipse; (3-D Special 11,14,19); 1 Sep 1986-3 Oct 1987

Issue	$Good	$Fine	$N.Mint	£Good	£Fine	£N.Mint
1 ND reprints 3 Stooges #2 (St.John); all isuues with bound-in 3-D glasses (25% less without glasses)	*$0.50*	*$1.50*	*$2.50*	£0.30	£0.90	£1.50
1 non 3-D issue ND scarce in the U.K.	*$0.60*	*$1.80*	*$3.00*	£0.40	£1.20	£2.00
2 ND reprints 3 Stooges #3 (St.John)	*$0.50*	*$1.50*	*$2.50*	£0.30	£0.90	£1.50
3 ND reprints 3 Stooges #1 (Jubilee)	*$0.50*	*$1.50*	*$2.50*	£0.30	£0.90	£1.50
Title Value:	*$2.10*	*$6.30*	*$10.50*	£1.30	£3.90	£6.50

3-D TRUE CRIME
3-D Zone,OS; 1 Jun 1992

Issue	$Good	$Fine	$N.Mint	£Good	£Fine	£N.Mint
1 ND three classic stories by Jack Cole that Dr. Frederick Wertham referred to in "Seduction of the Innocent", with 3-D glasses (25% less without glasses)	*$0.80*	*$2.40*	*$4.00*	£0.50	£1.50	£2.50
Title Value:	*$0.80*	*$2.40*	*$4.00*	£0.50	£1.50	£2.50

3-D ZONE PRESENTS
The 3-D Zone; 1 Feb 1987-21 Jun 1989

Issue	$Good	$Fine	$N.Mint	£Good	£Fine	£N.Mint
1 Wally Wood reprints from 1950's featuring Dr. Jekyll and Mr. Hyde; all issues come with bound-in 3-D glasses (25% less without glasses)	*$0.50*	*$1.50*	*$2.50*	£0.30	£0.90	£1.50
2 Weird Tales of Basil Wolverton	*$0.50*	*$1.50*	*$2.50*	£0.30	£0.90	£1.50
3 Picturescope Jungle Adventures, L.B. Cole reprint	*$0.50*	*$1.50*	*$2.50*	£0.30	£0.90	£1.50
4 Electric Fear by Brian Swift	*$0.50*	*$1.50*	*$2.50*	£0.30	£0.90	£1.50
5 Krazy Kat by George Herriman	*$0.50*	*$1.50*	*$2.50*	£0.30	£0.90	£1.50
6 Rat Fink by Ed Roth	*$0.50*	*$1.50*	*$2.50*	£0.30	£0.90	£1.50
7 Hollywood, colour 3-D photo-cover; photos of Jayne Mansfield, Jane Russell amongst others	*$0.50*	*$1.50*	*$2.50*	£0.30	£0.90	£1.50
8 High Seas by Joe Kubert	*$0.50*	*$1.50*	*$2.50*	£0.30	£0.90	£1.50
9 Red Mask by Frank Bolle	*$0.50*	*$1.50*	*$2.50*	£0.30	£0.90	£1.50
10 Jet; Bob Powell and Al Williamson reprints	*$0.50*	*$1.50*	*$2.50*	£0.30	£0.90	£1.50
11 Danse Macabre, Matt Fox art	*$0.50*	*$1.50*	*$2.50*	£0.30	£0.90	£1.50
12 Presidents; oversize issue (8"x10") with photos	*$0.50*	*$1.50*	*$2.50*	£0.30	£0.90	£1.50
13 Flash Gordon, oversize issue (8"x10"), Raymond reprints	*$0.50*	*$1.50*	*$2.50*	£0.30	£0.90	£1.50
14 Tyranostar	*$0.50*	*$1.50*	*$2.50*	£0.30	£0.90	£1.50
15 3-Dementia Comics; Kurtzman, Kubert, Engel, Foster, Scott Shaw art	*$0.50*	*$1.50*	*$2.50*	£0.30	£0.90	£1.50
16 Space Vixens, Dave Stevens cover	*$0.50*	*$1.50*	*$2.50*	£0.30	£0.90	£1.50
17 Thrilling Love; features Kamen, Feldstein, Wood, Frazetta art	*$0.50*	*$1.50*	*$2.50*	£0.30	£0.90	£1.50
18 Spacehawk by Basil Wolverton	*$0.50*	*$1.50*	*$2.50*	£0.30	£0.90	£1.50
19 Cracked Classics	*$0.50*	*$1.50*	*$2.50*	£0.30	£0.90	£1.50
20 Commander Battle & His Atomic Submarine by Michael Vance	*$0.50*	*$1.50*	*$2.50*	£0.30	£0.90	£1.50
21 The Deep, Deep Sleep by Steve Vance	*$0.50*	*$1.50*	*$2.50*	£0.30	£0.90	£1.50
Title Value:	*$10.50*	*$31.50*	*$52.50*	£6.30	£18.90	£31.50

Note: all the above came with bound-in 3-D glasses. Values would be approximately 25% less for copies without glasses. Note also that all are Non-Distributed on the news-stands in the U.K.

THREE-DIMENSIONAL ALIEN WORLDS
Pacific; 1 Jul 1984

Issue	$Good	$Fine	$N.Mint	£Good	£Fine	£N.Mint
1 ND Bolton, Dave Stevens art; 1st published Art Adams art (5pgs); with bound-in 3-D glasses (25% less without glasses)	*$1.00*	*$3.00*	*$5.00*	£0.70	£2.10	£3.50
1 2nd printing ND	*$0.90*	*$2.70*	*$4.50*	£0.60	£1.80	£3.00
Title Value:	*$1.90*	*$5.70*	*$9.50*	£1.30	£3.90	£6.50

THREE-DIMENSIONAL DNAGENTS
Eclipse; 1 Jan 1986

Issue	$Good	$Fine	$N.Mint	£Good	£Fine	£N.Mint
1 ND Mark Evanier script, features art by Jerry Ordway; glasses included (25% less without glasses)	*$0.50*	*$1.50*	*$2.50*	£0.30	£0.90	£1.50
Title Value:	*$0.50*	*$1.50*	*$2.50*	£0.30	£0.90	£1.50

THREE-DIMENSIONAL SEDUCTION OF THE INNOCENT

Eclipse; 1 Oct 1985-2 Apr 1986	$Good	$Fine	$N.Mint	£Good	£Fine	£N.Mint
1 ND pre-code reprints, Dave Stevens cover	$0.50	$1.50	$2.50	£0.30	£0.90	£1.50
1 non 3-D issue ND scarce in the U.K.	$0.60	$1.80	$3.00	£0.40	£1.20	£2.00
2 ND pre-code reprints	$0.50	$1.50	$2.50	£0.30	£0.90	£1.50
2 non 3-D issue ND scarce in the U.K.	$0.60	$1.80	$3.00	£0.40	£1.20	£2.00
Title Value:	$2.20	$6.60	$11.00	£1.40	£4.20	£7.00

3X3 EYES

Innovation,MS; 1 Aug 1991-5 Feb 1992	$Good	$Fine	$N.Mint	£Good	£Fine	£N.Mint
1 ND	$0.50	$1.50	$2.50	£0.30	£0.90	£1.50
1 2nd printing, ND (Mar 1992)	$0.40	$1.20	$2.00	£0.25	£0.75	£1.25
2-5 ND	$0.40	$1.20	$2.00	£0.25	£0.75	£1.25
Title Value:	$2.50	$7.50	$12.50	£1.55	£4.65	£7.75
3 x 3 Eyes (Feb 1995) Trade paperback reprints mini-series, black and white				£1.70	£5.10	£8.50

Note: this edition published by Dark Horse Comics

3X3 EYES: CURSE OF GESU

Dark Horse,MS; 1 Oct 1995-5 Feb 1996	$Good	$Fine	$N.Mint	£Good	£Fine	£N.Mint
1-5 ND Yuzo Takada script and art; black and white	$0.60	$1.80	$3.00	£0.40	£1.20	£2.00
Title Value:	$3.00	$9.00	$15.00	£2.00	£6.00	£10.00

THRESHERZ

Firstlight Comixx,MS; 1 Aug 1994-5 Dec 1994	$Good	$Fine	$N.Mint	£Good	£Fine	£N.Mint
1 ND holo-foil enhanced cover by Andy Smith	$0.50	$1.50	$2.50	£0.30	£0.90	£1.50
1 Gold Edition, ND, available to retailers with every 15 copies of #1	$1.00	$3.00	$5.00	£0.60	£1.80	£3.00
2-5 ND	$0.50	$1.50	$2.50	£0.30	£0.90	£1.50
Title Value:	$3.50	$10.50	$17.50	£2.10	£6.30	£10.50

THRILL-O-RAMA

Harvey; 1 Oct 1965-3 Dec 1966	$Good	$Fine	$N.Mint	£Good	£Fine	£N.Mint
1 rare although distributed in the U.K. Man in Black Called Fate by Bob Powell	$2.50	$7.50	$17.50	£1.75	£5.25	£12.50
2 rare although distributed in the U.K. Pirana begins (see The Phantom #46 for 1st appearance) and origin retold, 2pgs Clawfang, Williamson art	$2.10	$6.25	$15.00	£1.40	£4.25	£10.00
3 scarce in the U.K. Pirana, Man in Black Called Fate	$1.75	$5.25	$12.50	£1.05	£3.20	£7.50
Title Value:	$6.35	$19.00	$45.00	£4.20	£12.70	£30.00

THRILLER

DC Comics; 1 Nov 1983-12 Nov 1984	$Good	$Fine	$N.Mint	£Good	£Fine	£N.Mint
1 ND 1st appearance "7 Seconds"	$0.25	$0.75	$1.25	£0.15	£0.45	£0.75
2-12 ND	$0.25	$0.75	$1.25	£0.15	£0.45	£0.75
Title Value:	$3.00	$9.00	$15.00	£1.80	£5.40	£9.00

Note: all Deluxe Format Baxter paper.

THRILLING ADVENTURE STORIES

Atlas; 1 Feb 1975-2 Aug 1975	$Good	$Fine	$N.Mint	£Good	£Fine	£N.Mint
1 distributed in the U.K. 64pgs, Tigerman, Kromag the Killer, Doc Savage photo feature; Russ Heath art, black and white	$0.40	$1.25	$2.50	£0.25	£0.75	£1.50
2 distributed in the U.K. though scarce 64pgs, Tigerman, Kromag the Killer; Russ Heath, Walt Simonson and Alex Toth art and Neal Adams cover; black and white	$0.40	$1.25	$2.50	£0.30	£1.00	£2.00
Title Value:	$0.80	$2.50	$5.00	£0.55	£1.75	£3.50

THRILLING PLANET TALES

AC Comics,OS; 1 Jun 1991	$Good	$Fine	$N.Mint	£Good	£Fine	£N.Mint
1 ND 68pgs, reprints of classic Fiction House Planet Tales series, Murphy Anderson, Lee Elias, George Evans art featured; limited to 1,000 copies	$1.50	$4.50	$7.50	£1.00	£3.00	£5.00
Title Value:	$1.50	$4.50	$7.50	£1.00	£3.00	£5.00

THRILLING WONDER TALES

AC Comics; nn May 1991	$Good	$Fine	$N.Mint	£Good	£Fine	£N.Mint
nn ND classic sci-fi reprints featuring Kirby, Wood and Ayers art	$0.50	$1.50	$2.50	£0.30	£0.90	£1.50
Title Value:	$0.50	$1.50	$2.50	£0.30	£0.90	£1.50

THRILLKILLER

DC Comics/Elseworlds,MS; 1 Jan 1997-3 Mar 1997	$Good	$Fine	$N.Mint	£Good	£Fine	£N.Mint
1-3 ND Batgirl and Nightwing in a "what if?" story; Howard Chaykin script, Dan Brereton painted covers and art	$0.50	$1.50	$2.50	£0.30	£0.90	£1.50
Title Value:	$1.50	$4.50	$7.50	£0.90	£2.70	£4.50

THRILLOGY

Pacific; 1 Jan 1984	$Good	$Fine	$N.Mint	£Good	£Fine	£N.Mint
1 ND Tim Conrad art	$0.30	$0.90	$1.50	£0.20	£0.60	£1.00
Title Value:	$0.30	$0.90	$1.50	£0.20	£0.60	£1.00

THUMBSCREWS

Caliber Press; 1 Sep 1992-3 1992	$Good	$Fine	$N.Mint	£Good	£Fine	£N.Mint
1 ND 64pgs, horror anthology begins	$0.50	$1.50	$2.50	£0.30	£0.90	£1.50
2-3 ND 64pgs	$0.50	$1.50	$2.50	£0.30	£0.90	£1.50
Title Value:	$1.50	$4.50	$7.50	£0.90	£2.70	£4.50

THUN'DA TALES

Fantagraphics; 1 1987 (see Untamed Love)	$Good	$Fine	$N.Mint	£Good	£Fine	£N.Mint
1 ND Frank Frazetta reprint	$0.50	$1.50	$2.50	£0.30	£0.90	£1.50
Title Value:	$0.50	$1.50	$2.50	£0.30	£0.90	£1.50

THUNDER AGENTS

Tower; 1 Nov 1965-19 Nov 1968; 20 Nov 1969	$Good	$Fine	$N.Mint	£Good	£Fine	£N.Mint
1 DS	$15.50	$47.00	$110.00	£10.00	£30.00	£70.00
2 DS	$10.00	$30.00	$70.00	£6.75	£20.00	£47.50
3-5 DS	$6.75	$20.00	$47.50	£4.25	£12.50	£30.00
6-10 DS	$5.00	$15.00	$35.00	£3.20	£9.50	£22.50
11-15 DS	$3.90	$11.50	$27.50	£2.50	£7.50	£17.50
16-17 DS	$3.20	$9.50	$22.50	£2.10	£6.25	£15.00
18-19 rare although distributed in the U.K. DS	$3.20	$9.50	$22.50	£2.50	£7.50	£17.50
20 DS, all reprint	$2.85	$8.50	$20.00	£1.75	£5.25	£12.50
Title Value:	$105.90	$316.00	$745.00	£68.95	£205.25	£485.00

Note: Steve Ditko art in 6,7,12,16,18. Wally Wood art in most issues. All were distributed in the U.K. though patchily.

THUNDER AGENTS (2ND SERIES)

JC Comics Group,Magazine OS; 1 Feb 1982	$Good	$Fine	$N.Mint	£Good	£Fine	£N.Mint
1 scarce in the U.K. 48pgs, reprints 1st appearance of The Fly from Double Life of Private Strong #1 (Jun 1959) by Joe Simon & Jack Kirby, 1st professional work by Mark Texeira, Neal Adams reprint art (10pgs)	$1.50	$4.50	$7.50	£1.00	£3.00	£5.00
Title Value:	$1.50	$4.50	$7.50	£1.00	£3.00	£5.00

Note: Non-Distributed on the news-stands in the U.K.

THUNDER AGENTS (3RD SERIES)

JC Comics; 1 May 1983-2 Jan 1984	$Good	$Fine	$N.Mint	£Good	£Fine	£N.Mint
1 ND reprints of Wally Wood and Reed Crandall material; sub-titled "Hall of Fame featuring…"	$0.60	$1.80	$3.00	£0.30	£0.90	£1.50
2 ND new stories, intro Agent Vulcan; Murphy Anderson pin-up	$0.60	$1.80	$3.00	£0.30	£0.90	£1.50
Title Value:	$1.20	$3.60	$6.00	£0.60	£1.80	£3.00

Thor #337

Thrax #1

T.H.U.N.D.E.R. Agents #6

THUNDER AGENTS (4TH SERIES)

Maximum Comic Press; 1 Feb 1996-present

Issue	$Good	$Fine	$N.Mint	£Good	£Fine	£N.Mint
1 ND Rob Liefeld script, Chap Yaep art begins	$0.60	$1.80	$3.00	£0.40	£1.20	£2.00
2 ND	$0.60	$1.80	$3.00	£0.40	£1.20	£2.00
Title Value:	$1.20	$3.60	$6.00	£0.80	£2.40	£4.00

THUNDER AGENTS, WALLY WOOD'S

Deluxe Comics; 1 Nov 1984-5 Oct 1986

Issue	$Good	$Fine	$N.Mint	£Good	£Fine	£N.Mint
1 ND 48pgs, part Keith Giffen art	$0.50	$1.50	$2.50	£0.30	£0.90	£1.50
2 ND 48pgs, part George Perez art	$0.50	$1.50	$2.50	£0.30	£0.90	£1.50
3 ND 48pgs, Dave Cockrum, Keith Giffen, Steve Ditko art featured, George Perez cover	$0.50	$1.50	$2.50	£0.30	£0.90	£1.50
4 ND 48pgs	$0.50	$1.50	$2.50	£0.30	£0.90	£1.50
5 ND 48pgs, Jerry Ordway cover	$0.50	$1.50	$2.50	£0.30	£0.90	£1.50
Title Value:	$2.50	$7.50	$12.50	£1.50	£4.50	£7.50

THUNDERBOLT, PETER CANNON

Charlton; 1 Jan 1966; 51 Mar/Apr 1966-60 Nov 1967

(previously Son of Vulcan)

Issue	$Good	$Fine	$N.Mint	£Good	£Fine	£N.Mint
1 rare, distributed in the U.K. origin told	$1.75	$5.25	$12.50	£1.05	£3.20	£7.50
51-60 distributed in the U.K.	$1.05	$3.20	$7.50	£0.70	£2.10	£5.00
Title Value:	$12.25	$37.25	$87.50	£8.05	£24.20	£57.50

THUNDERBUNNY

Red Circle; 1 Jan 1984

Issue	$Good	$Fine	$N.Mint	£Good	£Fine	£N.Mint
1 ND	$0.40	$1.20	$2.00	£0.25	£0.75	£1.25
Title Value:	$0.40	$1.20	$2.00	£0.25	£0.75	£1.25

THUNDERBUNNY (2ND SERIES)

Warp/Apple; 1 Jun 1985-12 Nov 1987

Issue	$Good	$Fine	$N.Mint	£Good	£Fine	£N.Mint
1 ND origin retold	$0.30	$0.90	$1.50	£0.20	£0.60	£1.00
2-5 ND	$0.30	$0.90	$1.50	£0.20	£0.60	£1.00
6 ND last Warp issue	$0.30	$0.90	$1.50	£0.20	£0.60	£1.00
7-10 ND	$0.30	$0.90	$1.50	£0.20	£0.60	£1.00
11 ND THUNDER Agents appear	$0.30	$0.90	$1.50	£0.20	£0.60	£1.00
12 ND	$0.30	$0.90	$1.50	£0.20	£0.60	£1.00
Title Value:	$3.60	$10.80	$18.00	£2.40	£7.20	£12.00

THUNDERCATS

Marvel Comics Group/Star,TV; 1 Dec 1985-24 Jun 1988

Issue	$Good	$Fine	$N.Mint	£Good	£Fine	£N.Mint
1 ND	$0.15	$0.45	$0.75	£0.10	£0.30	£0.50
2 ND 65 and 75 cent covers are known to exist	$0.15	$0.45	$0.75	£0.10	£0.30	£0.50
3-24 ND	$0.15	$0.45	$0.75	£0.10	£0.30	£0.50
Title Value:	$3.60	$10.80	$18.00	£2.40	£7.20	£12.00

THUNDERGOD

Crusade Comics; 1 Jul 1996-present

Issue	$Good	$Fine	$N.Mint	£Good	£Fine	£N.Mint
1-3 ND Christopher Golden script, Albert Debnam art	$0.60	$1.80	$3.00	£0.40	£1.20	£2.00
Title Value:	$1.80	$5.40	$9.00	£1.20	£3.60	£6.00

THUNDERSTRIKE

Marvel Comics Group; 1 Jun 1993-24 Sep 1995

Issue	$Good	$Fine	$N.Mint	£Good	£Fine	£N.Mint
1 ND 48pgs, lightning pattern foil enhanced cover	$0.60	$1.80	$3.00	£0.40	£1.20	£2.00
2 ND Juggernaut appears	$0.30	$0.90	$1.50	£0.20	£0.60	£1.00
3 ND	$0.30	$0.90	$1.50	£0.20	£0.60	£1.00
4 ND Spiderman appears	$0.30	$0.90	$1.50	£0.20	£0.60	£1.00
5 ND Nick Fury and Shield appear	$0.30	$0.90	$1.50	£0.20	£0.60	£1.00
6-7 ND	$0.30	$0.90	$1.50	£0.20	£0.60	£1.00
8 ND with free Spiderman and his Deadly Foes card sheet	$0.30	$0.90	$1.50	£0.20	£0.60	£1.00
9 ND	$0.30	$0.90	$1.50	£0.20	£0.60	£1.00
10 ND Thor appears	$0.30	$0.90	$1.50	£0.20	£0.60	£1.00
11-19 ND	$0.30	$0.90	$1.50	£0.20	£0.60	£1.00
20 ND Black Panther guest-stars	$0.30	$0.90	$1.50	£0.20	£0.60	£1.00
21 ND War Machine, Ant-Man and She-Hulk appear	$0.30	$0.90	$1.50	£0.20	£0.60	£1.00
22 ND	$0.30	$0.90	$1.50	£0.20	£0.60	£1.00
23 ND The Avengers and Thor guest-star	$0.30	$0.90	$1.50	£0.20	£0.60	£1.00
24 ND Thunderstrike vs. Bloodaxe	$0.30	$0.90	$1.50	£0.20	£0.60	£1.00
Title Value:	$7.50	$22.50	$37.50	£5.00	£15.00	£25.00

THUNDERSTRIKE DOUBLE FEATURE

Marvel Comics Group,MS; 1 Oct 1994-4 Jan 1995

Issue	$Good	$Fine	$N.Mint	£Good	£Fine	£N.Mint
1 ND 48pgs, flip-book format; features Thunderstrike #13 plus Code: Blue	$0.50	$1.50	$2.50	£0.30	£0.90	£1.50
2 ND 48pgs, flip-book format; features Thunderstrike #14 plus Code: Blue	$0.50	$1.50	$2.50	£0.30	£0.90	£1.50
3 ND 48pgs, flip-book format; features Thunderstrike #15 plus Code: Blue	$0.50	$1.50	$2.50	£0.30	£0.90	£1.50
4 ND 48pgs, flip-book format; features Thunderstrike #16 plus Code: Blue	$0.50	$1.50	$2.50	£0.30	£0.90	£1.50
Title Value:	$2.00	$6.00	$10.00	£1.20	£3.60	£6.00

TICK SPECIAL EDITION, THE

New England Comics; 1,2 1988

Issue	$Good	$Fine	$N.Mint	£Good	£Fine	£N.Mint
1 ND 1st appearance The Tick	$13.00	$40.00	$80.00	£6.50	£20.00	£40.00
1 Reprise Edition, ND (Apr 1996), with new cover and ads disclaimer	$1.20	$3.60	$6.00	£0.80	£2.40	£4.00
2 ND	$11.50	$35.00	$70.00	£5.75	£17.50	£35.00
Title Value:	$25.70	$78.60	$156.00	£13.05	£39.90	£79.00

TICK'S GIANT CIRCUS OF THE MIGHTY, THE

New England Comics; 1 Apr 1992-3 1992

Issue	$Good	$Fine	$N.Mint	£Good	£Fine	£N.Mint
1-3 ND	$0.50	$1.50	$2.50	£0.30	£0.90	£1.50
Title Value:	$1.50	$4.50	$7.50	£0.90	£2.70	£4.50

TICK, THE

New England Comics; 1 Jun 1988-12 1993

Issue	$Good	$Fine	$N.Mint	£Good	£Fine	£N.Mint
1 black and white, reprints Special Edition 1 with minor changes; Ben Edlund script and art; slightly larger format 7.5" x 10.5"	$9.00	$28.00	$55.00	£4.15	£12.50	£25.00
1 2nd printing	$1.60	$4.80	$8.00	£0.90	£2.70	£4.50
1 3rd printing	$1.00	$3.00	$5.00	£0.50	£1.50	£2.50
1 4th printing	$0.50	$1.50	$2.50	£0.30	£0.90	£1.50
1 5th printing, (Apr 1991)	$0.50	$1.50	$2.50	£0.30	£0.90	£1.50
1 6th printing, (Apr 1995)	$0.50	$1.50	$2.50	£0.30	£0.90	£1.50
1 7th printing, (Mar 1996)	$0.55	$1.65	$2.75	£0.35	£1.05	£1.75
2 reprints Special Edition #2 with minor changes	$8.25	$25.00	$50.00	£2.90	£8.75	£17.50
2 2nd printing	$1.50	$4.50	$7.50	£0.50	£1.50	£2.50
2 3rd/4th printing	$0.50	$1.50	$2.50	£0.30	£0.90	£1.50
2 5th printing, (Jul 1991)	$0.50	$1.50	$2.50	£0.30	£0.90	£1.50
2 Un-Cut Edition, very rare in the U.K., rare in the U.S., available from New England Comics	$12.00	$36.00	$60.00	£8.00	£24.00	£40.00
3	$2.00	$6.00	$10.00	£1.20	£3.60	£6.00
3 2nd printing	$1.00	$3.00	$5.00	£0.50	£1.50	£2.50
3 3rd/4th printing	$0.50	$1.50	$2.50	£0.30	£0.90	£1.50
3 5th printing, (Oct 1993)	$0.50	$1.50	$2.50	£0.30	£0.90	£1.50
3 6th printing, (Apr 1995)	$0.50	$1.50	$2.50	£0.30	£0.90	£1.50
4	$2.00	$6.00	$10.00	£1.00	£3.00	£5.00
4 2nd printing	$0.60	$1.80	$3.00	£0.40	£1.20	£2.00
4 3rd/4th printing	$0.50	$1.50	$2.50	£0.30	£0.90	£1.50
4 5th printing, (Apr 1992)	$0.50	$1.50	$2.50	£0.30	£0.90	£1.50
5	$2.00	$6.00	$10.00	£1.00	£3.00	£5.00
5 2nd printing, (Aug 1992)	$0.50	$1.50	$2.50	£0.30	£0.90	£1.50
6	$1.50	$4.50	$7.50	£0.70	£2.10	£3.50
6 2nd printing, (Aug 1991)	$0.50	$1.50	$2.50	£0.30	£0.90	£1.50
6 3rd/4th printing	$0.50	$1.50	$2.50	£0.30	£0.90	£1.50
7 1st appearance Man-Eating Cow	$1.50	$4.50	$7.50	£0.70	£2.10	£3.50
7 2nd printing, (Nov 1991)	$0.50	$1.50	$2.50	£0.30	£0.90	£1.50
7 3rd printing	$0.50	$1.50	$2.50	£0.30	£0.90	£1.50
8	$1.00	$3.00	$5.00	£0.70	£2.10	£3.50
8 2nd printing, (Apr 1992)	$0.50	$1.50	$2.50	£0.30	£0.90	£1.50
8 3rd printing	$0.50	$1.50	$2.50	£0.30	£0.90	£1.50
8 printed without title logo scarce in the U.K.	$3.00	$9.00	$15.00	£1.20	£3.60	£6.00
9	$0.60	$1.80	$3.00	£0.40	£1.20	£2.00
9 2nd printing	$0.50	$1.50	$2.50	£0.30	£0.90	£1.50
10	$0.60	$1.80	$3.00	£0.40	£1.20	£2.00
10 2nd printing, ND (Mar 1996)	$0.50	$1.50	$2.50	£0.30	£0.90	£1.50
11	$0.60	$1.80	$3.00	£0.40	£1.20	£2.00
11 2nd printing	$0.50	$1.50	$2.50	£0.30	£0.90	£1.50
12	$0.60	$1.80	$3.00	£0.40	£1.20	£2.00
Title Value:	$60.90	$183.95	$323.25	£32.30	£97.00	£168.75

Note: all Non-Distributed on the news-stands in the U.K.

Item	£Good	£Fine	£N.Mint
Tick Omnibus: Sunday Through Wednesday, ND reprints #1-6 plus new story	£1.45	£4.35	£7.25
Tick Omnibus Limited Edition ND signed	£2.20	£6.60	£11.00
Tick Omnibus Vol. 2 ND collects issues #7-10	£1.45	£4.35	£7.25
Tick Omnibus Vol. 3 ND collects issues #11 and #12 plus 20pgs of sketches	£1.45	£4.35	£7.25
Tick Omnibus Vol. 4 ND collects issues #1-3 of Giant Circus of the Mighty	£1.45	£4.35	£7.25
Tick Omnibus Vol. 5 (Jun 1996) ND collects issues #9 and 10 of Paul the Samurai and Man-Eating Cow featuring The Tick	£1.45	£4.35	£7.25

Note: number 8 issued by New England Comics without a logo as a special issue for distributors and retailers

TICK, THE NEW

New England Comics; 1 Aug 1993-9 1995

Issue	$Good	$Fine	$N.Mint	£Good	£Fine	£N.Mint
1 ND pre-bagged with trading card; black and white begins	$0.70	$2.10	$3.50	£0.50	£1.50	£2.50
2 ND	$0.60	$1.80	$3.00	£0.40	£1.20	£2.00

	$Good	$Fine	$N.Mint	£Good	£Fine	£N.Mint
3 ND title becomes "The Tick: Karma Tornado"	$0.60	$1.80	$3.00	£0.40	£1.20	£2.00
4-9 ND	$0.60	$1.80	$3.00	£0.40	£1.20	£2.00
Title Value:	$5.50	$16.50	$27.50	£3.70	£11.10	£18.50
Tick Karma Tornado (Sep 1995) Trade paperback ND collects issues #1-5 with new Ben Edlund cover				£1.80	£5.40	£9.00
Tick Karma Tornado Vol. 2 (Mar 1996) ND collects issues #6-9 with new Ben Edlund cover				£1.80	£5.40	£9.00
TIGER GIRL						
Gold Key; 1 Sep 1968						
1 scarce, distributed in the U.K.	$3.90	$11.50	$27.50	£2.50	£7.50	£17.50
Title Value:	$3.90	$11.50	$27.50	£2.50	£7.50	£17.50
TIGER WOMAN, QUEST OF						
Millennium,OS; 1 Apr 1995						
1 ND Donald Marquez script and art	$0.50	$1.50	$2.50	£0.30	£0.90	£1.50
Title Value:	$0.50	$1.50	$2.50	£0.30	£0.90	£1.50
TIGER WOMAN, THE						
Millennium; 1 Sep 1994-2 1994						
1-2 ND Donald Marquez script, Brian Buniak art	$0.50	$1.50	$2.50	£0.30	£0.90	£1.50
Title Value:	$1.00	$3.00	$5.00	£0.60	£1.80	£3.00
TIGER-MAN						
Atlas; 1 Apr 1975-3 Sep 1975						
1	$0.25	$0.75	$1.50	£0.15	£0.50	£1.00
2-3 Steve Ditko art	$0.25	$0.75	$1.50	£0.15	£0.50	£1.00
Title Value:	$0.75	$2.25	$4.50	£0.45	£1.50	£3.00
TIGER-X						
Eternity; 1 Jun 1988-3 1989						
1-3 ND	$0.40	$1.20	$2.00	£0.25	£0.75	£1.25
Title Value:	$1.20	$3.60	$6.00	£0.75	£2.25	£3.75
Trade Paperback, reprints				£1.00	£3.00	£5.00
TIGER-X II						
Eternity; 1 1989-4 1990						
1-4 ND	$0.40	$1.20	$2.00	£0.25	£0.75	£1.25
Title Value:	$1.60	$4.80	$8.00	£1.00	£3.00	£5.00
TIGER-X SPECIAL						
Eternity; 1 1988						
1 ND	$0.40	$1.20	$2.00	£0.25	£0.75	£1.25
Title Value:	$0.40	$1.20	$2.00	£0.25	£0.75	£1.25
TIGERS OF TERRA						
Antarctic Press; 1 Jun 1994-present ?						
1-15 ND Ted Nomura script and art; black and white	$0.50	$1.50	$2.50	£0.30	£0.90	£1.50
16-17 ND Ted Nomura script and art; black and white	$0.55	$1.65	$2.75	£0.35	£1.05	£1.75
18-22 ND Ted Nomura script and art; black and white	$0.60	$1.80	$3.00	£0.40	£1.20	£2.00
Title Value:	$11.60	$34.80	$58.00	£7.20	£21.60	£36.00
Tigers of Terra Book 1 (Aug 1995) ND 104pgs, collects issues #1,2; black and white				£1.30	£3.90	£6.50
Tigers of Terra Book 2 (Dec 1995) ND collects issues #3 and 4 plus 8 new pages; black and white				£1.30	£3.90	£6.50
Tigers of Terra Book 3 (Apr 1996) ND collects issues #5 and 6 plus 8 new pages; black and white				£1.30	£3.90	£6.50
TIGERS OF TERRA COLOR SPECIAL						
Antarctic Press,OS; 1 Aug 1993						
1 ND black and white	$0.60	$1.80	$3.00	£0.40	£1.20	£2.00
Title Value:	$0.60	$1.80	$3.00	£0.40	£1.20	£2.00
TIGERS OF TERRA TECHNICAL MANUAL						
Antarctic Press; 1 Dec 1995-2 1996						
1-2 ND information and statistics; black and white	$0.60	$1.80	$3.00	£0.40	£1.20	£2.00
Title Value:	$1.20	$3.60	$6.00	£0.80	£2.40	£4.00
TIGRESS, THE						
Hero; 1 Aug 1992-7 1993						
1-5 ND black and white	$0.40	$1.20	$2.00	£0.25	£0.75	£1.25
6-7 ND 44pgs, black and white	$0.50	$1.50	$2.50	£0.30	£0.90	£1.50
Title Value:	$3.00	$9.00	$15.00	£1.85	£5.55	£9.25
TIM HOLT WESTERN ANNUAL						
AC Comics,OS; 1 1991						
1 ND 52pgs, black and white photo cover and black and white reprint art by Frank Bolle, scripted by Gardner Fox; Limited Collectors Edition blazon on cover	$0.50	$1.50	$2.50	£0.30	£0.90	£1.50
Title Value:	$0.50	$1.50	$2.50	£0.30	£0.90	£1.50
TIMBER WOLF						
DC Comics,MS; 1 Nov 1992-5 Mar 1993						
(see Adventure Comics #327)						
1-5	$0.25	$0.75	$1.25	£0.15	£0.45	£0.75
Title Value:	$1.25	$3.75	$6.25	£0.75	£2.25	£3.75
TIME BANDITS						
Marvel Comics Group,OS Film; 1 1982						
1 ND 52pgs, adapts film	$0.30	$0.90	$1.50	£0.20	£0.60	£1.00
Title Value:	$0.30	$0.90	$1.50	£0.20	£0.60	£1.00
TIME BEAVERS						
First; Graphic Novel; nn 1985						
nn ND Tim Truman art	$1.50	$4.50	$7.50	£1.00	£3.00	£5.00
Title Value:	$1.50	$4.50	$7.50	£1.00	£3.00	£5.00
TIME BREAKERS						
DC Comics/Helix,MS; 1 Jan 1997-5 May 1997						
1-5 ND Rachel Pollack script, Chris Weston art	$0.45	$1.35	$2.25	£0.30	£0.90	£1.50
Title Value:	$2.25	$6.75	$11.75	£1.50	£4.50	£7.50
TIME COP MOVIE ADAPTATION						
Dark Horse,MS Film; 1,2 Sep 1994						
1-2 ND Ron Randall art, Denis Beauvais painted cover	$0.50	$1.50	$2.50	£0.30	£0.90	£1.50
Title Value:	$1.00	$3.00	$5.00	£0.60	£1.80	£3.00
TIME GATES						
Double Edge; 1 May 1991-4 Oct 1991						
1 ND dinosaur issue; black and white begins	$0.30	$0.90	$1.50	£0.20	£0.60	£1.00
2-4 ND	$0.30	$0.90	$1.50	£0.20	£0.60	£1.00
Title Value:	$1.20	$3.60	$6.00	£0.80	£2.40	£4.00
TIME MACHINE GRAPHIC NOVEL, THE						
Eternity,OS; 1 Aug 1991						
1 ND adaptation of classic sci-fi book	$1.50	$4.50	$7.50	£1.00	£3.00	£5.00
Title Value:	$1.50	$4.50	$7.50	£1.00	£3.00	£5.00
TIME MACHINE, THE						
Eternity,MS; 1 Apr 1990-3 May 1990						
1-3 ND adaptation of H.G. Wells classic; Bill Spangler black and white art	$0.40	$1.20	$2.00	£0.25	£0.75	£1.25
Title Value:	$1.20	$3.60	$6.00	£0.75	£2.25	£3.75
Note: issues 1,2 bi-weekly						
TIME MASTERS						
DC Comics,MS; 1 Feb 1990-8 Sep 1990						
(see Rip Hunter)						
1 Art Thibert art begins, Rip Hunter appears throughout	$0.25	$0.75	$1.25	£0.15	£0.45	£0.75
2 Superman appears	$0.25	$0.75	$1.25	£0.15	£0.45	£0.75
3 Jonah Hex appears	$0.25	$0.75	$1.25	£0.15	£0.45	£0.75
4 Tomahawk appears	$0.25	$0.75	$1.25	£0.15	£0.45	£0.75
5 Cave Carson appears	$0.25	$0.75	$1.25	£0.15	£0.45	£0.75
6 Dr. Fate appears	$0.25	$0.75	$1.25	£0.15	£0.45	£0.75
7 Arion appears	$0.25	$0.75	$1.25	£0.15	£0.45	£0.75
8 Vandal Savage appears	$0.25	$0.75	$1.25	£0.15	£0.45	£0.75
Title Value:	$2.00	$6.00	$10.00	£1.20	£3.60	£6.00
Note: Deluxe Format; series re-evaluates time-travel in the DC Universe.						
TIME TRIPPERS						
Snyder Inkworks; 1-3 Winter 1990						
1-3 ND black and white	$0.15	$0.45	$0.75	£0.10	£0.30	£0.50
Title Value:	$0.45	$1.35	$2.25	£0.30	£0.90	£1.50
TIME TUNNEL, THE						
Gold Key; 1 Feb 1967-2 Jul 1967						
1 distributed in the U.K. based on TV series	$7.00	$21.00	$50.00	£4.25	£12.50	£30.00
2 based on TV series	$5.50	$17.00	$40.00	£3.55	£10.50	£25.00
Title Value:	$12.50	$38.00	$90.00	£7.80	£23.00	£55.00
TIME TWISTERS						
Quality Comics; 1 Sep 1987-21 May 1989						
1 LD in the U.K. reprints from 2000 AD begin; early issues feature Alan Moore scripts	$0.25	$0.75	$1.25	£0.15	£0.45	£0.75
2-13 LD in the U.K.	$0.25	$0.75	$1.25	£0.15	£0.45	£0.75
14 LD in the U.K. Brian Bolland art (3pgs)	$0.30	$0.90	$1.50	£0.20	£0.60	£1.00
15-16 LD in the U.K. Jackson Guice cover	$0.25	$0.75	$1.25	£0.15	£0.45	£0.75
17-21 LD in the U.K.	$0.25	$0.75	$1.25	£0.15	£0.45	£0.75
Title Value:	$5.30	$15.90	$26.50	£3.20	£9.60	£16.00
TIME WARP						
DC Comics; 1 Oct/Nov 1979-5 Jun/Jul 1980						
1 ND scarce in the U.K. 68pgs	$0.60	$1.80	$3.00	£0.40	£1.20	£2.00
2-5 ND scarce in the U.K. 68pgs	$0.50	$1.50	$2.50	£0.30	£0.90	£1.50
Title Value:	$2.60	$7.80	$13.00	£1.60	£4.80	£8.00
ARTISTS						
Ditko art in 1-4. Nasser art in 4.						
TIMEDRIFTER						
Innovation; 1 Dec 1990-3 Feb 1991						
1-3 ND Gerard Jones script/art; black and white	$0.40	$1.20	$2.00	£0.25	£0.75	£1.25
Title Value:	$1.20	$3.60	$6.00	£0.75	£2.25	£3.75
TIMESPIRITS						
Marvel Comics Group/Epic,MS; 1 Jan 1985-8 Mar 1986						
1-8 ND	$0.40	$1.20	$2.00	£0.25	£0.75	£1.25
Title Value:	$3.20	$9.60	$16.00	£2.00	£6.00	£10.00
Note: all on Baxter paper, Mature Readers label. Williamson art in 4.						

TIMESTRYKE

Marvel UK,MS; 1 Dec 1993

Issue	$Good	$Fine	$N.Mint	£Good	£Fine	£N.Mint
1 red foil enhanced cover (cancelled after 1 issue)	*$0.40*	*$1.20*	*$2.00*	£0.25	£0.75	£1.25
Title Value:	*$0.40*	*$1.20*	*$2.00*	£0.25	£0.75	£1.25

TIMEWALKER

Valiant/Acclaim Comics; 0 Apr 1994; 1 Dec 1994-15 Jun 1995

Issue	$Good	$Fine	$N.Mint	£Good	£Fine	£N.Mint
0 origin told	*$0.40*	*$1.20*	*$2.00*	£0.25	£0.75	£1.25
1 spin-off from The Chaos Effect storyline	*$0.40*	*$1.20*	*$2.00*	£0.25	£0.75	£1.25
2-5	*$0.40*	*$1.20*	*$2.00*	£0.25	£0.75	£1.25
6-7 Harbinger Wars story	*$0.40*	*$1.20*	*$2.00*	£0.25	£0.75	£1.25
8 1st Acclaim Comics issue, Harbinger Wars story; bi-weekly	*$0.40*	*$1.20*	*$2.00*	£0.25	£0.75	£1.25
9 bi-weekly, leads into Timewalker #0	*$0.40*	*$1.20*	*$2.00*	£0.25	£0.75	£1.25
10-15 bi-weekly	*$0.40*	*$1.20*	*$2.00*	£0.25	£0.75	£1.25
Title Value:	*$6.40*	*$19.20*	*$32.00*	£4.00	£12.00	£20.00

Note: all Non-Distributed on the news-stands in the U.K.

Timewalker (May 1995)

	£Good	£Fine	£N.Mint
Trade paperback reprints early appearances from Archer & Armstrong #8, 10, 11 and Magnus #33	£1.30	£3.90	£6.50

TIMEWALKER YEARBOOK

Valiant; 1 May 1995

Issue	$Good	$Fine	$N.Mint	£Good	£Fine	£N.Mint
1 ND story continues from Magnus Robot Fighter #33	*$0.50*	*$1.50*	*$2.50*	£0.30	£0.90	£1.50
Title Value:	*$0.50*	*$1.50*	*$2.50*	£0.30	£0.90	£1.50

TINY TOON ADVENTURES

DC Comics,Magazine; 1 Oct 1990-5 1991

Issue	$Good	$Fine	$N.Mint	£Good	£Fine	£N.Mint
1 ND 32pgs, Bugs Bunny, Daffy Duck and other MGM cartoon characters	*$0.30*	*$0.90*	*$1.50*	£0.20	£0.60	£1.00
2 ND 32pgs, Winter theme	*$0.30*	*$0.90*	*$1.50*	£0.20	£0.60	£1.00
3-5 ND 32pgs	*$0.30*	*$0.90*	*$1.50*	£0.20	£0.60	£1.00
Title Value:	*$1.50*	*$4.50*	*$7.50*	£1.00	£3.00	£5.00

TION

Pink Egg Publishing; 1,2 1990

Issue	$Good	$Fine	$N.Mint	£Good	£Fine	£N.Mint
1-2 ND black and white	*$0.40*	*$1.20*	*$2.00*	£0.25	£0.75	£1.25
Title Value:	*$0.80*	*$2.40*	*$4.00*	£0.50	£1.50	£2.50

TITAN GRAPHIC NOVEL

Continuity,OS; 1 Jul 1992

Issue	$Good	$Fine	$N.Mint	£Good	£Fine	£N.Mint
1 ND 48pgs, Neal Adams cover	*$0.80*	*$2.40*	*$4.00*	£0.50	£1.50	£2.50
Title Value:	*$0.80*	*$2.40*	*$4.00*	£0.50	£1.50	£2.50

TITAN SPECIAL

Dark Horse/Comics Greatest World,OS; 1 May 1994

Issue	$Good	$Fine	$N.Mint	£Good	£Fine	£N.Mint
1 ND 48pgs, Bart Sears cover	*$0.80*	*$2.40*	*$4.00*	£0.50	£1.50	£2.50
Title Value:	*$0.80*	*$2.40*	*$4.00*	£0.50	£1.50	£2.50

TITANS SELL-OUT SPECIAL, THE

DC Comics,OS; 1 Dec 1992

Issue	$Good	$Fine	$N.Mint	£Good	£Fine	£N.Mint
1 ND 48pgs, Titans Sell-Out part 1, X-over Deathstroke the Terminator #17, (continuation of "Total Chaos" storyline); bound-in Nightwing poster	*$0.60*	*$1.80*	*$3.00*	£0.40	£1.20	£2.00
Title Value:	*$0.60*	*$1.80*	*$3.00*	£0.40	£1.20	£2.00

TMNT MUTANT UNIVERSE SOURCEBOOK

Archie,OS; 1 Jan 1993

Issue	$Good	$Fine	$N.Mint	£Good	£Fine	£N.Mint
1 ND 48pgs	*$0.40*	*$1.20*	*$2.00*	£0.25	£0.75	£1.25
Title Value:	*$0.40*	*$1.20*	*$2.00*	£0.25	£0.75	£1.25

TMNT PRESENT: DONATELLO & LEATHERHEAD

Archie,MS; 1 Jun 1993-3 Aug 1993

Issue	$Good	$Fine	$N.Mint	£Good	£Fine	£N.Mint
1-3 ND	*$0.25*	*$0.75*	*$1.25*	£0.15	£0.45	£0.75
Title Value:	*$0.75*	*$2.25*	*$3.75*	£0.45	£1.35	£2.25

TMNT PRESENTS: APRIL O'NEIL - THE MAY EAST SAGA

Archie,MS; 1 Mar 1993-3 May 1993

Issue	$Good	$Fine	$N.Mint	£Good	£Fine	£N.Mint
1-3 ND	*$0.25*	*$0.75*	*$1.25*	£0.15	£0.45	£0.75
Title Value:	*$0.75*	*$2.25*	*$3.75*	£0.45	£1.35	£2.25

TMNT PRESENTS: MERDUDE & MICHAELANGELO

Archie,MS; 1 Aug 1993-3 Nov 1993

Issue	$Good	$Fine	$N.Mint	£Good	£Fine	£N.Mint
1-3 ND	*$0.25*	*$0.75*	*$1.25*	£0.15	£0.45	£0.75
Title Value:	*$0.75*	*$2.25*	*$3.75*	£0.45	£1.35	£2.25

TMNT/SAVAGE DRAGON CROSS-OVER SPECIAL

Mirage Studios,OS; 1 Nov 1993

Issue	$Good	$Fine	$N.Mint	£Good	£Fine	£N.Mint
1 ND X-over with Savage Dragon #2, part Erik Larsen cover	*$0.50*	*$1.50*	*$2.50*	£0.30	£0.90	£1.50
Title Value:	*$0.50*	*$1.50*	*$2.50*	£0.30	£0.90	£1.50

TMNT\FLAMING CARROT CROSS-OVER: LAND OF GREEN FIRE

Mirage Studios,MS; 1 Jan 1994-4 Apr 1994

Issue	$Good	$Fine	$N.Mint	£Good	£Fine	£N.Mint
1-4 ND Bob Burden script	*$0.50*	*$1.50*	*$2.50*	£0.30	£0.90	£1.50
Title Value:	*$2.00*	*$6.00*	*$10.00*	£1.20	£3.60	£6.00

TO BE ANNOUNCED

Strawberry Jam; 1 1985-7 Jun 1987

Issue	$Good	$Fine	$N.Mint	£Good	£Fine	£N.Mint
1-7 ND	*$0.30*	*$0.90*	*$1.50*	£0.20	£0.60	£1.00
Title Value:	*$2.10*	*$6.30*	*$10.50*	£1.40	£4.20	£7.00

TO DIE FOR IN 3-D

Blackthorne; (3-D Series #64) 1 Spring 1989

Issue	$Good	$Fine	$N.Mint	£Good	£Fine	£N.Mint
1 ND	*$0.50*	*$1.50*	*$2.50*	£0.30	£0.90	£1.50
1 non 3-D issue ND	*$0.40*	*$1.20*	*$2.00*	£0.25	£0.75	£1.25
Title Value:	*$0.90*	*$2.70*	*$4.50*	£0.55	£1.65	£2.75

TOKA JUNGLE KING

Dell; 1 Aug/Oct 1964-10 Jan 1967

Issue	$Good	$Fine	$N.Mint	£Good	£Fine	£N.Mint
1 painted cover	*$3.20*	*$9.50*	*$22.50*	£2.10	£6.25	£15.00
2 painted cover	*$1.70*	*$5.00*	*$12.00*	£1.10	£3.40	£8.00
3 Frank Springer covers and art begin	*$1.40*	*$4.25*	*$10.00*	£0.90	£2.75	£6.50
4-5	*$1.40*	*$4.25*	*$10.00*	£0.90	£2.75	£6.50
6-10	*$1.10*	*$3.40*	*$8.00*	£0.70	£2.10	£5.00
Title Value:	*$14.60*	*$44.25*	*$104.50*	£9.40	£28.40	£67.50

Note: all Limited Distribution in the U.K.

TOM CORBETT, SPACE CADET

Eternity,MS; 1 Mar 1990-4 Jun 1990

Issue	$Good	$Fine	$N.Mint	£Good	£Fine	£N.Mint
1-4 ND	*$0.40*	*$1.20*	*$2.00*	£0.25	£0.75	£1.25
Title Value:	*$1.60*	*$4.80*	*$8.00*	£1.00	£3.00	£5.00

	£Good	£Fine	£N.Mint
Graphic Album: The Reconstructed Man, reprints issues Book I #1-4	£1.10	£3.30	£5.50

TOM CORBETT, SPACE CADET BOOK TWO

Eternity,MS; 1 Sep 1990-4 Dec 1990

Issue	$Good	$Fine	$N.Mint	£Good	£Fine	£N.Mint
1 ND new adventures based on 1950s CBS television series begin	*$0.40*	*$1.20*	*$2.00*	£0.25	£0.75	£1.25
2-4 ND	*$0.40*	*$1.20*	*$2.00*	£0.25	£0.75	£1.25
Title Value:	*$1.60*	*$4.80*	*$8.00*	£1.00	£3.00	£5.00

TOM CORBETT, THE ORIGINAL

Eternity,MS; 1 Sep 1990-5 Jan 1991

Issue	$Good	$Fine	$N.Mint	£Good	£Fine	£N.Mint
1 ND bi-weekly issues, reprints 1950s newspaper strip of popular TV series	*$0.50*	*$1.50*	*$2.50*	£0.30	£0.90	£1.50
2-5 ND	*$0.50*	*$1.50*	*$2.50*	£0.30	£0.90	£1.50
Title Value:	*$2.50*	*$7.50*	*$12.50*	£1.50	£4.50	£7.50

TOM KATZ

Sun Comic Publishing; 1 May 1993

Issue	$Good	$Fine	$N.Mint	£Good	£Fine	£N.Mint
1 ND	*$0.40*	*$1.20*	*$2.00*	£0.25	£0.75	£1.25
Title Value:	*$0.40*	*$1.20*	*$2.00*	£0.25	£0.75	£1.25

TOMAHAWK

National Periodical Publications; 65 Nov/Dec 1959-140 May/Jun 1972

(see Limited Collector's Edition #47, Unknown Soldier) (previous issues ND)

Issue	$Good	$Fine	$N.Mint	£Good	£Fine	£N.Mint
65-70 scarce in the U.K.	*$6.25*	*$19.00*	*$45.00*	£4.25	£12.50	£30.00
71-76 scarce in the U.K.	*$6.00*	*$18.00*	*$42.50*	£3.90	£11.50	£27.50
77 last 10 cents issue	*$6.00*	*$18.00*	*$42.50*	£3.90	£11.50	£27.50
78-80	*$5.00*	*$15.00*	*$35.00*	£3.20	£9.50	£22.50
81-90	*$4.25*	*$12.50*	*$30.00*	£2.50	£7.50	£17.50
91-100	*$2.85*	*$8.50*	*$20.00*	£1.75	£5.25	£12.50
101 becomes Tomahawk and his Rip Roaring Rangers	*$2.05*	*$6.25*	*$12.50*	£1.25	£3.75	£7.50
102-110	*$2.05*	*$6.25*	*$12.50*	£1.25	£3.75	£7.50
111-113	*$1.25*	*$3.75*	*$7.50*	£0.80	£2.50	£5.00
114 scarce in the U.K.	*$1.25*	*$3.75*	*$7.50*	£1.00	£3.00	£6.00
115	*$1.25*	*$3.75*	*$7.50*	£0.80	£2.50	£5.00
116 scarce in the U.K. Neal Adams cover	*$1.25*	*$3.75*	*$7.50*	£1.00	£3.00	£6.00
117-119 Neal Adams covers	*$1.25*	*$3.75*	*$7.50*	£0.80	£2.50	£5.00
120	*$1.25*	*$3.75*	*$7.50*	£0.80	£2.50	£5.00
121 Neal Adams cover	*$1.15*	*$3.50*	*$7.00*	£0.65	£2.00	£4.00
122	*$1.15*	*$3.50*	*$7.00*	£0.65	£2.00	£4.00
123-130 Neal Adams covers	*$1.15*	*$3.50*	*$7.00*	£0.65	£2.00	£4.00
131 Frazetta reprint, becomes Son of Tomahawk on cover	*$1.30*	*$4.00*	*$8.00*	£0.80	£2.50	£5.00
132-138	*$1.15*	*$3.50*	*$7.00*	£0.65	£2.00	£4.00
139 scarce in the U.K. 52pgs, Frazetta reprint	*$1.15*	*$3.50*	*$7.00*	£0.65	£2.00	£4.00
140 scarce in the U.K. 52pgs	*$1.15*	*$3.50*	*$7.00*	£0.65	£2.00	£4.00
Title Value:	*$221.65*	*$665.50*	*$1513.50*	£138.95	£415.50	£948.00

FEATURES

Firehair in 131 (2pgs), 132, 134, 136.

TOMB OF DARKNESS

Marvel Comics Group; 9 Jul 1974-23 Nov 1976

(formerly Beware)

Issue	$Good	$Fine	$N.Mint	£Good	£Fine	£N.Mint
9 ND early '60s horror reprints begin	*$0.50*	*$1.50*	*$3.00*	£0.25	£0.75	£1.50
10-20	*$0.30*	*$1.00*	*$2.00*	£0.20	£0.60	£1.25
21-22 ND	*$0.30*	*$1.00*	*$2.00*	£0.25	£0.75	£1.50
23	*$0.30*	*$1.00*	*$2.00*	£0.20	£0.60	£1.25
Title Value:	*$4.70*	*$15.50*	*$31.00*	£3.15	£9.45	£19.50

TOMB OF DRACULA

Marvel Comics Group; 1 Apr 1972-70 Aug 1979

Issue	$Good	$Fine	$N.Mint	£Good	£Fine	£N.Mint
1 ND	*$12.50*	*$38.00*	*$75.00*	£7.50	£22.50	£45.00
2 ND	*$7.50*	*$22.50*	*$45.00*	£3.75	£11.00	£22.50
3 ND	*$5.25*	*$16.00*	*$32.50*	£2.90	£8.75	£17.50
4-5 ND	*$5.00*	*$15.00*	*$30.00*	£2.50	£7.50	£15.00
6 ND Neal Adams cover	*$4.15*	*$12.50*	*$25.00*	£1.25	£3.75	£7.50
7-9	*$3.75*	*$11.00*	*$22.50*	£1.25	£3.75	£7.50
10 1st Blade the Vampire Slayer	*$4.15*	*$12.50*	*$25.00*	£1.65	£5.00	£10.00
11	*$2.50*	*$7.50*	*$15.00*	£0.80	£2.50	£5.00

	$Good	$Fine	$N.Mint	£Good	£Fine	£N.Mint
12 scarce in the U.K. Brunner cover	$2.50	$7.50	$15.00	£1.00	£3.00	£6.00
13 origin Blade	$2.50	$7.50	$15.00	£0.80	£2.50	£5.00
14-17	$2.50	$7.50	$15.00	£0.80	£2.50	£5.00
18 Werewolf By Night appears	$2.50	$7.50	$15.00	£0.80	£2.50	£5.00
19-20 ND	$2.50	$7.50	$15.00	£1.00	£3.00	£6.00
21-22 ND	$2.05	$6.25	$12.50	£0.65	£2.00	£4.00
23-28	$2.05	$6.25	$12.50	£0.55	£1.75	£3.50
29-30 ND	$2.05	$6.25	$12.50	£0.65	£2.00	£4.00
31-34 ND	$1.65	$5.00	$10.00	£0.55	£1.75	£3.50
35 ND Brother Voodoo appears	$1.65	$5.00	$10.00	£0.55	£1.75	£3.50
36-40 ND	$1.65	$5.00	$10.00	£0.55	£1.75	£3.50
41-42 ND	$1.25	$3.75	$7.50	£0.50	£1.50	£3.00
43 ND Bernie Wrightson cover art	$1.25	$3.75	$7.50	£0.50	£1.50	£3.00
44-49 ND	$1.25	$3.75	$7.50	£0.50	£1.50	£3.00
50 ND Silver Surfer appears	$1.65	$5.00	$10.00	£0.65	£2.00	£4.00
51-54 ND	$1.00	$3.00	$6.00	£0.50	£1.50	£3.00
55-62	$1.00	$3.00	$6.00	£0.40	£1.25	£2.50
63-66 ND	$0.80	$2.50	$5.00	£0.50	£1.50	£3.00
67 ND Lilith appears	$0.80	$2.50	$5.00	£0.50	£1.50	£3.00
68-69 ND	$0.80	$2.50	$5.00	£0.50	£1.50	£3.00
70 ND scarce in the U.K. 52pgs	$1.00	$3.00	$6.00	£0.55	£1.75	£3.50
Title Value:	$148.30	$447.25	$893.50	£60.20	£183.50	£367.50

TOMB OF DRACULA (2ND SERIES)

Marvel Comics Group,Magazine; 1 Nov 1979-6 Sep 1980

	$Good	$Fine	$N.Mint	£Good	£Fine	£N.Mint
1 ND Gene Colan art begins	$1.00	$3.00	$5.00	£0.70	£2.10	£3.50
2 ND Steve Ditko art	$0.90	$2.70	$4.50	£0.50	£1.50	£2.50
3 ND 2pgs Frank Miller art	$0.90	$2.70	$4.50	£0.50	£1.50	£2.50
4 ND Stephen King feature	$0.90	$2.70	$4.50	£0.50	£1.50	£2.50
5 ND	$0.90	$2.70	$4.50	£0.50	£1.50	£2.50
6 ND 12pgs Sienkiewicz art	$1.00	$3.00	$5.00	£0.60	£1.80	£3.00
Title Value:	$5.60	$16.80	$28.00	£3.30	£9.90	£16.50

TOMB OF DRACULA (LIMITED SERIES)

Marvel Comics Group/Epic,MS; 1 Nov 1991-4 Feb 1992

	$Good	$Fine	$N.Mint	£Good	£Fine	£N.Mint
1-4 ND Marv Wolfman script, Gene Colan art	$1.00	$3.00	$5.00	£0.60	£1.80	£3.00
Title Value:	$4.00	$12.00	$20.00	£2.40	£7.20	£12.00

TOMB OF DRACULA: HALLOWEEN MEGAZINE

Marvel Comics Group,OS; nn Dec 1996

	$Good	$Fine	$N.Mint	£Good	£Fine	£N.Mint
nn ND reprints Blade storyline from Tomb of Dracula in view of Blade movie from New Line Cinema – call me an old cynic but...	$0.80	$2.40	$4.00	£0.50	£1.50	£2.50
Title Value:	$0.80	$2.40	$4.00	£0.50	£1.50	£2.50

TOMMI GUN

London Night Studios; ½ Sep 1996; 1 May 1996-3 Aug 1996

	$Good	$Fine	$N.Mint	£Good	£Fine	£N.Mint
½ ND	$0.60	$1.80	$3.00	£0.40	£1.20	£2.00
1 ND Everette Hartsoe script, George Jeanty art; centrefold "glamour" poster	$0.50	$1.50	$2.50	£0.30	£0.90	£1.50
1 Naughty Platinum Edition, ND - cardstock nude cover and nude centrefold	$2.00	$6.00	$10.00	£1.30	£3.90	£6.50
2 ND centrefold poster	$0.60	$1.80	$3.00	£0.40	£1.20	£2.00
2 Nude Cover Edition ND	$1.00	$3.00	$5.00	£0.70	£2.10	£3.50
3 ND	$0.60	$1.80	$3.00	£0.40	£1.20	£2.00
Title Value:	$5.30	$15.90	$26.50	£3.50	£10.50	£17.50

TOMOE

Crusade Comics,MS; 0 Feb 1996; 1 Jul 1995-3 1996

	$Good	$Fine	$N.Mint	£Good	£Fine	£N.Mint
0 ND	$0.60	$1.80	$3.00	£0.40	£1.20	£2.00
0 Commemorative Edition, ND Jimmy Palmiotti and Amanda Conner cover	$4.00	$12.00	$20.00	£2.50	£7.50	£12.50
0 Variant Cover Edition, ND Bill Tucci cover	$1.50	$4.50	$7.50	£1.00	£3.00	£5.00
1 ND orders of Shi #6 split to contain an even number of Tomoe #1; same interior as Shi #6 but with cover featuring Tomoe	$1.40	$4.20	$7.00	£1.00	£3.00	£5.00
1 Commemorative Edition, ND features Tomoe on right of cover holding a fan, no logo or title, limited to 5,000 copies; black and white	$4.00	$12.00	$20.00	£2.50	£7.50	£12.50
2-3 ND	$0.60	$1.80	$3.00	£0.40	£1.20	£2.00
Title Value:	$12.70	$38.10	$63.50	£8.20	£24.60	£41.00

TOMOE/WITCHBLADE/MANGA SHI PREVIEW

Crusade Comics,OS; nn Jul 1996

	$Good	$Fine	$N.Mint	£Good	£Fine	£N.Mint
nn ND 16pgs, signed by Bill Tucci and Peter Gutierrez, limited to 1,000 copies; black and white	$2.50	$7.50	$12.50	£1.50	£4.50	£7.50
Title Value:	$2.50	$7.50	$12.50	£1.50	£4.50	£7.50

TOMOE/WITCHBLADE: FIRE SERMON

Crusade Comics; 1 Sep 1996

	$Good	$Fine	$N.Mint	£Good	£Fine	£N.Mint
1 ND 48pgs, Peter Gutierrez script, Jamal Igle art	$0.80	$2.40	$4.00	£0.50	£1.50	£2.50
1 Avalon Edition, ND new card-stock cover, gold foil logo; limited to 3,000 copies	$3.00	$9.00	$15.00	£3.00	£9.00	£15.00
Title Value:	$3.80	$11.40	$19.00	£3.50	£10.50	£17.50

TOMORROW KNIGHTS

Marvel Comics Group/Epic,MS; 1 Jun 1990-6 Mar 1991

	$Good	$Fine	$N.Mint	£Good	£Fine	£N.Mint
1-6 ND DS	$0.40	$1.20	$2.00	£0.25	£0.75	£1.25
Title Value:	$2.40	$7.20	$12.00	£1.50	£4.50	£7.50

Note: bi-monthly

TOMORROW MAN

Antarctic Press,OS; 1 Aug 1993

	$Good	$Fine	$N.Mint	£Good	£Fine	£N.Mint
1 ND 48pgs	$0.50	$1.50	$2.50	£0.30	£0.90	£1.50
Title Value:	$0.50	$1.50	$2.50	£0.30	£0.90	£1.50

TOMORROW MAN/KNIGHT HUNTER: LAST RITES

Antarctic Press,MS; 1 Aug 1994-6 Jun 1995

	$Good	$Fine	$N.Mint	£Good	£Fine	£N.Mint
1-6 ND Jochen Weltjens script, Bobby Padilla art	$0.50	$1.50	$2.50	£0.30	£0.90	£1.50
Title Value:	$3.00	$9.00	$15.00	£1.80	£5.40	£9.00

TONGUE LASH

Dark Horse,MS; 1 Aug 1996-2 Sep 1996

	$Good	$Fine	$N.Mint	£Good	£Fine	£N.Mint
1-2 ND Marc Lofficier script, Dave Taylor art	$0.60	$1.80	$3.00	£0.40	£1.20	£2.00
Title Value:	$1.20	$3.60	$6.00	£0.80	£2.40	£4.00

TOO MUCH COFFEE MAN

Adhesive Comics; 1 Jul 1993-present

	$Good	$Fine	$N.Mint	£Good	£Fine	£N.Mint
1 ND Shannon Wheeler script and art; black and white	$1.50	$4.50	$7.50	£0.50	£1.50	£2.50
1 2nd printing, ND (Mar 94)	$0.60	$1.80	$3.00	£0.40	£1.20	£2.00
2 ND Shannon Wheeler script and art; black and white	$1.00	$3.00	$5.00	£0.40	£1.20	£2.00
3-5 ND Shannon Wheeler script and art; black and white						

Toka, Jungle King #6

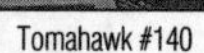
Tomahawk #140

Tomoe/Witchblade: Fire Sermon Avalon Edition

	$Good	$Fine	$N.Mint	£Good	£Fine	£N.Mint
	$0.60	$1.80	$3.00	£0.30	£0.90	£1.50
Title Value:	$4.90	$14.70	$24.50	£2.20	£6.60	£11.00
Too Much Coffee Man Collector's Pack (Mar 1996) ND collects issues #1-4 with signed postcard				£1.30	£3.90	£6.50

TOP CAT

Charlton; 1 Nov 1970-20 Nov 1973

	$Good	$Fine	$N.Mint	£Good	£Fine	£N.Mint
1 Ray Dirgo art begins	$5.75	$17.50	$35.00	£3.30	£10.00	£20.00
2-3	$3.30	$10.00	$20.00	£2.05	£6.25	£12.50
4-10	$2.90	$8.75	$17.50	£1.65	£5.00	£10.00
11-20	$2.50	$7.50	$15.00	£1.25	£3.75	£7.50
Title Value:	$57.65	$173.75	$347.50	£31.45	£95.00	£190.00

TOP COW SECRETS - SPECIAL WINTER LINGERIE EDITION

Image,OS; nn Dec 1995

	$Good	$Fine	$N.Mint	£Good	£Fine	£N.Mint
nn ND Cyblade, Witchblade, Velocity and other pin-ups, Marc Silvestri cover	$0.60	$1.80	$3.00	£0.40	£1.20	£2.00
Title Value:	$0.60	$1.80	$3.00	£0.40	£1.20	£2.00

TOP COW/BALLISTIC STUDIOS SWIMSUIT SPECIAL

Image,OS; 1 May 1995

	$Good	$Fine	$N.Mint	£Good	£Fine	£N.Mint
1 ND Marc Silvestri and co. and their pin-ups for Top Cow	$0.60	$1.80	$3.00	£0.40	£1.20	£2.00
Title Value:	$0.60	$1.80	$3.00	£0.40	£1.20	£2.00

TOP DOG, THE SECRET LIFE OF

Marvel Comics Group/Star; 1 Apr 1985-10 Oct 1986

	$Good	$Fine	$N.Mint	£Good	£Fine	£N.Mint
1-9 scarce in the U.K.	$0.15	$0.45	$0.75	£0.10	£0.30	£0.50
10 scarce in the U.K. Spiderman appears	$0.15	$0.45	$0.75	£0.10	£0.30	£0.50
Title Value:	$1.50	$4.50	$7.50	£1.00	£3.00	£5.00

TOPPS COMICS PRESENTS

Topps; 0 Aug 1993

	$Good	$Fine	$N.Mint	£Good	£Fine	£N.Mint
0 ND 16pgs, preview comic featuring Dracula vs. Zorro, Jack Kirby's TeenAgents, Silver Star and Bill The Galactic Hero; available for free from 1993 San Diego Comicon	$0.25	$0.75	$1.25	£0.15	£0.45	£0.75
Title Value:	$0.25	$0.75	$1.25	£0.15	£0.45	£0.75

TOR

DC Comics; 1 May/Jun 1975-6 Mar/Apr 1976

	$Good	$Fine	$N.Mint	£Good	£Fine	£N.Mint
1 new origin by Kubert	$0.50	$1.50	$3.00	£0.25	£0.75	£1.50
2 reprints original 1950s #1	$0.30	$1.00	$2.00	£0.15	£0.50	£1.00
3-6 all reprint	$0.30	$1.00	$2.00	£0.15	£0.50	£1.00
Title Value:	$2.00	$6.50	$13.00	£1.00	£3.25	£6.50

TOR

Marvel Comics Group,Magazine MS; 1 Jun 1993-4 Sep 1993

	$Good	$Fine	$N.Mint	£Good	£Fine	£N.Mint
1-4 ND Joe Kubert script and art	$1.00	$3.00	$5.00	£0.70	£2.10	£3.50
Title Value:	$4.00	$12.00	$20.00	£2.80	£8.40	£14.00

TOR 3-D

Eclipse; 1 Jul 1986-2 Aug 1986

	$Good	$Fine	$N.Mint	£Good	£Fine	£N.Mint
1 ND reprints 3-D Comics #1,#2 (St.John) by Joe Kubert; with bound-in 3-D glasses (25% less without glasses)	$0.50	$1.50	$2.50	£0.30	£0.90	£1.50
1 non 3-D issue ND	$0.60	$1.80	$3.00	£0.40	£1.20	£2.00
2 ND reprints 3-D Comics #1,#2 (St.John) by Joe Kubert; with bound-in 3-D glasses (25% less without glasses)	$0.50	$1.50	$2.50	£0.30	£0.90	£1.50
2 non 3-D issue ND scarce in the U.K.	$0.60	$1.80	$3.00	£0.40	£1.20	£2.00
Title Value:	$2.20	$6.60	$11.00	£1.40	£4.20	£7.00

TORCH OF LIBERTY SPECIAL, THE

Dark Horse,OS; 1 Dec 1994

	$Good	$Fine	$N.Mint	£Good	£Fine	£N.Mint
1 ND John Byrne script, Kieron Dwyer art; spin-off from Danger Unlimited	$0.50	$1.50	$2.50	£0.30	£0.90	£1.50
Title Value:	$0.50	$1.50	$2.50	£0.30	£0.90	£1.50

TORCHY

Innovation; 1 Spring 1991-5 Summer 1992

	$Good	$Fine	$N.Mint	£Good	£Fine	£N.Mint
1 ND Bill Ward reprints begin, black and white; quarterly frequency; Olivia de Berardinis painted cover; subtitled Summer Fun Special	$0.40	$1.20	$2.00	£0.25	£0.75	£1.25
2 ND Matt Thompson painted cover	$0.40	$1.20	$2.00	£0.25	£0.75	£1.25
3 ND Olivia de Berardinis painted cover	$0.40	$1.20	$2.00	£0.25	£0.75	£1.25
4 ND Brian Stelfreeze pianted cover	$0.40	$1.20	$2.00	£0.25	£0.75	£1.25
5 ND	$0.40	$1.20	$2.00	£0.25	£0.75	£1.25
Title Value:	$2.00	$6.00	$10.00	£1.25	£3.75	£6.25
Torchy the Blonde Bombshell Book One (Jan 1992) ND 100pgs, reprints 12 classic stories, new cover by Olivia de Berardinis; black and white				£0.90	£2.70	£4.50

TORG: REALITY STORM!

Adventure,MS; 1 Feb 1992-4 May 1992

	$Good	$Fine	$N.Mint	£Good	£Fine	£N.Mint
1-4 ND based on role-playing game	$0.40	$1.20	$2.00	£0.25	£0.75	£1.25
Title Value:	$1.60	$4.80	$8.00	£1.00	£3.00	£5.00

TORMENT

Aircel,MS; 1 Aug 1991-3 Oct 1991

	$Good	$Fine	$N.Mint	£Good	£Fine	£N.Mint
1-3 ND black and white	$0.40	$1.20	$2.00	£0.25	£0.75	£1.25
Title Value:	$1.20	$3.60	$6.00	£0.75	£2.25	£3.75

TORRID AFFAIRS

Eternity; 1 1988-5 1989

	$Good	$Fine	$N.Mint	£Good	£Fine	£N.Mint
1 ND 1950s romance reprints	$0.40	$1.20	$2.00	£0.25	£0.75	£1.25
2 "hot cover" ND	$0.40	$1.20	$2.00	£0.25	£0.75	£1.25
2 "tame "cover ND	$0.40	$1.20	$2.00	£0.25	£0.75	£1.25
3-5 ND	$0.40	$1.20	$2.00	£0.25	£0.75	£1.25
Title Value:	$2.40	$7.20	$12.00	£1.50	£4.50	£7.50

TORTURE

Cat Wild; 1 Jan 1991

	$Good	$Fine	$N.Mint	£Good	£Fine	£N.Mint
1 ND black and white	$0.40	$1.20	$2.00	£0.25	£0.75	£1.25
Title Value:	$0.40	$1.20	$2.00	£0.25	£0.75	£1.25

TOTAL CARNAGE

Dark Horse,OS; 1 Dec 1993

	$Good	$Fine	$N.Mint	£Good	£Fine	£N.Mint
1 ND 48pgs	$0.80	$2.40	$4.00	£0.50	£1.50	£2.50
Title Value:	$0.80	$2.40	$4.00	£0.50	£1.50	£2.50

TOTAL ECLIPSE

Eclipse; 1 May 1988-5 1989

	$Good	$Fine	$N.Mint	£Good	£Fine	£N.Mint
1-5 ND	$0.60	$1.80	$3.00	£0.40	£1.20	£2.00
Title Value:	$3.00	$9.00	$15.00	£2.00	£6.00	£10.00

TOTAL ECLIPSE: THE SERAPHIM OBJECTIVE

Eclipse,OS; 1 Nov 1988

	$Good	$Fine	$N.Mint	£Good	£Fine	£N.Mint
1 ND scarce in the U.K. Airboy, Valkyrie, Misery and The Heap appear; also features The Liberty Project	$0.60	$1.80	$3.00	£0.50	£1.50	£2.50
Title Value:	$0.60	$1.80	$3.00	£0.50	£1.50	£2.50

TOTAL JUSTICE

DC Comics,MS; 1-3 Nov 1996

	$Good	$Fine	$N.Mint	£Good	£Fine	£N.Mint
1-3 ND Justice League tie-in; weekly	$0.45	$1.35	$2.25	£0.30	£0.90	£1.50
Title Value:	$1.35	$4.05	$6.75	£0.90	£2.70	£4.50

TOTAL RECALL MOVIE ADAPTATION

DC Comics,OS; nn Aug 1990

	$Good	$Fine	$N.Mint	£Good	£Fine	£N.Mint
nn based on Arnold Schwarzenegger film	$0.40	$1.20	$2.00	£0.25	£0.75	£1.25
Title Value:	$0.40	$1.20	$2.00	£0.25	£0.75	£1.25

TOTAL WAR

Gold Key; 1 Jul 1965-2 Oct 1965

(becomes Mars Patrol Total War)

	$Good	$Fine	$N.Mint	£Good	£Fine	£N.Mint
1 scarce though distributed in the U.K. Wally Wood art and painted cover	$5.50	$17.00	$40.00	£3.55	£10.50	£25.00
2 scarce though distributed in the U.K. Wally Wood art and painted cover	$5.25	$16.00	$37.50	£3.20	£9.50	£22.50
Title Value:	$10.75	$33.00	$77.50	£6.75	£20.00	£47.50

TOTEM: SIGN OF THE WARDOG

Alpha Productions; 1 Jun 1991-5 1991

	$Good	$Fine	$N.Mint	£Good	£Fine	£N.Mint
1-5 ND black and white	$0.40	$1.20	$2.00	£0.25	£0.75	£1.25
Title Value:	$2.00	$6.00	$10.00	£1.25	£3.75	£6.25
Annual 1 (May 1994) 48pgs, black and white				£0.50	£1.50	£2.50

TOTEM: THE STEEL MOSQUITO

Alpha Productions; 1 Jul 1993

	$Good	$Fine	$N.Mint	£Good	£Fine	£N.Mint
1 ND	$0.40	$1.20	$2.00	£0.25	£0.75	£1.25
Title Value:	$0.40	$1.20	$2.00	£0.25	£0.75	£1.25

TOUCH OF SILVER, A

Image; 1 Jan 1997-present

	$Good	$Fine	$N.Mint	£Good	£Fine	£N.Mint
1 ND 24pgs, Jim Valentino script and art; black and white	$0.60	$1.80	$3.00	£0.40	£1.20	£2.00
Title Value:	$0.60	$1.80	$3.00	£0.40	£1.20	£2.00

TOWER OF SHADOWS

Marvel Comics Group; 1 Sep 1969-9 Jan 1971

(becomes Creatures on the Loose)

	$Good	$Fine	$N.Mint	£Good	£Fine	£N.Mint
1 scarce in the U.K. Steranko art	$3.20	$9.50	$22.50	£2.10	£6.25	£15.00
2 Neal Adams art (7pgs)	$2.50	$7.50	$15.00	£1.25	£3.75	£7.50
3 Barry Smith art (7pgs)	$2.05	$6.25	$12.50	£1.00	£3.00	£6.00
4 ND Gene Colan art	$1.65	$5.00	$10.00	£0.80	£2.50	£5.00
5 ND Barry Smith art, Wood inks	$2.05	$6.25	$12.50	£1.00	£3.00	£6.00
6 ND Wood art	$1.65	$5.00	$10.00	£0.80	£2.50	£5.00
7 ND Barry Smith art, Wood inks	$2.05	$6.25	$12.50	£1.00	£3.00	£6.00
8 ND Wood art	$1.65	$5.00	$10.00	£0.80	£2.50	£5.00
9 ND Wrightson cover	$1.30	$4.00	$8.00	£0.65	£2.00	£4.00
Title Value:	$18.10	$54.75	$113.00	£9.40	£28.50	£59.50

Note: back-up reprints in 6-9.

TOWER OF SHADOWS ANNUAL

Marvel Comics Group; 1 Dec 1971

	$Good	$Fine	$N.Mint	£Good	£Fine	£N.Mint
1 ND scarce in the U.K. all reprint including Neal Adams	$1.25	$3.75	$7.50	£0.75	£2.25	£4.50
Title Value:	$1.25	$3.75	$7.50	£0.75	£2.25	£4.50

TOXIC AVENGER

Marvel Comics Group; 1 Apr 1991-11 Feb 1992

	$Good	$Fine	$N.Mint	£Good	£Fine	£N.Mint
1 based on the cult Troma film series	$0.25	$0.75	$1.25	£0.15	£0.45	£0.75
2-10	$0.25	$0.75	$1.25	£0.15	£0.45	£0.75
11 nuclear explosion photo cover	$0.25	$0.75	$1.25	£0.15	£0.45	£0.75

	$Good	$Fine	$N.Mint	£Good	£Fine	£N.Mint
Title Value:	$2.75	$8.25	$13.75	£1.65	£4.95	£8.25

TOXIC CRUSADERS

Marvel Comics Group; 1 May 1992-8 Dec 1992

	$Good	$Fine	$N.Mint	£Good	£Fine	£N.Mint
1 anthology based on cartoon series featuring writing by Stan Lee and Steve Gerber, Sam Kieth cover	$0.25	$0.75	$1.25	£0.15	£0.45	£0.75
2-3 Sam Kieth cover	$0.25	$0.75	$1.25	£0.15	£0.45	£0.75
4 three stories	$0.25	$0.75	$1.25	£0.15	£0.45	£0.75
5	$0.25	$0.75	$1.25	£0.15	£0.45	£0.75
6 Captain Planet parody	$0.25	$0.75	$1.25	£0.15	£0.45	£0.75
7-8	$0.25	$0.75	$1.25	£0.15	£0.45	£0.75
Title Value:	$2.00	$6.00	$10.00	£1.20	£3.60	£6.00

TOXIC CRUSADERS (2ND SERIES)

Marvel Comics Group,MS; 1 Mar 1993-3 May 1993

	$Good	$Fine	$N.Mint	£Good	£Fine	£N.Mint
1 Steve Gerber script, based on US TV series	$0.25	$0.75	$1.25	£0.15	£0.45	£0.75
2-3 Jeremy Banx script	$0.25	$0.75	$1.25	£0.15	£0.45	£0.75
Title Value:	$0.75	$2.25	$3.75	£0.45	£1.35	£2.25

TOYBOY, JASON KRITER

Continuity; 1 Oct 1986-7 Mar 1989

	$Good	$Fine	$N.Mint	£Good	£Fine	£N.Mint
1 ND Neal Adams script and part pencils	$0.40	$1.20	$2.00	£0.25	£0.75	£1.25
2-3 ND Neal Adams cover	$0.40	$1.20	$2.00	£0.25	£0.75	£1.25
4-5 ND Neal Adams script and part art	$0.40	$1.20	$2.00	£0.25	£0.75	£1.25
6 ND	$0.40	$1.20	$2.00	£0.25	£0.75	£1.25
7 ND Neal Adams script, Michael Golden cover and art	$0.40	$1.20	$2.00	£0.25	£0.75	£1.25
Title Value:	$2.80	$8.40	$14.00	£1.75	£5.25	£8.75

TRACKER

Blackthorne,MS; 1 May 1988-4 Sep 1988

	$Good	$Fine	$N.Mint	£Good	£Fine	£N.Mint
1-4 ND	$0.40	$1.20	$2.00	£0.25	£0.75	£1.25
Title Value:	$1.60	$4.80	$8.00	£1.00	£3.00	£5.00

TRAGG AND THE SKY GODS

Gold Key; 1 Jun 1975-8 Feb 1977; Whitman; 9 May 1982

	$Good	$Fine	$N.Mint	£Good	£Fine	£N.Mint
1 scarce in the U.K. line-drawn and water-colour cover (most covers feature dinosaurs); origin and 1st appearance Tragg the Caveman	$0.50	$1.50	$3.00	£0.30	£1.00	£2.00
2 scarce in the U.K. line-drawn and water-colour cover	$0.30	$1.00	$2.00	£0.25	£0.75	£1.50
3 1st painted cover (ends #8)	$0.30	$1.00	$2.00	£0.20	£0.60	£1.25
4	$0.30	$1.00	$2.00	£0.20	£0.60	£1.25
5-8 Dan Spiegle art	$0.30	$1.00	$2.00	£0.20	£0.60	£1.25
9 scarce in the U.K. line-drawn cover	$0.30	$1.00	$2.00	£0.25	£0.75	£1.50
Title Value:	$2.90	$9.50	$19.00	£2.00	£6.10	£12.50

Note: all Limited Distribution in the U.K.

TRANCERS

Eternity; 1 Aug 1991-2 Sep 1991

	$Good	$Fine	$N.Mint	£Good	£Fine	£N.Mint
1-2 ND film adaptation; sub-titled "The Adventures of Jack Deth"	$0.40	$1.20	$2.00	£0.25	£0.75	£1.25
Title Value:	$0.80	$2.40	$4.00	£0.50	£1.50	£2.50
Prestige Edition (Nov 1991), collects first 2 issues squarebound				£0.65	£1.95	£3.25

TRANSFORMERS COMIC MAGAZINE, THE

Marvel Comics Group,Digest; 1 Oct 1986-11 Aug 1988

	$Good	$Fine	$N.Mint	£Good	£Fine	£N.Mint
1-11 ND	$0.25	$0.75	$1.25	£0.15	£0.45	£0.75
Title Value:	$2.75	$8.25	$13.75	£1.65	£4.95	£8.25

TRANSFORMERS IN 3-D

Blackthorne; (3-D Series #25,#29,#37); 1 1987-3 Apr 1988

	$Good	$Fine	$N.Mint	£Good	£Fine	£N.Mint
1 ND all with bound-in 3-D glasses (25% less without glasses)	$0.50	$1.50	$2.50	£0.30	£0.90	£1.50
2-3 ND	$0.50	$1.50	$2.50	£0.30	£0.90	£1.50
Title Value:	$1.50	$4.50	$7.50	£0.90	£2.70	£4.50

TRANSFORMERS UNIVERSE, THE

Marvel Comics Group,MS; 1 Dec 1986-4 Mar 1987

	$Good	$Fine	$N.Mint	£Good	£Fine	£N.Mint
1-4 ND guide to all the characters	$0.25	$0.75	$1.25	£0.15	£0.45	£0.75
Title Value:	$1.00	$3.00	$5.00	£0.60	£1.80	£3.00
Trade Paperback, 128pgs, reprints #1-4				£0.60	£1.80	£3.00

TRANSFORMERS, THE

Marvel Comics Group,TV Toy; 1 Sep 1984-80 Jul 1991

	$Good	$Fine	$N.Mint	£Good	£Fine	£N.Mint
1 ND	$0.30	$0.90	$1.50	£0.20	£0.60	£1.00
2 ND	$0.25	$0.75	$1.25	£0.15	£0.45	£0.75
3 ND Spiderman guest-stars	$0.25	$0.75	$1.25	£0.15	£0.45	£0.75
4-6	$0.25	$0.75	$1.25	£0.15	£0.45	£0.75
7-8 ND Kyle Baker inks	$0.25	$0.75	$1.25	£0.15	£0.45	£0.75
9-49	$0.25	$0.75	$1.25	£0.15	£0.45	£0.75
50 DS	$0.30	$0.90	$1.50	£0.20	£0.60	£1.00
51-61 ND	$0.25	$0.75	$1.25	£0.15	£0.45	£0.75
62-66 ND Matrix Quest story	$0.25	$0.75	$1.25	£0.15	£0.45	£0.75
67-74 ND	$0.25	$0.75	$1.25	£0.15	£0.45	£0.75
75 ND DS	$0.30	$0.90	$1.50	£0.20	£0.60	£1.00
76-80 ND	$0.25	$0.75	$1.25	£0.15	£0.45	£0.75
Title Value:	$20.15	$60.45	$100.75	£12.15	£36.45	£60.75

Note: first 4 issues titled "Limited Mini Series"; series carried on in order after 3 month gap. 2nd and 3rd prints of most early issues available (priced at about 60% of the above)

TRANSFORMERS: GENERATION 2

Marvel Comics Group; 1 Nov 1993-12 Oct 1994

	$Good	$Fine	$N.Mint	£Good	£Fine	£N.Mint
1 48pgs, Simon Furman and Derek Yaniger	$0.50	$1.50	$2.50	£0.30	£0.90	£1.50
1 Direct Market Edition, 48pgs,, foil stamped gatefold cover	$0.80	$2.40	$4.00	£0.50	£1.50	£2.50
2-11	$0.40	$1.20	$2.00	£0.25	£0.75	£1.25
12 48pgs	$0.50	$1.50	$2.50	£0.30	£0.90	£1.50
Title Value:	$5.80	$17.40	$29.00	£3.60	£10.80	£18.00

TRANSFORMERS: HEADMASTERS

Marvel Comics Group,MS; 1 Jul 1987-4 Oct 1987

	$Good	$Fine	$N.Mint	£Good	£Fine	£N.Mint
1-4 ND	$0.25	$0.75	$1.25	£0.15	£0.45	£0.75
Title Value:	$1.00	$3.00	$5.00	£0.60	£1.80	£3.00

TRANSFORMERS: THE MOVIE

Marvel Comics Group,MS; 1 Dec 1986-3 Feb 1987

	$Good	$Fine	$N.Mint	£Good	£Fine	£N.Mint
1-3 ND adapts animated film	$0.25	$0.75	$1.25	£0.15	£0.45	£0.75
Title Value:	$0.75	$2.25	$3.75	£0.45	£1.35	£2.25

TRANSIT

Vortex; 1 Apr 1987-5 1989

	$Good	$Fine	$N.Mint	£Good	£Fine	£N.Mint
1 ND Ted McKeever script and art begins; black and white	$0.50	$1.50	$2.50	£0.30	£0.90	£1.50
2-5 ND	$0.50	$1.50	$2.50	£0.30	£0.90	£1.50
Title Value:	$2.50	$7.50	$12.50	£1.50	£4.50	£7.50

TRANSYLVANIA SPECIAL EDITION

Continuity,OS; 1 Sep 1991

	$Good	$Fine	$N.Mint	£Good	£Fine	£N.Mint
1 ND 36pgs, Neal Adams script/art featuring Dracula, Frankenstein and Werewolf, originally serialized in Echo of Future Past	$1.00	$3.00	$5.00	£0.70	£2.10	£3.50
Title Value:	$1.00	$3.00	$5.00	£0.70	£2.10	£3.50

TRAPPED

Eclipse,OS; (Graphic Novel) 1 1993

	$Good	$Fine	$N.Mint	£Good	£Fine	£N.Mint
1 ND 80pgs, squarebound, based on Dean R. Koontz novel, painted art Anthony Bilau	$2.00	$6.00	$10.00	£1.40	£4.20	£7.00
Title Value:	$2.00	$6.00	$10.00	£1.40	£4.20	£7.00

TRAUMA CORPS

Anubis Press; 0 Jan 1994-2 1994

	$Good	$Fine	$N.Mint	£Good	£Fine	£N.Mint
0 ND black and white	$0.50	$1.50	$2.50	£0.30	£0.90	£1.50
1 ND foil enhanced cover	$0.50	$1.50	$2.50	£0.30	£0.90	£1.50
1 Ashcan Edition, ND (Nov 1994) - black and white; 5,000 copies	$0.50	$1.50	$2.50	£0.30	£0.90	£1.50
2 ND	$0.50	$1.50	$2.50	£0.30	£0.90	£1.50
Title Value:	$2.00	$6.00	$10.00	£1.20	£3.60	£6.00

TREKKER

Dark Horse; 1 May 1987-6 1988

	$Good	$Fine	$N.Mint	£Good	£Fine	£N.Mint
1-6 ND Ron Randall art; black and white	$0.50	$1.50	$2.50	£0.30	£0.90	£1.50
Title Value:	$3.00	$9.00	$15.00	£1.80	£5.40	£9.00
Trekker Collection (1988), reprints #1-4				£0.80	£2.40	£4.00
Trekker Color Special (1989)				£0.30	£0.90	£1.50

TRENCHER

Image; 1 May 1993-4 Oct 1993

	$Good	$Fine	$N.Mint	£Good	£Fine	£N.Mint
1 ND Keith Giffen script and art begins	$0.40	$1.20	$2.00	£0.25	£0.75	£1.25
2-4 ND	$0.40	$1.20	$2.00	£0.25	£0.75	£1.25
Title Value:	$1.60	$4.80	$8.00	£1.00	£3.00	£5.00

TRENCHER X-MAS BITES HOLIDAY BLOW-OUT

Blackball Comics,OS; 1 Dec 1993

	$Good	$Fine	$N.Mint	£Good	£Fine	£N.Mint
1 ND Keith Giffen script and art	$0.40	$1.20	$2.00	£0.25	£0.75	£1.25
Title Value:	$0.40	$1.20	$2.00	£0.25	£0.75	£1.25

TRIAD UNIVERSE

Triad Publishing; 1 Jul 1994

	$Good	$Fine	$N.Mint	£Good	£Fine	£N.Mint
1 ND Laurence Richardson art	$0.40	$1.20	$2.00	£0.25	£0.75	£1.25
Title Value:	$0.40	$1.20	$2.00	£0.25	£0.75	£1.25

TRIAL RUN

Miller Publishing; 1,2 1990

	$Good	$Fine	$N.Mint	£Good	£Fine	£N.Mint
1-2 ND smaller than regular comic size, black and white	$0.30	$0.90	$1.50	£0.20	£0.60	£1.00
Title Value:	$0.60	$1.80	$3.00	£0.40	£1.20	£2.00

TRIARCH

Caliber Press; 1 Jan 1991-4 1991

	$Good	$Fine	$N.Mint	£Good	£Fine	£N.Mint
1-4 ND	$0.40	$1.20	$2.00	£0.25	£0.75	£1.25
Title Value:	$1.60	$4.80	$8.00	£1.00	£3.00	£5.00

TRIBE

Image; 1 Apr 1993; Axis Comics; 2 Sep 1993-3 Apr 1994

	$Good	$Fine	$N.Mint	£Good	£Fine	£N.Mint
1 ND Larry Stroman art begins	$0.50	$1.50	$2.50	£0.30	£0.90	£1.50
1 Ivory Edition, ND - signed by Stroman and Johnson; limited to 10,000 copies	$0.70	$2.10	$3.50	£0.40	£1.20	£2.00
2-3 ND	$0.40	$1.20	$2.00	£0.25	£0.75	£1.25
Title Value:	$2.00	$6.00	$10.00	£1.20	£3.60	£6.00
Tribe, The Book (Feb 1994) Graphic Novel, 112pgs, reprints 3 issue series				£2.00	£6.00	£10.00

TRIBE (2ND SERIES)

Good Comics; 0 Oct 1996

0 ND Todd Johnson script, Larry Stroman art

	$Good	$Fine	$N.Mint	£Good	£Fine	£N.Mint
	$0.60	$1.80	$3.00	£0.40	£1.20	£2.00
Title Value:	$0.60	$1.80	$3.00	£0.40	£1.20	£2.00
TRICKSTER KING MONKEY						
Eastern; 1 May 1988						
1 ND scarce in the U.K.						
	$0.40	$1.20	$2.00	£0.25	£0.75	£1.25
Title Value:	$0.40	$1.20	$2.00	£0.25	£0.75	£1.25
TRIGGER TWINS						
DC Comics; 1 Mar/Apr 1973						
1 scarce in the U.K. reprints						
	$0.50	$1.50	$3.00	£0.25	£0.75	£1.50
Title Value:	$0.50	$1.50	$3.00	£0.25	£0.75	£1.50
TRINITY						
(See DC Universe: Trinity)						
TRIPLE-X						
Dark Horse,MS; 1 Dec 1994-7 Jun 1995						
1-7 ND 48pgs, Arnold and Jacob Pander script/art; black and white						
	$0.80	$2.40	$4.00	£0.50	£1.50	£2.50
Title Value:	$5.60	$16.80	$28.00	£3.50	£10.50	£17.50
TRIUMPH						
DC Comics,MS; 1 Jun 1995-4 Sep 1995						
1-4 Chris Priest script, Mike Miller art						
	$0.40	$1.20	$2.00	£0.25	£0.75	£1.25
Title Value:	$1.60	$4.80	$8.00	£1.00	£3.00	£5.00
TRIUMPHANT UNLEASHED						
Triumphant Comics; 0 Nov 1993						
0 ND	$0.40	$1.20	$2.00	£0.25	£0.75	£1.25
Title Value:	$0.40	$1.20	$2.00	£0.25	£0.75	£1.25
TROLL						
Image,OS; 1 Dec 1993						
1 ND Rob Liefeld script and Jeff Matsuda art begins						
	$0.50	$1.50	$2.50	£0.30	£0.90	£1.50
Title Value:	$0.50	$1.50	$2.50	£0.30	£0.90	£1.50
TROLL HALLOWEEN SPECIAL						
Image,OS; 1 Oct 1994						
1 ND	$0.60	$1.80	$3.00	£0.40	£1.20	£2.00
Title Value:	$0.60	$1.80	$3.00	£0.40	£1.20	£2.00
TROLL II						
Image; 1 Jul 1994						
1 ND 48pgs, squarebound, created by Rob Liefeld; Badrock guest-stars						
	$0.60	$1.80	$3.00	£0.40	£1.20	£2.00
Title Value:	$0.60	$1.80	$3.00	£0.40	£1.20	£2.00
TROLL STOCKING STUFFER						
Image,OS; 1 Dec 1994						
1 ND Giffen, Fleming and Nauck creative team						
	$0.60	$1.80	$3.00	£0.40	£1.20	£2.00
Title Value:	$0.60	$1.80	$3.00	£0.40	£1.20	£2.00
TROLL THANKSGIVING SPECIAL						
Image,OS; 1 Nov 1994						
1 ND Robert Loren Fleming and Jeff Matsuda						
	$0.60	$1.80	$3.00	£0.40	£1.20	£2.00
Title Value:	$0.60	$1.80	$3.00	£0.40	£1.20	£2.00
TROLL: ONCE A HERO						
Image,OS; 1 Aug 1994						
1 ND 48pgs, Troll in World War II						
	$0.50	$1.50	$2.50	£0.30	£0.90	£1.50
Title Value:	$0.50	$1.50	$2.50	£0.30	£0.90	£1.50
TROLLORDS (1ST SERIES)						
Tru Studios; 1 Feb 1986-15 1988						
1 ND black and white begins						
	$0.30	$0.90	$1.50	£0.20	£0.60	£1.00
1 2nd printing ND	$0.25	$0.75	$1.25	£0.15	£0.45	£0.75
2-15 ND	$0.30	$0.90	$1.50	£0.20	£0.60	£1.00
Title Value:	$4.75	$14.25	$23.75	£3.15	£9.45	£15.75
Special 1 (Feb 1987)				£0.30	£0.90	£1.50
TROLLORDS (2ND SERIES)						
Comico; 1 Nov 1988-4 May 1989						
1-4 ND colour	$0.30	$0.90	$1.50	£0.20	£0.60	£1.00
Title Value:	$1.20	$3.60	$6.00	£0.80	£2.40	£4.00
TROLLORDS SPECIAL						
Tru Studios; 1 Feb 1987						
1 ND sub-titled "Jerry's Big Fun Book"						
	$0.30	$0.90	$1.50	£0.20	£0.60	£1.00
Title Value:	$0.30	$0.90	$1.50	£0.20	£0.60	£1.00
TROLLORDS: DEATH AND KISSES						
Apple Comics; 1 Jun 1989-6 Apr 1990						
1-6 ND black and white						
	$0.40	$1.20	$2.00	£0.25	£0.75	£1.25
Title Value:	$2.40	$7.20	$12.00	£1.50	£4.50	£7.50
TROUBLE WITH GIRLS						
Malibu/Eternity; 1 Aug 1987-14 Jan 1989						
1 black and white begins						
	$0.50	$1.50	$2.50	£0.30	£0.90	£1.50
2 scarce in the U.K.						
	$0.40	$1.20	$2.00	£0.30	£0.90	£1.50
3-4	$0.40	$1.20	$2.00	£0.25	£0.75	£1.25
5 1st Eternity issue	$0.40	$1.20	$2.00	£0.25	£0.75	£1.25
6-14	$0.30	$0.90	$1.50	£0.20	£0.60	£1.00
Title Value:	$4.80	$14.40	$24.00	£3.15	£9.45	£15.75
Note: all Non-Distributed on the news-stands in the U.K.						
Graphic Novel 1 (Sep 1988), reprints #1-3				£0.90	£2.70	£4.50
Graphic Novel 2 (1989), reprints #4-6, new Gulacy cover				£0.90	£2.70	£4.50

	$Good	$Fine	$N.Mint	£Good	£Fine	£N.Mint
TROUBLE WITH GIRLS (2ND SERIES)						
Comico/Eternity; 1 Feb 1989-23 May 1991						
1-4 colour issues	$0.30	$0.90	$1.50	£0.20	£0.60	£1.00
5 1st Eternity issue, black and white begins						
	$0.30	$0.90	$1.50	£0.20	£0.60	£1.00
6-23	$0.30	$0.90	$1.50	£0.20	£0.60	£1.00
Title Value:	$6.90	$20.70	$34.50	£4.60	£13.80	£23.00
Note: all Non-Distributed on the news-stands in the U.K.						
TROUBLE WITH GIRLS ANNUAL						
Eternity; 1 1988						
1 ND 60pgs	$0.50	$1.50	$2.50	£0.30	£0.90	£1.50
Title Value:	$0.50	$1.50	$2.50	£0.30	£0.90	£1.50
TROUBLE WITH GIRLS XMAS SPECIAL						
Eternity,OS; 1 Feb 1992						
1 ND 40pgs	$0.50	$1.50	$2.50	£0.30	£0.90	£1.50
Title Value:	$0.50	$1.50	$2.50	£0.30	£0.90	£1.50
TROUBLE WITH GIRLS, THE						
Marvel Comics Group,MS; 1 Jun 1993-4 Sep 1993						
(see Eternity titles)						
1 ND embossed cover with metallic ink; all new stories						
	$0.40	$1.20	$2.00	£0.25	£0.75	£1.25
2-4 ND	$0.30	$0.90	$1.50	£0.20	£0.60	£1.00
Title Value:	$1.30	$3.90	$6.50	£0.85	£2.55	£4.25
TROUBLE WITH TIGERS						
Antarctic Press; 1,2 1992						
1-2 ND Ninja High School/Tigers of Terra X-over						
	$0.40	$1.20	$2.00	£0.25	£0.75	£1.25
Title Value:	$0.80	$2.40	$4.00	£0.50	£1.50	£2.50
TROUBLEMAKERS						
Acclaim Comics; 1 Mar 1997-present						
1 ND Fabian Nicieza script, Kenny Martinez and Anibal Rodriguez art						
	$0.50	$1.50	$2.50	£0.30	£0.90	£1.50
1 Painted Cover Variant ND						
	$0.50	$1.50	$2.50	£0.30	£0.90	£1.50
2 ND	$0.50	$1.50	$2.50	£0.30	£0.90	£1.50
Title Value:	$1.50	$4.50	$7.50	£0.90	£2.70	£4.50
TROUBLEMAN						
Image,MS; 1 Jun 1996-4 Sep 1996						
1-4 ND Michael Davis script, Chuck Drost art						
	$0.45	$1.35	$2.25	£0.30	£0.90	£1.50
Title Value:	$1.80	$5.40	$9.00	£1.20	£3.60	£6.00
TRUE 3-D						
Harvey; 1 Dec 1953-2 Feb 1954						
1 ND Powell art, with bound-in glasses (25% less without glasses)						
	$7.75	$23.50	$55.00	£5.00	£15.00	£35.00
2 ND very scarce in the U.K. Powell art, with bound-in glasses (25% less without glasses)						
	$7.00	$21.00	$50.00	£5.25	£16.00	£37.50
Title Value:	$14.75	$44.50	$105.00	£10.25	£31.00	£72.50
TRUE LOVE						
Eclipse; 1,2 Jan 1986						
1 ND 50s reprints, Dave Stevens cover						
	$0.40	$1.20	$2.00	£0.25	£0.75	£1.25
2 ND reprints, Brent Anderson cover						
	$0.40	$1.20	$2.00	£0.25	£0.75	£1.25
Title Value:	$0.80	$2.40	$4.00	£0.50	£1.50	£2.50
TRULY TASTELESS AND TACKY						
Caliber Press; 1 1992						
1 ND features cartoon jokes in the "Far Side" vein, black and white						
	$0.15	$0.45	$0.75	£0.10	£0.30	£0.50
Title Value:	$0.15	$0.45	$0.75	£0.10	£0.30	£0.50
TSR WORLDS ANNUAL						
DC Comics,OS; 1 Aug 1990						
1 ND intro Spelljammers						
	$0.40	$1.20	$2.00	£0.25	£0.75	£1.25
Title Value:	$0.40	$1.20	$2.00	£0.25	£0.75	£1.25
Note: ties in with Advanced Dugeons and Dragons, Forgotten Realms and Dragonlance.						
TUROK SON OF STONE						
Dell/Gold Key; 1 (Four Color #596) Dec 1954; 2 (Four Color #656) Oct 1955-130 Apr 1982						
(issues prior to "1st official distribution" all ND otherwise all distributed after that)						
1 very scarce in the U.K. (Four Color #596) 1st appearance Turok Son of Stone; painted covers begin						
	$120.00	$360.00	$850.00	£80.00	£240.00	£570.00
2 very scarce in the U.K. (Four Color #656) (Oct 1955)						
	$67.50	$205.00	$485.00	£46.00	£135.00	£325.00
3 scarce in the U.K. (Mar 1956)						
	$36.00	$105.00	$250.00	£23.50	£70.00	£165.00
4 scarce in the U.K. (Apr 1956)						
	$36.00	$105.00	$250.00	£23.50	£70.00	£165.00
5 scarce in the U.K.						
	$36.00	$105.00	$250.00	£23.50	£70.00	£165.00
6-10	$25.00	$75.00	$175.00	£16.00	£49.00	£115.00
11-15	$17.50	$52.50	$125.00	£11.50	£35.00	£82.50
16	$14.00	$43.00	$100.00	£9.50	£29.00	£67.50
1st official distribution in the U.K.						
17-20	$14.00	$43.00	$100.00	£9.50	£29.00	£67.50
21-30	$10.00	$30.00	$70.00	£6.50	£20.00	£47.00
31-40	$7.75	$23.50	$55.00	£5.25	£15.50	£37.00
41-50	$6.25	$19.00	$45.00	£4.25	£12.50	£30.00
51-60	$5.75	$17.50	$35.00	£3.30	£10.00	£20.00
61-62	$4.15	$12.50	$25.00	£2.50	£7.50	£15.00
63 line drawn cover						
	$4.15	$12.50	$25.00	£2.50	£7.50	£15.00
64-70	$4.15	$12.50	$25.00	£2.50	£7.50	£15.00

	$Good	$Fine	$N.Mint	£Good	£Fine	£N.Mint
71-80	*$3.30*	*$10.00*	*$20.00*	£1.65	£5.00	£10.00
81-90	*$2.50*	*$7.50*	*$15.00*	£1.25	£3.75	£7.50
91-99	*$2.05*	*$6.25*	*$12.50*	£0.80	£2.50	£5.00
100	*$2.50*	*$7.50*	*$15.00*	£1.00	£3.00	£6.00
101-110	*$1.65*	*$5.00*	*$10.00*	£0.80	£2.50	£5.00
111-113	*$1.65*	*$5.00*	*$10.00*	£0.65	£2.00	£4.00
114-115 48pgs	*$1.65*	*$5.00*	*$10.00*	£0.80	£2.50	£5.00
116-129	*$1.65*	*$5.00*	*$10.00*	£0.65	£2.00	£4.00
130 scarce in the U.K. line drawn cover						
	$1.65	*$5.00*	*$10.00*	£0.80	£2.50	£5.00
Title Value:	*$1045.45*	*$3146.25*	*$7162.50*	£658.15	£1984.50	£4564.00

Note: most scripts by Paul S. Newman and art by Jack Sparling and Alberto Giolitti.

TUROK SON OF STONE, THE ORIGINAL

Valiant/Western Publishing; 1 Apr 1995-4 Jul 1995

	$Good	$Fine	$N.Mint	£Good	£Fine	£N.Mint
1-4 ND reprints from the original Gold Key series featuring artwork by Alberto Gioletti						
	$0.50	*$1.50*	*$2.50*	£0.30	£0.90	£1.50
Title Value:	*$2.00*	*$6.00*	*$10.00*	£1.20	£3.60	£6.00

TUROK, DINOSAUR HUNTER

Valiant/Acclaim Comics; 0 Jul 1995; 1 Jun 1993-47 1996

	$Good	$Fine	$N.Mint	£Good	£Fine	£N.Mint
0 ND origin Turok and Andar						
	$0.40	*$1.20*	*$2.00*	£0.25	£0.75	£1.25
1 ND chromium embossed cover, Bart Sears art begins						
	$0.60	*$1.80*	*$3.00*	£0.40	£1.20	£2.00
1 Gold Edition ND	*$1.50*	*$4.50*	*$7.50*	£1.00	£3.00	£5.00
1 Valiant Validated Signature Series, ND (Feb 1994), signed by Randy Elliot and Bart Sears; limited to 5,300 copies with certificate and Mylar sleeve						
	$1.50	*$4.50*	*$7.50*	£1.00	£3.00	£5.00
2-3 ND	*$0.50*	*$1.50*	*$2.50*	£0.30	£0.90	£1.50
4 ND Tim Truman script						
	$0.50	*$1.50*	*$2.50*	£0.30	£0.90	£1.50
5-6 ND	*$0.50*	*$1.50*	*$2.50*	£0.30	£0.90	£1.50
7 ND Tim Truman script/art begins						
	$0.50	*$1.50*	*$2.50*	£0.30	£0.90	£1.50
8-10 ND	*$0.50*	*$1.50*	*$2.50*	£0.30	£0.90	£1.50
11 ND with free Upper Deck card bound-in at centre-fold						
	$0.40	*$1.20*	*$2.00*	£0.25	£0.75	£1.25
12-15 ND	*$0.40*	*$1.20*	*$2.00*	£0.25	£0.75	£1.25
16 ND Chaos Effect X-over						
	$0.40	*$1.20*	*$2.00*	£0.25	£0.75	£1.25
17-18 ND	*$0.40*	*$1.20*	*$2.00*	£0.25	£0.75	£1.25
19 ND X-O Manowar appears						
	$0.40	*$1.20*	*$2.00*	£0.25	£0.75	£1.25
20-24 ND	*$0.40*	*$1.20*	*$2.00*	£0.25	£0.75	£1.25
25 ND 1st Acclaim Comics issue; bi-weekly						
	$0.40	*$1.20*	*$2.00*	£0.25	£0.75	£1.25
26-28 ND bi-weekly						
	$0.40	*$1.20*	*$2.00*	£0.25	£0.75	£1.25
29-30 ND Mike Deodato Jnr. art; bi-weekly						
	$0.50	*$1.50*	*$2.50*	£0.30	£0.90	£1.50
31-33 ND Paul Gulacy art; bi-weekly						
	$0.50	*$1.50*	*$2.50*	£0.30	£0.90	£1.50
34-40 ND bi-weekly						
	$0.50	*$1.50*	*$2.50*	£0.30	£0.90	£1.50
41-42 ND Church of the Poison Mind story, Simon Furman script; bi-weekly						
	$0.50	*$1.50*	*$2.50*	£0.30	£0.90	£1.50
43-44 ND Mike Grell script						
	$0.50	*$1.50*	*$2.50*	£0.30	£0.90	£1.50
45-46 ND Tim Truman script, Jackson Guice art						
	$0.50	*$1.50*	*$2.50*	£0.30	£0.90	£1.50
47 ND	*$0.50*	*$1.50*	*$2.50*	£0.30	£0.90	£1.50
Title Value:	*$25.20*	*$75.60*	*$126.00*	£15.55	£46.65	£77.75

TUROK, DINOSAUR HUNTER YEARBOOK

Valiant; 1 Sep 1994; 2 Apr 1995

	$Good	$Fine	$N.Mint	£Good	£Fine	£N.Mint
1 ND Mike Baron script, Dave Cockrum pencils, Ganzalo Mayo inks; painted cover by Eric Hope						
	$0.80	*$2.40*	*$4.00*	£0.50	£1.50	£2.50
2 ND Mike Grell script, Mike Deodato Jnr. art; cover by Paul Smith and Bob Layton						
	$0.50	*$1.50*	*$2.50*	£0.30	£0.90	£1.50
Title Value:	*$1.30*	*$3.90*	*$6.50*	£0.80	£2.40	£4.00

TUROK, DINOSAUR HUNTER/SHAMAN'S TEARS

Acclaim Comics,MS; 1 Apr 1995-3 Jun 1995

	$Good	$Fine	$N.Mint	£Good	£Fine	£N.Mint
1-3 ND Mike Grell script and art with inks by Clarke Hawbaker						
	$0.50	*$1.50*	*$2.50*	£0.30	£0.90	£1.50
Title Value:	*$1.50*	*$4.50*	*$7.50*	£0.90	£2.70	£4.50

TUROK: THE EMPTY SOULS

Acclaim Comics; 1 Apr 1997-present

	$Good	$Fine	$N.Mint	£Good	£Fine	£N.Mint
1 ND 48pgs, Fabian Nicieza script, Rafael Kayanan art begins						
	$0.80	*$2.40*	*$4.00*	£0.50	£1.50	£2.50
Title Value:	*$0.80*	*$2.40*	*$4.00*	£0.50	£1.50	£2.50

TUROK: THE HUNTED

Acclaim Comics,MS; 1 Mar 1996-2 1996

	$Good	$Fine	$N.Mint	£Good	£Fine	£N.Mint
1-2 ND Mike Grell and Simon Furman script, Mike Deodato and Mozart Couto art						
	$0.50	*$1.50*	*$2.50*	£0.30	£0.90	£1.50
Title Value:	*$1.00*	*$3.00*	*$5.00*	£0.60	£1.80	£3.00

TURTLE SOUP

Mirage Studios,OS; 1 Sep 1987

(see Teenage Mutant Ninja Turtles)

	$Good	$Fine	$N.Mint	£Good	£Fine	£N.Mint
1 ND	*$0.50*	*$1.50*	*$2.50*	£0.30	£0.90	£1.50
Title Value:	*$0.50*	*$1.50*	*$2.50*	£0.30	£0.90	£1.50

TURTLE SOUP (2ND SERIES)

Mirage Studios,MS; 1 Nov 1991-4 Feb 1992

	$Good	$Fine	$N.Mint	£Good	£Fine	£N.Mint
1-4 ND colour	*$0.40*	*$1.20*	*$2.00*	£0.25	£0.75	£1.25
Title Value:	*$1.60*	*$4.80*	*$8.00*	£1.00	£3.00	£5.00
Turtle Soup Book I (1991), six stories by a variety of creators				£0.30	£0.90	£1.50

TV SCREEN CARTOONS

National Periodical Publications; 131 Nov/Dec 1959-138 Jan/Feb 1961

(previous issues ND as first official distribution in the U.K. was cover date November 1959)

	$Good	$Fine	$N.Mint	£Good	£Fine	£N.Mint
131-138 rare in the U.K, scarce in the U.S. Fox and The Crow featured						
	$10.00	*$30.00*	*$70.00*	£6.75	£20.00	£47.50
Title Value:	*$80.00*	*$240.00*	*$560.00*	£54.00	£160.00	£380.00

TV STARS

Marvel Comics Group,TV; 1 Aug 1978-4 Feb 1979

	$Good	$Fine	$N.Mint	£Good	£Fine	£N.Mint
1 ND scarce in the U.K. features Hanna-Barbera characters such as CB Bears and Undercover Elephant						
	$1.25	*$3.75*	*$7.50*	£0.65	£2.00	£4.00
2-4 ND scarce in the U.K. features Hanna-Barbera characters such as CB Bears and Undercover Elephant						
	$0.80	*$2.50*	*$5.00*	£0.40	£1.25	£2.50
Title Value:	*$3.65*	*$11.25*	*$22.50*	£1.85	£5.75	£11.50

21

Image,MS; 1 Feb 1996-3 Apr 1996

	$Good	$Fine	$N.Mint	£Good	£Fine	£N.Mint
1 ND Marc Silvestri script, Billy Tan art						
	$0.50	*$1.50*	*$2.50*	£0.30	£0.90	£1.50
1 Variant Cover Edition ND						
	$0.80	*$2.40*	*$4.00*	£0.60	£1.80	£3.00
2-3 ND	*$0.50*	*$1.50*	*$2.50*	£0.30	£0.90	£1.50
Title Value:	*$2.30*	*$6.90*	*$11.50*	£1.50	£4.50	£7.50
21 The Sage Begins (Jul 1996)						
Trade paperback ND collects issues #1-3, new cover				£1.30	£3.90	£6.50

22 BRIDES

Event Comics,MS; 1 May 1996-3 Jul 1996

	$Good	$Fine	$N.Mint	£Good	£Fine	£N.Mint
1 ND Fabian Niceiza script, Scott Lee and Jimmy Palmiotti art						
	$0.60	*$1.80*	*$3.00*	£0.40	£1.20	£2.00
1 Signed Edition, ND signed by Joe Quesada and Jimmy Palmiotti, no certificate						
	$2.00	*$6.00*	*$10.00*	£1.30	£3.90	£6.50

Tor (DC) #4

TSR Worlds Annual #1

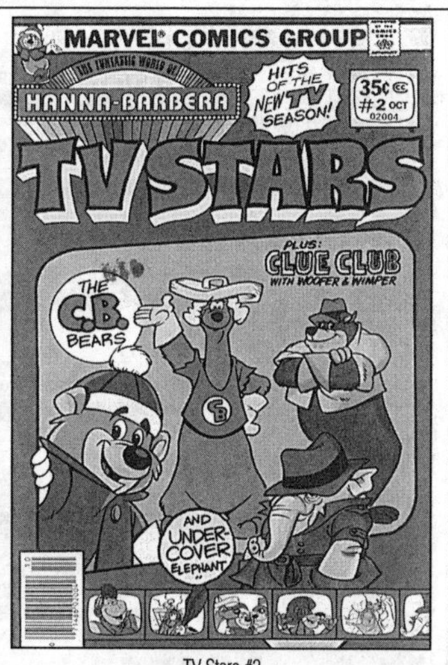

TV Stars #2

	$Good	$Fine	$N.Mint	£Good	£Fine	£N.Mint
2 ND Fabian Niceiza script, Scott Lee and Jimmy Palmiotti art						
	$0.60	*$1.80*	*$3.00*	£0.40	£1.20	£2.00
2 Signed Edition, ND signed by Joe Quesada and Jimmy Palmiotti						
	$2.00	*$6.00*	*$10.00*	£1.30	£3.90	£6.50
2 Variant Cover Edition, ND black cover, limited to 2% of print run						
	$1.00	*$3.00*	*$5.00*	£0.60	£1.80	£3.00
2 Variant Cover Edition Signed, ND signed by Joe Quesada and Jimmy Palmiotti, no certificate						
	$4.00	*$12.00*	*$20.00*	£3.00	£9.00	£15.00
3 ND Fabian Niceiza script, Scott Lee and Jimmy Palmiotti art						
	$0.60	*$1.80*	*$3.00*	£0.40	£1.20	£2.00
Title Value:	*$10.80*	*$32.40*	*$54.00*	£7.40	£22.20	£37.00

TWILIGHT

DC Comics,MS; 1 May 1991-3 Jul 1991

	$Good	$Fine	$N.Mint	£Good	£Fine	£N.Mint
1-3 ND 48pgs, features DC Space Heroes: Tommy Tomorrow, Star Rovers, Star Hawkins, Manhunter 2070, Ironwolf, Space Cabbie						
	$0.80	*$2.40*	*$4.00*	£0.50	£1.50	£2.50
Title Value:	*$2.40*	*$7.20*	*$12.00*	£1.50	£4.50	£7.50

Note: Prestige Format. Publication delayed from original solicitation.

TWILIGHT AVENGER

Elite; 1 Jul 1986-2 1987

	$Good	$Fine	$N.Mint	£Good	£Fine	£N.Mint
1-2 ND	*$0.40*	*$1.20*	*$2.00*	£0.25	£0.75	£1.25
Title Value:	*$0.80*	*$2.40*	*$4.00*	£0.50	£1.50	£2.50

TWILIGHT AVENGER (2ND SERIES)

Eternity; 1 1988-8 1989

	$Good	$Fine	$N.Mint	£Good	£Fine	£N.Mint
1-8 ND	*$0.40*	*$1.20*	*$2.00*	£0.25	£0.75	£1.25
Title Value:	*$3.20*	*$9.60*	*$16.00*	£2.00	£6.00	£10.00

TWILIGHT MAN

First,MS; 1 Feb 1989-4 May 1989

(see Sensei, Squalor)

	$Good	$Fine	$N.Mint	£Good	£Fine	£N.Mint
1 ND sub-titled "First Fiction Volume One"; glossy heavier stock paper covers						
	$0.40	*$1.20*	*$2.00*	£0.25	£0.75	£1.25
2-4 ND	*$0.40*	*$1.20*	*$2.00*	£0.25	£0.75	£1.25
Title Value:	*$1.60*	*$4.80*	*$8.00*	£1.00	£3.00	£5.00

TWILIGHT ZONE

Gold Key; 1 Nov 1962-91 Jun 1979; 92 May 1982

	$Good	$Fine	$N.Mint	£Good	£Fine	£N.Mint
1 scarce in the U.K.						
	$14.00	*$43.00*	*$100.00*	£10.00	£30.00	£70.00
2	*$10.00*	*$30.00*	*$70.00*	£6.25	£19.00	£45.00
3-4 Toth art	*$6.25*	*$19.00*	*$45.00*	£4.25	£12.50	£30.00
5	*$6.25*	*$19.00*	*$45.00*	£4.25	£12.50	£30.00
6-8	*$6.00*	*$18.00*	*$42.50*	£3.90	£11.50	£27.50
9 Toth art	*$6.00*	*$18.00*	*$42.50*	£3.90	£11.50	£27.50
10	*$6.00*	*$18.00*	*$42.50*	£3.90	£11.50	£27.50
11-15	*$4.60*	*$13.50*	*$32.50*	£3.20	£9.50	£22.50
16-20	*$3.20*	*$9.50*	*$22.50*	£2.10	£6.25	£15.00
21-25	*$2.90*	*$8.75*	*$17.50*	£1.65	£5.00	£10.00
26-30	*$2.05*	*$6.25*	*$12.50*	£1.25	£3.75	£7.50
31-40	*$1.25*	*$3.75*	*$7.50*	£0.80	£2.50	£5.00
41-50	*$0.80*	*$2.50*	*$5.00*	£0.55	£1.75	£3.50
51-60	*$0.65*	*$2.00*	*$4.00*	£0.40	£1.25	£2.50
61-70	*$0.50*	*$1.50*	*$3.00*	£0.30	£1.00	£2.00
71 reprint	*$0.40*	*$1.25*	*$2.50*	£0.25	£0.75	£1.50
72-80	*$0.40*	*$1.25*	*$2.50*	£0.25	£0.75	£1.50
81-82	*$0.30*	*$1.00*	*$2.00*	£0.20	£0.60	£1.25
83 48pgs	*$0.30*	*$1.00*	*$2.00*	£0.25	£0.75	£1.50
84 48pgs, new logo begins						
	$0.30	*$1.00*	*$2.00*	£0.25	£0.75	£1.50
85-91 48pgs	*$0.30*	*$1.00*	*$2.00*	£0.25	£0.75	£1.50
92	*$0.30*	*$0.90*	*$1.50*	£0.20	£0.60	£1.00
Title Value:	*$176.10*	*$531.90*	*$1186.00*	£115.35	£347.55	£779.50

Note: most issues distributed on the news-stands in the U.K.

TWILIGHT ZONE 3-D WINTER SPECIAL

Now Comics,OS; 1 May 1993

	$Good	$Fine	$N.Mint	£Good	£Fine	£N.Mint
1 ND pre-bagged with 3-D glasses (25% less without glasses)						
	$0.50	*$1.50*	*$2.50*	£0.30	£0.90	£1.50
Title Value:	*$0.50*	*$1.50*	*$2.50*	£0.30	£0.90	£1.50

TWILIGHT ZONE ANNIVERSARY SPECIAL

Now Comics,OS; 1 Nov 1992

	$Good	$Fine	$N.Mint	£Good	£Fine	£N.Mint
1 ND	*$0.50*	*$1.50*	*$2.50*	£0.30	£0.90	£1.50
Title Value:	*$0.50*	*$1.50*	*$2.50*	£0.30	£0.90	£1.50

TWILIGHT ZONE ANNUAL

Now Comics,OS; 1 Apr 1993

	$Good	$Fine	$N.Mint	£Good	£Fine	£N.Mint
1 ND two complete stories, no ads						
	$0.50	*$1.50*	*$2.50*	£0.30	£0.90	£1.50
Title Value:	*$0.50*	*$1.50*	*$2.50*	£0.30	£0.90	£1.50

TWILIGHT ZONE SCIENCE FICTION SPECIAL

Now Comics,OS; 1 Mar 1993

	$Good	$Fine	$N.Mint	£Good	£Fine	£N.Mint
1 ND 64pgs, pre-bagged with hologram badge						
	$0.60	*$1.80*	*$3.00*	£0.40	£1.20	£2.00
Title Value:	*$0.60*	*$1.80*	*$3.00*	£0.40	£1.20	£2.00

TWILIGHT ZONE WINTER SPECIAL

Now Comics,OS; 1 Apr 1993

	$Good	$Fine	$N.Mint	£Good	£Fine	£N.Mint
1 ND pre-bagged with 3-D glasses (25% less without glasses)						
	$0.60	*$1.80*	*$3.00*	£0.40	£1.20	£2.00
Title Value:	*$0.60*	*$1.80*	*$3.00*	£0.40	£1.20	£2.00

TWILIGHT ZONE, THE

Now Comics; 1 Nov 1990; 1 Oct 1991

	$Good	$Fine	$N.Mint	£Good	£Fine	£N.Mint
1 48pgs, Direct Sales Edition - Neal Adams art, Bill Sienkiewicz collage cover						
	$0.50	*$1.50*	*$2.50*	£0.30	£0.90	£1.50
1 Direct Sales Edition, , reprints 1990 one-shot with Neal Adams art and Sienkiewicz cover						
	$0.40	*$1.20*	*$2.00*	£0.25	£0.75	£1.25
1 Newstand Edition, reprints 1990 one-shot with Neal Adams cover						
	$0.50	*$1.50*	*$2.50*	£0.30	£0.90	£1.50
1 Premiere Collectors Edition, 32pgs, - pre-bagged, card cover with gold logo/upper and lower borders; Harlan Ellison interview, Neal Adams art and wraparound cover (25% less if un-bagged)						
	$0.60	*$1.80*	*$3.00*	£0.40	£1.20	£2.00
1 Premiere/Prestige Edition, 48pgs,, squarebound with extra Harlan Ellison text story, Neal Adams art and wraparound cover						
	$0.80	*$2.40*	*$4.00*	£0.50	£1.50	£2.50
Title Value:	*$2.80*	*$8.40*	*$14.00*	£1.75	£5.25	£8.75

Note; all Non-Distributed on the new-stands in the U.K.

TWILIGHT ZONE, THE (2ND SERIES)

Now Comics; 1 Nov 1991-16 1993

	$Good	$Fine	$N.Mint	£Good	£Fine	£N.Mint
1 Direct Sale Edition - non-code, Bruce Jones story						
	$0.40	*$1.20*	*$2.00*	£0.25	£0.75	£1.25
1 Newsstand Edition, code-approved, Bruce Jones story						
	$0.40	*$1.20*	*$2.00*	£0.25	£0.75	£1.25
2	*$0.40*	*$1.20*	*$2.00*	£0.25	£0.75	£1.25
3 dinosaur cover	*$0.40*	*$1.20*	*$2.00*	£0.25	£0.75	£1.25
4-8	*$0.40*	*$1.20*	*$2.00*	£0.25	£0.75	£1.25
9 3-D Special (Jul 1992) - pre-bagged with glasses and small hologram on cover (25 % less without glasses)						
	$0.60	*$1.80*	*$3.00*	£0.40	£1.20	£2.00
9 Prestige Edition, 48pgs, (Jul 1992) - squarebound, pre-bagged with 3-D glasses, 2 extra stories with different small hologram on cover (25% less without glasses)						
	$1.00	*$3.00*	*$5.00*	£0.70	£2.10	£3.50
10-16	*$0.40*	*$1.20*	*$2.00*	£0.25	£0.75	£1.25
Title Value:	*$8.00*	*$24.00*	*$40.00*	£5.10	£15.30	£25.50

Note: all Non-Distributed on the news-stands in the U.K.

TWILIGHT ZONE, THE (3RD SERIES)

Now Comics; 1 May 1993-6 1993

	$Good	$Fine	$N.Mint	£Good	£Fine	£N.Mint
1	*$0.50*	*$1.50*	*$2.50*	£0.30	£0.90	£1.50
2 computer-generated art, cover by Val Mayerik						
	$0.50	*$1.50*	*$2.50*	£0.30	£0.90	£1.50
2 titled "Twilght Zone Computer Special", with computer-generated cover art by John Picha						
	$0.50	*$1.50*	*$2.50*	£0.30	£0.90	£1.50
3-6	*$0.50*	*$1.50*	*$2.50*	£0.30	£0.90	£1.50
Title Value:	*$3.50*	*$10.50*	*$17.50*	£2.10	£6.30	£10.50

Note: all Non-Distributed on the news-stands in the U.K.

TWIST

Kitchen Sink; 1 Sep 1987-3 1989

	$Good	$Fine	$N.Mint	£Good	£Fine	£N.Mint
1 ND Wolverton, Clowes, Bagge, J.D.King art						
	$0.40	*$1.20*	*$2.00*	£0.25	£0.75	£1.25
2 ND Clowes, J.D.King, Bagge art						
	$0.40	*$1.20*	*$2.00*	£0.25	£0.75	£1.25
3 ND	*$0.40*	*$1.20*	*$2.00*	£0.25	£0.75	£1.25
Title Value:	*$1.20*	*$3.60*	*$6.00*	£0.75	£2.25	£3.75

TWISTED

Alchemy Studios; 1 Dec 1990

	$Good	$Fine	$N.Mint	£Good	£Fine	£N.Mint
1 ND horror/sci-fi/mystery anthology						
	$0.60	*$1.80*	*$3.00*	£0.40	£1.20	£2.00
Title Value:	*$0.60*	*$1.80*	*$3.00*	£0.40	£1.20	£2.00

TWISTED TALES

Pacific/Eclipse; 1 Nov 1982-10 Dec 1984

	$Good	$Fine	$N.Mint	£Good	£Fine	£N.Mint
1 Richard Corben, Bret Blevins, Tim Conrad art						
	$0.60	*$1.80*	*$3.00*	£0.40	£1.20	£2.00
2 Mike Ploog, Ken Steacy art; Berni Wrightson cover						
	$0.60	*$1.80*	*$3.00*	£0.40	£1.20	£2.00
3 Richard Corben, Doug Wildey, Bret Blevins art; Corben dinosaur cover						
	$0.50	*$1.50*	*$2.50*	£0.30	£0.90	£1.50
4 John Bolton, Don Lomax, Bruce Jones art; Bolton cover						
	$0.50	*$1.50*	*$2.50*	£0.30	£0.90	£1.50
5 Richard Corben, Bill Wray, Val Mayerik art; Corben cover						
	$0.50	*$1.50*	*$2.50*	£0.30	£0.90	£1.50
6 John Bolton, John Totleben art; Bolton cover						
	$0.50	*$1.50*	*$2.50*	£0.30	£0.90	£1.50
7	*$0.50*	*$1.50*	*$2.50*	£0.30	£0.90	£1.50
8 Butch Guice art	*$0.50*	*$1.50*	*$2.50*	£0.30	£0.90	£1.50
9	*$0.50*	*$1.50*	*$2.50*	£0.30	£0.90	£1.50
10 scarce in the U.K. 1st Eclipse issue; Berni Wrightson, Gray Morrrow, Rick Geary art						
	$0.60	*$1.80*	*$3.00*	£0.40	£1.20	£2.00
Title Value:	*$5.30*	*$15.90*	*$26.50*	£3.30	£9.90	£16.50

Note: all Non-Distributed on the news-stands in the U.K.

TWISTED TALES (2ND SERIES)

Eclipse; Graphic Novel 15; Nov 1987

	$Good	$Fine	$N.Mint	£Good	£Fine	£N.Mint
nn ND Dave Stevens cover						
	$1.00	*$3.00*	*$5.00*	£0.70	£2.10	£3.50
Title Value:	*$1.00*	*$3.00*	*$5.00*	£0.70	£2.10	£3.50

TWISTED TALES 3-D

Blackthorne; (3-D Series #7) 1 Aug 1986

	$Good	$Fine	$N.Mint	£Good	£Fine	£N.Mint
1 ND Corben, Totleben, Bolton art; with bound-in 3-D glasses (25% less without glasses)						
	$0.50	*$1.50*	*$2.50*	£0.30	£0.90	£1.50
Title Value:	*$0.50*	*$1.50*	*$2.50*	£0.30	£0.90	£1.50

TWISTED TALES OF BRUCE JONES

Eclipse,MS; 1 Feb 1986-4 May 1986

	$Good	$Fine	$N.Mint	£Good	£Fine	£N.Mint
1-4 ND Warren reprints in colour						
	$0.40	*$1.20*	*$2.00*	£0.25	£0.75	£1.25
Title Value:	*$1.60*	*$4.80*	*$8.00*	£1.00	£3.00	£5.00

TWISTER

Dark Horse/Harris Publications,MS; 1 Jan 1992-4 Apr 1992

	$Good	$Fine	$N.Mint	£Good	£Fine	£N.Mint
1 ND pre-bagged with "newspaper"						
	$0.60	*$1.80*	*$3.00*	£0.40	£1.20	£2.00
2-4 ND	*$0.60*	*$1.80*	*$3.00*	£0.40	£1.20	£2.00
Title Value:	*$2.40*	*$7.20*	*$12.00*	£1.60	£4.80	£8.00

TRADE PAPERBACKS, GRAPHIC NOVELS AND OTHER COLLECTIONS ARE PRICED IN POUNDS STERLING ONLY. CONVERT AT 1.5 FOR DOLLARS.

TWO THOUSAND MANIACS

Aircel,MS; 1 Sep 1991-3 Nov 1991

Issue	$Good	$Fine	$N.Mint	£Good	£Fine	£N.Mint
1-3 ND based on Herschell Gordon Lewis film, black and white						
	$0.25	*$0.75*	*$1.25*	£0.15	£0.45	£0.75
Title Value:	*$0.75*	*$2.25*	*$3.75*	£0.45	£1.35	£2.25

2001: A SPACE ODYSSEY

Marvel Comics Group; 1 Dec 1976-10 Sep 1977

Issue	$Good	$Fine	$N.Mint	£Good	£Fine	£N.Mint
1 Jack Kirby art	*$0.65*	*$2.00*	*$4.00*	£0.30	£1.00	£2.00
2-7 Jack Kirby art	*$0.50*	*$1.50*	*$3.00*	£0.25	£0.75	£1.50
8 origin and 1st appearance Mr. Machine (later Machine Man), Jack Kirby art						
	$0.55	*$1.75*	*$3.50*	£0.25	£0.85	£1.75
9-10 Mr. Machine appears, Jack Kirby art						
	$0.50	*$1.50*	*$3.00*	£0.25	£0.75	£1.50
Title Value:	*$5.20*	*$15.75*	*$31.50*	£2.55	£7.85	£15.75

2001: A SPACE ODYSSEY (TABLOID)

Marvel Comics Group,Tabloid OS; 1 Oct 1976

(see Marvel Treasury Special)

Issue	$Good	$Fine	$N.Mint	£Good	£Fine	£N.Mint
1 Jack Kirby art	*$0.80*	*$2.50*	*$5.00*	£0.40	£1.25	£2.50
Title Value:	*$0.80*	*$2.50*	*$5.00*	£0.40	£1.25	£2.50

2010

Marvel Comics Group,MS Film; 1 Apr 1985-2 May 1985

Issue	$Good	$Fine	$N.Mint	£Good	£Fine	£N.Mint
1-2 ND reprints Marvel Super Special #37						
	$0.25	*$0.75*	*$1.25*	£0.15	£0.45	£0.75
Title Value:	*$0.50*	*$1.50*	*$2.50*	£0.30	£0.90	£1.50

2001 NIGHTS

Viz,MS; 1 Oct 1990-10 1991

Issue	$Good	$Fine	$N.Mint	£Good	£Fine	£N.Mint
1-10 ND 64pgs, reprints Japanese material						
	$0.70	*$2.10*	*$3.50*	£0.50	£1.50	£2.50
Title Value:	*$7.00*	*$21.00*	*$35.00*	£5.00	£15.00	£25.00

Note: Premiere Format

2099 A.D.

Marvel Comics Group,OS; 1 May 1995

Issue	$Good	$Fine	$N.Mint	£Good	£Fine	£N.Mint
1 ND 48pgs, Spiderman, Punisher, Ghost Rider and X-Men appear; clear chromium cover						
	$0.80	*$2.40*	*$4.00*	£0.50	£1.50	£2.50
Title Value:	*$0.80*	*$2.40*	*$4.00*	£0.50	£1.50	£2.50

2099 APOCALYPSE

Marvel Comics Group,OS; 1 Dec 1995

Issue	$Good	$Fine	$N.Mint	£Good	£Fine	£N.Mint
1 ND 48pgs, the conclusion of One Nation Under Doom, leads into X-Nation and 2099 Genesis						
	$1.00	*$3.00*	*$5.00*	£0.60	£1.80	£3.00
Title Value:	*$1.00*	*$3.00*	*$5.00*	£0.60	£1.80	£3.00

2099 GENESIS

Marvel Comics Group,OS; 1 Jan 1996

Issue	$Good	$Fine	$N.Mint	£Good	£Fine	£N.Mint
1 ND 48pgs, continued from X-Men 2099 #28 and introducing Fantastic Four 2099; continued in Fantastic Four 2099 #1; Warren Ellis script, Dale Eaglesham and Scott Koblish art, chromium cover by Humberto Ramos						
	$1.00	*$3.00*	*$5.00*	£0.60	£1.80	£3.00
Title Value:	*$1.00*	*$3.00*	*$5.00*	£0.60	£1.80	£3.00

2099 MEGAHITS

Marvel Comics Group,OS; nn Dec 1995

Issue	$Good	$Fine	$N.Mint	£Good	£Fine	£N.Mint
nn ND boxed set of Doom , Punisher, Ravage, Spiderman and X-Men 2099 #1's						
	$1.80	*$5.25*	*$9.00*	£1.20	£3.60	£6.00
Title Value:	*$1.80*	*$5.25*	*$9.00*	£1.20	£3.60	£6.00

2099 SPECIAL: THE WORLD OF DOOM

Marvel Comics Group,OS; 1 May 1995

Issue	$Good	$Fine	$N.Mint	£Good	£Fine	£N.Mint
1 ND information and interviews concerning all aspects of the 2099 universe; painted cover by the Brothers Hildebrandt						
	$0.50	*$1.50*	*$2.50*	£0.30	£0.90	£1.50
Title Value:	*$0.50*	*$1.50*	*$2.50*	£0.30	£0.90	£1.50

2099 UNLIMITED

Marvel Comics Group; 1 Jul 1993-10 Oct 1995

Issue	$Good	$Fine	$N.Mint	£Good	£Fine	£N.Mint
1 ND 64pgs, introduces The Hulk of 2099; Spiderman 2099 back-ups begin						
	$0.80	*$2.40*	*$4.00*	£0.50	£1.50	£2.50
2-8 ND 64pgs	*$0.80*	*$2.40*	*$4.00*	£0.50	£1.50	£2.50
9 ND 64pgs, Joe Kubert cover						
	$0.80	*$2.40*	*$4.00*	£0.50	£1.50	£2.50
10 ND	*$0.80*	*$2.40*	*$4.00*	£0.50	£1.50	£2.50
Title Value:	*$8.00*	*$24.00*	*$40.00*	£5.00	£15.00	£25.00

2099: WORLD OF TOMORROW

Marvel Comics Group; 1 Sep 1996-present

Issue	$Good	$Fine	$N.Mint	£Good	£Fine	£N.Mint
1 ND 48pgs, Spiderman, X-Nation, Doom and X-Men 2099 all begin						
	$0.50	*$1.50*	*$2.50*	£0.30	£0.90	£1.50
2 ND 48pgs, with bound-in Overpower cards						
	$0.50	*$1.50*	*$2.50*	£0.30	£0.90	£1.50
3-7 ND 48pgs	*$0.50*	*$1.50*	*$2.50*	£0.30	£0.90	£1.50
Title Value:	*$3.50*	*$10.50*	*$17.50*	£2.10	£6.30	£10.50

TWO-FISTED ANNUAL

E.C. Comics; 1 1952-2 1953

Issue	$Good	$Fine	$N.Mint	£Good	£Fine	£N.Mint
1 scarce in the U.K. 128pgs, Kurtzman cover and art						
	$80.00	*$245.00*	*$575.00*	£52.50	£160.00	£375.00
2 very scarce in the U.K. 128pgs, Jack Davis cover and art						
	$57.50	*$175.00*	*$410.00*	£40.00	£120.00	£280.00
Title Value:	*$137.50*	*$420.00*	*$985.00*	£92.50	£280.00	£655.00

Note: both Non-Distributed on the news-stands in the U.K.

TWO-FISTED TALES

E.C. Comics; 18 Nov/Dec 1950-41 Feb/Mar 1955

Issue	$Good	$Fine	$N.Mint	£Good	£Fine	£N.Mint
18 Harvey Kurtzman covers begin (to #29); classic conflict covers begin						
	$92.50	*$275.00*	*$650.00*	£60.00	£185.00	£435.00
19	*$70.00*	*$210.00*	*$500.00*	£48.00	£140.00	£335.00
20	*$43.00*	*$125.00*	*$300.00*	£29.00	£85.00	£200.00
21 Kurtzman art	*$32.00*	*$95.00*	*$225.00*	£21.00	£62.50	£150.00
22	*$32.00*	*$95.00*	*$225.00*	£21.00	£62.50	£150.00
23-25	*$25.00*	*$75.00*	*$175.00*	£16.00	£49.00	£115.00
26-29	*$18.50*	*$55.00*	*$130.00*	£12.50	£38.00	£87.50
30 Jack Davis cover						
	$18.50	*$55.00*	*$130.00*	£12.50	£38.00	£87.50
31 Civil War issue, Kurtzman cover						
	$18.50	*$55.00*	*$130.00*	£12.50	£38.00	£87.50
32-33 Wood cover, Kubert art						
	$18.50	*$55.00*	*$130.00*	£12.50	£38.00	£87.50
34 Jack Davis cover						
	$18.50	*$55.00*	*$130.00*	£12.50	£38.00	£87.50
35 Civil War issue, Jack Davis cover						
	$18.50	*$55.00*	*$130.00*	£12.50	£38.00	£87.50
36-38	*$14.00*	*$43.00*	*$100.00*	£9.50	£29.00	£67.50
39 John Severin cover						
	$14.00	*$43.00*	*$100.00*	£9.50	£29.00	£67.50
40 George Evans cover						
	$14.00	*$43.00*	*$100.00*	£9.50	£29.00	£67.50
41	*$14.00*	*$43.00*	*$100.00*	£9.50	£29.00	£67.50
Title Value:	*$613.50*	*$1833.00*	*$4325.00*	£409.00	£1236.00	£2895.00

Note: all Non-Distributed on the news-stands in the U.K.

TWO-FISTED TALES (2ND SERIES)

Russ Cochran/EC Comics; 1 Oct 1992-present

Issue	$Good	$Fine	$N.Mint	£Good	£Fine	£N.Mint
1 ND reprints begin from original 1950s EC series with exact cover and interior reproduction						
	$0.40	*$1.20*	*$2.00*	£0.25	£0.75	£1.25
2-15 ND	*$0.40*	*$1.20*	*$2.00*	£0.25	£0.75	£1.25
16 ND	*$0.50*	*$1.50*	*$2.50*	£0.30	£0.90	£1.50
Title Value:	*$6.50*	*$19.50*	*$32.50*	£4.05	£12.15	£20.25
Two-Fisted Tales Annual #1 (Sep 1994)						
reprints issues #1-5 with covers				£1.20	£3.60	£6.00
Two-Fisted tales Annual #2 (Jan 1995)						
reprints issues #6-10 with covers				£1.20	£3.60	£6.00

TWO-FISTED TALES SPECIAL, THE NEW

Dark Horse,OS; 1 Aug 1994

Issue	$Good	$Fine	$N.Mint	£Good	£Fine	£N.Mint
1 ND 48pgs, new Kurtzman story plus reprints						
	$0.90	*$2.70*	*$4.50*	£0.60	£1.80	£3.00
Title Value:	*$0.90*	*$2.70*	*$4.50*	£0.60	£1.80	£3.00

TWO-GUN KID

Atlas/Marvel Comics Group; 54 Aug 1960-59 Apr 1961; 60 Nov 1962-92 Mar 1968; 93 Jul 1970-136 Apr 1977

(previous issues ND)

Issue	$Good	$Fine	$N.Mint	£Good	£Fine	£N.Mint
54	*$6.25*	*$19.00*	*$45.00*	£3.90	£11.50	£27.50
55-57	*$5.50*	*$17.00*	*$40.00*	£3.20	£9.50	£22.50
58 rare in the U.K. Jack Kirby art						
	$3.55	*$10.50*	*$25.00*	£2.10	£6.25	£15.00
59 rare in the U.K. last 10 cents issue						
	$3.55	*$10.50*	*$25.00*	£2.10	£6.25	£15.00
60 origin and 1st appearance of new Two-Gun Kid by Jack Kirby						
	$3.55	*$10.50*	*$25.00*	£2.10	£6.25	£15.00
61-65	*$2.10*	*$6.25*	*$15.00*	£1.40	£4.25	£10.00
66-70	*$1.75*	*$5.25*	*$12.50*	£1.05	£3.20	£7.50
71-72 rare in the U.K.						
	$1.75	*$5.25*	*$12.50*	£1.25	£3.85	£9.00
73-80	*$1.75*	*$5.25*	*$12.50*	£1.05	£3.20	£7.50
81-91	*$1.00*	*$3.00*	*$7.00*	£0.60	£1.90	£4.50
92 last new material						
	$1.00	*$3.00*	*$7.00*	£0.60	£1.90	£4.50
93-100	*$0.65*	*$2.00*	*$4.00*	£0.40	£1.25	£2.50
101 ND origin retold						
	$0.65	*$2.00*	*$4.00*	£0.40	£1.25	£2.50
102-109 ND	*$0.30*	*$1.00*	*$2.00*	£0.30	£1.00	£2.00
110 ND Williamson reprint						
	$0.30	*$1.00*	*$2.00*	£0.30	£1.00	£2.00
111-136 ND	*$0.25*	*$0.75*	*$1.50*	£0.25	£0.75	£1.50
Title Value:	*$97.20*	*$294.00*	*$667.00*	£62.95	£191.85	£439.00

Note: Kirby art in 54, 55, 57-62, 75-77.

TWO-GUN KID: SUNSET RIDERS

Marvel Comics Group,MS; 1 Nov 1995-2 Dec 1995

Issue	$Good	$Fine	$N.Mint	£Good	£Fine	£N.Mint
1-2 ND 64pgs, parchment paper cover						
	$1.40	*$4.20*	*$7.00*	£0.90	£2.70	£4.50
Title Value:	*$2.80*	*$8.40*	*$14.00*	£1.80	£5.40	£9.00

TYPHOID

Marvel Comics Group,MS; 1 Nov 1995-4 Feb 1996

Issue	$Good	$Fine	$N.Mint	£Good	£Fine	£N.Mint
1-4 ND Ann Nocenti script, John van Fleet art; UV coated covers						
	$0.80	*$2.40*	*$4.00*	£0.50	£1.50	£2.50
Title Value:	*$3.20*	*$9.60*	*$16.00*	£2.00	£6.00	£10.00

TYRANNOSAURUS REX

Monster Comics; 1 Jul 1991-3 1991

Issue	$Good	$Fine	$N.Mint	£Good	£Fine	£N.Mint
1-3 ND	*$0.40*	*$1.20*	*$2.00*	£0.25	£0.75	£1.25
Title Value:	*$1.20*	*$3.60*	*$6.00*	£0.75	£2.25	£3.75

TYRANT, S.R. BISSETTE'S

Spiderbaby Graphix; 1 Sep 1994-5 Mar 1996

Issue	$Good	$Fine	$N.Mint	£Good	£Fine	£N.Mint
1 ND black and white; Steve Bissette script and art on a dinosaur world epic						
	$0.80	*$2.40*	*$4.00*	£0.50	£1.50	£2.50
2-3 ND	*$0.60*	*$1.80*	*$3.00*	£0.40	£1.20	£2.00
3 Gold Edition ND	*$2.50*	*$7.50*	*$12.50*	£1.50	£4.50	£7.50
4-5 ND	*$0.60*	*$1.80*	*$3.00*	£0.40	£1.20	£2.00
Title Value:	*$5.70*	*$17.10*	*$28.50*	£3.60	£10.80	£18.00

U

UFO AND OUTER SPACE

Gold Key; 14 Jun 1978-25 Feb 1980

(previously UFO Flying Saucers)

	$Good	$Fine	$N.Mint	£Good	£Fine	£N.Mint
14 painted covers continue	$0.80	$2.50	$5.00	£0.40	£1.25	£2.50
15-20	$0.50	$1.50	$3.00	£0.30	£1.00	£2.00
21-25	$0.40	$1.25	$2.50	£0.25	£0.75	£1.50
Title Value:	$5.80	$17.75	$35.50	£3.45	£11.00	£22.00

Note: some issues are reprint. Limited Distribution in the U.K.

UFO FLYING SAUCERS

Gold Key; 1 Oct 1968-13 Jan 1977

(becomes UFO and Outer Space)

	$Good	$Fine	$N.Mint	£Good	£Fine	£N.Mint
1 scarce in the U.K. giant; painted covers begin	$3.20	$9.50	$22.50	£2.10	£6.25	£15.00
2	$2.05	$6.25	$12.50	£1.25	£3.75	£7.50
3	$1.65	$5.00	$10.00	£1.00	£3.00	£6.00
4-13	$1.25	$3.75	$7.50	£0.65	£2.00	£4.00
Title Value:	$19.40	$58.25	$120.00	£10.85	£33.00	£68.50

Note: some issues distributed in the U.K. and then only sporadically

ULTRA GIRL

Marvel Comics Group,MS; 1 Jan 1997-3 Mar 1997

	$Good	$Fine	$N.Mint	£Good	£Fine	£N.Mint
1-3 ND Barbara Kesel script, Leonard Kirk and Terry Pallot art	$0.30	$0.90	$1.50	£0.20	£0.60	£1.00
Title Value:	$0.90	$2.70	$4.50	£0.60	£1.80	£3.00

ULTRA KLUTZ

Onward; 1 Jun 1986-31 1993

	$Good	$Fine	$N.Mint	£Good	£Fine	£N.Mint
1-30 ND black and white	$0.30	$0.90	$1.50	£0.20	£0.60	£1.00
31 ND 48pgs, black and white	$0.40	$1.20	$2.00	£0.25	£0.75	£1.25
Title Value:	$9.40	$28.20	$47.00	£6.25	£18.75	£31.25

ULTRA KLUTZ (2ND SERIES)

Parody Press; 1 Aug 1993-11 1994

	$Good	$Fine	$N.Mint	£Good	£Fine	£N.Mint
1 ND reprints from first series begin (parodying Ultraman from Archie Comics)	$0.40	$1.20	$2.00	£0.25	£0.75	£1.25
1 Deluxe Edition, ND - silver foil embossed cover	$0.50	$1.50	$2.50	£0.30	£0.90	£1.50
2-11 ND	$0.40	$1.20	$2.00	£0.25	£0.75	£1.25
Title Value:	$4.90	$14.70	$24.50	£3.05	£9.15	£15.25

ULTRA X-MEN COLLECTION

Marvel Comics Group,MS; 1 Dec 1994-5 Apr 1995

	$Good	$Fine	$N.Mint	£Good	£Fine	£N.Mint
1-5 ND collects the set of Fleer Ultra X-Men trading cards, bound by a metallic ink gatefold cover	$0.60	$1.80	$3.00	£0.40	£1.20	£2.00
Title Value:	$3.00	$9.00	$15.00	£2.00	£6.00	£10.00

ULTRAFORCE

Malibu Ultraverse; 0 Sep/Oct 1994; 1 Aug 1994-10 Aug 1995

	$Good	$Fine	$N.Mint	£Good	£Fine	£N.Mint
0 reprints ashcan editions released with Wizard #35 and #36; prequel to Ultraforce #1	$0.50	$1.50	$2.50	£0.30	£0.90	£1.50
1 ND 40pgs, Prime, Prototype, Hardcase, Contrary, Topaz, Ghoul and Pixx begin; bound-in Prime/Ultraforce trading card, George Perez art	$0.50	$1.50	$2.50	£0.30	£0.90	£1.50
1 Ashcan Edition, ND (Jun 1994) - 16pgs interviews and sketches; black and white, limited to 25,000 copies	$0.30	$0.90	$1.50	£0.20	£0.60	£1.00
1 Gold Hologram Cover Edition, ND (Aug 1994)	$2.50	$7.50	$12.50	£1.50	£4.50	£7.50
1 Newstand Edition, ND less common variant cover; pre-bagged with Skybox trading card	$0.60	$1.80	$3.00	£0.40	£1.20	£2.00
2 ND	$0.50	$1.50	$2.50	£0.30	£0.90	£1.50
2 Variant Cover Edition, ND white cover featuring Prime; limited edition stamp on cover	$0.80	$2.40	$4.00	£0.60	£1.80	£3.00
3-5 ND	$0.50	$1.50	$2.50	£0.30	£0.90	£1.50
6-7 ND George Perez cover	$0.50	$1.50	$2.50	£0.30	£0.90	£1.50
8 ND Marvel's Black Knight appears, George Perez cover	$0.50	$1.50	$2.50	£0.30	£0.90	£1.50
9 ND Marvel's Black Knight appears, George Perez cover and art	$0.50	$1.50	$2.50	£0.30	£0.90	£1.50
10 ND 1st issue under Marvel Comics solicitation; Sersi (from Marvel's Avengers) appears, Eliminator appears; leads into Ultraforce/Avengers Prelude #1; George Perez cover	$0.50	$1.50	$2.50	£0.30	£0.90	£1.50
Title Value:	$9.70	$29.10	$48.50	£6.00	£18.00	£30.00

Note: all Non-Distributed on the news-stands in the U.K.

ULTRAFORCE (2ND SERIES)

Marvel Comics Group; 1 Dec 1995-present

	$Good	$Fine	$N.Mint	£Good	£Fine	£N.Mint
1 ND Warren Ellis script, Steve Butler and Dennis Jensen art, cover by Steve Butler and George Perez	$0.30	$0.90	$1.50	£0.20	£0.60	£1.00
1 Signed Limited Edition, ND (Mar 1996) - 2,000 copies with certificate	$1.50	$4.50	$7.50	£1.00	£3.00	£5.00
1 Variant Cover Edition, ND, computer painted art by Chuck Maiden	$0.50	$1.50	$2.50	£0.30	£0.90	£1.50
2 ND 1st appearance of Lament, flip-book format with Phoenix Ressurrection chapter	$0.30	$0.90	$1.50	£0.20	£0.60	£1.00
3 ND origin Wreckage	$0.30	$0.90	$1.50	£0.20	£0.60	£1.00
4-8 ND cover by Darick Robertson and George Perez	$0.30	$0.90	$1.50	£0.20	£0.60	£1.00
9 ND	$0.30	$0.90	$1.50	£0.20	£0.60	£1.00
10 ND Len Wein script and Mike Deodato art begin	$0.30	$0.90	$1.50	£0.20	£0.60	£1.00
11 ND	$0.30	$0.90	$1.50	£0.20	£0.60	£1.00
12 ND continued in Ultraverse Unlimited #2	$0.30	$0.90	$1.50	£0.20	£0.60	£1.00
13 ND new line up	$0.30	$0.90	$1.50	£0.20	£0.60	£1.00
14-15 ND Hardcase appears	$0.30	$0.90	$1.50	£0.20	£0.60	£1.00
Title Value:	$6.50	$19.50	$32.50	£4.30	£12.90	£21.50

ULTRAFORCE/AVENGERS

Malibu Ultraverse/Marvel Comics Group,OS; 1 Oct 1995

(see Avengers/Ultraforce)

	$Good	$Fine	$N.Mint	£Good	£Fine	£N.Mint
1 ND 48pgs, Warren Ellis script, George Perez wraparond cover and art; Loki appears	$0.80	$2.40	$4.00	£0.50	£1.50	£2.50
Title Value:	$0.80	$2.40	$4.00	£0.50	£1.50	£2.50

ULTRAFORCE/AVENGERS PRELUDE

Marvel Comics Group/Malibu Ultraverse,OS; 1 Sep 1995

	$Good	$Fine	$N.Mint	£Good	£Fine	£N.Mint
1 ND Ultraforce, Avengers, Loki and Adam Warlock appear (see also Eliminator #3 as Sersi returns with missing Infinity gem)	$0.50	$1.50	$2.50	£0.30	£0.90	£1.50
Title Value:	$0.50	$1.50	$2.50	£0.30	£0.90	£1.50

ULTRAFORCE: INFINITY

Marvel Comics Group,OS; nn Nov 1995

	$Good	$Fine	$N.Mint	£Good	£Fine	£N.Mint
nn ND Black September tie-in, intro the Fantastic Ultraforce Four	$0.50	$1.50	$2.50	£0.30	£0.90	£1.50
nn Variant Cover Edition ND 1 copy received for ever 5 copies of the regular issue ordered	$0.60	$1.80	$3.00	£0.40	£1.20	£2.00
Title Value:	$1.10	$3.30	$5.50	£0.70	£2.10	£3.50

ULTRAMAN

Harvey/Ultracomics; 1 Jul 1993-3 Sep 1993

	$Good	$Fine	$N.Mint	£Good	£Fine	£N.Mint
1-3 un-bagged/without trading card	$0.30	$0.90	$1.50	£0.20	£0.60	£1.00
1-3 Direct Market Edition, : pre-bagged with trading card; logo and all other cover deatails printed on the polybag; Ken Steacy painted cover	$0.40	$1.20	$2.00	£0.25	£0.75	£1.25
Title Value:	$2.10	$6.30	$10.50	£1.35	£4.05	£6.75

Note: all Non-Distributed on the news-stands in the U.K.

ULTRAMAN (2ND SERIES)

Nemesis Comics; -1 Mar 1994; 1 Apr 1994-5 1994

	$Good	$Fine	$N.Mint	£Good	£Fine	£N.Mint
-1 ND (issue #1 in indicia) Ernie Colon art begins	$0.30	$0.90	$1.50	£0.20	£0.60	£1.00
-1 Collectors Edition, ND - card-stock embossed cover	$0.40	$1.20	$2.00	£0.25	£0.75	£1.25
1 ND protective half-outer cover	$0.40	$1.20	$2.00	£0.25	£0.75	£1.25
2-5 ND	$0.40	$1.20	$2.00	£0.25	£0.75	£1.25
Title Value:	$2.70	$8.10	$13.50	£1.70	£5.10	£8.50

ULTRAMAN 3-D SPECIAL

Now Comics,OS; 1 Jul 1993

	$Good	$Fine	$N.Mint	£Good	£Fine	£N.Mint
1 ND hologravure process that does not need 3-D glasses	$0.50	$1.50	$2.50	£0.30	£0.90	£1.50
Title Value:	$0.50	$1.50	$2.50	£0.30	£0.90	£1.50

ULTRAMAN CLASSIC: BATTLE OF THE ULTRA-BROTHERS

Viz Communications,MS; 1 Feb 1994-5 Jul 1994

	$Good	$Fine	$N.Mint	£Good	£Fine	£N.Mint
1 ND 64pgs, squarebound, black and white	$0.80	$2.40	$4.00	£0.50	£1.50	£2.50
2-5 ND 64pgs, black and white	$0.80	$2.40	$4.00	£0.50	£1.50	£2.50
Title Value:	$4.00	$12.00	$20.00	£2.50	£7.50	£12.50

ULTRAVERSE DOUBLE FEATURE

Malibu Ultraverse; 1 Jan 1995

	$Good	$Fine	$N.Mint	£Good	£Fine	£N.Mint
1 ND 64pgs, Prime and Solitaire in separate stories	$0.60	$1.80	$3.00	£0.40	£1.20	£2.00
Title Value:	$0.60	$1.80	$3.00	£0.40	£1.20	£2.00

ULTRAVERSE ORIGINS

Malibu Ultraverse,OS; 1 Jan 1994

	$Good	$Fine	$N.Mint	£Good	£Fine	£N.Mint
1 ND origins of Ultraverse characters featuring art by Maguire, Bogdanove, Mike Zeck, Barry Windsor-Smith, George Perez, Hughes, Chaykin, Walt Simonson; gatefold cover by Joe Quesada	$0.30	$0.90	$1.50	£0.20	£0.60	£1.00
Title Value:	$0.30	$0.90	$1.50	£0.20	£0.60	£1.00

ULTRAVERSE PREMIERE

Malibu Ultraverse,OS; 0 Nov 1993

	$Good	$Fine	$N.Mint	£Good	£Fine	£N.Mint
0 ND collection of short stories featuring Prime, Strangers, Hardcase, Rune, Mantra and Freex; available through mail only with coupons sent in	$1.00	$3.00	$5.00	£0.60	£1.80	£3.00
Title Value:	$1.00	$3.00	$5.00	£0.60	£1.80	£3.00

ULTRAVERSE UNLIMITED

Marvel Comics Group; 1 Aug 1996-present

	$Good	$Fine	$N.Mint	£Good	£Fine	£N.Mint
1 ND 48pgs, Rune and Warlock appear, Kelley Jones cover	$0.50	$1.50	$2.50	£0.30	£0.90	£1.50
2 ND	$0.50	$1.50	$2.50	£0.30	£0.90	£1.50
Title Value:	$1.00	$3.00	$5.00	£0.60	£1.80	£3.00

ULTRAVERSE YEAR ONE

Malibu Ultraverse,OS; nn Sep 1994

	$Good	$Fine	$N.Mint	£Good	£Fine	£N.Mint
1 ND 48pgs, information and cover reproductions of Ultraverse characters and titles	$0.60	$1.80	$3.00	£0.40	£1.20	£2.00
Title Value:	$0.60	$1.80	$3.00	£0.40	£1.20	£2.00

ULTRAVERSE YEAR TWO

Marvel Comics Group/Malibu Ultraverse,OS; 1 Oct 1995

	$Good	$Fine	$N.Mint	£Good	£Fine	£N.Mint
1 ND 48pgs, information and cover reproductions concerning the inter-locking of Marvel and Ultraverse characters	$0.60	$1.80	$3.00	£0.40	£1.20	£2.00
Title Value:	$0.60	$1.80	$3.00	£0.40	£1.20	£2.00

ULTRAVERSE YEAR ZERO: THE DEATH OF THE SQUAD

Malibu Ultraverse,MS; 1 Apr 1995-4 Jul 1995

	$Good	$Fine	$N.Mint	£Good	£Fine	£N.Mint
1 ND chronicles events before Prime #1; Mantra back-up feature	$0.50	$1.50	$2.50	£0.30	£0.90	£1.50
2 ND chronicles events before Prime #1; Rune back-up feature	$0.50	$1.50	$2.50	£0.30	£0.90	£1.50
3 ND chronicles events before Prime #1; Codename: Firearm back-up feature						

	$Good	$Fine	$N.Mint	£Good	£Fine	£N.Mint
	$0.50	$1.50	$2.50	£0.30	£0.90	£1.50
Title Value:	$1.50	$4.50	$7.50	£0.90	£2.70	£4.50

ULTRAVERSE/MARVEL DREAM TEAM

Marvel Comics Group/Malibu Ultraverse,OS; 1 Sep 1995

	$Good	$Fine	$N.Mint	£Good	£Fine	£N.Mint
1 ND 48pgs, pin-ups of Marvel and Ultraverse characters; Shi by William Tucci also appears						
	$0.80	$2.40	$4.00	£0.50	£1.50	£2.50
Title Value:	$0.80	$2.40	$4.00	£0.50	£1.50	£2.50

ULTRAVERSE: FUTURE SHOCK

Marvel Comics Group,OS; nn Feb 1997

	$Good	$Fine	$N.Mint	£Good	£Fine	£N.Mint
nn ND 48pgs, Mark Paniccia script, Leonard Kirk and Terry Pallot art						
	$0.50	$1.50	$2.50	£0.30	£0.90	£1.50
Title Value:	$0.50	$1.50	$2.50	£0.30	£0.90	£1.50

UNCANNY ORIGINS

Marvel Comics Group; 1 Sep 1996-present

	$Good	$Fine	$N.Mint	£Good	£Fine	£N.Mint
1 ND origin of Cyclops retold						
	$0.20	$0.60	$1.00	£0.10	£0.35	£0.65
2 ND origin of Quicksilver retold						
	$0.20	$0.60	$1.00	£0.15	£0.45	£0.75
3 ND origin of The Angel retold						
	$0.20	$0.60	$1.00	£0.15	£0.45	£0.75
4 ND origin of Firelord retold						
	$0.20	$0.60	$1.00	£0.15	£0.45	£0.75
5 ND origin The Incredible Hulk retold						
	$0.20	$0.60	$1.00	£0.15	£0.45	£0.75
6 ND origin of The Beast retold						
	$0.20	$0.60	$1.00	£0.15	£0.45	£0.75
7 ND origin of Venom						
	$0.20	$0.60	$1.00	£0.15	£0.45	£0.75
Title Value:	$1.40	$4.20	$7.00	£1.00	£3.05	£5.15

UNCANNY TALES

Marvel Comics Group; 1 Dec 1973-12 Oct 1975

	$Good	$Fine	$N.Mint	£Good	£Fine	£N.Mint
1 ND scarce in the U.K. 50s/60s horror reprints begin						
	$0.65	$2.00	$4.00	£0.30	£1.00	£2.00
2-12 ND	$0.50	$1.50	$3.00	£0.25	£0.75	£1.50
Title Value:	$6.15	$18.50	$33.50	£3.05	£9.25	£18.50

Note: full title is Uncanny Tales From The Grave

UNCENSORED MOUSE

Eternity; 1,2 Apr 1989

	$Good	$Fine	$N.Mint	£Good	£Fine	£N.Mint
1 ND 40pgs, pre-bagged						
	$0.60	$1.80	$3.00	£0.40	£1.20	£2.00
2 scarce in both US and UK pre-bagged						
	$0.60	$1.80	$3.00	£0.50	£1.50	£2.50
Title Value:	$1.20	$3.60	$6.00	£0.90	£2.70	£4.50

Note: previously unpublished Mickey Mouse material with satirical or racist overtones. Sealed in plastic bags. Opened examples will bring 50% of the above values. Issue #2 is scarcer owing to legal problems with problems with Disney at the time and as such less were distributed in both the US and UK. Planned as an on-going series, it finished after just two issues.

UNCLE SCROOGE

Gladstone; 210 Oct 1986-242 1989; Disney; 243 Jun 1990-280 Jun 1993; Gladstone; 281 Jul 1993-present

	$Good	$Fine	$N.Mint	£Good	£Fine	£N.Mint
210 1st Gladstone issue, 75c, Barks reprints begin						
	$4.00	$12.00	$20.00	£1.20	£3.60	£6.00
211 scarce in the U.K. Prize of Pizarro						
	$2.50	$7.50	$12.50	£1.00	£3.00	£5.00
212-215	$2.50	$7.50	$12.50	£0.80	£2.40	£4.00
216 1st 95¢ issue	$2.00	$6.00	$10.00	£0.80	£2.40	£4.00
217-218	$2.00	$6.00	$10.00	£0.80	£2.40	£4.00
219 Son of the Sun by Rosa						
	$4.00	$12.00	$20.00	£1.20	£3.60	£6.00
220 Rosa 10pg story						
	$1.00	$3.00	$5.00	£0.60	£1.80	£3.00
221	$0.60	$1.80	$3.00	£0.40	£1.20	£2.00
222 Mysterious Island by Barks, includes restored panels & article						
	$0.60	$1.80	$3.00	£0.40	£1.20	£2.00
223	$0.60	$1.80	$3.00	£0.40	£1.20	£2.00
224 Cash Flow by Rosa						
	$0.60	$1.80	$3.00	£0.40	£1.20	£2.00
225	$0.60	$1.80	$3.00	£0.40	£1.20	£2.00
226 Paper Chase by Rosa						
	$0.60	$1.80	$3.00	£0.40	£1.20	£2.00
227 Fiscal Fitness by Rosa						
	$0.60	$1.80	$3.00	£0.40	£1.20	£2.00
228-230	$0.60	$1.80	$3.00	£0.40	£1.20	£2.00
231-240	$0.50	$1.50	$2.50	£0.30	£0.90	£1.50
241-242 68pgs	$0.60	$1.80	$3.00	£0.40	£1.20	£2.00
243 all new material begins						
	$0.50	$1.50	$2.50	£0.30	£0.90	£1.50
244-249	$0.50	$1.50	$2.50	£0.30	£0.90	£1.50
250 anniversary issue						
	$0.60	$1.80	$3.00	£0.40	£1.20	£2.00
251-254	$0.50	$1.50	$2.50	£0.30	£0.90	£1.50
255 classic The Flying Dutchman by Carl Barks						
	$0.50	$1.50	$2.50	£0.30	£0.90	£1.50
256-260	$0.50	$1.50	$2.50	£0.30	£0.90	£1.50
261-262 Return to Xanadu by Don Rosa						
	$0.50	$1.50	$2.50	£0.30	£0.90	£1.50
263-267	$0.50	$1.50	$2.50	£0.30	£0.90	£1.50
268 Carl Barks reprint						
	$0.50	$1.50	$2.50	£0.30	£0.90	£1.50
269-272	$0.50	$1.50	$2.50	£0.30	£0.90	£1.50
273-274 all Carl Barks issue						
	$0.50	$1.50	$2.50	£0.30	£0.90	£1.50
275 all Carl Barks issue plus Don Rosa poster						
	$0.50	$1.50	$2.50	£0.30	£0.90	£1.50
276-280 Carl Barks reprint						
	$0.50	$1.50	$2.50	£0.30	£0.90	£1.50
281 Carl Barks reprint; title noe re-published by Gladstone						
	$0.50	$1.50	$2.50	£0.30	£0.90	£1.50
282-284 Carl Barks reprint						
	$0.50	$1.50	$2.50	£0.30	£0.90	£1.50
285 The Life and Times of Scrooge McDuck begin (ends #297)						
	$1.20	$3.60	$6.00	£0.50	£1.50	£2.50
286-287	$0.70	$2.10	$3.50	£0.30	£0.90	£1.50
288 64pgs, Land Beneath the Ground by Barks						
	$0.80	$2.40	$4.00	£0.40	£1.20	£2.00
289-296	$0.70	$2.10	$3.50	£0.30	£0.90	£1.50
297-301	$0.40	$1.20	$2.00	£0.20	£0.60	£1.00
Title Value:	$71.80	$215.40	$355.00	£35.00	£105.00	£175.00

Note: all Non-Distributed on the news-stands in the U.K.

UNCLE SCROOGE ADVENTURES

Gladstone; 1 Nov 1987-21 May 1990; Gladstone/Disney; 22 Aug 1993-present

(formerly Gladstone title)

	$Good	$Fine	$N.Mint	£Good	£Fine	£N.Mint
1 McDuck of Arabia, Barks reprints begin						
	$1.30	$3.90	$6.50	£0.70	£2.10	£3.50
2-3	$0.80	$2.40	$4.00	£0.40	£1.20	£2.00
4 Golden River by Barks						
	$0.60	$1.80	$3.00	£0.30	£0.90	£1.50
5 Last Sled to Dawson by Rosa						
	$0.60	$1.80	$3.00	£0.30	£0.90	£1.50
6-8	$0.60	$1.80	$3.00	£0.30	£0.90	£1.50
9 Fortune on the Rocks by Rosa						
	$0.60	$1.80	$3.00	£0.30	£0.90	£1.50

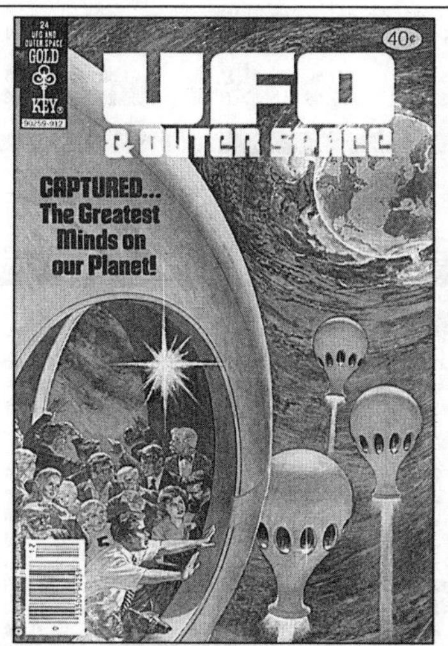

UFO and Outer Space #24

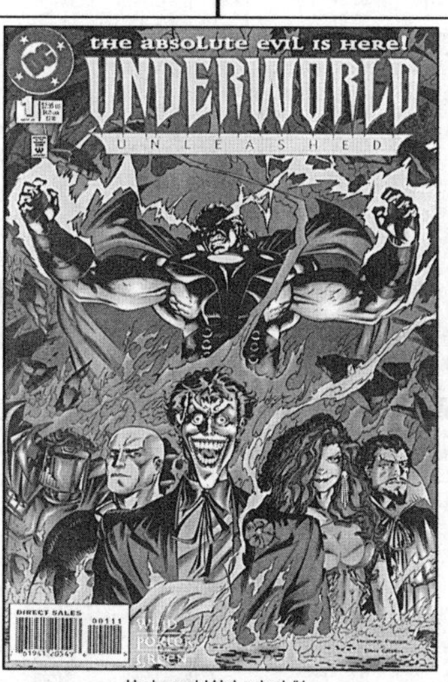

Underworld Unleashed #1

Unexpected #222

	$Good	$Fine	$N.Mint	£Good	£Fine	£N.Mint
10	$0.60	$1.80	$3.00	£0.30	£0.90	£1.50
11-19	$0.50	$1.50	$2.50	£0.25	£0.75	£1.25
20-21 64pgs	$0.50	$1.50	$2.50	£0.30	£0.90	£1.50
22 Carl Barks' "Prize of Pizarro" reprint	$0.40	$1.20	$2.00	£0.25	£0.75	£1.25
23 64pgs	$0.50	$1.50	$2.50	£0.30	£0.90	£1.50
24-25	$0.40	$1.20	$2.00	£0.25	£0.75	£1.25
26 64pgs, Back to Klondike reprinted	$0.60	$1.80	$3.00	£0.40	£1.20	£2.00
27-29	$0.40	$1.20	$2.00	£0.25	£0.75	£1.25
30 64pgs, Ramona Scarpa's "The Lentils of Babylon" begins	$0.60	$1.80	$3.00	£0.40	£1.20	£2.00
31-32	$0.40	$1.20	$2.00	£0.25	£0.75	£1.25
33 64pgs, new story called "Horsing Around With History" written by Carl Barks	$0.60	$1.80	$3.00	£0.40	£1.20	£2.00
34-36	$0.40	$1.20	$2.00	£0.25	£0.75	£1.25
37-43	$0.30	$0.90	$1.50	£0.20	£0.60	£1.00
Title Value:	$21.40	$64.20	$107.00	£12.10	£36.30	£60.50

Note: all Non-Distributed on the news-stands in the U.K.

UNCLE SCROOGE DIGEST

Gladstone; 1 1986-5 1987

	$Good	$Fine	$N.Mint	£Good	£Fine	£N.Mint
1 ND	$0.60	$1.80	$3.00	£0.30	£0.90	£1.50
2 ND Second Richest Duck by Barks	$0.70	$2.10	$3.50	£0.35	£1.05	£1.75
3-5 ND	$0.50	$1.50	$2.50	£0.30	£0.90	£1.50
Title Value:	$2.80	$8.40	$14.00	£1.55	£4.65	£7.75

UNCLE SCROOGE GOES TO DISNEYLAND

Gladstone; 1 1985

	$Good	$Fine	$N.Mint	£Good	£Fine	£N.Mint
1 ND 100pgs, 20pgs Carl Barks	$0.80	$2.40	$4.00	£0.50	£1.50	£2.50
Title Value:	$0.80	$2.40	$4.00	£0.50	£1.50	£2.50

UNCLE WALT'S COLLECTORY

Gladstone/Disney; 1 Jun 1995

	$Good	$Fine	$N.Mint	£Good	£Fine	£N.Mint
1 ND 48pgs, Don Rosa art	$0.50	$1.50	$2.50	£0.30	£0.90	£1.50
Title Value:	$0.50	$1.50	$2.50	£0.30	£0.90	£1.50

UNDERDOG

Charlton; 1 Nov 1970-10 Jan 1972

	$Good	$Fine	$N.Mint	£Good	£Fine	£N.Mint
1 scarce in the U.K. Frank Johnson art begins	$10.50	$33.00	$65.00	£6.25	£18.50	£37.50
2-3 scarce in the U.K.	$6.50	$20.00	$40.00	£3.30	£10.00	£20.00
4-10	$5.75	$17.50	$35.00	£2.50	£7.50	£15.00
Title Value:	$63.75	$195.50	$390.00	£30.35	£91.00	£182.50

Note: some issues distributed on the news-stands in the U.K.

UNDERDOG (2ND SERIES)

Gold Key/Whitman; 1 Mar 1975-23 Feb 1979

	$Good	$Fine	$N.Mint	£Good	£Fine	£N.Mint
1	$8.25	$25.00	$50.00	£3.75	£11.00	£22.50
2-3	$5.00	$15.00	$30.00	£2.50	£7.50	£15.00
4-10	$4.15	$12.50	$25.00	£2.05	£6.25	£12.50
11-20	$3.30	$10.00	$20.00	£1.65	£5.00	£10.00
21-23	$2.90	$8.75	$17.50	£1.25	£3.75	£7.50
Title Value:	$89.00	$268.75	$537.50	£43.35	£131.00	£262.50

Note: some issues distributed on the news-stands in the U.K.

UNDERDOG IN 3-D

Blackthorne; (3-D Series #43) 1 Jun 1988

	$Good	$Fine	$N.Mint	£Good	£Fine	£N.Mint
1 ND with bound-in 3-D glasses (25% less without glasses)	$0.50	$1.50	$2.50	£0.30	£0.90	£1.50
Title Value:	$0.50	$1.50	$2.50	£0.30	£0.90	£1.50

UNDERGROUND

Aircel,Magazine OS; 1 1987

	$Good	$Fine	$N.Mint	£Good	£Fine	£N.Mint
1 ND	$0.40	$1.20	$2.00	£0.25	£0.75	£1.25
Title Value:	$0.40	$1.20	$2.00	£0.25	£0.75	£1.25

UNDERSEA AGENT

Tower; 1 Jan 1966-6 Mar 1967

	$Good	$Fine	$N.Mint	£Good	£Fine	£N.Mint
1 distributed in the U.K. Giant	$7.00	$21.00	$50.00	£4.60	£13.50	£32.50
2-6 distributed in the U.K. Giant	$4.60	$13.50	$32.50	£2.85	£8.50	£20.00
Title Value:	$30.00	$88.50	$212.50	£18.85	£56.00	£132.50

UNDERWORLD

DC Comics,MS; 1 Dec 1987-4 Mar 1988

	$Good	$Fine	$N.Mint	£Good	£Fine	£N.Mint
1-4	$0.15	$0.45	$0.75	£0.10	£0.35	£0.60
Title Value:	$0.60	$1.80	$3.00	£0.40	£1.40	£2.40

UNDERWORLD UNLEASHED

DC Comics,MS; 1 Nov 1995-3 Jan 1996

	$Good	$Fine	$N.Mint	£Good	£Fine	£N.Mint
1-3 ND 48pgs, Neron and DC villains have their day; fluorescent ink covers	$0.60	$1.80	$3.00	£0.40	£1.20	£2.00
Title Value:	$1.80	$5.40	$9.00	£1.20	£3.60	£6.00

UNDERWORLD UNLEASHED TIE-INS

Underworld Unleashed concerns Neron, the ultimate demon who personifies the concept of evil in the DC Universe. As the villains achieve their aims and objectives so they become Neron's unwitting pawns. The tie-ins outside the 3 issue mini-series are as follows in order of publication:

Aquaman #14,
Azrael #10,
Damage #18,
Green Arrow #102,
Guy Gardner Warrior #36,
Manhunter #12,
Extreme Justice #10,
Flash #107,
Primal Force #13,
Spectre #35,
Green Lantern #68,
Hawkman #26,
Justice League America #105,
R.E.B.E.L.S. '95 #13,
Starman #13,
Detective Comics #691,
Fate #13,
Impulse #8,
The Ray #18,
Steel #21,
Catwoman #21,
Damage #19,
Green Arrow #103,
Guy Gardner: Warrior #37,
Robin #23,
Batman #525,
Extreme Justice #11,
Legion of Super-Heroes #75,
Primal Force #14,
Superboy #22,
Spectre #36,
Green Lantern #69,
Hawkman #27,
Justice League America #106,
R.E.B.E.L.S. '95 #14,
Adventures of Superman #530,
Detective Comics #692,
Fate #14,
Justice League Task Force #30,
Legionnaires #32,
Superman: The Man of Tomorrow #3,
The Ray #19.

Also included are Underworld Unleashed Specials:
Apokolips: Dark Uprising,
Batman - Devil's Asylum,
Abyss - Hell's Sentinel and **Patterns of Fear**.

UNDERWORLD UNLEASHED: ABYSS - HELL'S SENTINEL

DC Comics,OS; 1 Dec 1995

	$Good	$Fine	$N.Mint	£Good	£Fine	£N.Mint
1 ND 48pgs, Spectre, Fate, Zatanna, Deadman and Phantom Stranger appear with Sentinel (formerly the Golden Age Green Lantern)	$0.60	$1.80	$3.00	£0.40	£1.20	£2.00
Title Value:	$0.60	$1.80	$3.00	£0.40	£1.20	£2.00

UNDERWORLD UNLEASHED: APOKOLIPS - DARK UPRISING

DC Comics,OS; 1 Nov 1995

	$Good	$Fine	$N.Mint	£Good	£Fine	£N.Mint
1 ND 48pgs	$0.60	$1.80	$3.00	£0.40	£1.20	£2.00
Title Value:	$0.60	$1.80	$3.00	£0.40	£1.20	£2.00

UNDERWORLD UNLEASHED: BATMAN - DEVIL'S ASYLUM

DC Comics,OS; 1 Dec 1995

	$Good	$Fine	$N.Mint	£Good	£Fine	£N.Mint
1 ND Alan Grant script, Brian Stelfreeze art	$0.60	$1.80	$3.00	£0.40	£1.20	£2.00
Title Value:	$0.60	$1.80	$3.00	£0.40	£1.20	£2.00

UNDERWORLD UNLEASHED: PATTERNS OF FEAR

DC Comics,OS; 1 Dec 1995

	$Good	$Fine	$N.Mint	£Good	£Fine	£N.Mint
1 ND 48pgs, Barbara Gordon as Oracle assesses the new threat from DC villains as a result of Neron's work	$0.60	$1.80	$3.00	£0.40	£1.20	£2.00
Title Value:	$0.60	$1.80	$3.00	£0.40	£1.20	£2.00

UNEARTHLY SPECTACULARS

Harvey; 1 Oct 1965-3 Mar 1967

	$Good	$Fine	$N.Mint	£Good	£Fine	£N.Mint
1 rare in the U.K. Jack Quick Frost and Miracles Inc. begin	$2.50	$7.50	$17.50	£1.75	£5.25	£12.50
2 rare in the U.K. Giant, Wood art, Williamson art, Neal Adams art on advert	$3.90	$11.50	$27.50	£2.50	£7.50	£17.50
3 scarce in the U.K. Giant, Williamson art	$3.90	$11.50	$27.50	£2.50	£7.50	£17.50
Title Value:	$10.30	$30.50	$72.50	£6.75	£20.25	£47.50

Note: all distributed on the news-stands in the U.K.

UNEXPECTED SPECIAL, THE

DC Comics; nn 1977

(DC Special Series #4)

	$Good	$Fine	$N.Mint	£Good	£Fine	£N.Mint
nn ND 52pgs, Alex Nino art	$0.50	$1.50	$3.00	£0.30	£1.00	£2.00
Title Value:	$0.50	$1.50	$3.00	£0.30	£1.00	£2.00

UNEXPECTED, THE

National Periodical Publications; 105 Feb/Mar 1968-222 May 1982

(see Super DC Giant)
(previously Tales of the Unexpected)

	$Good	$Fine	$N.Mint	£Good	£Fine	£N.Mint
105	$3.55	$10.50	$25.00	£2.10	£6.25	£15.00
106 1st appearance Johnny Peril	$2.85	$8.50	$20.00	£1.75	£5.25	£12.50
107-112	$2.85	$8.50	$20.00	£1.40	£4.25	£10.00
113 last 12 cent issue	$2.85	$8.50	$20.00	£1.40	£4.25	£10.00
114-115	$1.65	$5.00	$10.00	£0.80	£2.50	£5.00
116 Wrightson art	$2.00	$6.00	$12.00	£1.00	£3.00	£6.00
117-118	$1.65	$5.00	$10.00	£0.80	£2.50	£5.00
119 Wrightson art	$2.00	$6.00	$12.00	£1.00	£3.00	£6.00
120	$1.65	$5.00	$10.00	£0.80	£2.50	£5.00
121 Wrightson art	$2.00	$6.00	$12.00	£1.00	£3.00	£6.00
122-125	$1.65	$5.00	$10.00	£0.80	£2.50	£5.00
126 52pgs	$1.30	$4.00	$8.00	£0.90	£2.75	£5.50

	$Good	$Fine	$N.Mint	£Good	£Fine	£N.Mint
127 52pgs	*$1.30*	*$4.00*	*$8.00*	£0.65	£2.00	£4.00
128 52pgs, Wrightson art	*$1.65*	*$5.00*	*$10.00*	£0.80	£2.50	£5.00
129-130 52pgs	*$1.30*	*$4.00*	*$8.00*	£0.65	£2.00	£4.00
131-132 52pgs	*$1.00*	*$3.00*	*$6.00*	£0.55	£1.75	£3.50
133 scarce in the U.K. 52pgs	*$1.00*	*$3.00*	*$6.00*	£0.65	£2.00	£4.00
134-136 52pgs	*$1.00*	*$3.00*	*$6.00*	£0.55	£1.75	£3.50
137-139	*$1.00*	*$3.00*	*$6.00*	£0.40	£1.25	£2.50
140 ND	*$1.00*	*$3.00*	*$6.00*	£0.50	£1.50	£3.00
141-156	*$0.80*	*$2.50*	*$5.00*	£0.30	£1.00	£2.00
157-162 100pgs	*$1.00*	*$3.00*	*$6.00*	£0.50	£1.50	£3.00
163-186	*$0.50*	*$1.50*	*$3.00*	£0.25	£0.75	£1.50
187-188 ND 44pgs	*$0.40*	*$1.25*	*$2.50*	£0.25	£0.85	£1.75
189-190 ND 68pgs	*$0.40*	*$1.25*	*$2.50*	£0.30	£1.00	£2.00
191 68pgs, Rogers art	*$0.40*	*$1.25*	*$2.50*	£0.25	£0.85	£1.75
192-195 ND 68pgs	*$0.40*	*$1.25*	*$2.50*	£0.30	£1.00	£2.00
196-200	*$0.40*	*$1.25*	*$2.50*	£0.20	£0.60	£1.25
201-202	*$0.40*	*$1.20*	*$2.00*	£0.20	£0.60	£1.00
203 Kaluta cover	*$0.40*	*$1.20*	*$2.00*	£0.20	£0.60	£1.00
204-222	*$0.40*	*$1.20*	*$2.00*	£0.20	£0.60	£1.00
Title Value:	*$109.25*	*$330.40*	*$665.00*	£54.35	£167.75	£346.50

ARTISTS

Ditko art in 189, 221. Kirby reprints in 127, 162. Nino art in 152, 159, 162. Wood art in 122 (inks), 137 (inks), 138. Wrightson reprint in 161.

FEATURES

Johnny Peril in 106-114, 117, 200, 205-213. Madame Xanadu in 190, 192, 194, 195.

REPRINT FEATURES

Johnny Peril in 127, 158. Various reprints in 126-136, 157-162.

UNICORN ISLE

Warp/Apple; 1 1986-5 1988

	$Good	$Fine	$N.Mint	£Good	£Fine	£N.Mint
1-5 ND	*$0.40*	*$1.20*	*$2.00*	£0.25	£0.75	£1.25
Title Value:	*$2.00*	*$6.00*	*$10.00*	£1.25	£3.75	£6.25

UNION

Image,MS; 0 Jul 1994; 1 Jun 1993-4 Feb 1994

	$Good	$Fine	$N.Mint	£Good	£Fine	£N.Mint
0 ND (Jul 1994)	*$0.50*	*$1.50*	*$2.50*	£0.30	£0.90	£1.50
0 Variant Cover Edition, ND Whilce Portacio cover art; cover forms larger picture when combined with the variant covers of Deathblow #5, Gen 13 #5, Kindred #3, Stormwatch #10, Team 7 #1, Wetworks #2, WildC.A.T.S #11	*$1.50*	*$4.50*	*$7.50*	£1.00	£3.00	£5.00
1 ND Direct Market Edition, Mark Texeira art begins, foil embossed cover	*$0.50*	*$1.50*	*$2.50*	£0.30	£0.90	£1.50
1 Newstand Edition, ND (no cover enhancement)	*$0.40*	*$1.20*	*$2.00*	£0.25	£0.75	£1.25
2-4 ND	*$0.40*	*$1.20*	*$2.00*	£0.25	£0.75	£1.25
Title Value:	*$4.10*	*$12.30*	*$20.50*	£2.60	£7.80	£13.00

Note: all Non-Distributed on the news-stands in the U.K.

UNION (2ND SERIES)

Image; 1 Feb 1995-12 Feb 1996

	$Good	$Fine	$N.Mint	£Good	£Fine	£N.Mint
1-3 ND Mike Heisler script and Ryan Benjamin art	*$0.50*	*$1.50*	*$2.50*	£0.30	£0.90	£1.50
4 ND Wildstorm Rising part 3, continued in Gen 13 #2; with two foil-bagged painted trading cards. Cover by Barry Windsor-Smith	*$0.50*	*$1.50*	*$2.50*	£0.30	£0.90	£1.50
4 Newstand Edition, ND, without trading cards	*$0.40*	*$1.20*	*$2.00*	£0.25	£0.75	£1.25
5-7 ND	*$0.50*	*$1.50*	*$2.50*	£0.30	£0.90	£1.50
8-9 ND Regal Vengeance story	*$0.50*	*$1.50*	*$2.50*	£0.30	£0.90	£1.50
10 ND Regal Vengeance story; Michael Golden cover	*$0.50*	*$1.50*	*$2.50*	£0.30	£0.90	£1.50
11-12 ND	*$0.50*	*$1.50*	*$2.50*	£0.30	£0.90	£1.50
Title Value:	*$6.40*	*$19.20*	*$32.00*	£3.85	£11.55	£19.25

UNION (3RD SERIES)

Image; 1 Jul 1996-present

	$Good	$Fine	$N.Mint	£Good	£Fine	£N.Mint
1 ND 24pgs, Mike Heisler script, Randy Green and Danny Bulandi art	*$0.35*	*$1.05*	*$1.75*	£0.25	£0.75	£1.25
2 ND	*$0.35*	*$1.05*	*$1.75*	£0.25	£0.75	£1.25
Title Value:	*$0.70*	*$2.10*	*$3.50*	£0.50	£1.50	£2.50

UNITY

The Unity series as written by Jim Shooter and drawn by Barry Windsor-Smith and Bob Layton defines the Valiant universe and how and where the titles and characters are related. Unity #0 was given away free by the distribution companies: retailers received 2 copies for every set of Unity chapters ordered. All 8 Valiant titles cover dated May and June 1992 had these chapters and the order is set out below. Unity #1 then concluded the 18 part story cover dated July 1992.

Chapter 1 - Unity #0
Chapter 2 - Eternal Warrior #1
Chapter 3 - Archer & Armstrong #1
Chapter 4 - Magnus Robot Fighter #15
Chapter 5 - X-O Manowar #7
Chapter 6 - Shadowman #4
Chapter 7 - Rai #6
Chapter 8 - Harbinger #8
Chapter 9 - Solar Man of the Atom #12
Chapter 10- Eternal Warrior #2
Chapter 11- Archer & Armstrong #2
Chapter 12- Magnus Robot Fighter #16
Chapter 13- X-O Manowar #8
Chapter 14- Shadowman #5
Chapter 15- Rai #7
Chapter 16- Harbinger #9
Chapter 17- Solar Man of the Atom #13
Chapter 18- Unity #1

UNITY (LIMITED SERIES)

Valiant; 0 May 1992-1 Oct 1992

	$Good	$Fine	$N.Mint	£Good	£Fine	£N.Mint
0 ND scarce in the U.K. 16pgs, originally given away free to retailers depending on the minimum order of all Valiant titles solicited for May cover date, Barry Windsor-Smith art	*$0.60*	*$1.80*	*$3.00*	£0.40	£1.20	£2.00
0 Gold Edition, ND retailer's "thankyou" from Valiant	*$1.50*	*$4.50*	*$7.50*	£1.00	£3.00	£5.00
0 Red Logo Edition, ND rare in the U.K., giveaway to U.S. retailers only	*$1.80*	*$5.25*	*$9.00*	£1.20	£3.60	£6.00
1 ND very scarce in the U.K. 16pgs, Unity: Epilogue; retailers quantities limited, depending on half the minimum order of all Valiant titles solicited for June cover date; cover/art by Barry Windsor-Smith	*$0.60*	*$1.80*	*$3.00*	£0.40	£1.20	£2.00
1 Gold Logo Premium, ND - retailer's "thankyou" from Valiant	*$1.50*	*$4.50*	*$7.50*	£1.00	£3.00	£5.00
1 Platinum Logo Premium, ND - retailer's "thankyou" from Valiant	*$1.80*	*$5.25*	*$9.00*	£1.20	£3.60	£6.00
Title Value:	*$7.80*	*$23.10*	*$39.00*	£5.20	£15.60	£26.00

	£Good	£Fine	£N.Mint
Unity Collection 1 (Jul 1992) very scarce in the U.K., collects the first set of Unity chapters with Frank Miller covers; Unity #0, Eternal Warrior #1, Archer & Armstrong #1, Magnus #15, X-O #6, Shadowman #4, Rai #5, Harbinger #8 and Solar #12. Frank Miller cover, signed by Jim Shooter and Bob Layton	£5.00	£15.00	£25.00
Unity Trade paperback 1 (1993) as above collects first four chapters of the Unity story but unsigned	£1.30	£3.90	£6.50
Unity Collection 2 (Aug 1992) very scarce in the U.K., collects the second set of Unity chapters with Walt Simonson covers: Eternal Warrior #2, Archer & Armstrong #2, Magnus #16, X-O #8, Shadowman #5, Rai #7, Harbinger #9, Solar #13 and Unity #1. Frank Miller cover, signed by Jim Shooter and Bob Layton	£5.00	£15.00	£25.00
Unity Trade paperback 2 (Oct 1994) as above collects chapters #5-9 of Unity story but unsigned	£1.30	£3.90	£6.50
Unity Trade paperback 3 (Nov 1994) collects chapters #10-14 of Unity story	£1.30	£3.90	£6.50
Unity Trade paperback 4 (Dec 1994) collects chapters #15-18 of Unity story	£1.30	£3.90	£6.50

UNITY: THE LOST CHAPTERS

Valiant,OS; 1 Feb 1995

	$Good	$Fine	$N.Mint	£Good	£Fine	£N.Mint
1 ND 48pgs, features X-O Manowar	*$0.50*	*$1.50*	*$2.50*	£0.30	£0.90	£1.50
Title Value:	*$0.50*	*$1.50*	*$2.50*	£0.30	£0.90	£1.50

UNIVERSAL INTERGALACTIC DISCOVERY CO.

Comico; 1 Apr 1992

	$Good	$Fine	$N.Mint	£Good	£Fine	£N.Mint
1 ND	*$0.40*	*$1.20*	*$2.00*	£0.25	£0.75	£1.25
Title Value:	*$0.40*	*$1.20*	*$2.00*	£0.25	£0.75	£1.25

UNIVERSAL MONSTERS

Dark Horse; 1 Jun 1993-4 Sep 1993

	$Good	$Fine	$N.Mint	£Good	£Fine	£N.Mint
1 ND 48pgs, squarebound, Frankenstein; adapted and painted by Denis Beauvais	*$1.00*	*$3.00*	*$5.00*	£0.70	£2.10	£3.50
2 ND 48pgs, squarebound, Creature From The Black Lagoon; Art Adams and Terry Austin art	*$1.00*	*$3.00*	*$5.00*	£0.70	£2.10	£3.50
3 ND 48pgs, squarebound, Dracula; Dan Vado script and Jonathan D. Smith art	*$1.00*	*$3.00*	*$5.00*	£0.70	£2.10	£3.50
4 ND 48pgs, squarebound, The Mummy; Dan Jolley script and Tony Harris art	*$1.00*	*$3.00*	*$5.00*	£0.70	£2.10	£3.50
Title Value:	*$4.00*	*$12.00*	*$20.00*	£2.80	£8.40	£14.00

UNIVERSAL PRESENTS DRACULA, THE MUMMY/OTHER STORIES

Dell,OS; 02-530-311 Sep/Nov 1963

	$Good	$Fine	$N.Mint	£Good	£Fine	£N.Mint
02-530-311 scarce in the U.K. 80pgs, all reprint from Dell Giants; distributed in some areas in the U.K.	*$30.00*	*$90.00*	*$210.00*	£20.00	£60.00	£140.00
Title Value:	*$30.00*	*$90.00*	*$210.00*	£20.00	£60.00	£140.00

UNIVERSAL SOLDIER

Now Comics,MS; 1 Sep 1992-3 Nov 1992

	$Good	$Fine	$N.Mint	£Good	£Fine	£N.Mint
1 ND based on film, pre-bagged with hologram cover	*$0.40*	*$1.20*	*$2.00*	£0.25	£0.75	£1.25
1 Newstand Edition, ND based on film, toned down issue, photo cover	*$0.30*	*$0.90*	*$1.50*	£0.20	£0.60	£1.00
2 ND pre-bagged	*$0.40*	*$1.20*	*$2.00*	£0.25	£0.75	£1.25
2 Newstand Edition ND	*$0.30*	*$0.90*	*$1.50*	£0.20	£0.60	£1.00
3 ND pre-bagged	*$0.40*	*$1.20*	*$2.00*	£0.25	£0.75	£1.25
3 Newstand Edition ND	*$0.30*	*$0.90*	*$1.50*	£0.20	£0.60	£1.00
Title Value:	*$2.10*	*$6.30*	*$10.50*	£1.35	£4.05	£6.75

UNKNOWN SOLDIER

DC Comics; 205 Apr/May 1977-268 Oct 1982

(see Brave and the Bold, DC Super-Stars)
(previously Star-Spangled War Stories)

	$Good	$Fine	$N.Mint	£Good	£Fine	£N.Mint
205	*$0.40*	*$1.20*	*$2.00*	£0.25	£0.75	£1.25
206-211	*$0.40*	*$1.20*	*$2.00*	£0.20	£0.60	£1.00
212-218 ND	*$0.40*	*$1.20*	*$2.00*	£0.25	£0.75	£1.25
219 ND 44pgs, Frank Miller art	*$0.50*	*$1.50*	*$2.50*	£0.30	£0.90	£1.50
220-221 ND 44pgs	*$0.50*	*$1.50*	*$2.50*	£0.30	£0.90	£1.50
222-250	*$0.40*	*$1.20*	*$2.00*	£0.20	£0.60	£1.00

Issue	$Good	$Fine	$N.Mint	£Good	£Fine	£N.Mint
251-253 Enemy Ace stories	*$0.40*	*$1.20*	*$2.00*	£0.20	£0.60	£1.00
254-256 Walt Simonson art, Capt. Fear	*$0.40*	*$1.20*	*$2.00*	£0.20	£0.60	£1.00
257-259	*$0.40*	*$1.20*	*$2.00*	£0.20	£0.60	£1.00
260-261 Enemy Ace stories	*$0.40*	*$1.20*	*$2.00*	£0.20	£0.60	£1.00
262-264	*$0.40*	*$1.20*	*$2.00*	£0.20	£0.60	£1.00
265-267 Enemy Ace stories	*$0.40*	*$1.20*	*$2.00*	£0.20	£0.60	£1.00
268	*$0.40*	*$1.20*	*$2.00*	£0.20	£0.60	£1.00
Title Value:	*$25.90*	*$77.70*	*$129.50*	£13.50	£40.50	£67.50

FEATURES

Andy Stewart Combat Nurse in 227, 228. Balloon Buster in 262-264. Captain Fear in 254-256. Capt. Storm in 257-259. Dateline: Frontline in 243-245, 254-256. Enemy Ace in 251-253, 260, 261, 265-267. Frogman (Robert Starr) in 219-221. Losers in 265. Lt. Larry Rock in 205-207. Mlle. Marie in 249. Ruptured Duck in 246-248. Tomahawk in 262-264. Unknown Soldier in all issues. Viking Commandos in 266, 267.

UNKNOWN SOLDIER (2ND SERIES)

DC Comics,MS; 1 Dec 1988-12 Nov 1989

Issue	$Good	$Fine	$N.Mint	£Good	£Fine	£N.Mint
1 LD in the U.K. origin retold	*$0.25*	*$0.75*	*$1.25*	£0.15	£0.45	£0.75
2-12 LD in the U.K.	*$0.25*	*$0.75*	*$1.25*	£0.15	£0.45	£0.75
Title Value:	*$3.00*	*$9.00*	*$15.00*	£1.80	£5.40	£9.00

Note: Mature Readers label

UNKNOWN SOLDIER (3RD SERIES)

DC Comics; 1 Apr 1997-present

Issue	$Good	$Fine	$N.Mint	£Good	£Fine	£N.Mint
1 ND Garth Ennis script	*$0.50*	*$1.50*	*$2.50*	£0.30	£0.90	£1.50
Title Value:	*$0.50*	*$1.50*	*$2.50*	£0.30	£0.90	£1.50

UNKNOWN WORLDS

ACG; 1 Aug 1960-57 Aug 1967

(all distributed in the U.K.)

Issue	$Good	$Fine	$N.Mint	£Good	£Fine	£N.Mint
1	*$19.00*	*$57.50*	*$135.00*	£12.00	£36.00	£85.00
2	*$12.00*	*$36.00*	*$85.00*	£7.75	£23.50	£55.00
3-5	*$10.50*	*$32.00*	*$75.00*	£7.00	£21.00	£50.00
6-10	*$7.75*	*$23.50*	*$55.00*	£5.00	£15.00	£35.00
11-20	*$6.25*	*$19.00*	*$45.00*	£3.90	£11.50	£27.50
21-30	*$4.60*	*$13.50*	*$32.50*	£2.85	£8.50	£20.00
31-40	*$3.90*	*$11.50*	*$27.50*	£2.50	£7.50	£17.50
41-50	*$3.55*	*$10.50*	*$25.00*	£2.10	£6.25	£15.00
51-57	*$3.20*	*$9.50*	*$22.50*	£1.75	£5.25	£12.50
Title Value:	*$306.65*	*$918.50*	*$2177.50*	£191.50	£571.75	£1352.50

Note: Magic Agent in 35,36,48,50,52,54,56

UNKNOWN WORLDS OF FRANK BRUNNER

Eclipse,MS; 1,2 Aug 1985

Issue	$Good	$Fine	$N.Mint	£Good	£Fine	£N.Mint
1-2 ND reprints in colour	*$0.40*	*$1.20*	*$2.00*	£0.25	£0.75	£1.25
Title Value:	*$0.80*	*$2.40*	*$4.00*	£0.50	£1.50	£2.50

UNKNOWN WORLDS OF SCIENCE FICTION

Marvel Comics Group,Magazine; 1 Jan 1975-6 Nov 1975

Issue	$Good	$Fine	$N.Mint	£Good	£Fine	£N.Mint
1 ND 80pgs, squarebound, scarce; Neal Adams, Williamson, Wood, Kaluta, Brunner reprints	*$0.80*	*$2.50*	*$5.00*	£0.65	£2.00	£4.00
2 ND 80pgs, squarebound, George Perez and Mike Kaluta art featured, Kaluta cover ("Iwo Jima" theme)	*$0.65*	*$2.00*	*$4.00*	£0.40	£1.25	£2.50
3 ND 80pgs, squarebound, George Perez and Alex Nino art featured	*$0.65*	*$2.00*	*$4.00*	£0.40	£1.25	£2.50
4 ND 80pgs, squarebound, Corben art featured, Frank Brunner cover	*$0.65*	*$2.00*	*$4.00*	£0.40	£1.25	£2.50
5 ND 72pgs, Howard Chaykin and Gray Morrow art featured	*$0.65*	*$2.00*	*$4.00*	£0.40	£1.25	£2.50
6 ND 72pgs, Alex Nino and Gene Colan art featured, Frank Brunner cover	*$0.65*	*$2.00*	*$4.00*	£0.40	£1.25	£2.50
Title Value:	*$4.05*	*$12.50*	*$25.00*	£2.65	£8.25	£16.50

ARTISTS

Brunner art in 2-4. Nino art in 3-6. Perez art in 2, 3.

UNKNOWN WORLDS OF SCIENCE FICTION SPECIAL

Marvel Comics Group,Magazine; 1 1976

Issue	$Good	$Fine	$N.Mint	£Good	£Fine	£N.Mint
1 ND scarce in the U.K. 96pgs, all reprint featuring Buscema, Giordano, Nino art	*$0.65*	*$2.00*	*$4.00*	£0.40	£1.25	£2.50
Title Value:	*$0.65*	*$2.00*	*$4.00*	£0.40	£1.25	£2.50

UNLEASHED

Triumphant Comics,OS; 1 Nov 1993

Issue	$Good	$Fine	$N.Mint	£Good	£Fine	£N.Mint
1 promotional giveaway, ND, serially numbered at top of page (80,000 copies printed); introduces the "Unleashed" X-over story	*$0.40*	*$1.20*	*$2.00*	£0.20	£0.60	£1.00
1 regular issue, ND 28,000 printed	*$0.40*	*$1.20*	*$2.00*	£0.20	£0.60	£1.00
Title Value:	*$0.80*	*$2.40*	*$4.00*	£0.40	£1.20	£2.00

UNTAMED

Marvel Comics Group/Epic,MS; 1 Jun 1993-3 Aug 1993

Issue	$Good	$Fine	$N.Mint	£Good	£Fine	£N.Mint
1-3 ND Neil Hansen script and art	*$0.40*	*$1.20*	*$2.00*	£0.25	£0.75	£1.25
Title Value:	*$1.20*	*$3.60*	*$6.00*	£0.75	£2.25	£3.75

UNTAMED LOVE

Fantagraphics; 1 Nov 1987

(see Thun'da Tales)

Issue	$Good	$Fine	$N.Mint	£Good	£Fine	£N.Mint
1 ND Frank Frazetta reprints	*$0.40*	*$1.20*	*$2.00*	£0.25	£0.75	£1.25
Title Value:	*$0.40*	*$1.20*	*$2.00*	£0.25	£0.75	£1.25

UNTOLD LEGEND OF THE BATMAN

(see Batman: Untold Legend of The)

UNTOUCHABLES

Eastern; 1 1988-8 1988

Issue	$Good	$Fine	$N.Mint	£Good	£Fine	£N.Mint
1-8 ND 20pgs	*$0.25*	*$0.75*	*$1.25*	£0.15	£0.45	£0.75
Title Value:	*$2.00*	*$6.00*	*$10.00*	£1.20	£3.60	£6.00

UNUSUAL TALES

Charlton; 1 Nov 1955-49 Mar/Apr 1965

(becomes Blue Beetle #50-54)

Issue	$Good	$Fine	$N.Mint	£Good	£Fine	£N.Mint
1 scarce in the U.K.	*$21.00*	*$62.50*	*$150.00*	£14.00	£43.00	£100.00
2 scarce in the U.K.	*$11.00*	*$34.00*	*$80.00*	£7.50	£22.50	£52.50
3-5 scarce in the U.K.	*$7.00*	*$21.00*	*$50.00*	£4.70	£14.00	£33.00
6 Steve Ditko cover art	*$8.50*	*$26.00*	*$60.00*	£5.50	£17.00	£40.00
7-8 Steve Ditko art	*$19.00*	*$57.50*	*$135.00*	£12.50	£39.00	£90.00
9 Steve Ditko art	*$20.00*	*$60.00*	*$140.00*	£13.00	£40.00	£92.50
10 Steve Ditko art	*$25.00*	*$75.00*	*$175.00*	£16.00	£49.00	£115.00
11 scarce in the U.K. 68pgs, Steve Ditko art	*$22.50*	*$67.50*	*$160.00*	£15.00	£45.00	£105.00
12 Steve Ditko art	*$14.00*	*$43.00*	*$100.00*	£9.50	£29.00	£67.50
13	*$5.50*	*$17.00*	*$40.00*	£3.85	£11.50	£27.00
14 Steve Ditko art	*$14.00*	*$43.00*	*$100.00*	£9.50	£29.00	£67.50
15 Steve Ditko art	*$15.50*	*$47.00*	*$110.00*	£10.00	£31.00	£72.50
16-17	*$5.00*	*$15.00*	*$35.00*	£3.35	£10.00	£23.50
1st official distribution in the U.K.						
18-20	*$5.00*	*$15.00*	*$35.00*	£3.35	£10.00	£23.50
21	*$3.55*	*$10.50*	*$25.00*	£2.35	£7.00	£16.50
22 Steve Ditko art	*$10.00*	*$30.00*	*$70.00*	£6.75	£20.00	£47.50
23 Steve Ditko cover art	*$10.00*	*$30.00*	*$70.00*	£6.75	£20.00	£47.50
24	*$3.55*	*$10.50*	*$25.00*	£2.10	£6.25	£15.00
25-27 Steve Ditko art	*$10.00*	*$30.00*	*$70.00*	£6.75	£20.00	£47.50
28	*$3.55*	*$10.50*	*$25.00*	£2.10	£6.25	£15.00
29 Steve Ditko art	*$10.00*	*$30.00*	*$70.00*	£6.75	£20.00	£47.50
30	*$3.55*	*$10.50*	*$25.00*	£2.10	£6.25	£15.00
31-49	*$3.20*	*$9.50*	*$22.50*	£1.75	£5.25	£12.50
Title Value:	*$376.00*	*$1130.50*	*$2635.00*	£242.10	£732.50	£1720.00

URBAN DECAY

Anubis Press,MS; 0 Jul 1994; 1 Jan 1994-4 Apr 1994

Issue	$Good	$Fine	$N.Mint	£Good	£Fine	£N.Mint
0 ND (Jul 1994) chromatix enhanced cover	*$0.50*	*$1.50*	*$2.50*	£0.30	£0.90	£1.50
0 Ashcan Edition, ND (Sep 1994) - 5,000 copies, black and white	*$0.60*	*$1.80*	*$3.00*	£0.40	£1.20	£2.00
1 ND Mark Texeira painted cover; b/w poster at centre-fold	*$0.50*	*$1.50*	*$2.50*	£0.30	£0.90	£1.50
1 Ashcan Edition, ND (Jan 1994)	*$0.60*	*$1.80*	*$3.00*	£0.40	£1.20	£2.00
2-4 ND	*$0.50*	*$1.50*	*$2.50*	£0.30	£0.90	£1.50
Title Value:	*$3.70*	*$11.10*	*$18.50*	£2.30	£6.90	£11.50

URBAN DECAY: CYBERJOCK

Anubis Press,OS; 1 Jul 1994

Issue	$Good	$Fine	$N.Mint	£Good	£Fine	£N.Mint
1 ND black and white	*$0.40*	*$1.20*	*$2.00*	£0.25	£0.75	£1.25
Title Value:	*$0.40*	*$1.20*	*$2.00*	£0.25	£0.75	£1.25

URBAN DECAY: FORK

Anubis Press; 0 Oct 1994; 1 Dec 1994

Issue	$Good	$Fine	$N.Mint	£Good	£Fine	£N.Mint
0 ND black and white	*$0.50*	*$1.50*	*$2.50*	£0.30	£0.90	£1.50
1 ND black and white	*$0.40*	*$1.20*	*$2.00*	£0.25	£0.75	£1.25
Title Value:	*$0.90*	*$2.70*	*$4.50*	£0.55	£1.65	£2.75

URBAN DECAY: KILLZONE

Anubis Press,OS; 1 Jan 1995

Issue	$Good	$Fine	$N.Mint	£Good	£Fine	£N.Mint
1 ND black and white	*$0.40*	*$1.20*	*$2.00*	£0.25	£0.75	£1.25
Title Value:	*$0.40*	*$1.20*	*$2.00*	£0.25	£0.75	£1.25

URBAN DECAY: KILLZONE ASHCAN EDITION

Anubis Press,OS; nn Aug 1994

Issue	$Good	$Fine	$N.Mint	£Good	£Fine	£N.Mint
1 ND black and white	*$0.50*	*$1.50*	*$2.50*	£0.30	£0.90	£1.50
Title Value:	*$0.50*	*$1.50*	*$2.50*	£0.30	£0.90	£1.50

URBAN DECAY: ZERO JOE

Anubis Press; 0 Feb 1995

Issue	$Good	$Fine	$N.Mint	£Good	£Fine	£N.Mint
0 ND black and white	*$0.50*	*$1.50*	*$2.50*	£0.30	£0.90	£1.50
Title Value:	*$0.50*	*$1.50*	*$2.50*	£0.30	£0.90	£1.50

URBAN LEGENDS

Dark Horse; 1 Jun 1993

Issue	$Good	$Fine	$N.Mint	£Good	£Fine	£N.Mint
1 ND humour anthology, Dan Clowes cover	*$0.60*	*$1.80*	*$3.00*	£0.40	£1.20	£2.00
Title Value:	*$0.60*	*$1.80*	*$3.00*	£0.40	£1.20	£2.00

	$Good	$Fine	$N.Mint	£Good	£Fine	£N.Mint
URTH 4						
Continuity; 1 May 1989-7 1991						
1-7 ND	***$0.30***	***$0.90***	***$1.50***	**£0.20**	**£0.60**	**£1.00**
Title Value:	***$2.10***	***$6.30***	***$10.50***	**£1.40**	**£4.20**	**£7.00**
URTH 4 (2ND SERIES)						
Continuity; 1 Sep 1992-4 1993						
(see Earth 4)						
1 ND Neal Adams cover	***$0.40***	***$1.20***	***$2.00***	**£0.25**	**£0.75**	**£1.25**
2-4 ND	***$0.40***	***$1.20***	***$2.00***	**£0.25**	**£0.75**	**£1.25**
Title Value:	***$1.60***	***$4.80***	***$8.00***	**£1.00**	**£3.00**	**£5.00**
US 1						
Marvel Comics Group, Toy; 1 May 1983-12 Oct 1984						
1-12 ND	***$0.15***	***$0.45***	***$0.75***	**£0.10**	**£0.35**	**£0.60**
Title Value:	***$1.80***	***$5.40***	***$9.00***	**£1.20**	**£4.20**	**£7.20**
US AIR FORCE COMICS						
Charlton; 1 Oct 1958-37 Mar/Apr 1965						
(becomes Army Attack 2nd Series)						
1 scarce in the U.K.	***$5.00***	***$15.00***	***$35.00***	**£3.55**	**£10.50**	**£25.00**
2	***$2.85***	***$8.50***	***$20.00***	**£1.75**	**£5.25**	**£12.50**
3-4	***$2.10***	***$6.25***	***$15.00***	**£1.40**	**£4.25**	**£10.00**
5-10	***$1.75***	***$5.25***	***$12.50***	**£1.10**	**£3.40**	**£8.00**
11-20	***$1.40***	***$4.25***	***$10.00***	**£0.85**	**£2.55**	**£6.00**
21-37	***$1.05***	***$3.20***	***$7.50***	**£0.70**	**£2.10**	**£5.00**
Title Value:	***$54.40***	***$164.40***	***$387.50***	**£35.10**	**£105.85**	**£250.50**
Note: all distributed on the newstands in the U.K.						
US FIGHTING AIR FORCE						
IW Super; 9 1964						
9 distributed in the U.K. reprints	***$0.80***	***$2.50***	***$5.00***	**£0.55**	**£1.75**	**£3.50**
Title Value:	***$0.80***	***$2.50***	***$5.00***	**£0.55**	**£1.75**	**£3.50**
USAGI YOJIMBO						
Fantagraphics; 1 Jun 1987-38 1993						
(see Critters)						
1 continues from Critters #14; black and white begins	***$0.60***	***$1.80***	***$3.00***	**£0.40**	**£1.20**	**£2.00**
1 2nd printing	***$0.50***	***$1.50***	***$2.50***	**£0.30**	**£0.90**	**£1.50**
2-9	***$0.50***	***$1.50***	***$2.50***	**£0.30**	**£0.90**	**£1.50**
10 Teenage Mutant Ninja Turtles appear	***$0.50***	***$1.50***	***$2.50***	**£0.30**	**£0.90**	**£1.50**
10 2nd printing	***$0.40***	***$1.20***	***$2.00***	**£0.25**	**£0.75**	**£1.25**
11-23	***$0.40***	***$1.20***	***$2.00***	**£0.25**	**£0.75**	**£1.25**
24 Lone Goat and Kid	***$0.40***	***$1.20***	***$2.00***	**£0.25**	**£0.75**	**£1.25**
25-32	***$0.40***	***$1.20***	***$2.00***	**£0.25**	**£0.75**	**£1.25**
33 Sergio Aragones script	***$0.40***	***$1.20***	***$2.00***	**£0.25**	**£0.75**	**£1.25**
34 $2.25 cover begins	***$0.45***	***$1.35***	***$2.25***	**£0.30**	**£0.90**	**£1.50**
35-38	***$0.45***	***$1.35***	***$2.25***	**£0.30**	**£0.90**	**£1.50**
Title Value:	***$17.45***	***$52.35***	***$87.25***	**£10.90**	**£32.70**	**£54.50**
Note: all Non-Distributed on the news-stands in the U.K.						
Book 1 ND reprints appearances prior to Usagi Yojimbo #1				£2.40	£7.20	£12.00
Book 1 ND 2nd, 3rd prints				£2.00	£5.00	£10.00
Book 1 ND 4th print (Mar 1993)				£1.60	£4.80	£8.00
Book 1 ND 5th print (Jun 1996)				£2.00	£6.00	£10.00
Book 1 Hardcover ND				£5.00	£15.00	£25.00
Book 2 ND reprints issues #1-6				£1.30	£3.90	£6.50
Book 2 (2nd print - Nov 1991) ND				£1.25	£3.75	£6.25
Book 2 Hardcover (Nov 1991)						
ND signed and numbered (1,000 copies)				£4.50	£13.50	£22.50
Book 3 ND reprints issues #7-12				£1.30	£3.90	£6.50
Book 3 2nd print (May 1995) ND				£1.80	£5.40	£9.00
Book 3 Hardcover (May 1995)						
ND signed and numbered (500 copies)				£5.00	£15.00	£25.00
Book 4 ND reprints issues #13-18				£1.30	£3.90	£6.50
Book 5 (Nov 1992) ND reprints issues #19-24				£1.30	£3.90	£6.50
Book 6, (Jul 1994 ND softcover				£1.70	£5.10	£8.50
Book 6, (Jul 1994) ND signed				£5.00	£15.00	£25.00
Color Special 1 ND				£0.35	£1.05	£1.75
Color Special 1 - Special Edition (Jun 1990)						
ND new cover. 2,000 copies				£0.55	£1.65	£2.75
USAGI YOJIMBO						
Dark Horse,MS; 1 Apr 1996-4 Jul 1996						
1-4 ND 24pgs, Stan Sakai script and art; black and white	***$0.60***	***$1.80***	***$3.00***	**£0.40**	**£1.20**	**£2.00**
Title Value:	***$2.40***	***$7.20***	***$12.00***	**£1.60**	**£4.80**	**£8.00**
USAGI YOJIMBO COLOUR SPECIAL						
Fantagraphics; 1 Nov 1989-3 1991						
1-3 ND 48pgs	***$0.50***	***$1.50***	***$2.50***	**£0.30**	**£0.90**	**£1.50**
Title Value:	***$1.50***	***$4.50***	***$7.50***	**£0.90**	**£2.70**	**£4.50**
USAGI YOJIMBO SUMMER SPECIAL						
Fantagraphics; 1 Spring 1987						
1 ND scarce in the U.K. reprints from Albedo	***$1.00***	***$3.00***	***$5.00***	**£0.60**	**£1.80**	**£3.00**
Title Value:	***$1.00***	***$3.00***	***$5.00***	**£0.60**	**£1.80**	**£3.00**
USAGI YOJIMBO VOLUME TWO						
Mirage Studios; 1 May 1993-16 1995						
1-2 ND Teenage Mutant Ninja Turtles appear	***$0.55***	***$1.65***	***$2.75***	**£0.35**	**£1.05**	**£1.75**
3-16 ND	***$0.55***	***$1.65***	***$2.75***	**£0.35**	**£1.05**	**£1.75**
Title Value:	***$8.80***	***$26.40***	***$44.00***	**£5.60**	**£16.80**	**£28.00**

V

	$Good	$Fine	$N.Mint	£Good	£Fine	£N.Mint
V						
DC Comics,TV; 1 Feb 1985-18 Jul 1986						
1-18 based upon TV movie and series	***$0.25***	***$0.75***	***$1.25***	**£0.15**	**£0.45**	**£0.75**
Title Value:	***$4.50***	***$13.50***	***$22.50***	**£2.70**	**£8.10**	**£13.50**
V FOR VENDETTA						
DC Comics,MS; 1 Sep 1988-10 Apr 1989						
1 ND David Lloyd art begins, Alan Moore script; reprints from British Warrior magazine	***$0.50***	***$1.50***	***$2.50***	**£0.40**	**£1.20**	**£2.00**
2-6 very LD	***$0.50***	***$1.50***	***$2.50***	**£0.30**	**£0.90**	**£1.50**
7 ND contains previously-unpublished story intended for cancelled Warrior magazine issue #27	***$0.50***	***$1.50***	***$2.50***	**£0.30**	**£0.90**	**£1.50**
8-10 ND all new material	***$0.50***	***$1.50***	***$2.50***	**£0.30**	**£0.90**	**£1.50**
Title Value:	***$5.00***	***$15.00***	***$25.00***	**£3.10**	**£9.30**	**£15.50**
Note: all Deluxe Format, Mature Readers						
Trade paperback (Jul 1990),						
288pgs, new cover painting and introduction by David Lloyd				£1.90	£5.70	£9.50
VALENTINO						
Renegade; 1 1985						
1 ND	***$0.40***	***$1.20***	***$2.00***	**£0.25**	**£0.75**	**£1.25**
Title Value:	***$0.40***	***$1.20***	***$2.00***	**£0.25**	**£0.75**	**£1.25**
VALENTINO TOO						
Renegade,OS; 1 1987						
1 ND	***$0.30***	***$0.90***	***$1.50***	**£0.20**	**£0.60**	**£1.00**

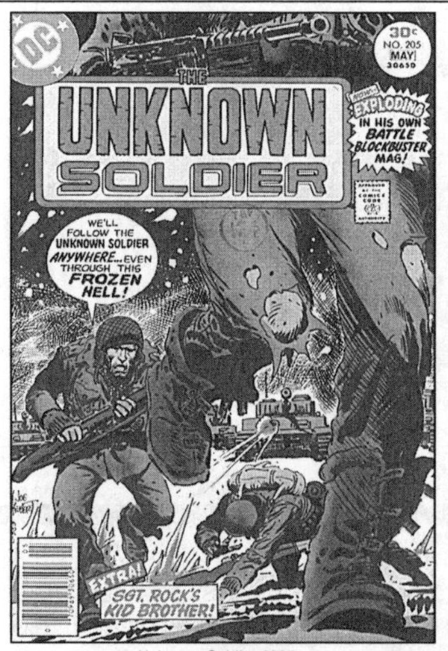

Unknown Soldier #205

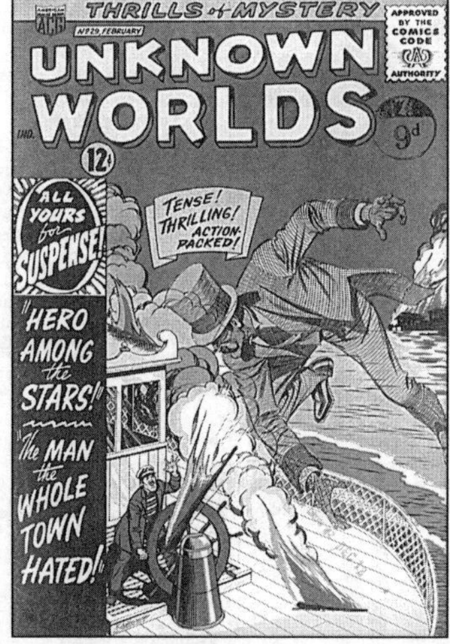

Unknown Worlds #29

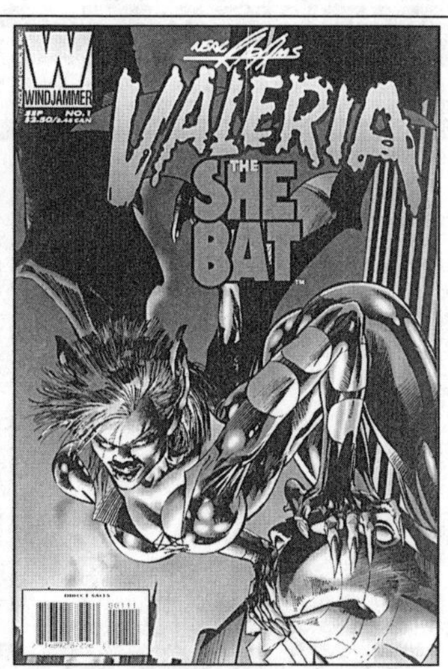

Valeria The She-Bat (2nd) #1

	$Good	$Fine	$N.Mint	£Good	£Fine	£N.Mint
Title Value:	$0.30	$0.90	$1.50	£0.20	£0.60	£1.00

VALERIA THE SHE-BAT

Continuity; 1 May 1993-5 Nov 1993

	$Good	$Fine	$N.Mint	£Good	£Fine	£N.Mint
1 ND script and art by Neal Adams, plastic acetate covers; available only to retailers ordering sufficient quantities of Deathwatch 2000 titles for May cover date	$1.00	$3.00	$5.00	£0.70	£2.10	£3.50
5 ND parchment embossed cover	$0.50	$1.50	$2.50	£0.30	£0.90	£1.50
Title Value:	$1.50	$4.50	$7.50	£1.00	£3.00	£5.00

Note: issues #2-4 do not exist

VALERIA, THE SHE-BAT (2ND SERIES)

Acclaim Comics/Windjammer,MS; 1,2 Sep 1995

	$Good	$Fine	$N.Mint	£Good	£Fine	£N.Mint
1-2 ND Neal Adams script and art with Peter Stone; reprints orginal series	$0.50	$1.50	$2.50	£0.30	£0.90	£1.50
Title Value:	$1.00	$3.00	$5.00	£0.60	£1.80	£3.00

VALIANT ERA COLLECTION

Valiant,OS; nn 1994

	$Good	$Fine	$N.Mint	£Good	£Fine	£N.Mint
1 ND Trade paperback reprinting Magnus #12, Shadowman #8, Solar #10,11, Eternal Warrior #4, 5. Pre-bagged with 8pg Valiant Era Special Edition	$2.50	$7.50	$12.50	£1.50	£4.50	£7.50
Title Value:	$2.50	$7.50	$12.50	£1.50	£4.50	£7.50

VALIANT READER - A GUIDE TO THE VALIANT UNIVERSE

Valiant; 1 Sep 1993; 2 Oct 1994

	$Good	$Fine	$N.Mint	£Good	£Fine	£N.Mint
1 ND a who's who of Valiant characters	$0.25	$0.75	$1.25	£0.15	£0.45	£0.75
2 ND details title histories from the beginning	$0.25	$0.75	$1.25	£0.15	£0.45	£0.75
Title Value:	$0.50	$1.50	$2.50	£0.30	£0.90	£1.50

VALIANT VISION STARTER KIT

Valiant,OS; 1 Jan 1994

	$Good	$Fine	$N.Mint	£Good	£Fine	£N.Mint
1 ND 8pg comic, poster and glasses; a 3-D effect on a comic that can be read quite normally without the glasses	$0.30	$0.90	$1.50	£0.20	£0.60	£1.00
Title Value:	$0.30	$0.90	$1.50	£0.20	£0.60	£1.00

VALIANT ZERO COLLECTION

Valiant; nn Apr 1995

	$Good	$Fine	$N.Mint	£Good	£Fine	£N.Mint
nn ND Trade paperback, 112pgs. Reprints Magnus, Harbinger, X-O, Archer & Armstrong and Armorines #0 issues	$2.00	$6.00	$10.00	£1.30	£3.90	£6.50
Title Value:	$2.00	$6.00	$10.00	£1.30	£3.90	£6.50

VALKYRIE

Marvel Comics Group,OS; nn Jan 1997

	$Good	$Fine	$N.Mint	£Good	£Fine	£N.Mint
nn ND 48pgs, J.M. DeMatteis script, Pablo Raimondi art	$0.60	$1.80	$3.00	£0.40	£1.20	£2.00
Title Value:	$0.60	$1.80	$3.00	£0.40	£1.20	£2.00

VALKYRIE (1ST SERIES)

Eclipse,MS; 1 May 1987-3 Aug 1987

	$Good	$Fine	$N.Mint	£Good	£Fine	£N.Mint
1 ND scarce in the U.K. Gulacy covers and art begin, colour; Air Fighters spin-off series	$0.50	$1.50	$2.50	£0.30	£0.90	£1.50
2-3 ND	$0.40	$1.20	$2.00	£0.25	£0.75	£1.25
Title Value:	$1.30	$3.90	$6.50	£0.80	£2.40	£4.00
Prisoner of the Past (Dec 1987) Trade paperback, reprints #1-3				£1.10	£3.30	£5.50

VALKYRIE (2ND SERIES)

Eclipse,MS; 1 Jul 1988-3 Sep 1988

	$Good	$Fine	$N.Mint	£Good	£Fine	£N.Mint
1-3 ND Brent Anderson art; Air Fighters spin-off series, colour	$0.40	$1.20	$2.00	£0.25	£0.75	£1.25
Title Value:	$1.20	$3.60	$6.00	£0.75	£2.25	£3.75

VALKYRIE!

Ken Pierce; nn 1982

	$Good	$Fine	$N.Mint	£Good	£Fine	£N.Mint
nn ND 84pgs, Trade paperback; Golden Age reprints from Airfighters and Airboy	$1.50	$4.50	$7.50	£1.00	£3.00	£5.00
Title Value:	$1.50	$4.50	$7.50	£1.00	£3.00	£5.00

VALLEY OF THE GWANGI

Dell/Movie Classics,OS Movie; 01-880-912 Dec 1969

	$Good	$Fine	$N.Mint	£Good	£Fine	£N.Mint
01-880-912 photo cover from film; distributed in the U.K. though thought to be sporadic in areas	$10.50	$32.00	$75.00	£7.00	£21.00	£50.00
Title Value:	$10.50	$32.00	$75.00	£7.00	£21.00	£50.00

VALOR

DC Comics; 1 Nov 1992-23 Sep 1994

	$Good	$Fine	$N.Mint	£Good	£Fine	£N.Mint
1 Eclipso: The Darkness Within spin-off begins with the former Mon-El	$0.25	$0.75	$1.25	£0.15	£0.45	£0.75
2 Supergirl appears	$0.25	$0.75	$1.25	£0.15	£0.45	£0.75
3-4 Lobo appears	$0.25	$0.75	$1.25	£0.15	£0.45	£0.75
5-7	$0.25	$0.75	$1.25	£0.15	£0.45	£0.75
8 Adam Hughes cover	$0.25	$0.75	$1.25	£0.15	£0.45	£0.75
9 Adam Hughes cover, Darkstar appears	$0.25	$0.75	$1.25	£0.15	£0.45	£0.75
10 Adam Hughes cover	$0.25	$0.75	$1.25	£0.15	£0.45	£0.75
11 Adam Hughes cover, new direction for title	$0.25	$0.75	$1.25	£0.15	£0.45	£0.75
12 Adam Hughes cover	$0.25	$0.75	$1.25	£0.15	£0.45	£0.75
13-16	$0.25	$0.75	$1.25	£0.15	£0.45	£0.75
17 Valor "dies"; prelude to Zero Hour mini-series	$0.25	$0.75	$1.25	£0.15	£0.45	£0.75
18-21	$0.25	$0.75	$1.25	£0.15	£0.45	£0.75
22 End of an Era part 2, continued in Legion of Super-Heroes #60	$0.25	$0.75	$1.25	£0.15	£0.45	£0.75
23 Zero Hour X-over; End of an Era part 5, continued in Legion of Super-Heroes #61	$0.25	$0.75	$1.25	£0.15	£0.45	£0.75
Title Value:	$5.75	$17.25	$28.75	£3.45	£10.35	£17.25

VAMPEROTICA

Brainstorm Comics; 1 1994-present

	$Good	$Fine	$N.Mint	£Good	£Fine	£N.Mint
1 ND adult material; black and white	$2.00	$6.00	$10.00	£1.00	£3.00	£5.00
1 2nd printing ND	$0.70	$2.10	$3.50	£0.50	£1.50	£2.50
1 3rd printing, ND (Dec 1994)	$0.60	$1.80	$3.00	£0.40	£1.20	£2.00
2 ND adult material; black and white	$1.50	$4.50	$7.50	£0.70	£2.10	£3.50
2 2nd printing, ND (Jan 1996)	$0.60	$1.80	$3.00	£0.40	£1.20	£2.00
3 ND adult material; black and white	$1.00	$3.00	$5.00	£0.50	£1.50	£2.50
3 2nd printing, ND (Mar 1996)	$0.60	$1.80	$3.00	£0.40	£1.20	£2.00
4 ND adult material; black and white	$0.60	$1.80	$3.00	£0.40	£1.20	£2.00
4 2nd printing, ND (Mar 1996)	$0.60	$1.80	$3.00	£0.40	£1.20	£2.00
5-20 ND adult material; black and white	$0.60	$1.80	$3.00	£0.40	£1.20	£2.00
Title Value:	$17.80	$53.40	$89.00	£11.10	£33.30	£55.50
Vamperotica: Red Reign (Feb 1996) Trade paperback ND reprints				£1.70	£5.10	£8.50

VAMPEROTICA ANNUAL

Brainstorm Comics; 1 Dec 1995

	$Good	$Fine	$N.Mint	£Good	£Fine	£N.Mint
1 ND previews Luxura #1	$0.60	$1.80	$3.00	£0.40	£1.20	£2.00
1 Gold Edition, ND gold foil cover	$1.00	$3.00	$5.00	£0.60	£1.80	£3.00
Title Value:	$1.60	$4.80	$8.00	£1.00	£3.00	£5.00

VAMPFIRE

Brainstorm Comics; 1 Sep 1996-present

	$Good	$Fine	$N.Mint	£Good	£Fine	£N.Mint
1-2 ND adult material; black and white	$0.60	$1.80	$3.00	£0.40	£1.20	£2.00
Title Value:	$1.20	$3.60	$6.00	£0.80	£2.40	£4.00

VAMPIRE COMPANION, THE

Innovation; 1 Jan 1991-4 1992

	$Good	$Fine	$N.Mint	£Good	£Fine	£N.Mint
1 ND articles/interview with Anne Rice	$0.60	$1.80	$3.00	£0.40	£1.20	£2.00
2-3 ND	$0.60	$1.80	$3.00	£0.40	£1.20	£2.00
4 ND John Bolton cover	$0.60	$1.80	$3.00	£0.40	£1.20	£2.00
Title Value:	$2.40	$7.20	$12.00	£1.60	£4.80	£8.00

VAMPIRE LESTAT, THE

Innovation,MS; 1 Jan 1990-12 Aug 1991

(see The Mummy)

	$Good	$Fine	$N.Mint	£Good	£Fine	£N.Mint
1 ND John Bolton covers begin	$6.00	$18.00	$30.00	£3.50	£10.50	£17.50
1 2nd printing ND	$0.80	$2.40	$4.00	£0.50	£1.50	£2.50
1 3rd printing ND	$0.60	$1.80	$3.00	£0.40	£1.20	£2.00
1 4th printing ND	$0.40	$1.20	$2.00	£0.25	£0.75	£1.25
2 ND	$3.00	$9.00	$15.00	£2.00	£6.00	£10.00
2 2nd printing ND	$0.80	$2.40	$4.00	£0.50	£1.50	£2.50
2 3rd printing ND	$0.40	$1.20	$2.00	£0.25	£0.75	£1.25
3 ND	$2.00	$6.00	$10.00	£1.00	£3.00	£5.00
3 2nd printing ND	$0.60	$1.80	$3.00	£0.40	£1.20	£2.00
4 ND	$1.50	$4.50	$7.50	£0.80	£2.40	£4.00
4 2nd printing ND	$0.50	$1.50	$2.50	£0.30	£0.90	£1.50
5 ND	$1.20	$3.60	$6.00	£0.70	£2.10	£3.50
5 2nd printing ND	$0.50	$1.50	$2.50	£0.30	£0.90	£1.50
6-8 ND	$1.00	$3.00	$5.00	£0.60	£1.80	£3.00
9 ND many copies were damaged at the time of printing hence a 2nd print was issued	$0.90	$2.70	$4.50	£0.60	£1.80	£3.00
9 2nd printing, ND (Jan 1992)	$0.50	$1.50	$2.50	£0.30	£0.90	£1.50
10-12 ND	$0.90	$2.70	$4.50	£0.60	£1.80	£3.00
Title Value:	$25.40	$76.20	$126.00	£15.40	£46.20	£77.00

Note: John Bolton covers

	$Good	$Fine	$N.Mint	£Good	£Fine	£N.Mint
Vampire Lestat Softcover (Nov 1991), reprints maxi-series				£3.10	£9.30	£15.50
Signed Edition (May 1993), signed in gold ink by Faye Perozich				£3.50	£10.50	£17.50
Vampire Lestat Hardcover (Jan 1992), reprints maxi-series, (4,500 copies)				£5.00	£15.00	£25.00
Signed Edition (May 1993), signed in gold ink by Faye Perozich				£6.00	£18.00	£30.00
Slipcase Set (Oct 1991), 12 issues plus 2 Vampire Companions in gold-embossed slipcase (2,000)				£7.00	£21.00	£35.00

VAMPIRE MIYU

Antarctic Press,MS; 1 Oct 1995-6 Mar 1996

	$Good	$Fine	$N.Mint	£Good	£Fine	£N.Mint
1-5 ND Harumi Kakinouchi script and art; black and white	$0.60	$1.80	$3.00	£0.40	£1.20	£2.00
6 ND 48pgs, Harumi Kakinouchi script and art; black and white	$0.80	$2.40	$4.00	£0.50	£1.50	£2.50
Title Value:	$3.80	$11.40	$19.00	£2.50	£7.50	£12.50

VAMPIRE TALES

Marvel Comics Group,Magazine; 1 Aug 1973-11 Jun 1975

	$Good	$Fine	$N.Mint	£Good	£Fine	£N.Mint
1 ND 72pgs, Morbius begins by Don McGregor	$4.55	$13.50	$27.50	£2.50	£7.50	£15.00
2 ND 72pgs, Steranko reprint	$2.05	$6.25	$12.50	£1.15	£3.50	£7.00

3 scarce in the U.K. 72pgs, Satana appears, Infantino reprint

SOME INDEPENDENT COMICS MAY NOT HAVE APPEARED ALTHOUGH THEY WERE ADVERTISED AND SOLICITED.

Issue	$Good	$Fine	$N.Mint	£Good	£Fine	£N.Mint
	$1.00	*$3.00*	*$6.00*	£0.55	£1.75	£3.50
4 72pgs, Boris painted cover						
	$1.00	*$3.00*	*$6.00*	£0.50	£1.50	£3.00
5 scarce in the U.K. 72pgs, Gulacy and Chaykin art, origin Morbius retold with Gil Kane art						
	$1.30	*$4.00*	*$8.00*	£0.80	£2.50	£5.00
6 72pgs, Boris painted cover, Lilith Daughter of Dracula appears, Steve Gerber script						
	$0.80	*$2.50*	*$5.00*	£0.50	£1.50	£3.00
7 72pgs, Gulacy and Chaykin art featured						
	$0.80	*$2.50*	*$5.00*	£0.50	£1.50	£3.00
8 72pgs, 1st Joe Staton art for Marvel on a short story ("The Vendetta"), Blade the Vampire-Slayer appears						
	$0.80	*$2.50*	*$5.00*	£0.50	£1.50	£3.00
9 72pgs, Blade the Vampire-Slayer appears, Jesus Blasco art on a short story, Russ Heath art (5pgs)						
	$0.80	*$2.50*	*$5.00*	£0.50	£1.50	£3.00
10 72pgs, Gulacy art (1pg)						
	$0.80	*$2.50*	*$5.00*	£0.50	£1.50	£3.00
11 72pgs	*$0.80*	*$2.50*	*$5.00*	£0.50	£1.50	£3.00
Title Value:	*$14.70*	*$44.75*	*$90.00*	£8.50	£25.75	£51.50

FEATURES
Blade in 8,9,10. Lilith in 6. Morbius in 1-5, 7, 8, 10, 11.
Note: a next issue was advertised but never appeared.

VAMPIRE TALES ANNUAL

Marvel Comics Group,Magazine; 1 Summer 1975

Issue	$Good	$Fine	$N.Mint	£Good	£Fine	£N.Mint
1 ND 88pgs, squarebound, all reprint featuring Russ Heath art						
	$0.80	*$2.50*	*$5.00*	£0.55	£1.75	£3.50
Title Value:	*$0.80*	*$2.50*	*$5.00*	£0.55	£1.75	£3.50

VAMPIRE VERSES

Cry For Dawn; 1 Aug 1995-4 1996 ?

Issue	$Good	$Fine	$N.Mint	£Good	£Fine	£N.Mint
1 ND 40pgs, Mike Bliss script, Frank Forte art; black and white						
	$1.20	*$3.60*	*$6.00*	£0.60	£1.80	£3.00
1 2nd printing, ND (Mar 1996)						
	$0.60	*$1.80*	*$3.00*	£0.40	£1.20	£2.00
2 ND	*$0.60*	*$1.80*	*$3.00*	£0.40	£1.20	£2.00
2 Variant Cover Edition, ND signed and numbered certificate; 1,000 copies						
	$2.00	*$6.00*	*$10.00*	£1.00	£3.00	£5.00
3-4 ND	*$0.60*	*$1.80*	*$3.00*	£0.40	£1.20	£2.00
4 Variant Cover Edition ND						
	$2.00	*$6.00*	*$10.00*	£1.00	£3.00	£5.00
Title Value:	*$7.60*	*$22.80*	*$38.00*	£4.20	£12.60	£21.00

VAMPIRELLA (1ST SERIES)

Warren; 1 Sep 1969-112 Sep 1983; 113 Jan 1988

Issue	$Good	$Fine	$N.Mint	£Good	£Fine	£N.Mint
1 ND Neal Adams art						
	$52.50	*$160.00*	*$375.00*	£29.00	£85.00	£200.00
2 distributed in the U.K.						
	$21.00	*$62.50*	*$150.00*	£12.50	£39.00	£90.00
3 ND rare in the U.K.						
	$50.00	*$150.00*	*$300.00*	£30.00	£90.00	£180.00
4-5 ND	*$12.00*	*$36.00*	*$85.00*	£7.00	£21.00	£50.00
6 distributed in the U.K.						
	$12.00	*$36.00*	*$85.00*	£6.25	£19.00	£45.00
7 ND	*$12.00*	*$36.00*	*$85.00*	£6.75	£20.00	£47.50
8 ND Vampirella begins						
	$12.50	*$39.00*	*$90.00*	£7.00	£21.00	£50.00
9 ND Barry Windsor Smith art						
	$10.00	*$30.00*	*$70.00*	£6.25	£19.00	£45.00
10 ND Neal Adams art, no Vampirella story						
	$5.75	*$17.50*	*$35.00*	£4.15	£12.50	£25.00
11-15 ND	*$8.25*	*$25.00*	*$50.00*	£5.00	£15.00	£30.00
16-18 ND	*$6.25*	*$18.50*	*$37.50*	£4.15	£12.50	£25.00
19 ND 1973 Annual; the classic Vampirella pose on cover						
	$7.50	*$22.50*	*$45.00*	£5.00	£15.00	£30.00
20 ND	*$6.25*	*$18.50*	*$37.50*	£4.15	£12.50	£25.00
21-25 ND	*$5.75*	*$17.50*	*$35.00*	£3.30	£10.00	£20.00
26 ND	*$5.00*	*$15.00*	*$30.00*	£2.90	£8.75	£17.50
27 ND 1974 Annual						
	$5.75	*$17.50*	*$35.00*	£3.30	£10.00	£20.00
28-30 ND	*$5.00*	*$15.00*	*$30.00*	£2.90	£8.75	£17.50
31-36 ND	*$4.55*	*$13.50*	*$27.50*	£2.50	£7.50	£15.00
37 ND 1975 Annual						
	$5.00	*$15.00*	*$30.00*	£2.90	£8.75	£17.50
38-40 ND	*$4.55*	*$13.50*	*$27.50*	£2.50	£7.50	£15.00
41-45 ND	*$4.15*	*$12.50*	*$25.00*	£2.05	£6.25	£12.50
46 ND origin retold						
	$4.55	*$13.50*	*$27.50*	£2.50	£7.50	£15.00
47-49 ND	*$4.15*	*$12.50*	*$25.00*	£2.05	£6.25	£12.50
50 ND Spirit appears						
	$4.15	*$12.50*	*$25.00*	£2.05	£6.25	£12.50
51-60 ND	*$3.30*	*$10.00*	*$20.00*	£1.65	£5.00	£10.00
61-70 ND	*$2.90*	*$8.75*	*$17.50*	£1.25	£3.75	£7.50
71-99 ND	*$2.50*	*$7.50*	*$15.00*	£1.00	£3.00	£6.00
100 ND origin retold						
	$6.50	*$20.00*	*$40.00*	£2.50	£7.50	£15.00
101-112 ND	*$5.00*	*$15.00*	*$30.00*	£1.15	£3.50	£7.00
113 very scarce in the U.K., scarce in the U.S.						
	$25.00	*$75.00*	*$150.00*	£13.00	£40.00	£80.00
Title Value:	*$641.85*	*$1932.00*	*$4025.00*	£327.55	£986.50	£2060.50

Note also: while it is known for sure that issues #2 and #6 were distributed on the news-stands in the U.K. it could be that some or many more issues were, even if in limited quantities

VAMPIRELLA (1ST SERIES) ANNUAL

Warren; 1 1972

Issue	$Good	$Fine	$N.Mint	£Good	£Fine	£N.Mint
1 scarce in the U.K. partly reprint; thought to be distributed in the U.K.						
	$36.00	*$105.00*	*$250.00*	£17.50	£52.50	£125.00
Title Value:	*$36.00*	*$105.00*	*$250.00*	£17.50	£52.50	£125.00

VAMPIRELLA (2ND SERIES)

Harris Publications/Dark Horse,MS; 1 Nov 1991-4 Jun 1992

Issue	$Good	$Fine	$N.Mint	£Good	£Fine	£N.Mint
1-4 ND sub-titled "Mourning in America"; Mike Kaluta covers						
	$1.00	*$3.00*	*$5.00*	£0.70	£2.10	£3.50
Title Value:	*$4.00*	*$12.00*	*$20.00*	£2.80	£8.40	£14.00
Vampirella (Feb 1994)						
Trade paperback reprints issues #1-4				£0.80	£2.40	£4.00

VAMPIRELLA (3RD SERIES)

Harris Comics,MS; 0 Dec 1994; 1 Nov 1992-5 Nov 1993

Issue	$Good	$Fine	$N.Mint	£Good	£Fine	£N.Mint
0 ND story bridges the gap between "Morning in America" and "Dracula War"						
	$0.80	*$2.40*	*$4.00*	£0.50	£1.50	£2.50
0 Gold Edition ND	*$8.00*	*$24.00*	*$40.00*	£3.50	£10.50	£17.50
0 Gold Signed & Numbered Edition, ND (Apr 1996), pre-bagged with certificate; limited to only 500 copies						
	$16.00	*$48.00*	*$80.00*	£7.00	£21.00	£35.00
0 Signed & Numbered Edition, ND (May 1995) - pre-bagged in mylar with certificate; limited to 2,500 copies						
	$3.00	*$9.00*	*$15.00*	£1.50	£4.50	£7.50
1 ND Adam Hughes cover; coupons begin for limited poster (ends #6)						
	$7.00	*$21.00*	*$35.00*	£4.00	£12.00	£20.00
1 2nd printing, ND Jun 1993						
	$1.50	*$4.50*	*$7.50*	£1.00	£3.00	£5.00
2 ND Adam Hughes cover						
	$5.00	*$15.00*	*$25.00*	£3.00	£9.00	£15.00
3 ND	*$3.00*	*$9.00*	*$15.00*	£2.00	£6.00	£10.00
4-5 ND	*$2.50*	*$7.50*	*$12.50*	£1.50	£4.50	£7.50
Title Value:	*$49.30*	*$147.90*	*$244.00*	£25.50	£76.50	£127.50

VAMPIRELLA 25TH ANNIVERSARY SPECIAL

Harris Comics,OS; nn Dec 1996

Issue	$Good	$Fine	$N.Mint	£Good	£Fine	£N.Mint
nn ND 48pgs, squarebound; homage issue featuring the talents of Mark Texeira, Grant Morrison, Jimmy Palmiotti and a painted cover by Frank Frazetta - what more could you ask?						
	$1.20	*$3.60*	*$6.00*	£0.80	£2.40	£4.00
Title Value:	*$1.20*	*$3.60*	*$6.00*	£0.80	£2.40	£4.00

VAMPIRELLA CLASSIC

Harris Comics; 1 Feb 1995-5 Nov 1995

Issue	$Good	$Fine	$N.Mint	£Good	£Fine	£N.Mint
1 ND classic Vampirella stories reprinted in colour; reprint of Frank Frazetta's cover to the original Vampirella Magazine #1						
	$0.60	*$1.80*	*$3.00*	£0.40	£1.20	£2.00
2-5 ND	*$0.60*	*$1.80*	*$3.00*	£0.40	£1.20	£2.00
Title Value:	*$3.00*	*$9.00*	*$15.00*	£2.00	£6.00	£10.00

VAMPIRELLA COMMEMORATIVE EDITION

Harris Comics,OS; 1 Nov 1996

Issue	$Good	$Fine	$N.Mint	£Good	£Fine	£N.Mint
1 ND card-stock cover, Kurt Busiek script, Louis Small Jnr and Jim Balent art						
	$0.60	*$1.80*	*$3.00*	£0.40	£1.20	£2.00
Title Value:	*$0.60*	*$1.80*	*$3.00*	£0.40	£1.20	£2.00

VAMPIRELLA LIVES

Harris Comics,MS; 1 Dec 1996-3 Feb 1997

Issue	$Good	$Fine	$N.Mint	£Good	£Fine	£N.Mint
1 Version A, ND Warren Ellis script, Amanda Connor and Jimmy Palmiotti art						
	$0.60	*$1.80*	*$3.00*	£0.40	£1.20	£2.00
1 Version B, ND photo cover						
	$0.70	*$2.10*	*$3.50*	£0.50	£1.50	£2.50
2-3 ND	*$0.60*	*$1.80*	*$3.00*	£0.40	£1.20	£2.00
Title Value:	*$2.50*	*$7.50*	*$12.50*	£1.70	£5.10	£8.50

VAMPIRELLA OF DRAKULON

Harris Comics; 0 Nov 1996; 1 Feb 1996-present

Issue	$Good	$Fine	$N.Mint	£Good	£Fine	£N.Mint
0 ND 24pgs, origin of Vampirella reprinted, script by Budd Lewis, art by Jose Gonzalez; card-stock cover, black and white						
	$0.60	*$1.80*	*$3.00*	£0.40	£1.20	£2.00
1 ND Michael Bair wraparound cover						
	$0.60	*$1.80*	*$3.00*	£0.40	£1.20	£2.00
1 Signed & Numbered Edition, ND signed by Michael Bair, in protective Mylar with certificate; limited to 500 copies						
	$3.00	*$9.00*	*$15.00*	£1.50	£4.50	£7.50
2-5 ND	*$0.60*	*$1.80*	*$3.00*	£0.40	£1.20	£2.00
Title Value:	*$6.60*	*$19.80*	*$33.00*	£3.90	£11.70	£19.50

VAMPIRELLA SPECIAL

Warren; nn 1977

Issue	$Good	$Fine	$N.Mint	£Good	£Fine	£N.Mint
nn ND reprints in colour; thought to be distributed in the U.K.						
	$5.00	*$15.00*	*$30.00*	£3.30	£10.00	£20.00
Title Value:	*$5.00*	*$15.00*	*$30.00*	£3.30	£10.00	£20.00

VAMPIRELLA STRIKES

Harris Comics; 1 Oct 1995-present

Issue	$Good	$Fine	$N.Mint	£Good	£Fine	£N.Mint
1 ND photo cover	*$0.60*	*$1.80*	*$3.00*	£0.40	£1.20	£2.00
1 Signed & Numbered Edition, ND (Oct 1995); pre-bagged with certificate - limited to 1,500 copies						
	$3.00	*$9.00*	*$15.00*	£1.50	£4.50	£7.50
1 Variant Cover Edition, ND features a different photo cover of Vampirella showing a rather toothsome young lady with arms raised; limited to 5,000 copies						
	$1.60	*$4.80*	*$8.00*	£0.80	£2.40	£4.00
1 Variant Cover Signed & Numbered Edition, ND signed by Ed McGuiness, in protective Mylar with certificate; 1,500 copies						
	$3.00	*$9.00*	*$15.00*	£2.00	£6.00	£10.00
2 ND Mike Deodato Jnr cover art						
	$0.60	*$1.80*	*$3.00*	£0.40	£1.20	£2.00
2 Signed & Numbered Edition, ND (Mar 1996), pre-bagged with signed and numbered cerificate; limited to 250 copies						
	$4.00	*$12.00*	*$20.00*	£2.50	£7.50	£12.50
3 ND	*$0.60*	*$1.80*	*$3.00*	£0.40	£1.20	£2.00
3 Signed & Numbered Edition, ND available in Mylar sleeve with certificate						
	$3.00	*$9.00*	*$15.00*	£1.50	£4.50	£7.50
4 ND	*$0.60*	*$1.80*	*$3.00*	£0.40	£1.20	£2.00
5 ND features The Eudaemon						
	$0.60	*$1.80*	*$3.00*	£0.40	£1.20	£2.00
6-7 ND	*$0.60*	*$1.80*	*$3.00*	£0.40	£1.20	£2.00
Title Value:	*$18.80*	*$56.40*	*$94.00*	£11.10	£33.30	£55.50

VAMPIRELLA'S SUMMER NIGHTS

Dark Horse/Harris Publications, OS; 1 Oct 1992

Issue	$Good	$Fine	$N.Mint	£Good	£Fine	£N.Mint
1 ND 48pgs	$0.80	$2.40	$4.00	£0.50	£1.50	£2.50
Title Value:	$0.80	$2.40	$4.00	£0.50	£1.50	£2.50

VAMPIRELLA, VENGEANCE OF

Harris Comics; 1 Feb 1994-25 Apr 1996

Issue	$Good	$Fine	$N.Mint	£Good	£Fine	£N.Mint
½ ND available with Wizard #55, issued in protective Mylar, with certificate	$3.00	$9.00	$15.00	£2.00	£6.00	£10.00
½ Platinum Edition, ND as abnove with platinum cover	$5.00	$15.00	$25.00	£3.00	£9.00	£15.00
1 ND Joe Quesada and Jimmy Palmiotti wraparound foil cover	$3.50	$10.50	$17.50	£2.00	£6.00	£10.00
1 2nd printing, ND Joe Quesada and Jimmy Palmiotti wraparound foil cover (Jun 1994)	$1.00	$3.00	$5.00	£0.80	£2.40	£4.00
1 Gold Edition ND	$6.00	$18.00	$30.00	£3.00	£9.00	£15.00
2 ND	$2.00	$6.00	$10.00	£1.20	£3.60	£6.00
3 ND	$1.20	$3.60	$6.00	£0.80	£2.40	£4.00
4-5 ND	$1.00	$3.00	$5.00	£0.70	£2.10	£3.50
6-7 ND	$0.80	$2.40	$4.00	£0.60	£1.80	£3.00
8 ND pre-bagged with Vampirella trading card	$0.80	$2.40	$4.00	£0.60	£1.80	£3.00
9-10 ND	$0.80	$2.40	$4.00	£0.50	£1.50	£2.50
11 ND pre-bagged with chase card	$0.60	$1.80	$3.00	£0.40	£1.20	£2.00
12-13 ND	$0.60	$1.80	$3.00	£0.40	£1.20	£2.00
14 ND The Mystery Walk; Vampirella's "secret" origin story begins; giant pull-out poster	$0.60	$1.80	$3.00	£0.40	£1.20	£2.00
14 Variant Cover Edition, ND Buzz art on cover, received for every 25 copies of the regular issue ordered	$3.50	$10.50	$17.50	£2.00	£6.00	£10.00
15 ND	$0.60	$1.80	$3.00	£0.40	£1.20	£2.00
15 Variant Cover Edition, ND Buzz art on cover, received for every 25 copies of the regular issue ordered	$3.50	$10.50	$17.50	£2.00	£6.00	£10.00
16 ND	$0.60	$1.80	$3.00	£0.40	£1.20	£2.00
16 Variant Cover Edition, ND Buzz art on cover, received for every 25 copies of the regular issue ordered	$3.50	$10.50	$17.50	£2.00	£6.00	£10.00
17 ND	$0.60	$1.80	$3.00	£0.40	£1.20	£2.00
17 Variant Cover Edition, ND Buzz art on cover, received for every 25 copies of the regular issue ordered	$3.50	$10.50	$17.50	£2.00	£6.00	£10.00
18 ND	$0.60	$1.80	$3.00	£0.40	£1.20	£2.00
18 Variant Cover Edition, ND Buzz art on cover, received for every 25 copies of the regular issue ordered	$3.50	$10.50	$17.50	£2.00	£6.00	£10.00
19 ND	$0.60	$1.80	$3.00	£0.40	£1.20	£2.00
19 Variant Cover Edition, ND Buzz art on cover, received for every 25 copies of the regular issue ordered	$3.50	$10.50	$17.50	£2.00	£6.00	£10.00
20-21 ND	$0.60	$1.80	$3.00	£0.40	£1.20	£2.00
22 ND cover by Gary Frank and Cam Smith	$0.60	$1.80	$3.00	£0.40	£1.20	£2.00
23 ND	$0.60	$1.80	$3.00	£0.40	£1.20	£2.00
24 ND Mike Deodato cover	$0.60	$1.80	$3.00	£0.40	£1.20	£2.00
25 ND red foil cover; story leads into Vampirella: Death & Destruction	$0.60	$1.80	$3.00	£0.40	£1.20	£2.00
25 2nd Signed & Numbered Edition, ND pre-bagged with certificate; limited to 1,500 copies; cover by Jae Lee	$6.00	$18.00	$30.00	£3.00	£9.00	£15.00
25 Signed & Numbered Edition, ND pre-bagged with certificate and signed by entire creative team; limited to 2,500 copies	$8.00	$24.00	$40.00	£4.00	£12.00	£20.00
Title Value:	$71.70	$215.10	$358.50	£42.00	£126.00	£210.00

VAMPIRELLA/SHADOWHAWK

(see Shadowhawk/Vampirella)

VAMPIRELLA: DEATH AND DESTRUCTION

Harris Comics, MS; 1 Jul 1996-3 Sep 1996

Issue	$Good	$Fine	$N.Mint	£Good	£Fine	£N.Mint
1 ND Amando Connor and Jimmy Palmiotti art	$0.60	$1.80	$3.00	£0.40	£1.20	£2.00
2 ND Amanda Connor and Jimmy Palmiotti art	$0.60	$1.80	$3.00	£0.40	£1.20	£2.00
3 ND	$0.60	$1.80	$3.00	£0.40	£1.20	£2.00
Title Value:	$1.80	$5.40	$9.00	£1.20	£3.60	£6.00

VAMPIRELLA: SAD WINGS OF DESTINY

Harris Comics, OS; 1 Sep 1996

Issue	$Good	$Fine	$N.Mint	£Good	£Fine	£N.Mint
1 ND card-stock cover; features work by Alan Davis & Mark Farmer, Gary Frank & Cam Smith, Jimmy Palmiotti and others	$0.80	$2.40	$4.00	£0.50	£1.50	£2.50
Title Value:	$0.80	$2.40	$4.00	£0.50	£1.50	£2.50

VAMPIRELLA: THE CULT OF CHAOS TRADE PAPERBACK

Dark Horse, OS; 1 Sep 1991

Issue	$Good	$Fine	$N.Mint	£Good	£Fine	£N.Mint
1 ND 142pgs, all reprint, new cover by Jim Steranko	$2.50	$7.50	$12.50	£1.50	£4.50	£7.50
Title Value:	$2.50	$7.50	$12.50	£1.50	£4.50	£7.50

VAMPIRELLA: TRANSCENDING TIME & SPACE TRADE PAPERBACK

Harris Comics, OS; nn 1994

Issue	$Good	$Fine	$N.Mint	£Good	£Fine	£N.Mint
nn ND 148pgs, black and white; reprints from original Vampirella series issues #17-23 with new cover by Dave Stevens	$2.50	$7.50	$12.50	£1.70	£5.00	£8.50
nn 2nd printing ND (Jan 1995)	$2.50	$7.50	$12.50	£1.70	£5.00	£8.50
Title Value:	$5.00	$15.00	$25.00	£3.40	£10.00	£17.00

VAMPRESS LUXURA, THE

Brainstorm Comics; 1 Feb 1996-present

Issue	$Good	$Fine	$N.Mint	£Good	£Fine	£N.Mint
1 ND Kirk Lindo script and art	$0.60	$1.80	$3.00	£0.40	£1.20	£2.00
1 Gold Edition, ND limited to 10,000 copies	$2.00	$6.00	$10.00	£1.30	£3.90	£6.50
1 Platinum Edition, ND (May 1996), Luxura in white satin; limited to 2,000 copies	$3.50	$10.50	$17.50	£2.00	£6.00	£10.00
Title Value:	$6.10	$18.30	$30.50	£3.70	£11.10	£18.50

VAMPS

DC Comics/Vertigo, MS; 1 Aug 1994-6 Jan 1995

Issue	$Good	$Fine	$N.Mint	£Good	£Fine	£N.Mint
1-6 Brian Bolland covers	$0.60	$1.80	$3.00	£0.40	£1.20	£2.00
Title Value:	$3.60	$10.80	$18.00	£2.40	£7.20	£12.00
Vamps (Feb 1996) Trade paperback reprints mini-series, new cover by William Simpson				£1.30	£3.90	£6.50

VAMPS: HOLLYWOOD & VEIN

DC Comics/Vertigo, MS; 1 Feb 1996-6 Jul 1996

Issue	$Good	$Fine	$N.Mint	£Good	£Fine	£N.Mint
1-6 ND Elaine Lee script, William Simpson art	$0.45	$1.35	$2.25	£0.30	£0.90	£1.50
Title Value:	$2.70	$8.10	$13.50	£1.80	£5.40	£9.00

VAMPYRE'S KISS BOOK 1

Aircel, MS; 1 Jun 1990-4 Sep 1990

Issue	$Good	$Fine	$N.Mint	£Good	£Fine	£N.Mint
1-4 ND Barry Blair script/art; black and white	$0.50	$1.50	$2.50	£0.30	£0.90	£1.50
Title Value:	$2.00	$6.00	$10.00	£1.20	£3.60	£6.00

Note: shipped pre-bagged. Issues 1,2 bi-weekly

Issue	$Good	$Fine	$N.Mint	£Good	£Fine	£N.Mint
Book I Set (Jun 1991), issues 1-4 pre-bagged				£1.10	£3.30	£5.50

VAMPYRE'S KISS BOOK 2

Aircel, MS; 1 Dec 1990-4 Mar 1991

Issue	$Good	$Fine	$N.Mint	£Good	£Fine	£N.Mint
1-4 ND Barry Blair script and art; black and white	$0.40	$1.20	$2.00	£0.25	£0.75	£1.25
Title Value:	$1.60	$4.80	$8.00	£1.00	£3.00	£5.00

VAMPYRE'S KISS BOOK 3

Aircel/Blair Grafix Productions, MS; 1 Oct 1991-4 Jan 1992

Issue	$Good	$Fine	$N.Mint	£Good	£Fine	£N.Mint
1-4 ND Barry Blair script and art; black and white	$0.40	$1.20	$2.00	£0.25	£0.75	£1.25
Title Value:	$1.60	$4.80	$8.00	£1.00	£3.00	£5.00

VAMPYRES

Eternity, MS; 1 Dec 1988-4 1989

Issue	$Good	$Fine	$N.Mint	£Good	£Fine	£N.Mint
1-4 ND black and white	$0.40	$1.20	$2.00	£0.25	£0.75	£1.25
Title Value:	$1.60	$4.80	$8.00	£1.00	£3.00	£5.00

VAMPYRES GRAPHIC NOVEL

Eternity, OS; 1 Aug 1991

Issue	$Good	$Fine	$N.Mint	£Good	£Fine	£N.Mint
1 ND anthology of tales	$1.50	$4.50	$7.50	£1.00	£3.00	£5.00
Title Value:	$1.50	$4.50	$7.50	£1.00	£3.00	£5.00

VANGUARD

Image; 1 Oct 1993-6 1994

(see Savage Dragon #2)

Issue	$Good	$Fine	$N.Mint	£Good	£Fine	£N.Mint
1 Erik Larsen co-creator; Tom Coker pencils, Jim Sinclair inks begin; gatefold cover. Supreme appears	$0.40	$1.20	$2.00	£0.25	£0.75	£1.25
2-3	$0.40	$1.20	$2.00	£0.25	£0.75	£1.25
4 Berzerker back-up	$0.40	$1.20	$2.00	£0.25	£0.75	£1.25
5 part Angel Medina art	$0.40	$1.20	$2.00	£0.25	£0.75	£1.25
6	$0.40	$1.20	$2.00	£0.25	£0.75	£1.25
Title Value:	$2.40	$7.20	$12.00	£1.50	£4.50	£7.50

Note: all Non-Distributed on the news-stands in the U.K.

VANGUARD (2ND SERIES)

Image, MS; 1 Sep 1995-4 Dec 1995

Issue	$Good	$Fine	$N.Mint	£Good	£Fine	£N.Mint
1 ND intro Amok, Scot Eaton art	$0.50	$1.50	$2.50	£0.30	£0.90	£1.50
2-3 ND	$0.50	$1.50	$2.50	£0.30	£0.90	£1.50
4 ND most Image characters appear	$0.50	$1.50	$2.50	£0.30	£0.90	£1.50
Title Value:	$2.00	$6.00	$10.00	£1.20	£3.60	£6.00

VANGUARD ILLUSTRATED

Pacific; 1 Nov 1983-7 Jul 1984

Issue	$Good	$Fine	$N.Mint	£Good	£Fine	£N.Mint
1 Legends of the Stargrazers with Tom Yeates art and cover; Mike Baron and Steve Rude back-up, Freakwave back-up by Milligan/McCarthy	$0.50	$1.50	$2.50	£0.30	£0.90	£1.50
2 Legends of the Stargrazers with Tom Yeates art and cover; Mike Baron and Steve Rude back-up, Freakwave back-up by Milligan/McCarthy; Dave Stevens cover	$0.50	$1.50	$2.50	£0.30	£0.90	£1.50
3 Mike Baron and Steve Rude story continues, Freakwave back-up by Milligan/McCarthy; Al Williamson cover	$0.50	$1.50	$2.50	£0.30	£0.90	£1.50
4 Geary, Rude art, Paul Neary back-up story/inks, Missing Man by Ditko pin-up page; Steve Rude cover	$0.50	$1.50	$2.50	£0.30	£0.90	£1.50
5 Burchett, Geary art; Kaluta cover	$0.50	$1.50	$2.50	£0.30	£0.90	£1.50
6 Peter Milligan story with George Freeman art, Perez art (4pg lead story)	$0.50	$1.50	$2.50	£0.30	£0.90	£1.50
7 1st appearance Mr. Monster by Gilbert, Goldyn appears; Kaluta cover	$1.00	$3.00	$5.00	£0.70	£2.10	£3.50
Title Value:	$4.00	$12.00	$20.00	£2.50	£7.50	£12.50

Note: all Non-Distributed on the news-stands in the U.K.

VANGUARD: STRANGE VISITORS

Image, MS; 1 Oct 1996-4 Jan 1997

Issue	$Good	$Fine	$N.Mint	£Good	£Fine	£N.Mint
1-4 ND Gary Carlson script, Scott Eaton and Bill Anderson art; black and white	$0.60	$1.80	$3.00	£0.40	£1.20	£2.00
Title Value:	$2.40	$7.20	$12.00	£1.60	£4.80	£8.00

VANITY

Pacific; 1 Jun 1984-2 Aug 1984

Issue	$Good	$Fine	$N.Mint	£Good	£Fine	£N.Mint
1-2 ND colour	$0.30	$0.90	$1.50	£0.20	£0.60	£1.00

	$Good	$Fine	$N.Mint	£Good	£Fine	£N.Mint
Title Value:	*$0.60*	*$1.80*	*$3.00*	£0.40	£1.20	£2.00
VARMINTS						
Blue Comet Press; 1 1987						
1 ND	*$0.40*	*$1.20*	*$2.00*	£0.25	£0.75	£1.25
Title Value:	*$0.40*	*$1.20*	*$2.00*	£0.25	£0.75	£1.25
VAULT OF EVIL						
Marvel Comics Group; 1 Feb 1973-23 Nov 1975						
1 ND horror reprints begin; Werewolf cover by Gil Kane	*$0.80*	*$2.50*	*$5.00*	£0.40	£1.25	£2.50
2-3 ND	*$0.50*	*$1.50*	*$3.00*	£0.30	£1.00	£2.00
4-22 ND	*$0.40*	*$1.25*	*$2.50*	£0.25	£0.75	£1.50
23	*$0.40*	*$1.25*	*$2.50*	£0.20	£0.60	£1.25
Title Value:	*$9.80*	*$30.50*	*$61.00*	£5.95	£18.10	£36.25
Note: Brunner covers on 3, 4.						
VAULT OF HORROR						
E.C. Comics; 12 Apr/May 1950-40 Dec/Jan 1954/55						
(formerly War Against Crime #1-11)						
12 very scarce in the U.K.	*$520.00*	*$1575.00*	*$4200.00*	£350.00	£1050.00	£2800.00
13 scarce in the U.K.	*$105.00*	*$315.00*	*$735.00*	£70.00	£210.00	£490.00
14	*$90.00*	*$270.00*	*$635.00*	£60.00	£180.00	£425.00
15	*$70.00*	*$210.00*	*$500.00*	£48.00	£140.00	£335.00
16	*$77.50*	*$235.00*	*$550.00*	£50.00	£155.00	£365.00
17-19	*$43.00*	*$125.00*	*$300.00*	£29.00	£85.00	£200.00
20-26	*$37.00*	*$110.00*	*$260.00*	£25.00	£75.00	£175.00
27-28	*$29.00*	*$85.00*	*$200.00*	£19.00	£57.50	£135.00
29 Ray Bradbury adaptation	*$29.00*	*$85.00*	*$200.00*	£19.00	£57.50	£135.00
30	*$29.00*	*$85.00*	*$200.00*	£19.00	£57.50	£135.00
31 Ray Bradbury adaptation	*$29.00*	*$85.00*	*$200.00*	£19.00	£57.50	£135.00
32-36	*$29.00*	*$85.00*	*$200.00*	£19.00	£57.50	£135.00
37 1st appearance of Drusilla (Vampirella clone!)	*$29.00*	*$85.00*	*$200.00*	£19.00	£57.50	£135.00
38-39	*$22.50*	*$67.50*	*$160.00*	£15.00	£45.00	£105.00
40 scarce in both US and UK	*$29.00*	*$85.00*	*$200.00*	£19.00	£57.50	£135.00
Title Value:	*$1643.50*	*$4905.00*	*$12060.00*	£1098.00	£3295.00	£8070.00
Note: all Non-Distributed on the news-stands in the U.K.						
VAULT OF HORROR (2ND SERIES)						
Gladstone; 1 Aug 1990-6 Jun 1991						
1 DS reprints Vault of Horror #34, Haunt of Fear #1	*$0.50*	*$1.50*	*$2.50*	£0.30	£0.90	£1.50
2 DS reprints Vault of Horror #27, Haunt of Fear #18	*$0.50*	*$1.50*	*$2.50*	£0.30	£0.90	£1.50
3 DS reprints Vault of Horror #13, Haunt of Fear #22	*$0.50*	*$1.50*	*$2.50*	£0.30	£0.90	£1.50
4 DS reprints Vault of Horror #23, Haunt of Fear #13	*$0.50*	*$1.50*	*$2.50*	£0.30	£0.90	£1.50
5 DS reprints Vault of Horror #19, Haunt of Fear #5	*$0.50*	*$1.50*	*$2.50*	£0.30	£0.90	£1.50
6 DS reprints Vault of Horror #32, Weird Fantasy #6	*$0.50*	*$1.50*	*$2.50*	£0.30	£0.90	£1.50
Title Value:	*$3.00*	*$9.00*	*$15.00*	£1.80	£5.40	£9.00
Note: issue #7 was advertised but never published.						
Note also: all Non-Distributed on the news-stands in the U.K.						
VAULT OF HORROR (3RD SERIES)						
Russ Cochran/EC Comics; 1 Sep 1991-5 May 1992						
1 reprints Vault of Horror #28, Weird Science #18	*$0.50*	*$1.50*	*$2.50*	£0.30	£0.90	£1.50

	$Good	$Fine	$N.Mint	£Good	£Fine	£N.Mint
2 reprints Vault of Horror #33, Weird Science #20	*$0.50*	*$1.50*	*$2.50*	£0.30	£0.90	£1.50
3 reprints Vault of Horror #26, Weird Science #7	*$0.50*	*$1.50*	*$2.50*	£0.30	£0.90	£1.50
4 reprints Vault of Horror #35, Weird Science #15	*$0.50*	*$1.50*	*$2.50*	£0.30	£0.90	£1.50
5 reprints Vault of Horror #18, Weird Science #11	*$0.50*	*$1.50*	*$2.50*	£0.30	£0.90	£1.50
Title Value:	*$2.50*	*$7.50*	*$12.50*	£1.50	£4.50	£7.50
Note: issues # 6 and 7 were advertised but never published.						
Note also: all Non-Distributed on the news-stands in the U.K.						
VAULT OF HORROR (4TH SERIES)						
Russ Cochran/EC Comics; 1 Oct 1992-present						
1 ND reprints begin from original 1950s EC series with exact cover and interior reproduction	*$0.40*	*$1.20*	*$2.00*	£0.25	£0.75	£1.25
2-15 ND	*$0.40*	*$1.20*	*$2.00*	£0.25	£0.75	£1.25
16 ND	*$0.50*	*$1.50*	*$2.50*	£0.30	£0.90	£1.50
Title Value:	*$6.50*	*$19.50*	*$32.50*	£4.05	£12.15	£20.25
Vault of Horror Annual #1 (Sep 1994) reprints issues #1-5 with covers				£1.20	£3.60	£6.00
Vault of Horror Annual #2 (Jan 1995) reprints issues #6-10 with covers				£1.20	£3.60	£6.00
VAULT OF SCREAMING HORROR						
Fantaco; 1 Oct 1993						
1 ND Gurchain Singh script and art	*$0.60*	*$1.80*	*$3.00*	£0.40	£1.20	£2.00
Title Value:	*$0.60*	*$1.80*	*$3.00*	£0.40	£1.20	£2.00
VECTOR						
Now Comics; 1 Jul 1986-3 Nov 1986						
1-3 ND computer artwork	*$0.30*	*$0.90*	*$1.50*	£0.20	£0.60	£1.00
Title Value:	*$0.90*	*$2.70*	*$4.50*	£0.60	£1.80	£3.00
VELOCITY						
Eclipse; 1 1991-6 1991						
1-6 ND Gary and Warren Pleece script/art	*$0.50*	*$1.50*	*$2.50*	£0.30	£0.90	£1.50
Title Value:	*$3.00*	*$9.00*	*$15.00*	£1.80	£5.40	£9.00
VELOCITY						
Image,MS; 1 Sep 1995-4 Dec 1995						
1-4 ND Kurt Busiek script, Anthony Chun and Aaron Sowd art	*$0.50*	*$1.50*	*$2.50*	£0.30	£0.90	£1.50
Title Value:	*$2.00*	*$6.00*	*$10.00*	£1.20	£3.60	£6.00
VELVET						
Adventure,MS; 1 Mar 1993-4 Jun 1993						
1-4 ND	*$0.40*	*$1.20*	*$2.00*	£0.25	£0.75	£1.25
Title Value:	*$1.60*	*$4.80*	*$8.00*	£1.00	£3.00	£5.00
VENGEANCE SQUAD						
Charlton; 1 Jul 1975-6 May 1976						
1 distributed in the U.K.	*$0.40*	*$1.25*	*$2.50*	£0.25	£0.75	£1.50
2 distributed in the U.K.	*$0.30*	*$1.00*	*$2.00*	£0.20	£0.60	£1.25
3 scarce, distributed in the U.K.	*$0.30*	*$1.00*	*$2.00*	£0.25	£0.75	£1.50
4-6 distributed in the U.K.	*$0.30*	*$1.00*	*$2.00*	£0.20	£0.60	£1.25
Title Value:	*$1.90*	*$6.25*	*$12.50*	£1.30	£3.90	£8.00
Note: Michael Mauser backups by Staton in all						
VENGER ROBO						
Viz Communications,MS; 1 Jan 1994-7 Jul 1994						
1-7 ND Go Nagi and Ken Ishikawa; black and white						

Valor #23

Vampirella (2nd) #4

Vamps #3

	$Good	$Fine	$N.Mint	£Good	£Fine	£N.Mint
	$0.50	$1.50	$2.50	£0.30	£0.90	£1.50
Title Value:	$3.50	$10.50	$17.50	£2.10	£6.30	£10.50

VENOM SUPER SIZE SPECIAL

Marvel Comics Group,OS; 1 Aug 1995

1 ND Planet of the Symbiotes part 3, continued in Spectacular Spiderman Super Size Special #1

	$Good	$Fine	$N.Mint	£Good	£Fine	£N.Mint
	$0.80	$2.40	$4.00	£0.50	£1.50	£2.50
Title Value:	$0.80	$2.40	$4.00	£0.50	£1.50	£2.50

VENOM-DEATHTRAP: THE VAULT

Marvel Comics Group,OS; 1 May 1993

1 ND 64pgs, bookshelf format, Ron Lim cover and art; reprints Marvel Graphic Novel

	$Good	$Fine	$N.Mint	£Good	£Fine	£N.Mint
	$1.40	$4.20	$7.00	£0.90	£2.70	£4.50
Title Value:	$1.40	$4.20	$7.00	£0.90	£2.70	£4.50

VENOM: ALONG CAME A SPIDER

Marvel Comics Group,MS; 1 Jan 1996-4 Apr 1996

1 ND 48pgs, Venom vs. the new Spiderman (Ben Reilly); Larry Hama script, Greg Luzniak art

	$Good	$Fine	$N.Mint	£Good	£Fine	£N.Mint
	$0.60	$1.80	$3.00	£0.40	£1.20	£2.00
2-4 ND	$0.60	$1.80	$3.00	£0.40	£1.20	£2.00
Title Value:	$2.40	$7.20	$12.00	£1.60	£4.80	£8.00

VENOM: CARNAGE UNLEASHED

Marvel Comics Group,MS; 1 Apr 1995-4 Jul 1995

1-4 ND Venom vs. Carnage; card-stock cover

	$Good	$Fine	$N.Mint	£Good	£Fine	£N.Mint
	$0.60	$1.80	$3.00	£0.40	£1.20	£2.00
Title Value:	$2.40	$7.20	$12.00	£1.60	£4.80	£8.00

Venom: Carnage Unleashed (Jun 1996)

	£Good	£Fine	£N.Mint
Trade paperback reprints mini-series	£1.70	£5.10	£8.50

VENOM: FUNERAL PYRE

Marvel Comics Group,MS; 1 Aug 1993-3 Oct 1993

1 ND Punisher guest-stars, bronze "flaming foil" holo-grafix cover

	$Good	$Fine	$N.Mint	£Good	£Fine	£N.Mint
	$0.60	$1.80	$3.00	£0.40	£1.20	£2.00

2-3 ND Punisher guest-stars, card stock cover

	$Good	$Fine	$N.Mint	£Good	£Fine	£N.Mint
	$0.60	$1.80	$3.00	£0.40	£1.20	£2.00
Title Value:	$1.80	$5.40	$9.00	£1.20	£3.60	£6.00

VENOM: LETHAL PROTECTOR

Marvel Comics Group,MS; 1 Feb 1993-6 Jul 1993

1 ND Spiderman appears, holo-grafix cover

	$Good	$Fine	$N.Mint	£Good	£Fine	£N.Mint
	$0.80	$2.40	$4.00	£0.50	£1.50	£2.50

1 Black Edition, ND - a misprint of the regular edition; approx. 650 copies in circulation but forgeries are known. Value given here is at best an estimate rather than based on actual sales

	$Good	$Fine	$N.Mint	£Good	£Fine	£N.Mint
	$20.00	$60.00	$100.00	£6.00	£18.00	£30.00

1 Gold Edition, ND - gold foil cover, available from Diamond Distributors for every 100 copies ordered of #1

	$Good	$Fine	$N.Mint	£Good	£Fine	£N.Mint
	$3.50	$10.50	$17.50	£2.00	£6.00	£10.00

2-6 ND Spiderman appears

	$Good	$Fine	$N.Mint	£Good	£Fine	£N.Mint
	$0.60	$1.80	$3.00	£0.40	£1.20	£2.00
Title Value:	$27.30	$81.90	$136.50	£10.50	£31.50	£52.50

Venom: Lethal Protector (Jul 1995)

	£Good	£Fine	£N.Mint
Trade paperback reprints mini-series	£2.00	£6.00	£10.00

VENOM: NIGHTS OF VENGEANCE

Marvel Comics Group,MS; 1 Aug 1994-4 Nov 1994

1 ND foil stamped neon ink cover, Ron Lim cover and art

	$Good	$Fine	$N.Mint	£Good	£Fine	£N.Mint
	$0.60	$1.80	$3.00	£0.40	£1.20	£2.00
2-4 ND	$0.60	$1.80	$3.00	£0.40	£1.20	£2.00
Title Value:	$2.40	$7.20	$12.00	£1.60	£4.80	£8.00

VENOM: ON TRIAL

Marvel Comics Group,MS; 1 Mar 1997-present

1-2 ND Larry Hama script, Josh Hood and Derek Fisher art

	$Good	$Fine	$N.Mint	£Good	£Fine	£N.Mint
	$0.40	$1.20	$2.00	£0.25	£0.75	£1.25
Title Value:	$0.80	$2.40	$2.00	£0.50	£1.50	£2.50

VENOM: SEPARATION ANXIETY

Marvel Comics Group,MS; 1 Dec 1994-4 Mar 1995

1 ND multi-level embossed cover

	$Good	$Fine	$N.Mint	£Good	£Fine	£N.Mint
	$0.60	$1.80	$3.00	£0.40	£1.20	£2.00

2-4 ND card-stock cover

	$Good	$Fine	$N.Mint	£Good	£Fine	£N.Mint
	$0.60	$1.80	$3.00	£0.40	£1.20	£2.00
Title Value:	$2.40	$7.20	$12.00	£1.60	£4.80	£8.00

Venom: Separation Anxiety (Jan 1996)

	£Good	£Fine	£N.Mint
Trade paperback reprints mini-series	£1.30	£3.90	£6.50

VENOM: SINNER TAKES ALL

Marvel Comics Group,MS; 1 Sep 1995-5 Dec 1995

1-5 ND 48pgs, Larry Hama script, Greg Luzniak art; Venom vs. the new Sin-Eater

	$Good	$Fine	$N.Mint	£Good	£Fine	£N.Mint
	$0.60	$1.80	$3.00	£0.40	£1.20	£2.00
Title Value:	$3.00	$9.00	$15.00	£2.00	£6.00	£10.00

VENOM: THE ENEMY WITHIN

Marvel Comics Group,MS; 1 Feb 1994-3 Apr 1994

1-3 ND Morbius and Demogoblin appear

	$Good	$Fine	$N.Mint	£Good	£Fine	£N.Mint
	$0.60	$1.80	$3.00	£0.40	£1.20	£2.00
Title Value:	$1.80	$5.40	$9.00	£1.20	£3.60	£6.00

VENOM: THE HUNGER

Marvel Comics Group,MS; 1 Aug 1996-4 Nov 1996

	$Good	$Fine	$N.Mint	£Good	£Fine	£N.Mint
1-4 ND	$0.40	$1.20	$2.00	£0.25	£0.75	£1.25
Title Value:	$1.60	$4.80	$8.00	£1.00	£3.00	£5.00

VENOM: THE HUNTED

Marvel Comics Group,MS; 1 May 1996-3 Jul 1996

1-3 ND Larry Hama script, Duncan Rouleau art

	$Good	$Fine	$N.Mint	£Good	£Fine	£N.Mint
	$0.60	$1.80	$3.00	£0.40	£1.20	£2.00
Title Value:	$1.80	$5.40	$9.00	£1.20	£3.60	£6.00

VENOM: THE MACE

Marvel Comics Group,MS; 1 May 1994-3 Jul 1994

1-3 ND Carl Potts script and Liam Sharp art

	$Good	$Fine	$N.Mint	£Good	£Fine	£N.Mint
	$0.60	$1.80	$3.00	£0.40	£1.20	£2.00
Title Value:	$1.80	$5.40	$9.00	£1.20	£3.60	£6.00

VENOM: THE MADNESS

Marvel Comics Group,MS; 1 Nov 1993-3 Jan 1994

1 ND Ann Nocenti script and Kelley Jones art begin; embossed cover

	$Good	$Fine	$N.Mint	£Good	£Fine	£N.Mint
	$0.60	$1.80	$3.00	£0.40	£1.20	£2.00
2-3 ND	$0.60	$1.80	$3.00	£0.40	£1.20	£2.00
Title Value:	$1.80	$5.40	$9.00	£1.20	£3.60	£6.00

VENOM: TOOTH & CLAW

Marvel Comics Group,MS; 1 Dec 1996-3 Feb 1997

1-3 ND Venom and Wolverine

	$Good	$Fine	$N.Mint	£Good	£Fine	£N.Mint
	$0.40	$1.20	$2.00	£0.25	£0.75	£1.25
Title Value:	$1.20	$3.60	$6.00	£0.75	£2.25	£3.75

VENTURE

AC Comics; 1 1986-5 1987

	$Good	$Fine	$N.Mint	£Good	£Fine	£N.Mint
1-4 ND	$0.40	$1.20	$2.00	£0.25	£0.75	£1.25

5 ND Cirocco, Nino art, Neal Adams cover

	$Good	$Fine	$N.Mint	£Good	£Fine	£N.Mint
	$0.40	$1.20	$2.00	£0.25	£0.75	£1.25
Title Value:	$2.00	$6.00	$10.00	£1.25	£3.75	£6.25

VENUS WARS

Dark Horse; 1 Apr 1991-14 Apr 1992

1 ND Yoshikazu Yashuhiko script/art begins, translated into English, black and white; 2 bound-in trading cards

	$Good	$Fine	$N.Mint	£Good	£Fine	£N.Mint
	$0.40	$1.20	$2.00	£0.25	£0.75	£1.25
2-11 ND	$0.40	$1.20	$2.00	£0.25	£0.75	£1.25
12 ND 48pgs	$0.50	$1.50	$2.50	£0.30	£0.90	£1.50
13-14 ND	$0.40	$1.20	$2.00	£0.25	£0.75	£1.25
Title Value:	$5.70	$17.10	$28.50	£3.55	£10.65	£17.75

Venus Wars Vol. 1 (Sep 1993) Trade paperback

	£Good	£Fine	£N.Mint
reprints series with painted cover by Yoshikazu Yasuhiko	£1.85	£5.55	£9.25

VENUS WARS II, THE

Dark Horse; 1 Jun 1992-15 Aug 1993

	$Good	$Fine	$N.Mint	£Good	£Fine	£N.Mint
1 ND 48pgs	$0.50	$1.50	$2.50	£0.30	£0.90	£1.50
2-8 ND	$0.40	$1.20	$2.00	£0.25	£0.75	£1.25
9-12 ND 40pgs	$0.50	$1.50	$2.50	£0.30	£0.90	£1.50
13-15 ND 32pgs	$0.40	$1.20	$2.00	£0.25	£0.75	£1.25
Title Value:	$6.50	$19.50	$32.50	£4.00	£12.00	£20.00

VERDICT: THE ACOLYTE

Caliber Press,OS; 1 Aug 1992

1 ND reprints from Caliber Presents

	$Good	$Fine	$N.Mint	£Good	£Fine	£N.Mint
	$0.60	$1.80	$3.00	£0.40	£1.20	£2.00
Title Value:	$0.60	$1.80	$3.00	£0.40	£1.20	£2.00

VERMILLION

DC Comics/Helix; 1 Oct 1996-present

1 ND Lucius Shepard script, Al Davison art, Mike Kaluta cover begins

	$Good	$Fine	$N.Mint	£Good	£Fine	£N.Mint
	$0.45	$1.35	$2.25	£0.30	£0.90	£1.50
2-6 ND	$0.45	$1.35	$2.25	£0.30	£0.90	£1.50
Title Value:	$2.70	$8.10	$14.00	£1.80	£5.40	£9.00

VEROTIKA

Verotik; 1 1995-present

	$Good	$Fine	$N.Mint	£Good	£Fine	£N.Mint
1 ND adult material	$2.00	$6.00	$10.00	£1.50	£4.50	£7.50
2 ND adult material	$1.40	$4.20	$7.00	£1.00	£3.00	£5.00

3-5 ND adult material

	$Good	$Fine	$N.Mint	£Good	£Fine	£N.Mint
	$0.80	$2.40	$4.00	£0.80	£2.40	£4.00

6-8 ND adult material

	$Good	$Fine	$N.Mint	£Good	£Fine	£N.Mint
	$0.60	$1.80	$3.00	£0.60	£1.80	£3.00

9-13 ND adult material

	$Good	$Fine	$N.Mint	£Good	£Fine	£N.Mint
	$0.60	$1.80	$3.00	£0.40	£1.20	£2.00
Title Value:	$10.60	$31.80	$53.00	£8.70	£26.10	£43.50

VERSION #1

Dark Horse,MS; 1 Dec 1992-8 Jul 1993

	$Good	$Fine	$N.Mint	£Good	£Fine	£N.Mint
1-8 ND	$0.50	$1.50	$2.50	£0.30	£0.90	£1.50
Title Value:	$4.00	$12.00	$20.00	£2.40	£7.20	£12.00

VERSION #2

Dark Horse,MS; 1 Aug 1993-7 Feb 1994

1-7 ND Hisashi Sakaguchi script and art

	$Good	$Fine	$N.Mint	£Good	£Fine	£N.Mint
	$0.50	$1.50	$2.50	£0.30	£0.90	£1.50
Title Value:	$3.50	$10.50	$17.50	£2.10	£6.30	£10.50

VERTIGO GALLERY: DREAMS AND NIGHTMARES

DC Comics/Vertigo,OS; 1 Oct 1995

1 ND pin-ups featuring past Vertigo characters, Dave McKean cover

	$Good	$Fine	$N.Mint	£Good	£Fine	£N.Mint
	$0.80	$2.40	$4.00	£0.50	£1.50	£2.50
Title Value:	$0.80	$2.40	$4.00	£0.50	£1.50	£2.50

VERTIGO JAM

DC Comics/Vertigo,OS; 1 Aug 1993

1 ND Sandman, Hellblazer, Shade, Animal Man, Doom Patrol, Kid Eternity stories

	$Good	$Fine	$N.Mint	£Good	£Fine	£N.Mint
	$0.80	$2.40	$4.00	£0.50	£1.50	£2.50
Title Value:	$0.80	$2.40	$4.00	£0.50	£1.50	£2.50

VERTIGO PREVIEW

DC Comics,OS; 1 Jan 1993

1 ND promo of Vertigo line of titles Sandman Mystery Theatre, Doom Patrol, Swamp Thing, Animal Man, Hellblazer and Shade

	$Good	$Fine	$N.Mint	£Good	£Fine	£N.Mint
	$0.30	$0.90	$1.50	£0.20	£0.60	£1.00
Title Value:	$0.30	$0.90	$1.50	£0.20	£0.60	£1.00

VERTIGO RAVE

DC Comics,OS; 1 Nov 1994

1 ND previews upcoming Vertigo titles for 1995

	$Good	$Fine	$N.Mint	£Good	£Fine	£N.Mint
	$0.25	$0.75	$1.25	£0.15	£0.45	£0.75
Title Value:	$0.25	$0.75	$1.25	£0.15	£0.45	£0.75

VERTIGO VERITE: GIRL

DC Comics/Vertigo,MS; 1 Jun 1996-3 Sep 1996

1-3 ND Peter Milligan script, Duncan Fegredo art and painted cover

	$Good	$Fine	$N.Mint	£Good	£Fine	£N.Mint
	$0.50	$1.50	$2.50	£0.30	£0.90	£1.50
Title Value:	$1.50	$4.50	$7.50	£0.90	£2.70	£4.50

VERTIGO VERITE: SEVEN MILES A SECOND

DC Comics/Vertigo,OS; nn May 1996

nn ND 64pgs, David Wojnarowicz script, James Romberger art

TRADE PAPERBACKS, GRAPHIC NOVELS AND OTHER COLLECTIONS ARE PRICED IN POUNDS STERLING ONLY. CONVERT AT 1.5 FOR DOLLARS.

	$Good	$Fine	$N.Mint	£Good	£Fine	£N.Mint
	$1.60	*$4.80*	*$8.00*	£1.10	£3.30	£5.50
Title Value:	*$1.60*	*$4.80*	*$8.00*	£1.10	£3.30	£5.50

VERTIGO VERITE: THE SYSTEM
DC Comics/Vertigo,MS; 1 May 1996-3 Jul 1996

	$Good	$Fine	$N.Mint	£Good	£Fine	£N.Mint
1-3 ND Peter Kuper painted art; no word balloons	*$0.60*	*$1.80*	*$3.00*	£0.40	£1.20	£2.00
Title Value:	*$1.80*	*$5.40*	*$9.00*	£1.20	£3.60	£6.00

VERTIGO VERITE: THE UNSEEN HAND
DC Comics/Vertigo,MS; 1 Sep 1996-4 Dec 1996

	$Good	$Fine	$N.Mint	£Good	£Fine	£N.Mint
1-4 ND Terry LaBan script	*$0.50*	*$1.50*	*$2.50*	£0.30	£0.90	£1.50
Title Value:	*$2.00*	*$6.00*	*$10.00*	£1.20	£3.60	£6.00

VERTIGO VISIONS: FEATURING..
(See Doctor Occult, Geek, The Phantom Stranger)

VERTIGO VOICES: THE EATERS
DC Comics/Vertigo,OS; 1 Nov 1995

	$Good	$Fine	$N.Mint	£Good	£Fine	£N.Mint
1 ND 64pgs, Peter Milligan script, Dean Ormston cover and art	*$1.00*	*$3.00*	*$5.00*	£0.60	£1.80	£3.00
Title Value:	*$1.00*	*$3.00*	*$5.00*	£0.60	£1.80	£3.00

VERY BEST OF DENNIS THE MENACE, THE
Marvel Comics Group,Digest; 1 Apr 1982-3 Aug 1982

	$Good	$Fine	$N.Mint	£Good	£Fine	£N.Mint
1-3 ND reprints	*$0.25*	*$0.75*	*$1.25*	£0.15	£0.45	£0.75
Title Value:	*$0.75*	*$2.25*	*$3.75*	£0.45	£1.35	£2.25

VERY BEST OF MARVEL TRADE PAPERBACK, THE
Marvel Comics Group; nn Sep 1991

	$Good	$Fine	$N.Mint	£Good	£Fine	£N.Mint
nn reprints selected classic stories including Fantastic Four #5, Daredevil #7 and Spiderman #39/40	*$2.50*	*$7.50*	*$12.50*	£1.70	£5.00	£8.50
nn 2nd printing (Sep 1992)	*$2.40*	*$7.00*	*$12.00*	£1.60	£4.80	£8.00
Title Value:	*$4.90*	*$14.50*	*$24.50*	£3.30	£9.80	£16.50

VIBRANIUM VENDETTA, THE
Marvel Comics Group; 1991

Cross-over storyline that ran throughout the following issues:
Amazing Spiderman Annual #25, Spectacular Spiderman Annual #11, Web of Spiderman Annual #7.

VIC AND BLOOD
Mad Dog Graphics,MS; 1 Oct 1987-2 Feb 1988

	$Good	$Fine	$N.Mint	£Good	£Fine	£N.Mint
1-2 ND Harlan Ellison script, Richard Corben art	*$0.50*	*$1.50*	*$2.50*	£0.30	£0.90	£1.50
Title Value:	*$1.00*	*$3.00*	*$5.00*	£0.60	£1.80	£3.00

VICKI
Atlas; 1 Feb 1975-4 Jul 1975

	$Good	$Fine	$N.Mint	£Good	£Fine	£N.Mint
1 LD in the U.K.	*$0.50*	*$1.50*	*$3.00*	£0.30	£1.00	£2.00
2-4 LD in the U.K.	*$0.40*	*$1.25*	*$2.50*	£0.25	£0.75	£1.50
Title Value:	*$1.70*	*$5.25*	*$10.50*	£1.05	£3.25	£6.50

VICKI VALENTINE
Renegade; 1 Jul 1985-4 1986

	$Good	$Fine	$N.Mint	£Good	£Fine	£N.Mint
1 ND Ellen Dolan, Mam'selle Poupee, Sophisticated Lady, Ms.Tree, Mike Mist, Rainbow, Amber cameos (1pg by Eisner, Valentino, Beatty, Meugniot); Deni Loubert appears	*$0.30*	*$0.90*	*$1.50*	£0.20	£0.60	£1.00
2-4 ND	*$0.30*	*$0.90*	*$1.50*	£0.20	£0.60	£1.00
Title Value:	*$1.20*	*$3.60*	*$6.00*	£0.80	£2.40	£4.00

VICTIMS
Eternity; 1 Dec 1988-5 1989

	$Good	$Fine	$N.Mint	£Good	£Fine	£N.Mint
1-5 ND black and white reprints	*$0.40*	*$1.20*	*$2.00*	£0.25	£0.75	£1.25
Title Value:	*$2.00*	*$6.00*	*$10.00*	£1.25	£3.75	£6.25

VICTOR VECTOR & YONDO
Fractal Comics; 1 Jul 1994-3 Sep 1994

	$Good	$Fine	$N.Mint	£Good	£Fine	£N.Mint
1-3 ND Ken Steacy script and art; based on CD-Rom characters	*$0.40*	*$1.20*	*$2.00*	£0.25	£0.75	£1.25
Title Value:	*$1.20*	*$3.60*	*$6.00*	£0.75	£2.25	£3.75

VICTORY
Topps,MS; 1 Jun 1994-5 Oct 1994

	$Good	$Fine	$N.Mint	£Good	£Fine	£N.Mint
1-5 ND Jack Kirby characters return! Captain Victory, Lady Lightning, Lord Ghost, Silverstar, Teenagants and Satan's Six	*$0.40*	*$1.20*	*$2.00*	£0.25	£0.75	£1.25
Title Value:	*$2.00*	*$6.00*	*$10.00*	£1.25	£3.75	£6.25

VIDEO JACK
Marvel Comics Group/Epic,MS; 1 Nov 1987-6 Nov 1988

	$Good	$Fine	$N.Mint	£Good	£Fine	£N.Mint
1-6 ND Giffen art	*$0.30*	*$0.90*	*$1.50*	£0.20	£0.60	£1.00
Title Value:	*$1.80*	*$5.40*	*$9.00*	£1.20	£3.60	£6.00

VIETNAM JOURNAL
Apple Comics; 1 Nov 1987-16 1989

	$Good	$Fine	$N.Mint	£Good	£Fine	£N.Mint
1 ND Don Lomax script/art begins	*$0.40*	*$1.20*	*$2.00*	£0.25	£0.75	£1.25
1 2nd printing ND	*$0.30*	*$0.90*	*$1.50*	£0.20	£0.60	£1.00
2-16 ND	*$0.40*	*$1.20*	*$2.00*	£0.25	£0.75	£1.25
Title Value:	*$6.70*	*$20.10*	*$33.50*	£4.20	£12.60	£21.00
Indian Country Trade paperback reprints issues #1-4 plus new story				£1.45	£4.35	£7.25
The Iron Triangle (Jan 1992) Trade paperback reprints issues #5-8				£1.40	£4.20	£7.00

VIETNAM JOURNAL: TET '68
Apple Comics,MS; 1 Sep 1991-5 1992

	$Good	$Fine	$N.Mint	£Good	£Fine	£N.Mint
1-5 ND Don Lomax script/art	*$0.40*	*$1.20*	*$2.00*	£0.25	£0.75	£1.25
Title Value:	*$2.00*	*$6.00*	*$10.00*	£1.25	£3.75	£6.25

VIETNAM JOURNAL: VALLEY OF DEATH
Apple Comics; 1 Mar 1994-2 1994

	$Good	$Fine	$N.Mint	£Good	£Fine	£N.Mint
1-2 ND Don Lomax script and art; black and white	*$0.40*	*$1.20*	*$2.00*	£0.25	£0.75	£1.25

	$Good	$Fine	$N.Mint	£Good	£Fine	£N.Mint
Title Value:	*$0.80*	*$2.40*	*$4.00*	£0.50	£1.50	£2.50

VIGIL: DESERT FOXES
Millennium,MS; 1 Jul 1995-2 Aug 1995

	$Good	$Fine	$N.Mint	£Good	£Fine	£N.Mint
1-2 ND black and white	*$0.60*	*$1.80*	*$3.00*	£0.40	£1.20	£2.00
Title Value:	*$1.20*	*$3.60*	*$6.00*	£0.80	£2.40	£4.00

VIGIL: FALL FROM GRACE
Innovation,MS; 1 Winter 1991-2 Spring 1992

	$Good	$Fine	$N.Mint	£Good	£Fine	£N.Mint
1-2 ND 48pgs, black and white	*$0.50*	*$1.50*	*$2.50*	£0.30	£0.90	£1.50
Title Value:	*$1.00*	*$3.00*	*$5.00*	£0.60	£1.80	£3.00

VIGIL: REBIRTH
Millennium; 1 Nov 1994-2 1995

	$Good	$Fine	$N.Mint	£Good	£Fine	£N.Mint
1-2 ND 48pgs, black and white	*$0.60*	*$1.80*	*$3.00*	£0.40	£1.20	£2.00
Title Value:	*$1.20*	*$3.60*	*$6.00*	£0.80	£2.40	£4.00

VIGIL: ROAD TRIPS
Millennium,OS; nn May 1996

	$Good	$Fine	$N.Mint	£Good	£Fine	£N.Mint
nn ND black and white	*$0.60*	*$1.80*	*$3.00*	£0.40	£1.20	£2.00
Title Value:	*$0.60*	*$1.80*	*$3.00*	£0.40	£1.20	£2.00

VIGIL: THE GOLDEN PARTS
Innovation,OS; 1 1992

	$Good	$Fine	$N.Mint	£Good	£Fine	£N.Mint
1 ND 48pgs, black and white	*$0.50*	*$1.50*	*$2.50*	£0.30	£0.90	£1.50
Title Value:	*$0.50*	*$1.50*	*$2.50*	£0.30	£0.90	£1.50

VIGILANTE ANNUAL, THE
DC Comics; 1 Oct 1985-2 Nov 1986

	$Good	$Fine	$N.Mint	£Good	£Fine	£N.Mint
1-2 ND	*$0.40*	*$1.20*	*$2.00*	£0.25	£0.75	£1.25
Title Value:	*$0.80*	*$2.40*	*$4.00*	£0.50	£1.50	£2.50

VIGILANTE, THE
DC Comics; 1 Oct 1983-50 Feb 1988

	$Good	$Fine	$N.Mint	£Good	£Fine	£N.Mint
1 ND origin	*$0.50*	*$1.50*	*$2.50*	£0.30	£0.90	£1.50
2 ND	*$0.40*	*$1.20*	*$2.00*	£0.25	£0.75	£1.25
3 ND Cyborg X-over	*$0.40*	*$1.20*	*$2.00*	£0.25	£0.75	£1.25
4-5 ND	*$0.40*	*$1.20*	*$2.00*	£0.25	£0.75	£1.25
6-7 ND origin	*$0.40*	*$1.20*	*$2.00*	£0.25	£0.75	£1.25
8-16 ND	*$0.40*	*$1.20*	*$2.00*	£0.25	£0.75	£1.25
17 ND Baikie art, Alan Moore script	*$0.60*	*$1.80*	*$3.00*	£0.40	£1.20	£2.00
18 ND Baikie art, Alan Moore script	*$0.50*	*$1.50*	*$2.50*	£0.30	£0.90	£1.50
19 ND	*$0.40*	*$1.20*	*$2.00*	£0.25	£0.75	£1.25
20 ND Nightwing X-over	*$0.40*	*$1.20*	*$2.00*	£0.25	£0.75	£1.25
21 ND Nightwing X-over	*$0.30*	*$0.90*	*$1.50*	£0.20	£0.60	£1.00
22-34 ND	*$0.30*	*$0.90*	*$1.50*	£0.20	£0.60	£1.00
35 ND John Byrne cover	*$0.30*	*$0.90*	*$1.50*	£0.20	£0.60	£1.00
36-46 ND	*$0.30*	*$0.90*	*$1.50*	£0.20	£0.60	£1.00
47 ND Batman appears	*$0.30*	*$0.90*	*$1.50*	£0.20	£0.60	£1.00
48-49 ND	*$0.30*	*$0.90*	*$1.50*	£0.20	£0.60	£1.00
50 ND scarce in the U.K. death (by suicide - 1st in comics?) of Vigilante	*$0.30*	*$0.90*	*$1.50*	£0.30	£0.90	£1.50
Title Value:	*$17.40*	*$52.20*	*$87.00*	£11.35	£34.05	£56.75

VIGILANTE: CITY LIGHTS, PRAIRIE JUSTICE
DC Comics,MS; 1 Nov 1995-4 Feb 1996

	$Good	$Fine	$N.Mint	£Good	£Fine	£N.Mint
1-4 ND Golden Age Vigilante appears, painted covers by Mark Chiarello	*$0.50*	*$1.50*	*$2.50*	£0.30	£0.90	£1.50
Title Value:	*$2.00*	*$6.00*	*$10.00*	£1.20	£3.60	£6.00

VIKING PRINCE GRAPHIC NOVEL
DC Comics; nn Aug 1991

	$Good	$Fine	$N.Mint	£Good	£Fine	£N.Mint
nn Hardcover ND 128pgs, Lee Marrs script, Bo Hampton painted art; introduction by Will Eisner	*$5.00*	*$15.00*	*$25.00*	£3.00	£9.00	£15.00
nn Softcover ND 128pgs, (Aug 1992)	*$2.90*	*$8.50*	*$14.50*	£1.90	£5.50	£9.50
Title Value:	*$7.90*	*$23.50*	*$39.50*	£4.90	£14.50	£24.50

VILLAINS & VIGILANTES
Eclipse,MS; 1 Feb 1987-4 Jul 1987

	$Good	$Fine	$N.Mint	£Good	£Fine	£N.Mint
1-4 ND Jeff Dee pencils, colour	*$0.40*	*$1.20*	*$2.00*	£0.25	£0.75	£1.25
Title Value:	*$1.60*	*$4.80*	*$8.00*	£1.00	£3.00	£5.00

VIOLATOR
Image,MS; 1 May 1994-3 Jul 1994

	$Good	$Fine	$N.Mint	£Good	£Fine	£N.Mint
1 ND Alan Moore script, Bart Sears pencils and Mark Pennington inks	*$0.80*	*$2.40*	*$4.00*	£0.50	£1.50	£2.50
2 ND Alan Moore script, Bart Sears pencils and Mark Pennington inks; Spawn appears	*$0.60*	*$1.80*	*$3.00*	£0.40	£1.20	£2.00
3 ND Alan Moore script, Bart Sears pencils and Mark Pennington inks; Violator vs. Spawn	*$0.60*	*$1.80*	*$3.00*	£0.40	£1.20	£2.00
Title Value:	*$2.00*	*$6.00*	*$10.00*	£1.30	£3.90	£6.50

VIOLATOR/BADROCK
Image,MS; 1 May 1995-4 Aug 1995

	$Good	$Fine	$N.Mint	£Good	£Fine	£N.Mint
1-4 ND Alan Moore script, Brian Denham and Jonathan Sibal art	*$0.50*	*$1.50*	*$2.50*	£0.30	£0.90	£1.50
Title Value:	*$2.00*	*$6.00*	*$10.00*	£1.20	£3.60	£6.00
Violator/Badrock (Dec 1995) Trade paperback collects issues #1-4, new Rob Liefeld cover				£1.30	£3.90	£6.50

VIOLENCE

London Night Studios; 1 Nov 1995	$Good	$Fine	$N.Mint	£Good	£Fine	£N.Mint
1 ND	*$0.60*	*$1.80*	*$3.00*	£0.40	£1.20	£2.00
Title Value:	*$0.60*	*$1.80*	*$3.00*	£0.40	£1.20	£2.00

VIOLENT CASES - AMERICAN EDITION

Tundra Publishing,OS; 1 Sep 1991	$Good	$Fine	$N.Mint	£Good	£Fine	£N.Mint
1 ND Neil Gaiman script, Dave McKean art	*$1.50*	*$4.50*	*$7.50*	£1.00	£3.00	£5.00
Title Value:	*$1.50*	*$4.50*	*$7.50*	£1.00	£3.00	£5.00

VIPER

DC Comics,MS; 1 Sep 1994-4 Oct 1994	$Good	$Fine	$N.Mint	£Good	£Fine	£N.Mint
1-4 ND based on US TV series; Howard Chaykin cover; bi-weekly	*$0.40*	*$1.20*	*$2.00*	£0.25	£0.75	£1.25
Title Value:	*$1.60*	*$4.80*	*$8.00*	£1.00	£3.00	£5.00

VIRTUA FIGHTER

Marvel Comics Group/Malibu Comics; 1 Aug 1995	$Good	$Fine	$N.Mint	£Good	£Fine	£N.Mint
1 ND based on Sega video game featuring Sarah	*$0.60*	*$1.80*	*$3.00*	£0.40	£1.20	£2.00
Title Value:	*$0.60*	*$1.80*	*$3.00*	£0.40	£1.20	£2.00

VIRUS

Dark Horse,MS; 1 Dec 1992-4 Mar 1994	$Good	$Fine	$N.Mint	£Good	£Fine	£N.Mint
1 ND Mike Ploog cover	*$0.50*	*$1.50*	*$2.50*	£0.30	£0.90	£1.50
2-4 ND	*$0.50*	*$1.50*	*$2.50*	£0.30	£0.90	£1.50
Title Value:	*$2.00*	*$6.00*	*$10.00*	£1.20	£3.60	£6.00
Virus (May 1995) Trade paperback collects four issue series with new cover				£2.30	£6.90	£11.50

VISION AND SCARLET WITCH, THE

Marvel Comics Group,MS; 1 Nov 1982-4 Feb 1983 (see Avengers, Marvel Fanfare, X-Men)	$Good	$Fine	$N.Mint	£Good	£Fine	£N.Mint
1-3 ND	*$0.30*	*$0.90*	*$1.50*	£0.20	£0.60	£1.00
4 ND Magneto confirmed as Scarlet Witch's and Quicksilver's father (see Avengers #187-#189 and X-Men #125)	*$0.40*	*$1.20*	*$2.00*	£0.25	£0.75	£1.25
Title Value:	*$1.30*	*$3.90*	*$6.50*	£0.85	£2.55	£4.25

VISION AND SCARLET WITCH, THE (2ND SERIES)

Marvel Comics Group,MS; 1 Oct 1985-12 Sep 1986	$Good	$Fine	$N.Mint	£Good	£Fine	£N.Mint
1 ND DS	*$0.30*	*$0.90*	*$1.50*	£0.20	£0.60	£1.00
2 ND West Coast Avengers X-over	*$0.25*	*$0.75*	*$1.25*	£0.15	£0.45	£0.75
3-11 ND	*$0.25*	*$0.75*	*$1.25*	£0.15	£0.45	£0.75
12 ND DS	*$0.30*	*$0.90*	*$1.50*	£0.20	£0.60	£1.00
Title Value:	*$3.10*	*$9.30*	*$15.50*	£1.90	£5.70	£9.50

VISION, THE

Marvel Comics Group,MS; 1 Nov 1994-4 Feb 1995	$Good	$Fine	$N.Mint	£Good	£Fine	£N.Mint
1-4 ND	*$0.40*	*$1.20*	*$2.00*	£0.25	£0.75	£1.25
Title Value:	*$1.60*	*$4.80*	*$8.00*	£1.00	£3.00	£5.00

VISIONARIES

Marvel Comics Group/Star; 1 Nov 1987-6 Nov 1988	$Good	$Fine	$N.Mint	£Good	£Fine	£N.Mint
1-6 ND	*$0.15*	*$0.45*	*$0.75*	£0.10	£0.35	£0.60
Title Value:	*$0.90*	*$2.70*	*$4.50*	£0.60	£2.10	£3.60

VISIONS

Visions,Fanzine; 1 1979-5 1981	$Good	$Fine	$N.Mint	£Good	£Fine	£N.Mint
1 ND scarce in the U.K. 1st appearance Flaming Carrot	*$10.00*	*$30.00*	*$60.00*	£6.50	£20.00	£40.00
2 ND scarce in the U.K. Flaming Carrot	*$5.00*	*$15.00*	*$30.00*	£3.30	£10.00	£20.00
3 ND scarce in the U.K. Flaming Carrot	*$2.90*	*$8.75*	*$17.50*	£2.05	£6.25	£12.50
4 ND scarce in the U.K. Flaming Carrot cover only	*$2.90*	*$8.75*	*$17.50*	£2.05	£6.25	£12.50
5 ND scarce in the U.K. 1pg Flaming Carrot	*$1.25*	*$3.75*	*$7.50*	£0.80	£2.50	£5.00
Title Value:	*$22.05*	*$66.25*	*$132.50*	£14.70	£45.00	£90.00

VISIONS: THE ART OF ARTHUR SUYDAM

Dark Horse,OS; nn May 1995	$Good	$Fine	$N.Mint	£Good	£Fine	£N.Mint
nn ND 128pgs, collection of illustrations with new Aliens cover painting	*$6.00*	*$18.00*	*$30.00*	£4.00	£12.00	£20.00
Title Value:	*$6.00*	*$18.00*	*$30.00*	£4.00	£12.00	£20.00

VISITOR VS. THE VALIANT UNIVERSE

Valiant,MS; 1,2 Mar 1995	$Good	$Fine	$N.Mint	£Good	£Fine	£N.Mint
1 ND Solar and Harada appear	*$0.40*	*$1.20*	*$2.00*	£0.25	£0.75	£1.25
2 ND X-O, Eternal Warrior, Geomancer and Magnus appear	*$0.40*	*$1.20*	*$2.00*	£0.25	£0.75	£1.25
Title Value:	*$0.80*	*$2.40*	*$4.00*	£0.50	£1.50	£2.50

VISITOR, THE

Valiant/Acclaim Comics; 1 Apr 1995-13 Nov 1995	$Good	$Fine	$N.Mint	£Good	£Fine	£N.Mint
1-3 ND Bernard Chang art	*$0.40*	*$1.20*	*$2.00*	£0.25	£0.75	£1.25
4 ND 1st Acclaim Comics issue, Bernard Chand art; bi-weekly	*$0.40*	*$1.20*	*$2.00*	£0.25	£0.75	£1.25
5 ND Bernard Chang art; bi-weekly	*$0.40*	*$1.20*	*$2.00*	£0.25	£0.75	£1.25
6-7 ND John Ross and Mike DeCarlo art; bi-weekly	*$0.40*	*$1.20*	*$2.00*	£0.25	£0.75	£1.25
8 ND John Ross art; The Visitor vs. The Harbinger; bi-weekly	*$0.40*	*$1.20*	*$2.00*	£0.25	£0.75	£1.25
9 ND John Ross art, The Harbinger appears; bi-weekly	*$0.40*	*$1.20*	*$2.00*	£0.25	£0.75	£1.25
10-11 ND bi-weekly	*$0.40*	*$1.20*	*$2.00*	£0.25	£0.75	£1.25
12 ND John Ross art; bi-weekly	*$0.40*	*$1.20*	*$2.00*	£0.25	£0.75	£1.25
13 ND bi-weekly	*$0.40*	*$1.20*	*$2.00*	£0.25	£0.75	£1.25
Title Value:	*$5.20*	*$15.60*	*$26.00*	£3.25	£9.75	£16.25

VOGUE

Image,MS; 1 Oct 1995-3 Dec 1995	$Good	$Fine	$N.Mint	£Good	£Fine	£N.Mint
1 ND	*$0.50*	*$1.50*	*$2.50*	£0.30	£0.90	£1.50
1 Variant Cover Edition ND	*$0.70*	*$2.10*	*$3.50*	£0.50	£1.50	£2.50
2-3 ND	*$0.50*	*$1.50*	*$2.50*	£0.30	£0.90	£1.50
Title Value:	*$2.20*	*$6.60*	*$11.00*	£1.40	£4.20	£7.00

VOID INDIGO

Marvel Comics Group/Epic,MS; 1 Nov 1984-2 Mar 1985 (see Marvel Graphic Novel)	$Good	$Fine	$N.Mint	£Good	£Fine	£N.Mint
1-2 ND	*$0.40*	*$1.20*	*$2.00*	£0.25	£0.75	£1.25
Title Value:	*$0.80*	*$2.40*	*$4.00*	£0.50	£1.50	£2.50

Note: Mature Readers label

VOLTAR

A Plus Comics; 1 Jan 1992	$Good	$Fine	$N.Mint	£Good	£Fine	£N.Mint
1 ND Alfredo Alcala art, reprint	*$0.40*	*$1.20*	*$2.00*	£0.25	£0.75	£1.25
Title Value:	*$0.40*	*$1.20*	*$2.00*	£0.25	£0.75	£1.25

VOLTRON

Modern,MS; 1-3 1984	$Good	$Fine	$N.Mint	£Good	£Fine	£N.Mint
1-3 ND Dick Ayers art	*$0.15*	*$0.45*	*$0.75*	£0.10	£0.30	£0.50
Title Value:	*$0.45*	*$1.35*	*$2.25*	£0.30	£0.90	£1.50

VON STRUCKER GAMBIT, THE

Marvel Comics Group; 1991

Cross-over storyline that ran throughout the following titles:
Daredevil Annual #7, Punisher Annual #4, Captain America Annual #10.

VOODOO/ZEALOT: SKIN TRADE

Image,OS; nn Aug 1995	$Good	$Fine	$N.Mint	£Good	£Fine	£N.Mint
nn ND 48pgs, Steve Seagle script, Michael Lopez art	*$1.00*	*$3.00*	*$5.00*	£0.70	£2.10	£3.50
Title Value:	*$1.00*	*$3.00*	*$5.00*	£0.70	£2.10	£3.50

VORTEX

Vortex; 1 Nov 1982-15 1988	$Good	$Fine	$N.Mint	£Good	£Fine	£N.Mint
1 ND scarce in the U.K.	*$1.00*	*$3.00*	*$5.00*	£0.70	£2.10	£3.50
2 ND 1st comic appearance Mr. X	*$0.80*	*$2.40*	*$4.00*	£0.50	£1.50	£2.50
3 ND	*$0.60*	*$1.80*	*$3.00*	£0.40	£1.20	£2.00
4-6 ND	*$0.50*	*$1.50*	*$2.50*	£0.30	£0.90	£1.50
7 ND Gilbert Hernandez story, Jaimie Hernandez cover	*$0.50*	*$1.50*	*$2.50*	£0.30	£0.90	£1.50
8-15 ND	*$0.50*	*$1.50*	*$2.50*	£0.30	£0.90	£1.50
Title Value:	*$8.40*	*$25.20*	*$42.00*	£5.20	£15.60	£26.00

VORTEX LIMITED SERIES

Comico,MS; 1 Sep 1991-4 Aug 1993	$Good	$Fine	$N.Mint	£Good	£Fine	£N.Mint
1-4 ND	*$0.40*	*$1.20*	*$2.00*	£0.25	£0.75	£1.25
Title Value:	*$1.60*	*$4.80*	*$8.00*	£1.00	£3.00	£5.00

VORTEX, OUT OF THE

Dark Horse/Comics Greatest World; 1 Oct 1993-12 Oct 1994	$Good	$Fine	$N.Mint	£Good	£Fine	£N.Mint
1 ND John Ostrander script begins; foil stamped cover	*$0.40*	*$1.20*	*$2.00*	£0.25	£0.75	£1.25
2-3 ND	*$0.40*	*$1.20*	*$2.00*	£0.25	£0.75	£1.25
4 ND Neal Barrett and Michael Eury script begins	*$0.40*	*$1.20*	*$2.00*	£0.25	£0.75	£1.25
5-12 ND	*$0.40*	*$1.20*	*$2.00*	£0.25	£0.75	£1.25
Title Value:	*$4.80*	*$14.40*	*$24.00*	£3.00	£9.00	£15.00

VORTEX: THE SECOND COMING

Entity Comics,MS; 1 Mar 1996-6 Aug 1996	$Good	$Fine	$N.Mint	£Good	£Fine	£N.Mint
1 ND Matt Martin script and art	*$0.60*	*$1.80*	*$3.00*	£0.40	£1.20	£2.00
1 Alternate Cover Edition, ND (Mar 1996), cover by Trent Kaniuga	*$0.60*	*$1.80*	*$3.00*	£0.40	£1.20	£2.00
2-4 ND	*$0.60*	*$1.80*	*$3.00*	£0.40	£1.20	£2.00
4 Crimson Limited Edition, ND, pre-bagged with certificate; limited to 5,000 copies	*$2.50*	*$7.50*	*$12.50*	£1.00	£3.00	£5.00
5-6 ND	*$0.60*	*$1.80*	*$3.00*	£0.40	£1.20	£2.00
Title Value:	*$6.70*	*$20.10*	*$33.50*	£3.80	£11.40	£19.00

VOYAGE TO THE BOTTOM OF THE SEA

Dell; 1 (Four Color 1230) 1961; 2 (10133-412) Gold Key 1961-16 Sep 1969	$Good	$Fine	$N.Mint	£Good	£Fine	£N.Mint
1 scarce in the U.K. (Four Color #1230) adapts film	*$15.00*	*$45.00*	*$105.00*	£10.00	£30.00	£70.00
1 issue #1 in indicia, , Dell cover number 10133-12	*$8.50*	*$26.00*	*$60.00*	£5.50	£17.00	£40.00
2	*$6.25*	*$19.00*	*$45.00*	£4.25	£12.50	£30.00
3 Alberto Gioletti art begins	*$5.50*	*$17.00*	*$40.00*	£3.55	£10.50	£25.00
4-5	*$5.50*	*$17.00*	*$40.00*	£3.55	£10.50	£25.00
6-10	*$4.25*	*$12.50*	*$30.00*	£2.85	£8.50	£20.00
11-14	*$3.90*	*$11.50*	*$27.50*	£2.50	£7.50	£17.50
15-16 all reprint	*$2.85*	*$8.50*	*$20.00*	£1.75	£5.25	£12.50
Title Value:	*$88.80*	*$266.50*	*$630.00*	£58.15	£174.00	£410.00

Note; all distributed on the news-stands in the U.K.

W

W

Good Comics; 1 Nov 1996-present

Issue	$Good	$Fine	$N.Mint	£Good	£Fine	£N.Mint
1 ND Joe Lalich and Pat Hatfield art	$0.40	$1.20	$2.00	£0.25	£0.75	£1.25
Title Value:	$0.40	$1.20	$2.00	£0.25	£0.75	£1.25

Note: series originally announced and solicited by Axis Comics.

WACKY SQUIRREL

Dark Horse; 1 Oct 1987-4 1988

Issue	$Good	$Fine	$N.Mint	£Good	£Fine	£N.Mint
1-4 ND	$0.40	$1.20	$2.00	£0.25	£0.75	£1.25
Title Value:	$1.60	$4.80	$8.00	£1.00	£3.00	£5.00

WACKY SQUIRREL'S HALLOWEEN ADVENTURE SPECIAL

Dark Horse,OS; nn 1987

Issue	$Good	$Fine	$N.Mint	£Good	£Fine	£N.Mint
nn ND Mr. Monster by Michael T. Gilbert appears	$0.40	$1.20	$2.00	£0.25	£0.75	£1.25
Title Value:	$0.40	$1.20	$2.00	£0.25	£0.75	£1.25

WACKY SQUIRREL'S SUMMER FUN SPECIAL

Dark Horse,OS; 1 Jul 1987

Issue	$Good	$Fine	$N.Mint	£Good	£Fine	£N.Mint
1 ND	$0.40	$1.20	$2.00	£0.25	£0.75	£1.25
Title Value:	$0.40	$1.20	$2.00	£0.25	£0.75	£1.25

WAGON TRAIN

Dell; 1 (Four Color #895) Mar 1958; 2 (Four Color #971); 3 (Four Color #1019) -13 Jun 1962

Issue	$Good	$Fine	$N.Mint	£Good	£Fine	£N.Mint
1 photo cover	$15.00	$45.00	$105.00	£10.00	£30.00	£70.00
2 photo cover	$8.50	$26.00	$60.00	£5.50	£17.00	£40.00
3 photo cover	$7.75	$23.50	$55.00	£5.25	£16.00	£37.50
4	$7.00	$21.00	$50.00	£5.00	£15.00	£35.00
5 Alex Toth art	$8.50	$26.00	$60.00	£5.50	£17.00	£40.00
6-13	$6.75	$20.00	$47.50	£4.60	£13.50	£32.50
Title Value:	$100.75	$301.50	$710.00	£68.05	£203.00	£482.50

Note: all distributed on the news-stands in the U.K.

WAGON TRAIN (2ND SERIES)

Gold Key; 1 Jan 1964-4 Oct 1964

Issue	$Good	$Fine	$N.Mint	£Good	£Fine	£N.Mint
1 LD in the U.K.	$4.25	$12.50	$30.00	£2.85	£8.50	£20.00
2-4 LD in the U.K.	$2.85	$8.50	$20.00	£2.00	£6.00	£14.00
Title Value:	$12.80	$38.00	$90.00	£8.85	£26.50	£62.00

WALKING DEAD, THE

Aircel; 1 Sep 1989

Issue	$Good	$Fine	$N.Mint	£Good	£Fine	£N.Mint
1 ND Jim Somerville script and art; black and white	$0.40	$1.20	$2.00	£0.20	£0.60	£1.00
Title Value:	$0.40	$1.20	$2.00	£0.20	£0.60	£1.00

WALLY THE WIZARD

Marvel Comics Group/Star; 1 Apr 1985-12 Mar 1986

Issue	$Good	$Fine	$N.Mint	£Good	£Fine	£N.Mint
1-12 scarce in the U.K.	$0.15	$0.45	$0.75	£0.10	£0.35	£0.60
Title Value:	$1.80	$5.40	$9.00	£1.20	£4.20	£7.20

WALLY WOOD'S WAR

ACG,OS; nn Jul 1995

Issue	$Good	$Fine	$N.Mint	£Good	£Fine	£N.Mint
nn ND reprints Wally Wood's rare D-Day stories from the 1960s	$0.50	$1.50	$2.50	£0.30	£0.90	£1.50
Title Value:	$0.50	$1.50	$2.50	£0.30	£0.90	£1.50

WALT DISNEY GIANT

Gladstone; 1 1995-7 1996

Issue	$Good	$Fine	$N.Mint	£Good	£Fine	£N.Mint
1 ND 48pgs, Carl Barks reprints begin	$0.50	$1.50	$2.50	£0.30	£0.90	£1.50
2-7 ND 48pgs	$0.45	$1.35	$2.25	£0.30	£0.90	£1.50
Title Value:	$3.20	$9.60	$16.00	£2.10	£6.30	£10.50

WALT DISNEY SHOWCASE

Gold Key; 1 Oct 1970-54 Jan 1980

Issue	$Good	$Fine	$N.Mint	£Good	£Fine	£N.Mint
1 scarce in the U.K. Boatniks; film adaptation with photo cover	$3.30	$10.00	$20.00	£1.65	£5.00	£10.00
2 Moby Duck	$2.00	$6.00	$12.00	£1.00	£3.00	£6.00
3 Bongo & Lumpjaw	$1.30	$4.00	$8.00	£0.50	£1.50	£3.00
4 Pluto	$1.65	$5.00	$10.00	£0.80	£2.50	£5.00
5 Million Dollar Duck; film adaptation	$2.50	$7.50	$15.00	£1.25	£3.75	£7.50
6 Bedknobs and Broomsticks; film adaptation	$2.50	$7.50	$15.00	£1.25	£3.75	£7.50
7 scarce in the U.K. Pluto	$1.30	$4.00	$8.00	£0.80	£2.50	£5.00
8 Daisy & Donald	$1.65	$5.00	$10.00	£0.80	£2.50	£5.00
9 101 Dalmatians; reprint from Four Color #1183	$2.05	$6.25	$12.50	£1.00	£3.00	£6.00
10 Napoleon & Samantha; film adaptation	$2.50	$7.50	$15.00	£1.25	£3.75	£7.50
11 Moby Duck	$1.30	$4.00	$8.00	£0.55	£1.75	£3.50
12 Dumbo; film adaptation reprint from Four Color #668	$1.65	$5.00	$10.00	£1.00	£3.00	£6.00
13 Pluto	$1.25	$3.75	$7.50	£0.50	£1.50	£3.00
14 The World's Greatest Athlete; film adaptation	$2.50	$7.50	$15.00	£1.25	£3.75	£7.50
15 Three Little Pigs	$1.25	$3.75	$7.50	£0.50	£1.50	£3.00
16 Aristocats; reprint	$2.50	$7.50	$15.00	£1.30	£4.00	£8.00
17 Mary Poppins; reprint	$2.50	$7.50	$15.00	£1.25	£3.75	£7.50
18 Gyro Gearloose; reprint	$4.15	$12.50	$25.00	£1.65	£5.00	£10.00
19 That Darn Cat; film adaptation reprint	$2.50	$7.50	$15.00	£1.25	£3.75	£7.50
20 Pluto	$1.25	$3.75	$7.50	£0.50	£1.50	£3.00
21 L'il Bad Wolf and The Three Little Pigs	$1.25	$3.75	$7.50	£0.50	£1.50	£3.00
22 Unbirthday Party with Alice in Wonderland; reprint	$2.05	$6.25	$12.50	£1.00	£3.00	£6.00
23 Pluto	$1.25	$3.75	$7.50	£0.50	£1.50	£3.00
24 Herbie Rides Again; film adaptation	$1.25	$3.75	$7.50	£0.80	£2.50	£5.00
25 Old Yeller; film adaptation reprint	$1.25	$3.75	$7.50	£0.50	£1.50	£3.00
26 Lt. Robin Crusoe USN; film adaptation reprint	$1.30	$4.00	$8.00	£0.50	£1.50	£3.00
27 The Island at the Top of the World; film adaptation	$2.05	$6.25	$12.50	£1.00	£3.00	£6.00
28 Brer Rabbit; reprint	$1.25	$3.75	$7.50	£0.50	£1.50	£3.00
29 Escape to Witch Mountain; film adaptation	$1.65	$5.00	$10.00	£0.80	£2.50	£5.00
30 Magica de Spell; reprint	$4.15	$12.50	$25.00	£1.65	£5.00	£10.00
31 Bambi; reprint	$2.05	$6.25	$12.50	£1.00	£3.00	£6.00
32 Spin & Marty; reprint	$2.05	$6.25	$12.50	£0.80	£2.50	£5.00
33 Pluto; reprint	$1.00	$3.00	$6.00	£0.40	£1.25	£2.50
34 Paul Revere's Ride; film adaptation	$1.00	$3.00	$6.00	£0.30	£1.00	£2.00
35 Goofy; reprint	$0.80	$2.50	$5.00	£0.30	£1.00	£2.00
36 Peter Pan; reprint						

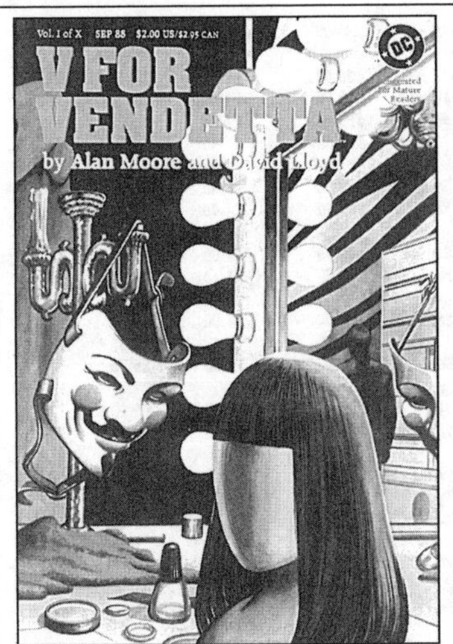

V For Vendetta #1

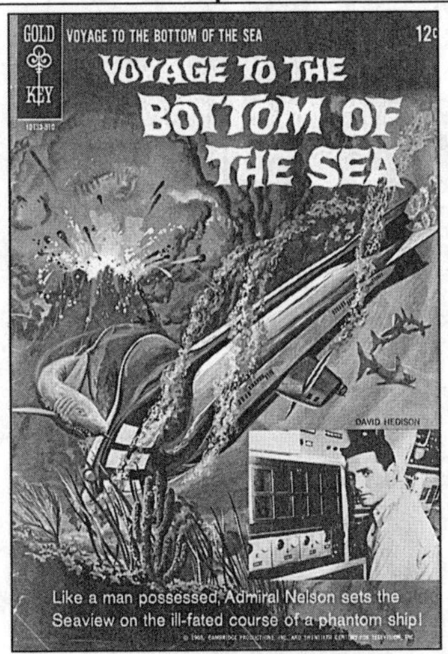

Voyage To The Bottom Of The Sea #3

Walt Disney's Comics & Stories #232

Issue	$Good	$Fine	$N.Mint	£Good	£Fine	£N.Mint
	$1.00	$3.00	$6.00	£0.40	£1.25	£2.50
37 Tinker Bell & Jiminy Cricket	$1.25	$3.75	$7.50	£0.80	£2.50	£5.00
38-39 Mickey & The Sleuth	$1.00	$3.00	$6.00	£0.40	£1.25	£2.50
40 The Rescuers; film adaptation	$1.25	$3.75	$7.50	£0.80	£2.50	£5.00
41 Herbie Goes to Monte Carlo; film adaptation	$1.25	$3.75	$7.50	£0.55	£1.75	£3.50
42 Mickey & The Sleuth	$0.80	$2.50	$5.00	£0.30	£1.00	£2.00
43 Pete's Dragon; film adaptation	$2.05	$6.25	$12.50	£1.00	£3.00	£6.00
44 64pgs, Return from Witch Mountain and In Search of the Castaways	$2.05	$6.25	$12.50	£1.00	£3.00	£6.00
45 scarce in the U.K. 64pgs, The Jungle Book; film adaptation reprint	$2.05	$6.25	$12.50	£1.25	£3.75	£7.50
46 64pgs, The Cat from Outer Space and The Shaggy Dog; film adaptations	$1.25	$3.75	$7.50	£0.55	£1.75	£3.50
47 64pgs, Mickey Mouse Surprise Party; reprint	$1.25	$3.75	$7.50	£0.40	£1.25	£2.50
48 64pgs, The Wonderful Adventures of Pinocchio; reprint from Four Color #1203	$1.25	$3.75	$7.50	£0.40	£1.25	£2.50
49 North Avenue Irregulars; film adaptation	$0.80	$2.40	$4.00	£0.30	£0.90	£1.50
50 Bedknobs and Broomsticks; reprints issue #6	$0.80	$2.40	$4.00	£0.30	£0.90	£1.50
51 101 Dalmatians; reprints issue #9	$0.80	$2.40	$4.00	£0.30	£0.90	£1.50
52 Unidentified Flying Oddball; film adaptation	$0.80	$2.40	$4.00	£0.30	£0.90	£1.50
53 The Scarecrow; film adaptation	$0.80	$2.40	$4.00	£0.30	£0.90	£1.50
54 scarce in the U.K. The Black Hole; film adaptation	$1.20	$3.60	$6.00	£0.50	£1.50	£2.50
Title Value:	$88.60	$267.60	$530.00	£40.85	£124.50	£247.00

WALT DISNEY SPRING FEVER

Disney,OS; 1 Apr 1991

Issue	$Good	$Fine	$N.Mint	£Good	£Fine	£N.Mint
1 ND 64pgs, features Donald Duck by Barks, Chip 'N Dale, Mickey Mouse, Goofy	$0.50	$1.50	$2.50	£0.30	£0.90	£1.50
Title Value:	$0.50	$1.50	$2.50	£0.30	£0.90	£1.50

WALT DISNEY'S AUTUMN ADVENTURES

Disney; 1 Oct 1990

Issue	$Good	$Fine	$N.Mint	£Good	£Fine	£N.Mint
1 ND 64pgs, Donald Duck, Pluto, Mickey Mouse, Goofy and others	$0.60	$1.80	$3.00	£0.40	£1.20	£2.00
Title Value:	$0.60	$1.80	$3.00	£0.40	£1.20	£2.00

Note: quarterly frequency

WALT DISNEY'S CHRISTMAS PARADE

Gladstone; 1 Winter 1988; 2 Winter 1989

Issue	$Good	$Fine	$N.Mint	£Good	£Fine	£N.Mint
1 ND 100pgs, squarebound, Barks reprint, painted Barks cover	$0.60	$1.80	$3.00	£0.40	£1.20	£2.00
2 ND 100pgs, squarebound	$0.60	$1.80	$3.00	£0.40	£1.20	£2.00
Title Value:	$1.20	$3.60	$6.00	£0.80	£2.40	£4.00

WALT DISNEY'S COMICS AND STORIES

Dell Publishing Company; Dell 1 Oct 1940-263 Aug 1962; Gold Key/Whitman; 264 Oct 1962- 510 1984; Gladstone; 511 Nov 1986-547 1989; Disney; 548 Jun 1990-585 Jun 1993; Gladstone; 586 Aug 1993-present

Issue	$Good	$Fine	$N.Mint	£Good	£Fine	£N.Mint
1 Donald Duck reprints by Al Taliaferro and Mickey Mouse reprints by Gottfredson begin; about 220 copies exist in any condition	$2000.00	$6000.00	$20000.00	£1325.00	£3950.00	£13300.00
2	$770.00	$2325.00	$7000.00	£510.00	£1550.00	£4650.00
3	$280.00	$840.00	$2250.00	£185.00	£560.00	£1500.00
4 Christmas cover	$185.00	$560.00	$1500.00	£125.00	£375.00	£1000.00
5	$130.00	$400.00	$1075.00	£90.00	£270.00	£720.00
6-10	$110.00	$335.00	$900.00	£75.00	£225.00	£600.00
11-14	$95.00	$290.00	$775.00	£65.00	£195.00	£520.00
15-17	$82.50	$250.00	$675.00	£55.00	£165.00	£450.00
18-21	$67.50	$205.00	$550.00	£46.00	£135.00	£365.00
22-30	$62.50	$185.00	$500.00	£42.00	£125.00	£335.00
31 original Donald Duck stories by Carl Barks begin (see Four Colour #9)	$360.00	$1075.00	$3250.00	£240.00	£720.00	£2175.00
32 Carl Barks art	$165.00	$500.00	$1350.00	£110.00	£335.00	£900.00
33 Carl Barks art	$125.00	$375.00	$1000.00	£82.50	£250.00	£670.00
34 Carl Barks art, Gremlins by Walt Kelly	$100.00	$300.00	$800.00	£65.00	£195.00	£530.00
35-36 Carl Barks art	$90.00	$270.00	$725.00	£60.00	£180.00	£485.00
37 Donald Duck by Jack Hannah	$48.00	$140.00	$385.00	£32.00	£95.00	£255.00
38 Carl Barks art	$57.50	$175.00	$475.00	£39.00	£115.00	£315.00
39 Christmas cover, Carl Barks art	$57.50	$175.00	$475.00	£39.00	£115.00	£315.00
40 no Carl Barks art; Walt Kelly art	$57.50	$175.00	$475.00	£39.00	£115.00	£315.00
41-50 Carl Barks art	$50.00	$150.00	$400.00	£34.00	£100.00	£270.00
51-60 Carl Barks art	$33.00	$97.50	$260.00	£21.50	£65.00	£175.00
61-68 Carl Barks art	$30.00	$90.00	$240.00	£20.00	£60.00	£160.00
69 Carl Barks art; my favourite cover	$30.00	$90.00	$240.00	£20.00	£60.00	£160.00
70 Carl Barks art	$30.00	$90.00	$240.00	£20.00	£60.00	£160.00
71-80 Carl Barks art	$21.50	$65.00	$175.00	£15.00	£45.00	£120.00
81-87 Carl Barks art	$20.00	$60.00	$160.00	£13.50	£41.00	£110.00
88 1st appearance Gladstone Gander, Carl Barks art	$25.00	$75.00	$200.00	£16.50	£50.00	£135.00
89-90 Carl Barks art	$20.00	$60.00	$160.00	£13.50	£41.00	£110.00
91-97 Carl Barks art	$16.00	$49.00	$130.00	£10.50	£33.00	£87.50
98 1st appearance of Uncle Scrooge in title, Carl Barks art	$35.00	$105.00	$280.00	£25.00	£75.00	£200.00
99 Carl Barks art	$16.00	$49.00	$130.00	£10.50	£33.00	£87.50
100 Carl Barks art	$22.50	$67.50	$180.00	£15.00	£45.00	£120.00
101-110 Carl Barks art	$15.50	$47.00	$125.00	£10.00	£31.00	£82.50
111 Carl Barks art	$13.00	$39.00	$105.00	£8.75	£26.00	£70.00
112 "drugs issue" (mentions ether), Carl Barks art	$13.00	$39.00	$105.00	£8.75	£26.00	£70.00
113 no Barks art	$6.25	$18.50	$50.00	£4.05	£12.00	£32.50
114 Carl Barks art	$13.00	$39.00	$105.00	£8.75	£26.00	£70.00
115-116 no Barks	$6.25	$18.50	$50.00	£4.05	£12.00	£32.50
117 Carl Barks art	$13.00	$39.00	$105.00	£8.75	£26.00	£70.00
118-123 no Barks	$6.25	$18.50	$50.00	£4.05	£12.00	£32.50
124 Carl Barks art	$11.00	$34.00	$90.00	£7.50	£22.50	£60.00
125 1st appearance Junior Woodchucks, Carl Barks art	$15.50	$47.00	$125.00	£10.00	£31.00	£82.50
126-131 Carl Barks art	$11.00	$34.00	$90.00	£7.50	£22.50	£60.00
132 Daisy Duck and Grandma Duck appear, Carl Barks art	$11.00	$34.00	$90.00	£7.50	£22.50	£60.00
133 Carl Barks art	$11.00	$34.00	$90.00	£7.50	£22.50	£60.00
134 1st appearance of The Beagle Boys, Carl Barks art	$25.00	$75.00	$200.00	£16.50	£50.00	£135.00
135-139 Carl Barks art	$11.00	$34.00	$90.00	£7.50	£22.50	£60.00
140 1st appearance Gyro Gearloose, Carl Barks art	$25.00	$75.00	$200.00	£16.50	£50.00	£135.00
141-150 Carl Barks art	$8.75	$26.00	$70.00	£5.75	£17.50	£47.50
151-170 Carl Barks art	$6.25	$18.50	$50.00	£4.05	£12.00	£32.50
171-199 Carl Barks art	$5.00	$15.00	$40.00	£3.40	£10.00	£27.50
200 Carl Barks art	$8.00	$24.00	$65.00	£5.50	£16.50	£45.00
201-240 Carl Barks art	$5.50	$17.00	$40.00	£3.90	£11.50	£27.50
241-266 Carl Barks art	$4.25	$12.50	$30.00	£2.50	£7.50	£17.50
267-268 Carl Bark art	$4.25	$12.50	$30.00	£2.50	£7.50	£17.50
269-283 Carl Barks art	$4.25	$12.50	$30.00	£2.50	£7.50	£17.50
284-285 no Barks	$2.10	$6.25	$15.00	£1.40	£4.25	£10.00
286 Barks stories	$2.85	$8.50	$20.00	£1.90	£5.75	£13.50
287 no Barks	$2.10	$6.25	$15.00	£1.40	£4.25	£10.00
288-289 Barks stories	$2.85	$8.50	$20.00	£1.90	£5.75	£13.50
290 Barks stories	$2.10	$6.25	$15.00	£1.40	£4.25	£10.00
291-294 Barks stories	$2.85	$8.50	$20.00	£1.90	£5.75	£13.50
295-296 no Barks	$2.10	$6.25	$15.00	£1.40	£4.25	£10.00
297-298 Barks stories	$2.85	$8.50	$20.00	£1.90	£5.75	£13.50
299-300 early Barks reprints	$2.85	$8.50	$20.00	£1.90	£5.75	£13.50
301-307 early Barks reprints	$3.30	$10.00	$20.00	£2.05	£6.25	£12.50
308 Barks stories	$3.30	$10.00	$20.00	£2.05	£6.25	£12.50
309-311 no Barks	$2.30	$7.00	$14.00	£1.50	£4.60	£9.25
312 last original stories	$3.30	$10.00	$20.00	£2.05	£6.25	£12.50
313-315 Barks reprints	$2.05	$6.25	$12.50	£1.00	£3.00	£6.00
316 Barks reprints; apparently the last issue published during the lifetime of Walt Disney	$2.05	$6.25	$12.50	£1.00	£3.00	£6.00
317-320 Barks reprints	$2.05	$6.25	$12.50	£1.00	£3.00	£6.00

VERY GENERAL PERCENTAGE CONVERSION CHART WHICH MAY BE USED TO CALCULATE LOW AND INBETWEEN GRADES:

	$Good	$Fine	$N.Mint	£Good	£Fine	£N.Mint
321-330 Barks reprints	*$2.05*	*$6.25*	*$12.50*	£0.80	£2.50	£5.00
331-350 Barks reprints	*$2.05*	*$6.25*	*$12.50*	£0.65	£2.00	£4.00
351-360 Barks reprints (with poster - 50% less without)	*$2.50*	*$7.50*	*$15.00*	£1.25	£3.75	£7.50
361-379 Barks reprint	*$2.05*	*$6.25*	*$12.50*	£0.65	£2.00	£4.00
380-400 Barks reprint	*$2.05*	*$6.25*	*$12.50*	£0.55	£1.75	£3.50
401-402 Barks reprint	*$2.50*	*$7.50*	*$12.50*	£0.60	£1.80	£3.00
403	*$2.50*	*$7.50*	*$12.50*	£0.60	£1.80	£3.00
404-415 Barks reprint	*$2.50*	*$7.50*	*$12.50*	£0.60	£1.80	£3.00
416-429 Barks reprint	*$2.50*	*$7.50*	*$12.50*	£0.40	£1.20	£2.00
430 no Barks	*$1.20*	*$3.60*	*$6.00*	£0.30	£0.90	£1.50
431 Barks reprint	*$1.50*	*$4.50*	*$7.50*	£0.40	£1.20	£2.00
432 no Barks	*$1.50*	*$4.50*	*$7.50*	£0.40	£1.20	£2.00
433	*$1.20*	*$3.60*	*$6.00*	£0.30	£0.90	£1.50
434-436 Barks reprint	*$1.50*	*$4.50*	*$7.50*	£0.40	£1.20	£2.00
437-438 no Barks	*$1.20*	*$3.60*	*$6.00*	£0.30	£0.90	£1.50
439-440 Barks reprint	*$1.50*	*$4.50*	*$7.50*	£0.40	£1.20	£2.00
441 no Barks	*$1.20*	*$3.60*	*$6.00*	£0.30	£0.90	£1.50
442-443 Barks reprint	*$1.50*	*$4.50*	*$7.50*	£0.40	£1.20	£2.00
444-445 no Barks	*$1.20*	*$3.60*	*$6.00*	£0.30	£0.90	£1.50
446-465 Barks reprint	*$1.00*	*$3.00*	*$5.00*	£0.25	£0.75	£1.25
466 no Barks	*$0.60*	*$1.80*	*$3.00*	£0.20	£0.60	£1.00
467-499 Barks reprint	*$1.00*	*$3.00*	*$5.00*	£0.25	£0.75	£1.25
500 Barks reprint	*$1.00*	*$3.00*	*$5.00*	£0.30	£0.90	£1.50
501-505 Barks reprint	*$1.00*	*$3.00*	*$5.00*	£0.25	£0.75	£1.25
506 no Barks	*$0.60*	*$1.80*	*$3.00*	£0.20	£0.60	£1.00
507-510 Barks reprint	*$1.00*	*$3.00*	*$5.00*	£0.25	£0.75	£1.25
511 1st Gladstone issue, 75c cover begins	*$4.00*	*$12.00*	*$20.00*	£0.80	£2.40	£4.00
512	*$2.50*	*$7.50*	*$12.50*	£0.40	£1.20	£2.00
513-516	*$2.50*	*$7.50*	*$12.50*	£0.30	£0.90	£1.50
517 1st 95¢ issue	*$0.60*	*$1.80*	*$3.00*	£0.30	£0.90	£1.50
518-520	*$0.60*	*$1.80*	*$3.00*	£0.30	£0.90	£1.50
521	*$0.60*	*$1.80*	*$3.00*	£0.25	£0.75	£1.25
522 reprints 1st appearance Huey, Dewey & Louie	*$0.60*	*$1.80*	*$3.00*	£0.25	£0.75	£1.25
523-524 Donald Duck by Rosa	*$1.50*	*$4.50*	*$7.50*	£0.25	£0.75	£1.25
525	*$0.60*	*$1.80*	*$3.00*	£0.25	£0.75	£1.25
526 Donald Duck by Rosa	*$0.60*	*$1.80*	*$3.00*	£0.25	£0.75	£1.25
527	*$0.60*	*$1.80*	*$3.00*	£0.25	£0.75	£1.25
528 Donald Duck by Rosa	*$0.60*	*$1.80*	*$3.00*	£0.25	£0.75	£1.25
529-530	*$0.60*	*$1.80*	*$3.00*	£0.25	£0.75	£1.25
531 Donald Duck by Rosa	*$0.60*	*$1.80*	*$3.00*	£0.25	£0.75	£1.25
532-545	*$0.60*	*$1.80*	*$3.00*	£0.25	£0.75	£1.25
546-547 98pgs	*$0.60*	*$1.80*	*$3.00*	£0.30	£0.90	£1.50
548 new material begins	*$0.40*	*$1.20*	*$2.00*	£0.25	£0.75	£1.25
549	*$0.40*	*$1.20*	*$2.00*	£0.25	£0.75	£1.25
550 48pgs, "new" Carl Barks story, unpublished for 30 years	*$0.55*	*$1.65*	*$2.75*	£0.35	£1.05	£1.75
551-560	*$0.40*	*$1.20*	*$2.00*	£0.25	£0.75	£1.25
561 early Barks illustrations feature begins	*$0.40*	*$1.20*	*$2.00*	£0.25	£0.75	£1.25
562-570	*$0.40*	*$1.20*	*$2.00*	£0.25	£0.75	£1.25
571 64pgs, Barks reprints, photo feature on Disney Legends Awards	*$0.60*	*$1.80*	*$3.00*	£0.40	£1.20	£2.00
572-573	*$0.40*	*$1.20*	*$2.00*	£0.25	£0.75	£1.25
574 64pgs, Barks reprints plus Disney Sunday pages	*$0.60*	*$1.80*	*$3.00*	£0.40	£1.20	£2.00
575-577 64pgs, Carl Barks reprints	*$0.60*	*$1.80*	*$3.00*	£0.40	£1.20	£2.00
578-579 Carl Barks reprints	*$0.40*	*$1.20*	*$2.00*	£0.25	£0.75	£1.25
580 64pgs, reprints Donald Duck's first appearance in the Silly Symphonies comic strip in 1934	*$0.60*	*$1.80*	*$3.00*	£0.40	£1.20	£2.00
581 Carl Barks reprints	*$0.40*	*$1.20*	*$2.00*	£0.25	£0.75	£1.25
582-583 64pgs, reprints "Three Caballeros" from Four Color #71	*$0.60*	*$1.80*	*$3.00*	£0.40	£1.20	£2.00
584 Carl Barks reprint	*$0.40*	*$1.20*	*$2.00*	£0.25	£0.75	£1.25
585 48pgs, "Mickey Mouse, Circus Roustabout" by Gottfredson and Taliaferro reprinted	*$0.50*	*$1.50*	*$2.50*	£0.30	£0.90	£1.50
586 Carl Barks reprint; title now re-published by Gladstone; part 1 of Gottfredson's "Lair of the Wolf Barker"	*$0.40*	*$1.20*	*$2.00*	£0.25	£0.75	£1.25
587 new 10pg story plus conclusion to Gottfredson's "Lair of the Wolf Barker"	*$0.40*	*$1.20*	*$2.00*	£0.25	£0.75	£1.25
588-592	*$0.40*	*$1.20*	*$2.00*	£0.25	£0.75	£1.25
593	*$0.50*	*$1.50*	*$2.50*	£0.30	£0.90	£1.50
594-598	*$0.40*	*$1.20*	*$2.00*	£0.25	£0.75	£1.25
599 $1.95 cover begins	*$0.40*	*$1.20*	*$2.00*	£0.25	£0.75	£1.25
600 48pgs, special reprints including Carl Barks' first ten page Duck story	*$0.60*	*$1.80*	*$3.00*	£0.40	£1.20	£2.00
601	*$0.30*	*$0.90*	*$1.50*	£0.20	£0.60	£1.00
602-604 64pgs	*$1.20*	*$3.60*	*$6.00*	£0.70	£2.10	£3.50
Title Value:	*$10000.20*	*$30099.25*	*$84175.75*	£6537.75	£19597.20	£55396.50

Note: all Non-Distributed on the news-stands in the U.K.

WALT DISNEY'S COMICS DIGEST

Gladstone; 1 1986-7 1987
(formerly Gladstone title)

	$Good	$Fine	$N.Mint	£Good	£Fine	£N.Mint
1 ND Three Caballeros	*$0.40*	*$1.20*	*$2.00*	£0.25	£0.75	£1.25
2-7 ND	*$0.40*	*$1.20*	*$2.00*	£0.25	£0.75	£1.25
Title Value:	*$2.80*	*$8.40*	*$14.00*	£1.75	£5.25	£8.75

WALT DISNEY'S SUMMER FUN

Disney,OS; 1 Jul 1991

	$Good	$Fine	$N.Mint	£Good	£Fine	£N.Mint
1 ND 64pgs, new stories plus Donald Duck by Barks reprint	*$0.50*	*$1.50*	*$2.50*	£0.30	£0.90	£1.50
Title Value:	*$0.50*	*$1.50*	*$2.50*	£0.30	£0.90	£1.50

WALT KELLY'S CHRISTMAS CLASSICS

Eclipse,OS; 1 Dec 1987
(Seduction of the Innocent #8)

	$Good	$Fine	$N.Mint	£Good	£Fine	£N.Mint
1 ND Steve Leiloha cover (in Walt Kelly style), colour	*$0.40*	*$1.20*	*$2.00*	£0.25	£0.75	£1.25
Title Value:	*$0.40*	*$1.20*	*$2.00*	£0.25	£0.75	£1.25

WALT KELLY'S SANTA CLAUS ADVENTURES

Innovation,OS; 1 Dec 1990

	$Good	$Fine	$N.Mint	£Good	£Fine	£N.Mint
1 ND 64pgs, squarebound	*$1.40*	*$4.20*	*$7.00*	£0.90	£2.70	£4.50
Title Value:	*$1.40*	*$4.20*	*$7.00*	£0.90	£2.70	£4.50

WALT KELLY'S SPRINGTIME TALES

Eclipse,OS; 1 Apr 1988
(Seduction of the Innocent #10)

	$Good	$Fine	$N.Mint	£Good	£Fine	£N.Mint
1 ND	*$0.50*	*$1.50*	*$2.50*	£0.30	£0.90	£1.50
Title Value:	*$0.50*	*$1.50*	*$2.50*	£0.30	£0.90	£1.50

WALTER: CAMPAIGN OF TERROR

Dark Horse,MS; 1 Feb 1996-4 May 1996

	$Good	$Fine	$N.Mint	£Good	£Fine	£N.Mint
1-4 ND The Mask's arch-ememy returns; John Arcudi script, Doug Mahnke and Keith Williams art	*$0.50*	*$1.50*	*$2.50*	£0.30	£0.90	£1.50
Title Value:	*$2.00*	*$6.00*	*$10.00*	£1.20	£3.60	£6.00

WANDERERS, THE

DC Comics; 1 Jun 1988-13 Apr 1989
(see Adventure Comics #375)

	$Good	$Fine	$N.Mint	£Good	£Fine	£N.Mint
1 LD in the U.K. origin & 1st appearance new team: Dartalon, Elvar, Psyche, Quantum Queen, Re-Animage, Aviax	*$0.25*	*$0.75*	*$1.25*	£0.20	£0.60	£1.00
2	*$0.25*	*$0.75*	*$1.25*	£0.15	£0.45	£0.75
3 Legion of Super-Heroes guest-star	*$0.25*	*$0.75*	*$1.25*	£0.15	£0.45	£0.75
4-13	*$0.25*	*$0.75*	*$1.25*	£0.15	£0.45	£0.75
Title Value:	*$3.25*	*$9.75*	*$16.25*	£2.00	£6.00	£10.00

Note: spin-off series from Legion of Super-Heroes, all Deluxe Format.

WANDERING STAR

Pen & Ink Comics; 1 1993-11 1996; Sirius Entertainment; 12 1996-present

	$Good	$Fine	$N.Mint	£Good	£Fine	£N.Mint
1 ND 24pgs, Teri Sue Wood script and art begins; black and white	*$2.50*	*$7.50*	*$12.50*	£1.20	£3.60	£6.00
1 2nd printing ND	*$0.80*	*$2.40*	*$4.00*	£0.40	£1.20	£2.00
1 3rd printing ND	*$0.60*	*$1.80*	*$3.00*	£0.30	£0.90	£1.50
2 ND 24pgs	*$1.50*	*$4.50*	*$7.50*	£0.70	£2.10	£3.50
3 ND 24pgs	*$0.80*	*$2.40*	*$4.00*	£0.50	£1.50	£2.50
4-16 ND 24pgs	*$0.50*	*$1.50*	*$2.50*	£0.30	£0.90	£1.50
Title Value:	*$12.70*	*$38.10*	*$63.50*	£7.00	£21.00	£35.00
Wandering Star (Nov 1994)						
Trade paperback ND collects issues #1-7				£1.50	£4.50	£7.50
2nd printing (1995)				£1.50	£4.50	£7.50

WANDERING STARS

Fantagraphics,OS; 1 Sep 1987

	$Good	$Fine	$N.Mint	£Good	£Fine	£N.Mint
1 ND Sam Keith cover and art	*$0.50*	*$1.50*	*$2.50*	£0.30	£0.90	£1.50
Title Value:	*$0.50*	*$1.50*	*$2.50*	£0.30	£0.90	£1.50

WANTED: THE WORLD'S MOST DANGEROUS VILLAINS

DC Comics; 1 Jul/Aug 1972-9 Aug/Sep 1973
(see DC Special)

	$Good	$Fine	$N.Mint	£Good	£Fine	£N.Mint
1 reprints Green Lantern #1	*$1.25*	*$3.75*	*$7.50*	£0.80	£2.50	£5.00
2 features 1940s Batman and Joker in reprint of Batman #25	*$1.25*	*$3.75*	*$7.50*	£0.80	£2.50	£5.00
3-8	*$0.80*	*$2.50*	*$5.00*	£0.55	£1.75	£3.50
9 Jack Kirby reprint	*$0.80*	*$2.50*	*$5.00*	£0.55	£1.75	£3.50
Title Value:	*$8.10*	*$25.00*	*$50.00*	£5.45	£17.25	£34.50

REPRINT FEATURES

Batman in 1, 2. Doll Man in 5. Dr.Fate in 3, 8. Green Arrow in 1. Green Lantern in 1, 5; GA Green Lantern

$Good $Fine $N.Mint £Good £Fine £N.Mint

in 4. Flash in 2, 8. GA Hawkman, Vigilante in 3. Kid Eternity in 4. Johnny Quick, Hourman in 7. Starman, Wildcat in 6. Superman, GA Sandman in 9.

WAR (1ST SERIES)

Charlton; 1 Jul 1975-48 Dec 1984

1 distributed in the U.K.
$0.40 $1.20 $2.00 **£0.25 £0.75 £1.25**
2-48 distributed in the U.K.
$0.30 $0.90 $1.50 **£0.20 £0.60 £1.00**
Title Value: *$14.50 $43.50 $72.50* **£9.65 £28.95 £48.25**

WAR (2ND SERIES)

A Plus Comics; 1 May 1991

1 ND 48pgs, ACG and Charlton war reprints, Wood and Glanzman art
$0.40 $1.20 $2.00 **£0.25 £0.75 £1.25**
Title Value: *$0.40 $1.20 $2.00* **£0.25 £0.75 £1.25**

WAR DANCER

Defiant; 1 Feb 1994-6 Jul 1994

1 ND Jim Shooter and Alan Weiss script, Alan Weiss art
$0.40 $1.20 $2.00 **£0.25 £0.75 £1.25**
2-6 ND *$0.40 $1.20 $2.00* **£0.25 £0.75 £1.25**
Title Value: *$2.40 $7.20 $12.00* **£1.50 £4.50 £7.50**
Note: issues #7-9 were advertised and solicited but never appeared

WAR HEROES

Charlton; 1 Feb 1963-27 Nov 1967

1 distributed in the U.K.
$2.85 $8.50 $20.00 **£1.75 £5.25 £12.50**
2 distributed in the U.K.
$2.10 $6.25 $15.00 **£1.40 £4.25 £10.00**
3 distributed in the U.K.
$1.75 $5.25 $12.50 **£1.05 £3.20 £7.50**
4-5 distributed in the U.K.
$1.40 $4.25 $10.00 **£0.85 £2.55 £6.00**
6-10 distributed in the U.K.
$1.10 $3.40 $8.00 **£0.70 £2.10 £5.00**
11-20 distributed in the U.K.
$0.85 $2.55 $6.00 **£0.55 £1.70 £4.00**
21-27 distributed in the U.K.
$0.70 $2.10 $5.00 **£0.50 £1.50 £3.50**
Title Value: *$28.40 $85.70 $202.50* **£18.40 £55.80 £131.50**

WAR HEROES CLASSICS

Lorne Harvey Publications/Recollections,OS; 1 Jun 1991

1 ND features Black Cat and Girl Commandoes, Paul Pelletier cover; black and white
$0.40 $1.20 $2.00 **£0.25 £0.75 £1.25**
Title Value: *$0.40 $1.20 $2.00* **£0.25 £0.75 £1.25**

WAR IS HELL

Marvel Comics Group; 1 Jan 1973-15 Oct 1975

1 ND '50s reprints begin; Al Williamson reprint
$0.50 $1.50 $3.00 **£0.30 £1.00 £2.00**
2 ND *$0.40 $1.25 $2.50* **£0.25 £0.75 £1.50**
3-6 ND *$0.30 $1.00 $2.00* **£0.20 £0.60 £1.25**
7-8 ND Sgt. Fury reprints
$0.30 $1.00 $2.00 **£0.20 £0.60 £1.25**
9-15 ND new stories
$0.30 $1.00 $2.00 **£0.20 £0.60 £1.25**
Title Value: *$4.80 $15.75 $31.50* **£3.15 £9.55 £19.75**

WAR MACHINE

Marvel Comics Group; 1 Feb 1994-25 Apr 1996

1 spin-off from Iron Man series: Jim Rhodes as War Machine
$0.30 $0.90 $1.50 **£0.20 £0.60 £1.00**
1 Ashcan Edition, ND (Apr 1994), 12pgs black and white; 75 cents sticker price on back cover
$0.30 $0.90 $1.50 **£0.20 £0.60 £1.00**
1 Collectors Edition, ND silver-etched foil image on black embossed cover
$0.60 $1.80 $3.00 **£0.40 £1.20 £2.00**
2 with free Spiderman's Amazing Powers card sheet
$0.30 $0.90 $1.50 **£0.20 £0.60 £1.00**
3 Nick Fury vs. War Machine
$0.30 $0.90 $1.50 **£0.20 £0.60 £1.00**
4-6 *$0.30 $0.90 $1.50* **£0.20 £0.60 £1.00**
7 Hawkeye guest-stars
$0.30 $0.90 $1.50 **£0.20 £0.60 £1.00**
8 *$0.30 $0.90 $1.50* **£0.20 £0.60 £1.00**
8 Collectors Edition, ND pre-bagged with acetate print from Marvel Action Hour TV series; neon ink cover; X-over Iron Man #310
$0.60 $1.80 $3.00 **£0.40 £1.20 £2.00**
9 Hands of the Mandarin part 2, continued in Iron Man #311
$0.30 $0.90 $1.50 **£0.20 £0.60 £1.00**
10 Hands of the Mandarin part 5, continued in Iron Man #312
$0.30 $0.90 $1.50 **£0.20 £0.60 £1.00**
11-13 *$0.30 $0.90 $1.50* **£0.20 £0.60 £1.00**
14 Force Works appear
$0.30 $0.90 $1.50 **£0.20 £0.60 £1.00**
15 48pgs, flip-book format, Captain America, Bucky and Nick Fury appear; continued in Iron Man #317
$0.50 $1.50 $2.50 **£0.30 £0.90 £1.50**
16 Captain America, Bucky and Nick Fury appear
$0.30 $0.90 $1.50 **£0.20 £0.60 £1.00**
17 *$0.30 $0.90 $1.50* **£0.20 £0.60 £1.00**
18 Avengers: The Crossing tie-in
$0.30 $0.90 $1.50 **£0.20 £0.60 £1.00**
19 Avengers: The Crossing tie-in, new armour, Hawkeye guest-stars
$0.30 $0.90 $1.50 **£0.20 £0.60 £1.00**
20-21 Avengers: The Crossing tie-in
$0.30 $0.90 $1.50 **£0.20 £0.60 £1.00**
22 new War Machine vs. new Iron Man
$0.30 $0.90 $1.50 **£0.20 £0.60 £1.00**
23 Avengers: Timeslide tie-in, continues in Iron Man #325
$0.30 $0.90 $1.50 **£0.20 £0.60 £1.00**
24 guest-starring The Avengers
$0.30 $0.90 $1.50 **£0.20 £0.60 £1.00**
25 *$0.30 $0.90 $1.50* **£0.20 £0.60 £1.00**
Title Value: *$9.20 $27.60 $46.00* **£6.10 £18.30 £30.50**

WAR MAN

Marvel Comics Group,MS; 1 Nov 1993-2 Dec 1993

1-2 Chuck Dixon and Juan Zanotto
$0.40 $1.20 $2.00 **£0.25 £0.75 £1.25**
Title Value: *$0.80 $2.40 $4.00* **£0.50 £1.50 £2.50**

WAR OF THE GODS

Cross-over series featuring the major DC characters in battle against the classical Gods brought to Earth under the spell of Circe. The cross-overs are listed below in chronological order around the core mini-series.

1) War of the Gods #1
2) Man of Steel #3
3) Wonder Woman (2nd Series) #58
4) Hawkworld #15
5) Legion '91 #31
6) Starman #38
7) Captain Atom #57
8) Dr. Fate #32
9) War of the Gods #2
10) Flash #55
11) Wonder Woman (2nd Series) #59
12) Hawkworld #16
13) Batman #470
14) Dr. Fate #33
15) Animal Man #40
16) Suicide Squad #58
17) War of the Gods #3
18) Wonder Woman (2nd Series) #60
19) Demon (2nd Series) #17
20) New Titans #81
21) War of the Gods #4
22) Wonder Woman (2nd Series) #61

WAR OF THE GODS (LIMITED SERIES)

DC Comics,MS; 1 Sep 1991-4 Jan 1992

1 George Perez script and art
$0.25 $0.75 $1.25 **£0.15 £0.45 £0.75**
1 Direct Sales Edition, ND of the above ("Collector's Edition" on cover of all direct sales editions), mini-posters included
$0.30 $0.90 $1.50 **£0.20 £0.60 £1.00**
2 George Perez script and art, Superman, Batman, Flash and many others heroes appear
$0.25 $0.75 $1.25 **£0.15 £0.45 £0.75**
2 Direct Sales Edition, ND of the above, yellow border cover, four glossy pin-up posters included
$0.30 $0.90 $1.50 **£0.20 £0.60 £1.00**
3 George Perez script and art, Lobo featured
$0.25 $0.75 $1.25 **£0.15 £0.45 £0.75**
3 Direct Sales Edition, ND of the above, four glossy pin-up posters included
$0.30 $0.90 $1.50 **£0.20 £0.60 £1.00**
4 George Perez script and art
$0.25 $0.75 $1.25 **£0.15 £0.45 £0.75**
4 Direct Sales Edition, ND of the above, four glossy pin-up posters included
$0.30 $0.90 $1.50 **£0.20 £0.60 £1.00**
Title Value: *$2.20 $6.60 $11.00* **£1.40 £4.20 £7.00**
Note: cross-over series with tie-ins across other DC titles

WAR OF THE WORLDS, THE

Caliber Comics; 1 1996-present

1-3 ND based on H.G. Wells' novel; painted covers by Gene Gonzales; black and white
$0.60 $1.80 $3.00 **£0.40 £1.20 £2.00**
Title Value: *$1.80 $5.40 $9.00* **£1.20 £3.60 £6.00**

WAR PARTY

Lightning Comics; 1 Oct 1994-2 1994

1-2 ND *$0.60 $1.80 $3.00* **£0.40 £1.20 £2.00**
Title Value: *$1.20 $3.60 $6.00* **£0.80 £2.40 £4.00**

WAR PARTY VS. DEATHMARK

Lightning Comics; 1 Mar 1995

1 ND black and white
$0.50 $1.50 $2.50 **£0.30 £0.90 £1.50**
Title Value: *$0.50 $1.50 $2.50* **£0.30 £0.90 £1.50**

WAR SIRENS & LIBERTY BELLES

Lorne-Harvey Publications/Recollectios,OS; nn 1991

nn ND 100pgs, squarebound, black and white Golden Age reprints featuring Black Cat, Rocket Girl and Girl Commandoes
$0.90 $2.70 $4.50 **£0.60 £1.80 £3.00**
Title Value: *$0.90 $2.70 $4.50* **£0.60 £1.80 £3.00**

WAR WAGON, THE

Dell/Movie Classics,OS Movie; 12-533-709 Sep 1967

12-533-709 distributed in the U.K. film adaptation with John Wayne
$11.00 $34.00 $80.00 **£7.00 £21.00 £50.00**
Title Value: *$11.00 $34.00 $80.00* **£7.00 £21.00 £50.00**

WAR, THE

DC Comics,MS; 1 Jun 1989-4 Sep 1989

1-4 ND 48pgs *$0.60 $1.80 $3.00* **£0.40 £1.20 £2.00**
Title Value: *$2.40 $7.20 $12.00* **£1.60 £4.80 £8.00**
Note: squarebound bookshelf format. The climax to all the New Universe stories

WARBLADE: ENDANGERED SPECIES

Image; 1 Jan 1995-4 Apr 1995

1 ND Warblade and Ripclaw; tri-fold cover
$0.60 $1.80 $3.00 **£0.40 £1.20 £2.00**

	$Good	$Fine	$N.Mint	£Good	£Fine	£N.Mint
2-4 ND Warblade and Ripclaw						
	$0.50	*$1.50*	*$2.50*	£0.30	£0.90	£1.50
Title Value:	*$2.10*	*$6.30*	*$10.50*	£1.30	£3.90	£6.50

WARCAT SPECIAL

Entity Comics; 1 May 1995

	$Good	$Fine	$N.Mint	£Good	£Fine	£N.Mint
1 ND Jason Raschack script, Raff Ienco art, foil-stamped cover						
	$0.50	*$1.50*	*$2.50*	£0.30	£0.90	£1.50
Title Value:	*$0.50*	*$1.50*	*$2.50*	£0.30	£0.90	£1.50

WARCHILD

Maximum Comic Press,MS; 0 Jul 1995; 1 Jan 1995-4 Oct 1995

	$Good	$Fine	$N.Mint	£Good	£Fine	£N.Mint
0 ND features work by Liefeld, Stephenson, Platt, Yaep and Matsuda						
	$0.50	*$1.50*	*$2.50*	£0.30	£0.90	£1.50
1 ND Rob Liefeld script, Eric Stephenson art (2 alternate covers)						
	$0.50	*$1.50*	*$2.50*	£0.30	£0.90	£1.50
1 Deluxe Reprint Edition, ND (Dec 1995), available with covers by Chuck Yaep and Rob Liefeld						
	$0.50	*$1.50*	*$2.50*	£0.30	£0.90	£1.50
2 ND Rob Liefeld script, Eric Stephenson art (2 alternate covers)						
	$0.50	*$1.50*	*$2.50*	£0.30	£0.90	£1.50
3 ND Rob Liefeld script, Eric Stephenson art (3 alternate covers)						
	$0.50	*$1.50*	*$2.50*	£0.30	£0.90	£1.50
4 ND Rob Liefeld script, Eric Stephenson art (2 alternate covers)						
	$0.50	*$1.50*	*$2.50*	£0.30	£0.90	£1.50
4 Variant Cover Edition ND						
	$0.60	*$1.80*	*$3.00*	£0.40	£1.20	£2.00
Title Value:	*$3.60*	*$10.80*	*$18.00*	£2.20	£6.60	£11.00
Warchild (Jan 1996)						
Trade paperback ND collects mini-series				£1.70	£5.10	£8.50

WARCHILD (2ND SERIES)

Maximum Comic Press,OS; 1 Mar 1996

	$Good	$Fine	$N.Mint	£Good	£Fine	£N.Mint
1 ND Alan Moore script, Rob Liefeld art						
	$0.50	*$1.50*	*$2.50*	£0.30	£0.90	£1.50
Title Value:	*$0.50*	*$1.50*	*$2.50*	£0.30	£0.90	£1.50

WARDRUMS

(see Journey: Wardrums)

WARFRONT

Harvey; 1 Sep 1951-39 Feb 1967

	$Good	$Fine	$N.Mint	£Good	£Fine	£N.Mint
1 ND scarce in the U.K.						
	$9.25	*$28.00*	*$75.00*	£6.25	£18.50	£50.00
2 ND scarce in the U.K.						
	$5.00	*$15.00*	*$40.00*	£3.10	£9.25	£25.00
3-10 ND	*$3.75*	*$11.00*	*$30.00*	£2.50	£7.50	£20.00
11-12 ND	*$2.50*	*$7.50*	*$20.00*	£1.55	£4.65	£12.50
13 ND Nostrand art						
	$6.25	*$18.50*	*$50.00*	£3.10	£9.25	£25.00
14 ND	*$2.50*	*$7.50*	*$20.00*	£1.55	£4.65	£12.50
15 ND	*$6.25*	*$18.50*	*$50.00*	£3.10	£9.25	£25.00
16-20 ND	*$2.50*	*$7.50*	*$20.00*	£1.55	£4.65	£12.50
21 ND	*$1.85*	*$5.50*	*$15.00*	£1.25	£3.75	£10.00
22 ND Nostrand art						
	$5.00	*$15.00*	*$40.00*	£2.50	£7.50	£20.00
23-27 ND	*$1.85*	*$5.50*	*$15.00*	£1.25	£3.75	£10.00
28 ND Jack Kirby cover						
	$5.00	*$15.00*	*$40.00*	£3.10	£9.25	£25.00
29 ND	*$1.85*	*$5.50*	*$15.00*	£1.25	£3.75	£10.00
30 ND Jack Kirby cover						
	$5.00	*$15.00*	*$40.00*	£3.10	£9.25	£25.00
31-33 ND	*$1.85*	*$5.50*	*$15.00*	£1.25	£3.75	£10.00
34 ND Jack Kirby cover						
	$4.35	*$13.00*	*$35.00*	£2.50	£7.50	£20.00
35 ND	*$1.85*	*$5.50*	*$15.00*	£1.25	£3.75	£10.00
36 distributed in the U.K. 1st appearance Dynamite Joe; Williamson art						
	$3.10	*$9.25*	*$25.00*	£1.25	£3.75	£10.00
37 distributed in the U.K. Wally Wood art						
	$3.10	*$9.25*	*$25.00*	£1.25	£3.75	£10.00
38-39 distributed in the U.K. some Wood art						
	$1.85	*$5.50*	*$15.00*	£1.25	£3.75	£10.00
Title Value:	*$126.35*	*$376.00*	*$1015.00*	£77.90	£233.20	£625.00

WARHEADS

Marvel UK; 1 Jun 1992-14 Aug 1993

(see Overkill in British section)

	$Good	$Fine	$N.Mint	£Good	£Fine	£N.Mint
1 Wolverine guest-stars, Nick Vince script and Gary Erskine art						
	$0.25	*$0.75*	*$1.25*	£0.15	£0.45	£0.75
2 Nick Fury and Shield appear						
	$0.25	*$0.75*	*$1.25*	£0.15	£0.45	£0.75
3 Nick Fury, Shield and Iron Man appear						
	$0.25	*$0.75*	*$1.25*	£0.15	£0.45	£0.75
4 X-Force appear	*$0.25*	*$0.75*	*$1.25*	£0.15	£0.45	£0.75
5 X-Force appear, Death's Head II cameo						
	$0.25	*$0.75*	*$1.25*	£0.15	£0.45	£0.75
6 Death's Head II appears						
	$0.25	*$0.75*	*$1.25*	£0.15	£0.45	£0.75
7 Death's Head II and Silver Surfer appear						
	$0.25	*$0.75*	*$1.25*	£0.15	£0.45	£0.75
8 X-Men and Silver Surfer appear						
	$0.25	*$0.75*	*$1.25*	£0.15	£0.45	£0.75
9-10	*$0.25*	*$0.75*	*$1.25*	£0.15	£0.45	£0.75
11 Mys-Tech Wars X-over, Death's Head II appears						
	$0.25	*$0.75*	*$1.25*	£0.15	£0.45	£0.75
12-14	*$0.25*	*$0.75*	*$1.25*	£0.15	£0.45	£0.75
Title Value:	*$3.50*	*$10.50*	*$17.50*	£2.10	£6.30	£10.50

WARHEADS: BLACK DAWN

Marvel UK,MS; 1 Jul 1993-2 Aug 1993

	$Good	$Fine	$N.Mint	£Good	£Fine	£N.Mint
1 David Hine art, red metallic cover and embossed logo						
	$0.40	*$1.20*	*$2.00*	£0.25	£0.75	£1.25
2	*$0.25*	*$0.75*	*$1.25*	£0.15	£0.45	£0.75
Title Value:	*$0.65*	*$1.95*	*$3.25*	£0.40	£1.20	£2.00

WARLASH

CFD Productions; 1 Oct 1995-2 1996 ?

	$Good	$Fine	$N.Mint	£Good	£Fine	£N.Mint
1-2 ND Frank Forte script, Rob Murdock art; black and white						
	$0.60	*$1.80*	*$3.00*	£0.40	£1.20	£2.00
Title Value:	*$1.20*	*$3.60*	*$6.00*	£0.80	£2.40	£4.00

WARLASH ASHCAN EDITION

Anubis Press; nn Sep 1994

	$Good	$Fine	$N.Mint	£Good	£Fine	£N.Mint
nn ND black and white						
	$0.50	*$1.50*	*$2.50*	£0.30	£0.90	£1.50
Title Value:	*$0.50*	*$1.50*	*$2.50*	£0.30	£0.90	£1.50

WARLOCK (1ST SERIES)

Marvel Comics Group; 1 Aug 1972-8 Oct 1973; 9 Oct 1975-15 Nov 1976

(see Fantastic Four #67, Strange Tales, Marvel Premiere)

	$Good	$Fine	$N.Mint	£Good	£Fine	£N.Mint
1 ND origin retold by Gil Kane						
	$5.00	*$15.00*	*$30.00*	£3.30	£10.00	£20.00
2 ND	*$2.05*	*$6.25*	*$12.50*	£1.25	£3.75	£7.50
3 ND	*$1.65*	*$5.00*	*$10.00*	£1.05	£3.25	£6.50
4 scarce in the U.K. Dr. Doom cameo						
	$1.30	*$4.00*	*$8.00*	£0.90	£2.75	£5.50
5 scarce in the U.K.						
	$1.30	*$4.00*	*$8.00*	£0.90	£2.75	£5.50
6-8 ND	*$1.25*	*$3.75*	*$7.50*	£0.80	£2.50	£5.00
9 2nd Thanos saga begins, Starlin story/art, continues from Strange Tales #181, Thanos cameo						
	$1.50	*$4.50*	*$9.00*	£1.00	£3.00	£6.00
10 Jim Starlin art, origin Thanos retold						
	$2.90	*$8.75*	*$17.50*	£1.25	£3.75	£7.50

Wanderers #1

Wanted #3

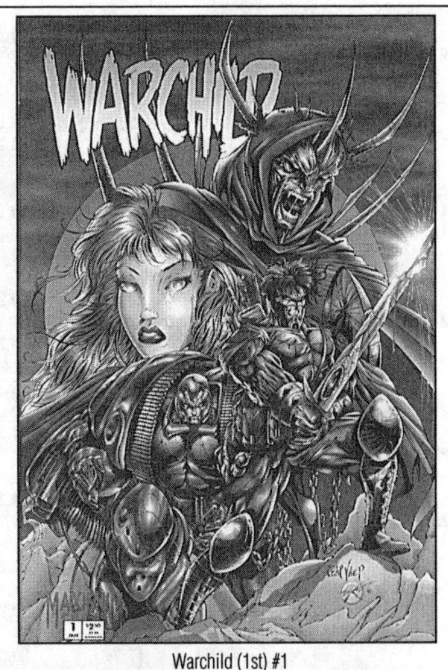

Warchild (1st) #1

Issue	$Good	$Fine	$N.Mint	£Good	£Fine	£N.Mint
11 Jim Starlin art, Thanos appears, Warlock "dies"	*$2.50*	*$7.50*	*$15.00*	£1.15	£3.50	£7.00
12-14 Jim Starlin art	*$1.50*	*$4.50*	*$9.00*	£0.75	£2.25	£4.50
15 origin Soul-Gem, Jim Starlin art, Thanos cover	*$2.05*	*$6.25*	*$12.50*	£1.15	£3.50	£7.00
Title Value:	*$28.50*	*$86.00*	*$172.00*	£16.60	£50.50	£101.00

WARLOCK (2ND SERIES)

Marvel Comics Group,MS; 1 Dec 1982-6 May 1983

Issue	$Good	$Fine	$N.Mint	£Good	£Fine	£N.Mint
1 ND reprints begin	*$0.80*	*$2.40*	*$4.00*	£0.50	£1.50	£2.50
2-6 ND	*$0.80*	*$2.40*	*$4.00*	£0.50	£1.50	£2.50
Title Value:	*$4.80*	*$14.40*	*$24.00*	£3.00	£9.00	£15.00

Note: reprints from Strange Tales #178-181, Warlock #9-15 by Starlin

WARLOCK (3RD SERIES)

Marvel Comics Group,MS; 1 May 1992-6 Oct 1992

Issue	$Good	$Fine	$N.Mint	£Good	£Fine	£N.Mint
1 ND reprints from Warlock Special Edition begin (1982/83 series)	*$0.50*	*$1.50*	*$2.50*	£0.30	£0.90	£1.50
2-5 ND	*$0.50*	*$1.50*	*$2.50*	£0.30	£0.90	£1.50
6 ND Warlock vs. Thanos, Avengers, Thing and Spiderman appear	*$0.50*	*$1.50*	*$2.50*	£0.30	£0.90	£1.50
Title Value:	*$3.00*	*$9.00*	*$15.00*	£1.80	£5.40	£9.00

WARLOCK 5

Aircel; 1 Nov 1986-22 1989

Issue	$Good	$Fine	$N.Mint	£Good	£Fine	£N.Mint
1 ND scarce in the U.K.	*$0.40*	*$1.20*	*$2.00*	£0.30	£0.90	£1.50
2 ND	*$0.40*	*$1.20*	*$2.00*	£0.25	£0.75	£1.25
3 ND very scarce in the U.K.	*$0.40*	*$1.20*	*$2.00*	£0.30	£0.90	£1.50
4 ND scarce in the U.K.	*$0.40*	*$1.20*	*$2.00*	£0.25	£0.75	£1.25
5 ND scarce in the U.K. robot skull cover	*$0.40*	*$1.20*	*$2.00*	£0.25	£0.75	£1.25
6 ND scarce in the U.K. misnumbered "5", woman on cover	*$0.40*	*$1.20*	*$2.00*	£0.25	£0.75	£1.25
7-9 ND scarce in the U.K.	*$0.40*	*$1.20*	*$2.00*	£0.25	£0.75	£1.25
10-15 ND	*$0.40*	*$1.20*	*$2.00*	£0.20	£0.60	£1.00
16-17 ND Dale Keown pencils	*$0.40*	*$1.20*	*$2.00*	£0.25	£0.75	£1.25
18-22 ND	*$0.40*	*$1.20*	*$2.00*	£0.20	£0.60	£1.00
Title Value:	*$8.80*	*$26.40*	*$44.00*	£5.05	£15.15	£25.25
Trade paperback 1, reprints issues #1-5				£0.80	£2.40	£4.00
Trade paperback 2, reprints issues #6-9				£0.80	£2.40	£4.00

WARLOCK 5 BOOK II

Aircel; 1 Jun 1989-7 1990

Issue	$Good	$Fine	$N.Mint	£Good	£Fine	£N.Mint
1-7 ND black and white	*$0.40*	*$1.20*	*$2.00*	£0.25	£0.75	£1.25
Title Value:	*$2.80*	*$8.40*	*$14.00*	£1.75	£5.25	£8.75
Graphic Album				£0.80	£2.40	£4.00

WARLOCK 5: THE GATHERING

Night Wynd; 1 Oct 1994-2 Jan 1994

Issue	$Good	$Fine	$N.Mint	£Good	£Fine	£N.Mint
1-2 ND Barry Blair script and art	*$0.40*	*$1.20*	*$2.00*	£0.25	£0.75	£1.25
Title Value:	*$0.80*	*$2.40*	*$4.00*	£0.50	£1.50	£2.50

WARLOCK AND THE INFINITY WATCH

Marvel Comics Group; 1 Feb 1992-42 Jul 1995

Issue	$Good	$Fine	$N.Mint	£Good	£Fine	£N.Mint
1 ND script by Jim Starlin, sequel to Infinity Gauntlet	*$0.50*	*$1.50*	*$2.50*	£0.30	£0.90	£1.50
2 ND	*$0.40*	*$1.20*	*$2.00*	£0.25	£0.75	£1.25
3-4 ND High Evolutionary appears	*$0.40*	*$1.20*	*$2.00*	£0.25	£0.75	£1.25
5-7 ND	*$0.40*	*$1.20*	*$2.00*	£0.25	£0.75	£1.25
8 ND Infinity War X-over, Thanos appears	*$0.40*	*$1.20*	*$2.00*	£0.25	£0.75	£1.25
9 ND Infinity War X-over, Galactus appears	*$0.40*	*$1.20*	*$2.00*	£0.25	£0.75	£1.25
10 ND Infinity War X-over, Thanos appears	*$0.40*	*$1.20*	*$2.00*	£0.25	£0.75	£1.25
11 ND	*$0.30*	*$0.90*	*$1.50*	£0.20	£0.60	£1.00
12-13 ND Hulk appears	*$0.30*	*$0.90*	*$1.50*	£0.20	£0.60	£1.00
14-17 ND	*$0.30*	*$0.90*	*$1.50*	£0.20	£0.60	£1.00
18 ND Reed Richards guest-stars	*$0.30*	*$0.90*	*$1.50*	£0.20	£0.60	£1.00
19-22 ND Infinity Crusade tie-in	*$0.30*	*$0.90*	*$1.50*	£0.20	£0.60	£1.00
23 ND Blood and Thunder part 4, Silver Surfer and Thor appear	*$0.30*	*$0.90*	*$1.50*	£0.20	£0.60	£1.00
24 ND Blood and Thunder part 8, Silver Surfer, Dr. Strange and Thor appear	*$0.30*	*$0.90*	*$1.50*	£0.20	£0.60	£1.00
25 ND Blood and Thunder part 12, Silver Surfer, Dr. Strange and Thor appear; embossed die-cut cover	*$0.50*	*$1.50*	*$2.50*	£0.30	£0.90	£1.50
26-27 ND	*$0.30*	*$0.90*	*$1.50*	£0.20	£0.60	£1.00
28 ND Giant Man, Black Widow, Thunderstrike, Hercules, Captain America and Vision appear	*$0.30*	*$0.90*	*$1.50*	£0.20	£0.60	£1.00
29-36 ND	*$0.30*	*$0.90*	*$1.50*	£0.20	£0.60	£1.00
37-39 ND Firelord appears	*$0.30*	*$0.90*	*$1.50*	£0.20	£0.60	£1.00
40 ND Thanos appears	*$0.30*	*$0.90*	*$1.50*	£0.20	£0.60	£1.00
41 ND Atlantis Rising tie-in	*$0.30*	*$0.90*	*$1.50*	£0.20	£0.60	£1.00
42 ND Atlantis Rising tie-in; leads into Curse of Rune #1 published by Malibu	*$0.30*	*$0.90*	*$1.50*	£0.20	£0.60	£1.00
Title Value:	*$13.90*	*$41.70*	*$69.50*	£9.05	£27.15	£45.25

WARLOCK CHRONICLES, THE

Marvel Comics Group; 1 Jul 1993-8 Feb 1994

Issue	$Good	$Fine	$N.Mint	£Good	£Fine	£N.Mint
1 Jim Starlin script begins, holo-grafix foil cover	*$0.50*	*$1.50*	*$2.50*	£0.30	£0.90	£1.50
2-5 Infinity Crusade X-over	*$0.40*	*$1.20*	*$2.00*	£0.25	£0.75	£1.25
6 Blood and Thunder part 3	*$0.40*	*$1.20*	*$2.00*	£0.25	£0.75	£1.25
7 Blood and Thunder part 7	*$0.40*	*$1.20*	*$2.00*	£0.25	£0.75	£1.25
8 Blood and Thunder part 11	*$0.40*	*$1.20*	*$2.00*	£0.25	£0.75	£1.25
Title Value:	*$3.30*	*$9.90*	*$16.50*	£2.05	£6.15	£10.25

WARLOCKS

Aircel; 1 Nov 1988-12 Oct 1989

Issue	$Good	$Fine	$N.Mint	£Good	£Fine	£N.Mint
1-12 ND Barry Blair script and art, black and white	*$0.40*	*$1.20*	*$2.00*	£0.25	£0.75	£1.25
Title Value:	*$4.80*	*$14.40*	*$24.00*	£3.00	£9.00	£15.00
Special Edition 1 (1989) 40pgs, reprints				£0.25	£0.75	£1.25

WARLORD (1ST SERIES)

DC Comics; 1 Jan/Feb 1976-2 Mar/Apr 1976; 3 Oct/Nov 1976-133 Winter 1988

(see DC Special Blue Ribbon Digest #10, First Issue Special #8)

Issue	$Good	$Fine	$N.Mint	£Good	£Fine	£N.Mint
1 scarce in the U.K. Mike Grell art, continues from First Issue Special #8	*$2.50*	*$7.50*	*$15.00*	£1.00	£3.00	£6.00
2 scarce in the U.K. 1st appearance Machiste	*$1.25*	*$3.75*	*$7.50*	£0.65	£2.00	£4.00
3-4 scarce in the U.K.	*$0.80*	*$2.50*	*$5.00*	£0.50	£1.50	£3.00
5 ND scarce in the U.K.	*$0.80*	*$2.50*	*$5.00*	£0.55	£1.75	£3.50
6-8 scarce in the U.K.	*$0.65*	*$2.00*	*$4.00*	£0.40	£1.25	£2.50
9 scarce in the U.K. new costume	*$0.65*	*$2.00*	*$4.00*	£0.40	£1.25	£2.50
10 ND	*$0.65*	*$2.00*	*$4.00*	£0.50	£1.50	£3.00
11 ND origin retold	*$0.50*	*$1.50*	*$3.00*	£0.30	£1.00	£2.00
12-14 ND	*$0.50*	*$1.50*	*$3.00*	£0.30	£1.00	£2.00
15 ND 44pgs, Tara returns, birth of Warlord's son	*$0.55*	*$1.75*	*$3.50*	£0.35	£1.10	£2.25
16-20 ND	*$0.40*	*$1.25*	*$2.50*	£0.25	£0.75	£1.50
21-27 ND	*$0.30*	*$1.00*	*$2.00*	£0.20	£0.60	£1.25
28 ND 1st Wizard World	*$0.30*	*$1.00*	*$2.00*	£0.20	£0.60	£1.25
29-30 ND	*$0.30*	*$1.00*	*$2.00*	£0.20	£0.60	£1.25
31 ND	*$0.30*	*$0.90*	*$1.50*	£0.20	£0.60	£1.00
32 ND 1st appearance Shakira	*$0.30*	*$0.90*	*$1.50*	£0.20	£0.60	£1.00
33-36 ND	*$0.30*	*$0.90*	*$1.50*	£0.20	£0.60	£1.00
37-39 ND Jim Starlin art on Omac back-up	*$0.40*	*$1.20*	*$2.00*	£0.25	£0.75	£1.25
40 ND new costume	*$0.30*	*$0.90*	*$1.50*	£0.20	£0.60	£1.00
41-47 ND	*$0.30*	*$0.90*	*$1.50*	£0.20	£0.60	£1.00
48 ND 52pgs, Arak Son of Thunder insert, Claw back-up	*$0.40*	*$1.20*	*$2.00*	£0.25	£0.75	£1.25
49 ND Claw back-up	*$0.30*	*$0.90*	*$1.50*	£0.20	£0.60	£1.00
50 ND	*$0.30*	*$0.90*	*$1.50*	£0.20	£0.60	£1.00
51 ND reprints #1	*$0.25*	*$0.75*	*$1.25*	£0.15	£0.45	£0.75
52 ND Dragonsword back-up	*$0.25*	*$0.75*	*$1.25*	£0.15	£0.45	£0.75
53 ND Mark Texeira art (1st pro work?), Dragonsword back-up	*$0.25*	*$0.75*	*$1.25*	£0.15	£0.45	£0.75
54 ND Mark Texeira art, Dragonsword back-up	*$0.25*	*$0.75*	*$1.25*	£0.15	£0.45	£0.75
55 ND Mark Texeira art, Arion back-up begins	*$0.25*	*$0.75*	*$1.25*	£0.15	£0.45	£0.75
56-58 ND Mark Texeira art	*$0.25*	*$0.75*	*$1.25*	£0.15	£0.45	£0.75
59 ND last Mike Grell art	*$0.25*	*$0.75*	*$1.25*	£0.15	£0.45	£0.75
60-62 ND	*$0.25*	*$0.75*	*$1.25*	£0.15	£0.45	£0.75
63 ND Barren Earth back-up starts, 16pg Masters of the Universe insert	*$0.25*	*$0.75*	*$1.25*	£0.15	£0.45	£0.75
64-70 ND	*$0.25*	*$0.75*	*$1.25*	£0.15	£0.45	£0.75
71 ND last Grell script	*$0.25*	*$0.75*	*$1.25*	£0.15	£0.45	£0.75
72-90 ND	*$0.25*	*$0.75*	*$1.25*	£0.15	£0.45	£0.75
91 ND origin retold	*$0.25*	*$0.75*	*$1.25*	£0.15	£0.45	£0.75
92-99 ND	*$0.25*	*$0.75*	*$1.25*	£0.15	£0.45	£0.75
100 ND DS painted cover	*$0.30*	*$0.90*	*$1.50*	£0.20	£0.60	£1.00
101-113 ND	*$0.25*	*$0.75*	*$1.25*	£0.15	£0.45	£0.75
114-115 ND Legends X-overs	*$0.25*	*$0.75*	*$1.25*	£0.15	£0.45	£0.75
116-119 ND	*$0.25*	*$0.75*	*$1.25*	£0.15	£0.45	£0.75
120-122 ND Art Thibert co-artist	*$0.25*	*$0.75*	*$1.25*	£0.15	£0.45	£0.75
123-130 ND	*$0.25*	*$0.75*	*$1.25*	£0.15	£0.45	£0.75

	$Good	$Fine	$N.Mint	£Good	£Fine	£N.Mint
131 ND Rob Liefeld art on insert story, 1st work at DC	*$0.30*	*$0.90*	*$1.50*	£0.20	£0.60	£1.00
132 ND	*$0.25*	*$0.75*	*$1.25*	£0.15	£0.45	£0.75
133 ND DS	*$0.30*	*$0.90*	*$1.50*	£0.20	£0.60	£1.00
Title Value:	*$44.25*	*$134.65*	*$242.00*	£26.90	£81.50	£146.75
Warlord Trade paperback (Jan 1992) ND reprints plus 9 new pages of story/art by Mike Grell				£2.50	£7.50	£12.50

FEATURES

Arion, Lord of Atlantis in 55-62. Claw in 48, 49. Dragonsword in 51-54. Omac in 37-39, 42-47. Wizard World in 28, 29, 40, 41.

WARLORD (1ST SERIES) ANNUAL

DC Comics; 1 Nov 1982-6 Nov 1987

	$Good	$Fine	$N.Mint	£Good	£Fine	£N.Mint
1 ND 52pgs, Mike Grell cover	*$0.30*	*$0.90*	*$1.50*	£0.20	£0.60	£1.00
2-5 ND	*$0.30*	*$0.90*	*$1.50*	£0.20	£0.60	£1.00
6 ND New Gods X-over	*$0.30*	*$0.90*	*$1.50*	£0.20	£0.60	£1.00
Title Value:	*$1.80*	*$5.40*	*$9.00*	£1.20	£3.60	£6.00

WARLORD (2ND SERIES)

DC Comics,MS; 1 Jan 1992-6 Jun 1992

	$Good	$Fine	$N.Mint	£Good	£Fine	£N.Mint
1-6 Mike Grell covers	*$0.30*	*$0.90*	*$1.50*	£0.20	£0.60	£1.00
Title Value:	*$1.80*	*$5.40*	*$9.00*	£1.20	£3.60	£6.00

WARP

First; 1 Mar 1983-19 1985

	$Good	$Fine	$N.Mint	£Good	£Fine	£N.Mint
1-16 ND Frank Brunner art	*$0.25*	*$0.75*	*$1.25*	£0.15	£0.45	£0.75
17-19 ND scarce in the U.K.	*$0.25*	*$0.75*	*$1.25*	£0.15	£0.45	£0.75
Title Value:	*$4.75*	*$14.25*	*$23.75*	£2.85	£8.55	£14.25

WARP GRAPHICS ANNUAL

Warp; 1 1986

	$Good	$Fine	$N.Mint	£Good	£Fine	£N.Mint
1 ND 64pgs, squarebound; includes new Elfquest story plus Mythadventures, A Distant Soil, Thunderbunny, Panda Khan, Blood of the Innocent, Captain Obese and Unicorn Isle	*$0.60*	*$1.80*	*$3.00*	£0.40	£1.20	£2.00
1 2nd printing ND	*$0.50*	*$1.50*	*$2.50*	£0.30	£0.90	£1.50
Title Value:	*$1.10*	*$3.30*	*$5.50*	£0.70	£2.10	£3.50

WARP SPECIAL

First; 1 Jul 1983-3 Jun 1984

	$Good	$Fine	$N.Mint	£Good	£Fine	£N.Mint
1 ND Chaykin art, features Chaos Prince of Madness origin	*$0.25*	*$0.75*	*$1.25*	£0.15	£0.45	£0.75
2 ND Silvestri/Gustovich art	*$0.25*	*$0.75*	*$1.25*	£0.15	£0.45	£0.75
3 ND Freeman art	*$0.25*	*$0.75*	*$1.25*	£0.15	£0.45	£0.75
Title Value:	*$0.75*	*$2.25*	*$3.75*	£0.45	£1.35	£2.25

WARPWALKING

Caliber Press,MS; 1 Jan 1992-4 Apr 1992

	$Good	$Fine	$N.Mint	£Good	£Fine	£N.Mint
1-4 ND	*$0.40*	*$1.20*	*$2.00*	£0.25	£0.75	£1.25
Title Value:	*$1.60*	*$4.80*	*$8.00*	£1.00	£3.00	£5.00

WARREN PRESENTS

Warren; 1 Jan 1979-12 1982

	$Good	$Fine	$N.Mint	£Good	£Fine	£N.Mint
1-12 ND	*$0.50*	*$1.50*	*$2.50*	£0.30	£0.90	£1.50
Title Value:	*$6.00*	*$18.00*	*$30.00*	£3.60	£10.80	£18.00

Note: most issues are reprint but not distributed in the U.K.

WARRIOR NUN AREALA

Antarctic Press,MS; 1 Dec 1994-3 Apr 1995

	$Good	$Fine	$N.Mint	£Good	£Fine	£N.Mint
1 ND Ben Dunn script and art	*$0.90*	*$2.70*	*$4.50*	£0.60	£1.80	£3.00
1 Signed & Numbered Edition, ND (May 1995) - limited to 5,000 copies	*$2.00*	*$6.00*	*$10.00*	£1.30	£3.90	£6.50
2-3 ND Ben Dunn script and art	*$0.60*	*$1.80*	*$3.00*	£0.40	£1.20	£2.00
Title Value:	*$4.10*	*$12.30*	*$20.50*	£2.70	£8.10	£13.50
Warrior Nun Areala (Jun 1995) ND Trade paperback reprints mini-series				£1.30	£3.90	£6.50
Warrior Nun Areala Vol. 1 Limited Edition Hardcover (Dec 1995) ND reprints mini-series, limited to 1,000 copies. Signed and numbered by Ben Dunn				£3.30	£9.90	£16.50

WARRIOR NUN AREALA AND AVENGELYNE

Antarctic Press,OS; 1 Dec 1996

	$Good	$Fine	$N.Mint	£Good	£Fine	£N.Mint
1 ND Fred Perry script, Ben Dunn art	*$0.60*	*$1.80*	*$3.00*	£0.40	£1.20	£2.00
Title Value:	*$0.60*	*$1.80*	*$3.00*	£0.40	£1.20	£2.00

WARRIOR NUN AREALA BOOK TWO

Antarctic Press,MS; 1 Aug 1995-6 Jun 1996

	$Good	$Fine	$N.Mint	£Good	£Fine	£N.Mint
1-5 ND Ben Dunn script and art	*$0.60*	*$1.80*	*$3.00*	£0.40	£1.20	£2.00
6 ND 40pgs, Ben Dunn script and art	*$0.70*	*$2.10*	*$3.50*	£0.50	£1.50	£2.50
Title Value:	*$3.70*	*$11.10*	*$18.50*	£2.50	£7.50	£12.50
Warrior Nun Areala Book Two Signed Edition (Apr 1996) with certificate, signed by Ben Dunn				£1.30	£3.90	£6.50

WARRIOR NUN AREALA VS. RAZOR

Antarctic Press; 1 May 1996

(see Razor vs. Areala Warrior Nun)

	$Good	$Fine	$N.Mint	£Good	£Fine	£N.Mint
1 ND 40pgs, Ben Dunn art	*$0.60*	*$1.80*	*$3.00*	£0.40	£1.20	£2.00
1 CD Soundtrack Edition, ND pre-bagged with CD soundtrack, new cover	*$2.00*	*$6.00*	*$10.00*	£1.30	£3.90	£6.50
Title Value:	*$2.60*	*$7.80*	*$13.00*	£1.70	£5.10	£8.50

WARRIOR NUN: PORTRAITS

Antarctic Press,OS; nn Mar 1996

	$Good	$Fine	$N.Mint	£Good	£Fine	£N.Mint
nn ND 40pgs, pin-ups by Everette Hartsoe, Bob Burden, Ron Lim and others	*$0.80*	*$2.40*	*$4.00*	£0.50	£1.50	£2.50
Title Value:	*$0.80*	*$2.40*	*$4.00*	£0.50	£1.50	£2.50

WARRIOR OF WAVERLY STREET, THE

Dark Horse,MS; 1 Nov 1996-2 Dec 1996

	$Good	$Fine	$N.Mint	£Good	£Fine	£N.Mint
1-2 ND Manny Coto script, John Stokes art	*$0.60*	*$1.80*	*$3.00*	£0.40	£1.20	£2.00
Title Value:	*$1.20*	*$3.60*	*$6.00*	£0.80	£2.40	£4.00

WARRIORS

Adventure; 1 Nov 1987-7 1988 ?

	$Good	$Fine	$N.Mint	£Good	£Fine	£N.Mint
1 ND Adam Hughes art	*$0.40*	*$1.20*	*$2.00*	£0.25	£0.75	£1.25
2-7 ND	*$0.40*	*$1.20*	*$2.00*	£0.25	£0.75	£1.25
Title Value:	*$2.80*	*$8.40*	*$14.00*	£1.75	£5.25	£8.75

WARRIORS OF PLASM

Defiant; 1 Aug 1993-15 Oct 1994

	$Good	$Fine	$N.Mint	£Good	£Fine	£N.Mint
1 ND Jim Shooter script and David Lapham art begins	*$0.30*	*$0.90*	*$1.50*	£0.20	£0.60	£1.00
2-12 ND	*$0.30*	*$0.90*	*$1.50*	£0.20	£0.60	£1.00
13 ND Schism X-over	*$0.30*	*$0.90*	*$1.50*	£0.20	£0.60	£1.00
14-15 ND	*$0.30*	*$0.90*	*$1.50*	£0.20	£0.60	£1.00
Title Value:	*$4.50*	*$13.50*	*$22.50*	£3.00	£9.00	£15.00
Warriors of Plasm (Feb 1994) Trade paperback reprints issues #1-4 and #0 plus sketches				£1.30	£3.90	£6.50

WARRIORS OF PLASM GRAPHIC NOVEL

Defiant; 1 Nov 1993

	$Good	$Fine	$N.Mint	£Good	£Fine	£N.Mint
1 ND 48pgs, squarebound; Len Wein and Dave Cockrum	*$0.80*	*$2.40*	*$4.00*	£0.50	£1.50	£2.50
Title Value:	*$0.80*	*$2.40*	*$4.00*	£0.50	£1.50	£2.50

WARSTRIKE

Malibu Ultraverse; 1 May 1994-7 Nov 1994

	$Good	$Fine	$N.Mint	£Good	£Fine	£N.Mint
1 ND Walt Simonson cover	*$0.40*	*$1.20*	*$2.00*	£0.25	£0.75	£1.25
2-7 ND	*$0.40*	*$1.20*	*$2.00*	£0.25	£0.75	£1.25
Title Value:	*$2.80*	*$8.40*	*$14.00*	£1.75	£5.25	£8.75

Note: all Non-Distributed on the news-stands in the U.K.

WARWORLD

Dark Horse,OS; 1 Feb 1989

	$Good	$Fine	$N.Mint	£Good	£Fine	£N.Mint
1 ND black and white	*$0.40*	*$1.20*	*$2.00*	£0.25	£0.75	£1.25
Title Value:	*$0.40*	*$1.20*	*$2.00*	£0.25	£0.75	£1.25

WARZONE

Entity Comics,MS; 1 Feb 1995-3 1995

	$Good	$Fine	$N.Mint	£Good	£Fine	£N.Mint
1-3 ND black and white	*$0.60*	*$1.80*	*$3.00*	£0.40	£1.20	£2.00
Title Value:	*$1.80*	*$5.40*	*$9.00*	£1.20	£3.60	£6.00

WASTELAND

DC Comics; 1 Dec 1987-18 Mar 1989

	$Good	$Fine	$N.Mint	£Good	£Fine	£N.Mint
1 LD in the U.K. David Lloyd art	*$0.30*	*$0.90*	*$1.50*	£0.20	£0.60	£1.00
2-4	*$0.30*	*$0.90*	*$1.50*	£0.20	£0.60	£1.00
5 George Freeman cover	*$0.30*	*$0.90*	*$1.50*	£0.20	£0.60	£1.00
5 cover numbered #6, (same story and art as above), Donald Simpson cover	*$0.30*	*$0.90*	*$1.50*	£0.20	£0.60	£1.00
6 ("The Real Number 6" on cover)	*$0.30*	*$0.90*	*$1.50*	£0.20	£0.60	£1.00
7-10	*$0.30*	*$0.90*	*$1.50*	£0.20	£0.60	£1.00
11 David Lloyd art	*$0.30*	*$0.90*	*$1.50*	£0.20	£0.60	£1.00
12-18	*$0.30*	*$0.90*	*$1.50*	£0.20	£0.60	£1.00
Title Value:	*$5.70*	*$17.10*	*$28.50*	£3.80	£11.40	£19.00

Note: all ND apart from #1, Mature Readers label, Deluxe Format. David Lloyd art featured.

WATCHMEN

DC Comics,MS; 1 May 1986-12 Aug 1987

(publication of last issue delayed)

	$Good	$Fine	$N.Mint	£Good	£Fine	£N.Mint
1 ND Dave Gibbons art begins, Alan Moore script and John Higgins colours	*$1.00*	*$3.00*	*$5.00*	£0.60	£1.80	£3.00
2-11 ND	*$0.70*	*$2.10*	*$3.50*	£0.40	£1.20	£2.00
12 ND	*$0.70*	*$2.10*	*$3.50*	£0.50	£1.50	£2.50
Title Value:	*$8.70*	*$26.10*	*$43.50*	£5.10	£15.30	£25.50

Note: all are Deluxe Format, Baxter Paper. All have Dave Gibbons art/Alan Moore script.

	£Good	£Fine	£N.Mint
DC Trade paperback ND reprints #1-12, new cover	£2.00	£6.00	£10.00
Warner Books Edition ND, cover as above	£2.00	£6.00	£10.00
Titan UK Edition Yellow Smiley cover	£1.80	£5.40	£9.00
(Note: 2nd printings available of all the above at 90% value)			
Limited Edition Hardback ND leather-bound with slipcase	£7.00	£21.00	£40.00

WAVEMAKERS

Blind Bat Press; 1 Jan 1990

	$Good	$Fine	$N.Mint	£Good	£Fine	£N.Mint
1 ND black and white	*$0.50*	*$1.50*	*$2.50*	£0.30	£0.90	£1.50
Title Value:	*$0.50*	*$1.50*	*$2.50*	£0.30	£0.90	£1.50

WAXWORK

Blackthorne; (3-D Series #55) 1 1988

	$Good	$Fine	$N.Mint	£Good	£Fine	£N.Mint
1 ND	*$0.50*	*$1.50*	*$2.50*	£0.30	£0.90	£1.50
1 non 3-D issue ND	*$0.40*	*$1.20*	*$2.00*	£0.25	£0.75	£1.25
Title Value:	*$0.90*	*$2.70*	*$4.50*	£0.55	£1.65	£2.75

WAY OUT STRIPS

Fantagraphics; 1 Feb 1994

	$Good	$Fine	$N.Mint	£Good	£Fine	£N.Mint
1 ND Carol Swain script and art; black and white	*$0.40*	*$1.20*	*$2.00*	£0.25	£0.75	£1.25

	$Good	$Fine	$N.Mint	£Good	£Fine	£N.Mint
Title Value:	$0.40	$1.20	$2.00	£0.25	£0.75	£1.25

WEAPON X

Marvel Comics Group; 1 Mar 1995-4 Jun 1995

(title previously called Wolverine)

Issue	$Good	$Fine	$N.Mint	£Good	£Fine	£N.Mint
1 ND Larry Hama script, Adam Kubert art	$0.80	$2.40	$4.00	£0.50	£1.50	£2.50
2-3 ND Larry Hama script, Adam Kubert art	$0.50	$1.50	$2.50	£0.30	£0.90	£1.50
4 ND Larry Hama script, Adam Kubert art; continued in X-Men: Omega	$0.50	$1.50	$2.50	£0.30	£0.90	£1.50
Title Value:	$2.30	$6.90	$11.50	£1.40	£4.20	£7.00
The Ultimate Weapon X (Jul 1995) ND 96pgs, Bookshelf Edtion collects issues #1-4 with etched gold cover				£1.20	£3.60	£6.00

WEAPON ZERO

Image; 0 Jun 1995-4 Oct 1995

Issue	$Good	$Fine	$N.Mint	£Good	£Fine	£N.Mint
0-4 ND Walt Simonson script, Joe Benitez art	$0.50	$1.50	$2.50	£0.30	£0.90	£1.50
Title Value:	$2.50	$7.50	$12.50	£1.50	£4.50	£7.50

WEAPON ZERO (2ND SERIES)

Image; 1 Mar 1996-present

Issue	$Good	$Fine	$N.Mint	£Good	£Fine	£N.Mint
1 ND Walt Simonson script, Joe Benitez art begins	$0.50	$1.50	$2.50	£0.30	£0.90	£1.50
2-9 ND	$0.50	$1.50	$2.50	£0.30	£0.90	£1.50
10 ND Devil's Reign Interlude	$0.50	$1.50	$2.50	£0.30	£0.90	£1.50
Title Value:	$5.00	$15.00	$25.00	£3.00	£9.00	£15.00

WEAPON ZERO T-MINUS

Image,MS; 4 May 1995-1 Aug 1995

Issue	$Good	$Fine	$N.Mint	£Good	£Fine	£N.Mint
1-4 ND Walt Simonson script, Joe Benitez and Batt art	$0.50	$1.50	$2.50	£0.30	£0.90	£1.50
Title Value:	$2.00	$6.00	$10.00	£1.20	£3.60	£6.00

WEAPON ZERO/SILVER SURFER

Marvel Comics Group/Top Cow Comics,OS; 1 Jan 1997

Issue	$Good	$Fine	$N.Mint	£Good	£Fine	£N.Mint
1 ND Devil's Reign part 1, continued in Ghost Rider/Cyblade; Walt Simonson script, Marc Silvestri cover	$0.60	$1.80	$3.00	£0.40	£1.20	£2.00
1 Variant Cover Edition, ND Garney/Wiacek cover; 25% of the print run	$1.00	$3.00	$5.00	£0.80	£2.40	£4.00
Title Value:	$1.60	$4.80	$8.00	£1.20	£3.60	£6.00

WEASEL PATROL

Eclipse,OS; 1 Apr 1989

Issue	$Good	$Fine	$N.Mint	£Good	£Fine	£N.Mint
1 ND	$0.40	$1.20	$2.00	£0.25	£0.75	£1.25
Title Value:	$0.40	$1.20	$2.00	£0.25	£0.75	£1.25

WEAVEWORLD

Marvel Comics Group/Epic,MS; 1 Dec 1991-3 Mar 1992

Issue	$Good	$Fine	$N.Mint	£Good	£Fine	£N.Mint
1-3 ND 48pgs, squarebound; adapts Clive Barker novel	$0.80	$2.40	$4.00	£0.50	£1.50	£2.50
Title Value:	$2.40	$7.20	$12.00	£1.50	£4.50	£7.50

WEB

DC Comics/Impact; 1 Sep 1991-14 Oct 1992

(see Comet, Fly, Jaguar, Shield)

Issue	$Good	$Fine	$N.Mint	£Good	£Fine	£N.Mint
1-8	$0.15	$0.45	$0.75	£0.10	£0.35	£0.60
9 previews Crusaders #1 (see Jaguar #9), trading cards included	$0.15	$0.45	$0.75	£0.10	£0.35	£0.60
10	$0.15	$0.45	$0.75	£0.10	£0.35	£0.60
11 $1.25 covers begin	$0.15	$0.45	$0.75	£0.10	£0.35	£0.60
12-14	$0.15	$0.45	$0.75	£0.10	£0.35	£0.60
Title Value:	$2.10	$6.30	$10.50	£1.40	£4.90	£8.40

Note: Archie character acquired by DC though events take place outside DC Universe continuity

WEB ANNUAL, THE

DC Comics/Impact; 1 May 1992

Issue	$Good	$Fine	$N.Mint	£Good	£Fine	£N.Mint
1 48pgs, Earthquest part 1, leads into Crusaders #1 (see other Impact annuals), includes trading cards	$0.30	$0.90	$1.50	£0.20	£0.60	£1.00
Title Value:	$0.30	$0.90	$1.50	£0.20	£0.60	£1.00

WEB OF HORROR

Major; 1 Dec 1969-3 Apr 1970

Issue	$Good	$Fine	$N.Mint	£Good	£Fine	£N.Mint
1 scarce in the U.K. Wrightson, Kaluta art	$5.25	$16.00	$37.50	£3.55	£10.50	£25.00
2 scarce in the U.K. Wrightson, Kaluta art	$5.00	$15.00	$30.00	£3.30	£10.00	£20.00
3 scarce in the U.K. Wrightson, Kaluta, Brunner	$5.00	$15.00	$30.00	£3.30	£10.00	£20.00
Title Value:	$15.25	$46.00	$97.50	£10.15	£30.50	£65.00

Note: all distributed on the news-stands in the U.K.

WEB OF SCARLET SPIDER

Marvel Comics Group; 1 Nov 1995-4 Jan 1996

Issue	$Good	$Fine	$N.Mint	£Good	£Fine	£N.Mint
1 ND Tom DeFalco script, Paris Karounos and Randy Emberlin art, continued in Amazing Scarlet Spider #1; metallic ink cover	$0.40	$1.20	$2.00	£0.25	£0.75	£1.25
2 ND continued in Amazing Scarlet Spider #2	$0.40	$1.20	$2.00	£0.25	£0.75	£1.25
3 ND continued in New Warriors #67	$0.40	$1.20	$2.00	£0.25	£0.75	£1.25
4 ND Nightmare in Scarlet part 3 (conclusion)	$0.40	$1.20	$2.00	£0.25	£0.75	£1.25
Title Value:	$1.60	$4.80	$8.00	£1.00	£3.00	£5.00

WEB OF SPIDERMAN SUPER-SIZE SPECIAL

Marvel Comics Group,OS; 1 Oct 1995

Issue	$Good	$Fine	$N.Mint	£Good	£Fine	£N.Mint
1 ND 64pgs, Planet of Symbiotes part 5 (conclusion); metallic ink cover	$0.80	$2.40	$4.00	£0.50	£1.50	£2.50
Title Value:	$0.80	$2.40	$4.00	£0.50	£1.50	£2.50

WEB OF SPIDERMAN, THE

Marvel Comics Group; 1 Apr 1985-129 Oct 1995

Issue	$Good	$Fine	$N.Mint	£Good	£Fine	£N.Mint
1 LD in the U.K. Charles Vess cover	$3.30	$10.00	$20.00	£1.30	£4.00	£8.00
2-3	$1.50	$4.50	$7.50	£0.80	£2.40	£4.00
4-5	$1.00	$3.00	$5.00	£0.60	£1.80	£3.00
6 Secret Wars X-over, Zeck art	$1.00	$3.00	$5.00	£0.60	£1.80	£3.00
7	$1.00	$3.00	$5.00	£0.60	£1.80	£3.00
8 Charles Vess cover	$1.00	$3.00	$5.00	£0.60	£1.80	£3.00
9	$1.00	$3.00	$5.00	£0.60	£1.80	£3.00
10 Dominic Fortune appears	$1.00	$3.00	$5.00	£0.60	£1.80	£3.00
11	$0.80	$2.40	$4.00	£0.50	£1.50	£2.50
12 Peter David story	$0.80	$2.40	$4.00	£0.50	£1.50	£2.50
13 Peter David story, Byrne cover	$0.80	$2.40	$4.00	£0.50	£1.50	£2.50
14-15 red costume returns	$0.80	$2.40	$4.00	£0.50	£1.50	£2.50
16-17 red costume returns	$0.80	$2.40	$4.00	£0.40	£1.20	£2.00
18 Venom's hand appears - 1st ever cameo appearance (see Amazing Spiderman #298-300)	$0.80	$2.40	$4.00	£0.40	£1.20	£2.00
19 1st appearance Solo	$0.80	$2.40	$4.00	£0.40	£1.20	£2.00
20-25	$0.80	$2.40	$4.00	£0.35	£1.05	£1.75
26 Charles Vess cover	$0.80	$2.40	$4.00	£0.35	£1.05	£1.75
27-28	$0.80	$2.40	$4.00	£0.35	£1.05	£1.75
29 Wolverine and Hobgoblin appear	$1.80	$5.25	$9.00	£0.90	£2.70	£4.50
30 origin Hobgoblin and The Rose	$1.80	$5.25	$9.00	£0.90	£2.70	£4.50
31 Kraven saga, Zeck art	$1.00	$3.00	$5.00	£0.60	£1.80	£3.00
32 Kraven saga, Zeck art	$1.00	$3.00	$5.00	£0.50	£1.50	£2.50
33 very LD	$0.60	$1.80	$3.00	£0.40	£1.20	£2.00
34 LD in the U.K.	$0.60	$1.80	$3.00	£0.35	£1.05	£1.75
35 LD in the U.K. 1st appearance Tarantula II	$0.60	$1.80	$3.00	£0.35	£1.05	£1.75
36 LD in the U.K. 1st appearance Tombstone	$0.60	$1.80	$3.00	£0.35	£1.05	£1.75
37	$0.60	$1.80	$3.00	£0.30	£0.90	£1.50
38 Hobgoblin appears	$1.00	$3.00	$5.00	£0.40	£1.20	£2.00
39	$0.50	$1.50	$2.50	£0.30	£0.90	£1.50
40 LD in the U.K.	$0.50	$1.50	$2.50	£0.35	£1.05	£1.75
41-45	$0.50	$1.50	$2.50	£0.30	£0.90	£1.50
46 Hulk appears	$0.50	$1.50	$2.50	£0.35	£1.05	£1.75
47 Inferno X-over, Hobgoblin II appears	$0.50	$1.50	$2.50	£0.35	£1.05	£1.75
48 Inferno X-over, origin Hobgoblin II (formerly Jack O'Lantern); X-over Spectacular Spiderman #147	$3.00	$9.00	$15.00	£0.60	£1.80	£3.00
49	$0.50	$1.50	$2.50	£0.30	£0.90	£1.50
50 DS Puma, Prowler, Rocket Racer, Sandman, Silver Sable, Will O' The Wisp appear	$0.50	$1.50	$2.50	£0.30	£0.90	£1.50
51-58	$0.40	$1.20	$2.00	£0.25	£0.75	£1.25
59 Dr. Doom appears; Acts of Vengeance tie-in (2nd part of Super Spidey Saga - see Spectacular Spiderman #158)	$0.80	$2.40	$4.00	£0.40	£1.20	£2.00
60 LD in the U.K. Goliath appears; Acts of Vengeance tie-in, Cosmic Spiderman	$0.60	$1.80	$3.00	£0.30	£0.90	£1.50
61 LD in the U.K. Wizard and Dragon Man appear; Acts of Vengeance tie-in, Cosmic Spiderman	$0.40	$1.20	$2.00	£0.25	£0.75	£1.25
62-63	$0.40	$1.20	$2.00	£0.20	£0.60	£1.00
64 Acts of Vengeance aftermath	$0.40	$1.20	$2.00	£0.20	£0.60	£1.00
65 Super Spidey Saga epilogue	$0.40	$1.20	$2.00	£0.20	£0.60	£1.00
66 Green Goblin appears	$0.40	$1.20	$2.00	£0.20	£0.60	£1.00
67 LD in the U.K. Green Goblin appears	$0.40	$1.20	$2.00	£0.25	£0.75	£1.25
68 ND	$0.40	$1.20	$2.00	£0.20	£0.60	£1.00
69 ND Spiderman vs Hulk	$0.40	$1.20	$2.00	£0.25	£0.75	£1.25
70 ND	$0.40	$1.20	$2.00	£0.20	£0.60	£1.00
71-72 ND Dominic Fortune appears	$0.30	$0.90	$1.50	£0.20	£0.60	£1.00
73 ND Human Torch/Sub-Mariner appear, John Byrne script	$0.30	$0.90	$1.50	£0.20	£0.60	£1.00
74-75 ND Colossus appears	$0.30	$0.90	$1.50	£0.20	£0.60	£1.00
76-77 ND	$0.30	$0.90	$1.50	£0.20	£0.60	£1.00
78 ND Cloak and Dagger appear	$0.30	$0.90	$1.50	£0.20	£0.60	£1.00
79 ND	$0.30	$0.90	$1.50	£0.20	£0.60	£1.00
80 ND Silvermane appears	$0.30	$0.90	$1.50	£0.20	£0.60	£1.00

	$Good	$Fine	$N.Mint	£Good	£Fine	£N.Mint
81-83 ND	*$0.30*	*$0.90*	*$1.50*	£0.20	£0.60	£1.00
84-88 ND Name of the Rose story, Hobgoblin appears	*$0.30*	*$0.90*	*$1.50*	£0.20	£0.60	£1.00
89 ND Name of the Rose story, The Rose becomes Blood Rose, Richard Fisk becomes the new Kingpin	*$0.30*	*$0.90*	*$1.50*	£0.20	£0.60	£1.00
90 ND pre-bagged 30th anniversary issue, hologram cover, gatefold poster	*$0.80*	*$2.40*	*$4.00*	£0.50	£1.50	£2.50
90 2nd printing, ND (Nov 1992) - gold foil hologram cover	*$0.60*	*$1.80*	*$3.00*	£0.40	£1.20	£2.00
91-92 ND	*$0.30*	*$0.90*	*$1.50*	£0.20	£0.60	£1.00
93 ND Moon Knight guest-stars	*$0.30*	*$0.90*	*$1.50*	£0.20	£0.60	£1.00
94 ND Infinity War X-over, Spiderman vs. Hobgoblin	*$0.30*	*$0.90*	*$1.50*	£0.20	£0.60	£1.00
95 ND Spirits of Venom part 1, continued in Spirits of Vengeance #5	*$0.30*	*$0.90*	*$1.50*	£0.20	£0.60	£1.00
96 ND Spirits of Venom part 3, Ghost Rider, John Blaze and Hobgoblin appear, concludes in Spirits of Vengeance #6; painted cover by Mark Texeira	*$0.30*	*$0.90*	*$1.50*	£0.20	£0.60	£1.00
97-99 ND	*$0.30*	*$0.90*	*$1.50*	£0.20	£0.60	£1.00
100 ND 48pgs, holo-grafix foil cover, 1st appearance Spider-armour	*$0.60*	*$1.80*	*$3.00*	£0.40	£1.20	£2.00
101 ND Maximum Carnage part 2, continued in Amazing Spiderman #378	*$0.30*	*$0.90*	*$1.50*	£0.20	£0.60	£1.00
102 ND Maximum Carnage part 6, continued in Amazing Spiderman #379	*$0.30*	*$0.90*	*$1.50*	£0.20	£0.60	£1.00
103 ND Maximum Carnage part 10, continued in Amazing Spiderman #380	*$0.30*	*$0.90*	*$1.50*	£0.20	£0.60	£1.00
104-106 ND Infinity Crusade X-over	*$0.30*	*$0.90*	*$1.50*	£0.20	£0.60	£1.00
106 pre-bagged, ND with copy of Dirt Magazine and audio cassette	*$0.60*	*$1.80*	*$3.00*	£0.40	£1.20	£2.00
107-108 ND Sandman appears	*$0.30*	*$0.90*	*$1.50*	£0.20	£0.60	£1.00
109-111 ND Lizard appears	*$0.30*	*$0.90*	*$1.50*	£0.20	£0.60	£1.00
112 ND Pursuit story, concluded in Spiderman #389	*$0.30*	*$0.90*	*$1.50*	£0.20	£0.60	£1.00
113 ND Gambit and Black Cat appear	*$0.30*	*$0.90*	*$1.50*	£0.20	£0.60	£1.00
113 Collectors Edition, ND, pre-bagged with 16pg preview and animation cel from Spiderman TV series; metallic ink cover	*$0.60*	*$1.80*	*$3.00*	£0.40	£1.20	£2.00
114-116 ND	*$0.30*	*$0.90*	*$1.50*	£0.20	£0.60	£1.00
117 ND Power and Responsibility part 1	*$0.30*	*$0.90*	*$1.50*	£0.20	£0.60	£1.00
117 Collectors Edition, Power and Responsibility part 1, foil stamped cover; incorporates 16pg flip book with second foil stamped cover; continued in Spiderman #394	*$0.60*	*$1.80*	*$3.00*	£0.40	£1.20	£2.00
118-119 ND Venom appears	*$0.30*	*$0.90*	*$1.50*	£0.20	£0.60	£1.00
119 pre-bagged, ND with copy of Marvel Milestone Edition of Amazing Spiderman #150	*$0.60*	*$1.80*	*$3.00*	£0.40	£1.20	£2.00
120 ND 48pgs, Web of Life part 1, continued in Spiderman #54	*$0.50*	*$1.50*	*$2.50*	£0.30	£0.90	£1.50
121 ND Web of Life part 3, continued in Spiderman #55	*$0.30*	*$0.90*	*$1.50*	£0.20	£0.60	£1.00
122-123 ND The Jackal appears	*$0.30*	*$0.90*	*$1.50*	£0.20	£0.60	£1.00
124 ND The Mark of Kaine part 1, continued in Amazing Spiderman #401	*$0.30*	*$0.90*	*$1.50*	£0.20	£0.60	£1.00
125 ND 48pgs, the return of the Gwen Stacy clone	*$0.60*	*$1.80*	*$3.00*	£0.40	£1.20	£2.00
125 Collectors Edition, ND 48pgs,, 3-D holodisk cover, Gwen Stacy clone	*$0.80*	*$2.40*	*$4.00*	£0.50	£1.50	£2.50
126 ND The Trial of Peter Parker part 1, continued in Amazing Spiderman #403	*$0.30*	*$0.90*	*$1.50*	£0.20	£0.60	£1.00
127 ND Maximum Clonage part 2, continued in Amazing Spiderman #404	*$0.30*	*$0.90*	*$1.50*	£0.20	£0.60	£1.00
128 ND Exiled part 1, continued in Amazing Spiderman #405	*$0.30*	*$0.90*	*$1.50*	£0.20	£0.60	£1.00
129 ND Timebomb part 2, continues in Amazing Spiderman #406	*$0.30*	*$0.90*	*$1.50*	£0.20	£0.60	£1.00
Title Value:	*$77.20*	*$231.40*	*$389.50*	£43.40	£130.30	£218.50

WEB OF THE SPIDERMAN ANNUAL, THE

Marvel Comics Group; 1 Sep 1985-10 1994

	$Good	$Fine	$N.Mint	£Good	£Fine	£N.Mint
1 ND	*$0.60*	*$1.80*	*$3.00*	£0.40	£1.20	£2.00
2 ND Arthur Adams art, New Mutants X-over	*$1.00*	*$3.00*	*$5.00*	£0.50	£1.50	£2.50
3 ND scarce in the U.K. all poster issue	*$0.60*	*$1.80*	*$3.00*	£0.40	£1.20	£2.00
4 ND squarebound, Evolutionary War, Ron Lim art	*$0.50*	*$1.50*	*$2.50*	£0.30	£0.90	£1.50
5 ND squarebound, Atlantis Attacks part 11, Fantastic Four appear	*$0.50*	*$1.50*	*$2.50*	£0.30	£0.90	£1.50
6 ND Spiderman's Totally Tiny Adventure part 3 Punisher appears	*$0.50*	*$1.50*	*$2.50*	£0.30	£0.90	£1.50
7 ND The Vibranium Vendetta part 3 (conclusion), Iron Man, Black Panther, Kingpin appear, origins retold of Green Goblin I & II plus Hobgoblin I & II and Venom	*$0.50*	*$1.50*	*$2.50*	£0.30	£0.90	£1.50
8 ND The Hero Killers part 3, New Warriors appear, Venom appears	*$0.50*	*$1.50*	*$2.50*	£0.30	£0.90	£1.50
9 ND 64pgs, pre-bagged with trading card introducing Cadre	*$0.60*	*$1.80*	*$3.00*	£0.40	£1.20	£2.00
10 ND 64pgs, Spiderman vs. Shriek	*$0.60*	*$1.80*	*$3.00*	£0.40	£1.20	£2.00
Title Value:	*$5.90*	*$17.70*	*$29.50*	£3.60	£10.80	£18.00

WEEZUL

Lightning Comics,OS; 1 Aug 1996

	$Good	$Fine	$N.Mint	£Good	£Fine	£N.Mint
1 ND Ale Garza and Cabin Boy art; black and white	*$0.55*	*$1.65*	*$2.75*	£0.35	£1.05	£1.75
Title Value:	*$0.55*	*$1.65*	*$2.75*	£0.35	£1.05	£1.75

WEIRD FALL

Antarctic Press; 1 Jul 1995-3 Nov 1995

	$Good	$Fine	$N.Mint	£Good	£Fine	£N.Mint
1-3 ND Matt Howarth script and art; black and white	*$0.50*	*$1.50*	*$2.50*	£0.30	£0.90	£1.50
Title Value:	*$1.50*	*$4.50*	*$7.50*	£0.90	£2.70	£4.50

WEIRD FANTASY (1ST SERIES)

E.C. Comics; 13 May/Jun 1950-22 Nov/Dec 1953

(formerly A Moon, A Girl, A Romance; becomes Weird Science Fantasy #23 on)

	$Good	$Fine	$N.Mint	£Good	£Fine	£N.Mint
1 number #13 on cover	*$185.00*	*$560.00*	*$1500.00*	£125.00	£375.00	£1000.00
2 number #14 on cover	*$82.50*	*$245.00*	*$580.00*	£55.00	£165.00	£385.00
3 number #15 on cover	*$62.50*	*$190.00*	*$450.00*	£43.00	£125.00	£300.00
4 number #16 on cover	*$62.50*	*$190.00*	*$450.00*	£43.00	£125.00	£300.00
5 number #17 on cover, Wally Wood art	*$55.00*	*$170.00*	*$400.00*	£38.00	£110.00	£265.00
6-10	*$41.00*	*$120.00*	*$285.00*	£27.00	£80.00	£190.00
11-13	*$34.00*	*$100.00*	*$235.00*	£22.00	£65.00	£155.00

Weapon Zero #1

Web of Scarlet Spider #1

Weird Mystery Tales #2

	$Good	$Fine	$N.Mint	£Good	£Fine	£N.Mint
14 Frazetta and Williamson art - 1st time at E.C.	*$48.00*	*$140.00*	*$335.00*	£32.00	£95.00	£225.00
15 Williamson art	*$32.00*	*$95.00*	*$225.00*	£21.00	£62.50	£150.00
16 Williamson art	*$31.00*	*$90.00*	*$215.00*	£20.50	£60.00	£145.00
17-19 Ray Bradbury adaptation	*$31.00*	*$90.00*	*$215.00*	£20.50	£60.00	£145.00
20 Frazetta and Williamson art	*$32.00*	*$95.00*	*$225.00*	£21.00	£62.50	£150.00
21 classic space girl-and-space monster cover by Frazetta and Williamson	*$48.00*	*$140.00*	*$335.00*	£32.00	£95.00	£225.00
22	*$22.50*	*$67.50*	*$160.00*	£15.00	£45.00	£105.00
Title Value:	*$1061.00*	*$3152.50*	*$7650.00*	£708.00	£2095.00	£5100.00

Note: all Non-Distributed on the news-stands in the U.K.

WEIRD FANTASY (2ND SERIES)

Russ Cochran/EC Comics; 1 Oct 1992-present

	$Good	$Fine	$N.Mint	£Good	£Fine	£N.Mint
1 ND reprints begin from original 1950s EC series with exact cover and interior reproduction	*$0.40*	*$1.20*	*$2.00*	£0.25	£0.75	£1.25
2-15 ND	*$0.40*	*$1.20*	*$2.00*	£0.25	£0.75	£1.25
16 ND	*$0.50*	*$1.50*	*$2.50*	£0.30	£0.90	£1.50
Title Value:	*$6.50*	*$19.50*	*$32.50*	£4.05	£12.15	£20.25
Weird Fantasy Annual #1 (Sep 1994) ND reprints issues #1-5 with covers				£1.20	£3.60	£6.00
Weird Fantasy Annual #2 (Jan 1995) ND reprints issues #6-10 with covers				£1.20	£3.60	£6.00
Weird Fantasy Annual #3 (Feb 1996) ND reprints issues #11-14 with covers				£1.20	£3.60	£6.00

WEIRD MYSTERY TALES

DC Comics; 1 Jul/Aug 1972-24 Nov 1975

(see DC 100 Page Super-Spectacular)

	$Good	$Fine	$N.Mint	£Good	£Fine	£N.Mint
1 scarce in the U.K. Bernie Wrightson splash-page, Jack Kirby art and Mike Kaluta cover	*$1.65*	*$5.00*	*$10.00*	£0.80	£2.50	£5.00
2-3 Jack Kirby art	*$0.65*	*$2.00*	*$4.00*	£0.40	£1.25	£2.50
4 2pgs Jim Starlin art	*$0.65*	*$2.00*	*$4.00*	£0.40	£1.25	£2.50
5-10	*$0.65*	*$2.00*	*$4.00*	£0.40	£1.25	£2.50
11-20	*$0.50*	*$1.50*	*$3.00*	£0.30	£1.00	£2.00
21-23 scarce in the U.K.	*$0.50*	*$1.50*	*$3.00*	£0.40	£1.25	£2.50
24 Kaluta art	*$0.50*	*$1.50*	*$3.00*	£0.40	£1.25	£2.50
Title Value:	*$14.50*	*$44.00*	*$88.00*	£9.00	£28.75	£57.50

ARTISTS

Nino art in 5, 6, 9, 13, 16, 21. Wood art in 23.

WEIRD ROMANCE

Eclipse; 1 Feb 1988

(Seduction of the Innocent #9)

	$Good	$Fine	$N.Mint	£Good	£Fine	£N.Mint
1 ND	*$0.40*	*$1.20*	*$2.00*	£0.25	£0.75	£1.25
Title Value:	*$0.40*	*$1.20*	*$2.00*	£0.25	£0.75	£1.25

WEIRD SCIENCE (1ST SERIES)

E.C. Comics; 1 May/Jun 1950-22 Nov/Dec 1953

(formerly Saddle Romances #1-11; becomes Weird Science-Fantasy #23 on)

	$Good	$Fine	$N.Mint	£Good	£Fine	£N.Mint
1 scarce in the U.K. has #12 on cover	*$225.00*	*$670.00*	*$1800.00*	£150.00	£450.00	£1200.00
2 scarce in the U.K. has #13 on cover; classic Feldstein flying saucer cover	*$92.50*	*$275.00*	*$650.00*	£60.00	£185.00	£435.00
3 scarce in the U.K. has #14 on cover	*$75.00*	*$225.00*	*$535.00*	£50.00	£150.00	£355.00
4 scarce in the U.K. has #15 on cover	*$75.00*	*$225.00*	*$535.00*	£50.00	£150.00	£355.00
5-10	*$50.00*	*$150.00*	*$350.00*	£34.00	£100.00	£235.00
11-14	*$34.00*	*$100.00*	*$235.00*	£22.00	£65.00	£155.00
15-16 Williamson art	*$36.00*	*$105.00*	*$250.00*	£23.50	£70.00	£165.00
17-18 Williamson art; Ray Bradbury adaptation	*$36.00*	*$105.00*	*$250.00*	£23.50	£70.00	£165.00
19-20 Ray Bradbury adaptation	*$45.00*	*$135.00*	*$315.00*	£30.00	£90.00	£210.00
21-22 Frazetta, Williamson, Wood art	*$46.00*	*$135.00*	*$325.00*	£31.00	£90.00	£215.00
Title Value:	*$1229.50*	*$3655.00*	*$8840.00*	£818.00	£2435.00	£5885.00

Note: all Non-Distributed on the news-stands in the U.K.

WEIRD SCIENCE (2ND SERIES)

Gladstone; 1 Sep 1990-4 Mar 1991

	$Good	$Fine	$N.Mint	£Good	£Fine	£N.Mint
1 ND 64pgs, reprints Weird Science #22, Weird Fantasy #1	*$0.50*	*$1.50*	*$2.50*	£0.30	£0.90	£1.50
2 ND 64pgs, reprints Weird Science #16, Weird Fantasy #7	*$0.50*	*$1.50*	*$2.50*	£0.30	£0.90	£1.50
3 ND 64pgs, reprints Weird Science #9	*$0.50*	*$1.50*	*$2.50*	£0.30	£0.90	£1.50
4 ND 64pgs, reprints	*$0.50*	*$1.50*	*$2.50*	£0.30	£0.90	£1.50
Title Value:	*$2.00*	*$6.00*	*$10.00*	£1.20	£3.60	£6.00

Note: reprints of 1950s sci-fi material featuring art by Wood, Feldstein, Kamen, Kurtzman and others. Bi-monthly

WEIRD SCIENCE (3RD SERIES)

Russ Cochran/EC Comics; 1 Sep 1992-present

	$Good	$Fine	$N.Mint	£Good	£Fine	£N.Mint
1 ND reprints begin from original 1950s EC series with exact cover and interior reproduction	*$0.40*	*$1.20*	*$2.00*	£0.25	£0.75	£1.25
2-15 ND	*$0.40*	*$1.20*	*$2.00*	£0.25	£0.75	£1.25
Title Value:	*$6.00*	*$18.00*	*$30.00*	£3.75	£11.25	£18.75
Weird Science Annual #1 (Aug 1994 ND reprints five stories with covers, softcover				£1.20	£3.60	£6.00
Weird Science Annual #2 ND reprints five stories with covers, softcover				£1.20	£3.60	£6.00
Weird Science Annual #3 (Dec 1995) ND reprints five stories with covers, softcover				£1.20	£3.60	£6.00

WEIRD SCIENCE-FANTASY (1ST SERIES)

EC Comics; 23 Mar 1954-29 Jun 1955

(formerly Weird Science. Becomes Incredible Science Fiction)

	$Good	$Fine	$N.Mint	£Good	£Fine	£N.Mint
23-24 Williamson, Wood art	*$28.00*	*$82.50*	*$225.00*	£18.50	£55.00	£150.00
25 Williamson, Wood art; Ray Bradbury adaptation	*$28.00*	*$82.50*	*$225.00*	£18.50	£55.00	£150.00
26 flying saucer special issue	*$28.00*	*$82.50*	*$225.00*	£18.50	£55.00	£150.00
27	*$28.00*	*$82.50*	*$225.00*	£18.50	£55.00	£150.00
28 Williamson, Wood art	*$28.00*	*$82.50*	*$225.00*	£18.50	£55.00	£150.00
29 Williamson, Wood art, Frazetta cover	*$47.00*	*$140.00*	*$375.00*	£31.00	£92.50	£250.00
Title Value:	*$215.00*	*$635.00*	*$1725.00*	£142.00	£422.50	£1150.00

Note: all Non-Distributed on the news-stands in the U.K.

WEIRD SCIENCE-FANTASY (1ST SERIES) ANNUAL

E.C. Comics; 1 1952-2 1953

	$Good	$Fine	$N.Mint	£Good	£Fine	£N.Mint
1 very scarce in the U.K.	*$175.00*	*$520.00*	*$1400.00*	£115.00	£355.00	£950.00
2 very scarce in the U.K.	*$115.00*	*$355.00*	*$950.00*	£80.00	£240.00	£650.00
Title Value:	*$290.00*	*$875.00*	*$2350.00*	£195.00	£595.00	£1600.00

WEIRD SCIENCE-FANTASY (2ND SERIES)

Russ Cochran/EC Comics; 1 Nov 1992-present ?

	$Good	$Fine	$N.Mint	£Good	£Fine	£N.Mint
1 ND reprints begin from original 1950s EC series with exact cover and interior reproduction	*$0.30*	*$0.90*	*$1.50*	£0.20	£0.60	£1.00
2-11 ND	*$0.30*	*$0.90*	*$1.50*	£0.20	£0.60	£1.00
Title Value:	*$3.30*	*$9.90*	*$16.50*	£2.20	£6.60	£11.00
Weird-Science Fantasy Annual #1 (Oct 1994) reprints issues #1-5 with covers				£1.20	£3.60	£6.00
Weird-Science Fantasy Annual #2 (Jul 1995) reprints issues #6-11 with covers				£1.70	£5.10	£8.50

WEIRD SUSPENSE

Atlas; 1 Feb 1975-3 Jul 1975

	$Good	$Fine	$N.Mint	£Good	£Fine	£N.Mint
1-3 distributed in the U.K. Tarantula appears	*$0.25*	*$0.75*	*$1.50*	£0.15	£0.50	£1.00
Title Value:	*$0.75*	*$2.25*	*$4.50*	£0.45	£1.50	£3.00

WEIRD TALES ILLUSTRATED

Millennium; 1 May 1992-2 1992

	$Good	$Fine	$N.Mint	£Good	£Fine	£N.Mint
1 ND John Bolton and Kelley Jones art featured	*$0.50*	*$1.50*	*$2.50*	£0.30	£0.90	£1.50
1 Deluxe Edition, ND, squarebound; as above plus art by Tim Vigil and P. Craig Russell, back cover also by John Bolton	*$0.60*	*$1.80*	*$3.00*	£0.40	£1.20	£2.00
2 ND John Bolton, Mike Mignola and P. Craig Russell art featured	*$0.50*	*$1.50*	*$2.50*	£0.30	£0.90	£1.50
Title Value:	*$1.60*	*$4.80*	*$8.00*	£1.00	£3.00	£5.00

WEIRD TALES OF THE MACABRE

Atlas; 1 Jan 1975-2 Mar 1975

	$Good	$Fine	$N.Mint	£Good	£Fine	£N.Mint
1 LD in the U.K. Pat Boyette and Ernie Colon art, Jeff Jones painted cover	*$0.30*	*$1.00*	*$2.00*	£0.30	£1.00	£2.00
2 LD in the U.K. Pat Boyette and John Severin art, Boris Vallejo painted cover	*$0.25*	*$0.75*	*$1.50*	£0.25	£0.75	£1.50
Title Value:	*$0.55*	*$1.75*	*$3.50*	£0.55	£1.75	£3.50

WEIRD WAR TALES

DC Comics; 1 Sep/Oct 1971-124 Jun 1983

	$Good	$Fine	$N.Mint	£Good	£Fine	£N.Mint
1 48pgs	*$2.05*	*$6.25*	*$12.50*	£1.25	£3.75	£7.50
2 48pgs	*$1.25*	*$3.75*	*$7.50*	£0.80	£2.50	£5.00
3 48pgs	*$1.00*	*$3.00*	*$6.00*	£0.65	£2.00	£4.00
4-5 48pgs	*$0.80*	*$2.50*	*$5.00*	£0.50	£1.50	£3.00
6-7	*$0.65*	*$2.00*	*$4.00*	£0.40	£1.25	£2.50
8 Neal Adams inks	*$1.15*	*$3.50*	*$7.00*	£0.55	£1.75	£3.50
9-10	*$0.65*	*$2.00*	*$4.00*	£0.40	£1.25	£2.50
11-30	*$0.55*	*$1.75*	*$3.50*	£0.30	£1.00	£2.00
31-35	*$0.50*	*$1.50*	*$3.00*	£0.25	£0.75	£1.50
36 64pgs	*$0.50*	*$1.50*	*$3.00*	£0.30	£1.00	£2.00
37-42	*$0.50*	*$1.50*	*$3.00*	£0.25	£0.75	£1.50
43 ND	*$0.50*	*$1.50*	*$3.00*	£0.25	£0.85	£1.75
44	*$0.50*	*$1.50*	*$3.00*	£0.25	£0.75	£1.50
45-50 scarce in the U.K.	*$0.50*	*$1.50*	*$3.00*	£0.25	£0.85	£1.75
51-52 scarce in the U.K. Rogers art	*$0.40*	*$1.25*	*$2.50*	£0.25	£0.85	£1.75
53-56	*$0.40*	*$1.25*	*$2.50*	£0.20	£0.60	£1.25
57 scarce in the U.K.	*$0.40*	*$1.25*	*$2.50*	£0.25	£0.75	£1.50
58-60	*$0.40*	*$1.25*	*$2.50*	£0.20	£0.60	£1.25
61 ND science-fiction special	*$0.40*	*$1.25*	*$2.50*	£0.20	£0.60	£1.25
62-63 ND	*$0.40*	*$1.25*	*$2.50*	£0.20	£0.60	£1.25
64 ND Frank Miller art	*$0.65*	*$2.00*	*$4.00*	£0.40	£1.25	£2.50
65-66 ND	*$0.40*	*$1.25*	*$2.50*	£0.20	£0.60	£1.25
67 ND 44pgs	*$0.40*	*$1.25*	*$2.50*	£0.25	£0.75	£1.50
68 ND 44pgs, Frank Miller art	*$0.65*	*$2.00*	*$4.00*	£0.40	£1.25	£2.50

Issue	$Good	$Fine	$N.Mint	£Good	£Fine	£N.Mint
69 ND 44pgs, science-fiction special	*$0.40*	*$1.25*	*$2.50*	£0.25	£0.75	£1.50
70-92	*$0.30*	*$1.00*	*$2.00*	£0.20	£0.60	£1.25
93 1st appearance Creature Commandoes	*$0.40*	*$1.20*	*$2.00*	£0.25	£0.75	£1.25
94-96	*$0.40*	*$1.20*	*$2.00*	£0.25	£0.75	£1.25
97 2nd appearance Creature Commandoes	*$0.40*	*$1.20*	*$2.00*	£0.25	£0.75	£1.25
98	*$0.40*	*$1.20*	*$2.00*	£0.25	£0.75	£1.25
99 dinosaur issue	*$0.40*	*$1.20*	*$2.00*	£0.25	£0.75	£1.25
100 Creature Commandoes full length story	*$0.40*	*$1.20*	*$2.00*	£0.25	£0.75	£1.25
101	*$0.30*	*$0.90*	*$1.50*	£0.20	£0.60	£1.00
102 Creature Commandoes	*$0.30*	*$0.90*	*$1.50*	£0.20	£0.60	£1.00
103-104	*$0.30*	*$0.90*	*$1.50*	£0.20	£0.60	£1.00
105 Creature Commandoes	*$0.30*	*$0.90*	*$1.50*	£0.20	£0.60	£1.00
106-107	*$0.30*	*$0.90*	*$1.50*	£0.20	£0.60	£1.00
108 Creature Commandoes become cover feature	*$0.30*	*$0.90*	*$1.50*	£0.20	£0.60	£1.00
109-110	*$0.30*	*$0.90*	*$1.50*	£0.20	£0.60	£1.00
111 G.I. Robot joins Creature Commandoes	*$0.30*	*$0.90*	*$1.50*	£0.20	£0.60	£1.00
112	*$0.30*	*$0.90*	*$1.50*	£0.20	£0.60	£1.00
113 G.I. Robot as cover feature	*$0.30*	*$0.90*	*$1.50*	£0.20	£0.60	£1.00
114	*$0.30*	*$0.90*	*$1.50*	£0.20	£0.60	£1.00
115-116 Gil Kane covers	*$0.30*	*$0.90*	*$1.50*	£0.20	£0.60	£1.00
117	*$0.30*	*$0.90*	*$1.50*	£0.20	£0.60	£1.00
118 Gil Kane cover	*$0.30*	*$0.90*	*$1.50*	£0.20	£0.60	£1.00
119	*$0.30*	*$0.90*	*$1.50*	£0.20	£0.60	£1.00
120 G.I. Robot as cover feature	*$0.30*	*$0.90*	*$1.50*	£0.20	£0.60	£1.00
121 last Creature Commandoes	*$0.30*	*$0.90*	*$1.50*	£0.20	£0.60	£1.00
122 G.I. Robot as cover feature (last appearance)	*$0.30*	*$0.90*	*$1.50*	£0.20	£0.60	£1.00
123-124	*$0.30*	*$0.90*	*$1.50*	£0.20	£0.60	£1.00
Title Value:	*$56.05*	*$173.95*	*$337.50*	£32.75	£101.80	£199.00

Note: #1-7, 36 are partly reprint.

ARTISTS

Ditko art in 46, 49, 95, 99, 104, 105, 106. Nino art in 9, 11, 13, 16, 23, 24, 25, 31, 36, 55, 61, 69, 70.

FEATURES

Creature Commandos in 93, 97, 102, 105, 108-110, 112, 114, 116. Creature Commandos/War That Time Forgot in 100. Creature Commandos/G.I.Robot in 111, 115. G.I.Robot in 108, 113, 116. War That Time Forgot in 94, 99, 10

WEIRD WESTERN TALES

DC Comics; 12 Jun/Jul 1972-70 Aug 1980

(previously All-Star Western)

Issue	$Good	$Fine	$N.Mint	£Good	£Fine	£N.Mint
12 52pgs, Neal Adams/Wrightson art, 3rd appearance Jonah Hex; Bat-Lash and Pow-Wow Smith reprints	*$4.15*	*$12.50*	*$25.00*	£2.50	£7.50	£15.00
13 Neal Adams art, 4th appearance Jonah Hex and 1st cover appearance	*$2.50*	*$7.50*	*$15.00*	£1.65	£5.00	£10.00
14 5th Jonah Hex appearace; Alex Toth art	*$1.65*	*$5.00*	*$10.00*	£1.05	£3.25	£6.50
15 Neal Adams art; no Jonah Hex	*$1.65*	*$5.00*	*$10.00*	£1.05	£3.25	£6.50
16-17 Jonah Hex	*$0.65*	*$2.00*	*$4.00*	£0.40	£1.25	£2.50
18 Jonah Hex regular series begins	*$1.50*	*$4.50*	*$9.00*	£0.80	£2.50	£5.00
19-28	*$0.65*	*$2.00*	*$4.00*	£0.40	£1.25	£2.50
29 origin Jonah Hex	*$1.25*	*$3.75*	*$7.50*	£0.80	£2.50	£5.00
30-37	*$0.65*	*$2.00*	*$4.00*	£0.40	£1.25	£2.50
38 scarce in the U.K. last Jonah Hex feature	*$0.65*	*$2.00*	*$4.00*	£0.50	£1.50	£3.00
39 origin and 1st appearance Scalp-Hunter; series begins	*$0.50*	*$1.50*	*$3.00*	£0.30	£1.00	£2.00
40-47	*$0.50*	*$1.50*	*$3.00*	£0.30	£1.00	£2.00
48-49 ND 44pgs	*$0.50*	*$1.50*	*$3.00*	£0.35	£1.10	£2.25
50-60	*$0.50*	*$1.50*	*$3.00*	£0.30	£1.00	£2.00
61-70	*$0.50*	*$1.50*	*$3.00*	£0.25	£0.75	£1.50
Title Value:	*$42.35*	*$128.25*	*$256.50*	£25.55	£80.20	£160.50

FEATURES

Cinnamon in 48, 49. El Diablo 12, 13, 15-17. Jonah Hex 12-14, 16-38. Scalphunter in 39-70.

REPRINT FEATURES

Bat Lash, Pow-Wow Smith in 12.

WEIRD WONDER TALES

Marvel Comics Group; 1 Dec 1973-22 May 1977

Issue	$Good	$Fine	$N.Mint	£Good	£Fine	£N.Mint
1 ND horror/fantasy reprints begin	*$0.80*	*$2.50*	*$5.00*	£0.40	£1.25	£2.50
2 ND	*$0.50*	*$1.50*	*$3.00*	£0.30	£1.00	£2.00
3-4 ND	*$0.40*	*$1.25*	*$2.50*	£0.25	£0.75	£1.50
5-11	*$0.40*	*$1.25*	*$2.50*	£0.20	£0.60	£1.25
12-16 ND	*$0.40*	*$1.25*	*$2.50*	£0.25	£0.75	£1.50
17 ND Jack Kirby cover	*$0.40*	*$1.25*	*$2.50*	£0.25	£0.75	£1.50
18 ND	*$0.40*	*$1.25*	*$2.50*	£0.25	£0.75	£1.50
19 ND reprints Dr. Droom origin and 1st appearance from Amazing Adventures (1st) #1 though re-named Dr. Druid; Jack Kirby and Steve Ditko back-up reprints; new Kirby cover	*$0.40*	*$1.25*	*$2.50*	£0.25	£0.75	£1.50
20 ND Dr. Druid (Droom) reprint by Kirby; new Jack Kirby cover	*$0.40*	*$1.25*	*$2.50*	£0.25	£0.75	£1.50
21 ND Dr. Druid (Droom) reprint	*$0.40*	*$1.25*	*$2.50*	£0.25	£0.75	£1.50
22 ND Dr. Druid (Droom) back-up reprints by Jack Kirby, with new Jack Kirby and John Byrne splash-page; Kubert back-up reprint	*$0.40*	*$1.25*	*$2.50*	£0.25	£0.75	£1.50
Title Value:	*$9.30*	*$29.00*	*$58.00*	£5.35	£16.20	£32.75

REPRINT FEATURES

Dr. Droom (re-named Dr.Druid) in 19-22. Venus in 16-18.

WEIRD WORLDS

DC Comics; 1 Sep 1972-9 Jan/Feb 1974; 10 Oct/Nov 1974

Issue	$Good	$Fine	$N.Mint	£Good	£Fine	£N.Mint
1 ND	*$1.15*	*$3.50*	*$7.00*	£0.65	£2.00	£4.00
2 part Neal Adams inks	*$0.80*	*$2.50*	*$5.00*	£0.50	£1.50	£3.00
3 part Neal Adams inks	*$0.50*	*$1.50*	*$3.00*	£0.30	£1.00	£2.00
4 Kaluta art	*$0.50*	*$1.50*	*$3.00*	£0.30	£1.00	£2.00
5-7	*$0.50*	*$1.50*	*$3.00*	£0.30	£1.00	£2.00
8-10 Chaykin art, Ironwolf	*$0.40*	*$1.25*	*$2.50*	£0.25	£0.75	£1.50
Title Value:	*$5.65*	*$17.25*	*$34.50*	£3.40	£10.75	£21.50

FEATURES

Iron Wolf in 8-10. John Carter of Mars in 1-7. Pellucidar in 1-7.

WEIRD, THE

DC Comics,MS; 1 Apr 1988-4 Jul 1988

Issue	$Good	$Fine	$N.Mint	£Good	£Fine	£N.Mint
1-4 LD in the U.K. Justice League X-over	*$0.50*	*$1.50*	*$2.50*	£0.30	£0.90	£1.50
Title Value:	*$2.00*	*$6.00*	*$10.00*	£1.20	£3.60	£6.00

Note: all 48pgs, Starlin scripts, Wrightson art

WELCOME BACK KOTTER

DC Comics,TV; 1 Nov 1976-10 Mar/Apr 1978

(see Limited Collector's Edition C-57)

Issue	$Good	$Fine	$N.Mint	£Good	£Fine	£N.Mint
1 scarce in the U.K.	*$0.30*	*$1.00*	*$2.00*	£0.20	£0.60	£1.25
2-10 scarce in the U.K.	*$0.25*	*$0.75*	*$1.50*	£0.15	£0.50	£1.00
Title Value:	*$2.55*	*$7.75*	*$15.50*	£1.55	£5.10	£10.25

Note: from US TV series.

WENDIGO, THE

Caliber Press,OS; 1 Dec 1991

Issue	$Good	$Fine	$N.Mint	£Good	£Fine	£N.Mint
1 ND film adaptation	*$0.50*	*$1.50*	*$2.50*	£0.30	£0.90	£1.50
Title Value:	*$0.50*	*$1.50*	*$2.50*	£0.30	£0.90	£1.50

WEREWOLF

Dell; 1 Dec 1966-3 Apr 1967

Issue	$Good	$Fine	$N.Mint	£Good	£Fine	£N.Mint
1 distributed in the U.K. Werewolf as secret agent begins	*$1.25*	*$3.85*	*$9.00*	£0.85	£2.55	£6.00
2 distributed in the U.K. origin	*$0.85*	*$2.55*	*$6.00*	£0.55	£1.70	£4.00
3 distributed in the U.K.	*$0.85*	*$2.55*	*$6.00*	£0.55	£1.70	£4.00
Title Value:	*$2.95*	*$8.95*	*$21.00*	£1.95	£5.95	£14.00

WEREWOLF BY NIGHT

Marvel Comics Group; 1 Sep 1972-43 Mar 1977

(see Marvel Spotlight)

Issue	$Good	$Fine	$N.Mint	£Good	£Fine	£N.Mint
1 ND scarce in the U.K. Ploog art	*$7.00*	*$21.00*	*$50.00*	£4.25	£12.50	£30.00
2 ND Ploog art	*$4.55*	*$13.50*	*$27.50*	£2.50	£7.50	£15.00
3 ND Ploog art	*$2.90*	*$8.75*	*$17.50*	£1.65	£5.00	£10.00
4-5 ND Ploog art	*$2.90*	*$8.75*	*$17.50*	£1.25	£3.75	£7.50
6-7 Ploog art	*$2.50*	*$7.50*	*$15.00*	£1.00	£3.00	£6.00
8-10	*$2.05*	*$6.25*	*$12.50*	£0.80	£2.50	£5.00
11-12	*$2.05*	*$6.25*	*$12.50*	£0.65	£2.00	£4.00
13-14 Ploog art	*$2.05*	*$6.25*	*$12.50*	£0.75	£2.25	£4.50
15 ND Werewolf vs. Dracula, Ploog art	*$2.05*	*$6.25*	*$12.50*	£0.80	£2.50	£5.00
16 ND Ploog art	*$2.05*	*$6.25*	*$12.50*	£0.75	£2.25	£4.50
17-18 ND	*$2.05*	*$6.25*	*$12.50*	£0.65	£2.00	£4.00
19 ND Werewolf vs. Dracula	*$2.05*	*$6.25*	*$12.50*	£0.65	£2.00	£4.00
20	*$2.05*	*$6.25*	*$12.50*	£0.55	£1.75	£3.50
21-31	*$1.30*	*$4.00*	*$8.00*	£0.50	£1.50	£3.00
32 1st appearance Moon Knight	*$8.25*	*$25.00*	*$50.00*	£2.50	£7.50	£15.00
33 2nd appearance Moon Knight	*$5.75*	*$17.50*	*$35.00*	£1.25	£3.75	£7.50
34-36	*$0.80*	*$2.50*	*$5.00*	£0.40	£1.25	£2.50
37 Moon Knight appears	*$1.30*	*$4.00*	*$8.00*	£0.50	£1.50	£3.00
38	*$0.80*	*$2.50*	*$5.00*	£0.40	£1.25	£2.50
39 Brother Voodoo appears	*$0.80*	*$2.50*	*$5.00*	£0.40	£1.25	£2.50
40 ND Brother Voodoo appears	*$0.65*	*$2.00*	*$4.00*	£0.30	£1.00	£2.00
41 Brother Voodoo appears	*$0.65*	*$2.00*	*$4.00*	£0.25	£0.75	£1.50
42-43 ND Iron Man appears	*$0.65*	*$2.00*	*$4.00*	£0.30	£1.00	£2.00
Title Value:	*$88.10*	*$268.00*	*$544.50*	£35.05	£106.25	£217.50

WEREWOLF GIANT SIZE

Marvel Comics Group; 2 Oct 1974-5 Jul 1975
(formerly Giant Size Creatures)

Issue	$Good	$Fine	$N.Mint	£Good	£Fine	£N.Mint
2 ND 68pgs, Frankenstein appears, Steve Ditko reprint	*$1.00*	*$3.00*	*$6.00*	£0.65	£2.00	£4.00
3 ND 68pgs	*$0.80*	*$2.50*	*$5.00*	£0.55	£1.75	£3.50
4 ND 68pgs, Morbius appears	*$1.00*	*$3.00*	*$6.00*	£0.65	£2.00	£4.00
5 ND 68pgs	*$0.80*	*$2.50*	*$5.00*	£0.55	£1.75	£3.50
Title Value:	*$3.60*	*$11.00*	*$22.00*	£2.40	£7.50	£15.00

WEREWOLF IN 3-D

Blackthorne; (3-D Series #61) 1 1988

Issue	$Good	$Fine	$N.Mint	£Good	£Fine	£N.Mint
1 ND with 3-D glases (25% less without glasses)	*$0.50*	*$1.50*	*$2.50*	£0.30	£0.90	£1.50
Title Value:	*$0.50*	*$1.50*	*$2.50*	£0.30	£0.90	£1.50

WEST COAST AVENGERS

Marvel Comics Group; 1 Oct 1985-102 Jan 1994

Issue	$Good	$Fine	$N.Mint	£Good	£Fine	£N.Mint
1 ND DS	*$0.50*	*$1.50*	*$2.50*	£0.60	£1.80	£3.00
2-9 ND	*$0.40*	*$1.20*	*$2.00*	£0.40	£1.20	£2.00
10 very LD Thing appears, X-over with Thing #36	*$0.40*	*$1.20*	*$2.00*	£0.40	£1.20	£2.00
11 LD in the U.K.	*$0.30*	*$0.90*	*$1.50*	£0.30	£0.90	£1.50
12-13	*$0.30*	*$0.90*	*$1.50*	£0.20	£0.60	£1.00
14 Daimon Hellstrom 1st called "Hellstorm"	*$0.30*	*$0.90*	*$1.50*	£0.20	£0.60	£1.00
15-19	*$0.30*	*$0.90*	*$1.50*	£0.20	£0.60	£1.00
20 Dr. Strange appears	*$0.30*	*$0.90*	*$1.50*	£0.20	£0.60	£1.00
21	*$0.30*	*$0.90*	*$1.50*	£0.20	£0.60	£1.00
22-23 Dr. Strange and Fantastic Four appear	*$0.30*	*$0.90*	*$1.50*	£0.20	£0.60	£1.00
24-26	*$0.30*	*$0.90*	*$1.50*	£0.20	£0.60	£1.00
27 LD in the U.K. Nick Fury appears	*$0.30*	*$0.90*	*$1.50*	£0.25	£0.75	£1.25
28 LD in the U.K.	*$0.30*	*$0.90*	*$1.50*	£0.25	£0.75	£1.25
29	*$0.30*	*$0.90*	*$1.50*	£0.20	£0.60	£1.00
30 LD in the U.K.	*$0.30*	*$0.90*	*$1.50*	£0.25	£0.75	£1.25
31-41	*$0.30*	*$0.90*	*$1.50*	£0.20	£0.60	£1.00
42 1st John Byrne art on West Coast Avengers; Visionquest begins	*$0.40*	*$1.20*	*$2.00*	£0.25	£0.75	£1.25
43-44 Visionquest; John Byrne art	*$0.30*	*$0.90*	*$1.50*	£0.20	£0.60	£1.00
45 Visionquest; 1st appearance new Vision; John Byrne art	*$0.30*	*$0.90*	*$1.50*	£0.20	£0.60	£1.00
46 1st Great Lakes Avengers; John Byrne art	*$0.30*	*$0.90*	*$1.50*	£0.20	£0.60	£1.00
47 title becomes "Avengers West Coast"; John Byrne art	*$0.30*	*$0.90*	*$1.50*	£0.20	£0.60	£1.00
48-49 John Byrne art	*$0.30*	*$0.90*	*$1.50*	£0.20	£0.60	£1.00
50 original Human Torch appears; John Byrne art	*$0.30*	*$0.90*	*$1.50*	£0.20	£0.60	£1.00
51-52 John Byrne art	*$0.30*	*$0.90*	*$1.50*	£0.20	£0.60	£1.00
53-54 Acts of Vengeance tie-in, John Byrne art	*$0.30*	*$0.90*	*$1.50*	£0.20	£0.60	£1.00
55 LD in the U.K. Acts of Vengeance tie-in, John Byrne art	*$0.30*	*$0.90*	*$1.50*	£0.25	£0.75	£1.25
56-57 John Byrne art	*$0.30*	*$0.90*	*$1.50*	£0.20	£0.60	£1.00
58-59	*$0.30*	*$0.90*	*$1.50*	£0.15	£0.45	£0.75
60-70 LD in the U.K.	*$0.30*	*$0.90*	*$1.50*	£0.20	£0.60	£1.00
71 ND Spiderwoman joins team	*$0.30*	*$0.90*	*$1.50*	£0.20	£0.60	£1.00
72-74 ND	*$0.30*	*$0.90*	*$1.50*	£0.20	£0.60	£1.00
75 ND DS Fantastic Four guest-star	*$0.40*	*$1.20*	*$2.00*	£0.25	£0.75	£1.25
76-78 ND	*$0.30*	*$0.90*	*$1.50*	£0.20	£0.60	£1.00
79 Dr. Strange appears; $1.25 cover begins	*$0.25*	*$0.75*	*$1.25*	£0.15	£0.45	£0.75
80 Galactic Storm part 2; Captain America, Rick Jones and Quasar appear	*$0.25*	*$0.75*	*$1.25*	£0.15	£0.45	£0.75
81 Galactic Storm part 9; Quasar appears	*$0.25*	*$0.75*	*$1.25*	£0.15	£0.45	£0.75
82 Galactic Storm part 16	*$0.25*	*$0.75*	*$1.25*	£0.15	£0.45	£0.75
83	*$0.25*	*$0.75*	*$1.25*	£0.15	£0.45	£0.75
84 Spiderman appears, origin Spiderwoman retold	*$0.25*	*$0.75*	*$1.25*	£0.15	£0.45	£0.75
85-86 Spiderman appears	*$0.25*	*$0.75*	*$1.25*	£0.15	£0.45	£0.75
87-88 Wolverine appears	*$0.25*	*$0.75*	*$1.25*	£0.15	£0.45	£0.75
89-93	*$0.25*	*$0.75*	*$1.25*	£0.15	£0.45	£0.75
94 Jim Rhodes as War Machine joins	*$0.25*	*$0.75*	*$1.25*	£0.15	£0.45	£0.75
95 Darkhawk guest-stars	*$0.25*	*$0.75*	*$1.25*	£0.15	£0.45	£0.75
96-97 Infinity Crusade tie-in	*$0.25*	*$0.75*	*$1.25*	£0.15	£0.45	£0.75
98-99	*$0.25*	*$0.75*	*$1.25*	£0.15	£0.45	£0.75
100 64pgs, red foil embossed cover, Mockingbird dies	*$0.80*	*$2.40*	*$4.00*	£0.50	£1.50	£2.50
101 Blood Ties part 3, X-Men and Magneto appear	*$0.40*	*$1.20*	*$2.00*	£0.40	£1.20	£2.00
102 leads into Force Works #1	*$0.30*	*$0.90*	*$1.50*	£0.30	£0.90	£1.50
Title Value:	*$31.45*	*$94.35*	*$157.25*	£22.45	£67.35	£112.25

WEST COAST AVENGERS ANNUAL

Marvel Comics Group; 1 Oct 1986-8 1993

Issue	$Good	$Fine	$N.Mint	£Good	£Fine	£N.Mint
1 ND	*$0.50*	*$1.50*	*$2.50*	£0.40	£1.20	£2.00
2 ND Silver Surfer X-over	*$0.50*	*$1.50*	*$2.50*	£0.30	£0.90	£1.50
3 ND 64pgs, squarebound, Evolutionary War, new Giant Man appears, Ron Lim art	*$0.50*	*$1.50*	*$2.50*	£0.30	£0.90	£1.50
4 ND squarebound, Atlantis Attacks part 12	*$0.50*	*$1.50*	*$2.50*	£0.30	£0.90	£1.50
5 ND The Terminus Factor part 4, continues in Avengers Annual #19	*$0.50*	*$1.50*	*$2.50*	£0.30	£0.90	£1.50
6 ND The Subterranean Odyssey part 5 (conclusion)	*$0.50*	*$1.50*	*$2.50*	£0.30	£0.90	£1.50
7 ND Assault On Armor City part 2, continues in Iron Man Annual #13, Darkhawk appears	*$0.50*	*$1.50*	*$2.50*	£0.30	£0.90	£1.50
8 ND 64pgs, pre-bagged with trading card introducing Raptor	*$0.60*	*$1.80*	*$3.00*	£0.40	£1.20	£2.00
Title Value:	*$4.10*	*$12.30*	*$20.50*	£2.60	£7.80	£13.00

WEST COAST AVENGERS, THE

Marvel Comics Group,MS; 1 Sep 1984-4 Dec 1984

Issue	$Good	$Fine	$N.Mint	£Good	£Fine	£N.Mint
1 ND Hawkeye, Mockingbird, Iron Man, Tigra, begin	*$0.60*	*$1.80*	*$3.00*	£0.50	£1.50	£2.50
2 ND	*$0.40*	*$1.20*	*$2.00*	£0.40	£1.20	£2.00
3 ND scarce in the U.K.	*$0.40*	*$1.20*	*$2.00*	£0.50	£1.50	£2.50
4 ND	*$0.40*	*$1.20*	*$2.00*	£0.40	£1.20	£2.00
Title Value:	*$1.80*	*$5.40*	*$9.00*	£1.80	£5.40	£9.00

WESTERN COMICS

National Periodical Publications; 78 Nov/Dec 1959-85 Jan/Feb 1961
(see Super DC Giant) (previous issues ND)

Issue	$Good	$Fine	$N.Mint	£Good	£Fine	£N.Mint
78-85 rare in the U.K. Matt Savage appears	*$7.75*	*$23.50*	*$55.00*	£5.25	£16.00	£37.50
Title Value:	*$62.00*	*$188.00*	*$440.00*	£42.00	£128.00	£300.00

WESTERN GUNFIGHTERS

Marvel Comics Group; 1 Aug 1970-33 Nov 1975

Issue	$Good	$Fine	$N.Mint	£Good	£Fine	£N.Mint
1 64pgs, Ghost Rider and Apache Kid plus other western heroes begin (all reprint)	*$1.00*	*$3.00*	*$6.00*	£0.65	£2.00	£4.00
2-3 64pgs	*$0.80*	*$2.50*	*$5.00*	£0.50	£1.50	£3.00
4 64pgs, Barry Windsor Smith art	*$0.80*	*$2.50*	*$5.00*	£0.50	£1.50	£3.00
5-6 64pgs	*$0.80*	*$2.50*	*$5.00*	£0.50	£1.50	£3.00
7 ND 48pgs	*$0.75*	*$2.25*	*$4.50*	£0.45	£1.35	£2.75
8-13 ND all reprint	*$0.65*	*$2.00*	*$4.00*	£0.40	£1.25	£2.50
14 ND all reprint, Steranko cover	*$0.65*	*$2.00*	*$4.00*	£0.40	£1.25	£2.50
15-20 ND all reprint	*$0.65*	*$2.00*	*$4.00*	£0.40	£1.25	£2.50
21-33 ND all reprint	*$0.55*	*$1.75*	*$3.50*	£0.30	£1.00	£2.00
Title Value:	*$21.35*	*$66.50*	*$133.00*	£12.70	£40.10	£80.25

Note: #1-7 are squarebound

ARTISTS

Steranko cover on 14. Williamson reprint in 18.

WESTERN KID, THE

Marvel Comics Group; 1 Dec 1971-5 Aug 1972

Issue	$Good	$Fine	$N.Mint	£Good	£Fine	£N.Mint
1 ND	*$0.80*	*$2.50*	*$5.00*	£0.55	£1.75	£3.50
2 ND	*$0.50*	*$1.50*	*$3.00*	£0.30	£1.00	£2.00
3 Williamson reprint	*$0.50*	*$1.50*	*$3.00*	£0.30	£1.00	£2.00
4-5 ND	*$0.50*	*$1.50*	*$3.00*	£0.30	£1.00	£2.00
Title Value:	*$2.80*	*$8.50*	*$17.00*	£1.75	£5.75	£11.50

WESTERN TEAM-UP

Marvel Comics Group,OS; 1 Nov 1973

Issue	$Good	$Fine	$N.Mint	£Good	£Fine	£N.Mint
1 ND scarce in the U.K. origin/1st appearance The Dakota Kid, rest reprint	*$0.50*	*$1.50*	*$3.00*	£0.50	£1.50	£3.00
Title Value:	*$0.50*	*$1.50*	*$3.00*	£0.50	£1.50	£3.00

WESTERNER, THE

I.W. Super; 15-17 1964

Issue	$Good	$Fine	$N.Mint	£Good	£Fine	£N.Mint
15-17 distributed in the U.K. reprints	*$0.85*	*$2.55*	*$6.00*	£0.55	£1.70	£4.00
Title Value:	*$2.55*	*$7.65*	*$18.00*	£1.65	£5.10	£12.00

WETWORKS

Image; 1 Jul 1994-present

Issue	$Good	$Fine	$N.Mint	£Good	£Fine	£N.Mint
1 ND Whilce Portacio with Brandon Choi	*$1.00*	*$3.00*	*$5.00*	£0.60	£1.80	£3.00
2 ND Whilce Portacio with Brandon Choi	*$0.80*	*$2.40*	*$4.00*	£0.50	£1.50	£2.50
2 Variant Cover Edition, ND cover forms larger picture when combined with variant covers of Deathblow #5, Gen 13 #5, Kindred #3, Stormwatch #10, Team 7 #1, Union #0, WildC.A.T.S. #11	*$1.50*	*$4.50*	*$7.50*	£1.00	£3.00	£5.00
3 ND Whilce Portacio with Brandon Choi	*$0.50*	*$1.50*	*$2.50*	£0.30	£0.90	£1.50
4-7 ND Whilce Portacio script and art	*$0.50*	*$1.50*	*$2.50*	£0.30	£0.90	£1.50

8 ND Wildstorm Rising part 7, continued in Backlash #8; with two foil-bagged painted trading cards.

Issue	$Good	$Fine	$N.Mint	£Good	£Fine	£N.Mint
Cover by Barry Windsor-Smith	$0.50	$1.50	$2.50	£0.30	£0.90	£1.50
8 Newstand Edition, ND (without trading cards)	$0.40	$1.20	$2.00	£0.25	£0.75	£1.25
9-10 ND Whilce Portacio script and art	$0.50	$1.50	$2.50	£0.30	£0.90	£1.50
11-15 ND	$0.50	$1.50	$2.50	£0.30	£0.90	£1.50
16 ND Fire From Heaven part 4, continued in Stormwatch #35	$0.50	$1.50	$2.50	£0.30	£0.90	£1.50
17 ND Fire From Heaven part 11, continued in Stormwatch #36	$0.50	$1.50	$2.50	£0.30	£0.90	£1.50
18-24 ND	$0.50	$1.50	$2.50	£0.30	£0.90	£1.50
Title Value:	$14.70	$44.10	$73.50	£8.95	£26.85	£44.75

WETWORKS SOURCEBOOK

Image; 1 Sep 1994

Issue	$Good	$Fine	$N.Mint	£Good	£Fine	£N.Mint
1 ND information and statistics about Wetworks characters	$0.50	$1.50	$2.50	£0.30	£0.90	£1.50
Title Value:	$0.50	$1.50	$2.50	£0.30	£0.90	£1.50

WHAT IF SPECIAL

Marvel Comics Group,OS; 1 Jun 1988

Issue	$Good	$Fine	$N.Mint	£Good	£Fine	£N.Mint
1 features Iron Man	$0.40	$1.20	$2.00	£0.25	£0.75	£1.25
Title Value:	$0.40	$1.20	$2.00	£0.25	£0.75	£1.25

WHAT IF...? (1ST SERIES)

Marvel Comics Group; 1 Feb 1977-47 Oct 1985

Issue	$Good	$Fine	$N.Mint	£Good	£Fine	£N.Mint
1 ND Spiderman, Fantastic Four	$3.30	$10.00	$20.00	£2.05	£6.25	£12.50
2 ND Hulk, origin Hulk retold	$2.50	$7.50	$15.00	£1.25	£3.75	£7.50
3 ND Avengers (vs. Hulk), Gil Kane/Janson art	$1.65	$5.00	$10.00	£1.00	£3.00	£6.00
4 ND Invaders	$1.65	$5.00	$10.00	£1.00	£3.00	£6.00
5 ND Captain America	$1.65	$5.00	$10.00	£1.00	£3.00	£6.00
6 ND Fantastic Four	$1.25	$3.75	$7.50	£0.80	£2.50	£5.00
7 ND Spiderman	$1.25	$3.75	$7.50	£0.80	£2.50	£5.00
8 ND Daredevil	$1.25	$3.75	$7.50	£0.80	£2.50	£5.00
9 ND Avengers	$1.25	$3.75	$7.50	£0.80	£2.50	£5.00
10 ND Thor	$1.25	$3.75	$7.50	£0.80	£2.50	£5.00
11 ND Jack Kirby art, Fantastic Four	$1.25	$3.75	$7.50	£0.80	£2.50	£5.00
12 ND Hulk	$1.00	$3.00	$5.00	£0.70	£2.10	£3.50
13 ND scarce in the U.K. Conan	$1.00	$3.00	$5.00	£0.70	£2.10	£3.50
14 ND Sgt. Fury	$1.00	$3.00	$5.00	£0.80	£2.40	£4.00
15 ND Nova	$1.00	$3.00	$5.00	£0.70	£2.10	£3.50
16 ND Master of Kung Fu	$1.00	$3.00	$5.00	£0.70	£2.10	£3.50
17 ND Captain Marvel, Spiderwoman, Ghost Rider	$1.50	$4.50	$7.50	£0.80	£2.40	£4.00
18 ND Dr. Strange	$1.00	$3.00	$5.00	£0.70	£2.10	£3.50
19 ND Spiderman	$1.00	$3.00	$5.00	£0.70	£2.10	£3.50
20 ND Avengers	$1.00	$3.00	$5.00	£0.70	£2.10	£3.50
21 Fantastic Four	$0.90	$2.70	$4.50	£0.60	£1.80	£3.00
22 ND Dr.Doom, origin retold	$0.90	$2.70	$4.50	£0.60	£1.80	£3.00
23 ND Hulk	$0.90	$2.70	$4.50	£0.60	£1.80	£3.00
24 ND Spiderman	$0.90	$2.70	$4.50	£0.60	£1.80	£3.00
25 ND Avengers	$0.90	$2.70	$4.50	£0.60	£1.80	£3.00
26 ND Captain America	$0.90	$2.70	$4.50	£0.60	£1.80	£3.00
27 ND X-Men "If Phoenix Had Not Died"; alternative to X-Men #137	$2.00	$6.00	$10.00	£0.80	£2.40	£4.00
28 ND Daredevil, Frank Miller art, Ghost Rider	$2.00	$6.00	$10.00	£1.00	£3.00	£5.00
29 ND Avengers, old X-Men appear, alternative to Avengers Annual #2, Golden cover	$0.90	$2.70	$4.50	£0.60	£1.80	£3.00
30 ND Spiderman	$2.00	$6.00	$10.00	£0.80	£2.40	£4.00
31 ND Wolverine/Hulk, X-Men/Magneto appear	$2.50	$7.50	$12.50	£1.00	£3.00	£5.00
32 ND Avengers	$0.80	$2.40	$4.00	£0.50	£1.50	£2.50
33 ND Galactus/Dazzler, Iron Man	$0.80	$2.40	$4.00	£0.50	£1.50	£2.50
34 ND Humour issue, Marvel crew each draw themselves, Frank Miller/Sienkiewicz art featured	$0.80	$2.40	$4.00	£0.50	£1.50	£2.50
35 ND Frank Miller art, Daredevil/Elektra	$0.90	$2.70	$4.50	£0.60	£1.80	£3.00
36 ND Fantastic Four, John Byrne art that reworks F.F. #1	$0.80	$2.40	$4.00	£0.50	£1.50	£2.50
37 ND The Beast/The Thing, Silver Surfer, old X-Men appear	$0.80	$2.40	$4.00	£0.50	£1.50	£2.50
38 ND Daredevil/Captain America, Vision/Scarlet Witch	$0.80	$2.40	$4.00	£0.50	£1.50	£2.50
39 ND Thor/Conan	$0.80	$2.40	$4.00	£0.50	£1.50	£2.50
40 ND Dr. Strange	$0.80	$2.40	$4.00	£0.50	£1.50	£2.50
41 ND Sub-Mariner	$0.70	$2.10	$3.50	£0.40	£1.20	£2.00
42 ND Invisible Girl, Fantastic Four	$0.70	$2.10	$3.50	£0.40	£1.20	£2.00
43 ND Conan	$0.70	$2.10	$3.50	£0.40	£1.20	£2.00
44 ND Captain America	$0.70	$2.10	$3.50	£0.40	£1.20	£2.00
45 ND Hulk	$0.70	$2.10	$3.50	£0.40	£1.20	£2.00
46 ND Spiderman	$0.70	$2.10	$3.50	£0.40	£1.20	£2.00
47 ND Thor	$0.70	$2.10	$3.50	£0.40	£1.20	£2.00
Title Value:	$54.75	$164.50	$292.50	£32.80	£99.10	£176.50

Note: all 52pgs.

Issue	$Good	$Fine	$N.Mint	£Good	£Fine	£N.Mint
Best of What If Trade paperback (Jan 1992) reprints seven stories, 192pgs				£1.60	£4.80	£8.00

WHAT IF...? (2ND SERIES)

Marvel Comics Group; 1 Jul 1989-present

Issue	$Good	$Fine	$N.Mint	£Good	£Fine	£N.Mint
1 ND Avengers/Evolutionary War	$0.80	$2.40	$4.00	£0.50	£1.50	£2.50
2 ND scarce in the U.K. Daredevil/Kingpin	$0.60	$1.80	$3.00	£0.40	£1.20	£2.00
3 ND Captain America	$0.50	$1.50	$2.50	£0.30	£0.90	£1.50
4 ND Spiderman's black costume	$0.50	$1.50	$2.50	£0.35	£1.05	£1.75
5 ND Wonderman/Vision/Avengers	$0.50	$1.50	$2.50	£0.30	£0.90	£1.50
6 ND X-Men, Ron Lim art	$0.70	$2.10	$3.50	£0.40	£1.20	£2.00
7 ND Wolverine, Rob Liefeld art	$0.90	$2.70	$4.50	£0.50	£1.50	£2.50
8 ND Iron Man	$0.40	$1.20	$2.00	£0.25	£0.75	£1.25
9 ND X-Men	$0.40	$1.20	$2.00	£0.30	£0.90	£1.50
10 ND Punisher	$0.40	$1.20	$2.00	£0.30	£0.90	£1.50
11 ND Fantastic Four	$0.40	$1.20	$2.00	£0.25	£0.75	£1.25
12 ND X-Men/Asgard	$0.40	$1.20	$2.00	£0.25	£0.75	£1.25

Weird Science (2nd) #1

Weird War Tales #93

Weird Western Tales #12

Issue	$Good	$Fine	$N.Mint	£Good	£Fine	£N.Mint
13 ND Professor Xavier	$0.40	$1.20	$2.00	£0.25	£0.75	£1.25
14 ND Captain Marvel	$0.40	$1.20	$2.00	£0.25	£0.75	£1.25
15 ND Fantastic Four	$0.40	$1.20	$2.00	£0.25	£0.75	£1.25
16 ND Wolverine/Conan	$0.60	$1.80	$3.00	£0.30	£0.90	£1.50
17 ND Kraven/Spiderman	$0.40	$1.20	$2.00	£0.25	£0.75	£1.25
18 ND Fantastic Four/Dr. Doom	$0.40	$1.20	$2.00	£0.25	£0.75	£1.25
19 ND The Vision	$0.40	$1.20	$2.00	£0.25	£0.75	£1.25
20-21 ND Spiderman/Mary-Jane Watson/Black Cat	$0.40	$1.20	$2.00	£0.25	£0.75	£1.25
22 ND Silver Surfer, Ron Lim art	$0.40	$1.20	$2.00	£0.25	£0.75	£1.25
23 ND X-Men	$0.40	$1.20	$2.00	£0.25	£0.75	£1.25
24 ND Wolverine as vampire, Dr. Strange's soul in Punisher	$0.40	$1.20	$2.00	£0.25	£0.75	£1.25
25 ND 40pgs, Atlantis Attacks	$0.40	$1.20	$2.00	£0.25	£0.75	£1.25
26 ND Punisher/Daredevil, guest-starring Spiderman, Kingpin, Cloak and Dagger	$0.30	$0.90	$1.50	£0.20	£0.60	£1.00
27 ND Sub-Mariner/Fantastic Four	$0.30	$0.90	$1.50	£0.20	£0.60	£1.00
28 ND DS Captain America, "Iwo Jima" cover (go and look it up)	$0.30	$0.90	$1.50	£0.20	£0.60	£1.00
29 ND Captain America/Avengers, continued from What If #28	$0.30	$0.90	$1.50	£0.20	£0.60	£1.00
30 ND 52pgs, Sue Richards	$0.40	$1.20	$2.00	£0.25	£0.75	£1.25
31 ND Spiderman	$0.30	$0.90	$1.50	£0.20	£0.60	£1.00
32 ND Phoenix, ties in with Days of Future Past story	$0.30	$0.90	$1.50	£0.20	£0.60	£1.00
33 ND Phoenix	$0.30	$0.90	$1.50	£0.20	£0.60	£1.00
34 ND all humour issue featuring The Watcher	$0.30	$0.90	$1.50	£0.20	£0.60	£1.00
35 ND Fantastic Four, ties in with What If (1st series) #1	$0.30	$0.90	$1.50	£0.20	£0.60	£1.00
36 ND Cosmic Avengers vs. Guardians of the Galaxy	$0.30	$0.90	$1.50	£0.20	£0.60	£1.00
37 ND X-Vampires vs. Dormammu	$0.30	$0.90	$1.50	£0.20	£0.60	£1.00
38 ND Thor, ties in to Thor #400	$0.30	$0.90	$1.50	£0.20	£0.60	£1.00
39 ND The Watcher	$0.30	$0.90	$1.50	£0.20	£0.60	£1.00
40 ND Storm, X-Men	$0.30	$0.90	$1.50	£0.20	£0.60	£1.00
41 ND Avengers vs. Galactus	$0.30	$0.90	$1.50	£0.20	£0.60	£1.00
42 ND follow-up to Amazing Spiderman #100-#102, Morbius appears	$0.30	$0.90	$1.50	£0.20	£0.60	£1.00
43 ND Wolverine marrying Mariko	$0.30	$0.90	$1.50	£0.20	£0.60	£1.00
44 ND Punisher Possessed By Venom	$0.30	$0.90	$1.50	£0.20	£0.60	£1.00
45 ND Barbara Ketch as Ghost Rider, Spiderman and Dr. Strange appear	$0.30	$0.90	$1.50	£0.20	£0.60	£1.00
46 ND Cable destroys the X-Men	$0.30	$0.90	$1.50	£0.20	£0.60	£1.00
47 ND X-Men, Avengers and Fantastic Four vs. Magneto	$0.30	$0.90	$1.50	£0.20	£0.60	£1.00
48 ND Daredevil saves Nuke	$0.30	$0.90	$1.50	£0.20	£0.60	£1.00
49 ND Silver Surfer and Infinity Gauntlet	$0.30	$0.90	$1.50	£0.20	£0.60	£1.00
50 ND DS Hulk kills Wolverine, silver-embossed logo	$0.60	$1.80	$3.00	£0.40	£1.20	£2.00
51 ND Punisher as Captain America	$0.30	$0.90	$1.50	£0.20	£0.60	£1.00
52 ND Hulk/Iron Man 2020/Spiderman	$0.30	$0.90	$1.50	£0.20	£0.60	£1.00
53 ND Dr. Doom as Dr. Strange	$0.30	$0.90	$1.50	£0.20	£0.60	£1.00
54 ND Death's Head I & II; Fantastic Four and Captain America appear	$0.30	$0.90	$1.50	£0.20	£0.60	£1.00
55-56 ND Avengers/Galactic Storm	$0.30	$0.90	$1.50	£0.20	£0.60	£1.00
57 ND Punisher/SHIELD	$0.30	$0.90	$1.50	£0.20	£0.60	£1.00
58 ND Punisher/Spiderman	$0.30	$0.90	$1.50	£0.20	£0.60	£1.00
59 ND Wolverine and Alpha Flight; Bryan Hitch art	$0.30	$0.90	$1.50	£0.20	£0.60	£1.00
60 ND three alternatives on the wedding of Scott Summers and Jean Grey; Bryan Hitch art	$0.30	$0.90	$1.50	£0.20	£0.60	£1.00
61 ND Spiderman; with free Spiderman and his Deadly Foes card sheet	$0.30	$0.90	$1.50	£0.20	£0.60	£1.00
62 ND Wolverine vs. Weapon X	$0.30	$0.90	$1.50	£0.20	£0.60	£1.00
63 ND Iron Man and War Machine	$0.30	$0.90	$1.50	£0.20	£0.60	£1.00
64 ND DS Iron Man with Magneto, Rhino and Electro	$0.30	$0.90	$1.50	£0.20	£0.60	£1.00
65 ND Archangel	$0.30	$0.90	$1.50	£0.20	£0.60	£1.00
66 ND Rogue and Avengers	$0.30	$0.90	$1.50	£0.20	£0.60	£1.00
67-68 ND Captain America	$0.30	$0.90	$1.50	£0.20	£0.60	£1.00
69 ND Stryfe/X-Men	$0.30	$0.90	$1.50	£0.20	£0.60	£1.00
70 ND Silver Surfer/Galactus	$0.30	$0.90	$1.50	£0.20	£0.60	£1.00
71 ND Hulk and Red Skull	$0.30	$0.90	$1.50	£0.20	£0.60	£1.00
72 ND Spiderman (alternate origin)	$0.30	$0.90	$1.50	£0.20	£0.60	£1.00
73 ND Daredevil/Kingpin	$0.30	$0.90	$1.50	£0.20	£0.60	£1.00
74 ND X-Men/Mr. Sinister	$0.30	$0.90	$1.50	£0.20	£0.60	£1.00
75 ND Generation X	$0.30	$0.90	$1.50	£0.20	£0.60	£1.00
76 ND Peter Parker/Spiderman	$0.30	$0.90	$1.50	£0.20	£0.60	£1.00
77 ND Legion/Magneto	$0.30	$0.90	$1.50	£0.20	£0.60	£1.00
78 ND Hulk, Spiderman, Ghost Rider and Wolverine	$0.30	$0.90	$1.50	£0.20	£0.60	£1.00
79 ND Storm as Phoenix; Wolverine, Black Panther and Dr. Doom appear	$0.30	$0.90	$1.50	£0.20	£0.60	£1.00
80 ND Hulk	$0.30	$0.90	$1.50	£0.20	£0.60	£1.00
81 ND X-Men and Galactus in the Age of Apocalypse	$0.30	$0.90	$1.50	£0.20	£0.60	£1.00
82 ND J. Jonah Jameson adopts Spiderman	$0.30	$0.90	$1.50	£0.20	£0.60	£1.00
83 ND Daredevil a disciple of Dr. Strange	$0.30	$0.90	$1.50	£0.20	£0.60	£1.00
84 ND Shard and Bishop	$0.30	$0.90	$1.50	£0.20	£0.60	£1.00
85 ND Magneto	$0.30	$0.90	$1.50	£0.20	£0.60	£1.00
86 ND Scarlet Spider kills Spiderman	$0.30	$0.90	$1.50	£0.20	£0.60	£1.00
87 ND Sabretooth slaughters the X-Men (do you feel that there's a pattern developing here?)	$0.30	$0.90	$1.50	£0.20	£0.60	£1.00
88 ND Spiderman mutates	$0.30	$0.90	$1.50	£0.20	£0.60	£1.00
89 ND Reed Richards betrays the Fantastic Four	$0.30	$0.90	$1.50	£0.20	£0.60	£1.00
90 ND Cyclops and Havok	$0.30	$0.90	$1.50	£0.20	£0.60	£1.00
91 ND The Incredible Hulk	$0.30	$0.90	$1.50	£0.20	£0.60	£1.00
92 ND Cannonball and Husk	$0.30	$0.90	$1.50	£0.20	£0.60	£1.00
93 ND Wolverine	$0.30	$0.90	$1.50	£0.20	£0.60	£1.00
94 ND Juggernaut and Professor X	$0.30	$0.90	$1.50	£0.20	£0.60	£1.00
95 ND Ghost Rider	$0.40	$1.20	$2.00	£0.25	£0.75	£1.25
Title Value:	**$33.40**	**$100.20**	**$167.00**	**£21.70**	**£65.10**	**£108.50**

WHAT THE -?!

Marvel Comics Group; 1 Aug 1988-4 Nov 1988; 5 1989-24 Dec 1992

Issue	$Good	$Fine	$N.Mint	£Good	£Fine	£N.Mint
1 ND Punisher	$0.40	$1.20	$2.00	£0.25	£0.75	£1.25
2 ND Superman/Fantastic Four by John Byrne, Wolverine by Mignola	$0.40	$1.20	$2.00	£0.25	£0.75	£1.25
3 ND 2pgs Batman/Joker by Todd McFarlane, X-Men/New Mutants/X-Factor by Kyle Baker	$0.40	$1.20	$2.00	£0.25	£0.75	£1.25
4 ND Archie, Lone Wolf	$0.40	$1.20	$2.00	£0.25	£0.75	£1.25
5 ND Hulk/Punisher/Wolverine, Erik Larsen art	$0.40	$1.20	$2.00	£0.25	£0.75	£1.25
6 ND Alpha Flight/Punisher by John Byrne	$0.30	$0.90	$1.50	£0.20	£0.60	£1.00
7 ND J.L.A/Alpha Flight/Hell-Cat	$0.30	$0.90	$1.50	£0.20	£0.60	£1.00
8 ND Forbush Man	$0.30	$0.90	$1.50	£0.20	£0.60	£1.00
9 ND Marvel Comics Presents featuring Wolverine/ Galactus; John Byrne cover	$0.30	$0.90	$1.50	£0.20	£0.60	£1.00
10 ND X-Men/Akira/Silver Surfer/Vision/Scarlet Witch	$0.30	$0.90	$1.50	£0.20	£0.60	£1.00
11 ND Daredevil/She-Hulk	$0.25	$0.75	$1.25	£0.15	£0.45	£0.75
12 ND Moanin' the Bavarian, John Byrne cover	$0.25	$0.75	$1.25	£0.15	£0.45	£0.75
13 ND Silver Burper, John Byrne cover	$0.25	$0.75	$1.25	£0.15	£0.45	£0.75
14 ND Spittle-Man	$0.25	$0.75	$1.25	£0.15	£0.45	£0.75
15 ND Wolverina, John Byrne cover	$0.25	$0.75	$1.25	£0.15	£0.45	£0.75
16 ND Dr. Octopus, The Watcher	$0.25	$0.75	$1.25	£0.15	£0.45	£0.75

VERY GENERAL PERCENTAGE CONVERSION CHART WHICH MAY BE USED TO CALCULATE LOW AND INBETWEEN GRADES:

Issue	$Good	$Fine	$N.Mint	£Good	£Fine	£N.Mint
17 ND Punisher and Wolverine parodies	$0.25	$0.75	$1.25	£0.15	£0.45	£0.75
18 ND Captain America and Star Trek parodies	$0.25	$0.75	$1.25	£0.15	£0.45	£0.75
19 ND Nick Fury parody	$0.25	$0.75	$1.25	£0.15	£0.45	£0.75
20 ND "Infinity Wart" X-over	$0.25	$0.75	$1.25	£0.15	£0.45	£0.75
21 ND Wolverine, She-Hulk, Ghost Rider parodies	$0.25	$0.75	$1.25	£0.15	£0.45	£0.75
22 ND X-Men	$0.25	$0.75	$1.25	£0.15	£0.45	£0.75
23 ND Super-Pro football parody	$0.25	$0.75	$1.25	£0.15	£0.45	£0.75
24 ND Halloween issue	$0.25	$0.75	$1.25	£0.15	£0.45	£0.75
Title Value:	$7.00	$21.00	$35.00	£4.35	£13.05	£21.75

Note: parody series like Not Brand Echh, originally announced as a mini-series. Published irregularly from #5 on until settling into bi-monthly frequency.

WHAT THE FALL SPECIAL

Marvel Comics Group,OS; 1 Sep 1993

Issue	$Good	$Fine	$N.Mint	£Good	£Fine	£N.Mint
1 ND 64pgs	$0.40	$1.20	$2.00	£0.25	£0.75	£1.25
Title Value:	$0.40	$1.20	$2.00	£0.25	£0.75	£1.25

WHAT THE SUMMER SPECIAL

Marvel Comics Group,OS; 1 Jun 1993

Issue	$Good	$Fine	$N.Mint	£Good	£Fine	£N.Mint
1 ND 64pgs, all X-Men parody issue	$0.40	$1.20	$2.00	£0.25	£0.75	£1.25
Title Value:	$0.40	$1.20	$2.00	£0.25	£0.75	£1.25

WHEEL OF WORLDS, NEIL GAIMAN'S

Tekno Comix; 0 Jul 1995; 1 Mar 1996

Issue	$Good	$Fine	$N.Mint	£Good	£Fine	£N.Mint
0 ND 48pgs, featuring Teknophage, Lady Justice, Mr. Hero and Adam Cain; featuring art by Bryan Talbot, Alan Craddock and Angus McKie	$0.40	$1.20	$2.00	£0.25	£0.75	£1.25
0 Direct Market Edition, ND 48pgs, (Jul 1995) - with double-sided poster and wraparound cover	$0.60	$1.80	$3.00	£0.40	£1.20	£2.00
1 ND 48pgs, Lady Justice appears	$0.65	$1.95	$3.25	£0.45	£1.35	£2.25
Title Value:	$1.65	$4.95	$8.25	£1.10	£3.30	£5.50

WHEELIE AND THE CHOPPER BUNCH

Charlton; 1 Jul 1975-7 Jul 1976

Issue	$Good	$Fine	$N.Mint	£Good	£Fine	£N.Mint
1 John Byrne art	$1.50	$4.50	$9.00	£1.00	£3.00	£6.00
2 John Byrne art	$1.00	$3.00	$6.00	£0.65	£2.00	£4.00
3-7 John Byrne art	$0.80	$2.50	$5.00	£0.55	£1.75	£3.50
Title Value:	$6.50	$20.00	$40.00	£4.40	£13.75	£27.50

Note: irregularly distributed on the news-stands in the U.K.

WHERE CREATURES ROAM

Marvel Comics Group; 1 Jul 1970-8 Sep 1971

Issue	$Good	$Fine	$N.Mint	£Good	£Fine	£N.Mint
1 ND reprints from pre-superhero Marvels begin; Steve Ditko and Jack Kirby reprints featured	$1.00	$3.00	$6.00	£0.65	£2.00	£4.00
2-4 ND	$0.65	$2.00	$4.00	£0.40	£1.25	£2.50
5-6	$0.65	$2.00	$4.00	£0.30	£1.00	£2.00
7-8 ND	$0.65	$2.00	$4.00	£0.40	£1.25	£2.50
Title Value:	$5.55	$17.00	$34.00	£3.25	£10.25	£20.50

Note: all horror/fantasy reprints. Kirby/Ditko art in most issues.

WHERE IN THE WORLD IS CARMEN SANDIEGO?

DC Comics; 1 Jun 1996-present

Issue	$Good	$Fine	$N.Mint	£Good	£Fine	£N.Mint
1-2 ND Barry Liebman script, Sean Taggart art; bi-monthly	$0.35	$1.05	$1.75	£0.25	£0.75	£1.25
3-4 ND Barry Liebmann script, Sean Taggart art; bi-monthly	$0.35	$1.05	$1.75	£0.25	£0.75	£1.25
Title Value:	$1.40	$4.20	$7.00	£1.00	£3.00	£5.00

WHERE MONSTERS DWELL

Marvel Comics Group; 1 Jan 1970-38 Oct 1975

Issue	$Good	$Fine	$N.Mint	£Good	£Fine	£N.Mint
1 ND horror/fantasy reprints from pre-superhero Marvels begin	$1.00	$3.00	$6.00	£0.65	£2.00	£4.00
2-5 ND	$0.65	$2.00	$4.00	£0.30	£1.00	£2.00
6-10	$0.55	$1.75	$3.50	£0.25	£0.85	£1.75
11	$0.50	$1.50	$3.00	£0.25	£0.75	£1.50
12 scarce in the U.K. 48pgs, squarebound	$0.50	$1.50	$3.00	£0.25	£0.85	£1.75
13 Gil Kane cover	$0.50	$1.50	$3.00	£0.25	£0.75	£1.50
14-15 Severin cover	$0.50	$1.50	$3.00	£0.25	£0.75	£1.50
16-20	$0.50	$1.50	$3.00	£0.25	£0.75	£1.50
21 reprints Strange Tales #89 - Fin Fang Foom	$0.40	$1.25	$2.50	£0.25	£0.75	£1.50
22-23	$0.40	$1.25	$2.50	£0.25	£0.75	£1.50
24 ND	$0.40	$1.25	$2.50	£0.25	£0.85	£1.75
25-27	$0.40	$1.25	$2.50	£0.25	£0.75	£1.50
28-29 ND	$0.40	$1.25	$2.50	£0.25	£0.85	£1.75
30	$0.40	$1.25	$2.50	£0.25	£0.75	£1.50
31 ND	$0.40	$1.25	$2.50	£0.25	£0.85	£1.75
32-37	$0.40	$1.25	$2.50	£0.25	£0.75	£1.50
38 ND Williamson art	$0.50	$1.50	$3.00	£0.25	£0.85	£1.75
Title Value:	$18.65	$57.50	$115.00	£10.10	£31.85	£64.25

Note: Kirby/Ditko art in most.

WHISPER (1ST SERIES)

Capital; 1 Dec 1983-2 Mar 1984

Issue	$Good	$Fine	$N.Mint	£Good	£Fine	£N.Mint
1 ND scarce in the U.K.	$0.60	$1.80	$3.00	£0.40	£1.20	£2.00
2 ND scarce in the U.K.	$0.50	$1.50	$2.50	£0.30	£0.90	£1.50
Title Value:	$1.10	$3.30	$5.50	£0.70	£2.10	£3.50

Note: Norm Breyfogle art

WHISPER (2ND SERIES)

First; 1 Jun 1986-37 Jun 1990

Issue	$Good	$Fine	$N.Mint	£Good	£Fine	£N.Mint
1 $1.25 cover begins	$0.30	$0.90	$1.50	£0.20	£0.60	£1.00
2	$0.30	$0.90	$1.50	£0.20	£0.60	£1.00
3-9 Norm Breyfogle cover and pencil art	$0.30	$0.90	$1.50	£0.20	£0.60	£1.00
10 Norm Breyfogle cover and pencil art; $1.75 cover begins	$0.30	$0.90	$1.50	£0.20	£0.60	£1.00
11 Norm Breyfogle cover and pencil art	$0.30	$0.90	$1.50	£0.20	£0.60	£1.00
12-17	$0.30	$0.90	$1.50	£0.20	£0.60	£1.00
18 $1.95 cover begins	$0.30	$0.90	$1.50	£0.20	£0.60	£1.00
19-37	$0.30	$0.90	$1.50	£0.20	£0.60	£1.00
Title Value:	$11.10	$33.30	$55.50	£7.40	£22.20	£37.00

Note: all Non-Distributed on the news-stands in the U.K.

WHISPER SPECIAL

First; 1 Nov 1985

Issue	$Good	$Fine	$N.Mint	£Good	£Fine	£N.Mint
1 ND 64pgs, Steven Grant script, Rich Larson art	$0.50	$1.50	$2.50	£0.30	£0.90	£1.50
Title Value:	$0.50	$1.50	$2.50	£0.30	£0.90	£1.50

WHITE DEVIL

Eternity,MS; 1 Aug 1990-6 1991

Issue	$Good	$Fine	$N.Mint	£Good	£Fine	£N.Mint
1-6 ND pre-bagged owing to sexual/violent content	$0.40	$1.20	$2.00	£0.25	£0.75	£1.25
Title Value:	$2.40	$7.20	$12.00	£1.50	£4.50	£7.50

WHITE FANG MOVIE ADAPTATION

Disney,OS; nn Feb 1991

Issue	$Good	$Fine	$N.Mint	£Good	£Fine	£N.Mint
nn ND 64pgs	$1.20	$3.60	$6.00	£0.80	£2.40	£4.00
Title Value:	$1.20	$3.60	$6.00	£0.80	£2.40	£4.00

Note: banned from sale in U.K.

WHITE LIKE SHE

Dark Horse,MS; 1 May 1994-4 Aug 1994

Issue	$Good	$Fine	$N.Mint	£Good	£Fine	£N.Mint
1-4 ND Bob Fingerman scipt/art; black and white	$0.60	$1.80	$3.00	£0.40	£1.20	£2.00
Title Value:	$2.40	$7.20	$12.00	£1.60	£4.80	£8.00

WHIZ COMICS

Fawcett; 1 (#2) Feb 1940-155 Jun 1953

(see Thrill Comics #1 and Flash Comics #1 in Top 50 Rarest section)

Issue	$Good	$Fine	$N.Mint	£Good	£Fine	£N.Mint
1 origin and 1st appearance (in general distribution) Captain Marvel; no number on cover, number 2 listed inside	$6400.00	$19200.00	$64000.00	£4250.00	£12800.00	£42750.00
2 no number on cover, number 3 listed inside	$550.00	$1650.00	$4400.00	£365.00	£1100.00	£2950.00
3 no number on cover, number 4 listed inside	$300.00	$900.00	$2400.00	£200.00	£600.00	£1600.00
4 scarce in the U.K. no number on cover, number 5 listed inside	$250.00	$750.00	$2000.00	£165.00	£495.00	£1325.00
5 scarce in the U.K.	$200.00	$600.00	$1600.00	£130.00	£400.00	£1075.00
6-10	$190.00	$570.00	$1350.00	£125.00	£385.00	£900.00
11-14	$125.00	$385.00	$900.00	£85.00	£255.00	£600.00
15 origin Sivana	$135.00	$415.00	$975.00	£92.50	£275.00	£650.00
16-18	$135.00	$415.00	$975.00	£92.50	£275.00	£650.00
19-20	$85.00	$255.00	$600.00	£55.00	£170.00	£400.00
21 1st appearance the Lieutenant Marvels	$100.00	$300.00	$700.00	£65.00	£195.00	£465.00
22-24	$77.50	$235.00	$550.00	£50.00	£155.00	£365.00
25 origin and 1st appearance Captain Marvel Jnr. (no mention on cover)	$680.00	$2050.00	$5500.00	£455.00	£1350.00	£3650.00
26-30	$67.50	$200.00	$475.00	£45.00	£135.00	£315.00
31-32	$55.00	$170.00	$400.00	£38.00	£110.00	£265.00
33 Captain Marvel and Spy Smasher team up (and on cover)	$67.50	$200.00	$475.00	£45.00	£135.00	£315.00
34	$45.00	$135.00	$315.00	£30.00	£90.00	£210.00
35 Captain Marvel and Spy Smasher team up (and on cover)	$50.00	$150.00	$360.00	£34.00	£100.00	£240.00
36-40	$45.00	$135.00	$315.00	£30.00	£90.00	£210.00
41 time travel story	$32.00	$95.00	$225.00	£21.00	£62.50	£150.00
42	$32.00	$95.00	$225.00	£21.00	£62.50	£150.00
43 Captain Marvel and Spy Smasher team up (and on cover)	$32.00	$95.00	$225.00	£21.00	£62.50	£150.00
44 patriotic cover, features The Life Story of Captain Marvel	$32.00	$95.00	$225.00	£21.00	£62.50	£150.00
45-50	$32.00	$95.00	$225.00	£21.00	£62.50	£150.00
51-60	$27.00	$80.00	$190.00	£17.50	£52.50	£125.00
61-70	$24.00	$72.50	$170.00	£16.00	£49.00	£115.00
71-80	$22.00	$65.00	$155.00	£15.00	£45.00	£105.00
81-90	$21.00	$62.50	$150.00	£14.00	£43.00	£100.00
91 infinity cover	$21.00	$62.50	$150.00	£14.00	£43.00	£100.00
92-99	$21.00	$62.50	$150.00	£14.00	£43.00	£100.00
100 anniversary issue	$25.00	$75.00	$175.00	£16.00	£49.00	£115.00
101-106	$20.00	$60.00	$140.00	£13.00	£40.00	£92.50
107 photo cover	$20.00	$60.00	$140.00	£13.00	£40.00	£92.50
108-110	$20.00	$60.00	$140.00	£13.00	£40.00	£92.50
111-130	$18.50	$55.00	$130.00	£12.50	£38.00	£87.50

Issue	$Good	$Fine	$N.Mint	£Good	£Fine	£N.Mint
131 dinosaur cover	*$18.50*	*$55.00*	*$130.00*	£12.50	£38.00	£87.50
132-152	*$18.50*	*$55.00*	*$130.00*	£12.50	£38.00	£87.50
153-155 very scarce in the U.K.	*$26.00*	*$77.50*	*$185.00*	£17.50	£52.50	£125.00
Title Value:	*$14236.50*	*$42745.00*	*$121440.00*	£9469.50	£28569.50	£81070.00

Note: like all Golden Age comics, these were not officially distributed on the news-stands in the U.K. but some came over with personnel movements during the Second World War and more regularly as bulk shipments through the news trade. There are many reports of the last 20 or so issues being available at coastal towns/seaside resorts like Blackpool and Brighton and copies have been known with British pence stamps

WHO IS THE CROOKED MAN?

Crusade Comics,MS; 1 Sep 1996-present

Issue	$Good	$Fine	$N.Mint	£Good	£Fine	£N.Mint
1 ND 40pgs, features The Martyr, Scarlet Seven and Garrison; black and white	*$0.70*	*$2.10*	*$3.50*	£0.50	£1.50	£2.50
Title Value:	*$0.70*	*$2.10*	*$3.50*	£0.50	£1.50	£2.50

WHO'S WHO

DC Comics,MS; 1 Mar 1985-26 1987

Issue	$Good	$Fine	$N.Mint	£Good	£Fine	£N.Mint
1 LD in the U.K. George Perez cover	*$0.25*	*$0.75*	*$1.25*	£0.20	£0.60	£1.00
2 LD scarce in the U.K. George Perez cover, Batman feature	*$0.25*	*$0.75*	*$1.25*	£0.25	£0.75	£1.25
3-10 LD in the U.K.	*$0.25*	*$0.75*	*$1.25*	£0.15	£0.45	£0.75
11 LD in the U.K. Joker feature	*$0.25*	*$0.75*	*$1.25*	£0.20	£0.60	£1.00
12-26 LD in the U.K.	*$0.25*	*$0.75*	*$1.25*	£0.15	£0.45	£0.75
Title Value:	*$6.50*	*$19.50*	*$32.50*	£4.10	£12.30	£20.50

Note: Issue #1 & #2 were printed from flexographic plates which tended to become clogged with paper-dust; many copies, especially of issue 1, have heavy ink blotches in the fine tints. All have wraparound covers.

WHO'S WHO (2ND SERIES)

DC Comics,MS; 1 Aug 1990-16 Feb 1992

Issue	$Good	$Fine	$N.Mint	£Good	£Fine	£N.Mint
1 ND 48pgs, Superman cover by Jerry Ordway, features pull-out poster of Atlantis	*$1.00*	*$3.00*	*$5.00*	£0.60	£1.80	£3.00
2 ND 48pgs, art by Arthur Adams/Adam Hughes featured, Flash cover	*$1.00*	*$3.00*	*$5.00*	£0.60	£1.80	£3.00
3 ND 48pgs, Arthur Adams/Adam Hughes art featured, Green Lantern cover	*$1.00*	*$3.00*	*$5.00*	£0.60	£1.80	£3.00
4 ND 48pgs, George Perez/Arthur Adams/Jerry Ordway art featured, Wonder Woman cover	*$1.00*	*$3.00*	*$5.00*	£0.60	£1.80	£3.00
5 ND 48pgs, Batmobile cover, Penguin/Riddler/Poison Ivy entries	*$1.00*	*$3.00*	*$5.00*	£0.60	£1.80	£3.00
6 ND 48pgs, Barbara Gordon/Huntress entries	*$1.00*	*$3.00*	*$5.00*	£0.60	£1.80	£3.00
7 ND 48pgs, Justice League of America cover, Captain Atom/Shade entries	*$1.00*	*$3.00*	*$5.00*	£0.60	£1.80	£3.00
8 ND 48pgs, Aqualad/Butcher/Spectre entries	*$1.00*	*$3.00*	*$5.00*	£0.60	£1.80	£3.00
9 ND 48pgs, Legion of Super-Heroes cover/entries plus Firehawk by Barry Kitson and Hugo Strange by George Perez	*$1.00*	*$3.00*	*$5.00*	£0.60	£1.80	£3.00
10 ND 48pgs, Robin cover, Flash entry by Carmine Infantino	*$1.00*	*$3.00*	*$5.00*	£0.60	£1.80	£3.00
11 ND 48pgs, Guy Gardner cover plus Legion '91	*$1.00*	*$3.00*	*$5.00*	£0.60	£1.80	£3.00
12 ND 48pgs, Aquaman cover plus Mera/Metal Men/Hawkwoman	*$1.00*	*$3.00*	*$5.00*	£0.60	£1.80	£3.00
13 ND 48pgs, Giffen and Stelfreeze art featured, Joker by Brian Bolland	*$1.00*	*$3.00*	*$5.00*	£0.60	£1.80	£3.00
14 ND 48pgs, New Teen Titans cover, Animal Man by Bolland	*$1.00*	*$3.00*	*$5.00*	£0.60	£1.80	£3.00
15 ND 48pgs, Swamp Thing by John Higgins, Doom Patrol	*$1.00*	*$3.00*	*$5.00*	£0.60	£1.80	£3.00
16 ND 56pgs, Catwoman by Brian Stelfreeze (Todd McFarlane missed the deadline), Legion of Super-Heroes	*$1.00*	*$3.00*	*$5.00*	£0.60	£1.80	£3.00
Title Value:	*$16.00*	*$48.00*	*$80.00*	£9.60	£28.80	£48.00

Note: all 48pgs graphic novel size, loose-leaf format featuring all statistical information on dozens of characters.

Note: Binder issued separately in Nov 1990, features cover illustration by George Perez. Binder 2 issued in April 1991 with the cover by Brian Bolland in larger size to contain more leaves

WHO'S WHO IN STAR TREK

DC Comics,MS; 1 Mar 1987-2 Apr 1987

Issue	$Good	$Fine	$N.Mint	£Good	£Fine	£N.Mint
1-2 scarce in the U.K.	*$0.60*	*$1.80*	*$3.00*	£0.30	£0.90	£1.50
Title Value:	*$1.20*	*$3.60*	*$6.00*	£0.60	£1.80	£3.00

Note: all wraparound covers

WHO'S WHO IN THE LEGION

DC Comics,MS; 1 May 1988-7 Nov 1988

Issue	$Good	$Fine	$N.Mint	£Good	£Fine	£N.Mint
1-7	*$0.30*	*$0.90*	*$1.50*	£0.20	£0.60	£1.00
Title Value:	*$2.10*	*$6.30*	*$10.50*	£1.40	£4.20	£7.00

Note: all wraparound covers

WHO'S WHO UPDATE '87

DC Comics,MS; 1 Aug 1987-5 Dec 1987

Issue	$Good	$Fine	$N.Mint	£Good	£Fine	£N.Mint
1 Batgirl/Batman feature	*$0.25*	*$0.75*	*$1.25*	£0.15	£0.45	£0.75
2-5	*$0.25*	*$0.75*	*$1.25*	£0.15	£0.45	£0.75
Title Value:	*$1.25*	*$3.75*	*$6.25*	£0.75	£2.25	£3.75

Note: all wraparound covers

WHO'S WHO UPDATE '88

DC Comics,MS; 1 Aug 1988-4 Nov 1988

Issue	$Good	$Fine	$N.Mint	£Good	£Fine	£N.Mint
1	*$0.25*	*$0.75*	*$1.25*	£0.15	£0.45	£0.75
2 Joker feature	*$0.25*	*$0.75*	*$1.25*	£0.15	£0.45	£0.75
3-4	*$0.25*	*$0.75*	*$1.25*	£0.15	£0.45	£0.75
Title Value:	*$1.00*	*$3.00*	*$5.00*	£0.60	£1.80	£3.00

Note: all wraparound covers

WHO'S WHO UPDATE '93

DC Comics; 1,2 Jan 1993

Issue	$Good	$Fine	$N.Mint	£Good	£Fine	£N.Mint
1-2 ND 48pgs, loose-leaf format, Travis Charest cover	*$1.00*	*$3.00*	*$5.00*	£0.60	£1.80	£3.00
Title Value:	*$2.00*	*$6.00*	*$10.00*	£1.20	£3.60	£6.00

WHODUNNIT?

Eclipse; 1 Jun 1986-3 Jan 1987

Issue	$Good	$Fine	$N.Mint	£Good	£Fine	£N.Mint
1-3 ND	*$0.40*	*$1.20*	*$2.00*	£0.25	£0.75	£1.25
Title Value:	*$1.20*	*$3.60*	*$6.00*	£0.75	£2.25	£3.75

WHY I HATE SATURN GRAPHIC ALBUM

DC Comics/Piranha Press,OS; 1 Jul 1990

Issue	$Good	$Fine	$N.Mint	£Good	£Fine	£N.Mint
1 ND 208pgs, script/art by Kyle Baker	*$2.50*	*$7.50*	*$12.50*	£1.70	£5.00	£8.50
1 2nd printing, ND (Oct 1991), new cover by Kyle Baker	*$2.40*	*$7.00*	*$12.00*	£1.60	£4.80	£8.00
Title Value:	*$4.90*	*$14.50*	*$24.50*	£3.30	£9.80	£16.50

WICKED

Millennium,MS; 1 Nov 1994-4 Jun 1995

Issue	$Good	$Fine	$N.Mint	£Good	£Fine	£N.Mint
1-4 ND Sean Shaw script and art; black and white	*$0.40*	*$1.20*	*$2.00*	£0.25	£0.75	£1.25
Title Value:	*$1.60*	*$4.80*	*$8.00*	£1.00	£3.00	£5.00

WIDOW: BOUND BY BLOOD

Ground Zero Comics,MS; 1 Aug 1996-5 Dec 1996

Issue	$Good	$Fine	$N.Mint	£Good	£Fine	£N.Mint
1 Version A, ND Mike Wolfer script and art; black and white	*$0.70*	*$2.10*	*$3.50*	£0.45	£1.35	£2.25
1 Version B, ND Mike Wolfer script and art; black and white	*$0.70*	*$2.10*	*$3.50*	£0.45	£1.35	£2.25
2-5 ND Mike Wolfer script and art; black and white	*$0.70*	*$2.10*	*$3.50*	£0.45	£1.35	£2.25
Title Value:	*$4.20*	*$12.60*	*$21.00*	£2.70	£8.10	£13.50

WIDOW: METAL GYPSIES

London Night Studios,MS; 1 Aug 1995-2 1995; Ground Zero Comics; 3 Mar 1996-present

Issue	$Good	$Fine	$N.Mint	£Good	£Fine	£N.Mint
1-3 ND Mike Wolfer script and art	*$0.60*	*$1.80*	*$3.00*	£0.40	£1.20	£2.00
Title Value:	*$1.80*	*$5.40*	*$9.00*	£1.20	£3.60	£6.00

WILD ANIMALS

Pacific; 1 Dec 1982

Issue	$Good	$Fine	$N.Mint	£Good	£Fine	£N.Mint
1 ND Scott Shaw, Larry Gonick, Sergio Aragones art	*$0.50*	*$1.50*	*$2.50*	£0.30	£0.90	£1.50
Title Value:	*$0.50*	*$1.50*	*$2.50*	£0.30	£0.90	£1.50

WILD CARDS

Marvel Comics Group/Epic,MS; 1 Sep 1990-4 Dec 1990

Issue	$Good	$Fine	$N.Mint	£Good	£Fine	£N.Mint
1-4 ND 48pgs, Barry Kitson/Jackson Guice art	*$0.50*	*$1.50*	*$2.50*	£0.30	£0.90	£1.50
Title Value:	*$2.00*	*$6.00*	*$10.00*	£1.20	£3.60	£6.00

Note: Bookshelf Format

Issue	$Good	$Fine	$N.Mint	£Good	£Fine	£N.Mint
Trade paperback (Oct 1991), reprints mini-series				£1.80	£5.40	£9.00

WILD DOG

DC Comics,MS; 1 Sep 1987-4 Dec 1987

(see Action Comics)

Issue	$Good	$Fine	$N.Mint	£Good	£Fine	£N.Mint
1-4	*$0.15*	*$0.45*	*$0.75*	£0.10	£0.35	£0.60
Title Value:	*$0.60*	*$1.80*	*$3.00*	£0.40	£1.40	£2.40

WILD DOG SPECIAL

DC Comics,OS; 1 Nov 1989

Issue	$Good	$Fine	$N.Mint	£Good	£Fine	£N.Mint
1 48pgs	*$0.25*	*$0.75*	*$1.25*	£0.15	£0.45	£0.75
Title Value:	*$0.25*	*$0.75*	*$1.25*	£0.15	£0.45	£0.75

WILD KNIGHTS

Eternity; 1 Aug 1988-10 May 1989

Issue	$Good	$Fine	$N.Mint	£Good	£Fine	£N.Mint
1-10 ND Evan Dorkin script, black and white	*$0.40*	*$1.20*	*$2.00*	£0.25	£0.75	£1.25
Title Value:	*$4.00*	*$12.00*	*$20.00*	£2.50	£7.50	£12.50

WILD THING

Marvel UK; 1 Apr 1993-9 Dec 1993

Issue	$Good	$Fine	$N.Mint	£Good	£Fine	£N.Mint
1 embossed cover	*$0.30*	*$0.90*	*$1.50*	£0.20	£0.60	£1.00
2	*$0.25*	*$0.75*	*$1.25*	£0.15	£0.45	£0.75
3 Shield appear	*$0.25*	*$0.75*	*$1.25*	£0.15	£0.45	£0.75
4-5	*$0.25*	*$0.75*	*$1.25*	£0.15	£0.45	£0.75
6 classic Spiderman villains appear including Dr. Octopus, Kraven, Electro and The Vulture	*$0.25*	*$0.75*	*$1.25*	£0.15	£0.45	£0.75
7-9	*$0.25*	*$0.75*	*$1.25*	£0.15	£0.45	£0.75
Title Value:	*$2.30*	*$6.90*	*$11.50*	£1.40	£4.20	£7.00

WILD THINGS

Metro Comics; 1,2 1986

Issue	$Good	$Fine	$N.Mint	£Good	£Fine	£N.Mint
1-2 ND John Workman art	*$0.40*	*$1.20*	*$2.00*	£0.25	£0.75	£1.25
Title Value:	*$0.80*	*$2.40*	*$4.00*	£0.50	£1.50	£2.50

WILD, THE

Eastern; 1 Oct 1988-4 1988

Issue	$Good	$Fine	$N.Mint	£Good	£Fine	£N.Mint
1-4 ND bi-weekly	*$0.30*	*$0.90*	*$1.50*	£0.20	£0.60	£1.00
Title Value:	*$1.20*	*$3.60*	*$6.00*	£0.80	£2.40	£4.00

WILD, WILD WEST, THE

Gold Key; 1 Jun 1966-7 Oct 1969

Issue	$Good	$Fine	$N.Mint	£Good	£Fine	£N.Mint
1 LD scarce in the U.K.	*$17.50*	*$52.50*	*$125.00*	£12.00	£36.00	£85.00
2 LD in the U.K.	*$12.50*	*$39.00*	*$90.00*	£8.50	£26.00	£60.00
3-7 LD in the U.K.	*$10.00*	*$30.00*	*$70.00*	£6.25	£19.00	£45.00
Title Value:	*$80.00*	*$241.50*	*$565.00*	£51.75	£157.00	£370.00

WILD, WILD WEST, THE (2ND SERIES)

Millennium,MS; 1 Oct 1990-4 Jan 1991

	$Good	$Fine	$N.Mint	£Good	£Fine	£N.Mint
1-4 ND Adam Hughes cover, colour	*$0.50*	*$1.50*	*$2.50*	£0.30	£0.90	£1.50
Title Value:	*$2.00*	*$6.00*	*$10.00*	£1.20	£3.60	£6.00

WILDBRATS

Fantagraphics,OS; 1 Sep 1992

	$Good	$Fine	$N.Mint	£Good	£Fine	£N.Mint
1 ND parody of Jim Lee's WildC.A.T.S. (Image)	*$0.40*	*$1.20*	*$2.00*	£0.25	£0.75	£1.25
Title Value:	*$0.40*	*$1.20*	*$2.00*	£0.25	£0.75	£1.25

WILDC.A.T.S

Image; 1 Aug 1992-present

	$Good	$Fine	$N.Mint	£Good	£Fine	£N.Mint
1 ND Jim Lee script/art, includes two trading cards; first appearance WildC.A.T.S.	*$1.00*	*$3.00*	*$5.00*	£0.50	£1.50	£2.50
1 Gold Edition ND	*$3.00*	*$9.00*	*$15.00*	£2.00	£6.00	£10.00
1 Gold Signed Edition, ND signed by Jim Lee	*$5.00*	*$15.00*	*$25.00*	£3.00	£9.00	£15.00
2 ND 1st appearance WetWorks in back-up feature; Jim Lee script/art, includes two trading cards, silver "prism" cover, contains Image #0 coupon 5	*$0.80*	*$2.40*	*$4.00*	£0.50	£1.50	£2.50
2 Newstand Edition, ND white background and black logo, with coupon	*$0.60*	*$1.80*	*$3.00*	£0.40	£1.20	£2.00
2 without coupon ND	*$0.60*	*$1.80*	*$3.00*	£0.40	£1.20	£2.00
3 ND previews Whilce Portacio's "Wetworks"	*$0.80*	*$2.40*	*$4.00*	£0.40	£1.20	£2.00
4 ND pre-bagged with trading card by Jim Lee; 1st appearance Tribe by Larry Stroman	*$0.80*	*$2.40*	*$4.00*	£0.40	£1.20	£2.00
4 Limited Edition, ND pre-bagged with extra trading card, limited to 2.5% of the total print run	*$1.20*	*$3.60*	*$6.00*	£0.80	£2.40	£4.00
5 ND two double gatefold pages	*$0.80*	*$2.40*	*$4.00*	£0.50	£1.50	£2.50
6-7 ND Killer Instinct story	*$0.80*	*$2.40*	*$4.00*	£0.50	£1.50	£2.50
7 Limited Edition, ND as above with additional silver outer card cover	*$3.00*	*$9.00*	*$15.00*	£2.00	£6.00	£10.00
8 ND unauthorised (?) cameos by Clark Kent and Lois Lane, Scott Summers and Jean Grey	*$0.80*	*$2.40*	*$4.00*	£0.50	£1.50	£2.50
9 ND	*$0.80*	*$2.40*	*$4.00*	£0.50	£1.50	£2.50
10 ND 1st appearance Huntsman	*$0.80*	*$2.40*	*$4.00*	£0.50	£1.50	£2.50
11 ND Huntsman appears	*$0.60*	*$1.80*	*$3.00*	£0.40	£1.20	£2.00
11 Variant Cover Edition, ND cover forms larger picture when combined with variant covers of Deathblow #5, Gen 13 #5, Kindred #3, Stormwatch #10, Team 7 #1, Wetworks #2	*$1.50*	*$4.50*	*$7.50*	£0.80	£2.40	£4.00
12-13 ND Huntsman appears	*$0.60*	*$1.80*	*$3.00*	£0.40	£1.20	£2.00
14 ND Image X Month tie-in	*$0.60*	*$1.80*	*$3.00*	£0.40	£1.20	£2.00
15 ND Travis Charest art	*$0.60*	*$1.80*	*$3.00*	£0.40	£1.20	£2.00
16-19 ND Travis Charest art	*$0.50*	*$1.50*	*$2.50*	£0.30	£0.90	£1.50
20 ND Wildstorm Rising part 2, continued in Union #4; with two foil-bagged painted trading cards. Cover by Barry Windsor-Smith, art by Travis Charest	*$0.50*	*$1.50*	*$2.50*	£0.30	£0.90	£1.50
20 Newstand Edition, ND without trading cards	*$0.40*	*$1.20*	*$2.00*	£0.25	£0.75	£1.25
21 ND Travis Charest art	*$0.50*	*$1.50*	*$2.50*	£0.30	£0.90	£1.50
22-24 ND Alan Moore script, Travis Charest art	*$0.50*	*$1.50*	*$2.50*	£0.30	£0.90	£1.50
25 ND 48pgs, Alan Moore script, Travis Charest art; wraparound chromium cover	*$1.00*	*$3.00*	*$5.00*	£0.70	£2.10	£3.50
26 ND Alan Moore script, Travis Charest art	*$0.50*	*$1.50*	*$2.50*	£0.30	£0.90	£1.50
27 ND Alan Moore script, Scott Clark art	*$0.50*	*$1.50*	*$2.50*	£0.30	£0.90	£1.50
28 ND Alan Moore script, Travis Charest art	*$0.50*	*$1.50*	*$2.50*	£0.30	£0.90	£1.50
29 ND Fire From Heaven part 7, continued in Deathblow #27	*$0.50*	*$1.50*	*$2.50*	£0.30	£0.90	£1.50
30 ND Fire From Heaven part 13, continued in Sigma #3	*$0.50*	*$1.50*	*$2.50*	£0.30	£0.90	£1.50
31-32 ND Alan Moore script, Jim Lee art	*$0.50*	*$1.50*	*$2.50*	£0.30	£0.90	£1.50
Title Value:	*$35.50*	*$106.50*	*$177.50*	£21.95	£65.85	£109.75
WildC.A.T.S (1994) Trade paperback						
ND 112pgs, reprints #1-4 pre-bagged with an issue #0				£1.30	£3.90	£6.50
WildC.A.T.S. #10-12: The Director's Cut (Aug 1994)						
ND three 64pg perfect bound editions, signed and numbered by Chris Claremont. 5,000 sets				£12.00	£36.00	£60.00
Way of the Coda: The Collected WildC.A.T.S. Vol. II (Aug 1996)						
Trade paperback ND 112pgs, reprints WildC.A.T.S Coda trilogy				£1.70	£5.10	£8.50

WILDC.A.T.S ADVENTURES

Image; 1 Sep 1994-10 Jun 1995

	$Good	$Fine	$N.Mint	£Good	£Fine	£N.Mint
1-10 ND based on US animated show	*$0.40*	*$1.20*	*$2.00*	£0.25	£0.75	£1.25
Title Value:	*$4.00*	*$12.00*	*$20.00*	£2.50	£7.50	£12.50

WILDC.A.T.S ADVENTURES SOURCEBOOK

Image; 1 Jan 1995

	$Good	$Fine	$N.Mint	£Good	£Fine	£N.Mint
1 ND information and statistics on the characters from the animated series; Jeff Smith cover	*$0.50*	*$1.50*	*$2.50*	£0.30	£0.90	£1.50
Title Value:	*$0.50*	*$1.50*	*$2.50*	£0.30	£0.90	£1.50

WILDC.A.T.S SOURCEBOOK

Image; 1 Sep 1993; 2 Oct 1994

	$Good	$Fine	$N.Mint	£Good	£Fine	£N.Mint
1-2 ND information and statistics about the WildC.A.T.S. team	*$0.50*	*$1.50*	*$2.50*	£0.30	£0.90	£1.50
Title Value:	*$1.00*	*$3.00*	*$5.00*	£0.60	£1.80	£3.00

WILDC.A.T.S SPECIAL

Image,OS; 1 Nov 1993

	$Good	$Fine	$N.Mint	£Good	£Fine	£N.Mint
1 ND Steve Gerber script, Travis Charest art	*$0.80*	*$2.40*	*$4.00*	£0.50	£1.50	£2.50
Title Value:	*$0.80*	*$2.40*	*$4.00*	£0.50	£1.50	£2.50

WILDC.A.T.S: TRILOGY

Image,MS; 1 Jun 1993-3 Aug 1993

	$Good	$Fine	$N.Mint	£Good	£Fine	£N.Mint
1-3 ND Jae Lee and Brandon Choi script/art	*$0.50*	*$1.50*	*$2.50*	£0.30	£0.90	£1.50
Title Value:	*$1.50*	*$4.50*	*$7.50*	£0.90	£2.70	£4.50

WILDSTAR

Image; 1 Sep 1995-present ?

	$Good	$Fine	$N.Mint	£Good	£Fine	£N.Mint
1-3 ND Al Gordon script, Chris Marrinan art	*$0.50*	*$1.50*	*$2.50*	£0.30	£0.90	£1.50
Title Value:	*$1.50*	*$4.50*	*$7.50*	£0.90	£2.70	£4.50

WILDSTAR: SKY ZERO

Image,MS; 1 Mar 1993-4 Nov 1993

	$Good	$Fine	$N.Mint	£Good	£Fine	£N.Mint
1 Jerry Ordway script and art begins	*$0.50*	*$1.50*	*$2.50*	£0.30	£0.90	£1.50
1 Gold Edition, (Mar 1993) - limited to 5,000 copies, embossed cover with gold logo and gold number/date box	*$2.00*	*$6.00*	*$10.00*	£1.20	£3.60	£6.00
2	*$0.40*	*$1.20*	*$2.00*	£0.25	£0.75	£1.25
3 Savage Dragon appears	*$0.40*	*$1.20*	*$2.00*	£0.25	£0.75	£1.25
Title Value:	*$3.30*	*$9.90*	*$16.50*	£2.00	£6.00	£10.00

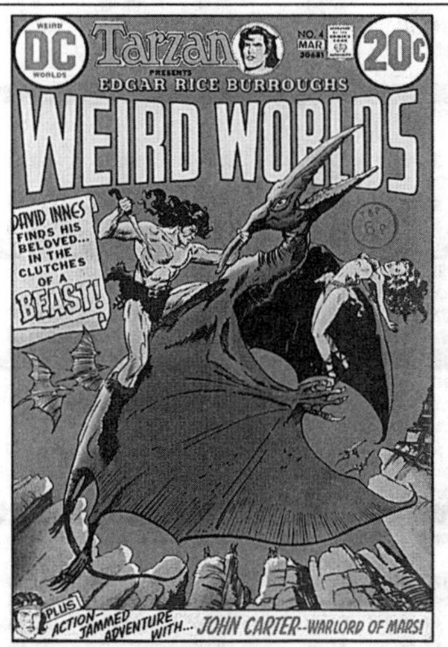

Weird Worlds #4

Welcome Back Kotter #8

Western Gun Fighters #3

	$Good	$Fine	$N.Mint	£Good	£Fine	£N.Mint
Note: all Non-Distributed on the news-stands in the U.K.						
Wildstar: Sky Zero (Aug 1994)						
Trade paperback reprints mini-series with 2 extra story pages				£1.70	£5.10	£8.50

WILDSTAR: THE SERIES - ASHCAN

	$Good	$Fine	$N.Mint	£Good	£Fine	£N.Mint
Image,OS; nn Aug 1995						
nn ND 16pgs, black and white	**$0.20**	**$0.60**	**$1.00**	**£0.15**	**£0.45**	**£0.75**
Title Value:	**$0.20**	**$0.60**	**$1.00**	**£0.15**	**£0.45**	**£0.75**

WILDSTORM

	$Good	$Fine	$N.Mint	£Good	£Fine	£N.Mint
Image,MS; 1 Aug 1995-4 Nov 1995						
1-4 ND	**$0.50**	**$1.50**	**$2.50**	**£0.30**	**£0.90**	**£1.50**
Title Value:	**$2.00**	**$6.00**	**$10.00**	**£1.20**	**£3.60**	**£6.00**

WILDSTORM RARITIES

	$Good	$Fine	$N.Mint	£Good	£Fine	£N.Mint
Image,OS; 1 Dec 1994						
1 ND Gen 13 appear	**$1.00**	**$3.00**	**$5.00**	**£0.70**	**£2.10**	**£3.50**
Title Value:	**$1.00**	**$3.00**	**$5.00**	**£0.70**	**£2.10**	**£3.50**

WILDSTORM RISING

	$Good	$Fine	$N.Mint	£Good	£Fine	£N.Mint
Image,MS; 1,10 May 1995						
1 ND James Robinson script, Barry Windsor-Smith cover and art; with two foil-bagged painted trading cards; story continued in WildC.A.T.S. #20	**$0.50**	**$1.50**	**$2.50**	**£0.30**	**£0.90**	**£1.50**
1 Newstand Edition, ND without trading cards	**$0.40**	**$1.20**	**$2.00**	**£0.25**	**£0.75**	**£1.25**
10 ND James Robinson script, Barry Windsor-Smith cover and art; with two foil-bagged painted trading cards	**$0.50**	**$1.50**	**$2.50**	**£0.30**	**£0.90**	**£1.50**
10 Newstand Edition, ND without trading cards	**$0.40**	**$1.20**	**$2.00**	**£0.25**	**£0.75**	**£1.25**
Title Value:	**$1.80**	**$5.40**	**$9.00**	**£1.10**	**£3.30**	**£5.50**

WILDSTORM RISING CHECKLIST

Cross-over series from Image by James Robison and Barry Windsor-Smith. The issue story order is as follows:

Prologue - Team 7 - Objective Hell #1
Part 1 - Wildstorm Rising Part 1
Part 2 - WildC.A.T.S. #20
Part 3 - Union #4
Part 4 - Gen 13 #2
Part 5 - Grifter #1
Part 6 - Deathblow #16
Part 7 - Wetworks #8
Part 8 - Backlash #8
Part 9 - Stormwatch #22
Part 10 - Wildstorm Rising Part 10

WILDSTORM RISING TRADE PAPERBACK

	$Good	$Fine	$N.Mint	£Good	£Fine	£N.Mint
Image,OS; nn Oct 1995						
nn ND	**$3.00**	**$9.00**	**$15.00**	**£2.00**	**£6.00**	**£10.00**
Title Value:	**$3.00**	**$9.00**	**$15.00**	**£2.00**	**£6.00**	**£10.00**

WILDSTORM SOURCEBOOK

	$Good	$Fine	$N.Mint	£Good	£Fine	£N.Mint
Image,OS; 1 May 1995						
1 ND guide to the Wildstorm Rising cross-over story	**$0.50**	**$1.50**	**$2.50**	**£0.30**	**£0.90**	**£1.50**
Title Value:	**$0.50**	**$1.50**	**$2.50**	**£0.30**	**£0.90**	**£1.50**

WILDSTORM SWIMSUIT SPECIAL

	$Good	$Fine	$N.Mint	£Good	£Fine	£N.Mint
Image,OS; 1 Dec 1994; 2 Aug 1995						
1 ND Jim Lee art featured	**$0.60**	**$1.80**	**$3.00**	**£0.40**	**£1.20**	**£2.00**
2 ND Jim Lee cover and featured in art	**$0.50**	**$1.50**	**$2.50**	**£0.30**	**£0.90**	**£1.50**
Title Value:	**$1.10**	**$3.30**	**$5.50**	**£0.70**	**£2.10**	**£3.50**

WILDSTORM UNIVERSE '97

	$Good	$Fine	$N.Mint	£Good	£Fine	£N.Mint
Image; 1 Dec 1996-present						
1-2 ND character profiles and statistics	**$0.50**	**$1.50**	**$2.50**	**£0.30**	**£0.90**	**£1.50**
Title Value:	**$1.00**	**$3.00**	**$5.00**	**£0.60**	**£1.80**	**£3.00**

WILDSTORM'S CHAMBER OF HORRORS

	$Good	$Fine	$N.Mint	£Good	£Fine	£N.Mint
Image,OS; 1 Oct 1995						
1 ND 48pgs, Simon Bisley cover	**$0.70**	**$2.10**	**$3.50**	**£0.50**	**£1.50**	**£2.50**
Title Value:	**$0.70**	**$2.10**	**$3.50**	**£0.50**	**£1.50**	**£2.50**

WILDSTORM'S WINTER WONDERFEST!

	$Good	$Fine	$N.Mint	£Good	£Fine	£N.Mint
Image,OS; 1 Dec 1995						
1 ND 48pgs, collection of stories featuring work by Steve Grant	**$0.70**	**$2.10**	**$3.50**	**£0.50**	**£1.50**	**£2.50**
Title Value:	**$0.70**	**$2.10**	**$3.50**	**£0.50**	**£1.50**	**£2.50**

WILL EISNER'S 3-D CLASSICS FEATURING THE SPIRIT

	$Good	$Fine	$N.Mint	£Good	£Fine	£N.Mint
Kitchen Sink,OS; 1 Dec 1985						
1 ND Spirit reprints, with 3-D glasses	**$0.60**	**$1.80**	**$3.00**	**£0.40**	**£1.20**	**£2.00**
Title Value:	**$0.60**	**$1.80**	**$3.00**	**£0.40**	**£1.20**	**£2.00**

WILL EISNER'S QUARTERLY

	$Good	$Fine	$N.Mint	£Good	£Fine	£N.Mint
Kitchen Sink,Magazine; 1 1984-8 1986						
1 ND	**$1.20**	**$3.60**	**$6.00**	**£0.80**	**£2.40**	**£4.00**
2-3 ND	**$0.90**	**$2.70**	**$4.50**	**£0.60**	**£1.80**	**£3.00**
4-6 ND giants, squarebound	**$1.20**	**$3.60**	**$6.00**	**£0.80**	**£2.40**	**£4.00**
7-8 ND	**$0.60**	**$1.80**	**$3.00**	**£0.40**	**£1.20**	**£2.00**
Title Value:	**$7.80**	**$23.40**	**$39.00**	**£5.20**	**£15.60**	**£26.00**

WILLOW

	$Good	$Fine	$N.Mint	£Good	£Fine	£N.Mint
Marvel Comics Group,MS Film; 1 Aug 1988-3 Oct 1988						
(see Marvel Graphic Novel)						
1-3 ND reprints Graphic Novel	**$0.15**	**$0.45**	**$0.75**	**£0.10**	**£0.35**	**£0.60**

	$Good	$Fine	$N.Mint	£Good	£Fine	£N.Mint
Title Value:	**$0.45**	**$1.35**	**$2.25**	**£0.30**	**£1.05**	**£1.80**

WIN A PRIZE COMICS

	$Good	$Fine	$N.Mint	£Good	£Fine	£N.Mint
Charlton; 1 Feb 1955-2 Apr 1955						
1 Edgar Allen Poe adaptation featured; lead story by Joe Simon and Jack Kirby (9pgs)	**$62.50**	**$185.00**	**$500.00**	**£44.00**	**£130.00**	**£350.00**
2 Joe Simon and Jack Kirby art (4pgs)	**$47.00**	**$140.00**	**$375.00**	**£31.00**	**£92.50**	**£250.00**
Title Value:	**$109.50**	**$325.00**	**$875.00**	**£75.00**	**£222.50**	**£600.00**
Note: both issues not distributed on the news-stands in the U.K.						

WINDY AND WILLY

	$Good	$Fine	$N.Mint	£Good	£Fine	£N.Mint
DC Comics; 1 May/Jun 1969-4 Nov/Dec 1969						
(see Showcase #81)						
1-4 very scarce in the U.K.	**$1.05**	**$3.20**	**$7.50**	**£0.55**	**£1.70**	**£4.00**
Title Value:	**$4.20**	**$12.80**	**$30.00**	**£2.20**	**£6.80**	**£16.00**
Note: reprints from 1950s/60s humour title with some art changes.						

WINGBIRD SPECIAL

	$Good	$Fine	$N.Mint	£Good	£Fine	£N.Mint
Verotik,OS; nn May 1996						
nn ND oversize squarebound collection; three stories plus pin-ups	**$2.00**	**$6.00**	**$10.00**	**£1.30**	**£3.90**	**£6.50**
Title Value:	**$2.00**	**$6.00**	**$10.00**	**£1.30**	**£3.90**	**£6.50**

WINTER WORLD

	$Good	$Fine	$N.Mint	£Good	£Fine	£N.Mint
Eclipse,MS; 1 Sep 1987-3 Mar 1988						
1 ND George Zaffino art begins, colour	**$0.40**	**$1.20**	**$2.00**	**£0.25**	**£0.75**	**£1.25**
2-3 ND scarce in the U.K.	**$0.40**	**$1.20**	**$2.00**	**£0.25**	**£0.75**	**£1.25**
Title Value:	**$1.20**	**$3.60**	**$6.00**	**£0.75**	**£2.25**	**£3.75**
Graphic Novel - Limited Edition, reprints issues #1-3, signed and numbered				£4.00	£12.00	£20.00

WISE SON: THE WHITE WOLF

	$Good	$Fine	$N.Mint	£Good	£Fine	£N.Mint
DC Comics/Milestone,MS; 1 Nov 1996-4 Feb 1997						
1-4 ND Blood Syndicate spin-off	**$0.50**	**$1.50**	**$2.50**	**£0.30**	**£0.90**	**£1.50**
Title Value:	**$2.00**	**$6.00**	**$10.00**	**£1.20**	**£3.60**	**£6.00**

WITCH HUNTER

	$Good	$Fine	$N.Mint	£Good	£Fine	£N.Mint
Marvel Comics Group/Ultraverse,OS; 1 Jun 1996						
1 ND Laurie Sutton script, Joyce Chin and Maria Beccari art	**$0.50**	**$1.50**	**$2.50**	**£0.30**	**£0.90**	**£1.50**
Title Value:	**$0.50**	**$1.50**	**$2.50**	**£0.30**	**£0.90**	**£1.50**

WITCHBLADE

	$Good	$Fine	$N.Mint	£Good	£Fine	£N.Mint
Image; ½ Feb 1996; 1 Oct 1995-present						
½ ND 12pgs, (Feb 1996), Mike Turner and Marc Silvestri cover, Adam McDaniel art; produced in conjunction with Overstreet's Fan magazine	**$5.00**	**$15.00**	**$25.00**	**£4.00**	**£12.00**	**£20.00**
1 ND Mike Turner art begin	**$4.00**	**$12.00**	**$20.00**	**£2.50**	**£7.50**	**£12.50**
2 ND	**$4.00**	**$12.00**	**$20.00**	**£2.40**	**£7.00**	**£12.00**
3 ND	**$2.50**	**$7.50**	**$12.50**	**£1.50**	**£4.50**	**£7.50**
4 ND	**$1.50**	**$4.50**	**$7.50**	**£1.00**	**£3.00**	**£5.00**
5 ND	**$1.00**	**$3.00**	**$5.00**	**£0.70**	**£2.10**	**£3.50**
6 ND	**$0.80**	**$2.40**	**$4.00**	**£0.50**	**£1.50**	**£2.50**
7 ND Ripclaw #7 preview by Garth Ennis	**$0.70**	**$2.10**	**$3.50**	**£0.40**	**£1.20**	**£2.00**
8 ND	**$0.70**	**$2.10**	**$3.50**	**£0.40**	**£1.20**	**£2.00**
9-10 ND	**$0.50**	**$1.50**	**$2.50**	**£0.30**	**£0.90**	**£1.50**
10 Dynamic Forces Edition, ND new cover by Michael Turner and D-Tron	**$3.00**	**$9.00**	**$15.00**	**£2.00**	**£6.00**	**£10.00**
10 Gold Variant Edition, ND gold foil logo; available from Top Cow Comics direct	**$4.00**	**$12.00**	**$20.00**	**£3.00**	**£9.00**	**£15.00**
10 Variant Cover Edition ND	**$2.00**	**$6.00**	**$10.00**	**£1.30**	**£3.90**	**£6.50**
11 ND	**$0.50**	**$1.50**	**$2.50**	**£0.30**	**£0.90**	**£1.50**
Title Value:	**$30.70**	**$92.10**	**$153.50**	**£20.60**	**£61.60**	**£103.00**
Witchblade Collected Edition #1 (Jul 1996) ND 48pgs squarebound, reprints #1 and #2				£0.65	£1.95	£3.25

WITCHBLADE, TALES OF THE

	$Good	$Fine	$N.Mint	£Good	£Fine	£N.Mint
Top Cow Productions; 1 Nov 1996-present						
1 ND Tony Daniel and Kevin Conrad cover and art	**$0.60**	**$1.80**	**$3.00**	**£0.40**	**£1.20**	**£2.00**
1 Alternate Cover Edition, ND Tony Daniel and Kevin Conrad art; Michael Turner cover	**$0.60**	**$1.80**	**$3.00**	**£0.40**	**£1.20**	**£2.00**
Title Value:	**$1.20**	**$3.60**	**$6.00**	**£0.80**	**£2.40**	**£4.00**

WITCHBLADE: WIZARD ACE EDITION

	$Good	$Fine	$N.Mint	£Good	£Fine	£N.Mint
Top Cow Productions,OS; 1 1996						
1 ND card-stock cover with acetate over-lay, Michael Turner art	**$4.00**	**$12.00**	**$20.00**	**£4.00**	**£12.00**	**£20.00**
Title Value:	**$4.00**	**$12.00**	**$20.00**	**£4.00**	**£12.00**	**£20.00**

WITCHCRAFT

	$Good	$Fine	$N.Mint	£Good	£Fine	£N.Mint
DC Comics/Vertigo,MS; 1 Jun 1994-3 Aug 1994						
1-3 48pgs, painted cover by Mike Kaluta; The Three Witches from Sandman (Mildred, Morganna and Cynthia)	**$0.60**	**$1.80**	**$3.00**	**£0.40**	**£1.20**	**£2.00**
Title Value:	**$1.80**	**$5.40**	**$9.00**	**£1.20**	**£3.60**	**£6.00**
Witchcraft (Nov 1996) Trade paperback collects mini-series, new painted cover by Mike Kaluta				£2.00	£6.00	£10.00

WITCHING HOUR

	$Good	$Fine	$N.Mint	£Good	£Fine	£N.Mint
National Periodical Publications/DC Comics; 1 Feb/Mar 1969-85 Oct 1978						
1 Neal Adams art (2pgs), part Toth art	**$4.15**	**$12.50**	**$25.00**	**£2.50**	**£7.50**	**£15.00**
2 Toth art	**$2.05**	**$6.25**	**$12.50**	**£1.25**	**£3.75**	**£7.50**
3 Wrightson art	**$1.65**	**$5.00**	**$10.00**	**£1.05**	**£3.25**	**£6.50**
4	**$1.25**	**$3.75**	**$7.50**	**£0.80**	**£2.50**	**£5.00**

	$Good	$Fine	$N.Mint	£Good	£Fine	£N.Mint
5 Wrightson art	*$1.65*	*$5.00*	*$10.00*	£1.05	£3.25	£6.50
6 Toth art	*$1.65*	*$5.00*	*$10.00*	£1.05	£3.25	£6.50
7 2pgs Kaluta art	*$1.25*	*$3.75*	*$7.50*	£0.80	£2.50	£5.00
8 Neal Adams art	*$1.50*	*$4.50*	*$9.00*	£1.00	£3.00	£6.00
9-10	*$1.25*	*$3.75*	*$7.50*	£0.65	£2.00	£4.00
11-12	*$1.00*	*$3.00*	*$6.00*	£0.55	£1.75	£3.50
13 Neal Adams art	*$1.15*	*$3.50*	*$7.00*	£0.75	£2.25	£4.50
14 Williamson, Jones art	*$1.15*	*$3.50*	*$7.00*	£0.75	£2.25	£4.50
15-20	*$0.50*	*$1.50*	*$3.00*	£0.50	£1.50	£3.00
21-25 52pgs	*$0.40*	*$1.25*	*$2.50*	£0.40	£1.25	£2.50
26 ND	*$0.40*	*$1.25*	*$2.50*	£0.45	£1.35	£2.75
27-30	*$0.40*	*$1.25*	*$2.50*	£0.40	£1.25	£2.50
31-37	*$0.30*	*$1.00*	*$2.00*	£0.30	£1.00	£2.00
38 100pgs	*$0.50*	*$1.50*	*$3.00*	£0.50	£1.50	£3.00
39-40	*$0.30*	*$1.00*	*$2.00*	£0.30	£1.00	£2.00
41-50	*$0.30*	*$1.00*	*$2.00*	£0.25	£0.75	£1.50
51-61	*$0.30*	*$1.00*	*$2.00*	£0.20	£0.60	£1.25
62-65	*$0.30*	*$1.00*	*$2.00*	£0.15	£0.50	£1.00
66-70 scarce in the U.K.	*$0.30*	*$1.00*	*$2.00*	£0.20	£0.60	£1.25
71-83	*$0.30*	*$1.00*	*$2.00*	£0.15	£0.50	£1.00
84-85 ND 44pgs	*$0.30*	*$1.00*	*$2.00*	£0.20	£0.60	£1.25
Title Value:	*$45.65*	*$143.25*	*$286.50*	£32.30	£99.90	£200.75

ARTISTS

Nino art in 31, 40, 45, 47. Wood art in 15.

WITCHING HOUR, ANNE RICE'S

Millennium,MS; 1 1992-5 1994 ?

	$Good	$Fine	$N.Mint	£Good	£Fine	£N.Mint
1 ND Duncan Eagleson script/art, John Bolton covers begin	*$1.00*	*$3.00*	*$5.00*	£0.60	£1.80	£3.00
1 Platinum Edition ND	*$2.50*	*$7.50*	*$12.50*	£1.50	£4.50	£7.50
2-5 ND	*$0.60*	*$1.80*	*$3.00*	£0.40	£1.20	£2.00
Title Value:	*$5.90*	*$17.70*	*$29.50*	£3.70	£11.10	£18.50

Note: #5 came out in Feb 1996 and issues #6 to #8 have been advertised and solicited but to date have not yet appeared. Only time will tell. Can I stand the suspense...

Anne Rice's The Witching Hour: The Beginning (Nov 1994)

	£Good	£Fine	£N.Mint
ND reprints issues #1-3, wraparound cover by John Bolton	£1.40	£4.20	£7.00

WITHIN OUR REACH

Marvel Comics Group; nn Jan 1991

	$Good	$Fine	$N.Mint	£Good	£Fine	£N.Mint
nn ND 80pgs, charity anthology including stories featuring Spiderman, Concrete (by Chadwick), Sherlock Holmes, Spiderman/Santa Claus cover by Norm Breyfogle	*$1.00*	*$3.00*	*$5.00*	£0.70	£2.10	£3.50
Title Value:	*$1.00*	*$3.00*	*$5.00*	£0.70	£2.10	£3.50

WIZARD OF FOURTH STREET

Dark Horse,MS; 1 Dec 1987-2 Mar 1988

	$Good	$Fine	$N.Mint	£Good	£Fine	£N.Mint
1 ND	*$0.30*	*$0.90*	*$1.50*	£0.20	£0.60	£1.00
2 ND scarce in the U.K.	*$0.30*	*$0.90*	*$1.50*	£0.25	£0.75	£1.25
Title Value:	*$0.60*	*$1.80*	*$3.00*	£0.45	£1.35	£2.25

Note: originally announced as a 6 issue mini-series

WIZARD'S TALE, THE

Eclipse,MS; 1 Dec 1993-3 Feb 1994

	$Good	$Fine	$N.Mint	£Good	£Fine	£N.Mint
1-3 ND 48pgs	*$1.00*	*$3.00*	*$5.00*	£0.60	£1.80	£3.00
Title Value:	*$3.00*	*$9.00*	*$15.00*	£1.80	£5.40	£9.00

WOLF & RED

Dark Horse,MS; 1 Apr 1995-3 Jun 1995

	$Good	$Fine	$N.Mint	£Good	£Fine	£N.Mint
1-3 ND based on Tex Avery cartoon characters	*$0.50*	*$1.50*	*$2.50*	£0.30	£0.90	£1.50
Title Value:	*$1.50*	*$4.50*	*$7.50*	£0.90	£2.70	£4.50

WOLFF & BYRD COUNSELORS OF THE MACABRE

Exhibit A Press; 1 Jun 1995-present

	$Good	$Fine	$N.Mint	£Good	£Fine	£N.Mint
1-11 ND	*$0.50*	*$1.50*	*$2.50*	£0.30	£0.90	£1.50
Title Value:	*$5.50*	*$16.50*	*$27.50*	£3.30	£9.90	£16.50

Wolff & Byrd, Counsellors of the Macabre Case Files Vol 1 (1996)

	£Good	£Fine	£N.Mint
Trade paperback ND 96pgs, collects issues #1-4	£1.30	£3.90	£6.50

Wolff & Byrd, Counsellors of the Macabre Case Files Vol. 11 (May 1996)

	£Good	£Fine	£N.Mint
Trade paperback ND 96pgs, collects issues #5-8	£1.30	£3.90	£6.50

WOLFMAN

Dell/Movie Classics,OS Movie; 12-922-308 Jun/Aug 1963

	$Good	$Fine	$N.Mint	£Good	£Fine	£N.Mint
19-922-308 (1st printing), scarce, distributed in the U.K. adapts film	*$5.00*	*$15.00*	*$35.00*	£2.10	£6.25	£15.00
12-922-308 (2nd printing), distributed in the U.K.	*$4.25*	*$12.50*	*$30.00*	£1.75	£5.25	£12.50
Title Value:	*$9.25*	*$27.50*	*$65.00*	£3.85	£11.50	£27.50

WOLFPACK

Marvel Comics Group,MS; 1 Feb 1988-12 Jul 1989

(see Marvel Graphic Novel)

	$Good	$Fine	$N.Mint	£Good	£Fine	£N.Mint
1-12 ND	*$0.25*	*$0.75*	*$1.25*	£0.15	£0.45	£0.75
Title Value:	*$3.00*	*$9.00*	*$15.00*	£1.80	£5.40	£9.00

WOLPH

Blackthorne,MS; 1 Jul 1987-4 Oct 1987

	$Good	$Fine	$N.Mint	£Good	£Fine	£N.Mint
1-4 ND	*$0.40*	*$1.20*	*$2.00*	£0.25	£0.75	£1.25
Title Value:	*$1.60*	*$4.80*	*$8.00*	£1.00	£3.00	£5.00

WOLVERINE

Marvel Comics Group; 1 Nov 1988-90 Feb 1995; 91 Jul 1995-present

(see Captain America Annual #8, Havok and..,Hulk and.., Kitty and.., Marvel Comics Presents, Marvel Fanfare, Marvel Team Up, Power Pack, Punisher War Journal #6,#7, Spiderman and.., X-Men)

(see Weapon X)

	$Good	$Fine	$N.Mint	£Good	£Fine	£N.Mint
1 ND	*$7.00*	*$21.00*	*$35.00*	£2.80	£8.25	£14.00
2 ND	*$4.00*	*$12.00*	*$20.00*	£1.40	£4.20	£7.00
3 ND	*$3.00*	*$9.00*	*$15.00*	£1.00	£3.00	£5.00
4 ND 1st appearance Roughouse and Bloodsport	*$2.50*	*$7.50*	*$12.50*	£0.90	£2.70	£4.50
5-6 ND	*$2.50*	*$7.50*	*$12.50*	£0.80	£2.40	£4.00
7-8 ND Hulk appears	*$2.50*	*$7.50*	*$12.50*	£0.80	£2.40	£4.00
9 ND Peter David script	*$2.50*	*$7.50*	*$12.50*	£0.80	£2.40	£4.00
10 ND scarce in the U.K. Sabretooth vs. Wolverine (chronologically their 1st battle)	*$6.00*	*$18.00*	*$30.00*	£4.00	£12.00	£20.00
11 ND bi-weekly issue, The Gehenna Stone story by Peter David begins	*$1.50*	*$4.50*	*$7.50*	£0.60	£1.80	£3.00
12-15 ND bi-weekly issue, The Gehenna Stone story	*$1.50*	*$4.50*	*$7.50*	£0.60	£1.80	£3.00
16 ND bi-weekly issue, The Gehenna Stone story	*$1.00*	*$3.00*	*$5.00*	£0.50	£1.50	£2.50
17 ND John Byrne co-art begins (to #23)	*$1.00*	*$3.00*	*$5.00*	£0.50	£1.50	£2.50
18 ND John Byrne art	*$1.00*	*$3.00*	*$5.00*	£0.40	£1.20	£2.00
19-20 ND Acts of Vengeance tie-in, John Byrne art	*$1.00*	*$3.00*	*$5.00*	£0.40	£1.20	£2.00
21-23 ND John Byrne art	*$0.80*	*$2.40*	*$4.00*	£0.40	£1.20	£2.00
24 ND Peter David script	*$0.80*	*$2.40*	*$4.00*	£0.40	£1.20	£2.00
25 ND	*$0.80*	*$2.40*	*$4.00*	£0.40	£1.20	£2.00
26 ND bi-weekly issues begin (end #31)	*$0.80*	*$2.40*	*$4.00*	£0.40	£1.20	£2.00
27-30 ND The Lazarus Project story, bi-weekly	*$0.80*	*$2.40*	*$4.00*	£0.40	£1.20	£2.00
31 ND bi-weekly	*$0.60*	*$1.80*	*$3.00*	£0.40	£1.20	£2.00
32-38 ND	*$0.60*	*$1.80*	*$3.00*	£0.40	£1.20	£2.00
39 ND Storm guest-stars	*$0.60*	*$1.80*	*$3.00*	£0.40	£1.20	£2.00
40 ND Wolverine vs. Wolverine clone	*$0.60*	*$1.80*	*$3.00*	£0.40	£1.20	£2.00
41 ND Sabretooth announces he's Wolverine's father, Cable appears, bi-weekly issue	*$1.20*	*$3.60*	*$6.00*	£0.80	£2.40	£4.00
41 2nd printing, ND Oct 1991, gold ink cover	*$0.60*	*$1.80*	*$3.00*	£0.40	£1.20	£2.00
42 ND Sabretooth proven not to be Wolverine's father, Cable appears, bi-weekly issue	*$1.00*	*$3.00*	*$5.00*	£0.70	£2.10	£3.50
42 2nd printing, ND (Dec 1991, gold ink cover)	*$0.40*	*$1.20*	*$2.00*	£0.25	£0.75	£1.25
43 ND Sabretooth father-saga concludes, bi-weekly issue	*$0.90*	*$2.70*	*$4.50*	£0.60	£1.80	£3.00
44 ND bi-weekly issue	*$0.60*	*$1.80*	*$3.00*	£0.40	£1.20	£2.00
45 ND Sabretooth appears, bi-weekly issue	*$0.60*	*$1.80*	*$3.00*	£0.40	£1.20	£2.00
46 ND Hunter in the Darkness story with Sabretooth concludes, bi-weekly issue	*$0.60*	*$1.80*	*$3.00*	£0.40	£1.20	£2.00
47 ND Hunter in the Darkness story epilogue	*$0.60*	*$1.80*	*$3.00*	£0.40	£1.20	£2.00
48 ND Weapon X sequel begins	*$0.60*	*$1.80*	*$3.00*	£0.40	£1.20	£2.00
49 ND Weapon X sequel; lead into true origin of Wolverine	*$0.60*	*$1.80*	*$3.00*	£0.40	£1.20	£2.00
50 ND die-cut cover (as if claws are ripping through), true origin of Wolverine revealed, Professor X, Nick Fury appear	*$0.80*	*$2.40*	*$4.00*	£0.50	£1.50	£2.50
51 ND Sabretooth appears, Andy Kubert art	*$0.60*	*$1.80*	*$3.00*	£0.40	£1.20	£2.00
52 ND	*$0.60*	*$1.80*	*$3.00*	£0.40	£1.20	£2.00
53 ND Spiral and Mystique appear	*$0.60*	*$1.80*	*$3.00*	£0.40	£1.20	£2.00
54 ND The Thing, Nick Fury and Gambit appear	*$0.60*	*$1.80*	*$3.00*	£0.40	£1.20	£2.00
55 ND Gambit appears	*$0.60*	*$1.80*	*$3.00*	£0.40	£1.20	£2.00
56 ND Sunfire guest stars, bi-weekly	*$0.60*	*$1.80*	*$3.00*	£0.40	£1.20	£2.00
57 ND Mariko dies, bi-weekly	*$0.60*	*$1.80*	*$3.00*	£0.40	£1.20	£2.00
58-59 ND Terror Inc., bi-weekly	*$0.60*	*$1.80*	*$3.00*	£0.40	£1.20	£2.00
60 ND Sabretooth appears, bi-weekly	*$0.60*	*$1.80*	*$3.00*	£0.40	£1.20	£2.00
61 ND bi-weekly	*$0.60*	*$1.80*	*$3.00*	£0.40	£1.20	£2.00
62-63 ND Sabretooth appears	*$0.60*	*$1.80*	*$3.00*	£0.40	£1.20	£2.00
64 ND	*$0.60*	*$1.80*	*$3.00*	£0.40	£1.20	£2.00
65 ND Professor X appears	*$0.60*	*$1.80*	*$3.00*	£0.40	£1.20	£2.00
66-68 ND X-Men appear, Texeira art	*$0.60*	*$1.80*	*$3.00*	£0.40	£1.20	£2.00
69 ND X-Men appear, Texeira art (tie-in to X-Men #300)	*$0.60*	*$1.80*	*$3.00*	£0.40	£1.20	£2.00
70-72 ND	*$0.60*	*$1.80*	*$3.00*	£0.40	£1.20	£2.00
73 ND Wolverine and Gambit vs. X-Cutioner	*$0.60*	*$1.80*	*$3.00*	£0.40	£1.20	£2.00
74 ND	*$0.60*	*$1.80*	*$3.00*	£0.40	£1.20	£2.00

	$Good	$Fine	$N.Mint	£Good	£Fine	£N.Mint
75 ND 48pgs, hologram cover, Wolverine loses his Adamantium skeleton						
	$1.50	*$4.50*	*$7.50*	£1.00	£3.00	£5.00
76 ND	*$0.50*	*$1.50*	*$2.50*	£0.30	£0.90	£1.50
77 ND Alpha Flight appears						
	$0.50	*$1.50*	*$2.50*	£0.30	£0.90	£1.50
78 ND	*$0.50*	*$1.50*	*$2.50*	£0.30	£0.90	£1.50
79 ND Wolverine now without his exo-skeleton..						
	$0.50	*$1.50*	*$2.50*	£0.30	£0.90	£1.50
80 ND Nightcrawler appears						
	$0.50	*$1.50*	*$2.50*	£0.30	£0.90	£1.50
81 ND Nightcrawler and Kitty Pryde appear						
	$0.50	*$1.50*	*$2.50*	£0.30	£0.90	£1.50
82-84 ND	*$0.50*	*$1.50*	*$2.50*	£0.30	£0.90	£1.50
85 ND Cable appears						
	$0.50	*$1.50*	*$2.50*	£0.35	£1.05	£1.75
85 Deluxe Edition, ND - foil stamped cover; Cable appears						
	$0.80	*$2.40*	*$4.00*	£0.50	£1.50	£2.50
86 ND	*$0.50*	*$1.50*	*$2.50*	£0.30	£0.90	£1.50
87 ND	*$0.40*	*$1.20*	*$2.00*	£0.25	£0.75	£1.25
87 Deluxe Edition, ND - printed on glossy stock paper						
	$0.50	*$1.50*	*$2.50*	£0.30	£0.90	£1.50
88 ND	*$0.40*	*$1.20*	*$2.00*	£0.25	£0.75	£1.25
88 Deluxe Edition, ND - printed on glossy stock paper; X-over with Ghost Rider #57						
	$0.50	*$1.50*	*$2.50*	£0.30	£0.90	£1.50
89 ND	*$0.40*	*$1.20*	*$2.00*	£0.25	£0.75	£1.25
89 Deluxe Edition, ND - printed on glossy stock paper with bound-in Fleer trading card						
	$0.50	*$1.50*	*$2.50*	£0.30	£0.90	£1.50
90 ND Wolverine vs. Sabretooth						
	$0.40	*$1.20*	*$2.00*	£0.25	£0.75	£1.25
90 Deluxe Edition, ND - printed on glossy paper with bound-in Fleer trading card; see Weapon X #1						
	$0.50	*$1.50*	*$2.50*	£0.30	£0.90	£1.50
91 ND continued from X-Men: Prime; Larry Hama script, Steve Skroce and Al Green art						
	$0.50	*$1.50*	*$2.50*	£0.30	£0.90	£1.50
92 ND Sabretooth appears, continued in X-Force #45						
	$0.50	*$1.50*	*$2.50*	£0.30	£0.90	£1.50
93-94 ND bi-weekly						
	$0.50	*$1.50*	*$2.50*	£0.30	£0.90	£1.50
95-99 ND	*$0.50*	*$1.50*	*$2.50*	£0.30	£0.90	£1.50
100 ND 48pgs, Wolverine rejects adamantium exo-skeleton						
	$1.20	*$3.60*	*$6.00*	£0.70	£2.10	£3.50
100 Collectors Edition, ND 48pgs, - foil hologram cover						
	$1.60	*$4.80*	*$8.00*	£1.00	£3.00	£5.00
101 ND Elektra guest-stars; bi-monthly						
	$0.40	*$1.20*	*$2.00*	£0.30	£0.90	£1.50
102-103 ND Elektra appears						
	$0.40	*$1.20*	*$2.00*	£0.30	£0.90	£1.50
104 ND 40pgs, Onslaught tie-in						
	$0.40	*$1.20*	*$2.00*	£0.30	£0.90	£1.50
105 ND Onslaught tie-in, Elektra appears						
	$0.40	*$1.20*	*$2.00*	£0.30	£0.90	£1.50
106 ND Elektra appears						
	$0.40	*$1.20*	*$2.00*	£0.30	£0.90	£1.50
107 ND prologue to Elektra #1						
	$0.40	*$1.20*	*$2.00*	£0.30	£0.90	£1.50
108-111 ND	*$0.40*	*$1.20*	*$2.00*	£0.30	£0.90	£1.50
Title Value:	*$107.50*	*$322.50*	*$537.50*	£57.30	£171.75	£286.50

Note: all high quality paper. John Byrne art from #17-23. Peter David script in 24.

	£Good	£Fine	£N.Mint
Wolverine: Weapon X Graphic Novel ND Hardcover, 128pgs, reprints Marvel Comics Presents #72-#84 by Barry Windsor-Smith	£2.50	£7.50	£12.50
Wolverine: Weapon X (Mar 1995) Trade paperback ND Softcover version of the above	£1.70	£5.10	£8.50
Wolverine: Triumphs & Tragedies (Dec 1995) Trade paperback ND 176pgs, reprints Wolverine's father saga	£2.20	£6.60	£11.00
The Essential Wolverine (Dec 1996) Trade paperback ND 528pgs, collects Wolverine #1-23 on newsprint, black and white	£1.70	£5.10	£8.50

WOLVERINE '95

Marvel Comics Group,OS; nn Sep 1995

	$Good	$Fine	$N.Mint	£Good	£Fine	£N.Mint
nn ND 64pgs, Nightcrawler, Deadpool and Maverick appear; Larry Hama script, J.H. Williams art						
	$0.80	*$2.40*	*$4.00*	£0.50	£1.50	£2.50
Title Value:	*$0.80*	*$2.40*	*$4.00*	£0.50	£1.50	£2.50

WOLVERINE '96

Marvel Comics Group,OS; nn Oct 1996

	$Good	$Fine	$N.Mint	£Good	£Fine	£N.Mint
nn ND 64pgs, Sunfire appears; Michael Golden cover						
	$0.60	*$1.80*	*$3.00*	£0.40	£1.20	£2.00
Title Value:	*$0.60*	*$1.80*	*$3.00*	£0.40	£1.20	£2.00

WOLVERINE (LIMITED SERIES)

Marvel Comics Group,MS; 1 Sep 1982-4 Dec 1982

(see Kitty Pryde and.., Marvel Comics Presents, Spiderman vs.., X-Men)

	$Good	$Fine	$N.Mint	£Good	£Fine	£N.Mint
1 ND Frank Miller art						
	$5.75	*$17.50*	*$35.00*	£2.50	£7.50	£15.00
2-3 ND Frank Miller art						
	$4.55	*$13.50*	*$27.50*	£1.65	£5.00	£10.00
4 ND scarce in the U.K. Frank Miller art						
	$5.00	*$15.00*	*$30.00*	£2.05	£6.25	£12.50
Title Value:	*$19.85*	*$59.50*	*$120.00*	£7.85	£23.75	£47.50

	£Good	£Fine	£N.Mint
Wolverine Trade paperback, reprints mini-series; Chris Claremont foreword, new Frank Miller cover	£1.00	£3.00	£5.00
(2nd print)	£0.80	£2.40	£4.00

WOLVERINE ENCYCLOPEDIA

Marvel Comics Group; 1 Jan 1997-present

	$Good	$Fine	$N.Mint	£Good	£Fine	£N.Mint
1 ND 48pgs, facts and figures, people and places; Adam Kubert cover						
	$1.20	*$3.60*	*$6.00*	£0.80	£2.40	£4.00
2 ND 48pgs, facts and figures, people and places; Anthony Winn cover						
	$1.20	*$3.60*	*$6.00*	£0.80	£2.40	£4.00
Title Value:	*$2.40*	*$7.20*	*$12.00*	£1.60	£4.80	£8.00

WOLVERINE IN GLOBAL JEOPARDY

Marvel Comics Group,OS; 1 Dec 1993

	$Good	$Fine	$N.Mint	£Good	£Fine	£N.Mint
1 ND co-produced with World Wildlife Fund featuring Ka-Zar, Namor and Shanna with Wolverine; card stock cover enhanced with separate colour ink						
	$0.60	*$1.80*	*$3.00*	£0.40	£1.20	£2.00
Title Value:	*$0.60*	*$1.80*	*$3.00*	£0.40	£1.20	£2.00

WOLVERINE SAGA, THE

Marvel Comics Group,MS; 1 Sep 1989-4 Dec 1989

	$Good	$Fine	$N.Mint	£Good	£Fine	£N.Mint
1 ND 48pgs, Liefeld cover						
	$0.80	*$2.40*	*$4.00*	£0.50	£1.50	£2.50
2-3 ND 48pgs	*$0.80*	*$2.40*	*$4.00*	£0.50	£1.50	£2.50
4 ND 48pgs, Kaluta cover						
	$0.80	*$2.40*	*$4.00*	£0.50	£1.50	£2.50
Title Value:	*$3.20*	*$9.60*	*$16.00*	£2.00	£6.00	£10.00

Note: all squarebound Bookshelf Format, uses text and art

WOLVERINE SPECIAL EDITION: THE JUNGLE ADVENTURE

Marvel Comics Group,OS; 1 Jan 1990

	$Good	$Fine	$N.Mint	£Good	£Fine	£N.Mint
1 ND 48pgs, Walt Simonson script, Mike Mignola art						
	$1.00	*$3.00*	*$5.00*	£0.70	£2.10	£3.50
Title Value:	*$1.00*	*$3.00*	*$5.00*	£0.70	£2.10	£3.50

Note: Bookshelf Format

WOLVERINE VS. SPIDERMAN

Marvel Comics Group,OS; 1 Mar 1995

	$Good	$Fine	$N.Mint	£Good	£Fine	£N.Mint
1 ND reprints Marvel Comics Presents #48-50 with Erik Larsen art						
	$0.50	*$1.50*	*$2.50*	£0.30	£0.90	£1.50
Title Value:	*$0.50*	*$1.50*	*$2.50*	£0.30	£0.90	£1.50

WOLVERINE/FURY: SCORPIO RISING

Marvel Comics Group,OS; 1 Dec 1994

	$Good	$Fine	$N.Mint	£Good	£Fine	£N.Mint
1 ND 48pgs, Howard Chaykin and Shawn McManus creative team						
	$1.20	*$3.60*	*$6.00*	£0.80	£2.40	£4.00
Title Value:	*$1.20*	*$3.60*	*$6.00*	£0.80	£2.40	£4.00

WOLVERINE/GAMBIT: VICTIMS

Marvel Comics Group,MS; 1 Sep 1995-4 Dec 1995

	$Good	$Fine	$N.Mint	£Good	£Fine	£N.Mint
1-4 ND Jeph Loeb script, Tim Sale art						
	$0.80	*$2.40*	*$4.00*	£0.50	£1.50	£2.50
Title Value:	*$3.20*	*$9.60*	*$16.00*	£2.00	£6.00	£10.00

	£Good	£Fine	£N.Mint
Wolverine/Gambit (Feb 1997) Trade paperback ND 96pgs, collects mini-series	£1.70	£5.10	£8.50

WOLVERINE/PUNISHER: DAMAGING EVIDENCE

Marvel Comics Group,MS; 1 Oct 1993-3 Dec 1993

	$Good	$Fine	$N.Mint	£Good	£Fine	£N.Mint
1-3 ND	*$0.40*	*$1.20*	*$2.00*	£0.25	£0.75	£1.25
Title Value:	*$1.20*	*$3.60*	*$6.00*	£0.75	£2.25	£3.75

WOLVERINE/TYPHOID MARY: TYPHOID'S KISS

Marvel Comics Group,OS; 1 Jul 1994

	$Good	$Fine	$N.Mint	£Good	£Fine	£N.Mint
1 ND 64pgs, reprints Marvel Comics Presents #108-116						
	$1.40	*$4.20*	*$7.00*	£0.90	£2.70	£4.50
Title Value:	*$1.40*	*$4.20*	*$7.00*	£0.90	£2.70	£4.50

WOLVERINE/WITCHBLADE

Top Cow/Marvel Comics Group,OS; 1 Mar 1997

	$Good	$Fine	$N.Mint	£Good	£Fine	£N.Mint
1 ND Devil's Reign part 5, continued in Witchblade/Elektra						
	$0.60	*$1.80*	*$3.00*	£0.40	£1.20	£2.00
Title Value:	*$0.60*	*$1.80*	*$3.00*	£0.40	£1.20	£2.00

WOLVERINE: BLOOD HUNGRY

Marvel Comics Group,OS; 1 Feb 1994

	$Good	$Fine	$N.Mint	£Good	£Fine	£N.Mint
1 ND 64pgs, Peter David script, Sam Kieth art and cover						
	$1.40	*$4.20*	*$7.00*	£0.90	£2.70	£4.50
Title Value:	*$1.40*	*$4.20*	*$7.00*	£0.90	£2.70	£4.50

WOLVERINE: BLOODLUST

Marvel Comics Group,OS; nn Jan 1991

	$Good	$Fine	$N.Mint	£Good	£Fine	£N.Mint
nn ND 48pgs, Alan Davis and Paul Neary script/art						
	$0.90	*$2.70*	*$4.50*	£0.60	£1.80	£3.00
Title Value:	*$0.90*	*$2.70*	*$4.50*	£0.60	£1.80	£3.00

WOLVERINE: BLOODY CHOICES

Marvel Comics Group,OS; 1 Jan 1994

	$Good	$Fine	$N.Mint	£Good	£Fine	£N.Mint
1 ND 64pgs, reprints Marvel Graphic Novel; Nick Fury appears						
	$1.50	*$4.50*	*$7.50*	£1.00	£3.00	£5.00
Title Value:	*$1.50*	*$4.50*	*$7.50*	£1.00	£3.00	£5.00

WOLVERINE: EVILUTION

Marvel Comics Group,OS; 1 Nov 1994

	$Good	$Fine	$N.Mint	£Good	£Fine	£N.Mint
1 ND 48pgs, Anne Nocenti script, Mark Texeira art						
	$1.20	*$3.60*	*$6.00*	£0.80	£2.40	£4.00
Title Value:	*$1.20*	*$3.60*	*$6.00*	£0.80	£2.40	£4.00

WOLVERINE: INNER FURY

Marvel Comics Group,OS; 1 Feb 1993

	$Good	$Fine	$N.Mint	£Good	£Fine	£N.Mint
1 ND 48pgs, Bill Sienkiewicz art						
	$1.20	*$3.60*	*$6.00*	£0.80	£2.40	£4.00
Title Value:	*$1.20*	*$3.60*	*$6.00*	£0.80	£2.40	£4.00

WOLVERINE: KILLING

Marvel Comics Group,OS; 1 Nov 1993

	$Good	$Fine	$N.Mint	£Good	£Fine	£N.Mint
1 ND 48pgs, John Reiber and Kent Williams						
	$1.20	*$3.60*	*$6.00*	£0.80	£2.40	£4.00
Title Value:	*$1.20*	*$3.60*	*$6.00*	£0.80	£2.40	£4.00

WOLVERINE: MARVEL COLLECTOR'S EDITION

Marvel Comics Group/Charleston Chew,OS; 1 Sep 1992

	$Good	$Fine	$N.Mint	£Good	£Fine	£N.Mint
1 ND scarce in the U.K. features solo stories of Wolverine and Ghost Rider backed on the flip-side with Spiderman and Silver Surfer, Sam Kieth cover and art featured;						
	$2.00	*$6.00*	*$10.00*	£1.20	£3.60	£6.00

	$Good	$Fine	$N.Mint	£Good	£Fine	£N.Mint
Title Value:	$2.00	$6.00	$10.00	£1.20	£3.60	£6.00

Note: this comic only distributed in U.S., made available by sending one wrapper from Charleston Chew Bar back to the confectionery company.

WOLVERINE: RAHNE FALL

Marvel Comics Group,OS; 1 Aug 1995

	$Good	$Fine	$N.Mint	£Good	£Fine	£N.Mint
1 ND 64pgs, Wolverine and Wolfsbane vs. Sabretooth	$1.40	$4.20	$7.00	£0.90	£2.70	£4.50
Title Value:	$1.40	$4.20	$7.00	£0.90	£2.70	£4.50

WOLVERINE: RAHNE OF TERRA

Marvel Comics Group,OS; 1 Nov 1991

	$Good	$Fine	$N.Mint	£Good	£Fine	£N.Mint
1 ND Peter David script, Andy Kubert art	$1.20	$3.60	$6.00	£0.80	£2.40	£4.00
1 2nd printing, ND Sep 1992	$1.00	$3.00	$5.00	£0.70	£2.10	£3.50
Title Value:	$2.20	$6.60	$11.00	£1.50	£4.50	£7.50

WOLVERINE: SAVE THE TIGER

Marvel Comics Group,OS; 1 Jul 1992

	$Good	$Fine	$N.Mint	£Good	£Fine	£N.Mint
1 ND 80pgs, reprints Marvel Comics Presents #1-10, new Sam Kieth cover	$0.60	$1.80	$3.00	£0.40	£1.20	£2.00
Title Value:	$0.60	$1.80	$3.00	£0.40	£1.20	£2.00

WONDER MAN

Marvel Comics Group,OS; 1 Mar 1986

	$Good	$Fine	$N.Mint	£Good	£Fine	£N.Mint
1 ND DS	$0.40	$1.20	$2.00	£0.25	£0.75	£1.25
Title Value:	$0.40	$1.20	$2.00	£0.25	£0.75	£1.25

WONDER MAN (2ND SERIES)

Marvel Comics Group; 1 Sep 1991-30 1994

	$Good	$Fine	$N.Mint	£Good	£Fine	£N.Mint
1 ND Gerard Jones' 1st Marvel work; bound-in gate-fold poster at centre-fold	$0.25	$0.75	$1.25	£0.15	£0.45	£0.75
2 ND Avengers West Coast appear	$0.25	$0.75	$1.25	£0.15	£0.45	£0.75
3-4 ND	$0.25	$0.75	$1.25	£0.15	£0.45	£0.75
5 ND Beast appears	$0.25	$0.75	$1.25	£0.15	£0.45	£0.75
6 ND Beast appears, $1.25 cover begins	$0.25	$0.75	$1.25	£0.15	£0.45	£0.75
7 ND Galactic Storm part 4, Hulk and Rick Jones appear	$0.25	$0.75	$1.25	£0.15	£0.45	£0.75
8 ND Galactic Storm part 11, Vision appears	$0.25	$0.75	$1.25	£0.15	£0.45	£0.75
9 ND Galactic Storm part 18	$0.25	$0.75	$1.25	£0.15	£0.45	£0.75
10 ND Galactic Storm: Aftermath, Avengers appear	$0.25	$0.75	$1.25	£0.15	£0.45	£0.75
11-12 ND	$0.25	$0.75	$1.25	£0.15	£0.45	£0.75
13 ND Infinity War X-over, Hercules and Thor appear	$0.25	$0.75	$1.25	£0.15	£0.45	£0.75
14 ND Infinity War X-over, Warlock and Thanos appear	$0.25	$0.75	$1.25	£0.15	£0.45	£0.75
15 ND Infinity War X-over, many Marvel characters appear	$0.25	$0.75	$1.25	£0.15	£0.45	£0.75
16-17 ND West Coast Avengers appear	$0.25	$0.75	$1.25	£0.15	£0.45	£0.75
18 ND Wonder Man vs. West Coast Avengers	$0.25	$0.75	$1.25	£0.15	£0.45	£0.75
19-21 ND	$0.25	$0.75	$1.25	£0.15	£0.45	£0.75
22 ND new direction for title: covers of #22-25 fit together as one image	$0.25	$0.75	$1.25	£0.15	£0.45	£0.75
23-24 ND	$0.25	$0.75	$1.25	£0.15	£0.45	£0.75
25 ND 48pgs, new costume; Scarlet Witch and Beast appear; embossed cover	$0.30	$0.90	$1.50	£0.20	£0.60	£1.00
26-27 ND Hulk appears	$0.25	$0.75	$1.25	£0.15	£0.45	£0.75
28 ND Thor and Asgard appear	$0.25	$0.75	$1.25	£0.15	£0.45	£0.75
29 ND Spiderman guest-stars	$0.25	$0.75	$1.25	£0.15	£0.45	£0.75
30 ND Iron Man appears	$0.25	$0.75	$1.25	£0.15	£0.45	£0.75
Title Value:	$7.55	$22.65	$37.75	£4.55	£13.65	£22.75

WONDER MAN ANNUAL

Marvel Comics Group; 1 Jul 1992-2 1993

	$Good	$Fine	$N.Mint	£Good	£Fine	£N.Mint
1 ND The System Bytes part 3, continued in Guardians of the Galaxy Annual #2	$0.30	$0.90	$1.50	£0.20	£0.60	£1.00
2 ND 64pgs, pre-bagged with trading card introducing Hit-Maker	$0.30	$0.90	$1.50	£0.20	£0.60	£1.00
Title Value:	$0.60	$1.80	$3.00	£0.40	£1.20	£2.00

WONDER WOMAN

National Periodical Publications/DC Comics; 1 Summer 1942-329 Feb 1986

(see Adventure, All New Collector's Edition, Best of DC #20, Brave and the Bold, DC Comics Presents, Famous First Edition, Justice League of America, Legend of Wonder Woman, Secret Origins, Secret Origins of Heroes, Super-Team Family, World's Finest Comics)

	$Good	$Fine	$N.Mint	£Good	£Fine	£N.Mint
1 origin retold from All Star Comics #8	$2000.00	$6000.00	$20000.00	£1325.00	£4000.00	£13350.00
2 1st appearance Mars, God of War	$290.00	$880.00	$2350.00	£195.00	£590.00	£1575.00
3	$180.00	$540.00	$1450.00	£120.00	£365.00	£975.00
4-5	$155.00	$465.00	$1250.00	£105.00	£315.00	£850.00
6 1st appearance The Cheetah, Cheetah cover	$125.00	$375.00	$1000.00	£82.50	£250.00	£675.00
7-10	$125.00	$375.00	$1000.00	£82.50	£250.00	£675.00
11-15	$110.00	$330.00	$775.00	£75.00	£225.00	£525.00
16-20	$100.00	$310.00	$725.00	£67.50	£205.00	£485.00
21-30	$95.00	$285.00	$675.00	£62.50	£190.00	£450.00
31-40	$60.00	$180.00	$425.00	£41.00	£120.00	£285.00
41-44	$43.00	$125.00	$300.00	£29.00	£85.00	£200.00
45 origin retold in more detail	$85.00	$255.00	$600.00	£55.00	£170.00	£400.00
46-47	$43.00	$125.00	$300.00	£29.00	£85.00	£200.00
48 Wonder Woman vs. Wonder Woman (robot)	$43.00	$125.00	$300.00	£29.00	£85.00	£200.00
49	$43.00	$125.00	$300.00	£29.00	£85.00	£200.00
50	$39.00	$115.00	$275.00	£26.00	£77.50	£185.00
51-58	$29.00	$85.00	$200.00	£19.00	£57.50	£135.00
59 last Golden Age logo	$29.00	$85.00	$200.00	£19.00	£57.50	£135.00
60	$29.00	$85.00	$200.00	£19.00	£57.50	£135.00
61-63	$25.00	$75.00	$175.00	£17.00	£50.00	£120.00
64 dinosaur cover	$25.00	$75.00	$175.00	£17.00	£50.00	£120.00
65-69	$25.00	$75.00	$175.00	£17.00	£50.00	£120.00
70 1st appearance Angle Man	$25.00	$75.00	$175.00	£17.00	£50.00	£120.00
71-72	$25.00	$75.00	$175.00	£17.00	£50.00	£120.00
73-79	$22.50	$67.50	$160.00	£15.50	£47.00	£110.00
80 1st appearance Invisible Plane	$22.50	$67.50	$160.00	£15.50	£47.00	£110.00
81-90	$22.50	$67.50	$160.00	£15.50	£47.00	£110.00
91-93	$17.50	$52.50	$125.00	£12.00	£36.00	£85.00
94 Robin Hood appears	$17.50	$52.50	$125.00	£12.00	£36.00	£85.00
95 atom bomb cover	$19.00	$57.50	$135.00	£12.50	£39.00	£90.00
96	$17.50	$52.50	$125.00	£12.00	£36.00	£85.00

Where Monsters Dwell #13

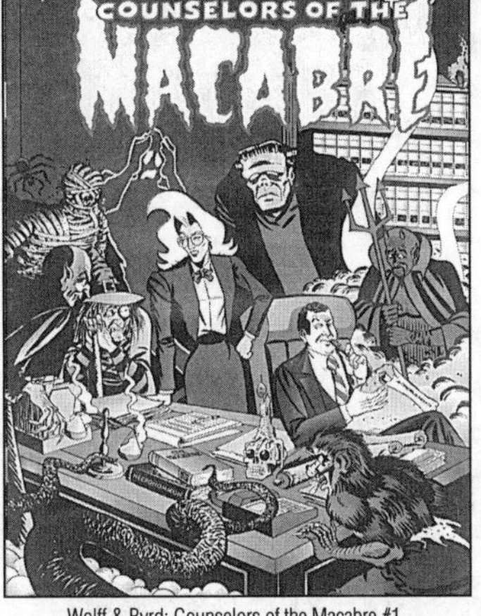

Wolff & Byrd: Counselors of the Macabre #1

Wolverine/Gambit: Victims #1

Issue	$Good	$Fine	$N.Mint	£Good	£Fine	£N.Mint
97 dinosaur cover	***$17.50***	***$52.50***	***$125.00***	**£12.00**	**£36.00**	**£85.00**
98 classic art team of Ross Andru and Mike Esposito begins	***$21.00***	***$62.50***	***$150.00***	**£14.00**	**£43.00**	**£100.00**
99 new facts revealed regarding Wonder Woman's origin and secret identity	***$17.50***	***$52.50***	***$125.00***	**£12.00**	**£36.00**	**£85.00**
100 special centennial story	***$18.50***	***$55.00***	***$150.00***	**£12.50**	**£38.00**	**£100.00**
101-104	***$16.00***	***$49.00***	***$115.00***	**£11.00**	**£33.00**	**£77.50**
105 very scarce in the U.K., scarce in the U.S. origin retold with new facts	***$75.00***	***$225.00***	***$600.00***	**£50.00**	**£150.00**	**£400.00**
[Prices may vary widely on this comic]						
106	***$16.00***	***$49.00***	***$115.00***	**£11.00**	**£33.00**	**£77.50**
107 1st Adventures of Wonder Girl, 1st Merboy, origin Wonder Woman's costume	***$16.00***	***$49.00***	***$115.00***	**£11.00**	**£33.00**	**£77.50**
108-109	***$16.00***	***$49.00***	***$115.00***	**£11.00**	**£33.00**	**£77.50**
1st official distribution in the U.K.						
110	***$16.00***	***$49.00***	***$115.00***	**£10.00**	**£30.00**	**£70.00**
111-120	***$11.00***	***$34.00***	***$80.00***	**£7.75**	**£23.50**	**£55.00**
121	***$8.50***	***$26.00***	***$60.00***	**£5.50**	**£17.00**	**£40.00**
122 1st appearance Wonder Tot	***$10.00***	***$30.00***	***$70.00***	**£6.25**	**£19.00**	**£45.00**
123	***$8.50***	***$26.00***	***$60.00***	**£5.50**	**£17.00**	**£40.00**
124 1st appearance Wonder Woman family	***$6.75***	***$20.00***	***$47.50***	**£4.60**	**£13.50**	**£32.50**
125	***$8.50***	***$26.00***	***$60.00***	**£5.50**	**£17.00**	**£40.00**
126 last 10 cents issue	***$8.50***	***$26.00***	***$60.00***	**£5.50**	**£17.00**	**£40.00**
127	***$5.25***	***$16.00***	***$37.50***	**£3.55**	**£10.50**	**£25.00**
128 origin Robot Plane	***$5.25***	***$16.00***	***$37.50***	**£3.55**	**£10.50**	**£25.00**
129-130	***$5.25***	***$16.00***	***$37.50***	**£3.55**	**£10.50**	**£25.00**
131-140	***$4.25***	***$12.50***	***$30.00***	**£2.85**	**£8.50**	**£20.00**
141-150	***$4.25***	***$12.50***	***$30.00***	**£2.50**	**£7.50**	**£17.50**
151-157	***$3.90***	***$11.50***	***$27.50***	**£2.10**	**£6.25**	**£15.00**
158 last Silver Age issue, indicia dated November 1965	***$3.90***	***$11.50***	***$27.50***	**£2.10**	**£6.25**	**£15.00**
159 origin retold	***$4.60***	***$13.50***	***$32.50***	**£2.85**	**£8.50**	**£20.00**
160-170	***$3.55***	***$10.50***	***$25.00***	**£1.75**	**£5.25**	**£12.50**
171-174	***$2.10***	***$6.25***	***$15.00***	**£1.10**	**£3.40**	**£8.00**
175 scarce in the U.K.	***$2.10***	***$6.25***	***$15.00***	**£1.25**	**£3.85**	**£9.00**
176-178	***$2.10***	***$6.25***	***$15.00***	**£1.05**	**£3.20**	**£7.50**
179 Wonder Woman loses powers, 1st appearance I-Ching; no costume worn now until re-intro of classic costume in #204; fab psychedelic groovy cover	***$2.85***	***$8.50***	***$20.00***	**£1.40**	**£4.25**	**£10.00**
180 death Steve Trevor	***$2.10***	***$6.25***	***$15.00***	**£1.05**	**£3.20**	**£7.50**
181-195	***$1.50***	***$4.50***	***$9.00***	**£0.80**	**£2.50**	**£5.00**
196 52pgs, origin and 1st appearance retold from All-Star Comics #8; extraordinary bondage cover featuring hot pants and sado-masochism!	***$2.50***	***$7.50***	***$15.00***	**£1.25**	**£3.75**	**£7.50**
197-198 52pgs	***$1.65***	***$5.00***	***$10.00***	**£0.90**	**£2.75**	**£5.50**
199-200 52pgs, Jeff Jones covers	***$1.65***	***$5.00***	***$10.00***	**£0.90**	**£2.75**	**£5.50**
201 scarce in the U.K. Wonder Woman vs. Catwoman	***$0.80***	***$2.50***	***$5.00***	**£0.55**	**£1.75**	**£3.50**
202 1st appearance Fafhrd & the Grey Mouser	***$0.80***	***$2.50***	***$5.00***	**£0.65**	**£2.00**	**£4.00**
203 Women's Lib issue	***$0.80***	***$2.50***	***$5.00***	**£0.40**	**£1.25**	**£2.50**
204 scarce in the U.K. 1st appearance Nubia; Wonder Woman regains powers/costume, I-Ching reprints	***$0.80***	***$2.50***	***$5.00***	**£0.55**	**£1.75**	**£3.50**
205	***$0.80***	***$2.50***	***$5.00***	**£0.40**	**£1.25**	**£2.50**
206 Wonder Woman vs. Nubia	***$0.80***	***$2.50***	***$5.00***	**£0.40**	**£1.25**	**£2.50**
207-210	***$0.80***	***$2.50***	***$5.00***	**£0.40**	**£1.25**	**£2.50**
211 100pgs, origin Robot Plane reprinted; Superman on cover and cameo appearance	***$0.80***	***$2.50***	***$5.00***	**£0.50**	**£1.50**	**£3.00**
212-213 Justice League of America guest-star	***$0.65***	***$2.00***	***$4.00***	**£0.40**	**£1.25**	**£2.50**
214 100pgs, Justice League of America guest-star	***$0.65***	***$2.00***	***$4.00***	**£0.55**	**£1.75**	**£3.50**
215 Justice League of America guest-star; Aquaman spotlighted	***$0.65***	***$2.00***	***$4.00***	**£0.40**	**£1.25**	**£2.50**
216 Justice League of America guest-star; Black Canary spotlighted	***$0.65***	***$2.00***	***$4.00***	**£0.40**	**£1.25**	**£2.50**
217 68pgs, Justice League of America guest-star	***$0.65***	***$2.00***	***$4.00***	**£0.50**	**£1.50**	**£3.00**
218-219 Justice League of America guest-star	***$0.65***	***$2.00***	***$4.00***	**£0.40**	**£1.25**	**£2.50**
220 ND Neal Adams inks, Justice League of America guest-star	***$0.65***	***$2.00***	***$4.00***	**£0.50**	**£1.50**	**£3.00**
221-222 Justice League of America guest-star	***$0.50***	***$1.50***	***$3.00***	**£0.30**	**£1.00**	**£2.00**
223 return of Steve Trevor (back from the dead again!)	***$0.50***	***$1.50***	***$3.00***	**£0.30**	**£1.00**	**£2.00**
224 ND	***$0.50***	***$1.50***	***$3.00***	**£0.35**	**£1.10**	**£2.25**
225-227	***$0.50***	***$1.50***	***$3.00***	**£0.30**	**£1.00**	**£2.00**
228 scarce in the U.K. both Wonder Women team-up, new WWII begins (ends #243)	***$0.50***	***$1.50***	***$3.00***	**£0.40**	**£1.25**	**£2.50**
229-230	***$0.50***	***$1.50***	***$3.00***	**£0.30**	**£1.00**	**£2.00**
231 scarce in the U.K.	***$0.30***	***$1.00***	***$2.00***	**£0.25**	**£0.85**	**£1.75**
232-236	***$0.30***	***$1.00***	***$2.00***	**£0.25**	**£0.75**	**£1.50**
237 origin retold	***$0.30***	***$1.00***	***$2.00***	**£0.25**	**£0.75**	**£1.50**
238-240	***$0.30***	***$1.00***	***$2.00***	**£0.25**	**£0.75**	**£1.50**
241 Spectre appears	***$0.30***	***$1.00***	***$2.00***	**£0.25**	**£0.75**	**£1.50**
242-246	***$0.30***	***$1.00***	***$2.00***	**£0.25**	**£0.75**	**£1.50**
247 scarce in the U.K. 44pgs, Tales of the Amazons back-up	***$0.30***	***$1.00***	***$2.00***	**£0.30**	**£1.00**	**£2.00**
248-249 ND 44pgs	***$0.40***	***$1.25***	***$2.50***	**£0.30**	**£1.00**	**£2.00**
250	***$0.30***	***$1.00***	***$2.00***	**£0.25**	**£0.75**	**£1.50**
251-264	***$0.30***	***$0.90***	***$1.50***	**£0.25**	**£0.75**	**£1.25**
265-266 Wonder Girl back-ups	***$0.30***	***$0.90***	***$1.50***	**£0.25**	**£0.75**	**£1.25**
267 Animal Man guest-stars, 1st Modern Age appearance	***$1.00***	***$3.00***	***$5.00***	**£0.40**	**£1.20**	**£2.00**
268 Animal Man guest-stars, 2nd Modern Age appearance	***$0.80***	***$2.40***	***$4.00***	**£0.30**	**£0.90**	**£1.50**
269 Wood part inks	***$0.30***	***$0.90***	***$1.50***	**£0.25**	**£0.75**	**£1.25**
270	***$0.30***	***$0.90***	***$1.50***	**£0.25**	**£0.75**	**£1.25**
271 1st Huntress back-up	***$0.30***	***$0.90***	***$1.50***	**£0.25**	**£0.75**	**£1.25**
272-279	***$0.30***	***$0.90***	***$1.50***	**£0.25**	**£0.75**	**£1.25**
280 Demon X-over	***$0.30***	***$0.90***	***$1.50***	**£0.25**	**£0.75**	**£1.25**
281-283 Joker appears	***$0.50***	***$1.50***	***$2.50***	**£0.30**	**£0.90**	**£1.50**
284-286	***$0.30***	***$0.90***	***$1.50***	**£0.25**	**£0.75**	**£1.25**
287 New Teen Titans X-over	***$0.30***	***$0.90***	***$1.50***	**£0.25**	**£0.75**	**£1.25**
288-290	***$0.30***	***$0.90***	***$1.50***	**£0.25**	**£0.75**	**£1.25**
291-293 3-part story; Huntress, Wonder Girl, Raven, Power Girl, Starfire, Black Canary, Supergirl, Phantom Lady, Madame Xanadu, Batgirl, Zatanna, Lois Lane guest-star	***$0.30***	***$0.90***	***$1.50***	**£0.25**	**£0.75**	**£1.25**
294-296	***$0.30***	***$0.90***	***$1.50***	**£0.25**	**£0.75**	**£1.25**
297 Kaluta cover	***$0.30***	***$0.90***	***$1.50***	**£0.25**	**£0.75**	**£1.25**
298-299	***$0.30***	***$0.90***	***$1.50***	**£0.25**	**£0.75**	**£1.25**
300 LD in the U.K. 76pgs, Giffen art, anniversary issue, Justice League of America/New Teen Titans appear	***$0.50***	***$1.50***	***$2.50***	**£0.40**	**£1.20**	**£2.00**
301-326	***$0.30***	***$0.90***	***$1.50***	**£0.20**	**£0.60**	**£1.00**
327-328 LD in the U.K. Crisis X-over	***$0.30***	***$0.90***	***$1.50***	**£0.20**	**£0.60**	**£1.00**
329 DS Crisis X-over	***$0.50***	***$1.50***	***$2.50***	**£0.30**	**£0.90**	**£1.50**
Title Value:	***$8314.70***	***$24965.95***	***$66074.00***	**£5548.25**	**£16700.90**	**£44233.50**

Note: Golden Age issues, that is 1940s/50s issues, were not available on the news-stand in the U.K. but some may have come over through personnel movement during the Second World War or as cheap ballast on ships, perhaps most likely in the late 1940s.

ARTISTS

Wood inks in 195,269.

FEATURES

Huntress in 271-287,289,290,294. Tales of the Amazons in 247-249. Wonder Woman in all "new look" Wonder Woman (without powers) in 178-203. Wonder Girl solo in 265,266.

Note: 191,196,199,200,211,214,217 are partially reprint. 197 and 198 are entirely reprint. 196 reprints origin from All-Star Comics 8 with alterations and text additions.

WONDER WOMAN (2ND SERIES)

DC Comics; 0 Oct 1994; 1 Feb 1987-present

Issue	$Good	$Fine	$N.Mint	£Good	£Fine	£N.Mint
0 (Oct 1994), Zero Hour X-over, origin retold	***$0.60***	***$1.80***	***$3.00***	**£0.40**	**£1.20**	**£2.00**
1 LD in the U.K. new origin by George Perez	***$0.60***	***$1.80***	***$3.00***	**£0.40**	**£1.20**	**£2.00**
2 George Perez art	***$0.50***	***$1.50***	***$2.50***	**£0.30**	**£0.90**	**£1.50**
3 George Perez art	***$0.40***	***$1.20***	***$2.00***	**£0.25**	**£0.75**	**£1.25**
4-7 George Perez art	***$0.30***	***$0.90***	***$1.50***	**£0.20**	**£0.60**	**£1.00**
8 Superman X-over, George Perez art	***$0.30***	***$0.90***	***$1.50***	**£0.20**	**£0.60**	**£1.00**
9 George Perez art	***$0.30***	***$0.90***	***$1.50***	**£0.20**	**£0.60**	**£1.00**
10 with triple foldout cover, Trial of the Gods begins; George Perez art	***$0.30***	***$0.90***	***$1.50***	**£0.20**	**£0.60**	**£1.00**
11 Trial of the Gods, George Perez art	***$0.30***	***$0.90***	***$1.50***	**£0.20**	**£0.60**	**£1.00**
12-13 Millennium X-over, George Perez art	***$0.30***	***$0.90***	***$1.50***	**£0.20**	**£0.60**	**£1.00**
14-24 George Perez art	***$0.30***	***$0.90***	***$1.50***	**£0.20**	**£0.60**	**£1.00**
25 Invasion X-over, George Perez cover and script	***$0.30***	***$0.90***	***$1.50***	**£0.20**	**£0.60**	**£1.00**
26 Invasion X-over, 16pg Bonus Book, George Perez cover	***$0.30***	***$0.90***	***$1.50***	**£0.20**	**£0.60**	**£1.00**
27-48 George Perez covers	***$0.30***	***$0.90***	***$1.50***	**£0.20**	**£0.60**	**£1.00**
49 guest-stars Superman, Guy Gardner, Captain Atom, Black Canary, Troia, Martian Manhunter in a retrospective on Wonder Woman; George Perez cover	***$0.30***	***$0.90***	***$1.50***	**£0.20**	**£0.60**	**£1.00**
50 LD in the U.K. DS, Superman, New Titans, Justice League appear; George Perez cover	***$0.40***	***$1.20***	***$2.00***	**£0.25**	**£0.75**	**£1.25**
51 Arkham Asylum featured, George Perez cover	***$0.30***	***$0.90***	***$1.50***	**£0.20**	**£0.60**	**£1.00**
52-57 George Perez covers						

	$Good	$Fine	$N.Mint	£Good	£Fine	£N.Mint
	$0.30	$0.90	$1.50	£0.20	£0.60	£1.00
58-61 War of the Gods tie-in						
	$0.30	$0.90	$1.50	£0.20	£0.60	£1.00
62 last George Perez script and cover						
	$0.30	$0.90	$1.50	£0.20	£0.60	£1.00
63 Brian Bolland covers begin; continued from Wonder Woman special						
	$0.30	$0.90	$1.50	£0.20	£0.60	£1.00
64-65	$0.30	$0.90	$1.50	£0.20	£0.60	£1.00
66-70 Exodus Into Space story						
	$0.30	$0.90	$1.50	£0.20	£0.60	£1.00
71 Wonder Woman returns to Earth after a year's absence						
	$0.30	$0.90	$1.50	£0.20	£0.60	£1.00
72 Wonder Woman's origin re-told						
	$0.30	$0.90	$1.50	£0.20	£0.60	£1.00
73-75	$0.30	$0.90	$1.50	£0.20	£0.60	£1.00
76 Dr. Fate guest-stars						
	$0.30	$0.90	$1.50	£0.20	£0.60	£1.00
77-84	$0.30	$0.90	$1.50	£0.20	£0.60	£1.00
85 1st Mike Deodato Wonder Woman						
	$1.50	$4.50	$7.50	£0.90	£2.70	£4.50
86-87	$0.60	$1.80	$3.00	£0.30	£0.90	£1.50
88 1st Christopher Priest script, Superman appears						
	$1.00	$3.00	$5.00	£0.70	£2.10	£3.50
89	$0.80	$2.40	$4.00	£0.50	£1.50	£2.50
90 1st appearance Artemis						
	$1.50	$4.50	$7.50	£0.80	£2.40	£4.00
91	$0.80	$2.40	$4.00	£0.50	£1.50	£2.50
92 Artemis becomes the new Wonder Woman						
	$0.80	$2.40	$4.00	£0.50	£1.50	£2.50
93 tie-in with Justice League America #95						
	$0.80	$2.40	$4.00	£0.50	£1.50	£2.50
94-95	$0.60	$1.80	$3.00	£0.40	£1.20	£2.00
96 The Joker appears						
	$0.60	$1.80	$3.00	£0.40	£1.20	£2.00
97-99	$0.60	$1.80	$3.00	£0.40	£1.20	£2.00
100 48pgs, Brian Bolland cover; Standard Edition, death of Artemis						
	$0.70	$2.10	$3.50	£0.50	£1.50	£2.50
100 Collectors Edition, 48pgs,, Brian Bolland cover; with holographic foil-stamped cover						
	$0.90	$2.70	$4.50	£0.60	£1.80	£3.00
101 John Byrne script and art begins and new direction for title						
	$0.40	$1.20	$2.00	£0.25	£0.75	£1.25
102-103 Darkseid appears						
	$0.40	$1.20	$2.00	£0.25	£0.75	£1.25
104-105	$0.40	$1.20	$2.00	£0.25	£0.75	£1.25
106 Demon and Phantom Stranger guest-star						
	$0.40	$1.20	$2.00	£0.25	£0.75	£1.25
107-108 Demon, Arion and Phantom Stranger guest-star						
	$0.40	$1.20	$2.00	£0.25	£0.75	£1.25
109 Wonder Woman vs."Barry Allen Flash"						
	$0.40	$1.20	$2.00	£0.25	£0.75	£1.25
110-111 Wonder Woman vs. Sinestro						
	$0.40	$1.20	$2.00	£0.25	£0.75	£1.25
112 Wonder Woman vs. Doomsday						
	$0.40	$1.20	$2.00	£0.25	£0.75	£1.25
113-117	$0.40	$1.20	$2.00	£0.25	£0.75	£1.25
118 ND Garcia Lopez covers begin						
	$0.40	$1.20	$2.00	£0.25	£0.75	£1.25
119 ND	$0.40	$1.20	$2.00	£0.25	£0.75	£1.25
Title Value:	$47.70	$143.10	$238.50	£30.85	£92.55	£154.25
Multi-Pack (1990)						
Three issues from #10-12 or #22-24 pre-bagged with illustrated header card; ND rare in the U.K.				£0.30	£0.90	£1.50
Wonder Woman: The Contest (1995)						
Trade paperback reprints issues #90, #0 and #91-93, new Mike Deodato cover				£1.30	£3.90	£6.50
Wonder Woman: The Challenge of Artemis (Jun 1996)						
Trade paperback reprints issues #95-100 with new Mike Deodato cover				£1.30	£3.90	£6.50

WONDER WOMAN ANNUAL

DC Comics; 1 1988-2 1989; 3-1992; 4 1995-present

	$Good	$Fine	$N.Mint	£Good	£Fine	£N.Mint
1 48pgs, George Perez, Art Adams, Brian Bolland, John Bolton, Garcia Lopez, Ross Andru, Curt Swan art						
	$0.50	$1.50	$2.50	£0.30	£0.90	£1.50
2 48pgs, part George Perez story and cover art Women writers/artists inc. Trina Robbins, Collen Doran and Lee Mars						
	$0.50	$1.50	$2.50	£0.30	£0.90	£1.50
3 64pgs, Eclipso: The Darkness Within tie-in						
	$0.50	$1.50	$2.50	£0.30	£0.90	£1.50
4 64pgs, Year One, script by Kate Worley, art by Brent Anderson						
	$0.80	$2.40	$4.00	£0.50	£1.50	£2.50
5 ND 48pgs, Legends of the Dead Earth story; John Byrne script, Dave Cockrum and Norm Breyfogle art						
	$0.60	$1.80	$3.00	£0.40	£1.20	£2.00
Title Value:	$2.90	$8.70	$14.50	£1.80	£5.40	£9.00

WONDER WOMAN BOOK AND RECORD SET

Power Records; PR-35 1974

	$Good	$Fine	$N.Mint	£Good	£Fine	£N.Mint
PR-35 scarce in the U.K. 20pg booklet with 45 rpm record						
	$1.25	$3.75	$7.50	£0.80	£2.50	£5.00
Title Value:	$1.25	$3.75	$7.50	£0.80	£2.50	£5.00

Note: item would be valued approximately 50% less without record

WONDER WOMAN GALLERY

DC Comics,OS; 1 Sep 1996

	$Good	$Fine	$N.Mint	£Good	£Fine	£N.Mint
1 ND pin-ups by John Byrne, George Perez, Alex Toth, Howard Chaykin and others						
	$0.70	$2.10	$3.50	£0.50	£1.50	£2.50
Title Value:	$0.70	$2.10	$3.50	£0.50	£1.50	£2.50

WONDER WOMAN PIZZA HUT GIVEAWAYS

DC Comics/Pizza Hut; 60, 62 Dec 1977

(see Batman, Superman)

	$Good	$Fine	$N.Mint	£Good	£Fine	£N.Mint
60 ND scarce in the U.K. original issue #60 reprinted in its entirety apart from different ads and Pizza Hut banner at top						
	$1.25	$3.75	$7.50	£1.00	£3.00	£6.00
62 ND scarce in the U.K. original issue #62 reprinted in its entirety apart from different ads and Pizza Hut banner at top						
	$1.25	$3.75	$7.50	£1.00	£3.00	£6.00
Title Value:	$2.50	$7.50	$15.00	£2.00	£6.00	£12.00

WONDER WOMAN PLUS #1

DC Comics,OS; 1 Jan 1997

	$Good	$Fine	$N.Mint	£Good	£Fine	£N.Mint
1 ND 48pgs, Wonder Woman and Jesse Quick; Mike Collins art						
	$0.60	$1.80	$3.00	£0.40	£1.20	£2.00
Title Value:	$0.60	$1.80	$3.00	£0.40	£1.20	£2.00

WONDER WOMAN SPECIAL

DC Comics,OS; 1 May 1992

	$Good	$Fine	$N.Mint	£Good	£Fine	£N.Mint
1 Deathstroke the Terminator appears, continued in Wonder Woman #63						
	$0.50	$1.50	$2.50	£0.30	£0.90	£1.50
Title Value:	$0.50	$1.50	$2.50	£0.30	£0.90	£1.50

WONDER WOMAN SPECTACULAR

DC Comics; nn 1978

(DC Special Series #9)

	$Good	$Fine	$N.Mint	£Good	£Fine	£N.Mint
nn ND 80pgs	$0.75	$2.25	$4.50	£0.50	£1.50	£3.00
Title Value:	$0.75	$2.25	$4.50	£0.50	£1.50	£3.00

WONDER WOMAN, THE LEGEND OF

DC Comics,MS; 1 May 1986-4 Aug 1986

	$Good	$Fine	$N.Mint	£Good	£Fine	£N.Mint
1-4 Trina Robbins art, Kurt Busiek script						
	$0.25	$0.75	$1.25	£0.15	£0.45	£0.75
Title Value:	$1.00	$3.00	$5.00	£0.60	£1.80	£3.00

WONDERWORLDS

Innovation,OS; 1 Feb 1992

	$Good	$Fine	$N.Mint	£Good	£Fine	£N.Mint
1 ND 100pgs, reprints						
	$0.60	$1.80	$3.00	£0.40	£1.20	£2.00
Title Value:	$0.60	$1.80	$3.00	£0.40	£1.20	£2.00

WORDSMITH

Renegade; 1 Aug 1985-12 Jan 1988

	$Good	$Fine	$N.Mint	£Good	£Fine	£N.Mint
1-12 ND	$0.30	$0.90	$1.50	£0.20	£0.60	£1.00
Title Value:	$3.60	$10.80	$18.00	£2.40	£7.20	£12.00
Collection 1, reprints issues #1-6				£1.65	£4.95	£8.25
Collection 2, reprints issues #7-12				£1.65	£4.95	£8.25

WORDSMITH (2ND SERIES)

Caliber Press; 1 Jan 1996-present ?

	$Good	$Fine	$N.Mint	£Good	£Fine	£N.Mint
1 ND 48pgs, Dave Darrigo script, R.G. Taylor art; black and white						
	$0.60	$1.80	$3.00	£0.40	£1.20	£2.00
2-4 ND	$0.60	$1.80	$3.00	£0.40	£1.20	£2.00
Title Value:	$2.40	$7.20	$12.00	£1.60	£4.80	£8.00

WORLD CHAMPION WRESTLING

Marvel Comics Group; 1 Apr 1992-12 Mar 1993

	$Good	$Fine	$N.Mint	£Good	£Fine	£N.Mint
1 based on WCW television wrestling stars, photo cover						
	$0.25	$0.75	$1.25	£0.15	£0.45	£0.75
2-12	$0.25	$0.75	$1.25	£0.15	£0.45	£0.75
Title Value:	$3.00	$9.00	$15.00	£1.80	£5.40	£9.00

WORLD OF GINGER FOX

Comico; Graphic Novel; nn Nov 1986

(see Ginger Fox)

	$Good	$Fine	$N.Mint	£Good	£Fine	£N.Mint
nn ND Mike Baron script, Mich O'Connell art						
	$1.80	$5.25	$9.00	£1.20	£3.60	£6.00
nn Limited Edition Hardback ND						
	$4.50	$13.50	$22.50	£3.00	£9.00	£15.00
Title Value:	$6.30	$18.75	$31.50	£4.20	£12.60	£21.00

WORLD OF KRYPTON

DC Comics,MS; 1 Jul 1979-3 Sep 1979

	$Good	$Fine	$N.Mint	£Good	£Fine	£N.Mint
1 ND Howard Chaykin pencils						
	$0.40	$1.25	$2.50	£0.25	£0.75	£1.50
2-3 ND	$0.40	$1.25	$2.50	£0.25	£0.75	£1.50
Title Value:	$1.20	$3.75	$7.50	£0.75	£2.25	£4.50

Note: 1st DC mini-series.

WORLD OF KRYPTON (2ND SERIES)

DC Comics,MS; 1 Dec 1987-4 Mar 1988

	$Good	$Fine	$N.Mint	£Good	£Fine	£N.Mint
1-2 John Byrne script and cover art, Mike Mignola art						
	$0.25	$0.75	$1.25	£0.15	£0.45	£0.75
3 ND John Byrne script and cover art, Mike Mignola art						
	$0.25	$0.75	$1.25	£0.20	£0.60	£1.00
4 John Byrne script and cover art, Mike Mignola art						
	$0.25	$0.75	$1.25	£0.15	£0.45	£0.75
Title Value:	$1.00	$3.00	$5.00	£0.65	£1.95	£3.25

WORLD OF METROPOLIS

DC Comics,MS; 1 Jun 1988-4 Sep 1988

	$Good	$Fine	$N.Mint	£Good	£Fine	£N.Mint
1-4 John Byrne cover art and script						
	$0.25	$0.75	$1.25	£0.15	£0.45	£0.75
Title Value:	$1.00	$3.00	$5.00	£0.60	£1.80	£3.00

Note: see World of Krypton (2nd), World of Smallville.

WORLD OF SMALLVILLE

DC Comics,MS; 1 Apr 1988-4 Jul 1988

	$Good	$Fine	$N.Mint	£Good	£Fine	£N.Mint
1-4 John Byrne cover art and script						
	$0.25	$0.75	$1.25	£0.15	£0.45	£0.75
Title Value:	$1.00	$3.00	$5.00	£0.60	£1.80	£3.00

Note: see World of Krypton (2nd Series), World of Metropolis.

WORLD OF WOOD

Eclipse,MS; 1 May 1986-4 Jun 1986; 5,6 1987

1 ND wrongly printed indicia, Dave Stevens cover

	$Good	$Fine	$N.Mint	£Good	£Fine	£N.Mint
	$0.40	*$1.20*	*$2.00*	£0.25	£0.75	£1.25
2 ND scarce in the U.K. Wood/Stevens cover	*$0.40*	*$1.20*	*$2.00*	£0.25	£0.75	£1.25
3 ND Wood, Blevins, Williamson cover	*$0.40*	*$1.20*	*$2.00*	£0.25	£0.75	£1.25
4-6 ND	*$0.40*	*$1.20*	*$2.00*	£0.25	£0.75	£1.25
Title Value:	*$2.40*	*$7.20*	*$12.00*	£1.50	£4.50	£7.50

WORLD OF YOUNG MASTER

New Comics Group; 1 Mar 1989

	$Good	$Fine	$N.Mint	£Good	£Fine	£N.Mint
1 ND intro The Demonblade	*$0.40*	*$1.20*	*$2.00*	£0.25	£0.75	£1.25
Title Value:	*$0.40*	*$1.20*	*$2.00*	£0.25	£0.75	£1.25

WORLD WITHOUT END

DC Comics,MS; 1 Dec 1990-6 Jun 1991

	$Good	$Fine	$N.Mint	£Good	£Fine	£N.Mint
1-6 ND 48pgs, Delano and Higgins script/art	*$0.50*	*$1.50*	*$2.50*	£0.30	£0.90	£1.50
Title Value:	*$3.00*	*$9.00*	*$15.00*	£1.80	£5.40	£9.00

Note: production delays between issue #4 and #5

WORLD WRESTLING FEDERATION BATTLEMANIA

Valiant,Magazine; 1 Sep 1991-9 Apr 1992

	$Good	$Fine	$N.Mint	£Good	£Fine	£N.Mint
1-9 ND	*$0.40*	*$1.20*	*$2.00*	£0.25	£0.75	£1.25
Title Value:	*$3.60*	*$10.80*	*$18.00*	£2.25	£6.75	£11.25

WORLD'S BEST COMICS

(see World's Finest Comics)

WORLD'S FINEST COMICS (1ST SERIES)

National Periodical Publications/DC Comics; 1 Spring 1941-323 Jan 1986

	$Good	$Fine	$N.Mint	£Good	£Fine	£N.Mint
1 (Spring 1941) titled "World's Best Comics", Superman and Batman begin in separate stories though they share the covers; the early covers are highly patriotic	*$1450.00*	*$4350.00*	*$14500.00*	£970.00	£2900.00	£9700.00
2	*$500.00*	*$1500.00*	*$4000.00*	£330.00	£990.00	£2650.00
3 origin and 1st appearance The Scarecrow	*$375.00*	*$1125.00*	*$3000.00*	£250.00	£750.00	£2000.00
4	*$265.00*	*$800.00*	*$2150.00*	£175.00	£530.00	£1425.00
5 (Spring 1942)	*$260.00*	*$780.00*	*$2100.00*	£175.00	£520.00	£1400.00
6-7 Joe Simon & Jack Kirby art	*$175.00*	*$530.00*	*$1425.00*	£115.00	£355.00	£950.00
8	*$165.00*	*$500.00*	*$1350.00*	£110.00	£335.00	£900.00
9 (Spring 1943) Hitler/Mussolini cover	*$170.00*	*$510.00*	*$1375.00*	£115.00	£345.00	£920.00
10	*$110.00*	*$335.00*	*$1125.00*	£75.00	£225.00	£750.00
11-12	*$150.00*	*$450.00*	*$1050.00*	£100.00	£300.00	£700.00
13 (Spring 1944)	*$150.00*	*$450.00*	*$1050.00*	£100.00	£300.00	£700.00
14-16	*$150.00*	*$450.00*	*$1050.00*	£100.00	£300.00	£700.00
17 (Spring 1945) last card covers	*$150.00*	*$450.00*	*$1050.00*	£100.00	£300.00	£700.00
[All the above are scarce in high grade - Very Fine+ or better]						
18-20	*$125.00*	*$385.00*	*$900.00*	£85.00	£255.00	£600.00
21 (Mar/Apr 1946)	*$95.00*	*$285.00*	*$675.00*	£62.50	£190.00	£450.00
22-25	*$95.00*	*$285.00*	*$675.00*	£62.50	£190.00	£450.00
26 (Jan/Feb 1947)	*$87.50*	*$265.00*	*$625.00*	£57.50	£175.00	£415.00
27-29	*$87.50*	*$265.00*	*$625.00*	£57.50	£175.00	£415.00
30 origin giant penny trophy in Batcave	*$87.50*	*$265.00*	*$625.00*	£57.50	£175.00	£415.00
31	*$77.50*	*$235.00*	*$550.00*	£50.00	£155.00	£365.00
32 (Jan/Feb 1948)	*$77.50*	*$235.00*	*$550.00*	£50.00	£155.00	£365.00
33-37	*$77.50*	*$235.00*	*$550.00*	£50.00	£155.00	£365.00
38 (Jan/Feb 1949)	*$77.50*	*$235.00*	*$550.00*	£50.00	£155.00	£365.00
39-40	*$77.50*	*$235.00*	*$550.00*	£50.00	£155.00	£365.00
41-42	*$62.50*	*$190.00*	*$450.00*	£43.00	£125.00	£300.00
43 (Dec/Jan 1950)	*$62.50*	*$190.00*	*$450.00*	£43.00	£125.00	£300.00
44-47	*$62.50*	*$190.00*	*$450.00*	£43.00	£125.00	£300.00
48 last square-bound	*$62.50*	*$190.00*	*$450.00*	£43.00	£125.00	£300.00
49 (Dec/Jan 1951)	*$62.50*	*$190.00*	*$450.00*	£43.00	£125.00	£300.00
50	*$62.50*	*$190.00*	*$450.00*	£43.00	£125.00	£300.00
51-54 scarce in both US and UK	*$60.00*	*$180.00*	*$425.00*	£41.00	£120.00	£285.00
55 (Dec/Jan 1952)	*$60.00*	*$180.00*	*$425.00*	£41.00	£120.00	£285.00
56-60	*$60.00*	*$180.00*	*$425.00*	£41.00	£120.00	£285.00
61	*$43.00*	*$125.00*	*$300.00*	£29.00	£85.00	£200.00
62 (Jan/Feb 1953)	*$43.00*	*$125.00*	*$300.00*	£29.00	£85.00	£200.00
63-64	*$43.00*	*$125.00*	*$300.00*	£29.00	£85.00	£200.00
65 scarce in both US and UK Tomahawk begins (end #101), origin of Superman briefly retold	*$77.50*	*$230.00*	*$625.00*	£50.00	£155.00	£415.00
66-67 scarce in the U.S, very scarce in the U.K.	*$52.50*	*$155.00*	*$425.00*	£36.00	£105.00	£285.00
68 scarce in the U.S, very scarce in the U.K. (Jan/Feb 1954)	*$52.50*	*$155.00*	*$425.00*	£36.00	£105.00	£285.00
69 scarce in the U.S, very scarce in the U.K.	*$52.50*	*$155.00*	*$425.00*	£36.00	£105.00	£285.00
70 scarce in the U.S, very scarce in the U.K. last 68pg issue	*$52.50*	*$155.00*	*$425.00*	£36.00	£105.00	£285.00
71 rare in the U.K., very scarce in the U.S. Superman and Batman regular team ups begin although they had always shared the cover	*$100.00*	*$300.00*	*$900.00*	£65.00	£200.00	£600.00
72-73 scarce in the U.S, very scarce in the U.K.	*$75.00*	*$225.00*	*$600.00*	£50.00	£150.00	£400.00
74 scarce in the U.S, very scarce in the U.K. (Jan/Feb 1955)	*$55.00*	*$165.00*	*$450.00*	£38.00	£110.00	£300.00
75 scarce in the U.S, very scarce in the U.K.	*$55.00*	*$165.00*	*$450.00*	£38.00	£110.00	£300.00
76 scarce in the U.K.	*$43.00*	*$125.00*	*$300.00*	£29.00	£85.00	£200.00
77 scarce in the U.K. The Super Batman	*$43.00*	*$125.00*	*$300.00*	£29.00	£85.00	£200.00
78-79 scarce in the U.K.	*$43.00*	*$125.00*	*$300.00*	£29.00	£85.00	£200.00
80 scarce in the U.K. (Jan/Feb 1956)	*$43.00*	*$125.00*	*$300.00*	£29.00	£85.00	£200.00
81-85	*$36.00*	*$105.00*	*$250.00*	£23.50	£70.00	£165.00
86 (Feb 1957)	*$36.00*	*$105.00*	*$250.00*	£23.50	£70.00	£165.00
87	*$36.00*	*$105.00*	*$250.00*	£23.50	£70.00	£165.00
88 1st Luthor-Joker team-up	*$36.00*	*$105.00*	*$250.00*	£23.50	£70.00	£165.00
89	*$36.00*	*$105.00*	*$250.00*	£23.50	£70.00	£165.00
90 The Super Batwoman	*$36.00*	*$105.00*	*$250.00*	£23.50	£70.00	£165.00
91	*$25.00*	*$75.00*	*$175.00*	£16.00	£49.00	£115.00
92 (Feb 1958)	*$25.00*	*$75.00*	*$175.00*	£16.00	£49.00	£115.00
93	*$25.00*	*$75.00*	*$175.00*	£16.00	£49.00	£115.00
94 scarce in the U.K. origin Superman/Batman team	*$67.50*	*$205.00*	*$550.00*	£46.00	£135.00	£365.00
95	*$25.00*	*$75.00*	*$175.00*	£15.50	£47.00	£110.00
96-98 Jack Kirby Green Arrow	*$25.00*	*$75.00*	*$175.00*	£15.50	£47.00	£110.00
99 (Feb 1959) Jack Kirby Green Arrow	*$25.00*	*$75.00*	*$175.00*	£15.50	£47.00	£110.00
100	*$44.00*	*$130.00*	*$305.00*	£25.00	£75.00	£175.00
101-104	*$17.00*	*$50.00*	*$120.00*	£11.00	£34.00	£80.00
1st official distribution in the U.K.						
105-106	*$17.00*	*$50.00*	*$120.00*	£10.50	£32.00	£75.00
107 (Feb 1960)	*$17.00*	*$50.00*	*$120.00*	£10.50	£32.00	£75.00
108-110	*$17.00*	*$50.00*	*$120.00*	£10.50	£32.00	£75.00
111-113	*$13.50*	*$41.00*	*$95.00*	£8.50	£26.00	£60.00
114 (Feb 1961)	*$13.50*	*$41.00*	*$95.00*	£8.50	£26.00	£60.00
115-120	*$13.50*	*$41.00*	*$95.00*	£8.50	£26.00	£60.00
121 last 10 cents issue	*$13.50*	*$41.00*	*$95.00*	£8.50	£26.00	£60.00
122	*$7.75*	*$23.50*	*$55.00*	£5.00	£15.00	£35.00
123 (Feb 1962)	*$7.75*	*$23.50*	*$55.00*	£5.00	£15.00	£35.00
124-128	*$7.75*	*$23.50*	*$55.00*	£5.00	£15.00	£35.00
129 Joker cover/story	*$8.50*	*$26.00*	*$60.00*	£5.50	£17.00	£40.00
130	*$7.75*	*$23.50*	*$55.00*	£5.00	£15.00	£35.00
131 (Feb 1963)	*$6.25*	*$19.00*	*$45.00*	£4.25	£12.50	£30.00
132-138	*$6.25*	*$19.00*	*$45.00*	£4.25	£12.50	£30.00
139 (Feb 1964)	*$6.25*	*$19.00*	*$45.00*	£4.25	£12.50	£30.00
140 Clayface appears	*$6.25*	*$19.00*	*$45.00*	£4.25	£12.50	£30.00
141	*$5.00*	*$15.00*	*$35.00*	£2.85	£8.50	£20.00
142 origin and 1st appearance Composite Superman	*$5.50*	*$17.00*	*$40.00*	£3.55	£10.50	£25.00
143	*$5.00*	*$15.00*	*$35.00*	£2.85	£8.50	£20.00
144 Clayface appears	*$5.00*	*$15.00*	*$35.00*	£2.85	£8.50	£20.00
145-146	*$5.00*	*$15.00*	*$35.00*	£2.85	£8.50	£20.00
147 (Feb 1965)	*$5.00*	*$15.00*	*$35.00*	£2.85	£8.50	£20.00
148-150	*$5.00*	*$15.00*	*$35.00*	£2.85	£8.50	£20.00
151-153	*$4.25*	*$12.50*	*$30.00*	£2.10	£6.25	£15.00
154 1st Sons of Superman/Batman; last Silver Age issue, indicia dated December 1965	*$4.25*	*$12.50*	*$30.00*	£2.10	£6.25	£15.00
155 (Feb 1966)	*$4.25*	*$12.50*	*$30.00*	£2.10	£6.25	£15.00
156 Joker cover/story; 1st appearance Bizarro Batman	*$12.50*	*$39.00*	*$90.00*	£5.50	£17.00	£40.00
157	*$4.25*	*$12.50*	*$30.00*	£2.10	£6.25	£15.00
158 Brainiac appears, origin Bottle City of Kandor retold	*$4.25*	*$12.50*	*$30.00*	£2.10	£6.25	£15.00
159-160	*$4.25*	*$12.50*	*$30.00*	£2.10	£6.25	£15.00
161 80pgs, Giant G-28	*$4.25*	*$12.50*	*$30.00*	£2.50	£7.50	£17.50
162-163	*$2.85*	*$8.50*	*$20.00*	£1.40	£4.25	£10.00
164 (Feb 1967) Brainiac appears	*$2.85*	*$8.50*	*$20.00*	£1.40	£4.25	£10.00
165	*$2.85*	*$8.50*	*$20.00*	£1.40	£4.25	£10.00
166 Joker cover/story	*$3.20*	*$9.50*	*$22.50*	£1.75	£5.25	£12.50
167 Brainiac and Supergirl appear	*$2.85*	*$8.50*	*$20.00*	£1.40	£4.25	£10.00
168 return and death of the Composite Superman	*$2.85*	*$8.50*	*$20.00*	£1.40	£4.25	£10.00
169 Batgirl (3rd appearance) and Supergirl appear (also in #176)	*$2.85*	*$8.50*	*$20.00*	£1.40	£4.25	£10.00
170 80pgs, Giant G-40	*$3.55*	*$10.50*	*$25.00*	£2.10	£6.25	£15.00
171	*$2.50*	*$7.50*	*$17.50*	£1.05	£3.20	£7.50

	$Good	$Fine	$N.Mint	£Good	£Fine	£N.Mint
172 Adult Legion appear						
	$2.50	*$7.50*	*$17.50*	£1.05	£3.20	£7.50
173 (Feb 1968)	*$2.50*	*$7.50*	*$17.50*	£1.05	£3.20	£7.50
174	*$2.50*	*$7.50*	*$17.50*	£1.05	£3.20	£7.50
175-176 reprints J'onn J'onzz origin from Detective #225, #226; Neal Adams art						
	$2.85	*$8.50*	*$20.00*	£1.25	£3.85	£9.00
177 Joker cover/story						
	$2.85	*$8.50*	*$20.00*	£1.25	£3.85	£9.00
178	*$2.50*	*$7.50*	*$17.50*	£1.05	£3.20	£7.50
179 80pgs, Giant G-52, reprints #94 and Superman #76						
	$2.85	*$8.50*	*$20.00*	£1.75	£5.25	£12.50
180	*$2.50*	*$7.50*	*$17.50*	£1.05	£3.20	£7.50
181	*$1.40*	*$4.25*	*$10.00*	£0.70	£2.10	£5.00
182 (Feb 1969)	*$1.40*	*$4.25*	*$10.00*	£0.70	£2.10	£5.00
183-187	*$1.40*	*$4.25*	*$10.00*	£0.70	£2.10	£5.00
188 scarce in the U.K. 80pgs, Giant G-64						
	$2.10	*$6.25*	*$15.00*	£1.40	£4.25	£10.00
189-190	*$1.40*	*$4.25*	*$10.00*	£0.70	£2.10	£5.00
191 (Feb 1970)	*$1.25*	*$3.75*	*$7.50*	£0.65	£2.00	£4.00
192-196	*$1.25*	*$3.75*	*$7.50*	£0.65	£2.00	£4.00
197 80pgs, Giant G-76						
	$2.50	*$7.50*	*$15.00*	£1.25	£3.75	£7.50
198 3rd Superman/Flash race (see Superman #199, Flash #175, Adv. Superman #463); Neal Adams cover						
	$10.50	*$32.00*	*$75.00*	£3.55	£10.50	£25.00
199 3rd Superman/Flash race continued (see Superman #199, Flash #175, Adv. Superman #463)						
	$10.50	*$32.00*	*$75.00*	£2.85	£8.50	£20.00
200 (Feb 1971) Superman/Batman regular team-ups end, Superman/Robin co-star; Neal Adams cover						
	$1.25	*$3.75*	*$7.50*	£0.65	£2.00	£4.00
201 Superman and Green Lantern, Neal Adams cover						
	$0.65	*$2.00*	*$4.00*	£0.40	£1.25	£2.50
202 Superman and Batman, Neal Adams cover						
	$0.65	*$2.00*	*$4.00*	£0.40	£1.25	£2.50
203 Superman and Aquaman, Neal Adams cover						
	$0.65	*$2.00*	*$4.00*	£0.40	£1.25	£2.50
204 52pgs, Superman and the new Wonder Woman (the 1970s version), Neal Adams cover						
	$1.00	*$3.00*	*$6.00*	£0.65	£2.00	£4.00
205 52pgs, Superman and The New Teen Titans, Neal Adams cover						
	$0.80	*$2.50*	*$5.00*	£0.55	£1.75	£3.50
206 80pgs, Giant G-88, reprints from World's Finest #118,#121, #130,#138						
	$1.25	*$3.75*	*$7.50*	£0.65	£2.00	£4.00
207 52pgs, Superman and Batman						
	$0.80	*$2.50*	*$5.00*	£0.55	£1.75	£3.50
208 52pgs, Superman and Dr. Fate, Neal Adams cover						
	$0.80	*$2.50*	*$5.00*	£0.55	£1.75	£3.50
209 52pgs, (Feb 1972) Superman and Hawkman, Neal Adams cover						
	$0.80	*$2.50*	*$5.00*	£0.55	£1.75	£3.50
210 52pgs, Superman and Green Arrow, Neal Adams cover						
	$0.80	*$2.50*	*$5.00*	£0.55	£1.75	£3.50
211 52pgs, Superman and Batman, Neal Adams cover						
	$0.80	*$2.50*	*$5.00*	£0.55	£1.75	£3.50
212 52pgs, Superman and Martian Manhunter						
	$0.80	*$2.50*	*$5.00*	£0.55	£1.75	£3.50
213 Superman and The Atom						
	$0.65	*$2.00*	*$4.00*	£0.30	£1.00	£2.00
214 Superman and The Vigilante						
	$0.65	*$2.00*	*$4.00*	£0.30	£1.00	£2.00
215 (Dec/Jan 1973) The Sons of Superman and Batman						
	$0.65	*$2.00*	*$4.00*	£0.30	£1.00	£2.00
216 The Sons of Superman and Batman						
	$0.65	*$2.00*	*$4.00*	£0.30	£1.00	£2.00
217 Superman, Batman and Metamporpho						

	$Good	$Fine	$N.Mint	£Good	£Fine	£N.Mint
	$0.65	*$2.00*	*$4.00*	£0.30	£1.00	£2.00
218 Superman and Batman resume regular team -ups						
	$0.65	*$2.00*	*$4.00*	£0.30	£1.00	£2.00
219-220	*$0.65*	*$2.00*	*$4.00*	£0.30	£1.00	£2.00
221 (Jan/Feb 1974)						
	$0.65	*$2.00*	*$4.00*	£0.30	£1.00	£2.00
222	*$0.65*	*$2.00*	*$4.00*	£0.30	£1.00	£2.00
223-226 100pgs	*$1.00*	*$3.00*	*$6.00*	£0.65	£2.00	£4.00
227 100pgs, (Jan 1975) Joker appears (cameo)						
	$1.00	*$3.00*	*$6.00*	£0.65	£2.00	£4.00
228 100pgs, The Sons of Superman and Batman co-star						
	$1.00	*$3.00*	*$6.00*	£0.65	£2.00	£4.00
229	*$0.65*	*$2.00*	*$4.00*	£0.30	£1.00	£2.00
230 scarce in the U.K. 68pgs, Neal Adams reprint						
	$0.80	*$2.50*	*$5.00*	£0.55	£1.75	£3.50
231 Green Arrow and Flash appear						
	$0.65	*$2.00*	*$4.00*	£0.30	£1.00	£2.00
232-233 scarce in the U.K.						
	$0.65	*$2.00*	*$4.00*	£0.40	£1.25	£2.50
234 LD in the U.K.	*$0.65*	*$2.00*	*$4.00*	£0.30	£1.00	£2.00
235 LD in the U.K. (Jan 1976)						
	$0.65	*$2.00*	*$4.00*	£0.30	£1.00	£2.00
236-242 LD in the U.K.						
	$0.65	*$2.00*	*$4.00*	£0.30	£1.00	£2.00
243 LD in the U.K. (Feb 1977)						
	$0.65	*$2.00*	*$4.00*	£0.30	£1.00	£2.00
244 ND 80pgs, Neal Adams cover						
	$0.75	*$2.25*	*$4.50*	£0.50	£1.50	£3.00
245 80pgs, Neal Adams cover art, no Comics Code Authority stamp (allegedly for violence)						
	$0.75	*$2.25*	*$4.50*	£0.40	£1.25	£2.50
246 ND 80pgs, Neal Adams cover						
	$0.75	*$2.25*	*$4.50*	£0.50	£1.50	£3.00
247 ND 80pgs	*$0.75*	*$2.25*	*$4.50*	£0.50	£1.50	£3.00
248 ND 80pgs, (Dec/Jan 1978)						
	$0.75	*$2.25*	*$4.50*	£0.50	£1.50	£3.00
249-252 ND 80pgs						
	$0.75	*$2.25*	*$4.50*	£0.50	£1.50	£3.00
253 68pgs	*$0.65*	*$2.00*	*$4.00*	£0.30	£1.00	£2.00
254 scarce in the U.K. 68pgs, (Dec/Jan 1979)						
	$0.65	*$2.00*	*$4.00*	£0.35	£1.10	£2.25
255-256 ND 68pgs						
	$0.65	*$2.00*	*$4.00*	£0.40	£1.25	£2.50
257 scarce in the U.K. 68pgs						
	$0.65	*$2.00*	*$4.00*	£0.35	£1.10	£2.25
258 ND 68pgs, Neal Adams cover						
	$0.65	*$2.00*	*$4.00*	£0.40	£1.25	£2.50
259 ND 68pgs, Rogers/Nasser art						
	$0.65	*$2.00*	*$4.00*	£0.35	£1.10	£2.25
260 ND 68pgs, (Dec/Jan 1980)						
	$0.65	*$2.00*	*$4.00*	£0.40	£1.25	£2.50
261-265 ND 68pgs						
	$0.65	*$2.00*	*$4.00*	£0.40	£1.25	£2.50
266 ND 52pgs, (Dec/Jan 1981)						
	$0.60	*$1.80*	*$3.00*	£0.40	£1.20	£2.00
267-269 ND 52pgs						
	$0.60	*$1.80*	*$3.00*	£0.40	£1.20	£2.00
270 ND 52pgs, Neal Adams cover						
	$0.60	*$1.80*	*$3.00*	£0.40	£1.20	£2.00
271 ND 52pgs, new origin Superman/Batman team; George perez cover art						
	$0.80	*$2.40*	*$4.00*	£0.50	£1.50	£2.50
272-274 52pgs	*$0.50*	*$1.50*	*$2.50*	£0.30	£0.90	£1.50

Wonder Woman (1st) #133

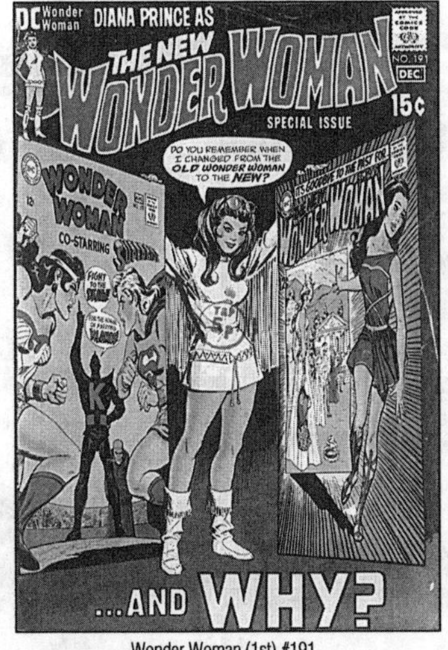

Wonder Woman (1st) #191

World's Finest #85

	$Good	$Fine	$N.Mint	£Good	£Fine	£N.Mint
275 52pgs, (Jan 1982)	*$0.50*	*$1.50*	*$2.50*	£0.30	£0.90	£1.50
276-278 52pgs, George Perez cover	*$0.50*	*$1.50*	*$2.50*	£0.30	£0.90	£1.50
279-282 52pgs	*$0.50*	*$1.50*	*$2.50*	£0.30	£0.90	£1.50
283 Composite Superman returns	*$0.40*	*$1.20*	*$2.00*	£0.25	£0.75	£1.25
284 Legion of Super-Heroes appears, Composite Superman appears	*$0.40*	*$1.20*	*$2.00*	£0.25	£0.75	£1.25
285-286	*$0.40*	*$1.20*	*$2.00*	£0.25	£0.75	£1.25
287 (Jan 1983)	*$0.40*	*$1.20*	*$2.00*	£0.25	£0.75	£1.25
288-298	*$0.40*	*$1.20*	*$2.00*	£0.25	£0.75	£1.25
299 (Jan 1984)	*$0.40*	*$1.20*	*$2.00*	£0.25	£0.75	£1.25
300 52pgs, Mark Texeira lead story, Teen Titans back-up by George Perez	*$0.60*	*$1.80*	*$3.00*	£0.40	£1.20	£2.00
301	*$0.40*	*$1.20*	*$2.00*	£0.20	£0.60	£1.00
302 Neal Adams reprint from World's Finest Comics #176	*$0.40*	*$1.20*	*$2.00*	£0.20	£0.60	£1.00
303-310	*$0.40*	*$1.20*	*$2.00*	£0.20	£0.60	£1.00
311 (Jan 1985)	*$0.40*	*$1.20*	*$2.00*	£0.20	£0.60	£1.00
312-321	*$0.40*	*$1.20*	*$2.00*	£0.20	£0.60	£1.00
322 Giffen art	*$0.40*	*$1.20*	*$2.00*	£0.20	£0.60	£1.00
323 (Jan 1986)	*$0.40*	*$1.20*	*$2.00*	£0.20	£0.60	£1.00
Title Value:	***$10471.35***	***$31454.45***	***$81509.50***	**£6921.05**	**£20765.10**	**£53909.50**

Note: like all Golden Age material, these comics were not available on the news-stands in the U.K. until cover date November 1959 but some Golden Age issues may have come to England as a result of personnel movements during the Second World War or as cheap ballast on ships.

Note: Joker covers and stories-129, 156, 166, 177. Bruce Wayne's older brother Thomas appears in 223, 227

ARTISTS

Ditko art in 249-255. Kirby reprints in 187, 197. Nasser art in 244-246, 259, 260.

FEATURES

Adam Strange in 263. Aquaman in 125-133, 135, 137, 139, 263, 264. Atom in 260. Black Canary in 244-249, 251-256, 262, 267. Black Lightning in 257-261. Captain Marvel/Marvel Family in 253-270, 272-282. Creeper in 249-255. Green Arrow in 107-134, 136, 138, 140, 244-249, 251-258, 261-266, 268-270, 272-282. Green Arrow/Hawkman in 259. Hawkman in 256-258, 261, 262, 264-270, 272-277, 279-282. Metamorpho in 218-220, 229. Plastic Man in 273. Red Tornado in 265-270, 272. Superman/Batman in 71-160, 162-169, 171-178, 180-187, 189-196, 202, 207, 211, 215-228, 230-249, 250 (guest starring Wonder Woman, Green Arrow, Black Canary), 251-282. Tommy Tomorrow in 107-124. Vigilante in 244-248. Wonder Woman in 244-249, 251, 252. Zatanna in 274-278.

Superman team-ups as follows:

Flash in 198, 199; Robin in 200; Green Lantern in 201; Aquaman in 203; Wonder Woman in 204; Teen Titans in 205; Dr.Fate in 208; Hawkman in 209; Green Arrow in 210; Manhunter From Mars in 212; Atom in 213; Vigilante in 214.

REPRINT FEATURES

Aquaman in 144, 146, 223, 228, 230. Batman in 209. Bizarro in 181 (origin). Black Canary in 225. Black Pirate, The King in 210. Captain Comet in 204. Challengers of the Unknown in 230. Congo Bill in 195. Congorilla in 148-151. Deadman in 223, 226. Eclipso in 226, 228. Ghost Patrol in 208. Green Arrow in 143, 145, 154, 159, 187, 204. Green Lantern in 174. Grim Ghost, Air Wave in 212. Harlequin in 211. Johnny Quick in 186, 198, 224. Lois Lane 141. Martian Manhunter in 175 (origin), 176, 184, 226, 227. Metamorpho in 224, 228. Rip Hunter in 225, 227. Robin in 190-193. Robotman 168, 208, 223, 226. Roy Raymond in 158, 166, 189. GA Sandman in 226. Silent Knight in 182, 205. Superboy in 146, 171. Superman in 142, 173, 178. Superman/Batman in 161, 170, 179, 180, 188, 206, 223-225, 228, 229. Superman/Batman/Green Arrow in 197. Tommy Tomorrow in 156, 162, 185. Tarantula in 207. Vigilante in 225, 227, 228.

WORLD'S FINEST COMICS (2ND SERIES)

DC Comics,MS; 1 Aug 1990-3 Oct 1990

	$Good	$Fine	$N.Mint	£Good	£Fine	£N.Mint
1 ND 48pgs, art by Steve Rude begins, script by Dave Gibbons	*$0.90*	*$2.70*	*$4.50*	£0.60	£1.80	£3.00
2-3 ND 48pgs	*$0.90*	*$2.70*	*$4.50*	£0.60	£1.80	£3.00
Title Value:	***$2.70***	***$8.10***	***$13.50***	**£1.80**	**£5.40**	**£9.00**
Multi-Pack (Nov 1991) ND, pre-bagged mini-series with illustrated header card				£1.50	£4.50	£7.50
Trade paperback (Jan 1993) 160pgs, reprints mini-series plus sketches by Steve Rude				£2.50	£7.50	£12.50

WORLD'S FINEST COMICS DIGEST

DC Comics,Digest; nn Feb 1981

(DC Special series #23)

	$Good	$Fine	$N.Mint	£Good	£Fine	£N.Mint
nn ND 68pgs	*$0.80*	*$2.40*	*$4.00*	£0.50	£1.50	£2.50
Title Value:	***$0.80***	***$2.40***	***$4.00***	**£0.50**	**£1.50**	**£2.50**

WORLD'S FINEST: SUPERBOY/ROBIN

DC Comics,MS; 1 Dec 1996-3 Feb 1997

	$Good	$Fine	$N.Mint	£Good	£Fine	£N.Mint
1-3 ND 48pgs, 1st meeting between Superboy and Robin as they battle Metallo and Poison Ivy	*$1.00*	*$3.00*	*$5.00*	£0.70	£2.10	£3.50
Title Value:	***$3.00***	***$9.00***	***$15.00***	**£2.10**	**£6.30**	**£10.50**

WORLD'S GREATEST SUPER HEROES

(see DC 100 Page Super Spectacular #6)

WORLD'S WORST COMICS AWARDS

Kitchen Sink,MS; 1 Feb 1991-2 Mar 1991

	$Good	$Fine	$N.Mint	£Good	£Fine	£N.Mint
1 ND scarce in the U.K. a look at the worst comics published in the last 25 years	*$0.50*	*$1.50*	*$2.50*	£0.35	£1.05	£1.75
2 ND	*$0.50*	*$1.50*	*$2.50*	£0.30	£0.90	£1.50
Title Value:	***$1.00***	***$3.00***	***$5.00***	**£0.65**	**£1.95**	**£3.25**

WORLDS COLLIDE

DC Comics/Milestone; 1 Jul 1994

	$Good	$Fine	$N.Mint	£Good	£Fine	£N.Mint
1 ND 48pgs	*$0.40*	*$1.20*	*$2.00*	£0.25	£0.75	£1.25
1 Collectors Edition, ND 48pgs, pre-bagged with sheet of vinyl clings; X-over between the regular DC universe and the Milestone universe; continued in Superboy #7	*$0.60*	*$1.80*	*$3.00*	£0.40	£1.20	£2.00
Title Value:	***$1.00***	***$3.00***	***$5.00***	**£0.65**	**£1.95**	**£3.25**

WORLDS OF H.P. LOVECRAFT, THE

Caliber Press; 1 1993

	$Good	$Fine	$N.Mint	£Good	£Fine	£N.Mint
1 ND Rob Davis art, black and white; adapts The Picture in the House	*$0.50*	*$1.50*	*$2.50*	£0.30	£0.90	£1.50
Title Value:	***$0.50***	***$1.50***	***$2.50***	**£0.30**	**£0.90**	**£1.50**

WORLDS UNKNOWN

Marvel Comics Group; 1 May 1973-8 Aug 1974

	$Good	$Fine	$N.Mint	£Good	£Fine	£N.Mint
1 ND scarce in the U.K. Harln Ellison story with art by Ralph Reese; also features Gil Kane art plus 1950s reprint	*$0.50*	*$1.50*	*$3.00*	£0.30	£1.00	£2.00
2 ND scarce in the U.K. features Gil Kane art; dinosaur cover	*$0.40*	*$1.25*	*$2.50*	£0.25	£0.75	£1.50
3 ND scarce in the U.K. full length adaptation of "Farewell To The Master" by Harry Bates which was to become the classic SF film The Day The Earth Stood Still	*$0.40*	*$1.25*	*$2.50*	£0.25	£0.75	£1.50
4 ND scarce in the U.K. adaptation of Fredric Brown story "Arena" by Buscema and Giordano plus 1950s reprint	*$0.40*	*$1.25*	*$2.50*	£0.25	£0.75	£1.50
5 ND scarce in the U.K. adaptation of A.E. Van Vogt's "Black Destroyer"	*$0.40*	*$1.25*	*$2.50*	£0.25	£0.75	£1.50
6 ND scarce in the U.K. adaptation of Theodore Sturgeon's "Killdozer"	*$0.40*	*$1.25*	*$2.50*	£0.25	£0.75	£1.50
7 ND adaptation of The Golden Voyage of Sinbad	*$0.40*	*$1.25*	*$2.50*	£0.20	£0.60	£1.25
8 adaptation of The Golden Voyage of Sinbad, classic Vince Coletta art	*$0.40*	*$1.25*	*$2.50*	£0.15	£0.50	£1.00
Title Value:	***$3.30***	***$10.25***	***$20.50***	**£1.90**	**£5.85**	**£11.75**

FEATURES

Science-fiction adaptations in 1-6. Sinbad in 7, 8. Back-up reprints in 1, 4.

WRATH

Malibu Ultraverse; 1 Jan 1994-9 Nov 1994

	$Good	$Fine	$N.Mint	£Good	£Fine	£N.Mint
1 ND Mike Barr script, James Pascoe art	*$0.40*	*$1.20*	*$2.00*	£0.25	£0.75	£1.25
2 ND Mantra guest-stars	*$0.40*	*$1.20*	*$2.00*	£0.25	£0.75	£1.25
3-4 ND	*$0.40*	*$1.20*	*$2.00*	£0.25	£0.75	£1.25
5 ND guest-starring Freex	*$0.40*	*$1.20*	*$2.00*	£0.25	£0.75	£1.25
6-7 ND	*$0.40*	*$1.20*	*$2.00*	£0.25	£0.75	£1.25
8 ND Warstrike and Mantra appear	*$0.40*	*$1.20*	*$2.00*	£0.25	£0.75	£1.25
9 ND Prime appears	*$0.40*	*$1.20*	*$2.00*	£0.25	£0.75	£1.25
Title Value:	***$3.60***	***$10.80***	***$18.00***	**£2.25**	**£6.75**	**£11.25**

WRATH OF THE SPECTRE

(see Spectre, Wrath of The)

WRATH, GIANT SIZE

Malibu Ultraverse; 1 Aug 1994

	$Good	$Fine	$N.Mint	£Good	£Fine	£N.Mint
1 ND 40pgs, Warstrike and Mantra appear	*$0.40*	*$1.20*	*$2.00*	£0.25	£0.75	£1.25
Title Value:	***$0.40***	***$1.20***	***$2.00***	**£0.25**	**£0.75**	**£1.25**

WULF THE BARBARIAN

Atlas; 1 Feb 1975-4 Sep 1975

	$Good	$Fine	$N.Mint	£Good	£Fine	£N.Mint
1 distributed in the U.K.	*$0.25*	*$0.75*	*$1.50*	£0.15	£0.50	£1.00
2 distributed in the U.K. Hama/Janson art	*$0.25*	*$0.75*	*$1.50*	£0.15	£0.50	£1.00
3 distributed in the U.K. Leo Summer art	*$0.25*	*$0.75*	*$1.50*	£0.15	£0.50	£1.00
4 distributed in the U.K.	*$0.25*	*$0.75*	*$1.50*	£0.15	£0.50	£1.00
Title Value:	***$1.00***	***$3.00***	***$6.00***	**£0.60**	**£2.00**	**£4.00**

WYATT EARP

Atlas/Marvel Comics Group; 29 Jun 1960; 30 Oct 1972-34 Jun 1973

(previous issues ND)

	$Good	$Fine	$N.Mint	£Good	£Fine	£N.Mint
29 Jack Kirby art	*$3.90*	*$11.50*	*$27.50*	£2.50	£7.50	£17.50
30-34 ND all reprints	*$0.50*	*$1.50*	*$3.00*	£0.30	£1.00	£2.00
Title Value:	***$6.40***	***$19.00***	***$42.50***	**£4.00**	**£12.50**	**£27.50**

Note: Williamson reprint in #30.

WYATT EARP, FRONTIER MARSHAL

Charlton; 12 Jan 1956-72 Dec 1967

	$Good	$Fine	$N.Mint	£Good	£Fine	£N.Mint
12 scarce in the U.K.	*$6.00*	*$18.00*	*$42.50*	£3.90	£11.50	£27.50
13-19	*$3.55*	*$10.50*	*$25.00*	£2.10	£6.25	£15.00
20 64pgs, Williamson art	*$7.75*	*$23.50*	*$55.00*	£5.00	£15.00	£35.00
21-26	*$2.10*	*$6.25*	*$15.00*	£1.40	£4.25	£10.00
1st official distribution in the U.K.						
27-30	*$2.10*	*$6.25*	*$15.00*	£1.40	£4.25	£10.00
31-50	*$1.40*	*$4.25*	*$10.00*	£1.05	£3.20	£7.50
51-72	*$1.05*	*$3.20*	*$7.50*	£0.70	£2.10	£5.00
Title Value:	***$110.70***	***$332.90***	***$787.50***	**£74.00**	**£222.95**	**£527.50**

Note: issues after about 1958 came to be distributed on the news-stands in the U.K.

WYNONNA EARP

Image; 1 Dec 1996-present

	$Good	$Fine	$N.Mint	£Good	£Fine	£N.Mint
1-3 ND Beau Smith script, Joyce Chin and Mark Irwin art begins	*$0.50*	*$1.50*	*$2.50*	£0.30	£0.90	£1.50
Title Value:	***$1.50***	***$4.50***	***$7.50***	**£0.90**	**£2.70**	**£4.50**

X

X

Dark Horse; 1 Jan 1994-25 Apr 1996

	$Good	$Fine	$N.Mint	£Good	£Fine	£N.Mint
1 ND Steven Grant script begins, red foil stamped logo	*$0.50*	*$1.50*	*$2.50*	£0.30	£0.90	£1.50

	$Good	$Fine	$N.Mint	£Good	£Fine	£N.Mint
2-17 ND	$0.50	$1.50	$2.50	£0.30	£0.90	£1.50
18-20 ND Predator X-over	$0.50	$1.50	$2.50	£0.30	£0.90	£1.50
21-24 ND Frank Miller cover	$0.50	$1.50	$2.50	£0.30	£0.90	£1.50
25 ND origin told; Frank Miller cover	$0.50	$1.50	$2.50	£0.30	£0.90	£1.50
Title Value:	$12.50	$37.50	$62.50	£7.50	£22.50	£37.50
X, THE MAN WITH X-RAY EYES						
Gold Key/Movie Comics,OS Movie; 10083-309 Sep 1963						
10083-309 distributed in the U.K. Ray Milland photo cover	$9.25	$28.00	$65.00	£5.50	£17.00	£40.00
Title Value:	$9.25	$28.00	$65.00	£5.50	£17.00	£40.00
X-1999						
Viz Communications,MS; 1 May 1995-6 Oct 1995						
1-6 ND Clamp script and art; black and white	$0.50	$1.50	$2.50	£0.30	£0.90	£1.50
Title Value:	$3.00	$9.00	$15.00	£1.80	£5.40	£9.00
X-CALIBRE						
Marvel Comics Group; 1 Mar 1995-4 Jun 1995						
(title previously called Excalibur)						
1 Warren Ellis script, Lashley and Wegrzyn art	$0.80	$2.40	$4.00	£0.50	£1.50	£2.50
2-3 Warren Ellis script, Lashley and Wegrzyn art	$0.50	$1.50	$2.50	£0.30	£0.90	£1.50
4 Warren Ellis script, Lashley and Wegrzyn art; continued in X-Men: Omega	$0.50	$1.50	$2.50	£0.30	£0.90	£1.50
Title Value:	$2.30	$6.90	$11.50	£1.40	£4.20	£7.00
The Ultimate X-Calibre (Jul 1995)						
96pgs, Bookshelf Edition collects issues #1-4 with etched gold cover				£1.20	£3.60	£6.00
X-FACTOR						
Marvel Comics Group; 1 Feb 1986-111 Feb 1995; 112 Jul 1995-present						
(see Avengers #263, Cloak and Dagger #18, Fantastic Four #286, Hulk #336, #337, Mephisto)						
(title becomes Factor X)						
1 LD in the U.K. DS Guice art begins (ends #7)	$2.50	$7.50	$12.50	£1.30	£3.90	£6.50
2 LD in the U.K. Mike Zeck cover	$1.50	$4.50	$7.50	£0.70	£2.10	£3.50
3-4	$1.00	$3.00	$5.00	£0.60	£1.80	£3.00
5 LD in the U.K. 1st appearance Apocalypse	$1.60	$4.80	$8.00	£0.80	£2.40	£4.00
6 LD in the U.K. 1st full appearance Apocalypse	$3.00	$9.00	$15.00	£1.00	£3.00	£5.00
7 LD in the U.K.	$0.80	$2.40	$4.00	£0.50	£1.50	£2.50
8	$0.80	$2.40	$4.00	£0.40	£1.20	£2.00
9 Mutant Massacre tie-in	$0.80	$2.40	$4.00	£0.40	£1.20	£2.00
10 Mutant Massacre tie-in, Walt Simonson art begins, Sabretooth appears	$0.80	$2.40	$4.00	£0.50	£1.50	£2.50
11 Mutant Massacre tie-in, Walt Simonson art	$0.60	$1.80	$3.00	£0.40	£1.20	£2.00
12 Mutant Massacre tie-in, Walt Simonson cover only (Silvestri art)	$0.60	$1.80	$3.00	£0.40	£1.20	£2.00
13-15 Walt Simonson art	$0.60	$1.80	$3.00	£0.40	£1.20	£2.00
16 Mazzucchelli art	$0.50	$1.50	$2.50	£0.30	£0.90	£1.50
17 Thor appears, Walt Simonson art	$0.50	$1.50	$2.50	£0.30	£0.90	£1.50
18-19 Walt Simonson art	$0.50	$1.50	$2.50	£0.30	£0.90	£1.50
20	$0.50	$1.50	$2.50	£0.30	£0.90	£1.50
21 Walt Simonson art	$0.50	$1.50	$2.50	£0.30	£0.90	£1.50
22	$0.50	$1.50	$2.50	£0.30	£0.90	£1.50
23 Fall of the Mutants, Walt Simonson art, Archangel cameo (1st appearance)	$1.20	$3.60	$6.00	£0.40	£1.20	£2.00
24 LD in the U.K. Walt Simonson art, Fall of the Mutants, 1st full appearance Archangel (formerly Angel of the X-Men); Apocalypse origin	$3.00	$9.00	$15.00	£1.00	£3.00	£5.00
25 DS Walt Simonson art, Fall of the Mutants	$0.90	$2.70	$4.50	£0.60	£1.80	£3.00
26 Walt Simonson art, Fall of the Mutants	$0.80	$2.40	$4.00	£0.50	£1.50	£2.50
27 LD in the U.K. Walt Simonson art	$0.50	$1.50	$2.50	£0.35	£1.05	£1.75
28-30 Walt Simonson art	$0.50	$1.50	$2.50	£0.30	£0.90	£1.50
31 Walt Simonson art	$0.40	$1.20	$2.00	£0.25	£0.75	£1.25
32 Avengers tie-in by Steve Lightle	$0.40	$1.20	$2.00	£0.25	£0.75	£1.25
33-34 Walt Simonson art	$0.40	$1.20	$2.00	£0.25	£0.75	£1.25
35	$0.40	$1.20	$2.00	£0.25	£0.75	£1.25
36-37 LD in the U.K. Inferno X-over, Walt Simonson art	$0.50	$1.50	$2.50	£0.30	£0.90	£1.50
38 LD in the U.K. DS Inferno X-over, X-Men appear, Walt Simonson art	$0.80	$2.40	$4.00	£0.50	£1.50	£2.50
39 LD in the U.K. Inferno X-over, X-Men appear, Walt Simonson art	$0.50	$1.50	$2.50	£0.30	£0.90	£1.50
40 Rob Liefeld cover and art	$0.80	$2.40	$4.00	£0.40	£1.20	£2.00

	$Good	$Fine	$N.Mint	£Good	£Fine	£N.Mint
41-42 Arthur Adams art	$0.40	$1.20	$2.00	£0.25	£0.75	£1.25
43 Judgement story begins (ends #50 with #47 as an interlude), Paul Smith art	$0.40	$1.20	$2.00	£0.25	£0.75	£1.25
44-46 Paul Smith art	$0.40	$1.20	$2.00	£0.25	£0.75	£1.25
47	$0.40	$1.20	$2.00	£0.25	£0.75	£1.25
48 Paul Smith art	$0.40	$1.20	$2.00	£0.25	£0.75	£1.25
49 Acts of Vengeance tie-in, Paul Smith art	$0.40	$1.20	$2.00	£0.25	£0.75	£1.25
50 LD in the U.K. DS Acts of Vengeance tie-in, McFarlane art, Liefeld cover	$0.60	$1.80	$3.00	£0.40	£1.20	£2.00
51-52 Sabretooth appears	$0.60	$1.80	$3.00	£0.40	£1.20	£2.00
53 Sabretooth appears, Cyclops proposes (and gets turned down)	$0.60	$1.80	$3.00	£0.40	£1.20	£2.00
54 1st appearance Crimson, Colossus appears	$0.30	$0.90	$1.50	£0.20	£0.60	£1.00
55 Peter David script	$0.30	$0.90	$1.50	£0.20	£0.60	£1.00
56	$0.30	$0.90	$1.50	£0.20	£0.60	£1.00
57 Andy Kubert art	$0.30	$0.90	$1.50	£0.20	£0.60	£1.00
58 Jon Bogdanove art	$0.30	$0.90	$1.50	£0.20	£0.60	£1.00
59	$0.30	$0.90	$1.50	£0.20	£0.60	£1.00
60 The X-Tinction Agenda part 3 (see X-Men #270 for start of story), Cable appears, Jon Bogdanove art	$1.50	$4.50	$7.50	£1.00	£3.00	£5.00
60 2nd printing, ND The X-Tinction Agenda part 3 (gold cover)	$0.60	$1.80	$3.00	£0.40	£1.20	£2.00
61 The X-Tinction Agenda part 6, Cable appears, Jon Bogdanove art	$1.00	$3.00	$5.00	£0.70	£2.10	£3.50
62 The X-Tinction Agenda part 9 (of 9), Cable appears, last Jon Bogdanove art	$1.00	$3.00	$5.00	£0.70	£2.10	£3.50
63 ND Whilce Portacio art begins	$1.20	$3.60	$6.00	£0.80	£2.40	£4.00
64-65 Whilce Portacio art	$0.80	$2.40	$4.00	£0.50	£1.50	£2.50
66-67 LD in the U.K. Whilce Portacio art	$0.60	$1.80	$3.00	£0.40	£1.20	£2.00
68 Nathan Summers appears, Whilce Portacio art	$0.60	$1.80	$3.00	£0.40	£1.20	£2.00
69 Whilce Portacio art	$0.30	$0.90	$1.50	£0.20	£0.60	£1.00
70 last "old" X-Factor, Peter David scripts begin	$0.30	$0.90	$1.50	£0.20	£0.60	£1.00
71 1st new X-Factor, Peter David script, 1st Larry Stroman art on title	$0.60	$1.80	$3.00	£0.40	£1.20	£2.00
71 2nd printing, ND Feb 1992	$0.40	$1.20	$2.00	£0.25	£0.75	£1.25
72-73 Peter David script, Larry Stroman art	$0.30	$0.90	$1.50	£0.20	£0.60	£1.00
74 Peter David script	$0.30	$0.90	$1.50	£0.20	£0.60	£1.00
75 LD in the U.K. DS, intro The Nasty Boys, Peter David script	$0.40	$1.20	$2.00	£0.25	£0.75	£1.25
76 Hulk appears, $1.25 cover begins	$0.30	$0.90	$1.50	£0.20	£0.60	£1.00
77	$0.30	$0.90	$1.50	£0.20	£0.60	£1.00
78 (see note below)	$0.30	$0.90	$1.50	£0.20	£0.60	£1.00
79-80	$0.30	$0.90	$1.50	£0.20	£0.60	£1.00
81 Brotherhood of Evil Mutants appear	$0.30	$0.90	$1.50	£0.20	£0.60	£1.00
82-83	$0.30	$0.90	$1.50	£0.20	£0.60	£1.00
84 X-Cutioner's Song part 2, pre-bagged with trading card, continued in X-Men #14	$0.40	$1.20	$2.00	£0.25	£0.75	£1.25
85 X-Cutioner's Song part 5, pre-bagged with trading card, continued in X-Men #15	$0.40	$1.20	$2.00	£0.25	£0.75	£1.25
86 X-Cutioner's Song part 10, pre-bagged with trading card, continued in X-Men #16	$0.30	$0.90	$1.50	£0.20	£0.60	£1.00
87-91 Joe Quesada art	$0.30	$0.90	$1.50	£0.20	£0.60	£1.00
92 DS, Joe Quesada art; hologram cover, Return of Magneto story begins	$0.90	$2.70	$4.50	£0.60	£1.80	£3.00
92 2nd printing, ND (Sep 1993)	$0.70	$2.10	$3.50	£0.45	£1.35	£2.25
93-94 Joe Quesada art	$0.30	$0.90	$1.50	£0.20	£0.60	£1.00
95-99	$0.30	$0.90	$1.50	£0.20	£0.60	£1.00
100 48pgs, death of Jaimie	$0.40	$1.20	$2.00	£0.25	£0.75	£1.25
100 Collectors Edition, 48pgs, red foil embossed cover, death of Jamie	$0.70	$2.10	$3.50	£0.45	£1.35	£2.25
101 ND	$0.30	$0.90	$1.50	£0.20	£0.60	£1.00
102 ND with free Spiderman vs. Venom card sheet	$0.30	$0.90	$1.50	£0.20	£0.60	£1.00
103-105 ND	$0.30	$0.90	$1.50	£0.20	£0.60	£1.00
106 ND	$0.40	$1.20	$2.00	£0.25	£0.75	£1.25
106 Deluxe Edition, ND foil stamped cover; Generation X tie-in	$0.60	$1.80	$3.00	£0.40	£1.20	£2.00
107-108 ND	$0.30	$0.90	$1.50	£0.20	£0.60	£1.00
108 Deluxe Edition, ND printed on glossy stock paper						

	$Good	$Fine	$N.Mint	£Good	£Fine	£N.Mint
	$0.40	$1.20	$2.00	£0.25	£0.75	£1.25
109 ND	$0.30	$0.90	$1.50	£0.20	£0.60	£1.00
109 Deluxe Edition, ND printed on glossy stock paper						
	$0.40	$1.20	$2.00	£0.25	£0.75	£1.25
110 ND	$0.30	$0.90	$1.50	£0.20	£0.60	£1.00
110 Deluxe Edition, ND printed on glossy stock paper						
	$0.40	$1.20	$2.00	£0.25	£0.75	£1.25
111 ND	$0.30	$0.90	$1.50	£0.20	£0.60	£1.00
111 Deluxe Edition, ND printed on glossy stock paper plus bound-in Fleer trading card						
	$0.40	$1.20	$2.00	£0.25	£0.75	£1.25
112 ND continued from X-Men: Prime; J.F. Moore script, Steve Epting and Al Milgrom art						
	$0.40	$1.20	$2.00	£0.25	£0.75	£1.25
113 ND Mystique guest-stars						
	$0.40	$1.20	$2.00	£0.25	£0.75	£1.25
114-116 ND	$0.40	$1.20	$2.00	£0.25	£0.75	£1.25
117 ND Cyclops appears, Havok leaves the team						
	$0.40	$1.20	$2.00	£0.25	£0.75	£1.25
118 ND	$0.40	$1.20	$2.00	£0.25	£0.75	£1.25
119 ND Sabretooth appears						
	$0.40	$1.20	$2.00	£0.25	£0.75	£1.25
120 ND	$0.40	$1.20	$2.00	£0.25	£0.75	£1.25
121 ND Sabretooth appears						
	$0.40	$1.20	$2.00	£0.25	£0.75	£1.25
122 ND Sabretooth joins X-Factor						
	$0.40	$1.20	$2.00	£0.25	£0.75	£1.25
123-124 ND new creative team of Howard Mackie and Jeff Matsuda						
	$0.40	$1.20	$2.00	£0.25	£0.75	£1.25
125 ND 48pgs, Onslaught tie-in						
	$0.60	$1.80	$3.00	£0.40	£1.20	£2.00
126 ND Onslaught tie-in						
	$0.40	$1.20	$2.00	£0.25	£0.75	£1.25
127 ND with bound-in Overpower cards						
	$0.40	$1.20	$2.00	£0.25	£0.75	£1.25
128-132 ND	$0.40	$1.20	$2.00	£0.25	£0.75	£1.25
Title Value:	$76.70	$230.10	$383.50	£45.95	£137.85	£229.75

Note: a cover-priced 70p edition has been reported as well as the regular 80p version. It is unknown how many copies there are but reports suggest it is very scarce in the U.K.

X-Men: Wrath of Apocalypse (Feb 1996)

	$Good	$Fine	$N.Mint	£Good	£Fine	£N.Mint
ND Trade paperback 96pgs, reprints X-Factor #65-68				£0.65	£1.95	£3.25

X-FACTOR ANNUAL

Marvel Comics Group; 1 Oct 1986-present

	$Good	$Fine	$N.Mint	£Good	£Fine	£N.Mint
1 ND	$0.60	$1.80	$3.00	£0.40	£1.20	£2.00
2 ND Adamsesque art by Grindberg						
	$0.50	$1.50	$2.50	£0.30	£0.90	£1.50
3 ND 64pgs, squarebound, Evolutionary War; Louise Simonson script						
	$0.50	$1.50	$2.50	£0.30	£0.90	£1.50
4 ND 64pgs, squarebound, Atlantis Attacks part 10, John Byrne art						
	$0.50	$1.50	$2.50	£0.30	£0.90	£1.50
5 ND 64pgs, squarebound, Days of Future Present part 2, continued in New Mutants Annual #6						
	$0.50	$1.50	$2.50	£0.30	£0.90	£1.50
6 ND 64pgs, squarebound, King of Pain part 4 (conclusion), Cable appears						
	$0.50	$1.50	$2.50	£0.30	£0.90	£1.50
7 ND 64pgs, squarebound, Shattershot part 3, continued in X-Force Annual #1						
	$0.50	$1.50	$2.50	£0.30	£0.90	£1.50
8 ND 64pgs, squarebound, pre-bagged with trading card introducing Charon						
	$0.60	$1.80	$3.00	£0.40	£1.20	£2.00
9 ND 64pgs, Professor X vs. Haven						
	$0.60	$1.80	$3.00	£0.40	£1.20	£2.00
Title Value:	$4.80	$14.40	$24.00	£3.00	£9.00	£15.00

X-FACTOR: PRISONER OF LOVE

Marvel Comics Group,OS; 1 Sep 1990

	$Good	$Fine	$N.Mint	£Good	£Fine	£N.Mint
1 ND 48pgs, The Beast in love by Jim Starlin/Jackson Guice						
	$0.90	$2.70	$4.50	£0.60	£1.80	£3.00
Title Value:	$0.90	$2.70	$4.50	£0.60	£1.80	£3.00

Note: Bookshelf Format

X-FILES

Topps; 0 May 1996; 1 Jan 1995-present

	$Good	$Fine	$N.Mint	£Good	£Fine	£N.Mint
-1 Silver Negative Edition, ND 16pgs, (Sep 1996) variant cover to the White Negative Edition						
	$3.00	$9.00	$15.00	£2.50	£7.50	£12.50
-1 White Negative Edition, ND 16pgs, (Sep 1996)						
	$2.00	$6.00	$10.00	£1.50	£4.50	£7.50
-2 Black Negative Edition, ND (Sep 1996)						
	$2.00	$6.00	$10.00	£1.50	£4.50	£7.50
-2 Red Negative Edition, ND (Sep 1996) variant cover to Black Negative Edition						
	$3.00	$9.00	$15.00	£2.50	£7.50	£12.50
½ ND 24pgs, available with Wizard #53, issued in protective Mylar with certificate						
	$4.00	$12.00	$20.00	£2.50	£7.50	£12.50
0 ND 48pgs, Roy Thomas script, John van Fleet art and painted cover						
	$1.00	$3.00	$5.00	£0.60	£1.80	£3.00
0 Variant Cover Edition A, ND Fox Mulder cover						
	$2.00	$6.00	$10.00	£2.00	£6.00	£10.00
0 Variant Cover Edition B, ND Dana Scully cover						
	$2.00	$6.00	$10.00	£2.00	£6.00	£10.00
1 ND Stefan Petrucha script and Charlie Adlard art begins; based on hit US (and UK!) TV show						
	$10.00	$30.00	$50.00	£8.00	£24.00	£40.00
1 2nd printing, ND serial number along top of comic up to 120,000						
	$1.00	$3.00	$5.00	£1.00	£3.00	£5.00
2 ND	$5.00	$15.00	$25.00	£3.00	£9.00	£15.00
2 2nd printing, ND serial number along top of comic						
	$0.60	$1.80	$3.00	£0.60	£1.80	£3.00
3 ND	$3.00	$9.00	$15.00	£1.50	£4.50	£7.50
3 2nd printing, ND serial number along top of comic						
	$0.60	$1.80	$3.00	£0.40	£1.20	£2.00
4 ND	$1.80	$5.25	$9.00	£1.20	£3.60	£6.00
4 2nd printing, ND (Apr 1996)						
	$0.60	$1.80	$3.00	£0.40	£1.20	£2.00
5 ND	$1.20	$3.60	$6.00	£0.80	£2.40	£4.00
6 ND $2.95 cover begins						
	$1.00	$3.00	$5.00	£0.60	£1.80	£3.00
7-9 ND	$0.80	$2.40	$4.00	£0.50	£1.50	£2.50
10 ND Feelings of Unreality story; bi-weekly						
	$0.80	$2.40	$4.00	£0.50	£1.50	£2.50
11 ND Feelings of Unreality story; bi-weekly						
	$0.60	$1.80	$3.00	£0.40	£1.20	£2.00
12 ND Feelings of Unreality story						
	$0.60	$1.80	$3.00	£0.40	£1.20	£2.00
13-14 ND	$0.60	$1.80	$3.00	£0.40	£1.20	£2.00
15-16 ND Home of the Brave story						
	$0.60	$1.80	$3.00	£0.40	£1.20	£2.00
17 ND	$0.60	$1.80	$3.00	£0.40	£1.20	£2.00
18 ND Night Lights story						
	$0.60	$1.80	$3.00	£0.40	£1.20	£2.00
19-26 ND	$0.60	$1.80	$3.00	£0.40	£1.20	£2.00
Title Value:	$56.60	$169.65	$283.00	£41.00	£123.00	£205.00

X-Files (Jul 1995)

	$Good	$Fine	$N.Mint	£Good	£Fine	£N.Mint
Trade paperback reprints issues #1-6				£2.70	£8.10	£13.50

X-FILES ANNUAL

Topps; 1 Aug 1995-present

	$Good	$Fine	$N.Mint	£Good	£Fine	£N.Mint
1 ND 48pgs, new double length story "Hallow Eve"; Stefan Petrucha script, Charlie Adlard art						
	$0.90	$2.70	$4.50	£0.70	£2.10	£3.50
2 ND John Rozum script, Gordon Purcell and Josef Rubenstein art						
	$0.80	$2.40	$4.00	£0.50	£1.50	£2.50
Title Value:	$1.70	$5.10	$8.50	£1.20	£3.60	£6.00

X-FILES COMICS DIGEST, THE

Topps,Digest; 1 Sep 1995-present

	$Good	$Fine	$N.Mint	£Good	£Fine	£N.Mint
1 ND 96pgs, Stefan Petrucha script, Charlie Adlard art; painted covers by Miran Kim begin; 9x7 digest size						
	$0.70	$2.10	$3.50	£0.60	£1.80	£3.00
2-3 ND 96pgs	$0.70	$2.10	$3.50	£0.50	£1.50	£2.50
Title Value:	$2.10	$6.30	$11.00	£1.60	£4.80	£8.00

X-FILES SPECIAL EDITION

Topps; 1 Jun 1995-present

	$Good	$Fine	$N.Mint	£Good	£Fine	£N.Mint
1 ND reprints issues #1-3, new cover by Miran Kim						
	$1.00	$3.00	$5.00	£0.70	£2.10	£3.50
2 ND reprints issues #4-6, new cover by Miran Kim						
	$1.00	$3.00	$5.00	£0.70	£2.10	£3.50
3 ND reprints issues #7-9, new cover by Miran Kim						
	$1.00	$3.00	$5.00	£0.70	£2.10	£3.50
4 ND reprints issues #10-12, new cover by Miran Kim						
	$1.00	$3.00	$5.00	£0.70	£2.10	£3.50
Title Value:	$4.00	$12.00	$20.00	£2.80	£8.40	£14.00

X-FORCE

Marvel Comics Group; 1 Aug 1991-43 Feb 1995; 44 Jul 1995-present

(title becomes Gambit & The X-Ternals)

	$Good	$Fine	$N.Mint	£Good	£Fine	£N.Mint
1 pre-bagged with one of the following trading cards: Cable, Shatterstar, Deadpool, Gideon/Sunspot, X-Force Team, Rob Liefeld art (Note: Cable card issue no longer valued higher than the others as it once was)						
	$0.60	$1.80	$3.00	£0.40	£1.20	£2.00
1 2nd printing, LD in the U.K. Aug 1991 - gold metallic ink cover						
	$0.40	$1.20	$2.00	£0.25	£0.75	£1.25
2 Juggernaut appears, Rob Liefeld art						
	$0.50	$1.50	$2.50	£0.30	£0.90	£1.50
3 Spiderman and Juggernaut appear, Rob Liefeld art						
	$0.40	$1.20	$2.00	£0.25	£0.75	£1.25
4 continued from Spiderman #16, entire issue printed sideways, Rob Liefeld art						
	$0.40	$1.20	$2.00	£0.25	£0.75	£1.25
5 Brotherhood of Evil Mutants appear, Rob Liefeld art						
	$0.40	$1.20	$2.00	£0.25	£0.75	£1.25
6 New Brotherhood of Evil Mutants appear, Rob Liefeld art						
	$0.30	$0.90	$1.50	£0.20	£0.60	£1.00
7 $1.25 cover begins, Rob Liefeld art						
	$0.30	$0.90	$1.50	£0.20	£0.60	£1.00
8 Rob Liefeld art on framing sequence, Mike Mignola art; part Cable origin						
	$0.30	$0.90	$1.50	£0.20	£0.60	£1.00
9-14 Rob Liefeld art						
	$0.30	$0.90	$1.50	£0.20	£0.60	£1.00
15 Cable leaves X-Force, Greg Capullo art begins						
	$0.30	$0.90	$1.50	£0.20	£0.60	£1.00
16 X-Cutioner's Song part 4, pre-bagged with trading card, continued in Uncanny X-Men #295						
	$0.30	$0.90	$1.50	£0.20	£0.60	£1.00
17 X-Cutioner's Song part 8, pre-bagged with trading card, continued in Uncanny X-Men #296						
	$0.30	$0.90	$1.50	£0.20	£0.60	£1.00
18 X-Cutioner's Song part 12 (conclusion), pre-bagged with trading card						
	$0.30	$0.90	$1.50	£0.20	£0.60	£1.00
19-20	$0.30	$0.90	$1.50	£0.20	£0.60	£1.00
21 X-Force vs. Iron Man						
	$0.30	$0.90	$1.50	£0.20	£0.60	£1.00
22-24	$0.30	$0.90	$1.50	£0.20	£0.60	£1.00
25 48pgs, wraparound cover with Cable hologram						
	$0.80	$2.40	$4.00	£0.50	£1.50	£2.50
26-31	$0.30	$0.90	$1.50	£0.20	£0.60	£1.00
32 continued in New Warriors #45						
	$0.30	$0.90	$1.50	£0.20	£0.60	£1.00
33 continued in New Warriors #46						
	$0.30	$0.90	$1.50	£0.20	£0.60	£1.00
34 with free Spiderman and his Deadly Foes card sheet						

$Good $Fine $N.Mint £Good £Fine £N.Mint

$0.30 $0.90 $1.50 £0.20 £0.60 £1.00
35-37 *$0.30 $0.90 $1.50* £0.20 £0.60 £1.00
38 ND *$0.40 $1.20 $2.00* £0.25 £0.75 £1.25
38 Deluxe Edition, ND foil stamped cover; leads into the creation of Generation X
$0.60 $1.80 $3.00 £0.40 £1.20 £2.00
39-40 ND *$0.30 $0.90 $1.50* £0.20 £0.60 £1.00
40 Deluxe Edition, ND printed on glossy stock paper
$0.40 $1.20 $2.00 £0.25 £0.75 £1.25
41 ND *$0.30 $0.90 $1.50* £0.20 £0.60 £1.00
41 Deluxe Edition, ND printed on glossy stock paper
$0.40 $1.20 $2.00 £0.25 £0.75 £1.25
42 ND *$0.30 $0.90 $1.50* £0.20 £0.60 £1.00
42 Deluxe Edition, ND printed on glossy stock paper
$0.40 $1.20 $2.00 £0.25 £0.75 £1.25
43 ND *$0.30 $0.90 $1.50* £0.20 £0.60 £1.00
43 Deluxe Edition, ND printed on glossy stock paper plus bound-in Fleer trading card; see Gambit & The X-Ternals #1
$0.40 $1.20 $2.00 £0.25 £0.75 £1.25
44 ND continued from X-Men: Prime; Jeph Loeb script, Adam Pollina art
$0.40 $1.20 $2.00 £0.25 £0.75 £1.25
45 ND *$0.40 $1.20 $2.00* £0,25 £0.75 £1.25
46 ND bi-weekly *$0.40 $1.20 $2.00* £0.25 £0.75 £1.25
47 ND Sabretooth appears, bi-weekly
$0.40 $1.20 $2.00 £0.25 £0.75 £1.25
48-49 ND *$0.40 $1.20 $2.00* £0.25 £0.75 £1.25
50 ND news-stand edition without cover enhancement
$0.60 $1.80 $3.00 £0.40 £1.20 £2.00
50 Collectors Edition, ND 48pgs, double gatefold prismatic foil cover
$0.80 $2.40 $4.00 £0.50 £1.50 £2.50
50 Variant Cover Edition, ND Rob Liefeld cover art; double gatefold prismatic foil cover
$1.00 $3.00 $5.00 £0.70 £2.10 £3.50
51-55 ND *$0.40 $1.20 $2.00* £0.25 £0.75 £1.25
56 ND 40pgs, Deadpool guest-stars
$0.40 $1.20 $2.00 £0.25 £0.75 £1.25
57 ND 40pgs, Onslaught tie-in, guest-starring X-Man
$0.40 $1.20 $2.00 £0.25 £0.75 £1.25
58 ND Onslaught tie-in
$0.40 $1.20 $2.00 £0.25 £0.75 £1.25
59 ND with bound-in Overpower cards
$0.40 $1.20 $2.00 £0.25 £0.75 £1.25
60 ND Longshot guest-stars
$0.40 $1.20 $2.00 £0.25 £0.75 £1.25
61-63 ND *$0.40 $1.20 $2.00* £0.25 £0.75 £1.25
64 ND S.H.I.E.L.D. appear
$0.40 $1.20 $2.00 £0.25 £0.75 £1.25
Title Value: *$27.30 $81.90 $136.50* £17.65 £52.95 £88.25

Note: The vast majority of distributed (U.K.) copies of issue #1 (possibly all issues) are defaced by a large white bar code sticker on the bag added by the distributor at a later date and are notoriously difficult to remove. Direct Sales issues do not have this.

Note also: black on white and white on black logos available on issue #1 have been reported but subject to confirmation.

X-Force & Spiderman: Sabotage (Jan 1993)
ND Trade paperback 64pgs, reprints X-Force #4, Spiderman #16 printed-sideways issues £0.85 £2.55 £4.25

X-FORCE ANNUAL

Marvel Comics Group; 1 May 1992-present
1 ND Shattershot part 4 (conclusion), continued from X-Factor Annual #7
$0.50 $1.50 $2.50 £0.30 £0.90 £1.50
2 ND 64pgs, pre-bagged with trading card, 1st appearance X-treme
$0.60 $1.80 $3.00 £0.40 £1.20 £2.00
3 ND 64pgs *$0.60 $1.80 $3.00* £0.40 £1.20 £2.00
Title Value: *$1.70 $5.10 $8.50* £1.10 £3.30 £5.50

X-FORCE MEGAZINE

(see New Mutants trade paperbacks)

X-FORCE/YOUNGBLOOD

Marvel Comics Group,OS; nn Oct 1996
nn ND squarebound; Eric Stephenson script, Stephen Platt and Marlo Alquiza art
$1.00 $3.00 $5.00 £0.70 £2.10 £3.50
Title Value: *$1.00 $3.00 $5.00* £0.70 £2.10 £3.50

X-MAN

Marvel Comics Group; 1 Mar 1995-present
(title previously called Cable)
1 ND Age of Apocalypse tie-in, Jeph Loeb script, Steve Skroce art
$1.20 $3.60 $6.00 £0.70 £2.10 £3.50
1 2nd printing ND *$0.50 $1.50 $2.50* £0.30 £0.90 £1.50
2-3 ND Jeph Loeb script, Steve Skroce art
$0.80 $2.40 $4.00 £0.50 £1.50 £2.50
4 ND Jeph Loeb script, Steve Skroce art; continued in X-Men: Omega
$0.60 $1.80 $3.00 £0.40 £1.20 £2.00
5 ND the character from the "After Xavier" alternate worlds storyline crosses over into the Marvel Universe
$0.60 $1.80 $3.00 £0.40 £1.20 £2.00
6-10 ND *$0.40 $1.20 $2.00* £0.30 £0.90 £1.50
11 ND *$0.40 $1.20 $2.00* £0.25 £0.75 £1.25
12 ND Excalibur guest-star
$0.40 $1.20 $2.00 £0.25 £0.75 £1.25
13-16 ND *$0.40 $1.20 $2.00* £0.25 £0.75 £1.25
17 ND 40pgs, Onslaught tie-in
$0.40 $1.20 $2.00 £0.25 £0.75 £1.25
18 ND 40pgs, Onslaught tie-in, guest-starring X-Force
$0.40 $1.20 $2.00 £0.25 £0.75 £1.25
19 ND Onslaught tie-in
$0.40 $1.20 $2.00 £0.25 £0.75 £1.25
20 ND The Abomination appears; with bound-in Overpower cards
$0.40 $1.20 $2.00 £0.25 £0.75 £1.25
21-22 ND *$0.40 $1.20 $2.00* £0.25 £0.75 £1.25
23 ND guest-starring Bishop, continued in X-Man '96
$0.40 $1.20 $2.00 £0.25 £0.75 £1.25
24 ND continued from Amazing Spiderman #428
$0.40 $1.20 $2.00 £0.25 £0.75 £1.25
25 ND 48pgs, Cyclops and Phoenix vs. Madelyne
$0.60 $1.80 $3.00 £0.40 £1.20 £2.00
Title Value: *$12.70 $38.10 $63.50* £8.20 £24.60 £41.00
The Ultimate X-Man (Jul 1995)
96pgs, Bookshelf Edition collects issues #1-4 with etched gold cover £1.20 £3.60 £6.00

X-MAN '96

Marvel Comics Group,OS; nn Jan 1997
nn ND Alan Davis and Mark Farmer cover and art
$0.60 $1.80 $3.00 £0.40 £1.20 £2.00
Title Value: *$0.60 $1.80 $3.00* £0.40 £1.20 £2.00

X-MEN

Marvel Comics Group; 1 Oct 1991-41 Feb 1995; 42 Jul 1995-present
(title becomes The Mutants: The Amazing X-Men)
1 cover A, featuring Storm, Jim Lee art
$0.50 $1.50 $2.50 £0.30 £0.90 £1.50
1 cover B, featuring Colossus, Jim Lee art
$0.50 $1.50 $2.50 £0.30 £0.90 £1.50
1 cover C, featuring Wolverine, Jim Lee art
$0.50 $1.50 $2.50 £0.30 £0.90 £1.50
1 cover D, featuring Magneto, Jim Lee art
$0.50 $1.50 $2.50 £0.30 £0.90 £1.50
1 cover E, double gatefold featuring all four covers as poster plus all pin-ups, heavier stock paper, Jim Lee art
$0.80 $2.40 $4.00 £0.50 £1.50 £2.50
2 Jim Lee art, Magneto story reference ties in with Defenders #16
$0.80 $2.40 $4.00 £0.30 £0.90 £1.50
3 Jim Lee art, last Claremont script
$0.80 $2.40 $4.00 £0.30 £0.90 £1.50
4 John Byrne script, Jim Lee plot and art, 1st appearance Omega Red
$0.80 $2.40 $4.00 £0.40 £1.20 £2.00
5 Longshot returns, John Byrne script, Jim Lee plot and art, 1st appearance Maverick
$0.80 $2.40 $4.00 £0.40 £1.20 £2.00
6 Sabretooth appears, Maverick appears
$0.60 $1.80 $3.00 £0.30 £0.90 £1.50
7 *$0.60 $1.80 $3.00* £0.30 £0.90 £1.50
8 last Jim Lee art, Ghost Rider appears
$0.60 $1.80 $3.00 £0.30 £0.90 £1.50
9 X-over with Ghost Rider #26, Wolverine vs. Ghost Rider
$0.60 $1.80 $3.00 £0.30 £0.90 £1.50
10 Longshot returns
$0.60 $1.80 $3.00 £0.30 £0.90 £1.50
11 Longshot vs. Mojo
$0.60 $1.80 $3.00 £0.30 £0.90 £1.50
11 Variant Cover Edition, ND scarce in the U.K. silver ink cover, issued with computer game
$3.00 $9.00 $15.00 £1.00 £3.00 £5.00
12-13 Thibert art *$0.60 $1.80 $3.00* £0.30 £0.90 £1.50
14 X-Cutioner's Song part 3, pre-bagged with trading card, continued in X-Force #16
$0.60 $1.80 $3.00 £0.30 £0.90 £1.50
15 X-Cutioner's Song part 6, pre-bagged with trading card, continued in X-Force #17
$0.60 $1.80 $3.00 £0.30 £0.90 £1.50
16 X-Cutioner's Song part 11, pre-bagged with trading card, continued in X-Force #18
$0.50 $1.50 $2.50 £0.30 £0.90 £1.50
17-19 Omega Red appears
$0.50 $1.50 $2.50 £0.30 £0.90 £1.50
20-24 *$0.50 $1.50 $2.50* £0.30 £0.90 £1.50
25 48pgs, hologram cover, Wolverine vs. Magneto
$0.90 $2.70 $4.50 £0.60 £1.80 £3.00
25 Black Edition, ND black and white cover, no date and price, Magneto figure in colour (produced in place of advertised Magneto Gold #0)
$4.50 $13.50 $22.50 £3.00 £9.00 £15.00
25 Gold Edition ND *$4.50 $13.50 $22.50* £3.00 £9.00 £15.00
26 Bloodties part 2 *$0.50 $1.50 $2.50* £0.30 £0.90 £1.50
27 *$0.50 $1.50 $2.50* £0.30 £0.90 £1.50
28-29 Sabretooth appears
$0.50 $1.50 $2.50 £0.30 £0.90 £1.50
30 wedding of Scott Summers and Jean Grey; with 3 card insert
$0.50 $1.50 $2.50 £0.30 £0.90 £1.50
31 *$0.40 $1.20 $2.00* £0.25 £0.75 £1.25
32 with free Spiderman's Amazing Powers card sheet
$0.40 $1.20 $2.00 £0.25 £0.75 £1.25
33-36 *$0.40 $1.20 $2.00* £0.25 £0.75 £1.25
36 Deluxe Edition, ND foil stamped cover; leads into the creation of Generation X
$0.60 $1.80 $3.00 £0.40 £1.20 £2.00
37 ND Andy Kubert art
$0.40 $1.20 $2.00 £0.25 £0.75 £1.25
37 Deluxe Edition, ND foil stamped cover
$0.60 $1.80 $3.00 £0.40 £1.20 £2.00
38 ND *$0.30 $0.90 $1.50* £0.20 £0.60 £1.00
38 Deluxe Edition, ND printed on glossy stock paper
$0.40 $1.20 $2.00 £0.25 £0.75 £1.25
39 ND *$0.30 $0.90 $1.50* £0.20 £0.60 £1.00
39 Deluxe Edition, ND printed on glossy stock paper
$0.40 $1.20 $2.00 £0.25 £0.75 £1.25
40 ND *$0.30 $0.90 $1.50* £0.20 £0.60 £1.00
40 Deluxe Edition, ND printed on glossy stock paper
$0.40 $1.20 $2.00 £0.25 £0.75 £1.25

	$Good	$Fine	$N.Mint	£Good	£Fine	£N.Mint
41 ND	$0.30	$0.90	$1.50	£0.20	£0.60	£1.00
41 Deluxe Edition, ND printed on glossy stock paper plus bound-in Fleer trading card; see Mutants: The Amazing X-Men #1	$0.40	$1.20	$2.00	£0.25	£0.75	£1.25
42 ND continued from X-Men: Prime; Fabian Nicieza script and Paul Smith art begins	$0.40	$1.20	$2.00	£0.25	£0.75	£1.25
43-44 ND	$0.40	$1.20	$2.00	£0.25	£0.75	£1.25
45 ND 48pgs, Rogue vs. Gambit; double gate-fold prismatic foil cover	$0.80	$2.40	$4.00	£0.50	£1.50	£2.50
46 ND	$0.40	$1.20	$2.00	£0.25	£0.75	£1.25
47 ND Dazzler guest stars	$0.40	$1.20	$2.00	£0.25	£0.75	£1.25
48 ND Sabretooth appears, continued in Sabretooth Special	$0.40	$1.20	$2.00	£0.25	£0.75	£1.25
49 ND	$0.40	$1.20	$2.00	£0.25	£0.75	£1.25
50 ND 48pgs	$0.60	$1.80	$3.00	£0.40	£1.20	£2.00
50 Collectors Edition, ND 48pgs, prismatic foil board cover	$0.80	$2.40	$4.00	£0.50	£1.50	£2.50
51 ND Mark Waid begins as regular scripter	$0.40	$1.20	$2.00	£0.25	£0.75	£1.25
52 ND	$0.40	$1.20	$2.00	£0.25	£0.75	£1.25
53 ND 1st appearance Onslaught	$0.80	$2.40	$4.00	£0.60	£1.80	£3.00
54 ND 40pgs, Onslaught tie-in	$0.70	$2.10	$3.50	£0.50	£1.50	£2.50
54 Collectors Edition, ND prismatic etched hologram cover; pre-bagged with certificate	$3.00	$9.00	$15.00	£2.00	£6.00	£10.00
55-56 ND 40pgs, Onslaught tie-in	$0.40	$1.20	$2.00	£0.25	£0.75	£1.25
57-61 ND	$0.40	$1.20	$2.00	£0.25	£0.75	£1.25
62 ND Master of Kung Fu appears	$0.40	$1.20	$2.00	£0.25	£0.75	£1.25
Title Value:	$52.20	$156.60	$261.00	£31.00	£93.00	£155.00
X-Men/Ghost Rider Trade paperback (Nov 1993) reprints X-Men #8,9 and Ghost Rider #26,27				£0.90	£1.80	£4.50
Magneto Returns (Oct 1995) Trade paperback reprints issues #1-7 featuring Jim Lee art				£2.00	£6.00	£10.00
X-Men Milestone (Nov 1995) boxed set collecting X-Men #25, Wolverine #75 and Excalibur #71 (all hologram covers), ND				£1.50	£4.50	£7.50
X-Men Collection (Dec 1995) boxed set collecting X-Men #27, X-Force #26-28, X-Men Annual #2; ND				£1.00	£3.00	£5.00
X-Men Greatest (Dec 1995) boxed set collecting Avengers #368/369, X-Men #26, Avengers West Coast #101 and Uncanny X-Men #307; ND				£1.00	£3.00	£5.00
X-MEN '95						
Marvel Comics Group,OS; nn Oct 1995						
nn ND 64pgs, J.M. DeMatteis script, Terry Dodson art spotlighting Mr. Sinister	$0.80	$2.40	$4.00	£0.50	£1.50	£2.50
Title Value:	$0.80	$2.40	$4.00	£0.50	£1.50	£2.50
X-MEN '96						
Marvel Comics Group,OS; nn Nov 1996						
nn ND 64pgs	$0.60	$1.80	$3.00	£0.40	£1.20	£2.00
Title Value:	$0.60	$1.80	$3.00	£0.40	£1.20	£2.00
X-MEN 2099						
Marvel Comics Group; 1 Oct 1993-35 Aug 1996						
1 ND blue foil embossed cover, Ron Lim and Adam Kubert art begins	$0.40	$1.20	$2.00	£0.25	£0.75	£1.25
1 Gold Edition, ND (Jan 1994) - 10 new pages, gold foil cover; limited to 15,000 copies	$4.00	$12.00	$20.00	£2.50	£7.50	£12.50
2-7 ND	$0.30	$0.90	$1.50	£0.20	£0.60	£1.00
8 ND with free Spiderman's Amazing Powers card sheet; $1.50 cover begin	$0.30	$0.90	$1.50	£0.20	£0.60	£1.00
9-13 ND	$0.30	$0.90	$1.50	£0.20	£0.60	£1.00
14 ND Loki appears	$0.30	$0.90	$1.50	£0.20	£0.60	£1.00
15-19 ND	$0.30	$0.90	$1.50	£0.20	£0.60	£1.00
20-22 ND	$0.40	$1.20	$2.00	£0.25	£0.75	£1.25
23-24 ND One Nation Under Doom	$0.40	$1.20	$2.00	£0.25	£0.75	£1.25
25 ND 48pgs, One Nation Under Doom	$0.50	$1.50	$2.50	£0.30	£0.90	£1.50
25 Collectors Edition, ND 48pgs,, One Nation Under Doom; enhanced cover	$0.80	$2.40	$4.00	£0.50	£1.50	£2.50
26 ND One Nation Under Doom	$0.40	$1.20	$2.00	£0.25	£0.75	£1.25
27 ND X-Nation, continued from 2099 Apocalypse and Doom 2099 #36	$0.40	$1.20	$2.00	£0.25	£0.75	£1.25
28 ND X-Nation, leads into 2099 Genesis	$0.40	$1.20	$2.00	£0.25	£0.75	£1.25
29 ND ties into X-Nation	$0.40	$1.20	$2.00	£0.25	£0.75	£1.25
30 ND X-Nation tie-in, continued from Doon 2099 #39	$0.40	$1.20	$2.00	£0.25	£0.75	£1.25
31-35 ND	$0.40	$1.20	$2.00	£0.25	£0.75	£1.25
Title Value:	$17.10	$51.30	$85.50	£10.90	£32.70	£54.50
X-MEN 2099 SPECIAL						
Marvel Comics Group; 1 Oct 1995						
1 ND 64pgs, painted cover by Brothers Hildebrandt	$0.80	$2.40	$4.00	£0.50	£1.50	£2.50
Title Value:	$0.80	$2.40	$4.00	£0.50	£1.50	£2.50
X-MEN 2099: OASIS						
Marvel Comics Group,OS; 1 Aug 1996						
1 ND 48pgs, John Francis Moore script, fully painted art by The Brothers Hildebrandt	$1.20	$3.60	$6.00	£0.80	£2.40	£4.00
Title Value:	$1.20	$3.60	$6.00	£0.80	£2.40	£4.00
X-MEN ADVENTURES SEASON II						
Marvel Comics Group; 1 Feb 1994-13 Feb 1995 (see X-Men: The Animated Series)						
1 ND based on the 2nd season of Fox TV's animated series	$0.30	$0.90	$1.50	£0.20	£0.60	£1.00
2-13 ND	$0.30	$0.90	$1.50	£0.20	£0.60	£1.00
Title Value:	$3.90	$11.70	$19.50	£2.60	£7.80	£13.00
X-MEN ADVENTURES SEASON III						
Marvel Comics Group; 1 Mar 1995-13 Apr 1996						
1-9 ND	$0.30	$0.90	$1.50	£0.20	£0.60	£1.00
10-13 ND The Dark Phoenix Saga	$0.30	$0.90	$1.50	£0.20	£0.60	£1.00
Title Value:	$3.90	$11.70	$19.50	£2.60	£7.80	£13.00
X-MEN AND ALPHA FLIGHT						
Marvel Comics Group,MS; 1 Jan 1986-2 Feb 1986 (see X-Men Annual #9)						
1-2 ND DS, Paul Smith art	$0.60	$1.80	$3.00	£0.40	£1.20	£2.00
Title Value:	$1.20	$3.60	$6.00	£0.80	£2.40	£4.00
X-MEN AND THE MICRONAUTS, THE						
Marvel Comics Group,MS; 1 Jan 1984-4 Apr 1984						
1-3 ND Guice art	$0.50	$1.50	$2.50	£0.30	£0.90	£1.50
4 ND	$0.50	$1.50	$2.50	£0.30	£0.90	£1.50
Title Value:	$2.00	$6.00	$10.00	£1.20	£3.60	£6.00
X-MEN ANNIVERSARY MAGAZINE						
Marvel Comics Group,Magazine OS; 1 Sep 1993						
1 ND 48pgs, cover inter-locks with Avengers Anniversary Magazine	$0.80	$2.40	$4.00	£0.50	£1.50	£2.50
Title Value:	$0.80	$2.40	$4.00	£0.50	£1.50	£2.50
X-MEN ANNUAL						
Marvel Comics Group; 1 May 1992-present						
1 ND Shattershot part 1, continued in Uncanny X-Men Annual #16, Jim Lee cover and art layouts	$0.50	$1.50	$2.50	£0.30	£0.90	£1.50
2 ND 64pgs, pre-bagged with trading card, 1st appearance Empyrean	$0.60	$1.80	$3.00	£0.40	£1.20	£2.00
3 ND 64pgs	$0.60	$1.80	$3.00	£0.40	£1.20	£2.00
Title Value:	$1.70	$5.10	$8.50	£1.10	£3.30	£5.50
X-MEN ARCHIVES: CAPTAIN BRITAIN						
Marvel Comics Group,MS; 1 Jul 1995-7 Jan 1996						
1-7 ND 48pgs, reprints; Dave Thorpe script, Alan Davis art; new Alan Davis covers	$0.60	$1.80	$3.00	£0.40	£1.20	£2.00
Title Value:	$4.20	$12.60	$21.00	£2.80	£8.40	£14.00
X-MEN ASHCAN						
Marvel Comics Group,OS; nn Jan 1995						
nn ND previews the major title changes for all the X-Men books for 1995	$0.15	$0.45	$0.75	£0.10	£0.30	£0.50
Title Value:	$0.15	$0.45	$0.75	£0.10	£0.30	£0.50
X-MEN ASHCAN EDITION						
Marvel Comics Group,OS; nn Aug 1994						
nn ND 16pgs, black and white, shorter history of the X-Men	$0.25	$0.75	$1.25	£0.15	£0.45	£0.75
Title Value:	$0.25	$0.75	$1.25	£0.15	£0.45	£0.75
X-MEN AT THE STATE FAIR OF TEXAS						
Marvel Comics Group; nn Oct 1983						
nn ND very scarce in the U.K. Dallas Times Herald Giveaway, paper cover	$4.00	$12.00	$20.00	£5.00	£15.00	£25.00
Title Value:	$4.00	$12.00	$20.00	£5.00	£15.00	£25.00
X-MEN CHRONICLES						
Fantaco; 1 Jul 1981						
1 ND story synopses and character details on early X-Men issue; intended as an on-going series	$0.60	$1.80	$3.00	£0.40	£1.20	£2.00
Title Value:	$0.60	$1.80	$3.00	£0.40	£1.20	£2.00
X-MEN CHRONICLES (2ND SERIES)						
Marvel Comics Group; 1 Mar 1995-2 Apr 1995 (title previously called X-Men Unlimited)						
1 ND Howard Mackie script, Ian Churchill art begins	$0.80	$2.40	$4.00	£0.50	£1.50	£2.50
2 ND	$0.80	$2.40	$4.00	£0.50	£1.50	£2.50
Title Value:	$1.60	$4.80	$8.00	£1.00	£3.00	£5.00
X-MEN CLASSICS						
Marvel Comics Group; 1 Dec 1983-3 Feb 1984						
1-3 ND Neal Adams reprints, Baxter paper	$1.00	$3.00	$5.00	£0.70	£2.10	£3.50
Title Value:	$3.00	$9.00	$15.00	£2.10	£6.30	£10.50
X-MEN FIRSTS						
Marvel Comics Group,OS; 1 Feb 1996						
1 ND 96pgs, reprints 1st appearances of Wolverine, Rogue, Gambit and Mr. Sinister	$1.00	$3.00	$5.00	£0.70	£2.10	£3.50
Title Value:	$1.00	$3.00	$5.00	£0.70	£2.10	£3.50
X-MEN GIANT SIZE						
Marvel Comics Group; 1 Summer 1975-2 Nov 1975						
1 ND 64pgs, 1st appearance of the new X-Men, 2nd full appearance Wolverine; back-up reprints X-Men #43, #47, #57. Gil Kane cover	$52.50	$155.00	$425.00	£33.00	£97.50	£260.00
1 Marvel Milestone Edition, ND (Oct 1991), reprints original issue with ads, silver border around cover	$0.90	$2.70	$4.50	£0.60	£1.80	£3.00
2 ND 64pgs, all Neal Adams reprints from X-Men #57-59						

	$Good	$Fine	$N.Mint	£Good	£Fine	£N.Mint
	$6.50	$20.00	$40.00	£4.15	£12.50	£25.00
Title Value:	$59.90	$177.70	$469.50	£37.75	£111.80	£288.00

X-MEN MEGAZINE

Marvel Comics Group,OS; nn Nov 1996

	$Good	$Fine	$N.Mint	£Good	£Fine	£N.Mint
nn ND 96pgs, reprints Uncanny X-Men #273-275						
	$0.80	$2.40	$4.00	£0.50	£1.50	£2.50
Title Value:	$0.80	$2.40	$4.00	£0.50	£1.50	£2.50

X-MEN RARITIES

Marvel Comics Group,OS; nn Oct 1995

	$Good	$Fine	$N.Mint	£Good	£Fine	£N.Mint
nn ND 64pgs, reprints "The Boy Who Could Fly" from Amazing Adult Fantasy #14 (1st reference to mutants), Classic X-Men #1 and Marvel Fanfare #40 to celebrate 20th anniversary of the new X-Men						
	$1.20	$3.60	$6.00	£0.80	£2.40	£4.00
Title Value:	$1.20	$3.60	$6.00	£0.80	£2.40	£4.00

X-MEN SPECIAL EDITION

Marvel Comics Group,OS; 1 Feb 1983

	$Good	$Fine	$N.Mint	£Good	£Fine	£N.Mint
1 ND scarce in the U.K. reprints Giant Size #1 plus one new Kitty Pryde story, Baxter paper						
	$2.00	$6.00	$10.00	£1.50	£4.50	£7.50
Title Value:	$2.00	$6.00	$10.00	£1.50	£4.50	£7.50

X-MEN SPECTACULAR

Marvel Comics Group,MS; 1-4 Jan 1995

	$Good	$Fine	$N.Mint	£Good	£Fine	£N.Mint
1-4 ND reprints from New Mutants #26-28 and X-Men #161; weekly issues						
	$0.50	$1.50	$2.50	£0.30	£0.90	£1.50
Title Value:	$2.00	$6.00	$10.00	£1.20	£3.60	£6.00

X-MEN SPOTLIGHT: THE STARJAMMERS

Marvel Comics Group,MS; 1 May 1990-2 Jun 1990

	$Good	$Fine	$N.Mint	£Good	£Fine	£N.Mint
1 ND 48pgs, squarebound; Dave Cockrum art begins						
	$0.90	$2.70	$4.50	£0.60	£1.80	£3.00
2 ND 48pgs, squarebound; Excalibur/X-Factor appear						
	$0.90	$2.70	$4.50	£0.60	£1.80	£3.00
Title Value:	$1.80	$5.40	$9.00	£1.20	£3.60	£6.00

X-MEN SURVIVAL GUIDE TO THE MANSION

Marvel Comics Group,OS; 1 Aug 1993

	$Good	$Fine	$N.Mint	£Good	£Fine	£N.Mint
1 ND scarce in the U.K. 48pgs, spiral-bound technical guide to the X-Men's mansion, Andy Kubert cover						
	$1.50	$4.50	$7.50	£1.50	£4.50	£7.50
Title Value:	$1.50	$4.50	$7.50	£1.50	£4.50	£7.50

X-MEN UNLIMITED

Marvel Comics Group; 1 Jun 1993-7 Dec 1994; 8 Oct 1995-present

(see X-Men Chronicles)

	$Good	$Fine	$N.Mint	£Good	£Fine	£N.Mint
1 ND 64pgs, high quality paper; Scott Lobdell script, Bachalo and Panosian art begins						
	$1.20	$3.60	$6.00	£0.70	£2.10	£3.50
2 ND 64pgs	$1.00	$3.00	$5.00	£0.60	£1.80	£3.00
3 ND 64pgs, Sabretooth appears						
	$1.20	$3.60	$6.00	£0.70	£2.10	£3.50
4 ND 64pgs	$0.80	$2.40	$4.00	£0.50	£1.50	£2.50
5 ND 64pgs, Liam Sharp art						
	$0.80	$2.40	$4.00	£0.50	£1.50	£2.50
6 ND 64pgs, Paul Smith art						
	$0.80	$2.40	$4.00	£0.50	£1.50	£2.50
7 ND 64pgs, John Romita Jnr. art						
	$0.80	$2.40	$4.00	£0.50	£1.50	£2.50
8 ND 64pgs, Gambit, Ice Man, Professor X and Jean Grey appear; Tom Grummett and Dan Lawlis art						
	$0.80	$2.40	$4.00	£0.50	£1.50	£2.50
9 ND Wolverine and Psylocke appear						
	$0.80	$2.40	$4.00	£0.50	£1.50	£2.50
10-11 ND	$0.80	$2.40	$4.00	£0.50	£1.50	£2.50
12 ND Juggernaut appears						
	$0.80	$2.40	$4.00	£0.50	£1.50	£2.50
13 ND 64pgs, George Perez script, Duncan Rouleau art						
	$0.60	$1.80	$3.00	£0.40	£1.20	£2.00
14 ND Onslaught: X-Men epilogue tie-in						
	$0.60	$1.80	$3.00	£0.40	£1.20	£2.00
Title Value:	$11.80	$35.40	$59.00	£7.30	£21.90	£36.50

X-MEN VISIONAIRES: ART OF ANDY & ADAM KUBERT

Marvel Comics Group,OS; nn Dec 1995

	$Good	$Fine	$N.Mint	£Good	£Fine	£N.Mint
nn ND 96pgs, four stories collected into one trade paperback						
	$1.80	$5.25	$9.00	£1.20	£3.60	£6.00
Title Value:	$1.80	$5.25	$9.00	£1.20	£3.60	£6.00

X-MEN VS. DRACULA

Marvel Comics Group,OS; 1 Dec 1993

	$Good	$Fine	$N.Mint	£Good	£Fine	£N.Mint
1 ND 48pgs, reprints X-Men Annual #6, new cover by Chris Sprouse/Terry Austin						
	$0.40	$1.20	$2.00	£0.25	£0.75	£1.25
Title Value:	$0.40	$1.20	$2.00	£0.25	£0.75	£1.25

X-MEN VS. THE AVENGERS

Marvel Comics Group,MS; 1 Apr 1987-4 Jul 1987

	$Good	$Fine	$N.Mint	£Good	£Fine	£N.Mint
1-4 ND	$0.50	$1.50	$2.50	£0.30	£0.90	£1.50
Title Value:	$2.00	$6.00	$10.00	£1.20	£3.60	£6.00
X-Men vs. The Avengers (Jun 1993)						
Trade paperback reprints 4 issue mini-series				£1.60	£4.80	£8.00

X-MEN VS. BROOD: DAY OF WRATH

Marvel Comics Group,MS; 1 Sep 1996-2 Oct 1996

	$Good	$Fine	$N.Mint	£Good	£Fine	£N.Mint
1-2 ND wraps up plotlines from X-Men #232-234; John Ostrander script, Bryan Hitch and Paul Neary art						
	$0.60	$1.80	$3.00	£0.40	£1.20	£2.00
Title Value:	$1.20	$3.60	$6.00	£0.80	£2.40	£4.00

X-MEN X-PLANATIONS

As part of a storyline called "The Age of Apocalypse", all the X-titles changed, causing some confusion for collectors and retailers alike. The basis of the change came about in X-Men: Alpha, which told of Professor Xavier's mutant son, Legion, going back in time and murdering him. Thus the X-Men were never formed and all the familiar X-titles ceased to exist for the four month duration of the story, culminating in X-Men: Omega. Below is a list of the pre X-Men: Alpha titles and their changes.

CABLE became **X-MAN**
EXCALIBUR became **X-CALIBRE**
GENERATION X became **THE MUTANTS: GENERATION NEXT**
UNCANNY X-MEN became **THE MUTANTS: THE ASTONISHING X-MEN**
WOLVERINE became **WEAPON X**
X-FACTOR became **FACTOR X**
X-FORCE became **GAMBIT & THE X-TERNALS**
X-MEN became **THE MUTANTS: THE AMAZING X-MEN**
X-MEN UNLIMITED became **X-MEN CHRONICLES**

X-MEN, THE ADVENTURES OF THE

Marvel Comics Group; 1 Apr 1996-present

	$Good	$Fine	$N.Mint	£Good	£Fine	£N.Mint
1 ND based on animated US TV show; Ralph Macchio script, Ben Herrera art						
	$0.20	$0.60	$1.00	£0.15	£0.45	£0.75
2 ND	$0.20	$0.60	$1.00	£0.15	£0.45	£0.75
3 ND continued in The Adventures of Spiderman #3						
	$0.20	$0.60	$1.00	£0.15	£0.45	£0.75
4 ND	$0.20	$0.60	$1.00	£0.15	£0.45	£0.75
5-6 ND Magneto appears						
	$0.20	$0.60	$1.00	£0.15	£0.45	£0.75
7 ND Sabretooth appears						
	$0.20	$0.60	$1.00	£0.15	£0.45	£0.75
8-10 ND	$0.20	$0.60	$1.00	£0.15	£0.45	£0.75
11 ND Man-Thing appears						
	$0.20	$0.60	$1.00	£0.15	£0.45	£0.75
12 ND	$0.20	$0.60	$1.00	£0.15	£0.45	£0.75
Title Value:	$2.40	$7.20	$12.00	£1.80	£5.40	£9.00

X-MEN, THE AMAZING

Marvel Comics Group; 1 Mar 1995-4 Jun 1995

(title previously called X-Men or X-Men [2nd Series])

	$Good	$Fine	$N.Mint	£Good	£Fine	£N.Mint
1 ND Fabian Nicieza script, Andy Kubert art						
	$0.80	$2.40	$4.00	£0.50	£1.50	£2.50
2-3 ND Fabian Nicieza script, Andy Kubert art						
	$0.50	$1.50	$2.50	£0.30	£0.90	£1.50
4 ND Fabian Nicieza script, Andy Kubert art; continued in X-Men: Omega						
	$0.50	$1.50	$2.50	£0.30	£0.90	£1.50
Title Value:	$2.30	$6.90	$11.50	£1.40	£4.20	£7.00
The Ultimate Amazing X-Men (Jul 1995)						
96pgs, Bookshelf Edition collects issues #1-4 with etched gold cover				£1.20	£3.60	£6.00

X-MEN, THE ASTONISHING

Marvel Comics Group; 1 Mar 1995-4 Jun 1995

(title previously called Uncanny X-Men or X-Men [1st Series])

	$Good	$Fine	$N.Mint	£Good	£Fine	£N.Mint
1 ND Scott Lobdell script, Madureira and Green art						
	$0.80	$2.40	$4.00	£0.50	£1.50	£2.50
2-3 ND Scott Lobdell script, Madureira and Green art						
	$0.50	$1.50	$2.50	£0.30	£0.90	£1.50
4 ND Scott Lobdell script, Madureira and Green art; continued in X-Men: Omega						
	$0.50	$1.50	$2.50	£0.30	£0.90	£1.50
Title Value:	$2.30	$6.90	$11.50	£1.40	£4.20	£7.00
The Ultimate Astonishing X-Men (Jul 1995)						
96pgs, Bookshelf Edition collects issues #1-4 with etched gold cover				£1.20	£3.60	£6.00

X-MEN, THE OFFICIAL MARVEL INDEX (1ST SERIES)

Marvel Comics Group,MS; 1 May 1987-7 Jul 1988

(see also The X-Men Chronicles)

	$Good	$Fine	$N.Mint	£Good	£Fine	£N.Mint
1 ND 48pgs, squarebound; information and colour cover reproductions X-Men #1-#23						
	$0.60	$1.80	$3.00	£0.40	£1.20	£2.00
2 ND 48pgs, squarebound; information and colour cover reproductions X-Men #24-#46, new Simonson cover						
	$0.60	$1.80	$3.00	£0.40	£1.20	£2.00
3 ND 48pgs, squarebound; information and colour cover reproductions X-Men #47-#66 plus Ka-Zar #2,#3 and Marvel Tales #30 (Angel appearances)						
	$0.60	$1.80	$3.00	£0.40	£1.20	£2.00
4 ND 48pgs, squarebound; information/colour cover repros X-Men #67-#96, Giant Size X-Men #1,#2, Annuals #1,#2, Amazing Adventures #11-#17, X-Men Classics and Classic X-Men #1-#3, Hulk vs. Wolverine #1						
	$0.60	$1.80	$3.00	£0.40	£1.20	£2.00
5 ND 48pgs, squarebound; information and colour cover reproductions X-Men #97-#108 and Classic X-Men #4-#14						
	$0.60	$1.80	$3.00	£0.40	£1.20	£2.00
6 ND 48pgs, squarebound; information and colour cover repros X-Men #109-#124, Classic X-Men #15-#19 and Marvel Treasury Edition #26						
	$0.60	$1.80	$3.00	£0.40	£1.20	£2.00
7 ND scarce in the U.K. 48pgs, squarebound; information and colour cover repros X-Men #125-#138, Amazing Adventures (3rd) #1-#14, Classic X-Men #20,#21, Marvel Treasury #27, Bizarre Adventures #27						
	$0.60	$1.80	$3.00	£0.50	£1.50	£2.50
Title Value:	$4.20	$12.60	$21.00	£2.90	£8.70	£14.50

Note: Volume 4 in Official Marvel Index series of 5.

X-MEN, THE OFFICIAL MARVEL INDEX (2ND SERIES)

Marvel Comics Group,MS; 1 Apr 1994-5 Aug 1994

	$Good	$Fine	$N.Mint	£Good	£Fine	£N.Mint
1 ND information and indexes on X-Men [1st Series] #1-51						
	$0.40	$1.20	$2.00	£0.25	£0.75	£1.25
2 ND information and indexes on issues #52-122						
	$0.40	$1.20	$2.00	£0.25	£0.75	£1.25
3 ND information and indexes on issues #123-177						
	$0.40	$1.20	$2.00	£0.25	£0.75	£1.25
4 ND information and indexes on issues #178-234						
	$0.40	$1.20	$2.00	£0.25	£0.75	£1.25
5 ND information and indexes on issues #235-287						
	$0.40	$1.20	$2.00	£0.25	£0.75	£1.25
Title Value:	$2.00	$6.00	$10.00	£1.25	£3.75	£6.25

X-MEN, THE UNCANNY

Marvel Comics Group; 1 Sep 1963-66 Mar 1970; 67 Dec 1970-93 Apr 1975; 94 Aug 1975-321 Feb 1995; 322 Jul 1995-present

(see The Mutants: The Astonishing X-Men) (title prefixed with "The Uncanny..." with issue #142)
(see Amazing Adventures, Bizarre Adventures 27, Classic X-Men, Heroes for Hope, Kitty Pryde, Marvel and DC Present, Marvel Fanfare, Marvel Graphic Novel, Marvel Team-Up, Marvel Triple Action, Nightcrawler, Official Marvel Index to.., Special Edition)

1 origin and 1st appearance of the X-Men (Angel, Beast, Cyclops, Iceman, Marvel Girl),

Issue	$Good	$Fine	$N.Mint	£Good	£Fine	£N.Mint
1st appearance Magneto	$520.00	$1550.00	$5750.00	£295.00	£880.00	£3250.00
[Scarce in high grade - Very Fine+ or better]						
1 Marvel Milestone Edition, ND (Sep 1991), reprints original issue with ads, silver border around cover	$0.60	$1.80	$3.00	£0.40	£1.20	£2.00
2 1st appearance The Vanisher	$185.00	$550.00	$1675.00	£95.00	£290.00	£875.00
3 (Jan 1964), 1st appearance The Blob	$80.00	$240.00	$650.00	£49.00	£145.00	£390.00
4 1st appearance of Quicksilver and the Scarlet Witch, 1st Brotherhood of Evil Mutants and 2nd appearance Magneto	$70.00	$215.00	$575.00	£44.00	£130.00	£350.00
5 less common in the U.K. 3rd appearance Magneto	$50.00	$150.00	$400.00	£33.00	£97.50	£265.00
6 scarce in the U.K. Sub-Mariner appears	$38.00	$110.00	$300.00	£23.50	£70.00	£190.00
7 scarce in the U.K. 1st appearance Cerebro, Magneto appears	$38.00	$110.00	$300.00	£22.50	£67.50	£180.00
8 rare in the U.K. 1st appearance Unus the Untouchable	$38.00	$110.00	$300.00	£26.00	£77.50	£210.00
9 scarce in the U.K. (Jan 1965), Avengers X-over, 1st appearance Lucifer	$38.00	$110.00	$300.00	£22.50	£67.50	£180.00
9 Marvel Milestone Edition, ND (Oct 1993)	$0.60	$1.80	$3.00	£0.40	£1.20	£2.00
10 1st Silver Age appearance Ka-Zar (unusually common in the U.K.!)	$43.00	$125.00	$300.00	£18.50	£55.00	£130.00
11 less common in the U.K. 1st appearance The Stranger	$29.00	$87.50	$235.00	£17.50	£52.50	£140.00
12 origin Professor X, origin and 1st appearance Juggernaut	$49.00	$145.00	$340.00	£22.50	£67.50	£160.00
13 Human Torch X-over, 1st full appearance Juggernaut	$29.00	$87.50	$235.00	£13.50	£41.00	£110.00
14 1st appearance Sentinels, 1st monthly issue	$29.00	$87.50	$235.00	£13.50	£41.00	£110.00
15 2nd appearance Sentinels, origin The Beast; last Silver Age issue indicia-dated December 1965	$34.00	$100.00	$235.00	£15.50	£47.00	£110.00
16 (Jan 1966), 3rd appearance Sentinels	$15.00	$45.00	$120.00	£7.50	£22.50	£60.00
17-18 Magneto appears	$15.00	$45.00	$120.00	£6.75	£20.50	£55.00
19 1st appearance Mimic (see Incredible Hulk #161)	$15.00	$45.00	$120.00	£7.50	£22.50	£60.00
20 explains how Professor X was crippled	$15.00	$45.00	$120.00	£6.75	£20.50	£55.00
21 Lucifer appears	$12.50	$39.00	$90.00	£6.25	£19.00	£45.00
22 Count Nefaria appears	$12.50	$39.00	$90.00	£6.25	£19.00	£45.00
23 Porcupine and Scarecrow appear	$12.50	$39.00	$90.00	£6.25	£19.00	£45.00
24 1st appearance The Locust	$12.50	$39.00	$90.00	£6.25	£19.00	£45.00
25-26 scarce in the U.K.	$12.50	$39.00	$90.00	£6.75	£20.00	£47.50
27 Spiderman appears	$12.50	$39.00	$90.00	£6.00	£18.00	£42.50
28 (Jan 1967), 1st appearance Banshee	$20.00	$60.00	$140.00	£8.50	£26.00	£60.00
28 Marvel Milestone Edition, ND (Nov 1994) - metallic ink cover	$0.60	$1.80	$3.00	£0.40	£1.20	£2.00
29 Mimic appears	$12.50	$39.00	$90.00	£5.25	£16.00	£37.50
30	$12.50	$39.00	$90.00	£5.25	£16.00	£37.50
31 1st appearance Cobalt Man	$9.25	$28.00	$65.00	£4.25	£12.50	£30.00
32 Juggernaut appears	$9.25	$28.00	$65.00	£4.25	£12.50	£30.00
33 Dr. Strange appears	$9.25	$28.00	$65.00	£4.60	£13.50	£32.50
34	$9.25	$28.00	$65.00	£3.90	£11.50	£27.50
35 Spiderman appears	$14.00	$43.00	$100.00	£6.25	£19.00	£45.00
36 1st appearance Mekano	$9.25	$28.00	$65.00	£3.90	£11.50	£27.50
37	$9.25	$28.00	$65.00	£3.90	£11.50	£27.50
38 X-Men origin feature begins (ends #57)	$12.00	$36.00	$85.00	£5.00	£15.00	£35.00
39 new costumes (3rd)	$9.25	$28.00	$65.00	£3.90	£11.50	£27.50
40 (Jan 1968)	$9.25	$28.00	$65.00	£3.90	£11.50	£27.50
41	$8.50	$26.00	$60.00	£3.55	£10.50	£25.00
42 death of Professor X (later revealed as Changeling disguised as Professor X)	$8.50	$26.00	$60.00	£3.55	£10.50	£25.00
43	$8.50	$26.00	$60.00	£3.55	£10.50	£25.00
44 GA Red Raven appears (1st time since Golden Age)	$8.50	$26.00	$60.00	£3.55	£10.50	£25.00
45 story continues in Avengers #53	$8.50	$26.00	$60.00	£3.55	£10.50	£25.00
46-48	$8.50	$26.00	$60.00	£3.20	£9.50	£22.50
49 Steranko cover, 1st appearance Lorna Dane	$8.50	$26.00	$60.00	£3.55	£10.50	£25.00
50 scarce in the U.K. Jim Steranko art	$10.00	$30.00	$70.00	£4.60	£13.50	£32.50
51 Jim Steranko art	$9.25	$28.00	$65.00	£3.90	£11.50	£27.50
52 (Jan 1969)	$6.25	$19.00	$45.00	£2.85	£8.50	£20.00
53 Barry Windsor Smith art, his first in comic books	$9.25	$28.00	$65.00	£3.90	£11.50	£27.50
54 1st Living Pharaoh, Barry Smith cover, 1st Alex Summers (later Havok)	$8.50	$26.00	$60.00	£3.40	£10.00	£24.00
55 Barry Smith cover	$8.50	$26.00	$60.00	£2.85	£8.50	£20.00
56 Neal Adams art, Pharaoh becomes Living Monolith, 1st appearance Havok	$8.50	$26.00	$60.00	£3.20	£9.50	£22.50
57 Neal Adams art, Sentinels story	$8.50	$26.00	$60.00	£3.20	£9.50	£22.50
58 Neal Adams art, Sentinels story, Havok appears	$11.00	$34.00	$80.00	£3.90	£11.50	£27.50
59 Neal Adams art, Sentinels story, Havok appears	$7.75	$23.50	$55.00	£3.20	£9.50	£22.50
60 Neal Adams art, 1st appearance Sauron	$7.75	$23.50	$55.00	£3.20	£9.50	£22.50
61 Neal Adams art	$7.75	$23.50	$55.00	£3.20	£9.50	£22.50
62-63 Neal Adams art, Ka-Zar X-over	$7.75	$23.50	$55.00	£3.20	£9.50	£22.50
64 (Jan 1970), 1st appearance Sunfire	$9.25	$28.00	$65.00	£2.85	£8.50	£20.00
65 Neal Adams art, Professor X returns	$7.75	$23.50	$55.00	£3.20	£9.50	£22.50
66 scarce in the U.K. X-Men vs. Hulk, last new story	$7.00	$21.00	$50.00	£2.85	£8.50	£20.00
67 scarce in the U.K. 52pgs, reprints #12,13	$4.25	$12.50	$30.00	£2.10	£6.25	£15.00
68 scarce in the U.K. 52pgs, (Feb 1971), reprints #14,15	$4.25	$12.50	$30.00	£2.10	£6.25	£15.00
69 52pgs, reprints #16,19	$4.25	$12.50	$30.00	£2.10	£6.25	£15.00
70 52pgs, reprints #17,18	$4.25	$12.50	$30.00	£2.10	£6.25	£15.00
71 ND reprints #20	$3.55	$10.50	$25.00	£2.10	£6.25	£15.00
72 ND 52pgs, reprints #21,24	$3.90	$11.50	$27.50	£2.35	£7.00	£16.50
73 scarce in the U.K. reprints #25	$3.55	$10.50	$25.00	£2.00	£6.00	£14.00
74 scarce in the U.K. (Feb 1972), reprints #26	$3.55	$10.50	$25.00	£2.00	£6.00	£14.00
75 scarce in the U.K. reprints #27	$3.55	$10.50	$25.00	£2.00	£6.00	£14.00
76 scarce in the U.K. reprints #28	$3.55	$10.50	$25.00	£2.00	£6.00	£14.00
77 scarce in the U.K. reprints #29	$3.55	$10.50	$25.00	£2.00	£6.00	£14.00
78 scarce in the U.K. reprints #30	$3.55	$10.50	$25.00	£2.00	£6.00	£14.00
79 scarce in the U.K. reprints #31	$3.55	$10.50	$25.00	£2.00	£6.00	£14.00
80 (Feb 1973), reprints #32	$3.55	$10.50	$25.00	£2.00	£6.00	£14.00
81 reprints #33	$3.20	$9.50	$22.50	£1.75	£5.25	£12.50
82 reprints #34	$3.20	$9.50	$22.50	£1.75	£5.25	£12.50
83 reprints #35 (Spiderman appearance)	$3.20	$9.50	$22.50	£1.75	£5.25	£12.50
84 reprints #36	$3.20	$9.50	$22.50	£1.75	£5.25	£12.50
85 reprints #37	$3.20	$9.50	$22.50	£1.75	£5.25	£12.50
86 (Feb 1974), reprints #38	$3.20	$9.50	$22.50	£1.75	£5.25	£12.50
87 ND rare in the U.K. reprints #39	$3.20	$9.50	$22.50	£2.25	£6.75	£16.00
88 ND rare in the U.K. reprints #40	$3.20	$9.50	$22.50	£2.25	£6.75	£16.00
89 reprints #41	$3.20	$9.50	$22.50	£1.40	£4.25	£10.00
90 reprints #42	$3.20	$9.50	$22.50	£1.40	£4.25	£10.00
91 reprints #43	$3.20	$9.50	$22.50	£1.40	£4.25	£10.00
92 (Feb 1975), reprints #44	$3.20	$9.50	$22.50	£1.25	£3.85	£9.00
93 reprints #45	$3.20	$9.50	$22.50	£1.25	£3.85	£9.00
94 ND New X-Men begin; Banshee, Colossus, Nightcrawler, Storm, Thunderbird, Wolverine become members; Gil Kane cover, story continues from Giant Size #1	$52.50	$155.00	$425.00	£33.00	£97.50	£260.00
95 ND Thunderbird dies	$10.50	$32.00	$75.00	£7.75	£23.50	£55.00
96 1st appearance Moira McTaggart	$8.50	$26.00	$60.00	£2.85	£8.50	£20.00
97 (Feb 1976), 1st appearance Lilandra	$8.50	$26.00	$60.00	£2.50	£7.50	£17.50
98 Sentinels; Stan Lee & Jack Kirby cameo	$8.50	$26.00	$60.00	£2.00	£6.00	£14.00
98 30 ¢ cover scarce in the U.K.	$8.50	$26.00	$60.00	£2.10	£6.25	£15.00
99 Sentinels appear	$8.50	$26.00	$60.00	£2.00	£6.00	£14.00
99 30 cents cover scarce in the U.K.	$8.50	$26.00	$60.00	£2.10	£6.25	£15.00

TRADE PAPERBACKS, GRAPHIC NOVELS AND OTHER COLLECTIONS ARE PRICED IN POUNDS STERLING ONLY. CONVERT AT 1.5 FOR DOLLARS.

SPECIALISTS
IN AMERICAN
COMICS & CARDS!
WHATEVER
COMICS
FROM X-FILES TO X-MEN
PROBABLY ONE OF THE BEST
STOCKED SHOPS THIS SIDE
OF LONDON.
2 BURGATE LANE
CANTERBURY, KENT, CTI 2HH
TEL: 01227 453226
5 MIDDLE ROW, HIGH STREET
MAIDSTONE, KENT, ME14 1TF
TEL: 01622 681041
OPEN MON-SAT 10am-5.30pm
VISA
IMPORT
COMICS
BACK
ISSUES
TRADING CARDS
COLLECTABLE
CARD GAMES
MERCHANDISE
MARVEL
COMICS
TM & © 1994 MARVEL ENTERTAINMENT GROUP, INC. ALL RIGHTS RESERVED.
9206-02R

	$Good	$Fine	$N.Mint	£Good	£Fine	£N.Mint
100 New X-Men vs Old X-Men, part origin Phoenix	*$9.25*	*$28.00*	*$65.00*	£2.25	£6.75	£16.00
101 1st appearance Phoenix	*$8.25*	*$25.00*	*$50.00*	£2.30	£7.00	£14.00
102 LD in the U.K. origin Storm	*$4.15*	*$12.50*	*$25.00*	£2.25	£6.75	£13.50
103 ND	*$4.15*	*$12.50*	*$25.00*	£2.30	£7.00	£14.00
104 ND Magneto re-appears (see Defenders #15, #16)	*$4.15*	*$12.50*	*$25.00*	£2.50	£7.50	£15.00
105 ND scarce in the U.K.	*$4.15*	*$12.50*	*$25.00*	£2.50	£7.50	£15.00
106-107 ND	*$4.15*	*$12.50*	*$25.00*	£2.30	£7.00	£14.00
108 1st John Byrne X-Men; Corbeau, Fantastic Four, Avengers, Beast cameos	*$7.50*	*$22.50*	*$45.00*	£2.50	£7.50	£15.00
109 (Feb 1978), 1st appearance Vindicator (Alpha Flight), John Byrne art	*$6.25*	*$18.50*	*$37.50*	£2.00	£6.00	£12.00
110 Phoenix joins team, no John Byrne art	*$3.75*	*$11.00*	*$22.50*	£1.05	£3.25	£6.50
111 John Byrne art	*$3.75*	*$11.00*	*$22.50*	£1.05	£3.25	£6.50
112 John Byrne art, George Perez cover	*$3.30*	*$10.00*	*$20.00*	£1.05	£3.25	£6.50
113 John Byrne art	*$3.30*	*$10.00*	*$20.00*	£1.05	£3.25	£6.50
114-116 Ka-Zar, Savage Land appear, John Byrne art	*$3.30*	*$10.00*	*$20.00*	£1.05	£3.25	£6.50
117 (Jan 1979), origin Professor X retold, John Byrne art	*$3.30*	*$10.00*	*$20.00*	£1.05	£3.25	£6.50
118-119 John Byrne art	*$3.30*	*$10.00*	*$20.00*	£1.05	£3.25	£6.50
120 1st appearance Alpha Flight (cameo), John Byrne art	*$6.25*	*$18.50*	*$37.50*	£2.65	£8.00	£16.00
121 ND John Byrne art, 1st full Alpha Flight story, Byrne cameo	*$7.50*	*$22.50*	*$45.00*	£5.00	£15.00	£30.00
122 ND John Byrne art	*$3.00*	*$9.00*	*$18.00*	£1.65	£5.00	£10.00
123 Colossus becomes Proletarian (for seven pages only!), John Byrne art	*$3.00*	*$9.00*	*$18.00*	£1.00	£3.00	£6.00
124-126 John Byrne art	*$3.00*	*$9.00*	*$18.00*	£1.00	£3.00	£6.00
127 1st appearance Proteus, John Byrne art	*$3.00*	*$9.00*	*$18.00*	£1.00	£3.00	£6.00
128 John Byrne art	*$3.00*	*$9.00*	*$18.00*	£1.00	£3.00	£6.00
129 (Jan 1980), 1st appearance Kitty Pryde, John Byrne art	*$4.30*	*$13.00*	*$26.00*	£1.25	£3.75	£7.50
130 1st appearance Dazzler, John Byrne art	*$3.75*	*$11.00*	*$22.50*	£1.25	£3.75	£7.50
131-132 John Byrne art	*$2.90*	*$8.75*	*$17.50*	£0.80	£2.50	£5.00
133 Wolverine goes solo, John Byrne art	*$2.90*	*$8.75*	*$17.50*	£1.30	£4.00	£8.00
134 John Byrne art	*$2.90*	*$8.75*	*$17.50*	£0.80	£2.50	£5.00
135 Dr. Strange, Spiderman, Silver Surfer cameos, John Byrne art	*$2.90*	*$8.75*	*$17.50*	£0.80	£2.50	£5.00
136 John Byrne art	*$2.90*	*$8.75*	*$17.50*	£0.80	£2.50	£5.00
137 ND DS, death of Phoenix; Recorder, Watcher appear, John Byrne art	*$3.30*	*$10.00*	*$20.00*	£1.30	£4.00	£8.00
138 X-Men's history re-capped, John Byrne art	*$2.90*	*$8.75*	*$17.50*	£1.30	£4.00	£8.00
139 Alpha Flight appears, Kitty Pryde joins, Wolverine's new costume, John Byrne art	*$5.00*	*$15.00*	*$30.00*	£1.25	£3.75	£7.50
140 Alpha Flight, Pierre Trudeau appear, brief origin Wolverine, John Byrne art	*$4.50*	*$13.50*	*$27.00*	£1.30	£4.00	£8.00
141 (Jan 1981), Days Of Future Past story, 1st new Phoenix (Rachel Summers), John Byrne art	*$4.50*	*$13.50*	*$27.00*	£1.50	£4.50	£9.00
142 ND Days Of Future Past story, X-Men all "die", John Byrne art; this is the first issue of "The Uncanny X-Men"	*$4.15*	*$12.50*	*$25.00*	£1.30	£4.00	£8.00
143 ND John Byrne art, "Alien" type story	*$2.00*	*$6.00*	*$12.00*	£0.80	£2.50	£5.00
144 Brent Anderson art (see note below)	*$1.50*	*$4.50*	*$9.00*	£0.55	£1.75	£3.50
145 old X-Men appear	*$1.50*	*$4.50*	*$9.00*	£0.55	£1.75	£3.50
146-147	*$1.50*	*$4.50*	*$9.00*	£0.55	£1.75	£3.50
148 Spiderwoman, Dazzler appear	*$1.50*	*$4.50*	*$9.00*	£0.55	£1.75	£3.50
149	*$1.50*	*$4.50*	*$9.00*	£0.55	£1.75	£3.50
150 DS Magneto appears	*$1.50*	*$4.50*	*$9.00*	£0.65	£2.00	£4.00
151-152	*$1.60*	*$4.80*	*$8.00*	£0.60	£1.80	£3.00
153 (Jan 1982)	*$1.60*	*$4.80*	*$8.00*	£0.60	£1.80	£3.00
154-156	*$1.60*	*$4.80*	*$8.00*	£0.60	£1.80	£3.00
157 Phoenix reborn	*$1.60*	*$4.80*	*$8.00*	£0.60	£1.80	£3.00
158 1st appearance Rogue in X-Men (see Avengers Annual #10)	*$3.00*	*$9.00*	*$15.00*	£1.00	£3.00	£5.00
159 Dracula vs. X-Men, Sienkiewicz art	*$1.50*	*$4.50*	*$7.50*	£0.60	£1.80	£3.00
160 Anderson art	*$1.50*	*$4.50*	*$7.50*	£0.60	£1.80	£3.00
161 origin Magneto	*$1.20*	*$3.60*	*$6.00*	£0.80	£2.40	£4.00
162 scarce in the U.K. Wolverine solo story	*$2.40*	*$7.00*	*$12.00*	£0.80	£2.40	£4.00
163 scarce in the U.K. 1st appearance Binary	*$1.20*	*$3.60*	*$6.00*	£0.80	£2.40	£4.00
164 scarce in the U.K. Carol Danvers as Binary	*$1.20*	*$3.60*	*$6.00*	£0.80	£2.40	£4.00
165 (Jan 1983), 1st Paul Smith art	*$2.00*	*$6.00*	*$10.00*	£0.90	£2.70	£4.50
166 DS, Paul Smith art	*$1.60*	*$4.80*	*$8.00*	£1.00	£3.00	£5.00
167 New Mutants X-over, Paul Smith art	*$1.20*	*$3.60*	*$6.00*	£0.90	£2.70	£4.50
168 1st Madelyne Pryor (see Avengers Annual #10), Paul Smith art	*$1.20*	*$3.60*	*$6.00*	£0.90	£2.70	£4.50
169-170 Paul Smith art	*$1.20*	*$3.60*	*$6.00*	£0.80	£2.40	£4.00
171 Rogue joins X-Men, Walt Simonson art	*$3.00*	*$9.00*	*$15.00*	£1.10	£3.30	£5.50
172 LD in the U.K. spotlight on Wolverine, Paul Smith art	*$1.20*	*$3.60*	*$6.00*	£1.10	£3.30	£5.50
173 Paul Smith art, Wolverine cover	*$1.20*	*$3.60*	*$6.00*	£1.10	£3.30	£5.50
174 "Phoenix" cameo, Paul Smith art	*$1.20*	*$3.60*	*$6.00*	£0.80	£2.40	£4.00
175 DS, anniversary, "Phoenix" returns, part Paul Smith cover/art (rest Romita)	*$2.00*	*$6.00*	*$10.00*	£1.10	£3.30	£5.50
176 LD in the U.K.	*$1.20*	*$3.60*	*$6.00*	£0.70	£2.10	£3.50
177 LD in the U.K. (Jan 1984)	*$1.20*	*$3.60*	*$6.00*	£0.70	£2.10	£3.50
178-183 LD in the U.K.	*$1.20*	*$3.60*	*$6.00*	£0.70	£2.10	£3.50
184 LD in the U.K. 1st appearance Forge	*$1.50*	*$4.50*	*$7.50*	£0.70	£2.10	£3.50
185 LD in the U.K. Storm loses powers, Rogue appears	*$1.20*	*$3.60*	*$6.00*	£0.80	£2.40	£4.00
186 DS Barry Smith art	*$1.20*	*$3.60*	*$6.00*	£0.50	£1.50	£2.50
187-188	*$1.00*	*$3.00*	*$5.00*	£0.40	£1.20	£2.00
189 (Jan 1985)	*$1.00*	*$3.00*	*$5.00*	£0.40	£1.20	£2.00
190-192	*$1.00*	*$3.00*	*$5.00*	£0.40	£1.20	£2.00
193 DS 100th anniversary issue	*$1.80*	*$5.25*	*$9.00*	£0.70	£2.10	£3.50
194 Juggernaut appears, John Romita Jnr. art	*$1.00*	*$3.00*	*$5.00*	£0.50	£1.50	£2.50
195 Power Pack X-over	*$1.00*	*$3.00*	*$5.00*	£0.50	£1.50	£2.50
196 LD in the U.K. Secret Wars X-over	*$1.00*	*$3.00*	*$5.00*	£0.60	£1.80	£3.00
197 LD in the U.K. Juggernaut appears, John Romita Jnr. art	*$1.00*	*$3.00*	*$5.00*	£0.60	£1.80	£3.00
198 Barry Smith art	*$1.00*	*$3.00*	*$5.00*	£0.50	£1.50	£2.50
199 very LD	*$1.00*	*$3.00*	*$5.00*	£0.80	£2.40	£4.00
200 LD in the U.K. DS Magneto on trial	*$2.00*	*$6.00*	*$10.00*	£1.00	£3.00	£5.00
201 very LD (Jan 1986), 1st appearance Cyclop's son Nathan Summers; Whilce Portacio inks (1st work on X-Men)	*$4.00*	*$12.00*	*$20.00*	£1.20	£3.60	£6.00
202-203 LD in the U.K. Secret Wars X-over	*$1.60*	*$4.80*	*$8.00*	£0.80	£2.40	£4.00
204	*$1.60*	*$4.80*	*$8.00*	£0.60	£1.80	£3.00
205 Barry Smith art, solo Wolverine story	*$4.00*	*$12.00*	*$20.00*	£1.50	£4.50	£7.50
206	*$1.60*	*$4.80*	*$8.00*	£0.60	£1.80	£3.00
207 Wolverine cover/story	*$1.60*	*$4.80*	*$8.00*	£0.70	£2.10	£3.50
208-209	*$1.60*	*$4.80*	*$8.00*	£0.60	£1.80	£3.00
210 Mutant Massacre tie-in	*$4.00*	*$12.00*	*$20.00*	£1.70	£5.00	£8.50
211 Mutant Massacre tie-in, Colossus kills	*$4.00*	*$12.00*	*$20.00*	£1.70	£5.00	£8.50
212 Mutant Massacre tie-in, Wolverine and Sabretooth battle	*$5.50*	*$16.50*	*$27.50*	£2.00	£6.00	£10.00
213 (Jan 1987), Mutant Massacre tie-in, Davis/Neary art, Wolverine and Sabretooth battle	*$5.50*	*$16.50*	*$27.50*	£2.20	£6.50	£11.00
214 Barry Smith art	*$1.20*	*$3.60*	*$6.00*	£0.60	£1.80	£3.00
215 Alan Davis art	*$1.20*	*$3.60*	*$6.00*	£0.50	£1.50	£2.50
216-217	*$1.20*	*$3.60*	*$6.00*	£0.30	£0.90	£1.50
218 Art Adams cover	*$1.20*	*$3.60*	*$6.00*	£0.30	£0.90	£1.50
219 Havok joins the X-Men, Sabretooth appears	*$1.20*	*$3.60*	*$6.00*	£0.40	£1.20	£2.00
220-221	*$1.20*	*$3.60*	*$6.00*	£0.30	£0.90	£1.50
222 Wolverine battles Sabretooth cover and story	*$3.00*	*$9.00*	*$15.00*	£0.80	£2.40	£4.00
223	*$1.20*	*$3.60*	*$6.00*	£0.40	£1.20	£2.00
224 LD in the U.K.	*$1.20*	*$3.60*	*$6.00*	£0.50	£1.50	£2.50

Issue	$Good	$Fine	$N.Mint	£Good	£Fine	£N.Mint
225 (Jan 1988), Fall of the Mutants	$2.00	$6.00	$10.00	£0.60	£1.80	£3.00
226 LD in the U.K. DS Fall of Mutants	$2.00	$6.00	$10.00	£0.70	£2.10	£3.50
227 Fall of the Mutants	$2.00	$6.00	$10.00	£0.60	£1.80	£3.00
228-232	$1.20	$3.60	$6.00	£0.40	£1.20	£2.00
233 LD in the U.K. Wolverine temporaily transformed into alien Brood member	$1.20	$3.60	$6.00	£0.50	£1.50	£2.50
234 Wolverine temporaily transformed into alien Brood member	$1.20	$3.60	$6.00	£0.40	£1.20	£2.00
235-238	$1.20	$3.60	$6.00	£0.35	£1.05	£1.75
239 Inferno X-over	$1.20	$3.60	$6.00	£0.40	£1.20	£2.00
240 (Jan 1989), Inferno X-over, Sabretooth appears	$1.60	$4.80	$8.00	£0.40	£1.20	£2.00
241 Inferno X-over	$1.20	$3.60	$6.00	£0.35	£1.05	£1.75
242 LD in the U.K. DS Inferno X-over, X-Factor appear	$1.20	$3.60	$6.00	£0.50	£1.50	£2.50
243 Inferno X-over, Sabretooth appears	$1.00	$3.00	$5.00	£0.40	£1.20	£2.00
244 1st appearance Jubilee	$4.00	$12.00	$20.00	£0.60	£1.80	£3.00
245 Rob Liefeld's 2nd X-book, only part art	$0.80	$2.40	$4.00	£0.40	£1.20	£2.00
246-247	$1.00	$3.00	$5.00	£0.30	£0.90	£1.50
248 1st Jim Lee art on X-Men	$4.50	$13.50	$22.50	£1.00	£3.00	£5.00
248 2nd printing, ND (Jun 1992) - gold cover	$0.50	$1.50	$2.50	£0.30	£0.90	£1.50
249	$0.60	$1.80	$3.00	£0.30	£0.90	£1.50
250 Ka-Zar appears	$0.60	$1.80	$3.00	£0.30	£0.90	£1.50
251-252 bi-weekly issue	$0.60	$1.80	$3.00	£0.30	£0.90	£1.50
253-255 bi-weekly issue	$1.00	$3.00	$5.00	£0.40	£1.20	£2.00
256 Acts of Vengeance tie-in, Jim Lee art	$2.00	$6.00	$10.00	£0.80	£2.40	£4.00
257 (Jan 1990), Acts of Vengeance tie-in, Jim Lee art	$2.00	$6.00	$10.00	£0.80	£2.40	£4.00
258 Acts of Vengeance tie-in, Wolverine cover and story, Jim Lee art	$2.40	$7.00	$12.00	£1.00	£3.00	£5.00
259 LD in the U.K.	$1.00	$3.00	$5.00	£0.40	£1.20	£2.00
260-262	$0.60	$1.80	$3.00	£0.30	£0.90	£1.50
263-265 bi-weekly issue	$0.60	$1.80	$3.00	£0.30	£0.90	£1.50
266 1st full appearance Gambit (see Annual #14), bi-weekly issue	$8.00	$24.00	$40.00	£2.50	£7.50	£12.50
267 LD in the U.K. Jim Lee art run begins	$3.00	$9.00	$15.00	£1.00	£3.00	£5.00
268 Captain America/Black Widow appear, Jim Lee/Scott Williams art begins, Wolverine cover, last bi-weekly issue	$4.00	$12.00	$20.00	£1.20	£3.60	£6.00
269 LD in the U.K. Jim Lee art	$1.20	$3.60	$6.00	£0.80	£2.40	£4.00
270 LD in the U.K. The X-Tinction Agenda part 1 (of 9; see New Mutants/X-Factor), Jim Lee art	$2.00	$6.00	$10.00	£0.90	£2.70	£4.50
270 2nd printing, ND The X-Tinction Agenda part 1 (gold ink cover)	$0.80	$2.40	$4.00	£0.50	£1.50	£2.50
271 The X-Tinction Agenda part 4, Jim Lee art	$1.50	$4.50	$7.50	£0.60	£1.80	£3.00
272 (Jan 1991), The X-Tinction Agenda part 7, Jim Lee art	$1.50	$4.50	$7.50	£0.60	£1.80	£3.00
273 X-Factor/New Mutants appear, many artists including Jim Lee and John Byrne	$1.30	$3.90	$6.50	£0.60	£1.80	£3.00
274 Jim Lee art	$1.20	$3.60	$6.00	£0.50	£1.50	£2.50
275 DS Jim Lee art, gatefold cover	$1.30	$3.90	$6.50	£0.60	£1.80	£3.00
275 2nd printing, ND gold ink cover	$0.50	$1.50	$2.50	£0.30	£0.90	£1.50
276-277 Jim Lee art	$0.60	$1.80	$3.00	£0.40	£1.20	£2.00
278 Paul Smith art	$0.60	$1.80	$3.00	£0.30	£0.90	£1.50
279 the lead into the new X-Men #1	$0.60	$1.80	$3.00	£0.30	£0.90	£1.50
280 X-over X-Factor #70, Andy Kubert art	$0.60	$1.80	$3.00	£0.30	£0.90	£1.50
281 ties into X-Men (2nd series) #1, new line-up revealed: Storm, Marvel Girl, Archangel, Ice man, Colossus, Whilce Portacio pencils, Thibert inks, John Byrne scripts begin	$1.40	$4.20	$7.00	£0.50	£1.50	£2.50
281 2nd printing, ND scarce in the U.K. red ink cover	$0.55	$1.65	$2.75	£0.35	£1.05	£1.75
282 John Byrne script, 1st appearance Bishop (on last page), Whilce Portacio pencils, Thibert inks	$2.00	$6.00	$10.00	£0.60	£1.80	£3.00
282 2nd printing, ND gold cover; inside back cover shows how 2nd print #281 should have originally been presented, a combination of gold and red)	$0.60	$1.80	$3.00	£0.40	£1.20	£2.00
283 1st full appearance Bishop, John Byrne script, Whilce Portacio pencils, Thibert inks	$2.80	$8.25	$14.00	£0.60	£1.80	£3.00
284 John Byrne script, Portacio pencils, Thibert inks	$0.50	$1.50	$2.50	£0.30	£0.90	£1.50
285 John Byrne script, Portacio art, $1,25 cover begins	$0.50	$1.50	$2.50	£0.20	£0.60	£1.00
286 John Byrne script, Lee and Portacio plot and pencils, Thibert co-pencils	$0.50	$1.50	$2.50	£0.20	£0.60	£1.00
287-288 John Byrne script, Portacio art, Bishop appears	$0.50	$1.50	$2.50	£0.20	£0.60	£1.00
289 John Byrne script, Portacio art, Bishop appears and joins team	$0.50	$1.50	$2.50	£0.20	£0.60	£1.00
290-292 Whilce Portacio art	$0.50	$1.50	$2.50	£0.20	£0.60	£1.00
293	$0.50	$1.50	$2.50	£0.20	£0.60	£1.00
294 X-Cutioner's Song part #1, pre-bagged and includes Marvel trading card, continues in X-Factor #84	$0.50	$1.50	$2.50	£0.25	£0.75	£1.25
295 X-Cutioner's Song part 5, pre-bagged and includes Marvel trading card, continues in X-Factor #85	$0.50	$1.50	$2.50	£0.20	£0.60	£1.00
296 X-Cutioner's Song part 9, pre-bagged and includes Marvel trading card, continues in X-Factor #86	$0.40	$1.20	$2.00	£0.20	£0.60	£1.00
297-299	$0.40	$1.20	$2.00	£0.20	£0.60	£1.00
300 64pgs, squarebound, anniversary issue, silver holo-grafix foil cover	$1.00	$3.00	$5.00	£0.50	£1.50	£2.50
301-303	$0.30	$0.90	$1.50	£0.20	£0.60	£1.00
304 LD in the U.K. 64pgs, 30th anniversary issue; Magneto returns, Magneto hologram cover	$1.00	$3.00	$5.00	£0.60	£1.80	£3.00
305	$0.30	$0.90	$1.50	£0.20	£0.60	£1.00
306 X-Cutioner vs. Archangel	$0.30	$0.90	$1.50	£0.20	£0.60	£1.00
307 Bloodties part 4; Spiderwoman, Crystal and Quicksilver appear	$0.30	$0.90	$1.50	£0.20	£0.60	£1.00
308 Jean Grey proposes to Scott Summers (see X-Men 2nd Series #30)						

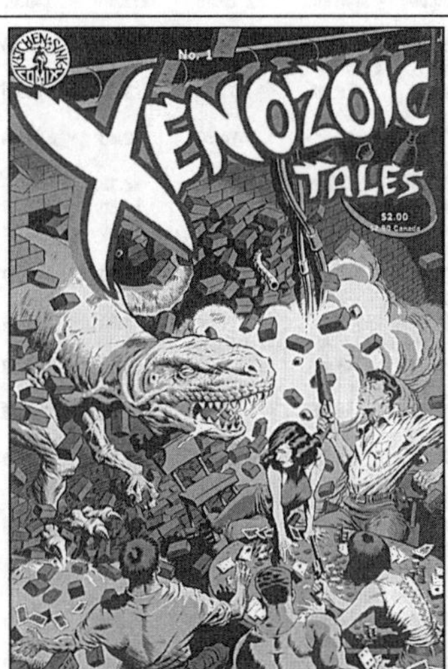

Xenozoic Tales #1

X-Files #2

X-Men: Rarities

EXTREMELY HIGH GRADE COPIES MAY COMMAND MULTIPLES OF GUIDE ALTHOUGH THIS IS MORE PREVELANT IN THE US THAN IN THE UK

	$Good	$Fine	$N.Mint	£Good	£Fine	£N.Mint
	$0.30	$0.90	$1.50	£0.20	£0.60	£1.00
309 Magneto cameo						
	$0.30	$0.90	$1.50	£0.20	£0.60	£1.00
310 Sabretooth and Cable appear; 3 bound-in trading cards						
	$0.60	$1.80	$3.00	£0.30	£0.90	£1.50
311	$0.30	$0.90	$1.50	£0.20	£0.60	£1.00
312 with free Spiderman's Amazing Powers card sheet						
	$0.30	$0.90	$1.50	£0.20	£0.60	£1.00
313-316	$0.30	$0.90	$1.50	£0.20	£0.60	£1.00
316 Deluxe Edition, LD in the U.K. foil stamped cover						
	$0.60	$1.80	$3.00	£0.40	£1.20	£2.00
317 ND	$0.30	$0.90	$1.50	£0.20	£0.60	£1.00
317 Deluxe Edition, ND foil stamped cover						
	$0.60	$1.80	$3.00	£0.40	£1.20	£2.00
318 ND	$0.30	$0.90	$1.50	£0.20	£0.60	£1.00
318 Deluxe Edition, ND printed on glossy stock paper						
	$0.40	$1.20	$2.00	£0.25	£0.75	£1.25
319 ND	$0.30	$0.90	$1.50	£0.20	£0.60	£1.00
319 Deluxe Edition, ND printed on glossy stock paper						
	$0.40	$1.20	$2.00	£0.25	£0.75	£1.25
320 ND (Jan 1995)	$0.30	$0.90	$1.50	£0.20	£0.60	£1.00
320 Deluxe Edition, ND printed on glossy stock paper						
	$0.40	$1.20	$2.00	£0.25	£0.75	£1.25
321 ND	$0.30	$0.90	$1.50	£0.20	£0.60	£1.00
321 Deluxe Edition, ND printed on glossy stock paper plus bound-in Fleer trading card; see Mutants: The Astonishing X-Men #1						
	$0.40	$1.20	$2.00	£0.25	£0.75	£1.25
322 ND continued from X-Men: Prime; Scott Lobdell script, Tom Grummett art						
	$0.40	$1.20	$2.00	£0.25	£0.75	£1.25
323-324 ND	$0.40	$1.20	$2.00	£0.25	£0.75	£1.25
325 ND 48pgs, 20th anniversary of the new X-Men; double gate-fold prismatic foil cover						
	$0.80	$2.40	$4.00	£0.50	£1.50	£2.50
326 ND Sabretooth appears						
	$0.40	$1.20	$2.00	£0.30	£0.90	£1.50
327 ND Magneto appears						
	$0.40	$1.20	$2.00	£0.30	£0.90	£1.50
328 ND Sabretooth appears, continued in X-Men #48						
	$0.40	$1.20	$2.00	£0.30	£0.90	£1.50
329 ND Dr. Strange appears						
	$0.40	$1.20	$2.00	£0.30	£0.90	£1.50
330-331 ND	$0.40	$1.20	$2.00	£0.30	£0.90	£1.50
332 ND continued from Wolverine #100						
	$0.40	$1.20	$2.00	£0.30	£0.90	£1.50
333 ND	$0.40	$1.20	$2.00	£0.30	£0.90	£1.50
334 ND 40pgs, Onslaught tie-in						
	$0.40	$1.20	$2.00	£0.30	£0.90	£1.50
335 ND 40pgs, Onslaught tie-in, The Avengers appear						
	$0.40	$1.20	$2.00	£0.30	£0.90	£1.50
336 ND Onslaught tie-in						
	$0.40	$1.20	$2.00	£0.30	£0.90	£1.50
337 ND	$0.40	$1.20	$2.00	£0.25	£0.75	£1.25
338 ND The Angel returns						
	$0.40	$1.20	$2.00	£0.25	£0.75	£1.25
339-342 ND	$0.40	$1.20	$2.00	£0.25	£0.75	£1.25
342 Variant Cover Edition, ND Rogue cover; 25% of print run						
	$1.00	$3.00	$5.00	£0.50	£1.50	£2.50
Title Value:	$2435.30	$7297.30	$19512.25	£1221.75	£3658.75	£10037.50

Note: issue 144 often turns up ink-smudged: near mint copies are scarce in both the U.S and U.K.

ARTISTS

Kirby art in #1-11, lay-outs in 12-17. Cockrum art in #94-105, 107, 145-158.

FEATURES

Origins as follows: Angel in #54-56; Beast in #48-53; Cyclops in #39-43; Iceman in #44-47; Marvel Girl in #57.

	£Good	£Fine	£N.Mint
X-Men: Asgardian Wars (Apr 1989)			
Trade paperback ND reprints X-Men Annual #9, X-Men/Alpha Flight mini-series, New Mutants Special #1 with Art Adams and Paul Smith art	£1.80	£5.40	£9.00
X-Men: Phoenix Saga			
Trade paperback ND 192pgs, reprints #129-137	£1.40	£4.20	£7.00
(2nd - 5th printings)	£1.25	£3.75	£6.25
(6th printing - Nov 1990)	£1.20	£3.60	£6.00
(7th printing - Nov 1994)	£1.20	£3.60	£6.00
X-Men: Savage Land			
Trade paperback ND reprints Marvel Fanfare #1-4	£1.00	£3.00	£5.00
(2nd print that emphasizes "X-Men" more. Oct 1989)	£0.90	£2.70	£4.50
X-Men: Days of Future Past			
Trade paperback ND 48pgs, reprints X-Men #141,#142 featuring Claremont script, Byrne/Austin art	£0.60	£1.80	£3.00
(2nd print - Nov 1990)	£0.50	£1.50	£2.50
(3rd print - Mar 1995)	£0.80	£2.40	£4.00
X-Men: Days of Future Present			
Trade paperback ND 160pgs, reprints storyline from Fantastic Four Annual #23, X-Men Annual #14, X-Factor Annual #5, New Mutants Annual #10. Mike Mignola cover	£1.80	£5.40	£9.00
(2nd print - Mar 1995)	£2.00	£6.00	£10.00
X-Men: From The Ashes			
Trade paperback ND reprints X-Men #165-175	£1.80	£5.40	£9.00
(2nd print - May 1993)	£1.75	£5.25	£8.75
(3rd print - Nov 1994)	£1.70	£5.10	£8.50
X-Men: X-Tinction Agenda			
Trade paperback (Dec 1992)			
ND reprints X-Men #270-272, X-Factor #60-62, New Mutants #95-97 special "enhanced" cover	£3.00	£9.00	£15.00
(2nd print - Jun 1993)	£2.80	£8.40	£14.00
(3rd print - Nov 1994)	£2.75	£8.25	£13.75
X-Men: The X-Cutioner's Song (Jun 1994)			
Trade paperback			
ND reprints X-Cutioner's Song storyline, metal foil stamped cover	£3.20	£9.60	£16.00
Greatest Battles of the X-Men (Oct 1994)			
Trade paperback ND 176pgs, reprints	£2.00	£6.00	£10.00
Marvel Limited: The Best of Chris Claremont X-Men (Dec 1994)			
230pgs, leather-bound hardcover with foil stamping; classic reprints	£3.00	£9.00	£15.00
X-Men: Fatal Attractions (Feb 1995)			
Trade paperback ND 160pgs, reprints "Fatal Attractions" story from 1993	£2.40	£7.20	£12.00
X-Men: The Coming of Bishop (Apr 1995)			
Trade paperback ND reprints origin and 1st appearance of Bishop	£1.70	£5.10	£8.50
X-Men Spotlight (Nov 1995)			
ND boxed set collecting Uncanny X-Men #304, X-Force #25 and X-Factor #92 (all hologram covers)	£1.50	£4.50	£7.50
X-Men: Legion Quest (Jan 1996)			
Trade paperback ND 88pgs, reprints Legion Quest saga; gold foil etched cover	£1.20	£3.60	£6.00
X-Men: Dawn of the Age of Apocalypse (Jan 1996)			
Trade paperback ND 96pgs, reprints Cable #20 and X-Men: Alpha	£1.20	£3.60	£6.00
X-Men: Twilight of the Age of Apocalypse (Feb 1996)			
Trade paperback ND 96pgs, reprints X-Universe #1,2 and X-Men: Omega	£1.20	£3.60	£6.00
X-Men: Danger Room Battle Archives (Aug 1996)			
Trade paperback ND 224pgs, classic reprints featuring art by George Perez, John Byrne and Art Adams	£3.00	£9.00	£15.00
X-Men Visionaries: Neal Adams Collection (Sep 1996)			
Trade paperback ND 208pgs, reprints Neal Adams' run on X-Men from #56-63	£3.00	£9.00	£15.00
X-Men: Mutant Massacre (Nov 1996)			
Trade paperback ND 256pgs, reprints X-Men #210-213, New Mutants #46, Thor #373,374, Power Pack #27, X-Factor #9-11	£3.30	£9.90	£16.50
The Essential X-Men (Dec 1996)			
Trade paperback ND 528pgs, collects Giant Size X-Men #1 and X-Men #94-119 on newsprint	£1.70	£5.10	£8.50
X-Men: Mutations (Dec 1996)			
Trade paperback			
ND collects moments of change for the X-Men such as Amazing Adventures #11, X-Factor #24 and Uncanny X-Men #256-258	£2.70	£8.10	£13.50
X-Men: Inferno (Jan 1997)			
Trade paperback ND 352pgs, collects X-Men #239-243, New Mutants #71-73, X-Factor #36-39	£3.30	£9.90	£16.50

X-MEN, THE UNCANNY '95

Marvel Comics Group,OS; nn Nov 1995

	$Good	$Fine	$N.Mint	£Good	£Fine	£N.Mint
nn ND 64pgs, Terry Kavanagh script, Bryan Hitch art; Cannonball and Husk appear						
	$0.80	$2.40	$4.00	£0.50	£1.50	£2.50
Title Value:	$0.80	$2.40	$4.00	£0.50	£1.50	£2.50

X-MEN, THE UNCANNY '96

Marvel Comics Group,OS; nn Sep 1996

	$Good	$Fine	$N.Mint	£Good	£Fine	£N.Mint
nn ND 64pgs, Bishop and Shard appear						
	$0.60	$1.80	$3.00	£0.40	£1.20	£2.00
Title Value:	$0.60	$1.80	$3.00	£0.40	£1.20	£2.00

X-MEN, THE UNCANNY ANNUAL

Marvel Comics Group; 1 1970-2 1971; 3 1979-18 1994

(see X-Men, The Uncanny '95,96))

	$Good	$Fine	$N.Mint	£Good	£Fine	£N.Mint
1 52pgs, scarce, reprints X-Men #9, #11						
	$10.00	$30.00	$70.00	£6.25	£19.00	£45.00
2 ND 52pgs, scarce, reprints X-Men #22, #23						
	$8.50	$26.00	$60.00	£5.50	£17.00	£40.00
3 ND 52pgs, Arkon appears, George Perez art						
	$3.30	$10.00	$20.00	£1.65	£5.00	£10.00
4 ND 52pgs, Dr.Strange appears, John Romita Jnr art						
	$2.00	$6.00	$10.00	£1.00	£3.00	£5.00
5 ND 52pgs, Anderson art						
	$1.50	$4.50	$7.50	£0.80	£2.40	£4.00
6 ND Dracula, Lilith appear, Sienkiewicz art						
	$1.00	$3.00	$5.00	£0.70	£2.10	£3.50
7 ND Golden art	$1.00	$3.00	$5.00	£0.60	£1.80	£3.00
8 ND	$0.90	$2.70	$4.50	£0.50	£1.50	£2.50
9 ND Arthur Adams art (see X-Men/Alpha Flight #1 & #2)						
	$2.50	$7.50	$12.50	£1.00	£3.00	£5.00
10 ND Arthur Adams art, Longshot joins X-Men						
	$2.00	$6.00	$10.00	£1.00	£3.00	£5.00
11 ND Davis/Neary art, Captain Britain, Meggan, Psylocke (Excalibur) appear						
	$0.80	$2.40	$4.00	£0.50	£1.50	£2.50
12 ND squarebound, Evolutionary War, Art Adams art						
	$0.60	$1.80	$3.00	£0.40	£1.20	£2.00
13 ND squarebound, Atlantis Attacks part 3						
	$0.60	$1.80	$3.00	£0.40	£1.20	£2.00
14 ND Days of Future Present conclusion, continued from New Mutants Annual #6, Cable appears, 1st appearance Gambit (cameo - chronologically his 2nd appearance) - see X-Men #266						
	$2.00	$6.00	$10.00	£0.80	£2.40	£4.00
15 ND King of Pain part 3, continued in X-Factor Annual #6; origin retold						
	$0.80	$2.40	$4.00	£0.40	£1.20	£2.00
16 ND Shattershot part 2, continued in X-Factor Annual #7, Jae Lee art						
	$0.60	$1.80	$3.00	£0.40	£1.20	£2.00
17 ND 64pgs, pre-bagged with trading card introducing X-Cutioner						
	$0.60	$1.80	$3.00	£0.40	£1.20	£2.00
18 ND 64pgs, Sabretooth and Caliban appear						

VERY GENERAL PERCENTAGE CONVERSION CHART WHICH MAY BE USED TO CALCULATE LOW AND INBETWEEN GRADES:

Issue	$Good	$Fine	$N.Mint	£Good	£Fine	£N.Mint
	$0.60	$1.80	$3.00	£0.40	£1.20	£2.00
Title Value:	$39.30	$118.50	$237.50	£22.70	£68.90	£141.50

Note: this Marvel annual becomes a dated yearbook, that is, Uncanny X-Men '95, '96 etc.

X-MEN/CLANDESTINE

Marvel Comics Group,MS; 1 Oct 1996-2 Nov 1996

Issue	$Good	$Fine	$N.Mint	£Good	£Fine	£N.Mint
1-2 ND 48pgs, Alan Davis script and art	$0.60	$1.80	$3.00	£0.40	£1.20	£2.00
Title Value:	$1.20	$3.60	$6.00	£0.80	£2.40	£4.00

X-MEN: ALPHA

Marvel Comics Group,OS; 1 Feb 1995

Issue	$Good	$Fine	$N.Mint	£Good	£Fine	£N.Mint
1 ND 48pgs, the death of Professor X; chromium cover	$1.50	$4.50	$7.50	£1.00	£3.00	£5.00
1 Gold Edition, ND 48pgs, (Apr 1995) - gold chromium wraparound cover	$8.00	$24.00	$40.00	£5.00	£15.00	£25.00
Title Value:	$9.50	$28.50	$47.50	£6.00	£18.00	£30.00

X-MEN: ASKANI'S SON

Marvel Comics Group,MS; 1 Jan 1996-4 May 1996

Issue	$Good	$Fine	$N.Mint	£Good	£Fine	£N.Mint
1 ND Scott Lobdell script, Gene Ha art; the sequel to The Adventures of Cyclops & Phoenix, UV coated cover	$0.60	$1.80	$3.00	£0.40	£1.20	£2.00
2-4 ND UV coated cover	$0.60	$1.80	$3.00	£0.40	£1.20	£2.00
Title Value:	$2.40	$7.20	$12.00	£1.60	£4.80	£8.00

X-MEN: BOOKS OF ASKANI

Marvel Comics Group,OS; 1 Feb 1996

Issue	$Good	$Fine	$N.Mint	£Good	£Fine	£N.Mint
1 ND painted portraits by John Bolton, Bill Sienkiewicz and others	$0.60	$1.80	$3.00	£0.40	£1.20	£2.00
Title Value:	$0.60	$1.80	$3.00	£0.40	£1.20	£2.00

X-MEN: EARTHFALL

Marvel Comics Group,OS; nn Sep 1996

Issue	$Good	$Fine	$N.Mint	£Good	£Fine	£N.Mint
nn ND 64pgs, reprints Uncanny X-Men #232-234	$0.60	$1.80	$3.00	£0.40	£1.20	£2.00
Title Value:	$0.60	$1.80	$3.00	£0.40	£1.20	£2.00

X-MEN: GOD LOVES, MAN KILLS

Marvel Comics Group,OS; 1 Oct 1994

Issue	$Good	$Fine	$N.Mint	£Good	£Fine	£N.Mint
1 ND 64pgs, reprints Marvel Graphic Novel #5	$1.20	$3.60	$6.00	£0.80	£2.40	£4.00
Title Value:	$1.20	$3.60	$6.00	£0.80	£2.40	£4.00

X-MEN: MARVEL COLLECTOR'S EDITION

Marvel Comics Group,OS; 1 Oct 1993

Issue	$Good	$Fine	$N.Mint	£Good	£Fine	£N.Mint
1 ND scarce in the U.K. 16pgs, Magneto appears; available in conjunction with Stridex Acne Medication	$2.00	$6.00	$10.00	£1.50	£4.50	£7.50
Title Value:	$2.00	$6.00	$10.00	£1.50	£4.50	£7.50

X-MEN: OMEGA

Marvel Comics Group,OS; 1 Jun 1995

Issue	$Good	$Fine	$N.Mint	£Good	£Fine	£N.Mint
1 ND 48pgs, the conclusion to The Age of Xavier storyline; chromium cover	$1.50	$4.50	$7.50	£1.00	£3.00	£5.00
1 Gold Edition, ND 48pgs, (Jul 1995)	$8.00	$24.00	$40.00	£5.00	£15.00	£25.00
Title Value:	$9.50	$28.50	$47.50	£6.00	£18.00	£30.00

X-MEN: PRIME

Marvel Comics Group,OS; 1 Jul 1995

Issue	$Good	$Fine	$N.Mint	£Good	£Fine	£N.Mint
1 ND 48pgs, all the plotlines of the current X-titles converge and re-start here; Scott Lobdell and Fabian Nicieza script, Bryan Hitch art	$1.50	$4.50	$7.50	£1.00	£3.00	£5.00
Title Value:	$1.50	$4.50	$7.50	£1.00	£3.00	£5.00

X-MEN: PRYDE & WISDOM

Marvel Comics Group,MS; 1 Sep 1996-3 Nov 1996

Issue	$Good	$Fine	$N.Mint	£Good	£Fine	£N.Mint
1-3 ND Warren Ellis script, Terry Dodson and Karl Story art	$0.40	$1.20	$2.00	£0.25	£0.75	£1.25
Title Value:	$1.20	$3.60	$6.00	£0.75	£2.25	£3.75

X-MEN: RISE OF THE APOCALYPSE

Marvel Comics Group,MS; 1 Oct 1996-4 Jan 1997

Issue	$Good	$Fine	$N.Mint	£Good	£Fine	£N.Mint
1-4 ND the origin of Apocalypse; Adam Polllina and Cam Smith art	$0.40	$1.20	$2.00	£0.25	£0.75	£1.25
Title Value:	$1.60	$4.80	$8.00	£1.00	£3.00	£5.00

X-MEN: THE ANIMATED SERIES

Marvel Comics Group; 1 Nov 1992-15 Jan 1994

(see X-Men Adventures Season II)

Issue	$Good	$Fine	$N.Mint	£Good	£Fine	£N.Mint
1 ND based on US cartoon series, styled in the image of the original new X-Men from Uncanny X-Men #94	$0.80	$2.40	$4.00	£0.50	£1.50	£2.50
2 ND	$0.60	$1.80	$3.00	£0.40	£1.20	£2.00
3 ND title changed to "X-Men Adventures"; Magneto appears	$0.50	$1.50	$2.50	£0.30	£0.90	£1.50
4 ND Magneto appears	$0.50	$1.50	$2.50	£0.30	£0.90	£1.50
5 ND	$0.50	$1.50	$2.50	£0.30	£0.90	£1.50
6 ND	$0.40	$1.20	$2.00	£0.25	£0.75	£1.25
7 ND Cable appears	$0.40	$1.20	$2.00	£0.25	£0.75	£1.25
8-9 ND	$0.40	$1.20	$2.00	£0.25	£0.75	£1.25
10 ND Archangel guest-stars	$0.40	$1.20	$2.00	£0.25	£0.75	£1.25
11-14 ND	$0.40	$1.20	$2.00	£0.25	£0.75	£1.25
15 ND 48pgs, eight page pin-up gallery	$0.50	$1.50	$2.50	£0.30	£0.90	£1.50
Title Value:	$7.00	$21.00	$35.00	£4.35	£13.05	£21.75
X-Men Adventures Vol. 1 (Feb 1994) Trade paperback 96pgs, reprints issues #1-4				£0.60	£1.80	£3.00
X-Men Adventures Volume 2 (Jul 1994) Trade paperback reprints issues #5-8				£0.60	£1.80	£3.00
X-Men Adventures Volume 3 (Dec 1994) Trade paperback reprints issues #9-12				£0.80	£2.40	£4.00
X-Men Adventures Volume 4 (Jul 1995) Trade paperback reprints issues #13-16				£0.80	£2.40	£4.00

X-MEN: THE EARLY YEARS

Marvel Comics Group; 1 May 1994-17 Sep 1995

Issue	$Good	$Fine	$N.Mint	£Good	£Fine	£N.Mint
1 ND reprints begin from Uncanny X-Men #1 by Stan Lee and Jack Kirby	$0.30	$0.90	$1.50	£0.20	£0.60	£1.00
2-16 ND	$0.30	$0.90	$1.50	£0.20	£0.60	£1.00
17 ND 48pgs, reprints Uncanny X-Men #17 and #18	$0.50	$1.50	$2.50	£0.30	£0.90	£1.50
Title Value:	$5.30	$15.90	$26.50	£3.50	£10.50	£17.50

X-MEN: THE MANY LOVES OF JEAN & SCOTT

Marvel Comics Group,Magazine OS; 1 Mar 1994

Issue	$Good	$Fine	$N.Mint	£Good	£Fine	£N.Mint
1 ND wedding album issue with new stories, reprints and pin-ups	$0.60	$1.80	$3.00	£0.40	£1.20	£2.00
Title Value:	$0.60	$1.80	$3.00	£0.40	£1.20	£2.00

X-MEN: YEAR OF THE MUTANTS COLLECTORS' REVIEW

Marvel Comics Group,OS; 1 Feb 1995

Issue	$Good	$Fine	$N.Mint	£Good	£Fine	£N.Mint
1 ND 48pgs, flip-book format; information on current creators and characters	$0.40	$1.20	$2.00	£0.25	£0.75	£1.25
Title Value:	$0.40	$1.20	$2.00	£0.25	£0.75	£1.25

X-NATION 2099

Marvel Comics Group; 1 Mar 1996-6 Aug 1996

Issue	$Good	$Fine	$N.Mint	£Good	£Fine	£N.Mint
1 ND Tom Peyer script, Humberto Ramos and Jimmy Palmiotti art; wrapawround chromium cover	$0.80	$2.40	$4.00	£0.50	£1.50	£2.50
2-4 ND	$0.40	$1.20	$2.00	£0.25	£0.75	£1.25
5 ND Exodus guest-stars	$0.40	$1.20	$2.00	£0.25	£0.75	£1.25
6 ND	$0.40	$1.20	$2.00	£0.25	£0.75	£1.25
Title Value:	$2.80	$8.40	$14.00	£1.75	£5.25	£8.75

X-O MANOWAR

Valiant/Acclaim Comics; 0 Jul 1993; 1 Feb 1992-68 Sep 1996

Issue	$Good	$Fine	$N.Mint	£Good	£Fine	£N.Mint
½ ND produced in conjunction with Wizard Comics; issued in a Wizard protective Mylar with certificate of authenticity	$1.00	$3.00	$5.00	£1.00	£3.00	£5.00
½ Gold Edition, ND as above, but with gold logo	$1.50	$4.50	$7.50	£1.50	£4.50	£7.50
0 ND (Jul 1993), origin re-told and expanded, part Joe Quesada completely foil cover enhanced with metallic inks	$0.60	$1.80	$3.00	£0.40	£1.20	£2.00
0 Gold Edition ND	$3.00	$9.00	$15.00	£1.50	£4.50	£7.50
0 Valiant Validated Signature Series, ND (Feb 1994), signed by Joe Quesada and Jimmy Palmiotti; limited to 5,300 copies with certificate in Mylar sleeve	$1.50	$4.50	$7.50	£1.00	£3.00	£5.00
1 ND origin	$2.00	$6.00	$10.00	£1.40	£4.20	£7.00
2 ND origin	$1.50	$4.50	$7.50	£1.00	£3.00	£5.00
3 ND Harada appears	$1.50	$4.50	$7.50	£1.00	£3.00	£5.00
4 ND Harbinger appears; 1st appearance (cameo) Jack Boniface (later Shadowman)	$1.50	$4.50	$7.50	£1.00	£3.00	£5.00
5 ND	$1.00	$3.00	$5.00	£0.60	£1.80	£3.00
6 ND part Steve Ditko art	$1.00	$3.00	$5.00	£0.60	£1.80	£3.00
7 ND Unity: Chapter 5	$0.60	$1.80	$3.00	£0.40	£1.20	£2.00
8 ND Unity: Chapter 13, Harbinger appears, Walt Simonson cover	$0.60	$1.80	$3.00	£0.40	£1.20	£2.00
9-10 ND	$0.50	$1.50	$2.50	£0.30	£0.90	£1.50
11 ND Solar appears	$0.50	$1.50	$2.50	£0.30	£0.90	£1.50
12 ND continues in Solar, Man of the Atom #17	$0.50	$1.50	$2.50	£0.30	£0.90	£1.50
13 ND	$0.50	$1.50	$2.50	£0.30	£0.90	£1.50
14 ND Turok appears	$0.50	$1.50	$2.50	£0.30	£0.90	£1.50
14 Valiant Validated Signature Series, ND (Dec 1993) - signed set of issues #14 and #15, limited to 5,000 sets; signed in gold ink on cover by Bart Sears	$1.80	$5.25	$9.00	£1.20	£3.60	£6.00
15 ND Turok appears	$0.50	$1.50	$2.50	£0.30	£0.90	£1.50
15 Pink Logo Edition, ND issued free with a box of Ultra-Pro mylar comic sleeves (Jul 1993)	$0.60	$1.80	$3.00	£0.40	£1.20	£2.00
16-18 ND	$0.50	$1.50	$2.50	£0.30	£0.90	£1.50
19 ND Randy Cartier becomes X-O, She God of War	$0.50	$1.50	$2.50	£0.30	£0.90	£1.50
20 ND	$0.50	$1.50	$2.50	£0.30	£0.90	£1.50
21-23 ND	$0.40	$1.20	$2.00	£0.25	£0.75	£1.25
24 ND Cameo appearance of Armorines, the real X-O returns...	$0.40	$1.20	$2.00	£0.25	£0.75	£1.25
25 ND Armorines #0 insert included	$0.40	$1.20	$2.00	£0.25	£0.75	£1.25
26 ND	$0.40	$1.20	$2.00	£0.25	£0.75	£1.25
27 ND Turok guest-stars	$0.40	$1.20	$2.00	£0.25	£0.75	£1.25
28 ND	$0.40	$1.20	$2.00	£0.25	£0.75	£1.25
29 ND Turok guest-stars	$0.40	$1.20	$2.00	£0.25	£0.75	£1.25
30 ND Solar appears	$0.40	$1.20	$2.00	£0.25	£0.75	£1.25
31-32 ND	$0.40	$1.20	$2.00	£0.25	£0.75	£1.25
33 ND Chaos Effect tie-in	$0.40	$1.20	$2.00	£0.25	£0.75	£1.25
34-36 ND	$0.40	$1.20	$2.00	£0.25	£0.75	£1.25

	$Good	$Fine	$N.Mint	£Good	£Fine	£N.Mint
37-40 ND The Wolfbridge Affair, weekly issue						
	$0.40	*$1.20*	*$2.00*	£0.25	£0.75	£1.25
41-43 ND	*$0.40*	*$1.20*	*$2.00*	£0.25	£0.75	£1.25
44 ND 1st Acclaim Comics issue, Bart Sears art; bi-weekly						
	$0.50	*$1.50*	*$2.50*	£0.30	£0.90	£1.50
45 ND Bart Sears art; bi-weekly						
	$0.50	*$1.50*	*$2.50*	£0.30	£0.90	£1.50
46-47 ND bi-weekly						
	$0.50	*$1.50*	*$2.50*	£0.30	£0.90	£1.50
48 ND Bart Sears art; bi-weekly						
	$0.50	*$1.50*	*$2.50*	£0.30	£0.90	£1.50
49 ND bi-weekly	*$0.50*	*$1.50*	*$2.50*	£0.30	£0.90	£1.50
50 50-X, ND story continued in #50-O						
	$0.50	*$1.50*	*$2.50*	£0.30	£0.90	£1.50
50 50-O, ND	*$0.50*	*$1.50*	*$2.50*	£0.30	£0.90	£1.50
51-60 ND bi-weekly						
	$0.50	*$1.50*	*$2.50*	£0.30	£0.90	£1.50
61-62 ND Keith Giffen script; bi-weekly						
	$0.50	*$1.50*	*$2.50*	£0.30	£0.90	£1.50
63 ND Keith Giffen script, Bart Sears art; bi-weekly						
	$0.50	*$1.50*	*$2.50*	£0.30	£0.90	£1.50
64 ND Keith Giffen script; bi-weekly						
	$0.50	*$1.50*	*$2.50*	£0.30	£0.90	£1.50
65 ND Keith Giffen script						
	$0.50	*$1.50*	*$2.50*	£0.30	£0.90	£1.50
66-67 ND	*$0.50*	*$1.50*	*$2.50*	£0.30	£0.90	£1.50
68 ND Jackson Guice art						
	$0.50	*$1.50*	*$2.50*	£0.30	£0.90	£1.50
Title Value:	*$47.90*	*$143.55*	*$239.50*	£30.55	£91.65	£152.75
X-O Manowar (Jul 1993)						
ND Trade paperback, reprints issues #1-4 with new 8pg						
X-O Manowar Sourcebook, new cover by Bob Layton				£1.35	£4.05	£6.75
Bart Sears' X-O Manowar Hardcover (Apr 1995)						
ND collects all Bart Sears' work on the title including special issues				£2.40	£7.20	£12.00

X-O MANOWAR (2ND SERIES)

Acclaim Comics; 1 Feb 1997-present

	$Good	$Fine	$N.Mint	£Good	£Fine	£N.Mint
1 ND Mark Waid and Brian Augustyn script, Sean Chen and Tom Ryder art begins						
	$0.50	*$1.50*	*$2.50*	£0.30	£0.90	£1.50
2-4 ND	*$0.50*	*$1.50*	*$2.50*	£0.30	£0.90	£1.50
Title Value:	*$2.00*	*$6.00*	*$10.00*	£1.20	£3.60	£6.00

X-O MANOWAR YEARBOOK

Valiant/Acclaim Comics; 1 Apr 1995

	$Good	$Fine	$N.Mint	£Good	£Fine	£N.Mint
1 ND Bryan Hitch cover						
	$0.60	*$1.80*	*$3.00*	£0.40	£1.20	£2.00
Title Value:	*$0.60*	*$1.80*	*$3.00*	£0.40	£1.20	£2.00

X-O MANOWAR/IRON MAN HEAVY METAL CROSSOVER

Acclaim Comics,MS; nn Oct 1996

	$Good	$Fine	$N.Mint	£Good	£Fine	£N.Mint
nn ND Fabian Niceiza script and Andy Smith art						
	$0.50	*$1.50*	*$2.50*	£0.30	£0.90	£1.50
Title Value:	*$0.50*	*$1.50*	*$2.50*	£0.30	£0.90	£1.50

X-PATROL

Marvel Comics Group/Amalgam,OS; 1 Apr 1996

	$Good	$Fine	$N.Mint	£Good	£Fine	£N.Mint
1 ND a Marvel/DC amalgamation of X-Men and Doom Patrol; Karl Kesel script, Roger Cruz and Jon Holdredge art						
	$0.40	*$1.20*	*$2.00*	£0.30	£0.90	£1.50
Title Value:	*$0.40*	*$1.20*	*$2.00*	£0.30	£0.90	£1.50

X-TERMINATORS

Marvel Comics Group,MS; 1 Oct 1988-4 Jan 1989

	$Good	$Fine	$N.Mint	£Good	£Fine	£N.Mint
1 ND 1st appearance N'astirh; Inferno tie-in						
	$0.60	*$1.80*	*$3.00*	£0.30	£0.90	£1.50
2-3 Inferno tie-in	*$0.40*	*$1.20*	*$2.00*	£0.25	£0.75	£1.25
4 co-stars New Mutants, Inferno tie-in						
	$0.40	*$1.20*	*$2.00*	£0.25	£0.75	£1.25
Title Value:	*$1.80*	*$5.40*	*$9.00*	£1.05	£3.15	£5.25

X-THIEVES

Fictioneer; 7 Apr 1988-10 1988

	$Good	$Fine	$N.Mint	£Good	£Fine	£N.Mint
(previously Aristocratic...)						
7-10 ND	*$0.40*	*$1.20*	*$2.00*	£0.25	£0.75	£1.25
Title Value:	*$1.60*	*$4.80*	*$8.00*	£1.00	£3.00	£5.00

X-UNIVERSE

Marvel Comics Group,MS; 1 May 1995-2 Jun 1995

	$Good	$Fine	$N.Mint	£Good	£Fine	£N.Mint
1-2 ND Ben Grimm, Sue Storm, Bruce Banner and Gwen Stacy appear; foil-stamped card-stock cover						
	$0.80	*$2.40*	*$4.00*	£0.50	£1.50	£2.50
Title Value:	*$1.60*	*$4.80*	*$8.00*	£1.00	£3.00	£5.00

X.S.E.

Marvel Comics Group,MS; 1 Nov 1996-4 Feb 1997

	$Good	$Fine	$N.Mint	£Good	£Fine	£N.Mint
1-4 ND Bishop and Shard - more information on their backgrounds and origins						
	$0.40	*$1.20*	*$2.00*	£0.25	£0.75	£1.25
Title Value:	*$1.60*	*$4.80*	*$8.00*	£1.00	£3.00	£5.00

X: ONE SHOT TO THE HEAD

Dark Horse,OS; 1 Aug 1994

	$Good	$Fine	$N.Mint	£Good	£Fine	£N.Mint
1 ND collects the early appearances from Dark Horse Comics #8-10						
	$0.50	*$1.50*	*$2.50*	£0.30	£0.90	£1.50
Title Value:	*$0.50*	*$1.50*	*$2.50*	£0.30	£0.90	£1.50

XANADU: HELIA'S TALE

Eclipse; 1 1988

	$Good	$Fine	$N.Mint	£Good	£Fine	£N.Mint
1 ND	*$0.40*	*$1.20*	*$2.00*	£0.25	£0.75	£1.25
Title Value:	*$0.40*	*$1.20*	*$2.00*	£0.25	£0.75	£1.25

XANDER IN LOST UNIVERSE, GENE RODDENBERRY'S

Tekno Comix; 1 Dec 1995-6 Jan 1996; Big Entertainment; 7 Apr 1996-8 May 1996

	$Good	$Fine	$N.Mint	£Good	£Fine	£N.Mint
1-3 ND Jae Lee cover						
	$0.45	*$1.35*	*$2.25*	£0.30	£0.90	£1.50
4 ND pre-bagged with back-issue Tekno comic; Jae Lee cover						
	$0.45	*$1.35*	*$2.25*	£0.30	£0.90	£1.50
5 ND Jae Lee cover	*$0.45*	*$1.35*	*$2.25*	£0.30	£0.90	£1.50
6-8 ND	*$0.45*	*$1.35*	*$2.25*	£0.30	£0.90	£1.50
Title Value:	*$3.60*	*$10.80*	*$18.00*	£2.40	£7.20	£12.00

XANDER IN LOST UNIVERSE, GENE RODDENBERRY'S (2ND SERIES)

Big Entertainment,MS; 1 Jun 1996-4 Sep 1996

	$Good	$Fine	$N.Mint	£Good	£Fine	£N.Mint
1-4 ND Primortals feature throughout						
	$0.45	*$1.35*	*$2.25*	£0.30	£0.90	£1.50
Title Value:	*$1.80*	*$5.40*	*$9.00*	£1.20	£3.60	£6.00

XAVIER INSTITUTE ALUMNI YEARBOOK, THE

Marvel Comics Group,OS; nn Feb 1997

	$Good	$Fine	$N.Mint	£Good	£Fine	£N.Mint
nn ND 48pgs, Peter Sanderson script						
	$0.40	*$1.20*	*$2.00*	£0.25	£0.75	£1.25
Title Value:	*$0.40*	*$1.20*	*$2.00*	£0.25	£0.75	£1.25

XENOBROOD

DC Comics,MS; 0 Oct 1994; 1 Nov 1994-6 Apr 1995

	$Good	$Fine	$N.Mint	£Good	£Fine	£N.Mint
0 (Oct 1994) Zero Hour X-over, origin						
	$0.40	*$1.20*	*$2.00*	£0.25	£0.75	£1.25
1-2	*$0.30*	*$0.90*	*$1.50*	£0.20	£0.60	£1.00
3-4 Superman appears						
	$0.30	*$0.90*	*$1.50*	£0.20	£0.60	£1.00
5-6	*$0.30*	*$0.90*	*$1.50*	£0.20	£0.60	£1.00
Title Value:	*$2.20*	*$6.60*	*$11.00*	£1.45	£4.35	£7.25

XENON

Eclipse; 1 Dec 1987-23 1989

	$Good	$Fine	$N.Mint	£Good	£Fine	£N.Mint
1-23 ND Masaomi Kamzaki script/art (translated Japanese reprint); black and white						
	$0.30	*$0.90*	*$1.50*	£0.20	£0.60	£1.00
Title Value:	*$6.90*	*$20.70*	*$34.50*	£4.60	£13.80	£23.00
Heavy Metal Warrior Part 1 (Aug 1991), reprints				£1.60	£4.80	£8.00
Heavy Metal Warrior Part 2 (Oct 1992), reprints				£1.85	£5.55	£9.25
Heavy Metal Warrior Part 3 (Dec 1992), reprints				£1.85	£5.55	£9.25
Heavy Metal Warrior Part 4 (Feb 1993), reprints				£1.85	£5.55	£9.25

XENOTECH

Mirage/Next Comics; 1 Aug 1994-3 1994

	$Good	$Fine	$N.Mint	£Good	£Fine	£N.Mint
1 ND Michael Doohey script, Robert Jones art begins						
	$0.50	*$1.50*	*$2.50*	£0.30	£0.90	£1.50
2 ND	*$0.50*	*$1.50*	*$2.50*	£0.30	£0.90	£1.50
3 ND with two bound-in trading cards						
	$0.50	*$1.50*	*$2.50*	£0.30	£0.90	£1.50
Title Value:	*$1.50*	*$4.50*	*$7.50*	£0.90	£2.70	£4.50

XENOZOIC TALES

Kitchen Sink; 1 Feb 1987-12 1990; 13 Dec 1994; 14 Oct 1996-present

	$Good	$Fine	$N.Mint	£Good	£Fine	£N.Mint
(see Death Rattle #7)						
1 ND Mark Schultz script and art begins; black and white						
	$0.30	*$0.90*	*$1.50*	£0.20	£0.60	£1.00
1 2nd printing, ND (Jan 1989)						
	$0.25	*$0.75*	*$1.25*	£0.15	£0.45	£0.75
2 ND	*$0.30*	*$0.90*	*$1.50*	£0.20	£0.60	£1.00
2 2nd printing ND	*$0.25*	*$0.75*	*$1.25*	£0.15	£0.45	£0.75
3-11 ND	*$0.30*	*$0.90*	*$1.50*	£0.20	£0.60	£1.00
12 ND delayed issue with new format paper stock and heavier stock cover						
	$0.40	*$1.20*	*$2.00*	£0.25	£0.75	£1.25
13 ND Mark Schultz script and art returns; black and white						
	$0.50	*$1.50*	*$2.50*	£0.30	£0.90	£1.50
14 ND Mark Schultz script and art; black and white with card-stock cover						
	$0.60	*$1.80*	*$3.00*	£0.40	£1.20	£2.00
Title Value:	*$5.30*	*$15.90*	*$26.50*	£3.45	£10.35	£17.25
Xenozoic Tales: Cadillacs and Dinosaurs						
Trade paperback reprints Xenozoic Tales #1-4 plus first story						
from Death Rattle #8. 136pgs, black and white				£2.00	£6.00	£10.00
Note: five printings are available that sell for about the same value						

XIMOS

Triumphant Comics; 1 Feb 1994-2 1994

	$Good	$Fine	$N.Mint	£Good	£Fine	£N.Mint
1-2 ND	*$0.40*	*$1.20*	*$2.00*	£0.25	£0.75	£1.25
Title Value:	*$0.80*	*$2.40*	*$4.00*	£0.50	£1.50	£2.50

XIMOS: VIOLENT PAST

Triumphant Comics,MS; 1,2 Mar 1994

	$Good	$Fine	$N.Mint	£Good	£Fine	£N.Mint
1-2 ND	*$0.40*	*$1.20*	*$2.00*	£0.25	£0.75	£1.25
Title Value:	*$0.80*	*$2.40*	*$4.00*	£0.50	£1.50	£2.50

XOMBI

DC Comics/Milestone; 0 Jan 1994; 1 Jun 1994-21 Feb 1996

	$Good	$Fine	$N.Mint	£Good	£Fine	£N.Mint
0 (Jan 1994) Denys Cowan and Jimmy Palmiotti art begins; spot varnished cover by Walt Simonson						
	$0.40	*$1.20*	*$2.00*	£0.25	£0.75	£1.25
1 John Byrne cover	*$0.40*	*$1.20*	*$2.00*	£0.25	£0.75	£1.25
2-12	*$0.40*	*$1.20*	*$2.00*	£0.25	£0.75	£1.25
13 becomes a Mature Readers title						
	$0.40	*$1.20*	*$2.00*	£0.25	£0.75	£1.25
14-16	*$0.40*	*$1.20*	*$2.00*	£0.25	£0.75	£1.25
17 special price of 99 cents						
	$0.20	*$0.60*	*$1.00*	£0.10	£0.35	£0.65
18 Howard Chaykin cover						
	$0.40	*$1.20*	*$2.00*	£0.25	£0.75	£1.25
19-21	*$0.40*	*$1.20*	*$2.00*	£0.25	£0.75	£1.25
Title Value:	*$8.60*	*$25.80*	*$43.00*	£5.35	£16.10	£26.90

Y

YAKUZA

Eternity; 1 Sep 1987-5 1988

	$Good	$Fine	$N.Mint	£Good	£Fine	£N.Mint
1-5 ND	*$0.40*	*$1.20*	*$2.00*	£0.25	£0.75	£1.25

TRADE PAPERBACKS, GRAPHIC NOVELS AND OTHER COLLECTIONS ARE PRICED IN POUNDS STERLING ONLY. CONVERT AT 1.5 FOR DOLLARS.

	$Good	$Fine	$N.Mint	£Good	£Fine	£N.Mint
Title Value:	$2.00	$6.00	$10.00	£1.25	£3.75	£6.25
YANG						
Charlton; 1 Nov 1973-13 May 1976; 14 Sep 1985-17 Jan 1986						
(see House of Yang)						
1 distributed in the U.K.	$0.75	$2.25	$4.50	£0.50	£1.50	£3.00
2 distributed in the U.K.	$0.50	$1.50	$3.00	£0.30	£1.00	£2.00
3-13 distributed in the U.K.	$0.40	$1.25	$2.50	£0.25	£0.75	£1.50
14-17 distributed in the U.K.	$0.40	$1.20	$2.00	£0.25	£0.75	£1.25
Title Value:	$7.25	$22.30	$43.00	£4.55	£13.75	£26.50
YARN MAN						
Kitchen Sink; 1 Oct 1989						
1 ND	$0.40	$1.20	$2.00	£0.25	£0.75	£1.25
Title Value:	$0.40	$1.20	$2.00	£0.25	£0.75	£1.25
YATTERING AND JACK HARDCOVER, THE						
Eclipse,OS; 1 Feb 1992						
1 ND 64pgs, adaptation of Clive Barker story by Steve Niles and John Bolton	$4.50	$13.50	$22.50	£3.00	£9.00	£15.00
Title Value:	$4.50	$13.50	$22.50	£3.00	£9.00	£15.00
YELLOW SUBMARINE						
Gold Key/Movie Comics,OS Movie; 35000-902 Feb 1969						
35000-902 scarce though distributed in the U.K. 64pgs, adapts film	$31.00	$90.00	$215.00	£20.50	£60.00	£145.00
Title Value:	$31.00	$90.00	$215.00	£20.50	£60.00	£145.00
Note: comes with pull-out poster that would lose up to 50% of the value if missing						
YOGI BEAR						
Charlton; 1 Nov 1970-35 Jan 1976						
1 scarce, distributed in the U.K. Ray Dirgo art	$4.15	$12.50	$25.00	£2.50	£7.50	£15.00
2	$2.50	$7.50	$15.00	£1.50	£4.50	£9.00
3-6	$2.00	$6.00	$12.00	£1.00	£3.00	£6.00
7 Summer Fun Giant	$2.50	$7.50	$15.00	£1.25	£3.75	£7.50
8-10	$2.00	$6.00	$12.00	£0.80	£2.50	£5.00
11-30	$1.65	$5.00	$10.00	£0.65	£2.00	£4.00
31-35	$1.25	$3.75	$7.50	£0.55	£1.75	£3.50
Title Value:	$62.40	$188.25	$376.50	£27.40	£84.00	£168.00
YOGI BEAR, HANNA-BARBERA'S						
Marvel Comics Group; 1 Nov 1977-9 Mar 1979						
1 ND	$0.40	$1.25	$2.50	£0.25	£0.75	£1.50
2-9 ND	$0.30	$1.00	$2.00	£0.20	£0.60	£1.25
Title Value:	$2.80	$9.25	$18.50	£1.85	£5.55	£11.50
YOU'RE UNDER ARREST						
Dark Horse,MS; 1 Dec 1995-8 Jul 1996						
1-8 ND Kosuke Fujishima script and art; black and white	$0.60	$1.80	$3.00	£0.40	£1.20	£2.00
Title Value:	$4.80	$14.40	$24.00	£3.20	£9.60	£16.00
YOUNG ALL-STARS						
DC Comics; 1 Jun 1987-31 Oct 1989						
1-7	$0.25	$0.75	$1.25	£0.15	£0.45	£0.75
8 unofficial Millennium X-over	$0.25	$0.75	$1.25	£0.15	£0.45	£0.75
9 Millennium X-over	$0.25	$0.75	$1.25	£0.15	£0.45	£0.75
10-14	$0.25	$0.75	$1.25	£0.15	£0.45	£0.75
15 LD in the U.K.	$0.25	$0.75	$1.25	£0.20	£0.60	£1.00
16-22	$0.25	$0.75	$1.25	£0.15	£0.45	£0.75
23 intro The Squire, Phantasmo, Fireball and Kuei the Man Demon	$0.25	$0.75	$1.25	£0.15	£0.45	£0.75
24-31	$0.25	$0.75	$1.25	£0.15	£0.45	£0.75
Title Value:	$7.75	$23.25	$38.75	£4.70	£14.10	£23.50
Note: Deluxe Format Baxter paper						
YOUNG ALL-STARS ANNUAL						
DC Comics; 1 1988						
1 48pgs	$0.30	$0.90	$1.50	£0.20	£0.60	£1.00
Title Value:	$0.30	$0.90	$1.50	£0.20	£0.60	£1.00
YOUNG DRACULA: DIARY OF A VAMPIRE						
Caliber Press,MS; 1 Mar 1993-3 Jul 1993						
1-3 ND 48pgs	$0.60	$1.80	$3.00	£0.40	£1.20	£2.00
Title Value:	$1.80	$5.40	$9.00	£1.20	£3.60	£6.00
YOUNG GUN						
AC Comics,OS; 1 1992						
1 ND black and white	$0.40	$1.20	$2.00	£0.25	£0.75	£1.25
Title Value:	$0.40	$1.20	$2.00	£0.25	£0.75	£1.25
YOUNG INDIANA JONES CHRONICLES, THE						
Dark Horse; 1 Feb 1992-12 Jan 1993						
1 ND based on TV series, Dan Barry script/pencils, Frank Springer inks begin	$0.50	$1.50	$2.50	£0.30	£0.90	£1.50
2 ND Dan Barry script/art/cover	$0.50	$1.50	$2.50	£0.30	£0.90	£1.50
3-4 ND Dan Barry and Gray Morrow script/art	$0.50	$1.50	$2.50	£0.30	£0.90	£1.50
5-12 ND Dan Barry script/art/cover	$0.50	$1.50	$2.50	£0.30	£0.90	£1.50
Title Value:	$6.00	$18.00	$30.00	£3.60	£10.80	£18.00
YOUNG LOVE						
National Periodical Publications/DC Comics; 39 Sep/Oct 1963-120 Winter 1975/6; 121 Oct 1976-126 Jul 1977						
(#1-38 published by Prize Features)						
39 scarce in the U.K.	$3.90	$11.50	$27.50	£2.50	£7.50	£17.50
40-50 scarce in the U.K.	$2.50	$7.50	$17.50	£1.40	£4.25	£10.00
51-60	$2.10	$6.25	$15.00	£1.05	£3.20	£7.50
61-63	$2.10	$6.25	$15.00	£1.00	£3.00	£7.00
64 Joe Simon & Jack Kirby art	$2.50	$7.50	$17.50	£1.05	£3.20	£7.50
65-70	$2.10	$6.25	$15.00	£1.00	£3.00	£7.00
71-72	$1.65	$5.00	$10.00	£0.80	£2.50	£5.00
73 Alex Toth art	$1.65	$5.00	$10.00	£1.00	£3.00	£6.00
74-77	$1.65	$5.00	$10.00	£0.80	£2.50	£5.00
78-79 Alex Toth art	$1.65	$5.00	$10.00	£1.00	£3.00	£6.00
80	$1.65	$5.00	$10.00	£0.80	£2.50	£5.00
81-90	$1.25	$3.75	$7.50	£0.55	£1.75	£3.50
91-100	$0.80	$2.50	$5.00	£0.40	£1.25	£2.50
101-106	$0.50	$1.50	$3.00	£0.30	£1.00	£2.00
107-114 scarce in the U.K. 100pgs	$0.65	$2.00	$4.00	£0.40	£1.25	£2.50
115-121	$0.50	$1.50	$3.00	£0.30	£1.00	£2.00
122 Alex Toth art	$0.50	$1.50	$3.00	£0.30	£1.00	£2.00
123-126	$0.50	$1.50	$3.00	£0.30	£1.00	£2.00
Title Value:	$125.00	$375.75	$833.50	£65.15	£200.95	£442.00
YOUNG MASTER						
New Comics Group; 1 Nov 1987-9 1989						
(becomes The Master)						
1 ND Hama script/Meyerick art begins	$0.40	$1.20	$2.00	£0.25	£0.75	£1.25

Yang #2

Young Love #67

Zen Intergalactic Ninja Color Deluxe #1

	$Good	$Fine	$N.Mint	£Good	£Fine	£N.Mint
2-9 ND	$0.40	$1.20	$2.00	£0.25	£0.75	£1.25
Title Value:	$3.60	$10.80	$18.00	£2.25	£6.75	£11.25

YOUNG ROMANCE COMICS

National Periodical Publications; 125 Aug/Sep 1963/1964-208 Nov/Dec 1975
(previous issues published by Prize/Headline and ND)

	$Good	$Fine	$N.Mint	£Good	£Fine	£N.Mint
125 scarce in the U.K.	$4.60	$13.50	$32.50	£2.85	£8.50	£20.00
126-135 scarce in the U.K.	$2.85	$8.50	$20.00	£1.75	£5.25	£12.50
136-140	$2.50	$7.50	$17.50	£1.40	£4.25	£10.00
141-150	$2.10	$6.25	$15.00	£1.05	£3.20	£7.50
151-160	$2.10	$6.25	$15.00	£0.85	£2.55	£6.00
161-170	$1.25	$3.75	$7.50	£0.80	£2.50	£5.00
171-190	$1.00	$3.00	$6.00	£0.55	£1.75	£3.50
191-196	$1.00	$3.00	$6.00	£0.40	£1.25	£2.50
197-204 less common in the U.K. 100pgs	$1.00	$3.00	$6.00	£0.50	£1.50	£3.00
205-208	$0.80	$2.50	$5.00	£0.40	£1.25	£2.50
Title Value:	$137.30	$410.50	$881.50	£73.35	£224.25	£499.00

YOUNG ZEN INTERGALACTIC NINJA SPECIAL: CITY OF DEATH

Entity Comics,OS; 1 1994

	$Good	$Fine	$N.Mint	£Good	£Fine	£N.Mint
1 ND gold foil stamped cover	$0.80	$2.40	$4.00	£0.50	£1.50	£2.50
Title Value:	$0.80	$2.40	$4.00	£0.50	£1.50	£2.50

YOUNGBLOOD (1ST SERIES)

Image; 0 Dec 1992; 1 Apr 1992-10 1995

	$Good	$Fine	$N.Mint	£Good	£Fine	£N.Mint
0 (Dec 1992), origin Youngblood team, includes two trading cards and Image #0 coupon 7	$0.60	$1.80	$3.00	£0.40	£1.20	£2.00
0 Gold Edition	$2.00	$6.00	$10.00	£1.30	£3.90	£6.50
0 Gold Signed Edition	$2.50	$7.50	$12.50	£1.50	£4.50	£7.50
0 without coupon	$0.50	$1.50	$2.50	£0.30	£0.90	£1.50
1 Rob Liefeld script/art, includes two trading cards; 1st appearance Riptide, Die Hard, Badrock, Vogue, Chapel, Shaft	$0.60	$1.80	$3.00	£0.50	£1.50	£2.50
1 2nd printing, no trading cards	$0.50	$1.50	$2.50	£0.30	£0.90	£1.50
1 Silent Edition, (Jun 1994), without word balloons; card-stock cover	$1.00	$3.00	$5.00	£0.70	£2.10	£3.50
2 Rob Liefeld script/art, includes two trading cards; 1st appearance Shadowhawk	$0.90	$2.70	$4.50	£0.50	£1.50	£2.50
3 Rob Liefeld script/art, includes two trading cards; 1st appearance Supreme	$0.60	$1.80	$3.00	£0.40	£1.20	£2.00
4 Rob Liefeld script/art, includes two trading cards, glow-in-the-dark cover; 1st appearance Pitt	$0.60	$1.80	$3.00	£0.40	£1.20	£2.00
5	$0.60	$1.80	$3.00	£0.40	£1.20	£2.00
6 48pgs, story continued from Team Youngblood #9	$0.60	$1.80	$3.00	£0.40	£1.20	£2.00
7	$0.50	$1.50	$2.50	£0.30	£0.90	£1.50
8 Chapel vs. Spawn	$0.50	$1.50	$2.50	£0.30	£0.90	£1.50
9 Image X Month tie-in	$0.50	$1.50	$2.50	£0.30	£0.90	£1.50
10 Chapel commits suicide	$0.50	$1.50	$2.50	£0.30	£0.90	£1.50
Title Value:	$13.00	$39.00	$65.00	£8.30	£24.90	£41.50

Note: originally a 3 issue series was expanded into 4. The new issue 3 has expanded contents from issue 2 and the new issue 4 contains what was originally issue 3. All Non-Distributed on the news-stands in the U.K.

	$Good	$Fine	$N.Mint	£Good	£Fine	£N.Mint
Youngblood (Jan 1995) Trade paperback reprints issues #1-5, re-dialogued				£2.20	£6.60	£11.00
Youngblood (Feb 1996) Trade paperback ND repackaged collection of issues #6-8,10 and Team Youngblood #9-11				£2.20	£6.60	£11.00

YOUNGBLOOD (2ND SERIES)

Image; 1 Sep 1995-present

	$Good	$Fine	$N.Mint	£Good	£Fine	£N.Mint
1 ND Rob Liefeld and Eric Stephenson script, Roger Cruz and Danny Miki art begins	$0.50	$1.50	$2.50	£0.30	£0.90	£1.50
2 ND	$0.50	$1.50	$2.50	£0.30	£0.90	£1.50
3 ND Extreme Babewatch tie-in; 4 alternate covers available (distributed in equal quantities)	$0.50	$1.50	$2.50	£0.30	£0.90	£1.50
4 ND Extreme Destroyer part 4, continued in Glory #9; pre-bagged with trading card; Rob Liefeld script, Roger Cruz and Danny Miki art	$0.50	$1.50	$2.50	£0.30	£0.90	£1.50
5 ND	$0.50	$1.50	$2.50	£0.30	£0.90	£1.50
6 ND Rage of Angels tie-in	$0.50	$1.50	$2.50	£0.30	£0.90	£1.50
7 ND Shadowhunt part 3, continued in Team Youngblood #22	$0.50	$1.50	$2.50	£0.30	£0.90	£1.50
8-9 ND	$0.50	$1.50	$2.50	£0.30	£0.90	£1.50
10 ND flip-side preview of Blindside #1	$0.50	$1.50	$2.50	£0.30	£0.90	£1.50
11-14 ND	$0.50	$1.50	$2.50	£0.30	£0.90	£1.50
Title Value:	$7.00	$21.00	$35.00	£4.20	£12.60	£21.00

YOUNGBLOOD YEAR ONE

Image; 1 Nov 1994-2 1995

	$Good	$Fine	$N.Mint	£Good	£Fine	£N.Mint
1 ND Rob Liefeld script, Danny Miki art, cover by George Perez	$0.50	$1.50	$2.50	£0.30	£0.90	£1.50
2 ND Liefeld and Miki	$0.50	$1.50	$2.50	£0.30	£0.90	£1.50
Title Value:	$1.00	$3.00	$5.00	£0.60	£1.80	£3.00

YOUNGBLOOD YEARBOOK

Image,OS; 1 Jul 1993

	$Good	$Fine	$N.Mint	£Good	£Fine	£N.Mint
1 ND Chap Yaep and Norm Rapmund art; four-page fold-out	$0.50	$1.50	$2.50	£0.30	£0.90	£1.50
Title Value:	$0.50	$1.50	$2.50	£0.30	£0.90	£1.50

YOUNGBLOOD/X-FORCE

Image,OS; 1 Jul 1996

	$Good	$Fine	$N.Mint	£Good	£Fine	£N.Mint
1 ND 48pgs, squarebound; Eric Stephenson script, Roger Cruz and Lary Stucker art, Rob Liefeld cover with black background	$1.00	$3.00	$5.00	£0.65	£1.95	£3.25
1 Alternate cover, ND as above with alternate Rob Liefeld cover showing team picture with Youngblood and Cable in close-up; 50% allocation	$1.00	$3.00	$5.00	£0.65	£1.95	£3.25
Title Value:	$2.00	$6.00	$10.00	£1.30	£3.90	£6.50

YOUNGBLOOD: BATTLEZONE

Image; 1 May 1993; 2 Jul 1994

	$Good	$Fine	$N.Mint	£Good	£Fine	£N.Mint
1-2 ND information and specifications of Youngblood weaponry and vehicles etc; Liefeld cover	$0.50	$1.50	$2.50	£0.30	£0.90	£1.50
Title Value:	$1.00	$3.00	$5.00	£0.60	£1.80	£3.00

YOUNGBLOOD: STRIKE FILE

Image; 1 Apr 1993-11 Feb 1995

	$Good	$Fine	$N.Mint	£Good	£Fine	£N.Mint
1 Rob Liefeld script and art begins, 1st appearance Glory	$0.60	$1.80	$3.00	£0.40	£1.20	£2.00
1 Gold Edition	$1.20	$3.60	$6.00	£0.80	£2.40	£4.00
2-5	$0.40	$1.20	$2.00	£0.25	£0.75	£1.25
6 flip-book format featuring two stories with Badrock and Masada	$0.50	$1.50	$2.50	£0.30	£0.90	£1.50
7 flip-book format featuring two stories with Troll and Die Hard	$0.50	$1.50	$2.50	£0.30	£0.90	£1.50
8 flip-book format featuring two stories with Shaft and Dutch	$0.50	$1.50	$2.50	£0.30	£0.90	£1.50
9	$0.50	$1.50	$2.50	£0.30	£0.90	£1.50
10 1st appearance the Bloodpool	$0.50	$1.50	$2.50	£0.30	£0.90	£1.50
11 Extreme Sacrifice tie-in; origins of Link and Crypt	$0.50	$1.50	$2.50	£0.30	£0.90	£1.50
Title Value:	$6.40	$19.20	$32.00	£4.00	£12.00	£20.00

YUMMY FUR

Vortex/Drawn & Quarterly; 1 Dec 1986-32 1994

	$Good	$Fine	$N.Mint	£Good	£Fine	£N.Mint
1 reprints Chester Brown mini-comics #1 (originally published from July 1983 to September 1985)	$1.40	$4.20	$7.00	£0.60	£1.80	£3.00
2 reprints Chester Brown mini-comics #2 (originally published from July 1983 to September 1985)	$1.00	$3.00	$5.00	£0.40	£1.20	£2.00
3 reprints Chester Brown mini-comics #3 (originally published from July 1983 to September 1985)	$0.80	$2.40	$4.00	£0.40	£1.20	£2.00
4 new material begins	$0.60	$1.80	$3.00	£0.30	£0.90	£1.50
5-8	$0.60	$1.80	$3.00	£0.30	£0.90	£1.50
9 very scarce in the U.K.	$0.50	$1.50	$2.50	£0.50	£1.50	£2.50
10-26	$0.50	$1.50	$2.50	£0.30	£0.90	£1.50
27 last Vortex issue	$0.50	$1.50	$2.50	£0.30	£0.90	£1.50
28-31	$0.50	$1.50	$2.50	£0.30	£0.90	£1.50
32 $2.95 cover	$0.60	$1.80	$3.00	£0.40	£1.20	£2.00
Title Value:	$18.30	$54.90	$90.00	£10.40	£31.20	£52.00

Note: all Non-Distributed on the news-stands in the U.K.

	$Good	$Fine	$N.Mint	£Good	£Fine	£N.Mint
Book 1 (Aug 1990), reprints issues #1-12 plus new story				£1.00	£3.00	£5.00

YUPPIES FROM HELL

Marvel Comics Group,OS; 1 Feb 1989

	$Good	$Fine	$N.Mint	£Good	£Fine	£N.Mint
1 ND black and white social satire by Barbara Slate	$0.70	$2.10	$3.50	£0.50	£1.50	£2.50
1 2nd printing, ND (Jan 1991) black and white social satire by Barbara Slate	$0.60	$1.80	$3.00	£0.40	£1.20	£2.00
Title Value:	$1.30	$3.90	$6.50	£0.90	£2.70	£4.50

YUPPIES FROM HELL

Marvel Comics Group,OS; 1 Apr 1992

	$Good	$Fine	$N.Mint	£Good	£Fine	£N.Mint
1 ND Barbara Slate script/art	$0.50	$1.50	$2.50	£0.30	£0.90	£1.50
Title Value:	$0.50	$1.50	$2.50	£0.30	£0.90	£1.50

YUPPIES FROM HELL, SON OF

Marvel Comics Group,OS; 1 Jan 1991

	$Good	$Fine	$N.Mint	£Good	£Fine	£N.Mint
1 ND Barbara Slate continues the satire	$0.50	$1.50	$2.50	£0.30	£0.90	£1.50
Title Value:	$0.50	$1.50	$2.50	£0.30	£0.90	£1.50

Z

ZAMINDAR

Innovation; 1 Jan 1994-2 Feb 1994

	$Good	$Fine	$N.Mint	£Good	£Fine	£N.Mint
1-2 ND adaptation of sci-fi film	$0.50	$1.50	$2.50	£0.30	£0.90	£1.50
Title Value:	$1.00	$3.00	$5.00	£0.60	£1.80	£3.00

ZAP

Last Gasp; 1 1990-12 1990

	$Good	$Fine	$N.Mint	£Good	£Fine	£N.Mint
1-12 reprints of 1960s comics inc. covers featuring "underground" material by Robert Crumb et al.	$0.40	$1.20	$2.00	£0.25	£0.75	£1.25
Title Value:	$4.80	$14.40	$24.00	£3.00	£9.00	£15.00

Note: all Non-Distributed on the news-stands in the U.K.

ZATANNA

DC Comics,MS; 1 Jul 1993-4 Oct 1993

	$Good	$Fine	$N.Mint	£Good	£Fine	£N.Mint
1	$0.40	$1.20	$2.00	£0.25	£0.75	£1.25
2 new costume	$0.40	$1.20	$2.00	£0.25	£0.75	£1.25

	$Good	$Fine	$N.Mint	£Good	£Fine	£N.Mint
3-4	*$0.40*	*$1.20*	*$2.00*	£0.25	£0.75	£1.25
Title Value:	*$1.60*	*$4.80*	*$8.00*	£1.00	£3.00	£5.00
ZATANNA SPECIAL						
DC Comics,OS; 1 Apr 1987						
1 64pgs, Gray Morrow art, no ads						
	$0.30	*$0.90*	*$1.50*	£0.20	£0.60	£1.00
Title Value:	*$0.30*	*$0.90*	*$1.50*	£0.20	£0.60	£1.00
ZEALOT						
Image,MS; 1 Aug 1995-3 Oct 1995						
1 ND Ron Marz script, Terry Shoemaker and Jon Holdredge art						
	$0.60	*$1.80*	*$3.00*	£0.40	£1.20	£2.00
2-3 ND	*$0.50*	*$1.50*	*$2.50*	£0.30	£0.90	£1.50
Title Value:	*$1.60*	*$4.80*	*$8.00*	£1.00	£3.00	£5.00
ZELL, SWORDANCER						
Thoughts and Images; 1 1986						
1 ND	*$0.40*	*$1.20*	*$2.00*	£0.25	£0.75	£1.25
Title Value:	*$0.40*	*$1.20*	*$2.00*	£0.25	£0.75	£1.25
ZEN INTERGALACTIC NINJA						
Archie; 1 May 1992-3 Jul 1992						
1-3 ND	*$0.50*	*$1.50*	*$2.50*	£0.30	£0.90	£1.50
Title Value:	*$1.50*	*$4.50*	*$7.50*	£0.90	£2.70	£4.50
ZEN INTERGALACTIC NINJA (2ND SERIES)						
Zen Comics; 0 Jun/Jul 1993; 1 Aug 1993-5 1994						
0 ND (Jun/Jul 1993) - available direct only from publishers; gold embossed cover, black and white interior						
	$1.50	*$4.50*	*$7.50*	£1.00	£3.00	£5.00
0 Signed & Numbered Edition, ND (Mar 1996), pre-bagged with signed and numbered certificate; celebrates the 1st appearance of Nira X						
	$3.50	*$10.50*	*$17.50*	£2.00	£6.00	£10.00
1 ND Stern, Andru and Eposito begin						
	$0.50	*$1.50*	*$2.50*	£0.30	£0.90	£1.50
1 2nd printing, ND (1992)						
	$0.30	*$0.90*	*$1.50*	£0.20	£0.60	£1.00
2 ND	*$0.50*	*$1.50*	*$2.50*	£0.30	£0.90	£1.50
2 2nd printing, ND (1992)						
	$0.30	*$0.90*	*$1.50*	£0.20	£0.60	£1.00
3 ND	*$0.50*	*$1.50*	*$2.50*	£0.30	£0.90	£1.50
3 2nd printing ND	*$0.30*	*$0.90*	*$1.50*	£0.20	£0.60	£1.00
4-5 ND	*$0.50*	*$1.50*	*$2.50*	£0.30	£0.90	£1.50
Title Value:	*$8.40*	*$25.20*	*$42.00*	£5.10	£15.30	£25.50
ZEN INTERGALACTIC NINJA - MILESTONE						
Entity Comics,MS; 1 Mar 1994-3 Jul 1994						
1 ND reprints Defend the Earth story; Ross Andru and Mike Esposito art						
	$0.50	*$1.50*	*$2.50*	£0.30	£0.90	£1.50
1 Gold Edition, ND (Mar 1994) with new gold foil stamped cover						
	$0.60	*$1.80*	*$3.00*	£0.40	£1.20	£2.00
2-3 ND reprints Defend the Earth story; Ross Andru and Mike Esposito art						
	$0.50	*$1.50*	*$2.50*	£0.30	£0.90	£1.50
Title Value:	*$2.10*	*$6.30*	*$10.50*	£1.30	£3.90	£6.50
Note: reprints "Defend the Earth" series originally published by Archie						
ZEN INTERGALACTIC NINJA APRIL FOOL'S SPECIAL						
Entity Comics,OS; 1 Apr 1994						
1 ND black and white						
	$0.50	*$1.50*	*$2.50*	£0.30	£0.90	£1.50
Title Value:	*$0.50*	*$1.50*	*$2.50*	£0.30	£0.90	£1.50
ZEN INTERGALACTIC NINJA COLOUR DELUXE						
Entity Comics; 0 1994; 1 Mar 1994-7 Feb 1995						
0 ND Jae Lee cover art						
	$0.50	*$1.50*	*$2.50*	£0.30	£0.90	£1.50
1 ND	*$0.50*	*$1.50*	*$2.50*	£0.30	£0.90	£1.50
1 pre-bagged, ND with chromium trading card						
	$0.80	*$2.40*	*$4.00*	£0.50	£1.50	£2.50
2 ND	*$0.50*	*$1.50*	*$2.50*	£0.30	£0.90	£1.50
2 pre-bagged, ND with chromium trading card						
	$0.80	*$2.40*	*$4.00*	£0.50	£1.50	£2.50
3 ND 3-part Fire Upon The Earth story concludes						
	$0.50	*$1.50*	*$2.50*	£0.30	£0.90	£1.50
4-6 ND Battle Beyond the Ozone story						
	$0.50	*$1.50*	*$2.50*	£0.30	£0.90	£1.50
7 ND Battle Beyond the Ozone story; foil-enhanced cover						
	$0.50	*$1.50*	*$2.50*	£0.30	£0.90	£1.50
Title Value:	*$5.60*	*$16.80*	*$28.00*	£3.40	£10.20	£17.00
Zen Intergalactic Ninja: A Fire Upon The Earth (Dec 1994)						
Trade paperback, reprints issues #0-3, foil-stamped cover				£1.70	£5.10	£8.50
ZEN INTERGALACTIC NINJA COLOUR DELUXE (2ND SERIES)						
Entity Comics; 1 Mar 1995-5 1996 ?						
1-2 ND Roger Stern script, Joe Orbeta art						
	$0.50	*$1.50*	*$2.50*	£0.30	£0.90	£1.50
2 Deluxe Edition, ND (May 1995) - pre-bagged with interactive plastic phone card						
	$1.00	*$3.00*	*$5.00*	£0.65	£1.95	£3.25
3-4 ND Roger Stern script, Joe Orbeta art						
	$0.50	*$1.50*	*$2.50*	£0.30	£0.90	£1.50
5 ND	*$0.50*	*$1.50*	*$2.50*	£0.30	£0.90	£1.50
Title Value:	*$3.50*	*$10.50*	*$17.50*	£2.15	£6.45	£10.75
ZEN INTERGALACTIC NINJA EARTH-DAY ANNUAL						
Zen Comics; 1 Jun 1993						
1 ND metallic cover by Sam Keith						
	$0.60	*$1.80*	*$3.00*	£0.40	£1.20	£2.00
Title Value:	*$0.60*	*$1.80*	*$3.00*	£0.40	£1.20	£2.00
ZEN INTERGALACTIC NINJA LEGENDS						
Entity Comics,OS; nn May 1996						
nn ND reprints 1st appearance of Nira X from 1993						
	$0.60	*$1.80*	*$3.00*	£0.40	£1.20	£2.00
Title Value:	*$0.60*	*$1.80*	*$3.00*	£0.40	£1.20	£2.00
ZEN INTERGALACTIC NINJA SPECIAL, THE ART OF						
Entity Comics,OS; 1 Jun 1994						
1 ND pin-ups collection; part Frank Brunner cover						
	$0.60	*$1.80*	*$3.00*	£0.40	£1.20	£2.00
1 2nd printing, ND (Jan 1995)						
	$0.60	*$1.80*	*$3.00*	£0.40	£1.20	£2.00
Title Value:	*$1.20*	*$3.60*	*$6.00*	£0.80	£2.40	£4.00
ZEN INTERGALACTIC NINJA SPRING SPECTACULAR						
Entity Comics,OS; 1 Apr 1994						
1 ND Hearn Cho script/art; black and white						
	$0.50	*$1.50*	*$2.50*	£0.30	£0.90	£1.50
Title Value:	*$0.50*	*$1.50*	*$2.50*	£0.30	£0.90	£1.50
ZEN INTERGALACTIC NINJA SUMMER SPECIAL: VIDEO WARRIOR						
Entity Comics,OS; 1 Jun 1994						
1 ND prismatic vortex holo-foil enhanced cover (!)						
	$0.60	*$1.80*	*$3.00*	£0.40	£1.20	£2.00
Title Value:	*$0.60*	*$1.80*	*$3.00*	£0.40	£1.20	£2.00
ZEN INTERGALACTIC NINJA XMAS SPECIAL						
Zen Comics,OS; 1 Feb 1993						
1 ND	*$0.50*	*$1.50*	*$2.50*	£0.30	£0.90	£1.50
1 Collectors Edition, ND, foil-stamped cover limited to 1,000 copies						
	$0.80	*$2.40*	*$4.00*	£0.50	£1.50	£2.50
Title Value:	*$1.30*	*$3.90*	*$6.50*	£0.80	£2.40	£4.00
ZEN INTERGALACTIC NINJA: MISTRESS OF CHAOS						
Entity Comics,OS; 1 May 1994						
1 ND Steve Stern text with Bill Maus illustrations; card stock cover						
	$0.50	*$1.50*	*$2.50*	£0.30	£0.90	£1.50
Title Value:	*$0.50*	*$1.50*	*$2.50*	£0.30	£0.90	£1.50
ZEN INTERGALACTIC NINJA: STAR QUEST						
Entity Comics; 1 Mar 1994-11 1996 ?						
1-11 ND gold foil enhanced cover						
	$0.60	*$1.80*	*$3.00*	£0.40	£1.20	£2.00
Title Value:	*$6.60*	*$19.80*	*$33.00*	£4.40	£13.20	£22.00
Zen Intergalactic Ninja: Starquest (Jan 1995)						
Trade paperback, reprints issues #1-4 with foil-stamped cover				£0.90	£2.70	£4.50
ZEN INTERGALACTIC NINJA: THE HUNTED						
Entity Comics,MS; 1 Nov 1993-3 Jan 1994						
1 ND Bill Maus script and art, silver foil stamped cover						
	$0.60	*$1.80*	*$3.00*	£0.40	£1.20	£2.00
1 Collectors Edition, ND, Bill Maus script and art, silver foil stamped cover; pre-bagged with chromium trading card by Sam Keith						
	$0.80	*$2.40*	*$4.00*	£0.50	£1.50	£2.50
2-3 ND Bill Maus script and art, silver foil stamped cover						
	$0.60	*$1.80*	*$3.00*	£0.40	£1.20	£2.00
Title Value:	*$2.60*	*$7.80*	*$13.00*	£1.70	£5.10	£8.50
Zen Intergalactic Ninja: The Hunted (Oct 1994)						
Trade paperback, collects mini-series plus Nira X preview				£0.90	£2.70	£4.50
Signed & Numbered Hardcover (Oct 1994)				£4.00	£12.00	£20.00
ZEN YEARBOOK: HAZARDOUS DUTY						
Entity Comics; 1 Dec 1994						
1 ND foil-stamped enhanced cover						
	$0.60	*$1.80*	*$3.00*	£0.40	£1.20	£2.00
Title Value:	*$0.60*	*$1.80*	*$3.00*	£0.40	£1.20	£2.00
ZERO HOUR						
DC Comics,MS; 0 Sep 1994-4 Sep 1994						
(see Zero Issues in 40 individual DC titles)						
4 Zero Hour: Crisis in Time part 1; Dan Jurgens and Jerry Ordway creative team						
	$0.50	*$1.50*	*$2.50*	£0.30	£0.90	£1.50
3 Zero Hour: Crisis in Time part 2						
	$0.50	*$1.50*	*$2.50*	£0.30	£0.90	£1.50
2 Zero Hour: Crisis in Time part 3, birth of Power Girl's child						
	$0.50	*$1.50*	*$2.50*	£0.30	£0.90	£1.50
1 Zero Hour: Crisis in Time part 4						
	$0.50	*$1.50*	*$2.50*	£0.30	£0.90	£1.50
0 gatefold Time-line chart						
	$0.50	*$1.50*	*$2.50*	£0.30	£0.90	£1.50
Title Value:	*$2.50*	*$7.50*	*$12.50*	£1.50	£4.50	£7.50

ZERO ISSUES

As part of DC Comics "Zero Hour mini-series, most of the main DC titles of the time had special "0" issues, usually re-telling origins and acting as jumping-on points for new readers. Distinguished by some excellent cover art, the Zero Issues are as follows in alphabetical order:

Action Comics #0
Adventures of Superman #0
Anima #0
Aquaman #0
Batman #0
Batman: Legends of the Dark Knight #0
Batman: Shadow of the Bat #0
Catwoman #0
Damage #0
Darkstars #0
Deathstroke the Hunted #0
Demon #0
Detective Comics #0
Fate #0
Flash #0
Green Arrow #0
Green Lantern #0
Gunfire #0
Guy Gardner, Warrior #0
Hawkman #0

	$Good	$Fine	$N.Mint	£Good	£Fine	£N.Mint
Justice League of America #0						
Justice League Task Force #0						
Legionnaires #0						
Legion of Super-Heroes #0						
Lobo #0						
Manhunter #0						
New Titans #0						
Outsiders #0						
Primal Force #0						
Ray #0						
Rebels '94 #0						
Robin #0						
Spectre #0						
Starman #0						
Steel #0						
Superboy #0						
Superman #0						
Superman: The Man of Steel #0						
Wonder Woman #0						
Xenobrood #0						
ZERO PATROL						
Continuity; 1 Nov 1984-10 1992						
1-2 Neal Adams script, cover and part art, Megalith backup	*$0.30*	*$0.90*	*$1.50*	£0.20	£0.60	£1.00
3 part Neal Adams art	*$0.30*	*$0.90*	*$1.50*	£0.20	£0.60	£1.00
4 part Neal Adams script, art and cover	*$0.30*	*$0.90*	*$1.50*	£0.20	£0.60	£1.00
5 part Neal Adams art	*$0.30*	*$0.90*	*$1.50*	£0.20	£0.60	£1.00
6-10	*$0.30*	*$0.90*	*$1.50*	£0.20	£0.60	£1.00
Title Value:	*$3.00*	*$9.00*	*$15.00*	£2.00	£6.00	£10.00
Note: all Non-Distributed on the news-stands in the U.K.						
ZERO TOLERANCE						
First,MS; 1 Oct 1990-4 Jan 1991						
1-4 ND Tim Vigil pencils, Tim Tyler inks	*$0.40*	*$1.20*	*$2.00*	£0.25	£0.75	£1.25
Title Value:	*$1.60*	*$4.80*	*$8.00*	£1.00	£3.00	£5.00
ZETRAMAN						
Antarctic Press,MS; 1 Sep 1991-3 Feb 1992						
1-3 ND	*$0.40*	*$1.20*	*$2.00*	£0.25	£0.75	£1.25
Title Value:	*$1.20*	*$3.60*	*$6.00*	£0.75	£2.25	£3.75
ZETRAMAN 2						
Antarctic Press,MS; 1 Oct 1993-2 Dec 1994; 3 Aug 1995						
1-3 ND	*$0.40*	*$1.20*	*$2.00*	£0.25	£0.75	£1.25
Title Value:	*$1.20*	*$3.60*	*$6.00*	£0.75	£2.25	£3.75
ZILLION						
Eternity; 1 Apr 1993-6 Sep 1993						
1 ND Tom Mason script and Harrison Fong art begins, plastic coated covers; black and white	*$0.40*	*$1.20*	*$2.00*	£0.25	£0.75	£1.25
2-6 ND	*$0.40*	*$1.20*	*$2.00*	£0.25	£0.75	£1.25
Title Value:	*$2.40*	*$7.20*	*$12.00*	£1.50	£4.50	£7.50
ZIPPY QUARTERLY						
Fantagraphics,Magazine; 1 Mar 1993-12 1996 ?						
1-3 ND 48pgs	*$0.90*	*$2.70*	*$4.50*	£0.60	£1.80	£3.00
4-11 ND 32pgs	*$0.80*	*$2.40*	*$4.00*	£0.50	£1.50	£2.50
12 ND	*$0.60*	*$1.80*	*$3.00*	£0.40	£1.20	£2.00
Title Value:	*$9.70*	*$29.10*	*$48.50*	£6.20	£18.60	£31.00
ZOMBIE WAR						
Fantaco/Tundra,MS; 1 Jun 1992-2 Aug 1992						
1-2 ND co-scripted by Kevin Eastman	*$0.50*	*$1.50*	*$2.50*	£0.30	£0.90	£1.50
Title Value:	*$1.00*	*$3.00*	*$5.00*	£0.60	£1.80	£3.00
ZONE						
Dark Horse,OS; 1 Jun 1990						
1 ND ties up plot from Dark Horse Presents	*$0.40*	*$1.20*	*$2.00*	£0.25	£0.75	£1.25
Title Value:	*$0.40*	*$1.20*	*$2.00*	£0.25	£0.75	£1.25
ZONE CONTINUUM						
Caliber Press,MS; 1 Aug 1992-2 Sep 1992						
1-2 ND Bruce Zick script/art, black and white	*$0.40*	*$1.20*	*$2.00*	£0.25	£0.75	£1.25
Title Value:	*$0.80*	*$2.40*	*$4.00*	£0.50	£1.50	£2.50
ZONE CONTINUUM (2ND SERIES)						
Caliber Press; 1 Mar 1994-2 Dec 1994						
1-2 ND Bruce Zick script and art, black and white	*$0.50*	*$1.50*	*$2.50*	£0.30	£0.90	£1.50
Title Value:	*$1.00*	*$3.00*	*$5.00*	£0.60	£1.80	£3.00
ZOONIVERSE						
Eclipse,MS; 1 Aug 1986-6 Jun 1987						
1-4 ND	*$0.30*	*$0.90*	*$1.50*	£0.20	£0.60	£1.00
5 ND rare in the U.K. (never imported into U.K. comic shops? Therefore rare?)	*$0.30*	*$0.90*	*$1.50*	£0.25	£0.75	£1.25
6 ND	*$0.30*	*$0.90*	*$1.50*	£0.20	£0.60	£1.00
Title Value:	*$1.80*	*$5.40*	*$9.00*	£1.25	£3.75	£6.25
ZORRO						
Marvel Comics Group,MS; 1 Dec 1990-12 Dec 1991						
1-11 based on US TV series	*$0.25*	*$0.75*	*$1.25*	£0.15	£0.45	£0.75
12 based on US TV series, Alex Toth cover	*$0.25*	*$0.75*	*$1.25*	£0.15	£0.45	£0.75
Title Value:	*$3.00*	*$9.00*	*$15.00*	£1.80	£5.40	£9.00

	$Good	$Fine	$N.Mint	£Good	£Fine	£N.Mint
Note: produced by Marvel UK but printed in America, based on televsion show.						
ZORRO						
Topps; 0 Jan 1994; 1 Jan 1994-11 Dec 1994						
0 (Jan 1994) Don McGregor and Mike Mayhew; Brian Stelfreeze cover; promotional free issue	*$0.60*	*$1.80*	*$3.00*	£0.30	£0.90	£1.50
1 Frank Miller cover	*$0.50*	*$1.50*	*$2.50*	£0.30	£0.90	£1.50
2 1st appearance Lady Rawhide (not in costume), Jae Lee cover	*$0.50*	*$1.50*	*$2.50*	£0.30	£0.90	£1.50
3 1st appearance Lady Rawhide, Adam Hughes cover	*$2.50*	*$7.50*	*$12.50*	£1.30	£3.90	£6.50
4 Mike Grell cover	*$0.50*	*$1.50*	*$2.50*	£0.30	£0.90	£1.50
5 Lady Rawhide appears, Keith Giffen/Joe Sinnott cover	*$1.20*	*$3.60*	*$6.00*	£0.80	£2.40	£4.00
6 Mike Mignola cover	*$0.50*	*$1.50*	*$2.50*	£0.30	£0.90	£1.50
7 Paul Gulacy cover	*$0.50*	*$1.50*	*$2.50*	£0.30	£0.90	£1.50
8 George Perez cover	*$0.50*	*$1.50*	*$2.50*	£0.30	£0.90	£1.50
9 Lady Rawhide appears (and on cover)	*$0.80*	*$2.40*	*$4.00*	£0.50	£1.50	£2.50
10 Lady Rawhide appears	*$0.80*	*$2.40*	*$4.00*	£0.50	£1.50	£2.50
11 Joseph Michael Linsner cover art, Lady Rawhide appears (and on cover)	*$1.00*	*$3.00*	*$5.00*	£0.60	£1.80	£3.00
Title Value:	*$9.90*	*$29.70*	*$49.50*	£5.80	£17.40	£29.00
Note: all Non-Distributed on the news-stands in the U.K.						
ZOT IN DIMENSION 10 AND A HALF						
Not Available,Mini-comic; 1 Jun 1986						
1 ND 8pgs, orange paper, Matt Feazell art	*$0.30*	*$0.90*	*$1.50*	£0.20	£0.60	£1.00
1 2nd printing ND	*$0.25*	*$0.75*	*$1.25*	£0.15	£0.45	£0.75
Title Value:	*$0.55*	*$1.65*	*$2.75*	£0.35	£1.05	£1.75
ZOT!						
Eclipse; 1 Apr 1984-36 Jul 1991						
1 ND Scott McLoud story/art begins	*$0.80*	*$2.40*	*$4.00*	£0.40	£1.20	£2.00
2-9 ND	*$0.60*	*$1.80*	*$3.00*	£0.30	£0.90	£1.50
10 ND last colour issue	*$0.50*	*$1.50*	*$2.50*	£0.30	£0.90	£1.50
11 ND black and white begins	*$0.40*	*$1.20*	*$2.00*	£0.25	£0.75	£1.25
12-14 ND	*$0.40*	*$1.20*	*$2.00*	£0.25	£0.75	£1.25
14½ ND by Matt Feazell	*$0.40*	*$1.20*	*$2.00*	£0.25	£0.75	£1.25
15-35 ND	*$0.40*	*$1.20*	*$2.00*	£0.25	£0.75	£1.25
36 ND 48pgs	*$0.50*	*$1.50*	*$2.50*	£0.30	£0.90	£1.50
Title Value:	*$17.00*	*$51.00*	*$81.50*	£9.90	£29.70	£49.50
Book 1, reprints #1-4 (1989)				£1.45	£4.35	£7.25
Book 2, reprints #5-10 (1990)				£1.90	£5.70	£9.50
Hardcover Book 2				£5.00	£15.00	£25.00
ZULU						
Dell/Movie Classics,OS Movie; 12-950-410 Aug/Oct 1964						
12-950-410 distributed in the U.K. film adaptation; photo cover	*$10.50*	*$32.00*	*$75.00*	£5.50	£17.00	£40.00
Title Value:	*$10.50*	*$32.00*	*$75.00*	£5.50	£17.00	£40.00

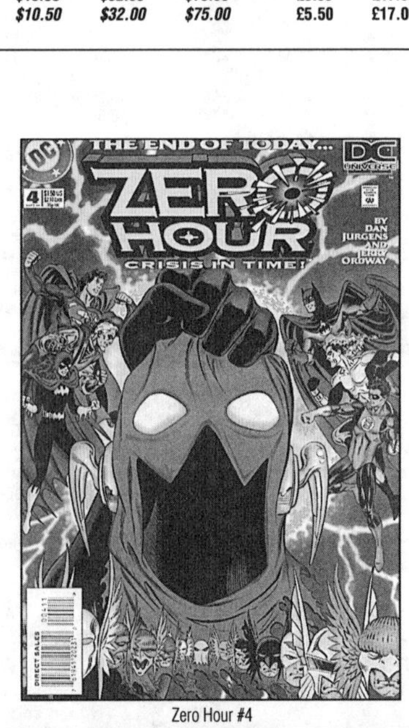

Zero Hour #4

VERY GENERAL PERCENTAGE CONVERSION CHART WHICH MAY BE USED TO CALCULATE LOW AND INBETWEEN GRADES:

THE BRITISH AND AMERICAN MARKET

A Comparison

IT IS OFTEN SAID, more so here on the British side of the Atlantic than on the American, that the British comics scene, market and latterly industry is a mirror-image of America only on a smaller scale. As a certain Asgardian might quoth *"I say thee nay!"* or at least I hope to show throughout the course of this article that our green and sceptr'd isle has its own unique historical traditions, distribution patterns and consequently collecting habits. Where once it might have been thought that the British and American markets were gradually converging, the gap between the two markets is in the process of ever-widening in terms of speculative interest, pricing resistance and ultimately marketplace structure as I also hope to show.

One of the most fundamental differences between the U.K. and U.S. markets is that of comics history and traditions. In Great Britain we did not have a "Golden Age" (apart from the historical one of Queen Elizabeth I, Shakespeare and Raleigh, Drake and the Armada). The Golden Age of American comics (1938-1945) is almost completely unknown to and even ignored by many U.K. collectors. It is almost completely unknown to the general population who have their own memories of the comics they read as children back in the 1930s and 1940s. In fact Great Britain only just caught on to the next phase of American comic development, the Silver Age, after it had been well underway. As is generally regarded, Showcase #4 cover-dated September/October 1956 ushered in the Silver Age of American comics wherein Golden Age heroes were updated for a new generation of readers and super-heroes with super-powers became once more the dominant genre. It may not be widely known to American collectors and dealers but American comic books were not officially distributed in Great Britain until as late as the first couple of months of 1960 (issues cover-dated November 1959), mostly DCs with some Atlas, Archies, Charltons, Harveys and ACGs. There was some limited distribution of romance, war and funny animal titles from late 1957, presumably as market-testers, the most popular of those being Charlton war titles catering to a market stimulated in part by the pocket sized War Picture Library and Battle Picture Library by Fleetway, publisher of today's 2000 AD comic.

While the transatlantic time-lag between actual distribution of American comics is more than twenty years, happily the same cannot be said for the establishment of a back-issue market. It may have begun in the United States before it did in the U.K. but thanks to certain pioneering individuals, the basis for markets that could at least be compared was established. There were isolated collectors up and down the U.K. who began to correspond and to trade comics with each other in the early 1960s as had begun in the States in the late 1950s. The establishment of fanzines were only a few years apart if one compares Jerry Bails' Alter Ego #1 in 1960 and in the U.K. Frank Dobson's Fantasy Advertiser #1 and Dez Skinn's interestingly-named Derinn Comicollector #1 in 1965. Comic book conventions seemed to have started at around the same time with Phil Seuling's New York convention in 1968 and Phil Clark's convention in Birmingham in the same year. When Bob Overstreet started his Comic Book Price Guide in 1970, British collector and dealer Alan Austin produced his first price guide in 1975, researched at source from his own massive collection and painstakingly typed out by hand with addenda at the back for titles he missed out along the way – no luxuries like a computer or word processor here! Alan's book represents an important pedigree of U.K. price guides that this present Guide is directly descended from. As such, the general pattern seemed to be that events in the awareness of the collectibility of back issues that happened in the States were mirrored over in the U.K. after some increasingly short time delay but the advantage in America was the much broader range and age of back issues available. By the mid 1960s, these isolated British collectors had five or six years' worth of distributed American comics to consider: their U.S. counterparts had more than twenty five. The beauty for collectors of American comics in the U.K. was that sets were entirely possible to put together, at least of Marvel comics. A DC comics fan was faced with the prospect of some very high numbers with the first distributed issues of Action Comics at #258 and Detective Comics at #272 for example. British comics were equally daunting with 52 issues a year rather than twelve and generally being larger in size and even then being available in a wide variety of sizes, there were (and still are!) inevitable storage problems. It is no wonder that the collecting of American comics in general and some especially caught on so well in the U.K., presaged by the black and white album and comic reprints throughout the 1940s and 1950s.

Back-issue collecting of American comics had the perfect platform in the 1950s. In October 1951 the first Superman Annual from Atlas Publishing appeared. This collected the first six Australian issues that had appeared from July to December 1950 published by K.G. Murray for distribution by Atlas. The reprints from National Periodical Publications were black and white only and took their content from issues of late 1940s Superman, Action and World's Finest Comics. The cover was taken from the famous origin issue of Superman #53. Batman, Superboy and SuperAdventure Annuals followed along with monthly comics of the same titles. One hundred page reprint comics also appeared such as All Favourites, Hundred Comics and Superman Supacomics. By the end of the 1950s, there were not many National Periodical/DC comics characters that British youngsters had not seen. More importantly it got regular buyers into the habit of the monthly comic book so that when the originals arrived at the newsagents at the beginning of 1960, now they could read the adventures of familiar characters in full colour. Not surprisingly these British and Australian reprints are fast becoming very sought after for their unusual reprints and many original covers. Interestingly the process was reversed in the 1960s for Marvel comics as the colour originals were reprinted in black and white form by Alan Class titles like Astounding Stories and Secrets of the Unknown and Odhams Press titles like Pow! and Smash!

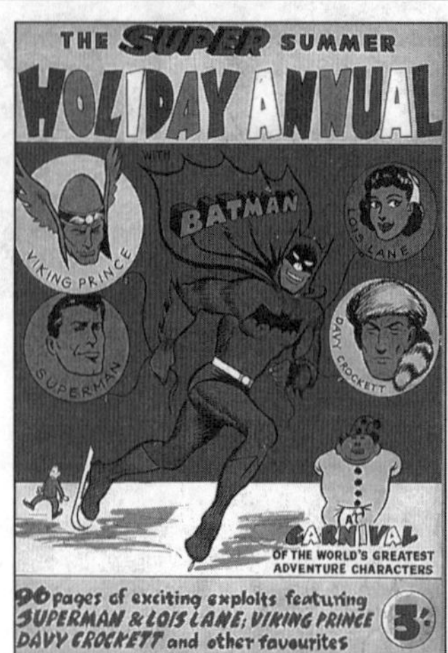

The Super Summer Holiday Annual

Five Score Comic Monthly #69

Mighty Comic #41

Superman #105

Superboy # 67

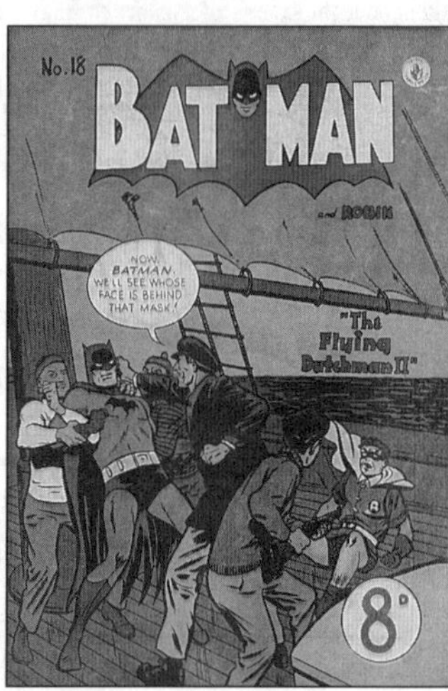

Batman #18

Super Adventure Comic #99

Super Adventure Annual 1958-59 (1st)

Superman Annual #1 (1951)

A SELECTION OF ATLAS COMICS AND ANNUALS, AVAILABLE IN THE U.K. THROUGHOUT THE 1950S AND THE EARLY 1960S WITH A WIDE VARIETY OF REPRINT MATERIAL BEFORE THE "REAL THING" BEGAN TO BE DISTRIBUTED WITH COVER DATE NOVEMBER 1959

The second fundamental difference is the weekly format established from the very beginning by British comics and the monthly magazine format favoured in America. One obvious reason must be the relative sizes of the countries. For America to base a comic distribution service on a weekly basis would have meant an extremely sophisticated distribution network in those early days. And on a more basic economic level, a shelf-life of a month (or more) was more attractive than a week, given the number of days it would take to get comics out to the furthest parts of the country by road. It is interesting to consider that though the British invented the very word itself when it first appeared in dictionaries in the 1780s as "comick" meaning satirical broadsheet paper with amusing stories and caricature illustrations, aimed at an adult audience and it was the British who developed the comic for a younger audience in the 1890s with Comic Cuts and the like, it was the Americans who took the genre and made it their own in the late 1920s when a month's worth of Sunday Funnies could be collected together and bound with cardboard covers. And there the American comic stayed and flourished right through the Thirties, Forties and Fifties while the British tradition carried on as it had done, almost unchanged during the same period.

Up until official distribution at the beginning of 1960, the staple diet of every school-boy (not discounting publications like June, Girl and Schoolfriend for the school-girl market) were weekly comics like The Dandy (first issue 14th December 1937 and still going today) or The Beano (first issue 30th July 1938 and likewise still going strong) which are even today still very much in the tradition of the finite one page jolly jape story. There were very few continuing dramatic stories with developing characters in this type of comic from the 1930s to the 1950s though the 1960s saw the rise and (some British collectors would argue) peak of this phenomenon, possibly owing to American influence. The other alternative was the generic term "Boys Papers" like The Rover or The Wizard, mostly text stories with illustrations dealing with stories based on school dormitory antics and castaways on desert islands, war hero exploits or tales of the athletes and other sportsmen. The outstanding exception to all this was The Eagle comic (first issue dated 14th April 1950) featuring Dan Dare Pilot of the Future as drawn in full colour by Frank Hampson. With its rocket ships and ray guns, futuristic cityscapes and the dreaded Mekon as principal foe, the Dan Dare strip freely borrowed from the American tradition of dashing heroes and outer space exploits though his firm square-set jaw and very British exclamations ("Cheerio!" and "Great Heavens!") planted him solidly in the British Royal Air Force world and vocabulary of the Second World War. Not a super power or a flapping cape to be seen. The brightly-costumed hero was relegated to decidedly second-raters like Electroman and Masterman though the one major exception to this was Marvelman, produced by Mick Anglo and Roy Parker from their tiny studio in Gower Street in London from 1954 to 1963 though the character, it could be argued, was an obvious derivative of Fawcett's Captain Marvel.

It was against this background that the American monthly comic book appeared, first in dribs and drabs and then in official distribution.

Their full colour glossy covers and colour interiors were a sharp contrast to the duller newsprint quality of virtually all British weeklies, most of which were black and white interiors or at best occasional spot colour.

Distribution of American comics, even when it was official, was patchy at first and very often the sea-side towns of Brighton and Bournemouth, Blackpool and Southend had ample supplies for holidaying youngsters with extra pocket money to spend, supplies that tended to get no further inland. Distribution to Scotland, however, has always been somewhat better from the start and as DCs seemed to be in the greatest supply, the marked fondness for mainstay characters like Superman and Batman still survives today in those areas.

While it was mentioned earlier that no Golden Age comics were distributed in Great Britain on an official scale, it is certain that some found their way over with visiting friends or relatives from the U.S. and indeed many thousands of comics came with the arrival of G.I.s stationed in Britain during the War. Areas where there are U.S.A.F. bases such as Norwich in the county of Norfolk north-east of London are generally good for turning up older, pre-distribution issues as these have been gradually disseminated throughout the county since the War. I myself have seen a copy of Action Comics #1 with an old sixpence stamp on it. It is highly unlikely that there is anything vaguely approaching a treasure trove of Golden Age comics to be found in this country, certainly not on the pedigree scale of some of the American finds such as The Edgar Church Collection. The dream of finding a box of Detective 27s in an old lady's attic will have to remain, as Charles Dickens would be wont to say, "...charming food for contemplation".

A number of early (pre-distribution) Batman and Detective Comics have been known with Popular Book Centre Stamps on the front cover for example. These PBC shops were more prevalent in the late 1940s and 1950s though the chain still survives today. The mainstay of their stock was cheap paperbacks and pornographic magazines and thus the inclusion of American comics associated them with literature that was liable to corrupt, a stigma attached to the American comic for a very long time. This attitude was not helped by the appearance in unusually large quantities of EC comics in the early 1950s, the first occasion of anything like mass-exposure to the American comic. Though short-lived in Britain, these comics were quickly banned, leading to the Children and Young Person (Harmful Publications) Act of 1955 and found themselves consigned to the same pornographic shelves in adult corner bookshops. The Popular Book Centre stamp is usually a very large diamond shape in the middle of the cover with the re-sale price, usually threepence or sixpence (these coins are no longer in circulation and then would have been worth about 4 cents and 7 cents respectively) scrawled in biro or felt tip pen in the box provided. These Popular Bookshop Centre-stamped copies were the scourge of those early collectors in Britain in the 1960s. Great for reading value but not so great for those interested in high grade copies.

The first American comic books to be distributed usually had the English price of ninepence stamped anywhere on the front cover. This stamp was done in ink and could often be in a neat circle on an unobtrusive part of the cover. More infuriatingly, it could be very heavy, even smudged and right on the face of a leading character or right in the middle of a clear expanse of cover so as to be all the more obvious. Occasionally the inking would be so heavy as to bleed through to the inside front cover.

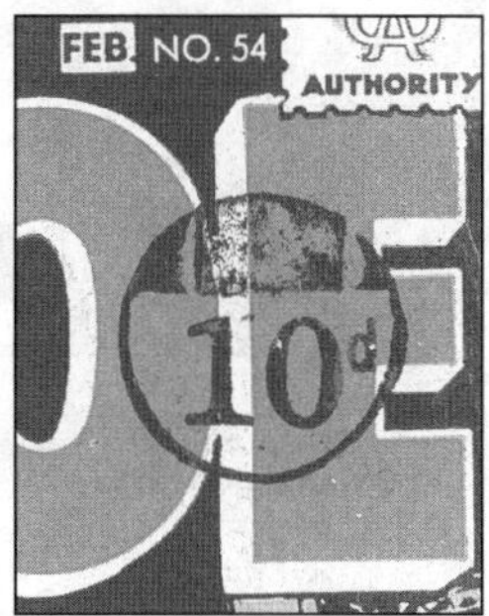

A PENCE STAMP IN DETAIL.
A fairly typical example although there were many variations.

The very early Marvels more sensibly had the English price printed where the cents price would have been, ninepence from 1961 to mid 1964, tenpence from 1965 to 1967 and one shilling until decimalization in 1971 when it became six new pence or "6p". This gradually rose up to 15p until the practice of dual-pricing in the early 1980s. More confusing still, the "sell-by" month was removed for these exported copies as by the time they arrived on the British news-stands, it was already the actual month (and sometimes later) that was printed inside the comic. Nervous distributors felt that it would give a very limited shelf-life to a publication if the cover month was left on. Classic examples of this would be a Fantastic Four #1 with the "NOV" missing from a British-priced pence copy or the "AUG" missing from a British-priced Amazing Fantasy #15. Interestingly, the earliest distributed westerns, romance and war titles had the U.S. indicia removed inside and in its place had emblazoned "Exclusively distributed in the U.K. by Thorpe and Porter".

AMAZING SPIDERMAN #1 –
Cents copy of Amazing Spiderman compared to a Pence copy (see below). Note that the covers are identical apart from the "9d" in place of the "12¢" and the cover month of "MAR" missing under the number 1.

This has lead to the question of cents copies versus pence copies for collectors in the U.K. Many collectors feel that as American comics they should have the original American price while others, content in their nostalgia, prefer the pence pricing as that is what they remember as children. The debate still continues as a matter of personal choice but for those who wish to invest their money in higher grade copies, particularly of key issues, only cents will do. For lower grade ordinary issues with no key significance, the cents/pence distinction becomes negligible. In a sense the pence copies are much rarer than cents copies as only a small fraction of the entire print run (2%?), usually at the end when the black cover plates were changed, were set aside for foreign distribution. Some would claim that this meant lesser clarity of printing quality as the inks became faded and the plates would start to show wear and as such a non-cents copy is necessarily of inferior production quality. Recent ideas have suggested that at the beginning of official distribution in early 1960, the pence-priced copies were produced first as there was a set number ordered by cautious British wholesalers, unsure as how how these new-fangled American comics would sell against the British weeklies which were cheaper (The Dandy and The Beano were 2 old/pre-decimalization pence at the time or just under 3 cents as opposed to 10 cents cover price for American comics to give some price perspective). It is possible therefore that mid Silver Age DCs and the very first Marvel comics are of a better quality of printing than the American cents-priced copies.

The actual process of printing renders these ideas doubtful as it would mean restarting the printing presses after an initial short run-time.

Either way, in this current age of collecting cover variants, American collectors and dealers may care to consider the possibilities of The British Cover Variant Edition of, say, an Amazing Spiderman #1 or a Superman Annual #1. They are certainly much rarer and the early Marvels do have these interesting printing variations. Most collectors in the U.K. cannot understand why most Americans consider these pence copies as inferior reprints. They were printed on the same day, in the same place, on the same paper using the same original artwork. When the finite resource of very high grade cent copies key issues runs out, if it hasn't done so already, where else can collectors turn in order to buy unrestored high grades? Surely the condition of the comic is more important? There is an argument for the attraction and genuine rarity value of a Near Mint unrestored pence copy of Amazing Fantasy #15 in the marketplace if only Fine and Very Fine cents copies are otherwise available. More and more pence-priced copies of Silver Age Marvels seem to be appearing on American dealers' mail order lists and are priced at about 75% of a similar grade cents copy. It would be interesting to find out how well they sell. It is still a remarkable fact of luck or foresight that a key issue survives in perfect condition whether it be a cents or pence copy, perhaps more so for "British copies" as there were far fewer pence copies produced in the first place.

Even today in Great Britain there is necessarily a greater supply of pence copies of Silver Age/1960s material in spite of the increasing amounts cents copies brought over by British dealers visiting American conventions in recent years. It will be some time, if ever, before there are equal amounts of cents and pence copies of Silver Age books in the U.K.

TALES OF SUSPENSE #59
An example of a comic made Scarce in the U.K. by a quirk of distribution at the time

Distribution throughout the 1960s and 1970s was handled by a company called Thorpe and Porter and the T & P stamp or later on the white sticker with the T & P in the symbol of an indian tent (or teepee – get it?) became what most British collectors fondly remember. While gaining in frequency and reliability, occasionally hiccups in distribution occurred. A national dock strike at the beginning of 1965 meant that for at least two (and possibly three) months Marvels in particular only came over in very limited quantities as most were turned away to be delivered to other parts of the Commonwealth, mostly South Africa and Australia. Issues across all the Marvel titles starting with cover-date Oct 1964 (in one instance Sept 1964, that of Two-Gun Kid #71) and ending with cover-date Jan 1965 are in generally short supply with cover date Dec 1964 being what seems to be the height of the dock strike as most of those issues are traditionally rare. As the dock strike gradually lessened so the issue numbers became very scarce or scarce and issues cover-dated Feb and Mar 1965 are increasingly found to be less common that otherwise thought. Issues of note affected by this dock strike in the U.K. market are: **Amazing Spiderman #18,#19** and to a lesser extent **#20**; **Avengers #9-11** and to a lesser extent **#12**; **Daredevil #4,5**; **Fantastic Four #32,#33** and to a lesser extent **#34**; **Journey into Mystery #109-112**; **Kid Colt, Outlaw #119, 120**; **Rawhide Kid #43**; **Sgt. Fury #11-13**; **Strange Tales #126,#127** and to a lesser extent **#128**; **Tales of Suspense #58-60**; **Tales to Astonish #60-63**; **Two-Gun Kid #71-73**; **X-Men #8,9**. DCs of the same cover-dates do not seem to be as unusually rare or scarce.

THE FIRST OVERSTREET PRICE GUIDE IN 1970.
(Special note: Cover © Copyright Overstreet Publications)

There is another peculiarity to Marvel comics in the U.K. market. As the majority of issues in the 1960s and early 1970s were shipped by sea, very often bundles of them got water-stained and at worst completely water-soaked. Though sea-shipping still continues today, there must have been an unusually high proportion of un-seaworthy vessels in the early 1970s as Marvels in particular suffer from this severe fault. Amazing Spidermans from #105 to 110 and later on from #120-129 and Iron Mans from #42 to 44 are notoriously regular sufferers when they surface in indigenous collections. One wonders how many hundreds even thousands of copies have been rendered completely uncollectible in this way.

It is perhaps the history and establishment of Price Guides that cause the markets in the U.K. and U.S. to differ most significantly. In my opinion, one of the most important books about comics ever written appeared in 1970. Two hundred and twenty eight pages long with a handful of adverts at the back, typed out rather than type-set, a few mistakes like Batman #46 being the famous origin cover and story rather than #47 and with what were then ground-breaking prices like Action Comics #1 at $300 in Mint, Detective #27 at $275 and Showcase #4 at $12! The first Comic Book Price Guide by Bob Overstreet had a 1,000 print run, an innocuous white cover and sold for $5. The first edition sold out and a second print run of 800 with a blue cover soon followed. The book did two very important things: it immediately established a market value for American comics the moment that prices were seen in black and white and thereby sowed the seed for speculative interest in the buying and selling of comics. It also, and perhaps more importantly, established a pricing structure centred around the three grades of Good, Fine and Mint. The ratios between the three were roughly 1 to 1.5 to 2 (a little different to some of today's ratios of 1 to 3 to 15!). The concept of the condition being the major factor of value was now set in stone. In 1982, Bob Overstreet with Jon Warren brought out a Price Update as a supplement to the Comic Book Price Guide #12 and the structure of the American market was complete. Dealers and collectors alike could look forward to a regular price increase in most cases (decreases some of the time) and report on the the constant shifting state of the back issue industry. In the years that have followed, some would argue that such a system leads to a healthy and sustainable growth in the market year on year while others would make accusations of unnecessary hype and ever spiralling multiples of Guide. Either way, it is clear that the structure of the American market is more sophisticated in certain areas.

THE FIRST OVERSTREET UPDATE IN 1982.
(Special note: Cover © Copyright Overstreet Publications)

Twenty six years later, the Overstreet Guide is still going strong when other American guides have come and gone. While values are set and shown to evolve every year for the American market, it is becoming increasingly clear that those same prices cannot be applied issue for issue to the British market. Different traditions. Different distribution patterns. Different character popularity. Different size of collector interest. Different general awareness. And different attitude to realistic levels of prices.

When Alan Austin produced his first Price Guide in 1975, the current Overstreet Guide of the time was number 4 with number 5 just about to come out. Interesting examples of price comparison would be X-Men #1 priced at $10 in Mint and Fantastic Four #1 priced at $70. Alan adopted more or less the same ratio splits as Overstreet between Good, Fine and Mint (which would seem logical at the time) and his pricing seems very consistent. He priced X-Men #1 at £3.50 (when $10 converted at the then exchange rate of 2.40 would have been £4.16) and Fantastic Four #1 at £25 ($70 converted at 2.40 being £29.16). It would not surprise me in the least if Alan had completely ignored the Overstreet price and came up with those values independently. He just knew the market rate for comics like that in this country. In his introduction he wrote about seeing "a trend back towards more reasonable prices" and twenty one years later I hope that this Guide will echo that same sentiment.

No. 1. A SPLENDID TOY MODEL GIVEN FREE WITH THIS NUMBER. 1d

THE RAINBOW 1d

No. 1. Vol. 1. PRICE ONE PENNY. February 14, 1914.

THE JOLLY ADVENTURES OF THE BRUIN BOYS.—THEIR SNOW-MAN HAS A WARM TIME.

1. There was a great surprise awaiting the boys at Mrs. Bruin's Boarding-School when they awoke the other morning. "Look!" cried Tiger Tim excitedly. "It has been snowing in the night! Isn't it grand!" "I wish we could go out," grumbled Willie Ostrich. "It will all have melted away by the time we've finished our lessons."

2. "I know!" exclaimed Tim. "Let's dress and go up on the roof before Mrs. Bruin gets up! We can have some fine fun up there." The other boys thought it a jolly fine idea, too, and in less than half a minute they were climbing through the roof door. "Come along, boys!" piped Joey, the parrot. "Who'll take me on for a snowball fight?"

3. But Tiger Tim had a better idea than that. "Let's make a snow-man," he said. "He'll look fine sitting up here on the chimney!" So they all set to work, and this is the beauty they made. "Now, that's what I call a real work of art!" cried Jumbo, as Tim put on the finishing-touch. "Well done, sir! You ought to get a medal for that!" "Bravo, Tim!" chimed in Joey. "That's the coolest piece of work I've seen for a long time!"

4. But while all this was going on Mrs. Bruin was busy down in the kitchen below, preparing breakfast for her pupils, and as soon as the fire began to burn up, down the chimney came a great heap of snow—plomp!—which put the fire out. "Goodness me!" she exclaimed, with a start. "I've never known it to snow such large flakes as this before! What ever can be the cause of it all?"

5. And she promptly went up on to the roof to find out. Meanwhile, the naughty boys were wondering what had become of their snow-man. "He needn't have left us in such a hurry," cried Georgie Giraffe, who was looking down the chimney for him. "He has done the disappearing trick, if you ask me!" "I wish I could do the same," groaned Jumbo, who just then spotted their teacher. "Oh dear! We're in for it now, I can see!"

6. And Jumbo had guessed quite right, for Mrs. Bruin pretty quickly had them downstairs again, and they had to put up with a cold breakfast. "Isn't she cool to us this morning!" remarked Jacko. "Yes, and so is everything else," agreed Fido. "Cold tea, eh! Bur-r-h!" Anyway, Mrs. Bruin made up for it by giving them all a good dinner, because they promised to be good in future. Do you think they will be? We shall see next week!

THE RAINBOW #1 – WIDELY ACKNOWLEDGED TO BE THE FIRST PARTICULARLY FORMATTED CHILDREN'S COMIC

British Comics

AN INTRODUCTION TO BRITISH COMICS

Cut a collector of British comics and you will find nostalgia flowing in his veins: the memory of a scene, or a certain character, or the excellence of an anonymous artist are all spurs that will turn a reader into a collector. Traditionally, British comics have been aimed at a young audience up to the age of fourteen, and the influence of comics in those formative years is incalculable; that such disposable ephemera would be of any interest to you after that age (or whatever age you gave up reading comics, after all, it's kid's stuff, isn't it?) is difficult to imagine, yet the past few years have seen a change towards comics and to comic collecting.

A combination of events have given the public a greater awareness of comics: the arrival of graphic novels such as **The Dark Knight Returns** (1986) and **Watchmen** (1988), neither of which were available through general retailers in their original formats, caused a stir in the British media. Comics, it was said, were not necessarily 'kid's stuff' any longer, and the publicity machine which rolled in their wake spotlighted the adult direction comics can take. The emphasis was on the very differences between recent titles such as **Crisis** and **Revolver** and the traditional British comic, yet the collecting of the latter also took an upswing around the same time, probably due to the interest in, and the coverage given to, the anniversaries of **The Dandy**, **The Beano** and **Eagle** in that period (1987-90). For a change these comics received a great deal of serious attention in the press, where comics only seem to be mentioned when they are the target of some pressure group trying to get them banned for promoting violence and sado-masochism.

A history of British comics would require a book in itself: an albeit short but representative history by Lew Stringer appeared in **The Comics Journal 122**, June 1988 (an issue which covered many aspects of British comics). Rather than repeat the information available there, this introduction will try to cover some of the various collectable aspects of British comics.

The direction of collecting has changed greatly over the years. There will always be the hard-core of fans who will collect the comics they read as a child, but as time marches on, comics published early in the century drift into obscurity, the realm of specialists and completists. The British 'Golden Age' comics of the thirties, with the advent of the 1d provincial comics and the ever present comics of the Amalgamated Press such as **Comic Cuts**, **Illustrated Chips** and **Puck** still attract collectors. The thirties also saw the first photogravure comic in the shape of **Mickey Mouse Weekly** (1936) and the birth of **The Dandy** (1937) and **The Beano** (1938). Pre-war comics such as these are very rare and probably command the highest prices of all British comics; who can tell how many copies were pulped during the wartime when paper was at a premium.

Perhaps the greatest nostalgia generator of them all appeared in 1950 to herald the arrival of the 'Silver Age' – **Eagle**. The brainchild of Marcus Morris and artist Frank Hampson, **Eagle** introduced 'Dan Dare' in its first issue. Hampson's perfectionist attitude to the strip assured Dare a place in the history books as Britain's most fondly remembered hero. His other strips were drawn with the same loving care for detail, making them equally collectable.

Hampson spearheads the group of artists whose every page is collected rather than specific characters they may have worked on, although (as with Hampson) they may be remembered for one strip above all others. In this group would be such artists as Frank Bellamy whose work for **Eagle** included biographical strips such as 'The Happy Warrior' (Winston Churchill) and 'Montgomery of Alamein', adventure strips 'Fraser of Africa' and 'Heros the Spartan', and 'Dan Dare' himself. Bellamy also did numerous other notable strips such as 'Thunderbirds' in **TV Century 21** and 'Garth' in the **Daily Mirror** newspaper.

Don Lawrence is best remembered for 'The Rise and Fall of the Trigan Empire' which first appeared in **Ranger** and later in the educational weekly **Look and Learn**. His earlier work on 'Olac the Gladiator' in **Tiger** and 'Karl the Viking' in **Lion** continue to prove popular, particularly in Europe where Lawrence has chronicled the adventures of 'Storm' for the past fourteen years.

Ron Embleton's career ranged from the one-off comics of the late forties, through classic strips such as 'Wrath of the Gods' in **Boys' World** and 'Wulf the Briton' in **Express Weekly**, 'Stingray' and 'Captain Scarlet' in **TV Century 21**, all the way to 'Oh Wicked Wanda' and 'Sweet Chastity' in **Penthouse**.

Also in the group of particularly collected artists would be the classic artists of the early days such as Tom Browne, Percy Cocking, Bertie Brown and Roy Wilson; the artists who made D.C. Thomson's comics amongst the most widely read by children, Dudley D. Watkins, Paddy Brennan and the stars of the fifties funny strips, Leo Baxendale and Ken Reid; the great adventure artists of Amalgamated Press, Eric Parker, H.M. Brock, Hugh McNeil, Derek Eyles, and later Joe Colquhoun and Denis McLoughlin. The traditional anonymity of British comics has meant that many names are still unknown, and the use of European and South American artists (amongst the most notable being Hugo Pratt, Jesus Blasco, Alberto Breccia, Esteban Maroto, Enric Sio and Solano Lopez) via agencies has further complicated the issue of who did which strip. The re-introduction of credits in **2000AD** has led to greater interest in the artists themselves, and the work of Brian Bolland, Dave Gibbons, Simon Bisley and others who have found work and wider recognition in America, have built up followers in great numbers.

Nostalgia isn't limited to the comics themselves. Film, radio and TV have all created memorable characters which have made the translation into strip form. **Film Fun**, **Radio Fun** and later **TV Comic** all plundered their respective media for inspiration and not only for particular characters: the artists and actors themselves were often the heroes of the strips, ranging from Harold Lloyd (under the guise of 'Winkle') to Big Daddy (the wrestler). Most of the characters starred in humour strips, but adventure strips based on TV shows are particularly sought after. The Gerry Anderson puppet shows inspired their own comic in **TV Century 21**, whilst The Avengers, The Man From U.N.C.L.E., Danger Man and many others continue to grow in popularity long after their respective shows have ceased production. Dr Who has had one of the longest and varied careers in British comics and still appears today.

One area in which British and American comics have differed greatly is in the genre of the costumed superhero. Whilst the heroes and supergroups have crossed the Atlantic, notable in the Power Comics of the sixties, **Smash!**, **Pow!**, **Terrific** and **Fantastic**, and via the British end of Marvel Comics, there have been few home-grown successes. The earliest weekly costumed hero was 'The Amazing Mr X' in **Dandy 1944**, although there had been occasional short lived strips earlier, an example being William Ward's macabre, Batman inspired, 'The Bat' who appeared in **Thrill Comics** and **Extra Fun** in 1940. The most successful was Marvelman, produced by Mick Anglo's Gower Street Studios between 1954 and 1963, although he was a derivative of the American character Captain Marvel. 'Marvelman' was revived in 1982 in **Warrior** with writer Alan Moore at the helm. Moore was also writing 'Captain Britain' for Marvel UK (at various times in **Marvel Super-Heroes**, **The Daredevils** and **The Mighty World of Marvel**), another strip which had American origins, albeit that it was created and originally written and drawn by Americans for the British market. Both characters subsequently made successful moves to America in *Miracleman* and *Excalibur*.

The British comic at its conception was designed for adults, using the strips to caricature and satirize popular figures of the time, yet it is now predominantly a form of children's entertainment. That doesn't mean that adult comics ceased to exist, for in the early seventies there was a thriving underground movement led by **Cyclops**, **Nasty Tales**, **Cozmic Comix** and the many other comix that were published by the Ar-Zak group. These and the adult orientated comics that followed, such as **Graphixus**, **Near Myths** and more recently **Knockabout**, nurtured the talents of many new artists, amongst them Brian Bolland, Dave Gibbons, Bryan Talbot and Hunt Emerson.

Also aimed at the more adult end of the market (with varying degrees of success) were the independents which sprung up in the recent past. These have been helped by the distribution services and specialist shops which have grown up around the comics industry. Amongst the more notable titles to appear in the past ten years were **Deadface** from Harrier, **Redfox** and **The Adventures of Luther Arkwright** from Valkyrie and the graphic novel **Violent Cases** from Escape. The Fast Fiction group published and distributed numerous small-press comics, whilst the (admittedly patchy) growth of the graphic novel led to more appearances of comics in regular retail outlets and booksellers, which have previously only carried juvenile material to any great extent.

1996: THE YEAR IN REVIEW

Tom Browne was one of the first superstars of comics. Born in 1870, at the age of 11 he became an errand boy, first for a milliner's and later in the lace market in his native Nottingham. At 14 he became apprenticed to a local firm of lithographic printers, serving the full seven year term, unpaid. To live, he sold cartoons; the first appeared in **Scraps** in 1889 and was, prophetically, entitled "He knew how to do it!". The eight-panel strip earned him thirty shillings.

In 1895, Browne set up a studio in London from which he would draw six or more comic sets, jokes, illustrations and full-page features for magazines, postcards and posters for theatrical productions a week. On trips to America he sold sketches and cartoons to the **New York Herald**, the **New York Times** and the **Chicago Tribune**; he was a co-founder of the London Sketch Club and served as its President; was elected to the Royal Society of British Artists, Royal Institute of Painters in Water Colour, and exhibited at the Royal Academy.

Browne is remembered today by three distinct groups whose paths rarely, if ever, cross: as a cartoonist, as a postcard artist and as a comic strip artist. In comics he completely dominated the field between 1896 and 1900, drawing the cover strips for five titles; and it was Browne who created comics' first dynamic duo.

On May 16, 1896 – and thus celebrating their 100th anniversary – **Illustrated Chips** #298 ran a six panel cover strip by Browne entitled 'Innocents on the River'. Its stars, Weary Waddles and Tired Timmy are first introduced at the side of a rowing boat, the caption: "I say, Timmy, a great idea has hit me in the head. If we catch that horse we can make him tow us in this boat." Timmy, plump and patched and wearing a hat that looks as if it was attacked with a can-opener, thinks it a noble scheme, and his rake-thin, top-hatted partner grabs the horse ("How's this," he says, riding back. "Ye'd take me for a Dragooner in the Queen's Bodyguard, wouldn't ye?"), and, by panel four the horse is trotting along the bank, towing the boat; W.W. lays back, lazily trailing his hand in the river, for all the world a Toff, with his thin-stemmed pipe, being punted along the Cam. For T.T. it "reminds me of the old days at Oxford."

Being a gag strip, they languish naively, ignoring the oars, oblivious - until it's too late - as their horse takes a rise along the towpath where a bridge spans the river. "Great Pip!" yells W.W. as he realises. "Whoa, you brute!" shouts T.T, as the boat is dragged up the brickwork of the bridge and the two are unceremoniously dumped.

Six panels of unsophisticated humour, you may think. But still clever. Those who 'read' comics (thesis writers take note) could make a lot of Browne's understated and sublime final caption; not a descriptive, as most captions had to be, no sound effects, but a subtle punch line: "And then they got out and walked."

The Don Quixote and Sancho Panza of comics were too good to drop. Five weeks later they scored another cover, and soon after became the regular front men of **Chips**; in all, the adventures of 'The World Famous Tramps' – Weary Willie and Tired Tim, as they were renamed - would run from issue 310 (August 8th, 1896) until the very last issue of **Chips**, issue 2997 (September 12th, 1953).

They long outlived their creator: Tom Browne, R.I., died in 1910 at the early age of 39 and was buried with military honours at Shooter's Hill. Tim's paunch swelled in girth but Willie never put on an ounce and his trousers were permanently ripped across one knee - so much for 'modern' fashion. Many artists would tell their tales (including Freddie Compton, Walter Bell and, the duo's most long-standing resident artist, Percy Cocking), but Willie and Tim remained much the same for 57 years.

What can we take away from this? I'm not a great one for metaphores or parables (I prefer accuracy to allegory), but if you look closely at Browne and his characters, although they were created 100 years ago, there are resonances that echo down the century. For instance, Browne became a star of the comics when there were maybe a couple of dozen titles...well, there aren't many more than that today. Although famous as a comic artist, he worked in other media, as many artists do today. I think the primary difference between then and now is that many (most?) of today's artists grew up on comics and targetted comics as a career, whereas Browne trained as a lithographic printer and comics were a means to an end, although that's not to say that he put any less energy into his comic sets than he did his watercolours. Nowadays, with the market contracting rather than expanding (as it was 100 years ago), the newcomer cannot grow with a new title but must battle the established hand for a chance to show his talent. In the 1890s, the market for reading material was expanding rapidly to accomodate the newly literate, and comics were just part of that growth. Nowadays, computers and computer games are a 6 billion pound industry that has all but taken the place that publishing and magazines held 100 years ago as the tool of education and entertainment.

Is there a moral that can be taken from Weary Waddles and Tired Timmie, the two innocents on the river? Something along the lines of "You can take a horse to water..." maybe? You can create comics cheaply – and, however expensive you may think they are, they're still a damn sight cheaper than a computer game – but you can't force people to buy them. Is there something to be said about their leisurely cruise comics have had in the past century? That perhaps comics have languished too long believing in their own infallibility and not kept their eyes open for dangers ahead? Or that industry is taking a surprise bath? That comics are water under the bridge?

This isn't a solo game. You can think up your own analogies. There are no prizes. I think most of us can see that comics have hit the brickwork and those who work in the industry are taking a ducking. Comics have reached a bridge they can't pass.

One more? We're up a creek and sod the paddles – where's the boat?

Britain's comic industry has taken hit after hit in recent years. We're down to essentially four companies still producing comics that would be of interest to the traditional boys market. D.C. Thomson now leads the field in numbers, publishing 12 titles (one up on last year, having added **Classics from the Comics**, a reprint monthly). Fleetway Editions recently lost two reprint titles, **Classic Judge Dredd** and **Classic 2000AD**, taking their output down to 7, below both Marvel UK and Titan Magazines, who both clock in with 8 titles apiece. Under the heading 'The Rest' are five adult humour titles – **Smut, Spit, Sweet F.A., Zit and Viz** – and the junior activity magazine **I Love to Read Batman** from Redan. Roughly 40 titles, of which 25 contain original material. About 20 of them aim for what was the core market of 14–16 year-olds; about a dozen are TV or movie related; 4 are aimed squarely at schoolgirls.

The target audience for comics is now polarised four ways that can be roughly broken down as: nursery comics (5-year-olds and under), juvenile comics (5–11-year-olds), 'teenage' comics (12 to 16-year-olds) and adult comics (17-years plus). Of these, the adult comics can be dealt with as a separate entity: I don't think anyone would disagree that the adult humour titles are generally read by non-comic fans who would rarely find them so stimulating that they head off for the nearest comic shop and pick up Vertigo titles. They are a breed unto themselves (the comics and the fans). The comics that bear the brunt of an older (14-years plus) readership, therefore, are limited to those titles that are principally magazines, in which category we count **Doctor Who Magazine, Star Trek Monthly, Star Wars: The Official Magazine, X-Files** and **Manga Mania**. With most being reprint titles, and **Doctor Who Magazine** only carrying one short strip nowadays, the marketplace for older comic readers is catered for by those perennial favourites, **2000AD** and **Judge Dredd Megazine**. And, boy, have they come in for some stick this past year.

2000AD celebrated its millennial issue with a return to basics following the misfortune of the Judge Dredd movie. Any hopes of riding in Stallone's slipstream to a brighter future were cruelly dashed by the runaway success of Batman Forever, released two weeks earlier, the same-day release of Apollo 13 (both of which went on to gross over $150 million), and a critical press. 2000AD's junior title, **Lawman of the Future** survived only 22 issues, and as the millennium approached, **2000AD** and the **Judge Dredd Megazine** switched editors, John Tomlinson for David Bishop, both under Steve MacManus...then cut back to Bishop and MacManus.

The two instigated their 'back to basics' policy of strong stories, led by the creator-owned 'Mazeworld' by Alan Grant and Arthur Ranson, with a rotating pair of classic characters - 'Slaine' and 'Rogue Trooper' - supporting the backbone of the paper, 'Judge Dredd'. Perhaps the biggest visible change in the paper was the disappearance of Tharg, whose editorial hand and Betelgeusian philosophy had carried the magazine through over 1,000 issues: a crisis on his homeworld forced him to return to Quaxxann...or did he? For the new management are a group of covert operatives known only as Vector 13. Did Tharg retire, or was he retired?

The character editor is one of those traditions that refuses to die completely. From the days of 'Mr. Chip's Chat' and the inky, misspelled efforts of various 'Orfice' Boys, it's not a great step to the superheroic 'Big E' of Tornado, the Action Man of Action (who has since taken over the fabled position of Old Wooden Leg), and Vector 13. This air of unbreakable traditionalism, anthology formats, and 'Great News Pals' rhetoric still holds sway.

Still, it avoids direct conflict with readers, which broke out in the **Judge Dredd Megazine** in August when the paper began running 20 pages of reprints out of 52 pages, almost as many reprint pages as new stories: new story art clocked in at 23 pages that issue. The anger was directed at David Bishop and 'Dreddlines', the paper's letter pages, proved a lively forum for the pros and cons, with openly aggressive correspondents Matt Nixon and 'Sloano' taking on...well, just about everybody. Flame wars are not what you expect from British comics.

Will the problem be solved by the recent slimlining of the paper - down to 44 pages total, but now with 30 pages of new story and art for the same price? The first issue began what perhaps the paper needs most: a genuine epic for its readers to get their teeth into. The honour of starting the paper's renaissance should have rested with 'America II', the long-awaited sequel to John Wagner and Colin MacNeil's 1990 highlight in modern Dredd history; it should have created a major buzz, but generated little more that a hum. And is it just me who thinks that Colin MacNeil has turned into Gary Erskine?

Despite all the complaints, **2000AD** and the **Megazine** remain the pinnacle of British boys' comics, and attract some excellent artists. With Dermot Power riding high as artist on 'Slaine' (always 2000AD's reward of excellence), and Paul Johnson back in the fold, there is still space for upcoming talents, honing their art, ready for that leap across the Atlantic, taking some genuine storytelling talent with them. The ability to tell a story is something too many young American artists are ignorant of, but something that British audiences demand. That shows most clearly in the popularity of certain American comics in the UK which cannot sustain a home audience. Expect Steve Sampson, Jim Murray and Jason Brashill to start picking up dollar cheques soon (and, lads, don't forget there's a five pound standing charge at banks for dollar cheques, so try and get cheques made out in sterling, eh?).

Distribution in the UK is dominated by the newsagent chain, W.H. Smiths, who control up to 75% of the news outlets in the UK not only by dominating town centre locations, railway stations (this latter right was secured way back in 1848) and most busy thoroughfares, but also via distribution to smaller outlets and cornershops. Smiths brought in a new policy this Spring – without informing the magazine publishers who generate the majority of Smiths' vast profits – not to carry magazines that sell less than 10 copies in a shop. Smiths already split magazines into three streams: a must-carry stream, a recommended stream, and a selection to be decided by local managers (usually of local interest titles). This new policy has proven highly damaging to niche market titles since – whilst magazines can be ordered through Smiths – it is only newsstand exposure that can allow impulse purchasing; nowadays, the only way to raise the readership is a continual string of 'boom' issues – those with free gifts and giveaways – which Smiths will generally take (with the caveat that they can also decide the suitability and safety of every free gift).

With such control over the market, Smiths can also control other factors: it is they who essentially decide the initial print run on a magazine and the concept of a magazine slowly growing in stature is now a thing of the past. It must be an instant hit to be carried beyond its first issue, and – not surprisingly – the attrition rate of titles is phenomenal.

The industry remains in the hands of the publishers already established. And none come bigger than newspaper giants D.C. Thomson, whose **Beano** and **Dandy** continue to sell over a million copies a week between them, institutions amongst children and university students.

A 13-episode 'Dennis the Menace' animated TV show launched in May 1996, screening on Tuesdays at 4.10pm, racked up an audience of 2.1 million (or 50.3% of the market), and 35 licenses for the property were issued for everything from bed linen to bubblebath. Polygram released two volumes of videos in October following on from previous releases, The Beano Video in 1993 and Beano Video Stars in 1994; the latter sold over a quarter of a million copies and picked up the Best Children's Special award at the 1995 British Animation Awards. This new-found TV stardom will help sustain Dennis and the **Beano**, apt in the year Dennis celebrated his silver anniversary. Twenty five years of menacing has done nothing to tame the wild child of British comics, even as the title approaches pensionable age (**Dandy**, the older of Thomson's titles by seven months, reaches 60 in December 1997).

Another celebration for Thomson was the 2000th edition of **Bunty** in the spring of '96, an astonishing run that began way back in 1958. Long before Disney got their animators to work, Thomson's were regaling their readers with the adventures of 'Pocahontas' and a pre-Dredd Ron Smith chronicled 'The Dancing Life of Moira Kent'. **Bunty** still runs the ever-popular school soap 'The Comp' which began life in **Nikki** in 1985. Girls' comics are now limited to two titles, plus two spin-off pocket library series, and whilst both **Bunty** and **Mandy** still clearly deliver to their audience, you have to wonder what happened to the halcyon days of forty-five years ago when **School Friend** was Britain's million-plus-copy best-selling adventure comic – beating even the mighty **Eagle**. The boys' comic market has claimed its audience was hijacked by the computer games industry, but it seems that girls have disappeared in even greater numbers. Where did they go? Or was it simply the case that most girls' comics turned into photo pop mags and as the comic strips disappeared, the audience did not complain? This could well be the case if the recent example of **Barbie** is anything to go by: when switched from a comic into a magazine, sales trebled.

The legacy girls' comics left behind, oddly, was an invigorated boys' comic market: many of the creators associated with **2000AD** in its golden years worked in the girls' market (which could boast such diverse talents as John Wagner, Pat Mills, Jim Baikie and Kev O'Neill at various times), and the sensibilities of telling a story and creating characters rubbed off. It's an influence that we should perhaps mourn the loss of; I would not like to lose that unique flavour to British comics. God forbid we ever need nude cover variants to sell a comic.

Another doomed arena for comics seems to be the traditional juvenile funnies. While **Beano** and **Dandy** gain acres of free publicity from merchandise, Fleetway's Buster has been in steady decline for some years, reducing its costs this year by reducing the number of new strips, Lew Stringer's 'Tom Thug' being one of the casualties. It seems unlikely that **Buster** will survive much longer (even Fleetway's reprint humour titles seem to have disappeared). Stringer tried his own title, **Yampy Tales**, but this also folded after three issues due to lack of distribution.

D.C. Thomson are one of the few companies to continue issuing annuals (along with World International); both Fleetway and Marvel UK failed to bring out any of the traditional bumper hardbacks. In this case, it was the low profit margins offered to Britain's corner-shop retailers that caused their downfall. One notable specialised title appeared this Christmas when Thomson used the 60th anniversary of the Sunday Post to produce a retrospective **The Broons and Oor Wullie** book.

Despite this seeming lack of enthusiasm in a nation (supposedly) of shopkeepers to actually stock comics, the youth market is still said to be worth £140 million, and that's attractive to any publisher, but with the distribution system stacked against them, few publishers will risk an entirely new venture in the risky, quirky and unpredictable children's market unless they can tie their product to a television show in some way. For example, one of the most successful launches in 1996 was **Rug Rats** from Marvel, with sales of over 100,000 per issue and a schedule that jumped from four weekly to fortnightly within a few issues.

Marvel UK, as was, ceased to exist as a separate entity. In its place was Panini UK Ltd., a division of Panini s.p.a. of Modena, Italy. Marvel Comics is now one of three divisions (the others being Panini Stickers and Cards and Marvel International Distribution), and now sets its crosshairs solely on the junior UK markets from its offices in Tunbridge Wells. The move from London and a programme of cautious expansion has meant that Panini was one of the few branches of the giant Marvel Entertainment Group that has not gone into Chapter 11 bankruptcy.

Under new managing director Richard Maskell, Marvel have retained their most popular reprint titles – **Amazing X-Men**, **Astonishing Spider-Man**, **Essential X-Men**, and **Spectacular Spider-Man** – and dropped a number of low sellers – recent casualties include **Beavis and Butt-Head** and **Power Rangers**. In the summer, Maskell announced Marvel's intention to concentrate on the younger audience, adding **Action Man** and **Rug Rats** to their output soon after. Superheroes, however, have not been forgotten, and the latest title launched is a US-sized gathering of strips, **Wolverine Unleashed**. It's a shining example of Sod's Law that, as their American owner struggles along uncertainly, the British Marvel Comics appears to be at its most stable for some years.

Where Marvel are treading fearfully, Titan Magazines has rushed in to fill the void. On the backbone of **Star Trek Monthly** and **Star Wars: The Official Magazine**, and under the guidance of ex-**Doctor Who Monthly** editor John Freeman, Titan Magazines have rapidly expanded into the TV spin-off market that their parent, Titan Books, has been successfully ploughing for many years.

Three launches based on cartoons, **The Mask Adventures**, **The Real Adventures of Jonny Quest** and **Gargoyles** proved popular with younger fans. Titan's expansion behind the magazine front included the launching of a number of official fan clubs, including Britain's fastest rising club for, not surprisingly, **The X-Files**. The show's transfer to BBC1 immediately added 3 million viewers (apparently incapable of finding BBC2 on their remotes). The show became the most popular American show on British TV, with an average audience of 9.05 million viewers (for comparison, The New Adventures of Superman averaged 7.88

million, Baywatch 6.8 million and Friends 4.55 million).

A spin-off magazine, reprinting the strips published in the USA by Topps, was a soaraway success for Manga Publishing, best-known until the launch of **X-Files** for **Manga Mania**. Launched by Dick Hansom, who left the company during 1996 to pursue his interests in the theatre, **Manga Mania** had faltered with the last episodes of Katsuhiro Otomo's *Akira*; an unsteady and relentless line-up of cyberpunk and babes-with-guns strips – the most popular genres in Manga's anime video line – prompted a reworking of the title by editor Cefn Ridout. A heavy dose of Hong Kong action and body horror movies spilled into the magazine, upsetting manga traditionalists, who had already lost **Anime FX** earlier in the year. Whether it would have succeeded is a moot point, as more changes were in the wind for Manga; news of the takeover filtered onto the grapevine in September, but was only confirmed in October.

New owners Titan were clearly in the market for the **X-Files** magazine and graphic novels that can be spun-off from the title. **Manga Mania** continues under the newly announced editorship of Helen McCarthy, and the recent launch of the fortnightly **Space: Above and Beyond** to coincide with the shows appearance on terrestrial TV boosts the company's portfolio to eight titles, although mostly reprint, and mostly with the built-in time bomb of all TV tie-ins: you only attract fans of the show, and you tend to lose them when the show goes off the air. The most popular TV show tie-in comics in the UK have consistently been anthology titles that rotate characters: **TV Comic** and **Look-In** both achieved incredible runs (33 and 23 years respectively) where more specifically targetted titles wither and die without the support of their broadcast parents.

So much for Britain's big four.

But what happened to the small presses? Poor distribution and relatively high printing costs in the UK seem to dampen most enthusiasm, although there have been one or two successes recently. Two, in fact. **Strangehaven** by Gary Spencer Millidge has found itself nominated for a slew of well-deserved awards, although its survival was put in doubt by the bankruptcy of Capital Distributors. Millidge has, however, weathered the storm and continues to self-publish. Meanwhile, Heretic Press' **Six Degrees**, was given a boost by no less a patron of the arts than Dave Sim. Again, a hiccup in distribution with issue 3 could have put Martin Shipp & Marc Laming's title out of business; again, they battled on and weathered the storm, perhaps proving that even in today's climate of uncertainty, quality will out.

Talking of whom...

Comics International, the newspaper of the British comics' industry, experimented with cover design and took everyone by surprise by publishing a flip-book issue, backing issue 67 with **Warrior 1996 Spring Special** featuring two strips, 'The Liberators' and 'Big Ben', the latter ending with a hopeful "to be continued." Whilst it did little more than rescue twelve-year-old artwork from oblivion, it did start up – once again – the rumour that **Warrior** would return, or Comics International's supremo Dez Skinn would be returning to the world of editing comics, although he seemed to rule out the idea in a reply to repeated requests favouring **Warrior**'s swift return: the costs had been looked into, and the figures simply didn't favour a launch.

British fans have been well served this past year. **Panelhouse**, **Comics Forum**, **Vicious** and **Trip Wire** have between them shown that fandom is still feisty and thriving. Hurling the occasional spiky barb at the industry has always been the realm of fanzines (look at the titles of those last two named), but the industry has rarely been hurt – and can benefit heavily – by having a mirror held up to itself. Fanzines and small press publications offer a network of communication that is sometimes lacking between fans.

With the demise of the Glasgow Comic Art Convention, the main Rusty Staples' sponsored UK Comic Art Convention moved to March and lost its trade day when it was announced that DC could not attend. However, the US convention that clashed was aborted, which meant that some of DC's convention team did arrive, and without formal panels to attend found the convention far more relaxing. The year's UKCAC Awards went to a diverse, although not thoroughly unexpected, group: Best Writer: Garth Ennis (*Preacher*); Best Artist: Steve Dillon (*Preacher*); Best Writer/Artist: Frank Miller (*Sin City*); Best Auxiliary Contributor: Matt Hollingworth (Colourist – *Preacher*); Best Newcomer: Alex Ronald (**Judge Dredd: Lawman of the Future**); Best Publisher: DC; Best Graphic Novel: *Stuck Rubber Baby* by Howard Cruse; Best Book Collection: *The Tale of One Bad Rat* by Bryan Talbot; Best Ongoing Publication: **2000AD**; Best New Publication: *Preacher* (DC); Special Achievement Award: Alan Moore.

Both the annual Caption event and Independents Day at Page 45 concentrated on the smaller press market, with Stephen Holland (no relation to this writer) attracting a wide-ranging group of talents from Dave Sim & Gerhard, Gary Spencer Millidge, Jeremy Dennis and Ed Hillyer (Ilya, current *Vertigo Verite* artist, but a long-time small press champion) to the latter.

Outside of the regular comic marketplace and fan networks, Britain's most famous comic character, Dan Dare, returned to full-colour glory (drawn by Syd Jordan, of 'Jeff Hawke' fame) in the pages of **The Planet on Sunday**, and promptly disappeared again when the returns for the first issue proved that eco-awareness was not on most people's agendas on a Sunday morning.

A 30-minute pilot show, Comicana, appeared on Sky's Sci-Fi Channel on September 10, hosted by this volume's editor, Duncan McAlpine, a step towards a hoped for regular slot that will be beamed across Europe. The opportunities for comics to expand beyond print media have never been so close: with digital television just around the corner, there is every chance for well-known, and even a few obscure, comic characters to become stars of their own shows. Egmont Publications, owners of Fleetway Editions, set up Fleetway Film and TV in late 1996 to develop some of their characters in this direction. And in the wake of the disappointing returns from Judge Dredd, they are said to be keen to involve original creators in any developments. The rewards are potentially great, and it should allow those creators to augment their salaries from the declining comic field. In Britain, most of our top echelon of talent has been lured across the Atlantic by the money and market available in the USA. Time was when those creators would be able to return to the UK to produce more arty fare using the filthy lucre earned from the mainstream American publishers. Alan Moore is still one of the few following this policy, producing *From Hell*, *Lost Girls* and other stories on the back of Image hackery (bar *Supreme* which, on early showings, could well be the place for Moore to pick up the gauntlet he originally threw down with 'Marvelman'); Moore even had time to produce his first book, a collection of thematically related short stories published by Victor Gollancz in October. Bryan Talbot has also used mainstream success to finance something heartfelt in *The Tale of One Bad Rat*, even the Pleece Brothers returned to their roots with a new issue of **Velocity**.

I very much doubt if the digital revolution will wipe comics from the newsstands. In the 1950s, some feared that television would destroy the public's ability to read books, yet today there are more titles published each year than ever before. It will be one more change that realigns an industry which has already proved its ability to adapt and survive. Comics were at their peak in the late 1930s, both here and in America, and sixty years later they're still with us. Although doomsayers may say that the British comics industry risks being dragged off to some shallow grave, scuffing its heels in the gravel, it has a tenacity that will see comics survive into the new millennium. Perhaps not as you or I know them, but they'll still be here.

ACKNOWLEDGEMENTS

Once again I have to thank my colleagues and fellow collectors who have helped the section grow in accuracy. My sincere thanks go to everyone who has helped in the past eight years, and whilst singling out names seems a little unfair, the annual list was getting a little unweildy, so I'd like to particularly thank John and Sue Allen-Clark, David Ashford, Mike Bentley, Howard Corn of *Eagle Times*, Bill Lofts, Ray Moore, Lance Rickman, and Bryon Whitworth of *The Comic Journal*. Research isn't done in isolation, and I have to thank all those other historians, researchers, dealers and retailers who have, by their previous efforts, made my job somewhat easier.

PRICING

British comics are often graded differently to American comics and many American comic grades will have little meaning. In the main, we have listed only one price corresponding to an American grade of Very Fine: complete, clean, with no major defects, sometimes referred to as British Grade A.

As ever, we leave you with this very important note: the prices listed here are just a guide based upon averages of sales we have noted from dealers. They were not issued to us on tablets of stone, and this is not a bible. The person who decides on whether a price is right is you, the buyer, and a combination of opportunity, desire and cashflow.

When selling comics, the rule of thumb is: don't presume that two contemporary papers have the same value to a collector. Prices depend on two things: supply and demand. You may be able to supply the rarest comic in the world, but it's only 'worth' what you're asking if somebody wants to buy it at that price.

Steve Holland, Colchester, Feb 1997

BRITISH COMICS

Points to Remember

- THIS BOOK IS ONLY A GUIDE AND SHOULD BE TREATED AS ONLY A GUIDE.
- COMICS SHOULD BE VERY STRICTLY GRADED, EVEN UNDER-GRADED, TO ENSURE CORRECT VALUATION
- WHEN GRADING A COMIC, THE WHOLE COMIC MUST BE GRADED, NOT JUST THE COVER. START FROM THE INSIDE AND WORK OUT.
- FOR THE BRITISH COMICS SECTION, A SINGLE NEAR MINT PRICE HAS BEEN GIVEN. HOWEVER, BRITISH COMICS ARE OFTEN GRADED DIFFERENTLY FROM AMERICAN COMICS AND THE TOP GRADE OF BRITISH COMIC IS GENERALLY REFERRED TO AS "GRADE A" IN BRITISH COLLECTING TERMS, THAT IS COMPLETE, FLAT, CLEAN AND WITH NO MAJOR DEFECTS. PLEASE THEN REFER TO PERCENTAGE CHARTS AT THE BOTTOM OF EACH PAGE. OWING TO PAPER QUALITY AND AN ASSORTMENT OF SHAPES AND SIZES BRITISH COMICS AND ANNUALS IN PERFECT NEAR MINT CONDITION ARE EXTREMELY UNUSUAL. THIS PARTICULAR GRADE IS SOMETIMES REFERRED TO IN BRITISH TERMS AS "EXCELLENT".
- PRICES OF COMICS ARE CALCULATED AND SET AT TIME OF GOING TO PRESS ONLY. PLEASE ALLOW FOR A PERCENTAGE INCREASE AT LEAST IN LINE WITH INFLATION THROUGHOUT THE YEAR. THIS PERCENTAGE MAY BE MUCH HIGHER FOR OLDER, SCARCER OR IMPORTANT ISSUES.
- SOME COMICS, PARTICULARLY RARE AND "KEY" ISSUES, MAY FETCH PREMIUM PRICES IN HIGH GRADE CONDITION, IN EXCEPTIONAL CIRCUMSTANCES THESE MAY BE CALCULATED IN MULTIPLES OF GUIDE (1.25, 1.5, 2.0 times Guide – SEE RELEVANT SECTION IN THE GENERAL INTRODUCTION). FOR THOSE NEW TO COLLECTING, IT IS ADVISED TO SEEK PROFESSIONAL OPINIONS
- SCARCE, RARE AND VERY RARE HAVE BEEN USED SPARINGLY. THEY MUST NOT BE OVER-USED OR USED CASUALLY.
- THIS BOOK MUST AT ALL TIMES BE USED WITH COMMON SENSE AND FLEXIBILITY OF INTERPRETATION WITH REGARD TO PRICES.

N.MINT

A1

Atomeka Press; 1 May 1989-6a, Mar 1992

1 96pgs; Moore, Gaiman, Milligan scripts, Windsor-Smith, Leach, Campbell, Bolton, McKeever, Bolland, Parkhouse, Sienkiewicz, McKean, Motter, Gibbons, McCarthy, Fabry art; strips include Warpsmith, Deadface, Bojeffries Saga, Mr X, Flaming Carrot £5.00
2 128pgs; Moore, Milligan scripts, Pedro Henry text, Lloyd, Hewlett, Parkhouse, Bolton, Michael T. Gilbert, Fabry, Bond, Windsor-Smith, Bisley, McKeever, Campbell art; strips include Mr Monster, Deadface, Mr X (montage), Bojeffries, Pressbutton text £5.00
3 80pgs; Morrison, Moore scripts, Campbell, Bolland, McKean, Fabry, Bond, Bolton, Parkhouse, Moebius art £3.50
4 96pgs; James Robinson, Moore scripts, Hewlett, Fabry, Moebius, Sienkiewicz, Bolton, Parkhouse art £3.50
5 96pgs; Gaiman, Milligan scripts, Fabry, Ewins, Joe Kubert, Lloyd art, Jeff Hawke by Sydney Jordan & Goring/Rich £4.50
6a 72pgs; Tank Girl by Hewlett, Campbell, Fabry art £3.00
The A1 True Life Bikini Confidential No.1 (1990) A.Moore, S.Moore scripts, Milligan text, Gilbert, Bolland, Hewlett, Jackson, Parkhouse, Leach art £4.00
Note: Issue 6b was announced but not released.

AARGH!

Mad Love; Oct 1988

nn Anti Clause 28 benefit comic; Moore, Gaiman scripts, Talbot, O'Neill, Sim/ Gerhardt, Spiegelman, Bissette, Emerson, Gibbons, Leach, Sienkiewicz, Miller art, McKean cover £3.50

A.B.C. WARRIORS

Fleetway-Quality; 1 1990-8 1991

1 2000AD reprints begin £1.25
2-8 £1.00

A.B.C. WARRIORS, THE

Titan (Best of 2000AD); 1983-1988; 1991

Book One £4.50
Book Two £4.50
Book Three Bisley, S.M.S. art £5.00
Book Four Bisley S.M.S. art £5.00
The Black Hole (Oct 1991) reprints books 3 & 4 £8.00

A.B.C. WARRIORS (2000AD BOOKS)

Mandarin; Sep 1992

Khronicles of Khaos 2000AD reprints, Kevin Walker art £7.00

ABSLOM DAAK: DALEK KILLER

Marvel; 1990

nn reprints from Dr Who Weekly, Dillon, Lloyd art newly coloured £6.00

ACCIDENT MAN

Apocalypse (Apocalypse Presents); Jun 1991-Aug 1991

nn reprints from Toxic 1-6, Martin Emond art £2.50
nn reprints from Toxic, Duke Mighton art £2.50
Note: new series later published by Dark Horse (USA).

ACE

Harrier; 1 1987

1 Eddie Campbell art £1.00

ACTION

IPC; 14th Feb 1976-16th Oct 1976, 36 unnumbered issues; 23rd Oct 1976 (not distributed)

14 Feb 1976 Dredger by Horacio Altuna, Hellman of Hammer Force by Mike Dorey, Blackjack by Leopoldo Sanchez, Play Till You Drop by Barrie Mitchell, Hook Jaw by Ramon Sola, Sport's Not For Losers by Dudley Wynn, The Coffin Sub by Angelo Todaro, The Running Man by Lalia all begin £4.00
14 Feb 1976 with free gift (Red Arrow plane) £5.00
21 Feb-9 Oct 1976 £2.00
16 Oct 1976 last issue of original run £3.00
23 Oct 1976 withdrawn from sale because of violent content, some copies printed for editorial checking, very rare £25.00

FREE GIFT ISSUES

14 Feb 1976 Red Arrow plane 21 Feb 1976 Hook Jaw Transfer, 28 Feb 1976 16 Soccer Cards, 29 Mar 1976 Invasion (game).

CHRONOLOGY

3 Apr 1976 last Coffin Sub. 24 Apr 1976 last Play Till You Drop, Green's Grudge War by Belardinelli starts. 1 May 1976 last Sport's Not For Losers, no Hook Jaw, Look Out For Lefty by Barrie Mitchell starts. 8 May 1976 Death Game 1999 by Costa begins, no Hook Jaw. 12 Jun 1976 last Running Man. 19 Jun 1976 Hell's Highway by Mike White begins. 4 Sep 1976 last Blackjack. 11 Sep 1976 Kid's Rule OK by Mike White begins. 25 Sep 1976 Probationer by Tom Hirst begins.

ARTISTS/FEATURES

Horacio Altuna in 14 Feb-9 May 1976. Massimo Belardinelli in 24 Apr-18 Sep 1976. Ricardo Villagran in 19 Jun, 17 Jul, 14 Aug-21 Aug, 4 Sep, 18 Sep-25 Sep, 16 Oct 1976.

ACTION (NEW SERIES)

IPC; 4th Dec 1976-12th Nov 1977, 50 unnumbered issues (joins Battle Action)

4 Dec 1976 Dredger by Ricardo Villagran, Spinball (ex-Death Game 1999) by Costa, Look Out For Lefty by Tony Harding, Hookjaw by John Stokes, Hell's Highway by Mike White revived £2.00
11 Dec 1976-10 Sep 1977 £0.75
17 Sep 1977 Spinball retitled The Spinball Slaves £0.75
24 Sep-12 Nov 1977 £0.75

ARTISTS/FEATURES

Massimo Belardinelli in 4 Dec-18 Dec 1976. Jesus Blasco in 29 Jan-5 Feb 1977, 19 Feb-26 Feb 1977. Ron Turner in 17 Sep-12 Nov 1977. Ricardo Villagran in 4 Dec-11 Dec 1976, 8 Jan 1977, 22 Jan 1977.

ACTION ANNUAL

IPC; 1977-1985

1977-1978 £2.50
1979 Spinball by Brian Bolland £3.00
1980-1985 £2.00

ACTION COMICS

Miller; 1 1958-2 1958

1 68pgs; reprints from A1 Comics (Magazine Enterprises) £6.00
2 reprints incl. Ghost Rider by Powell, Frazetta art £4.00

ACTION DOUBLE DOUBLE COMICS

Thorpe & Porter; 1 1967-4 1968

1 bound-together remaindered copies of selected DC and Marvel comics, with new line drawn covers £2.50

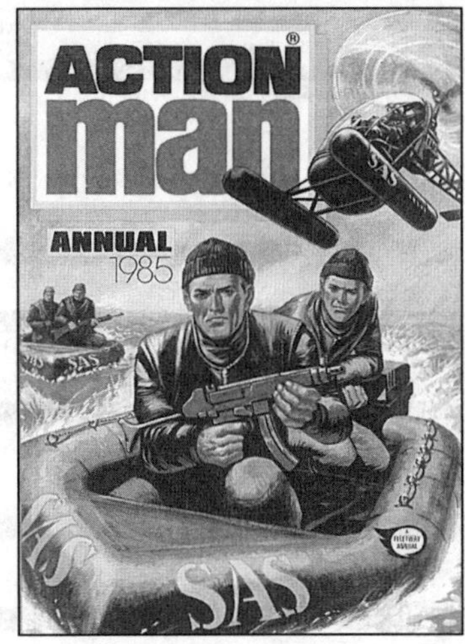

Action Man Annual 1985

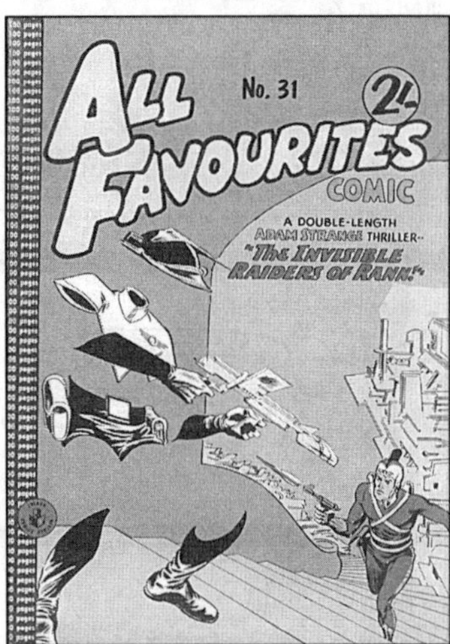

All Favourites Comic #31

Astounding Stories #94

N.MINT

2-4 £2.00
Note: contents varied from one copy to the next; an example of issue 4, for instance, contains reprints of Action Comics #350, Fantastic Four #65 and Avengers #47.

ACTION FORCE
Marvel; 1 7th Mar 1987-50 13th Feb 1988 (joins Transformers)
1 Action Force based on toy-line begins £1.00
2-13,16,18-22,24-43,47-50 £0.50
14-15 Steve Yeowell art £0.50
17 Masters of Kung Fu by Grant Morrison and Steve Yeowell £0.50
23 Brett Ewins art £0.50
44-46 Mike Collins art £0.50

ACTION FORCE ANNUAL
Marvel; 1988
1989 GI Joe reprints; original text story by Abnett/J. Paris £2.50

ACTION FORCE MINI-COMIC
IPC/CPG Products; 1 16th Jul 1983-5 10th Sep 1983 (givaway in Battle, Eagle, Tiger)
1,5 8pgs; Ron Turner art £0.50
2-4 Vano art £0.30

ACTION FORCE MONTHLY
Marvel; 1 Jun 1988-15 Aug 1989
1 £1.20
2,4-15 £0.80
3 Grant Morrison script £0.80

ACTION MAN
Northern & Shell; 1 29th Jun 1995-6 1995
1 24pgs; Mike McKone, Simon Fraser art £0.75
2-6 £0.50

ACTION MAN ANNUAL
IPC; 1985
1985 £2.50

ACTION PICTURE LIBRARY
IPC; 1 Aug 1969-30 Oct 1970
1 60pgs pocket size £3.00
2-14 £1.00
15-30 68pgs; back-up stories begin £1.00
ARTISTS/FEATURES
1 Wildcat by Redondo. 2 The Doom Machine. 3 Tiger Trap. 4 At Gunpoint. 5 Voodoo!. 6 Taken For A Ride. 7 Wall of Death. 8 Terror of the Deep by Carlos Pino. 9 Atom Pirates. 10 Frontier Fury. 11 Back From the Dead. 12 Scorpion Island. 13 Hunter!. 14 Blood Heat by Carlos Pino. 15 The Destroyer. 16 Sabotage!. 17 Scoop!. 18 Gang-Buster by Henares. 19 Cue For Murder. 20 The Supermen. 21 Mob Rule. 22 Sky-Jack!. 23 Rats of London. 24 The Bandit. 25 Time Fuse. 26 Sea Hunt. 27 The Mercenaries. 28 Salvage. 29 The Shore-Busters. 30 The Faceless Ones by Eustaquio Segrelles.

ACTION SERIES
Miller; 1-12 1958
1 68pgs; Ghost Riders, Magazine Enterprises reprints begin £6.00
2 Prairie Guns £4.00
3 B-Bar-B Riders £4.00
4 Red Mask, Frank Frazetta art £4.00
5 Thunda, Bob Powell art £4.00
6 Cave Girl, Bob Powell art £4.00
8 Cave Girl, Frank Frazetta art £4.00
9 Lone Vigilante £4.00
10 Kid Cowboy £4.00
11,12 Dan Adams, Fawcett reprints (from Gene Autrey) £5.00

ACTION SERIES
Young World (Gold Token); 1 Jul 1964-12 Sep 1964
1,8 Secret Agent X9, US newspaper reprints begin £3.00
2 Big Ben Bolt £2.00
3,10 Flash Gordon £3.00
4 Tim Tyler £2.00
5,12 Brick Bradford £2.00
6 Mandrake the Magician £2.00
7,11 Ripcord £2.00

ACTION SPECIAL
IPC; May 1976-May 1980
1976-1978 titled Action Summer Special £1.50
1979 titled Action Holiday Special £1.50
1980 titled Action Holiday Special; Erik the Viking reprint by Lawrence £1.75

ACTION STREAMLINE COMICS
Streamline; nn 1950s
nn 68pgs; US reprints £5.00

ACTION 21
Engale; 1 Jul 1988-10 Oct 1989
1 Stingray by Ron Embleton, Captain Scarlet by Embleton, Thunderbirds by Bellamy, Fireball XL5 by Mike Noble, Lady Penelope by Eric Eden, Zero-X by Mike Noble - all TV Century 21 reprints begin £2.50
2 Secret Agent X by Rab Hamilton reprints begin £2.00
3-7 £2.00
8 Angels by Jon Davis reprints from Lady Penelope begin £2.00
9-10 £2.00

ADVENTURE DOUBLE DOUBLE COMICS
Thorpe & Porter; 1-3 1967
1 bound-together remainders of DC and Marvel comics, some with new line drawn covers £2.50
2-3 £2.00
Note: contents varied from one copy to the next; an example of issue 3, for instance, reprints Adventure Comics #355, World's Finest #163, Wonder Woman #163 and Aquaman #28

ADVENTURES INTO THE UNKNOWN
Arnold Book Co./Thorpe & Porter; 1 1950-?, 163+ issues
1 68pgs; very scarce; American Comics Group reprints £12.50
2-5 £5.00
6-163? £2.50

N.MINT

ADVENTURES INTO WEIRD WORLDS
Thorpe & Porter; 1 1952-?
1 68pgs; rare; Marvel reprints £20.00
2-5 very scarce £10.00
6-20 scarce £5.00
21-? £2.50

ADVENTURES OF BLONDIE AND DAGWOOD
Associated Newspapers; nn Feb 1957
nn - 84pgs; reprints American newspaper strip by Chic Young £5.00

ADVENTURES OF FAT FREDDY'S CAT
Hassle Free Press; 1 1978-5 1979
1-5 reprints US underground strips by Gilbert Shelton £4.00

ADVENTURES OF LUTHER ARKWRIGHT, THE
Book 1: Rat Trap (Never Ltd, Dec 1982) Bryan Talbot script/art begins, most copies have binding defects and loose pages £8.00
Book 1: Rat Trap (Valkyrie, Nov 1989) £4.50
Book 2: Transfiguration (Valkyrie, Dec 1987) £6.00
Book 3: Gotterdammerung (Valkyrie, Jun 1989) £6.00

ADVENTURES OF LUTHER ARKWRIGHT, THE
Valkyrie; 1 Oct 1987-10 Apr 1989
1 Bryan Talbot script/art begins £2.50
2-7 £1.50
8-9 all new material (first publication of Book 3) £1.75
10 ARKeology; contributions by Talbot, Gaiman & McKean, Morrison £2.00

AIR ACE PICTURE LIBRARY
Fleetway/IPC; 1 Jan 1960-545 Nov 1970
1 60pgs pocket size; Target Top Secret by Solano Lopez £12.50
2 £5.00
3-50 £2.00
51-199 £1.00
200-399 £0.75
400 mostly reprints from hereon £0.50
401-545 68pgs from 492, most have back-up strips £0.50
ARTISTS/FEATURES
1 Target Top Secret by Solano Lopez. 2 Out of the Sun. 3 Torpedo Strike by Luis Ramos?. 4 Mission Completed. 5 Sky High by Solano Lopez. 6 MacGregor's Crew by Solano Lopez. 7 Seek and Strike by Mike Western. 8 Hurribombers. 9 Endless Battle by Solano Lopez. 10 Objective Destroyed by Ian Kennedy. 11 Scramble! by Ferdinando Tacconi. 12 Tiger in the Sky by Solano Lopez.Other issues incl. art by Luis Bermejo. Kurt Caesar. Joe Colquhoun in 35. Fernando Fernandez. Ian Kennedy. Solano Lopez. Jose Ortiz. Ferdinando Tacconi. Ron Turner in 141,450. Mike Western in 7,23,46.

AIR ACE PICTURE LIBRARY HOLIDAY SPECIAL
Fleetway/IPC; May 1969-1979?
1969 224pgs; reprints from Air Ace Picture Library begin £2.00
1970-1979 later issues 192pgs £1.00

AIRBOY COMICS
Streamline/United Anglo-American; 1951 (5+ issues)
nn 28pgs; reprints from Hillman £9.00
nn 36pgs £9.00
3-5 £6.00

AIRBOY COMICS
Thorpe & Porter; 1 1953
1 68pgs; reprints from Hillman £8.00

AJAX ADVENTURE ANNUAL
Popular Press; 1950s
nn incl. Dollman, Plastic Man reprints by Lloyd Cole; McLoughlin cover £7.50

AKIRA
Mandarin; Jan 1995
Book 1 320pgs; Katsuhiro Otomo reprints £11.00

ALAN MOORE'S SHOCKING FUTURES
Titan (Best of 2000AD); Nov 1986
nn 2000AD reprints by Alan Moore £5.00

ALAN MOORE'S TWISTED TIMES
Titan (Best of 2000AD); Jan 1987
nn 2000AD reprints by Alan Moore £4.50

ALEC
Escape; Jul 1984-Sep 1986/ Acme; Jun 1990
Episodes in the Life of Alec McGarry 36pgs (1,000 copies) £5.00
Love and Beerglasses £3.00
Doggie in the Window £2.50
The Complete Alec (Acme) 144pgs £8.00
Note: all Eddie Campbell script/art. Later episodes published by Fantagraphics and Dark Horse (USA)

ALIAS SMITH AND JONES
World; 1976-1977
1976 64pgs; 4 strips + 2 text stories £3.00
1977 64pgs; 3 strips + 6 text stories £2.50

ALICE IN WONDERLAND
Miller; nn Nov 1941
nn 20pgs small square; reprints from US newspaper strip redrawn by British artist £3.00

ALIEN 3
Dark Horse; 1 Aug 1992-3 Sep 1992
1-3 reprints US movie adaptation with new text features £1.50

ALIENS
(see also Superman)
Titan; 1990-present
Aliens Book 1 (1990) Dark Horse reprints begin £7.00
Aliens Book 2 (1990) £7.50
Aliens: Earth War (1992) £9.00
Aliens versus Predator (1992) £10.00
Aliens: Genocide (Apr 1993) £9.00
Aliens: Hive (1993) Kelley Jones art £9.00
Aliens: Newt's Tale (Nov 1994) retells Aliens movie from Newt's perspective 7.00
Aliens: Rogue (Nov 1994) Will Simpson art £9.00

N.MINT

Aliens/Predator: War (Aug 1996) £13.00
Aliens: Stronghold (Oct 1996) £10.00
Aliens: Outbreak (Oct 1996) £12.00

ALIENS
Trident/Dark Horse; 1 Feb 1991-17 Jun 1992
1 Aliens, Predator, Aliens vs Predator reprints begin £1.75
2-16 £1.50
17 published by Dark Horse; Bisley art £1.50

ALIENS (NEW SERIES)
Dark Horse; v2:1 Jul 1992-22 Apr 1994
1 Aliens: Hive (ends 9), Predator: Cold War (ends 8) reprints begin, Bolton cover £1.50
2-8 Newt's Tale reprints £1.50
9 Aliens: Sacrifice by Milligan & Johnson begins, Colonial Marines reprints begin, free Aliens: Countdown comic pt.1 £1.50
10 Aliens: Countdown comic pt.2, Tribes reprints begin (ends 16), Johnson art £1.50
11-12 Johnson art ends £1.50
12 Aliens: Horror Show begins (ends 14), Roach art £1.50
13 Aliens: Holy War by Mike Cook & Christian Gorny begins, Roach art £1.50
14 Roach art ends £1.50
15 Aliens: Backsplash begins (ends 16) £1.50
16-17,19-22 £1.50
18 Renegade by Chris Claremont £1.50

ALIENS VS PREDATOR: THE DEADLIEST OF THE SPECIES
Boxtree; Apr-Nov 1995
Aliens vs Predator Book 1 (Apr 1995) Dark Horse reprints by Chris Claremont, Jackson Guice, Eduardo Barreto £10.00
Aliens vs Predator Book 2 (Nov 1995) £10.00

ALL ACTION COMIC
Moring; nn 1956?
nn 68pgs, softcover; McLoughlin, Turner, Embleton reprints £10.00

ALL FAVOURITES
(see Century Comic, Five-Score Comic Monthly, Mighty Comic)
K.G. Murray (Australia); 1 mid-1950s-31? early-1960s
1 rare; 100pgs, squarebound; Mational Periodical Publications reprints, incl. Tomahawk, Tommy Tomorrow, Mr. District Attorney, Congo Bill, Johnny Thunder, Wonder Woman £75.00
2 rare £50.00
3-5 very scarce £40.00
6-10 scarce £35.00
11-31? scarce £30.00
Note: issues beyond #31 are thought to exist. Later issues incl. Atom, Viking Prince, Adam Strange, etc

ALL FAVOURITES (2ND SERIES)
K.G. Murray (Australia); 1 late 1960s-? early 1970s
1 US reprints £20.00
2-? £12.00

ALL TOP COMICS
Streamline/United Anglo-American; nn 1949
nn 28pgs; reprints from Fox £6.00

AMAZING STORIES
Alan Class; nn 196?-?
nn 68pgs; reprints from American Comics Group £12.00
2-10 scarce £5.00
11-? £2.50

AMAZING STORIES OF SUSPENSE
Alan Class; 1 196?-?
1-? 68pgs; incl. Ditko Captain Atom art £2.50

AMAZING WORLD OF DOCTOR WHO
PBS; 1976
nn reprints stories from Dr. Who Annual 1976, Daleks from TV21 £10.00

AMERICA
Fleetway; 1991
nn 64pgs; Judge Dredd Megazine reprints by John Wagner & Colin MacNeil £5.00

AMERICAN COMIC ANNUAL
Miller; nn 1943
nn 68pgs; reprints US newspaper strips £5.00

AMERICAN EAGLE WESTERN
Strato; 1 1954?
1 US reprints; John Severin cover £6.00

ANDERSON PSI DIVISION
(see Judge Anderson)
Fleetway; 1991
Shamballa (1991) 64pgs; 2000AD reprints by Alan Grant & Arthur Ranson £3.00
Note: heavily remaindered in 1994

ANDY CAPP
(see also Laugh Again with Andy Capp)
Mirror; 1958-present
(1) The Andy Capp Book (1958) reprints Daily Mirror strip by Reg Smythe £15.00
(2) Andy Capp's Spring Tonic (1959) bottle shaped £7.50
(3) Life With Andy Capp (1959) £7.50
(4) Andy Capp's Spring Collection (1960) £6.00
(5) Best of Andy Capp (1960) 1st oblong £5.00
(6) Laugh With Andy Capp (1961) £5.00
(7) World of Andy Capp (1961) £4.00
(8) More Andy Capp (1962) £4.00
(9) Andy Capp, I Must Be Dreaming (1962) £4.00
(10) Andy Capp Picks His Favourites (1963) £4.00
(11) Happy Days With Andy Capp (1963) £4.00
(12) Laugh At Life With Andy Capp (1964) £4.00
(13) Andy Capp and Florrie (1964) £3.00
(14) All the Best From Andy Capp (1965) £3.00
(15) (Andy in wash-tub) £3.00
(16) (Carving on tree) £3.00
(17) (Andy heading goal) £3.00
18-20 numbered inside £2.50
21-46 £2.50
47-49,51-53 copyright dated annually, cy1983 onwards £2.50
50 Andy Capp Strikes Gold! £2.50
The World of Andy Capp (1980-1986) magazine format £3.00
This Is Your Life Andy Capp (1986) £3.00
The Cream of Andy Capp (Mirror, 1965) hardcover, issued with dw £10.00
You're A Star Andy Capp (Mirror, Mar 1988) £2.00
The World of Andy Capp (Titan, Oct 1990) £9.00
Don't Wait Up (Ravette, Apr 1992) £3.00
After A Few (Ravette, Apr 1992) £3.00

ANDY DEVINE
Miller; 50 1950-?
50 reprints from Fawcett £5.00
51-? £2.50

ANGELS ANNUAL, THE
Century 21; 1967
1967 scarce £12.00

ANGELS STORYBOOK, THE
Century 21; A2 1968
A2 £9.00

ARIZONA KID, THE
Streamline/United Anglo-American; 1 1952
1 28pgs; reprints from Marvel £3.00

ARTHUR ASKEY'S ANNUAL
D.C. Thomson; 1940
(1940) very scarce £40.00
Note: no more issued, although more were planned

ASTERIX
Brockhampton Press/ Hodder & Stoughton; 1969-present
Asterix the Gaul (Brockhampton, 1969) French reprints begin £10.00
Asterix and Cleopatra (Brockhampton, 1969) £10.00
Asterix the Gladiator (Brockhampton, 1969) £10.00
Asterix in Britain (Brockhampton, 1970) £8.00
Asterix the Legionary (Brockhampton, 1970) £8.00
Asterix in Spain (Brockhampton, 1971) £5.00
Asterix and the Big Fight (Brockhampton, 1971) £5.00
Asterix and the Roman Agent (Brockhampton, 1972) £5.00
Asterix and the Olympic Games (Brockhampton, 1972) £5.00
Asterix in Switzerland (Brockhampton, 1973) £5.00
The Mansions of the Gods (Brockhampton, 1973) £5.00
Asterix and the Laurel Wreath (Brockhampton, 1974) £5.00
Asterix and the Goths (Brockhampton, 1974) £5.00
Asterix and the Soothsayer (Brockhampton, 1975) £5.00
Asterix and the Golden Sickle (Hodder, 1975) £3.00
Asterix and the Great Crossing (Hodder, 1976) £3.00
Asterix and the Cauldron (Hodder, 1976) £3.00
Asterix and the Chieftain's Shield (Hodder, 1977) £3.00
Asterix and Caesar's Gift (Hodder, 1977) £3.00
Asterix and the Normans (Hodder, 1978) £3.00
The Twelve Tasks of Asterix (Hodder, 1978) based on the film £3.00
Obelix and Co. (Hodder, 1979) £3.00
Asterix and the Banquet (Hodder, 1979) £3.00
Asterix in Corsica (Hodder, 1979) £3.00
Asterix in Belgium (Hodder, 1980) £3.00
Asterix and the Black Gold (Hodder, 1982) £3.00
Asterix and Son (Hodder, 1983) £3.00
Asterix versus Caesar (Hodder, 1986) based on the film £3.00
Asterix and the Magic Carpet (Hodder, 1988) £3.00
How Obelix Fell into the Magic Potion When He was a Little Boy (Hodder, 1989) £3.00
Asterix and the Secret Weapon (Hodder, 1992) cased £6.00
Asterix and the Secret Weapon (Hodder, 1993) softcover £4.00
Operation Getafix: Book of the Film (Hodder, 1990) £1.50
Asterix the Gaul (contains: Asterix in Britain, Asterix in Switzerland, Asterix the Gaul) £4.00
Asterix and the Romans (contains: Asterix the Legionary, Asterix & the Chieftain's Shield, The Mansions of the Gods, Asterix in Belgium) (Hodder, 1986) £4.00
Asterix the Brave (contains: Asterix and the Golden Sickle, Asterix and the Cauldron, Asterix and the Normans, Asterix and the Great Crossing) (Hodder, 1987) £4.00
Note: omnibus editions heavily remaindered in 1995

ASTERIX ADVENTURE GAMES BOOKS
Hodder & Stoughton; 1986-present
Asterix to the Rescue (1986) £2.00
The Meeting of the Chieftains (1989) £2.00
Idol of the Gauls (Apr 1990) £2.00

ASTONISHING STORIES
Alan Class; nn 196?-?
nn 68pgs; reprints from American Comics Group, Atlas £10.00
2-5 scarce £5.00
6-? £2.50

ASTOUNDING COMIC ADVENTURES
(see Super Duper Comics)

ASTOUNDING
Streamline; nn 1952
nn £8.00

ASTOUNDING STORIES
Alan Class; 1 Feb 1966-195 Apr 1989
1 68pgs; reprints from Marvel, American Comics Group, Archie £3.50
2 £2.00
3-5 £1.50
6-195 £1.00

N.MINT

AVALON

Harrier; 1 Oct 1986-14 Mar 1988
1 Phil Elliott art £1.00
2-14 £0.60

AVENGERS

(see also New Avengers Annual, TV Crimebusters)
Souvenir/Atlas; 1967-1969
1967 Diana Rigg £20.00
1968 Linda Thorson £12.50
1969 Linda Thorson, scarce £15.00

AVENGERS, THE

Thorpe & Porter; 1 1966
1 68pgs, Diana Rigg; Mick Anglo art, very scarce £50.00
Note: an American comic John Steed - Emma Peel (Gold Key, 1968) is given inside as Avengers No.1, the title changed to avoid copyright problems with Marvel; this has nothing to do with the above title, the strips being coloured reprints from TV Comic (qv).

AVENGERS, THE

Marvel; 1 22nd Sep 1973-147 14th Jul 1976 (joins Mighty World of Marvel)
1 36pgs; The Avengers, Doctor Strange reprints begin £2.00
1 with free gift (sheet of transfers) £4.00
2 £1.50
2 with free gift (Avengers Wonder Weapon) £3.00
3-27,29-94 £1.00
28 1st "Avengers & Master of Kung Fu" £1.25
95 1st "Avengers & Savage Sword of Conan" £1.25
96-147 £1.00

AVENGERS ANNUAL, THE

Marvel/World Distributors; 1974-1977
cover year 1975 80pgs; reprints #110-112; colour £6.00
1976 64pgs; reprints #83-85; colour £5.00
1977 80pgs; reprints #143, Giant Size Conan #1, Conan #39,57; colour £4.00
1978 reprints #59-60, Conan #24; colour £3.50

AVENGERS TREASURY

Marvel; nn 1982
nn 56pgs; US reprints, Dave Gibbons cover £1.50

AVENGERS WINTER SPECIAL

Marvel; nn Nov 1982
nn US reprints £1.25

B

BAD COMPANY

Titan (Best of 2000AD); Aug 1987-Dec 1988
Book One 2000AD reprints by Milligan & Ewins/McCarthy begin £4.50
Book Two £4.50
Book Three The Bewilderness £4.50
Book Four The Krool Heart £4.50

BARBARIENNE

(see Cuirass)
Harrier; 1 Mar 1987-8 Nov 1988
1 28pgs; Nick Neocleus art £1.50
2-5 28pgs; Nick Neocleous art 2-4, John Marshall art 5 £1.25
6-8 36pgs titled Barbarienne Versus Cuirass; John Marshall art £1.00

BAREFOOT GEN

Penguin; 1989, 1990
Barefoot Gen reprints Hadashi no Gen by Keiji Nakazawa £5.00
Barefoot Gen, new edition (1995) with intro by Art Spiegelman £8.00
Barefoot Gen: The Day After £4.00
Barefoot Gen: The Day After new edition (1995) £8.00

BASH STREET KIDS BOOK

D.C. Thomson; Sep 1979-present (bi-annual at first, now annual)
1980 £10.00
1982 £7.50
1984 £7.50
1986 £6.00
1989 £5.00
1990-1996 £3.00

BASH STREET KIDS SUMMER SPECIAL

D.C. Thomson; 1994-present
1994 £1.50
1995 £1.00

BATMAN

K.G. Murray (Australia); 1 1950?-125? 1962?
1 very rare; b/w reprints of original Batman and Detective Comics £150.00
2 very rare £75.00
3-5 rare £35.00
6-10 very scarce £20.00
11-50 £15.00
51-125? £12.50

BATMAN

Four Square Books (NEL); 1966
Batman paperback format reprints, origin by Bob Kane £5.00
Batman versus The Penguin £5.00
Batman versus The Joker £5.00
Batman versus The Catwoman £5.00
Titan reprints, each £1.50

BATMAN (TRADE PAPERBACKS)

Titan Books; 1986-present
The Dark Knight Returns (1986) Miller story/art £9.00
Year One (1988) Miller story, Mazzuchelli art £6.00
The Killing Joke (1988) by Moore & Bolland £2.50
Year Two (1989) Davis/McFarlane art £6.00
Vow From the Grave (1989) £6.00
Gotham By Gaslight (1989) £2.50
The Joker's Revenge (1989) £6.00
Challenge of the Man-Bat (1989) £6.00
A Death in the Family (1989) Death of Robin £2.50
The Demon Awakes (1989) £6.00
Arkham Asylum (1989) hardback, by Morrison & McKean £15.00
Arkham Asylum (1990) softcover £9.00
Digital Justice (1990) hardback £15.00
The Frightened City (1990) £6.00
Red Water, Crimson Death (1990) £6.00
Batman 3-D (1990) £5.50
The Cult (1991) £8.50
Gothic (Aug 1991) Legends of the Dark Knight 6-10 reprints £8.50
Batman versus Predator (Jul 1992) by Gibbons & Kubert/Kubert £8.00
Red Rain (Jul 1992) Moench/Jones/Jones III £6.00
Shaman (Feb 1993) Legends of the Dark Knight reprints £8.00
Sword of Azrael (1993) Joe Quesada art £6.00
Venom (Sep 1993) Legends of the Dark Knight reprints £6.50
Knightfall: Broken Bat (Nov 1993) 288pgs; Batman, Detective reprints £8.00
Knightfall: Who Rules the Night (Nov 1993) 296pgs; Batman, Detective, Showcase, Shadow of the Bat reprints £8.00
Collected Legends of the Dark Knight (Apr 1994) Legends/Dark Knight reprints £8.50
Ten Nights of the Beast (Aug 1994) reprints Batman #417-420, Jim Aparo art £4.00
Dark Joker - The Wild (Sep 1994) Elseworlds novel, Kelley Jones art £6.00
The Last Angel (Nov 1994) Lee Moder/Scott Hanna art £8.00
Castle of the Bat (Dec 1994) Bo Hampton art £4.00
Batman featuring Two-Face and The Ridder (Aug 1995) Bob Kane, Sam Kieth art £9.00
Batman vs Predator II: Bloodmatch (Dec 1995) Paul Gulacy art £5.00
Batman: The Last Arkham (Jan 1996) Norm Breyfogle art £9.00
Superman/Batman: Alternate Histories (May 1996) reprints various annuals £10.00
Contagion (Jun 1996) reprints crossover series £9.00

BATMAN ADVENTURES

(see Batman: The Collected Adventures)
Fleetway Editions; 1 Mar 1993-?
1 DC reprints begin £1.20
2-? £0.50

BATMAN ALBUM

(publisher?); 1-2
1-2 64pgs, card covers £25.00

BATMAN AND SUPERMAN

Fleetway Editions; 1 Mar 1994-? 1995?
1 Batman, Superman reprints begin, Who's Who in Superman booklet £1.20
2 Knightfall continued from Batman Special #4 £1.00
3-? £0.75

BATMAN ANNUAL/BATMAN OFFICIAL ANNUAL

Atlas/Top Sellers/London Editions/World/Fleetway; 1960-1994?
1960-61 scarce, b/w reprints; also incl. John Jones, Kit Carson £100.00
1961-62 £50.00
1962-63 also incl. Roy Raymond, Congorilla £30.00
1963-64 £20.00
1964-65 £15.00
1965-66 80pgs; monochrome colour throughout £12.50
1967 also incl. John Jones £12.50
1968 Top Sellers; Adam West cover; reprints incl. Detective #345 £15.00
1969 Top Sellers; Batman and Robin in Batmobile cover; light blue back cover,1960s DC reprints £12.50
1970 Top Sellers; titled Batman Bumper Book £9.00
1971 Top Sellers; titled Batman Bumper Book, feature on John Steed/Emma Peel Avengers £9.00
1972 Brown Watson Ltd; titled Batman and Robin Annual #1; reprints Detective Comics #404 with Neal Adams art £6.00
1973-1978 £5.00
1979 Egmont; entitled Batman Official Annual (to 1985?); incl. origin of Batman by Kane £5.00
1980 Egmont; reprints Team-Up, plus from 1950s £5.00
1981 Egmont; reprints Batman/Swamp Thing x-over (Swamp Thing #7), Wrightson art £5.00
1982 London Editions; 78pgs; Bolland cover, Arthur Ranson end-papers £6.00
1983, 1986-1988 £4.00
1984 London Editions; 64pgs; Dave Gibbons cover £5.00
1985 London Editions; 64pgs; Alan Moore + Jamie Delano text stories, Alan Davis illos, Talbot cover £6.00
1989 London Editions; reprints Detective #570, Alan Davis art £3.50
1990,1992,1994-present £3.00
1991 World; reprints Detective #474-476, Marshall Rogers art £3.00
1993 Fleetway; reprints Batman #460-461, plus classic from 1945 £3.00

BATMAN DOUBLE DOUBLE COMICS

Thorpe & Porter; nn 1967
nn bound-together remaindered copies of Batman #188, #189, #196 with new line-drawn cover £5.00

BATMAN/JUDGE DREDD: JUDGEMENT ON GOTHAM

Fleetway/DC, Mandarin (2000AD Books); 1991, 1992
nn (Dec 1991) 64pgs softcover; Batman vs Judge Dredd by Wagner/Grant & Bisley £5.00
nn (Jan 1992) news-stand magazine edition £3.00
nn Mandarin (Sep 1992) softcover £6.00

BATMAN/JUDGE DREDD: THE ULTIMATE RIDDLE

Fleetway, Hamlyn (2000AD Books); 1995, 1996
nn (1995) magazine sized DC reprint by Wagner/Grant, Critchlow & Power £3.00
nn Hamlyn (Jul 1996) softcover £7.00

BATMAN/JUDGE DREDD: VENDETTA IN GOTHAM

Fleetway, Mandarin (2000AD Books); 1993, 1995
nn (Nov 1993) by Wagner/Grant & Cam Kennedy, DC reprint, Mignola cover; magazine format £3.00
nn Mandarin (May 1995) softcover £6.00

BATMAN MONTHLY

London Editions/Fleetway Editions; 1 Aug 1990-55 Feb 1993; (becomes Batman Monthly (New Series))
1 US reprints begin £2.00

	N.MINT
2-3	£1.25
4-10,12-23	£1.00
11 Batman 50th Anniversary issue	£1.25
24-29	£0.85
30-55	£0.85

BATMAN MONTHLY (NEW SERIES)

Fleetway Editions; Vol 2. No.1 Mar 1993-11 Jan 1994 (becomes Batman & Superman)

1 Batman: Year One by Miller reprints	£1.25
2 Miller art, Year One concludes	£1.00
3-11	£1.00

BATMAN POCKET BOOK

Egmont/Methuen; 1 1978-9? 1980

1 100pgs; pocket size; US reprints begin; colour	£1.25
2 Joker cover, Marshal Rogers art	£1.25
3-9?	£1.00

BATMAN SPECIAL EDITION

Fleetway Editions; 4 Spring 1994-5?

4 Knightfall reprints begin, continued in Batman & Superman	£1.25
5 features Joker reprints	£1.00

BATMAN STORY BOOK ANNUAL

World; 1967-1970

1967 6 text stories	£10.00
1968 11 text stories	£10.00
1969 13 text stories	£8.00
1970 11 text stories	£8.00

BATMAN: THE COLLECTED ADVENTURES

Titan; Dec 1993-Jul 1994

Volume 1 144pgs; reprints Batman Adventures 1-6	£4.00
Volume 2 reprints Batman Adventures 7-12	£4.00

BATMAN WITH ROBIN THE BOY WONDER STORY BOOK ANNUAL

World Distributors; 1966-1969

1966 96pgs; 6 stories, all text	£8.00
1967 11 stories by Douglas Enefer, illus. by John Leeder	£7.50
1968, 1969 13/11 stories, all text	£6.00

BATMAN WORLD ADVENTURE LIBRARY

World Distributors; 1 Nov 1966-10 Aug 1967

1 68pgs pocket size; text stories	£5.00
2-10	£3.50

BATTLE ACTION/BATTLE ACTION FORCE

(see Battle Picture Weekly)

BATTLE PICTURE LIBRARY

Fleetway/IPC; 1 Jan 1961-1706 Dec 1984

1 60pgs pocket size; The Rats of Tobruk	£12.50
2	£8.00
3-20	£5.00
21-50	£2.50
51-350	£1.00
351-528 mostly reprints from hereon	£0.75
529-1706 68pgs	£0.60

ARTISTS/FEATURES

1 The Rats of Tobruk by Renzo Calegari. 2 Devils' Cauldron by Luis Bermejo. 3 Trained To Kill by Fred T. Holmes. 4 Island of Guilt. 5 The Ghost Battalion by Aldoma Puig. 6 The Silver Plated Luger by Roberto Diso. 7 Killer At Large by Jose Bielsa. 8 Tough Company by Annibale Casabianca. 9 Crack-Up! by John Severin. 10 Achtung - Kommando by Fred T. Holmes. 11 Battle Shock. 12 Blood on the Sand by Leo Duranona. Other issues incl. art by Luis Bermejo, Gino D'Antonio, Victor de la Fuente, Ian Kennedy, Solano Lopez, Jorge Moliterni, Jose Ortiz, Aldomo Puig, Ferdinando Tacconi, et al. Hugo Pratt in 62. Ron Turner in 869,875-876,987,1041,1086,1161,1415,1487, 1536,1566,1630,1639,1640-1642,1655.

BATTLE PICTURE LIBRARY HOLIDAY SPECIAL

Fleetway/IPC; 1964-1982?

1964 224pgs; reprints from picture libraries	£3.50
1965-1974	£2.00
1975-1982 later issues 192pgs	£1.00

BATTLE PICTURE WEEKLY

IPC; 8th Mar 1975-23rd Jan 1988, 673 unnumbered issues (joins Eagle)

No.1 D-Day Dawson by Casabianca, Rat Pack by Ezquerra, Day of the Eagle by Pat Wright begin	£3.00
No.1 with free gift (Combat Stickers)	£6.00
No.2 - 15 Mar 1975	£2.00
No.2 with free gift (30" x 20" poster)	£4.00
No.3 - 22 Mar 1975	£1.25
No.3 with free gift (20 Battle Swap Cards)	£2.50
29 Mar 1975-16 Oct 1976	£0.75
23 Oct 1976 1st Battle Picture Weekly and Valiant	£1.00
30 Oct 1976-12 Nov 1977	£0.75
19 Nov 1977 1st Battle Action; Dredger, Spinball Wars by Ron Turner begin	£0.75
26 Nov 1977-16 Dec 1978	£0.75
199 (23 Dec 1978) last Colquhoun Johnny Red	£0.75
200 (6 Jan 1979) Charley's War by Pat Mills & Joe Colquhoun, H.M.S. Nightshade by John Wagner & Mike Western begin, 1st John Cooper Johnny Red	£1.25
13 Jan 1979-1 Oct 1983	£0.75
8 Oct 1983 Action Force toy tie-in begins	£0.55
15 Oct 1983-19 Jan 1985	£0.55
26 Jan 1985 last WWI Charley's War by Mills & Colquhoun	£0.55
2 Feb 1985 1st WWII Charley's War by Scott Goodall & Colquhoun	£0.45
9 Feb 1985-26 Jul 1986, 23 Aug-28 Sep 1986, 8 Nov 1986	£0.45
2 Aug-16 Aug 1986 Manhatten Transfer by Pete Milligan & E.B. Romero	£0.45
4 Oct 1986 last Charley's War	£0.45
11 Oct 1986 censored Charley's War reprints begin	£0.40
18 Oct-1 Nov 1986, 15 Nov-22 Nov 1986 Milligan scripts	£0.45
29 Nov 1986 Action Force end, Milligan script	£0.45
6 Dec 1986-17 Jan 1987, 31 Jan 1987-23 Jan 1988	£0.40
24 Jan 1987 1st Battle With Storm Force, Storm Force begins	£0.40

Avengers Annual 1977

Batman #50

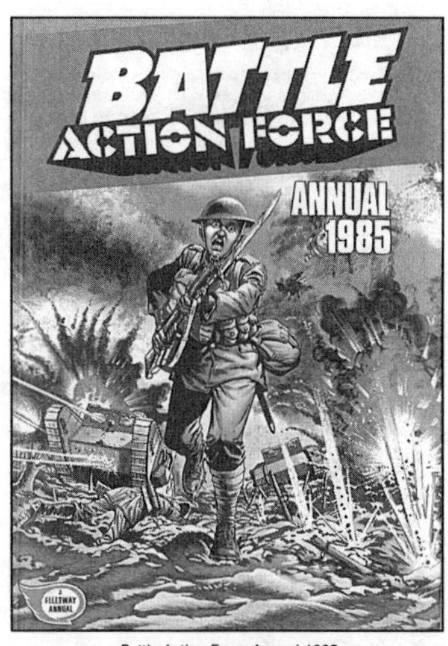

Battle Action Force Annual 1985

N.MINT

ARTISTS/FEATURES

Belardinelli in various 1975-1977 (Rat Pack). Joe Colquhoun in 23 Oct 1976-22 Jan 1977 (Soldier Sharp), 29 Jan-23 Dec 1978 (Johnny Red), 6 Jan 1979-4 Oct 1986 (Charley's War), plus various features. Carlos Ezquerra in 8 Mar-15 Mar 1975, 19 Jul 1975-23 Aug 1975, 27 Sep 1975, 18 Oct 1975, 22 Nov 1975, 20 Dec 1975 (Rat Pack), 10 Jan-27 Mar 1976, 15 May 1976-23 Apr 1977, 29 Jan-23 Apr 1977, 19 Nov 1977-10 Jun 1978 (Major Eazy), 4 Jun-17 Sep 1977 (El Mestizo), plus various short stories. Ron Turner 19 Nov 1977-3 Nov 1979 (Spinball Wars), 8 Dec 1979-28 Jan 1984 (numerous short stories), 3 Dec 1983-7 Jan 1984 (Codename: Sky Raider), 24 Mar-21 Apr 1984 (Sea Fury), 30 Jun-4 Aug 1984 (Death Castle)

Note: no issue dated 30 Dec 1978.

BATTLE PICTURE WEEKLY ANNUAL

Fleetway, 1976-1988

	N.MINT
1976-1982	£2.50
1983,1984 becomes Battle Annual	£2.00
1985-1987 becomes Battle Action Force Annual	£2.00
1988 becomes Battle Annual	£1.50

ARTISTS/FEATURES

Joe Colquhoun (Charley's War) in 1982-1983. Cam Kennedy in 1981,1983,1984.

BATTLER BRITTON

Fleetway; 1960-1961

	N.MINT
1960 hardcover, with dust-jacket	£5.00
1960 without dust-jacket	£2.00
Book Two (1961) hardcover, with dust-jacket	£5.00
Book Two without dust-jacket	£2.00

BATTLER BRITTON PICTURE LIBRARY HOLIDAY SPECIAL

IPC; 1978-1982; Ron Phillips 1988

	N.MINT
1978 192pgs; Air Ace Picture Library reprints begin	£1.50
1979-1982	£1.25
1988	£1.00

BATTLESTAR GALACTICA

Grandreams; 1978

	N.MINT
nn hardback, John Higgins art	£2.50

BATTLETIDE

(see main American comics section) (see also Death's Head II, Motormouth)

BATTLETIDE II: DEATH'S HEAD II & KILLPOWER

(see main American comics section)

BEANO/DANDY – INTRODUCTION

THE COW-PIE DIET OR QUO VADIS DENNIS? – A SHORT HISTORY OF THE DANDY AND BEANO

Ask anyone in Britain aged between six and sixty to name a weekly comic and their answer is almost certain to be either the Dandy or Beano. Go further and ask them to name a comic character and more often than not it will be either Desperate Dan or Korky the Cat or Lord Snooty or Dennis the Menace. For the better part of six decades, the Dandy and Beano have reigned supreme as the quintessential British comic titles. So well loved are they that they are now part of the common cultural iconography which all of us on our tight little island share. A fundamental part of the toys in all our attics.

Their success has been astonishing and even more surprising when one considers that for nearly fifty years they were essentially self promoting as their publishers D.C. Thomson of Dundee assiduously refused all merchandising rights. Half a century passed before the toys, games, sweets, soft furnishings and even TV shows arrived, providing the comics with an even greater capacity still to infiltrate the lives of their readers. If Disney has Mickey Mouse and Donald Duck, then D.C. Thomson have now got their own multi-media giants in the form of Desperate Dan and the ultimate franchising favourite Dennis the Menace.

In collecting circles, the Dandy and Beano also leave all the rest behind, holding all records for prices realised. Whether it be a £4000 first Dandy book, a £4200 first Beano comic or a rare piece of artwork by the comics' most celebrated artist Dudley D. Watkins, which recently went for £2500, nothing can match them. After sixty years, the vein of nostalgia, a major factor in British comic collecting, runs deep and as each title continues to prosper, future generations are also guaranteed to try and reclaim a piece of their past by tumbling into the cosy comic vortex of the Dandy and Beano's yesterdays.

In short, the Dandy and Beano were and are the best that British comicdom has to offer and what follows is a brief synopsis of the story so far.

THE DANDY

The remarkable success story of Britain's greatest comic papers The Dandy and The Beano began innocuously enough in the first week of December 1937 as the gathering clouds of war loomed ever darker over Britain and mainland Europe. For in that week was launched the new 28pg Dandy 'comic' complete with free 'Express Whistler'. It being the first such comic weekly published by the Scottish based D.C. Thomson & Co, a firm eager to branch out and consolidate the success they had had since the 1920s in the boy's story paper market with their 'Big Five' text titles Adventure, Rover, Wizard, Skipper and Hotspur.

Within the Dandy's pages were to be found an eclectic mix of comic and adventure strips and a full twelve pages devoted to text stories, the latter being a common feature in almost all British comics up until the 1950s. Here we met for the first time the snooping eavesdropper Keyhole Kate, the guzzling gourmand Hungry Horace and Freddy the Fearless Fly forever outwitting his arch adversary Septimus Spider, all destined for long comic careers under the pen of Allan Marley (1895-1960), while thrills were provided by adventure strips set in the Andes and the Wild West, and in text stories set in mythical lands where magic held sway. But most of all, we were introduced to Korky the Cat and Desperate Dan who, sixty years on, still grace the Dandy's pages every week.

Korky the Cat was the Dandy's up front figurehead and cover star for forty seven years, who became the epitome of anthropomorphism by degrees. He began life as a dumb, fish obsessed feline who, as the years went by became a house owning, verbally articulate bon viveur whose major worries were his three nephews, the Kits, and the mice who plagued his otherwise smart home. An undoubted hybrid of Disney's Mickey and Donald, but leavened with some of D.C. Thomson's own editorial style.

Without doubt though, the Dandy's greatest single contribution to comicdom's Hall of Fame is Desperate Dan, scripted from the start by Dandy editor Albert Baines (1913-1983) and drawn for over thirty years by Britain's most renowned comic strip artist Dudley D. Watkins (1907-1969). Like Korky, Desperate Dan developed his personality in stages in response to changes in the environment around him. At first he was simply the toughest guy in the Western cow-town of Cactusville, but then his Aunt Aggie came to stay, complete with her recipe for his favourite food, huge cow pies with horns and tail peeping out of the pastry, and he was transformed into a rather over-grown schoolboy with more muscles than sense. His intelligence was further tested to the limit when his wily nephew and niece Danny and Katey eventually came to stay and the town of Cactusville itself developed alarmingly surreal tendencies. Retaining its hitching rails, its sheriff and its western style jail, but also acquiring the tram lines, gas lamps and postal pillar-boxes of a typical British town; a disorientating mid-Atlantic amalgam perfectly suited as a backdrop to Dan's equally arcane adventures. With his own books, wide range of related merchandise and even his own Dandy Pie-Eaters Club, Dan has proved himself to be the Dandy's most popular character, a prime example perhaps of what the rest of the world sometimes perceived as a British bias towards whimsicality and a love for the curiously absurd.

A year after its inception, the Dandy comic spawned its first annual appropriately named the Dandy Monster Comic, a title it would retain for its first fourteen editions. Things were looking good for the Dandy, but then, nine months later, the war intervened. In the early years of the war, lack of wood pulp arriving from Scandinavia dramatically reduced the supplies of available paper and drastic measures were employed to keep publications afloat. For many comics, it simply proved to be the end of the road as their paper quota was ploughed into keeping more viable titles going. The Dandy and The Beano were two such titles who survived, but even then only in a much reduced fortnightly form.

Not too surprisingly, the war also affected the contents of the comics. The Dandy, in part, reflecting the greater global concerns going on around it as many of its characters were shown 'doing their bit' for the war effort, with even Desperate Dan, presumably an American citizen, tweaking Hitler's moustache as early as 1939, long before the US officially entered the war in December 1941. Hitler and Goering themselves became the 'heroes' of their very own Dandy comic strip titled 'Addy and Hermy - the Nasty Nazis'.

Before too long however, it was deemed that escapism was a far better tool for weekly comics to employ and slowly the war ceased to be mentioned except in ads exhorting readers to give up their comics to salvage for the war effort (a very successful ad campaign which goes some way to explain why early issues of the Dandy and Beano are now so scarce and fetch anything from £50 to £100 per issue). So, in the place of the harsh realities of the war-time world, we had the distanced medieval landscape of Dudley Watkins' Peter Pye, Dick Whittington and Daddy Longlegs and the bucolic trappings of life on a border hill farm in the adventures of the Dandy's wonder dog Black Bob.

Inspired to some degree by Eric Knight's 'Lassie Come Home', Black Bob first appeared in the Dandy in 1944. A black and white border collie rather than the long-haired variety, he would star in the Dandy for a total of 38 years and also feature as the eponymous hero of eight books, published irregularly between 1950 and 1965, with most artwork supplied by Thomson staff artist Jack Prout.

In the immediate post-war period, and it must be remembered that thanks to the continuing paper shortages it wasn't until 1949 that a regular weekly but more slimline 12-page Dandy was once again available, the two most telling artists recruited to the Dandy's ranks were Paddy Brennan and Bill Holroyd; Brennan inheriting the adventure strip mantle left by Dudley Watkins when the pressure of other work left him unavailable for such assignments, and Holroyd a versatile artist whose main forte was the light comic adventure strip. Both men would play a key role in deciding the Dandy's look for the next thirty years.

After the relative quiet of the 1950s, the 1960s were something of a watershed for the Dandy too, as telling new strips bolstered its success – the perpetually scruffy Dirty Dick and Winker Watson, the champion wangler of Greytowers school, both drawn by Eric Roberts; the food obsessed schoolteacher Greedy Pigg drawn by George Martin; Corporal Clott by the truly marvellous David Law and Ali-Ha-Ha and the Forty Thieves and Big Head and Thick Head drawn by the master of facial expressions, Ken Reid. The sixties also saw the first appearance of that now regular summer-time treat, the 32 page tabloid-sized Dandy Summer Special from 1964, a combined Dandy/Beano edition having been published the previous year.

Since the sixties ceased to swing, much has also happened. Comic strips have come and gone and adventure strips have gone, never to return. Comedy is all these days. Full colour graces every page as does gravure printing and since 1983 there has been the twice monthly digest sized Dandy Comic Libraries. The Dandy may not be what it once was, that which so makes British comics collectors drool with nostalgic anticipation, but then that is not the whole point. It is still a highly viable commodity and whether now travelling in a different direction or not, its continuing high profile image, like that of the Beano, still shows that it is certainly going somewhere.

THE BEANO

The first issue of the Beano was published in July 1938 and naturally much of its publishing history is intertwined with that of the Dandy, both leading parallel lives and sharing many artists in common, Dudley Watkins in particular. Fronted by Big Eggo the ostrich, the first issue contained a pleasing mix of fun and thrills with Hairy Dan, Rip Van Wink, Tom Thumb, the Wild Boy of the Woods and most importantly Lord Snooty and his Pals. It was another one of those endemically British comic strips that you couldn't imagine appearing anywhere else, let alone succeeding to the remarkable extent that it did.

Snooty was actually Lord Marmaduke of Binkerton and his pals were the socially challenged kids from Ash Can Alley. A pretty motley crew of social misfits, they very soon took up residence with Snooty in Binkerton Castle, where Dudley Watkins deftly depicted the mayhem they created. With its seemingly endless opportunities for fun and slap-up feeds in palatial surroundings, the Snooty strip tapped the core of many a fantasy of childhood wish-fulfilment and in several long series, occupied the Beano's pages for something over fifty years, in the process becoming the nearest the Beano has yet achieved to an ever present character.

In late 1939, the first Beano Book was published, alas soon followed by the paper restrictions which similarly disrupted the Dandy's schedule. Disruptions or not though, there was still the need to provide the young reader with some respite from the drab daily round up of wartime Britain and so was devised perhaps the most fondly remembered light adventure strip ever published in a British comic - Jimmy and his Magic Patch. Debuting in the Beano in Jan 1944 and originally drawn with great style by the ubiquitous Dudley Watkins, the Magic Patch was a superlative piece of whimsy. Jimmy Watson was a young lad who saved an old gypsy woman's cat from the attentions of a vicious dog and got his short trousers torn for his pains. Suitably grateful, the old woman then mended his pants with a piece of magic carpet and from then on he had the power to travel back through time to any event in history he chose. On and off for fifteen years, Jimmy's time travelling adventures would enthral Beano readers.

In the late 1940s, the most significant change in the Beano was the arrival of a new cover star in the furry shape of Dudley Watkins' Biffo the Bear in 1948. Biffo was the nearest the Beano ever got to emulating the success of the Dandy's Korky the Cat and spent 26 years as the comic's front 'man'.

In contrast to the Dandy, which maintained a number of its original characters throughout the 1940s and 1950s, by 1949 the Beano had none of its original crew left, with even Lord Snooty leaving for an eighteen month sabbatical. As a consequence, the Beano spent the 1950s reinventing itself and so successful was it that in the process a new dawn broke over British comicdom with the Beano at its heart.

The modern age of British comics most certainly had its genesis in the Beano in the 1950s. It was here that the traditionally funny most evidently gave way to the zanily anarchic, and all thanks to the brilliant Beano scriptwriters, particularly Walter Fearn, and three marvellous artists, David Law (1907–1971), Ken Reid (1919–1987) and Leo Baxendale (1931–). The absolute starting point for the 'new age' was March 1951 when, in a small half page strip, we were given our first view of a spiky-haired lad much given to acts of mischievous malevolence, Dennis the Menace, drawn by David Law. It is difficult to explain the success that he has had in the last 45 years, but in his usual garb of red and black hooped jersey and short black trousers, Dennis is certainly the mega-star of modern British comics. Having had his own book since 1956, he is now also the star of a TV cartoon series, several videos and a plethora of Menace merchandise, much of the associated material also featuring his pet dog Gnasher, who he teamed up with in 1968, and his less than fearsome adversary Walter the Softy.

Another current Beano favourite, the devilishly devious Roger the Dodger, arrived in 1953 with artwork by Ken Reid, the same artist responsible for Jonah five years later. Only running for a handful of years, the sea-going jinx is still fondly remembered as the Beano's most goonish star, extracting from Ken Reid some of his finest artwork.

A perfect counter-balance to Reid's artwork was that of new kid on the block Leo Baxendale, who created Dennis the Menace's female alter-ego Minnie the Minx in 1953 and the terminally manic Bash St. Kids in 1954. In his ten-year stint on the Beano, Baxendale's strips came to top the popularity polls and his artistic style proved to be a seminal influence on British comic art for the next twenty years, much imitated but never bettered.

In the wake of the Beano's comic strip revolution in the 1950s, its adventure strip output began to take a back seat before it was finally ousted from the comic altogether in 1975, but nonetheless some of its more serious contributions are still worthy of a mention. Most notable are the underwater exploits of the one man fish shaped submarine, The Iron Fish, General Jumbo in command of his own miniature mechanical army, the young crime fighting cycle team, The Q Bikes, and last but not least, the Beano's very own schoolboy turned super-hero, Billy The Cat.

Since the mid 1960s the Beano has developed further outlets for its characters including, in line with the Dandy, a yearly Summer Special, a regular book devoted solely to the Bash St. Kids, the twice monthly Beano Comic Library, the Beano Calendar and the monthly Beano Special/Beano Super Stars, produced in full colour on quality paper.

Still, these publications are only the tip of the Beano's merchandising iceberg, as its characters have proven themselves very saleable commodities in areas far removed from the printed page. Dennis the Menace has his own cartoon show on TV, but at a price, as the Dennis in the weekly comic has been redrawn to match up with the animated Dennis' celluloid limitations. This may not please us comic collecting purists, but then comics are not about nostalgia to the companies who produce them. They look to the future and whether we choose to follow them or not, Dennis and the rest of the Beano entourage are moving on.

© Ray Moore, 1997

BEANO BOOK, THE

D.C. Thomson; Sep 1939-present

	GOOD	FINE	N.MINT
(1940) (Big Eggo and others on see-saw supported by Pansy Potter)	£375.00	£1125.00	£3000.00

Note: A copy in fn+ was sold at auction in March 1996 for an auction record price of £4000. As there have been no further sales recorded at this price, it must be considered a one-off sale price rather than a "going rate".

	GOOD	FINE	N.MINT
(1941) (Large eggs with characters emerging, Big Eggo's head peering through)	£170.00	£510.00	£1200.00
(1942) (Lord Snooty playing bagpipes)	£85.00	£255.00	£600.00
(1943) becomes Magic Beano Book (Big Eggo and Koko lead in three-legged race)	£70.00	£210.00	£500.00
(1944) (Eggo and Koko in pillow fight on a pole)	£55.00	£170.00	£400.00
(1945) (Big Eggo and other characters playing leap-frog)	£55.00	£170.00	£400.00
(1946) (Big Eggo pulling other characters in a cart)	£43.00	£125.00	£300.00
(1947) (Hairy Dan on Pansy Potter's shoulders looking into Big Eggo's mouth)	£29.00	£85.00	£200.00
(1948) (Big Eggo and the other characters playing musical instruments)	£29.00	£85.00	£200.00
(1949) (Biffo, Big Eggo and others gathered around Maxy's Taxi)	£21.00	£62.50	£150.00
(1950) (Biffo painting portraits of others , Big Eggo peering round canvas)	£17.00	£50.00	£120.00
(1951) reverts to Beano Book (Biffo riding a mechanical horse)	£14.00	£43.00	£100.00
(1952) Biffo nailing pictures of characters to cover)	£11.00	£34.00	£80.00
(1953) (Jack Flash carries characters on trips to the moon)	£10.00	£30.00	£70.00
(1954) (Biffo hanging from a tree with a monkey sawing the branch, Dennis with lobster)	£10.00	£30.00	£70.00
(1955) (Policeman falling in a river where Biffo and Dennis are fishing)	£10.00	£30.00	£70.00
(1956) (Biffo in captain's hat watching other characters, Dennis in plane)	£8.50	£26.00	£60.00
(1957) (Dennis scoring a goal with the ball rebounding off other characters)	£8.50	£26.00	£60.00
(1958) (Biffo juggling, Dennis releasing bees from a hive)	£8.50	£26.00	£60.00
(1959) (Dennis playing leap-frog with a goat about to butt him)	£8.50	£26.00	£60.00
(1960) (Biffo doing jig-saw puzzle of other characers)	£6.25	£19.00	£45.00
(1961) (Biffo in large letters, characters at top and bottom of cover)	£6.50	£20.00	£40.00
(1962) (Jonah dancing on the mast of a sinking ship with SOS flag)	£6.50	£20.00	£40.00
(1963) (Bash Street kids on large swing tied to Beano logo)	£5.00	£15.00	£30.00
(1964) (Biffo in circus ring with bar-bells, tickled by Buster with feather)	£5.00	£15.00	£30.00
(1965) (Minnie and Little Plum blowing up balloon shaped like Biffo's head)	£5.00	£15.00	£30.00
1966 1st dated on cover	£3.30	£10.00	£20.00
1967	£2.50	£7.50	£15.00
1968,1969	£2.05	£6.25	£12.50
1970	£1.65	£5.00	£10.00
1971-1975	£1.00	£3.00	£6.00
1976-1980	£1.00	£3.00	£5.00
1981-1989	£0.80	£2.40	£4.00
1990-1997	£0.60	£1.80	£3.00
Title Value:	**£1085.15**	**£3261.45**	**£7990.50**

BEANO COMIC, THE

D.C. Thomson; 1 30th Jul 1938-present (2845 issues to Jan 1997)

	GOOD	FINE	N.MINT
1	£340.00	£1025.00	£2750.00

Note: a copy was sold at auction in September 1995 for £4200 representing the highest price paid for a British comic. As there have been no further sales recorded at this price, it must be considered a one-off sale price rather than a "going rate". Having said that, the company responsible for the auction has stated that there were several serious bidders over the £3,000 mark. The position of the Guide at this point in time is one of healthy caution

	GOOD	FINE	N.MINT
1 facsimile	£5.00	£15.00	£25.00
2	£285.00	£850.00	£2000.00
3	£110.00	£340.00	£800.00
4	£70.00	£210.00	£500.00
5-10	£38.00	£110.00	£300.00
11-25	£25.00	£75.00	£200.00
1939 issues	£15.50	£47.00	£125.00
1940 issues	£10.00	£30.00	£80.00
1941-1943 issues	£7.50	£22.50	£60.00
1944-1945 issues	£6.25	£18.50	£50.00
1946-1948 issues	£4.35	£13.00	£35.00
1949-1951 issues	£3.10	£9.25	£25.00
1952-1954 issues	£1.85	£5.50	£15.00
1955-1958 issues	£1.25	£3.75	£10.00
1959-1960 issues	£1.05	£3.20	£7.50
1961-1963 issues	£0.70	£2.10	£5.00
1964-1966 issues	£0.40	£1.25	£3.00
1967-1969 issues	£0.25	£0.85	£2.00
1970-1975 issues	£0.20	£0.60	£1.25
1976-1980 issues	£0.15	£0.50	£1.00
1981-1990 issues	£0.10	£0.35	£0.60
1991-1997 issues	£0.05	£0.20	£0.40
Title Value:	**£1465.70**	**£4383.55**	**£11295.75**

Note: issue 1660 (11 May 1974) was accidentally mis-numbered 1659.

CHRONOLOGY

1 1st Lord Snooty by Watkins. 21 (17 Dec 1938) 1st Pansy Potter by McNeill. 130 (18 Jan 1941) 1st Tom Thumb by Watkins. 200 (27 Feb 1943) 1st Shipwrecked Circus by Watkins. 222 (1 Jan 1944) 1st Jimmy and his Magic Patch by Watkins. 240 (9 Sep 1944) 1st Strang the Terrible by Watkins. 327 (24 Jan 1948) 1st Biffo the Bear by Watkins. 413 (17 Jun 1950) title shortened to Beano. 452 (17 Mar 1951) 1st Dennis the Menace by David Law. 561 (18 Apr 1953) 1st Roger the Dodger by Ken Reid. 583 (19 Sep 1953) 1st General Jumbo by Paddy Brennan. 586 (10 Oct 1953) 1st Little Plum by Leo Baxendale. 596 (19 Dec 1953) 1st Minnie the Minx by Baxendale. 604 (13 Feb 1954) 1st When the Bell Rings by Baxendale (becomes The Bash Street Kids from 1 Dec 1956). 680 (30 Jul 1955) 1st Grandpa by Reid. 817 (15 Mar 1958) 1st Jonah by Reid. 881 (6 Jun 1959) 1st Three Bears by Baxendale. 1139 (16 May 1964) 1st Billy Whizz by Malcolm Judge. 1289 (1 Apr 1967) 1st Billy the Cat by David Sutherland. 1363 (31 Aug 1968) 1st Gnasher (in Dennis the Menace). 1553 (22 Apr 1972) 1st Babyface Finlayson by Ron Spencer. 1678 (14 Sep 1974) 1st Dennis the Menace front cover. 2674 (16 Oct 1993) 1st all colour issue.

ARTISTS

Leo Baxendale in 586-1045. Paddy Brennan in 400-505,516-536,553-567,583-599,642-654,664-683,701-723,740-768,789-801,891-903,1068-1094. David Law in 452-1462. Allan Morley in 1-35,69-335,337-475. Ken Reid in 561-1152. Dudley D.Watkins in 1-1422.

BEANO COMIC LIBRARY

D.C. Thomson; 1 Apr 1982-present (356 to Jan 1997)

	N.MINT
1 pocket size; King Dennis the Menace by David Gudgeon	£5.00
2-10	£2.00
11-100	£1.00
101-332	£0.50

BEANO SUMMER SPECIAL, THE

(see also Dandy-Beano Summer Special)

D.C. Thomson; Jun 1964-present

	N.MINT
1964	£50.00
1965	£30.00
1966-1969	£15.00
1970-1975	£10.00
1976-1979	£5.50
1980-1989	£3.00
1990-1996	£1.25

BEANO SUPER STARS, THE

D.C. Thomson; 1 1992-present (61 to Jan 1997)

	N.MINT
1 Dennis the Menace	£1.25
2 The Bash Street Kids	£1.10
3 Minnie the Minx	£1.10
4 Roger the Dodger	£1.10
5-45	£1.00

BEAVIS AND BUTT-HEAD

Titan; 1994-present

	N.MINT
Greatest Hits	£6.00
Trashcan Edition	£7.00
Holidazed and Confused (Jul 1995)	£7.00
Wanted (Mar 1996)	£7.00

BEAVIS AND BUTT-HEAD

Marvel; 1 1994-present?

	N.MINT
1 reprints US strips based on TV show	£1.00
2-20	£0.35

BEEZER, THE

(see also The Best of Beezer Quarterly)

D.C. Thomson; 1 21st Jan 1956-1809 15th Sep 1990 (becomes The Beezer and Topper)

	N.MINT
1 tabloid size	£125.00
1 with free gift (The Whiz Bang)	£200.00
2	£40.00
3	£15.00
1956 issues	£12.50
1957-1959 issues	£6.00
1960-1965 issues	£3.50
1966-1969 issues	£2.50
1970-1977 issues	£1.25
1978-1981 issues	£0.75
1981-1990 small size issues	£0.50

CHRONOLOGY

1 1st Ginger by Watkins, Lone Wolfe by Ron Smith, Pop, Dick and Harry by Tom Bannister, Nosey Parker by Allan Morley, Banana Bunch by Baxendale. 34 (8 Sep 1956) 1st Baby Crockett by Bill Ritchie. 103 (4 Jan 1958) 1st Cap'n'Hand by David Law. 148 (15 Nov 1958) 1st Colonel Blink by Tom Bannister. 171 (25 Apr 1959) 1st Showboat Circus by Paddy Brennan. 210 (23 Jan 1960) 1st The Badd Lads by Malcolm Judge. 322 (17 Mar 1962) 1st Numbskulls by Malcolm Judge. 577 (4 Feb 1967) 1st Smiffy by Bill Ritchie. 788 (20 Feb 1971) 1st Barny's Barmy Army by Ken Hunter. 1079 (18 Sep 1976) 1st "Beezer and Cracker". 1207 (3 Mar 1979) 1st "Beezer and Plug". 1315 (28 Mar 1981) 1st small size.

ARTISTS

Leo Baxendale in 1-436. Paddy Brennan in 171-211,726-760,1079-1206. David Law in 103-147. Allan Morley in 1-13. Ron Smith in 103-147,165-169,284-329,445-557,584-605,1044-1099. Dudley D.Watkins in 1-718 (719-737 contain Watkins Ginger reprints).

BEEZER AND TOPPER, THE

D.C. Thomson; 1 22nd Sep 1990-21st Aug 1993, 153 issues

	N.MINT
1	£1.00
2-15	£0.35
16-67	£0.25
68-153	£0.20

BEEZER AND TOPPER SUMMER SPECIAL, THE

(see The Beezer Summer Special)

BEEZER BOOK, THE

D.C. Thomson; Sep 1957-present

	N.MINT
(1958) (Characters climbing up steep stairway)	£100.00
(1959) (Stepladder, balloon, bicycle holding up logo)	£45.00
(1960) (Head and shoulders of Baby Crockett)	£30.00
(1961) (Globe wearing a school cap, characters in corners)	£25.00
(1962) (Old locomotive with characters)	£20.00
(1963) (Two pirates in the logo, aeroplane at top of cover)	£17.50

	N.MINT
(1964) (Large head/shoulders of decorated man, logo on hat)	£15.00
(1965) (Colonel Blink with drum about to walk into manhole)	£12.50
1966 1st dated on cover	£10.00
1967-1969	£8.00
1970-1979	£5.00
1980-1989	£3.00
1990-1996	£2.50
1997	£3.50

BEEZER SUMMER SPECIAL, THE

D.C. Thomson; Jun 1973-present

1973	£5.00
1974-1979	£3.00
1980-1989	£1.50
1990-1992	£1.00
1993 Beezer & Topper Summer Special	£0.90
1994-1995	£0.90

BERYL THE PERIL

D.C. Thomson; Sep 1958-Sep 1987 (bi-annual to 1979, irregular thereon)

(1959) (Beryl appears out of hole she has cut in cover with saw)	£100.00
(1961) (Beryl dressed as a cowboy, riding a pneumatic drill)	£40.00
(1963) (Beryl wearing boxing gloves, attacking teacher shaped punch bag)	£30.00
(1965) (Beryl pulling tiger by rope away from circus)	£25.00
1967-1969 dated on cover	£15.00
1971-1979	£7.50
1981-1988	£3.00

BEST OF 2000AD

IPC/Fleetway; 1 Oct 1985-119 Aug 1995 (becomes Classic 2000AD)

1 Strontium Dog, Judge Dredd; 2000AD reprints begin	£8.00
2	£5.00
3,5 Nemesis	£3.50
4	£3.25
6-8 Nemesis; 8 D.R. & Quinch	£2.50
9-11 Robo-Hunter	£2.00
12 Robo-Hunter	£2.50
13-14 A.B.C. Warriors	£1.75
15-16 Strontium Dog	£1.75
17-18 D.R. & Quinch	£2.00
19 D.R. & Quinch, Slaine	£2.00
20-22 Slaine	£1.50
23-25,29-32	£1.25
26 Robo-Hunter	£1.25
27-28 Harry 20	£1.25
33-34,36-37 Slaine	£1.50
35,41,46-47,49,53-55	£1.25
38-39,43-45,48,56 Nemesis	£1.25
40,42 Halo Jones	£2.00
50,57 Strontium Dog	£1.25
51-52 Robo-Hunter	£1.20
58,60-64	£1.20
59 Slaine	£1.20
65 Rogue Trooper, Halo Jones	£1.20
66 Halo Jones	£1.20
67-74,77-80	£1.20
75-76 Robo-Hunter	£1.20
81 Slaine the King, new Fabry cover	£1.75
82-83 Skizz Book 1. 83 A.B.C. Warriors	£1.50
84 Ace Trucking Co.	£1.20
85 Robo-Hunter, free poster	£1.20
86 Robo-Hunter	£1.10
87-88 Strontium Dog	£1.10
89,92 Ace Trucking Co	£1.10
90 Rogue Trooper	£1.10
91 The Dead	£1.10
93 Slaine, Ace Trucking	£1.20
94-95 Rogue Trooper	£1.00
96-98 Strontium Dog	£1.00
99 Zenith	£1.20
100-119	£1.25

BIG NUMBERS

Mad Love; 1 Apr 1990-2 Aug 1990

1 44pgs large square; Alan Moore & Bill Sienkiewicz	£3.50
2	£3.50

BIG ONE, THE

Fleetway; 17th Oct 1964-20th Feb 1965, 19 unnumbered issues (joins Buster)

17 Oct 1964 scarce; 12pgs, large (14.5x21.5"); various retitled humour strips by Eric Roberts, Reg Parlett, Hugh McNeill, Roy Wilson, etc. begin	£75.00
No. 1 - 17 Oct 1964 scarce; with free gift (Sharps Super Kreem Toffee Bar)	£100.00
No. 2 - 24 Oct 1964 scarce	£20.00
No. 3 - 1 Nov 1964 scarce	£10.00
8 Nov 1964-20 Feb 1965 scarce	£5.00

BIGGLES ANNUAL

World; 1980

1980 scarce	£6.00

BILLY THE KID ADVENTURE MAGAZINE

World Distributors; 1 1953-76 1959

1 36pgs; reprints from Toby	£5.00
2-10	£4.00
11-76 36pgs/68pgs; incl. Williamson, Frazetta art	£3.00

BIONIC WOMAN ANNUAL

Grandreams; 1977-1978

1977-1978 Ian Gibson art	£3.00

BIRTHDAY BOOK FOR BOYS

Fleetway; 1972

	N.MINT
1972 reprints strips from Buster, Valiant and Tiger including Fishboy and Galaxus	£2.50

BISLEY'S SCRAPBOOK

Atomeka; 1 Sep 1993

1 with double cover	£3.00
1 with single cover	£2.50

BLAAM!

Willyprods; preview 1988; 1 Sep 1988-3 Feb 1989

Preview free with Heartbreak Hotel No.5, Fegredo art	£0.75
1 Neil Gaiman script (10,000 copies)	£1.50
2-3	£0.30

BLACK AXE

(see main American comics section)

BLACK BOB BOOK

D.C. Thomson; 1950-1965 (irregular)

1950 oblong format begins; Jack Prout art (back cover: Bob on top of mountain with shepherd coming up hill towards him)	£40.00
1951 (bc: on hilltop with small boy looking down at sheep)	£27.50
1953 (bc: Bob with two birds perched on foodbowl)	£25.00
1955 (bc: oval inset of Bob pulling girl and puppy in bath tub through snow)	£25.00
1957 (bc: Bob on mountain being patted on head)	£20.00
1959 (bc: Bob with three other dogs)	£15.00
1961 (fc: six evenly spaced heads)	£7.50
1965 regular format (Bob surrounded by silver cups)	£7.50

Note: fc of all but 1961 is single head shot of Bob, so bc descriptions are given.

BLACK DIAMOND WESTERN

Pemberton; nn 1951-33 1954

nn 36pgs; reprints from Lev Gleason begin	£5.00
2-33 28pgs; incl. Dick Rockwell, Charles Biro, Al Luster, Basil Wolverton reprints	£3.00

BLACK DRAGON, THE

Titan; May 1996

nn 208pgs; reprints Marvel series by Chris Claremont & John Bolton in b&w	£9.00

BLACKHAWK

Boardman/Popular; 11 1949-61 1953, 15 issues variously numbered

11,18,20,21,25,27,28,32,40,42,44 12pgs; reprints from Quality, incl. Reed Crandell art	£8.00
15 second strip redrawn by Denis McLoughlin	£12.00
47,57,59,61 28pgs	£6.00

BLACKHAWK

Strato; 1 1956-36 1958

1 68pgs; reprints from Quality	£6.00
2-36	£4.00

BLACK MAGIC

Arnold Book Co.; 1 1952-16 1954

1-14,16 68pgs; reprints from Prize Publishing	£6.00
15 reprints stories from Eerie & Crime SuspenStories cited in US and UK horror campaign	£15.00

BLACK MAGIC ALBUM

Arnold Book Co; 1-2 1954

1 160pgs; reprints from Prize, cited in UK horror campaign	£18.00
2 reprints from Prize	£10.00

BLACK ORCHID

Titan; Aug 1991

nn reprints Black Orchid #1-3 by Neil Gaiman & Dave McKean	£11.00

BLAKE'S SEVEN

Marvel; 1 Oct 1981-23 Aug 1983

1 Blake's 7 by Ian Kennedy begins	£10.00
1 with free gift (iron on transfer)	£15.00
2	£5.00
3-20,22	£3.50
21 no Blake's 7 strip	£3.50
23 double sized issue	£5.00

ARTISTS/FEATURES

Artists include Ian Kennedy, David Lloyd, Steve Dillon, Mick Austin, Phil Gascoine.

BLAKE'S SEVEN ANNUAL

World Distributors; 1978-1979, 1981

1978-1979	£5.00
1981 smaller print run	£7.00

BLAKE'S SEVEN SPECIALS

Marvel; May 1981-Nov 1982, 1994

Summer Special 1981	£4.00
Summer Special 1982	£3.00
Winter Special 1982	£2.50
Winter Special 1994	£2.50

BLAST!

(see also Lazerus Churchyard, Sherlock Holmes, White Trash)

John Brown; 1 Jun 1991-7 Dec 1991

1 Mr Monster by Gilbert & Bisley, Concrete by Paul Chadwick, Torpedo reprints by Abuli & Bernet, Axel Pressbutton by Henry & Dillon, Junior by Bagge, Lazarus Churchyard by Warren Ellis & D'Israeli begins	£2.00
2 Big Berta by Yan Shimony begins, Concrete, Mr. Monster reprints	£1.50
3-6	£1.50
7 White Trash by Gordon Rennie & Martin Emond, Sherlock Holmes by Rennie & Woodrow Phoenix begin	£1.50

BLOCKBUSTER

Marvel; 1 Jun 1981-9 Feb 1982

1 Iron Fist, The Inhumans, Omega reprints begin	£1.50
2-9	£1.00

BLOCKBUSTER WINTER SPECIAL

Marvel; Nov 1980

nn 52pgs; reprints	£1.75

BLOODSEED

(see main American section)

	N.MINT
BLUE BEETLE	
Streamline/United Anglo-American; 1-nn 1950, 2 issues	
1 28pgs; reprints from Fox	£8.50
nn 28pgs	£6.00
BLUE BEETLE	
Miller; 1-3? 1950s	
1-3 28pgs; reprints from Fox	£5.00
BLUE PETER ANNUAL	
IPC/BBC; 1 1965-present?	
1 scarce	£90.00
2	£30.00
3-5	£15.00
6-10	£7.50
11-20	£5.00
21-31	£3.00
BLUE PETER HOLIDAY SPECIAL	
IPC/BBC; 1976	
1976 40pgs	£2.00
BOGIE MAN, THE	
(see also Toxic)	
Fat Man Press; 1 Sep 1989-4 Sep 1990 (released late)	
1 Bogie Man by John Wagner/Alan Grant & Robin Smith begins	£2.00
2-4	£1.50
The Bogie Man (1991) trade paperback, collects 1-4	£3.50
The Bogie Man (Apocalypse Presents, Jul 1991) Toxic reprints, Kennedy art	£1.50
The Manhatten Project (Apocalypse Presents, Sep 1991) Toxic reprints, Smith art	£1.50
The Manhatten Project (Tundra, Jul 1992) revised version	£3.00
BOGIE MAN, THE: CHINATOON	
Atomeka; 1 Mar 1993-4 Jun 1993	
1 by John Wagner/Alan Grant & Robin Smith	£1.80
2-4	£1.50
Chinatoon (Atomeka, Oct 1993) collects 1-4	£3.50
BONANZA	
Top Sellers; 1970-1971 (8+ issues)	
1 36pgs; reprints from Dell	£3.00
2-? US reprints, later issues feature original material	£1.00
BONANZA	
Purnell; 1962-1969	
1962 Text stories, illus. by Desmond Walduck & Eric Dadswell	£4.00
1963 Text stories, illus. by Leo Rawlings & R. Simonette	£3.50
1964 Stories by Basil Deakin, illus. by Leo Rawlings & R. Walker	£3.50
1965,1967	£3.00
1966,1968 Stories by Basil Deakin, illus. by Barrie Mitchell	£2.50
1969 Stories by Basil Deakin, illus by Barrie Mitchell, McLoughlin cover	£3.00
Note: the 1966 annual appears to have 2 variant editions with identical contents but two different covers, the first showing 4 characters on horseback, the second 3 characters standing	
BONANZA	
World Distributors; 1963-1969	
1963 Dell/Gold Key (#1110-606) reprints	£5.00
1964-1966	£3.50
1967 Stories and features by J.L. Morrissey, M. Broadley, and J.W. Elliott	£3.00
1968 illus by Walt Howarth	£3.00
1969	£3.00
BONANZA COMIC ALBUM	
World Distributors; 1 1965	
1 softcover; reprints incl. Dell Bonanza #7	£4.00
BONANZA WORLD ADVENTURE LIBRARY	
World Distributors; 1 Jun 1967-3 Aug 1967	
1 68pgs; The Ponderosa Ranch, reprints from Dell	£3.00
2-3	£2.50
BONNY ANNUAL	
Gerald Swan; Oct 1949-Sep 1955	
nn 149pgs	£3.50
1951-1956	£3.00
BOOK OF REDFOX, THE	
Harrier/Valkyrie; 1986-1989	
Book 1 (Harrier) reprints Redfox 1-4, Bolland cover	£3.00
Book 1 (Valkyrie) recoloured cover	£4.00
Book 2 (Valkyrie) reprints Redfox 5-10, Fabry cover	£4.00
BOOK OF SPACE ADVENTURES	
Atlas Publishing; 1962?	
1962 scarce, factual text with Space Ace strip	£10.00
Note: interior title Boys' Book of Space	
BOOKS OF MAGIC, THE	
Titan; Feb 1993, Mar 1995	
The Books of Magic (Feb 1993) reprints The Books of Magic #1-4 by Neil Gaiman	£13.00
Bindings (Mar 1995) reprints ongoing series #1-4 by John Ney Rieber	£8.00
BOYS' WORLD	
Longacre; v1,1 26th Jan 1963-v2,40 3rd Oct 1964, 89 issues (joins Eagle)	
Vol 1,1 Pike Mason by Tom Tully & Luis Bermejo, John Brody by Colin Andrew, Wrath of the Gods by Michael Moorcock & Ron Embleton all begin	£12.50
Vol.1,1 with free gift (Pathfinder Watch Compass)	£25.00
2	£7.50
2-10, 12-23,25-45,47-49	£5.00
11 1st Merlo the Magician text story by Harry Harrison	£5.00
24 1st Iron Man by Gerry Embleton (later by Martin Salvador), Brett Million (The Angry Planet, partly based on Deathworld by Harry Harrison) by H.K. Bulmer & Frank Langford, 1st Merlo the Magician picture strip by Garcia Pizarro, 1st John Burns Wrath of the Gods, 1st Brian Lewis John Brody	£5.50
46 1st Frank Bellamy Brett Million (The Ghost World)	£5.00
Vol 2,1-17	£3.50
18 1st Raff Regan	£2.50

Biggles Annual

Book of Space Adventures

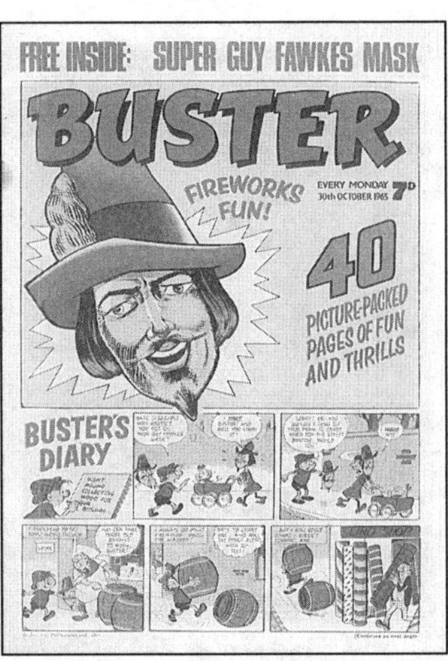

Buster 30/10/65

	N.MINT
19-40	£2.50

BOYS' WORLD ANNUAL

Odhams; 1963-1971

1964 Don Harley, Brian Lewis art	£6.00
1965 John Burns, Gerry Embleton art, Ron Embleton, Don Harley, Bellamy illos	£5.00
1966 Ron Embleton, Don Harley art, Bellamy illos	£4.00
1967 John Burns art, R.Embleton, Lawrence illos	£3.00
1968 Don Lawrence art	£3.00
1969 Lawrence, Kieth Watson, Frank Humphris illos	£3.00
1970 Don Harley art, R.Embleton illos	£3.00
1971 Lawrence art, Bellamy illos	£3.50
1972 Lawrence, Humphris illos	£3.00

BRAINSTORM!

Alchemy Publications; Dec 1982

nn Bryan Talbot art, Chester P. Hackenbush reprints	£15.00

BRAINSTORM COMIX

Alchemy; Nov 1975-Sum 1977

1-2 Chester Hackenbush by Talbot	£12.00
3 titled Mixed Bunch No.1; "The Papist Affair" (early version of Luther Arkwright) by Talbot, Emerson art	£15.00
4 titled Brainstorm Comix No 3; Hackenbush by Talbot	£12.00
5 titled Brainstorm Fantasy Comix No.1; Higgins, Talbot art	£10.00
6 titled Amazing Rock & Roll Adventures; "The Omega Report" by Talbot	£10.00

BRAVE AND THE BOLD ANNUAL, THE

Thorpe & Porter; 1967

1967 scarce; bound-together remaindered copies of selected DC comics incl. Brave & Bold #56	£25.00

BRICKMAN

Harrier; 1 Dec 1986

1 Lew Stringer, Gibbons, O'Neill, Collins/Farmer art	£1.50

BRONCO BILL COMIC

Donald Peters; 23/2 1950

23/2 36pgs; reprints US newspaper strip by Harry O'Neill	£3.50

BRONCO BILL WESTERN COMIC

Donald Peters; 1 1951-17 1952?

1-17 28pgs; reprints US newspaper strip by Harry O'Neill	£3.00

BRONCO KIDS WILD WEST YARNS

Purnell; 1950s

nn annnual, 2 strips, 15 text stories	£2.00

BRONCO LAYNE

World Distributors; 1959-1964

1959 Stories by Joe Morrissey	£4.00
1960 Stories by Joe Morrissey, illus. by Walt Howarth	£3.50
1961-1962,1964	£3.00
1963 Stories by Joe Morrissey; incl. Dell reprints	£3.00

BROONS, THE

D.C. Thomson; Sep 1940-present (bi-annual)

1940 (Faces of family, each named) Dudley D. Watkins art begins	£500.00
1942 (head/shoulders of Maw/Paw in oval with family around them, yellow b/g)	£325.00
1948 (Paw reading newspaper, Maw with tea tray, yellow b/g)	£150.00
1952 (Family sitting round table smiling at reader)	£100.00
1954 (Maw/Paw doing Highland Fling, tartan b/g)	£75.00
1956 (Family looking out of large window)	£60.00
1958 (Family playing board games on table and floor, tartan b/g)	£40.00
1960 (Family at dinner table, calendar reads 25 Jan, tartan b/g)	£35.00
1962 (Family at home, woman reading story to child on lap, tartan b/g)	£30.00
1964 (Family perched on mountain top waving, tartan b/g)	£30.00
1966-1970 (copyright dated, e.g. cy1965 for 1966)	£20.00
1972-1980 last Watkins	£15.00
1982-1989	£4.50
1992,1994,1996	£3.00

BULLETMAN

Arnold Book Co.; 10 1951, 1 issue

10 24pgs; reprints from Fawcett	£10.00
10, Facsimile (1995)	£5.00

BURGLAR BILL

Trident; 1 Dec 1990

1 Paul Grist art and script	£1.00

BUSTER

Fleetway/IPC/Fleetway; 28th May 1960-present

No.1 - 28 May 1960 Buster by Bill Titcombe, Phantom Force Five by Eric Bradbury, Sea Hawk by Eric Parker all begin	£50.00
No.1 with free gift (Buster's Balloon Beeper)	£80.00
4 Jun 1960	£25.00
11 Jun 1960	£12.50
18 Jun 1960-18 Feb 1961	£6.00
25 Feb 1961 1st Buster & Radio Fun; Superman newspaper reprints begin	£7.50
4 Mar 1961-18 Mar 1961	£5.00
18 Mar 1961 with free gift (3 Men in Danger photocards)	£6.00
25 Mar 1961-8 Sep 1962	£3.00
15 Sep 1962 1st Buster & Film Fun; Nick Shannan (Johnny Wingco reprints from Knockout) by Mike Western begins	£4.00
22 Sep 1962-20 Feb 1965	£2.50
27 Feb 1965 1st Buster & Big One; The Toys of Doom by Solano Lopez begins	£4.00
6 Mar-29 May 1965	£2.50
5 Jun 1965 1st smaller size	£2.00
12 Jun 1965-6 Nov 1965	£2.00
6 Nov 1965 with free gift (The Buster Guy Fawkes Banger)	£5.00
13 Nov 1965-5 Nov 1966	£1.50
12 Nov 1966 Galaxus - The Thing From Outer Space by Solano Lopez begins	£2.00
19 Nov 1966-13 Jan 1968	£1.50
20 Jan 1968 1st "Buster and Giggle", Fishboy by John Stokes begins	£2.00
27 Jan 1968-26 Sep 1971	£1.50
2 Oct 1971 1st "Buster and Jet", Faceache by Ken Reid begins	£1.50
9 Oct 1971-15 Jun 1974	£0.75
22 Jun 1974-7 Apr 1990	£0.50
14 Apr 1990-13 Jan 1995	£0.30
20 Jan 1995-present fortnightly	£0.40

CHRONOLOGY

20 Oct 1960 Maxwell Hawke by Bradbury begins. 22 Jun 1974 1st "Buster and Cor!!". 6 Nov 1976 1st "Buster and Monster Fun". 6 Feb 1982 1st "Buster and Jackpot". 2 Jun 1984 1st "Buster and School Fun". 19 Sep 1987 1st "Buster and Nipper". 29 Oct 1988 1st "Buster and Oink!" (not given on cover). 14 Apr 1990 1st full colour. 3 Nov 1990 1st "Buster and Whizzer & Chips". 25 Dec 1993/1 Jan 1994 Double Number. 17 Dec/29 Dec 1995 Double Number. **Note: no issues dated 29 Jun-3 Aug 1974**

BUSTER ADVENTURE LIBRARY

Fleetway; 1 Jul 1966-36 Dec 1967

1 John Steel reprints begin (odd numbers to 25)	£3.50
2 Robin Hood reprints begin (all even numbers)	£2.50
3-26,28,30,32,34,36	£2.00
27,29,31,33,35 Rick Random reprints	£3.00

ARTISTS/FEATURES

1 Dateline for Danger (TPL355) by Lopez Espi. 2 Robin Hood's Challenge. 3 Catch Me A Killer (TPL363) by Luis Bermejo. 4 Robin Hood's Peril. 5 Showdown (TPL367) by Reg Bunn. 6 Robin Hood At Bay (TPL122, 2 stories) by Reg Bunn, Pat Nicolle. 7 Death Deals A Joker. 8 Sword of Robin Hood (TPL287, 2 stories) by Nadir Quinto, Martin Salvador. 9 Terror Calls the Tune (TPL371) by Luis Bermejo. 10 Robin Hood and the Beast of Rockspur. 11 Tomorrow You Die! (TPL379) by Luis Bermejo. 12 Robin Hood the Valiant (TPL275, 3 stories) by Guido Buzzelli, Nadir Quinto. 13 Death Shadows the Hunter (TPL395) by Luis Bermejo. 14 Robin Hood and the Seal of Doom (TPL226?). 15 Savage Waterfront (TPL403) by Luis Bermejo. 16 Prince of Sherwood (TPL170, 3 stories) by Reg Bunn, Angel Pardo. 17 Dead Man's Tale (TPL399) by Alberto Breccia. 18 Robin Hood and the Hunted Thief. 19 The Big Fix (TPL431) by Luis Bermejo. 20 Robin Hood the Bold. 21 Who Is My Enemy? (TPL431) by Erio Nicolo. 22 Robin Hood & the Castle of Fear. 23 Invitation to Death (TPL427). 24 Courage of Robin Hood (TPL303, 2 stories) incl. Martin Salvador. 25 The Devil of Antiga by Erio Nicolo. 26 Rally to Robin Hood (TPL186,134, 3 stories) by Angel Pardo, Reg Bunn. 27 Terror From Space (SDL143) by Ron Turner. 28 Ho For Robin Hood (TPL174, 3 stories) by Arthur Horowicz, Guido Buzzelli. 29 Killer in Space (SDL44) by Ron Turner. 30 Robin Hood, Freedom Fighter. 31 Kidnappers From Mars (SDL31) by Ron Turner. 32 Robin Hood the Magnificent. 33 Death Planet (SDL48) by Bill Lacey. 34 Vengeance Arrow (TPL198, 3 stories) by Angel Pardo, Nadir Quinto, Reg Bunn. 35 Emperor of the Moon (SDL49) by Ron Turner. 36 The Justice of Robin Hood.

BUSTER AND MONSTER FUN HOLIDAY BOOK

Fleetway; 1990-1994

1990-1994	£1.00

BUSTER BOOK

(see also Buster Book of Thrills)

Fleetway; 1962-1994

1962 softback	£25.00
1963 softback	£15.00
1964-1965 softback	£10.00
1966-1969	£6.00
1970-1973	£4.00
1974-1979	£3.50
1980-1989	£3.00
1990-1994	£2.50

BUSTER BOOK OF GAGS

Fleetway; 1969

1969 very scarce	£7.50

BUSTER BOOK OF SPOOKY STORIES

Fleetway; 1974-1975

1975-1976 Eric Bradbury, Carlos Cruz reprints	£4.00

BUSTER BOOK OF THRILLS

Fleetway; 1962

1962 softback, scarce; Ron Turner Rick Random reprint	£30.00

BY THE TIME I GET TO WAGGA WAGGA

Harrier; 1 May 1987

1 Eddie Campbell art	£1.00

C

CAPTAIN AMERICA

Miller; 1 1954-?

1-? 28pgs; reprints from Marvel	£6.00

CAPTAIN AMERICA

Marvel; 1 25th Feb 1981-59 3rd Apr 1982

1 32pgs; Captain America, Iron Man, Defenders, Dazzler reprints begin	£1.50
1 with free gift (Superhero sticker)	£3.00
2	£1.25
2 with free gift (Superhero sticker)	£2.50
3-5	£1.00
6-20,22-36	£0.75
21 1st "Captain America and Marvel Action"; Captain America, Thor, Iron Man, Dazzler, Fantastic Four	£0.75
37 1st "Captain America and Marvel Super Adventures"; glossy cover, 8pgs colour	£1.25
37 with free gift (Captain Britain mask)	£2.50
38-49,51-59	£0.75
50 reprints Captain America #241	£1.00

CAPTAIN AMERICA SUMMER SPECIAL

Marvel; nn May 1981

nn 52pgs; reprints	£0.40

CAPTAIN AMERICA COLLECTORS EDITION

Marvel/Grandreams; 1981

1981 US reprints, Sterenko colour art from Captain America #110-111, 113	£3.00

CAPTAIN BRITAIN

Marvel; 1 13th Oct 1976-39 6th Jul 1977 (joins Super Spider-Man)

1 Captain Britain by Chris Claremont & Herbe Trimpe/Fred Kida begins	£2.50
1 with free gift (Captain Britain mask)	£4.00
2	£1.25
3-6,8-10	£1.00
7 Howard the Duck pull-out comic	£1.25

N.MINT

11-16,19-23 Gary Friedrich scripts £0.75
17 free comic insert; some pages from issue 18 printed in error £1.25
18 colour pages reprinted from 17 £1.00
24-39 glossy cover issues, various creators £1.00

CAPTAIN BRITAIN
Marvel; 1986
nn 192pgs; Jamie Delano & Alan Davis reprints £6.00

CAPTAIN BRITAIN ANNUAL
Marvel; 1978
1978 £2.50

CAPTAIN BRITAIN MONTHLY
Marvel; 1 Jan 1985-14 Feb 1986
1 Captain Britain by Jamie Delano & Alan Davis, Freefall Warriors by Steve Parkhouse begin, Abslom Daak, Nightraven reprints begin £5.00
2,4 £3.50
3 Mike Collins Captain Britain script £3.50
5 Space Thieves by David Harper & Barry Kitson begins £3.50
6-10,13 £3.00
11 The Cherubin by Mike Collins & Mark Farmer £3.00
12 Black Knight reprints begin £3.00
14 Grant Morrison text story £3.00

CAPTAIN BRITAIN SUMMER SPECIAL
Marvel; Jun 1980-May 1983, Oct 1992
1980 52pgs, reprints £1.50
1981 52pgs, reprints £1.50
1983 £1.50
Autumn Special 1992 Alan Davis reprints £1.00

CAPTAIN MARVEL
Miller; nn Dec 1944
nn 68pgs; Fawcett reprints £50.00

CAPTAIN MARVEL ADVENTURES
Miller; 1946-27th Jan 1954 (becomes Marvelman)
Note: Miller published a number of different series of Captain Marvel, all based on the Fawcett comics; variations in format are listed below.
54 16pgs, photogravure £20.00
55-58,64,66 16pgs, photogravure £12.50
nn 16pgs, red/blue letterpress (15? issues) £10.00
50 (Apr 1950)-**84** 36/24pgs £8.00
v1:1 (19 Aug 1953)-**24** (27 Jan 1954) 28pgs £8.00
Captain Marvel Colouring Book (Miller, 1948) £18.00

CAPTAIN MARVEL ANNUAL
Miller; Sep 1953
1954 32pgs spiral bound £25.00

CAPTAIN MARVEL BOOK OF KNOWLEDGE
Miller; 1950s
nn 1/- £15.00

CAPTAIN MARVEL JR
Miller; 1945-27th Jan 1954 (becomes Young Marvelman)
Note: Miller published a number of different series of Captain Marvel Jr., all based on the Fawcett comics; variations in format are listed below.
nn (24),33,37,40,50,58 16pgs, photogravure (6+ issues) £12.50
50 (May 1950)-**85** 24/36pgs £8.00
v1:1 (19 Aug 1953)-**24** (27 Jan 1954) 28pgs £8.00

CAPTAIN MARVEL JR ANNUAL
Miller; Sep 1953
1954 32pgs spiral bound £25.00

CAPTAIN MIDNIGHT
Miller/Arnold Book Co.; 1946-Jul 1963 (54? issues)
Note: Miller published a number of different series of Captain Midnight, all based on the Fawcett comics; variations in format are listed below.
10,11,12 photogravure £12.50
42 16pgs, photogravure £10.00
43 68pgs, photogravure £10.00
44,48 £10.00
100-139 28pgs £6.00
1 (Aug 1962)-**12** (Jul 1963) 28pgs £5.00

CAPTAIN MIRACLE
Anglo; 1 Oct 1960-9 Jun 1961
1 28pgs; rejigged Marvelman reprints £4.00
2-5,7-9 Don Lawrence art £3.50
6 title given as Invincible on cover; Don Lawrence art £4.00

CAPTAIN SCARLET
Ravette; Oct 1993
Spectrum is Green TV21 reprints £3.00
Indestructible TV21 reprints £3.00

CAPTAIN SCARLET AND THE MYSTERONS
Fleetway; 1 23rd Oct 1993-14 6th May 1994 (joins Thunderbirds)
1 Captain Scarlet TV21 reprints and original material begins, Angels, Zero X reprints begin £1.00
2-14 £0.85

CAPTAIN SCARLET AND THE MYSTERONS STORYBOOK
Century 21; 1967
1967 £20.00

CAPTAIN SCARLET ANNUAL
City; 1967-1968
1967 Ron Turner art £15.00
1968 Ron Turner art £10.00

CAPTAIN SCARLET ANNUAL, THE OFFICIAL
Grandreams; cy1993
1993 £4.75

CAPTAIN SCARLET/THUNDERBIRDS ANNUAL
City; 1969
1969 slightly oversize format £20.00

N.MINT

CASPER THE FRIENDLY GHOST
Streamline/United Anglo-American; 1 1953
1 28pgs; reprints from Harvey £2.50

CASPER THE FRIENDLY GHOST
Top Sellers; 1 1973-? 1974
1-? 36pgs; reprints from Harvey £1.00

CASTLE OF HORROR
Portman; 1 Sep 1978-?
1-? 68pgs; reprints from Marvel £1.50

CENTURY COMIC
(see All Favourites, Five-Score Comic Monthly, Mighty Comic)
K.G. Murray (Australia); 1 late-1950s-92? mid-1960s
1 rare; 100pgs squarebound; b/w National Periodical reprints, incl. Pow-Wow Smith, Congo Bill, Tomahawk, Rex the Wonder Dog, Binky, Superman, Aquaman £75.00
2 rare £50.00
3-5 very scarce £40.00
6-10 very scarce £35.00
11-92? scarce £30.00
Note: later issues feature Batman, Lois Lane, Tommy Tomorrow, etc.

CHALLENGERS OF THE UNKNOWN
Strato; 1-4 1960
1-4 reprints from National Periodical Publications £3.00

CHAMPION
Fleetway; 26th Feb 1966-4th Jun 1966, 15 unnumbered issues (joins Lion)
No.1 - 26 Feb 1966 Jet Jordan, School For Spacemen, Return of the Stormtroopers by Eric Bradbury, When the Sky Turned Green by Carlos Cruz begin £15.00
No.1 with free gift (Screamer Balloon) £25.00
No 2 - 5 Mar 1966 £7.50
12 Mar-4 Jun 1966 £5.00

CHAMPION THE WONDER HORSE
Daily Mirror; Aug 1957-1962
1957 scarce £6.00
1958 Stories by Arthur Groom, illus. by John Pollack £4.00
1959 Stories by Arthur Groom, illus. by John Burns £4.00
1960 Stories by Arthur Groom, illus. by Michael Godfrey £3.50
1961 Stories by Arthur Groom, illus. by Michael Godfrey £3.50
1962 £3.00

CHAMPION THE WONDER HORSE
Purnell; 1959
1959 Text stories, John Burns frontis £4.00

CHAMPION THE WONDER HORSE COMIC ANNUAL
World Distributors; undated-1959?
nd "Trail to Danger" (1st story) £4.00
1954 Dell reprints £3.50
1955-1959 £2.50

CHARLIE'S ANGELS ANNUAL
Stafford Pemberton; 1978-1981
1978-1981 £2.00

CHEYENNE ANNUAL
World Distributors; 1960-1964
1960 stories by Joe Morrissey; "Trial by Water" (1st story) £5.00
1961 stories by Joe Morrissey; "Bounty Hunter" (1st story) £4.00
1962 (blue background) stories by Joe Morrissey; Dell/Gold Key reprints £4.00
1962 (orange background) £4.00
1963 Dell reprints £3.50
1964 Dell reprints £3.50

CHEYENNE ADVENTURE STORIES
Adprint; 1961
1961 stories by John Stanstead, illus. by Desmond Walduck £5.00

CHEYENNE COMIC ALBUM
World Distributors; 1 1958,1964
1 "The Captives" (1st story) £5.00
1964 Dell/Gold Key reprints £4.00
Note: Other editions probably exist

CHEYENNE, A TELEVISION STORY BOOK
New Town Printers; 1961-1962
1961 "Moose Jaw Trail" (1st story) £5.00
1962 "The Kiowa Trial" (1st story) £4.00
1963 £4.00

CHEYENNE KID
Miller; 1 1957-18 1958
1 28pgs; Charlton reprints, incl. Williamson/Torres art in some issues £4.00
2-18 £2.50

CHEYENNE WESTERN ALBUM
G.T. Ltd.; 1959?
nn reprints Kit Carson, Lucky Logan, Davy Crockett, Buck Jones £5.00

CHICKS' OWN, THE
Amalgamated Press; 1 25th Sep 1920-1605 9th Mar 1957 (joins Playhour)
1 12pgs tabloid; Dicky the Duck by Arthur White begins £50.00
1920 issues £15.00
1921-1939 incl. White, Hugh O'Neill, Philip Swinnerton art £5.00
1940-1951 8pgs; becomes fortnightly £2.50
1952-1957 12pgs, reverts to weekly £2.00
CHRONONLOGY
21 Apr 1934 1st "Chicks' Own & Bo Peep". 12 Aug 1939 1st "Chicks' Own & Happy Days". 31 May 1941 1st "Chicks' Own & Bubbles". 27 Oct 1951 reverts to weekly schedule. 9 Jun 1956 becomes all picture.

CHICKS' OWN ANNUAL
Amalgamated Press; 1924-1957
1924 scarce £50.00
1925 £40.00
1926-1930 £30.00
1931-1940 £20.00

N.MINT

1941-1950 £15.00
1951-1957 £10.00
Note: early editions are tabloid size

CHILLER POCKET BOOK
Marvel; 1 Mar 1980-28 Jul 1982
1 52pgs small; Dracula, Satana reprints begin £1.00
2-8,10-19,21-28 £0.40
9,20 100pgs; Xmas double numbers £0.80

CHOPPER
Fleetway; Aug 1990
Song of the Surfer 2000AD reprints by John Wagner & Colin MacNeil £6.00

CHRONICLES OF GENGHIS GRIMTOAD, THE
Marvel; Oct 1990
nn reprints from Strip by Wagner/Grant & Gibson £6.00

CHRONICLES OF JUDGE DREDD, THE
(see The Complete Judge Dredd)
Titan; 1981-1990
1 Judge Dredd, 2000AD reprints begin, Bolland art £6.00
1 hardback £12.00
2-3 The Cursed Earth Part One/Two £5.00
2-3 hardback £10.00
4-5 Judge Caligula Book One/Two £5.00
4-5 hardback £10.00
6 Judge Dredd 2 McMahon art £5.00
6 hardback £10.00
7 Judge Death, Bolland art £5.00
7 hardback £10.00
8-10 Judge Child Book One/Two/Three £5.00
11 Judge Dredd 3, McMahon art £5.00
12 Block Mania £4.50
13-14 Apocalypse War Book One/Two £5.00
15-23 Judge Dredd 4-12 £4.50
24 City of the Damned £5.00
25-34 Judge Dredd 13-22 £4.50
35-37 Judge Dredd in Oz Book One/Two/Three £5.00
38-40 Judge Dredd 23-25 £5.00
41-42 Judge Dredd 26-27 £5.50
43-45 Mega-City Vice 1,2,3 £5.50
46 Destiny's Angels £5.50
Note: numbering comes from Titan adverts and was dropped on later issues.

CHRONICLES OF ULLAH, THE
Magpie Graphics; 1 Apr 1992-7 Sep 1993
1 Of Beggars & Kings begins £1.00
2-7 £0.75

CISCO KID, THE
World Distributors; 1 1952-51 1955
1 36pgs; reprints from Dell begin £10.00
2-48 £5.00
49-51 28pgs £5.00

THE CISCO KID COMIC ALBUM
World Distributors; 1 1953?-3 1955?
1 £5.00
2-3 £4.00

CITY, THE
Pan; 1994
nn James Herbert 'Rats' graphic novel £5.00

CLASH OF THE TITANS
Independant Television; nn Jul 1981
nn 64pgs; Look-In Special, reprints US strip based on film £1.00

CLASSIC ACTION HOLIDAY SPECIAL
Fleetway; Jun 1990
nn new stories featuring classic Fleetway characters incl. Kelley's Eye by John Cooper, Robot Archie by Sandy James, The Steel Claw by Vano, Jet Ace Logan by John Gillatt, Johnny Cougar by Sandy James £0.75

A CLASSIC IN PICTURES
Amex; 1-12 1949
1-12 each £8.00
ARTISTS/FEATURES
1 Oliver Twist by C.L. Doughty. 2 Ivanhoe by F.A. Philpott. 3 Macbeth by F.A. Philpott. 4 Westward Ho by Colin Merritt. 5 Treasure Island by Colin Merritt. 6 A Tale of Two Cities. 7 The Three Musketeers. 8 Lorna Doone by C.L. Doughty. 9 Henry V by F.A. Philpott. 10 Barnaby Rudge. 11 Mutiny on the Bounty by Colin Merritt. 12 Julius Caesar by F.A. Philpott.
Note: this series was reprinted by Philipp Marx under their Bairns Books imprint as Famous Stories In Pictures (qv)

CLASSIC JUDGE DREDD
(see The Complete Judge Dredd)
Fleetway; 1 Aug 1995-18 Jan 1997
1 2000AD reprints begin, Midnight Surfer £1.50
2-18 £1.25

CLASSIC 2000AD (PREVIOUSLY THE BEST OF 2000AD)
Fleetway Editions; 1 Sep 1995-15 Jan 1997
1 reprints America by Wagner & McNeil £1.50
2,4-15 £1.50
3 reprints Shamballa by Grant & Ranson £1.50

CLASSICS ILLUSTRATED
(see Double Duo, Illustrated Library of..., World Illustrated)
Thorpe & Porter; 1952-1962, 167 issues
Note: the original American issue number is given in parentheses. Classics Illustrated were reprinted and reissued many times, and a second price for later printings is given, although some titles were printed in up to 10 different editions and some later or more common printings may be worth less. A comprehensive guide to printing details can be found in The Complete Guide to Classics Illustrated by Dan Malan

N.MINT

1 Huckleberry Finn by Mark Twain; David Gantz art (19) £7.00
later printings £3.00
2 20,000 Leagues Under the Sea by Jules Verne; Henry C. Kiefer art (47) £7.00
later printings £3.00
3 Mysterious Island by Jules Verne; Robert Hayward Webb & David Heames art (34) £7.00
later printings £3.00
4 Macbeth by William Shakespeare; Alex A. Blum art (128) £7.00
later printings £3.00
5 Moby Dick by Herman Melville; Norman Nodel art (5) £7.00
later printings £3.00
6 A Tale Of Two Cities by Charles Dickens; Joe Orlando art (6) £6.00
later printings £3.00
(see also Giant Classics Series, below)
7 Robin Hood Fred Eng art (7) £5.00
later printings £3.00
(see also Giant Classics Series, below)
8 The Odyssey by Homer; Alex A. Blum art (81) £7.00
later printings £3.00
9 Caesar's Conquests by Julius Caesar; Joe Orlando art (130) £7.00
later printings £3.00
10 Robinson Crusoe by Daniel Defoe; Sam Citron art (10) £6.00
later printings £3.00
(see also Giant Classics Series, below)
11 The Time Machine by H.G. Wells; Lou Cameron art (133) £6.00
later printings £3.00
12 The Dark Frigate by Charles Boardman Hawes; Norman Nodel art (132) £6.00
later printings £3.00
13 Romeo and Juliet by William Shakespeare; George Evans art (134) £7.00
later printing £3.00
Note: number duplicated in Super Deluxe Classics Series, see below
14 Westward Ho! by Charles Kingsley; Allen Simon art (14) £25.00
later printings, new British cover £40.00
(see also Super Deluxe Classics, below)
15 Uncle Tom's Cabin by Harriet Beecher Stowe; Rolland Livingstone art (15) £6.00
later printings £3.00
(see also One Shilling Series and Deluxe Series, below)
16 Gulliver's Travels by Jonathan Swift; Lillian Chestney art (16) £9.00
(see also Popular Classics Series, below)
17 The Deerslayer by James Fenimore Cooper; Louis Zansky art (17), new British cover £30.00
(see also Popular Classics Series, below)
18 Waterloo by Erckmann-Chatrian; Graham Ingels art (135) £6.00
later printings £3.00
Note: number duplicated in One Shilling Series and Deluxe series, below
19 The Covered Wagon by Emerson Hough; Norman Nodel art (131) £7.00
later printings £3.00
20 Ivanhoe by Sir Walter Scott; Edd Ashe art (2) £6.00
later printings £3.00
21 The Count of Monte Cristo by Alexandre Dumas; Allen Simon art (3) £6.00
later printings £3.00
22 The Pathfinder by James Fenimore Cooper; Louis Zansky art (22) £5.00
later printings, new British cover £40.00
(see also Popular Classics Series, below)
23 Oliver Twist by Charles Dickens; Arnold Hicks art (23) £8.00
later printings £5.00
24 Journey to the Centre of the Earth by Jules Verne; Norman Nodel art (138) £6.00
later printing £3.00
25 Two Years Before the Mast by Richard Henry Dana; Robert Hayward Webb & David Heames art (25) £8.00
later printings £4.00
(see also Super Deluxe Classics, below)
26 The Little Savage by Frederick Marryat; George Evans art (137) £6.00
later printings £3.00
27 The Spy by James Fenimore Cooper; Arnold Hicks art (51) £6.00
later printings £3.00
28 The Lady of the Lake by Sir Walter Scott; Henry C. Kiefer art (75) £6.00
later printing £3.00
29 The Prince and the Pauper by Mark Twain; Arnold Hicks art (29) £6.00
later printings £3.00
30 A Connecticut Yankee in King Arthur's Court by Mark Twain; Jack Hearne art. (24) £6.00
later printings £3.00
31 The Black Arrow by Robert Louis Stevenson; Arnold Hicks art (31) £8.00
later printings £4.00
32 Lorna Doone by R.D. Blackmore; Matt Baker art (32) £8.00
later printings £4.00
33 The Adventures of Tom Sawyer by Mark Twain; Aldo Rubano art (50) £6.00
later printings £3.00
34 The Sea Wolf by Jack London; Alex A. Blum art (85) £6.00
later printings £4.00
35 Jane Eyre by Charlotte Bronte; Harley M. Griffiths art (39) £6.00
later printings £3.00
36 The Man in the Iron Mask by Alexandre Dumas; Henry C. Kiefer art (54) £6.00
later printings £3.00
37 The Pioneers by James Fenimore Cooper; Rudolph Palais art (37) £7.00
later printings, new British cover £30.00
(see also Popular Classics Series, below)
38 The House of Seven Gables by Nathaniel Hawthorne; Harley M. Griffiths art (52) £6.00
later printings £3.00
39 The Scottish Chiefs by Jane Porter; Alex A. Blum art (67) £6.00
later printings £3.00
40 Benjamin Franklin by Franklin; Alex A. Blum art (65) £8.00
later printings £3.00

	N.MINT
Note: number duplicated in Super Deluxe Classics, below	
41 The Pilot by James Fenimore Cooper; Alex A. Blum art (70)	£9.00
later printings	£4.00
42 Swiss Family Robinson by Johann Wyss; Henry C. Kiefer art (42)	£10.00
later printings	£4.00
43 A Midsummer Night's Dream by William Shakespeare; Alex A. Blum art (87)	£6.00
later printings	£4.00
44 Puddn'head Wilson by Samuel L. Clemens; Henry C. Kiefer art. (93)	£6.00
later printings	£5.00
45 The Bottle Imp by Robert Louis Stevenson; Lou Cameron art (116)	£6.00
later printings	£5.00
46 Kidnapped by Robert Louis Stevenson; Robert H. Webb art (46)	£8.00
later printings	£4.00
47 In the Reign of Terror by G.A. Henty; George Evans art (139)	£6.00
later printings	£3.00
48 David Copperfield by Charles Dickens; Henry C. Kiefer art (48)	£7.00
later printings	£3.00
49 Alice in Wonderland by Lewis Carroll; Alex A. Blum art (49)	£8.00
later printings	£4.00
(see also Popular Classics Series, below)	
50 Castle Dangerous by Sir Walter Scott; Stan Campbell art (141)	£6.00
later printings	£3.00
51 Lord Jim by Joseph Conrad; advertised, but not published in UK	–
52 The First Men in the Moon by H.G. Wells; George Woodbridge art (144)	£6.00
later printings	£3.00
53 A Christmas Carol by Charles Dickens; Henry C. Kiefer art (53)	£18.00
later printings, new British cover	£100.00
54 With Fire and Sword by Henryk Sienkiewicz; George Woodbridge art (146)	£6.00
later printings	£3.00
55 Silas Marner by George Eliot; Henry C. Kiefer art (55)	£6.00
later printings	£3.00
56 The Hunchback of Notre Dame by Victor Hugo. Allen Simon art. (18)	£5.00
later printing	£5.00
(see also One Shilling Series and Deluxe Series, below)	
56a The Corsican Brothers by Alexandre Dumas; Allen Simon art (20)	£20.00
later printing, new British cover	£25.00
57 The Song of Hiawatha by Henry Wadsworth Longfellow; Alex A. Blum art (57)	£9.00
later printings	£4.00
58 The Prairie by James Fenimore Cooper; Rudolph Palais art (58)	£5.00
later printings	£3.00
(see also Popular Classics Series, below)	
59 Ben Hur by Lew Wallace; Joe Orlando art (147)	£6.00
later printings	£3.00
60 Black Beauty by Anna Sewell; August M. Groehlich art (60)	£7.00
(see also Popular Classics Series, below)	
61 The Buccaneer; based on film; George Evans & Bob Jenney art (148)	£6.00
later printing	£3.00
62 Western Stories by Bret Harte (contains The Luck of Roaring Lamp, The Outcasts of Poker Flat); Henry C. Kiefer art (62)	£6.00
later printings	£3.00
63 Off on a Comet by Jules Verne; Gerald McCann art (149)	£6.00
later printing	£3.00
64 Treasure Island by Robert Louis Stephenson; Alex A. Blum art (64)	£5.00
later printings	£3.00
(see also Popular Classics Series, below)	
65 The King of the Mountains by Edmond About; Norman Nodel art (127)	£6.00
later printings	£3.00
66 The Last of the Mohicans by James Fenimore Cooper; Ray Ramsey art (4)	£6.00
later printings	£3.00
67 The Three Musketeers by Alexandre Dumas; Malcolm Kildare art (1)	£6.00
68 Julius Caesar by William Shakespeare; Henry C. Kiefer art (68)	£5.00
later printings	£4.00
(see also Popular Classics Series, below)	
69 Around the World in Eighty Days by Jules Verne; Henry C. Kiefer art (69)	£7.00
later printings	£4.00
70 The Virginian by Owen Wister; Norman Nodel art (150)	£6.00
later printing	£3.00
71 The Man Who Laughs by Victor Hugo; Alex A. Blum art (71)	£12.00
later printing	£9.00
72 The Oregon Trail by Francis Parkman; Henry C. Kiefer art (72)	£9.00
later printings	£5.00
73 The Black Tulip by Alexandre Dumas; Alex A. Blum art (73)	£25.00
later printings, new British cover	£35.00
74 Mr. Midshipman Easy by Frederick Marryat; Alex A. Blum art (74)	£25.00
later printings, new British cover	£125.00
(see also Super Deluxe Classics, below)	
75 On Jungle Trails by Frank Buck; Norman Nodel art (140)	£6.00
later printing	£4.00
76 Rip Van Winkle (and The Headless Horseman) by Washington Irving; Rolland Livingstone art (12)	£6.00
later printings	£3.00
77 The Iliad by Homer; Alex A. Blum art; new British cover (77)	£25.00
later printings	£23.00
later printings with US cover	£7.00
(see also Popular Classics Series, below)	
78 Joan of Arc Henry C. Kiefer art (78)	£6.00
later printings	£3.00
(see also One Shilling Series and Deluxe Series, below)	
79 Cyrano De Bergerac by Edmond Rostand; Alex A. Blum art (79)	£10.00
80 White Fang by Jack London; Alex A. Blum art (80)	£6.00
later printings	£3.00
81 The Adventures of Marco Polo Homer Fleming art (27)	£7.00

Classics Illustrated #1

CLASSICS
Illustrated
Featuring Stories by the World's Greatest Authors
No. 11 1'3
THE TIME MACHINE
H. G. WELLS

Classics Illustrated #11

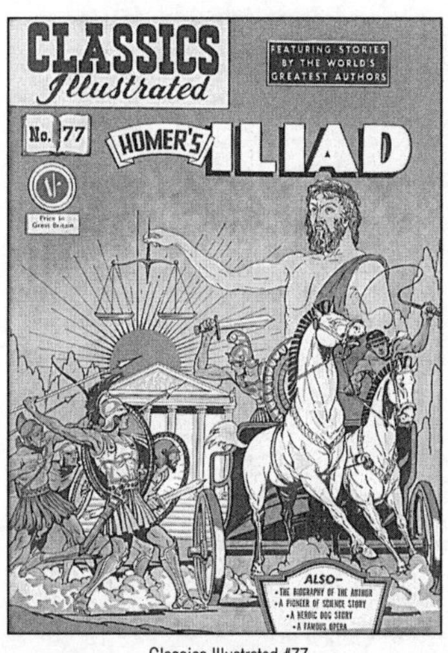

Classics Illustrated #77

N.MINT

later printings £4.00
82 The Master of Ballantrae by Robert Louis Stevenson; L.M. Dresser art (82) £4.00
later printings £3.00
later printings, new British cover £25.00
(see also One Shilling Series and Deluxe series, below)
83 Won By the Sword by G.A. Henty; John Tartaglione art (151) £7.00
later printings £4.00
84 The Gold Bug and other stories by Edgar Allan Poe; British originated art by Mick Anglo £85.00
85 Dr Jekyll and Mr Hyde by Robert Louis Stevenson; Arnold Hicks art (13) £7.00
later printings £7.00
86 Under Two Flags by Ouida; Maurice Del Bourgo art (86) £7.00
later printings £3.00
87 Abraham Lincoln Norman Nodel art (142) £6.00
later printings £6.00
88 Men Of Iron by Howard Pyle; L.M. Dresser (88) £7.00
later printings £3.00
89 Crime and Punishment by Feodor Dostoevsky; Rudolf Palais art (89) £6.00
later printings £3.00
(see also One Shilling Series and Deluxe Series, below)
90 Green Mansions by W.H. Hudson; Alex A. Blum art (90) £7.00
later printing £6.00
91 The Call of the Wild by Jack London; Maurice Del Bourgo art (91) £7.00
later printings £3.00
92 Les Miserables by Victor Hugo; Rolland Livingstone art (9) £8.00
93 Wild Animals I Have Known by Ernest Thomson Seton; L.B. Cole art (152) £6.00
later printing £4.00
94 David Balfour by Robert Louis Stevenson; Rudolf Palais art (94) £7.00
later printing £3.00
95 The Crisis by Winston Churchill; George Evans art (145) £8.00
96 Daniel Boone by John Bakeless; Alex A. Blum art (96) £7.00
later printings £5.00
97 King Solomon's Mines by H. Rider Haggard; Henry C. Kiefer art (97) £7.00
later printings £5.00
98 The Red Badge of Courage by Stephen Crane; Gustav Shrotter & Maurice Del Bourgo art (98) £6.00
later printings £3.00
99 Hamlet by William Shakespeare; Alex A. Blum art (99) £7.00
later printings £3.00
100 Mutiny on the Bounty by Charles Nordhoff & James Norman Hall; M. Waldinge art (100) £7.00
later printings £5.00
101 William Tell by Frederick Schiller; Maurice Del Bourgo art (101) £5.00
later printings £3.00
(see also One Shilling Series)
102 The Moonstone by William Wilkie Collins; Don Rico art (30) £7.00
103 Men Against the Sea by Charles Nordhoff & James Norman Hall; Rudolf Palais art (103) £7.00
later printings £5.00
104 Bring 'em Back Alive by Frank Buck with Edward Anthony; Henry C. Kiefer art (104) £7.00
later printings £5.00
(see also One Shilling Series and Deluxe Series, below)
105 From the Earth to the Moon by Jules Verne. Alex A. Blum art. (105) £7.00
later printings £3.00
106 Buffalo Bill Maurice Del Bourgo art (106) £5.00
later printings £3.00
(see also One Shilling Series and Deluxe Series, below)
107 King of the Khyber Rifles by Talbot Mundy; Seymour Moskowitz art (107) £7.00
later printings £3.00
(see also Deluxe Series, below)
108 Knights of the Round Table Alex A. Blum art (108) £7.00
later printings £5.00
(see also Deluxe Series, below)
109 Pitcairn's Island by Charles Nordhoff & James Norman Hall; Rudolf Palais art (109) £7.00
later printing £4.00
110 Michael Strogoff by Jules Verne; Arnold Hicks art (28) £7.00
later printing £4.00
111 The Talisman by Sir Walter Scott; Henry C. Kiefer art (111) £7.00
later printing £5.00
112 The Adventures of Kit Carson Rudolf Palais art (112) £7.00
later printing £5.00
(see also Deluxe Series, below)
113 The Forty-Five Guardsmen by Alexandre Dumas; Maurice Del Bourgo art (113) £7.00
later printings £3.00
114 The Red Rover by James Fenimore Cooper; Peter Costanza art (114) £7.00
later printings £5.00
115 How I Found Livingstone by Sir Henry M. Stanley; S.Trapani, Ted Galindo & Dick Giordano art (115) £7.00
later printings £5.00
116 Typee by Herman Melville; Ezra Whiteman art (36) £7.00
later printing, British originated art by Luis Dominguez £40.00
117 Twenty Years After by Alexandre Dumas; Robert C. Burns art (41) £7.00
118 Rob Roy by Sir Walter Scott; Rudolf & Walter Palais art (118) £7.00
later printings £4.00
119 Soldiers of Fortune by Richard Harding Davis; Kurt P. Shaffenberger art (119) £7.00
later printings £3.00
120 The Hurricane by Charles Nordhoff & James Norman Hall; Lou Cameron art (120) £7.00
later printings £3.00
121 Wild Bill Hickok Medio Iorio & S. Trapani art (121) £7.00
later printings £5.00
122 The Mutineers by Charles Boardman Hawes; Peter Costanza art (122) £7.00
later printings £3.00
123 Fang and Claw by Frank Buck; Lin Streeter art (123) £7.00
later printings £5.00
124 The War of the Worlds by H.G. Wells; Lou Cameron art (124) £7.00
later printings £5.00

N.MINT

125 The Ox-bow Incident Norman Nodel art (125) £7.00
later printings £3.00
126 The Downfall by Emile Zola; Lou Cameron art (126) £7.00
later printings £3.00
127 The Invisible Man by H.G. Wells; Norman Nodel art (153) £7.00
later printing £6.00
128 Wuthering Heights by Emily Bronte; Henry C. Kiefer art (59) £7.00
later printings £6.00
129 Davy Crockett Lou Cameron art (129) £7.00
later printings £4.00
130 The Woman in White by Wilkie Collins; Alex A. Blum art (61) £6.00
later printing £5.00
131 The Man Without a Country by Edward Everett Hale; Henry C. Kiefer art (63) £6.00
later printing, alternative cover £7.00
132 The Conspiracy of Pontiac by Francis Parkman; Gerald McCann art (154) £6.00
later printing £3.00
133 The Lion of the North by G.A. Henty; Norman Nodel art (155) £6.00
later printing £3.00
134 The Conquest of Mexico by Bernal Diaz Del Castillo; Bruno Premiani art (156) £6.00
later printing £3.00
135 Great Expectations by Charles Dickens; Henry C. Kiefer art (43) £90.00
later printing, new British cover £90.00
136 Lives of the Hunted by Ernest Thompson Seton; Norman Nodel art (157) £6.00
137 The Conspirators by Alexandre Dumas; Gerald McCann art (158) £6.00
138 Don Quixote by Miguel de Cervantes; Louis Zansky art (11) £8.00
139 The Octopus by Frank Norris; Gray Morrow & George Evans art (159) £6.00
139a The Food of the Gods by H.G. Wells; Tony Tallarico art (160) £6.00
139b Cleopatra by H. Rider Haggard; Norman Nodel art (161) £6.00
140 Robur the Conqueror by Jules Verne; Don Perlin art (162) £7.00
later printings £6.00
141 Master of the World by Jules Verne; Gray Morrow art (163) £7.00
142 The Cossack Chief by Nikolai Gogol; Sidney Miller art (164) £7.00
143 Sail With the Devil based on "Captain Singleton's Adventures" by Daniel Defoe; British originated art by Norman Light £75.00
144 The Queen's Necklace by Alexandre Dumas; Gray Morrow art (165) £7.00
145 Tigers and Traitors by Jules Verne; Norman Nodel art (166) £9.00
146 Adventures of Baron Munchausen British originated art by Denis Gifford £75.00
147 Through the Looking Glass by Lewis Carroll; British originated art by Jennifer H. Robertson £75.00
148 Nights of Terror by Collins/Dickens; British originated art by Mick Anglo £75.00
149 The Gorilla Hunters by R.M. Ballantyne; British originated art £75.00
150 The Canterville Ghost by Oscar Wilde; British originated art by Mick Anglo £75.00
151 Tom Brown's Schooldays by Thomas Hughes; Homer Fleming art (45) £9.00
152 The Toilers of the Sea by Victor Hugo; August M. Froehlich art (56) £9.00
153 The Last Days of Pompeii by Edward Bulwer Lytton; Henry C. Kiefer art (35) £9.00
154 The Arabian Nights Lillian Chestney art (8) £20.00
155 Adventures of Cellini by Benvenuto Cellini; A.M. Frochlich art (38) £9.00
156 The Dog Crusoe by R.M. Ballentyne; British originated art by Norman Light £75.00
157 The Queen of Spades by Alexander Pushkin; British originated art £75.00
158 Faust by Johann W. Von Goeth; (167) £12.00
158a Doctor No by Ian Fleming; Norman Nodel art; 1st publication, originally commissioned for Dell Movie Classic £175.00
159 Master and Man by Count Leo Tolstoy; British originated art £75.00
160 In Freedom's Cause by G.A. Henty; George Evans & Reed Crandall art (168) £30.00
161 The Aeneid by Virgil; British originated art £125.00
162 Saga of the North by Pierre Loti; British originated art by Tomas Porto £80.00
163 The Argonauts by Appolonius; British originated art £185.00

Note: The US main series #95 (All Quiet on the Western Front) and #110 (A Study in Scarlet) were distributed in the UK by Thorpe & Porter. The following numbers were not reprinted from the US series: 21 (3 Famous Mysteries), 26 (Frankenstein), 33 (The Adventures of Sherlock Holmes, 44 (Mysteries of Paris, 66 (The Cloister and the Hearth, 76 (The Prisoner of Zenda), 83 (The Jungle Book), 92 (The Courtship of Miles Standish, 102 (The White Company), 117 (Captains Courageous), 143 (Kim), 167 (Faust) and 169 (Negro Americans).

CLASSICS ILLUSTRATED DELUXE SERIES

Thorpe & Porter; 1952, 10 issues
Note: Priced 2/6, hardcover, unnumbered
Uncle Tom's Cabin £65.00
Hunchback of Notre Dame (see main series #56) £65.00
Note: number duplicated in main series, reprinted as main series #56
Joan of Arc (see main series #78) £65.00
Master of Ballantrae (see main series #82) £65.00
Crime and Punishment (see main series #89) £65.00
Bring 'em Back Alive (see main series #104) £65.00
Buffalo Bill (see main series #106) £65.00
King of the Khyber Rifles (see main series #107) £75.00
Knight of the Round Table (see main series #108) £65.00
Kit Carson (see main series #112) £65.00

CLASSICS ILLUSTRATED: GIANT CLASSICS SERIES

Thorpe & Porter; May 1952-1952, 4 issues
Note: Priced 2/-, US numbering
2 Ivanhoe (see main series #20) £17.00
Note: number duplicated in main series, reprinted as main series #20
6 A Tale of Two Cities (see main series #6) £17.00
7 Robin Hood (see main series #7) £17.00
10 Robinson Crusoe (see main series #10) £17.00

CLASSICS ILLUSTRATED JUNIOR SERIES

Thorpe & Porter; 501 1955-516 1956, 14 issues
Note: Priced 1/3, US numbering
501 Snow White and the Seven Dwarfs Jennifer H. Robertson art begins £10.00
502 The Ugly Duckling £8.00
503 Cinderella £7.00
504 The Pied Piper £7.00
505 The Sleeping Beauty £7.00

	N.MINT
506 The Three Little Pigs	£7.00
507 Jack and the Beanstalk	£7.00
508 Goldilocks	£7.00
509 Beauty and the Beast	£7.00
510 Little Red Riding Hood	£7.00
511 Puss in Boots	£7.00
512 Rumpelstiltskin	£7.00
513 Pinocchio	£7.00
516 Aladdin and his Lamp	£7.00

CLASSICS ILLUSTRATED: ONE SHILLING SERIES

Thorpe & Porter; 1952, 8 issues
Note: Priced 1/-, US numbering

15 Uncle Tom's Cabin (see main series #15)	£14.00
18 The Hunchback of Notre Dame (see main series #56)	£14.00
Note: number duplicated in main series, reprinted as main series #56	
78 Joan of Arc (see main series #78)	£14.00
82 The Master of Ballantrae (see main series #82)	£10.00
89 Crime and Punishment (see main series #89)	£8.00
101 William Tell (see main series #101)	£7.00
104 Bring 'em Back Alive (see main series #104)	£7.00
106 Buffalo Bill (see main series #106)	£7.00

CLASSICS ILLUSTRATED POPULAR CLASSICS SERIES

Thorpe & Porter; Oct 1951-Mar 1952, 10 issues
Note: Priced 1/3, US numbering, US line covers

16 Gulliver's Travels by Jonathan Swift (Nov 1951) Lillian Chestney art	£19.00
17 The Deerslayer by James Fenimore Cooper (Mar 1952) Louis Zansky art	£19.00
22 The Pathfinder by James Fenimore Cooper (Feb 1952) Louis Zansky art	£19.00
37 The Pioneers by James Fenimore Cooper (Feb 1952) Rudolph Palais art	£19.00
49 Alice in Wonderland by Lewis Carroll (Oct 1951) Alex A. Blum art	£25.00
58 The Prairie by James Fenimore Cooper (Mar 1952) Rudolph Palais art	£19.00
60 Black Beauty by Anna Sewell (Nov 1951) August M. Groehlich art	£19.00
64 Treasure Island by Robert Louis Stephenson (Jan 1952) Alex A. Blum art	£19.00
68 Julius Caesar by William Shakespeare (Oct 1951) Henry C. Kiefer art	£20.00
77 The Iliad by Homer (Jan 1952) Alex A. Blum art	£19.00

CLASSICS ILLUSTRATED: SUPER DELUXE CLASSICS

Thorpe & Porter; May 1952-1953, 5 issue
Note: Priced 1/6, US numbering

13 Dr Jekyll and Mr Hyde (see main series #85)	£17.00
later printing	£8.00
Note: number duplicated in main series, reprinted as main series #85	
14 Westward Ho (see also main series 14)	£30.00
25 Two Years Before the Mast (see main series #25)	£14.00
40 Mysteries by Edgar Allan Poe; contains: The Pit and the Pendulum, A.M. Frochlich art; The Adventures of Hans Pfall, Henry C. Kiefer art; The Fall of the House of Usher, H.M. Griffiths art	£30.00
Note: number duplicated in main series	
74 Mr Midshipman Easy (see main series #74)	£30.00

CODENAME: GENETIX

(see main American comics section)

COLLECTED ADVENTURES OF FAT FREDDY'S CAT

(no imprint); 1975

nn 36pgs; Shelton reprints	£3.00

COLLECTED JUDGE CALIGULA, THE

Titan; nn 1991

nn 144pgs; 2000AD reprints by Wagner, Bolland & McMahon	£6.00

COMBAT COMIC ALBUM

World Distributors; 1 1965

1 64pgs, Dell reprints in colour	£4.00

COMBAT PICTURE ANNUAL

Micron; 1961

1961 254pgs; reprints from Combat Picture Library plus new text	£2.00
Note: issued in dust jacket which will double price if intact	

COMBAT PICTURE LIBRARY

Micron/Smith; 1 Mar 1959-1212 Jun 1985

1 68pgs pocket size; Sea Hunt	£5.00
2	£2.50
3-5	£1.25
6-250	£1.00
251-1212	£0.50

COMET, THE

(titled The Comet/Comet Comic/The Comet Adventure Weekly/Comet Weekly)
Allen/Amalgamated; 1 20th Sep 1946-17th Oct 1959, 580 issues, numbered to 566 (joins Tiger)

1	£40.00
2	£15.00
3-5	£10.00
6-14	£7.50
15 (4 Apr 1947) 1st photogravure issue	£6.00
16-75,77-112	£6.00
76 (13 Aug 1949) Thunderbolt Jaxon begins	£6.00
113 (16 Sep 1950) Kit Carson begins	£6.00
114-192	£6.00
193 (29 Mar 1952) 1st comic-book format issue	£5.00
194-246,248-263,265-269,271-273	£5.00
247 (11 Apr 1953) Dick Barton begins (ends 273)	£5.00
264 (8 Aug 1953) Strongbow the Mighty begins	£5.00
270 (19 Sep 1953) Claude Duval begins	£5.00
274-518	£4.00
519 1st letterpress issue	£3.00
520-564	£3.00
16 May 1959 1st unnumbered issue	£3.00
23 May-17 Oct 1959	£3.00
Note: one un-numbered/undated issue appeared between 27 Jun-15 Aug 1959.	

COMIC CUTS

Harmsworth/Amalgamated; 1 17th May 1890-12th Sep 1953 (joins Knockout)

	N.MINT
1 8pgs tabloid; reprints cartoons from American magazines	£250.00
1890-1895	£60.00
1896-1900	£30.00
1901-1920	£8.00
1921-1940	£6.00
1941-1950	£5.00
1951-1953	£2.50

CHRONOLOGY

331 (Sep 1896) first full colour British comic. 4 Feb 1928 1st "Comic Cuts & Golden Penny". 4 Nov 1939 1st "Comic Cuts & Jolly Comic. 25 May 1940 1st "Comic Cuts & Larks".

ARTISTS/FEATURES

Early artists include Jack Yeats, Tom Browne, Percy Cocking, etc. Later issues incl. Ron Embleton (Forgotten City, Mohawk Trails, Tom O'London). James Holdaway (Cal McCord). Ken Reid (Super Sam, Foxy, Billy Boffin).

COMIC RELIEF COMIC, THE

Fleetway; Mar 1991

nn 56pgs; Benefit comic, Baikie, Bisley, Bond, Dillon, Emerson, Gibbons, Hewlett, Lloyd, Parkhouse, Phillips, Pleece, Ranson, Ridgway, Talbot, Viz team, Yeowell et al art; features Lenny Henry, Jonathan Ross, Griff Rees-Jones, Rowan Atkinson	£1.50

COMMANDO LIBRARY

D.C. Thomson; 1 Jul 1961-present (3018 to Jan 1997)

1 68pgs pocket size; Walk or Die	£10.00
2	£5.00
3-5	£3.00
6-100	£2.00
101-250	£1.00
251-500	£0.75
501-1000	£0.50
1001-3018	£0.25

ARTISTS/FEATURES

1 Walk or Die by Amador Garcia. 2 They Called Him Coward by Armando Banato. 3 A Guy Needs Guts by C.T. Rigby. 4 Mercy For None by Gordon Livingstone. 5 Hellfire Landing by Ortiz. 6 They Came By Night by Ros. 7 The Ship They Couldn't Sink by Savi. 8 Red Runs the River by Rafael Auraleon. 9 Jungle Fury! by Madaigan. 10 Hun Bait by Gordon Livingstone. 11 Closer Than Brothers by Ortiz. 12 The Desperate Days by Gordon Livingstone.Cam Kennedy in 417,604,642,666,702,729,825,878,2172. John Ridgway in 546,572,748,818, 833,1021,1054,1134,1385,1448,1604,1698. Saichann in 2247.

COMPLETE FANTASTIC FOUR, THE

Marvel; 1 28th Sep 1977-53 8th Jun 1979 (joins Mighty World of Marvel)

1 36pgs; FF reprints begin	£1.50
1 with free gift (plastic model Boing 747)	£2.00
2	£1.25
2 with free gift (Maze Game)	£1.50
3-53	£0.75

COMPLETE JUDGE DREDD, THE

Fleetway; 1 Feb 1992-42 Jul 1995 (becomes Classic Judge Dredd)

1 Judge Dredd reprints from 2000AD begin	£5.00
2	£3.00
3	£2.50
4-5	£2.25
6-15	£2.00
16-25	£1.75
26-42	£1.50

COMPLETE JUDGE DREDD, THE

(see The Collected Judge Caligula)
Titan; 1994-1995

The Complete Judge Dredd in Oz (Jun 1994) 240pgs; by Wagner/Grant, Robinson, Dillon, Simpson, etc.	£11.00
The Complete Judge Dredd in the Cursed Earth (Jul 1994) 160pgs; by Mills, McMahon, Bolland	£10.00
The Complete Apocalypse War (Apr 1995) by Wagner/Grant, Ezquerra, McMahon, Bolland etc.	£11.00
Classic Judge Dredd (Jul 1995) by Wagner & Bolland	£10.00
The Complete Judge Child Quest (Jul 1995) by Wagner/Grant, Bolland, McMahon, Smith	£11.00
Judge Dredd and the Angel Gang (Jul 1995) by Wagner/Grant, Ezquerra, McMahon, Smith	£10.00

COMPLETE JUDGE DREDD SPECIAL EDITION, THE

Fleetway Editions; 1 1994-2 1995

1 132pgs; 2000AD group reprints	£2.50
2	£2.50

COMPLETE SPIDER-MAN, THE

Marvel; 1 1990-24 Sep 1992 (continued as The Exploits of Spider-Man)

1 Spider-Man reprints begin, all four US titles	£2.00
1 with free gift (iron-on Spider-Man patch)	£4.00
2	£1.50
3-24 incl. Larsen art	£1.00

CONAN THE BARBARIAN POCKET BOOK

Marvel; 1 11th Sep 1980-13 12th Nov 1981

1 52pgs small; Conan by Barry Windsor-Smith reprints begin	£1.00
2,4-13	£0.50
3 100pgs double issue	£1.00

CONAN WINTER SPECIAL

Marvel; nn Nov 1982

nn Conan reprints	£1.00

CONQUEROR

Harrier; Preview Jun 1984; 1 Aug 1984-9 Dec 1985 (joins Swiftsure)

Preview Dave Harwood art begins (in all issues)	£0.75
1 Harwood/Bolland cover	£0.60
2 Eddie Campbell art, Gibbons cover	£0.50
3 Collins/Farmer art	£0.50
4 Eddie Campbell script	£0.50
5-9	£0.50

N.MINT

CONQUEROR SPECIAL
Harrier; 1 Feb 1987
1 Harwood art £0.75

CONQUEROR UNIVERSE
Harrier; 1 Dec 1985
1 Collins/Roach, Harwood, O'Donnell art £1.00

COR!!
IPC; 6th Jun 1970-15th Jun 1974 (196? issues)
No.1 - 6 Jun 1970 Gus Gorilla by Alf Saporito, Tomboy by Brian Lewis, Ivor Lott & Tony Broke by Reg Parlett begin £5.00
No.1 with free gift (fruit juice sachet) £10.00
No.2 - 13 Jun 1970 £2.50
No.2 with free gift (2 instant picture sheets/Super Anglo Bubble Gum) £5.00
13 Jun 1970-15 Jun 1974 £0.75
ARTISTS/FEATURES
Joe Colquhoun (The Chameleon, The Goodies). Ron Turner (Robby Hood).

COR!! ANNUAL
Fleetway; 1972-1976
1972 £3.50
1973-1976 £3.00

COR!! BOOK OF GAGS
IPC; 1977
1977 scarce £5.00

COR!! SUMMER SPECIAL
IPC; 1972-1974
1972-1974 £2.00

COUNTDOWN
Polystyle; 1 20th Feb 1971-58 24th Mar 1972 (becomes TV Action)
1 24pgs numbered in reverse; Dr Who by Harry Lindfield, Thunderbirds, Captain Scarlet, UFO begin, 1st Countdown by John Burns £25.00
1 with free gift (poster) £40.00
2 Joe 90, Secret Service begin £10.00
3 Jon Pertwee cover £15.00
4-8 £7.50
9-15 £5.00
16-30 £4.00
31-34,36-43,45-58 £4.00
35 Persuaders by Lindfield begins £4.00
44 Thunderbirds by Don Harley begins (original material) £4.00
ARTISTS/FEATURES
Features and artists rotated regularly; artists included Harry Lindfield, Frank Langford, John Burns, Gerry Haylock, Jon Davis, Brian Lewis, Martin Asbury, Don Harley in various issues; some Gerry Anderson material was reprinted from TV Century 21, including Thunderbirds, Stingray, Fireball XL5.

COUNTDOWN ANNUAL
Polystyle; 1972-1973
1972 features include UFO, Thunderbirds, Captain Scarlet, Countdown, The Secret Service, Joe 90, Dr Who by Jim Baikie £12.50
1973 titled "Countdown for TV Action"; features include UFO, Thunderbirds by Ron Turner, The Persuaders, Captain Scarlet, Dr Who by Frank Langford £8.50

COUNTDOWN HOLIDAY SPECIAL
Polystyle; 1971
nn 48pgs; Hampson Fireball XL5 reprints, scarce £8.00

COUNTDOWN WITH TV ACTION HOLIDAY SPECIAL
Polystyle; Mar 1972
nn 48pgs £6.00

COWBOY COMICS/COWBOY PICTURE LIBRARY
Amalgamated Press; 1 Apr 1950-468 Sep 1962
1 Buck Jones - the Fighting Sheriff by Geoff Campion £75.00
2 £30.00
3-5 £25.00
6-20 £20.00
21-50 £15.00
51-204 £8.00
205-468 titled Cowboy Picture Library £4.00
ARTISTS/FEATURES
Jesus Blasco in 265,276,300,305,316,318,329,341,353,357,377,386,389,401,413,446,457, Reg Bunn. Alberto Breccia in 402,410,439,450,468. Steve Chapman. Arturo Del Castillo in 455,463,467. Gerry Embleton. Ron Embleton in 104,106,107,109,115,121,127,137,143, 245. Eric Parker. Carlos V. Roume in 358, 378, 388, 398, 404, 405, 412, 424, 432, 451, 459. Jose Luis Salinas (Cisco Kid reprint) in 55. Tony Weare in 83, 129, 144.

CREEPY WORLDS
Alan Class; 1 Aug 1962-249 Apr 1989
1 64pgs; US reprints begin £15.00
2 £7.50
3-5 £5.00
6-50 £2.50
51-249 £1.50

CRIME DOES NOT PAY
Arnold Book Co.; 1950, 2 unnumbered issues
nn 12pgs green/orange gravure; Lev Gleason reprints £8.00
nn 36pgs full colour cover £8.00

CRIME DOES NOT PAY
Pemberton; 1-6 1951
1-6 36pgs; Lev Gleason reprints £6.00

CRISIS
(see For A Few Troubles More, New Statesmen, Third World War, Troubled Souls, True Faith)
Fleetway; 1 17th Sep 1987-63 Oct 1991
1 Third World War by Pat Mills & Carlos Ezquerra, New Statesmen by John Smith & Jim Baikie begin £1.50
2-3 £1.00
4-10 £0.90
11-13,16-20 £0.80
14 New Statesmen ends £0.80

N.MINT

15 Troubled Souls by Garth Ennis & John McCrea, Sticky Fingers by Myra Hancock & David Hine begin £0.90
21 no Troubled Souls £0.75
22 no Sticky Fingers £0.75
23-26 £0.75
27 Troubled Souls. Sticky Fingers both end £0.75
28 New Statesman Prologue, Angels Amongst Us by Philip Bond begins £0.80
29 True Faith by Garth Ennis & Warren Pleece begins £0.80
30 more scarce, new strip Skin advertised but did not appear £1.00
31-38 £0.80
39 Amnesty International issue £1.00
40 Third World War Book 3, For A Few Troubles More by Ennis & McCrea, Reflexions by Oscar Zarate begin £1.00
41,43 £1.00
42,45 China in Crisis by Tony Allen & David Hine £1.00
44 David Lloyd art £1.00
46-49 The New Adventures of Hitler by Grant Morrison & Steve Yeowell £1.00
50 1st monthly; Straightgate by Smith & Phillips, Milo Manara art £1.75
51 Alberto Breccia art £1.75
52 Amnesty International followup, Fabry art, Sinner by Sampayo & Munoz reprints begin £1.75
53 Straightgate, Third World War both end £1.75
54 Insider by Mark Miller & Paul Grist, The General & the Priest by Igor Goldkind & Jim Baikie begin £1.75
55 First Crisis & Revolver, Dan Dare by Morrison & Rian Hughes £1.75
55-59 £1.75
60 1st magazine size; Trip to Tulum by Fellini & Manara begins £1.75
61-63 Manara art, 63 incl. Operation Massacre by Solano Lopez £1.75
ARTISTS/FEATURES
Jim Baikie in 1-4,9-12,28,54-55. Philip Bond in 28-37. Alberto Breccia reprint in 51. Al Davison in 34,62. Gary Erskine in 56-61. Carlos Ezquerra in 1-6,9-14,17-18,20-21. Glenn Fabry in 39,52. Duncan Fegredo in 7-8,19,26. John Hicklenton in 16,25,29,35,53. Paul Johnson in 51,54. David Lloyd in 37,44. Brendan McCarthy in 15-24. John McCrea in 15-20,22-27,31,40-43,45-46. Jose Munoz reprint in 52-55. Sean Phillips in 5-6,13-14, 22-24,27,31,33-34,39,50-53. Warren Pleece in 29-38,41,49. Richard Piers Rayner in 30,38. Steve Yeowell in 46-49. Oscar Zarate in 40-63.

CRYING FREEMAN
Manga; Sep 1995-Jan 1996
Vol.1: Portrait of a Killer Kazuo Koike & Ryoichi Ikegami reprints begin £8.00
Vol.2 (Jan 1996) £8.00

CUIRASS
(see also Barbarienne)
Harrier; 1 May 1988
1 36pgs; John Marshall art £1.50

CYBERSPACE 3000
(see main American comics section)

D

DAILY MIRROR BOOK OF GARTH
IPC; 1975-1976
1975 annual size, Bellamy art £3.50
1976 small oblong; Bellamy art £4.50

DAILY STRIPS
(see Garth, Romeo Brown)

DALEK ANNUAL
World Distributors; 1976-1979
1976,1977 £10.00
1978,1979 £6.00

DALEK BOOK, THE
Souvenir; 1964
nn very scarce £50.00

DALEK OUTER SPACE BOOK, THE
Souvenir; 1965
nn very scarce £60.00

DALEK WORLD, THE
Souvenir; 1966
nn scarce £40.00

DAN DARE ANNUAL
Fleetway; 1974, 1979-1980, 1987, 1991
1974 Red Moon Mystery/Safari in Space edited Hampson reprints, scarce £7.50
1979,1980 includes Judge Dredd strips £4.00
1987 Ian Kennedy, Ron Turner, Garry Leach art £2.00
1991 Don Harley, Keith Page art £3.50

DAN DARE HOLIDAY SPECIAL
Fleetway; nn May 1990
nn Dan Dare by John Ridgway, Ian Kennedy, Mekon by Alan Langford £1.00

DAN DARE, PILOT OF THE FUTURE
Dragon's Dream; 1979-1982
Vol 1 The Man From Nowhere additional art by Don Harley £5.00
Vol 2 Rogue Planet £4.50
Vol 3 Reign of the Robots £4.00
Vol 1-3 hardback editions, scarce, each £10.00

DAN DARE, PILOT OF THE FUTURE
Hamlyn; 1981
nn Dan Dare reprints from Eagle Annual £5.00

DAN DARE, PILOT OF THE FUTURE DELUXE COLLECTOR'S EDITION
Hawk Books; 1 1987-12 Dec 1995
Vol 1 (1987) hardback £20.00
Vol 1 (1988) softback £10.00
Vol 2 (1988) Red Moon Mystery/Marooned on Mercury hardback £20.00
Vol 2 reprint (1995) £18.00
Vol 3 (1989) Operation Saturn/The Double Headed Eagle £18.00
Vol 4 (1990) Prisoners of Space/Operation Triceratops £16.00
Vol 5 (1991) The Man From Nowhere £13.00

	GOOD	FINE	N.MINT
Vol 6 (1992) Rogue Planet			£18.00
Vol 7 (1993) Reign of the Robots/The Ship That Lived			£19.00
Vol 8 (1993) The Phantom Fleet			£18.00
Vol 9 (1994) Terra Nova Trilogy			£19.00
Vol 10 (Nov 1994) Project Nimbus, Frank Bellamy art			£19.00
Vol 11 (1995) The Solid Space Mystery, Keith Watson art			£19.00
Vol 12 (Dec 1995) The Final Volume, Watson art			£25.00

DAN DARE POSTER MAGAZINE

IPC; 1 Jun 1977

	GOOD	FINE	N.MINT
1 Dave Gibbons art			£1.50

DAN DARE SPACE ANNUAL

Longacre; 1963

	GOOD	FINE	N.MINT
1963 Eric Eden art			£25.00

DAN DARE SPACE BOOK

Hulton; Apr 1953

	GOOD	FINE	N.MINT
nn scarce; ed. by Marcus Morris & Frank Hampson, Hampson, Cornwell art			£80.00

DAN LENO'S COMIC JOURNAL

C.A. Pearson; 1 26th Feb 1898-93 2nd Dec 1899

	GOOD	FINE	N.MINT
1 8pgs; first UK comic to feature a real person, music hall comedian Dan Leno by Tom Browne			£45.00
2-93			£10.00

DANCES WITH DEMONS

(see main American comics section)

DANDY AND BEANO PRESENT AN ALPHABET OF FUN

D.C. Thomson; 1996

	GOOD	FINE	N.MINT
1996 annual style hardcover			£2.50

DANDY BOOK, THE

D.C. Thomson; Sep 1938-present

	GOOD	FINE	N.MINT
1939 titled Dandy Monster Comic (Korky the Cat in foreground pointing to other characters each named, Jimmy/Grockle in right bottom corner)	£310.00	£930.00	£2500.00

Note: A copy was sold at auction in March 1996 for an auction record price of £4000. As there have been no further sales recorded at this price, it must be considered a one-off sale price rather than a "going rate".

	GOOD	FINE	N.MINT
1940 (Korky hanging from trapeze in circus)	£110.00	£340.00	£800.00
1941 (Korky leading musical procession of other characters)	£85.00	£255.00	£600.00
1942 (Desperate Dan towing the other characters in a boat)	£70.00	£210.00	£500.00
1943 (characters all riding bikes, Despertae Dan in a steamroller)	£70.00	£210.00	£500.00
1944 (Korky sailing through net on a ball kicked by Desperate dan)	£36.00	£105.00	£250.00
1945 (Korky ski-ing, Desperate Dan using two tree-trunks as skis)	£29.00	£85.00	£200.00
1946 (characters in star-shaped frames watched by a bell-boy)	£21.00	£62.50	£150.00
1947 (Korky being tossed in a blanket by other characters)	£17.50	£52.50	£125.00
1948 (Korky as puppeteer using other characters as puppets)	£17.50	£52.50	£125.00
1949 (Korky in top hat smoking a cigar with Desperate Dan carrying luggage)	£14.00	£43.00	£100.00
1950 (Korky in bathing costume on beach pouring hot water into the sea)	£14.00	£43.00	£100.00
1951 (Korky as ringmaster in circus, Despertae Dan holding up an elephant)	£11.00	£34.00	£80.00
1952 (Korky painting clockwork model, model Desperate Dan pushing paint off shelf)	£11.00	£34.00	£80.00
1953 becomes Dandy Book; (six frames, Korky trickes mice out of a feed)	£6.25	£19.00	£45.00
1954 (four frames; Korky coceals stolen fish under a top hat)	£6.25	£19.00	£45.00
1955 (four frames; Korky uses tail to fish under No Fishing sign)	£6.25	£19.00	£45.00
1956 (four frames; Korky painting sign over Korky's Joke Shop)	£5.00	£15.00	£35.00
1957 (three frames; Korky with four anglers in a railway carriage)	£5.00	£15.00	£35.00
1958 (three frames; Korky feeds fish with iron filings then catches them with a magnet)	£5.00	£15.00	£35.00
1959 (three frames; Korky sailing in canoe then in umbrella)	£5.00	£15.00	£35.00
1960 (three frames; Korky uses chained pillar box to keep food safe from mice)	£5.00	£15.00	£35.00
1961 less common in the U.K. (three frames; Korky balancing egg on nose)	£5.00	£15.00	£30.00
1962 (three frames; Korky frying bacon & egg under a lamp-post)	£4.15	£12.50	£25.00
1963 (four frames; Korky looking through port-hole, wearing a sailer suit)	£4.15	£12.50	£25.00
1964 (three frames; Korky sitting in a deck-chair, eating a pie)	£4.15	£12.50	£25.00
1965 (two frames; Korky pouring itching powder on a pantomime horse)	£3.30	£10.00	£20.00
1966 1st dated on cover	£3.30	£10.00	£20.00
1967-1969	£2.90	£8.75	£17.50
1970	£1.65	£5.00	£10.00
1971-1975	£1.25	£3.75	£7.50
1976-1979	£1.00	£3.00	£5.00
1980-1989	£0.60	£1.80	£3.00
1990-1996	£0.50	£1.50	£2.50
Title Value:	**£913.90**	**£2751.50**	**£6732.50**

DANDY COMIC, THE

D.C. Thomson; 1 4th Dec 1937-present (2880 issues to Jan 1997)

	GOOD	FINE	N.MINT
1 very rare in the U.K. (believed only 30/40 copies in any condition)	£200.00	£600.00	£2000.00

Note: An issue was sold at auction recently for £2,300, but as no further sales have been made at this price it must be considered a one-off sales price rather than the "going rate". Note also: owing to the quality of paper, issues above VFN condition are virtually unknown. A copy of issue #1 with the free gift has never been sold

	GOOD	FINE	N.MINT
2 rare in the U.K.	£100.00	£300.00	£800.00
3 very scarce in the U.K.	£62.50	£185.00	£500.00
4 very scarce in the U.K.	£44.00	£130.00	£350.00
5-10 scarce in the U.K.	£28.00	£82.50	£225.00
11-25	£18.50	£55.00	£150.00
1938 remaining issues	£15.50	£47.00	£125.00
1939 issues	£12.50	£38.00	£100.00
1940 issues	£9.25	£28.00	£75.00
1941 issues	£6.25	£18.50	£50.00
1942-1943 issues	£5.00	£15.00	£40.00
1944-1945 issues	£3.75	£11.00	£30.00
1946-1947 issues	£2.50	£7.50	£20.00
1948-1949 issues	£1.85	£5.50	£15.00

Century Comic #92

Dandy #1326

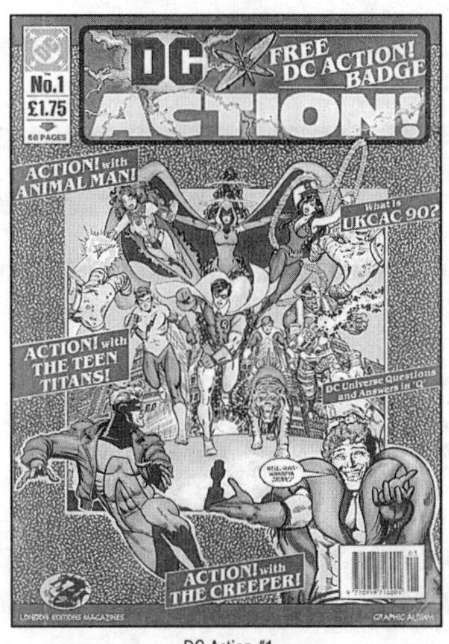

DC Action #1

	GOOD	FINE	N.MINT
1950-1951 issues	£1.50	£4.50	£12.00
1952-1954 issues	£0.90	£2.80	£7.50
1955-1958 issues	£0.60	£1.85	£5.00
1959-1960 issues	£0.50	£1.50	£3.50
1961-1963 issues	£0.35	£1.05	£2.50
1964-1966 issues	£0.25	£0.85	£2.00
1967-1969 issues	£0.20	£0.60	£1.50
1970-1975 issues	£0.15	£0.50	£1.00
1976-1980 issues	£0.10	£0.30	£0.60
1981-1990 issues	£0.05	£0.20	£0.40
1991-1996 issues	£0.05	£0.20	£0.35
Title Value:	**£913.25**	**£2719.85**	**£7741.35**

CHRONOLOGY

1 1st Korky the Cat by James Crichton, Keyhole Kate by Allan Morley Desperate Dan by Dudley Watkins, Jimmy and his Grockle by James Clark, Smarty Grandpa by Watkins. 207 (7 Feb 1942) 1st Peter Pye by Watkins. 227 (14 Nov 1942) 1st Dick Whittington by Watkins. 272 (12 Aug 1944) 1st The Amazing Mr X by Jack Glass (1st British costumed crimefighter serial). 280 (25 Nov 1944) 1st Black Bob text story. 285 (3 Feb 1945) 1st Danny Longlegs by Watkins. 447 (17 Jun 1950) title shortened to Dandy. 603 (13 Jun 1953) 1st Westward Ho by Paddy Brennan. 721 (17 Sep 1955) 1st all-picture issue. 754 (5 May 1956) 1st Black Bob picture strip by Jack Prout. 990 (12 Nov 1960) 1st Corporal Clott by David Law. 1000 (21 Jan 1961) Special issue. 1455 (11 Oct 1960) Dudley Watkins Desperate Dan reprints begin. 2000 (22 Mar 1980) Special issue. 2287 (21 Sep 1985) 1st "Dandy and Nutty". 2345 (1 Nov 1986) 1st "Dandy and Hoot". 2704 (18 Sep 1993) 1st all colour issue.

ARTISTS

Paddy Brennan in 408-437,445-675,707-735,750-773,861-880,967-1076,1087-1103,1310-1319,1451-1493,1529-1544,1590-1617,1662-1679,1976-2031. David Law in 990-1496. Allan Morley in 1-860. Ken Reid in 676-731,760-1187. Ron Smith in 665-728. Dudley D. Watkins in 1-1454 (1455-2148 contain Watkins Desperate Dan reprints with occasional originals by others, notably in 2000.

DANDY-BEANO SUMMER SPECIAL

D.C. Thomson; 1963

1963 32pgs, scarce (Desperate Dan eating pie, Dennis about to hit him) £60.00

Note: This was the first British summer special title to be published and started a grand tradition followed by most other titles. Split to become Beano Summer Special and Dandy Summer Special

DANDY COMIC LIBRARY

D.C. Thomson; 1 Apr 1983-present (332 issues to Jan 1997)

1 64pgs pocket size; Rodeo Round-Up (Desperate Dan) by Ken Harrison £3.00
2-5 £1.25
6-332 £0.50

DANDY SUMMER SPECIAL

D.C. Thomson; 1964-present

1964 32pgs; (Korky riding a red/white polka dot inflatable horse) £30.00
1965 £15.00
1966 £10.00
1967-1969 £7.50
1970-1975 £4.00
1976-1085 £2.50
1986-1996 £1.25

DANGER MAN

Thorpe & Porter; 1 1966

1 68pgs; Mick Anglo art £12.00

DANGER MAN

Young World Productions (Top TV Series); 1-2 1965

1 Kingdom of Fear 48pgs, hardback £15.00
2 War Against the Mafia 48pgs, hardback £12.50

DANGER MAN ANNUAL

Atlas/World Distributors; 1964-1966

1964 (Atlas) £12.00
1965,1966 (World Distributors) £8.00

DANGER MAN TELEVISION STORY BOOK

PBS; 1965

1965 hardback £9.00

DARE

Fleetway; Oct 1991

nn Morrison & Hughes reprints from Revolver/Crisis £2.50

Note: Common; widely remaindered in 1994

DAREDEVIL

Pemberton; 1 1951-7 1952

1 28pgs; Lev Gleason Daredevil Comics reprints begin £10.00
2-7 £6.00

DAREDEVIL

Miller; 1-3? 1953

1-3? 36pgs; Lev Gleason Daredevil Comics reprints begin £5.00

DAREDEVIL WINTER SPECIAL

Marvel; nn Nov 1982

nn 52pgs; Marvel reprints, John Higgins cover £1.25

DAREDEVILS, THE

Marvel; 1 Jan 1983-11 Nov 1983 (joins Mighty World of Marvel)

1 Captain Britain by Alan Moore & Alan Davis begins, Spider-Man, Miller Daredevil reprints begin £6.00
1 with free gift (metal Daredevils badge) £7.50
2-5 last Spider-Man £4.00
6 incorporated Marvel Super-Heroes; Night Raven text stories by Moore, Dr. Who back-up reprints by Moore begin £4.00
7,9 £3.50
8 Grit (Daredevil satire) by Moore & Collins/Farmer £3.50
10 scarcer; Crusader reprint by Alan Davis (1st professional strip) £5.00
11 scarcer; Night Raven text by Jamie Delano £4.00

Note: 1,2,4-11 had pull-out posters, if intact issues are worth 10-20% more, 5,7,10,11 by Alan Davis. Alan Moore articles in 1,3-6

DARK ANGEL

(see Hell's Angel in main American comics section)

DARK GUARD

(see main American comics section)

N.MINT

DC ACTION

London Editions; 1 Jan 1990-6 Nov 1990

1 New Teen Titans, Animal Man by Morrison DC reprints begin £2.00
2-6 £1.75

DEADFACE

Harrier; 1 Apr 1987-8 Oct 1988

1 Eddie Campbell story/art begins £1.50
2-3 £1.25
4-8 Campbell/Hillyer art £1.00

Note: A collected edition was issued by Dark Horse (US).

DEADLINE

Portobello Project; v1:1 1987

v1:1 Nick Abadzis art £0.75

DEADLINE

Tom Astor; 1 Oct 1988-71 Oct/Nov 1995

1 Tank Girl by Alan Martin & Jamie Hewlett, Sharp by Steve Dillon, Beryl the Bitch by Julie Hollings, Wired World by Philip Bond, Johnny Nemo by Pete Milligan & Brett Ewins all begin, Milligan text £3.00
2 Hugo Tate by Nick Abadzis begins, Milligan text £2.50
3 Double number; B-Bop and Lula by Steve Dillon begins £2.75
4 £2.00
5 Johnny Nemo text story £2.00
6 Hot Triggers by Philip Bond, Timulo by D'Israeli begin, £2.00
7 Temptation by Glenn Dakin begins £2.00
8-12 £1.80
13 Atomic Baby by Rob Moran begins £1.80
14 Double number £2.50
15-18 £1.60
19 1st 76pgs & colour strips, Fabry art £1.80
20-22 £1.80
23 Halloween number; last Wired World £1.80
24 last Timulo, Planet Swerve by Alan Martin & Glyn Dillon begins £1.70
25 Double number; fold-out cover; Bond art £2.00
26 Fireball by Jamie Hewlett begins, numbering on cover becomes irregular £1.70
Feb-May 1991, Aug-Nov 1991 £1.70
Jul 1991 Cheekie Wee Budgie Boy by Glynn Dillon begins £1.70
Dec 1991/Jan 1992 Double number, Hugo Tate returns £2.50
Feb-Mar 1992 £2.00
Apr 1992 free tape, Tank Girl returns £2.00
May 1992 Love & Rockets reprints begin £2.00
Jun-Nov 1992 £2.00
Dec/Jan 1992/93 (47) Double number £2.50
Feb-Mar 1993 £2.00
Apr 1993 50th issue, Tank Girl, Wired World, Johnny Nemo, Hugo Tate, Several Colours Later by Pleece Brother begins £2.00
May-Aug 1993 Several Colours Later £2.00
Sep-Nov 1993 Oct. cover by Glenn Fabry, Nov. cover by John Bolton £2.00
Dec 1993/Jan 1994 Double number, Brian Bolland cover & poster £2.50
Feb-Apr 1994 £2.50
May 1994 Exit by Nabiel Kanan reprints begin £2.50
Jun/Jul 1994 1st bi-monthly issue £2.50
Aug/Sep 1994-Oct/Nov 1995 £2.50

DEATH OF SUPERMAN, THE

(see Superman in main American comics section)

DEATH METAL

(see main American comics section)

DEATH METAL VS GENETIX

(see main American comics section)

DEATH: THE HIGH COST OF LIVING

Titan; Jun 1994

nn reprints Vertigo series by Neil Gaiman, Chris Bachalo & Mark Buckingham £8.00

DEATH 3

(see main American comics section)

DEATH WRECK

(see main American comics section)

DEATH'S HEAD

(see main American comics section)

DEATH'S HEAD II (LIMITED SERIES)

(see main American comics section)

DEATH'S HEAD II (ONGOING SERIES)

(see main American comics section)

DEATH'S HEAD II AND DIE CUT

(see main American comics section)

DEATH'S HEAD II AND KILLPOWER

(see main American comics section)

DEATH'S HEAD II GOLD

(see main American comics section)

DEATHWATCH

Harrier; 1 Jul 1987

1 28pgs; Art Wetherell art £0.60

DEEP SPACE NINE

Boxtree; Jul 1994-present

Stowaway/Old Wounds (Jul 1994) reprints Malibu series £8.00
Emancipation and Beyond (Aug 1994) Malibu reprints £8.00
Requiem (Apr 1995) Malibu reprints £8.00
Hearts and Minds Malibu reprints £8.00
Dax's Comet (Feb 1996) Malibu reprints £9.00

DEMON

Portman; 1 1978-?

1 68pgs, Satana by Esteban Moroto, Romita, Colan Infantino and Blasco reprints £1.25
2-? £1.00

N.MINT

DENNIS THE MENACE BOOK

D.C. Thomson; Sep 1955-present (bi-annual, later annual)

1956 (Dennis holding tin of paint) £150.00
1958 (Dennis whizzing downhill on a go-kart flooring people on the way) £80.00
1960 (Dennis underwater in flippers using pincers on swimmer's toe) £50.00
1962 (Dennis holding giant caricature head of himself over his own head) £25.00
1964 (Dennis bursting through black/red sheet) £20.00
1966,1968 dated on cover £15.00
1970-1978 £7.50
1980-1990 £3.00
1991-1994 £2.50

DESPERATE DAN BOOK

D.C. Thomson; 1953, 1978, 1990-1992

1954 Dudley Watkins art £150.00
1979 £5.00
1991-1993 £3.00

DICE MAN

IPC; 1 Jan 1986-5 Oct 1986

1 Judge Dredd by Talbot, Nemesis by O'Neill, Slaine by David Lloyd £2.50
2 ABC Warriors by Dillon, Diceman by Graham Manley, Slaine by Nik Williams £2.00
3 Rogue Trooper by Collins/Farmer, Diceman by Ridgway, Torquemada by Talbot, more scarce £2.25
4 Diceman by Dillon, Slaine by Collins/Farmer £2.00
5 Rogue Trooper by Collins, Ronald Reagan by Hunt Emerson, Diceman by Dillon £1.75

DICK TRACY

Streamline/United Anglo-American; 1 1953-?

1 28pgs; reprints American newspaper strip £8.00
2-? £5.00

DICK TURPIN ANNUAL

Grandreams; 1980

1980 Felix Carrion art £1.50

DIE CUT VS G-FORCE

(see main American comics section)

DIGITEK

(see Overkill, main American comics section)

DIRTY PAIR

Manga; Sep 1995-Jan 1996

Biohazards (Sep 1995) Toren Smith & Adam Warren Dark Horse reprints £8.00
Dangerous Acquaintances (Jan 1996) £8.00

DISNEY MAGAZINE

House of Grolier; 1-4? 1978

1-4? 32pgs giveaway; US reprints £1.25

DISNEY MAGAZINE

London Editions/Fleetway; 1 Feb 1982-12 Feb 1983 (provincial); 1 Mar 1983-?

1-12 32pgs; European reprints, provincial release £0.50
1-? national release £0.25

DISNEY MIRROR

Daily Mirror; 1 2nd Mar 1991-162? 2nd Apr 1994

1-98,100-113 8pgs half tabloid giveaway with Daily Mirror £0.20
99 (16 Jan 1993) printed tabloid size as part of TV weekly supplement £0.20
114 (1 May 1993) first regular tabloid, loose £0.20
115-162? £0.10

DISNEY TIME

IPC; 1 29th Jan 1977-21 18th Jun 1977

1 16pgs £1.50
2-21 £1.25

DISNEY TIME SPECIALS

IPC; May 1977-Aug 1977

Funtime Special £1.50
Holiday Special £1.25
Summer Special £1.00

DISNEYLAND

IPC; 1 27th Feb 1971-298 13th Nov 1976 (joins Mickey Mouse)

1 20pgs; Basil Reynolds, Roland Davies art, various Disney characters £3.50
1 with free gift (Merry-Go-Round mobile) £6.00
2 £1.50
3-298 incl. Hugh McNeil art £0.75

Note: incorporates Sunny Stories (26 Jun 1971), Once Upon A Time (29 Apr 1972), Now I Know (20 Oct 1973)

DISNEYLAND SPECIALS

IPC; 1971-1980

Fun Time Special 1971-1978 £0.75
Christmas Special 1971-1976 £0.75
Springtime Special 1972-1978 £0.75
Holiday Special 1972-1980 £0.75
Summer Special 1972-1980 £0.75
Autumn Special 1973 £0.75
Fun Time Spring Special 1979 £0.75

DIXON OF DOCK GREEN

C.A. Pearson (TV Picture Stories); 1 Nov 1959-6 Mar 1960

1 68pgs pocket size £6.00
2-6 £4.00

ARTISTS/FEATURES

1 A Whiff of Garlic. 2 Bracelets for the Groom. 3 The Hell. 4 The Gent From Siberia. 5 A Little Bit of French. 6 The Case of Mrs. X.

DOCTOR WHO

(see also The Mark of Mandragora)

DOCTOR WHO AND THE INVASION FROM SPACE

World Distributors; 1965

1965 scarce £50.00

DOCTOR WHO ANNUAL/ YEARBOOK

(see also K-9 Annual)

World Distributors/Marvel; 1965-present

1965 Hartnell £20.00
1966 Hartnell, scarce £35.00
1967 1st Troughton £40.00
1968 Troughton, Cyberman cover, scarce £50.00
1969 Troughton, photo cover £30.00
1970 1st Pertwee, white and pink spines known £30.00
1973 1st coverdated; Pertwee £10.00
1974,1975 Pertwee £7.50
1976 1st Tom Baker £4.00
1977-1980 Tom Baker £3.50
1981 Tom Baker, some issued without coverdate £3.00
1982 Tom Baker/Davidson £2.75
1983,1984 Davidson £2.75
1985-1987 Colin Baker £2.75
1991-1996 (Marvel) becomes Dr. Who Yearbook £2.50

Note: mostly text material with 1 or 2 strips.

DOCTOR WHO CLASSIC COMICS

Marvel; 1 9th Dec 1992-27 7th Dec 1994

1 52pgs; reprints from TV Comic, Countdown & TV Century 21 begin £2.50
2-8 £2.50
9 reprints Dell movie adaptation Dr. Who and the Daleks, Giordano/Trapini art, Gibbons art £2.50
10-11 Tides of Time by Gibbons reprint £2.50
12-27 £2.50

DOCTOR WHO CLASSIC COMICS AUTUMN HOLIDAY SPECIAL

Marvel; Sep 1993

(1993) Evening's Empire, Richard Piers Raynor art £2.50

DOCTOR WHO COMIC

(see Mighty Midget)

DOCTOR WHO MONTHLY

(see Doctor Who Weekly)

DOCTOR WHO SPECIALS

Polystyle/Marvel; May 1974-1993

Holiday 1974 48pgs £5.00
Winter 1977 £3.50
Summer 1980 52pgs; Gibbons reprints £3.00
Very Best of Doctor Who (1981) all reprints, Moore script, Neary art £3.00
Winter 1981 £2.50
Summer 1982 incl. poster £2.50
Winter 1982 Pertwee interview, incl. poster £2.25
Summer 1983 McMahon, Dillon reprints, incl. poster £2.00
Winter 1983 producers special £2.00
Summer 1984 merchandise special £2.00
Winter 1984 archives special £2.00
Summer 1985 £1.50
Winter 1985 £1.50
Summer 1986 historical stories £1.25
Autumn 1986 Tom Baker special £1.50
Autumn 1987 designers special £1.25
25th Anniversary Special (Nov 1988) £2.50
It's Bigger on the Inside (Nov 1988) £2.00
DWM 10th Anniversary Special (1989) £2.00
Summer 1991 (Jul 1991) location listings £2.25
Winter 1991 (Nov 1991) UNIT special £2.25
Holiday 1992 Sarah Jane Smith special £2.25
Summer 1993 Daleks special £2.25

DOCTOR WHO SPECIAL: JOURNEY THROUGH TIME

Galley Press; 1986?

nn 192pgs, hardback £7.50

DOCTOR WHO. THE AMAZING WORLD OF

BBC; 1976

1976 Jon Pertwee cover £15.00

DOCTOR WHO: VOYAGER

Marvel; 1989

nn Steve Parkhouse & John Ridgeway reprints £5.00

DOCTOR WHO WEEKLY/MONTHLY/MAGAZINE

Marvel; Dr. Who Weekly 1 17th Oct 1979-43 6th Aug 1980; Dr. Who Monthly 44 Sep 1980-present (244 issues to Dec 1996)

1 Dr. Who by Dave Gibbons begins £5.00
1 with free gift (transfer) £7.50
2 £3.50
2 with free gift (transfer) £6.00
3-16,19-25 £2.50
17 Paul Neary art, 1st Abslom Daak back-up by Steve Moore & Steve Dillon £3.00
18 Neary art £3.00
26-34 Gibbons art, covers not numbered £2.00
35-38,40-43 Alan Moore back-up scripts, Gibbons art £2.00
39 Gibbons art £2.00
44 becomes Dr. Who Monthly, Gibbons art £4.00
45-46 Gibbons art £2.50
47,51,57 Gibbons art, A.Moore back-up scripts £2.00
48-49,52-55,60 Gibbons art £2.00
50,61,68-69 Gibbons art, incl. poster £2.00
56 1st Freefall Warriors (in Dr. Who strip) by Gibbons £2.00
58-59 McMahon art £2.00
62-67 Gibbons art £2.00
70-73,75-83 incl. poster £1.50
74,76-82 £1.50
84 Freefall Warriors back-up by Gibbons £1.50
85 incl. poster, no Dr. Who main strip £1.50
86 Steve Dillon art £1.50
87 Dillon art, incl. poster £1.50
88-99 Ridgway art £1.25

100 Ridgway art £1.75
101-102,104-110 Ridgway art £1.25
103,111,118,120,123,130 Ridgway art, incl. poster £1.50
112-117,119,121-122,124,127-129,131-135 Ridgway art £1.25
122-123 Berni Resaurant giveaways ("Free" corner flash on cover) £1.10
125-126 Ridgway art £1.40
136-138 £1.20
139-144 140 Higgins art, 143-144 Ridgway art £1.25
145-146 £1.25
147 Sleeze Brothers in Dr. Who strip £1.25
148-153 £1.25
154-166 157-161 incl. Ridgway art, 164-166 incl. Arthur Ranson art £1.50
167 double issue; free Flexi-Disc £2.00
168-173 £1.75
174-179 £2.00
180 52pgs; Rayner art, Daleks reprints from TV21 begin £2.25
181-183 £2.25
184-189 free postcards £2.50
190,193-199 £2.50
191-192 Ridgway art £2.50
200 Anniversary issue, fold out, wraparound cover £2.50
201-206 £2.50
207 30th Anniversary issue, Ridgway art, wraparound cover £2.50
208-233 £2.50
234-244 £2.95
Doctor Who Adventure Comics (1986) 145mm x 105mm reprints (free with Golden Wonder Crisps) 1-6 each £0.60
Doctor Who Collected Comics (1986) reprints 87-88,95-97 £1.25

ARTISTS/FEATURES

(Dr. Who) Colin Andrew in 193-196,203-206. Dave Gibbons in 1-16,19-57,60-69. John Higgins in 140. Mike McMahon (pencils) in 58-59. Paul Neary in 17-18. Arthur Ranson in 164-166. John Ridgway in 88-126,143-144,157-161,191-192,207 (pencils in 127-132). Jamie Delano script in 114-116,123-126. Steve Moore script in 35-55. Grant Morrison script in 118-119,127-129,139. Steve Parkhouse script in 56-84,86-99. (back-ups) Steve Dillon in 6,7,9-11,13-14,17-20,23-24,27-29. David Lloyd in 15-16,21-22,25-26,30-46,51,57,59,184 (rpt). Mike McMahon in 56. Paul Neary/David Lloyd in 1-4. Paul Neary in 5,8,12. TV21 Dalek reprints in 33-42,180-193 (Richard Jennings), 53-56,58-66,68 (Turner).

DOLLMAN
R.& L.Locker; nn Aug 1949
nn 36pgs; Quality reprint £5.00

DOLLMAN
Popular; 6 Sep 1951, 1 issue
6 36pgs; Quality reprint £5.00

DOMU
Mandarin; Jan 1995
nn Katsuhiro Otomo manga reprints £9.00

DONALD AND MICKEY
IPC; 1 4th Mar 1972-182 29th Aug 1974 (becomes Mickey & Donald)
1 24pgs; American Disney reprints £2.00
2-182 titled Donald & Mickey & Goofy from 18 May 1974 £0.50

DONALD AND MICKEY SPECIALS
IPC; Jun 1972-Jun 1975
Holiday Special 1972-1975 £0.75
Fun Time Extra 1972-1975 £0.75
Christmas Special 1972-1974 £0.75

DONALD DUCK
IPC; 1 27th Sep 1975-18 24th Jan 1976 (joins Mickey Mouse)
1 32pgs; American Disney reprints £1.25
2-18 £0.50

DONALD DUCK CHRISTMAS SPECIAL
IPC; nn Nov 1975
nn 48pgs; American Disney reprints £0.75

DONALD DUCK FUN LIBRARY
Egmont/Purnell 1 Apr 1978-?
1 100pgs small size; foreign reprints £0.75
2-? £0.50

DOUBLE DUO
Williams; nn 1976-12 1977, numbered from 9 onwards
(1) 68pgs; The Open Boat/The Denver Express, reprints Classics Illustrated (European issues) £14.00
(2) March of 10,000/Ship to Buenos Aires £14.00
(3) Voyage to the Far East/The Brigands £14.00
(4) Attack on Mill/Escape of Incas £14.00
(5) Conquest-Peru/Wandering Horsemen £14.00
(6) The Blue Hotel/A Terrible Revenge £14.00
(7) Battle-Jerusalem/Castle Ontranto £14.00
(8) Uncharted Waters/The Burma Road £14.00
9 Death-Capt. Cook/Young Carthaginian £14.00
10 Quest for the Holy Grail/Seven Who Were Hanged £14.00
11 Wreck of Sao Joao/Warlord-Mexico £14.00
12 Martin Eden/Apostle of the Indies £14.00

DOWN WITH CRIME
Arnold Book Co.; 50-56 1952
50-56 28pgs; Fawcett reprints, incl. material cited in POP & UK campaign £10.00

D.R. & QUINCH'S TOTALLY AWESOME GUIDE TO LIFE
Titan (Best of 2000AD); 1986
nn 2000AD reprints by Moore & Davis £5.00

DRACULA
Top Sellers; nn 1962
nn 68pgs; Dell Movie Classics reprint, adapts Dracula film £2.50

DRACULA
New English Library; 1 30th Sep 1972-12 24th Feb 1973
1 24pgs; Spanish reprints £1.50
2-12 £0.75

DRACULA
Titan; Jan 1993
nn reprints Topps Dracula #1-4, movie adaptation, Mignola art £8.00

DRACULA
Dark Horse; 1 19th Jan 1993-9 Aug 1993
1 Bram Stoker's Dracula movie adaptation reprint begins, Mignola art £1.25
2-5 movie adaptation. 4 - 1st Vampirella reprints £1.25
6-9 Vlad the Impaler reprints, Maroto art £1.50

DRACULA COMICS SPECIAL
Quality; 1 Apr 1974
1 reprints Paul Neary, John Bolton strips from House of Hammer £2.00

DRACULA LIVES
Marvel; 1 26th Oct 1974-87 16th Jun 1976 (joins Planet of the Apes)
1 36pgs; Dracula, Werewolf By Night reprints begin £1.50
2 £1.25
3-5 £1.00
4-59 £0.60
60-87 title becomes Dracula Lives featuring the Legion of Monsters £0.50

DRACULA LIVES SPECIAL
World Distributors; 1 1976
1 68pgs; Marvel reprints £1.50

DRACULA SUMMER SPECIAL
Marvel; May 1982
nn 48pgs; reprints £1.25

DRACULA'S SPINECHILLERS ANNUAL
World International; 1982
1982 reprints Paul Neary Dracula, Blas Gallego Twins of Evil strips from House of Hammer £2.00

DRAGON'S CLAWS
(see main American comics section)

DRAGONSLAYER
Marvel; 1982
nn 52pgs; reprints adaptation of Disney film £1.25

E

EAGLE
Hulton/Longacre/Odhams/IPC; Volume 1 No. 1 14th Apr 1950-Volume 20 No. 17 26th Apr 1969 (987 issues; joins Lion)

Volume 1			
1 1st appearance Dan Dare, Pilot of the Future by Frank Hampson, PC 49 by Alan Stranks & Strom Gould, Rob Conway, Tommy Walls, The Great Adventurer (all by Hampson) all begin	£28.00	£82.50	£225.00
2	£10.00	£30.00	£70.00
3	£4.25	£12.50	£30.00
4	£3.55	£10.50	£25.00
5	£2.85	£8.50	£20.00
6-10	£2.10	£6.25	£15.00
11-35	£1.40	£4.25	£10.00
36	£1.05	£3.20	£7.50
37 Riders of the Range by Charles Chilton & Jack Daniel begins	£1.05	£3.20	£7.50
38-52	£1.05	£3.20	£7.50
Volume Value:	**£112.00**	**£335.90**	**£822.50**
Volume 2			
1-10	£0.85	£2.55	£6.00
11-52	£0.70	£2.10	£5.00
Volume Value:	**£37.90**	**£113.70**	**£270.00**
Volume 3			
1-4	£0.70	£2.10	£5.00
5 Luck of the Legion by Geoffrey Bond and Martin Aitchison begins	£0.70	£2.10	£5.00
6-52	£0.70	£2.10	£5.00
Volume Value:	**£36.40**	**£109.20**	**£260.00**
Volume 4			
1-25	£0.55	£1.70	£4.00
26 Storm Nelson by Edward Trice and Richard Jennings begins	£0.55	£1.70	£4.00
27-38	£0.55	£1.70	£4.00
Volume Value:	**£20.90**	**£64.60**	**£152.00**
Volume 5			
1-53	£0.55	£1.75	£3.50
Volume Value:	**£29.15**	**£92.75**	**£185.50**
Volume 6			
1-3	£0.55	£1.75	£3.50
4 Jack O'Lantern by George Beardmore and Robert Ayton begins	£0.55	£1.75	£3.50
5-52	£0.55	£1.75	£3.50
Volume Value:	**£28.60**	**£91.00**	**£182.00**
Volume 7			
1-52	£0.55	£1.75	£3.50
Volume Value:	**£28.60**	**£91.00**	**£182.00**
Volume 8			
1-10	£0.55	£1.75	£3.50
11 last PC 49	£0.55	£1.75	£3.50
12 Mark Question by Stranks and Harry Lindfield begins	£0.55	£1.75	£3.50
13-52	£0.55	£1.75	£3.50
Volume Value:	**£28.60**	**£91.00**	**£182.00**
Volume 9			
1-29	£0.55	£1.75	£3.50
30 last Mark Question	£0.55	£1.75	£3.50
31 Cavendish Brown MS by Bill Wellings and Pat Williams	£0.55	£1.75	£3.50
32-52	£0.55	£1.75	£3.50
Volume Value:	**£28.60**	**£91.00**	**£182.00**
Volume 10			
1	£0.55	£1.75	£3.50
3 last Cavendish Brown	£0.55	£1.75	£3.50

			N.MINT
4 They Showed The Way by Peter Simpson and Pat Williams begins	£0.55	£1.75	£3.50
5-26	£0.55	£1.75	£3.50
27 undated; last Dan Dare by Frank Hampson; no speech balloons on cover	£0.65	£2.00	£4.00
28 1st Dan Dare by Frank Bellamy	£0.65	£2.00	£4.00
29-45	£0.55	£1.75	£3.50
Volume Value:	**£24.40**	**£77.50**	**£155.00**
Volume 11			
1-10	£0.50	£1.50	£3.00
11 They Showed The Way ends	£0.50	£1.50	£3.00
12 Knights of the Raod by George Beardmore and Gerald Haylock begins	£0.50	£1.50	£3.00
13-27	£0.50	£1.50	£3.00
28 last Bellamy Dan Dare	£0.50	£1.50	£3.00
29 1st Dan Dare by Don Harley and Bruce Cornwell	£0.55	£1.75	£3.50
30 £0.50	£1.50	£3.00	
31 last Jack O'Lantern	£0.50	£1.50	£3.00
32 Fraser of Africa by Frank Bellamy begins	£0.50	£1.50	£3.00
33-53	£0.50	£1.50	£3.00
Volume Value:	**£26.55**	**£79.75**	**£159.50**
Volume 12			
1-31	£0.40	£1.25	£2.50
32 last Fraser of Africa	£0.40	£1.25	£2.50
33 Danger Unlimited by Aitchison begins	£0.40	£1.25	£2.50
34-52	£0.30	£1.00	£2.00
Volume Value:	**£18.60**	**£59.25**	**£118.50**
Volume 13			
1-8	£0.30	£1.00	£2.00
9 Riders of the Range, Knights of the Road, Danger Unlimited, Storm Nelson end	£0.30	£1.00	£2.00
10 Montgomery of Alamein by Bellamy, Vengeance Trail by Jesus Blasco, Sgt. Bruce CID by Jim Edgar & Paul Travillion, Dan Dare by Keith Watson all begin	£0.30	£1.00	£2.00
11-27	£0.30	£1.00	£2.00
28 Lt. Hornblower by Aitchison begins	£0.30	£1.00	£2.00
29	£0.30	£1.00	£2.00
30 Island of Fire by Jennings begins	£0.30	£1.00	£2.00
31-32	£0.30	£1.00	£2.00
33 Hornblower strip changes title to Captain Hornblower	£0.30	£1.00	£2.00
34-41	£0.30	£1.00	£2.00
42 Mann of Battle by Brian Lewis begins, Island of Fire ends	£0.30	£1.00	£2.00
43 Heros the Spartan by Bellamy begins, Sgt. Bruce becomes Can You Catch A Crook?	£0.30	£1.00	£2.00
44-52	£0.30	£1.00	£2.00
Volume Value:	**£15.60**	**£52.00**	**£104.00**
Volume 14			
1-8	£0.30	£1.00	£2.00
9 last Hornblower	£0.30	£1.00	£2.00
10 1st "Eagle and Swift"; Blackbow the Cheyenne by Victor de la Fuente, Beast in Loch Craggon by John McClusky begin	£0.30	£1.00	£2.00
11-52	£0.25	£0.85	£1.75
Volume Value:	**£13.50**	**£45.70**	**£93.50**
Volume 15			
1-4	£0.30	£0.90	£1.50
5 last Mann of Battle	£0.30	£0.90	£1.50
6 Johnny Frog by Ron Embleton begins	£0.30	£0.90	£1.50
7-22	£0.30	£0.90	£1.50
23 Cornelius Dimworthy by Sam Fair begins	£0.30	£0.90	£1.50
24-40	£0.30	£0.90	£1.50
41 1st "Eagle and Boys' World"; Iron Man by Martin Salvador, Raff Regan, Wrath of the Gods by Moorcock and John Burns begin	£0.40	£1.20	£2.00
41 with free gift, (4 Olympic Medals in packet)	£1.00	£3.00	£5.00
42-43	£0.30	£0.90	£1.50
44 With free supplement of Indoor Games	£0.30	£0.90	£1.50
45-52	£0.30	£0.90	£1.50
Volume Value:	**£16.70**	**£50.10**	**£83.50**
Volume 16			
1-52	£0.30	£0.90	£1.50
Volume Value:	**£15.60**	**£46.80**	**£78.00**
Volume 17			
1-53	£0.30	£0.90	£1.50
Volume Value:	**£15.90**	**£47.70**	**£79.50**
Volume 18			
1 last original Dan Dare (except Vol. 18 No. 52-Vol. 19. No. 3)	£0.30	£0.90	£1.50
2 Frank Hampson Dan Dare reprints begin (from Vol. 5 No. 22 on)	£0.30	£0.90	£1.50
3-52	£0.30	£0.90	£1.50
Volume Value:	**£15.60**	**£46.80**	**£78.00**
Volume 19			
1-52	£0.30	£0.90	£1.50
Volume Value:	**£15.60**	**£46.80**	**£78.00**
Volume 20			
1-17	£0.30	£0.90	£1.50
Volume Value:	**£5.10**	**£15.30**	**£25.50**
TITLE VALUE:	**£533.90**	**£1647.85**	**£3471.00**
The Best of Eagle Ed. by Marcus Morris (Michael Joseph/Edbury Press, 1977)			£5.00
The Eagle Book of Cutaways Ed. by Denis Gifford (Webb & Bower/Michael Joseph, 1988)			£2.50

ARTISTS/FEATURES

Martin Aitchison in v3:5-v12:37 (Luck of the Legion), v12:33-v13:9 (Danger Unlimited), v13:10-29 (The Lost World), v13:28-v14:9 (Lt./Capt.Hornblower). Frank Bellamy in v8:40-v9:36 (The Happy Warrior), v9:37-v10:15 (The Shepherd King), v10:16-23 (The Travels of Marco Polo), v10:28-v11:28 (Dan Dare; some pages by Harley/ Cornwell, Gerald Palmer), v11:32-v12:32 (Fraser of Africa), v13:10-27 (Montgomery of Alemein), v13:43-v14:43, v15:23-42, v16:9-30 (Heros the Spartan). Jesus Blasco in v13:10-28 (Venegance Trail). Ron Embleton in v15:6-39 (Johnny Frog). Frank Hampson in v1:1-v10:27 (Dan Dare: Note that assistants included Don Harley, Bruce Cornwell, Eric Eden and Keith Watson; some issues have finished art by Harold Johns, Desmond Walduck, based

Eagle Volume 10 #45

Eagle Volume 15 #44

Express Weekly #74

N.MINT

on Hampson roughs. Dan Dare reprints by Hampson in v18:2-v18:51, v19:4-v20:17), v1:1-43 (The Great Adventurer; some assisted by Joscelyn Thomas), v1:1-2 (Rob Conway), v1:1-7 (Tommy Walls; some episodes assisted or wholly by Bruce Cornwell), v11:10-v12:14 (The Road Of Courage; assisted by Joan Porter). Frank Humphris in v3:7-v4:22, v4:38-v7:35, v7:45-v8:50, v8:52-v12:18, v12:21-v13:9 (Riders of the Range), v13:35-41 (The Devil's Henchman), v14:24-v17:35, v17:39-v20:17 (Blackbow the Cheyenne). Don Lawrence v17:35-38 (Blackbow the Cheyenne). Norman Williams in v2:7-v8:11 (numerous back-cover biographies).

EAGLE (NEW SERIES)

IPC/Fleetway; 1 27th Mar 1982-Jan 1994, 506 issues; 1-3,99,100,127-158,163-344 numbered, all others dated only)

	N.MINT
1 mostly photo-strips; Doomlord, Dan Dare picture strip by Gerry Embleton, The Tower King picture strip by Jose Ortiz all begin	£2.00
1 with free gift (Space Spinner)	£3.00
2-4 Sep 1982,18 Sep 1982-19 Feb 1983	£0.75
11 Sep 1982 House of Daemon by Ortiz begins	£0.75
26 Feb 1983 The Fifth Horseman by Ortiz begins	£0.50
5 Mar-17 Sep 1983	£0.50
24 Sep 1983 1st all-picture strip issue, Doomlord continues by Heinzl, Fists of Danny Pike by John Burns begins	£0.30
1 Oct 1983-2 Jun 1984	£0.30
9 Jun 1984 Bloodfang by Baikie begins	£0.30
16 Jun 1984-127 (25th Aug 1984)	£0.30
128 (1 Sep 1984) 1st "Eagle and Scream"; Thirteenth Floor by Ortiz begins	£0.30
129-30 Mar 1985	£0.30
6 Apr 1985 1st "Eagle and Tiger"; Death Wish by Vanyo begins	£0.30
13 Apr 1985-216,218-220,222-231	£0.30
217 (17 May 1986) Ant Wars (2000AD reprints) begins	£0.30
233-258,260-284,286-305	£0.30
259 (7 Mar 1987) new look; Comrade Bronski by Carlos Ezquerra, Survival by Ortiz begin	£0.30
285 (5 Sep 1987) Mach Zero (2000AD reprints) begins	£0.30
306 (30 Jan 1988) 1st Eagle and Battle; Charley's War (censored Battle Action reprints) by Mills and Colquhoun begins	£0.30
307-344 (22 Oct 1988)	£0.30
29 Oct 1988 1st "Eagle and Mask"	£0.30
6 Nov 1988-1 Apr 1989,15 Apr-19 Aug 1989,21 Oct 1989-21 Apr 1990	£0.30
8 Apr 1989 1st "Eagle and Wildcat"	£0.30
26 Aug-14 Oct 1989 old look Dan Dare by Keith Watson begins	£0.75
28 Apr 1990 new look; Ghost World by Eric Bradbury, Dark Angels by Solano Lopez begin	£0.40
5 May 1990-1 Sep 1990, 15 Sep-8 Dec 1990	£0.30
8 Sep 1990 Beast by Eric Bradbury begins	£0.30
15 Dec 1990-19 Jan 1991 John Burns Dan Dare	£0.30
26 Jan 1991-6 Apr 1991	£0.30
May 1991-Jan 1994 becomes monthly, mostly reprints	£0.40

ARTISTS/FEATURES

Jim Baikie in 9 Jun 1984-127 (Bloodfang). Massimo Belardinelli in 206-210 (1pg Alien art feature), 251,252 (Mach 1 reprints). John Burns in 24 Sep 1983-21 Jul 1984, 18 Aug 1984-151 (Fists of Danny Pike), 221-257 (Dole Busters), 15 Dec 90-19 Jan 1991. Carlos Ezquerra in 259-262,264,267-268,272-275. Frank Hampson in 4 Dec-11 Dec 1982 (Dan Dare reprints). Cam Kennedy in 15 Oct 1983-7 Jan 1984, 7 Apr 1984, 18 Aug 1984, 145 (Amstor Computer). Jose Ortiz in 27 Mar-4 Sep 1982 (The Tower King), 11 Sep 1982-12 Feb 1983 (House of Daemon), 26 Feb-16 Jul 1983 (Fifth Horseman), 24 Sep 1983, 17 Dec 1983, 99 (11 Feb 1984) (The Amstor Computer), 18 Feb-31 Mar 1984 (News Team), 8 Dec 1984 (Bloodfang), 128-258 (The Thirteenth Floor), 259-319 (Survival), 332-343 (Kid Cops), 8 Apr-22 Apr 1989, 13 Jun-12 Aug 1989 (Kitten Magee). Keith Watson 26 Aug-14 Oct 1989, 3 Feb-10 Mar 1990, 9 Jun-16 Jun 1990 (Dan Dare).

EAGLE ANNUAL

Hulton/Longacre/Odhams/Fleetway; 1 (Sep 1951)-1975, 1983-1994?

	N.MINT
1 scarce, Dan Dare by Frank Hampson/Harold Johns	£45.00
2 Dare by Harold Johns/Greta Tomlinson	£15.00
2 with dust wrapper	£25.00
3 Dare by Don Harley	£10.00
3 with dust wrapper	£15.00
4 Dare by Harold Johns	£10.00
4 with dust wrapper	£12.50
5-7,9	£7.50
8 Dare by Hampson/Harley	£7.50
10 1st with date on cover	£6.00
11,12 last numbered, last with dust jackets	£6.00
1964-1965	£5.00
1966 Heros the Spartan by Bellamy	£5.00
1967-1975	£3.00
1983-1992 some incl. Ron Turner art	£2.50
Best of Eagle Annual edited by Denis Gifford (Webb & Bower, 1989)	£10.00

Note: copies of 5-12 with dustwrappers command L2.00-3.00 higher. Also note that there was no dustwrapper on the first annual.

EAGLE BOOKS

	N.MINT
Eagle Book of Adventure Stories (Hulton, Dec 1950)	£15.00
Eagle Book of Adventure Stories (Hulton, Sep 1951) 2nd edition	£6.00
Eagle Book of Aircraft by John W.R. Taylor (Hulton, Oct 1953)	£10.00
Eagle Book of Aircraft revised (Aug 1957)	£6.00
Eagle New Book of Aircraft 3rd edition (1960)	£4.00
Eagle Book of Amazing Stories 1973 (1972)	£3.00
Eagle Book of Amazing Stories 1974 (1973)	£3.00
Eagle Book of Balsa Models by Bill Dean (Hulton, Oct 1954)	£8.00
Eagle Book of Cars and Motor Sport	£10.00
Eagle Book of Exploring the Arts (Longacre, 1961) dust wrapper	£25.00
Eagle Book of Exploring the Universe (Hulton, 1960) dust wrapper	£25.00
Eagle Book of Fighting Services (1962)	£8.00
Eagle Book of Hobbies (1958)	£10.00
Eagle Book of How It Works (1962)	£10.00
Eagle Book of Magic (Hulton, 1955) landscape, incl. press-outs	£35.00
Eagle Book of Model Aircraft (1959)	£10.00
Eagle Book of Model Boats (1960)	£8.00
Eagle Book of Model Cars (1961)	£8.00
Eagle Book of Modern Adventurers (Hulton, Oct 1952)	£10.00
Eagle Book of Modern Adventurers (Apr 1957) 2nd edition	£5.00
Eagle Book of Modern Wonders (Hulton, Sep 1955)	£10.00
Eagle Book of Modern Wonders revised (Aug 1957)	£6.00
Eagle Book of Police and Detection (1960)	£10.00
Eagle Book of Records and Champions (Hulton, Oct 1950) scarce	£30.00
Eagle Book of Records and Champions revised (1959)	£15.00
Eagle Book of Rockets and Space Travel (1961)	£15.00
Eagle Book of Ships and Boats (1959)	£12.50
Eagle Book of Spacecraft Models (1960)	£10.00
Eagle Book of Trains by Cecil J. Allen (Hulton, Oct 1953)	£10.00
Eagle Book of Trains revised (Aug 1957)	£6.00
Eagle Book of Trains 3rd edition (1960)	£5.00
Eagle New Book of Trains 4th edition (1963)	£4.00
Eagle/Girl Book of Exploring the Arts	£7.50
Eagle/Girl Book of the Universe	£7.50
I Want To Be...: An Eagle Book of Careers (Hulton, Jul 1957)	£4.00

EAGLE CLASSICS

(see Fraser of Africa, Harris Tweed, P.C. 49, Riders of the Range)

EAGLE EXTRA

Hulton; 11th Sep 1953-13th Nov 1953 (10 issues)

	N.MINT
11 Sep 1953-13 Nov 1953 4pg supplement in Eagle	£3.00

EAGLE HOLIDAY SPECIAL

IPC/Fleetway; 1983-present

	N.MINT
1983-1992 Ron Turner Dan Dare in 1985-86	£1.00

EAGLE PICTURE LIBRARY

IPC; 1 May 1985-14 Nov 1985

	N.MINT
1 Talisman of Doom by Joe Colquhoun (reprints Saber from Tiger)	£1.00
2-14 reprints	£0.25

ARTISTS/FEATURES

1 Talisman of Doom (Saber) by Joe Colquhoun. 2 Murder in Space (Jet Ace Logan) by Brian Lewis. 3 The Black Archer by Eric Bradbury. 4 Rebels of Rome (Olac) by Ruggero Giovannini. 5 Terror of the Deep. 6 Black Archer vs The Weatherman by John Gillatt. 7 Public Enemy No.1 (Thesbius) by John Gillatt. 8 The Schoolboy Commandos. 9 The Red Knight of Morda (Maroc the Mighty) by Don Lawrence. 10 Company of Thieves (Thesbius) by John Gillatt. 11 The Asssassins (Olac) by Ruggero Giovannini. 12 Janus Stark. 13 Hunter's Moon by Graham Coton. 13 The Metal Monsters. All stories are adapted reprints from Tiger, Lion and Valiant.

EAGLE SPECIAL

Odhams; 1962, 1966

	N.MINT
1962 Holiday Extra, 48pgs, Dan Dare by Harold Johns	£15.00
1966 Summer Special, 48pgs, Dan Dare by Bruce Maraffa	£10.00

EAGLE SPORTS ANNUAL

Hulton; 1 Oct 1952-1973

	N.MINT
1 (Oct 1952)	£15.00
1 with dust wrapper	£20.00
2 (Sep 1953)	£8.00
3-5	£7.50
6-8	£6.00
1961-1965	£5.00
1966-1970	£4.00
1971-1973	£2.50

ECLIPSE GRAPHIC NOVELS

HarperCollins/Eclipse Publishing; Jan 1993-1994

	N.MINT
The Yattering and Jack (Jan 1993) Clive Barker adaptation, Bolton art	£7.00
Dragonflight (Jan 1993) Anne McCaffrey adaptation	£8.00
Trapped (Apr 1993) Dean R. Koontz adaptation	£7.00
Revelations (May 1993) Clive Barker adaptation	£7.00
Dread (Jun 1993) Clive Barker adaptation, Dan Brereton art	£7.00
Miracleman: The Golden Age by Neil Gaiman & Mark Buckingham, reprints Miracleman #17-22	£9.00
The Life of Death Clive Barker adaptation	£7.00

EERIE

Gold Star; 1-4 1972

	N.MINT
1-4 52pgs; Warren reprints	£1.00

EERIE COMICS

Thorpe & Porter; 1 Oct 1951-2? 1952

	N.MINT
1 68pgs; Avon reprints begin, incl. strips from Out of This World, cited in UK horror campaign	£20.00
2	£12.50

EERIE TALES

Alan Class; 1 1962-?

	N.MINT
1 68pgs; American reprints begin, very scarce	£12.50
2 scarce	£6.00
3-5	£4.00
6-?	£1.50

EMERGENCY WARD 10

C.A. Pearson (TV Picture Stories); 1 Jun 1958-21 May 1960

	N.MINT
1 68pgs pocket size	£5.00
2-21	£2.50

ARTISTS/FEATURES

1 Calling Nurse Roberts. 2 Calling Nurse Young. 3 A Date For Carole. 4 O'Meara Makes Amends. 5 The Cocktail Party. 6 Trouble For Simon. 7 Coming Sister. 8 Night Duty. 9 The Casting Vote. 10 The Daily Round. 11 The Rivals. 12 Checkmate. 13 The Contract. 15 Night Falls on Oxbridge. 16 Carole's Dilemma. 18 A Very Special Baby. 19 Nurse Roberts' Evening Out. 21 Two Lives On His Hands.

ENIGMA

Titan; Nov 1995

	N.MINT
nn 192pgs; reprints Vertigo series by Pete Milligan & Duncan Fegredo	£12.50

EPIC

(see Lion Summer Spectacular: Epic)

ESCAPE

Escape/Titan; 1 Mar 1983-19 Sep 1990

	N.MINT
1 scarce (1,000 copies) issued with postcards & badge; digest size	£5.00
2 (2,000 copies) 8pg 3-D section & glasses	£3.00
3,4	£2.00
5-7 last digest issues	£1.50
8,9 magazine size	£2.00

N.MINT

10 1st Titan issue, squarebound; 20pg Munoz £2.50
11 1st Mr Mamoulian by Bolland £2.25
12-14,17,19 Bolland art £2.25
18 Bolland, Chaykin, Eisner, Sienkiewicz art £2.25
15-16 more scarce £2.50

ARTISTS

Steve Bissette in 17. Simon Bisley in 15. Brian Bolland in 11-19. Philip Bond in 14-15. Eddie Campbell in 1-4,6-11. Howard Chaykin in 18. Steve Ditko in 17. Will Eisner in 18. Hernandez Bros in 16. Jamie Hewlett in 15. Ted McKeever in 16. Bill Sienkiewicz in 18.

ESCAPE EXHIBITION SUPPLEMENTS

Escape/Titan; 1987-1991
Cosmic Iconoclasm (1987) £0.95
The Black Island (Mar 1988) Britain in Bandes Dessinees 12pgs £0.75
Strip Search (1989) £1.50
Strip Search 2 (Feb 1991) 64pgs £1.00

EUREKA

Ron Tiner; v3:1 1972
v3:1 Dave Gibbons, Ron Tiner art, Jeff Hawke by Sydney Jordan reprint £2.00

EXIT

N.Khan; 1 1992-8 1994
1 Exit by Nabiel Khan begins £3.50
2-8 £2.00
Note: reprinted in Deadline

EXPLOITS OF SPIDER-MAN, THE

Marvel; 1 21st Oct 1992-40 1995
1 Spider-Man, Motormouth reprints begin £2.00
2-3 £1.00
4-40 £0.75

EXPRESS ANNUAL

Beaverbrook; 1 (1956)-1960 (becomes TV Express Annual)
1 undated (1956) Jet Morgan by Tacconi, Biggles text by W.E. Johns £10.00
nn undated (1957) Wulf the Briton by Embleton £7.50
1959,1960 Wulf the Briton by Embleton £6.00

EXPRESS WEEKLY

Beaverbrook; first appeared in 1954 as a newspaper for children, converted to a comic with issue 39; Junior Express Weekly: 39 18th Jun 1955-73 11th Feb 1956 (35 issues); Express Weekly: 74 18th Feb 1956-285 20th Apr 1960 (212 issues) (becomes TV Express)
39 Wyatt Earp by Harry Bishop, Mark Fury by Raffaele Paparella begin £35.00
40 £10.00
41-49,51-73 £5.00
50 Jeff Hawke by Ferdinando Tacconi begins £5.00
74 becomes Express Weekly; Rex Keene by Bishop begins, 1st full-colour Mark Fury by Peter Jackson £15.00
74 with free gift (Super Book of Racing Cars) £25.00
75-83,85-107,109-114,116-119,121-139 £5.00
84 Jet Morgan by Charles Chilton & Tacconi begins £7.50
108 Freedom is the Prize by Giovannini begins (1st appearence of Wulf the Briton) £5.00
115 1st "Express and Rocket" £5.00
120 1st Wulf the Briton strip £7.50
140-285 Ron Embleton Wulf the Briton £3.00

F

FABULOUS FURRY FREAK BROTHERS

Hassle Free Press/Knockabout; 1 1976-12 1992
1 44pgs; Gilbert Shelton underground reprints £3.00
2-4 £2.00
5-12 £1.50

THE FALL GUY ANNUAL

Grandreams; 1981-1983
1981 (blue cover, 1981 for 1982) £1.50
1981 (red cover, 1982 for 1983) David Lloyd art £1.50
1981 (yellow cover, 1983 for 1984) David Lloyd art £1.50

FALLING IN LOVE

Trent; 1-8 1955
1 68pgs; National Periodical Publications reprints £2.50
2-8 £1.50

FANTASTIC

Odhams; 1 18th Feb 1967-89 26th Oct 1968
1 Thor (from Journey Into Mystery #83), X-Men (from X-Men #1), Iron Man (from Tales of Suspense #83) reprints begin, Missing Link by Luis Bermejo begins £7.50
1 with free gift (plastic pennant/wallet) £12.50
2 £5.00
2 with free gift (Stick-on scars) £7.50
3 £3.00
3 with free gift (Fantastic Bubble Gum £6.00
4-10,12-15,17-30 £2.50
11 no X-Men story £1.50
16 Missing Link becomes Johnny Future £1.50
31-50,53-69,71-89 £1.00
51 Iron Man reprints, Johnny Future end £1.00
52 1st "Fantastic and Terrific"; Avengers (from Avengers #26), Dr. Strange (from Strange Tales #151) reprints begin £1.00
70 Hulk (from Hulk #1) reprints begin £2.00

FANTASTIC ANNUAL

Odhams; 1968-1970
1968 reprints Journey Into Mystery #109, X-Men #3, TOS #41 (Dr Strange) £6.00
1969 reprints X-Men #24, TOS #68 (Iron Man), JIM #112 (Thor vs Hulk) £4.00
1970 reprints X-Men #40, FF Ann #2, TOS #60 (Iron Man) £4.00

FANTASTIC FOUR

Marvel; 1 6th Oct 1982-29 20th Apr 1983
1 24pgs; FF reprints begin £1.50
1 with free gift (Fantastic Four press-out boomerang) £2.50
2 £1.25
2 with free gift (Pt 1 of Fantasti-Car) £2.50
3-4 £1.00
3-4 with free gift (Pts 2-3 of Fantasti-Car) £2.00
5-29 18-19 incl. Spider-Man origin £0.75
Note: some issues include posters by British artists, namely Mick Austin in 8,10,12, Alan Davis in 2,7,12,14, Paul Neary in 15.

FANTASTIC FOUR ANNUAL

Grandreams; 1979-1981
1979 reprints FF Ann #4,11, Jack Kirby art £4.00
1980 reprints FF #185-186 £3.00
1981 reprints incl. FF #26 (with X-Men), GS #4 £3.00

FANTASTIC FOUR COMIC ANNUAL

World Distributors; 1969-1970
1970 reprints FF #22-24,81 £5.00
1971 reprints FF #84-87 £5.00

FANTASTIC FOUR FULL COLOUR COMIC ALBUM

World Distributors; 1970
1 64pgs; reprints FF #51,53,60 £4.00

FANTASTIC FOUR POCKET BOOK

Marvel; 1 Apr 1980-28 Jul 1982
1 52pgs small; FF reprints begin from #43 £1.00
2-3,5-19,21-28 £0.60
4 reprints ff #48 (1st Silver Surfer) £1.00
20 100pgs double number £1.25

FANTASTIC FOUR SPECIALS

Marvel; Oct 1981-Oct 1983
Winter Special 1981,1983 £1.25
Summer Special 1982 £1.00

FANTASTIC FOUR TELEVISION PICTURE STORY BOOK, THE

P.B.S.; 1969
1969 scarce, reprints FF #54,56,59 £5.00

FANTASTIC FOUR, THE COMPLETE

(see Complete Fantastic Four)

FANTASTIC SERIES/STUPENDOUS SERIES

Fleetway (A Fleetway Super Library); 1 Jan 1967-26 Jan 1968
1 132pgs, Steel Claw by Carlos Cruz (in all odd numbers) £6.00
2 The Spider (in all even numbers) £4.00
3-26 title becomes Stupendous Series £3.00

ARTISTS/FEATURES

1 The Raiders of Fear by Carlos Cruz. 2 The Professor of Power by Marcuzzi. 3 The Waves of Peril by Massimo Belardinelli. 4 Crime Unlimited by Giorgio Trevisan. 5 The Cold Trail by Jesus Blasco. 6 The Bubbles of Doom by Ogeras. 7 Snake Island. 8 The Man Who Stole New York by Marcuzzi. 9 Forbidden Territory by Massimo Belardinelli. 10 The Chessman by Marcuzzi. 11 The Blinding Light. 12 The Animator by Romagnoli. 13 City Beneath the Sand by Jesus Blasco. 14 The Scarecrow's Revenge by Francisco Cueto. 15 The Formula of Fear by Massimo Belardinelli. 16 Mr Stonehart by Ogeras. 17 Treason By Request. 18 Dr Argo's Challenge by Marcuzzi. 19 The March of the Guerillas. 20 The Immortals by Francisco Cueto. 21 Operation Floodtide by Carlos Cruz. 22 The Shriveller by Marcuzzi. 23 The Torum Experiment by Carlos Cruz. 24 The Melody of Crime by Giorgio Trevisan. 25 The Phantom Pirate. 26 Child's Play by Francisco Cueto.

FANTASTIC SUMMER SPECIAL

Odhams; 1968
1968 56pgs; reprints £6.00
Note: full title is Smash! Pow! Its Fantastic Summer Special

FANTASTIC TALES

Top Sellers; 1-20 1963
1 68pgs; American reprints £2.50
2-20 £1.50

FAT FREDDY'S COMICS AND STORIES

(see Famous Tales of Fat Freddy's Cat)
Knockabout; 1984
nn 36pgs; Gilbert Shelton u/g reprints £2.00

FAWCETT MOVIE COMIC

(see The Thundering Trail)
Miller; 50 1951-62 1952 (13 issues)
50 36pgs; Monte Hale in The Old Frontier by Bob Powell (9), adapts film £10.00
51-62 £7.50

FEATURES

51 The Missourians (Monte Hale, 10). 52 Rustlers on Horseback (Rocky Lane, 12). 53 The Thundering Trail (Lash LaRou, 11). 54 Warpath (13). 55 The Last Outpost (14). 56 Man from Planet 'X' by Kurt Schaffenberger (15). (57 ?10 Tall Men?, 16). 58 The Brigand by Kurt Schaffenberger (Brave Warriors, 18). 59 Rose of Cimarron (17). 60 Carbine Williams by Peter Costanza (19). (61 ?Ivanhoe?, 20).

FAWCETT'S FUNNY ANIMALS

Miller; Dec 1945-1952
nn 68pgs photogravure; subtitled American Comic Annual, Fawcett reprints £8.00
28,39,etc 16/12pgs red/green photogravure £6.00
P448 16pgs red/green letterpress £5.00
50-57 (1951-52) 28pgs £5.00

FEATURE COMICS

T.V. Boardman; 29 1940-33 1941 (5 issues)
29 36pgs; Quality reprints £8.00
30-33 20pgs £5.00

FEATURE STORIES MAGAZINE

Streamline; 1 1951
1 28pgs; Fox reprints £4.00

FIGHT COMICS

Streamline; 1 1949
1 36pgs; Fiction House reprints £4.00

FIGHT COMICS

Cartoon Art; 1 1950
1 36pgs; Fiction House reprints £4.00

N.MINT

FIGHT COMICS
Trent; 1-2 1960
1-2 68pgs; Fiction House reprints £3.00

FIGHT COMICS - ATTACK
Cartoon Art; 1 1951
1 68pgs; Fiction House reprints £4.00

FIGHTIN' AIR FORCE
Miller; 1-3 1956
1-3 28pgs; Charlton reprints £3.50

FIGHTIN' NAVY
Miller; 1-3 1956
1-3 28pgs; Charlton reprints £3.50

FIGHTING OUTLAWS
Streamline; 1-10 1950s
1-10 reprints £3.50

FILM FUN
Amalgamated Press/Fleetway; 1 17th Jan 1920-8th Sep 1962 (2225 issues, numbered to 2052, joins Buster)
1 Winkle by Tom Radford begins £400.00
2 £175.00
3-10 £120.00
11-100 £45.00
101-999 £22.50
1000-1300 £10.00
1301-2052 £6.50
23 May 1959 1st unnumbered £5.00
30 May 1959-6 Jun 1959 £3.00
13 Jun 1959 title changes to Film Fun and Thrills; Scoop Donovan by Geoff Campion begins £3.00
20 Jun 1959-8 Sep 1962 £2.50
ARTISTS/FEATURES
Early artists include Tom Radford, George Wakefield, Alex Akerbladh, etc. Later artists incl. Arturo Del Castillo (Ringo, Three Musketeers) 5 Mar 1960-27 May 1961. Ron Turner (Scoop Donovan).

FILM FUN ANNUAL
Amalgamated Press; 1938-1961
1938 £175.00
1939 £110.00
1940-1944 £75.00
1945-1950 £40.00
1951-1955 £20.00
1956-1958 £15.00
1959-1961 £7.50

FIREBALL XL5 ANNUAL
Century 21; 1963-1966
1963 scarce £35.00
1964 £25.00
1965-1966 £15.00

FIREBALL XL5: A LITTLE GOLDEN BOOK
Golden Press; 1964
1964 £15.00

FIREHAIR COMICS
Streamline; 1 1950
1 28pgs; Fiction House reprints £4.00

FIRKIN
Virgin; Oct 1985
nn 100pgs; Hunt Emerson art, reprints The Firkin Version from Fiesta £5.00

FIRKIN
Knockabout; 1 Oct 1989-7?
1 Firkin reprints by Tym Manley & Hunt Emerson £1.50
2 £1.50
3-7 £1.95

FIRST LOVE
Strato; 1 1959-18 1961?
1-18 68pgs; Harvey reprints £1.50

FITNESS AND SUN
(see Sun)

FIVE-SCORE COMIC MONTHLY
(see All Favourites)
K.G. Murray (Australia); 1 late-1950s- 83? early 1960s
1 rare; 100pgs squarebound; b/w reprints from National Periodicals incl. Doom Patrol, Superboy, Jimmy Olsen, Straight Arrow, Pow-Wow Smith £75.00
2 rare £50.00
3-5 very scarce £40.00
6-10 scarce £35.00
11-83? scarce £30.00
Note: further issues are thought to exist.

FLASH, THE
Top Sellers; 1-5 1962
1 68pgs; The Flash, Wonder Woman reprints £10.00
2-5 £5.00

FLASH GORDON
World Distributors; 1-3 1953
1 36pgs; US reprints £10.00
2-3 £4.00

FLASH GORDON
World Distributors; 1-7 1959
1 68pgs, pocket size; American newspaper strip reprints by Dan Barry £8.00
2-6 Dan Barry reprints £4.00
7 Al Williamson reprints

FLASH GORDON
Miller; 1-5 1962
1 68pgs, pocket size; American newspaper strip reprints by Dan Barry £7.50
2-5 £3.00

N.MINT

FLASH GORDON ANNUAL
World Distributors/Brown Watson/World; 1966-1967, 1976, 1978, 1980
cover year 1967,1968 £5.00
1976 Charlton reprints, plus John Bolton, Pat Boyette art £4.00
1978 John Bolton art £3.00
1980 Charlton reprints by Reed Crandall £2.00

FLASH GORDON WORLD ADVENTURE LIBRARY
World Distributors; 1 Jan 1967-8 Aug 1967
1 68pgs pocket size; American newspaper strip reprints by Dan Barry £3.50
2-8 £3.00

FLASH STREAMLINE COMICS
Streamline; nn 1951?
nn 68pages; US reprints £3.00

FLEETWAY SUPER LIBRARY, A
(see Fantastic Series)

FLINTSTONES MINI-COMIC
City; 6th Mar 1965
nn supplement to Huckleberry Hound Weekly £2.00

FLYING A'S RANGE RIDER
World Distributors; 1 1954-17 1955
1 28pgs; Dell reprints, based on TV series £10.00
2-17 £5.00

FLYING A'S RANGE RIDER TV BUMPER BOOK
New Town Press; 1959
1959 Stories by Joe Morrissey £4.00

FLYING ACES
Streamline; 1956 (2 unnumbered issues)
nn 28pgs; Key Publications reprint £5.00
nn 68pgs £4.00

FOOD FOR THOUGHT
Flying Pig; Apr 1985
nn Band Aid benefit comic, Cold Snap by Moore & Talbot, Nemesis by Mills & O'Neil, Alec by Campbell, Slaine by Mills & Pugh, Emerson, Gibbons, Davis, Elliott, Gibson, Lloyd, Baikie art £2.50

FOR A FEW TROUBLES MORE
(see also Troubled Souls)
Fleetway; Oct 1990
nn trade paperback; Crisis reprints by Garth Ennis & John McCrea £4.00

FOR YOUR EYES ONLY
Marvel; Jul 1981
nn 64pgs; movie adaptation by Steve Moore & Paul Neary £1.50

FOR YOUR EYES ONLY SPECIAL
Grandreams; 1981
1981 £2.50

FORBIDDEN WORLDS
Strato; 1 195?-145 196?
1 68pgs; ACG reprints, very scarce £15.00
2 scarce £8.00
3-5 scarce £5.00
6-10 £3.50
2-145 £2.50

FORCES IN COMBAT
Marvel; 1 15th May 1980-37 21st Jan 1981 (joins Future Tense)
1 32pgs; Sgt Fury, Rom (from #1), Rawhide Kid, Machine Man (Ditko art), Kull, Master of Kung Fu reprints begin £1.25
1 with free gift (Matilda tank sticker) £2.00
2 £1.00
2 with free gift (Hurricane sticker) £1.50
3 £1.00
3 with free gift (King George V Battleship sticker) £1.50
4-37 £0.75
Note: issues 1-13 reprint Embleton's Wulf the Briton from Express Weekly

FOUR FEATHER FALLS
Collins; 1960-1962
1960 entitled Television's Four Feather Falls £25.00
1961 entitled Tex Tucker's Four Feather Falls £15.00
1962 entitled Four Feather Falls £12.50

FOX AND CROW
Top Sellers; 1 1970-?
1-? 36pgs; DC Comics reprints £2.00

FRANK BUCK
Streamline; 1 1950
1 28pgs; Fox reprints, Wood art £8.00

FRANK FAZAKERLY
Preston SF Group; Jul 1991
nn 24pgs; Bryan Talbot reprints from Ad Astra; signed/numbered 1000 copies £2.00

FRANKENSTEIN
Top Sellers; nn 1963
nn 68pgs; Dell reprints £12.50

FRANKENSTEIN COMICS
Arnold Book Co.; 1-5 1951
1 68pgs; reprints various US strips incl. Airboy Comics £12.50
2 £8.00
3 titled Frankenstein Magazine £6.00
4 titled Frankenstein £6.00
5 titled The Monster of Frankenstein £6.00

FRANTIC
Marvel; 1 Mar 1980-18 Jul 1981 (joins Marvel Madhouse)
1 36pgs; Marvel reprints £1.25
2-18 £0.60

FRANTIC SPECIALS
Marvel; May 1979-Oct 1979
Summer Special 52pgs, Mork & Mindy, Superman, M.A.S.H., Bionic Woman £0.75

	N.MINT
Winter Special	£0.60
FREDDY'S NIGHTMARES	
Trident; 1 (Jan 1992)-?	
1 based on movies; Nightmare on Elm Street reprints from Innovation, Marvel	£1.50
2-?	£1.25
FROGMAN COMICS	
Thorpe & Porter; 1-4 1952	
1 68pgs; Hillman reprints	£7.50
2-4	££5.00
FROLICOMIC, THE	
Martin & Reid; 1-4 1949	
1-4 8pgs; full colour photogravure on alternate pages, Frank Minnitt art	£3.00
FRONTIER TRAIL	
Miller; 50 1958-?	
50 28pgs; Ajax reprints begin	£5.00
51-?	£2.50
FRONTIER WESTERN	
Miller; 1 1956-13 1957	
1 28pgs; Atlas reprints begin	£5.00
2-13	£2.50
FURY	
Marvel; 1 16th Mar 1977-25 31st Aug 1977 (joins Mighty World of Marvel)	
1 Sgt. Fury reprints begin, Williamson art	£1.00
2-25	£0.50
FUTURE TENSE	
Marvel; 1 5th Nov 1980-41 Jan 1982	
1 Micronauts, Paladin, Warlock and Starlord reprints begin	£1.25
2-3	££1.00
4-5	£0.75
6 Star Trek: The Motion Picture adaptation reprints begin	£1.00
7-12 Star Trek adaptation	£0.75
13 1st Future Tense & Forces in Combat; non-movie Star Trek reprints (to 33)	£0.60
14-19	£0.50
20 1st Future Tense & Valour; Conan the Barbarian begins	£0.60
21-34	£0.50
35 last weekly issue (1st Jul 1981); Conan ends	£0.50
36 1st monthly issue (Aug 1981), 52pgs; Star Trek returns	£1.25
37-41	£0.75
Note: 1-3 have cut-out parts to build a spaceship with instructions in #3	
G	
!GAG!	
Gag; 1 Dec 1984; Harrier; 1 Jan 1987-7 1989	
1 A4 8pgs, Elliott, Dakin, Campbell art	£0.80
1-3 1st Harrier issues, 28pgs, Campbell art	£0.60
4-7 magazine format	£0.80
GARTH	
(see also Daily Mirror Book For Boys, Daily Mirror Book of Garth)	
Titan; 1 Jan 1985-2 Aug 1985	
Book One: The Cloud of Balthus newspaper strip reprints by Edgar & Bellamy	£5.00
Book Two: The Women of Galba Bellamy art	£5.00
GARTH (DAILY STRIPS)	
(see also Romeo Brown)	
John Dakin; 1979-1981	
1 The Bride of Jenghis Khan, Bellamy art; A5 size	£1.00
3 The Spanish Lady, Bellamy art; first A4 size	£1.00
4 Sapphire, Martin Asbury art	£1.00
5 Night of the Knives, Dowling art	£2.00
7 The Doomsmen, Bellamy art	£1.00
nn Mr. Rubio Calls, Asbury art	£1.00
GARTH - MAN OF MYSTERY	
Daily Mirror; 1946	
nn 36pgs small oblong; Steve Dowling art	£30.00
GARTH/ROMEO BROWN	
Daily Mirror; 1958	
nn 128pgs oblong flip-book; Garth and the Last Goddess by Dowling; two Romeo Brown stories by O'Donnell & Holdaway	£15.00
GEMINI MAN ANNUAL	
Grandreams; 1977	
1977 Ian Gibson art	£2.00
GENE DOGS	
(see main American comics section)	
GENETIX	
(see main American comics section)	
GENGHIS GRIMTOAD	
(see The Chronicles of Genghis Grimtoad, Strip)	
GERRY ANDERSON'S THUNDERBIRDS	
(see Thunderbirds Specials)	
GHOST RIDER	
Boxtree; Mar 1995	
Ghost Rider/Wolverine/Punisher: The Dark Design Marvel reprints	£8.00
GHOST RIDER SPECIAL	
Marvel; Oct 1992	
nn 36pgs; reprints Ghost Rider 4, Marvel Holiday Special 1	£1.00
GHOST RIDERS	
(see Action Series)	
GHOST STORIES COMIC ALBUM	
World Distributors; 1 1965	
1 64pgs; Dell reprints in colour	£4.00
GHOSTLY WEIRD STORIES	
Arnold Book Co.; 1 1954	

Fightin' Navy #2

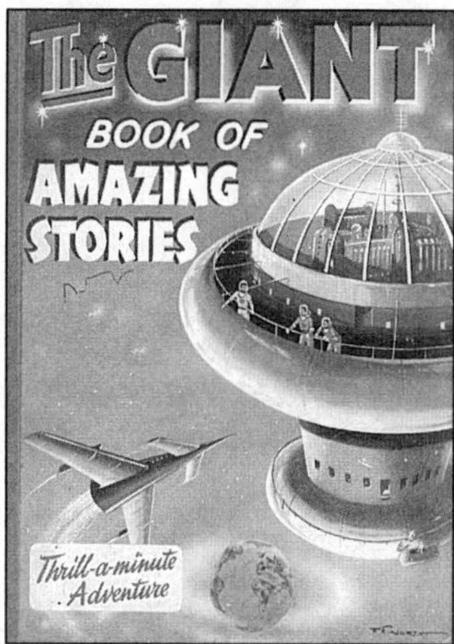

Giant Book of Amazing Stories

Giggle 20/05/67

	N.MINT
1 68pgs; Star reprints, cited in UK horror campaign	£10.00
GIANT BOOK OF AMAZING STORIES	
The Children's Press; nn 1952	
1952 scarce, softcover; text stories with Rex Strong strips	£12.00
GIANT CLASSICS ILLUSTRATED	
(see Classics Illustrated)	
GIANT COMIC	
World Distributors; 1 1956-20 1957	
1,5,13,17 Black Diamond Western, Lev Gleason reprints	£5.00
2,6,10,14,18 All Star Western, National Periodical reprints	£5.00
3,7,9,11,15,19 Turok, Son of Stone, Dell reprints	£6.50
4,8,12,16,20 Fast Action Western	£5.00
Note: 68pgs; reprints of American and Australian comicbooks	
GIANT WAR PICTURE LIBRARY	
Fleetway; 1 Jun 1964-76 Dec 1965	
1 68pgs, 13.5" tall format	£10.00
2	£6.00
3-50	£4.00
51-76	£3.00
GIGGLE	
Fleetway; 29th Apr 1967-13th Jan 1968 (38 issues, joins Buster)	
No.1 - 29 Apr 1967 Giggle by Alf Saporito, Buck Bingo (Lucky Luke) reprints begin	£25.00
No.1 with free gift (Giggle Balloon)	£40.00
No. 2 - 6 May 1967	£7.50
No. 2 with free gift (The Giggle Twizzler)	£15.00
13 May 1967	£2.50
20 May-9 Sep 1967	£1.25
16 Sep 1967-13 Jan 1968 smaller size	£0.75
GILES ANNUAL	
Express; 1 1946-44 1992	
1 reprints Giles cartoons from Sunday Express (later from Daily Express)	£250.00
2	£180.00
3	£150.00
4,5	£125.00
6	£50.00
7 first laminated covers	£25.00
8-9	£18.00
10-13	£15.00
14-19	£10.00
20-24	£5.00
25-29	£4.00
30-34	£3.00
35-39	£2.00
40-43	£1.50
44 all reprints from earlier editions	£1.50
Giles Nurse Special (1975)	£12.50
The Giles Family (Headline, Oct 1993) edited by Peter Tory	£14.00
Giles Classics '94 (1993) reprints	£3.00
GIRL	
Hulton/Longacre; Vol 1:1 2nd Nov 1951-Vol 13:14 3rd Oct 1964 (643 issues, joins Princess)	
Vol 1:1 Kitty Hawke by Ray Bailey, Penny Wise by Norman Pett, Lettice Leefe by John Ryan begin	£35.00
Vol 1:2	£10.00
Vol 1:3-52	£3.50
Vol 2:1-62	£2.50
Vol 3:1-Vol 6:52	£2.50
Vol 7:1-Vol 9:11	£2.00
Vol 9:12-Vol 12:5 Longacre issues	£1.75
Vol 12:6-Vol 13:14 smaller size	£1.00
GIRL ANNUAL	
Hulton/Longacre; 1 1952-1964	
1 published 1952 for 1953, undated	£10.00
2-10	£5.00
1963-1965	£3.00
The Best of Girl Annual 1952-1959, edited by Denis Gifford (Webb & Bower, 1990) 3.00	
GIRL FROM U.N.C.L.E. ANNUAL, THE	
World Distributors; 1967-1969	
1967	£6.00
1968-1969	£5.00
GIVE ME LIBERTY	
(see also Martha Washington Goes to War)	
Penguin; 1991	
nn Frank Miller & Dave Gibbons, hardcover	£15.00
nn softcover	£9.00
GRAPHIXUS	
Graphic Eye; 1 Feb 1977-6 Mar 1979, 5b Spr 1979	
1 Matthews art, Higgins cover	£5.00
2 Matthews, Emerson, Leach art	£4.00
3 Matthews, Whitaker art, Little Nympho by Bolland	£6.00
4,6	£4.00
5 Bolland, Higgins art	£6.00
5b (Alternative Series Imprint 1)	£1.50
GREEN HORNET ANNUAL, THE	
World Distributors; 1966-1967	
1966	£20.00
1967	£15.00
GREEN LANTERN ANNUAL	
World Distributors (?); 1967	
1967 very scarce; bound-together remaindered copies of Green Lantern #51, Tales of the Unexpected #96, Lois Lane #72, House of Secrets #78, Batman #190, Superboy #136	£25.00
GREMLINS	
Marvel; Nov 1984	
nn 68pgs; American reprint based on film	£1.00

	N.MINT
GRUN	
Harrier; 1 Jun 1987-4 Dec 1987	
1-4 Paul Marshall art	£0.65
GUNHAWK, THE	
Streamline; nn-2 1951	
nn 28pgs; Marvel reprints	£3.00
2	£2.50
GUNS OF FACT AND FICTION	
United Anglo-American; 1951	
nn 36pgs; reprints A.1 #13 (Magazine Enterprises); cited in SOTI & UK horror campaign	£12.00
GUNSMOKE	
Top Sellers; 1 1970-? 1971	
1 36pgs; Dell reprints; based on TV series	£1.00
2-?	£0.50
GUNSMOKE PICTURE AND STORY ALBUM	
Mellifont; W3 1950s	
W3 96pgs	£3.00
GUNSMOKE TRAIL	
Miller; 1-4 1957	
1-4 28pgs; Ajax-Farrell Publishing Co. reprints	£4.00
GUNSMOKE WESTERN	
Miller; 1 1955-23 1956	
1 28pgs; Atlas/Marvel reprints	£6.00
2-23	£4.00

H

	N.MINT
HALLS OF HORROR	
(see House of Hammer; for Halls of Horror Winter Special see HoH No.24)	
HALO JONES	
Titan (Best of 2000AD); Aug 1986-Oct 1986, 1992	
Book One 2000AD reprints by Moore & Gibson begin	£5.00
Book Two	£5.00
Book Three	£5.00
The Complete Halo Jones	£10.00
HARD BOILED DEFECTIVE STORIES	
Penguin; Mar 1990	
nn reprints Charles Burns strips from Raw	£8.00
HARDY BOYS/NANCY DREW MYSTERIES ANNUAL	
Grandreams; 1979	
1979	£1.50
HAROLD HARE'S OWN PAPER	
Fleetway; 14th Nov 1959-4th Apr 1964 (230 issues; joins Playhour)	
No.1 - 14 Nov 1959 Harold Hare by Hugh McNeill begins	£35.00
No.1 with free gift (Mask and Balloon)	£50.00
21 Nov 1959	£5.00
28 Nov 1959-4 Apr 1964 incl. Philip Mendoza art	£1.00
Note: a collector recently paid £135 by postal auction for a copy of #1 with the free gift.	
CHRONOLOGY	
29 Apr 1961: incorporates Walt Disney's Weekly. Title later changed to Harold Hare, and drops to smaller size.	
HARRIER PREVIEW	
Harrier; 1 Mar 1988	
1 previews of Cuirass and Night Bird	£0.30
HAUNT OF FEAR	
Strato; 1 1952	
1 EC reprints	£15.00
HAUNT OF FEAR, THE	
Arnold Book Co.; 1 1954	
1 68pgs; Haunt of Fear 23, Crime SuspenStories 14 reprints, widely cited in UK horror campaign	£25.00
HAVOC	
Marvel; 1 13th Jul 1991-9 7th Sep 1991	
1 36pgs; Robocop, Ghost Rider, Deathlok, Conan, Starslammers reprints begin	£1.25
2-9	£0.75
HAWKEYE AND THE LAST OF THE MOHICANS	
C.A. Pearson (TV Picture Stories); 1 Jun 1958-6 May 1959	
1 68pgs pocket size	£5.00
2-6	£3.00
ARTISTS/FEATURES	
1 The Long Rifles. 2 The Renegade. 3 La Salle's Treasure by Terry Aspin. 4 Revenge by Terry Aspin. 5 The Wild One. 6 The Reckoning.	
HAWKEYE AND THE LAST OF THE MOHICANS ANNUAL	
Adprint; 1 1958-nn 1959	
1 (cy1958) text stories by Michael Holt; illus. by George Shaw	£5.00
nn (cy1959) text stories by David Roberts; illus. by Ron Embleton	£5.00
HEARTBREAK HOTEL	
Willyprods; 1 Jan 1988-6 Nov/Dec 1988	
1 LD, Trina Robbins text, Alan Moore, Gibbons art, flexidisc (1,000)	£2.50
1 LD, no flexidisc (9,000)	£1.75
2 LD, scarce, O'Neill, Talbot, Emerson art, flexidisc (1,000)	£2.50
2 LD, scarce, no flexidisc	£2.00
3 LD, Fabry, Elliott art, flexidisc	£1.75
3 LD, no flexidisc	£1.50
4 Clive Barker text, Grant Morrison, Elliott art, flexidisc	£1.75
4 no flexidisc	£1.50
5 Trina Robbins art, 8pg Blaam! preview	£1.50
6 Dave McKean art	£1.50
HEART THROBS	
Fleetway (Xpresso); Aug 1991	
nn 84pgs; European reprints by Max Cabanes	£3.50
HEART TO HEART	
(see Magic Moment Romance, Twin Hearts)	
K.G. Murray (Australia); 1 1958-?	

N.MINT

1 very rare; 100pgs squarebound; b/w romance reprints from National Periodical Publications; priced at 1 shilling £75.00
2-? £40.00
Note: further issues likely to exist

HELL-FIRE RAIDERS
Alan Class; 1966
nn 68pgs; Fawcett reprints featuring Tom Mix, Tex Ritter and Lash LaRue £2.50

HELL'S ANGEL
(see Overkill, main American comics section)

HEROES OF THE WEST
Miller; 150-158 1959 (previously Western Hero)
150 28pgs; Fawcett reprints £5.00
151-158 incl. Bobby Benson, Presto Kid reprints £3.00

HEWLIGAN'S HAIRCUT
Fleetway; Jul 1991
nn 2000AD reprints by Pete Milligan & Jamie Hewlett £3.50

HI-YO SILVER
World Distributors; 1-9 1953
1 36pgs; Dell reprints £6.00
2-9 £4.00

HIGH CHAPARRAL ANNUAL, THE
World Distributors; 1969-1973
1969-1972 mainly text stories £4.00
1973 £3.00

HOMER THE HAPPY GHOST
Miller; 1 1955
1 28pgs; Atlas reprints (colophon gives Charlton) £3.00

HOODED HORSEMAN, THE
Streamline; 1953 (2 issues)
nn 28pgs; American Comic Group reprints £5.00
nn 68pgs £5.00

HOOKS DEVLIN
Cartoon Art; 1 1950
1 16pgs; Fiction House reprints £3.00

HOOT GIBSON
Streamline/United Anglo-American; 1-6 1950
1-6 28pgs; Fox reprints, incl. Wood art £7.50

HORNET, THE
D.C. Thomson; 1 14th Sep 1963-648 7th Feb 1975 (joins The Hotspur)
1 £25.00
1 with free gift (balsa wood Kestrel glider) £40.00
2 £7.50
3 £4.00
4-5 £1.25
6-52,54-98,100-648 £0.50
53 The Truth About Wilson begins £0.50
99 V For Vengeance (Deathless Men) by F.A. Philpott begins £0.50

HOT ROD AND SPEEDWAY COMICS
United Anglo-American; 1 1953
1 28pgs; Hillman reprints £3.00

HOT ROD COMICS
Arnold Book Co.; 1-4 1952
1-4 28pgs; Fawcett reprints, Bob Powell art £4.00

HOT RODS AND RACING CARS
Miller; 50-51 1953
50-51 28pgs; Charlton reprints £3.00

HOTSPUR, THE
D.C. Thomson; 1 2nd Sep 1933-1197 17th Oct 1959 (becomes The New Hotspur, below)
1 scarce £75.00
1 facsimile £5.00
2 scarce £50.00
3 £25.00
1933 issues £20.00
1934-1940 issues £12.50
1941-1950 issues £7.50
1951-1955 issues £5.00
1956-1959 issues £3.00

HOTSPUR, THE
(titled The New Hotspur/The Hotspur; see The Air Flights of Flyer Hart)
D.C. Thomson; 1 24th Oct 1959-1110 24th Jan 1981 (joins Victor)
1 Johnny Jett the Super Boy by Dudley Watkins reprints, Coral Island by Bill Holroyd begin £25.00
1 with free gift (Jumping frog) £35.00
2 £6.00
3 £2.50
4-101,103-173 £1.00
102 The Wolf of Kabul by J.T. Higson begins £0.60
174 1st "The Hotspur"; Limpalong Leslie by Bert van de Put begins £1.00
175-299,301-335,337-779,781-851 £0.40
300 Zigimar - the Master Spy by Terry Patrick begins £0.40
336 Spring Heeled Jack by Steve Chapman begins £0.40
780 Nick Jolly by Ron Smith begins £0.40
852 1st "Hotspur & Hornet"; King Cobra by Ron Smith begins £0.40
853-1058 £0.25
1059 1st "Hotspur & The Crunch"; Starhawk begins £0.25
1060-1071,1073-1110 £0.25
1072 The Doom Wardens by Alcatena begins £0.25
ARTISTS/FEATURES
Alcatena in 1072-1083,1095,1100,1102. Dave Gibbons in 882-889,941-949.

HOTSPUR BOOK FOR BOYS, THE
D.C. Thomson; 1935-1949, 1965-1980
(1935) (Teacher (Big Stiff) showing boys seated on ground a sum on blackboard) £75.00
(1936) (Teacher with three Eskimo boys sitting on ground) £50.00
(1937) (Teacher & boys from Westmore Academy shipwrecked on island) £25.00
(1938) (Teacher tied to a post, Chinese attacking in foreground with boys coming to rescue with cricket bats) £20.00
(1939) (Teacher tied up - is there a theme developing here? - by two indians, one on horseback) £20.00
(1940) (Young boy on a scrambling bike (No.26) in race) £20.00
(1941) (Young Indian boy with a tiger alarming teacher) £15.00
(1943) (Teacher on ladder painting red wall in a room where a sweep's brush is coming down the chimney) £15.00
(1949) (Iron Teacher being held by a tank with a flexible claw) £10.00
1966 first dated £6.00
1967-1969 £4.00
1970-1974 £3.00
1975-1981 £2.50
Note: no annuals issued 1942, 1944-48.

HOTSPUR CHRISTMAS SPECIAL
D.C. Thomson; 22nd Dec 1973
nn 8pg supplement to Hotspur £4.00

HOUSE OF HAMMER/HALLS OF HORROR
(see also Dracula's Spinechillers Annual)
General Book Distribution/Top Sellers/Quality; 1 Oct 1976-30 Nov 1984 (joins Warrior)
1 Dracula by Neary, 1st Captain Kronos by Gibson £5.00
2-3 Curse of Frankenstein by Cuyas, Gibson art, rare £6.00
4 Legend of the Seven Golden Vampires by Brian Lewis, Bolton art, v rare £10.00
5 Moon Zero Two by Neary, v rare £10.00
6 Dracula, Prince of Darkness by Bolton, v rare £12.00
7 Twins of Evil by Blas Gallego, 1pg Gibbons art £3.00
8 Quatermass Xperiment by Lewis, Father Shandor by Bolton £4.00
9 Quatermass Xperiment by Lewis £3.00
10 Curse of the Werewolf by Bolton £5.00
11,12 The Gorgon by Trev Goring/Cuyas £4.00
13 Plague of Zombies by Goring/Bolland £5.00
14 Million Years BC by Bolton £4.00
15 Mummy's Shroud by Dave Jackson, Gibbons reprint £2.00
16 Star Wars issue; Shandor by Bolton, Pat Wright art £4.00
17 title becomes Halls of Horror; Vampire Circus by Bolland £6.00
18 Frankenstein, Dracula, Werewolf by Neal Adams, rare £5.00
19 Reptile by Lewis £2.00
20 Captain Kronos, Vampire Hunter £3.00
21 Shandor by Bolton, Berni Wrightson back-up £2.00
22 The Mummy by Dave Jackson £2.00
23 Quatermass 2 by David Lloyd, Gibbons back-up £2.00
Winter Special 1982 (24) Brian Lewis art £4.00
25 Monster Club reprint by Bolton, pull out poster £5.00
26 Monster Club by Bolton, Lloyd £2.00
27-28 Bride of Dracula by John Stokes £1.50
29 Night Holds Terror by Lewis £1.50
30 no strips £2.00

HUCKLEBERRY HOUND AND YOGI BEAR EXTRA
City Magazines; 1963
Summer Extra 48pgs £2.00
Winter Extra £2.00

HUCKLEBERRY HOUND MINI-COMIC
City Magazines; 20th Feb 1965
nn 16pgs; supplement to Huckleberry Hound Weekly £1.00

HUCKLEBERRY HOUND EXTRA
City Magaines; 1964-1965
Winter Extra (1964) 48pgs £2.00
Summer Extra (1965) 40pgs £2.00

HUCKLEBERRY HOUND WEEKLY
(see Flintstones Mini-Comic, Huckleberry Hound Mini-Comic)
City Magazines/Robert Hayward; 1 7th Oct 1961-308 28th Aug 1967
1 Hanna-Barbera characters, incl. Huckleberry Hound, Mr Jinks, Pixie & Dixie, Yogi Bear, Flintstones, etc £5.00
2-283 some incl. Top Cat £1.50
284-308 (Hayward) some incl. Space Ghost £1.00

HULK ANNUAL/INCREDIBLE HULK ANNUAL
Marvel/Grandreams; 1977-1984
1977 reprints origin from Hulk #1, Hulk #6 (Ditko art), Tales to Astonish #62 (1st Leader); colour £5.00
1978 64pgs; reprints Hulk/Sub-Mariner from Ann #1; colour £4.00
1979 1st Grandreams; Bill Bixby cover, strips & stories based on tv show, b/w reprint from Hulk #1, John Higgins art, titled Incredible Hulk Annual £3.00
1980 1st Marvel/Grandreams; Lou Ferrigno cover, strips & stories based on tv show, b/w reprint from Hulk #3, David Lloyd art, titled Hulk Annual £3.00
1981 £3.00
(1982) reprints Hulk #127,129,184 £3.00
1983 reprints Hulk Ann #5 £3.00
1984 reprints What If #12, Hulk #104 £3.00

HULK COMIC
Marvel; 1 7th Mar 1979-63 15th May 1980 (joins Spiderman Weekly)
1 Hulk by Dave Gibbons, Black Knight by Steve Parkhouse & John Stokes, Nick Fury by Steve Moore & Steve Dillon (1st pro work), Night Raven by Steve Parkhouse & David Lloyd all begin £3.50
1 with free gift (Hulk sticker album) £6.00
2 £1.50
2 with free gift (Hulk stickers) £3.00
3-14 £2.00
15-19 John Bolton Night Raven £2.50
20-30 £1.00
31 Captain Britain origin reprinted £1.25
32-41 incl. Black Knight origin reprints £1.00
42-46 original Black Knight stories returns £1.00
47 title becomes The Incredible Hulk Weekly £0.75

N.MINT

48 UK Antman strip by Steve Moore & Steve Dillon £0.95
49-63 £0.75

HULK POCKET BOOK
Marvel; 1 Sep 1980-13 Nov 1981
1 52pgs; Incredible Hulk reprints begin from Hulk #1 (origin); b/w £1.25
1 reprints Incredible Hulk #3-4 £1.00
3 100pgs double-number £1.25
4-13 £0.75

HULK POP-UP BOOK
Piccollo; 1981
nn 12pgs £4.00

HUNDRED COMIC MONTHLY
(see All Favourites, Century Comic, Five-Score Comic Monthly)
K.G. Murray (Australia); 1 mid-1950s-100? mid-1960s
1 rare; 100pgs squarebound; b/w reprints from National Periodicals incl. Tommy Tomorrow, Aquaman, J'onn J'onzz Manhunter from Mars, Flash, Buzzy, Congo Bill, Vigilante; priced at 2 shillings £75.00
2 rare £50.00
3-5 very scarce £40.00
6-10 scarce £35.00
11-100? scarce £30.00
Note: later issues incl. Wonder Woman, Challengers of the Unknown, etc. Further editions thought to exist.

HURRICANE
Fleetway; 29th Feb 1964-8th May 1965 (63 unnumbered issues)
No.1 - 29 Feb 1964 Typhoon Tracy, Skid Solo, Sword for hire by Alberto Giolitti all begin £15.00
No.1 with free gift (T.S.R.2 flying model) £30.00
No. 2 - 7 Mar 1964 £6.00
No. 3 - 14 Mar 1964 £3.00
21 Mar-27 Jun 1964 £2.00
4 Jul 1964 Black Avenger (reprints Billy the Kid from Sun) by Campion, "Hurry" of the Hammers (reprints "Roy of the Rovers" from Tiger) by Colquhoun begin £1.00
11 Jul 1964-8 May 1965 £1.00

I

I LOVE LUCY
World Distributors; 1-16 1954
1-16 28pgs; Dell reprints £5.00

I LOVE YOU
Miller; 1 1955-23 1956
1-23 68pgs; Charlton reprints £3.00

I WANTED BOTH MEN
Streamline; nn 1950s
nn 28pgs; Fox reprints £4.00

I WAS A CHEAT
Streamline; nn 1950s
nn US reprints £4.00

IBIS THE INVINCIBLE
Miller; nn 1950
nn 16pgs; Fawcett reprints £8.00

ILLUSTRATED LIBRARY OF GREAT...STORIES
(see Classics Illustrated)
Thorpe & Porter; Oct 1952; 2 titles
Note: Priced 7/6. Reprints issues of Classics Illustrated (qv), original issue numbers in parenthesis
Great Adventure Stories contains 20,000 Leagues Under the Sea (2), Robin Hood (7); Robinson Crusoe (10) £75.00
Great Indian Stories contains The Pioneers (17); The Pathfinders (22); The Last of the Mohicans (37); The Deerslayer (58) £75.00
Note: A third title, Exciting Mystery Stories (to contain The Moonstone, The Sign of the 4, The Murders in the Rue Mogue, The Flayed Hand, The Pit and the Pendulum, The Fall of the House of Usher, The Adventures of Hans Pfall, and Dr Jekyl and Mr Hyde) was advertised but not issued

IMMORTALIS
(see main American comics section)

INCOMPLETE DEATH'S HEAD, THE
(see main American comics section)

INCREDIBLE HULK!, THE
Marvel; 1 21st Mar 1982-27 29th Sep 1982 (joins Spiderman)
1 32pgs; Hulk reprints begin, Wolverine (What If) reprint, Brian Bolland centre-fold poster; b/w with 8pgs colour £1.50
1 with free gift (cut-out walking Hulk) £3.00
2-3 £1.00
2-3 with free gift (Lou Ferrigno poster) £2.00
4-17,22-26 £0.75
18-21 4-part X-Men poster as centre-fold £1.00
27 repro of Hulk #1 cover as centre-fold poster £1.00

INCREDIBLE HULK ANNUAL, THE
(see Hulk Annual)

INCREDIBLE HULK PRESENTS, THE
Marvel; 1-12 1980s
1 Hulk, Dr. Who, Action Force, Indiana Jones begin £1.20
2-12 £1.00

INCREDIBLE HULK SPECIALS
Marvel; 1982
Summer Special reprints Hulk vs Sasquatch, Lou Ferrigno centre-fold poster £1.50
Winter Special Steve Ditko art, Earl Norem painted cover £1.25

INDIAN CHIEF
World Distributors; 1 1953-31 1954
1 36pgs; Dell reprints £5.00
2-31 £2.50

N.MINT

INDIAN FIGHTER
Streamline; 1951 (2 unnumbered issues)
nn 28pgs; Youthful Magazines reprints, censored by removal of panels £4.00
nn 68pgs £3.00

INDIAN WARRIORS
Streamline; nn 1951
nn 28pgs; Star Publications reprints £2.00

INDIANA JONES
Marvel; 1 Oct 1984-11 Aug 1985 (joins Spiderman)
1 Temple of Doom based on Spielberg & Lucas film; US reprints £1.00
2-11 £0.50

INDIANA JONES WINTER SPECIAL
Marvel; Nov 1984
nn reprints £1.00

INDIANS
Streamline; 1-25? 1953
1 28pgs; Fiction House reprints £3.00
2-25 £2.50

IN ORBIT
Turtun & Co.; nn early 1960s
nn Sheriff and Electroman reprints £5.00

INTIMATE LOVE
World Distributors; 1-6 1953
1-6 28pgs; Standard Comics reprints £1.50

J

JACE PEARSON OF THE TEXAS RANGERS
World Distributors; 1 1953-21 1954
1 36pgs; Dell reprints begin £5.00
2-21 £2.50

JAG
Fleetway/IPC; 4th May 1968-29th Mar 1969 (48 unnumbered issues; joins Tiger)
No.1 - 4 May 1968 16pgs large size; The Mouse Patrol by Eric Bradbury, The Indestructable Man by Jesus Blasco, Custer by Geoff Campion begin £10.00
No.1 with free gift (Bobby Moore's Book of the F.A. Cup) £20.00
2-3 - 11 May-18 May 1968 £5.00
2-3 with free gift (Soccer Wall Chart) £7.50
18 May 1968-15 Feb 1969 £3.00
22 Feb-29 Mar 1969 32pgs smaller size £2.50

JAG ANNUAL
Fleetway; 1969-1973
1969 scarce £3.50
1970-1973 £2.50

JAG SOCCER SPECIAL
Fleetway; 1970?
1970? scarce £3.00

JAMES BOND
Titan; Jun 1987-Jul 1990
The Living Daylights (Jun 1987) newspaper reprints by Jim Lawrence & Yaroslav Horak £5.00
Octopussy (Mar 1988) £5.00
The Spy Who Loved Me (1989) £5.50
Casino Royale (Jul 1990) by Anthony Hearne & John McClusky £5.50

JAMES BOND 007 ANNUAL
World Distributors; 1966
1966 scarce; photo features on Thunderball £25.00

JAMES BOND: LICENCE TO KILL
(see main American comics section)

JAMES BOND: PERMISSION TO DIE
(see main American comics section)

JAMES BOND: SERPENT'S TOOTH
(see main American comics section)

JAMES BOND: A SILENT ARMAGEDDON
(see main American comics section)

JET
IPC; 1st May 1971-25th Sep 1971 (22 unnumbered issues; joins Buster)
1 Von Hoffman's Invasion by Eric Bradbury, The Sludgemouth Sloggers by Douglas Maxted, Bala the Briton, Carno's Cadets by Solano Lopez, The Kids From Stalag 41 by Tony Goffe, Faceache by Ken Reid begin £7.50
1 with free gift (Monster Wasp) £10.00
8 May-25 Sep 1971 £2.00

JOE 90
Fleetway; 1 29 July 1994-7 21st October 1994 (joins Thunderbirds)
1 Joe 90: Top Secret reprints begin £1.50
2-7 £0.75

JOE 90 ANNUAL
(see also Joe 90: Top Secret Comic Annual)
City; 1968-1969
1968 Ron Turner art £12.00
1969 white cover £8.00

JOE 90 STORYBOOK
City; 1968-1969 (4 issues, unnumbered)
Joseph Nineski (1968) £5.00
Appointment with Death (1968) £4.50
Double Agent (1968) £4.50
The Cracksman (1969) £4.00

JOE 90: TOP SECRET
City; 1 18th Jan 1969-34 6th Sep 1969 (joins TV 21 & Joe 90)
1 scarce, Joe 90 by Keith Watson, Star Trek by Harry Lindfield, The Champions by Jon Davis, Land of the Giants by Gerry Haylock begin £35.00
1 with free gift (Mac's Jet Car kit) £60.00
2 £10.00

	N.MINT
3	£6.00
4-5	£4.00
6-34	£2.50
JOE 90: TOP SECRET COMIC ANNUAL	
(see also Joe 90 Annual)	
City; 1969	
1969 red cover; Joe 90, Star Trek, Land of the Giants, Champions, Ron Turner art	£10.00
JOE PALOOKA	
Streamline; 1 Mar 1953-?	
1 28pgs; Harvey Publications reprints	£4.00
2-?	£2.00
JOE PALOOKA'S HUMPHREY	
United Anglo-American; 1 1950-13 1951	
1 28pgs; Harvey Publications reprints	£3.00
2-13	£1.50
JOE YANK	
Cartoon Arts; 1 1954?	
1 Magazine Enterprises reprints	£4.00
JOHN CARTER OF MARS	
World Distributors; 1-2 1953	
1-2 28pgs; Dell 4-colour reprints	£6.00
JOHN WAYNE ADVENTURE ANNUAL	
World Distributors; Sep 1953-1959	
1953-1959	£6.00
JOHN WAYNE ADVENTURE COMICS	
Pemberton/World Distributors; 1 Aug 1952-82 1958	
1 28pgs; Toby Press reprints	£10.00
2	£5.00
3-77 incl. Williamson,Frazetta art	£3.00
78-82 68pgs	£4.00
JOHNNY MACK BROWN	
World Distributors; 1 1954-21 1955	
1 28pgs; Dell 4-colour reprints	£12.00
2-21	£7.50
JO-JO CONGO KING	
Streamline; 1 1950	
1 28pgs; Fox Syndicate reprints	£4.00
JOKER SPECIAL	
London Editions; nn 1990	
nn US reprints	£1.50
JOURNEY INTO DANGER	
Miller; 1-8 1957	
1 68pgs; Atlas reprints	£5.00
2-8	£3.00
JUDGE ANDERSON	
(see also Anderson Psi Division)	
Titan (Best of 2000AD); Oct 1987-Feb 1990, Jul 1995	
Book 1 Ewins art	£4.50
Book 2 Ewins art	£4.50
Book 3 Kitson art	£4.50
Book 4 Roach art	£5.50
Book 5 Austin, Ranson art	£5.50
The Collected Judge Anderson (Jul 1995) reprints Books 1-3	£10.00
JUDGE ANDERSON	
Mandarin/Hamlyn; May 1995, Jul 1996	
Childhood's End (May 1995) Megazine reprint by Alan Grant & Kevin Walker	£7.00
Satan (Jul 1996) Megazine reprint by Grant & Arthur Ranson	£10.00
JUDGE DREDD	
(see also America, The Chronicles of Judge Dredd, The Complete Judge Dredd, Judgement on Gotham, 2000AD, Vendetta in Gotham)	
JUDGE DREDD	
(see also main American comics section)	
Eagle/Quality; 1 Sep 1983-35 Sep 1986	
1 2000AD reprints begin	£6.00
2-3	£2.50
4-5,9-10	£1.75
6-8	£1.50
11-14	£1.25
15-33	£1.00
34-35 Quality issues	£1.00
Note: Bolland, McMahon, Kennedy covers	
JUDGE DREDD	
Fleetway; Apr 1990-1991	
Curse of the Spider Woman (Apr 1990) 2000AD reprints in full colour begin	£4.50
Judge Child Quest (Jan 1991) 160pgs; newly coloured Bolland, McMahon reprints	£8.00
Tale of the Dead Man (1991)	£6.00
JUDGE DREDD (DEFINITIVE EDITIONS)	
Fleetway; Oct 1990-1991	
Future Crime (Oct 1990) incl. Bolland reprints	£4.50
Bad Science (1990) incl. McMahon reprints	£4.50
Hall of Justice (1991) incl. Gibson reprints	£4.50
Metal Fatigue (1991) incl. Ranson reprints	£4.50
JUDGE DREDD (OFFICIAL MOVIE ADAPTATION)	
Fleetway Editions; Jul 1995	
nn 64pgs; movie adapted by Andrew Helfer & Carlos Ezquerra	£3.00
JUDGE DREDD (2000AD BOOKS)	
Mandarin/Hamlyn; Sep 1992-present	
Democracy Now! (Sep 1992) 2000AD reprints, Jeff Anderson, John Burns art	£5.00
Raptaur (Sep 1992) Megazine reprints, Dean Ormston art	£6.00
Top Dog (Mar 1993) JD Annual, 2000AD reprints, Colin MacNeil, Burns art	£6.00
Heavy Metal Dredd (Mar 1993) Rock Power reprints, Bisley art	£5.00
Tales of the Damned (Sep 1993) 2000AD, Megazine reprints, Burns, Sean Phillips art	£6.00

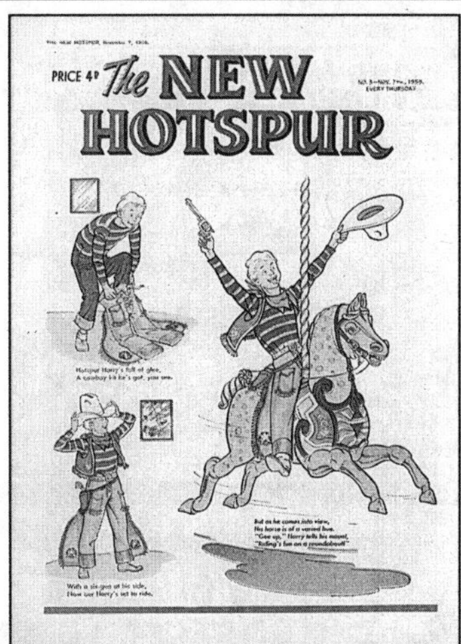

The New Hotspur #3

Hundred Comic Monthly #8

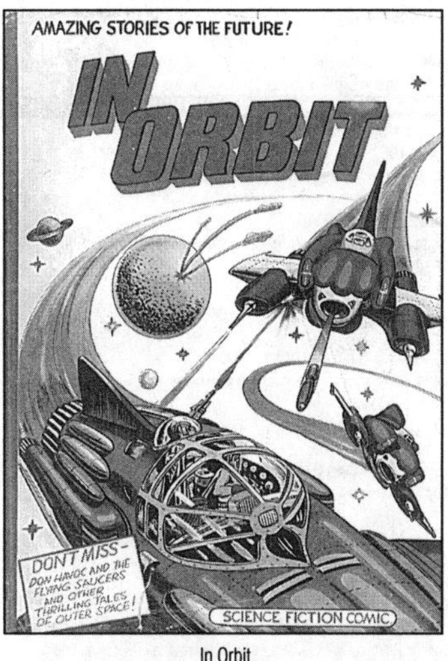

In Orbit

	N.MINT
Mechanismo (Sep 1993) Megazine reprints, McNeil, Doherty art	£8.00
Book of the Dead (May 1995) 2000AD reprints by Morrison/Millar & Power	£6.00
Babes in Arms (May 1995) 2000AD reprints, Greg Staples art	£8.00
The Three Amigos (Jul 1996) Megazine reprints, Trevor Hairsine art	£8.00

JUDGE DREDD ANNUAL/YEARBOOK

Fleetway; 1981-1994

	N.MINT
1981 Mike McMahon art, 1st Dredd story (previously unused) by Ezquerra	£10.00
1982 McMahon art	£8.00
1983 Ezquerra art	£5.00
1984 Ezquerra art	£5.00
1985 Ezquerra art	£4.00
1986	£4.00
1987 Gibson, McCarthy/Riot, Talbot art	£4.50
1988 Higgins art	£4.50
1989 Ezquerra art	£4.50
1990 Arthur Ranson art	£4.00
1991 Sean Phillips, Gibson art	£3.50
1992 becomes Judge Dredd Yearbook, Geoff Senior art	£5.00
1993 Steve Yeowell, Simon Hunter art	£6.00
1994 McMahon, Dean Ormston, Peart art	£6.00
1995 Sean Phillips, Chris Halls, Trevor Hairsine art	£4.00

JUDGE DREDD COLLECTION, THE

IPC/Fleetway nn 1985-5 1989

	N.MINT
nn reprints Wagner/Grant & Smith newspaper strip from the Star begin	£2.95
2-4	£2.25
5 Fat City	£2.50
Judge Dredd Mega Collection (Oct 1990); hardcover	£7.00

JUDGE DREDD CRIME FILES

Titan; 1 Jul 1989-4 Oct 1989

	N.MINT
1-4 2000AD Annual, Judge Dredd Annual reprints	£3.50

JUDGE DREDD: LAWMAN OF THE FUTURE

Fleetway Editions; 1 28th Jul 1995-23 31st May 1996

	N.MINT
1 Dredd for younger audience in movie costume begins; 3 x Dredd stories	£1.00
2-23	£1.00

JUDGE DREDD MEGA-SPECIAL

Fleetway; 1 1988-present (8 to date)

	N.MINT
1 John Higgins, Casanovas, Will Simpson art, Bolland cover	£2.75
2 Kev Hopgood, Mick Austin art, McCarthy cover	£2.50
3 Cliff Robinson, David Roach, Ron Smith art	£1.00
4 Glyn Dillon, John McCrae, Ian Gibson, Shaky Kane, Phillips art	£1.75
5 Steve Yeowell art	£1.75
6 Paul Grist, Siku, Shaky Kane art	£1.75
7 Adrian Salmon/Jim Vickers Sin City parody, Steve Sampson art	£1.75
8 Raptour by Grant, Sammy Martini & John Cromer (Ormston/Luke)	£2.00

JUDGE DREDD MEGAZINE

(see America, Young Death)

Fleetway; 1 Oct 1990-20 May 1992 (continued as New Series)

	N.MINT
1 Judge Dredd by Alan Grant & Jim Baikie, Chopper by Garth Ennis & John McCrea, Young Death by Brian Skuter & Peter Doherty, America by John Wagner & Colin MacNeil, Beyond Our Kenny by Wagner & Cam Kennedy	£6.00
2-3	£4.00
4 Al's Baby by Wagner & Ezquerra begins	£3.75
5-6	£3.50
7 Sean Phillips art	£3.50
8 Red Razers by Mark Millar & Steve Yeowell begins, Phillips art	£2.50
9 Armitage by Dave Stone & Sean Phillips begins	£2.50
10-13	£2.50
14 Judge Dredd (Rock Power) Bisley reprints, free poster	£2.00
15 free Dredd poster by Bisley, Middenface McNulty by McCrea begins	£2.00
16 Brit-Cit Babes by Wagner & Steve Sampson begins, Bisley art	£2.00
17 Bisley art	£2.00
18-20 19 incl. Bisley art, 20 incl. Sam Kieth Judge Dredd	£2.00

ARTISTS/FEATURES

Jim Baikie in 1-5. Simon Bisley reprints in 14,16,19. Peter Doherty in 1-12. Carlos Ezquerra in 4-15. Glen Fabry reprint in 17. John Hicklenton in 7-9,17. Sam Kieth in 20. Cam Kennedy in 1-3. John McCrea in 1-6,15-20. Colin MacNeil in 1-7,18. Dean Ormston in 6,11-17. Sean Phillips in 7-14. Steve Sampson in 16-20. Will Simpson in 10. Steve Yeowell in 8-15.

JUDGE DREDD MEGAZINE (2ND SERIES, FORTNIGHTLY)

(see Devlin Waugh: Swimming in Blood)

Fleetway; 1 2nd May 1992-83 7 Jul 1995 (continued as new series)

	N.MINT
1 Armageddon by Grant & Ezquerra, Devlin Waugh by Smith & Phillips begin	£4.00
2	£3.00
3-9 Judgement Day crossover with 2000AD	£2.25
10 first new size, Calhab Justice by Ridgway, Judge Anderson by Ranson	£2.00
11-12	£2.00
13 Mechanismo by Wagner & MacNeil begins (ends 17)	£2.00
14 Judge Anderson by Ranson	£2.00
15,17-21	£2.00
16 Blood on the Bib by Wagner & Ezquerra begins (ends 24)	£2.00
22 Mechanismo returns, Doherty art, Judge Anderson by Ranson	£1.75
23-25	£1.75
26 Devlin Waugh meets Dredd, Phillips art	£1.75
27 Anderson by Kev Walker begins (to 34)	£1.75
28 Harke & Burr by Si Spencer & Dean Ormston begins	£1.75
29 Missionary Man by Gordon Rennie & Frank Quitely begins	£1.75
30,32-34	
31 Brit-Cit Brute by Robbie Morrison & Nick Percival, Armitage Flashback by Stone & Adlard begin, Calhab Justice returns	£1.75
35 Hershey & Steel by Stone & Adlard begins	£1.75
36 Chopper by Ennis & Martin Emond	£1.75
37 Mechanismo: Body Count by Wagner & Manuel Benet (ends 43), Shimura by Robbie Morrison & Quitely, Return of the Taxidermist by Wagner & Ian Gibson all begin, free poster featuring Judge Anderson story by Mark Harrison	£2.50
37 without poster	£1.50
38-40	£1.75
41 The Creep by Si Spencer & Kevin Cullen begins	£1.75
42-43 43 incl. Missionary Man	£1.75
44 Calhab Justice returns, Pan-African Judges begins	£1.75
45-49	£1.75
50 Judge Anderson: Postcards from the Edge (ends 60), Shimura by Colin McNeil (ends 55), Missionary Man by Quitely (ends 55) return	£1.75
51-52	£1.50
53-54 Mike McMahon Dredd	£1.50
55 Harmony by Chris Standley & Trevor Hairsine begins, McMahon Dredd, Missionary Man continues (ends 59)	£1.50
56 Karyn by John Freeman & Adrian Salmon begins; McMahon Dredd	£1.50
57 Dredd: Wilderlands Prologue by Wagner & Peter Doherty	£1.50
58 Dredd: The Tenth Planet by Wagner & Ezquerra begins (ends 62)	£1.50
59-60	£1.50
61 Brit-Cit Brute, O'Rork begin, Bisley Heavy Metal Dredd reprint	£1.50
62 Bisley Heavy Metal Dredd reprint	£1.50
63 Dredd: Wilderlands by Wagner & Hairsine begins (ends 27; 2000AD x-over), Missionary Man (to 66) and Armitage (to 71) return, Son of Mean Machine begins by Wagner & Carl Critchlow begins (ends 72)	£1.50
64 Free Femme Fatale pin-up booklet	£1.50
65-69,71	£1.50
70 68pgs; 2 x Dredd	£2.25
72 Shimura returns (to 77)	£1.60
73 Maelstrom by Robbie Morrison & Colin McNeil begins (ends 80), Anderson Psi (to 80), Harmony (to 76) return	£1.60
74-80	£1.60
81 Missionary Man returns (to 83)	£1.60
82-83	£1.60

ARTISTS/FEATURES

Charlie Adlard in 10-21,31-33,35-36. Carl Critchlow in 63-72. Martin Emond in 36. Carlos Ezquerra in 1-7, 10-11, 16-24, 58-62. Charlie Gillespie in 52, 58, 64-71, 77-80, 82-83. Trevor Hairsine in 55-60, 63-67. Chris Halls in 7. Shaky Kane in 2-9. Mike McMahon 53-56. Colin MacNeil in 12-17, 44-45, 50-55, 63, 73-80. Dean Ormston in 4-6, 8-9, 13, 28, 40-42, 47-49, 70. Frank Quitely in 29-30, 37-39, 50-55. Sean Phillips in 1-9, 26. Arthur Ranson in 10, 14, 22-24, 53. John Ridgway in 10-13, 18, 64-66. David Roach in 8. Steve Sampson in 50, 59, 73-77, 83.

JUDGE DREDD MEGAZINE (3RD SERIES, FORTNIGHTLY)

Fleetway; 1 21 July 1995-present

	N.MINT
1 Dredd by Paul Johnson, Harmony by Sampson (to 6), Missionary Man (to 3), Anderson Psi (to 7) by Ranson return	£2.00
2 Dredd: Three Amigos by Wagner & Hairsine begins	£1.80
3-5,7-8,10-13	£1.80
6 5th Anniversary issue; Pan-African Judges return	£1.80
9 Judge Hershey returns	£1.80
14 1st monthly issue; Anderson by Ranson, Shimura returns (to 17)	£2.00
15-16	£2.00
17 Missionary Man returns	£2.00
18 Harmony by Samson returns (to 19)	£2.00
19 Dredd/Shimura team-up	£2.00
20 New Look issue; America: Fading of the Light by Wagner & MacNeil (to 25), Holocaust 12 by Standley /Smith & Murray begins (to 23), Dredd reprints begin	£2.00
21-22,24-25	£2.00
24 The Inspectre by Jim Campbell & Kevin Walker begins (to 25)	£2.00
26 44pgs; Dredd: Fetish by Smith & Siku begins	£2.00

ARTISTS/FEATURES

Trevor Hairsine in 2-7. Paul Johnson in 1. Mike McMahon in 3. Colin McNeil 20-25. Dean Ormston in 4-7. Frank Quitely 21. Arthur Ranson in 1-7,14. Steve Sampson in 1-6,8-10,18-19,24-25. Kevin Walker 23-25.

JUDGE DREDD, THE COMPLETE

(see Complete Judge Dredd)

JUDGE DREDD: THE EARLY CASES

Eagle; 1 Feb 1986-6 Jul 1986

	N.MINT
1-6 2000AD reprints, Bolland covers	£1.50

JUDGE DREDD: THE JUDGE CHILD QUEST

(see The Chronicles of Judge Dredd)

Eagle; 1 Aug 1984-5 Dec 1985

	N.MINT
1-5 2000AD reprints, Bolland covers	£1.35

JUDGE DREDD/LOBO: PSYCHO BIKERS VS MUTANTS FROM HELL

Fleetway Editions; Dec 1995

	N.MINT
nn 48pgs; by Alan Grant/Val Semeiks/John Dell; Bisley cover	£3.00

JUDGE DREDD'S CRIME FILES

Eagle; 1 Aug 1986-6 Jan 1987

	N.MINT
1-6 2000AD reprints	£1.50

JUDGE DREDD'S HARDCASE PAPERS

Fleetway; 1 May 1991-4 Aug 1991

	N.MINT
1-4 2000AD reprints	£4.00

JUDGEMENT ON GOTHAM

(see Batman/Judge Dredd: Judgement on Gotham)

JUGHEAD

Thorpe & Porter; 1 1950s-?

	N.MINT
1 Archie reprints	£3.00
2-?	£1.50

JUNGLE

Streamline; nn 1950

	N.MINT
nn 28pgs; Fox reprints	£4.00

JUNGLE COMICS

Streamline; 1 1949-4 1950

	N.MINT
1-4 36pgs; Fiction House reprints	£3.00

JUNGLE COMICS

Thorpe & Porter; 1 1952-? (27+ issues)

	N.MINT
1 28pgs; Fiction House reprints	£3.00
2-27?	£2.50

	N.MINT
JUNGLE JIM	
World Distributors; 1-10 1955	
1 28pgs; Dell 4-colour reprints	£5.00
2-10	£3.00
JUNGLE LIL	
Streamline; nn 1951	
nn 28pgs; Fox Publishing reprints	£4.00
JUNGLE THRILLS	
Streamline; nn 1952	
nn 28pgs; Fox Publishing reprints	£4.00
JUNIOR EXPRESS WEEKLY	
(see Express Weekly)	
JUNIOR SPIDER-MAN SUMMER SPECIAL	
Marvel; nn May 1983	
nn reprints	£1.00
JURASSIC PARK	
Dark Horse; 1 (8 Jul 1993)-15 Oct 1994	
1-5 36pgs; Topps reprints of Spielberg movie adaptation, Kane/Perez art	£1.25
6 Raptor by Englehart & Gil, Age of Reptiles by Richard Delgado reprints begin	£1.00
7-9	£1.00
10 (May 1994)	£0.95
11 28pgs (released Jun 1994)	£0.95
12-15	£0.95
JURASSIC PARK	
Titan; Nov 1993	
nn Topps reprints of Spielberg movie adaptation, Kane/Perez art	£6.00
JURASSIC PARK ANNUAL	
Grandreams; 1993	
1993 film tie-in	£4.75
JUST DENNIS	
Alan Class; 1 1965	
1 68pgs; Hallden reprints	£3.00
JUSTICE TRAPS THE GUILTY	
United Anglo-American; 1 1949	
1 Prize Publications reprint	£5.00
JUSTICE TRAPS THE GUILTY	
Arnold Book Co./Thorpe & Porter; 1 1951-43 1954	
1 68pgs; Prize Publications reprints	£8.00
2-28	£5.00
29-43 Thorpe & Porter issues	£4.00
JUSTICE TRAPS THE GUILTY	
Top Sellers; 1-8 1960s	
1-8 Prize Publications reprints	£3.00
JUSTICE LEAGUE DOUBLE-DOUBLE COMICS	
Thorpe & Porter; 2 1967	
2 bound together remainders of selected DC comics incl. JLA #45,50,51	£4.50

K

	N.MINT
KAANGA	
Thorpe & Porter; 1 1952-? (20+ issues)	
1 28pgs; Fiction House reprints	£4.00
2-20?	£2.50
KALGAN THE GOLDEN	
Harrier; 1 Mar 1988	
1 Ron Turner art	£0.75
KANE	
Dancing Elephant Press; 1 Apr 1993-present (14 to Aug 1996)	
1 28pgs; Paul Grist art	£3.00
1 second printing; different cover	£1.80
2	£2.00
3-14 32pgs	£1.80
KID COLT OUTLAW	
Miller; 50-52 1951	
50-52 28pgs; Atlas reprints	£5.00
KID COLT OUTLAW	
Strato/Top Sellers; 1-58 1950s	
1 68pgs; Atlas reprints	£6.00
2-58	£4.00
KID COLT WESTERN COMICS	
Thorpe & Porter; 1-7 1952	
1-7 68pgs; Atlas reprints	£5.00
KID COWBOY	
(see Action Series)	
KID ETERNITY	
T.V. Boardman; 1-3 1949	
1-3 36pgs; Quality reprints	£8.00
KID MONTANA	
Miller; 50-59 1959	
50-59 36pgs; Charlton Comics reprints	£3.50
KID SLADE GUNFIGHTER	
Strato/Top Sellers; 1-7 1957	
1-7 Atlas reprints from Kid Slade Gunfighter and Kid Colt Outlaw	£3.00
KILLPOWER: THE EARLY YEARS	
(see main American comics section)	
KING KONG	
Top Sellers; 1970	
nn 68pgs; Giant Classics Album reprint from Western Publishing; based on film	£2.00
KING OF THE ROYAL MOUNTED (ZANE GREY'S...)	
World Distributors; 1-21 1953	
1-21 28pgs; Dell reprints	£4.00

	N.MINT
KING OF THE ROYAL MOUNTED	
Miller; 1 1962-15 1963	
1-15 68pgs; reprints King Features syndicated strip by Jim Gary	£3.00
KISS OF DEATH	
(see also Last Kiss)	
Acme Press; 1 Apr 1987-2 Jun 1987 (3 not issued)	
1 John Watkiss art begins	£0.75
2	£0.60
Note: 3 issue mini-series, third issue later appeared as The Last Kiss	
KIT CARSON COMICS	
Thorpe & Porter; 1 1952	
1 68pgs; Avon reprints	£5.00
KNIGHT RIDER ANNUAL	
Grandreams; 1982-1983 (both copyright 1982)	
1982 David Lloyd art	£2.00
1983 Jim Eldridge art	£1.50
KNIGHTS OF PENDRAGON, THE	
(see main American comics section)	
K-9 ANNUAL	
World; 1983	
1983 scarce	£5.00
KNOCKABOUT COMICS	
Knockabout; nn 1980-14 1987	
nn Emerson, Graham Manley art	£3.00
2 Talbot, Manley, Emerson art	£2.50
3-5	£1.50
6 Dan Maniac by Mike Matthews begins	£3.50
7,9-11	£3.00
8 Peter Pank by Max begins	£3.00
12 Jack Alarum by Graham Higgins begins	£4.00
13	£4.00
14	£4.50
KNOCKABOUT TRIAL SPECIAL	
Knockabout; 1984	
nn hardback; Moore text, Emerson, Bolland, Gibbons, Talbot art	£5.00
KNOCKOUT	
Amalgamated/Fleetway; 1 4th Mar 1939-16th Feb 1963 (1231 issues, numbered to 1054, joins Valiant)	
1 titled The Knock-Out Comic; Billy Bunter by Charles E. Chapman, Sexton Blake by Jos Walker, Deed-a-Day Danny by Hugh McNeill, Our Ernie by C.E. Holt begin	£300.00
2	£150.00
3-5	£100.00
6-11	£75.00
12 1st McNeill Our Ernie, 1st Frank Minnitt Billy Bunter	£75.00
13-65	£50.00
66 1st "Knock-Out and Magnet"	£35.00
67-193	£25.00
194 Gulliver's Travels by Eric Parker begins	£20.00
195-213,215-269,271-308,310-349	£20.00
214 Arabian Nights by Parker begins	£20.00
270 Mr. Midshipman Easy by Parker begins	£20.00
309 Children of the New Forest by Parker begins	£20.00
350 Kidnapped by Parker begins	£20.00
351-387,389-408,410-430,432-460	£15.00
388 Three Musketeers by Parker begins	£15.00
409 Westward Ho! by Parker begins	£15.00
431 The Phantom Sheriff by Parker begins (later by D.C. Eyles)	£15.00
461 Tough Tod and Happy Annie by McNeill begins	£15.00
462-473,475-489,491-505,507-532,534-561	£10.00
474 Black Arrow by Parker begins	£10.00
490 Dick Turpin's Ride to York by Eyles begins	£10.00
506 Capt. Flame by Sep E. Scott begins	£10.00
533 Captain Kidd by T. Heath-Robinson begins	£10.00
562 Kit Carson by Parker begins (later by Ian Kennedy, Don Lawrence, etc)	£5.00
563	£5.00
564 Breed of the Brudenells by H.M.Brock begins	£5.00
565-606	£4.00
607-610 jointly numbered issue	£4.00
611-615 un-dated issues (1950)	£4.00
616-617 jointly numbered issue	£4.00
618-759,761-814,816-868	£3.50
760 1st "Knockout and Comic Cuts"	£3.50
815 Johnny Winco by Mike Western begins	£3.50
869 Davy Crockett by Kennedy and others begins	£3.50
870-887,895-1053	£3.00
888-894 combined issue dated 3rd Mar-14th Apr 1956	£3.00
1054 last numbered issue	£3.00
16 May 1959-20 Jun 1959,nn,22 Aug 1959-3 Jun 1961	£3.00
10 Jun 1961 title becomes Billy Bunter's Knockout	£3.00
17 Jun 1961-14 Jul 1962	£3.00
21 Jul 1962 1st new look; Kelly's Eye by Solano Lopez begins	£2.50
28 Jul 1962-16 Feb 1963	£2.50
Note: no issues dated 14 Oct-23 Dec 1950 (numbered 607-617), one un-numbered/undated issue published between 27 Jun-15 Aug 1959.	
KNOCKOUT (2ND SERIES)	
IPC; 12th Jun 1971-23rd Jun 1973; 105 issues (joins Whizzer and Chips)	
No. 1–12 Jun 1971	£2.00
1 with free gift	£4.00
No. 2–19 Jun 1971	£1.50
2 with free gift (Super Shaking Skeleton)	£3.00
26 Jun 1971-23 Jun 1973	£0.60
KNOCKOUT FUN BOOK/ ANNUAL	
Amalgamated/Fleetway; 1941-1962,1978	

	N.MINT
1941	£150.00
1942	£100.00
1943	£80.00
1944,1945	£60.00
1946-1948	£30.00
1949-1951	£20.00
1952-1956	£10.00
1957-1959 becomes Knockout Annual	£8.00
1960-1962	£7.50
1978	£2.50

KONA COMIC ALBUM

World Distributors; 1 1965

1 64pgs; Dell colour reprints	£4.00

KORAK SON OF TARZAN

Williams; 1 1971-44? 1974

1 36pgs; Dell reprints	£3.00
2-44	£2.00

KORAK SON OF TARZAN BUMPER ALBUM

Top Sellers; 1973

nn 52pgs; National Periodicals reprints	£2.50

KUNG FU

Brown Watson; 1974

1974 Stories by Steve Moore, illus. by Desmond Walduck, Melvyn Powell	£3.50

L

LADY PENELOPE

City; 1 22nd Jan 1966-122 18th May 1968; becomes Penelope 123 25th May 1968-204 13th Dec 1969 (joins Princess Tina)

1 scarce, Perils of Parker by Peter Ford, Man From UNCLE, Lady Penelope by Frank Langford, Space Family Robinson by John Burns begin	£40.00
1 with free gift (Signet Ring)	£60.00
2	£20.00
3-5	£10.00
6-10	£7.50
11-50	£5.00
51-122	£2.50
123 title becomes Penelope	£1.00
124-204	£0.50

ARTISTS/FEATURES

John Burns in 1-52,60-65. Ron Embleton in 39-52.

LADY PENELOPE ANNUAL

City; 1966-1968 (becomes Penelope Annual)

1966	£15.00
1967-1968	£10.00

LADY PENELOPE SUMMER EXTRA

City; 1966

1966 very scarce	£25.00

LANCE O'CASEY

Arnold Book Co.; 10 1951

10 Fawcett reprints incl. strips from Funny Animals	£3.00

LANCER ANNUAL

World Distributors; 1970

1970 96pgs; Dell strip reprints plus text stories	£3.00

LAND OF THE GIANTS ANNUAL

World Distributors; 1968-1969

1969 "Crash Into the Unknown" (1st story)	£10.00
1970 "Two in a Trap" (1st story)	£7.50

LAND OF THE GIANTS TELEVISION STORY BOOK

PBS; 1969

1969 "Countdown to Escape" (1st story)	£5.00

LARAMIE ANNUAL/ LARAMIE

World Distributors/ Dean; 1961-1964

1961 Stories by Alex Gifford, illus. by Patrick Williams	£5.00
1962 Stories by Gordon Grimsley, illus. by Alex Henderson	£4.00
1963 Stories by Gordon Grimsley, illus. by John Burns	£3.00
1964 Dean; illus. by John Burns	£3.00

LARADO ANNUAL

World Distributors; 1966

1966 96pgs; Western/Dell strip reprints, plus text stories	£3.00

LASH LARUE WESTERN

Miller; 50 Sep 1950-125 1959, 76 issues

50 36pgs; Fawcett reprints	£5.00
51-125 reduced to 28pgs, later issues reprinted from Charlton	£3.00

LASSIE (M.G.M.'S...)

World Distributors; 1 Oct 1952-18 1954

1 36pgs; Dell reprints	£2.50
2-18 later issues 28pgs	£1.50

LAST KISS

(see also Kiss of Death)

Acme Press/Eclipse International; Mar 1989

nn 52pgs; John Watkiss art	£2.00

LAZARUS CHURCHYARD

Tundra; 1 Jun 1992-3 Nov 1992

1 The Virtual Kiss by Warren Ellis & D'Israeli, Blast reprints	£2.50
2 Goodnight Ladies mostly original material	£2.25
3 Inspector Sleep new material	£2.25

LIEUTENANT BLUEBERRY

Egmont/Methuen; 1977-1978

1 Fort Navajo (1977) 52pgs; Jean Giraud (Moebius) reprints	£3.00
2 Thunder in the West (1977)	£3.00
3 Lone Eagle (1978)	£3.00
4 Mission to Mexico (1978)	£3.00

LION

Amalgamated/Fleetway/IPC; 1 23rd Feb 1952-18th May 1974 (1136 issues, numbered to 378; joins Valiant)

	N.MINT
1 Captain Condor by Frank S. Pepper & Ronald Forbes, Sandy Dean, Jungle Robot (early Robot Archie) by F.A. Philpott	£75.00
2	£25.00
3-5	£15.00
6-30	£7.50
31-100	£4.00
101-212,218-256	£3.00
213-217 jointly numbered issue dated 17 Mar-14 Apr 1956	£3.00
257 1st Archie the Robot	£3.00
258-283	£3.00
284 Paddy Payne begins	£2.50
285-17 Oct 1959, 2 Nov 1959-22 Oct 1960	£2.50
24 Oct 1959 1st "Lion and Sun"	£3.50
29 Oct 1960 Sword of Eingar (1st Karl the Viking story) by Don Lawrence begins	£2.50
5 Nov 1960-26 Sep 1964,10 Oct 1964-19 Jun 1965,3 Jul 1965-4 Jun 1966	£2.50
3 Oct 1964 Hand of Zar (1st Maroc the Mighty story) by Don Lawrence begins	£2.50
26 Jun 1965 The Spider by Reg Bunn begins (created by Jerry Siegel)	£2.50
11 Jun 1966 1st "Lion and Champion"; Danger Man by Jesus Blasco begins	£2.00
18 Jun 1966-26 Apr 1969	£2.00
3 May 1969 1st "Lion and Eagle"; Hampson Dan Dare reprints begin	£1.50
10 May 1969-13 Mar 1971	£1.00
20 Mar 1971 1st "Lion and Thunder"; Fury's Family by McLoughlin begins	£0.75
27 Mar 1971-18 May 1974	£0.75

ARTISTS

Jesus Blasco in 11 Jun-3 Sep 1966. Joe Colquhoun in ?? Mar 1959-7 Mar 1964, 15 May-18 Sep 1965. Don Lawrence in 28 Oct 1960-10 Aug 1963, 23 Nov 1963-3 Jul 1965. Denis McLoughlin in 20 Mar-21 Oct 1971.

Note: two un-numbered/undated issues published between 27 Jun-29 Aug 1959, no issues dated 21 Nov 1970-30 Jan 1971, 26 Jan 1974, 9 Feb 1974, 23 Feb 1974, 9 Mar 1974, 23 Mar 1974.

LION ANNUAL

Amalgamated/Fleetway; 1954-1983

1954	£20.00
1955	£12.50
1956-1958	£7.50
1959-1964	£5.00
1965 Karl the Viking by Don Lawrence	£4.00
1966-1968	£4.00
1969-1975	£3.00
1976-1983	£2.50

LION BOOK OF...

Fleetway; 1961-1969

War Adventures 1962	£4.00
Speed 1963	£3.50
How It Works 1968	£3.00
Great Conquerors 1970	£3.00
Motor Racing 1970	£3.00

LION PICTURE LIBRARY

Fleetway/IPC; 1 Oct 1963-136 May 1969

1 60pgs; Paddy Payne,Rocket Buster (reprint from Lion)	£5.00
2-50	£2.50
51-136 reprints from Air Ace, Battle, War Picture Libraries	£1.00

ARTISTS/FEATURES

Robot Archie in 2,4,8. Captain Condor by Frank Pepper & Ron Forbes in 6,9. Joe Colquhoun art in 11,13,15,17,20,27,31.

LION SUMMER SPECIAL

Fleetway; 1968-1980

1968-1970 96pgs	£5.00
1971-1973 title becomes Lion and Thunder Summer Special	£3.00
1974-1980 title becomes Lion Holiday Special 80pgs	£2.00

LION SUMMER SPECTACULAR: EPIC

Fleetway; 1967

nn movie adaptions incl. Tobruk, Run of the Arrow, Quo Vadis, The Lost World, The Four Feathers, reprints from Film Fun, Thriller Picture Library; Batman, You Only Live Twice, Thunderbirds Are Go! photo features	£7.50

LITTLE LULU

World Distributors; 1-3 1955

1-3 28pgs; Dell reprints	£1.25

LITTLE MAX COMICS

United Anglo-American; 1-4 1953

1-4 28pgs; Harvey Publications reprints	£2.50

LOBO: THE LAST CZARNIAN

Titan; nn 1992

nn reprints DC series by Alan Grant & Simon Bisley	£6.00

LOGAN'S RUN ANNUAL

Brown Watson; 1978

1978 based on film; David Lloyd art	£3.50

LONDON'S DARK

Escape/Titan; Apr 1989

nn James Robinson & Paul Johnson	£4.00

LONE RANGER

World Distributors; 1 Jan 1953-66 Jun 1958

1 36pgs; Dell reprints	£5.00
2-61	£3.00
62-66 68pg issues	£4.00

LONE RANGER

Top Sellers; 1 1970-?

1 36pgs; Dell reprints	£1.50
2-?	£1.00

N.MINT

LONE RANGER
Egmont-Methuen; 1-2 1977
1-2 100pgs; Dell reprints £1.00

LONE RANGER, THE
World Distributors; Aug 1964-1969
1964 Stories by Douglas Enefer, J.L. Morrissey, M. Broadley, J.W. Elliott, illus. by Walter J. Howarth, "Enter Lone Ranger and Tonto" (1st story) £4.00
(1965-1967) some issues undated £4.00
1968 "The Silver Bullet" (1st story) £3.00
1969 "The Deserted Stage Station" (1st story) £2.00

LONE RANGER, THE
Brown Watson; 1975
1975 "The Story of the Lone Ranger" (1st story) £2.00

LONE RANGER ADVENTURE STORIES
Adprint; 1957-1960
1957 text/photos, Lone Ranger movie adapted by Arthur Groom £6.00
2 (1958) all text, stories by Richard Lewis, illus. by Don Lawrence £3.00
1959 all text, stories by Richard Lewis, illus. by Don Lawrence £3.00
1960 all text, stories by David Roberts, illus. by Eric Dadswell £3.50

LONE RANGER COMIC ALBUM, THE/ LONE RANGER ALBUM
World Distributors; 1 1950-5 1954; 1 Mar 1957
1-5 £5.00
(1957) The Lone Ranger Album £4.00

LONE RANGER TELEVISION STORY BOOK, THE
PBS; 1963, 1967
1963 "Silver Bullets" (1st story) £5.00
1967 The Lone Range Television Picture Story Book, "The Trap" (1st story) 3.00

LONE VIGILANTE
(see Action Series)

LONG BOW
Atlas Publishing; 1 Sep 1960-31 1964
1 28pgs; Fiction House reprints £2.50
2-31 later issues incl. Firehair reprints £1.50

LONG JOHN SILVER
Miller; 1-2 1956
1-2 28pgs; Charlton Comics reprints £4.00

LOOK AND LEARN
Fleetway/IPC; 1 20th Jan 1962-1049 17th Apr 1982 (see Picture Classics)
1 Prince Charles cover £3.00
2 £2.00
3-30 £1.50
31-176,178-231 £1.00
177 article about Gerry Anderson £2.00
232 scarce; 1st "Look and Learn and Ranger"; Trigan Empire by Mike Butterworth & Don Lawrence begins £3.00
233-382 Lawrence art £1.50
383-390 Ron Embleton Trigan Empire £1.25
391-752 Lawrence art £0.50
753 1st Oliver Frey Trigan Empire £0.25
754-853,855-1049 £0.25
854 1st Gerry Wood Trigan Empire £0.25
Note: many text features were illustrated by notable artists including Frank Bellamy, Luis Bermejo, C.L. Doughty, Ron Embleton, Peter Jackson, Eric Parker, Ferdinando Tacconi, etc

LOOK AND LEARN BOOK FOR BOYS
Amalgamated Press; 1962-? (1980s)
1962 scarce £7.50
1962 with dust wrapper £10.00
1963-1965 £5.00
1966-1969 £4.00
1970s £3.00
1980s £2.00

LOOK AND LEARN BOOK OF THE TRIGAN EMPIRE
(see also Tales of the Trigan Empire, The Trigan Empire)
Fleetway; 1973
nn reprints Trigan Empire by Don Lawrence from Ranger/Look & Learn £5.00

LOOK AND LEARN BOOKS
IPC; 1967-1972
1001 Questions and Answers (5 editions, 1968-1972), each £2.00
The Wonders of Nature (5 editions, 1967-1971), each £2.00
Railway Wonders of the World (1974) £2.50
Speed & Power (1978) £2.50

LOOK AND LEARN HOLIDAY SPECIAL
IPC; nn Apr 1976
nn 52pgs £0.75

LOOK AND LEARN SUMMER EXTRA
IPC; 1963
1963 scarce; subtitled On Your Holidays £7.50

LOOK-IN
Independent Television; 9th Jan 1971-1994
9 Jan 71 Leslie Crowther by Tom Kerr, Freewheelers by Vincente Alcazar, Timeslip by Mike Noble begin £5.00
1971-1973 £1.50
1974-1977 £0.75
1978-1982 £0.50
1982-1994 £0.35

ARTISTS
Martin Asbury (Kung Fu, Six-Million Dollar Man, Dick Turpin, Battlestar Galactica, Buck Rogers in the 25th Century). Jim Baikie (Chips, Charlie's Angels, Terrahawks, The Fall Guy). John Bolton (The Bionic Woman, 18 Mar 1978-19 May 1979). John Burns (The Tomorrow People, The Bionic Woman, How the West was Won). Ian Gibson (Bionic Action). Tom Kerr (Crowther in Trouble, Doctor in Charge, The Fenn Street Gang). Brian Lewis (Mark Strong, Les Dawson is Superflop, Jason King, The Marked Man). Mike Noble (Timeslip, Follyfoot, The Tomorrow People, Black Beauty, Space 1999, Man From Atlantis, Enid Blyton's Famous Five, Worzel Gummidge, Star Fleet,

Jag #2

Knockout (2nd) #2

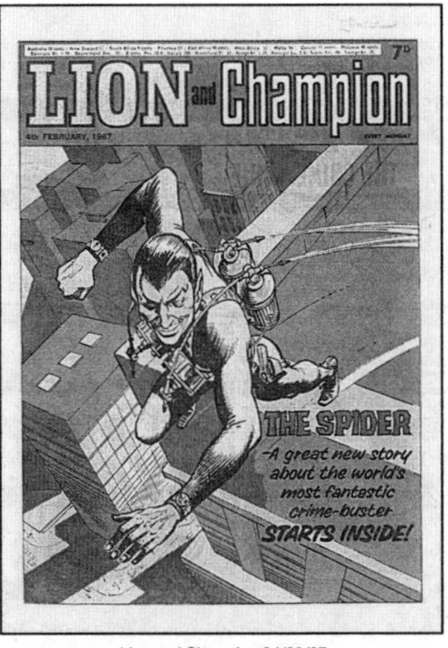

Lion and Champion 04/02/67

N.MINT

Robin of Sherwood). Harry North (Doctor on the Go, No.73). Arthur Ranson (Les Dawson, Michael Bentine's Potty Time, Just William, The Bionic Woman, Logan's Run, Worzel Gummidge, Chips, Sapphire and Steel, Further Adventures of Oliver Twist, Elvis the Story, The Story of the Beatles, Danger Mouse, Alias the Jester).

LOOK-IN SPECIALS
(see also Clash of the Titans)
Independant Television; 1973-1984
Follyfoot Special (1973) Mike Noble art £1.00
Danger Mouse Special (1982) £0.50
Madabout Special (1984) £0.35

LOOK-IN SUMMER EXTRA
Independant Television; 1974-?
1974-? £0.50

LOOK KIDDIES!
Gerald Swan; nn Oct 1948
nn 36pgs £3.00

LOONEY TUNES
World Distributors; 1 1953
1 28pgs; Dell reprints £2.00

LORDS OF MISRULE, THE
Atomeka; Mar 1993
nn by John Tomlinson & Gary Erskine, Bisley cover £4.50

LORNA THE JUNGLE GIRL
Miller; 1-9 1952
1-9 28pgs; Atlas reprints, incl. Frazetta art £4.00

LOST WORLD COMICS
Cartoon Art; 1 1950
1 84pgs; Ficton House reprints £4.00

LOVE AFFAIR
Miller; 1-3 1950s
1-3 68pgs; Fawcett (?) reprints £1.50

LOVERS
Miller; 1-12 1956
1-12 28pgs; Marvel reprints £1.50

LUCIFER
Trident; 1 Jul 1990-3 Sep 1990
1 Lucifer by Eddie Campbell & Paul Grist begins £1.25
2-3 £1.10

M

MAD MAGAZINE
Thorpe & Porter/Suron Enterprises/Fleetway; 1 Oct 1959-381 Jan 1994
1 32pgs; classic satire magazine begins featuring Alfred E. Neuman character on cover; reprints material beginning from about issue #22 or 23 of the American edition £100.00
2 £50.00
3-5 £30.00
6-9 £15.00
10 2/- cover price begins £15.00
11-20 £10.00
21-50 £5.00
51-100 £2.50
101-200 £2.00
201-300 £1.50
301-381 £1.50

MAGIC COMIC, THE
D.C. Thomson; 1 22nd Jul 1939-80 25th Jan 1941
1 Koko the Pup by E.H. Banger, Dolly Dimple by Allan Morley, Peter Piper by Dudley Watkins £350.00
1 facsimile £2.50
2 £175.00
3-10 £85.00
11-30 £45.00
31-47,49-60,62-70,72-80 £22.50
48 Dirty Dick by Morley begins £22.50
61 Gulliver by Watkins begins £22.50
71 Bandy Legs by Roland Davies begins £22.50
ARTISTS/FEATURES
Roland Davies in 71-80. Allan Morley in 1-80. Dudley D. Watkins in 1-80.

MAGIC FUN BOOK
D.C. Thomson; Sep 1939-Sep 1940 (joined Magic Beano Book)
1940 (Koko leading other characters skating across icy pond), very scarce £800.00
1941 (Koko doing strongman act with Tootsy McTurk on his shoulders), very scarce £700.00

MAGIC MOMENT ROMANCES
(see Heart to Heart, Twin Hearts)
K.G. Murray (Australia); 1 1958-?
1 very rare; 100pgs squarebound; b/w romance reprints from National £75.00
2-? £40.00

MAKABRE
Apocalypse (Apocalypse Presents); nn Oct 1991
nn Toxic reprints, Alcatena art £1.50

MAN ELF
(see The Saga of the Man Elf)

MAN FROM U.N.C.L.E. ALL COLOUR COMIC ALBUM, THE
World Distributors; 1 1966
1 softcover £5.00

MAN FROM U.N.C.L.E. ANNUAL, THE
World Distributors; 1966-1969
1966 £5.00
1967-1969 £4.00

MAN FROM U.N.C.L.E. TELEVISION STORYBOOK, THE
PBS; 1967-1968
1967-1968 £5.00

N.MINT

MAN FROM U.N.C.L.E. WORLD ADVENTURE LIBRARY, THE
World Distributors; 1-14 1966
1 US reprints begin, Don Heck art £8.00
2,4 US reprints, Sekowsky art £5.00
3 US reprint £5.00
5-14 UK originals by Mick Anglo, etc £3.00

MANDRAKE THE MAGICIAN
(see also Action Series)
Miller; 1 1961-24 1962
1 68pgs; reprints American newspaper strip by Lee Falk & Phil Davis £3.00
2-24 £1.50

MANDRAKE THE MAGICIAN WORLD ADVENTURE LIBRARY
World Distributors; 1 Jan 1967-8 Aug 1967
1 68pgs pocket size; Aftermath, reprints American newspaper strip by Lee Falk & Phil Davis £2.50
2-8 £1.50

MANGA HEROES
Manga Publishing; 1 Feb 1995-4 May 1995
1 Timecop, reprints Dark Horse movie adaptation £2.00
2-3 Appleseed; reprints Book 2 by Masamune Shirow £2.00
4 GenoCyber; manga reprint by Tony Takezaki £2.00

MANGA MANIA
Dark Horse/Manga Publishing/Titan Magazines; v1:1 Jul 1993-present (40 to Jan 1997)
v1:1 Godzilla, Akira, Appleseed reprints begin £2.25
v1:2-8,10 £2.00
v1:9 Dirty Pair, Demon reprints begin £2.00
v1:11 1st Manga Entertainment issue; with free Skyblazer Comic £2.00
v1:12 Dominion by Masamune Shirow reprints begin £2.00
v1:13,15 £2.00
v1:14 Hellhounds by Maroru Oshi & Kamui Fujiwara reprints begin £2.00
16 New Look; Bubblegum Crisis by Adam Warren reprints begin £2.00
17-19,21,23-24 £2.00
20 Silent Mobius by Kia Asamiya reprints begin £2.00
22 Firetripper by Rumiko Takahashi reprints begin £2.00
25 1st larger size; Free Dirty Pair poster mag; Dirty Pair by Adam Warren reprints begin £3.00
25 without poster mag £1.25
26-28,30-37 £2.50
29 Appleseed: Side Story reprints begin £2.50
38 New Look; Gunsmith Cats reprints begin; more text material £2.50
39 (Oct 1996) last Manga Publishing Ltd. issue £2.50
40 (Jan/Feb 1997) 1st Titan Magazines issue £2.95

MANHUNT
Streamline; 1-4 1951
1-4 36pgs; reprints Secret Agent X9 from American newspaper, cited in UK horror campaign £10.00

MANHUNT
World Distributors; 1-6 1959
1-6 28pgs; reprints Secret Agent X9 from American newspaper £6.00

MARINES IN ACTION
Streamline; nn 1955
nn 28pgs; Atlas reprints £2.50

MARINES IN BATTLE
Streamline; nn 1955
nn 28pgs; Atlas reprints £2.50

MARS COMICS
Streamline; nn 1950
nn 28pgs; reprints Planet Comics from Fiction House £8.00

MARSHAL LAW
Apocalypse; 1 Nov 1990, nn Mar 1991
1 48pgs; Kingdom of the Blind by Pat Mills & Kev O'Neill £1.50
nn 48pgs; Marshal Law Takes Manhattan £1.50
Note: Available in U.K. and American size

MARTHA WASHINGTON GOES TO WAR
(see also Give Me Liberty)
Titan; Mar 1996
nn by Frank Miller & Dave Gibbons £9.00

MARTIN KANE, PRIVATE EYE
Streamline; 1 c1950
1 reprints from Fox Features, Wood art £6.00

MARVEL ACTION
Marvel; 1 1st Apr 1981-15 8th Jul 1981 (joins Captain America)
1 Thor, Dr. Strange, Fantastic Four reprints begin £1.50
1 with free gift (Fantastic Four Super-Hero sticker) £3.00
2 £1.00
2 with free gift (Thor Super-Hero sticker) £2.00
3 £0.75
3 with free gift (Dr Strange Super-Hero sticker) £1.50
4-15 £0.60

MARVEL ANNUAL
Fleetway/World Distributors; 1972-1975,1978
cover year 1973 128pgs; reprints Hulk #2,5, Conan #5, Spider-Man #2,20 Secrets of Spider-Man (Ann #1), FF #7, £6.00
1974 128pgs; origins of Daredevil (#1), Hulk (#1), and Giant Man, reprints Spider-Man #8, Fantastic Four #12 £5.00
1975 80pgs; 1st World Distributors; reprints Hulk #164-166, Tales To Astonish #93, Silver Surfer £4.00
1976 64pgs; reprints Hulk (MTU #27), Hulk/Surfer/Namor (Submariner #34-35) £4.00
1979 64pgs; reprints Daredevil/Black Panther team-up £3.50

MARVEL CLASSICS COMICS
Marvel; 1 Oct 1981-12 Mar 1982
1-12 52pgs; Marvel reprints £0.75

MARVEL COMIC
(previously Mighty World of Marvel)
Marvel; 330 24th Jan 1979-352 25th Jul 1979 (joins Spider-Man, see also Marvel Super Heroes)
330 X-Men reprints £1.25

N.MINT

331-352 £0.75

MARVEL COMIC ANNUAL

World Distributors; 1969-1971

1969 scarce; reprints Journey Into Mystery #98, Hulk #4, Spider-Man #27, plus GA Captain America and Sub-Mariner £7.50

1970 reprints Journey Into Mystery 105, Hulk #4, Spider-Man #23, plus Captain America, Sub-Mariner, Thor, Iron Man £6.00

1971 reprints Thor #165, Captain America #100, TOS #98-99, plus Inhumans, Hulk (from Tales to Astonish) £6.00

MARVEL FAMILY, THE

Miller; nn (3 issues) 1949; 50 1950-89 1953 (30 issues)

nn-nn 16pgs 2-tone gravure £12.00

50-70 32pgs 2-tone gravure £8.00

71-89 28pgs smaller size £6.00

MARVEL MADHOUSE

Marvel; 1 Jun 1981-17 Oct 1982

1 36pgs £1.00

2-17 Dicky Howett art £0.40

MARVEL STORYBOOK ANNUAL

World Distributors; 1968

1968 scarce; text stories featuring Captain America, Spider-Man, Thor, Hulk, Sub-Mariner, Iron Man, Ant Man, Doctor Strange and Fantastic Four by Enefer, Tyson, Elliott £5.00

MARVEL SUPER ADVENTURE

Marvel; 1 6th May 1981-26 28th Oct 1981 (joins Captain America)

1 32pgs; Daredevil (from DD #42), Black Panther (Kirby art) reprints begin £1.50

1 with free gift (Daredevil iron-on transfer) £3.00

2-7,9-26 £0.75

8 reprints Daredevil #53 (origin retold) £1.00

MARVEL SUPER ADVENTURE WINTER SPECIAL

Marvel; nn Dec 1980

nn 52pgs; reprints featuring The Defenders (origin retold), Iron Fist and GA Sub-Mariner; b/w £1.25

MARVEL SUPER HEROES

(previously Marvel Comic)

Marvel 353 Sep 1979-397 May 1983 (joins Daredevil)

353-372 52pgs; X-Men, Ms Marvel, Avengers reprints begin £1.50

373 1st new look issue £1.50

374-376 £1.25

377 1st new look Captain Britain by Alan Davis £7.50

378-386 Davis art £5.00

387-388 1st Alan Moore Captain Britain script, Davis art £6.00

389-397 £3.00

Note: some issues have Alan Moore Night Raven text stories

MARVEL SUPER HEROES AND THE OCCULT

Marvel; nn Nov 1980

nn 64pgs; reprints featuring Human Torch, Dr. Doom, Iron Man, Dr. Strange; b/w with 6pgs colour £1.00

MARVEL SUPERHEROES ANNUAL

(see also The Superheroes Annual)

Marvel/Grandreams; 1980,1990-1993

1980 64pgs; reprints X-Men #1, Ms Marvel #5, Avengers #157; colour £4.00

1990 Marvel; 96pgs; reprints Spider-Man & His Amazing Friends #1, FF #232, X-Men, Hulk #340; McFarlane, Byrne art £3.50

1991 64pgs; reprints Hulk #314, Spider-Man vs Doc Octopus; Breyfogle art £3.00

1992 64pgs; reprints Iron Man, FF, X-Men stories £3.00

1993 64pgs; reprints X-Men, She Hulk, DD, Iron Man stories £3.00

MARVEL SUPERHEROES OMNIBUS

Marvel; 1986-1987

1986 Spider-Man, Iron Man, Hulk, Captain America, X-Men reprints £3.00

1987 Amazing Spider-Man #282, Iron Man #217, Incredible Hulk #314, Captain America #291, Uncanny X-Men #213 reprints £3.50

MARVEL SUPER HEROES SPRING SPECIAL

Marvel; nn Feb 1994

nn 32pgs; Iron Man, Thing, Black Widow, Daredevil reprints; colour £1.25

MARVEL SUPER HEROES SUMMER SPECIAL

Marvel; nn May 1979

nn 52pgs; reprints from Fantastic Four, Silver Surfer, Dr. Strange; b/w £1.25

MARVEL TALES

Miller; 1-7 1959

1-7 68pgs; Atlas pre-Code reprints £4.00

MARVEL TEAM-UP

Marvel; 1 11th Sep 1980-25 4th Mar 1981 (joins Spider-Man)

1 32pgs; Spider-Man & Daredevil, Ms. Marvel, Morbius the Living Vampire, Fantastic Four reprints begin £1.25

1 with free gift (Spider-Man & Daredevil Super-Hero stickers) £2.50

2 £1.00

2 with free gift (Ms. Marvel & Spider-Man Super-Hero stickers) £2.00

3 £0.75

3 with free gift (Fantastic Four Super-Hero stickers) £1.50

4-25 £0.60

MARVEL TEAM-UP WINTER SPECIAL

Marvel; nn Nov 1980

nn 52pgs; reprints featuring Fantastic Four, Red Sonja, Storm/Black Panther; b/w £1.25

MARVELMAN

(previously Captain Marvel)

Miller; 25 3rd Feb 1954-370 Feb 1963 (346 issues)

25 Marvelman by Mick Anglo & Roy Parker begins £25.00

26-30 £12.50

31 1st James Bleach Marvelman £7.50

32 1st Don Lawrence Marvelman £15.00

33-50 £7.50

51-100 £6.00

101,103-335 £4.00

102 Kid Marvelman by Don Lawrence begins £3.00

N.MINT

336-370 monthly issues, mostly reprints £2.50

Magician colouring book £15.00

Giant Flower colouring book £15.00

MARVELMAN ANNUAL

Miller; 1954-1961, 1963

1954 softcover, rare; Marvelman standing on cover £50.00

1955 softcover, very rare; Marvelman flying on cover £75.00

1956 £30.00

1957-1960 hardback £20.00

1961 title becomes Marvelman Adventures; card cover, Marvelman appears with Captain Marvel's face and cape £15.00

1963 scarce, card cover £25.00

MARVELMAN FAMILY

Miller; 1 Oct 1956-30 Nov 1959

1 Marvelman Family by Don Lawrence, Marvelman by Kurt (James Bleach), Young Marvelman by Leo Rawlings begin £15.00

2-11 £7.50

12 1st George Parlett Young Marvelman £6.50

13 1st Norman Light Marvelman £5.50

14 1st Arthur Whitworth Marvelman £5.50

15 1st Bill Merrill reprint by Ron Embleton £5.50

16-30 £4.50

MARVELMAN FAMILY ANNUAL

Miller; 1963

1963 scarce £30.00

MARVELMAN JR., ANNUAL

(see also Young Marvelman Annual)

Miller; 1963

1963 scarce, features Young Marvelman £27.50

MARVELMAN SPECIAL

Quality; 1 May 1984

1 reprints Anglo Marvelman with new framing sequence by Alan Moore & Alan Davis, Big Ben by Ian Gibson £1.75

MARY MARVEL

Miller; 11 1947?

11 16pgs gravure; Fawcett reprints £10.00

MASKED RAIDER

World Distributors; 1-4 1955

1-4 28pgs; Charlton Comics reprints £5.00

MASKED RAIDER

Miller; 50 1957-66 1958

50 28pgs; Charlton Comics reprints £5.00

51-66 £3.00

MASKED RIDERS OF THE RANGE

Cartoon Art; nn 1952

nn 20pgs; Magazine Enterprises reprints £5.00

MASTER COMICS

Miller; 1945-1958 (102 issues)

nn,nn,**49,55,58,74,84,106,107** (1945) 16pgs 2-tone gravure; Fawcett reprints £10.00

nn (1946) 36pgs larger size £6.00

50-142 (1950-1958) 28pgs £3.50

MASTERMAN COMIC

Streamline; 1 Nov 1952-Aug 1953 (10 issues, mostly unnumbered)

1 28pgs; Masterman by Joe Colquhoun begins £15.00

Dec 1952-Aug 1953 some incl. reprints from Will Rogers (Fox Publishing), Real Clue Comics (Hillman) £7.50

MATT SLADE GUNFIGHTER

Strato; 1-5 1957

1-5 68pgs; reprints from Kid Slade Gunfighter (Atlas), All Star Western (National Periodical Publications) £5.00

MAUS

Penguin/Andre Deutsch; 1987, 1992

Maus (Penguin, 1987) 160pgs; art spiegelman story/art US reprints begin £6.00

Maus II (Andre Deutsch, Mar 1992) 136pgs, hardcover £14.00

Maus II (Penguin, Mar 1992) £9.00

MAVERICK ANNUAL

World Distributors; 1961-1962

1961 text stories by Douglas Enefer £5.00

1962 text stories by Douglas Enefer £5.00

MAVERICK ANNUAL

Grandreams; 1981

1981 based on TV series £3.00

MAVERICK MARSHAL

Miller; 50-52 1959

50-52 28pgs; Charlton Comics reprints £4.00

MAVERICK TELEVISION STORY BOOK

New Town; 1960-1962

1960-1962 £4.00

MAX

Macmillan; 1954-1961?

Max (Macmillan, 1954) reprints Max by Giovannetti from Punch £5.00

Nothing But Max (Macmillan, 1959) £4.00

Max Presents (Macmillan, 1961?) £4.00

The Penguin Max (Penguin, 1962) softcover £1.00

MERLIN AND EXCALIBUR IN QUEST OF THE KING

Marvel; nn Jul 1981

nn American reprint £1.00

METAL MEN ANNUAL

(see Brave & Bold Annual, Green Lantern Annual)

Thorpe & Porter; 1967

1967 scarce, bound together remaindered copies of selected DC comics incl. Metal Men #20,25, Superman #190, Batman #181, Tomohawk 108, Bob Hope #104 £25.00

MICKEY MOUSE HOLIDAY SPECIAL

Willbank; 1936-1938 (3 issues)

	N.MINT
1936 64pgs; Basil Reynolds, Reg Carter art	£50.00
1937-1938 Reg Perrott, Basil Reynolds art	£40.00

MICKEY MOUSE SPECIALS

IPC; May 1976-Jun 1980 (10 issues)

	N.MINT
Fun Time Extra 1976,1977,1978,1979	£0.60
Holiday Special 1976,1977,1978	£0.60
Summer Special 1979,1980	£0.60
Fun Time Holiday Special 1980	£0.60

MICKEY MOUSE WEEKLY

Willbank/Odhams; (1) 8th Feb 1936-(920) 28th Dec 1957 (numbered inside only; splits into two comics, Zip and Walt Disney's Mickey Mouse)

	N.MINT
1	£200.00
2	£100.00
3-5	£75.00
6-10	£50.00
11-47	£25.00
1937-1939 issues	£15.00
1940-1945 issues	£7.50
1946-1950 issues	£5.00
1951-1953 issues	£2.50
1954-1957 issues	£2.00

CHRONOLOGY

25 May 1940: page count reduced to 8. 5 Jul 1940: page size reduced. 13 Sep 1940: title shortened to Mickey Mouse, publication reduced to fortnightly. 11 Apr 1942: size reduced again. 25 Dec 1948: size enlarged. 3 Sep 1949: page count increased to 12. 4 Mar 1950: title retuned to Mickey Mouse Weekly, weekly publication resumed. 21 Oct 1950: size increases. 1 Oct 1955: title changed to Walt Disney's Mickey's Weekly.

ARTISTS/FEATURES

Frank Bellamy in 25 Jul 1953-26 Jun 1954 (Monty Carstairs), plus occasional Walt Disney's Living World. Ron Embleton in various (Roger's Rangers, Strongbow the Mighty). James Holdaway (Davy Crockett). Reg Perrott in various (Road to Rome, White Cloud, Song of the Sword, Sir Roger de Coverlet, White King of Arabia). Tony Weare in various (Pride of the Circus, Billy Brave, Savage Splendour, Robin Alone).

MICKEY MOUSE ANNUAL

Dean & Son; 1931-1965

	N.MINT
1931	£200.00
1932	£125.00
1933	£100.00
1934-1940	£75.00
1941-1943	£50.00
1946-1949	£25.00
1950-1959	£12.50
1960-1965	£7.50

MICKEY MOUSE XMAS SPECIAL

Willbank; nn 1939

	N.MINT
nn 72pgs; Basil Reynolds, Alan Philpott, reprint art	£75.00

MIDNIGHT SURFER SPECIAL

(see also Strontium Dog Special)

Quality; 2 1986

	N.MINT
2 2000AD reprints, Cam Kennedy art	£1.50

MIGHTY ATOM, THE

Denlee Publishing Co. (S.D.Frances); nn 1948

	N.MINT
nn 16pgs; Philip Mendoza art	£15.00

MIGHTY COMIC

K.G. Murray (Australia); 1 late 1950s-41? early 1960s

	N.MINT
1 rare; 100pgs squarebound; b/w reprints from National Periodicals incl. Tomahawk, Congo Bill, Wonder Woman, Mr. District Attorney, Robin Hood, Viking Prince	£75.00
2 rare	£50.00
3-5 very scarce	£40.00
6-10 scarce	£35.00
11-41? scarce	£30.00

Note: Later issues incl. Justice League of America, Eclipso, Mark Merlin, Adam Strange and others

MIGHTY MIDGET

Polystyle; 1 18th Sep 1976-2 25th Sep 1976

	N.MINT
1 16pgs; Dr Who	£7.50
2 16pgs; Star Trek	£5.00

Note: published as supplements to TV Comic

MIGHTY THOR, THE

Marvel; 1 20th Apr 1983-39 11th Jan 1984; joins Spiderman

	N.MINT
1 Thor reprints begin	£1.25
1 with free gift (red plastic spinner)	£3.00
2	£1.00
2 with free gift (Thor sticker)	£2.00
3,5-19	£0.75
4 John Higgins cover	£1.00
20 1st "Mighty Thor & Original X-Men"	£1.00
21-39	£0.75

MIGHTY WARRIORS ANNUAL

(World?); 1978

	N.MINT
1979 Dr. Solar, Dagar, Magnus reprints from Gold Key	£5.00

MIGHTY WORLD OF MARVEL, THE

Marvel; 1 7th Oct 1972-329 17th Jan 1979 (becomes Marvel Comic)

	N.MINT
1 Hulk, Fantastic Four, Amazing Spider-Man reprints begin	£6.00
1 with free gift (Green-skinned monster T-shirt transfer)	£12.00
2	£2.00
3	£1.50
4-18	£1.25
19 last Spider-Man	£1.25
20 Daredevil reprints begin	£1.25
21-45,47-48,50-66	£1.00
46 Avengers reprints begin	£1.00
49 X-Men reprints begin	£1.00
67 new look	£1.00
68-198	£0.75
199 1st "Mighty World of Marvel & Avengers"	£1.00
200-230,232-257	£0.75
231 1st "Mighty World of Marvel & Planet of the Apes"	£1.00
258 1st "Mighty World of Marvel & Fury"	£0.75
259-297,299-329	£0.60
298 1st "Mighty World of Marvel & Fantastic Four"	£0.75

MIGHTY WORLD OF MARVEL (2ND SERIES)

Marvel; 1 Jun 1983-17 Oct 1984 (joins Savage Sword of Conan)

	N.MINT
1 X-Men (ends #6), Vision & Scarlet Witch (ends #4) reprints begin	£5.00
1 with free gift (X-Men Mighty World of Marvel sticker)	£7.50
2-4,6	£3.00
5 Miller Wolverine reprints begin (ends #8)	£3.00
7 1st "Mighty World of Marvel and Daredevils"; Captain Britain by Moore & Davis, Night Raven text by Jamie Delano begin, 1st Showcase	£6.00
8,10-12 Davis art	£3.50
9 Cloak and Dagger reprints begin (ends #12)	£3.00
13 X-Men and Micronauts reprints begin (ends #16), last Moore Captain Britain	£3.00
14,15 1st Davis script/art on Captain Britain	£3.00
16 last Captain Britain, Davis script/art	£2.50
17 Magik reprint, last issue	£1.25

MIGHTY WORLD OF MARVEL ANNUAL

Marvel; 1977-1979

	N.MINT
1977 80pgs; reprints Hulk #179, FF #123,166, Man-Thing; colour	£4.50
1978 64pgs; Captain Marvel, Luke Cage reprints, Hulk featured; Daredevil cover by Brodsky/Adams; colour	£4.00
1979 reprints DD Annual #4, DD #140; colour	£3.50

MIGHTY WORLD OF MARVEL SUMMER SPECIAL

Marvel; nn Jun 1983

	N.MINT
nn 48pgs; US reprints of Thor and Hulk, b/w; Garry Leach painted cover and Thor centre-fold poster	£1.25

MIKE BARNETT MAN AGAINST CRIME

Miller/Arnold Book Co.; 50-55 1952

	N.MINT
50 28pgs; Fawcett reprints	£10.00
51-55	£7.50

MIRACLEMAN

(see Eclipse Graphic Novels, Marvelman, Marvelman Special, Warrior)

MIRACLE MAN

Top Sellers; 1965, 13? issues

	N.MINT
1-13 68pgs; Spanish reprints. Some incl. Blackhawk reprints from US	£1.50

MONSTER FUN COMIC

IPC; 1 14th Jun 1975-nn 29th Sep 1976 (joins Buster)

	N.MINT
No. 1 - 14th Jun 1975 Kid Kong by Robert Nixon begins	£1.50
1 with free gift (Plate Wobbler)	£3.00
No. 2 - 21 Jun 1975	£1.25
No. 2 with free gift (Spider Ring)	£2.50
28 Jun 1975-29 Sep 1976	£0.50

MONSTER FUN COMIC SUMMER SPECIAL

IPC; nn 1976

	N.MINT
nn 64pgs	£1.00

MONSTER MASSACRE

Tundra (Atomeka); Jul-Aug 1993

	N.MINT
Monster Massacre (Jul 1993) Bisley, O'Neill, Braithwaite/Gibbons art	£5.00
Carnosaur Carnage (Aug 1993) Kev Walker, John McCrea art	£3.25

MONSTER MASSACRE

Blackball Comics; 1 Apr 1994

	N.MINT
1 Bisley, O'Neill, Keith Giffen, James O'Barr art	£2.00

MONSTER OF FRANKENSTEIN, THE

(see Frankenstein Comic)

MONSTER RUPERT ANNUAL

Sampson Low; 1931-1934, 1948-1950

	N.MINT
1931 (Rupert and wolf)	£200.00
1932 (Rupert sitting on log)	£180.00
1933 (Rupert and bird)	£180.00
1934 (Rupert and young boy in storeroom)	£180.00
1948 (Rupert sitting on log) dustjacket	£35.00
1949 (Rupert and fox) dustjacket	£35.00
1950 (Rupert assisting young boy out of hole) dustjacket	£35.00

MONTE HALE WESTERN

Miller; Sep 1950, 1 unnumbered issue; 50 Jun 1951-118 1959

	N.MINT
nn 16pgs, 2-tone gravure; Fawcett reprints	£10.00
50-118 36pgs/24pgs; monthly series	£5.00

MORNINGSTAR

Trident; 1 1990

	N.MINT
Book One: Black Dog Nigel Kitching art	£1.25

MOTION PICTURE COMICS

Miller; 50 Mar 1951-60 1952

	N.MINT
50 36pgs; Code of the Silver Sage (Rocky Lane, 102), Fawcett reprints based on movie	£10.00
51-59 later issues 24pgs	£7.50

FEATURES

51 Covered Wagon Raid (Rocky Lane, 103). 52 Vigilante Hideout by Bob Powell (Rocky Lane, 104). 53 The Red Badge of Courage by Bob Powell (104). 54 The Texas Rangers (105). 55 Frisco Tornado (107), 56 Mask of the Avenger (108). 57 Rough Rider of Durango (Rocky Lane, 109). 58 When Worlds Collide by Williamson/Evans (110). 59 The Vanishing Outpost (Lash LaRue, 111). 59 Brave Warrior (112). 60 Walk East on Beacon by Kurt Schaffenberger (113).

MOTORMOUTH

(see main American Section)

MOVIE CLASSICS

World Distributors; 1 1955-88 1960

	N.MINT
1 36pgs; Sir Walter Raleigh, Dell reprints	£12.00
2-88	£6.00

	N.MINT
MR. DISTRICT ATTORNEY	
Thorpe & Porter; 1-23 1953	
1 68pgs; National Comics reprints based on TV series	£10.00
2-23	£5.00
MR. PUNCH	
Victor Gollancz; Oct 1994	
nn 96pgs; by Neil Gaiman & Dave McKean; hardcover	£15.00
nn softcover	£8.00
MUMMY, THE	
Top Sellers; nn 1963	
nn 68pgs; Dell reprints	£2.00
MYS-TECH WARS	
(see main American section)	
MYSTERIES OF UNEXPLORED WORLDS	
Miller; 1 1956	
1 68pgs; Charlton reprints	£5.00
MYSTERY COMICS	
T.V. Boardman; 7 1940-11 1941, 5 issues	
7 36pgs; reprints from Smash Comics (Quality)	£6.00
8-11 20pgs	£3.50
MYSTERY IN SPACE	
Miller; 1 1952-9 1954	
1 28pgs; National Periodical Publications reprints	£12.50
2-9	£6.00
MYSTERY IN SPACE	
Strato Publications; 1 1954-13 1955	
1 68pgs; National Periodical Publications reprints	£7.50
2-13	£5.00
MYSTIC	
Miller; 1 1961-66 1966	
1-66 68pgs; incl. reprints from Atlas, Marvel, EC etc.	£2.50

N

NATURE BOY	
Miller; 1-3 1957	
1-3 28pgs; Charlton reprints	£2.50
NEAR MYTHS	
Galaxy Media; 1 Sep 1978-5 Apr 1980	
1 Luther Arkwright by Bryan Talbot, Tales From the Edge by Graham Manley begin	£6.00
2 Bryan Talbot art, Grant Morrison 1st appearence	£4.00
3 Gideon Stargrave by Grant Morrison begins, Talbot art	£4.00
4 Thiirania by Tony O'Donnell begins, Morrison, Talbot art	£4.00
5 Morrison, Talbot, Hunt Emerson art	£4.00
NEMESIS	
Titan (Best of 2000AD); 1984-Aug 1989, 1992	
Book One O'Neill art	£5.00
Book Two O'Neill art	£5.00
Book Three Talbot art	£5.00
Book Four Talbot art	£5.00
Book Five Talbot art	£5.00
Book Six O'Neill, Talbot art	£5.00
Book Seven Hicklenton art	£5.00
Book Eight Roach art	£4.50
Book Nine Hicklenton art	£5.50
Nemesis the Beginning (1992) reprints Book One, Book Two	£9.00
NEMESIS THE WARLOCK	
Eagle; 1 Sep 1984-7 Mar 1985	
1 2000AD reprints, partly redrawn and resized by Kevin O'Neill	£1.50
2-7	£1.25
NEW AVENGERS ANNUAL	
(see also Avengers Annual)	
Brown Watson; 1977-1978	
1977 features New Avengers (Steed, Gambit, Purdie), Bolton art	£4.00
1978 Bolton art	£3.25
NEW HOTSPUR, THE	
(see The Hotspur)	
NEW STATESMEN	
Fleetway; 1 1989-5 Jul 1990	
1,4 54pgs squarebound; Crisis reprints by Smith & Baikie begin	£1.75
2,5 Baikie, Phillips art	£1.75
3 Phillips, Fegrado art	£1.75
The Complete New Statesmen (Fleetway)	£8.00
NICK HAZARD	
(see JRF Presents)	
Harrier; 1 Jan 1988	
1 Ron Turner art	£0.75
NIGHTRAVEN: THE COLLECTED STORIES	
Marvel; 1990	
nn Hulk Comic reprints by Jamie Delano, David Lloyd & John Bolton, newly coloured	£4.50
NIGHTRAVEN: HOUSE OF CARDS	
Marvel; 1991, 1992	
nn (1991) large pb format, by Jamie Delano & David Lloyd	£7.00
nn (1992) prestige format, new Lloyd cover	£3.50
NIGHT VISION	
Atomeka; 1993	
nn by David Quinn & Hannibal King, John Bolton cover & poster	£2.50
NO HIDING PLACE ANNUAL	
World Distributors; 1966	
1966 "The Voice" (1st story)	£3.00
NYOKA THE JUNGLE GIRL	
(see Further Adventures of Nyoka the Jungle Girl)	

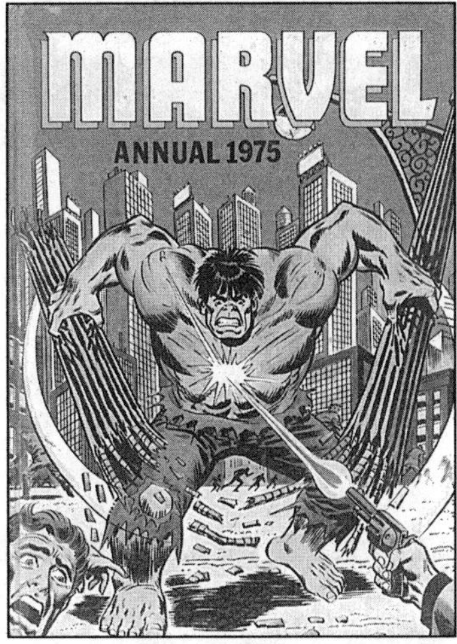

Marvel Annual 1975

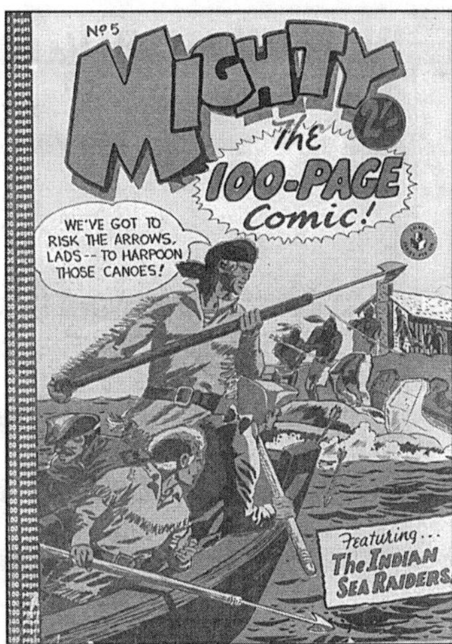

Mighty Comic #5

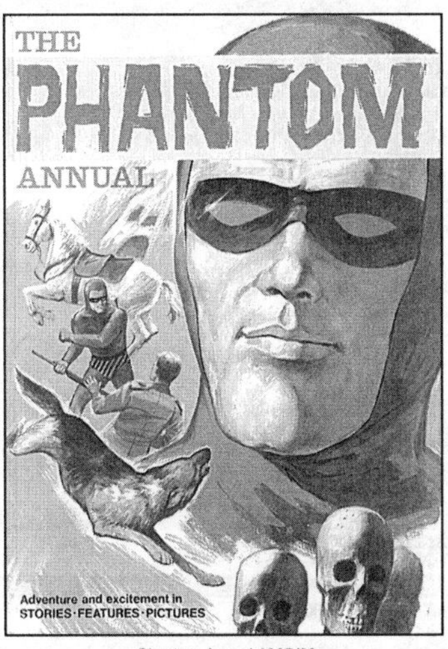

Phantom Annual 1967/68

N.MINT

Miller; 1950, 1 unnumbered issue; 50 Jun 1951-118 1959
nn 16pgs, 2-tone gravure; Fawcett reprints £8.00
50-118 £5.00

O

OOR WULLIE
D.C. Thomson; 1941-present (bi-annual)
1941 (large pic of Wullie sitting on bucket) Dudley D. Watkins art begins £300.00
1943 (Wullie stood next to bucket, hands in pockets, satchel over shoulder) £250.00
1949 (head/shoulders shot of Wullie against red background) £100.00
1951 (16 different facial expressions) £75.00
1953 (12 frames featuring Wullie in dunces cap, etc) £75.00
1955 (Wullie reading copy of "Oor Wullie" with same picture on cover) £40.00
1957 (Snowman of Wullie sitting on a bucket, cabin in background) £40.00
1959 (Wullie with paint and brush behind wall with body painted on it) £25.00
1961 (Wullie eating breakfast made to look like face) £25.00
1963 (Wullie walking by wall casting policeman shaped shadow) £20.00
1965 (Wullie on knees polishing bucket) £20.00
1967-1971 (copyright dated, i.e. cy1966 for 1967) £10.00
1973-1979 £5.00
1981-1989 £2.50
1991,1993 £2.50
1995,1997 £2.00

OOR WULLIE SUMMER FUN SPECIAL
D.C. Thomson; Jun 1980-1994
1980 36pgs £2.00
1981-1993 £1.00
1994 published only as a supplement to the Sunday Post Summer Special £1.20

ORIGINAL X-MEN
Marvel; 1 27th Apr 83-17 23rd May 83 (joins The Mighty Thor)
1 X-Men reprints from X-Men #1 £2.00
2-17 X-Men reprints £1.50

OUTER LIMITS ANNUAL, THE
World Distributors; 1966-1967
1966 scarce, Dell reprints; rocket cover £10.00
1967 scarce, Dell reprints £7.50

OUT OF THIS WORLD
Strato Publications/Thorpe & Porter; 1 Oct 1951-22 1953
1 68pgs; reprints various US strips £25.00
2 £12.50
3 £7.50
4-5 £5.00
6-22 incl. Captain Midnight, Captain Video, etc. £3.00

OUT OF THIS WORLD
Alan Class; nn 1960s; 1 196?- ; 1 197?-
nn 68pgs; Charlton reprints £20.00
1-? £12.50
1-? 52pgs; Class series £2.00

OUTER SPACE
Miller; 1-4? 1958
1-4? 68pgs; Charlton reprints £3.00

OUTER SPACE
G.T. Ltd; 1959?
nn 96pgs, card cover; Captain Future by Norman Light, Embleton reprints £10.00

OUTER SPACE
Alan Class; 1-9 1961
1 68pgs; Charlton reprints £2.50
2-9 £1.50

OUTLAWS WESTERN STORIES
Streamline; 1-2 1954
1-2 28pgs; US reprints £2.50

OVERKILL
(see Black Axe, Death's Head II (limited, ongoing), Digitek, Hell's Angel, Knights of Pendragon, Motormouth, Super Soldiers, Warheads)
Marvel; 1 24th Apr 1992-52 24th Aug 1994
1 32pgs; Hell's Angel by Bernie Jaye & Geoff Senior/Cam Smith, Warheads by Nick Vince & Gary Erskine, Knights of Pendragon by Dan Abnett/John Tomlinson & Phil Gascoine/Adolfo Buylla, Motormouth by Graham Marks & Gary Frank/Cam Smith £0.75
2-11 £0.55
12 Death's Head II (mini-series) reprints begin £0.60
13-14,17-20 Death's Head II £0.60
15-16 Death's Head II, Gary Erskine art £0.60
21 £0.60
22 Death's Head II (ongoing) reprints begin, Liam Sharp art £0.60
22-29,31 Death's Head II, Sharp art £0.60
30 Black Axe, Super Soldiers reprints begin, Liam Sharp art £0.60
32-42 Death's Head II £0.60
43 first monthly; Dark Guard, Wild Thing begin £1.00
44-52 £1.00
Note: Early issues also published as a separate titles by Marvel with additional pages for American market. From around issue 12 the full stories were published.

P

P.C. 49
Hawk (Eagle Classics); 1990
nn reprints Alan Stranks & John Worsley strip from Eagle £5.00

P.C. 49 ANNUALS
Juvenile/Preview/Dakers; 1951-1955
P.C. 49 (Juvenile, 1951) £10.00
On Duty With P.C. 49 (Juvenile, 1952) £10.00

N.MINT

On the Beat with P.C. 49 (Juvenile, Sep 1953) text stories, Worsley illus. £10.00
Eagle Strip Cartoon Book No.1 (Preview, Oct 1953) Eagle Worsley reprints £10.00
Eagle Strip Cartoon Book No.2 (Preview, Sep 1954) Eagle Wosley reprints £10.00
P.C. 49 Annual 1955 (Dakers, Aug 1955) text stories, Worsley illus. £10.00
Note: All annuals except strip books issued in dust jackets. Price halved if dust-jacket missing

PENELOPE
(see Lady Penelope)

PENELOPE ANNUAL
(previously Lady Penelope Annual)
Century 21/IPC; 1969-1971
1969 Gerry Anderson related material £7.50
1971-1972 no Anderson related material £1.50

PHANTOM, THE
(see The Phantom World Adventure Library, TV Tornado)
Miller; 1 1959-18 1961
1 68pgs; reprints American newspaper strip by Lee Falk £5.00

PHANTOM, THE
Wolf Publishing; 1 Jul 1992-11 May 1993
1 32pgs; reprints Swedish strip by Tierres & Felmang £1.00
2-11 £1.00

PHANTOM ANNUAL, THE
World Distributors; 1967-68
copyright year 1967-68 text stories and strips £4.00

PHANTOM WORLD ADVENTURE LIBRARY, THE
(see The Phantom, TV Tornado)
World Distributors; 1 Jan 1967-8 Aug 1967
1 68pgs pocket size; The Deadly Catch, reprints Gold Key/King strips £6.00
2-8 reprints £4.00

PLANET COMICS
Cartoon Art Productions; nn 1950
nn 28pgs; Fiction House reprints £6.00

PLANET COMICS
R. & L. Locker; 1-5 1951
1-2 68pgs; Fiction House reprints, cited in UK horror campaign £15.00
3-5 £6.00

PLANET OF THE APES
Marvel; 1 26th Oct 1974-123 23rd Feb 1977, 123 numbered issues
(joins Mighty World of Marvel)
1 Planet of the Apes film adaptation reprints begin £1.50
1 with free gift (colour Apes poster) £3.00
2 Planet of the Apes adaptation, Ka-Zar back-up begins (later back-ups incl. Gulliver Jones, Dr. Doom, Warlock, etc) £1.25
3-11 Planet of the Apes adaptation £1.00
12-34 £1.00
35-46 Beneath the Planet of the Apes adaptation £1.00
47-48 £0.75
50-62 Escape from the Planet of the Apes adaptation £0.75
63-74 Conquest of the Planet of the Apes adaptation £0.60
75-87 £0.50
88 1st "Planet of the Apes & Dracula Lives", Spider-Man appears £1.00
89-107 £0.50
108-123 Battle for the Planet of the Apes (cont. in Mighty World of Marvel) £0.50
Note: some later stories reprint other titles with ape heads drawn on

PLANET STORIES
Atlas; 1 Jun 1961-?
1-? 28pgs; Fiction House reprints £6.00

PLASTIC MAN
Popular; 2 Mar 1951-(various numbers)
2 36pgs; Quality reprints £12.00
5,60 £10.00

POLICE COMIC
Archer Press (King Comic Series); 1-6 1953
1-6 68pgs; Quality reprints £8.00

POPEYE
Pembertons; 1 1950-19 1951
1-19 28pgs; Dell reprints, Bud Sagendorf art £8.00

POPEYE
World Distributors; 1-7 1957
1-7 28pgs; Western Printing reprints, Bud Sagendorf art £7.50

POPEYE
Miller; 1 1959-30 1963
1-30 28pgs; reprints King Features syndicated strip by Bela Zaboly £5.00

POPEYE
Hawk Books; nn 1995
nn 128pgs, hardcover; edited by Mike Higgs £15.00

POW!
Odhams; 1 21st Jan 1967-86 7th Sep 1968 (joins Smash!)
1 Spider-Man (from Spider-Man #1), Nick Fury Agent of S.H.I.E.L.D. (from Strange Tales #135), reprints begin, The Python by Borrell, Jack Magic, Dolls of St. Dominics, The Group, Dare-a-Day Davy by Ken Reid begin £25.00
1 with free gift (Spider-Matic Gun and ammo) £50.00
2 £10.00
2 with free gift (iron-on Spider-Man transfer) £20.00
3-9 £3.00
10,34,35 no The Python £2.00
11 no Jack Magic £2.00
12-16 £2.00
17 last Jack Magic £2.00
18 The Cloak by Mike Higgs begins £2.00
19-33,36-42,45-51 £2.00
43 last The Python £2.00
44 Experiment X by Ed Feito begins £2.00

	N.MINT
52 Fantastic Four (from FF27) reprints begin, last Nick Fury, The Group	£2.50
53 1st "Pow! and Wham!"; Two Faces of Janus by Ayhan, George's Germs by Cyril Price begin	£2.50
54-68,70-86	£1.50
69 last Experiment X	£1.50

POW! ANNUAL
Odhams; 1968-1972 (joins Wham! Annual)

1968 reprints from Amazing Spider-Man #1, Nick Fury from Strange Tales #135	£6.00
1969	£5.50
1970-1972	£4.50

PREDATOR
(see also Aliens, Batman vs Predator)
Titan

Predator (1990) Dark Horse reprints	£7.50
Predator: Big Game (1992) Dark Horse reprints, Evan Dorkin art	£7.50
Predator: Cold War (Feb 1995) Dark Horse reprints, Ron Randall art	£9.00

PROJECT SWORD
City; 1968

1968 annual for planned TV series which never appeared	£12.50

PROTECTORS ANNUAL
Polystyle; 1973

1974 based on TV series starring Robert Vaughn	£6.00

PSSST!
Never/Artpool; Dummy 1981; 1 Jan 1982-10 Oct 1982

Dummy scarce; previews some material, bulked out with blank pages	£4.00
1 Paul Johnson, Bob Wakelin art	£2.00
2 Bryan Talbot Luthor Arkwright begins, Rob Moran art	£3.50
3 Talbot, John Higgins art	£2.00
4 Talbot, Angus McKie art	£2.00
5 Talbot, Moran art	£2.00
6 Talbot art, Temptation by Glenn Dakin begins	£2.00
7 Talbot, David Jackson, Mike Matthews art	£2.00
8 Talbot, McKie, Johnson art	£2.00
9 Talbot, McKie art	£2.00
10 Talbot, Higgins, Johnson, McKie art	£2.00

Note: each issue included a free poster which if intact will command 25% higher price

PUNISHER AUTUMN SPECIAL, THE
Marvel; Oct 1992

1992 36pgs; reprints from Punisher Summer Special 1, Mark Texiera art	£1.00

Q

QUESTPROBE
Marvel; 1 Jun 1984

1 US reprint, based on computer game	£3.00

QUICK TRIGGER WESTERN
Miller; 1-8? 1956

1-8 28pgs, Atlas/Marvel reprints	£3.00

R

RACE FOR THE MOON
Alan Class; nn 1959

nn 68pgs; Harvey reprints	£5.00

RACE FOR THE MOON
Strato Publications/Top Sellers; 1 1959?-23 1960

1 68pgs; various reprints from Harvey, National Periodicals, A.C.G. etc.	£12.50
2	£7.50
3-5 incl. Kirby reprints	£6.00
6-23 incl. Kirby, Ditko reprints	£2.50

RACE INTO SPACE
Alan Class; 1-14? 1961

1 68pgs; DC reprints	£8.00
2-14?	£5.00

RADIO FUN
Amalgamated Press; 1 15th Oct 1938-nn 18th Feb 1961, 1167 issues, mostly numbered (joins Buster)

1 George the Jolly Geegee by Roy Wilson, Flanagan & Allen by Alex Akerbladh begin	£300.00
2	£150.00
3-5	£100.00
6-11	£80.00
12-53	£50.00
54-64	£40.00
1941-1945	£25.00
1946-1950	£10.00
1951-1955	£5.00
1956-1959	£3.00
1960-1961	£2.50

CHRONOLOGY
19 Sep 1953: 1st "Radio Fun & Wonder". 22 Aug 1959: title becomes Radio Fun and Adventures.
ARTISTS/FEATURES
Artists incl. Bertie Brown, George Heath (The Falcon, etc.), John Jukes, Hugh McNeill (Jack O'Justice), Roy Wilson. Superman newspaper strip reprints 1959-60.

RADIO FUN ANNUAL
Amalgamated Press; 1940-1960

1940 scarce	£150.00
1941 scarce	£100.00
1942-1944	£60.00
1945-1947	£45.00
1948-1949	£30.00
1950-1955	£15.00
1956-1960	£7.50

RAIDERS OF THE LOST ARK
Marvel; 1981

	N.MINT
1981 reprints film adaptation	£2.50

RAMAR OF THE JUNGLE
Miller; 1-4 1959

1-4 28pgs; Charlton reprints (1956)	£4.00

RAMPAGE
Marvel; 1 19th Oct 1977-77 31st May 1978 (continued as Rampage Monthly)

1 The Defenders and Nova (origin) reprints begin	£1.50
1 with free gift (plastic Concorde model)	£3.00
2 Nova origin concluded	£1.25
2 with free gift (plastic Stratocruiser)	£2.50
3-5 complete Defenders stories begin	£1.00
6-77	£0.60

RAMPAGE MONTHLY/MAGAZINE
(previously Rampage)
Marvel; 1 Jul 1978-54 Dec 1982 (joins Marvel Super Heroes)

1 Hulk, X-Men, Dr. Strange reprints begin	£2.00
2-5	£1.50
6-27,29-39,42-54	£1.25
28 1st new look issue; John Byrne's X-Men reprints, Thing team-ups and Luke Cage reprints all begin	£1.50
40 Timesmasher by Paul Neary & Mick Austin begins	£1.55
41 The Origin of the Crusader by Alan Davis	£2.50

RANGER
Fleetway; 18th Sep 1965-18th Jun 1966 (40 unnumbered issues, joins Look and Learn)

No. 1 - 18 Sep 1965 Rise and Fall of the Trigan Empire by Mike Butterworth & Don Lawrence, Rob Riley by Jesus Blasco begin	£7.50
No.1 with free gift (Space chart)	£15.00
25 Sep 1965-18 Jun 1966	£3.00

RANGER ANNUAL
Fleetway; 1968-1969

1968,1969	£8.00

RANGERS COMICS
Cartoon Art; nn 1950

nn 20pgs; Fiction House reprints	£4.00

RANGERS COMICS
Thorpe & Porter; 1 1952-?

1 28pgs; Fiction House reprints	£4.00
2-?	£3.00

RANMA ½
Boxtree; Dec 1994

Volume 1 Rumiko Takahashi manga reprints begin	£6.00
Volume 2	£6.00

R.D.H. COMIX
R.D.Harwood; Sep 1971

nn Brian Bolland art	£10.00

REAL CLUE CRIME STORIES
Streamline/United Anglo-American; 1-2 1951

1-2 36pgs; Hillman Periodicals reprints	£4.00

REAL LIFE STORIES
Cartoon Art; 1 1955?

1 Magazine Enterprises reprints	£4.00

REAL WESTERN HERO
Arnold Book Co.; 70 1949, 1 issue (continued as Western Hero)

70 32pgs; Fawcett reprints	£3.00

RED DWARF SMEGAZINE
Fleetway Editions; 1 Mar 1992-14 Apr 1993; Vol 2:1 May 1993-9 Jan 1994

1 40pgs; based on TV series, Alan Burrows art	£7.50
2	£5.00
3-5	£4.00
6-10	£3.00
11-14	£2.00
Vol 2:1 48pgs; new look	£3.50
2-8	£2.00
9 64-page special	£2.25

REDFOX
(see The Book of Redfox)
Harrier/Valkyrie; 1 Jan 1986-20 Jun 1989

1 Fox art begins	£5.00
1 second printing	£1.00
2 scarce	£4.50
3	£2.00
4	£1.50
5	£0.85
6-11,16 Fox/Harwood art	£0.75
12-13,15 Fox/O'Donnell art	£0.75
14 Meadows/O'Donnell art	£0.75
17-19	£0.60
20 partly by Gaiman & SMS (5pgs)	£1.50

RED HAWK
Cartoon Art; 1 1953

1 28pgs; Magazine Enterprises reprints	£4.00

RED MASK
(see Action Series)

REGAL COMIC
Miller; nn 1950s

nn 28pgs; Fawcett reprints from Bill Boyd, etc	£3.00

REN AND STIMPY
Marvel; 1 1994-16 1996

1 reprints US strips based on TV show	£1.00
2-16	£0.35

N.MINT

REN AND STIMPY SHOW, THE
Titan
Pick of the Litter £7.00
Tastes Like Chicken £7.00

RETURN OF THE JEDI
(see Star Wars)

REVOLVER
(see Dare)
Fleetway; 1 Jul 1990-7 Jan 1991 (joins Crisis)
1 Purple Days by Charles Shaar Murray & Floyd Hughes, Dare by Grant Morrison & Rian Hughes, Happenstance & Kismet by Paul Neary & Steve Parkhouse, Rogan Gosh by Pete Milligan & Brendan McCarthy, Dire Streets by Julie Hollings begin £2.00
2,5 £1.65
3 Fabry art £1.65
4 Al Davison, Pleece art, no Dire Streets £1.65
6 Rogan Gosh ends £1.65
7 Sean Phillips, McCarthy art £1.65
Horror Special (1990) Gaiman script, Bolton, Pleece, Simpson art £2.50
Romance Special (Mar 1991) Bolland cover, Phillips, Fabry, D'Israeli art £2.00

RINGO KID WESTERN
Miller; 1 1955-17 1956
1-17 28pgs; Atlas reprints £3.50

RIP CARSON
Cartoon Art; 1 1950
1 16pgs; Fiction House reprints £4.00

RIP CARSON
United Anglo-American; nn 1951
nn 28pgs; Fiction House reprints £4.00

ROBIN HOOD
World Distributors; 1-4 1955
1-4 28pgs; American reprints £5.00

ROBIN HOOD
(some issues titled Robin Hood Tales)
Miller; 1 1957-34 1959
1 Colin Andrew art £5.00
2-34 some issues repinted from Charlton Comics, National Comics, others British originals £2.50

ROBIN HOOD AND HIS MERRY MEN
Streamline; 1956, 2 unnumbered issues
nn 28pgs; Charlton reprints £2.50
nn 52pgs £3.00

ROBIN HOOD ANNUAL
(see also The Adventures of Robin Hood Annual)
Amalgamated Press; 1957-1960
1957 £10.00
1958-1960 £10.00

ROBOCOP MOVIE SPECIAL
Marvel; Mar 1988
nn movie adaptation £0.75

ROBO HUNTER
(see Sam Slade, Robo Hunter)
Titan (Best of 2000AD); 1982-Mar 1985
Book One 2000AD reprints by Ian Gibson begin £3.50
Book Two £4.50
Book Three £4.00
Book Four £4.00

ROBO HUNTER
Eagle; 1 Apr 1984-5 Dec 1985
1 2000AD reprints by Ian Gibson £1.25
2-5 £1.00

RO-BUSTERS
Titan (Best of 2000AD); 1983
Book One £4.50
Book Two £4.00

ROCKET
News of the World/Eric Bemrose; 1 21st Apr 1956-32 24th Nov 1956 (joins Express Weekly)
1 Captain Falcon by Frank Black, Seabed Citadel by Ley Kenyon begin, Flash Gordon, Johnny Hazard, Brick Bradford US reprints begin £25.00
2 £12.50
3 £7.50
4-10 £5.00
11-31 £3.00
32 last issue, includes pages introducing stories from Express Weekly £3.00

ROCKETSHIP X
United Anglo-American; nn 1951
nn 28pgs; Fox Features reprints £6.00

ROCKY LANE ANNUAL
Miller; 1957?-1960?
nn £6.00
nn £6.00
3-4 £5.00

ROCKY LANE WESTERN
Miller; nn 1950?; 50 Jun 1950-139 1959, 90 issues
nn 12pgs gravure; Fawcett reprints £10.00
50 monthly publication £7.50
51-139 £5.00

ROD CAMERON WESTERN
Miller; various series 1950-1960
50 (1950?) £10.00
51-57 £6.00
1 (1950) 32pgs gravure; Fawcett reprints £8.00
2-8 (1950-51?) 32pgs gravure, larger size £5.00
50-64 (Oct 1951-1953) 24pgs £3.00
1-3 (1960) 68pgs; incl. reprints from Bob Steele, Young Eagle etc. £2.50

ROGUE TROOPER
Titan (Best of 2000AD); 1984-Apr 1988
Book One Gibbons, Wilson art £4.50
Book Two Gibbons, Wilson, Kennedy art £4.50
Book Three Wilson, Ewins art £5.00
Book Four £5.00
Book Five £5.00
Book Six £5.00
Rogue Trooper's Future Wars £5.50

ROGUE TROOPER ACTION SPECIAL
Fleetway; Jul 1996
1996 Braithwaite, Tappin art, Gibbons cover £2.50

ROGUE TROOPER ANNUAL
Fleetway; 1991
1991 Dillon, Hicklenton art, features new Rogue Trooper £4.00

ROGUE TROOPER POSTER PROG
Fleetway Editions; 1 1994
1 Poster with story £1.00

ROM SUMMER SPECIAL
Marvel; 1982
1982 48pgs; US reprints; centre-fold poster is often missing £1.00

ROOKIE COP
Miller; 1 1956-?
1-? 28pgs; Charlton reprints £3.00

ROVER, THE
D.C. Thomson; 1 4th Mar 1922-1855 31st Dec 1961 (becomes Rover and Adventure)
1 very scarce; story paper with only a few comic strips £100.00
2 scarce £50.00
3 £30.00
1922 issues £20.00
1923-1930 issues £15.00
1931-1940 issues £10.00
1941-1950 issues £7.50
1951-1955 issues £5.00
1956-1959 issues £3.00
1960-1969 issues £2.00
1970-1973 issues £1.50
CHRONOLOGY:
21 Jan 1961: 1st "Rover & Adventure". 23rd Nov 1963: 1st "Rover & Wizard".

ROVER AND ADVENTURE, THE
D.C. Thomson; 1 21st Jan 1961-626 13th Jan 1973 (joins Wizard)
1 story paper £15.00
2 £6.00
3-5 £3.00
1961 issues £2.00
1962-1969 issues £1.00
1970-1973 issues £0.50

ROVER BOOK FOR BOYS, THE
D.C. Thomson; 1926-1959
(1926) (Boy in cross-country race jumping stream) £50.00
(1927) (Cowboy mounting a bucking bronco) £35.00
(1928) (Two boys in blazers driving an open-top car carrying camping gear) £30.00
(1929) (Two boys in white shirts riding camels in desert) £25.00
(1930) (Young man pulling two friends along road in a rickshaw) £25.00
(1931) (Motor boat towing skiing boys) £20.00
(1932) (Two boy hikers and dog trying to hitch a lift from a farmer) £20.00
(1933) (Man on motor cycle trying to lassoo a galloping zebra) £20.00
(1934) (Two naval men, one holding a rabbit) £20.00
(1935) (Two naval men laughing at two chinamen - one in a barber's chair has been shorn) £20.00
(1936) (Two boys in tropical gear watch a dinosaur) £17.50
(1937) (A cowboy playing football bursts the ball on his spur) £17.50
(1938) (A cowboy with his tooth tied with rope while another holding the other end rides off on horseback) £17.50
(1939) (Two lumberjacks joust whilst riding a log on a river) £17.50
(1940) (Mountie riding a moose jumps over snow-covered cliff to avoid wolves) £17.50
(1941) (Lumberjack riding a log down a chute being passed by a man on skis) £15.00
(1942) (Two men in tropical gear playing darts surprised as a spear hits the bullseye of the target) £15.00
(1950) (Blacksmith repairing robot with a screwdriver) scarce £20.00
(1956) (Globe in centre of cover with characters in stars at each corner) £12.50
(1957) (Five horizontal divisions, five pictures, top pic of a plane) £10.00
(1958) (Five horizontal divisions, four pictures, top pic of an indian firing an arrow) £10.00
(1959) (Airliner crossing over mountains, someone firing arrows at eagles below) scarce £15.00
Note: no editions published for 1943-49, 1951-55.

ROVER MIDGET COMIC, THE
D.C. Thomson; nn 11th Feb 1933
nn 32pgs giveaway with The Rover; Dudley Watkins, Allan Morley art £4.00

ROVER SUMMER FUN BOOK, THE
D.C. Thomson; nn 6th Jun 1936
nn 8pgs giveaway with The Rover; Dudley Watkins, Allan Morley art £4.00

ROY OF THE ROVERS ANNUAL
Amalgamated Press/Fleetway/IPC; 1958-1990s
1958 £20.00
1959 £15.00
1960-1965 £10.00
1966-1969 £6.00
1970-1979 £3.00
1980s/1990s £2.00

RUPERT
The Adventures of Rupert the Little Lost Bear (Nelson, 1921) £400.00
The Little Bear and the Fairy Child (Nelson, 1922) £350.00
Margot the Midget and Little Bear's Christmas (Nelson, 1922) £350.00

			N.MINT
The Little Bear and the Ogres (Nelson, 1922)			£350.00
RUPERT BOOKS			
Oldbourne Book Co.; 1960 (2 titles)			
Rupert and the Pink Letter			£20.00
Rupert and Dickory Dock			£20.00
RUPERT ACTIVITY BOOK			
Oldbourne Book Co.; 1959 (2 issues)			
1-2			£60.00
RUPERT ADVENTURE BOOK			
Beaverbrook Newspapers; 1-2 1975			
1 Rupert in Mysteryland 32pgs; reprints			£3.50
2 Rupert at Rocky Bay			£3.50
RUPERT ADVENTURE SERIES			
Express; 1 Sep 1948-50 Jun 1963			
1 Rupert & Snuffy; reprints begin			£50.00
2 reprints			£25.00
3-5 reprints			£20.00
6-25 reprints			£15.00
25-39 new material			£25.00
40-45 new material, more scarce			£45.00
46-48 new material, more scarce			£55.00
49 new marterial, scarce			£80.00
50 new material, scarce			£90.00
RUPERT AND HIS WONDERFUL BOOTS			
Sampson Low; Aug 1946			
nn boot-shaped book			£125.00
RUPERT ANNUAL			
(see Monster Rupert Annual)			
Express; 1936-1994			
1936 full title The Adventures of Rupert; red cloth boards and red spine; price 2/6d; cover shows Rupert sitting down eating; very scarce with dust-jacket	£330.00	£1000.00	£2000.00
Note: Only 15-20 known copies exist with dustjacket, all in poor to fine condition with prices at auction rising to £2,250 in very fine condition. Prices can vary widely on this book			
1936 without dust-jacket	£65.00	£200.00	£400.00
1937 full title More Adventures of Rupert; cover shows Rupert and friends on a stone-arch bridge, Rupert waving a stick	£46.00	£135.00	£275.00
1938 full title The New Rupert Book; cover shows Rupert and friends up a tree, Rupert is waving	£38.00	£110.00	£225.00
1939 full title The Adventures of Rupert; cover shows Rupert and friends chasing a monkey who is flying a kite	£33.00	£100.00	£200.00
194 1st in colour; full title Rupert's Adventure Book; price 3/-; cover shows Rupert scribbling with a pencil/crayon, looking over his shoulder	£52.50	£160.00	£325.00
1941 full title The Rupert Book; price 3/6d; cover shows Rupert in the foreground waving a paddle with Algy in the background in a boat	£46.00	£135.00	£275.00
1942 1st soft cover; full title More Adventures of Rupert; cover shows Rupert and friends sitting on the battlements of a castle waving; very scarce in the U.K.	£75.00	£225.00	£450.00
1943 full title More Rupert Adventures; Rupert holding a lantern reaching for a butterfly while his friends watch	£38.00	£110.00	£225.00
1944 full title Rupert in More Adventures; Rupert waving from the branches of a tree with his friends; Tiger Lily is in bottom left	£30.00	£90.00	£180.00
1945	£25.00	£75.00	£150.00
1946	£16.50	£50.00	£100.00
1947-1949 last softcovers	£12.50	£38.00	£75.00
1950-1953	£10.00	£30.00	£60.00
1954-1956	£9.00	£28.00	£55.00
1957-1959	£7.50	£22.50	£45.00
1960-1966 magic painting done	£4.15	£12.50	£25.00
1960-1966 magic painting not done	£12.50	£38.00	£75.00
1967-1968 magic painting done	£3.00	£9.00	£18.00
1967-1968 magic painting not done	£6.50	£20.00	£40.00
1969-1980	£0.80	£2.50	£5.00
1981-1984	£0.80	£2.40	£4.00
1985 anniversary issue	£1.00	£3.00	£5.00
1986-1990	£0.80	£2.40	£4.00
1991-1994	£0.60	£1.80	£3.00
Title Value:	**£864.15**	**£2600.10**	**£5219.00**
Facsimile 1936 (Hawk)			£25.00
Facsimile 1937-1938 (Hawk)			£20.00
Facsimile 1939-42 (Hawk)			£12.00
Facsimile 1943 (Hawk, 1995)			£18.00
RUPERT COLOUR LIBRARY			
Purnell; nn 1976			
nn			£2.00
RUPERT CUT-OUT AND STORY BOOK			
Sampson Low; 1949-1950			
Rupert and Edward and the Circus (1949)			£100.00
Rupert and the Snowman (1950)			£150.00
Rupert			£60.00
The Monster Rupert (1950) 200 cut-outs			£50.00
The Monster Rupert (1953) revised reprint of above, 120 cut-outs			£30.00
Note: Cut-outs must be intact			
RUPERT FORTNIGHTLY			
Celebrity Publications; 1 18th Oct 1989-20 20th Oct 1990			
1			£1.50
2-20			£1.00
RUPERT HOLIDAY SPECIAL			
Polystyle; 1979-1981			
1979 48pgs; Alfred Bestell reprints begin			£1.50
1980-1981			£1.00

Scorcher #2

Score 'N' Roar #1

Scream #1

N.MINT

RUPERT SUMMER SPECIAL
Marvel; May 1983
nn 52pgs; reprints £1.00

RUPERT LITTLE BEAR
Sampson Low, 1925-1927, 6 volumes
1-6 Mary Tourtel art £300.00

RUPERT LITTLE BEAR LIBRARY
Sampson Low; 1928-1937, 46 volumes
1 Rupert and the Enchanted Princess (1928) £25.00
2 Rupert and the Black Dwarf (1928) £25.00
3 Rupert and his Pet Monkey (1928) £25.00
4 Rupert and his friend Margot (1928) £25.00
5 Rupert in the Wood of Mystery (1929) £25.00
6 Further Adventures of Rupert (1929) £25.00
7 Rupert and the Three Robbers (1929) £25.00
8 Rupert, the Knight and the Lady, and Rupert and the Wise Goat's Birthday Cake £25.00
9 Rupert and the Circus Clown (1929) £25.00
10 Rupert and the Magic Hat (1929) £25.00
11 Rupert and the Little Prince (1930) £25.00
12 Rupert and King Pippin (1930) £25.00
13 Rupert and the Wilful Prince (1930) £25.00
14 Rupert's Mysterious Flight (1930) £25.00
15 Rupert In Trouble Again, and Rupert and the Fancy Dress Party (1930) £25.00
16 Rupert and the Wooden Soldiers, and Rupert's Christmas Adventure (1930) £25.00
17 Rupert and the Old Man of the Sea (1931) £25.00
18 Rupert and Algy at Hawthorne Farm (1931) £25.00
19 Rupert and the Magic Whistle (1931) £25.00
20 Rupert Gets Stolen (1931) £25.00
21 Rupert and the Wonderful Boots (1931) £25.00
22 Rupert and the Christmas Fairies and Rupert and Bill Badger's Picnic Party £25.00
23 Rupert and his Pet Monkey Again, and Beppo Back with Rupert (1932) £25.00
24 Rupert and the Robber Wolf (1932) £25.00
25 Rupert's Latest Adventure (1932) £25.00
26 Rupert and Prince Humpty Dumpty (1932) £25.00
27 Rupert's Holiday Adventure, Rupert's Message to Father Christmas, and Rupert's New Year's Eve Party (1932) £25.00
28 Rupert's Christmas Tree, and Rupert's Picnic Party (1932) £25.00
29 Rupert, the Witch and Tabitha (1933) £25.00
30 Rupert Goes Hiking (1933) £25.00
31 Rupert and Willy Wispe (1933) £25.00
32 Rupert, Margot and the Bandits, and Rupert at School (1933) £25.00
33 Rupert and the Magic Toy Man (1933) £25.00
34 Rupert and Bill Keep Shop, and Rupert's Christmas Thrills (1933) £25.00
35 Rupert Rupert and Algernon, and Rupert and the White Dove (1934) £25.00
36 Rupert and Beppo Again (1934) £25.00
37 Rupert and Dapple (1934) £25.00
38 Rupert and Bill's Aeroplane Adventure (1934) £25.00
39 Rupert and the Magician's Umbrella (1934) £25.00
40 Rupert and Bill and the Pirates (1935) £25.00
41 Rupert at the Seaside, and Rupert and Bingo (1935) £25.00
42 Rupert Gets Captured, and Rupert and the Snow Babe's Christmas Adventures (1935) £25.00
43 Rupert, The Manikin and the Black Knight (1935) £25.00
44 Rupert and the Greedy Princess (1935) £25.00
45 Rupert and Bill's Seaside Holiday, and Rupert and the Twins' Birthday Cake (1946) £25.00
46 Rupert and Edward and the Circus, and Rupert and the Snowman (1936) £25.00
Note: These 46 titles were reissued many times, priced variously at 6d, 9d, 1/- and 1/3, and are generally in the £10-20 range. 18 titles were reissued in 1970s under the same title and are usually priced £3-5.

RUPERT LITTLE BEAR'S ADVENTURES
Sampson Low, 1924-1925, 3 volumes
1-3 Mary Tourtel art £300.00

RUPERT STORY BOOK
Sampson Low; 1938-1940
The Rupert Story Book (1938) Mary Tourtel art £150.00
Rupert Little Bear - More Stories (1939) £150.00
Rupert Again (1940) £150.00

RUPERT TV PLAYBOOKS
Stanfield; 1975
Rupert Goes to the Moon 16pgs £2.00
Rupert and the Blue Mist £2.00
Rupert the Postman £2.00
Rupert and the Magician's Hat £2.00

RUPERT TV STORYBOOKS
Stanfield; 1-6 1978
1-6 28pgs; Mick Wells art £1.00

RUPERT WEEKLY
Marvel; 1 20th Oct 1982-100 15th Sep 1984
1 £3.00
2-5 £1.50
2-100 £1.00

RUPERT'S FAMOUS YELLOW LIBRARY
Sampson Low Marston; 1949
Rupert and his Friend Margo 20pgs; Mary Tourtel Daily Express reprints £45.00
Rupert the Knight and the Lady £45.00

S

SABRETOOTH
Boxtree; Mar 1995
Death Hunt (1995) reprints Marvel mini-series by Larry Hama & Mark Texeira £7.00

SAD SACK
Top Sellers; 1 1973-?
1-? 36pgs; Harvey reprints £1.50

SAGA OF THE MAN ELF, THE
Trident Comics; 1 Aug 1989-5 1990
1 Man Elf by Guy Lawley & Steve Whitaker begins; uses characters by Moorcock £1.25
2 £1.10
3-5 Richard Western art £1.10

SAINT, THE
Top Sellers; 1-5 1966
1-5 68pgs; American reprints based on Leslie Charteris character £4.00

SAINT ANNUAL
World Distributors/Stafford; 1968-1970, 1979-1980
1968-1970 Roger Moore £5.00
1979,1980 titled Return of the Saint Annual, Ian Ogilvy £2.00

SAINT ANNUAL, THE
PBS; 1973
1973 Roger Moore £3.00

SAINT DETECTIVE CASES, THE
Thorpe & Porter; 1 Oct 1951-4? 1952
1 68pgs; Avon reprints £7.50
2-4 £5.00

SAINT TELEVISION STORY BOOK, THE
PBS; 1971
1971 £3.50

SANDMAN
Titan; Jun 1990-present
Preludes and Nocturnes (Oct 1991) reprints Sandman 1-8 £10.00
The Doll's House (Jun 1990) reprints Sandman 9-16 £9.00
Dream Country (Jul 1992) reprints Sandman 17-20 £7.00
Season of Mists (Sep 1992) reprints Sandman 21-28 £9.00
A Game of You (Sep 1993) reprints Sandman 32-37 £9.00
Fables and Reflections (Jan 1994) reprints Sandman 29-31,38-40,50, Special 1 £12.50
Brief Lives (Jan 1995) reprints Sandman 41-49 £12.50
World's End (Jun 1995) reprints Sandman 51-56 £12.50
The Kindly Ones (Apr 1996) hardcover; reprints Sandman 57-69 £25.00

SAVAGE ACTION
Marvel; 1 Nov 1979-15 Jan 1982
1 Punisher, Dominic Fortune, Moon Knight reprints begin, Night Raven text stories by Maxwell Grant (Alan McKenzie) begin £1.50
2-15 £1.25

SAVAGE SWORD OF CONAN
Marvel; 1 8th Mar 1975-18 5th Jul 1975 (joins The Avengers)
1 Conan by Barry Smith, King Kull reprints begin £5.00
2 £2.50
3-18 £1.25

SAVAGE SWORD OF CONAN
Marvel; 1 Nov 1977-93 Jul 1985
1 52pgs; Conan reprints by Thomas & Buscema/Alcala begin £3.00
2-12,14-84 £1.50
13 new cover format; 1st Red Sonja reprint £2.00
85-93 "Savage Sword of Conan and Mighty World of Marvel"; Night Raven text stories by Jamie Delano £1.50
ARTISTS
Artists on Conan reprints include Neal Adams, John Buscema, Gil Kane, etc.

SAVIOUR
Trident Comics; 1 Dec 1989-5 1990
1 Saviour by Mark Millar & Daniel Vallely begins £1.50
2-5 Nigel Kitching art £1.00
Saviour 128pgs; trade paperback; collects 1-5 £4.00

SCAVENGERS
(see Spellbinders)

SCHOOLBOY'S ALBUM
Gerald Swan; Nov 1943-Sep 1956
1944 £8.00
1945-1946 £7.50
1947-1957 £6.00

SCORCHER
IPC Magazines; 10th Jan 1970-26th Jun 1971, 70? issues
No. 1 - 10th Jan 1970 Royal's Rangers by Leslie Branton, Sub by Ken Reid, Billy's Boots, Paxton's Powerhouse by Barnie Mitchell all begin £2.00
No. 1 with free gift £4.00
No. 2 - 17 Jan 1970 £1.50
No. 2 with free gift (Super Soccer Wall Chart) £3.00
24 Jan 1970-26 Jun 1971 £0.75

SCORCHER AND SCORE
IPC Magazines; 3rd Jul 1971-5th Oct 1974, 167? issues (joins Tiger)
No. 1 - 3 Jul 1971 Jack of United, Jimmy of City, Billy's Boots, Manager Matt by Ken Reid all begin £1.50
10 Jul 1971-5 Oct 1974 £0.50

SCORE 'N ROAR
IPC Magazines; 19th Sep 1970-26th Jun 1971, 41 issues
(becomes Scorcher and Score)
No. 1 - 19 Sep 1970 Jack of United, Jimmy of City, Peter the Cat all begin £1.50
No. 1 with free gift (Football League Ladders) £5.00
26 Sep 1970-26 Jun 1971 £0.50

SCREAM!
IPC Magazines; 1 24th Mar 1984-15 30th Jun 1984
1 Monster by Alan Moore and Heinz (only Moore issue), The Thirteenth Floor by Ian Holland (Wagner/Grant) and Ortiz begin £1.50
1 with free gift (plastic vampire teeth - cover often damaged by sellotape) £3.00
2-3, 5-6, 8-15 £0.40
4 Cam Kennedy art £0.75
7 Brendan McCarthy art £0.75

SECOND CITY
Harrier; 1 Nov 1986-4 May 1987

	N.MINT
1 Phil Elliot art begins	£1.00
2-4	£0.80

SECRET AGENT X9

(see Action Series)

SECRET WARS

(title varies: Secret Wars/Secret Wars Featuring Zoids/Secret Wars II)

Marvel; 1 27th Apr 1985-80 10th Jan 1987

	N.MINT
1 32pgs; Secret Wars reprints begin	£1.50
1 with free gift (Secret Wars rub-down transfers)	£3.00
2	£1.25
2 with free gift (Captain America sticker) poster centrefold	£2.50
3	£1.00
3 with free gift (Dr. Doom sticker)	£2.00
4-18	£0.75
19 24pgs; Zoids toy tie-in strip by Ian Rimmer & Kev Hopgood begins	£0.75
20-34 features Zoids	£0.75
35-80 titled Secret Wars II	£0.60

SECRET WARS

Marvel/Grandreams; 1986

	N.MINT
1986 reprints Secret Wars #1, Marvel Team-Up #7	£2.00

SECRET WARS WINTER SPECIAL

Marvel; Oct 1985

	N.MINT
nn reprints	£1.25

SECRET WARS II SPECIAL

Marvel; Mar 1986

	N.MINT
nn reprints	£1.00

SECRETS OF THE UNKNOWN

Alan Class; 1 Oct 1962-249 Mar 1989

	N.MINT
1 68pgs; reprints from Atlas, Marvel, Charlton, A.C.G. etc; very scarce	£20.00
2 scarce	£10.00
3-5	£6.00
6-10	£4.00
11-50	£2.50
51-200	£1.50
201-249	£1.25

77 SUNSET STRIP COMIC ALBUM

World Distributors; 1 cy1963?

	N.MINT
1 98pgs softcover; Dell reprints	£10.00

SEX WARRIOR

Apocalypse; nn Nov 1991

	N.MINT
nn Toxic! reprints by Will Simpson	£1.50

Note: Sex Warrior later published in US by Dark Horse

SHADOW, THE

Boxtree; 1994

	N.MINT
nn reprints Dark Horse movie adaptation, Michael Kaluta art	£7.00

SHADOWMEN, THE

Trident; 1 May 1990-2 1990

	N.MINT
1 28pgs; by Mark Millar & Andrew Hope/Ben Dilworth	£1.00
2	£0.85

SHADOW RIDERS

Marvel; 1 Jun 1993-4 Sep 1993

	N.MINT
1 Ross Dearsley art, guest stars Cable; embossed cover	£1.75
2 guest stars Ghost Rider	£1.50
3-4 guest stars Cable	£1.20

SHIVER AND SHAKE

IPC Magazines; 10th Mar 1973-5th Oct 1974, 83 issues

	N.MINT
No. 1 - 10 Mar 1973 Frankie Stein by Robert Nixon, Scream Inn by Brian Walker begin	£3.00
1 with free gift (1 of practical jokes)	£6.00
17 Mar 1973	£1.25
24 Mar 1973-5 Oct 1974	£0.50

ARTISTS/FEATURES

Leo Baxendale (Sweeney Toddler reprints), Ken Reid (Creepy Creations), Ron Turner (Malice in Wonderland)

SHOCKWAVE

London Editions; 1 (2 Mar 1991)-4 (16 May 1991)

	N.MINT
1 Animal Man (to 2), Hellblazer, Black Orchid reprints begin	£1.25
2	£1.00
3-4 Catwoman Year One reprints begin	£1.00

SIGNAL TO NOISE

Victor Gollancz; Jul 1992

	N.MINT
nn graphic novel by Neil Gaiman & Dave McKean, hardback	£15.00
nn paperback	£10.00

SILVER SURFER WINTER SPECIAL

Marvel; Nov 1982

	N.MINT
nn 52pgs; reprints	£1.25

SIN CITY

H. Bunch; 1 Nov 1973

	N.MINT
1 Dave Gibbons art	£2.50

SIN CITY

Titan Books; 1993-1995

	N.MINT
Sin City (Jan 1993) Frank Miller art/story	£8.00
A Dame to Kill For (Jan 1995) Miller art/story	£9.00
The Big Fat Kill (Dec 1995) Miller art/story; hardcover	£17.00

SKIN

Tundra Publishing UK; nn Aug 1992

	N.MINT
nn - graphic novel by Pete Milligan, Brendan McCarthy and Carol Swain	£4.00

SKIZZ

Titan; Mar 1989

	N.MINT
nn 2000AD reprints by Alan Moore & Jim Baikie	£7.00

SKIZZ II: ALIEN CULTURES

Mandarin (2000AD Books); Sep 1993

	N.MINT
nn 2000AD reprints, Baikie story & art	£6.00

SLAINE

Titan (Best of 2000AD); 1985-1987, 1990

	N.MINT
Book One	£4.50
Slaine Gaming Book	£4.50
Slaine the King Fabry art	£4.50
Slaine the King Special Edition (1990)	£6.00
The Collected Slaine (Sep 1993)	£9.00

SLAINE: DEMON KILLER

Hamlyn; Jul 1996

	N.MINT
Slaine: Demon Killer Glenn Fabry, Dermot Power reprints from 2000AD	£11.00

SLAINE THE HORNED GOD

Fleetway/Mandarin (2000AD Books); 1 Nov 1989-3 Mar 1991; Sep 1993

	N.MINT
Volume 1 (1989) Pat Mills & Simon Bisley reprints from 2000AD	£4.50
Volume 2 (1990) Slaine reprints	£4.50
Volume 3 (1991) Slaine reprints	£4.50
Slaine the Horned God (Mandarin, 1993) hardcover	£17.00
Slaine the Horned God (Mandarin, 1993) softcover	£13.00

SLEEZE BROTHERS, THE

Marvel; 1 Aug 1989-6 Jan 1990

	N.MINT
1 Sleeze Brothers by John Carnell & Andy Lanning/Stephen Baskerville begins	£0.75
2-6	£0.60
The Sleeze Brothers File (1990) incl. previously unpublished 8pg story	£8.50

SLEEZE BROTHERS SPECIAL, THE

Marvel; 1 1991

	N.MINT
1 48pgs; previously unpublished material	£1.00

SMALL KILLING, A

Victor Gollancz; Sep 1991

	N.MINT
nn (hardback) Alan Moore & Oscar Zarate	£15.00
nn (paperback)	£9.00

SMASH!

Odhams/IPC; 1 5th Feb 1966-3rd Apr 1971 (257 issues, numbered to 162)

	N.MINT
1 Bad Penny, The Nervs, The Swotts & the Blotts, Grimley Feendish - all by Leo Baxendale, Space Jinx by Brian Lewis, Queen of the Seas by Ken Reid begin	£35.00
1 with free gift (Big Bang Gun)	£60.00
2	£10.00
3-8,10-14,17-19	£3.50
9 Legend Testers by Jordi Bernet, Moon Madness by Lewis begin	£3.50
15 It's the Rubberman begins	£3.50
16 Hulk (from Hulk #2) reprints begin	£3.50
20 Batman Sunday newspaper reprints begin	£3.50
21-26,28-35	£3.50
27 Fantastic Four (from FF #1) reprints begin	£4.00
36 Avengers (from Avengers #4) reprints begin (ends #38)	£4.00
37 no Hulk	£3.00
38 British original Hulk strip (one-off), scarce	£10.00
39-75,77-136	£1.50
76 Daredevil (from DD #2) reprints begin	£1.50
137 1st "Smash! and Pow!"; Spider-Man (from Spider-Man #34) reprints begin, The Cloak by Mike Higgs begins	£1.50
138-143,145-162	£1.25
144 1st "Smash! and Pow! Incorperating Fantastic"; Thor (from Thor #140) reprints begin	£1.50
15th Mar '69 1st IPC issue, new look; Cursitor Doom by Eric Bradbury begins	£2.00
as above with free gift (Secret Codemaster card)	£4.00
22nd Mar '69-26th Apr '69,10th May 69-3rd Apr '71	£1.00
3rd May '69 Eric the Viking by Don Lawrence (reprints Karl the Viking from Lion) begin	£1.00

SMASH! ANNUAL

Odhams/Fleetway; 1967-1976

	N.MINT
1967	£6.00
1968-1970	£4.50
1971 softcover	£3.50
1972-1976	£2.00

SMASH! HOLIDAY SPECIAL

IPC; 1969-1970

	N.MINT
1969 96pgs	£4.50
1970 96pgs	£3.50

SOLO

City; 1 18th Feb 1967-31 16th Sep 1967 (joins TV Tornado)

	N.MINT
1 very scarce; Sgt. Bilko by Tom Kerr, Man From UNCLE by Paul Trevillion begin	£30.00
1 with free gift (Solar Saucer)	£60.00
2 scarce	£15.00
3-5	£10.00
6-18	£7.50
19 Mark of the Mysterons by Don Harley, Project SWORD begin	£10.00
20-31 very scarce	£7.50

FEATURES

all issues contain Walt Disney based strips (reprinted from Gold Key).

SOLTHENIS, THE

The Rogues' Gallery; 1 Sep 1987

	N.MINT
1 Richard Piers Rayner script & art	£2.00

SOMETIME STORIES

Hourglass Comics; 1 May 1977

	N.MINT
1 32pgs; McCarthy/Ewins art	£4.00

SONIC THE COMIC

Fleetway Editions; 1 29th May 1993-present (95 issues to Jan 1997)

	N.MINT
1 Sonic the Hedgehog by Alan McKenzie & Anthony Williams begins, John Howard, Mike White art	£0.75
2-57	£0.50
58 (18th Aug 1995) 1st New Look	£0.95
59-95	£0.50

SPACE ACE

Atlas; 1 Aug 1960-32 Mar 1963

	N.MINT
1 Ron Turner art	£12.00
2-13 Ron Turner art	£8.00

N.MINT

14-32 £1.50

SPACE ADVENTURES
Miller; 1-? 1950s
1 68pgs pocket size; The Unknown Element, Charlton reprint £8.00
2-? £6.00

SPACE ADVENTURES
Miller; 50 1953-?57
50-57? 28pgs; Charlton reprints £8.00

SPACE ADVENTURES PRESENTS SPACE TRIP TO THE MOON
Alan Class; 1 1961
1 68pgs; Charlton reprints (1959), Ditko art £8.00

SPACE COMICS
Arnold Book Co.; 50 Jun 1953-81 1954
50 Captain Valiant by Mick Anglo begins £10.00
51-54 monthly issues £8.00
55-81 weekly issues, from 28 Nov 1953 £6.00

SPACE COMICS OMNIBUS
Arnold Book Co.; nn 1954
nn Space Comics 55-60 rebound in new cover £10.00

SPACE COMMANDER KERRY
Miller; 50 Aug 1953-55 Jan 1954, 6 issues
50 Space Commander Kerry by Mick Anglo begins £10.00
51-55 £8.00

SPACE COMMANDO COMICS
Miller; 50 Sep 1953-59 Jun 1954, 10 issues
50 Sparky Malone by Mick Anglo begins £10.00
51-59 £8.00

SPACE FAMILY ROBINSON ANNUAL
World Distributors; 1967
1967 £12.00

SPACEMAN
Gould-Light; 1 1953-15 1954
1 28pgs; Ron Embleton, Norman Light art begins £25.00
2-15 £15.00

SPACEMAN COMICS
Cartoon Art; nn 1950
nn 28pgs; Fiction House reprints from Planet Comics £6.00

SPACE 1999 ANNUAL
World Distributors/World & Whitman; 1975-1979
1975 £6.00
1976-1978 £5.00
1979 more scarce £7.50

SPACE PATROL
Young World; 12 Jun 1964, 24 Dec 1964 (2 issues)
12,24 Space Patrol by R. Paul Hoye, based on TV series £6.00
Note: part of Super Mag series

SPACE PICTURE LIBRARY HOLIDAY SPECIAL
IPC; 1977-1981 (5 issues)
1977-1979 192pgs pocket size; Kurt Caesar Jet Ace Logan reprints £1.50
1980-1981 Ron Turner Rick Random/Jet Ace Logan reprints £1.50

SPACE PRECINCT
Manga Publishing; 1 31st Oct 1995-6 Mar 1996
1 based on Gerry Anderson TV series; John Erasmus art £1.25
2-3 Erasmus, David Hine art £1.25
4-6 £1.00

SPACE PRECINCT
Manga Publishing; Dec 1995
Vol.1: The Last Warrior (Dec 1995) 48pgs; Space Precinct reprints, Erasmus art £5.00

SPACE PRECINCT ANNUAL
Grandreams; 1995
1995 £5.00

SPACE SQUADRON
Streamline; 1-2 1951
1-2 28pgs; Atlas reprints £6.00

SPACEWAYS COMIC ANNUAL
Moring; 1953-1955
1953-1954 Denis McLoughlin reprints 52,50,54,30 £10.00
1955 titled The New Spaceways Comic Annual No.1 £8.00
Note: all have McLoughlin Swift Morgan, Roy Carson reprints

SPARKY
D.C. Thomson; 1 23rd Jan 1965-16th Jul 1977 (652 issues, joins Topper)
1 Keyhole Kate by George Drysdale, Wee Tusky by Jack Monk, Hungry Horace by George Drysdale, Sparky by Ron Spencer all begin £25.00
1 with free gift (The Flying Snorter balloon) £50.00
2 £5.00
3 £2.50
30 Jan 1965-25 Jan 1970, 8 Feb 1970-16 Jul 1977 £1.00
1 Feb 1970 I Spy by Les Barton begins £1.00

SPARKY BOOK, THE
D.C. Thomson; 1968-1980
1968 £5.00
1969-1970 £3.50
1971-1980 £2.50

SPELLBINDERS/SCAVENGERS
Quality; 1 Dec 1986-25 1989
1-6 52pgs; Slaine, Amadeus Wolf (Cursitor Doom from Smash!), Nemesis reprints begin £1.25
7-12 £1.00
13 titled Spellbinders featuring Scavengers £1.00
14-25 titled Scavengers £1.00

SPELLBOUND
Miller; 1 1961-66 1966
1 68pgs; Atlas reprints £5.00
2-5 £3.00
6-66 incl. Human Torch, Thor, Avengers, etc., Ditko art £2.50
Note: later (?) issues incl. occasional Fawcett reprints

SPELLBOUND ALBUM
Miller; nn 1964
nn scarce; 64pgs; Atlas reprints £10.00

SPELLBOUND MAGAZINE
Cartoon Art; nn 1952
nn 68pgs; Magazine Enterprises reprints, cited in UK horror campaign £6.00

SPIDER-MAN
Boxtree; Dec 1994
The Return of the Sinister Six (Dec 1994) Erik Larsen reprints £10.00
Revenge of the Sinister Six (Mar 1995) Erik Larsen reprints £9.00
Spider-Man's Greatest Villains (Feb 1996) various Marvel reprints £10.00
Chance Encounter (May 1996) Todd McFarlane reprints £9.00
Silver Sable (May 1996) Todd McFarlane reprints £9.00

SPIDER-MAN AND HULK OMNIBUS
Marvel/Grandreams; 1983
1983 128pgs; reprints Peter Parker Ann #2, Hulk 127,129,183 £3.00

SPIDER-MAN ANNUAL
World Distributors/Marvel-Grandreams/Marvel; 1974-1986, 1990-1992
1975 80pgs; reprints Amazing Spiderman #129-131 (Punisher), Tales To Astonish #57 £6.00
1976 reprints Spiderman #1, Amazing Spiderman #8, Team-Up #20 £6.00
1977 reprints Spiderman Giant Size #3-4 (Doc Savage/Punisher) £5.00
1978 reprints Amazing Spiderman Annual #5, Amazing Spiderman #11 £4.00
1979 reprints Amazing Spiderman Annual #4 £3.00
copyrigh year 1979 1st Grandreams; reprints Amazing Spiderman #165-166 £3.00
cy1980 Marvel/Grandreams; reprints Peter Parker #20-21 £3.00
cy1981 white cover; reprints Spiderman #48-49 £3.00
cy1982 blue/photo insert cover; reprints Peter Parker Ann #4 £3.00
cy1983 Death of Gwen Stacey, Green Goblin from Amazing Spiderman #121-122 £3.00
cy1984 reprints Amazing Spiderman 226-227 £3.00
cy1985 orange b/g cover; reprints Amazing Spideman #3, Team-Up #106 £3.00
cy1986 reprints Amazing Spiderman #269-270 £3.00
1990 reprints Amazing Spiderman #204-305; McFarlane art £3.00
1991 reprints Amazing Spiderman #260-261 £2.50
1992 reprints Marvel Fanfare #47 £2.50

SPIDER-MAN COMICS WEEKLY
Marvel; 1 17th Feb 1973-666 14th Dec 1985
1 Spider-Man, The Mighty Thor (origin) reprints begin £5.00
1 with free gift (Spider-Man mask) £10.00
2 £3.50
3-5 £2.50
6-49 £1.25
50 The Invincible Iron Man reprints begin £1.25
51-157 £1.00
158 1st titled "Super Spider-Man with the Super-Heroes", 1st landscape issue; X-Men reprints begin £0.75
159-161,163-198,200-204,206-228,230,255-299,301-310,312-333 £0.75
162,205 Frank Hampson centre-spread art £2.50
199 1st titled "Super Spider-Man and the Titans"; The Avengers, Captain America reprints begin £0.75
229 reverts to standard format £0.75
231 1st titled "Super Spider-Man and Captain Britain"; original Captain Britain strip, Fantastic Four reprints begin £1.00
232-247 feature original Captain Britain strips £1.00
248-253 feature reprint Captain Britain (from Marvel Team-Up #65-66) £1.25
254 Captain America reprints begin £0.75
300 Spiderman origin retold £1.25
311 1st titled "Spider-Man Comic"; Nova, Sub-Mariner reprints begin £0.75
334 1st titled "The Spectacular Spider-Man Weekly"; Daredevil reprints begin £0.75
335-375,377-449,451-499,501-528 £0.60
376 1st titled "Spider-Man and Hulk Weekly"; Hulk reprints begin £0.75
450 1st titled "Super Spider-Man TV Comic" £0.60
500 Hulk reprints return £0.60
529 Fantastic Four reprints return £0.60
530-552,554-606,611-633 £0.60
553 1st titled "Spider-Man and his Amazing Friends" £0.60
607-610 feature original Spiderman strip by Mike Collins, Jerry Paris, Barry Kitson, Mark Farmer in various combinations £1.00
634 1st titled "Spider-Man Comic" £0.50
635-651,653-666 £0.50
652 1st titled "Spidey Comic" £0.50
ARTISTS/FEATURES
Some issues contained original British material including posters by Mick Austin in 500, John Higgins in 482.

SPIDER-MAN AND ZOIDS
Marvel; 1 3rd Mar 1986-51 16th Feb 1987
1 £1.00
2-14,16-51 £0.50
15 incorporates Star Wars £1.00
ARTISTS
Artists include Kev Hopgood, Steve Parkhouse, John Ridgway, Geoff Senior, Ron Smith, Steve Yeowell. Some scripts by Grant Morrison.

SPIDER-MAN POCKET BOOK
Marvel; 1 Mar 1980-28 Jul 1982
1 52pgs small; US reprints £1.00
2-8,10-19,21-28 £0.75
9,20 100pgs; double size Xmas numbers £1.25
Note: the story from issue #28 was continued in The Daredevils (qv).

SPIDER-MAN SPECIALS
Marvel; May 1979-May 1987; 1992
Summer Special 1979 Spider-Man origin from Amazing Fantasy #15 £2.50
Winter Special 1979,1980,1981,1982,1983,1984,1985 £1.25
Summer Special 1980,1981,1982,1983,1984,1985,1986,1987 £1.25

N.MINT

Holiday Special 1992 30th Anniversary special, Marvel Comics Presents reprints £1.25

SPIDERWOMAN

Marvel/Grandreams; 1983
1983 reprints Spiderwoman #21 £2.50

STAR HEROES

Marvel; nn Oct 1979
nn 52pgs; US reprints £1.00

STAR HEROES POCKET BOOK

Marvel; 1 Mar 1980-13 May 1981; continued as X-Men Pocket Book
1 52pgs pocket size; Battlestar Galactica, Micronauts reprints begin £1.00
2-8 £0.50
9 100pgs double issue £1.00
10 X-Men origin story £1.00
11-13 X-Men reprints £0.75

STARLORD

IPC; 1 13th May 1978-7th Oct 1978 (22 mostly unnumbered issues; joins 2000AD)
1 Planet of the Damned, Timequake by Ian Kennedy, Strontium Dog by Ezquerra, Ro-Busters by Carlos Pino begin £3.00
1 with free gift (Starlord badge) £5.00
2 Mind Wars begins £2.00
2 with free gift (Space Calculator) £4.00
27 May 1978 Gibbons art £1.50
3 Jun-15 Jul 1978, 29 Jul-5 Aug 1978 £1.25
22 Jul 1978, 26 Aug 1978 no Strontium Dog £1.25
12 Aug 1978 Holocaust begins £1.25
2 Sep-7 Oct 1978 £1.25

ARTISTS/FEATURES

Carlos Ezquerra in 13 May-15 Jul 1978, 29 Jul-16 Aug 1978, 30 Sep-7 Oct 1978 (Strontium Dog). Dave Gibbons in 27 May 1978 (Ro-Busters). Ian Gibson in 9-16 Sep 1978 (Strontium Dog). Ian Kennedy in 13 May 1978, 27 May 1978 (Timequake), 10-17 Jun 1978, 5-12 Aug 1978 (Ro-Busters). Brendan McCarthy in 2 Sep 1978 (Strontium Dog).

STARLORD ANNUAL

Fleetway; 1980-1982
1980 Strontium Dog by Brendan McCarthy £3.00
1981-1982 £2.50

STARLORD SUMMER SPECIAL

IPC; Jul 1978
1978 48pgs £1.50

STAR TREK

(see Mighty Midget)

STAR TREK/ THE FINAL FRONTIER

Trident/Phoenix; 1 Mar 1992-?
1 DC reprints £1.25
2-10 £1.00
11-20 £0.80
21-? unofficial magazine £0.75

STAR TREK

Titan; Sep 1992-present
The Modala Imperative (Sep 1992) DC reprints begin £9.00
Debt of Honour (Nov 1992) Adam Hughes art £7.00
Who Killed Captain Kirk (Aug 1993) £9.00
Tests of Courage (Oct 1994) reprints The Tabukan Syndrome (ST #35-40) £10.00
Ashes of Eden (Jul 1995) co-written by William Shatner £10.00

STAR TREK ANNUAL

World Distributors; 1968-1976
1968 scarce; Gold Key reprints begin £15.00
copyright year 1968/69 1st story "Invasion of the City Builders" £8.50
cy1969/70 1st story "When Planets Collide" £6.00
1972-1975 dated on cover £5.00
1976-1977 £3.00

STAR TREK COMIC ALBUM

World Distributors; 1974
1974 scarce; reprints Gold Key comics in b/w, designed as colouring book £7.50

STAR TREK MONTHLY

Titan; 1 Mar 1995-present (10 to Dec 1995)
1 magazine format; DC/Malibu ST:NG/DS9 crossover reprints begin £2.00
2-10 £2.00

STAR TREK SPECIAL

Polystyle/IPC/Marvel; 1975-1982
Winter Special (Polystyle, 1975) £2.50
Special (IPC, 1978) £2.00
Summer Special (Marvel, 1979) £2.00
Summer Special (Marvel, 1981) £1.50
Winter Special (Marvel, 1982) £1.50

STAR TREK: THE NEXT GENERATION

Titan; Apr 1993-present
The Star Lost (Apr 1993) DC reprints £8.00
The Best of Star Trek: The Next Generation (Feb 1994) £10.00
Beginnings (Aug 1995) £9.00

STAR TREK: THE NEXT GENERATION/DEEP SPACE NINE

Titan; Aug 1995
Crossover (Aug 1995) DC/Malibu reprints £8.00

STAR TREK: DEEP SPACE NINE

Boxtree; Jul 1994-present
Deep Space Nine/Emancipation (Jul 1994) Malibu reprints £8.00
Emancipation and Beyond (Aug 1994) £8.00
Hearts and Minds (Jun 1995) £9.00
The Maquis (Apr 1996) reprints The Maquis: Soldier of Peace mini-series £9.00
Shanghaied (Apr 1996) £9.00

STAR WARS

(title varies: Star Wars Weekly/ Star Wars: The Empire Strikes Back/ Star Wars: The Empire Strikes Back Monthly/ Star Wars: The Return of the Jedi) (joins Spider-Man and Zoids)

Smash Holiday Special 1970

Space Story Omnibus

Sparky #303

	N.MINT
Marvel; 1 8th Feb 1978-171 Jul 1983; 1 22nd Jun 1983-155 31st May 1986	
1 28pgs; Star Wars movie adaptation begins	£6.00
1 with free gift (cut out Star Wars X-Wing fighter)	£12.00
2 Star Wars movie adaptation	£3.00
2 with free gift (cut out Star Wars T.I.E. fighter	£6.00
3-12 Star Wars movie adaptation	£2.00
13 reprints by Roy Thomas & Howard Chaykin begin	£1.50
14,16-44,46-50	£1.50
15 Starlord reprints by Claremont & Byrne begin	£1.50
45 Warlock reprints begin	£1.50
51 The Micronauts reprints begin	£1.50
52-72,74-88,90-117	£1.25
73 The Guardians of the Galaxy reprints begin	£1.25
89 Deathlok reprints begin	£1.25
118 (29 May 1980) becomes Star Wars: The Empire Strikes Back, movie reprints begin	£1.50
119-134 Empire Strikes Back reprints	£1.25
135 No movie reprint, Killraven reprints begin	£1.25
136-138 movie reprints	£1.25
139 (23 Oct 1980) last weekly issue	£1.25
140 (Nov 1980) becomes monthly	£1.50
141-150,152,157-158,160-170	£1.50
151 "The Pandora Effect" by Alan Moore & Adolfo Buylla	£2.50
153 "Dark Knights Deviltry" by Steve Moore & Alan Davis	£2.50
154,155,159 Alan Moore back-ups	£2.50
156 Alan Moore & Alan Davis backup	£2.50
171 (Jul 1983) last monthly issue	£1.00
1 (22 Jun 1983) becomes Star Wars: Return of the Jedi	£1.25
2-5	£1.00
6-155	£0.75

STAR WARS

Dark Horse; 1 Oct 1992-10 Jul 1993	
1 Star Wars: Dark Empire by Veitch & Kennedy, Indiana Jones reprints begin	£1.75
2-6 Dark Empire reprints	£1.50
7 Tales of the Jedi, Classic Star Wars reprints begin	£1.50
8-10	£1.50

STAR WARS

Boxtree	
Dark Empire (Jul 1994) Dark Horse reprints; Cam Kennedy art	£10.00
Tales of the Jedi (Jan 1995) Dark Horse reprints; David Roach art	£10.00
A New Hope (Apr 1995) reprints movie adaptation	£8.00
The Empire Stikes Back (Apr 1995) reprints movie adaptation	£8.00
Return of the Jedi (Apr 1995) reprints movie adaptation	£8.00
Droids (Jul 1995) Dark Horse reprints	£9.00
Dark Lords of Sith Book 1 (Jul 1995) Dark Horse reprints	£11.00
Classic Star Wars Book 1	£11.00
Classic Star Wars Book 2 (Nov 1995)	£11.00
Classic Star Wars Book 3 (Nov 1995)	£11.00
River of Chaos (Mar 1996)	£9.00

STAR WARS ANNUAL

Brown Watson; 1978	
1978 reprints Marvel film adaptaion in colour & b/w	£5.00

STAR WARS ANNUALS

Marvel/Grandreams; 1980, 1984	
Star Wars: The Empire Strikes Back (1980) reprints Marvel film adaptation	£2.50
Star Wars: Return of the Jedi (1984) reprints Marvel film adaptation	£2.50
Star Wars Special Edition reprints both of the above in one collected edition produced exclusively for BHS	£5.00

STAR WARS SPECIALS

Marvel; May 1983-Jun 1985	
Summer Special 1983 Alan Moore, Steve Moore script reprints, Alan Davis, John Stokes art reprints	£1.50
Winter Special 1983,1984	£1.25
Summer Special 1984,1985	£1.25

STEEL CLAW

Quality; 1 Dec 1986-4 Mar 1987	
1-3 Jesus Blasco reprints from Valiant with new framing sequence begin	£1.00
4 52pgs	£1.00

STINGRAY

Ravette; 1992	
Battle Stations (1992) TV Century 21 reprints by Embleton	£4.00
Stand By For Action (1992)	£4.00

STINGRAY ANNUAL

City/Fleetway; 1965-1966, 1992-1993	
1965	£15.00
1966	£10.00
1993-1994	£4.50

STINGRAY MONTHLY

(see Stingray: The Comic)

STINGRAY SUMMER SPECIAL

Polystyle; Jun 1983	
1983 48pgs, reprints, Brian Lewis, Rab Hamilton art	£2.00

STINGRAY TELEVISION STORY BOOK

PBS; 1965	
1965	£15.00

STINGRAY: THE COMIC/STINGRAY MONTHLY

Fleetway; 1 10th Oct 1992-24 18 Oct 1993; v2:1 Oct 1993-8 May 1994 (joins Thunderbirds)	
1 Stingray reprints from TV Century 21 by Ron Embleton	£1.25
2-3,5-8	£0.75
4 1st original stories	£1.00
9-24	£0.75
v2:1 monthly	£1.00
v2:2-8	£0.75

STORMWATCHER

	N.MINT
Acme Press/Eclipse; 1 Apr 1989-4 Dec 1989	
1 Stormwatcher by Alan Cowsill/'Ian Abbinnett' & Andrew Currie begins	£1.25
2-4	£1.00

STRAIGHT ARROW

Compix/Cartoon Art; 1 1952-20 195?	
1 24pgs; Magazine Enterprises reprints	£3.00
2-20	£2.50

STRAIGHT ARROW

World Distributors; 1-20? 1950s	
1-20 68pgs	£4.00

STRANGE ADVENTURES

KG Murray (Australia); 1 late 1950s-43 early 1960s	
1 very rare	£75.00
2 rare	£40.00
3-5 very scarce	£25.00
6-10 scarce	£20.00
11-43 scarce	£15.00

STRANGE ADVENTURES DOUBLE DOUBLE COMIC

Thorpe & Porter; 1 1967	
1 rebound remainder copies of DC Comics	£2.00

Note: contents vary from one copy to another; an example examined, for instance, contains Challengers of the Unknown and Doctor Strange.

STRANGE EMBRACE

Atomeka; 1 Apr 1993-4 1993	
1 David Hine art & story	£2.50
2-4	£2.00

STRANGEHAVEN

Abiogenesis Press; 1 Jun 1995-present	
1 Gary Spencer Millidge story and art; black and white	£4.00
2-6	£2.50

STRANGE WORLDS

Thorpe & Porter; 1 Oct 1951-200?	
1 68pgs; Avon reprints; scarce	£25.00
2	£12.50
3-5	£6.00
6-10	£3.00
11-100	£2.00
101-200	£1.25

STRIP

(see The Chronicles of Genghis Grimtoad, Storm)

Marvel; 1 17th Feb 1990-20 10th November 1990	
1 Marshal Law reprints by Mills & O'Neill, Genghis Grimtoad by Wagner/Grant & Gibson, Man From Cancer by Dakin & Elliott begin	£1.25
2 Storm reprints by Martin Lodewijk & Don Lawrence begin (to 7)	£1.00
3-5,7	£1.00
6 badly printed issue, lower distribution	£1.25
6 special complimentary reissue (yellow cover)	£0.75
8 Thorgal reprints by Rosinski & Van Hamme begin (ends 13)	£1.00
9 Free reissue of #6	£1.00
9 without reissue	£0.50
10-11,15	£1.00
12 last Marshal Law, McCrea art	£1.00
13 Death's Head by Furman & Senior begins (ends 15)	£1.00
14 Storm: The Labyrinth of Death begins	£1.00
16 The Punisher reprints begin	£1.00
17-20 Punisher reprints; #18. Bisley cover	£1.00

STRONTIUM DOG

Eagle; 1 Dec 1985-4 Mar 1986	
1-4 2000AD reprints by Ezquerra	£1.25

STRONTIUM DOG

Quality; ??	
1-4 2000AD reprints by Ezquerra	£1.25

STRONTIUM DOG

Titan (Best of 2000AD); 1985	
nn Ezquerra reprints	£5.00

STRONTIUM DOG SPECIAL

Quality; 1 1986 (numbering continued by Midnight Surfer Special)	
1 2000AD reprints by Ezquerra	£1.25

ST. SWITHIN'S DAY

Trident Comics; Apr 1990	
nn Trident reprints by Grant Morrison & Paul Grist, newly coloured	£3.00

STUPENDOUS SERIES

(see Fantastic Series)

SUDDENLY AT TWO O'CLOCK IN THE MORNING

Last Minute Productions; Jul 1974	
nn Bolland art, very rare (50 copies)	£35.00

SUGARVIRUS

Atomeka; 1993	
nn 48pgs; by Warren Ellis & Martin Chaplin/Garry Marshall, John Bolton cover & poster	£2.50

SUPACOMIC SUMMER GIFT BOOK

Atlas Publishing; 1 late 1950s	
1 96pgs, softcover, scarce; b/w reprints featuring Superman, Jimmy Olsen, Silent Knight and Buffalo Bill	£25.00

SUPERADVENTURE ANNUAL

Atlas/Top Sellers; 1958-1972	
1958-59 160pgs; incl. Batman, Tommy Tomorrow, Congo Bill, Wyoming Kid, Aquaman	£45.00
1959-60 160pgs; 22 DC reprints incl. Johnny Quick, Congo Bill, Aquaman, Daniel Boone, Tommy Tomorrow	£30.00
1960-61 (Space Ranger cover) 160pgs; incl.	£20.00
(1961-62)? (Flash cover) incl. Flash, Aquaman, Tommy Tomorrow, Congo Bill	£17.50
1962-63 100pgs; incl. Jimmy Olsen, Superboy, Aquaman, Flash, Tommy Tomorrow	£15.00

N.MINT

1963-64 100pgs; incl. Aquaman, Flash, Tommy Tomorrow, Jimmy Olsen £15.00
1964-65 62pgs; incl. Flash, Jimmy Olsen, Tommy Tomorrow, Aquaman £15.00
1967 78pgs; incl. Flash, Tommy Tomorrow, Green Arrow, Jimmy Olsen; recoloured £15.00
1968-1969 £10.00
1970 entitled Superadventure Bumper Book; scarce; incl. Batman, Superman, Supergirl, Superboy, Legion of Super-Heroes; colour £15.00
(1971) 1st Top Sellers £8.00
(1972) (Superman blasted by flying saucer cover) £8.00

SUPER ADVENTURE COMIC

Atlas; 1 1950?-120? 1959?
1 entitled Adventure Comics starring Superboy; very rare; b/w reprints of Superman, Superboy and Batman from 1940s/50s; new line drawn covers £125.00
2 very rare £70.00
3-4 rare £35.00
5 1st entitled Super Adventure Comic; rare £30.00
6-10 scarce £25.00
11-50 £15.00
51-120? £10.00
Note: A second series running to at least 59 issues was published in the late 1960s-early 1970s with the cover emblem Planet Comics. These mostly featured Justice League and Green Lantern reprints in b/w

SUPERBOY

K.G. Murray (Australia); 1 early 1950s-137? early 1960s
1 very rare, National Periodical Publications reprints in b/w; some new line-drawn covers £125.00
2 very rare £75.00
3-5 rare £35.00
6-10 very scarce £25.00
11-50 £15.00
51-100 £12.50
101-137? £10.00

SUPERBOY ANNUAL

Atlas; 1953-1967?
1953-54 192pgs; 17 reprints £50.00
1954/55 £30.00
1955-56, 1956/57 £25.00
1957/58 titled Superboy Adventure Book; 17 stories, plus Rex the Wonder Dog reprints £25.00
1958-59 18 reprints, plus Rex reprints £20.00
1959-60 18 reprints, incl. Adventure #247, plus Rex £20.00
1960-61 16 reprints, plus Rex, Detective Chimp £17.50
1961-62 19 reprints, plus Rex, Detective Chimp £15.00
1962-63 120gs; 12 reprints, incl. Adventure #267, plus Rex £15.00
1963/64-1964/65 £15.00
1965-66 96pgs; 8 reprints, plus Rex £10.00
1967 11 stories, plus Detective Chimp £10.00

SUPERBOY DOUBLE DOUBLE COMICS

Thorpe & Porter; 1-2 1967
1 bound together remainders of selected DC Comics £5.00
2 £5.00
Note: contents varied from one copy to the next; an example of #1 above, for example, includes Superboy #132,#135 and Green Lantern #53.

SUPERCAR ANNUAL

Collins; 1961-1963
1961 entitled Mike Mercury in Supercar £35.00
1962-1963 £25.00

SUPERCAR (A LITTLE GOLDEN BOOK)

Golden Press; 1962
1962 scarce, by G. Sherman £15.00

SUPER D.C.

Top Sellers; 1 Jun 1969-14 Jul 1970
1 40pgs; Superman, Batman, Superboy, Jimmy Olsen, Lois Lane reprints; styled very much like TV Tornado £15.00
1 with free gift (Batman poster, wristwatch calendar, Superman Magic Disc) £30.00
2 scarce £7.00
3-5 £4.00
6-14 £3.00

SUPER D.C. BUMPER BOOK

Top Sellers; 1970
1970 1960s DC reprints, Superman, Batman, plus 3 new text stories £10.00

SUPER DETECTIVE LIBRARY

Amalgamated; 1 Mar 1953-188 Dec 1960
1 Meet the Saint (reprints American newspaper strip) £50.00
2 £30.00
3-5 £22.50
6-50 £15.00
51-100 £10.00
101-150 £7.50
151-188 £5.00

ARTISTS/FEATURES
Rick Random by Bill Lacey in 37,48,75, by Ron Turner in 44, 49, 64, 66, 70, 79, 83, 90, 97, 101, 111, 115, 123, 127, 129, 133, 137, 143, 153, 163, by others in 53, 91, 105, 139. Rip Kirby by Alex Raymond American newspaper reprints in 120, 122, 124, 126, 128, 130, 132, 134, 136, 138, 140, 142, 144, 146, 148, 150, 152 ,154. Buck Ryan by Jack Monk British newspaper reprints in 156, 158, 159, 162, 164, 166, 168, 170, 174, 176, 178, 180, 182, 184, 186. The Saint by John Spranger American newspaper reprints in 1, 5, 11, 33, 59, UK originals in 15,28,38. Alberto Breccia in 172. Ron Embleton in 58,72. Ron Turner in 55, 109, 169, 177, 183, 188, see also Rick Random above.

SUPER FUNNIES

T.V. Boardman; 29 1940-33 1941, 5 issues
29 36pgs; Quality reprints from Feature Comics £6.00
30-33 20pgs £4.00

SUPER HERO FUN AND GAMES

Marvel; 1 Mar 1979-18 Aug 1980
1-18 puzzles and games featuring Marvel characters £0.75
Note: worth less if any puzzles or games begun or defaced

N.MINT

SUPER HERO FUN AND GAMES WINTER SPECIAL

Marvel; Winter 1979
Winter 1979 £0.75

SUPER-HEROES, THE

Marvel; 1 8th Mar 1975-50 14th Feb 1976 (joins Spider-Man)
1 Silver Surfer, X-Men reprints begin, both from #1 £2.00
1 with free gift (Silver Surfer poster) £3.50
2 Silver Surfer, X-Men origin reprints £1.50
3-22,24-30 Silver Surfer reprints £1.25
23 Doc Savage reprints begin £1.25
31 The Cats reprints begin £1.00
32-40,42-44,46-48,50 £1.00
41 The Scarecrow reprints begin £1.00
45 The Thing reprints begin £1.00
49 Black Knight reprints begin £1.00

SUPERHEROES ANNUAL (MARVEL PRESENTS THE...)

(see also Marvel Superheroes Annual)
Brown Watson; 1978
1978 reprints Thor #231, ASM #155, Silver Surfer £5.00

SUPERHEROES ANNUAL, THE

London Editions; 1982-1984
1982 reprints Detective #327, JLA #70, Superman, Batman; Bolland pin-up £5.00
1983 reprints JLA #138, Atom, Batman; new Wonder Woman text story by Kelvin Gosnell; Talbot end-papers £4.00
1984 reprints JLA #202, Superman, Atom, Batman; Moore/Talbot text story; Talbot end-papers £4.00

SUPER HEROES MONTHLY

Egmont/London Editions; v1:1 Sep 1980-v2:7 Apr 1982 (19 issues)
Vol 1:1 52pgs; Superman, Batman, Wonder Woman reprints £5.00
Vol 1:2 Superman origin from Action Comics #1, Leach cover £3.00
Vol 1:3 reprints Batman #251 Joker by Neal Adams £3.00
Vol 1:4 reprints Detective #400 Man-Bat by Adams £2.50
Vol 1:5-6 Adams Batman reprints £2.00
Vol 1:7 Superman II movie, Superman #76 (Batman/Superman) £2.00
Vol 1:8 Flash origin from Showcase 4, Adams Batman reprint £5.00
Vol 1:9 Marshal Rogers Batman reprint £2.00
Vol 1:10 Captain Cold and The Huntress origins £2.00
Vol 1:11 Silver age Hawkman origin from Brave & Bold #34, Talbot cover £4.00
Vol 1:12 Adams Batman, Kubert Hawkman £2.00
Vol 2:1 Flash from Showcase #13 £3.00
Vol 2:2 Solomon Grundy origin, Swamp Thing £2.00
Vol 2:3 Frank Miller Batman reprint, Talbot cover £2.50
Vol 2:4 Kubert Hawkman from Brave & Bold #35, Talbot cover £2.50
Vol 2:5-7 incl. Kubert Hawkman £2.00

SUPER HORSE

(see Blue Bolt series)

SUPERMAN

K.G. Murray (Australia); 1 1946-137? 1962?
1 very rare; b/w reprints from Superman and Action Comics plus Green Arrow and Johnny Quick alternating £150.00
2 very rare £80.00
3-5 very scarce £35.00
6-10 scarce £25.00
11-50 £15.00
51-100 £12.50
101-137? £10.00

SUPERMAN

Titan; Dec 1992-present
The Death of Superman (Dec 1992) 168pgs; reprints Doomsday storyline £3.50
World Without Superman (1993) reprints Funeral For A Friend £5.00
The Return of Superman (Nov 1993) 480pgs; reprints Reign of the Supermen £9.00
Time and Time Again (Sep 1994) reprints various issues from 1991 £5.00
The Man of Steel (Feb 1995) reprints John Byrne Superman 1-6 £6.00
Kal (Feb 1995) Elseworlds graphic novel by Dave Gibbons & Jose Luis Garcia-Lopez £4.00
Eradication (Jan 1996) reprints various issues from 1989 £9.00
Superman/Batman: Alternate Histories (May 1996) reprints various Annuals £10.00
Superman Aliens (Aug 1996) DC/Dark Horse mini-series reprints by Dan Jurgens & Kevin Nowlan £10.00
Krisis of the Krimson Kryptonite (Oct 1996) reprints various issues from 1990 £9.00

SUPERMAN

Health Education Council; 1 Feb 1981-2 Oct 1982
1 (AS26) 8pgs; anti-smoking promo £0.60
2 (AS30) 8pgs; anti-smoking promo £0.50

SUPERMAN/THE ADVENTURES OF SUPERMAN

London Editions/Fleetway Editions; 1 16th Jun 1988-57 Mar 1993; 1 Apr 1993-15 Jan 1994 (joins Batman)
1 US reprints begin; fortnightly publication £1.00
2-19 £0.60
20-34 monthly publication £0.80
35-57 bi-monthly publication £0.85
1-15 New series; fortnightly, later monthly £1.00

SUPERMAN AND BATMAN ANNUAL

Brown Watson; 1974-1978
1974 1960s/70s DC reprints; colour £5.00
1975-1976 1970s DC reprints; colour £4.00
1977-1978 1970s DC reprints; part colour; Bolton illus £5.00

SUPERMAN AND SPIDER-MAN

Marvel; 1982
nn 68pgs; US reprints £1.50

SUPERMAN ANNUAL/SUPERMAN OFFICIAL ANNUAL

Atlas/Top Sellers/Fleetway; Oct 1951-present
1951 entitled Superman Bumper Edition; 192pgs; very rare; reprints US strips in b/w incl. origin and strips from 1947-48 Superman, Action, World's Finest; cover from Superman #53 £125.00
Note: Printed in Australia and published by K.G. Murray for distribution by Atlas; collects

	N.MINT
first six Australian issues (Jul-Dec 1950).	
1952 1st entitled Superman Annual; 16 stories from 1947-50 Superman, Action; cover from Action Comics #137	£60.00
1953-54 1st to use split year on title page; 16 stories from 1947-49 Superman, Action, World's Finest	£40.00
1954-55 14 Superman stories, 2 Batman stories	£30.00
1955-56 1st Superman Adventure Book; 1st cardboard spine; incl. 4 Captain Comet stories by Murphy Anderson	£25.00
1956-57 17 stories, 14 featuring Superman's Pal Jimmy Olsen by Curt Swan	£20.00
1957-58 160pgs; 5/6 price	£20.00
1958-59 160pgs; 6/- price; reverts to Annual; incl. Vigilante by Dan Barry	£20.00
1959-60 to 1960-1 incl. Green Arrow	£20.00
1961-62 incl. Jimmy Olsen, Lois Lane, Green Arrow, art by Jack Kirby	£15.00
1962-63 1st partly in full colour; smaller size; 7/6 price	£13.50
1963-64 3 stories in colour	£12.50
1964-65 reverts to larger size	£12.00
1965-66 (1966)	£10.00
1967 96pgs; 7 stories, 4 in colour	£9.00
1968 96pgs; 10 stories, 4 in colour	£9.00
1969 Top Sellers; (red cover) incl. Superman, Superman/Batman	£8.00
1970 Top Sellers; (yellow cover) incl. Superman, Superman/Batman	£8.00
1971 Top Sellers; titled Superman Giant Bumper Book; 1960s reprints plus 3 text stories including 1 Batman	£6.00
1972 1st Brown and Watson; reprints plus text stories	£6.00
1973/74-1978 BECAME SUPERMAN AND BATMAN ANNUAL (see title entry above)	
1979 Superman Official Annual; Egmont; 64pgs; 1960s/70s DC reprints; colour	£4.00
1980 64pgs; 1970s DC reprints; colour	£3.00
1981 London Editions; 64pgs; 1970s DC reprints; Kev O'Neill cover; colour	£3.00
1982 64pgs; DC reprints; colour; Steve Dillon end-papers	£3.00
1983 reprints DC Presents #27-29; Bolland cover, Gibbons end-papers	£4.00
1984 reprints DC Presents, Jim Starlin art; Talbot cover	£3.50
1985 1970s/80s DC reprints; Alan Moore & Delano text stories	£3.50
1986 1970/80s DC reprints; G. Morrison & P. Milligan text stories	£3.00
1987-present	£3.00

SUPERMAN POCKETBOOK

Egmont/Methuen; 1 Apr 1978-3?	
1 100pgs; DC reprints	£2.00
2-3	£1.00
Note: almost certinly more exist	

SUPERMAN SPECTACULAR

London Editions; nn Mar 1982	
nn 52pgs; Superman reprints incl. Superman Red/Superman Blue	£1.50

SUPERMAN STORY BOOK ANNUAL

World Distributors; 1967-1969	
1967 14 text stories	£12.00
1968 13 text stories	£10.00
1969 11 text stories	£8.00

SUPERMAN'S SUPACOMIC

(see All Favourites, Five-Score Comic Monthly, Century Comics, Hundred Comic Monthly)

K.G. Murray (Australia); 1 1958-56? mid-1960s	
1 rare; 100pgs squarebound; b/w National reprints incl. Superman, Superboy, Jimmy Olsen, Lois Lane, Batman	£100.00
2 rare	£60.00
3-5 very scarce	£45.00
6-10 scarce	£40.00
11-56?	£35.00

Note: later issues incl. Supergirl, Legion of Super-Heroes, etc. More editions are thought to exist.

SUPER MOUSE

Alan Class; 1 1950s	
1 68pgs; Charlton reprints	£5.00

SUPERNATURALS

Fleetway; 1 31st October 1987-?	
No. 1 - 31 Oct 1987	£0.60
No. 1 with free gift (Double Skull Mask)	£1.00

SUPER PICTURE SPECIAL

IPC; Jul 1969	
nn 448pgs; picture library reprints incl. Turner Rick Random	£6.00

SUPER SOLDIERS

(see main American section)

SUPER SUMMER HOLIDAY ANNUAL

Atlas Publishing; early 1960s	
nn very scarce; 64pgs; b/w reprints incl. Batman, Viking Prince, Superman and Lois Lane, Davy Crockett	£40.00

SUPER THRILL ALBUM

G.T. Ltd; 1959?	
nn card cover; McLoughlin cover	£10.00

SUPERTHRILLER/SUPER THRILLER COMIC

(previously The Thriller)

Foldes/ World Distributors; 5 1948-33 195? (becomes Western Super Thriller)	
5 12pgs; Rex Hart art	£7.50
nn (6) 20pgs; C. Purvis art	£5.00
7-33 incl. James Bleach, Terrence Patrick, John Compare art	£3.00

SUPERTHRILLER ANNUAL

World Distributors; Aug 1957	
1957	£4.00

SUSPENSE STORIES

Alan Class; 1 May 1963-241 Mar 1989	
1 68pgs; Atlas reprints; very rare	£25.00
2 very rare	£15.00
3-5 rare	£10.00
6-20 scarce	£5.00
21-50	£2.50
51-200	£1.50
201-241	£1.25

SWEETMEATS

Atomeka; Mar 1993	
nn by Steve Tanner & Pete Venters; John Bolton cover & poster	£2.50

SWIFT

Hulton/Longacre; v1:1 20th Mar 1954-v10:9 2nd Mar 1963 (462 issues; joins Eagle)	
Vol 1:1 Tarna the Jungle Boy by Harry Bishop, Nicky Nobody, Tom Tex, Paul English by Georgio Bellavitis	£20.00
2	£10.00
3-5	£5.00
6-29,31-41	£2.50
30 Swiss Family Robinson	£2.50
Vol 2:1-30,32,34-53	£2.00
31 King Arthur and his Knights by Frank Bellamy begins	£2.00
33 Cliff McCoy by James Holdaway begins	£2.00
Vol 3:1-12,14-18,20-52	£2.00
13 Red Rider by James Holdaway begins	£2.00
19 Robin Hood by Frank Bellamy	£2.00
Vol 4:1-33	£2.00
34-50,52	£1.50
51 Dixon of Dock Green begins	£1.50
Vol 5:1-52	£1.25
Vol 6:1-34	£1.25
35 1st "Swift and Zip"; Wells Fargo by Don Lawrence begins	£1.25
36-45	£1.25
Vol 7:1-53	£1.25
Vol 8:1-40 Pony Express by Don Lawrence	£1.25
41-52	£1.00
Vol 9:1-52	£1.00
Vol 10:1-9	£1.00

ARTISTS/FEATURES

Frank Hampson (covers) v8:29, v9:2.

SWIFT ANNUAL

Hulton/Longacre; 1955-1963	
1955 blue cover	£12.50
1956	£7.50
1957-1959	£5.00
1960-1963 Don Lawrence art	£3.00

SWIFTSURE

Harrier; 1 May 1985-16 Sep 1987	
1 Lieut. Fl'ff, Dandy in the Underworld, Ram Assassin, Rock Solid, Codename Andromeda all begin	£1.50
2-3,6	£1.00
4-5 Fl'ff by Mike Collins	£1.00
7 combines with Conqueror	£1.00
8,11-13 Fl'ff by Steve Yeowell	£1.00
9 Redfox origin story by Fox	£1.75
10,14-16	£1.00

T

T-MAN FIGHTER OF CRIME

Archer Press (King Comic Series); 1-6 1953	
1-6 68pgs; Quality reprints	£6.00

TALE OF ONE BAD RAT, THE

Titan; Jan 1996	
nn by Bryan Talbot	£10.00

TALES FROM THE CRYPT

Arnold Book Co.; 1-2 1954	
1-2 68pgs; E.C. reprints, cited in UK horror campaign	£15.00

TALES FROM THE FRIDGE

H. Bunch (Cozmic); nn Mar 1974	
nn 36pgs; Kitchen Sink reprints	£2.00

TALES FROM THE TRIGAN EMPIRE

(see also Look and Learn Book of The Trigan Empire, The Trigan Empire)

Hawk Books; 1989	
nn hardcover; Trigan Empire by Don Lawrence reprints	£18.00

TALES OF ACTION

Alan Class; 1-2 1960s	
1 68pgs; reprints Sgt. Fury #1	£6.00
2	£2.00

TALES OF DREAD ALBUM

G.T. Ltd.; nn Jan 1959	
nn - card cover	£6.00

TALES OF TERROR

Portman; 1 Sep 1978-?	
1 68pgs; Marvel reprints	£1.50
2-?	£0.75

TALES OF THE MYSTERIOUS TRAVELLOR

G.T. Ltd.; 1959?	
nn 96pgs, card cover; Ditko, Colan etc, Charlton reprints	£6.00

TALES OF THE SUPERNATURAL

Alan Class; 1 1960s	
1 68pgs; US reprints	£5.00

TALES OF THE UNDERWORLD

Alan Class; 1-5 1960	
1 68pgs; Charlton reprints	£5.00
2-5	£3.50

TANK GIRL

Penguin; 1990, 1995-1996	
Tank Girl (Aug 1990) Martin & Hewlett reprints from Deadline	£6.00
Tank Girl (Jan 1995) new colour edition of above	£9.00

	N.MINT
Tank Girl 2 (Apr 1995) Deadline reprints in colour	£9.00
Tank Girl: The Movie (May 1995) Graphic novelisation by Pete Milligan & Andy Pritchett, Bolton cover	£6.00
Tank Girl 3 (Dec 1996) Deadline reprints in colour	£10.00
TANK GIRL	
Manga Publishing; 1 Jul 1995-8 Feb 1995	
1 68pgs; Tank Girl: The Odyssey reprints, Fireball, Booga by Philip Bond	£2.20
2-8	£2.00
TAPPING THE VEIN	
Titan; 1 Sep 1990-2 Oct 1990	
1 reprints Eclipse prestige format adaptations of Clive Barker stories, Scott Hampton, P. Craig Russell art, John Bolton cover	£4.50
2 Klaus Janson, John Bolton art, Scott Hampton cover	£4.50
TARGET	
Target Publications; 1 15th Jun 1935-176 22nd Oct 1938 (joins Target and Rocket)	
1 8pgs on green paper; Bert Hill, Harry Banger art	£35.00
2 8pgs	£10.00
3-5 8pgs	£7.50
6-112,131-176 8pgs	£5.00
113-130 12pgs	£5.00
TARZAN ADVENTURES	
Westworld; Tarzan: The Grand Adventure Comic v1:1 15th Sep 1951-v2:36 3rd Apr 1953 (59 issues); Tarzan Adventures v3:1 8th Apr 1953-v9:32 26th Dec 1959 (342 issues)	
Vol 1:1 Tarzan reprints begins (by Foster, Hogarth, etc.)	£15.00
2-23? published fortnightly	£7.50
Vol 2:1-36 (1 Aug 1952-3 Apr 1953) published weekly	£4.00
Vol 3:1-52 becomes Tarzan Adventures	£3.00
Vol 4:1-52 incl. James Bleach, Wally Robertson art	£3.00
Vol 5:1-50	£3.00
Vol 6:1-52	£3.00
Vol 7:1-52 1st edited by Michael Moorcock, incl. James Cawthorn art	£3.00
Vol 8:1-52 incl. Luis Bermejo, Lopez Espi art	£3.00
Vol 9:1-32 incl. Kimo Budesca art	£2.50
Note: began as a British edition of a French magazine which reprinted Tarzan from the American newspaper strip. Later issues had numerous filler text stories including tales by Moorcock which will command a higher price than other issues.	
TARZAN ANNUAL	
World Distributors/Brown Watson; 1965-1969, 1977	
1965 Gold Key reprints	£3.00
1966-1969 Gold Key reprints	£2.50
1977 reprints with new text	£2.50
TARZAN COMIC	
Donald F. Peters; v1:1 1950-v2:15 Oct 1951	
Vol 1:1-4 68pgs; reprints Tarzan newspaper strip	£5.00
Vol 2:1-15 36pgs	£4.00
TARZAN OF THE APES	
Top Sellers; 1 1970-? 1971; 1 1971-100 1975	
1 36pgs; monthly; Western Publishing reprints begin	£1.50
2-?	£0.75
1 36pgs; fortnightly	£1.50
2-100	£0.75
TARZAN OF THE APES	
Top Sellers; 1972	
nn 260pgs pocket size; Dell/Gold Key reprints	£1.00
TARZAN SPECIAL	
Byblos; May 1978-Nov 1981	
Summer Special 1978 68pgs; US reprints	£1.00
Summer Special 1979-1981 52pgs	£0.75
Autumn Special 1979-1980	£0.75
Winter Special 1979-1981	£0.75
Spring Special 1980	£0.75
TARZAN OF THE APES SPECIAL SUPER ADVENTURE	
Williams; 1-2 1972	
1-2 52pgs; Dell reprints	£1.00
TARZAN: THE GRAND ADVENTURE COMIC	
(see Tarzan Adventures)	
TARZAN WEEKLY	
Byblos; 1 11th Jun 1977-?	
1 (11 Jun 1977) Tarzan reprints, also incl. Ramon Sola/Ian Gibson art	£1.50
1 with free gift (Super Survival Kit Bag)	£3.00
2 (18 Jun 1977) with centre-fold poster (sometimes missing)	£0.75
25 Jun 1977-?	£0.50
TARZAN WORLD ADVENTURE LIBRARY	
World Distributors; 1 May 1967-4 Aug 1967	
1 68pgs pocket size; Men of the Deep, Western Publishing reprints	£3.00
2-4	£2.00
TELEVISION FAVOURITES COMIC	
World Distributors; 1 Jan 1958-18 1959	
1 28pgs; Dell reprints	£10.00
2-17	£4.00
18 68pgs	£5.00
TELL ME WHY	
Fleetway; 1 31st Aug 1968-82 21st Nov 1970 (joins World of Wonder)	
1 24pgs, junior Look & Learn	£2.00
2-82	£0.60
TELL ME WHY ANNUAL	
Fleetway; 1970-1973	
1970-1973	£2.00
TERMINATOR, THE	
Trident/ Dark Horse; 1 Oct 1991-17 Feb 1993	
1 Dark Horse reprints begin	£1.50
2-12	£1.00

Strange Adventures #43

Superboy Annual 1963–64

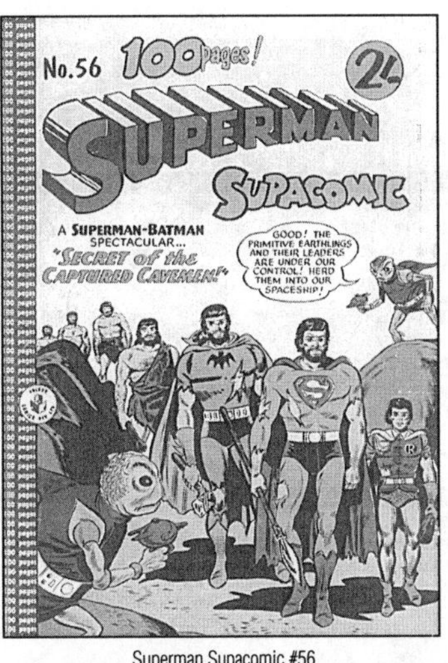

Superman Supacomic #56

N.MINT

13 1st Dark Horse issue £1.50
14 52pgs; RoboCop vs Terminator reprints begin £1.50
15-17 RoboCop vs Terminator £1.50

TERMINATOR
Titan; 1991?
Terminator: Tempest Now Comics reprints £7.50

TERRAHAWKS ANNUAL
World; 1983-1984
1983,1984 based on Gerry Anderson series £3.00

TERRIFIC
Odhams; 1 15th Apr 1967-43 3rd Feb 1968
1 Sub-Mariner (from Tales to Astonish #70), Avengers (from Avengers #6), Dr. Strange (from Strange Tales #115) reprints begin £5.00
1 with free gift (iron-on Iron Man transfer) £10.00
2 £2.50
2 with free gift (Iron Man missile launcher) £5.00
3 Living Dolls begins £1.25
4-22,24-43 £1.00
23 Giant Man (from Tales to Astonish #49) reprints begin £1.00

TERRIFIC ANNUAL
Odhams; 1969
1969 £3.00

TEX RITTER WESTERN
Miller; 50 1951-99 1959, 49 issues
50 36pgs; Fawcett reprints £10.00
51-99 28pgs £5.00

TEXAS KID COMICS
Thorpe & Porter; 1-2 1952
1-2 68pgs; Atlas reprints £4.00

TEXAS RANGERS IN ACTION
Miller; 1-16 1959
1-16 28pgs; Charlton reprints £3.00

THING IS BIG BEN, THE
Marvel; 1 28th Mar 84-18 19th Jul 84 (joins Spider-Man)
1 The Thing, Iron Man, Captain America reprints begin £1.00
2-13,15-18 £0.25
14 John Higgins cover £0.25

THING IS BIG BEN SUMMER SPECIAL, THE
Marvel; 1984
1984 52pgs; reprints The Thing, X-Men £1.25

THIRD WORLD WAR
Fleetway-Quality; 1 Sep 1990-6 1991
1 32pgs; Crisis reprints by Mills & Ezquerra begin £1.50
2-6 £1.25

THRILLER COMICS/THRILLER PICTURE LIBRARY
Amalgamated/Fleetway; 1 Nov 1951-450 May 1963
1 The Three Musketeers by W. Bryce-Hamilton £300.00
Note: The first issue is very rare but prices vary greatly, with sales in 1995 including vg copies at both £200 and £80.
1 facsimile £5.00
2 Dick Turpin, Derek Eyles, Stephen Chapman, Colin Merritt art £125.00
3 Treasure Island by Michael Hubbard £75.00
4-5 £50.00
6-10 £25.00
11-30 £20.00
Note: The first 30 or so issues are at least very scarce and virtually all copies from the series suffer from rusty staples. Copies that are completely flat and free from rust may fetch up to 25% more
31-50 £15.00
51-100 £10.00
101-162,164-200 £7.50
163 becomes Thriller Picture Library £7.50
201-300 £5.00
301-450 £4.00
ARTISTS
Alberto Breccia in 348, 376. Jesus Blasco in 143, 262, 291, 299. H.M. Brock in 22, 25, 47, 81, 102, 109, 189. C.L. Doughty in 37, 44, 85, 92, 94, 101, 121, 137, 141, 153, 177, 178, 185, 192, 199, 214, 223. Derek Eyles in 2, 4, 110, 139, 159, 175. Hugh McNeill in 117, 239, 247. J. Miller-Watt in 145, 183. Eric Parker in 14, 18, 38, 43, 67, 79, 89, 180, 188, 208, 335. Alberto Salinas in 445. Sep E. Scott in 13, 28, 31, 41, 53, 73, 116, 118, 134, 156. Ron Turner in 418, 442.

THUNDER
IPC; 17th Oct 1970-13th Mar 1971 (22 unnumbered issues; joins Lion)
No. 1 - 17 Oct 1970 Fury's Family by Denis McLoughlin, Adam Eterno by Tom Kerr begin £5.00
1 with free gift (Jumping Kangaroo) £10.00
No. 2 - 24 Oct 1970 £2.50
2 with free gift (Black Max Bat) £5.00
No. 3 - 31 Oct 1970 £2.00
3 with free gift (15 Little Peelers stickers) £4.00
7 Nov1970-13 Mar 1971 £1.50

THUNDER ANNUAL
IPC; 1972-1974
1972 £2.50
1973 Denis McLoughlin art £3.00
1974 £2.50

THUNDERBIRDS
Ravette; Feb 1992-1992
Thunderbirds to the Rescue 48pgs; Bellamy TV21 reprints £4.00
Thunderbirds in Space Bellamy reprints £4.00
Danger Zone Bellamy reprints £4.00
Lift Off Bellamy reprints £4.00
In Action Bellamy reprints £4.00
Shockwave Bellamy reprints £4.00

N.MINT

THUNDERBIRDS ANNUAL
(see also The Official Thunderbirds Annual, below)
City/Century 21/Purnell; 1966-1968, 1971-1972
1966 £25.00
1967 £15.00
1968 £12.50
1971 £6.00
1972 (Purnell) more scarce, Ron Turner art £8.50
Note: for 1969 see Captain Scarlet and Thunderbirds Annual

THUNDERBIRDS ANNUAL, THE OFFICIAL
Grandreams; 1992-present?
1992 £4.50
1993 £4.75

THUNDERBIRDS ARE GO
(Alan Fennell); 1 13th May 1995-13 Dec 1995)
1 TV 21, Lady Penelope reprints £1.00
2-13 £0.75

THUNDERBIRDS EXTRA
City; Mar 1966
1966 Ron Turner, Brian Lewis art £30.00

THUNDERBIRDS HOLIDAY SPECIAL
Fleetway Editions; Apr 1992-Apr 1993
1992 48pgs; Frank Bellamy, Don Harley reprints £1.50
1993 48pgs; Frank Bellamy, Don Lawrence reprints £1.35

THUNDERBIRDS SPECIAL
Polystyle; 1971, 1982-1984
1971 titled Gerry Anderson's Thunderbirds; reprints TV21 Spring Extra: Thunderbirds £6.00
1982 reprints from Annuals, Ron Turner art £1.50
1983 repints from Countdown Don Harley, Frank Langford art £1.50
1984 reprints £1.25

THUNDERBIRDS TELEVISION STORYBOOK
PBS; 1966
1966 £15.00

THUNDERBIRDS THE COMIC/THE NEW THUNDERBIRDS COMIC
Fleetway; 1 19th Oct 1991-91 Apr 1995
1 Frank Bellamy Thunderbirds reprints from TV21 begin £2.00
2-8 £1.50
9 Lady Penelope reprints by Eric Eden begin £1.00
10-14 £0.75
15-34 £0.70
35 Fireball XL5 reprints by Graham Coton begin £0.75
36-47,49-56,59-66 £0.75
48 John Cooper Thunderbirds reprints from TV21 & Joe 90 begin £0.75
57-58 Frank Hampson Lady Penelope reprints from TV21 £0.85
67 1st retitled "The New Thunderbirds featuring Captain Scarlet and Stingray" £0.85
68-79 £1.00
80 Joe 90, Agent 21 both begin £1.15
81-91 £1.15
Thunderbirds Poster Magazine 1-9 (Feb 1992-1993) 1,3,5 incl. 7pg strip £0.95
Thunderbirds The Collection (Mar 1992) collects 1-3 £2.00

THUNDERBIRDS 2086
Grandreams; 1983
1983 based on Japanese TV series £3.00

THUNDERCATS
Marvel; 1 16th Mar 1989-129 12th Jan 1991
1 Thundercats begins, based on TV cartoon series £0.50
2-129 £0.25

THE THUNDERING TRAIL
(see Fawcett Movie Comic)
Miller; nn 1950s
nn one-shot £10.00

TIGER
Amalgamated/Fleetway/IPC; 1 11th Sep 1954-30th Mar 1985 (1555 issues, numbered to 245; joins Eagle)
1 Roy of the Rovers by "Stewart Colwyn" (Frank Pepper) & Joe Colquhoun begins £60.00
2 £30.00
3-5 £15.00
6-10 £12.50
11-50 £7.50
51-77,85-100 £4.00
78-84 jointly numbered issue dated 3 Mar-14 Apr 1956 £4.00
101-14 Oct 1959 £3.00
21 Oct 1959 1st "Tiger and Comet"; Jet Ace Logan by Pepper & John Gillatt begins £3.50
21 Oct 1959 with free gift (football photos) £7.00
28 Oct 1959-24 Mar 1962 £2.50
31 Mar 1962 Johnny Cougar by Geoff Campion begins £2.00
7 Apr 1962-2 May 1964, 16 May 1964-8 May 1965 £2.00
9 May 1964 Casey and the Champ by Joe Colquhoun begins £2.00
15 May 1965 1st "Tiger and Hurricane"; Val Venture by Jesus Blasco begins £1.50
22 May 1965-2 Apr 1966, 16 Apr 1966-10 Jun 1967, 24 Jun 1967-29 Mar 1969 £1.50
9 Apr 1966 Robot Builders by Carlos Cruz begins (later by Ron Turner) £1.50
17 Jun 1967 Saber, King of the Jungle by Colquhoun begins (later by McLoughlin) £1.50
14 Oct 1967 Peg-Leg's Flying Penguins by Colquhoun begins £1.50
5 Apr 1969 1st "Tiger and Jag" £1.00
12 Apr 1969-25 Oct 1980 £0.75
1 Nov 1980 1st "Tiger and Speed"; Death Wish by Vano, Topps on Two Wheels by Mike Western begin £0.50
8 Nov 1980-30 Mar 1985 £0.50
Note: two un-numbered/ undated issues appeared between 27th Jun-22nd Aug '59, fortnightly schedule Mar-Apr '74.

TIGER ANNUAL
Amalgamated/Fleetway; 1957-1987
1957 £10.00

	N.MINT
1958-1959	£6.00
1960-1965	£5.00
1966-1969	£4.00
1970-1980	£3.00
1981-1987	£2.00

TIGER HOLIDAY SPECIAL

I.P.C. Magazines; Jun 1971-

	N.MINT
1971-1973 96pgs	£3.00
1974-1975 80pgs	£2.00
1976-? 64pgs	£1.00

TIGER SPORTS LIBRARY

Fleetway; 1 Jul 1961-12 Dec 1961

	N.MINT
1 68pgs; Come on Carford by Alfredo Marculeta	£4.00
2-12 Carford on all odd numbers, Bradmere in all even numbers	£3.00

ARTISTS/FEATURES

1 Come On Carford by Alfredo Marculeta. 2 Shoot, Cannon! by Fred T. Holmes. 3 Danger Mark. 4 Bird on the Wing by Loredano Ugolini. 5 Private 'Jankers' - Inside Right by Josep Marti. 6 The Unknown Quantity by Giorgio Trevisan. 7 Hit and Run. 8 The Luck of the Bounce by Fred T. Holmes. 9 The Big Deal. 10 Heads...You Lose. 11 Rush-Tactics by Josep Marti. 12 Clash of Giants.

Note: 13 and 14 advertised but thought not to have appeared

TINTIN

Methuen; 1958-1965

	N.MINT
The Crab with the Golden Claws (1958)	£25.00
King Ottokar's Sceptre (1958)	£20.00
The Secret of the Unicorn (1959)	£15.00
Red Rackham's Treasure (1959)	£12.50
Destination Moon (1959)	£12.50
Explorers on the Moon (1959)	£12.50
The Calculus Affair (1960)	£10.00
The Red Sea Sharks (1960)	£10.00
The Shooting Star (1961)	£10.00
The Seven Crystal Balls (1962)	£7.50
Prisoners of the Sun (1962)	£7.50
TinTin in Tibet (1962)	£12.50
The Castafiore Emerald (1963)	£10.00
TinTin and The Golden Fleece (1965) film adaptation	£12.50
The Black Island (1966)	£12.50
TinTin and The Blue Oranges (1967) film adaptation	£10.00
Flight 714 (1968)	£7.50
Cigars of the Pharoah (1971)	£7.50
Land of Black Gold (1972)	£7.50
TinTin and The Lake of Sharks (1973) film adaptation	£10.00
The Broken Ear (1975)	£6.00
TinTin and the Picaros (1976)	£5.00
TinTin in America (1978)	£5.00
The Blue Lotus (1983)	£4.00
The Making of TinTin I (1983)	£8.00
The Making of TinTin II (1985)	£8.00
TinTin in the Land of the Soviets (Les Editions du Petit Vingtieme, 1989)	£10.00

TITANS

Marvel; 1 25th Oct 1975-58 24th Nov 1976 (joins Super Spider-Man)

	N.MINT
1 36pgs oblong; Captain America, Sub-Mariner, Inhumans, Nick Fury, Captain Marvel reprints begin	£1.25
2	£1.00
3-10	£0.75
11-12 Emergency issues, page count/price down, no glossy cover	£0.75
13 X-Men reprints begin	£0.75
14-25,27-30,32-52,54-58	£0.75
26 X-Men origin story reprints	£0.75
31 Ghost Rider reprints begin	£0.75
53 Avengers reprints begin	£0.75

TITANS ANNUAL, THE

World Distributors; 1977-1978

	N.MINT
1977 reprints Submariner #72, X-Men #40,42,57, plus Captain America	£5.00
1978 reprints FF Ann #6, plus Black Widow	£3.00

TITANS POCKET BOOK

Marvel; 1 25th Sep 1980-13 12th Nov 1981

	N.MINT
1 52pgs pocket size; Thor, Captain America, Iron Man origins begin; Tales of Suspense #40 reprinted; b/w	£1.00
2	£1.00
3 100pgs double issue	£1.25
4-13	£0.60

TOM AND JERRY

Thorpe & Porter; 1 Jan 1953-4 1953

	N.MINT
1-4 36pgs; Dell reprints	£2.00

TOM AND JERRY SPECIALS

World/Polystyle; May 1973-Jul 1984

	N.MINT
Summer Special 1973-1974 32pgs	£0.70
Holiday Special 1975-1984 48pgs	£0.60
Winter Special 1976-1979 48pgs	£0.50

TOM AND JERRY WEEKLY

Spotlight Publications; 13th Oct 1973-3rd Aug 1974, 43 issues (joins TV Comic)

	N.MINT
13 Oct 1973 24pgs; Dell reprints	£1.00
20 Oct 1973-3 Aug 1974	£0.35

TOM CORBETT SPACE CADET

World Distributors; 1 Apr 1953-9 Dec 1953

	N.MINT
1 36pgs; Dell reprints	£4.00
2-9	£2.50

TOMAHAWK

Strato; 1 1954-40 1957

	N.MINT
1 68pgs; National Periodical Publications reprints	£4.00
2-40	£3.00

TONTO

World Distributors; 1 1953-32 1955

	N.MINT
1 28pgs; Dell reprints	£5.00
2-32	£2.50

TOPPER

(see also The Best of Topper Quarterly)

D.C. Thomson; 1 7th Feb 1953-1963 15th Sep 1990 (joins The Beezer and Topper)

	N.MINT
1 tabloid size	£125.00
1 with free gift (The Big Crack Bang)	£150.00
2	£35.00
3	£15.00
1953-1955 issues	£7.50
1956-1959 issues	£5.00
1960-1965 issues	£3.00
1966-1969 issues	£1.50
1970-1979 issues	£0.75
1980-1990 issues	£0.50

CHRONOLOGY

1 Micky the Monkey by Dudley Watkins, The Fighting Frasers by Bill Holroyd, Beryl the Peril by David Law, Flip McCoy by Paddy Brennan all begin, Treasure Island by Watkins reprints (from People's Journal) begin. 31 (3 Sep 1953) Kidnapped by Watkins reprints begin. 55 (20 Feb 1954) Robinson Crusoe by Watkins reprints begin. 95 (7 Nov 1954) King Solomon's Mines by Watkins begins. 140 (8 Oct 1955) Allan Quatermain by Watkins begins. 251 (23 Nov 1957) Oliver Twist by Watkins reprints begin. 1145 (11 Jan 1975) 1st "Topper and Buzz". 1277 (23 Jul 1977) 1st "Topper and Sparky". 1440 1st small size

ARTISTS/FEATURES

Paddy Brennan in 1-80,124-158,193-282,342-363,471-489,574-779,868-901,979-1152,1153-1175,1202,1529-1631. David Law in 1-912. Allan Morley in 2-227. Dudley D. Watkins in 1-873.

TOPPER BOOK

D.C. Thomson; 1955-present

	N.MINT
1955 landscape format begins (5 strips of 25 characters, last is panda)	£70.00
1956 (Dartboard design, logo in centre, characters in middle band)	£40.00
1957 (25 squares, each with character or object)	£32.50
1958 (20 diagonal diamond divisions each with different character)	£30.00
1959 (Captain Bungle holds rifle with monkey sitting on barrel aiming catapault)	£30.00
1960 (Logo diagonally down from left to right with various heads)	£20.00
1961 (Figaro and horse laughing whilst reading Topper Book)	£15.00
1962 (Character heads with their names, Beryl the Peril top right)	£12.50
1963 (Julius Cheeser sits in deck chair on box surrounded by drawing pins) 12.50	
1964 (Foxy with gun in back held by chicken)	£12.50
1965 (2 frames, Figaro holding up cowboy, cowboy lighting firework)	£12.50
1966 (4 frames, Tom Cat and Julius Cheeser and a fire-cracker)	£10.00
1967-1968 regular annual format begins, cover dated	£10.00
1969-1970	£7.50
1971-1979	£5.00
1980-1996	£2.50

TOPPER PICTURE BOOK

D.C. Thomson; Apr 1954

	N.MINT
nn scarce	£80.00

TOPPER SUMMER SPECIAL

D.C. Thomson; 1983-May 1992

	N.MINT
1983-1985	£2.50
1986-1989	£1.50
1990-1992	£1.00

TORCHY GIFTBOOK

Daily Mirror; 1960-1964

	N.MINT
nn undated (1960) features Gerry Anderson's Torchy by Roberta Leigh	£15.00
cy1961-cy1964 stories by Roberta Leigh	£10.00

TORNADO

IPC; 1 24th Mar 1979-22 18th Aug 1979 (joins 2000AD)

	N.MINT
1 Victor Drago by Mike Dorey, Mind of Wolfie Smith by Vano, Angry Planet by Belardinelli, The Tale of Benkie by Steve Moore & Musquera, Captain Klepp by Kev O'Neill begin	£3.00
2,5-7,9-22	£1.00
3 Storm by Musquerra begins	£1.00
4 Blackhawk by Alfonso Azpiri begins	£1.00
8 Cam Kennedy Storm begins	£1.00

Note: many issues have photos of Dave Gibbons dressed as editor Big E. Fab!

TORNADO ANNUAL

Fleetway; 1979-1980

	N.MINT
cover year 1980-1981	£2.00

TORNADO SUMMER SPECIAL

IPC; Jun 1979

	N.MINT
1979 64pgs	£1.00

TOTAL CARNAGE

Dark Horse; 1 Apr 1993-10 Jan 1994

	N.MINT
1 Batman vs Predator, Army of Darkness, The Mask, Grendel: War Child reprints begin	£1.50
2-8,10	£1.50
9 Aliens/Predator: Deadliest of the Species by Claremont & Gulacy reprints begin	£1.50

TOXIC!

(see Accident Man, Bogie Man, Makabre, Marshal Law, Sex Warrior)

Apocalypse Ltd.; 1 28 Mar 1991-31 4th Oct 1991

	N.MINT
1 Marshal Law by Mills & O'Neill, Accident Man by Mills/Skinner & Martin Emond, Mutomaniac by Mills & McMahon all begin, Bisley art	£1.00
2 Bogie Man by Wagner/Grant & Cam Kennedy begins	£1.00
3-6,8,10 10 incl. Arthur Ranson art	£1.00
7 Makabre by Grant & Alcatena begins	£1.00
9 Sex Warrior by Will Simpson begins	£1.00
11 Bogie Man by Wagner/Grant & Robin Smith begins	£1.00
12 Psycho-Killer begins	£1.00
13 Coffin begins	£1.00
14,16-24,26-29,31	£1.00
15 Dinner Ladies From Hell begins	£1.00
25 Detritus Rex, T-Bone begin	£1.00

N.MINT

30 The Road to Hell by Colin McNeil begins £1.00

TRANSFORMERS

Marvel; 1 20th Sep 1984-332 1991

1 all American reprints £1.00
2-8 US reprints £0.60
9-10 1st original British strip by Parkhouse & Ridgway £1.00
11-12 Mike Collins art £0.75
13-112,114-152,154-332 £0.30
113 1st Deaths Head £4.00
153 incorporates Action Force £0.30

ARTISTS

Artists include Mike Collins, Barry Kitson, John Ridgway, Geoff Senior, Will Simpson, Ron Smith in 82, John Stokes, etc.

TRANSFORMERS

Fleetway; 1 1994-4 (Dec 1994)

1-4 £0.50

TRIDENT

(see St. Swithin's Day)

Trident Comics; 1 Aug 1989-8 1990

1 50pgs; Light Brigade by Neil Gaiman & Nigel Kitching, Bacchus by Eddie Campbell, St. Swithin's Day by Grant Morrison & Paul Grist, Dom Zombi by Dominic Regan all begin £2.00
2-4 Grant Morrison script, Campbell art £1.75
5 Campbell art £2.25
6 Light Brigade by Rob Moran, Campbell art £2.25
7 Phil Elliott art, 1st Shadows by Vincent Danks/Steve Pini £2.25
8 £2.25

TRIGAN EMPIRE, THE

(see also Look and Learn Book of the Trigan Empire, Tales of the Trigan Empire)

Hamlyn; 1978

nn 192pgs hardback; reprints Trigan Empire by Don Lawrence from Ranger/Look & Learn £8.00

TRIGGER

(see Roy Rogers' Trigger)

TRIUMPH

Amalgamated Press; 1 18th Oct 1924-814 25th May 1940 (joins The Champion)

1 story paper for boys, no strips £25.00
2-767 story paper £3.00
768-814 more scarce; incl. Superman reprints, Nat Brand, Stanley White art £4.00

Note: there were 21 issues (#772–793) with the Superman strip, 4 of which had Superman on the cover and one of these was based on Action Comics #1. These 4 would be valued more highly than the others. Was this the first U.K. appearance of Superman? A set of these sold in 1994 for £1,500. As such each individual issue carrying the Superman strip would be valued at over £70 but this must be approached with caution as this sale could be regarded as a one-off. It may also be noted that this set also had quite rusty staples so were hardly Near Mint. Another set of the 21 appeared at a San Diego Comicon and I recall a sticker price of $6,000. I believe it sold for considerably less.

TRIUMPH ANNUAL

Amalgamated Press; 1937-1941

1937 scarce; cover shows giant robot about to club two explorers £40.00
1938 £25.00
1939-1941 £20.00

TROUBLED SOULS

(see also For A Few Troubles More)

Fleetway; Feb 1990

nn 96pgs trade paperback; Crisis reprints by Garth Ennis & John McCrea £6.50

TRUE FAITH

Fleetway; Oct 1990

nn trade paperback; Crisis reprints by Garth Ennis & Warren Pleece, withdrawn by publishers in Dec 1990 £6.00

TV ACTION

(previously Countdown)

Polystyle; 59 1st Apr 1972-132 25th Aug 1973 (joins TV Comic)

59 Dr. Who by Gerry Haylock, The Persuaders by Harry Lindfield, Thunderbirds by Don Harley, Stingray reprints by Ron Embleton continued, Tightrope by Stanley Houghton, UFO, Hawaii Five-O by Leslie Branton, Countdown by John Burns begin £15.00
60,64-69 £7.00
61 last original Thunderbirds, Stingray reprints £5.00
62 1st original Stingray by Harley £3.50
63 Embleton Captain Scarlet reprints begin £3.50
70 last Captain Scarlet (returns 78-82) £3.50
71 1st Bellamy Thunderbirds reprint, last Stingray, 1st Burns UFO £3.50
72 1st Noble Fireball XL5 reprint £3.50
73-76 £3.50
77 last Thunderbirds £3.50
78-82 £3.00
83 1st Noble Zero X reprint £3.00
84-87 £3.00
88 Mission Impossible by Burns begins £2.50
89-100 £2.50
101 1st "Big Story" £2.50
102 Dad's Army by Peter Ford begins £2.50
103 Alias Smith and Jones by Colin Andrews begins £2.50
104 The Protectors by Jose Ortiz begins £2.50
105 Cannon by Martin Asbury begins £2.50
106-132 £2.00

TV ACTION & COUNTDOWN HOLIDAY SPECIAL

Polystyle; 1972

1972 48pgs £6.00

TV ACTION ANNUAL

Polystyle; 1973-1974

1973,1974 £6.00

TV ACTION HOLIDAY SPECIAL

Polystyle; Mar 1973

1973 48pgs; Martin Asbury art £3.50

N.MINT

TV CENTURY 21 – INTRODUCTION

INTO THE 21st CENTURY

"It's the 21st Century. You are sitting in the control cabin of Stingray. Next to you is Captain Troy Tempest. You are travelling at 600 knots. You reach Marineville, and a supersonic helicopter transports you inland, swooping low over the metal roads, the fantastic buildings and cities of 2065. This is the world of TV21."

With those words, editor Alan Fennell introduced the readers of 1965 to the world of 2065, and the comic called TV Century 21. It was a world familiar to anyone with access to a TV set, and on the front cover of the first issue blazed the banner 'With Gerry Anderson's Stingray, Fireball XL5 and Supercar'.

If you bought TV21 issue number one on January 20th 1965, you probably knew exactly what those names meant. Only the night before, TV viewers in the Midlands had seen an episode of Stingray, while in the North, it was broadcast that evening. London viewers would have to be content with a repeat of Fireball XL5.

As a spin off, TV21 was a perfect complement to the TV shows. Posing as a newspaper of the future, with its tabloid-like front pages and its illusion of continuity, TV21 gave the television characters a life beyond the TV screen. At a time when most viewers owned black and white TV sets, TV21 literally put the characters into another dimension. Ron Embleton's Stingray was tasteful and robust, Frank Bellamy's Thunderbirds was at the forefront of British comics' design. Mike Noble's Fireball XL5 transformed the spacemen into the spiritual sons of the frontier heroes. Humans and spacecraft were depicted with the same mechanical precision. Explosions spat off the page. Space had a frosty depth.

TV21 was first published in 1965, but its roots lay with TV Comic, where assistant editor Alan Fennell was providing comic strip adaptations of Gerry Anderson's Four Feather Falls and Supercar. At a time when many British strips were often heavily captioned to placate parents who thought "there wasn't enough reading" in comics, Fennell's work was finely balanced. There was enough verbal information to stop the reader getting bored, and the kind of visuals that kept the reader interested.

Anderson was impressed enough to ask him for scripts for his next series, Fireball XL5, and as the two got to know each other, so the concept of a comic based on the output of Anderson's AP Films began to emerge. By the time Stingray was on the air - with many episodes written by Fennell- a dummy of the proposed comic had been produced.

Called Century 21 (also the original proposed title of Fireball XL5), it was hawked around Fleet Street until City Magazines, part of the News of the World empire, agreed to handle production and distribution. Another subsidiary, Eric Bemrose Ltd, would provide printing facilities.

In the final months of 1964, 'TV' had been added to Century 21's title, and most of the staff and freelancers were assembled. Dennis Hooper was recruited as Art Director, along with designer Peter Corri. Hooper also provided some scripts for various strips and collaborated with office manager Tod Sullivan on the covers. Sullivan also contributed scripts, notably for Secret Agent 21. Script editing was provided by Angus Allan, whose wife Gillian also edited the text features and front page news stories.

In terms of artists, Frank Bellamy was approached for Stingray but was still contracted to Eagle, so Dennis Hooper turned to Ron Embleton, who had previously drawn Biggles, Battleground, Colonel Pinto and Wulf the Briton for Express Weekly. Graham Coton provided artwork for Fireball XL5, but was replaced after six issues by Mike Noble, whose previous work had included The Lone Ranger for TV Comic.

Thanks to TV21's connections with AP Films, Fennell didn't have to rely on publicity stills for his front pages. He could arrange with special effects supervisor Derek Meddings to have model shots set up to tie in with comic scripts. More often than not he could also use Stills Photographer Doug Luke's action shots of the TV episodes during production. Thus the Fireflash airliner, or the Sidewinder army vehicle could appear in a Stingray strip or on the cover, or Lady Penelope and Parker could appear in the comic nine months before their TV appearances, either in stills or drawn by Eric Eden.

Apart from The Daleks (drawn by Richard Jennings, Eric Eden and Ron Turner, and written by David Whittaker), the rest of the strips were in black and white. These included Supercar, by Bruno Marraffa and Toledano, Burke's Law and Secret Agent 21.

As TV21's 'host', Agent 21 occupied a two-page feature in which readers' letters and photos were printed and toys offered as competition prizes. In issue 21, one of the pages was taken over by a comic strip drawn by Rab Hamilton. Combined with Sullivan's sparse narration, Hamilton's monochrome art evoked the mood of Le Carre fused with the gadgetry of James Bond. Set 'in the past' of the 2040s, the long running strip laid much of the groundwork for the world of the 21st century.

ATV finally broadcast Thunderbirds in September 1965. The following January, Frank Bellamy's strip commenced in TV21, replacing Lady Penelope who transferred to her own comic, edited by Gillian Allan. Although ostensibly a 'girls' comic', it had an appeal that crossed the sexes. Aside from the title strip drawn by Frank Langford, The Man from UNCLE, Bewitched, Beverly Hillbillies and Marina all put in an appearance, along with Space Family Robinson, based on the Gold Key characters, and later The Angels, from Captain Scarlet.

In TV21, new strips came and went. Supercar and Burke's Law were replaced by the Munsters, an extra page of Agent 21's adventures and a dull industrial espionage story by Don Harley called The Investigator. This was later dropped in favour of the far superior Catch or Kill strip by Angus Allan and John Burns.

By the end of 1966, AP Films had been renamed Century 21, and United Artists had financed Thunderbirds Are Go. To publicise the film, the Daily Mail ran a comic strip by Don Lawrence and Alan Fennell, while TV21 published a four-part photostrip movie adaptation.

When the photostrip ended, the adventures of the Zero X spaceship continued in comic strip format. Angus Allan and Mike Noble transferred from Fireball XL5, working on stories that were faithful to the tone of the movie. So while XL5 travelled at the speed of light or beyond, Zero X took weeks to cross the Solar System.

At the end of 1967, more changes to the comic's line up, and to Century 21 Publishing had taken place. In TV21, Don Lawrence took over Fireball X15 on the back page, a spot formerly occupied by the Daleks for two years. New humour strips appeared briefly in this period, including R.E.Cord, Wright C.H.A.R.L.I.E. (drawn by Brian Lewis) and Sergeant Bilko by Tom Kerr.

On the publishing front, new comics were launched. Aside from the numerous annuals and storybooks (some of which were packaged by World Distributors), new publications included Candy, aimed at the nursery audience, and Solo, which began by reprinting Disney material but later featured a strip by Don Harley called The Mark of The Mysterons. Although set in the 1960s and having virtually no connection with Captain Scarlet, it did nonetheless help publicise the new TV series which debuted in TV21 in September 1967. Ron Embleton, Mike Noble, Jim and Keith Watson, along with Don Harley and John Cooper all illustrated that strip at some point, with Frank Bellamy providing occasional covers. Solo itself was merged with City Magazine's TV Tornado after 30 issues in 1967, and the Mysterons strip, now set in the 21st century, related the Mysterons' attempts to conquer the rest of the universe whilst continuing their 'war of nerves' with Earth.

In January 1968, TV21 was revamped. The newspaper front page was diminished to a headline and publicity photo, along with the first three panels of the Captain Scarlet strip. During the coming year, Fireball and Stingray would be phased out in favour of new features like the apocalyptic Project Sword, and later on, strips brought in from TV Tornado, which merged with TV21 in September 1968 after 88 issues. Soon, The Saint, Tarzan and Department S would all be jostling for space alongside the remaining Anderson strips, and they would be joined in 1969 by articles on football and space exploration.

With the cancellation of Solo and TV Tornado, everyone seemed eager to launch a new comic. Joe 90 Top Secret, launched in January 1969, faced the unfortunate situation where there was more confidence in the planned back up strips than there was in the title character. The problems were compounded when it was discovered that few readers would know what one of those strips - Star Trek - would be about. The BBC had bought the series, but didn't screen it until six months after the comic was launched.

By mid 1969, the recession that had hit Britain at the end of the '60s finally hit Century 21. In an effort to cut costs, TV21 and Penelope both reduced their page sizes and colour material, and weaker titles like Joe 90 Top Secret were soon floundering. Century 21 sold its merchandising arms to concentrate on TV and film production only, and the publishing side of the business was gradually wound down. On September 6th, 1969, TV21 and Joe 90 Top Secret merged, and shortly afterwards, City Magazines took over the sole production of the comic

After 242 issues, TV21 was renumbered, and gradually the Anderson content was reduced. Star Trek became the cover feature, with artwork supplied by Mike Noble, Ron Turner, Harold Johns and Carlos Pino, succeeding that of Harry Lindfield and Jim Baikie. In July 1971, the comics were sold to IPC. Candy was merged with Jack and Jill, Penelope with Princess Tina and on September 25th, TV21 was merged with Valiant, after 105 issues.

By this time, new magazines were competing for TV21's former readership. Dennis Hooper went on to edit Countdown, using a combination of reprints from TV21 and new material including Doctor Who. Alan Fennell created Look-In, which in its various guises, survived until earlier 1995.

Reprints from TV21 continued to appear occasionally in the '70s and '80s, mainly in the form of Dalek Annuals publishing the Ron Turner and Richard Jennings strips, or Polystyle Thunderbirds and Stingray Specials, where the Countdown and TV21 strips barely survived the cheap printing process used. Finally, in 1989, Action 21 was published by Engale Marketing in Blackpool, combining strips from TV21 and Lady Penelope in a full colour monthly. It lasted only ten issues, killed by spiralling print costs and distribution problems.

With the revived popularity of Thunderbirds broadcast by the BBC in 1991, the strips from TV21 made an appearance again, this time courtesy of Fleetway. In all, four titles were published, all edited by Alan Fennell. Thunderbirds The Comic survived the longest, with Joe 90 repeating history with an even shorter run than its 1960s counterpart.

Looking back it's hard to say what exactly makes a comic memorable. British comics are generally aimed at children and the best ones encourage reader participation through the editorial pages. Both Eagle and TV21 went to great lengths to involve the readership in the stories and characters, often through the letters and club pages, with varying degrees of success. Children can put a lot of themselves into a well produced comic, inventing a surprising amount of background detail about their favourite heroes.

TV21 recognised that contribution, but didn't short change the reader. A lot went into the stories about the future, but TV21 didn't ignore the present either. Alan Fennell's script for the Thunderbirds Nicaraguan story reflects a period in 1966 when the Somosa family was still in power, and America's President Johnston was considering using atomic bombs to carve a canal through that country. The TV21 storyline highlights the injustices which the Nicaraguan farmers were suffering, just as they were in real life.

TV21 had high production standards, common to many comics of the period, standards that offered artists the chance to do their best - standards that demanded the best. Backed by Associated Television, it reflected the flair of the shows that inspired it.

In the skies of the 1960s, TV21 blazed briefly. But it blazed bright.

© Graham Bleathman, 1995

TV CENTURY 21

City; 1 23rd Jan 1965-242 20th Sep 1969 (joins TV 21 and Joe 90)

	GOOD	FINE	N.MINT
1 Burke's Law by Pat Williams, Fireball XL5 by Graham Coton, Stingray by Ron Embleton, Lady Penelope by Eric Eden, The Daleks by Terry Nation and Richard Jennings begin **(Note: interior coupon often clipped. Beware!)**	£18.50	£55.00	£150.00
1 with free gift, (Secret Decoder)	£25.00	£75.00	£200.00
2	£8.50	£26.00	£60.00
3 Dalek cover	£10.00	£30.00	£70.00
4	£4.25	£12.50	£30.00
5	£2.85	£8.50	£20.00
6 1st Fireball XL5 by Mike Noble	£2.10	£6.25	£15.00
7-10	£1.40	£4.25	£10.00
11-20	£1.05	£3.20	£7.50
21 Secret Agent 21 by Rab Hamilton begins	£1.05	£3.20	£7.50
22-39	£0.85	£2.55	£6.00
40-43 Fireball XL5 by Frank Bellamy	£1.05	£3.20	£7.50
44-49	£0.85	£2.55	£6.00
50 1st Daleks by Ron Turner	£0.85	£2.55	£6.00
51	£1.00	£3.00	£5.00
52 Get Smart, The Munsters by Trevillion, Thunderbirds by Frank Bellamy all begin	£0.85	£2.55	£6.00
53-70	£0.70	£2.10	£5.00
71 last Ron Embleton Stingray (Gerry Embleton art from #72)	£0.70	£2.10	£5.00
72	£0.55	£1.70	£4.00
73 The Investigator by Don Harley begins	£0.55	£1.70	£4.00
74-89	£0.55	£1.70	£4.00
90 Catch or Kill by John Burns begins	£0.55	£1.70	£4.00
91-92	£0.55	£1.70	£4.00
93-98 Don Harley Thunderbirds art	£0.55	£1.70	£4.00
99	£0.55	£1.70	£4.00
100	£0.70	£2.10	£5.00
101-104 Thunderbirds Are Go! photo story fom the movie. #104 last Daleks	£0.55	£1.70	£4.00
105 Zero X by Mike Noble begins	£0.70	£2.10	£5.00
106-108	£0.55	£1.70	£4.00
109 1st Don Lawrence Fireball XL5	£0.70	£2.10	£5.00
110-131	£0.55	£1.70	£4.00
132 Front Page by John Burns begins	£0.40	£1.25	£3.00
133-140	£0.40	£1.25	£3.00
141 Captain Scarlet by Ron Embleton begins	£0.55	£1.70	£4.00
142-153	£0.40	£1.25	£3.00
154 title becomes TV 21	£0.40	£1.25	£3.00
155-167	£0.40	£1.25	£3.00
168 Project Sword text stories by Angus Allen begin	£0.40	£1.25	£3.00
169-184	£0.40	£1.25	£3.00
185-186 Frank Bellamy Captain Scarlet covers	£0.50	£1.50	£3.50
187-189	£0.40	£1.25	£3.00
190 1st "TV 21 & TV Tornado"; Tarzan and The Saint both begin	£0.50	£1.50	£3.50
191	£0.40	£1.25	£3.00
192-193 Frank Bellamy Captain Scarlet covers	£0.50	£1.50	£3.50
194-199	£0.40	£1.25	£3.00
200	£0.50	£1.50	£3.50
201-209	£0.40	£1.25	£3.00
210 Frank Bellamy Captain Scarlet covers	£0.50	£1.50	£3.50
211-225	£0.40	£1.25	£3.00
226-241 less common in the U.K.	£0.50	£1.50	£3.50
242 scarce in the U.K.	£0.55	£1.70	£4.00

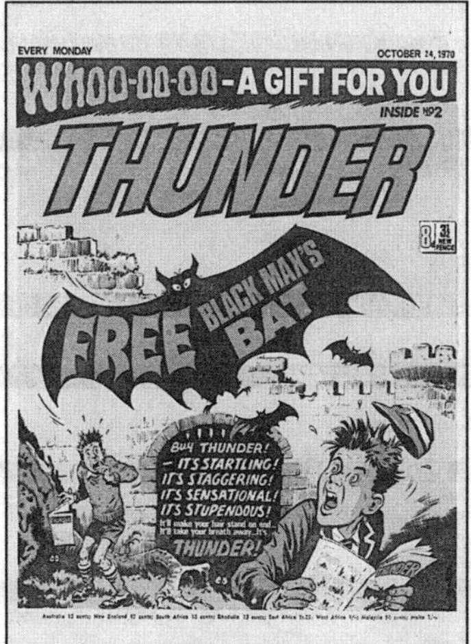

Thunder #2

TV Century 21 #2

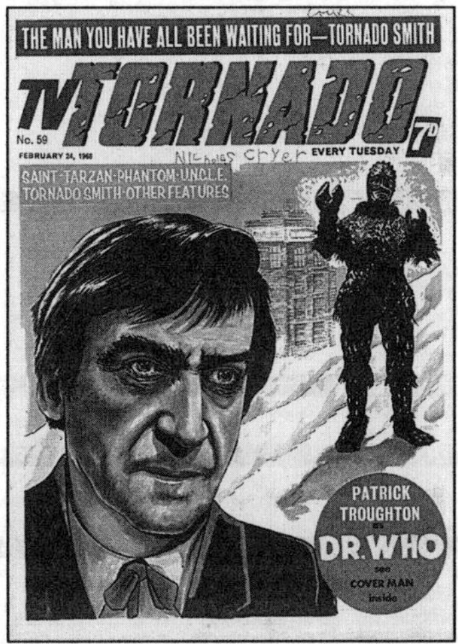

TV Tornado #59

GOOD FINE N.MINT

Title Value: **£209.40 £636.05 £1543.00**

ARTISTS

Frank Bellamy in 52-92,99-242. John Burns in 90-114,119-154. Ron Embleton in 1-57,62-71,141-157. Frank Hampson in 40-43. Don Lawrence in 109-140. Mike Noble in 6-39,44-86,90-100,105-130,135-154,158-166,172-179,182-184,187-189,194-241. Ron Turner in 50-51,59-104. Keith Watson in 167-169,180-181,190-191,199-200,205-206. Mike Western in 7.

TV CENTURY 21 ANNUAL

City/Fleetway; 1965-1973

1965 £22.00
1966 £15.00
1967 £12.50
1968-1969 becomes TV 21 Annual £7.50
1970-1973 no Gerry Anderson material £2.50

TV CENTURY 21 INTERNATIONAL EXTRA

City; 1965

1965 48pgs; scarce, Ron Turner art £32.50

TV CENTURY 21 STINGRAY SPECIAL

City; 1965

1965 48pgs; Ron Turner, Ron Embleton art £27.50
1965 with free gift (WASP and Stingray badges) £50.00

TV CENTURY 21 SUMMER EXTRA

City; 1965-May 1966

1965 48pgs; Lady Penelope by Hampson, Ron Embleton art £27.50
1965 with free gift (Cosmic Capers Kit) £50.00
1966 Don Harley art £22.50

TV COMIC

News of the World/Beaverbrook/TV/Polystyle; 1 9th Nov 1951-1697 29th Jun 1984

1 Muffin the Mule by Neville Main, Tom Puss (Dutch reprints) by Marten Toonder, Prince Valiant (US reprints) by Hal Foster begin £60.00
2 £25.00
3-5 £12.50
6-15 £10.00
16-25 £5.00
26-50 £3.00
51-200 £2.00
201-438,440-482 £1.50
439 Four Feather Falls by Main begins £1.50
483 Supercar by H. Watts begins £3.00
484-507,509-564,566-673 £3.00
508 Range Rider by Ron Embleton begins £3.00
565 Fireball XL5 by Main begins £3.00
674-719 Dr Who by Main (later by Bill Mevin, John Canning) £3.00
720 The Avengers by Pat Williams begins, Dr. Who £3.00
721-999 Dr Who £3.00
1000-1132 £1.75
1133-1291 Dr Who returns by Gerry Haylock (later by Martin Asbury, Canning) £1.50
1292 title becomes "Mighty TV Comic", 1st tabloid format, Dr Who £1.50
1293-1385 tabloid format, Dr Who £1.00
1386-1392 Dr Who reprints, redrawn as Tom Baker £1.00
1393 1st "TV Comic incorporating Target", standard format, Dr. Who reprints £1.00
1395-1430 Dr. Who reprints £1.00
1431-1697 £0.50

TV COMIC ANNUAL

News of the World/Beaverbrook/TV Publications/Polystyle; 1954-1985?

1954 scarce £35.00
1955 £18.00
1956-1959 £10.00
1960-1964 £7.50
1965 (TV) Fireball XL5, Supercar £8.50
1966 Troughton Dr Who by Neville Main £8.00
1967 Avengers (Diana Rigg) strip, Dr Who by John Canning £7.00
1968 Troughton Dr Who & Daleks by Pat Williams, Adam Adament text story £8.50
1969 (Polystyle) Troughton Dr Who, Skippy text story £6.00
cy1970-cy1971 Pertwee Dr Who, Avengers (Tara King) text stories £3.25
1972,1974 £3.00
1973 Avengers (Tara King) £4.00
1975-1977 Tom Baker Dr Who £2.50
1978 Tom Baker Dr Who £2.25
cy1978 titled New Mighty TV Comic Annual; Tom Baker Dr Who £2.25
cy1979-cy1980 incl. Dr Who £1.50
cy1981-cy1984 £1.25

TV COMIC HOLIDAY SPECIAL

TV/Polystyle; Jun 1963-Apr 1984

1963-1964 £3.00
1965 Troughton Dr Who by Neville Main £5.00
1966-1970 Dr Who £2.50
1971-1973 £1.00
1974-1978 Dr Who £1.50
1979-1984 £0.75

TV COMIC SUMMER SPECIAL

TV; 1962 (becomes TV Comic Holiday Special)

1962 48pgs; reprints £4.00

TV CRIMEBUSTERS

TV; 1962

nn hardback, scarce features Dangerman, Avengers (Steed and David Keel), Persuers, Dixon of Dock Green, Four Just Men, Charlie Chan; all are a mixture of artwork and photographs £25.00

TV EXPRESS

(previously Express Weekly)

TV; 286 23rd Apr 1960-375 6th Jan 1962 (90 issues, joins TV Comic)

286 Battleground by Embleton, Wulf the Briton by Embleton £5.00
287 £3.00
288-305,307-331,333-346,348-375 £2.50

N.MINT

306 Biggles by Embleton begins £2.50
332 Col. Pinto by Embleton begins £2.50
347 Danger Man text stories begin £2.50

ARTISTS

Ron Embleton in 286-371.

TV EXPRESS ANNUAL

(previously Express Annual)

TV; 1961-1962

1961 Wulf the Briton by Embleton £5.00
1962 Biggles by Embleton £6.00

TV FAN

(see TV Fun)

TV FEATURES

Anglo; 1 Nov 1960-8 Jun 1961

1-8 28pgs; Miller reprints £3.00

TV FUN/TV FAN

Amalgamated/Fleetway; 1 19th Sep 1953-333 30th Jan 1960 (joins Valentine)

1 Arthur Askey by Arthur Martin, The House with Red Shutters by George Heath begin £30.00
2 £15.00
3-5 £7.50
6-15 £5.00
16-50 £3.00
51-150 £2.50
151-312 £2.00
313 title becomes TV Fan £1.75
314-333 £1.75

ARTISTS

George Heath art in most issues (The House with Red Shutters, I Vow Vengeance, Our 'Tec Teaser, Cal Conway's Son, The Under-Sea Pirates, Roar with the Lyons, A Texan in the Big City, Family Theatre).

TV FUN ANNUAL

Amalgamated; 1957-1960

1957 £6.00
1958-1960 £5.00

TV HEROES

Miller; 1 Jul 1958-26 Aug 1960

1 Robin Hood, Last of the Mohicans, Wyatt Earp begin £5.00
2-7 £3.00
8 1st Mick Anglo edited issue £3.00
9-25 £2.00
26 Don Lawrence reprints £3.00

Note: Although subtitled "Your Favourite TV Stars and Others in Action" a disclaimer noted that "there is no connection between this magazine and the transmission of any television programme"

TV LAND

TV 1 1st Jan 1960-68 16th Jan 1962 (joins TV Comic)

1 Gerry Anderson's Twizzle, Yogi bear, Larry the Lamb by Neville Main £2.00
2-68 £1.00

TV PHOTO STORIES

C.A. Pearson; 1 Jan 1960-6 Mar 1960

1,5 OSS £5.00
2,6 William Tell £5.00
3 Dial 999 £5.00
4 Buccaneers £5.00

Note: all photo-strips

TV PICTURE STORIES

(C.A. Pearson; inter-related series of digest sized comics, numbered as a series on cover to 12, inside from 13. Each series was also numbered independently. See Adventures of Robin Hood, The Buccaneers, Dixon of Dock Green, Emergency Ward 10, Hawkeye and the Last of the Mohicans, Highway Patrol, Murder Bag, New Adventures of Charlie Chan, O.S.S., Sheriff of Cochise, Sword of Freedom, William Tell)

TV TORNADO

City; 1 14th Jan 1967-88 14th Sep 1968 (joins TV 21)

1 Voyage to the Bottom of the Sea by Mick Anglo, Tarzan by Harry Bishop, Bonanza, Gold key reprints (Phantom, Flash Gordon, Lone Ranger), Batman, Superman begin £30.00
1 with free gift (Bat Parachute) £75.00
2 £15.00
2 with free gift (TV Tornado Magic Cards) £30.00
3 £7.50
4-6,8-14,16-35 £5.00
7 Green Hornet, Magnus Robot Fighter reprints begin £5.00
15 The Saint by Bishop begins £5.00
36 Mysterons begin £5.00
37 1st "TV Tornado & Solo" £5.00
38-47,49-57,60-63,65-88 £4.00
48 The Prisoner cover £20.00
58 2pgs Troughton Dr.Who photo feature £25.00
58 with free gift (blue plastic boomerang) £40.00
59 Troughton/Ice Warriors cover £20.00
64 Patrick MacNee Avengers cover £25.00

TV TORNADO ANNUAL

City; 1967-1970

1967 96pgs; Tarzan, UNCLE, Green Hornet, Bonanza, Magnus strips £5.50
1968 Phantom, UNCLE, Tarzan, Saint, Magnus strips, MacNee photo £4.50
1969 Magnus, UNCLE, Lone Ranger, Tarzan, Saint strips £3.50
1970 Lone Ranger, Tarzan, Saint strips £3.50

TV TOYLAND

Fleetway Publications; 28th May 1966-23rd Feb 1968 (92 issues, joins Playhour)

28 May 1966 Champion the Wonder Horse, Leslie Crowther by Leslie Branton, Magic Roundabout, Rolf Harris by Philip Mendoza all start £2.00
4 Jun 1966-23 Feb 1968 £0.35

TV 21

(see TV Century 21)

TV 21 & JOE 90

City/IPC; 1 27th Sep 1969-105 25th Sep 1971 (joins Valiant)

	N.MINT
1 Tarzan by Don Lawrence, The Saint by Alcazar/Pino, Star Trek by Harry Lindfield, Joe 90 by Michael Strand, Thunderbirds by Frank Bellamy begin	£15.00
1 with free gift (Soccer Stars Portraits)	£30.00
2	£7.50
3	£6.00
4 last Bellamy Thunderbirds	£5.00
5-35,37	£2.50
36 Last Joe 90	£2.50
38 last Thunderbirds, no further Anderson material	£2.50
39-57,62-105	£1.50
58-61 Ron Turner Star Trek art	£1.50

ARTISTS/FEATURES

Frank Bellamy in 1-4. Don Lawrence in 1-6,8-24,39-40,43-46,48,51. Mike Noble in 33-57. Ron Turner in 58-61.

TV 21 SPRING EXTRA: THUNDERBIRDS

City; Mar 1967

	N.MINT
1967 48pgs; Ron Turner, Brian Lewis, Don Harley art	£20.00

TWILIGHT ZONE ANNUAL

World Distributors; 1965

	N.MINT
1965 scarce; Dell reprints in colour	£5.00

TWILIGHT ZONE COMIC ALBUM

World Distributors; 1 1964

	N.MINT
1 scarce; 64pgs; b/w Dell reprints	£4.00

TWIZZLE ADVENTURE STORIES

Birn Brothers; 1958, 1960

	N.MINT
1958 stories by Roberta Leigh	£12.50
1960 entitled More Twizzle Adventure Stories, stories by Roberta Leigh	£10.00

TWIZZLE STORY BOOK

Birn Brothers; 1960

	N.MINT
1960	£10.00

TWO GUN KID

World Distributors; 1 1950-?

	N.MINT
1- 36pgs; Atlas reprints	£3.00

TWO GUN KID

Miller; 1 1955-38 1959?

	N.MINT
1 28pgs; Atlas reprints	£4.00
2-38	£2.00

TWO GUN WESTERN

United Anglo-American; 1 1951-9? 195?

	N.MINT
1 28pgs; Atlas reprints	£3.00
2-9	£2.00

TWO GUN WESTERN

Arnold Book Co.; 1 1952

	N.MINT
1 28pgs; Atlas reprints	£4.00

2000AD – INTRODUCTION

MILLENNIUM FEVER

Cast the spotlight of history on the greatest of Britain's comics and the cold light reveals their humble beginnings. We know, for instance, that the iconic Dan Dare and Eagle began life on Frank Hampson's kitchen table in Southport; that Dan became the hero of the fifties and ushered in the Silver Age of British comics is now a matter of record. With hindsight, we know that Pat Mills and John Wagner were destined for greater things but, 22-years ago, the creators of Judge Dredd, Slaine, the A.B.C. Warriors, Robo-Hunter and countless other top strips, were fresh out of D.C. Thomson's fiction department and beginning their comic careers hacking out 'Tomboy' and 'Jack Pott' humour strips for I.P.C. from a garden shed in Dundee.

In the early 1970s, with the traditional British boys' comic dying on its feet, Mills and Wagner were part of a renaissance that actually began in I.P.C.'s girls' titles, Tammy and Sandie. 'Ella on Easy Street' and 'Back Stab Ballerina' ushered in a new realism in comics, the "soap opera element," as Mills calls it. Out of that was to come the new, realistic war comic Battle Picture Weekly, created by Mills and Wagner and launched in 1975.

In 1976 IPC Magazines launched a wild-child on the news-stands called Action. The winning formula was to take themes that were popular in film and television as a meter for kids' tastes and turn them into colourful, kinetic comic strips. Many saw Action as anti-authoritarian, vicious and dangerous, but it was lifeblood to its audience: against all the odds, the circulation began to rise as word spread about the comic with attitude.

Once the shape of Action had been moulded and an editor appointed, Mills was invited to create another new title, and was given unprecedented freedom by I.P.C.'s management. The idea for a science fiction comic came from Kelvin Gosnell, fresh out of the company's Competitions Department but destined to be 2000AD's first editor. Gosnell had read an article about SF movies being made in Hollywood. Films such as Rollerball and Logan's Run mixed futuristic adventure with violence in the style of Mills' new vision for comics, and with Star Wars and Close Encounters of the Third Kind on the horizon, a science fiction comic was potentially a winner.

The idea evolved into the seminal 2000AD, a distillation of film and television hits and potential hits, processed by Mills and further distorted with a futuristic twist. If Action was the punk of I.P.C.'s comics, 2000AD was Death Race 2000, filled with gutsy, bloody stories that struck a nerve.

When Programme 1 of 2000AD welcomed us into the future on February 26, 1977, it didn't look much like The Galaxy's Greatest Comic of nowadays. Although Tharg, his Nerve Centre and his Betelgeusian catchphrases were present, Judge Dredd didn't arrive until Programme 2 (the familiar 'Prog' abbreviation didn't occur until May 21, Prog 13). Now, nineteen years on, 2000AD is entering a new millennium, but it still has echoes of those early issues: "If you have something and its foundations are strong and solid, you'll always return to those foundations," says Mills. "You'll go off occasionally on different tangents as you reflect the tastes of the times, but you always come back to the bedrock of the characters, the basic fabric. At times, 2000AD has been more rock orientated, more political, and has gone through phases of being very fan conscious - it was all the taste of the times.

"For example, now you've got 'Vector 13' which clearly reflects interest in The X-Files. We had the equivalent years back: we had 'Harlem Heroes' which reflected the interest at the time in things like Rollerball and Death Race 2000."

"I think of 'Vector 13' as a combination of The X-Files and Rod Serling's Twilight Zone," says group editor Steve MacManus. "The thing about 2000AD was that once it had ridden on the back of Star Wars, we second guessed Hollywood all the way and we had nothing to rip off because we'd got there first. The Japanese have a saying: 'If it's good, how can we make it better?' I'm sure that's the philosophy that Pat applied to, say, The Six Million Dollar Man in M.A.C.H. 1 and he did make it so much better. 'Man Activated by Compu-puncture Hyperpower' - what a great concept! - which, without the Six Million Dollar Man, Pat maybe wouldn't have bothered to look at [the idea of] an indestructible man."

MacManus, a sub-editor on Action, joined 2000AD a year and a half into its existence from Starlord, and still retains every ounce of enthusiasm for his eighteen years on the title. "What was nice was that having joined on Prog 76, there was so much to look forward to: 'Robo-Hunter' appeared and 2000 was being merged with Starlord. That's why I joined. You merge a comic and one of the two subs has to go."

Things have changed from the distant days when Tharg rocketed his comic out of King's Reach Towers. Or have they? "Next year is twenty years on and it's going to be a year of science fiction; that's a nice echo. On his noticeboard, David [Bishop]'s got a snap of an old Starlord cover of the Washington Monument being snapped in two by a UFO being chased by American pilots. The thing about science fiction is that its cyclical."

Things may be coming back to basics but 2000AD has matured over the years. "From a production point of view, you could say a lot of the things we had hoped to get in the early days, we've finally succeeded in getting," says Pat Mills. "Glossy covers, full colour in a lot of cases and I can tell you, its been a bloody long, hard slog and fight to get that. I think there is better continuity of artwork and arguably some of the stories have become more sophisticated. I think that's the standard answer, but I don't think that's entirely true. I think there are stories going back some years that would compete pretty well with today's stories. Things are a little more sophisticated than they have been, but the basic rules that applied then apply now."

"If you look at the first issues, it's predominantly filled with Spanish artists," says current editor David Bishop. "I don't think any artist got work from us in the first two years without coming through an agency; now, of course, agencies are very much in the minority. Most people come to us through the post or at conventions and that's how people break through these days. In terms of writers, frequently the best of the writers around twenty years ago are the best of the writers today, Wagner and Mills being the obvious ones from the first couple of years and Alan Grant, who came in on stream later. So, to a large extent I think the writing has definitely improved: in the early days, 2000AD was virtually written by committee.

"We do have a situation with 2000AD where we're about to go full circle. If you consider, in 1976 the reason 2000AD was launched, one of the deciding factors, was the Alexander Walker article in the Evening Standard about how all these science fiction movies were going to be the rage in 1977, with Star Wars and even the director of Jaws, Stephen Spielberg was going to do a movie about UFOs - which of course was Close Encounters. Now, twenty years later, you've got Independence Day, Mars Attacks! and a very long article in the Sunday Times recently about the wealth of science fiction; it's hip again for TV and film and all we're going to see over the next year is more SF, with millennium fever and all that. It feels like we've turned the clock back to 1976. Star Wars is on the horizon, the Sex Pistols are touring again…

"The only difference maybe is that in the Seventies, 2000AD was the new kid on the block," says Macmanus. "Twenty years on we're the old man on the block, but pumped full of rejuve drugs."

David Bishop neatly summarises 2000AD's place in the scheme of things when he casually remarks "Imagine if 2000AD never existed. I think you would struggle to name any British writer or artist over the past twenty years who didn't get their showcase on 2000AD. The exception would be Neil Gaiman, I think he wrote one and a half 'Future Shocks' for us and then cut straight to the chase, because he went into almost self publishing when he did Violent Cases, and Jamie Hewlett with Deadline... Not all these creators needed 2000AD because talent will out, but for the past twenty years, almost all the best writers and artists have sprung from the pages of 2000AD. So finding that talent, nurturing that talent and tearfully waving it goodbye as it crosses the pond has been 2000's role, to create the people who now sit around the bar at UKCAC. Without 2000AD, you could probably argue the case that there'd be no Vertigo. Without Vertigo, you wouldn't have Paradox and so many other things."

2000AD

IPC/Fleetway: 1 26th Feb 1977-present (1028 issues to Jan 1997)

(see A.B.C. Warriors, Alan Moore's Shocking Futures, Alan Moore's Twisted Times, America, Anderson Psi Division, Bad Company, Best of 2000AD, Chopper, Complete Judge Dredd, Halo Jones, Judge Anderson, Judge Dredd, Killing Time, Midnight Surfer Special, Nemesis, Robo Hunter, Ro-Busters, Rogue Trooper, Slaine, Spellbinders, Strontium Dog, The VC's, Zenith)

(Note: all distributed on the newstands in the U.K.)

	GOOD	FINE	N.MINT
1 Invasion by Blasco, Flesh by Boix, Mach 1 by Enio (ends #64, not in #47-51), Harlem Globetrotters by Gibbons; revived Dan Dare by Belardinelli begins (ends #20)	£10.00	£30.00	£60.00
1 with free gift, (space spinner) Note: attached by sellotape to front cover which stains over the years	£13.00	£40.00	£80.00
2 1st appearance of Judge Dredd by Alan Grant, John Wagner and Steve McMahon	£11.50	£35.00	£70.00
2 with free gift, (bionic stickers)	£15.00	£45.00	£90.00
3 McMahon Judge Dredd	£4.15	£12.50	£25.00
3 with free gift, (survival manual)	£5.75	£17.50	£35.00
4 McMahon Judge Dredd	£2.50	£7.50	£15.00
5 1st appearance of Judge Dredd by Carlos Ezquerra	£2.05	£6.25	£12.50
6-7 McMahon Judge Dredd	£1.65	£5.00	£10.00
8 1st appearance Judge Dredd by Belardinelli	£1.65	£5.00	£10.00
9 1st Turner Judge Dredd, Robot Wars begin	£1.25	£3.75	£7.50
10	£1.25	£3.75	£7.50
11-12	£1.00	£3.00	£6.00
13 1st appearance of Walter the Wobot	£1.00	£3.00	£6.00
14 1st Gibson Judge Dredd	£1.00	£3.00	£6.00
15	£1.00	£3.00	£6.00
16-17 Robot Wars end	£1.00	£3.00	£6.00
18	£0.80	£2.50	£5.00
19 Flesh ends; 1st John Cooper Dredd	£0.80	£2.50	£5.00
20 1st appearance Max Normal	£0.80	£2.50	£5.00
21-23	£0.80	£2.50	£5.00
24 Kev O'Neill art	£0.80	£2.50	£5.00
25 1st Tharg's Future Shocks	£0.80	£2.50	£5.00
26-27 last Harlem Heroes	£0.75	£2.25	£4.50
28 1st appearance Dan Dare by Dave Gibbons	£0.80	£2.50	£5.00
29-32	£0.65	£2.00	£4.00
33 Ewins/McCarthy art	£0.65	£2.00	£4.00
34-35	£0.65	£2.00	£4.00
36 1st story credits; Inferno by Belardinelli begins (ends #75)	£0.65	£2.00	£4.00
37-39	£0.65	£2.00	£4.00
40 Bill Ward Judge Dredd	£0.65	£2.00	£4.00
41 1st Judge Dredd by Brian Bolland	£1.00	£3.00	£6.00
42-46	£0.55	£1.75	£3.50
47 Bolland art	£0.65	£2.00	£4.00
48-49	£0.55	£1.75	£3.50
50 Bolland art; Walter the Wobot by Gibson begins (ends #61)	£0.65	£2.00	£4.00
51 Bolland art; Invasion ends	£0.70	£2.10	£3.50
52 1st appearance of Walter the Wobot by Brian Bolland; Future Shock story also by Bolland	£0.80	£2.40	£4.00
53-59 Bolland art	£0.70	£2.10	£3.50
60 Bolland art; 1st Lewis Dan Dare	£0.60	£1.80	£3.00

	GOOD	FINE	N.MINT
61 Bolland art; Cursed Earth story begins (ends #85)	£0.60	£1.80	£3.00
62-64 Bolland art	£0.60	£1.80	£3.00
65 Bolland art; Mach Zero begins (ends #75)	£0.60	£1.80	£3.00
66-70 Bolland art	£0.60	£1.80	£3.00
71 Burger Wars story; Ant Wars begins (ends #85)	£1.20	£3.60	£6.00
72 scarce in the U.K. Burger Wars	£1.20	£3.60	£6.00
73-75 scarce in the U.K.	£1.00	£3.00	£5.00
76 scarce in the U.K. Robo-Hunter by Gibson begins (ends #85)	£1.00	£3.00	£5.00
77-78 scarce in the U.K. Jolly Green Giant by Bolland	£1.50	£4.50	£7.50
79-80 Goring and Garry Leach art on Dan Dare begins	£0.50	£1.50	£2.50
81-82 Bolland, Leach art	£0.50	£1.50	£2.50
83 Leach art	£0.40	£1.20	£2.00
84 1st Walter the Wobot by McCarthy; Gibbons, Leach art	£0.40	£1.20	£2.00
85 Gibson Dan Dare ends (returns #100)	£0.40	£1.20	£2.00
86 1st "2000AD and Starlord"; Bolland art, Day The Law Died (Judge Caligula) (ends #108),Strontium Dog by Carlos Ezquerra (ends #94), Flesh II by Belardinelli (ends #99), Ro-Busters by Gibbons (ends #115 and not in #102) all begin	£0.60	£1.80	£3.00
87 Bolland art	£0.50	£1.50	£2.50
88-91	£0.40	£1.20	£2.00
92-93 Ewins art	£0.40	£1.20	£2.00
94-95 Bolland, Leach art	£0.50	£1.50	£2.50
96-97	£0.40	£1.20	£2.00
98 Bolland art	£0.50	£1.50	£2.50
99	£0.40	£1.20	£2.00
100 Robo-Hunter returns (ends #112), Dan Dare returns (ends #126)	£0.80	£2.40	£4.00
101-102 Bolland art	£0.50	£1.50	£2.50
103 Leach, O'Neill art	£0.30	£0.90	£1.50
104 Strontium Dog returns (ends #118), O'Neill art; 1st Ron Smith Judge Dredd	£0.30	£0.90	£1.50
105-108	£0.30	£0.90	£1.50
109 no Judge Dredd	£0.30	£0.90	£1.50
110 Bolland art	£0.40	£1.20	£2.00
111-112	£0.30	£0.90	£1.50
113 1st Rick Random by Steve Moore and Ron Turner (ends #118)	£0.30	£0.90	£1.50
114-118	£0.30	£0.90	£1.50
119 ABC Warriors by O'Neill (ends #139) and Disaster 1990 by Carlos Pino (ends #139) both begin	£0.30	£0.90	£1.50
120 Bolland art	£0.40	£1.20	£2.00
121	£0.30	£0.90	£1.50
122 Bolland art	£0.40	£1.20	£2.00
123-126	£0.30	£0.90	£1.50
127 1st "2000AD and Tornado"; Blackhawk by Belardinelli (ends #161, not in #129), The Mind of Wolfie Smith by Gibson (ends #145), Captain Klep by O'Neill all begin, Bolland art also	£0.60	£1.80	£3.00
128-137	£0.30	£0.90	£1.50
138 Leach, McMahon art	£0.40	£1.20	£2.00
139	£0.30	£0.90	£1.50
140 Stainless Steel Rat by Ezquerra (ends #151 and VC's by McMahon (ends #175, not in #144, #166-167, #170) both begin	£0.40	£1.20	£2.00
141	£0.30	£0.90	£1.50
142-143 Cam Kennedy art	£0.30	£0.90	£1.50
144	£0.30	£0.90	£1.50
145 Leach, McMahon art	£0.40	£1.20	£2.00
146-147 Cam Kennedy art	£0.30	£0.90	£1.50
148 Leach art	£0.30	£0.90	£1.50
149 Bolland Judge Death begins (ends #151), 1st appearance Judge Anderson, Leach art	£0.80	£2.40	£4.00
150-151 Bolland art	£0.60	£1.80	£3.00
152 Kennedy art, Robo-Hunter returns (ends #174), Fiends of the Eastern Front by Ezquerra begins (ends #161)	£0.30	£0.90	£1.50
153	£0.30	£0.90	£1.50
154 Leach art	£0.35	£1.05	£1.75
155 Leach art, no Judge Dredd	£0.30	£0.90	£1.50
156 Judge Child begins (ends #181); Bolland art	£0.50	£1.50	£2.50
157-160 Kennedy art	£0.30	£0.90	£1.50
161 Leach, McMahon art	£0.30	£0.90	£1.50
162 Mach Zero returns (ends #165), Wolfie Smith returns (ends #177); Bolland, Kennedy art	£0.50	£1.50	£2.50
163-164 Kennedy art	£0.30	£0.90	£1.50
165 Leach art	£0.30	£0.90	£1.50
166 Stainless Steel Rat Saves the World by Ezquerra (ends #177)	£0.30	£0.90	£1.50
167 1st appearance Nemesis (Terror Tube) by O'Neill	£0.40	£1.20	£2.00
168 Leach art	£0.30	£0.90	£1.50
169	£0.30	£0.90	£1.50
170 scarce in the U.K. Alan Moore script, McMahon art	£0.40	£1.20	£2.00
171	£0.30	£0.90	£1.50
172-173 Bolland art	£0.40	£1.20	£2.00
174-177	£0.30	£0.90	£1.50
178 Mean Arena by John Richardson (ends #187, not in #181), Meltdown Man by Belardinelli (ends #227), Dash Decent by O'Neill (ends #198, not in #180), Nemesis (Killer Watt) by O'Neill (ends #179) all begin; Strontium Dog returns (ends #233, not in #198,199, #207-209)	£0.30	£0.90	£1.50
178 with free badge	£0.60	£1.80	£3.00
179-181	£0.30	£0.90	£1.50
182 Bolland art	£0.40	£1.20	£2.00
183-188	£0.30	£0.90	£1.50
189 Alan Moore script	£0.35	£1.05	£1.75
190-196	£0.30	£0.90	£1.50
197 Mean Arena returns (ends #202), Bolland cover	£0.30	£0.90	£1.50
198-199	£0.30	£0.90	£1.50

	GOOD	FINE	N.MINT
200	£0.50	£1.50	£2.50
201-204	£0.30	£0.90	£1.50
205 1st Steve Dillon Judge Dredd; Gary Leach art featured	£0.40	£1.20	£2.00
206-207 Unamerican Grafitti (1st appearance Chopper) by Ron Smith	£0.40	£1.20	£2.00
208	£0.30	£0.90	£1.50
209 Alan Moore script, 1st Colin Wilson Judge Dredd	£0.35	£1.05	£1.75
210-213	£0.30	£0.90	£1.50
214 Alan Moore script	£0.30	£0.90	£1.50
215 Gary Leach art	£0.30	£0.90	£1.50
216	£0.30	£0.90	£1.50
217 Alan Moore script	£0.30	£0.90	£1.50
218 Colin Wilson art	£0.30	£0.90	£1.50
219 Alan Moore script, Gary Leach and Colin Wilson art	£0.35	£1.05	£1.75
220-221	£0.30	£0.90	£1.50
222 Nemesis Book 1 begins by Kev O'Neill (ends #244, not in #234-237), Colin Wilson art	£0.30	£0.90	£1.50
223	£0.30	£0.90	£1.50
224 Judge Death Lives by Brian Bolland begins	£0.70	£2.10	£3.50
225 Brian Bolland and Colin Wilson art	£0.60	£1.80	£3.00
226 Brian Bolland and Gary Leach art	£0.60	£1.80	£3.00
227 Brian Bolland art	£0.60	£1.80	£3.00
228 Brian Bolland art; Rogue Trooper by Dave Gibbons begins (to #392, not in #244-245, #259, #263-264, #302, #356-357, #365)	£0.70	£2.10	£3.50
229-230 Colin Wilson art	£0.30	£0.90	£1.50
231	£0.25	£0.75	£1.25
232 less common in the U.K. Ace Trucking Co. by Belardinelli begins (to #293, not in #237-238, #286-287)	£0.40	£1.20	£2.00
233	£0.25	£0.75	£1.25
234 Alan Moore script	£0.30	£0.90	£1.50
235 less common in the U.K.	£0.35	£1.05	£1.75
236 McMahon Block Mania begins (ends #244)	£0.25	£0.75	£1.25
237 Alan Moore script	£0.30	£0.90	£1.50
238 scarce in the U.K. Alan Moore script	£0.40	£1.20	£2.00
239	£0.25	£0.75	£1.25
240 scarce in the U.K. Alan Moore script	£0.40	£1.20	£2.00
241-243	£0.25	£0.75	£1.25
244 Brian Bolland art	£0.40	£1.20	£2.00
245 Alan Moore script, Carlos Ezquerra Apocalypse War begins (ends #267)	£0.30	£0.90	£1.50
246 Alan Moore script, Nemesis Book 2 by Redondo begins (ends #257)	£0.30	£0.90	£1.50
247 Alan Moore script	£0.30	£0.90	£1.50
248	£0.25	£0.75	£1.25
249 Alan Moore script	£0.30	£0.90	£1.50
250	£0.25	£0.75	£1.25
251-254 Alan Moore scripts	£0.30	£0.90	£1.50
255-256	£0.25	£0.75	£1.25
257 Alan Moore script, Bryan Talbot art	£0.30	£0.90	£1.50
258	£0.25	£0.75	£1.25
259 Robo-Hunter returns (to #288, not in #273-274)	£0.25	£0.75	£1.25
260-264	£0.25	£0.75	£1.25
265 Alan Moore script, Dave Gibbons art	£0.30	£0.90	£1.50
266	£0.25	£0.75	£1.25
267 Alan Moore script, Dave Gibbons art	£0.30	£0.90	£1.50
268 Alan Moore script	£0.30	£0.90	£1.50
269 Alan Moore script, Dave Gibbons art	£0.30	£0.90	£1.50
270-273 Alan Moore scripts	£0.30	£0.90	£1.50
274-277	£0.25	£0.75	£1.25
278-286 Alan Moore scripts	£0.30	£0.90	£1.50
287 Harry Twenty by Alan Davis begins (ends #307)	£0.25	£0.75	£1.25
288-290 Alan Davis art	£0.25	£0.75	£1.25
291 Alan Moore script, Alan Davis art	£0.30	£0.90	£1.50
292 Alan Davis art; Robo-Hunter returns (to #334, not in #308-311)	£0.25	£0.75	£1.25
293-297 Alan Davis art	£0.25	£0.75	£1.25
298-299 Alan Moore script, Alan Davis art	£0.30	£0.90	£1.50
300 Alan Davis art	£0.50	£1.50	£2.50
301-307 Alan Davis art	£0.25	£0.75	£1.25
308 Skizz by Alan Moore and Jim Baikie begins (ends #330)	£0.30	£0.90	£1.50
309-316 Alan Moore scripts	£0.30	£0.90	£1.50
317 1st appearance D.R. and Quinch by Alan Moore and Alan Davis in a Future Shock story	£0.40	£1.20	£2.00
318-321 Alan Moore scripts	£0.30	£0.90	£1.50
322 Alan Moore script, Alan Davis art	£0.30	£0.90	£1.50
323-329 Alan Moore scripts	£0.30	£0.90	£1.50
330 Alan Moore script, Slaine by Angie Mills begins (to #367)	£0.30	£0.90	£1.50
331-332 Alan Moore scripts	£0.30	£0.90	£1.50
333-334	£0.25	£0.75	£1.25
335 1st McMahon Slaine; Nemesis Book 3 by Kev O'Neill begins (ends #349), Strontium Dog returns (to #385, not in #346-349, #360-362)	£0.40	£1.20	£2.00
336-349	£0.25	£0.75	£1.25
350 D.R. and Quinch by Alan Moore and Alan Davis returns (to #367, not in #360-362)	£0.40	£1.20	£2.00
351-359 Alan Moore scripts, Alan Davis and Mike McMahon art	£0.30	£0.90	£1.50
360-363	£0.25	£0.75	£1.25
364-367 Alan Moore scripts, Alan Davis art	£0.30	£0.90	£1.50
368-375	£0.25	£0.75	£1.25
376 Halo Jones Book 1 by Alan Moore and Ian Gibson begins (ends #385)	£0.40	£1.20	£2.00
377 Alan Moore script, Dredd Angel by Ron Smith returns (ends #383)	£0.30	£0.90	£1.50
378 Alan Moore script, AceTrucking Co. returns (to #400, not in #391)	£0.30	£0.90	£1.50
379-385 Alan Moore scripts	£0.30	£0.90	£1.50
386	£0.25	£0.75	£1.25

	GOOD	FINE	N.MINT
387 Nemesis Book 4 by Kev O'Neill begins (ends #406)	£0.25	£0.75	£1.25
388 Kev O'Neill art	£0.25	£0.75	£1.25
389-392 Bryan Talbot art on Nemesis	£0.25	£0.75	£1.25
393 Bryan Talbot art; City of the Damned begins (ends #406), Stainless Steel Rat for President by Carlos Ezquerra (ends #404)	£0.25	£0.75	£1.25
394-399 Bryan Talbot art on Nemesis	£0.25	£0.75	£1.25
400 Bryan Talbot art	£0.50	£1.50	£2.50
401 Bryan Talbot art; Rogue Trooper returns (ends #432)	£0.20	£0.60	£1.00
402-404 Bryan Talbot art on Nemesis	£0.20	£0.60	£1.00
405 Alan Moore script as Halo Jones Book 2 begins (ends #415); Bryan Talbot art	£0.30	£0.90	£1.50
406 Alan Moore script, Bryan Talbot art	£0.30	£0.90	£1.50
407-410 Alan Moore scripts	£0.30	£0.90	£1.50
411 Alan Moore script, Slaine returns by Glenn Fabry (to #434, not in #429-430)	£0.30	£0.90	£1.50
412 Alan Moore script, Glenn Fabry art	£0.30	£0.90	£1.50
413-415 Alan Moore scripts	£0.30	£0.90	£1.50
416 Anderson Psi Division by Brett Ewins begins (to #427), Strontium Dog returns (to #434)	£0.25	£0.75	£1.25
417-418 less common in the U.K.	£0.30	£0.90	£1.50
419 scarce in the U.K. Glenn Fabry art	£0.40	£1.20	£2.00
420-421 Glenn Fabry art	£0.30	£0.90	£1.50
422	£0.20	£0.60	£1.00
423 less common in the U.K.	£0.30	£0.90	£1.50
424 Midnight Surfer by Cam Kennedy begins (ends #430)	£0.25	£0.75	£1.25
425-426 less common in the U.K.	£0.30	£0.90	£1.50
427 scarce in the U.K. Glenn Fabry art	£0.40	£1.20	£2.00
428 Glenn Fabry art; Ace Trucking Co. returns (to #433)	£0.30	£0.90	£1.50
429-430	£0.20	£0.60	£1.00
431 Glenn Fabry and Bryan Talbot art	£0.30	£0.90	£1.50
432-434	£0.20	£0.60	£1.00
435 Nemesis Book 5 by Bryan Talbot begins (ends #445), Robo-Hunter returns (to #443)	£0.25	£0.75	£1.25
436-442 Bryan Talbot art	£0.20	£0.60	£1.00
443 Bryan Talbot art, last Robo-Hunter	£0.20	£0.60	£1.00
444 Bryan Talbot art, Rogue Trooper returns (to 449)	£0.20	£0.60	£1.00
445 Bryan Talbot art, Strontium Dog returns (to #587, not in #468, #500-504, #530-531, #537-539, #554-559, #574-577)	£0.20	£0.60	£1.00
446	£0.20	£0.60	£1.00
447 Slaine by Glenn Fabry returns	£0.25	£0.75	£1.25
448 Glenn Fabry art	£0.25	£0.75	£1.25
449-450	£0.20	£0.60	£1.00
451 Alan Moore script; Halo Jones Book 3 begins (ends #466), Ace Trucking Co. returns (ends #498, not in #473-474)	£0.30	£0.90	£1.50
452-455	£0.25	£0.75	£1.25
456 1st John Higgins Judge Dredd	£0.30	£0.90	£1.50
457-458	£0.25	£0.75	£1.25
459 Bryan Talbot art	£0.25	£0.75	£1.25
460-463	£0.25	£0.75	£1.25
464 1st Barry Kitson Judge Dredd	£0.30	£0.90	£1.50
465-467	£0.25	£0.75	£1.25
468 Bad City Blues by Robin Smith begins (ends #477), Sooner or Later by Brendan McCarthy and Riot begin (both end #499), Judge Anderson returns (to #499)	£0.30	£0.90	£1.50
469-473	£0.25	£0.75	£1.25
474-475 Kev O'Neill art	£0.25	£0.75	£1.25
476-481	£0.25	£0.75	£1.25
482 Nemesis Book 6 by Bryan Talbot begins (ends #504, not in #488-499)	£0.25	£0.75	£1.25
483 Metalzoic by Kev O'Neill begins (ends #492); (see DC Graphic Novel)	£0.25	£0.75	£1.25
484 Fists of Stan Lee by Barry Kitson (intro Deathfist)	£0.25	£0.75	£1.25
485-491	£0.25	£0.75	£1.25
492 Garry Leach art	£0.25	£0.75	£1.25
493 Slaine returns by Mike Collins and Mark Farmer	£0.25	£0.75	£1.25
494	£0.25	£0.75	£1.25
495 Rogue Trooper returns (to #499)	£0.25	£0.75	£1.25
496-499	£0.25	£0.75	£1.25
500 scarce in the U.K. wraparound glossy cover; Bad Company by Brett Ewins and Brendan McCarthy begins (to #519), Tharg's Head Revisited by Pat Mills and Alan Moore with Dave Gibbons, Mike McMahon, Cam Kennedy, Ian Gibson and Kev O'Neill	£1.00	£3.00	£5.00
501-503 Glenn Fabry and Bryan Talbot art	£0.25	£0.75	£1.25
504 Glenn Fabry and Kev O'Neill art	£0.25	£0.75	£1.25
505-508 Glenn Fabry art	£0.25	£0.75	£1.25
509	£0.20	£0.60	£1.00
510 1st The Dead by Pete Milligan and Belardinelli (ends ##579)	£0.25	£0.75	£1.25
511-512	£0.20	£0.60	£1.00
513 The Comeback (Jaxon Prince) by Garry Leach	£0.25	£0.75	£1.25
514-516	£0.20	£0.60	£1.00
517-519 Glenn Fabry art	£0.25	£0.75	£1.25
520 scarce in the U.K. 10th Birthday issue and 1st new look; Rogue Trooper by Steve Dillon (to #531), Anderson by Barry Kitson (to #532), Torquemada the God by Kev O'Neill begins (ends #524)	£0.50	£1.50	£2.50
521-524 Kev O'Neill art	£0.20	£0.60	£1.00
525 D.R. and Quinch agony page by Jamie Delano and Alan Davis with Mark Farmer begins (ends #534, not in #531)	£0.20	£0.60	£1.00
526-534	£0.20	£0.60	£1.00
535 Zenith Book 1 by Grant Morrison and Steve Yeowell begins (ends #550)	£0.25	£0.75	£1.25
536 scarce in the U.K.	£0.30	£0.90	£1.50
537-539	£0.20	£0.60	£1.00
540 scarce in the U.K.	£0.30	£0.90	£1.50
541 LD in the U.K.	£0.25	£0.75	£1.25

2000AD #2

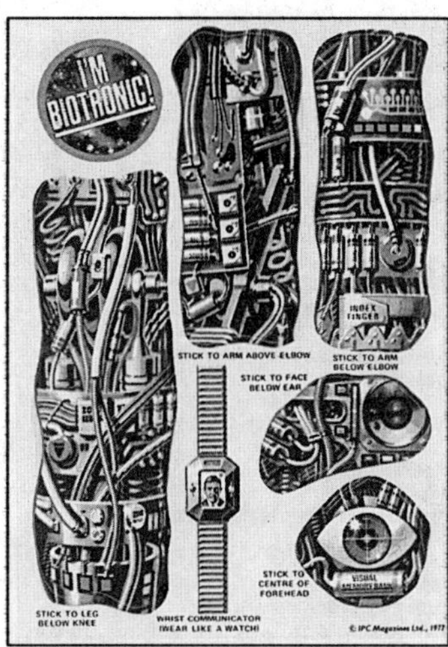

2000AD #2 (Bionic stickers)

2000AD #50

	GOOD	FINE	N.MINT
542 LD in the U.K. Freaks by Pete Milligan and John Higgins begins (ends #547)	£0.25	£0.75	£1.25
543 LD scarce in the U.K.	£0.25	£0.80	£1.40
544	£0.20	£0.60	£1.00
545 scarce in the U.K. Dredd in Oz begins (ends #570)	£0.30	£0.90	£1.50
546 Nemesis Book 7 by John Hinckleton begins (ends #557)	£0.20	£0.60	£1.00
547 scarce in the U.K.	£0.30	£0.90	£1.50
548 scarce in the U.K. Bad Company returns (to #557)	£0.30	£0.90	£1.50
549-553	£0.20	£0.60	£1.00
554 scarce in the U.K.	£0.30	£0.90	£1.50
555 scarce in the U.K. ABC Warriors return by Simon Bisley	£0.40	£1.20	£2.00
556-557	£0.20	£0.60	£1.00
558 Zenith "Interlude" begins (ends #559), Nemesis Book 8 by Davis Roach begins (ends #566)	£0.20	£0.60	£1.00
559	£0.20	£0.60	£1.00
560-561 scarce in the U.K.	£0.30	£0.90	£1.50
562	£0.20	£0.60	£1.00
563-565 scarce in the U.K.	£0.30	£0.90	£1.50
566-570	£0.20	£0.60	£1.00
571 Summer Magic by John Ridgway begins (ends #577)	£0.20	£0.60	£1.00
572	£0.20	£0.60	£1.00
573 ABC Warriors returns (ends #581)	£0.20	£0.60	£1.00
574-575	£0.20	£0.60	£1.00
576 Bad Company returns (ends #585)	£0.20	£0.60	£1.00
577 Glenn Fabry art	£0.25	£0.75	£1.25
578-581	£0.20	£0.60	£1.00
582 Slaine by Glenn Fabry	£0.25	£0.75	£1.25
583-584	£0.20	£0.60	£1.00
585 Judge Dredd by Alan Davis and Mark Farmer	£0.25	£0.75	£1.25
586 Nemesis Book 9 by John Hinckleton begins (ends #593)	£0.20	£0.60	£1.00
587-588	£0.20	£0.60	£1.00
589 new look and format; Slaine by Glenn Fabry returns (to #591), Zenith Book 2 begins (ends #606), Rogue Trooper returns	£0.25	£0.75	£1.25
590-591 Glenn Fabry art	£0.25	£0.75	£1.25
592-593	£0.20	£0.60	£1.00
594 Chopper by Colin MacNeil begins	£0.20	£0.60	£1.00
595-597	£0.20	£0.60	£1.00
598 Rogue Trooper returns (to #603)	£0.20	£0.60	£1.00
599	£0.20	£0.60	£1.00
600 Glenn Fabry art, Strontium Dog returns (to #606)	£0.30	£0.90	£1.50
601 Bad Company UKCAC story	£0.20	£0.60	£1.00
602-604	£0.15	£0.45	£0.80
605 Nemesis Book 9 returns (to #608)	£0.15	£0.45	£0.80
606	£0.15	£0.45	£0.80
607 Anderson returns (to #622, not in #610-611)	£0.15	£0.45	£0.80
608-613	£0.15	£0.45	£0.80
614 Swifty's Return by Pete Milligan and Jamie Hewlett (ends #617)	£0.15	£0.45	£0.80
615 Strontium Dog returns (to #621)	£0.15	£0.45	£0.80
616-618	£0.15	£0.45	£0.80
619 Medivac 318 by Hilary Robinson & Nigel Dobbyns begins (to #624)	£0.15	£0.45	£0.80
620-623	£0.15	£0.45	£0.80
624 Rogue Trooper retuns (to #635, not in #631-632)	£0.15	£0.45	£0.80
625	£0.15	£0.45	£0.80
626 Slaine the Horned God by Simon Bisley begins (to #635), Zenith Book 3 begins (to #634)	£0.60	£1.80	£3.00
627-629 Simon Bisley art	£0.50	£1.50	£2.50
630-634 Simon Bisley art	£0.40	£1.20	£2.00
635 Medivac returns (to #640, Anderson returns (to #647); Simon Bisley art	£0.40	£1.20	£2.00
636 Strontium Dog returns (to #647, not in #642-644)	£0.15	£0.45	£0.80
637-649	£0.15	£0.45	£0.80
650 new look Rogue Trooper by Dave Gibbons and Will Simpson begins (to #663), Deadman by Ridgway begins (to #662, continued in Judge Dredd), Slaine by Simon Bisley returns (to #656), Zenith returns (to #662)	£0.40	£1.20	£2.00
651-653 Simon Bisley art	£0.30	£0.90	£1.50
654 Chopper returns (to #665); Simon Bisley art	£0.30	£0.90	£1.50
655-656 Simon Bisley art	£0.30	£0.90	£1.50
657 Anderson returns (to #659)	£0.15	£0.45	£0.80
658-661	£0.15	£0.45	£0.80
662 Slaine by Simon Bisley returns (to #664), Tale of the Deadman (Dredd) begins	£0.30	£0.90	£1.50
663-664 Simon Bisley art	£0.25	£0.75	£1.25
665-666	£0.15	£0.45	£0.80
667 Rogue Trooper returns (to #671), Zenith returns (to #670)	£0.15	£0.45	£0.80
668 Dredd takes a long walk...	£0.15	£0.45	£0.80
669 Anderson returns (to #670)	£0.15	£0.45	£0.80
670	£0.15	£0.45	£0.80
671 new look Harlem's heroes by Michael Fleischer and Steve Dillon/ Kev Walker begins (to #705, not in #677-682, #700)	£0.20	£0.60	£1.00
672 Shadows by Pete Milligan and Richard Elson begins (ends #681)	£0.15	£0.45	£0.80
673	£0.15	£0.45	£0.80
674 Necropolis (Dredd) begins (ends #699)	£0.15	£0.45	£0.80
675-677	£0.15	£0.45	£0.80
678 Indigo Prime by John Smith and Chris Weston begins (to #682, not in #679)	£0.15	£0.45	£0.80
679-681	£0.15	£0.45	£0.80
682 Strontium Dog returns by Colin MacNeil (ends #687)	£0.15	£0.45	£0.80
683 Rogue Trooper returns (ends #687), Medivac returns (to #694)	£0.15	£0.45	£0.80
684-686	£0.15	£0.45	£0.80
687 death of Johnny Alpha in Strontium Dog	£0.20	£0.60	£1.00
688 Slaine by Simon Bisley returns (to#698)	£0.20	£0.60	£1.00

	GOOD	FINE	N.MINT
689-696 Simon Bisley art	£0.20	£0.60	£1.00
697 less common in the U.K. Simon Bisley art	£0.25	£0.75	£1.25
698 Simon Bisley art	£0.20	£0.60	£1.00
699	£0.15	£0.45	£0.80
700 Time Flies by Garth Ennis and Philip Bond (ends #711) and Hewligan's Haircut by Pete Milligan and Jamie Hewlett (ends #707) both begin, Nemesis & Deadlock one-off, Anderson by Arthur Ranson returns (to #711)	£0.40	£1.20	£2.00
701	£0.25	£0.75	£1.25
702-711	£0.20	£0.60	£1.00
712 Anderson by David Roach (ends #717) and Rogue Trooper both return	£0.15	£0.45	£0.80
713-717	£0.15	£0.45	£0.80
718-719 Danzig's Inferno by John Smith and Sean Philips	£0.15	£0.45	£0.80
720-722	£0.15	£0.45	£0.80
723 Robo-Hunter by Casanovas (to #734), Nemesis and Deadlock by Carl Critchlow (ends #729), Bix Barton (to #728) all return; Tao de Moto begins (ends #749); free Mega-Scan (poster)	£0.20	£0.60	£1.00
724-725 free Mega-Scan by Simon Bisley (Slaine, #724), Ian Gibson (Halo Jones, #725)	£0.20	£0.60	£1.00
726-729	£0.15	£0.45	£0.80
730 Rogue Trooper returns (to #741), Mean Machine by Richard Dolan begins (ends #736)	£0.15	£0.45	£0.80
731-734	£0.15	£0.45	£0.80
735 Killing Time by John Smith and Chris Weston (to #744)	£0.15	£0.45	£0.80
736	£0.15	£0.45	£0.80
737 Bix Barton returns (to #741)	£0.15	£0.45	£0.80
738-739	£0.15	£0.45	£0.80
740 Glenn Fabry Dredd	£0.20	£0.60	£1.00
741-743	£0.15	£0.45	£0.80
744 Revere by John Smith and Simon Harrison begins (to #749)	£0.20	£0.60	£1.00
745-749	£0.15	£0.45	£0.80
750 Democracy storyline in Dredd begins (to #756), Sam Slade returns (to #759), Strontium Dogs by Steve Pugh (ends #761), ABC Warriors by Kevin Walker (to #757); free data-chips (cards)	£0.25	£0.75	£1.25
751-752 free data-chips	£0.20	£0.60	£1.00
753-757	£0.15	£0.45	£0.80
758 Anderson by David Roach returns (ends #763)	£0.15	£0.45	£0.80
759-761	£0.15	£0.45	£0.80
762 Durham Red begins by Carlos Ezquerra (ends #773)	£0.15	£0.45	£0.80
763-766	£0.15	£0.45	£0.80
767 Skizz by Jim Baikie returns	£0.15	£0.45	£0.80
768-769	£0.15	£0.45	£0.80
770 Finn by Pat Mills and Jim Elston begins (to #779)	£0.15	£0.45	£0.80
771-779	£0.15	£0.45	£0.80
780 ABC Warriors by Kevin Walker returns (to #784), Rogue Trooper returns (to #791), The Button man by John Wagner and Arthur Ranson begins (ends #791)	£0.15	£0.45	£0.80
781-785	£0.15	£0.45	£0.80
786 Judgement Day (Judge Dredd Megazine cross-over) begins (ends #799)	£0.15	£0.45	£0.80
787 ABC Warriors by Kevin Walker returns (to #790)	£0.15	£0.45	£0.80
788-790	£0.15	£0.45	£0.80
791 Zenith returns (to #808)	£0.15	£0.45	£0.80
792 Sam Slade returns (to #802)	£0.15	£0.45	£0.80
793-799	£0.15	£0.45	£0.80
800 Flesh: Legend of Shamana begins (to #808), The Night Walker (Luke Kirby) begins (to #812)	£0.25	£0.75	£1.25
801-806	£0.15	£0.45	£0.80
807 Finn returns (to #816)	£0.15	£0.45	£0.80
808	£0.15	£0.45	£0.80
809 Revere returns (to #814)	£0.15	£0.45	£0.80
810-814 John Burns Dredd; Sam Slade returns in #813 (to #816)	£0.15	£0.45	£0.80
815 Brigand Doom returns (to #818)	£0.15	£0.45	£0.80
816	£0.15	£0.45	£0.80
817 John McCrea Dredd; Strontium Dogs returns (to #824), Flesh returns (to #825)	£0.15	£0.45	£0.80
818 John Higgins Dredd	£0.15	£0.45	£0.80
819 Colin MacNeil Dredd, Sam Slade returns (to #822)	£0.15	£0.45	£0.80
820	£0.15	£0.45	£0.80
821 Kelly's Eye by Alan McKenzie and Brett Ewins begins (to #830)	£0.15	£0.45	£0.80
822-827	£0.15	£0.45	£0.80
828 Bad Company returns (to #837), Firekind by John Smith and Paul Marshal begins (ends #840)	£0.15	£0.45	£0.80
829-833	£0.15	£0.45	£0.80
834 Purgatory by Mark Millar and Carlos Ezquerra begins (to #841)	£0.15	£0.45	£0.80
835-841	£0.15	£0.45	£0.80
842 Dredd: Inferno by Grant Morrison and Carlos Ezquerra (to #853), Big Dave by Morrison/Millar and Parkhouse, Slaughterbowl by Smith and Peart, Really & Truly by Morrison and Hughes, Maniac 5 by Millar and Yeowell all begin (and all end #849)	£0.20	£0.60	£1.00
843-849	£0.15	£0.45	£0.80
850 Strontium Dogs, Rogue Trooper, Luke Kirby by Ridgway, Slaine by Staples, return (all end #851)	£0.15	£0.45	£0.80
851	£0.15	£0.45	£0.80
852 Mean Arena by McKenzie and Williams begins, Tyranny Rex by Smith and Buckingham (to #859), Sam Slade by Hogan and Hughes (to #854), Slaine: Demon Killer by Mills and Fabry (to #859) return	£0.25	£0.75	£1.25
853-854 Glenn Fabry art	£0.20	£0.60	£1.00
855 Strontium Dogs returns (to #866)	£0.15	£0.45	£0.80
856-858 Glenn Fabry art	£0.20	£0.60	£1.00
859 Judge Dredd: Book of the Dead by Morrison/Millar and Power			

	GOOD	FINE	N.MINT
begins (to #866)	£0.15	£0.45	£0.80
860	£0.15	£0.45	£0.80
861 Cannon Fodder by Mark Millar and Chris Weston begins (ends #867)	£0.15	£0.45	£0.80
862-866	£0.15	£0.45	£0.80
867 Soul Gun Warrior by Shaky 2000 (to #872), Mother Earth by Bernie Jaye and Paul Neary/Cliff Robertson (ends #872), Revere Book III by Smith and Harrison begin (ends #872)	£0.15	£0.45	£0.80
868	£0.15	£0.45	£0.80
869 Big Dave returns (to #872)	£0.15	£0.45	£0.80
870-872	£0.15	£0.45	£0.80
873 Luke Kirby (to #877), Tyranny Rex, Rogue Trooper return, Dinosty by Mills and Clint Langley begins	£0.15	£0.45	£0.80
874-877	£0.15	£0.45	£0.80
878 The Grudge-Father by Mark Millar and Jim McCarthy begins (to #883)	£0.15	£0.45	£0.80
879-883	£0.15	£0.45	£0.80
884 John Higgins Dredd, Luke Kirby returns	£0.15	£0.45	£0.80
885 Bradley returns	£0.15	£0.45	£0.80
886-888	£0.15	£0.45	£0.80
889 Slaine by Dermot Power (to #889), Rogue Trooper (to #891) return, Mambo by David Hine begins (to #896)	£0.15	£0.45	£0.80
890	£0.15	£0.45	£0.80
891 Mark Harrison Dredd (to #894, story continued in Megazine #57)	£0.15	£0.45	£0.80
892-895	£0.15	£0.45	£0.80
896 Rogue Trooper returns (to #899)	£0.15	£0.45	£0.80
897 Strontium Dogs, Brigand Doom return (both to #899)	£0.15	£0.45	£0.80
898-899	£0.15	£0.45	£0.80
900 28pg Judge Dredd/Rogue Trooper cross-over story	£0.20	£0.60	£1.00
901 Dredd: Judge Death the True Story by Wagner & Gibson (to #902), Durham Red by Mark Harrison, Rogue trooper, Bradley, Nemesis return (all to #903)	£0.15	£0.45	£0.80
902	£0.15	£0.45	£0.80
903 John Burns Dredd	£0.15	£0.45	£0.80
904 Dredd: Wilderlands by Wagner & Ezquerra (to #914, Megazine cross-over. 13 by Mick Austin); Big Dave (to #907), ABC Warriors by Walker (to #911), Sam Slade (to #911) all return; The Button Man II by Wagner & Ranson begins (ends #919)	£0.15	£0.45	£0.80
905-907	£0.15	£0.45	£0.80
908 Red Razors by Millar & Nigel Dobbyn begins (ends #917)	£0.15	£0.45	£0.80
909-911	£0.15	£0.45	£0.80
912 Skizz III by Jim Baikie begins (ends #927), Bix Barton returns (to #917)	£0.15	£0.45	£0.80
913-917	£0.15	£0.45	£0.80
918 The Corps by Garth Ennis and Paul Marshall begins (ends #923)	£0.15	£0.45	£0.80
919 John Burns Dredd, Colin MacNeil pencils on The Corps begin	£0.15	£0.45	£0.80
920 52pgs, 18pg Dredd story by Ross Dearsley & Dermot Power, Soul Gun Assassin by Shaky kane (ends #925), Burns art also	£0.20	£0.60	£1.00
921-923	£0.15	£0.45	£0.80
924 Finn by Mills/Skinner & Liam Sharp returns (to #927; originally painted for Crisis)	£0.15	£0.45	£0.80
925-927	£0.15	£0.45	£0.80
928 Star Trek cover; Dredd: Crusade by Millar/Morrison & Austin begins (ends #937), Rogue Trooper (to #931), Finn by Mills/Skinner & Paul Staples (to #937), Harlem's Heroes (to #939) all return	£0.15	£0.45	£0.80
929-931	£0.15	£0.45	£0.80
932 Brigand Doom returns	£0.15	£0.45	£0.80
933-935	£0.15	£0.45	£0.80
936 Paul Johnson art	£0.15	£0.45	£0.80
937 Rogue Trooper, Strontium Dogs return (both to #939)	£0.15	£0.45	£0.80
938-939	£0.15	£0.45	£0.80
940 new look, Sylvester Stallone cover; Mambo by David Hine (to #947), Strontium Dogs by Simon Harrison (to #947), Finn by Staples (to #949), The Grudge-Father (to #945) all return	£0.20	£0.60	£1.00
941-945	£0.15	£0.45	£0.80
946 Rogue Trooper returns (to #949)	£0.15	£0.45	£0.80
947	£0.15	£0.45	£0.80
948 Tracer by Dave Stone & Paul Peart begins (ends #949)	£0.15	£0.45	£0.80
949	£0.15	£0.45	£0.80
950 new look, 44pgs; Judge Dredd x 2 begins (including The Return of Rico by Pat Mills and paul Johnson), Rogue Troopers by Charlie Adlard, Slaine by Greg Staples (to #956) returns	£0.20	£0.60	£1.00
951 Vector 13 begins	£0.20	£0.60	£1.00
952	£0.20	£0.60	£1.00
953 Chris Foss Dredd & cover; Janus: Psi Division by Grant Morrison/ Maggie Knight & Paul Johnson	£0.20	£0.60	£1.00
954 Foss cover; John Burns Dredd, Luke Kirby returns (to #963)	£0.20	£0.60	£1.00
955 Foss cover; John Higgins Dredd	£0.20	£0.60	£1.00
956 Maniac 5 by Steve Yeowell returns (to #963)	£0.20	£0.60	£1.00
957 Strontium Dogs one-off by Simon Harrison	£0.20	£0.60	£1.00
958 Slaine by Clint Langley returns (to #963)	£0.20	£0.60	£1.00
959 John Burns Dredd	£0.20	£0.60	£1.00
960 Durham Red by Simon Harrison returns (to #963), Dredd: Hammerstein by Mills/Skinner & Jason Brashill begins (to #963), Burns Dredd	£0.20	£0.60	£1.00
961-963 John Burns Dredd, Simon Harrison art	£0.20	£0.60	£1.00
964 Rogue Trooper, Chopper by John Higgins, ABC Warriors by Kev Walker return, PARAsites begins	£0.20	£0.60	£1.00
965-967	£0.20	£0.60	£1.00
968 Steve Yeowell Dredd	£0.20	£0.60	£1.00
969	£0.20	£0.60	£1.00
970 Dredd: The Pit by Wagner/Ezquerra begins	£0.20	£0.60	£1.00
971-972	£0.20	£0.60	£1.00
973 Flash returns by White/Abnett/Erskine (to #979)	£0.20	£0.60	£1.00
974	£0.20	£0.60	£1.00
975 Darkness Visible by Abadzis & Ridgway begins (to #979)	£0.20	£0.60	£1.00
976 Venus Blue Genes begins	£0.20	£0.60	£1.00
977-979	£0.20	£0.60	£1.00
980 Janus: Psi by Mark Millar and Paul Johnson begins	£0.20	£0.60	£1.00
981 Sinister Dexter begins (to 995, exc. 987)	£0.20	£0.60	£1.00
982-992	£0.20	£0.60	£1.00
993 Strontium Dogs by Trevor Hairsine returns (to 999)	£0.20	£0.60	£1.00
994-999	£0.20	£0.60	£1.00
1000 Slaine, Durham Red, (to 1006) return, Outlaw begins (to 1013)	£0.25	£0.75	£1.25
1001 Slaine: The Treasures of Britain by Mills/Power begins (to 1010), Black Light by Abnett/White/Burns begins (to 1013)	£0.20	£0.60	£1.00
1002-1006	£0.20	£0.60	£1.00
1007 Rogue Trooper returns	£0.20	£0.60	£1.00
1008-1010	£0.20	£0.60	£1.00
1011 Slaine: The Cloak of Fear by Mills/Tappin (to 1012)	£0.20	£0.60	£1.00
1012 Hairsine art	£0.20	£0.60	£1.00
1013 Tharg announces his departure to Quaxxann	£0.20	£0.60	£1.00
1014 Mazeworld by Grant & Ranson begins (to 1023), Mambo returns (to 1022) with X-Files series 2 trading cards pack on cover	£0.20	£0.65	£1.10
1015 Time Flies by Ennis and Bond returns (to 1023)	£0.20	£0.65	£1.10
1016-1020	£0.20	£0.65	£1.10
1021 Havok advertising brochure begins (to 1028)	£0.20	£0.65	£1.10
1022	£0.20	£0.65	£1.10
1023 44pgs, Sam Slade one-off, Sinister Dexter returns	£0.20	£0.65	£1.10
1024 Slaine, Janus Psi, Vector 13 return	£0.20	£0.65	£1.10
1025-1028	£0.20	£0.65	£1.10
Title Value:	**£351.45**	**£1059.50**	**£1882.85**

Note: issues 1-35 were uncredited, the main artists as follows: Dan Dare: Massimo Belardinelli in 1-23, Dave Gibbons in 28-35; Flesh by Juan Boix, Ramon Sola in 1-19; Harlem Heroes by Gibbons in 1-27; Judge Dredd by Belardinelli in 8, John Cooper in 19, Carlos Ezquerra in 5,10, Ian Gibson in 14,17,22,25,27,29,31,33,35, Mike McMahon in 2-4,6-7,12,15,18,20,23-24,26,28,30,32,34, Ron Turner in 9,11,13,16,21; various Kevin O'Neill art in 24,28; Brian Bolland covers on 11,13,19,20,23,27,30.

ARTISTS/FEATURES

Mick Austin in 612-613, 625-626, 629, 635, 639, 717, 746, 832-834, 840. Jim Baikie in 308-330, 369, 546, 569-573, 626, 658, 767-775, 912-927. Massimo Belardinelli in 1-24, 36-75, 86-97, 116, 127-128, 130-131, 134-142, 145-161, 178-227, 232-236, 244-285, 288-293, 296-297, 306-312, 314, 331-334, 337-344, 360-367, 370, 374-375, 378-390, 392-393, 396-400, 407, 424, 428-433, 437-447, 451-472, 475-483, 485-498, 510-519, 525-538, 551, 554, 557-558, 563, 565, 569, 570, 572, 591, 607, 616-617, 641-646, 670, 672, 760. Simon Bisley in 555-558, 563-566, 577-581, 626-635, 650-656, 662-664, 688-698. Jesus Blasco in 1-3. Brian Bolland in 41, 47, 50-61, 65, 67-70, 77-78, 81-82, 86-87, 94-95, 98, 101, 102, 110, 120, 122-123, 127, 149-151, 156, 162, 172-173, 182, 224-228, 244. Philip Bond in 700-711, 1015-1019. John Bums in 738, 754-756, 762-765, 810-814, 903, 919-920, 954. Mike Collins in 372, 493-499, 529-530, 539, 637 (script only in 509, 544, 554, 611, 636, 638). Carl Critchlow in 700, 723-729, 748, 800-808, 817-825, 829. Dave D'Antiques in 518, 524, 603, 608, 625, 632, 643, 664, 706-711, 717-722, 764-769, 771-773, 815-818. Alan Davis in 287-307, 317, 322, 350-359, 363-367, 509, 525-530, 532-534, 585. Steve Dillon in 189-190, 200, 205, 219-223, 242-243, 305-307, 322-328, 353, 374-375, 379-380, 393, 397-399, 404-405, 409, 442-443, 450, 479, 495-499, 505, 511-512, 520-531, 535-539, 561, 566-572, 574-575, 578, 582-584, 589, 598-600, (601 inks), 602-603, 609-610, 702-705 (624-630, 633-635, 671-676, 683-699, 701-703, 783-785 pencils). Gary Erskine in 741. Brett Ewins (often with Brendan McCarthy) in 37-38, 53-54, 88, 92-93, 96, 105, 113-115, 124, 161, 175, 206, 216, 260-261, 273-274, 286, 290-292, 299-301, 311-315, 323-326, 335-340, 359-363, 390-392, 500-519, 521, 523-524, 548-557, 576-585, 601, 750-759, 821-831, 841. Carlos Ezquerra in 5, 10, 34, 86-94, 102, 104-118, 140-162, 166-197, 200-206, 210-221, 224-233, 245-267, 269-272, 275-277, 281-288, 291-294, 296-297, 304, 308-314, 319-321, 331-345, 350-359, 363-385, 393-404, 416-434, 438-439, 445-467, 469-499, 505-529, 532-536, 544-553, 560-573, 638, 640, 651-655, 657-659, 669-699, 711-715, 719-720, 733-735, 762-773, 788-791, 794-797, 799, 815, 842-854, 867-871. Glenn Fabry in 411-412, 419-421, 427-428, 431, 447-448, 458-460, 500-508, 577, 579, 582, 589-591, 577, 600, 740, 852-858. Dave Gibbons art in 1-60, 64-78, 84-87, 91, 98-107, 109-126, 130-131, 157, 176, 181, 183-184, 196, 228-232, 234, 239-240, 249-250, 265, 267, 269, 310, 500. Script in 650-653, 667-671, 683-687. Ian Gibson in 14, 17, 22, 25, 27, 29, 31, 33, 35-36, 38, 42, 45-46, 48-51, 53-56, 76-84, 100-112, 116, 119-120, 127-130, 152-174, 188, 190-191, 195, 198-199, 201, 203-204, 208-209, 214, 220-223, 239-243, 259-272, 275-281, 283-288, 292-307, 312-442, 451-466, 468-469, 476, 496-498, 500, 521, 578-581, 780-782, 901-902. Simon Harrison in 522, 532-533, 539, 544-545, 552, 554, 559, 568, 580-583, 600-606, 615-621, 636-641, 645-647, 660-661, 666, 670, 682, 744-749, 795-799, 809-814, 885. Jamie Hewlett in 614-617, 700-707. John Hicklenton in 488, 515, 546-557, 586-593, 605-608. John Higgins in 108, 176, 202, 217, 241, 247-248, 252-253, 256, 272, 278, 289-290, 298, 309, 327, 434, 436, 456, 460, 471, 480, 494-495, 504, 531-533, 542-547, 564-565, 620-621, 650, 818, 884. Rian Hughes in 774-779, 842-849, 852-854. Cam Kennedy in 142-143, 146-153, 156-160, 163-164, 169, 265, 271, 278-284, 286-288, 293, 298, 304-310, 316-322, 327-332, 342-347, 350-355, 358-364, 366-377, 381-392, 401-406, 416, 418, 424-429, 435, 437, 440-441, 451-455, 458, 461-463, 466-467, 477-479, 500, 507-510, 514, 521, 643-645, 718. Barry Kitson in 437, 440, 464-465, 473, 475, 481-482, 484, 491, 493, 501, 506, 520-531, 540-541, 557, 566-568, 587, 629-630. Garry Leach in 58, 94-95, 103, 138, 141, 145, 148, 154-155, 161-162, 165, 168, 205, 215, 219, 492, 513, 520, 547-550. Brendan McCarthy (often with Brett Ewins) in 37-38, 54, 84-85, 88, 93, 105, 120, 127-128, 146, 166, 391-392, 468-501, 519, 549, 551-552, 558-560, 614. John McCrea in 817. Mike McMahon in 2-4, 6-7, 12, 15, 18, 20, 23-24, 26, 28, 30, 32, 34, 37, 39, 43-44, 58-64, 66-68, 70-76, 79-80, 83, 85, 89-91, 96-97, 99-100, 105-108, 113-115, 121-122, 125-126, 129, 132-133, 137-140, 144-145, 147, 160-161, 163, 166, 170-171, 176-178, 183-185, 193-196, 236-237, 245, 335-336, 345-359, 500. Colin MacNeil in 508-509, 526, 540-543, 578-579, 594-597, 608-611, 627-628, 636, 654-665, 736, 819. Paul Marshall in 625, 627, 638, 647, 649, 657, 671, 828-840, 856-859, 1017-1024+. Kevin O'Neill in 24, 28, 36, 41-49, 88, 90, 103-104, 111-112, 119, 123, 127-128, 167, 178-179, 181-198, 222-233, 238-240, 243-244, 335-349, 387-388, 430, 474-475, 483-492, 500, 520-524. Sean Phillips in 718-719, 800-803. Dermot Power in 722, 746-748, 760, 837-839, 859-866, 889-896, 1001-1010. Arthur Ranson in 635-644, 700-711, 720, 742, 780-791, 904-919, 1014-1023. John Ridgway in 377, 491, 525-526, 571-577, 588-591, 597, 605-606, 650-662, 708-716, 723-730, 800-812, 850-851. David Roach in 529-530, 539, 558-566, 614-622, 645-647, 669-670, 712-717, 758-763. Liam Sharp in 531, 534, 542-544, 575-576, 592-594, 599, 6632-634, 642, 924-927. William Simpson in 525, 535, 555-556, 561-563, 583-584, 586, 595-598, 603-604, 612, 623-625, 629-631, 637-643, 650-653, 662-665, 667-671, 683-687. Greg Staples in 761, 776-779, 804-807, 824-825, 830, 839, 850-851, 1019-1020. Joe Staton in 133. Bryan Talbot in 257, 389-406, 431, 435-445, 459, 482-487, 500-504. Kevin Walker in 594, 596, 599, 610, 612, 614, (624-630, 633-635, 671-676, 683-692, 696-699, 701-702 inks), 703, (704 pencils), 750-757, 780-784, 787-790. Colin Wilson in 209-210, 218-219, 229-230, 236-238, 241, 246-248, 251-253, 257-277, 285, 289. Steve Yeowell in 535-550, 558-559, 589-606, 626-634, 650-662, 667, 710, 716, 791-808, 842-849, 968.

2000AD ACTION SPECIAL

Fleetway Editions; Apr 1992

1992 new stories featuring classic Fleetway characters incl. Steel Claw by Sean Phillips, Cursitor Doom by Jim Baikie, Kelly's Eye by Brett Ewins, Mytek the Mighty by Shaky Kane,

N.MINT

The Spider by John Higgins/David Hine, Doctor Sin by John Burns £2.00

2000AD ANNUAL/YEARBOOK
Fleetway; 1977-1994

1978 Dredd by McMahon, O'Neill art £10.00
1979 Dredd by McCarthy, Ewins art £8.00
1980 Dredd by David Jackson £7.50
1981 Dredd by Ewins £4.00
1982 Dredd by Bolland, Moore script £4.50
1983 Dredd by "Emberton" (Gibson), Moore script, O'Neill art £3.50
1984 Moore script, Gibson art £3.50
1985 Dredd by Gibson, Moore script £3.50
1986 Dredd by Gibson, Cam Kennedy art £3.25
1987 Dredd by Talbot, Romero art £3.25
1988 Dredd by McCarthy/Riot/Ewins, O'Neill art £3.75
1989 Dredd by Higgins, Steve Parkhouse art £3.00
1990 Dredd by Hopgood, Morrison script £3.50
1991 Dredd, John Smith text story £3.50
1992 becomes 2000AD Yearbook, Dredd by Kennedy, Glen Fabry Slaine £5.00
1993 Dredd by Ewins, Ezquerra, Phillips art £6.00
1994 Dredd by Burns, Staples, Hughes, Marshall, Parkhouse art £6.00
1995 Dredd by Baikie £4.00

2000AD SCI-FI SPECIAL
(previously 2000AD Summer Special Supercomic)
IPC; nn May 1978-present

1978 Dredd by "Subliminal Kid" (McCarthy), Leach, O'Neill art, Ron Turner Rick Random reprint £6.00
1979 Dredd by Ewins, Leach art £4.50
1980 Dredd by Dillon, Moore script £4.00
1981 Dredd by Colin Wilson, Nemesis by O'Neill £3.50
1982 Dredd by Casanovas, Blackhawk by Joe Staton £3.25
1983 Dredd by John Byrne £2.75
1984 Dredd by Cliff Robinson, Ewins art £2.50
1985 Dredd by Cam Kennedy, D.R. and Quinch by Moore and Davis, McCarthy art £2.25
1986 Dredd by Dillon Fabry art £2.25
1987 Dredd by Collins/Farmer £1.75
1988 Dredd by Phil Elliott £1.50
1989 no Dredd, Judge Corey by Mick Austin £1.25
1990 Dredd reprint by Cam Kennedy, Bix Barton by Milligan & Jim McCarthy £1.25
1991 Dredd by Dermot Power, D'Antiques art £1.25
1992 Ridgway, Ewins, Phillips art £1.50
16 first numbered; D'Antiques, Hine, Beeston/MacNeil art £1.50
17 Dredd by Peter Doherty £1.50
18 Dredd by Paul Peart; Dredd movie feature £1.75
1996 Dredd by C.Bravery/Jack Couvela; Vector 13 supplement £2.00

2000AD SUMMER SPECIAL SUPERCOMIC
IPC; nn Jun 1977 (continues as 2000AD Sci-Fi Special)

nn scarce, Dredd by Kevin O'Neill £9.00

2000AD MONTHLY
Eagle/Quality; 1 Apr 1985-6 Sep 1985

1-4 £1.00
5, 6 Quality issues £0.90

2000AD PRESENTS/2000AD SHOWCASE
Quality/Fleetway-Quality; 1 Apr 1986-54 Nov 1990

1 £1.25
2-24 £0.80
25-26 becomes 2000AD Showcase £0.75
27/28 jointly numbered issue £0.75
29/30 jointly numbered issue; Zenith begins £0.75
31-45 features Zenith £0.75
46-54 £0.75

2000AD WINTER SPECIAL
Fleetway; 1 1988-present

1 Zenith by Morrison & Carmona, Dredd by Vanyo, Strontium Dog, Judge Anderson by Gibson, Rogue Trooper by Moore reprint £2.50
2 Dredd by Arthur Ranson, Rogue Trooper by Steve Dillon & Chris Weston £2.25
3 Dredd by Brett Ewins, Milligan, Smith scripts, Ezquerra art, Bisley cover 2.25
4 Dredd by Greg Staples, Walker, Weston art £2.25
5 Dredd by Paul Marshall, Morrison script, Ezquerra, MacNeil art £2.35
Alternity (1995) alternative worlds, incl. Judge Dredd, medievil Dredd £2.75

TWIN HEARTS
K.G. Murray (Australia); 1 1958-?

1 very rare, 100pgs squarebound begin; b/w romance reprints from National Periodical Publications; priced at 1 shilling £75.00
2-? £40.00

U

UFO ANNUAL
Polystyle; 1970

1971 £8.00

UNCANNY TALES
Alan Class; 1 May 1963-?

1 68pgs; various reprints from Atlas, Marval, Fawcett, etc.; scarce £12.00
2-? £2.50

UNCENSORED LOVE
Alan Class; 1 1960s

1 68pgs; US reprints £3.50

UNUSUAL TALES
Alexander Moring; 1 1959

1 36pgs; Charlton reprints £4.00

UNUSUAL TALES
Alan Class; 1 196?-?

1 68pgs; Charlton reprints £12.00

N.MINT

2-? £3.00

V

V FOR VENDETTA
Titan; 1990

nn reprints V For Vendetta 1-10 by Alan Moore & David Lloyd £10.00

VALIANT
Fleetway/IPC: 6th Oct 1962-16th Oct 1976 (713 unnumbered issues, joins Battle)

1 (6 Oct 1962) Captain Hurricane, Steel Claw by Ken Bulmer & Jesus Blasco, To Glory We Steer by Parker, Jack O'Justice (Dick Turpin reprints from Sun) begin £25.00
1 with free gift (League Ladders & Pocket Rocket) £60.00
13 Oct 1962 £10.00
20 Oct 1962 £5.00
27 Oct 1962-16 Feb 1963 £3.50
23 Feb 1963 1st "Valiant and also Knockout"; Kelly's Eye by Lopez £2.00
2 Mar 1963-21 Mar 1964, 4 Apr 1964-17 Sep 1964, 1 Oct 1964-1 Oct 1966 £2.00
28 Mar 1964 Wild Wonders by Tom Tully & Mike Western begins £2.00
24 Sep 1964 Mytek the Mighty by Bradbury begins £2.00
8 Oct 1966 House of Dolmann by Bradbury begins, 1st Bill Lacey Mytek £1.50
15 Oct 1966-6 Jan 1968, 20 Jan 1968-24 Feb 1968 £1.25
13 Jan 1968 Sexton Blake (from TV series) by Eric Dadswell begins £1.25
2 Mar 1968 Raven on the Wing by Solano Lopez begins £1.25
9 Mar 1968-9 May 1970, 30 May 1970-3 Apr 1971 £1.00
16 May 1970 last Steel Claw £1.00
23 May 1970 Slave of the Screamer by Tully & Blasco begins £1.00
10 Apr 1971 1st "Valiant and Smash!" £0.85
17 Apr 1971-29 May 1971, 12 Jun 1971-25 Sep 1971 £0.85
5 Jun 1971 Return of the Claw begins £0.85
2 Oct 1971 1st "Valiant and TV21"; Star Trek by John Stokes begins £0.75
9 Oct 1971-22 Dec 1973, 5 Jan 1974-18 May 1974 £0.75
29 Dec 1973 last Star Trek £0.75
18 May 1974 last Kelly's Eye, Raven, Wild Wonders £0.75
25 May 1974 1st "Valiant and Lion" £0.50
1 Jun 1974-13 Dec 1975, 27 Dec 1975-3 Apr 1976, 17 Apr 1976-16 Oct 1976 £0.40
20 Dec 1975 Death Wish (some by Ian Gibson), One-Eyed Jack by John Cooper begin £0.40
10 Apr 1976 1st "Valiant and Vulcan" (features Vulcan mini-comic) £0.40

ARTISTS/FEATURES
Jesus Blasco in 6 Oct 1962-13 Apr 1968, 2 May 1970 (Steel Claw), 23 May 1970-3 Apr 1971 (Slave of the Screamer), 5 Jun 1971-27 Oct 1973 (Return of the Claw).
Note: jointly dated issue 6/13 Jun 1970, no issues dated 21 Nov 1970-30 Jan 1971, 19 Jan 1974, 2 Feb 1974, 16 Feb 1974, 6 Jul-27 Jul 1974.

VALIANT ANNUAL
Fleetway; 1964-1984

1964 £15.00
1965 Blasco art £12.50
1966 Blasco art £8.00
1967-1969 £5.00
1970-1979 £3.00
1980-1984 £2.00

VALIANT BOOK OF...
Fleetway; 1967, 1968, 1971, 1972, 1975

Pirates (1967) oversize £5.00
TV's Sexton Blake 1969 £12.50
Conquest of the Air 1972 £2.50
Sports 1973 £2.50
Magic and Mystery 1976 £5.00
Weapons and War 1976 £2.50

VALIANT PICTURE LIBRARY
Fleetway; 1 Jun 1963-144 May 1969

1 60pgs pocket size; War Eagle by Ferdinando Tacconi (reprint from Comet) £3.00
2-5 incl. reprints from Thriller Picture Library £2.00
6-49 incl. reprints from Thriller Picture Library £1.50
50-144 mostly reprints from Air Ace, Battle, War picture libraries £1.00

ARTISTS
Luis Bermejo. Robert Forrest. Solano Lopez. Hugh McNeill in 9.

VALIANT SPACE SPECIAL
Fleetway; 1967-1968

1967 incl. Steel Claw £7.50
1968 incl. Steel Claw, scarce £10.00

VALIANT STORY OF THE WEST
Fleetway; 1-2 Apr 1966

1 Westward Ho! £3.00
2 The Far Frontier £3.00
Note: Reprints Italian series Storia Del West by Gino D'Antonio & Renato Polese

VALIANT SUMMER SPECIAL
Fleetway/I.P.C. Magazines; 1966-1980

1966 96pgs £10.00
1967-1969 96pgs £7.50
1970-1973 96pgs £5.00
1974-1976 80pgs £4.00
1977-1980 64pgs £2.50

VALOUR
Marvel; 1 5th Nov 1980-19 11th Mar 1981 (joins Future Tense)

1 32pgs; Conan, Dr. Strange, Devil Dinosaur, Tales of Asgard reprints begin; slightly larger size than following issues £1.25
1 with free gift (Devil Dinosaur jigsaw piece) £2.50
2-3 £0.75
2-3 with free gifts (Devil Dinosaur jigsaw piece) £1.50
2-19 £0.45

VALOUR WINTER SPECIAL
Marvel; Nov 1980

	N.MINT
nn 64pgs; Thor and Dr Strange reprints in b/w, colour centre-fold poster and pin-ups	£1.25
VAMPIRELLA	
I.P.C. Magazines; 1 Feb 1975-4 May 1975	
1-4 48pgs; Warren reprints	£1.50
VAMPS	
Titan; Mar 1996	
nn 144pgs; reprints Vertigo series by Lee & Simpson	£9.00
VAULT OF HORROR	
Arnold Book Co.; 1 1954	
1 68pgs; E.C. reprints, cited in UK horror campaign	£45.00
Note: This is a minimum expected price as no known copies exist. The title was advertised in other Arnold publications, and cited in contemporary newspapers, and it is thought that nearly all copies were pulped during the 1950s horror comics clampdown.	
VCS, THE	
Titan (Best of 2000AD); 1987	
Book One	£4.50
Book Two	£5.00
VELOCITY	
Warren & Garry Pleece; 1 1988-5?	
1-5 all material by Warren & Garry Pleece	£1.50
VENDETTA ON GOTHAM	
(see Batman/Judge Dredd: Vendetta on Gotham)	
VIC TORRY AND HIS FLYING SAUCER	
Miller; 1 1950	
1 32pgs; Fawcett reprints, Bob Powell art	£20.00
VICTOR, THE	
D.C. Thomson; 1 25th Feb 1961-1657 21st November 1992	
1 scarce; I Flew With Braddock by Keith Shone begins	£25.00
1 very scarce; with free gift (Super Squirt Ring)	£50.00
2 H.K. Rodd The Wonder Man begins	£10.00
2 with free gift (Sportsman's Wallet and team photo Man Utd. & Wolves)	£20.00
3-5	£5.00
6-10	£2.25
11-57, 59-70, 72-108	£1.00
58 The Smasher by F.A. Philpott begins	£1.00
71 The Tough of the Tracks by Peter Sutherland begins	£1.00
109 Morgyn the Mighty by Ted Kearon begins	£0.60
110-624	£0.50
625 Cadman by Mike Dorey begins	£0.50
626-660, 662-1115, 1117-1657	£0.30
661 The Hammer Man by Ted Rawlings begins	£0.30
1116 The Rule of Rogat by Alcatena begins	£0.30
ARTISTS	
Alcatena in 1116-1131, 1211-1226, 1284-1299, 1338-1359, 1456-1472, 1485-1494, 1527-1538, 1570-1588, 1611-1618, 1632-1635, 1653-1657.	
VICTOR BOOK FOR BOYS, THE	
D.C. Thomson; 1964-1992	
(1964) (some commandos leaving a boat at St. Nazair)	£15.00
(1965) (two canoes each with two commandos)	£10.00
1966	£7.50
1967-1969 first dated	£5.00
1970-1975	£3.00
1976-1992	£2.00
VICTOR FOR BOYS SUMMER SPECIAL	
D.C. Thomson; 1967-1992	
1967 32pgs; dinosaur cover	£3.00
1968-1970	£1.50
1971-1975	£0.75
1975-1992	£0.50
VIOLENT CASES	
Escape; Oct 1987	
nn Neil Gaiman & Dave McKean	£5.00
nn (Titan, Jul 1991) colour edition	£5.00
VIZ COMIC	
Viz Comics/John Brown; 1 Dec 1979-present (81 to Dec 1996/Jan 1997)	
1 12pgs, rare (150 copies)	£100.00
2 16pgs, rare	£65.00
3 scarce	£45.00
4 scarce	£30.00
5-9 scarce	£20.00
10-15	£8.00
16-19	£6.00
20-24	£4.00
25-31	£2.50
32-39	£2.00
40-45	£1.50
46-59	£1.00
60-81	£1.25
Best of Viz 1-4 (Nov 1983), 20pgs	£10.00
Viz Monster Sex Remix (May 1985), best of 5-6	£7.50
Viz Big Hard One hardback, best of 1-12	£5.50
Viz Big Hard One softback	£5.00
Viz Big Hard One Number Two hardback, best of 13-18	£6.00
Viz Big Pink Stiff One (1988) hardback, best of 19-25	£6.00
Viz The Dog's Bollocks (1989) hardback, best of 26-31	£6.00
Viz Book of Crap Jokes hardback (small)	£4.00
The Spunky Parts (1990) hardback, best of 32-37	£7.00
Billy the Fish Football Yearbook (1990)	£3.50
Pathetic Sharks Bumper Special (Jun 1991)	£3.00
The Sausage Sandwich (1991) hardback, best of 38-42	£7.00
The Fish Supper (1992) hardback, best of 43-47	£7.00
Bumper Book of Absolute Shite For Older Boys and Girls (1993) hardback	£6.00

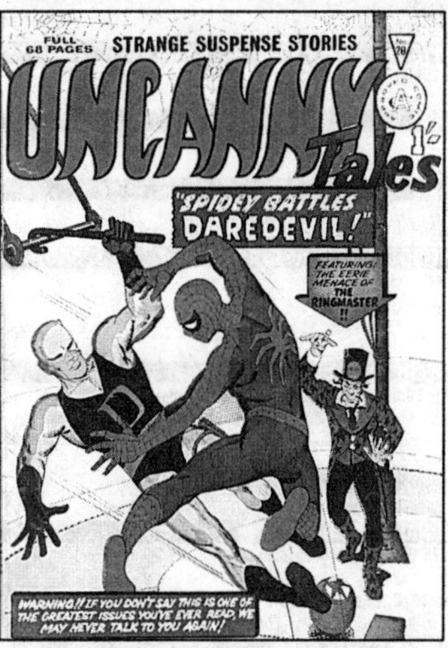

Uncanny Tales #28

Victor #15

Walt Disney Series #1

N.MINT

The Porky Chopper (1993) hardback, best of 48-52 £7.00
The Big Bell End (1995) hardback, best of 58-62 £8.00

VIZ HOLIDAY SPECIAL
John Brown; Jul 1988
1988 softback £4.00

VOLTRON ANNUAL
World; 1987
1987 Japanese anime robot £2.00

VOODOO
Miller; 1-8 1961
1-8 68pgs; Atlas reprints £5.00

VOYAGE TO THE BOTTOM OF THE SEA ANNUAL
World Distributors; 1965-1967
cy1965 £10.00
cy1966 £10.00
cy1967 £8.00

VULCAN (SCOTTISH EDITION)
IPC: 1st Mar 1975-20th Sep 1975 (30 unnumbered issues)
1 Mar 1975 Mytek the Mighty by Bradbury, The Spider by Reg Bunn, Saber, King of the Jungle by Colquhoun, The Trigan Empire by Don Lawrence, The Steel Claw by Jesus Blasco, Kelly's Eye by Solano Lopez, Robot Archie by Bert Bus reprints all begin £4.00
8 Mar-19 Apr, 3 May-20 Sep 1975 £2.00
26 Apr 1975 McLoughlin Saber reprints begin £2.00

VULCAN (NATIONAL EDITION)
IPC: 27th Sep 1975-3rd Apr 1976 (28 unnumbered issues, joins Valiant)
27 Sep 1975 reprints continue from Scotish edition £1.50
4 Oct 1975-17 Jan 1976, 7 Feb-3 Apr 1976 £1.00
24 Jan 1976 Ron Embleton Trigon Empire reprints £1.00

VULCAN ANNUAL
Fleetway; 1977
1977 softback, Don Lawrence reprints £6.00

VULCAN HOLIDAY SPECIAL
IPC; Jun 1976
1976 64pgs; McLoughlin, Blasco reprints £3.50

VULCAN MINI-COMIC
IPC; 10th Apr 1976-24th Apr 1976 (3 unnumbered issues, supplement to Valiant)
nn severely edited reprints £0.25

W

WALT DISNEY SERIES
World Distributors; 1 1956-52 1957
1 36pgs; Dell reprints £4.00
2-52 £2.00
FEATURES
Chip 'n' Dale in 12, 20, 31, 38, 50. Donald Duck in 2, 6, 10.14.17, 28, 32, 37, 47. Goofy in 3, 7, 11, 15, 18, 36. Jiminy Cricket in 16. Lady & the Tramp in 4, 8. Mickey Mouse in 1, 5, 9, 13, 21, 27, 35, 40, 51. Pluto in 19, 49. Scamp in 24, 25, 34, 45. Uncle Scrooge in 22, 52.

WALT DISNEY'S MICKEY MOUSE
Walt Disney Productions; 1 4th Jan 1958-56 19th Jan 1959 (becomes Walt Disney's Weekly)
1 12pgs gravure; features Disney characters £4.00
2-56 £2.00

WALT DISNEY'S NOW I KNOW
IPC; 1-26 1972
1 £2.50
2-26 £1.00

WALT DISNEY'S PICTURE TREASURY
IPC; 1972-1976
Snow White 32pgs £0.50
Robin Hood £0.50
Peter Pan £0.50
Lady and the Tramp 48pgs £0.50
Jungle Book £0.50

WALT DISNEY'S UNCLE REMUS AND HIS TALES OF BRER RABBIT
Collins; 1947
nn 16pgs; Dell reprints adapting Song of the South £3.00

WALT DISNEY'S WEEKLY
Walt Disney Productions; 1 26th Jan 1959-118 24th Apr 1961 (joins Harold Hare's Own Paper)
1 16pgs gravure; features Disney features £3.00
2-118 £1.50

WAR
Miller; 1 1961-11 1962
1-11 52pgs; Atlas War Comics reprints £2.00

WAR AT SEA
Miller; 1 1958-?
1 28pgs; Charlton reprints £2.00

WAR AT SEA PICTURE LIBRARY
Fleetway Publications; 1 Feb 1962-36 Jul 1963
1 68pgs pocket size; Devil's Cargo by Farrugia £3.00
2-36 £1.50
ARTISTS/FEATURES
1 Devil's Cargo by Farrugia. 2 Killer Fish by Gino D'Antonio. 3 The Nelso Touch by Jose Ortiz. 4 Escort by Gino D'Antonio. 5 Engage the Enemy by Farrugia. 6 The Long Haul by Juan Zanotto. 7 I Vow Vengeance by Gino D'Antonio. 8 Leatherneck by Victor de la Fuente. 9 Down Ramps. 10 Man of War. 11 Repel Borders by Roberto Diso. 12 Torpedo Run by Jorge Macabich. 13 The Navy Way by Aldoma Puig. 14 Ram - and Wreck by John Gillatt. 15 Crash Dive by Roberto Diso. 16 Destroyer by Farrugia. 17 To Strike Unseen. 18 Q-Ship. 19 Close Quarters by Solano Lopez. 20 Mosquito Navy. 21 The Thunder of Guns by Nevio Zeccara. 22 False Colours by Jesus Blasco. 23 Clear for Action by Renzo Calegari. 24 Flight Deck by Solano Lopez. 25 The Blind Eye by Giorgio Trevisan. 26 Ship-o-the-Line by Farrugia. 27 Errand of Mercy. 28 Sea Devil by John Gillatt. 29 Storm Centre. 30 The Savage Deep by Farrugia. 31 Fire All Guns. 32 Shock Wave. 33 Hazard Below by Jorge Moliterni. 34 Battle Stations by Hugo Pratt. 35 Wolf Pack. 36 Colours Flying.

N.MINT

WAR PICTURE LIBRARY
Amalgamated/Fleetway/IPC; 1 Sep 1958-2103 Dec 1984
1 60pgs pocket size; Fight Back to Dunkirk by Nevio Zeccara £15.00
2 £10.00
3-5 £7.50
6-20 £5.00
21-50 £2.50
51-571 £1.00
572-2103 68pgs; mostly reprints £0.75
ARTISTS/FEATURES
1 Fight Back to Dunkirk by Nevio Zeccara. 2 Wings of Victory (2 stories) by Nevio Zeccara. 3 Action Stations by Renzo Calegari. 4 The Gallant Few by Renzo Calegari. 5 The Ship That Ran Away by Renzo Calegari. 6 For Valour (3 stories) by Nevio Zeccara, Reg Bunn. 7 The Red Devils by Gino D'Antonio. 8 Wings Over the Navy by Fred T. Holmes. 9 Bombs Away by Renzo Calegari. 10 Up Periscope by Nevio Zeccara. 11 Tracy of Tobruk by Renzo Calegari. 12 Course For Danger by Fred T. Holmes. Artists include Gino D'Antonio. Victor de la Fuente. Fernando Fernandez. Ian Kennedy. Solano Lopez. Hugo Pratt in 25, 40, 50, 58, 62, 91, 92, 133, 791, 992, 1102. Ferdinando Tacconi. Ron Turner in 1047, 1147, 1206, 1218, 1231, 1243, 1291, 1338, 1362, 1399, 1764, 1797, 1805, 1809, 1950, 1962, 1980, 2010, 2058.

WAR PICTURE LIBRARY HOLIDAY SPECIAL
I.P.C. Magazines; Jul 1963-?
1963 224pgs £3.00
1964-1969 £2.00
1970-present £1.25

WARHEADS
(see Overkill)
Marvel; 1 Jun 1992-14 Aug 1993
1 1st appearance Warheads, Wolverine guests, Gary Erskine art £1.50
2 Gary Erskine art £1.20
3 Iron Man guests £1.20
4-5 X-Force guest £1.20
6-7 £1.20
8 X-Men, Silver Surfer guest £1.20
9-10, 12-14 £1.20
11 MyS-TECH Wars x-over, Death's Head II guests £1.20

WARHEADS: BLACK DAWN
Marvel; 1 Jul 1993-2 Aug 1993
1-2 Charlie Adlard art £1.20

WARLORD
D.C. Thomson; 1 28th Sep 1974-627 27th Sep 1986 (joins Victor)
1 Union Jack Jackson by Carlos Cruz, Bomber Braddock, Code-Name Warlord, Young Wolf begin £1.50
1 with free gift (8 golden replica medals) £3.00
2-5 £0.75
6-17, 19-120, 122-219 £0.50
18 Drake of E-Boat Alley by Ron Smith begins £0.50
121 Killer Kane by Colin Andrew begins £0.50
220 1st "Warlord and Bullet"; Fireball begins £0.30
221-450, 452-627 £0.30
451 Sabor's Army by Alcatena begins £0.30
ARTISTS
Alcatena in 451-466. Belardinelli in 403, 479, 482, 484, 486, 492, 500, 503. Denis McLoughlin in 248-257, 267-299, 353-363. Ron Smith in 3, 10, 17-36, 75 (some stories reprinted later).

WARLORD BOOK FOR BOYS
D.C. Thomson; 1976-1984
1976 £3.00
1977-1980 £2.50
1981-1984 £2.00

WARLORD PETER FLINT SPECIAL
D.C. Thomson; 1976
nn 32pgs tabloid £0.75

WARLORD SUMMER SPECIAL
D.C. Thomson; 1975-?
1975 32pgs tabloid £1.25
1976-1980 32pgs £0.75
1981-? 36pgs £0.50

WARRIOR
Derek G. Skinn/Penwith Publications; 1 1974-6 1975
1 Wrath of the Gods, Kelpie the Boy Wizard both by John Burns, Erik the Viking by Don Lawrence, Heros the Spartan by Frank Bellamy, Olac the Gladiator by Don Lawrence, Black Axe by Tom Kerr, all reprints £2.50
2 Thong by Steve Parkhouse begins £1.25
3-4 £1.25
5 Horatius, the Hero of Rome by Del Castillo begins, McKie art £1.25
6 Swordspell by Booth & Jackson begins (continued in Fantasy Advertiser) £1.25

WARRIOR
Quality: 1 Mar 1982-26 Feb 1985, 1996 Spring Special
1 1st modern Marvelman (later Miracleman) by Alan Moore & Garry Leach, Laser Eraser and Pressbutton by Pedro Henry (Steve Moore) & Steve Dillon, V For Vendetta by Alan Moore & Dave Lloyd, Spiral Path by Parkhouse, Legend of Prester John by S. Moore & Bolton, Father Shandor reprints by Steve Moore & Bolton begin, 2pg by Gibbons £5.00
2 Madman by Paul Neary begins £3.50
3 1st Zirk by Henry and Bolland £3.50
4 52pgs; "Summer Special", Marvelman by A. Moore, Dillon, Neary & Davis, Golden Amazon by Lloyd, Pressbutton origin by Henry & David Jackson £3.50
5 new Shandor series by S. Moore & Jackson begins, 1st Neary & Austin Madman £3.50
6 1st Davis/Leach Marvelman, Gibbons reprint £3.00
7 last Madman (story incomplete) £5.00
8 1st Davis Marvelman, Hunt Emerson art £3.00
9-10 Warpsmith by Moore & Leach £3.00
11 Laser Eraser ends £2.50
12 last Spiral Path, Bojeffries Saga by Moore & Parkhouse begins, Young Marvelman by Moore & Ridgway £2.50
13 Bojeffries ends, Zirk by Henry & Leach £2.50
14 Twilight World by S.Moore & Jim Baikie begins, Ektryn by Henry & Cam Kennedy £2.00

N.MINT

15 Laser Eraser returns (one isssue only, story unfinished) £2.00
16 Laser Eraser reprint from Sounds £2.00
17 no Marvelman, V, Shandor £2.00
18 Parkhouse, Asbury reprints from Halls of Horror £2.00
19 Bojeffries returns (ends 20), Big Ben by Skinn & William Simpson begins, no Marvelman £2.50
20 V filler by Lloyd & Tony Weare £2.50
21 Marvelman ends (unfinished) under threat of legal action from Marvel Comics, 1st Davis Laser Eraser/Pressbutton £2.50
22 1st Bogey European reprint by Segura & Sanchez, no Shandor, Laser Eraser £2.00
23 1st John Ridgway Shandor £2.50
24 no Bogey £2.50
25 Ektryn by Kennedy, Shandor by John Stokes; Laser Eraser ends £2.50
26 Garry Leach Zirk, Liberators by Morrison & Ridgway; scarce £3.00
1996 Spring Special published as a flip-book with Comics International #67 (Apr 1996) incl. concluding episode of The Liberators by Morrison & Ridgway £1.00

ARTISTS

Horacio Altuna in 25-26. Martin Asbury in 18. Jim Baikie in 14-17. Brian Bolland in 3. John Bolton in 1-3. Alan Davis 4, 8-11, 13-16, 18, 20-21, 24-25 (pencils 6-7). Steve Dillon in 1-11, 15. Hunt Emerson in 8. Dave Gibbons in 1, 6. David Jackson in 4-10, 13-21. Cam Kennedy in 14, 25. Garry Leach in 1-3, 5, 9-10, 13, 26 (inks 6-7). David Lloyd in 1-16, 18-26. Steve Parkhouse in 1-2, 4-8, 12-13, 18-20 (pencils 3, 9-12). John Ridgway in 12-13, 17, 22-24, 26 (inks 9-12). William Simpson in 19-24 (pencils 25-26). Alan Moore script in 1-26. Steve Moore script in 1-21, 23-26. Grant Morrison script in 26. Steve Parkhouse script in 1-13, 17-18.

WARRIOR WOMEN
Marvel; Jun 1980
nn 52pgs; US reprints £1.00

WATCHMEN
Titan; 1988
nn reprints Watchmen 1-12 by Alan Moore & Dave Gibbons £11.00

WEIRD PLANETS
Alan Class; 1 1962-21 1963
1 68pgs; various reprints from Atlas, Charlton , A.C.G., etc £12.50
2-5 £6.00
6-10 £4.00
11-21 £2.50

WEIRD WORLDS
Thorpe & Porter; 1 Mar 1953-?
1 68pgs; Atlas reprints £12.50
2-5 £5.00
6-20 £2.50
21-? £1.50

WEREWOLF
Marvel; Oct 1981
nn 52pgs; US reprints £1.00

WESTERN CLASSICS
World Distributors; 1 Feb 1958-40?
1 36pgs; Gunsmoke, Dell reprints £5.00
2-40 incl. various western reprints £3.00

WESTERN CLASSICS
Top Sellers; 1 1972
1 36pgs; Dell reprints £2.00
2-? £0.75

WESTERN COMIC ALBUM
World Distributors; Sep 1955-Sep 1957
nn £4.50
2-3 £4.00

WESTERN GUNFIGHTERS SPECIALS
Marvel; Jun 1980-Oct 1981
Summer Special 1980 Bellamy cover, Barry Smith, Kirby, Williamson reprints £1.25
Summer Special 1981 £1.00
Winter Special 1981 £0.75

WESTERN HERO
Miller; 50 Sep 1950-149 1959, 100 issues (became Heroes of the West)
50 28pgs; Fawcett reprints £5.00
51-149 £3.00

WESTERN KID
Miller; 1-12 1955
1 28pgs; Atlas reprints £4.00
2-12 £2.00

WESTERN KILLERS
Streamline; 1950s
nn 6d £5.00
nn 1/- £4.00

WESTERN OUTLAWS
Miller; 1-2 1954
1-2 28pgs; Marvel reprints £4.00

WESTERN OUTLAWS
Gerald Swan; 1-8 1954
1 36pgs; US reprints £3.00
2-8 £2.00

WESTERN OUTLAWS
Streamline; 1-nn 1955
1-2, nn 28pgs; reprints from Prize Westerns (Prize), Red Hawk (ME) £3.00

WESTERN ROUGH RIDERS
Streamline; 1955, 2 unnumbered issues
nn 28pgs; Stanmor Publications reprints £5.00
nn 68pgs £5.00

WESTERN ROUND-UP ANNUAL
World Distributors; 1955-Aug 1958
cy1955 £5.00
(1956) Gene Autry, Roy Rogers, Johnny Mack Brown, Dale Evans; Dell reprints £5.00
cy1957 Gene Autry, Roy Rogers, Range Rider; Dell reprints £5.00
cy1958 Wells Fargo, Wagon Train, Range Rider; Dell reprints £5.00

WESTERN ROUNDUP COMIC
World Distributors; 1 Jan 1955-40 1958
1 28pgs; Dell reprints £5.00
2-40 £3.00

WESTERN STARS COMIC
Miller; 1 1952-17 1958
1 68pgs; Fawcett reprints, incl. Ken Maynard, Hopalong Cassidy, Tom Mix, etc. £10.00
2-17 £5.00

WESTERN SUPER THRILLER COMICS
World Distributors; 34 195?-82 195? (previously Super Thriller)
34-82 incl. James Bleach, Terrence Patrick, Gerry Embleton art £5.00

WESTERN TALES
World Distributors; 1 1955
1 28pgs; Harvey Publications reprints £5.00

WESTERN TALES
United Anglo-American; 1-2 1956
1-2 28pgs; Harvey Publications reprints £4.00

WESTERN THRILLER
Streamline; 1 1955
1 68pgs; various reprints from Prize Publications, Fiction House £5.00

WESTERN THRILLERS
Streamline; 1 1950
1 28pgs; Fox Features reprints £4.00

WESTERN TRAILS
Miller; 1-5 1957
1-5 28pgs; Atlas reprints £3.00

WHAM!
Odhams: 1 20th Jun 1964-187 13th Jan 1968 (joins Pow!)
1 General Nitt, The Tiddlers, Eagle Eye, Biff, Pest of The West, George's Germs (all by Baxendale), Kelpie the Boy Wizard by Ken Mennell & John Burns begin £25.00
1 with free gift (Wham! Gun) £50.00
2 £12.50
3 £7.50
4 Frankie Stein by Ken Reid begins £6.00
5-10 £5.00
11-36 £4.00
37 Johnny Straight by Don Lawrence (Wells Fargo reprints from Zip) begin £3.00
38-50 £3.00
51-111 £2.00
112 Fantastic Four reprints begin £2.00
113-187 £1.50

WHAM! ANNUAL
Odhams; 1966-1974
1966 £7.50
1967-1969 £5.00
1970-1972 £3.00
1973-1974 titled Wham! and Pow! Annual £2.50

WHITE TRASH
Tundra (Atomeka); 1 Sep 1992-4 Jun 1993
1 1st edition, 200 copies; Blast reprints by Gordon Rennie & Martin Emond £5.00
1 2nd edition, revised lyrics £3.00
2-4 £3.00
Note: first edition of first issue was pulped when Elvis Presley Estate objected to Presley lyrics being used, only 200 copies bound.

WHIZ COMICS
Miller; (1) nn 1945; (2) 60-76; (3) 50 Jun 1950-130 1959
nn 16pgs gravure; Fawcett reprints begin; Captain Marvel: "Sivana's Twin" (from #59) £20.00
nn "Seven League Boots" (from #64) £20.00
nn "Lamp of Diogenes" (from #65) £20.00
60-70 16pgs gravure £10.00
71-76 16pgs letterpress £8.00
50-69 28pgs large gravure £5.00
70-88 28pgs smaller format £5.00
89-130 28pgs; no Captain Marvel £3.00

WILBUR COMICS
Gerald Swan; 1 1952-?
1 36pgs; Archie reprints £2.50
2-? £1.50

WILD BILL ELLIOTT COMICS
World Distributors; 1 1954-18 1955
1 28pgs; Dell reprints £5.00
2-18 £3.00

WILD BILL HICKOK AND JINGLES
Miller; 1 1959-16 1960
1 28pgs; Dell reprints based on TV series £5.00
2-16 £3.00

WILD BILL HICKOK COMICS
Thorpe & Porter; 1 Dec 1952-14 1954
1 68pgs; Avon Periodicals reprints from Wild Bill Hickok Comics, and Jesse James Comic £4.00
2-14 £3.00

WILD FRONTIER
Miller; 1 1955-? 1956
1 28pgs; Charlton reprints £2.50
2-? £1.50

WILD PALMS
Arrow; Nov 1993
nn 72pgs; by Bruce Wagner & Julian Allen, reprints from Details £8.00
Note: reprints strip which formed the basis for Oliver Stone TV series

WILD THING
(see main American section)

WILD WEST COMIC ANNUAL
World Distributors; 1952-1960?

N.MINT

cy1952 John Wayne, Buffalo Bill, etc; Western Publishing reprints £4.00
cy1953 Wild Bill Pecos, Lobo the Wolf Boy, Black Diamond reprints £4.00
cy1954-cy1960 £4.00

WILD WEST PICTURE LIBRARY
Fleetway; 1 May 1966-114 Jan 1971
1 60pgs pocket size; Gun Rule £3.00
2-92 £1.50
93-114 68pgs £1.00
ARTISTS/FEATURES
1 Gun Rule. 2 Twisted Trails by Robert Forrest. 3 Call of the Wild. 4 Death in Ambush. 5 Outlaw Gold. 6 Cattle Drive. Many issues reprint Kit Carson, Buck Jones, etc stories from Cowboy Comics with the lead character's name changed; artists include Jesus Blasco in 66, 73, 76, 78, 86, 100. Carlos V. Roume. Jose Luis Salinas in 109.

WILD WEST PICTURE LIBRARY HOLIDAY SPECIAL
I.P.C. Magazines/ Fleetway Publications; 1973-?
1973 192pgs; reprints £1.50
1974- £1.00

WILD WESTERN
Streamline; 1 1951
1 28pgs; reprints from Prize Western (Prize) £4.00

WILD WESTERN
Miller; 1-9 1955
1 28pgs; Atlas/Marvel reprints £5.00
2-9 £4.00

WILL ROGERS WESTERN COMIC
United Anglo-American; 1950, 2 unnumbered issues
nn-nn 28pgs; Fox Features reprints £5.00

WILLIAM TELL
(see TV Photo Stories)
C.A. Pearson (TV Picture Stories); 1 Feb 1959-3 Jun 1959
1 68pgs pocket size; The Assassins £5.00
2-3 £3.00
ARTISTS/FEATURES
1 The Assassins. 2 The Bear. 3 The Prisoner.

WINGS COMICS
Cartoon Art; 1950
nn Fiction House reprints £4.00

WINGS COMICS
Streamline; 1951, 2 unnumbered issues
nn-nn 28pgs; Fiction House reprints £4.00

WINGS COMICS
Trent; 1-3 1953?
1-3 68pgs; Fiction House reprints £3.50

WIZARD, THE
D.C. Thomson; 1 23rd Sep 1922-1970 16th Nov 1963 (joins Rover)
1 very scarce £75.00
2 scarce £50.00
3-5 £30.00
1922 issues £25.00
1923 issues £20.00
1924-1930 issues £15.00
1931-1935 issues £10.00
1936-1940 issues £7.50
1941-1950 issues £5.00
1951-1955 issues £4.00
1956-1959 issues £3.00
1960-1963 issues £2.00

WIZARD
D.C. Thomson; 1 14th Feb 1970-24th Jun 1978 (435 issues, numbered to 153; joins Victor)
1 Soldiers of the Jet Age by Martin Asbury begins £3.00
1 with free gift (Sure-Shot Shooter) £6.00
2-5 £1.00
6-13 Jan 1974, 27 Jan-13 Jul 1974 £0.75
20 Jan 1974 1st "Wizard and Rover" £0.75
20 Jul 1974 The Wriggling Wrecker by Dave Gibbons begins £1.25
27 Jul 1974-24 Jun 1978 incl. some Gibbons, Bolland art £0.30
ARTISTS/FEATURES
Martin Asbury (Soldiers of the Jet Age 1-23, 41-54, The Crimson Claw 26-34, The River Raiders 56-70, The Secret War of Deep 16 134-146, Big River Bill 2 Oct 1976-22 Jan 1971). Brian Bolland (The Box 25 Sep 1976). Paddy Brennan (Longlegs the Desert Wild Boy 19 May-17 Nov 1973 reprint, King Solomon's Mines 23 Feb-17 Aug 1974, reprint). Carlos Ezquerra (Chained to His Sword 25 Sep 1976-1 Jan 1977, The Wrong Face of Fear 19 Nov 1977). Dave Gibbons (The Wriggling Wrecker 20 Jul-21 Dec 1974, Year of the Shark Men 24 Apr-10 Jul 1976, The Deathless Army 14 Aug 1976, The Last Torpedo 28 Aug 1976, The Flying Tripehound 18 Dec 1976-12 Feb 1977, Cat and Mouse 13 Aug-15 Oct 1977, 3 Dec 1977, 17 Dec-24 Dec 1977). Denis McLoughlin (Power the Danger Ranger 18 May-20 Jul 1974, Terror of the Tall Tower 28 Sep 1974-25 Jan 1975, Black Jaguar 25 Jan 1975, It's Only Zeke 1 Feb-29 Mar 1975, Sign of the Shark 14 Jun-25 Oct 1975, The Frozen Man 29 Nov 1975-17 Apr 1976, Frankie and Johnnie 16 Oct 1976-1 Jan 1977, etc).

WIZARD BOOK FOR BOYS, THE
D.C. Thomson; Aut 1935-Aut 1941, Aut 1948
(1936) scarce £75.00
(1937) £35.00
(1938) £25.00
(1939) £20.00
(1940) £15.00
(1941) £15.00
(1942) £15.00
(1949) £12.50
Note: no annuals issued for 1943-1948

WIZARD HOLIDAY BOOK
D.C. Thomson; Aut 1937-Aut 1938
(1938) scarce, softcover (seaside scene) £50.00
(1939) scarce, softcover (railway scene) £40.00

N.MINT

WIZARD MIDGET COMIC
D.C. Thomson; 11th Sep 1954
nn 32pgs giveaway with Wizard; incl. The Truth About Wilson, Limpalong Leslie £3.00

WONDERMAN
(see Oh Boy! Comics, Wonderman)
Paget; 1 1948-24 1951
1 8pgs; Wonderman by Mick Anglo begins £7.50
2-3, 5-7 £5.00
4 more common £3.00
8-15, 21, 23-24 12pgs £4.00
16-20 16pgs £4.00
nn (22) titled Oh Boy! and Wonderman; H. Stanley White Tornado £4.00

WONDER WOMAN
Titan; Apr 1995
The Contest DC reprints by William Messner-Loebs & Mike Deodato £6.00

WONDER WOMAN OFFICIAL ANNUAL
Egmont/London Editions; 1980-1982
1980 Egmont; DC reprints; Brian Bolland end-papers £3.00
1981 Egmont; DC reprints; Brian Bolland cover, Garry Leach end-papers £3.00
1982 London Editions; DC reprints £2.00

WORLD ADVENTURE LIBRARY SERIES
(see Bonanza, Flash Gordon, The Man From U.N.C.L.E., Mandrake the Magician, The Phantom, Tarzan.)
Note: Batman World Adventure Library and Superman World Adventure Library contain text stories, not comic strips)

WORLD ILLUSTRATED
Thorpe & Porter; 1 1953-34 1963
1 52pgs; Flight (US #8), Gilberton reprints from The World Around Us, new cover £15.00
2 Pirates (7) £10.00
3 Horses (3) £7.50
4 Prehistoric Animals (15) £8.00
5 Space (5) £7.00
6 Dogs (1) £7.00
7 The F.B.I. (6) £7.00
8 The Crusades (16) £7.00
9 Scientists (18) £7.00
10 French Revolution (14) £8.00
11 The Jungle (19) £8.00
12 Communications (20) £7.00
13 Ghosts (24) £7.00
14 Great Explorers (23) £7.00
15 Magic (25) £8.00
16 High Adventure (27) £7.00
17 Whaling (28) £7.00
18 The Vikings (29) £7.00
19 Underwater Adventure (30) £7.00
20 Hunting (31) new cover £9.00
21 Gold and Glory (32) new cover £9.00
22 Spies (35) £7.00
23 Fishing (34) £7.00
24 Famous Teens (33) £7.00
25 Fight for Life (36) £7.00
26 Day of Fury (new) mostly US art £25.00
27 Boating (22) £7.00
28 The Sea (new) mostly US art £15.00
29 Great Escapes (new) £15.00
30 Life/Planets (new) mostly US art £15.00
31 North West Passage (new) £15.00
32 Golden Horde (new) £15.00
33 The Cossacks (new) mostly US art £15.00
34 Disasters (new) £20.00
Note: Follows European series

WORLD WITHOUT SUPERMAN
(see Superman)

WORLD'S FINEST
Titan; Jan 1993
nn reprints World's Finest 1-3 by Dave Gibbons, Rude/Kesel art £9.00

WOW!
IPC Magazines; 1 5th Jun 1982-25th Jun 1983
No. 1 - 5 Jun 1982 £1.25
No. 1 with free gift (1 of 4 Funny Face Makers) £3.00
No. 2 - 12 Jun 1982 £1.00
No. 2 with free gift (Rubber Spider) £2.00
19 Jun 1982-25 Jun 1983 £0.60

WYATT EARP
Miller; 1 1957-44 1960
1 28pgs; Charlton reprints £5.00
2-44 £3.00

X

X-FILES, THE
Manga Publishing/Titan Magazines; 1 Jun 1995-present (21 issues to Jan 1997)
1 Topps Comics reprints begin, Charlie Adlard art £12.50
1 with free gift (X-Files badge) £15.00
1 'gold' reprint (May 1996) £5.00
2 £8.00
2 with free gift (post-cards) £10.00
3,4 £5.00
5,6 £3.50
7 free Book of the Unexplained supplement £2.50
8-10 £2.00
11-18 £1.50

	N.MINT
19 1st Titan issue (Nov 1996)	£1.50
20-21	£1.50

X-FILES, THE

Manga Publishing/Titan Books; Nov 1995-present	
Firebird (Nov 1995) 148pgs; reprints X-Files 1-6	£10.00
Project Aquarius (Jul 1996)	£10.00
Dead to the World (Oct 1996)	£7.00
The Haunting (Dec 1996)	£10.00

X-FILES SPECIAL EDITION, THE

Manga Publishing; 1 Win 1996-2 1996	
1-2 Magazine with 10-pg reprint strip	£2.25

X-MEN

Boxtree; Jun 1994-present	
Wolverine (Jun 1994) Chris Claremont & Frank Miller reprints	£7.00
X-Men & Ghost Rider: Brood Trouble in the Big Easy (Jun 1994)	£5.25
God Loves, Man Kills (Dec 1994) Chris Claremont & Brent Anderson reprints	£6.00
Gambit (Aug 1995) Howard Mackie, Lee Weeks, Klaus Janson reprints	£8.00
The Adventures of Cyclops and Phoenix (Dec 1995) Scott Lobdell & Gene Ha	£9.00
Executions Book 1 (Feb 1996) Claremont/Lee reprints	£9.00
Executions Book 2 (Feb 1996) Claremont/Lee reprints	£9.00
Generation X (May 1996) reprints Generation X #1-4 by Lobdell & Bachalo	£10.00
Bishop: The Mountjoy Crisis (May 1996)	£10.00

X-MEN COLLECTOR'S EDITION

Grandreams; 1981-1982	
cy1981 red cover; Uncanny X-Men #56, 58, Neal Adams art; colour	£3.50
cy1982 yellow cover; reprints Uncanny X-Men #61-63, Neal Adams art; colour	£3.00

X-MEN POCKET BOOK (PREVIOUSLY STAR HEROES POCKET BOOK)

Marvel; 14 Jun 1981-28 Aug 1982	
14-19, 21-28 52pgs, small size; X-Men reprints	£0.50
20 100pgs; double size Xmas number	£1.00

X-MEN, THE ORIGINAL

Marvel; 1 27th Apr 1983-17 23rd May 1983	
1 reprints begin from X-Men #1; colour	£2.00
1 with free gift (red/yellow or red/blue plastic gun)	£4.00
2-3	£1.25
2-3 with free gift (X-Men stickers)	£3.00
4-17	£1.00

X-MEN WINTER SPECIAL

Marvel; Oct 1981-Nov 1982	
1981-1982 52pgs; reprints	£1.25

Y

YOUNG DEATH

Mandarin (2000AD Books); Sep 1992	
nn Judge Dredd Megazine reprints, Peter Doherty art	£7.00

YOUNG EAGLE

Arnold Book Co./ Miller; (1) 1 1951-8 1952; (2) 50 1955-58 1956	
1-8 (Arnold) 24pgs; Fawcett reprints	£5.00
50-58 (Miller) 28pgs	£3.00

YOUNG MARVELMAN

Miller: 25 3rd Feb 1954-370 Feb 1963 (346 issues)	
25 Young Marvelman by George Parlett begins	£12.50
26, 28-36, 38-50	£5.00
27 1st James Bleach Y.Marvelman	£5.00
37 1st Marvelman/Y.Marvelman team-up	£5.00
51-100	£3.50
101-335	£2.75
336-370 monthly issues, mostly reprints	£2.50
The Reindeer colouring book	£12.50
In Space	£12.50

YOUNG MARVELMAN ANNUAL

(see Marvelman Jr. Annual)	
Miller: 1954-1961	
1954 scarce, softcover, (Y.Marvelman shaking hands with alien)	£40.00
1955 scarce, softcover, (Y.Marvelman and Dagger)	£35.00
1956 hardcover, slightly smaller format begins	£25.00
1957-1960	£15.00
1961 card cover, becomes "Young Marvelman Adventures"; Young Marvelman appears with Cap. Marvel Jr.'s cape	£12.50

Z

Z-CARS ANNUAL

World Distributors; 1963-1966	
cy1963 stories/features by Ian Kennedy Martin based on TV series	£5.00
cy1964-cy1966 mostly stories by Ian Kennedy Martin	£4.00

ZAZA THE MYSTIC

Miller; 1 1956-?	
1 28pgs; Charlton reprints	£5.00
2-?	£3.00

ZENITH

Titan (Best of 2000AD); Apr 1988-Aug 1990	
Book One	£5.00
Book Two	£5.00
Book Three	£5.00
Book Four	£5.95
Book Five	£5.50

ZIP

Odhams; 4th Jan 1958-3rd Oct 1959 (85 unnumbered issues; joins Swift)	N.MINT
1 (4 Jan 1958) Strongbow the Mighty by Ron Embleton, Wells Fargo by Don Lawrence begin	£10.00
1 with free gift	£20.00
11 Jan 1958	£5.00
18 Jan-8 Mar 1958	£2.50
15 Mar 1958 1st Gerry Embleton Strongbow	£2.50
22 Mar-1 Nov 1958	£2.00
8 Nov 1958 last Strongbow	£2.00
15 Nov 1958 Nigel Tawney by Redvers Blake, Captain Morgan by Colin Andrew begin	£1.50
22 Nov 1958-27 Jun 1959, 22 Aug-3 Oct 1959	£1.50
Note: no issues were published dated 4 Jul-15 Aug 1959	

ZOMBIE

Miller; 1-8 c1961	
1-8 68pgs; E.C. reprints	£3.00

ZORRO

S.N.P.I./ Miller; 50 Feb 1952-87 1955	
50 24pgs; French reprints	£4.00
51-87	£2.00

ZORRO

World Distributors; 1 1955-6 195?	
1 28pgs; Return of Zorro, Dell reprints based on Walt Disney film and television	£5.00
2-6	£3.00

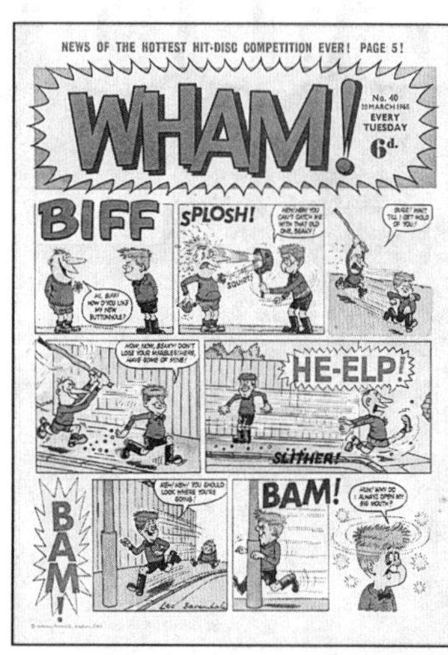

Wham! #40

X-Files (Manga) #1

Advertisers Index & Advertisements

ADVERTISERS INDEX

As a free service to all our advertisers, below is a list of shops and publishers, publications and services. As a collector it is important to shop around and compare so don't be afraid of trying new retailers or services to the ones you are already using. And you might try the American advertisers who often have a different range of comics.

OPPOSITE FANTASTIC FOUR
ACTIVE IMAGES
430 Colorado Avenue #301,
Santa Monica,
CA 90401USA
(001) 310 458 9094
Fax: (001) 310 451 9761

A3
ALTERED IMAGES
3 Eagle Star House,
299-301 High Street,
Sutton, Surrey SM1 1LG
(0181) 770 3815
Fax: (01372) 720753

A12
AMERICAN DREAM
17 Pickwick Road,
Corsham, Wilts SN13 9BQ
(01249) 70647

72 Walcot Street,
Bath BA1 5BD

A14
ARCHIVE COLLECTIONS
328 High Street,
Orpington,
Kent BR6 0NQ
(01689) 824489

A1
AVALON COMICS & COLLECTIBLES
P.O. Box 234
Boston
MA 02123
USA
(617) 262 5544
Fax: (617) 948 2300

OPPOSITE THE X-FILES
BOOK & COMIC EXCHANGE
14 Pembridge Road,
Notting Hill Gate,
London W11
(0171) 229 8420

A13
CALAMITY COMICS
160 Station Road,
Harrow,
Middlesex HA1 2RH
(0181) 427 3831

90 Queens Road,
Watford,
Herts WD1 2LA
(01923) 249 293

INSIDE FRONT COVER
CARDS INC
2 Handford Court,
Garston Lane,
Watford,
Herts WD2 6EJ
(01923) 894 405
Fax: (01923) 894 447

OPPOSITE SPIDERMAN
COMIC BOOK POSTAL AUCTIONS LTD
40-42 Osnaburgh Street,
London NW1 3ND
(0171) 586 3007
Fax: (0171) 586 0945

A15
CONQUISTADOR
(Mail Order only)
158 Kent House Road,
Beckenham, Kent BR3 1JY
Tel/fax: (0181) 659 9714

COLOUR SECTION
DC COMICS INC
1700 Broadway,
New York NY 10019
U.S.A.
(001) (212) 636 5400

BACK COVER
DIAMOND COMIC DISTRIBUTORS, INC
Unit 1, Empson Street,
London E3 3LT
(0171) 538 8300
Fax: (0171) 987 6744

US:
(001) 410 560 7100
Fax: (001) 410 560 7148

OPPOSITE US SECTION & A11
FORBIDDEN PLANET
30 Penn Street,
Bristol BS1 3AS
(01179) 298692
Fax: (01179) 300150

31 Cross Cheaping,
Coventry CV1 1HF
(01203) 229672
Fax: (01203) 230041

92 Bold Street,
Liverpool L1 4HR
(0151) 707 1491
Fax: (0151) 707 3471

59 Grainger Street,
Newcastle NE1 5JE
(0191) 261 9173
Fax: (0191) 233 1516

60 Burleigh Street,
Cambridge CB1 1DJ
(01223) 301666
Fax: (01223) 516717

175 North End,
Croydon CR0 1TP
(0181) 688 7190
Fax: (0181) 681 5189

71 New Oxford Street,
London WC1A 1DG
(0171) 836 4179
Fax: (0171) 240 7118

TRADING CARD SECTION
FIRST CHOICE CARDS
11 Keith Ave
Liverpool
L4 5SL
01704 548629

A13
GALAXY 4
493 Glossop Road,
Broom Hill,
Sheffield S10 2QE
(0114) 268 49 76

A8
GARY DOLGOFF COMICS
P.O. Box #507
Northampton
Mass 01061-0507
USA
(718) 596 5719
Fax: (718) 858 5475

A5
HARLEY YEE
PO Box 51758
Livonia
MI 48151-5758
USA
(800) 731 1029
(313) 421 7921
Fax: (313) 421 7928

OPPOSITE X-MEN
INCOGNITO COMICS
1-2 The Friars,
Canterbury,
Kent ME14 1EB
Tel/fax: (01227) 785898

21 Union Street,
Maidstone,
Kent ME14 1EB.
Tel/fax: (01622) 683642

A4
JOSEPH KOCH
206 41st Street,
Brooklyn, NY 11232
USA
(001) 718 768 8571
Fax: (001) 718 768 8918

A6 & 7
JUST COMICS
(Dept PG)
2 Crossmead Avenue,
Greenford,
Middlesex UB6 9TY

A15
KEN HARMAN
(0181) 771 8756

A11
KRAKKERS
5 Bath Place
Taunton
Somerset TA1 4ER
(01823) 335 057

COLOUR SECTION
MERLIN PUBLISHING
18 Vincent Avenue,
Crownhill,
Milton Keynes,
MK8 0AW
(01908) 561588
Fax: (01908) 565773

***OPPOSITE LADY DEATH* & A9**
MIGHTY WORLD OF COMICANA
125 East Barnet Road,
Barnet,
Herts, EN4 8RF
(0181) 449 2991
Fax: (0181) 449 3152
Mail Order: (0181) 449 5535

***OPPOSITE CONTENTS* & A10**
PRICE GUIDE PRODUCTIONS
PO Box 2541,
London N16 0LT
(0181) 809 3437
Fax: (0181) 449 3152

A12
PURPLE HAZE
38 Eastlake Walk,
Drake Circus Shopping Centre, Plymouth,
Devon PL1 1BX
(01752) 254136

A2
SHEFFIELD SPACE CENTRE
33 The Wicker,
Sheffield S3 8HS
(01742) 758905

A16
SILVER ACRE COMICS
(Mail Order only)
PO Box 114
Chester CH2 4WQ
(07000) 266 427
Fax: (01244) 300 815

COLOUR SECTION
TITAN BOOKS
42-44 Dolben Street
London SE1 0UP

Enquiries:
(0171) 620 0200
Fax: (0171) 620 0032

Trade Orders UK (Diamond):
(0171) 538 8300
Fax: (0171) 987 6744

Mail Order UK:
(01536) 763 631
Fax: (01536) 760 306

OPPOSITE X-FILES (UK SECTION)
TITAN MAGAZINES
42-44 Dolben Street
London SE1 0UP

Enquiries:
(0171) 620 0200
Fax: (0171) 620 0032

Trade Orders UK (Diamond):
(0171) 538 8300
Fax: (0171) 987 6744

Mail Order UK:
(01536) 763 631
Fax: (01536) 760 306

OPPOSITE X-MEN
WHATEVER COMICS
2 Burgate Lane,
Canterbury ,
Kent CT1 2HH
(01227) 453226

5 Middle Row,
High Street,
Maidstone,
Kent ME14 1TF
(01622) 681041

AVALON

COMICS & COLLECTIBLES

In our seven years we have gained one of the best reputations in the business, for:

Grading
Plain dealing
Fairness to beginners
Choice selection
Super service

And we have consistently issued one of the best catalogs in the business!

68 jam-packed pages
150 photographs

Featuring over 15,000 comic books from 1933-1975, and choice memorabilia from 1880-1980.

Character & personality items
Vintage Superman collectibles
Disneyana
Cowboy & Western items
Movie posters
Antique advertising
Premiums, Pulps
Big Little books
Cardboard & Hardcover books
& much, much more!

Please sign up to receive our catalogs!

Send your name, address and $2. (in the U.S. and Canada, $3. foreign) to get our current and next catalogs, or send $5. to receive our current and next three catalogs ($7. foreign).

Avalon Comics
P.O. Box 234
Boston, MA 02123
Phone: (617) 262-5544
Fax: (617) 948-2300

Larry Curcio, proprietor
Overstreet Senior Advisor 1994-1996
Comic's Buyers Guide Customer
Service Award Winner 1990-1996

TRANSFORM YOUR DEAD STOCK ....

JOSEPH KOCH'S AVALANCHE PRESENTS

2 000 000 COMICS & MAGAZINES FOR SALE OR TRADE

Over the last 20 years we have shipped over 1 000 000 comics, magazines, and related items to the United Kingdom, Ireland, and the continent.

Our 150 page tabloid sized **AVALANCHE OF WONDER** catalgue is larger than say, the *Daily Sport*, or - to be more upscale - Hamburg's *Die Zeit.* Our trade and overstock alone would fill most convention halls. The **AVALANCHE** lists everything from individual comics to bagged sets to small collections to entire inventories.

Not only do we sell. *We love to trade.* Check out the trade value of your loose ends by consulting the list of categories below. Notice that we find almost anything acceptable except heavy duplication or books of the last 15 years (but we'll even make offers on those as well).

We have been shipping to the United Kingdom, Ireland, & the continent for years and may be able to make special shipping arrangements to & from your nearest port, airport, or place of business. Conversely, we are always looking for any new shipping arrangements you may suggest.

Send $3.00 (or its local equivalent in pounds, DM, francs etc) to the address below & we will rush you our latest **SALE/ TRADE AVALANCHE.** ***And remember, if you're in New York, call for an appointment to visit the warehouse.***

WE WILL TRADE FOR YOUR LOOSE ENDS, SURPLUS, ETC Got some stray comics, books, or magazines? Trade them to us. Trade values given in 1st column are against material listed in overstock section at right. Trade values listed in 2 right hand columns refer to pages in our 150 page catalogue (send $3.00; $4.00 via phone & charge card). Trades from catalogue will require alternate choices. If trading from overstock list at right, simply invoice your books in accordance with category list below and ship. All trade prices based on F or better condition; items in good to very good will trade for 50% of listed value; items in fair (must be complete with cover) will trade for 25% of listed value; if sending more than 5 of an issue, fax 1st;
Questions? Fax us with your questions & fax number and we will get back to you.

WE WILL TRADE FOR	Overstock at Right	Pages A2-A8, F1-f17 X1-X3	Pages M1-M3
1930'S-1940'S COMICS	30.00	20.00	15.00
10 CENT COVER COMICS			
PRE CODE HORROR, ATLAS	15.00	10.00	6.00
DC,MOVIE/TV ADAPTATION COMICS	10.00	8.00	6.00
ALL OTHERS	8.00	6.00	4.50
12-15 CENT COVER COMICS			
MOVIE/TV ADAPTATION COMICS	8.00	6.00	4.00
DELL/GOLD KEY, DC	4.00	3.00	2.00
CHARLTON, ARCHIE, HARVEY	2.00	1.50	1.00
ALL OTHERS	1.50	1.00	-
20-50 CENT COVER COMICS			
HANNA BARBERA	2.00	1.50	1.00
DC WAR, ROMANCE	2.00	1.50	1.00
DC/MARVEL HORROR	1.50	-	-
FUNNY ANIMAL, WESTERN	1.50	-	-
MARVEL ROMANCE, UNDERGROUNDS	1.50	1.00	-
ALL OTHERS	1.00	-	-
ADULT (XXX) INDEPENDENTS	1.50	1.00	
COMIC FORMAT MAGAZINES THROUGH 1980			
VAMPIRELLA	5.00	3.50	2.50
CREEPY,EERIE,2000 AD	2.50	1.50	1.00
ALL OTHER HUMOR, HORROR,DR WHO	1.75	1.25	1.00
MARVEL MAGAZINES; ALL OTHER	1.50	-	-
COMIC DIGESTS,BRITISH WEEKLIES	1.00	-	-
TRADE PAPERBACKS	3.00	2.00	1.50
GRAPHIC NOVELS,BRITISH ANNUALS	2.00	1.50	1.00
PAPERBACKS, MOVIE/TV TIE-INS			
COMIC/CARTOON PB'S	0.50	-	-
SCI-FI (60 CENT COVER OR LESS)	0.50	-	-
MONSTER/SCI-FI FILM MAGAZINES			
75 CENT COVER OR LESS	3.00	2.00	1.50
ALL OTHERS	1.00	-	-
REVIEWS, JOURNALS, FANZINES			
PRE 1980'S	1.50	1.00	
1980 TO PRESENT	1.00	-	-

CHOOSE FROM over a million items available in trade. **LIST ADVERTISED IN CBG #1115, PAGE 63 IS STILL VALID.**

OVERSTOCK TRADE/CASH 1st price is trade value against first column prices at right; 2nd price is cash price (postpaid). All vf-nm unless noted

		Trade	Cash
SANDMAN 19 error ed	50 for	500.00	200.00
SPAWN 8	50 for	100.00	40.00
MAXX 1	50 for	75.00	35.00
X Lot: X FACTOR,X FORCE,WOLVERINE,X MEN (max 20 of an issue)	2000 for	2500.00	725.00
1994 collection (900+ comics,all different,all 1994,50% Marvel,35% DC)	ONLY	1500.00	625.00
XXX COMICS (Adults only); 20@ of 20 different issues	400 for	600.00	195.00
MENS ADVENTURE COMICS 1	50 for	500.00	200.00
MONSTER WORLD 1 F-VF	10 for	150.00	45. 00
SAVAGE SWORD OF CONAN 16	10 for	100.00	40.00
X MEN 150	50 fo	200.00	80.00
COMICO PRIMER 2 (1st Grendel)	10 for	750.00	350.00
VAMPIRELLA (1969 Warren) 6 - the original series !!!	10 for	350.00	150.00
BLAZING COMBAT (1965-1966) 3 F-VF	10 for	150.00	65.00
VAMPIRELLA (1992 HARRIS) 4	20 for	125.00	60.00

Design your own lot from the categories given below; our choice of issue numbers, allow up 20 of an issue, minimum lot size 1000 comics; most books will be from the last five years; you may mix or you may trade for one category exclusively: **1.50 per book in trade, 40c in cash.**

BATMAN titles & appearances • SUPERMAN titles & appearances
ENHANCED Covers • SPIDERMAN titles • 1995 COVER DATES

SPECIAL TRADE TERMS FOR ITEMS RETAILING AT $25.00 OR MORE

WRITE FOR CURRENT TRADE FORMULAS ON HIGH TICKET ITEMS

JOSEPH KOCH 206 41st ST.
BROOKLYN NY 11232
Tel: 718 - 768 - 8571 Fax: 718 - 768 - 8918

BACK ISSUES!

To celebrate our team-up with Titan Books, Price Guide Productions is pleased to present back copies of all the Price Guides produced from #2 to date (#1 sold out), in mint, unsigned, signed and special editions. Who knows? These variations may themselves become collector's items! They make fascinating reading and comparing and stocks are limited. ***Please enclose a flat fee of £2.50 per order for postage and packing. Cheques/PO's payable to Price Guide Productions.***

Nº 2 (1990)

Simon Bisley cover featuring Spiderman and the Punisher! Interior pin-ups by Ewins & Lloyd, Kitson and Ridgeway; first typeset Guide in the new familiar format. The days when Iron Man #55 was £4.00 and New Mutants #87 wasn't even out yet! **£6.95**
Special signed and hand-stamped edition **£7.95**

Nº 3 (1991)

Dave Gibbons cover featuring Judge Dredd and Dan Dare. New features include the famous First Appearance Index and Artist Gallery featuring Philips & Kane, Higgins & Hughes **£7.95**
Special signed and hand-stamped edition **£8.95**
Signed and numbered Limited Edition. Only 250 of these were produced and some very low numbers (25-100) have been kept back for a first come, first served basis **£9.95**
Numbers #1–#10 also available **please enquire**

Nº 4 (1992)

Sean Philips cover featuring the "girlfriends" of Dredd and Dare—Judge Anderson and Dr. Jocelyn Peabody! Special colour section for the first time and many new features **£8.95**
Signed by author and cover artist **£9.95**
Special signed and hand-stamped edition **£9.95**
Signed and numbered Limited Edition. Only 50 of these were produced, signed by the author and cover artist **£10.95**
Numbers #1–#5 available **please enquire**

Nº 5 (1993)

Liam Sharpe cover featuring the unlikely team-up of Death's Head (a robot) and Magnus Robot Fighter **£9.95**
Signed by author and cover artist **£10.95**
Special signed and hand-stamped edition **£10.95**
Signed and numbered Limited Edition. Only 50 of these were produced, signed by the author and cover artist **£11.95**
Numbers #1–#5 available **please enquire**

Nº 6 (1994)

John Bolton cover featuring a specially created character called "Liliana", one in a long line of vampiresses from the depths of the artist's imagination **£10.95**
Signed by author and cover artist **£11.95**
Special signed and hand-stamped edition **£11.95**
Signed and numbered Limited Edition. Only 50 of these were produced, signed by the author and cover artist **£12.95**
Numbers #1–#5 available **please enquire**

Guide #7 (1996) with a stunning Sabretooth cover by Gary Frank. First dual priced edition with prices in pounds and dollars **£12.95**
Special signed (by author) edition with dedication of your choice **£13.95**

Price Guide Productions • P.O. Box 10793 • London N10 3NF

PRICE GUIDE PRODUCTIONS VALUATION SERVICE

PRICE GUIDE PRODUCTIONS are pleased to announce the continuation of their exclusive Comics Valuation Service. With the publication of the new 1997/98 Edition of the Official Comic Book Price Guide, collectors everywhere will see for themselves just how valuable comic books can be. Sizeable collections can add up to a great deal of money and uninsured collections are at constant risk. This valuation may help to influence your insurance company.

Price Guide Productions can offer a valuation service which is fast, efficient and authentic. DUNCAN MCALPINE, author of The Comic Book Price Guide for Great Britain will value your comics if they are individually listed out (groups if they are runs of the same sort of comic *i.e. Conan #60-70 or Batman #120-130*), if they are strictly graded and if a sample can be shown should he think it necessary.

These will then be typed out in order and arranged on computer print-out with a headed certificate from Price Guide Productions to indicate in writing the official valuation at the time of writing plus a clause to allow for inflationary rise throughout the next twelve months plus comments and advice on your collection and how best to improve it.

The cost of this service is structured as follows to make for a fairer fee, no matter how large or small the collection:-

Flat fee for a Total Collection not exceeding 250 comics.....£25
Extra fee for every 50 additional comics or part thereof.......£10

Damned Fine Comics Shops, but don't take our word for it just look what some of our customers say . . .

" I REALLY LIKE THE FACT THAT THEY GET IMPORT COMICS TWICE WEEKLY" — *Arnold Schwarzenegger*

"*!!*?!*??!!!*/! $%!!* AND !**?! OFF!! — *Quentin Tarrantino*

" THEIR FINE SELECTION OF GRAPHIC NOVELS AND BOOKS IS SECOND TO NONE" — *Bruce Willis*

"NO IT'S NOT A WIG !!!!" — *William Shatner*

" THE BEST BACK ISSUE SECTION I'VE EVER SEEN" — *Sharon Stone*

160 Station Road
Harrow, Middlesex HA1 2RH
0181 427 3831

90 Queens Road
Watford, Herts WD1 2LA
01923 249 293

SHEFFIELDS NEWEST SCI-FI, CULT TV, FILM & COMIC SHOP

NEW & SECOND HAND COMICS

WEEKLY IMPORTS OF ALL MAJOR, DC, INDEPENDENT AND MARVEL TITLES, PLUS BACK ISSUES FROM 1960'S TO THE PRESENT)

A wide range of new and secondhand paperbacks, annuals, videos,toys, magazines and memorabilia.

493 GLOSSOP ROAD
BROOM HILL
SHEFFIELD
S10 2QE

GALAXY4

FOR MAIL ORDER send 2 1st class stamps

0114 268 49 76

Abelé Design Services 0191 417 57 66

DR WHO STAR TREK STAR WARS

THE
COMIC
BOOK
PRICE GUIDE

SILVER ACRE COMICS

OWNERS OF 1930s - 1940s - 1950s - 1960s COMIC BOOKS: LOOK NO FURTHER!

$ I'M BUYING $

Call everyone else first, then call us for your highest offer. I am always paying top cash for any pre-1969 comics. No matter what title or condition, whether you have one comic or a warehouse full, I've got thousands of £s to spend.

Before your sell – THINK!

We offer: immediate cash, we will travel anywhere to view collections, high percentage of guide paid, experience no heavy handed dealing. We are happy to compete with any large American dealers – fax them first.

We are building a reputation, not running a race!

We also need: all pre-1975 comics – pre-superhero Marvels, westerns, EC, horror, crime, Classics Illustrated, Dell, Gold Key, photo covers and any or all your Golden Age books.

WE OFFER:

1) Massive 1/2 of a million comics from 1930s to 1996 from Detective #1 to Spawn #4 from Star Wars to 2000 AD.

2) Accuracy grading, all books are guaranteed to be in the stated grade and an unconditioned 7 day return option.

3) FAST dependable and reputable mail order service.

4) There is NO MINIMUM mail order.

5) Time payments, we offer several types of payment plans, to assist you in obtaining the more expensive books.

6) Wants list service, send us a list of the comics you need, and we will do our best to locate them for you, with no obligation for you to buy.

7) If required, we will sell comics on a consignment basis for you. Low commission around 10% or less.

Worldwide mail order service, do you live in Ireland, Scotland, Holland, Japan. Fax me your wants list or sale list, we are in London every 14 days. We also sell comic supplies, bags, boards, boxes, mylars, all prices on request.

TRY US NOW

MasterCard

SILVER ACRE COMICS

PO Box 114, CHESTER CH2 4WQ. Tel: 07000 266 427. Fax: 01244 300815

International Customers Phone: 01244 300 165

PHONE, VISA ORDERS/ENQUIRIES WELCOMED.